TWENTIETH-CENTURY
CRIME AND MYSTERY
WRITERS

Twentieth-Century Writers Series

Twentieth-Century Children's Writers

Twentieth-Century Crime and Mystery Writers

Twentieth-Century Science-Fiction Writers

Twentieth-Century Romance and Historical Writers

Twentieth-Century Western Writers

TWENTIETH-CENTURY CRIME AND MYSTERY WRITERS

THIRD EDITION

PREFACE TO THE FIRST EDITION
JOHN M. REILLY

PREFACE TO THE THIRD EDITION
KATHLEEN GREGORY KLEIN

EDITOR
LESLEY HENDERSON

St J
St James Press

Chicago and London

For information, write:
ST. JAMES PRESS
233 East Ontario Street
Chicago, Illinois 60611
U.S.A.

or

2–6 Boundary Row
London SE1 8HP
England.

British Library Cataloguing in Publication Data
20th-century crime and mystery writers.—3rd ed.
  1. Crime fiction in English—critical studies
  I. Henderson, Lesley II. Twentieth-century crime and mystery writers
823.0872

  ISBN 1-55862-031-1
  Library of Congress Catalog Card Number: 90-63662

First edition published 1980; second edition 1985.

CONTENTS

PREFACE
to the first edition

The art of crime and mystery literature conceals a paradox. If we were not so captivated by the entertainment, we might pause to wonder how it can be that stories devoted to the spectacle of violent crime neither disturb nor horrify us. Thomas De Quincey, in his essay "On Murder Considered as One of the Fine Arts," was the first to note the aesthetic value of well-accomplished, and appropriately reported, homicide. Read today, De Quincey's essay confirms more than a century of fiction. Imaginary tales of crime provide a sensation of incongruity when victims meet their death in libraries, clubs, and private houses, or they offer the satisfaction of probability when violence occurs in society's back-alleys; but these accounts of murder engender no anxiety. In the same way, death by poison, strangulation, firearms, the blunt instrument, bladed weapons, explosives, and bizarre devices illustrate the range of human invention available, on the one hand to culprits who spill the blood of family and friends for the simple motives of greed, hate, or lust, and on the other hand to killers who undertake murder as a simple job of work; but, if the writing is skillful, we appreciate the ingenuity more than the perversity. At once predictable in their formularized representation of crime and resolution and cunning in their craft, stories of crime and mystery could scarcely be more entertaining, and less likely to remind their readers of the sin of Cain.

Evidently, though, reading crime and mystery fiction is one thing, explaining it another. The thrill of danger evaded, ratification of fantasy, satisfaction with a witty or tough style, the grace and idiosyncrasy of character keep us reading, but when challenged to justify a taste for literature that is, after all, devoted to anti-social violence, one reader will speak of the attraction of the riddle to be solved, while another reader, no more or less sophisticated, will say the tale of crime is realistic. The first explanation has the advantage of paying some attention to the special craft of crime fiction, and the second acknowledges a sense of the tale's origin, but neither gives a satisfactory account of the genre.

Authoritative precedence for both of these popular justifications can be found in the words of the genre's ablest writers. Among the so-called Golden Age authors there are R. Austin Freeman whose "The Art of the Detective Story" inveighs against sensationalism that distracts from a controlled effect of a detection puzzle; S.S. Van Dine whose "Twenty Rules for Writing Detective Stories" prescribe rational limits to the means of detection, thereby advancing the dogma of plausibility; Ronald A. Knox whose "Ten Commandments of Detection" anathematizes hackneyed devices and asserts the obligation to challenge a reader with details that, properly arranged, constitute a rational solution to mystery. In support of realism there is Raymond Chandler, a master of narrative artifice, insisting in "The Simple Art of Murder" that his own type of mystery—what we have learned to call hardboiled—is distinguished by typical murder, actual speech, and normal setting. Evidently, though, the character of the detective may be other than life-like, for Chandler describes him in the remarkable conclusion to his essay as though he were the hero of a medieval romance, armored with honor and pride, searching for hidden truth.

Chandler's effort, or anyone else's for that matter, to champion the crime and mystery story as essentially realistic confuses subject with treatment. With all narrative, mystery and crime fiction shares the necessity of supplying the illusion that the story conforms to a reality other than the text. Just as setting gives the plot a place to happen. and character allows for description of action, a fictional crime and the usually dominant detective are necessities of story-telling more than reflections of actuality. The account of a crime in, say, a newspaper article contrives to establish raw fear of criminal violence. In other words the conventions of reportage function to diminish the distance between readers and the threat of actuality. In contrast, mystery fiction thrills rather than threatens, because such motifs as the perversity of human invention when bent to violence, or the evident similarity of motives shared among likely suspects and the guilty, are contained within a design of plot in which we are always sensitive to the artist's hand. Theme, event, character—all these affirm the literary form rather than reconstruct actuality. Crime and mystery literature, thus, displaces the subject of violence with patterns of story-telling that, even in tales of mean streets, work against our receiving them as direct commentary on real life.

Other reading may urge utilitarian goals. History, current affairs, and biography, like the newspaper report of crime, are to help us understand how the world works. The "classics" are to inform us of life philosophically, or so it is said, and if they do not accomplish that, then they will improve our taste. But we consume crime and mystery stories, apart from a natural curiosity about the outcome of the plot, in the way we exercise for the pleasure of physical activity. If ever there were art read for its own sake, this is it.

Because it has been so often repeated, the claim that the essence of the genre is an intellectual puzzle seems much harder to deny than the allegation of realism. One thinks, for example, of the mystery book reviewers' habit of appraising a novel in terms of the surprises it contains and conspicuously refusing to divulge a book's ending so as not to spoil the reader's encounter with the criminal problem; or of the author Ellery Queen's practice of halting a story to challenge the reader to match wits with the detective Ellery Queen; or of the 101 times some fellow mystery fan has announced that he knew the killer at least as soon as the fictional detective. The weight of such testimony is intimidating, but it simply cannot be conclusive. Most of the puzzles, if abstracted from their tales, have practically no intrinsic interest, and, what is more, may be as available to ridicule as Chandler found the puzzle in *The Red House Mystery*. Of course ridicule is not the point either. Illogic in the way Mark Ablett (or is it his brother Robert?) is killed makes little difference, for the book interests us above all else because of its good-natured play on the manners and character of Great Detectives; that is to say, the rendering of the tale interests us in the Ablett case despite its flimsy riddle.

The dominance of the tale over its subject was announced as long ago as 1913, in E.C. Bentley's novel *Trent's Last Case*. Bentley has been praised for many contributions to the craft of detective story writing, but so far as I remember never for the implied statement of the writer's business contained in his story of a crime that has three solutions. Readers will remember that the detective Philip Trent first accounts for Sigsbee Manderson's death in an extended analysis that is then overturned by testimony that uses the same facts to produce a different explanation. Later, in the final pages of the book, the facts are once again reinterpreted when the murderer confesses. All three solutions are valid. The third solution contains the same evidence as the first or second and is no truer, even though a fictional character, at Bentley's bidding, certifies its accuracy by owning up to the crime. What, then, is the significance of the puzzle? It is a literary device like any other. What is more, the reduction of the puzzle to a device carries with it the suggestion that our knowledge of the laws of evidence, or of the objective reality on which we base our notions of the truth, becomes decidedly secondary when we read a novel of mystery. Its primary field of reference is literature, the previous experience we have had with similar stories that allows us to see that tales of crime justify themselves.

In denying that crime and mystery fiction is either realistic or an intellectual puzzle, I want to be careful not to endorse a third popular view which holds that the genre is fundamentally a literature of escape designed to be positively irrelevant to real experience. That idea is untenable because in its own non-realistic way crime and mystery fiction bears a definite relationship to history.

With all popular culture crime and mystery literature shares an origin in the technology that makes possible economical reproduction and wide distribution of printed texts to a literate, largely urban audience. Readily acquired in a money market, crime and mystery books, which can be collected in impressive numbers or disposed of after they are read, are examples of culture as commodity. Among the jumble of commodities available to a modern consumer, it has special significance for being the result of the manifestly modern interest in social control. Although literary concern for justice is universal, stories grounded in plots devoted to unraveling the mystery surrounding crimes originate only with the consciousness among the populations of large, urban settings that neither traditional associations of family, clan, and village, nor the ideal of self-reliant individualism are practical means of protecting the peace of all and the property of the privileged. On the streets, as well as in the courts, state power enforces order, more or less with the consent of the governed. Thus, crime has become a social issue, and in the anonymity of the city its solution and control, a problem. This is what is meant when historians of crime fiction remark that its prerequisites were public sympathy for law and order and the creation of official police.

Crime and mystery fiction, however, is no more a problem literature than it is a puzzle literature. It approaches its subject obliquely, conveying attitudes through the contrivance of technique and affirming with the inherent order of plot a myth of the resolution of the criminal issue. Of course, the foundation of the genre is the criminal event, and without minimizing or explaining away the differences among the types of crime story, it can be said that the plot is normally arranged to represent clarification of the mystery surrounding the event; thus, there are, at the very least, two imperatives. One is a character who works as an expositor of crime. The detective, amateur or professional, is the most familiar agent of rationalization, but a group of investigators, as in the police procedural novel, a Raffles-like rogue or his counterparts in the caper story, the spy, even the Gothic heroine—all these have as their literary motive the reduction of threatening events to a rational system of explanation. Inevitably, the implicit effect when this motive becomes plot is the conviction that there is a means to control and direct events, temporarily if not most of the time.

Authors whom the critics classify as classic—the creators of a Golden Age in detective fiction—direct their art to the creation of settings and characters that idealize the achievement of rationality as though it were a norm of civilized society and crime a brief eruption of behavior that, akin to evil, is nevertheless controllable. In contrast to this social conservatism, the later variations manifest in hard-boiled writing and allied types insist by their fictional settings and characters that the social environment is corrupt. Still, they, too, have plots which include an agent who provides a tentative explanation of crime. Therefore, a second generic imperative is met in the "tough" examples of the genre as well as in the comedic classic examples—the effect of closure, an explanation of crime that brings the story to an end with a neat conclusiveness that rarely appears in actual life.

These necessities of plot, together with other conventions of the idealized world of crime and mystery fiction, reveal their origin in a middle-class culture that sees reality in terms of personality. That culture's literature characteristically projects the issues involved in a matter like crime as problems to be managed, that is, solved, by remarkable individuals who will reveal that the predominant motive for everyone's behavior is personal. The genres of middle-class literature, including crime and mystery fiction, thus provide ways of perceiving reality, ways that interpret also, though in no way revealing themselves through direct social commentary. Development of new varieties in the genre, most strikingly the hard-boiled departure, signal a partial rejection of the received ways of interpreting reality; however, complete repudiation would result in a new genre altogether. Sometimes that may happen, but in the meantime the seemingly endless possibilities for character types, the rising fortunes of the thriller, the maturing of the police story, and the insistence of some contemporary authors on writing novels that almost abandon detection characterize a vital form with a long history before it.

Customarily we trace a literary history such as I have been outlining through accounts of the work of significant authors, and that is a major purpose of this book. The critical essays on William Godwin, Edgar Allan Poe, Charles Dickens, Emile Gaboriau, Anna Katharine Green, Arthur Conan Doyle, and others describe the foundation of crime and mystery fiction by discussing the techniques and conventions invented by the parents of the genre. Similarly, analyses of such Golden Age writers as E.C. Bentley, Agatha Christie, Dorothy L. Sayers, Anthony Berkeley, S.S. Van Dine, Ellery Queen, John Dickson Carr, and many more will indicate how the patterns of that version of the mystery story formed. The studies of Carroll John Daly, Erle Stanley Gardner, George Harmon Coxe, Steve Fisher, Bruno Fischer, and, of course, Dashiell Hammett and Raymond Chandler will do the same for the American invention of the hard-boiled or tough-guy writing. Essays on John Buchan, Erskine Childers, Ian Fleming, Martha Albrand, Helen MacInnes, Geoffrey Household, Len Deighton, John le Carré and their fellow authors of thrillers and spy stories will illustrate the traditions of that type. The same task is accomplished for the police procedural novel by the essays on Maurice Procter, Hillary Waugh, Ed McBain, Lawrence Treat, and more. And there are other vantage points too. The reader of this volume will find the special significance of the short story illustrated in essays on contributors to the dime weeklies, the pulp magazines, as well as the band of contemporary writers whose work regularly appears in such remaining magazines of short fiction as *Ellery Queen's Mystery Magazine*; the phenomenon of the bestseller described in such essays as those on Edgar Wallace, John Creasey, and Mickey Spillane, to name only a few of these remarkable writers; the appearance of fiction that may be considered as efforts to re-define the genre receives analysis in essays on Patricia Highsmith, Julian Symons, Brian Garfield, and others. These highly selective examples hardly do justice to the information available in the critical essays. They omit, for instance, reference to the authors whose work sustains the genre by creation of freshly compelling series characters, or those who enrich the tradition by inventive variations on the basic conventions, or the authors writing in other languages whose books become English classics in translation. Perhaps the examples are sufficient, though, to show that the more than 700 critical articles, in addition to their value as analyses of individual writers, also constitute a collective essay in literary history. All that leaves to be done here in the preface is to add a few remarks on background.

The great matter of crime first reached a popular audience through the medium of writing that purported to be more or less the truth about thief-catching and criminal investigation. Precedence goes to the French author François Eugène Vidocq whose memoirs appeared in 1829. Evidently the widely circulated English translation of Vidocq encouraged others, and in the later 19th century recollections of detective and police work flooded from the presses. The most familiar of these memoirists is Allan Pinkerton whose name, if not his writing, still has household currency. The veracity of Pinkerton and his contemporaries need not concern us, but the construction of their works must, for the simple reason that they read very much like fiction. The detective author presides over his narrative, imparting the authority of experience to his pronouncements on crime, selecting events to testify about his skill in detection, and dramatizing the achievements of a singular individual in combat with criminals. Typically a memoir contains a sequence of formularized steps: the detective meets his client, he undertakes an investigation that may require the use of disguises and other ingenuities, he passes through a climactic adventure, and provides a summary that suggests the obligatory scene in fiction where the sleuth assembles suspects and proceeds to retrace the steps of his inquiry. The fact that detective memoirists found a model for their reports in the devices of fiction rather than in the forms of autobiographical writing was lucky, because it meant that, besides meeting a rising interest in the subject of crime and helping to build a consensus on the social importance of the detective, their books also helped to prepare the audience for the entirely imaginative creations that would flower at the end of the century.

Yet another literary type contributing to the development of crime and mystery fiction was the romantic adventure. As Dorothy L. Sayers observed in the introduction to her *Great Short Stories of Detection, Mystery, and Horror* the huge popularity of James Fenimore Cooper, among others, helped to stimulate the intention of adapting the excitement of tracking and hunting to the routine of criminal investigation. "In the 'sixties," she writes, "the generation who had read Fenimore Cooper in boyhood turned, as novelists and readers, to tracing the spoor of the criminal upon their own native heath." An interesting combination of such a source with the memoir appears in the books that Julian Hawthorne, son of the American romancer, wrote in the 1880's about Thomas Byrnes, Chief of New York detectives. The stories purport to be from Byrnes's diaries of day-to-day police experience, but in the plotting they include attenuated love stories and a whirlwind of events surrounding international conspiracies and high society figures. Over all rears Byrnes as an executive armchair detective dispatching his amateur aides to their adventures in criminal apprehension. In its own wonderful way the hodge-podge of forms and types in Hawthorne's stories illustrates the new genre constituting itself out of usable parts of its predecessors. A still clearer portrayal of the significance of romantic adventure to crime and mystery writing might be offered by anyone who recalls the stories about Nick Carter, Sexton Blake, or their brothers in derring-do, Doc Savage and The Shadow, but that is unnecessary, for we have reached the heart of the matter.

Our literature of crime and mystery is a species of adventure tale, the oldest class of narrative. Its central characters whose names—Sherlock Holmes, Perry Mason—rather than the authors' specify the tale, just as Robin Hood or King Arthur specify theirs, are modern heroes. Whether they are sleuths or the pursued, elite or typical, men or women, these characters live in the popular imagination as both representatives of modern life and its ideal. Their narratives, whose plots oscillate between stressing the accomplishments of intellectual force and featuring the protagonist facing tests of physical peril, transform the mundane subject of crime into material with an aura of the extraordinary.

If such descriptions of the crime and mystery story as I have given stress its fixed form, it is because I am intrigued by the idea that when we "discover" a new author our eagerness to read seems to be a desire to see how this new author will solve not criminal problems, but the technical problems involved in telling a crime story. Our enthusiasm for a new detective character, a novel investigative method, setting, or turn in the plot is a response to craft. But despite the repetition of stories that permits one to see their fixed form, the genre of crime and mystery writing is marked by great vigor. This vigor ought to be kept in mind, because it is due to the grand and simple fact that this fiction tells us stories, an ability which in other realms of literature has suffered decline. Mind you, stories need not be new to be interesting. Possibly they need not even be about anything in particular so far as theme goes or what we usually think of as meaning. We tell anecdotes all the time for the purpose of establishing human community; any information the anecdotes contain is secondary. It is the act of the telling that we love.

Finally, then, it is the narrative impulse of crime and mystery writing that accounts for the paradox of violent entertainment and explains how a form that originated in the distinctive circumstances of Victorian middle-class culture retains the power to affect us. Through the ability to simulate compelling experience, writers of crime and mystery fiction have created a nearly autonomous world. As readers we are proprietary about the world, since we know it so well. And we keep reading, sure that world can delight us again. And again.

JOHN M. REILLY

PREFACE
to the third edition

This third edition of *Twentieth-Century Crime and Mystery Writers* provides an opportunity to ask, not so much what crime fiction is, as what is currently happening within the genre. Detective fiction has for so long been described as a conservative genre or an economic commodity by Marxists, and as escapist entertainment by critics of "high culture," that these labels have assumed a life of their own. They said: "Formulaic." Now, to some extent, earlier dismissals of the conventions underpinning mystery fiction have been replaced by a fascination with the ways in which authors and readers attempt to re-invent the formula. And while many literary critics use detective fiction to illustrate their various theories, rather than to illuminate the novels, some of the most provocative questions being asked today are focussed directly on the texts. Critics wonder whether the genre really is what it purports to be, whether it does what it promises, and whether it can be as neatly packaged as earlier claims would suggest. Widespread interest among academics, avid fans, and casual readers in the workings of the genre has generated new journals, review and fan newsletters, as well as scholarly books. But do the novels support the original assumptions, or are there critics, readers, and fans who read different crime and mystery fiction in different ways?

Segregated from "high culture" by generations of critics and reviewers, popular fiction studies are now reconsidering the use of a formula—which results in pigeonholing—as an all-purpose explanation for the genre's success. Questions of pleasure, the relationship between book and reader, and the manipulation of the formula all cross the boundary between high and popular culture. For fans of detective fiction, the pleasure of reading may seem to be a given one, but as John M. Reilly points out in the preface to earlier editions of this volume, what arouses that pleasure is still not entirely clear. Reader-response criticism demonstrates how each reader creates her or his own version of a novel in the process of reading: no book is exactly the same for each reader. And so, the reader who picks up Agatha Christie for her details of British country life reads with a different eye to that of one whose attention is drawn by the puzzle of the plot. Focussing on different aspects of the novel, each reader both discovers and creates a different pleasure. The choices readers make among the sub-categories of crime fiction—preferring classical, hard-boiled, espionage, or psychological formats—are another version of the pleasure principle which is part of the reading process. Sales data from the last 20 years reveal that crime fiction accounts for 20 per cent of all books sold in England and the United States; but who are the readers and why do they read? Because attempts to determine how pleasure is produced still focus on the text itself, there has been no ethnographic description of crime fiction readers like the one of romance fiction audiences which Janice Radway provides in *Reading the Romance*. Yet readers' desires, both obvious and covert, provoke change and demand continuity equally in the genre. Consequently, the apparent fixity of the formula, and much touted conservatism of both structure and content, are coming under scrutiny as novels themselves mix the familiar with a new emphasis on variety.

The idea of difference as a cultural, academic and literary motif of the past 25 years (from the mid-1960's to the 1990's), covering a range from Civil rights movements to feminism to cultural diversity, is one feature which has moved crime and mystery fiction off its definitional pedestal. Some of these issues have already been debated to some extent, but often they have been subsumed under the wider categorization and generic definitions of crime fiction. Of course, the idea of diversity has always been around: the earliest detective dime novels blatantly marketed "the boy detective," "the bowery detective," "the lady detective," and even "the dog detective." Raising these issues may be like trying to solve the chicken and egg riddle: sometimes new types of fiction draw attention, sell well, and so provide the impetus for additional publication. This cyclical pattern of increasing production and popularity is certainly true of female—as well as ethnic—detectives.

This diversity comes out of literary criticism, social conditions, and the historical parameters of the genre to assume new importance. The strongest example of this is the increase, in number and importance, of women detectives. While there have always been Miss Marple, the Mary Roberts Rinehart heroines, Miss Silver, Nora Charles, and Honey West to refer back to as examples, they were as often as not the product of male writers, and frequently shared the stage with male inspectors, sidekicks, or husbands. The fact that they were female was emphasized in stereotypical ways: in nosey, spinsterish prying; in sexy, bombshell posturing; or in innocent, girlish foolishness. They very often solved the crimes they were investigating through skill, intuition, or luck. But taken collectively, they were not taken seriously. They provided no significant model for a type of detective, as Sherlock Holmes or Sam Spade had done.

Coincidentally, it would seem, three books about women detectives or authors were published in 1988. Adding to *Crime on her Mind* (1975) and *The Lady Detects* (1981), *Silk Stalkings* (Susan Nichols and Victoria Thompson) is a readers' guide to selected women writers who have created male and female series characters. *The Women Detectives: Gender and Genre* (Kathleen Gregory Klein) traces the development of the woman private eye from her first appearance in 1864, contrasting these portrayals with the changing roles of women historically, and the growth of detective fiction as a genre. Maureen T. Reddy's *Sisters in Crime* traces a line of progress in the presentation of women detectives, beginning with the Gothic strand in the late 19th century, and covering amateur, classical, lesbian, hard-boiled, and feminist detectives. Added to these is the collection

Gender, Genre and Narrative Pleasure (edited by Derek Longhurst), whose five central essays call into question the criteria for masculinity which have been adopted in detective fiction. These latter three demonstrate the extent to which standard definitions of detective fiction are being queried, challenged, or discarded when feminist critics refuse to accept any analysis which is not gender-conscious. This has led in turn to reconsiderations of Marxist analysis, to racial, ethnic, and preference-conscious analysis, and—in consequence—to new kinds of novels as well.

The presence of women detectives has never been a simple matter of role reversal: since their earliest appearance, women have been a challenge to either the scientific, rationalist model of investigation first practiced by Dupin and Holmes, or the active, instructive style of the hard-boiled detectives. Women characters who tried to work in the style of men were neatly undercut by their authors, whereas those writers who created a distinctly feminine style for their protagonists often showed that the women could not actually complete the job. The new women detectives—amateurs, police, and private eyes—of the 1970's and 1980's were predominantly created by women writers who tried to break the male/female dichotomy by creating characters who function in the male heroic role of detective, while behaving in female—though not stereotyped feminine—ways. Authors like Marcia Muller, Nancy Pickard, Mary Wings, Antonia Fraser, Gwen Moffat, and others invent detectives who maintain multiple roles, carefully meshing disparate characters with crime solving. Although amateurs, these women do not merely stumble over unexpected corpses, but work in contexts where death is plausible. With their working-class police women—although they are subordinate to male heroes and male superiors on the force—P.D. James and Elizabeth George have redefined the police-detective series.

Beyond that, a growing number of novels featuring women detectives consciously and carefully tell women's stories through feminocentric plots and structures which challenge the generic restrictions. Feminist critic and detective novelist Carolyn Heilbrun/Amanda Cross says that the work of a woman detective is to "deconstruct . . . the patriarchy." Crime, in this formulation, does not simply focus on an individual murder, but also examines the social structures which support the powerful and those who victimize minorities. Writers like Cross, Barbara Wilson, Sara Paretsky, Sue Grafton, Katherine V. Forrest, and others create interrogative texts which urge the reader to solve not only the problems of the crime, but also the problems of the social system. They provide an explicit and persuasive awareness of the gender inequality which pervades contemporary life, persisting despite the hopeful promise of a competent woman doing what is still often called "men's work." The tensions between the demands of the detective novel and the feminist ideology—which goes beyond the creation of a woman detective—require a careful balancing act: these authors are attempting to recreate the genre, effecting changes in form and content.

Another aspect of the difference is the use of the non-generic detective: not White, not upper or middle class, and not educated, as well as not being male. These detectives are marked less by the eccentricities of a Lord Peter Wimsey or a Nero Wolfe than by their minority status, which offers them special insights in the resolution of certain crimes. Harry Kemmelman's orthodox rabbi detective tumbles from problems with his congregation into crime solving: his faculty of Talmudic reasoning leads him to see from a perspective not shared by other characters in the novels. Dave Brandstetter, Joseph Hansen's gay detective, and many of the lesbian detectives created in the 1980's, like Barbara Wilson's Pam Nielson, use their awareness of homosexual culture to hone in on clues not apparent to outsiders. Tony Hillerman's Native American police officers draw on their ethnic unity with the community in which they work to resolve both civil and cultural crimes. Emphasizing the bi-culturalism which allows ethnic and minority detectives to cross from one world to another, John Ball's black detective Virgil Tibbs is successful in both the Black community and White Californian society: he acts as a translator between the two, making the unknown comprehensible. Less emphatic about the ethnic angle as a crime-solving strategy—but growing from the same impulse—are the Armenian, Hispanic, Slavic, and Asian detectives. With these detectives from the cultural minorities come different kinds of crime, settings, criminals, and social observations. Katherine V. Forrest's lesbian police officer, Kate Delafield, recognizes parallels between the McCarthy investigations of the 1950's and the homophobia of the 1980's—not a far-fetched or startling comparison, but one which enriches the texture of the novel. Just as British Golden Age novels and early hard-boiled incursions into Hollywood are considered by some to be among the finest social documents of the period, so readers now enter worlds otherwise closed to them because of their own social placement. And the crimes, although they still involve murder, now include rape, prostitution, racism and sexism, as well as the more familiar types of institutional corruption. In some novels (more typically those coming from small presses which focus on women's issues, lesbian and gay concerns, socialism, or internationalism), moral and ethical dilemmas are built into mystery and detection, sometimes subordinating the latter. In the best of these novels, readers can find the tensions of generic tradition and changing practice exposed. Frequently, the refusal to resolve them is deliberate.

It would be a mistake to forget that continuity has as strong a position as change in the history of crime and mystery fiction. In this reference guide to some 700 authors, the familiar names remain; many of the new entries are well-known names—Sara Paretsky, Sue Grafton, Tom Clancy, Martha Grimes, Michael Dibdin, Scott Turow, Andrew Vachss, Jeremiah Healy, Thomas Harris—and it is easy to forget how new their careers are. With an average of five well-received books each, series characters, numerous prizes, and growing reputations, they represent the future as well as the present. Their work sends readers back to the models they imitate or reject, and to their contemporaries and successors.

KATHLEEN GREGORY KLEIN

READING LIST

Adams, Donald K., editor, *The Mystery and Detection Annual* (for 1972 and 1973). Beverly Hills, California, Donald Adams, 1972–73.

Adey, Robert C.S., *Locked Rooms and Other Impossible Crimes*. London, Ferret Fantasy, 1979.

Aisenberg, Nadya, *A Common Spring: Crime Novel and Classic*. Bowling Green, Ohio, Popular Press, 1979.

Albert, Walter, *Detective and Mystery Fiction: An International Bibliography of Secondary Sources*. Madison, Indiana, Brownstone, 1984.

Allen, Dick, and David Chacko, editors, *Detective Fiction: Crime and Consequences*. New York, Harcourt Brace, 1974.

Altick, Richard, *Victorian Studies in Scarlet*. New York, Norton, 1970; London, Dent, 1972.

Amis, Kingsley, *What Became of Jane Austen? and Other Questions*. London, Cape, 1970; New York, Harcourt Brace, 1971.

Anderson, Cynthia S., *Western and Hard-Boiled Detective Fiction in America*. London, Macmillan, 1987.

Apostolou, John L., and Martin H. Greenberg, *Japanese Stories of Crime and Detection*. New York, Dembner, 1987.

Atkins, John, *The British Spy Novel: Styles in Treachery*. London, Calder, and New York, Riverrun, 1984.

Bakerman, Jane S., editor, *And Then There Were Nine: More Women of Mystery*. Bowling Green, Ohio, Popular Press, 1984.

Ball, John, editor, *The Mystery Story*. San Diego, University of California Extension, 1976; London, Penguin, 1978.

Bargainnier, Earl F., editor, *Ten Women of Mystery*. Bowling Green, Ohio, Popular Press, 1981.

Bargainnier, Earl F., editor, *Twelve Englishmen of Mystery*. Bowling Green, Ohio, Popular Press, 1984.

Bargainnier, Earl F., *Comic Crime*. Bowling Green, Ohio, Popular Press, 1987.

Barnes, Melvyn, *Best Detective Fiction: A Guide from Godwin to the Present*. London, Clive Bingley, and Hamden, Connecticut, Linnet, 1975.

Barnes, Melvyn, *Murder in Print: A Guide to Two Centuries of Crime Fiction*. Lydeard St. Lawrence, Somerset, Barn Owl, 1986.

Barzun, Jacques, editor, *The Delights of Detection*. New York, Criterion, 1961.

Barzun, Jacques, and Wendell Hertig Taylor, *A Book of Prefaces to Fifty Classics of Crime Fiction 1900–50*. New York, Garland, 1976.

Barzun, Jacques, and Wendell Hertig Taylor, *A Catalogue of Crime*. New York, Harper, 1971.

Becker, Jens Peter, *Der Englische Spionageroman*. Munich, Goldmann, 1973.

Becker, Jens Peter, and Paul G. Buchloh, editors, *Der Detektiverzählung auf der Spur*. Darmstadt, Wissenschaftliche Buchgesellschaft, 1977.

Bell, Ian A., and Graham Daldry, editors, *Watching the Detectives: Essays on Crime Fiction*. London, Macmillan, 1990.

Benstock, Bernard, editor, *Essays on Detective Fiction*. London, Macmillan, 1983; as *Art in Crime Writing*, New York, St. Martin's Press, 1983.

Benstock, Bernard, and Thomas F. Staley, editors, *Dictionary of Literary Biography No. 70: British Mystery Writers 1860–1919*. Detroit, Michigan, Gale, 1988.

Benstock, Bernard, and Thomas F. Staley, editors, *Dictionary of Literary Biography No. 77: British Mystery Writers 1920–39*. Detroit, Michigan, Gale, 1989.

Benstock, Bernard, and Thomas F. Staley, editors, *Dictionary of Literary Biography No. 87: British Mystery and Thriller Writers Since 1940*. Detroit, Michigan, Gale, 1989.

Best Detective Stories of the Year. New York, Dutton, 1945–81; continued as *The Year's Best Mystery and Suspense Stories*, New York, Walker, 1982-84. (Annual volumes have been edited by David C. Cooke, Brett Halliday, Anthony Boucher, Allen J. Hubin, and Edward D. Hoch.)

Binyon, T.J., *Murder Will Out: The Detective in Fiction*. Oxford, Oxford University Press, 1989.

Birkhead, Edith, *The Tale of Terror: A Study of the Gothic Romance*. London, Constable, 1921; New York, Russell, 1963.

Block, Lawrence, *Writing the Novel: From Plot to Print*. Cincinnati, Writer's Digest, 1979.

Bloom, Clive, editor, *Nineteenth-Century Suspense: From Poe to Conan Doyle*. London, Macmillan, and New York, St. Martin's Press, 1988.

Bloom, Clive, editor, *Twentieth-Century Suspense: The Thriller Comes of Age*. London, Macmillan, 1990.

Bloom, Clive, editor, *Spy Thrillers from Buchan to le Carré*. London, Macmillan, 1990.

Boileau-Narcejac, *Le Roman policier*. Paris, Payot, 1964; revised edition, Paris, Presses Universitaires de France, 1982.

Borowitz, Albert, *Innocence and Arsenic: Studies in Crime and Literature*. New York, Harper, 1977.

Bourgeau, Art, *The Mystery Lover's Companion*. New York, Crown, 1986.

Brean, Herbert, editor, *The Mystery Writer's Handbook*. New York, Harper, 1956; revised edition, edited by Lawrence Treat, Cincinnati, Writer's Digest, 1976.

Breen, Jon L., *The Girl in the Pictorial Wrapper: An Index to Reviews of Paperback Original Novels in the New York Times' "Criminals at Large" Column 1953–1970*. Dominguez Hills, California State College Library, 1972; revised edition, 1973.

Breen, Jon L., *What about Murder? A Guide to Books about Mystery and Detective Fiction*. Metuchen, New Jersey, Scarecrow Press, 1981.

Breen, Jon L., *Novel Verdicts: A Critical Guide to Courtroom Fiction*. Metuchen, New Jersey, Scarecrow Press, 1984.

Breen, Jon L., and Martin H. Greenberg, editors, *Murder Off the Rack: Critical Studies of Ten Paperbacks*. Metuchen, New Jersey, Scarecrow Press, 1989.

Briney, R. E., and Francis M. Nevins, Jr., editors, *Multiplying Villainies: Selected Mystery Criticism 1942–1968*, by Anthony Boucher. Boston, Bouchercon, 1973.

Browne, Ray B., *Heroes and Humanities: Detective Fiction and Popular Culture*. Bowling Green, Ohio, Popular Press, 1987.

Buchloh, Paul. G., and Jens Peter Becker, *Der Detektivroman: Studien zur Geschichte und Form der Englischen und Amerikanischen Detektivliteratur*. Darmstadt, Wissenschaftliche Buchgesellschaft, 1973; revised edition, 1978.

Budd, Elaine, *13 Mistresses of Murder*. New York, Ungar, 1986.

Burack, A.S., editor, *Writing Detective and Mystery Fiction*. Boston, The Writer, 1945; revised edition, 1967.

Burack, A.S., editor, *Writing Suspense and Mystery Fiction*. Boston, The Writer, 1977.

Butler, William Vivian, *The Durable Desperadoes*. London, Macmillan, 1973.

Byrnes, Thomas F., *Professional Criminals of America*. New York, Cassell, 1886; revised edition, New York, Dillingham, 1895.

Carr, Helen, editor, *From My Guy to Sci-Fi: Genre and Women's Writing in the Postmodern World*. London, Pandora Press, 1989.

Carr, John C., *The Craft of Crime: Conversations with Crime Writers*. Boston, Houghton Mifflin, 1983.

Carter, John, *Books and Book-Collectors*. London, Hart Davis, 1956; Cleveland, World, 1957.

Carter, John, editor, *New Paths in Book-Collecting*. London, Constable, and New York, Scribner, 1934.

Cawelti, John G., *Adventure, Mystery, and Romance: Formula Stories as Art and Popular Culture*. Chicago, University of Chicago Press, 1976.

Cawelti, John G., and Bruce A. Rosenburg, *The Spy Story*. Chicago, University of Chicago Press, 1987.

Champigny, Robert, *What Will Have Happened: A Philosophical and Technical Essay on Mystery Stories*. Bloomington, Indiana University Press, 1977.

Chandler, Frank Wadleigh, *The Literature of Roguery*. London, Constable, and Boston, Houghton Mifflin, 2 vols., 1907.

Charney, Hanna, *The Detective Novel of Manners: Hedonism, Morality, and the Life of Reason*. Rutherford, New Jersey, Fairleigh Dickinson University Press, and London, Associated University Presses, 1981.

Clark, William J., *An Author Index to Doc Savage Magazine*. Los Angeles, M and B, 1971.

Conquest, John, *Trouble Is Their Business: Private Eyes in Fiction, Film and Television 1927–1988*. New York, Garland, 1990.

Cook, Michael L., *Murder by Mail: Inside the Mystery Book Clubs, with Complete Checklist*. Evansville, Indiana, Cook, 1979.

Cook, Michael L., *Monthly Murders: A Checklist and Chronological Listing of Fiction in the Digest-Size Magazines in the United States and England*. Westport, Connecticut, Greenwood Press, 1982.

Cook, Michael L., editor, *Mystery, Detective, and Espionage Magazines*. Westport, Connecticut, Greenwood Press, 1983.

Cook, Michael L., *Mystery Fanfare: A Composite Annotated Index to Mystery and Related Fanzines 1963–1981*. Bowling Green, Ohio, Popular Press, 1983.

Cook, Michael L., *Dime Novel Roundup: Annotated Index 1931–1981*. Bowling Green, Ohio, Popular Press, 1983.

Cook, Michael L., and Stephen T. Miller, *Mystery, Detective, and Espionage Fiction: A Checklist of Fiction in U.S. Pulp Magazines 1915–1974*. New York, Garland, 2 vols., 1988.

Cooper-Clark, Diana, *Designs of Darkness: Interviews with Detective Novelists*. Bowling Green, Ohio, Popular Press, 1983.

Craig, Patricia, and Mary Cadogan, *The Lady Investigates: Women Detectives and Spies in Fiction*. London, Gollancz, 1981; New York, St. Martin's Press, 1982.

Craig, Patricia, editor, *The Oxford Book of Detective Stories*. Oxford, Oxford University Press, 1990.

Crime Writers Association of Great Britain, anthologies edited by members, since 1953.

Davis, David Brian, *Homicide in American Fiction 1798–1860*. Ithaca, New York, Cornell University Press, 1957.

Denning, Michael, *Cover Stories: Narrative and Ideology in the British Spy Thriller*. London, Routledge, 1987.

Depken, F., *Sherlock Holmes, Raffles, und Ihre Vorbilder*. Heidelberg, Winter, 1914.

De Quincey, Thomas, "On Murder Considered as One of the Fine Arts" (1827), in *The Collected Writings of Thomas De Quincey*, edited by David Masson, vol. 13. London, Black, 1889–90.

de Vries, P.H., *Poe and After: The Detective Story Investigated*. Amsterdam, Bakker, 1956.

Disher, M. Willson, *Melodrama: Plots That Thrilled*. New York, Macmillan, and London, Rockliff, 1954.

Docherty, Brian, editor, *American Crime Fiction: Studies in the Genre*. London, Macmillan, and New York, St. Martin's Press, 1988.

Donaldson, Betty, and Norman Donaldson, *How Did They Die?* New York, St. Martin's Press, 1980.

Dove, George N., *The Police Procedural*. Bowling Green, Ohio, Popular Press, 1982.

Dove, George N., and Earl Bargainnier, editors, *Cops and Constables: American and British Fictional Policemen*. Bowling Green, Ohio, Popular Press, 1986.

Eames, Hugh, *Sleuths, Inc.: Studies of Problem Solvers, Doyle, Simenon, Hammett, Ambler, Chandler*. Philadelphia, Lippincott, 1978.

East, Andy, *The Cold War File*. Metuchen, New Jersey, Scarecrow Press, 1983.

Epstein, H., *Der Detektivroman der Unterschicht*. Frankfurt, Neuer Frankfurter Verlag, 1930.

Everson, William K., *The Detective in Film*. Secaucus, New Jersey, Citadel, 1972.

Fleenor, Juliann, editor, *The Female Gothic*. Montreal, Eden Press, 1983.

Afrikaans from 1951–1971. Johannesburg, University of the Witwatersrand, 1972.

Geherin, David, *The American Private Eye: The Image in Fiction*. New York, Ungar, 1984.

Geherin, David, *Sons of Sam Spade: The Private-Eye Novel in the 70's*. New York, Ungar, 1980.

Gilbert, Elliot L., editor, *The World of Mystery Fiction*. San Diego, University of California Extension, 1978.

Gilbert, Michael, editor, *Crime in Good Company: Essays on Criminals and Crime-Writing*. London, Constable, 1959.

Glover, Dorothy, and Graham Greene, *Victorian Detective Fiction: A Catalogue*. London, Bodley Head, 1966.

Goulart, Ron, *Cheap Thrills: An Informal History of the Pulp Magazines*. New Rochelle, New York, Arlington House, 1972.

Goulart, Ron, *The Dime Detectives*. New York, Mysterious Press, 1988.

Goulart, Ron, editor, *The Hardboiled Dicks: An Anthology and Study of Pulp Detective Fiction*. Los Angeles, Sherbourne Press, 1965; London, Boardman, 1967.

Graves, Robert, and Alan Hodge, *The Long Week-end*. London, Faber, 1940; New York, Macmillan, 1941.

Jen Green, editor, *Reader, I Murdered Him*. London, Women's Press, 1989.

Greene, Graham, and Hugh Greene, editors, *The Spy's Bedside Book*. London, Hart Davis, 1957.

Greene, Hugh, editor, *The American Rivals of Sherlock Holmes*. London, Bodley Head, and New York, Pantheon, 1976.

Greene, Hugh, editor, *The Crooked Counties*. London, Bodley Head, 1973; as *The Further Rivals of Sherlock Holmes*, New York, Pantheon, 1973.

Greene, Hugh, editor, *More Rivals of Sherlock Holmes: Cosmopolitan Crimes*. London, Bodley Head, 1971; as *Cosmopolitan Crimes: Foreign Rivals of Sherlock Holmes*, New York, Pantheon, 1971.

Greene, Hugh, editor, *The Rivals of Sherlock Holmes*. London, Bodley Head, and New York, Pantheon, 1970.

Gribbon, Lenore S., *Who's Whodunit: A List of 3218 Detective Story Writers and Their 1100 Pseudonyms*. Chapel Hill, University of North Carolina Library, 1968.

Grossvogel, David, I., *Mystery and Its Fictions: From Oedipus to Agatha Christie*. Baltimore, Johns Hopkins University Press, 1979.

Gruber, Frank, *The Pulp Jungle*. Los Angeles, Sherbourne Press, 1967.

Hackett, Alice Payne, and James Henry Burke, *80 Years of Best Sellers 1895–1975*. New York, Bowker, 1977.

Hagemann, E.R., *A Comprehensive Index to Black Mask 1920–1951*. Bowling Green, Ohio, Popular Press, 1982.

Hagen, Ordean, *Who Done It? A Guide to Detective, Mystery, and Suspense Fiction*. New York, Bowker, 1969.

Haining, Peter, editor, *The Fantastic Pulps*. London, Gollancz, and New York, St. Martin's Press, 1975.

Haining, Peter, *Mystery! An Illustrated History of Crime and Detective Fiction*. London, Souvenir Press, 1977; New York, Stein and Day, 1982.

Haining, Peter, *The Penny Dreadful*. London, Gollancz, 1975.

Hall, Stuart, and Paddy Whannel, *The Popular Arts*. London, Hutchinson, 1964; New York, Pantheon, 1965.

Hamilton, Cynthia, *Western and Hard-Boiled Detective Fiction in America: From High Noon to Midnight*. Iowa City, University of Iowa Press, and London, Macmillan, 1987.

the Detective Story. New York, Appleton Century, 1941; London, Davis, 1942; revised edition, New York, Biblo and Tannen, 1968.

Haycraft, Howard, editor, *The Art of the Mystery Story: A Collection of Critical Essays*. New York, Simon and Schuster, 1946.

Hedman-Morelius, Iwan, *Deckare och Thrillers pa Svenska, 1864–1973*. Strangäs, Sweden, DAST, 1974.

Henderson, Lesley, editor, *Twentieth-Century Romance and Historical Writers*. London and Chicago, St. James Press, 1990.

Herman, Linda, and Beth Stiel, *Corpus Delicti of Mystery Fiction: A Guide to the Body of the Case*. Metuchen, New Jersey, Scarecrow Press, 1974.

Hersey, Harold Brainerd, *Pulpwood Editor: The Fabulous World of the Thriller Magazines Revealed by a Veteran Editor and Publisher*. New York, Stokes, 1937.

Highsmith, Patricia, *Plotting and Writing Suspense Fiction*. Boston, The Writer, 1966; London, Poplar Press, 1983.

Hinckley, Karen, and Barbara Hinckley, *American Best Sellers: A Reader's Guide to Popular Fiction*. Bloomington, Indiana University Press, 1989.

Hirsch, Foster, *The Dark Side of the Screen: Film Noir*. New York, Da Capo Press, 1983.

Hogarth, Basil, *Writing Thrillers for Profit: A Practical Guide*. London, A. & C. Black, 1936.

Hoppenstand, Gary, and Ray B. Browne, *The Defective Detective in the Pulps*. Bowling Green, Ohio, Popular Press, 1983.

Hoppenstand, Gary, editor, *The Dime Novel Detective*. Bowling Green, Ohio, Popular Press, 1983.

Hoppenstand, Gary, *In Search of the Paper Tiger: A Sociological Perspective of Myth, Formula and the Mystery Genre in the Entertainment Print Mass Medium*. Bowling Green, Ohio, Popular Press, 1987.

Hoveyda, Fereydoren, *Histoire du Roman Policier*. Paris, Pavillon, 1955.

Hubin, Allen, J., *The Bibliography of Crime Fiction 1749–1975*. San Diego, University of California Extension, 1979; revised edition, as *Crime Fiction 1749–1980: A Comprehensive Bibliography*, New York, Garland, 1984.

Hubin, Allen J., *1981–1985 Supplement to Crime Fiction, 1749–1980*. New York, Garland, 1988.

Inge, M. Thomas, editor, *Handbook of American Popular Culture 1* (includes "Guide to Detective Fiction" by Larry N. Landrum). Westport, Connecticut, Greenwood Press, 1979.

Ivy, Randolph, *The Victorian Sensation Novel* (unpublished dissertation). Chicago, University of Chicago, 1974.

Johannsen, Albert, *The House of Beadle and Adams and Its Dime and Nickel Novels*. Norman, University of Oklahoma Press, 3 vols., 1950.

Johnson, Timothy W., and Julia Johnson, editors, *Crime Fiction Criticism: An Annotated Bibliography*. New York, Garland, 1981.

Jones, Robert Kenneth, *The Shudder Pulps: A History of the Weird Menace Magazines of the 1930's*. West Linn, Oregon, FAX, 1975.

Jute, André, *Writing a Thriller*. London, A. & C. Black, 1986; New York, St. Martin's Press, 1987.

Keating, H.R.F., *Murder Must Appetize*. London, Lemon Tree Press, 1975; New York, Mysterious Press, 1981.

Keating, H.R.F., editor, *Crime Writers: Reflections on Crime Fiction*. London, BBC Publications, 1978.

Keating, H.R.F., editor, *Whodunit? A Guide to Crime, Suspense, and Spy Fiction*. London, Winward, and New York, Van Nostrand, 1982.

Keating, H.R.F., *Writing Crime Fiction*. London, A. & C. Black, 1986; New York, St. Martin's Press, 1987.

Keating, H.R.F., *Crime and Mystery: The 100 Best Books*. London, Xanadu, and New York, Carroll and Graf, 1987.

Keating, H.R.F., *The Bedside Companion to Crime*. London, O'Mara, 1989; New York, Mysterious Press, 1990.

Klein, Kathleen Gregory, *The Woman Detective: Gender and Genre*. Champaign, Illinois University Press, 1988.

Knight, Stephen, *Form and Ideology in Crime Fiction*. London, Macmillan, and Bloomington, Indiana University Press, 1980.

Knox, Ronald A., and Henry Harrington, editors, *The Best Detective Stories of the Year 1928*. London, Faber, 1929; as *The Best English Detective Stories of 1928*, New York, Liveright, 1929.

Knox, Ronald A., *Literary Distractions*. London and New York, Sheed and Ward, 1958.

Knudson, Richard L., *The Whole Spy Catalogue: An Espionage Lover's Guide*. New York, St. Martin's Press, 1986.

Koontz, Dean R., *How to Write Best-Selling Fiction*. Cincinnati, Writer's Digest, and London, Poplar Press, 1981.

Koontz, Dean R., *Writing Popular Fiction*. Cincinnati, Writer's Digest, 1973.

Kramer, John E., Jr., and John E. Kramer, III, *College Mystery Novels: An Annotated Guide to Professional Series Character Sleuths*. New York, Garland, 1983.

Lacassin, Francis, *Mythologie du Roman Policier*. Paris, Union Générale d'Editions, 2 vols., 1974.

LaCombe, Alain, *Le Roman Noir Américain*. Paris, 10/18, 1975.

la Cour, Tage, and Harald Mogensen, *The Murder Book: An Illustrated History of the Detective Story*. London, Allen and Unwin, and New York, Herder, 1971.

Lambert, Gavin, *The Dangerous Edge*. London, Barrie and Jenkins, 1975; New York, Grossman, 1976.

Landrum, Larry N., Pat Browne, and Ray B. Browne, editors, *Dimensions of Detective Fiction*. Bowling Green, Ohio, Popular Press, 1976.

Larmoth, Jeanine, *Murder on the Menu*. New York, Scribner, 1972.

Leavis, Q.D., *Fiction and the Reading Public*. London, Chatto and Windus, 1932; New York, Russell, 1965.

Leham, David, *The Perfect Murder: A Study in Detection*. New York, Free Press, 1989.

Lindsay, Ethel, *Here Be Mystery and Murder*. Privately printed, 1983.

Lins, Álvaro, *No Mundo do Romance Policial*. Rio de Janeiro, Ministério do Educacão, 1953.

Lofts, W.O.G., and Derek Adley, *The Men Behind Boys' Fiction*. London, Baker, 1970.

Lundin, Bo, *Svenska Deckere/The Swedish Crime Story*. Uppsala, Tidskriften Jury, 1981.

Madden, David, editor, *Tough Guy Writers of the Thirties*. Carbondale, Southern Illinois University Press, 1968.

Mandell, Ernest, *Delightful Murder: A Social History of the Crime Story*. London, Pluto Press, 1984; Minneapolis, University of Minnesota Press, 1985.

Mann, Jessica, *Deadlier Than the Male: An Investigation into Feminine Crime Writing*. Newton Abbot, Devon, David and Charles, and New York, Macmillan, 1981.

Margolies, Edward, *Which Way Did He Go? The Private Eye in Dashiell Hammett, Raymond Chandler, Chester Himes, and Ross Macdonald*. New York, Holmes and Meier, 1982.

Marsch, Edgar, *Die Kriminalerzählung: Theorie, Geschichte, Analyse*. Munich, Winkler, 1972.

Martienssen, Anthony, *Crime and the Police*. London, Secker and Warburg, 1951.

Mason, Bobbie Anne, *The Girl Sleuth: A Feminist Guide*. Old Westbury, New York, Feminist Press, 1975.

McCleary, G.F., *On Detective Fiction and Other Things*. London, Hollis and Carter, 1960.

McCormick, Donald, *Who's Who in Spy Fiction*. London, Elm Tree, and New York, Taplinger, 1977.

McSherry, Frank D., Jr., *Studies in Scarlet: Essays on Murder and Detective Fiction*. San Bernardino, California, Borgo Press, 1985.

Meet the Detective (broadcasts by 10 authors). London, Allen and Unwin and New York, Telegraph Press, 1935.

Melling, John Kennedy, editor, *The Crime Writer's Practical Handbook of Technical Information*. Bath, Avon, Crime Writers Association, 1989.

Menendez, Albert J., *The Subject Is Murder: A Selective Guide to Mystery Fiction*. New York, Garland, 1986.

Merry, Bruce, *Anatomy of the Spy Thriller*. Dublin, Gill and Macmillan, 1977.

Messac, Regis, *Le "Detective Novel" et L'Influence de la Pensée Scientifique*. Paris, Champion, 1929.

Meyers, Richard, *TV Detectives*. San Diego, A.S. Barnes, and London, Tantivy Press, 1982.

Mooney, Joan M., "Best-Selling American Detective Fiction," in *Armchair Detective* (White Bear Lake, Minnesota), 9 issues, January 1970–1973.

Morland, Nigel, *How to Write Detective Novels*. London, Allen and Unwin, 1936.

Morland, Nigel, *Who's Who in Crime Fiction*. London, Elm Tree, 1980.

Most, Glenn W., and William W. Stowe, editors, *The Poetics of Murder: Detective Fiction and Literary Theory*. New York, Harcourt Brace, 1983.

Mott, Frank Luther, *Golden Multitudes: The Story of Best Sellers in the United States*. New York, Macmillan, 1947.

Mundell, E.H., and G. Jay Rausch, *The Detective Short Story: A Bibliography and Index*. Manhattan, Kansas State University Library, 1974.

Murch, A.E., *The Development of the Detective Novel*. London, Peter Owen, and New York, Philosophical Library, 1958.

Murder Manual: A Handbook for Mystery Story Writers. East San Diego, Wight House, 1936.

Mussell, Kay J., *Women's Gothic and Romantic Fiction: A Reference Guide*. Westport, Connecticut, Greenwood Press, 1981.

Mystery Writers of America, Annual Short Story Collections, edited by members since 1946.

Narcejac, Thomas, *Une Machine à Lire: Le Roman Policier*. Paris, Denoël Gonthier, 1975.

Nevins, Francis M., Jr., editor, *The Mystery Writer's Art*. Bowling Green, Ohio, Popular Press, 1971.

Nichols, Victoria, and Susan Thompson, *Silk Stalkings: When Women Write of Murder: A Survey of Series Characters Created by Women Authors in Crime and Mystery Fiction*. Berkeley, California, Black Lizard, 1988.

Nieminski, John, *EQMM350: An Author/Title Index to Ellery Queen's Mystery Magazine, Fall 1941 through January 1973*. White Bear Lake, Minnesota, Armchair Detective Press, 1974.

Nieminski, John, *The Saint Magazine Index: Authors and Titles Spring 1953–October 1967*. Evansville, Indiana, Cook and McDowell, 1980.

Nixon, Joan Lowery, *Writing Mysteries for Young People*. Boston, The Writer, 1977.

Noel, Mary, *Villains Galore: The Heyday of the Popular Story Weekly*. New York, Macmillan, 1954.

Nye, Russel B., *The Unembarrassed Muse: The Popular Arts in America*. New York, Dial Press, 1970.

O'Brien, Geoffrey, *Hardboiled America: The Lurid Years of Paperbacks*. New York, Van Nostrand, 1981.

Odell, Robin, *Jack the Ripper in Fact and Fiction*. London, Harrap, 1965.

Olderr, Steven, *Mystery Index: Subjects, Settings, and Sleuths of 10,000 Titles*. Chicago, American Library Association, 1987.

Oleskiw, Susan, *A Reader's Guide to the Classic British Mystery*. Boston, G.K. Hall, 1988; London, Blanford Press, 1989.

The 100 Best Crime Stories. London, Sunday Times, 1959.

Ousby, Ian, *Bloodhounds of Heaven: The Detective in English Fiction from Godwin to Doyle*. Cambridge, Massachusetts, Harvard University Press, 1976.

Overton, Grant, *Cargoes for Crusoes*. New York, Appleton, 1924.

Palmer, Jerry, *Thrillers: Genesis and Structure of a Popular Genre*. London, Arnold, and New York, St. Martin's Press, 1979.

Panek, LeRoy Lad, *Watteau's Shepherds: The Detective Novel in Britain 1914–1940*. Bowling Green, Ohio, Popular Press, 1979.

Panek, LeRoy Lad, *The Special Branch: The British Spy Novel 1890–1980*. Bowling Green, Ohio, Popular Press, 1981.

Panek, LeRoy Lad, *An Introduction to the Detective Story*. Bowling Green, Popular Press, 1987.

Parish, James Robert, and Michael R. Pitts, *The Great Spy Pictures*. Metuchen, New Jersey, Scarecrow Press, 1974.

Pate, Janet, *The Black Book of Villains*. Newton Abbot, Devon, David and Charles, 1975.

Pate, Janet, *The Book of Sleuths*. London, New English Library, and Chicago, Contemporary, 1977.

Pearson, Edmund, *Dime Novels; or, Following an Old Trail in Popular Literature*. Boston, Little Brown, 1929.

Penzler, Otto, *The Private Lives of Private Eyes, Spies, Crime Fighters, and Other Good Guys*. New York, Grosset and Dunlap, 1977.

Penzler, Otto, editor, *The Great Detectives*. Boston, Little Brown, 1978.

Peterson, Audrey, *Victorian Masters of Mystery*. New York, Ungar, 1983.

Phillips, Walter C., *Dickens, Reade, and Collins: Sensation Novelists*. New York, Columbia University Press, 1919.

Pike, B.A., and John Cooper, *Detective Fiction: The Collector's Guide*. Lydeard St. Lawrence, Somerset, Barn Owl, 1988.

Pitts, Michael R., *Famous Movie Detectives*. Metuchen, New Jersey, Scarecrow Press, 1979.

Porter, Dennis, *The Pursuit of Crime: Art and Ideology in Detective Fiction*. New Haven, Connecticut, Yale University Press, 1981.

Prager, Arthur, *Rascals at Large; or, The Clue in the Old Nostalgia*. New York, Doubleday, 1971.

Pronzini, Bill, *Gun in Cheek*. New York, Coward McCann, 1982.

Quayle, Eric, *The Collector's Book of Detective Fiction*. London, Studio Vista, 1972.

Queen, Ellery, *The Detective Short Story: A Bibliography*. Boston, Little Brown, 1942.

Queen, Ellery, *In the Queen's Parlor and Other Leaves from the Editors' Notebook*. New York, Simon and Schuster, and London, Gollancz, 1957.

Queen, Ellery, *Queen's Quorum: A History of the Detective-Crime Short Story as Revealed by the 106 Most Important Books Published in This Field since 1845*. Boston, Little Brown, 1951; London, Gollancz, 1953; revised edition, New York, Biblo and Tannen, 1969.

Radcliffe, Elsa J., *Gothic Novels of the Twentieth Century: An Annotated Bibliography*. Metuchen, New Jersey, Scarecrow Press, 1979.

Rader, Barbara A., and Howard G. Zettler, editors, *The Sleuth and the Scholar: Origins, Evolution and Current Trends in Detective Fiction*. Westport, Connecticut, Greenwood Press, 1988.

Randall, David A., editor, *The First Hundred Years of Detective Fiction, 1841–1941*. Bloomington, Indiana University Lilly Library, 1973.

Reddy, Maureen T., *Sisters in Crime: Feminism and the Crime Novel*. New York, Continuum, 1988.

Reinert, Claus, *Das Unheimliche und die Detektivliteratur: Entwurfe, Poetolog*. Bonn, Bouvier, 1973.

Reynolds, Quentin, *The Fiction Factory; or, From Pulp Row to Quality Street: The Story of 100 Years of Publishing at Street and Smith*. New York, Random House, 1955.

Richardson, Maurice, editor, *Novels of Mystery from the Victorian Age*. London, Pilot Press, and New York, Duell, 1946.

Rodell, Marie, *Mystery Fiction: Theory and Technique*. New York, Duell, 1943; revised edition, New York, Hermitage House, 1952; London, Hammond, 1954.

Routley, Erik, *The Puritan Pleasures of the Detective Story: A Personal Monograph*. London, Gollancz, 1972.

Ruehlmann, William, *Saint with a Gun: The Unlawful American Private Eye*. New York, New York University Press, 1974.

Ruhm, Herbert, editor, *The Hard-Boiled Detective: Stories from Black Mask Magazine, 1920–1951*. New York, Vintage, 1977; London, Coronet, 1979.

Sandoe, James, *The Hard-Boiled Dick: A Personal Checklist*. Chicago, Arthur Lovell, 1952.

Sandoe, James, editor, *Murder: Plain and Fanciful, with Some Milder Malefactions*. New York, Sheridan House, 1948.

Sauerberg, Lars Ole, *Secret Agents in Fiction: Ian Fleming, John le Carré, and Len Deighton*. London, Macmillan, 1984; New York, St. Martin's Press, 1985.

Sayers, Dorothy L., editor, *Great Short Stories of Detection, Mystery and Horror*. London, Gollancz, 3 vols., 1928–34; as *The Omnibus of Crime*, New York, Payson and Clarke, 1929; *Second* and *Third Omnibus*, New York, Coward McCann, 1932–35.

Sayers, Dorothy L., editor, *Tales of Detection*. London, Dent, 1936.

Sayers, Dorothy L., *Unpopular Opinions*. London, Gollancz, 1946; New York, Harcourt Brace, 1947.

Schönhaar, Rainer, *Novelle und Kriminalschema: Ein Struktur-modell Deutscher Erzahlkunst um 1800*. Berlin, Gehlen, 1969.

Schreuders, Piet, *Paperbacks USA*. San Diego, Blue Dolphin, 1982.

Schwartz, Saul, *The Detective Story: An Introduction to the Whodunit*. Skokie, Illinois, National Textbook Company, 1976.

Scott, Sutherland, *Blood in Their Ink: The March of the Modern Mystery Novel*. London, Stanley Paul, 1953.

Scribner's Detective Fiction: A Collection of First and a Few Early Editions. New York, Scribner, 1934.

Semple, Linda, *A Suitable Job for a Woman: Women Mystery Writers*. London, Pandora Press, 1990.

Shaw, Joseph T., editor, *The Hardboiled Omnibus: Early Stories from Black Mask*. New York, Simon and Schuster, 1946.

Skene Melvin, David, and Ann Skene Melvin, editors, *Crime, Detective, Espionage, Mystery, and Thriller Fiction and Film: A Comprehensive Bibliography of Critical Writing Through 1979.* Westport, Connecticut, Greenwood Press, 1980.

Skinner, Robert E., *The Hard-Boiled Explicator: A Guide to the Study of Dashiell Hammett, Raymond Chandler and Ross Macdonald.* Metuchen, New Jersey, Scarecrow Press, 1985.

Skinner, Robert E., *The New Hard-Boiled Dicks: A Personal Checklist.* San Bernardino, California, Borgo Press, 1987.

Slung, Michele, editor, *Crime on Her Mind: Fifteen Stories of Female Sleuths from the Victorian Era to the Forties.* New York, Pantheon, 1975; London, Joseph, 1976.

Smith, Curtis C., editor, *Twentieth-Century Science-Fiction Writers,* London, Macmillan, and New York, St. Martin's Press, 1981.

Smith, Myron J., Jr., *Cloak-and-Dagger Bibliography: An Annotated Guide to Spy Fiction 1937–1975.* Metuchen, New Jersey, Scarecrow Press, 1976; revised edition, as *Cloak and Dagger Fiction: An Annotated Guide to Spy Thrillers,* Santa Barbara, California, and Oxford, ABC-CLIO, 1982.

Solmes, Alwyn, *The English Policeman 1871–1935.* London, Allen and Unwin, 1935.

Spencer, William David, *Mysterium and Mystery: The Clerical Crime Novel.* Ann Arbor, Michigan, UMI Research, 1989.

Steinbrunner, Chris, and others, *Detectionary: A Bibliographical Dictionary of the Leading Characters in Detective and Mystery Fiction.* Lock Haven, Pennsylvania, Hammerhill Paper, 1971; revised edition, New York, Overlook Press, 1977.

Steinbrunner, Chris, and Otto Penzler, *Encyclopedia of Mystery and Detection.* New York, McGraw Hill, and London, Routledge, 1976.

Stevenson, W.B., *Detective Fiction.* Cambridge, Cambridge University Press, 1958.

Stewart, A.W., *Alias J.J. Connington.* London, Hollis and Carter, 1947.

Stewart, R. F., *. . . and Always a Detective: Chapters on the History of Detective Fiction.* Newton Abbot, Devon, David and Charles, 1980.

Stilwell, Steven, A., *The Armchair Detective Index (Volumes 1–10) 1967-1977.* New York, Armchair Detective, 1979.

Symons, Julian, *Bloody Murder.* London, Faber, 1972; as *Mortal Consequences,* New York, Harper, 1972; revised edition, as *Bloody Murder,* London, Penguin, and New York, Viking 1985.

Symons, Julian, *Critical Observations.* London, Faber, and New Haven, Connecticut, Ticknor and Fields, 1981.

Symons, Julian, *Critical Occasions.* London, Hamish Hamilton, 1966.

Symons, Julian, *The Detective Story in Britain.* London, Longman, 1962.

Symons, Julian, *The Modern Crime Story.* Edinburgh, Tragara Press, 1980.

Talburt, Nancy Ellen, and Lyna Lee Montgomery, editors, *A Mystery Reader.* New York Scribner, 1975.

Thomas, Gilbert, *How to Enjoy Detective Fiction.* London, Rockliff, 1947.

Thomson, H. Douglas, *Masters of Mystery: A Study of the Detective Story.* London, Collins, 1931.

Turner, Robert, *Some of My Best Friends Are Writers, But I Wouldn't Want My Daughter to Marry One.* Los Angeles, Sherbourne Press, 1970.

Tuska, Jon, *The Detective in Hollywood.* New York, Doubleday, 1978.

Tymn, Marshall B., editor, *Horror Literature: A Core Collection and Reference Guide.* New York, Bowker, 1981.

Usborne, Richard, *Clubland Heroes: A Nostalgic Study of Some Recurrent Characters in the Romantic Fiction of Dornford Yates, John Buchan and Sapper.* London, Constable, 1953; revised edition, London, Barrie and Jenkins, 1975.

Van Dover, J.K., *Murder in the Millions: Erle Stanley Gardner, Mickey Spillane, Ian Fleming.* New York, Ungar, 1984.

Vinson, James, and D.L. Kirkpatrick, editors, *Twentieth-Century Western Writers.* London, Macmillan, and Detroit, Gale, 1983.

Vogt, Jochen, editor, *Der Kriminalroman: Zur Theorie und Geschichte einer Galtung.* Munich, Fink, 2 vols., 1971.

Watson, Colin, *Snobbery with Violence: Crime Stories and Their Audience.* London, Eyre and Spottiswoode, 1971; New York, St. Martin's Press, 1972; revised edition, London, Eyre Methuen, 1979.

Wells, Carolyn, *The Technique of the Mystery Story.* Springfield, Massachusetts, Home Correspondence School, 1913; revised edition, 1929.

Wilson, Edmund, *A Literary Chronicle 1920–1950.* New York, Doubleday, 1956.

Winks, Robin W., editor, *Detective Fiction: A Collection of Critical Essays.* Englewood Cliffs, New Jersey, Prentice Hall, 1980.

Winks, Robin W., editor, *The Historian as Detective: Essays on Evidence.* New York, Harper, 1969.

Winks, Robin W., *Modus Operandi: An Excursion into Detective Fiction.* Boston, Godine, 1982.

Winks, Robin W., editor, *Colloquium on Crime: Eleven Renowned Mystery Writers Discuss Their Work.* New York, Scribner, 1986.

Winn, Dilys, editor, *Murder Ink: The Mystery Reader's Companion.* New York, Workman, 1977; Newton Abbott, Devon, Westbridge, 1978; revised edition, Workman, 1984, London, Souvenir Press, 1985.

Winn, Dilys, editor, *Murderess Ink: The Better Half of the Mystery.* New York, Workman, 1979.

Woeller, Waltraud, and Bruce Cassiday, *The Literature of Crime and Detection: An Illustrated History from Antiquity to the Present.* New York, Ungar, 1988.

Wölcken, Fritz, *Der Literaiesche Mord: Eine Untersuchung über die English und Amerikanische Detektivliteratur.* Nuremberg, Nest Verlag, 1953.

Wright, Willard Huntington, editor, *The Great Detective Stories: A Chronological Anthology.* New York, Scribner, 1927.

Wrong, E.M., editor, *Crime and Detection.* London and New York, Oxford University Press, 1926.

Yates, Donald A., editor, *Antologia del Cuento Policial Hispanoamericano.* Mexico City, Ediciones de Andrea, 1964.

Yates, Donald A., editor and translator, *Latin Blood: The Best Crime and Detective Stories of Spanish America.* New York, Herder, 1972.

EDITOR'S NOTE

The selection of writers included in this book is based upon the recommendations of the advisers listed on page xxi.

The main part of the book covers English-language writers of crime and mystery fiction whose work appeared during or since the time of Sir Arthur Conan Doyle. Appendices include selective representations of authors preceding Doyle and foreign-language writers whose books have a large audience in English translation.

The entry for each writer in the main part of the book consists of a biography, a bibliography, and a signed critical essay. Living authors were invited to add a comment on their work. The bibliographies list writings according to the categories of crime fiction and other publications. In addition, crime writing is further sub-divided into lists of works published under pseudonyms. Series characters are indicated for novels and short story collections. Original British and United States editions of all books have been listed; other editions are listed only if they are the first editions. As a rule all uncollected crime short stories published since the entrant's last collection have been listed; exceptions occur when a writer's reputation is based largely on short stories; in those cases where a story has been published in a magazine and later in an anthology, we have tended to list the anthology.

Entries include notations of available bibliographies, manuscript collections, and book-length critical studies. Other critical materials appear in the Reading List of secondary works on the genre.

We would like to thank the entrants and contributors for their patience and cooperation in helping us compile this book.

ADVISERS

Walter Albert
Jane S. Bakerman
John Ball
Melvyn Barnes
Ian A. Bell
Manfred A. Bertram
T.J. Binyon
E.F. Bleiler
Jon L. Breen
Jan Broberg
John G. Cawelti
Michael Collins
Kathy B. Daniel
George N. Dove
David Geherin
Jen Green
George Grella
L.T. Hergenhan
Edward D. Hoch

C. Hugh Holman
Allen J. Hubin
Maxim Jakubowski
A. Norman Jeffares
H.R.F. Keating
H.M. Klein
Kathleen Gregory Klein
William Malloy
Marcia Muller
Francis M. Nevins, Jr.
Susan Oleskiw
Robert B. Parker
Otto Penzler
Bill Pronzini
Janet A. Rudolph
Linda Semple
Michele Slung
Ralph Spurrier
Donald A. Yates

CONTRIBUTORS

Robert C.S. Adey
Jack Adrian
Walter Albert
Martha Alderson
Pearl G. Aldrich
Kenneth D. Alley
John L. Apostolou
Arthur Nicholas Athanason
Newton Baird
Susan Baker
Jane S. Bakerman
John Ball
Jeff Banks
Robert Barnard
Melvyn Barnes
Carol Barry
Jacques Baudou
Jens Peter Becker
Mary Helen Becker
Jeanne F. Bedell
Ian A. Bell
Carol Ann Bergmann
E.F. Bleiler
Ellen H. Bleiler
Helga Borck
David A. Bowman
Jon L. Breen
R.E. Briney
Jan Broberg
Richard Brown
Frank Campenni
Peter Caracciolo
Richard C. Carpenter
Dale Carter
Steven Carter
Donna Casella-Kern

Neysa Chouteau
Carol Cleveland
Don Cole
Max Allan Collins
Michael Collins
J. Randolph Cox
Patricia Craig
Bill Crider
GraceAnne A. DeCandido
Mary Jean DeMarr
Frank Denton
Betty Donaldson
Norman Donaldson
George N. Dove
Bernard A. Drew
Fred Dueren
Elizabeth F. Duke
Wayne D. Dundee
Andy East
Martin Edwards
Jeanne Carter Emmons
Elizabeth Evans
Sue Feder
Karl G. Fredriksson
Lilian Fredriksson
Larry L. French
David Geherin
Curtis S. Gibson
Elliot L. Gilbert
James Gindin
Greg Goode
Ed Gorman
Jane Gottschalk
George Grella
Larry E. Grimes
Mary Ann Grochowski

Mary Groff
E.R. Hagemann
Carol M. Harper
Herbert Harris
John Harwood
Barrie Hayne
Joanne Harack Hayne
Reginald Hill
Barbara Hinckley
Karen Hinckley
Edward D. Hoch
Naomi Hoida
C. Hugh Holman
Jim Huang
Dorothy B. Hughes
Donald C. Ireland
Maxim Jakubowski
Trevor James
A. Norman Jeffares
David K. Jeffrey
Nancy C. Joyner
Roz Kaveney
H.R.F. Keating
George Kelley
R. Gordon Kelly
Burton Kendle
Daniel P. King
Margaret J. King
H.M. Klein
Kathleen Gregory Klein
Rex E. Klett
Marvin Lachman
Larry N. Landrum
Richard G. La Porte
Margaret B. Lewis
Peter Lewis
Shelley Lowenkopf
Bo Lundin
Andrew Macdonald
Gina Macdonald
Kathleen L. Maio
William Malloy
Ann Massa
James R. McCahery
Frances D. McConachie
Ian McMechan
Frank D. McSherry, Jr.
Robert H. Meier
John Kennedy Melling
Stephen Mertz
Jeffrey Meyerson
D.A. Miller
Roda M. Morrison
Marcia Muller
Will Murray
Kay Mussell

John M. Muste
Ellen A. Nehr
Francis M. Nevins. Jr.
Frank Occhiogrosso
Susan Oleskiw
Ian Ousby
Robert B. Parker
Donald J. Pattow
Michael Pettengell
B.A. Pike
Philip Plowden
Bill Pronzini
Elmer Pry
Lyn Pykett
L.M. Quinn
Katherine M. Restaino
Judith Rhodes
Gillian Rodgerson
Trevor Royle
Seymour Rudin
Janet A. Rudolph
Sharon A. Russell
Joan M. Saliskas
Art Scott
Linda Semple
Charles Shibuk
Robert E. Skinner
Michele Slung
Christopher Smith
Dan Smith
Penny Smith
John Snyder
Ralph Spurrier
Katherine Staples
Jane W. Stedman
T.R. Steiner
Carol Simpson Stern
Steven A. Stilwell
Nancy Ellen Talburt
Anna-Marie Taylor
George J. Thompson
June Thomson
Guy M. Townsend
James L. Traylor
J.K. Van Dover
Donald C. Wall
Marilyn Wallace
Carol Washburne
William Weaver
John A. Weigel
John S. Whitley
John Williams
Neville W. Wood
George Woodcock
Donald A. Yates

TWENTIETH-CENTURY
CRIME AND MYSTERY
WRITERS

Edward S. Aarons
Cleve F. Adams
Harold Adams
Herbert Adams
Joan Aiken
Catherine Aird
Marvin Albert
Martha Albrand
David Alexander
Ted Allbeury
Michael Allegretto
Margery Allingham
Eric Ambler
Delano Ames
Frederick Irving Anderson
James Anderson
Evelyn Anthony
Peter Antony
William Ard
Tom Ardies
Charlotte Armstrong
Isaac Asimov
Philip Atlee
Pierre Audemars
Paul Auster
Michael Avallone

Marian Babson
Desmond Bagley
H.C. Bailey
John Ball
Willis Todhunter Ballard
Bill S. Ballinger
Edwin Balmer and William MacHarg
William Bankier
John Franklin Bardin
Robert Barnard
Linda Barnes
Robert Barr
Richard Barth
George Baxt
K.K. Beck
Francis Beeding
Noel Behn
Josephine Bell
George Bellairs
Robert Leslie Bellem
Margot Bennett
Ben Benson
E.C. Bentley
Evelyn Berckman
Anthony Berkeley
Earl Derr Biggers
John Bingham
Gavin Black
Lionel Black
John Blackburn
Charity Blackstock
Algernon Blackwood
Nicholas Blake
Robert Bloch
Lawrence G. Blochman
Lawrence Block
John and Emery Bonett
J.S. Borthwick
Anthony Boucher
Edgar Box

Rick Boyer
Leigh Brackett
Ernest Bramah
Pamela Branch
Christianna Brand
H.C. Branson
Lilian Jackson Braun
Herbert Brean
Jon L. Breen
Simon Brett
Gil Brewer
William Brittain
Carter Brown
Fredric Brown
Gerald A. Browne
Howard Browne
Leo Bruce
Eric Bruton
John Buchan
William F. Buckley, Jr.
James Lee Burke
John Burke
Thomas Burke
W.J. Burley
W.R. Burnett
Rex Burns
Roger Busby
Christopher Bush
Gwendoline Butler
Max Byrd

Alan Caillou
James M. Cain
Paul Cain
Robert Campbell
Joanna Cannan
Victor Canning
Harry Carmichael
Carol Carnac
Glyn Carr
John Dickson Carr
Vera Caspary
Sarah Caudwell
Henry Cecil
Peter Chambers
John Newton Chance
Raymond Chandler
Leslie Charteris
Jerome Charyn
James Hadley Chase
Thomas Chastain
George C. Chesbro
G.K. Chesterton
Peter Cheyney
Erskine Childers
Agatha Christie
Tom Clancy
Douglas Clark
Mary Higgins Clark
Anna Clarke
Clyde B. Clason
Jon Cleary
Brian Cleeve
Ann Cleeves
Francis Clifford
V.C. Clinton-Baddeley
Andrew Coburn

Liza Cody
Anthea Cohen
Octavus Roy Cohen
G.D.H. and Margaret Cole
Manning Coles
John Collier
Max Allan Collins
Michael Collins
Richard Condon
J.J. Connington
K.C. Constantine
Brian Cooper
Basil Copper
Peter Corris
Desmond Cory
Stephen Coulter
S.H. Courtier
William R. Cox
George Harmon Coxe
Jonathan Craig
Frances Crane
John Creasey
Michael Crichton
Bill Crider
Edmund Crispin
Freeman Wills Crofts
Amanda Cross
Ken Crossen
James Crumley
Guy Cullingford
E. V. Cunningham
Ursula Curtiss
Clare Curzon
Clive Cussler

Carroll John Daly
Elizabeth Daly
Norman A. Daniels
Jocelyn Davey
Lionel Davidson
L.P. Davies
Dorothy Salisbury Davis
Frederick C. Davis
Kenn Davis
S.F.X. Dean
William L. DeAndrea
Len Deighton
Lillian de la Torre
Nelson DeMille
Richard Deming
Lester Dent
August Derleth
Thomas B. Dewey
Eileen Dewhurst
Colin Dexter
Michael Dibdin
Peter Dickinson
Doris Miles Disney
Dorothy Cameron Disney
Stephen Dobyns
David Dodge
Dick Donovan
Arthur Conan Doyle
Peter Driscoll
June Drummond
Daphne du Maurier
Susan Dunlap

Dorothy Dunnett
Francis Durbridge

Mignon G. Eberhart
Clive Egleton
Aaron J. Elkins
Stanley Ellin
James Ellroy
Earl W. Emerson
Howard Engel
Paul E. Erdman
Margaret Erskine
Loren D. Estleman
Helen Eustis

Gerard Fairlie
Katharine Farrer
Kenneth Fearing
Elizabeth Fenwick
Elizabeth Ferrars
Robert Finnegan
Jack Finney
Bruno Fischer
Robert L. Fish
Steve Fisher
Mary Fitt
Ian Fleming
Joan Fleming
David Fletcher
J.S. Fletcher
Lucille Fletcher
Fletcher Flora
Ken Follett
Hulbert Footner
Colin Forbes
Stanton Forbes
Leslie Ford
Katherine V. Forrest
Richard Forrest
Frederick Forsyth
James M. Fox
Dick Francis
Anthea Fraser
Antonia Fraser
James Fraser
Nicolas Freeling
R. Austin Freeman
Brian Freemantle
Celia Fremlin
Kinky Friedman
Roy Fuller
Jacques Futrelle

Reg Gadney
Sarah Gainham
Erle Stanley Gardner
John Gardner
Brian Garfield
Andrew Garve
Jonathan Gash
William Campbell Gault
Elizabeth George
Walter B. Gibson
Val Gielgud
Thomas Gifford
Anthony Gilbert
Michael Gilbert

B.M. Gill
Bartholomew Gill
Dorothy Gilman
E.X. Giroux
John Godey
Donald Goines
David Goodis
The Gordons
Joe Gores
Ed Gorman
Paula Gosling
Ron Goulart
Bruce Graeme
C.W. Grafton
Sue Grafton
Caroline Graham
Winston Graham
Bill Granger
Lesley Grant-Adamson
Dulcie Gray
Andrew M. Greeley
Anna Katharine Green
Graham Greene
Stephen Greenleaf
Leonard Gribble
Edward Grierson
Frank Gruber

William Haggard
Adam Hall
William H. Hallahan
Brett Halliday
Donald Hamilton
Patrick Hamilton
Dashiell Hammett
Gerald Hammond
Joseph Hansen
Thomas W. Hanshew
Cyril Hare
Robert Harling
Joyce Harrington
William Harrington
Herbert Harris
Thomas Harris
Timothy Harris
Michael Harrison
Ray Harrison
Carolyn G. Hart
Frances Noyes Hart
Simon Harvester
Joseph Hayes
S.T. Haymon
Matthew Head
Tim Heald
Jeremiah Healy
H.F. Heard
Mark Hebden
Joe L. Hensley
Joan Hess
Georgette Heyer
Carl Hiaasen
George V. Higgins
Jack Higgins
Patricia Highsmith
Reginald Hill
Tony Hillerman
John Buxton Hilton

Chester Himes
Edward D. Hoch
Anne Hocking
William Hope Hodgson
Elisabeth Sanxay Holding
James Holding
Timothy Holme
Victoria Holt
Leonard Holton
Geoffrey Homes
Joseph Hone
Sydney Horler
Doug Hornig
E.W. Hornung
S.B. Hough
Geoffrey Household
Clark Howard
Richard Hoyt
P.M. Hubbard
Dorothy B. Hughes
Richard Hull
Fergus Hume
E. Howard Hunt
Alan Hunter
Elspeth Huxley

Hammond Innes
Michael Innes
Robert Irvine

P.D. James
Charlotte Jay
Roderic Jeffries
Selwyn Jepson
F. Tennyson Jesse
Richard Jessup
Veronica Parker Johns
E. Richard Johnson
Velda Johnston

Lucille Kallen
Stuart M. Kaminsky
Frank Kane
Henry Kane
Dan Kavanagh
H.R.F. Keating
Harry Stephen Keeler
Day Keene
Faye Kellerman
Jonathan Kellerman
Mary Kelly
Harry Kemelman
Baynard H. Kendrick
Milward Kennedy
Tony Kenrick
Michael Kenyon
Gerald Kersh
William X. Kienzle
Rufus King
C.H.B. Kitchin
Clifford Knight
Kathleen Moore Knight
Bill Knox
Ronald A. Knox
Dean R. Koontz
Thomas Kyd
Duncan Kyle

Ed Lacy
Derek Lambert
Jane Langton
Joe R. Lansdale
Emma Lathen
Jonathan Latimer
Hilda Lawrence
James Leasor
John le Carré
Anthony Lejeune
Elizabeth Lemarchand
Elmore Leonard
William Le Queux
Ira Levin
Michael Z. Lewin
Roy Lewis
Elizabeth Linington
Robert Littell
Nancy Livingston
Dick Lochte
Richard and Frances Lockridge
Philip Loraine
Peter Lovesey
Marie Belloc Lowndes
Nicholas Luard
Robert Ludlum
Edgar Lustgarten
John Lutz
Gavin Lyall
Arthur Lyons

John D. MacDonald
Philip MacDonald
Ross Macdonald
Helen MacInnes
Donald MacKenzie
Alistair MacLean
Charlotte MacLeod
John Malcolm
Arthur Maling
Barry N. Malzberg
Jessica Mann
Dan J. Marlowe
Derek Marlowe
Stephen Marlowe
John P. Marquand
Ngaio Marsh
William Marshall
A.E.W. Mason
F. Van Wyck Mason
John Masterman
Harold Q. Masur
Lia Matera
Berkely Mather
W. Somerset Maugham
Frank McAuliffe
Ed McBain
Charles McCarry
Helen McCloy
James McClure
Horace McCoy
Philip McCutchan
Gregory Mcdonald
Patricia McGerr
Edmund McGirr
William P. McGivern
Jill McGown

Paul McGuire
William McIlvanney
Ralph McInerny
Mary McMullen
Mark McShane
L.T. Meade
M.R.D. Meek
James Melville
Nicholas Meyer
Laurence Meynell
Margaret Millar
Wade Miller
A.A. Milne
John Milne
Gladys Mitchell
James Mitchell
Gwen Moffat
Susan Moody
Anne Morice
Nigel Morland
Arthur Morrison
L.A. Morse
John Mortimer
Patricia Moyes
Marcia Muller
Warren Murphy and Richard Sapir
Max Murray

Magdalen Nabb
Frederick Nebel
Richard Neely
Margot Neville
Francis M. Nevins, Jr.
Bernard Newman
G.F. Newman
Beverley Nichols
Helen Nielsen
William F. Nolan
Gil North

Lillian O'Donnell
Peter O'Donnell
William O'Farrell
Lenore Glen Offord
Joan O'Hagan
Anthony Oliver
D.B. Olsen
Carol Ann O'Marie
E. Phillips Oppenheim
Baroness Orczy
Roger Ormerod

Frank L. Packard
Marco Page
Stuart Palmer
Sara Paretsky
Robert B. Parker
Frank Parrish
Elliot Paul
Laurence Payne
Don Pendleton
Hugh Pentecost
Barry Perowne
Anne Perry
Ritchie Perry
Elizabeth Peters
Ellis Peters

Gerald Petievich
Eden Phillpotts
Nancy Pickard
Evelyn Piper
Joyce Porter
Melville Davisson Post
Raymond Postgate
Jean Potts
James Powell
Talmage Powell
Richard S. Prather
Anthony Price
J.B. Priestley
Allan Prior
Maurice Procter
Bill Pronzini
Milton Propper
E.R. Punshon
Philip Purser

Ellery Queen
Patrick Quentin

Peter Rabe
Sheila Radley
Hugh C. Rae
Robert J. Randisi
Julian Rathbone
Clayton Rawson
Derek Raymond
Arthur B. Reeve
Helen Reilly
Ruth Rendell
Herbert Resnicow
William J. Reynolds
John Rhode
Craig Rice
Mary Roberts Rinehart
Jack Ritchie
James Hall Roberts
Les Roberts
Willo Davis Roberts
Joel Townsley Rogers
Sax Rohmer
Kelley Roos
Richard Rosen
Angus Ross
Jonathan Ross
Holly Roth
Kenneth Royce
Martin Russell
Douglas Rutherford

Richard Sale
Lawrence Sanders
Sapper
Eric Sauter
Ernest Savage
Dorothy L. Sayers
Margaret Scherf
Mark Schorr
Jack S. Scott
Mabel Seeley
Francis Selwyn
David Serafin
Gerald Seymour
Joseph Shearing

John Sherwood
M.P. Shiel
Roger L. Simon
Dorothy Simpson
George Sims
Henry Slesar
Gillian Slovo
Julie Smith
Kay Nolte Smith
Martin Cruz Smith
Shelley Smith
Nancy Spain
Bart Spicer
Mickey Spillane
Vincent Starrett
Kurt Steel
Aaron Marc Stein
Stewart Sterling
Richard Martin Stern
Mary Stewart
Rex Stout
J.F. Straker
John Stephen Strange
T.S. Stribling
Ian Stuart
Jean Stubbs
Jeremy Sturrock
Julian Symons

William G. Tapply
Andrew Taylor
Phoebe Atwood Taylor
Josephine Tey
Lee Thayer
Ross Thomas
Jim Thompson
Basil Thomson
June Thomson
Newton Thornburg
Ernest Tidyman
Arthur Train
Lawrence Treat
John Trench
John Trenhaile
Trevanian
Miles Tripp
Peter Turnbull
Scott Turow
Robert Twohy
Nedra Tyre

Dorothy Uhnak
Michael Underwood
Arthur W. Upfield

Andrew Vachss
Jonathan Valin
John Holbrook Vance
Louis Joseph Vance
Janwillem van de Wetering
S.S. Van Dine
Peter Van Greenaway
Gerald Verner
Roy C. Vickers

Henry Wade
John Wainwright

Hannah Wakefield
Edgar Wallace
Marilyn Wallace
Thomas Walsh
Joseph Wambaugh
Thurman Warriner
Colin Watson
Hillary Waugh
Jack Webb
John Welcome
Carolyn Wells
Patricia Wentworth
Donald E. Westlake
Peter Whalley
Carolyn Wheat
Dennis Wheatley
Jon Manchip White
Lionel White
Teri White
Raoul Whitfield
Phyllis A. Whitney
Harry Whittington

Colin Wilcox
Charles Williams
David Williams
Valentine Williams
Ted Willis
Cecil M. Wills
Barbara Wilson
Colin Wilson
Mary Wings
Pauline Glen Winslow
Ted Wood
Sara Woods
Cornell Woolrich
Richard Wormser
Eric Wright
L.R. Wright

Dornford Yates
Andrew York
Margaret Yorke
P.B. Yuill

NINETEENTH-CENTURY WRITERS

Mary Elizabeth Braddon
Wilkie Collins
Charles Dickens
William Godwin
Sheridan Le Fanu

Edgar Allan Poe
Richmond
Waters
Mrs. Henry Wood
Israel Zangwill

FOREIGN-LANGUAGE WRITERS

Pierre Boileau and Thomas Narcejac
Jorge Luis Borges
Friedrich Dürrenmatt
Émile Gaboriau
Sebastien Japrisot
Hans Hellmut Kirst
Maurice Leblanc
Gaston Leroux
Seicho Matsumoto

Hubert Monteilhet
Shizuko Natsuki
Poul Ørum
Alain Robbe-Grillet
Leonardo Sciascia
Georges Simenon
Masako Togawa
Robert H. van Gulik
Per Wahlöö and Maj Sjöwall

Writers not included in this volume who appear in previous editions:

Grant Allen
Kingsley Amis
Frank Arthur
John Austwick
Nina Bawden
E.F. Benson
Nicolas Bentley
Phyllis Bentley
Kenneth Benton
Andrew Bergman
Suzanne Blanc
M. M'Donnell Bodkin

John Boland
Miriam Borgenicht
Pierre Boulle
Jack Boyle
Ray Bradbury
Caryl Brahms
Max Brand
John G. Brandon
Michael Brett
Ann Bridge
Victor Bridges
Lynn Brock

John Bude
Gelett Burgess
Michel Butor
Janet Caird
Edward Candy
A.H.Z. Carr
Margaret Carr
Heron Carvic
G. Belton Cobb
A.E. Coppard
Alec Coppel
Mark Corrigan
Patrick Cosgrave
Frances Cowen
Marten Cumberland
Roald Dahl
Clemence Dane
Glyn Daniel
Roland Daniel
Mildred Davis
Amber Dean
Miriam Allen deFord
Ovid Demaris
Hugh Desmond
D.M. Devine
Frederic Van Rensselear Dey
Adam Diment
Hildegarde Dolson
Madelaine Duke
John Gregory Dunne
Wessel Ebersohn
Dorothy Eden
Robert Eustace
William Faulkner
Ruth Fenisong
A. Fielding
Nigel Fitzgerald
Pat Flower
Rae Foley
Sydney Fowler
Samuel Fuller
Dorothy Gardiner
Catherine Gaskin
Arthur G. Goldstein
Joseph Harrington
Rosemary Harris
Macdonald Hastings

Wallace Hildick
Cornelius Hirschberg
C. Hugh Holman
Stanley Hyland
Jack Iams
John N. Ianuzzi
Stuart Jackman
Shirley Jackson
Cora Jarrett
Hamilton Jobson
Clarence Budington Kelland
Richard Keverne
C. Daly King
Henry Klinger
Arthur La Bern
Constance and Gwyneth Little
Ivy Litvinov
Nora Lofts
George Markstein
Robin Maugham
Brown Meggs
James Norman
Emma Page
Max Pemberton
Ludovic Peters
Zelda Popkin
E. and M.A. Radford
S.S. Rafferty
Marion Randolph
Ishmael Reed
Ray Russell
R.T.M. Scott
Nevil Shute
Helen Simpson
Christopher St. John Sprigg
Bram Stoker
Margaret Summerton
Glen Trevor
C.E. Vulliamy
R.A.J. Walling
Patrick Wayland
Carolyn Weston
Ethel Lina White
Victor L. Whitechurch
William Wiegand
Jacqueline Wilson

A

AARONS, Edward S(idney). Also wrote as Paul Ayres; Edward Ronns. American. Born in Philadelphia, Pennsylvania, in 1916. Educated at Columbia University, New York, degrees in ancient history and literature. Served in the United States Coast Guard, 1941–45: Chief Petty Officer. Married 1) Ruth Ives (died); 2) Grace Dyer. Worked as millhand, salesman, fisherman, and as reporter on Philadelphia newspaper. Full-time writer from 1945. Lived in Connecticut. *Died 16 June 1975.*

CRIME PUBLICATIONS

Novels (series: Sam Durell in all Assignment books)

Nightmare. Philadelphia, McKay, 1948.
Dead Heat (as Paul Ayres). Drexel Hill, Pennsylvania, Bell, 1950.
Escape to Love. New York, Fawcett, 1952; London, Fawcett, 1957.
Come Back, My Love. New York, Fawcett, 1953; London, Fawcett, 1954.
The Sinners. New York, Fawcett, 1953; London, Fawcett, 1954.
Girl on the Run. New York, Fawcett, 1954; London, Fawcett, 1956.
Assignment to Disaster. New York, Fawcett, 1955; London, Fawcett, 1956.
Assignment—Suicide. New York, Fawcett, 1956; London, Fawcett, 1958.
Assignment—Treason. New York, Fawcett, 1956; London, Fawcett, 1957.
Assignment—Budapest. New York, Fawcett, 1957; London, Fawcett, 1959.
Assignment—Stella Marni. New York, Fawcett, 1957; London, Fawcett, 1958.
Assignment—Angelina. New York, Fawcett, 1958; London, Fawcett, 1959.
Assignment—Madeleine. New York, Fawcett, 1958; London, Muller, 1960.
Assignment—Carlotta Cortez. New York, Fawcett, 1959; London, Muller, 1960.
Assignment—Helene. New York, Fawcett, 1959; London, Muller, 1960.
Assignment—Lili Lamaris. New York, Fawcett, 1959; London, Muller, 1960.
Assignment—Mara Tirana. New York, Fawcett, 1960; London, Fawcett, 1962.
Hell to Eternity (novelization of screenplay). New York, Fawcett, and London, Muller, 1960.
Assignment—Zoraya. New York, Fawcett, 1960, London, Muller, 1961.
Assignment—Ankara. New York, Fawcett, 1961; London, Muller, 1962.
Assignment—Lowlands. New York, Fawcett, 1961; London, Muller, 1962.
The Defenders (novelization of television play). New York, Fawcett, 1961; London, Jenkins, 1962.
Assignment—Burma Girl. New York, Fawcett, 1961; London, Muller, 1962.
Assignment—Karachi. New York, Fawcett, 1962; London, Muller, 1963.

Assignment—Sorrento Siren. New York, Fawcett, and London, Muller, 1963.
Assignment—Manchurian Doll. New York, Fawcett, 1963; London, Muller, 1964.
Assignment—Sulu Sea. New York, Fawcett, 1964.
Assignment—The Girl in the Gondola. New York, Fawcett, 1964; London, Hodder and Stoughton, 1969.
Assignment—The Cairo Dancers. New York, Fawcett, 1965.
Assignment—Palermo. New York, Fawcett, 1966; London, Hodder and Stoughton, 1967.
Assignment—Cong Hai Kill. New York, Fawcett, 1966.
Assignment—School for Spies. New York, Fawcett, 1966; London, Hodder and Stoughton, 1967.
Assignment—Black Viking. New York, Fawcett, 1967; London, Hodder and Stoughton, 1968.
Assignment—Moon Girl. New York, Fawcett, 1968.
Assignment—Nuclear Nude. New York, Fawcett, 1968; London, Hodder and Stoughton, 1969.
Assignment—Peking. New York, Fawcett, 1969; London, Hodder and Stoughton, 1970.
Assignment—Star Stealers. New York, Fawcett, and London, Hodder and Stoughton, 1970.
Assignment—White Rajah. New York, Fawcett, and London, Hodder and Stoughton, 1970.
Assignment—Tokyo. New York, Fawcett, and London, Hodder and Stoughton, 1971.
Assignment—Bangkok. New York, Fawcett, and London, Hodder and Stoughton, 1972.
Assignment—Golden Girl. New York, Fawcett, and London, Hodder and Stoughton, 1972.
Assignment—Maltese Maiden. New York, Fawcett, 1972; London, Hodder and Stoughton, 1973.
Assignment—Ceylon. New York, Fawcett, 1973; London, Hodder and Stoughton, 1974.
Assignment—Silver Scorpion. New York, Fawcett, 1973; London, Hodder and Stoughton, 1974.
Assignment—Amazon Queen. New York, Fawcett, 1974; London, Hodder and Stoughton, 1975.
Assignment—Sumatra. New York, Fawcett, 1974; London, Hodder and Stoughton, 1975.
Assignment—Black Gold. New York, Fawcett, 1975; London, Hodder and Stoughton, 1977.
Assignment—Quayle Question. New York, Fawcett, 1975; London, Hodder and Stoughton, 1976.
Assignment—Afghan Dragon. New York, Fawcett, 1976; London, Coronet, 1979.

Novels as Edward Ronns (series: Jerry Benedict)

Death in a Lighthouse. New York, Phoenix Press, 1938; as *The Cowl of Doom,* n.p., Hangman's House, 1946.
Murder Money. New York, Phoenix Press, 1938; as *$1,000,000 in Corpses,* n.p., Best Detective Selections, 1943.
The Corpse Hangs High. New York, Phoenix Press, 1939.
No Place to Live (Benedict). Philadelphia, McKay, 1947; London, Boardman, 1950; as *Lady, The Guy Is Dead,* New York, Avon, 1950.
Terror in the Town. Philadelphia, McKay, 1947.
Gift of Death (Benedict). Philadelphia, McKay, 1948.
The Art Studio Murders. Kingston, New York, Quin, 1950.

Catspaw Ordeal. New York, Fawcett, 1950; London, Gaywood, 1953.

Dark Memory. Kingston, New York, Quin, 1950.

Million Dollar Murder. New York, Fawcett, 1950; London, Fawcett, 1952.

State Department Murders. New York, Fawcett, 1950; London, Fawcett, 1958.

The Decoy. New York, Fawcett, 1951.

I Can't Stop Running. New York, Fawcett, 1951; London, Moring, 1958.

Don't Cry, Beloved. New York, Fawcett, 1952.

Passage to Terror. New York, Fawcett, 1952; London, Moring, 1958.

Dark Destiny. Hasbrouck Heights, New Jersey, Graphic, 1953.

The Net. Hasbrouck Heights, New Jersey, Graphic, 1953.

Say It with Murder. Hasbrouck Heights, New Jersey, Graphic, 1954; London, Red Seal, 1960.

They All Ran Away. Hasbrouck Heights, New Jersey, Graphic, 1955.

Point of Peril. New York, Curl, 1956; London, Red Seal, 1960.

Death Is My Shadow. New York, Curl, 1957.

Pickup Alley (novelization of screenplay). New York, Avon, 1957.

Gang Rumble. New York, Avon, 1958; London, Red Seal, 1960.

The Lady Takes a Flyer (novelization of screenplay). New York, Avon, 1958.

The Big Bedroom. New York, Pyramid, 1959.

The Black Orchid (novelization of screenplay). New York, Pyramid, and London, Panther, 1959.

But Not for Me (novelization of screenplay). New York, Pyramid, 1959; London, World Distributors, 1960.

The Glass Cage. New York, Pyramid, 1962.

Uncollected Short Story

"Nightmare," in *Two Complete Detective Books* (New York), March 1949.

Uncollected Short Stories as Edward Ronns

"Death in a Dory," in *Detective Story Magazine* (New York), July 1944.

"Night of Fear," in *Detective Story Magazine* (New York), October 1944.

"A Day's Haul," in *Detective Story Magazine* (New York), September 1945.

"The Trap," in *The Shadow* (New York), November 1945.

"A Corpse for Carol," in *The Shadow* (New York), December 1945.

"Terror in the Town," in *Detective Story Magazine* (New York), February 1946.

"Eyes in the Night," in *Detective Story Magazine* (New York), February 1947.

"Night Blind," in *Detective Story Magazine* (New York), December 1947.

"Woolsey's Trip," in *Doc Savage* (New York), September–October 1948.

"Noose Around My Neck," in *Scarab* (New York), November 1950.

"The Clay Pigeons," in *Scarab* (New York), January 1951.

"We've Got Time," in *The Saint* (New York), June–July 1953.

"Deadly Curves," in *Mercury* (New York), December 1955.

*   *   *

Edward S. Aaron's most successful creation was the *Assignment* series, featuring durable Sam Durell of the CIA "K" section. In the 20 odd years he was operative, Durell aged little, his thick black hair showing gray at the temples only toward the end. Early in the series, he had served with G-2 and the OSS, but no mention was been made of organizations which would date him. Still a Yalie, however, Durell prefers dark blue or gray suits, white shirts with button-down collars, and solid neckties. He was reared by his grandfather, a riverboat captain who taught him his gambler's instincts and ways aboard an old paddlewheeler in the Delta's Bayou Peche Rouge. Thus Durell's code name—Cajun.

The *Assignment* series is characteristically humorless and tough-minded. Durell claims to be a coldly objective man, calculating odds and consequences, placing his patriotic duty to job and country before the lives of his cohorts. His actions, however, contradict these claims; despite his rhetoric, he has always instinctively and impetuously attempted to rescue his underlings—at least the women among them—from the villain's schemes and clutches, no matter the consequences. Violence in the series is frequent, explicit, and brutal. Characters are tortured and slaughtered by villains in a variety of arcane ways. Durell's violence, by contrast, is straightforward; he kills quickly with fists, knives, guns, and bombs. Durell himself absorbs an astonishing amount of punishment. He is beaten and knocked unconscious at least twice in every novel, coming to a climactic confrontation with the arch-villain bloody but unbowed, although at the arch-villain's mercy. Indeed, in *The Girl in the Gondola* Durell allows himself to be tortured in order to buy time for the successful completion of a mission. There, too, Aarons deals most interestingly with the psychic effects of violence, linking Durell's apparent emotional coldness with his violence. In that novel, the scars on Durell's body and on his woman's symbolically measure the losses his job has caused. As always, however, Durell finds the reservoir of strength necessary to overcome both his own pain and the enemy.

The arch-villains of the series represent a threat at least to an entire country—to Algeria, for example, in *Madeleine*, to the U.S. in *Angelina* and *Stella Marni*, to Thailand in *Cong Hai Kill*, and to an African nation in *Black Gold*—if not to the world—*The Girl in the Gondola*, *Star Stealers*, and *Amazon Queen*. The villains are typically either sadistic barbarians of incredible physical strength—L'Heureux in *Madeleine*, Slago in *Angelina*, Agpak terrorists in *Black Gold*—or the cunning and nasty brain behind such brawn—Dr. Von Handel in *Star Stealers*, Paio Chu in *Cong Hai Kill*. Occasionally, the villain will be a combination of the two—Dinov in *The Girl in the Gondola*, Agosto in *Amazon Queen*. Early in the series, the villains were sometimes women—Jessie Corbin in *Angelina*, and Stella Marni in the book of that name.

Later, however, the women in the series have been pliant and accessible ladies of considerable class and background or pliant and accessible females of, shall I say, rather less breeding. Instead of faulting Aarons for what may seem on its face a chauvinistic divisiveness, I would congratulate him for his creation of women of the first type. His "ladies," while hardly saintly virgins, are in fact competent and determined people with intelligence and power. In various novels such women as Queen Salduva of Pakuru, the wealthy owner of an electronics industry, and the widow of Italy's Defense Minister have been Durell's lovely and loving helpmates, despite his more or less regular attachment to Deirdre Padgett, also a "lady," coming from a wealthy family on Maryland's Eastern Shore. Deirdre was a newspaper reporter before joining the CIA, and she figures in occasional novels as a tough and cunning operative who accompanies Durell on his adventures.

The novels are generally as topical as yesterday's newspaper. Aarons wrote, for example, of the Algerian conflict, Cold War tensions, the Chinese influence in Albania, spy satellites, the Indo-China wars, and the oil crisis. His formula was to open each novel with a chapter of violence and mystery, introduce Durell, situate him in a foreign country and direct him through a series of false leads and traitors until he meets the arch-villain and emerges triumphantly from his confrontation with a shaky peace and the lady.

—David K. Jeffrey

————

ABBEY, Kieran. *See* **REILLY, Helen.**

————

ACRE, Stephen. *See* **GRUBER, Frank.**

————

ADAMS, Andy. *See* **GIBSON, Walter B.**

————

ADAMS, Cleve F(ranklin). Also wrote as Franklin Charles; John Spain. American. Born in Chicago, Illinois, in 1895. Married, one child. Worked as a copper miner, detective, life insurance executive, art director for films and operated a chain of candy stores before becoming a full-time writer in the late 1930's. *Died 28 December 1949.*

CRIME PUBLICATIONS

Novels (series: Rex McBride; John J. Shannon)

And Sudden Death (McBride). New York, Dutton, 1940.
Sabotage (McBride). New York, Dutton, 1940; as *Death Before Breakfast*, New York, Mystery Novel of the Month, 1942; as *Death at the Dam*, London, Cassell, 1946.
The Black Door. New York, Dutton, 1941.
Decoy (McBride). New York, Dutton, 1941.
The Vice Czar Murders (as Franklin Charles; with Robert Leslie Bellem). New York, Funk and Wagnalls, 1941.
The Private Eye (Shannon). New York, Reynal, 1942.
What Price Murder. New York, Dutton, 1942.
Up Jumped the Devil (McBride). New York, Reynal, 1943; as *Murder All Over*, New York, New American Library, 1950.
The Crooking Finger (McBride). New York, Reynal, 1944.
Contraband. New York, Knopf, 1950; as *Borderline Cases*, London, Cassell, 1952.
No Wings on a Cop (Shannon), expanded by Robert Leslie Bellem. Kingston, New York, Quin, 1950.
Shady Lady (McBride). New York, Ace, 1955.

Novels as John Spain (series: Bill Rye)

Dig Me a Grave (Rye). New York, Dutton, 1942; London, Corgi, 1952.
Death Is Like That (Rye). New York, Dutton, 1943.
The Evil Star. New York, Dutton, 1944; London, Swan, 1950.

Uncollected Short Stories

"Inspector Thomas Wins a Hat," in *Clues* (New York), February 1933.
"Racket Trap," in *Clues* (New York), November 1933.
"Twenty-Eight Grand," in *All Detective Magazine* (New York), May 1934.
"Page Violet McDade," in *Clues* (New York), January 1935.
"Shrinking Violet," in *Clues* (New York), July 1935.
"Mexican Bargain," in *Clues* (New York), August 1935.
"Framing the Picture," in *Clues* (New York), November 1935.
"Vision of Violet," in *Clues* (New York), February 1936.
"Flowers for Violet," in *Clues* (New York), May 1936.
"The Voice," in *Clues* (New York), September 1936.
"Compromising Violet," in *Clues* (New York), October 1936.
"Important Money," in *Clues* (New York), December 1936.
"Violet to Orchid," in *Clues* (New York), February 1937.
"No Match for a Murder," in *Sure-Fire Detective Magazine* (Springfield, Massachusetts), February 1937.
"A Copper Calls His Shots," in *Headquarters Detectives* (Springfield, Massachusetts), March 1937.
"Corpse's Understudy," in *Sure-Fire Detective Magazine* (Springfield, Massachusetts), April 1937.
"Default with Doom," in *Ten Detective Aces* (Springfield, Massachusetts), April 1937.
"Murder City," in *Clues* (New York), April 1937.
"Ring Around the Rackets," in *Sure-Fire Detective Magazine* (Springfield, Massachusetts), June 1937.
"She-Devil," in *Clues* (New York), June 1937.
"Dime a Death," in *Ten Detective Aces* (Springfield, Massachusetts), July 1937.
"The Back Door," in *Clues* (New York), September 1937.
"Double Shuffle," in *Detective Fiction Weekly* (New York), 11 September 1937.
"Private War," in *Detective Fiction Weekly* (New York), 2 October 1937.
"Death's Five Brothers," in *Ten Detective Aces* (Springfield, Massachusetts), October 1937.
"Money No Object," in *Detective Fiction Weekly* (New York), 13 November 1937.
"Pattern of Panic," in *Double Detective* (New York), November 1937.
"Bloody Bullets," in *Clues* (New York), November 1937.
"The Heel," in *Detective Fiction Weekly* (New York), 11 December 1937.
"The Girl from Frisco," in *Detective Fiction Weekly* (New York), 1 January 1938.
"Tragedy of Errors," in *Double Detective* (New York), January 1938.
"Racket Buster," in *Clues* (New York), January 1938.
"Traffic Case," in *Detective Fiction Weekly* (New York), 12 February 1938.
"Murder Takes a Trade," in *Detective Fiction Weekly* (New York), 5 March 1938.
"Punk," in *Detective Fiction Weekly* (New York), 19 March 1938.
"Gentleman's Agreement," in *Clues* (New York), March 1938.
"This Is Murder," in *Double Detective* (New York), April 1938.

"Jigsaw," in *Detective Fiction Weekly* (New York), 11 June 1938.

"The Man Who Limped," in *Double Detective* (New York), June 1938.

"Flatfoot," in *Double Detective* (New York), July 1938.

"Give the Guy Rope," in *Detective Fiction Weekly* (New York), 20 August 1938.

"Song of Hate," in *Double Detective* (New York), August 1938.

"Guardian Angel," in *Detective Fiction Weekly* (New York), 10 September 1938.

"Kidnappers Make Good Corpses," in *Top-Notch Detective* (Chicago), September 1938.

"Burn a Feather," in *Detective Fiction Weekly* (New York), 29 October 1938.

"Frame for a Lady," in *Popular Detective* (New York), October 1938.

"Inside Straight," in *Detective Fiction Weekly* (New York), 5 November 1938.

"Speak No Evil," in *Collier's* (Springfield, Ohio), 26 November 1938.

"Murder Is Serious," in *Star Detective Magazine* (Chicago), November 1938.

"Homing Pigeon," in *Detective Fiction Weekly* (New York), 10 December 1938.

"Murder Goes Unshod," in *Detective Fiction Weekly* (New York), 17 December 1938.

"Mannequin for a Morgue," in *Double Detective* (New York), December 1938.

"Corpse C.O.D.," in *Ten Detective Aces* (Springfield, Massachusetts), January 1939.

"Help! Murder! Police!," in *Argosy* (New York), 4, 11, and 18 February 1939.

"Sabotage," in *Detective Fiction Weekly* (New York), March–April 1939.

"The Knife," in *Double Detective* (New York), April 1939.

"Cops Are Sissies," in *Detective Tales* (New York), May 1939.

"The Jade Ring," in *Detective Fiction Weekly* (New York), 24 June 1939.

"Smart Guy," in *Detective Fiction Weekly* (New York), 12 August 1939.

"Exit with Bullets," in *Double Detective* (New York), August 1939.

"Contraband," in *Detective Fiction Weekly* (New York), 9 September 1939.

"The Lady Was a Tramp," in *Double Detective* (New York), October 1939.

"Greek Meets Greek," in *Double Detective* (New York), November 1939.

"Homicide—Honolulu Bound," in *Detective Fiction Weekly* (New York), December 1939–January 1940.

"Exodus," in *Detective Fiction Weekly* (New York), 13 January 1940.

"Death Strikes a Chord," in *Detective Fiction Weekly* (New York), 13 January 1940.

"Triple Threat," in *Detective Story Magazine* (New York), April 1940.

"The Key," in *Black Mask* (New York), July 1940.

"The Dead Can't Vote," in *Detective Fiction Weekly* (New York), 3 August 1940.

"Clean Sweep," in *Detective Fiction Weekly* (New York), 24 August 1940.

"Passage for Satan," In *Argosy* (New York), 14 September 1940.

"That Certain Feeling," in *Black Mask* (New York), September 1940.

"Backfire," in *Detective Fiction Weekly* (New York), 30 November 1940.

"The Red Carnation," in *Detective Story Magazine* (New York), November 1940.

"Murder While You Wait," in *Dime Detective* (New York), December 1940.

"Sinners Three," in *Argosy* (New York), 18 January 1941.

"The Aunt of Sigma Chi," in *Black Mask* (New York), January 1941.

"Decoy," in *Detective Fiction Weekly* (New York), 25 January–1 March 1941.

"Murder Ad Lib," in *Detective Fiction Weekly* (New York), 17 May 1941.

"Night in Sinaloa," in *Argosy* (New York), 31 May 1941.

"Murder Parade," in *Black Mask* (New York), May 1941.

"Nobody Loves Cops," in *Black Mask* (New York), July 1941.

"Forty Pains" in *Dime Detective Magazine* (Chicago), July 1941.

"Kill and Let Kill," in *Dime Detective Magazine* (Chicago), February 1942.

"Herrings Are Red," in *Black Mask* (New York), March 1942.

"The Private Eye," in *Two Complete Detective Books* (New York), November 1944.

"The Crooking Finger," in *Detective Novel Magazine* (New York), December 1948.

"Too Fair to Die," in *Two Complete Detective Books* (New York), March 1951.

"What Price Murder," in *Thrilling Detective* (New York), June 1951.

OTHER PUBLICATIONS

Other

"Motivation in Mystery Fiction," in *The Writer* (Boston), April 1942.

*

Bibliography: by Francis M. Nevins, Jr., and William J. Clark, in "The World of Cleve Adams" by Nevins, in *Armchair Detective* (White Bear Lake, Minnesota), May 1975.

*   *   *

After working at a variety of jobs, Cleve F. Adams began writing mystery fiction for the pulp magazines around 1934, almost simultaneously with Raymond Chandler and Cornell Woolrich, and like them he turned to novels at the end of the 1930's and produced most of his books in a frenzy of activity during the early 1940's. Although the books are little read today, in his own style Adams captured the gray and gritty feel of the time as powerfully as Chandler, and created as enduring an image of the private detective.

The Adams private eye—who has many names but is usually called Rex McBride—is a sort of prophecy of the Humphrey Bogart persona. But unlike Bogey, whose apparent hard shell hid a sentimental heart, the Adams protagonist's apparent soft heart is itself a shell concealing a brutal and cynical core. He is slim and dark, with a wolfishly satanic look and a capacity for deep brooding silences, sudden ribald laughter, fierce rages, aloof arrogance. He is a supreme male chauvinist, with a penchant for slapping his girlfriends around and chasing other women. He is a fascist ("An American Gestapo is goddam well what we need"), a racist (throwing around terms like spic, wop, nigger, and kike as casually as he shoots people), a cynic and a hypocrite, but a sentimental ballad can bring tears to his eyes. Chandler said of the private eye that "He is the hero, he is everything," but Adams's aim is to debunk this knightly image and reduce the eye to a royal ass and a cosmic oaf. In Adams's cynical world there is no hero, and the detective is as rotten as everyone else, just tougher and luckier.

Almost all of Adams's novels feature a good girl, a bad girl, a gambling czar, a good gray police captain, a sadistic Homicide dick, a corrupt politician, hired goons, a pompous businessman or government official, and a Runyonesque cabbie who miraculously pops up to pull the eye out of jams. Every book contains a smoke-ring blowing scene, some drunk scenes, at least two beatings, and a confrontation between the detective and each woman in the tale, one of whom is usually the murderer. Adams recycles the same descriptions and lines of dialogue tirelessly, and he was so fond of Dashiell Hammett's novels that he filched the storyline of *Red Harvest* three times and of *The Glass Key* twice, although Adams's versions collapse whenever he tries to explain his chaotic plots. And yet for all his faults he was a genius at juggling disparate groups of shady characters each with a separate greedy objective, and his books boil over with breathless raw readability. His last and best novel, *Shady Lady,* is rich in character sketches and powerfully understated scenes which suggest that, had he lived longer, he might have grown into a writer rivaling Chandler.

—Francis M. Nevins, Jr.

ADAMS, Harold.   American.   Born in Clerk, South Dakota, 20 February 1923. Educated at the University of Minnesota, Minneapolis, B.A. in English Literature 1950. Served in the United States Army, 1943–44. Married Betty Skogsberg in 1949 (divorced 1965); one daughter. Warehouse manager, The Sloan Company, St. Paul, Minnesota, 1953–57; assistant manager, Better Business Bureau of Minneapolis, 1957–65; Executive Director, Charities Review Council of Minnesota, 1965–88. Since 1988 full-time writer. Agent: Ivy Fischer Stone, Fifi Oscard Associates, 19 West 44th Street, New York, New York 10036. Address: 12916 Greenwood Road, Minnetonka, Minnesota 55343, U.S.A.

CRIME PUBLICATIONS

Novels (series Kyle Champion; Carl Wilcox)

Murder (Wilcox).   New York, Charter, 1981; Bath, Avon, Chivers, 1989.
Paint the Town Red (Wilcox).   New York, Charter, 1983.
The Missing Moon (Wilcox).   New York, Charter, 1983.
The Naked Liar (Wilcox).   New York, Mysterious Press, 1985; Bath, Avon, Chivers, 1986.
The Fourth Widow (Wilcox).   New York, Mysterious Press, 1986.
The Barbed Wire Noose (Wilcox).   New York, Mysterious Press, 1987; Bath, Avon, Chivers, 1990.
When Rich Men Die (Champion).   New York, Doubleday, 1987.
The Man Who Met the Train (Wilcox).   New York, Mysterious Press, 1988.
The Man Who Missed the Party (Wilcox).   New York, Mysterious Press, 1989.

*

Harold Adams comments:
The Carl Wilcox series takes place for the most part in small towns of South Dakota. The hero is a former cowboy, soldier, rustler, housepainter, convict, and brawler. He began doing murder investigations in self defense, became good at it and winds up occasionally making money at it but depends on his skills as a sign painter for more or less steady employment. His parents own the Wilcox Hotel in Corden, a town of approximately 1,300 people, and he regularly returns there to work temporarily helping out his father. The father/son relationship is primarily negative. He doesn't get along much better with his mother and considers his parents hopeless puritans.

In the later books he drinks less and doesn't fight quite as often. His fondness for women never wavers or weakens. He has high albeit flexible principles and no pretensions about his skills as a Sherlock Holmes or Dupin. He solves crimes by talking with people involved and depending on his instincts about suspects and their motivations. I think these stories are funny.

Kyle Champion is a contemporary character with a background in Better Business Bureau work, investigative work for television, and a brief career as a news anchor man with a television station in Minneapolis. His first experience in murder investigation takes him to Mexico. In books not yet published he goes to France and then northern Minnesota. His techniques are not far removed from those of Carl Wilcox but he uses them in a more subtle fashion and is more inclined to out-think than out-fight his opponents.

*   *   *

The image of the canny rustic has a long tradition in mystery fiction. Pastoral detective heroes have ranged from the transcendental (Melville Davisson Post's Uncle Abner) to the cartoonish (Arthur Train's Ephraim Tutt). The preponderance of these characters, however, belong to the cozy, puzzle-oriented school of crime fiction. When Hammett and his successors turned the focus from untraceable poisons, jewel-encrusted daggers, and British country estates to murder as the hood in the street would commit it, the locus of modern detective fiction became the mean streets of urban America. Adhering to this sensibility, and searching for novel settings outside the hard-boiled school's "golden triangle" of New York, Los Angeles, and San Francisco, today's crime writers began casting about. In the past decade or two, we have seen hard-boiled private eyes and hard-bitten homicide detectives working such out-of-the-way locales as Hong Kong, Amsterdam, Mexico City, Osaka, and Akron, Ohio.

In a 1981 paperback original entitled, straightforwardly enough, *Murder,* Harold Adams placed the best aspects of the citified investigator into a bucolic setting. His detective, Carl Wilcox, combines the tough, street-smart attributes of the urban private eye with the shrewdness of the archetypical rural Yankee peddler. Not that Corden, South Dakota, the setting for nearly all the Wilcox novels, is a Sylvan paradise. It is a high and bare land of dust storms, relentless heat and cold, populated by farmers of dour, presbyterian mien who work long and miserable hours to scratch a living out of the hardscrabble earth. Adams's chosen time period—the height of the Great Depression—accentuates the bleakness and sense of despair. The Carl Wilcox series has been compared by reviewers to the work of crime fiction's prime existentialists, James M. Cain and Jim Thompson.

But even though his surroundings are conductive to brooding and despair, Carl Wilcox is no nihilist. Among the upstanding citizens of tiny Corden, Wilcox is rather a flamboyant embarrassment, someone from whom to keep the children—particularly the teenage daughters. Though possessed of the personal moral code endemic to Chandler's ilk—which drives him to seek justice for the oppressed and powerless, and allows the reader to side with him over his calvinistic fellow Cordenites—Wilcox is direct and crude of speech, a drinker, a loafer, and a womanizer.

In the first few novels Wilcox is driven to detective work only because, as a recent ex-convict, he is likely to be the first suspected and accused of the killing. By *The Man Who Met the Train,* however, his reputation as a sleuth leads the masters—judge and banker—of the town of Toqueville (another dusty Dakota town, not far from Corden either in miles or attitude) to hire Wilcox to help in the investigation of a local murder. Thus, by default, Wilcox joins the ranks of the professional private investigators.

Even in the beginning, however, Wilcox the amateur sleuth conducts himself more like a Philip Marlowe than a Philo Vance. He asks questions, gets a variety of answers, must determine which of them are lies. Material clues—fingerprints and such—play a small role in the episodes. It's unlikely that anyone in Corden would know what to do with them. Wilcox, though small of stature, is handy with his fists. Near the end of each novel, he finds himself fighting for his life—and, carrying no gun or knife, must improvise against his aggressors. He has dispatched murderous opponents with such weapons as a 10-foot ladder, a toilet tank cover, and a six-foot length of dead cornstalk.

The greatest strength of the Wilcox series lies in Adams's laconic prose style, perfectly suited to his prosaic Dakota landscape, salt-of-the-earth characters, and appropriately simple mystery plots (yes, a farmer *would* commit murder with a pitchfork and hide the corpse under hay). Adams imbues ne'er-do-well Wilcox with a great deal of charm, turns even characters who appear briefly into three-dimensional beings, and has the happy gift of creating wisecracks that succeed.

An inherent problem in any small-town mystery series—with such a limited population, how long before homicide decimates the village?—is neatly sidestepped by Adams. In *Paint the Town Red,* Chicago mobsters arrive to recover loot stashed in Corden; a perfect hiding place, because no one wants to visit there. In *The Missing Moon,* the moonshiner who services the entire countryside is accused of murder when found asleep beside a freshly-dead corpse. And in *The Man Who Missed the Party,* the tenth reunion of Corden High's class of 1924 brings victims and suspects to town from as far away as Minneapolis.

The Adams novels may also be read with a healthy nostalgic appreciation. Adams spent his boyhood in this milieu and, although Corden is by no stretch of imagination a place any reader would want to live, the books brilliantly delineate a time before the small western and Midwestern farming communities withered away, bled by declining populations and failing businesses along Main Street. If the mysteries in the Carl Wilcox novels were not as fine as they are, Adams would still be remembered for what he remembers.

—William Malloy

———

ADAMS, Herbert. Also wrote as Jonathan Gray. British. Born in London 1874. Married Jessie Louise Cooper. Member of the Surveyors Institute. Died in 1958 (?)

CRIME PUBLICATIONS

Novels (series: Major Roger Bennion; Jimmie Haswell)

The Secret of the Bogey House (Haswell). London, Methuen, 1924; Philadelphia, Lippincott, 1925.
By Order of the Five. London, Methuen, 1925.
The Sloane Square Mystery. London, Methuen, 1925; New York, Dial Press, 1926.
The Crooked Lip (Haswell). London, Methuen, and Philadelphia, Lippincott, 1926.
Comrade Jill. London, Methuen, 1926; Philadelphia, Lippincott, 1927.
The Queen's Gate Mystery (Haswell). London, Methuen, and Philadelphia, Lippincott, 1927.
The Empty Bed (Haswell). London, Methuen, and Philadelphia, Lippincott, 1928.
Exit the Skeleton (Bennion). London, Macdonald, 1928.
Rogues Fall Out (Bennion). London, Methuen, and Philadelphia, Lippincott, 1928.
A Lady so Innocent. London, Methuen, 1929.
Caroline Ormsby's Crime. London, Methuen, and Philadelphia, Lippincott, 1929.
Oddways. Philadelphia, Lippincott, 1929; London, Methuen, 1930.
The Crime in the Dutch Garden (Haswell). Philadelphia, Lippincott, 1930; London, Methuen, 1931.
The Golden Ape (Haswell). London, Methuen, and Philadelphia, Lippincott, 1930.
The Paulton Plot (Haswell). Philadelphia, Lippincott, 1931; London, Methuen, 1932.
Queen's Mate. London, Methuen, and Philadelphia, Lippincott, 1931.
The Woman in Black (Haswell). Philadelphia, Lippincott, 1932; London, Methuen, 1933.
John Brand's Will. London, Methuen, 1933; as *The Golf House Murder,* Philadelphia, Lippincott, 1933.
The Strange Murder of Hatton. Philadelphia, Lippincott, 1933; as *The Knife,* London, Collins, 1934.
Safety Last (as Jonathan Gray). London, Muller, 1934.
Mystery and Minette. London, Collins, and Philadelphia, Lippincott, 1934.
The Body in the Bunker. London, Collins, and Philadelphia, Lippincott, 1935.
Fate Laughs. London, Collins, and Philadelphia, Lippincott, 1935.
Death Off the Fairway (Bennion). London, Collins, 1936.
A Word of Six Letters. London, Collins, 1936; as *Murder Without Risk!* Philadelphia, Lippincott, 1936.
The Old Jew Mystery (Bennion). London, Collins, 1936.
A Single Hair (Bennion). London, Collins, 1937.
The Owl (as Jonathan Gray). London, Harrap, and Philadelphia, Lippincott, 1937.
The Bluff. London, Collins, 1938.
The Dammed Spot (Bennion). London, Collins, 1938.
Black Death (Bennion). London, Collins, 1939.
The Nineteenth Hole Mystery (Bennion). London, Collins, 1939.
The Case of the Stolen Bridegroom (Bennion). London, Collins, 1940.
The Chief Witness (Bennion). London, Collins, 1940.
Roger Bennion's Double. London, Collins, 1940.
Stab in the Back (Bennion). London, Collins, 1941.
The Araway Oath (Bennion). London, Collins, 1942.
Signal for Invasion (Bennion). London, Collins, 1942.
Victory Song (Bennion). London, Collins, 1943.
The Scarlet Feather. London, Cherry Tree Books, 1943.

Four Winds (Bennion). London, Collins, 1944.
The Writing on the Wall (Bennion). London, Collins, 1945.
Welcome Home! (Bennion). London, Macdonald, 1946.
Diamonds Are Trumps (Bennion). London, Macdonald, 1947.
Crime Wave at Little Cornford (Bennion). London, Macdonald, 1948.
One to Play. London, Macdonald, 1949.
The Dean's Daughters (Bennion). London, Macdonald, 1950.
The Sleeping Draught (Bennion). London, Macdonald, 1951.
The Spectre in Brown (Bennion). London, Macdonald, 1953.
Slippery Dick (Bennion). London, Macdonald, 1954.
The Judas Kiss (Bennion). London, Macdonald, 1955.
Death on the First Tee (Bennion). London, Macdonald, 1957.
Death of a Viewer (Bennion). London, Macdonald, 1958.

OTHER PUBLICATIONS

Novel

A Virtue of Necessary. London, Greening, 1899.

Short Stories

The Perfect Round: Tales of the Links. London, Methuen, 1927.

* * *

Herbert Adams published his first mystery novel in 1924 and his last in 1958, spanning over 30 years working within the mystery genre in which many writers took the form in several new directions. Adams, however, remained true to the basic formula he developed in the 1920's, and his books are remarkably consistent in quality. In every story there is a murder but also a love story, a good deal of sentiment, and a number of platitudes, depending on the political or economic situation at the time. Adams also indulges in occasional digressions into areas of personal interest, such as cricket or golf. These criticisms notwithstanding, there are also good plots with complications, reversals, surprises occurring regularly, a group of young men and women, and a few minor characters who are an interesting contrast even if presented as caricatures. Adams's novels were well received in the early years of his career, in the 1920's and 1930's, but tended to be less noticed by reviewers thereafter. Regardless of the lack of official notice, Adams's books have always enjoyed a loyal audience.

Adams has two amateur detectives: Jimmie Haswell, a barrister, and Major Roger Bennion. Both men could certainly be described as honorable, but neither one is the scrupulously honest pursuer of truth many readers have come to expect from the amateur sleuth in the British mystery. In at least one instance Bennion lets a suspect withhold information from the police on her actions during a critical time, thereby protecting the woman in question but doing little to advance the police investigation. Both Haswell and Bennion ultimately marry women who were suspects in one of their investigations.

The chief pleasure in Adams's mysteries is the precision with which he poses the issue—a person is murdered and someone is guilty—and seeks a solution (finding the murderer). Good people may be involved, the crime may in fact be partly accidental, but no one walks away from responsibility. Bennion might at times be more chivalrous than ethical, but Adams plays it straight to the end.

Adams begins many of his stories with a murder occurring suddenly and giving no possible clue as to the identity of the murderer. In *The Crooked Lip* a businessman takes his daughter, a young woman, on her first trip through Britain, traveling by train. Haswell and his friend strike up a conversation with the father and daughter, and invite them to dinner in the dining car. The daughter accepts and on their return the three young people find the businessman dead. The device of several young people working together to solve a murder by tracing backward someone's life, moving through several levels of society, from high to low, to do so, remains characteristic of Adams's stories.

In *Diamonds Are Trumps* Adams begins with an ingenious device but parts of the story are marred by the propaganda and platitudes typical of the work of less-talented writers during the war years. Vernon Trask, a young man who fought in Burma, stands in the dock convicted of the murder of his friend, Bill Glanville, another soldier in Burma. When he is asked by the judge if he has anything to say before sentencing, he announces that he is not Vernon Trask; he is Bill Glanville, the man thought to be dead. The judge, of course cannot pass sentence and the effort to prove the man's identity brings in Roger Bennion and leads to the unraveling of the events that brought one of the army buddies to his death.

One of Adams's most successful novels is *The Dean's Daughters.* The Right Reverend Cardale, dean of Fenchester cathedral, has three strong minded daughters. The oldest, Suzanne, is standing for Parliament as a socialist; Rosemary wants to become a professional dancer and is studying with a Frenchman who just happens to have been her mother's dance teacher many years before; and Ruth, the youngest, is studying law by day and going in disguise to meetings of the Communist Party by night. Mrs. Cardale also has a problem: the dance teacher is blackmailing her and she is afraid of what will happen to her home and her husband's career. When the teacher is found murdered, all three daughters are suspected, as are their assorted friends.

Despite the changes in the mystery novel that left Adams's works dated, his stories contain a cleanness of vision and integrity of form that makes them attractive to many readers. Both Bennion and Haswell may be sometimes weak in the exercise of detection and ratiocination, but they move among the suspects until the murderer is found, letting the surface plot play itself out while the murder investigation goes on underneath.

—Susan Oleskiw

———

AIKEN, Joan (Delano). British. Born in Rye, Sussex, 4 September 1924; daughter of the writer Conrad Aiken; sister of the writer Jane Aiken Hodge. Educated at Wychwood School, Oxford, 1936–40. Married 1) Ronald George Brown in 1945 (died 1955), one son and one daughter; 2) Julius Goldstein in 1976. Worked for the BBC, 1942–43; information officer, then librarian, United Nations Information Centre, London, 1943–49; sub-editor and features editor, *Argosy,* London, 1955–60; copywriter, J. Walter Thompson, London, 1960–61. Recipient: *Guardian* award, 1969; Mystery Writers of America Edgar Allan Poe award, 1972. Agent: A.M. Heath Ltd., 79 St. Martin's Lane, London WC2N 4AA; or, Brandt and Brandt, 1501 Broadway, New York, New York 10036, U.S.A. Address: The Hermitage, East Street, Petworth, West Sussex GU28 OAB, England.

CRIME PUBLICATIONS

Novels

The Silence of Herondale. New York, Doubleday, 1964; London, Gollancz, 1965.
The Fortune Hunters. New York, Doubleday, 1965.
Trouble with Product X. London, Gollancz, 1966; as *Beware of the Banquet,* New York, Doubleday, 1966.
Hate Begins at Home. London, Gollancz, 1967; as *Dark Interval,* New York, Doubleday, 1967.
The Ribs of Death. London, Gollancz, 1967; as *The Crystal Crow,* New York, Doubleday, 1968.
The Embroidered Sunset. London, Gollancz, and New York, Doubleday, 1970.
Died on a Rainy Sunday. London, Gollancz, and New York, Holt Rinehart, 1972.
The Butterfly Picnic. London, Gollancz, 1972; as *A Cluster of Separate Sparks,* New York, Doubleday, 1972.
Last Movement. London, Gollancz, and New York, Doubleday, 1977.
Foul Matter. London, Gollancz, and New York, Doubleday, 1983.
A Fit of Shivers. London, Gollancz, 1990.

Short Stories

The Windscreen Weepers and Other Tales of Horror and Suspense. London, Gollancz, 1969.

Uncollected Short Stories

"Old Firkin," in *Twilight Zone,* April 1982.
"Picnic Area," in *Twilight Zone,* July 1982.
"Something Very Obsessional," in *Ellery Queen's Mystery Magazine* (New York), November 1982.
"Black Cliffs," in *Ellery Queen's Prime Crimes,* New York, 1983.

OTHER PUBLICATIONS

Novels

Voices in an Empty House. London, Gollancz, and New York, Doubleday, 1975.
Castle Barebane. London, Gollancz, and New York, Viking Press, 1976.
The Five-Minute Marriage. London, Gollancz, 1977; New York, Doubleday, 1978.
The Smile of the Stranger. London, Gollancz, and New York, Doubleday, 1978.
The Lightning Tree. London, Gollancz, 1980; as *The Weeping Ash,* New York, Doubleday, 1980.
The Young Lady from Paris. London, Gollancz, 1982; as *The Girl from Paris,* New York, Doubleday, 1982.
Mansfield Revisited. London, Gollancz, 1984; New York, Doubleday, 1985.
Deception. London, Gollancz, 1987; as *If I Were You,* New York, Doubleday, 1987.
Blackground. London, Gollancz, and New York, Doubleday, 1989.

Fiction (for children)

All You've Ever Wanted and Other Stories. London, Cape, 1953.
More Than You Bargained For and Other Stories. London, Cape, 1955; New York, Abelard Schuman, 1957.

The Kingdom and the Cave. London, Abelard Schuman, 1960; New York, Doubleday, 1974.
The Wolves of Willoughby Chase. London, Cape, 1962; New York, Doubleday, 1963.
Black Hearts in Battersea. New York, Doubleday, 1964; London, Cape, 1965.
Nightbirds on Nantucket. London, Cape, and New York, Doubleday, 1966.
The Whispering Mountain. London, Cape, 1968; New York, Doubleday, 1969.
A Necklace of Raindrops and Other Stories. London, Cape, and New York, Doubleday, 1968.
Armitage, Armitage, Fly Away Home. New York, Doubleday, 1968.
A Small Pinch of Weather and Other Stories. London, Cape, 1969.
Night Fall. London, Macmillan, 1969; New York, Holt Rinehart, 1971.
Smoke from Cromwell's Time and Other Stories. New York, Doubleday, 1970.
The Green Flash and Other Tales of Horror, Suspense, and Fantasy. New York, Holt Rinehart, 1971.
The Cuckoo Tree. London, Cape, and New York, Doubleday, 1971.
The Kingdom under the Sea and Other Stories. London, Cape, 1971.
All and More. London, Cape, 1971.
A Harp of Fishbones and Other Stories. London, Cape, 1972.
Arabel's Raven. London, BBC Publications, 1972; New York, Doubleday, 1974.
The Escaped Black Mamba. London, BBC Publications, 1973; as *Arabel and the Escaped Black Mamba,* London, BBC Publications, 1984.
All But a Few. London, Penguin, 1974.
The Bread Bin. London, BBC Publications, 1974.
Midnight Is a Place. London, Cape, and New York, Viking Press, 1974.
Not What You Expected: A Collection of Short Stories. New York, Doubleday, 1974.
Mortimer's Tie. London, BBC Publications, 1976.
A Bundle of Nerves: Stories of Horror, Suspense, and Fantasy. London, Gollancz, 1976.
The Faithless Lollybird and Other Stories. London, Cape, 1977; New York, Doubleday, 1978.
The Far Forests: Tales of Romance, Fantasy, and Suspense. New York, Viking Press, 1977.
Go Saddle the Sea. New York, Doubleday, 1977; London, Cape, 1978.
Tale of a One-Way Street and Other Stories. London, Cape, 1978; New York, Doubleday, 1979.
Mice and Mendelson, music by John Sebastian Brown. London, Cape, 1978.
Mortimer and the Sword Excalibur. London, BBC Publications, 1979.
The Spiral Stair. London, BBC Publications, 1979.
A Touch of Chill: Stories of Horror, Suspense, and Fantasy. London, Gollancz, 1979; New York, Delacorte Press, 1980.
Arabel and Mortimer (includes *Mortimer's Tie, The Spiral Stair, Mortimer and the Sword Excalibur*). London, Cape, 1980; New York, Doubleday, 1981.
The Shadow Guests. London, Cape, and New York, Delacorte Press, 1980.
Mortimer's Portrait on Glass. London, BBC Publications, 1980.
Mr. Jones's Disappearing Taxi. London, BBC Publications, 1980.

The Stolen Lake. London, Cape and New York, Delacorte Press, 1981.
A Whisper in the Night: Stories of Horror, Suspense, and Fantasy. London, Gollancz, 1982.
Mortimer's Cross. London, Cape, 1983.
Bridle the Wind. London, Cape, and New York, Delacorte Press, 1983.
The Kitchen Warriors. London, BBC Publications, 1983.
Up the Chimney Down and Other Stories. London, Cape, 1984.
Fog Hounds, Wind Cat, Sea Mice. London, Macmillan, 1984.
Mortimer Says Nothing and Other Stories. London, Cape, 1985; New York, Harper, 1987.
The Last Slice of the Rainbow and Other Stories. London, Cape, 1985; New York, Harper, 1988.
Dido and Pa. London, Cape, and New York, Delacorte Press, 1986.
Past Eight O'Clock: Goodnight Stories. London, Cape, 1986.
A Goose on Your Grave. London, Gollancz, 1987.
The Moon's Revenge. London, Cape, and New York, Knopf, 1987.
The Teeth of the Gale. London, Cape, and New York, Harper, 1988.
The Erl King's Daughter. London, Heinemann, 1988.
Voices. London, Hippo, and New York, Scholastic, 1988.
Give Yourself a Fright: Thirteen Tales of the Supernatural. New York, Delacorte Press, 1989.
Night Fall. London, Macmillan, 1989.

Plays (for children)

Winterthing, music by John Sebastian Brown (produced Albany, New York, 1977). New York, Holt Rinehart, 1972; included in *Winterthing, and the Mooncusser's Daughter,* 1973.
Winterthing, and the Mooncusser's Daughter, music by John Sebastian Brown. London, Cape, 1973; *The Mooncusser's Daughter* published separately, New York, Viking Press, 1974.
Street, music by John Sebastian Brown (produced London, 1977). New York, Viking Press, 1978.
Moon Mill (produced London, 1982).

Television Plays: *The Dark Streets of Kimballs Green,* 1976; *The Apple of Trouble,* 1977; *Midnight Is a Place* (serial), from her own story, 1977; *The Rose of Puddle Fratrum,* 1978; *Armitage, Armitage, Fly Away Home,* from her own story, 1978.

Verse (for children)

The Skin Spinners. New York, Viking Press, 1976.

Other

The Way to Write for Children. London, Elm Tree, 1982; New York, St. Martin's Press, 1983.

Translator, *The Angel Inn,* by Comtesse de Ségur. London, Cape, 1976; Owings Mills, Maryland, Stemmer House, 1978.

* * *

Joan Aiken is a highly respected writer of children's fiction who turned to the adult novel in 1964 with excellent results. Her first three gothic romances followed the conventional plot: the damsels-in-distress won through to happy endings with the right young men. But even in these relatively unremarkable books, there were signs that Aiken would find the forms too confining for her imagination, which is full of highly plausible fantasies and horrors. In *Trouble with Product X,* for instance, one of the major secondary characters is a four-month-old baby girl who is the heiress to a fabulous perfume formula which gets eaten by Cornish slugs. *Hate Begins at Home,* her next book, is described on the cover as a "modern novel with gothic suspense," and in fact the elements of horror almost overwhelm the heroine and the book. The issue of the heroine's survival is left in doubt until the last sentence. There followed two of Aiken's best and most characteristic books. They are indefinable as to genre and reach denouements determined only by the logic of the characters she has created and the situations she has placed them in.

The Ribs of Death gives us as heroine a very young novelist who lives with a horrible female saint. This couple is juxtaposed with a psychotic female doctor and her brother, whom she has placed under a false medical death sentence. Several other characters with various mental problems, including schizophrenia and depression, wander about, together with an escaped leopard. The plot proceeds through various quotidian horrors to a final passage of mayhem and a bleak ending. The young innocents have survived the destruction, but their fragile intimacy is dead. *The Embroidered Sunset* has just as diverse and engaging a cast of characters as its predecessor. The heroine is a young woman with a talent for the piano, a nasty step-father, a weak heart, and a dedicated appreciation for the art of Aunt Fennel Culpepper, who may or may not be her companion of many years. Dr. Adnan, a lively young Turkish doctor, and Max Benovek, a dying pianist, both come to the rescue of the heroine, but they arrive an hour after the heroine's heart has worn out.

How Aiken makes these characters and plots both moving and credible is something of a mystery. One attractive quality of Aiken's heroes and heroines is their high threshold for self-pity. They may have a great many burdens to bear, but they don't shift them onto others, and Aiken's incident-filled plots leave them little time for brooding. Her short stories, collected in *The Green Flash* and *The Far Forests,* flash with wit, and fantasy, and the peculiar wisdom of this very individual writer.

—Carol Cleveland

———

AIRD, Catherine. Pseudonym for Kinn Hamilton McIntosh. British. Born in Huddersfield, Yorkshire, 20 June 1930. Educated at Waverley School and Greenhead High School, both in Huddersfield. Since 1975, chair of the Finance Committee, Girl Guides Association, London. Agent: Aitken and Stone Ltd., 29 Fernshaw Road, London SW10 0TG. Address: Invergordon, 1 Sturry Hill, Sturry, Canterbury, Kent CT2 0NG, England.

CRIME PUBLICATIONS

Novels (series: Inspector C.D. Sloan in all books except *A Most Contagious Game*)

The Religious Body. London, Macdonald, and New York, Doubleday, 1966.
A Most Contagious Game. London, Macdonald, and New York, Doubleday, 1967.
Henrietta Who? London, Macdonald, and New York, Doubleday, 1968.
The Complete Steel. London, Macdonald, 1969; as *The Stately Home Murder,* New York, Doubleday, 1970.

A Late Phoenix. London, Collins, and New York, Doubleday, 1971.
His Burial Too. London, Collins, and New York, Doubleday, 1973.
Slight Mourning. London, Collins, 1975; New York, Doubleday, 1976.
Parting Breath. London, Collins, 1977; New York, Doubleday, 1978.
Some Died Eloquent. London, Collins, 1979; New York, Doubleday, 1980.
Passing Strange. London, Collins, 1980; New York, Doubleday, 1981.
Last Respects. London, Collins, and New York, Doubleday, 1982.
Harm's Way. London, Collins, and New York, Doubleday, 1984.
A Dead Liberty. London, Collins, 1986; New York, Doubleday, 1987.
The Body Politic. London, Macmillan, 1990.

Uncollected Short Stories

"The Scales of Justice," in *Argosy* (New York), February 1974.
"Home Is the Hunter," in *John Creasey's Crime Collection,* edited by Herbert Harris. London, Gollancz, 1988.

OTHER PUBLICATIONS

Play

The Story of Sturry (*son et lumiére* script; produced Sturry, 1973).

Other

"Gervase Fen and the Teacake School" and "Benefit of Clergy," in *Murder Ink: The Mystery Reader's Companion,* edited by Dilys Winn. New York, Workman, 1977.

Editor, *Sturry: The Changing Scene.* Privately printed, 1972.
Editor, *Fordwich, The Lost Port.* Privately printed, 1975.
Editor, *Chislet and Westbere, Villages of the Stour Lathe.* Privately printed, 1979.
Editor, *The Six Preachers of Canterbury Cathedral.* Privately printed, 1982.
Editor, *Hoath and Hern: The Last of the Forest.* Privately printed, 1984.

*   *   *

All but one of Catherine Aird's novels are police procedurals featuring the same group of detectives and set in the same imaginary county—Calleshire. In the exception, *A Most Contagious Game,* an amateur detective solves a 100-year-old murder by using church records. Aird's first novel, *The Religious Body,* contains a map of Calleshire, showing the geographical features and all locations used in subsequent books: the villages, farms, schools, industrial sites, and the three major towns: Calleford with the minster on the River Calle, Luston with all the factories, and Berebury, where the hospital and police headquarters are located.

The Religious Body (suggested, Aird says, by a visit to a convent where she was fascinated by its total silence) establishes Aird's narrative method—incremental repetition—and complete characterizations for each detective, none of whom ever changes.

The main character, Inspector C.D. Sloan, "—Christopher Dennis to his wife and family—. . .inevitably known as "Seedy" to his friends," was born and bred in a Calleshire village and attended a school that apparently offered a university education, given the range of authors he quotes. He is intuitive, sensitive, and kind. "[Sloan] was head of the tiny Criminal Investigation Department of the Berebury Division of the Calleshire Police Force and thus responsible to Superintendent Leeyes."

Superintendent Leeyes, rather stupid and lazy ("The superintendent. . .seldom stepped out of his office. . .but was all in favor of everyone else's doing so."), is a font of stereotypical attitudes and esoteric lore. His conversations with Sloan wander through numerous by-paths, with Sloan "hanging on to the shreds of his patience with an effort."

The two who complete the series quartet are Detective Constable William Crosby, known throughout the force as the "Defective Constable" whose promotion from the uniformed branch was said to be the result of a typist's error, and Dr. Dabbe, the pathologist, whose black humor frequently slows his diagnoses.

The stories move by conversations, usually between Sloan and Leeyes. The following example, typical of them all, also illustrates Aird's method of inserting ironic comments.

In *A Dead Liberty,* Leeyes and Sloan are recapitulating a murder case that has gone to trial and unexpectedly runs into difficulties because the young woman charged with the crime refuses to speak. Sloan must appear in court because the inspector who handled the investigation was later severely brain damaged in a battle with two villains.

"'What killed Carline?' [Leeyes asked.]
'Poison,' [Sloan replied.]
'A woman's way,' mused Leeyes. It was a response that would have upset a great many campaigners for Women's Liberation. . .
'Who was [the victim], then?' asked Leeyes. . .
'A young man who worked for her father's firm.'
'One of the old stories?' enquired Leeyes. . .'Him wanting to marry the boss's daughter and Daddy telling her she must and her not being keen.'
'No, sir, it wasn't like that at all.' There was a certain simplicity about famous legends that didn't equate with life.
'Sloan,' said Leeyes unexpectedly, 'you know there's a time in every fairy story when the frog turns into the prince?'
'Ye-es,' agreed Sloan warily. The superintendent's discursiveness could lead anywhere. Anywhere at all.
'They've just discovered that there are some of those funny inheritance things—DNA molecules—in the phosphate in the skin of the frog. . .Funny, that. . .Especially when you think how often it was the frog that got turned into a prince.'"

The Complete Steel published in the States as *The Stately Home Murder,* deserves special mention; it's an *opera bouffe,* complete with dotty aunts and cousins, three generations of a titled family, including a son born on the wrong side of the blanket—all, in effect, singing *fortissimo.* It's all very funny, particularly the identity of the villain, and it's both a departure and a *tour de force* for Aird. The book is marred only by the silly but conventional attitude that to be born penniless in a village cottage without plumbing is nobler than to be born wealthy in a stately home.

Aird's tone is smiling, good-natured, good-mannered, but invincibly smug, the smugness of "How very, very English" of the middle-class. It's amusing, frequently used to deflate pomposity, but ultimately somewhat irritating to readers in other countries whose middle-class smugness turns on different qualities.

However, Aird's books are satisfying reads; the mysteries

fascinating, the detectives entertaining and endearing, the locale effectively cohesive.

—Pearl G. Aldrich

————

ALBERT, Marvin (Hubert). Also writes as Mike Barone; Al Conroy; Albert Conroy; Ian MacAlister; Nick Quarry; Anthony Rome. American. Born in Philadelphia, Pennsylvania, in 1924. Served as a Chief Radio Officer on Liberty ships during World War II. Married 1) Vivian Coleman (marriage dissolved); 2) the artist Xenia Klar in 1986. Has had several editorial jobs, including copy writer for Philadelphia *Record,* magazine editor, researcher for *Look* magazine, New York, and television scriptwriter. Recipient: Mystery Writers of America special Edgar Allan Poe award, 1975. Lives in France. Address: c/o Macmillan Publishers Ltd., 4 Little Essex Street, London WC2R 3LF, England.

CRIME PUBLICATIONS

Novels (Series: Pierre-Ange Sawyer)

Party Girl. New York, Fawcett, 1958; London, Fawcett, 1959.
The Pink Panther (novelization of screenplay). New York, Bantam, 1964.
Goodbye Charlie (novelization of screenplay). New York, Dell, 1964.
Crazy Joe (as Mike Barone; novelization of screenplay). New York, Bantam, 1974.
The Gargoyle Conspiracy. New York, Doubleday, and London, Deutsch, 1975.
The Dark Goddess. New York, Doubleday, and London, Deutsch, 1978.
The Medusa Complex. New York, Arbor House, 1981.
Hidden Lives. New York, Delacorte Press, 1981.
Operation Lila. New York, Arbor House, 1983.
Stone Angel (Sawyer). New York, Fawcett, 1986; London, Macmillan, 1987.
Back in the Real World (Sawyer). New York, Fawcett, 1986; London, Macmillan, 1987.
Get Off at Babylon (Sawyer). New York, Fawcett, 1987; London, Macmillan, 1988.
Long Teeth (Sawyer). New York, Fawcett, 1987; London, Macmillan, 1988.
The Untouchables (novelization of screenplay). New York, Ballantine, 1987; London, Severn House, 1988.
The Last Smile (Sawyer). New York, Fawcett, 1988; London, Macmillan, 1989.
The Midnight Sister (Sawyer). New York, Fawcett, and London, Macmillan, 1989.
Bimbo Heaven (Sawyer). New York, Fawcett, and London, Macmillan, 1990.

Novels as Albert Conroy

The Road's End. New York, Fawcett, 1952; London, Fawcett, 1960.
The Chiselers. New York, Fawcett, 1953.
Nice Guys Finish Dead. New York, Fawcett, 1957; London, Fawcett, 1958.
Murder in Room 13. New York, Fawcett, 1958; London, Fawcett, 1960.

The Mob Says Murder. New York, Fawcett, 1958; London, Fawcett, 1960.
Mr. Lucky (novelization of television series). New York, Dell, 1960.
Devil in Dungarees. New York, Crest, 1960.
The Looters. New York, Crest, 1961.

Novels as Nick Quarry (series: Jake Barrow)

Trail of a Tramp (Barrow). New York, Fawcett, 1958; London, Muller, 1960.
The Hoods Come Calling (Barrow). New York, Fawcett, 1958; London, Fawcett, 1959.
The Girl with No Place to Hide (Barrow). New York, Fawcett, 1959; London, Muller, 1961.
No Chance in Hell (Barrow). New York, Fawcett, 1960; London, Muller, 1962.
Till It Hurts. New York, Fawcett, 1960; London, Muller, 1962.
Some Die Hard. New York, Fawcett, 1961; London, Muller, 1963.
The Don Is Dead. New York, Fawcett, and London, Coronet, 1972.
The Vendetta. New York, Fawcett, 1972.

Novels as Anthony Rome (series: Tony Rome in all books)

Miami Mayhem New York, Pocket Books, 1960; London, Hale, 1961; as *Tony Rome* (as Marvin Albert), New York, Dell, 1967.
The Lady in Cement. New York, Pocket Books, 1961; London, Hale, 1962.
My Kind of Game. New York, Dell, 1962.

Novels as Al Conroy (series: Johnny Morini in all books)

Death Grip! New York, Lancer, 1972.
Soldato! New York, Lancer, 1972.
Blood Run. New York, Lancer, 1973.
Murder Mission! New York, Lancer, 1973.
Strangle Hold! New York, Lancer, 1973.

Novels as Ian MacAlister

Driscoll's Diamonds. New York, Fawcett, 1973; London, Coronet, 1974.
Skylark Mission. New York, Fawcett, 1973; London, Coronet, 1974.
Strike Force 7. New York, Fawcett, 1974; London, Coronet, 1975.
Valley of the Assassins. New York, Fawcett, 1975; London, Coronet, 1976.

OTHER PUBLICATIONS

Novels

Lie Down with Lions. New York, Fawcett, 1955; London, Miller, 1957.
The Law and Jake Wade. New York, Fawcett, 1956; London, Fawcett, 1957.
Apache Rising. New York, Fawcett, 1957; as *Duel at Diablo,* London, Coronet, 1966.
The Bounty Killer. New York, Fawcett, 1958; London, Fawcett, 1959.
Renegade Posse. New York, Fawcett, 1958; London, Muller, 1960.

That Jane from Maine. New York, Fawcett, 1959; London, Muller, 1960.

Pillow Talk (novelization of screenplay). New York, Fawcett, 1959; London, Muller, 1960.

Rider from Wind River. New York, Fawcett, 1959; London, Muller, 1960.

The Reformed Gun. New York, Fawcett, 1959; London, Muller, 1960.

All the Young Men (novelization of screenplay). New York, Pocket Books, 1960.

Come September. New York, Dell, 1961.

Lover Come Back (novelization of screenplay). New York, Fawcett, 1962.

The VIP's (novelization of screenplay). New York, Dell, 1963.

Move Over, Darling. New York, Dell, 1963.

Palm Springs Week-end. New York, Dell, 1963.

Under the Yum Yum Tree (novelization of screenplay). New York, Dell, 1963.

The Outrage (novelization of screenplay). New York, Pocket Books, 1964.

Honeymoon Hotel. New York, Dell, 1964.

Posse at High Pass. New York, Fawcett, 1964.

What's New, Pussycat? (novelization of screenplay). New York, Dell, and London, Mayflower, 1965.

Strange Bedfellows (novelization of screenplay). New York, Pyramid, 1965.

Do Not Disturb. New York, Dell, 1965.

The Great Race. New York, Dell, 1965.

A Very Special Favor (novelization of screenplay). New York, Dell, 1965.

Novels as Al Conroy

Clayburn. New York, Dell, 1961.
Last Train to Bannock. New York, Dell, 1963.
Three Ride North. New York, Dell, 1964.
The Man in Black. New York, Dell, 1965.

Plays

Screenplays: *Duel at Diablo,* with Michel M. Grilikhes, 1966; *Rough Night in Jericho,* with Sydney Boehm, 1967; *Lady in Cement,* with Jack Guss, 1968; *A Twist of Sand,* 1968.

Other

Broadsides and Boarders (naval history). New York, Appleton Century, 1957; London, Harrap, 1958.

The Long White Road: Sir Ernest Shackleton's Antarctic Adventures (for children). New York, McKay, 1957; London, Lutterworth Press, 1960.

Becoming a Mother, with Theodore R. Seidman. New York, Fawcett, 1958; revised edition, 1963.

The Divorce: A Re-Examination of the Great Tudor Controversy. New York, Simon and Schuster, 1965; London, Harrap, 1966.

*   *   *

Marvin Albert is a prolific writer of mysteries, suspense fiction, westerns, and novelizations of screenplays. After 40 years of writing, Albert is now producing a contemporary suspense series of high quality—the Stone Angel books—and getting the critical recognition that had escaped him for most of his long career.

In *Stone Angel,* Peter Sawyer narrates his story in a sophisticated style while the French setting is captured perfectly. Sawyer is a hybrid: son of an American pilot shot down over France during World War II and a mother who achieved fame as a French resistance fighter. Sawyer was raised by his grandparents in Chicago, but spent summers with his brilliant, scholarly mother in France learning to speak perfect French. His mother named him Pierre-Ange—Peter or Pete in English, Stone Angel in French.

After a successful career as an investigator in America, Sawyer leaves the States to pursue a career in France as an escape from some unpleasant activities for which powerful figures in Washington still hold grudges against him. Sawyer partners himself with the aged Fritz Donhoff—his surrogate father—who has invaluable contacts worldwide.

In the first book of the series, Sawyer is hired by a wealthy American couple to find their daughter, a spoiled teenager who's supposed to be taking classes in Paris. Sawyer discovers that the daughter, Sarah Byrnes, has taken up with a young man who may be a terrorist. Sayer locates Sarah leaving the young man's apartment, is attacked by other terrorists, and is left for dead. The plot is satisfactorily complex as Sawyer follows the clues that lead back to World War II and the aristocratic Lemaire family, whose Champagne empire may be about to fall.

The second book, *Back in the Real World,* builds on the success of the first. When Sawyer drops by his friend Frank Crowley's house and finds the murdered bodies of Frank's wife and another private detective, he gets embroiled in a complex plot dealing with the French fashion industry and a rogue French intelligence agent who is heavily involved in blackmail. Only Sawyer can solve the puzzle of the murders before his friend Frank Crowley is condemned to death.

Get Off at Babylon is the most unconventional Sawyer thriller. Former Grand Prix champion racer Egon Mulhausser hires Sawyer to find his daughter, Odile Garnier. Sawyer discovers that Odile is a drug addict who has ripped off a drug shipment belonging to crime boss Fulvio Callega. Callega puts out a contract on Odile, and Sawyer is in a desperate race against time to find Odile before someone kills her. The search takes Sawyer into the underground caverns beneath Paris to a unique, eerie world few know exists. Sawyer's search is filled with tension, and his plan to save Odile from Callega's contract is particularly clever.

Albert's longest and most successful Stone Angel book is *Long Teeth.* Sawyer is hired to deliver the ransom for the kidnapped wife of industrialist Karl Malo. But through the exchange, Sayer gets involved with the Malo family's problems as he investigates Malo's brilliant son, Alexandre, his secretive daughter, Claudette, and his too-good-to-be-true son-in-law, Jean-Noel. Together with the appearance of ex-CIA agent Johnny Duncan, Sawyer's analytical skills are tested to their limits sorting out the plots and counterplots surrounding Karl Malo's empire.

The Last Smile begins with Sawyer learning that his partner, Fritz Donhoff, has been shot. Sawyer investigates the case Fritz was working on before his near-fatal ambush and is drawn into a multi-million dollar plot to smuggle Etruscan artwork out of Italy to an American buyer in France.

The Midnight Sister is the name of a secret criminal society dealing in drugs, murder, and illegal aliens. When Sawyer's lover, lawyer Arlette Alfani, is framed by a former client, psychopathic killer and jewel thief Andre Colin, Sawyer needs to find the evidence to clear her. His search leads him to Colin's former girlfriend, and a typical Albert race against death ensues in an abandoned World War II French fortress while the murderous members of the Midnight Sister hunt them down.

The latest Peter Sawyer thriller, *Bimbo Heaven,* begins with a beautiful woman stepping out of the water at Sawyer's house on the Riviera and hiring him to deliver a letter. Sawyer's attempt to deliver the letter involves him in murder, blackmail, diamonds worth millions, and a bloody shootout in the Sahara desert.

Unfortunately, many of Albert's other works are out-of-print. His novels written as Albert Conroy are well done, as is his High Adventure series written under the pseudonym of Ian MacAlister which features exotic settings and furious action characteristic of the later Stone Angel books.

Perhaps because of the continued popularity of the Frank Sinatra movies on which they are based, Albert's Tony Rome books—*Miami Mayhem, The Lady in Cement,* and *My Kind of Game*—are reprinted periodically. Tony Rome is a Miami cop who's a compulsive gambler. Rome's father, also on the Miami police force, exposed the crooked dealings of a powerful politician. In retaliation, information about Rome's father's embarrassing activities to raise money for his dying wife was released to the press. Rome's father committed suicide and Tony Rome quit the force. Now Rome lives on a boat, *Straight Pass,* he won in a card game and solves cases to get the money for another run at breaking the bank at Las Vegas.

Albert is a supreme professional writer. He writes in many genres and styles but all his books are consistently excellent with well developed characters, detailed settings, and strong plots.

—George Kelley

ALBRAND, Martha. Pseudonym for Heidi Huberta Freybe; also wrote as Katrin Holland; Christine Lambert. American. Born in Rostock, Germany, 8 September 1914, emigrated to U.S. in 1937: naturalized, 1947. Educated privately and in public and private schools in Italy, France, Switzerland, and England; attended the University of Zurich. Married 1) Joseph M. Loewengard in 1932 (died); 2) Sydney J. Lamon in 1957 (died). Full-time writer. Recipient: Grand Prix de Littérature Policière, 1950. Ph.D.: Colorado State Christian College, 1972. Member, American Academy of Achievement, 1975. *Died 24 June 1981.*

CRIME PUBLICATIONS

Novels

No Surrender. Boston, Little Brown, 1942; London, Chatto and Windus, 1943.
Without Orders. Boston, Little Brown, 1943; London, Chatto and Windus, 1944.
Endure No Longer. Boston, Little Brown, 1944; London, Chatto and Windus, 1945.
None Shall Know. Boston, Little Brown, 1945; London, Chatto and Windus, 1946.
Remembered Anger. Boston, Little Brown, 1946.
Whispering Hill. New York, Random House, 1947; London, Chatto and Windus, 1948.
After Midnight. New York, Random House, and London, Chatto and Windus, 1949.
Wait for the Dawn. New York, Random House, and London, Chatto and Windus, 1950.
Desperate Moment. New York, Random House, and London, Chatto and Windus, 1951.

The Hunted Woman. New York, Random House, 1952; London, Hodder and Stoughton, 1953.
Nightmare in Copenhagen. New York, Random House, and London, Hodder and Stoughton, 1954.
The Mask of Alexander. New York, Random House, 1955; London, Hodder and Stoughton, 1956.
The Linden Affair. New York, Random House, 1956; as *The Story That Could Not Be Told,* London, Hodder and Stoughton, 1956.
A Day in Monte Carlo. New York, Random House, and London, Hodder and Stoughton, 1959.
Meet Me Tonight. New York, Random House, 1960; London, Hodder and Stoughton, 1961; as *Return to Terror,* New York, Ace, 1964.
A Call from Austria. New York, Random House, and London, Hodder and Stoughton, 1963.
A Door Fell Shut. New York, New American Library, and London, Hodder and Stoughton, 1966.
Rhine Replica. New York, Random House, 1969; London, Hodder and Stoughton, 1970.
Manhattan North. New York, Coward McCann, 1971; London, Hodder and Stoughton, 1972.
Zürich AZ/900. New York, Holt Rinehart, 1974; London, Hodder and Stoughton, 1975.
A Taste of Terror. London, Hodder and Stoughton, 1976; New York, Putnam, 1977.
Intermission. London, Hodder and Stoughton, 1978; as *Final Encore,* New York, St. Martin's Press, 1978.

OTHER PUBLICATIONS

Novels

The Obsession of Emmet Booth. New York, Random House, 1957; London, Gollancz, 1958.
The Ball (as Christine Lambert). New York, Atheneum, 1964.
A Sudden Woman (as Christine Lambert). New York, Atheneum, 1964.

Novels as Katrin Holland

Man Spricht über Jacqueline. Berlin, Ullstein, 1930.
Wie macht Man das Nur! (for children). Oldenburg, Stalling, 1930.
Indisches Abendteuer. Ahrbeck, Knorr and Hirth, 1932.
Unterwegs zu Alexander. Berlin, Ullstein, 1932.
Die Silberne Wolke. Berlin, Ullstein, 1933; as *The Silver Cloud,* London, Nicholson and Watson, 1936.
Ein Mädchen fiel vom Himmel. Berlin, Ullstein, 1933; as *Girl Tumbles Out of the Sky,* London, Nicholson and Watson, 1934.
Jutta von Tilseck. Ahrbeck, Knorr and Hirth, 1933.
Babbett auf Gottes Gnaden. Berlin, Ullstein, 1934.
Das Frauenhaus. Zurich, Orell Füssli, 1935; as *Youth Breaks In,* London, Nicholson and Watson, 1935.
Das Mädchen, das niemand Mochte (for children). Berlin, Ullstein, 1935.
Sandro Irrt sich. Zurich, Orell Füssli, 1936.
Einsamer Himmel. Zurich, Orell Füssli, 1938.
Carlotta Torrensani. Zurich, Orell Füssli, 1938.
Vierzehn Tage mit Edith. Zurich, Orell Füssli, 1939.
Helene. Zurich, Orell Füssli, 1940.

Play

Television Play: *Nightmare in Copenhagen.*

*

Manuscript Collection: Mugar Memorial Library, Boston University.

Martha Albrand commented (1980):

My early novels published in Germany reflect the interest and concern of a young female writer with the romantic influences of that period. They were successful because the reading public in Germany wanted, besides a good story, a plot with which they could temporarily exit from reality.

But my first book published in America, *No Surrender,* changed my writing wittingly and unwittingly. It was a story of the Dutch underground fictionalized but basically as I'd known it firsthand. I considered it a novel, but the public again dictated its whim, for they saw the book as a suspense story. Because it was my initial exposure in America, I was labeled a suspense writer and more was expected to follow, particularly since the book was so successful. Therefore, the majority of my books published in America have been in the genre of suspense.

I found the genre to be a workable vehicle for my major concern as an author, namely the theme of personal freedom. Although this concept has frequently been politically realized in many of my books, I do not believe it is the only freedom valuable to the individual and have explored a variety of other freedoms, both in my suspense novels and in my non-suspense works.

Because I have traveled extensively most of my life and lived in many countries, I have always felt it important for people of different nationalities to become more knowledgeable of one another. And I have incorporated this philosophy into my writing.

I am primarily a storyteller. As a storyteller I must first decide if I want to tell the story through sheer development of action or through the development of characters or both. The latter requires the least artificial plot and is the most comfortable for me. I live with my characters—get to know them—before I actually start writing. Once I begin, the characters often dictate their personalities as well as the direction of the story. When I have completed the first draft, I must eliminate the unnecessary. Though all writing is a process of elimination, it is of the utmost importance in a suspense novel.

*   *   *

The strength of Martha Albrand's novels of suspense, most reviewers have agreed, is the superb sense of milieu and background in each of her books, as well as the way in which the setting contributes to the development of believable and interesting characters. Her first few novels in English were timely evocations of the crisis in Europe during World War II. Two novels of the underground were published in 1942 and 1943, although the former, *No Surrender,* was somewhat more favorably reviewed than the latter, *Without Orders,* which was described by the *New York Times* as a long novel "written in a hurry." *Endure No Longer,* a novel of pre-war Germany, analyzes the class structure in order to understand the causes of Germany's disaster. Immediately following the war, Albrand shifted her interest to postwar intrigue, concentrating on the aftermath of Nazism and the growing realization of the threat of communism to ordinary European citizens.

Albrand has been known as the author of novels of international intrigue, but she also evidenced a consistent concern with the issues of domestic mystery; in *Whispering Hill* and *The Obsession of Emmet Booth,* the sensitive portrayal of emotional horrors inflicted in the name of love is especially well realized. Even in her international mysteries, however, the element of subtle torment in personal relationships is a constant theme.

Because Albrand was always interested in the contemporary world, her novels over the years changed in theme and focus. Although some of the earlier books are still popular enough to be in print, the later ones do not merely rework her earlier interests. *A Call from Austria* is about the discovery of a long-hidden Nazi treasure, still being used to fund nefarious projects. *Manhattan North* is a mystery about the murder of a Supreme Court Justice. *Zürich AZ/900* is about the attempt to steal an innovative treatment for arteriosclerosis in order to save the life of a Latin American dictator. Although background and situations change, however, most of her novels of suspense delineate the ways in which political considerations and conditions can affect and victimize individuals.

Critics are not always kind to Albrand, citing occasionally her haste and her tendency to melodrama. Readers, however, have responded for years to her fast-paced and complex plots. Consistently offering suspense and intrigue, she rarely repeats herself. Although she always solves the mystery, she does not always end the story as neatly. Exigencies of plot determine the fate of characters. Taken as a whole, her long career may have produced few classics of the genre, but it has contributed a variety of sophisticated suspense novels for her fans.

—Kay Mussell

————

ALDING, Peter. *See* **JEFFRIES, Roderic.**

————

ALEXANDER, David. American. Born in Shelbyville, Kentucky, 21 April 1907. Educated at the University of Kentucky, Lexington, 1926–28; Columbia University, New York, 1928. Served in the United States Army, 1943–45. Married Alice Le Mere in 1930. Advertising manager, Franco-Belgique Tours, New York, 1928–30; managing editor and columnist, New York *Morning Telegraph,* 1930–40; publicity director, California Jockey Club, San Mateo, 1941–43; freelance writer from 1945. Racing columnist, *Blood-Horse* and *Thoroughbred Record,* both Lexington. Recipient: Boys' Clubs of America award, 1964. *Died 21 March 1973.*

CRIME PUBLICATIONS

Novels (series: Bert Hardin; Marty Land; Lieutenant Romano; Tommy Twotoes and Terry Rooke)

Murder in Black and White (Twotoes and Rooke; Romano). New York, Random House, 1951; London, Hammond, 1954.
Most Men Don't Kill (Twotoes and Rooke; Romano). New York, Random House, 1951; London, Hammond, 1953; as *The Corpse in My Bed,* New York, Ace, 1954.

Murder Points a Finger (Romano). New York, Random House, 1953; London, Boardman, 1955.

Terror on Broadway (Hardin). New York, Random House, 1954; London, Boardman, 1956.

Paint the Town Black (Hardin). New York, Random House, 1954; London, Boardman, 1957.

Shoot a Sitting Duck (Hardin; Romano). New York, Random House, 1955; London, Boardman, 1957.

The Murder of Whistler's Brother (Hardin; Romano). New York, Random House, 1956; London, Boardman, 1958.

Die, Little Goose (Hardin; Romano). New York, Random House, 1956; London, Boardman, 1957.

The Death of Humpty-Dumpty (Hardin; Romano). New York, Random House, 1957; London, Boardman, 1959.

Hush-a-Bye Murder (Hardin; Romano). New York, Random House, 1957; London, Boardman, 1958.

The Madhouse in Washington Square. Philadelphia, Lippincott, 1958; London, Boardman, 1959.

Dead, Man, Dead (Hardin; Romano). Philadelphia, Lippincott, 1959; London, Boardman, 1960.

Pennies from Hell. Philadelphia, Lippincott, 1960; London, Boardman, 1961.

The Death of Daddy-O (Land). Philadelphia, Lippincott, and London, Boardman, 1960.

Bloodstain (Land). Philadelphia, Lippincott, 1961; London, Boardman, 1962.

Short Stories

Hangman's Dozen. New York, Roy, and London, Boardman, 1961.

Uncollected Short Story

"Coffee and—," in *Crime for Two,* edited by Frances and Richard Lockridge. Philadelphia, Lippincott, 1955; London, Macdonald, 1957.

OTHER PUBLICATIONS

Other

Panic! The Life and Times of the Wall Street Crash. Evanston, Illinois, Regency, 1962.

The History and Romance of the Horse. New York, Cooper Square, 1963; revised edition, 1965.

The Red Coat Mystery (for children). Indianapolis, Bobbs Merrill, 1966.

A Sound of Horses: The World of Racing from Eclipse to Kelso. Indianapolis, Bobbs Merrill, 1966.

Editor, *Tales for a Rainy Night: Eighteen Stories by the Mystery Writers of America.* New York, Holt Rinehart, 1961; London, Dobson, 1967.

* * *

David Alexander is an underrated writer, at least in part because he had an idiosyncratic, sometimes self-consciously poetic and mannered style that some readers find off-putting. But his plots are unusual and compelling, as are his offbeat, colorful characters; and the best of his work has undeniable power.

His eight novels featuring Bart Hardin, columnist for the sporting newspaper the *Broadway Times,* are expert portraits of New York's Broadway and Times Square in the 1950's. The best of these are probably the first, *Terror on Broadway,* which involves Hardin with a Ripper-style killer who leaves calling cards on his victims reading "Compliments of Waldo"; *Shoot a Sitting Duck,* in which kidnapping and murder in a flea circus combine to spoil Hardin's Christmas eve; and *Dead, Man, Dead,* which has a calypso theme and such oddball characters as a half-mad ventriloquist and his pair of hideous dummies, Hunch and Trudy.

Alexander also created two other series of two books each. The first features the detective duo of Tommy Twotoes, an eccentric penguin fancier, and private eye Terry Rooke; although *Most Men Don't Kill* and *Murder in Black and White* are enjoyable and amusing, they are not up to the quality of the Hardin novels. The same is true of *The Death of Daddy-O* and *Bloodstain,* the two mysteries starring Broadway lawyer Marty Land (who also appears in the Hardin series).

Of Alexander's three non-series novels, the best by far is *The Madhouse in Washington Square.* This may, in fact, be his best novel overall—in strong contradiction to Barzun and Taylor's unjustifiable dismissal of it as "close to unreadable" in *A Catalogue of Crime. Madhouse* centers on a Greenwich Village bar of the same name and its collection of screwball patrons, headed by John Cossack, "a painter of barber poles. . .a barroom porter, a manufacturer of bombs, and something of a philosopher." In this novel, and others, Alexander has the rare ability to make the reader care for people whose lives and actions are far beyond the limits of rational behavior, and his treatment of them is compassionate as well as humorous.

Alexander was an even better short-story writer than he was a novelist, as his one collection, *Hangman's Dozen,* proves. This is a truly heterogenous gathering, illustrating the range and depth of Alexander's talent. Among its 13 stories are "The Man Who Went to Taltavul's," which won a prize in one of Ellery Queen's annual contests, and "Uncle Tom," a devastating indictment of bigotry and racial injustice in the South.

—Bill Pronzini

ALLARDYCE, Paula. *See* **BLACKSTOCK, Charity.**

ALLBEURY, Ted (Theodore Edward le Bouthillier Allbeury). Also writes as Richard Butler; Patrick Kelly. British. Born in Stockport, Cheshire, 24 October 1917. Educated at Slade Primary School, Erdington, Birmingham; King Edward's Grammar School, Aston, Birmingham. Served in the Intelligence Corps, 1940–47: Lt. Colonel. Married Grazyna Maria Felinska in 1971; two daughters, and two children by two previous marriages. Foundry worker and junior draughtsman before the war; worked in sales and advertising after the war: Creative director, Walter George, London, 1950–57; managing director, W.J. Southcombe, London, 1957–62; managing director of Pirate Radio Station, Radio 390, 1964–67. Co-founder, Allbeury Coombs & Partners, Tunbridge Wells, Kent, 1964–81. Member, TVS Supervisory Board. Agents: Carole Blake and Julian Friedmann, Blake Friedmann Literary Agency, 37–41 Gower Street, London WC1E 6HH. Address: Cheriton House, Furnace Lane, Lamberhurst, Kent, England.

CRIME PUBLICATIONS

Novels (series: Tad Anders)

A Choice of Enemies. New York, St. Martin's Press, 1972; London, Davies, 1973.

Snowball (Anders). London, Davies, and Philadelphia, Lippincott, 1974.

Palomino Blonde. London, Davies, 1975, New York, Harper 1983; as *Omega Minus,* New York, Viking Press, 1975.

The Special Collection. London, Davies, 1975.

Where All the Girls Are Sweeter (as Richard Butler). London, Davies, 1975.

Italian Assets (as Richard Butler). London, Davies, 1976.

Moscow Quadrille. London, Davies, 1976.

The Only Good German. London, Davies, 1976; as *Mission Berlin,* New York, Walker, 1986.

The Man with the President's Mind. London, Davies, 1977; New York, Simon and Schuster, 1978.

The Lantern Network. London, Davies, 1978; New York, Mysterious Press, 1989.

The Alpha List. London, Hart Davis MacGibbon, 1979; New York, Methuen, 1980.

Consequence of Fear. London, Hart Davis MacGibbon, 1979; as *Smokescreen,* New York, Medallion, 1986.

The Twentieth Day of January. London, Granada, 1980.

Codeword Cromwell (as Patrick Kelly). London, Granada, 1980.

The Reaper, London, Granada, 1980; as *The Stalking Angel,* New York, Mysterious Press, 1988.

The Other Side of Silence. London, Granada, and New York, Scribner, 1981.

The Secret Whispers. London, Granada, 1981; New York, Medallion, 1987.

The Lonely Margins (as Patrick Kelly). London, Granada, 1981.

Shadow of Shadows. London, Granada, and New York, Scribner, 1982.

All Our Tomorrows. London, Granada, 1982; New York, Mysterious Press, 1989.

Pay Any Price. London, Granada, 1983.

The Girl from Addis. London, Granada, 1984.

The Judas Factor (Anders). London, New English Library, 1984; New York, Mysterious Press, 1988.

No Place to Hide. London, New English Library, 1984.

Children of Tender Years. London, New English Library, and New York, Beaufort, 1985.

The Choice. London, New English Library, 1986.

The Seeds of Treason. London, New English Library, 1986; New York, Mysterious Press, 1987.

The Crossing. London, New English Library, 1987.

A Wilderness of Mirrors. London, New English Library, 1988.

Deep Purple. London, New English Library, 1989; New York, Mysterious Press, 1990.

A Time Without Shadows. London, New English Library, 1990.

Short Stories

Other Kinds of Treason. London, Hodder and Stoughton, 1990.

OTHER PUBLICATIONS

Plays

Radio Plays: *Long Ago and Far Away,* 1981; *The Other Side of Silence,* 1982; *Time Spent in Reconnaissance,* 1983; *Pay Any Price,* 1983; *Music of a Small Life,* 1983; *The Way We Live,* 1983; *No Place to Hide,* 1984; *The Lonely Margins,* 1987.

Other

"Memoirs of an Ex-Spy," in *Murder Ink: The Mystery Reader's Companion,* edited by Dilys Winn. New York, Workman, 1977.

*

Manuscript Collection: Mugar Memorial Library, Boston University.

Ted Allbeury comments:

I have tried in my novels to show that people employed in espionage or in intelligence work have private lives, and that their work affects their lives. The man who is tough in his intelligence work may compensate by always picking lame ducks so far as his ladies are concerned. Although so far I have had the nicest of reviews in all countries, there is sometimes a comment that my books have sad endings. This, of course, is deliberate. I believe that all wars have sad endings for both losers and winners, and that those who are concerned with espionage and counter espionage tend to have sad endings even in peace time. In the real-life recruitment of intelligence agents, to want to do that kind of work would be considered a disadvantage. It is reckoned that it is better to use men who feel some doubt about the morality of what they are doing. This, naturally, has some disadvantages in operational terms, but it also has the advantage of avoiding excessive use of power. I have tried to get this over in my books. Although most of my books are anti-communist and anti-KGB, I have nevertheless tried to paint a fairly full picture of Russian life and the life of a typical KGB man, and tried also to show their point of view. Reviewers have praised my novels for having authenticity, and I expect that this flows from my having done this type of work. But I hope that the authenticity has been provided in a fairly subtle way, as I dislike undue dwelling on hardware, organisation, and method. I didn't start writing until I was 54, and I had no particular ambition to be a writer, but starting late in life gives one a store of incident, characters, and location which is a great help. Like most writers, I concentrated on plot and action in my early books, and I hope that in my later books the characters themselves are more deeply and better explored. Having a full-time job and writing two novels a year required a very strict discipline, but each source of income gave me a feeling of independence of the other, and that made the routine full-time job more tolerable. Nowadays I am even more fortunate in being able to write full time.

*   *   *

Ted Allbeury has been lauded by peers Len Deighton, Desmond Bagley, and Anthony Price, and has become known as the spy writer's spy writer. He has mastered the many facets of the spy novel, as well as the craft of the novel itself. In humanity of tone, depth of character, and variety of plot, he is unmatched by any spy writer. The humanity in Allbeury's writing was bought with a tragic price—his four-year old daughter was kidnapped in 1970 and remained missing for years. To express his love and concern for her, he wrote his first novel, *A Choice of Enemies*. With heartfelt *roman á clef* figures of Allbeury's daughter and wife, *A Choice of Enemies* depicts the perils of the espionage profession for those who love. The book's compassionate outlook and portrayal of a man's dismal treatment by his own intelligence service make it a feeling man's *Spy Who Came In from the Cold*.

Through the years, Allbeury has refined his feel for the people in and around the enterprise of espionage. In several books, including *A Choice of Enemies*, romantic love comes into direct conflict with the requirements of the Service. Allbeury picks on the evils of the profession in *No Place to Hide*, in which a killer-for-hire has a crisis of conscience and tries to begin life over with a new lover. In *A Wilderness of Mirrors*, when SIS officer Robert Thornton's East Berlin operation crumbles around him, he finds that to control further damage in the way ordered by his superiors would threaten a woman he loves. Allbeury's fair-minded treatment of Thornton's heroism and the human costs of espionage make this gripping novel everything that Graham Greene's *The Human Factor* should have been.

Although Allbeury's books are justly praised for their realism, they do not sag with over-written secrets about tradecraft. Instead, they penetrate the shadowy themes of espionage in a clean, lucid prose style reminiscent of Ross MacDonald. The earlier novels bristle with plot and hi-tech background and the later ones focus on character and history, but with fluent writing and fascinating themes throughout.

In several books Allbeury ingeniously develops the labyrinthine connections between Soviet communism and World War II, where modern spies are forced to resurrect their wartime allegiances. In *Snowball*, the Polish-British agent Tad Anders investigates a clever KGB propaganda operation that asserts a World War II collusion between the U.S. and Hitler. *The Only Good German* tells of a right-wing German organization with inevitable links to Naziism. In *The Secret Whispers*, a tragic German agent, who made it through World War II in England, gets collared into service for his British masters. *The Special Collection* is a conspiracy thriller about a Russian operation to bring industrial chaos to Britain, with the key being Russia's involvement in Germany during World War II. In *The Judas Factor*, Tad Anders from *Snowball* is pulled back into the Secret Service to hunt for a Soviet assassin in East Berlin. *Children of Tender Years* tells in an amazingly unhackneyed way of an MI6 agent being sent to Germany to investigate outbreaks of antisemitism—40 years after his family perished in the Nazi death camps.

At the expense of plot, some of the more implausible books explore the deviousness of psychological operations. Allbeury examines several techniques, such as thought-copying in *The Man With the President's Mind*, indoctrination and impersonation in *The Twentieth Day of January*, and Richard Condon's famous *Manchurian Candidate* motif of murder by mind control in *Pay Any Price*.

Historical and political topics are obligatory for the serious espionage writer and have been used by Allbeury in his strongest novels. In *The Lantern Network*, a contemporary SIS agent investigates the World War II activities of the French Resistance. In *The Alpha List*, a sleek first-person tale structured like a private eye novel, an Intelligence man investigates the life of his childhood friend who is suspected of betraying his country to the Russians. Allbeury's motifs of betrayal and character study are refined in *The Other Side of Silence*, his finest novel. A fictional essay on the Kim Philby defection, it presents layer by layer the inquiry of a naive young SIS employee into the reasons for Philby's betrayal. The theme in *Consequence of Fear* is a supposedly accidental series of Russian nuclear explosions in the Urals in 1956. *All Our Tomorrows* speculates on Britain's capitulation to a Soviet takeover, and is Allbeury's hat in the ring with George Orwell's *1984* and Deighton's *SS-GB*. *The Crossing* is Allbeury's fictional essay on the United States' puzzling efforts to retrieve Francis Gary Powers, the American pilot captured by the Russians in 1960. And the recent *Time Without Shadows* looks into a charge that Britain sabotaged a spy network in France during World War II to placate Russia.

Although *Codeword Cromwell* and *The Lonely Margins*, written as Patrick Kelly, differ little from the books under Allbeury's own name, the two-book Max Farne series under the Richard Butler penname is unique in the Allbeury corpus. Set in Santa Margherita on the Italian Riviera, *Where All the Girls Are Sweeter* and *Italian Assets* take luxury boat salesman Farne back to the seaside village where he fought with the Resistance decades before in World War II. Written in a simple pastoral style with an integral sense of place, the Max Farne books are to the Italian seacoast what Gavin Black's splendid thrillers are to the Far East.

With over 30 original and well-respected novels in 18 years, Allbeury has become one of the finest, most consistent, and most inventive modern espionage craftsmen in the English language.

—Greg Goode

ALLEGRETTO, Michael. American. Born in Florida, in 1944. Educated at Colorado School of Mines, Golden 1962–64; University of Denver, Colorado 1965; Santa Monica City College, California 1970; University of Colorado, Denver, 1972. Has had a variety of jobs including civil draughtsman, surveyor, bookseller, school bus driver, silk screen printer, and technical writer. Recipient: Private Eye Writers of America Shamus award, 1987. Agent: Dominick Abel Literary Agency Inc., 498 West End Avenue, New York, New York 10024. Address: 3929 Stuart Street, Denver, Colorado 80212, U.S.A.

CRIME PUBLICATIONS

Novels (series: Jacob Lomax)

Death on the Rocks (Lomax). New York, Scribner, 1987; London, Macmillan, 1988.
Blood Stone (Lomax). New York, Scribner, 1988; London, Macmillan, 1989.
The Dead of Winter (Lomax). New York, Scribner, 1989.
Night of Reunion. New York, Scribner, 1990.

Uncollected Short Story

"The Bookie's Daughter," in *Justice for Hire* edited by Robert J. Randisi. New York, St. Martin's Press, 1990.

*

Michael Allegretto comments:
My series character, Jacob Lomax, follows in the footsteps of the classic fictional private eyes—tough, tenacious, laconic, and wry, with a well-developed sense of justice (and humor). His investigations center about Denver, Colorado, and involve people as varied as the geography: mountains and plains, city and suburb.

My non-series fiction is criminous, but as different from Lomax as I can make it: psychological suspense involving ordinary people forced into extraordinarily dangerous situations.

*   *   *

In Jacob Lomax, Michael Allegretto has developed something more than the run-of-the-mill cop turned private eye. First of all, the scene is Denver, Colorado, not known as one of the hot beds of crime like La-La Land, the Vieux Carre or Manhattan Island. In the second place, Lomax is not case hardened to the point that one or two more dead bodies don't raise his hackles a bit. But most of all, Jacob Lomax is the decade's white-hatted shamus; as up-to-date as a news release.

As he tells of his adventures in the classic first-person narrative style of Raymond Chandler's Philip Marlowe stories, Lomax looks at the criminal, the victim, and the innocent bystander with the same penetrating eye, for they may switch from one to another in the flick of a phrase. The descriptions are wry and the similes are provocative. Allegretto is a fluent writer with a good ear for the current sound of the spoken word. If he errs at all in this field, it is by alluding to personalities that may be more transient in the public eye than his books.

Allegretto has an excellent heritage on which to base the character of Lomax. Although his own father was a member of the Denver Police Department for many years and served as a detective, Allegretto did not use him as model but based Lomax on a separate set of characteristics; "he is not a father figure". Although a steady diet of crime at the dinner table is not a requirement for writing good crime fiction, it certainly helps with the atmosphere. The Denver locale gives Allegretto an opportunity to mix urban and rural scenes in his stories more easily than an author with a private eye character in New York City where even some of the suburbs are full-fledged urban ghettos. The western mountain feeling is strong in Lomax as shown by his dealing with his clients, the authorities and his adversaries.

The Lomax character, morose and introverted in the first book as a reaction to the violent death of his wife, develops into a much more open person with the ability to share more of his activities than the "loner" type he was. His life style is loose and his eating and sleeping habits are casual. These attributes are, in essence, Allegretto's statement of individuality, not only for Lomax, but for himself as a writer.

Although Allegretto has only published three Lomax novels and a short story in the same vein, he is already well established in the publishing world. In a change of pace that every artist needs before he is hopelessly typecast, Allegretto's fourth novel *Night of Reunion* is concerned with the impact of a psychotically driven woman's revenge on a prosaically average family in the prosaically average community of Colorado Springs. The psychotic mind is more hinted at than delved into in this third-person narrative style. Allegretto avoids the obvious problem of sinking into a bog of nonrational thought and follows the weavings of the disturbed mind by skimming the surface for traces of memories and actions that directly influence the flow of action in the story.

All the private eyes that walk the mean streets of any town owe their souls to Raymond Chandler to some extent. It is that higher urge to right wrongs, rescue damsels, and tilt at windmills that put them in the profession to begin with and no amount of physical pain, mental anguish, and lack of financial security will drive them out or hold them back.

It may be difficult to walk the path beaten by the great and near-great writers of crime fiction but Allegretto carries on with enough verve and originality to be recognized. There is no guarantee of fame or fortune in the history of crime literature, so only time will tell how Jacob Lomax will fare.

—Richard G. La Porte

———

ALLINGHAM, Margery (Louise). Also wrote as Maxwell March. British. Born in London, 20 May 1904; daughter of the writer H.J. Allingham. Educated at Perse High School for Girls, Cambridge; Polytechnic of Speech Training. Married the artist and editor Philip Youngman Carter in 1927. *Died 30 June 1966.*

CRIME PUBLICATIONS

Novels (series: Albert Campion)

The White Cottage Mystery. London, Jarrolds, 1928.
The Crime at Black Dudley (Campion). London, Jarrolds, 1929; as *The Black Dudley Murder*, New York, Doubleday, 1930.
Mystery Mile (Campion). London, Jarrolds, and New York, Doubleday, 1930.
Look to the Lady (Campion). London, Jarrolds, 1931; as *The Gyrth Chalice Mystery*, New York, Doubleday, 1931.
Police at the Funeral (Campion). London, Heinemann, 1931; New York, Doubleday, 1932.
Sweet Danger (Campion). London, Heinemann, 1933; as *Kingdom of Death*, New York, Doubleday, 1933; as *The Fear Sign*, New York, Macfadden 1933.
Other Man's Danger (as Maxwell March). London, Collins, 1933; as *The Man of Dangerous Secrets,* New York, Doubleday, 1933.
Death of a Ghost (Campion). London, Heinemann, and New York, Doubleday, 1934.
Rogue's Holiday (as Maxwell March). London, Collins, and New York, Doubleday, 1935.
Flowers for the Judge (Campion). London, Heinemann, and New York, Doubleday, 1936; as *Legacy in Blood*, New York, American Mercury, 1949.
Six Against the Yard, with others. London, Selwyn and Blount, 1936; as *Six Against Scotland Yard*, New York, Doubleday, 1936.
The Shadow in the House (as Maxwell March). London, Collins, and New York, Doubleday, 1936.
Dancers in Mourning (Campion). London, Heinemann, and New York, Doubleday, 1937; as *Who Killed Chloe?*, New York, Avon, 1943.
The Case of the Late Pig (Campion). London, Hodder and Stoughton, 1937.
Mr. Campion, Criminologist (includes *The Case of the Late Pig* and stories). New York, Doubleday, 1937.
The Fashion in Shrouds (Campion). London, Heinemann, and New York, Doubleday, 1938.
Black Plumes. London, Heinemann, and New York, Doubleday, 1940.
Traitor's Purse (Campion). London, Heinemann, and New York, Doubleday, 1941; as *The Sabotage Murder Mystery*, New York, Avon, 1943.
Coroner's Pidgin (Campion). London, Heinemann, 1945; as *Pearls Before Swine*, New York, Doubleday, 1945.
More Work for the Undertaker (Campion). London, Heinemann, 1948; New York, Doubleday, 1949.

Deadly Duo (2 novelets). New York, Doubleday, 1949; as *Take Two at Bedtime,* Kingswood, Surrey, World's Work, 1950.

The Tiger in the Smoke (Campion). London, Chatto and Windus, and New York, Doubleday, 1952.

No Love Lost (2 novelets). Kingswood, Surrey, World's Work, and New York, Doubleday, 1954.

The Beckoning Lady (Campion). London, Chatto and Windus, 1955; as *The Estate of the Beckoning Lady,* New York, Doubleday, 1955.

Hide My Eyes (Campion). London, Chatto and Windus, 1958; as *Tether's End,* New York, Doubleday, 1958; as *Ten Were Missing,* New York, Dell, 1959.

The China Governess (Campion). New York, Doubleday, 1962; London, Chatto and Windus, 1963.

The Mysterious Mr. Campion (omnibus). London, Chatto and Windus, 1963.

The Mind Readers (Campion). London, Chatto and Windus, and New York, Morrow, 1965.

Mr. Campion's Lady (omnibus, with stories). London, Chatto and Windus, 1965.

Cargo of Eagles (Campion; completed by Youngman Carter). London, Chatto and Windus, and New York, Morrow, 1968.

Short Stories

Mr. Campion and Others. London, Heinemann, 1939; augmented edition, London, Penguin, 1950.

Wanted: Someone Innocent (novelet and stories). N.p., Pony Books, 1946.

The Case Book of Mr. Campion, edited by Ellery Queen. New York, American Mercury, 1947.

The Allingham Case-Book. London, Chatto and Windus, and New York, Morrow, 1969.

The Allingham Minibus. London, Chatto and Windus, and New York, Morrow, 1973.

OTHER PUBLICATIONS

Novels

Blackkerchief Dick: A Tale of Mersea Island. London, Hodder and Stoughton, and New York, Doubleday, 1923.

Dance of the Years. London, Joseph, 1943; as *The Gallantrys,* Boston, Little Brown, 1943.

Plays

Dido and Aeneas (produced London, 1922).

Water in a Sieve London, French, 1925.

Other

The Oaken Heart. London, Joseph, and New York, Doubleday, 1941.

*

Critical Studies: *Campion's Career: A Study of the Novels of Margery Allingham* by B.A. Pike, Bowling Green, Ohio, Bowling Green University Press, 1987; *Ink in Her Blood: The Life and Crime Fiction of Margery Allingham* by Richard Martin, Ann Arbor, Michigan, UMI Research Press, 1988.

* * *

A cook-book phrase perhaps best describes the writings of Margery Allingham: boil until a rich consistency is reached. To

some extent in everything she wrote and in her best books from start to finish she created worlds of her own, rich and romantic yet springing undeniably from the actual world in which she lived.

She had an extraordinary energy of observation that took objects and made them almost into people, forcing life as it is to marry with her high romantic outlook. As early as *Mystery Mile,* she could say of London that it "seemed to be huddled round his hotel room as if it were trying to squeeze the life out of it," and as late as *More Work for the Undertaker* we find the casual phrase "On the desk the telephone squatted patiently." The everyday was surely and simply made into something supercharged.

And if her energy made things into people, of her people it made beings at once recognisable as belonging to the world of which she wrote (chiefly teeming London and the mysterious salt-marshes of Essex) and at the same time demons or gods. Take Campion's faithful valet, Magersfontein Lugg: the very name combines verisimilitude (people were named after battles) and the tuppence, nay fourpence, coloured. Or take that splendid creation, the Scotland Yard man Charlie Luke. Hear him describe a local doctor: "Comes out of his flat nagged to a rag in the mornings and goes down into his surgery-room with a shop front like a laundry. Seven-and-six for a visit, half-a-dollar for a squint at your tonsils or a thorough once-over if he isn't sure, and a bottle of muck which does you good. Stooping. Back like a camel...." Charlie Luke, Margery Allingham continues, "talked with his whole body. When he described Doctor Smith's back his own arched. When he mentioned the shop front he squared it with his hands." It is a marvellously energetic portrait.

Allied to that superabundance of energy was a gift for the topsy-turvy. She had but to make a bishop visit a smart London restaurant (in *Coroner's Pidgin*) to remark, "It was typical of him that at that moment it was not he, but the Minoan, which appeared a little out of place." Such a thought process derived from her strong intuitive intelligence which over the years she came to bring to bear on a widening spectrum of human activity. It seems, in fact, to have been the experience of the 1939–45 war in England, during which she tackled a variety of jobs grimmer than writing, that moved her sympathies a vital layer deeper making her able to write, still within the confines of the crime novel, of evil and the great issues.

As early as 1936, however, she had produced in *Flowers for the Judge* a murder story that kept in all the dull bits that the crime writers of that age (and a good many even 40 years later) omitted and, so infusing was her energy, that they read as grippingly as any smelly red herring trailed across lesser pages.

Her development is interestingly reflected in her handling of Albert Campion. Originally he was pretty much of a caricature, a cleverly updated version of Baroness Orczy's Scarlet Pimpernel, the indolent man-about-town who in reality...(and is as well probably related to the Royal Family). But as the books she wrote became more serious, moving away from the skillfully fabricated romance, that two-dimensional detective became more and more of a hindrance. So gradually she froze him out until he was little more than a pair of observing eyes. Then came the trauma of the war. And in the post-war books Campion is quite a different figure, even physically. "There were new lines on his over-thin face and with their appearance some of his old misleading vacancy of expression had vanished." He became, in fact, Margery Allingham speaking.

In the post-war books her extraordinary energy expressed itself in a splendid certainty that marks every line she wrote. Pen in hand, she was afraid of no one. Cheerfully she labelled a county family as "frightful females who smell like puppies' breath." As confidently, she created a figure of real evil in the criminal Jack Havoc of *The Tiger in the Smoke*. She could write without straining of love and of death, death as a reality rather than that "body with a neat hole in the forehead" beloved of the straightforward whodunit writers.

She could compose a poem to put into the mouth of a character, and it is no bad creation. She could write a *Times* obituary that actually read like words from that august newspaper (reproducing newspaper extracts is a feat which seems to fox almost every crime writer who tackles it, including those who have been journalists). She could produce a learned lecture joke that was exactly what such a curious piece of humour should be. And in *The Beckoning Lady* she casually invents a remark for Queen Victoria to have made of an ancestor that might have issued primly from the royal lips themselves.

Increasingly in the later books that strong female intelligence enabled her to say much that is penetrating and wise about men and women, perhaps especially women. And it is this which gives to these books (from which, alas, one must except the posthumously published *Cargo of Eagles*) a universality which some 30 years after the earliest of them was written makes them still immensely readable and is likely to make them readable 100 years after their publication.

—H.R.F. Keating

AMBLER, Eric. Also wrote as Eliot Reed (with Charles Rodda). British. Born in London, 28 June 1909. Educated at Colfe's Grammar School, London; London University, 1925–28. Served in the Royal Artillery, 1940–46; assistant director of army kinematography, 1944–46: Lieutenant Colonel; Bronze Star (USA). Married 1) Louise Crombie in 1939 (divorced 1958); 2) the writer Joan Harrison in 1958. Engineering apprentice, 1928; advertising copywriter, 1929–37; director of an advertising agency, 1937–38. Created *Checkmate* TV series, 1959. Recipient: Crime Writers Association Gold Dagger award, 1959, 1962, 1967, 1972, Diamond Dagger award, 1986; Mystery Writers of America Edgar Allan Poe award, 1964, and Grand Master award, 1975; Svenska Deckarakademins Grand Master, 1975; Grand Prix de Littérature Policière, 1976. O.B.E. (Officer, Order of the British Empire), 1981. Agent: Campbell Thomson and McLaughlin Ltd., 31 Newington Green, London N16 9PU, England.

CRIME PUBLICATIONS

Novels (series: Arthur Abdel Simpson)

The Dark Frontier. London, Hodder and Stoughton, 1936; New York, Mysterious Press, 1990.
Uncommon Danger. London, Hodder and Stoughton, 1937; as *Background to Danger*, New York, Knopf, 1937.
Epitaph for a Spy. London, Hodder and Stoughton, 1938; New York, Knopf, 1952; revised edition, London, Hodder and Stoughton, 1966.
Cause for Alarm. London, Hodder and Stoughton, 1938; New York, Knopf, 1939.
The Mask of Dimitrios. London, Hodder and Stoughton, 1939; as *A Coffin for Dimitrios*, New York, Knopf, 1939.
Journey into Fear. London, Hodder and Stoughton, and New York, Knopf, 1940.

Judgment on Deltchev. London, Hodder and Stoughton, and New York, Knopf, 1951.
The Schirmer Inheritance. London, Heinemann, and New York, Knopf, 1953.
The Night-Comers. London, Heinemann, 1956; as *State of Siege*, New York, Knopf, 1956.
Passage of Arms. London, Heinemann, 1959; New York, Knopf, 1960.
The Light of Day (Simpson). London, Heinemann, 1962; New York, Knopf, 1963; as *Topkapi*, New York, Bantam, 1964.
A Kind of Anger. London, Bodley Head, and New York, Atheneum, 1964.
Dirty Story (Simpson). London, Bodley Head, and New York, Atheneum, 1967.
The Intercom Conspiracy. New York, Atheneum, 1969; London, Weidenfeld and Nicolson, 1970.
The Levanter. London, Weidenfeld and Nicolson, and New York, Atheneum, 1972.
Doctor Frigo. London, Weidenfeld and Nicolson, and New York, Atheneum, 1974.
Send No More Roses. London, Weidenfeld and Nicolson, 1977; as *The Siege of the Villa Lipp*, New York, Random House, 1977; London, Prior, 1978.
The Care of Time. London, Weidenfeld and Nicolson, and New York, Farrar Straus Giroux, 1981.

Novels as Eliot Reed (with Charles Rodda)

Skytip. New York, Doubleday, 1950; London, Hodder and Stoughton, 1951.
Tender to Danger. New York, Doubleday, 1951; as *Tender to Moonlight*, London, Hodder and Stoughton 1952.
The Maras Affair. London, Collins, and New York, Doubleday, 1953.
Charter to Danger. London, Collins, 1954.
Passport to Panic. London, Collins, 1958.

Short Stories

Waiting for Orders. New York, Mysterious Press, 1990.

OTHER PUBLICATIONS

Plays

Screenplays: *The Way Ahead*, with Peter Ustinov, 1944; *United States*, 1945; *The October Man*, 1947; *The Passionate Friends* (*One Woman's Story*), 1949; *Highly Dangerous*, 1950; *The Magic Box*, 1951; *Gigolo and Gigolette*, in *Encore*, 1951; *The Card* (*The Promoter*), 1952; *Rough Shoot* (*Shoot First*), 1953; *The Cruel Sea*, 1953; *Lease of Life*, 1954; *The Purple Plain*, 1954; *Yangtse Incident* (*Battle Hell*), 1957; *A Night to Remember*, 1958; *The Wreck of the Mary Deare*, 1960; *Love Hate Love*, 1970.

Other

The Ability to Kill and Other Pieces. London, Bodley Head, 1963; New York, Mysterious Press, 1987.
"Introduction" to *The Adventures of Sherlock Holmes*, by Arthur Conan Doyle. London, Murray-Cape, 1974.
"A Better Sort of Rubbish: An Inquiry into the State of the Thriller," in *The Times* (London), 30 November 1974.
Here Lies: An Autobiography. London, Weidenfeld and Nicolson, 1985; New York, Farrar Straus Giroux, 1986.

Editor, *To Catch a Spy: An Anthology of Favorite Spy Stories*. London, Bodley Head, 1964; New York, Atheneum, 1965.

*

Manuscript Collection: Mugar Memorial Library, Boston University.

Eric Ambler comments:

I am sometimes asked, by assistant professors of Eng. Lit. and others with theses to write, to tell them what makes me tick. I always reply unhelpfully. Most of my books have been in print more or less continuously since they were written. I would not like to upset that apple cart by explaining myself. A reasonable explanation would probably read like an extract from Krafft-Ebing's case book. No suspense at all and very old hat.

*   *   *

During a career that has spanned almost 60 years, Eric Ambler has established himself as a giant among thriller writers. His reputation as one of the most innovative, original, and influential thriller writers of the 20th century is thoroughly deserved, and few novelists have done as much to bridge the gap between "popular" and "serious" literature as he has done since the 1930's.

While studying engineering and later working in advertising, Ambler tried his hand at writing plays in the early 1930's. Dissatisfied with his attempts, he turned to the thriller because it presented a literary challenge to him. Although he read thrillers, he realized that the genre largely merited its position as one of the lowest sub-literary forms and "had nowhere to go but up." He consciously set out to redeem the form by raising it from the "pulp" level of writers like Sapper and transforming it into a vehicle for serious political ideas. With the six novels he published in quick succession between 1936 and 1940, Ambler achieved this aim, demonstrating that thriller conventions were not incompatible with good prose, complex narrative structures, and subtlety of thought. In rewriting the genre Ambler also reversed its political basis. The formulaic, cliché-ridden thriller he inherited from the 1920's and 1930's was characterized by a right-wing ideology endorsing nationalism, xenophobia, and even fascism. Ambler's sympathies at the time were with the socialist Left, and consequently his novels, with their Marxist overtones, were almost heretical. This was a major breakthrough in that, after Ambler, the thriller could no longer be stereotyped. The wide gap separating thrillers from "literary" novels began to narrow, leading to the situation today in which there is a significant overlap between "popular" and "serious" fiction.

Ambler began his first novel, *The Dark Frontier,* with the intention of parodying the typical thriller, but ended up with an alternative, leftist form of thriller containing elements of fantasy as well as burlesque and parody. Prophetic about nuclear weapons, *The Dark Frontier* is a pioneering experiment rather than an accomplished work of fiction, but it pointed the way forward for Ambler. In his second novel, *Uncommon Danger (Background to Danger),* he concentrated on a realistic narrative of adventure and suspense set in contemporary Central Europe. At the heart of the story is Desmond Kenton, the first of a number of typical Ambler heroes or antiheroes notable for their ordinariness rather than any exceptional or superhuman qualities. It is by being in the wrong place at the wrong time that Kenton finds himself involved in a complex political conspiracy threatening European stability, and he has to choose between helping the sympathetic Russian spies, Andreas and Tamara Valeshoff, or the fascistic agents of ruthless multinational capitalism, which is vigorously satirized. Kenton eventually sides with the Valeshoffs to scupper an ingenious pro-Nazi scheme. The Valeshoffs reappear in Ambler's fourth novel, *Cause for Alarm,* in which another

English innocent abroad, Nicholas Marlow, is caught between them and the forces of fascism, this time in Mussolini's Italy. Ambler again makes use of the pursuit-and-escape device of the thriller, but his adaptation of such formulaic ingredients is even more original than in *Uncommon Danger,* as Andreas and Marlow succeed in outmanoeuvring a Nazi agent so as to cause a temporary rift in the Rome-Berlin Axis of Hitler and Mussolini.

Between the two Valeshoff novels, Ambler attempted a different reworking of elements of popular literature in *Epitaph for a Spy,* an unorthodox blend of Golden Age mystery and spy fiction, set in a hotel in the south of France. Ambler retains the closed-world puzzle of English classical detective fiction, but the object of the investigation is a spy working for Italy, not a murderer, and the totally incompetent "detective" is another of Ambler's innocents, a lonely Hungarian refugee, who is forced by the French police to help their enquiries after he is wrongly suspected of being a spy himself. The political content is less than in Ambler's other early novels, but the plight of members of the anti-Nazi resistance is movingly presented through a German communist being hunted by the Gestapo.

Of the six novels constituting Ambler's first phase, the best is his fifth, *The Mask of Dimitrios (A Coffin for Dimitrios),* which has become a landmark in the history of the thriller. Ambler knew that he "was breaking new ground with it," abandoning the straightforward narrative structures based on adventure and detection he had been employing. Instead he attempted a complex, interlocking double narrative, about the detective novelist Charles Latimer's quest in various parts of Europe for information concerning Dimitrios, and about the world of Dimitrios himself. Latimer's interest in fiction introduces an important element of self-reflexivity into the novel, while Dimitrios's life story between 1922 and 1938 appears in fragments, by means of assorted interviews and letters. As with Modernist texts, the reader has to piece together the criminal career of Dimitrios, blackmailer, drug-runner, and murderer turned successful businessman. Dimitrios emerges as symbolic of the destructive forces threatening civilization because of the fusion of monopolistic capitalism and fascist politics during the interwar years. He is, in a sense, the shadow cast by Hitler. With its historical sweep and its intricate narrative, *The Mask of Dimitrios* is a turning point in literary history: the point at which the thriller successfully aspires to the condition of art.

Before World War II brought Ambler's career as a novelist to a temporary halt in 1940, he completed his sixth novel, *Journey into Fear.* In this novel Ambler's English innocent abroad is an armaments engineer who finds himself targeted for assassination by Nazi agents because he possesses some top-secret information about the war effort. With its detailed scrutiny of a mind under stress in the closed world of a ship in the Mediterranean, *Journey into Fear* is the most psychological of Ambler's early novels as well as the most patriotic. It is marked by a shift in Ambler's political stance following the notorious Non-Aggression Pact between Hitler's Germany and Stalin's Soviet Union in August 1939 and the ensuing outbreak of war. Instead of being a capitalist evil, the British military-industrial complex now becomes a necessity in the struggle against totalitarian tyranny.

During the war Ambler worked for the army's film-making unit, and this experience prepared him for his successful career, mainly as a prolific scriptwriter, in the British film industry between 1946 and 1958. He then went to Hollywood, but his experience there turned out to be more frustrating than fruitful, and he returned to Europe after 10 years. Despite his heavy involvement in cinema after the war, Ambler eventually returned to fiction in 1951 with one of his most ambitious novels, *Judgment on Deltchev.* At the same time he began a collaboration with Charles Rodda to write fiction using the name Eliot Reed; five of these novels appeared between 1950 and 1958, but even at the outset Ambler was the lesser partner and his involvement soon waned to zero. In *Judgment on Deltchev*, the first of 12 extremely varied postwar novels, Ambler adapts the thriller format to explore the Stalinist show trials taking place throughout Eastern Europe after the communists seized power. With its lament for the fate of liberal democracy and its indictment of the crimes committed in the name of socialism, the novel is a seminal work in the history of Cold War literature, but Ambler himself did not pursue this path.

After the comparatively lightweight *The Schirmer Inheritance*, which concerns a complex investigation into the German past in order to solve a major inheritance problem in the USA, Ambler turned his attention to the political conflicts accompanying decolonization in South-East Asia in both *The Night-Comers* (*State of Siege*) and the richer and more rewarding *Passage of Arms*. What is new in *Passage of Arms* is the strong element of comedy—a wry comedy of character rather than a knockabout comedy of situation. Ambler had previously used parody, irony, caricature, and satire, but had not revealed a gift for comic yet sympathetic characterization.

In his next novel, *The Light of Day,* written during his Hollywood years, he goes even further in blending comic and thriller elements to produce a genuine comedy thriller set in Greece and Turkey. The narrator, Arthur Abdel Simpson, is one of Ambler's most memorable creations, an outrageous Falstaffian rogue and petty crook who never has any difficulty in proving to himself that black is white. Forced to help the Turkish police under threat of serious charges, he eventually thwarts, more by accident than design, an extremely ingenious robbery of royal treasures from Istanbul by a sophisticated international gang. Ambler planned a trilogy featuring Simpson, but wrote only one sequel to *The Light of Day*, the inferior *Dirty Story*. Dealing with Simpson's comic adventures as a reluctant mercenary in decolonized Africa, this novel continues Ambler's exploration of the close relationship between big business and crime in *A Kind of Anger*, published between the two Simpson books in the mid-1960s. An exciting narrative of pursuit, duplicity, and doublecrossing, set mainly in the south of France but dealing with international political intrigue involving the Kurdish minority in Iraq, *A Kind of Anger* is Ambler's first novel in which an intimate relationship between a man and a woman is central, determining the course of the action. Although not well received when published, it contains one of Ambler's most interesting psychological studies, that of the Dutch narrator Piet Maas, who begins as a suicidal, existential antihero but is transformed by his love for Lucia Bernardi into a man of heroic action.

The Intercom Conspiracy comes closer to being a Cold War spy novel than any of his other books, but it would be misleading to call it one. In some ways it radically subverts the spy novel, exposing the Cold War intelligence game as little more than a paranoid fantasy. Presented in an unusual narrative form as a dossierlike assembly of letters, interviews, and documents, *The Intercom Conspiracy* is about a brilliant money-making scam directed against both the CIA and the KGB by two disillusioned NATO intelligence officers from small countries, who manipulate the central character, a Canadian journalist in Geneva, into achieving their goal without realizing what he is doing. In writing about Israel and the Palestinian question in *The Levanter*, Ambler again handles his subject by focusing on the unenviable predicament of someone unintentionally caught up in a conspiracy, this time a British businessman long resident in the Middle East. The publication of *The Levanter* virtually coincided with the

massacre of Israeli athletes by Palestinians belonging to Black September at the Munich Olympics in 1972, thus making the novel highly topical.

A more impressive achievement is *Doctor Frigo,* Ambler's most politically profound novel since *Judgment on Deltchev* and one of his two or three best. Whereas individuals triumph over powerful groups in such novels as *A Kind of Anger, The Intercom Conspiracy,* and *The Levanter,* there is no comparable victory for Ernesto Castillo, the central character in *Doctor Frigo* (his nickname). The son of an assassinated President, Castillo is ruthlessly pressured by Latin American political machiavels and French intelligence to lend his name and support to a coup in his native country, wholly against his better judgment. The coup succeeds, but there is little hope that it will achieve any significant transformation.

In *Send No More Roses* (*The Siege of the Villa Lipp*) Ambler explores the extraordinarily lucrative world of white-collar crime by using a narrator, Firman, labelled as an "Able Criminal" by a leading criminologist. Centred on the siege (of the American title) in the south of France, the novel takes the form of Firman's defence of his imaginative financial activities during a career begun in World War II, and it poses the question of whether there is any difference between an "able criminal" and an "able businessman" in a society encouraging individual initiative and endorsing enterprise culture. Ambler's most recent novel, *The Care of Time,* appeared in 1981, and deals with the threats posed by chemical weapons and the mental instability of an autocratic Arab ruler. It was, therefore, obliquely prophetic of the Gulf War between Iraq and Iran during the 1980's.

The Care of Time is not one of Ambler's best books, but it confirms his lifelong commitment to providing entertainment and good storytelling while using such thriller ingredients as melodrama, suspense, and mystery to treat serious themes, thus bridging the gap between the "popular" and the "literary." Ambler, currently working on the sequel to the first volume of his autobiography *Here Lies,* is a true novelist as well as being a thriller writer.

—Peter Lewis

———

AMES, Delano. American. Born in Knox County, Ohio, 29 May 1906. Educated at Yale University, New Haven, Connecticut. Married 1) the writer Maysie Grieg; 2) Kit Woodward. Lived for many years in England. Address: c/o Harper and Row, 10 East 53rd Street, New York, New York 10022, U.S.A.

CRIME PUBLICATIONS

Novels (series: Jane and Dagobert Brown; Juan Llorca)

They Journey by Night. London, Hodder and Stoughton, 1932; as *Not in Utter Nakedness,* New York, Dial Press, 1932.
No Traveller Returns. London, Nicholson and Watson, 1934.
The Cornish Coast Conspiracy. London, Amalgamated Press, 1942.
He Found Himself Murdered. London, Swan, 1947.
She Shall Have Murder (Brown). London, Hodder and Stoughton, 1948; New York, Rinehart, 1949.
Murder Begins at Home (Brown). London, Hodder and Stoughton, 1949; New York, Rinehart, 1950.

Corpse Diplomatique (Brown). London, Hodder and Stoughton, 1950; New York, Rinehart, 1951.
Death of a Fellow Traveller (Brown). London, Hodder and Stoughton, 1950; as *Nobody Wore Black,* New York, Dell, 1951.
The Body on Page One (Brown). London, Hodder and Stoughton, and New York, Rinehart, 1951.
Murder, Maestro, Please (Brown). London, Hodder and Stoughton, and New York, Rinehart, 1952.
No Mourning for the Matador (Brown). London, Hodder and Stoughton, and New York, Washburn, 1953.
Crime, Gentlemen, Please (Brown). London, Hodder and Stoughton, 1954; as *Coffin for Christopher,* New York, Washburn, 1954.
Landscape with Corpse (Brown). London, Hodder and Stoughton, and New York, Washburn, 1955.
Crime Out of Mind (Brown). London, Hodder and Stoughton, and New York, Washburn, 1956.
She Wouldn't Say Who (Brown). London, Hodder and Stoughton, 1957; New York, Washburn, 1958.
Lucky Jane (Brown). London, Hodder and Stoughton, 1959; as *For Old Crime's Sake,* Philadelphia, Lippincott, 1959.
The Man in the Tricorn Hat (Llorca). London, Methuen, 1960; Chicago, Regnery, 1966.
The Man with Three Jaguars (Llorca). London, Methuen, 1961; Chicago, Regnery, 1967.
The Man with Three Chins (Llorca). London, Methuen, 1965; Chicago, Regnery, 1968.
The Man with Three Passports (Llorca). London, Methuen, 1967.

OTHER PUBLICATIONS

Novels

Uneasily to Bed. London, Grayson, 1934.
A Double Bed on Olympus. London, Grayson, 1936.
A Night in Casablanca (novelization of screenplay). London, Hollywood Publications, 1947.
School for Secrets (novelization of screenplay). London, World Film Publications, 1947.

Other

Contract Bridge Rhymes. London, Ritz, 1933.

Translator, *History of the Piano,* by Ernest Closson. London, Elek, 1947.
Translator, with Kit Ames, *Meet a Body,* by Jacques Decrest. London, Hammond, 1953.
Translator, *The Missing Formula,* by Jacques Decrest. London, Hammond, 1956.
Translator, *The Suspect,* by Mario Lacruz. London, Methuen, 1956.
Translator, with Richard Aldington, *Larousse Encyclopedia of Mythology,* edited by Félix Guirand. London, Batchworth Press, 1959; revised edition, as *New Larousse Encyclopedia of Mythology,* London, Hamlyn, 1969; selection, as *Greek Mythology,* Hamlyn, 1963.
Translator, *The Eyes of the Proud,* by Mercedes Salisachs. London, Methuen, 1960.
Translator, with Geoffrey Sainsbury, *Larousse Encyclopedia of Ancient and Medieval History,* edited by Marcel Dunan. London, Hamlyn, 1963.
Translator, *Larousse Encyclopedia of Modern History from 1500 to the Present Day,* edited by Marcel Dunan. London, Hamlyn, 1964; revised edition, 1972.

Translator, *Egyptian Mythology,* from text by J. Viau. London, Hamlyn, 1965.
Translator, *Larousse Science of Life: A Study of Biology, Sex, Genetics, Heredity, and Evolution,* by Jean Rostand and Andrée Tétry. London, Hamlyn, 1971.

*   *   *

The 12 adventures of Dagobert and Jane Brown are, at times, exasperatingly British, even when they take place in France, Switzerland, or America. Although written over many years, they represent only a short period of time in the characters' lives. Delano Ames uses Jane Hamish (later Brown) as the first-person narrator of all the books. Jane's purpose seems to be to help the reader understand Dagobert's way of thinking—although it isn't entirely clear to her either. Dagobert, the black sheep son of a titled family, will do almost anything to avoid work. Jane, on the other hand, is a hard-working clerk typist in a small office—at least during their first meeting and courtship.

This series won't make much sense unless the reader has read *She Shall Have Murder* which sets the stage for all following adventures with Dagobert's questionable contention that he can solve a murder even before the crime itself has been committed. Jane has become fond of one of her law firm's clients and when the woman is found dead (of gas fumes in her flat), Jane wonders out loud to Dagobert if that is actually what happened. Fumbling through a disguise as a meter reader and having Jane go through her employer's correspondence for clues, Dagobert creates a situation which almost gets them both killed. At his suggestion, Jane gives up her job and writes up the case, thereby becoming the sole support of the couple. They start on a merry married life where Jane does all the work and Dagobert wanders through vague attempts at scholarly occupations, taking up esoteric subjects that require travel to places so small that one would need a magnifying glass to find them on a map.

In one book, *Lucky Jane,* Jane wins a contest that Dagobert has entered for her, and sets off to attend the wedding of very minor royalty on a Mediterranean island, with her husband hitchhiking along behind on a motor cycle across most of France. The contest winners, riding in a Rolls-Royce, keep dying during stopovers on the trip; it is only the last scene, on board the prospective bridegroom's yacht, that eliminates nearly all of the suspects. Jane's gushy "isn't he wonderful" attitude is a little hard to take after more than one book, and the mystery solutions aren't always explained.

The four books about Juan Llorca, especially *The Man in the Tricorn Hat,* are much more successful, since Ames exploits, with loving care, the atmosphere, language, climate, and living conditions in Spain. He manages to portray the life of British expatriates who are living on reduced incomes (but with inflated aspirations) in a land of inexpensive household help. Since these people have brought with them old family problems and relationships, and they are chafing at an insular way of life, murder is almost bound to happen. Llorca is an interesting, and sometimes dashing hero, and it is to be regretted that there weren't more of this series.

—Ellen A. Nehr

————

AMOS, Alan. *See* **KNIGHT, Kathleen Moore.**

————

ANDERSON, Frederick Irving. American. Born in Aurora, Illinois, 14 November 1877. Educated in public schools; Wharton School, University of Pennsylvania, Philadelphia, graduated 1899. Married Emma Helen de Zouche in 1908 (died 1937). Worked as a journalist on the Aurora *News,* 1895–96, and New York *World,* 1898–1908. Freelance writer from 1910. *Died 24 December 1947.*

CRIME PUBLICATIONS

Novel

The Notorious Sophie Lang. London, Heinemann, 1925.

Short Stories

The Adventures of the Infallible Godahl. New York, Crowell, 1914.
The Book of Murder. New York, Dutton, 1930.

Uncollected Short Stories

"Madame the Cat," in *Best American Mystery Stories of the Year,* edited by Carolyn Wells. New York, Day, 1931.
"The Unknown Man," in *Ellery Queen's Mystery Magazine* (New York), July 1942.
"The Phantom Guest," in *Ellery Queen's Mystery Magazine* (New York), Winter 1942.
"The Jorgensen Plates," in *Female of the Species,* edited by Ellery Queen. Boston, Little Brown, 1943; as *Ladies of Crime,* London, Faber, 1947.
"The Signed Masterpiece," in *Ellery Queen's Mystery Magazine* (New York), November 1943.
"Murder in Triplicate," in *Ellery Queen's Mystery Magazine* (New York), December 1946.
"The Phantom Alibi," in *Ellery Queen's Mystery Magazine* (New York), November 1947.
"The Purple Flame," in *Ellery Queen's Mystery Magazine* (New York), January 1949.
"The Man from the Death House," in *Ellery Queen's Mystery Magazine* (New York), January 1951.
"The Door Key," in *Ellery Queen's Mystery Magazine* (New York), March 1952.
"The Half-Way House," in *Anthology 1963 Mid-Year,* edited by Ellery Queen. New York, Davis, 1963.

OTHER PUBLICATIONS

Other

The Farmer of To-morrow. New York, Macmillan, 1913.
Electricity for the Farm. New York, Macmillan, 1915.

* * *

Frederick Irving Anderson, although a fairly prolific writer for the American slick magazines, is represented by only three fiction books, the first and third of which are among the rarest collector's items.

The Adventures of the Infallible Godahl narrates six adventures of a remarkable master thief. An interesting touch is that Godahl employs the unwitting Oliver Armiston, a famous writer of detective stories, to plan his greatest coup. Because of this, Armiston retired from authorship. In *The Book of Murder* Armiston is again employed, but now by the great Deputy Parr of the New York police, for assistance in unusual crimes.

Together they work through eight cases, all of which are characterized by a Baghdadian zest. The two remaining stories in the book are concerned with crime in a rural setting, with other detective figures. In *The Notorious Sophie Lang,* an episodic novel, the most brilliantly conceived female criminal in the literature leads Parr and Armiston a long and frustrating chase through insurance fraud, murder, a gem robbery, and other crimes. Sophie is always more than a match for them.

Anderson has never achieved the recognition that he deserves. He was probably the only detective story writer to capture successfully the pre-*Titanic* syndrome of ultra-sophistication mingled with vulgarity, refinement with crude greed, hedonism with a zest for cultural color. He brought a certain Stevensonian glamor and fairytale quality into even police routine. His stories are intelligent, original, well-crafted, excellent in characterization, and often brilliant stylistically.

—E.F. Bleiler

———

ANDERSON, James. British. Educated at grammar school and at Reading University, B.A. in history. Has worked as salesman, copywriter, and journalist. Address: 4 Church Road, Penarth, South Glamorgan, Wales.

CRIME PUBLICATIONS

Novels (series: Mikael Petros; Inspector Wilkins)

Assassin (Petros). London, Constable, 1969; New York, Simon and Schuster, 1970.
The Alpha List. London, Constable, 1972; New York, Walker, 1973.
The Abolition of Death (Petros). London, Constable, 1974; New York, Walker, 1975.
The Affair of the Blood-Stained Egg Cosy (Wilkins). London, Constable, 1975; New York, McKay, 1977.
Appearance of Evil. London, Constable, 1977.
Angel of Death. London, Constable, 1978.
Assault and Matrimony. London, Muller, 1980; New York, Doubleday, 1981.
Auriol. London, Muller, 1982.
The Affair of the Mutilated Mink Coat (Wilkins). New York, Avon, 1982.
The Murder of Sherlock Holmes. London, W.H. Allen, and New York, Avon, 1985.
Hooray for Homicide. London, W.H. Allen, and New York, Avon, 1985.
Lovers and Other Killers. London, W.H. Allen, and New York, Avon, 1986.
Additional Evidence. New York, Doubleday, 1988.

* * *

Few writers are gifted with the range of skill James Anderson exhibits in his novels. He is best known in the United States for *Assault and Matrimony,* his hilarious tale of a husband and wife whose long simmering dissatisfactions with their marriage are brought to a boil when they learn that the house next door will soon have new occupants. The novel was made into a television movie.

In *The Affair of the Blood-Stained Egg Cosy* (the title alone is perfection) Anderson has produced a classic tale recalling the

Golden Age of the mystery novel. It is set in the 1930's, and the earl and countess of Burford invite a number of guests to their country home, Alderley; the earl's brother also entertains a few diplomats who discreetly conduct a little business. The mix also includes a Texas millionaire, a young woman of gentle birth but no money, an exotic but mysterious European baroness, and a jewel thief. Anderson plays out hilariously all the cliché's of the Golden Age mystery. At the opening of a sequel, *The Affair of the Mutilated Mink Coat,* the earl and countess of Burford allude to the disastrous events in the earlier book by commenting on their bad luck with large houseparties; they are resigned to smaller parties and prepare themselves for what they expect to be a tame gathering: a film idol and producer scouting for a location for a film, a cousin and her husband recently arrived from Australia, and the countess's daughter and her two beaus, from whom she hopes to make a final choice. Inspector Wilkins appears in both novels, and occasionally takes the unusual stance of asking helpful suspects if they could keep their information to themselves and save him a lot of bother. The tone Anderson strikes in these three cozies is superb.

In sharp contrast to his cozies are Anderson's three political thrillers, two of which follow the pursuits of Mikael Petros. In *Assassin,* Petros, a man who spent 12 years in the military before resigning and drifting for another three years, is facing execution in a fictitious European country. Only days before his execution he is offered the chance to live if he will assassinate the leader of a neighboring country to which Petros's country is closely tied. Petros agrees, but to ensure his compliance he is injected with a poison that will prove fatal unless he receives an antidote in 12 weeks. Since Petros does not know what poison was used, he must meet the deadline set by his captors. In *The Abolition of Death,* Petros is living safely outside his native land, having served a sentence for the assassination, but he still feels condemned by all those around him. He is given a chance to redeem himself by carrying out a secret mission for his new country: a scientist in Europe has learned how to stop the aging process and is about to hand over this knowledge to a dictator. In these two novels Anderson occasionally suggests he is poised for a leap into science fiction, but he adheres instead to the form of a political thriller. The tautness of the suspense holds until the very end in *Appearance of Evil,* in which an embittered librarian, Matt Greenwood, feels compelled to leave his job at a small U.S. college to travel to England to stop a murder he is certain is inevitable. The tying-up at the end is convincing until the last line of the book, which is painfully disappointing.

Anderson has also turned his pen to the police procedural and straight novel of detection. In *Additional Evidence,* Stephen Grant, a literary agent, is arrested for the murder of his mistress, Linda Matthews. Stephen's wife, Alison, sets out to prove his innocence. She joins forces with Linda's brother, who happens to be a detective chief inspector with Scotland Yard. The novel teeters between hard-nosed investigation and comedy, particularly in the interplay between Inspector Bidwell and Sergeant Primrose, then settles down into a police procedural. There is no inconsistency in *Angel of Death,* a stunner of a tale about George Roussos, a rich Greek shipping magnate with an aristocratic British wife, his second, a spoiled teenage daughter being raised by her fanatical grandmother, and an enemy who is threatening to kidnap the daughter. The plot is superb. *The Alpha List* sits on the line between a police procedural and a novel of detection, and is the least satisfying of Anderson's work. The story begins with Inspector Palmer tracking down a blackmailer who has put a twist into his line of business.

Anderson devises clever plots, draws strong characters, and has a knack for finding the humor in any situation, but the last can be a weakness as well as a strength. Although his best novels tend to be those in which he gives full play to his sense of humor, his suspense or thriller tales are equally good until undermined by his failure to curb his humor. *Appearance of Evil* is too fine a story of deception, fear, and illusion to fail at the end because of one misplaced jocular line, and *Additional Evidence* is too good a murder puzzle to be confused by the comedy between the police officers, who deserve a book of their own.

—Susan Oleskiw

ANMAR, Frank. *See* **NOLAN, Willam F.**

ANDRESS, Lesley. *See* **SANDERS, Lawrence.**

ANTHONY, Evelyn. Pseudonym for Evelyn Bridget Patricia Ward-Thomas, née Stephens. British. Born in London, 3 July 1928. Educated at Convent of the Sacred Heart, Roehampton, to 1944, and privately. Married Michael Ward-Thomas in 1955; two daughters and four sons. Recipient: *Yorkshire Post* award, 1973. Agent: A.P. Watt Ltd., 20 John Street, London WC1N 2DL. Address: Horham Hall, Thaxted, Essex, England.

CRIME PUBLICATIONS

Novels (series: Davina Graham)

The Rendezvous. London, Hutchinson, 1967; New York, Coward McCann, 1968.
The Legend. London, Hutchinson, and New York, Coward McCann, 1969.
The Assassin. London, Hutchinson, and New York, Coward McCann, 1970.
The Tamarind Seed. London, Hutchinson, and New York, Coward McCann, 1971.
The Poellenberg Inheritance. London, Hutchinson, and New York, Coward McCann 1972.
The Occupying Power. London, Hutchinson, 1973; as *Stranger at the Gates,* New York, Coward McCann, 1973.
The Malaspiga Exit. London, Hutchinson, 1974; as *Mission to Malaspiga,* New York, Coward McCann, 1974.
The Persian Ransom. London, Hutchinson, 1975; as *The Persian Price,* New York, Coward McCann, 1975.
The Silver Falcon. London, Hutchinson, and New York, Coward McCann, 1977.
The Return. London, Hutchinson, and New York, Coward McCann, 1978.
The Grave of Truth. London, Hutchinson, 1979; as *The Janus Imperative,* New York, Coward McCann, 1980.
The Defector (Graham). London, Hutchinson, 1980; New York, Coward McCann, 1981.
The Avenue of the Dead (Graham). London, Hutchinson, 1981; New York, Coward McCann, 1982.

Albatross (Graham). London, Hutchinson, 1982; New York, Putnam, 1983.

The Company of Saints (Graham). London, Hutchinson, 1983; New York, Putnam, 1984.

Voices on the Wind. London, Century Hutchinson, and New York, Putnam, 1985.

No Enemy But Time. London, Century Hutchinson, 1987; as *A Place to Hide*, New York, Putnam, 1987.

OTHER PUBLICATIONS

Novels

Imperial Highness. London, Museum Press, 1953; as *Rebel Princess*, New York, Crowell, 1953.

Curse Not the King. London, Museum Press, 1954; as *Royal Intrigue*, New York, Crowell, 1954.

Far Flies the Eagle. New York, Crowell, 1955.

Anne Boleyn. London, Museum Press, and New York, Crowell, 1957.

Victoria and Albert. New York, Crowell, 1958; as *Victoria*, London, Museum Press, 1959.

Elizabeth. London, Museum Press, 1960; as *All the Queen's Men*, New York, Crowell, 1960.

Charles the King. London, Museum Press, and New York, Doubleday, 1961.

Clandara. London, Hurst and Blackett, and New York, Doubleday, 1963.

The Heiress. London, Hurst and Blackett; as *The French Bride*. New York, Doubleday, 1964; London, Arrow, 1966.

Valentina. London, Hurst and Blackett, and New York, Doubleday, 1966.

Anne of Austria. London, Hurst and Blackett, 1968; as *The Cardinal and the Queen*, New York, Coward McCann, 1968.

The House of Vandekar. London, Century Hutchinson, and New York, Putnam, 1988.

The Scarlet Thread. London, Century Hutchinson, 1989; New York, Harper, 1990.

*

Evelyn Anthony comments:
I love my work, and so long as it pleases my readers, that is all the incentive I need.

* * *

Evelyn Anthony's novels of suspense often begin with a situation out of recent history or headlines then develop into the type of international love story for which she is well known. *The Rendezvous, The Poellenberg Inheritance,* and *The Occupying Power* all concern Nazi war criminals trying to escape punishment. *The Legend, The Defector,* and *The Tamarind Seed* are about Russian spies and defectors. *The Assassin* takes place in the midst of an American election with a bizarre Russian plot that is unwittingly financed by an American millionaire. *The Malaspiga Exit* uncovers an international drug and art smuggling ring. *The Persian Ransom* is about a Palestine Liberation Organization kidnapping. In *No Enemy But Time,* the heroine tries to save her half-brother from his enemies in the Irish Republican Army. Anthony's most highly praised work, however, has been her recent series of four novels (*The Defector, The Avenue of the Dead, Albatross,* and *The Company of Saints*) featuring Davina Graham, an attractive and capable British intelligence officer.

Although the initial events in Anthony's novels may be motivated by recognizable historical or current events, the action of her plots often involves more romance than intrigue. The villains may be evil in themselves, but political realities also pose an almost insurmountable threat to the lovers. In *The Rendezvous, The Legend,* and *The Persian Ransom,* one of the lovers is killed; in other books, they are united, even if their happiness means fleeing respectable society. Anthony's lovers in each novel are immediately identifiable to the reader by the strong and immutable sexual attraction they feel for each other. No matter how the book ends, the characters have no choice but to be motivated and controlled by that attraction.

Anthony is interested in victim psychology, a subject she handles with great skill; she sometimes depicts lovers whose relationship develops out of a captor-captive situation. *The Persian Ransom* is the most thorough evocation of the theme; the victim and one of her kidnappers fall in love and he turns against his fellows to help her escape. In *The Rendezvous,* a former Nazi has a love affair with a woman he had interrogated during the war; because he had been kind to her then, she loves him despite her terror-filled memories. In *The Defector* (the first Davina Graham book) and in *The Tamarind Seed* (filmed with Julie Andrews and Omar Sharif), the heroine falls in love with a defecting Russian spy she has been assigned to help to hide from his former Soviet colleagues who are trying to kill him. In both novels, Anthony's heroines must contend with their feelings for the hero while owing ultimate loyalty to their country. Her handling of the cultural differences between the lovers is sensitive and engaging.

In the Davina Graham books, Anthony develops espionage themes similar to those of John le Carré. After Davina marries the defector Ivan Sasanov, he is assassinated by Soviet operatives and Davina must locate the British traitor responsible for his death. Despite her family's disapproval and her personal sorrow, she continues her espionage work, pitting herself successfully against the leader of the KGB. Eventually, she earns promotion to head of the British intelligence service.

—Kay Mussell

———

ANTONY, Peter. Pseudonym for the twin brothers Anthony and Peter Shaffer. British. **SHAFFER, Anthony (Joshua):** Born in Liverpool, Lancashire, 15 May 1926. Educated at St. Paul's School, London; Trinity College, Cambridge (editor, *Granta*), graduated 1950. Married 1) Carolyn Soley; two daughters; 2) the actress Diane Cilento in 1985. Barrister, 1951–55; journalist, 1956–58; partner in advertising film production agency, 1959–69. Recipient: Tony award, 1971; Mystery Writers of America Edgar Allan Poe award, for screenplay, 1973. Lives in Wiltshire. Agent: Peters, Fraser and Dunlop, 5th Floor, The Chambers, Chelsea Harbour, Lots Road, London SW10 0XF, England. **SHAFFER, Peter (Levin):** Born in Liverpool, Lancashire, 15 May 1926. Educated at preparatory school in Liverpool; Hall School, London; St. Paul's School, London; Trinity College, Cambridge, 1947–50, B.A. in history 1950. Conscript coalminer, Chislet colliery, Kent, 1944–47. Worked in Doubleday bookstore, an airline terminal at Grand Central Station, Lord and Taylors department store, and in the acquisition department, New York Public Library, all New York 1951–54; staff member Boosey and Hawkes, music publishers, London, 1954–55; literary critic, *Truth*, 1956–57; music critic, *Time and Tide*, 1961–62 both London. Recipient (for drama): *Evening Standard* award, 1958, 1980; New York Drama Critics Circle award, 1960, 1975; Tony award, 1975, 1981; Outer Critics Circle award, 1981; Vernon Rice award, 1981; Oscar, for screenplay, 1985. C.B.E. (Commander, Order of the British Empire), 1987. Lives in New York City. Agent: Macnaughton Lowe Representation, 200 Fulham Road, London SW10 9PN, England; or, Robert Lantz, The Lantz Office, 888 Seventh Avenue, New York, New York 10106, U.S.A.

CRIME PUBLICATIONS

Novels (series: Mr. Verity)

The Woman in the Wardrobe (Verity).   London, Evans, 1951.
How Doth the Little Crocodile? (Verity).   London, Evans, 1952; as Anthony and Peter Shaffer, New York, Macmillan, 1957.
Withered Murder (as Anthony and Peter Shaffer).   London, Gollancz, 1955; New York, Macmillan, 1956.
Absolution (novelization of screenplay; by Anthony Shaffer). London, Corgi, 1979.

Uncollected Short Story

"Before and After," in *London Mystery Magazine*, June 1953.

OTHER PUBLICATIONS

Novel by Anthony Shaffer

The Wicker Man (novelization of screenplay), with Robin Hardy.   New York, Crown, 1978; London, Hamlyn, 1979.

Plays by Anthony Shaffer

The Savage Parade (produced London, 1963; as *This Savage Parade*, produced London, 1987).
Sleuth (produced London and New York, 1970). New York, Dodd Mead, 1970; London, Calder and Boyars, ˙1971.
Murderer (produced Brighton and London, 1975). London, Boyars, 1979.
Widow's Weeds (produced Brisbane, South Australia, 1977; Plymouth, 1987).
Whodunnit (as *The Case of the Oily Levantine*, produced Guildford, Surrey, 1977; London, 1979, revised version, as *Whodunnit*, produced New York, 1982; Brighton, 1987). New York, French, 1983.

Screenplays: *Mr. Forbush and the Penguins*, 1971; *Frenzy*, 1972; *Sleuth*, 1973; *The Wicker Man*, 1973; *Masada*, 1974; *The Moonstone*, 1975; *Death on the Nile*, 1978; *Absolution*, 1981; *Evil Under the Sun*, 1982.

Television Play: *Pig in the Middle.*

Plays by Peter Shaffer

Five Finger Exercise (produced London, 1958; New York, 1959). London, Hamish Hamilton, 1958; New York, Harcourt Brace, 1959.
The Private Ear and The Public Eye (produced London, 1962; New York, 1963). London, Hamish Hamilton, 1962; New York, Stein and Day, 1964.
The Merry Roosters' Panto, with the Theatre Workshop (produced London, 1963; as *It's About Cinderella*, produced London, 1969).
Sketch in *The Establishment* (produced New York, 1963).

The Royal Hunt of the Sun: A Play Concerning the Conquest of Peru (produced Chichester and London, 1964; New York, 1965). London, Hamish Hamilton, and New York, Stein and Day, 1965.
Black Comedy (produced Chichester 1965; London, 1966; New York, 1967). Included in *Black Comedy, Including White Lies*, 1967.
White Lies (produced New York, 1967). Included in *Black Comedy, Including White Lies*, 1967; as *White Liars* (produced London, 1968), London, French, 1967; revised version, (produced London and New York, 1976).
Black Comedy, Including White Lies: Two Plays. New York, Stein and Day, 1967; as *White Liars, Black Comedy: Two Plays*, London, Hamish Hamilton, 1968.
Shrivings (as *The Battle of Shrivings*, produced London, 1970; revised version, as *Shrivings*, produced York, 1975). London, Deutsch, 1974; with *Equus*, New York, Atheneum, 1974.
Equus (produced London, 1973; New York, 1974). London, Deutsch, 1973; with *Shrivings*, New York, Atheneum, 1974.
Amadeus (produced London, 1979). London, Deutsch, 1980; revised version (produced New York, 1980; London, 1981), New York, Harper, and London, Penguin, 1981.
The Collected Plays of Peter Shaffer (revised texts; includes *Five Finger Exercise, The Private Ear, The Public Eye, The Royal Hunt of the Sun, White Liars, Black Comedy, Equus, Shrivings, Amadeus*). New York, Harmony, 1982.
Black Mischief (produced Bristol, 1983).
Yonadab (produced London, 1985).
Lettice and Lovage (produced Bath and London, 1987). London, Deutsch, 1988; revised version, produced London, 1988.

Screenplays: *Lord of the Flies*, with Peter Brook, 1963; *The Public Eye* (*Follow Me!*), 1972; *Equus*, 1977; *Amadeus*, 1984.

Radio Plays: *Alexander the Corrector*, 1946; *The Prodigal Father*, 1957; *Whom Do I Have the Honour of Addressing?*, 1989.

Television Plays: *The Salt Land*, 1955; *Balance of Terror*, 1957.

*

Bibliography: *Peter and Anthony Shaffer: A Reference Guide* by Dennis A. Klein, Boston, Hall, 1982.

Critical Studies: *Peter Shaffer* by John Russell Taylor, London, Longman, 1974; *Peter Shaffer* by Dennis A. Klein, Boston, Twayne, 1979; *File on Shaffer* edited by Virginia Cooke and Malcolm Page, London, Methuen, 1987; *Peter Shaffer: Roles, Rites and Rituals in the Theater* by Gene A. Plunka, Teaneck, New Jersey, Fairleigh Dickinson University Press, 1988.

*   *   *

In the first of their three books, *The Woman in the Wardrobe*, the Shaffer brothers set the scene in a seaside resort and introduce their detective, Mr. Verity. (In the last book his name was inexplicably changed to Fathom.) There is in the literature a long tradition of eccentric detectives, and Verity is true to that tradition. He is described as "an immense man, just tall enough to carry his breadth majestically. His face was sharp, smooth and teak-brown; his blue eyes small and of a startling brilliance. He wore a fine chestnut Van-Dyck and an habitual cloak in winter, all of which lent him in equal proportions the roles of a corpulent Satyr and an elderly Laughing Cavalier." His passions were twofold, black Cuban cigars and collecting statuary. He made constant use, we are told, of a huge purple bathing costume purchased in 1924 from a fruit merchant in Beirut. But the Shaffers do not maroon their strangely behaved detective in a world of normal people. He is quickly joined by Detective Inspector Rambler, a man almost as large and unusual as himself, and, in the first book only, by an irritating Richard Tudor, a latter-day pretender to the throne. Equally odd characters appear in the later books.

For their main themes the authors also choose from the classical repertory. Two of the books present problems of impossible crime after the manner of Edgar Allan Poe, while the other is concerned with that fine old detective story institution, the Criminologists' Club, established for the discussion of crime considered as a fine art.

It is not then the basic ingredients of the Shaffers' books which make them stand out from the rest; it is the manner in which they handle those ingredients. Take first the plots. Locked-room murders and murder clubs were hardly new departures; indeed the literature of the 1920's and 1930's abounded with them. Yet most of those books are now forgotten, and deservedly so because they were generally dull, wordy affairs with no vestige of originality in problem or solution. In comparison the Shaffers shine. Their first book somehow manages to invest that hardy perennial, the locked-room murder, with a brilliant original tongue-in-cheek solution which a hundred other authors had overlooked. In fact this book may well be the best locked-room novel written in the last 40 years. Their second contains a devious and diabolical plot of multiple murder to which a solution of equal merit is provided, while their third returns unashamedly to impossible crime and sets down yet another new and ingenious explanation.

Finally in considering the success of the novels there is another major factor which must not be overlooked, their humour. They are witty, full of telling observations and apt descriptions, and best of all they display their writers' rare ability to poke gentle fun at the time-worn form, and incidentally at themselves. There can be no doubt that the authors are devotees of the detective novel, but there can also be no doubt that they have never taken the subject or themselves too seriously. The result is a small but heady brew of the highest quality.

—Robert C.S. Adey

ARD, William (Thomas). Also wrote as Ben Kerr; Mike Moran; Jonas Ward; Thomas Wills. American. Born in Brooklyn, New York, 7 July 1922. Educated at Dartmouth College, Hanover, New Hampshire, graduated 1944. Served in the United States Marine Corps, 1944–45: medical discharge. Married Eileen Kovara in 1945; one daughter and one son. Copywriter, Buchanan Advertising Agency, New York; publicity writer, Warner Brothers New York office; freelance writer from 1950; lived in Clearwater, Florida, from 1953. *Died 12 March 1960.*

CRIME PUBLICATIONS

Novels (series: Timothy Dane; Danny Fontaine; Lou Largo)

The Perfect Frame (Dane).   New York, Mill, 1951; London, Hammond, 1953.

.38 (Dane).   New York, Rinehart, 1952; as *You Can't Stop Me,* New York, Popular Library, 1953; as *This Is Murder,* London, Hammond, 1954.
The Diary (Dane).   New York, Rinehart, 1952; London, Hammond, 1954.
You'll Get Yours (as Thomas Wills).   New York, Lion, 1952.
A Girl for Danny.   New York, Popular Library, 1953.
A Private Party (Dane).   New York, Rinehart, 1953; as *Rogue's Murder,* London, Hammond, 1955.
Double Cross (as Mike Moran).   New York, Popular Library, 1953.
Don't Come Crying to Me (Dane).   New York, Rinehart, 1954.
No Angels for Me.   New York, Popular Library, 1954.
Mr. Trouble (Dane).   New York, Rinehart, 1954.
Hell Is a City (Dane).   New York, Rinehart, 1955.
Mine to Avenge (as Thomas Wills).   New York, Fawcett, 1955; London, Fawcett, 1956.
Cry Scandal (Dane).   New York, Rinehart, 1956; London, Digit, 1960.
The Root of His Evil (Dane).   New York, Rinehart, 1957; London, Boardman, 1958; as *Deadly Beloved,* New York, Dell, 1958.
All I Can Get (Largo).   Derby, Connecticut, Monarch, 1959.
As Bad as I Am.   New York, Rinehart, 1959; London, Boardman, 1960; as *Wanted: Danny Fontaine,* New York, Dell, 1960.
Like Ice She Was (Largo).   Derby, Connecticut, Monarch, 1960.
When She Was Bad (Fontaine).   New York, Dell, 1960.
The Sins of Billy Serene.   Derby, Connecticut, Monarch, 1960.
The Naked and the Innocent.   London, Digit, 1960.

Novels as Ben Kerr

Shakedown.   New York, Holt, 1952.
Down I Go.   New York, Popular Library, 1955.
Damned If He Does.   New York, Popular Library, 1956.
I Fear You Not.   New York, Popular Library, 1956; London, Digit, 1960.
Club 17.   New York, Popular Library, 1957.
The Blonde and Johnny Malloy.   New York, Popular Library, 1958.

OTHER PUBLICATIONS

Novels as Jonas Ward

The Name's Buchanan.   New York, Fawcett, 1956; London, Fawcett, 1958.
Buchanan Says No.   New York, Fawcett, 1957; London, Fawcett, 1958.
One-Man Massacre.   New York, Fawcett, 1958; London, Fawcett, 1959.
Buchanan Gets Mad.   New York, Fawcett, 1958; London, Fawcett, 1960.
Buchanan's Revenge.   New York, Fawcett, and London, Muller, 1960.
Buchanan on the Prod, completed by Robert Silverberg.   New York, Fawcett, 1960; London, Muller, 1961.

*

Bibliography: by Francis M. Nevins, Jr., in *Armchair Detective* 15 (New York), no. 2, 1982.

*   *   *

In the early 1950's, when the nation's political and cultural life were dominated by Joe McCarthy and HUAC and its crime fiction by the bloody exploits of Mike Hammer, Ard and a few others carried on the Hammett-Chandler tradition and rejected Mickey Spillane's formula of sadism-snigger-and-sleaze. In Ard's world the private eye stands for personal and political decency, a clear line is drawn between dramatically justified violence and gratuitous brutality, and sex is seen as a restoration of oneself and a friendly caring for another. But the strongest influence on Ard was neither Hammett nor Chandler but John O'Hara, whom he mentions several times and to whom Ard owes his simple yet vivid style, his flashbacks to explore characters' social and economic roots, and his recurring theme of the man who drops ethnicity to achieve success. What makes Ard unique is that despite the trappings of dark alleys, ganglords, crooked cops and pols, and sinister roadhouses, his heart was with movies and stage musicals and Broadway nightspots. He loved everyone and everything in the world of popular entertainment and bathed its every aspect in a soft romantic glow. The same romanticism permeates Ard's main series character, private eye Timothy Dane, who is a shamus like no other in fiction: young, naive, tender with women, inept at machismo, incapable of escaping tight spots singlehanded, resorting to violence rarely. There is about Dane a sweetness, a delicate simplicity as incongruous as it is memorable.

The most powerful and exciting Dane novel, *Hell Is a City,* takes place in a nightmare New York where the mayor, the police commissioner, and most of the officials are corruptly allied with the mobs and determined to win the upcoming city elections. When a young Latino shoots the Brooklyn vice cop who was about to rape the boy's sister, the municipal bosses use their puppets in the news media to portray the case as the coldblooded murder of a heroic officer and put out word to shoot on sight whoever might contradict the party line. Brought in by a crusading newspaper editor, Dane finds himself in the classic *roman noir* situation: knowing the truth no one else will believe, threatened on all sides by killers with badges and without, hounded through city streets dark with something more than night. With its sharply drawn characters, pulsating pace and terrifying premise, this book could easily have been a masterpiece, were it not for a grotesquely bad denouement. In *As Bad as I Am,* a later Dane-less novel, Ard reworked the same storyline to better effect but without the raw nightmarish tension of *Hell Is a City.*

He was far from a model of all the literary virtues. Writing at white heat and not always taking time to revise, he could perpetrate such ghastly clinkers as: "There were audible gasps when Mike Carhart's rippling muscles strode from the wings." His style was readable and efficient but his work lacks the hauntingly quotable lines so common in Chandler and Ross Macdonald. His plots tend to fall apart under scrutiny, especially when he toyed with motifs from classical detective fiction. He unwittingly recycled certain character names over and over, so that his novels contain a small army of hoodlums called Stix Larsen and sleuths named Barney Glines. But even his worst efforts are enjoyable, and his best are miracles of storytelling economy, blending tough-guy elements with singular warmth and tenderness. His death of cancer at the age of 37 silenced one of the most distinctive voices in the history of the private-eye novel.

—Francis M. Nevins, Jr.

ARDEN, William. *See* **COLLINS, Michael.**

ARDIES, Tom. American. Born in Seattle, Washington, 5 August 1931. Educated at Daniel McIntyre Collegiate Institute, Winnipeg, Manitoba. Served in the United States Air Force. Married Sharon Bernard in 1963; two children. Reporter, columnist, and editorial writer, Vancouver *Sun,* 1950–64; telegraph editor, Honolulu *Star Bulletin,* 1964–65. Special Assistant to Governor of Guam, 1965–67. Address: 3985 Lakeside Road, Penticton, British Columbia, Canada.

CRIME PUBLICATIONS

Novels (series: Charlie Sparrow)

Their Man in the White House (Sparrow). New York, Doubleday, and London, Macmillan, 1971.
This Suitcase Is Going to Explode (Sparrow). New York, Doubleday, and London, Macmillan, 1972.
Pandemic (Sparrow). New York, Doubleday, 1973; London, Angus and Robertson, 1974.
Kosygin Is Coming. New York, Doubleday, 1974; London, Angus and Robertson, 1975; as *Russian Roulette,* London, Panther, 1975.
Palm Springs. New York, Doubleday, 1978.

OTHER PUBLICATIONS

Novel

In a Lady's Service. New York, Doubleday, 1976; London, Panther, 1978.

Play

Screenplay: *Russian Roulette,* with Stanley Mann, 1975.

*   *   *

Tom Ardies's early novels, *Their Man in the White House, This Suitcase Is Going to Explode,* and *Pandemic,* are facile tales of counter-espionage whose plots follow a "minutes to midnight" pattern, culminating in dramatic, but implausible, climaxes.

Charlie Sparrow is their hero: a handsome, cocky spy, good with women, and always the victor, be it pitting his will against his superiors, the CIA, and the fanatical enemy to save the nation from World War III, as in one book, or preventing the outbreak of a flu-virus pandemic, as in another. Sparrow descends from the chivalric and outlaw traditions, a kind of modern knight errant and Dick Turpin. Capable of ball-breaking when he needs valuable information fast, a stud with women, he is, nonetheless, the democratic hero, an individualist, crude, but governed by a moral code that demands that fanatics who use cloning, lobotomies, or nuclear reactions for evil ends be defeated.

Kosygin Is Coming and *In a Lady's Service,* a spy story and a spoof, are Ardies's best novels. Earlier, detailed accounts of germ warfare and the Manhattan project did not lend plausibility to his plots. In *Kosygin Is Coming,* he used the Warren Commission report to give his story an inferior version of the chilling relevance Robert Ludlum brilliantly accomplishes. In his spoof, his journalistic tidbits yield a Dip Threat, Mission-Impossible-like directives, and a ludicrous parody of his own plots. In both, the plots are tighter, complications more zany, and characters more convincing. Shaver, the bungling cop suspended from the Royal Canadian Mounted police who foils the KGB and CIA, and Buchanan, a ne'er-do-well in Mexico who disguises himself as a pansy, a gigolo, and a remittance man, are among his best characters.

—Carol Simpson Stern

———————

ARMSTRONG, Charlotte. Also wrote as Jo Valentine. American. Born in Vulcan, Michigan, in 1905. Educated at the University of Wisconsin, Madison; Barnard College, New York, B.A. 1925. Married Jack Lewi; one daughter and two sons. Worked in the *New York Times* advertising department, as a fashion reporter for *Breath of the Avenue* (a buyer's guide), and in an accounting firm. Recipient: Mystery Writers of America Edgar Allan Poe award, 1956. *Died 18 July 1969.*

CRIME PUBLICATIONS

Novels (series: MacDougal Duff)

Lay On, Mac Duff! (Duff). New York, Coward McCann, 1942; London, Gifford, 1943.
The Case of the Weird Sisters (Duff). New York, Coward McCann, and London, Gifford, 1943.
The Innocent Flower (Duff). New York, Coward McCann, 1945; as *Death Filled the Glass,* London, Cherry Tree Books, 1945.
The Unsuspected. New York, Coward McCann, 1946; London, Harrap, 1947.
The Chocolate Cobweb. New York, Coward McCann, 1948; London, Davies, 1952.
Mischief. New York, Coward McCann, 1950; London, Davies, 1951.
The Black-Eyed Stranger. New York, Coward McCann, 1951; London, Davies, 1952.
Catch-as-Catch-Can. New York, Coward McCann, 1952; London, Davies, 1953; as *Walk Out on Death,* New York, Pocket Books, 1954.
The Trouble in Thor (as Jo Valentine). New York, Coward McCann, and London, Davies, 1953; as *And Sometimes Death,* New York, Pocket Books, 1955.
The Better to Eat You. New York, Coward McCann, and London, Davies, 1954; as *Murder's Nest,* New York, Pocket Books, 1955.
The Dream Walker. New York, Coward McCann, and London, Davies, 1955; as *Alibi for Murder,* New York, Pocket Books, 1956.
A Dram of Poison. New York, Coward McCann, and London, Davies, 1956.
The Seventeen Widows of Sans Souci. New York, Coward McCann, and London, Davies, 1959.
Duo: The Girl with a Secret, Incident at a Corner. New York, Coward McCann, 1959; London, Davies, 1960.
Something Blue. New York, Ace, 1962.
Then Came Two Women. New York, Ace, 1962.
Who's Been Sitting in My Chair? New York, Ace, 1963.

A Little Less Than Kind. New York, Coward McCann, 1963; London, Collins, 1964.
The Mark of the Hand. New York, Ace, 1963.
The One-Faced Girl. New York, Ace, 1963.
The Witch's House. New York, Coward McCann, 1963; London, Collins, 1964.
The Turret Room. New York, Coward McCann, and London, Collins, 1965.
Dream of Fair Woman. New York, Coward McCann, and London, Collins, 1966.
The Gift Shop. New York, Coward McCann, and London, Collins, 1967.
Lemon in the Basket. New York, Coward McCann, 1967; London, Collins, 1968.
The Balloon Man. New York, Coward McCann, and London, Collins, 1968.
Seven Seats to the Moon. New York, Coward McCann, and London, Collins, 1969.
The Protégé. New York, Coward McCann, and London, Collins, 1970.

Short Stories

The Albatross. New York, Coward McCann, 1957; London, Davies, 1958; selection, as *Mask of Evil,* New York, Fawcett, 1958.
I See You. New York, Coward McCann, 1966.

Uncollected Short Stories

"A Gun Is a Nervous Thing," in *Ellery Queen's Anthology 1964.* New York, Davies, 1963.
"More Than One Kind of Luck," in *Ellery Queen's Mystery Magazine* (New York), December 1967.
"The Splintered Monday," in *Ellery Queen's All-Star Lineup.* New York, New American Library, 1967.
"The Cool Ones," in *Ellery Queen's Mystery Parade.* New York, New American Library, 1968.
"The Light Next Door," in *Ellery Queen's Mystery Magazine* (New York), January 1969.
"Night Call," in *Ellery Queen's Mystery Magazine* (New York), April 1969.
"From Out of the Garden," in *Ellery Queen's Murder Menu.* Cleveland, World, 1969.
"The Second Commandmant," in *Ellery Queen's Aces of Mystery.* New York, Davis, 1975.

OTHER PUBLICATIONS

Plays

The Happiest Days (produced New York, 1939).
Ring Around Elizabeth (produced New York, 1940). New York, French, 1942.

Screenplays: *The Unsuspected,* 1947; *Don't Bother to Knock,* 1952.

Television Plays: scripts for *Alfred Hitchcock Presents* series, 1955–61.

*

Manuscript Collection: Mugar Memorial Library, Boston University.

*   *   *

Charlotte Armstrong was one of America's most energetic practical moralists, who masqueraded for 28 years as a successful suspense novelist. The best of her work still packs a high degree of tension into the plot. Armstrong was an expert at creating a situation in which an innocent is threatened, setting a rescue effort in motion, and then manipulating the world of ordinary events into a crescendo of perfectly maddening delays and mishaps. *Catch-as-Catch-Can, The Gift Shop,* and *The Witch's House* are good examples of her technique.

As a moralist, she was not insensitive to the psychology of groups or individuals. But she had a distaste for looking at abnormal psychology in as much depth as Margaret Millar or Patricia Highsmith. Armstrong was a competent observer with such insights as are available to the intelligent adult, and a vigorous expositor of her findings. One of her early successes was *The Unsuspected;* it is built around a convincing portrait of a modern Svengali, who hypnotizes by projecting an uncritical love, in a commanding beautiful voice. Luther Grandison has even convinced the richer of his two wards that she is ugly, so that she will believe that he loves her despite her lack of beauty. *The Witch's House,* though not first rate Armstrong, has a good study of an adolescent girl who has retreated to a world of fantasy because the adults around her don't trouble to introduce her to the real one. Her isolation and self-dramatization are ludicrous and faintly frightening. In *A Little Less Than Kind,* Armstrong reveals a positive dislike of coddling the emotionally ill by using too much understanding. The book reworks *Hamlet* by taking the premise that if Hamlet believed on insufficient evidence that his father had been murdered then he was neurotic, and very destructive. The book is unsuccessful because Ladd Cunningham, the Hamlet figure, is one of Armstrong's flimsiest characters. He reveals her lack of patience with those who, for whatever reason, refuse to *think.*

The kind of psychology that Armstrong did grasp was that of sane and decent people. In most of her best work, it is the people who live as though their behavior mattered who manage to get themselves out of some very tight places, or to save the innocents who are threatened by the forces of evil. Again and again, the good prevail because they come up with the understanding, the courage, the resourcefulness, or the friends that tip the balance. The evil doers include the greedy, the manipulators, the plotters, and, above all, those who lie to themselves as well as others. In *The Seventeen Widows of Sans Souci* one of the characters coins the term "li-ee," to describe those who force others to lie to them by giving the impression that anything but a sanitized version of reality would kill them. The hard core "li-ee" in that novel proves to be a very dangerous friend.

The best of Armstrong's novels and stories discuss practical moral problems, and even philosophical ones, while the plot holds the reader in suspense. In *A Dram of Poison,* one of her best, a group of people discuss the questions of free will and determinism with great relish while trying to find a dose of poison disguised as olive oil before someone cooks dinner with it. The enemy of life and health in this novel is an amateur psychologist who manages to convince her brother and his young wife that they are variously doomed, of destructive impulses, and that the love they have discovered for each other, but not had a chance to declare, is futile. The cast of characters who joins this couple in the search for the poison includes a blond nurse who is anything but dumb, a ruminative bus driver, a portly society matron with the mind of a general and the heart of a woman, and several other non-conformists. These good samaritans throw the newlyweds back into each other's arms, after they have settled the hash of irresponsible psychologizers, determinists, and all those who stereotype large or small groups of people.

Armstrong was quite aware of the power of the wealthy and the injustice they can inflict on the poor who get in their way. The hero of *The Turret Room* has already suffered grossly at the hands of his wife's family when he returns to their house at the opening of the book. He walks into trouble, because another crime has just been committed which the Whitmans would love to pin on him, as they did once before, because it is so much more convenient than finding out where the blame really lies. Fortunately, a young woman who does social work and feels for the underdog comes to his rescue. In *The Balloon Man,* the heroine is a young woman who simply wants to get out of a bad marriage with custody of her young son. She is a fine example of the Armstrong heroine, penniless, but bright, resourceful, and determined. The man her father-in-law hires to defame her is shrewd, imaginative, and nervy, but he is just outmatched. Both these novels have convincing casts and plots timed to the split second. And they are largely unmarred by the sentimentality that is the defect of Armstrong's literary virtues. There is a distinct coyness in the handling of dialogue and character in *The Witch's House* and *Lemon in the Basket,* as well as in the earlier gothic romances like *The Chocolate Cobweb* and *The Better to Eat You.*

Although Armstrong's short story "The Enemy" won the *Ellery Queen Mystery Magazine* contest, that story is surpassed by four others in the volume in which it is collected, including the title novelette, "The Albatross." That story, and "Laugh It Off," "Miss Murphy," and "Ride with the Executioner" are all built around encounters with society's misfits. They are shocking, tightly plotted, and very convincing. Two stories from a later collection, "How They Met," and the title story, "I See You," are unconventional and beautiful love stories.

—Carol Cleveland

————

ARNEY, James. *See* **RUSSELL, Martin.**

————

ASHDOWN, Clifford. *See* **FREEMAN, R. Austin.**

————

ASHE, Douglas. *See* **BARDIN, John Franklin.**

————

ASHE, Gordon, *See* **CREASEY, John.**

————

ASHE, Mary Ann. *See* **BRAND, Christianna.**

————

ASHFORD, Jeffrey. *See* **JEFFRIES, Roderic.**

————

ASIMOV, Isaac. Also writes as Dr. A.; Paul French. American. Born in Petrovichi, Russia, 2 January 1920; emigrated to the United States in 1923; naturalized, 1928. Educated at Columbia University, New York, B.S. 1939, M.A. 1941, Ph.D. in chemistry 1948. Served in the United States Army, 1945–46. Married 1) Gertrude Blugerman in 1942 (divorced 1973), one son and one daughter; 2) Janet Opal Jeppson in 1973. Instructor in biochemistry, 1949–51, Assistant Professor, 1951–55, Associate Professor, 1955–79, and since 1979 Professor, Boston University School of Medicine. Recipient: Edison Foundation National Mass Media award, 1958; Blakeslee award, for non-fiction, 1960; American Chemical Society James T. Grady award, 1965; American Association for the Advancement of Science-Westinghouse Science Writing award, 1967; Hugo award, 1973, 1977, 1983; Science Fiction Writers award, 1973; Locus award, 1981; Washington *Post* Children's Book Guild award, for non-fiction, 1985. Address: 10 West 66th Street, Apartment 33-A, New York, New York 10023, U.S.A.

CRIME PUBLICATIONS

Novels (series: Elijah Baley)

The Caves of Steel (Baley). New York, Doubleday, and London, Boardman, 1954.
The Naked Sun (Baley). New York, Doubleday, 1957; London, Joseph, 1958.
The Death Dealers. New York, Avon, 1958; as *A Whiff of Death,* New York, Walker, and London, Gollancz, 1968.
The Robot Novels (includes *The Caves of Steel* and *The Naked Sun*). New York, Doubleday, 1971.
Murder at the ABA. New York, Doubleday, 1976; as *Authorized Murder,* London, Gollancz, 1976.
The Robots of Dawn (Baley). New York, Doubleday, 1983; London, Granada, 1984.
Robots and Empire (Baley). New York, Doubleday, and London, Granada, 1985.

Short Stories

Asimov's Mysteries. New York, Doubleday, and London, Rapp and Whiting, 1968.
Tales of the Black Widowers. New York, Doubleday, 1974; London, Gollancz, 1975.
More Tales of the Black Widowers. New York, Doubleday, 1976; London, Gollancz, 1977.
Casebook of the Black Widowers. New York, Doubleday, and London, Gollancz, 1980.
The Union Club Mysteries. New York, Doubleday, 1983; London, Gollancz, 1985.
Banquets of the Black Widowers. New York, Doubleday, 1984.
Puzzles for the Black Widowers. New York, Doubleday, 1990.

OTHER PUBLICATIONS

Novels

Pebble in the Sky. New York, Doubleday, 1950; London, Sidgwick and Jackson, 1968.

The Stars, Like Dust. New York, Doubleday, 1951; London, Panther, 1958; abridged edition, as *The Rebellious Stars,* New York, Ace, 1954.
Foundation. New York, Gnome Press, 1951; London, Weidenfeld and Nicolson, 1953; abridged edition, as *The Thousand-Year Plan,* New York, Ace, 1955.
Foundation and Empire. New York, Gnome Press, 1952; London, Panther, 1962; as *The Man Who Upset the Universe,* New York, Ace, 1955.
The Currents of Space. New York, Doubleday, 1952; London, Boardman, 1955.
Second Foundation. New York, Gnome Press, 1953.
The End of Eternity. New York, Doubleday, 1955; London, Panther, 1958.
Fantastic Voyage (novelization of screenplay). Boston, Houghton Mifflin, and London, Dobson, 1966.
The Gods Themselves. New York, Doubleday, and London, Gollancz, 1972.
The Collected Fiction: The Far Ends of Time and Earth, Prisoners of the Stars. New York, Doubleday, 2 vols., 1979.
Foundation's Edge. New York, Doubleday, 1982; London, Granada, 1983.
Foundation and Earth. New York, Doubleday, and London, Grafton, 1986.
Fantastic Voyage II: Destination Brain. New York, Doubleday, and London, Grafton, 1987.
Prelude to Foundation. New York, Doubleday, and London, Grafton, 1988.
Azazel. New York, Doubleday, 1988; London, Doubleday, 1989.
Nemesis. New York, Doubleday, 1989, and London, Doubleday, 1989.
Nightfall, with Robert Silverberg. London, Gollancz, 1990.

Short Stories

I, Robot. New York, Gnome Press, 1950; London, Grayson, 1952.
The Martian Way and Other Stories. New York, Doubleday, 1955; London, Dobson, 1964.
Earth Is Room Enough. New York, Doubleday, 1957; London, Panther, 1960.
Nine Tomorrows: Tales of the Near Future. New York, Doubleday, 1959; London, Dobson, 1963.
The Rest of the Robots. New York, Doubleday, 1964.
Through a Glass, Clearly. London, New English Library, 1967.
Nightfall and Other Stories. New York, Doubleday, 1969; London, Rapp and Whiting, 1970.
The Early Asimov; or, Eleven Years of Trying. New York, Doubleday, 1972.
The Best of Isaac Asimov (*1939–1972*). London, Sidgwick and Jackson, 1973; New York, Doubleday, 1974.
Have You Seen These? Cambridge, Massachusetts, NESFA, 1974.
The Heavenly Host. New York, Walker, 1975.
Buy Jupiter and Other Stories. New York, Doubleday, 1975; London, Gollancz, 1976.
The Dream, Benjamin's Dream, Benjamin's Bicentennial Blast. Privately printed, 1976.
The Bicentennial Man and Other Stories. New York, Doubleday, and London, Gollancz, 1976.
Good Taste. Topeka, Kansas, Apocalypse Press, 1976.
The Complete Robot. New York, Doubleday, and London, Granada, 1982.
The Winds of Change and Other Stories. New York, Doubleday, and London, Granada, 1983.

The Edge of Tomorrow (stories and essays).   New York, Tor, 1985; London, Harrap, 1986.

Alternative Asimov's.   New York, Doubleday, 1986.

Robot Dreams.   New York, Berkley, 1986; London, Gollancz, 1987.

The Best Science Fiction of Isaac Asimov.   New York, Doubleday, 1986; London, Grafton, 1987.

The Best Mysteries of Isaac Asimov.   New York, Doubleday, 1986; London, Grafton, 1987.

The Asimov Chronicles: Fifty Years of Isaac Asimov, edited by Martin H. Greenberg.   New York, Dark Harvest, 1989.

Robot Visions.   New York, New American Library, 1990.

Verse

Lecherous Limericks.   New York, Walker, 1975; London, Corgi, 1977.

More Lecherous Limericks.   New York, Walker, 1976.

Still More Lecherous Limericks.   New York, Walker, 1977.

Asimov's Sherlockian Limericks.   New York, Mysterious Press, 1978.

Limericks: Too Gross, with John Ciardi.   New York, Norton, 1978.

A Grossery of Limericks, with John Ciardi.   New York, Norton, 1981.

Limericks for Children.   New York, Caedmon, 1984.

Other (fiction for children) as Paul French

David Starr, Space Ranger.   New York, Doubleday, 1952; Kingswood, Surrey, World's Work, 1953.

Lucky Starr and the Pirates of the Asteroids.   New York, Doubleday, 1953; Kingswood, Surrey, World's Work, 1954.

Lucky Starr and the Oceans of Venus.   New York, Doubleday, 1954; as *The Oceans of Venus,* as Isaac Asimov, London, New English Library, 1973.

Lucky Starr and the Big Sun of Mercury.   New York, Doubleday, 1956; as *The Big Sun of Mercury,* as Isaac Asimov, London, New English Library, 1974.

Lucky Starr and the Moons of Jupiter.   New York, Doubleday, 1957; as *The Moons of Jupiter,* as Isaac Asimov, London, New English Library, 1974.

Lucky Starr and the Rings of Saturn.   New York, Doubleday, 1958; as *The Rings of Saturn* (as Isaac Asimov), London, New English Library, 1974.

Other

Biochemistry and Human Metabolism, with Burnham Walker and William C. Boyd.   Baltimore, Williams and Wilkens, 1952; revised edition, 1954, 1957; London, Ballière Tindall and Cox, 1955.

Chemicals of Life: Enzymes, Vitamins, Hormones.   New York, Abelard Schuman, 1954; London, Bell, 1956.

Races and People, with William C. Boyd.   New York, Abelard Schuman, 1955; London, Abelard Schuman, 1958.

Chemistry and Human Health, with Burnham Walker and M.K. Nicholas.   New York, McGraw Hill, 1956.

Inside the Atom.   New York, Abelard Schuman, 1956; revised edition, New York and London, Abelard Schuman, 1958, 1961, 1966, 1974.

Building Blocks of the Universe.   New York, Abelard Schuman, 1957; London, Abelard Schuman, 1958; revised edition 1961, 1974.

Only a Trillion.   London, Abelard Schuman, 1957; New York, Abelard Schuman, 1958; as *Marvels of Science,* New York, Collier, 1962.

The World of Carbon.   New York and London, Abelard Schuman, 1958; revised edition, New York, Collier, 1962.

The World of Nitrogen.   New York and London, Abelard Schuman, 1958; revised edition, New York, Collier, 1962.

The Clock We Live On.   New York and London, Abelard Schuman, 1959; revised edition, New York, Collier, 1962; Abelard Schuman, 1965.

The Living River.   New York and London, Abelard Schuman, 1959; revised edition, as *The Bloodstream: River of Life,* New York, Collier, 1961.

Realm of Numbers.   Boston, Houghton Mifflin, 1959; London, Gollancz, 1963.

Words of Science and the History Behind Them.   Boston, Houghton Mifflin, 1959; London, Harrap, 1974.

Breakthroughs in Science (for children).   Boston, Houghton Mifflin, 1960.

The Intelligent Man's Guide to Science.   New York, Basic Books, 2 vols., 1960; revised edition, as *The New Intelligent Man's Guide to Science,* 1 vol., 1965; London, Nelson, 1967; as *Asimov's Guide to Science,* New York, Basic Books, 1972; London, Penguin, 2 vols., 1975; as *Asimov's New Guide to Science,* Basic Books, 1984.

The Kingdom of the Sun.   New York and London, Abelard Schuman, 1960; revised edition, New York, Collier, 1962; Abelard Schuman, 1963.

Realm of Measure.   Boston, Houghton Mifflin, 1960.

Satellites in Outer Space (for children).   New York, Random House, 1960; revised edition, 1964, 1973.

The Double Planet.   New York, Abelard Schuman, 1960; London, Abelard Schuman, 1962; revised edition, 1966.

The Wellsprings of Life.   New York and London, Abelard Schuman, 1960.

Realm of Algebra.   Boston, Houghton Mifflin, 1961; London, Gollancz, 1964.

Words from the Myths.   Boston, Houghton Mifflin, 1961; London, Faber, 1963.

Fact and Fancy.   New York, Doubleday, 1962.

Life and Energy.   New York, Doubleday, 1962; London, Dobson, 1963.

The Search for the Elements.   New York, Basic Books, 1962.

Words in Genesis.   Boston, Houghton Mifflin, 1962.

Words on the Map.   Boston, Houghton Mifflin, 1962.

View from a Height.   New York, Doubleday, 1963; London, Dobson, 1964.

The Genetic Code.   New York, Orion Press, 1963; London Murray, 1964.

The Human Body: Its Structure and Operation.   Boston, Houghton Mifflin, 1963; London, Nelson, 1965.

The Kite That Won the Revolution.   Boston, Houghton Mifflin, 1963.

Words from the Exodus.   Boston, Houghton Mifflin, 1963.

Adding a Dimension: 17 Essays on the History of Science.   New York, Doubleday, 1964; London, Dobson, 1966.

The Human Brain: Its Capacities and Functions.   Boston, Houghton Mifflin, 1964; London, Nelson, 1965.

Quick and Easy Math.   Boston, Houghton Mifflin, 1964; London, Whiting and Wheaton, 1967.

A Short History of Biology.   Garden City, New York, Natural History Press, 1964; London, Nelson, 1965.

Planets for Man, with Stephen H. Dole.   New York, Random House, 1964.

Asimov's Biographical Encyclopedia of Science and Technology.   New York, Doubleday, 1964; London, Allen and Unwin, 1966; revised edition, Doubleday, 1972, 1982; London, Pan, 1975.

An Easy Introduction to the Slide Rule.   Boston, Houghton Mifflin, 1965; London, Whiting and Wheaton, 1967.

The Greeks: A Great Adventure. Boston, Houghton Mifflin, 1965.

Of Time and Space and Other Things. New York, Doubleday, 1965; London, Dobson, 1967.

A Short History of Chemistry. New York, Doubleday, 1965; London, Heinemann, 1972.

The Neutrino: Ghost Particle of the Atom. New York, Doubleday, and London, Dobson, 1966.

The Genetic Effects of Radiation, with Theodosius Dobzhansky. Washington, D.C., Atomic Energy Commission, 1966.

The Noble Gases. New York, Basic Books, 1966.

The Roman Republic. Boston, Houghton Mifflin, 1966.

From Earth to Heaven. New York, Doubleday, 1966.

Understanding Physics. New York, Walker, 3 vols., 1966; London, Allen and Unwin, 3 vols., 1967; as *The History of Physics,* Walker, 1 vol., 1984.

The Universe: From Flat Earth to Quasar. New York, Walker, 1966; London, Penguin, 1967; revised edition, Walker and Penguin, 1971; revised edition, as *The Universe: From Flat Earth to Black Holes—and Beyond,* Walker, 1980, Penguin, 1983.

The Roman Empire. Boston, Houghton Mifflin, 1967.

The Moon (for children). Chicago, Follett, 1967; London, University of London Press, 1969.

Is Anyone There? (essays). New York, Doubleday, 1967; London, Rapp and Whiting, 1968.

To the Ends of the Universe. New York, Walker, 1967; revised edition 1976.

The Egyptians. Boston, Houghton Mifflin, 1967.

Mars (for children). Chicago, Follett, 1967; London, University of London Press, 1971.

From Earth to Heaven: 17 Essays on Science. New York, Doubleday, 1967; London, Dobson, 1968.

Environments Out There. New York, Abelard Schuman, 1967; London, Abelard Schuman, 1968.

Science, Numbers and I: Essays on Science. New York, Doubleday, 1968; London, Rapp and Whiting, 1969.

The Near East: 10,000 Years of History. Boston, Houghton Mifflin, 1968.

Asimov's Guide to the Bible: The Old Testament, The New Testament. New York, Doubleday, 2 vols., 1968–69.

The Dark Ages. Boston, Houghton Mifflin, 1968.

Galaxies (for children). Chicago, Follett, 1968; London, University of London Press, 1971.

Stars (for children). Chicago, Follett, 1968; London, University of London Press, 1971.

Words from History. Boston, Houghton Mifflin, 1968.

The Shaping of England. Boston, Houghton Mifflin, 1969.

Photosynthesis. New York, Basic Books, 1969. London, Allen and Unwin, 1970.

Twentieth Century Discovery (for children). New York, Doubleday, and London, Macdonald, 1969.

Opus 100 (selection). Boston, Houghton Mifflin, 1969.

ABC's of Space (for children). New York, Walker, 1969.

Great Ideas of Science (for children). Boston, Houghton Mifflin, 1969.

To the Solar System and Back. New York, Doubleday, 1970.

Asimov's Guide to Shakespeare: The Greek, Roman and Italian Plays, The English Plays. New York, Doubleday, 2 vols., 1970.

Constantinople. Boston, Houghton Mifflin, 1970.

ABC's of the Ocean (for children). New York, Walker, 1970.

Light (for children). Chicago, Follett, 1970.

The Best New Thing (for children). Cleveland, World, 1971.

The Stars in Their Courses. New York, Doubleday, 1971; London, White Lion, 1974.

The Space Dictionary. New York, Starline, 1971.

What Makes the Sun Shine? Boston, Little Brown, 1971.

The Isaac Asimov Treasury of Humor. Boston, Houghton Mifflin, 1971; London, Vallentine Mitchell, 1972.

The Sensuous Dirty Old Man (as Dr. A.). New York, Walker, 1971.

The Land of Canaan. Boston, Houghton Mifflin, 1971.

ABC's of the Earth (for children). New York, Walker, 1971.

More Words of Science. Boston, Houghton Mifflin, 1972.

Electricity and Man. Washington, D.C., Atomic Energy Commission, 1972.

The Shaping of France. Boston, Houghton Mifflin, 1972.

Asimov's Annotated "Don Juan." New York, Doubleday, 1972.

ABC's of Ecology (for children). New York, Walker, 1972.

The Story of Ruth. New York, Doubleday, 1972.

Worlds Within Worlds. Washington, D.C., Atomic Energy Commission, 1972.

The Left Hand of the Electron (essays). New York, Doubleday, 1972; London, White Lion, 1975.

Ginn Science Program. Boston, Ginn, 5 vols., 1972–73.

How Did We Find Out about Dinosaurs [*the Earth Is Round, Electricity, Vitamins, Germs, Comets, Energy, Atoms, Nuclear Power, Numbers, Outer Space, Earthquakes, Black Holes, Our Human Roots, Antarctica, Coal, Solar Power, Volcanoes, Life in the Deep Sea, Our Genes, the Universe, Computers, Robots, the Atmosphere, DNA, the Speed of Light, Blood, Sunshine, the Brain, Super Conductivity, Microwaves, Photosynthesis*] (for children). New York, Walker, 32 vols., 1973–89; 6 vols. published London, White Lion, 1975–76; 1 vol., published London, Pan, 1980; 7 vols. Published (as *How We Found Out. . .* series), London, Longman, 1982.

The Tragedy of the Moon (essays). New York, Doubleday, 1973; London, Abelard Schuman, 1974.

Comets and Meteors (for children). Chicago, Follett, 1973.

The Sun (for children). Chicago, Follett, 1973.

The Shaping of North America from the Earliest Times to 1763. Boston, Houghton Mifflin, 1973; London, Dobson, 1975.

Please Explain (for children). Boston, Houghton Mifflin, 1973; London, Abelard Schuman, 1975.

Physical Science Today. Del Mar, California, CRM, 1973.

Jupiter the Largest Planet (for children). New York, Lothrop, 1973; revised edition, 1976.

Today, Tomorrow, and. . . New York, Doubleday, 1973; London, Abelard Schuman, 1974; as *Towards Tomorrow,* London, Hodder and Stoughton, 1977.

The Birth of the United States 1763–1816. Boston, Houghton Mifflin, 1974.

Earth: Our Crowded Spaceship. New York, Day, and London, Abelard Schuman, 1974.

Asimov on Chemistry. New York, Doubleday, 1974; London, Macdonald and Jane's, 1975.

Asimov on Astronomy. New York, Doubleday, and London, Macdonald, 1974.

Asimov's Annotated "Paradise Lost." New York, Doubleday, 1974.

Our World in Space. Greenwich, Connecticut, New York Graphic Society, and Cambridge, Patrick Stephens, 1974.

The Solar System (for children). Chicago, Follett, 1975.

Birth and Death of the Universe. New York, Walker, 1975.

Of Matters Great and Small. New York, Doubleday, 1975.

Our Federal Union: The United States from 1816 to 1865. Boston, Houghton Mifflin, and London, Dobson, 1975.

The Ends of the Earth: The Polar Regions of the World. New York, Weybright and Talley, 1975.

Eyes on the Universe: A History of the Telescope. Boston, Houghton Mifflin, 1975; London, Deutsch, 1976.

Science Past—Science Future. New York, Doubleday, 1975.

The Heavenly Host (for children).   New York, Walker, 1975;
London, Penguin, 1978.
Alpha Centauri, The Nearest Star (for children).   New York,
Lothrop, 1976.
I, Rabbi (for children).   New York, Walker, 1976.
Asimov on Physics.   New York, Doubleday, 1976.
The Planet That Wasn't.   New York, Doubleday, 1976;
London, Sphere, 1977.
The Collapsing Universe: The Story of the Black Holes.   New
York, Walker, and London, Hutchinson, 1977.
Asimov on Numbers.   New York, Doubleday, 1977.
The Beginning and the End.   New York, Doubleday, 1977.
Familiar Poems Annotated.   New York, Doubleday, 1977.
The Golden Door: The United States from 1865 to 1918.
Boston, Houghton Mifflin, and London, Dobson, 1977.
The Key Word and Other Mysteries (for children).   New York,
Walker, 1977.
Mars, The Red Planet (for children).   New York, Lothrop,
1977.
Life and Time.   New York, Doubleday, 1978.
Quasar, Quasar, Burning Bright.   New York, Doubleday, 1978.
Animals of the Bible (for children).   New York, Doubleday,
1978.
Isaac Asimov's Book of Facts.   New York, Grosset and
Dunlap, 1979; London, Hodder and Stoughton, 1980;
abridged edition (for children), as *Would You Believe?* and
More...Would You Believe?, Grosset and Dunlap, 2 vols.,
1981–82.
Extraterrestrial Civilizations.   New York, Crown, 1979; Lon-
don, Robson, 1980.
A Choice of Catastrophes.   New York, Simon and Schuster,
1979; London, Hutchinson, 1980.
Saturn and Beyond.   New York, Lothrop, 1979.
Opus 200 (selection).   Boston, Houghton Mifflin, 1979.
*In Memory Yet Green: The Autobiography of Isaac Asimov 1920–
1954.*   New York, Doubleday, 1979.
The Road to Infinity.   New York, Doubleday, 1979.
Opus (includes *Opus 100* and *Opus 200*).   London, Deutsch,
1980.
In Joy Still Felt: The Autobiography of Isaac Asimov 1954–1978.
New York, Doubleday, 1980.
The Annotated Gulliver's Travels.   New York, Potter, 1980.
Change! Seventy-One Glimpses of the Future.   Boston,
Houghton Mifflin, 1981.
Visions of the Universe, paintings by Kazuaki Iwasaki.
Montrose, California, Cosmos Store, 1981.
Asimov on Science Fiction.   New York, Doubleday, 1981;
London, Granada, 1983.
Venus, Near Neighbor of the Sun (for children).   New York,
Lothrop, 1981.
The Sun Shines Bright.   New York, Doubleday, 1981; London,
Granada, 1984.
In the Beginning: Science Faces God in the Book of Genesis.
New York, Crown, and London, New English Library, 1981.
*Exploring the Earth and the Cosmos: The Growth and Future of
Human Knowledge.*   New York, Crown, 1982; London,
Allen Lane, 1983.
Counting the Eons.   New York, Doubleday, 1983; London,
Granada, 1984.
The Measure of the Universe.   New York, Herder, 1983.
The Roving Mind.   Buffalo, New York, Prometheus, 1983;
Oxford, Oxford University Press, 1987.
Those Amazing Electronic Thinking Machines! (for children).
New York, Watts, 1983.
Norby the Mixed-Up Robot (for children), with Janet Asimov.
New York, Walker, 1983; London, Methuen, 1984.

X Stands for Unknown (essays).   New York, Doubleday, 1984;
London, Granada, 1985.
Opus 300.   Boston, Houghton Mifflin, 1984; London, Hale,
1985.
Norby's Other Secret (for children), with Janet Asimov.   New
York, Walker, 1984; London, Methuen, 1985.
Robots: Where the Machine Ends and Life Begins, with Karen A.
Frenkel.   New York, Crown, 1985.
The Exploding Suns: The Secrets of the Supernovas.   New
York, Dutton, and London, Joseph, 1985.
Asimov's Guide to Halley's Comet.   New York, Walker, and
London, Panther, 1985.
The Subatomic Monster: Essays on Science.   New York,
Doubleday, 1985; London, Grafton, 1986.
Norby and the Lost Princess (for children), with Janet Asimov.
New York, Walker, 1985.
Norby and the Invaders (for children), with Janet Asimov.
New York, Walker, 1985.
The Dangers of Intelligence and Other Science Essays.   Boston,
Houghton Mifflin, 1986.
Norby and the Queen's Necklace (for children), with Janet
Asimov.   New York, Walker, 1986.
Future Days: A Nineteenth-Century Vision of the Year 2000.
New York, Holt, and London, Virgin, 1986.
*Wonderful Worldwide Science Bazaar: Seventy-two Up-to-Date
Reports on the State of Everything from Inside the Atom to
Outside the Universe.*   Boston, Houghton Mifflin, 1986.
Bare Bones: Dinosaur (for children), with David Hawcock.
New York, Holt, 1986; London, Methuen, 1987.
As Far as Human Eye Could See (essays).   New York,
Doubleday, 1987; London, Grafton, 1988.
Past, Present and Future (essays).   Buffalo, New York,
Prometheus, 1987.
*Beginnings: The Story of Origins—of Mankind, Life, the Earth,
the Universe.*   New York, Walker, 1987.
How to Enjoy Writing: A Book of Aid and Comfort.   New York,
Walker, 1987.
Norby Finds a Villain (for children), with Janet Asimov.   New
York, Walker, 1987.
Asimov's Annotated Gilbert and Sullivan.   New York, Double-
day, 1988.
Relativity of Wrong: Essays on the Solar System and Beyond.
New York, Doubleday, 1988; Oxford, Oxford University
Press, 1989.
Library of the Universe (*Did Comets Kill the Dinosaurs; The
Asteroids; Ancient Astronomy; Is There Life on Other
Planets?; Jupiter, the Spotted Giant; Mercury, the Quick
Planet; How Was the Universe Born?; Saturn, the Ringed
Beauty; The Space Spotter's Guide; Unidentified Flying
Objects; Earth, Our Home Base; The Birth and Death of the
Stars; Science Fiction, Science Fact; Space Garbage; Astron-
omy Today; Comets and Meteors, Mythology of the Universe;
Pluto, A Double Planet?*   Milwaukee, Stevens, 18 vols.,
1988–90.
The Tyrannosaurus Prescription and 100 Other Essays.   Buffalo,
New York, Prometheus, 1989.
Asimov's Galaxy: Reflections on Science Fiction.   New York,
Doubleday, 1989.
Asimov on Science: A Thirty Year Retrospective.   New York,
Doubleday, 1989.
*Asimov's Chronology of Science and Discovery: How Science Has
Shaped the World and How the World Has Affected Science
from 4,000,000 B.C. to the Present.*   New York, Harper,
1989.
Norby and Yobo's Great Adventure (for children), with Janet
Asimov.   New York, Walker, 1989.

Norby Down to Earth (for children), with Janet Asimov. New York, Walker, 1989.

Think About Space: Where Have We Been and Where Are We Going (for children), with Frank White. New York, Walker, 1989.

All the Troubles of the World (for children). Mankato, Minnesota, Creative Education, 1989.

Robbie (for children). Mankato, Minnesota, Creative Education, 1989.

Franchise (for children). Mankato, Minnesota, Creative Education, 1989.

Sally (for children). Mankato, Minnesota, Creative Education, 1989.

Norby and the Oldest Dragon (for children), with Janet Asimov. New York, Walker, 1990.

Editor, *Soviet Science Fiction* [and *More Soviet Science Fiction*]. New York, Collier, 2 vols., 1962.

Editor, *The Hugo Winners 1–5.* New York, Doubleday, 5 vols., 1962–86, *1* and *3,* London, Dobson, 2 vols., 1963–67; *2,* London, Sphere, 1973.

Editor, with Groff Conklin, *Fifty Short Science Fiction Tales.* New York, Collier, 1963.

Editor, *Tomorrow's Children: 18 Tales of Fantasy and Science Fiction.* New York, Doubleday, 1966; London, Futura, 1974.

Editor, *Where Do We Go From Here?* New York, Doubleday, 1971; London, Joseph, 1973.

Editor, *Nebula Award Stories 8.* New York, Harper, and London, Gollancz, 1973.

Editor, *Before the Golden Age: A Science Fiction Anthology of the 1930's.* New York, Doubleday, and London, Robson, 1974.

Editor, with Martin H. Greenberg and Joseph D. Olander, *100 Great Science Fiction Short-Short Stories.* New York, Doubleday, and London, Robson, 1978.

Editor, with Martin H. Greenberg and Charles G. Waugh, *The Science Fictional Solar System.* New York, Harper, 1979; London, Sidgwick and Jackson, 1980.

Editor, with Martin H. Greenberg and Charles G. Waugh, *Thirteen Crimes of Science Fiction.* New York, Doubleday, 1979.

Editor, with Martin H. Greenberg, *The Great SF Stories 1–18.* New York, DAW, 18 vols., 1979–88.

Editor, with Martin H. Greenberg and Joseph D. Olander, *Microcosmic Tales: 100 Wondrous Science Fiction Short-Short Stories.* New York, Taplinger, 1980.

Editor, with Martin H. Greenberg and Joseph D. Olander, *Space Mail 1.* New York, Fawcett, 1980.

Editor, with Martin H. Greenberg and Joseph D. Olander, *The Future in Question.* New York, Fawcett, 1980.

Editor, with Alice Laurance, *Who Done It?* Boston, Houghton Mifflin, 1980.

Editor, with Martin H. Greenberg and Charles G. Waugh, *The Seven Deadly Sins of Science Fiction.* New York, Fawcett, 1980.

Editor, with Martin H. Greenberg and Joseph D. Olander, *Miniature Mysteries: 100 Malicious Little Mystery Stories.* New York, Taplinger, 1981.

Editor, with Martin H. Greenberg and Charles G. Waugh, *Science Fiction Shorts* series (for children; includes *After the End, Thinking Machines, Travels Through Time, Wild Inventions, Mad Scientists, Mutants, Tomorrow's TV, Earth Invaded, Bug Awful, Children of the Future, The Immortals, Time Warps*). Milwaukee, Raintree, 12 vols., 1981–84.

Editor, *Fantastic Creatures.* New York, Watts, 1981.

Editor, with Charles G. Waugh and Martin H. Greenberg, *The Best Science Fiction* [*Fantasy, Horror and Supernatural*] *of the 19th Century.* New York, Beaufort, 3 vols., 1981–83; *Science Fiction* London, Gollancz, 1983; *Fantasy* and *Horror and Supernatural,* London, Robson, 2 vols., 1985.

Editor, *Asimov's Marvels of Science Fiction.* London, Hale, 1981.

Editor, with Carol-Lynn Rössell Waugh and Martin H. Greenberg, *The Twelve Crimes of Christmas.* New York, Avon, 1981.

Editor, with Charles G. Waugh and Martin H. Greenberg, *The Seven Cardinal Virtues of Science Fiction.* New York, Fawcett, 1981.

Editor, with Martin H. Greenberg and Charles G. Waugh, *TV: 2000.* New York, Fawcett, 1982.

Editor, with Martin H. Greenberg and Charles G. Waugh, *Last Man on Earth,* New York, Fawcett, 1982.

Editor, with Charles G. Waugh and Martin H. Greenberg, *Tantalizing Locked Room Mysteries.* New York, Walker, 1982.

Editor, with J.O. Jeppson, *Laughing Space: Funny Science Fiction.* Boston, Houghton Mifflin, and London, Robson, 1982.

Editor, with Alice Laurance, *Speculations.* Boston, Houghton Mifflin, 1982.

Editor, with Charles G. Waugh and Martin H. Greenberg, *Science Fiction A to Z: A Dictionary of the Great Themes of Science Fiction.* Boston, Houghton Mifflin, 1982.

Editor, with Martin H. Greenberg and Charles G. Waugh, *Flying Saucers.* New York, Fawcett, 1982.

Editor, with Martin H. Greenberg and Charles G. Waugh, *Dragon Tales.* New York, Fawcett, 1982.

Editor, *Asimov's Worlds of Science Fiction.* London, Hale, 1982.

Editor, with Martin H. Greenberg and Charles G. Waugh, *Hallucination Orbit: Psychology in Science Fiction.* New York, Farrar Straus, 1983.

Editor, with Martin H. Greenberg and Charles G. Waugh, *Magical Worlds of Fantasy* series (*Wizards, Witches*). New York, New American Library, 2 vols., 1983–84; as *Magical Worlds of Fantasy: Witches and Wizards,* New York, Bonanza, 1 vol., 1985.

Editor, with Martin H. Greenberg and Charles G. Waugh, *Caught in the Organ Draft: Biology in Science Fiction.* New York, Farrar Straus, 1983.

Editor, *The Big Apple Mysteries.* New York, Avon, 1983.

Editor, with George R.R. Martin and Martin H. Greenberg, *The Science Fiction Weight-Loss Book.* New York, Crown, 1983.

Editor, with Martin H. Greenberg and Charles G. Waugh, *Starships.* New York, Fawcett, 1983.

Editor, *Asimov's Wonders of the World.* London, Hale, 1983.

Editor, with George Zebrowski and Martin H. Greenberg, *Creations: The Quest for Origins in Story and Science.* New York, Crown, 1983; London, Harrap, 1984.

Editor, with Martin H. Greenberg and Charles G. Waugh, *Computer Crimes and Capers.* Chicago, Academy, 1983; London, Viking, 1985.

Editor, with Patricia S. Warrick and Martin H. Greenberg, *Machines That Think.* New York, Holt Rinehart, and London, Allen Lane, 1984.

Editor, with Terry Carr and Martin H. Greenberg, *100 Great Fantasy Short Stories.* New York, Doubleday, and London, Robson, 1984.

Editor, with Martin H. Greenberg and Charles G. Waugh, *The Great Science Fiction Firsts.* New York, Beaufort, 1984; London, Robson, 1985.

Editor, with others, *Murder on the Menu,* New York, Avon, 1984.

Editor, with Martin H. Greenberg and Charles G. Waugh, *Sherlock Holmes Through Time and Space.* New York, Bluejay, 1984; London, Severn House, 1985.

Editor, with Martin H. Greenberg, *Isaac Asimov's Wonderful World of Science Fiction 2: The Science Fictional Olympics,* New York, New American Library, 1984.

Editor, with Martin H. Greenberg and Charles G. Waugh, *Young Mutants, Extraterrestials, Ghosts, Monsters, Star Travelers, Witches and Warlocks* (for children). New York, Harper, 6 vols., 1984–87.

Editor, with Martin H. Greenberg, *Election Day 2084: A Science Fiction Anthology on the Politics of the Future.* Buffalo, New York, Prometheus, 1984.

Editor, with Martin H. Greenberg and Charles G. Waugh, *Baker's Dozen: 13 Short Fantasy Novels.* New York, Greenwich House, 1984.

Editor, with Martin H. Greenberg and Charles G. Waugh. *Amazing Stories: 60 Years of the Best Science Fiction.* Lake Geneva, Wisconsin, TRS, 1985.

Editor, *Living in the Future.* New York, Beaufort, 1985.

Editor, with Martin H. Greenberg and Charles G. Waugh, *Great Science Fiction Stories by the World's Great Scientists.* New York, Fine, 1985.

Editor, with Martin H. Greenberg and Charles G. Waugh, *Giants.* New York, New American Library, 1985.

Editor, with Martin H. Greenberg and Charles G. Waugh, *Comets.* New American Library, 1986.

Editor, with Martin H. Greenberg and Charles G. Waugh, *Mythical Beasties.* New American Library, 1986; as *Mythic Beasts,* London, Robinson, 1988.

Editor, *The Mammoth Book of Short Fantasy Novels.* London, Robinson, 1986.

Editor, *The Mammoth Book of Short Science Fiction Novels.* London, Robinson, 1986.

Editor, *The Dark Void.* London, Severn House, 1987.

Editor, *Beyond the Stars.* London, Severn House, 1987.

Editor, with Carol-Lynn Rössell Waugh and Martin H. Greenberg, *Hound Dunnit.* New York, Carroll and Graf, 1987; London, Robson, 1988.

Editor, with Martin H. Greenberg and Charles G. Waugh, *Cosmic Knights.* London, Robinson, 1987.

Editor, with Martin H. Greenberg and Charles G. Waugh, *The Best Crime Stories of the 19th Century.* New York, Dember, 1988; London, Robson, 1989.

Editor, with Jason A. Shulman, *Book of Science and Nature Quotations.* New York, Weidenfeld and Nicolson, 1988.

Editor, with Martin H. Greenberg and Charles G. Waugh, *Ghosts.* London, Collins, 1988.

Editor, with Martin H. Greenberg and Charles G. Waugh, *The Best Detective Stories of the 19th Century.* New York, Dember, 1988.

Editor, with Martin H. Greenberg and Charles G. Waugh, *The Mammoth Book of Classic Science Fiction: Short Novels of the 1930's.* New York, Carroll and Graf, and London, Robinson, 1988.

Editor, with Martin H. Greenberg and Charles G. Waugh, *The Mammoth Book of Golden Age Science Fiction: Short Novels of the 1940's.* New York, Carroll and Graf, and London, Robinson, 1989.

Editor, with Martin H. Greenberg and Charles G. Waugh, *Curses.* New York, New American Library, 1989.

Editor, with Martin H. Greenberg and Charles G. Waugh, *Monsters.* New York, New American Library, 1988; London, Robinson, 1989.

Editor, with Martin H. Greenberg and Charles G. Waugh, *Tales of the Occult.* Buffalo, New York, Prometheus, 1989.

Editor, with Martin H. Greenberg and Charles G. Waugh, *Robots.* London, Robinson, 1989.

Editor, *The New Hugo Winners.* New York, Wynwood Press, 1989.

Editor, with Martin H. Greenberg and Charles G. Waugh, *The Mammoth Book of Vintage Science Fiction: Short Novels of the 1950's.* London, Robinson, 1990.

*

Bibliography: *Isaac Asimov: A Checklist of Works Published in the United States March 1939–May 1972* by Marjorie M. Miller, Kent, Ohio, Kent State University Press, 1972; in *Joy Still Felt,* 1980.

Manuscript Collection: Mugar Memorial Library, Boston University.

Critical Studies: *Asimov Analyzed* by Neil Goble, Baltimore, Mirage Press, 1972; *Isaac Asimov* edited by Joseph D. Olander and Martin H. Greenberg, New York, Taplinger, and Edinburgh, Harris, 1977; *Isaac Asimov* by Jean Fiedler and Jim Mele, New York, Ungar, 1982.

Isaac Asimov comments:

As I look over this bibliography I am taken aback at the work that had to be done to compile it and I am absolutely appalled at myself for having made the work necessary. Had I known at the start that the time would come when these pages would be put together, listing my 298 books (and still going upward at my usual book a month) I'd have gone into something less onerous—like ditch-digging.—But I'm just kidding when I say that. I love to write and when you no longer see words spouting out of my typewriter/word procesor, you will know that I am not only dead, but have been dead for three days.

* * *

Both science fiction and detective fiction by Isaac Asimov unite in revealing in the author a fondness for the fact, a delight in reasoning from careful observation, and an absorption in cause and effect. Several different types of mystery occur in his writings.

The Black Widowers tales illustrate the author's inventiveness in meeting the stringent requirements of the armchair formula. At club meetings guests pose problems which are solved by the least likely detective in so distinguished a company, the waiter, Henry. Puzzle is all—club members are characterized only by a few habits, a common misogyny, and a consistent truculence. But with the clever juxtaposition of elaborate false solutions against the simple, correct ones furnished by Henry, the stories please and often surprise. The imaginative variations on the traditional use and misuse of clues are not uniformly surprising, fair, or successful in matching the resolution to the build up, yet the average in quality is high, and particularly good are the simple reversal in "No Smoking," the familiar clue in "The Biological Clock," the Ackroydal note of "The Obvious Factor," and the Sherlockian elements of "The Ultimate Clue."

More than a little of Archie Goodwin flavors the bantam bristlings of Darius Just, the five-foot-five novelist who narrates and does the sleuthing in *Murder at the ABA.* This breezy venture into a parodic approximation of the hard-boiled tradition provides clues for the reader and also exhibits the slangy wise-cracks, sexual adventure, and fuller characterization of that tradition. Direct addresses by Just to the reader, resembling Asimov's earlier Forewords and Afterwords to stories, are part of the chatty and consciously clever texture of the novel in which Asimov himself plays a minor role.

Asimov's most original contribution to mystery fiction is the subject matter of the future worlds, worlds containing such denizens as the rabbit-eared, rock-eating *silicony* and the robot. Stories set against this scene include armchair investigations by the extra-terrologist Dr. Wendell Urth; two inverted stories in which the crime is seen by the reader who then follows the efforts of a detective at reconstruction ("The Singing Bell" and "The Dust of Death"); and a handful of other mysteries involving less detection. Among the latter are "The Billiard Ball," which utilizes the theory of relativity in a murder method, and "I'm at Marsport Without Hilda," which manages to satirize and emulate James Bond-like adventure in a Mars setting.

The Caves of Steel has a startling innovation: the first robot detective. Assigned to partner an Earth policeman, R. Daneel Olivaw might have become the ultimate detective. Instead, the author chose to show human intelligence superior to that of the perfectly logical, but unreasonable, robot. Nevertheless, as a Watson-figure R. Daneel is a superior invention. Detection by Elijah "Lije" Baley and the robot contains classic patterns, following Sherlock Holmes at every turn and resembling the work of such early police detectives as Josephine Tey's Alan Grant rather than that in a police-procedural novel. Biblical allusion and dystopian and even Swiftian elements in the depiction of the earthmen's agoraphobia and the spacers' revulsion at "seeing" complement detection. While *The Caves of Steel* and its sequel, *The Naked Sun,* contain excellent detection, they are primarily utopian science fiction, inasmuch as the solution to the crime is less significant than the reestablishment of the potentiality of Earth's political and cultural vitality.

Consistent with the bulk of detective fiction, that by Isaac Asimov leaves unattempted analyses of emotional and philosophic issues, development of three-dimensional character, and stylistic innovation. Unlike much such writing, however, his is intelligent, varied, sound in construction and enlivened by humor, energy, and a love of paradox and pun: his works consistently interest and entertain.

—Nancy Ellen Talburt

———

ATKEY, Philip. *See* **PEROWNE, Barry.**

———

ATLEE, Philip. Pseudonym for James Atlee Phillips. Born in 1915.

CRIME PUBLICATIONS

Novels (series: Joe Gall in all books)

The Green Wound. New York, Fawcett, 1963; London, Muller, 1964; as *The Green Wound Contract,* New York, Fawcett, 1967.

The Silken Baroness. New York, Fawcett, 1963; as *The Silken Baroness Contract,* New York, Fawcett, 1966; London, Hodder and Stoughton, 1967.
The Death Bird Contract. New York, Fawcett, 1966; London, Hodder and Stoughton, 1968.
The Irish Beauty Contract. New York, Fawcett, 1966; London, Hodder and Stoughton, 1968.
The Paper Pistol Contract. New York, Fawcett, 1966; London, Hodder and Stoughton, 1968.
The Star Ruby Contract. New York, Fawcett, 1967; London, Hodder and Stoughton, 1969.
The Skeleton Coast Contract. New York, Fawcett, 1968.
The Rockabye Contract. New York, Fawcett, 1968.
The Ill Wind Contract. New York, Fawcett, 1969.
The Trembling Earth Contract. New York, Fawcett, 1969; London, Hodder and Stoughton, 1970.
The Fer-de-Lance Contract. New York, Fawcett, 1970.
The Canadian Bomber Contract. New York, Fawcett, 1971.
The White Wolverine Contract. New York, Fawcett, 1971.
The Judah Lion Contract. New York, Fawcett, 1972.
The Kiwi Contract. New York, Fawcett, 1972.
The Shankhill Road Contract. New York, Fawcett, 1973.
The Spice Route Contract. New York, Fawcett, 1973.
The Kowloon Contract. New York, Fawcett, 1974.
The Underground Cities Contract. New York, Fawcett, 1974.
The Black Venus Contract. New York, Fawcett, 1975.
The Makassar Strait Contract. New York, Fawcett, 1976.
The Last Domino Contract. New York, Fawcett, 1976.

Novels as James Atlee Phillips

The Case of the Shivering Chorus Girls. New York, Coward McCann, 1942; London, Lane, 1950.
Suitable for Framing. New York, Macmillan, 1949; London, Lane, 1952.
Pagoda. New York, Macmillan, 1951; London, Lane, 1953.
The Deadly Mermaid. New York, Dell, 1954.

OTHER PUBLICATIONS

Novels

The Inheritors. New York, Dial Press, 1940.
The Naked Year. New York, Lion, 1954.

*   *   *

When James Atlee Phillips became Philip Atlee for the purpose of selling a paperback original novel about an attempt by Black militants to take over a Southern town in 1963, he brought a lot of his old writing self—the self that had produced in *Suitable for Framing* what many people still regard as the best American crime novel of 1949. He borrowed the opening scene, one of the most spectacular in modern popular fiction, from that book. He borrowed his lead character, Joe Gall, from *Pagoda,* which he had published two years later; finally, he added to Gall's background a considerable amount of detail he had created for the unnamed hero of his first real spy book, *The Deadly Mermaid.* Further fleshing out of Gall, who had begun his fictional life as a convincing soldier of fortune, involved a topical reference to the Bay of Pigs incident as an explanation for his forced early retirement from the CIA and a very important switch of point of view so that Gall narrated his own adventure. The overall result was a hero who could be appealing as well as a more believable American equivalent of James Bond.

Gall returned soon in several later adventures, ending with the aptly named *The Last Domino Contract*. During the 13 years of the Fawcett Gold Medal series, various gimmicks were tried (such as the brief use of "The Nullifier" as a Gall *nom-de-guerre*) but generally the books centered on character. Beginning as one of the most interesting heroes of action fiction, Gall went on to become even more so. Kelly Wu, the exotic Canadian Chinese heroine of *The White Wolverine Contract* and *The Kowloon Contract*, became Gall's common law wife and presided over the "clapboard castle" in the Arkansas Ozarks, which had always been his home-base. Padraic O'Connell, adopted by Gall as an autistic victim of the Northern Ireland Civil War at the end of *The Shankhill Road Contract*, benefited from a surprisingly near-normal later childhood. Most importantly, this "family" seems to have given Gall a growing maturity and sense of responsibility.

His withdrawal from spying at the end of the particularly bitter "final" book in the series is quite credible, but only because of the gradual development of his socio-political conscience. Thus, while the first half dozen books, with their exotic villains and extravagant gimmickry, remind the reader of Ian Fleming, the last half dozen are more comparable to Deighton and le Carré. Yet Gall is as convincing and compelling at the end as he was at the beginning. Atlee's achievement in this series may well be regarded by future generations as the best American espionage series of the latter half of the 20th century.

—Jeff Banks

AUDEMARS, Pierre. Also wrote as Peter Hodemart. British. Born in London, 25 December 1909. Served in the British army, 1940–46: Lieutenant. Married Joan Wood; two sons. Salesman, Louis Audemars & Co., watch imports, London, 1928–39; manager, Camerer Cuss & Co., jewellers, London, 1949–56; sales manager, Zenith Watch Co. Ltd., London, 1960–76. *Died in August 1989.*

CRIME PUBLICATIONS

Novels (series: Monsieur Pinaud; Hercule Renard)

Hercule and the Gods. London, Pilot Press, 1944; New York, Rinehart, 1946.
The Temptations of Hercule. London, Pilot Press, 1945.
When the Gods Laughed. Hounslow, Middlesex, Foster, 1946.
The Obligations of Hercule. London, Sampson Low, 1947.
The Confessions of Hercule. London, Sampson Low, 1947.
The Thieves of Enchantment. London, Chambers, 1956.
The Two Imposters (Pinaud). London, Long, 1958.
The Fire and the Clay (Pinaud). London, Long, 1959.
The Turns of Time (Pinaud). London, Long, 1961; New York, Harper, 1962.
The Crown of Night (Pinaud). London, Long, and New York, Harper, 1962.
The Dream and the Dead (Pinaud). London, Long, 1963.
The Wings of Darkness (Pinaud). London, Long, 1963; as *The Street of Grass*, New York, Harper, 1963.
Fair Maids Missing (Pinaud). London, Long, 1964; New York, Doubleday, 1965.
Dead with Sorrow (Pinaud). London, Long, 1965; as *A Woven Web*, New York, Doubleday, 1965.

Time of Temptation (Pinaud). London, Long, and New York, Doubleday, 1966.
A Thorn in the Dust (Pinaud). London, Long, 1967.
The Veins of Compassion (Pinaud). London, Long, 1967.
The White Leaves of Death (Pinaud). London, Long, 1968.
The Flame in the Mist (Pinaud). London, Long, 1969; New York, Curtis, 1971.
A Host for Dying (Pinaud). London, Long, 1970; New York, Curtis, 1972.
Stolen Like Magic Away (Pinaud). London, Long, 1971.
The Delicate Dust of Death (Pinaud). London, Long, 1973.
No Tears for the Dead (Pinaud). London, Long, 1974.
Nightmare in Rust (Pinaud). London, Long, 1975.
And One for the Dead (Pinaud). London, Long, 1975; New York, Walker, 1981.
The Healing Hands of Death (Pinaud). London, Long, and Salem, New Hampshire, Hutchinson, 1977.
Now Dead Is Any Man (Pinaud). London, Long, 1978; New York, Walker, 1980.
A Sad and Savage Dying (Pinaud). London, Long, 1978.
Slay Me a Sinner (Pinaud). London, Long, 1979; New York, Walker, 1980.
Gone to Her Death (Pinaud). London, Hale, and New York, Walker, 1981.
The Bitter Path of Death (Pinaud). London, Hale, 1982; New York, Walker, 1983.
The Red Rust of Death (Pinaud). London, Hale, 1983.
A Small Slain Body (Pinaud). London, Hale, 1985.

Short Story

Fate and Fernand. London, Vallancey Press, 1945.

Uncollected Short Story

"Hercule and Jou-Jou," in *Murder Plain and Fanciful*, edited by James Sandoe. New York, Sheridan House, 1948.

OTHER PUBLICATIONS

Novels

Night Without Darkness. London, Selwyn and Blount, 1936.
Wrath of the Valley (as Peter Hodemart). London, Rockliff, 1947.

*   *   *

Pierre Audemars wrote 33 suspense tales. They are set in France, a mythical France created by the author, in which the forces of evil are frequently rooted in ancient families whose character and power were established in the Middle Ages. The mythical quality is underlined by what would otherwise seem to be inexplicable geographical dislocations—placing the Gorges du Tarn, for example, in Haute Savoie.

Audemars invariably writes well, lightly manipulating narrative devices which many writers would hesitate to employ. In *Hercule and the Gods,* his first novel, a railway passenger is told a tale by the French laborer Hercule, so that there are two first person narrators. What could be cumbersome and distracting to the reader is instead cleverly handled. Hercule's language is sprinkled with French expressions and consistently seems to have been somewhat awkwardly translated from the French. The author manages all this admirably, enhancing the atmosphere as well as the humor, which in this book ranges from broad farce to rather subtle word play.

Hercule's cousin, an actor, impersonates Pinaud, "the greatest detective in France."

In most of Audemars's suspense novels, the hero is Inspector Pinaud of the French Sûreté. Pinaud is very fond of good food and fine wine. He loves fast cars and is often shown at the wheel of a powerful Sûreté car or an interesting antique or hand-built model. He is highly susceptible to attractive women, and in practically every adventure encounters a lovely nude female, a bit of fortune much envied by M. le Chef, Pinaud's boss. For all that, Pinaud is the antithesis of a James Bond. He is a conscientious family man who nearly always resists the temptations lavished upon him, despite the torments of his carnal thoughts. He and his wife Germaine have two daughters. They struggle against poverty and are often separated because of his work, reminding the mystery fan, in this respect, of Marric's George Gideon and Kate. Constantly chafed by the injustice of a system which pays him only a pittance for his brilliance and dedication, Pinaud has, nevertheless, an almost feudal obligation to M. le Chef, though he is well aware that the loyalty is not reciprocated. Our hero is a philosopher, a great sympathizer with all the unfortunate and downtrodden, and a firm believer in a higher law which "worked, granted—but not always, and not often enough, not irrevocably, not consistently, and not inevitably...," so that Pinaud continues to seek justice. He sometimes sees himself as a medieval knight, rescuing maidens and righting wrongs.

Pinaud's cases are related by a detached, somewhat tongue-in-cheek narrator who refers to the great detective's unpublished (and published) memoirs. The stories begin in a stylized manner—"In the days when M. Pinaud's fame had grown to such an extent that no one ever dared to question his veracity...," or "In the days when M. Pinaud was younger and leaner than one would ever have believed possible (considering the gargantuan majesty of his present appearance) and when his utterance and pronouncements rang more with the certainty of his own convictions than with the complacency of universal acclaim...." If Pinaud's cases seem most often to deal with narcotics and white slavery, or the murder of young girls, they are told in such a way that the gruesome details do not offend (not too much, anyway, nor for long). He is characterized by sardonic humor, intrepid self-confidence, and much information—he declares, for instance, that a great detective "must know something about everything. Not everything about everything. And certainly not something about something. But something about everything."

Audemars, whose sense of humor is delectable, wrote suspense fiction that is original and intriguing. Any reader who has not yet met M. Pinaud would do well to make his acquaintance.

—Mary Helen Becker

AUSTER, Paul. Has also written as Paul Benjamin. Born in Newark, New Jersey, 3 February 1947. Educated at Columbia University, New York, B.A. 1969, M.A. 1970. Married 1) Lydia Davis in 1974; 2) Siri Hustvedt in 1981; two children. Has had a variety of jobs including merchant seaman, census taker, and tutor. Since 1986 teacher of creative writing, Princeton University, New Jersey. Recipient: Poetry grant, Ingram Merrill Foundation, 1975, 1982; PEN Translation Center grant, 1977; National Endowment for the Arts fellowship (for poetry), 1979, and for creative writing, 1985. Address: c/o Viking Books, 40 West 23rd Street, New York, New York 10001, U.S.A.

CRIME PUBLICATIONS

Novels (series: The New York Trilogy)

Squeeze Play (as Paul Benjamin). London, Alpha-Omega, 1982; New York, Avon, 1984.
The New York Trilogy. London, Faber, 1987.
  City of Glass. Los Angeles, Sun and Moon Press, 1985.
  Ghosts. Los Angeles, Sun and Moon Press, 1986.
  The Locked Room. Los Angeles, Sun and Moon Press, 1987.

OTHER PUBLICATIONS

Novels

In the Country of Last Things. New York, Viking, 1987; London, Faber, 1988.
Moon Palace. New York, Viking, 1989; London, Faber, 1990.

Play

Eclipse. (produced New York, 1977).

Verse

Unearth: Poems 1970–72. Weston, Connecticut, Living Hand, 1974.
Wall Writing: Poems 1971–75. Berkeley, California, Figures, 1976.
Facing the Music. New York, Station Hill, 1980.
Disappearances. New York, Overlook Press, 1988.

Other

White Spaces. New York, Station Hill, 1980.
The Art of Hunger and Other Essays. London, Menard Press, 1982.
The Invention of Solitude. New York, Sun, 1982; London, Faber, 1988.
Ground Work: Selected Poems and Essays 1970–1979. London, Faber, 1990.

Editor, *The Random House Book of Twentieth-Century French Poetry.* London, Random House, 1982; New York, Vintage, 1984.
Editor and translator, *The Notebooks of Joseph Joubert: A Selection.* San Francisco, North Point Press, 1983.

Translator, *A Little Anthology of Surrealist Poems.* New York, Siamese Banana Press, 1972.
Translator, *Fits and Starts: Selected Poems of Jacques Dupin.* Weston, Connecticut, Living Hand, 1974.
Translator, with Lydia Davis, *Arabs and Israelis: A Dialogue,* by Saul Friedlander and Mahmoud Hussein, New York, Holmes and Meier, 1975.
Translator, *The Uninhabited: Selected Poems of André de Bouchet.* Weston, Connecticut, Living Hand, 1976.
Translator, with Lydia Davis, *Jean-Paul Sartre: Life Situations.* New York, Pantheon, 1977; as *Sartre in the Seventies: Interviews and Essays.* London, Deutsch, 1978.
Translator, with Lydia Davis, *China: The People's Republic 1949–76,* by Jean Chesneaux, New York, Pantheon, 1979.
Translator, with Françoise Le Barbier and Marie-Claire Bergère, *China From the 1911 Revolution to Liberation.* New York, Pantheon, 1979.
Translator, *A Tomb for Anatole,* by Stéphane Mallarmé, San Francisco, North Point Press, 1983.

Translator, *Vicious Circles,* by Maurice Blanchot. New York, Station Hill, 1985.

Translator, *On the High Wire,* by Philippe Petit. New York, Random House, 1985.

Translator, with Margit Rowell, *Joan Miró: Selected Writings.* Boston, G.K. Hall, 1986.

* * *

Although *City of Glass,* part one of *The New York Trilogy,* was shortlisted for the 1985 Edgar Allan Poe award for best novel (won by L.R. Wright for *The Suspect*) and the pseudonymous *Squeeze Play* was similarly shortlisted for the 1983 Private Eye Writers of America Shamus award, Paul Auster is anything but a typical crime writer.

Squeeze Play comes off as a classic exercise in style, featuring New York investigator Max Klein, a rough diamond down-on-his-luck dick operating from a familiar rundown office on Broadway. Previously a college baseball player, Klein gets himself involved with the political ambitions of a former baseball star and his sexy, luscious wife. The occasional sparsity and minimalism of the style reflects Auster's origins in poetry, essays and translation work and prefigures the brilliant pared to the bone conceits of *The New York Trilogy.* Here, Auster attempts a unique metaphysical deconstruction in three parts of the mystery novel, twisting and turning many of the conventions of the genre on a literary Mobius Strip which literally falls back on itself with devilish cleverness. As Elmore Leonard aptly remarked: "(Auster) uses the bare bones of the genre to get to the essence of good writing...mystery as metaphor."

The three independent novels that constitute Auster's trilogy juggle in an hallucinatory manner with voyeurism, questions of identity and obsession. In *City of Glass,* a writer of detective stories gets a strange phone call and becomes enmeshed in a mysterious many-layered case which changes his life and his sense of identity. In *Ghosts,* Blue, a student of Brown, is hired by White to spy on Black; the potent imagery of film noir is given maddening illogical twists as the plot turns into an urban nightmare. With the final volume *The Locked Room,* a nameless narrator embarks on a puzzling search for a missing novelist and ends up assuming his identity and appropriating his wife and works. All three novels mirror each other in uncanny ways (Auster even appears as a nebulous character himself, but then is it the Paul Auster we know?) and form a grand mosaic of exhilarating question marks multiplied to infinity.

Auster's venture into the crime and mystery field might well be a self-evident experimental dead end, but it is a one-off magnificent venture epitomised by the Washington *Post* Book World reviewer who classified it as a "post-existentialist private eye...It's as if Kafka has gotten hooked on the gumshoe genre and penned his own ever-spiraling version."

Although *The New York Trilogy* has brought Auster much acclaim (he was previously better known as an essayist and editor of *The Random House Book of Twentieth-Century French Poetry,* his later novels have been outside the crime and mystery genre.

—Maxim Jakubowski

———

AVELLANO, Albert. *See* **MARLOWE, Dan J.**

———

AVALLONE, Michael (Angelo, Jr.). Also writes as Nick Carter; Troy Conway; Priscilla Dalton; Mark Dane; Jean-Anne de Pre; Dora Highland; Stuart Jason; Steve Michaels; Dorothea Nile; Edwina Noone; Vance Stanton; Sidney Stuart; Max Walker; Lee Davis Willoughby. American. Born in Manhattan, New York, 27 October 1924. Educated at Theodore Roosevelt High School, Bronx, New York. Served in the United States Army, 1943–46: Sergeant. Married 1) Lucille Asero in 1949, one son; 2) Fran Weinstein in 1960, one daughter and one son. Worked as stationery salesman, 1946–55; editor for Republic Features, New York, 1956–58; editor for Cape Magazines, New York, 1958–60. Since 1955 guest lecturer in New York and New Jersey schools. Chairman, television committee, 1963–65, and movie committee, 1965–70, Mystery Writers of America. Agent: Susan Crawford-Neister, Box 198, Evans Road, Barnstead, New Hampshire 03218. Address: 80 Hilltop Boulevard, East Brunswick, New Jersey 08816, U.S.A.

CRIME PUBLICATIONS

Novels (series: April Dancer; Ed Noon; Satan Sleuth)

The Tall Dolores (Noon). New York, Holt Rinehart, 1953; London, Barker, 1956.

The Spitting Image (Noon). New York, Holt Rinehart, 1953; London, Barker, 1957.

Dead Game (Noon). New York, Holt Rinehart, 1954; London, W.H. Allen, 1959.

Violence in Velvet (Noon). New York, New American Library, 1956; London, W.H. Allen, 1958.

The Case of the Bouncing Betty (Noon). New York, Ace, 1957; London, W.H. Allen, 1959.

The Case of the Violent Virgin (Noon). New York, Ace, 1957; London, W. H. Allen, 1960.

The Crazy Mixed-Up Corpse (Noon). New York, Fawcett, 1957; London, Fawcett, 1959.

The Voodoo Murders (Noon). New York, Fawcett, 1957; London, Fawcett, 1959.

Meanwhile Back at the Morgue (Noon). New York, Fawcett, 1960; London, Muller, 1961.

The Alarming Clock (Noon). London, W.H. Allen, 1961; New York, Curtis, 1973.

The Bedroom Bolero (Noon). New York, Belmont, 1963; as *The Bolero Murders,* London, Hale, 1972.

The Main Attraction (novelization of screenplay; as Steve Michaels). New York, Belmont, 1963.

The Living Bomb (Noon). London, W.H. Allen, 1963; New York, Curtis, 1972.

There Is Something about a Dame (Noon). New York, Belmont, 1963.

Shock Corridor (novelization of screenplay). New York, Belmont, 1963.

The Doctor's Wife. Beacon, New York, Beacon Signal, 1963.

Lust Is No Lady (Noon). New York, Belmont, 1964; as *The Brutal Kook,* London, W.H. Allen, 1965.

Felicia (novelization of screenplay; as Mark Dane). New York, Belmont, 1964.

The Thousand Coffins Affair. New York, Ace, and London, New English Library, 1965.

The Birds of a Feather Affair (Dancer). New York, New American Library, 1966; London, New English Library, 1967.

The Blazing Affair (Dancer). New York, New American Library, 1966.

The Fat Death (Noon). London, W.H. Allen, 1966; New York, Curtis, 1972.

Kaleidoscope (novelization of screenplay). New York, Popular Library, 1966.
The February Doll Murders (Noon). London, W.H. Allen, 1966; New York, New American Library, 1967.
Madame X (novelization of screenplay). New York, Popular Library, 1966.
The Felony Squad. New York, Popular Library, 1967.
The Man from AVON. New York, Avon, 1967.
Assassins Don't Die in Bed (Noon). New York, New American Library, 1968.
The Coffin Things. New York, Lancer, 1968.
Hawaii Five-O. New York, New American Library, 1968.
The Incident (novelization of screenplay). New York, New American Library, 1968.
The Horrible Man (Noon). London, Hale, 1968; New York, Curtis, 1972.
Mannix. New York, Popular Library, 1968.
The Flower-Covered Corpse (Noon). London, Hale, 1969; New York, Curtis, 1972.
The Doomsday Bag (Noon). New York, New American Library, 1969; as *Killer's Highway,* London, Hale, 1970.
Hawaii Five-O : Terror in the Sun. New York, New American Library, 1969.
The Killing Star. London, Hale, 1969.
Missing! New York, New American Library, 1969.
A Bullet for Pretty Boy (novelization of screenplay). New York, Curtis, 1970.
One More Time (novelization of screenplay). New York, Popular Library, 1970.
Death Dives Deep (Noon). New York, New American Library, and London, Hale, 1971.
Little Miss Murder (Noon). New York, New American Library, 1971; as *The Ultimate Client,* London, Hale, 1971.
When Were You Born? Paris, Gallimard, 1971.
The Night Before Chaos. Paris, Gallimard, 1971.
Shoot It Again, Sam (Noon). New York, Curtis, 1972; as *The Moving Graveyard,* London, Hale, 1973.
The Girl in the Cockpit (Noon). New York, Curtis, 1972; London, Hale, 1974.
London, Bloody London. New York, Curtis, 1972; as *Ed Noon in London,* London, Hale, 1974.
Kill Her—You'll Like It! (Noon). New York, Curtis, 1973; London, Hale, 1974.
The Hot Body (Noon). New York, Curtis, 1973.
Killer on the Keys (Noon). New York, Curtis, 1973.
The X-Rated Corpse (Noon). New York, Curtis, 1973.
153 Oakland Street (as Dora Highland). New York, Popular Library, 1973.
Death Is a Dark Man (as Dora Highland). New York, Popular Library, 1974.
Fallen Angel (Satan). New York, Warner, 1974; London, New English Library, 1976.
The Werewolf Walks Tonight (Satan). New York, Warner, 1974.
Devil, Devil (Satan). New York, Warner, 1975; London, New English Library, 1976.
Only One More Miracle. New York, Scholastic, 1975.
The Big Stiffs (Noon). London, Hale, 1977.
Dark on Monday (Noon). London, Hale, 1978.
Charlie Chan and the Curse of the Dragon Queen (novelization of screenplay). New York, Pinnacle, 1981.
The Cannonball Run (novelization of screenplay). New York, Nordon, 1981.
Friday the Thirteenth Part Three (novelization of screenplay). New York, Nordon, 1982.

Novels as Nick Carter (with Valerie Moolman)

The China Doll. New York, Award, 1964; London, Digit, 1965.
Run Spy Run. New York, Award, 1964; London, Tandem, 1969.
Saigon. New York, Award, 1964; London, Digit, 1965.

Novels as Sidney Stuart

The Night Walker (novelization of screenplay). New York, Award, 1964.
Young Dillinger (novelization of screenplay). New York, Belmont, 1965.
The Beast with Red Hands. New York, Popular Library, 1973.

Novels as Priscilla Dalton (Gothics)

The Darkening Willows. New York, Paperback Library, 1965.
90 Gramercy Park. New York, Paperback Library, 1965.
The Silent, Silken Shadows. New York, Paperback Library, 1965.

Novels as Edwina Noone (Gothics)

Corridor of Whispers. New York, Ace, 1965.
Dark Cypress. New York, Ace, 1965.
Heirloom of Tragedy. New York, Lancer, 1965.
Daughter of Darkness. New York, New American Library, 1966.
The Second Secret. New York, Belmont, 1966.
The Victorian Crown. New York, Belmont, 1966.
Seacliffe. New York, New American Library, 1968.
The Cloisonne Vase. New York, Curtis, 1970.
The Craghold Legacy. New York, Beagle, 1971.
The Craghold Creatures. New York, Beagle, 1972.
The Craghold Curse. New York, Beagle, 1972.
The Craghold Crypt. New York, Beagle, 1973.

Novels as Dorothea Nile (Gothics)

The Evil Men Do. New York, Tower, 1966.
Mistress of Farrondale. New York, Tower, 1966.
Terror at Deepcliff. New York, Tower, 1966.
The Vampire Cameo. New York, Lancer, 1968.
The Third Shadow. New York, Avon, 1973.

Novels as Jean-Anne de Pre (Gothics)

A Sound of Dying Roses. New York, Popular Library, 1971.
The Third Woman. New York, Popular Library, 1971; London, Sphere, 1973.
Aquarius, My Evil. New York, Popular Library, 1972.
Die, Jessica, Die. New York, Popular Library, 1972.
Warlock's Woman. New York, Popular Library, 1973.

Novels as Vance Stanton

Keith Partridge, Master Spy. New York, Curtis, 1971.
The Fat and Skinny Murder Myster. New York, Curtis, 1972.
The Walking Fingers. New York, Curtis, 1972.
Who's That Laughing in the Grave?. New York, Curtis, 1972.

Novels as Stuart Jason (series: The Butcher in all books)

The Judas Judge. New York, Pinnacle, 1979.
Slaughter in September. New York, Pinnacle, 1979.
Death in Yellow. New York, Pinnacle, 1980.
Kill Them Silently. New York, Pinnacle, 1980.
Coffin Corner, U.S.A. New York, Pinnacle, 1981.
The Hoodoo Horror. New York, Pinnacle, 1981.
Go Die in Afghanistan. New York, Pinnacle, 1982.
The Man from White Hat. New York, Pinnacle, 1982.
Gotham Gore. New York, Pinnacle, 1982.

Short Stories

Tales of the Frightened. New York, Belmont, 1963.
Where Monsters Walk. New York, Scholastic, 1978.
Five Minute Mysteries. New York, Scholastic, 1978.
CB Logbook of the White Knight. New York, Scholastic, 1978.

Uncollected Short Stories

"Better Off Dead," in *Private Eye* (New York), July 1953.
"The Man Who Walked on Air," in *Weird Tales* (New York), July 1953.
"Accident Report," in *The Saint* (New York), June 1956.
"The Curse of Cleopatra," in *Tales of the Frightened* (New York), September 1956.
"The Stop at Nothing," in *Tales of the Frightened* (New York), September 1956.
"White Legs" (as Mark Dane), in *Tales of the Frightened* (New York), August 1957.
"The Man Who Thought He Was Poe," in *Tales of the Frightened* (New York), August 1957.
"The Killer Was Anonymous," in *Mike Shayne Mystery Magazine* (New York), October 1961.
"The Ten Percent Kill," in *Mike Shayne Mystery Magazine* (New York), November 1961.
"Dark on Monday," in *Mike Shayne Mystery Magazine* (New York), February 1962.
"Murder Has Only One Act," in *Mike Shayne Mystery Magazine* (New York), May 1962.
"MS. Found in an Attic," in *The Saint* (New York), September 1962.
"Open Season on Cops," in *Mike Shayne Mystery Magazine* (New York), September 1962.
"The Sound of Murder," in *Mike Shayne Mystery Magazine* (New York), January 1963.
"Another Beautiful Client," in *Mike Shayne Mystery Magazine* (New York), June 1963.
"The Case of the Arabella Nude," in *Mike Shayne Mystery Magazine* (New York), July 1963.
"Oliver's Twist," in *Mike Shayne Mystery Magazine* (New York), October 1963.
"The Unguessable Bullet," in *The Saint* (London), December 1963.
"Murder at the Ball Park," in *Mike Shayne Mystery Magazine* (New York), December 1963.
"A Frame Has Four Sides," in *Mike Shayne Mystery Magazine* (New York), January 1964.
"Trouble at Travers Pharmacy," in *Mike Shayne Mystery Magazine* (New York), June 1964.
"The Gun Next Door," in *Mike Shayne Mystery Magazine* (New York), September 1964.
"Camoflage," in *The Saint* (London), November 1964.
"The Scar," in *Mike Shayne Mystery Magazine* (New York), December 1964.

"Take Me Out to the Ball Game," *Ellery Queen's Mystery Magazine* (New York), December 1964.
"A Letter from Ed Noon," in *Mike Shayne Mystery Magazine* (New York), March 1965.
"The Thing in Evening Dress," in *Mike Shayne Mystery Magazine* (New York), May 1965.
"Murder the Leader," in *Mike Shayne Mystery Magazine* (New York), October 1965.
"Some People Kill People," in *Mike Shayne Mystery Magazine* (New York), September 1966.
"Great Night for a Murder," in *Shell Scott Mystery Magazine* (New York), September 1966.
"Seven of Intrex," in *The Saint* (London), September 1966.
"Send a Man from Intrex," in *The Saint* (New York), January 1967.
"Corpes Are for Killing," in *Mike Shayne Mystery Magazine* (New York), March 1967.
"Seven Miles from Intrex," in *The Saint* (London), May 1967.
"Address: Intrex, Saigon," in *The Saint* (London), October 1967.
"The Ugly Penny Murder," in *Mike Shayne Mystery Magazine* (New York), July 1968.
"The Missing Gabriel Horn," in *Mike Shayne Mystery Magazine* (New York), May 1969.
"A Bullet for Big Nick," in *Mike Shayne Mystery Magazine* (Los Angeles), December 1971.
"Violin Solo for a Corpse," in *Mike Shayne Mystery Magazine,* (Los Angeles), May 1974.
"Queen's Quisine," in *Ellery Queen's Mystery Magazine* (New York), August 1974.
"The Dakar Diamond Caper," in *Mike Shayne Mystery Magazine* (Los Angeles), January 1976.
"The Marquee Alibi," in *Mystery Monthly* (New York), November 1976.
"Perfect Crime," in *Ellery Queen's Mystery Magazine* (New York), May 1978.
"The Fourth Homer," in *Mike Shayne Mystery Magazine* (Los Angeles), November 1979.
"The Little Dread Schoolhouse," in *Skullduggery* (Owensboro, Kentucky), January 1980.
"Sweet Violets," in *Mike Shayne Mystery Magazine* (Los Angeles), October 1980.
"The Real Gone Horn," in *Mike Shayne Mystery Magazine* (Los Angeles), November 1980.
"Courtroom Killer," in *Mike Shayne Mystery Magazine* (Los Angeles), December 1980.
"The Circus Catch," in *Woman's World,* February 1981.
"The Painting at the Wrights," in *Weirdbook,* April 1981.
"MS. Found in a Crypt," in *Mike Shayne Mystery Magazine* (Los Angeles), July 1981.
"You Can't Kiss a Corpse," in *Mike Shayne Mystery Magazine* (Los Angeles), November 1981.
"Conversation While Prying," in *Mike Shayne Mystery Magazine* (New York), 1984.
"Walter Ego," in *The New Black Mask.* San Diego, California, Harcourt Brace Jovanovich, 1987.

OTHER PUBLICATIONS

Novels

All the Way. New York, Midwood, 1960.
The Little Black Book. New York, Midwood, 1961.
Stag Stripper. New York, Midwood, 1961.
Women in Prison. New York, Midwood, 1961.
Flight Hostess Rogers. New York, Midwood, 1962.

Never Love a Call Girl. New York, Midwood, 1962.
The Platinum Trap. New York, Midwood, 1962.
Sex Kitten. New York, Midwood, 1962.
Sinners in White. New York, Midwood, 1962.
Lust at Leisure. Beacon, New York, Beacon Signal, 1963.
And Sex Walked In. Beacon, New York, Beacon Signal, 1963.
Station Six—Sahara (novelization of screenplay). New York, Popular Library, 1964.
Krakatoa, East of Java (novelization of screenplay). New York, New American Library, 1969.
Beneath the Planet of the Apes (novelization of screenplay). New York, New American Library, 1970.
The Doctors. New York, Popular Library, 1970.
Hornets' Nest (novelization of screenplay). New York, Popular Library, 1970.
The Haunted Hall. New York, Curtis, 1970.
Keith, The Hero. New York, Curtis, 1970.
The Partridge Family. New York, Curtis, 1970.
The Last Escape (as Max Walker). New York, Popular Library, 1970.
Love Comes to Keith Partridge. New York, Curtis, 1973.
The Girls in Television. New York, Ace, 1974.
Carquake. London, Star, 1977.
Name That Movie. New York, Scholastic, 1978.
Son of Name That Movie. New York, Scholastic, 1978.
The Gunfighters (as Lee Davis Willoughby). New York, Dell, 1981.
A Woman Called Golda (novelization of screenplay). New York, Nordon, 1982.
Red Roses Forever (as Lee Davis Willoughby). New York, Dell, 1983.

Novels as Troy Conway

Come One, Come All. New York, Paperback Library, 1968.
The Man-Eater. New York, Paperback Library, 1968.
The Big Broad Jump. New York, Paperback Library, 1969.
A Good Peace. New York, Paperback Library, 1969.
Had Any Lately?. New York, Paperback Library, 1969.
I'd Rather Fight than Swish. New York, Paperback Library, 1969.
The Blow-Your-Mind Job. New York, Paperback Library, 1970.
The Cunning Linguist. New York, Paperback Library, 1970.
All Screwed Up. New York, Paperback Library, 1971.
The Penetrator. New York, Paperback Library, 1971.
A Stiff Proposition. New York, Paperback Library, 1971.

Other

Editor, *Edwina Noone's Gothic Sampler*. New York, Fawcett, 1966.

*

Bibliography: "Michael Avallone: A Checklist" by Stephen Mertz, in *Armchair Detective* (White Bear Lake, Minnesota), February 1976.

Manuscript Collection: Mugar Memorial Library, Boston University.

Michael Avallone comments:
    A professional writer should be able to write anything from a garden seed catalogue to the Bible. Writing is the Last Frontier of Individualism left in a 1984 world, for it is the art form that demands the *least* collaboration.

* * *

    Since 1953 Michael Avallone has ground out countless short stories and over 150 paperback novels—private eye tales, Gothics under female bylines, juveniles, erotics, espionage thrillers, movie and TV tie-in books. But unlike most purveyors of drugstore fiction, Avallone is a true *auteur,* with a unique personality discernible throughout his work.
    He is best known for the 30 novels about his fantasy alter ego, Ed Noon, New York private detective, movie and baseball nut, lover of luscious women and lousy jokes ("Hi, Noon!" his friends greet him), and personal investigator for a disgraced recent president of the United States. The key to the Nooniverse is its creator's passion for old movies. He is so immersed in Hollywood's output of the 1930's and 1940's that fragments from dozens of those flicks leap from his cine-satiated mind to his pages and fill them with jumbled, raucous, and frenetic life. The fun of reading Avallone lies in encountering the most film-intoxicated man alive.
    By normal standards every Nooner is an inept mess. Avallone's chaotic plots, all of them dealing with the quest for some McGuffin or other, are literally improvised as he goes along, and his style is an ungrammatical, mispelled, brain-jangling approximation of English. "My stunned intellect, the one that found death in his own backyard with him standing only feet away, hard to swallow in a hurry, found the answer." "She had tremendous hips and breasts encased in a silly short black fur jacket and calf-high boots." When the plot squeaks to a halt, have a black dwarf enter the room walking on his hands with a .45 in each foot. Make the language do flipflops, mangle the metaphors like a trash compactor, slap down as many allusions to characters and incidents and lines and settings from old movies as the page can hold, spice with gobs of revulsion at hippies, perverts, Commies, pacifists, dissidents, militant blacks, liberated women, longhairs and pointyheads, and all other traitors to the John Wayne ethos. With this recipe Avallone has inadvertently created a private Nooniverse.
    If any of his books is Avallone's testament it's *Shoot It Again, Sam,* in which the President orders Noon to accompany a dead Hollywood star's body on a transcontinental train ride. While the "corpse" sits up in its coffin, Chinese agents raid the train, kidnap Noon, and use brainwashers made up to look like Gable, Cagney, and Lorre to convince Noon that he is none other than Sam Spade (as portrayed by Bogart of course). It's all part of the screwiest assassination plot ever concocted by a movie maniac. Whatever else might be said about Avallone, one must say what Casper Gutman said to Spade in *The Maltese Falcon:* "By Gad, sir, you're a character, that you are!"

—Francis M. Nevins, Jr.

———

AXTON, David. *See* **KOONTZ, Dean R.**

———

AYRES, Paul. *See* **AARONS, Edward S.**

———

B

BABSON, Marian. American. Born in Salem, Massachusetts. Has lived in London since 1960. Secretary, Crime Writers Association 1976–78. Recipient: Crime Writers Association Special award, 1985. Address: c/o Collins, 8 Grafton Street, London W1X 3LA, England.

CRIME PUBLICATIONS

Novels (series: Trixie Dolan and Evangeline Sinclair; Douglas Perkins and Gerry Tate)

Cover-Up Story (Perkins). London, Collins, 1971; New York, St. Martin's Press, 1988.
Murder on Show (Perkins). London, Collins, 1972; as *Murder at the Cat Show*, New York, St. Martin's Press, 1989.
Pretty Lady. London, Collins, 1973.
The Stalking Lamb. London, Collins, 1974.
Unfair Exchange. London, Collins, 1974; New York, Walker, 1986.
Murder Sails at Midnight. London, Collins, 1975; New York, Bantam, 1989.
There Must Be Some Mistake. London, Collins, 1975; New York, St. Martin's Press, 1987.
Untimely Guest. London, Collins, 1976.
The Lord Mayor of Death. London, Collins, 1977; New York, Walker, 1979.
Murder, Murder, Little Star. London, Collins, 1977; New York, Walker, 1980.
Tightrope for Three. London, Collins, 1978; New York, Walker, 1990.
So Soon Done For. London, Collins, 1979; New York, Walker, 1988.
The Twelve Deaths of Christmas. London, Collins, 1979; New York, Walker, 1980.
Dangerous to Know. London, Collins, 1980; New York, Walker, 1981.
Queue Here for Murder. London, Collins, 1980; as *Line Up for Murder*, New York, Walker, 1981.
Bejewelled Death. London, Collins, 1981; New York, Walker, 1982.
Death Warmed Up. London, Collins, and New York, Walker, 1982.
Death Beside the Seaside. London, Collins, 1982; as *Death Beside the Sea*, New York, Walker, 1983.
A Fool for Murder. London, Collins, 1983; New York, Walker, 1984.
The Cruise of a Deathtime. London, Collins, 1983; New York, Walker, 1984.
A Trail of Ashes. London, Collins, 1984; New York, Walker, 1985.
Death Swap. London, Collins, 1984; New York, Walker, 1985.
Death in Fashion. London, Collins, 1985; New York, Walker, 1986.
Weekend for Murder. London, Collins, 1985; as *Murder on a Mystery Tour*, New York, Walker, 1987.
Reel Murder (Dolan and Sinclair). London, Collins, 1986; New York, St. Martin's Press, 1987.
Fatal Fortune. London, Collins, 1987.
Guilty Party. London, Collins, 1988.
Encore Murder (Dolan and Sinclair). London, Collins, 1989.
Tourists Are for Trapping (Perkins and Tate). New York, St. Martin's Press, 1989.
In the Teeth of Adversity (Perkins and Tate). New York, St. Martin's Press, 1990.

*

Marian Babson comments:
I have always enjoyed reading mystery novels; I enjoy writing them. (It's even more enjoyable since they started selling.) My favourites are straight suspense and crime-with-comedy, and I alternate between the two. Which is not to say that I might not do something completely different at any time. I don't think writers ought to be too predictable. I also think they ought to let their work speak for them.

*   *   *

Marian Babson is a skilled and versatile writer of mystery and suspense novels that are remarkably even in their high quality. Her books are always tautly plotted, with believable and interesting characters, and are written in a smooth and polished style.

Babson began her career in the traditional detective story genre. Douglas Perkins, partner in a publicity firm, becomes entangled in mysteries as he attempts to publicize a troupe of "hillbilly" musicians and a cat show, respectively, and then to counter the negative publicity caused by the murders which he must investigate. Perkins is a rather conventional amateur detective, and his novels, *Cover-Up Story* and *Murder on Show*, are creditable examples of the genre as well as being amusingly satirical treatments of the worlds of popular music and of cat fanciers.

With *Pretty Lady*, Babson turned to suspense and found her true voice. Here, typically, she creates a helpless character who is innocently drawn into a net of terror and learns about the darker side of human nature. This novel effectively uses a mentally retarded adult man for the creation of extreme tension. In *The Stalking Lamb*, an American high-school girl, visiting England for the first time, because of her naiveté and trustfulness is victimized and then terrorized by an English tough.

Babson's versatility is one of her great strengths. She can compel either terror or laughter. The Douglas Perkins mysteries are fine examples of the comic mystery, and the following novels brought her control of suspense and terror to maturity. *Queue Here for Murder* takes as its subject a group of intent shoppers waiting for a famous annual department store sale and satirizes amusingly both the shopping custom and the heterogeneous characters in line. *Weekend for Murder* (*Murder on a Mystery Tour*) uses the fad for "mystery weekends" to gather a number of eccentrics who play out a contemporary version of the conventional English country-house murder plot.

A number of Babson's novels center around particular professions. The world of entertainment (popular music, theater, film) serves as backdrop in such novels as *Cover-Up Story*, *Reel Murder* (about a fading, elderly film actress), and *Murder, Murder, Little Star* (which depicts an amusingly portrayed bratty child movie star). The world of the high fashion industry serves as setting for *Death in Fashion*, and other novels illuminate additional aspects of contemporary London life.

Babson is particularly adroit at portraying children and young people. Twinkle, the child star of *Murder, Murder, Little Star,* is a case in point, and the terror felt by the likable protagonist of *The Stalking Lamb* is made excruciating for the reader because of her innocence and goodness. Two precocious youngsters, in *Bejewelled Death,* unwittingly set into action a comic chase in which the children become full partners; this funny and good-natured novel is made especially delightful by the children's charmingly depicted ingenuity and high spirits.

Babson shows great skill in her manipulation of chronology and of narrative methods. She upsets chronology to good effect in *The Stalking Lamb,* contrasting the protagonist's withdrawn and defeated mental state after her initial victimization with the high spirits and innocence that had allowed her to become a victim. In *The Lord Mayor of Death,* the point of view shifts among a variety of characters involved in the festivities surrounding a parade and celebration. As the narrative moves from one character to another, the danger is gradually clarified and fears for a small child's safety become intense. A powerful study in obsession and terror, *The Lord Mayor of Death* is tightly plotted and skillfully crafted.

A native of the United States, Babson has long lived and worked in England, the setting for most of her novels. However, she has made significant use of American characters, generally treating them sympathetically, though Black Bart, leader of the hillbilly troupe in *Cover-Up Story,* represents evil. Her naive innocents often are Americans visiting in England, as in *The Stalking Lamb, Death Swap, Bejewelled Death,* and *Death Beside the Seaside,* in all of which appealing young American women surmount danger partly through their courage and shrewdness.

A particularly interesting experiment using both American and English backgrounds and characters is a pair of books, *Death Swap,* set in England, and *A Trail of Ashes,* set in New England. An English and an American family trade homes for a summer, and each novel follows one family's holiday and their subsequent involvement in murder in alien surroundings. Both settings are well evoked, and the frustrations, fears, and delights of parents and children in both families are clearly and amusingly depicted.

Babson's skill at characterization and plotting, her variety of settings and backgrounds, her control of a mixture of themes and tones, and her finely crafted style place her at the forefront of contemporary crime fiction writers. Though some of her novels are highly comic, even farcical, while others are terrifying, each is a gripping tale about believable characters.

—Mary Jean DeMarr

BAGBY, George. *See* **STEIN, Aaron Marc.**

BAGLEY, Desmond. British. Born Simon Bagley in Kendal, Westmorland, 29 October 1923. Left school at 14. Married Joan Margaret Brown in 1960. Worked in the aircraft industry, 1940–46; worked in Uganda, 1947, Kenya, 1948, Rhodesia, 1949; worked for the South African Broadcasting Corporation, Durban, 1951–52; editor of house magazine for Masonite (Africa) Ltd., 1953; film critic, *Rand Daily Mail,* Johannesburg, 1958–62; writer for Filmlets Ltd., Johannesburg, 1960–61. *Died 12 April 1983.*

CRIME PUBLICATIONS

Novels (series Slade)

The Golden Keel.   London, Collins, 1963; New York, Doubleday, 1964.
High Citadel.   London, Collins, and New York, Doubleday, 1965.
Wyatt's Hurricane.   London, Collins, and New York, Doubleday, 1966.
Landslide.   London, Collins, and New York, Doubleday, 1967.
The Vivero Letter.   London, Collins, and New York, Doubleday, 1968.
The Spoilers.   London, Collins, 1969; New York, Doubleday, 1970.
Running Blind (Slade).   London, Collins, 1970; New York, Doubleday, 1971.
The Freedom Trap (Slade).   London, Collins, 1971; New York, Doubleday, 1972; as *The Mackintosh Man,* New York, Crest, 1973.
The Tightrope Men.   London, Collins, and New York, Doubleday, 1973.
The Snow Tiger.   London, Collins, and New York, Doubleday, 1975.
The Enemy.   London, Collins, 1977; New York, Doubleday, 1978.
Flyaway.   London, Collins, 1978; New York, Doubleday, 1979.
Bahama Crisis.   London, Collins, 1980; New York, Summit, 1983.
Windfall.   London, Collins, and New York, Summit, 1982.
The Legacy.   London, Collins, 1982.
Night of Error.   London, Collins, 1984; New York, St. Martin's Press, 1987.
Juggernaut.   London, Collins, 1985; New York, St. Martin's Press, 1987.

Uncollected Short Stories

"My Old Man's Trumpet," in *Argosy* (London), January 1957.
"A Matter of Mouths," in *Winter's Crimes 8,* edited by Hilary Watson.   London, Macmillan, 1976.

OTHER PUBLICATIONS

Other

"The Circumstances Surrounding the Crime," in *I, Witness: True Personal Encounters with Crime by Members of the Mystery Writers of America,* edited by Brian Garfield. New York, Times Books, 1978.

*   *   *

Desmond Bagley's untimely death in 1983 ended a writing career spanning two decades which saw him rise steadily into the premier division of British thriller writers and brought him into serious contention for the number one spot. More consistently lively than Innes, less mechanical then MacLean, he created fast-moving stories in which the action is underpinned but never overwhelmed by detailed technical expertise and rich local colour. Like all the great adventure/thriller writers from Haggard via Buchan to the moderns, he was more interested in movement than shape, and occasionally (as, for example, in *The Spoilers*) the reader may experience a sense almost of dislocation as the narrative is wrenched in an unexpected direction. But the sheer momentum of his writing is always more than enough to carry the reader happily through to the end.

There has to be more than action, of course, and with Bagley the "more" was never just tossed in as a make-weight. His books are as international in their settings as in their success, and he has the priceless ability to conjure up the feel of places as various and remote as the Mexican jungle (*The Vivero Letter*), the peaks of the Andes (*High Citadel*), the Icelandic wastes (*Running Blind*), and the Kenyan savannah (*Windfall*). He makes the terrain work for him. What the reader gets is never simply a tourist's-eye view of a place, but the living reality.

The same attention to detail is apparent in the technical backgrounds of the stories. It's reasonable to expect a thriller writer to sound as knowledgeable about weapons as Bagley does in, say, his description of Fleet's rifle in *Running Blind*, but it takes a scrupulous craftsman to dig as deep as he obviously did into such esoteric areas of knowledge as computer technology and genetic engineering (*The Enemy*), the history of bronze mirrors (*The Vivero Letter*), the causes and behaviour of hurricanes (*Wyatt's Hurricane*), earth tremors (*Landslide*), and avalanches (*The Snow Tiger*). And it takes a percipient artist to resist the temptation to overload his book with the results of his researchers and instead include precisely that amount which is interesting, informative, and authentic.

This same economy, however, is not always happy in its results when applied to characterization, and at the fringes of his books this often tends to be merely functional. For all that, he was remarkably adept at whittling out heroes who are both identifiable and identifiable with. Both the main prototypes of thriller hero are used—the professional agent/investigator (as in *The Enemy* and *Windfall*) with all the requisite physical and mental ingenuity of his training, and the ordinary, or at least non-specialist man facing a challenge cast down equally by external circumstance and internal self-discovery (as in *Bahama Crisis* and *The Snow Tiger*). His favoured method of storytelling was the first-person narrative, permitting him to involve the reader as closely as possible in the excitement of life-or-death decisions and explosive action, but that he had no difficulty working to the different demands of third-person and multi-viewpoint narratives is evident in books such as *The Spoilers* and *The Snow Tiger*. Indeed, in the latter, set in the framework of a Commission of Enquiry into an avalanche disaster, he brought off a *tour de force* which may perhaps survive at his most substantial work.

Bagley will probably not be remembered for giving the genre any substantial new direction, but as long as meticulous craftsmanship and honest entertainment are valued, and as long as action, authenticity, and expertise still make up the strong framework of the good adventure/thriller, Desmond Bagley's books will surely be read.

—Reginald Hill

BAILEY, H(enry) C(hristopher). British. Born in London, 1 February 1878. Educated at City of London School; Corpus Christi College, Oxford (Scholar), B.A. 1901. Married Lydia Haden Janet Guest in 1908; two daughters. Drama critic, war correspondent, and leader writer, *Daily Telegraph,* London, 1901–46. *Died 24 March 1961.*

CRIME PUBLICATIONS

Novels (series: Joshua Clunk; Reggie Fortune)

Garstons (Clunk).   London, Methuen, 1930; as *The Garston Murder Case,* New York, Doubleday, 1930.
The Red Castle (Clunk).   London, Ward Lock, 1932; as *The Red Castle Mystery,* New York, Doubleday, 1932.
The Man in the Cape.   London, Benn, 1933.
Shadow on the Wall (Fortune).   London, Gollancz, and New York, Doubleday, 1934.
The Sullen Sky Mystery (Clunk).   London, Gollancz, and New York, Doubleday, 1935.
Black Land, White Land (Fortune).   London, Gollancz, and New York, Doubleday, 1937.
Clunk's Claimant.   London, Gollancz, 1937; as *The Twittering Bird Mystery,* New York, Doubleday, 1937.
The Great Game (Fortune; Clunk).   London, Gollancz, and New York, Doubleday, 1939.
The Veron Mystery.   London, Gollancz, 1939; as *Mr. Clunk's Text,* New York, Doubleday, 1939.
The Bishop's Crime (Fortune).   London, Gollancz, 1940; New York, Doubleday, 1941.
The Little Captain (Clunk).   London, Gollancz, 1941; as *Orphan Ann,* New York, Doubleday, 1941.
Dead Man's Shoes (Clunk).   London, Gollancz, 1942; as *Nobody's Vineyard,* New York, Doubleday, 1942.
No Murder (Fortune).   London, Gollancz, 1942; as *The Apprehensive Dog,* New York, Doubleday, 1942.
Mr. Fortune Finds a Pig.   London, Gollancz, and New York, Doubleday, 1943.
Slippery Ann (Clunk).   London, Gollancz, 1944; as *The Queen of Spades,* New York, Doubleday, 1944.
The Cat's Whisker (Fortune).   New York, Doubleday, 1944; as *Dead Man's Effects,* London, Macdonald, 1945.
The Wrong Man (Clunk; Fortune).   New York, Doubleday, 1945; London, Macdonald, 1946.
The Life Sentence (Fortune).   London, Macdonald, and New York, Doubleday, 1946.
Honour among Thieves (Fortune).   London, Macdonald, and New York, Doubleday, 1947.
Saving a Rope (Fortune).   London, Macdonald, 1948; as *Save a Rope,* New York, Doubleday, 1948.
Shrouded Death (Clunk).   London, Macdonald, 1950.

Short Stories

Call Mr. Fortune.   London, Methuen, 1920; New York, Dutton, 1921.
Mr. Fortune's Practice.   London, Methuen, 1923; New York, Dutton, 1924.
Mr. Fortune's Trials.   London, Methuen, 1925; New York, Dutton, 1926.
Mr. Fortune, Please.   London, Methuen, and New York, Dutton, 1928.
Mr. Fortune Speaking.   London, Ward Lock, 1930; New York, Dutton, 1931.
Mr. Fortune Explains.   London, Ward Lock, 1930; New York, Dutton, 1931.
Case for Mr. Fortune.   London, Ward Lock, and New York, Doubleday, 1932.
Mr. Fortune Wonders.   London, Ward Lock, and New York, Doubleday, 1933.

Mr. Fortune Objects. London, Gollancz, and New York, Doubleday, 1935.
A Clue for Mr. Fortune. London, Gollancz, and New York, Doubleday, 1936.
Mr. Fortune's Case Book (omnibus). London, Methuen, 1936.
This Is Mr. Fortune. London, Gollancz, and New York, Doubleday, 1938.
Mr. Fortune Here. London, Gollancz, and New York, Doubleday, 1940.
Meet Mr. Fortune (selection). New York, Doubleday, 1942.
The Best of Mr. Fortune. New York, Pocket Books, 1943.

Uncollected Short Story

"The Thistle Down," in *The Queen's Book of the Red Cross.* London, Hodder and Stoughton, 1939.

OTHER PUBLICATIONS

Novels

My Lady of Orange. London and New York, Longman, 1901.
Karl of Erbach. New York, Longman, 1902; London, Longman, 1903.
The Master of Gray. London and New York, Longman, 1903.
Rimingtons. London, Chapman and Hall, 1904.
Beaujeu. London, Murray, 1905.
Under Castle Walls. New York, Appleton, 1906; as *Springtime,* London, Murray, 1907.
Raoul, Gentleman of Fortune. London, Hutchinson, 1907; as *A Gentleman of Fortune,* New York, Appleton, 1907.
The God of Clay. London, Hutchinson, and New York, Brentano's, 1908.
Colonel Stow. London, Hutchinson, 1908; as *Colonel Greatheart,* Indianapolis, Bobbs Merrill, 1908.
Storm and Treasure. London, Methuen, and New York, Brentano's, 1910.
The Lonely Queen. London, Methuen, and New York, Doran, 1911.
The Suburban. London, Methuen, 1912.
The Sea Captain. New York, Doran, 1913; London, Methuen, 1914.
The Gentleman Adventurer. London, Methuen, 1914; New York, Doran, 1915.
The Highwayman. London, Methuen, 1915; New York, Dutton, 1918.
The Gamesters. London, Methuen, 1916; New York, Dutton, 1919.
The Young Lovers. London, Methuen, 1917; New York, Dutton, 1929.
The Pillar of Fire. London, Methuen, 1918.
Barry Leroy. London, Methuen, 1919; New York, Dutton, 1920.
His Serene Highness. London, Methuen, 1920; New York, Dutton, 1922.
The Fool. London, Methuen, 1921.
The Plot. London, Methuen, 1922.
The Rebel. London, Methuen, 1923.
Knight at Arms. London, Methuen, 1924; New York, Dutton, 1925.
The Golden Fleece. London, Methuen, 1925.
The Merchant Prince. London, Methuen, 1926; New York, Dutton, 1929.
Bonaventure. London, Methuen, 1927.
Judy Bovenden. London, Methuen, 1928.
Mr. Cardonnel. London, Ward Lock, 1931.
The Bottle Party. New York, Doubleday, 1940.

Play

The White Hawk, with David Kimball, adaptation of the novel *Beaujeu* by Bailey (produced London, 1909).

Other

Forty Years After: The Story of the Franco-German War, 1870. London, Hodder and Stoughton, 1914.
The Roman Eagles (for children). London, Gill, 1929.

*   *   *

One of the Big Five of British mystery writers of the Golden Age, H.C. Bailey has been praised for his puzzles, and many readers delight in his style and characterization. Readers who do not delight usually dislike his major detectives. Is Reggie Fortune "intolerably facetious and whimsical" (Julian Symons) or engagingly benevolent? Is Joshua Clunk a villainous Christian or do his ends justify the means? Critics take sides: detectives are fair game.

More disturbing is the critical inaccuracy of categorizing the well-known Fortune as an intuitive detective. In mild protest, Bailey's Introduction to *Meet Mr. Fortune* informs readers that Reginald Fortune intended to continue in his father's suburban medical practice after studies at Oxford and Vienna. But his testimony in cases arising from the practice made his powers of inference from "slight obscure facts" known to the CID, which drafted him as scientific advisor. A "natural man," Reginald would disclaim any abnormal powers, insists Bailey. Unfortunately for Fortune, the intuitive label persists. Readers, if not critics, however, recognize Fortune's observation and inference. The Hon. Sidney Lomas is his chief, Supt. Bell his admiring colleague, and Inspector Underwood Fortune's choice for a co-worker. Plump, fair, and clean-shaven, the fastidious Fortune looks cherubically youthful even as he ages. He is fond of children and cats, and enjoys his garden and laboratory. Devoted to his wife, Joan, he is a gourmet who can demand lunch after a gory autopsy with the directness of a child. He knows himself. "That's what I'm for. Compellin' the official mind to think." "I'm on the side of those who are wronged. I'm for the weak." The weak are frequently children. He is also for his own justice—not always the legal one.

No authorial biography is provided for Joshua Clunk, but novels reveal that he continued in Covent Garden family quarters for Clunk & Clunk, a law practice in which he is the only Clunk remaining, "a block off the old chip." He deploys a loyal staff in investigating, and lives cozily with Mrs. Clunk in a suburb. Like Fortune, Clunk is plump and fond of children. His method is similar to Fortune's. "Apply your mind!" However, Clunk is of coarser clay. Prominent gray eyes in an ivory-yellow face match his moustache and whiskers. Quantity rather than quality pleases his palate and sucking sweets is his oral vice (no alcohol). Amiable Fortune quotes literature, but affable Clunk croons hymns, quotes the Bible, and runs Gospel Hall. He has an eye for a fee, though frequently there is none, and he is reputed to thwart justice and keep criminals in business. He is also for his own justice—not always the legal one. Clunk criticism is also misleading, especially concerning his relationship with Superintendent Bell.

Obviously Bailey uses the same police personnel in each series and occasionally Fortune and Clunk appear in the same novel. In *The Great Game,* Reggie's case, Clunk represents a client; squeaking, he establishes doubt about police evidence and gets an open verdict. The lawyer and the doctor exchange greetings after the episode. In *The Wrong Man,* Clunk's case, Inspector Underwood calls Reggie, asking about digitalis.

Reggie is plaintive: "I cannot tell you whether an overdose in him was murder, suicide, or accident. Your job." A post-mortem is requested.

The Bailey canon? Rarely is any author's work of uniform calibre, and Bailey's, though readable and fair, has its gems. Anthologists and readers select favorites from the tales of Mr. Fortune. A choice few illustrate different situations. "The Hermit Crab" is atypical, a Wodehousian romp, with working girls of the 1920's discomfiting Reggie. "The Yellow Slugs" is "Not nice. No." Called in by Bell on a case of near-drowned children, Reggie finds poor people; a boy and a girl are the real victims, not the corpse; the title is a physical clue. Initially reluctant to go with his wife to a girls' school for "The Greek Play," Reggie finds snobbery and criminous action, not only on stage. He uses medical knowledge to frustrate murder, and wit and physical exertion to conclude the action. Many readers choose *The Bishop's Crime* as the best Fortune novel, a case begun when Reggie finds a mixture of old mortar, red sandstone, and limestone under the fingernails of a tramp found dead. This leads him to his sister and thence to Badon Cathedral for goings-on he suspects if the Bishop does not. Assisted by Inspector Underwood and later by Bell, Reggie uses his knowledge of Dante to reach the solution, and he confronts the whodunits. In *Slippery Ann,* Clunk gets a client acquitted but immediately initiates additional inquiry. This leads him to Sturton, a seaport town, where he uses his operatives, John Scott, a one-armed veteran, and Miss Jones. Both novels demonstrate the superior wit of the detective, his physical activity, and his own kind of justice. For leisurely reading, Mr. Fortune is good fortune, Joshua Clunk fit the battle of whodunit, and the Hon. Victoria Pumphrey, in a single tale, is victorious as a charming lady detective. Bailey entertains.

—Jane Gottschalk

BAKER, Asa. *See* **HALLIDAY, Brett.**

BALL, John (Dudley, Jr.). American. Born in Schenectady, New York, 8 July 1911. Educated at Carroll College, Waukesha, Wisconsin, B.A. 1934. Served in the United States Army Air Corps 1942–45 Lieutenant Colonel; former Command Pilot in the Civil Air Patrol. Married Patricia Hamilton in 1942; one son. Staff member, *Fortune* magazine, New York, 1937–40; assistant curator, Hayden Planetarium, New York, 1940–41; staff member, Columbia Records, 1945–47; music editor, Brooklyn *Eagle,* 1946–51; commercial pilot from 1947; commentator, WOL radio, Washington, D.C., 1948–49; columnist, New York *World Telegram,* 1951–52; director of public relations, Institute of the Aerospace Sciences, Los Angeles, 1958–61; editor-in-chief, DMS (aerospace) News Service, Beverly Hills, California, 1961–63. Chairman of the Board and editor-in-chief, Mystery Library of the University of California, San Diego Extension. Full-time writer from 1958. Recipient: Mystery Writers of America Edgar Allan Poe award, 1965; Crime Writers Association Gold Dagger, 1966. D.H.L.: Carroll College, 1978. *Died 15 October 1988.*

CRIME PUBLICATIONS

Novels (series: Jack Tallon; Virgil Tibbs)

In the Heat of the Night (Tibbs). New York, Harper, 1965; London, Joseph, 1966.
The Cool Cottontail (*Tibbs*). New York, Harper, 1966; London, Joseph, 1967.
Johnny Get Your Gun. Boston, Little Brown, 1969; London, Joseph, 1970; revised edition, as *Death for a Playmate,* New York, Bantam, 1972.
The First Team. Boston, Little Brown, 1971; London, Joseph, 1973.
Five Pieces of Jade (Tibbs). Boston, Little Brown, and London, Joseph, 1972.
Mark One—The Dummy. Boston, Little Brown, 1974.
The Eyes of Buddha (Tibbs). Boston, Little Brown, and London, Joseph, 1976.
Police Chief (Tallon). New York, Doubleday, 1977; London, Hale, 1982.
The Killing in the Market, with Bevan Smith. New York, Doubleday, 1978; London, Hamlyn, 1980.
The Murder Children. New York, Dodd Mead, 1979.
Then Came Violence (Tibbs). New York, Doubleday, 1980; London, Joseph, 1981.
Trouble for Tallon. New York, Doubleday, 1981; London, Hale, 1982.
Chief Tallon and the S.O.R. New York, Dodd Mead, 1984.
Singapore (Tibbs). New York, Dodd Mead, 1986.
The Kiwi Target. New York, Dodd Mead, 1988.
The Van. New York, St. Martin's Press, 1989.

Short Story

The Upright Corpse. Privately printed, 1979.

Uncollected Short Stories

"The Sixth Armando," in *Blue Book* (New York), March 1955.
"The Case of the Elderly Actor," in *Baker Street Journal* (Morristown, New Jersey), October 1959.
"The Ripe Moment," in *Baker Street Journal* (Morristown, New Jersey), September 1968.
"One for Virgil Tibbs," in *Ellery Queen's Mystery Magazine* (New York), January 1976.
"The Man Who Liked Baseball," in *Ellery Queen's Mystery Magazine* (New York), October 1977.
"Fido," in *Cop Cade.* New York, Doubleday, 1978.
"Virgil Tibbs and the Cocktail Napkin," in *Ellery Queen's Scenes of the Crime.* New York, Davis, 1979.
"Full Circle" in *Ellery Queen's Veils of Mystery.* New York, Davis, 1980.
"Appointment with the Governor," in *Who Done It?,* edited by Alice Laurance and Isaac Asimov. Boston, Houghton Mifflin, 1980.
"Virgil Tibbs and the Fallen Body," in *Ellery Queen's Eyewitnesses.* New York, Davis, 1982.

OTHER PUBLICATIONS

Novels

Rescue Mission. New York, Harper, 1966.
Miss 1000 Spring Blossoms. Boston, Little Brown, 1968.
Last Plane Out. New York, Harper, 1970.
The Fourteenth Point. Boston, Little Brown, 1973.
The Winds of Mitamura. Boston, Little Brown, 1975.
Phase Three Alert. Boston, Little Brown, 1977.

Other

The Phonograph Record Industry. Boston, Bellman, 1947.
Records for Pleasure. New Brunswick, New Jersey, Rutgers University Press, 1947.
Operation Springboard (for children). New York, Duell, 1958; as *Operation Space,* London, Hutchinson, 1960.
Spacemaster I (for children). New York, Duell, 1960.
Edwards: Flight Test Center of the U.S.A.F. New York, Duell, 1962.
Judo Boy (for children). New York, Duell, 1964.
Arctic Showdown (for children). New York, Duell, 1966.
Dragon Hotel (travel). New York, Walker Wetherhill, 1969.
Ananda, Where Yoga Lives. Bowling Green, Ohio, Popular Press, 1982.

Editor, *The Mystery Story*. San Diego, University of California, 1976; London, Penguin, 1978.
Editor, *Cop Cade*. New York, Doubleday, 1978.
Editor, with Jon L. Breen, *Murder, California Style*. New York, St. Martin's Press, 1987.

*

Manuscript Collection: Mugar Memorial Library, Boston University.

John Ball commented (1984):

For as long as I have been writing, I have been doing the books that I genuinely wanted to create; I have never tried to fit into market trends and I have undertaken some projects that I felt sure would not return the time and research costs I would have to invest. *The Fourteenth Point* is an example: to the best of my knowledge no one had ever written a novel based on the religions of the world. The idea appealed to me immensely and I did it—after two trips around the world and visits with religious leaders and institutions in a great many different countries.

To me research and accuracy are prime essentials. I will never make up facts to suit a plot idea if the actual data are available. If they conflict with the plot idea, then it will have to be modified or abandoned. I have a strong personal distaste for writing, no matter how good in itself, which irresponsibly describes places the author has never seen, or which is totally careless in supplying technical data. People believe what they read in books and I want mine to be as accurately informative as I can make them. I determined on this policy in high school when I found that all of the supposed "science" I had read in the Tom Swift books, and had so carefully learned, was the author's own invention. He let me down and I won't do it to others.

I am not a "message" author, but I believe in building books on ideas. For example, the idea behind *In the Heat of the Night* is that in any group of men a WASP is not necessarily the best qualified person present. *The Cool Cottontail* is built on the theme "Don't judge minorities until you know what you're talking about." This gives me a satisfaction in my work and the sales records seem to indicate that the public approves of this approach.

*   *   *

John Ball, a writer whose varied background and eclectic interests are reflected in his books, is best known for those mysteries featuring the Negro detective Virgil Tibbs, a homicide specialist who works out of the police department in Pasadena, California. Following the well-deserved commercial and critical success of the first in the series, *In the Heat of the Night,* Ball wrote several more novels featuring Tibbs, some of them quite good and others less so. Problematical in the subsequent stories, unfortunately, is the color of Tibbs's skin. What was integral to the narrative in the original is generally incidental to the best of those that follow and merely serves as a vehicle for Ball's social commentary which, admirable though it may be, is rarely pertinent and usually distracting. Happily enough, Ball's strengths as a writer far outweigh his occasional lapses, and the Tibbs series as a whole is a substantial and significant contribution to the genre. Notably good are *Five Pieces of Jade*, in which Tibbs unravels what seems to be the ritual murder of an elderly Chinese-American importer, and *The Cool Cottontail*, an involved but credible homicide case in the environs of a nudist resort in the Southern California mountains. Forensic work plays a critical part in the solutions of these cases and nobody writes about that sadly neglected end of the business better than Ball. Less satisfying but engaging nonetheless is *The Eyes of Buddha*, which takes Tibbs from the discovery of a year-old corpse in Pasadena to Katmandu in search of a missing heiress. The central premise and cast of characters are only marginally believable, but the procedural work is thorough and convincing. Not as well conceived, or as carefully written, are *Then Came Violence*, an uncharacteristically loose saga of urban vigilantism, and *Johnny Get Your Gun*, which features a nearly ludicrous cameo performance by movie cowboy Gene Autry and the California Angels baseball team.

The Killing in the Market, co-written with Bevan Smith, is arguably the purest entertainment of Ball's mysteries and the one which most adheres to a traditional format. The New York Stock Exchange serves much the same function as one of Agatha Christie's country houses in this story of fraud and revenge, and motives for murder abound. As ever, Ball knows whereof he writes—in this case the financial milieu of Wall Street—and he presents the reader with a palatable lesson in insider trading as the generous and oftentimes funny mayhem ensues.

But comedy is not a hallmark of Ball's mysteries, nor does it seem to coincide with his vision. On the contrary, the genre provided him with a venue to exercise his fascination with the machinery of society and the displacement of individuals within it. That is what characterizes and, in fact, informs his stories. As his cops discern the significant in the minutiae of their casework, Ball recognized, and displayed in bold relief, the dangers of the seemingly commonplace. Victims and villains alike, his players are unwitting participants in a larger tragedy.

—Curtis S. Gibson

————

BALLARD, K.G. *See* **ROTH, Holly.**

————

BALLARD, P.D. *See* **BALLARD, Willis Todhunter.**

————

BALLARD, Willis Todhunter. Also wrote as Brian Agar; P.D. Ballard; Parker Bonner; Sam Bowie; Walt Bruce; Nick Carter; Hunter D'Allard; Brian Fox; John Grange; Harrison Hunt; John Hunter; Willard Kilgore; Neil MacNeil; Clint Reno; John Shepherd; Jack Slade; Clay Turner. American. Born in Cleveland, Ohio, 13 December 1903. Educated at Westtown Preparatory School; Wilmington College, Ohio, B.S. 1926. Married Phoebe Dwiggin in 1936; one son. Recipient: Western Writers of America Spur award, 1965. *Died 27 December 1980.*

CRIME PUBLICATIONS

Novels (series: Lieutenant Max Hunter; Bill Lennox)

Say Yes to Murder (Lennox). New York, Putnam, 1942; as *The Demise of a Louse* (as John Shepherd), New York, Belmont, 1962.
Murder Can't Stop (Lennox). Philadelphia, McKay, 1946.
Murder Picks the Jury (as Harrison Hunt, with Norbert Davis). New York, Curl, 1947.
Dealing Out Death (Lennox). Philadelphia, McKay, 1948.
Walk in Fear. New York, Fawcett, 1952; London, Red Seal, 1957.
Chance Elson. New York, Pocket Books, 1958.
Lights, Camera, Murder (Lennox; as John Shepherd). New York, Belmont, 1960.
Pretty Miss Murder (Hunter). New York, Permabooks, 1961.
The Seven Sisters (Hunter). New York, Permabooks, 1962.
Three for the Money (Hunter). New York, Permabooks, 1963.
Murder Las Vegas Style (Lennox). New York, Tower, 1967.
The Kremlin File (as Nick Carter). New York, Award, 1973; London, Tandem, 1976.

Novels as Neil MacNeil (series: Tony Costaine and Bert McCall in all books)

Death Takes on Option. New York, Fawcett, 1958; London, Fawcett, 1960.
Third on a Seesaw. New York, Fawcett, 1959; London, Muller, 1961.
Two Guns for Hire. New York, Fawcett, 1959; London, Muller, 1960.
Hot Dam. New York, Fawcett, and London, Muller, 1960.
The Death Ride. New York, Fawcett, 1960; London, Muller, 1962.
Mexican Slay Ride. New York, Fawcett, 1962; London, Muller, 1963.
The Spy Catchers. New York, Fawcett, 1966.

Novels as P.D. Ballard

Age of the Junkman. New York, Fawcett, 1963; London, Muller, 1964.
End of a Millionaire. New York, Fawcett, 1964.
Brothers in Blood. New York, Fawcett, 1972.
Angel of Death New York, Fawcett, 1974.
The Death Brokers. New York, Fawcett, 1974.

Uncollected Short Stories

"A Little Different," in *Black Mask* (New York), September 1933.
"Three Reasons," in *Underworld Novelettes,* Winter 1933.
"A Million Dollar Tramp," in *Black Mask* (New York), October 1933.

"Positively the Best Liar," in *Black Mask* (New York), November 1933.
"Trouble-Hunted," in *Black Mask* (New York), January 1934.
"A Busy Day," in *Underworld Novelettes,* March 1934.
"Tears Don't Help," in *Black Mask* (New York), April 1934.
"That's Hollywood," in *Black Mask* (New York), May 1934.
"Whatta Guy," in *Black Mask* (New York), July 1934.
"Crime's Web," in *Black Mask* (New York), September 1934.
"Snatching Is Dynamite," in *Black Mask* (New York), October 1934.
"In Dead Man's Alley," in *Black Mask* (New York), November 1934.
"Murdered in Reno," in *Super Detective* (New York), November 1934.
"Murder Isn't Legal," in *Black Mask* (New York), December 1934.
"Confession Means Death," in *Black Mask* (New York), February 1935.
"Gamblers Don't Win," in *Black Mask* (New York), April 1935.
"Dead Men Don't Walk," in *Underworld Novelettes,* May 1935.
"Phantom Clue," in *Phantom Detective* (New York), May 1935.
"Night Club Murder," in *Underworld Novelettes,* June 1935.
"Night Is for Dying," in *New Detective* (Kokomo, Indiana), June 1935.
"Bodyguard," in *New Detective,* June 1935.
"Murder Makes a Difference," in *Black Mask* (New York), June 1935.
"Killer's Bait," in *The Underworld Detective* (Springfield, Massachusetts), July 1935.
"You Never Know about Women," in *Black Mask* (New York), October 1935.
"After Breakfast," in *Black Mask* (New York), December 1935.
"Numbers with Lead," in *Black Mask* (New York), January 1936.
"Blood on the Moon," in *Black Mask* (New York), April 1936.
"Blackmailers Die Hard," in *Black Mask* (New York), May 1936.
"Death in the Patio," in *Clues* (New York), May 1936.
"How about Murder," in *Underworld Novelettes,* July 1936.
"Fugitive from Justice," in *Black Mask* (New York), August 1936.
"There's No Excuse for Murder," in *Black Mask* (New York), September 1936.
"A Ride in the Rain," in *Black Mask* (New York), October 1936.
"Contact Man," in *Feds* (New York), October 1936.
"Whipsawed," in *Black Mask* (New York), December 1936.
"This Is Murder," in *Black Mask* (New York), March 1937.
"Stones of Death," in *Black Mask* (New York), April 1937.
"Call a Dead Man," in *Black Mask* (New York), May 1937.
"Cop's Choice," in *This Week,* 20 June 1937.
"Fortune Deals Death," in *Black Mask* (New York), July 1937.
"Friends Sometimes Kill," in *Black Mask* (New York), November 1937.
"Only Proof Counts," in *Black Mask* (New York), December 1937.
"Masquerading Corpse," in *Ace G-Man* (Chicago), January–February 1938.
"G-Man on the Dodge," in *Ace G-Man* (Chicago), March–April 1938.
"Never Trust a Cop," in *Captain Satan* (Chicago), May 1938.
"Case of the Cluttered Corpses," in *10 Detective Aces* (Springfield, Massachusetts), June 1938.

"Live Bait for Suckers," in *Ace G-Man* (Chicago), June–July 1938.

"Lady, Don't Die," in *10 Detective Aces* (Springfield, Massachusetts), September 1938.

"Special Agent from Hell," in *Ace G-Man* (Chicago), September–October 1938.

"Murder on Approval," in *Ace G-Man* (Chicago), September–October 1938.

"Homicide Blues," in *10 Detective Aces* (Springfield, Massachusetts), October 1938.

"Death Is on Board," in *Detective Tales* (Springfield, Massachusetts), October 1938.

"Drake Deals Death," in *Crime Busters* (New York), October 1938.

"Nosey Guy," in *Double Action Detective* (Holyoke, Massachusetts), October 1938.

"Mobster Guns," in *Black Mask* (New York), November 1938.

"The Devil's Warehouse," in *Detective Yarns* (Holyoke, Massachusetts) December 1938.

"Stooge for Murder," in *10 Detective Aces* (Springfield, Massachusetts), December 1938.

"Death Holds the Stakes," in *Thrilling Detective* (New York), January 1939.

"Murder Merchant," in *Variety Detective* (Springfield, Massachusetts), February 1939.

"No Parole from Death," in *Black Mask* (New York), February 1939.

"Decoy Dame," in *10 Detective Aces* (Springfield, Massachusetts), February 1939.

"Tickets for Murder," in *Crime Busters* (New York), February 1939.

"Letter of the Law," in *Detective Short Stories* (New York), March 1939.

"G-Man Corpse Catcher," in *Ace G-Man* (Chicago), March–April 1939.

"Death Doubles on Red," in *10 Story Detective* (Springfield, Massachusetts), March–April 1939.

"Rogue's Gallery Galahad," in *Top-Notch Detective* (Chicago), March 1939.

"Suicide for Killers," in *Crime Busters* (New York), April 1939.

"Hell's Hangover," in *10 Detective Aces* (Springfield, Massachusetts), April 1939.

"No Escape from the Dead," in *Thrilling Mystery* (New York), May 1939.

"Wise Girl," in *Crime Busters* (New York), May 1939.

"More Than Blood," in *Popular Detective* (New York), June 1939.

"The Whole Scenario," in *Thrilling Detective* (New York), June 1939.

"Death in the Zoo," in *Black Mask* (New York), July 1939.

"Blind Date with Death," in *Crime Busters* (New York), August 1939.

"Women Are Funny," in *Popular Detective* (New York), August 1939.

"Routine with Death," in *Variety Detective* (Springfield, Massachusetts), August 1939.

"Five-Star Fraud," in *10 Detective Aces* (Springfield, Massachusetts), September 1939.

"The Name Is Kelly," in *Thrilling Detective* (New York), September 1939.

"The Phantom Strikes Back," in *Phantom Detective* (New York), October 1939.

"Not Too Blind," in *Popular Detective* (New York), November 1939.

"Scars of Murder," in *Black Mask* (New York), November 1939.

"Women's Work," in *Crime Busters* (New York), November 1939.

"Murder's No Accident," in *Popular Detective* (New York), January 1940.

"Murders Aren't Nice," in *Mystery Magazine* (New York), February 1940.

"Engraving for Death," in *Popular Detective* (New York), February 1940.

"Sauce for a Rat," in *Popular Detective* (New York), February 1940.

"Murder in the Mirror," in *Thrilling Detective* (New York), March 1940.

"Odds on Death," in *Mystery Magazine* (New York), April 1940.

"I Stole a Horse," in *Mystery Magazine* (New York), June 1940.

"Bridge of Death," in *Strange Detective Mysteries* (Chicago), July 1940.

"Black Gold Doom," in *10 Detective Aces* (Springfield, Massachusetts), August 1940.

"Pictures for Murder," in *Black Mask* (New York), September 1940.

"Murder Tavern," in *Dime Mystery* (Kokomo, Indiana), September 1940.

"Wired for Death," in *Mystery Magazine* (New York), November 1940.

"Thirty Miles to Albuquerque," in *Black Mask* (New York), March 1941.

"The Lady with the Light Blue Hair," in *Black Mask* (New York), January 1941.

"Heads It's Murder," in *Popular Detective* (New York), February 1941.

"Dancer Kills a Horse," in *Argosy* (New York), 3 February 1941.

"The Alibi That Was Too Air Tight," in *Detective Short Stories* (New York), February 1941.

"The Body in Drawer 13," in *Lone Wolf Detective* (Springfield, Massachusetts), February 1941.

"You Can't Forget Murder," in *Mystery Magazine* (New York), March 1941.

"Four Killers and a Kid," in *Detective Short Stories* (New York), April 1941.

"The Masked Detective Bets on Death," in *Black Bat Detective* (New York), May 1941.

"Not in the Script," in *Black Mask* (New York), July 1941.

"Flames of Death," in *Mystery Magazine* (New York), July 1941.

"He's in the Death House," in *Popular Detective* (New York), August 1941.

"Water for the San Pasquel," in *10 Story Detective* (Springfield, Massachusetts), September 1941.

"The Diamond Bride," in *Thrilling Detective* (New York), September 1941.

"Kidnapped for What," in *Popular Detective* (New York), September 1941.

"Murder Is a Swell Idea," in *Black Mask* (New York), November 1941.

"Death Deals in Diamonds," in *Thrilling Detective* (New York), December 1941.

"Eight Hours to Doom," in *Dime Detective* (Kokomo, Indiana), December 1941.

"Shark Bait," in *Popular Detective* (New York), December 1941.

"Death Comes with the Fog," in *Mystery Magazine* (New York), December 1941.

"Key to Murder," in *Thrilling Detective* (New York), January 1942.

"Men with Guns," in *Mystery Magazine* (New York), January 1942.

"And Here Comes Murder," in *Popular Detective* (New York), January 1942.

"The Corpse That Died Twice," in *Exciting Mystery* (New York), Winter 1942.

"The Colt and the Killer," in *Black Mask* (New York), February 1942.

"Murder's Not My Line," in *Big Book Detective* (Chicago), February 1942.

"Death Writes the Bond," in *Mystery Magazine* (New York), March 1942.

"Lights, Action—Killer!," in *Black Mask* (New York), May 1942.

"Murder Merry Go Round," in *All Star Detective* (Chicago), May 1942.

"Homicide House," in *Flynn's Detective Fiction* (New York), May 1942.

"A Toast to Crime," in *Mystery Magazine* (New York), May 1942.

"Preview to Crime," in *10 Detective Aces* (Springfield, Massachusetts), June 1942.

"A Horse on Death," in *Mystery Magazine* (New York), July 1942.

"Referred to Death," in *Crack Detective* (Holyoke, Massachusetts), July 1942.

"Contract with Death," in *10 Detective Aces* (Springfield, Massachusetts), August 1942.

"Deep in the Heart of Murder," in *New Detective* (New York), September 1942.

"Death Takes a Vacancy," in *Thrilling Detective* (New York), September 1942.

"Hell Is My Hangout," in *10 Detective Aces* (Springfield, Massachusetts), September 1942.

"Death Wears a Horseshoe," in *Mystery Magazine* (New York), September 1942.

"Combination with Murder," in *Flynn's Detective Fiction* (New York), October 1942.

"Ninety-six Hours to Kill," in *New Detective* (New York), November 1942.

"Murder Takes the Stage," with Norbert Davis, in *Detective Story* (New York), November 1942.

"Death Knows No Dimout," in *10 Detective Aces* (Springfield, Massachusetts), December 1942.

"The Con Man and the Cop," in *Black Mask* (New York), December 1942.

"Murder Takes Priority," in *Thrilling Detective* (New York), December 1942.

"You Gotta Have Homicides," in *Thrilling Detective* (New York), January 1943.

"Look for a Luscious Redhead," in *Detective Short Stories* (New York), January 1943.

"There's that Corpse Again," in *10 Detective Aces* (Springfield, Massachusetts), February 1943.

"Murder Warden," in *Dime Detective* (Kokomo, Indiana), March 1943.

"Just One More Case Uncle Sam," in *Mammoth Detective* (Chicago), March 1943.

"Countess and the Killer," in *10 Detective Aces* (Springfield, Massachusetts), April 1943.

"Death Rides Iron Horses," in *Mystery Magazine* (New York), May 1943.

"All Set for a Death Rehearsal," in *10 Story Detective* (Springfield, Massachusetts), May 1943.

"Mister Six Foot Deep," in *Dime Detective* (Kokomo, Indiana), June 1943.

"The Man Who Was Killed Twice," in *10 Detective Aces* (Springfield, Massachusetts), July 1943.

"I've Seen That Corpse Before," in *Detective Tales* (Chicago), October 1943.

"New Orleans Limited," in *Shadow Mystery* (New York), October 1943.

"Front Page Obituary," in *Detective Tales* (Chicago), November 1943.

"I'm a Dead Man," in *Mammoth Detective* (Chicago), November 1943.

"Death on the Way," in *10 Detective Aces* (Springfield, Massachusetts), December 1943.

"Hearse Ride to Murder," in *Dime Mystery* (Kokomo, Indiana), March 1944.

"My Kingdom for a Corpse," in *10 Detective Aces* (Springfield, Massachusetts), April 1944.

"Sing for Your Slaughter," in *Black Mask* (New York), July 1944.

"The Knave of Diamonds," in *10 Story Detective* (Springfield, Massachusetts), December 1944.

"Murder Calls the Tune," in *Thrilling Detective* (New York), February 1945.

"The Accidental Clue," with Norbert Davis, in *Detective Story* (New York), March 1945.

"Murder Has Green Eyes," in *Detective Tales* (New York), April 1945.

"It Could Happen to You," in *Detective Tales* (New York), May 1945.

"Dressed to Kill," in *Black Mask* (New York), May 1945.

"The Very Silent Partner," in *Detective Tales* (New York), June 1945.

"The Noose Hangs High," in *Super Detective* (New York), June 1945.

"Head South to Murder," in *Detective Tales* (New York), July 1945.

"Case of the Climbing Corpse," in *Detective Tales,* September 1945.

"Murder's Mandate," in *Thrilling Detective* (New York), September 1945.

"Death Is Like That," in *New Detective* (Kokomo, Indiana), September 1945.

"All's Fair in Murder," in *Dime Detective* (Kokomo, Indiana), September 1945.

"Hide Out in Hell," in *Detective Tales* (New York), December 1945.

"Mary Took a Little Lam," in *Super Detective* (New York), January 1946.

"The Second Act Is Murder," in *Thrilling Detective* (New York), January 1946.

"Don't Turn on Me," in *New Detective* (Kokomo, Indiana), January 1946.

"Make-up for Murder," in *New Detective* (Kokomo, Indiana), January 1946.

"Murder the Girl Said," in *Detective Tales* (New York), May 1946.

"Murder Stakes the Claim," in *Detective Tales* (New York), June 1946.

"Dig Your Own Murder," in *Dime Mystery* (Kokomo, Indiana), September 1946.

"Don't Look Now—It's Murder," in *Detective Tales* (New York), October 1946.

"The Model in the Morgue," in *Detective Tales* (New York), December 1946.

"Accent on Trouble," in *New Detective* (Kokomo, Indiana), March 1947.

"Bury Me Not," in *New Detective* (Kokomo, Indiana), July 1947.
"Blood on the Stars," in *Dime Detective* (Kokomo, Indiana), July 1947.
"A Dame Called Flame," in *Detective Tales* (New York), September 1947.
"Death Before Breakfast," in *New Detective* (Kokomo, Indiana), November 1947.
"Slay Ride," in *Private Detective* (New York), November 1947.
"Having a Wonderful Crime," in *Detective Tales* (New York), December 1947.
"The Dead Don't Care," in *Dime Detective* (Kokomo, Indiana), January 1948.
"I Could Kill You" (as Willard Kilgore), in *Shadow Mystery* (New York), February–March 1948.
"No Body Knows," in *Detective Novel* (New York), Spring 1948.
"Stand-In for a Corpse," in *10 Detective Aces* (Springfield, Massachusetts), March 1948.
"Lady Fingers," in *10 Detective Aces* (Springfield, Massachusetts), April 1948.
"Don't Bury Me Yet," in *Black Book Detective* (Chicago), April 1948.
"Ruckus in Reno," in *10 Detective Aces* (Springfield, Massachusetts), September 1948.
"Let's Have Some Murder," in *Thrilling Detective* (New York), February 1949.

Uncollected Short Stories as John Grange, with Robert Leslie Bellem.

"Hell's Ice Box," in *Super Detective* (New York), July 1942.
"Days of Death," in *Super Detective* (New York), August 1942.
"Caribbean Cask," in *Super Detective* (New York), November 1942.
"Murder Between Shifts," in *Super Detective* (New York), December 1942.
"Cauldron of Death," in *Super Detective* (New York), January 1943.
"Murder's Migrants," in *Super Detective* (New York), February 1943.
"Death Is a Flying Dutchman," in *Super Detective* (New York), March 1943.
"Homicide Heiress," in *Super Detective* (New York), April 1943.
"Curse of the Masters," in *Super Detective* (New York), May 1943.
"Pipeline to Murder," in *Super Detective* (New York), August 1943.

Uncollected Short Stories as Walt Bruce

"Sinister House," in *Popular Detective* (New York), October 1942.
"Camelback Kill," in *Popular Detective* (New York), February 1943.
"Lion's Loot," in *Popular Detective* (New York), June 1943.
"Blackmail Clinic," in *Popular Detective* (New York), December 1943.
"Corpse Cargo," in *Popular Detective* (New York), August 1944.

Uncollected Short Stories as Parker Bonner

"Murder on the Meter," in *Detective Tales* (Chicago), August 1945.
"The Clock Reads Death," in *Detective Tales* (Chicago), July 1946.

"Redheads Is Poison," in *Detective Tales* (Chicago), August 1946.
"Toehold on a Torpedo," in *Detective Tales* (Chicago), December 1946.
"Hymie's Christmas Carol," in *Detective Tales* (Chicago), January 1947.
"Red Hot Ice," in *Detective Tales* (Chicago), January 1947.
"Hell on Wheels," in *Detective Tales* (Chicago), May 1947.
"Can't Keep a Dead Man Down," in *Detective Tales* (Chicago), October 1947.
"Hymie on the Spot," in *Detective Tales* (Chicago), January 1948.
"Hymie and the Homemade Lettuce," in *Detective Tales* (Chicago), February 1948.
"Hymie and the Double-Dome," in *Detective Tales* (Chicago), May 1948.

OTHER PUBLICATIONS

Novels

Two-Edged Vengeance. New York, Macmillan, 1951; as *The Circle C Feud.* London, Sampson Low, 1952.
Incident at Sun Mountain. Boston, Houghton Mifflin, 1952; London, Rich and Cowan, 1954.
West of Quarantine. Boston, Houghton Mifflin, 1953; London, Rich and Cowan, 1954.
High Iron. Boston, Houghton Mifflin, 1953; London, Rich and Cowan, 1955.
Showdown, with James C. Lynch. New York, Popular Library, 1953.
Rawhide Gunman. New York, Popular Library, 1954.
Trigger Trail. New York, Popular Library, 1955.
Blizzard Range. New York, Popular Library, 1955.
The Package Deal. New York, Appleton Century Crofts, 1956; London, Corgi, 1959.
Gunman from Texas. New York, Popular Library, 1956.
Guns of the Lawless. New York, Popular Library, 1956.
Roundup. New York, Popular Library, 1957.
Trail Town Marshal. New York, Popular Library, 1957.
Saddle Tramp. New York, Popular Library, 1958.
Fury in the Heart. Derby, Connecticut, Monarch, 1959.
Trouble on the Massacre. New York, Popular Library, 1959.
The Long Trail Back. New York, Doubleday, 1960; London, Jenkins, 1961.
The Night Riders. New York, Doubleday, 1961; London, Jenkins, 1962.
Have Love, Will Share (as Brian Agar). Derby, Connecticut, Monarch, 1961.
The Long Sword (as Hunter D'Allard). New York, Avon, 1962.
Gopher Gold. New York, Doubleday, 1962; as *Gold Fever in Gopher,* London, Jenkins, 1962.
Westward the Monitors Roar. New York, Doubleday, and London, Jenkins, 1963; as *Fight or Die,* New York, Belmont, 1977.
Desperation Valley. New York, Macmillan, 1964.
Gold in California! New York, Doubleday, 1965.
The Sex Web (as Brian Agar). N.p., Soft Cover Library, 1967.
The Californian. New York, Doubleday, 1971.
Nowhere Left to Run. New York, Doubleday, 1972.
Loco and the Wolf. New York, Doubleday, 1973.
Home to Texas. New York, Doubleday, 1974; London, Hale, 1977.
Sierra Massacre (as Clint Reno). New York, Fawcett, 1974.

Sun Mountain Slaughter (as Clint Reno).   New York, Fawcett, 1974.

Trails of Rage.   New York, Doubleday, 1975; London, Prior, 1976.

Sheriff of Tombstone.   New York, Doubleday, 1977; London, Prior, 1978.

Novels as John Hunter

West of Justice.   Boston, Houghton Mifflin, 1954.
Ride the Wind South.   New York, Permabooks, 1957.
The Marshal from Deadwood.   New York, Permabooks, 1958.
Badlands Buccaneer.   New York, Pocket Books, 1959; London, Ward Lock, 1961.
Desperation Valley.   New York, Macmillan, 1964.
Duke.   New York, Popular Library, 1965.
The Man from Yuma.   New York, Berkley, 1965.
A Canyon Called Death.   New York, Berkley, 1968.
Death in the Mountain.   New York, Ballantine, 1969.
Lost Valley.   New York, Ballantine, 1971.
Hell Hole.   New York, Ballantine, 1972.
The Burning Land.   New York, Ballantine, 1973; London, Gold Lion, 1975.
Gambler's Gun.   New York, Ballantine, 1973; London, White Lion, 1976.
The Higraders.   New York, Ballantine, 1974.
This Range Is Mine.   New York, Ballantine, 1975; London, Hale, 1977.
Manhunt.   New York, Ballantine, 1975.

Novels as Parker Bonner

Superstition Range.   New York, Popular Library, 1953.
Outlaw Brand.   New York, Popular Library, 1954.
Tough in the Saddle.   Derby, Connecticut, Monarch, 1964.
Applegate's Gold.   New York, Avon, 1967.
Plunder Canyon.   New York, Paperback Library, 1968.
The Town Tamer.   New York, Paperback Library, 1968.
Look to Your Guns.   New York, Paperback Library, 1969.
Borders to Cross.   New York, Paperback Library, 1969.

Novels as Sam Bowie

Thunderhead Range.   Derby, Connecticut, Monarch, 1959.
Gunlock.   New York, Award, and London, Tandem, 1968.
Canyon War.   New York, Ace, 1969.
Chisum.   New York, Ace, 1970.
The Train Robbers.   New York, Ace, 1973.

Novels as Jack Slade

Lassiter.   New York, Tower, 1967.
Bandido.   New York, Tower, 1968.
The Man from Cheyenne.   New York, Tower, 1968.

Novels as Clay Turner

Give a Man a Gun.   New York, Paperback Library, 1971.
Gold Goes to the Mountain.   New York, Paperback Library, 1974.
Go West, Ben Gold!   New York, Paperback Library, 1974.

Novels as Brian Fox

A Dollar to Die For.   New York, Award, 1968.
The Wild Bunch.   New York, Award, 1969.
Outlaw Trail.   New York, Award, 1969.
Unholy Angel.   New York, Award, 1969.

Sabata.   New York, Award, 1970.
Dead Ringer.   New York, Award, 1971.
Apache Gold.   New York, Award, 1971.
Dragooned.   New York, Award, 1971.
Return of Sabata.   New York, Award, 1972.
Bearcats!   New York, Award, 1973.

Other

The Man Who Stole a University (for children), with Phoebe Ballard.   New York, Doubleday, 1967.
How to Defend Yourself, Your Family, and Your Home.   New York, Mckay, 1967.

Editor, *A Western Bonanza.*   New York, Doubleday, 1969.

*

Manuscript Collection: University of Oregon Library, Eugene.

Critical Studies: interview with Stephen Mertz, in *Armchair Detective* (White Bear Lake, Minnesota), 1979; *Hollywood Troubleshooter: W.T. Ballard's Bill Lennox* edited by James L. Traylor, Bowling Green, Ohio, Popular Press, 1984.

*   *   *

Willis Todhunter Ballard was part of the second wave of famous and influential *Black Mask* contributors. His first *Black Mask* short story—"A Little Different"—appeared in the September 1933 issue. It features Bill Lennox, a trouble shooter for the fictitious General Consolidated Studios. Lennox was patterned after Ballard's friend Jim Lawson who repeatedly rescued the son of Universal Pictures' Carl Laemmle when he was in trouble with the police.

Lennox is not a private eye. Still, he became one of the most popular characters in *Black Mask,* appearing 27 times between 1933 and 1942. There is a sense of immediacy with Lennox; the reader likes him. He's hardboiled enough to satisfy the confines of the genre, yet he has a respect for women which is atypical of the normal pulp orientation.

One of Ballard's achievements as a pulp writer was his ability to portray realistically a sense of love between characters. Lennox is as warm a pulp character as can be found. He romances Nancy Hobbs, obeying all the dicta against a hardboiled character's marriage, yet still revealing a commitment which is the characteristic element of a hardboiled Ballard protagonist (whether PI, cop, or an ordinary guy who becomes unknowingly trapped in a tough situation).

After publishing short stories for about 10 years, Ballard wrote *Say Yes to Murder,* the first of four Lennox novels. *Say Yes to Murder* set the standard for the Hollywood murder mystery. By careful depiction of scene and close emphasis on character, Ballard created a cast of characters which became clichés of the movie industry: the crusty studio head, the long-suffering girl friend, even cops who are less condescending than usual. *Dealing Out Death* is the best Lennox novel. It is more mysterious in execution, more believable because of its finely honed dialogue, and has the never-never land of Las Vegas as an appropriate background for mirth and murder.

Between the late 1940's and the middle 1960's, Ballard worked primarily writing western novels, and crime and western short stories (at least until the pulps died in the early 1950's) and scripts for movies and television. Ballard and his close friend Robert Leslie Bellem, famous for creating Dan Turner, Hollywood Detective, collaborated on many projects. In adjoining offices in Pasadena, they worked on novelettes and screenplays. Ballard created several long-running series characters for the pulps: Red Drake, a race track PI and prototype for Dick Francis's Sid Halley, appeared in *Black Mask, Crime Busters,* and *Mystery Magazine;* Hymie Beerman, the wisecracking Bronx cabbie who appeared (as by Parker Bonner) in *Detective Tales* in the late 1940's; Dr. Zeng Tse-Lin, the almost superhuman hero of *Popular Detective* (published as by Walt Bruce); and Jim Anthony, the ethnic troubleshooter of *Super Detective* that was published as by John Grange but actually written by Ballard and Bellem. In the 1950's and 1960's Ballard and Bellem wrote for *Superman, Wild Bill Hickok, Cowboy G Men, Death Valley Days, Dick Tracy* and *Manhunt.*

After having written only western novels through most of the 1950's, Ballard reentered the crime market in the late 1950's. His Tony Costaine and Bert McCall thrillers—written under the pen name Neil MacNeil for Gold Medal—recapture the spark of the early Lennox cases with their realistic sexual relationships and broad range of characters. They have a definite western flavor and are great fun to read because of intricate and engaging plotting and the repartee between the two PI's.

At the same time Ballard was also writing a series of paperback originals about Max Hunter, a Las Vegas police lieutenant. These are written in the first person and approach the ethos of the world-weary PI. The characters in this series are closer to the actual human condition than in the Costaine/McCall books and the books resemble Ballard's crime stories: smooth in presentation but complicated with regard to plot. Although all three of the Hunter series reveal a humane quality, the first *Pretty Miss Murder,* which presents a variation on the Laura theme, is most enjoyable.

Ballard's last private eye novel, *Murder Las Vegas Style,* has been seriously neglected by hard-boiled critics. The story returns the reader to familiar *Black Mask* territory with its PI, mysterious and untrustworthy women, and fast, violent action. Mark Foran, an LA PI who's over his head in the Vegas whirl, is not a typical Ballard character. He's an amalgam of Ballard's entire crime-writing career, a worldly innocent who faces the classic pulp dilemma: easy money and the resulting corruption. It is the epitome of Ballard's crime-writing career.

Ballard wrote convincingly in many styles and from different viewpoints. He was extremely prolific, writing hundreds of short stories for the pulp and slick magazines, numerous screenplays and teleplays and almost one hundred western and mystery novels (under at least 20 pennames). Although he never won an MWA award, he did win the Western Writers of America Spur Award in 1965 for the best novel of the year, *Gold in California.* His crime novels are always rewarding; he had the ability to engage the reader with his characters, making the reader care what happened to them—crook, cop, or PI. Ballard wrote some near-classic detective novels, ones which played an unacknowledged role in the development of the hard-boiled detective tradition.

—James L. Traylor

BALLINGER, Bill S. (William Sanborn Ballinger). Also wrote as Frederic Freyer; B.X. Sanborn. American. Born in Oskaloosa, Iowa, 13 March 1912. Educated at the University of Wisconsin, Madison, B.S. 1934. Married 1) Geraldine Taylor in 1936 (divorced 1948), two sons 2) Laura Dunham in 1949 (died 1962), 2 daughters; 3) Lucille Rambeau in 1964, one step-daughter, and one step-son. Worked in advertising; radio and television writer, 1934–77; Associate Professor of Writing, California State University, Northridge, 1977–79. Executive Vice-President, Mystery Writers of America, 1957; member of the board of directors, Health and Welfare Plan and Pension Plan, 1977–78, and President of Federal Credit Union, 1978–79, Writers Guild of America. Recipient: Presses de la Cité Prix Roman Policier, 1953; Mystery Writers of America Edgar Allan Poe award, for television play, 1960. LL.D.: Northern Colleges of the Phillippines, 1940. Guest of Honor, Bouchercon II writing conference, 1971. *Died 23 March 1980.*

CRIME PUBLICATIONS

Novels (series: Barr Breed; Joaquin Hawks)

The Body in the Bed (Breed). New York, Harper, 1948; London, World Distributors, 1960.
The Body Beautiful (Breed). New York, Harper, 1949; London, World Distributors, 1960.
Portrait in Smoke. New York, Harper, 1950; London, Reinhardt and Evans, 1951; as *The Deadlier Sex,* London, Corgi, 1958.
The Darkening Door. New York, Harper, 1952.
Rafferty. New York, Harper, and London, Reinhardt and Evans, 1953; as *The Beautiful Trap,* New York, New American Library, 1955.
The Black, Black Hearse (as Frederic Freyer). New York, St. Martin's Press, 1955; London, Hale, 1956; as *The Case of the Black, Black Hearse,* New York, Avon, 1955.
The Tooth and the Nail. New York, Harper, and London, Reinhardt and Evans, 1955.
The Longest Second. New York, Harper, 1957; London, Reinhardt and Evans, 1958.
The Wife of the Red-Haired Man. New York, Harper, and London, Reinhardt and Evans, 1957.
Beacon in the Night. New York, Harper, 1958; London, Boardman, 1960.
Formula for Murder. New York, New American Library, 1958.
The Doom-Maker (as B.X. Sanborn). New York, Dutton, and London, Boardman, 1959; as *The Blonde on Borrowed Time,* Rockville Centre, New York, Zenith, 1960.
The Fourth of Forever. New York, Harper, and London, Boardman, 1963.
The Chinese Mask (Hawks). New York, New American Library, 1965.
Not I, Said the Vixen. New York, Fawcett, 1965.
The Spy in Bangkok (Hawks). New York, New American Library, 1965.
The Spy in the Jungle (Hawks). New York, New American Library, 1965.
The Heir Hunters. New York, Harper, 1966; London, Boardman, 1967.
The Spy at Angkor Wat (Hawks). New York, New American Library, 1966.
The Spy in the Java Sea (Hawks). New York, New American Library, 1966.
The Source of Fear. New York, New American Library, 1968; London, Hale, 1971.
The 49 Days of Death. Los Angeles, Sherbourne Press, 1969.
Heist Me Higher. New York, New American Library, 1969; London, Hale, 1971.

The Lopsided Man. New York, Pyramid, 1969.
Triptych (omnibus). Los Angeles, Sherbourne Press, 1971.
The Corsican. New York, Dodd Mead, 1974; London, Hale, 1976.
The Law (novelization of television play). New York, Warner, 1975.

Uncollected Short Stories

"The Private Affair," in *Sleuth* (New York), October 1958.
"You Better Be Right," in *Sleuth* (New York), December 1958.
"Save Me in San Salvador," in *Mike Shayne Mystery Magazine* (New York), August 1959.

OTHER PUBLICATIONS

Novel

The Ultimate Warrior (novelization of screenplay). New York, Warner, 1975; London, Star, 1976.

Plays

Screenplays: *The Strangler*, 1964; *Operation CIA*, with Peter J. Oppenheimer, 1966.

Television Plays: *The Hero, Road Hog, Dry Run, The Day of the Bullet, Escape to Sonoita* (with James A. Howard), and *Deathmate*, in *Alfred Hitchcock Presents* series, 1955–61, *The Mice* (with Joseph Stefano), in *The Outer Limits* series, 1963–64, and some 150 other scripts for *I Spy, Mickey Spillane's Mike Hammer, M. Squad, Ironside,* and *Cannon* series.

Other

Lost City of Stone. New York, Simon and Schuster, 1978.
The California Story: Credit Union's First Fifty Years. Dubuque, Iowa, Kendall Hunt, 1979.

*

Manuscript Collection: Mugar Memorial Library, Boston University.

Bill S. Ballinger commented (1980):

I consider myself, primarily, a story-teller. To me the story *is* the thing. Although I usually try to make a point, as all good stories should, I stay away from moralizing and propaganda. Usually, I also try to include some material—"information"—which may be of extra interest to my reader. I have always enjoyed a good plot, the thrill of plotting. Nothing is more pleasant than to receive a letter saying—"You out-guessed me." Although I have been writing for 50 years—first as a "stringer" for newspapers—I intend to keep on with my books.

*   *   *

Bill S. Ballinger began his career writing conventional and clearly derivative hard-boiled detective fiction. His first novel, *The Body in the Bed,* featured a private eye named Barr Breed and the resemblances between this book and the *Maltese Falcon* go well beyond the fact that their heroes share tough, alliterative, single-syllable names. They extend to the important presence of an antique wooden statue, and to the central role of a woman who is less innocent than she appears to be; in both novels, incidentally, the novelists violate one of the cardinal unwritten rules of this genre by sending their detectives to bed with the murderess. *The Body in the Bed* is

somewhat over-complicated and hides too many clues from the reader, but its Chicago setting, its violence, and its emphasis on sex mark it as a typical example of the hard-boiled novel from the period just after World War II.

Ballinger soon abandoned the conventional detective novel, however, and from the early 1950's concentrated on novels about many different kinds of crime; he also moved away from the first-person narration of the private eye genre. Instead, Ballinger specialized in a multi-leveled kind of narration, typified by what is perhaps his best-known book, *The Wife of the Red-Haired Man.* Beginning with an Enoch Arden situation, this novel involves the murder of the second husband by the first, and the subsequent flight of the murderer and the wife from New York to Williamsburg to Kansas City to New Orleans and finally to a small village in Ireland. Chapters telling this story from an omniscient viewpoint alternate with the first-person narration of the detective who is leading the search for the couple. The wife is the most interesting of the characters; she manages the flight, holds her companion together when his fear would betray them, and in the end arranges for him to be killed to save him from what he fears the most, a return to prison. The gimmick in the novel (later copied by others) is that the reader does not know until the final page that the detective, who feels a mystical kinship with the fleeing killer, is black.

The same kind of divided narrative is used in *The Tooth and the Nail.* Here the first-person protagonist is a magician whose wife is murdered and who sets out to find the killer and wreak vengeance. The alternating narrative tells, somewhat tediously, the story of a murder trial in which the identity of the accused is kept hidden from the reader. In the end, we learn that the avenger has faked a murder and successfully framed his wife's murderer for the apparent crime. Like many of Ballinger's novels, this one is flawed by an improbability in the early stages—in this case, the fact that the magician has no good reason for withholding what he knows from the police when his wife is murdered. Later in his career, Ballinger used narratives which shift focus among several characters; in *Beacon in the Night,* the survivors of a criminal network compete with each other for a map purported to show rich Albanian oil deposits. In spite of a too-conventional love triangle, this novel generates a good deal of suspense.

Ballinger's novels are entertainments which often include a puzzle, but they are seldom mystery stories. Typically, they include a considerable amount of bloodshed but (except for the early private eye stories) very little sex, and there is not much character development: the revelation of the racial background of the detective in *The Wife of the Red-Haired Man* is a surprise because we have been allowed to learn very little about the characters. And all of the novels are flawed by a prose which is characteristically wooden, interspersed occasionally with purple descriptions of scenery or exhaustive details, always irrelevant to the narrative; and there is too much twisted syntax, along with occasional blunders in language. But in the best of his novels, Ballinger does generate considerable suspense.

—John M. Muste

BALMER, Edwin. Collaborated with William MacHarg. American. Born in Chicago, Illinois, 26 July 1883. Educated at Northwestern University, Evanston, Illinois, A.B. 1902 (Phi Beta Kappa); Harvard University, Cambridge, Massachusetts, A.M. 1903. Married 1) Katharine MacHarg in 1909 (died

1925), two daughters and one son; 2) Grace A. Kee in 1927. Reporter, Chicago *Tribune*, 1903; associated with Graham Taylor in publishing *The Commons*, New York, 1904–05; editor, 1927–49, and associate publisher, 1949–53, *Red Book* magazine. *Died 21 March 1959.*

Crime Publications

Novels with William MacHarg

The Surakarta. Boston, Small Maynard, 1913.
The Blind Man's Eyes. Boston, Little Brown, and London, Nash, 1916.
The Indian Drum. Boston, Little Brown, 1917; London, Stanley Paul, 1919.

Novels by Edwin Balmer

Waylaid by Wireless. Boston, Small Maynard, 1909.
Ruth of the U.S.A. Chicago, McClurg, 1919.
Her Great Moment. London, Stanley Paul, 1921.
The Breath of Scandal. Boston, Little Brown, 1922; London, Arnold, 1923.
Keeban. Boston, Little Brown, and London, Arnold, 1923.
That Royle Girl. New York, Dodd Mead, 1925.
Dangerous Business. New York, Dodd Mead, 1927; London, Long, 1928.
Flying Death. New York, Dodd Mead, 1927.
Dragons Drive You. New York, Dodd Mead, 1934.
The Torn Letter. New York, Dodd Mead, 1941; London, Nicholson and Watson, 1943.
The Candle of the Wicked. New York, Longman, 1956.

Novels with Philip Wylie

Five Fatal Words. New York, Land and Smith, 1932; London, Stanley Paul, 1933.
The Golden Hoard. New York, Stokes, 1934.
The Shield of Silence. New York, Stokes, 1936; London, Collins, 1937.

Short Stories with William MacHarg

The Achievements of Luther Trant. Boston, Small Maynard, 1910.

Short Stories by William MacHarg

The Affairs of O'Malley. New York, Dial Press, 1940; as *Smart Guy*, New York, Popular Library, 1951.

Uncollected Short Stories by William MacHarg

"Unwilling Witness," in *Mystery Books Magazine* (New York), August 1945.
"Broadway Murder," in *Ellery Queen's Mystery Magazine* (New York), February 1946.
"No Clues," in *Ellery Queen's Mystery Magazine* (New York), July 1946.
"The Important Point," in *Fourth Mystery Companion*, edited by Abraham Louis Furman. New York, Lantern Press, 1946.
"Hidden Evidence," in *Best Detective Stories of the Year 1947*, edited by David Coxe Cooke. New York, Dutton, 1947.
"Information Obtained," in *Fireside Mystery Book*, edited by Frank Owen. New York, Lantern Press, 1947.

"Lost Girl," in *Ellery Queen's Mystery Magazine* (New York), January 1948.
"The Widow's Share," in *The Saint* (New York), January 1955.
"Deceiving Clothes," in *The Saint* (New York), March 1955.
"The Murder Trap," in *The Saint* (New York), July 1955.
"The Murderer's Ring," in *The Saint* (New York), May 1956.
"The Vanishing Man," in *The Saint* (New York), September 1956.
"Green Paint and Neat Knots," in *The Saint* (New York), March 1957.
"The Soiled Diamonds," in *The Saint* (New York), February 1959.
"Manhattan Murder," in *Ellery Queen's Mystery Magazine* (New York), August 1965.
"East Side Homicide," in *Ellery Queen's Mystery Magazine* (New York), April 1966.
"Tell 'em at Headquarters," in *Ellery Queen's Mystery Magazine* (New York), February 1968.
"Murder Makes It Worse," in *Ellery Queen's Mystery Magazine* (New York), September 1970.

Other Publications

Novels

A Wild-Goose Chase. New York, Duffield, 1915.
Resurrection Rock. Boston, Little Brown, and London, Hodder and Stoughton, 1920.
Fidelia. New York, Dodd Mead, 1924.
In His Hands. New York, Longman, 1954.
With All the World Away. New York, Longman, 1958.

Novels with Philip Wylie

When Worlds Collide. New York, Stokes, and London, Stanley Paul, 1933.
After Worlds Collide. New York, Stokes, and London, Stanley Paul, 1934.

Other

The Science of Advertising. Chicago, Wallace Press, 1909.

* * *

Edwin Balmer and William MacHarg, one-time reporters on the Chicago *Tribune* and successful career writers of popular fiction, collaborated on several mystery-adventures. The best-remembered of them, *The Achievements of Luther Trant*, introduces psychology as a means of detection when an upright student of "the methods of Freud and Jung" uses word association, memory tests, and several elaborate prototypes of the lie detector to solve crimes. In *The Blind Man's Eyes* an attempt is made on the life of a prominent blind lawyer who depends on his daughter and his secretary as his "eyes." He himself discovers the criminals, one of whom must be one of his trusted "eyes." *The Indian Drum* is a tale of crime, romance, hidden identity, and adventure in a prosperous Great Lakes shipping firm.

The characters and values of the Balmer-MacHarg collaborations much resemble those of other popular adventures of the period. The distinction between good and evil is always clear, despite the development of psychology as a theme. Detective heroes are compassionate, cleancut, and men of action; criminal villains, whether the motivation for their crimes is conscious or unconscious, are self-centered, sneering, and cynical.

—Katherine Staples

———

BANKIER, William (John). Canadian. Born in Belleville, Ontario, 3 July 1928. Educated at Belleville Collegiate. Married Phyllis Rochlin in 1952 (died 1985); two daughters; 2) Felice Nelson. Bellboy, Queen's Hotel, and radio announcer, CJBQ, both Belleville; advertising copywriter for 25 years, ending as creative director, Maclaren Advertising Ltd., Montreal, 1974; then freelance writer in England: wrote 40 romantic novelets for *Woman's Weekly* library under pseudonyms of Phyllis Thurlow, Belinda Ballantine, and Edna Kingston, 1974–79. Agent: Curtis Brown Ltd., 10 Astor Place, New York, New York 10003, U.S.A.

Crime Publications

Uncollected Short Stories

"What Happened in Act One," in *Ellery Queen's Mystery Mix.* New York, Random House, 1963; London, Gollancz, 1964.
"The Gag of the Century," in *Ellery Queen's Mystery Magazine* (New York), February 1965.
"Traffic Violation," in *Ellery Queen's Mystery Magazine* (New York), September 1967.
"One Clear Sweet Clue," in *Ellery Queen's Headliners.* Cleveland, World, 1971; London, Gollancz 1972.
"My Brother's Killer," in *Ellery Queen's Mystery Magazine* (New York), April 1973.
"A Bad Scene," in *Ellery Queen's Mystery Magazine* (New York), July 1973.
"By the Neck until Dead," in *Ellery Queen's Mystery Magazine* (New York), January 1974.
"The Big Bunco," in *Ellery Queen's Mystery Magazine* (New York), November 1974.
"C'est Voulu," in *Ellery Queen's Mystery Magazine* (New York), January 1975.
"Dangerous Enterprises," in *Ellery Queen's Mystery Magazine* (New York), September 1975.
"The Road Without a Name," in *Ellery Queen's Giants of Mystery.* New York, Davis, 1976; London, Gollancz, 1977.
"What Really Happened?," in *Ellery Queen's Mystery Magazine* (New York), July 1976.
"To Kill an Angel," in *Ellery Queen's Mystery Magazine* (New York), August 1976.
"IOU One Life," in *Ellery Queen's Mystery Magazine* (New York), September 1976.
"The Window," in *Alfred Hitchcock's Tales to Take Your Breath Away,* edited by Eleanor Sullivan. New York, Dial Press, 1977.
"Den of Thieves," in *Alfred Hitchcock's Mystery Magazine* (New York), January 1977.
"The Final Twist," in *Ellery Queen's Mystery Magazine* (New York), January 1977.
"Rapunzel, Rapunzel," in *Alfred Hitchcock's Mystery Magazine* (New York), March 1977.
"A Lovely Bottle of Wine," in *Alfred Hitchcock's Mystery Magazine* (New York), April 1977.
"Laughing Chaz," in *Alfred Hitchcock's Mystery Magazine* (New York), June 1977.

"The Voice of Doreen Gray," in *Ellery Queen's Mystery Magazine* (New York), August 1977.
"Wednesday Night at the Forum," in *Alfred Hitchcock's Mystery Magazine* (New York), August 1977.
"In the House Next Door," in *Ellery Queen's Mystery Magazine* (New York), September 1977.
"The Rescue of Professor Parkindon," in *Ellery Queen's Mystery Magazine* (New York), October 1977.
"Policeman's Lot," in *Ellery Queen's Masks of Mystery.* New York, Davis, 1978; London, Gollancz, 1979.
"The Immortal Quest," in *Alfred Hitchcock's Mystery Magazine* (New York), January 1978.
"Who Steals My Face?" in *Alfred Hitchcock's Mystery Magazine* (New York), February 1978.
"The Main Event," in *Ellery Queen's Mystery Magazine* (New York), February 1978.
"The Prodigal Brother," in *Alfred Hitchcock's Mystery Magazine* (New York), March 1978.
"A Hint of Danger," in *Ellery Queen's Mystery Magazine* (New York), April 1978.
"The Eye of the Beholder," in *Alfred Hitchcock's Mystery Magazine* (New York), April 1978.
"Lorenzo the Inventor," in *Alfred Hitchcock's Mystery Magazine* (New York), May 1978.
"The Last Act Was Deadly," in *Alfred Hitchcock's Mystery Magazine* (New York), June 1978.
"A Game of Errors," in *Alfred Hitchcock's Mystery Magazine* (New York), September 1978.
"Lost and Found," In *Alfred Hitchcock's Mystery Magazine* (New York), November 1978.
"The Mystery of the Missing Penelope," in *Ellery Queen's Mystery Magazine* (New York), December 1978.
"The Dream of Hopeless White," in *Alfred Hitchcock's Mystery Magazine* (New York), December 1978.
"Devil's Advocate," in *Ellery Queen's Mystery Magazine* (New York), February 1979.
"Rock's Last Role," in *Alfred Hitchcock's Mystery Magazine* (New York), March 1979.
"The Piper's Caper," in *Ellery Queen's Mystery Magazine* (New York), March 1979.
"The Trial of Judge Axminster," in *Alfred Hitchcock's Mystery Magazine* (New York), April 1979.
"Girls, Like White Birds," in *Ellery Queen's Mystery Magazine* (New York), April 1979.
"Fear and Trembling," in *Alfred Hitchcock's Mystery Magazine* (New York), June 1979.
"The Woman in the Control Room," in *Ellery Queen's Mystery Magazine* (New York), July 1979.
"The Man of the Hour," in *Alfred Hitchcock's Mystery Magazine* (New York), July 1979.
"Is There a Killer in the House?," in *Alfred Hitchcock's Mystery Magazine* (New York), August 1979.
"Cattle Call," in *Ellery Queen's Mystery Magazine* (New York), September 1979.
"Duffy's Last Contract," in *Alfred Hitchcock's Mystery Magazine* (New York), September 1979.
"The Impossible Scheme," in *Alfred Hitchcock's Mystery Magazine* (New York), October 1979.
"A Funny Thing Happened," in *Alfred Hitchcock's Mystery Magazine* (New York), November 1979.
"My Name is Lorenzo, Goodbye," in *Alfred Hitchcock's Mystery Magazine* (New York), December 1979.
"The Mystery of the Missing Guy," in *Ellery Queen's Mystery Magazine* (New York), December 1979.
"Making a Killing with Mama Cass," in *Alfred Hitchcock's Mystery Magazine* (New York), 30 January 1980.

"Dr. Temple Is Dead," in *Ellery Queen's Mystery Magazine* (New York), 11 February 1980.

"The Missing Missile," in *Alfred Hitchcock's Mystery Magazine* (New York), 27 February 1980.

"The Last One to Know," in *Alfred Hitchcock's Mystery Magazine* (New York), 26 March 1980.

"Nothing to Lose," in *Alfred Hitchcock's Mystery Magazine* (New York), 23 April 1980.

"Brough, as in Rough," in *Alfred Hitchcock's Mystery Magazine* (New York), 21 May 1980.

"Events at Headland Cottage," in *Ellery Queen's Mystery Magazine* (New York), 30 June 1980.

"You Get What You Deserve," in *Alfred Hitchcock's Mystery Magazine* (New York), 16 July 1980.

"Defensive Moves," in *Alfred Hitchcock's Mystery Magazine* (New York), 13 August 1980.

"The Solid-Gold Lie," in *Alfred Hitchcock's Mystery Magazine* (New York), 1 October 1980.

"Paid in Advance," in *Ellery Queen's Mystery Magazine* (New York), 6 October 1980.

"Crazy Old Woman," in *Alfred Hitchcock's Mystery Magazine* (New York), 19 November 1980.

"The Choirboy," in *Best Detective Stories of the Year 1981,* edited by Edward D. Hoch. New York, Dutton, 1981.

"Happiness You Can Count On," in *Ellery Queen's Mystery Magazine* (New York), 1 January 1981.

"A Woman Waits for Me," in *Ellery Queen's Mystery Magazine* (New York), 25 March 1981.

"Concerto for Violence and Orchestra," in *Ellery Queen's Mystery Magazine* (New York), 17 June 1981.

"Only If You Get Caught," in *Ellery Queen's Mystery Magazine* (New York), 7 October 1981.

"A Fierceness Deep Inside," in *Ellery Queen's Mystery Magazine* (New York), 2 December 1981.

"Funny Man," in *Ellery Queen's Mystery Magazine* (New York), 27 January 1982.

"Where Will It All End," in *Ellery Queen's Mystery Magazine* (New York), September 1982.

"Doors," in *Ellery Queen's Mystery Magazine* (New York), October 1982.

"Breaking Free," in *Ellery Queen's Mystery Magazine* (New York), March 1983.

"Silently, In the Dead of Night," in *Ellery Queen's Mystery Magazine* (New York), January 1984.

"Her Voice on the Phone Was Magic," in *Ellery Queen's Mystery Magazine* (New York), February 1984.

"Forged Laughter," in *Ellery Queen's Mystery Magazine* (New York), March 1984.

"Appointment in Baytown," in *Ellery Queen's Mystery Magazine* (New York), April 1984.

"Nice One," in *Ellery Queen's Mystery Magazine* (New York), June 1984.

"The Right Physical Type," in *Ellery Queen's Mystery Magazine* (New York), July 1984.

"The Collaborators," in *Ellery Queen's Mystery Magazine* (New York), August 1984.

"The Maggie File," in *Ellery Queen's Mystery Magazine* (New York), September 1984.

"The Broken Contract," in *Ellery Queen's Mystery Magazine* (New York), October 1984.

"Dead Women Sell No Tales," in *Ellery Queen's Mystery Magazine* (New York), November 1984.

"Arrivals and Departures, in *Ellery Queen's Mystery Magazine* (New York), December 1984.

"If Cats Could Speak," in *Ellery Queen's Mystery Magazine* (New York), December 1984.

"A Bucket of Ice-Cold Life," in *Ellery Queen's Mystery Magazine* (New York), January 1985.

"Cutting It Close," in *Ellery Queen's Mystery Magazine* (New York), February 1985.

"Dead Like Dogs," in *Ellery Queen's Mystery Magazine* (New York), April 1985.

"Baytown's Loss," in *Ellery Queen's Mystery Magazine* (New York), March 1985.

"Doctor Workman," in *Ellery Queen's Mystery Magazine* (New York), March 1985.

"Murder in the Cards," in *Ellery Queen's Mystery Magazine* (New York), June 1985.

"The Joke That Died," in *Ellery Queen's Mystery Magazine* (New York), July 1985.

"Zut, Alors, Josie," in *Ellery Queen's Mystery Magazine* (New York), August 1985.

"Brent's Experiment," in *Ellery Queen's Mystery Magazine* (New York), September 1985

"Baytown's Gain," in *Ellery Queen's Mystery Magazine* (New York), October 1985.

"Mean Characters," in *Ellery Queen's Mystery Magazine* (New York), November 1985.

"For Old Time's Sake," in *Ellery Queen's Mystery Magazine* (New York), December 1985.

"Safe as Houses," in *Ellery Queen's Mystery Magazine* (New York), January 1986.

"Veronica's Husband," in *Ellery Queen's Mystery Magazine* (New York), February 1986.

"Information Leading To," in *Ellery Queen's Mystery Magazine* (New York), March 1986.

"A Visit to Rip-Off City," in *Ellery Queen's Mystery Magazine* (New York), April 1986.

"One Consideration with Another," in *Ellery Queen's Mystery Magazine* (New York), May 1986.

"The Road to Ste. Agathe," in *Ellery Queen's Mystery Magazine* (New York), June 1986.

"Never Leave Me, Dawn Patrol," in *Ellery Queen's Mystery Magazine* (New York), July 1986.

"The Paternity Thing," in *Ellery Queen's Mystery Magazine* (New York), August 1986.

"You Never Know Your Luck," in *Ellery Queen's Mystery Magazine* (New York), September 1986.

"The Prize in the Pack," in *Ellery Queen's Mystery Magazine* (New York), October 1986.

"The Good Old Days By the Sea," in *Ellery Queen's Mystery Magazine* (New York), November, 1986.

"Fear Is a Killer," in *Ellery Queen's Mystery Magazine* (New York), December 1986.

"The Body in the Car," in *Ellery Queen's Mystery Magazine* (New York), January 1987.

"The Rescue of 'Two-Kinds' Tuttle," in *Ellery Queen's Mystery Magazine* (New York), February 1987.

"The Brass Cat Is Not for Sale," in *Ellery Queen's Mystery Magazine* (New York), March 1987.

"Legacy from a Bad Actor," in *Ellery Queen's Mystery Magazine* (New York), April 1987.

"Oil and Water," in *Ellery Queen's Mystery Magazine* (New York), June 1987.

"Wimbledon Fortnight," in *Ellery Queen's Mystery Magazine* (New York), July 1987.

"Where the Bodies Are Buried," in *Ellery Queen's Mystery Magazine* (New York), September 1987.

"Saved from Deep Water," in *Ellery Queen's Mystery Magazine* (New York), October 1987.

"We Only Live Once," in *Ellery Queen's Mystery Magazine* (New York), December 1987.

"The Parking Lot Dream," in *Ellery Queen's Mystery Magazine* (New York), January 1988.

"Stolen Careers," in *Ellery Queen's Mystery Magazine* (New York), February 1988.

"Losers," in *Ellery Queen's Mystery Magazine* (New York), May 1988.

"How Dangerous Is Your Brother," in *Ellery Queen's Mystery Magazine* (New York), September 1988.

"One Day at a Time," in *Ellery Queen's Mystery Magazine* (New York), October 1988.

"Coming Clean," in *Ellery Queen's Mystery Magazine* (New York), November 1988.

"Two Bards with One Stone," in *Ellery Queen's Mystery Magazine* (New York), December 1988.

"Cross Words," in *Ellery Queen's Mystery Magazine* (New York), January 1989.

"The Hitman's Daughter," in *Ellery Queen's Mystery Magazine* (New York), March 1989.

"The Baytown Follies," in *Ellery Queen's Mystery Magazine* (New York), April 1989.

"Norris Farmer's Secret," in *Ellery Queen's Mystery Magazine* (New York), May 1989.

"The Coward He'd Always Been," in *Ellery Queen's Mystery Magazine* (New York), July 1989.

"The Lottery Ticket," in *Ellery Queen's Mystery Magazine* (New York), July 1989.

"Pop Goes the Weasel," in *Ellery Queen's Mystery Magazine* (New York), September 1989.

"The Fifty-Pound Rip-Off," in *Ellery Queen's Mystery Magazine* (New York), October 1989.

"The Drop," in *Ellery Queen's Mystery Magazine* (New York), November 1989.

"Shorty,"in *Ellery Queen's Mystery Magazine* (New York), March 1990.

"All the Little Pussycats," in *Ellery Queen's Mystery Magazine* (New York), August 1990.

OTHER PUBLICATIONS

Plays

Radio Plays: *The Night Stan Kenton Died*, 1982 (UK); plays in Montreal.

Television Plays: a dozen plays, in Montreal.

*   *   *

One of the most prolific of mystery short story writers, William Bankier is known for his use of unusual subject matter and locales. Ellery Queen said, "No one in the genre writes about music better than William Bankier," and that is not surprising, considering Bankier's life-long love affair with music. "The Dog Who Hated Jazz" shows Bankier's special understanding and love of jazz. "Gunfight at the O'Shea Chorale," is as clever as its title, artfully using rivalries in an amateur group giving its annual performance at the Kiwanis Karnival. Another ingenious Bankier title is "Concerto for Violence and Orchestra," introducing a story about the "theft" of a dance band. Integral to the plot is the conflict between disco and old-fashioned dance music. "The Choirboy," another story of musical conflict, is about a pop singer who has the number one hit on the Canadian charts but is unhappy because he is "conspiring to produce rubbish." Probably his best, but certainly his most unusual, music story is "The Woman in the Control Room." Again, there is a conflict between two types of music, atonal modern versus classical 19th-century symphonic.

Out of such an unlikely subject, Bankier has fashioned a brilliant mystery *tour de force*.

Bankier has worked in Canadian advertising and combines that field with music in "Making a Killing with Mama Cass." Because he loved her music, ". . .a huge, pure voice soaring over the others like a silver-belled horn," an advertising salesman suggests a movie be made from her life, but his idea is stolen. It is set in Montreal, one of many Canadian locales Bankier has brought alive in the mystery. "Wednesday Night at the Forum" tells of Montreal before the referendum which threatened to separate Quebec from the rest of Canada. In this story of politics and kidnapping, Bankier uses the Canadian sports scene as background and metaphor. A hockey star vanishes in "The Missing Missile," and a Montreal radio station hires Bankier's occasional series detective, a former magician Harry Lawson, called "Praw" since the days a circus barker introduced him as "the Prawfessah." The Lawson stories entertain, but they are Bankier below his best, as if the restrictions of clues, detection, and a recurrent character inhibit'his imagination.

Since his first story in *Ellery Queen's Mystery Magazine*, "What Happened in Act One," imagination and originality have been Bankier hallmarks. His debut, like many subsequent stories, is set in a bar, and it shows his inventiveness and ear for how people talk when they have been drinking. "The Event" is probably Bankier's most preposterous story, about con men and a Russian boxer called "Battleship Potemkin." It includes a plot to sell Montreal's Jacques Cartier Bridge.

Though much of Bankier's work is lighthearted, he just as often writes of people going through crises. An excellent example of the Bankier human-interest story is "Traffic Violation" in which a policeman, whose child needs expensive medical treatment, is offered $20,000 to ignore an illegal left turn. In "Child of Another Time," a man discovers who was responsible for the death of his baby many years ago. The protagonist in "Dangerous Enterprise" is a former baseball player, his life now in shambles, who must make a crucial decision. Similarly placed at the brink is the Canadian emigré in "The Last One to Know." He has been seduced by a glamorous British television actress and asked to kill her husband.

Bankier crams so many interesting characters and plot twists into his short stories that one wishes he would occasionally permit himself the opportunity for fuller development that the greater length of a novel would afford.

—Marvin Lachman

———

BARBETTE, Jay. *See* **SPICER, Bart.**

———

BARCLAY, Bennett. *See* **CROSSEN, Ken.**

———

BARDIN, John Franklin. Also wrote as Douglas Ashe; Gregory Tree. American. Born in Cincinnati, Ohio, 30 November 1916. Educated at Walnut Hills High School,

Cincinnati. Married 1) Rhea Schooler Yalowich in 1943; one daughter and one son; 2) Phyllida Korman in 1966. Vice-President and Director of Edwin Bird Wilson Inc., New York, 1944–63; Instructor, New School for Social Research, New York, 1961–66; senior editor, *Coronet* magazine, New York, 1968–72; managing editor, *Today's Health* magazine, Chicago, 1972–73; managing editor of magazines published by the American Bar Association, 1973–74. *Died 9 July 1981.*

CRIME PUBLICATIONS

Novels

The Deadly Percheron. New York, Dodd Mead, 1946; London, Gollancz, 1947.
The Last of Philip Banter. London, Gollancz, and New York, Dodd Mead, 1947.
Devil Take the Blue-Tail Fly. London, Gollancz, 1948; New York, Macfadden, 1967.
A Shroud for Grandmama (as Douglas Ashe). New York, Scribner, and London, Gollancz, 1951; as *The Longstreet Legacy,* New York, Paperback Library, 1970.
Purloining Tiny. New York, Harper, 1978.

Novels as Gregory Tree (series: Bill Bradley and Noel Mayberry in first two books)

The Case Against Myself. New York, Scribner, 1950; London, Gollancz, 1951.
The Case Against Butterfly. New York, Scribner, 1951.
So Young to Die. New York, Scribner, and London, Gollancz, 1953.

OTHER PUBLICATIONS

Novels

The Burning Glass. New York, Scribner, and London, Gollancz, 1950.
Christmas Comes But Once a Year. New York, Scribner, and London, Davies, 1954.

*

John Franklin Bardin commented (1980):
 A novel is a detector of mined experience. As a soldier walks a mined field with a contraption in front of him that buzzes when it's over a mine, so a novelist, such as I, elaborates a contraption that when the reader experiences it may warn him of the mines of his own emotions. I draw no distinction between the novel and the detective novel: there are only good and bad novels. I have tried to make each of my novels different from all the rest, better to explore other mine fields.

* * *

John Franklin Bardin's career as a writer of mystery stories was an unusual one. In a three-year period (1946–1948) he published three interesting novels. *The Deadly Percheron, The Last of Philip Banter,* and *Devil Take the Blue-Tail Fly.* Later he wrote other novels, including several orthodox and rather dull crime novels under the pseudonym of Gregory Tree, but the three earlier novels were long out of print and have only recently been reprinted in England, due to the patient efforts of Julian Symons.

Bardin's three novels have close affinities with the Hollywood "film noir" of the 1940's combining eerily mysterious occurrences with an interest in abnormal psychology and dreams, and an almost Gothic sense of the ways in which the past interpenetrates the present. As Symons points out in his Introduction to the Penguin edition, the first two are flawed by a need to provide a surprising ending which, inevitably, fails to surprise; but the third is a brilliant study of the disintegration of an artist where the mystery elements are effortlessly carried by the confusions inherent in the central character's disturbed mind. As in the film noir, all three novels derive much of their power from a continuing sense that the real, "normal" world is always in danger of being overturned by a parallel shadow world of guilt, perversion, and lack of control, a situation that receives its final, terrifying statement in the use of the "split personality" in the closing pages of *Blue-Tail Fly.* It is a pity that Bardin did not see fit to work this rich vein over a longer period.

—John S. Whitley

———

BARKER, DUDLEY. *See* **BLACK, Lionel.**

———

BARNARD, Robert. British. Born in Burnham-on-Crouch, Essex, 23 November 1936. Educated at Royal Grammar School, Colchester, Essex, 1948–56; Balliol College, Oxford (exhibitioner), B.A. 1959; University of Bergen, Norway, Ph.D. 1972. Married Mary Louise Tabor in 1963. Lecturer in English, University of New England, Armidale, New South Wales, 1961–66; Lecturer, later Senior Lecturer in English, University of Bergen, 1966–76; Professor of English, University of Tromsø, Norway, 1976–84. Agent: Peters, Fraser and Dunlop, 5th Floor, The Chambers, Chelsea Harbour, Lots Road, London SW10 0XF; or, Sterling Lord Literistic Inc., 1 Madison Avenue, New York, New York 10010, U.S.A. Address: Hazeldene, Houghley Lane, Leeds, Yorkshire LS13 2DT, England.

CRIME PUBLICATIONS

Novels (series: Charlie Peace; Perry Trethowan)

Death of an Old Goat. London, Collins, 1974; New York, Walker, 1977.
A Little Local Murder. London, Collins, 1976; New York, Scribner, 1983.
Death on the High C's. London, Collins, 1977; New York, Walker, 1978.
Blood Brotherhood. London, Collins, 1977; New York, Walker, 1978.
Unruly Son. London, Collins, 1978; as *Death of a Mystery Writer,* New York, Scribner, 1979.
Posthumous Papers. London, Collins, 1979; as *Death of a Literary Widow,* New York, Scribner, 1980.
Death in a Cold Climate. London, Collins, 1980; New York, Scribner, 1981.
Mother's Boys. London, Collins, 1981; as *Death of a Perfect Mother,* New York, Scribner, 1981.

Sheer Torture (Trethowan). London, Collins, 1981; as *Death by Sheer Torture,* New York, Scribner, 1982.

Death and the Princess (Trethowan). London, Collins, and New York, Scribner, 1982.

The Missing Brontë (Trethowan). London, Collins, 1983; as *The Case of the Missing Brontë,* New York, Scribner, 1983.

Little Victims. London, Collins, 1983; as *School for Murder,* New York, Scribner, 1984.

A Corpse in a Gilded Cage. London, Collins, and New York, Scribner, 1984.

Out of the Blackout. London, Collins, and New York, Scribner, 1985.

The Disposal of the Living. London, Collins, 1985; as *Fête Fatale,* New York, Scribner, 1985.

Political Suicide. London, Collins, and New York, Scribner, 1986.

Bodies (Trethowan and Peace). London, Collins, and New York, Scribner, 1986.

Death in Purple Prose (Trethowan and Peace). London, Collins, 1987; as *The Cherry Blossom Corpse,* New York, Scribner, 1987.

The Skeleton in the Grass. London, Collins, 1987; New York, Scribner, 1988.

At Death's Door. London, Collins, and New York, Scribner, 1988.

Death and the Chaste Apprentice (Peace). London, Collins, and New York, Scribner, 1989.

A City of Strangers. London, Bantam, and New York, Scribner, 1990.

Short Stories

Death of a Salesperson and Other Untimely Exits. London, Collins, 1989; New York, Scribner, 1990.

Uncollected Short Stories

"Happy Christmas," in *Ellery Queen's Prime Crimes 4,* New York, Davis, 1986.

"Perfect Honeymoon," in *Ellery Queen's Mystery Magazine* (New York), August 1987.

"More Final than Divorce," in *Ellery Queen's Mystery Magazine* (New York), October 1988.

"The Face of Violence," in *Ellery Queen's Mystery Magazine* (New York), February 1989.

"Not Much of a Life," in *Ellery Queen's Mystery Magazine* (New York), March 1989.

"Post Mortem," in *Ellery Queen's Mystery Magazine* (New York), May 1989.

"Divine Anger," in *Ellery Queen's Mystery Magazine* (New York), July 1989.

"A Good Turn," in *Ellery Queen's Mystery Magazine* (New York), December 1989.

"The Nick of Time," in *Ellery Queen's Mystery Magazine* (New York), January 1990.

OTHER PUBLICATIONS

Other

Imagery and Theme in the Novels of Dickens. Oslo, Universitetsforlaget, and New York, Humanities Press, 1974.

A Talent to Deceive: An Appreciation of Agatha Christie. London, Collins, and New York, Dodd Mead, 1980.

A Short History of English Literature. Oslo, Universitetsforlaget, 1984.

*

Robert Barnard comments:

I write only to entertain. I think that in travelling "from the detective story to the crime novel" (to use Julian Symons's phrase) mysteries have lost a lot of sparkle and accumulated a lot of dullness. My books are old-fashioned, though I think some of them contain more humour than most of the "Golden Age" writers usually put in. Among the writers I admire most are Christie, Allingham, Rendell, and Margaret Millar.

*   *   *

Robert Barnard is recognized as one of the leading practitioners of the pure detective story to debut in the past 20 years. His allegiance to the formal puzzle is expressed in *A Talent to Deceive,* the finest critical study extant of Agatha Christie, and in many ways his own books fit right in with the cozy, comfortable school of British detective fiction she best exemplified. His crimes usually take place in incongruously respectable settings and involve a closed circle of suspects, with the emphasis on verbal jousting rather than violent physical action. But Barnard's biting wit, his darkly satirical world-view, and his telling insights into character set him apart from the kind of writers usually called cozy.

Barnard's first two novels give an indication of what is to come. *Death of an Old Goat* is set at an Australian university, where an elderly visiting professor from Oxford gets not quite the reception he expected. Inspector Royle, who rivals Joyce Porter's Dover for undiluted obnoxiousness, does the detecting. In *A Little Local Murder,* the English village of Twytching is to be immortalized in a radio broadcast to be produced for airing in the American city of Twytching, Wisconsin, and the local citizens hilariously jockey for position on the program. Each book has a grim and shocking ending that is all the more effective for its contrast to the comedic tone of the rest of the novel.

In subsequent books, Barnard uses the mystery form to satirize aspects of religion (in *Blood Brotherhood,* depicting an amusing variety of clerical types), the book world (in *Unruly Son* and *Posthumous Papers,* the latter including an especially wicked caricature of an American scholar), education (in *Little Victims,* centering on a hopelessly mediocre English prep school and introducing one of the great schoolboy villains in Hilary Frome), politics (in *Political Suicide,* its plague-on-all-your-houses viewpoint sometimes concealing the author's left-wing views in an election satire comparable to Edmund Crispin's *Buried for Pleasure*), and theatre (in *Death and the Chaste Apprentice,* set at the Ketterick Arts Festival).

Death in a Cold Climate, concerning the murder of an Englishman in Tromsø, Norway, gives a strong sense of how somber and depressing a Scandinavian winter can be, while providing the customary well-constructed plot and incisive social commentary. *Death in a Cold Climate*'s Inspector Fagermo is one of several Barnard sleuths who are interesting and individual enough to be potential series detectives. But only Perry Trethowan, the Scotland Yard detective introduced in *Sheer Torture,* comes back for encores.

In his first case, Trethowan must investigate a murder in his own rather embarrassing family of crazy British eccentrics. His father has been found dead, wearing spangled tights in a medieval torture machine called a strappado. Perry becomes a royal bodyguard in *Death and the Princess,* a relatively weak

Barnard entry from a plot standpoint but one with much telling satire on the institution of royalty. The fifth and most recent in the series, *Death in Purple Prose* (*The Cherry Blossom Corpse,*) finds Trethowan in attendance at a convention of WARN (World Association of Romantic Novelists.)

A Barnard book without humor is unimaginable, but he has departed from the essentially comic detective novel in two books that have several other features in common and must be counted among his best. *Out of the Blackout* begins with an irresistible mystery situation: in 1941, one of a group of London children evacuated to the town of Yeasdon is a boy of about five who calls himself Simon Thorn—but there is no record of who he really is or where he came from. Through the decades to follow, Simon tries to trace his own roots, and the final revelation does not arrive until 1982. *The Skeleton in the Grass* is set in 1936, when young Sarah Causeley takes a job as governess with the Hallam family, pacifist landed gentry who are harassed for their political beliefs. Apart from their richly detailed setting in the recent past, the two books share an emphasis on politics, with much background on the English fascists who sprang up in the 1930's and a theme of contrasting happy and unhappy families: in *Out of the Blackout*, the unhappy family is in the forefront, in *The Skeleton in the Grass* the happy one, but Barnard's treatment of the two situations is anything but simple.

In recent years, Barnard has proved as capable at short-story lengths as in novels. Most of the 16 tales gathered in *Death of a Salesperson and Other Untimely Exits* are ironic crime stories in the TV-Hitchcock vein rather than detective stories. They sometimes have a theme of future danger clear to the reader but unknown (or ignored) by the characters (e.g. "A Business Partnership" and "Little Terror"). Among the highlights are "Daylight Robbery," a typically pointed satire on both the art world and the stately home business, and "The Oxford Way of Death," a grimly amusing picture of petrified academia.

—Jon L. Breen

———

BARNAO, Jack. *See* **WOOD, Ted.**

———

BARNES, Julian. *See* **KAVANAGH, Dan.**

———

BARNES, Linda (Joyce, née Appelblatt). American. Born in Detroit, Michigan, 6 June 1949. Educated at Boston University School of Fine and Applied Art, B.F.A. in theatre (cum laude) 1971. Married Richard A. Barnes in 1970; one son. Teacher of theatre, Chelmsford High School, Chelmsford, Massachusetts, 1971–76; drama director, Lexington public schools, Lexington, Massachusetts, 1977–78. Recipient: Anthony award for short story, 1986; American Mystery award for private eye novel 1987. Agent: Gina Maccoby, 1123 Broadway, Suite 1000, New York, New York 10010. Address: 56 Seaver Street, Brookline, Massachusetts 02346. U.S.A.

CRIME PUBLICATIONS

Novels (series: Carlotta Carlyle; Michael Spraggue)

Blood Will Have Blood (Spraggue).   New York, Avon, 1982.
Bitter Finish (Spraggue).   New York, St. Martin's Press, and London, Severn House, 1983.
Dead Heat (Spraggue).   New York, St. Martin's Press, and London, Severn House, 1984.
Cities of the Dead (Spraggue).   New York, St. Martin's Press, and London, Severn House, 1986.
A Trouble of Fools (Carlyle).   New York, St. Martin's Press, 1987; London, Hodder and Stoughton, 1988.
The Snake Tattoo (Carlyle).   New York, St. Martin's Press, and London, Hodder and Stoughton, 1989.
Coyote (Carlyle).   New York, Delacorte Press, 1990, and London, Hodder and Stoughton, 1991.

Uncollected Short Story

"Lucky Benny," in *New Black Mask*. San Diego, California, Harcourt Brace Jovanovich, 1986.

OTHER PUBLICATIONS

Plays

Wings.   Boston, Baker, 1973.
Prometheus.   Boston, Baker, 1974.

*

Linda Barnes comments:

I consider my four Spraggue novels to be my apprentice work. At the time I began the series, I was seeking a detective who was neither a wealthy British dilettante nor a tough American woman-hater. I created Michael Spraggue—wealthy, ex-private eye, actor, feminist—a "mid-Atlantic" detective. Because I had chosen to make Spraggue an amateur, I had the continuing problem of involving him legitimately in his cases. I solved this by killing off many of his friends and relatives. His subsequent depression became difficult to deal with and I sought a new hero.

I had always wanted to write a female first-person detective novel. I hesitated because I was told by publishing insiders that my envisioned "semi-tough" woman would never sell. Still, Carlotta Carlyle—ex-cop, part-time cab driver, licensed private eye—was on my mind, and in between Spraggue novels I auditioned her in a short story, "Lucky Penny," which languished unsold for over a year. In 1986, I sent it along to my new agent as an afterthought. She promptly sold it, and it quickly garnered more attention and critical acclaim than all the Spraggue books to date.

I enjoy Carlotta for her voice, her independence, and her relationships with those she loves.

*   *   *

As Sara Paretsky is to Chicago, so Linda Barnes is to Boston, She has created two series characters based in that city: part-time actor/sleuth Michael Spraggue and ex-cop/cab driver/private eye Carlotta Carlyle. The Spraggue novels are standard whodunnits with added interest in their theatre settings and more unusual places such as during the Boston marathon. The Carlotta novels are like Paretsky's in that there is an underlying feminism which informs their action and plot without being as explicit as, for example, Barbara Wilson.

Barnes's novels are particularly strong on supporting characters—another thing she shares with Paretsky. In the Spraggue novels, she furnishes him with an especially engaging Watson-figure: his elderly aunt Mary Spraggue Hillman still acute and formidable in mind and body and useful for her contacts in Boston high society. But it is in the Carlotta novels that her flair for memorable characters comes into its own, Gloria, the wheelchair-bound controller of a cab firm; Carlotta's punk flatmate Roz with her wild hair and wilder affairs; Lieutenant Moody "one of the few honest cops in Boston;" Sam Gianelli, occasional lover of Carlotta and heir to a Mafia family.

As well as consistently excellent plots Barnes has the rare facility of writing believable sexual relationships for her characters—a particularly rare skill among writers with female sleuths. However the tendency of both Spraggue and Carlotta to get involved with suspects and other shady characters should perhaps not be encouraged.

The only question mark against Barnes's writing is in the characterisation of her sleuths, Both Spraggue and Carlotta have personal habits and tics which are repeated a little too often: Spraggue is forever fighting with his aunt over his reluctance to accept his house—in which she lives—and his inheritance; Carlotta frequently takes refuge in her blues guitar playing; nice character touches but they would be more effective if used more sparingly.

As is true of the best writers using urban settings, the city itself becomes an important character. Boston is portrayed with affection but also with an understanding of its geography, politics, people, and problems. The reader learns much from both series about the difficulties of parking a car. Unfortunately, this means that when transplanted, as Spraggue is in *Cities of the Dead* set in New Orleans, the sense of place is not so keen and the novel is inferior.

—Linda Semple

BARONE, Mike. *See* **ALBERT, Marvin.**

BARR, Robert. Also wrote as Luke Sharp. Born in Glasgow, Scotland, 16 September 1850; moved to Canada at age 4. Educated at Normal School, Toronto. Married Eva Bennett in 1876; two children. School headmaster, Windsor, Ontario, 1876; editorial staff member, Detroit *Free Press* 1875–76; moved to England in 1881 as British editor of the *Free Press*; founding editor, with Jerome K. Jerome, 1892–97, and with others, 1897–1911, *The Idler*, London. Honorary Chief of a Canadian Iroquois tribe. *Died 21/22 October 1912.*

CRIME PUBLICATIONS

Novels

The Face and the Mask. London, Hutchinson, 1894; New York, Stokes, 1895.
A Woman Intervenes; or, The Mistress of the Mine. London, Chatto and Windus, and New York, Stokes, 1896.

The Mutable Many. New York, Stokes, 1896; London, Methuen, 1897.
Jennie Baxter, Journalist. London, Methuen, and New York, Stokes, 1899.
The King Dines. London, McClure, 1901; as *A Prince of Good Fellows.* London, Chatto and Windus, and New York, McClure, 1902.
Over the Border. London, Isbister, and New York, Stokes, 1903.
A Chicago Princess. New York, Stokes, 1904; as *The Tempestuous Petticoat,* London, Methuen, 1905.
A Rock in the Baltic. New York, Authors and Newspapers, 1906; London, Hurst and Blackett, 1907.
The Watermead Affair. Philadelphia, Altemus, 1906.
The Girl in the Case. London, Nash, 1910.
Lady Eleanor, Lawbreaker. Chicago, Rand McNally, 1911.

Short Stories

From Whose Bourne? London, Chatto and Windus, 1893; New York, Stokes, 1896.
Revenge! London, Chatto and Windus, and New York, Stokes, 1896.
The Strong Arm. New York, Stokes, 1899; London, Methuen, 1900; selection, as *Gentlemen, the King!,* Stokes, n.d.
The Woman Wins. New York, Stokes, 1904; as *The Lady Electra,* London, Methuen, 1904.
The Triumphs of Eugène Valmont. London, Hurst and Blackett, and New York, Stokes, 1906.
Tales of Two Continents. London, Mills and Boon, 1920.
The Adventures of Sherlaw Kombs. Boulder, Colorado, Aspen Press, 1979.

OTHER PUBLICATIONS

Novels

In the Midst of Alarms. London, Methuen, and New York, Stokes, 1894.
One Day's Courtship, and The Heralds of Fame. New York, Stokes, 1896.
Tekla: A Romance of Love and War. New York, Stokes, 1898; as *The Countess Tekla,* London, Methuen, 1899.
The Victors: A Romance of Yesterday Morning and This Afternoon. New York, Stokes, 1901; London, Methuen, 1902.
The O'Ruddy, with Stephen Crane. New York, Stokes, 1903; London, Methuen, 1904.
The Speculations of John Steele. London, Chatto and Windus, and New York, Stokes, 1905.
The Measure of the Rule. London, Constable, 1907; New York, Appleton, 1908.
Young Lord Stranleigh. London, Ward Lock, and New York, Appleton, 1908.
Stranleigh's Millions. London, Nash, 1909.
Cardillac. London, Mills and Boon, and New York, Stokes, 1909.
The Sword Maker. London, Mills and Boon, and New York, Stokes, 1910.
Lord Stranleigh, Philanthropist. London, Ward Lock, 1911.
The Palace of Logs. London, Mills and Boon, 1912.
My Enemy Jones: An Extravaganza. London, Nash, 1913; as *Unsentimental Journey,* London, Hodder and Stoughton, 1913.
A Woman in a Thousand. London, Hodder and Stoughton, 1913.
Lord Stranleigh Abroad. London, Ward Lock, 1913.

Short Stories

Strange Happenings (as Luke Sharp). London, Dunkerley, 1883.
In a Steamer Chair and Other Shipboard Stories. London, Chatto and Windus, and New York, Cassell, 1892.
The Helping Hand and Other Stories. London, Mills and Boon, 1920.

Plays

An Evening's Romance, with Cosmo Hamilton, from the novel *Tekla* by Barr (produced Hartlepool, County Durham, 1901).
The Conspiracy, with S. Lewis Ransom (produced Dublin, 1907; London, 1908). Published in *Short Modern Plays 2,* edited by S. R. Littlewood, London, Macmillan, 1939.
Lady Eleanor, Lawbreaker, from his own novel (produced Liverpool, 1912).
The Hanging Outlook, with J.S. Judd (produced London, 1912).

Other

The Unchanging East. London, Chatto and Windus, 1 vol., and Boston, Page, 2 vols., 1900.
I Travel the Road. London, Quality Press, 1945.

*

Manuscript Collections: Crane Collection, Butler Library, Columbia University, New York; Regional History Department, University of Western Ontario.

* * *

Despite the large amount of fiction that Robert Barr wrote—adventure stories, westerns, romances, science-fiction, supernatural fiction, topical fiction—he is likely to be remembered only for a single book and a short parody. The book is *The Triumphs of Eugéne Valmont* (1906) and the parody is "The Great Pegram Mystery."

Before book publication the great French detective Eugéne Valmont appeared in such periodicals as the *Windsor Magazine* and *Pearson's Magazine* in Great Britain, and the *Saturday Evening Post* in the United States. Valmont narrates his own adventures, and the amusing personality that emerges is that of an amiable, witty, intelligent, resourceful, but vain, self-dramatizing, and slightly unscrupulous investigator. He writes in a mildly Gallic English, strong enough to be piquant, but not exaggerated or stagey. It has been pointed out by several authorities that Agatha Christie's Hercule Poirot shares quite a bit with Valmont.

The Triumphs of Eugéne Valmont contains eight short stories and nouvelles, linked together by the reflections and recollections of Valmont. In the first story, "The Mystery of the 500 Diamonds," Valmont explains how he came to be a private detective domiciled in England. As head of the Paris police, he had set out to guard a gem auction and had failed badly. The failure could have been forgiven, but the incident brought newspaper ridicule on the ministry, and Valmont was fired. After some difficulty in adjusting to British ways, he eventually became a highly successful society detective.

The other stories in the book vary greatly in quality. Three are excellent. "Lord Chizlerigg's Missing Fortune" involves finding a large inheritance hidden by an eccentric nobleman; "The Absent-Minded Coterie," which is often anthologized, brilliantly describes a new sort of crime; "The Clue of the Silver Spoons" pits Valmont against a kleptomaniac. These stories are nicely written, original in idea, and dominated by the strong

personality of Valmont. The other stories, unfortunately, are not up to the same level, and one of them, "The Liberation of Wyoming Ed," is even a misplaced western story.

Barr's second work of quality is "The Great Pegram Mystery, which was first published in *The Idler* as "The Adventures of Sherlaw Kombs" by Luke Sharp. It is one of the earliest and best parodies of Doyle's work. Holmes's mannerisms are nicely hit off, and the case is an amusing debacle.

Much of Barr's other crime fiction belongs to a hybrid form that includes a considerable amount of supernaturalism. *From Whose Bourne?* is an odd mixture of ghosts, humor, crime detection, and romance. William Brenton, a prosperous resident of Cincinnati, suddenly awakens in the spirit world and learns that he is dead. He can see what is happening in the real world, though he can do nothing directly, and is shocked to learn that his wife is being charged with his murder. To save her he invokes the aid of the ghost of Gaboriau's great detective M. LeCocq (*sic*), who muddles things badly. A more efficient investigation in the world of the living solves the mystery. The story is original in idea, but undistinguished.

Several short stories mingle crime with supernaturalism. "Share and Share Alike" (*In a Steamer Chair and Other Shipboard Stories*) describes a murder aboard ship, in which the dead man has some say as to what happens. "The Vengeance of the Dead" (*Revenge!*) invokes contemporary occultism to give a new twist to a crime. A disembodied spirit slips into a temporarily unoccupied human body (its real owner is out wandering in the astral world) commits a murder, then slips out again, leaving the body and its returned owner in a terrible situation.

Much of Barr's sensational fiction contains crime elements, but it would be stretching to describe these, since they are now deservedly forgotten.

It is a just evaluation to say that Barr is a one-book author. Although *The Triumphs of Eugéne Valmont* has several of the finest stories of the period, Barr's other work in mystery fiction is on the trivial side. It is lamentable that Barr did not recognize Valmont's potentialities and continue his adventures. As it is, the safest judgment on Barr is that he devised a first-rate detective, but in the long run did not know what to do with him.

—E.F. Bleiler

BARRY, Mike. *See* **MALZBERG, Barry N.**

BARTH, Richard. American. Born in South Orange, New Jersey, 27 March 1943. Educated at Riverdale Country School, New Jersey, graduated, 1960; Amherst College, Massachusetts, 1960–64, B.A. (cum laude) in economics 1964; Pratt Institute, Brooklyn, New York, M.F.A. 1973. Served with the United States Army Reserves, 1964–70. Married Ilene Kleinman in 1969; two children. Vice President, Barth Smelting Company, New Jersey, 1965–72. Since 1973 Assistant Professor of jewelry design, Fashion Institute of Technology, New York. Has had several individual and group shows of sculpture and jewelry, 1973–83. Agent: Esther Newburg, International Creative Management, 40 West 57th Street, New York, New York 10019. Address: 239 Central Park West, New York, New York, 11704, U.S.A.

CRIME PUBLICATIONS

Novels (series: Rag Bag Clan in all books)

A Rag Bag Clan. New York, Dial Press, 1978; London, Gollancz, 1979.
A Ragged Plot. New York, Dial Press, 1981; London, Gollancz, 1984.
One Dollar Death. New York, Dial Press, 1982; London, Gollancz, 1985.
The Condo Kill. New York, Scribner, 1985; as *The Co-op Kill,* London, Gollancz, 1986.
Deadly Climate. New York, St. Martin's Press, 1988.
Blood Doesn't Tell. New York, St. Martin's Press, 1989.
Furnished for Murder. New York, St. Martin's Press, 1990.

Uncollected Short Stories

"The Bungling Bank Robber," "Frozen in Time," "One Good Crime Deserves Another," in *Women's World* (New Jersey), 1983–85.

OTHER PUBLICATIONS

Screenplay

A Small Killing (from his novel *A Rag Bag Clan*), 1982.

*

Richard Barth comments:
  Too often detective fiction glorifies the role of a single individual in solving the riddles involved in the case. I thought I'd take a different approach and have a group of people help solve the mystery, and a group that are mutually dependent because all they have is each other. So I made them all in their seventies, gave them quirky personalities, appointed one of them their leader, and let them have some fun. In the process, so did I.

*   *   *

Little old ladies aren't what they used to be. They may remain widowed, but a cadre of eccentric friends keep them busy and far from lonely. No longer content to sit and knit, they lead full and active lives, right down to breaking-and-entering to obtain clues. Margaret Binton is the quintessential modern little old lady who first appears Richard Barth's novel *The Rag Bag Clan.*

Having not yet begun her career in crime detection, Binton often volunteered her services at a neighborhood center—"You know how I spend my days when I'm not at the center?...At my knitting group...in a kind of coma. Nothing ever changes. A lot of dull old women, dry, dust, just like the old Victorian building we meet in. All they ever talk about is their grandchildren." Her work brought Binton into contact with a "shopping bag lady" who was murdered, apparently a professional job. When thousands of dollars are found near her body, the police suspect that the woman had been a drug courier. No stranger to scavengers—being a good friend of one—Binton convinces the police to use her as a decoy. ("...this would be kind of an adventure for me....And I'd feel good about it, like I was being useful.") Dressing herself as a bag lady, she wanders New York City's Upper West Side until she finds the killer with the help of some friends.

Having decided that pitting her wits against bad guys is even more fun than doing crossword puzzles, she finds herself involved in the investigation of the murder of a neighborhood gardener which has something to do with a major diamond heist. Barth seems more comfortable exploring the eccentricities of the elderly; the numerous young people involved in *A Ragged Plot* aren't terribly convincing characters, making this one of the least successful books of the series.

One Dollar Death is less well known and the hardest of the series to locate. Binton's friends from the first book are much more in evidence and, although Margaret remains the brains of the group, this marks the start of some clearly ensemble efforts. In this one Binton finds herself somewhat off her turf, investigating the murder of a friend in Sotheby's. When she learns the friend's coin was worth a great deal of money, she ventures into the world of coin collecting. Unfortunately, the local precinct cops neither know nor appreciate her very much, and Binton actually finds herself suspected of murder.

In *The Condo Kill.* Binton becomes involved in some deadly real estate dealing. The owner of an old tenement building wants to demolish it and build a luxury condominium. Margaret, appalled to hear of the escalating harassment of the last two tenants, offers her help. This is an all-too-familiar tale of greed in the big city, and real news stories give lie to the thought that this is melodramatic fiction.

In the fifth book in the series Binton and her friends find a *Deadly Climate* in beautiful downtown Miami Beach. Having won an unwanted recreational vehicle in a church lottery, she agrees to take her friends on a brief vacation to sand and surf before she sells it. Upon arriving, sightseeing plans change when they sight the old folks sitting on porches and waiting to die. She offers their services as the Dream-trippers Coach and Excursions in an attempt to get them out into the sunshine, but finds one home peculiarly opposed to their efforts. To find out what is really going on they have one of their party take up residence. Although the ending is atypical and overblown, the depiction of the ghetto of the aging is depressingly accurate.

Blood Doesn't Tell is the most compelling book of the series. Binton finds herself coming up against the entire bureaucracy of New York City as she seeks to protect the interests of a 15-month old white baby soon to be up for adoption. The little boy is about to be smothered in red tape and ripped apart by people who have more than his best interests at heart.

The manipulation of the weak and defenseless is a common theme in Barth's books, whether it be evil and for personal gain, or by the simple ignorance of a severely overburdened system. Barth tells us that the solutions are to be found in one's personal community and refusal to pull down the windowshades.

Characters develop slowly in Barth's series, and are defined chiefly by their eccentricities. Nevertheless, one has come to learn a great deal about Margaret Binton and her companions over the years, and the changing face of the neighborhood is lovingly and accurately portrayed throughout. Binton could give some of her younger competition a good run for the money, and her appeal crosses the line between British cozy and American softboiled very nicely. Long may she sleuth!

—Sue Feder

———

BAX, Roger. *See* **GARVE, Andrew.**

———

BAXT, George. American. Born in Brooklyn, New York, 11 June 1923. Educated at City College of New York, 1940; Brooklyn College, 1941. Address: 340 West 55th Street, New York, New York 10019, U.S.A.

CRIME PUBLICATIONS

Novels (series: Pharoah Love; Sylvia Plotkin and Max Van Larsen)

A Queer Kind of Death (Love). New York, Simon and Schuster, 1966; London, Cape, 1967.
Swing Low, Sweet Harriet (Love). New York, Simon and Schuster, 1967.
A Parade of Cockeyed Creatures; or, Did Someone Murder Our Wandering Boy? (Plotkin and Van Larsen). New York, Random House, 1967; London, Cape, 1968.
Topsy and Evil (Love). New York, Simon and Schuster, 1968.
"I!" Said the Demon (Plotkin and Van Larsen). New York, Random House, and London, Cape, 1969.
The Affair at Royalties. London, Macmillan, 1971; New York, Scribner, 1972.
Burning Sappho. New York, Macmillan, and London, Macmillan, 1972.
The Neon Graveyard. New York, St. Martin's Press, 1979.
Process of Elimination. New York, St. Martin's Press, 1984.
The Dorothy Parker Murder Case. New York, St. Martin's Press, 1984; London, Collins, 1985.
The Alfred Hitchcock Murder Case. New York, St. Martin's Press, 1986.
Satan Is a Woman. New York, International Polygonics, 1987.
The Tallulah Bankhead Murder Case. New York, St. Martin's Press, 1987.
Who's Next? New York, International Polygonics, 1988.

Uncollected Short Stories

"So Much Like Me," in Winter's Crimes 4, edited by George Hardinge. London, Macmillan, 1972.
"Cut from the Same Cloth," in Ellery Queen's Mystery Magazine (New York), 10 September 1980.
"What'sisname," in Ellery Queen's Mystery Magazine (New York), 22 April 1981.
"Show Me a Hero," in Ellery Queen's Mystery Magazine (New York), 15 July 1981.
"What You Been Up to Lately," in The Year's Best Mystery and Suspense Stories 1982, edited by Edward D. Hoch. New York, Walker, 1982.
"Show Business," in Ellery Queen's Mystery Magazine (New York), 1 January 1982.
"Play 'Lover' for Me," in Ellery Queen's Mystery Magazine (New York), 24 February 1982.
"Writer's Block," in Ellery Queen's Mystery Magazine (New York), May 1982.
"The Woman I Envied," in Ellery Queen's Mystery Magazine (New York), June 1982.
"Clap Hands, There Goes Charlie," in Ellery Queen's Mystery Magazine (New York), August 1982.
"I Wish He Hadn't Said That," in Ellery Queen's Mystery Magazine (New York), November 1982.
"Mary, Mary, Quite Contrary," in Ellery Queen's Mystery Magazine (New York), March 1983.
"The Vulture Within," in Ellery Queen's Mystery Magazine (New York), June 1983.

"Cauldron Boil, Cauldron Bubble," in Ellery Queen's Mystery Magazine (New York), November 1983.
"Call Him Ishmael," in Ellery Queen's Mystery Magazine (New York), July 1984.
"Gertrude and Alice and Spite and Malice," in Ellery Queen's Mystery Magazine (New York), August 1984.

OTHER PUBLICATIONS

Plays

Screenplays: Circus of Horrors, 1960; The City of the Dead (Horror Hotel), 1960; The Shadow of the Cat, 1961; Payroll, 1961; Night of the Eagle (Burn Witch Burn), with Charles Beaumont and Richard Matheson, 1962; Strangler's Web, 1965; Thunder in Dixie, 1965; Vampire Circus, with Judson Kinberg and Wilbur Stark, 1971; Beyond the Fog, with Jim O'Connolly, 1981.

*

Manuscript Collection: Mugar Memorial Library, Boston University.

*   *   *

George Baxt exploded across the skies of mystery fiction like a particularly bright meteor in 1966 with the launching of an excellent series. His brief career was so brilliant that it will take those of us who seek among more enduring stars for his equal long to forget him.

The pair of good, solid books which detail the adventures of Sylvia Plotkin and Max Van Larsen account for part of his total output, but it is the remainder, the Pharoah (sic) Love trilogy, upon which his fame does and will depend. These began with his first, and best known, work, A Queer Kind of Death, a quite satisfactory murder-puzzle solved by police detective Love. But the book is no more a police procedural novel than are the Columbo television movies. What makes it unique is its verisimilitude-laden portrayal of the homosexual underground of New York City. Victim, murderer, and detective all belong to this milieu; the presentation mixes irony and clinical objectivity without losing sympathy, a feat in the realm of style and tone analogous to juggling while walking on eggshells.

That book was universally and deservedly praised by reviewers, but the inevitable sequel was even better. In Swing Low, Sweet Harriet, Baxt emerged as one of the finest of modern satirists, with the homosexual scene and Busby Berkeley musicals as the chief of his many targets. In the last series book, Topsy and Evil, Love surrendered center stage to another black detective (Satan Stagg), but he remained a major figure nevertheless.

Mystery lovers should read the trilogy in proper sequence if possible, but they should read it!

—Jeff Banks

———————

BECK, K.K. Pseudonym for Kathrine Marris. American. Married Ernest Marris; three children. Advertising copy writer. Lives in Seattle, Washington. Address: c/o Walker and Company, 720 Fifth Avenue, New York, New York 10019, U.S.A.

Novels

Death in a Deckchair.   New York, Walker, 1984.
Murder in a Mummy Case.   New York, Walker, 1986.
The Body in the Volvo.   New York, Walker, 1987.
Young Mrs. Cavendish and the Kaiser's Men.   New York, Walker, 1987.
Unwanted Attentions.   New York, Walker, 1988.
Peril Under the Palms.   New York, Walker, 1989.

*   *   *

Versatile and beguiling are two of the attributes justifiably used when describing the works appearing under the name of K. K. Beck. Her first book, *Death in a Deck Chair*, chronicles the initial adventure of the 19-year-old Iris Cooper who, with her wealthy Aunt Hermione, is on the final voyage on their round-the-world tour on board the *Irenia* from Southampton to Montreal. By setting the trip, the crime and the mode of transportation in the mid-1920's Beck sets a carefully calculated mark on that decade of American life. Iris and brash neophyte newspaper reporter, Jack Clancy, solve a murder and part, seemingly forever, when the ship docks. *Murder in a Mummy Case* has a San Francisco Peninsula background as Iris, now at Stanford University, is invited by a new boyfriend to visit his wealthy family during a short vacation. He keeps a real mummy in the house and even the butler is somewhat eccentric. The complications intensify when another visitor is murdered. Jack Clancy just happens to be working on a San Francisco paper so the pair play sleuth again. The atmosphere, language, fads, and costumes of the pre-depression era are all presented in a matter-of-fact manner and with an authentic twist. There are unsavory characters in the novel and a few more eccentric individuals than the plot can support successfully but the attention to detail is impressive. The last Cooper/Clancy investigation takes place in Hawaii in *Peril Under the Palms* where a Bostonian matron searching for missionary ancestors is killed by a blow from a coconut while sitting under a palm tree. The social attitudes of the major characters is somewhat simplistic but Beck's penchant for historical accuracy and crisp dialogue exert a strong appeal.

Beck's major work *Young Mrs. Cavendish and the Kaiser's Men* is a judiciously combined historical romance, thriller, detective story, and is a prime exponent of the journalistic approach to fiction which was popular just prior to America's entry into World War I. The plot has more twists than a triple braided noose. Here Beck researched how life was being lived in 1916. Well constructed with great technical proficiency Beck uses several unusual variants of conflict within society as seen from the point of view of Maude Cavandish, the young divorcee, who earns her living as the society columnist for the *San Francisco Globe*. Maude, who is bringing up her harum-scarum younger brother, holds down a full time job and aspires to be another Nellie Bly. She is kidnapped when mistaken for a debutante daughter of a scientist, manages to escape, writes up her adventures and doesn't get the hoped for by-line. The adventures which follow involve her brother George, a Baron who has a small vineyard in the Napa Valley, the debutante again and a young aircraft designer and pilot. Newspaper women were still unique during that period and the world of flying with its experimental devices was even more strange. There is a visual vividness in all parts of this book and the flights of the zeppelins are especially realistic and electrifying.

The Body in the Volvo is a leap into current times, academic skullduggery, and the mystique of a small business in Seattle. The first chapter presents the effect of scholarly malice that changes the liveliness of academic life to unemployment when Professor Charles Carstairs is denied tenure by Dr. Bateman. At the same time Charles's Uncle Cosmo wins the lottery and turns Cosmo's Car Center, over to him. Cosmo takes off and Charles is alone with an almost bankrupt business. Since the complete lack of any records and Cosmo's indifferent credit rating puts Charles in a financial bind he hires Sylvia Snow, a bookkeeper with artist leanings, to try and make some sense of the business. The body of Dr. Bateman shows up at the garage in the welded trunk of a Volvo that was supposed to be sent to the wrecking yard. Charles, his mechanics, his customers, the scams in the car repair business, and threats by two detectives from the homicide division who are sure he killed the department head, are just a few of the off-the-wall characters that enliven this exercise in mystery and misfortune.

Beck deftly fashions her characters and presents them fully designed into a world that is just different enough to qualify for unique status. She has shown the variety of locales and eras with which she is familiar in the Cooper and Mrs. Cavendish books and her transformation into a "serious" novelist with the haunting *Unwanted Attentions* was a surprise to some of her readers who were not expecting a novel of such intensity and psychological menace.

By cleverly presenting so many different aspects of the mystery, Beck keeps her readers surprised, tantalized and entertained.

—Ellen A. Nehr

BEEDING, Francis. Pseudonym for John Leslie Palmer and Hilary Aidan St. George Saunders; also wrote as David Pilgrim; Palmer also wrote as Christopher Haddon; Saunders also wrote as Barum Browne and as Cornelius Cofyn.   British.
PALMER, John Leslie: Born in 1885. Educated at Balliol College, Oxford (Brackenbury Scholar). Married Mildred Hodson Woodfield in 1911; one son and one daughter. Drama critic and assistant editor, *Saturday Review of Literature*, London, 1910–15; drama critic, *Evening Standard*, London, 1916–19; served in the War Trade Intelligence Department, 1915–19; member of the British Delegation to the Paris Peace Conference, 1919; staff member, Permanent Secretariat of the League of Nations, 1920–39. *Died 5 August 1944.*
SAUNDERS, Hilary Aidan St. George: Born 14 January 1898. Educated at Balliol College, Oxford. Served in the Welsh Guard, 1916–19: Military Cross, 1919; worked for the Air Ministry during World War II. Married 1) Helen Foley (died 1917); 2) Joan Bedford. Staff member, Permanent Secretariat of the League of Nations, 1920–37; private secretary to Fridtjof Nansen, 1921–23; librarian of the House of Commons, 1946–50. *Died 16 December 1951.*

Novels (series: Colonel Alastair Granby; Professor Kreutzemark; Inspector George Martin)

The Seven Sleepers (Kreutzemark).   London, Hutchinson, and Boston, Little Brown, 1925.

The Little White Hag. London, Hutchinson, and Boston, Little Brown, 1926.

The Hidden Kingdom (Kreutzemark). London, Hodder and Stoughton, and Boston, Little Brown, 1927.

The House of Dr. Edwardes. London, Hodder and Stoughton, 1927; Boston, Little Brown, 1928; as *Spellbound,* Cleveland, World, 1945.

The Six Proud Walkers (Granby). London, Hodder and Stoughton, and Boston, Little Brown, 1928.

The Five Flamboys (Granby). London, Hodder and Stoughton, and Boston, Little Brown, 1929.

Pretty Sinister (Granby). London, Hodder and Stoughton, and Boston, Little Brown, 1929.

The Four Armourers (Granby). London, Hodder and Stoughton, and Boston, Little Brown, 1930.

The League of Discontent (Granby). London, Hodder and Stoughton, and Boston, Little Brown, 1930.

Death Walks in Eastrepps. London, Hodder and Stoughton, and New York, Mystery League, 1931.

The Three Fishers. London, Hodder and Stoughton, and Boston, Little Brown, 1931.

Murder Intended. London, Hodder and Stoughton, and Boston, Little Brown, 1932.

Take It Crooked (Granby). London, Hodder and Stoughton, and Boston, Little Brown, 1932.

The Emerald Clasp. London, Hodder and Stoughton, and Boston, Little Brown, 1933.

The Two Undertakers (Granby). London, Hodder and Stoughton, and Boston, Little Brown, 1933.

The One Sane Man (Granby). London, Hodder and Stoughton, Boston, Little Brown, 1934.

Mr. Bobadil. London, Hodder and Stoughton, 1934; as *The Street of the Serpents,* New York, Harper, 1934.

Death in Four Letters. London, Hodder and Stoughton, and New York, Harper, 1935.

The Norwich Victims (Martin). London, Hodder and Stoughton, and New York, Harper, 1935.

The Eight Crooked Trenches (Granby). London, Hodder and Stoughton, and New York, Harper, 1936; as *Coffin for One,* New York, Avon, 1943.

The Nine Waxed Faces (Granby). London, Hodder and Stoughton, and New York, Harper, 1936.

The Erring Under-Secretary. London, Hodder and Stoughton, 1937.

Hell Let Loose (Granby). London, Hodder and Stoughton, and New York, Harper, 1937.

No Fury (Martin). London, Hodder and Stoughton, 1937; as *Murdered: One by One,* New York, Harper, 1937.

The Big Fish. London, Hodder and Stoughton, 1938; as *Heads Off at Midnight,* New York, Harper, 1938.

The Black Arrows (Granby). London, Hodder and Stoughton, and New York, Harper, 1938.

The Ten Holy Terrors (Granby). London, Hodder and Stoughton, and New York, Harper, 1939.

He Could Not Have Slipped (Martin). London, Hodder and Stoughton, and New York, Harper, 1939.

Not a Bad Show (Granby). London, Hodder and Stoughton, 1940; as *The Secret Weapon,* New York, Harper, 1940.

Eleven Were Brave (Granby). London, Hodder and Stoughton, 1940; New York, Harper, 1941.

The Twelve Disguises (Granby). London, Hodder and Stoughton, and New York, Harper, 1942.

There Are Thirteen (Granby). London, Hodder and Stoughton, and New York, Harper, 1946.

Novels by Palmer

Under the Long Barrow (as Christopher Haddon). London, Gollancz, 1939; as *The Man in the Purple Gown,* New York, Dodd Mead, 1939.

Mandragora. London, Gollancz, 1940; as *The Man with Two Names,* New York, Dodd Mead, 1940.

Novels by Saunders

The Devil and X.Y.Z. (with Geoffrey Dennis, as Barum Browne). London, Gollancz, and New York, Doubleday, 1931.

The Death-Riders (with John de Vere Loder, as Cornelius Cofyn). London, Gollancz, and New York, Knopf, 1935.

The Sleeping Bacchus. London, Joseph, 1951.

Uncollected Short Stories

"Death by Judicial Hanging," in *My Best Thriller.* London, Faber, 1933.

"The Woman He Had to Kill," in *Mystery* (Chicago), June 1934.

"Condemned!" in *Mystery* (Chicago), June 1935.

"Me Ne Frego," in *Detective Stories of Today,* edited by Raymond Postgate. London, Faber, 1940.

OTHER PUBLICATIONS

Novels as David Pilgrim

So Great a Man. London, Macmillan, and New York, Harper, 1937.

No Common Glory. London, Macmillan, and New York, Harper, 1941.

The Great Design. London, Macmillan, and New York, Harper, 1944.

The Emperor's Servant. London, Macmillan, 1946.

OTHER PUBLICATIONS by Palmer

Novels

Peter Paragon: A Tale of Youth. London, Secker, and New York, Dodd Mead, 1915.

The King's Men. London, Secker, and New York, Putman, 1916.

The Happy Fool. London, Christophers, and New York, Harcourt Brace, 1922.

Looking after Joan. London, Christophers, and New York, Harcourt Brace, 1923.

Jennifer. London, Christophers, and New York, Harcourt Brace, 1926.

Timothy. London, Eyre and Spottiswoode, 1931; New York, Doubleday, 1932.

Play

Over the Hills (produced London, 1912). London, Sidgwick and Jackson, 1914.

Other

The Censor and the Theatres. London, Unwin, 1912; New York, Kennerley, 1913.

The Comedy of Manners. London, Bell, 1913.

The Future of the Theatre. London, Bell, 1913.

Comedy. London, Secker, and New York, Doran, 1914.
Bernard Shaw: An Epitaph. London, Richards, 1915; as *George Bernard Shaw, Harlequin or Patriot?,* New York, Century, 1915.
Rudyard Kipling. London, Nisbet, 1915; New York, Holt, 1925(?).
Studies in the Contemporary Theatre. London, Secker, and Boston, Little Brown, 1927.
Molière: His Life and Works. London, Bell, and New York, Brewer and Warren, 1930.
Ben Jonson. London, Routledge, and New York, Viking Press, 1934.
The Hesperides: A Looking-Glass Fugue. London, Secker and Warburg, 1936.
Political [Comic] Characters of Shakespeare. London, Macmillan, 2 vols., 1945–46; New York, St. Martin's Press, 1961.

OTHER PUBLICATIONS by Saunders

Other

The Battle of Britain, August–October 1940: An Air Ministry Record. London, Ministry of Information, 1941.
Bomber Command: The Air Ministry's Account of Bomber Command's Offensive Against the Axis. London, Ministry of Information, 1941.
Combined Operations, 1940–1942. London, His Majesty's Stationery Office, 1943; as *Combined Operations: The Official Story of the Commandos,* New York, Macmillan, 1943.
Return at Dawn: The Official Story of the New Zealand Bomber Squadron of the R.A.F. Wellington, New Zealand Tourist and Publicity Department, 1943.
Pioneers! O Pioneers! London and New York, Macmillan, 1944.
Per Ardua: The Rise of British Air Power, 1911–1939. London, Oxford University Press, 1944.
Ford at War. London, Harrison, 1946.
The Left Hand Shakes: The Boy Scout Movement During the War. London, Collins, 1948.
Valiant Voyaging: A Short History of the British India Steam Navigation Company in the Second World War. London, Faber, 1948.
The Green Beret: The Story of the Commandos, 1940–1945. London, Joseph, 1949.
The Middlesex Hospital, 1745–1948. London, Parrish, 1949.
The Red Cross and the White: A Short History of the Joint War Organization of the British Red Cross Society and the Order of St. John of Jerusalem. London, Hollis and Carter, 1949.
The Red Beret: The Story of the Parachute Regiment at War. London, Joseph, 1951.
Westminster Hall. London, Joseph, 1951.
Royal Air Force, 1939–1945, with Denis Richards. London, Her Majesty's Stationery Office, 3 vols., 1954.

*   *   *

Francis Beeding and David Pilgrim were the shared pseudonyms of two English writers, John Leslie Palmer and Hilary Aidan St. George Saunders, who met shortly after 1920 in Geneva where they were both serving in the League of Nations Permanent Secretariat. Their acquaintanceship soon developed into a literary collaboration that lasted for years and eventually produced some 50 detective novels and thrillers by

which they are best known. When Palmer and Saunders resigned from the League in 1939, they had published as Francis Beeding almost a score of thrillers about the espionage adventures of Colonel Alastair Granby, D.S.O., of the British Intelligence Service and a number of exceptionally fine *romans policiers.*

Saunders once explained the success of their collaboration by saying, "Palmer can't be troubled with description and narrative, and I'm no good at creating characters or dialogue." Their literary aim, it has been said, was to take as contemporary a situation as possible and deal with it in a way that did not run absolutely counter to the rules of plausibility. Their pseudonymous anonymity permitted them the freedom to be as extravagant as they wished in their presentation of issues and their invention of incidents.

Of all Palmer and Saunder's collaborative detective novels, *Death Walks in Eastrepps* is today the best known—and by common consent the best written and conceived. Set in the quiet English seacoast village of Eastrepps, this fast-paced detective story of multiple brutal murder is a "page-turner" beyond compare filled with mounting, almost unendurable suspense. Considered by Vincent Starrett "one of the ten greatest detective novels" ever written, *Death Walks in Eastrepps* boasts a unique crime motive, an impressive gallery of engaging characters, a superb and highly satisfying surprise-ending, and a dramatic Old Bailey courtroom sequence that ranks with Agatha Christie's *Witness for the Prosecution.*

Other successes by this talented team are *The House of Dr. Edwardes,* a detective novel filmed by Alfred Hitchcock as *Spellbound,* and *The Norwich Victims,* a thriller, filmed by Emlyn Williams as *Dead Men Tell No Tales.*

—Arthur Nicholas Athanason

BEHN, Noel. American. Born in Chicago, Illinois, 6 January 1928. Educated at the University of Wyoming, Laramie, 1946–47; Stanford University, California, B.A. 1950; University of Paris, 1950–51. Served in the United States Army Counter Intelligence, 1952–54. Married Jo Ann Le Compte in 1956 (divorced 1961). Producer at East Chop Playhouse, Martha's Vineyard, Massachusetts, Summer 1954; co-manager, Flint Musical Tent Theatre, Michigan, Summer 1955; producer and operator of Cherry Lane Theatre, New York, 1956–61 producer at Edgewater Beach Playhouse, Chicago, Summers 1957–60. Recipient: Obie award, 1958. Address: 73 Horatio Street, New York, New York 10014, U.S.A.

CRIME PUBLICATIONS

Novels

The Kremlin Letter. New York, Simon and Schuster, and London, W.H. Allen, 1966.
The Shadowboxer. New York, Simon and Schuster, 1969; London, Hart Davis, 1970.
Seven Silent Men. New York, Arbor House, and London, Pan, 1984

OTHER PUBLICATIONS

Other

Big Stick-Up at Brink's! New York, Putnam, 1977; as
*Brink's!: It Took Six Years and Eleven Men to Steal 2,700,000
Dollars!* London, W.H. Allen, 1977.

*   *   *

Noel Behn's first espionage thriller, *The Kremlin Letter,* was
widely reviewed; the *New York Times* and *Time* magazine
harshly condemned Behn's explicit depiction of sex and sadism
and remarked on the improbable premise of the plot. That a
team of American agents could be put into Russia, make their
way unnoticed to Moscow and there live undetected for weeks
while they set about locating and retrieving an indiscreet letter
sent to a Russian official by Western politicians seems no less
improbable now than it did in 1966, although Behn deserves
high marks for the novel's circumstantiality of setting and
detail. But a decade of revelations about the conduct of covert
operations by the FBI and the CIA ought to vindicate Behn
from the charge of having exaggerated the conscience-numbing
amorality of intelligence operations. Behn's nominal hero,
Charles Rone, has two distinguishing qualities: his photographic memory and his alleged willingness to let another
person die in his place if need be. His fellow operatives have
compatible talents and values. Skilled in motivating betrayal,
they routinely resort to violence, sex, drugs—whatever
works.

The Shadowboxer, Behn's second thriller, is set in Germany
in 1944 and depicts, with the same thumb-in-the-eye realism,
characters and scenes that are, if possible, more despicable
than those in *The Kremlin Letter.* Eric Spangler, the shadowboxer of the title, is a tormented, enigmatic agent with an
uncanny ability to get into and out of concentration camps at
will. He is treacherously used by his American masters to
further the establishment of a provisional German government. Spangler, however, is less a character in his own right
than a device by means of which Behn can make his point: that
in their ruthless expediency, the Americans are indistinguishable from their German counterparts who are administering
the death camps. *The Kremlin Letter* and *The Shadowboxer* are
books infused with undisguised anger and revulsion. When
Behn returned to writing in 1977, after an eight-year silence, it
was not to the espionage novel but to the non-fiction novel and
an account of the Brink's robbery. With *Seven Silent Men* Behn
moved into the field of the caper novel producing a fine novel of
suspense with an ingenious plot and infused with humor.

—R. Gordon Kelly

———

BELL, Josephine. Pseudonym for Doris Bell Ball, née
Collier. British. Born in Manchester, Lancashire, 8 Decem-
ber 1897. Educated at Godolphin School, Salisbury. 1910–16;
Newnham College, Cambridge, 1916–19; University College
Hospital, London, M.R.C.S., L.R.C.P. 1922, M.B., B.S. 1924.
Married Norman Dyer Ball in 1923 (died 1936); one son and
three daughters. Practiced medicine with her husband in
Greenwich and London, 1927–35, and in Guildford, Surrey,
1936–54; member of the Management Committee, St. Luke's
Hospital, 1954–62. Co-founder, Crime Writers Association,
1953, chairwoman, 1959–60. *Died 24 April 1987.*

CRIME PUBLICATIONS

Novels (series: Dr. Henry Frost; Inspector Steven Mitchell;
Amy Tupper; Claude Warrington-Reeve; Dr. David
Wintringham)

Murder in Hospital (Wintringham; Mitchell). London, Long-
man, 1937.
Death on the Borough Council (Wintringham). London,
Longman, 1937.
Fall over Cliff (Wintringham; Mitchell). London, Longman,
1938; New York, Macmillan, 1956.
The Port of London Murders (Mitchell). London, Longman,
1938; New York, Macmillan, 1958.
Death at Half-Term (Wintringham; Mitchell). London, Long-
man, 1939; as *Curtain Call for a Corpse,* New York,
Macmillan, 1965.
From Natural Causes (Wintringham). London, Longman,
1939.
All Is Vanity (Wintringham). London, Longman, 1940.
Trouble at Wrekin Farm (Wintringham). London, Longman,
1942.
Death at the Medical Board (Wintringham). London, Long-
man, 1944; New York, Ballantine, 1964.
Death in Clairvoyance (Wintringham; Mitchell). London,
Longman, 1949.
The Summer School Mystery (Wintringham; Mitchell). Lon-
don, Methuen, 1950.
The Backing Winds. London, Methuen, 1951.
To Let, Furnished. London, Methuen, 1952; as *Stranger on a
Cliff,* New York, Ace, 1964.
Bones in the Barrow (Wintringham; Mitchell). London,
Methuen, 1953; New York, Macmillan, 1955.
Fires at Fairlawn (Wintringham). London, Methuen, 1954.
Death in Retirement (Wintringham). London, Methuen, and
New York, Macmillan, 1956.
The China Roundabout (Wintringham; Mitchell). London,
Hodder and Stoughton, 1956; as *Murder on the Merry-Go-
Round,* New York, Ballantine, 1965.
Double Doom. London, Hodder and Stoughton, 1957; New
York, Macmillan, 1958.
The Seeing Eye (Wintringham; Mitchell). London, Hodder
and Stoughton, 1958.
The House above the River. London, Hodder and Stoughton,
1959.
Easy Prey (Warrington-Reeve; Mitchell). London, Hodder
and Stoughton, and New York, Macmillan, 1959.
A Well-Known Face (Warrington-Reeve; Mitchell). London,
Hodder and Stoughton, and New York, Washburn, 1960.
New People at the Hollies. London, Hodder and Stoughton,
and New York, Macmillan, 1961.
Adventure with Crime. London, Hodder and Stoughton, 1962.
A Flat Tyre in Fulham (Warrington-Reeve; Mitchell). Lon-
don, Hodder and Stoughton, 1963; as *Fiasco in Fulham,* New
York, Macmillan, 1963; as *Room for a Body,* New York,
Ballantine, 1964.
The Hunter and the Trapped. London, Hodder and Stoughton,
1963.
The Upfold Witch (Frost). London, Hodder and Stoughton,
and New York, Macmillan, 1964.
The Alien. London, Bles, 1964.
No Escape. London, Hodder and Stoughton, 1965; New
York, Macmillan, 1966.
Death on the Reserve (Frost). London, Hodder and Stoughton,
and New York, Macmillan, 1966.
The Catalyst. London, Hodder and Stoughton, 1966; New
York, Macmillan, 1967.

Death of a Con Man.   London, Hodder and Stoughton, and
  Philadelphia, Lippincott, 1968.
The Fennister Affair.   London, Hodder and Stoughton, 1969;
  New York, Stein and Day, 1977.
The Wilberforce Legacy.   London, Hodder and Stoughton, and
  New York, Walker, 1969.
A Hydra with Six Heads.   London, Hodder and Stoughton,
  1970; New York, Stein and Day, 1977.
A Hole in the Ground.   London, Hodder and Stoughton, 1971;
  New York, Ace, 1973.
Death of a Poison-Tongue.   London, Hodder and Stoughton,
  1972; New York, Stein and Day, 1977.
A Pigeon among the Cats.   London, Hodder and Stoughton,
  1974; New York, Stein and Day, 1977.
Victim.   London, Hodder and Stoughton, 1975; New York,
  Walker, 1976.
The Trouble in Hunter Ward.   London, Hodder and Stoughton,
  1976; New York, Walker, 1977.
Such a Nice Client.   London, Hodder and Stoughton, 1977; as
  Stroke of Death, New York, Walker, 1977.
A Swan-Song Betrayed.   London, Hodder and Stoughton,
  1978; as *Treachery in Type,* New York, Walker, 1980.
Wolf! Wolf! (Tupper).   London, Hodder and Stoughton, 1979;
  New York, Walker, 1980.
A Question of Inheritance (Tupper).   London, Hodder and
  Stoughton, 1980; New York, Walker, 1981.
The Innocent.   London, Hodder and Stoughton, 1982; as *A
  Deadly Place to Stay,* New York, Walker, 1983.

Uncollected Short Stories

"The Case of the Faulty Drier," "Gale Warning," "Death in
  Ambrose Ward," "The Thimble River Murder," and "Death
  in a Cage," in *The Evening Standard Detective Book.* Lon-
  don, Gollancz, 1950.
"The Surgeon's Towel," in *The Evening Standard* (London), 29
  June 1950.
"The Case of the Murdered Cellist," in *The Evening Standard,*
  19 October 1950.
"The Fatal Concerto," in *The Evening Standard* (London), 27
  December 1950.
"The Dead Bed," in *The Evening Standard* (London), 17
  January 1951.
"Dead Man's Mouth," in *The Evening Standard* (London), 18
  May 1951.
"Man Overboard," in *The Evening Standard* (London), 3 July
  1951.
"The Missing Key," in *The Evening Standard* (London), 6
  September 1951.
"Yacht in Distress," in *The Evening Standard* (London), 28
  September 1951.
"The Packet Boat Murder," in *The Evening Standard Detective
  Book,* 2nd series.   London, Gollancz, 1951.
"Money Box Murder," in *The Evening Standard* (London), 23
  February 1952.
"Death in a Crystal," in *The Evening Standard* (London), 26
  April 1952.
"Man in the Water," in *The Evening Standard* (London), 27
  May 1953.
"Easy Money," in *The Evening Standard* (London), 11 January
  1954.
"A Question of Fouling," in *John Creasey Mystery Magazine*
  (London), January 1957.
"You Need the Luck for the Job," in *John Creasey Mystery
  Magazine* (London), September, 1958.
"The Sea Decides," in *Planned Departures,* edited by Elizabeth
  Ferrars.   London, Hodder and Stoughton, 1958.

"Wash, Set, and Murder," *in The Mystery Bedside Book.* edited
  by John Creasey.   London, Hodder and Stoughton, 1960.
"A Case of Hiccups," in *The Evening News* (London), 10 July
  1961.
"A Case of Fugue," in *Crime Writer's Choice,* edited by Roy
  Vickers.   London, Hodder and Stoughton, 1964.
"Murder Delayed," in *Crimes Across the Sea,* edited by John
  Creasey.   London, Longman, and New York, Harper, 1964.
"Experiment," in *The Saint* (New York), October 1965.
"The Commuters," in *John Creasey's Mystery Bedside Book,*
  edited by Herbert Harris.   London, Hodder and Stoughton,
  1966.
"The Alibi," in *John Creasey's Bedside Book 1975,* edited by
  Herbert Harris, London, Hodder and Stoughton, 1974.
"The Unfinished Heart," in *John Creasey's Mystery Bedside
  Book 1974,* edited by Herbert Harris.   London, Hodder and
  Stoughton, 1973.
"The Carol Singers," in *John Creasey's Crime Collection 1979,*
  edited by Herbert Harris.   London, Gollancz, 1979.

OTHER PUBLICATIONS

Novels

The Bottom of the Well.   London, Longman, 1940.
Martin Croft.   London, Longman, 1941.
Alvina Foster.   London, Longman, 1943.
Compassionate Adventure.   London, Longman, 1946.
Total War at Haverington.   London, Longman, 1947.
Wonderful Mrs. Marriott.   London, Longman, 1948.
The Whirlpool.   London, Methuen, 1949.
Cage-Birds.   London, Methuen, 1953.
Two Ways to Love.   London, Methuen, 1954.
Hell's Pavement.   London, Methuen, 1955.
The Convalescent.   London, Bles, 1960.
Safety First.   London, Bles, 1962.
Tudor Pilgrimage.   London, Bles, 1967.
Jacobean Adventure.   London, Bles, 1969.
Over the Seas.   London, Bles, 1970.
The Dark and the Light.   London, Bles, 1971.
To Serve a Queen.   London, Bles, 1972.
In the King's Absence.   London, Bles, 1973.
A Question of Loyalties.   London, Bles, 1974.

Other

Crime in Our Time.   London, Nicholas Vane, 1961;   New
  York, Abelard Schuman, 1962.

*   *   *

A requisite of the detective novel is someone who detects.
Yet Josephine Bell's novels—traditional, numerous, and a
product of the golden age of such fiction—omit the Great
Detective. Since characters impressive in their variety, vitality,
and realistic naturalism are one of Bell's accomplishments, it is
perhaps not unexpected that her works fail to utilize a central
series figure. Barzun and Taylor observe that Bell "has written
more than she should if she had any hope of becoming a
classic," but it is possible that her choice not to use a highly
visible continuing figure bears the main responsibility for her
lesser reputation.

Bell is a decidedly competent craftsman. Her writing is
seamless (never drawing attention through stylistic eccentricity), quietly ironic, economic without terseness, and mildly
flavored with effective humor. Third-person narration is the
rule. Authorial comment is seldom intrusive but often

foreshadows or underscores. Narrative is more prevalent than dialogue, but the characters' lines, when spoken, ring true. Like Ross Macdonald, whom she does not otherwise resemble, she has a good sense of domestic conflict, effectively sketching out the difficulties of living with tedious, humorless, quarrelsome family members one must not only endure but for whom one tries to care.

Bell's early works are traditional. Dr. David Wintringham appears destined to become a strong detective figure. However, it is Inspector Mitchell of Scotland Yard (who appears in the same novels, as well as those featuring the barrister Warrington-Reeve) who comes up with the crucial clues which are the result of painstaking detection or the correct interpretation of what his amateur colleague has discovered. Early works such as *Death at Half-Term* and *Fall over Cliff* as well as later ones such as *A Flat Tyre in Fulham* and *The China Roundabout* follow this pattern and are effective puzzles, though the last one resembles the thriller.

Consistent throughout the novels is the figure of the young, idealistic, overworked, and underpaid physician. Hospital routine and personnel figure prominently. Also consistent is the love affair involving a young career girl on whom the work, in the absence of a series figure, often focuses. Criminals are usually evil, rather than simply misguided, and include both amateurs and professionals. The strongest passion presented is hatred, and sexual desire is sordid, heartless, and often deadly. The weakest aspect of Bell's art is plotting. Action is sometimes insufficient to sustain the interest and suspects too few to provide the suspense necessary for a strong conclusion.

Bell writes novels which fit into a number a categories, although in few cases is the fit exact. The isolated heroine with a tragic past and the brooding figure of the principal male character place *To Let, Furnished* squarely in the gothic tradition of *Jane Eyre* and *Rebecca*. Notable departures from this formula, however, include the facts that the heroine is forty, and the mother of two, and that the mansion is in perfect repair. A feature of *Double Doom,* a kind of mystery melodrama, is one of the author's most unusual characters, the 38-year-old Joyce Morley who has a mental age of 120.

Two other works of particular interest are *The Catalyst,* a domestic tragedy in which young lovers serve as chorus and detective, and *Death in Retirement,* a classic mystery centering on Dr. Clayton, one of Miss Bell's most fascinating older women. In both, characterization is absorbing, pace good, and conclusion equal to the development. *Bones in the Barrow* is a good example of the unvarnished, even grisly, presentation of the facts of a crime and of the communal method, including police procedure, of getting at the truth. There is an unusual love story, as well. Later novels, especially those of the 1970's, tend to be thrillers rather than puzzles. *Such a Nice Client* is essentially a thesis novel, making a strong indictment of the simplistic views of social workers.

Bell has a distinctive voice, and among her novels are those whose combination of qualities will please most readers and whose characters will be hard to forget.

—Nancy Ellen Talburt

———

BELLAIRS, George. Pseudonym for Harold Blundell. British. Born in Heywood, Lancashire 19 April 1902. Educated at Heywood Grammar School; London School of Economics, B.Sc. 1928. Married Gwladys Mabel Robert in 1930. Banker: superintendent of branches, Manchester, 1949–53, and chief of the Manchester office, 1953–62, Martins' Bank. Member of the board, United Manchester Hospitals and Manchester Royal Infirmary. M.A.: University of Manchester, 1958. *Died 18 April 1982.*

CRIME PUBLICATIONS

Novels (Series: Thomas Littlejohn in all books except *Turmoil in Zion*)

Littlejohn on Leave. London, Gifford, 1941.
Death of a Busybody. London, Gifford, 1942; New York, Macmillan, 1943.
The Dead Shall Be Raised. London, Gifford, 1942; as *Murder Will Speak,* New York, Macmillan, 1943.
The Four Unfaithful Servants. London, Gifford, 1942.
Calamity at Harwood. London, Gifford, 1943; New York, Macmillan, 1945.
The Murder of a Quack. London, Gifford, 1943; New York, Macmillan, 1944.
Turmoil in Zion. London, Gifford, 1943; as *Death Stops the Frolic,* New York, Macmillan, 1944.
Death in the Night Watches. London, Gifford, 1945; New York, Macmillan, 1946.
He'd Rather Be Dead. London, Gifford, 1945.
The Case of the Scared Rabbits. London, Gifford, 1946.
The Crime at Halfpenny Bridge. London, Gifford, 1946.
The Case of the Seven Whistlers. London, Gifford, and New York, Macmillan, 1948.
Death on the Last Train. London, Gifford, 1948; New York, Macmillan, 1949.
Outrage on Gallows Hill. New York, Book Club Edition, 1948; London, Gifford, 1949.
The Case of the Demented Spiv. London, Gifford, 1949; New York, Macmillan, 1950.
The Case of the Famished Parson. London, Gifford, and New York, Macmillan, 1949.
The Case of the Headless Jesuit. London, Gifford, 1950; as *Death Brings in the New Year,* New York, Macmillan, 1951.
Dead March for Penelope Blow. London, Gifford, and New York, Macmillan, 1951; as *Dead March for Penelope.* London, Viking, 1956.
Crime in Leper's Hollow. London, Gifford, 1952.
Death in Dark Glasses. London, Gifford, and New York, Macmillan, 1952.
Half-Mast for the Deemster. London, Gifford, 1953.
A Knife for Harry Dodd. London, Gifford, 1953.
Corpses in Enderby. London, Gifford, 1954.
The Cursing Stones Murder. London, Gifford, 1954.
Death in Room Five. London, Gifford, 1955.
Death Drops the Pilot. London, Gifford, 1956.
Death Treads Softly. London, Gifford, 1956.
Death in Desolation. London, Gifford, 1957.
Death in High Provence. London, Gifford, 1957.
Death Sends for the Doctor. London, Gifford, 1957.
Corpse at the Carnival. London, Gifford, 1958.
Murder Makes Mistakes. London, Gifford, 1958.
Bones in the Wilderness. London, Gifford, 1958.
Toll the Bell for Murder. London, Gifford, 1959.
Death in Despair. London, Gifford, 1960.
Death in the Fearful Night. London, Gifford, 1960.
The Body in the Dumb River. London, Gifford, 1961; as *Murder Masquerade,* New York, Tower, 1981.
Death of a Tin God. London, Gifford, 1961.
Death Before Breakfast. London, Gifford, and New York, British Book Centre, 1962.
The Tormentors. London, Gifford, 1962.

Death in the Wasteland.   London, Gifford, 1963; New York,
     British Book Centre, 1964.
Death of a Shadow.   London, Gifford, 1964.
Death Spins the Wheel.   London, Gifford, 1965.
Intruder in the Dark.   London, Gifford, 1966.
Surfeit of Suspects.   London, Gifford, 1966.
Stranger Among the Dead.   London, Gifford, 1966.
Single Ticket to Death.   London, Gifford, 1967.
Fatal Alibi.   London, Gifford, 1968.
Murder Gone Mad.   London, Gifford, 1968.
The Night They Killed Joss Varran.   London, Gifford, 1970.
Tycoon's Death-Bed.   London, Gifford, 1970.
Pomeroy, Deceased.   London, Gifford, 1971.
Murder Adrift.   London, Gifford, 1972.
Devious Murder.   London, Gifford, 1973; New York, Walker,
     1980.
Fear Around About.   London, Gifford, 1975; New York,
     Walker, 1981.
Close All Roads to Sospel.   London, Gifford, 1976; as *All
     Roads to Sospel.*   New York, Walker, 1981.
Downhill Ride of Leeman Popple.   London, Gifford, 1978.
Old Man Dies.   London, Gifford, 1980.

* * *

George Bellairs is the pseudonym of Harold Blundell, an
English banker. After he retired in 1962, Blundell devoted most
of his time to writing: he published more than 50 books—his
first novel was published in 1941—and almost all of the novels
feature Inspector (later Chief Superintendent) Littlejohn. The
early books in the Littlejohn series featured wildly eccentric
characters who were supposed to add comedy to the mystery
plot but too often these attempts at humor misfire. The
strongest Littlejohn books are the ones with the fewest colorful
characters.

Death in High Provence and *Death Before Breakfast* are the
among the best of Bellair's novels. In *Death in High Provence*
the scenes of France are a perfect backdrop to Littlejohn's
assisting the French police investigation into a mysterious
death. *Death Before Breakfast* features some of Bellair's best
plotting as Littlejohn solves the mystery of a man found dead in
a gutter.

Of the later Littlejohn books, *Murder Adrift* stands out for its
solid plotting and strong characterizations. Chief Superintendent Littlejohn and his new assistant Hopkinson are sent to
Fordinghurst to investigate the murder of Heck Todd who was
found dead in his boat at sea. The Todd family secrets hold the
clues to Littlejohn's solving the murder.

One of the more unusual cases in the series is *Devious Murder.*
While walking his dog, Littlejohn discovers the body of Charles
Blunt, one of the most renowned thieves in Europe. Littlejohn,
with Superintendent Cromwell, investigate this curious death
and discover that Blunt was about to rob the Havenith
diamonds from the wife of an American millionaire. But
why was Blunt killed on the eve of his greatest crime and who
did it? Littlejohn's keen sense of logic pieces the puzzle
together.

Some of the best Littlejohn mysteries are set in France. *Close
all Roads to Sospel* begins with Littlejohn vacationing at the
residence of his close friend, Jerome Dorange, Commissaire of
the Nice Sûreté. But the discovery of two murder victims and
the stranding of a Peace group in the mountains near Sospel
leads Littlejohn into joining his host in an investigation that
culminates in a suspenseful chase scene through the Alpes
Maritimes.

Blundell's prolific output as Bellairs results in a varying range
of quality. Some of the Littlejohn books are weakly plotted and

tediously written like *Death on the Last Train* or *The Case of the
Headless Jesuit.* Others like *The Case of the Demented Spiv* and
Death in the Wasteland are unspectacular but competently
written. Some, like *Calamity at Harwood, The Murder of a
Quack,* and *The Night They Killed Joss Varran* are first-rate
mysteries.

—George Kelley

————

BELLEM, Robert Leslie. Also wrote as Franklin Charles (with
Cleve F. Adams); John Grange (with Willis Todhunter
Ballard); John A. Saxon.   American.   Born in Philadelphia,
Pennsylvania, in 1902. Reporter in 1920's, then freelance
writer; staff member, Frank Armer's Culture Publications
(later Trojan Publications), from 1933, and edited *Dan Turner,
Hollywood Detective* (later *Hollywood Detective*), from 1942 to
the early 1950's; also radio and television writer. *Died in 1968.*

Crime Publications

Novels

Blue Murder.   New York, Phoenix Press, 1938.
The Vice Czar Murders (as Franklin Charles; with Cleve F.
     Adams).   New York, Funk and Wagnalls, 1941.
Half-Past Mortem (as John A. Saxon).   New York, Mill, 1947;
     London, Foulsham, 1949.
The Window with the Sleeping Nude.   Kingston, New York,
     Quin, 1950.
No Wings on a Cop (expanded by Bellem from story by Cleve F.
     Adams).   Kingston, New York, Quin, 1950.

Short Stories

Dan Turner, Hollywood Detective, edited by John Wooley.
     Bowling Green, Ohio, Popular Press, 1983.

Uncollected Short Stories

"Lights Outs," in *Real Detective* (Chicago), August–September
     1926.
"Open-and-Shut" in *Real Detective* (Chicago), January 1928.
"The Flowers of Enchantment," in *Tales of Magic and Mystery*
     (Camden, New Jersey), April 1928.
"The Old Timer," in *Real Detective* Tales and Mystery Stories
     (Chicago), September 1930.
"Gorilla Justice," in *Underworld Magazine* (Springfield,
     Massachusetts), May 1931.
"Gangster Gloves," in *Racketeer* (Springfield, Massachusetts),
     July–August 1931.
"Pineapples!," in *Greater Gangster* (Springfield Massachu-
     setts), July 1933.
"Crimson Crisis," in *Greater Gangster* (Springfield Massachu-
     setts), January 1934.
"The Shanghai Jester," in *Spicy Detective* (Wilmington,
     Delaware), April 1934.
"Murder by Proxy," in *Spicy Detective* (Wilmington, Dela-
     ware), June 1934.
"Diamonds of Death," in *Spicy Detective* (Wilmington,
     Delaware), July 1934.
"The Shanghai Jester," in *Spicy Adventure* (Wilmington,
     Delaware), July 1934.
"Dead Man's Bed," in *Spicy Detective* (Wilmington, Dela-
     ware), August 1934.

"Murder in the Stratosphere," in *Complete Detective Novel Magazine* (New York), September 1934.

"Sleeping Dogs," in *Spicy Detective* (Wilmington, Delaware), September 1934.

"Murder at Malibu," in *Spicy Detective* (Wilmington, Delaware), October 1934.

"Murder for Fame," in *Spicy Detective* (Wilmington, Delaware), November 1934.

"The Claws of the Dragon," in *Spicy Adventure* (Wilmington, Delaware), November 1934.

"Girl with Green Eyes," in *Spicy Detective* (Wilmington, Delaware), December 1934.

"The House of the Gilded Buddha," in *Spicy Adventure* (Wilmington, Delaware), December 1934.

"Temple of Death," in *Spicy Adventure* (Wilmington, Delaware), January 1935.

"The Corpse in the Cabinet," in *Spicy Detective* (Wilmington, Delaware), January 1935.

"Death on Location," in *Spicy Detective* (Wilmington, Delaware), February 1935.

"The Pool of Piranhas," in *Spicy Adventure* (Wilmington, Delaware), February 1935.

"The Crimson Flame," in *Spicy Adventure* (Wilmington, Delaware), March 1935.

"The Horoscope Case," in *Spicy Detective* (Wilmington, Delaware), March 1935.

"Adventure's End," in *Spicy Adventure* (Wilmington, Delaware), April 1935.

"Bullet from Nowhere," in *Spicy Detective* (Wilmington, Delaware), April 1935.

"Caspian Contraband," in *Spicy Adventure* (Wilmington, Delaware), May 1935.

"Temporary Corpse," in *Spicy Detective* (Wilmington, Delaware), May 1935.

"Fangs of the Bat," in *Spicy Mystery* (Wilmington, Delaware), June 1935.

"Fortune's Rogue," in *Spicy Adventure* (Wilmington, Delaware), June 1935.

"Murder Masquerade," in *Spicy Detective* (Wilmington, Delaware), June 1935.

"Tuareg Treasure," in *Spicy Adventure* (Wilmington, Delaware), June 1935.

"Daughter of the Damned," in *Spicy Adventure* (Wilmington, Delaware), July 1935.

"Five-Grand Fee," in *Spicy Detective* (Wilmington, Delaware), July 1935.

"The Broken Tael," in *Spicy Adventure* (Wilmington, Delaware), August 1935.

"The Executioner," in *Spicy Mystery* (Wilmington, Delaware), August 1935.

"Two-Time Corpse," in *Spicy Detective* (Wilmington, Delaware), August 1935.

"Master of Death," in *Spicy Mystery* (Wilmington, Delaware), September 1935.

"Sister of Judas," in *Spicy Adventure* (Wilmington, Delaware), September 1935.

"Voice from Beyond," in *Spicy Detective* (Wilmington, Delaware), September 1935.

"Command to Kill," in *Spicy Mystery* (Wilmington, Delaware), October 1935.

"Dead Man's Diamonds," in *Spicy Adventure* (Wilmington, Delaware), October 1935.

"Death's Bright Halo," in *Spicy Detective* (Wilmington, Delaware), October 1935.

"Beyond Justice," in *Spicy Detective* (Wilmington, Delaware), November 1935.

"The Man Who Was Not," in *Spicy Mystery* (Wilmington, Delaware), November 1935.

"Murder's Message," in *Spicy Detective* (Wilmington, Delaware), December 1935.

"The Crimson Crone," in *Spicy Mystery* (Wilmington, Delaware), December 1935.

"The Vengeance of Setep Re," in *Spicy Adventure* (Wilmington, Delaware), December 1935.

"A Comet Passes," in *Spicy Detective* (Wilmington, Delaware), January 1936.

"Crimson Treasure," in *Spicy Adventure* (Wilmington, Delaware), January 1936.

"Labyrinth of Monsters," in *Spicy Mystery* (Wilmington, Delaware), January 1936.

"Blood Pearls," in *Spicy Adventure* (Wilmington, Delaware), February 1936.

"Cool Her Off," in *Spicy Detective* (Wilmington, Delaware), February 1936.

"Fifty Grand in Pearls," in *Thrilling Detective* (New York), February 1936.

"Shadows Pass," in *Spicy Mystery* (Wilmington, Delaware), February 1936.

"A Million in Celluloid," in *Spicy Detective* (Wilmington, Delaware), March 1936.

"Beyond the Veil," in *Spicy Mystery* (Wilmington, Delaware), March 1936.

"Gongs of the Jungle" in *Spicy Adventure* (Wilmington, Delaware), March 1936.

"Green Ticket," in *Spicy Detective* (Wilmington, Delaware), April 1936.

"Taupoo Dance," in *Spicy Mystery* (Wilmington, Delaware), April 1936.

"Tryst with Death," in *Spicy Adventure* (Wilmington, Delaware), April 1936.

"Cavern of the Faceless," in *Spicy Mystery stories* (Wilmington, Delaware), May 1936.

"Cooked!," in *Spicy Detective* (Wilmington, Delaware), May 1936.

"In Debt to the Devil," in *Spicy Adventure* (Wilmington, Delaware), May 1936.

"Surgeon of Souls," in *Spicy Mystery* (Wilmington, Delaware), June 1936.

"The Million Buck Snatch," in *Spicy Detective* (Wilmington, Delaware), June 1936.

"Death's Nocturne," in *Spicy Mystery* (Wilmington, Delaware), July 1936.

"The Camera Guy," in *Spicy Adventure* (Wilmington, Delaware), July 1936.

"The Second Dagger," in *Spicy Detective* (Wilmington, Delaware), July 1936.

"Dead Man's Head," in *Spicy Detective* (Wilmington, Delaware), August 1936.

"Luck of the Pipers," in *Spicy Adventure* (Wilmington, Delaware), August 1936.

"Reunion Beyond," in *Spicy Mystery* (Wilmington, Delaware), August 1936.

"Carboy of Death," in *Spicy Adventure* (Wilmington, Delaware), September 1936.

"Falling Star," in *Spicy Detective* (Wilmington, Delaware), September 1936.

"Flowers of Desire," in *Spicy Mystery* (Wilmington, Delaware), September 1936.

"Brunette Bait," in *Spicy Adventure* (Wilmington, Delaware), October 1936.

"Silver Green Spectre," in *Spicy Detective* (Wilmington, Delaware), October 1936.

"From the Sea," in *Spicy Mystery* (Wilmington, Delaware), November 1936.

"Murder for Metrovox," in *Spicy Detective* (Wilmington, Delaware), November 1936.

"The Power-Smashers," in *Spicy Adventure* (Wilmington, Delaware), November 1936.

"Crooner's Caress," in *Spicy Detective* (Wilmington, Delaware), December 1936.

"Midnight Legion," in *Spicy Adventure* (Wilmington, Delaware), December 1936.

"The Moon-God Takes," in *Spicy Mystery* (Wilmington, Delaware), December 1936.

"Bastions of Badajos," in *Spicy Adventure* (Wilmington, Delaware), January 1937.

"I Am a Monster," in *Spicy Mystery* (Wilmington, Delaware), January 1937.

"Unfinished Melody," in *Spicy Detective* (Wilmington, Delaware), January 1937.

"Death's Diary!" in *Spicy Detective* (Wilmington, Delaware), February 1937.

"Flame Demon," in *Spicy Mystery* (Wilmington, Delaware), February 1937.

"Jail-Break," in *Spicy Adventure* (Wilmington, Delaware), February 1937.

"Bitter Reckoning," in *Spicy Mystery* (Wilmington, Delaware), March 1937.

"Gallows Still," in *Spicy Detective* (Wilmington, Delaware), March 1937.

"Killer's Luck," in *True Gang Life* (New York), March 1937.

"Log Jam," in *Spicy Adventure* (Wilmington, Delaware), March 1937.

"Death for a Name," in *Spicy Detective* (Wilmington, Delaware), April 1937.

"Lynch Legacy," in *Spicy Adventure* (Wilmington, Delaware), April 1937.

"Gypsum Blizzard," in *Spicy Detective* (Wilmington, Delaware), May 1937.

"Shawl of Shaloor," in *Spicy Mystery* (Wilmington, Delaware), May 1937.

"Teeth of the Tiger," in *Modern Adventures* (Philadelphia, Penna), May 1937.

"The House of 7 Dragons," in *Spicy Adventure* (Wilmington, Delaware), May 1937.

"Born to Be Hanged," in *True Gang Life* (New York), June 1937.

"Death's Agent," in *Spicy Detective* (Wilmington, Delaware), June 1937.

"Ghoul's Trap," in *Spicy Mystery* (Wilmington, Delaware), June 1937.

"Murder on the Sound Stage," in *Private Detective* (New York), June 1937.

"Better Than Perfect," in *Detective and Murder Mysteries* (Philadelphia, Pennsylvania), July 1937.

"Corpse in the Closet," in *Spicy Detective* (Wilmington, Delaware), July 1937.

"Death Mask," in *Private Detective* (New York), July 1937.

"Mademoiselle Firebrand," in *Modern Adventures* (Philadelphia, Pennsylvania), July 1937.

"Thirty Seconds," in *Spicy Mystery* (Wilmington, Delaware), July 1937.

"Blondes Make Mistakes," in *Private Detective* (New York), August 1937.

"Death's Detour," in *Spicy Mystery* (Wilmington, Delaware), August 1937.

"For Valour," in *Spicy Adventure* (Wilmington, Delaware), August 1937.

"Hop Cargo," in *Spicy Adventure* (Wilmington, Delaware), August 1937.

"Star Chamber," in *Spicy Detective* (Wilmington, Delaware), August 1937.

"Frozen Fire," in *Spicy Adventure* (Wilmington, Delaware), September 1937.

"Murderer's Error," in *Spicy Detective* (Wilmington, Delaware), September 1937.

"The Dark Tower," in *Spicy Mystery* (Wilmington, Delaware), September 1937.

"Perjury's Playback," in *Private Detective* (New York), October 1937.

"Royal Badger," in *Spicy Adventure* (Wilmington, Delaware), October 1937.

"Veiled Lady," in *Spicy Detective* (Wilmington, Delaware), October 1937.

"Find That Corpse," in *Spicy Detective* (Wilmington, Delaware), November 1937.

"Heritage of Madness," in *Spicy Mystery* (Wilmington, Delaware), November 1937.

"Storm Warning," in *Spicy Adventure* (Wilmington, Delaware), November 1937.

"Gallows Heritage," in *Spicy Mystery* (Wilmington, Delaware), December 1937.

"Hate's Harvest," in *Spicy Detective* (Wilmington, Delaware), December 1937.

"Murder's Malice," in *Private Detective* (New York), December 1937.

"Yoke of the Yogi," in *Spicy Adventure* (Wilmington, Delaware), December 1937.

"Dark Star of Death," in *Spicy Detective* (Wilmington, Delaware), January 1938.

"Hawke's Vengeance," in *Spicy Adventure* (Wilmington, Delaware), January 1938.

"The Soul Eater," in *Spicy Mystery* (Wilmington, Delaware), January 1938.

"Dealer in Death," in *Spicy Mystery* (Wilmington, Delaware), February 1938.

"F.B.I. Spells T.N.T.," in *Romantic Detective* (Chicago), February 1938.

"Killer's Quota," in *Spicy Detective* (Wilmington, Delaware), February 1938.

"Gems for General Sheng," in *Spicy Adventure* (Wilmington, Delaware), March 1938.

"Telephone Tryst," in *Spicy Detective* (Wilmington, Delaware), March 1938.

"Death on Display," in *Private Detective* (New York), April 1938.

"Formula for Death," in *Spicy Adventure* (Wilmington, Delaware), April 1938.

"Mirror Magic," in *Spicy Mystery* (Wilmington, Delaware), April 1938.

"Silverscreen Shakedown," in *Spicy Detective* (Wilmington, Delaware), April 1938.

"Brunette Bump-Off," in *Spicy Detective* (Wilmington, Delaware), May 1938.

"Shadow from Eleusis," in *Spicy Mystery* (Wilmington, Delaware), May 1938.

"Singapore Salvage," in *Spicy Adventure* (Wilmington, Delaware), May 1938.

"Badge of Valor," in *Thrilling Detective* (New York), June 1938.

"Color Scheme," in *Spicy Detective* (Wilmington, Delaware), June 1938.

"Fiend's Feast," in *Spicy Mystery* (Wilmington, Delaware), June 1938.

"Killer's Island," in *Spicy Adventure* (Wilmington, Delaware), June 1938.

"Scarlet Shakedown," in *Private Detective* (New York), June 1938.

"Branded Flesh," in *Private Detective* (New York), July 1938.

"Happy Doomsday to You," in *Popular Detective* (New York), July 1938.

"Killer's Harvest," in *Spicy Detective* (Wilmington, Delaware), July 1938.

"The Road Home," in *Spicy Adventure* (Wilmington, Delaware), July 1938.

"Bullet Bait," in *Private Detective* (New York), August 1938.

"Island of Dogs," in *Spicy Adventure* (Wilmington, Delaware), August 1938.

"Pleasure Peddler," in *Spicy Detective* (Wilmington, Delaware), August 1938.

"Princess of Dreams," in *Spicy Mystery* (Wilmington, Delaware), August 1938.

"Alimony League," in *Spicy Detective* (Wilmington, Delaware), September 1938.

"Hostage to Vengeance," in *Spicy Adventure* (Wilmington, Delaware), September 1938.

"Registered Killer," in *Private Detective* (New York), September 1938.

"Double Kick Back," in *Romantic Detective* (Chicago), October 1938.

"Dummy Kill," in *Spicy Detective* (Wilmington, Delaware), October 1938.

"Strange Journey," in *Spicy Mystery* (Wilmington, Delaware), October 1938.

"Torture-Feature," in *Detective Short Stories* (Chicago), October 1938.

"Blackmail From Beyond," in *Spicy Detective* (Wilmington, Delaware), November 1938.

"Vengeance is Mine," in *Private Detective* (New York), November 1938.

"Dark Eyes of Hell," in *Spicy Mystery* (Wilmington, Delaware), December 1938.

"Death's High Parallel," in *Spicy Detective* (Wilmington, Delaware), December 1938.

"Too Many Alibis," in *Private Detective* (New York), December 1938.

"Danger to Share," in *Spicy Adventure* (Wilmington, Delaware), January 1939.

"Final Fade-Out," in *Spicy Detective* (Wilmington, Delaware), January 1939.

"Reservation Racket," in *Private Detective* (New York), January 1939.

"Copra Squeeze," in *Spicy Adventure* (Wilmington, Delaware), February 1939.

"Crimson Quest," in *Spicy Detective* (Wilmington, Delaware), February 1939.

"Kill That Headline," in *Romantic Detective* (Chicago), February 1939.

"Crime Conqueror," in *Candid Detective* (New York), March 1939.

"Gentleman's Code," in *Spicy Detective* (Wilmington, Delaware), March 1939.

"Program for Plunder," in *Secret Agent X Detective* (Springfield, Massachusetts), March 1939.

"Rebels Rifles," in *Spicy Adventure* (Wilmington, Delaware), March 1939.

"Death Makes Demands," in *Private Detective* (New York), April 1939.

"Design for Dying," in *Spicy Detective* (Wilmington, Delaware), April 1939.

"Forged Warrant," in *Spicy Adventure* (Wilmington, Delaware), April 1939.

"The Devil's Whipping Post," in *Spicy Mystery* (Wilmington, Delaware), April 1939.

"Death Tank," in *Spicy Detective* (Wilmington, Delaware), May 1939.

"Ticket to Hell," in *Spicy Adventure* (Wilmington, Delaware), May 1939.

"Blackbirder's Pearls," in *Spicy Adventure* (Wilmington, Delaware), June 1939.

"Death on Ice," in *Spicy Detective* (Wilmington, Delaware), June 1939.

"Portals of Peril," in *Spicy Mystery* (Wilmington, Delaware), June 1939.

"Dog Eat Dog," in *Spicy Detective* (Wilmington, Delaware), July 1939.

"Photograph Finish," in *Spicy Detective* (Wilmington, Delaware), August 1939.

"Reckoning from Beyond," in *Spicy Mystery* (Wilmington, Delaware), August 1939.

"Sandakan Shake-Up," in *Spicy Adventure* (Wilmington, Delaware), August 1939.

"The Thing in the Shaft," in *Uncanny Tales* (Chicago), August 1939.

"Check-Up" in *Thrilling Detective* (New York), September 1939.

"Lure of the Green Hell," in *Detective and Murder Mysteries* (Holyoke, Massachusetts), September 1939.

"Rifle Mike," in *Spicy Detective* (Wilmington, Delaware), September 1939.

"The Long Journey," in *Spicy Adventure* (Wilmington, Delaware), September 1939.

"War Plans Divided," in *Thrilling Spy Stories* (New York), Fall 1939.

"Daughter of Pharaoh," in *Spicy Mystery* (Wilmington, Delaware), October 1939.

"Fall Guy," in *Private Detective* (New York), October 1939.

"Night Beat," in *Detective Fiction Weekly* (New York), 21 October 1939.

"Peril's Highway," in *Spicy Adventure* (Wilmington, Delaware), October 1939.

"Serpent's Tooth," in *Spicy Detective* (Wilmington, Delaware), October 1939.

"Suicide Masquerade," in *Detective Yarns* (Holyoke, Massachusetts), October 1939.

"Triple Cross," in *Thrilling Detective* (New York), October 1939.

"Bund Blockade," in *Spicy Detective* (Wilmington, Delaware), November 1939.

"Guard Me from a Rub-Out," in *Detective and Murder Mysteries* (Holyoke, Massachusetts), November 1939.

"Never-Never Corpses," in *Spicy Adventure* (Wilmington, Delaware), November 1939.

"Wooed by a Werewolf," in *Uncanny Tales* (Chicago), November 1939.

"Contract to Kill," in *Spicy Detective* (Wilmington, Delaware), December 1939.

"Cuban Contraband," in *Spicy Adventure* (Wilmington, Delaware), December 1939.

"Thunderheads of Greed," in *Spicy Mystery* (Wilmington, Delaware), December 1939.

"Blood Debt," in *Thrilling Detective* (New York), January 1940.

"Skyrocket's Husband," in *Spicy Detective* (Wilmington, Delaware), January 1940.

"The Vintage of Vengeance," in *Spicy Adventure* (Wilmington, Delaware), January 1940.

"Badger Bump," in *Spicy Detective* (Wilmington, Delaware), February 1940.

"Payable in Steel," in *Spicy Adventure* (Wilmington, Delaware), February 1940.

"Back Home to Hell," in *Sinister Stories* (Chicago), March 1940.

"Blood for the Vampire Dead," in *Mystery Tales* (Chicago), March 1940.

"Monster's Menace," in *Spicy Detective* (Wilmington, Delaware), March 1940.

"Sonance Sinister," in *Spicy Mystery* (Wilmington, Delaware), March 1940.

"Vain Victory," in *Spicy Adventure* (Wilmington, Delaware), March 1940.

"A Fool About Women," in *Spicy Adventure* (Wilmington, Delaware), April 1940.

"Curse of the Lovely Torso," in *Uncanny Tales* (Chicago), March 1940.

"Half An Inch," in *Popular Detective* (New York), April 1940.

"Murder Claws," in *Spicy Detective* (Wilmington, Delaware), April 1940.

"Peril for Sale," in *Detective Dime Novels* (New York), April 1940.

"Mistress Death-Kiss," in *Spicy Adventure* (Wilmington, Delaware), May 1940.

"Murder Montage," in *Spicy Detective* (Wilmington, Delaware), May 1940.

"Danger's Delegate," in *Red Star Detective* (New York), June 1940.

"Death's Test Pilot," in *Thrilling Spy Stories* (New York), Summer 1940.

"Drunk, Disorderly, and Dead," in *Private Detective* (New York), June 1940.

"Elemental Vengeance," in *Spicy Mystery* (Wilmington, Delaware), June 1940.

"Killer's Clinic," in *Detective Novels Magazine* (New York), June 1940.

"The Cock Crows Murder," in *Ghost, Super-Detective* (New York), Summer 1940.

"Thug's Threshold," in *Spicy Detective* (Wilmington, Delaware), June 1940.

"Created He Them," in *Spicy Adventure* (Wilmington, Delaware), July 1940.

"Death Dubbed In," in *Spicy Detective* (Wilmington, Delaware), July 1940.

"Johnny on the Spot," in *Thrilling Detective* (New York), July 1940.

"Crimson Ritual," in *Spicy Detective* (Wilmington, Delaware), August 1940.

"Hazard's Harvest," in *Red Star Detective* (New York), August 1940.

"Loot for the Lords of Doom," in *Spicy Adventure* (Wilmington, Delaware), August 1940.

"Cokey's Perfect Plan," in *Thrilling Detective* (New York), September 1940.

"Death's Blue Discs," in *Spicy Detective* (Wilmington, Delaware), September 1940.

"Jeopardy's Jackpot," in *Red Star Detective* (New York), October 1940.

"Murdered Man's Mission," in *Spicy Adventure* (Wilmington, Delaware), October 1940.

"Murder's Escorts," in *Spicy Detective* (Wilmington, Delaware), October 1940.

"Rose Pearl," in *Spicy Mystery* (Wilmington, Delaware), October 1940.

"Agents of Wrath," in *Super Detective* (New York), November 1940.

"Enough Glory," in *Fifth Column* (New York), November 1940.

"Peril's Partners," in *Spicy Adventure* (Wilmington, Delaware), November 1940.

"Premiere in Purgatory," in *Spicy Detective* (Wilmington, Delaware), November 1940.

"Agents of Doom," in *Detective Novels Magazine* (New York), December 1940.

"Valor's Volunteer," in *Thrilling Spy Stories* (New York), Winter 1940.

"Murder's Middleman," in *Spicy Detective* (Wilmington, Delaware), January 1941.

"Prisoners on Proteus," in *Spicy Adventure* (Wilmington, Delaware), January 1941.

"Bargain in Blackmail," in *Super Detective* (New York), February 1941.

"Cat Act," in *Spicy Detective* (Wilmington, Delaware), February 1941.

"High Heels," in *Private Detective* (New York), February 1941.

"Mesa of Madness," in *Spicy Mystery* (Wilmington, Delaware), February 1941.

"Tropic Talisman," in *Spicy Adventure* (Wilmington, Delaware), February 1941.

"Reckoning in Red," in *Spicy Detective* (Wilmington, Delaware), March 1941.

"Welcome to Hell," in *Spicy Mystery* (Wilmington, Delaware), March 1941.

"A Hero Comes Home," in *Spicy Mystery* (Wilmington, Delaware), April 1941.

"Danger Delivered C.O.D." in *Private Detective* (New York), April 1941.

"Killer's Cue," in *Spicy Detective* (Wilmington, Delaware), April 1941.

"Low Bridge," in *Super Detective* (New York), April 1941.

"Murder's Ten Percent," in *Spicy Detective* (Wilmington, Delaware), April 1941.

"Sun-Death's Daughter," in *Spicy Adventure* (Wilmington, Delaware), April 1941.

"Future Book," in *Spicy Detective* (Wilmington, Delaware), May 1941.

"Pearl of Hell," in *Spicy Adventure* (Wilmington, Delaware), May 1941.

"Property of Death," in *Spicy Detective* (Wilmington, Delaware), June 1941.

"You're So Dead," in *Hollywood Detective* (Springfield, Massachusetts), June 1941.

"Chaos and Back," in *Spicy Adventure* (Wilmington, Delaware), July 1941.

"Death by Arrangement," in *Spicy Detective* (Wilmington, Delaware), July 1941.

"Lanimea Salvage," in *Stirring Adventures* (New York), July 1941.

"Risks Redoubled," in *Double Detective* (New York), August 1941.

"Witch Hunt," in *Spicy Detective* (Wilmington, Delaware), August 1941.

"You Are a Murderer!," in *Spicy Mystery* (Wilmington, Delaware), August 1941.

"Barmecide Bride," in *Spicy Detective* (Wilmington, Delaware), September 1941.

"Silver Scales of Justice," in *Spicy Adventure* (Wilmington, Delaware), September 1941.

"Melody of Vengeance," in *Spicy Mystery* (Wilmington, Delaware), October 1941.

"Shanghai Sellout," in *Spicy Adventure* (Wilmington, Delaware), October 1941.

"Picture Frame," in *Spicy Detective* (Wilmington, Delaware), November 1941.

"The Sign of the Song," in *Spicy Mystery* (Wilmington, Delaware), November 1941.

"Crimson Comedy," in *Spicy Detective* (Wilmington, Delaware), December 1941.

"Death's Convoy," in *Spicy Mystery* (Wilmington, Delaware), December 1941.

"X-B 391-A," in *Spicy Adventure* (Wilmington, Delaware), December 1941.

"A Comet Passes," in *Dan Turner, Hollywood Detective* (Wilmington, Delaware), January 1942.

"Bullet From Nowhere," in *Dan Turner, Hollywood Detective* (Wilmington, Delaware), January 1942.

"Burma Booty," in *Spicy Adventure* (Wilmington, Delaware), January 1942.

"Cooked!," in *Dan Turner, Hollywood Detective* (Wilmington, Delaware), January 1942.

"Death Dance," in *Spicy Detective* (Wilmington, Delaware), January 1942.

"Million Buck Snatch," in *Dan Turner, Hollywood Detective* (Wilmington, Delaware), January 1942.

"Murder on the Sound Stage," in *Dan Turner, Hollywood Detective* (Wilmington, Delaware), January 1942.

"Murder's Messenger," in *Dan Turner, Hollywood Detective* (Wilmington, Delaware), January 1942.

"The Horoscope Case," in *Dan Turner, Hollywood Detective* (Wilmington, Delaware), January 1942.

"Death in the Doghouse," in *Spicy Detective* (Wilmington, Delaware), February 1942.

"Corpse Cross," in *Private Detective* (New York), March 1942.

"Mistress of Fury," in *Spicy Adventure* (Wilmington, Delaware), March 1942.

"Shouldn't Happen to a Dog," in *Spicy Detective* (Wilmington, Delaware), March 1942.

"Beyond Justice," in *Dan Turner, Hollywood Detective* (Wilmington, Delaware), April 1942.

"Crimson Reckoning," in *Super Detective* (New York), April 1942.

"Death on Location," in *Dan Turner, Hollywood Detective* (Wilmington, Delaware), April 1942.

"Forever Vengeance," in *Spicy Mystery* (Wilmington, Delaware), April 1942.

"Gas-House Still," in *Dan Turner, Hollywood Detective* (Wilmington, Delaware), April 1942.

"Murder Done Twice," in *Dan Turner, Hollywood Detective* (Wilmington, Delaware), April 1942.

"Murderer's Error," in *Dan Turner, Hollywood Detective* (Wilmington, Delaware), April 1942.

"Murder for Fame," in *Dan Turner, Hollywood Detective* (Wilmington, Delaware), April 1942.

"Payoff on Peril," in *Spicy Detective* (Wilmington, Delaware), April 1942.

"Star Chamber," in *Dan Turner, Hollywood Detective* (Wilmington, Delaware), April 1942.

"Ace in the Hole," in *Spicy Detective* (Wilmington, Delaware), May 1942.

"Murder's Remake," in *Private Detective* (New York), May 1942.

"No Questions," in *Mammoth Detective* (Chicago), May 1942.

"Killer's Keepsake," in *Spicy Detective* (Wilmington, Delaware), June 1942.

"Blonde Motive," in *Dan Turner, Hollywood Detective* (Wilmington, Delaware), July 1942.

"Blackmail Book," in *Dan Turner, Hollywood Detective* (Wilmington, Delaware), July 1942.

"Blizzard in August," in *Dan Turner, Hollywood Detective* (Wilmington, Delaware), July 1942.

"Death Drop," in *Dan Turner, Hollywood Detective* (Wilmington, Delaware), July 1942.

"Killer's Pocket," in *Private Detective* (New York), July 1942.

"Lady Scarface," in *Dan Turner, Hollywood Detective* (Wilmington, Delaware), July 1942.

"Puzzle in Purple," in *Spicy Detective* (Wilmington, Delaware), July 1942.

"Ramsomed Remainders," in *Dan Turner, Hollywood Detective* (Wilmington, Delaware), July 1942.

"Spur of the Moment," in *Dan Turner, Hollywood Detective* (Wilmington, Delaware), July 1942.

"Voice from Beyond," in *Dan Turner, Hollywood Detective* (Wilmington, Delaware), July 1942.

"Forgery's Foil," in *Spicy Detective* (Wilmington, Delaware), August 1942.

"Tide of Triumph," in *Spicy Adventure* (Wilmington, Delaware), August 1942.

"Death in the Draft," in *Spicy Detective* (Wilmington, Delaware), September 1942.

"Hot Skins," in *Mammoth Detective* (Chicago), September 1942.

"Black Light Payoff" in *Private Detective* (New York), September 1942.

"Death's Dark Star," in *Dan Turner, Hollywood Detective* (Wilmington, Delaware), October 1942.

"Dummy Kill," in *Dan Turner, Hollywood Detective* (Wilmington, Delaware), October 1942.

"Four Minutes Past Nine," in *Dan Turner, Hollywood Detective* (Wilmington, Delaware), October 1942.

"Homicide Haunt," in *Dan Turner, Hollywood Detective* (Wilmington, Delaware), October 1942.

"Judas Jewels," in *Dan Turner, Hollywood Detective* (Wilmington, Delaware), October 1942.

"Last Round," in *Spicy Mystery* (Wilmington, Delaware), October 1942.

"Phantom Fangs," in *Spicy Detective* (Wilmington, Delaware), October 1942.

"Telephone Tangle," in *Dan Turner, Hollywood Detective* (Wilmington, Delaware), October 1942.

"Trahua Treasure," in *Spicy Adventure* (Wilmington, Delaware), October 1942.

"Riddle in Red," in *Spicy Detective* (Wilmington, Delaware), November 1942.

"Will for a Killer," in *Super Detective* (New York), November 1942.

"Years That Are Not,'" in *Spicy Mystery* (Wilmington, Delaware), November 1942.

"Broken Melody," in *Dan Turner, Hollywood Detective* (Wilmington, Delaware), December 1942.

"Corpse By Mistake," in *Dan Turner, Hollywood Detective* (Wilmington, Delaware), December 1942.

"Daughter of Murder," in *Dan Turner, Hollywood Detective* (Wilmington, Delaware), December 1942.

"Killers Union," in *Dan Turner, Hollywood Detective* (Wilmington, Delaware), December 1942.

"League of Leeches," in *Dan Turner, Hollywood Detective* (Wilmington, Delaware), December 1942.

"Malibu Mess," in *Dan Turner, Hollywood Detective* (Wilmington, Delaware), December 1942.

"Petticoat Payoff," in *Spicy Detective* (Wilmington, Delaware), December 1942.

"The Color of Murder," in *Dan Turner, Hollywood Detective* (Wilmington, Delaware), December 1942.

"Dark Miracle," in *Speed Mystery* (Springfield Massachusetts), January 1943.

"Eyes of the Dead," in *Dan Turner, Hollywood Detective* (Wilmington, Delaware), January 1943.

"Glittering Clue," in *Dan Turner, Hollywood Detective* (Wilmington, Delaware), January 1943.

"Headed for Nowhere," in *Mammoth Detective* (Chicago), January 1943.

"Headlines in Hell," in *Dan Turner, Hollywood Detective* (Wilmington, Delaware), January 1943.

"Homicide Parallel," in *Dan Turner, Hollywood Detective* (Wilmington, Delaware), January 1943.

"Murder in Yellow," in *Dan Turner, Hollywood Detective* (Wilmington, Delaware), January 1943.

"Riddle of the Rain," in *Speed Detective* (Springfield, Massachusetts), January 1943.

"Sleeping Dogs," in *Dan Turner, Hollywood Detective* (Wilmington, Delaware), January 1943.

"Snake Tangle," in *Dan Turner, Hollywood Detective* (Wilmington, Delaware), January 1943.

"The Murdered Mummy," in *Dan Turner, Hollywood Detective* (Wilmington, Delaware), January 1943.

"Arrow From Nowhere," in *Dan Turner, Hollywood Detective* (Wilmington, Delaware), February 1943.

"Feature Snatch," in *Dan Turner, Hollywood Detective* (Wilmington, Delaware), February 1943.

"Heads You Lose," in *Dan Turner, Hollywood Detective* (Wilmington, Delaware), February 1943.

"Homicide Hunch," in *Dan Turner, Hollywood Detective* (Wilmington, Delaware), February 1943.

"Monsters Meet," in *Speed Adventure* (Springfield, Massachusetts), February 1943.

"Murder's Blue Motive," in *Dan Turner, Hollywood Detective* (Wilmington, Delaware), February 1943.

"Phony Shakedown," in *Dan Turner, Hollywood Detective* (Wilmington, Delaware), February 1943.

"The Case of the Vanishing Limousine," in *Dan Turner, Hollywood Detective* (Wilmington, Delaware), February 1943.

"The Dame Dies Twice," in *Speed Detective* (Springfield, Massachusetts), February 1943.

"Alibi in Reverse," in *Mammoth Detective Stories* (Chicago), March 1943.

"Dead Man's Shakedown," in *Dan Turner, Hollywood Detective* (Wilmington, Delaware), March 1943.

"Gentleman's Jackpot," in *Speed Detective* (Springfield, Massachusetts), March 1943.

"Killer's Investment," in *Dan Turner, Hollywood Detective* (Wilmington, Delaware), March 1943.

"Russian Run-Around," in *Dan Turner, Hollywood Detective* (Wilmington, Delaware), March 1943.

"Satan's Shrine," in *Dan Turner, Hollywood Detective* (Wilmington, Delaware), March 1943.

"Sing Me a Song of Murder," in *Dan Turner, Hollywood Detective* (Wilmington, Delaware), March 1943.

"The Case of the Slain Gorilla," in *Dan Turner, Hollywood Detective* (Wilmington, Delaware), March 1943.

"Water Cooled," in *Dan Turner, Hollywood Detective* (Wilmington, Delaware), March 1943.

"Three Blond Mice," in *Speed Detective* (Springfield, Massachusetts), April 1943.

"Dead Man's Guilt," in *Dan Turner, Hollywood Detective* (Wilmington, Delaware), May 1943.

"Death's Escort," in *Dan Turner, Hollywood Detective* (Wilmington, Delaware), May 1943.

"Dissolve Shot," in *Dan Turner, Hollywood Detective* (Wilmington, Delaware), May 1943.

"Kiss the Corpse Goodbye," in *Dan Turner, Hollywood Detective* (Wilmington, Delaware), May 1943.

"Monter's Malice," in *Dan Turner, Hollywood Detective* (Wilmington, Delaware), May 1943.

"Shakedown Sham," in *Dan Turner, Hollywood Detective* (Wilmington, Delaware), May 1943.

"Star Dice," in *Speed Detective* (Springfield, Massachusetts), May 1943.

"Home Is the Hunter," in *Private Detective* (New York), June 1943.

"Hurry with the Hearse," in *Speed Detective* (Springfield, Massachusetts), June 1943.

"Bund Bump," in *Dan Turner, Hollywood Detective* (Wilmington, Delaware), July 1943.

"Cast for Killing," in *Dan Turner, Hollywood Detective* (Wilmington, Delaware), July 1943.

"Check Tangle," in *Dan Turner, Hollywood Detective* (Wilmington, Delaware), July 1943.

"Death's Blind Date," in *Dan Turner, Hollywood Detective* (Wilmington, Delaware), July 1943.

"Homicide Bite," in *Dan Turner, Hollywood Detective* (Wilmington, Delaware), July 1943.

"Homicide Dodge," in *Private Detective* (New York), July 1943.

"Murder Tank," in *Dan Turner, Hollywood Detective* (Wilmington, Delaware), July 1943.

"Murder with Music," in *Dan Turner, Hollywood Detective* (Wilmington, Delaware), July 1943.

"Shooting Schedule," in *Speed Detective* (Springfield, Massachusetts), July 1943.

"Murder on Furlough," in *Private Detective* (New York), August 1943.

"Sisterhood of Fear," in *Mammoth Detective* (Chicago), August 1943.

"Taps for a Trumpeter," in *Speed Detective* (Springfield, Massachusetts), August 1943.

"Corpse on Ice," in *Hollywood Detective* (Springfield, Massachusetts), September 1943.

"Death Begins at Forty," in *Hollywood Detective* (Springfield, Massachusetts), September 1943.

"Dump the Jackpot," in *Speed Detective* (Springfield, Massachusetts), September 1943.

"Harvest of Hate," in *Hollywood Detective* (Springfield, Massachusetts), September 1943.

"Dead Man's Code," in *Hollywood Detective* (Springfield, Massachusetts), October 1943.

"Homicide Highball," in *Hollywood Detective* (Springfield, Massachusetts), October 1943.

"King-Size Kill," in *Hollywood Detective* (Springfield, Massachusetts), October 1943.

"Murder Off the Record," in *Hollywood Detective* (Springfield, Massachusetts), October 1943.

"Murder Rations," in *Super Detective* (New York), October 1943.

"Cat Act," in *Hollywood Detective* (Springfield, Massachusetts), November 1943.

"Copper's Comeback," in *Private Detective* (New York), November 1943.

"Death's Dress Rehearsal," in *Hollywood Detective* (Springfield, Massachusetts), November 1943.

"Half-Size Homicide," in *Speed Detective* (Springfield, Massachusetts), November 1943.

"A Corpse Can't Croon," in *Private Detective* (New York), December 1943.

"The Lake of the Left-Hand Moon," in *Hollywood Detective* (Springfield, Massachusetts), December 1943.

"Coffin Frame," in *Speed Detective* (Springfield, Massachusetts), January 1944.

"Dead Heat," in *Hollywood Detective* (Springfield, Massachusetts), January 1944.

"Focus on Death," in *Hollywood Detective* (Springfield, Massachusetts), January 1944.

"Melodies of Murder," in *Hollywood Detective* (Springfield, Massachusetts), January 1944.

"The Cat Mew's Murder," in *Speed Mystery* (Springfield, Massachusetts), January 1944.

"The Tree of the Pointing Finger," in *Hollywood Detective* (Springfield, Massachusetts), January 1944.

"Widow by Proxy," in *Hollywood Detective* (Springfield, Massachusetts), January 1944.

"Killer's Legacy," in *Hollywood Detective* (Springfield, Massachusetts), February 1944.

"Over the Hill to the Death House," in *Hollywood Detective* (Springfield, Massachusetts), February 1944.

"The Vanishing Vampire," in *Hollywood Detective* (Springfield, Massachusetts), February 1944.

"Death's Wife," in *Private Detective* (New York), March 1944.

"Killer's Cure," in *Hollywood Detective* (Springfield, Massachusetts), March 1944.

"Odds on the Eight-Ball," in *Hollywood Detective* (Springfield, Massachusetts), March 1944.

"Killer, Come Back to Me," in *Private Detective* (New York), April 1944.

"Pistol-Packing Premiere," in *Hollywood Detective* (Springfield, Massachusetts), April 1944.

"Five o'Clock Shadow," in *Speed Detective* (Springfield, Massachusetts), May 1944.

"Heel's Blood," in *Hollywood Detective* (Springfield, Massachusetts), May 1944.

"Killer's Contract," in *Hollywood Detective* (Springfield, Massachusetts), May 1944.

"Special Effect," in *Private Detective* (New York), May 1944.

"Sleep for a Dreamer," in *Hollywood Detective* (Springfield, Massachusetts), June 1944.

"Dan Turner Deals an Ace," in *Hollywood Detective* (Springfield, Massachusetts), July 1944.

"Death Buys Black Gas," in *Private Detective* (New York), July 1944.

"Kidnap Ticket," in *Hollywood Detective* (Springfield, Massachusetts), July 1944.

"Murder's Mouthpiece," in *Hollywood Detective* (Springfield, Massachusetts), August 1944.

"Death in the Risk Racket," in *Hollywood Detective* (Springfield, Massachusetts), September 1944.

"The Bride Wore Black," in *Super Detective* (New York), September 1944.

"Home Is the Killer," in *Hollywood Detective* (Springfield, Massachusetts), October 1944.

"Killer's Clue," in *Hollywood Detective* (Springfield, Massachusetts), October 1944.

"Murder on Wings," in *Hollywood Detective* (Springfield, Massachusetts), October 1944.

"Stars Die at Night," in *Speed Detective* (Springfield, Massachusetts), October 1944.

"Clever Corpse," in *Hollywood Detective* (Springfield, Massachusetts), November 1944.

"Remake for Death," in *Hollywood Detective* (Springfield, Massachusetts), November 1944.

"Cue for a Killing," in *Hollywood Detective* (Springfield, Massachusetts), December 1944.

"Deathbed Caper," in *Hollywood Detective* (Springfield, Massachusetts), December 1944.

"Heel's Heritage," in *Hollywood Detective* (Springfield, Massachusetts), December 1944.

"Murder by the Book," in *Hollywood Detective* (Springfield, Massachusetts), December 1944.

"Trump for the Ace," in *Speed Detective* (Springfield, Massachusetts), December 1944.

"Homicide Legacy," in *Hollywood Detective* (Springfield, Massachusetts), February 1945.

"Killer's Cross-Up," in *Private Detective* (New York), February 1945.

"Morgue Case," in *Speed Detective* (Springfield, Massachusetts), February 1945.

"Murder Has Four Letters," in *Hollywood Detective* (Springfield, Massachusetts), February 1945.

"Death in the Cast," in *Hollywood Detective* (Springfield, Massachusetts), March 1945.

"Death Is Where You Find It," in *Hollywood Detective* (Springfield, Massachusetts), March 1945.

"Cameo Code," in *Hollywood Detective* (Springfield, Massachusetts), April 1945.

"Comet's Consort," in *Hollywood Detective* (Springfield, Massachusetts), April 1945.

"Die, Witch, Die!," in *Hollywood Detective* (Springfield, Massachusetts), April 1945.

"Screen-Test Kill," in *Hollywood Detective* (Springfield, Massachusetts), April 1945.

"Snatch Buster," in *Speed Detective* (Springfield, Massachusetts), April 1945.

"Suicide Stunt," in *Speed Detective* (Springfield, Massachusetts), April 1945.

"Cure for a Quisling," in *Hollywood Detective* (Springfield, Massachusetts), May 1945.

"Dead Ringer," in *Hollywood Detective* (Springfield, Massachusetts), May 1945.

"The Big Cut," in *Hollywood Detective* (Springfield, Massachusetts), May 1945.

"Dead Mike," in *Super Detective* (New York), June 1945.

"Dolly Shot," in *Speed Detective* (Springfield, Massachusetts), June 1945.

"Homicide Flash," in *Hollywood Detective* (Springfield, Massachusetts), June 1945.

"Death in a Crystal Casket," in *Street and Smith's Detective Story Magazine* (New York), June 1945.

"The Dead Don't Dream," in *Hollywood Detective* (Springfield, Massachusetts), July 1945.

"Funeral Fade-Out," in *Speed Detective* (Springfield, Massachusetts), August 1945.

"Pin-Up Corpse," in *Hollywood Detective* (Springfield, Massachusetts), August 1945.

"Bury the Badger," in *Speed Detective* (Springfield, Massachusetts), October 1945.

"Crazy for the Kill," in *Hollywood Detective* (Springfield, Massachusetts), October 1945.

"Frame Around a Fall Guy," in *Hollywood Detective* (Springfield, Massachusetts), October 1945.

"The Lady Regrets," in *Hollywood Detective* (Springfield, Massachusetts), October 1945.

"Double Switch," in *Private Detective* (New York), November 1945.

"Coffin for a Coward," in *Hollywood Detective* (Springfield, Massachusetts), December 1945.

"Death in the Groove," in *Speed Detective* (Springfield, Massachusetts), December 1945.

"Dog's Life," in *Hollywood Detective* (Springfield, Massachusetts), December 1945.

"Poison Payoff," in *Hollywood Detective* (Springfield, Massachusetts), December 1945.

"Ruby Ransom," in *Hollywood Detective* (Springfield, Massachusetts), December 1945.

"The Book of the Phantom Bullet," in *Hollywood Detective* (Springfield, Massachusetts), December 1945.

"Green Heat," in *Hollywood Detective* (Springfield, Massachusetts), February 1946.

"Homicide Surprise," in *Speed Detective* (Springfield, Massachusetts), February 1946.

"Kill Me Again!," in *Hollywood Detective* (Springfield, Massachusetts), February 1946.

"Murder—N.S.F.," in *Hollywood Detective* (Springfield, Massachusetts), February 1946.

"Red Night," in *Hollywood Detective* (Springfield, Massachusetts), February 1946.

"Syndicate Snatch," in *Hollywood Detective* (Springfield, Massachusetts), February 1946.

"The Hot Rock," in *Private Detective* (New York), February 1946.

"Don't Change Hearses," in *Super Detective* (New York), March 1946.

"Arrangement for Murder," in *Hollywood Detective* (Springfield, Massachusetts), April 1946.

"Fangs for the Memory," in *Hollywood Detective* (Springfield, Massachusetts), April 1946.

"Freak Snow," in *Hollywood Detective* (Springfield, Massachusetts), April 1946.

"Homicide's Partner," in *Hollywood Detective* (Springfield, Massachusetts), April 1946.

"Murder from Music," in *Hollywood Detective* (Springfield, Massachusetts), April 1946.

"Gold-Badge of Courage," in *Speed Detective* (Springfield, Massachusetts), May 1946.

"Dirge for a Phony," in *Hollywood Detective* (Springfield, Massachusetts), July 1946.

"Half-Past Dead," in *Super Detective* (New York), July 1946.

"Key to the Kill," in *Hollywood Detective* (Springfield, Massachusetts), July 1946.

"Reunion with Murder," in *Private Detective* (New York), July 1946.

"Serial Kill," in *Hollywood Detective* (Springfield, Massachusetts), July 1946.

"The Queen Was in Her Coffin," in *Hollywood Detective* (Springfield, Massachusetts), July 1946.

"Latin Blood," in *Speed Detective* (Springfield, Massachusetts), August 1946.

"Fall Guy for a Forgery," in *Hollywood Detective* (Springfield, Massachusetts), September 1946.

"Homicide Gotfoot," in *Hollywood Detective* (Springfield, Massachusetts), September 1946.

"Slow Burn," in *Hollywood Detective* (Springfield, Massachusetts), September 1946.

"Spare the Rod," in *Private Detective* (New York), September 1946.

"Wolf Trap," in *Speed Detective* (Springfield, Massachusetts), October 1946.

"Careless Corpse," in *Hollywood Detective* (Springfield, Massachusetts), November 1946.

"Murder's Monogram," in *Super Detective* (New York), November 1946.

"The Riddle of Thumbs a Ride," in *Hollywood Detective* (Springfield, Massachusetts), November 1946.

"Treachery Pulls the Trigger," in *Hollywood Detective* (Springfield, Massachusetts), November 1946.

"Come Die for Me," in *Speed Detective* (Springfield, Massachusetts), December 1946.

"Gun from Gotham," in *Rue Morgue 1*, edited by Rex Stout and Louis Greenfield. New York, Creative Age Press, 1946.

"The Phantom Bullet," in *The Saint's Choice 6* (Hollywood), 1946.

"Death's Autograph," in *Hollywood Detective* (Springfield, Massachusetts), January 1947.

"Hair of the Dog," in *Hollywood Detective* (Springfield, Massachusetts), January 1947.

"Murder Strikes Back," in *Hollywood Detective* (Springfield, Massachusetts), January 1947.

"Slay It Isn't So!," in *Hollywood Detective* (Springfield, Massachusetts), January 1947.

"Homicide Honeymoon," in *Speed Detective* (Springfield, Massachusetts), February 1947.

"Death Watch," in *Super Detective* (New York), March 1947.

"Encore for Death," in *Hollywood Detective* (Springfield, Massachusetts), June 1947.

"Don't Go Near the Slaughter," in *Hollywood Detective* (Springfield, Massachusetts), September 1947.

"Lethal Lullaby," in *Hollywood Detective* (Springfield, Massachusetts), September 1947.

"Murder Follows Me!," in *Hollywood Detective* (Springfield, Massachusetts), September 1947.

"I'll Take That Rap," in *Popular Detective* (New York), January 1948.

"Suicide Scenario," in *Thrilling Detective* (New York), February 1948.

"Mahatma of Mayhem," in *Thrilling Detective* (New York), April 1948.

"Death Ends the Scene," in *Hollywood Detective* (Springfield, Massachusetts), May 1948.

"Hanging Frame," in *G-Men Detective* (New York), May 1948.

"Killer's Disease," in *Private Detective* (New York), May 1948.

"Wired Alibi," in *Hollywood Detective* (Springfield, Massachusetts), May 1948.

"No Reprieve for the Killer," in *Black Book Detective Magazine* (Chicago), June 1948.

"Cinema Corpse," in *Hollywood Detective* (Springfield, Massachusetts), August 1948.

"The 9th Doll," in *Thrilling Detective* (New York), August 1948.

"Secret Circuit," in *Super Detective* (New York), September 1948.

"Homicide Spike," in *Hollywood Detective* (Springfield, Massachusetts), November 1948.

"Off-Stage Murder," in *Hollywood Detective* (Springfield, Massachusetts), November 1948.

"Serenade with Slugs," in *Thrilling Detective* (New York), December 1948.

"Knife in the Dark," in *G-Men Detective* (New York), January 1949.

"Keys to a Killer," in *Thrilling Detective* (New York), February 1949.

"Make with the Mayhem," in *Hollywood Detective* (Springfield, Massachusetts), February 1949.

"Murder Muscles In," in *Hollywood Detective* (Springfield, Massachusetts), February 1949.

"Gray Steel," in *The Phantom Detective* (New York), Spring 1949.

"Murder Tune," in *Super Detective* (New York), March 1949.

"Homicide Shaft," in *Thrilling Detective* (New York), April 1949.

"Body in the Closet," in *Hollywood Detective* (Springfield, Massachusetts), June 1949.

"Homicide's Hallmark," in *Detective Novel Magazine* (New York), Summer 1949.

"Killer's Ruse," in *Super Detective* (New York), June 1949.

"Kill with a Kiss!," in *Hollywood Detective* (Springfield, Massachusetts), June 1949.

"Murder on the Meter," in *Private Detective* (New York), June 1949.

"Preview of Murder," in *Thrilling Detective* (New York), June 1949.

"Slayer's Serenade," in *Hollywood Detective* (Springfield, Massachusetts), June 1949.

"Triple-Edged Murder," in *Hollywood Detective* (Springfield, Massachusetts), June 1949.

"Puzzle in Peril," in *Thrilling Detective* (New York), October 1949.

"Music of Doom," in *Hollywood Detective* (Springfield, Massachusetts), December 1949.

"Nameless Dread of the Savage Sirens," in *Book of Terror* (New York and Toronto), December 1949.

"Starring—Death!," in *Hollywood Detective* (Springfield, Massachusetts), December 1949.

"Quickie Kill," in *Hollywood Detective* (Springfield, Massachusetts), January 1950.

"Terror on the Doorstep," in *Hollywood Detective* (Springfield, Massachusetts), January 1950.

"Blind Man's Fluff," in *Thrilling Detective* (New York), February 1950.

"Death on the Set," in *Hollywood Detective* (Springfield, Massachusetts), February 1950.

"Model for a Corpse," in *Hollywood Detective* (Springfield, Massachusetts), February 1950.

"Through Fire," in *Spicy Mystery* (Wilmington, Delaware), February 1950.

"Any Number Can Slay," in *Hollywood Detective* (Springfield, Massachusetts), March 1950.

"Doom on File," in *Hollywood Detective* (Springfield, Massachusetts), March 1950.

"Action! Camera! Drop Dead!," in *Hollywood Detective* (Springfield, Massachusetts), April 1950.

"Movie Mad—Murder Mad," in *Hollywood Detective* (Springfield, Massachusetts), April 1950.

"Shakedown Legacy," in *Super Detective* (New York), April 1950.

"Cast as a Corpse," in *Hollywood Detective* (Springfield, Massachusetts), May 1950.

"Screen Test for Murder," in *Hollywood Detective* (Springfield, Massachusetts), May 1950.

"Cast for Murder," in *Hollywood Detective* (Springfield, Massachusetts), June 1950.

"Cutie in a Coffin," in *Hollywood Detective* (Springfield, Massachusetts), June 1950.

"Diamonds of Death," in *Hollywood Detective* (Springfield, Massachusetts), August 1950.

"Murder Steals the Scene," in *Thrilling Detective* (New York), August 1950.

"Murder Wears Makeup," in *Hollywood Detective* (Springfield, Massachusetts), August 1950.

"Curtains for a Corpse," in *Hollywood Detective* (New York), October 1950.

"Death in the Spotlight," in *Hollywood Detective* (New York), October 1950.

"Shells of Justice," in *Thrilling Detective* (New York), October 1950.

"The Doomed Quartet," in *Hollywood Detective* (New York), October 1950.

"The Glass Noose," in *Phantom Detective* (New York), Winter 1952.

"Hang My Killer High," in *Top Detective Annual* (New York), 1953.

"Death Draws a Picture," in *Phantom* (London), February 1962.

"Death's Passport," in *The Pulps: Fifty Years of American Pop Culture,* edited by Tony Goodstone, New York, Chelsea House, 1970.

"The Lake of the Left-Hand Moon," in *The American Detective,* edited by William Kitteredge and Steven M. Krauzer. New York, New American Library, 1978.

Uncollected Short Stories as John Grange, with Willis Todhunter Ballard

"Hell's Ice Box," in *Super Detective* (New York), July 1942.

"Days of Death," in *Super Detective* (New York), August 1942.

"Caribbean Cask," in *Super Detective* (New York), November 1942.

"Murder Between Shifts," in *Super Detective* (New York), December 1942.

"Cauldron of Death," in *Super Detective* (New York), January 1943.

"Murder's Migrants," in *Super Detective* (New York), February 1943.

"Death Is a Flying Dutchman," in *Super Detective* (New York), March 1943.

"Homicide Heiress," in *Super Detective* (New York), April 1943.

"Curse of the Masters," in *Super Detective* (New York), May 1943.

"Pipeline to Murder," in *Super Detective* (New York), August 1943.

OTHER PUBLICATIONS

Plays

Radio Plays: for *Boris Karloff's Creeps by Night.*

Television Plays: for *The Lone Ranger, Superman, Broken Arrow, Perry Mason, 77 Sunset Strip, Death Valley Days, Tarzan, and The FBI* series.

*

Bibliography: "The Further Adventures of Robert Leslie Bellem; or, The Bellem-Adams Connection" by Steven Mertz, in *Xenophile* (St. Louis), March-April 1978.

Manuscript Collection: University of California at Los Angeles.

*　　*　　*

Thanks to Raymond Chandler, the private eye became firmly established in the role of Arthurian knight errant, but if Philip Marlowe is Sir Galahad, then Robert Leslie Bellem's Dan Turner is the court jester. In hundreds of Dan Turner pulp stories published between 1934 and 1950, Bellem combined the standard elements of the hard-boiled tale with a zany style to create one of the most offbeat series in the history of the genre.

Known as "Hollywood's hottest hawkshaw," Turner worked mainly for clients from the movie industry, beautiful starlets being his favorites. With a minimum of detective work but a maximum of wisecracks, scotch (always Vat 69), and romantic dalliances, Turner somehow always managed to nab the guilty party at the conclusion of each of his adventures. His crime-solving and amorous escapades made him one of the most popular of all pulp private eyes: following his debut in the June 1934 issue of *Spicy Detective* (a pulp that perfected the formula of blending tough-guy talk with sexual innuendo), he went on to appear in every issue of that magazine (whose name was later changed under pressure to the tamer *Speed Detective*) until its demise in 1947. He also starred in his own magazine, *Dan*

Turner, Hollywood Detective (later just *Hollywood Detective*), which ran between 1942 and 1950 and which often featured as many as five Turner tales in a single issue.

What elevates the Turner stories above their often silly plots and paper-thin characterizations is Bellem's genius in taking the traditional elements of the hard-boiled tale and pushing them to their limits (and beyond). Bellem mastered the tough-guy idiom but refused to take it as seriously as his predecessors (especially Carroll John Daly). In his clever hands, each Turner story becomes essentially a linguistic (and comic) variation on the hard-boiled tale, his style, an inventive concoction of slang, wisecracks, and colorful colloquialisms, transcending mere parody to become the main focus of interest itself rather than just a vehicle for the action or a simple exercise in satiric imitation.

Bellem was certainly no follower of Joseph T. Shaw's famous admonition to his *Black Mask* writers to "prune and cut"; embellish was his motto, especially in the frequent eye-popping descriptions of female pulchritude (standard in a Turner story). His adjectival extravagance notwithstanding, Bellem's narratives race by a breakneck speed, propelled by a headlong rush of words and an overabundance of alliterative phrases ("The pooch yelped piteously as the porky slob's brogan booted him in the brisket"). Private eyes normally employ slang, but few do it so relentlessly as Turner, who never chooses a simple word where he can find a more colorful one: cigarettes become "gaspers," women "wrens" and "cupcakes," breasts "whatcha-callems," and "thingumbobs," guns "roscoes" and "rodneys" that bark "Chow-Chow" and sneeze "Ka-Chowp! Chowp! Chowp!" Bellem even rivals Chandler in the use of colorful similes, especially in his descriptions of the corpses that litter his stories (e.g. "dead as a Hitler promise"; "dead as a cannibal's conscience"; "deader than the chicken in a hard-boiled egg").

Dan Turner wasn't Bellem's only creation; under his own name as well as several wacky pseudonyms (Jerome Severs Perry, Justin Case, Ellery Watson Calder, Harcourt Weems, among others), he cranked out perhaps as many as 3000 stories, many featuring private eyes cut from the same cloth as Turner, though none equalled Turner's popularity or his unique brand of zaniness. While it would be inaccurate to include Bellem in a list of the most talented pulp writers of the 1930's and 1940's, his linguistic flair, narrative energy, and sheer comic exuberance nevertheless resulted in one of the most entertaining of all pulp mystery series.

—David Geherin

———

BENJAMIN, Paul. *See* **AUSTER, Paul.**

———

BENNETT, John. *See* **LUTZ, John.**

———

BENNETT, Margot. British. Born in Lenzie, Scotland, in 1912. Educated at schools in Scotland and Australia. Married Richard Bennett in 1938; one daughter and three sons. Worked as an advertising copywriter in Sydney and London in the 1930's. Nurse in Spanish Civil War. Recipient: Crime Writers Association award, 1958. *Died 6 December 1980.*

CRIME PUBLICATIONS

Novels (series: John Davies)

Time to Change Hats (Davies). London, Nicholson and Watson, 1945; New York, Doubleday, 1946.
Away Went the Little Fish (Davies). London, Nicholson and Watson, and New York, Doubleday, 1946.
The Golden Pebble. London, Nicholson and Watson, 1948.
The Widow of Bath. London, Eyre and Spottiswoode, and New York, Doubleday, 1952.
Farewell Crown and Good-Bye King. London, Eyre and Spottiswoode, 1953; New York, Walker, 1961.
The Man Who Didn't Fly. London, Eyre and Spottiswoode, 1955; New York, Harper, 1956.
Someone from the Past. London, Eyre and Spottiswoode, and New York, Dutton, 1958.
That Summer's Earthquake. London, Eyre and Spottiswoode, 1964.

Uncollected Short Stories

"An Old-Fashioned Poker for My Uncle's Head," in *Magazine of Fantasy and Science Fiction* (New York), 1946.
"No Bath for the Browns," in *Alfred Hitchcock Presents: Stories Not for the Nervous.* New York, Random House, 1965.

OTHER PUBLICATIONS

Novels

The Long Way Back. London, Lane, 1954; New York, Coward McCann, 1955.
The Furious Masters. London, Eyre and Spottiswoode, 1968.

Plays

Screenplays: *The Crowning Touch*, 1959; *The Man Who Liked Funerals*, 1959.

Television Plays: *Emergency Ward Ten* series (20 episodes); *The Sun Divorce*, 1956; *The Widow of Bath*, from her own novel, 1959; *The Third Man* series (2 episodes), 1960; *Maigret* series (8 episodes), 1960–64; *They Met in a City* series (1 episode), 1961; *Killer in the Band*, 1962; *The Flying Swan* series (1 episode), 1965; *The Big Spender*, 1965; *The Tungsten Ring*, 1966; *Honey Lane* series (7 episodes), 1968.

Other

The Intelligent Woman's Guide to Atomic Radiation. London, Penguin, 1964.

*

Margot Bennett commented (1980):
When I wrote my first book, *Time to Change Hats*, I tried the novelty of combining comedy with the obligatory murder. This gave me a good start—but the book was too long. *The Widow of Bath* has an entirely plausible and novel plot, but it was low on comedy and had too many twists. My best books were the last two. *The Man Who Didn't Fly* has an unusual plot and a set of

people I believed in. In the same way, *Someone from the Past* had five characters that I might have met anywhere. The best of all my people was the girl Nancy. She was kind and cruel, and loyal and bitchy. She was a ready liar, with a sharp tongue, but she was brave and real. All through my books, the best I have done is to make the people real.

* * *

Margot Bennett's work is impossible to categorise; indeed not one of her books can be described as classic detection or thriller or psychological suspense story; they each display a rare mixture of these elements, and may be enjoyed as much by the reader who is fascinated by the puzzles as by the reader whose interest mainly lies in the examination of human relationships leading to a criminal situation.

Her early detective novels demonstrated conclusively that the mystery factor need not stifle the social background or the development of strong character studies. The unsettled post-war atmosphere, the desperate struggle to build new relationships between people, and many other nuances show the deft skill of Margot Bennett's writing. Of her work following *Time to Change Hats* and *Away Went the Little Fish*, it is no easy task to decide upon pride of place between *The Widow of Bath* and *The Man Who Didn't Fly*.

The Widow of Bath has as its central character Hugh Everton, betrayed and imprisoned in the past and gradually adjusting his life to a stagnant respectability as a reporter for a restaurant guide. Alternatively, the central character might be Lucy, the wife of Mr. Justice Bath; she is completely without scruples, of a physical perfection which ensnares everyone with whom she comes into contact, and whom Everton has found to be "luxurious, greedy, mercenary, unscrupulous, selfish, faithless, ambitious and lax." Then again, in spite of the fact that the elderly judge is shot in the early pages, his incorruptibility and his need for a legally clear conscience are dominant features of the book. Bennett gives considerable weight to each of her characters; there is not a cardboard figure among them. This applies also to the hangers-on in the judge's retinue, the evil Atkinson who has reappeared with Lucy from Everton's past, and the oily public-school figure of the necrophile Cady. The background and atmosphere of a seedy resort, used as the centre of a vile criminal activity stemming directly from the aftermath of war, is conveyed to perfection. The mystery of the judge's death, and a further murder, exists almost as a parallel plot to the main mystery of what is actually going on in the town. In due course, however, they are beautifully dovetailed.

The Man Who Didn't Fly is, yet again, a novel of character. The fact that four men set off to fly to Ireland, but only three are on the plane when it crashes, is the basis of a most original mystery—which one did not fly? was he murdered? and if so who murdered him? This would in itself have made a sufficiently acceptable plot for many crime writers, but Bennett shows us the events leading up to the flight and portrays the relationships between the principal characters with a dexterity possessed by few novelists.

Throughout her regrettably short list of books, Bennett's technical originality and literary craftsmanship depict love and hate, absurdity and helplessness, humour and suspense. She does it by using a devastating wit, a capacity for crackling dialogue and repartee, and an incredible facility for summing up a person or place or situation with an exquisitely apt stroke of her pen.

—Melvyn Barnes

BENSON, Ben(jamin). American. Born in Boston, Massachusetts, in 1915. Educated at Suffolk University Law School, Boston. Served in the United States Army, 1943–45: Purple Heart, two battle stars; seriously wounded and confined to hospital for three years; began writing as therapy. Married; one daughter. Tea salesman; self-employed writer after 1949. Member, Board of Directors, Mystery Writers of America. *Died 29 April 1959.*

CRIME PUBLICATIONS

Novels (series: Trooper Ralph Lindsay; Detective Inspector Wade Paris)

Beware the Pale Horse (Paris). New York, Mill, 1951; London, Muller, 1952.
Alibi at Dusk (Paris). New York, Mill, 1951; London, Corgi, 1952.
Lily in Her Coffin (Paris). New York, Mill, 1952; London, Boardman, 1954.
Stamped for Murder (Paris). New York, Mill, 1952; London, Gannet, 1955.
Target in Taffeta (Paris). New York, Mill, 1953; London, Collins, 1955.
The Venus Death (Lindsay). New York, Mill, 1953; London, Muller, 1954.
The Girl in the Cage (Lindsay). New York, Mill, 1954; London, Collins, 1955.
The Burning Fuse (Paris). New York, Mill, 1954; London, Collins, 1956.
Broken Shield (Lindsay). New York, Mill, 1955; London, Collins, 1957.
The Silver Cobweb (Lindsay). New York, Mill, 1955; London, Collins, 1956.
The Ninth Hour (Paris). New York, Mill, 1956; London, Collins, 1957.
The Black Mirror. New York, Mill, 1957; London, Collins, 1958.
The Running Man (Lindsay). New York, Mill, 1957; London, Collins, 1958.
The Affair of the Exotic Dancer (Paris). New York, Mill, 1958.
The Blonde in Black (Paris). New York, Mill, 1958; London, Collins, 1959.
The End of Violence (Lindsay). New York, Mill, and London, Collins, 1959.
Seven Steps East (Lindsay). New York, Mill, 1959.
The Frightened Ladies (novelets). New York, Mill, 1960.
The Huntress Is Dead (Paris). New York, Mill, 1960.

Uncollected Short Stories

"Night-Blooming Cereus," in *Street and Smith's Detective Story Magazine* (New York), May 1947.
"Killer in the House," in *Butcher, Baker, Murder-Maker.* New York, Knopf, 1954.
"The Big Kiss-Off," in *Eat, Drink, and Be Buried,* edited by Rex Stout. New York, Viking Press, 1956; as *For Tomorrow We Die,* London, Macdonald, 1958.
"Somebody Has to Make a Move," in *The Second Mystery Bedside Book,* edited by John Creasey. London, Hodder and Stoughton, 1961.

Other

Hoboes of America: Sensational Life Story and Epic of Life on the Road, by Hobo Benson. New York, Hobo News, 1942.

* * *

Writers of police procedural mysteries—e.g., Ed McBain, Elizabeth Linington, and John Creasey—have written mostly of urban crime. Ben Benson is an exception, generally avoiding the city in his two series about Wade Paris and Ralph Lindsay of the Massachusetts State Police. Benson's protagonists even appear uncomfortable in cities. In *Stamped for Murder* Paris is uncharacteristically careless, obeying the instructions of an anonymous phone caller in "Eastern City" (Benson's Boston) to go to a crowded nightclub, where he is stabbed. Lindsay seems out of place in Times Square where he trails a suspect during *The Running Man.*

It was more than his rural settings that set Benson apart from his competitors. They adopted a documentary approach, often including facsimiles of police records—e.g., fingerprint cards and arrest sheets. They used criminal argot and usually had their detectives juggle several cases at the same time. Though Benson had done considerable research (with the full cooperation of the Massachusetts Police), he never attempted to overwhelm the reader with details. His realism was achieved more subtly by authentic bits of dialogue and shared thoughts that rang true, what Anthony Boucher called, "a sympathetic comprehension of the policeman-as-human being," praising *Target in Taffeta* for its "reader-character intimacy." If it was less realistic of Benson to have his policemen work on only one case at a time, it also allowed the reader to care more about its resolution.

Benson was especially good at depicting young people, and the immaturity and vulnerability of his rookie State Trooper, Ralph Lindsay, adds to the interest of his series. He is quick to lose his temper and become emotionally involved with suspects, permitting himself in *The End of Violence* to be accused of police brutality. He is occasionally rebellious against authority, and intolerant of the older trooper who does not wear his uniform as smartly as he does. But he is always brave and dedicated, willingly posing as a juvenile delinquent in *The Girl in the Cage* to get evidence against a brutal young gang.

Dubbed "Old Icewater" by his colleagues, Wade Paris is much more mature and almost invulnerable. He is very cool under stress, as in *The Ninth Hour,* in which he must free hostages taken during an attempted prison break, and "Somebody Has to Make a Move," where he keeps vigil outside a house in which a cop-killer is trapped. In addition to being patient and fearless, Paris seldom shows fatigue. He is careful not to become involved with suspects, thus appearing immune to the charms of attractive females. His traits led the critic Avis De Voto to say, "We'd enjoy seeing Paris develop a few human weaknesses."

Yet, Paris is not without emotion, either personally or professionally. True, his sex life is treated discreetly, in keeping with his times. He reacts angrily to political pressure and the argument that, since the "people" pay his salary, he must treat them obsequiously rather than with his customary firm politeness.

It would have been interesting to see how Paris and Lindsay might have developed. However, Benson's untimely death ended a career of considerable achievement and even greater promise.

—Marvin Lachman

———

BENTLEY, E(dmund) C(lerihew). British. Born in Shepherds Bush, London, 10 July 1875. Educated at St. Paul's School, London; Merton College, Oxford 1894–98 (scholar; President, Oxford Union, 1898), B.A.; Inner Temple, London, called to the Bar, 1902. Married Violet Boileau in 1902 (died 1949); two sons, including the writer Nicolas Bentley. Staff member, *Daily News,* London, 1902–12; leader writer, *Daily Telegraph,* 1912–34; retired in 1934, but returned as Chief Literary Critic, *Daily Telegraph,* 1940–47. *Died 30 March 1956.*

CRIME PUBLICATIONS

Novels (series: Philip Trent)

Trent's Last Case. London, Nelson, 1913; as *The Woman in Black,* New York, Century, 1913; revised edition, New York and London, Knopf, 1929.
Trent's Own Case, with H. Warner Allen. London, Constable, and New York, Knopf, 1936.
Elephant's Work: An Enigma. London, Hodder and Stoughton, and New York, Knopf, 1950; as *The Chill,* New York, Dell, 1953.
The Scoop, and Behind the Screen, with others. London, Gollancz, 1983.

Short Stories

Trent Intervenes. London, Nelson, and New York, Knopf, 1938.

Uncollected Short Stories

"Greedy Night," in *Stories of Detection,* edited by R. W. Jepson. London, Longman, 1939.
"The Ministering Angel," in *To the Queen's Taste,* edited by Ellery Queen. Boston, Little Brown, 1946.
"The Genuine Tabard," in *Ellery Queen's Mystery Magazine* (New York), November 1950.
"The Sweet Shot," in *Ellery Queen's Mystery Magazine* (New York), July 1952.
"The Feeble Folk," in *Ellery Queen's Mystery Magazine* (New York), March 1953.

OTHER PUBLICATIONS

Verse

Biography for Beginners (as E. Clerihew). London, Laurie, 1905.
More Biography. London, Methuen, 1929.
Baseless Biography. London, Constable, 1939.
Clerihews Complete. London, Laurie, 1951; as *The Complete Clerihews,* New York, Oxford University Press, 1981.

Other

Peace Year in the City, 1918–1919: An Account of the Outstanding Events in the City of London During Peace Year. Privately printed, 1920.
Those Days: An Autobiography. London, Constable, 1940.
Far Horizon: A Biography of Hester Dowden, Medium and Psychic Investigator. London and New York, Rider, 1951.

Editor, *More Than Somewhat,* by Damon Runyon. London, Constable, 1937.
Editor, *Damon Runyon Presents Futhermore.* London, Constable, 1938.
Editor, *The Best of Runyon.* New York, Stokes, 1938.
Editor, *The Second Century of Detective Stories.* London, Hutchinson, 1938.

* * *

Most writers who attempt novels usually improve their skills with time and experience. E.C. Bentley, with over a decade of professional journalism and a book of nonsense verse behind him, reversed this process with his first novel, *Trent's Last Case.* I venture to suggest that not only is this work the best "first" produced by anyone writing in the mystery genre, but that it is also one of the best mystery novels of all time.

The detective story in those days—particularly in the novel form—was in a virtual state of wilderness. In his autobiography, *Those Days,* Bentley stated that *Trent's Last Case* was a conscious reaction against the sterility and artificiality into which much of the detection writing of the day had sunk. "It does not seem to have been noticed that *Trent's Last Case* is not so much a detective story as an exposure of detective stories. . . it should be possible, I thought, to write a detective story in which the detective was recognizable as a human being." Bentley's attempt to "expose" the detective story was ineffective and ignored by most commentators, who have viewed this novel in a serious and straightforward manner. In terms of the characterizations in *Trent's Last Case,* Bentley was closer to the mark. His central character, Philip Trent, a youngish, untidy-looking artist, has been retained by a prominent London newspaper to investigate the sensational murder of a wealthy financier. Trent, unlike Dupin or Sherlock Holmes, is fallible. During his investigation he falls in love with the victim's widow—who is also the chief suspect. When he concludes his efforts, he discovers that his ingenious solution is completely wrong.

The popularity of *Trent's Last Case* through the years has been awesome. It has generated 3 film versions, a radio dramatization, and many reprints. Now, after the passage of over 60 years, Bentley's unprecedented masterpiece remains mint-fresh, witty, literate, immensely appealing, and an exhilarating reading experience. Unquestionably, *Trent's Last Case* is a great and enduring detective novel.

Bentley's demanding journalistic career, unfortunately, left little opportunity for further crime fiction efforts for too many years. A breakthrough came with a short story "Greedy Night," a take-off on Dorothy L. Sayer's novel *Gaudy Night,* and features Lord Peter Wimsey. Ellery Queen called it "the finest detective parody of our time." A long awaited and hoped for sequel to *Trent's Last Case* was finally published in 1936. *Trent's Own Case* was written in collaboration with H(erbert) Warner Allen—a writer with several minor mystery novels to his credit. It starts with the discovery of an elderly philanthropist found shot in the back in his bedroom, and the only clue points straight to Philip Trent. *Trent's Own Case,* it must be admitted, is hardly the equal of its illustrious predecessor, but it

is an excellent detective novel of considerable skill and depth. *Trent Intervenes* is a collection of 12 short stories that displays its author's ability to perform notable work in the short form. Several of these stories have become anthology favorites. "The Ministering Angel" is an uncollected Trent short story which Ellery Queen thought one of Bentley's most satisfying efforts.

Bentley's last novel, *Elephant's Work,* concerns a protagonist whose pursuit of a master criminal is complicated by his own amnesia. Its creation was inspired by John Buchan in 1916, and is dedicated to his memory. Many detective story writers, including Allingham, Blake, and Innes, turned their attention to the thriller form at the start of World War II. Here, belatedly, is Bentley's sole essay in this genre. Most of the reviewers thought it was below standard, but it is a literate, exciting, and highly readable thriller that is not unworthy of Bentley's talent.

—Charles Shibuk

BENTON, John L. *See* **DANIELS, Norman A.**

BERCKMAN, Evelyn (Domenica). American. Born in Philadelphia, Pennsylvania, 18 October 1900. Educated at Columbia University, New York. Concert pianist and composer: compositions include the ballets *From the Odyssey* and *County Fair* and other works. Lived in London after 1960. *Died 18 September 1978.*

CRIME PUBLICATIONS

Novels

The Evil of Time. New York, Dodd Mead, 1954; London, Eyre and Spottiswoode, 1955.
The Beckoning Dream. New York, Dodd Mead, 1955; London, Eyre and Spottiswoode, 1956; as *Worse Than Murder,* New York, Dell, 1957.
The Strange Bedfellow. New York, Dodd Mead, 1956; London, Eyre and Spottiswoode, 1957; as *Jewel of Death,* New York, Pyramid, 1968.
The Blind Villain. New York, Dodd Mead, and London, Eyre and Spottiswoode, 1957; as *House of Terror,* New York, Dell, 1960; as *A Hidden Malice,* New York, Belmont, n.d.
The Hovering Darkness. New York, Dodd Mead, 1957; London, Eyre and Spottiswoode, 1958.
No Known Grave. New York, Dodd Mead, 1958; London, Eyre and Spottiswoode, 1959.
Lament for Four Brides. New York, Dodd Mead, 1959; London, Eyre and Spottiswoode, 1960.
Do You Know This Voice? New York, Dodd Mead, 1960; London, Eyre and Spottiswoode, 1961.
Blind-Girl's-Buff. New York, Dodd Mead, and London, Eyre and Spottiswoode, 1962.
A Thing That Happens to You. New York, Dodd Mead, 1964; as *Keys from a Window,* London, Eyre and Spottiswoode, 1965.
A Simple Case of Ill-Will. London, Eyre and Spottiswoode, 1964; New York, Dodd Mead, 1965.

Stalemate. London, Eyre and Spottiswoode, and New York, Doubleday, 1966.

A Case in Nullity. London, Eyre and Spottiswoode, 1967; New York, Doubleday, 1968.

The Heir of Starvelings. New York, Doubleday, 1967; London, Eyre and Spottiswoode, 1968.

The Long Arm of the Prince. London, Hale, 1968.

She Asked for It. New York, Doubleday, 1969; London, Hamish Hamilton, 1970.

The Voice of Air. New York, Doubleday, 1970; London, Hale, 1971.

A Finger to Her Lips. London, Hale, and New York, Doubleday, 1971.

The Stake in the Game. London, Hamish Hamilton, 1971; New York, Doubleday, 1973.

The Fourth Man on the Rope. London, Hamish Hamilton, and New York, Doubleday, 1972.

The Victorian Album. London, Hamish Hamilton, and New York, Doubleday, 1973.

Wait. London, Hamish Hamilton, 1973; as *Wait, Just You Wait,* New York, Doubleday, 1973.

Indecent Exposure. London, Hamish Hamilton, 1975; as *The Nightmare Chase,* New York, Doubleday, 1975.

The Blessed Plot. London, Hamish Hamilton, 1976; as *The Crown Estate,* New York, Doubleday, 1976.

Be All and End All. London, Hamish Hamilton, 1976; as *Journey's End,* New York, Doubleday, 1977.

OTHER PUBLICATIONS

Other

Nelson's Dear Lord: A Portrait of St. Vincent. London, Macmillan, 1962.

The Hidden Navy. London, Hamish Hamilton, 1973.

Creators and Destroyers of the English Navy. London, Hamish Hamilton, 1974.

Victims of Piracy: The Admiralty Court 1575–1678. London, Hamish Hamilton, 1979.

*

Manuscript Collection: Mugar Memorial Library, Boston University.

* * *

Evelyn Berckman's modest output was a most acceptable mixture of the classic style and the psychological thriller, with attention to detail and careful literary craftsmanship. She showed herself at home with the more conventional detective themes—one recalls *A Simple Case of Ill-Will,* where quarrels at a bridge club lead to foul play, with some neat character sketches along the way. She was equally at home in the gothic style—*The Heir of Starvelings,* with her genteel heroine surrounded by an atmosphere of menace, not only displays her ability to out-write many of today's so-called gothic novelists, but shows very clearly the painstaking research which is one of her most enduring features.

The Victorian Album, perhaps her most interesting work, illustrates her multi-faceted talents; in a strange and eerie mixture of detection and the supernatural, combined with a strong line of suspense, we share the innermost thoughts of a latent medium impelled by an old album she finds in her attic to delve back into a Victorian murder. We see initial curiosity

turn into inexorable pursuit of truth, leading to a disturbing climax.

A consistent feature of Berckman's novels was her ability to present credible characters. In some she explores complex emotional relationships, like the ménage of the ageing actress in *She Asked for It,* while some others stem from her interest in art, history, and archaeology without leaving an impression of mustiness.

Berckman's multiplicity of talents and styles makes it impossible to "type-cast" her in any one area of crime fiction, which might account for her undeserved neglect by historians of the genre.

—Melvyn Barnes

———

BERKELEY, Anthony. Pseudonym for A(nthony) B(erkeley) Cox; also wrote as Francis Iles; A. Monmouth Platts. British. Born in Watford, Hertfordshire, 5 July 1893. Educated at Sherborne School; University College, London. Served in the British Army during World War I. Married Helen Macgregor in 1932 (died). Contributor to *Punch* and *The Humorist,* London, and reviewer for *John O'London's Weekly,* 1938, and, as Francis Iles, reviewer, London *Daily Telegraph,* in the 1930's, *Sunday Times,* London, after World War II, and *Manchester Guardian,* later *Guardian,* from mid-1950's to 1970. *Died 9 March 1971.*

CRIME PUBLICATIONS

Novels (series: Ambrose Chitterwick; Roger Sheringham)

The Layton Court Mystery (Sheringham; published anonymously). London, Jenkins, 1925; New York, Doubleday, 1929.

The Wychford Poisoning Case (Sheringham). London, Collins, 1926; New York, Doubleday, 1930.

Roger Sheringham and the Vane Mystery. London, Collins, 1927; as *The Mystery at Lovers' Cave,* New York, Simon and Schuster, 1927.

Mr. Priestley's Problem (as A.B. Cox). London, Collins, 1927; as *The Amateur Crime,* New York, Doubleday, 1928.

Cicely Disappears (as A. Monmouth Platts). London, Long, 1927.

The Silk Stocking Murders (Sheringham). London, Collins, and New York, Doubleday, 1928.

The Piccadilly Murder (Chitterwick). London, Collins, 1929; New York, Doubleday, 1930.

The Poisoned Chocolates Case (Sheringham; Chitterwick). London, Collins, and New York, Doubleday, 1929.

The Second Shot (Sheringham). London, Hodder and Stoughton, 1930; New York, Doubleday, 1931.

Top Storey Murder (Sheringham). London, Hodder and Stoughton, and New York, Doubleday, 1931.

The Floating Admiral, with others. London, Hodder and Stoughton, 1931; New York, Doubleday, 1932.

Murder in the Basement (Sheringham). London, Hodder and Stoughton, and New York, Doubleday, 1932.

Ask a Policeman, with others. London, Barker, and New York, Morrow, 1933.

Jumping Jenny (Sheringham). London, Hodder and Stoughton, 1933; as *Dead Mrs. Stratton,* New York, Doubleday, 1933; London, Hogarth Press, 1984.

Panic Party (Sheringham). London, Hodder and Stoughton, 1934; as *Mr. Pidgeon's Island,* New York, Doubleday, 1934.

Six Against the Yard, with others. London, Selwyn and Blount, 1936; as *Six Against Scotland Yard,* New York, Doubleday, 1936.

Trial and Error (Chitterwick). London, Hodder and Stoughton, and New York, Doubleday, 1937.

Not to Be Taken. London, Hodder and Stoughton, 1938; as *A Puzzle in Poison,* New York, Doubleday, 1938.

Death in the House. London, Hodder and Stoughton, and New York, Doubleday, 1939.

The Scoop, and Behind the Screen, with others. London, Gollancz, 1983.

Novels as Francis Iles

Malice Aforethought. London, Gollancz, and New York, Harper, 1931.

Before the Fact. London, Gollancz, and New York, Doubleday, 1932; revised edition, London, Pan, 1958.

As for the Woman. London, Jarrolds, and New York, Doubleday, 1939.

Uncollected Short Stories

"The Avenging Chance," in *The Best Detective Stories of the Year 1929.* London, Faber, 1930; as *The Best English Detective Stories of the Year,* edited by Ronald Knox and H. Harrington, New York, Liveright, 1930.

"Perfect Alibi," in *Radio Times* (London), 1 August 1930.

"Mr. Simpson Goes to the Dogs," in *Strand* (London), June 1934.

"Publicity Heroine," in *Missing from Their Homes.* London, Hutchinson, 1936.

"Outside the Law," in *Fifty Masterpieces of Mystery.* London, Odhams Press, 1937.

"White Butterfly," in *Fifty Famous Detectives of Fiction.* London, Odhams Press, 1938.

"The Wrong Jar," in *Detective Stories of Today,* edited by Raymond Postgate. London, Faber, 1940.

"Mr. Bearstowe Says...," in *The Saturday Book 3,* edited by Leonard Russell. London, Hutchinson, 1943.

"The Policeman Only Taps Once," in *Ellery Queen's Mystery Magazine* (New York), June 1951.

Uncollected Short Stories as Francis Iles

"Dark Journey," in *A Century of Horror Stories,* edited by Dennis Wheatley. London, Hutchinson, 1935.

"Sense of Humour," in *Strand* (London), October 1935.

"It Takes Two to Make a Hero," in *The Saturday Book 3,* edited by Leonard Russell. London, Hutchinson, 1943; revised edition, as "The Coward," in *Ellery Queen's Mystery Magazine* (New York), January 1953.

"Outside the Law," in *Ellery Queen's Mystery Magazine* (New York), June 1949.

OTHER PUBLICATIONS as A.B. COX

Novels

The Family Witch: An Essay in Absurdity. London, Jenkins, 1925.

The Professor on Paws. London, Collins, 1926; New York, Dial Press, 1927.

Short Stories

Brenda Entertains. London, Jenkins, 1925.

Play

Mr. Priestley's Adventure, adaptation of his own novel (produced Brighton, 1928; as *Mr. Priestley's Night Out,* produced London, 1928; also produced as *Mr. Priestley's Problem* and *Handcuffs for Two*).

Other

Jugged Journalism (sketches). London, Jenkins, 1925.

O England! London, Hamish Hamilton, 1934.

A Pocketful of One Hundred New Limericks. Privately printed, 1960.

*

Bibliography: "A Bibliography of the Works of Anthony Berkeley Cox (Francis Iles)," by Paul R. Moy, in *The Armchair Detective* No. 14 Summer 1981.

*   *   *

A.B. Cox wrote as both Anthony Berkeley and Francis Iles, in the latter case producing work which ensured him a distinguished place in the history of the crime novel as we know it today.

The typical detective novel of the 1920's was, on the whole, somewhat staid. It contained all the expected ingredients of systematic investigation, methodical questioning of suspects, examination of small clues, and so on. In this scene, like a herald of the Golden Age of detection, came "Anthony Berkeley" with his detective Roger Sheringham. His debut in 1925 with *The Layton Court Mystery* (published anonymously, but soon followed by many others under the Berkeley name) was praised by Howard Haycraft as bringing a "naturalistic quality that was a welcome and needed relief." In Roger Sheringham, Berkeley introduced an amateur detective who was loquacious, conceited, occasionally downright offensive, on good terms with the police, and something of a man-about-town with contacts in all the right places.

Infallibility was not one of Sheringham's virtues. In *The Poisoned Chocolates Case,* Chief Inspector Moresby of Scotland Yard (a regular Berkeley character) recounts a murder case to the assembled members of the Crimes Circle, who then in turn produce alternative solutions. Berkeley developed the novel from his short story "The Avenging Chance," a brilliant model of construction which has appeared in many anthologies. The novel stands on its own, however, as a clear demonstration of Berkeley's ingenious mind. It also shows his satirical bent, as he lampoons the Great Detective syndrome and pokes gentle fun at the London Detection Club (of which he was Honorary Secretary). The debunking of Sheringham is a nice touch, it being unusual for writers of the time to portray their detective heroes as anything other than invincible, and the triumph of the hen-pecked little Ambrose Chitterwick is nothing short of a brainwave. Chitterwick appeared in other Berkeley novels, but never to such magnificent effect. *The Poisoned Chocolates Case* is a classic.

Berkeley's tendency to laugh behind his own hand at the rather stuffy conventions of detective fiction was evident throughout his books. So too was his penchant for the farcical, as seen in *Mr. Priestley's Problem* or in that delicious scene toward the end of *Trial and Error* when mild-mannered Mr. Lawrence Todhunter punches the hangman on the chin. To such examples may be added the pastiche short story "Holmes and the Dasher" (*Jugged Journalism*) and his collaboration with other members of The Detection Club in *Ask a Policeman*.

There are many admirable facets to Berkeley. One recalls his ability to enlist our sympathy for the murderer, often by creating murder victims so disagreeable that we feel bumping-off to be too good for them. He was also able to portray chinless young men and flappers, so shallow and superficial in many novels and plays of the time, yet inject into them such life that they emerged from the pages as credible characters. His talent sometimes extended to producing a moving study which we feel to be an "inverted" crime novel, then stunning the reader with an entirely unpredictable ending which turns the whole thing into a "whodunit." His sound knowledge of police procedure, and his mastery of legal points, indicated an interest in criminology which showed through many of the novels, and was evident also in his reconstructions of famous crimes. Particularly noteworthy are his second novel, *The Wychford Poisoning Case* based on the Florence Maybrick affair.

It was in 1930, in his preface to *The Second Shot*, that Berkeley asserted his significant views on the likely future pattern of crime fiction. He felt that "the detective story is in the process of developing into the novel. . . holding its readers less by mathematical than psychological ties. The puzzle element will no doubt remain, but it will become a puzzle of character rather than a puzzle of time, place, motive, and opportunity." *The Second Shot* was not itself a particularly good example of what Berkeley was suggesting, but his ideas were fully developed one year later (as Francis Iles) with the masterpiece *Malice Aforethought*. From the first page, we know that Dr. Bickleigh intends to murder his wife—just as on the first page of Iles's second book, *Before the Fact*, we are told that Lina Aysgarth's husband is a murderer.

This was something different, with the mind of the murderer established as more important that his identity. We are shown murder not as a sensational subject, but planned in the cosy drawing-rooms of English suburbia or at tennis parties. With a nice mixture of cynicism and realism Iles allows us to accompany the murderer, or the victim, through a succession of twists and turns which make his plots even more enthralling than those of the classic detective novel. The reader finds it impossible not to identify himself with the protagonist—certainly in Bickleigh's case—and not to feel personally the pressures and fears. The Iles novels are, however, very far from the documentary crime novel or the police procedural story which later writers developed from his ideas. He shows, with stunning panache, that there are countless ways of shocking the reader while completely eliminating the "whodunit" element.

Iles was the innovator, the father of those techniques so evident in much of today's crime fiction; Berkeley was the dry-humoured, literary, clever exponent of detective novels in which he rebelled against the stolid conventions. Cox, the man behind both, will for long remain a key figure in the history of the genre.

—Melvyn Barnes

———

BETTERIDGE, Don. *See* **NEWMAN, Bernard.**

———

BIGGERS, Earl Derr. American. Born in Warren, Ohio, 26 August 1884. Educated at Harvard University, Cambridge, Massachusetts, B.A. 1907. Married Eleanor Ladd in 1912; one son. Began career in journalism as staff member, Boston *Traveler*, 1907. *Died 5 April 1933.*

CRIME PUBLICATIONS

Novels (series: Detective Sergeant/Inspector Charlie Chan)

Seven Keys to Baldpate. Indianapolis, Bobbs Merrill, 1913; London, Mills and Boon, 1914.
Love Insurance. Indianapolis, Bobbs Merrill, 1914.
Inside the Lines, with Robert Welles Ritchie. Indianapolis, Bobbs Merrill, 1915.
The Agony Column. Indianapolis, Bobbs Merrill, 1916; as *Second Floor Mystery,* New York, Grosset and Dunlap, 1930.
The House Without a Key (Chan). Indianapolis, Bobbs Merrill, 1925; London, Harrap, 1926.
The Chinese Parrot (Chan). Indianapolis, Bobbs Merrill, 1926; London, Harrap, 1927.
Fifty Candles. Indianapolis, Bobbs Merrill, 1926.
Behind That Curtain (Chan). Indianapolis, Bobbs Merrill, and London, Harrap, 1928.
The Black Camel (Chan). Indianapolis, Bobbs Merrill, 1929; London, Cassell, 1930.
Charlie Chan Carries On. Indianapolis, Bobbs Merrill, 1930; London, Cassell, 1931.
Keeper of the Keys (Chan). Indianapolis, Bobbs Merrill, and London, Cassell, 1932.

Short Stories

Earl Derr Biggers Tells Ten Stories. Indianapolis, Bobbs Merrill, 1933.

OTHER PUBLICATIONS

Plays

If You're Only Human (produced 1912).
Inside the Lines (produced Baltimore and New York, 1915; London, 1917). Indianapolis, Bobbs Merrill, 1915; London, French, 1924.
A Cure for Curables, with Lawrence Whitman, adaptation of a story by Cora Harris (produced New York, 1918).
See-Saw, music by Louis A. Hirsch (produced New York, 1919).
Three's a Crowd, with Christopher Morley (produced New York, 1919; London, 1923).
The Ruling Passion, in *Reference Scenarios.* Hollywood, Palmer Institute of Authorship, 1924.

*   *   *

Earl Derr Biggers began as a newspaper columnist and playwright, and wrote his first successful mystery novel, *Seven Keys to Baldpate*, in 1913, followed by other mystery-romances cast in the melodramatic mold. But his contribution to the mystery-detective genre is his detective, Charlie Chan. Based on an actual Honolulu police detective, Chan was introduced in 1925 as a marked departure from the clichés of the sinister Chinese villain with *The House Without a Key* (often considered the best of the series), followed by five additional Chan novels, all initially published as serials in *The Saturday Evening Post*. The unassuming sleuth and his adventures were immediately successful and a sizeable "industry" of radio dramas, comic strips, and films grew up around the Chan character, manners, and methods. Chan soon acquired international repute, becoming, for better or for worse, the household name for any Chinese.

A member of the Honolulu Police Department, Chan works both in and away from Hawaii to build his reputation of tenacious sagacity in solving his baffling cases, crowded with suspects of every description. The pudgy, keen-eyed sleuth is a student of Chinese philosophy and in his terse, stilted, pidgin style quotes Confucian aphorisms to fit every occasion: "Eggs shouldn't dance with stones"; "The fool in a hurry drinks his tea with the fork." Chan's hybrid cultural character of race and national affiliation (Chinese, Chinese-Hawaiian, and assimilated American) brings to these puzzles—themselves compounds of national, cultural, ethnic, and generational elements—resources of cross-cultural acumen going beyond the more obvious Asian-American connections. In *The Chinese Parrot* Chan goes to California to look into the murder of a Chinese cook on a ranch. *Behind That Curtain* connects two killings sixteen years apart—one in London, one in San Francisco—through the only clue: a pair of Chinese slippers embroidered with Chinese characters. The setting of *The Black Camel* is Waikiki Beach, the scene of the crime in the stabbing of a famous film actress. *Charlie Chan Carries On* features ship-board suspense as Chan pursues a murderer on a round-the-world cruise in its final lap between San Francisco and Honolulu. The final adventure, *Keeper of the Keys,* takes Chan to Lake Tahoe where a flamboyant opera prima donna has been murdered; in this story Chan is able to discern motives because of his familiarity with differences between Chinese and American codes of justice.

Chan lore has recently begun to take on new meaning with the emergence of the study of popular culture as an academic subject. As a Chinese on the side of law and order, Chan was in part designed to counteract the image of the sinister or deviously clever Oriental which had dominated foreign adventure novels from the 19th century: E. Harcourt Burrage's Chinese Ching Ching, Sax Rohmer's Dr. Fu Manchu, and the Yellow Menace figures of *Detective Comics*. Chan's amiable if enigmatic persona prepared the way for other favorable images of the Oriental, which included Hugh Wiley's James Lee Wong, John Marquand's Mr. Moto, and Robert van Gulik's revival of the 7th century magistrate Judge Dee. Chan is a well-rounded figure, meditating and discoursing on questions of justice, liberty, right, tradition, and cultural identity, as well as on a range of ethical problems which often focus on racism. But it is the persistent polarity of Eastern and Western values that makes Chan such an intriguing man in terms of cross-cultural interaction. His cases interweave with the ambiguity and ambivalence of his cultural identity as an Americanized Chinese, and his struggle to maintain his traditional heritage under pressure of demands from a modern Western environment. The cross-cultural detective, manifest in such new creations as Harry Kemelman's Rabbi David Small, Arthur Upfield's Aboriginal police inspector Napoleon Bonaparte, and H.R.F. Keating's Indian C.I.D. Inspector Ghote have in common a venerable ancestor in Charlie Chan.

—Margaret J. King

BINGHAM, John (Michael Ward, Lord Clanmorris). British. Born in York, 3 November 1908. Educated at Cheltenham College, and in France and Germany. Served in the Royal Engineers, 1939–40. Married Madeleine Ebel in 1934 (died 1988); one son and one daughter, the writer Charlotte Bingham. Worked in the War Office, 1940–46, with the Control Commission in Germany, 1946–48, and in the Ministry of Defence, 1950–77. Reporter, Hull *Daily Mail*, after 1931, and picture editor and feature writer for *Sunday Dispatch,* London Chairman, Crime Writers Association, London, 1971–72. *Died 6 August 1988.*

CRIME PUBLICATIONS

Novels (series: Brock; Ducane)

My Name Is Michael Sibley. London, Gollancz, and New York, Dodd Mead, 1952.
Five Roundabouts to Heaven. London, Gollancz, 1953; as *The Tender Poisoner*, New York, Dodd Mead, 1953.
The Third Skin. London, Gollancz, and New York, Dodd Mead, 1954; as *Murder Is a Witch*, New York, Dell, 1957.
The Paton Street Case. London, Gollancz, 1955; as *Inspector Morgan's Dilemma*, New York, Dodd Mead, 1956.
Murder off the Record. New York, Dodd Mead, 1957; as *Marion*, London, Gollancz, 1958.
Murder Plan Six. London, Gollancz, 1958; New York, Dodd Mead, 1959.
Night's Black Agent. London, Gollancz, and New York, Dodd Mead, 1961.
A Case of Libel. London, Gollancz, 1963.
A Fragment of Fear. London, Gollancz, 1965; New York, Dutton, 1966.
The Double Agent (Ducane). London, Gollancz, 1967; New York, Dutton, 1967.
I Love, I Kill. London, Gollancz, 1968; as *Good Old Charlie*, New York, Simon and Schuster, 1969.
Vulture in the Sun (Ducane). London, Gollancz, 1971.
God's Defector. London, Macmillan, 1976; as *Ministry of Death*, New York, Walker, 1977.
The Marriage Bureau Murders. London, Macmillan, 1977.
Deadly Picnic. London, Macmillan, 1980; New York, State Mutual, 1982.
Brock. London, Gollancz, 1981.
Brock and the Defector. London, Gollancz, and New York, Doubleday, 1982.

Uncollected Short Stories

"A Smile for a Killer," in *Suspense* (London), September 1959.
"Murderer at Large," in *Ellery Queen's Mystery Magazine* (New York), January 1961.
"The Hangman's Fish," in *Ellery Queen's Mystery Magazine* (New York), March 1965.

OTHER PUBLICATIONS

Play

Radio Play: *Not My Pigeon,* 1977.

Other

The Hunting Down of Peter Manuel, Glasgow Multiple Murderer, with William Muncie. London, Macmillan, 1973.

*

John Bingham commented (1984):

I am not so much interested in who committed, say, the murder, but in the psychological build-up, whether the murder will, in fact, be committed, and whether the criminal will be caught. I do not describe sadistic scenes in detail, since I think this is pandering to only a section of the reading public, probably offends and upsets a larger section, and may spark off imitative action among some. Similarly, I do not describe sexual matters for the first two of the above reasons, and in any case it is better to imply certain events and allow the reader to use his or her own imagination: a description which might excite one reader may bore another. This assumption is based on the reasonable theory that the readers know what sex is all about.

Any small contribution I may have made in the crime novel field is partly due, I think, to fairly new and accurate descriptions of some police interrogation methods, and set a trend which was subsequently developed and bore fruit in some well-known and popular television series and characterisations, showing police officers and their methods as they often are. I have evolved no brilliant amateur detectives who solve crimes better than the police, because they do not exist, and, not having the same organisation, scientific equipment, and records, could not exist; nor are my detectives bumbling, amusing, sadistic, stupid, or whimsical. Most of them are overworked and human, and involved in normal hopes for promotion and normal family life.

*   *   *

"The world's full of people taking chances," a spymaster called Vandoren remarks sardonically to one of his agents in the closing pages of *God's Defector.* Vandoren, who appears earlier as Ducane in *The Double Agent* and *Vulture in the Sun,* is John Bingham's version of the chief of Britain's Secret Intelligence Service—the counterpart of Maugham's "R," Fleming's "M," and le Carré's "Control." "A concentrated force of pure ferocity, easily misinterpreted as malevolence," Vandoren is engaged in plotting the death of a Conservative MP turned traitor. His retort, meant to rebuke the agent who objects to his plan, is a particularly apt gloss on Bingham's work as a whole; for in his dozen crime novels and espionage thrillers written over a 25-year period, Bingham has drawn a compelling picture of a dangerous world full of people taking chances. Life, Bingham's novels suggest, is an exceedingly dangerous business—and not just for traitorous MP's. Especially for the unwary, the foolish, or those inclined to take the seemingly easy way out—but for the cunning, the cautious, and the farsighted as well—destruction lies all too close at hand. Unlike most mystery writers, who celebrate the sufficiency of rationality in a deceptive and dangerous world, Bingham explores the limits, the vulnerability of rational procedures.

The world of Bingham's fiction is a menacing one, in part, because there are some very nasty predators abroad in it. Men like Green, the blackmailing villain of *Night's Black Agent,* and Robert Draper, the murderer in *The Paton Street Case,* are quintessentially evil—brutal, vicious, cunning, sadistic, preternaturally alert both to potential danger and to the weaknesses of their prey. Both are nondescript in appearance—epitomizing the "banality of evil"—and utterly conscienceless; their criminality is simply a given. In other cases Bingham makes a gesture in the direction of explanation: in *The Marriage Bureau Murders* Shaw's criminal aggression can be traced to a destructive marriage. In other novels, the predators are foreign intelligence agents out to protect themselves from exposure, whether at the hands of persistent curious amateurs or opposing agents. Explicit in *A Fragment of Fear,* the division of the world into the hunters and the hunted is implicit throughout Bingham's work, especially since *Night's Black Agent,* published in 1961.

Bingham's is a dangerous world, too, because of the unsettling ease with which hatred, malice, or treachery can dissemble, even among friends of long standing, as in Bingham's first novel, *My Name Is Michael Sibley,* where the narrator successfully conceals for years his hatred of a bullying former schoolmate. In *I Love, I Kill,* the narrator comes to hate Paul King, who has stolen his girl from him and married her, but he feigns friendship for King and devotes himself to furthering King's acting career, convinced that if King becomes successful he will eventually divorce his wife, leaving her free to marry Charlie. In *Five Roundabouts to Heaven,* a married man plots the poisoning of his wife so that he can be free to marry a younger woman.

Throughout Bingham's fiction, the most trivial or ordinary acts turn out to have dangerous, even fatal, consequences. Sometimes it is years before the danger is precipitated; on other occasions the slip leads immediately to trouble. In *The Marriage Bureau Murders,* Sidney Shaw's ex-wife continues to carry his picture in her purse—and as a direct result Shaw is murdered. In *The Paton Street Case,* Chief Detective Inspector David Morgan decides, out of consideration for the person, to delay the arrest of a suspect until the last possible moment—and it leads to two unnecessary deaths. In *Five Roundabouts to Heaven* a woman, stirring in her sleep and reaching out for her husband, precipitates his decision to poison her. An indiscreet conversation in a pub years earlier leads the police to suspect Charles Maither of murder in *Good Old Charlie.* A boy, bullied at school, buys a knuckleduster and continues to carry it as a talisman into manhood but is seen disposing of it in a trash container following the fatal bludgeoning of a friend (*My Name Is Michael Sibley*). The act becomes a damaging bit of circumstantial evidence as the police build a plausible but false case against him.

In Bingham's world, the police are more likely to be part of what threatens the individual rather than a source of aid and protection. In *The Paton Street Case* Inspector Morgan, though portrayed sympathetically, disastrously mishandles the case. In *A Fragment of Fear,* however, it is stolid, suspicious, unimaginative policemen who endanger the narrator by refusing him needed protection, and in *My Name Is Michael Sibley* the narrator finds himself interrogated by officers whose principal interest is in closing out cases rather than discovering the truth of the matter. The murder in that novel remains unsolved at the end.

Luck has a great deal to do, finally, with survival in Bingham's world. Few characters, by means of their own exertions, can evade the determined efforts of the predators. James Compton (in *A Fragment of Fear*) survives only because Special Branch agents happen to pick up his captors before they can dispose of him. "We live in dangerous times," Compton concludes, reflecting on his ordeal. "All one can do is to keep the spear ready, and a feeble thing it is, touch the amulet, and hope for the best, and trust that, as in my case, the tribe can after all protect not only the tribe but the individual."

Bingham was one of the more original writers of suspense fiction to appear in the last 25 years. He was also one of the most varied. His absorption with character, his interest in the effects of crime, and his stunning descriptions of police interrogations, at which he must be acknowledged a master, distinguish his work. And equally to his credit, his novels do little to celebrate or perpetuate the exaggerated claims for functional rationality and the abductive method that characterize mystery fiction as a whole, particularly that part that is misleadingly termed "detection."

—R. Gordon Kelly

BIRKEN, Dolan. *See* **OLSEN, D.B.**

BLACK, Gavin. Pseudonym for Oswald (Morris) Wynd. Scottish. Born in Tokyo, Japan, 4 July 1913. Educated at American School, Tokyo; Atlantic City High School, New Jersey; Edinburgh University. Served in the British army, 1940–45; Lieutenant mentioned in despatches. Married Janet Muir. Since 1946 freelance writer. Agent: Curtis Brown Ltd., 575 Madison Avenue, New York, New York 10022, U.S.A.; or, Campbell Thomson and McLaughlin Ltd., 31 Newington Green, London N16 9 PU, England. Address: St. Adrian's Crail, Fife KY10 3SU, Scotland.

CRIME PUBLICATIONS

Novels (series Paul Harris in all books except *The Fatal Shadow*)

Suddenly, At Singapore.... London, Collins, 1961.
Dead Man Calling. London, Collins, and New York, Random House, 1962.
A Dragon for Christmas. London, Collins, and New York, Harper, 1963.
The Eyes Around Me. London, Collins, and New York, Harper, 1964.
You Want to Die, Johnny? London, Collins, and New York, Harper, 1966.
A Wind of Death. London, Collins, and New York, Harper, 1967.
The Cold Jungle. London, Collins, and New York, Harper, 1969.
A Time for Pirates. London, Collins, and New York, Harper, 1971.
The Bitter Tea. New York, Harper, 1972; London, Collins, 1973.
The Golden Cockatrice. London, Collins, 1974; New York, Harper, 1975.
A Big Wind for Summer. London, Collins, 1975; New York, Harper, 1976; as *Gale Force,* London, Fontana, 1978.
A Moon for Killers. London, Collins, 1976; as *Killer Moon,* London, Fontana, 1977.

Night Run from Java. London, Collins, 1979.
The Fatal Shadow. London, Collins, 1983.

Novels as Oswald Wynd

Death the Red Flower. London, Cassell, and New York, Harcourt Brace, 1965.
Walk Softly, Men Praying. London, Cassell, and New York, Harcourt Brace, 1967.
Sumatra Seven Zero. London, Cassell, and New York, Harcourt Brace, 1968.

OTHER PUBLICATIONS

Novels

Black Fountains. New York, Doubleday, 1947; London, Home and Van Thal, 1948.
Red Sun South. New York, Doubleday, 1948.
The Stubborn Flower. London, Joseph, 1949; as *Friend of the Family,* New York, Doubleday, 1949.
When Ape Is King. London, Home and Van Thal, 1949.
The Gentle Pirate. New York, Doubleday, 1951.
Stars in the Heather. Edinburgh, Blackwood, 1956.
Moon of the Tiger. London, Cassell, and New York, Doubleday, 1958.
Summer Can't Last. London, Cassell, 1960.
The Devil Came on Sunday. London, Cassell, and New York, Doubleday, 1961.
A Walk in the Long Dark Night. London, Cassell, 1962.
The Hawser Pirates. London, Cassell, and New York, Harcourt Brace, 1970.
The Forty Days. London, Collins, 1972; New York, Harcourt Brace, 1973.
The Ginger Tree. London, Collins, and New York, Harper, 1977.
The Blazing Air. New Haven, Connecticut, Ticknor and Fields, 1981.

Plays

Radio Plays: *Tomorrow All My Hopes,* 1951; *Satan and a House in the Country,* 1951; *Anna from the Jungle,* 1952; *A Medal for the Poachers,* 1954.

Television Play: *Killer Lie Waiting,* 1963; *The Ginger Tree* (from his own novel), 1989.

*

Manuscript Collection: Mugar Memorial Library, Boston University.

Gavin Black comments:
I really can't think of much to say about my suspense product; you either like it or you don't. Fortunately quite a few people seem to like it, but I can't do the bang bang action stuff which makes for the really big sales. Can't read the products of the boys who do it so successfully. I like characters who at least vaguely resemble human beings.

*   *   *

Gavin Black is a Scotsman who knows and writes of the Far East quite as if he were a native of Malaysia. In *A Dragon for Christmas,* one of the most entertaining as well as thought-provoking mysteries of its year, Black took the reader into

Red China, not with spies and counter-spies, but with a nice, sensible young fellow, Paul Harris, whose project was to sell to the Chinese engines for their river boats. Another salesman, the pragmatic and mysterious Mr. Kishimura, is also on his way to China. However, he has another reason for his voyage: his partner has vanished there and he intends to find out why. The story moves at a quick pace, and is witty, wise, and quietly probing without interrupting the suspense.

A like pattern was followed in subsequent books. The Scotsman in a foreign place was always basic, whether being harried in Hong Kong as in *The Eyes Around Me,* or taking Malaysian citizenship as his business prospered and he made his home there. In these years, newsmen covering the Far East were aware of the undercurrents marking troubles to come, and other novelists, like William J. Lederer, Eugene Burdick, and Graham Greene, were writing about the Far East. Meanwhile Black was adroitly educating his readers as to what was happening and about to happen.

In *A Big Wind for Summer* Paul Harris has returned to Scotland. Instead of the islands of Malaysia, he was travelling to the Outer Hebrides, which could become just as well known and as beautifully explored as the others.

—Dorothy B. Hughes

BLACK, Lionel. Pseudonym for Dudley Barker; also wrote as Anthony Matthews. British. Born in London, 25 March 1910. Educated at Bournemouth School, 1920–29; Oriel College, Oxford, B.A. 1933. Served in the Royal Air Force, 1941–45: Wing Commander, mentioned in despatches. Married Muriel Irene Griffiths in 1935; one son and one daughter. Reporter and news editor, *Evening Standard,* London, 1933–39; reporter and features editor, *Daily Herald,* London, 1940–41, 1945–54; associate editor, *John Bull,* London, 1954–59; staff member of Curtis Brown Ltd., literary agents, London, 1960–65. From 1965 freelance writer and broadcaster. *Died in 1980.*

CRIME PUBLICATIONS

Novels (series: Superintendent Francis Foy; Emma Greaves; Kate Theobald)

A Provincial Crime. London, Cassell, 1960.
Chance to Die (Greaves). London, Cassell, 1965.
The Bait (Greaves). London, Cassell, 1966.
Two Ladies in Verona (Greaves). London, Cassell, 1967; as *The Lady Is a Spy,* New York, Paperback Library, 1969.
Outbreak. London, Cassell, and New York, Stein and Day, 1968.
Swinging Murder (Theobald). London, Cassell, 1969; (as Anthony Matthews) New York, Walker, 1969.
Breakaway (Foy). London, Collins, 1970; as *Flood,* New York, Stein and Day, 1971.
Death Has Green Fingers (Theobald). London, Collins, 1971; (as Anthony Matthews) New York, Walker, 1971.
Ransom for a Nude (Foy). London, Collins, and New York, Stein and Day, 1972.
The Life and Death of Peter Wade (Foy). London, Collins, 1973; New York, Stein and Day, 1974.
Death by Hoax (Theobald). London, Collins, 1974; New York, Avon, 1978.

Arafat Is Next! New York, Stein and Day, and London, Collins, 1975.
A Healthy Way to Die (Theobald). London, Collins, 1976; New York, Avon, 1979.
The Foursome. London, Collins, 1978.
The Penny Murders (Theobald). London, Collins, and New York, Avon, 1979.
The Eve of the Wedding (Theobald). London, Collins, 1980; New York, Avon, 1981.
The Rumanian Circle. London, Collins, 1981.

OTHER PUBLICATIONS as Dudley Barker

Novels

A Few of the People. London, Jarrolds, 1946.
Grandfather's House. London, Heinemann, 1951.
The Voice. London, Heinemann, 1953.
Green and Pleasant Land. London, Heinemann, 1955; as *This Green and Pleasant Land,* New York, Holt, 1956.
Toby Pinn. London, Heinemann, 1956.
Private Company. London, Longman, 1959.
The Ladder. London, Cassell, 1968.
A Pillar of Rest. London, Cassell, 1970.

Plays

Radio Plays: *Visiting Airman*, 1960; *Obedience Test,* 1961.

Other

Laughter in Court (sketches). London, Methuen, 1935.
Palmer, The Rugeley Poisoner. London, Duckworth, 1935.
Lord Darling's Famous Cases. London, Hutchinson, 1936.
Coastal Command at War, with Gordon Campbell and Tom Guthrie (as Tom Dudley-Gordon). Cairo, Schindler, and London, Jarrolds, 1943; as *I Seek My Prey in the Waters,* New York, Doubleday, 1943.
Harvest Home: The Official Story of the Great Floods of 1947 and Their Sequel. London, His Majesty's Stationery Office, 1947.
People for the Commonwealth: The Case for Mass Migration. London, Werner Laurie, 1948.
Berlin Air Lift: An Account of the British Contribution. London, His Majesty's Stationery Office, 1949.
Grivas: Portrait of a Terrorist. London, Cresset Press, 1959; New York, Harcourt Brace, 1960.
The Commonwealth We Live In. London, Her Majesty's Stationery Office, 1960.
The Young Man's Guide to Journalism. London, Hamish Hamilton, 1963.
The Man of Principle: A View of John Galsworthy. London, Heinemann, and New York, British Book Centre, 1963.
British Aid to Developing Nations. London, Her Majesty's Stationery Office, 1964.
Swaziland. London, Her Majesty's Stationery Office, 1965.
Writer by Trade: A View of Arnold Bennett. London, Allen and Unwin, and New York, Atheneum, 1966.
Prominent Edwardians. London, Allen and Unwin, and New York, Atheneum, 1969.
G.K. Chesterton: A Biography. London, Constable, and New York, Stein and Day, 1973.

*

Lionel Black commented (1980):

I write as well as I can, and hope that, at least, it's always a professional job.

* * *

Lionel Black is the pseudonym under which Dudley Barker, a newspaper writer, editor, novelist, biographer, and prolifically knowledgeable explainer of England to the English dating from his R.A.F. service during World War II, wrote 17 mystery novels between 1960 and 1981. Three of the early mystery novels had a series character named Emma Greaves; others were self-contained, relying more on subject matter than on character. In 1969 Barker introduced Kate Theobald, a newspaper reporter, in *Swinging Murder*. Intrepid, intuitive, and independent, Kate is helped by her husband Henry, a logical barrister with long-standing helpful contacts within the English establishment. Kate works on the fringes of legality, never really violating the law but often defying the advice or wishes of detective inspectors, Roger Wake in the country or Aloysius Comfort in London, who are "not all that fond of the Press." She is also frequently helped by other reporters, like stringers from her own newspaper or a reporter named Dereck Andrews (at work on a long study of Samuel Beckett) who is not in competition because he works for a Sunday paper and she for a daily. In exemplifying the problems and the curiosity of the press at its most involved and imaginative level, Kate often is in danger, mugged or captured until rescued by Henry or the police. Although not infallible, she is likely to arrive at the truth, at considerable risk to herself, just one step before the more authorized and thorough agents of society's morality.

The Black novels show a conventional generic interest in detective fiction. Numbers of them center on confined settings, carefully described: *Death Has Green Fingers* takes place in an old village concerned with rose growing and its new university; *Breakaway* takes place in the isolation of the English fen country; *The Eve of the Wedding* uses a Victorian Gothic mansion overlooking Wimbledon Common, a vast house with a legend of poltergeists. *The Penny Murders,* focussing on the death of a coin collector, poses the problems of the locked-room mystery, although it does not solve the crime in those terms. Even more interesting is the author's searching interest in process, in how something works. The reader is given extensive information on breeding hybrid roses (*Death Has Green Fingers*), dismantling explosive devices and booby traps (*Death by Hoax*), both arcane numismatic lore and the process of counterfeiting coins (*The Penny Murders*), and the legal system in all the novels. Often beginning with a conventionally impossible problem like breeding a blue rose or finding a 1933 or 1954 penny (years in which none was minted, although dies were cast), the author supplies extensive and fascinating information on the subject, giving the novels the additional appeal of well-researched and skillfully presented journalism.

Victims and criminals alike are, in Black's fiction, accorded little sympathy or psychological depth. Most often, the victim is one who has corrupted the legitimate process, a thief, blackmailer, or forger, and the killer has sufficient motive, although, at times, as in *The Eve of the Wedding,* in which an eccentric pair of siblings kill their unscrupulous nephew to preserve their own amiably obsolescent way of life, the implications about crime seem rather trivial. Often, as in *Death Has Green Fingers* or *Death by Hoax*, the killer is herself or himself killed before the crime is solved, the second murder committed by menacing thugs brought into the confined setting from the more anarchic outside world. Detective Inspector Wade explains to Kate in *Death by Hoax:*

Most murderers in this country are not dangerous, except of course to the victim. They're domestic—husband, wife, lover, mistress. And most are committed on impulse by somebody who would certainly never commit murder again. But there's another kind of murder, now widespread, of which until lately we have seen very little in England— ruthless, violent, sometimes political as in the Irish or the Palestinian troubles, sometimes simply criminal, as quite often in the United States.

These second kinds of murder, more random and menacing, are brought in only near the ends of novels, most often not integrated very closely or convincingly with the plots. They lurk vaguely outside the principal interest and distinction of the fiction, the intelligent and responsible journalism that explains a profession or a process.

—James Gindin

_____

BLACK, Mansell. *See* **HALL, Adam.**

_____

BLACKBURN, John (Fenwick). British. Born in Corbridge on Tyne, Northumberland, 26 June 1923; brother of the writer Thomas Blackburn. Educated at Haileybury College, 1937–40; Durham University, B.A. 1949. Served as a radio officer in the merchant navy, 1942–45. Married Joan Mary Clift in 1950. Has worked as a lorry driver, schoolmaster in London, 1949–51, and Berlin, 1951–52; Director, Red Lion Books, London, 1952–59. Ran a book shop with his wife in Richmond, Surrey. Agent: A.M. Heath & Co. Ltd., 79 St. Martin's Lane, London WC2N 4AA, England.

CRIME PUBLICATIONS

Novels (series: General Charles Kirk)

A Scent of New-Mown Hay (Kirk). London, Secker and Warburg, and New York, Mill, 1958; as *The Reluctant Spy,* London, Lancer, 1966.
A Sour Apple Tree (Kirk). London, Secker and Warburg, 1958; New York, Mill, 1959.
Broken Boy (Kirk). London, Secker and Warburg, 1959; New York, Mill, 1962.
Dead Man Running. London, Secker and Warburg, 1960; New York, Mill, 1961.
The Gaunt Woman (Kirk). London, Cape, and New York, Mill, 1962.
Blue Octavo. London, Cape, 1963; as *Bound to Kill,* New York, Mill, 1963.
Colonel Bogus (Kirk). London, Cape, 1964; as *Packed for Murder,* New York, Mill, 1964.
The Winds of Midnight. London, Cape, 1964; as *Murder at Midnight,* New York, Mill, 1964.
A Ring of Roses (Kirk). London, Cape, 1965; as *A Wreath of Roses,* New York, Mill, 1965.
Children of the Night. London, Cape, 1966; New York, Putnam, 1969.
The Flame and the Wind. London, Cape, 1967.
Nothing But the Night. London, Cape, 1968.
The Young Man from Lima (Kirk). London, Cape, 1968.

Bury Him Darkly. London, Cape, 1969; New York, Putnam, 1970.
Blow the House Down. London, Cape, 1970.
The Household Traitors. London, Cape, 1971.
Devil Daddy. London, Cape, 1972.
For Fear of Little Men. London, Cape, 1972.
Deep among the Dead Men. London, Cape, 1973.
Our Lady of Pain. London, Cape, 1974.
Mister Brown's Bodies. London, Cape, 1975.
The Face of the Lion. London, Cape, 1976.
The Cyclops Goblet. London, Cape, 1977.
Dead Man's Handle. London, Cape, 1978.
The Sins of the Father. London, Cape, 1979.
A Beastly Business. London, Hale, 1982.
A Book of the Dead. London, Hale, 1984.
The Bad Penny. London, Hale, 1985.

Uncollected Short Stories

"Johnny Cut-Throat," in *The Devil's Kisses.* London, Corgi, 1976.
"The Final Trick," in *The Taste of Fear,* edited by Hugh Lamb. New York, Taplinger, 1976.
"Dad," in *Return from the Grave,* edited by Hugh Lamb. New York, Taplinger, 1977.

*

Manuscript Collection: Mugar Memorial Library, Boston University.

*   *   *

John Blackburn has gained, over a period of 27 years, a solid reputation in the mystery, suspense, and espionage field: He is known as a stylish, genuinely chilling author. He has successfully wed the thriller with aspects of the super-scientific or the supernatural. His characters must directly confront objects of horror. These devils do not loom vaguely in the background, but seem unstoppable and are among the most malevolent portrayals in the genre.

Blackburn's first novel, *A Scent of New-Mown Hay,* creates a sustained nightmare in which the survivor of a Nazi concentration camp loses a biological weapon which threatens both Russia and England. What begins as a routine investigation turns into a matter of life and death. The novel has been praised for its explicit detail, but criticized for having too much science and not enough detection. General Kirk and the British Foreign Office Intelligence, featured in several other novels, appear here for the first time.

In *Children of the Night,* Blackburn has a tightly plotted story of nature-gone-daft. The setting of the Yorkshire moors is suitably forbidding. *Dead Man Running* begins with the protagonist taking a prosaic business trip to Russia. It quickly turns into a nightmare: he is accused of murder, branded as a traitor, and becomes a hunted man. This novel also introduces the engaging J. Moldon Mott, explorer and big-game hunter turned amateur detective.

Broken Boy is a sinister and macabre tale involving underground rituals, the revival of an unholy religion, and a cult of women, seeking revenge. Here, too, Blackburn weaves in espionage. In *Colonel Bogus,* Blackburn uses his first-hand knowledge of the used book business in a tale of intrigue and assassination.

The author uses a contemporary version of the Black Death in *A Ring of Roses.* A small English boy lost in East Germany is infected with the bubonic plague and carries it to West Germany and England. Countries suspect each other until intelligence departments cooperate to track down the scientist-priest responsible.

Bury Him Darkly is a supernatural horror story which is one of Blackburn's most successful novels. An unremarkable 18th-century gentleman had a period of intense creativity in his last years, and commanded that his last journals be buried with him. Events leading to the opening of his tomb make a remarkable story, a gripping, elemental confrontation of good and evil, though the climax does not reach the level of the build-up.

Blackburn has achieved a substantial following. He can be depended upon to sustain swift, sure, exciting, and absorbing stories with some characters who are off-beat and bizarre. They will almost assuredly deal with super-science or the supernatural, often verging on the occult. They have been labelled science fiction as often as thriller or mystery. Critics occasionally feel that the climaxes do not live up to the rest of the book, that essential clues sometimes come much too late, or that the author has not been totally fair in his misdirection. His faults, however, are far outweighed by his accomplishments. In style, Blackburn has been compared to John Buchan and Geoffrey Household, in plot to John Creasey. No matter the comparisons, Blackburn is undoubtedly one of England's best practicing novelist in the tradition of the thriller/fantasy novel.

—Frank Denton

———

BLACKSTOCK, Charity. Pseudonym for Ursula Torday; also writes as Paula Allardyce; Lee Blackstock; Charlotte Keppel. British. Born in London. Educated at Kensington High School, London; Lady Margaret Hall, Oxford, B.A. in English; London School of Economics, social science certificate. Worked as a typist at the National Central Library, London. Recipient: Romantic Novelists Association Major award, 1961. Agent: Andrew Hewson, John Johnson Literary Agency, 45–47 Clerkenwell Road, London EC1R OHT, Address: Balcombe Place, Balcolmbe, West Sussex RH17 6QJ, England.

CRIME PUBLICATIONS

Novels

Dewey Death. London, Heinemann, 1956; with *The Foggy, Foggy Dew,* New York, British Book Centre, 1959.
Miss Fenny. London, Hodder and Stoughton, 1957; as *The Woman in the Woods* (as Lee Blackstock), New York, Doubleday, 1958.
The Foggy, Foggy Dew. London, Hodder and Stoughton, 1958; with *Dewey Death,* New York, British Book Centre, 1959.
All Men Are Murderers (as Lee Blackstock). New York, Doubleday, 1958; as *The Shadow of Murder* (as Charity Blackstock), London, Hodder and Stoughton, 1959.
The Bitter Conquest. London, Hodder and Stoughton, 1959; New York, Ballantine, 1964.
The Briar Patch. London, Hodder and Stoughton, 1960; as *Young Lucifer,* Philadelphia, Lippincott, 1960.
The Exorcism. London, Hodder and Stoughton, 1961; as *A House Possessed,* Philadelphia, Lippincott, 1962.
The Gallant. London, Hodder and Stoughton, 1962; New York, Ballantine, 1966.

Mr. Christopoulos. London, Hodder and Stoughton, 1963; New York, British Book Centre, 1964.

The Factor's Wife. London, Hodder and Stoughton, 1964; as *The English Wife,* New York, Coward McCann, 1964.

When the Sun Goes Down. London, Hodder and Stoughton, 1965; as *Monkey on a Chain,* New York, Coward McCann, 1965.

The Knock at Midnight. London, Hodder and Stoughton, 1966; New York, Coward McCann, 1967.

Party in Dolly Creek. London, Hodder and Stoughton, 1967; as *The Widow,* New York, Coward McCann, 1967.

The Melon in the Cornfield. London, Hodder and Stoughton, 1969; as *The Lemmings,* New York, Coward McCann, 1969.

Ghost Town. London, Hodder and Stoughton, and New York, Coward McCann, 1976.

I Met Murder on the Way. London, Hodder and Stoughton, 1977; as *The Shirt Front,* New York, Coward McCann, 1977.

Miss Charley. London, Hodder and Stoughton, 1979.

With Fondest Thoughts. London, Hodder and Stoughton, 1980.

Novels as Paula Allardyce

After the Lady. London, Ward Lock, 1954.

The Doctor's Daughter. London, Ward Lock, 1955.

A Game of Hazard. London, Ward Lock, 1955.

Adam and Evelina. London, Ward Lock, 1956.

The Man of Wrath. London, Ward Lock, 1956.

The Lady and the Pirate. London, Ward Lock, 1957.

Southarn Folly. London, Ward Lock, 1957.

Beloved Enemy. London, Ward Lock, 1958.

My Dear Miss Emma. London, Ward Lock, 1958; Chicago, Playboy Press, 1980.

Death, My Lover. London, Ward Lock, 1959.

A Marriage Has Been Arranged. London, Ward Lock, 1959.

Johnny Danger. London, Ward Lock, 1960; as *The Rebel Lover,* Chicago, Playboy Press, 1979.

Witches' Sabbath. London, Ward Lock, 1961; New York, Macmillan, 1962.

The Gentle Highwayman. London, Ward Lock, 1961.

Adam's Rib. London, Hodder and Stoughton, 1963; as *Legacy of Pride,* New York, Dell, 1975.

The Respectable Miss Parkington-Smith. London, Hodder and Stoughton, 1964; as *Paradise Row,* New York, Dell, 1976.

The Ghost of Archie Gilroy. London, Hodder and Stoughton, 1970; as *Shadowed Love,* New York, Dell, 1977.

Haunting Me. London, Hodder and Stoughton, 1978; New York, St. Martin's Press, 1979.

Novels as Charlotte Keppel

Madam, You Must Die. London, Hodder and Stoughton, 1975; as *Loving Sands, Deadly Sands,* New York, Delacorte Press, 1975.

My Name Is Clary Brown. New York, Random House, 1976; as *When I Say Goodbye, I'm Clary Brown,* London, Hodder and Stoughton, 1977.

I Could Be Good to You. London, Hutchinson, and New York, St. Martin's Press, 1980.

The Villains. Loughton, Essex, Piatkus, 1980; New York, St. Martin's Press, 1982.

The Ghosts of Fontenoy. Loughton, Essex, Piatkus, 1981.

OTHER PUBLICATIONS

Novels

The Daughter. New York, Coward McCann, 1970; London, Hodder and Stoughton, 1971.

The Encounter. New York, Coward McCann, 1971; Loughton, Essex, Piatkus, 1981.

The Jungle. London, Hodder and Stoughton, and New York, Coward McCann, 1972.

The Lonely Strangers. New York, Coward McCann, 1972; London, Hodder and Stoughton, 1973.

People in Glass Houses. London, Hodder and Stoughton, and New York, Coward McCann, 1975.

Dream Towers. London, Hodder and Stoughton, 1981.

Novels as Ursula Torday

The Ballad-Maker of Paris. London, Allan, 1935.

No Peace for the Wicked. London, Nelson, 1937.

The Mirror of the Sun. London, Nelson, 1938.

Novels as Paula Allardyce

Octavia; or, The Trials of a Romantic Novelist. London, Hodder and Stoughton, 1965; New York, Dell, 1977.

The Moonlighters. London, Hodder and Stoughton, 1966; as *Gentleman Rogue,* New York, Dell, 1975.

Six Passengers for the "Sweet Bird." London, Hodder and Stoughton, 1967.

Waiting at the Church. London, Hodder and Stoughton, 1968; as *Emily,* New York, Dell, 1976.

Miss Jonas's Boy. London, Hodder and Stoughton, 1972; as *Eliza,* New York, Dell, 1975.

The Gentle Sex. London, Hodder and Stoughton, 1974; as *The Carradine Affair,* New York, Pocket Books, 1976.

Miss Philadelphia Smith. London, Hodder and Stoughton, 1977.

The Rogue's Lady. Chicago, Playboy Press, 1979.

The Vixen's Revenge. Chicago, Playboy Press, 1980.

Other

The Children. Boston, Little Brown, 1966; as *Wednesday's Children,* London, Hutchinson, 1967.

*   *   *

The strengths of Charity Blackstock's fiction in the mystery and crime traditions are mainly in the former, although *Miss Fenny* is a competent example of the latter and a useful demonstration of her capacity for delineation of character and the skillful use of setting. While there are suspense and violence in her mystery fiction, these elements of the thriller are subordinate to an interest in the emotions of the protagonists. For the impatient reader these emotions appear to be longueurs; indeed, this is a point where Blackstock's strategy is not always fortunate.

Settings and character types are varied but the essential theme of Blackstock's fiction is, in the great tradition of crime and thriller writing, the perennial conflict of good and evil. Here of course differentiation is necessary: her interest is such that narrative action is subordinated to character self-discovery and conflict is internalised. Related to this is Blackstock's interest in aspects of evil, particularly guilt and hatred, which remains as a constant feature of the works. Against evil she sets the human virtues, particularly love, and human relationships form a crucible through which the protagonist generally gains a type of wisdom or essential experience. For example *I Met Murder on the Way* has a background of spies, murder, and conspiracy, but the emotional centre is young Victoria Katona and her love for the obviously untrustworthy Zoltan. In this battle of evil and virtue it is Victoria's emotions which are the effective arena. For all this her disillusionment does not destroy her and after misadventures and sustained emotional traumas there is a satisfactory ending.

Blackstock's "endings" may appear too satisfactory, the warmth and human wisdom just a little too facile. In part this reflects her treatment of evil which usually appears too stereotyped and with little exploration of motivation; as a consequence virtue as it appears is difficult to define. An example of this is *Mr. Christopoulos* where Christopoulos himself is simply an occasion to explore metaphysical and human questions about evil: central though he is, he remains an enigma and the question of moral attitudes towards him, while equally central, remains superficial. Here Blackstock shows evil to be "triumphant" though morally rejected and even, in a metaphysical sense, overcome by forces of conscience and human decency.

—Trevor James

———

BLACKSTOCK, Lee. *See* **BLACKSTOCK, Charity.**

———

BLACKWOOD, Algernon (Henry). British. Born in Kent, 14 March 1869. Educated at Moravian School, Germany; Wellington College; Edinburgh University. Ran a hotel and was a farmer in Canada; staff member, *Canadian Methodist Magazine,* Toronto, New York *Evening Sun* and New York *Times;* private secretary to James Speyer, New York; returned to England in 1899, and worked briefly in the dried milk business; appeared on television, 1947–51. Recipient: Television Society Silver Medal, 1948. C.B.E. (Commander, Order of the British Empire), 1949. *Died 10 December 1951.*

Crime Publications

Short Stories (series: John Silence)

The Listener and Other Stories. London, Nash, 1907; New York, Vaughan, 1914.
John Silence, Physician Extraordinary. London, Nash, 1908; Boston, Luce, 1909.
Day and Night Stories (Silence). London, Cassell, and New York, Dutton, 1917; as *Tales of the Mysterious and Macabre,* London, Spring, 1968.

Other Publications

Novels

Jimbo: A Fantasy. London and New York, Macmillan, 1909.
The Human Chord. London and New York, Macmillan, 1910.
The Centaur. London and New York, Macmillan, 1911.
Julius Le Vallon. London, Cassell, and New York, Dutton, 1916.
The Wave: An Egyptian Aftermath. London, Macmillan, and New York, Dutton, 1916.
The Garden of Survival. London, Macmillan, and New York, Dutton, 1918.
The Promise of Air. London, Macmillan, and New York, Dutton, 1918.

The Bright Messenger. London, Cassell, 1921; New York, Dutton, 1922.
Dudley and Gilderoy: A Nonsense. London, Benn, and New York, Dutton, 1929.

Short Stories

The Empty House and Other Ghost Stories. London, Nash, 1906; New York, Vaughan, 1915.
The Lost Valley and Other Stories. London, Nash, 1910; New York, Vaughan, 1914.
Pan's Garden. London and New York, Macmillan, 1912.
Incredible Adventures. London and New York, Macmillan, 1914.
Ten Minute Stories. London, Murray, and New York, Dutton, 1914.
The Wolves of God and Other Fey Stories, with Wilfred Wilson. London, Cassell, and New York, Dutton, 1921.
Tongues of Fire and Other Sketches. London, Jenkins, 1924; New York, Dutton, 1925.
The Dance of Death and Other Tales. London, Jenkins, 1927; New York, Dial Press, 1928.
Ancient Sorceries and Other Tales. London, Collins, 1927.
Full Circle (story). London, Mathews and Marrot, 1929.
Strange Stories. London, Heinemann, 1929.
(*Stories.*) London, Harrap, 1930.
The Willows and Other Queer Tales. London, Collins, 1932.
Shocks. London, Grayson, 1935; New York, Dutton, 1936.
The Tales of Algernon Blackwood. London, Secker and Warburg, 1938; New York, Dutton, 1939.
Selected Tales: Stories of the Supernatural and the Uncanny. London, Penguin, 1942.
The Doll and One Other. Sauk City, Wisconsin, Arkham House, 1946.
Tales of the Uncanny and Supernatural. London, Nevill, 1949.
In the Realm of Terror: 8 Haunting Tales. New York, Pantheon, 1957.
Selected Tales. London, Baker, 1964; as *Tales of Terror and the Unknown,* New York, Dutton, 1965; as *The Insanity of Jones and Other Stories,* London, Penguin, 1966.
Ancient Sorceries and Other Stories. London, Penguin, 1968.
Tales of the Supernatural, edited by Mike Ashley. Woodbridge, Suffolk, Bookmasters, 1983.
The Magic Mirror: Lost Supernatural and Mystery Stories, edited by Mike Ashley. Wellingborough, Northhamptonshire, Thorsons, 1989.

Plays

The Starlight Express, with Violet Pearn, adaptation of the story *A Prisoner in Fairyland* by Blackwood (produced London, 1915).
Karma: A Re-incarnation Play, with Violet Pearn. London, Macmillan, and New York, Dutton, 1918.
Through the Crack, with Violet Pearn (produced London, 1920). London and New York, French, 1920.
The Crossing, with Bertram Forsyth (produced London, 1920).
The Halfway House, with Elaine Ainley (produced London, 1921).
Max Hensig, with Kinsey Peile (produced London, 1929).

Other (for children)

The Education of Uncle Paul. London, Macmillan, 1909; New York, Holt, 1910.
A Prisoner of Fairyland: The Book That "Uncle Paul" Wrote. London and New York, Macmillan, 1913.
The Extra Day. London and New York, Macmillan, 1915.

Episodes Before Thirty (autobiography). London, Cassell, 1923; New York, Dutton, 1924; as *Adventures Before Thirty*, London, Cape, 1934.
Sambo and Snitch. Oxford, Blackwell, and New York, Appleton, 1927.
Mr. Cupboard. Oxford, Blackwell, 1928.
By Underground. Oxford, Blackwell, 1930.
The Italian Conjuror. Oxford, Blackwell, 1932.
Maria—of England—in the Rain. Oxford, Blackwell, 1933.
The Fruit Stoners. London, Grayson, 1934; New York, Dutton, 1935.
Sergeant Poppett and Policeman James. Oxford, Blackwell, 1934.
How the Circus Came to Tea. Oxford, Blackwell, 1936.

*

Bibliography: *Blackwood's Books: A Bibliography Devoted to Algernon Blackwood* by John Robert Colombo, Willowdale, Ontario, Hounslow Press, 1981.

* * *

Algernon Blackwood, generally considered the foremost Edwardian author of supernatural fiction, wrote only one true mystery/detective story, "Max Hensig" (aka "Max Hensig, Bacteriologist"), which appeared in *The Listener and Other Stories.* It is based loosely on the historic Carlyle Harris murder case, which Blackwood covered as a police reporter for the New York *Times.* In the story, the reporter Williams has the misfortune to antagonize Hensig, who is being tried for the murder of his wife. Hensig, who is found not guilty, is a vain and vindictive man and he wants his revenge on the reporter who wrote unfavorably about him. The story soon turns into a cat-and-mouse game as Hensig stalks Williams, and Williams, perforce, must pretend ignorance in an attempt to trap Hensig. Noteworthy in the story is the excellent local color of the New York tenderloin and the description of the ways of the New York reporters, a drunken, irresponsible lot. "Max Hensig" is a fine story, and it makes one regret that Blackwood did not do more in this vein.

Much better known than "Max Hensig" are the stories about Dr. John Silence, who is one of the outstanding occult detectives of the century. Obviously based in part on Sheridan Le Fanu's Dr. Hellelius in *In a Glass Darkly* (1872), Silence is a physician who specializes in nervous disorders, particularly those due to supernatural causes. He appears in six cases, five of which are presented in *John Silence, Physician Extraordinary,* while the sixth, "A Victim of Higher Space," appears in *Day and Night Stories.* Blackwood uses two narrative approaches. In one a patient comes to Dr. Silence for a consultation, much as a client might visit Sherlock Holmes, and Silence uncovers the problem and solves it. In the second group someone undergoes a supernatural experience and Silence either explains it or resolves it. It has been claimed that the stories of this second group were not originally centered on Silence, but were later adapted to his personality.

In "A Psychical Invasion" a young writer of humor pleads for help against psychic attacks that are being made against him by a dead woman. The writer had lowered his psychic defenses with hashish, and now everything that he writes is colored by the dead woman's warped mind. Silence encounters the woman's spirit and overcomes it in a psychic battle. Unusual in the story is the early description of synesthesia resulting from the hallucinogen that Silence takes to enter the dead witch's level. In "The Nemesis of Fire" Silence is called in to explain the mysterious fires that have been breaking out in Colonel Wragge's estate. The solution to the problem is a fire elemental, and the reason for its appearance is connected with ancient Egyptian magic. In the third case book story, "A Victim of Higher Space," a patient complains that he keeps slipping into the fourth dimension. Indeed, the man disappears while stating his problem to Silence. The doctor can help him, but Blackwood unfortunately does not give details. This story, together with several others that are not mystery stories, is based on the contemporary interest in the fourth dimension. Blackwood had apparently explored the concept both in terms of non-Euclidean geometry and Charles Hinton's visualizing exercises.

In three stories Silence only comments or resolves. In "Ancient Sorceries" the protagonist has a remarkable experience amid a witch cult in a small town in Northern France, and in "Secret Worship" a former student, on returning to a school in the Black Forest where he had studied as a boy, discovers the survival of the wicked dead, the Black Mass, and devil worship. Silence comes along at the right moment to save him. The last story, "The Camp of the Dog," is a fairly routine werewolf story.

At least four of the Silence stories can be classed among Blackwood's best work. Although the doctor is perhaps colorless if compared with Carnacki or Jules de Grandin, his adventures are fully imagined. The subject matter, drawn in part from Blackwood's long studies and his association with the Hermetic Order of the Golden Dawn, is colorful and unusual.

There are occasional crime elements in other stories. "A Suspicious Gift" (*The Empty House*) tells of a murder frame much like the one that Blackwood almost fell into during his down-and-out days in New York. "Accessory Before the Fact" (*Ten Minute Stories*) is concerned with a man who has a premonitory vision of a murder, meets the criminals before the crime takes place, and does nothing about it. It is a very effective story. Several other stories reveal murders or suicides in the past that are brought to light by supernatural experiences, but these lie too far afield to describe.

—E.F. Bleiler

BLAISDELL, ANNE. *See* **LININGTON, Elizabeth.**

BLAKE, Nicholas. Pseudonym for C(ecil) Day Lewis. British. Born in Ballintubbert, Queen's County (now County Laois), Ireland, 27 April 1904; brought to England in 1905. Educated at Wilkie's Preparatory School, London, 1912–17; Sherborne School, Dorset, 1917–23; Wadham College, Oxford, 1923–27, B.A. 1927, M.A. Served as an Editor in the Ministry of Information, London, 1941–46. Married 1) Mary King in 1928 (divorced 1951), two sons; also one other son; 2) Jill Balcon in 1951, one daughter and one son, the actor Daniel Day Lewis. Assistant master, Summer Fields School, Oxford, 1927–28; master, Larchfield School, Helensburgh, Dunbartonshire, 1928–30, and Cheltenham Junior School, Gloucestershire, 1930–35; reader, John Lehmann Ltd., publishers, London, 1946; reader from 1946, and Director from 1954, Chatto and Windus, publishers, London. Professor of Poetry, Oxford University, 1951–56; Norton Professor of Poetry, Harvard

University, Cambridge, Massachusetts, 1964–65. Clark Lecturer, 1946, and Sidgwick Lecturer, 1956; Cambridge University; Warton Lecturer, British Academy, London, 1951; Byron Lecturer, University of Nottingham, 1952; Chancellor Dunning Lecturer, Queen's University, Kingston, Ontario, 1954; Compton Lecturer, University of Hull, Yorkshire, 1968. Member, Arts Council of Great Britain, 1962–67; chairman of the Poetry, later Literature, Panel. Honorary Fellow, Wadham College, 1968. D. Litt: University of Exeter, 1965; University of Hull, 1970; Litt.D.: Trinity College, Dublin, 1968: Fellow; 1944, Vice-President, 1959, and Companion of Literature, 1965, Royal Society of Literature; Honorary Member, American Academy, 1966; Member, Irish Academy of Letters, 1968. C.B.E. (Commander, Order of the British Empire), 1950. Poet Laureate, 1968. *Died 22 May 1972.*

CRIME PUBLICATIONS

Novels (series: Nigel Strangeways)

A Question of Proof (Strangeways).   London, Collins, and New York, Harper, 1935.
Thou Shell of Death (Strangeways).   London, Collins, 1936; as *Shell of Death,* New York, Harper, 1936.
There's Trouble Brewing (Strangeways).   London, Collins, and New York, Harper, 1937.
The Beast Must Die (Strangeways).   London, Collins, and New York, Harper, 1938.
The Smiler with the Knife (Strangeways).   London, Collins, and New York, Harper, 1938.
Malice in Wonderland (Strangeways).   London, Collins, 1940; as *The Summer Camp Mystery,* New York, Harper, 1940; as *Malice with Murder,* New York, Pyramid, 1964.
The Case of the Abominable Snowman (Strangeways).   London, Collins, 1941; as *The Corpse in the Snowman,* New York, Harper, 1941.
Minute for Murder (Strangeways).   London, Collins, 1947; New York, Harper, 1948.
Head of a Traveller (Strangeways).   London, Collins, and New York, Harper, 1949.
The Dreadful Hollow (Strangeways).   London, Collins, and New York, Harper, 1953.
The Whisper in the Gloom (Strangeways).   London, Collins, and New York, Harper, 1954; as *Catch and Kill,* New York, Bestseller, 1955.
A Tangled Web.   London, Collins, and New York, Harper, 1956; as *Death and Daisy Bland,* New York, Dell, 1960.
End of Chapter (Strangeways).   London, Collins, and New York, Harper, 1957.
A Penknife in My Heart.   London, Collins, 1958; New York, Harper, 1959.
The Widow's Cruise (Strangeways).   London, Collins, and New York, Harper, 1959.
The Worm of Death (Strangeways).   London, Collins, and New York, Harper, 1961.
The Deadly Joker.   London, Collins, 1963.
The Sad Variety (Strangeways).   London, Collins, and New York, Harper, 1964.
The Morning after Death (Strangeways).   London, Collins, and New York, Harper, 1966.
The Private Wound.   London, Collins, and New York, Harper, 1968.

Uncollected Short Stories

"A Slice of Bad Luck," in *Detection Medley,* edited by John Rhode.   London, Hutchinson, 1939; abridged edition, as *Line Up,* New York, Dodd Mead, 1940.
"The Assassin's Club," in *Murder for the Millions,* edited by Frank Owen.   New York, Fell, 1946.
"It Fell to Earth," in *Armchair Detective Reader,* edited by Ernest Dudley.   London, Boardman, 1948.
"A Study in White," in *Queen's Awards,* 4th series, edited by Ellery Queen.   Boston, Little Brown, and London, Gollancz, 1949.
"Mr. Prendergast and the Orange," in *Great Stories of Detection,* edited by R.C. Bull.   London, Barker, 1960.
"Conscience Money," in *Ellery Queen's Mystery Magazine* (New York), January 1962.
"Sometimes the Blind," in *The Saint* (New York), January 1964.
"Long Shot," in *Twentieth Anniversary Annual,* edited by Ellery Queen.   New York, Random House, 1965.

OTHER PUBLICATIONS as C. Day Lewis

Novels

The Friendly Tree.   London, Cape, 1936; New York, Harper, 1937.
Starting Point.   London, Cape, 1937; New York, Harper, 1938.
Child of Misfortune.   London, Cape, 1939.

Plays

Screenplays (documentaries): *The Colliers,* 1939; *The Green Girdle,* 1940.

Radio Play: *Calling James Braithwaite, 1940.*

Verse

Beechen Vigil and Other Poems.   London, Fortune Press, 1925.
Country Comets.   London, Hopkinson, 1928.
Transitional Poem.   London, Hogarth Press, 1929.
From Feathers to Iron.   London, Hogarth Press, 1931.
The Magnetic Mountain.   London, Hogarth Press, 1933.
Collected Poems 1929–1933.   London, Hogarth Press, 1935; with *A Hope for Poetry,* New York, Random House, 1935.
A Time to Dance and Other Poems.   London, Hogarth Press, 1935.
Noah and the Waters.   London, Hogarth Press, 1936.
A Time to Dance, Noah and the Waters, and Other Poems with an Essay, Revolution in Writing.   New York, Random House, 1936.
Overtures to Death and Other Poems.   London, Cape, 1938.
Poems in Wartime.   London, Cape, 1940.
Selected Poems.   London, Hogarth Press, 1940.
Word over All.   London, Cape, 1943; New York, Transatlantic, 1944.
(Poems).   London, Eyre and Spottiswoode, 1943.
Short Is the Time: Poems 1936–1943 (includes *Overtures to Death* and *Word over All*).   New York, Oxford University Press, 1945.
Poems 1943–1947.   London, Cape, and New York, Oxford University Press, 1948.
Collected Poems 1929–1936.   London, Hogarth Press, 1949.
Selected Poems.   London, Penguin, 1951; revised edition, 1957, 1969, 1974.

An Italian Visit. London, Cape, and New York, Harper, 1953.
Collected Poems. London, Cape-Hogarth Press, 1954.
Christmas Eve. London, Faber, 1954.
The Newborn: D.M.B., 29th April, 1957. London, Favil Press of Kensington, 1957.
Pegasus and Other Poems. London, Cape, 1957; New York, Harper, 1958.
The Gate and Other Poems. London, Cape, 1962.
Requiem for the Living. New York, Harper, 1964.
On Not Saying Everything. Privately printed, 1964.
A Marriage Song for Albert and Barbara. Privately printed, 1965.
The Room and Other Poems. London, Cape, 1965.
C. Day Lewis: Selections from His Poetry, edited by Patric Dickinson. London, Chatto and Windus, 1967.
Selected Poems. New York, Harper, 1967.
The Abbey That Refused to Die: A Poem. County Mayo, Ireland, Ballintubber Abbey, 1967.
The Whispering Roots. London, Cape, 1970; as *The Whispering Roots and Other Poems,* New York, Harper, 1970.
Going My Way. London, Poem-of-the-Month Club, 1970.
Poems of C. Day Lewis 1925–1972, edited by Ian Parsons. London, Cape-Hogarth Press, 1977.
Posthumous Poems. Andoversford, Gloucestershire, Whittington Press, 1979.

Recording: *Poems,* Argo, 1974.

Other

Dick Willoughby (for children). Oxford, Blackwell, 1933; New York, Random House, 1938.
A Hope for Poetry. Oxford, Blackwell, 1934; with *Collected Poems,* New York, Random House, 1935.
Revolution in Writing. London, Hogarth Press, 1935; New York, Random House, 1936.
Imagination and Thinking, with L. Susan Stebbing. London, British Institute of Adult Education, 1936.
We're Not Going to Do Nothing: A Reply to Mr. Aldous Huxley's Pamphlet "What Are You Going to Do about It?" London, Left Review, 1936.
Poetry for You: A Book for Boys and Girls on the Enjoyment of Poetry. Oxford, Blackwell, 1944; New York, Oxford University Press, 1947.
The Poetic Image. London, Cape, and New York, Oxford University Press, 1947.
Enjoying Poetry: A Reader's Guide. London, National Book League, 1947.
The Colloquial Element in English Poetry. Newcastle-upon-Tyne, Literary and Philosophical Society, 1947.
The Otterbury Incident (for children). London, Putnam, 1948; New York, Viking Press, 1949.
The Poet's Task. Oxford, Clarendon Press, 1951.
The Grand Manner. Nottingham, University of Nottingham, 1952.
The Lyrical Poetry of Thomas Hardy. London, Oxford University Press, 1953.
Notable Images of Virtue: Emily Brontë, George Meredith, W.B. Yeats. Toronto, Ryerson Press, 1954.
The Poet's Way of Knowledge. Cambridge, University Press, 1957.
The Buried Day (autobiography). London, Chatto and Windus, and New York, Harper, 1960.
The Lyric Impulse. Cambridge, Massachusetts, Harvard University Press, and London, Chatto and Windus, 1965.
Thomas Hardy, with R.A. Scott-James. London, Longman, 1965.

A Need for Poetry? Hull, University of Hull, 1968.
On Translating Poetry: A Lecture. Abingdon-on-Thames, Berkshire, Abbey Press, 1970.

Editor, with W.H. Auden, *Oxford Poetry 1927.* Oxford, Blackwell, 1927.
Editor, with John Lehmann and T.A. Jackson, *A Writer in Arms,* by Ralph Fox. London, Lawrence and Wishart, 1937.
Editor, *The Echoing Green: An Anthology of Verse* (for children). Oxford, Blackwell, 3 vols., 1937.
Editor, *The Mind in Chains: Socialism and the Cultural Revolution.* London, Muller, 1937.
Editor, with Charles Fenby, *Anatomy of Oxford: An Anthology.* London, Cape, 1938.
Editor, with L.A.G. Strong, *A New Anthology of Modern Verse 1920–1940.* London, Methuen, 1941.
Editor, with others, *Orion 2–3.* London, Nicholson and Watson, 2 vols., 1945–46.
Editor, *The Golden Treasury of the Best Songs and Lyrical Poems in the English Language,* by Francis Turner Palgrave. London, Collins, 1954.
Editor, with John Lehmann, *The Chatto Book of Modern Poetry 1915–1955.* London, Chatto and Windus, 1956.
Editor, with Kathleen Nott and Thomas Blackburn, *New Poems 1957.* London, Joseph, 1957.
Editor, *A Book of English Lyrics.* London, Chatto and Windus, 1961; as *English Lyric Poems 1500–1900,* New York, Appleton Century Crofts, 1961.
Editor, *The Collected Poems of Wilfred Owen.* London, Chatto and Windus, 1963; New York, New Directions, 1964.
Editor, *The Midnight Skaters: Poems for Young Readers,* by Edmund Blunden. London, Bodley Head, 1968.
Editor, *The Poems of Robert Browning.* Cambridge, Limited Editions Club, 1969; New York, Heritage Press, 1971.
Editor, *A Choice of Keats's Verse.* London, Faber, 1971.
Editor, *Crabbe.* London, Penguin, 1973.
Editor, *A Lasting Joy: An Anthology.* London, Allen and Unwin, 1973.

Translator, *The Georgics of Virgil.* London, Cape, 1940; New York, Oxford University Press, 1947.
Translator, *The Graveyard by the Sea,* by Paul Valéry. London, Secker and Warburg, 1947.
Translator, *The Aeneid of Virgil.* London, Hogarth Press, and New York, Oxford University Press, 1952.
Translator, *The Eclogues of Virgil.* London, Cape, 1963; with *The Georgics,* New York, Doubleday, 1964.
Translator, with Mátyás Sárközi, *The Tomtit in the Rain: Traditional Hungarian Rhymes,* by Erzsi Gazdas. London, Chatto and Windus, 1971.

*

Bibliography: *C. Day Lewis, The Poet Laureate: A Bibliography* by Geoffrey Handley-Taylor and Timothy d'Arch Smith, London and Chicago, St. James Press, 1968.

Manuscript Collections: New York Public Library; State University of New York, Buffalo; British Library, London; University of Liverpool.

Critical Studies: *C. Day Lewis* by Clifford Dyment, London, Longman, 1955, revised edition, 1963; *C. Day Lewis* by Joseph N. Riddel, New York, Twayne, 1971; *C. Day-Lewis: An English Literary Life* by Sean Day-Lewis, London, Weidenfeld and Nicolson, 1980.

Theatrical Activities:

Actor: **Radio**—Tom Moore in *Blame Not the Bard,* 1942.

*   *   *

Under the pseudonym of Nicholas Blake, Cecil Day Lewis, the poet and novelist who was Poet Laureate from 1968 until his death in 1972, wrote 20 detective novels. His detective, the urbane, cultivated, amateur Nigel Strangeways, an Oxford graduate of many skills and no profession, through his many acquaintances just happens to be on or familiar with the scene before the crime is committed. Strangeways works well, with mutual respect, with Inspector Blount, the blunt hard-headed Scotsman in charge of the investigations for Scotland Yard. The novels are full of literary references, ranging from Shakespeare and the classics to more recent poetry like that of Blake, Keats, Arthur Hugh Clough, and A.E. Housman. Puns and literary digressions are frequent, particularly in the more heavily written early novels. One of these, *Thou Shell of Death,* set in a country house on a cold Christmas week-end, even updates a famous and intricate literary plot. A former World War I flying ace, embittered by his past, and ill, stages his own suicide to look like murder to incriminate enemies from his distant Irish past, enemies themselves destroyed in the course of the novel. This is a contemporary version of Cyril Tourneur's gory 1607 play, *The Revenger's Tragedy.* Themes are frequently those central to classical and Elizabethan literature. Plots, often complicated with multiple murders or with murders faked to look like suicide, gradually reveal the past, dig down to discover basic corruptions of the family unit or sibling rivalries. There is, over the course of the novels published between 1935 and 1968, a gradual, uneven progression from the novels based on one sibling protecting the other to preserve a sense of family to one sibling destroying another out of jealousy. In the best of the novels, *The Case of the Abominable Snowman,* set in a country house, *Minute for Murder,* which takes place in the government ministry for propaganda at the end of World War II, and *End of Chapter,* set in a publishing house, the murderer is a complex and tragic figure, torn between protection and revenge or unable to choose between what represents active life and what represents peaceful death.

The novels pay strict attention to the passing of years. Nigel Strangeways ages and changes, and the texture of topic reference, like comments on Marx Brothers' films in the 1930's, dates each novel fairly accurately. In the novels from the 1930's, possible psychological explanations are likely to be put down as accounting for behavior by "glands," and the few characters of proletarian origin are straightforwardly defiant of arid convention and admirably honest. Over the years, Nigel Strangeways gradually becomes more hospitable to deepening psychological explanations, and the defiant artists from the working classes, although never maimed enough to become the criminals, are seen less idealistically. A novel from the mid-1950's, *The Whisper in the Gloom,* centers on saving talks, designed to assuage the Cold War, between the Russians and the British from the murderous plots of an unscrupulous leader of cartels who makes millions from the Cold War. This novel, like some of the others, is more a story of action and adventure than an exercise in detection; others, like *Minute for Murder* or, another novel set in a country house owned by a complicated poet, *Head of a Traveller,* advance the story through a more intricately executed series of clues and events. Sometimes, the characters are stereotyped, like the academic Americans in *The Morning after Death;* often, the typology is only a superficial view and the characters grow into more complex figures, particularly the gentle poets, the thwarted intellectuals, the

repressed siblings, and the sexy and forward women. The range and variety of characters, all seen through the sensitive, shrewd, and sophisticated judgement of Nigel Strangeways, are, perhaps, the fiction's principal fascination.

—James Gindin

————

BLAKE, Patrick. *See* **EGLETON, Clive.**

————

BLAKE, Sexton. *See* **BRANDON, John G.**

————

BLEECK, Oliver. *See* **THOMAS, Ross.**

————

BLOCH, Robert (Albert). Also writes as Collier Young. American. Born in Chicago, Illinois, 5 April 1917. Educated in public schools in Maywood, Illinois, and Milwaukee. Married 1) Marion Holcombe; one daughter; 2) Eleanor Alexander in 1964. Copywriter, Gustav Marx Advertising Agency, Milwaukee, 1943–53. President, Mystery Writers of America, 1970–71. Recipient: Evans Memorial award, 1959; Hugo award, 1959; Ann Radcliffe award, 1960, 1966; Mystery Writers of America Edgar Allan Poe award, 1960; Trieste Film Festival award, 1965; Convention du Cinéma Fantastique de Paris prize, 1973; World Fantasy Convention award, 1975. Guest of Honor, World Science Fiction Convention, 1948, 1973; World Fantasy Convention, 1975; Bouchercon I, 1971. Agent: Kirby McCauley Ltd., 425 Park Avenue South, New York, New York 10016. Address: Shapiro Lichtman Talent Agency, 8827 Beverly Boulevard, Los Angeles, California 90067, U.S.A.

CRIME PUBLICATIONS

Novels

The Scarf. New York, Dial Press, 1947; as *The Scarf of Passion,* New York, Avon, 1948; revised edition, New York, Fawcett, 1966; London, New English Library, 1972.
The Kidnapper. New York, Lion, 1954.
Spiderweb. New York, Ace, 1954.
The Will to Kill. New York, Ace, 1954..
Shooting Star. New York, Ace, 1958.
Psycho. New York, Simon and Schuster, 1959; London, Hale, 1960.
The Dead Beat. New York, Simon and Schuster, 1960; London, Hale, 1961.
Firebug. Evanston, Illinois, Regency, 1961; London, Corgi, 1977.
The Couch (novelization of screenplay). New York, Fawcett, 1962.

Terror. New York, Belmont, 1962; London, Corgi, 1964.
The Star Stalker. New York, Pyramid, 1968.
The Todd Dossier (as Collier Young). New York, Delacorte Press, and London, Macmillan, 1969.
Night-World. New York, Simon and Schuster, 1972; London, Hale, 1974.
American Gothic. New York, Simon and Schuster, 1974; London, W.H. Allen, 1975.
There Is a Serpent in Eden. New York, Zebra, 1979; as *The Cunning Serpent*, 1981.
Psycho II. New York, Warner, 1982; London, Corgi, 1982.
The Night of the Ripper. New York, Doubleday, 1984; London, Hale, 1986.
Lori. New York, Tor, 1989.
Psycho House. New York, Tor, 1990.
The Jekyll Legacy with Andre Norton. New York, Tor, 1990.

Short Stories

The Opener of the Way. Sauk City, Wisconsin, Arkham House, 1945; London, Spearman, 1974; selection, as *House of the Hatchet*, London, Panther, 1976.
Terror in the Night and Other Stories. New York, Ace, 1958.
Pleasant Dreams—Nightmares. Sauk City, Wisconsin, Arkham House, 1960; London, Whiting and Wheaton, 1967; as *Nightmares,* New York, Belmont, 1961.
Blood Runs Cold. New York, Simon and Schuster, 1961; London, Hale, 1963.
More Nightmares. New York, Belmont, 1962.
Yours Truly, Jack the Ripper: Tales of Horror. New York, Belmont, 1962; as *The House of the Hatchet and Other Tales of Horror*, London, Tandem, 1965.
Atoms and Evil. New York, Fawcett, 1962; London, Muller, 1963.
Horror-7. New York, Belmont, 1963; London, Corgi, 1965.
Bogey Men. New York, Pyramid, 1963.
Tales in a Jugular Vein. New York, Pyramid, 1965; London, Sphere, 1970.
The Skull of the Marquis de Sade and Other Stories. New York, Pyramid, 1965; London, Hale, 1975.
Chamber of Horrors. New York, Award, 1966; London, Corgi, 1977.
The Living Demons. New York, Belmont, 1967; London, Sphere, 1970.
This Crowded Earth, and Ladies' Day. New York, Belmont, 1968.
Fear Today—Gone Tomorrow. New York, Award, 1971.
Cold Chills. New York, Doubleday, 1977; London, Hale, 1978.
The King of Terrors. New York, Mysterious Press, 1977; London, Hale, 1978.
Out of the Mouths of Graves. New York, Mysterious Press, 1979; London, Hale, 1980.
Such Stuff as Screams Are Made Of. New York, Ballantine, 1979; London, Hale, 1980.
The Selected Stories of Robert Bloch. Los Angeles, California, Underwood Miller, 3 vols., 1987.
Midnight Pleasures. New York, Doubleday, 1987.
Fear and Trembling. New York, Tor, 1989.

OTHER PUBLICATIONS

Novels

It's All in Your Mind. New York, Curtis, 1971.
Sneak Preview. New York, Paperback Library, 1971.
Reunion with Tomorrow. New York, Pinn, 1978.

Strange Eons. Browns Mills, New Jersey, Whispers Press, 1979.
Unholy Trinity: Three Novels of Suspense (includes *The Scarf, The Dead Beat, The Couch*). Santa Cruz, California, Scream Press, 1986.
Screams (includes *The Will to Kill, Firebug, The Star Stalker*). Los Angeles, California, Underwood Miller, 1989.

Short Stories

Sea-Kissed. London, Utopian, 1945.
Dragons and Nightmares. Baltimore, Mirage Press, 1969.
Bloch and Bradbury, with Ray Bradbury. New York, Tower, 1969; as *Fever Dream and Other Fantasies*, London, Sphere, 1970.
The Best of Robert Bloch. New York, Ballantine, 1977.
Mysteries of the Worm. New York, Zebra, 1979.
Lost in Time and Space with Lefty Feep, edited by John Stanley. Pacifico, California, Creatures at Large, 1987.

Plays

Screenplays: *The Couch*, with Owen Crump and Blake Edwards, 1962; *The Cabinet of Caligari*, 1962; *Strait-Jacket*, 1964; *The Night Walker*, 1964; *The Psychopath*, 1966; *The Deadly Bees*, with Anthony Marriott, 1967; *Torture Garden*, 1967; *The House That Dripped Blood*, 1970; *Asylum*, 1972; *The Amazing Captain Nemo*, with others, 1979.

Radio Plays: *Stay Tuned for Terror* series (39 scripts), 1944–45.

Television Plays: *The Cuckoo Clock, The Greatest Monster of Them All, A Change of Heart, The Landlady, The Sorcerer's Apprentice, The Gloating Place, Bad Actor,* and *The Big Kick,* in *Alfred Hitchcock Presents*, 1955–61; *The Cheaters, The Devil's Ticket, A Good Imagination, The Grim Reaper, The Weird Tailor, Waxworks, Till Death Do Us Part,* and *Man of Mystery,* in *Thriller*, 1960–61; scripts for *Lock-Up*, 1960, *I Spy*, 1964, *Run for Your Life*, 1965, *Star Trek*, 1966–67, *Journey to the Unknown*, 1968, and *Night Gallery*, 1971; *The Cat Creature*, 1973; *The Dead Don't Die*, 1975; *Beetles*, 1987.

Other

The Eighth Stage of Fandom: Selections from 25 Years of Fan Writing, edited by Earl Kemp. Chicago, Advent, 1962.
The Laughter of a Ghoul: What Every Young Ghoul Should Know. West Warwick, Rhode Island, Necronomicon Press, 1977.

Editor, *The Best of Fredric Brown.* New York, Ballantine, 1977.

*

Bibliography: in *The Robert Bloch Fanzine* (Los Altos, California), 1973.

Manuscript Collection: University of Wyoming Library, Laramie.

Critical Study: *Robert Bloch* by Randall Di Larson, Mercer Island, Washington, Starmont House, 1986.

Robert Bloch comments:
    I have been a professional writer since the age of 17 and it's too late for me to reform now. About all I can do is to scrawl on the wall in red letters, "Stop me before I write more!"

But, judging from current production, the output will continue—which statement can be regarded either as a promise or a warning.

There's very little to be said about—or for—my work. I consider my writing to be an "entertainment," as Graham Greene so aptly designated his novels in the genre. What the reader considers it to be is his problem.

* * *

One of Robert Bloch's most frequently quoted lines is his claim "I have the heart of a small boy; I keep it in a jar on my desk." This gruesome word-play is characteristic of a large part of Bloch's writing. Many of his stories stem from a stock phrase or cliché carried to a grisly extreme, or a pun given a macabre new interpretation. Bloch's ability to generate chills when playing things straight (if that is the appropriate word) is just as impressive. Many of his stories deal with one or another form of psychopathology, and their impact is in no way diminished by the author's disclaimer of specialized knowledge in this area.

Bloch began writing stories while still in high school, and at the age of 17 made his first professional sale to *Weird Tales* magazine. Many of his early stories (such as those collected in *The Opener of the Way*) show the unmistakable influence of the weird-fiction writer H.P. Lovecraft, with whom Bloch had corresponded since 1932. Gradually Bloch developed a voice of his own. He branched out into humorous fantasy, science fiction, and stories of crime and suspense, although *Weird Tales* continued to publish much of his best work. A very successful story from that magazine was "Yours Truly, Jack the Ripper," which told of the search for Jack the Ripper, believed to have preserved his youth through supernatural means and to be haunting the streets of modern Chicago.

Bloch's first novel appeared in 1947. *The Scarf* is the first-person narrative of a psychopathic strangler. It is told in a terse, conversational style far removed from the mannered prose of the Lovecraft imitations or the manic slang of Bloch's humorous fantasies. In its original version, the conclusion shows the narrator coming to a realization of his condition, and generates a certain sympathy for him. In 1966 a revised version of the novel was prepared for paperback publication. Here the last few pages were replaced by new text, tightening up the original ending and putting the narrator's obsession in an altogether more chilling perspective.

Seven years passed before the publication of Bloch's next book. In 1954 three novels appeared. The best of these, and one of the author's own favorites among his work, is *The Kidnapper,* another first-person narrative of a psychopath, cold, clinical, and unsparingly honest in treatment. *Spiderweb* is the story of a phony California cult, and *The Will to Kill* tells of a Korean War veteran searching for the secret of his periodic mental blackouts. *Shooting Star* is a Hollywood private eye novel.

The watershed of Bloch's career came in 1959: a novel whose impact (helped in no small measure by Alfred Hitchcock's stunning film version) has caused Bloch to become permanently labeled as "the author of *Psycho.*" This story of Norman Bates and the odd events at his isolated motel has had a profound effect on both written and filmed suspense stories ever since. By the time of the film's release, Bloch had already moved to Hollywood and was at work on a number of television and film assignments but the success of *Psycho* undoubtedly opened further doors for him. Since 1959 he has supplied stories or scripts for a dozen films and some seventy-five teleplays, as well as 14 novels and many stories.

Bloch has returned to the world of *Psycho* twice in subsequent years. If the original novel dealt with the violence in a particular individual, *Psycho II* (unrelated to the film of the same title) deals with the violence in society, and *Psycho House* with the exploitation of violence. Both books are smoothly done and full of surprises, but neither one has the impact of the initial novel. Bloch's first novel after *Psycho* was, understandably, something of a let-down. *The Dead Beat* told of an attractive but dangerous young con-man and his effect on the family that befriended him. *Firebug* was the story of a murderous pyromaniac; *The Couch* was the novelization of a screenplay about a mass murderer; *Terror* was a tale of Indian Thuggee in contemporary Chicago. *Night-World* is a story of the search for an escaped madman. *American Gothic* is based on the murderous career of Herman W. Mudgett in Chicago in the 1890's.

Not quite a part of the crime genre, despite its title, is *The Star Stalker,* an excellent novel set in Hollywood during the last days of silent movies.

—R.E. Briney

BLOCHMAN, Lawrence G(oldtree). American. Born in San Diego, California, 17 February 1900. Educated at the University of California, Berkeley, A.B. 1921; Armed Forces Institute of Pathology, Certificate in Forensic Pathology 1952. Worked in the Office of War Information, 1941–46. Married Marguerite Maillard in 1926. Assistant night editor, *Japan Advertiser,* Tokyo, 1921; staff writer, *South China Morning Post,* Hong Kong, 1922; feature writer, *Englishman,* Calcutta, 1922–23; assistant night editor and editor of Riviera supplement, Chicago *Tribune,* European edition, 1923–25; editorial writer, Paris *Times,* 1925–27; freelance writer, 1928–33; script writer, Universal Pictures, 1933–34; freelance writer from 1946. Consultant, Commission on Government Security, 1957, and United States Information Agency, 1962–67. President, Mystery Writers of America, 1948–49. Recipient: Mystery Writers of America Edgar Allan Poe award, 1950, Special award, 1958. *Died 22 January 1975.*

CRIME PUBLICATIONS

Novels (series: Inspector Leonidas Prike)

Bombay Mail (Prike). Boston, Little Brown, and London, Collins, 1934.
Bengal Fire (Prike). London, Collins, 1937; New York, Dell, 1948.
Red Snow at Darjeeling (Prike). London, Collins, 1938; New York, Great American Publications, 1960.
Midnight Sailing. New York, Harcourt Brace, 1938; London, Collins, 1939.
Blow-Down. New York, Harcourt Brace, 1939; London, Collins, 1940.
Wives to Burn. New York, Harcourt Brace, and London, Collins, 1940.
See You at the Morgue. New York, Duell, 1941; London, Cassell, 1946.
Death Walks in Marble Halls. New York, Dell, 1951.
Pursuit. Kingston, New York, Quin, 1951; as *Menace,* London, Comyns, 1951.
Rather Cool for Mayhem. Philadelphia, Lippincott, 1951; London, Cassell, 1952.
Recipe for Homicide. Philadelphia, Lippincott, 1952; London, Hammond, 1954.

Short Stories

Diagnosis: Homicide. Philadelphia, Lippincott, 1950.
Clues for Dr. Coffee. Philadelphia, Lippincott, 1964.

Uncollected Short Stories

"Death by Drowning," in *Ellery Queen's Mystery Magazine* (New York), April 1965.
"The Traitor," in *Intrigue* (New York), October 1965.
"The Mad Yogi of Zara Pore," in *The Saint* (New York), December 1965.
"The Man Who Lost His Taste," in *Ellery Queen's Anthology 1966.* New York, Davis, 1965.
"Toast to Victory," in *The Saint Magazine Reader,* edited by Leslie Charteris and Hans S. Santesson. New York, Doubleday, 1966.
"Dr. Coffee and the Philanderer's Brain," in *Ellery Queen's All-Star Lineup.* New York, New American Library, 1967.
"The Case of Poetic Justice," in *Ellery Queen's Mid-Year Anthology 1968.* New York, Davis, 1968.
"Reprieve," in *The Locked Room Reader,* edited by Hans S. Santesson. New York, Random House, 1968.
"Dr. Coffee and the Amateur Angel," in *Ellery Queen's Mystery Magazine* (New York), October 1971.
"Dr. Coffee and the Pardell Case," in *Ellery Queen's Mystery Magazine* (New York), June 1972.
"Dr. Coffee and the Other Twin," in *Ellery Queen's Mystery Magazine* (New York), May 1973.
"Whatever Happened to Big Joe?" in *Ellery Queen's Mystery Magazine* (New York), July 1973.
"The Hate Collector," in *Mike Shane Mystery Magazine* (New York), March 1974.
"Dr. Coffee and the Whiz Kid," in *Killers of the Mind,* edited by Lucy Freeman. New York, Random House, 1974.
"Missing: One Stage-Struck Hippie," in *Ellery Queen's Aces of Mystery.* New York, Davis, 1975.
"Catfish Story," in *The Edgar Winners,* edited by Bill Pronzini. New York, Random House, 1980.

OTHER PUBLICATIONS

Play

Screenplay: *Quiet, Please, Murder,* with John Larkin, 1943.

Other

Here's How! A Round-the-World Bar Book. New York, New American Library, 1957.
Doctor Squibb: The Life and Times of a Rugged Idealist. New York, Simon and Schuster, 1958.
My Daughter Maria Callas, with Evangelia Callas. New York, Fleet, 1960; London, Frewin, 1967.
Alone No Longer, with Stanley Stein. New York, Funk and Wagnalls, 1963.
Are You Misunderstood?, with Harlan Logan. New York, Funk and Wagnalls, 1965.
The Power of Life or Death, with Michael V. DiSalle. New York, Random House, 1965.
Second Choice, with Michael V. DiSalle. New York, Hawthorn, 1966.
Understanding Your Body. New York, Crowell Collier, 1968.
Wake Up Your Body. New York, McKay, 1969.
Help Without Psychoanalysis, with Herbert Fensterheim. New York, Stein and Day, 1971.

Mister Mayor, with A.J. Cervantes. Los Angeles, Nash, 1974.

Translator, *The Unknown Warriors: A Personal Account of the French Resistance,* by Pierre Guillain de Bénouville. New York, Simon and Schuster, 1949.
Translator, *In Search of Man,* by André Missenard. New York, Hawthorn, 1957.
Translator, *The Heroes of God,* by Henri Daniel-Rops. Kingswood, Surrey, World's Work, 1959.
Translator, *The Shorter Cases of Inspector Maigret,* by Simenon. New York, Doubleday, 1959.
Translator, *Three Beds in Manhattan,* by Simenon. London, Hamish Hamilton, 1976.

*

Manuscript Collection: University of Wyoming Library, Laramie.

* * *

Lawrence G. Blochman was a journalist first and a mystery novelist second. It would require the most serious of mystery scholars to recall Blochman's fictional sleuths. Anthony Boucher noted, however, that "Blochman has single-handed created enough series detectives to fill an anthology by themselves." Blochman's specialties were the knowledge of police routine and an intimate acquaintance with India, and his very first published mystery short story ("The Fifty-Carat Jinx") contained both elements. He credited the mechanics of the detective story to Charles G. Booth, though neither Booth nor Blochman is mentioned in Haycraft's *Murder for Pleasure* or Symons's *Bloody Murder.*

The foregoing is not intended to diminish the quality and value of a Blochman mystery novel, but to emphasize the point that the man never attained the fame he deserved. He is perhaps best known for his first mystery novel, *Bombay Mail.* It featured Inspector Leonidas Prike of the C.I.D., British Secret Service in India, who was described as small, dynamic, efficient, and, when on a case, interested only in the facts. The story features one of the more famous mystery motifs, a railroad train carrying a host of interesting characters.

Blochman's most famous detective, however, was Dr. Daniel Webster Coffee, a famous pathologist, who appeared in only one novel, *Recipe for Homicide,* but in a large number of short stories. A television series, *Diagnosis: Unknown,* also featured him. Blochman's most famous short story is "Red Wine," in which the temperature of the table wine served at a jungle outpost is a vital point.

—Larry L. French

BLOCK, Lawrence. Also writes as Chip Harrison; Paul Kavanagh. American. Born in Buffalo, New York, 24 June 1938. Educated at Antioch College, Yellow Springs, Ohio, 1955–59. Married 1) Loretta Ann Kallett in 1960 (divorced 1973), three daughters; 2) Lynne Wood in 1983. Editor, Scott Meredith Inc., New York, 1957–58, and Whitman Publishing Company, Racine, Wisconsin, 1964–66. Since 1977 corresponding editor, *Writer's Digest.* Recipient: Nero Wolfe award, 1979; Private Eye Writers of America Shamus award, 1983, 1985; Mystery Writers of American Edgar Allan Poe award 1985. Agent: Knox Burger, 39½ Washington Square South, New York, New York 10012, U.S.A.

CRIME PUBLICATIONS

Novels (series: Leo Haig; Bernie Rhodenbarr; Matthew Scudder; Evan Tanner)

Death Pulls a Double Cross. New York, Fawcett, 1961; as *Coward's Kiss*, New York, Foul Play Press, 1987.
Mona. New York, Fawcett, 1961; London, Muller, 1963.
The Case of the Pornographic Photos (novelization of television play). New York, Belmont, 1961; London, Consul, 1965; as *You Could Call it Murder*, New York, Foul Play Press, 1987.
The Girl With the Long Green Heart. New York, Fawcett, 1965; London, Muller, 1967.
The Thief Who Couldn't Sleep (Tanner). New York, Fawcett, 1966.
The Cancelled Czech (Tanner). New York, Fawcett, 1966.
Deadly Honeymoon. New York, Macmillan, 1967; London, Hale, 1981.
Tanner's Twelve Swingers. New York, Fawcett, 1967; London, Coronet, 1968.
Two for Tanner. New York, Fawcett, 1967.
Here Comes a Hero (Tanner). New York, Fawcett, 1968.
Tanner's Tiger. New York, Fawcett, 1968.
After the First Death. New York, Macmillan, 1969; London, Hale, 1981.
The Specialists. New York, Fawcett, 1969; London, Hale, 1980.
Me Tanner, You Jane. New York, Macmillan, 1970.
Make Out With Murder (Haig; as Chip Harrison). New York, Fawcett, 1974; as *Five Little Rich Girls* (as Lawrence Block), London, Allison and Busby, 1986.
The Topless Tulip Caper (Haig; as Chip Harrison). New York, Fawcett, 1975; London, Allison and Busby, 1984.
In the Midst of Death (Scudder). New York, Dell, 1976; London, Hale, 1979.
Sins of the Fathers (Scudder). New York, Dell, 1976; London, Hale, 1979.
Time to Murder and Create (Scudder). New York, Dell, 1977; London, Hale, 1979.
Burglars Can't Be Choosers (Rhodenbarr). New York, Random House, 1977; London, Hale, 1978.
The Burglar in the Closet (Rhodenbarr). New York, Random House, 1978; London, Hale, 1980.
The Burglar Who Liked to Quote Kipling (Rhodenbarr). New York, Random House, 1979; London, Hale, 1981.
Ariel. New York, Arbor House, 1980; London, Hale, 1981.
The Burglar Who Studied Spinoza (Rhodenbarr). New York, Random House, 1981; London, Hale, 1982.
A Stab in the Dark (Scudder). New York, Arbor House, 1981; London, Hale, 1982.
Eight Million Ways to Die (Scudder). New York, Arbor House, 1982; London, Hale, 1983.
The Burglar Who Painted Like Mondrian (Rhodenbarr). New York, Arbor House, 1983; London, Gollancz, 1984.
When the Sacred Ginmill Closes (Scudder). New York, Arbor House, 1986; London, Macmillan, 1987.
Into the Night (completion of the novel by Cornell Woolrich). New York, Mysterious Press, 1987; London, Simon and Schuster, 1989.
Random Walk. New York, Tor, 1988.
Out on the Cutting Edge (Scudder). New York, Morrow, 1989.
A Ticket to the Boneyard (Scudder). New York, Morrow, 1990.

Novels as Paul Kavanagh

Such Men Are Dangerous. New York, Macmillan, 1969; London, Hodder and Stoughton, 1971.
The Triumph of Evil. Cleveland, World, 1971; London, Hodder and Stoughton, 1972.
Not Comin' Home to You. New York, Putnam, 1974; London, Hodder and Stoughton, 1976.

Short Stories

Sometimes They Bite. New York, Arbor House, 1983.
Like a Lamb to the Slaughter. New York, Arbor House, 1984.

Uncollected Short Story

"The Ehrengraf Alternative," in *Ellery Queen's Mystery Magazine* (New York), May 1984.

OTHER PUBLICATIONS

Novels

No Score (as Chip Harrison). New York, Fawcett, 1970.
Ronald Rabbit Is a Dirty Old Man. New York, Geis, 1971.
Chip Harrison Scores Again (as Chip Harrison). New York, Fawcett, 1971.
Code of Arms, with Harold King. New York, Coward McCann, 1981.
Introducing Chip Harrison (omnibus). Woodstock, Vermont, Countryman Press, 1984.

Other

Swiss Shooting Talers and Medals, with Delbert Ray Krause. Racine, Wisconsin, Whitman, 1965.
Writing the Novel: From Plot to Print. Cincinnati, Writer's digest, 1979; London, Poplar Press, 1986.
Telling Lies for Fun and Profit: A Manual for Fiction Writers. New York, Arbor House, 1981.
Real Food Places, with Cheryl Morrison. Pennsylvania, Rodale Press, 1981.
Spider, Spin Me a Web: Lawrence Block on Writing Fiction. Cincinnati, Writer's Digest, 1988.

Ghost Writer: *Babe in the Woods* by William Ard, 1960.

*

Bibliography: "Lawrence Block: Annotated Checklist of Tanner Series Books," by Jeff Banks, in *Mystery Nook* (Wheaton, Maryland). May 1975.

Manuscript Collection: University of Oregon, Eugene.

*   *   *

Lawrence Block won the Nero Wolfe award for Best Mystery of 1979 with *The Burglar Who Liked to Quote Kipling.* Although the adventures of Bernie Rhodenbarr, professional burglar and bibliophile, are popular among mystery readers, Block's more gritty, hard-hitting Matt Scudder novels contain his best writing.

The Matt Scudder novels began as a series of paperbacks written in the mid 1970's. But only when the series reached hardcover with the fourth book, *A Stab in the Dark,* did critical acclaim and increased sales result.

In *Sins of the Fathers,* Scudder investigates the savage murder of a Greenwich Village hooker. Her homosexual roommate is accused of the crime and when he hangs himself in his jail cell the police close the case. But Scudder knows the murderer is still loose and continues his own investigation. Block sets the scene of Scudder as an ex-cop who accidentally killed an innocent bystander. The guilt drives Scudder to leave the police force, leave his family, and become an alcoholic. Yet, from time to time, Scudder is asked to investigate cases the police have no interest in. When he's paid, Scudder gives 10 per cent of the money to the nearest church—his way of tithing.

In *Time to Murder and Create,* Scudder receives a letter from a man who fears he's about to be murdered. The letter names three suspects. Then Scudder discovers his client has already been murdered. Scudder makes himself the bait to draw out the murderer. In *In the Midst of Death,* Scudder is hired by a corrupt cop who's accused of murdering his girl friend. This is the weakest book in the series.

The fifth book in the series, *Eight Million Ways to Die* was a breakthrough book for Block. The book was critically acclaimed and was made into a movie starring Jeff Bridges. The most successful book in the Scudder series is *When the Sacred Ginmill Closes.* The action is based in the summer of 1975 when Scudder was still an alcoholic. The scenes of Scudder and his friends in the bars, ginmills, and after hours clubs with lots of broads and lots of booze possess a clammy realism which is perfect for the settings of Scudder's investigations.

In *Out on the Cutting Edge.* Scudder is hired by the father of a young Indiana girl who came to New York City to be a star, but then mysteriously disappears. The search takes Scudder into the glitting world of show business and leads him to a woman who once was a member of a radical group. The plot and subplots neatly come together in this satisfying novel.

The Burglar books are Block's most popular series. In *Burglars Can't Be Choosers,* Block introduces Bernie Rhodenbarr, professional burglar, who finds a body in the apartment he's burglarizing. This is all done with flair and fun. Although the writing is pure confection, Block's skills at plotting and characterization are strong.

The Burglar Who Liked to Quote Kipling features Bernie and his bookstore near Greenwich Village. Bernie's hired to steal a rare edition of Kipling—only a single volume exists—located in a millionaire's private library. Bernie steals the book but gets involved in murder and has to solve the case in order to clear himself. This is the best of the Burglar series.

The Burglar Who Studied Spinoza features Bernie stealing a coin collection. But things go wrong: most of the collection has already been stolen before Bernie gets there. However, Bernie steals the remaining 1913 Liberty Head V-Nickel. Yet, when Bernie's fence tries to sell the coin, he's murdered and Bernie has to solve another murder before he's the murderer's next victim.

The Burglar Who Painted Like Mondrian is the last Burglar book and shows signs of Block's interest flagging with the series. However, the novel is worth reading for Block's depiction of the New York City landscape and people.

Block had early success with the original paperback Evan Tanner series which featured an agent who had permanent insomnia. The Tanner novels have the lightness and fun of the later Burglar books but with international settings. The second Tanner novel, *The Canceled Czech,* features Tanner engineering a kidnapping in Czechoslovakia. *Tanner's Twelve Swingers,* revolves around Tanner's drunken promise to smuggle himself into Russia and rescue his friend's girlfriend. Tanner does indeed smuggle himself into Russia and finds the girl but she won't leave without her sister and her sister won't leave without

her 10 girlfriends who are on the Olympic team. So Tanner is faced with the impossible mission of smuggling a whole group of people to America past Communist security. This is the cleverest novel in the series.

The highlight of the fourth Tanner novel, *Two for Tanner,* is Tanner's escape from guerrillas who want to chop off his head. *Tanner's Tiger,* involves the assassination attempt on the Queen of England while, *Here Comes a Hero,* has Tanner exploring Far Eastern brothels.

Block has written much of his work under pseudonyms. Notable for their excellence are the Paul Kavanagh books and the Chip Harrison series.

The Paul Kavanagh books are suspenseful and violent, showing the tough, gritty kind of writing Block later used in the Matt Scudder novels. *Such Men Are Dangerous* is a caper novel where the object of the plot is to steal $2 million worth of advanced guerrilla warfare weapons. *The Triumph of Evil* concerns political assassination. *Not Comin' Home to You* is the story of a young couple on a killing spree.

The Chip Harrison books, *Make Out With Murder,* and *The Topless* are affectionate spoofs of Rex Stout's Nero Wolfe mysteries written in the breezy style of the Burglar books.

Less successful are Block's non-series novels. *Code of Arms* written with Harold King is a disappointing war novel. *Random Walk* features one of the scariest serial killers in recent years, but the impact is lost amid a tangled muddle of "New Age" phenomena like a mass migration and psychic powers and spiritual healing. *Into the Night*—a fragment of a novel never finished by Cornell Woolrich—was completed by Block but failed to gather much critical interest.

Much more successful are Block's short story collections: *Sometimes They Bite* and *Like A Lamb to Slaughter.* Included are stories about Matt Scudder and Chip Harrison, as well as non-series characters. Block displays mastery of the short story with gems like "A Bad Night for Burglars" and "Click!"

Also useful for learning how Block creates his works are the *Writer's Digest* essay collections: *Writing the Novel: From Plot to Print, Telling Lies for Fun and Profit,* and *Spider, Spin Me a Web: Lawrence Block on Writing Fiction.* Block discusses his writing techniques and tells why he chooses to create certain effects and characters in his work. These books are highly recommended for readers interested in the methods of a professional fiction writer.

—George Kelley

———

BLOOD, Matthew. *See* **HALLIDAY, Brett.**

———

BONETT, John and Emery. Pseudonyms for John H.A. Coulson and Felicity Winifred Carter. British. **COULSON, John H(ubert) A(rthur):** Born in Benton, Northumberland, 10 August 1906. Educated at Durham School. Served in the Admiralty, 1940–45. Married Felicity Carter in 1939; one son. Banker, 1924–37, company secretary, 1937–39, and sales promotion executive, 1945–63. **CARTER, Felicity Winifred:** Born in Sheffield, Yorkshire, 2 December 1906. Agent: Curtis Brown Ltd., 162-168 Regent Street, London WIR 5TB, England. Address: Las Adelfos 6 Calpe, Alicante, Spain.

CRIME PUBLICATIONS

Novels (series: Inspector Borges; Professor Mandrake)

Dead Lion (Mandrake). London, Joseph, and New York, Doubleday, 1949.
A Banner for Pegasus (Mandrake). London, Joseph, 1951; as *Not in the Script*, New York, Doubleday, 1951.
No Grave for a Lady (Mandrake). New York, Doubleday, 1959; London, Joseph, 1960.
Better Dead (Borges). London, Joseph, 1964; as *Better Off Dead*, New York, Doubleday, 1964.
The Private Face of Murder (Borges). London, Joseph, and New York, Doubleday, 1966.
This Side Murder? (Borges). London, Joseph, 1967; as *Murder on the Costa Brava,* New York, Walker, 1968.
The Sound of Murder (Borges). London, Harrap, 1970; New York, Walker, 1971.
No Time to Kill (Borges). London, Harrap, and New York, Walker, 1972.
Perish the Thought (Borges). London, Hale, 1984.

Novels by Emery Bonett

Never Go Dark (as Felicity Carter). London, Heinemann, 1940.
Make Do with Spring. London, Heinemann, 1941.
The High Pavement. London, Heinemann, 1944; as *Old Mrs. Camelot,* Philadelphia, Blakiston, 1944.

OTHER PUBLICATIONS by Emery Bonett

Novel

A Girl Must Live. London, Barker, 1936.

Plays

One Fine Day (broadcast 1944). Published in *Radio Theatre,* edited by Val Gielgud, London, Macdonald, 1946.
The Puppet Master, in *5 Radio Plays.* London, Vox Mundi, 1948.

Screenplays: *The Glass Mountain,* with others, 1949; *Children Galore,* with John Bonett and Peter Plaskett, 1954; *One Exciting Night* (*You Can't Do Without Love*), with others, 1954.

Radio Play: *One Fine Day,* 1944.

*   *   *

John and Emery Bonett are not your average husband and wife mystery team. For one thing, they sound like a brother team. For another, they never created the alter-ego husband and wife sleuth team we associate with the Lockridges and other mystery mates like "Kelley Roos." What the Bonetts have created is two vastly different series sleuths in a modest number of solidly constructed classic puzzles.

Felicity Carter was the first novelist in the family, beginning her career, with some success, before her marriage to John Coulson in 1939. But it is their work together that brought recognition in the mystery field. Their first collaborative novel appeared under Felicity Coulson's pseudonym of Emery Bonett. *High Pavement* is a first-person narrative by Robina Adams who comes to the small "two-bomb town" to work for the war effort and to reestablish herself with her lost lover. Her search for a suitable billet indirectly leads to a murder, which she and her no-longer-lost love successfully investigate. While a charming mystery, with the romance nicely tied to the puzzle, *The High Pavement* is an effort totally unlike the Bonetts' later work.

Five years after the appearance of *The High Pavement,* the first book credited to John and Emery Bonett appeared. Entitled *Dead Lion,* it is a considerable achievement. Again, it is a first-person narrative (this time told by the victim's nephew), and again romance plays a part. In fact, in *Dead Lion,* the new-found love of Simon Crane for one of the major suspects is crucial to the plot. The victim, a literary critic of great repute but no compassion, is a fascinating figure. The emotional savagery of his numerous relationships with women creates they plenty of suspects and sophisticated commentary on sexual politics. And, peppering the plot, the little details of post-war life (e.g., the challenge of shopping for and cooking with limited rations) give the book a wonderful texture.

The most notable thing about *Dead Lion* is, however, its introduction of the Bonetts' first series character, Professor Mandrake. This "old, fat, singularly ugly man" makes a memorable detective. By trade he is an anthropologist, author, and radio (later television) personality. By avocation he is an avuncular meddler, gleeful over any chance to play mastermind or, on occasion, cupid. Mandrake reappears in *A Banner for Pegasus,* the Bonetts' most famous mystery. When movie folk come to sleepy Steeple Tottering to film a local legend on location, there is a clash of cultures—and a corpse. The authors' own experience in the British film industry adds a nice touch of authenticity to their satire of the movie biz and village life. And it is the benevolent bite of their storytelling that makes *A Banner for Pegasus* a classic.

Mandrake appears once more in another agreeable tale, *No Grave for a Lady.* But when the Bonetts settled on the Costa Brava of Spain in the 1960's, they left the professor in England and created a new sleuth suited to their new home. Inspector Salvador Borges of the Brigade of Criminal Investigation is a much more elusive character than the homely professor. He is a handsome and very businesslike professional who reveals little of himself in the five mysteries in which he appears. Even a trip to England (in *The Sound of Murder*) exposes little of the man beyond his skill at English.

The Borges books are well-constructed and readable, but have few of the charms of the Mandrake books. In them, the formula shows. The victims and the suspects resemble stock characters. The young love is extraneous to the plot and has the appearance of being tacked on. Most maddening of all, the Bonetts never use their Spanish locale and Spanish sleuth as an opportunity to show some of the contrasts and conflicts between Anglo and Iberian culture. Borges might as well be in Scotland Yard.

—Kathleen L. Maio

BONNER, Parker. *See* **BALLARD, Willis Todhunter.**

BORTHWICK, J.S. American. Address: c/o St. Martin's Press, 175 Fifth Avenue, New York, New York, 10010 U.S.A.

CRIME PUBLICATIONS

Novels (series: Sarah Deane in all books)

The Case of the Hook-Billed Kites. New York, St. Martin's Press, 1982.
The Down East Murders. New York, St. Martin's Press, 1985.
The Student Body. New York, St. Martin's Press, 1986.
Bodies of Water. New York, St. Martin's Press, 1990.

* * *

J.S. Borthwick's books are vigorous mysteries in the high literate tradition, and even their presentation recalls the palmy days of the form, with maps and lists of characters as preliminaries. They are substantial narratives, crowded and closely-wrought, and each with a particular expertise appropriate to its setting, whether a nature reserve, an offshore island, a college English department or an 80-foot cruising sloop. Borthwick sustains a vivacious manner with every sign of ease and her dialogue is a continual source of pleasure.

All four novels to date feature Sarah Deane, a young teacher, and Alex Mackenzie, a slightly older doctor. Though not especially close at first, they are living together by the start of their third investigation and announce their wedding at the end of their fourth. Since two earlier liaisons have ended in trauma for Sarah, she is slower than Alex to commit herself. Her first lover has died in a car accident and her second is one of the victims in *The Case of the Hook-Billed Kites.* This novel is set among birdwatchers in a Texan nature reserve, where the movements of the eponymous kites prove crucial to the murder investigation. The action hinges on a drug being questionably marketed as a cure for cancer without its side-effects having been properly determined. The narrative method is traditional and reliable: the people are assembled, the victim is discovered and speculation and investigation run their course. Three women have established reason to dislike Sarah's dead lover, her predecessor in his affections and two elderly tour-guides ousted from their teaching posts by his reforming zeal. Other motives emerge as the action proceeds and the pattern begins to change when a second victim is found. Matters are resolved in a curious coda to the main action, in which a too-knowing "wunderkind" finds his life in danger.

The Down East Murders is set in Maine, partly on Weymouth Island off the coast and partly in adjacent coastal towns. The account of a close-knit rural community is meticulous and wholly convincing: the author lives on the Maine coast and it shows. Her exposition is precise and unhurried, as much concerned with manoeuvring the characters into position and establishing their potential as with the groundwork of the mystery: indeed, they are one and the same.

A series of art thefts launches the action, which deepens and darkens when a car runs into the sea and the elderly couple inside are drowned. The third victim is a turbulent local painter, whose body is washed ashore after a storm, and the intended fourth is the tenacious daughter of the drowned couple, who barely survives a terrible fall. Sarah sifts all the "quips and cranks, the oddities and contradictions" that she encounters, reaching thereby some dangerous conclusions; and though she puts herself repeatedly at risk, her procedures bear logical scrutiny and are not merely melodramatic.

The Student Body is also set in Maine, at Bowmouth College, in the depths of winter. The cold is a permanent presence and

snow and ice help to shape the course of events: the first victim is entombed in an ice-sculpture of a Viking ship and the second dies during a night of appalling weather, when staff and students are forced to bed down within the college itself. Both are members of the English department, the one a student, the other the departmental secretary. Attention focuses on the teaching staff, who are divertingly drawn, with much satirical comment on their professional and personal activities.

The victims shared singleness of purpose and neither is much mourned: the student because, though she was awesomely gifted, her intolerance and ruthless candour have made her a communal thorn in the flesh; the secretary because she has been an office tyrant, with a finger in every pie and a keen eye to self-aggrandisement. She also proves to have been playing a far deeper game than the essentially innocent student.

Bodies of Water takes Sarah and Alex on a luxurious cruise of the Maine coastal waters, but the mysterious death of one of their company destroys all hopes of plain sailing. Though the dead man was disturbing and destructive, he was so in a riveting way; and he is dispatched too soon for the good of the narrative, which is blander than usual and might have gained from more of his particular pungency. Sarah muses on his death and suffers from one of its consequences, but is more concerned with a putative traffic in drugs than with attempting to establish how and why he died. Her performance is her least distinguished since the trauma of Texas, and though she blunders into an assortment of truths she fails dismally to apportion their significance. Despite its characteristic elegance and some beguiling hints and echoes, the mystery also seems lacking in assurance and purpose.

—B.A. Pike

BOSTON, Charles, K. *See* **GRUBER, Frank.**

BOUCHER, Anthony. Pseudonym for William Anthony Parker White; also wrote as Theo Durrant; H.H. Holmes. American. Born in Oakland, California, 21 August 1911. Educated at Pasadena Junior College, California, 1928–30; University of Southern California, Los Angeles, B.A. 1932; University of California, Berkeley, M.A. 1934. Married Phyllis May Price in 1938; two sons. Theatre and music critic, *United Progressive News,* Los Angeles, 1935–37; science fiction and mystery reviewer, San Francisco *Chronicle,* 1942–47; mystery reviewer, *Ellery Queen's Mystery Magazine,* 1948–50 and 1957–68, and *New York Times Book Review,* 1951–68; fantasy book reviewer, as H.H. Holmes, for Chicago *Sun-Times,* 1949–50, and New York *Herald Tribune,* 1951–63; reviewer for *Opera News,* 1961–68. Editor, with J. Francis McComas, 1949–54, and alone, 1954–58, *Magazine of Fantasy and Science Fiction,* New York; editor, *True Crime Detective,* 1952–53; edited the Mercury Mysteries, 1952–55, Dell Great Mystery Library, 1957–60, and Collier Mystery Classics, 1962–68. Originated *Great Voices* program of historical recordings, Pacifica Radio, Berkeley, 1949–68. President, Mystery Writers of America, 1951. Recipient: Mystery Writers of America Edgar Allan Poe award, for non-fiction, 1946, 1950, 1953. *Died 29 April 1968.*

CRIME PUBLICATIONS

Novels (series: Fergus O'Breen)

The Case of the Seven of Calvary.   New York, Simon and
    Schuster, and London, Hamish Hamilton, 1937.
The Case of the Crumpled Knave (O'Breen).   New York, Simon
    and Schuster, and London, Harrap, 1939.
The Case of the Baker Street Irregulars (O'Breen).   New York,
    Simon and Schuster, 1940; as *Blood on Baker Street,* New
    York, Mercury, 1953.
The Case of the Solid Key (O'Breen).   New York, Simon and
    Schuster, 1941.
The Case of the Seven Sneezes (O'Breen).   New York, Simon
    and Schuster, 1942; London, United Authors, 1946.
The Marble Forest (as Theo Durrant, with others).   New York,
    Knopf, and London, Wingate, 1951; as *The Big Fear,* New
    York, Popular Library, 1953.
*The Case of the Seven of Calvary, Nine Times Nine, Rocket to the
    Morgue, The Case of the Crumpled Knave.*   London, Zomba,
    1984.

Novels as H.H. Holmes (series: Sister Ursula in both books)

Nine Times Nine.   New York, Duell, 1940.
Rocket to the Morgue.   New York, Duell, 1942.

Short Stories

*Exeunt Murderers: The Best Mystery Stories of Anthony
    Boucher,* edited by Francis M. Nevins, Jr. and Martin H.
    Greenberg.   Carbondale, Southern Illinois University
    Press, 1983.

OTHER PUBLICATIONS

Short Stories

Far and Away: Eleven Fantasy and Science-Fiction Stories.
    New York, Ballantine, 1955.
*The Compleat Werewolf and Other Stories of Fantasy and Science
    Fiction.*   New York, Simon and Schuster, 1969; London,
    W.H. Allen, 1970.

Plays

Radio Plays: for *Sherlock Holmes* and *The Case Book of Gregory
    Hood* series, 1945–48.

Other

Ellery Queen: A Double Profile.   Boston, Little Brown, 1951.
*Multiple Villainies: Selected Mystery Criticism, 1942–
    1968.*   Boston, Bouchercon, 1973.
*Sincerely, Tony/Faithfully, Vincent: The Correspondence of
    Anthony Boucher and Vincent Starrett,* edited by Robert W.
    Hahn.   Chicago, Catullus Press, 1975.

Editor, *The Pocket Book of True Crime Stories.*   New York,
    Pocket Books, 1943.
Editor, *Great American Detective Stories.*   Cleveland, World,
    1945.
Editor, *Four and Twenty Bloodhounds.*   New York, Simon and
    Schuster, 1950; London, Hammond, 1951.
Editor, *The Best from Fantasy and Science Fiction.*   Boston,
    Little Brown, 2 vols., 1952–53; New York, Doubleday, 6
    vols., 1954–59.

Editor, *A Treasury of Great Science Fiction.*   New York,
    Doubleday, 1959.
Editor, *The Quality of Murder.*   New York, Dutton, 1962.
Editor, *The Quintessence of Queen: Best Prize Stories from 12
    Years of Ellery Queen's Mystery Magazine.*   New York,
    Random House, 1962; as *A Magnum of Mysteries,* London,
    Gollancz, 1963.
Editor, *Best Detective Stories of the Year: 18th* [through *23rd*]
    Annual Collection.   New York, Dutton, and London, Board-
    man, 6 vols., 1963–68.

*

Bibliography: "Anthony Boucher Bibliography" by J.R.
Christopher, Dean W. Dickensheet, and R.E. Briney, in
Armchair Detective (White Bear Lake, Minnesota), nos. 2, 3, 4,
1969.

*   *   *

Anthony Boucher's twin careers as author and as critic of
mystery fiction are remarkable not only for their duration and
quality but also for the fact that they represented only half of
the activities of this productive and versatile man. He was
equally active in the fields of science fiction and fantasy (being
one of the founding editors of *The Magazine of Fantasy and
Science Fiction*), and was an authority on opera and other vocal
music, a teacher, and a radio and television personality.

Boucher made his first professional sale (at 16) to *Weird Tales*
magazine: a short ghost story parody. The first of his seven
mystery novels, *The Case of the Seven of Calvary,* appeared in
1937. Like its successors, this is a fair-play puzzle story in the
classic pattern of John Dickson Carr and Ellery Queen,
intricately constructed and told with wit and style. It is,
unfortunately the only recorded case of armchair detective Dr.
John Ashwin, Professor of Sanskrit at the University of
California. *The Case of the Crumpled Knave* introduced the
brash and very Irish private detective Fergus O'Breen and
Detective Lt. Jackson of the Los Angeles police. Separately or
together, O'Breen and Jackson appeared in three further
novels. In *The Case of the Baker Street Irregulars* a screen-writer
working on a Sherlock Holmes film is murdered. The identity
of the person who solves the crime is of almost as much interest
here as the identity of the murderer. *The Case of the Solid Key* is
a locked-room murder among a crowd of Hollywood personalities. *The Case of the Seven Sneezes* is an isolated-house-party
murder with roots in an ugly crime 25 years in the past.

In the early 1940's Boucher's interest in fantasy fiction
revived, and soon he was writing stories for the fantasy and
science fiction magazines along with his detective novels. He
delighted in mixing genres, and characters from his crime
fiction pop up frequently in his fantasy stories: Fergus O'Breen
in "The Compleat Werewolf" and Martin Lamb (from *The
Case of the Seven of Calvary*) in "The Anomaly of the Empty
Man."

With the Boucher name tied up by contractual obligations,
the author chose the byline H.H. Holmes (the alias of a
notorious 19th-century mass murderer) for *Nine Times Nine.*
This is a locked-room murder investigated by Sister Ursula of
the (fictional) Order of Martha of Bethany. It contains a
discussion of locked-room methods building on the famous
"Locked Room Lecture" in John Dickson Carr's *The Three
Coffins.* The only other H.H. Holmes novel is *Rocket to the
Morgue,* another locked room mystery and a *roman à clef* in
which many of Boucher's science fiction writer friends

appear in disguise. Among Boucher's finely crafted mystery short stories, the best remembered are those featuring Nick Noble, an ex-policeman and dipsomaniac who served as armchair detective in some very odd problems.

Boucher's twenty-six year span of reviewing mystery fiction began in 1941. In 1951 he began writing the "Criminals at Large" column in the Sunday *New York Times Book Review*. In this widely circulated forum he built up the remarkable record of more than 850 weekly columns, notable for his breadth of taste and his attention to new writers and to paperback as well as hardcover books. During these years he was surely the most influential as well as the most popular American critic of mystery and detective fiction.

After his death, Boucher's friends and admirers established the tradition of sponsoring in his memory an annual convention of mystery enthusiasts. The fourth of these "Bouchercons," held in Boston in 1973, published a memorial volume of his mystery criticism under the title *Multiplying Villainies*.

—R.E. Briney

BOWEN, Marjorie. *See* **SHEARING, Joseph.**

BOWIE, Sam. *See* **BALLARD, Willis Todhunter.**

BOX, Edgar. Pseudonym for Gore Vidal (Eugene Luther Vidal, Jr.) American. Born in West Point, New York, 3 October 1925. Educated at Los Alamos School, New Mexico, 1939–40; Phillips Exeter Academy, New Hampshire, 1940–43. Served in the United States Army, 1943–46: Warrant Officer. Editor, E.P. Dutton, publishers, New York, 1946. Member, Advisory Board, *Partisan Review,* New Brunswick, New Jersey, 1960–71; Democratic-Liberal candidate for Congress, New York, 1960; member, President's Advisory Committee on the Arts, 1961–63; co-chairman, New Party, 1968–71. Recipient: Mystery Writers of America award, for television play, 1954; National Book Critics Circle award, for criticism, 1983. Address: La Rondinaia, Ravello, 84010 Salerno, Italy; or c/o Random House Inc., 201 East 50th Street, New York, New York 10022, U.S.A.

CRIME PUBLICATIONS

Novels (series: Peter Cutler Sergeant in all books)

Death in the Fifth Position. New York, Dutton, 1952; London, Heinemann, 1954.
Death Before Bedtime. New York, Dutton, 1953; London, Heinemann, 1954.
Death Likes it Hot. New York, Dutton, 1954; London, Heinemann, 1955.

OTHER PUBLICATIONS as Gore Vidal

Novels

Williwaw. New York, Dutton, 1946; London, Panther, 1965.
In a Yellow Wood. New York, Dutton, 1947; London, New English Library, 1967.
The City and the Pillar. New York, Dutton, 1948; London, Lehmann, 1949; revised edition, Dutton, and London, Heinemann, 1965.
The Season of Comfort. New York, Dutton, 1949.
Dark Green, Bright Red. New York, Dutton, and London, Lehmann, 1950.
A Search for the King: A Twelfth Century Legend. New York, Dutton, 1950; London, New English Library, 1967.
The Judgment of Paris. New York, Dutton, 1952; London, Heinemann, 1953; revised edition, Boston, Little Brown, 1965; Heinemann, 1966.
Messiah. New York, Dutton, 1954; London, Heinemann, 1955; revised edition, Boston, Little Brown, 1965; Heinemann, 1968.
Three: Williwaw, A Thirsty Evil, Julian the Apostate. New York, New American Library, 1962.
Julian. Boston, Little Brown, and London, Heinemann, 1964.
Washington, D.C. Boston, Little Brown, and London, Heinemann, 1967.
Myra Breckinridge. Boston, Little Brown, and London, Blond, 1968.
Two Sisters: A Memoir in the Form of a Novel. Boston, Little Brown, and London, Heinemann, 1970.
Burr. New York, Random House, 1973; London, Heinemann, 1974.
Myron. New York, Random House, 1974; London, Heinemann, 1975.
1876. New York, Random House, and London, Heinemann, 1976.
Kalki. New York, Random House, and London, Heinemann, 1978.
Creation. New York, Random House, and London, Heinemann, 1981.
Duluth. New York, Random House, and London, Heinemann, 1983.
Lincoln. New York, Random House, and London, Heinemann, 1984.
Empire. New York, Random House, and London, Deutsch, 1987.
Hollywood. New York, New York, Random House, 1990.

Short Stories

A Thirsty Evil: Seven Short Stories. New York, Zero Press, 1956; London, Heinemann, 1958.

Plays

Visit to a Small Planet (televised, 1955). Included in *Visit to a Small Planet and Other Television Plays,* 1956; revised version (produced New York, 1957; London, 1960), Boston, Little Brown, 1957; in *Three Plays,* 1962.
Honor (televised, 1956). Published in *Television Plays for Writers: Eight Television Plays,* edited by A.S. Burack, Boston, The Writer, 1957; revised version, as *On the March to the Sea: A Southron Comedy* (produced Bonn, Germany, 1961), in *Three Plays,* 1962.
Visit to a Small Planet and Other Television Plays (includes *Barn Burning, Dark Possessions, The Death of Billy the Kid, A Sense of Justice, Smoke, Summer Pavilion, The Turn of the Screw*). Boston, Little Brown, 1956.

The Best Man: A Play about Politics (produced New York, 1960). Boston, Little Brown, 1960; in *Three Plays,* 1962.
Three Plays (includes *Visit to a Small Planet, The Best Man, On the March to the Sea*). London, Heinemann, 1962.
Romulus: A New Comedy, adaptation of a play by Friedrich Dürrenmatt (produced New York, 1962). New York, Dramatists Play Service, 1962.
Weekend (produced New York, 1968). New York, Dramatists Play Service, 1968.
An Evening with Richard Nixon and. . . (produced New York, 1972). New York, Random House, 1972.

Screenplays: *The Catered Affair,* 1956; *I Accuse,* 1958; *The Scapegoat,* with Robert Hamer, 1959; *Suddenly Last Summer,* with Tennessee Williams, 1960; *The Best Man,* 1964; *Is Paris Burning?,* with Francis Ford Coppola, 1966; *Last of the Mobile Hot-Shots,* 1970; *The Sicilian,* 1970.

Television Plays: *Barn Burning,* from the story by Faulkner, 1954; *Dark Possession,* 1954; *Smoke,* from the story by Faulkner, 1954; *Visit to a Small Planet,* 1955; *The Death of Billy the Kid,* 1955; *A Sense of Justice,* 1955; *Summer Pavilion,* 1955; *The Turn of the Screw,* from the story by Henry James, 1955; *Honor,* 1956; *The Indestructible Mr. Gore,* 1960; *Vidal in Venice* (documentary), 1985; *Dress Gray,* from the novel by Lucian K. Truscott IV, 1986.

Other

Rocking the Boat (essays). Boston, Little Brown, 1962; London, Heinemann, 1963.
Sex, Death, and Money (essays). New York, Bantam, 1968.
Reflections upon a Sinking Ship (essays). Boston, Little Brown, and London, Heinemann, 1969.
Homage to Daniel Shays: Collected Essays 1952–1972. New York, Random House, 1972; as *Collected Essays 1952–1972,* London, Heinemann, 1974.
Matters of Fact and of Fiction: Essays 1973–1976. New York, Random House, and London, Heinemann, 1977.
Great American Families, with others. New York, Norton, and London, Times Books, 1977.
Sex Is Politics and Vice Versa. Los Angeles, Sylvester and Orphanos, 1979.
Views from a Window: Conversations with Gore Vidal, with Robert J. Stanton. Secaucus, New Jersey, Stuart, 1980.
The Second American Revolution and Other Essays 1976–1982. New York, Random House, 1982; as *Pink Triangle and Yellow Star and Other Essays,* London, Heinemann, 1982.
Vidal in Venice, edited by George Armstrong, photographs by Tore Gill. New York, Summit, and London, Weidenfeld and Nicolson, 1985.
Armageddon? Essays 1983–1987. London, Deutsch, 1987; as *Time for a Change,* New York, Random House, 1988.

Editor, *Best Television Plays.* New York, Ballantine, 1956.

*

Bibliography: *Gore Vidal: A Primary and Secondary Bibliography* by Robert J. Stanton, Boston, Hall, and London, Prior, 1978.

Manuscript Collection: University of Wisconsin, Madison.

Critical Studies: *Gore Vidal* by Ray Lewis White, New York, Twayne, 1968; *The Apostate Angel: A Critical Study of Gore*

Vidal by Bernard F. Dick, New York, Random House, 1974; *Gore Vidal* by Robert F. Kiernan, New York, Ungar, 1982.

Theatrical Activities:

Actor: **Film**—*Roma* (*Fellini Roma*), 1972.

*   *   *

In the early 1950's, at the end of his first period as a novelist and the beginning of his career as a writer of live television drama, Gore Vidal turned briefly to the detective story. Under the pseudonym Edgar Box he published a trilogy of mystery novels narrated by and starring Peter Cutler Sargeant II, young public relations expert, sexual gymnast (exclusively hetero), and amateur sleuth. The books were reprinted regularly in paperback over the next quarter century, often with a glowing encomium from Vidal himself emblazoned on their covers. Judged as formal detective novels all three are mediocre, but Vidal's guided tour through the worlds of art, politics, and high society entertains us royally with countless gleefully sardonic jabs at every target in sight.

In *Death in the Fifth Position* Sargeant is hired to procure favorable media coverage for a ballet company which is being harassed by a right-wing veteran's group for having a "Communist" choreographer. Then the company's prima ballerina is murdered onstage, and we are treated to pages of superb satire about professional dancers and their hangers-on and much tedious speculation about homicidal motives, interspersed with two more gruesome deaths. *Death Before Bedtime* finds Sargeant in Washington as public relations adviser to an ultra-conservative senator angling for the Presidential nomination—until he's blown to bits by a gunpowder charge in his fireplace. Once again a lackluster detective plot is saved by Vidal's mocking gibes at politics, journalism, sex, and society. And in *Death Likes it Hot* Sargeant is invited to a weekend house party at a Long Island beachfront mansion and encounters tangled emotions and murder among a cast of ludicrous plutocrats and talentless pseudo-artists. Its fairly complex plot, a few deft clues and a dramatic climax make this the best mystery of the trio, but as usual it's the pungent satire that brings the book to life.

Clever deductions, fair play with the reader, and the Christie-Queen bag of tricks are not Vidal's strong points. But his mastery of the language did not fail him even in these mysteries that he himself regarded merely as potboilers, and his tone of cynical good-humored tolerance towards an American populated exclusively by crooks, opportunists, and buffoons is the closest approximation to the authentic spirit of H.L. Mencken that readers of mystery fiction are ever likely to experience.

—Francis M. Nevins, Jr.

————

BOYD, Frank. *See* **KANE, Frank.**

————

BOYER, Rick (Richard Lewis). American. Born in Evanston, Illinois, 13 October 1943. Educated at Evanston Township High School, graduated 1961; Denison University,

Granville, Ohio, B.A. in English 1965; University of Iowa, Iowa City, M.F.A. 1968. Married Elaine Edythe Smudsky in 1968 (divorced 1985); two sons. English teacher, New Trier Township High School, 1968–70; textbook representative, 1971–73, and acquisitions editor, 1973–78, Little Brown and Company, Boston, Massachusetts, Full-time writer, 1978–88. Since 1978, founding partner, Places Rated Partnership, Asheville, North Carolina. Currently Assistant Professor of English, Western Carolina University, Cullowhee, North Carolina. Recipient: Mystery Writers of America Edgar Allan Poe award, 1982. Agent: Helen Rees Agency, 308 Commonwealth Avenue, Boston, Massachusetts 02116. Address: 18 Colonial Place, Asheville, North Carolina 28804, U.S.A.

CRIME PUBLICATIONS

Novels (series: Doctor Charlie Adams in all books except *The Giant Rat of Sumatra*)

The Giant Rat of Sumatra. New York, Warner, 1976; London, W.H. Allen, 1977.
Billingsate Shoal. Boston, Houghton Mifflin, 1982; London, Gollancz, 1985.
The Penny Ferry. Boston, Houghton Mifflin, 1984; London, Gollancz, 1985.
The Daisy Ducks. Boston, Houghton Mifflin, 1986.
Moscow Metal. Boston, Houghton Mifflin, 1987; London, Gollancz, 1988.
The Whale's Footprint. Boston, Houghton Mifflin, 1988.
Gone to Earth. New York, Fawcett, 1990.

OTHER PUBLICATIONS

Other

Places Rated Almanac, with D. Savageau. Chicago, Rand McNally, 1981.

*

Rick Boyer comments:

While I enjoy reading all sorts of fiction and have read quite a few of the "great classics," the storytelling fiction of the late 19th and early 20th centuries has been my favorite through the years. Storytelling (as opposed to *writing*), especially as it reached its apex of development in England at the turn of the century with such authors as Conan Doyle, Stevenson, Kipling, Conrad, Wodehouse, *et. al.,* is what I like to read and what I like to write. In this form, one doesn't have to fret about coming off the Mount with the Stone Tablets of Truth; one merely has to keep the reader turning the pages. However, one soon discovers that good readers are a fussy bunch, and giving them a good "read" is perhaps more demanding than it seems at the outset.

I have always been a great admirer of the British and their tradition of story-telling, especially in suspense/adventure novels. I also think that this quality of the written word is reflected in British portrayals of such works on the screen and television.

Doc Adams is my attempt to create a character who mirrors—in his socio-economic class and in his lifestyle and tastes—the readers of suspense and thriller books (who, surveys show, are the top 2–5% of the population in income, education, and intelligence). Doc's occasional spells of malaise and depression stem from the unescapable conclusion that life in a developed country in the late 20th century is woefully void of

risk and adventure, while it seems heaped with anxiety, self-centeredness, materialism, and other petty pastimes. He therefore longs for some sort of escape from this tedious treadmill (the parallels with Sherlock Holmes and Doctor Watson might be obvious here). Doc usually gets relief from his boredom; the trouble is, it's usually quite a bit more than he's bargained for.

*   *   *

Rick Boyer's series character, Doctor Charles Adams, has one of the more unusual jobs in the genre. He's an oral surgeon, with a lucrative practice in the well-to-do suburban community of Concord, Massachusetts. Doc's property is large enough to include a small greenhouse, a Japanese tea-house (plus bonsai garden) and an atelier in which his wife Mary throws pottery. He also has a house on Cape Cod, overlooking the bay. He owns an Audi, a Scout and a BMW motorcycle (". . .adventure on wheels. A rolling death wish."), not to mention the boat. His practice leaves him plenty of time to take off. Doc Adams lives well.

But all those trappings of success aren't enough. Exasperated by his yearning for excitement, Mary challenges Doc with this summation of their life: "for most people having a nice house, a good family and friends, a good career in medicine, plenty of money . . . is enough. Hell, Charlie, it's *more* than *enough*. I mean, you've got everything." Doc replies, "I know. That's my problem," adding "I think we need to have adventures." At another point, he says that life has lost its challenge. However good he is at his work, he knows perfectly well that it's boring. The strength of Rick Boyer's novels is that while Doc's lifestyle isn't average, he remains a figure with whom the average person can identify. His adventures are demanding, but for the most part, Boyer successfully puts us in Doc's shoes and allows us to come along as participants rather than mere observers.

Doc's concern for those around him is the key to our identification with him. All but one of the novels is primarily driven by a friend or family member; important secondary ingredients are Doc's curiosity and his tenacity. In the first Doc Adams novel, the Edgar award winning *Billingsate Shoal,* Doc observes a stranded fishing boat from his deck of his Cape Cod cottage. He signals it to determine if it needs help, and calls the coast guard. He figures he's done his duty, but later in the day he sees the boat again in Wellfleet harbor. An acquaintance is scuba diving in the harbor; he suggests that his friend run out to the boat to see if he can figure out what's wrong with it. When the diver is later found dead, Doc feels responsible: he feels sure that it was the investigation of the boat which caused the death. The investigation becomes quite complicated and rather dangerous, but Doc doesn't let go. He must find his friend's killer. His persistence and his sense of justice are powerful. It's also more fun than oral surgery.

Doc Adams' other adventures flow from similar roots. In *The Whale's Footprint,* for example, a houseguest is murdered and Doc's son is suspected. Mary's brother, a state police officer, gets Doc appointed temporary coroner to allow him to participate in the investigation. This is a difficult book to enjoy; as soon as Boyer gets the story moving, he stops it for a sailing trip or, later in the book, for a whale-watch. But in spite of the pacing problems, *The Whale's Footprint* is remarkably enjoyable, with a warm tone and driven by strong family feelings which go beyond Doc's immediate problem of clearing his son.

Sometimes, Doc's involvement in the case is hard to credit. In *Moscow Metal,* Doc learns that a neighbor, a scientist at Lincoln Labs, may also be a KGB spy. Though he's warned off by Liatus Roantis, a friend who didn't forget his lethal training when he left Vietnam, Doc persists in helping Emil Haszmanay elude both the KGB's assassins and the American intelligence officers who want to question him. It's incredible that any ordinary oral surgeon would willingly battle the KGB, but Boyer skillfully focuses Doc's concern on Haszmanay as a person, rather than a pawn in an intelligence game.

Boyer is less successful in *The Daisy Ducks*, in which Roantis is shot, apparently by a member of his Vietnam war team. Doc scouts the surviving members of The Daisy Ducks, and ends up participating in a commando raid to rescue a kidnapped woman. There's no mystery in *The Daisy Ducks* beyond the sudden improvement in Doc's combat skills and in his perception. In *Billingsgate Shoal*, a bad guy is able to surprise Doc by waiting in the back seat of his car and knocking him out as he gets in. In *The Daisy Ducks*, Doc is asleep in a trailer when he's awakened by the presence of an onlooker—outside the vehicle! Late in this book, he tells us that "there are limits to my foolishness," but we're hard pressed to find any this time out.

There are other excesses in Boyer's work. Like the occasional exaggeration in Doc's physical abilities, Doc's investigative abilities are sometimes too good to be true. Concord Police Chief Brian Hannon, also a family friend, tells Doc that he likes "the way you notice things." An FBI agent tells him that he has very good powers of observation. At times, the praise is simply too thick. Another problem lies in the circle of people around Doc, which includes a mercenary, a brother-in-law who's a state cop, a family friend who's a police chief, and a psychiatrist who offers a quick diagnosis when it's convenient to the story. It's apparently not enough that Doc, like most amateur detectives, has one connection to the police; Boyer has to give him two. Mercenary Liatus Roantis is awfully handy to have around, always eager to help Doc with a covert surveillance raid on a private island or watching a closely guarded estate. Jim and Janice DeGroot, a couple with whom the Adams family socializes frequently, round out the regular cast; Janice's flirtation with Doc gets the both of them into trouble—sometimes credibly, sometimes not.

While these people might be unbelievable as a group, as individuals they're distinct and well-drawn, as are all the others Doc runs across in the course of the series. Boyer knows New England, and he does an especially fine job of portraying the rich ethnic diversity of the area. *The Penny Ferry*—perhaps the best book in the series—is especially strong in this regard, as it explores the Italian community and the legacy of the Sacco and Vanzetti execution.

Prior to beginning the Doc Adams series, Boyer penned a competent, though not entirely authentic, Sherlock Holmes pastiche, *The Giant Rat of Sumatra*. The story, inspired by *The Hound of the Baskervilles*, offers some intriguing hints of the direction Boyer's writing would take, including, of course, the curious parallel of the two medical men who shun their practices in order to pursue challenging, exciting and entertaining adventures.

—Jim Huang

BRACKETT, Leigh (Douglass). American. Born in Los Angeles, California, 7 December 1915. Married the writer Edmond Hamilton in 1946 (died 1977). Freelance writer from 1939. Recipient: Jules Verne award; Western Writers of America Spur award, 1964. *Died 24 March 1978.*

CRIME PUBLICATIONS

Novels

No Good from a Corpse. New York, Coward McCann, 1944; London, Simon and Schuster, 1989.
Stranger at Home (ghost-written for George Sanders). New York, Simon and Schuster, 1946; London, Pilot Press, 1947.
The Tiger among Us. New York, Doubleday, 1957; London, Boardman, 1958; as *Fear No Evil,* London, Corgi, 1960; as *13 West Street,* New York, Bantam, 1962.
An Eye for an Eye. New York, Doubleday, 1957; London, Boardman, 1958.
Silent Partner. New York, Putnam, 1969.

OTHER PUBLICATIONS

Novels

Shadow over Mars. London, Consul, 1951; as *The Nemesis from Terra,* New York, Ace, 1961.
The Starmen. New York, Gnome Press, 1952; London, Museum Press, 1954; abridged edition as *The Galactic Breed,* New York, Ace, 1955; original version, as *The Starmen of Llyrdis,* New York, Ballantine, 1976.
The Sword of Rhiannon. New York, Ace, 1953; London, Boardman, 1956.
The Big Jump. New York, Ace, 1955.
The Long Tomorrow. New York, Doubleday, 1955.
Rio Bravo (novelization of screenplay). New York, Bantam, and London, Corgi, 1959.
Follow the Free Wind. New York, Doubleday, 1963.
Alpha Centauri—or Die! New York, Ace, 1963.
People of the Talisman, The Secret of Sinharat. New York, Ace, 1964.
The Ginger Star. New York, Ballantine, 1974; London, Sphere, 1976.
The Book of Skaith. New York, Doubleday, 1976.
  The Hounds of Skaith. New York, Ballantine, 1974; London, Sphere, 1976.
  The Reavers of Skaith. New York, Ballantine, 1976.
Eric John Stark, Outlaw of Mars. New York, Ballantine, 1982.

Short Stories

The Coming of the Terrans. New York, Ace, 1967.
The Halfling and Other Stories. New York, Ace, 1973.
The Best of Leigh Brackett. New York, Doubleday, 1977.

Plays

Screenplays: *The Vampire's Ghost,* with John K. Butler, 1945; *Crime Doctor's Manhunt,* with Eric Taylor, 1946; *The Big Sleep,* with William Faulkner and Jules Furthman, 1946; *Rio Bravo,* with Jules Furthman and B.H. McCampbell, 1959; *Gold of the Seven Saints,* with Leonard Freeman, 1961; *Hatari!,* with Harry Kurnitz, 1962; *El Dorado,* 1967; *Rio Lobo,* with Burton Wohl, 1970; *The Long Goodbye,* 1973; *Star Wars II: The Empire Strikes Back,* 1980.

Television Plays: for *Checkmate* and *Suspense* series, and *Terror at Northfield* for *Alfred Hitchcock* series.

Other

Star Wars, "The Empire Strikes Back" Story Book. London, Fontana, 1980.

Editor, *Strange Adventures in Other Worlds*. New York, Ballantine, 1975.
Editor, *The Best of Edmond Hamilton*. New York, Ballantine, 1977.

*

Manuscript Collection: Special Collections, Eastern New Mexico University Library, Portales.

*   *   *

Leigh Brackett's reputation as a writer of crime and mystery fiction is based on a slim output of five novels, a few screenplays, and some television scripts for the *Alfred Hitchcock* and *Checkmate* series. While her major work was in the field of science and fantasy fiction (over 200 titles), she also distinguished herself with Westerns, including the screenplays for *Rio Bravo, Rio Lobo,* and *El Dorado,* as well as a novel about a black mountain man, *Follow the Free Wind* (Spur award). Brackett was a writer who loved her work, who wrote well in a variety of genres, and who had the gift of writing novels with the qualities of screenplays and screenplays verging on novels; her output is consistent in its careful development of character, straightforward storylines with interesting but not improbable twists, fastmoving dialogue, well-placed suspense, and good timing. She acknowledged Chandler and Hammett as major influences on her work, a debt evident in her first mystery novel, *No Good from a Corpse.*

No Good from a Corpse, a story about a hard-boiled detective, Edmond Clive, in Southern California who is determined to clear an innocent man of the murder of his girlfriend, led to Brackett's most famous screen credit. When Howard Hawks read *No Good from a Corpse,* he told his assistant to get Leigh Brackett as a screenwriter for *The Big Sleep.* Hawks assumed Brackett was a man, but despite his mistake, he still wanted her to join William Faulkner in writing the screenplay of Chandler's novel. Brackett understood the tradition of the hard-boiled detective, and, in particular, the essence of Phillip Marlowe. Her account of working on *The Big Sleep* with Faulkner and Hawks is fascinating; she and Faulkner worked independently on separate chapters of the Chandler novel and submitted them directly to Hawks without seeing each other's work. Hawks then created the film from these individual efforts. It is no wonder that this method, combined with the novel's ambiguities, caused Humphrey Bogart to ask the question no one could answer, "Who killed Owen Taylor?" The picture was criticized by a number of reviewers for its excessive violence—perhaps the very reason Hawks chose Brackett for the assignment. *No Good from a Corpse* was also noted for the same touch. 25 years later Brackett accepted a second Chandler assignment for *The Long Goodbye,* starring Elliott Gould as Philip Marlowe and directed by Robert Altman. The transformation of the novel into a screenplay posed many problems, some of which were connected with the novel's introspective nature and others with references that Altman felt dated the work. Brackett, sensitive to the criticism that the film was not the book, did not consider the film a "sacrilege" of the novel, and she doubted that "Chandler himself would have regarded every aspect of his work as Holy Writ."

Brackett's second novel, *Stranger at Home,* was ghost-written for George Sanders. A disguised credit appears in the novel's dedication to "Leigh Brackett Whom I Have Never Met." The storyline about Michael Vickers who disappears for four years, is presumed dead, and returns to Hollywood to find out which of his business associates and friends tried to kill him gains interesting twists because of the interaction between Vickers

and his wife. The book deals with things Brackett knows well—the L.A. landscape, the movies, and the private-eye tradition. Reviews were mixed probably because of a bias towards Sanders. One critic said it was not like his earlier work, *Crime on My Hands* (credit for that one belongs to Craig Rice and Cleve Cartmill).

1957 was a significant year for Brackett with the publication of *An Eye for an Eye* and *The Tiger among Us. An Eye for an Eye,* which became the basis for the television series *Markham,* is an exciting tale of revenge in which an alcoholic, bitter over his wife's divorce, decides to kidnap the lawyer's wife as a hostage. *The Tiger among Us* is Brackett's best book. Another variation of the vengeance motif, Brackett's novel unfolds a story of suspense and violence about Walter Sherris, the victim of a brutal beating and robbery by a group of teenagers. Sherris, in his efforts to track down his attackers, becomes the symbol of the decent man wavering on the edge of lawlessness. Brackett provides insights about juvenile delinquency, but with the suspense of the hunt and the violent action, she manages to avoid writing a social tract. Several critics saw the novel's potential as a film which it did become in 1962 as *13 West Street,* starring Alan Ladd.

Silent Partner, Brackett's final mystery novel, a tale of espionage, murder, and romance set in Los Angeles, London, and Iran, captures the cinematic quality of Brackett's work. The novel's diverse elements—smuggling, gun battles, imprisonment in a remote Iranian village, exciting car chases, and attempts by fanatics to overthrow the Shah of Iran—could have degenerated into Hollywood clichés and stereotypes, but the artistry of Leigh Brackett prevented that. In *Silent Partner* as in all her novels and screenplays, Brackett wrote stories using much physical violence, but the violence is never the major focus. Brackett uses violence in many ways—to explore a man's reaction to violence or his ability to withstand it, to move a story along, but in her writing, violence never supplants a good story well told.

—Katherine M. Restaino

BRAMAH, Ernest (Ernest Bramah Smith). British. Facts of his life are uncertain: born near Manchester, Lancashire, 20 March 1868. Educated at Manchester Grammar School. Married Lucie Maisie Barker in 1897. Farmer for 3 years; worked on a provincial newspaper, then secretary to Jerome K. Jerome, and staff member on Jerome's magazine *To-day*; editor, *The Minster,* London, 1895–96. *Died 27 June 1942.*

CRIME PUBLICATIONS

Novel (series: Max Carrados)

The Bravo of London (Carrados). London, Cassell, 1934.

Short Stories (series: Max Carrados in all books)

Max Carrados. London, Methuen, 1914; Westport, Connecticut, Hyperion, 1975.
The Eyes of Max Carrados. London, Grant Richards, 1923; New York, Doran, 1924.
The Specimen Case. London, Hodder and Stoughton, 1924; New York, Doran, 1925.
Max Carrados Mysteries. London, Hodder and Stoughton, 1927; Baltimore, Penguin, 1964.

Best Max Carrados Detective Stories, edited by E.F. Bleiler. New York, Dover, 1972.

OTHER PUBLICATIONS

Novel

What Might Have Been: The Story of a Social War. London, Murray, 1907; as *The Secret of the League,* London, Nelson, 1909.

Short Stories

The Wallet of Kai Lung. London, Grant Richards, and Boston, Page, 1900.
The Mirror of Kong Ho. London, Chapman and Hall, 1905; New York, Doubleday, 1930.
Kai Lung's Golden Hours. London, Grant Richards, 1922; New York, Doran, 1923.
The Story of Wan and the Remarkable Shrub and The Story of Ching-Kwei and the Destinies. New York, Doubleday, 1927; in *Kai Lung Unrolls His Mat,* 1928.
Kai Lung Unrolls His Mat. London, Richards Press, and New York, Doubleday, 1928.
A Little Flutter. London, Cassell, 1930.
The Moon of Much Gladness. London, Cassell, 1932; as *The Return of Kai Lung,* New York, Sheridan 1938.
Kai Lung Beneath the Mulberry Tree. London, Richards Press, 1940.

Other

English Farming and Why I Turned It Up. London, Leadenhall, 1894.
A Guide to the Varieties and Rarity of English Regal Copper Coins: Charles II-Victoria, 1671–1860. London, Methuen, 1929.

*

Bibliography: "Some Uncollected Authors," in *Book Collector 13* (London), 1964, and "A Bramah Biographer's Dilemma," in *American Book Collector 15* (Chicago), 1965, both by William White.

Manuscript Collections: Humanities Research Center, University of Texas, Austin; University of Illinois Library.

* * *

The reclusive creator of fiction's most successful blind detective, Ernest Bramah made his mark with his first Kai Lung book, which has been praised by a small but distinguished band of readers ever since. It and its successors concern an itinerant story-teller and are written with great felicity in a mock-Chinese idiom, but the books featuring Kai Lung are quite rich, and too long an exposure is not unlike a surfeit of wedding-cake. By contrast, the stories about the blind detective, Max Carrados, are among the most readable in the genre. Ellery Queen rated the first collection as one of the 10 best volumes in the field, and a *Times* reviewer of the final collection recommended it be read "twice running—the first time quickly to reach the solution, the second, slowly, to appreciate neatness of adjustments and subtleties of diction." The single Carrados tale, "The Bunch of Violets," included in *The Specimen Case,* is of indifferent quality, and the

Carrados novel, *The Bravo of London,* is uneven and disappointing, exhibiting the hero in a quite unmemorable way. The best works occur in the three volumes of short stories.

"The Coin of Dionysius," the opening episode of *Max Carrados,* finds Louis Carlyle, the capable, unimaginative inquiry agent, appealing for help to the blind amateur. Carlyle is surprised to recognize him as an old acquaintance, Max Wynn, who, in the years since their last meeting, has had the misfortune to be struck blind but the good luck to inherit—on condition he change his name to that of his American benefactor—enough money to make him independent. Carrados is able to solve Carlyle's case without leaving his study. And so the partnership is born.

"The Knight's Cross Signal Problem" concerns a railway crash in which 27 people have died. The engine driver has been suspended, but Carrados clears his name, unmasks the real culprit, and dispenses his own justice. The third case, "The Tragedy at Brookbend Cottage," is perhaps the best of all. Max foils a husband's elaborate plot to electrocute his wife, only to have the affair end—quite plausibly—in utter tragedy. "The Clever Mrs. Straithwaite" shows us that Carrados is very much at ease in a domestic setting especially when, as here, crosscurrents must be navigated and cross-purposes resolved. In this tale of a make-believe jewel theft the dialogue of the spoiled wife is a delight. In "The Tilling Shaw Mystery" Bramah again succeeds in breaking new ground. Carrados, upon investigation, declines to aid an attractive young client. Yet he solves her wider problem, rearranges her life, and gains a devoted friend. In this affair, as in most others, the detection is less important than the atmosphere, the characterization, and the fine writing.

The Eyes of Max Carrados opens with a long introduction in which Bramah defends the plausibility of his character's exploits by cataloguing those of real blind persons. But he is not quite convincing. That Carrados can read the morning headlines with his fingertips we may perhaps accept, but not that he can instantly recognize acquaintances before they speak and discover vital hairs on a raspberry cane. It would have been well if more use had been made of Parkinson, the butlering servant with outstanding powers of observation. E.F. Bleiler has sapiently described Max as "a blind man who can see perfectly well." Such is the impression he makes. Reminders of his supposed handicap do nevertheless remind us how important the other four senses can be, especially when highly developed.

This collection of stories is less successful than its predecessor. Bramah's lack of scientific knowledge reduces him to inventing a new anaesthetic and a new toadstool poison. The best of the nine tales is "The Ghost of Massingham Mansions," the opening of which displays the disparate temperaments of the satirical Carrados and the naive Carlyle to excellent effect. Of the eight stories in *Max Carrados Mysteries,* the best are perhaps "The Holloway Flat Tragedy," a rare homicide case, and "The Vanished Petition Crown," in which the blind sleuth brings a crooked coin-dealer to book. But a choice is difficult; all the tales are dominated by Carrados's personality, and every line is marked by the meticulous touch of a rare literary craftsman.

—Norman Donaldson

———

BRANCH, Pamela (Jean). British. Born in Ceylon in 1902. Educated in England and Paris; Royal Academy of Dramatic

Art, London. Had a variety of jobs and travelled extensively in Europe, India, the Middle East, and Africa. *Died in 1967.*

CRIME PUBLICATIONS

Novels

The Wooden Overcoat. London, Hale, 1951.
Lion in the Cellar. London, Hale, 1951.
Murder Every Monday. London, Hale, 1954.
Murder's Little Sister. London, Hale, 1959.

*   *   *

It is unfortunate that most of Pamela Branch's smart, sophisticated writing is out of print. But her first book, *The Wooden Overcoat* apparently written in a monastery in Cyprus, has been re-issued in the Penguin green classics series and her exploration of the seedy world of publishing, *Murder's Little Sister* is published by Pandora in its Classic Women Crime Writers Series.

Branch's writing gives a strong sense of 1950's London on various levels of the social scale. The wacky goings-on in *The Wooden Overcoat* concern Fan and Bertha in their first venture as landladies. They have the misfortune of owning a house next door to a club for acquitted murderers. Their house is also overrun with rats, necessitating numerous visits from Mr Beesum, an exterminator who loves his work. When the house is littered with corpses, not all of them rodents, they begin to suspect each other, their husbands, Marleen their charmless char, and especially the creepy neighbours.

The humour in Branch's books lies in the situations, the outrageous characters and in the dialogue which almost makes sense but not quite. This is life viewed through a fun-house distorting mirror where the ordinary suddenly becomes bizarre and then ordinary again. The sweetly chummy relationship between Fan and her friend Rex, a classic straight woman/gay man friendship, is a high point of *The Wooden Overcoat.* Their nonsensical conversations as they attempt to dispose of bodies whilst secretly suspecting each other of murder, are really funny as are the midnight maneouvres in which the neighbouring households go to war. Ultimately, it is a very silly book but the writing is seamless and witty and the denouement makes it all worthwhile.

Although not quite as amusing as *The Wooden Overcoat, Murder's Little Sister* is also permeated with death. Enid Marley wants revenge on her wayward husband, so she attempts suicide. Unfortunately for all concerned, she survives. Her actions do however boost the circulation of *You,* the no-hope magazine she writes for. Branch's drawing of the various people involved in publishing *You* must have come from either first-hand knowledge or good informants. All the second-guessing, back-stabbing, and ego-boosting banality is present as the magazine exploits the attempted suicide or possible attempted murder of its star, and universally loathed, columnist. Things go from weird to worse as Enid's readers revolt and she is blamed for various deaths and misadventures because of advice she has given in her column.

Branch does not write classic "crime novels" in that the mystery is really secondary to the farce in her work. But what she does, she does well and her books are worth seeking out.

—Gillian Rodgerson

———

BRAND, (Mary) Christianna (née Milne). Also wrote as Mary Ann Ashe; Annabel Jones; Mary Roland; China Thompson. British. Born in Malaya, 17 December 1907; lived in India as a child. Educated at a Franciscan convent, Taunton, Somerset. Married Roland S. Lewis in 1939; one adopted daughter. Worked as governess, receptionist, dancer, model, salesperson, and secretary. Chairwoman, Crime Writers Association, London, 1972–73. *Died 11 March 1988.*

CRIME PUBLICATIONS

Novels (series: Inspector Charlesworth; Inspector Chucky; Inspector Cockrill)

Death in High Heels (Charlesworth). London, Lane, 1941; New York, Scribner, 1954.
Heads You Lose (Cockrill). London, Lane, 1941; New York, Dodd Mead, 1942.
Green for Danger (Cockrill). New York, Dodd Mead, 1944; London, Lane, 1945.
The Crooked Wreath (Cockrill). New York, Dodd Mead, 1946; as *Suddenly at His Residence,* London, Lane, 1947.
Death of Jezebel (Chucky; Cockrill). New York, Dodd Mead, 1948; London, Lane, 1949.
Cat and Mouse (Chucky). London, Joseph, and New York, Knopf, 1950.
London Particular (Charlesworth; Cockrill). London, Joseph, 1952; as *Fog of Doubt,* New York, Scribner, 1953.
Tour de Force (Cockrill). London, Joseph, and New York, Scribner, 1955.
The Three-Cornered Halo (Cockrill). London, Joseph, and New York, Scribner, 1957.
Starrbelow (as China Thompson). London, Hutchinson, and New York, Scribner, 1958.
Court of Foxes. London, Joseph, 1969; Northridge, California, Brooke House, 1977.
Alas, For Her That Met Me! (as Mary Ann Ashe). London, Star, 1976.
A Ring of Roses (Chucky; as Mary Ann Ashe). London, Star, 1977; as Christianna Brand, London, W.H. Allen, 1977.
The Honey Harlot. London, W.H. Allen, 1978.
The Rose in Darkness (Charlesworth). London, Joseph, 1979.
The Brides of Aberdar. London, Joseph, 1982; New York, St. Martin's Press, 1983.
Crime on the Coast, and No Flowers by Request, with others. London, Gollancz, 1984.

Short Stories

What Dread Hand? London, Joseph, 1968.
Brand X. London, Joseph, 1974.
Buffet for Unwelcome Guests: The Best Short Stories of Christianna Brand, edited by Francis M. Nevins, Jr., and Martin H. Greenberg. Carbondale, Southern Illinois University Press, 1983.

Uncollected Short Stories

"The Last Short Story," in *Ellery Queen's Mystery Magazine* (New York), January 1973.
"The Kissing Cousin," in *Woman* (London), 2 June 1973.
"Over My Dead Body," in *Ellery Queen's Mystery Magazine* (New York), August 1979.
"Cloud Nine," in *Verdict of Thirteen,* edited by Julian Symons. London, Faber, and New York, Harper, 1979.
"A Piece of Cake," in *Ellery Queen's Mystery Magazine* (New York), January 1983.

"And She Smiled at Me," in *Ellery Queen's Mystery Magazine* (New York), May 1983.
"The Widow," in *The Saint* (New York), June 1984.
"The Rocking Chair," in *The Saint* (New York), August 1984.
"The Man on the Roof," in *Ellery Queen's Mystery Magazine* (New York), October 1984.

OTHER PUBLICATIONS

Novels

The Single Pilgrim (as Mary Roland). London, Sampson Low, and New York, Crowell, 1946.
The Radiant Dove (as Annabel Jones). London, Joseph, 1974; New York, St. Martin's Press, 1975.

Plays

Secret People (screenplay), with others, in *Making a Film,* edited by Lindsay Anderson. London, Allen and Unwin, and New York, Macmillan, 1952.

Screenplays: *Death in High Heels,* 1947; *The Mark of Cain,* with W.P. Lipscomb and Francis Cowdry, 1948; *Secret People,* with others, 1952.

Other

Danger Unlimited (for children). New York, Dodd Mead, 1948; as *Welcome to Danger,* London, Foley House Press, 1950.
Heavens Knows Who. London, Joseph, and New York, Scribner, 1960.
Nurse Matilda (for children). Leicester, Brockhampton Press, and New York, Dutton, 1964.
Nurse Matilda Goes to Town (for children). Leicester, Brockhampton Press, 1967; New York, Dutton, 1968.
Nurse Matilda Goes to Hospital (for children). London, Hodder and Stoughton, and New York, Dutton, 1974.
"Inspector Cockrill," in *The Great Detectives,* edited by Otto Penzler. Boston, Little Brown, 1978.

Editor, *Naughty Children: An Anthology.* London, Gollancz, 1962; New York, Dutton, 1963.

*

Bibliography: "The Works of Christianna Brand" by Otto Penzler, in *Green for Danger,* San Diego, University of California Extension, 1978.

Christianna Brand commented (1984):
I have written in all eight detective stories of which I can say that I am really proud. I write a few "mainstreym" novels also, but crime novels are my real interest. I write them for no reason more pretentious than simply to entertain. I try to include, within the regulation puzzle form, good and interesting characterization, dialogue, and background: having written a scene containing the necessary "clues," I will go back over it and try to make it interesting in itself, so that readers not interested in crime fiction might read the books for their own sakes, as novels. I write with enormous respect for correctness and style, endlessly altering and fiddling with my work and with scrupulous fairness in the puzzle aspect. But all that being said, I make no claim to do anything other than entertain.

*　*　*

Perhaps best known for her detective stories featuring Inspector Cockrill of the Kent County Police, Christianna Brand was the author of a number of mystery or suspense stories and novels. *The Three-Cornered Halo,* described by the author as a "mystery-comedy," takes place on an imaginary island (also the setting for *Tour de Force*) and features Inspector Cockrill's sister, Henrietta. This novel, which contains strong fantasy elements, embodies the essence of the author's claim to distinction: a sense of humour, conveyed in a witty style which allows the reader to see the absurdities of human behavior without losing track of the essential seriousness of the plot. *Green for Danger,* set in a military hospital during World War II, presents one of the most ingenious murders ever devised: a patient is killed on the operating table under the eyes of seven witnesses. *Heads You Lose,* in which Inspector Cockrill made his first appearance, is the story of a jealous spinster who declares that she "wouldn't be caught dead in a ditch" wearing a particular hat. She is murdered, and her severed head, complete with hat, is found in a ditch.

Brand's lightness of touch should not be confused with a lack of seriousness. *Cat and Mouse* is included in Julian Symons's list of the 100 best crime stories because, he says, "the author seems here to take her characters just a little more seriously than usual." In fact, she invariably takes her characters seriously; it is the absurdity of their situations which she observes and documents with telling irony. Her surprise endings, reminiscent of the final "turn of the screw" in an O. Henry story, are much admired; *London Particular* reveals the criminal's method in the last line. It is a tribute to Brand's skill at characterization that her endings are as convincing as they are ingenious.

Inspector Cockrill is in the tradition of the eccentric, omniscient private detective rather than that of the realistic police procedural. Shrewd, irascible, and shabbily dressed, his fingers stained dark from rolling cigarettes, Cockrill is a *deus ex machina* who manages, by virtue of acute powers of observation, to ferret out the real criminal from a confusing collection of suspects. The reader derives great satisfaction from trying to outwit the Inspector; that he rarely succeeds in doing so is the result of the author's subtlety in planting false clues, dropping apparent red herrings in unlikely places, and providing a convincing cast of Least Likely Persons from which to choose.

In her shorter mystery fiction, collected in *What Dread Hand?* and *Brand X,* Brand was particularly adept at the intricate plotting for which she is well known. The stories are almost uniformly satisfying, whether or not they feature Inspector Cockrill. Of her long suspense novels without the serial detective, *Death in High Heels,* about murder in a chic London fashion house, and *Cat and Mouse,* a gothic suspense story, are especially noteworthy.

—Joanne Harack Hayne

———

BRANDT, Tom *See* **DEWEY, Thomas B.**

———

BRANSON, H(enry) C(lay). American. Born in Battle Creek, Michigan. Educated at Princeton University, New Jersey, 1924; University of Michigan, Ann Arbor, B.A. 1937. Married; three daughters.

CRIME PUBLICATIONS

Novels (series: John Bent in all books)

I'll Eat You Last. New York, Simon and Schuster, 1941;
 London, Lane, 1943; as *I'll Kill You Last,* New York, Mystery
 Novel of the Month, 1942.
The Pricking Thumb. New York, Simon and Schuster, 1942;
 London, Lane, 1949.
Case of the Giant Killer. New York, Simon and Schuster,
 1944; London, Lane, 1949.
The Fearful Passage. New York, Simon and Schuster, 1945;
 London, Lane, 1950.
Last Year's Blood. New York, Simon and Schuster, 1947;
 London, Lane, 1950.
The Leaden Bubble. New York, Simon and Schuster, 1949;
 London, Lane, 1951.
Beggar's Choice. New York, Simon and Schuster, 1953.

OTHER PUBLICATIONS

Novel

Salisbury Plain. New York, Dutton, 1965.

* * *

Henry Clay Branson derived from his father not only his
substantial American name but also a solid midwestern
upbringing. Branson had read Doyle as a boy, followed Philo
Vance's cases in Paris in the pages of *Scribner's Magazine,* and
was one of the most familiar of card-holders at the Ann Arbor
Public Library, where he withdrew and consumed hundreds of
mystery stories. Following a period of physical and emotional
crisis, he considered: perhaps he could write detective fiction.

John Bent, Branson's series detective, is a physician by
training, but does not practice in the stories. He is low-keyed,
humane, likeable, self-assured, and wise. He is singularly
observant and frank to the point of being out-spoken—this
being perhaps his only vice outside the pleasures of drinking
and smoking to which he is openly devoted. We know little
more about him. Branson takes a similar approach to the
locales of his books. One is never sure precisely where the
action is taking place. In his mind, Branson sees all of his
stories laid out in and around Battle Creek, Jackson, and
Kalamazoo, Michigan. But geography is always vague for his
readers. Praise for most of Branson's work has been general
and widespread. People and the tangles they involve themselves in are what interest Branson, and consequently the stress
in the Bent novels is on plotting. Analyzing behavior and
discerning motivations are the detective's strong suits. In these
respects he has won his place among the best.

—Donald A. Yates

BRAUN, Lilian Jackson. American. Address: c/o The
Putnam Berkley Group Inc., 200 Madison Avenue, New York,
New York 10016, U.S.A.

CRIME PUBLICATIONS

Novels (series: Jim Qwilleran in all books)

The Cat Who Could Read Backwards. New York, Dutton,
 1966; London, Collins, 1967.
The Cat Who Ate Danish Modern. New York, Dutton, 1967;
 London, Collins, 1968.
The Cat Who Turned On and Off. New York, Dutton, and
 London, Collins, 1968.
The Cat Who Saw Red. New York, Jove, 1986.
The Cat Who Played Brahms. New York, Jove, 1987.
The Cat Who Played Post Office. New York, Jove, 1987.
The Cat Who Knew Shakespeare. New York, Jove, 1988.
The Cat Who Sniffed Glue. New York, Putnam, 1988.
The Cat Who Went Underground. New York, Putnam, 1989.
The Cat Who Talked to Ghosts. New York, Putnam, 1990.
The Cat Who Lived High. New York, Putnam, 1990.

Short Stories

The Cat Who Had 14 Tales. New York, Jove, 1988.

* * *

Lilian Jackson Braun has written a well-crafted, witty, and
highly entertaining series called *The Cat Who....* These books
tell the adventures of amateur detective Jim Qwilleran and his
two Siamese cats, Koko and Yum Yum.

Qwilleran (known to his friends as Qwill) from the unusual
spelling of his name to his unpretentious life style is a well-
defined and likable character. Qwilleran is a middle-aged,
slightly rumpled bachelor newspaperman with an oversized
mustache and an overactive curiosity. The Siamese cats, Koko
and Yum Yum, are likable and smart but not supernatural.
They do catlike things which are interpreted by Qwilleran as
clues in solving crimes, but he is always willing to give them the
credit for the solutions. Thus, the premise of cats "solving
mysteries" is not as far-fetched as the series title would imply.

Anyone who has ever shared life with a pet will understand
and appreciate Qwilleran's fondness and indulgence of his cats.
Readers who may be ambivalent about cats can still appreciate
their entertaining antics.

Braun's only book not in the Qwilleran series is a collection of
short stories *The Cat Who Had 14 Tales.* In the novels the cats
Koko and Yum Yum seem real because Qwilleran tells their
story, whereas the short stories are weakened because some of
the cats are given human thought processes and even narrate
their own stories.

Among Braun's cast of memorable supporting characters
who grow and reappear like old friends throughout the series
are Iris Cobb, Qwilleran's landlady during his stay in Junktown
(*The Cat Who Turned On and Off*); Polly Duncan, Pickax City's
librarian and one of Qwilleran's romantic interests; Melinda
Goodwinter, local doctor and member of the famous Goodwinter family; Alexander and Penelope Goodwinter of the
Pickax City law firm of Goodwinter and Goodwinter. These
and other supporting characters are clearly defined. They often
have major roles in the plot but some of them become victims or
villains and disappear from the series.

Braun's plots are always original. The murder victims are the
rich and famous as well as the poor. The murders are both
surprising and shocking, but the dialogue, the local color, and
the characters make up more of the story than the act of murder
itself. Braun is a master of using words to draw visual images of
the people, the places, and the cats such as this description of
the two Siamese from *The Cat Who Saw Red:* "Waiting for

him, they looked like two loaves of homemade bread. They sat facing the door—two bundles of pale toasty fur with brown legs tucked out of sight." The dialogue is witty, from the good-natured bantering between the newspapermen at the Press Club to the conversations with the Moose County locals where every greeting begins with a discussion of the weather.

In the first book in the series, *The Cat Who Could Read Backwards,* Qwilleran, a former big city crime reporter, down on his luck after a nasty divorce and a bout with drinking, lands a job as a features writer with a midwestern newspaper, the *Daily Fluxion,* where he discovers his boyhood chum, Arch Riker, is the features editor and his new boss. Qwilleran is assigned to cover the local art beat even though he is a novice on the subject. Quickly he discovers the underlying jealousies and rivalries among the artists and the *Fluxion*'s own mysterious art critic, George Bonifield Mountclemens III. When an artist is found murdered, Qwilleran's natural curiosity as well as his previous crime reporting experience draws him into the investigation.

Murder seems to follow Qwilleran on his assignment as a features writer. His writing assignments take him into the world of interior decorating (*The Cat Who Ate Danish Modern*), antiques and antique dealers (*The Cat Who Turned On and Off*), and gourmet dining (*The Cat Who Saw Red*).

In *The Cat Who Played Brahms,* Braun switches locales and takes Qwilleran to Mooseville ("400 miles north of every-where") on a summer vacation at the cottage of rich and eccentric old family friend "Aunt" Fanny Klingenschoen. This book is especially rich in local color and conversation. Qwilleran plans to spend a quiet summer writing a book, but strange things start happening and he and the cats spend their time detecting instead of writing.

After unexpectedly inheriting a huge fortune, Qwilleran and the cats move to Pickax City (in Moose County) and take up residence in their inherited mansion. When his curiosity leads him to start asking questions about the disappearance of one of the mansion's maids five years earlier, he uncovers secrets that some of the townspeople would rather forget. (*The Cat Who Played Post Office*) Qwilleran investigates the accident that claimed the life of the *Pickax Picayune*'s eccentric publisher in *The Cat Who Knew Shakespeare.* The Pickax Theatre Club's opening performance is cancelled because of murder in *The Cat Who Sniffed Glue.* Qwilleran is back in Mooseville at the summer cottage in *The Cat Who Went Underground* and discovers what appears to be a vendetta against handymen. In *The Cat Who Talked to Ghosts,* Qwilleran investigates ghosts haunting the Goodwinter Farm Museum only to find skeletons in prominent families' closets.

Braun's mysteries have a thoroughly original and likable sleuth team in Jim Qwilleran and the Siamese cats, Koko and Yum Yum. The Siamese cats with their elegance and exuberance are a perfect foil to Qwilleran's staid personality. Readers can enjoy Braun's books not only for their mystery plots but as stories of witty and entertaining characters, local color, and of course, the antics of the cats.

—Carol Barry

BREAN, Herbert. American. Born in Detroit, Michigan, 10 December 1907. Educated at University of Detroit High School; University of Michigan, Ann Arbor, A.B. 1929. Married Dorothy Skeman in 1934; two daughters. Staff member, United Press, New York, 1929, and in Detroit an assistant bureau manager; writer for Detroit *Times,* for 10 years; Detroit *Time* and *Life* news bureau chief, 1943–44, then in New York as a *Life* editor, and staff writer, 1953–62. Public Relations consultant to General Motors. President of Mystery Writers of America, 1967. Fellow, International Institute of Arts and Letters. *Died 7 May 1973.*

CRIME PUBLICATIONS

Novels (series: William Deacon; Reynold Frame)

Wilders Walk Away (Frame). New York, Morrow, 1948; London, Heinemann, 1949.
The Darker the Night (Frame). New York, Morrow, 1949; London, Heinemann, 1950.
Hardly a Man Is Now Alive (Frame). New York, Morrow, 1950; London, Heinemann, 1952; as *Murder Now and Then,* London, Macmillan, 1965.
The Clock Strikes Thirteen (Frame). New York, Morrow, 1952; London, Heinemann, 1954.
A Matter of Fact. New York, Morrow, 1956; as *Collar for the Killer,* London, Heinemann, 1957; as *Dead Sure,* New York, Dell, 1958.
The Traces of Brillhart (Deacon). New York, Harper, 1960; London, Heinemann, 1961.
The Traces of Merrilee (Deacon). New York, Morrow, 1966.

Uncollected Short Stories

"The Hooded Hawk," in *American Magazine* (Springfield, Ohio), November 1949.
"Nine Hours Late on Opening Run," in *Ellery Queen's Mystery Magazine* (New York), December 1957.
"Then They Came Running," in *Ellery Queen's 14th Mystery Annual.* New York, Random House, 1959; London, Collins, 1961.
"Something White in the Night," in *Crimes Across the Sea,* edited by John Creasey. New York, Harper, and London, Longman, 1964.
"Incident at Mardi's," in *Alfred Hitchcock's Mystery Magazine* (New York), January 1966.

OTHER PUBLICATIONS

Other

How to Stop Smoking. New York, Vanguard Press, 1951; Kingswood, Surrey, World's Work, 1952; revised edition, Vanguard Press, 1958.
How to Stop Drinking. New York, Holt Rinehart, 1958; as *A Handbook for Drinkers—and for Those Who Want to Stop,* New York, Collier, 1963.
The Life Treasury of American Folklore. New York, Time, 1961.
The Music of Life, with the editors of *Life.* New York, Time, 1962.
The Only Diet That Works. New York, Morrow, 1965.

Editor, *The Mystery Writers' Handbook.* New York, Harper, 1956.

*

Manuscript Collection: Mugar Memorial Library, Boston University.

* * *

Herbert Brean, newspaperman, magazine writer, and author of 12 books, perfected his craft throughout his professional life. During his years on the Detroit *Times,* he began to write detective stories for pulp magazines. After moving to New York to work on *Life* magazine, he fulfilled his ambition to write a mystery novel with *Wilders Walk Away* in 1948, the first of seven he was to produce.

Part of Brean's boyhood was spent in Vermont, his father's home territory, and the setting for his first mystery. The narrator Reynold Frame, a magazine free-lancer in the town of Wilders Lane to do a story, meets the town's oldest family, who still live in their ancestral home surrounded by heirlooms. Plagued with vanishing menfolk since the 1775 disappearance of Jonathan Wilder, the family is in trouble again when Constance Wilder's young sister goes missing, as does an aunt soon after. Secret compartments and passages, murder both contemporary and remote, and a Revolutionary War treasure are parts of this story.

Frame appears again in *Hardly a Man Is Now Alive,* set in Concord, Massachusetts. Frame finds himself among an odd group, and in an atmosphere seemingly conducive to supernatural manifestations. Once again present-day crimes are mixed up with old ones. A mystery of the American Revolution is cleared up, a 19th-century literary puzzle is solved, and a modern murderer is exposed. A venerable citizen of 104 who knew Emerson and who had heard about the battles of Lexington and Concord from an eyewitness is a pivotal character. Concord lore from the Revolutionary period and from its literary heyday of the next century are cleverly interwoven to create a delightful tale.

The Clock Strikes Thirteen, another Frame novel, takes place on an island off the coast of Maine where a team of scientists is engaged in research on germ warfare. When the book appeared it contained information that was only beginning to be known to the public. *A Matter of Fact* is an excellent police procedural in which the attitudes and motivations of several officers are explored in depth. A young detective is tormented by guilt because of evidence tampered with by an unlucky colleague about to retire. The New York setting and the climate in which the police must work are thoughtfully portrayed.

In *The Traces of Brillhart,* the narrator-hero is journalist William Deacon. Deacon's girlfriend (an independent young woman with a Phi Beta Kappa key and a Ph.D. in chemistry) and their friends the Dolans help him straighten things out. Supposedly murdered, Brillhart, a contemptible character from the popular music industry, returns from the dead only to be murdered definitely. *The Traces of Merrilee* is set on a luxury liner on which Deacon, his girl, and the Dolans share an elegant suite. Deacon has been hired to look after Merrilee Moore, an insecure but legendary movie star reminiscent of Marilyn Monroe. A campaign of terror is waged to keep her from making a movie. In this last crime novel Brean is at his best. Deacon, modest and slightly self-mocking, is a thoroughly likable fellow. His encounters with the lovely Merrilee—every man's fantasy—are done with just the right touch.

Many mystery authors have used quotations from other works as chapter headings, and Brean follows this tradition. An original feature of his books, however, is his use of footnotes to provide additional information bearing on his story, to illuminate background, and to distinguish fact from fiction. Intelligent, with a lively curiosity and an unusual fund of knowledge about many things, Brean includes much fascinating material in his mysteries. His interests in music, travel, and good food are obvious, as is that in scientific developments in such fields as parapsychology and microbiology. Herbert Brean was witty, urbane, civilized, and created characters worthy of their author.

—Mary Helen Becker

BREEN, Jon L(inn). American. Born in Montgomery, Alabama, 8 November 1943. Educated at Pepperdine College (now University), Los Angeles, B.A. 1965; University of Southern California, Los Angeles, M.S. in library science 1966. Served in the United States Army, 1967–69. Married Rita A. Gunson in 1970. Sports broadcaster, Radio KWAV, Los Angeles, 1963–65; librarian, California State University, Long Beach, 1966–67, California State University, Dominguez Hills, 1969–75, and since 1975 Rio Hondo College, Whittier, California. Mystery book reviewer, *Wilson Library Bulletin,* 1972–83, and *Ellery Queen's Mystery Magazine,* 1977–83, both New York. Recipient: Mystery Writers of America Edgar Allan Poe award, for non-fiction, 1981, 1984. Address: 10642 La Bahia Avenue, Fountain Valley, California 92708, U.S.A.

CRIME PUBLICATIONS

Novels (series: Jerry Brogan; Rachel Hennings)

Listen for the Click (Brogan). New York, Walker, 1983; as *Vicar's Roses,* London, Macmillan, 1984.
The Gathering Place. (Hennings). New York, Walker, and London, Macmillan, 1984.
Triple Crown (Brogan). London, Macmillan, 1985; New York, Walker, 1986.
Touch of the Past (Hennings). New York, Walker, 1988; London, Macmillan, 1989.
Loose Lips (Brogan). New York, Simon and Schuster, and London, Macmillan, 1990.

Short Stories

Hair of the Sleuthhound: Parodies of Mystery Fiction. Metuchen, New Jersey, Scarecrow Press, 1982.

Uncollected Short Stories

"The Idea Man," in *The Queen Canon Bibliophile* (Oneida Castle, New York), August 1969.
"Horsehide Sleuth," in *Ellery Queen's Mystery Magazine* (New York), November 1971.
"The Fortune Cookie," in *Ellery Queen's Mystery Bag.* New York, World, 1972; London, Gollancz, 1973.
"The Body in the Bullpen," in *Ellery Queen's Mystery Magazine* (New York), May 1972.
"The Babe Ruth Murder Case," in *Ellery Queen's Mystery Magazine* (New York), June 1972.
"Fall of a Hero," in *Ellery Queen's Mystery Magazine* (New York), November 1972.
"Old-Timer's Game," in *Ellery Queen's Mystery Magazine* (New York), April 1973.
"Malice at the Mike," in *Ellery Queen's Mystery Magazine* (New York), October 1973.
"C.I.A.: The Swedish Boot Mystery," in *Ellery Queen's Mystery Magazine* (New York), November 1973.
"Designated Murderer," in *Ellery Queen's Mystery Magazine* (New York), July 1974.

"The Vanity Murder Case," in *Ellery Queen's Aces of Mystery*. New York, Davis, 1975.

"The Adventure of the Disoriented Detective," in *Ellery Queen's Mystery Magazine* (New York), September 1976.

"The Pun Detective," in *Ellery Queen's Mystery Magazine* (New York), April 1977.

"The Clara Long Case," *Alfred Hitchcock's Mystery Magazine* (New York), July 1977.

"Diamond Dick," in *Masterpieces of Mystery: Detective Directory: Part Two,* edited by Ellery Queen. New York, Davis, 1978.

"The Auteur Theory," in *Alfred Hitchcock's Mystery Magazine* (New York), January 1978.

"The Pun Detective and the Great Seal Mystery," in *Cloak and Dagger* (Englewood Cliffs, New Jersey), 7 April 1978.

"Revival in Eastport,"in *Ellery Queen's Mystery Magazine* (New York), February 1979.

"Match Race," in *Ellery Queen's Mystery Magazine* (New York), June 1979.

"Affirmative Action," in *Mike Shayne Mystery Magazine* (Los Angeles), January 1980.

"The Threat of Nostalgia," in *Skullduggery* (Owensboro, Kentucky), May 1980.

"A Quiet Death," in *Mike Shayne Mystery Magazine* (Los Angeles), November 1980.

"The Flying Thief of Oz," in *Ellery Queen's Doors to Mystery*. New York, Davis, 1981.

"Silver Spectre," in *Best Detective Stories of the Year 1981,* edited by Edward D. Hoch. New York, Dutton, 1981.

"The Number 12 Jinx," in *All But Impossible!,* edited by Edward D. Hoch. New Haven, Connecticut, Ticknor and Fields, 1981.

"The Old Radio Puzzle," in *Black Cat 5* (Toronto), 1982.

"The Pun Detective and the Danny Boy Killer," in *Mike Shayne Mystery Magazine* (Los Angeles), March 1982.

"The World's Champion Lovers," in *Mike Shayne Mystery Magazine* (Los Angeles), July 1983.

"Instant Replay," in *Ellery Queen's Mystery Magazine* (New York), May 1984.

"Spirit Recording," in *Ellery Queen's Mystery Magazine* (New York), Mid-December 1984.

"A Thumb on the Scales," in *Winter Crimes 17,* edited by George Harding. London, Macmillan, 1985.

"A Piece of the Auction," in *Ellery Queen's Mystery Magazine* (New York), July 1986.

"The Straight and Narrow," in *Ellery Queen's Mystery Magazine* (New York), Mid-December 1986.

"Starstruck," in *Murder in Los Angeles,* edited by Bill Adler and D. C. Fontana. New York, Morrow, 1987.

"All-Star Team," in *Murder California Style,* edited by Jon L. Breen and John Ball. New York, St. Martin's Press, 1987.

"The Adventure of the Unique Holmes," in *The New Adventures of Sherlock Holmes,* edited by Martin H Greenberg and Carol-Lynn Rössel Waugh. New York, Carroll and Graf, 1987.

"The Big Nap," in *Hardboiled* (Rockford, Illinois), Summer-Fall 1987.

"Streak to Death," in *The Second Black Lizard Anthology of Crime Fiction,* edited by Edward Gorman. Berkeley, California, Black Lizard Press, 1987.

"Captain Benvolio Bullhorner," in *Detective Story Magazine* (New York), August 1989.

OTHER PUBLICATIONS

Other

"Charlie Chan in Qui Nhon," in *Armchair Detective* (White Bear Lake, Minnesota), January 1969.

"About the Murders of Anthony Abbot," in *Armchair Detective* (White Bear Lake, Minnesota), October 1969.

A Little Fleshed Up Around the Crook of the Elbow: A Selected Bibliography of Some Literary Parodies. Dominguez Hills, California State College Library, 1970.

"On Carolyn Wells," in *Armchair Detective* (White Bear Lake, Minnesota), January 1970.

"The Invisible Man Revisited," in *Armchair Detective* (White Bear Lake, Minnesota), April 1971.

"Detective Fiction and the Turf," in *Armchair Detective* (White Bear Lake, Minnesota), October 1971.

The Girl in the Pictorial Wrapper: An Index to Reviews of Paperback Original Novels in the New York Times' "Criminals at Large" Column 1953–1970. Dominguez Hills, California State College Library, 1972; revised edition, 1973.

"On Lee Thayer," in *Armchair Detective* (White Bear Lake, Minnesota), April 1972.

The Mystery of Racing," in *Thoroughbred Record* (Lexington, Kentucky), 27 October 1973.

"Who Killed Charlie Chan?" in *Armchair Detective* (White Bear Lake, Minnesota), February 1974.

"Charlie Chan: The Man Behind the Curtain," in *Views and Reviews* (Milwaukee), Fall 1974.

"Murder Number One: Earl Derr Biggers," in *New Republic* (Washington, D.C.), 30 July 1977.

"Reviewing Mysteries," in *Book Reviewing,* edited by Sylvia E. Kamerman. Boston, The Writer, 1978.

"On Science Fiction Detective Stories," in *Isaac Asimov's Science Fiction Magazine* (New York), June 1979.

"Cortland Fitzsimmons and the Sports Mystery," in *Armchair Detective* (New York), Spring 1981.

What about Murder? A Guide to Books about Mystery and Detective Fiction. Metuchen, New Jersey, Scarecrow Press, 1981.

"The Classical Detective Novel in America," in *AB Bookman's Weekly* (Clifton, New Jersey), 16 April 1984.

Novel Verdicts: A Critical Guide to Courtroom Fiction. Metuchen, New Jersey, Scarecrow Press, 1984.

Editor, with Rita A. Breen, *American Murders: 11 Rediscovered Short Novels from the American Magazine 1934–54.* New York, Garland, 1986.

Editor, with John Ball, *Murder California Style: A Collection of Short Stories by the Southern California Chapter of Mystery Writers of America.* New York, St. Martin's Press, 1987.

Editor, with Martin H. Greenberg, *Murder Off the Rack: Critical Studies of Ten Paperbacks.* Metuchen, New Jersey, Scarecrow Press, 1989.

*

Jon L. Breen comments:

My enthusiasm for mysteries dates back to hearing "Mr. Chameleon" and "Hearthstone of the Death Squad" on the radio, and an element of nostalgia seems to run through most of my stories. In detective fiction, I most appreciate the labyrinthine puzzle plots of Ellery Queen, John Dickson Carr, and Agatha Christie, and (as perhaps logically follows) I find that the hardest kind of story to write. As detective-story backgrounds, I am especially fond of sports, courtrooms, religion, show business (especially of the early 20th century), the book world, and such relatively slow modes of transportation as ships and trains. What I haven't yet used from the above list I probably will, and what I have I probably will again. My strong points seem to be humor and the ability to create likeable characters. My weak points I won't enumerate, just in case they are less obvious to others than they are to me.

*   *   *

Jon L. Breen's contributions to the mystery field fall neatly into four categories: book reviews and critical work, short parodies of other writers, "serious" short mysteries, and detective novels. His periodical articles and regular review columns for *Wilson Library Bulletin* and *Ellery Queen's Mystery Magazine* rank with the finest mystery criticism since the death of Anthony Boucher, and his reference volumes *What About Murder?* and *Novel Verdicts* are indispensable guides, the one to earlier nonfiction books on the genre, the other to courtroom crime fiction. His parodies, collected in *Hair of the Sleuthhound*, are masterpieces of this most difficult form, capturing in about 10 pages apiece both what is memorable and what is laughable in the styles and shticks of Van Dine, Queen, Carr, Christie, McBain, MacDonald, Macdonald and the outrageous Avallone. His "straight" short mysteries—including the cases of umpire-detective Ed Gorgon and some fine pastiches of Earl Derr Biggers' Charlie Chan—reflect Breen's love of the old-fashioned whodunit and of horse-racing, baseball and other sports. If he sometimes mirrors too faithfully the dullness of style and characterization of the mid-level Golden Age detective writers, his best tales spring from premises worthy of Carr or Queen.

Breen's novels, like his short stories, pay homage both to sports and to Golden Age traditions. His first, third and fifth full-length mysteries feature racetrack announcer Jerry Brogan while his second and fourth deal with bookshop owner Rachel Hennings. Both characters prove themselves as amateur detectives in cases that spring from their occupations. In *Listen for the Click* Brogan becomes involved when a jockey is shot to death in riding silks at the foot of a bronze horse statue, and in *Triple Crown* he looks into a series of deaths connected with the Big Three turf contests of the title. *The Gathering Place* opens with Rachel inheriting a bookshop and moving to Los Angeles, where she finds romance, murder and an uncanny ability to duplicate the signatures of dead authors. Clearly Breen agrees with Rachel that old books are ikons and old bookshops temples. Indeed friendly ghosts hover about Rachel's premises like guardian angels, or fugitives from a Spielberg supernatural fantasy. But in *Touch of the Past* the lady is on her own, exploring the murder of a long-forgotten mystery writer who for reasons unknown had surrounded himself with hundreds of artifacts from the year 1937. All of Breen's novels to date feature neat plots, likable people, unpretentious prose, a soft-spoken leisurely ambience—precisely as if the ghost of Earl Derr Biggers were hovering over his disciple's word processor.

—Francis M. Nevins, Jr.

———

BRETT, Michael. *See* **TRIPP, Miles.**

———

BRETT, Simon (Anthony Lee). British. Born in Worcester Park, Surrey, 28 October 1945. Educated at Dulwich College, London, 1956–64; Wadham College, Oxford (President, Oxford University Dramatic Society), B.A. (honours) in English 1967. Married Lucy Victoria McLaren in 1971; one daughter and two sons. Radio producer, BBC, London, 1967–77; producer, London Weekend Television, 1977–79. Chairman, Crime Writers Association, 1986–87. Recipient: Writers Guild of Great Britain radio award, 1973; Broadcasting Press Guild award, 1987. Agent: Michael Motley Ltd., 78 Gloucester Terrace, London W2 3HH. Address: Frith House, Burpham, Arundel BN18 9RR, England.

CRIME PUBLICATIONS

Novels (series: Charles Paris; Mrs. Pargeter)

Cast, In Order of Disappearance (Paris).   London, Gollancz, 1975; New York, Scribner, 1976.
So Much Blood (Paris).   London, Gollancz, 1976; New York, Scribner, 1977.
Star Trap (Paris).   London, Gollancz, 1977; New York, Scribner, 1978.
An Amateur Corpse. (Paris).   London, Gollancz, and New York, Scribner, 1978.
A Comedian Dies (Paris).   London, Gollancz, and New York, Scribner, 1979.
The Dead Side of the Mike (Paris).   London, Gollancz, and New York, Scribner, 1980.
Situation Tragedy (Paris).   London, Gollancz, and New York, Scribner, 1981.
Murder Unprompted (Paris).   London, Gollancz, and New York, Scribner, 1982.
Murder in the Title (Paris).   London, Gollancz, and New York, Scribner, 1983.
Not Dead, Only Resting (Paris).   London, Gollancz, and New York, Scribner, 1984.
A Shock to the System.   London, Macmillan, 1984; New York, Scribner, 1985.
Dead Giveaway (Paris).   London, Gollancz, 1985; New York, Scribner, 1986.
Dead Romantic.   London, Macmillan, 1985; New York, Scribner, 1986.
A Nice Class of Corpse (Pargeter).   London, Macmillan, 1986; New York, Scribner, 1987.
Shock to the System.   New York, Dell, 1987.
What Bloody Man Is That? (Paris).   London, Gollancz, and New York, Scribner, 1987.
Mrs. Presumed Dead (Pargeter).   London, Macmillan, 1988; New York, Scribner, 1989.
A Series of Murders (Paris).   London, Gollancz, and New York, Scribner, 1989.

Short Stories

A Box of Tricks.   London, Gollancz, 1985; as *Tickled to Death*, New York, Scribner, 1985.

OTHER PUBLICATIONS

Novel

After Henry (novelization of radio series).   London, Viking, 1987.

Plays

Mrs. Gladys Moxon (produced London, 1970).
Did You Sleep Well, and A Good Day at the Office (produced London, 1971).
Third Person (produced London, 1972).
Drake's Dream, music and lyrics by Lynne and Richard Riley (produced Worthing, Sussex, and London, 1977).

Radio Plays: *Semi-Circles* series, 1982; *Gothic Romances,* 1982; *A Matter of Life and Death,* 1982; *Cast, In Order of Disappearance,* from his own novel, 1984; *So Much Blood,* from his own novel, 1985; *After Henry,* 1985; *Molesworth* series, 1987.

Television Plays: *The Crime of the Dancing Duchess,* 1983; *A Promising Death,* 1983; *After Henry* series, 1988–1990

Other

Frank Muir Goes into.... London, Robson, 1978; *Second, Third,* and *Fourth* books, 3 vols., 1979–81.
Frank Muir on Children. London, Heinemann, 1980.
Molesworth Rites Again. London, Hutchinson, 1983.
The Childowner's Handbook. London, Allen and Unwin, 1983.
Bad Form or, How Not to Get Invited Back. London, Elm Tree, 1984.
People Spotting: The Human Species Laid Bare. London, Elm Tree, 1985.
The Wastepaper Basket Archive. London, Sidgwick and Jackson, 1986.
The Three Detectives and the Missing Superstar (for children). New York, Scribner, and London, Scholastic Hippo, 1986.
The Three Detectives and the Knight in Armour (for children). New York, Scribner, 1987.
The Booker Book (on the Booker Prize). London, Sidgwick and Jackson, 1989.

Editor, *The Faber Book of Useful Verse.* London, Faber, 1981.
Editor, with Frank Muir, *Frank Muir Presents the Book of Comedy Sketches.* London, Elm Tree, 1982.
Editor, *Take a Spare Truss: Tips for Nineteenth Century Travellers.* London, Elm Tree, 1983.
Editor, *The Faber Book of Parodies.* London, Faber, 1984.
Editor, *The Faber Book of Diaries.* London, Faber, 1989.

Manuscript Collection: Mugar Memorial Library, Boston University.

*

Simon Brett comments:

In the Charles Paris books I am able to combine two of my major interests, the theatre and crime, together, I hope, with a dash of humour. They are written solely to entertain. Through short stories, however, I have been able to explore other kinds of crime-writing and, though I will never abandon Charles Paris (I'm far too fond of him—anyway, no one else ever gives him any work), I hope in the future to continue to extend the range of my crime fiction.

*   *   *

Simon Brett's Charles Paris detective stories *are* the insider's view of show business and the middleaged actor Paris himself, a discontent with bourgeois settling, for whom the stage represents constant promise of a brave new world. Boredom makes Charles, like Sherlock Holmes, anxious. Nothing combats it for long—not sex, not detection, not even acting, and everyday professional practice is much more boring than exhilarating. With his talisman, a large Bell's whisky, Charles can anesthetize dullness and for the moment also evade the guilt for freedom that often vexes this very decent libertine.

Brett's representation of contemporary British Boz Arts from the high West End to the desert of television sitcoms and game shows is acid and ceaselessly fascinating. The seedy rehearsal room in London's warehouse district, the desperate artiness of provincial amateur companies, the barracudas of TV production, the compulsory hardboiled argot of the young, the untiring inventive bitchiness of British theater people. Of this world, Brett has given us a vivid fictional encyclopedia.

A few individual characters repeat from book to book: Charles's Watson, a successful London solicitor always willing to table his lucrative practice when the game's afoot; his incompetent agent; his admirable, undivorced, all-but-ex-wife and their numbingly boring yuppy daughter and son-in-law. Most, however, are types, like the interchangeable beautiful horny ingenues whom Charles beds and the university mates who have, unlike the often "resting" actor, achieved fame and fortune in respectable professions. The typical dramatis personae of various showbusiness "venues" also tend to be undistinguishable from one another, except sometimes the featured players, of whatever sex, all infected with lust for power and overweening pride, usually proportionate to their trashiness as performers.

Although Brett always provides something of an investigative plot, that is the weakest element of these novels. One readily accepts that Charles, a curious combination of inexperienced amateur detective and occasional hardboiled rake, often bungles through drunkenness, sexual distraction or just inattentiveness. However, it is usually difficult to work up interest in what happens to Brett's cast of indistinct suspects or in the mechanical operations of the plot. The red herrings usually remain just cold fish.

The best Paris mysteries in texture, wit and even plotting are those about the theater, perhaps because, unlike broadcasting, the variety show or popular music, has tradition, some standards other than money and survival and a degree of seriousness. (This is not to say that there aren't flashes of brilliance in the other books, notably the constantly funny music-hall veteran of *A Comedian Dies.*) Although the plot of *What Bloody Man is That?* with its short list of suspects readily may be seen through, the book succeeds because of the variety and richness of the theater. High jinks during rehearsals and performances are combined with a send-up of Royal Shakespeare pomposity and representation of a fascinatingly obnoxious old actor-queen. Brett's "production" of Shakespeare is brilliant. The novel is crammed with Shakespearean text and issues of interpretation. Charles and his fellow professionals know the plays intimately, can quote ad lib whole passages, remember the details of their every appearance in Shakespeare. The play here, *Macbeth,* has a reputation for calamitous production that several detective stories before Brett's have exploited. Of many Shakespearean mysteries by writers as diverse as Ngaio Marsh, Michael Innes and M.M. Kaye, to name a few, *What Bloody Man is That?* for its knowledge without pretension and brisk economy seems to me the best.

With good sense, Brett has allowed Charles to age. A certain James Bond-ish stud quality has given way to banked fires and even (gasp!) occasional impotence. The figure of his career appears ever more ambiguous; Charles now speculates about the closing scenes. Where some Paris novels of the late 1970's and early 1980's suffered from the growing mechanicality that afflicts any series, the latest, *A Series of Murders,* implies a modest new turn. Here, the venue is a television series based on the novels of a fictional Golden Age mistress of mystery. Brett's untypical invoking of detective-fiction tradition contributes to an interesting psychology and motivation of crime and an engagingly knotty plot. As in a Christie novel there is a mounting rhythm of murder, and the sudden twists at the close appear to be Brett's homage to and even imitation of classic Christie.

One hopes that Brett will carry Charles into his sunset years, as Christie and Cyril Hare among others carried their distinctive creations. Although he has left the precincts of Paris several times for individual mysteries and lately two books about the widow Mrs. Pargeter—Jane Marple if she had flourished in boudoirs and among criminals—so far none has approached the distinction of the Paris mysteries.

—T.R. Steiner

BREWER, Gil. Also wrote as Eric Fitzgerald; Bailey Morgan. American. Served in the United States Army during World War II. Worked as warehouseman, gas station attendant, cannery worker, and book seller. Lived in Florida. *Died 9 January 1983.*

CRIME PUBLICATIONS

Novels (series: Al Mundy)

13 French Street. New York, Fawcett, 1951; London, New Fiction Press, 1952.
Satan Is a Woman. New York, Fawcett, 1951; London, New Fiction Press, 1952.
So Rich, So Dead. New York, Fawcett, 1951; London, New Fiction Press, 1952.
Flight to Darkness. New York, Fawcett, 1952.
Hell's Our Destination. New York, Fawcett, 1953; London, Fawcett, 1955.
A Killer Is Loose. New York, Fawcett, 1954; London, Moring, 1956.
Some Must Die. New York, Fawcett, 1954; London, Moring, 1956.
The Squeeze. New York, Ace, 1955.
77 Rue Paradis. New York, Fawcett, 1955; London, Red Seal, 1959.
And the Girl Screamed. New York, Fawcett, 1956; London, Fawcett, 1959.
The Angry Dream. New York, Bouregy, 1957; as *The Girl from Hateville*, Rockville Centre, New York, Zenith, 1958.
The Brat. New York, Fawcett, 1957; London, Fawcett, 1958.
Little Tramp. New York, Fawcett, 1957; London, Red Seal, 1959.
The Bitch. New York, Avon, 1958.
The Red Scarf. New York, Bouregy, 1958; London, Digit, 1959.
The Vengeful Virgin. New York, Fawcett, 1958; London, Muller, 1960.
Wild. New York, Fawcett, 1958; London, Fawcett, 1959.
Sugar. New York, Avon, 1959.
Wild to Possess. Derby, Connecticut, Monarch, 1959.
Angel. New York, Avon, 1960.
The Three-Way Split. New York, Fawcett, 1960.
Backwoods Teaser. New York, Fawcett, 1960.

Nude on Thin Ice. New York, Avon, 1960.
Appointment in Hell. Derby, Connecticut, Monarch, 1961.
A Taste of Sin. New York, Berkley, 1961.
Memory of Passion. New York, Lancer, 1963.
Play It Hard. Derby, Connecticut, Monarch, 1964.
The Hungry One. New York, Fawcett, 1966.
Sin for Me. New York, Banner, 1967.
The Tease. New York, Banner, 1967.
The Devil in Davos (Mundy; novelization of television play). New York, Ace, 1969.
Mediterranean Caper (Mundy; novelization of television play). New York, Ace, 1969.
Appointment in Cairo (Mundy; novelization of television play). New York, Ace, 1970.

Uncollected Short Stories

"The Quest of the Silver Cloud," in *Zeppelin Stories* (New York), April 1929.
"The Gorilla of the Gasbags," in *Zeppelin Stories* (New York), June 1929.
"The Derelict Dirigible," in *Zeppelin Stories* (New York), July 1929.
"Just Plain Dumb," in *Detective Fiction Weekly* (New York), 14 June 1930.
"The Second Ride," in *Gun Molls Magazine* (New York), October 1930.
"Gumming the Works," in *Gangster Stories* (New York), July 1931.
"The Black Widow," in *Detective Action Stories* (Chicago), October 1931.
"Hot Money," in *Underworld Romances* (New York), November 1931.
"The Yellow Finger," in *Detective Action Stories* (Chicago), February 1932.
"Trail of the Ant," in *Detective Fiction* (Kokomo, Indiana), February 1932.
"The House of Blades," in *Detective Action Stories* (Chicago), April 1932.
"The Dynamite Dick," in *Gang World* (Chicago), June 1932.
"The Flying Butcher," in *Dare-Devil Aces* (Chicago), June 1932.
"The Black Circus," in *Dare-Devil Aces* (Chicago), August 1932.
"The Death Ace," in *Dare-Devil Aces* (Chicago), September 1932.
"The Gang Grinder," in *Gang World* (Chicago), September 1932.
"Tip and Double-Cross," in *Thrilling Detective* (New York), December 1933.
"With This Gun," in *Detective Tales,* March 1951.
"It's Always too Late," in *Detective Fiction* (Kokoma, Indiana), April 1951.
"Final Appearance," in *Detective Tales,* October 1951.
"Moonshine," in *Manhunt* (New York), March 1955.
"I Saw Her Die," in *Manhunt* (New York), October 1955.
"The Red Scarf," in *Mercury Mystery Book Magazine* (New York), November 1955.
"They'll Find Us," in *Accused* (New York), January 1956.
"Fog," in *Manhunt* (New York), February 1956.
"Home," in *Accused* (New York), March 1956.
"The Gesture," in *The Saint* (New York), March 1956.
"Come Across," in *Manhunt* (New York), April 1956.
"Goodbye, Jeannie," in *Accused* (New York), May 1956.
"Matinee," in *Manhunt* (New York), October 1956.
"The Tormentors," in *Manhunt* (New York), November 1956.
"The Axe Is Ready," in *Trapped* (New York), December 1956.

"Die, Darling, Die," in *The Hardboiled Lineup,* edited by Harry Widmer.   New York, Lion, 1956.
"On a Sunday Afternoon," in *Manhunt* (New York), January 1957.
"Prowler!," in *Manhunt* (New York), May 1957.
"I'll Be in the Bedroom," in *Trapped* (New York), June 1957.
"Bothered," in *Manhunt* (New York), July 1957.
"Old Times," in *Murder* (New York), July 1957.
"That Damned Piper," in *Pursued* (New York), July 1957.
"The Glass Eye," in *Guilty* (New York), September 1957.
"Meet Me in the Dark," in *Manhunt* (New York), February 1958.
"Sauce for the Goose," in *Bad Girls,* edited by Leo Margulies. New York, Fawcett, 1958.
"Getaway Money," in *Guilty* (New York), November 1958.
"Teen-Age Casanova," in *Young and Deadly,* edited by Leo Margulies.   New York, Fawcett, 1959.
"Redheads Die Slowly," in *Mystery Tales* (New York), April 1959.
"This Petty Pace," in *Mystery Tales* (New York), June 1959.
"Harlot House," in *Mystery Tales* (New York), August 1959.
"Cop," in *Mike Shayne Mystery Magazine* (New York), July 1968.
"Sympathy," in *Mike Shayne Mystery Magazine* (New York), June 1969.
"Trick," in *Alfred Hitchcock's Mystery Magazine* (New York), November 1969.
"Small Bite," in *Alfred Hitchcock's Mystery Magazine* (New York), February 1970.
"Goodbye Now," in *Alfred Hitchcock's Get Me to the Wake on Time.*   New York, Dell, 1970.
"Token," in *Mike Shayne Mystery Magazine* (Los Angeles), June 1972.
"Peccadillo," in *Mike Shayne Mystery Magazine* (Los Angeles), May 1973.
"Apologize," in *Mike Shayne Mystery Magazine* (Los Angeles), February 1974.
"Investment," in *Mike Shayne Mystery Magazine* (Los Angeles), March 1974.
"Blue Moon," in *Mike Shayne Mystery Magazine* (Los Angeles), April 1974.
"Mother," in *Mike Shayne Mystery Magazine* (Los Angeles), July 1974.
"Deadly Little Green Eyes," in *Mike Shayne Mystery Magazine* (Los Angeles), February 1975.
"Cave in the Rain," in *87th Precinct* (Los Angeles), April 1975.
"Love-Lark," in *Executioner* (Los Angeles), April 1975.
"The Gentle Touch," in *Executioner* (Los Angeles), May 1975.
"The Waking Dream," in *87th Precinct* (Los Angeles), May 1975.
"Upriver," in *87th Precinct* (Los Angeles), June 1975.
"Love Bait," in *Executioner* (Los Angeles), June 1975.
"The Getaway," in *Mystery Monthly* (New York), June 1976.
"The Thinking Child," in *Mystery Monthly* (New York), September 1976.
"Swamp Tale," in *Mystery Monthly* (New York), December 1976.
"Hit," in *Alfred Hitchcock's Mystery Magazine* (New York), March 1977.
"Family," in *Alfred Hitchcock's Mystery Magazine* (New York), March 1978.
"The Closed Room," in *Alfred Hitchcock's Mystery Magazine* (New York), April 1979.

Uncollected Short Stories as Bailey Morgan

"Dig That Crazy Corpse," in *Pursuit* (New York), March 1955.
"Sudden Justice," in *Hunted* (New York), April 1955.
"My Lady Is a Tramp," in *Pursuit* (New York), May 1955.
"Gigolo," in *Pursuit* (New York), July 1955.
"Death in Bloom," in *Pursuit* (New York), September 1955.
"Hammer," in *Hunted* (New York), October 1955.
"Speak No Evil," in *Pursuit* (New York), November 1955.
"Don't Do That," in *Hunted* (New York), December 1955.
"Wife Sitter," in *Pursuit* (New York), July 1956.
"Cold Rain," in *Pursuit* (New York), September 1956.
"Whiskey," in *Pursuit* (New York), November 1956.

Uncollected Short Stories as Eric Fitzgerald

"Death Comes Last," in *Hunted* (New York), October 1955.
"Sauce for the Goose," in *Pursuit* (New York), January 1956.
"The Black Suitcase," in *Hunted* (New York), February 1956.
"Home-Again Blues," in *Pursuit* (New York), March 1956.
"Alligator," in *Hunted* (New York), April 1956.
"Cut Bait," in *Pursuit* (New York), May 1956.
"Return to Yesterday," in *Pursuit* (New York), July 1956.
"The Screamer," in *Pursuit* (New York), September 1956.

*   *   *

With the publication of his first novel, *13 French Street,* in 1951, Gil Brewer began a successful career as one of the leading writers of paperback originals.

Most of his 30 crime novels for Fawcett Gold Medal, Avon, Monarch, and others are built around a similar and classical theme: an ordinary man who becomes involved with, and is often corrupted and destroyed by, an evil or designing woman. (Most of his books—just as most of those by softcover "rivals" John D. MacDonald, Harry Whittington, and Day Keene—are set in the cities, small towns, and back-country areas of Florida.) His style is simple and direct, with sharp dialogue and considerable passion and intensity; at times it takes on an almost Hemingwayesque flavor, as in one of his best works, *The Three-Way Split,* where it is so reminiscent of Hemingway's *To Have and Have Not* that it approaches pastiche.

Other well-crafted Brewer books include *13 French Street, A Killer Is Loose, Some Must Die,* and *And the Girl Screamed.* But his most accomplished work is one of two hardcovers, *The Red Scarf*—a tense story of a motel owner caught up in a web of greed, treachery, and violence made all the more complex by his own weakness.

While he was producing novels Brewer also found time to write many short stories for the last of the detective pulps in the early 1950's and for later magazines.

—Bill Pronzini

BRITTAIN, William. Also writes as James Knox.   American. Born in Rochester, New York, 16 December 1930. Educated at Colgate University, Hamilton, New York 1948–50; Brockport State Teachers College (now State University College), New York, B.S. 1952; Hofstra University, Hempstead, New York, M.S. 1959. Married Virginia Connorton in 1954; one daughter and one son. Teacher, Leroy Central Schools, New York, 1952–54. English Teacher, Lawrence Junior High School, New York,

1954–86. Address: 17 Wisteria Drive, Asheville, North Carolina 28804, U.S.A.

CRIME PUBLICATIONS

Uncollected Short Stories

"Joshua," in *Alfred Hitchcock's Mystery Magazine* (New York), October 1964.
"The Man Who Read John Dickson Carr," and "The Man Who Read Ellery Queen," in *Ellery Queen's Crime Carousel*. New York, New American Library, 1966.
"The Man Who Didn't Read," in *Ellery Queen's Mystery Magazine* (New York), May 1966.
"Mr. Lightning" (as James Knox), in *Ellery Queen's Mystery Magazine* (New York), July 1966.
"The Woman Who Read Rex Stout," in *Ellery Queen's Mystery Magazine* (New York), July 1966.
"The Boy Who Read Agatha Christie," in *Ellery Queen's Mystery Magazine* (New York), December 1966.
"Mr. Strang Gives a Lecture," in *Ellery Queen's Mystery Magazine* (New York), March 1967.
"Mr. Strang Performs an Experiment," in *Ellery Queen's Mystery Parade*. New York, New American Library, 1968.
"Mr. Strang Sees a Play," in *Ellery Queen's Mystery Magazine* (New York), March 1968.
"The Zaretski Chain," in *Ellery Queen's Mystery Magazine* (New York), June 1968.
"The Last Word" (as James Knox), in *Ellery Queen's Mystery Magazine* (New York), June 1968.
"Mr. Strang Takes a Field Trip," in *Ellery Queen's Mystery Magazine* (New York), December 1968.
"The Man Who Read Sir Arthur Conan Doyle," in *Ellery Queen's Murder Menu*. Cleveland, World, 1969.
"The Second Sign in the Melon Patch," in *Ellery Queen's Mystery Magazine* (New York), January 1969.
"Mr. Strang Pulls a Switch," in *Ellery Queen's Mystery Magazine* (New York), June 1969.
"That Day on the Knob," in *Ellery Queen's Mystery Magazine* (New York), September 1969.
"Hand," in *Alfred Hitchcock's Mystery Magazine* (New York), October 1969.
"Mr. Strang Finds the Answers," in *Rogue's Gallery*, edited by Walter Gibson. New York, Doubleday, 1970.
"Just About Average," in *Alfred Hitchcock's Mystery Magazine* (New York), June 1970.
"A Gallon of Gas," in *Alfred Hitchcock's Mystery Magazine* (New York), April 1971.
"Mr. Strang Lifts a Glass," in *Ellery Queen's Mystery Magazine* (New York), May 1971.
"Mr. Strang Finds an Angle," in *Ellery Queen's Mystery Magazine* (New York), June 1971.
"Mr. Strang Hunts a Bear," in *Ellery Queen's Mystery Magazine* (New York), November 1971.
"Falling Object," in *Ellery Queen's Mystery Bag*. Cleveland, World, 1972.
"The Driver," in *Alfred Hitchcock's Mystery Magazine* (New York), January 1972.
"Mr. Strang Checks a Record," in *Ellery Queen's Mystery Magazine* (New York), February 1972.
"Wynken, Blynken and Nod," in *Ellery Queen's Mystery Magazine* (New York), April 1972.
"The Artificial Liar," in *Alfred Hitchcock's Mystery Magazine* (New York), April 1972.
"Mr. Strang Finds a Car," in *Ellery Queen's Mystery Magazine* (New York), July 1972.

"Mr. Strang Makes a Snowman," in *Ellery Queen's Mystery Magazine* (New York), December 1972.
"Mr. Strang Amends a Legend," in *Ellery Queen's Mystery Magazine* (New York), February 1973.
"The Sonic Boomer," in *Alfred Hitchcock's Mystery Magazine* (New York), February 1973.
"The Scarab Ring," in *Alfred Hitchcock's Mystery Magazine* (New York), May 1973.
"Mr. Strang Invents a Strange Device," in *Ellery Queen's Mystery Magazine* (New York), June 1973.
"A State of Preparedness," in *Alfred Hitchcock's Mystery Magazine* (New York), September 1973.
"Mr. Strang Follows Through," in *Ellery Queen's Mystery Magazine* (New York), September 1973.
"The Button," in *Alfred Hitchcock's Mystery Magazine* (New York), October 1973.
"The Platt Avenue Irregulars," in *Alfred Hitchcock's Mystery Magazine* (New York), November 1973.
"Mr. Strang Discovers a Bug," in *Ellery Queen's Mystery Magazine* (New York), November 1973.
"Mr. Strang under Arrest," in *Ellery Queen's Mystery Magazine* (New York), February 1974.
"He Can't Die Screaming," in *Ellery Queen's Mystery Magazine* (New York), February 1974.
"Waiting for Harry," in *Alfred Hitchcock's Mystery Magazine* (New York), March 1974.
"The Man Who Read Dashiell Hammett," in *Ellery Queen's Mystery Magazine* (New York), May 1974.
"The Impossible Footprint," in *Alfred Hitchcock's Mystery Magazine* (New York), November 1974.
"I'm Back, Little Sister," in *Alfred Hitchcock's Mystery Magazine* (New York), December 1974.
"The Man Who Read Georges Simenon," in *Ellery Queen's Mystery Magazine* (New York), January 1975.
"The Girl Who Read John Creasey," in *Ellery Queen's Mystery Magazine* (New York), March 1975.
"Aunt Abigail's Wall Safe," in *Alfred Hitchcock's Mystery Magazine* (New York), May 1975.
"Mr. Strang and the Cat Lady," in *Ellery Queen's Mystery Magazine* (New York), May 1975.
"Yellowbelly," in *Alfred Hitchcock's Mystery Magazine* (New York), October 1975.
"Mr. Strang, Armchair Detective," in *Ellery Queen's Mystery Magazine* (New York), December 1975.
"Mr. Strang Picks Up the Pieces," in *Best Detective Stories of the Year 1976*, edited by Edward D. Hoch. New York, Dutton, 1976.
"Historical Errors," in *Alfred Hitchcock's Mystery Magazine* (New York), February 1976.
"A Private Little War," in *Alfred Hitchcock's Mystery Magazine* (New York), May 1976.
"Mr. Strang Battles a Deadline," in *Ellery Queen's Mystery Magazine* (New York), June 1976.
"One Big Happy Family," in *Alfred Hitchcock's Mystery Magazine* (New York), September 1976.
"Mr. Strang Accepts a Challenge," in *Ellery Queen's Mystery Magazine* (New York), November 1976.
"The Ferret Man," in *Antaeus* (New York), Spring–Summer 1977.
"The Man Who Read G.K. Chesterton," in *Ellery Queen's Who's Who of Whodunits*. New York, Davis, 1977.
"Mr. Strang Takes a Hand," in *Masterpieces of Mystery—Part II*, edited by Ellery Queen. New York, Davis, 1978.
"Mr. Strang Buys a Big H," in *Ellery Queen's Mystery Magazine* (New York), April 1978.
"The Men Who Read Isaac Asimov," in *Ellery Queen's Mystery Magazine* (New York), May 1978.

"Mr. Strang Unlocks a Door," in *Ellery Queen's Mystery Magazine* (New York), June 1981.

"Mr. Strang Interprets a Picture," in *Ellery Queen's Mystery Magazine* (New York), August 1981.

"Mr. Strang Grasps at Straws," in *Ellery Queen's Mystery Magazine* (New York), November 1981.

"The Second Reason," in *Ellery Queen's Maze of Mysteries.* New York, Davis, 1982.

"Mr. Strang and the Lost Ship," in *Ellery Queen's Mystery Magazine* (New York), June 1982.

"Mr. Strang Takes a Partner," in *Ellery Queen's Mystery Magazine* (New York), Mid-July 1982.

"Mr. Strang Studies Exhibit A," in *Ellery Queen's Mystery Magazine* (New York), October 1982.

"Mr. Strang and the Purloined Memo," in *Ellery Queen's Mystery Magazine* (New York), February 1983.

"Mr. Strang Takes a Tour," in *Ellery Queen's Mystery Magazine* (New York), Mid-July 1983.

OTHER PUBLICATIONS

Other

Survival Outdoors. Derby, Connecticut, Monarch, 1977.

All the Money in the World (for children). New York, Harper, 1979.

Devil's Donkey (for children). New York, Harper, 1981.

The Wish-Giver (for children). New York, Harper, 1983.

Who Knew There'd Be Ghosts? (for children). New York, Harper, 1985.

Dr. Dedd's Wagon of Wonders (for children). New York, Harper, 1987.

The Fantastic Freshman (for children). New York, Harper, 1988.

My Buddy, the King (for children). New York, Harper, 1989.

*

Manuscript Collection: University of Wyoming, Laramie.

William Brittain comments:

Much of my mystery writing consists of two series, "The Man Who Read..." and the Mr. Strang stories. Both series first appeared in the *Ellery Queen's Mystery Magazine,* and they were begun with the help and encouragement of Frederic Dannay. Since Mr. Strang, like me, is a teacher, I often find the germ of a story idea coming from commonplace happenings during my teaching day. However, unlike Aldershot High school, where Mr. Strang holds sway, the school where I teach can hardly be considered a hotbed of crime.

One of the fringe benefits of my writing has been the opportunity to meet other mystery writers, primarily through the Mystery Writers of America. And in total antithesis to the literary violence they so lovingly create, they're some of the friendliest and most helpful and obliging people it has been my pleasure to know.

* * *

William Brittain's mystery writing has thus far been confined to the short story field, where he has produced two series of interest. The earliest of these, which might be called "The Man Who Read..." series, began with "The Man Who Read John Dickson Carr." A pastiche of Carr's plots and style, it involves a murderer who is inspired to devise an intricate locked-room problem. He kills his victim and escapes from the room, but makes one mistake. The story is one of Brittain's best. It was followed by other stories using a similar technique and involving sleuths or criminals who were readers of Ellery Queen, Agatha Christie, Arthur Conan Doyle, Rex Stout, G.K. Chesterton, Isaac Asimov, and others. There was even one story titled "The Man Who Didn't Read."

A longer series with greater potential has been built around Mr. Strang, a high school science teacher in a school which must be fashioned just a bit after the one in which Brittain himself teaches. The first of these stories was "Mr. Strang Gives a Lecture," in which the teacher's car is used in a holdup. Mr. Strang examines the car and finds evidence of the criminal's identity. In "Mr. Strang Picks Up the Pieces" the teacher discovers how the window of a jewelery store could be broken by a seemingly invisible weapon. Often in his cases Mr. Strang comes to the aid of a student falsely accused of a crime. The result is a portrait of modern high school life combined with a solid mystery plot.

—Edward D. Hoch

———

BROWN, Carter. Pseudonym for Alan Geoffrey Yates; also writes as Caroline Farr. Australian. Born in London, 1 August 1923; became Australian citizen in 1948. Educated at schools in Essex. Served in the Royal Navy, 1942–46: Lieutenant. Married Denise Sinclair Mackellar; one daughter and three sons. Sound recordist, Gaumont-British Films, London, 1946–48; salesman in Sydney, Australia, 1948–51; public relations staff member, Qantas Empire Airways, Sydney, 1951–53. Full-time writer from 1953. *Died 5 May 1985.*

CRIME PUBLICATIONS

Novels as Carter Brown, Peter Carter Brown, and Peter Carter-Brown (series: Larry Baker; Danny Boyd; Paul Donavan; Rick Holman; Andy Kane; Randy Roberts; Mavis Seidlitz; Al Wheeler)

Venus Unarmed. Sydney, Transport, 1953.

The Mermaid Murmurs Murder. Sydney, Transport, 1953.

The Lady Is Chased. Sydney, Transport, 1953.

The Frame Is Beautiful. Sydney, Transport, 1953.

Fraulein Is Feline. Sydney, Transport, 1953.

Wreath for Rebecca. Sydney, Transport, 1953(?).

The Black Widow Weeps. Sydney, Transport, 1953(?).

Penthouse Passout. Sydney, Transport, 1953(?); as *Hot Seat for a Honey,* Sydney, Horwitz, 1956.

Shady Lady. Sydney, Transport, 1953(?).

Strip Without Tease. Sydney, Transport, 1953(?).

Trouble Is a Dame. Sydney, Transport, 1953(?).

Lethal in Love. Sydney, Transport, 1953(?); as *The Minx Is Murder,* Sydney, Horwitz, 1957.

Murder—Paris Fashion. Sydney, Transport, 1954.

Nemesis Wore Nylons. Sydney, Transport, 1954.

Maid for Murder. Sydney, Transport, 1954.

Murder Is My Mistress. Sydney, Associated General Publications, 1954; revised edition, as *The Savage Salome* (Boyd), Sydney, Horwitz, and New York, New American Library, 1961.

Homicide Hoyden. Sydney, Horwitz, 1954.

A Morgue Amour. Sydney, Horwitz, 1954.

The Killer Is Kissable. Sydney, Horwitz, 1955.

Curtains for a Chorine. Sydney, Horwitz, 1955.

Shamus, Your Slip Is Showing. Sydney, Horwitz, 1955.

Cutie Cashed His Chips. Sydney, Horwitz, 1955; revised edition, as *The Million Dollar Babe,* New York, New American Library, 1961.

Honey, Here's Your Hearse! (Seidlitz). Sydney, Horwitz, 1955.

The Two-Timing Blonde. Sydney, Horwitz, 1955.

Sob-Sister Cries Murder. Sydney, Horwitz, 1955.

The Blonde (Wheeler). Sydney, Horwitz, 1955; New York, New American Library, 1958; London, New English Library, 1964.

Curves for the Coroner. Sydney, Horwitz, 1955.

Miss Called Murder. Sydney, Horwitz, 1955.

Swan Song for a Siren. Sydney, Horwitz, 1955; revised edition, as *Charlie Sent Me!* (Baker), Horwitz, and New York, New American Library, 1963; London, New English Library, 1965.

A Bullet for My Baby (Seidlitz). Sydney, Horwitz, 1955.

Kiss and Kill. Sydney, Horwitz, 1955.

Kiss Me Deadly. Sydney, Horwitz, 1955.

The Wench Is Wicked. Sydney, Horwitz, 1955.

Shroud for My Sugar. Sydney, Horwitz, 1955.

Lead Astray. Sydney, Horwitz, 1955.

Lipstick Larceny. Sydney, Horwitz, 1955.

The Hoodlum Was a Honey. Sydney, Horwitz, 1956.

Murder by Miss-Demeanor. Sydney, Horwitz, 1956.

Darling You're Doomed. Sydney, Horwitz, 1956.

No Halo for Hedy. Sydney, Horwitz, 1956.

Donna Died Laughing. Sydney, Horwitz, 1956.

Blonde, Beautiful, and—Blam! Sydney, Horwitz, 1956.

Strictly for Felony. Sydney, Horwitz, 1956.

Booty for a Babe. Sydney, Horwitz, 1956.

Delilah Was Deadly. Sydney, Horwitz, 1956.

Blonde Verdict (Wheeler). Sydney, Horwitz, 1956.

The Eve of His Dying. Sydney, Horwitz, 1956.

Model of No Virtue. Sydney, Horwitz, 1956.

My Darling Is Deadpan. Sydney, Horwitz, 1956.

The Bribe Was Beautiful. Sydney, Horwitz, 1956.

Death of a Doll. Sydney, Horwitz, 1956; revised edition (Holman), 1960; as *The Ever-Loving Blues,* New York, New American Library, 1961.

The Lady Has No Convictions. Sydney, Horwitz, 1956.

Baby, You're Guilt-Edged. Sydney, Horwitz, 1956.

No Harp for My Angel. Sydney, Horwitz, 1956.

Hi-Jack for a Jill. Sydney, Horwitz, 1956.

Bid the Babe By-By. Sydney, Horwitz, 1956.

Meet Murder, My Angel. Sydney, Horwitz, 1956.

Caress Before Killing. Sydney, Horwitz, 1956.

Sweetheart, This Is Homicide. Sydney, Horwitz, 1956.

That's Piracy, My Pet. Sydney, Horwitz, 1957; revised edition, as *Bird in a Guilt-Edged Cage* (Kane), 1963; as *The Guilt-Edged Cage,* New York, New American Library, 1962; London, New English Library, 1963.

Last Note for a Lovely. Sydney, Horwitz, 1957.

Blonde, Bad, and Beautiful. Sydney, Horwitz, 1957(?); revised edition, as *The Hong Kong Caper* (Kane), Horwitz, and New York, New American Library, 1962; London, New English Library, 1963.

Doll for the Big House. Sydney, Horwitz, 1957; revised edition, as *The Bombshell* (Wheeler), Horwitz, and New York, New American Library, 1960; London, New English Library, 1968.

Stripper, You've Sinned. Sydney, Horwitz, 1957(?).

Madam, You're Mayhem. Sydney, Horwitz, 1957.

Good Morning, Mavis (Seidlitz). Sydney, Horwitz, 1957(?).

Sinner, You Slay Me! Sydney, Horwitz, 1957.

No Law Against Angels. Sydney, Horwitz, 1957; revised edition, as *The Body* (Wheeler), New York, New American Library, 1958; London, New English Library, 1963.

Wreath for a Redhead. Sydney, Horwitz, 1957.

The Unorthodox Corpse. Sydney, Horwitz, 1957; revised edition (Wheeler), Horwitz, and New York, New American Library, 1961.

Ten Grand Tallulah and Temptation. Sydney, Horwitz, 1957.

Cutie Wins a Corpse. Sydney, Horwitz, 1957; revised edition, as *Graves, I Dig!,* Horwitz, and New York, New American Library, 1960.

Eve, It's Extortion. Sydney, Horwitz, 1957; revised edition, as *Walk Softly Witch!* (Wheeler), Horwitz, 1959; as *The Victim,* New York, New American Library, 1959.

Bella Donna Was Poison. Sydney, Horwitz, 1957.

Murder Wears a Mantilla. Sydney, Horwitz, 1957; revised edition (Seidlitz), New York, New American Library, and London, New English Library, 1962.

Chorine Makes a Killing (Wheeler). Sydney, Horwitz, 1957.

So Lovely She Lies. Sydney, Horwitz, 1958.

Ice-Cold in Ermine. Sydney, Horwitz, 1958.

Goddess Gone Bad. Sydney, Horwitz, 1958.

No Body She Knows. Sydney, Horwitz, 1958; with *Slaughter in Satin,* 1960.

The Blonde (Wheeler). Sydney, Horwitz, and New York, New American Library, 1958; London, New English Library, 1964.

Cutie Takes the Count. Sydney, Horwitz, 1958.

No Future, Fair Lady. Sydney, Horwitz, 1958.

Hi-Fi Fadeout. Sydney, Horwitz, 1958.

Widow Bewitched. Sydney, Horwitz, 1958.

Luck Was No Lady. Sydney, Horwitz, 1958(?).

A Siren Sounds Off. Sydney, Horwitz, 1958; with *Moonshine Momma,* 1960; revised edition, as *The Myopic Mermaid,* New York, New American Library, 1961.

Tempt a Tigress. Sydney, Horwitz, 1958(?).

The Charmer Chased. Sydney, Horwitz, 1958(?).

High Fashion in Homicide. Sydney, Horwitz, 1958.

Deadly Miss. Sydney, Horwitz, 1958.

Sinfully Yours. Sydney, Horwitz, 1958(?).

Death on the Downbeat. Sydney, Horwitz, 1958; revised edition, as *The Corpse* (Wheeler), New York, New American Library, 1958; London, New English Library, 1963.

The Lover (Wheeler). Sydney, Horwitz, 1958; New York, New American Library, 1959; London, New English Library, 1963.

The Mistress (Wheeler). Sydney, Horwitz, 1958; New York, New American Library, 1959; London, New English Library, 1963.

The Loving and the Dead (Seidlitz). Sydney, Horwitz, and New York, New American Library, 1959; London, New English Library, 1966.

So Deadly, Sinner! (Boyd). Sydney, Horwitz, 1959; as *Walk Softly, Witch,* New York, New American Library, 1959; London, New English Library, 1965.

The Passionate (Wheeler). Sydney, Horwitz, and New York, New American Library, 1959; London, New English Library, 1966.

None But the Lethal Heart (Seidlitz). Sydney, Horwitz, and New York, New American Library, 1959; London, New English Library, 1967; as *The Fabulous,* Horwitz, 1961.

The Wanton (Wheeler). Sydney, Horwitz, and New York, New American Library, 1959; London, New English Library, 1968.

Suddenly by Violence (Boyd). Sydney, Horwitz, and New York, New American Library, 1959.

The Dame (Wheeler). Sydney, Horwitz, and New York, New American Library, 1959; London, New English Library, 1966.

Terror Comes Creeping (Boyd). Sydney, Horwitz, and New York, New American Library, 1959; London, New English Library, 1967.

The Desired (Wheeler). Sydney, Horwitz, 1959; New York, New American Library, 1960; London, New English Library, 1966.

The Wayward Wahine (Boyd). Sydney, Horwitz, and New York, New American Library, 1960; London, New English Library, 1966; as *The Wayward*, Horwitz, 1962.

Tomorrow Is Murder (Seidlitz). Sydney, Horwitz, and New York, New American Library, 1960.

The Temptress (Wheeler). Sydney, Horwitz, and New York, New American Library, 1960; London, New English Library, 1964.

The Brazen (Wheeler). Sydney, Horwitz, and New York, New American Library, 1960; London, New English Library, 1962.

The Dream Is Deadly (Boyd). Sydney, Horwitz, and New York, New American Library, 1960; London, New English Library, 1962.

Lament for a Lousy Lover (Seidlitz, Wheeler). New York, New American Library, 1960; London, New English Library, 1968.

The Stripper (Wheeler). Sydney, Horwitz, and New York, New American Library, 1961; London, New English Library, 1962.

The Tigress (Wheeler). Sydney, Horwitz, and New York, New American Library, 1961; as *Wildcat*, London, New English Library, 1962.

The Exotic (Wheeler). Sydney, Horwitz, and New York, New American Library, 1961; London, New English Library, 1962.

The Seductress (Boyd). Sydney, Horwitz, 1961; as *The Sad-Eyed Seductress*, New York, New American Library, 1961; London, New English Library, 1962.

Zelda (Holman). Sydney, Horwitz, and New York, New American Library, 1961; London, New English Library, 1962.

Angel! (Wheeler). Sydney, Horwitz, New York, New American Library, and London, New English Library, 1962.

The Ice-Cold Nude (Boyd). Sydney, Horwitz, New York, New American Library, and London, New English Library, 1962.

The Hellcat (Wheeler). Sydney, Horwitz, New York, New American Library, and London, New English Library, 1962.

Murder in the Harem Club (Holman). Sydney, Horwitz, 1962; as *Murder in the Key Club*, New York, New American Library, and London, New English Library, 1962.

The Lady Is Transparent (Wheeler). Sydney, Horwitz, and New York, New American Library, 1962; London, New English Library, 1963.

The Dumdum Murder (Wheeler). Sydney, Horwitz, and New York, New American Library, 1962; London, New English Library, 1963.

Lover, Don't Come Back! (Boyd). Sydney, Horwitz, and New York, New American Library, 1962; London, New English Library, 1963.

The Murder among Us (Holman). Sydney, Horwitz, and New York, New American Library, 1962; London, New English Library, 1964.

Blonde on the Rocks (Holman). Sydney, Horwitz, and New York, New American Library, 1963; London, New English Library, 1964.

Girl in a Shroud (Wheeler). Sydney, Horwitz, and New York, New American Library, 1963; London, New English Library, 1964.

The Sinners (Wheeler). Sydney, Horwitz, 1963; as *The Girl Who Was Possessed*, New York, New American Library, and London, New English Library, 1963.

The Jade-Eyed Jinx (Holman). Sydney, Horwitz, 1963; as *The Jade-Eyed Jungle*, New York, New American Library, 1963; London, New English Library, 1964.

The Lady Is Not Available (Wheeler). Sydney, Horwitz, 1963; as *The Lady Is Available*, New York, New American Library, 1963; London, New English Library, 1964.

Nymph to the Slaughter (Boyd). Sydney, Horwitz, and New York, New American Library, 1963; London, New English Library, 1964.

The Passionate Pagan (Boyd). Sydney, Horwitz, and New York, New American Library, 1963; London, New English Library, 1964.

The Ballad of Loving Jenny (Holman). Sydney, Horwitz, 1963; as *The White Bikini*, New York, New American Library, 1963; London, New English Library, 1965.

The Scarlet Flush. Sydney, Horwitz, and New York, New American Library, 1963; London, New English Library, 1965.

The Silken Nightmare (Boyd). Sydney, Horwitz, and New York, New American Library, 1963; London, New English Library, 1964.

The Wind-Up Doll (Holman). Sydney, Horwitz, 1963; New York, New American Library, 1964; London, New English Library, 1965.

The Dance of Death (Wheeler). Sydney, Horwitz, and New York, New American Library, 1964; London, New English Library, 1965.

The Never-Was Girl (Holman). Sydney, Horwitz, and New York, New American Library, 1964; London, New English Library, 1965.

The Vixen (Wheeler). Sydney, Horwitz, 1964; as *The Velvet Vixen*, New York, New American Library, 1964; London, New English Library, 1965.

The Bump and Grind Murders (Seidlitz). New York, New American Library, 1964; London, New English Library, 1965.

Murder Is a Package Deal (Holman). Sydney, Horwitz, and New York, New American Library, 1964; London, New English Library, 1965.

Who Killed Dr. Sex? (Holman). New York, New American Library, 1964; London, New English Library, 1965.

Catch Me a Phoenix! (Boyd). Sydney, Horwitz, and New York, New American Library, 1965; London, New English Library, 1966.

Yogi Shrouds Yolanda, and Poison Ivy. Sydney, Horwitz, 1965.

A Corpse for Christmas (Wheeler). Sydney, Horwitz, and New York, New American Library, 1965; London, New English Library, 1966.

No Blonde Is an Island (Baker). Sydney, Horwitz, New York, New American Library, and London, New English Library, 1965.

Nude—with a View (Holman). Sydney, Horwitz, and New York, New American Library, 1965; London, New English Library, 1966.

The Girl from Outer Space (Holman). New York, New American Library, 1965; London, New English Library, 1966.

Homicide Harem, and Felon Angel. Sydney, Horwitz, 1965.

The Sometime Wife (Boyd). New York, New American Library, 1965; London, New English Library, 1966.

The Hammer of Thor (Wheeler). New York, New American Library, 1965.

Blonde on a Broomstick (Holman). Sydney, Horwitz, New York, New American Library, and London, New English Library, 1966.

So What Killed the Vampire? (Baker). Sydney, Horwitz, and New York, New American Library, 1966; London, New English Library, 1967.

Play Now—Kill Later (Holman). Sydney, Horwitz, and New York, New American Library, 1966.

The Black Lace Hangover (Boyd). Sydney, Horwitz, and New York, New American Library, 1966; London, New English Library, 1969.

No Tears from the Widow (Holman). Sydney, Horwitz, and New York, New American Library, 1966; London, New English Library, 1968.

Target for Their Dark Desire (Wheeler). New York, New American Library, 1966; London, New English Library, 1968.

The Deadly Kitten (Holman). New York, New American Library, 1967.

House of Sorcery (Boyd). New York, New American Library, 1967; London, New English Library, 1968.

No Time for Leola (Holman). Sydney, Horwitz, and New York, New American Library, 1967.

The Plush-Lined Coffin (Wheeler). Sydney, Horwitz, and New York, New American Library, 1967; London, New English Library, 1968.

Seidlitz and the Super-Spy. Sydney, Horwitz, and New York, New American Library, 1967; as *The Super-Spy,* London, New English Library, 1968.

Until Temptation Do Us Part (Wheeler). Sydney, Horwitz, and New York, New American Library, 1967; London, New English Library, 1968.

The Deep Cold Green (Wheeler). Sydney, Horwitz, and New York, New American Library, 1968.

The Mini-Murders (Boyd). Sydney, Horwitz, and New York, New American Library, 1968.

Had I But Groaned (Baker). Sydney, Horwitz, and New York, New American Library, 1968; as *The Witches,* London, New English Library, 1969.

Die Anytime, After Tuesday! (Holman). Sydney, Horwitz, and New York, New American Library, 1969.

The Flagellator (Holman). Sydney, Horwitz, and New York, New American Library, 1969.

Murder Is the Message (Boyd). New York, New American Library, 1969.

Only the Very Rich? (Boyd). Sydney, Horwitz, and New York, New American Library, 1969.

The Steaked-Blonde Slave (Holman). New York, New New American Library, 1969.

The Up-Tight Blonde (Wheeler). New York, New American Library, 1969.

Burden of Guilt (Wheeler). New York, New American Library, 1970.

The Coffin Bird (Boyd). New York, New American Library, 1970.

A Good Year for Dwarfs? (Holman). New York, New American Library, 1970.

The Hang-Up Kid (Holman). Sydney, Horwitz, and New York, New American Library, 1970.

True Son of the Beast! (Baker). New York, New American Library, 1970.

Where Did Charity Go? (Holman). New York, New American Library, 1970.

The Coven (Holman). Sydney, Horwitz, and New York, New American Library, 1971.

The Creative Murders (Wheeler). Sydney, Horwitz, and New York, New American Library, 1971.

The Invisible Flamini (Holman). New York, New American Library, 1971.

Murder in the Family Way (Roberts). New York, New American Library, 1971.

The Sex Clinic (Boyd). Sydney, Horwitz, 1971; New York, New American Library, 1972.

W.H.O.R.E. (Wheeler). New York, New American Library, 1971.

The Clown (Wheeler). New York, New American Library, 1972.

The Angry Amazons (Roberts, Boyd). Sydney, Horwitz, and New York, New American Library, 1972.

The Aseptic Murders (Wheeler). Sydney, Horwitz, and New York, New American Library, 1972.

Murder Is So Nostalgic (Seidlitz). New York, New American Library, 1972.

The Pornbroker (Holman). Sydney, Horwitz, and New York, New American Library, 1972.

The Seven Sirens (Roberts). Sydney, Horwitz, and New York, New American Library, 1972.

The Born Loser (Wheeler). Sydney, Horwitz, and New York, New American Library, 1973.

Manhattan Cowboy (Boyd). Sydney, Horwitz, and New York, New American Library, 1973.

The Master (Holman). Sydney, Horwitz, and New York, New American Library, 1973.

Murder on High (Roberts). Sydney, Horwitz, and New York, New American Library, 1973.

So Move the Body (Boyd). Sydney, Horwitz, and New York, New American Library, 1973.

Phreak-Out! (Holman). New York, New American Library, 1973.

Night Wheeler. New York, New American Library, 1974.

Donavan. Sydney, Horwitz, and New York, New American Library, 1974.

And the Undead Sing (Seidlitz). New York, New American Library, 1974.

Negative in Blue (Holman). New York, New American Library, 1974.

The Star-Crossed Lover (Holman). New York, New American Library, 1974.

Wheeler Fortune. New York, New American Library, 1974.

Donavan's Day. Sydney, Horwitz, and New York, New American Library, 1975.

The Early Boyd. Sydney, Horwitz, and New York, New American Library, 1975.

The Iron Maiden (Baker). Sydney, Horwitz, and New York, New American Library, 1975.

Ride the Roller Coaster (Holman). Sydney, Horwitz, and New York, New American Library, 1975.

Wheeler, Dealer! Sydney, Horwitz, and New York, New American Library, 1975.

Sex Trap (Roberts). Sydney, Horwitz, and New York, New American Library, 1975.

The Savage Sisters. New York, New American Library, 1976.

Chinese Donavan. Sydney, Horwitz, and New York, New American Library, 1976.

The Dream Merchant (Wheeler). New York, New American Library, 1976.

The Pipes Are Calling (Boyd). New York, New American Library, 1976.

Remember Maybelle? (Holman). Sydney, Horwitz, and New York, New American Library, 1976.

Busted Wheeler. Sydney, Horwitz, New York, Belmont, and London, Corgi, 1979.

Donavan's Delight. Sydney, Horwitz, New York, Belmont, and London, Corgi, 1979.
The Rip-Off (Boyd). New York, Belmont, and London, Corgi, 1979.
The Spanking Girls (Wheeler). Sydney, Horwitz, New York, Belmont, and London, Corgi, 1979.
The Strawberry Blonde Jungle (Boyd). Sydney, Horwitz, New York, New American Library, and London, Corgi, 1979.
See It Again, Sam (Holman). Sydney, Horwitz, New York, New American Library, and London, Corgi, 1979.
Death to a Downbeat (Boyd). Sydney, Horwitz, and New York, Tower, 1980.
Model for Murder (Wheeler). Sydney, Horwitz, and New York, Tower, 1980.
The Phantom Lady (Holman). Sydney, Horwitz, and New York, Tower, 1980.
The Swingers (Holman). Sydney, Horwitz, and New York, Tower, 1980.
Kiss Michelle Goodbye. New York, Tower, 1981.
The Wicked Widow. New York, Tower, 1981.

Novels as Caroline Farr

The House of Tomba. Sydney, Horwitz, and New York, New American Library, 1966.
The Intruder. Sydney, Horwitz, 1966.
Mansion of Evil. New York, New American Library, 1966.
Mansion of Peril. Sydney, Horwitz, 1966; New York, New American Library, 1967.
Villa of Shadow. Sydney, Horwitz, 1966.
Web of Horror. Sydney, Horwitz, and New York, New American Library, 1966; as *A Castle in Spain,* New American Library, 1967.
Granite Folly. Sydney, Horwitz, and New York, New American Library, 1967.
The Secret of the Chateau. New York, New American Library, 1967.
So Near and Yet. New York, New American Library, 1967.
Witch's Hammer. Sydney, Horwitz, and New York, New American Library, 1967.
House of Destiny. New York, New American Library, 1970.
Terror on Duncan Island. New York, New American Library, 1971.
Dark Citadel. New York, New American Library, 1971.
The Secret of Castle Ferrara. New York, New American Library, 1971.
The Castle in Canada. New York, New American Library, 1972.
The Towers of Fear. New York, New American Library, 1972.
House of Dark Illusions. New York, New American Library, 1973.
The Possessed. Sydney, Horwitz, 1973.
House of Secrets. New York, New American Library, 1973.
Dark Mansion. New York, New American Library, 1974.
The House on the Cliffs. New York, New American Library, 1974.
Mansion Malevolent. New York, New American Library, 1974.
Castle of Terror. Sydney, Horwitz, and New York, New American Library, 1975.
The Scream in the Storm. New York, New American Library, 1975.
Chateau of Wolves. New York, New American Library, 1976.
Mansion of Menace. New York, New American Library, 1976.

The House at Landsdowne. Sydney, Horwitz, and New York, New American Library, 1977.
House of Treachery. New York, New American Library, 1977.
Ravensnet. New York, New American Library, 1977.
Heiress of Fear. Sydney, Horwitz, and New York, New American Library, 1978.
Heiress to Corsair Keep. Sydney, Horwitz, and New York, New American Library, 1978.
House of Valhalla. New York, New American Library, 1978.
Island of Evil. Sydney, Horwitz, 1978; New York, New American Library, 1979.
Sinister House. Sydney, Horwitz, and New York, New American Library, 1978.
Castle on the Loch. Sydney, Horwitz, 1979.
Castle on the Rhine. Sydney, Horwitz, and New York, New American Library, 1979.
Room of Secrets. Sydney, Horwitz, and New York, New American Library, 1979.
Secret at Ravenswood. Sydney, Horwitz, and New York, New American Library, 1980.

OTHER PUBLICATIONS

Novel

The Cold Dark Hours (as A.G. Yates). Sydney, Horwitz, New York, New American Library, and London, Barker, 1958.

* * *

The astonishingly prolific Australian paperback writer Alan G. Yates, writing as Carter Brown, produced a series of books which for some 30 years have been happily devoured by a huge and faithful reading public. At the same time, however, the Brown books have been consistently ignored by most critics of the mystery genre despite their status as a genuine publishing phenomenon, with sales in the tens—perhaps hundreds—of millions of copies. That the Brown books have been slighted is not too surprising, since they exhibit no pretentions to being other than lightweight, breezy mystery entertainment, to read in one sitting and forgotten. They also suffer the stigma of being paperback originals, and their sheer number invites easy dismissal as hack potboilers. Only Anthony Boucher, that most exceptional and unstuffy mystery critic, gave the Carter Brown books a fair hearing in his review columns.

That the Brown books were and still are so popular with a large segment of the mystery reading public is testimony to the durability of a mystery sub-genre which seemingly perished in the late 1940's, with the demise of the pulp magazines. The Brown books are the direct descendants of the "spicy" detective pulps like *Hollywood Detective* and *Spicy Detective,* which occupied the opposite end of the respectability scale from the revered *Black Mask,* Yates hews to the conventions of that school closely, following in the footsteps of Robert Leslie Bellem, master of that particular style of pulp writing; Brown's private eye heroes are, likewise, close cousins to Bellem's creation. Dan Turner, the ultimate "Hollywood dick." Richard S. Prather's Shell Scott series—like the Browns, hugely popular and critically slighted—belongs to this same school.

The hallmarks of the Carter Brown style are brevity, simple plotting, fast pace, much breezy slang (Yates exhibited a rather shaky grasp of American slang in the early books), broad humor, lots of action and a liberal strewing of corpses. Above all there is the spicy element: lots of girls, all gorgeous and impossibly endowed (no female is introduced in a Brown book without her breasts being also introduced and described in the same paragraph). The sex is lighthearted, of the "leer and lights out" variety—up to 1973 at least, when explicit sex scenes were incorporated to disastrous effect. The settings are invariably among the rich and glamorous, most often denizens of the Hollywood film colony. No "mean streets" are to be found in a Carter Brown book.

Brown has worked this formula with a varied cast of series characters, the most noteworthy of which are Al Wheeler, a homicide lieutenant with the sheriff's department of the fictional Pine City, near Los Angeles; Rick Holman, a Hollywood private eye and saviour of blackmailed film starlets; Randy Roberts, lawyer and skirt-chaser based in San Francisco; and Larry Baker, Hollywood scriptwriter, who, accompanied by his perpetually drunk partner Boris Slivka, is saddled with the most bizarre cases to be found in all of Brown, usually involving strange cultists of some sort. There is also a female lead character, private detective Mavis Seidlitz, a sort of cross between Gracie Allen and Candy Christian, whose pulchritudinous assets far outweigh her mental equipment.

The Brown books are indeed formula potboilers, and can be cruelly picked apart on grounds of sloppy plotting, minimal characterization, uninspired prose and, of course, unbelievability (the plots and characters have tended to become sillier over the years). Yet the formula has proven consistently popular; this canny mixture of action, sex, and humor, with its attendant refusal to be taken at all seriously, is escapism pure and simple.

—Art Scott

* * *

BROWN, Fredric. American. Born in Cincinnati, Ohio, 29 October 1906. Educated at University of Cincinnati night school; Hanover College, Indiana, 1 year. Married 1) Helen Ruth Brown in 1929 (divorced 1947), two sons; 2) Elizabeth Charlier in 1948. Office worker, 1924–36; proofreader, Milwaukee *Journal*; freelance writer after 1947. Recipient: Mystery Writers of America Edgar Allan Poe award, 1948. *Died 11 March 1972.*

CRIME PUBLICATIONS

Novels (series: Ed and Am Hunter)

The Fabulous Clipjoint (Hunter). New York, Dutton, 1947; London, Boardman, 1949.
The Dead Ringer (Hunter). New York, Dutton, 1948; London, Boardman, 1950.
Murder Can Be Fun. New York, Dutton, 1948; London, Boardman, 1951; as *A Plot for Murder,* New York, Bantam, 1949.
The Bloody Moonlight (Hunter). New York, Dutton, 1949; as *Murder in Moonlight,* London, Boardman, 1950.
The Screaming Mimi. New York, Dutton, 1949; London, Boardman, 1950.
Compliments of a Fiend (Hunter). New York, Dutton, 1950; London, Boardman, 1951.
Here Comes a Candle. New York, Dutton, 1950; London, Boardman, 1951.
Night of the Jabberwock. New York, Dutton, and London, Boardman, 1951.
The Case of the Dancing Sandwiches. New York, Dell, 1951.

Death Has Many Doors (Hunter). New York, Dutton, 1951; London, Boardman, 1952.
The Far Cry. New York, Dutton, 1951; London, Boardman, 1952.
The Deep End. New York, Dutton, 1952; London, Boardman, 1953.
We All Killed Grandma. New York, Dutton, 1952; London, Boardman, 1953.
Madball. New York, Dell, 1953; London, Muller, 1962.
His Name Was Death. New York, Dutton, 1954; London, Boardman, 1955.
The Wench Is Dead. New York, Dutton, 1955.
The Lenient Beast. New York, Dutton, 1956; London, Boardman, 1957.
One for the Road. New York, Dutton, 1958; London, Boardman, 1959.
Knock Three-One-Two. New York, Dutton, and London, Boardman, 1959.
The Late Lamented (Hunter). New York, Dutton, and London, Boardman, 1959.
The Murderers. New York, Dutton, 1961; London, Boardman, 1962.
The Five-Day Nightmare. New York, Dutton, 1962; London, Boardman, 1963.
Mrs. Murphy's Underpants (Hunter). New York, Dutton, 1963; London, Boardman, 1965.

Short Stories

Mostly Murder: Eighteen Stories. New York, Dutton, 1953; London, Boardman, 1954.
Nightmares and Geezenstacks: 47 Stories. New York, Bantam, 1961; London, Corgi, 1962.
The Shaggy Dog and Other Murders. New York, Dutton, 1963; London, Boardman, 1964.
Carnival of Crime: The Best Mystery Stories of Fredric Brown, edited by Francis M. Nevins, Jr., and Martin H. Greenberg. Carbondale, Southern Illinois University Press, 1985.

Uncollected Short Stories

"Why, Benny, Why?" in *Ellery Queen's 20th Anniversary Annual.* New York, Random House, 1965; London, Gollancz, 1966.
"Homicide Sanitarium," in *Fredric Brown in the Detective Pulps* (San Antonio, California), vol. 1 1984.
"Before She Kills," in *Fredric Brown in the Detective Pulps* (San Diego, California), vol. 2 1984,
"Madman's Holiday," in *Fredric Brown in the Detective Pulps* (Volcano, Hawaii), vol. 3 1985.
"The Case of the Dancing Sandwiches," in *Fredric Brown in the Detective Pulps* (Volcano, Hawaii), vol. 4 1985.
"The Freak Show Murders," in *Fredric Brown in the Detective Pulps* (Belen, New Mexico), vol. 5 1985.
"Thirty Corpses Every Day," in *Fredric Brown in the Detective Pulps* (Belen, New Mexico), vol. 6 1985.
"Pardon My Goulish Laughter," in *Fredric Brown in the Detective Pulps* (n.p.), vol. 7 1986.
"Red Is the Hue of Hell," in *Fredric Brown in the Detective Pulps* (Miami Beach, Florida), vol. 8 1986.
"Sex Life on the Planet Mars," in *Fredric Brown in the Detective Pulps* (Miami Beach, Florida), vol. 10 1986.
"Brother Monster," in *Fredric Brown in the Detective Pulps* (Miami Beach, Florida), vol. 9 1987.
"Nightmare in Darkness," in *Fredric Brown in the Detective Pulps* (Miami Beach, Florida), vol. 11 1987.

"Who Was That Blonde I Saw You Kill last Night?," in *Fredric Brown in the Detective Pulps* (Miami Beach, Florida), vol. 12 1988.
"Three Corpse Parley," in *Fredric Brown in the Detective Pulps* (Missoula, Montana), vol. 13 1988.
"Selling Death Short," in *Fredric Brown in the Detective Pulps* (Missoula, Montana), vol. 14 1988.
"Whispering Death," in *Fredric Brown in the Detective Pulps* (Missoula, Montana), vol. 15 1989
"Happy Ending," in *Fredric Brown in the Detective Pulps* (Missoula, Montana), vol. 16 1990.

OTHER PUBLICATIONS

Novels

What Mad Universe. New York, Dutton, 1949; London, Boardman, 1951.
The Lights in the Sky Are Stars. New York, Dutton, 1953; as *Project Jupiter*, London, Boardman, 1954.
Martians, Go Home. New York, Dutton, 1955.
Rogue in Space. New York, Dutton, 1957.
The Office. New York, Dutton, 1958.
The Mind Thing. New York, Bantam, 1961.

Short Stories

Space on My Hands. Chicago, Shasta, 1951; London, Corgi, 1953.
Angels and Spaceships. New York, Dutton, 1954; London, Gollancz, 1955; as *Star Shine*, New York, Bantam, 1956.
Honeymoon in Hell. New York, Bantam, 1958.
Daymares. New York, Lancer, 1968.
Paradox Lost and Twelve Other Great Science Fiction Stories. New York, Random House, 1973; London, Hale, 1975.
The Best of Fredric Brown, edited by Robert Bloch. New York, Ballantine, 1977.

Plays

Television Plays: for *Alfred Hitchcock* series.

Other

"Where Do You Get Your Plot?" in *The Mystery Writers' Handbook,* edited by Herbert Brean. New York, Harper, 1956.
Mitkey Astromouse (for children). New York, Quist, 1971.

Editor, with Mack Reynolds, *Science-Fiction Carnival.* Chicago, Shasta, 1953.

*

Bibliography: *A Key to Fredric Brown's Wonderland: A Study and an Annotated Bibliographical Checklist* by Newton Baird, Georgetown, California, Talisman, 1981.

*　*　*

The essence of the work of Fredric Brown is uniqueness. One of the most ingenious writers of his time, he wrote mysteries with a lucid style that disguised complex plots and themes. Sometimes he wrote science fiction, he said, to overcome the "too real" aspect of detective fiction. Fantasy, mystery, psychology, and science are often mixed in his stories, along with uses of classic literature, like that of Lewis Carroll in *Night*

of the Jabberwock. The Office, his only "straight" novel, is a blend of realism and mystery, based on his experiences in a Cincinnati office. "Star Spangled Night," his only "straight" short work, is an inspiring tale of an ancestor's role in the War of 1812.

Self-taught, he wrote for the pulps. His first full-length mystery, *The Fabulous Clipjoint,* one of seven books dealing with Ed and Am Hunter, an amateur detective team, combines youthful idealism with the logic of a retired circus performer. Other mysteries go beyond the series in invention, especially *The Deep End, The Screaming Mimi, Knock Three-One-Two,* and *The Far Cry,* but *The Fabulous Clipjoint* remained his favorite. A forerunner in plot and theme of later work, the title expresses a paradox that he projected in much of his work. Chicago, the setting, is both "clipjoint" and "fabulous" in its hero's perception. Ayn Rand thought Brown ingenious, but commented on his "malevolent sense of life." Anthony Boucher praised him but noted this novel was "sordidly compelling." Sometimes Brown brought his experience to a positive resolution: when Ed Hunter solves his father's murder, he no longer sees a clipjoint, but the skyline "looking like fingers reaching to the sky."

My own study of Brown traces the conflict of the romantic versus the naturalistic in his work. This conflict may have influenced him to experiment frequently with point-of-view to improve everyday perception. One experiment with narrative point-of-view is *The Lenient Beast,* with five first person points-of-view. A procedural novel about a killer who murders out of his own perception of "mercy," it makes the conventional procedural detective plot seem tame and static. One novel has 10 third person points-of-view. The paradoxical aesthetics in his work may have been responsible for his mix of hero and anti-hero, and his inability to create a viable romantic detective.

A story of extreme malevolence, set in a mental institution, is "Come and Go Mad," which creates an intolerable state of existence in which human volition is a fallacy. Crag, in the novel *Rogue in Space,* is half-hero, half-criminal. He creates an uncorrupted new planet in order to reconcile the dichotomy in his nature.

The Screaming Mimi, his best known work, uses symbolic horror to heighten the suspense of a reporter's search for a "ripper" killer. A revision of the beauty and beast allegory, beauty and beast succumb together to evil. *The Deep End* begins with the death of a boy under the wheels of a roller coaster car, and penetrates both the detective's and the killer's disturbed minds in a Conradian duality. Trauma is symbolized in the ascending and descending roller coaster "deep end" that haunts the reporter-detective's mind. *The Far Cry* is his *tour de force*. It probes a love/hate perplex to one of mystery writing's most startling endings, but the horror almost spoils the achievement.

Knock Three-One-Two is a mystery about a liquor salesman with a gambling habit who happens to observe a killer who terrorizes an entire city. The reader is kept guessing as to the identity of the killer. Competent and incompetent characters are woven into plot and subplot, including a mentally retarded news vendor who wants to be identified as a killer. The novel's theme, derived from the irrationality or rationality of eight points-of-view, is that objectivity brings light (reason or good) to darkness (irrationality or evil) when disturbed perceptions are brought into focus. In fact, the overall theme of much of Brown's fiction concerns the struggle to understand existence and achieve happiness. His larger meaning is the end benefit of his easy-to-read entertainments.

The best expressions of his ingenuity and imagination are in some of his short stories, particularly the collection *Nightmares and Geezenstacks,* a delightful potpourri of innocent and ribald humor, expectation and surprise. Other collections are mixed in quality, but *The Shaggy Dog and Other Murders,* containing stories like "Little Boy Lost" and "Good Night, Good Knight," deserves attention. "Knock," his most famous story, and many others among his best can be found in the collections *Paradox Lost* and *The Best of Fredric Brown.*

Everyday characters and conventional villainy dominate his lesser work, like *Murder Can Be Fun* or a failed experiment, *Here Comes a Candle,* but plot invention removes them from the conventional, and a "thinking-ahead" pace makes them highly readable. A sense of unlimited invention comes from a reading of his varied work, and one is reminded of O. Henry and his mind of a million inventions. But Fredric Brown is really one of a kind. His view of a paradoxical existence is capsulated in the science fiction story "Paradox Lost," set in a classroom of bewildering modern philosophy. A student crosses over from reality to fantasy and fulfills his dreams in an invisible world. Brown portrayed a world that always betrayed and terrified idealists, making them yearn for a place that inspired rather than suppressed freedom and adventure. In his detective novels and mysteries his characters sometimes found that what they had hoped for proved more horrifying than what they had to begin with. In his fantasies, through "loopholes in reality," happiness is achieved. So this unique writer wrote for his own time and the future.

—Newton Baird

BROWNE, Barum. *See* **BEEDING, Francis.**

BROWNE, Gerald A(ustin). American. Address: c/o Arbor House, 105 Madison Avenue, New York, New York 10016, U.S.A.

CRIME PUBLICATIONS

Novels

11 Harrowhouse. New York, Arbor House, 1972; London, Deutsch, 1973.
Hazard. New York, Arbor House, 1973; London, Hart Davis, 1974.
Green Ice. New York, Delacorte Press, 1976; London, Hart Davis, 1978.
19 Purchase Street. New York, Arbor House, 1982; London, Lane, 1983.
Stone 588. New York, Arbor House, 1985; London, Viking, 1986.

OTHER PUBLICATIONS

Novels

It's All Zoo. New York, Doubleday, 1968.
Slide. New York, Arbor House, 1976.
Hot Siberian. New York, Arbor House, 1989.

* * *

11 Harrowhouse contains all the elements that have become the stock of Gerald Browne's novels. At the time of its publication in 1972 it was compared with Frederick Forsyth's *The Day of the Jackal.* In a number of important aspects the comparison doesn't quite fit. The stories deal with different matters and Browne's novel does not center around a figure of the international importance of DeGaulle. But the books are comparable in the kind of treatment they give to place and to the scope of their action. In addition, the international diamond monopoly, known as The System and housed at 11 Harrowhouse, lends itself to the kind of international intrigue and conspiracy that figure in *The Day of the Jackal.*

Browne's fascination with the world of the diamond, the polyhedron crystal whose value is maintained by ruthless manipulation of the market, is one that organizes the bulk of his novels. If it is not the diamond, it is the emerald that excites his imagination and provides the kind of situation and characters which are ideally suited for extravagant capers, high living, rough sex, and intoxicating addictions—all subjects in which he revels in his fiction. *11 Harrowhouse, Green Ice, Stone 588,* and most recently, *Hot Siberian,* each take as their subject a precious gem and intrigues of international scope surrounding the mining and marketing of them. Men murder for the gems; international conspiracies abound, and greed, lust, and money fuel his tales. These subjects allow him to depict a world of wealth and leisure. They let him travel to London, Switzerland, the Riviera, Bogota, Columbia, and New York. He catalogues the auction houses, the fashionable districts, the poshest stores, and the most labyrinthine vaults as his characters participate in heists and double-crosses, pursuing each other across continents, even to the bitter climes of Siberia.

Browne is a fan of films. No novel is written without frequent mention of James Cagney, Cary Grant, Humphrey Bogart, and other unforgettable stars of film. Some of his novels are the very stuff of the disaster film. *Slide* is a kind of *Airport* or *Hotel.* In *Slide* the story is structured around a fissure which becomes a rupture in the earth so deep that a portion of the Californian coast begins to slip, immersing all that comes in its path in mountains of mud. A seaside supermarket on the Pacific Coast Highway near Laguna beach is covered and all the characters in it (a cast of 14 originally) face a horrible death, buried alive in mud. His cast of characters is as stock as the cast of *Hotel* or *Airport.* He has all the ingredients—a distinguished yuppy architect, diagnosed with lymphomic cancer; a film mogul who likes to hit his actress wife; a recently divorced woman who has taken advantage of all the most sophisticated operations plastic surgery can offer—liposuction, silicon injections, cellulose removal, a nose-job and rebuilt eyes and jaw; an angry young revolver-swinging man, and a newly-wed couple embarking on their honeymoon. These characters provide Browne with an opportunity to show us all the excesses of our consumer culture.

In novels like *Green Ice, 11 Harrowhouse,* and *Hot Siberian* Browne parades his cast of sophisticates before us. They are greedy, swinging, muddled psychologically, some of them perverted. They want the most expensive playtoys; they drive Daimlers and Bentleys, and Rolls Royces and they buy their clothes from exclusive stores off London's Bond Street. Their monetary thefts involve gems priced at in excess of 33 million dollars. Their life stories are for the most part messy. The elements of suspense in the story are not what it is really about. What it actually gives its readership is an opportunity to escape and live figuratively for a while with people whose tinselled lives mask despair. We see the jet-set; the man and the women in the fast-track. the workaholic; and a few ordinary types. Disaster brings out the best and worst of their characters and Browne can offer his own homespun brand of moral justice.

Very often he kills off his central couple in a quick and violent manner right at the end of the novel.

Browne is also deft at writing a literature of travel. His descriptions of London's Mayfair, or the Tower of London, or Curzon Square and the fashionable Jermyn and Bond Street please both the reader who has traveled to these places and the reader who has only heard about them. Browne's fiction is made for our high-tech, ultra-sophisticated, media-hyped public. Reading it you think that you are browsing through the pages of *Vogue Magazine* or a Tiffany catalogue; or, perhaps, as in *Hot Siberian,* you are sitting in the auction rooms of Sotheby's, watching the auction of a miniature, carved white chalcedony mouse made by one of the workman of Fabergé, a rarity usually found only in the palace of Czar Nicholas or in Buckingham Palace.

Probably the most constant element in Browne's fiction is his appetite to describe sex in all its colorations. Frankly, he is quite good at it, often finding the right combination of pornographic language and dizzying, intoxicating detail to excite his reader. All his stories feature a dazzling couple—the man less wealthy than the woman whom he desires. Usually the woman is unavailable, either married or if unmarried, unable to remarry without forfeiting vast wealth bestowed upon her by a recently dead husband whose hand reaches beyond the grave in the form of a will which disinherits her if she remarries. The women are always chic and sophisticated, restless, eager for excitement, gamblers many times. Their appetite for all kinds of sex in all kinds of positions and places gives Browne innumerable opportunities to practice his sexual prose. The portraits would offend feminists, particularly because he panders to all the so-called male fantasies, making women their object, forcing them into submissions while affecting to grant them a sort of dominance, relishing his portraits of the multi-orgasmic woman, but always making them hungry for marriage and love. Lesbianism, sadomasochism, pornography, and homosexuality are features of all his books. He is shameless in exploiting these features which guarantee the sales of his books.

Browne is equally drawn to other kinds of kinkiness—extra-sensory perception, mediums, rebirthing, and recollections of earlier lives. Similarly he has an affinity for particularly offensive forms of violence and rather gross methods of smuggling. In one novel diamonds are smuggled in small blue packets placed in the cavities of dead men by a devious mortician. He also has a continental flair for character. His young Russian trader in the diamond export agency, his portrait of Arab extremists in *Hazard;* his intelligent agent trained in extra-sensory perception; and mercenaries from Columbia all contribute to his thrillers.

Browne's novels are fast-paced, spicy, if not downright raunchy at times; startling in the unexpected and sometimes brutal turns in their plots. They are also full of specialized knowledge about the gem trade, or mud slides, or the mafia, or the world of the auction houses, or the origins of the thalmic stem of the brain. Browne's novels offer entertaining reading, not particularly challenging, but never dull.

—Carol Simpson Stern

BROWNE, Howard. Also writes as John Evans. American. Born in Omaha, Nebraska, 15 April 1908. Married 1) Esther Levy in 1931 (divorced 1959); 2) Doris Kaye in 1959; one son and two daughters. Department store credit manager, Chicago, 1929–41; magazine editor, Ziff-Davis, publishers, Chicago and New York, 1941–56; executive story consultant, 20th-Century Fox Television Studios, and story editor for *Kraft Mystery Theater, The Virginian,* and *Longstreet* television series, all Hollywood; Instructor, University of California, San Diego, from 1973. Recipient: Private Eye Writers of American Life Achievement award, 1985. Agent: Harold Greene Agency, 8455 Beverly Boulevard, Los Angeles, California 90048. Address: 3303 La Costa Avenue, Carlsbad, California 92009, U.S.A.

CRIME PUBLICATIONS

Novels (series: Paul Pine)

Thin Air. New York, Simon and Schuster, 1954; London, Gollancz, 1955.
The Taste of Ashes (Pine). New York, Simon and Schuster, 1957; London, Gollancz, 1958.
Pork City. New York, St. Martin's Press, and London, W.H. Allen, 1988.

Novels as John Evans (series: Paul Pine)

Halo in Blood (Pine). Indianapolis, Bobbs Merrill, 1946. Harpenden, Hertfordshire, No Exit Press, 1988.
If You Have Tears. New York, Mystery House, 1947; as *Lona,* New York, Lion, 1952.
Halo for Satan (Pine). Indianapolis, Bobbs Merrill, 1948; London, Boardman, 1949.
Halo in Brass (Pine). Indianapolis, Bobbs Merrill, 1949; London, Foulsham, 1951.
The Paper Gun (Pine). New York, Macmillan, 1985.

Uncollected Short Story as John Evans

"So Dark for April," in *My Favorite Mystery Stories,* edited by Maureen Daly. New York, Dodd Mead, 1966.

OTHER PUBLICATIONS

Novel

Warrior of the Dawn. Chicago, Reilly and Lee, 1943.

Plays

Screenplays: *Portrait of a Mobster,* 1961; *The St. Valentine's Day Massacre,* 1967; *A Bowl of Cherries,* 1969; *Capone,* 1975.

Television Plays: 127 episodes of *Cheyenne, 77 Sunset Strip, Playhouse 90, The Virginian, The Bold Ones, Alias Smith and Jones, Destry, Mission Impossible, Longstreet, Asphalt Jungle, West World, Colombo, Simon and Simon,* and other series.

*

Manuscript Collections: University of Wyoming, Laramie; Mugar Memorial Library, Boston University

Howard Browne comments:
    While my highschool teachers were extolling the virtues and values of reading the classics, I was out behind the barn deep in *Flynn's Detective Weekly* and similar character-warping pulp-magazine publications. "Craig Kennedy" and "Jimmie Dale" I found far more engrossing then, say, Richard III—and a lot easier to read. The English mysteries, with their accent on clues

instead of character, left me cold; the fact that "Lady Van de Meer's lorgnette was found four yards west of the sundial, proving the butler was in East Hampton on the night of the murder" might be fine for a puzzle buff but not something designed to keep me up nights. In short, I'll take Raymond Chandler over Agatha Christie, Robert Parker over S.S. Van Dine. Any day.

The writing style of my first books was heavily influenced, to put it mildly, by Raymond Chandler and James M. Cain. In fact, if there had been no "Philip Marlowe" there could have no "Paul Pine." Other authors whose works had much to do with my approach to writing were Mark Twain and John O'Hara.

*　*　*

In the 1940's, Howard Browne not only contributed numerous short stories and novelettes to the Ziff-Davis line of pulps (*Mammoth Detective, Mammoth Mystery,* etc.), but for five years was the managing editor of the Chicago-based chain publisher's science-fiction magazines *Amazing Stories* and *Fantastic Adventures.* In 1952 he became editor of Ziff-Davis's sf/fantasy digest *Fantastic,* and of two other short-lived digests, *Conflict* (detective and mystery) and *Tales of the Sea* (sea adventure stories).

Halo in Blood, Browne's first mystery novel, was published in 1946 under the pseudonym John Evans; this and the two "Halo" novels which followed it feature Chicago private detective Paul Pine, one of the best of the plethora of tough-guy heroes from that era. Although the Pine novels are solidly in the tradition of Raymond Chandler, they have a complexity and character all their own and are too well-crafted to be mere imitations. They also deal with subject matter which was provocative and then-controversial: *Halo for Satan* concerns an ancient manuscript purportedly in the handwriting of Christ which triggers some highly unChristian behavior; *Halo in Brass* has to do with lesbianism. A fourth Pine adventure, *The Taste of Ashes,* was published eight years after the last "Halo" book, under Browne's own name. This offbeat, violent, exciting tale also contains a theme previously considered too controversial for mysteries—child molestation—and is surely the cream of the series.

The fifth Pine novel, *The Paper Gun,* is a work-in-progress, not a full-fledged novel. This story of the murder of a teenage girl from Missouri that triggers three other violent killings in a 24 hour period is only 35,000 words in length, and while it marginally stands on its own, its denouement is clearly tacked on. In his forward to the book (which also includes the only Paul Pine short story, "So Dark for April"), the author says that the reason he has yet to complete *The Paper Gun* is "not that I ran into a dead end or a terminal case of writer's block; it's simply that—even with a completely detailed synopsis on paper—I lost interest in the private eye genre."

Browne's first complete new novel in 30 years, *Pork City,* is totally different from anything else he has written. Set in Chicago in the early 1930's, it is the fact-based story of the broad-daylight slaying of Chicago *Tribune* reporter Jake Lingle and its resounding repercussions. Authentic in detail, filled with fascinating insights into the prohibition era and with such other real-life characters as Al Capone, Bugs Moran, and the man who colluded in the killing of Lingle, *Tribune* owner Robert Rutherford McCormick, *Pork City* is Browne's magnum opus.

—Bill Pronzini

———

BROWNING, Sterry. *See* **GRIBBLE, Leonard.**

———

BRUCE, Leo. Pseudonym for Rupert Croft-Cooke. British. Born in Edenbridge, Kent, 20 June 1903. Educated at Tonbridge School, Kent; Wellington College, now Wrekin College; University of Buenos Aires, 1923–26. Served in Field Security, 1939–46: Captain; British Empire Medal. Founding editor, *La Estrella,* Buenos Aires, 1923–24; antiquarian bookseller, 1929–31; Lecturer, Institute Montana, Zugerberg, Switzerland, 1931; book critic, *The Sketch,* London, 1946–53. *Died 10 June 1979.*

CRIME PUBLICATIONS

Novels (series: Sergeant William Beef; Carolus Deene)

Release the Lions. London, Jarrolds, 1933; New York, Dodd Mead, 1934.
Case for Three Detectives (Beef). London, Bles, 1936; New York, Stokes, 1937.
Case Without a Corpse (Beef). London, Bles, and New York, Stokes, 1937.
Case with Four Clowns (Beef). London, Davies, and New York, Stokes, 1939.
Case with No Conclusion (Beef). London, Bles, 1939, Chicago, Academy, 1984.
Case with Ropes and Rings (Beef). London, Nicholson and Watson, 1940; Chicago, Academy, 1980.
Case for Sergeant Beef. London, Nicholson and Watson, 1947; Chicago, Academy, 1980.
Neck and Neck (Beef). London, Gollancz, 1951; Chicago, Academy, 1980.
Cold Blood (Beef). London, Gollancz, 1952; Chicago, Academy, 1980.
At Death's Door (Deene). London, Hamish Hamilton, 1955.
Dead for a Ducat (Deene). London, Davies, 1956.
Death of Cold (Deene). London, Davies, 1956.
Dead Man's Shoes (Deene). London, Davies, 1958; Chicago, Academy, 1987.
A Louse for the Hangman (Deene). London, Davies, 1958.
Our Jubilee Is Death (Deene). London, Davies, 1959; Chicago, Academy, 1986.
Furious Old Women (Deene). London, Davies, 1960; Chicago, Academy, 1983.
Jack on the Gallows Tree (Deene). London, Davies, 1960; Chicago, Academy, 1983.
Die All, Die Merrily (Deene). London, Davies, 1961; Chicago, Academy, 1987.
A Bone and a Hank of Hair (Deene). London, Davies, 1961.
Nothing Like Blood (Deene). London, Davies, 1962; Chicago, Academy, 1985.
Crack of Doom (Deene). London, Davies, 1963; as *Such Is Death,* New York, British Book Centre, 1963.
Death in Albert Park (Deene). London, W.H. Allen, 1964; New York, Scribner, 1979.
Death at Hallows End (Deene). London, W.H. Allen, 1965; New York, British Book Centre, 1966.
Death on the Black Sands (Deene). London, W.H. Allen, 1966.
Death of a Commuter (Deene). London, W.H. Allen, 1967; Chicago Academy, 1988.

Death at St. Asprey's School (Deene).   London, W.H. Allen, 1967; Chicago, Academy, 1984.
Death on Romney Marsh (Deene).   London, W.H. Allen, 1968.
Death with Blue Ribbon (Deene).   London, W.H. Allen, 1969; Chicago, Academy, 1989.
Death on Allhallowe'en (Deene).   London, W.H. Allen, 1970; Chicago, Academy, 1988.
Death by the Lake (Deene).   London, W.H. Allen, 1971.
Death in the Middle Watch (Deene).   London, ·W.H. Allen, 1974.
Death of a Bovver Boy (Deene).   London, W.H. Allen, 1974.

Novels as Rupert Croft-Cooke

Seven Thunders.   London, Macmillan, and New York, St. Martin's Press, 1955.
Thief.   London, Eyre and Spottiswoode, 1960; New York, Doubleday, 1961.
Clash by Night.   London, Eyre and Spottiswoode, 1962.
Paper Albatross.   London, Eyre and Spottiswoode, 1965; New York, Abelard Schuman, 1968.
Three in a Cell.   London, Eyre and Spottiswoode, 1968.
Nasty Piece of Work.   London, Eyre Methuen, 1973.

Short Stories as Rupert Croft-Cooke

Pharaoh and His Waggons and Other Stories.   London, Jarrolds, 1937.

Uncollected Short Stories

"Holiday Task," in *The Evening Standard* (London), 13 May 1950.
"The Doctor's Wife," in *The Evening Standard* (London), 10 October 1950.
"Beef and Spiders," in *The Evening Standard* (London), November 1950.
"Bloody Moon," in *Giant Detective Annual.*   New York, Best Books, 1950.
"Death in the Garden," in *The Evening Standard Detective Book.*   London, Gollancz, 1950.
"Summons to Death," in *The Evening Standard* (London), 1 March 1951.
"The Chicken and the Egg," in *The Evening Standard* (London), 29 May 1951.
"On the Spot," in *Magpie* (London), June 1951.
"Blunt Instrument," in *The Evening Standard* (London), 19 July 1951.
"I, Said the Sparrow," in *The Evening Standard* (London), 6 October 1951.
"Murder in Miniature," in *The Evening Standard Detective Book,* 2nd series.   London, Gollancz, 1951.
"A Piece of Paper," in *The Evening Standard* (London), 30 January 1952.
"Letter of the Law," in *The Evening Standard* (London), 30 September 1952.
"A Glass of Sherry," in *The Evening Standard* (London), 7 October 1952.
"The Scene of the Crime," in *The Evening Standard* (London), 10 October 1952.
"Murder in Reverse," in *The Evening Standard* (London), 27 December 1952.
"Woman in the Taxi," in *The Evening Standard* (London), 16 January 1953.
"The Nine Fifty-five," in *The Evening Standard* (London), 17 February 1953.
"Person or Persons," in *The Evening Standard* (London), 4 March 1953.

"The Wrong Moment," in *The Evening Standard* (London), 18 March 1953.
"A Box of Capsules," in *The Evening Standard* (London), 19 April 1953.
"Blind Witness," in *The Evening Standard* (London), 22 May 1953.
"Deceased Wife's Sister," in *The Evening Standard* (London), 10 June 1953.
"Riverside Night," in *The Evening Standard* (London), 22 July 1953.
"Rufus—the Murderer," in *The Evening Standard* (London), 24 August 1955.
"The Marsh Light," in *The Evening Standard* (London), 2 June 1956.
"A Stiff Drink," in *The Evening Standard* (London), 16 July 1956.
"Into Thin Air," in *The Evening Standard* (London), 29 August 1956.
"A Case for the Flies," in *The Evening Standard* (London), 19 November 1956.

OTHER PUBLICATIONS as Rupert Croft-Cooke

Novels

Troubadour.   London, Chapman and Hall, 1930.
Give Him the Earth.   London, Chapman and Hall, 1930; New York, Knopf, 1931.
Night Out.   London, Jarrolds, and New York, Dial Press, 1932.
Cosmopolis.   London, Jarrolds, 1932; New York, Dial Press, 1933.
Her Mexican Lover.   London, Mellifont Press, 1934.
Picaro.   London, Jarrolds, and New York, Dodd Mead, 1934.
Shoulder the Sky.   London, Jarrolds, 1934.
Blind Gunner.   London, Jarrolds, 1935.
Crusade.   London, Jarrolds, 1936.
Kingdom Come.   London, Jarrolds, 1936.
Rule, Britannia.   London, Jarrolds, 1938.
Same Way Home.   London, Jarrolds, 1939; New York, Macmillan, 1940.
Glorious.   London, Jarrolds, 1940.
Ladies Gay.   London, Macdonald, 1946.
Octopus.   London, Jarrolds, 1946; as *Miss Allick,* New York, Holt, 1947.
Wilkie.   London, Macdonald, 1948; as *Another Sun, Another Home,* New York, Holt, 1949.
The White Mountain.   London, Falcon Press, 1949.
Brass Farthing.   London, Laurie, 1950.
Three Names for Nicholas.   London, Macmillan, 1951.
Nine Days with Edward.   London, Macmillan, 1952.
Harvest Moon.   London, Macmillan, and New York, St. Martin's Press, 1953.
Fall of Man.   London, Macmillan, 1955.
Barbary Night.   London, Eyre and Spottiswoode, 1958.
Wolf from the Door.   London, W.H. Allen, 1969.
Exiles.   London, W.H. Allen, 1970.
Under the Rose Garden.   London, W.H. Allen, 1971.
While the Iron's Hot.   London, W.H. Allen, 1971.
Conduct Unbecoming.   London, W.H. Allen, 1975.

Short Stories

A Football for the Brigadier and Other Stories. London, Laurie, 1950.

Plays

Banquo's Chair. London, Deane, 1930.
Tap Three Times. London, French, 1934.
Deliberate Accident (produced London, 1934).
Gala Night at The Willows, with G.B. Stern. London, Deane, 1950.

Radio Plays: *You Bet Your Life,* with Beverley Nichols, 1938; *Peter the Painter,* 1946; *Theft,* 1963.

Verse

Songs of a Sussex Tramp. Steyning, Sussex, Vine Press, 1922.
Tonbridge School. Tonbridge, Kent, Free Press, 1923.
Songs South of the Line. London, Lincoln Torrey, 1925.
The Viking. Privately printed, 1926.
Some Poems. Rochester, Kent, Galleon Press, 1929.
Tales of a Wicked Uncle. London, Cape, 1963.

Other

How Psychology Can Help. London, Daniel, 1927.
Darts. London, Bles, 1936.
God in Ruins: A Passing Commentary. London, Fortune Press, 1936.
The World Is Young. London, Hodder and Stoughton, 1937; as *Escape to the Andes,* New York, Messner, 1938.
How to Get More Out of Life. London, Bles, 1938.
The Man in Europe Street (travel). London, Rich and Cowan, and New York, Putnam, 1938.
The Circus Has No Home. London, Methuen, 1941; revised edition, London, Falcon Press, 1950.
How to Enjoy Travel Abroad. London, Rockliff, 1948.
The Moon in My Pocket: Life with the Romanies. London, Sampson Low, 1948.
Rudyard Kipling. London, Home and Van Thal, and Denver, Swallow, 1948.
Cities, with Noël Barber. London, Wingate, 1951.
The Sawdust Ring, with W.S. Meadmore. London, Odhams Press, 1951.
Buffalo Bill: The Legend, The Man of Action, The Showman, with W.S. Meadmore. London, Sidgwick and Jackson, 1952.
The Life for Me (memoirs). London, Macmillan, 1952; New York, St. Martin's Press, 1953.
The Blood-Red Island (memoirs). London, Staples Press, 1953.
A Few Gypsies. London, Putnam, 1955.
Sherry. London, Putnam, 1955; New York, Knopf, 1956.
The Verdict of You All (memoirs). London, Secker and Warburg, 1955.
The Tangerine House (memoirs). London, Macmillan, and New York, St. Martin's Press, 1956.
Port. London, Putnam, 1957.
The Gardens of Camelot (memoirs). London, Putnam, 1958.
The Quest for Quixote. London, Secker and Warburg, 1959; as *Through Spain with Don Quixote,* New York, Knopf, 1960.
Smiling Damned Villain: The True Story of Paul Axel Lund. London, Secker and Warburg, 1959.
The Altar in the Loft (memoirs). London, Putnam, 1960.
English Cooking: A New Approach. London, W.H. Allen, 1960.
The Drums of Morning (memoirs). London, Putnam, 1961.

Madeira. London, Putnam, 1961.
The Glittering Pastures (memoirs). London, Putnam, 1962.
Wine and Other Drinks. London, Collins, 1962.
Bosie: The Story of Lord Alfred Douglas, His Friends and Enemies. London, W.H. Allen, 1963; Indianapolis, Bobbs Merrill, 1964.
Cooking for Pleasure. London, Collins, 1963.
The Numbers Came (memoirs). London, Putnam, 1963.
The Last of Spring (memoirs). London, Putnam, 1964.
The Wintry Sea (memoirs). London, W.H. Allen, 1964.
The Gorgeous East: One Man's India. London, W.H. Allen, 1965.
The Purple Streak (memoirs). London, W.H. Allen, 1966.
The Wild Hills (memoirs). London, W.H. Allen, 1966.
Feasting with Tigers: A New Consideration of Some Late Victorian Writers. London, W.H. Allen, 1967; New York, Holt Rinehart, 1968.
The Happy Highways (memoirs). London, W.H. Allen, 1967.
The Ghost of June: A Return to England and the West. London, W.H. Allen, 1968.
Exotic Food: Three Hundred of the Most Unusual Dishes in Western Cookery. London, Allen and Unwin, 1969; New York, Herder, 1971.
The Licentious Soldiery (memoirs). London, W.H. Allen, 1971.
The Unrecorded Life of Oscar Wilde. London, W.H. Allen, and New York, McKay, 1972.
The Dogs of Peace (memoirs). London, W.H. Allen, 1973.
The Caves of Hercules (memoirs). London, W.H. Allen, 1974.
The Long Way Home (memoirs). London, W.H. Allen, 1974.
Circus: A World History, with Peter Cotes. London, Elek, 1976; New York, Macmillan, 1977.
The Green, Green Grass (memoirs). London, W.H. Allen, 1977.

Editor, *Major Road Ahead: A Young Man's Ultimatum.* London, Methuen, 1939.
Editor, *The Circus Book.* London, Sampson Low, 1948.

Translator, *The Last Days of Madrid: The End of the Second Spanish Republic,* by Segismundo Casado. London, Davies, 1939.

*

Manuscript Collection: Humanities Research Center, University of Texas, Austin.

* * *

Leo Bruce (pseudonym of Rupert Croft-Cooke) is a major British detective story writer of salient merit. His fertility of invention in devising puzzles that reach totally unexpected conclusions is exceptional. His subtlety is outstanding, and his efforts at misdirection are worthy of Agatha Christie.

Bruce's highly-praised, *Case for Three Detectives,* pits his first series detective, the plebeian Sergeant William Beef, against Lord Simon Plimsoll, M. Amer Picon, and Monsignor Smith (alias Wimsey, Poirot, and Brown) in a problem involving a locked-room murder. Beef solves this, and other cunningly devised crime problems such as those told in *Case Without a Corpse, Case with Ropes and Rings,* and *Neck and Neck.* His early successes persuade Beef to leave the police force and set up on his own as a private inquiry agent.

His exploits are chronicled by the irascible Lionel Townsend, who would much rather work with and narrate the exploits of a more aristocratic sleuth such as Lord Peter Wimsey. Townsend's patience is often tried when Beef abandons his interest in a crime problem in favor of drinking copious amounts of beer and indulging in a few innocent games of darts at any nearby pub. The friction and byplay (which is not up to the highest level of Stout's Wolfe-Goodwin team) will often go too far and cut to the bone. Bruce continued this series until *Cold Blood*, in which Beef places his life in jeopardy in order to solve the murder of a millionaire who is dispatched by a croquet mallet. Beef solves this case, but is abandoned by his creator for no explicable reason.

Bruce tightened his prose style, dispensed with a Watson-narrator, and introduced the less colorful Carolus Deene in *At Death's Door*. Deene (who is preferred to Beef by Jacques Barzun and Wendell Hertig Taylor) is a laconic ex-commando who serves as Senior History Master at Queen's School, Newminster, and solves crime problems as a hobby. During his investigations, Deene often has to cope with the efforts of his headmaster and his housekeeper who try to dissuade him, and his least-favorite student, the odious Rupert Priggley, who always seeks to encourage him. *A Bone and a Hank of Hair, Furious Old Women, Jack on the Gallows Tree*, and *Nothing Like Blood* are among the best Deene narratives.

—Charles Shibuk

———

BRUCE, Walt. *See* **BALLARD, Willis Todhunter.**

———

BRUTON, Eric (Moore). British. Born in London in 1915. Educated privately. Served as an engineering officer in the Royal Air Force, 1940–46. Married Anne Valerie Britton (died 1976). Ran a riding school; visiting lecturer, Sir John Cass College, London; jeweller: director, Diamond Boutique Ltd. and Things and Ideas Ltd; managing director, N.A.G. Press Ltd, later Eric Bruton Associates; consultant, *Retail Jeweller*, London. Liveryman, Company of Clockmakers and Company of Turners; Freeman, Company of Goldsmiths; Fellow, British Horological Institute and Gemmological Association of Great Britain; President, National Association of Goldsmiths, 1983–85. Recipient: American Watchmakers Institute award, 1968; Hannemann award, for non-fiction, 1981. Agent: Elaine Greene Ltd., 37 A Goldhawk Road, London, W12 8QQ. Address: The House by the Pond, Great Bentley, Colchester CO7 8QG, England.

CRIME PUBLICATIONS

Novels (series: Inspector George Judd)

Death in Ten Point Bold. London, Jenkins, 1957.
Die, Darling, Die. London, Boardman, 1959.
Violent Brothers. London, Boardman, 1960.
The Hold Out. London, Boardman, 1961.
King Diamond. London, Boardman, 1961.
The Devil's Pawn. London, Boardman, 1962.
The Laughing Policeman (Judd). London, Boardman, 1963.
The Finsbury Mob (Judd). London, Boardman, 1964.
The Smithfield Slayer (Judd). London, Boardman, 1965.

The Wicked Saint (Judd). London, Boardman, 1965.
The Firebug (Judd). London, Boardman, 1967.

Uncollected Short Story

"Waxing of a Drone," in *John Creasey's Mystery Bedside Book,* edited by Herbert Harris. London, Hodder and Stoughton, 1966.

OTHER PUBLICATIONS

Other

The True Book about Clocks (for children). London, Muller, 1957.
The True Book about Diamonds (for children). London, Muller, 1961.
Automation (for children). London, Muller, 1962.
Dictionary of Clocks and Watches. London, Arco, 1962; New York, Archer House, 1963.
The Longcase Clock. London, Arco, 1964; New York, Praeger, 1968; revised edition, London, Hart Davis MacGibbon, 1976; New York, Scribner, 1979.
Clocks and Watches 1400–1900. London, Barker, and New York, Praeger, 1967.
Clocks and Watches. London, Hamlyn, 1968.
Diamonds. London, N.A.G. Press, 1970; Philadelphia, Chilton, 1971; revised edition, 1978.
Hallmarks and Date Letters on Gold and Silver, revised edition. London, N.A.G. Press, 1970.
Antique Clocks and Clock Collecting. London, Hamlyn, 1974.
The History of Clocks and Watches. London, Orbis, 1979; New York, Rizzoli, 1980.
The Wetherfield Collection of Clocks: A Guide to Dating English Antique Clocks. London, N.A.G. Press, 1981.
Legendary Gems: or Gems that Made History. Philadelphia, Chilton, and London, N.A.G. Press, 1986.
Clock and Watch Dictionary. London, N.A.G. Press, 1990.

*   *   *

The opening paragraph to Eric Bruton's first crime novel, *Death in Ten Point Bold,* gives the clue to the early success enjoyed by this fastidious and craftsmanlike writer. The book is set in the Fleet Street offices of a woman's weekly magazine, and Bruton immediately conjures up the hectic pace of a busy newspaper going to press. So immediate is the sensation and so accurate the delineation of the office atmosphere that the reader cannot but help feel that he or she has been granted privileged access to the action that is about to unfold. What follows next, though, is something of a let-down. A terrified scream reveals a dead member of staff with the single word "murder" written beside this desk, and a young artist, Steven Kelly, sets out to make his own enquiries. The resulting denouement is typical of many British crime mysteries of the 1950's and is reminiscent of the work of Freeman Wills Crofts, but the strengths of the novel's narrative line and the concern with accuracy of detail were sufficient to herald the arrival of a new talent.

In his fourth novel, *The Hold Out,* Bruton began the first of a series of novels concerned with the operations of London's police force, on which his reputation ultimately depends. (The series was not officially named until the publication of his next novel.) It introduces a thoroughly modern criminal, an ex-World War II pilot disenchanted with the world of the early 1950's who takes a woman hostage and lays siege to the police from the top of a London monument. Unable to persuade him to come down peacefully, the police have to use all their prowess in psychological warfare to deal with the case, and as a result the novel is a model of professional police procedure. No less enticing is the background of London itself which comes to life as a character in its own right in this moving human drama. Its success persuaded Bruton to begin a series of novels, centering on the City of London Police, and the first of their number, *The Laughing Policeman,* introduces the reader to the men of "A" division based at Moor Lane police station in the City. It is dedicated to Detective Chief Inspector Tom Grealey (who also wrote crime fiction under the pseudonym of Louis Southworth) who provided Bruton with knowledge of police procedures and with information from his work in police training. The plot is simple enough: two crimes which seem to be unrelated until by sifting through the mass of available evidence and by patient examination in the forensic laboratory the police come closer to finding a solution. All the while the hum-drum day-to-day work of the police station continues apace as the detectives take up the challenge of the seemingly intractable problem that has been thrown at them.

Detective Inspector Judd who strides patiently through the series is a policeman cast entirely in the traditional British mould; patient, hard-working, and with a touch of cynicism that keeps his feet firmly on the ground. He is the obvious model for countless successors in later novels and in film and television. However antiquated in his outlook Judd might appear to a new generation of readers, the criminals who harass him move with the times, and it is a feature of Bruton's later novels that the events they describe are thoroughly contemporary. *The Firebug* concerns itself with an arsonist at large in London and shows Bruton at his most refined: the dialogue is convincing, the characters well drawn, and the plot suitably taut as Judd wades his way through the evidence to get his man.

In recent years, Bruton, a master horologist, has turned his talents to writing books about antique clocks and jewelry. It is to be hoped that he will turn his pen again to the creation of more London police novels and resuscitate the formidable Inspector Judd.

—Trevor Royle

———

BUCHAN, John; 1st Baron Tweedsmuir of Elsfield. British. Born in Broughton Green, Peebles-shire, 26 August 1875. Educated at Hutchison Grammar School, Glasgow; University of Glasgow; Brasenose College, Oxford (scholar, 1895; Stanhope prize, 1897; Newdigate prize, 1898; President of the Union, 1899), B.A. (honours) 1899; Middle Temple, London, called to the Bar, 1901. Served on the Headquarters Staff of the British Army in France, as temporary Lieutenant Colonel, 1916–17; Director of Information under the Prime Minister, 1917–18. Married Susan Charlotte Grosvenor in 1907; three sons and one daughter. Private secretary to the High Commissioner for South Africa, Lord Milner, 1901–03; director, Nelson, publishers, London, from 1903, and Reuters, London, 1919; Conservative Member of Parliament for the Scottish Universities, 1927–35; Lord High Commissioner, Church of Scotland, 1933, 1934; Governor-General of Canada, 1935–40; Privy Councillor, 1937. Curator, Oxford University Chest, 1924–30; President, Scottish History Society, 1929–33; bencher, Middle Temple, 1935; Chancellor, University of Edinburgh, 1937–40; Justice of the Peace, Peebles-shire and Oxfordshire. Recipient: James Tait Black Memorial prize, 1929. D.C.L.: Oxford University; LL.D.: University of

Glasgow; University of St. Andrews; University of Edinburgh; McGill University, Montreal; University of Toronto; University of Manitoba, Winnipeg; Harvard University, Cambridge, Massachusetts; Yale University, New Haven, Connecticut; D. Litt.: Columbia University, New York; University of British Columbia, Vancouver; McMaster University, Hamilton, Ontario. Honorary Fellow, Brasenose College, Oxford. Companion of Honour, 1932; created Baron Tweedsmuir, 1935; G.C.M.G. (Knight Grand Cross, Order of St. Michael and St. George), 1935; G.C.V.O. (Knight Grand Cross, Royal Victorian Order), 1939. *Died 11 February 1940.*

CRIME PUBLICATIONS

Novels (series: Richard Hannay; Sir Edward Leithen; Dickson Mc'Cunn)

The Thirty-Nine Steps (Hannay). Edinburgh, Blackwood, 1915; New York, Doran, 1916.
The Power-House (Leithen). Edinburgh, Blackwood, and New York, Doran, 1916.
Greenmantle (Hannay). London, Hodder and Stoughton, and New York, Doran, 1916.
Mr. Standfast (Hannay). London, Hodder and Stoughton, and New York, Doran, 1919.
Huntingtower (Mc'Cunn). London, Hodder and Stoughton, and New York, Doran, 1922.
The Three Hostages (Hannay). London, Hodder and Stoughton, and Boston, Houghton Mifflin, 1924.
John Macnab (Leithen). London, Hodder and Stoughton, and Boston, Houghton Mifflin, 1925.
The Dancing Floor (Leithen). London, Hodder and Stoughton, and Boston, Houghton Mifflin, 1926.
The Courts of the Morning. London, Hodder and Stoughton, and Boston, Houghton Mifflin, 1929.
Castle Gay (Mc'Cunn). London, Hodder and Stoughton, and Boston, Houghton Mifflin, 1929.
A Prince of the Captivity. London, Hodder and Stoughton, and Boston, Houghton Mifflin, 1933.
The House of the Four Winds (Mc'Cunn). London, Hodder and Stoughton, and Boston, Houghton Mifflin, 1935.
The Island of Sheep (Hannay). London, Hodder and Stoughton, 1936; as *The Man from the Norlands,* Boston, Houghton Mifflin, 1936.
Sick Heart River (Leithen). London, Hodder and Stoughton, 1941; as *Mountain Meadow,* Boston, Houghton Mifflin, 1941.

Short Stories

The Watcher by the Threshold and Other Tales. Edinburgh, Blackwood, 1902; augmented edition, New York, Doran, 1918.
The Moon Endureth: Tales and Fancies. Edinburgh, Blackwood, and New York, Sturgis, 1912.
The Runagates Club. London, Hodder and Stoughton, and Boston, Houghton Mifflin, 1928.
The Gap in the Curtain. London, Hodder and Stoughton, and Boston, Houghton Mifflin, 1932.
The Best Short Stories of John Buchan, edited by David Daniell. London, Joseph, 2 vols., 1980–82.

OTHER PUBLICATIONS

Novels

Sir Quixote of the Moors, Being Some Account of an Episode in the Life of the Sieur de Rohaine. London, Unwin, and New York, Holt, 1895.

John Burnet of Barns. London, Lane, and New York, Dodd Mead, 1898.

A Lost Lady of Old Years. London, Lane, 1899.

The Half-Hearted. London, Isbister, and Boston, Houghton Mifflin, 1900.

Prester John. London, Nelson, 1910; as *The Great Diamond Pipe,* New York, Dodd Mead, 1911.

Salute to Adventurers. London, Nelson, and Boston, Houghton Mifflin, 1915.

Midwinter: Certain Travellers in Old England. London, Hodder and Stoughton, and New York, Doran, 1923.

Witch Wood. London, Hodder and Stoughton, and Boston, Houghton Mifflin, 1927.

The Blanket of the Dark. London, Hodder and Stoughton, and Boston, Houghton Mifflin, 1931.

The Free Fishers. London, Hodder and Stoughton, and Boston, Houghton Mifflin, 1934.

The Long Traverse. London, Hodder and Stoughton, 1941; as *Lake of Gold,* Boston, Houghton Mifflin, 1941.

Short Stories

Grey Weather: Moorland Tales of My Own People. London, Lane, 1899.

Ordeal by Marriage: An Eclogue. London, R. Clay, 1915.

The Path of the King. London, Hodder and Stoughton, and New York, Doran, 1921.

Play

Screenplay: *The Battles of Coronel and Falkland Islands,* with Harry Engholm and Merritt Crawford, 1927.

Verse

The Pilgrim Fathers. Oxford, Blackwell, 1898.

Poems, Scots and English. London, Jack, 1917; revised edition, London, Nelson, 1936.

Other

Scholar Gipsies. London, Lane, and New York, Macmillan, 1896.

Sir Walter Raleigh. Oxford, Blackwell, 1897.

Brasenose College. London, Robinson, 1898.

The African Colony: Studies in the Reconstruction. Edinburgh, Blackwell, 1903.

The Law Relating to the Taxation of Foreign Income. London, Stevens, 1905.

A Lodge in the Wilderness. Edinburgh, Blackwood, 1906.

Some Eighteenth Century Byways and Other Essays. Edinburgh, Blackwood, 1908.

Sir Walter Raleigh (for children). London, Nelson, and New York, Holt, 1911.

What the Home Rule Bill Means (speech). Peebles, Smythe, 1912.

The Marquis of Montrose. London, Nelson, and New York, Scribner, 1913.

Andrew Jameson, Lord Ardwall. Edinburgh, Blackwood, 1913.

Britain's War by Land. London, Oxford University Press, 1915.

Nelson's History of the War. London, Nelson, 24 vols., 1915–19; as *A History of the Great War,* 4 vols., 1921–22.

The Achievement of France. London, Methuen, 1915.

The Future of the War (speech). London, Boyle Son and Watchurst, 1916.

The Purpose of War (speech). London, Dent, 1916.

These for Remembrance. Privately printed, 1919; London, Buchan and Enright, 1987.

The Island of Sheep, with Susan Buchan (as Cadmus and Harmonia). London, Hodder and Stoughton, 1919; Boston, Houghton Mifflin, 1920.

The Battle-Honours of Scotland 1914–1918. Glasgow, Outram, 1919.

The History of the South African Forces in France. London, Nelson, 1920.

Francis and Riversdale Grenfell: A Memoir. London, Nelson, 1920.

A Book of Escapes and Hurried Journeys. London, Nelson, 1922; Boston, Houghton Mifflin, 1923.

The Last Secrets: The Final Mysteries of Exploration. London, Nelson, 1923; Boston, Houghton Mifflin, 1924.

The Memoir of Sir Walter Scott (speech). Privately printed, 1923.

Days to Remember: The British Empire in the Great War, with Henry Newbolt. London, Nelson, 1923.

Some Notes on Sir Walter Scott (speech). London, Oxford University Press, 1924.

Lord Minto: A Memoir. London, Nelson, 1924.

The History of the Royal Scots Fusiliers (1678–1918). London, Nelson, 1925.

The Man and the Book: Sir Walter Raleigh. London, Nelson, 1925.

Two Ordeals of Democracy (lecture). Boston, Houghton Mifflin, 1925.

Homilies and Recreations. London, Nelson, 1926; Freeport, New York, Books for Libraries, 1969.

The Fifteenth—Scottish—Division 1914–1919, with John Stewart. Edinburgh, Blackwood, 1926.

To the Electors of the Scottish Universities (speech). Glasgow, Anderson, 1927.

The Causal and the Casual in History (lecture). Cambridge, University Press, and New York, Macmillan, 1929.

What the Union of the Churches Means to Scotland. Edinburgh, McNivern and Wallace, 1929.

Montrose and Leadership (lecture). London, Oxford University Press, 1930.

The Revision of Dogmas (lecture). Ashridge, Wisconsin, Ashridge Journal, 1930.

Lord Rosebery 1847–1930. London, Oxford University Press, 1930.

The Novel and the Fairy Tale. London, Oxford University Press, 1931.

Sir Walter Scott. London, Cassell, and New York, Coward McCann, 1932.

The Magic Walking-Stick (for children). London, Hodder and Stoughton, and Boston, Houghton Mifflin, 1932.

Julius Caesar. London, Davies, and New York, Appleton, 1932.

The Massacre of Glencoe. London, Davies, and New York, Putnam, 1933.

Andrew Lang and the Border (lecture). London, Oxford University Press, 1933.

The Margins of Life (speech). London, Birkbeck College, 1933.

The Principles of Social Service (lecture). Glasgow, Glasgow Society of Social Service, 1934(?).
The Scottish Church and the Empire (speech). Glasgow, Church of Scotland Commission on Colonial Churches, 1934.
Gordon at Khartoum. London, Davies, 1934.
Oliver Cromwell. London, Hodder and Stoughton, and Boston, Houghton Mifflin, 1934.
Men and Deeds. London, Davies, 1935; Freeport, New York, Books for Libraries, 1969.
The King's Grace 1910–35 (on George V). London, Hodder and Stoughton, 1935; as *The People's King,* Boston, Houghton Mifflin, 1935.
An Address [The Western Mind]. Montreal, McGill University, 1935.
Address [A University's Bequest to Youth]. Toronto, Victoria University, 1936.
Augustus. London, Hodder and Stoughton, and Boston, Houghton Mifflin, 1937.
The Interpreter's House (speech). London, Hodder and Stoughton, 1938.
Presbyterianism Yesterday, Today, and Tomorrow. Edinburgh, Church of Scotland, 1938.
Memory Hold-the-Door. London, Hodder and Stoughton, 1940; as *Pilgrim's War: An Essay in Recollection,* Boston, Houghton Mifflin, 1940.
Comments and Characters, edited by W. Forbes Gray. London, Nelson, 1940; Freeport, New York, Books for Libraries, 1970.
Canadian Occasions (lectures). London, Hodder and Stoughton, 1940.
The Clearing House: A Survey of One Man's Mind, edited by Lady Tweedsmuir. London, Hodder and Stoughton, 1946.
Life's Adventure: Extracts from the Works of John Buchan, edited by Lady Tweedsmuir. London, Hodder and Stoughton, 1947.

Editor, *Essays and Apothegms,* by Francis Bacon. London, Scott, 1894.
Editor, *Musa Piscatrix.* London, Lane, and Chicago, McClurg, 1896.
Editor, *The Compleat Angler,* by Izaak Walton. London, Methuen, 1901.
Editor, *The Long Road to Victory.* London, Nelson, 1920.
Editor, *Great Hours in Sport.* London, Nelson, 1921.
Editor, *Miscellanies, Literary and Historical,* by Archibald Primrose, Earl of Rosebery. London, Hodder and Stoughton, 1921.
Editor, *A History of English Literature.* London, Nelson, 1923; New York, Ronald Press, 1938.
Editor, *The Nations of Today; A New History of the World.* London, Hodder and Stoughton, and Boston, Houghton Mifflin, 12 vols., 1923–24.
Editor, *The Northern Muse: An Anthology of Scots Vernacular Poetry.* London, Nelson, 1924.
Editor, *Modern Short Stories.* London, Nelson, 1926.
Editor, *Essays and Studies 12.* Oxford, Clarendon Press, 1926.
Editor, *South Africa.* London, British Empire Educational Press, 1928.
Editor, *The Teaching of History.* London, Nelson, 11 vols., 1928–30.
Editor, *The Poetry of Neil Munro.* Edinburgh, Blackwood, 1931.

*

Bibliography: *John Buchan: A Bibliography* by Archibald Hanna, Jr., Hamden, Connecticut, Shoe String Press, 1953; by J. Randolph Cox, in *English Literature in Transition* (Tempe, Arizona), 1966–67; *The First Editions of John Buchan: A Collector's Bibliography* by Robert G. Blanchard, Hamden, Connecticut, Archon, 1981.

Manuscript Collections: National Library of Scotland, Edinburgh; Edinburgh University Library; Douglas Library, Queen's University, Kingston, Ontario.

Critical Studies: *The Interpreter's House: A Critical Assessment of John Buchan* by David Daniell, London, Nelson, 1975; *John Buchan and His World* by Janet Adam Smith, London, Thames and Hudson, 1979; *John Buchan: A Memoir* by William Buchan, London, Buchan and Enright, 1982.

*   *   *

In recent years the critical biographies of Janet Adam Smith and David Daniell have gone a long way towards separating John Buchan from such less enduringly serious writers as Sapper and E. Phillips Oppenheim; but to claim a place for Buchan beside his fellow Scotsmen Walter Scott and Stevenson is to go too far. Buchan writes a good literary English, there is nothing of the "racism" and jingoism which is so strong in Sapper, and his narrative gift is at least commensurate with his and Oppenheim's. But he continues to be read primarily as a writer of thrillers ("shockers," as he himself called them), however literate, well-constructed, and intellectual they may be.

Buchan's life was acted out on an even larger stage than his fictional heroes trod. One of Lord Milner's Young Men reconstructing South Africa after the Boer War, Buchan held various high intelligence postings during World War 1 and died as Governor-General of Canada during World War II. He wrote history and biography, literary criticism (most notably his work on Scott), historical fiction, and at the end a very moving autobiography, *Memory Hold-the-Door.* His best thrillers divide between those featuring Richard Hannay and those featuring the lawyer Edward Leithen. Into these two most lasting of his character creations Buchan put the two sides of himself; the man of action and the man of contemplation. While Hannay's novels are some of the finest examples of the novels of intrigue, Leithen's, in their greater psychological depth and their distillation of Buchan's own thought, may ultimately be the more rewarding.

One quality Buchan does have in common with the thriller writers of his generation, those who mixed snobbery with violence (and there is little of either in Buchan), is his presentation of his heroes as men's men, reserved in female company. Leithen is a bachelor, and Hannay professes to know about as much of woman's ways "as I know about the Chinese language" (Buchan himself said that he could as well fly to the moon as draw a fictional woman). While the good heroines are maternal, such a woman as Hilda von Einem in *Greenmantle,* akin to Doyle's Irene Adler, is both idealized and terrifying. It is the very feminine qualities of Buchan's most convincing villain, Dominic Medina in *The Three Hostages,* which make him so threatening, and charge the relationship between him and Hannay with the same kind of power as binds Holmes to Moriarty, Bulldog Drummond to Carl Peterson, Nayland Smith to Fu Manchu, and so on.

The real antagonist in Buchan's fiction are the forces of irrationality, wherever embodied, which stalk a fragile civilization, and so far is Buchan from mere national hatred that he drew a sympathetic portrait of the Kaiser in *Greenmantle,* at the drew a sympathetic portrait of the Kaiser in *Greenmantle,* at the height of the War. His principal villains are those who seek to subject the minds and wills of others to theirs, like the protean villain of *The Thirty-Nine Steps,* Hilda von Einem, and Dominic Medina.

Buchan is an accurate commentator on contemporary public affairs, even in his shockers. Such a seeming excursion into the supernatural as *The Gap in the Curtain* (a number of people are given a glimpse of the *Times,* a year hence) has much to teach about coming to terms with death, as well as being laden with some sharp satire of politics and business. Finally, while it is right to be wary of absolutely equating the dying Leithen in *Sick Heart River* with Buchan himself, it is in this last novel that one finds his final thoughts distilled; it is the last testament of a supremely humane man.

—Barrie Hayne

BUCKLEY, William F(rank), Jr.   American.   Born in New York City, 24 November 1925. Educated privately at home and in France and England; Millbrook School, New York, graduated 1943; University of Mexico, Mexico City, 1943–44; Yale University, New Haven, Connecticut, B.A. (honors) 1950. Served in the United States Army, 1944–46: 2nd Lieutenant. Married Patricia Austin Taylor in 1950; one son. Instructor in Spanish, Yale University, 1947–51; associate editor, *American Mercury,* New York, 1952; freelance writer and lecturer, 1952–55. Since 1955, founding editor, *National Review,* New York; since 1962, syndicated columnist ("On the Right"); since 1966, host, *Firing Line* television program. Lecturer, New School for Social Research, New York, 1967–68; chairman of the board, Starr Broadcasting Group Inc., 1969–78 member, U.S. National Advisory Commission on Information, 1969–72; public member of U.S. delegation to the United Nations, New York, 1973; Froman Distinguished Professor, Russell Sage College, Troy, New York, 1973. Conservative Party candidate for mayor of New York City, 1965. Recipient: University of Southern California award, for journalism, 1968; Emmy award, for television, 1969; Bellarmine Medal, 1977; American Book award, 1980. L.H.D.: Seton Hall University, South Orange, New Jersey, 1966; Niagara University, New York, 1967; Mount Saint Mary's College, Emmitsburg, Maryland, 1969; College of William and Mary, Williamsburg, Virginia, 1981; Colby College, Waterville, Maine, 1985. LL.D.: St. Peter's College, Jersey City, New Jersey, 1969; Syracuse University, New York, 1969; Ursinus College, Collegeville, Pennsylvania, 1969; Lehigh University, Bethlehem, Pennsylvania, 1970; Lafayette College, Easton, Pennsylvania, 1972; Saint Anselm's College, Manchester, New Hampshire, 1973; Saint Bonaventure University, New York, 1974; Notre Dame University, Indiana, 1978; New York Law School, 1981; D.Sc.O.: Curry College, Milton, Massachusetts, 1970; Litt.D.: Saint Vincent College, Latrobe, Pennsylvania, 1971; Fairleigh Dickinson University, Rutherford, New Jersey, 1973; Alfred University, New York, 1974; William Jewell College, Liberty, Missouri, 1985; Albertus Magnus College, New Haven, Connecticut, 1987; College of St. Thomas, St. Paul, Minnesota, 1987; Bowling Green State University, Ohio, 1987. Address: National Review, 150 East 35th Street, New York, New York 10016, U.S.A.

CRIME PUBLICATIONS

Novels (series: Blackford Oakes in all books)

Saving the Queen.   New York, Doubleday, and London, W.H. Allen, 1976.
Stained Glass.   New York, Doubleday, 1978; London, Penguin, 1979.
Who's on First?   New York, Doubleday, and London, Allen Lane, 1980.
Marco Polo, If You Can.   New York, Doubleday, and London, Allen Lane, 1982.
The Story of Henri Tod.   New York, Doubleday, and London, Allen Lane, 1984.
See You Later, Alligator.   New York, Doubleday, 1985; London, Century, 1986.
High Jinx.   New York, Doubleday, and London, Century, 1986.
Mongoose, R.I.P.   New York, Random House, and London, Muller, 1988.

OTHER PUBLICATIONS

Play

Stained Glass, from his own novel (produced Louisville, Kentucky, 1989).

Other

God and Man at Yale: The Superstitions of "Academic Freedom."   Chicago, Regnery, 1951.
McCarthy and His Enemies: The Record and Its Meaning, with L. Brent Bozell.   Chicago, Regnery, 1954.
Up from Liberalism.   New York, McDowell Obolensky, 1959.
The Committee and Its Critics: A Calm Review of the House Committee on Un-American Activities, with others.   New York, Putnam, 1962.
Rumbles Left and Right: A Book about Troublesome People and Ideas.   New York, Putnam, 1963.
The Unmaking of a Mayor.   New York, Viking Press, 1966.
The Jeweler's Eye: A Book of Irresistible Political Reflections.   New York, Putnam, 1968.
Quotations from Chairman Bill: The Best of William F. Buckley, Jr., edited by David Franke.   New Rochelle, New York, Arlington House, 1970.
The Governor Listeth: A Book of Inspired Political Revelations.   New York, Putnam, 1970.
Cruising Speed: A Documentary.   New York, Putnam, 1971.
Taiwan: The West Berlin of China.   Jamaica, New York, St. John's University Center of Asian Studies, 1971.
Inveighing We Will Go.   New York, Putnam, 1972.
Four Reforms: A Guide for the Seventies.   New York, Putnam, 1973.
United Nations Journal: A Delegate's Odyssey.   New York, Putnam, 1974; London, Joseph, 1975.
The Assault on the Free Market (lecture).   Manhattan, Kansas State University, 1974.
Execution Eve and Other Contemporary Ballads.   New York, Putnam, 1975.
Airborne: A Sentimental Journey.   New York, Macmillan, 1976.
A Hymnal: The Controversial Arts.   New York, Putnam, 1978.
Atlantic High: A Celebration.   New York, Doubleday, 1982.
Overdrive: A Personal Documentary.   New York, Doubleday, 1983.
Right Reason.   New York, Doubleday, 1985.

The Temptation of Wilfred Malachey (for children). New York, Workman, 1985.
Racing Through Paradise: A Pacific Passage. New York, Random House, 1987.
On the Firing Line: The Public Life of Our Public Figures. New York, Random House, 1989.

Editor, *Odyssey of a Friend: Whittaker Chambers' Letters to William F. Buckley, Jr., 1954–1961.* Privately printed, 1969; New York, Putnam, 1970.
Editor, with Charles R. Kesler, *Did You Ever See a Dream Walking? American Conservative Thought in the Twentieth Century.* Indianapolis, Bobbs Merrill, 1970; revised edition as *Keep Taking the Tablets: Modern American Conservative Thought.* New York, Perennial, 1988.
Editor, with Stuart W. Little, *The Buckley-Little Catalogue 1984–87.*

*

Critical Studies: *William F. Buckley, Jr.,* by Mark Royden Winchell, Boston, Twayne, 1984; *William F. Buckley, Jr.: Patron Saint of the Conservatives* by John B. Judis, New York, Simon and Schuster, 1988.

* * *

William F. Buckley, Jr., a leading conservative spokesman and editor of the *National Review,* is also the author of best-selling spy novels. His hero is Blackford ("Blacky") Oakes, who, like Buckley himself at one time in his life, is a CIA agent recruited from Yale. Young Blacky is handsome, privileged, and urbane. He thinks for himself and gets into scrapes from time to time, but his patriotism and hatred of communism are not to be questioned.

Buckley's stories are Cold War vignettes, set in the Eisenhower and Kennedy years and fashioned from well-known historical events. Even *Mongoose R.I.P.,* published in the time of *glasnost,* returns to the early 1960's and the height of the Cold War. What happened in the Kremlin after the death of Stalin? What followed the CIA attempt to assassinate Castro? Was the U.S. spy plane shot down by the Russians part of a deliberate American plot? Buckley weaves fanciful but plausible accounts around these real events. Another feature of a Buckley story is the imaginary conversations of such historical figures as Khrushchev, Castro, Eisenhower, and Kennedy. So, in *The Story of Henri Tod* Khrushchev negotiates with the East German leader, and Kennedy tries to guess what the two are doing while he muses about sailing, Cape Cod, and why he dislikes de Gaulle. The titles are also distinctive, carrying on the spirit of wit and whimsy found in the characters' conversations. *Saving the Queen* and *Mongoose R.I.P.* are examples in point. *Marco Polo if You Can* provides a Buckley reader with the greatest challenge and is one of the most opaque titles ever found in a best seller.

These stories, however, for all their wit and originality, are not for those who insist on action or suspense. In *The Story of Henri Tod,* for example, Blacky's role is minimal. Readers are told, through flashbacks, the story of Tod and his sister, who were orphaned during the Nazi regime. The time shifts in the narrative help link the Nazi and communist enemies, whom Blacky and Tod are fighting against. Even in *High Jinx,* one of the more active of the Blackford Oakes's adventures, there is much less espionage than talk. Blacky finds a clue at the beginning of the story, recognizes the traitor by coincidence on the street, meets once with his Russian counterpart who helps him, and plays a role in the investigation at the end. He also

talks to friends and superiors about various subjects not related to spying, visits his mother, and chats with the Queen of England. Although Buckley often arranges surprise endings—a character is shot or a case suddenly connects up with a famous international event—the author does not attempt to build suspense. So, in *High Jinx* while Blacky and his superiors are trying to find the traitor who has destroyed a secret commando mission, the readers know who the traitor is.

A Buckley narrative is trim and readable. The plot is simple despite the many characters and shifts in point of view. Yet, for all the light banter and sprightly pace, there is often a somber framing supplied by introductory and concluding events. In one book, a group of soldiers Blacky has trained with is suddenly annihilated. In another, a man is shot and killed at the very point of gaining freedom. Typically, Blacky is faced with a moral choice involving a matter of life or death. This framing serves to remind readers, at both the beginning and end of the novel, why such a charming and talented hero has chosen this particular job.

See You Later Alligator is an example of Buckley at his best. He gives full portraits of Cuba's Fidel Castro and the revolutionary leader Che Guevara, describing the way they address crowds and their style and impact on people. Buckley also relates how his hero passes the time waiting to speak to Guevara:

> Blackford had packed six detective stories in Spanish and a Spanish-English dictionary and—for this he thanked God for the forethought—a paperback containing the ten tragedies of Shakespeare. So he spent the afternoon with Hercule Poirot tracking down the butler or whoever or whomever, as Agatha Christie would have put it, and the early evening with King Lear; had dinner (just this side of inedible), drank more rum than he normally would have, did some push-ups, and asked Velasco what he was thinking about.

Yet, *See You Later Alligator* has a more serious tone than many of these novels. It is Blacky, in fact, who must tell the American president about the Russian missiles in Cuba. He himself faces a death sentence, while another character in prison is led past six soldiers, apparently loitering, and suddenly finds death by firing squad. At the same time, *See You Later Alligator* displays all the familiar components of the Buckley craft: the same hero, setting, and simple plot, an amusing title and a famous event. Like many other authors of mystery and suspense, Buckley develops a popular formula that readers can recognize and come to expect.

—Barbara Hinckley

———

BURGESS, Trevor. *See* **HALL, Adam.**

———

BURKE, James Lee. American. Born in Houston, Texas, 5 December 1936. Educated at the University of Southestern Louisiana, Lafayette, 1955–57; University of Missouri, Columbia, B.A. in English 1959, M.A. in English 1960. Married Pearl Pai in 1960; four children. English Instructor, University of Southwestern Louisiana, Lafayette, University of Montana,

Missoula, and Miami-Dade Community College, Florida; social worker, Los Angeles, 1962–64, reporter, Lafayette, 1964; worked for the United States Forest Service, Kentucky, 1965–66. Currently part-time Professor, Wichita State University, Kansas. Recipient. National Endowment grant, 1977; John Simon Guggenheim fellowship, 1989; Mystery Writers of America Edgar Allan Poe award, 1989. Agent: Philip Spitzer, 788 Ninth Avenue, New York, New York 10019. Address: 11100 Grant Creek Road, Missoula, Montana 59802, U.S.A.

CRIME PUBLICATIONS

Novels (series: Dave Robicheaux in all books)

The Neon Rain.   New York, Holt, 1987; London, Mysterious Press, 1989.
Heaven's Prisoners.   New York, Holt, 1988; London, Mysterious Press, 1989.
Black Cherry Blues.   Boston, Little Brown, 1989.
A Morning for Flamingoes.   Boston, Little Brown, 1990.

OTHER PUBLICATIONS

Novels

Half of Paradise.   Boston, Houghton Mifflin, 1965.
To the Bright and Shining Sun.   New York, Scribner, 1970.
Lay Down My Sword and Shield.   New York, Crowell, 1971.
Two for Texas.   New York, Pocket Books, 1983.
The Lost Get-Back Boogie.   Baton Rouge, Louisiana State University Press, 1986.

Short Stories

The Convict.   Baton Rogue, Louisiana State University Press, 1985.

*

James Lee Burke comments:

I try to write everyday and in some way make the world a better place through my art. I believe that whatever degree of talent I possess is a gift and must be treated as such. To misuse one's talent, to be cavalier about it, to set it aside because of fear or sloth is unpardonable. In my view good and evil are very real elements in the world, and the forces which represent each are in constant struggle against one another. As William Faulkner and George Orwell both suggested, the artist has an obligation to give voice to those people who have none, and ultimately the artist must tell the truth about the period in which he lives and expose those who would exploit their fellowmen and make the earth an intolerable place. I take great happiness in being part of that struggle. I hope that my work will be remembered because it details the lives of people who possess both courage and compassion. It is those two virtues, I feel, that enable us to make art greater than the creation of one individual.

*   *   *

James Lee Burke is the author of a crime series set in New Orleans and Southern Louisiana's bayou country. Burke's protagonist in the series is Dave Robicheaux, a Cajun and a recovering alcoholic, who resigns from the New Orleans Police Department at the end of *The Neon Rain* and investigates crimes in which he becomes inadvertently involved in *Heaven's Prisoners* and *Black Cherry Blues*. Burke is a writer of extraordinary talent and power, a writer whose novels reveal interests which are both Southern and international; the novels convey Burke's affection for Cajun country, customs, people, and speech, while they also reveal his disdain for America's misadventures in Vietnam and Central America. At the same time, the novels are well-plotted, suspenseful, and action-packed; their characters are complicated and psychologically real; their violence shocks and horrifies.

In *The Neon Rain* Burke introduces many of the characters who will figure in the series. Burke's protagonist, Dave Robicheaux, is a graduate of the University of Southwestern Louisiana with a degree in English, a Vietnam veteran haunted by memories of the war, an alcoholic recovering from his past bad behavior and failed marriage, and a 14-year veteran of the New Orleans Police Department. His partner is Cletus Purcel, a loutish, heavy-drinking redneck, corrupt, tough, and wildly funny. Robicheaux's brother, Jimmie, owns a New Orleans bar/restaurant and has connections with the Mafia. During the course of the novel, Robicheaux meets and falls in love with Annie Ballard, a cellist and social worker. Burke's villains here (some of whom recur as types if not as individuals) include a Mafia don, a Nicaraguan drug lord, a retired general involved in arms smuggling and right-wing causes, four sociopathic hitmen, and an assortment of sleazy lowlifes connected to the New Orleans rackets. Aware that America's political alliances in the past several years have been what might charitably be called tangled, Robicheaux also suspects the involvement of agents of the federal government in his case.

That case, the most complicated of the series, opens when Robicheaux discovers the drowned body of a Negro prostitute in a bayou while he is fly-fishing. This invasion of violence into an Edenic environment is a characteristic opening. Robicheaux's concern with the murder leads him to Didoni Giaconi, Julio Segura, and General Abshire, and also to his brutalization at the hands of three hitmen, the murder of a federal agent, the attempted murder of Robicheaux's brother, Robicheaux's shooting of Segura and one of the hitmen and his arrest of another, and to Purcel's flight to Guatemala after he murders another of the hitman for money. Burke's treatment of violence shocks because he handles it as a matter of fact. His humanistic Robicheaux, who retains ethical and religious ideals despite his experiences on the street and in Vietnam, contrasts with the cynical Purcel, who believes that criminals are "human garbage" to be humiliated and exterminated. Neither view seems viable, and at the novel's conclusion Robicheaux resigns from the department and returns to the bayou country in which he was raised, while Purcel flees one step ahead of the law. The novel was a strong debut.

Heaven's Prisoners is an even better novel, its plot more tightly focused, its violence truly stunning, and its concentration on Robicheaux's attempts to cope with his losses poignant and moving. The novel begins with Robicheaux, now the owner of a bait and boat-rental business near New Iberia, Louisiana, trawling for shrimp in the Gulf of Mexico with Annie, now his wife. When a small plane crashes near them and Robicheaux rescues a child from the wreck, he and Annie unofficially adopt the girl, whom Robicheaux names Alafair, after his mother. His report of the incident, however, arouses the interest of Immigration officials and agents of the DEA. His own interest in the incident leads to his brutal humiliation by two sociopathic hitmen and, eventually, to Annie's murder. Liquor assuages his grief only temporarily; indeed, because he is an alcoholic, liquor only creates other problems. Drying out, working out, wrestling with his desire for another drink, and exacting revenge and some measure of justice in the last half of the book, Robicheaux is a deeply tormented character, by turns pitiful and pitiable, sensitive yet strong. Burke's ear for dialogue is acute; his rendering of Cajun and black dialects is never condescending. *Heaven's Prisoners* is an exceptional novel, one which other critics have accurately claimed expands the genre.

In *Black Cherry Blues* Robicheaux continues to wrestle with his grief; both Annie and his father, an oilrigger killed years before, visit him in his sleep and in waking dreams. Trouble finds him in the person of his college roommate, Dixie Lee Pugh, a former rhythm and blues singer, battered by his predilection for drugs and alcohol, now working as an oil leaseman in Montana for Star Drilling, the company on whose rig Robicheaux's father was killed. Pugh asks for advice after he overhears two other leasemen discussing murder, and Robicheaux gradually becomes more and more enmeshed until his own troubles outweigh Pugh's. Accused of murdering one of the two leasemen after he receives a mailed threat against Alafair, Robicheaux and the girl follow the other, a sociopath named Mapes, to Montana. There Robicheaux discovers that Pugh's oil-leasing involves Sally Dio, a Mafioso with whom Pugh has done time in a Texas prison. Dio also employs as head of security Cletus Purcel, back from Guatemala, the murder charge against him dropped. Burke's handling of Robicheaux's gradual reconciliation with Purcel, of their partnership, admiration, and low, is one of a fine novel's finest points. Still loud, crude, and mean, Purcel also has a rough sensitivity and outrageous humor that make him a fascinating original. Purcel's vengeful "justice" on Sally Dio forms as satisfactory a conclusion to that aspect of the plot as Robicheaux's extrication from his own legal difficulties involving Mapes. Robicheaux and Purcel are at least as interesting a pair of alter egos as Robert B. Parker's Spenser and Hawk—and Purcel gives Burke's pair the coarser, funnier edge.

Burke began his career as a writer of "serious" novels, but he has found a wide audience and popular success as a writer of "series" novels. The novels in the Robicheaux series reveal Burke's intelligence, lyrical/poetic eye for setting, concern for psychological realism in character, strong plotting, political concern, and traditional values. One can only hope that he will continue the series and achieve the same high quality he has risen to in these novels.

—David K. Jeffrey

BURKE, John (Frederick). Also writes as Jonathan Burke; Owen Burke; Harriet Esmond (in collaboration with his wife); Jonathan George; Joanna Jones; Robert Miall; Sara Morris; Martin Sands. British. Born in Rye, Sussex, 8 March 1922. Educated at Holt High School, Liverpool. Served in the Royal Air Force, Royal Electrical and Mechanical Engineers, and Royal Marines 1942–47: Sergeant. Married 1) Joan Morris in 1941 (divorced 1963), five daughters; 2) Jean Williams in 1963, two sons. Associate editor, 1953–56, and production manager, 1956–57, Museum Press, London; editorial manager, Books for Pleasure Group, London, 1957–58; public relations and publications executive, Shell International Petroleum, London, 1959–63; story editor, Twentieth Century-Fox, London, 1963–65; Director, Lom Associates Ltd., literary agency, London, 1965. Since 1966 freelance writer. Recipient: Rockfeller Foundation Atlantic award, 1949. Agent: David Higham Associates Ltd., 5-8 Lower John Street, London W1R 4HA, or, Harold Ober Associates Inc., 40 East 49th Street, New York,

New York 10017, U.S.A. Address: 8 North Parade, Southwold, Suffolk IP18 6LP, England.

CRIME PUBLICATIONS

Novels as John and Jonathan Burke (series: The Bill; Dr. Caspian; Mike Merriman)

The Poison Cupboard. London, Secker and Warburg, 1956.
Corpse to Copenhagen. London, Amalgamated Press, 1957.
Echo of Barbara. London, Long, 1959.
Fear by Instalments (Merriman). London, Long, 1960.
Teach Yourself Treachery. London, Long, 1962.
Deadly Downbeat (Merriman). London, Long, 1962.
The Man Who Finally Died (novelization of screenplay). London, Pan, 1963.
Guilty Party (novelization of stage play). London, Elek, 1963.
The Twisted Tongues. London, Long, 1964; as *Echo of Treason,* New York, Dodd Mead, 1966.
Only the Ruthless Can Play. London, Long, 1965.
The Weekend Girls. London, Long, 1966; New York, Doubleday, 1967; as *Goodbye, Gillian,* New York, Ace, n.d.
Gossip to the Grave. London, Long, 1967; as *The Gossip Truth,* New York, Doubleday, 1968.
Maroc 7 (novelization of screenplay; as Martin Sands). London, Pan, 1967.
Someone Lying, Someone Dying. London, Long, 1968.
Rob the Lady. London, Long, 1969.
Four Stars for Danger. London, Long, 1970.
Strange Report (novelization of television play). London, Hodder and Stoughton, and New York, Lancer, 1970.
The Killdog (with George Theiner, as Jonathan George). London, Macmillan, and New York, Doubleday, 1970.
Dead Letters (as Jonathan George). London, Macmillan, 1972.
The Devil's Footsteps (Caspian). London, Weidenfeld and Nicolson, and New York, Coward McCann, 1976.
The Black Charade (Caspian). London, Weidenfeld and Nicolson, and New York, Coward McCann, 1977.
Ladygrove (Caspian). London, Weidenfeld and Nicolson, and New York, Coward McCann, 1978.
The Bill [*2, 3, 4*] (novelizations of television series). First two vols., London, Thames Methuen, 1985–87, last two vols, London, Thames Mandarin, 1989–90.
The Fourth Floor (novelization of television series). London, Methuen, 1986.
King and Castle (novelization of television series). London, Methuen, 1986.

Novels as Harriet Esmond

Darsham's Tower. New York, Delacorte Press, 1973; as *Darsham's Folly,* London, Collins, 1974.
The Eye Stones. London, Collins, and New York, Delacorte Press, 1975.
The Florian Signet. London, Collins, and New York, Fawcett, 1977.

Uncollected Short Stories

"Party Games," in *6th Pan Book of Horror Stories,* edited by Herbert Van Thal. London, Pan, 1965.
"The Calculated Nightmare," in *John Creasey's Mystery Bedside Book,* edited by Herbert Harris. London, Hodder and Stoughton, 1967.
"Miss Mouse and Mrs. Mouse," in *Ellery Queen's Mystery Magazine* (New York), November 1968.

"Don't You Dare," in *Splinters*, edited by Alex Hamilton. London, Hutchinson, 1968; New York, Walker, 1969.

"A Comedy of Terrors," in *9th Pan Book of Horror Stories*, edited by Herbert Van Thal. London, Pan, 1968.

"Be Our Guest," in *More Tales of Unease*, edited by John Burke. London, Pan, 1969.

"The Tourists," in *Tandem Horror 3*. London, Tandem, 1969.

"Casualty," in *The Sixth Ghost Book*. London, Barrie and Jenkins, 1971.

"Flitting Tenant," in *The Seventh Ghost Book*. London, Barrie and Jenkins, 1971.

"The Loiterers," in *The Eighth Ghost Book*. London, Barrie and Jenkins, 1972.

"False Harmonic," in *The Ninth Ghost Book*, edited by Rosemary Timperley. London, Barrie and Jenkins, 1973.

"Leave of Absence," in *The Tenth Ghost Book*, edited by Aidan Chambers. London, Barrie and Jenkins, 1975.

"The Custodian," in *The Eleventh Ghost Book*, edited by Aidan Chambers. London, Barrie and Jenkins, 1976.

"And Cannot Come Again," in *New Tales of Unease*, edited by John Burke. London, Pan, 1976.

"Lucille Would Have Known," in *New Terrors*. London, Pan, 1979.

OTHER PUBLICATIONS

Novels as J.F. John and Jonathan Burke

Swift Summer. London, Laurie, 1949.
Another Chorus. London, Laurie, 1949.
These Haunted Streets. London, Laurie, 1950.
The Outward Walls. London, Laurie, 1952.
Chastity House. London, Laurie, 1952.
Dark Gateway. London, Panther, 1953.
The Echoing World. London, Panther, 1954.
Twilight of Reason. London, Panther, 1954.
Pattern of Shadows. London, Panther, 1954.
Hotel Cosmos. London, Panther, 1954.
Deep Freeze. London, Panther, 1955.
Revolt of the Humans. London, Panther, 1955.
Pursuit Through Time. London, Ward Lock, 1956.
The Entertainer (novelization of stage play). London, Four Square, 1960.
Look Back in Anger (novelization of stage play). London, Four Square, 1960.
A Widow for the Winter (as Sara Morris). London, Barker, 1961.
The Lion of Sparta (novelization of screenplay). London, Pan, 1961; as *The 300 Spartans*, New York, New American Library, 1961.
Flame in the Streets (novelization of screenplay). London, Four Square, 1961.
The Angry Silence (novelization of screenplay). London, Hodder and Stoughton, 1961.
The Boys (novelization of screenplay). London, Pan, 1962.
Private Potter (novelization of screenplay). London, Pan, 1962.
The World Ten Times Over (novelization of screenplay). London, Pan, 1962.
The System (novelization of screenplay). London, Pan, 1964.
A Hard Day's Night (novelization of screenplay). New York, Dell, 1964; London, Pan, 1977.
That Magnificent Air Race (novelization of screenplay). London, Pan, 1965; as *Those Magnificent Men and Their Flying Machines*, New York, Pocket Books, 1965.
The Trap (novelization of screenplay). London, Pan, 1966.
The Suburbs of Pleasure. London, Secker and Warburg, and New York, Delacorte Press, 1967.
Till Death Us Do Part (novelization of television play). London, Pan, 1967.
The Jokers (novelization of screenplay; as Martin Sands). London, Pan, 1967.
Privilege (novelization of screenplay). London, Pan, and New York, Avon, 1967.
Chitty Chitty Bang Bang: The Story of the Film. London, Pan, 1968.
Smashing Time (novelization of screenplay). London, Pan, 1968.
Moon Zero Two: The Story of the Film. London, Pan, 1969.
The Smashing Bird I Used to Know (novelization of screenplay). London, Pan, 1969.
All the Right Noises (novelization of screenplay). London, Hodder and Stoughton, 1970.
Expo 80. London, Cassell, 1972.
Luke's Kingdom (novelization of television play). London, Fontana, 1976.
The Prince Regent (novelization of television play). London, Fontana, 1979.
The Figurehead (as Owen Burke). London, Collins, and New York, Coward McCann, 1979.

Novels as Joanna Jones

Nurse Is a Neighbour. London, Joseph, 1958.
Nurse on the District. London, Joseph, 1959.
The Artless Flat-Hunter. London, Pelham, 1963.
The Artless Commuter. London, Pelham, 1965.

Novels as Robert Miall (novelizations of screenplays and television plays)

UFO 1–2. London, Pan, 2 vols., 1971.
Jason King. London, Pan, 1972.
Kill Jason King! London, Pan, 1972.
The Protectors. London, Pan, 1973.
The Adventurer. London, Pan, 1973.

Short Stories as John and Jonathan Burke

Alien Landscape: Science Fiction Stories. London, Museum Press, 1955.
Dr. Terror's House of Horrors (adaptation of screenplay). London, Pan, 1965.
The Hammer Horror Omnibus. London, Pan, 1966.
The Power Game (adaptation of screenplays). London, Pan, 1966.
The Second Hammer Horror Film Omnibus. London, Pan, 1967.

Plays

Screenplay: *The Sorcerers*, with Michael Reeves and Tom Baker, 1967.

Radio Plays: *The Prodigal Pupil*, 1949; *The Man in the Ditch*, 1958; *Across Miss Desmond's Desk*, 1961.

Television Plays: *Safe Conduct*, 1965; *Calculated Nightmare*, from his own story, 1970; *Miss Mouse*, from his own story, 1972.

Other

The Happy Invaders: A Picture of Denmark in Springtime, with William Luscombe. London, Hale, 1956.

Suffolk. London, Batsford, 1971.
England in Colour. London, Batsford, and New York, Hastings House, 1972.
Sussex. London, Batsford, 1974.
An Illustrated History of England. London, Collins, 1974; New York, McKay, 1976.
English Villages. London, Batsford, 1975.
South East England (for children). London, Faber, 1975.
Suffolk in Photographs, photographs by Anthony Kersting. London, Batsford, 1976.
Czechoslovakia. London, Batsford, 1976.
Historic Britain. London, Batsford, 1977.
Life in the Castle in Mediaeval England. London, Batsford, and Totowa, New Jersey, Rowman and Littlefield, 1978.
Life in the Villa in Roman Britain. London, Batsford, 1978.
Look Back on England. London, Orbis, 1980.
The English Inn. London, Batsford, and New York, Holmes and Meier, 1981.
Musical Landscapes. Exeter, Webb and Bower, and New York, Holt Rinehart, 1983.
Roman England. London, Weidenfeld and Nicolson, 1983.
The Illustrated History of Music. London, Sphere, 1988.
A Traveller's History of Scotland. London, Murray, 1990.

Editor, *Tales of Unease.* London, Pan, 1966; New York, Doubleday, 1969.
Editor, *More Tales of Unease.* London, Pan, 1969.
Editor, *New Tales of Unease.* London, Pan, 1976.
Editor, *Beautiful Britain.* London, Batsford, 1976.

Translator, *The West Face,* by Guido Magnone. London, Museum Press, 1955.
Translator, *The Spark and the Flame,* by F.B. Muus. London, Museum Press, 1957.
Translator, with Eiler Hansen, *The Moon of Beauty,* by Jørgen Andersen-Rosendal. London, Museum Press, 1957.
Translator, with Eiler Hansen, *The Happy Lagoons: The World of Queen Salote,* by J<TO>rgen Andersen-Rosendal. London, Jarrolds, 1961.

*

John Burke comments:

Coming as I do from a long line of master carpenters, I have always considered it complimentary rather than derogatory to be called a "competent craftsman." This does not mean that I have ever consciously devoted myself to hack-work. A good carpenter should be able to make, for the pleasure and use of the people who want to buy it, a good kitchen table which will stand without wobbling and which is free from awkward corners or splintered edges. He may now and then, by refining his craft, aspire to become a Chippendale; but should remain proud of his well-proportioned kitchen tables. In writing thrillers and science-fiction I have rarely used extravagant ideas but tried rather to produce a tightly-knit, credible narrative. And in my other novels—which I refuse to refer to as "straight" or "serious" since I don't think of crime fiction or science-fiction as bent or frivolous—I have planned ahead just as carefully.

I cannot start a story of any kind until I know the setting in which the characters are to live and move. My wife and I cannot write our Victorian Gothic suspense novels (in collaboration as Harriet Esmond) without having stayed in, and explored, the region concerned.

I have always been more interested in the psychological suspense story rather than the detective, spy, or thick-ear picaresque rampage. The element of suspense should, I think,

be present in other fictional genres as well: self-indulgent semi-autobiographical novelists insult their readers by supposing that their own personal problems are enough in themselves to carry a story. No matter what its theme, every novel, modern or historical, should to some extent be a mystery story— mysterious to the reader, but not to the carpenter who is planning and polishing the last raw snags off it.

* * *

John Burke, man of many aliases, is both prolific and versatile, a writer of thrillers, science fiction, Victorian romantic suspense, novelizations of plays and films, an anthologist, and a short-story writer (his best story, "The Calculated Nightmare," becoming a TV play). His memorable crime novel *Echo of Barbara* became a successful motion-picture, and other thrillers, such as *Deadly Downbeat, Fear by Instalments, The Twisted Tongues, The Weekend Girls, Four Stars for Danger,* and *The Killdog,* followed. These novels were for the most part suspense stories and psychological thrillers, and one, *Twisted Tongues,* was a thriller in the international-political-power-game genre some years ahead of others in similar vein.

Most recently Burke has concentrated on novelizations of television series. *The Bill,* adapted from a popular television series of the same name, focuses on Sun Hill Police Station in London's East End. Burke depicts solid police work coupled with personal tensions which together provide a realistic view of a working police station.

—Herbert Harris

————

BURKE, Noel. *See* **OLSEN, D.B.**

————

BURKE, Thomas. British. Born in London, in 1886. Educated at an orphanage after age 9. Served in the American division of the Ministry of Information during World War I. Married Winifred Wells (i.e., the writer Clare Cameron) in 1918. Left school at 14: worked in a boarding house and in an office, age 15–19; secretary in a theatre; bookseller's assistant; worked in Frank Casenove's literary agency, 1907–14. *Died 22 September 1945.*

CRIME PUBLICATIONS

Novels

Murder at Elstree: or, Mr. Thurtell and His Gig. London, Longman, 1936.
Abduction: A Story of Limehouse. London, Jenkins, 1939.

Short Stories (series: Quong Lee)

Limehouse Nights: Tales of Chinatown (Quong). London, Richards, 1916; New York, McBride, 1917; selections, as *Broken Blossoms,* Richards, 1920, and *In Chinatown,* Richards, 1921.
Whispering Windows: Tales of the Waterside. London, Richards, 1921; as *More Limehouse Nights,* New York, Doran, 1921.

East of Mansion House. New York, Doran, 1926; London, Cassell, 1928.
The Bloomsbury Wonder. London, Mandrake Press, 1929.
The Pleasantries of Old Quong. London, Constable, and New York, Macmillan, 1931; as *A Tea-Shop in Limehouse,* Boston, Little Brown, 1931.
Night Pieces: Eighteen Tales. London, Constable, 1935; New York, Appleton, 1936.
Dark Nights. London, Jenkins, 1944.
The Best Stories of Thomas Burke, edited by John Gawsworth. London, Phoenix House, 1950.

OTHER PUBLICATIONS

Novels

Twinkletoes: A Tale of Chinatown. London, Richards, 1917; New York, McBride, 1918.
The Sun in Splendour. New York, Doran, 1926; London, Constable, 1927.
The Flower of Life. London, Constable; 1929; New York, Doubleday, 1930.
The Winsome Wench: The Story of a London Inn, 1825–1900. London, Routledge, 1938.

Short Story

The Wind and the Rain: A Book of Confessions. London, Butterworth, and New York, Doran, 1924.

Play

Radio Play: *The Hands of Mr. Ottermole.*

Verse

Verses. Privately printed, 1910.
Pavements and Pastures: A Book of Songs. Privately printed, 1912.
London Lamps: A Book of Songs. London, Richards, 1917; New York, McBride, 1919.
The Song Book of Quong Lee of Limehouse. London, Allen and Unwin, and New York, Holt, 1920.

Other

Kiddie Land (verse for children), with Margaret G. Hays. London, Dean, 1913.
Nights in Town: A London Autobiography (essays). London, Allen and Unwin, 1915; as *Nights in London,* New York, Holt, 1916.
Out and About: A Note-Book of London in War-Time. London, Allen and Unwin, 1919; as *Out and About in London,* New York, Holt, 1919.
The Outer Circle: Rambles in Remote London. London, Allen and Unwin, and New York, Doran, 1921.
The London Spy: A Book of Town Travels. London Butterworth, and New York, Doran, 1922.
(Essays). London, Harrap, 1928.
The English Inn. London, Longman, 1930; revised edition. London, Jenkins, 1947.
Go, Lovely Rose. New York, Sesphra Library, 1931.
The Maid's Head, Norwich. London, True Temperance Association, 1931.
An Old London Alehouse: The Anchor, at Bankside. London, True Temperance Association, 1932.

City of Encounters: A London Divertissement. London, Constable and Boston, Little Brown, 1932.
The Real East End. London, Constable, 1932.
The Beauty of England. London, Harrap, 1933; New York, McBride, 1934.
London in My Time. London, Rich and Cowan, 1934; New York, Loring and Mussey, 1935.
Billy and Beryl in Chinatown [*Old London, Soho*] (for children). London, Harrap, 3 vols., 1935–36.
Vagabond Minstrel: The Adventures of Thomas Dermody. London, Longman, 1936.
Will Someone Lead Me to a Pub? Being a Note upon Certain of the Taverns, Old and New, of London. London, Routledge, 1936.
Dinner Is Served! or, Eating round the World in London. London, Routledge, 1937.
Living in Bloomsbury. London, Allen and Unwin, 1939.
The Streets of London Through the Centuries. London, Batsford, and New York, Scribner, 1940.
The First Noel. London, Wakeham, 1940.
English Night-Life, From Norman Curfew to Present Black-Out. London, Batsford, 1941; New York, Scribner, 1946.
Victorian Grotesque. London, Jenkins, 1941.
Travel in England from Pilgrim to Pack-Horse to Light Car and Plane. London, Batsford, 1943; New York, Scribner, 1946.
English Inns. London, Collins, 1943.
The English and Their Country. London, Longman, 1945.
The English Townsman, As He Was and as He Is. London, Batsford, 1946; New York, Scribner, 1947.
Son of London. London, Jenkins, 1946.

Editor, *The Small People: A Little Book of Verse about Children for Their Elders.* London, Chapman and Hall, 1910.
Editor, *An Artist's Day Book: A Treasury of Good Counsel from the Great Masters in the Arts for Their Disciples.* London, Herbert and Daniel, 1911; selections, as *Life and Art* and *Truth and Beauty,* London, Cape, 2 vols., 1921; Boston, Humphries, 2 vols., 1937.
Editor, *The Charm of the West Country.* Bristol, Arrowsmith, 1913.
Editor, *Children in Verse: Fifty Songs of Playful Childhood.* London, Duckworth, 1913.
Editor, *The Contented Mind: An Anthology of Optimism.* London, Truslove and Hanson, 1914.
Editor, *The Charm of England.* London, Truslove and Hanson, 1914.
Editor, *The German Army from Within,* by B.G. Baker. London, Hodder and Stoughton, and New York, Doran, 1914.
Editor, *The Book of the Inn.* London, Constable, and New York, Doran, 1927.
Editor, *The Ecstasies of Thomas De Quincey.* London, Harrap, 1928; New York, Doubleday, 1929.

*

Bibliography: in *Ten Contemporaries,* 2nd series, by John Gawsworth, London, Benn, 1933.

*   *   *

Although best known for his exotic tales of London's Chinatown, *Limehouse Nights* and its sequels, Thomas Burke wrote more than 30 books, many of them evocative descriptions of London, its streets, its inns, and particularly its East End where he grew up. Orphaned in infancy, Burke lived the first nine years of his life with an uncle in the London working-class district of Poplar, not far from Limehouse and the teeming Thames River docks. Fascinated at an early age with the life of the East End streets, he gained more of an education from observing the flotsam and jetsam of humanity there than he did from books and formal schooling. During these years, his best friend was an elderly Chinaman, the original model for the character of Quong Lee, the Chinatown philosopher in *Limehouse Nights,* whose tea-shop in Limehouse he would visit in secret to receive bits of ginger and a knowledge of "all the beauty and all the evil of the heart of Asia; its cruelty, its grace and its wisdom." "In that shop," Burke wrote, "I knew what some people seek in church and others seek in taverns." Several years later, when his aged friend was deported for having operated an opium den, Burke was inspired to write the first of his collection of short stories about Limehouse. To Burke, whose literary credo was "to tell a story as ably as Ambrose Bierce and to see and write as clearly as Stephen Crane," *Limehouse Nights* was "admittedly violent stuff written hastily," as a means of "simply telling tales." But it firmly established his literary reputation in Britain, and the film adaptation of the first tale in the collection under the title of *Broken Blossoms* extended the boundaries of his reputation internationally.

Among Burke's many tales of terror, superstition, human passion, and borderline mystery-detection, at least three are genuine and noteworthy contributions to detective fiction: "The Hands of Mr. Ottermole" and "Murder under the Crooked Spire," two short stories with anonymous detectives, and *Murder at Elstree; or, Mr. Thurtell and His Gig,* a novelette based on the murder of Mr. William Weare in 1821 by Messrs. Thurtell and Hunt, chronicled in George Borrow's *Celebrated Trials and Remarkable Cases of Criminal Jurisprudence.* Undoubtedly, however, "The Hands of Mr. Ottermole," a fictional reworking *par excellence* of the Jack-the-Ripper story in the original East End setting, replete with foggy, gaslit streets and strangled corpses, is Burke's detective fiction masterpiece. In this multiple murder tale of rushing terror, Burke conjures an air of black magic mixed with mass paranoia and transforms a pair of human hands—"those appendages that are a symbol for our moments of trust and affection and salutation"—into two "five-tentacled members" of brutal and wanton murder. In 1949, a board of eminent critics including Anthony Boucher, John Dickson Carr, and Ellery Queen selected "The Hands of Mr. Ottermole" as the "greatest mystery story of all time."

—Arthur Nicholas Athanason

BURLEY, W(illiam) J(ohn). British. Born in Falmouth, Cornwall, 1 August 1914. Educated at County Technical School; trained as gas engineer (Keam Scholar), qualified 1936; Balliol College, Oxford (Herbertson Prize, 1952), 1950–53, B.A. 1953. Married Muriel Wolsey in 1938; two sons. Engineer and manager for South Western Gas and Water Corporation Ltd., in southwest England, 1936–50; head of Biology Department, Richmond Grammar School, Surrey, 1953–55; head of Biology, 1955–59, and Tutor, 1959–74, Newquay School, Cornwall. Since 1974 fulltime writer. Agent: Victor Gollancz Ltd., 14 Henrietta Street, London WC2E 8QJ. Address: St. Patricks, Holywell, Newquay, Cornwall, TR8 5PT England.

CRIME PUBLICATIONS

Novels (series: Henry Pym; Superintendent Charles Wycliffe)

A Taste of Power (Pym). London, Gollancz, 1966.
Three-Toed Pussy (Wycliffe). London, Gollancz, 1968.
Death in Willow Pattern (Pym). London, Gollancz, 1969; New York, Walker, 1970.
To Kill a Cat (Wycliffe). London, Gollancz, and New York, Walker, 1970.
Guilt Edged (Wycliffe). London, Gollancz, 1971; New York, Walker, 1972.
Death in a Salubrious Place (Wycliffe). London, Gollancz, and New York, Walker, 1973.
Death in Stanley Street (Wycliffe). London, Gollancz, and New York, Walker, 1974.
Wycliffe and the Pea-Green Boat. London, Gollancz, and New York, Walker, 1975.
Wycliffe and the Schoolgirls. London, Gollancz, and New York, Walker, 1976.
The Schoolmaster. London, Gollancz, and New York, Walker, 1977.
Wycliffe and the Scapegoat. London, Gollancz, 1978; New York, Doubleday, 1979.
Charles and Elizabeth. London, Gollancz, 1979; New York, Walker, 1981.
Wycliffe in Paul's Court. London, Gollancz, and New York, Doubleday, 1980.
The House of Care. London, Gollancz, 1981; New York, Walker, 1982.
Wycliffe's Wild Goose Chase. London, Gollancz, and New York, Doubleday, 1982.
Wycliffe and the Beales. London, Gollancz, 1983; New York, Doubleday, 1984.
Wycliffe and the Four Jacks. London, Gollancz, 1985; New York, Doubleday, 1986.
Wycliffe and the Quiet Virgin. London, Gollancz, and New York, Doubleday, 1986.
Wycliffe and the Windsor Blue. London, Gollancz, and New York, Doubleday, 1987.
Wycliffe and the Tangled Web. London, Gollancz, 1988; New York, Doubleday, 1989.
Wycliffe and the Cycle of Death. London, Gollancz, 1990.

OTHER PUBLICATIONS

Novel

The Sixth Day. London, Gollancz, 1978.

Other

Centenary History of the City of Truro. Truro, Blackford, 1977.

*

W.J. Burley comments:

I started to write crime fiction in 1966 after being greatly impressed by a belated introduction to the work of Simenon. My first three novels were attempts to find my feet and a publisher. I was lucky, for all three were published by Gollancz. In my fourth—*To Kill a Cat*—I tried to establish my detective, Charles Wycliffe, as a recognizable character round whom I could write a series of novels. I wanted him to be diligent but compassionate, earnest but with a wry sense of humour, and sufficiently idiosyncratic to be interesting. My next five books exploited the Wycliffe character and three of them, *Guilt*

Edged, Wycliffe and the Pea-Green Boat, and *Wycliffe and the Schoolgirls,* adopted a more psychological approach. This trend culminated in *The Schoolmaster,* a non-Wycliffe crime story which tells how a sensitive, introspective schoolmaster with a load of guilt finds his way to some sort of salvation.

Most of my books are set in the far southwest, and they are concerned with the tensions which arise within small groups of people who live or work together in close proximity—the family in a country house; the partners in a family business; the people living in a village street or a town square. My criminals are never professionals but ordinary people who feel driven by repressed emotions of fear, hatred, or jealousy to commit crimes which in other circumstances they would find unthinkable. In my more recent books I have used actual locations in Cornwall and Devon, confusing the topography slightly in order to avoid the risk of seeming to represent actual people.

* * *

W.J. Burley started writing fiction relatively late in life, but he has experimented with a variety of genres. His work includes mysteries in two series, gothic novels, and science fiction. Burley's best-known work is his series featuring Superintendent Charles Wycliffe of the area CID, in the West Country, an area Burley knows well. Wycliffe is introduced in *Three-Toed Pussy,* which concerns the violent death of a promiscuous young woman in a quiet Cornish village. The suspects, like most of the other residents of the area, are an intellectual lot; far more literary than one might expect in such a remote location. Wycliffe's approach is to learn as much as he can about the victim and the suspects, letting the investigation of the crime recede in favor of a close look at the varieties of human beings the village sets before us. He is especially interested in the pressures on people from living in close proximity and repressing the feelings of resentment, jealousy, or greed. Wycliffe is a fully realized series character, and we get to know his wife, Helen, and their two children.

Burley's first novel in the series defines the formula he uses for most of the Wycliffe novels: the death of an attractive young woman and the residents' perception of the attractive woman as a danger to the community. Unfortunately, Burley's repeated use of a young woman as the murder victim gives a sameness to his mystery novels that cannot be alleviated by varying the range of suspects. In *To Kill a Cat,* Wycliffe is on vacation at the coast when he becomes involved in the investigation of the murder of an elegant young woman who was staying in a sleazy boarding house. In *Guilt Edged,* Wycliffe investigates the death of the wife of a prominent businessman. In *Death in a Salubrious Place,* a young woman is murdered and the villagers want to blame the outsider in their midst, a pop singer. In *Death in Stanley Street,* the victim is an intelligent, educated, and expensive, prostitute who also runs a real estate business.

Burley explores a variation on his formula in the subsequent five books: the inevitability of violence arising from fervent emotions in small, closed communities. In *Wycliffe and the Pea-Green Boat,* two cousins commit murder 20 years apart. In the 1950's the two cousins are attracted to the same woman, and one murders her out of jealousy; 20 years later the other cousin is accused of murdering his father out of greed. In *Wycliffe and the Schoolgirls,* two women are murdered, and their only apparent connection is that they knew each other as schoolgirls. In *Wycliffe and the Scapegoat,* a man estranged from family and community disappears, just before Halloween.

In *Wycliffe in Paul's Court,* the tensions in the neighborhood of Paul's Court are exacerbated by an attractive woman who sunbathes in the nude; then her teenage daughter disappears—

and is later found dead. Soon after, another neighbor is found dead. In *Wycliffe's Wild Goose Chase,* Wycliffe finds a stolen gun, which leads unexpectedly to a murder and an earlier suicide.

In some of his more recent novels, Burley relaxes his formula and lets the characters play out their lives; these are among his better stories. In *Wycliffe and the Beales,* we watch odd-job man Bunny Newcombe change from a decent villager to a tramp, after his mother's death. In *Wycliffe and the Windsor Blue,* Burley draws with sympathy the complex characters of the heirs and relatives of Edwin Garland, an artist who dies suddenly. Burley studies the effects of a deep sense of guilt on a man in *The Schoolmaster,* which is not part of the Wycliffe series.

When all his books are viewed chronologically, Burley's gothic tales, *Charles and Elizabeth* and *The House of Care,* can be seen to complement the deepening psychological focus of the later Wycliffe books. Neither one of the gothic novels is outstanding, and the second one could easily have been a straight police procedural, but both exhibit a skill in developing atmosphere and suspense.

Burley began his career with another series character Dr. Henry Pym, a zoologist at the Huntley-May Grammar School who investigates a spate of poison-pen letters in *A Taste of Power* and *Death in Willow Pattern.* Pym's training as a zoologist affords him ample opportunity to cogitate on the human species, a trait more fully developed in Superintendent Wycliffe.

Burley is interested in exploring the possibilities of the genre. His recognizable style displays an overriding concern with emotions worked out in the confined communities in Devon and Cornwall, and a pervading interest in the psychological profiles of characters. Only occasionally does Burley reveal his other interests in zoology, archaeology, art, or bibliophilism.

—Susan Oleskiw

BURNETT, W(illiam) R(iley). Also wrote as John Monahan; James Updyke. American. Born in Springfield, Ohio, 25 November 1899. Educated at Miami Military Institute, Germantown, Ohio; Ohio State University, Columbus, 1919–20. Married 1) Marjorie Louise Barton in 1921; 2) Whitney Forbes Johnston in 1943; two sons. Statistician, State of Ohio, 1921–27; full-time writer from 1927. Recipient: O. Henry Memorial award, 1930; Mystery Writers of America Edgar Allan Poe award, for screenplay, 1951, and Grand Master award, 1980; Writers Guild of America award, for screenplay, 1963. *Died 25 April 1982.*

<small>CRIME PUBLICATIONS</small>

Novels

Little Caesar. New York, Dial Press, and London, Cape, 1929.
The Silver Eagle. New York, Dial Press, 1931; London, Heinemann, 1932.
Dark Hazard. New York, Harper, 1933; London, Heinemann, 1934.
High Sierra. New York, Knopf, and London, Heinemann, 1940.

The Quick Brown Fox. New York, Knopf, 1942; London, Heinemann, 1943.

Nobody Lives Forever. New York, Knopf, 1943; London, Heinemann, 1944.

Tomorrow's Another Day. New York, Knopf, 1945; London, Heinemann, 1946.

Romelle. New York, Knopf, 1946; London, Heinemann, 1947.

The Asphalt Jungle. New York, Knopf, 1949; London, Macdonald, 1950.

Little Men, Big World. New York, Knopf, 1951; London, Macdonald, 1952.

Vanity Row. New York, Knopf, 1952; London, Macdonald, 1953.

Big Stan (as John Monahan). New York, Fawcett, 1953; London, Fawcett, 1955.

Underdog. New York, Knopf, and London, Macdonald, 1957.

Conant. New York, Popular Library, 1961.

Round the Clock at Volari's. New York, Fawcett, 1961.

The Widow Barony. London, Macdonald, 1962.

The Cool Man. New York, Fawcett, 1968.

Good-bye Chicago. New York, St. Martin's Press, 1981; London, Hale, 1982.

Uncollected Short Stories

"Dressing Up," in *O. Henry Memorial Award Prize Stories of 1930.* New York, Doubleday, 1930.

"Ivory Tower," in *Best American Short Stories of 1946,* edited by Martha Foley. Boston, Houghton Mifflin, 1946.

"Round Trip," in *Ellery Queen's Mystery Magazine* (New York), December 1950.

"Traveling Light," in *Ellery Queen's Mystery Magazine* (New York), September 1951.

"Nobody's All Bad," in *Ellery Queen's Mystery Magazine* (New York), December 1953.

"Vanishing Act," in *Manhunt Detective Story Monthly* (New York), November 1955.

"The Night of the Gran Baile Massacre," in *Ellery Queen's Mystery Magazine* (New York), July 1965.

"The Hunted," in *Mike Shane Mystery Magazine* (New York), July 1971.

OTHER PUBLICATIONS

Novels

Iron Man. New York, Dial Press, and London, Heinemann, 1930.

Saint Johnson. New York, Dial Press, 1930; London, Heinemann, 1931.

The Giant Swing. New York, Harper, 1932; London, Heinemann, 1933.

Goodbye to the Past: Scenes from the Life of William Meadows. New York, Harper, 1934; London, Heinemann, 1935.

The Goodhues of Sinking Creek. New York, Harper, 1934.

King Cole. New York, Harper, 1936; as *Six Days' Grace,* London, Heinemann, 1937.

The Dark Command: A Kansas Iliad. New York, Knopf, and London, Heinemann, 1938.

Stretch Dawson. New York, Fawcett, 1950; London, Muller, 1960.

Adobe Walls. New York, Knopf, 1953; London, Macdonald, 1954.

Captain Lightfoot. New York, Knopf, 1954; London, Macdonald, 1955.

It's Always Four O'Clock (as James Updyke). New York, Random House, 1956.

Pale Moon. New York, Knopf, 1956; London, Macdonald, 1957.

Bitter Ground. New York, Knopf, and London, Macdonald, 1958.

Mi Amigo. New York, Knopf, 1959; London, Macdonald, 1960.

The Goldseekers. New York, Doubleday, 1962; London, Macdonald, 1963.

Sergeants Three (novelization of screenplay). New York, Pocket Books, 1962.

The Abilene Samson. New York, Pocket Books, 1963.

The Winning of Mickey Free. New York, Bantam, 1965.

Plays

Screenplays: *The Finger Points,* with John Monk Saunders, 1931; *The Beast of the City,* 1932; *Scarface, The Shame of the Nation,* 1932; *Some Blondes Are Dangerous,* with Lester Cole, 1937; *King of the Underworld,* with George Bricker and Vincent Sherman, 1938; *High Sierra,* with John Huston, 1941; *This Gun For Hire,* with Albert Maltz, 1941; *The Get-Away,* with Wells Root and J. Walter Ruben, 1941; *Wake Island,* with Frank Butler, 1942; *Crash Dive,* with Jo Swerling, 1943; *Action in the North Atlantic,* with others, 1943; *Background to Danger,* 1943; *San Antonio,* with Alan LeMay, 1945; *Nobody Lives Forever,* 1946; *Belle Starr's Daughter,* 1948; *Yellow Sky,* with Lamar Trotti, 1949; *The Iron Man,* with George Zuckerman and Borden Chase, 1951; *Vendetta,* with Peter O'Crotty, 1951; *The Racket,* with William Wister Haines, 1951; *Dangerous Mission,* with others, 1954; *Captain Lightfoot,* with Oscar Brodney, 1955; *Illegal,* with James R. Webb and Frank Collins, 1955; *I Died a Thousand Times,* 1955; *Accused of Murder,* with Robert Creighton Williams, 1957; *September Storm,* with Steve Fisher, 1961; *Sergeants 3,* 1962; *The Great Escape,* with James Clavell, 1963.

Television Play: *Debt of Honor* (*Naked City* series), 1958–62.

Other

The Roar of the Crowd (on baseball). New York, Potter, 1965.

* * *

If his novels were to be judged solely for their influence, W.R. Burnett would undeniably be numbered among the most important writers of his time. His works may fall short of greatness, but they deserve more critical attention than they now receive. Three were transformed into major genre movies, pictures that either established or extended the possibilities of their particular kind—*Little Caesar, High Sierra,* and *The Asphalt Jungle.* His novels are not mysteries, but crime novels, powerful, accurate cynical explorations of criminals in their own environment; at their best they are important additions to the honor roll of hard-boiled fiction that includes such writers as Dashiell Hammett, Horace McCoy, and James M. Cain, as well as Hemingway and the early Faulkner. Their terse, clipped style, their close attention to the observed reality of modern urban society, their concentration on the hard surfaces of things, and especially their cinematic urgency and immediacy not only make them easily adaptable to the screen, but place them squarely in the tradition of Thirties naturalism.

Little Caesar and *The Asphalt Jungle,* separated by two decades, are Burnett's major achievements. The first, for all practical purposes, created the gangster as the appropriate figure for his time; the second did for the big caper novel what Walpole did for the Gothic romance. *Little Caesar,* the story of the rise and fall of Rico Cesare Bandello, introduced the major and minor elements that soon became commonplace in the form—the ambitious Italian who rises from petty hoodlum to leader of a gang through ruthlessness and treachery, the world of urban violence that fosters criminal activity, the necessary defeat of the protagonist at the peak of his success. He established the dominant iconography of sleek cars and flashy clothes, bootleg liquor and tommyguns, the atmospheres of dance halls and saloons, brothels and speakeasies, the gilded seediness of city life in what used to be called the underworld. Most of all, *Little Caesar* made the gangster one of the generative symbols of the 1930's—the small, dark, menacingly self-controlled man whose parabolic trajectory and anarchic rebellion against the existing social order reflected ironically the aspirations and dissatisfactions of Americans everywhere in a harsh and difficult time. As a novel, *Little Caesar* influenced William Faulkner's *Sanctuary* and Graham Greene's *Brighton Rock.* As a film it turned the gangster movie into one of the richest and most significant American genres, engendering some remarkable offspring—*Public Enemy, The Roaring Twenties, White Heat,* and *The Godfather*—and energizing the careers of, for example, Edward G. Robinson, Jimmy Cagney, George Raft, and Humphrey Bogart.

Although it lacks some of the relentless pacing and the bleak atmospherics of *Little Caesar, The Asphalt Jungle* may be even more original as a fictional achievement. It is generally credited with being the first built around the complicated crime involving an enormous quantity of loot. It focuses less on one dominating figure and more on the collective entity required to pull off the crime. In the process of showing the necessary interactions of a team of specialists working together, the book comments on the changes in American society between 1929 and 1949; the movement from individualism to group endeavor indicates the evolution of crime from a relatively simple act of free enterprise to a complex corporate action. Crime, we understand, parallels its culture, a much more sophisticated and intricate business than in the days of Little Caesar and more insidious in its evolution from rebellion to cooperation. The big caper novel revolves around the inevitable collision of two organizations—the criminals and the policemen—which, though in some ways similar, must ultimately be opposed; the intercutting between the two sets up the tension and ambivalence that cause the reader to divide his loyalties and at some point root for the bad guys. The novel also originated that important sense of mechanism—the caper as a brilliant, thoroughly planned, rigidly timed scheme depending on absolute adherence to its details. Burnett's novel, and all the big capers that follow it, shows the folly of such schemes—technology cannot triumph over the imponderable absurdities of human behavior: someone acts unpredictably or some trivial chance occurrence intervenes, and the whole structure of delusion collapses.

Burnett is an important and original writer whose credentials must be recognized and respected: he may be the single most successful writer on the notion of the criminal as the emblem of an era. He provides some of the most dynamic and apposite metaphors for the life of America in the twentieth century. The fact that his metaphors derive from a context of violence and treachery, rebellion and disorder, the violation and corruption of the law, should not shock any alert, informed observer; his

world demonstrates Burnett's profound and accurate insight into his country and his age.

—George Grella

BURNS, Rex (Raoul Stephen Sehler). American. Born in San Diego, California, 13 June 1935. Educated at Stanford University, California, B.A. in English and Creative Writing, 1958; University of Minnesota, Minneapolis, M.A. in English, 1963, Ph.D. in American Studies 1965. Served in the United States Marine Corps, 1958–61: Captain. Married 1) Emily Sweitzer in 1959 (divorced 1984), three sons; 2) Terry Fostvedt in 1987, three sons and two daughters. Assistant Professor, Central Missouri State University, Warrensburg, 1965–68; Associate Professor, 1968–75 and since 1975 Professor, University of Colorado, Denver. Fulbright lecturer in Greece, 1969–70, and Argentina, 1977. Recipient: Mystery Writers of America Edgar Allan Poe award, 1976. Agent: Brandt and Brandt, 1501 Broadway, New York, New York 10036. Address: 1017 Vivian Circle, Boulder, Colorado 80303, U.S.A.

CRIME PUBLICATIONS

Novels (series: Gabriel Wager in all books except *Suicide Season*)

The Alvarez Journal. New York, Harper, 1975; London, Hale, 1976.
The Farnsworth Score. New York, Harper, 1977; London, Hale, 1978.
Speak for the Dead. New York, Harper, 1978; London, Hale, 1980.
Angle of Attack. New York, Harper, 1979; London, Hale, 1980.
The Avenging Angel. New York, Viking Press, 1983.
Strip Search. New York, Viking, 1984; London, Penguin 1985.
Ground Money. New York, Viking, 1986; London, Penguin, 1988.
Suicide Season. New York, Viking, 1987; London, Penguin, 1988.
The Killing Zone. New York, Viking, 1988; London, Penguin, 1989.

OTHER PUBLICATIONS

Other

Success in America: The Yeoman Dream and the Industrial Revolution. Amherst, University of Massachusetts Press, 1975.
"Writing the Police Procedural," in *The Writer* (Boston), July 1977.
"The Reality of the Lie," in *Colorado Quote* (Denver), December 1978.
"Plot and Life in the Police Procedural," in *The Writer* (Boston), March 1981.
"Description and Narration," in *The Writer* (Boston), March 1984.
"Characterization," in *The Writer* (Boston), May 1988.

*

Rex Burns comments:

I try to do two things: create life and make the reader ask: "What happens next?" anything else—themes, patterns etc.— is of lesser importance, and primarily for my own pleasure.

* * *

Detective Gabriel Wager of the Denver Police Department, who is featured in the series of police stories by Rex Burns, belongs to a minority of mystery series protagonists whose attitudes and personal qualities undergo marked changes from one story to another. Wager, who is half Anglo and half Chicano, suffers some sharp disappointments in the first two novels of the series as a result of his mixed heritage, and he undergoes considerable emotional trauma from an earlier unsuccessful marriage. Later, however, he has matured to the point where he can take an objective view toward those Hispanics who regard him as a traitor to "his people," and he also comes to realize that he gave up a bad marriage in order to be a good cop. Wager has learned some valuable lessons about the weapons available to the police detective: in one story he humiliates a reporter who had made him look bad in a newspaper account, and in *Angle of Attack* he exercises the ultimate clout in setting up for death a particularly nasty character who can not be convinced by legal processes.

One special strength of the series is Burn's knowledge of police methods and his ability to incorporate them into the fabric of the narratives. In *Speak for the Dead,* for example, some really impressive technology accomplishes the almost impossible identifications of a murder victim and in *The Killing Zone* Burns uses his knowledge of police investigative procedure to good effect as Wager investigates what appears to be a racist murder. Burn's understanding of the police mentality also lends credibility to the stories, as it does in *The Avenging Angel* when Wager, overwhelmed with work in a complicated investigation, must take time to fill out an administrative time-study form, and he wonders how soon the police department will be solving forms instead of crimes.

In *The Suicide Season* Burns introduces Devlin Kirk, an ex-Stanford Law School drop-out, ex-secret service agent now running his own company specializing in industrial surveillance. Kirk is drawn into the world of industrial espionage in this fast-paced tale of corrution. Burns is a careful craftsman who knows how to integrate theme, character, and suspense elements into a unified while, as he does in *The Avenging Angel,* in which the menace of the fanatic lynch-gang, Wager's disclaimed sense of guilt over his earlier engineering of a murder, and a half-concealed terror in the community combine to produce a particularly effective climax.

—George N. Dove

———

BURTON, ANNE. See **WOODS, Sara.**

———

BURTON, Miles. See **RHODE, John.**

———

BUSBY, Roger (Charles). British. Born in Leicester, 24 July 1941. Educated at Bishop Vesey's Grammar School for Boys; Aston University, Birmingham, certificate in journalism, 1968. Married Maureen-Jeanette Busby in 1968. Journalist, Caters News Agency, Birmingham, 1959–66, and Birmingham *Evening Mail,* 1966–73. Since 1973 force information officer, Devon and Cornwall Constabulary, Exeter. Recipient: Crime Writers Association Police Review award, 1987. Address: c/o William Collins and Sons, 8 Grafton Street, London W1X 3LA, England. Address: Sunnymoor, Bridford, near Exeter EX6 7HS, England.

CRIME PUBLICATIONS

Novels (series: Detective Inspector Leric)

Main Line Kill, with Gerald Holtham. London, Cassell, and New York, Walker, 1968.
Robbery Blue (Leric). London, Collins, 1969.
The Frighteners (Leric). London, Collins, 1970.
Deadlock (Leric). London, Collins, 1971.
A Reasonable Man (Leric). London, Collins, 1972.
Pattern of Violence (Leric). London, Collins, 1973.
New Face in Hell. London, Collins, 1976.
Garvey's Code. London, Collins, 1978.
The Negotiator. London, Collins, 1984.
The Hunter. London, Collins, 1985; New York, Doubleday, 1989.
Snow Man. London, Collins, 1987; New York, Doubleday, 1989.

Short Stories

Fading Blue. London, Police Review, 1984.

*

Roger Busby comments:

My novels are police stories through which I endeavor to produce the authentic flavour of criminal investigation. I hope that they give the reader an insight into the world of the British police within the dramatic framework of crime fiction. For any chronicle of police work would be a pale shadow without drawing upon the character and psychology of both the detectives and the criminals, the principal protagonists of the drama. My emphasis, therefore, is on characterization rather than the mechanics of the plot. If, on reaching the last page, the reader feels he or she has experienced the unique atmosphere of the police environment, then I have achieved my purpose.

* * *

Roger Busby is one of the best practitioners of the police procedural novel. A journalist-crime reporter for many years, he has obviously used his experience to provide very accurate background information. Although the reader has little detection to do, he is kept alert by taut plots; Busby's characters are very believable and the portrayals well-written.

Busby's first novel, *Main Line Kill*, was written in collaboration with Gerald Holtham and received general acclaim. The first novel under his own name was *Robbery Blue*, and he kept to a subject well known to him. The narrative of this book is exciting and the portrayal of characters, be they police or villains, convincing. Inspector Leric made his first appearance in *Robbery Blue*, and his down-to-earth appraisal of both villains and his own superiors made him an obvious character for featuring in future books.

Unlike those of some writers, Busby's books seem to get better and better, and, although still concentrating upon police procedurals, he varies his themes sufficiently to satisfy even the most demanding of readers. Although most of his books are set in the midlands, his stories both north and south of this location do not lose their authenticity. In *Snow Man* three detectives are trapped in nightmares from their past. An undercover policewoman dies in a booby-trapped Devon farmhouse and the three men's paths cross as together they attempt to smash an international crime cartel bent on flooding Britain with cocaine. The investigations take them to the Bavarian Alps as they plan to trap the drug-runners. Bush has created a gripping tale of top-level police intrigue smoothly incorporating his knowledge of police methods into this chilling tale of fear and paranoia.

—Donald C. Ireland

BUSH, Christopher. Pseudonym for Charlie Christmas Bush; also wrote as Michael Home. British. Born in East Anglia, in 1888(?): birth date unrecorded. Educated at Thetford Grammar School, Norfolk; King's College, London, B.A. (honours) in modern languages. Served in both world wars: Major. Schoolmaster before becoming a full-time writer. *Died 21 September 1973.*

CRIME PUBLICATIONS

Novels (series: Ludovic Travers in all books)

The Plumley Inheritance. London, Jarrolds, 1926.
The Perfect Murder Case. London, Heinemann, and New York, Doubleday, 1929.
Murder at Fenwold. London, Heinemann, 1930; as *The Death of Cosmo Revere*, New York, Doubleday, 1930.
Dead Man Twice. London, Heinemann, and New York, Doubleday, 1930.
Dancing Death. London, Heinemann, and New York, Doubleday, 1931.
Dead Man's Music. London, Heinemann, 1931; New York, Doubleday, 1932.
Cut Throat. London, Heinemann, and New York, Morrow, 1932.
The Case of the Unfortunate Village. London, Cassell, 1932.
The Case of the Three Strange Faces. London, Heinemann, 1933; as *The Crank in the Corner*, New York, Morrow, 1933.

The Case of the April Fools. London, Cassell, and New York, Morrow, 1933.
The Case of the Dead Shepherd. London, Cassell, 1934; as *The Tea Tray Murders,* New York, Morrow, 1934.
The Case of the 100% Alibis. London, Cassell, 1934; as *The Kitchen Cake Murder,* New York, Morrow, 1934.
The Case of the Chinese Gong. London, Cassell,. and New York, Holt, 1935.
The Case of the Bonfire Body. London, Cassell, 1936; as *The Body in the Bonfire,* New York, Morrow, 1936.
The Case of the Monday Murders. London, Cassell, 1936; as *Murder on Mondays,* New York, Holt, 1936.
The Case of the Hanging Rope. London, Cassell, 1937; as *The Wedding Night Murder,* New York, Holt, 1937.
The Case of the Missing Minutes. London, Cassell, 1937; as *Eight O'Clock Alibi,* New York, Holt, 1937.
The Case of the Tudor Queen. London, Cassell, and New York, Holt, 1938.
The Case of the Leaning Man. London, Cassell, 1938; as *The Leaning Man,* New York, Holt, 1938.
The Case of the Green Felt Hat. London, Cassell, and New York, Holt, 1939.
The Case of the Flying Ass. London, Cassell, 1939.
The Case of the Climbing Rat. London, Cassell, 1940.
The Case of the Murdered Major. London, Cassell, 1941.
The Case of the Fighting Soldier. London, Cassell, 1942.
The Case of the Kidnapped Colonel. London, Cassell, 1942.
The Case of the Magic Mirror. London, Cassell, 1943.
The Case of the Running Mouse. London, Cassell, 1944.
The Case of the Platinum Blonde. London, Cassell, 1944; New York, Macmillan, 1949.
The Case of the Corporal's Leave. London, Cassell, 1945.
The Case of the Second Chance. London, Cassell, 1946; New York, Macmillan, 1947.
The Case of the Missing Men. London, Macdonald, 1946; New York, Macmillan, 1947.
The Case of the Curious Client. London, Macdonald, 1947; New York, Macmillan, 1948.
The Case of the Haven Hotel. London, Macdonald, 1948.
The Case of the Housekeeper's Hair. London, Macdonald, 1948; New York, Macmillan, 1949.
The Case of the Seven Bells. London, Macdonald, 1949; New York, Macmillan, 1950.
The Case of the Purloined Picture. London, Macdonald, 1949; New York, Macmillan, 1951.
The Case of the Happy Warrior. London, Macdonald, 1950; as *The Case of the Frightened Manequin,* New York, Macmillan, 1951.
The Case of the Fourth Detective. London, Macdonald, 1951.
The Case of the Corner Cottage, London, Macdonald, 1951; New York, Macmillan, 1952.
The Case of the Happy Medium. London, Macdonald, and New York, Macmillan, 1952.
The Case of the Counterfeit Colonel. London, Macdonald, 1952, New York, Macmillan, 1953.
The Case of the Burnt Bohemian. London, Macdonald, 1953; New York, Macmillan, 1954.
The Case of the Silken Petticoat. London, Macdonald, 1953; New York, Macmillan, 1954.
The Case of the Three Lost Letters. London, Macdonald, 1953; New York, Macmillan, 1955.
The Case of the Red Brunette. London, Macdonald, 1954; New York, Macmillan, 1955.
The Case of the Amateur Actor. London, Macdonald, 1955; New York, Macmillan, 1956.
The Case of the Benevolent Bookie. London, Macdonald, 1955; New York, Macmillan, 1956.

The Case of the Extra Man. London, Macdonald, 1956; New York, Macmillan, 1957.

The Case of the Flowery Corpse. London, Macdonald, 1956; New York, Macmillan, 1957.

The Case of the Russian Cross. London, Macdonald, 1957; New York, Macmillan, 1958.

The Case of the Treble Twist. London, Macdonald, 1958; as *The Case of the Triple Twist,* New York, Macmillan, 1958.

The Case of the Running Man, London, Macdonald, 1958; New York, Macmillan, 1959.

The Case of the Careless Thief. London, Macdonald, 1959; New York, Macmillan, 1960.

The Case of the Sapphire Brooch. London, Macdonald, 1960; New York, Macmillan, 1961.

The Case of the Extra Grave. London, Macdonald, 1961; New York, Macmillan, 1962.

The Case of the Dead Man Gone. London, Macdonald, and New York, Macmillan, 1962.

The Case of the Three-Ring Puzzle. London, Macdonald, 1962; New York, Macmillan, 1963.

The Case of the Heavenly Twin. London, Macdonald, 1963; New York, Macmillan, 1964.

The Case of the Grand Alliance. London, Macdonald, 1964; New York, Macmillan, 1965.

The Case of the Good Employer. London, Macdonald, 1966; New York, Macmillan, 1967.

The Case of the Deadly Diamonds. London, Macdonald, 1967; New York, Macmillan, 1969.

The Case of the Prodigal Daughter. London, Macdonald, 1968; New York, Macmillan, 1969.

Novels as Michael Home

The Questing Man. London, Rich and Cowan, 1936.
The Harvest Is Past. London, Rich and Cowan, 1937.
July at Fritham. London, Rich and Cowan, 1938.
City of the Soul. London, Methuen, 1943.
The Cypress Road. London, Methuen, 1945.
The Strange Prisoner (with John Benham). London, Methuen, 1947.
No Snow in Latching. London, Methuen, 1949.
The Soundless Years. London, Methuen, 1951.
The Auber File (with John Benham). London, Methuen, 1953.
That Was Yesterday. London, Methuen, 1955.

Uncollected Short Stories

"The Hampstead Murder," in *A Century of Detective Stories.* London, Hutchinson, 1935.

"A Drop Too Much," in *Fifty Famous Detectives of Fiction.* London, Odhams Press, 1938.

"The Holly Bears a Berry: A Ludovic Travers Story," in *Illustrated London News,* 15 November 1951.

"Tears for the Jury," in *The Saint* (New York), June 1956.

"Wings of Death," in *The Saint* (New York), October 1956.

"Murder of a Maharajah," in *The Saint* (New York), February 1957.

OTHER PUBLICATIONS as Michael Home

Novels

Return. New York, Morrow, 1933; as *God and the Rabbit,* London, Rich and Cowan, 1934.

This String First. London, Rich and Cowan, 1935.

The Place of Little Birds. London, Methuen, 1941; as *Attack in the Desert,* New York, Morrow, 1942.

The House of Shade. London, Methuen, and New York, Morrow, 1942.

Grain of the Wood. London, Methuen, 1950; New York, Macmillan, 1951.

The Brackenford Story. London, Methuen, and New York, Macmillan, 1952.

Other

David. London, Rich and Cowan, 1937.
Autumn Fields. London, Methuen, 1944.
Spring Sowing. London, Methuen, 1946.
Winter Harvest: A Norfolk Boyhood. London, Macdonald, 1967.

* * *

Christopher Bush published 63 detective novels in the classic English mould, the first in 1926 and the last over 40 years later, in 1968. He also wrote a miscellany of works under a pseudonym, including six thrillers, but these are subsidiary to the extraordinary series on which his primary reputation rests. No-one who delights in true detective fiction will wish to disregard his work. Anthony Shaffer saw it as "nourishing to the addict" and coined the aphorism: "A Bush in the hand is worth two of any other bird."

From the outset Bush showed himself aware of his duty to tease and intrigue the reader and he rang the changes on the tricks of his trade most divertingly over the years. The novels are remarkable for their ingenuity, their complexity and their concentrated focus on the matter in hand. They tend to be unsensational, unfolding with scrupulous logic and eschewing extremes of melodrama and fast or violent action. They are absorbing rather than thrilling, their appeal is more to the intellect than to the headier emotions. They also have a certain staid wit, a wry, understated quality that led one reviewer to welcome an addition to the canon as "another dry sherry from Christopher Bush."

The books are very much of their period and occupy a masculine world in which class distinctions are unquestioned, foreigners are automatically suspect and women know and keep their place. Their style is easy and urbane, continually cajoling and buttonholing the reader. The aim is direct and unaffected: to give us the facts, to invite us to interpret them correctly and yet to ensure that we do not do so until the author is ready to explain. Though the plot itself need not be very complicated, its presentation invariably is. The action often advances in meticulously defined phases and certain cases are brought to a point of terminal exhaustion, only to be revived after an interval, by a new development or a fresh insight.

Bush was a master of the false alibi, a recurring device that came to be a welcome characteristic of much of his fiction. He developed considerable resource in the adroit manipulation of time and drew on a formidable array of tricks with clocks and telephones to construct and demolish fantastical alibis. The earlier books, in particular, contain some remarkable inventive flights and achieve, at their best, an exuberant fancy wholly in the spirit of the Golden Age. The later books are generally less ornate, the effects less dazzling, the narratives more spare. They remain, nonetheless, exemplary in their dedication to the cause of teasing and pleasing the reader.

Throughout the long series the same detective investigates, an amiable, unassuming toff named Ludovic Travers. He is the quintessential good chap of English detective fiction, though blessedly free of any compulsion to show us how tough he is. He represents brain rather than brawn and from his first appearance as a young veteran of World War I reveals himself as above all else intelligent. Though astute he is modest, with an endearing habit of signalling to the reader by removing his glasses when "on the edge of discovery." Like Dr. Watson, he does not allow his marriage to interfere with his yen for a mystery, and though his wife Bernice even participates in a case on occasion, she obligingly spends much of her time visiting friends and relations.

A successful writer with considerable private means, Travers works for occupation only and becomes involved in criminal investigation because he cannot resist a mystery. He works as a financial adviser after World War I and becomes the proprietor of the Broad Street Detective Agency after World War II. He is well-connected and moves easily through his world in his various roles, professionally at ease with finance and personally with art and antiques. The theatre is another recurrent motif: his wife was a speciality dancer and her father a famous actor-manager. Travers's war activities give rise to a run of military investigations and a number of cases take him to France.

In his first case Travers occupies a secondary position as a friend of the protagonist, but as his career advances he assumes increasing dominance until established as the controlling intelligence and eventually the narrator. He quickly finds favour at Scotland Yard and works consistently, though not invariably, with the police (the more plausibly, perhaps, because he is also a nephew of the Assistant Commissioner). His chief associate is a Yard superintendent, George Wharton, more familiarly known as 'the Old General'. An entertaining compound of zealot and charlatan, Travers contributes richly to the undercurrent of gaiety that runs through the series and is much missed after his retirement. His replacement is Chief-Inspector Jewle, who is no less efficient but much less engaging.

—B.A. Pike

————

BUTLER, Gwendoline (née Williams). Also writes as Jennie Melville. British. Born in London. Educated at Haberdashers' Aske's Hatcham Girls' School, London, 1939–42; Lady Margaret Hall, Oxford, 1944–49, B.A. in modern history 1949. Married Lionel Butler in 1949 (died 1981); one daughter. Taught at two Oxford colleges for a short time. Recipient: Crime Writers Association Silver Dagger award, 1973; Romantic Novelists Association Major award, 1981. Agent: Vanessa Holt, Vanessa Holt Associates, 59 Crescent Road, Leigh-on-Sea, Essex SS9 2PF. Address: 32 Harvest Road, Englefield Green, Surrey, England.

CRIME PUBLICATIONS

Novels (series: Inspector John Coffin; Inspector/Superintendent William Winter)

Receipt for Murder. London, Bles, 1956.
Dead in a Row (Coffin; Winter). London, Bles, 1957.
The Dull Dead (Coffin; Winter). London, Bles, 1958; New York, Walker, 1962.
The Murdering Kind (Coffin; Winter). London, Bles, 1958; New York, Roy, 1964.
The Interloper. London, Bles, 1959.
Death Lives Next Door (Coffin). London, Bles, 1960; as *Dine and Be Dead,* New York, Macmillan, 1960.
Make Me a Murderer (Coffin). London, Bles, 1961.

Coffin in Oxford. London, Bles, 1962.
Coffin for Baby. London, Bles, and New York, Walker, 1963.
Coffin Waiting. London, Bles, 1963; New York, Walker, 1965.
Coffin in Malta. London, Bles, 1964; New York, Walker, 1965.
A Nameless Coffin. London, Bles, 1966; New York, Walker, 1967.
Coffin Following. London, Bles, 1968.
Coffin's Dark Number. London, Bles, 1969.
A Coffin from the Past. London, Bles, 1970.
A Coffin for Pandora. London, Macmillan, 1973; as *Olivia,* New York, Coward McCann, 1974.
A Coffin for the Canary. London, Macmillan, 1974; as *Sarsen Place,* New York, Coward McCann, 1974.
The Vesey Inheritance. New York, Coward McCann, 1975; London, Macmillan, 1976.
The Brides of Friedberg. London, Macmillan, 1977; as *Meadowsweet,* New York, Coward McCann, 1977.
The Red Staircase. New York, Coward McCann, 1979; London, Collins, 1980.
Coffin on the Water. London, Collins, 1986; New York, St. Martin's Press, 1989.
Coffin in Fashion. London, Collins, 1987; New York, St. Martin's Press, 1990.
Coffin Underground. London, Collins, 1988; New York, St. Martin's Press, 1989.
Coffin in the Black Museum. London, Collins, 1989.
Coffin and the Paper Man. London, Collins, 1990.

Novels as Jennie Melville (series: Chairman Daniels)

Come Home and Be Killed (Daniels). London, Joseph, 1962; New York, British Book Centre, 1964.
Burning Is a Substitute for Loving (Daniels). London, Joseph, 1963; New York, British Book Centre, 1964.
Murderers' Houses (Daniels). London, Joseph, 1964.
There Lies Your Love (Daniels). London, Joseph, 1965.
Nell Alone (Daniels). London, Joseph, 1966.
A Different Kind of Summer (Daniels). London, Joseph, 1967.
The Hunter in the Shadows. London, Hodder and Stoughton, 1969; New York, McKay, 1970.
A New Kind of Killer, An Old Kind of Death (Daniels). London, Hodder and Stoughton, 1970; as *A New Kind of Killer,* New York, McKay, 1971.
The Summer Assassin. London, Hodder and Stoughton, 1971.
Ironwood. London, Hodder and Stoughton, and New York, McKay, 1972.
Nun's Castle. New York, McKay, 1973; London, Hodder and Stoughton, 1974.
Raven's Forge. London, Macmillan, and New York, McKay, 1975.
Dragon's Eye. New York, Simon and Schuster, 1976; London, Macmillan, 1977.
Axwater. London, Macmillan, 1978; as *Tarot's Tower,* New York, Simon and Schuster, 1978.
Murder Has a Pretty Face (Daniels). London, Macmillan, 1981; New York, St. Martin's Press, 1989.
The Painted Castle. London, Macmillan, 1982.
The Hand of Glass. London, Macmillan, 1983.
Listen to the Children. London, Macmillan, 1986.
Death in the Garden. London, Macmillan, 1987; as *Murder in the Garden,* New York, St. Martin's Press, 1990.
Windsor Red. London, Macmillan, and New York, St. Martin's Press, 1988.
A Cure for Dying. London, Macmillan, 1989.
Witching Murder. London, Macmillan, 1990.

Making Good Blood (Daniels). New York, St. Martin's Press, 1990.

Uncollected Short Stories

"The Sisterhood," in *Ellery Queen's Murder Menu.* Cleveland, World, 1969.
"Time Bomb," in *Winter's Crimes 4,* edited by George Hardinge. London, Macmillan, 1972.
"Older Than the Rocks," in *Winter's Crimes 6,* edited by George Hardinge. London, Macmillan, 1974.
"Hand in Glove" (as Jennie Melville), in *Winter's Crimes 6,* edited by George Hardinge. London, Macmillan, 1974.
"North Wind," in *Winter's Crimes 11,* edited by George Hardinge. London, Macmillan, and New York, St. Martin's Press, 1978.
"The Rogue's Twist," in *Verdict of Thirteen,* edited by Julian Symons, London, Faber, and New York, Harper, 1979.

OTHER PUBLICATIONS

Novel

Albion Walk. New York, Coward McCann, 1982; London, Collins, 1983; as *Cavalcade,* London, Fontana, 1984.

Play

Radio Play: *Nell Alone,* from her own novel, 1968.

* * *

In British crime-writing, Gwendoline Butler is regarded as a considerable find, and her work deserved its 1973 Silver Dagger. Her prize-winning book, *A Coffin for Pandora,* was set in Oxford (where she lived for some time both as university student and teacher), but the Oxford of the 1880's, the formative years of the British CID, in which a young governess becomes involved in a kidnapping and a murder. It was one of several Victorian mysteries which she has written about, brilliantly evoking the sights and sounds of the turn-of-the-century period.

Strangely enough, *A Coffin for Pandora* had nothing to do with the popular character she created, Inspector Coffin, a contemporary policeman with his "manor" in South London. Coffin is an excellent and unusual creation, a tough, self-educated man with a habit of getting involved in bizarre cases involving elderly women. Coffin and his unimaginative assistant, Sergeant Dove, are memorable characters. They appear in many of her crime novels, including *A Coffin from the Past* (an ingenious story of the murder of an M.P. and his secretary in a house where murder was committed in another century) *A Coffin for the Canary* (with a numbing shock ending) and *Coffin and the Paper Man* (an investigation of disturbing deaths and messages from the mysterious paper man). She is able to create an atmosphere of subliminal evil and corruption (the "smell of something nasty") while achieving an intimate chatty style. Her earlier novels were all able to haunt readers with a chilling and eerie unreality. With *A Coffin for Pandora* Butler proved that she could be a "gothic" novelist of considerable power as well as the author of the popular Inspector Coffin detective stories with their devious twists. Since her debut in 1956 she has produced well over 40 novels, and has seen much of her work serialised in magazines and dramatised.

—Herbert Harris

As Jennie Melville, Gwendoline Butler writes novels in two categories: the straightforward detective stories featuring policewoman Charmian Daniels and the neo-Gothic thrillers each with its first-person narrator and romantic setting. In the latter, the protagonist is usually a young girl in threatened circumstances, caught up in a sequence of mysterious events, under a near-fatal misapprehension about her own affairs, unable to locate the true source of menace. Someone wishes her ill, generally for economic reasons; someone else has nothing but her good at heart, and often she is hopelessly confused between the two. The lover/killer figure is a favourite motif of Melville's: naturally, since it provides a focus for the tensions of the plot and takes to its most obvious extreme the concept of fear as an erotic force ("You could say for those weeks I was two people; one screaming, the other hopelessly in love," the heroine of *Ironwood* remarks, making an apt comment on the genre). It is used most effectively, however, in an early (1964) detective novel, *Murderers' House,* in which the apparent roles of the central characters are reversed, with a great deal of subtlety and low-key humour.

The romantic thrillers are competent and interesting but lack the more original qualities of the Chairman Daniels stories with their flippant narrative tone, their quirks and eccentricities of plot and characterization. Homicidal madness is brought down to suburban level and given a squalid, ludicrous, or grotesque form. Character is established economically, usually by means of a half-mocking assessment—often one of the subject's own phrases which is taken over by the author and repeated until its implications are embedded in the reader's consciousness: for instance Charmian's assistant Chris is a girl who lives "a life and a half." The stories are not without defects: the narrative occasionally reads like a television script and the jaunty, joking style can easily shade into glibness. But they are always cleverly constructed, grounded in an acute sense of the sinister possibilities inherent in the most commonplace situations, and presented with assurance.

—Patricia Craig

———

BUTLER, Richard. *See* **ALLBEURY, Ted.**

———

BYRD, Max. American. Born in Atlanta Georgia, 11 April 1942. Educated at Harvard University, Cambridge, Massachusetts, B.A. (magna cum laude) in history and literature 1964; Ph.D 1970; King's College, Cambridge, 1964–65. Married Brookes Clyde Byrd in 1965; one daughter and one son. Assistant Professor of English, 1970–75, and Associate Professor, 1975–76; Yale University, New Haven, Connecticut; Associate Professor, 1976–81, and since 1981 Professor, University of California, Davis. Recipient: Private Eye Writers of America Shamus award, 1982. Agent: Virginia Barber Literary Agency, 353 West 21st Street, New York, New York 10011. Address: 43,329 Walnut Lane, Davis, California, 95616, U.S.A.

CRIME PUBLICATIONS

Novels (series: Mike Haller)

California Thriller (Haller). New York, Bantam, 1981; London, Allison and Busby 1984.
Fly Away, Jill (Haller).   New York, Bantam, 1981; London, Allison and Busby, 1984.
Finders Weepers (Haller).   New York, Bantam, 1983; London, Allison and Busby, 1985.
Target of Opportunity. London, Joseph, and New York, Bantam, 1988.
Fuse Time. New York, Bantam, 1991.

OTHER PUBLICATIONS

Other

Visits to Bedlam: Madness and Literature in the Eighteenth Century. Columbia, University of South Carolina Press, 1974.
London Transformed: Images of the City in the 18th Century. New Haven, Connecticut, Yale University Press, 1978.
Tristram Shandy. London, Allen and Unwin, 1985.

Editor, *Daniel Defoe: A Collection of Critical Essays.* Englewood Cliffs, New Jersey, Prentice Hall, 1976.

*

Max Byrd comments:

I like the extraordinary variety of characters (under stress) natural to a crime story. I also like the variety of social and economic classes that the crime novel so often brings into a single design. Similarly, I try to take advantage of the unusual range of styles available in such variety, where slang can be placed within or next to classically balanced English (the mysterious effect of vitality within form that P.G. Wodehouse pulls off). In this tradition the writers that I perhaps admire most are Raymond Chandler, Dick Francis, and John Le Carré. I *dislike* the idea that crime fiction is inherently less serious or interesting than other kinds of fiction—the late Ross MacDonald used to say that the first detective writer was Sophocles.

* * *

On the opening page of *California Thriller,* the debut appearance of San Francisco private eye Mike Haller, Max Byrd pays homage to Raymond Chandler. Haller places a martini olive between his teeth and then pulls a little pink sword out of it "like a plastic Excalibur," reminding us that the spirit of Philip Marlowe, the private eye as knight errant, lives on. A transplanted Bostonian with a psychologist girl friend and a habit of making literary allusions, Haller also inescapably reminds the reader of Robert B. Parker's Spenser. (Haller's name also bears a close resemblance to Mike Hammer, but he has nothing else in common with Spillane's sadistic hero.) But as Byrd's three novels amply demonstrate, he isn't simply writing pale imitations of Chandler or Parker: his novels are

among the most interesting of the newer crop of private-eye books.

Byrd openly invites comparison with Parker. (Interestingly, both began as English Professors; Byrd still teaches at the University of California at Davis.) His novels are filled with several direct and indirect allusions to the Spenser books. But Haller isn't Spenser. He is neither as macho nor as violent. His code is simpler and less subject to constant re-examination. He lacks Spenser's self-confidence, usually proceeding with caution rather than bravado. Dinah Farrell, his girlfriend, resembles Susan Silverman, especially in her role as analyst of his character, though she is less adulatory than Susan often is. Haller's sidekick is no superhero like Hawk but a grandfatherly retired Irish cop by the name of Fred. The similarities to Spenser are enjoyable to note, but Haller is well-developed enough as a character to stand on his own.

Haller describes himself as a specialist in missing persons, though he usually ends up involved in much bigger crimes. In *California Thriller*, the mysterious disappearance of a local newspaper columnist eventually exposes a maniacal plot cooked up by a biochemist and a right-wing zealot to control the behavior of the masses. In *Fly Away, Jill*, a runaway wife leads Haller on a trail first to England and then to France, where he discovers an international drug-smuggling operation. In *Finders Weepers,* the job of trying to locate a hooker named as heir in a will leads to the loss of his license, after which his problems only worsen. But thanks to a reporter's persistence (his previous occupation) and a private-eye's determination, he searches until he gets to the bottom of things.

Haller is witty, clever, and literate. He has a finely developed sense of humor, though he doesn't feel compelled to fill each page with wisecracks. He has a Chandleresque knack for comic hyperbole and a flair for the eye-catching simile. He is also fond of puns: watching the oil-rich clientele stroll through the lobby of a plush hotel prompts him to quip, "Sheik, rattle, and roll." Haller's narration is fun to read.

Byrd's skillful use of the San Francisco setting is also noteworthy. His rich, atmospheric portrait of the city, from its famous landmarks and popular tourist attractions to the sordid underbelly of its back streets, provides a colorful backdrop for the action. Sending a very American private eye to a foreign country can be a chancy proposition, but Byrd manages it expertly in *Fly Away, Jill,* where Haller traces a missing woman to her native England. (Byrd himself studied at Cambridge after his graduation from Harvard and he writes about London and the surrounding area with authority.) An interesting feature of this novel is Haller's commentary about the many cultural differences between England and the U.S.

Despite a promising beginning (three books in two years), the Haller series appears to have ended prematurely. Nonetheless, readers looking for literate and entertaining mysteries and a character in the Philip Marlowe tradition won't be disappointed in any of Byrd's three series novels.

—David Geherin

C

CAILLOU, Alan. Pseudonym for Alan Lyle-Smythe. American. Born in Redhill, Surrey, England, 9 November 1914; naturalized American citizen, 1978. Studied acting at the Oscar Lewis Academy. Served in the British Army, 1939–41, and the Intelligence Corps in Africa, Italy, and Yugoslavia, 1941–45; captured and escaped twice: M.B.E. (Member, Order of the British Empire), Military Cross. Married Aliza Sverdlova in 1939; one daughter. Officer, Palestine Police, Jerusalem and Haifa, 1936–39; Commissioner for the Reserved Areas Police in Ethiopia and Somalia, 1945–47; district officer, guide-interpreter, hunter, trapper, and actor in Africa, 1947–52. Actor and writer in Canada, 1952–57, and since 1957 in California. Author of romantic novels. Recipient: Mystery Writers of America Edgar Allan Poe award, 1970. Agent: Reece Halsey Agency, 8733 Sunset Boulevard, Los Angeles, California 90069; or, Scott Meredith Literary Agency Inc., 845 Third Avenue, New York, New York 10022. Address: 55 Grasshopper Lane, Sedona, Arizona 86366, U.S.A.

CRIME PUBLICATIONS

Novels (series: Mike Benasque; Cabot Cain; Colonel Tobin)

Rogue's Gambit. London, Davies, 1955.
Alien Virus. London, Davies, 1957; as *Cairo Cabal*, New York, Pinnacle, 1974.
The Mindanao Pearl. London, Davies, 1959; New York, Pinnacle, 1973.
The Plotters (Benasque). London, Davies, and New York, Harper, 1960.
Marseilles (Benasque). New York, Pocket Books, 1964.
A Journey to Orassia. New York, Doubleday, 1965; London, W.H. Allen, 1966.
Who'll Buy My Evil? (Benasque). New York, Pocket Books, 1966.
Assault on Kolchak (Cain). New York, Avon, 1969.
Assault on Loveless (Cain). New York, Avon, 1969.
Assault on Ming (Cain). New York, Avon, 1970.
The Dead Sea Submarine (Tobin). New York, Pinnacle, 1971; London, New English Library, 1973.
Terror in Rio (Tobin). New York, Pinnacle, 1971; London, New English Library, 1973.
Congo War-Cry (Tobin). New York, Pinnacle, 1971.
Afghan Onslaught (Tobin). New York, Pinnacle, 1971.
Assault on Fellawi (Cain). New York, Avon, 1972.
Assault on Agathon (Cain). New York, Avon, 1972.
Swamp War (Tobin). New York, Pinnacle, 1973.
Death Charge (Tobin). New York, Pinnacle, 1973.
The Garonsky Missile (Tobin). New York, Pinnacle, 1973.
Assault on Aimata (Cain). New York, Avon, 1975.
Diamonds Wild (Benasque). New York, Avon, 1979.

OTHER PUBLICATIONS

Novels

The Walls of Jolo. New York, Appleton Century Crofts, 1960; London, Davies, 1961.
Rampage. New York, Appleton Century Crofts, 1961; London, Davies, 1962.
Field of Women. New York, Appleton Century Crofts, 1963.
The Hot Sun of Africa. New York, New American Library, 1964; London, W.H. Allen, 1965.
Khartoum New York, New American Library, 1966.
Charge of the Light Brigade. New York, Pyramid, 1968.
Bichu the Jaguar. Cleveland, World, 1969; London, Hodder and Stoughton, 1970.
The Cheetahs (as Alan Lyle-Smythe). Cleveland, World, 1970; London, Hodder and Stoughton, 1972.
Joshua's People. New York, Pinnacle, 1982.
The House on Curzon Street. New York, Morrow, 1983.
The Prophetess. New York, Pinnacle, 1983.
The Shepherd and the Giant. New York, Pinnacle, 1985.
The League of Hawks. New York, Lorevan, 1986.
The Swords of God. New York, Lorevan, 1987.

Plays

Screenplays: *The Plotters*, 1962; *Village of the Giants*, with Bert I. Gordon, 1965; *Clarence, The Cross-Eyed Lion*, with Art Arthur and Marshall Thompson, 1965; *The Losers*, 1970; *Evel Knievel*, with John Milius, 1972; *Assault on Agathon*, 1974; *Thermoliath*, 1975; *Kingdom of the Spiders*, with Richard Robinson, 1977; *Tennessee Work Farm*, 1978; *Devilfish*, with Bert I. Gordon, 1978.

Television Plays and Documentaries: about 80 in Canada and the US, including episodes for *The 6 Million Dollar Man, The Man from U.N.C.L.E., The Rogues, Voyage to the Bottom of the Sea, Thriller, Behind Closed Doors, The Man from Atlantis, The Fugitive, Flipper, Daktari, Bus Stop, 77 Sunset Strip, The Bob Cummings Show, The Outlaws, Bulldog Drummond,* and *Cannonball,* series.

Other

The Shakespeare Festival: A Short History of Canada's First Shakespeare Festival, 1949–54, with Arnold M. Walter and Frank Chappell. Toronto, Ryerson Press, 1954.
The World Is Six Feet Square (autobiography). London, Davies, 1954; New York, Norton, 1955.
Sheba Slept Here (autobiography). New York, Abelard Schuman, 1973.
South from Khartoum: The Story of Emin Pasha. New York, Hawthorn, 1974.

*

Theatrical Activities:

Director: **Films**—*The Star of India; The Good Life.*

Actor: **Films**—*The Fiercest Heart*, 1961; *Pirates of Tortuga*, 1961; *Five Weeks in a Balloon*, 1962; *It Happened in Athens*, 1962; *Clarence, The Cross-Eyed Lion*, 1965; *The Rare Breed*, 1966; *Hellfighters*, 1968; *Sole Survivor*, 1969; *Search for Eden*, 1979; *Centennial*, 1979; **Television**—in some 80 plays.

Alan Caillou comments:

Many years ago, in a period of doubt (I supose all writers suffer this once in a while), I asked the then head of New American Library, Victor Weybright, "What kind of market an I really writing for—or *should* I be writing for?" I did not know at the time that the question was a foolish one, and he took me up on it immediately: "Write what you enjoy writing," he said, "if enough people are of similar persuasion, you will make a living of some sort. . . ."

The effect of this sound advice, which of course I took, was that I never really specialised in any particular type of writing. I derive most pleasure, perhaps, from working on the kind of book that is loosely classed as "mystery-adventure-suspense." But following my personal tastes in other directions as well, I find that I have written at least one love story, two autobiographies, a biography, and three novels about animals as well as an historical novel once in a while. This does have its disadvantages. It must be that on occasion a reader picks up a book by a writer he knows to write in his own preferred category, and, finding the book is outside that category, therefore feels cheated; and this is regrettable.

Over the years that sound advice referred to above may have lost some of its value. There seems a tendency—at least in America—to take a peek at the current market before starting work. Today, it seems, one is expected to ask "Would you like a book about this or that?" One even finds oneself submitting *outlines*—and I am quite sure that this is not a healthy trend. I do not believe Victor Hugo ever asked his public (represented by the Sales Department and the Distributors), "Should I kill off Jean Valjean around chapter 27? Or shall I let him live happily ever after?" But that's the kind of thing we are headed for, if we don't fight it.

*   *   *

Alan Caillou's best work has been in paperback novels of intrigue and adventure, beginning with the Mike Benasque novels (*Marseilles, Who'll Buy My Evil?*). The well-rendered international settings, the smooth first-person narratives, and the occasional telling insights into human nature and politics combine to make the stories quite entertaining. But Benasque, a journalist by profession, is caught up in intrigue and violence more or less against his will, unlike Cabot Cain of Caillou's very good *Assault* series. Cain is a huge (6 feet 7 inches, 210 pounds) athletic genius (degrees in microbiology, petrology, automotive engineering, etc.). He is also an engaging adventurer who deals in likelihoods rather than facts, usually very successfully, and—though always his own man—works closely with Interpol and his good friend Colonel Matthias Fenrek. Cain's exploits take him all over the globe, and as usual Caillou's use of local color is excellent. Customs, historical background, landmarks, and even linguistic niceties are described with seemingly easy familiarity.

Caillou's series, subtitled "The Private Army of Colonel Tobin," allows him to make full use of his knowledge of history and military tactics. The books feature a group of mercenary soldiers, under the direction of Colonel Tobin, which fights only for the right causes. Again the settings range over the world, from the Sinai Desert to Cambodia. In the sixth book of the series, *Death Charge*, Caillou pulls the unusual stunt of having several major characters killed; and for the subsequent novel, *The Garonsky Missile*, the subtitle was changed to "Tobin's Commando," with the Colonel's son taking charge of the remainder of the troops.

—Bill Crider

———

CAIN, James M(allahan). American. Born in Annapolis, Maryland, 1 July 1892. Educated at Washington College, Chesterton, Maryland, B.A. 1910, M.A. 1917. Served in the United States Army during World War I (editor-in-chief of *Lorraine Cross*, 79th Division newspaper). Married 1) Mary Rebecca Clough in 1920 (divorced 1927); 2) Elina Sjösted Tyszecha in 1927 (divorced 1942); 3) the actress Aileen Pringle in 1944 (divorced 1947); 4) Florence Macbeth Whitwell in 1947 (died 1966). Reporter, Baltimore *American*, 1917–18 and Baltimore *Sun*, 1919–23; Professor of Journalism, St. John's College, Annapolis, 1923–24; editorial writer, New York *World*, 1924–31; screenwriter, 1932–48. Recipient: Mystery Writers of America Grand Master award, 1970. *Died 27 October 1977.*

CRIME PUBLICATIONS

Novels

The Postman Always Rings Twice. New York, Knopf, and London, Cape, 1934.
Serenade. New York, Knopf, 1937; London, Cape, 1938.
Mildred Pierce. New York, Knopf, 1941; London, Hale, 1943.
Love's Lovely Counterfeit. New York, Knopf, 1942; in *Three of Hearts*, 1949.
Three of a Kind: Career in C Major, The Embezzler, Double Indemnity. New York, Knopf, 1944; London, Hale, 1956; *Career in C Major* and *The Embezzler* published as *Everybody Does It*, New York, New American Library, 1949.
Past All Dishonor. New York, Knopf, 1946; in *Three of Hearts*, 1949.
The Butterfly. New York, Knopf, 1947; in *Three of Hearts*, 1949.
Sinful Woman. New York, Avon, 1948; with *Jealous Woman*, London, Hale, 1955.
The Moth. New York, Knopf, 1948; London, Hale, 1950.
Three of Hearts (omnibus). London, Hale, 1949.
Jealous Woman. New York, Avon, 1950; London, Hale, 1955.
The Root of His Evil. New York, Avon, 1952; London, Hale, 1954; as *Shameless*, New York, Avon, 1958.
Galatea. New York, Knopf, 1953; London, Hale, 1954.
Mignon. New York, Dial Press, 1962; London, Hale, 1963.
The Magician's Wife. New York, Dial Press, 1965; London, Hale, 1966.
Rainbow's End. New York, Mason Charter, and London, W.H. Allen, 1975.
The Institute. New York, Mason Charter, 1976; London, Hale, 1977.
Cloud Nine. New York, Mysterious Press, 1984; London, Hale, 1985.
The Enchanted Isle. New York, Mysterious Press, 1985.

Short Stories

Career in C Major and Other Stories. New York, Avon, 1943.

The Baby in the Icebox and Other Short Fiction, edited by Roy Hoopes. New York, Holt Rinehart, 1981; London, Hale, 1982.

Uncollected Short Stories

"The Girl in the Story," in *For Men Only*, edited by James M. Cain. Cleveland, World, 1944.
"It Was the Cat," in *Continent's End: A Collection of California Writing*, edited J.H. Jackson. New York, McGraw Hill, 1944.
"Brush Fire," in *Fourth Round*, edited by Charles Grayson. New York, Holt Rinehart, 1952.
"Pay-Off Girl," in *Ellery Queen's Mystery Magazine* (New York), February 1955.
"Visitor," in *Esquire* (New York), September 1961.

OTHER PUBLICATIONS

Short Stories

Career in C Major and Other Fiction, edited by Roy Hoopes. New York, McGraw Hill, 1986.

Plays

Hero; *Hemp*; *Red, White and Blue*; *Trial by Jury*; *Theological Interlude*; *Citizenship*; *Will of the People* (short plays), in *American Mercury* 6 to 29 (New York), 1926–29.
The Postman Always Rings Twice, from his own novel (produced 1936).
Algiers (screenplay), with John Howard Lawson, in *Foremost Films of 1938*, edited by Frank Vreeland. Toronto, Pitman, 1939.

Screenplays: *Algiers*, with John Howard Lawson, 1938; *Stand Up and Fight*, with Jane Murfin and Harvey Ferguson, 1939; *When Tomorrow Comes*, with Dwight Taylor, 1939; *Gypsy Wildcat*, with James Hogan and Gene Lewis, 1944; *Everybody Does It*, with Nunnally Johnson, 1949.

Other

Our Government. New York, Knopf, and London, Allen and Unwin, 1930.
60 Years of Journalism, edited by Roy Hoopes. Bowling Green, Ohio, Popular Press, 1986.

Editor, with Malcolm Gilbert, *79th Division Headquarters Troop: A Record.* Privately printed, 1919.
Editor, *For Men Only: A Collection of Short Stories.* Cleveland, World, 1944.

*

Critical Studies: by Joyce Carol Oates, in *Tough Guy Writers of the Thirties*, edited by David Madden, Carbondale, Southern Illinois University Press, 1968, *Cain*, New York, Twayne, 1970 and *Cain's Craft*, Metuchen, New Jersey, Scarecrow Press, 1985, both by Madden; *Cain: The Biography of James M. Cain* by Roy Hoopes, New York, Holt Rinehart, 1982, revised edition, Carbondale, Southern Illinois University Press, 1987.

* * *

James M. Cain once remarked that he belonged "to no school, hard-boiled or otherwise, and I believe these so-called schools exist mainly in the imagination of critics." Be that as it may, Cain's first novel, *The Postman Always Rings Twice*, is generally taken to be a high point of hard-boiled writing, partly because of its frank treatment of sex and violence and partly because of its spare, basic style which, like Hemingway's, eschews abstractions and adjectival modification. Its immediacy is enhanced by the directness of its first-person narrative, which is confessional in a specific as well as general sense, since its hero, Frank Chambers, is writing his story in a death cell, and which possesses the sleeve-holding, hypnotic power of an Ancient Mariner's tale.

Unlike a number of his tough-writing contemporaries, Cain offers the reader little direct social criticism. Exceptions might include *Love's Lovely Counterfeit*, with a brutal picture of a corrupt, crime-ridden town in the manner of Hammett's *Red Harvest* and McCoy's *No Pockets in a Shroud;* his historical novels, *Past All Dishonor* and *Mignon*, which both deal in some ways with conflicts between social duties and personal desires; and *Mildred Pierce*, which offers fascinating observations on the lacunae between myth and reality in the American view of the middle-class woman. Yet if there is little direct social comment the very insistence of Cain's plot patterns carries a set of popular mythic meanings which, in a Jungian sense, may offer readers as telling a series of truths about American society as the more obvious social realism of Dreiser and Sinclair Lewis.

The Postman Always Rings Twice can be seen, alongside McCoy's *They Shoot Horses, Don't They?* and O'Hara's *Hope of Heaven*, as a Depression-view of the end of an American dream. Cora has come to California from a small Iowa town to become a Hollywood star; Frank is a bum with no more horizons to reach. Their sordid story provides an ironic comment on their desire for love and respectability. The plot pattern of *Postman* is one that Cain has endlessly modified and reused in his subsequent fiction. A man meets a woman, succumbs to her charms, becomes involved in dangerous, often criminal activity as a result and is frequently destroyed or, at least, loses the woman. This is the patten of *Serenade, Double Indemnity, The Butterfly, The Magician's Wife*, and *The Institute*, as well as several others. While his men may try to act out large Romantic notions, his women frequently represent earthy reality, and confront the hero with basic, primitive urges involving sex, money, violence, and food. Sex and violence are inextricably linked in *Postman* when Frank and Cora make love beside the body of the murdered Greek; sex and food coalesce in a remarkable scene in the church in *Serenade*, and sex fuels the murderous fraud which unites Walter Huff and Phyllis Nirdlinger in *Double Indemnity*. Like Daisy Buchanan in *The Great Gatsby*, these women represent a bedrock of reality against which the Romantic dream must fall, and, like Brigid O'Shaughnessy in Hammett's *The Maltese Falcon*, they can also demonstrate a bewildering unpredictability and dishonesty. In other words, Cain's repeated plot patterns emphasize the basic conflicts in the American psyche between the dream of Romance and the dream of realistic success.

Cain rarely writes mystery novels (perhaps only *Jealous Woman* properly comes into this category) so that murder and crime become, in his work, not something which can be solved and hence disposed of in a cleansing motion, but part of the unalterable series of events usually set in motion by a meeting between man and woman which can exert the same relentless grip (on both protagonists and readers) as Fate in Greek tragedy or Chance in the novels of Thomas Hardy. Part of Cain's power comes from his ability to show the fragility of order and common-sense.

Cain had a long writing career (despite being over 40 when his first novel was published) and the repetitive nature of his plots and language has worked against his overall achievement. His novels are usually well-researched but there is little interaction between his central protagonists and their social setting, and he is so concerned with the way in which characters show themselves in action that he pays much less attention to motivation than he should. Despite these caveats, Cain *was* a prime influence on Camus's *L'Etranger* and showed himself to be one of the foremost storytellers in American popular literature, demonstrating from the outset of his career a mastery of place, set scenes, and first-person narrative.

—John S. Whitley

CAIN, Paul. Pseudonym for George Carrol Sims; also wrote as Peter Ruric. American. Born in Des Moines, Iowa, 30 May 1902. Married three times, had two sons. Lived in Los Angeles after 1923: freelance writer. *Died 23 June 1966.*

CRIME PUBLICATIONS

Novel

Fast One. New York, Doubleday, 1933; London, Constable, 1936.

Short Stories

Seven Slayers. Hollywood, Saint Enterprises, 1946; Harpenden, Hertfordshire, No Exit Press, 1988.

Uncollected Short Stories

"Hunch," in *Black Mask* (New York), March 1934.
"Trouble-Chaser," in *Black Mask* (New York), April 1934.
"Chinaman's Chance," in *Black Mask* (New York), September 1935.
"555," in *Detective Fiction Weekly* (New York), 14 December 1935.
"Death Song," in *Black Mask* (New York), January 1936.
"Sockdolager," in *Star Detective Magazine*, April 1936.
"Dutch Treat," in *Black Mask* (New York), December 1936.
"The Tasting Machine" (as Peter Ruric), in *Gourmet* (New York), November–December 1949.

OTHER PUBLICATIONS as Peter Ruric

Plays

Screenplays: *Gambling Ship*, with others, 1933; *Black Cat*, 1934; *Affairs of a Gentleman*, 1934; *Grand Central Murders*, 1942; *Mademoiselle Fifi*, with others, 1944.

Television Play: *The Lady in Yellow*, 1960.

* * *

Paul Cain-Peter Ruric—Cain for his fiction, Ruric for his film work—was born George Sims. He is known for his only novel, *Fast One*, one of the toughest tough-guy and most brutal gangster story ever written. Set in Depression Los Angeles, it has a surreal quality that is positively hypnotic. Once read, the saga of gunman-gambler Gerry Kells and his dipsomaniacal

lover, S. Grandqueist (she has no first name), is not soon forgotten—if ever. The pace is incredible and the complex plot defies summary.

45 years after its first publication, the book was reprinted by Southern Illinois University Press as a "Lost Book." Paul Cain was "a man who emerged from nowhere," then "disappeared." Thus began Cain's reputation as the "lost man" of the Black Mask school. Much of this mystery was by Cain's own whimsical design, and the rest a result of four decades of his drifting in-and-out of Hollywood, a town not known for its foothold on reality.

Cain was born George Carrol Sims in Des Moines, Iowa, in 1902. It's unknown when he moved to Los Angeles but in 1923 he was listed as an art decorator in the Los Angeles City Directory. He then appeared as a production assistant in Joseph Von Sternberg's first film, *Salvation Hunters* (1925), under the name George Ruric. That same year he further changed his name to Peter Ruric while suggesting to a chorus girl that she change hers from Myrna Williams to Myrna Loy.

In the late 1920's he moved to New York where he began writing as Paul Cain for *Black Mask*. Why he moved or chose the hardboiled genre is unknown. His output included the stories that would later become *Fast One*. In 1932, he returned to Hollywood because Cary Grant was making *Gambling Ship*, a film loosely based on the *Fast One* stories. The film sale inspired Ruric to pull together a novel, and *Fast One* was published in 1933. The book was attacked by one reviewer for being "a ceaseless welter of bloodshed . . . saturnalia of black-and-blue passion, bloodlust, death." While the *Saturday Review of Literature* called it: "The hardest-boiled year of a decade. So H.b. it gets funny. But it moves like a machine-gun. Zowie!"

Regardless of these opinions, the book made no impression on the public and disappeared. The next year, as Peter Ruric, he wrote his best and most flamboyant script, *The Black Cat*—a Boris Karloff picture about a coven of Bauhaus Satanists. The film's co-star, Bella Lugosi, and Ruric became friends and roamed Hollywood together. During this time, he continued writing as Paul Cain for *Black Mask*, but never pulled together another novel. In 1936, like other writers, he stopped writing for the magazine when editor Joseph Shaw resigned.

Paul Cain published two minor stories in two minor magazines, then gave up the pulps forever. Years later in 1948, Joseph Shaw edited *The Hard-boiled Omnibus*, and that motived Ruric to publish *Seven Slayers*, a paperback collection of Paul Cain's best Black Mask work, now over 15 years old.

In addition to the two Cain titles, Peter Ruric claimed in various resumés to have written such works as *Hypersensualism: A Practical Philosophy for Acrobats* and *The Ecstasy Department*. No evidence has been found to indicate that these works exist. Ruric's only other published works are two rambunctious contributions to *Gourmet* magazine made in 1949 and 1951.

From the mid 1930's until his death, Ruric traveled extensively between Hollywood, New York, Europe, and North Africa. He also married at least three times. In 1940, his first marriage made the Los Angeles papers when his wife leapt three-stories from their Hollywood apartment after a drunken quarrel. She survived, but her jump ended the marriage. His second wife is unknown—but relatives remember being told she was either a scriptwriter or an Italian actress. In the early 1950's, he moved to Mallorca, Spain; a sun-soaked haven for penniless writers. There he married an American student. The couple drifted to North Africa before moving to Laguna Beach, California. They had two sons, then divorced in the late 1950's.

Ruric returned to Hollywood to try writing for television, but got little work. His last six years remain particularly opaque. We only know for sure that he died of cancer on 23 June 1966 in

Los Angeles, the city he evoked so brilliantly in *Fast One.* Ironically, after his death, this "man who disappeared"— didn't. His ashes were kept in storage unclaimed for two years until a woman had them shipped to her in Hawaii. Who she was and where Ruric's remains are now is unknown.

In his brief prime, Paul Cain had been favorably compared with Dashiell Hammett and Raoul Whitfield and declared worthy to be in their company. Ironically, he was also confused with James M. Cain—one reviewer speculating that *The Postman Always Rings Twice* was written by "that mysterious bearded gentleman who wrote *A Fast One.*" So *Fast One* it is. Now collected by aficionados and the knowledgeable, it remains what Raymond Chandler called "some kind of high point in the ultra hard-boiled manner."

—E.R. Hagemann and David A. Bowman

————

CAINE, Peter. *See* **HORNIG, Doug.**

————

CALLAS, Theo. *See* **CORY, Desmond.**

————

CAMPBELL, Margaret. *See* **Shearing, Joseph.**

————

CAMPBELL, R. Wright. *See* **CAMPBELL, Robert.**

————

CAMPBELL, Robert (Wright). Also writes as R. Wright Campbell; F.G. Clinton. American. Born in Newark, New Jersey, 9 June 1927. Educated at the Pratt Institute, Brooklyn, New York 1944–47, certificate in illustration, 1947. Served in the United States Army 1950–52. Freelance illustrator, 1947–50. Recipient: Mystery Writers of America Edgar Allan Poe award, 1987. Agent: JET Associates, 124 East 84th Street, New York, New York 10028. Address: c/o Poseidon Press, 1340 North Alameda, Las Cruces, New Mexico 88001, U.S.A.

CRIME PUBLICATIONS

Novels (series: Jimmy Flannery; Jake Hatch; Whistler)

The Tin Cop (as F.G. Clinton). New York, Pinnacle, 1983.
The Junkyard Dog (Flannery). New York, New American Library, 1986.
In La-La Land We Trust (Whistler). New York, Mysterious Press, 1986.
The 600-Pound Gorilla (Flannery). New York, New American Library, 1987.

Hip-Deep in Alligators (Flannery). New York, New American Library, 1987.
Alice in La-La Land (Whistler). New York, Poseidon Press, 1987.
Thinning the Turkey Herd (Flannery). New York, New American Library, 1988.
Cat's Meow (Flannery). New York, New American Library, 1988.
Plugged Nickle (Hatch). New York, Pocket Books, 1988.
Juice. New York, Poseidon Press, 1989.
Red Cent (Hatch). New York, Pocket Books, 1989.
Sweet La-la Land (Whistler). New York. Poseidon Press, 1990.

Novels as R. Wright Campbell

The Spy Who Sat and Waited. New York, Putnam, 1975; London, Weidenfeld and Nicolson, 1976.
Circus Couronne. New York, Putnam, 1977.
Killer of Kings. Indianapolis, Bobbs Merrill, and London, Sidgwick and Jackson, 1979.
Malloy's Subway. New York, Atheneum, 1981; London, Hale, 1982.
Honor. New York, Tor, 1987.

OTHER PUBLICATIONS

Novels as R. Wright Campbell

Where Pigeons Go to Die. New York, Rawson, 1978; London, Sidgwick and Jackson, 1979.
Fat Tuesday. Newhaven, Connecticut, Ticknor and Fields, 1983.

Plays

Wordsmith (produced 1977).

Screenplays: *Five Guns West*, 1955; *Naked Paradise*, 1957; *Gun for a Coward*, 1957; *Quantez*, 1957; *Man of a Thousand Faces*, 1957; *Machine Gun Kelley*, 1958; *A New World*, 1958; *Teenage Caveman* (*Out of the Darkness*), 1958; *The Night Fighters*, 1960; *The Young Racers*, 1963; *The Masque of the Red Death*, 1964; *The Secret Invasion*, 1964; *Hell's Angels on Wheels*, 1967; *Captain Nemo and the Underwater City*, 1969.

Television Plays: scripts for *Medic*, *Mavrick*, *Cheyenne*, *Mr. Garland*, *Twelve O'Clock High*, *The Loretta Young Show*, *The Star and the Story*, *Marcus Welby M.D.*, *Harry O*, series.

*   *   *

Robert Campbell came to the writing of crime fiction after a long and successful career scripting "B" movies including *Hell's Angels on Wheels* and *The Masque of the Red Death*. Perhaps because of his experience in motion pictures, one can often see a cinematic approach in his many thrillers and crime stories. However, his real strength as a writer lies in his characterizations and his uncanny ear for the diversity of American speech. In this latter he has proven himself the equal of Raymond Chandler and Elmore Leonard.

Like Leonard, Campbell had been successfully writing non-series thrillers for a number of years before he first gained a measure of critical appreciation. *The Junkyard Dog*, the first in his Jimmy Flannery series won an Edgar Allen Poe award, bringing him to the attention of critics and mystery readers alike.

Campbell's early work is both diverse and colorful, making use of a vast array of unusual backdrops and often peopled with a veritable mosaic of characters. His first book (published as R. Wright Campbell) *The Spy Who Sat and Waited*, concerns a German spy placed in the Orkney Islands as a sleeper to work against the Allies in World War II. *Killer of Kings* seems to have presaged the victimization of movie and television actors by obsessed madmen. In this story, the protagonist-villain's hatred of a particular star prompts him to attempt a massacre in the Dorothy Chandler Pavilion.

Although not strictly a crime novel, *Fat Tuesday* is certainly Campbell's darkest work to date and is the closest he has come to writing a serious novel. Set in New Orleans at the time of World War I, Campbell tells the story of a New York journalist who comes to look for his missing daughter. Rich in historical background and imagery, the story is a moody masterpiece of a man slowly caught up in and defeated by the sinful malaise with which he is surrounded. In it, one can see the beginnings of Campbell's obsession with decadence and moral decay, things he later artfully depicts in his La-La Land series.

Ironically, it is for work that is much lighter in dramatic weight that Campbell has finally begun to be recognized. Virtually all of his work since 1986 has been expressed in a more traditional crime or mystery format with a recurring cast of characters. Campbell has thus far created three series detectives, none of whom resembles the other in occupation or personality. The first of these is Jimmy Flannery, a precinct captain in the crumbling but still powerful Chicago Democratic machine. Short, stocky, red-headed, and bearing a resemblance to James Cagney, Flannery speaks in a rich, Runyonesque dialect which makes up in descriptive color what it may lack in grammar and syntax.

Although Flannery maintains a loyalty to his party and the old-time political bosses which still dominate it, he has no real interest in politics and remains part of the machine simply to help his neighbors. Usually this neighborly interest in his precinct is the catalyst for his involvement in a murder investigation.

The most interesting aspect of Flannery's character is that although he is admittedly blue-collar, Flannery is amazingly liberal in his outlook and interests. *In The Junkyard Dog*, for example, Flannery gets involved in a case because of his anger at the death of an innocent little girl during the bombing of an abortion clinic. In *The 600-Pound Gorilla*, a government cover-up of the murder of two homosexuals so enrages him that he risks his life and his job to publicly back a lesbian candidate for alderman. Campbell's movie background is especially evident here, for although the stories take place in modern times, Flannery's 12th Precinct seems more like the set from the back lot at Republic or RKO during the 1930's.

The complete opposite of Jimmy Flannery's urban dream-world is the glittery, sleazy, and nightmarish backdrop for the three La-La Land stories. Told in the third person and set in modern-day Hollywood, the books relate the adventures of Whistler, a tough, laconic, but sentimental private detective who hangs out in a diner at the corner of Hollywood and Vine.

Whistler is an aging adventurer who came to Hollywood in his youth looking for excitement and romance and who remains there, even though he has no illusions about the filth hiding beneath the neon-lit surface of his city. In each of his adventures thus far, Whistler comes into the case because of his attraction to what he perceives is a damsel in distress, but who turns out instead to be shrewd, manipulative, and dangerous.

The Jake Hatch series, which has not commanded much in the way of critical interest, is concerned with the adventures of a skirt-chasing railroad man. Overall, they are less interesting than *Juice*, a non-series novel about a ruthless loan shark

named Puffy Pachulo, and Panama Heath, a tough vice detective. This particular story owes a great deal to Elmore Leonard and successfully imitates Leonard's dark humor, colorful characterizations and rich urban patois.

Campbell is a prolific writer with a natural ear for dialog. His boundless imagination, coupled with the sheer zest of his writing is bound to place him in the front rank of American hard-boiled writers in the coming years.

—Robert E. Skinner

———

CANADAY, John. *See* **HEAD, Matthew.**

———

CANNAN, Joanna (Maxwell). British. Born in Oxford, in 1898. Educated at Wychwood School, Oxford, and in Paris. Married H.J. Pullein-Thompson in 1918 (died 1957); three daughters, the writers Diana, Christine, and Josephine Pullein-Thompson, and one son, the writer Denis Cannan. *Died 22 April 1961.*

CRIME PUBLICATIONS

Novels (series: Inspector Guy Northeast; Inspector Ronald Price)

The Simple Pass On. London, Benn, 1929; as *Orphan of Mars*, Indianapolis, Bobbs Merrill, 1930.
No Walls of Jasper. London, Benn, 1930; New York, Doubleday, 1931.
Under Proof. London, Hodder and Stoughton, 1934.
A Hand to Burn. London, Hodder and Stoughton, 1936.
Frightened Angels. London, Gollancz, and New York, Harper, 1936.
They Rang Up the Police (Northeast). London, Gollancz, 1939.
Death at The Dog (Northeast). London, Gollancz, 1940; New York, Reynal, 1941.
Murder Included (Price). London, Gollancz, 1950; as *Poisonous Relations*, New York, Morrow, 1950; as *The Taste of Murder*, New York, Dell, 1951.
Body in the Beck (Price). London, Gollancz, 1952; New York, Garland, 1983.
Long Shadows (Price). London, Gollancz, 1955.
And Be a Villain (Price). London, Gollancz, 1958.
All Is Discovered (Price). London, Gollancz, 1962.

OTHER PUBLICATIONS

Novels

The Misty Valley. London, First Novel Library, 1922; New York, Doran, 1924.
Wild Berry Wine. London, Unwin, and New York, Stokes, 1925.
The Lady of the Heights. London, Unwin, 1926.
Sheila Both-Ways. London, Benn, 1928; New York, Stokes, 1939.

Ithuriel's Hour.   London, Hodder and Stoughton, 1931; New
    York, Doubleday, 1932.
High Table.   London, Benn, and New York, Doubleday, 1931.
Snow in Harvest.   London, Hodder and Stoughton, 1932.
North Wall.   London, Hodder and Stoughton, 1933.
The Hills Sleep On.   London, Hodder and Stoughton, 1935.
Pray Do Not Venture.   London, Gollancz, 1937.
Princes in the Land.   London, Gollancz, 1938.
Idle Apprentice.   London, Gollancz, 1940.
Blind Messenger.   London, Gollancz, 1941.
Little I Understood.   London, Gollancz, 1948.
The Hour of the Angel; Ithuriel's Hour.   London, Pan, 1949.
And All I Learned.   London, Gollancz, 1952.
People to Be Found.   London, Gollancz, 1956.

Other

A Pony for Jean (for children).   London, Lane, 1936; New
    York, Scribner, 1937.
We Met Our Cousins (for children).   London, Collins, 1937;
    New York, Dodd Mead, 1938.
Another Pony for Jean (for children).   London, Collins, 1938.
London Pride (for children).   London, Collins, 1939.
More Ponies for Jean (for children).   London, Collins, 1943.
They Bought Her a Pony (for children).   London, Collins, 1944.
Hamish: The Story of a Shetland Pony (for children).   London,
    Penguin, 1944.
I Wrote a Pony Book (for children).   London, Collins, 1950.
Gaze at the Moon (for children).   London, Collins, 1957.

Editor, with M.D. and May W. Cannan, *The Tripled Crown: A
    Book of English, Scotch and Irish Verse for the Age of Six to
    Sixteen.*   London, Frowde, 1908.

                    *   *   *

Joanna Cannan wrote some detective fiction as well as many
novels and a number of pony books for girls. "The trouble
about detective stories is that they're not the least like life.
People find a corpse and make no more fuss than if it was a
dead rabbit," says Delia Cathcart on the first page of *They
Rang Up the Police;* it is a significant remark since the corpse
found later in the story is Delia's own, and certainly its
discovery leaves no one broken-hearted. Four women, a mother
and three middle-aged daughters, live at Marley Grange in the
usual state of cloying emotional dependence that can only lead
to disaster. Underneath the facade of sweetness and affection a
great deal of nastiness is secreting. The perpetrator of the
murderous attack on Delia is her younger sister, "the home
bird," "the poor baby," "silly timid me." The narrative irony is
just a little too emphatic to be convincing.

Guy Northeast is the C.I.D. Inspector who solves the
mystery of Marley Grange. His next case (*Death at The Dog*)
takes him to a country pub in wartime England where he
proceeds to develop a profitless infatuation for one of his
suspects. Cressy Hardwick is a writer, spirited, humane, and
just sufficiently disreputable to captivate the plodding young
detective. It is Cressy who clarifies one of the author's policies
when she declares: "I believe I know what my mistake was
now...I mean, in my detective novel, I tried to make my
detective a brilliant kind of person—like Dr. Priestley, only
young and attractive....."

This is a mistake that Cannan never makes. In fact there is
something subversive and interesting about her refusal to
glorify her detectives, though the impulse towards realism is in
the end self-defeating, largely because it isn't carried far
enough. The fantasy-detectives—Sayers's Lord Peter Wimsey,

Allingham's Albert Campion and so on—have a quality of style
that balances the obvious exaggerations; industrious, painstaking policemen like Freeman Wills Crofts's Inspector French
depend for their impact upon a detailed and meticulous
narrative approach. Cannan, however, has lumbered her
sleuths somewhat gratuitously with many squalid defects and
deficiencies. The mundane workings of their minds are
revealed to the reader as they go through the process of
suspecting the wrong people, antagonizing their colleagues,
and generally making themselves obnoxious. Guy Northeast
isn't exactly a dashing figure, but Cannan's Inspector Ronald
Price is positively shoddy and unprepossessing. To complete
the picture he is provided with an intolerable wife and a couple
of awful children; and one novel at least (*All Is Discovered*) is
taken up with low-key observations of domestic friction:
"Valerie's rat-like face appeared at a window in the thatch.
'Your dinner's in the oven and if it's all dried up it's your own
fault,' she screamed."

"The cankerous malignity of the domestically oppressed" is a
quality that interests the author as a source of criminal
derangement. The phrase occurs in what is probably her best
detective novel, *Murder Included*, where the usual sequence of
crimes is reversed, with unquestionable logic. The book
contains another version of the only character who merits
narrative approval: the slightly jaded, fastidious woman writer
with inner resources of vitality and subtle charm. On the whole,
the novels are competent rather than brilliant but they do show
an admirable grasp of the technical principles of the genre.

—Patricia Craig

                    ————

CANNING, Victor.   Also wrote as Alan Gould. British.
Born in Plymouth, Devon, 11 June 1911. Educated at Plymouth
Technical College and Oxford Central School. Served in the
Royal Artillery, 1940–46: Major. Recipient: Crime Writers
Association Silver Dagger award, 1972. Married 1) Phyllis
McEwen in 1934; 2) Adria Irving-Bell in 1976. Clerk prior to
1934. *Died 21 February 1986.*

Crime Publications

Novels (series: Rex Carver)

The Chasm.   London, Hodder and Stoughton, and New York,
    Mill, 1947.
Panthers' Moon.   London, Hodder and Stoughton, and New
    York, Mill, 1948.
The Golden Salamander.   London, Hodder and Stoughton, and
    New York, Mill, 1949.
A Forest of Eyes.   London, Hodder and Stoughton, and New
    York, Mill, 1950.
Venetian Bird.   London, Hodder and Stoughton, 1951; as *Bird
    of Prey*, New York, Mill, 1951.
The House of the Seven Flies.   London, Hodder and Stoughton,
    and New York, Mill, 1952.
The Man from the "Turkish Slave."   London, Hodder and
    Stoughton, and New York, Sloane, 1954.
A Handful of Silver.   New York, Sloane, 1954; as *Castle
    Minerva*, London, Hodder and Stoughton, 1955.
His Bones Are Coral.   London, Hodder and Stoughton, 1955;
    as *Twist of the Knife*, New York, Sloane, 1955; as *The Shark
    Run*, London, New English Library, 1968.

The Hidden Face. London, Hodder and Stoughton, 1956; as *Burden of Proof*, New York, Sloane, 1956.

The Manasco Road. London, Hodder and Stoughton, and New York, Sloane, 1957; as *The Forbidden Road*, New York, Permabooks, 1959.

The Dragon Tree. London, Hodder and Stoughton, and New York, Sloane, 1958; as *The Captives of Mora Island*, New York, Permabooks, 1959.

The Burning Eye. London, Hodder and Stoughton, and New York, Sloane, 1960.

A Delivery of Furies. London, Hodder and Stoughton, and New York, Sloane, 1961.

Black Flamingo. London, Hodder and Stoughton, 1962; New York, Sloane, 1963.

The Limbo Line. London, Heinemann, 1963; New York, Sloane, 1964.

The Scorpio Letters. London, Heinemann, and New York, Sloane, 1964.

The Whip Hand (Carver). London, Heinemann, and New York, Sloane, 1965.

Doubled in Diamonds (Carver). London, Heinemann, 1966; New York, Morrow, 1967.

The Python Project (Carver). London, Heinemann, 1967; New York, Morrow, 1968.

The Melting Man (Carver). London, Heinemann, 1968; New York, Morrow, 1969.

Queen's Pawn. London, Heinemann, 1969; New York, Morrow, 1970.

The Great Affair. London, Heinemann, 1969; New York, Morrow, 1970.

Firecrest. London, Heinemann, 1971; New York, Morrow, 1972.

The Rainbird Pattern. London, Heinemann, 1972; New York, Morrow; 1973; as *Family Plot*, New York, Award, 1976.

The Finger of Saturn. London, Heinemann, 1973; New York, Morrow, 1974.

The Mask of Memory. London, Heinemann, 1974; New York, Morrow, 1975.

The Kingsford Mark. London, Heinemann, 1975; New York, Morrow, 1976.

Birdcage. London, Heinemann, 1978; New York, Morrow, 1979.

The Satan Sampler. London, Heinemann, 1979; New York, Morrow, 1980.

Fall from Grace. London, Heinemann, 1980; New York, Morrow, 1981.

The Boy on Platform One. London, Heinemann, 1981; as *Memory Boy*, New York, Morrow, 1981.

Vanishing Point. London, Heinemann, 1982; New York, Morrow, 1983.

Birds of a Feather. London, Heinemann, and New York, Morrow, 1985.

Table Number Seven. London, Heinemann, 1987.

Short Stories

Young Man on a Bicycle and Other Stories. London, Hodder and Stoughton, 1958; as *Oasis Nine: Four Short Novels*, New York, Sloane, 1959.

Delay on Turtle and Other Stories. London, New English Library, 1962.

Uncollected Short Stories

"Star Stuff," in *Ellery Queen's Mystery Magazine* (New York), June 1962.

"The Sunday Fishing Club," in *To Be Read Before Midnight*, edited by Ellery Queen. New York, Random House, 1962; London, New English Library, 1967.

"The Carnation Mystery," in *Ellery Queen's Mystery Magazine* (New York), January 1963.

"A Stroke of Genius," in *Ellery Queen's Mystery Magazine* (New York), February 1965.

"Flint's Diamonds," in *Alfred Hitchcock Presents: Stories That Scared Even Me.* New York, Random House, 1967.

"A Question of Character," in *John Creasey's Mystery Bedside Book 1970*, edited by Herbert Harris. London, Hodder and Stoughton, 1969.

"The Botany Pattern," in *Anthology 1970 Mid-Year*, edited by Ellery Queen. New York, Davis, 1970.

"Disappearing Trick," in *John Creasey's Mystery Bedside Book 1971*, edited by Herbert Harris. London, Hodder and Stoughton, 1970.

"Baskets of Apples and Roses," in *Ellery Queen's Doors to Mystery.* New York, Davis, 1981.

OTHER PUBLICATIONS

Novels

Mr. Finchley Discovers His England. London, Hodder and Stoughton, 1934; as *Mr. Finchley's Holiday*, New York, Reynal, 1935.

Polycarp's Progress. London, Hodder and Stoughton, 1935.

Fly Away Paul. London, Hodder and Stoughton, and New York, Reynal, 1936.

Matthew Silverman. London, Hodder and Stoughton, 1937.

Mr. Finchley Goes to Paris. London, Hodder and Stoughton, and New York, Carrick and Evans, 1938.

Fountain Inn. London, Hodder and Stoughton, 1939.

Mr. Finchley Takes the Road. London, Hodder and Stoughton, 1940.

Green Battlefield. London, Hodder and Stoughton, 1943.

The Runaways. London, Heinemann, and New York, Morrow, 1972.

Flight of the Grey Goose. London, Heinemann, and New York, Morrow, 1973.

The Painted Tent. London, Heinemann, and New York, Morrow, 1974.

The Crimson Chalice. London, Heinemann, 1976; New York, Morrow, 1978.

The Doomsday Carrier. London, Heinemann, 1976; New York, Morrow, 1977.

The Circle of the Gods. London, Heinemann, 1977.

The Immortal Wound. London, Heinemann, 1978.

Raven's Wind. London, Heinemann, and New York, Morrow, 1983.

Novels as Alan Gould

Two Men Fought. London, Collins, 1936.

Mercy Lane. London, Collins, 1937.

Sanctuary from the Dragon. London, Collins, 1938.

Every Creature of God Is Good. London, Hodder and Stoughton, 1939.

The Viaduct. London, Hodder and Stoughton, 1939.

Atlantic Company. London, Hodder and Stoughton, 1940.

Plays

Screenplays: *Golden Salamander*, with Ronald Neame, 1950; *Venetian Bird* (*The Assassin*), 1952.

Television Plays: *Curtain of Fear*, 1964; *Breaking Point*, 1966; *This Way to Murder*, 1967; *Cuculus Canorum*, 1972.

Radio Plays: *London Fox*, 1982; *Loud Sing Cuckoo*; *The Return of Uncle Arthur*, 1984.

Other

Everyman's England. London, Hodder and Stoughton, 1936.

*   *   *

Victor Canning wrote more than 50 novels. He began his career as a skillful writer about the countryside, an aspect which continued throughout his work. After World War II he turned his attention almost exclusively to spy and espionage thrillers. The reputation he gained was solidly established on his ability as a story teller. An inveterate traveler with an eye for local color and detail, Canning used many locales for his stories. Canning's essential ingredients are excitement, suspense, and realism. His conflicts of personality are always convincing. His characters are real people involved in a steadily moving story, and he has a fine ear for dialogue. Although some stories may be quieter than others, they are always full of contrasts and reverses. He also used a generous dollop of humor, a trait not often found in spy and espionage stories.

In *Panthers' Moon* two magnificent black panthers are loose in the Alps. In one's collar is a precious microfilm, and the hunters become the hunted. In *The House of the Seven Flies* the secret of a quarter of a million pounds worth of diamonds is contained in the cryptic phrase of the title. One man is given the phrase but no clue to its meaning. In *The Burning Eye* Canning used a smelly Somali port, a conglomeration of marooned passengers, and an American engineer facing the local sultan in a struggle for oil. Canning juggles two plots in *The Rainbird Pattern*, the principal one concerning the kidnapping of the Archbishop of Canterbury. In *The Finger of Saturn* a country squire's wife returns after a two-year disappearance with no memory. The squire reverts to a calculating primitive as he uncovers a conspiracy to establish a world supremacy.

Canning's private investigator, Rex Carver, works both for himself and for British Intelligence in trailing two women across Europe in *The Whip Hand*. The settings of Paris, the Dalmatian coast, and Austria are marvelously done. Carver appears in several other novels.

In *Fall from Grace* Canning shows that he is a realist with few illusions. A selfish and immoral rogue falls in love with a Bishop's gardener, but fights a losing battle against temptation and greed, attempts blackmail, and destroys all he has gained. In *The Boy on Platform One* we find an appealing, yet unsentimental portrait of a 14-year old with total recall of anything he hears aloud. He is recruited by British Intelligence to listen to a list of traitors recited by a French count. The murder of the count sends the boy and his father into hiding. *Vanishing Point* is another example of Canning's elegant writing and suave wit. An art dealer learns that he has English parents. He is unaware that a portrait of his father contains documents implicating highly placed English gentlemen. Soon "Birdcage," a devious undercover agency, is seeking him, along with the Mafia and the security service of another country.

Dorothy B. Hughes, the noted mystery critic, called Canning the post-war successor to Eric Ambler in writing about the confidential agent. He can never be accused of writing the same book twice. Canning's name is synonymous with the best in international intrigue.

—Frank Denton

———

CANNON, Curt, *See* **McBAIN, Ed.**

———

CARLISLE, Clark. *See* **HOLDING, James.**

———

CARMICHAEL, Harry. Pseudonym for Leopold Horace Ognall; also wrote as Hartley Howard. British. Born in Montreal, Canada, 20 June 1908. Educated at Rutherglen Academy, Lanarkshire, to age 13. Married Cecilia Jacobson in 1932; two sons and one daughter. Journalist in Glasgow, Leeds, and Manchester, and worked as an efficiency engineer and in a mail order firm before 1939. *Died in April 1979.*

CRIME PUBLICATIONS

Novels (series: John Piper; Quinn)

Death Leaves a Diary (Piper; Quinn). London, Collins, 1952.
The Vanishing Track (Piper). London, Collins, 1952.
Deadly Night-Cap (Piper; Quinn). London, Collins, 1953.
School for Murder (Piper). London, Collins, 1953.
Death Counts Three (Piper). London, Collins, 1954; as *The Screaming Rabbit*, New York, Simon and Schuster, 1955.
Why Kill Johnny? (Piper; Quinn). London, Collins, 1954.
Noose for a Lady (Piper; Quinn). London, Collins, 1955.
Money for Murder (Piper; Quinn). London, Collins, 1955.
Justice Enough (Piper; Quinn). London, Collins, 1956.
The Dead of the Night (Piper; Quinn). London, Collins, 1956.
Emergency Exit (Piper). London, Collins, 1957.
Put Out That Star (Piper; Quinn). London, Collins, 1957; as *Into Thin Air*, New York, Doubleday, 1958.
A Question of Time. London, Collins, 1958.
James Knowland, Deceased (Piper; Quinn). London, Collins, 1958.
. . . Or Be He Dead (Piper; Quinn). New York, Doubleday, 1958; London, Collins, 1959.
Stranglehold (Piper; Quinn). London, Collins, 1959; as *Marked Man*, New York, Doubleday, 1959.
The Seeds of Hate (Piper; Quinn). London, Collins, 1959.
Requiem for Charles (Piper; Quinn). London, Collins, 1960; as *The Late Unlamented*, New York, Doubleday, 1961.
Alibi (Piper; Quinn). London, Collins, 1961; New York, Macmillan, 1962.
Confession. London, Collins, 1961.
The Link (Piper; Quinn). London, Collins, 1962.
Of Unsound Mind (Piper; Quinn). London, Collins, and New York, Doubleday, 1962.
Vendetta (Piper; Quinn). London, Collins, and New York, Macmillan, 1963.
Flashback (Piper; Quinn). London, Collins, 1964.

Safe Secret (Piper; Quinn). London, Collins, 1964; New York, Macmillan, 1965.
Post Mortem (Piper; Quinn). London, Collins, 1965; New York, Doubleday, 1966.
Suicide Clause (Piper; Quinn). London, Collins, 1966.
Murder by Proxy (Piper; Quinn). London, Collins, 1967.
The Condemned. London, Collins, 1967.
A Slightly Bitter Taste (Quinn). London, Collins, 1968.
Remote Control (Piper; Quinn). London, Collins, 1970; New York, McCall, 1971.
Death Trap (Piper; Quinn). London, Collins, 1970; New York, McCall, 1971.
Most Deadly Hate (Piper; Quinn). London, Collins, 1971; New York, Saturday Review Press, 1974.
The Quiet Woman (Piper; Quinn). London, Collins, 1971; New York, Saturday Review Press, 1972.
Naked to the Grave (Piper; Quinn). London, Collins, 1972; New York, Saturday Review Press, 1973.
Too Late for Tears (Piper; Quinn). London, Collins, 1973; New York, Saturday Review Press, 1975.
Candles for the Dead (Piper; Quinn). London, Collins, 1973; New York, Saturday Review Press, 1976.
The Motive (Piper; Quinn). London, Collins, 1974; New York, Dutton, 1977.
False Evidence (Piper; Quinn). London, Collins, 1976; New York, Dutton, 1977.
A Grave for Two (Piper; Quinn). London, Collins, 1977.
Life Cycle (Piper; Quinn). London, Collins, 1978.

Novels as Hartley Howard (series: Glenn Bowman; Philip Scott)

The Last Appointment (Bowman). London, Collins, 1951.
The Last Deception (Bowman). London, Collins, 1951.
The Last Vanity (Bowman). London, Collins, 1952.
Death of Cecilia (Bowman). London, Collins, 1952.
The Other Side of the Door (Bowman). London, Collins, 1953.
Bowman Strikes Again. London, Collins, 1953.
Bowman on Broadway. London, Collins, 1954.
Bowman at a Venture. London, Collins, 1954.
Sleep for the Wicked (Bowman). London, Collins, 1955.
No Target for Bowman. London, Collins, 1955.
The Bowman Touch. London, Collins, 1956.
A Hearse for Cinderella (Bowman). London, Collins, 1956.
The Long Night (Bowman). London, Collins, 1957.
Key to the Morgue (Bowman). London, Collins, 1957.
The Big Snatch (Bowman). London, Collins, 1958.
Sleep, My Pretty One (Bowman). London, Collins, 1958.
Deadline (Bowman). London, Collins, 1959.
The Armitage Secret (Bowman). London, Collins, 1959.
Fall Guy (Bowman). London, Collins, 1960.
Extortion (Bowman). London, Collins, 1960.
Time Bomb (Bowman). London, Collins, 1961.
I'm No Hero (Bowman). London, Collins, 1961.
Count Down (Bowman). London, Collins, 1962.
Double Finesse. London, Collins, 1962.
The Stretton Case. London, Collins, 1963.
Department K (Scott). London, Collins, 1964; as *Assignment K*, New York, Pyramid, 1968.
Out of the Fire. London, Collins, 1965.
Portrait of a Beautiful Harlot (Bowman). London, Collins, 1966.
Counterfeit. London, Collins, 1966.
Routine Investigation (Bowman). London, Collins, 1967.
The Eye of the Hurricane (Scott). London, Collins, 1968.
The Secret of Simon Cornell (Bowman). London, Collins, 1969.

Cry on My Shoulder (Bowman). London, Collins, 1970.
Room 37 (Bowman). London, Collins, 1970.
Million Dollar Snapshot (Bowman). London, Collins, 1971.
Murder One (Bowman). London, Collins, 1971.
Epitaph for Joanna (Bowman). London, Collins, 1972.
Nice Day for a Funeral (Bowman). London, Collins, 1972.
Highway to Murder (Bowman). London, Collins, 1973.
Dead Drunk (Bowman). London, Collins, 1974.
Treble Cross (Bowman). London, Collins, 1975.
Payoff (Bowman). London, Collins, 1976.
One-Way Ticket (Bowman). London, Collins, 1978.
The Sealed Envelope (Bowman). London, Collins, 1979.

*

Harry Carmichael commented (1979):

It is difficult for me to make any valid statement on my own work. I am a slave to accuracy of detail, prefer the classic type of detective fiction to the cops-and-robbers type, and labour hard in the interests of originality. Because I have written so many novels, my main problem nowadays is to avoid self-plagiarization.

* * *

Although he steadily produced mysteries for over 25 years, Harry Carmichael wrote his best work in his last decade. He uses all the tricks of deception and misdirection to produce highly British, traditional works in a modern setting. Insurance assessor John Piper and crime reporter Quinn are his series detectives. Once they are introduced into a story virtually everything is seen from their viewpoint, sometimes resulting in a stiff, dry narrative of events.

In the late 1950's and 1960's Carmichael concentrated on building the characters and personalities of Piper and Quinn. Quinn has never been a particularly likeable person. He's brash, obnoxious, drinks too much, always has a flippant reply. His clothes need pressing, his hair is uncombed. He started as a general reporter for the *Morning Post*, and eventually earned a daily spot with "Quinn's Column on Crime." By the 1970's his unpleasantness had been toned down—he drinks less and is more responsible—and he became the primary detective, calling on Piper for consultation. In contrast, Piper is always neat, polite, quiet: a perfect gentleman. Quinn's inferiority complex is sharpened by Piper's assurance and outward infallibility. But Piper has his own problems—the death of his wife, and his consequent guilt—in the earlier books. Finally, in *Death Trap*, he remarried and settled down to a normal life.

Piper and Quinn's relationship is very close; they understand and tolerate each other in a perfect stereotype of masculine comradeship and solidarity. That relationship plays a strong part in their work as investigators. They work individually, then meet to discuss their findings and continually rehash and rearrange the pieces of the puzzle. They both act more as agitators and catalysts than as detectives. They question and prod endlessly, often unwilling to accept a police solution of accident or suicide. The killer frequently gives himself away while trying to avoid their questions and traps. On the cases that they do work together, they usually arrive at the solution at the same time, but by different routes, Quinn by physical aggression, Piper by psychological cornering.

Carmichael's plots present a consistently pessimistic view of married life. What appears to be a proper, content, happy life is a mask for greed, infidelity, jealousy, and duplicity. *Put Out That Star, Candles for the Dead, False Evidence, Most Deadly Hate, The Quiet Woman,* and others follow this pattern. One spouse is plotting an escape from an intolerable situation. A secondary motive of monetary gain is often involved. Just as often there is a complication: the spouse's new lover is planning his own double-cross, the unwanted spouse learns of the scheme, or an outside force throws the plan off track. A life of sordid cheapness, selfishness, and vindictiveness underlies the placid London suburbs.

Based on ratiocination rather than adventure, Carmichael's books are a holdover from the late Golden Age. There are no bizarre or impossible crimes, but an elaborate scheme and series of events build up to a puzzle story that will, more often than not, deceive the reader.

—Fred Dueren

CARNAC, Carol. Pseudonym for Edith Caroline Rivett; also wrote as E.C.R. Lorac. British. Born in Hendon, London, in 1894. Educated at South Hampstead High School; Central School of Arts and Crafts, London. Member of the Detection Club. *Died 2 July 1958.*

CRIME PUBLICATIONS

Novels (series: Chief Inspector Julian Rivers; Inspector Ryvet)

Triple Death (Ryvet). London, Butterworth, 1936.
The Missing Rope (Ryvet). London, Skeffington, 1937.
Murder at Mornington (Ryvet). London, Skeffington, 1937.
When the Devil Was Sick (Ryvet). London, Davies, 1939.
The Case of the First-Class Carriage (Ryvet). London, Davies, 1939.
Death in the Diving-Pool (Ryvet). London, Davies, 1940.
A Double for Detection (Rivers). London, Macdonald, 1945.
The Striped Suitcase (Rivers). London, Macdonald, 1946; New York, Doubleday, 1947.
Clue Sinister (Rivers). London, Macdonald, 1947.
Over the Garden Wall (Rivers). London, Macdonald, 1948; New York, Doubleday, 1949.
Upstairs, Downstairs (Rivers). London, Macdonald, 1950; as *Upstairs and Downstairs*, New York, Doubleday, 1950.
Copy for Crime (Rivers). London, Macdonald, 1950; New York, Doubleday, 1951.
It's Her Own Funeral (Rivers). London, Collins, 1951; New York, Doubleday, 1952.
Crossed Skies (Rivers). London, Collins, 1952.
Murder as a Fine Art (Rivers). London, Collins, 1953.
A Policeman at the Door (Rivers). London, Collins, 1953; New York, Doubleday, 1954.
Impact of Evidence (Rivers). London, Collins, and New York, Doubleday, 1954.
Murder among Members (Rivers). London, Collins, 1955.
Rigging the Evidence (Rivers). London, Collins, 1955.
The Double Turn (Rivers). London, Collins, 1956; as *The Late Miss Trimming*, New York, Doubleday, 1957.
The Burning Question. London, Collins, 1957.
Long Shadows (Rivers). London, Collins, 1958; as *Affair at Helen's Court*, New York, Doubleday, 1958.
Death of a Lady Killer. London, Collins, 1959.

Novels as E. C. R. Lorac (series: Inspector/Superintendent MacDonald)

The Murder on the Burrows (MacDonald). London, Sampson Low, 1931; New York, Macaulay, 1932.

The Affair at Thor's Head (MacDonald). London, Sampson Low, 1932.
The Greenwell Mystery (MacDonald). London, Sampson Low, 1932; New York, Macaulay, 1934.
Death on the Oxford Road (MacDonald). London, Sampson Low, 1933.
The Case of Colonel Marchand (MacDonald). London, Sampson Low, and New York, Macaulay, 1933.
Murder in St. John's Wood (MacDonald). London, Sampson Low, and New York, Macaulay, 1934.
Murder in Chelsea (MacDonald). London, Sampson Low, 1934; New York, Macaulay, 1935.
The Organ Speaks (MacDonald). London, Sampson Low, 1935.
Death of an Author. London, Sampson Low, 1935; New York, Macaulay, 1937.
Crime Counter Crime (MacDonald). London, Collins, 1936.
A Pall for a Painter (MacDonald). London, Collins, 1936.
Post after Post-Mortem (MacDonald). London, Collins, 1936.
These Names Make Clues (MacDonald). London, Collins, 1937.
Bats in the Belfry (MacDonald). London, Collins, and New York, Macaulay, 1937.
The Devil and the C.I.D. (MacDonald). London, Collins, 1938.
Slippery Staircase (MacDonald). London, Collins, 1938.
Black Beadle (MacDonald). London, Collins, 1939.
John Brown's Body (MacDonald). London, Collins, 1939.
Tryst for a Tragedy (MacDonald). London, Collins, 1940.
Death at Dyke's Corner (MacDonald). London, Collins, 1940.
Case in the Clinic (MacDonald). London, Collins, 1941.
Rope's End, Rogue's End (MacDonald). London, Collins, 1942.
The Sixteenth Stair (MacDonald). London, Collins, 1942.
Death Came Softly. London, Collins, and New York, Arcadia House, 1943.
Fell Murder (MacDonald). London, Collins, 1944.
Checkmate to Murder (MacDonald). London, Collins, and New York, Arcadia House, 1944.
Murder by Matchlight (MacDonald). London, Collins, 1945; New York, Arcadia House, 1946.
Fire in the Thatch (MacDonald). London, Collins, and New York, Arcadia House, 1946.
The Theft of the Iron Dogs (MacDonald). London, Collins, 1946; as *Murderer's Mistake*, New York, Curl, 1947.
Relative to Poison (MacDonald). London, Collins, 1947; New York, Doubleday, 1948.
Death Before Dinner (MacDonald). London, Collins, 1948; as *A Screen for Murder*, New York, Doubleday, 1948.
Part for a Poisoner (MacDonald). London, Collins, 1948; as *Place for a Poisoner*, New York, Doubleday, 1949.
Still Waters (MacDonald). London, Collins, 1949.
Policeman in the Precinct (MacDonald). London, Collins, 1949; as *And Then Put Out the Light*, New York, Doubleday, 1950.
Accident by Design (MacDonald). London, Collins, 1950; New York, Doubleday, 1951.
Murder of a Martinet (MacDonald). London, Collins, 1951; as *I Could Murder Her*, New York, Doubleday, 1951.
The Dog It Was That Died (MacDonald). London, Collins, and New York, Doubleday, 1952.
Murder in the Mill-Race (MacDonald). London, Collins, 1952; as *Speak Justly of the Dead*, New York, Doubleday, 1953.
Crook o'Lune (MacDonald). London, Collins, 1953; as *Shepherd's Crook*, New York, Doubleday, 1953.
Let Well Alone (MacDonald). London, Collins, 1954.

Shroud of Darkness (MacDonald). London, Collins, and New York, Doubleday, 1954.
Ask a Policeman (MacDonald). London, Collins, 1955.
Murder in Vienna (MacDonald). London, Collins, 1956.
Dangerous Domicile (MacDonald). London, Collins, 1957.
Picture of Death (MacDonald). London, Collins, 1957.
Murder on a Monument (MacDonald). London, Collins, 1958.
Death in Triplicate (MacDonald). London, Collins, 1958; as *People Will Talk*, New York, Doubleday, 1958.
Dishonour among Thieves (MacDonald). London, Collins, 1959; as *The Last Escape*, New York, Doubleday, 1959.
No Flowers by Request, and Crime on the Coast, with others. London, Gollancz, 1984.

Uncollected Short Stories as E.C.R. Lorac

"The Live Wire," in *Detection Medley*. London, Hutchinson, 1939.
"Remember to Ring Twice," in *The Evening Standard* (London), 7 June 1950.
"Chance Is a Great Thing," in *The Evening Standard* (London), 8 August, 1950.
"Death at the Bridge Table," in *The Evening Standard* (London), 11 October 1950; as "A Bit of Wire-Pulling," in *The Evening Standard Detective Book*, 2nd series. London, Gollancz, 1951.
"Permanent Policeman," in *The Evening Standard* (London), 18 June 1951.

OTHER PUBLICATIONS

Novels as Carol Rivett

Outer Circle. London, Hodder and Stoughton, 1939.
Time Remembered. London, Hodder and Stoughton, 1940.

* * *

Edith Caroline Rivett published more than 70 books under the pseudonyms of Carol Carnac and E. C. R. Lorac.

The Murder on the Burrows, published under the Lorac pseudonym, was her first novel, and introduced Inspector MacDonald, a "London Scot" whose father was a newspaper man. After serving with the first battalion of the London Scottish from 1914 to 1919, MacDonald joined the Metropolitan Police. A bachelor, he lived with an old batman. Although MacDonald appears in many Lorac novels, there is little physical description of him. It can be gleaned from a careful reading that he is physically active, lean, tall, with a penchant for walking the English countryside though a most expert driver when the occasion demands one. His assistant, Reeves, is a bit more colorful, dark, married, easy-going, less dignified, able to disguise himself as one of the "common" folk, and a very able detective. The pair make a formidable team capable of unscrambling even the most twisted circumstances and finding the most well hidden motives.

Inspector Julian Rivers, in the Carnac series, is remarkably like Inspector MacDonald, although more meditative and less inclined to romping through the bush. He leaves that task to his lively assistant, Inspector Lancing, who was a student of "home accidents" which were of the "you never can tell" category. Rivers is from a genteel family; he is an art connoisseur and a romantic. Lancing, a commoner by birth, energetic and enthusiastic, is a perfect complement to Rivers. Other novels written under the Carnac pseudonym which do not feature Inspector Rivers are less interesting with little detection and more obscure plotting.

The author's chief weakness lies in the lack of description given to her characters. They emerge virtually faceless and consequently are quite easily forgotten. In contrast, surprisingly vivid descriptions are always given to the villains, who are promptly murdered off. Usually, the first person murdered in the novels is an embodiment of evil, a hypocritical religious fanatic in several instances, such as *The Double Turn, Murder in the Mill-Race*, or *Policeman in the Precinct*. Subsequent murders of innocent people are only necessitated to cover up the first crime. Another frequent plot device is to take a supposedly accidental death and have MacDonald, or Inspector Rivers, with the aid of their respective assistants, deduce through a complex system of circumstances and plot twists that the death was actually due to murder. Although the manner in which the CID becomes involved in these "accidental deaths" seems a trifle farfetched at times, the plotting and detection which subsequently follow are consistently well done.

—Mary Ann Grochowski

———

CARR, Glyn. Pseudonym for Frank Showell Styles. British. Born in Four Oaks, Warwickshire, 14 March 1908. Educated at Bishop Vesey's Grammar School, Sutton Coldfield. Served in the Royal Navy, 1939–46: Commander. Married Kathleen Jane Humphreys in 1954; two daughters and one son. Clerk, 1924–34; tramp, 1934–37; freelance journalist, 1937–39; led expeditions to the Arctic, 1952 and 1953, and to the Himalayas, 1954. Since 1946 full-time writer. Fellow, Royal Geographical Society. Agent: Curtis Brown Ltd., 162–168 Regent Street, London W1R 5TA, England. Address: Trwyn Cae Iago, Borthy-Gest, Porthmadog, Gwynedd LL49 9TW, Wales.

CRIME PUBLICATIONS

Novels (series: Sir Abercrombie Lewker in all books)

Death on Milestone Buttress. London, Bles, 1951.
Murder on the Matterhorn. London, Bles, 1951; New York, Dutton, 1953.
The Youth Hostel Murders. London, Bles, 1952; New York, Dutton, 1953.
The Corpse in the Crevasse. London, Bles, 1952.
Death under Snowdon. London, Bles, 1952.
A Corpse at Camp Two. London, Bles, 1954.
Murder of an Owl. London, Bles, 1956.
The Ice Axe Murders. London, Bles, 1958.
Swing Away, Climber. London, Bles, and New York, Washburn, 1959.
Holiday with Murder. London, Bles, 1960.
Death Finds a Foothold. London, Bles, 1961; New York, Garland, 1983.
Lewker in Norway. London, Bles, 1963.
Death of a Weirdy. London, Bles, 1965.
Lewker in Tirol. London, Bles, 1967.
Fat Man's Agony. London, Bles, 1969.

Novels as Showell Styles (series: Sir Abercrombie Lewker)

Traitor's Mountain (Lewker). London, Selwyn and Blount, 1945; New York, Macmillan, 1946.
Kidnap Castle. London, Selwyn and Blount, 1947.
Hammer Island (Lewker). London, Selwyn and Blount, 1947.

Dark Hazard. London, Selwyn and Blount, 1948.
The Rising of the Lark. London, Selwyn and Blount, 1948.

OTHER PUBLICATIONS as Showell Styles

Novels

Sir Devil. London, Selwyn and Blount, 1949.
Path to Glory. London, Faber, 1951.
Land from the Sea. London, Faber, 1952.
Mr. Nelson's Ladies. London, Faber, 1953.
The Frigate Captain. London, Faber, 1954; New York, Vanguard Press, 1956; as *The Sea Lord*, New York, Ballantine, n.d.
His Was the Fire. London, Faber, 1956.
Tiger Patrol. London, Collins, 1957.
The Admiral's Fancy. London, Faber, 1958.
Tiger Patrol Wins Through. London, Collins, 1958.
The Tiger Patrol at Sea. London, Collins, 1959.
Wolfe Commands You. London, Faber, 1959.
Shadow Buttress. London, Faber, 1959.
The Flying Ensign. London, Faber, 1960; as *Greencoats Against Napoleon*, New York, Vanguard Press, 1960.
The Sea Officer. London, Faber, 1961; New York, Macmillan, 1962.
Tiger Patrol Presses On. London, Collins, 1961.
Gentleman Johnny. London, Faber, 1962.
Byrd of the 95th. London, Faber, 1962; as *Thunder over Spain*, New York, Vanguard Press, 1962.
H.M.S. Diamond Rock. London, Faber, 1963.
A Necklace of Glaciers. London, Gollancz, 1963.
Number Two-Ninety. London, Faber, 1966; as *Confederate Raider*, New York, Washburn, 1967.
A Tent on Top. London, Gollancz, 1971.
"Vincey Joe" at Quiberon. London, Faber, 1971.
Admiral of England. London, Faber, 1973.
A Sword for Mr. Fitton. London, Faber, 1975.
Mr. Fitton's Commission. London, Faber, 1977.
The Baltic Convoy. London, Faber, 1979.
A Kiss for Captain Hardy. London, Faber, 1979.
Centurion Comes Home. London, Faber, 1980.
The Quarterdeck Ladder. London, Kimber, 1982.
Seven-Gun Broadside. London, Kimber, 1982.
The Malta Frigate. London, Kimber, 1983; New York, Walker, 1986.
Mutiny in the Caribbean. London, Kimber, 1984.
Stella and the Fireships. London, Kimber, 1985.
The Lee Shore. London, Kimber, 1986.
Gun-Brig Captain. London, Kimber, 1987.
H.M.S. Cracker. London, Kimber, 1988.

Plays

Two Longer Plays for Juniors (Prince George's Dragon and *May Eve).* London, Blackie, 1938.

Radio Play: *The Shop in the Mountain*, from his own novel, 1966.

Other

Walks and Climbs in Malta. Valetta, Progressive Press, 1944.
A Climber in Wales. Birmingham, Cornish Brothers, 1949.
The Mountaineer's Week-End Book. London, Seeley Service, 1951.
Mountains of the Midnight Sun. London, Hurst and Blackett, 1954.

Introduction to Mountaineering. London, Seeley Service, 1955.
The Moated Mountain. London, Hurst and Blackett, 1955.
The Lost Glacier (for children). London, Hart Davis, 1955; New York, Vanguard Press, 1956.
Kami the Sherpa (for children). Leicester, Brockhampton Press, 1957; as *Sherpa Adventure*, New York, Vanguard Press, 1960.
Midshipman Quinn (for children). London, Faber, and New York, Vanguard Press, 1957.
The Camper's and Tramper's Weekend Book. London, Seeley Service, 1957.
How Mountains Are Climbed. London, Routledge, 1958.
Introduction to Caravanning. London, Seeley Service, 1958.
How Underground Britain Is Explored. London, Routledge, 1958.
Getting to Know Mountains, edited by Jack Cox. London, Newnes, 1958.
Quinn of the "Fury" (for children). London, Faber, 1958; New York, Vanguard Press, 1961.
The Battle of Cotton (for children). London, Constable, 1959.
The Battle of Steam (for children). London, Constable, 1960.
The Lost Pothole (for children). Leicester, Brockhampton Press, 1961.
The Shop in the Mountain (for children). London, Gollancz, and New York, Vanguard Press, 1961.
Midshipman Quinn Wins Through (for children). London, Faber, 1961; as *Midshipman Quinn and Denise the Spy*, New York, Vanguard Press, 1961.
The Ladder of Snow (for children). London, Gollancz, 1962.
Look at Mountains. London, Hamish Hamilton, 1962.
Greenhorn's Cruise (for children). Leicester, Brockhampton Press, and Princeton, New Jersey, Van Nostrand, 1964.
The Camp in the Hills (for children). London, Benn, 1964.
Modern Mountaineering. London, Faber, 1964.
Blue Remembered Hills. London, Faber, 1965.
Quinn at Trafalgar (for children). London, Faber, and New York, Vanguard Press, 1965.
Red for Adventure (for children). Leicester, Brockhampton Press, 1965.
Mr. Fiddle (for children). London, Hamish Hamilton, 1965.
The Foundations of Climbing. London, Stanley Paul, 1966; as *The Arrow Book of Climbing*, London, Arrow, 1967.
Wolf Club Island (for children). Leicester, Brockhampton Press, 1966.
The Pass of Morning (for children). London, Gollancz, and New York, Washburn, 1966.
Mr. Fiddle's Pig (for children). London, Hamish Hamilton, 1966.
Mallory of Everest. London, Hamish Hamilton, and New York, Macmillan, 1967.
The Sea Cub (for children). Leicester, Brockhampton Press, 1967.
On Top of the World: An Illustrated History of Mountaineering and Mountaineers. London, Hamish Hamilton, and New York, Macmillan, 1967.
Mr. Fiddle's Band (for children). London, Hamish Hamilton, 1967.
Rock and Rope. London, Faber, 1967.
Indestructible Jones (for children). London, Faber, 1967; New York, Washburn, 1969.
The Climber's Bedside Book. London, Faber, 1968.
Sea Road to Camperdown (for children). London, Faber, 1968.
Journey with a Secret (for children). London, Gollancz, 1968; New York, Meredith Press, 1969.
A Case for Mr. Fiddle (for children). London, Hamish Hamilton, 1969.
Jones's Private Navy (for children). London, Faber, 1969.

First Up Everest.   London, Hamish Hamilton, and New York, Coward McCann, 1969.

First on the Summits.   London, Gollancz, 1970.

The Forbidden Frontiers: A Survey of India from 1765 to 1949.   London, Hamish Hamilton, 1970.

Welsh Walks and Legends.   Cardiff, John Jones, 2 vols., 1972–77; revised edition, London, Mayflower, 1979; Chicago, Academy, 1982.

Snowdon Range.   Reading, Berkshire, Gaston's Alpine Books, 1973.

The Mountains of North Wales.   London, Gollancz, 1973.

Glyder Range.   Reading, Berkshire, Gaston's Alpine Books, 1974.

Backpacking: A Comprehensive Guide.   London, Macmillan, 1976; New York, McKay, 1977.

Backpacking in Alps and Pyrenees.   London, Gollancz, 1976.

Backpacking in Wales.   London, Hale, 1977.

Snowdonia National Park.   Exeter, Devon, Webb and Bower, 1987.

Editor, *Men and Mountaineering: An Anthology of Writings by Climbers.*   London, Hamish Hamilton, and New York, David White, 1968.

Translator, *White Fury*, by Raymond Lambert and Claude Kogan.   London, Hurst and Blackett, 1956.

*

Glyn Carr comments:

My pompous actor-manager detective Sir Abercrombie Lewker stumped and boomed his way through 15 novels almost by accident. By predilection I am a writer of historical novels and children's books, but my lifelong recreation has been mountaineering and rock-climbing. One day on a particular "pitch" of the classic rock-climb called Milestone Buttress, it struck me how easy it would be to arrange an undetectable murder in that place, and by way of experiment I worked out the system and wove a thinnish plot round it. Bles published the book and wanted more of the same sort. So a further 14 novels under the pseudonym Glyn Carr were written and published—until, ways of slaughtering people on steep rock-faces being limited, they had to stop.

I enjoy the whodunits of other writers (particularly those of Michael Innes, Margery Allingham, and William Haggard), but I have not myself the whodunit mind. I believe the people who read my Glyn Carr books are people who themselves know the mountains and climbs I described—always with assiduous care for topography and mountain atmosphere—and enjoy a fictional, perhaps exciting, return to their old haunts.

*   *   *

Glyn Carr is the pseudonym of Frank Showell Styles, a noted explorer and author of many works on the subject of mountaineering. Many of Carr's detective novels are set in exotic locales such as the Nepal Himalayas (*A Corpse at Camp Two*), Innsbruck (*The Corpse in the Crevasse*), Wales (*Death under Snowdon, Murder of an Owl, Death of a Weirdy, Swing Away, Climber*), and Majorca (*Holiday with Murder*); *Lewker in Tirol, Lewker in Norway*, and *Murder on the Matterhorn* speak for themselves. Many also feature mountaineering as an integral part of their plot and puzzle. This is especially true of *A Corpse at Camp Two, Murder of an Owl*, and *Swing Away, Climber*.

Carr's series detective, Sir Abercrombie Lewker (nicknamed "filthy"), is a famous actor-manager and interpreter of Shakespeare. He is bald and squat, with heavy jowls and a pouchy face. A pompous, perhaps unattractive person, his most impressive feature is his voice which booms constantly—often with a Shakespearean quotation. He seems the least likely person to have climbed Chomolu, a 24,000 foot peak in the Himalayas, when he was over 50 years of age. Lewker has been a passionate mountain climber for many years, and his flair for detection may have been acquired as the result of his training in the Special Commando Branch of Intelligence during World War II. Obviously, Lewker's interest and ability make him the right man to solve crime problems set in mountainous regions.

Carr's narratives are well-written and characterized. His puzzles usually involve maps, timetables, and "perfect" alibis in the demanding tradition of Freeman Wills Crofts. Clues may be found among rocks, cliffs, precipices, and crevasses. Mountaineering equipment such as nailed boots, pitons, climbing ropes, and snaplinks must also be carefully scrutinized.

In *Murder of an Owl*, Lewker sums up a murderer he had encountered in *Death on Milestone Buttress* by stating, "He even had the effrontery to use the hills themselves as the means and mechanism of murder." This statement might also be applicable to Carr himself.

—Charles Shibuk

———

CARR, John Dickson. Also wrote as Carr Dickson; Carter Dickson; Roger Fairbairn.   American.   Born in Uniontown, Pennsylvania, 30 November 1906. Educated at the Hill School; Haverford College, Pennsylvania, 1928; studied abroad. Married Clarice Cleaves in 1931; three daughters. Lived in England, 1932–48; wrote for the BBC during World War II. Reviewer, *Ellery Queen's Mystery Magazine*, 1969–77. President, Mystery Writers of America, 1949. Recipient: *Ellery Queen's Mystery Magazine* award (twice); Mystery Writers of America Edgar Allan Poe award, 1949, 1969, and Grand Master award, 1962. *Died 27 February 1977.*

CRIME PUBLICATIONS

Novels (series: Henri Bencolin; Patrick Butler; Dr. Gideon Fell)

It Walks by Night (Bencolin).   New York, Harper, 1930; London, Hamish Hamilton, 1976.

Castle Skull (Bencolin).   New York, Harper, 1931; London, Severn House, 1976.

The Lost Gallows (Bencolin).   New York, Harper, 1931; London, Severn House, 1976.

Poison in Jest.   New York, Harper, and London, Hamish Hamilton, 1932.

The Corpse in the Waxworks (Bencolin).   New York, Harper, 1932; as *The Waxworks Murder*, London, Hamish Hamilton, 1932.

Hag's Nook (Fell).   New York, Harper, and London, Hamish Hamilton, 1933.

The Mad Hatter Mystery (Fell).   New York, Harper, and London, Hamish Hamilton, 1933.

The Blind Barber (Fell).   New York, Harper, and London, Hamish Hamilton, 1934.

The Eight of Swords (Fell).   New York, Harper, and London, Hamish Hamilton, 1934.

Devil Kinsmere (as Roger Fairbairn). New York, Harper, and London, Hamish Hamilton, 1934; revised edition, as *Most Secret*, 1964.

Death-Watch (Fell). New York, Harper, and London, Hamish Hamilton, 1935.

The Three Coffins (Fell). New York, Harper, 1935; as *The Hollow Man*, London, Hamish Hamilton, 1935.

The Arabian Nights Murder (Fell). New York, Harper, and London, Hamish Hamilton, 1936.

The Burning Court. New York, Harper, and London, Hamish Hamilton, 1937.

The Four False Weapons, Being the Return of Bencolin. New York, Harper, 1937; London, Hamish Hamilton, 1938.

To Wake the Dead (Fell). London, Hamish Hamilton, 1937; New York, Harper, 1938.

The Crooked Hinge (Fell). New York, Harper, and London, Hamish Hamilton, 1938.

The Problem of the Green Capsule (Fell). New York, Harper, 1939; as *The Black Spectacles*, London, Hamish Hamilton, 1939.

The Problem of the Wire Cage (Fell). New York, Harper, 1939; London, Hamish Hamilton, 1940.

The Man Who Could Not Shudder (Fell). New York, Harper, and London, Hamish Hamilton, 1940.

The Case of the Constant Suicides (Fell). New York, Harper, and London, Hamish Hamilton, 1941.

Death Turns the Tables (Fell). New York, Harper, 1941; as *The Seat of the Scornful*, London, Hamish Hamilton, 1942.

The Emperor's Snuffbox. New York, Harper, 1942; London, Hamish Hamilton, 1943.

Till Death Do Us Part (Fell). New York, Harper, and London, Hamish Hamilton, 1944.

He Who Whispers (Fell). New York, Harper, and London, Hamish Hamilton, 1946.

The Sleeping Sphinx (Fell). New York, Harper, and London, Hamish Hamilton, 1947.

The Dead Man's Knock (Fell). New York, Harper, and London, Hamish Hamilton, 1948.

Below Suspicion (Fell, Butler). New York, Harper, 1949; London, Hamish Hamilton, 1950.

The Bride of Newgate. New York, Harper, and London, Hamish Hamilton, 1950.

The Devil in Velvet. New York, Harper, and London, Hamish Hamilton, 1951.

The Nine Wrong Answers. New York, Harper, and London, Hamish Hamilton, 1952.

Captain Cut-Throat. New York, Harper, and London, Hamish Hamilton, 1955.

Patrick Butler for the Defense. New York, Harper, and London, Hamish Hamilton, 1956.

Fire, Burn! New York, Harper, and London, Hamish Hamilton, 1957.

Scandal at High Chimneys: A Victorian Melodrama. New York, Harper, and London, Hamish Hamilton, 1959.

In Spite of Thunder (Fell). New York, Harper, and London, Hamish Hamilton, 1960.

The Witch of the Lowtide: An Edwardian Melodrama. New York, Harper, and London, Hamish Hamilton, 1961.

The Demoniacs. New York, Harper, and London, Hamish Hamilton, 1962.

The House at Satan's Elbow (Fell). New York, Harper, and London, Hamish Hamilton, 1965.

Panic in Box C (Fell). New York, Harper, and London, Hamish Hamilton, 1966.

Dark of the Moon (Fell). New York, Harper, 1967; London, Hamish Hamilton, 1968.

Papa La-Bas. New York, Harper, 1968; London, Hamish Hamilton, 1969.

The Ghosts' High Noon. New York, Harper, 1969; London, Hamish Hamilton, 1970.

Deadly Hall. New York, Harper, and London, Hamish Hamilton, 1971.

The Hungry Goblin: A Victorian Detective Novel. New York, Harper, and London, Hamish Hamilton, 1972.

No Flowers by Request, and Crime on the Coast, with others. London, Gollancz, 1984.

Novels as Carter Dickson (series: Sir Henry Merrivale)

The Bowstring Murders (as Carr Dickson). New York, Morrow, 1933; London, Heinemann, 1934.

The Plague Court Murders (Merrivale). New York, Morrow, 1934; London, Heinemann, 1935.

The White Priory Murders (Merrivale). New York, Morrow, 1934; London, Heinemann, 1935.

The Red Widow Murders (Merrivale). New York, Morrow, and London, Heinemann, 1935.

The Unicorn Murders (Merrivale). New York, Morrow, 1935; London, Heinemann, 1936.

The Magic Lantern Murders (Merrivale). London, Heinemann, 1936; as *The Punch and Judy Murder*, New York, Morrow, 1937.

The Third Bullet (novelet). London, Hodder and Stoughton, 1937.

The Peacock Feather Murders (Merrivale). New York, Morrow, 1937; as *The Ten Teacups*, London, Heinemann, 1937.

Death in Five Boxes (Merrivale). New York, Morrow, and London, Heinemann, 1938.

The Judas Window (Merrivale). New York, Morrow, and London, Heinemann, 1938; as *The Crossbow Murder*, New York, Berkley, 1964.

Drop to His Death, with John Rhode. London, Heinemann, 1939; as *Fatal Descent*, New York, Dodd Mead, 1939.

The Reader Is Warned (Merrivale). New York, Morrow, and London, Heinemann, 1939.

And So to Murder (Merrivale). New York, Morrow, 1940; London, Heinemann, 1941.

Nine—and Death Makes Ten (Merrivale). New York, Morrow, 1940; as *Murder in the Submarine Zone*, London, Heinemann, 1950; as *Murder in the Atlantic*, Cleveland, World, 1959.

Seeing Is Believing (Merrivale). New York, Morrow, 1941; London, Heinemann, 1942; as *Cross of Murder*, Cleveland, World, 1959.

The Gilded Man (Merrivale). New York, Morrow, and London, Heinemann, 1942; as *Death and the Gilded Man*, New York, Pocket Books, 1947.

She Died a Lady (Merrivale). New York, Morrow, and London, Heinemann, 1943.

He Wouldn't Kill Patience (Merrivale). New York, Morrow, and London, Heinemann, 1944.

The Curse of the Bronze Lamp (Merrivale). New York, Morrow, 1945; as *Lord of the Sorcerers*, London, Heinemann, 1946.

My Late Wives (Merrivale). New York, Morrow, 1946; London, Heinemann, 1947.

The Skeleton in the Clock (Merrivale). New York, Morrow, 1948; London, Heinemann, 1949.

A Graveyard to Let (Merrivale). New York, Morrow, 1949; London, Heinemann, 1950.

Night at the Mocking Widow (Merrivale). New York, Morrow, 1950; London, Heinemann, 1951.

Behind the Crimson Blind (Merrivale). New York, Morrow, and London, Heinemann, 1952.
The Cavalier's Cup (Merrivale). New York, Morrow, 1953; London, Heinemann, 1954.
Fear Is the Same. New York, Morrow, and London, Heinemann, 1956.

Short Stories

The Department of Queer Complaints (as Carter Dickson). New York, Morrow, and London, Heinemann, 1940; reprinted in part as *Scotland Yard: Department of Queer Complaints*, New York, Dell, 1944.
Dr. Fell, Detective, and Other Stories. New York, Spivak, 1947.
The Third Bullet and Other Stories. New York, Harper, and London, Hamish Hamilton, 1954.
The Exploits of Sherlock Holmes, with Adrian Conan Doyle. New York, Random House, and London, Murray, 1954.
The Men Who Explained Miracles. New York, Harper, 1963; London, Hamish Hamilton, 1964.
The Door to Doom and Other Detections, edited by Douglas C. Greene. New York, Harper, 1980; London, Hamish Hamilton, 1981.

Uncollected Short Story

"Detective's Day Off," in *Crime at Christmas*, edited by Jack Adrian. Wellingborough, Northamptonshire, Equation, 1988.

Other Publications

Plays

The Dead Sleep Lightly (radio plays), edited by Douglas G. Greene. New York, Doubleday, 1983.

Radio Plays: *Appointment with Fear* series, 1940's, and *Suspense* series; *The Man Without a Body*, 1943.

Other

The Murder of Sir Edmund Godfrey. New York, Harper, and London, Hamish Hamilton, 1936.
The Life of Sir Arthur Conan Doyle. New York, Harper, and London, Murray, 1949.

Editor, *Maiden Murders.* New York, Harper, 1952.
Editor, *Great Stories*, by Arthur Conan Doyle. London, Murray, and New York, British Book Centre, 1959.

*

Bibliography: "The Books of John Dickson Carr/Carter Dickson" by R.E. Briney, in *The Crooked Hinge*, San Diego, University of California Extension, 1976.

* * *

In John Dickson Carr's first novel, *It Walks by Night*, there is a passage from a play ascribed to one of the characters: "The art of the murderer my dear Maurot, is the same as the art of the magician. And the art of the magician does not lie in any such nonsense as 'the hand is quicker than the eye,' but consists simply in directing your attention to the wrong place. He will cause you to be watching one hand, while with the other hand, unseen though in full view, he produces his effect." This is also

the art of the mystery writer as practiced for more than 40 years by John Dickson Carr. Additional facets of his talent were perfected through the years—the meticulous historical reconstructions; the broad, sometimes farcical humor; the expert deployment of bizarre incident and eerie atmosphere; the occasional touch of outright fantasy—but the fundamental framework was always the same: the ingeniously plotted murder puzzle, set forth with all the illusionist's skill at deception. Carr's particular forte was the "miracle problem" or "impossible crime" with its primary sub-category, the locked-room murder. He compiled a longer list of variations on this theme than any other author, and even included an analytical lecture on the subject in one of his novels (the famous "Locked Room Lecture" in *The Three Coffins*).

50 out of Carr's 70 mystery novels belong to series featuring one of three continuing detective characters. The first of these detectives, introduced in *It Walks by Night*, was the flamboyant Parisian *juge d'instruction*, Henri Bencolin. Bencolin's cases include an impossible murder in a gambling club—the victim, seen to enter an empty room with all entrances under observation, is subsequently found there, beheaded; the stabbing of a young girl in a wax museum; and multiple deaths in a macabre castle on the Rhine. The books do not have the discipline and polish of Carr's best mysteries, and lack the overt humor often present in later work. But all of the author's other hallmarks are present, including his fondness for "bad" women in place of *ingénues*.

Four Bencolin novels and one non-series mystery, *Poison in Jest*, appeared in rapid succession. It became obvious that Carr's output was more than his original publishers were prepared to handle. A second publisher was more than happy to take the overflow, under a new byline. Carr's most durable detective, the bulky and bibulous Dr. Gideon Fell, was introduced in *Hag's Nook*. Modelled in appearance and mannerisms on G.K. Chesterton, whom Carr admired, Dr. Fell appeared in some 23 novels. Among the notable Dr. Fell novels are *The Blind Barber*, and all-stops-out farce about murder on an ocean liner; *The Three Coffins*, which contains two "impossible" murders and the celebrated "Locked Room Lecture"; *The Crooked Hinge*, one of the most audacious mystery puzzles ever written; *The Problem of the Wire Cage*, in which a man is found strangled in the middle of a wet clay tennis court, with only his own footprints leading out to the body; *He Who Whispers*, with its brooding atmosphere and hints of vampires; and *Below Suspicion*, in which murder is mixed with modern Satanism. Dr. Fell's last appearance was in *Dark of the Moon*, in which he unmasked a murderer in Carr's adopted city of Charleston, South Carolina.

A year after the introduction of Dr. Fell, the equally imposing bulk of Sir Henry Merrivale ("H.M.") hove into view in *The Plague Court Murders* under the Carter Dickson byline. More broadly drawn than Gideon Fell, and prone to fits of childishness and ill-temper, H.M. was equally astute at unravelling intricate crimes. Almost all of his cases are "impossible" crimes. *The Peacock Feather Murders* and *The Judas Window* are justly regarded as classics of the locked-room story. In *The Curse of the Bronze Lamp* and *A Graveyard to Let* there are miraculous disappearances to rival any produced by stage illusionists. H.M. is an openly comic figure, but even in the midst of the funny scenes the author keeps the demands of his plot in mind. In one story, H.M.'s majestic progress along the pavement comes to an abrupt halt when he slips on a banana peel. His classic prat-fall is funny in context, but it also serves to distract the reader's attention from a revealing conversation taking place in the foreground. One of the funniest scenes in all of Carr/Dickson's books occurs in the opening pages of *Night at the Mocking Widow* when H.M.'s suitcase on wheels gets away from him and is chased down a village street by a pack of dogs. This is pure slapstick, like something from a Laurel and Hardy comedy; but the climax of the scene provides H.M. with a significant clue to later crimes. H.M. ultimately bows out (at least in book length) in a blaze of comic glory in *The Cavalier's Cup*, which reads like a cross between P.G. Wodehouse and Thorne Smith, but still has a substantial crime puzzle at its core.

A small number of Carr's contemporary detective novels fall outside his established series. Of these, undoubtedly the best is *The Burning Court*. In this astonishing tour de force, the narrator discovers that his wife has the name and the appearance of a notorious poisoner, executed some 75 years previously. What is he to think when new deaths by poison begin to occur?

In 1928, before he turned to detective fiction, Carr had written a historical romance "with lots of Gadzookses and swordplay." The story was never published, and the manuscript was destroyed. But in 1934, while the Fell and H.M. series were just getting off the ground, he published a historical novel called *Devil Kinsmere* under the pseudonym Roger Fairbairn. 30 years later, the book was rewritten and published as *Most Secret* under Carr's own name. Carr published no historical fiction, as such, between 1934 and 1950, although in 1936 he wrote *The Murder of Sir Edmund Godfrey*, a fascinating account of an actual crime from the late seventeenth century. In 1950, Carr produced *The Bride of Newgate*, the first of a series of historical romances that were also detective novels. The second of these, *The Devil in Velvet*, sold better than any of Carr's other novels. Here the historical setting and the murder puzzle were augmented by deal-with-the-Devil and time-travel fantasy themes. Two subsequent historical mysteries, *Fear Is the Same* and *Fire, Burn!*, also involved time-travel, much in the manner of John Balderston's stage drama *Berkeley Square*. Carr's historical novels culminated with *The Hungry Goblin*, a Victorian mystery in which the role of the detective was played by the writer Wilkie Collins.

In addition to his novels, Carr wrote a highly successful *Life of Sir Arthur Conan Doyle*, as well as numerous short stories and radio plays. His short fiction ranged from pulp-magazine melodrama to classic puzzle stories, from the fantasy of "New Murders for Old" to the prize-winning and often reprinted "The Gentleman from Paris." Nine of the short stories featured another series detective, Colonel March of the Department of Queer Complaints. Carr also collaborated with Adrian Conan Doyle, Sir Arthur's youngest son, on six Sherlock Holmes pastiches, *The Exploits of Sherlock Holmes*.

In recent years the researches of Douglas G. Greene have uncovered many early stories published in Carr's college magazine, *The Haverfordian*. These include several stories about Henri Bencolin, including a short version of the first Bencolin novel. In these earliest works, many of Carr's characteristic themes and techniques are already visible. A vigorous reprinting program is bringing most of Carr's works back into print; the first book-length critical study has appeared; and an authorized biography is in progress.

—R.E. Briney

CARR, Philippa. *See* **HOLT, Victoria.**

CARROLL, John D. *See* **DALY, Carroll John.**

CARTER, Felicity. *See* **BONETT, John and Emery.**

CARTER, Nick *See* **AVALLONE, Michael; BALLARD, Willis Todhunter; CHASTAIN, Thomas; COLLINS, Michael; CRIDER, Bill; RANDISI, Robert J.; SMITH, Martin Cruz; WHITE, Lionel.**

CASPARY, Vera. American. Born in Chicago, Illinois, 13 November 1904. Educated in public schools in Chicago. Married the film producer Isadore G. Goldsmith in 1949 (died 1964). Worked as stenographer; copy writer; director of mail order school; editor of *Dance* magazine, 1925–27. Freelance author and screen writer after 1927. Recipient: Screen Writers Guild award, 1950. *Died 13 June 1987*

CRIME PUBLICATIONS

Novels

Laura. Boston, Houghton Mifflin, 1943; London, Eyre and Spottiswoode, 1944.
Bedelia. Boston, Houghton Mifflin, and London, Eyre and Spottiswoode, 1945.
The Murder in the Stork Club. New York, Black, 1946; as *The Lady in Mink*, London, Gordon Martin, 1946.
Stranger Than Truth. New York, Random House, 1946; London, Eyre and Spottiswoode, 1947.
The Weeping and the Laughter. Boston, Little Brown, 1950; as *The Death Wish*, London, Eyre and Spottiswoode, 1951.
Thelma. Boston, Little Brown, 1952; London, W.H. Allen, 1953.
False Face. London, W.H. Allen, 1954.
The Husband. New York, Harper, and London, W.H. Allen, 1957.
Evvie. New York, Harper, and London, W.H. Allen, 1960.
A Chosen Sparrow. New York, Putnam, and London, W.H. Allen, 1964.
The Man Who Loved His Wife. New York, Putnam, and London, W.H. Allen, 1966.
The Rosecrest Cell. New York, Putnam, 1967; London, W.H. Allen, 1968.
Final Portrait. London, W.H. Allen, 1971.
Ruth. New York, Pocket Books, 1972.
Elizabeth X. London, W.H. Allen, 1978; as *The Secret of Elizabeth*, New York, Pocket Books, 1979.

Uncollected Short Story

"Sugar and Spice," in *Ellery Queen's Mystery Magazine* (New York), October 1948.

OTHER PUBLICATIONS

Novels

The White Girl.   New York, Sears, 1929.
Ladies and Gents.   New York, Century, 1929.
Music in the Street.   New York, Sears, 1930.
Thicker Than Water.   New York, Liveright, 1932.
The Dreamers.   New York, Pocket Books, 1975.

Plays

Blind Mice, with Winifred Lenihan (produced New York, 1930).
Geraniums in My Window, with Samuel Ornitz (produced New York, 1934).
Laura, with George Sklar, adaptation of the novel by Caspary (produced London, 1945; New York, 1947). New York, Dramatists Play Service, 1945; London, English Theatre Guild, 1952.
Wedding in Paris, music by Hans May, lyrics by Sonny Miller (produced London, 1954).   New York, French, 1956.

Screenplays: *I'll Love You Always*, 1935; *Easy Living*, with Preston Sturges, 1937; *Scandal Street*, with Bertram Millhauser and Eddie Welch, 1938; *Service Deluxe*, with others, 1938; *Sing, Dance, Plenty Hot*, with others, 1940; *Lady from Louisiana*, with others, 1941; *Lady Bodyguard*, with Edmund L. Hartmann and Art Arthur, 1942; *Claudia and David*, with Rose Franken and William Brown Meloney, 1946; *Bedelia*, with others, 1946; *Out of the Blue*, with Walter Bullock and Edward Eliscu, 1947; *A Letter to Three Wives*, with Joseph L. Mankiewicz, 1949; *Three Husbands*, with Edward Eliscu, 1950; *I Can Get It for You Wholesale*, with Abraham Polonsky, 1951; *The Blue Gardenia*, with Charles Hoffman, 1953; *Give a Girl a Break*, with Albert Hackett and Frances Goodrich, 1954; *Les Girls*, with John Patrick, 1957; *Bachelor in Paradise*, with Valentine Davies and Hal Kanter, 1961.

Other

The Secrets of Grown-Ups (autobiography).   New York, McGraw Hill, 1979.

*   *   *

Best known for her mystery novels, Vera Caspary also wrote screenplays and non-mysteries. In all her fiction, she employs a taut, gritty style whose even, unjudgmental tone is almost Naturalistic. All the novels reveal her accurate ear for clipped, brisk dialogue, one of her strongest techniques, for this device conveys clearly and without burdensome modifiers the tone, mood, and tension of men and women under threat. Another Caspary strength is her understanding of the herd instinct of frightened human beings. The books explore the likely and unlikely alliances her characters make in the face of terror or in response to police investigations. The impulse to resist the investigator, to protect one's own circle, is strong in her mystery protagonists, and this impulse lends a realistic complication to the plots.

Evvie is a good example of all these factors and, as is typical of Caspary's mysteries, is essentially a personality study. Both the victim, Evvie Ashton, and the narrator, Louise Goodman, consider themselves emancipated women, and the two range through widely varied social levels of prohibition-era Chicago, believing their friendship to be the one constant in a world of shifting familial and sexual alliances. When Evvie takes a lover whose identity she keeps secret, however, new pressures threaten their relationship. Evvie's murder, while certainly central to the plot, is but one incident in Louise's sustained attempt to come to terms with herself, her friend, and with Evvie's lover. The results are greatly satisfying to both the mystery fan and to the general reader.

Caspary's best known work, *Laura*, is also a personality study. Here, the policeman-detective is a sympathetic character who falls in love with the victim during the investigation. As in *Stranger Than Truth*, *Final Portrait*, and *The Husband*, Caspary effectively employs multiple points of view. *Laura* is brilliantly constructed, and the reader shares the characters' fascination with Laura's vivid, appealing personality. Actually, *Laura* examines the American Dream from a new, revealing angle. The unreality of the Dream is clearly symbolized by the novel's cleverly constructed double climax. Deservedly, *Laura* is a mystery classic.

The plots of *Bedelia* and *The Man Who Loved His Wife* hinge on personalities which lack some civilizing factor, for each centers around a person who allows one emotion to govern his behavior and to overshadow concern for family and friends. In *Bedelia*, Charlie Horst seeks to discover the true character of his seemingly ideal wife. Equally fascinating are the alterations in Charlie himself as he changes from enchanted lover to judge. In *The Man Who Loved His Wife*, jealous Fletcher Strode plans his suicide to look like murder. By means of a carefully crafted diary in which his fantasies are recorded as fact, he posthumously accuses his wife of infidelity, always considered a strong motive for murder. The strange crime is in itself a powerful complication, but Caspary's sure touch with personality development and revelation carries the novel.

Equally compelling is *False Face*, the story of the abduction of Nina Redfield who, though a successful teacher and seemingly a mature, competent adult, is emotionally adolescent. Nina has remained entranced with her school beau, Nick Brazza, a dangerous criminal whom she romanticizes. The plot moves briskly along, aided by the portrait of Nina's friend, brassy Flo Allen, who contrasts nicely with the protagonist. As usual, the novel is flavored by a new romance. In this variation of the maturation tale, Caspary deftly creates an intriguing mystery.

A careful writer who vividly depicts both character and setting, Caspary achieved powerful plots with unusual climaxes in her excellent novels. Despite her consistent use of similar themes, motifs, and devices, each plot is a unique contribution to the genre.

—Jane S. Bakerman

———

CAUDWELL, Sarah. Pseudonym for Sarah Cockburn.   Born in 1939: daughter of the writer Claud Cockburn. Has worked as a barrister. Address: c/o William Collins Ltd., 8 Grafton Street, London W1X 3LA, England.

CRIME PUBLICATIONS

Novels (series: Hilary Tamar in all books)

Thus Was Adonis Murdered.   London, Collins, and New York, Scribner 1981.
The Shortest Way to Hades.   London, Collins, 1984; New York, Scribner, 1985.

The Sirens Sang of Murder. London, Collins, and New York, Delacorte Press, 1989.

* * *

"They are a decorative little group—it would be a difficult taste that was pleased by none of them." Sarah Caudwell's description of the junior members of the Chancery Bar at 62 and 63 New Square, Lincoln's Inn, captures precisely the tone that imbues her writing: arch, lapidary, and erotically ambiguous. Her cast of characters is a beguiling group, inhabiting the three intellectual and civilized mysteries she has thus far produced.

The basic cast numbers six: four barristers at number 62, Cantrip, Ragwort, Selena, and the somewhat older Timothy; Julia, who does tax and finance law next door; and Oxford professor and narrator Hilary Tamar. Michael Cantrip and Desmond Ragwort share an office: Cantrip is dark, Byronic, and carries with him an air of charming dissoluteness. He is the butt of much teasing as the Cambridge man in a sea of Oxford graduates. Ragwort is a beautiful young man of autumnal coloring and apallingly high principles. Selena Jardine abides in the next office, a pretty woman with the face of a Persian cat and a voice other advocates envy—hymettus honey and lemon, says an admirer. Julia Larwood, while lovely and possessed of a voluptuous figure, is a master of tax law but a complete muddle at the minutiae of everyday existence. Professor Tamar was Timothy Shepherd's tutor at Oxford, and Timothy's function is generally to be out of town so that Hilary can come house-sit in London and solve the mysteries besetting the young barristers. Locales become comfortably familiar: Timothy's flat, the junior members' chambers (called the Nursery by some), the Corkscrew for drinking, and Guido's for dinner.

Tamar is a specialist in medieval English law. It is a tribute to Caudwell's construction of plot and delineation of character that many readers may not realize till well into the novels that Tamar's gender is never indicated. It is a further tribute that while it adds to the piquancy of the story to set one wondering, it is so smoothly integrated that it scarce matters. Tamar is something of a prig and something of a genius, and the professor's acumen is woefully underappreciated by the young members of Lincoln's Inn.

While Caudwell's stories are contemporary in tone, there is no concern in them for some of the darker themes favored by some current writers: there is generous consumption of alchohol and cigarettes, and more than a fair amount of double entendre and cheerful promiscuity. Indeed, the sexual ambiguity of Professor Tamar is reflected in any number of liaisons and semi-relationships in the series. Julia, whose affair with Cantrip ended in a disastrous April fool's joke, has a weakness for lovely male profiles. She also persists in announcing that Ragwort (the beautiful and virtuous) is the only man she would consider marrying. Julia is, however, not above letting undesirable pursuers believe her interest is piqued only by other women. This affords Cantrip the opportunity to loudly and rather publicly dissuade one undesirable pursuer from such an opinion based, of course, on Cantrip's own experience (*The Sirens Sang of Murder*). Ragwort, virtue notwithstanding, in the course of duty might encourage a classmate of clearly homosexual bent to continue an acquaintance in the hope of eliciting his help in solving one mystery (*Thus Was Adonis Murdered*).

Caudwell is mistress of the hilarious set piece. In *The Shortest Way to Hodes* Selena and Julia (in one of the funniest scenes ever imagined into the mystery genre) attend what turns out to be an orgy where they are expected to perform together. Instead Selena whips out her Jane Austen and reads throughout the accompanying scene of writhing bodies and suggestive costumes. Another set piece in *The Sirens Sang of Murder*, inducing equal parts merriment and terror, concerns the activities of Cantrip's uncle Colonel Hereward Cantrip, Julia *in décolleté*, and a helicopter.

All three novels follow an intricate but most elegant pattern. One of the members of the group finds it necessary to go to an exotic locale (Venice, Greece, the Cayman Islands) to solve a work-related case or to rescue a colleague. Much of the action is described in letters sent back to London, and the solution comes from Hilary's knowledge of obscure sections of ancient English law and ability to put together small, variegated bits of gossip and information into a whole that reveals the truth.

Thus Was Adonis Murdered, the first in the series, introduces this enchanting coterie. Julia goes on holiday to Venice with the Art Lovers Tour, where she seeks to drown her sorrows with the Inland Revenue in pursuit of "a picaresque series of attempted seductions." The seduction of the lovely Ned, however, ends in his murder, and Julia is the accused. A series of ever-more frantic letters to Selena tracks seduction, betrayal, and a certain amount of multisexual eroticism.

The Shortest Way to Hades finds the members of 62 New Square dealing with the complicated inheritance of a family with British and Greek roots. A cousin of the heiress dies from a fall over a balcony; the court rules death by misadventure. The poor unlikeable victim is little mourned, but Julia suspects murder for what seems like the flimsiest of reasons and no motive at all. Selena and her companion take a sailing holiday in the Greek islands, where many of the protagonists come together in a most tangled series of events. Professor Tamar finds it necessary to travel to Greece to unravel them.

Cantrip, in pursuit of business, goes off to the Cayman Islands, Monaco, and motors through much of France in the trunk of a car in *The Sirens Sang of Murder*. The center of an international tax planning trust and some very old fashioned ideas of honor and chivalry comprise the making of a murder case which Hilary solves, in part, by astute examination of the handwriting on checkbook stubs.

Caudwell's luscious prose is funny, charming, literate, and sexy—but not easy. Her plots are complex and her references esoteric enough to demand that close attention be paid. That attention is amply rewarded, however, by acquaintance with the delicious and sensuous young persons of Lincoln's Inn, with whom one quickly becomes on intimate terms. One hopes for a long series of novels narrated by the ambiguous professor Tamar.

—GraceAnne A. DeCandido and Helga Borck

CECIL, Henry. Pseudonym for Henry Cecil Leon; also wrote as Clifford Maxwell. British. Born in London, 19 September 1902. Educated at St. Paul's School, London; King's College, Cambridge; Gray's Inn, London: called to the Bar 1923. Served in the 1/5 Queen's Regiment, 1939–45: Military Cross, 1942. Married 1) Lettice Mabel Apperly in 1935 (died 1950); 2) Barbara Jeanne Ovenden in 1954; one stepson. County Court Judge, 1949–67. Chairman, British Copyright Council, 1973–76. *Died in May 1976.*

CRIME PUBLICATIONS

Novels (series: Colonel Brain; Ambrose Low; Roger Thursby)

The Painswick Line. London, Chapman and Hall, 1951.
No Bail for the Judge (Brain; Low). London, Chapman and
    Hall, and New York, Harper, 1952.
Ways and Means. London, Chapman and Hall, 1952.
Natural Causes. London, Chapman and Hall, 1953.
According to the Evidence (Brain; Low). London, Chapman
    and Hall, and New York, Harper, 1954.
Brothers in Law (Thursby). London, Joseph, and New York,
    Harper, 1955.
Friends at Court (Thursby). London, Joseph, 1956; New
    York, Harper, 1957.
Much in Evidence. London, Joseph, 1957; as *The Long Arm*,
    New York, Harper, 1957.
Sober as a Judge (Thursby). London, Joseph, and New York,
    Harper, 1958.
Settled Out of Court. London, Joseph, and New York,
    Harper, 1959.
Alibi for a Judge. London, Joseph, 1960.
Daughters in Law. London, Joseph, and New York, Harper,
    1961.
Unlawful Occasions. London, Joseph, 1962.
Independent Witness. London, Joseph, 1963.
Fathers in Law. London, Joseph, 1965; as *A Child Divided*,
    New York, Harper, 1965.
The Asking Price. London, Joseph, and New York, Harper,
    1966.
A Woman Named Anne. London, Joseph, and New York,
    Harper, 1967.
No Fear or Favour. London, Joseph, 1968; as *The Blackmail-
    ers*, New York, Simon and Schuster, 1969.
Tell You What I'll Do. London, Joseph, and New York,
    Simon and Schuster, 1969.
Juror in Waiting. London, Joseph, 1970.
The Buttercup Spell. London, Joseph, 1971.
The Wanted Man. London, Joseph, 1972.
Truth with Her Boots On. London, Joseph, 1974.
Cross Purposes. London, Joseph, 1976.
Hunt the Slipper. London, Joseph, 1977.

Short Stories

Full Circle. London, Chapman and Hall, 1948.
Portrait of a Judge and Other Stories. London, Joseph, 1964;
    New York, Harper, 1965.
Brief Tales from the Bench. London, BBC Publications, 1968;
    New York, Simon and Schuster, 1972.

OTHER PUBLICATIONS

Plays

Brothers-in-Law, with Ted Willis, adaptation of the novel by
    Cecil (produced Wimbledon, Surrey, 1959). London,
    French, 1959.
Settled Out of Court, with William Saroyan, adaptation of the
    novel by Cecil (produced London, 1960). London, French,
    1962.
Alibi for a Judge, with Felicity Douglas and Basil Dawson,
    adaptation of the novel by Cecil (produced London,
    1965). London, French, 1967.
According to the Evidence, with Felicity Douglas and Basil
    Dawson, adaptation of the novel by Cecil (produced London,
    1967). London, French, 1968.

No Fear or Favour (produced Birmingham, 1967).
Hugo, with C.E. Webber (produced London, 1969).
A Woman Named Anne, adaptation of his own novel (produced
    Edinburgh, 1969; London 1970).
The Tilted Scales (produced Guildford, Surrey, 1971).

Radio Plays: *Independent Witness*, 1958; *A Matter for Speculation*, 1965; *Fathers in Law*, from his own novel, 1965; *Brief Tales
from the Bench*, 1967; *Contempt of Court*, 1967; *The Buttercup
Spell*, from his own novel, 1972.

Television Plays: *The Painswick Line*, from his own novel,
1963; *Mr. Justice Duncannon* (series), with Frank Muir and
Denis Norden, 1963.

Other

Brief to Counsel. London, Joseph, 1958; New York, Harper,
    1959; revised edition, Joseph, 1972.
I Married the Girl (as Clifford Maxwell). London, Joseph,
    1960.
Not Such an Ass. London, Hutchinson, 1961.
Tipping the Scales. London, Hutchinson, 1964.
Know about English Law. London, Blackie, 1965; revised
    edition, as *Learn about English Law*, London, Luscombe
    Press, 1974.
A Matter of Speculation: The Case of Lord Cochrane. London,
    Hutchinson, 1965.
The English Judge. London, Stevens, 1970; revised edition,
    London, Arrow, 1972.
Just Within the Law (autobiography). London, Hutchinson,
    1975.

Editor, *Trial of Walter Graham Rowland*. Newton Abbot,
Devon, David and Charles, 1975.

*

Manuscript Collection: McMaster University, Hamilton,
Ontario.

*   *   *

Mystery literature abounds with excellent writers who,
because they are stereotyped as "mystery writers," fail to
acquire the larger audience they deserve. Henry Cecil is one of
these writers. Cecil wrote a number of works, of which almost
all manage to keep a fine balance; while they are thoughtful
and thought-provoking, they maintain a healthy view of
society's more curious foibles. Though one might not always
agree with Cecil's views, he is always provocative and
entertaining.
    Cecil's fiction deals with the law, though not all of his works
are mysteries. And the mysteries are not all of a piece. Some are
suspense novels, some are puzzling murder mysteries, and some
are just puzzles. *Tell You What I'll Do* is a typical (if any Cecil
novel can be called typical) suspense story about a con-man
who commits crimes in order to be put in prison. Though it is
one of Cecil's lighter works, it is stylish and incorporates both
humor and social criticism in an attempt to argue for prison
reform.
    Cecil's murder mysteries are equally distinguished by skilful
style, appropriate comic relief, an uncanny ear for dialogue and
the rhythms of speech, deftly handled detail, and a consistently
unique (and often refreshing) perspective.
    Some of Cecil's more memorable murder mysteries are those
starring Ambrose Low, an ex-criminal, and Colonel Brain, an
ex-army officer. In the inverted tale *No Bail for the Judge*, the

unframing of Sir Edwin Prout provides the basis for an enlightening story. An even stronger work, also involving Low and Brain, is *According to the Evidence*, in which Cecil raises fundamental questions about the legal system while telling a good story. It is fascinating to watch Low get Alec Moreland acquitted of murdering a murderer—and even more fascinating to find out who did it.

Those murder mysteries not including Low and Brain are also skilfully crafted and entertaining. In *The Asking Price*, for example, 52-year-old Ronald Holbrook is accused of murdering his 17-year-old fiancée. The detail is superb, the character study of Holbrook is concise, and the humorous anecdotes are both amusing and relevant to the story. This novel does seem to be more cynical than Cecil's earlier works; the social criticism is more biting, there are no heroes, the solution is very sardonic.

As effective and fascinating as Cecil's mysteries are, it is his marginal mysteries, his puzzles, that are truly extraordinary. In *A Women Named Anne*, for example, there is no detection, no murder, no violence—yet the novel is absolutely spellbinding. Almost all the story takes place in a courtroom, where Michael Amberley is being divorced by his wife. The exchanges crackle, the dialogue is witty and quick, the plot is inspired. The characters are colorful, three-dimensional, and seemingly sketched with ease.

Cecil is an excellent model for a would-be writer, or for many already established writers. He is a skilful author who clearly cares for the language. He has a good eye for detail, he often has strong female characters, and, though he is obviously very knowledgeable about law and the legal system, he is never (well, almost never) pedantic. Though he has strong feelings, they are tempered with a humaneness and humor that are rare today. He should be read.

—Donald J. Pattow

CHABER, M.E. *See* **CROSSEN, Ken.**

CHALLIS, Mary. *See* **WOODS, Sara.**

CHALLIS, Simon, *See* **CHAMBERS, Peter.**

CHAMBERS, Peter. Also writes as Simon Challis; Peter Chester; Philip Daniels; Dennis Phillips. British. Born in London, 17 August 1924. Educated at Westminster City School, London, 1935–40. Served in the Royal Air Force, 1942–47. Married 1) Irene Cooney in 1946, one son and one daughter; 2) Kathleen June Sonia Blake in 1954, two sons and one daughter. Former professional jazz musician; has worked as a senior manager in nationalized industry. Executive councillor, Writers Guild of Great Britain, London, 1982–1987; chairman, Crime Writers Association, London, 1984–85. Since 1983

Director, and since 1990 honourary treasurer, Author's Licencing and Collecting Society, London. Address: Hillcrest House, 94 Highfield Lane, Maidenhead, Berkshire SL6 3PF, England.

<small>CRIME PUBLICATIONS</small>

Novels (series: Mark Preston in all books except *The Day the Thames Caught Fire*.)

Murder Is for Keeps. London, Hale, 1961; New York, Abelard Schuman, 1962.
Wreath for a Redhead. London, Hale, and New York, Abelard Schuman, 1962.
The Big Goodbye. London, Hale, 1962.
Dames Can Be Deadly. London, Hale, and New York, Abelard Schuman, 1963.
Down-Beat Kill. London, Hale, 1963; New York, Abelard Schuman, 1964.
Lady, This Is Murder. London, Hale, 1963; New York, Roy, 1964.
This'll Kill You. London, Hale, and New York, Roy, 1964.
Nobody Lives Forever. London, Hale, 1964.
You're Better Off Dead. London, Hale, 1965.
Always Take the Big Ones. London, Hale, 1965.
No Gold When You Go. London, Hale, 1966.
Don't Bother to Knock. London, Hale, and New York, Roy, 1966.
The Bad Die Young. London, Hale, and New York, Roy, 1967.
The Blonde Wore Black. London, Hale, and New York, Roy, 1968.
No Peace for the Wicked. London, Hale, and New York, Roy, 1968.
Speak Ill of the Dead. London, Hale, 1968.
Death on a Quiet Beach (as Simon Challis). London, Hale, 1968.
Revenge Incorporated (as Dennis Phillips). London, Hale, 1970.
They Call It Murder. London, Hale, 1973.
Somebody Has to Lose. London, Hale, 1975.
The Deader They Fall. London, Hale, 1979.
Lady, You're Killing Me. London, Hale, 1979.
The Day of the Big Dollar. London, Hale, 1979.
The Beautiful Golden Frame. London, Hale, 1980.
Nothing Personal. London, Hale, 1980.
The Deep Blue Cradle. London, Hale, 1980.
A Long Time Dead. London, Hale, 1981.
The Lady Who Never Was. London, Hale, 1981.
Female—Handle With Care. London, Hale, 1981.
Murder Is Its Own Reward. London, Hale, 1982.
The Highly Explosive Case. London, Hale, 1982.
A Miniature Murder Mystery. London, Hale, 1982.
Jail Bait. London, Hale, 1983.
Dragons Can Be Dangerous. London, Hale, 1983.
Bomb-Scare Flight 147. London, Hale, 1984.
The Moving Picture Writes. London, Hale, 1984.
The Vanishing Holes Murders. London, Hale, 1985.
The Day the Thames Caught Fire. Bath, Avon, Chivers, 1989; New York, St. Martin's Press, 1990.

Novels as Peter Chester

Killing Comes Easy. London, Jenkins, and New York, Roy, 1958.
Murder Forestalled. London, Jenkins, and New York, Roy, 1960.

The Pay-Grab Murders. London, Jenkins, and New York, Roy, 1962.
Blueprint for Larceny. London, Jenkins, 1963.
The Traitors. London, Jenkins, 1964.

Novels as Philip Daniels

Goldmine-London W1. London, Hale, 1979.
The Scarred Man. London, Hale, 1980.
The Nice Quiet Girl. London, Hale, 1980.
Alibi of Guilt. London, Hale, 1980; New York, Lorevan, 1986.
Foolproof. London, Hale, 1981.
Suspicious. London, Hale, 1981.
The Inconvenient Corpse. London, Hale, 1982.
A Genteel Little Murder. London, Hale, 1982; Chicago, Academy, 1986.
Nice Knight for Murder. London, Hale, 1982; New York, Lorevan, 1986.
The Dracula Murders. London, Hale, 1983; New York, Lorevan, 1986.
Cinderella Spy. London, Hale, 1984; New York, Lorevan, 1986.
Enquiries Are Proceeding. London, Hale, 1986.
The Hunting of Mr. Gloves. Bolton, Lancashire, Anderson, 1986; New York, St. Martin's Press, 1989.

Uncollected Short Stories

"Just Bad Luck," in *Titbits* (London), 1983.
"It Don't Seem Right," in *Titbits* (London), 1983.
"Freddy the Gent," in *Titbits* (London), Summer 1984.
"Cash Card Clue," in *Sporting Post* (Glasgow), 1986.
"Small World," in *Crime and Mystery Monthly* (London), 1990.

*

Peter Chambers comments:

As an impressionable boy I had two great escape routes from the harsh realities of 1930's London. One was the public library, and the other the cinema. Not only could I read about Nick Charles, Sherlock Holmes, Philo Vance and of course the incomparable Philip Marlowe, but also see and hear them, along with Perry Mason, Poirot, Miss Withers and all the others. In retrospect, I suppose they must have represented the modern morality tale. It was enormously comforting to know that once *Our Hero* has appeared, the days of the bad guys are numbered. The locales might vary, from the night clubs and racetracks of one type of investigator to the village inns and gloomy churchyards of another, but the format was basically unchanged. Good would inevitably triumph and we knew it.

I loved them all, along with the supporting cast of shady lawyers, gold-diggers, scribes (thank you Mr. Runyon), the spinster ladies and the nervous vicars. I owe those printed pages and flickering images a very large debt.

*   *   *

A leading American reviewer wrote (1990), "Whether writing as himself or as Philip Daniels, Chambers is one of the more prolific and inventive of English mystery authors." Peter Chambers may be English, but his private-eye books, which feature the laconic Mark Preston, are as American as bourbon on the rocks. He has the rare distinction of being one of the few writers whose thrillers, set in the Californian town of Monkton City, are enjoyed by his many readers on both sides of the Atlantic—no mean achievement when even the smallest detail of language and background has to be accurate, and Chambers carries it off with authenticity and real panache.

Chambers's novels are in the best tradition of the Raymond Chandler school of thriller writing; dry and witty in tone, racy in style, moving swiftly between locales, whether it is a sleazy night-club in down-town Monkton City or the exclusive homes of the rich and influential. It is a world of professional gangsters, beautiful women and millionaires in which Preston, a natural loner, moves with an easy, wise-cracking assurance. As a character, he is likeable and believable. It is also refreshing, in an age where gratuitous sex and violence tend to figure too largely in books, films, and television, to find a hero who, though hard-nosed, is not foul-mouthed, and who, like Chandler's Philip Marlowe, possesses his own brand of morality and integrity.

The plots are fast-moving, the dialogue crisp and sharp, and in unravelling the central mystery or crime, Chambers carries his readers along with him in his search for the truth with pace and skill. A specialist knowledge of guns and the California setting add their own flavour to his tough stylish fiction.

The Philip Daniels novels are in complete contrast, and essentially English both in their setting and treatment. They also range over a wide field of social backgrounds and environments. Some stories are detailed studies of day-by-day middle-class family and business life, with an underlying sense of brooding boredom and potential eruption. Others are concerned with ordinary people precipitated suddenly into bizarre situations where the normal civilised rules have no application. As one critic noted, "(Daniels) approaches comparison with the classic suspense studies of Margaret Millar." The Daniels stories are as different from the Chambers series as chalk is from cheese, and it is astonishing that they should originate from the same pen. If, as I said, Chambers is as American as bourbon on the rocks, it is only fair to say that Daniels is as English as tea in the vicarage.

With some writers of fiction it is a sad fact that their work, being essentially of its day, does not survive the passage of the years. This cannot be said of Chambers, now in the fourth decade of his writing career. Many of the earliest books are currently re-appearing as reprints, large-print editions and in the newly-arrived "talking-book" format. The appeal of the stories, and the story-telling, is clearly timeless. It is also universal, as witness the translations into almost every European language.

In addition to the reading public, Chambers's fellow-writers have also good reason to be grateful to him for the large amount of work he has done on their behalf in his spare time. A former chairman of The Crime Writers Association, he also served for several years as chairman of the Books Committee of the Writers Guild of Great Britain, and as a member of the board of directors of the Authors Licencing and Collecting Society, which recently appointed him as honorary treasurer. Readers of the Black Dagger series of reprinted crime classics may not be aware that the series was Chambers's brain child.

Happily, he is still producing regular work. With 60 titles already published, his schedule provides for one new title each year from each name, and I, along with a legion of others, will be looking out for them.

—June Thomson

———

CHANCE, John Newton. Also wrote as J. Drummond; John Lymington; David C. Newton. British. Born in London, in 1911. Educated at Streatham Hill College and privately. Served in the Royal Air Force during World War II. *Died 3 August 1983.*

CRIME PUBLICATIONS

Novels (series: Superintendent Black; Jonathan Blake; Chance; Mr. DeHavilland; Jason; John Marsh)

Murder in Oils. London, Gollancz, 1935.
Wheels in the Forest (DeHavilland; Black). London, Gollancz, 1935.
The Devil Drives. London, Gollancz, 1936.
Maiden Possessed (DeHavilland). London, Gollancz, 1937.
Rhapsody in Fear. London, Gollancz, 1937.
Death of an Innocent (DeHavilland; Black). London, Gollancz, 1938.
The Devil in Greenlands. London, Gollancz, 1939.
The Ghost of Truth (Black). London, Gollancz, 1939.
The Screaming Fog (Chance). London, Macdonald, 1944; as *Death Stalks the Cobbled Square*, New York, McBride, 1946.
The Red Knight (Chance; Black; DeHavilland). London, Macdonald, and New York, Macmillan, 1945.
The Eye in Darkness (Chance). London, Macdonald, 1946.
The Knight and the Castle (DeHavilland). London, Macdonald, 1946.
The Black Highway (DeHavilland). London, Macdonald, 1947.
Coven Gibbet. London, Macdonald, 1948.
The Brandy Pole (DeHavilland). London, Macdonald, 1949.
The Night of the Full Moon (DeHavilland). London, Macdonald, 1950.
Aunt Miranda's Murder. London, Macdonald, and New York, Dodd Mead, 1951.
The Man in My Shoes (Chance). London, Macdonald, 1952.
The Twopenny Box. London, Macdonald, 1952.
The Jason Affair. London, Macdonald, 1953; as *Up to Her Neck*, New York, Popular Library, 1955.
The Randy Inheritance. London, Macdonald, 1953.
Jason and the Sleep Game. London, Macdonald, 1954.
The Jason Murders. London, Macdonald, 1954.
Jason Goes West. London, Macdonald, 1955.
The Last Seven Hours. London, Macdonald, 1956.
A Shadow Called Janet. London, Macdonald, 1956.
Dead Man's Knock. London, Hale, 1957.
The Little Crime. London, Hale, 1957.
Affair with a Rich Girl. London, Hale, 1958.
The Man with Three Witches. London, Hale, 1958.
The Fatal Fascination. London, Hale, 1959.
The Man with No Face. London, Hale, 1959.
Alarm at Black Brake. London, Hale, 1960.
Lady in a Frame. London, Hale, 1960.
Import of Evil. London, Hale, 1961.
The Night of the Settlement. London, Hale, 1961.
Triangle of Fear. London, Hale, 1962.
The Man Behind Me. London, Hale, 1963.
The Forest Affair (DeHavilland). London, Hale, 1963.
Commission for Disaster. London, Hale, 1964.
Death under Desolate. London, Hale, 1964.
Stormlight (DeHavilland). London, Hale, 1966.
The Affair at Dead End (Blake). London, Hale, 1966.
The Double Death (Blake). London, Hale, 1966.
The Case of the Death Computer (Marsh). London, Hale, 1967.
The Case of the Fear Makers (Marsh). London, Hale, 1967.
The Death Women (Blake). London, Hale, 1967.
The Hurricane Drift (Blake). London, Hale, 1967.
The Mask of Pursuit (Blake). London, Hale, 1967.

The Thug Executive (Marsh). London, Hale, 1967.
Dead Man's Shoes (Blake). London, Hale, 1968.
Death of the Wild Bird (Blake). London, Hale, 1968.
Fate of the Lying Jade (Blake). London, Hale, 1968.
The Halloween Murders. London, Hale, 1968.
Mantrap (Blake). London, Hale, 1968.
The Rogue Aunt (Blake). London, Hale, 1968.
The Abel Coincidence (Blake). London, Hale, 1969.
The Ice Maidens (Blake). London, Hale, 1969.
Involvement in Austria (Blake). London, Hale, 1969.
The Killer Reaction (Blake). London, Hale, 1969.
The Killing Experiment (Blake). London, Hale, 1969.
The Mists of Treason (Blake). London, Hale, 1970.
A Ring of Liars (Blake). London, Hale, 1970.
Three Masks of Death (Blake). London, Hale, 1970.
The Mirror Train (Blake). London, Hale, 1970.
The Cat Watchers (Blake). London, Hale, 1971.
The Faces of a Bad Girl (Blake). London, Hale, 1971.
A Wreath of Bones (Blake). London, Hale, 1971.
A Bad Dream of Death (Blake). London, Hale, 1972.
Last Train to Limbo (Blake). London, Hale, 1972.
The Man with Two Heads (Blake). London, Hale, 1972.
The Dead Tale-Tellers (Blake): London, Hale, 1972.
The Farm Villains (Blake). London, Hale, 1973.
The Grab Operators (Blake). London, Hale, 1973.
The Love-Hate Relationship. London, Hale, 1973.
The Girl in the Crime Belt (Blake). London, Hale, 1974.
The Shadow of the Killer (Blake). London, Hale, 1974.
The Starfish Affair (Blake). London, Hale, 1974.
The Canterbury Kilgrims (Blake). London, Hale, 1974.
Hill Fog (Blake). London, Hale, 1975.
The Devil's Edge. London, Hale, 1975.
The Monstrous Regiment. London, Hale, 1975.
The Murder Maker. London, Hale, 1976.
Return to Death Valley. London, Hale, 1976.
A Fall-Out of Thieves. London, Hale, 1976.
The Laxham Haunting (as John Lymington). London, Hodder and Stoughton, 1976.
The Frightened Fisherman. London, Hale, 1976.
The House of the Dead Ones. London, Hale, 1977.
Motive for a Kill. London, Hale, 1977.
The Ducrow Folly. London, Hale, 1978.
End of an Iron Man. London, Hale, 1978.
A Drop of Hot Gold. London, Hale, 1979.
Thieves' Kitchen. London, Hale, 1979.
The Guilty Witness. London, Hale, 1979.
A Place Called Skull. London, Hale, 1980.
The Death Watch Ladies. London, Hale, 1980.
The Mayhem Madchen. London, Hale, 1980.
The Black Widow. London, Hale, 1981.
The Death Importer. London, Hale, 1981.
The Mystery of Enda Favell. London, Hale, 1981.
Madman's Will. London, Hale, 1982.
The Hunting of Mr. Exe. London, Hale, 1982.
The Shadow in Pursuit. London, Hale, 1982.
The Traditional Murders. London, Hale, 1983.
The Death Chemist. London, Hale, 1983.
Terror Train. London, Hale, 1983.
Looking for Samson. London, Hale, 1984.
Nobody's Supposed to Murder the Butler. London, Hale, 1984.
The Bad Circle. London, Hale, 1985.
The Time Bomb. London, Hale, 1985.
The Woman Hater. London, Hale, 1986.
The Psychic Trap. London, Hale, 1986.
Spy on a Spider. London, Hale, 1987.
The Hit Man. London, Hale, 1987.
The Hiller Weapon. London, Hale, 1987.

The Smiling Cadaver. London, Hale, 1987.
The Reluctant Agent. London, Hale, 1988.
The Shadow Before. London, Hale, 1988.
The Offshore Conspiracy. London, Hale, 1988.
The Man on the Cliff. London, Hale, 1988.
A Confusion of Eyes. London, Hale, 1989.
The Running of the Spies. London, Hale, 1989.
A Tale of Tangled Ladies. London, Hale, 1989.

Novels as J. Drummond (series: Sexton Blake in all books)

The Essex Road Crime. London, Amalgamated Press, 1944.
The Manor House Menace. London, Amalgamated Press, 1944.
The Painted Dagger. London, Amalgamated Press, 1944.
The Riddle of the Leather Bottle. London, Amalgamated Press, 1944.
The Tragic Case of the Station Master's Legacy. London, Amalgamated Press, 1944.
At Sixty Miles an Hour. London, Amalgamated Press, 1945.
The House on the Hill. London, Amalgamated Press, 1945.
The Riddle of the Mummy Case. London, Amalgamated Press, 1945.
The Mystery of the Deserted Camp. London, Amalgamated Press, 1948.
The Town of Shadows. London, Amalgamated Press, 1948.
The Case of the "Dead" Spy. London, Amalgamated Press, 1949.
The Riddle of the Receiver's Hoard. London, Amalgamated Press, 1949.
The Secret of the Living Skeleton. London, Amalgamated Press, 1949.
The South Coast Mystery. London, Amalgamated Press, 1949.
The Case of L.A.C. Dickson. London, Amalgamated Press, 1950.
The Mystery of the Haunted Square. London, Amalgamated Press, 1950.
The House in the Woods. London, Amalgamated Press, 1950.
The Secret of the Sixty Steps. London, Amalgamated Press, 1951.
The Case of the Man with No Name. London, Amalgamated Press, 1951.
Hated by All! London, Amalgamated Press, 1951.
The Mystery of the Sabotaged Jet. London, Amalgamated Press, 1951.
The House on the River. London, Amalgamated Press, 1952.
The Mystery of the Five Guilty Men. London, Amalgamated Press, 1954.
The Case of the Two-Faced Swindler. London, Amalgamated Press, 1955.
The Teddy-Boy Mystery. London, Amalgamated Press, 1955.

Uncollected Short Stories

"No One Came," in *London Mystery Magazine,* December 1958.
"The Long Walk," in *London Mystery Magazine,* March 1959.

OTHER PUBLICATIONS

Novels as John Lymington

Night of the Big Heat. London, Corgi, 1959; New York, Dutton 1960.
The Giant Stumbles. London, Hodder and Stoughton, 1960.

The Grey Ones. London, Hodder and Stoughton, 1960.
The Coming of the Strangers. London, Hodder and Stoughton, 1961; New York, Manor 1978.
A Sword above the Night. London, Hodder and Stoughton, 1962.
The Screaming Face. London, Hodder and Stoughton, 1963; New York, Manor, 1978.
The Sleep Eaters. London, Hodder and Stoughton, 1963; New York, Manor, 1978.
Froomb! London, Hodder and Stoughton, 1964; New York, Doubleday, 1966.
The Star Witches. London, Hodder and Stoughton, 1965; New York, Manor, 1978.
The Green Drift. London, Hodder and Stoughton, 1965; as *The Night Spiders,* New York, Doubleday, 1967.
Ten Million Years to Friday. London, Hodder and Stoughton, 1967.
The Nowhere Place. London, Hodder and Stoughton, 1969.
Give Daddy the Knife, Darling. London, Hodder and Stoughton, 1969.
The Year Dot. London, Hodder and Stoughton, 1972.
The Hole in the World. London, Hodder and Stoughton, 1974.
A Spider in the Bath. London, Hodder and Stoughton, 1975.
Starseed on Eye Moor. London, Hodder and Stoughton, 1977.
The Waking of the Stone. London, Hodder and Stoughton, 1978.
The Grey Ones, A Sword above the Night. New York, Manor 1978.
A Caller from Overspace. London, Hodder and Stoughton, 1979.
Voyage of the Eighth Mind. London, Hodder and Stoughton, 1980.
The Power Ball. London, Hale, 1981.
The Terror Version. London, Hale, 1982.
The Vale of the Sad Banana. London, Hale, 1984.

Short Stories

The Night Spiders (as John Lymington). London, Corgi, 1964.

Other

The Black Ghost (for children; as David C. Newton). London, Oxford University Press, 1947.
The Dangerous Road (for children; as David C. Newton). London, Oxford University Press, 1948.
Bunst and the Brown Voice [*the Bold, and the Secret Six, and the Flying Eye*] (for children). London, Oxford University Press, 4 vols., 1950–53.
The Jennifer Jigsaw (for children), with Shirley Newton Chance. London, Oxford University Press, 1951.
Yellow Belly (autobiography). London, Hale, 1959.
The Crimes at Rillington Place: A Novelist's Reconstruction. London, Hodder and Stoughton, 1961.

*   *   *

Under a variety of pseudonyms, John Newton Chance was one of the more prolific detective-thriller writers of the mid-20th century. His early novels gained much critical acclaim, yet his work as a whole has been largely shunned by later commentators, who, if they mention him at all, usually relegate him to a footnote on "pot-boilers." Possibly the later work can be placed in this category, but to ignore the books published from the 1930's to the 1950's would be a mistake; the thrillers of the 1940's are particularly rich in atmosphere.

Eerie and bizarre situations abound: the flight through the

plague-pits in *Screaming Fog;* the entrance of the garrulous vicar through the French windows in *The Red Knight;* the discovery of a body among the dismembered figures in a waxworks modelling-room at night in *The Eye in Darkness.* To offset this, Chance injects much lively dialogue into his stories, and fills them with a host of Dickensian (indeed, Chaucerian) characters, many of whom are not what they seem.

Probably his most sustained creative effort is to be found in the 25 thrillers he wrote (1944–55) for the Sexton Blake Library under the name John Drummond. Especially good are *The Manor House Menace, The Town of Shadows, The Mystery of the Haunted Square,* and *The House on the River*—though all are worth reading.

In later years he channelled his energies into a series of excellent psychological SF novels. Also of interest are a reconstruction of the Christie/Evans case *The Crimes at Rillington Place; The Night Spiders,* a collection of weird stories under the John Lymington pseudonym; and the highly readable account of his wartime and writing experiences, *Yellow Belly.*

—Jack Adrian

CHANDLER, Raymond (Thornton). American. Born in Chicago, Illinois, 23 July 1888; moved to England with his mother: naturalized British subject, 1907; again became an American citizen, 1956. Educated in a local school in Upper Norwood, London; Dulwich College, London, 1900–05; studied in France and Germany, 1905–07. Served in the Gordon Highlanders, Canadian Army, 1917–18, and in the Royal Air Force, 1918–19. Married Pearl Cecily Hurlburt in 1924 (died 1954). Worked in the supply and accounting departments of the Admiralty, London, 1907; reporter for the *Daily Express,* London, and the *Western Gazette,* Bristol, 1908–12; returned to the United States, 1912; worked in St. Louis, then on a ranch and in a sporting goods firm in California; accountant and bookkeeper at the Los Angeles Creamery, 1912–17; worked in a bank in San Francisco, 1919; worked for the *Daily Express,* Los Angeles, 1919; bookkeeper, then auditor, Dabney Oil Syndicate, Los Angeles, 1922–32; full-time writer from 1933. President, Mystery Writers of America, 1959. Recipient: Mystery Writers of America Edgar Allan Poe award, for screenplay, 1946, for novel, 1954. *Died 26 March 1959.*

CRIME PUBLICATIONS

Novels (series: Philip Marlowe in all books)

The Big Sleep. New York, Knopf, and London, Hamish Hamilton, 1939.
Farewell, My Lovely. New York, Knopf, and London, Hamish Hamilton, 1940.
The High Window. New York, Knopf, 1942; London, Hamish Hamilton, 1943.
The Lady in the Lake. New York, Knopf, 1943; London, Hamish Hamilton, 1944.
The Little Sister. London, Hamish Hamilton, and Boston, Houghton Mifflin, 1949; as *Marlowe,* New York, Pocket Books, 1969.
The Long Goodbye. London, Hamish Hamilton, 1953; Boston, Houghton Mifflin, 1954.

Playback. London, Hamish Hamilton, and Boston, Houghton Mifflin, 1958.
Poodle Springs (unfinished). In *Raymond Chandler Speaking,* 1962; completed by Robert B. Parker, New York, Putnam, 1989; London, Macdonald, 1990.

Short Stories

Five Murders. New York, Avon, 1944.
Five Sinister Characters. New York, Avon 1945.
Finger Man and Other Stories. New York, Avon, 1946.
Red Wind. Cleveland, World, 1946.
Spanish Blood. Cleveland, World, 1946.
The Simple Art of Murder. Boston, Houghton Mifflin, and London, Hamish Hamilton, 1950; as *Trouble Is My Business, Pick-Up on Noon Street,* and *The Simple Art of Murder,* New York, Pocket Books, 3 vols., 1951–53.
Smart Aleck Kill. London, Hamish Hamilton, 1953.
Pearls Are a Nuisance. London, Hamish Hamilton, 1953.
Killer in the Rain, edited by Philip Durham. Boston, Houghton Mifflin, and London, Hamish Hamilton, 1964.
The Smell of Fear. London, Hamish Hamilton, 1965.
The Midnight Raymond Chandler (omnibus), edited by Joan Kahn. Boston, Houghton Mifflin, 1971.

Uncollected Short Story

"Professor Bingo's Snuff," in *Park East* (New York), June–August 1951.

OTHER PUBLICATIONS

Plays

Double Indemnity, with Billy Wilder, in *Best Film Plays 1945,* edited by John Gassner and Dudley Nichols. New York, Crown, 1946.
The Blue Dahlia (screenplay), edited by Matthew J. Bruccoli. Carbondale, Southern Illinois University Press, and London, Elm Tree, 1976.
Raymond Chandler's Unknown Thriller: The Screenplay of Playback. New York, Mysterious Press, and London, Harrap, 1985.

Screenplays: *And Now Tomorrow,* with Frank Partos, 1944; *Double Indemnity,* with Billy Wilder, 1944; *The Unseen,* with Hagar Wilde and Ken Englund, 1945; *The Blue Dahlia,* 1946; *Strangers on a Train,* with Czenzi Ormonde and Whitfield Cook, 1951.

Other

Raymond Chandler Speaking, edited by Dorothy Gardiner and Kathrine Sorley Walker. Boston, Houghton Mifflin, and London, Hamish Hamilton, 1962.
Chandler Before Marlowe, edited by Matthew J. Bruccoli. Columbia, University of South Carolina Press, 1973.
The Notebooks of Raymond Chandler, and English Summer: a Gothic Romance, edited by Frank MacShane. New York, Ecco Press, 1976; London, Weidenfeld and Nicolson, 1977.
"Farewell My Hollywood," in *Antaeus* (New York), Autumn 1976.
Raymond Chandler and James M. Fox: Letters. Privately printed, 1979.
Selected Letters, edited by Frank MacShane. New York, Columbia University Press, and London, Cape, 1981.

*

Bibliography: *Raymond Chandler: A Descriptive Bibliography* by Matthew J. Bruccoli, Pittsburgh, University of Pittsburgh Press, and London, Fefler and Simons, 1979.

Manuscript Collection: Department of Special Collections, University of California Research Library, Los Angeles.

Critical Studies: *Down These Mean Streets a Man Must Go: Raymond Chandler's Knight* by Philip Durham, Chapel Hill, University of North Carolina Press, 1963; *The Life of Raymond Chandler* by Frank MacShane, New York, Dutton, and London, Cape, 1976; *The World of Raymond Chandler* edited by Miriam Gross, London, Weidenfeld and Nicolson, 1977, New York, A and W, 1978; *Raymond Chandler* by Jerry Speir, New York, Ungar, 1981; *Chandlertown: The Los Angeles of Philip Marlowe* by Edward Thorpe, London, Hutchinson, 1983; *Raymond Chandler* by William Marling, Boston, Twayne, 1986.

*   *   *

Chandler's novels are one of the halfdozen landmarks of detective fiction. Philip Marlowe is almost as well known as Holmes or Hamlet while the volume of criticism about Chandler probably exceeds that about Conan Doyle. The novels have been touted by some critics not only as detective classics but also classics of 20th-century American literature.

They derived from the new popular crime fiction of the 1920's and 1930's—realistic stories about gangsters and hardboiled detectives—most by unremembered hacks but some by talented young writers like Dashiell Hammett and James M. Cain. Chandler, who 20 years earlier had abandoned a fledgling career as a London man of letters, came to write hardboiled fiction fortuitously. After an intense self-directed apprenticeship, he gradually turned the genre to his distinctive ends. No earlier hardboiled writer had presented such vivid, evocative images of city life and of nature. Although writers like Ernest Hemingway, Ring Lardner and Hammett had been developing a trenchant comic American written lingo, Chandler intensified and further stylized it, particularly with the comic similes and litotes that became trademarks of his style. If hardboiled fiction always was, paradoxically, romance, Chandler made it even more romantic.

According to Chesterton, detective fiction expresses the "poetry" of modern city life. By universal accord, Chandler is the poet laureate of Los Angeles, the provincial city of the 1930's and 1940's that was metamorphosing into the sprawling gasoline-powered metropolis. Though Chandler captures both its incarnations, he is especially poignant on the earlier Los Angeles of red cars and tree-shaded streets and on distinctive Southern California atmospheres. We encounter here the first of many paradoxes about Chandler. Despite his loving construction of Los Angeles, he maintained a sense of his British difference, especially in the face of what he regarded to be crass, polyglot American culture. A second paradox opposes his practice of the hardboiled to what Julian Symons calls Chandler's "romantic aestheticism." Eric Homberger rightly sees him as "a man divided."

Central to the novels—though certainly not "everything," as Chandler claimed the hero to be—is Marlowe, who almost immediately became the model hardboiled detective. He has the hardboiled toughness and something of hardboiled libertinism. However, even the most casual reader quickly realizes that Marlowe is a "romantic," as he ironically names himself, a modern knight, descendant of the stained-glass Medieval figure above General Sternwood's door. From the Sternwood sisters in *The Big Sleep* to Eileen Wade in *The Long Good-bye*, Marlowe keeps saving distressed damsels (even if nearly all

turn out to be loathly ladies) and opposes the corruption that he constantly encounters with a stern, though not puritanical, moral code. Chandler fills his Los Angeles scenes with other memorable characters as well: Moose Malloy (the lovestruck hulk of *Farewell, My Lovely*), Harry Jones (the courageous "little man" of *The Big Sleep*), the feral Carmen Sternwood. . . .

Some admirers of Chandler believe that his best work is in the early books, what Lawrence Clark Powell calls, "the 'big four' of his brief prime." *The Big Sleep* is, indeed, a classic almost without flaw. In *Farewell, My Lovely*, the opening dozen or so chapters—the introduction of Malloy, the vignettes of the black district—equal anything in Chandler's writing for invention, setting of scene, development of plot and suspense. However, neither *The Lady in the Lake* nor *The High Window* has the invention or tight plotting of the next book, *The Little Sister*. Rather than "falling" and "sputtering" in *The Little Sister* and *The Long Goodbye*, as Powell would have it, Chandler kept consolidating his ground and launching beyond it.

The Long Goodbye seems to me not only Chandler's best but the masterwork of hardboiled detective-fiction, providing an image of how much can be done with the genre. Several years before writing it, Chandler had revealed in the manifesto-like essay of 1945, "The Simple Art of Murder," a literary and critical sophistication that must have surprised his typical reader. It made apparent that he had read widely in not only detective stories but also modern literature and that he had reflected on issues of form and literary art. He argues that although there is "precious little" art anywhere it is not restricted to particular "high" genres. Detective story has a real art, not in complications of whodunit but in the "effect of movement, intrigue, cross-purposes and the gradual elucidation of character" that characterizes all good fiction. The unsimple art of detective fiction implied throughout the essay Chandler realizes in *The Long Goodbye*.

As always in his novels, the narrative proceeds by two apparently unrelated plots which inexorably come together. In the first, Marlowe tries to clear Terry Lennox of his wife's murder. Marlowe's curious comradeship with the paradoxical Terry, alternately a man of authentic style and a drunken wastrel, seems to rewrite the male bonding of Hemingway's *The Sun Also Rises*, turning Hemingway's pastoral into a dark tale of betrayal. Chandler also rewrites *The Great Gatsby*. In Harlan Potter, his daughters, and the public men he owns there is a Fitzgeraldian fascination with the ultra rich and powerful that may be found in all Chandler's novels. More pointedly, Terry with his mysterious past, wartime heroism and many-faced ambiguity reiterates Gatsby himself.

In the second plot Marlowe undertakes the job of finding and then protecting the writer, Roger Wade. Like Terry, Wade is an especially useful figure for Chandler's various symbolism. As a successful writer of popular fiction and an alcoholic, he stands an ambiguous distance from the alcoholic Chandler—Chandler's double but also someone "worse." Marlowe scathingly criticizes Wade for his self-indulgent collapse, but he also sympathizes, accepts him and finally revenges his murder.

The solution to the mystery lies in Britain and the past, in which Terry was once a British soldier—like Chandler—and the now, Eileen Wade his wife. For the first time in fiction Chandler turns to his roots, and returns the hardboiled to something like the British "classic" form of detective fiction. For all the book's dense representation and symbolism, it is also a more intense whodunit than the earlier novels. It appears that Chandler took to heart criticisms of his earlier weak plotting and of his lush romanticism. If he too much yearned after rare ideals and snobbishly associated personal value with British civility, such romanticism in the murderer, Eileen, is corroded by irony. She associates her beloved dream of past perfection with Britain and rejects the "sordid" present of America. Her spoiled, embittered idealism negates life; it licenses indifference and murder. Even more than Eileen, Marlowe finds the world fraudulent. The last tenable ideal, friendship, is betrayed by Terry. But Marlowe soldiers on, and nothing can make him say goodbye to his spare code.

With the popularity of hardboiled detective fiction it was probably inevitable that a writer of genius would follow Hammett in upgrading the form. Chandler's ambitions for the Marlowe saga may have crystallized as early as *Farewell, My Lovely*. There, Marlowe jokingly calls a police detective, "Hemingway," and continues to make taunting references to the overly plain style. Chandler cared passionately both about his art and his reputation. Although in the decade before his death he began to enjoy recognition, it was nothing like the later canonization. Whatever Chandler's ultimate status in American letters, for modern detective story his blend of realism, romance, verbal wit, and satire bordering on tragedy has proven to be the archetype.

—T.R. Steiner

———

CHARLES, Franklin. *See* **ADAMS, Cleve F.; BELLEM, Robert Leslie.**

———

CHARLES, Will. *See* **WILLEFORD, Charles.**

———

CHARTERIS, Leslie. Born Leslie Charles Bowyer Yin; adopted the name Charteris legally in 1926. American. Born in Singapore, 12 May 1907; naturalized American citizen, 1946. Educated privately; Falconbury School, Purley, Surrey, 1919–22; Rossall School, Fleetwood, Lancashire, 1922–24; King's College, Cambridge, 1925–26. Married 1) Pauline Schishkin in 1931 (divorced 1937), one daughter; 2) Barbara Meyer in 1938 (divorced 1943; 3) Elizabeth Bryant Borst in 1943 (divorced 1951); 4) Audrey Long in 1952. Worked at odd jobs in England, France, and Malaya until 1935; lived in America after 1935. Writer and journalist: wrote syndicated comic strip *Secret Agent X-9*, in mid-1930's, and *Saint*, 1945–55; editor, *Suspense* magazine, 1946–47, and *The Saint Detective Magazine*, later *The Saint Mystery Magazine*, 1953–67; columnist, *Gourmet Magazine*, 1966–68; editorial consultant, *The New Saint Magazine*, 1984–85, Fellow, Royal Society of Arts. Address: c/o Thompson Levett & Co., 3-4 Great Marlborough Street, London W1V 2AR, England.

CRIME PUBLICATIONS

Novels (series: Simon Templar, The Saint)

X Esquire. London, Ward Lock, 1927.
The White Rider. London, Ward Lock, 1928; New York, Doubleday, 1930.

Meet the Tiger (Saint). London, Ward Lock, 1928; New York, Doubleday, 1929.
Daredevil. London, Ward Lock, and New York, Doubleday, 1929.
The Bandit. London, Ward Lock, and New York, Doubleday, 1929.
The Last Hero. London, Hodder and Stoughton, and New York, Doubleday, 1930; as *The Saint Closes the Case,* New York, Sun Dial Press, 1941.
Enter the Saint (3 novelets). London, Hodder and Stoughton, 1930; New York, Doubleday, 1931.
Knight Templar. London, Hodder and Stoughton, 1930; as *The Avenging Saint,* New York, Doubleday, 1931.
Featuring the Saint (3 novelets). London, Hodder and Stoughton, 1931.
Alias the Saint (3 novelets). London, Hodder and Stoughton, 1931.
Wanted for Murder (combines *Featuring the Saint* and *Alias the Saint*). New York, Doubleday, 1931.
She Was a Lady. London, Hodder and Stoughton, 1931; as *Angels of Doom,* New York, Doubleday, 1932; as *The Saint Meets His Match,* New York, Sun Dial Press, 1941.
The Holy Terror (3 novelets). London, Hodder and Stoughton, 1932; as *The Saint Versus Scotland Yard,* New York, Doubleday, 1932.
Getaway. London, Hodder and Stoughton, 1932; as *The Saint's Getaway,* New York, Doubleday, 1933.
Once More the Saint (3 novelets). London, Hodder and Stoughton, 1933; as *The Saint and Mr. Teal,* New York, Doubleday, 1933.
The Misfortunes of Mr. Teal (3 novelets). London, Hodder and Stoughton, and New York, Doubleday, 1934; as *The Saint in London,* New York, Sun Dial Press, 1941.
The Saint Goes On (3 novelets). London, Hodder and Stoughton, 1934; New York, Doubleday, 1935.
The Saint in New York. London, Hodder and Stoughton, and New York, Doubleday, 1935.
The Saint Overboard. London, Hodder and Stoughton, and New York, Doubleday, 1936; as *The Pirate Saint,* New York, Triangle, 1941.
The Ace of Knaves (3 novelets). London, Hodder and Stoughton, and New York, Doubleday, 1937; as *The Saint in Action,* New York, Sun Dial Press, 1938.
Thieves' Picnic. London, Hodder and Stoughton, and New York, Doubleday, 1937; as *The Saint Bids Diamonds,* New York, Triangle, 1942.
Prelude for War. London, Hodder and Stoughton, and New York, Doubleday, 1938; as *The Saint Plays with Fire,* New York, Triangle, 1942.
Follow the Saint (3 novelets). New York, Doubleday, 1938; London, Hodder and Stoughton, 1939.
The Saint in Miami. New York, Doubleday, 1940; London, Hodder and Stoughton, 1941.
The Saint Goes West. New York, Doubleday, and London, Hodder and Stoughton, 1942.
The Saint Steps In. New York, Doubleday, 1943; London, Hodder and Stoughton, 1944.
The Saint on Guard (2 novelets). New York, Doubleday, 1944; London, Hodder and Stoughton, 1945; 1 novelet published as *The Saint and the Sizzling Saboteur,* New York, Avon, 1956.
Lady on a Train (novelization of screenplay). Los Angeles, Shaw Press, 1945.
The Saint Sees It Through. New York, Doubleday, 1946; London, Hodder and Stoughton, 1947.
Call for the Saint (2 novelets). New York, Doubleday, and London, Hodder and Stoughton, 1948.

Arrest the Saint (omnibus). New York, Permabooks, 1951.
Vendetta for the Saint. New York, Doubleday, 1964; London, Hodder and Stoughton, 1965.
The Saint in Pursuit (novelization of comic strip). New York, Doubleday, 1970; London, Hodder and Stoughton, 1971.

Short Stories (series: Simon Templar, The Saint)

The Brighter Buccaneer. London, Hodder and Stoughton, and New York, Doubleday, 1933.
Boodle. London, Hodder and Stoughton, 1934; as *The Saint Intervenes*, New York, Doubleday, 1934.
The Happy Highwayman. New York, Doubleday, and London, Hodder and Stoughton, 1939.
The Saint at Large. New York, Sun Dial Press, 1943.
Saint Errant. New York, Doubleday, 1948; London, Hodder and Stoughton, 1949.
The Saint in Europe. New York, Doubleday, 1953; London, Hodder and Stoughton, 1954.
The Saint on the Spanish Main. New York, Doubleday, and London, Hodder and Stoughton, 1955.
The Saint Around the World. New York, Doubleday, 1956; London, Hodder and Stoughton, 1957.
Thanks to the Saint. New York, Doubleday, 1957; London, Hodder and Stoughton, 1958.
Señor Saint. New York, Doubleday, 1958; London, Hodder and Stoughton, 1959.
Concerning the Saint. New York, Avon, 1958.
The Saint to the Rescue. New York, Doubleday, 1959; London, Hodder and Stoughton, 1961.
The Saint Cleans Up. New York, Avon, 1959.
Trust the Saint. New York, Doubleday, and London, Hodder and Stoughton, 1962.
The Saint in the Sun. New York, Doubleday, 1963; London, Hodder and Stoughton, 1964.
The Fantastic Saint, edited by Martin H. Greenberg and Charles G. Waugh. New York, Doubleday, 1982; London, Hodder and Stoughton, 1983.

OTHER PUBLICATIONS

Plays

Screenplays: *Midnight Club*, with Seton I. Miller, 1933; *The Saint's Double Trouble*, with Ben Holmes, 1940; *The Saint's Vacation*, with Jeffrey Dell, 1941; *The Saint in Palm Springs*, with Jerry Cady, 1941; *Lady on a Train*, with Edmund Beloin and Robert O'Brien, 1945; *River Gang*, with others, 1945; *Two Smart People*, with others, 1946; *Tarzan and the Huntress*, with Jerry Grushkind and Rowland Leigh, 1947.

Radio Plays: *Sherlock Holmes* series, with Denis Green.

Other

Spanish for Fun. London, Hodder and Stoughton, 1964.
Paleneo: A Universal Sign Language. London, Hodder and Stoughton, 1972.

Editor, *The Saint's Choice of Humorous Crime.* Los Angeles, Shaw Press, 1945.
Editor, *The Saint's Choice of Impossible Crime.* Los Angeles, Bond Charteris, 1945.
Editor, *The Saint's Choice of Hollywood Crime.* Los Angeles, Saint Enterprises, 1946.
Editor, *The Saint Mystery Library.* New York, Great American Publications, 13 vols., 1959–60.

Editor, with Hans Santesson, *The Saint Magazine Reader.* New York, Doubleday, 1966; as *The Saint's Choice*, London, Hodder and Stoughton, 1967.

Translator, *Juan Belmonte, Killer of Bulls: The Autobiography of a Matador*, by Belmonte and Manuel Chaves Nogales. New York, Doubleday, and London, Heinemann, 1937.

*

Bibliography: *Leslie Charteris och Helgonet under 5 Decennium* by Jan Alexandersson and Iwan Hedman, Strängnäs, DAST Magazine, 1972.

Manuscript Collection: Mugar Memorial Library, Boston University.

Critical Study: *The Saint and Leslie Charteris* by W.O.G. Lofts and Derek Adley, London, Hutchinson, 1971, Bowling Green, Ohio, Popular Press, 1972.

*   *   *

Thriller fiction in England in the 1920's and early 1930's was full of rich young men of the officer class, who returned from the War, found peace too peaceful, gathered their old trench-mates around them, and declared themselves Gentleman Outlaws at war with boredom, officialdom, and—more often than not—democracy. There is a strong smell of latent fascism in their exploits: they had put themselves not only outside, but above, the law, were self-proclaimed judges and enthusiastic executioners of unwanted foreigners, communists, Jews, and other possible enemies of Good Old England as it once was and forever should be.

Leslie Charteris started his Saint saga, about the brilliant buccaneer Simon Templar, in that literary climate when, after a couple of false starts, he began writing Saint stories for *The Thriller* in 1930. He conformed to most of the unspoken rules of the genre when he wrote about dealing out private justice, making fun of Scotland Yard (personified by Inspector Claude Eustace Teal), and collecting wealth—"boodle"—from people not fit to be so filthy rich. But, like the Saint, Charteris in those days was a bit of an outlaw and an outsider, never quite at home among the clubland gentlemen, and wryly modifying the clichés of the popular thriller to suit his own, sometimes surprising, ends. The Saint has no war record, a classless, romantic past only hinted at, and nothing but caustic contempt for chauvinism, pride of birth, public school, and the ruling classes.

Sapper's Bulldog Drummond flogged Jews "within an inch of their lives," but Charteris lets the Saint use the whip on an underpaying and knighted lorry magnate to teach him respect for work. He praises Roosevelt's New Deal, and once he even exposes a fox-hunting and noble sportsman as the murderer of a pale, left-wing poet. There is no doubt about his sympathies—and still less doubt that they were not shared by the majority of thriller writers of the day. Yet he kept himself within the limits of the society around him, and was never a revolutionary. Charteris enjoyed himself by tickling the feet of the upright citizen with furled umbrella (as he once defined his readers), but he was never ready to cut off his head.

Charteris's prose in those days was carefree, lighthearted, sometimes Wodehousian. The stories are full not only of an outsider's social comments, but of experiments by a self-confident and amused writer in how far he can lead his reader by the nose. The tongue-in-cheek commentaries often have little to do with the plot, and include long nonsense poems and extemporized limericks—but the reader tended to fall under the Charteris charm.

In the 1930's Charteris moved to the United States, and in *The Saint in Miami* (1940), he moved the whole group, Templar and his loyal gang, across the Atlantic. But hereafter we meet a new Saint. If being the center of a group of idle, rich, and admiring followers is a British ideal, the hard-working, half-anonymous lone ranger is an American one. During the War, the Saint worked as an undercover agent for a government department, and his loyalties are more to democracy than to economic systems. After the War, Charteris for nearly 30 years sent the Saint around the world as a lonely, solitary traveller with a new hotel room, a new heroine, and a new adventure in each short story, and in the single full-length novel from the period, *Vendetta for the Saint*. The timeless, always 35-year-old Gentleman Outlaw is still an outlaw, but depends more on his own legend than on actual lawbreaking to keep alive. He accepts rather than seeks out adventure, seemingly more interested in good food and luxury surroundings than in the adventure itself; the caustic comments have disappeared. Many of the stories based on the television series were written by Fleming Lee and others, and merely touched up by Charteris before publication; for an old Saint fan, reading them is like chewing plastic beef: an artificial product only superficially similar to the real thing. *The Saint in Pursuit*, based on an old comic strip, was slightly better.

The literary idea of a hero outside the law is an old and honored one: Robin Hood is a venerable ancestor, Raffles, Arsène Lupin, and Chesterton's Flambeau older cousins, and Spillane's Mike Hammer a young relative. In the best Charteris stories, that tradition is free from its fascist overtones and loaded with witty humor, fast story-telling, and a refreshing outlook on the world of crime, the ruling classes, and romantic heroes. "Maybe I am a crook," said the Saint once; "But in between times I'm something more. In my simple way I am a kind of justice. . . ." There was a time when one could almost believe him.

—Bo Lundin

———

CHARYN, Jerome. American. Born in New York City, 13 May 1937. Educated at Columbia University, New York, B.A. (cum laude) 1959 (Phi Beta Kappa). Married Marlene Phillips in 1965 (divorced). Recreation leader, New York City Department of Parks, early 1960's; English teacher, High School of Music and Art, and School of Performing Arts, both New York, 1962–64; Lecturer in English, City College, New York, 1965; Assistant Professor of English, Stanford University, California, 1965–68; Assistant Professor, 1968–72, Associate Professor, 1972–78, and Professor of English, 1978–80, Herbert Lehman College, City University of New York; Mellon Visiting Professor of English, Rice University, Houston, 1979. Visiting Professor, 1980, and since 1981, Lecturer in Creative Writing, Princeton University, New Jersey. Founding editor, *Dutton Review*, New York, 1970–72; executive editor, *Fiction*, New York, 1970–75. Visiting Distinguished Professor of English, City College of New York, 1988–89. Since 1984, Member of the Executive Board, PEN American Center, since 1988 of the International Association of Crime Writers, and since 1989 of Mystery Writers of America. Since 1986 member of Playwright/Director Unit, The Actors Studio, New York. Recipient: National Endowment for the Arts grant, 1979, 1984; Rosenthal Foundation award, 1981; Guggenheim

grant, 1982 Chevalier de e'Ordre des Arts et des lettres, 1989. Address: 302 West 12th Street, Apartment 10-C, New York, New York 10014, U.S.A.; and 68 Avenue de Saxe, Paris 75015, France.

CRIME PUBLICATIONS

Novels (series: Sidney Holden; Isaac Sidel)

The Franklin Scare. New York, Arbor House, 1977.
The Isaac Quartet (Sidel). London, Zomba, 1984.
    Blue Eyes. New York, Simon and Schuster, 1975.
    Marilyn the Wild. New York, Arbor House, 1976; London, Bloomsbury, 1990.
    The Education of Patrick Silver. New York, Arbor House, 1976.
    Secret Isaac. New York, Arbor House, 1978.
War Cries Over Avenue C. New York, Fine, 1985; London, Abacus, 1986.
Paradise Man (Holden). New York, Fine, 1987; London, Joseph, 1988.
The Good Policeman (Sidel). New York, Mysterious Press, 1990; London, Bloomsbury, 1991.

Uncollected Short Stories

"The Blue Book of Crime," in *The New Black Mask*. San Diego, California, Harcourt Brace Jovanovich, 1986.
"Fantômas in New York," in *A Matter of Crime*. San Diego, California, Harcourt Brace Jovanovich, 1988.
"Young Isaac," in *The Armchair Detective* (New York), Summer, 1990.

OTHER PUBLICATIONS

Novels

Once Upon a Droshky. New York, McGraw Hill, 1964.
On the Darkening Green. New York, McGraw Hill, 1965.
Going to Jerusalem. New York, Viking Press, 1967; London, Cape, 1968.
American Scrapbook. New York, Viking Press, 1969.
Eisenhower, My Eisenhower. New York, Holt Rinehart, 1971.
The Tar Baby. New York, Holt Rinehart, 1973.
The Seventh Babe. New York, Arbor House, 1979.
The Catfish Man: A Conjured Life. New York, Arbor House, 1980.
Darlin' Bill: A Love Story of the Wild West. New York, Arbor House, 1980.
Panna Maria. New York, Arbor House, 1982.
Pinocchio's Nose. New York, Arbor House, 1983.
The Magician's Wife. Tournai, Belgium, Casterman, 1986; New York, Catalan, 1987; London, Titan, 1988.

Short Stories

The Man Who Grew Younger and Other Stories. New York, Harper, 1967.

Other

Metropolis: New York as Myth, Marketplace, and Magical Land. New York, Putnam, 1986; London, Abacus, 1988.
Movieland: Hollywood and the Great American Dream Culture. New York, Putnam, 1989.

Editor, *The Single Voice: An Anthology of Contemporary Fiction.* New York, Collier, 1969.
Editor, *The Troubled Vision: An Anthology of Contemporary Short Novels and Passages.* New York, Collier, 1970.

*

Critical Studies: introductions by Charyn to *The Single Voice*, 1969, and *The Troubled Vision*, 1970; "Notes on the Rhetoric of Anti-Realist Fiction" by Albert Guerard, in *Tri-Quarterly* (Evanston, Illinois), Spring 1974; "Jerome Charyn: Artist as Mytholept" by Robert L. Patten, in *Novel* (Providence, Rhode Island), Fall 1984; "Exploding the Genre: The Crime Fiction of Jerome Charyn" by Mike Woolf, in *American Crime Fiction*, London, Macmillan, 1988.

Jerome Charyn comments:

I do not think of myself as a "genre" writer. My own crazy wanderings have led me toward the crime novel. Where else could I go? New York is my heartland, and the heart of New York is crime. It's into this maddening heart that I have tried to enter, not as a sociologist, not as a judge, but as a participant in the city's merciless magic. I am the cops. I am the bad guys. New York is a great city because it has no real ruling class other than the streets. And it is the anarchy of the streets that I write about. That's where my music comes from. That is the only vocabulary I have ever had. I'm the urban tar baby, the ghetto brat whose mother, father, brother, sister are New York.

*   *   *

Jerome Charyn is a prose poet who writes crime novels. He leaves lovely bits and pieces of remarkable scenes in the mind, yet carries the reader forward with narratives of potent intensity. He is a writer of police fantasies, not procedurals. To read a Charyn novel is to enter an alternate universe; the reader is cued early on by the Charyn style that he ain't in Kansas anymore. The author moves easily from a flowing, rhythmic stream of words on one page, to a nervous, fidgeting, blurting rush on the next. But always, Charyn's words are imaginatively and attractively tied together, flavored by quirky juxtapositions and sparked by a demonic sense of humor.

A New Yorker, Charyn reflects the energy of his native city, and nearly every one of his crime-related works is set within the Five Boroughs (the exception is *The Franklin Scare*, his historical novel set in 1940's Washington D.C.). The chaotic atmosphere of New York City, the feeling that "anything can happen and usually does," speeds the cascading fairy-tale plots the author favors.

The journeyman Charyn reader may be intimidated by the author's seeming irrationalities. In *The Franklin Scare*, how much of the information conveyed is real? President Roosevelt *did* make a wartime trip to Hawaii, and rumor *did* have it that he sent a U.S. Navy Battleship back to pick up Fala, his pet Scottish terrier. But did FDR really reserve his closest confidences for a strange sailor who served as his personal barber—Oliver Beebe, the protagonist of the novel? In the autobiographical *The Catfish Man*, Charyn claims to have begun his writing career as an author of pirate adventure stories for pulp magazines, to have been a weightlifter in his teenage years, and to have been doubles ping pong champion of Manhattan's West Side; his partner was an odd, obsessed 12-year-old who treated him with disdain. Questioned, the author admits never to have written for the pulps, and that the youth never existed. (Charyn—almost skeletal today—did, however, lift weights as a boy.) Be on guard—like B. Traven, the enigmatic author of *The Death Ship* and *Treasure of the Sierra Madre*, Charyn delights in warping the truth for his own purposes.

The centerpiece of Charyn's work as a crime novelist is the "Isaac Quartet," four novels written during the 1970's which feature Isaac Sidel, deputy police commissioner of New York City. The first of the four, *Blue Eyes*, centers on the sensitive, shotgun-toting cop Manfred Coen—a protegé of Isaac, who appears in the novel as a sort of sinister back-room chief and puppetmaster. Isaac's machinations cause Coen's death by the end of the book, and Isaac takes over as the central figure for the next three novels: *Marilyn the Wild*, *The Education of Patrick Silver*, and *Secret Isaac*. It is clear that Charyn found Isaac the more compelling character.

As Isaac moves to center stage, he becomes a more human, sympathetic character. He acquires the sort of idiosyncrasies which link him to the great tradition of eccentric detective heroes; Charyn calls him at one point "a Sherlock Holmes with a tapeworm instead of a fiddle." (During the events of the "Quartet," Isaac is given a tapeworm by his archenemies, the Guzmann crime family of the Bronx. Forever after, Isaac carries a bottle of milk in his coat pocket to appease the worm, and stop it from tearing at his insides. At times, the worm represents Isaac's conscience—but the metaphor varies from scene to scene at Charyn's whim.)

In 1990, Charyn returned to Isaac after a long hiatus. With the extra 12 years of development under his belt, the author made *The Good Policeman* the finest of the Isaac novels. The plot is clever and complex, the offbeat stylistic exuberance is under firm control, and the cast of characters is marvelously eccentric. The Christy Mathewson Club, an exclusive Manhattan brotherhood which collects memorabilia on pre-World War II baseball and which figures largely in the criminal goings-on of the plot, is typical of Charyn's brilliantly lunatic creations.

Charyn originally conceived Isaac as a father figure in 1974. They become contemporaries in age in *The Good Policeman*—and Charyn's view of "the Commish" changes accordingly. The author plans a new "Isaac Quartet" for the 1990's.

The highly spiced crime narratives of Jerome Charyn may be an acquired taste; those looking for a new Chandler, Sayers, or McBain had better keep looking. Charyn is a true original—and one who never repeats himself. But once the adventurous reader allows himself to enter Charyn's dangerously enchanted "forest" of New York City, he will find fruit unlike any other in crime fiction.

—William Malloy

CHASE, James Hadley. Pseudonym for René Brabazon Raymond; also wrote as James L. Docherty; Ambrose Grant; Raymond Marshall. British. Born in London, 24 December 1906. Educated at King's School, Rochester, Kent; Reading Grammar School; Hastings University School. Editor of Royal Air Force Journal: Squadron Leader. Married Sylvia Ray, one son. Encyclopedia salesman, then worked for Simpkin Marshall wholesale booksellers in the late 1920's and 1930's. *Died 5 February 1985.*

CRIME PUBLICATIONS

Novels (series: Al Barney; Dave Fenner; Mark Girland; Steve Harmas; Vic Malloy; Herman Radnitz; Helga Rolfe; Lu Silk; Frank Terrell)

No Orchids for Miss Blandish (Fenner). London, Jarrolds, 1939; New York, Howell Soskin, 1942; as *The Villain and the Virgin*, New York, Avon, 1948; revised edition, London, Panther, and Avon, 1961.

The Dead Stay Dumb. London, Jarrolds, 1939; as *Kiss My Fist!*, New York, Eton, 1952.

He Won't Need It Now (as James L. Docherty). London, Rich and Cowan, 1939.

Twelve Chinks and a Woman (Fenner). London, Jarrolds, 1940; New York, Howell Soskin, 1941; revised edition, as *12 Chinamen and a Woman*, London, Novel Library, 1950; as *The Doll's Bad News*, London, Panther, 1970.

Miss Callaghan Comes to Grief. London, Jarrolds, 1941.

Miss Shumway Waves a Wand. London, Jarrolds, 1944.

Eve. London, Jarrolds, 1945.

More Deadly Than the Male (as Ambrose Grant). London, Eyre and Spottiswoode, 1946.

I'll Get You for This. London, Jarrolds, 1946; New York, Avon, 1951.

The Flesh of the Orchid. London, Jarrolds, 1948; New York, Pocket Books, 1972.

You Never Know with Women. London, Jarrolds, 1949; New York, Pocket Books, 1972.

You're Lonely When You're Dead (Malloy). London, Hale, 1949; New York, Duell, 1950.

Figure It Out for Yourself (Malloy). London, Hale, 1950; New York, Duell, 1951; as *The Marijuana Mob*, New York, Eton, 1952.

Lay Her among the Lilies (Malloy). London, Hale, 1950; as *Too Dangerous To Be Free*, New York, Duell, 1951.

Strictly for Cash. London, Hale, 1951; New York, Pocket Books, 1973.

The Fast Buck. London, Hale, 1952.

The Double Shuffle (Harmas). London, Hale, 1952; New York, Dutton, 1953.

This Way for a Shroud. London, Hale, 1953.

I'll Bury My Dead. London, Hale, 1953; New York, Dutton, 1954.

Tiger by the Tail. London, Hale, 1954.

Safer Dead. London, Hale, 1954; as *Dead Ringer*, New York, Ace, 1955.

You've Got It Coming. London, Hale, 1955; New York, Pocket Books, 1973; revised edition, Hale, 1975.

There's Always a Price Tag (Harmas). London, Hale, 1956; New York, Pocket Books, 1973.

The Guilty Are Afraid. London, Hale, 1957; New York, New American Library, 1959.

Not Safe to Be Free. London, Hale, 1958; as *The Case of the Strangled Starlet*, New York, New American Library, 1958.

Shock Treatment (Harmas). London, Hale, and New York, New American Library, 1959.

The World in My Pocket. London, Hale, 1959; New York, Popular Library, 1962.

What's Better Than Money? London, Hale, 1960; New York, Pocket Books, 1972.

Come Easy—Go Easy. London, Hale, 1960; New York, Pocket Books, 1974.

A Lotus for Miss Quon. London, Hale, 1961.

Just Another Sucker. London, Hale, 1961; New York Pocket Books, 1974.

I Would Rather Stay Poor. London, Hale, 1962; New York, Pocket Books, 1974.

A Coffin from Hong Kong. London, Hale, 1962.

Tell It to the Birds (Harmas). London, Hale, 1963; New York, Pocket Books, 1974.

One Bright Summer Morning. London, Hale, 1963; New York, Pocket Books, 1974.

The Soft Centre (Terrell). London, Hale, 1964.

This Is for Real (Girland; Radnitz). London, Hale, 1965; New York, Walker, 1967.

The Way the Cookie Crumbles (Terrell). London, Hale, 1965; New York, Pocket Books, 1974.

Cade. London, Hale, 1966; New York, Pocket Books, 1973.

You Have Yourself a Deal (Girland). London, Hale, 1966; New York, Walker, 1968.

Well Now, My Pretty— (Terrell). London, Hale, 1967; New York, Pocket Books, 1972.

Have This One on Me (Girland). London, Hale, 1967.

An Ear to the Ground (Barney; Harmas; Terrell). London, Hale, 1968.

Believed Violent (Girland; Radnitz; Silk; Terrell). London, Hale, 1968.

The Vulture Is a Patient Bird. London, Hale, 1969.

The Whiff of Money (Girland; Radnitz; Silk). London, Hale, 1969; New York, Pocket Books, 1972.

There's a Hippie on the Highway (Terrell). London, Hale, 1970.

Like a Hole in the Head. London, Hale, 1970.

Want to Stay Alive? London, Hale, 1971.

An Ace up My Sleeve (Rolfe). London, Hale, 1971.

Just a Matter of Time. London, Hale, 1972.

You're Dead Without Money (Barney; Radnitz). London, Hale, 1972.

Knock, Knock! Who's There? London, Hale, 1973.

Have a Change of Scene. London, Hale, 1973.

Three of Spades (omnibus). London, Hale, 1974.

Goldfish Have No Hiding Place. London, Hale, 1974.

So What Happens To Me? London, Hale, 1974.

Believe This, You'll Believe Anything. London, Hale, 1975.

The Joker in the Pack (Rolfe). London, Hale, 1975.

Do Me a Favour—Drop Dead. London, Hale, 1976.

I Hold the Four Aces (Rolfe). London, Hale, 1977.

Meet Mark Girland (omnibus). London, Hale, 1977.

My Laugh Comes Last. London, Hale, 1977.

Consider Yourself Dead. London, Hale, 1978.

You Must Be Kidding. London, Hale, 1979.

A Can of Worms. London, Hale, 1979.

You Can Say That Again. London, Hale, 1980.

Try This One for Size. London, Hale, 1980.

Hand Me a Fig-Leaf. London, Hale, 1981.

We'll Share a Double Funeral. London, Hale, 1982.

Have a Nice Night. London, Hale, 1982.

Not My Thing. London, Hale, 1983.

Hit Them Where It Hurts. London, Hale, 1984.

Meet Helga Rolfe (includes *An Ace Up My Sleeve, The Joker in the Pack, I Hold Four Aces*). London, Hale, 1984.

Get a Load of This. London, Hale, 1984.

Novels as Raymond Marshall (series: Brick-Top Corrigan; Don Micklem)

Lady—Here's Your Wreath. London, Jarrolds, 1940.

Just the Way It Is. London, Jarrolds, 1944.

Blondes' Requiem. London, Jarrolds, 1945; New York, Crown, 1946.

Make the Corpse Walk. London, Jarrolds, 1946.

No Business of Mine. London, Jarrolds, 1947.

Trusted Like the Fox. London, Jarrolds, 1948.

The Paw in the Bottle. London, Jarrolds, 1949.

Mallory (Corrigan). London, Jarrolds, 1950.

In a Vain Shadow. London, Jarrolds, 1951; as James Hadley Chase, London, Hale, 1977.

But a Short Time to Live. London, Jarrolds, 1951.

Why Pick on Me? (Corrigan). London, Jarrolds, 1951.

The Wary Transgressor. London, Jarrolds, 1952.

The Things Men Do. London, Jarrolds, 1953.
Mission to Venice (Micklem). London, Hale, 1954.
The Sucker Punch. London, Jarrolds, 1954.
Mission to Siena (Micklem). London, Hale, 1955.
The Pickup. Toronto, Harlequin, 1955.
Ruthless. Toronto, Harlequin, 1955.
You Find Him—I'll Fix Him. London, Hale, 1956.
Never Trust a Woman. Toronto, Harlequin, 1957.
Hit and Run. London, Hale, 1958; as James Hadley Chase,
London, Hale, 1977.

OTHER PUBLICATIONS

Plays

Get a Load of This, with Arthur Macrea, music and lyrics by
Manning Sherwin and Val Guest (produced London, 1941).
No Orchids for Miss Blandish, with Robert Nesbitt, adaptation
of the novel by Chase (produced London, 1942).
Last Page (produced London, 1946). London, French, 1947.

Other

Editor (as René Raymond), with David Langdon, *Slipstream:
A Royal Air Force Anthology.* London, Eyre and Spottiswoode, 1946.

*

James Hadley Chase commented (1984):
There are authors who like to talk about themselves and their
work. I don't. If an author's work sells steadily and well,
worldwide, he should not need to waste time giving press
interviews, writing introductions, or bothering about what
critics have to say. My job is to write a book for a wide variety
of readers. I do this job conscientiously. An introduction to my
work would certainly not be of use to my general readers. They
couldn't care less. All they are asking for is a good read: that is
what I try to give them.

*   *   *

James Hadley Chase has the dubious distinction of being a
very prolific English author who wrote more than 80 novels
almost exclusively about American characters in American
settings in spite of having made very few trips to the United
States, and then visiting only the atypical locales of Florida and
New Orleans. Most of the author's knowledge of America was
derived from encyclopedias, detailed maps, and slang dictio-
naries. Often referred to in the past as "the king" of thriller
writers by both English and Continental critics, Chase propels
the reader through complex, intricate plots with gaudy,
explosive characters and a fast-moving, hard-boiled style.
Chase was working for a book wholesaler in London when he
wrote his first extremely popular mystery novel, *No Orchids for
Miss Blandish*. An heiress is kidnapped by a mob of ruthless
gangsters. Dave Fenner, an ex-reporter turned private eye, is
the hero of this tale. Fenner stars again in *Twelve Chinks and a
Woman*.
The world of the novels written as Raymond Marshall,
sometimes about Brick-Top Corrigan, an unscrupulous private
eye, or Don Micklem, a millionaire playboy, is the same hard-
boiled, explosive, violent, and fast-paced world of the Chase
novels.
Two of the prominent Chase characters are Vic Malloy, a
California private eye, and Mark Girland, a former CIA agent

who sells his services to support his tastes in women. Girland is
occasionally engaged by the head of the Paris branch of the
CIA; in *You Have Yourself a Deal*, the appearance of a
beautiful amnesiac with three Chinese symbols tattooed on her
left buttock signals the involvement of Girland in a dangerous
caper fraught with Russian and Chinese agents, brutal methods
of information seeking, and beautiful girls.
Ingeniously plotted insurance frauds are the subjects of the
Chase novels starring Maddux and his chief investigator Steve
Harmas, whose beautiful wife, Helen, often provides valuable
assistance. In *Tell It to the Birds* Harmas uncovers an intricate
murder scheme involving a sadistic husband, a prostitute, a
pimp, and an amoral insurance salesman. In *The Double Shuffle*
Harmas and his wife investigate two unusual insurance policies
which could cost Harmas's company, National Fidelity,
650,000 dollars. Twins, one of whom is an exotic dancer who
enjoys "kissing" a pet cobra, a kidnapped movie star, an ex-
con, and a snake island make intriguing ingredients for a
chilling thriller. The facts that the insurance frauds are highly
questionable, that the settings do not much resemble the
California locale on which they are based, and that the
characters retain a 1930's image can all be overlooked when the
reader has been captured by the fast-paced action and thrill-a-
minute dialogue of the Chase style.

—Mary Ann Grochowski

———————

CHASTAIN, Thomas. Also wrote as Nick Carter. American.
Worked as newspaper reporter and editor. President, Mystery
Writers of America, 1989. Address: c/o William Morrow Inc.,
105 Madison Avenue, New York, New York 10016 U.S.A.

CRIME PUBLICATIONS

Novels (series: Inspector Max Kauffman; Perry Mason; J.T.
Spanner)

Death Stalk. New York, Award, 1971.
Assassination Brigade (as Nick Carter). New York, Award,
1973; London, Tandem, 1974.
Pandora's Box (Kauffman; Spanner). New York, Mason and
Lipscomb, 1974; London, Cassell, 1975.
911 (Kauffman). New York, Mason Charter, 1976; as *The
Christmas Bomber*, London, Cassell, 1976.
Vital Statistics (Spanner). New York, Times Books, 1977.
High Voltage (Kauffman). New York, Doubleday, 1979;
London, Hale, 1980.
The Diamond Exchange (Kauffman). New York, Doubleday,
and London, Hale, 1981.
Nightscape. New York, Atheneum, 1982.
*Who Killed the Robins Family? And Where and When and Why
and How Did They Die?* New York, Morrow, 1983.
The Revenge of the Robins Family, with Bill Adler. New York,
Morrow, 1984.
The Picture-Perfect Murders, with Bill Adler. New York,
Morrow, 1987.
Where the Truth Lies, with Helen Hayes. New York, Morrow,
1988.
The Case of Too Many Murders (Mason). New York, Morrow,
1989.
The Case of the Burning Bequest (Mason). New York,
Morrow, 1990.

Uncollected Short Story

"Directed Verdict," in *Murder in Manhattan*, edited by Bill Adler and D.C. Fontana. New York, Morrow, 1986.

OTHER PUBLICATIONS

Novel

Judgment Day. New York, Doubleday, 1962.

*   *   *

Thomas Chastain is best known for his two bestsellers—*Who Killed the Robins Family?* and its sequel *The Revenge of the Robins Family*—based on an idea created by literary agent Bill Adler. Adler's idea was clever: the book's publisher, William Morrow, would offer $10,000 to the reader who came up with the best solution to the eight murders in *Who Killed the Robins Family?*

One by one, Chastain kills off the eight members of the wealthy Robins family; aboard a yacht in the South Pacific, on the Orient Express, and in a series of equally exotic locales. The methods range from the conventional to the bizarre. Chastain provides an endless stream of red herrings, motives, and opportunities for the murders.

Although *Who Killed the Robins Family?*, *The Revenge of the Robins Family*, and *The Picture-Perfect Murders* are all gimmick books, Chastain does a professional job in writing a classic mystery novel in the tradition of Agatha Christie with one exception: the readers must deduce the solutions of the murders themselves. Adler and Chastain's solutions were kept in the U.S. Safety Deposit Corporation in New York and the solutions were added to the paperback editions after the contest was over.

However, the reading public soon tired of these types of gimmick novels, and Chastain returned to writing mysteries—with a twist. He wrote a novel with Helen Hayes called *Where the Truth Lies* and then did an exceptional job capturing Erle Stanley Gardner's writing style in creating a new Perry Mason mystery, *The Case of Too Many Murders*.

The Case of Too Many Murders is the first new Perry Mason mystery in 20 years. Perry Mason returns with Della Street and Paul Drake, Jr. to defend the wife of a businessman who is accused of murdering her husband. This has all the elements of the winning Perry Mason formula: a twisting plot, mysterious clues, and a courtroom finale that solves the case.

Before the instant fame and success of *Who Killed the Robins Family?* and its sequels, Chastain was known for a series of competent police procedurals featuring New York City's Deputy Chief Inspector Max Kauffman. The exceptional aspect of the series is Chastain's use of caper novel elements to generate the plots.

The first book in the series, *Pandora's Box*, introduces J.T. Spanner, a private detective. Spanner discovers an informant who claims a multi-million-dollar heist is about to occur. He turns the informant over to Max Kauffman, but finds himself involved in the case as Kauffman's investigation fails to prevent the theft of priceless paintings from the Metropolitan Museum. The caper is clever and Chastain's handling of the intricate plot is deft, but the shattering conclusion is an unexpected bonus.

911 is less successful. A psychopath sets off a bomb a day while Kauffman receives daily conversations with the man who calls and taunts him on the 911 line. Aspects of Kauffman's personality are central to this book: his personal wealth and his mistress. Unfortunately, these are not enough to sustain a weak plot.

J.T. Spanner takes center stage while Kauffman is in the background in *Vital Statistics*. Spanner almost runs over the mutilated body of a young girl tossed from the car in front of him. The body is hijacked before it can reach the morgue; this chain of events sets Spanner into action, investigating singles bars, sex clubs, and discovering the bizarre plot.

Max Kauffman returns as the main protagonist in *High Voltage*. A band of daring criminals threatens to cause a massive blackout of New York City unless they receive a three-million-dollar ransom. They arrange a series of small blackouts to prove they can do it. Kauffman comes up with a plan to con the criminals, but he has to make the money drop himself. *High Voltage* is the best book in the series.

In *The Diamond Exchange* the caper is large-scale: a group of thieves take over a precinct, and using police uniforms and police cars, pull off a 25-million-dollar heist. Along with the caper, Kauffman also has to deal with a series of rape-murders, a police corruption case, and his own complicated personal life. The resolutions leave the series open for additional books.

The best of Chastain's non-series novels is *Nightscape*, in which a mother of a lost child discovers a pack of wild children who roam the night streets and parks of New York City. Chastain manages to make the situation and the lead character believable and sympathetic. Chastain's best paperback original is *Death Stalk* where three young couples vacationing on the Salmon River find themselves terrorized by a band of escaped convicts. Chastain's first novel, *Judgment Day*, is his weakest; as Walker Percy said of the book, "Any novel beginning with a lynching sets heavy odds against itself...."

—George Kelley

CHESBRO, George C(lark). Also writes as David Cross. American. Born in Washington, D.C., 4 June 1940. Educated at Syracuse University, New York, 1958–62, B.S. in special education. Married 1) Donna Troch in 1960 (divorced 1964), one son; 2) Oranus Ravar in 1966 (divorced 1990). Teacher of special education, 1962–79; Writer in Residence, Rockland Center for the Arts, New York, 1987–88; Visiting Lecturer, Matsu-Susitna College, Alaska University, 1989–90. Since 1980 member of the board of directors, Mystery Writers of America. Agent: Mel Berger, William Morris Agency Inc., 1350 Avenue of the Americas, New York, New York 10019. Address: 15 Orchard Street, Nyack, New York 10960, U.S.A.

CRIME PUBLICATIONS

Novels (series: Dr. Robert Frederickson, Mango in all books except *Bone*)

Shadow of a Broken Man. New York, Simon and Schuster, 1977; London, Severn House, 1981.
City of Whispering Stone, New York, Simon and Schuster, 1978; London, Severn House, 1981.
An Affair of Sorcerers. New York, Simon and Schuster, 1979; London, Severn House, 1980.
The Beasts of Valhalla. New York, Atheneum, 1985; London, Grafton, 1986.

Two Songs This Archangel Sings.   New York, Atheneum, 1986.
The Cold Smell of Sacred Stone.   New York, Atheneum, 1988.
Second Horseman Out of Eden.   New York, Atheneum, 1989.
Bone.   New York, Mysterious Press, 1989.
The Language of Cannibals.   New York, Mysterious Press, 1990.

Short Stories

In the House of Secret Enemies.   New York, Mysterious Press, 1990.

Uncollected Short Stories

"Broken Pattern," in *Alfred Hitchcock's Mystery Magazine* (New York), April 1972.
"The Club of Venice," in *Mike Shane Mystery Magazine* (New York), March 1973.
"Four Knights' Game," in *Alfred Hitchcock's Mystery Magazine* (New York), September 1974.
"King's Indian Defense," in *Alfred Hitchcock's Mystery Magazine* (New York), December 1974.
"The Dragon Variation," in *Alfred Hitchcock's Mystery Magazine* (New York), August 1975.
"House of Rain," in *Mystery Monthly* (New York), November 1976.
"Key 16: The Tower," in *Syracuse University Magazine* (New York), June, 1989

OTHER PUBLICATIONS

Novels

King's Gambit.   London, New English Library, 1976.
Turn Loose the Dragons.   New York, Ballantine, 1982; London, Severn House, 1983.
Veil.   New York, Mysterious Press, 1986.
The Golden Child (novelization of screenplay).   New York, Pocket Books, 1986; London, Severn House, 1987.
Chant (as David Cross).   New York, Berkley, 1986.
Chant: Silent Killer (as David Cross).   New York, Berkley, 1986.
Chant: Code of Blood (as David Cross).   New York, Berkley, 1987.
Jungle of Steel and Stone.   New York, Mysterious Press, 1988.

Other

"The Birth of a Series Character," in *The Writer* (Boston), March 1989.

*

George C. Chesbro comments:

Any reader approaching my fictional world will very quickly discover that at the core of my work is a certain dwarf private investigator, Dr. Robert Frederickson, AKA "Mongo"—a name derived from his days as a circus headliner. Why a dwarf? Although I have often endeavoured to respond to that question, I have never been sure that I know the answer. If there is any "secret" to Mongo's appeal, it may be that all of us, from time to time, feel like dwarves in a world of giants, in imminent danger of being spiritually, emotionally, even physically crushed by events, situations, people, the weight of our lives. If Mongo can survive, so can we.

*   *   *

Even in the pandemonium of its recent years, with hundreds of authors turning their attention to the crime tale, the mystery genre has maintained a certain purity of form. Authors have conservatively settled into subgenres—the cozy, the hard-boiled, the thriller—barricaded the doors, and looked askance at those who challenged the status quo.

George C. Chesbro is one of the few writers to pull aspects of other popular fiction genres into the realm of the classic private eye novel. As a result, Chesbro's novels pop up in science fiction and fantasy listings as well as in mystery. He is one of the few critically successful "crossover acts" in modern crime writing.

A master raconteur, Chesbro doesn't take himself too seriously; within the structure of the private eye form, he seems willing to try anything. Widely-read and inquisitive, Chesbro delights in shoehorning newly-acquired bits of arcane information into his books, building whole plots on such outré devices as clashes between urban ceremonial magicians (*An Affair of Sorcerers*), world Armageddon and the preservation of the "chosen people" in artificial biospheres (*Second Horseman Out of Eden*) or genetic mutation begetting monsters (the novels of the "Valhalla Trilogy,") Chesbro's novels exhibit a wild imagination, and the sort of delight in flamboyant storytelling rarely seen since Lord Dunsany's travel tales of Joseph Jorkens and the heyday of the pulp magazines (in Chesbro's case, comparison may be made to *Weird Tales* as well as to *Black Mask*). This sly attitude of genre leg-pulling can inflame the private eye purist. To confront a mainstream crime writer and ask his opinion of Chesbro's work is to invite raised eyebrows and an icy-toned "Isn't he the man who writes about the *dwarf??*"

Yes, he is. Chesbro's primary detective creation, Dr. Robert Frederickson, known to his friends as "Mongo," is an ex-circus headliner (an acrobat) turned professor of criminology at a leading and unnamed New York City university. By the time of *Second Horseman Out of Eden*, Mongo has left academia in order to open the Frederickson and Frederickson investigation agency in partnership with his normal-sized brother, Garth. Mongo has been called "one of the great characters of recent mystery fiction" by *Ellery Queen's Mystery Magazine*; he is a profoundly human protagonist who is rendered an alien by his dwarfism. A liberal humanist by personal philosophy, Mongo remains an outsider to the common run of humanity.

Throughout the series, however, whether earning his bread as a professor or professional investigator, Mongo takes on the classic role of the private eye with the author's own personal twist—hired to take on seemingly earthbound detecting jobs, Mongo's cases quickly expand into worldwide conspiracies involving advanced science or the supernatural. (Chesbro himself argues against supernatural readings—Garth in *The Cold Smell of Sacred Stone* does not actually perform miracles; the witches and warlocks in *An Affair of Sorcerers* do not perform actual magic. Yet Chesbro writes so strongly about the occult that the effect on the reader is as if supernatural events have actually occured. The author cites the axiom "You should be careful about what you choose to believe, because what you believe is what you become.")

The first novel of the Mongo series, *Shadow of a Broken Man*, is one of the more impressive debuts in modern mystery fiction. The complex plot revolves around an architect long thought dead, but whose unmistakably brilliant work has oddly been continuing. The "Valhalla Trilogy" (consisting of *The Beasts of Valhalla*, *Two Songs This Archangel Sings*, and *The Cold Smell of Sacred Stone*) sees both Mongo and Garth subjected to DNA tampering, resulting in their physical degeneration into subhuman life forms; when the process is reversed, a side effect leaves Garth with a profound psychological shift and deep empathic powers—he eventually becomes the center of a worldwide cult which considers him the new Messiah. Though Garth denies Godhood and the cult is dissolved by the end of the final novel of the trilogy, he retains empathic talents which continue to figure in the series. Over these three novels, Garth transcends the role of sidekick and becomes a fully-defined and fascinating character, a true brother to Mongo.

One of Chesbro's Mongoless novels, the thriller *Bone*, provides a fine example of the author's charmingly quirky, complex imagination. The novel is set among New York's homeless population and concerns a protagonist with a case of double amnesia: an unknown trauma has cleared his memory; he has gone about some mysterious business as a street person for a full year when another trauma blanks him again. He is an amnesiac with not one but *two* lives to recover. In addition to these problems, of course, he has a few more necessary in a thriller: a gang of murderous teenage thugs he has wronged during the past year wants to kill him, and the police are convinced that he is responsible for a series of beheadings of homeless people during that same year. Of course, he might be—he has no idea *what* he was doing then. How's that for complexity?

"Humanity may be an extinct species," says Chesbro; and this is the philosophy behind the heinous conspiracies and galloping entertainment of the novels. Though a strong liberal humanist himself, Chesbro expresses essentially a pessimistic worldview; the self-destructive qualities of the human race—expressed through global pollution, tribalism (both religious and nationalist), and the relentless advance of weapons technology—play a large role in his work. Though Mongo and Garth have managed to save the planet on several occasions, there will never be a shortage of nefarious evildoers for them to vanquish.

—William Malloy

———

CHESTER, Peter. *See* **CHAMBERS, Peter.**

———

CHESTERTON, G(ilbert) K(eith). British. Born in Kensington, London, 29 May 1874. Educated at Colet Court School, London; St. Paul's School, London (editor, *The Debater*, 1891–93), 1887–92; drawing school, St. John's Wood. London, 1892; Slade School of Art, London, 1893–96. Married Frances Alice Blogg in 1901. Worked for the London publishers Redway, 1896, and T. Fisher Unwin, 1896–1902; contributor, *Daily News*, London, 1901–13, and the *Illustrated London News*, 1905–36; co-editor, *Eye Witness*, London, 1911–12, and editor, *New Witness*, 1916–23; regular contributor to the *Daily Herald*, London, 1913–14; leader of the Distributist movement after the war, and subsequently President of the Distributist League; convert to Roman Catholicism, 1922; editor, with H. Jackson and R.B. Johnson, Readers' Classics series, 1922; editor, *G.K.'s Weekly*, 1925–36; Lecturer, Notre Dame University, Indiana, 1930; radio broadcaster BBC, 1930's. Also an illustrator; illustrated some of his own works and books by Hilaire Belloc and E.C. Bentley. President, Detection Club, 1928. Honorary degrees: Edinburgh, Dublin and Notre Dame universities. Fellow, Royal Society of Literature. Knight Commander with Star, Order of St. Gregory the Great, 1934. *Died 14 June 1936.*

CRIME PUBLICATIONS

Novel

The Man Who Was Thursday: A Nightmare. Bristol, Arrowsmith, and New York, Dodd Mead, 1908.

Short Stories (series: Father Brown)

The Club of Queer Trades. London and New York, Harper, 1905.
The Innocence of Father Brown. London, Cassell, and New York, Lane, 1911; as *The Annotated Innocence of Father Brown*, edited by Martin Gardner, New York, Oxford University Press, 1987.
The Wisdom of Father Brown. London, Cassell, 1914; New York, Lane, 1915.
The Man Who Knew Too Much and Other Stories. London, Cassell, and New York, Harper, 1922.
The Incredulity of Father Brown. London, Cassell, and New York, Dodd Mead, 1926.
The Secret of Father Brown. London, Cassell, and New York, Harper, 1927.
The Poet and the Lunatic: Episodes in the Life of Gabriel Gale. London, Cassell, and New York, Dodd Mead, 1929.
The Moderate Murderer, and the Honest Quack. New York, Dodd Mead, 1929.
The Ecstatic Thief. New York, Dodd Mead, 1930.
Four Faultless Felons. London, Cassell, and New York, Dodd Mead, 1930.
The Floating Admiral, with others. London, Hodder and Stoughton, 1931; New York, Doubleday, 1932.
The Scandal of Father Brown. London, Cassell, and New York, Dodd Mead, 1935.
The Paradoxes of Mr. Pond. London, Cassell, 1936; New York, Dodd Mead, 1937.
The Vampire of the Village. Privately printed, 1947.
Father Brown: Selected Stories, edited by Ronald Knox. London, Oxford University Press, 1955.
The Father Brown Omnibus. New York, Dodd Mead, 1983.
Thirteen Detectives: Classic Mystery Stories, edited by Marie Smith. London, Xanadu, 1987.
The Best of Father Brown, edited by H.R.F. Keating. London, Dent, 1987.

Uncollected Short Story

"Dr. Hyde, Detective" ["The White Pillar Murders"], in *To the Queen's Taste*, edited by Ellery Queen. Boston, Little Brown, 1946.

OTHER PUBLICATIONS

Novels

The Napoleon of Notting Hill. London and New York, Lane, 1904.
The Ball and the Cross. New York, Lane, 1909; London, Wells Gardner, 1910.
Manalive. London, Nelson, and New York, Lane, 1912.
The Flying Inn. London, Methuen, and New York, Lane, 1914.
The Return of Don Quixote. London, Chatto and Windus, and New York, Dodd Mead, 1927.

Short Stories

The Tremendous Adventures of Major Brown. London, Shurmer Sibthorp, 1903.
The Perishing of the Pendragons. New York, Paget, 1914.
Tales of the Long Bow. London, Cassell, and New York, Dodd Mead, 1925.
The Sword of Wood. London, Elkin Mathews, 1928.
Stories. London, Harrap, 1928.
The Coloured Lands (includes non-fiction). London and New York, Sheed and Ward, 1938.
Selected Stories, edited by Kingsley Amis. London, Faber, 1972.
Daylight and Nightmare: Uncollected Stories and Fables, edited by Marie Smith. London, Xanadu, and New York, Dodd Mead, 1986.

Plays

Magic: A Fantastic Comedy (produced Eastbourne and London, 1913; New York, 1917). London, Martin Secker, and New York, Putnam, 1913.
The Judgment of Dr. Johnson (produced London, 1932). London, Sheed and Ward, 1927; New York, Putnam, 1928.
The Surprise (produced Hull, 1953). London, Sheed and Ward, 1953.

Verse

Greybeards at Play: Literature and Art for Old Gentlemen: Rhymes and Sketches. London, R. Brimley Johnson, 1900.
The Wild Knight and Other Poems. London, Richards, 1900; revised edition, London, Dent, and New York, Dutton, 1914.
The Ballad of the White Horse. London, Methuen, and New York, Lane, 1911.
Poems. London, Burns Oates, 1915; New York, Lane, 1916.
Wine, Water, and Song. London, Methuen, 1915.
A Poem. Privately printed, 1915.
Old King Cole. Privately printed, 1920.
The Ballad of St. Barbara and Other Verses. London, Palmer, 1922; New York, Putnam, 1923.
(Poems). London, Benn, and New York, Stokes, 1925.
The Queen of Seven Swords. London, Sheed and Ward, 1926.
The Collected Poems of G.K. Chesterton. London, Palmer, 1927; revised edition, New York, Dodd Mead, 1932.
Gloria in Profundis. London, Faber and Gwyer, and New York, Rudge, 1927.
Ubi Ecclesia. London, Faber, 1929.
The Grave of Arthur. London, Faber, 1930.
Greybeards at Play and Other Comic Verse, edited by John Sullivan. London, Elek, 1974.
Collected Nonsense and Light Verse, edited by Marie Smith. London, Xanadu, and New York, Dodd Mead, 1987.

Other

The Defendant. London, R. Brimley Johnson, 1901; New York, Dodd Mead, 1902.
Twelve Types. London, Humphreys, 1902; augmented edition, as *Varied Types*, New York, Dodd Mead, 1903; selections as *Five Types*, Humphreys, 1910; New York, Holt, 1911; and as *Simplicity and Tolstoy*, Humphreys, 1912.
Thomas Carlyle. London, Hodder and Stoughton, 1902; New York, Pott, n.d.

Robert Louis Stevenson, with W. Robertson Nicoll. London, Hodder and Stoughton, and New York, Pott, 1903.
Leo Tolstoy, with G.H. Perris and Edward Garnett. London, Hodder and Stoughton, and New York, Pott, 1903.
Charles Dickens, with F.G. Kitton. London, Hodder and Stoughton, and New York, Pott, 1903.
Robert Browning. London and New York, Macmillan, 1903.
Tennyson, with Richard Garnett. London, Hodder and Stoughton, 1903; New York, Pott, n.d.
Thackeray, with Lewis Melville. London, Hodder and Stoughton, and New York, Pott, 1903.
G.F. Watts. London, Duckworth, and New York, Dutton, 1904.
Heretics. London and New York, Lane, 1905.
Charles Dickens. London, Methuen, and New York, Dodd Mead, 1906.
All Things Considered. London, Methuen, and New York, Lane, 1908.
Orthodoxy. London and New York, Lane, 1908.
George Bernard Shaw. London and New York, Lane, 1909; revised edition, London, Lane, 1935.
Tremendous Trifles. London, Methuen, and New York, Dodd Mead, 1909.
What's Wrong with the World. London, Cassell, and New York, Dodd Mead, 1910.
Alarms and Discursions. London, Methuen, 1910; New York, Dodd Mead, 1911.
William Blake. London, Duckworth, and New York, Dutton, 1910.
The Ultimate Lie. Privately printed, 1910.
A Chesterton Calendar. London, Kegan Paul, 1911; as *Wit and Wisdom of G.K. Chesterton*, New York, Dodd Mead, 1911; as *Chesterton Day by Day*, Kegan Paul, 1912.
Appreciations and Criticisms of the Works of Charles Dickens. London, Dent, and New York, Dutton, 1911.
A Defence of Nonsense and Other Essays. New York, Dodd Mead, 1911.
The Future of Religion: Mr. G.K. Chesterton's Reply to Mr. Bernard Shaw. Privately printed, 1911.
The Conversion of an Anarchist. New York, Paget, 1912.
A Miscellany of Men. London, Methuen, and New York, Dodd Mead, 1912.
The Victorian Age in Literature. London, Williams and Norgate, and New York, Holt, 1913.
Thoughts from Chesterton, edited by Elsie E. Morton. London, Harrap, 1913.
The Barbarism of Berlin. London, Cassell, 1914.
London, photographs by Alvin Langdon Coburn. Privately printed, 1914.
Prussian Versus Belgian Culture. Edinburgh, Belgian Relief and Reconstruction Fund, 1914.
Letters to an Old Garibaldian. London, Methuen, 1915; with *The Barbarism of Berlin*, as *The Appetite of Tyranny*, New York, Dodd Mead, 1915.
The So-Called Belgian Bargain. London, National War Aims Committee, 1915.
The Crimes of England. London, Palmer and Hayward, 1915; New York, Lane, 1916.
Divorce Versus Democracy. London, Society of SS. Peter and Paul, 1916.
Temperance and the Great Alliance. London, True Temperance Association, 1916.
The G.K. Chesterton Calendar, edited by H. Cecil Palmer. London, Palmer and Hayward, 1916.
A Shilling for My Thoughts, edited by E.V. Lucas. London, Methuen, 1916.
Lord Kitchener. Privately printed, 1917.

A Short History of England. London, Chatto and Windus, and New York, Lane, 1917.

Utopia of Usurers and Other Essays. New York, Boni and Liveright, 1917.

How to Help Annexation. London, Hayman Christy and Lilly, 1918.

Irish Impressions. London, Collins, and New York, Lane, 1920.

The Superstition of Divorce. London, Chatto and Windus, and New York, Lane, 1920.

Charles Dickens Fifty Years After. Privately printed, 1920.

The Uses of Diversity: A Book of Essays. London, Methuen, 1920; New York, Dodd Mead, 1921.

The New Jerusalem. London, Hodder and Stoughton, 1920; New York, Doran, 1921.

Eugenics and Other Evils. London, Cassell, 1922; New York, Dodd Mead, 1927.

What I Saw in America. London, Hodder and Stoughton, and New York, Dodd Mead, 1922.

Fancies Versus Fads. London, Methuen, and New York, Dodd Mead, 1923.

St. Francis of Assisi. London, Hodder and Stoughton, 1923; New York, Dodd Mead, 1924.

The End of the Roman Road: A Pageant of Wayfarers. London, Classic Press, 1924.

The Superstitions of the Sceptic (lecture). Cambridge, Heffer, and St. Louis, Herder, 1925.

The Everlasting Man. London, Hodder and Stoughton, and New York, Dodd Mead, 1925.

William Cobbett. London, Hodder and Stoughton, 1925; New York, Dodd Mead, 1926.

The Outline of Sanity. London, Methuen, 1926; New York, Dodd Mead, 1927.

The Catholic Church and Conversion. New York, Macmillan, 1926; London, Burns Oates, 1927.

Selected Works (Minerva Edition). London, Methuen, 9 vols., 1926.

A Gleaming Cohort, Being Selections from the Works of G.K. Chesterton, edited by E.V. Lucas. London, Methuen, 1926.

Social Reform Versus Birth Control. London, Simpkin Marshall, 1927.

Culture and the Coming Peril (lecture). London, University of London Press, 1927.

Robert Louis Stevenson. London, Hodder and Stoughton, 1927; New York, Dodd Mead, 1928.

Generally Speaking: A Book of Essays. London, Methuen, and New York, Dodd Mead, 1928.

(Essays). London, Harrap, 1928.

Do We Agree? A Debate, with G.B. Shaw. London, Palmer, and Hartford, Connecticut, Mitchell, 1928.

A Chesterton Catholic Anthology, edited by Patrick Braybrooke. London, Burns Oates, and New York, Kenedy, 1928.

The Thing (essays). London, Sheed and Ward, 1929.

G.K.C. a M.C., Being a Collection of Thirty-Seven Introductions, edited by J.P. de Fonseka. London, Methuen, 1929.

The Resurrection of Rome. London, Hodder and Stoughton, and New York, Dodd Mead, 1930.

Come to Think of It: A Book of Essays. London, Methuen, 1930; New York, Dodd Mead, 1931.

The Turkey and the Turk. Ditchling, Sussex, St. Dominic's Press, 1930.

At the Sign of the World's End. Palo Alto, California, Harvest Press, 1930.

Is There a Return to Religion? with E. Haldeman-Julius. Girard, Kansas, Haldeman Julius, 1931.

All Is Grist: A Book of Essays. London, Methuen, 1931; New York, Dodd Mead, 1932.

Chaucer. London, Faber, and New York, Farrar Rinehart, 1932.

Sidelights on New London and Newer York and Other Essays. London, Sheed and Ward, and New York, Dodd Mead, 1932.

Christendom in Dublin. London, Sheed and Ward, 1932; New York, Sheed and Ward, 1933.

All I Survey: A Book of Essays. London, Methuen, and New York, Dodd Mead, 1933.

St. Thomas Aquinas. London, Hodder and Stoughton, and New York, Sheed and Ward, 1933.

G.K. Chesterton (selected humour), edited by E.V. Knox. London, Methuen, 1933; as *Running after One's Hat and Other Whimsies,* New York, McBride, 1933.

Avowals and Denials: A Book of Essays. London, Methuen, 1934; New York, Dodd Mead, 1935.

The Well and the Shallows. London and New York, Sheed and Ward, 1935.

Explaining the English. London, British Council, 1935.

Stories, Essays and Poems. London, Dent, 1935.

As I Was Saying: A Book of Essays. London, Methuen, and New York, Dodd Mead, 1936.

Autobiography. London, Hutchinson, and New York, Sheed and Ward, 1936.

The Man Who Was Chesterton, edited by Raymond T. Bond. New York, Dodd Mead, 1937.

Essays, edited by John Guest. London, Collins, 1939.

The End of the Armistice, edited by F.J. Sheed. London and New York, Sheed and Ward, 1940.

Selected Essays, edited by Dorothy Collins. London, Methuen, 1949.

The Common Man. London and New York, Sheed and Ward, 1950.

Essays, edited by K.E. Whitehorn. London, Methuen, 1953.

A Handful of Authors: Essays on Books and Writers, edited by Dorothy Collins. London and New York, Sheed and Ward, 1953.

The Glass Walking-Stick and Other Essays from the Illustrated London News 1905–1936, edited by Dorothy Collins. London, Methuen, 1955.

G.K. Chesterton: An Anthology, edited by D.B. Wyndham Lewis. London and New York, Oxford University Press, 1957.

Essays and Poems, edited by Wilfrid Sheed. London, Penguin, 1958.

Lunacy and Letters (essays), edited by Dorothy Collins. London and New York, Sheed and Ward, 1958.

Where All Roads Lead. London, Catholic Truth Society, 1961.

The Man Who Was Orthodox: A Selection from the Uncollected Writings of G.K. Chesterton, edited by A.L. Maycock. London, Dobson, 1963.

The Spice of Life and Other Essays, edited by Dorothy Collins. Beaconsfield, Buckinghamshire, Finlayson, 1964; Philadelphia, Dufour, 1966.

G.K. Chesterton: A Selection from His Non-Fictional Prose, edited by W.H. Auden. London, Faber, 1970.

Chesterton on Shakespeare, edited by Dorothy Collins. Henley on Thames, Oxfordshire, and Chester Springs, Pennsylvania, Dufour, 1971.

The Apostle and the Wild Ducks, and Other Essays, edited by Dorothy Collins. London, Elek, 1975.

The Spirit of Christmas: Stories, Poems, Essays, edited by Marie Smith. London, Xanadu, 1984; New York, Dodd Mead, 1985.

As I Was Saying: A Chesterton Reader, edited by Robert Knille. Grand Rapids, Michigan, Eerdmans, and Exeter, Paternoster, 1985.

The Bodley Head G.K. Chesterton, edited by P.J. Kavanagh. London, Bodley Head, 1985; as *The Essential Chesterton*, Oxford, Oxford University Press, 1987.
Collected Works, edited by Denis J. Conlon. Harrison, New York, Ignatius Press, 1986–87; San Francisco, Ignatius Press, 1989.

Editor, *Thackeray* (selections). London, Bell, 1909.
Editor, with Alice Meynell, *Samuel Johnson* (selections). London, Herbert and Daniel, 1911.
Editor, *Essays by Divers Hands 6*. London, Oxford University Press, 1926.
Editor, *G.K.'s* (miscellany from *G.K.'s Weekly*). London, Rich and Cowan, 1934.

*

Bibliography: *Chesterton: A Bibliography* by John Sullivan. London, University of London Press, 1958, supplement, 1968, and *Chesterton 3: A Bibliographical Postscript*, Bedford, Vintage, 1980.

Manuscript Collections: Humanities Research Center, University of Texas, Austin; John Carroll University Library, Cleveland, Ohio.

Critical Studies: *Paradox in Chesterton* by Hugh Kenner, New York, Sheed and Ward, 1947; *Chesterton: Man and Mask* by Garry Wills, New York, Sheed and Ward, 1961; *G.K. Chesterton: A Bibliography* by Dudley Barker, London, Constable, 1973; *G.K. Chesterton* by Lawrence J. Clipper, New York, Twayne, 1974; *Chesterton: A Centennial Appraisal* edited by John Sullivan, New York, Barnes and Noble, 1974; *The Novels of G.K. Chesterton: A Study in Art and Propaganda* by Ian Boyd, New York, Barnes and Noble, and London, Elek, 1975; *Chesterton: The Critical Judgments 1900–1937*, edited by D.J. Conlon 1976; *Chesterton: Explorations in Allegory* by Lynette Hunter, London, Macmillan, 1979. *The Outline of Sanity: A Biography of G.K. Chesterton* by Alzina Stone Dale, Grand Rapids, Michigan, Eerdmans, 1982; *G.K. Chesterton* by Michael Ffinch, London, Weidenfeld and Nicolson, 1986; *G.K. Chesterton: A Critical Study* by K. Dwarakanath, New Delhi, Classical, 1986; *G.K. Chesterton: A Half Century of Views*, edited by D.J. Conlon, Oxford and New York, Oxford University Press, 1987; *Gilbert: The Man Who Was G.K. Chesterton*, edited by Michael Coren, London, Cape, 1989: New York, Paragon, 1990.

*   *   *

G.K. Chesterton, very much a figure of the first third of the 20th century, was a spouting volcano of fire-dazzling words who appears to have left solely mounds of dead ashes—with one notable exception, his still glowingly alive detective stories about the little, modest Catholic priest Father Brown. Ironically, many of these he regarded as pot-boilers. Told his bank balance had shrunk to a mere hundred pounds, he would say "That means Father Brown again." Yet the best of these stories are among the peaks of crime fiction.

What the Father Brown stories interrupted, and partly paid for, was polemical journalism, debating (his encounters with Shaw were legendary), poetry, literary and art criticism, and novels. But the stories frequently rose above these hazards, as well as the hazard of the form they took, the moral paradox. The chief reason they did so was that Chesterton wrote with immense verve and splendid vividness (not for nothing was he an artist, trained at the prestigious Slade School). A strong

subsidiary reason was his greedy delight in the detective genre. The pockets of the enveloping cape he wore were apt to be stuffed with what he called "penny dreadfuls" and some of his stories are of a devilish, or god-like, detective ingenuity (how is it that there is one corpse but two heads in "The Secret Garden"?; what is the answer to "The Invisible Man"?; what is the significance of "The Queer Feet"?). It is fitting that when the Detection Club was founded in London in 1928 he was elected its first President.

In an essay written 10 years before Father Brown was brought to life he said, in his typically over-the-top manner, that the detective was "the original and poetic figure, while the burglars and footpads are merely placid old cosmic conservatives, happy in the immemorial respectability of apes and wolves." The words give an immediate flavour of Chesterton's endemic paradox-making.

Indeed, Father Brown's very origin sprang from a paradox. Chesterton had become acquainted with a Father O'Connor and had been deeply impressed one morning by his knowledge, gained in the confessional, of the evil in man. At lunch some students had been delighted by the priest's intelligent conversation but afterwards deplored the way he must be living in protected ignorance. Out of this contrast Chesterton evolved his clumsy bumbler with a face "as round and dull as a Norfolk dumpling," a seeming innocent who could see further into mysteries than any policeman, though in the stories written after Chesterton had become a Catholic himself (in 1922) his hero tends to be simply an astute investigator.

Father Brown's method at his best, however, was to put himself heart and soul—I use the words advisedly—into the minds of suspects. With a murderer he plunges down "till I have bent myself into the posture of his hunched and peering hatred." Thus Chesterton makes his hero at once, and unbeknowingly, that archetype, The Great Detective. He is Poe's Dupin seeking night solitude to penetrate at once the mystery of a mere crime and of the human contradiction. He is Sherlock Holmes, pipe-smoke wreathed and plunging, or Maigret as enveloped in tobacco clouds.

It should be added that stories in *The Club of Queer Trades* and in *The Man Who Knew Too Much* and *Four Faultless Felons* come more or less into the crime field and have their virtues. And there is the thriller novel *The Man Who Was Thursday*, which with *Napoleon of Notting Hill*, is an exception, though neglected, to my dictum that only the Father Brown stories still glow with life. But *Thursday*, despite all its seven main characters turning out to be detectives, hardly puts its crime content first. Chesterton's fame still rests on the priest with "the harmless, human name of Brown" and it will endure.

—H.R.F. Keating

———

CHEYNEY, Peter (Reginald Southouse Cheyney). Also wrote as Harold Brust. British. Born in London in 1896. Trained as a lawyer; worked as songwriter, bookmaker, journalist, and politician. *Died 26 June 1951.*

<small>CRIME PUBLICATIONS</small>

Novels (series: Slim Callaghan; Lemmy Caution; Michael Kells; Everard Peter Quayle; Johnny Vallon)

This Man Is Dangerous (Caution). London, Collins, 1936; New York, Coward McCann, 1938.

Poison Ivy (Caution). London, Collins, 1937.

Dames Don't Care (Caution). London, Collins, 1937; New York, Coward McCann, 1938.

Can Ladies Kill? (Caution). London, Collins, 1938.

The Urgent Hangman (Callaghan). London, Collins, 1938; New York, Coward McCann, 1939.

Don't Get Me Wrong (Caution). London, Collins, 1939.

Dangerous Curves. London, Collins, 1939; as *Callaghan*, New York, Belmont, 1973.

Another Little Drink. London, Collins, 1940; as *A Trap for Bellamy*, New York, Dodd Mead, 1941; as *Premeditated Murder*, New York, Avon, 1943.

You'd Be Surprised (Caution). London, Collins, 1940.

You Can't Keep the Change (Callaghan). London, Collins, 1940; New York, Dodd Mead, 1944.

Your Deal, My Lovely (Caution). London, Collins, 1941.

It Couldn't Matter Less (Callaghan). London, Collins, 1941; New York, Arcadia House, 1943; as *Set-Up for Murder*, New York, Pyramid, 1950.

Never a Dull Moment (Caution). London, Collins, 1942.

Dark Duet. London, Collins, 1942; New York, Dodd Mead, 1943; as *The Counter Spy Murders*, New York, Avon, 1944.

Sorry You've Been Troubled (Callaghan). London, Collins, 1942; as *Farewell to the Admiral*, New York, Dodd Mead, 1943.

The Unscrupulous Mr. Callaghan. New York, Handi-Books, 1943.

You Can Always Duck (Caution). London, Collins, 1943.

The Stars Are Dark (Quayle). London, Collins, and New York, Dodd Mead, 1943; as *The London Spy Murders*, New York, Avon, 1944.

They Never Say When (Callaghan). London, Collins, 1944; New York, Dodd Mead, 1945.

The Dark Street (Quayle). London, Collins, and New York, Dodd Mead, 1944; as *The Dark Street Murders*, New York, Avon, 1946.

Sinister Errand (Kells). London, Collins, and New York, Dodd Mead, 1945; as *Sinister Murders*, New York, Avon, 1957.

I'll Say She Does! (Caution). London, Collins, 1945; New York, Dodd Mead, 1946.

Dark Hero. London, Collins, and New York, Dodd Mead, 1946.

Uneasy Terms (Callaghan). London, Collins, 1946; New York, Dodd Mead, 1947.

The Curiosity of Etienne MacGregor. London, Locke, 1947; as *The Sweetheart of the Razors*, London, New English Library, 1962.

Dark Interlude (Quayle). London, Collins, and New York, Dodd Mead, 1947; as *The Terrible Night*, New York, Avon, 1959.

Dance Without Music. London, Collins, 1947; New York, Dodd Mead, 1948.

Try Anything Twice. London, Collins, and New York, Dodd Mead, 1948; as *Undressed to Kill*, New York, Avon, 1959.

Dark Wanton (Quayle). London, Collins, 1948; New York, Dodd Mead, 1949.

You Can Call It a Day (Vallon). London, Collins, 1949; as *The Man Nobody Saw*, New York, Dodd Mead, 1949.

One of Those Things. London, Collins, 1949; New York, Dodd Mead, 1950; as *Mistress Murder*, New York, Avon, 1951.

Lady, Behave! (Vallon). London, Collins, 1950; as *Lady Beware*, New York, Dodd Mead, 1950.

Dark Bahama (Vallon). London, Collins, 1950; New York, Dodd Mead, 1951; as *I'll Bring Her Back*, New York, Eton, 1952.

Ladies Won't Wait (Kells). London, Collins, and New York, Dodd Mead, 1951; as *Cocktails and the Killer*, New York, Avon, 1957.

Short Stories (series: Alonzo MacTavish)

You Can't Hit a Woman and Other Stories. London, Collins, 1937.

Knave Takes Queen. London, Collins, 1939.

Mister Caution—Mister Callaghan. London, Collins, 1941.

Adventures of Alonzo MacTavish. London, Todd, 1943.

Alonzo MacTavish Again. London, Todd, 1943.

Love with a Gun and Other Stories. London, Todd, 1943.

The Murder of Alonzo. London, Todd, 1943.

Account Rendered. London, Vallancey Press, 1944.

The Adventures of Julia. Brighton, Poynings Press, 1945; as *The Adventures of Julia and Two Other Spy Stories*, London, Todd, 1954; as *The Killing Game*, New York, Belmont, 1975.

Dance Without Music. London, Vallancey Press, 1945.

Escape for Sandra. Brighton, Poynings Press, 1945.

Night Club. Brighton, Poynings Press, 1945; as *Dressed to Kill*, London, Todd, 1952.

A Tough Spot for Cupid and Other Stories. London, Vallancey Press, 1945.

You Can't Trust Duchesses and Other Stories. London, Vallancey Press, 1945.

G Man at the Yard. Brighton, Poynings Press, 1946.

Date after Dark and Other Stories. London, Todd, 1946.

He Walked in Her Sleep and Other Stories (MacTavish). London, Todd, 1946; as *MacTavish*, New York, Belmont, 1973.

The Man with Two Wives and Other Stories. London, Todd, 1946.

A Spot of Murder and Other Stories. London, Todd, 1946.

Time for Caution. Hounslow, Middlesex, Foster, 1946.

Vengeance with a Twist and Other Stories. London, Vallancey Press, 1946.

Lady in Green and Other Stories. London, Bantam, 1947.

A Matter of Luck and Other Stories. London, Bantam, 1947.

Cocktail for Cupid and Other Stories. London, Bantam, 1948.

Cocktail Party and Other Stories. London, Bantam, 1948.

Fast Work and Other Stories. London, Bantam, 1948.

Information Received and Other Stories. London, Bantam, 1948.

The Unhappy Lady and Other Stories. London, Bantam, 1948.

The Lady in Tears and Other Stories. London, Bantam, 1949.

Velvet Johnnie and Other Stories. London, Collins, 1952.

Calling Mr. Callaghan. London, Todd, 1953.

The Best Stories of Peter Cheyney, edited by Viola G. Garvin. London, Faber, 1954.

The Mystery Blues and Other Stories. London, Todd, 1954; as *Fast Work*, London, Four Square, 1964.

OTHER PUBLICATIONS

Plays

Screenplay: *Wife of General Ling*, with others, 1937.

Radio Plays: *The Adventures of Alonzo MacTavish* (serial), 1939; *The Callaghan Touch* (serial), 1941; *Knave Takes Queen*, 1941; *The Key*, 1941; *The Lady Talks*, 1942; *Again—Callaghan*, 1942; *The Perfumed Murder*, 1943; *Concerto for Crooks*, 1943;

Parisian Ghost, 1943; *The Callaghan Come-Back* (serial), 1943; *The Adventures of Julia*, 1945; *Way Out*, 1945; *Pay-Off for Cupid*, 1946; *Duet for Crooks*, 1946.

Other

Three Character Sketches.   London, Reynolds, 1927.
"I Guarded Kings": The Memoirs of a Political Police Officer (as Harold Brust).   London, Stanley Paul, 1935.
In Plain Clothes: Further Memoirs of a Political Police Officer (as Harold Brust).   London, Stanley Paul, 1937.
Making Crime Pay (miscellany).   London, Faber, 1944.
No Ordinary Cheyney (stories and sketches).   London, Faber, 1948.

Editor, *Best Stories of the Underworld.*   London, Faber, 1942.

*

Critical Study: *Peter Cheyney, Prince of Hokum* by Michael Harrison, London, Spearman, 1954.

*   *   *

Peter Cheyney was an Englishman whose specialty was ersatz hard-boiled "American"-style thrillers aimed primarily at British and European audiences, although by the mid-1940's he had acquired a considerable following in America as well.

Cheyney's earliest fiction works were short stories and serials for British magazines and newspapers in the early 1930's. His initial series character, who never appeared in a novel, was a debonair rogue named Alonzo MacTavish. The MacTavish tales offer early, well-done examples of Cheyney's affinity for intricate plots concerning opposing criminal factions who try to outwit each other through an intricate web of double- and triple-crosses. This became a common plot element throughout the Cheyney canon. The character and style of the MacTavish stories were more than a little influenced by the Saint adventures by Leslie Charteris, and were gathered together in a volume entitled *He Walked in Her Sleep.*

For his first novel, *This Man Is Dangerous*, Cheyney turned to the American detective pulp magazine for his inspiration, primarily to the work of Carroll John Daly and Robert Leslie Bellem, with an occasional nod to Jonathan Latimer. Cheyney's first novel introduced Lemmy Caution, a tough American G-man who narrates his own adventures in the present tense. Caution went on to appear in several more novels as well as a handful of short stories and radio dramas, with the plotting mannerisms of the MacTavish stories now set against the constant rattling of pistols and tommyguns. Unfortunately, Cheyney's American underworld milieu in most of these books is far from convincing; his attempts at tough guy dialogue are uniformly unintentionally hilarious, far closer to Damon Runyon than anything actually spoken by such hard-boiled types ("Carson, a New York 'G' man, was takin' it all down in shorthand, after which this palooka passes out and hands in his dinner pail before he comes around again, an' so that is that, an' where do you go from there?").

Cheyney was the first British thriller writer to attempt to write in a purely American vein, and the cynicism and graphic violence of the Caution books, which far exceeded even that of the earlier Bulldog Drummond tales by Sapper, both shocked and dismayed many British readers and critics. Yet the best of the Caution books—such as the first, as well as *Can Ladies Kill?* and *You'd Be Surprised*—served as interesting examples of

Cheyney's singular gifts for breakneck pace, colorful characterization, wit, and intricacy of plotting. The Caution series also served to launch Cheyney's career as one of the most popular storytellers of his time, and his time, and his success inspired a long line of British hard-boiled writers such as James Hadley Chase, Hartley Howard, Peter Chambers, Hank Janson, and Carter Brown.

For his next series, about private eye Slim Callaghan, Cheyney again switched influences, this time to two more American detective writers, borrowing the understated prose style of Dashiell Hammett and the slightly tipsy humor of Cleve F. Adams. Cheyney also wisely shifted the setting of the Callaghan books to London, drawing on his first-hand knowledge of that city's West End gambling club and crime scene which he had acquired during his years as a journalist before turning to fiction. The Callaghan books were every bit as popular as the Caution tales and indicated a maturing of Cheyney's talents as a writer, with the frantic nonstop action of the Caution novels giving way to a more subtle approach. *The Urgent Hangman* and *Dangerous Curves* are both fine examples of the Callaghan series. Cheyney also employed a similar tone and style in a number of non-series private eye books, the best of these being *Another Little Drink* and *Dance Without Music.*

Cheyney's most original, and most critically acclaimed, work was his so-called "Dark" series of espionage novels, all of which feature the word dark in the title, concerning a top secret British counter-intelligence unit operating against Nazi agents in war-time England and abroad. Cheyney's cross-doublecross plotting technique reached its zenith in these uncompromising studies of the cold-blooded world of spies and double agents. With their vivid characterizations, effective low-key writing style, and well-maintained building of suspense, the first two books of this series, *Dark Duet* and *The Stars Are Dark*, represent Cheyney at the very top of his form.

—Stephen Mertz

———

CHILDERS, (Robert) Erskine.   British.   Born in London, 25 June 1870. Educated at Haileybury College; Trinity College, Cambridge, B.A. 1893. Married Mary Alden Osgood in 1904; two sons. Served in the City Imperial Volunteer Battery of the Honourable Artillery Company during the Boer War; in the Royal Naval Air Service during World War I: Lieutenant-Commander; mentioned in despatches; Distinguished Service Cross. Clerk in the House of Commons, 1895–1910; settled in Dublin in 1919, and fought for Home Rule; elected to the Dail Eireann, for County Wicklow, 1921; principal secretary to delegation for Irish-UK treaty; joined the Irish Republican Army after the establishment of the Irish Free State: court-martialled and executed, 1922. *Died 24 November 1922.*

CRIME PUBLICATIONS

Novel

The Riddle of the Sands: A Record of Secret Service Recently Achieved.   London, Smith Elder, 1903; New York, Dodd Mead, 1915.

OTHER PUBLICATIONS

Other

In the Ranks of the C.I.V.: A Narrative and Diary of Personal Experiences with the C.I.V. Battery (Honourable Artillery Company) in South Africa. London, Smith Elder, 1900.
The H.A.C. in South Africa: A Record of the Services Rendered in the South African War by Members of the Honourable Artillery Company, with Basil Williams. London, Smith Elder, 1903.
The Times History of the War in South Africa, vol. 5. London, Sampson Low, 1907.
War and the Arme Blanche. London, Arnold, 1910.
German Influence on British Cavalry. London, Arnold, 1911.
The Framework of Home Rule. London, Arnold, 1911.
The Form and Purpose of Home Rule: A Lecture. Dublin, Ponsonby, 1912.
Military Rule in Ireland. Dublin, Talbot Press, 1920.
Is Ireland a Danger to England? Dublin, Woodgrange Press, 1921.
What the Treaty Means. Dublin, Republic of Ireland, 1922.
Clause by Clause: A Comparison Between the "Treaty" and Document No. 2. Dublin, Republic of Ireland, 1922.
A Thirst for the Sea: The Sailing Adventures of Erskine Childers, edited by Hugh and Robin Popham. London, Stanford Maritime, 1979.

Editor, with Alfred O'Rahilly, *Who Burnt Cork City? A Tale of Arson, Loot, and Murder.* Dublin, Irish Labour Party and Trade Union Congress, 1921.

*

Bibliography: *A Bibliography of the Books of Erskine Childers* by P.S. O'Hegarty, privately printed, 1948.

Critical Studies: *Damned Englishman: A Study of Erskine Childers* by Tom Cox, Hicksville, New York, Exposition Press, 1975; *The Zeal of the Convert* by Burke Wilkinson, Washington, D.C., Luce, 1976; *The Riddle of Erskine Childers* by Andrew Boyle, London, Hutchinson, 1977.

* * *

The Riddle of the Sands, which has survived as a fine tale of mystery and adventure, began life as a novel with a serious purpose. Erskine Childers, a man of considerable intellectual powers who knew something of the process of government and had seen active service in the Boer War, was convinced that at the end of the Victorian era Britain was entering upon a period when its supremacy as a world power would come under threat. In particular, he felt that there was much complacency in the easy assumption that her sea power, unchallenged since the Battle of Trafalgar, could always protect the island from invasion and guarantee the trade routes by which food and raw materials were brought in and by which manufactured goods were exported to the rest of the world. He was impressed by the growth in German naval power and commercial development under Kaiser Wilhelm, and it is noteworthy that though he is scathing in the novel about any sort of treachery by renegade Britons, he is open in his admiration for the efficiency of a younger power which seeks its own advancement. A country, he implies, is entitled to win its way in the world, and what angers him is not so much Germany's ambition as the laziness which he thinks may cost Britain dear.

The idea that the swarms of torpedo boats might dash out from the muddy waters behind the West Frisian islands to harry the British fleet or that an invading army might embark in shallow-draft barges to cross the North Sea and fall upon unsuspecting Lincolnshire can hardly be expected to make today's readers hold their breath. But *The Riddle of the Sands* still commands attention. Childers tells his story with great skill. He presents it solemnly as a true account of real-life events which he has written up in the form of a novel simply in order to ensure that it is read by as large a number of people as possible. The pretension to veracity is backed by a high degree of realism in details of every sort. At one level the novel reads like an account by one of those intrepid Victorian and Edwardian yachtsmen, like R.T. McMullen of *Down Channel* fame, who, dispensing with the cumbersome luxury of paid hands, cruised long distances single-handed or with one companion. This is a story of charts marked with soundings and there is much talk of galvanised rigging-screws and retractable centre-boards that allow the cutter *Dulcibella* to rest comfortably on the mud when the tide is low. All this has the ring of truth, and it is a fact that there are entries in Childers's log of his cruises to the Frisian Islands and the Baltic in his yacht the *Vixen* which are remarkably similar to passages in the novel.

The two heroes are fairly obviously reflections of two sides of Childers's character, and again it can be argued that they seem so real because the author has followed the sound practice of basing his fiction on his own experience. The owner and skipper of the *Dulcibella* is Davies, a very private person. He is an excellent sailor, and his ambition is to serve his country in some way. He is moved by evidence of Prussian devotion to duty, is excited by the mere sight of even German warships, and dreams of saving Britain from disaster by showing how her supposed impregnability may be undermined. After his suspicions have been aroused and his boat has been damaged, he invites Carruthers to join him. Now, Carruthers is a more conventional person, a Foreign Office clerk of high intelligence and with an understandable tendency to object to the discomforts of a small yacht at the end of the season and to pooh-pooh Davies's seemingly far-fetched interpretations of events. We tend to identify with him, perhaps even thinking he is a little too sceptical, a little too hard on Davies (for, in best public school tradition the pair continue to refer to one another by surname). By the time Carruthers is convinced, we are fully prepared to take his word for it, especially as it is he who solves the mystery.

The Riddle of the Sands is like a maze. The journeys through the muddy channels, once even over the sands left bare at low tide, as the salt winds blow are one symbol of it. Another is the complex web of human relationships, with even a little coy love interest added for good measure at the publisher's insistence. It is only at the very end that at last we see how everything fits together, and even then we are allowed only a glimpse, which leaves us, as we started, with questions in our mind.

—Christopher Smith

———

CHRISTIE, (Dame) Agatha (Mary Clarissa, née Miller). Also wrote as Mary Westmacott. British. Born in Torquay, Devon, 15 September 1890. Educated privately at home; studied singing and piano in Paris. Married 1) Colonel Archibald Christie in 1914 (divorced, 1928, died 1962), one daughter; 2) the archaeologist Max Mallowan in 1930 (died 1978). Served as a Voluntary Aid Detachment nurse in a Red Cross hospital in Torquay during World War I, and worked in the dispensary of University College Hospital, London, during World War II; also assisted her husband on excavations in Iraq and Syria and on the Assyrian cities. President, Detection Club. Recipient: Mystery Writers of America Grand Master award, 1954; New York Drama Critics Circle award, 1955. D.Litt.: University of Exeter, 1961. Fellow, Royal Society of Literature, 1950. C.B.E. (Commander, Order of the British Empire), 1956; D.B.E. (Dame Commander, Order of the British Empire), 1971. *Died 12 January 1976.*

CRIME PUBLICATIONS

Novels (series: Superintendent Battle; Tuppence and Tommy Beresford; Jane Marple; Hercule Poirot; Colonel Race)

The Mysterious Affair at Styles (Poirot). London, Lane, 1920; New York, Dodd Mead, 1927.

The Secret Adversary (Beresfords). London, Lane, and New York, Dodd Mead, 1922.

The Murder on the Links (Poirot). London, Lane, and New York, Dodd Mead, 1923.

The Man in the Brown Suit (Race). London, Lane, and New York, Dodd Mead, 1924.

The Secret of Chimneys (Battle). London, Lane, and New York, Dodd Mead, 1925.

The Murder of Roger Ackroyd (Poirot). London, Collins, and New York, Dodd Mead, 1926.

The Big Four (Poirot). London, Collins, and New York, Dodd Mead 1927.

The Mystery of the Blue Train (Poirot). London, Collins, and New York, Dodd Mead, 1928.

The Seven Dials Mystery (Battle). London, Collins, and New York, Dodd Mead, 1929.

The Murder at the Vicarage (Marple). London, Collins, and New York, Dodd Mead, 1930.

The Floating Admiral, with others. London, Hodder and Stoughton, 1931; New York, Doubleday, 1932.

The Sittaford Mystery. London, Collins, 1931; as *The Murder at Hazelmoor*, New York, Dodd Mead, 1931.

Peril at End House (Poirot). London, Collins, and New York, Dodd Mead, 1932.

Lord Edgware Dies (Poirot). London, Collins, 1933; as *Thirteen at Dinner*, New York, Dodd Mead, 1933.

Why Didn't They Ask Evans? London, Collins, 1934; as *The Boomerang Clue*, New York, Dodd Mead, 1935.

Murder on the Orient Express (Poirot). London, Collins, 1934; as *Murder in the Calais Coach*, New York, Dodd Mead, 1934.

Murder in Three Acts. New York, Dodd Mead, 1934; as *Three Act Tragedy*, London, Collins, 1935.

Death in the Clouds (Poirot). London, Collins, 1935; as *Death in the Air*, New York, Dodd Mead, 1935.

The A.B.C. Murders (Poirot). London, Collins, and New York, Dodd Mead, 1936; as *The Alphabet Murders*, New York, Pocket Books, 1966.

Cards on the Table (Battle; Poirot; Race). London, Collins, 1936; New York, Dodd Mead, 1937.

Murder in Mesopotamia (Poirot). London, Collins, and New York, Dodd Mead, 1936.

Death on the Nile (Poirot). London, Collins, 1937; New York, Dodd Mead, 1938.

Dumb Witness. London, Collins, 1937; as *Poirot Loses a Client*, New York, Dodd Mead, 1937.

Appointment with Death (Poirot). London, Collins, and New York, Dodd Mead, 1938.

Hercule Poirot's Christmas. London, Collins, 1938; as *Murder for Christmas*, New York, Dodd Mead, 1939; as *A Holiday for Murder*, New York, Avon, 1947.

Murder Is Easy (Battle). London, Collins, 1939; as *Easy to Kill*, New York, Dodd Mead, 1939.

Ten Little Niggers. London, Collins, 1939; as *And Then There Were None*, New York, Dodd Mead, 1940; as *Ten Little Indians*, New York, Pocket Books, 1965.

One, Two, Buckle My Shoe (Poirot). London, Collins, 1940; as *The Patriotic Murders*, New York, Dodd Mead, 1941; as *An Overdose of Death*, New York, Dell, 1953.

Sad Cypress (Poirot). London, Collins, and New York, Dodd Mead, 1940.

Evil under the Sun (Poirot). London, Collins, and New York, Dodd Mead, 1941.

N or M? (Beresfords). London, Collins, and New York, Dodd Mead, 1941.

The Body in the Library (Marple). London, Collins, and New York, Dodd Mead, 1942.

The Moving Finger (Marple). New York, Dodd Mead, 1942; London, Collins, 1943.

Five Little Pigs (Poirot). London, Collins, 1942; as *Murder in Retrospect*, New York, Dodd Mead 1942.

Death Comes as the End. New York, Dodd Mead, 1944; London, Collins, 1945.

Towards Zero (Battle). London, Collins, and New York, Dodd Mead, 1944.

Sparkling Cyanide. London, Collins, 1945; as *Remembered Death*, New York, Dodd Mead 1945.

The Hollow (Poirot). London, Collins, and New York, Dodd Mead, 1946; as *Murder after Hours*, New York, Dell, 1954.

Taken at the Flood (Poirot). London, Collins, 1948; as *There Is a Tide. . .*, New York, Dodd Mead, 1948.

Crooked House. London, Collins, and New York, Dodd Mead, 1949.

A Murder Is Announced (Marple). London, Collins, and New York, Dodd Mead, 1950.

They Came to Baghdad. London, Collins, and New York, Dodd Mead, 1951.

They Do It with Mirrors (Marple). London, Collins, 1952; as *Murder with Mirrors*, New York, Dodd Mead, 1952.

Mrs. McGinty's Dead (Poirot). London, Collins, and New York, Dodd Mead, 1952; as *Blood Will Tell*, New York, Detective Book Club, 1952.

After the Funeral (Poirot). London, Collins, 1953; as *Funerals Are Fatal*, New York, Dodd Mead, 1953; as *Murder at the Gallop*, London, Fontana, 1963.

A Pocket Full of Rye (Marple). London, Collins, 1953; New York, Dodd Mead, 1954.

Destination Unknown. London, Collins, 1954; as *So Many Steps to Death*, New York, Dodd Mead, 1955.

Hickory, Dickory, Dock (Poirot). London, Collins, 1955; as *Hickory, Dickory, Death*, New York, Dodd Mead, 1955.

Dead Man's Folly (Poirot). London, Collins, and New York, Dodd Mead, 1956.

4:50 from Paddington (Marple). London, Collins, 1957; as *What Mrs. McGillicuddy Saw!*, New York, Dodd Mead, 1957; as *Murder She Said*, New York, Pocket Books, 1961.

Ordeal by Innocence. London, Collins, 1958; New York, Dodd Mead, 1959.

Cat among the Pigeons (Poirot). London, Collins, 1959; New York, Dodd Mead, 1960.

The Pale Horse. London, Collins, 1961; New York, Dodd Mead, 1962.

The Mirror Crack'd from Side to Side (Marple). London, Collins, 1962; as *The Mirror Crack'd*, New York, Dodd Mead, 1963.

The Clocks (Poirot). London, Collins, 1963; New York, Dodd Mead, 1964.

A Caribbean Mystery (Marple). London, Collins, 1964; New York, Dodd Mead, 1965.

At Bertram's Hotel (Marple). London, Collins, 1965; New York, Dodd Mead, 1966.

Third Girl (Poirot). London, Collins, 1966; New York, Dodd Mead, 1967.

Endless Night. London, Collins, 1967; New York, Dodd Mead, 1968.

By the Pricking of My Thumbs (Beresfords). London, Collins, and New York, Dodd Mead, 1968.

Hallowe'en Party (Poirot). London, Collins, and New York, Dodd Mead, 1969.

Passenger to Frankfurt. London, Collins, and New York, Dodd Mead, 1970.

Nemesis (Marple). London, Collins, and New York, Dodd Mead, 1971.

Elephants Can Remember (Poirot). London, Collins, and New York, Dodd Mead, 1972.

Postern of Fate (Beresfords). London, Collins, and New York, Dodd Mead, 1973.

Curtain: Hercule Poirot's Last Case. London, Collins, and New York, Dodd Mead, 1975.

Sleeping Murder (Marple). London, Collins, and New York, Dodd Mead, 1976.

The Scoop, and Behind the Screen, with others. London, Gollancz, and New York, Harper, 1983.

Short Stories (series: Jane Marple; Hercule Poirot)

Poirot Investigates. London, Lane, 1924; New York, Dodd Mead, 1925.

Partners in Crime. London, Collins, and New York, Dodd Mead, 1929; reprinted in part as *The Sunningdale Mystery*, Collins, 1933.

The Under Dog. London, Readers Library, 1929.

The Mysterious Mr. Quin. London, Collins, and New York, Dodd Mead, 1930.

The Thirteen Problems. London, Collins, 1932; as *The Tuesday Club Murders*, New York, Dodd Mead, 1933; selection, as *The Mystery of the Blue Geranium and Other Tuesday Club Murders*, New York, Bantam, 1940.

The Hound of Death and Other Stories. London, Odhams, 1933.

Parker Pyne Investigates. London, Collins, 1934; as *Mr. Parker Pyne, Detective*, New York, Dodd Mead, 1934.

The Listerdale Mystery and Other Stories. London, Collins, 1934.

Murder in the Mews and Three Other Poirot Cases. London, Collins, 1937; as *Dead Man's Mirror and Other Stories*, New York, Dodd Mead, 1937.

The Regatta Mystery and Other Stories. New York, Dodd Mead, 1939.

The Mystery of the Baghdad Chest. Los Angeles, Bantam, 1943.

The Mystery of the Crime in Cabin 66. Los Angeles, Bantam, 1943.

Poirot and the Regatta Mystery. Los Angeles, Bantam, 1943.

Poirot on Holiday. London, Todd, 1943.

Problem at Pollensa Bay, and Christmas Adventure. London, Todd, 1943.

The Veiled Lady, and The Mystery of the Baghdad Chest. London, Todd, 1944.

Poirot Knows the Murderer. London, Todd, 1946.

Poirot Lends a Hand. London, Todd, 1946.

The Labours of Hercules. London, Collins, and New York, Dodd Mead, 1947.

The Witness for the Prosecution and Other Stories. New York, Dodd Mead, 1948.

The Mousetrap and Other Stories. New York, Dell, 1949; as *Three Blind Mice and Other Stories*, New York, Dodd Mead, 1950.

The Under Dog and Other Stories. New York, Dodd Mead, 1951.

The Adventure of the Christmas Pudding, and Selection of Entrées. London, Collins, 1960.

Double Sin and Other Stories. New York, Dodd Mead, 1961.

13 for Luck! A Selection of Mystery Stories for Young Readers. New York, Dodd Mead, 1961; London, Collins, 1966.

Surprise! Surprise! A Collection of Mystery Stories with Unexpected Endings, edited by Raymond T. Bond. New York, Dodd Mead, 1965.

Star over Bethlehem and Other Stories (as Agatha Christie Mallowan). London, Collins, and New York, Dodd Mead, 1965.

13 Clues for Miss Marple. New York, Dodd Mead, 1966.

The Golden Ball and Other Stories. New York, Dodd Mead, 1971.

Poirot's Early Cases. London, Collins, 1974; as *Hercule Poirot's Early Cases*, New York, Dodd Mead, 1974.

Miss Marple's Final Cases and Two Other Stories. London, Collins, 1979.

The Agatha Christie Hour. London, Collins, 1982.

Hercule Poirot's Casebook: Fifty Stories. New York, Dodd Mead, 1984.

Miss Marple: Complete Short Stories. New York, Dodd Mead, 1985.

Uncollected Short Stories

"Within a Wall," in *Royal Magazine* (London), October 1925.

"The House of Dreams," in *Sovereign Magazine* (London), January 1926.

"The Lonely God," in *Royal Magazine* (London), July 1926.

"The Edge," in *Pearson's Magazine* (London), February, 1927.

"The Stolen Ghost," in *Sovereign Magazine* (London), March 1927.

"The Harlequin Tea Set," in *Winter's Crimes 3*, edited by George Hardinge. London, Macmillan, 1971.

OTHER PUBLICATIONS

Novels as Mary Westmacott

Giant's Bread. London, Collins, and New York, Doubleday, 1930.

Unfinished Portrait. London, Collins, and New York, Doubleday, 1934.

Absent in the Spring. London, Collins, and New York, Farrar and Rinehart, 1944.

The Rose and the Yew Tree. London, Heinemann, and New York, Rinehart, 1948.

A Daughter's a Daughter. London, Heinemann, 1952; New York, Dell, 1963.

The Burden. London, Heinemann 1956; New York, Dell, 1963.

Plays

Black Coffee (produced London, 1930). London, Ashley, and Boston, Baker, 1934.

Ten Little Niggers, adaptation of her own novel (produced Wimbledon and London, 1943). London, French, 1944; as

Ten Little Indians (produced New York, 1944), New York, French, 1946.

Appointment with Death, adaptation of her own novel (produced Glasgow and London, 1945). London, French, 1956; in *The Mousetrap and Other Plays*, 1978.

Murder on the Nile, adaptation of her novel *Death on the Nile* (as *Little Horizon*, produced Wimbledon, 1945; as *Murder on the Nile*, produced London and New York, 1946). London and New York, French, 1948.

The Hollow, adaptation of her own novel (produced Cambridge and London, 1951; Princeton, New Jersey, 1952; New York, 1978). London and New York, French, 1952.

The Mousetrap, adaptation of her story "Three Blind Mice" (broadcast 1952; produced Nottingham and London, 1952; New York, 1960). London and New York, French, 1954.

Witness for the Prosecution, adaptation of her own story (produced Nottingham and London, 1953; New York, 1954). London and New York, French, 1954.

Spider's Web (produced Nottingham and London, 1954; New York, 1974). London and New York, French, 1957.

Towards Zero, with Gerald Verner, adaptation of the novel by Christie (produced Nottingham and London, 1956). New York, Dramatists Play Service, 1957; London, French, 1958.

Verdict (produced Wolverhampton and London, 1958). London, French, 1958; in *The Mousetrap and Other Plays*, 1978.

The Unexpected Guest (produced Bristol and London, 1958). London, French, 1958; in *The Mousetrap and Other Plays*, 1978.

Go Back for Murder, adaptation of her novel *Five Little Pigs* (produced Edinburgh and London, 1960) London, French, 1960; in *The Mousetrap and Other Plays*, 1978.

Rule of Three: Afternoon at the Seaside, The Patient, The Rats (produced Aberdeen and London, 1962; *The Rats* produced New York, 1974; *The Patient* produced New York, 1978). London, French, 3 vols., 1963.

Fiddlers Three (produced Southsea, 1971; London, 1972).

Akhnaton (as *Akhnaton and Nefertiti*, produced New York, 1979; as *Akhnaton*, produced London, 1980). London, Collins, and New York, Dodd Mead, 1973.

The Mousetrap and Other Plays (includes *Witness for the Prosecution, Ten Little Indians, Appointment with Death, The Hollow, Towards Zero, Verdict, Go Back for Murder*). New York, Dodd Mead, 1978.

Radio Plays: *The Mousetrap*, 1952; *Personal Call*, 1960.

Verse

The Road of Dreams. London, Bles, 1925.
Poems. London, Collins, and New York, Dodd Mead, 1973.

Other

Come, Tell Me How You Live (travel). London, Collins, and New York, Dodd Mead, 1946; revised edition, 1975.
An Autobiography. London, Collins, and New York, Dodd Mead, 1977.

*

Critical Studies: *Studies in Agatha Christie's Writings* by Frank Behre, Gothenburg, Universitetet, 1967; *Agatha Christie: Mistress of Mystery* by G.C. Ramsey, New York, Dodd Mead, 1967, revised edition, London, Collins, 1968; *The Mysterious World of Agatha Christie*, New York, Award, 1975; *An Agatha Christie Chronology* by Nancy Blue Wynne, New York, Ace,

1976; *The Agatha Christie Mystery* by Derrick Murdoch, Toronto, Pagurian Press, 1976; *Agatha Christie: First Lady of Crime* edited by H.R.F. Keating, London, Weidenfeld and Nicolson, and New York, Holt Rinehart, 1977; *The Mystery of Agatha Christie* by Gwyn Robyns, New York, Doubleday, 1978; *The Bedside, Bathtub, and Armchair Companion to Agatha Christie* edited by Dick Riley and Pam McAllister, New York, Ungar, 1979, London, Angus and Robertson, 1983; revised edition, Ungar, 1986; *A Talent to Deceive: An Appreciation of Agatha Christie* (includes bibliography by Louise Barnard) by Robert Barnard, London, Collins, and New York, Dodd Mead, 1980; *The Agatha Christie Who's Who* by Randall Toye, New York, Holt Rinehart, and London, Muller, 1980; *The Gentle Art of Murder: The Detective Fiction of Agatha Christie* by Earl F. Bargainnier, Bowling Green, Ohio, Bowling Green University Press, 1981; *Murder She Wrote: A Study of Agatha Christie's Detective Fiction* by Patricia D. Maida and Nicholas B. Spornick, Bowling Green, Ohio, Bowling Green University Press, 1982; *The Life and Crimes of Agatha Christie* by Charles Osborne, London, Collins, 1982, New York, Holt Rinehart, 1983; *The Agatha Christie Companion: The Complete Guide to Agatha Christie's Life and Work* by Dennis Sanders and Len Lovallo, New York, Delacorte Press, 1984, London, W.H. Allen, 1985; *Agatha Christie: A Biography* by Janet Morgan, London, Cape, 1984, New York, Knopf, 1985; *The Life and Times of Miss Jane Marple*, New York, Dodd Mead, 1985 and *The Life and Times of Hercule Poirot*, New York, Putnam, and London, Pavilion, 1990, both by Anne Hart; *An A to Z of the Novels and Short Stories of Agatha Christie* by Ben Morselt, Phoenix, Arizona, Phoenix, 1986.

*   *   *

Shortly after the end of World War I an aspirant to the then increasingly popular ranks of detective-story writers sent a manuscript to a London publisher. It was returned. Five more times it went off, and five more times it came back. But at last a seventh publisher, John Lane at the Bodley Head, accepted it and in 1920 *The Mysterious Affair at Styles* by Agatha Christie first introduced the world to Hercule Poirot. The book was a modest success. Others followed. Gradually Christie began to emerge as a leader in the genre, and eventually the regular stream of Christie books took off (about the time of World War II). By the end of her life she had become a name known from China (where they were apt to call her a running-dog of imperialism) to Nicaragua (where the magnificent moustaches of Hercule Poirot decorated a postage stamp) and she was selling more books than anyone in the genre. But to acknowledge the hugeness of her sales is not to disparage her achievement. A vessel that can take such a hurricane in her sails and keep upright must be a sturdy barque, and Agatha Christie's books—set aside some weak performances in a total of over 80—are well-built craft indeed.

She developed and continued to keep a wonderful ingenuity of plot. She knew the rules of the game and worked out every possible variation of them delightfully to trick her readers. The least likely person, the very least likely person, the person already cleared, the apparently unbreakable alibi, the unimpeachable witness who for a very good reason proves not to be, the murder committed after the "corpse" has been seen—all these, and more, she cunningly employed. She had a dazzling ingenuity in the planting of clues and the trailing of red herrings, the basis of her particular patch in the great field of crime-writing. Does she need to establish that the butler is short-sighted (and so did not see the person he swore he had)? Poirot makes great play over asking whether a date has been torn off a wall-calendar. The butler crosses the room to give him his answer. Poor deluded readers puzzle away about the significance of dates while the true clue has been quietly dropped into their laps.

But if she was a mistress of complication, she was also a mistress of simplicity. The actual writing of her complicated stories was always marvellously simple. A great deal of what she had to tell her reader she told in dialogue. She had a good ear (she had had an excellent musical education, good enough to consider—had she not been a very private person—concert careers both as pianist and singer) and she catches exactly the tone of her middle-class English characters, though with servants and lower-class "extras" she is a little apt to caricature. And here is another clue to her success. She was an upper-middle-class English lady and, almost always, she wrote only about upper-middle-class English life. She had the modesty to know her limits, and the sense to stick to them.

But despite this social limitation her books are loved world-wide. This is because she was an ordinary person herself and took for her characters what was ordinary, shared-by-everyone about them. Miss Marple is the most ordinary of old ladies, triumphing as a detective frequently by seeing the ordinary (the butcher boy's deceit) in the act of murder or by finding clues during the everyday process of gossip and tittle-tattle. Poirot, who on the surface might appear quite extraordinary, is in fact no more than a gathering together of all the simple eccentricities the ordinary person would expect, though they are seen with a warm enjoyment.

In short, Christie's prime virtue is her unoriginality in everything bar plot. But hers is an unoriginality presented always with exceptional rightness. Other unoriginal crime writers produce books in which uninteresting people say uninteresting things and try to make up for it often by frantic activity. Christie gives us ordinary, not wildly exciting, people, but by describing them with exact rightness she makes them clear and clean to every reader. Nothing clogs. Her timing is unostentatiously right. This is what makes her such a good storyteller: you get the right piece of information at exactly the right moment. And you never get digressions, those bits of cleverness that tempt other writers.

I see her as a clown in the circus, an entertainer connected to her audience by an invisible magic link. She produces for them things that are quite simple but are nonetheless welcome, welcome to the ordinary spectator and welcome to the spectator more used to the complexities of the drama (provided only that he is willing to sink some prejudices). Out of the conical white cap with its big black bobbles comes the expected, long waited-for check silk handkerchief—at exactly the right moment, and in neatly the *unexpected* colour. We burst out clapping. And so we should.

—H.R.F. Keating

CIRCUS, Anthony. *See* **HOCH, Edward D.**

CLARK, Al C. *See* **GOINES, Donald.**

CLARK, Curt. *See* **WESTLAKE, Donald E.**

CLANCY, Tom. American. Born in Maryland in 1947. Married; four children. Address: c/o Putnam, 200 Madison Avenue, New York, New York 10016, U.S.A.

CRIME PUBLICATIONS

Novels (series: Jack Ryan in all books except *Red Storm Rising*)

The Hunt for Red October. Annapolis, Maryland, Naval Institute Press, 1984; London, Collins, 1985.
Red Storm Rising. New York, Putnam, 1986.
Patriot Games. New York, Putnam, and London, Collins, 1987.
The Cardinal of the Kremlin. New York, Putnam, and London, Collins, 1988.
Clear and Present Danger. New York, Putnam, and London, Collins, 1989.

* * *

Tom Clancy's first novel, *The Hunt for Red October*, catapulted his name to the top of the lists as a first-rate writer of suspense fiction in the tradition of Frederick Forsyth, Robert Ludlum, and John le Carré. Clancy's books, aside from *The Cardinal of the Kremlin*, are not structured around spies, moles, and espionage in the way that is typical of these writers; rather they rival these masters' tales in their ability to harness a vast array of highly technical detail and construct a gripping account of a chase, vividly capturing the geopolitical ramifications of the kernel incident which gives rise to the plot. Like Forsyth, Ludlum and le Carré, Clancy writes with immediacy, precision, and a wealth of information. His zeal to research his subject thoroughly enabled him to write a novel which brilliantly captures the reality of submarine warfare in a nuclear age, and handles detail with such specificity that it won the admiration of the U.S. Naval Institute, making them his first publisher.

His first novel recounts the 18-day hunt for *Red October*, a Soviet ballistic-missile submarine, commanded by a Lithuanian-born Soviet commander, Marko Ramius, who plans to defect and deliver to the Americans the world's most advanced submarine—one capable of nearly silent running, making detection by sonar or acoustical buoys strewn in the bottle-necks of the oceans nearly impossible. Jack Ryan, the protagonist of all but one of Clancy's books, is a young American analyst working for the CIA. He is called upon to assist the Americans in fathoming the motives of the Russian defector and interpreting his thoughts and strategies in order to find him and bring his submarine into the Norfolk naval base without being discovered. The defection of Ramius has caused the Russians to send attack submarines and surface ships into American waters with orders to find and destroy the submarine. The presence of the Soviet Atlantic fleet in American waters creates a potentially explosive situation which could easily trigger a nuclear war. The novel traces the intricacy of the diplomatic maneuverings of the two governments as both attempt to navigate the crisis, each intent upon their own purposes, but each anxious to avoid war. It also follows, day by day, hour by hour, the cunning unfolding of the treasonous plot of Ramius who is determined to outwit the

Russian *zampolit* who has been assigned to his ship to further the interests of the Communist Party by serving as a propagandist and a political check on the navy. He also must outwit both the agent of the main political administration who has orders to scuttle the ship in a case of true emergency, as well as the majority of the crew of his vessel, except his 10 carefully chosen senior officers. The novel charts the course of his submarine as Ramius takes it through Arctic waters, across the North Atlantic, and into American coastal waters, deftly evading the Soviet subs sent in pursuit of him as well as the American crafts sent to assist him, who, too, must avoid an incident with the Soviet fleet.

This novel won rave reviews when it first appeared. The strength of the book lies not in Clancy's delineation of character, nor, actually, in his treatment of the tensions between East and West, Soviet and capitalist. There his treatment is too stereotyped to be taken very seriously. His constant propagandistic attacks upon the ethics and judgment of the Communist Party and their colossal bureaucratic inefficiencies are heavy-handed. What is marvelous are Clancy's descriptions of the technology of submarine warfare and the depth of his understanding of naval armaments, submarine detection systems, and codes of conduct that govern the relationship between officers and crews on board U.S. and Soviet submarines. I cannot think of a writer in the suspense traditions that has such mastery of tactics and instruments. His book is replete with descriptions of the interior of submarines, the missile room, the business end of a boomer, and thermonuclear warheads. There are abundant descriptions of sonar detection systems, high-frequency pinging, and propulsion sounds. He makes underwater submarine warfare seem completely real. In many ways his writing gives me the sort of pleasure derived from reading John Keegan's *The Face of Battle* where the battles of Agincourt, Waterloo, and the Somme are vividly reconstructed by a writer expert in battle and a lecturer in military history at Sandhurst. His accounts of the tactics of the two Soviet commanders and the commander of the *U.S.S. Dallas*, an American attack submarine, are stunningly realistic. The authenticity of the book reminds me of *Das Boat*, a remarkable German film about submarine warfare during World War II. Both the movie and Clancy's book make you believe that you are on the submarine, executing the maneuvers, living in close quarters, and discovering the critical role that patience plays in the life of a submarine commander.

Recently, a movie has been made of the book but it does not begin to do justice to the novel's plot. Even though it has the advantage of the visual medium to lend authenticity to Clancy's prose, it is less taut than the book and omits entirely the exciting conclusion when the Americans outsmart the Soviets and safely bring the submarine into their own shipyard after having reported that it has been accidentally scuttled by its own charges during the midst of the American rescue action.

Clancy's second novel, *Red Storm Rising*, is his most technical and his most ambitious. It opens with a terrorist attack upon one of the world's largest refining complexes located in western Siberia. Its destruction deprives Russia of more than a third of its petroleum holdings, throwing the Politburo into a crisis and precipitating *Red Storm*, a plan for a mechanized attack on West Germany and the Low Countries. The book ambitiously charts how such a war would be fought. It is a war game on a vast scale, involving a Soviet attack upon NATO, which necessitates Russia's invasion of Iceland (a land free of any conquering forces for more than 1000 years); a submarine battle between the Allies and the Soviets in the North Atlantic; and fierce land campaigns to seize Germany. All this is but a plan on the part of the Russians to enable them ultimately to seize the petroleum supplies they desperately need

from the Persian Gulf without risk of interference by the NATO forces. As in *The Hunt for Red October*, Clancy writes of the internecine struggles between rival interests in the Politburo, as well as between the KGB and the military. He describes submarine warfare, air warfare in the age of nuclear missiles, Miniature Homing Vehicles, sidewinders, SAMs, mobile anti-aircraft guns and stealth technology as well as the nature of tank warfare as it would be experienced were World War III to break out. The book takes the principal players terrifyingly close to unleashing a nuclear war. Its conclusion cleverly plots the defeat of the corrupt KGB officer who was willing to stage the killing of children in order to give credibility to the Politburo's act of aggression against the Germans. This novel more than any other written by Clancy is the most authentic in its detailed account of modern warfare.

Patriot Games takes its impulse from a detail first provided in *The Hunt for Red October*. In Clancy's first novel we learn that Jack Ryan had received an honorary knighthood as a reward for having "broken up a terrorist incident that had erupted around him in St. James's Park, London." *Patriot Games* shows us Ryan as the innocent American abroad, visiting with his talented wife, Caroline, known as Cathy, a liberated woman, instructor in opthalmic surgery, and a classical pianist. Traveling with them is their four-year-old daughter, Sally. Ryan is immediately caught up in a terrorist episode executed by the Ulster Liberation Army, a Maoist fringe group which has broken off from the Provisional Irish Republican Army. The ULA relishes commiting deeds more dastardly than the killing of Lord Mountbatten. They are well-trained and well-organized fanatics, specializing in high-risk, high-profile operations and second only to the Lebanese terrorists.

At the novel's opening, Ryan bravely prevents the assassination of the Prince and Princess of Wales. Soon he finds himself brought into a American-British intelligence effort, working with the CIA and C-13, the Anti-Terrorist Branch of Scotland Yard, to identify the leadership of the ULA and arrest its members. Ryan is pursued by the vindictive terrorists back to the United States where they mount a full attack upon him when he is entertaining the Prince and his wife in his home. The plot also requires that C-13 discover the identity of the man with high-level clearance who is giving the terrorists information regarding the whereabouts of the royal family. This novel represents a change of pace for Clancy and allows him to try his hand at capturing the dialogue of the American abroad and delineating the character of Kevin Joseph O'Donnell and Sean Miller, two ruthless and amoral terrorists. The early dialogue of Ryan's blunt talking to His Highness is embarrassingly bad. As the book progresses, however, the portrait of the terrorists improves and Clancy again shows his skill at narrating the maneuvers of those involved in terrorist operations. Like le Carré in *The Little Drummer Girl*, Clancy explores the ambivalence that underlies political interactions, particularly the kind of patriot games in which men use the tactics of professional soldiers to commit acts, such as the murder of children and innocent civilians, which the professional army likes to imagine it does not do.

In *The Cardinal of the Kremlin* Clancy moves within the genre of suspense fiction to develop the novel of espionage, counter-espionage, spies, and spy-catchers. Gaining skill in developing characters, he crafts two characters with considerable success. One is the Cardinal, Colonel Mikhail Semyonovich Filitov, a three-time hero of the Soviet Union, a hero at Stalingrad, a fighter at Minsk, Vyasma, and outside of Russia when the Russians stopped the fascists, and a man who has served for 30 years as a spy for the West. His cunning and courage coupled with his extraordinary military record make his treacherous behavior intolerable to the Soviets. The other, known as the

Archer, is a man who leads a small band of *Mudjaheddin* and fights the Soviets with a fanaticism that chills even the most seasoned reader of spy thrillers. The story again uses Ryan and draws considerably upon the material of *The Hunt for Red October*. In fact, Ramius assists the CIA in their rescue mission carried out in Baltic waters to take the wife and child of the deputy director of the KGB to America where they join the deputy director himself who has chosen enforced defection rather than certain death at the hands of the Soviets. This plot is structured around armament negotiations between the Soviets and the Americans and it is the mechanics of Star-Wars that dominate the tale. Again, the choice of topic is timely: its plot is set against the background of *Perestroika* and Reagan's dream of Star Wars. Clancy's treatment of the arms race and the tensions between Russia and the U.S. follow the same lines as in the other novels. He also draws on material from insider trading scandals to flesh out Ryan's background and provide grist for the plot. In this novel the Russians attempt to get Ryan to defect, believing information planted by the CIA that Ryan will become the victim of inside-trading scandals and rivalries amongst top presidential advisors. Ryan uses the situation to his own advantage, snatching the Cardinal from the Russians and also, in a surprise ending, bringing about the defection of the head of the KGB.

Clancy's most recent novel, *Clear and Present Danger*, finds its subject in the drug-wars played out in the United States and Columbia. The assassination of three American officials by the Columbian druglords causes some of the advisors for the United States President to decide to use the War Powers Acts to their own advantage. They plan covert activities, using the most sophisticated military equipment and personnel, to be used in Columbia to incite the druglords into wars with each other and to destroy air fields and cocaine-making plants in South America. The president's officials argue that the drug-smuggling operations in South America provide a clear and present danger to the United States, and they urge the President to approve operation SHOWBOAT as an act of National Security, justified under the Special and Hazardous Operation Rule which does not require the approval of Congress. One government mission aborts the laundering of $600,000,000 by one of the leaders of the Medillin cartel and seizes the money from banks located in over 26 countries around the world. The plot also revolves around the corruption of highly placed U.S. government officials, reminding the readers of the book of some of the excesses of the Iran/Contra Scandal. In this novel, Ryan is serving as Acting Deputy Director of Intelligence and yet the covert operations in South America are not made known to him. Much of the plot involves Ryan's discovery of the illegal covert activities and the rescue mission he initiates to bring the operations to a halt and rescue the military men who have been abandoned by the government officials whose policies have placed them there.

At present, Clancy's novels have reached sales in excess of 15,000,000 copies. His ability to construct a tight plot and immerse the reader in a wealth of detail—a kind of how-to of armaments, star wars, guerilla tactics, terrorist operations, and the techniques of counterespionage—appeals to the American appetite to grasp how something is done. His mastery of technical information alone and his lucid account of it in an eminently readable prose account for a large part of his success. He is also a good spinner of tales and the topical nature of the subjects he chooses—East-West tensions, drug-trafficking, insider-trading scandals—guarantee him a large readership. At present, he is one of the most popular writers of suspense fiction on the scene.

—Carol Simpson Stern

CLARK, Douglas (Malcolm Jackson). Also writes as James Ditton; Peter Hosier. British. Born in Lincolnshire, 1 December 1919. Educated at the University of London. Served in the British Army, 1939–56: with Royal Horse Artillery during World War II; in Amphibious Warfare unit, 1945–56. Married Dorothea Patricia Clark in 1953; two sons. Since 1956 has worked for a pharmaceutical company, first as promotion copywriter, currently as executive. Agent: John Farquharson Ltd., 162–168 Regent Street, London W1R 5TB, England.

Crime Publications

Novels (series: Inspector/Chief Superintendent George Masters and Chief Inspector Green in all books)

Nobody's Perfect.   London, Cassell, and New York, Stein and Day, 1969.
Death after Evensong.   London, Cassell, 1969; New York, Stein and Day 1970.
Deadly Pattern.   London, Cassell, and New York, Stein and Day, 1970.
Sweet Poison.   London, Cassell, 1970.
Sick to Death.   London, Cassell, and New York, Stein and Day, 1971.
Premedicated Murder.   London, Gollancz, 1975; New York, Scribner, 1976.
Dread and Water.   London, Gollancz, 1976; New York, Harper, 1984.
Table d'Hote.   London, Gollancz, 1977; New York, Harper, 1984.
The Gimmel Flask.   London, Gollancz, 1977; New York, Dell, 1982.
The Libertines.   London, Gollancz, 1978.
Heberden's Seat.   London, Gollancz, 1979; New York, Harper, 1984.
Poacher's Bag.   London, Gollancz, 1980; New York, Harper, 1983.
Golden Rain.   London, Gollancz, 1980; New York, Dell, 1982.
Roast Eggs.   London, Gollancz, and Boston, Little Brown, 1981.
The Longest Pleasure.   London, Gollancz, 1981; New York, Harper, 1984.
Shelf Life.   London, Gollancz, 1982; New York, Harper, 1983.
Doone Walk.   London, Gollancz, 1982.
Vicious Circle.   London, Gollancz, 1983; New York, Harper, 1985.
The Monday Theory.   London, Gollancz, 1983; New York, Harper, 1985.
Bouquet Garni.   London, Gollancz, 1984.
Dead Letter.   London, Gollancz, 1984; New York, Harper, 1985.
Jewelled Eye.   London, Gollancz, 1985; New York, Harper, 1988.
Performance.   London, Gollancz, 1985; New York, Harper, 1986.

Storm Centre. London, Gollancz, 1986; New York, Harper, 1988.
The Big Grouse. London, Gollancz, 1986.
Plain Sailing. London, Gollancz, 1987; New York, Harper, 1988.

Novels as James Ditton

You're Fairly Welcome. London, Hale, 1973.
The Bigger They Are. London, Hale, 1973.
Escapemanship. London, Hale, 1975.
Copley's Hunch. London, Gollancz, 1980.

OTHER PUBLICATIONS

Novel as Peter Hosier

The Miracle Makers. London, Cassell, 1971.

Plays

Radio Plays: for *Saturday Night Theatre* and *Afternoon Theatre* series.

Other

Suez Touchdown: A Soldier's Tale (as D.M.J. Clark). London, Davies, 1964.

*

Douglas Clark comments:

The majority of my books are in the Masters and Green series and are intended for readers who like fictional policemen as opposed to private eyes, and who prefer to read stories that contain little or nothing in the way of bad language, violence, or torrid sex. The books are for the most part medical mysteries and I try to make their appeal lie in the technical problems they present to lay policemen, and, consequently, to the reader. I aim to rely on medical fact (as opposed to fiction) to make the plots credible, which—thank heaven—medical and pharmaceutical publications have said, from time to time, they are.

*   *   *

Douglas Clark's medical mysteries usually focus on a fictional police detective team from Scotland Yard, inspectors Masters and Green and sergeants Reed and Berger, careful investigators of means, motive, state of mind, and personality.

Methodical and thorough, Chief Superintendent George Masters and Chief Inspector Bill Green very politely pry and ask disconcerting but insightful questions. Pompous, recalcitrant witnesses yield to their authority, as do witnesses protecting others. The detectives remain very closed about their actual suspicions, so that part of the pleasure of the books derives from trying to guess the direction of the investigation from the direction of their questions—though sometimes these intentionally misdirect. *Dread and Water*, in which high-security nuclear research physicists meet "accidental" mountaineering deaths, exemplifies effective interrogation to reveal character.

Masters, challenged by the technical details of cases, carries with him a small library of toxicology books, "recipe books" for murder suggesting possibilities experts ignore. For example, the medical experts in *Vicious Circle* name prescribed digitalis the means, but Masters and Green find the common lily of the valley easily yields herbal cardiac glycosides, whose taste,

colors, and chemical presence certain meals would hide. Seemingly innocent inquiries about local gardens, local foods, and folk medicine point to this source of glycosides and to the "excited" psychosis of a trapped and thwarted individual as the cause of murder. The solution to two murders in *Herberden's Seat* depends on traces of etorphine and angles of lens refraction, while in *The Gimmel Flask*, who murdered the senior partner of an esteemed English auction house depends on who had access to a rare poison served in a rare flask. In *Golden Rain*, laburnum seeds in the pepper drum kill a beautiful headmistress, and in *The Monday Theory* arsine, from iron pyrites common to Sussex beaches, kills a contrary London newspaper columnist and her lover. Frequently, suspected suicide proves to be murder.

Clark's reliance on careful scientific detail, particularly pharmaceutical, is both his weakness and his forte. At times his plot stops dead for a lecture as in *The Longest Pleasure*. Brilliant police guesswork about calculated outbreaks of botulism from meat tins uncovers a technician determined to bring down a large grocery chain. The puzzle is to prove how. However, at every stage of the pathological and chemical investigation, we learn all about *clostridium botulinum*, so that the technical overwhelms the plot, even at the denouement.

Despite depicting a clever scheme for the murder of a young soprano, *Performance* also becomes bogged down in lecture, while *Sick to Death* is medically precise about diabetes, diabetic comas, insulin, and zinc sulphate, but overwhelming. In contrast, in *Nobody's Perfect* the technical details enhance the mystery and direct the focus and method of the investigation. The action takes place inside a pharmaceutical company where drugs and their workings are familiar to the staff, but ironically the murder depends on limited knowledge of medical reactions rather than professional knowledge. In *Shelf Life* a simple case—a disorderly teenage drunk who dies in his jail cell—proves complex, and good pharmacology vindicates the police and exposes a devious killer. At his best Clark uses technical detail to add interest, to enhance his puzzle, and to make credible and natural his *recherché* modes of murder.

In determining what makes a seeming suicide or accident really murder and how that murder was perpetrated, the detectives find "saintly" sinners, sinning "saints", and friends or relatives who know more than they say. In *Death after Evensong* the supposedly kind and benevolent village vicar proves to be much unloved and the motives for murdering him multiple, but the hole through his heart reveals no trace of a bullet, and the story of how and why proves masterful. The detectives seek a fatal flaw, ask themselves how they would react in similar circumstances, and then look for behavior that breaks their expectations. In *Deadly Pattern* the discovery of four respectable, middle-class wives, buried in the sand dunes of a tiny resort, reveals a deadly pattern that allows Masters and Green to uncover a fifth body, anticipate a sixth, and unravel a psychotic antagonism extending from the fifth-form school days. The final section of each novel is a clearly reasoned, concise, and humane explanation of the step-by-step process of logic and investigation that leads to the final arrest, at times with a recommendation for how the case might best be handled in court.

Throughout the series, friction between the impertinent and self-assertive Green and the suave and self-contained Masters is vital to Clark's method. Green initially feels antagonistic toward Masters because of his youth, his education, his polished style, his politics, and (more importantly) his promotion over him, but gradually comes to respect and appreciate him. The movement is from a non-integrated team engaged in one-up-manship to a smoothly functioning unit acting for best effect. Dislike mellows, particularly after Masters protects Green from forced retirement. In *Sick to Death*, Masters and Green are supposedly not on speaking terms, but engage in congenial conversations about the insulin murder of an enchanting beauty. Green's love of plain food, plain language, and apt quotes endear, but his snap judgments based on left-wing political views grate. In *Premedicated Murder*, the plot of revenge delayed 30 years is ingenious, as is the idea of multiple murder plans, each going awry, and of victim and villain proving quite different from what they seem, but Green's "sneers" jar. Clark's later works handle the relationship better, as when, in *Jewelled Eye*, Masters heads a new crime-busting network and maps out the script that Green ably and companionably follows to recover a biotechnician kidnapped by an international ring of industrial spies and Libyan terrorists.

Table d'Hote reveals Clark at his best. Masters falls in love with (and later marries) the prime suspect—Wanda Mace, the lover of the victim's husband, and the hostess whose dinner kills the victim. Sexual tension adds an extra edge to an ingenious plot with unexpected but plausible twists, particularly a menu which spells death for anyone on anti-depressants. As is usual in Clark's novels simple solutions prove erroneous and reality is a complex tangle of emotions and desires. In another well-designed tale, *Roast Eggs*, Masters and Green join the plot just when a respected engineer is to be acquitted for murdering his wife by arson. With only the trial record to go on, they hypothesize a scenario and engineer a dramatic court incident that induces hysterical aphasia in the accused. Such armchair detection works well in *Poacher's Bag*, with Masters and Green's quiet weekend turned busman's holiday as they solve a recent murder case.

Ultimately it is the strict medical fact, the ingenious murder methods, the very English village relationships, and the psychology of close interpersonal contacts that make Clark's plots credible and enjoyable.

—Gina Macdonald

CLARK, Mary Higgins. American. Born in New York City, 24 December 1929. Educated at Villa Maria Academy; Ward Secretarial School; Fordham University, Bronx, New York, B.A. (summa cum laude) 1979. Married 1) Warren F. Clark in 1949 (died 1964), three daughters and two sons; 2) Raymond Charles Ploetz in 1978. Advertising assistant, Remington Rand, New York, 1946; stewardess, Pan American Airlines, 1949–50; radio scriptwriter and producer for Robert G. Jennings, 1965–70; partner and vice president, Aerial Communications, 1970–80. Since 1980 creative director and chair of the board, D.J. Clark Enterprises, New York. President, Mystery Writers of America. Recipient: Grand Prix de Littérature Policière (France), 1980. Agent: Gene Winick McIntosh and Otis Inc., 475 Fifth Avenue, New York, New York 10017. Address: 200 Central Park South, New York, New York 10019, U.S.A.

CRIME PUBLICATIONS

Novels

Where Are the Children? New York, Simon and Schuster, and London, Talmy Franklin, 1975.

A Stranger Is Watching. New York, Simon and Schuster, and London, Collins, 1978.
The Cradle Will Fall. New York, Simon and Schuster, and London, Collins, 1980.
A Cry in the Night. New York, Simon and Schuster, 1982; London, Collins, 1983.
Stillwatch. New York, Simon and Schuster, and London, Collins, 1984.
Weep No More, My Lady. New York, Simon and Schuster, and London, Collins, 1987.
While My Pretty One Sleeps. New York, Simon and Schuster, and London, Century, 1989.

Short Stories
The Anastasia Syndrome and Other Stories. New York, Simon and Schuster, 1989; London, Century, 1990.

Uncollected Short Story

"Death on the Cape," in *Woman's Day* (New York), 1989.

OTHER PUBLICATIONS

Other

Aspire to the Heavens: A Portrait of George Washington (for children). New York, Meredith Press, 1969.

Editor, *Murder on the Aisle.* New York, Simon and Schuster, 1987.

*　　*　　*

Following a couple of early suspense stories in women's magazines during the 1950's, Mary Higgins Clark turned her attention to other types of writing. It was not until 1975 that she returned to the suspense field with her highly successful novel, *Where Are the Children?* Though set on Cape Cod, the book seems to have been inspired by the Alice Crimmins case in 1965, in which a Queens, N.Y. mother reported the disappearance of her two small children. They were later found murdered, and after an extensive investigation and two lengthy trials, Alice Crimmins herself was convicted of killing her own children, apparently to prevent her estranged husband from getting custody of them.

The immediate popularity of *Where Are the Children?* might have surprised traditional mystery readers, because the plot of the book is quite different from the real-life Crimmins case and in fact the reader knows the identity of the true villain from the beginning. But it is the suspense rather than the mystery that makes the book so compulsively readable. The idea of children in jeopardy strikes a responsive chord with women readers—and with a great many men as well.

Clark's second suspense novel, *A Stranger Is Watching*, worked a variation on the theme. Here a child has witnessed a murder for which a possibly innocent man stands convicted. Both the child and a woman journalist in love with the boy's father are kidnapped and hidden away beneath New York's Grand Central Station. The suspense of a bomb about to explode, used so effectively by writers as varied as Wilkie Collins and Cornell Woolrich, is brought into play again here.

With her third suspense novel, *The Cradle Will Fall*, Clark expanded her horizons considerably to produce a medical thriller of mounting tension. Its heroine, Katie DeMaio, is a prosecutor in a small New Jersey town who is briefly hospitalized following a minor auto accident. In the night she thinks she sees the familiar figure of Dr. Edgar Highley, a distinguished obstetrician, carring a woman's body to his car. More deaths follow as Katie tries to convince people of what she saw and gather evidence against the doctor. The plot and its motivation are somewhat reminiscent of the sort of hospital thrillers Robin Cook excels at, but Clark produces a few new twists of her own.

She continued to improve with her fourth novel, *A Cry in the Night*, which could trace its roots back through literature to the Brontës. The story of a young woman who marries a man without really knowing him, and then goes off to live in an isolated house, is one of the classic themes of fiction. There is the usual suspense, but by witholding more from the reader Clark creates a greater degree of mystery as well. Readers may be reminded of the Brontës, and even Robert Bloch, though the ending—with children in jeopardy—is pure Mary Higgins Clark.

With *Stillwatch*, her next novel, she turned to the political thriller with a glamorous Washington setting. Television journalist Pat Traymore makes an attractive heroine as she digs into her own past life and discovers a secret that may influence the President's decision to nominate Senator Abigail Jennings as the first woman Vice President of the United States.

Even more glamorous is the setting of Clark's sixth novel *Weep No More, My Lady*, which takes place mainly at the luxurious Cypress Point Spa in Pebble Beach, California. The heroine here, Elizabeth Lange, is haunted by the death of her actress sister, who died mysteriously in a plunge from the balcony of her Manhattan penthouse. If the novel has a weakness, it is the too-obvious placement of a key clue to the killer's identity. Readers of the paperback edition should not be bothered by this, since the author used some judicious editing to make the clue less obvious in the reprint.

If her three most recent novels could be said to represent Clark's glamour period, *While My Pretty One Sleeps* is the best of them. Its New York setting, centered around the Manhattan fashion industry, comes vividly alive, and an excellent clue is there for the clever reader to spot.

Clark's first collection of stories, *The Anastasia Syndrome*, opens with the title novella, a suspenseful fantasy that may not appeal to her regular readers. It's followed, however, by four very good novelettes, one of them a Christmas story about a child in danger. Three of these were annual contributions to *Woman's Day*. An excellent 1989 contribution to the same magazine, "Death on the Cape," remains uncollected.

—Edward D. Hoch

CLARKE, Anna. British. Born in Cape Town, South Africa, 28 April 1919. Educated at schools in Cape Town, Oxford, and Montreal; University of London external B.Sc. in economics 1945; Open University, 1971–74; University of Sussex, Brighton, M.A. 1975. Divorced. Private secretary, Victor Gollancz, publishers, London, 1947–50, and Eyre and Spottiswoode, publishers, London, 1951–53; administrative secretary, British Association for American Studies, London, 1956–63. Agent: Wendy Lipkind, 165 East 66th Street, New York, New York 10021, U.S.A. Address: 17 Cobden Road, Brighton, Sussex BN2 2T2, England.

CRIME PUBLICATIONS

Novels (series: Professor Paula Glenning)

The Darkened Room. London, Long, 1968.
A Mind to Murder. London, Chatto and Windus, 1971.
The End of a Shadow. London, Chatto and Windus, 1972.
Plot Counter-Plot. London, Collins, 1974; New York, Walker, 1975.
My Search for Ruth. London, Collins, 1975; New York, Richardson Steirman Black, 1988.
Legacy of Evil. London, Collins, 1976.
The Deathless and the Dead. London, Collins, 1976; as *This Downhill Path*, New York, McKay, 1977.
The Lady in Black. London, Collins, 1977; New York, McKay, 1978.
Letter from the Dead. London, Collins, 1977; New York, Doubleday, 1981.
One of Us Must Die. London, Collins, 1977; New York, Doubleday, 1980.
The Poisoned Web. London, Collins, 1979; New York, St. Martin's Press, 1982.
Poison Parsley. London, Collins, 1979.
Last Voyage. London, Collins, 1980; New York, St. Martin's Press, 1982.
Game, Set, and Danger. New York, Doubleday, 1981; London, Hale, 1983.
Desire to Kill. New York, Doubleday, 1982; London, Hale, 1983.
We the Bereaved. New York, Doubleday, 1982; London, Hale, 1984.
Soon She Must Die. New York, Doubleday, 1984; London, Hale, 1985.
Last Judgement (Glenning). New York, Doubleday, 1985; London, Hale, 1986.
Cabin 3033 (Glenning). New York, Doubleday, 1986; Bath, Avon, Chivers, 1988.
The Mystery Lady (Glenning). New York, Doubleday, 1986; London, Severn House, 1988.
Last Seen in London (Glenning). New York, Doubleday, 1987.
Murder in Writing (Glenning). New York, Doubleday, 1988.
The Whitelands Affair (Glenning). New York, Doubleday, 1989.

Uncollected Short Stories

"Caesar's Wife," in *Ellery Queen's Mystery Magazine* (New York), May 1983.
"The Laburnum Tree," in *Ellery Queen's Mystery Magazine* (New York), August 1983.
"Outside the Law," in *Ellery Queen's Mystery Magazine* (New York), May 1984.
"Triangle at Sea," in *Ellery Queen's Mystery Magazine* (New York), December 1984.
"The Silver Teapot," in *Ellery Queen's Mystery Magazine* (New York), September 1985.
"Mr. Mundon's Memoirs," in *Ellery Queen's Mystery Magazine* (New York), May 1985.
"The Secret Path," in *Ellery Queen's Mystery Magazine* (New York), March 1987.
"The Mystery of Percy's Heart," in *Ellery Queen's Mystery Magazine* (New York), August 1989.

*

Manuscript Collection: Mugar Memorial Library, Boston University.

Anna Clarke comments:

It is difficult to say anything about my own writing because I have never taken it very seriously except as a source of income and a mental release from the frustrations of life. I have turned into an obsessional spinner of stories, going on with them in my own mind even when not writing them down, but I only started writing late in life and should never have done so if a very long and severe illness had not destroyed my chosen career. I should have been a mathematician, and am even now more interested in maths than in fiction. I don't know whether the love of pattern and order and an eye for similarities that form the love of mathematics have any influence on what I write. I never plan a novel and have no idea when I start how it is going to develop and end. This is the only way I can keep up my interest enough to finish it—not knowing myself "whodunit"! But it always seems to fall into some sort of pattern and to conclude at about the same length, so there must be a connection. There is certainly a connection between what I write and the fact that I was cured of my illness by a long and deep Freudian analysis and that I have done a lot of work on psycho-analytical writings. As far as I have any conscious feeling about writing novels at all beyond the obsessional story-telling, I am interested in the workings of the human mind and their effect on character and action. And I only took to writing mystery and suspense stories because nobody wanted to publish the straight novels that I was writing.

*   *   *

Anna Clarke's crime fiction gives the whole genre an interesting twist for she moves detecting away from the mystery of the criminal mind to the mystery of writing itself. She writes crime fiction on the edge of metafiction without either calling undue attention to this act or stretching the genre beyond its give.

An early example of this aspect of her work is found in *Plot Counter-Plot*, in which an established and successful suspense novelist, Helen Mitchell, engages in a literary and love affair with a young, unsuccessful author named Brent Ashwood. Clarke holds metafiction and the crime genre together nicely in this novel as she plays plot in the literary sense against plot in the criminal sense. Brent resolves to steal Helen's novel (after all, it is about him and so, in a fashion, is his) and to pass it off as an autobiographical novel of his own. Helen discovers his plot to steal her plot and decides to kill Brent. In both senses, plot thickens and counter-plot grows bolder. Fiction imitates life imitates fiction imitates. . .and the denouement is superb.

For Clarke, aesthetic considerations and the literary act become one with the presentation and solution of a crime. Indeed, literary concerns and aesthetic sensibility are the primary instruments for penetrating mystery in Clarke's fiction. *My Search for Ruth* is particularly interesting as an illustration of the way in which literary pursuit yields up the subtle mysteries of the self to those possessed of literary sensibility. Ruth writes for us a chronicle of her search for identity. Like Hitchcock's Marnie, Ruth follows a single image through a maze of violence and death, until that image is so embellished as to show forth the truth of her identity. This image is presented on the first page of the novel:

The head in the wall; that was the first of my memories. It had a grinning red face, surrounded by hair sticking up in all directions like Shockheaded Peter, and it shot out of the shadows by the side of the fireplace in my Aunt Bessie's little living room and remained twisting about as if it belonged to some monstrous being that was striving to break through the brown wallpaper and run rampant through the house, leaving in its wake a horror beyond what the timid mind could bear.

Ruth possesses a fine literary sense and was raised and educated by literary people; but her search for her parents and her attempt to understand the image that contains the essential truth about her life cause her to reject a university education and life as a scholar in favor of a compulsive, personal, primary encounter with the stuff of literature itself—image, character, plot. *The Deathless and the Dead* continues Clarke's pattern of building crime fiction around literary activity. With a nod backward to Dorothy Sayers, Edmund Crispin, and Michael Crispin, Clarke gives us John Broom, a young scholar-sleuth who is studying the life and death of a minor 19th-century poet, Emily Witherington. Through his pursuit of a ribbon-tied cache of old letters, the mysteries of Emily's life and death, the criminal mind, and literary research all unfold. This tale of crime and its detection is a roaring good one, but the better mystery is the one which unfolds as literary sensibility gives life and order to the world by shaping fact, fear, and fantasy into a complete and coherent biography.

With only a little tinkering, Clarke shaped from *The Deathless and the Dead* a most successful series of academic crime novels. So far there are six books in the series. Professor Paula Glenning of Princess Elizabeth College, University of London, appears in them all. She teaches modern English literature and is author of a highly acclaimed literary biography. In the best of the series, *Last Judgment*, *The Mystery Lady*, and *Murder in Writing*, Clarke continues to explore metafictional issues. In the first book of the series, *Last Judgment*, two English professors position themselves unsuccessfully to gain sole rights to the literary remains of a great novelist, G.E. Goff. As they jockey for position, the untold story of G.E. Goff unfolds before us. The fiction Clarke writes is the biography neither scholar produces. Quite literally, their dreams for literary triumph go up in flames. One of these scholars, James Goff, grandson of the famous novelist, is salvaged from this book to become Paula Glenning's Watson, friend, and lover.

Paula Glenning doesn't take charge of Clarke's series until *Cabin 3033*, figuring as third fiddle to James Goff and Richard Grieve in *Last Judgment*. But it is not until *The Mystery Lady* that Clarke succeeds in pairing Glenning and Goff to produce a truly satisfying Paula Glenning novel. In it, Paula is signed to write the biography of popular novelist, Rosie O'Grady. Author Clarke sends author Glenning in search of author O'Grady who may well be the creation of yet another author and never an author herself. Needless to say, Paula and James discover crime and concealment aplenty as they try to sort fact from fiction in their attempt to identify the real Rosie O'Grady. Crime and metafiction indeed.

Nowhere is writing itself better used as the subject and vehicle of Clarke's novels than in *Murder in Writing*. Paula visits a friend who teaches creative writing at a local manor house to a cast of characters who become suspects in a murder mystery perhaps orchestrated in the writing seminar itself. Though the theme is post-modern, the plot and setting are vintage Agatha Christie—small village, closed society, a cast of eccentrics, murder on the manor grounds. Clarke's ability to deal with contemporary aesthetics in the shell of Golden Age crime fiction is a hallmark of her best work.

The Whitelands Affair is a wonderful example of this mix. Though not preachy, the novel, like most in the Paula Glenning series, is concerned with feminist issues and makes conscious nods to the life and work of Virginia Woolf and to Edward Albee's play, "Who's Afraid of Virginia Woolf. It is also written in meticulous detail according to the outline set down by W.H. Auden in "The Guilty Vicarage." Her clever concern for the literariness of the genre she has mastered makes Clarke a most special practitioner of mystery writing. Her talent is immense. She breathes a true creator's breath into old conventions and clichés precisely because, as a writer of mysteries, she is bold enough to fashion them from the mystery of writing itself.

—Larry E. Grimes

CLASON, Clyde B.   American.   Born in Denver, Colorado, in 1903. Worked as advertising copywriter and trade paper editor in Chicago.

CRIME PUBLICATIONS

Novels (series: Theocritus Lucius Westborough in all books)

The Fifth Tumbler.   New York, Doubleday, 1936; London, Heinemann, 1937.
The Death Angel.   New York, Doubleday, 1936; London, Heinemann, 1937.
Blind Drifts.   New York, Doubleday, 1937.
The Purple Parrot.   New York, Doubleday, and London, Heinemann, 1937.
The Man from Tibet.   New York, Doubleday, and London, Heinemann, 1938.
The Whispering Ear.   New York, Doubleday, 1938; London, Heinemann, 1939.
Murder Gone Minoan.   New York, Doubleday, 1939; as *Clue to the Labyrinth*, London, Heinemann, 1939.
Dragon's Cave.   New York, Doubleday, 1939; London, Heinemann, 1940.
Poison Jasmine.   New York, Doubleday, 1940.
Green Shiver.   New York, Doubleday, 1941; London, Heinemann, 1948.

OTHER PUBLICATIONS

Novels

Ark of Venus.   New York, Knopf, 1955.
I Am Lucifer: Confessions of the Devil.   Philadelphia, Muhlenberg Press, 1960; London, Hodder and Stoughton, 1961.

Other

The Story of Period Furniture.   Chicago, Nutshell, 1925.
Evolution of Architecture.   Chicago, Nutshell, n.d.
How to Write Stories That Sell.   Chicago, Nutshell, n.d.
Exploring the Distant Stars: Thrilling Adventures in Our Galaxy and Beyond.   New York, Putnam, 1958.
Men, Planets, and Stars (for children).   New York, Putnam, 1959.
This Rock Exists.   London, Davies, 1962.
The Delights of the Slide Rule.   New York, Crowell, 1964.

*   *   *

Clyde B. Clason is in many ways a typical figure among traditional American detective novelists of the 1930's. The puzzle is very much the center of his novels, with most characters sketched just fully enough to be told apart. From his

first novel, *The Fifth Tumbler*, he frequently displays an enthusiasm for the locked rooms and impossible crimes of Carr and Rawson. His novels are often illustrated with maps of the murder scene. Like many American puzzle-makers of the 1930's, he was heavily influenced by the intellectual and informational content of S.S. Van Dine's Philo Vance novels. Thus, he offers a considerable display of erudition on various arcane subjects, usually relevant to the mystery at hand. Though Clason generally shuns footnotes, except to plug his earlier books, he goes Van Dine's apparatus one better by including a three-page bibliography at the beginning of *The Man from Tibet*.

Clason's continuing sleuth, initially a Chicago resident but later pursuing crime in California, is the elderly Roman Empire scholar Theocritus Lucius Westborough, a stock character in some respects but ultimately a well-realized individual. The detective's police friend, Lieutenant John Mack, is a notably rude cop when dealing with suspects, but Westborough himself is mild and likeable, far from the abrasive intellect of Philo Vance or the irascible personalities of scholar-sleuths like John Rhode's Dr. Priestley or Jacques Futrelle's Thinking Machine. For all his age, Westborough is no armchair detective and does not shun strenuous physical activity in the pursuit of truth. His customary ornate and pedantic speaking style serves his creator well in the melodramatic murder-spotting scenes. No real lover of the standard between-World-Wars detective novel can resist a line like this one, from *Blind Drifts*: "Guard the door please, Mr. Williams! Mr. McKenzie's murderer, Mrs. Edmonds' assailant, the man in whose hands the unlucky Seaver was as putty, is now in this room."

Westborough solves his first case, *The Fifth Tumbler*, when impossible murder strikes among the inhabitants of the residential hotel where he lives. The novel's complicated plot is nicely worked out and plays fair with the reader to an admirable extent. The same can be said for the subsequent Chicago case, *The Purple Parrot*, concerning a nutty will in which the only bequest to the decedent's granddaughter is the vanished bird of the title.

Blind Drifts is not one of the best Clason novels—the plot is far-fetched and over-elaborate, and the killer stands out rather obviously—but it includes one of his most unusual and successfully exploited backgrounds: a working gold mine in Colorado. *The Man from Tibet* is probably the author's high-water mark, including both his best locked room (pronounced "highly original and practicable" by impossible-crime specialist Robert C.S. Adey) and one of his most impressive displays of scholarship, on Tibetan art and religion. *Dragon's Cave*, about the murder of a weapons collector, involves the solving of a cryptogram and has a nicely managed Least Suspected Person solution.

Clason is a highly entertaining writer and a conscientious builder of puzzle plots. His main fault is that, in going for the spectacular, dazzling solution, he sometimes builds too tricky and too elaborate a deductive edifice. But two of the greatest puzzle-spinners of them all, Queen and Carr, have sometimes been accused of the same fault, one that would be more than welcome in a few more contemporary writers of detective fiction.

—Jon L. Breen

CLEARY, Jon (Stephen).   Australian.   Born in Sydney, New South Wales, 22 November 1917. Educated at Marist Brothers

School, Randwick, New South Wales, 1924–32. Served in the Australian Imperial Forces in the Middle East and New Guinea, 1940–45: Lieutenant. Married Constantine Joy Lucas in 1946; two daughters. Prior to 1939 worked as a commercial traveller, bush worker, and commercial artist. Since 1945 full-time writer. Journalist, Government of Australia News and Information Bureau, in London, 1948–49, and in New York, 1949–51. Recipient: Australian Broadcasting Commission prize, for radio drama, 1944; Australian Section prize, *New York Herald Tribune* World Short Story Contest, 1950; Mystery Writers of America Edgar Allan Poe award, 1974. Lives in New South Wales. Agent: John Farquharson Ltd., 162–168 Regent Street, London W1R 5TB. Address: c/o William Collins Ltd., 8 Grafton Street, London W1X 3LA, England.

CRIME PUBLICATIONS

Novels (series: Scobie Malone)

You Can't See Around Corners. New York, Scribner, 1947; London, Eyre and Spottiswoode, 1949.
The Long Shadow. London, Laurie, 1949.
Just Let Me Be. London, Laurie, 1950.
The Climate of Courage. London, Collins, 1954; as *Naked in the Night*, New York, Popular Library, 1955.
Justin Bayard. London, Collins, 1955; New York, Morrow, 1956; as *Dust in the Sun*, New York, Popular Library, 1957.
North from Thursday. London, Collins, 1960; New York, Morrow, 1961.
Forests of the Night. New York, Morrow, and London, Collins, 1963.
A Flight of Chariots. New York, Morrow, 1963; London, Collins, 1964.
The Fall of an Eagle. New York, Morrow, 1964; London, Collins, 1965.
The Pulse of Danger. New York, Morrow, and London, Collins, 1966.
The High Commissioner (Malone). New York, Morrow, and London, Collins, 1966.
The Long Pursuit. New York, Morrow, and London, Collins, 1967.
Season of Doubt. New York, Morrow, and London, Collins, 1968.
Helga's Web (Malone). New York, Morrow, and London, Collins, 1970.
The Liberators. New York, Morrow, 1971; as *Mask of the Andes*, London, Collins, 1971.
Ransom (Malone). New York, Morrow, and London, Collins, 1973.
Peter's Pence. New York, Morrow, and London, Collins, 1974.
The Safe House. New York, Morrow, and London, Collins, 1975.
A Sound of Lightning. New York, Morrow, and London, Collins, 1976.
High Road to China. New York, Morrow, and London, Collins, 1977.
Vortex. London, Collins, 1977; New York, Morrow, 1978.
Dragons at the Party (Malone). London, Collins, 1987; New York, Morrow, 1988.
Now and Then, Amen (Malone). London, Collins, 1988; New York, Morrow, 1989.
Babylon South (Malone). London, Collins, 1989; New York, Morrow, 1990.

Murder Song (Malone). London, Collins, and New York, Morrow, 1990.

Short Stories

These Small Glories. Sydney, Angus and Robertson, 1946.

OTHER PUBLICATIONS

Novels

The Sundowners. New York, Scribner, and London, Laurie, 1952.
The Green Helmet. London, Collins, 1957; New York, Morrow, 1958.
Back of Sunset. New York, Morrow, and London, Collins, 1959.
The Country of Marriage. New York, Morrow, and London, Collins, 1962.
Remember Jack Hoxie. New York, Morrow, and London, Collins, 1969.
The Ninth Marquess. New York, Morrow, 1972; as *Man's Estate*, London, Collins, 1972.
The Beaufort Sisters. New York, Morrow, and London, Collins, 1979.
A Very Private War. New York, Morrow, and London, Collins, 1980.
The Golden Sabre. New York, Morrow, and London, Collins, 1981.
The Faraway Drums. London, Collins, 1981; New York, Morrow, 1982.
Spearfield's Daughter. London, Collins, 1982; New York, Morrow, 1983.
The Phoenix Tree. London, Collins, 1984.
City of Fading Light. London, Collins, 1985; New York, Morrow, 1986.

Short Stories

Pillar of Salt. Sydney, Horwitz, 1963.

Plays

Strike Me Lucky (produced Bromley, Kent, 1963).

Screenplays: *The Siege of Pinchgut*, with Harry Watt and Alexander Baron, 1959; *The Green Helmet*, 1961; *The Sundowners*, 1961; *Sidecar Racers* (*Sidecar Boys*), 1975.

Radio Play: *Safe Horizon*, 1944.

Television Play: *Just Let Me Be* (UK), 1957; *Spearfield's Daughter* (from his own novel), 1988.

*   *   *

John Cleary's writing, now recognized and respected by over two generations of avid readers, embodies the sterling qualities of masterful storytelling, stage setting, and character delineation. Though a superb hand at any of these could attract attention, Cleary manages to imbue his works—both general fiction and mystery—with an energetic presence combining all three. His prose, while carefully composed, quick-moving, and easy-to-read, lacks a sense of literary craftsmanship; however, his works are broader than they are deep and are meant to be read purely for entertainment.

By the time Cleary introduced his important series detective Scobie Malone in *The High Commissioner*, he was well acquainted with mystery writing. Malone appears again in *Ransom*, but *Now and Then, Amen*, firmly secured the character's niche among crime detectives. As in many of his novels, Cleary hooks the reader with an opening ploy; in this case, a nun is found murdered on the front steps of Sydney's most notorious and exclusive brothel. While rooted firmly in Australia, Malone's search for clues takes him into sordid familial backgrounds and dubious business transactions both there and abroad.

In *Dragons at the Party*, the fourth Scobie Malone novel, police establish the identity of a hired assassin early in the plot. The victims, though, innocent bystanders, shrink in significance compared to a Marcos-like exiled leader, his ex-dancer wife, and Australian political archrivals. Here again, Cleary's eye for character and his ability to capture salient features in a few lines are readily apparent. Malone's search for the terrorist murderer continues, displayed against a panoramic backdrop of Sydney's bicentennial celebration and a wild brush fire on the outskirts of town.

Scobie Malone, as a strong, magnetic protagonist, jousts for position in Cleary's canon with other personalities like Cornelius Mullane (*A Very Private War*), Eve Tozer (*High Road to China*), and Matt Cabell (*The Golden Sabre*). All of these fascinating, colorful characters—sometimes reckless, sometimes wronged, but always plucky—provide slightly larger-than-life ideals for audience consumption.

Earlier novels featured less elevated principal characters. *Season of Doubt*, for example, fairly typical for Cleary, features a more subdued leading man and occurs in Beirut during the Middle East crisis of 1967. To a situation already ripe with tension and conflict, the author adds an American Embassy official/narrator affected by anti-American demonstrators, an Arab-French mistress, and a second-hand arms dealer. Detailed descriptions contribute richness to a plot that seldom sits still. Action and suspense also permeate *The Long Pursuit*, another adventure novel set in desperate times and faraway places. As a motley crew of international mix tries to escape 1942 Japanese-controlled Singapore and Sumatra by ship, they encounter everything from bullets to shark-infested waters. This work, like so many of Cleary's, contains moments of humor which leaven the serious content.

Since 1980, this heroism of the individual has expanded in scope. Exotic backdrops continue; however, the stories become more bizarre and the characters a bit more idiosyncratic. Action in *The Faraway Drums*, for example, occurs in early 20th century British India. Eve Tozer's search for her kidnapped father takes her across China in 1920, while events in *The Golden Sabre* hurtle through Revolutionary Russia. These works evidence an increased flair for high adventure and intrigue; and with the accompaniment of exaggerated protagonists, they satisfy the reader's taste for escapist fare.

Cleary's most recent books seem to offer a different kind of escape, but they never lose the basis in reality that marks all his novels. The locales may be exotic, but Cleary has researched or experienced the place and the tradition. Certainly he knows his native Australia and his home city of Sydney. Widely travelled, Cleary spends a great deal of time in Europe, Africa, Asia, and the United States, all of which he has used as locations for his stories. More importantly, he gives life to these settings with his characterization. Because of Cleary's gift, his audience can experience vicariously, empathize with fascinating characters, and participate in "historical" events.

—Rex E. Klett

———

CLEEVE, Brian (Brendan Talbot). Irish. Born in Thorpe Bay, Essex, England, 22 November 1921. Educated at Selwyn House, Broadstairs, Kent, 1930–35; St. Edward's School, Oxford, 1935–38; University of South Africa, Johannesburg, 1951–53, B.A. 1953; National University of Ireland, Dublin, 1954–56, Ph.D. 1956. Served in the British Merchant Navy, 1939–45. Married Veronica McAdie in 1945; two daughters. Freelance journalist in South Africa, 1948–54, and in Ireland since 1954. Broadcaster, Radio Telefis Eireann, Dublin, 1962–72. Address: 60 Heytesbury Lane, Ballsbridge, Dublin 4, Ireland.

CRIME PUBLICATIONS

Novels (series: Sean Ryan)

Birth of a Dark Soul. London, Jarrolds, 1953; as *The Night Winds*, Boston, Houghton Mifflin, 1954.
Assignment to Vengeance. London, Hammond, 1961.
Death of a Painted Lady. London, Hammond, 1962; New York, Random House, 1963.
Death of a Wicked Servant. London, Hammond, 1963; New York, Random House, 1964.
Vote X for Treason (Ryan). London, Collins, 1964; New York, Random House, 1965; as *Counterspy*, London, Lancer, 1966.
Dark Blood, Dark Terror (Ryan). New York, Random House, 1965; London, Hammond, 1966.
The Judas Goat (Ryan). London, Hammond, 1966; as *Vice Isn't Private*, New York, Random House, 1966.
Violent Death of a Bitter Englishman (Ryan). New York, Random House, 1967; London, Corgi, 1969.
You Must Never Go Back. New York, Random House, 1968.
Exit from Prague. London, Corgi, 1970; as *Escape from Prague*, New York, Pinnacle, 1973.
Tread Softly in This Place. London, Cassell, and New York, Day, 1972.

Uncollected Short Stories

"Death," in *London Mystery Magazine*, September 1953.
"Vendetta!," in *Suspense* (London), March 1961.
"Foxer," in *Best Detective Stories of the Year 1966*, edited by Anthony Boucher. New York, Dutton, 1966.
"The Devil Finds Work for Jake O'Hara," in *Ellery Queen's Mystery Magazine* (New York), December 1969.

OTHER PUBLICATIONS

Novels

The Far Hills. London, Jarrolds, 1952.
Portrait of My City. London, Jarrolds, 1952.
Cry of Morning. London, Joseph, 1971; as *The Triumph of O'Rourke*, New York, Doubleday, 1972.
The Dark Side of the Sun. London, Cassell, 1973.
A Question of Inheritance. London, Cassell, 1974; as *For Love of Crannagh Castle*, New York, Dutton, 1975.
Sara. London, Cassell, and New York, Coward McCann, 1976.
Kate. London, Cassell, and New York, Coward McCann, 1977.
Judith. London, Cassell, and New York, Coward McCann, 1978.

Hester. London, Cassell, 1979; New York, Coward McCann, 1980.

Short Stories

The Horse Thieves of Ballysaggert and Other Stories. Cork, Mercier Press, 1966.

Other

Colonial Policies in Africa. Johannesburg, St. Benedict's House, 1954.
Dictionary of Irish Writers. Cork, Mercier Press, 3 vols., 1967–71; as *A Biographical Dictionary of Irish Writers*, Mullingar, Westmeath, Lilliput Press, and New York, St. Martin's Press, 1 vol., 1985.
The House on the Rock. London, Watkins, 1980.
The Seven Mansions. London, Watkins, 1980; New York, State Mutual, 1981.
1938: A World Vanishing. London, Buchan and Enright, and New York, State Mutual, 1982.
The Fourth Mary. Dublin, Co-op, 1982.
A View of the Irish. London, Buchan and Enright, 1983.

Editor, *W.B. Yeats and the Designing of Ireland's Coinage.* Dublin, Dolmen Press, 1972.

*

Manuscript Collection: Mugar Memorial Library, Boston University.

Brian Cleeve comments:

Crime and thriller stories have always appealed to me for the same reason that fairy stories do, and folk tales and myths. They deal directly with the conflict between good and evil, and for that reason touch the most fundamental levels of human experience. In my own crime and thriller novels I *tried*—I only wish I had succeeded—to deal with this theme as seriously as it should be dealt with. I wish that publishers and novel readers were willing to accept serious work in these categories—and I wish too that the whole concept of categories for fiction could be thrown away.

* * *

Brian Cleeve's Irish novels put to rest romanticized myths of an idyllic Ireland with Seal Queens and Martyrs, yet show how these have shaped modern Irish goals and actions. Cleeve sees inevitable contradictions and self-destructive extremes in the Irish character: legendary ancestry versus present economic deprivation, repressive puritanical training versus retaliatory drunkenness and lechery, rigid conservative Catholicism versus socialist/communist sympathies, an ancient system of clans and feuds versus modern community and democracy, tight lips to strangers versus continual gossip and rumor among friends, a xenophobic love of rural Ireland and its ancient manor houses versus a desire for the wealth foreign developers bring. Cleeve's digressive sagas suggest the subtle class and racial tensions that influence the thoughts, actions, goals, and transformations of a number of families or individuals from diverse social levels: itinerants (particularly tinkers), gentry, clergy, Anglo-Irish, peasant families with noble ancestry. In *Tread Softly in This Place* developers blame a costly prank by local xenophobes on IRA commandos and expect plots everywhere, which causes local radicals to mount a real raid. *Death of a Painted Lady*, a more traditional tale of promiscuity,

drunkenness, and sadism in the art world that lead to rape, murder, robbery, and the conviction of an innocent man, focuses on the hypocrisies of Dublin characters from tramp to art critic—all in or around the scene of the crime at the crucial moment.

Cleeve's spy series follow the checkered career of Sean Ryan, an impetuous ex-Irish revolutionary turned cynic, recruited from prison by Major Courtney of British Intelligence to infiltrate and investigate groups whose plans threaten the security of England. Usually these are large-scale operations to seize or keep power: a Home Secretary who destroys his own agents to conceal his kinky sex habits (*The Judas Goat*); a group of reactionary Lords and MP's who use commandos and teddy boys trained in health clubs and a secret oil agreement with Iraq to precipitate a change of government (*Vote X for Treason*); another fascist organization that plots to seize power on a racist wave to eliminate coloreds in England on funds extorted from them by protection rackets (*Violent Death of a Bitter Englishman*); an Afrikaner task force using Ryan's agency as a front for their plot to assassinate the South African Prime Minister (*Dark Blood, Dark Terror*). The sadistic directors of these diabolical schemes employ hideous physical punishment to break and eliminate opponents: crucifixion, castration, electroshock, drugs. To counter his own deep-seated fear of torture and personal injury, Ryan resorts to equally violent methods with the tools at hand—a tank of boiling coffee in the face, gasoline to produce a human torch, deadly karate chops, sudden blows with spike, mace, or board. But the villain's violence is planned and savoured while Ryan's is a spontaneous instinct to save himself and the innocents he seeks to protect (usually a pliable, clinging female). Always Ryan suffers from guilt about his cruel temper, and doubts the worth of his cause since another evil group quickly replaces the one destroyed; he also questions his status in an organization in which, as an Irishman, he can never fully belong.

Cleeve's other short stories and novels vary from straightforward adventure like *You Must Never Go Back*, in which a young man returns to the scene of his parents' murder to put to rest childhood nightmares, only to find Italian murderers ready to finish the job, to romantic intrigue like *Kate, Sara*, and *Judith*, Regency novels focusing on women who survive revolution, prison, poverty, and heartbreak.

—Gina Macdonald

CLEEVES, Ann (née Richardson). British. Born in Hereford, 24 October 1954. Educated at Barnstaple Grammar School, Devon, 1967–72; Liverpool University, 1977–79, diploma in social work. Married Tim Cleeves in 1977; two daughters. Child care officer, Camden Social Services, London, 1973–75; bird observatory cook, Fair Isle, Scotland, 1975–76; auxiliary coastguard, 1977–81; probation officer, 1981–83, both Wirral, Cheshire. Agent: Murray Pollinger, 222 Old Brompton Road, London, SW5 OBZ. Address: 19 Holywell Dene Road, Holywell, Whitley Bay, Northumberland NE25 OLB, England.

CRIME PUBLICATIONS

Novels (series: George Palmer-Jones in all books except *A Lesson in Dying*)

A Bird in the Hand. London, Century, and New York, Fawcett, 1986.
Come Death and High Water. London, Century, and New York, Fawcett, 1987.
Murder in Paradise. London, Century, 1988; New York, Fawcett, 1989.
A Prey to Murder. London, Century, and New York, Fawcett, 1989.
A Lesson in Dying. London, Century, 1990.

*

Ann Cleeves comments:

Detail is very important in detective fiction, in natural history it's crucial. George Palmer-Jones is a retired civil servant and amateur ornithologist with an eye for detail. The books in which he appears have a background in natural history and conservation with subjects as different as twitching—the obsessive search for rare birds—to the theft of birds of prey. Place is often an integral part of the action. My husband works for the Royal Society for the Protection of Birds and I take care in getting detail right too.

A Lesson in Dying begins a new series set firmly in my home county of Northumberland. Inspector Ramsay is a local man, lonely, stubborn, and aloof. His work will take him, in future novels, from the docks and industry of the Tyne to the Scottish borders.

*   *   *

Ann Cleeves is a gifted recruit to the traditional detective novel, incisive in manner and with acute insight into character. She respects the convention and pays scrupulous attention to the fundamental need to keep the reader guessing. She shows an impressive ability to shape the various tensions within a community into an absorbing and satisfying pattern.

Four of her novels feature George Palmer-Jones, a retired Home Office official married to a former social worker. His natural authority is augmented by his professional past and the reputation persisting from it; yet he suffers from self-doubt and is subject to "depression and lethargy." He finds difficulty in adjusting to retirement and misses the structure and discipline of professional life. Eventually he establishes an "advice agency" for the families of missing teenagers.

It is his secondary reputation as a seasoned ornithologist that involves him in crime. In *A Bird in the Hand* Palmer-Jones joins a community of birdwatchers, some of whom are willing to travel any distance at a moment's notice to encounter a rare breed. Such enthusiasm amounts to obsession, a force sufficiently strong to turn a man's mind, to "alter mood, sense, even personality, like a drug." George must consider whether it also has "the power to make a person mad enough to commit murder." The victim's influence was strong in the community and his complex personality takes shape as the action proceeds. Enmities surface, associations breed suspicion: one man was his rival in love, another sought the same job, a third lost status by his ascendancy. A revealing slant on the victim determines a part of the truth and a rare bird contributes fittingly to the final resolution.

Come Death and High Water opens in classic style as a number of people prepare to gather at a nature reserve off the Devon coast. No sooner are they assembled than the owner of the island announces his intention to sell out: not surprisingly, he is dead by the following morning. Suspicion spreads impartially through the company and the despatch of a second victim contracts the closed circle even further. The island community is established with a keen eye for vagaries of

character and the puckish eccentricity of the first victim is especially attractive. Despite his death, his influence persists and the design is enhanced by encounters with his family on the mainland. Palmer-Jones appears as if on cue and solves the case with close and subtle reasoning: even the clumsy stowage of a net has its relevance for him.

Murder in Paradise takes him to the remote island of Kinness in the Western Isles of Scotland. The closed community opens to admit a bride from the mainland and she becomes the principal witness, both of the life on the island and of the course of the investigation. Her young sister-in-law dies during her wedding feast and the second victim soon after she has enjoyed his hospitality. She and Palmer-Jones observe and ponder—on a cryptic message, an inscription on a gravestone, the dispositions of a will, and the odd maturity of a small boy. George pursues the secret known to the first victim and the treasured scarf she was wearing when she died: rightly, since both prove crucial. The rhythm of life on the island is finely evoked and a marvellous sense of shared tradition emerges. Despite this, most of the principals are driven to some degree, by unease at best, by neurosis at worst. The stability of the community is continually threatened, not just by the murders but more subtly by the need for change, the lure of the mainland, the betrayals of temperament and "the philosophy of keeping up appearances."

A Prey to Murder is set in and around a Shropshire hotel, where the owner, a small-scale matriarch, dies by violence (rather too soon for her to have made her full impact as the subtle tyrant she proves to have been). Her murder seems a dreadful side-effect of an illicit trade in birds of prey and much time and energy are expended on the pursuit of the prime suspect. The narrative is less various than its predecessors, more concentrated and direct, though no less intelligent. Much of the investigation is conducted by an ebullient Welsh policeman, with George rather uncomfortably in tow. His wife Molly makes her own enquiries at the hotel and it is she who provokes the violent climax. Molly's relationship with George undergoes some stress during the action, sufficient to threaten their marriage but not permanently to injure it.

A Lesson in Dying introduces Inspector Stephen Ramsay, an impulsive, even reckless policeman, disliked by his colleagues and prone to serious error. He investigates the murder of a blackmailer among a village community in Northumberland, disregarding those who had reason to wish him dead and arresting instead his innocent wife, with disastrous consequences. Though stylish and absorbing, the narrative strains credibility at times, besides promising rather more than it achieves. Diversionary tactics fail adequately to conceal the killer, whose eventual collapse is shocking and demeaning.

Cleeves intends to develop both her detectives and on her current form will continue to command attention. She may even establish a significant reputation: at her best she is already exceptional.

—B.A. Pike

———

CLIFFORD, Francis. Pseudonym for Arthur Leonard Bell Thompson. British. Born in Bristol, 1 December 1917. Educated at Christ's Hospital, Horsham, Sussex, 1928–35. Served in the Burma Rifles, 1939–43, and as Special Operations Executive, 1943–45: Distinguished Service Order. Married 1) Majorie Bennett in 1944 (marriage dissolved), one son; 2) Josephine Bridget Devereux in 1955, one son. Commercial assistant in the rice trade, London, 1935–38, and Burma, 1938–39; industrial journalist in the steel industry, London, 1946–59. Recipient: Crime Writers Association Silver Dagger award, 1969, 1974. *Died 24 August 1975.*

CRIME PUBLICATIONS

Novels

The Trembling Earth. London, Hamish Hamilton, 1955.
Overdue. London, Hamish Hamilton, 1957; New York, Dutton, 1958.
Act of Mercy. London, Hamish Hamilton, and New York, Coward McCann, 1960; as *Guns of Darkness*, New York, Dell, 1962.
Time Is an Ambush. London, Hodder and Stoughton, 1962.
The Green Fields of Eden. London, Hodder and Stoughton, and New York, Coward McCann, 1963.
The Hunting-Ground. London, Hodder and Stoughton, and New York, Coward McCann, 1964.
The Third Side of the Coin. London, Hodder and Stoughton, and New York, Coward McCann, 1965.
The Naked Runner. London, Hodder and Stoughton, and New York, Coward McCann, 1966.
Spanish Duet: Two Novels of Suspense (includes *The Trembling Earth and Time Is an Ambush*). New York, Coward McCann, 1966.
All Men are Lonely Now. London, Hodder and Stoughton, and New York, Coward McCann, 1967.
Another Way of Dying. London, Hodder and Stoughton, 1968; New York, Coward McCann, 1969.
The Blind Side. London, Hodder and Stoughton, and New York, Coward McCann, 1971.
A Wild Justice. London, Hodder and Stoughton, and New York, Coward McCann, 1972.
Amigo, Amigo. London, Hodder and Stoughton, and New York, Coward McCann 1973.
The Grosvenor Square Goodbye. London, Hodder and Stoughton, 1974; as *Goodbye and Amen*, New York, Coward McCann, 1974.
Drummer in the Dark. London, Hodder and Stoughton, and New York, Harcourt Brace, 1976.

Short Stories

Ten Minutes on a June Morning and Other Stories. London, Hodder and Stoughton, 1977.

OTHER PUBLICATIONS

Novels

Honour the Shrine. London, Cape, 1953.
Something to Love. London, Hamish Hamilton, 1958.
A Battle Is Fought to Be Won. London, Hamish Hamilton, 1960; New York, Coward McCann, 1961.

Other

Desperate Journey. London, Hodder and Stoughton, 1979.

*   *   *

"Only during strain—a moral, a physical, or a psychological strain—do you get to know your own character; that's my experience from the war—it is only under such circumstances

that the right character of a man emerges." These remarks were made by Francis Clifford when I interviewed him in London more than 20 years ago, and they explain very much in his novels.

Clifford's first novels were war novels set in southeast Asia, and they are still very readable especially as they seem based on his own adventures during World War II, when he belonged to the Special Operations Executive, first in India and later in London. His favourite among these books was *A Battle Is Fought to Be Won*, which he considered his most honest war novel.

But there is no doubt that his later thrillers are of much greater importance, for example, *The Green Fields of Eden* with its portrait of an Englishman with a serious disease living on a tropical island where he is confronted with a hired killer, and *The Naked Runner*, which is written in the same vein as the novels by Len Deighton and John le Carré. In my opinion however, the most ambitious novels by Clifford are *All Men Are Lonely Now*, *The Blind Side*, and *Amigo, Amigo*. These form a trilogy in which he deals with the moral dilemmas of man varied in three extremely fascinating ways. The courses of events in the books are different, as are the geographical backgrounds—England, Biafra, and Central America—but the theme is the same: the demands of loyalty and the stress that loyalty may lead to.

Ernest Hemingway was among Clifford's literary favourites and also—naturally enough—Graham Greene. Clifford, in fact, was the only thriller writer of the 1960's and 1970's who continued the tradition of Graham Greene as seen in such works as *The Power and the Glory* and *The Heart of the Matter*. Religion is a recurrent theme in some of Clifford's novels—and it is probably not mere chance that, like Greene, he converted to catholicism.

To be sure, some of Clifford's novels are somewhat superficial, with rather impersonally constructed scenes of suspense, but this can not conceal the fact that in many ways he is a greater artist than most of his contemporaries.

—Jan Broberg

_____

CLINTON, F.G. *See* **CAMPBELL, Robert.**

_____

CLINTON-BADDELEY, V(ictor Vaughan Reynolds Geraint) C(linton). British. Born in Budleigh Salterton, Devon, in 1900; brother of the actresses Angela and Hermione Baddeley. Educated at Sherborne School, Dorset; Jesus College, Cambridge, M.A. Editor in the modern history section of the Encyclopaedia Britannica; actor: toured in the U.S.A. with Ben Greet Company; gave many poetry readings and ran Jupiter Records which specialised in poetry recordings. *Died 6 August 1970.*

CRIME PUBLICATIONS

Novels (series: Dr. R.V. Davie in all books)

Death's Bright Dart. London, Gollancz, 1967; New York, Morrow, 1970.

My Foe Outstretch'd Beneath the Tree. London, Gollancz, and New York, Morrow, 1968.
Only a Matter of Time. London, Gollancz, 1969; New York, Morrow, 1970.
No Case for the Police. London, Gollancz, and New York, Morrow, 1970.
To Study a Long Silence, completed by Mark Goullet. London, Gollancz, 1972; New York, Harper, 1984.

OTHER PUBLICATIONS

Plays

Behind the Beyond, adaptation of the story by Stephen Leacock (produced London, 1926). London, Gowans and Gray, and Boston, Baker, 1932.
The Cup That Cheers, with Joyce Dennys (produced 1927). London, Gowans and Gray, and Boston, Baker, 1934.
Aladdin; or, Love Will Find Out the Way, music by Walter Leigh (produced London, 1931). London, Westminster Press, 1931.
The Split in the Cabinet, adaptation of a story by Stephen Leacock (produced London, 1931). London, Gowans and Gray, 1938.
The Billiard Room Mystery; or, Who D'You Think Did It?, adaptation of a story by Stephen Leacock (produced Cambridge, 1931). London, Gowans and Gray, and Boston, Baker, 1934.
The Pride of the Regiment; or, Cashiered for His Country: An Operetta, with Scobie Mackenzie, music by Walter Leigh (also director: produced London, 1932). London, Westminster Press, 1932.
Winsome Winnie: A Romantic Drama, adaptation of the story by Stephen Leacock (broadcast, 1944). London, Gowans and Gray, 1932.
Jolly Roger; or, The Admiral's Daughter: A Comic Opera, with Scobie Mackenzie, music by Walter Leigh (produced London, 1933). London, Boosey, 1933.
Nichevo, with Scobie Mackenzie (produced London, 1934). London, French, 1938.
Cinderella: A Cynical Pantomine, music by Walter Leigh. London, French, 1935.
The Babes in the Wood: A Cynical Pantomime. London, French, 1935.
Sherborne Story: A Chronicle Play. Winchester, Warren, 1950.
Jack and the Beanstalk; or, Love Conquers All, music by Gavin Gordon (broadcast, 1952). London, French, 1953.
Dick Whittington; or, Love Is the Key That Opens Every Door, music by Gavin Gordon. London, French, 1959.
Sleeping Beauty, music by Julian Leigh and Courtney Kenny. London, French, 1959.

Screenplay: *Born That Way*, with Diana Bourbon, 1936.

Radio Plays: *Nicholas Nickleby*, from the novel by Dickens, 1929; *Mr. Pickwick's a Hundred Years Old*, 1936; *Up the Garden* (Parts 2 and 3), 1938; *Mr. Pickwick*, 1939; *Winsome Winnie*, 1944; *Stephen Leacock*, 1944; *Bardell v. Pickwick*, from *The Pickwick Papers* by Dickens, 1946; *Thomas Campion*, 1946; *A Tale of Two Cities*, from the novel by Dickens, 1947; *Jack and the Beanstalk*, 1952; *Benevolent Teachers of Youth 1820–1840*, 1955.

Verse

Songs from the Festival Revue. Cambridge, Arliss, 1931.

Other

Devon. London, A. and C. Black, 1935.
Words for Music (essays). Cambridge, University Press, 1941.
The Burlesque Tradition in the English Theatre after 1660. London, Methuen, 1952; New York, Bloom, 1971.
All Right on the Night (on the Georgian theatre). London, Putnam, 1954.
Some Pantomime Pedigrees. London, Society for Theatre Research, 1963.

Editor, *The What D'Ye Call It: An Opera by Phyllis Tate, based on the Tragi-Comi-Pastoral Farce by John Gay.* London, Oxford University Press, 1966.

*

Theatrical Activities:

Director: **Play**—*The Pride of the Regiment*, London, 1932.

Actor: **Plays**—John Williams in *Water* by Molly Marshall-Hale, London, 1929; Francisco and Rosencrantz in *Hamlet* by Shakespeare, London, 1930; Perriton in *The Split in the Cabinet*, London, 1931; Pontius Pilate in *Judas* by R.V. Ratti, London, 1931; Abanazar in *Aladdin*, London, 1931; General Sir Joshua Blazes in *The Pride of the Regiment*, London, 1932; Jens Schelotrup in *The Witch* by John Masefield, London, 1933; Julian Cleveland in *Cock Robin* by Elmer Rice and Philip Barry, London, 1933; The Abbot in *Montebanks* by Frank Birch, London, 1934; Semyon Semyonitch Kristoffy in *Nichevo*, London, 1934; roles in *Victoria Regina* by Laurence Housman, London, 1935.

*   *   *

The five mysteries that V.C. Clinton-Baddeley wrote are special treats. At a time when many writers were turning away from the classical, fair-play detective story, Clinton-Baddeley was demonstrating that the form still had considerable life left in it. More than that, however, mystery readers should be thankful to Clinton-Baddeley for creating one of the most personable, believable, and downright likeable amateur detectives in the history of the genre. Indeed, Dr. R.V. Davie of St. Nicholas College, Cambridge, is so delightful that the reader easily overlooks the occasional flaws in the stories as detective tales. In his seventies, Dr. Davie is blessed with good health, a superb memory, and an ever-active mind which puzzles out patterns in wallpaper and carpets when it is not busy remembering how things were and how they have changed. He is ever being reminded of sights and events of his long-distant youth, not in the manner of one hungering disconsolately after a never-again-to-be-experienced past, but, rather, in the manner of a collector, for whom the possession of memories is a pleasure second only to the making of them. Dr. Davie uses the experiences of his seven decades, his understanding of human nature and behavior, and his keen intelligence to ferret out solutions to problems which have baffled the police or, in one instance, have been dismissed by the police as not being crimes at all. Clinton-Baddeley writes delightful dialogue, and this, combined with his knack for creating entertaining characters, insures a pleasant read from first page to last. His books are witty, literate, and superb.

—Guy M. Townsend

———

COBURN, Andrew. American. Born in Exeter, New Hampshire, 1 May 1932. Educated at Suffolk University, Boston, 1954–58. Served in the United States Army, 1951–54: Staff Sergeant. Married to Bernadine Coburn; four daughters. Worked at a variety of jobs, including bank trainee and fur salesman; feature writer, and later police reporter, suburban editor, and city editor, Lawrence *Eagle-Tribune*, Massachusetts, 1963–73; book reviewer and part-time copy editor, Boston *Globe*, 1973–78; political columnist for several Massachusetts newspapers, 1978–81. Since 1981 full-time writer. Recipient: Saxton Fellowship, 1966; five journalism awards from United Press International and Associated Press. Honorary doctorate, Merrimack College, North Andover, Massachusetts, 1987. Agent: Nikki Smith, Smith Skolnik Literary Management, 23 East 10th Street, New York, New York 10003. Address: 3 Farrwood Drive, Andover, Massachusetts 01810, U.S.A.

CRIME PUBLICATIONS

Novels (series: Rita Gardella O'Dea)

The Trespassers. Boston, Houghton Mifflin, 1974.
The Babysitter. New York, Norton, 1979; London, Secker and Warburg, 1980.
Off Duty. New York, Norton, 1980; London, Secker and Warburg, 1981.
Company Secrets. London, Secker and Warburg, 1982.
Widow's Walk. London, Secker and Warburg, 1984.
Sweetheart (O'Dea). New York, Macmillan, and London, Secker and Warburg, 1985.
Love Nest (O'Dea). New York, Macmillan, and London, Secker and Warburg, 1987.
Goldilocks (O'Dea). New York, Scribner, 1989; London, Secker and Warburg, 1990.

*

Andrew Coburn comments:
During my years as a newsman my closest friends were criminals, police officers, and trial lawyers. In each was something of the other, and at times the dividing lines were too thin to see. In all of them were elements of the actor, entertainer, the comedian, the tragedian. Some were Shakespearian, the criminal no less than the lawyer performing on the courtroom stage. In more formidable ways they seemed a breed apart from the rest of us, in the same manner that professional soldiers living on the edge have little in common with civilians. Soldiers speak their own peculiar language. Cops, criminals, and lawyers share a common one. Yet they share with all of us the same concerns for their children, the same black sense of aloneness when lying awake at three in the morning.

These are the thoughts that I bring to my fiction, which I write like a newsman, preparing no drafts, instead creating a page at a time, sometimes rewriting that page several times, structuring as I go along. No character is real until he casts a shadow of his own, until he takes a step I did not plan, until he goes to the bathroom without first raising his hand. I know I have a novel when I am all the characters, but the characters are not me.

*   *   *

Andrew Coburn turned relatively late in life to the writing of suspense fiction, but his first novel, *The Trespassers*, gave ample evidence of the promise that was to burgeon in his flawlessly plotted *Off Duty*. *Off Duty* is set in Boston; the texture of its world is reminiscent of Dashiell Hammett's fiction, though its sensibility and imagery owe more to Raymond Chandler. Frank Chase, its central character, has started a new life in a smart Boston suburb, and a new career away from the police drug squad he has served for so many years. From that quiet, almost understated, beginning the novel is plunged into blackness when Chase's wife wakes one morning to find a badly multilated corpse lying on their lawn, an image designed to shatter the calm of their new-found domesticity. In a series of rapid, almost cinematic, flash-backs to Chase's college days and his early years in the police force, Coburn builds up a composite picture of his hero's life, his relationship to his wife, Ida, and of her previous marriage to Rupert Goetz, a classmate and fellow cop. The polarities created by that triangular relationship and the competitiveness engendered by the parallel careers of the two policemen create a tension in the novel that gives it its mainspring. Although he is now free of the police force, the murder plunges Chase back into the shady world of drug-trafficking, petty crooks, informers, and Mafia kingpins, shifting the story into a cat-and-mouse game between the good cop and the bad cop. An authentic aura of evil permeates the novel; the crisp dialogue carries the action along apace as the two protagonists face up to the final test when loyalty becomes more important than matters of right and wrong.

Boston, too, is the setting of *The Babysitter*; in the suburb of Ballardville, "a town of twelve thousand, a bedroom of Boston," Coburn begins *in medias res*, with two agents questioning John Wright about the bloodthirsty murder of his babysitter Paula Aherne during the course of the previous evening. The murderer seems to have made off with the Wright's baby leaving neither ransom note nor much evidence, and the police appear to be only interested in investigating the babysitter's mysterious past. In defiance of the instructions given to them by the police and the FBI, the Wrights set out on a quest to find their kidnapped baby, a journey that takes them into the nightmare world of the derelict North End where death and violence become constant companions. The plot is intricate, resulting from a complex situation where good often merges into evil, but Coburn is careful to place his reader between the innocence of the Wrights and the tragic loss of their child as the novel marches towards a terrifying conclusion. The plot structure, the characterisation, and the quality of his prose have given Coburn's novels a distinctive flavour: those and his ability to create a malevolent mood have made him one of the most promising newcomers to suspense fiction.

—Trevor Royle

CODY, Liza. A pseudonym. British. Born in London, 11 April 1944. Educated at Lady Eleanor Holles School; City and Guilds of London Art School; Royal Academy School of Art, all London. One daughter. Has worked as a painter, a studio technician at Madame Tussauds, London, and a graphic designer. Recipient: Crime Writers Association John Creasey award, 1980. Agent: Felicity Bryan, 2A North Parade, Banbury Road, Oxford OX2 6PE, England.

CRIME PUBLICATIONS

Novels (series: Anna Lee, in all books except *Rift*)

Dupe.   London, Collins, 1980; New York, Scribner, 1983.
Bad Company.   London, Collins, and New York, Scribner, 1982.
Stalker.   London, Collins, and New York, Scribner, 1984.
Headcase.   London, Collins, 1985; New York, Scribner, 1986.
Under Contract.   London, Collins, 1986; New York, Scribner, 1987.
Rift.   London, Collins, 1988; New York, Scribner, 1989.

Uncollected Short Stories

"K.K.," in *Murder and Company*.   London, Pandora Press, 1988.
"The Uniform," in *New Crimes*, edited by Maxim Jakubowski.   London, Robinson, 1989; New York, Carroll and Graf, 1990.
"Lucky Dip," in *The Eye of a Woman*.   New York, Delacorte Press, 1990.

*   *   *

Anna Lee, of Brierly Security, a London detective agency, is the protagonist of Liza Cody's excellent series. Staunchly independent but capable of strong allegiances and warm friendships, Anna balances cleverly between cynical humility toward her pompous employer, Martin Brierly, and outright disdain for his office manager, bossy, intrusive Beryl Doyle. Several fellow operatives figure in various of Anna's adventures, but her friendship with valued colleague Bernie Schiller and his wife, Syl, extends well beyond professional support. Similarly, Anna's abrasively loving relationship with downstairs neighbors Selwyn and Bea Price shows her supportiveness and loyalty. These associations demonstrate Anna's ability to sustain family-like ties, even though she remains aloof from her relatives, one of several qualities which place her among the "new breed" of hard-boiled private eyes who conduct complex but generally positive personal lives.

The Prices and the Schillers also lend continuity, an important factor in light of Cody's interest in open endings: the puzzles are always solved, but in the interest of realism, the consequences of both crime and solution are often left partially unresolved. Moreover, in the best private-eye tradition, some characters, especially friends and lovers, disappear from Anna's circle. Such devices also suggest that Anna Lee's life goes on *between* as well as *during* the novels, another nice realistic touch.

Anna's first case, *Dupe*, concerns the death of ambitious Dierdre Jackson. To discover the truth about Dierdre's death, Anna must, of course, uncover the secrets of her life, thereby learning a great deal about various London film subcultures—and discovering that placid, seemingly subservient housewives can be keenly astute. Critical response to *Dupe* was positive, and Cody's reputation has been enhanced with each new title.

Bad Company extends a pattern introduced in *Dupe*; Anna's cases often involve youngsters who need protection not only from some criminal involvement but also from their careless friends or families. In Cody's work, as in Ross Macdonald's and Robert B. Parker's, the disaffected teenager symbolizes familial and societal dysfunction. Kidnapped when she tries to stop the abduction of young Verity Hewit, Anna feeds her resolve by taunting their dangerously amateurish captors and by persistent efforts toward escape. The action switches between those scenes and the search conducted by other Brierly staffers, and the results of both crime and search are tantalizingly yet satisfyingly ironic.

At heart, Anna Lee is a devoted urbanite, a fact very clearly demonstrated in *Stalker*, when the case takes her into wildest Somerset where glimpses of the countryside delight readers if not Anna. Here, her rescue of an injured young horsewoman complicates an assignment already more dangerous than it appears. Three beautifully realized adult characters—Flora, a reclusive animal-lover; Donald Parrish, the local deer stalker; and Ian Olsen, the attractive entrepreneur who becomes Anna's lover, enhance this novel.

When Anna investigates the disappearance of Thea Hahn, a 16-year-old genius, she becomes involved with young Sam Tulloch, a teenager who is the most mature member of his immediate family, and with gentle-giant Quex, a rigger from the North Sea oil fields. With Quex's help, she supports Thea during a mental breakdown while she helps Sam through the early days after his father's murder. Certainly, the mystery puzzle is gripping in *Headcase*, but the interplay between characters is equally compelling.

Music is a frequent motif in the Anna Lee novels, and in *Under Contract*, the rock-concert circuit dominates the scene. Shona Una, a popular singer on the verge of superstardom, has received threatening letters, and her volatile life-style complicates Anna's attempts to protect her. Shona's entourage is a closed but very mobile circle of suspects to whom Anna's professional expertise means little. Utterly worldly, they are nevertheless disconnected from the real world, setting their own rules, scorning, often exploiting, outsiders. Fate toys cruelly with the denizens of Anna's world, making for bittersweet endings, and the denouements of *Stalker*, *Headcase*, and *Under Contract* depict various characters' grace under such pressure particularly well.

In 1988, Cody interrupted her popular series to publish *Rift*, a remarkable novel in which crime and its consequences are complications to the plot rather than its driving force. Though readers may miss Cody's familiar cast of characters, this tale of Fay Jassahn's miserable pleasure trip through Africa's Rift Valley where she confronts violent death, famine, war, theft, and a sense of total alienation is in no way a disappointing change of direction. Ethiopia, its climate, people, and internal troubles become a compelling background for Fay's maturation journey in which her physical endurance, ethics, and spirit are sorely tested. *Rift* depicts a young woman with far more courage and determination than she realizes, who loses confidence in the trappings of "civilization" but gains useful self-knowledge and deepened social awareness. In *Rift*, as in the Anna Lee novels, sound plotting, astute characterization, touches of humor, and thoughtful assessment of our times make for very good reading.

—Jane S. Bakerman

————

COE, Tucker. *See* **WESTLAKE, Donald E.**

————

COFFEY, Brian. *See* **KOONTZ, Dean R.**

————

COFFIN, Geoffrey. *See* **MASON, F. Van Wyck.**

COFFIN, Peter. *See* **LATIMER, Jonathan.**

COFYN, Cornelius. *See* **BEEDING, Francis.**

COHEN, Anthea. Pseudonym for Doris Simpson.   British. Born in Guilford, Surrey, 26 August, 1913. Educated at convent school, Northampton. Married Mark Simpson in 1947. State Registered Nurse, worked in hospitals in Leicester, Chelsea and Ryde, Isle of Wight, until 1970. Agent: Vanessa Holt, 1 Old Compton Street, London W1V 5PH. Address: 3 Camden Court, Dover Street, Ryde, Isle of Wight.

CRIME PUBLICATIONS

Novels (series: Agnes Carmichael in all books)

Angel Without Mercy.   London, Quartet, 1982; New York, Doubleday, 1984.
Angel of Vengeance.   London, Quartet, 1983; New York, Doubleday, 1984.
Angel of Death.   London, Quartet, 1983; New York, Doubleday, 1985.
Fallen Angel.   London, Quartet, 1984.
Guardian Angel.   London, Quartet, and New York, Doubleday, 1985.
Hell's Angel.   London, Quartet, 1986.
Ministering Angel.   London, Quartet, 1987.
Destroying Angel.   London, Quartet, 1988.
Angel Dust.   London, Quartet, 1989.

OTHER PUBLICATIONS

Novels

Dangerous Love.   London, Pan, 1984.
Substance and Shadows.   London, Pan, 1986.

Other

Be Patient: Your Life in Their Hands.   London, Butterworth, 1967.
Popular Hospital Misconceptions.   London, International Publishing Corporation, 1969.

*

Anthea Cohen comments:
Agnes Carmichael is the heroine, or anti-heroine, of all my Angel books—she kills when she thinks it necessary to rescue a victim. My public lending right is high and my Angel books in the libraries are worn out with reading.

*   *   *

Anthea Cohen's Angel series is a study of the obsessive and psychotic personality of one woman, Agnes Carmichael, as told from Agnes's point of view. In the course of her life, from her childhood in an orphanage and throughout her career as a nurse, she solves all her problems by simply disposing of anyone unfortunate enough to stand in her way. The unwitting victims may have directly thwarted her ambitions, for example Nurse Pearson who is strangled because she is having an affair with the object of Agnes's affections, or they may merely have a annoyed her in some small way on an already bad day. The outcome is always the same—another unsolved crime for the police and a re-established sense of power for the homely and introverted nurse.

This predictability is the main weakness of the series. Agnes is rarely in danger of discovery and as a consequence the plotting of the novels is often repetitious. Nothing ever happens to seriously threaten Agnes's secret life, nor does her personality change in any way. In common with the classic serial killers of both fiction and true crime, as opposed to those who impulsively succumb to a one-off momentary crime of passion, she is completely amoral and guilt-free to begin with, and remains so to the end. However what is lost in drama and excitement is more than made up for by Cohen's carefully observed psychological insights.

The books are structured so that each individual episode reveals a different aspect of Agnes's character. She appears to be a heartless spinster who is untouched by her colleagues' problems, and yet undertakes to solve them in her own way. Nurse Jones's bedridden and demanding mother is one victim of Agnes's "helpfulness." Dismayed by the way in which she treats her daughter, Agnes quietly does away with her by slipping 10 Nembutal tablets into an evening drink. She justifies her actions afterwards by telling herself that she has just freed Jones from a lifetime of slavery, and yet at the time of the murder she was entirely self-focussed. The old lady and her complaining had driven her to distraction and she simply wanted to keep her quiet.

Agnes is so single minded in her actions and in pursuit of what she wants that she always exhibits an air of icy calm. She prepares her methods of murder with the planning and care of a housewife baking a cake which she already knows will be a success since she has practised it so often. These are the times, outside of her job, that she feels totally self-assured and in command of her world. She replaces the empty capsules to allay suspicion, and she brazens her way out of Jones's feeble questions regarding the circumstances of her mother's death. She is rather disappointed at Jones's lack of appreciation for her new found freedom, and with the smug egocentricity of the socially alienated she attributes it to Jones's stupidity. A portrait is gradually built up of a predominantly insecure personality who manipulates her surroundings in order to assuage her powerlessness.

On the other hand she does appear to have one or two genuinely tender moments. She cares deeply for her patients' welfare, and cannot tolerate unkindness on the part of her nurses, but on closer examination this is yet another manifestation of her dark side. She fulfils the role of nurse because it is such a clearly defined one, not because of her sensitivity to suffering. She reprimands her nurses for failing in their duty only because it reflects badly on her personally, and on her adopted image. Carmichael is not the possessor of a divided personality, an angel one moment and a devil the next—she knows exactly what she is only too well, and how hard she must try to maintain the illusion to the world of being otherwise.

Crime is not central to the books. It is instead merely an adjunct to Cohen's chief preoccupation, the inner workings of the mind of a psychopath. Her books are more accurately thrillers, in the sense that they deal with the murderer's motivation and method rather then the detective's logic and deduction. It is a perspective which sets Cohen apart as an original and refreshing writer in this genre.

—L.M. Quinn

———

COHEN, Octavus Roy. American. Born in Charleston, South Carolina, 26 June 1891. Educated at Porter Military Academy, Charleston; Clemson Agricultural College, South Carolina, B.S. 1911; studied law in his father's office, and admitted to the South Carolina Bar, 1913. Served in the United States Naval Reserve, 1939–40: Lieutenant. Married Inez Lopez in 1914; one son. Civil engineer, Tennessee Coal Iron and Railroad Company, 1909–10; newspaperman for Birmingham *Ledger*, Charleston *News and Courier*, Bayonne *Times*, New Jersey, and Newark *Morning Star*, before practising law, Charleston, 1913–15. Self-employed writer after 1915. Litt. D.: Birmingham Southern College, 1927. *Died 6 January 1959.*

CRIME PUBLICATIONS

Novels (series: David Carroll; Max Gold; Jim Hanvey; Lt. Marty Walsh)

The Other Woman, with J.U. Giesy. New York, Macaulay, 1917; London, Wells Gardner, 1920.
The Crimson Alibi (Carroll). New York, Dodd Mead, and London, Nash, 1919.
Gray Dusk (Carroll). New York, Dodd Mead, and London, Nash, 1920.
Six Seconds of Darkness (Carroll). New York, Dodd Mead, and London, Nash, 1921.
Midnight (Carroll). New York, Dodd Mead, and London, Nash, 1922.
The Iron Chalice. Boston, Little Brown, 1925; London, Cassell, 1926.
The Outer Gate. Boston, Little Brown, and London, Hodder and Stoughton, 1927.
The May Day Mystery (Hanvey). New York, Appleton, 1929.
The Backstage Mystery (Hanvey). New York, Appleton, 1930; as *Curtain at Eight*, New York, Grosset and Dunlap, 1933.
Star of Earth (Hanvey). New York, Appleton, 1932.
The Townsend Murder Mystery (novelization of radio play). New York, Appleton Century, 1933.
Child of Evil. New York, Appleton Century, 1936.
I Love You Again. New York, Appleton Century, 1937; as *There's Always Time to Die*, New York, Popular Library, 1949.
East of Broadway. New York, Appleton Century, 1938.
Strange Honeymoon. New York, Appleton Century, 1939.
Romance in Crimson. New York, Appleton Century, 1940; as *Murder in Season*, New York, Popular Library, 1946.
Lady in Armor. New York, Appleton Century, 1941.
Sound of Revelry. New York, Macmillan, 1943; London, Hale, 1945.
Romance in the First Degree. New York, Macmillan, 1944; London, Hale, 1951.
Danger in Paradise (Gold). New York, Macmillan, 1945; London, Hale, 1949.

Dangerous Lady. New York, Macmillan, 1946; London, Barker, 1948.
Love Has No Alibi (Gold). New York, Macmillan, 1946; London, Hale, 1952.
Don't Ever Love Me (Gold). New York, Macmillan, 1947; London, Barker, 1948.
My Love Wears Black (Walsh). New York, Macmillan, 1948; London, Barker, 1949.
More Beautiful Than Murder (Walsh). New York, Macmillan, 1948; London, Barker, 1950.
A Bullet for My Love (Walsh). New York, Macmillan, 1950; London, Barker, 1951.
The Corpse That Walked. New York, Fawcett, 1951; London, Red Seal, 1957.
Lost Lady. New York, Fawcett, 1951; London, Fawcett, 1953.
Love Can Be Dangerous. New York, Macmillan, and London, Barker, 1955; as *The Intruder*, Hasbrouck Heights, New Jersey, Graphic, 1956.

Short Stories (series: Florian Slappey)

Jim Hanvey, Detective. New York, Dodd Mead, 1923; London, Nash, 1924.
Detours. Boston, Little Brown, 1927.
Florian Slappey Goes Abroad. Boston, Little Brown, 1928.
Cameos. New York, Appleton, 1931.
Scrambled Yeggs. New York, Appleton Century, 1934.
Florian Slappey. New York, Appleton Century, 1938.

Uncollected Short Stories

"Always Trust a Cop," in *Queen's Awards, Seventh Series*, edited by Ellery Queen. Boston, Little Brown, 1952; London, Gollancz, 1954.
"Let Me Kill You Sweetheart," in *The Saint* (New York), October–November 1953.
"The Midway Murder," in *The Saint* (New York), May 1954.
"Sweet Music and Murder," in *The Saint* (New York), January 1955.
"The Bridal-Night Murder," in *The Saint* (New York), September 1956.
"Double Jeopardy," in *The Saint* (New York), December 1957.

OTHER PUBLICATIONS

Novels

Polished Ebony. New York, Dodd Mead, 1919.
Come Seven. New York, Dodd Mead, 1920.
Sunclouds. New York, Dodd Mead, 1924; London, Hodder and Stoughton, 1925.
The Other Tomorrow. New York, Appleton, 1927.
The Light Shines Through. Boston, Little Brown, 1928.
Spring Tide. New York, Appleton, 1928.
The Valley of Olympus. New York, Appleton, 1929.
Epic Peters, Pullman Porter. New York, Appleton, 1930.
Lilies of the Alley. New York, Appleton, 1931.
Scarlet Woman. New York, Appleton Century, 1934.
Transient Lady. New York, Appleton Century, 1934.
Back to Nature. New York, Appleton Century, 1935.
With Benefit of Clergy. New York, Appleton Century, 1935.
Kid Tinsel. New York, Appleton Century, 1941.
Borrasca. New York, Macmillan, 1953; London, Barker, 1954.

Short Stories

Highly Colored.   New York, Dodd Mead, 1921.
Assorted Chocolates.   New York, Dodd Mead, 1922; London, Hodder and Stoughton, 1925.
Dark Days and White Knights.   New York, Dodd Mead, 1923.
Bigger and Blacker.   Boston, Little Brown, 1925.
Black and Blue.   Boston, Little Brown, 1926.
Carbon Copies.   New York, Appleton, 1932.

Plays

The Crimson Alibi (produced New York, 1919).
Come Seven, adaptation of his own novel (produced New York, 1920).   New York, Longman, 1927.
The Melancholy Dane, in *The Appleton Book of Short Plays*, 2nd series, edited by Kenyon Nicholson.   New York, Appleton, 1927.

Other Plays: *The Scourge*, 1920; *Shadows*, 1920; *Every Saturday Night*, 1921; *Alias Mrs. Roberts*, 1928.

Radio Plays: *Amos 'n' Andy* series, 1945–46.

*   *   *

A prolific American author of countless short stories and many detective novels, Octavus Roy Cohen is best known for the creation of his extremely soft-hearted and amiable detective, Jim Hanvey, who first appeared in *Jim Hanvey, Detective*. This book was later nominated by Ellery Queen as a book of historical value with a high quality of literary style.

A man of immense proportions, wearing clothes that always seemed too large, Jim Hanvey had remarkable fishlike eyes and always sported a gold toothpick attached to his vest by a long gold chain. It had been given to him as a token of good will by a crook he had sent up for a long stretch. Reformed criminals were some of Hanvey's closest allies, but he was relentless in their pursuit should they ever go astray.

One other noteworthy character introduced by Cohen was Florian Slappey, the opposite of Jim Hanvey in almost every respect, the Black Beau Brummell of Birmingham, Alabama, meticulous in dress, and manner. His witty and humorous adventures are related in two collections of stories, *Florian Slappey Goes Abroad* and *Florian Slappey*.

Cohen's literary style is smooth, his characters romanticized but credible, and his suspenseful plots are varied. The settings range from Broadway to Hollywood with a few, like *I Love You Again*, set in Cohen's native South.

—Mary Ann Grochowski

————

COLE, G.D.H. and Margaret. British. **COLE, G(eorge) D(ouglas) H(oward):** Born 25 September 1889. Educated at St. Paul's School, London; Balliol College, Oxford (Domus and Jenkyns exhibitioner). Head of Research Department, Amalgamated Society of Engineers, 1914–18, and trade union economic adviser during World War I; Head of Nuffield College Social Reconstruction Survey during World War II. Married Margaret Isabel Postgate in 1918; one son and two daughters. Fellow, Magdalen College, Oxford, 1912–19; Deputy Professor of Philosophy, Armstrong College, University of Durham, 1913–14; Head of Tutorial Classes Department, University of London, 1919–25; Fellow, University

College, Oxford, and University Reader in Economics, 1925–44; Fellow, All Souls College, Oxford, 1944–57; Chichele Professor of Social and Political Theory, Oxford University, 1944–57; Sub-Warden, later Fellow, and from 1957, Research Fellow, Nuffield College, Oxford. Associated from 1912 with the Workers' Educational Association: vice-president for some years, and acting president for one year; Director of Labour Party Research from 1918; staff member, *New Statesman*, London, 1918 to the 1940's; general editor, Oxford Studies in Economics and Hutchinson's University Library. President, University Socialist Federation; Founding President, Association of Tutors in Adult Education; Chairman, 1939–46 and 1948–50, and President, 1952–59, Fabian Society. Honorary Fellow, University College and Balliol College, Oxford. *Died 15 January 1959.* **COLE, Margaret (Isabel, née Postgate):** Born in Cambridge, 6 May 1893; sister of Raymond Postgate, *q.v.* Educated at Roedean School, Brighton; Girton College, Cambridge, B.A. (honours) in classics 1914. Married G.D.H. Cole in 1918 (died 1959); one son and two daughters. Classical Mistress, St. Paul's Girls' School, London, 1914–16; assistant secretary, Labour Research Department, London, 1917–25; Lecturer, University Tutorial classes, London, 1925–49, and Cambridge, 1941–44. Honorary Secretary, New Fabian Research Bureau, 1935–39; Honorary Secretary, 1939–53, Chairman, 1955, and President from 1963, Fabian Society; Member of the Education Committee, 1943–65 (Chairman, Further Education Committee, 1951–60 and 1961–65), and Alderman, 1952–65, London County Council; Member of the Education Committee and Vice-Chairman of the Further and Higher Education Sub-Committee, Inner London Education Authority, 1965–67; Chairman, Geffrye Museum, Sidney Webb College of Education, and Battersea College of Education, all London. Honorary Fellow, London School of Economics. Fellow, Royal Historical Society. O.B.E. (Officer, Order of the British Empire), 1965; D.B.E. (Dame Commander, Order of the British Empire), 1970. *Died 7 May 1980.* The Coles: editor, *The Guildsman*, later *The Guild Socialist*, London, 1916–23.

CRIME PUBLICATIONS

Novels (series: Everard Blatchington; Dr. Benjamin Tancred; Superintendent Henry Wilson)

The Brooklyn Murders (Wilson; by G.D.H. Cole alone).   London, Collins, 1923; New York, Seltzer, 1924.
The Death of a Millionaire (Wilson).   London, Collins, and New York, Macmillan, 1925.
The Blatchington Tangle (Blatchington, Wilson).   London, Collins, and New York, Macmillan, 1926.
The Murder at Crome House.   London, Collins, and New York, Macmillan, 1927.
The Man from the River (Wilson).   London, Collins, and New York, Macmillan, 1928.
Poison in the Garden Suburb (Wilson).   London, Collins, and New York, Payson and Clarke, 1929.
Burglars in Bucks (Blatchington; Wilson).   London, Collins, 1930; as *The Berkshire Mystery*, New York, Brewer and Warren, 1930.
Corpse in Canonicals (Wilson).   London, Collins, 1930; as *Corpse in the Constable's Garden*, New York, Morrow, 1931; Collins, 1933.
The Great Southern Mystery (Wilson).   London, Collins, 1931; as *The Walking Corpse*, New York, Morrow, 1931.
The Floating Admiral, with others.   London, Hodder and Stoughton, 1931; New York, Doubleday, 1932.

Dead Man's Watch (Wilson). London, Collins, 1931; New York, Doubleday, 1932.
Death of a Star. London, Collins, 1932; New York, Doubleday, 1933.
The Affair at Aliquid. London, Collins, 1933.
End of an Ancient Mariner (Wilson). London, Collins, 1933; New York, Doubleday, 1934.
Death in the Quarry (Wilson, Blatchington). London, Collins, and New York, Doubleday, 1934.
Murder in Four Parts. London, Collins, 1934.
Big Business Murder (Wilson). London, Collins, and New York, Doubleday, 1935.
Dr. Tancred Begins; or, The Pendexter Saga, First Canto (Wilson). London, Collins, and New York, Doubleday, 1935.
Scandal at School (Blatchington). London, Collins, 1935; as *The Sleeping Death*, New York, Doubleday, 1936.
Last Will and Testament; or The Pendexter Saga, Second (and Last) Canto (Tancred; Wilson). London, Collins, and New York, Doubleday, 1936.
The Brothers Sackville (Wilson). London, Collins, 1936; New York, Macmillan, 1937.
Disgrace to the College. London, Hodder and Stoughton, 1937.
The Missing Aunt (Wilson). London, Collins, 1937; New York, Macmillan, 1938.
Off With Her Head! (Wilson). London, Collins, 1938; New York, Macmillan, 1939.
Double Blackmail (Wilson). London, Collins, and New York, Macmillan, 1939.
Greek Tragedy (Wilson). London, Collins, 1939; New York, Macmillan, 1940.
Murder at the Munition Works (Wilson). London, Collins, and New York, Macmillan, 1940.
Counterpoint Murder (Wilson). London, Collins, 1940; New York, Macmillan, 1941.
Knife in the Dark (Wilson). London, Collins, 1941; New York, Macmillan, 1942.
Toper's End (Wilson). London, Collins, and New York, Macmillan, 1942.

Short Stories (series: Superintendent Henry Wilson)

Superintendent Wilson's Holiday. London, Collins, 1928; New York, Payson and Clarke, 1929.
A Lesson in Crime and Other Stories. London, Collins, 1933.
Mrs. Warrender's Profession. London, Collins, 1938; New York, Macmillan, 1939.
Wilson and Some Others. London, Collins, 1940.
Death in the Tankard (story). London, Todd, 1943.
Strychnine Tonic, and A Dose of Cyanide. London, Todd, 1943.
Birthday Gifts and Other Stories. London, Todd, 1946.

OTHER PUBLICATIONS by G.D.H. Cole

Verse

The Record. Privately printed, 1912.
New Beginnings, and The Record. Oxford, Blackwell, 1914.
The Crooked World. London, Gollancz, 1933.

Other

The Greater Unionism, with William Mellor. Manchester, National Labour Press, 1913.
The World of Labour: A Discussion of the Present and Future of Trade Unionism. London, Bell, 1913; revised edition, 1915.

Labour in War Time. London, Bell, 1915.
Trade Unionism in War Time, with William Mellor. London, Limit, 1915(?).
Some Problems of Urban and Rural Industry, with others. Oxford, Council of Ruskin College, 1917.
The Principles of Socialism: A Syllabus, revised edition. London, University Socialist Federation, 1917.
Self-Government in Industry. London, Bell, 1917; revised edition, 1920; Freeport, New York, Books for Libraries, 1971.
The British Labour Movement: A Syllabus for Study Circles. London, University Socialist Federation, 1917; revised edition, 1922; New York, Workers Education Bureau of America, 1924.
Trade Unionism on the Railways: Its History and Problems, with R. Page Arnot. London, Allen and Unwin, 1917.
An Introduction to Trade Unionism. London, Allen and Unwin, 1918; as *Organised Labour*, 1924; revised edition, 1929.
Labour in the Commonwealth: A Book for the Younger Generation. London, Headley, 1918; New York, Huebsch, 1920.
The Meaning of Industrial Freedom, with William Mellor. London, Allen and Unwin, 1918.
The Payment of Wages: A Study in Payment by Results under the Wage-System. London, Allen and Unwin, 1918; revised edition, 1928.
Workers' Control in Industry. London, Independent Labour Party, 1919.
Chaos and Order in Industry. London, Methuen, and New York, Stokes, 1920.
Democracy in Industry (lecture). Manchester, Manchester University Press, 1920.
Guild Socialism. London, Fabian Publications, 1920; New York, Stokes, 1921.
Guild Socialism Re-Stated. London, Parsons, 1920.
Social Theory. London, Methuen, and New York, Stokes, 1920; revised edition, Methuen, 1921.
Unemployment and Industrial Maintenance. London, Labour Publishing Company, 1921.
The Future of Local Government. London, Cassell, 1921.
Guild Socialism: A Plan for Economic Democracy. New York, Stokes, 1921.
English Economic History. London, Labour Research Department, 1922(?)
Labour in the Coal-Mining Industry 1914–1921. Oxford, Clarendon Press, 1923.
Unemployment: A Study Syllabus. London, Labour Research Department, 1923.
Out of Work: An Introduction to the Study of Unemployment. London, Labour Publishing Company, and New York, Knopf, 1923.
National Government and Inflation: Six Little Talks on Politics. London, Society for Socialist Inquiry, n.d.
Trade Unionism and Munitions. Oxford, Clarendon Press, 1923.
Rents, Rings, and Houses, with Margaret Cole. London, Labour Publishing Company, 1923.
Workshop Organisation. Oxford, Clarendon Press, 1923.
British Trade Unionism: Problems and Policy. London, Labour Research Department, 1923.
The Life of William Cobbett. London, Collins, and New York, Harcourt Brace, 1924; revised edition, London, Home and Van Thal, 1947; New York, Russell and Russell, 1971.
The Place of the Workers' Educational Association in Working Class Education. Leicester, Blackfriars Press, 1924(?).

Robert Owen. London, Benn, and Boston, Little Brown, 1925; as *The Life of Robert Owen*, London, Macmillan, 1930; Hamden, Connecticut, Archon Books, 1966.

William Cobbett. London, Fabian Publications, 1925; Folcroft, Pennsylvania, Folcroft Editions, 1973.

A Short History of the British Working Class Movement. London, Allen and Unwin, 3 vols., 1925–27; New York, Macmillan, 2 vols., 1927; revised edition, Allen and Unwin, 1937, 1948; Macmillan, 1938.

Industrial Policy for Socialists: A Syllabus. London, Independent Labour Party Information Committe, 1926.

A Select List of Books on Economic and Social History, with H.L. Beales. London, Tutors' Association, 1927.

The Economic System. London, Longman, 1927.

What to Read on English Economic History. Leeds, Leeds Public Libraries, 1928.

The Next Ten Years of British Social and Economic Policy. London, Macmillan, 1929; New York, Garland, 1985.

Politics and Literature. London, Hogarth Press, and New York, Harcourt Brace, 1929.

Gold, Credit and Employment: Four Essays for Laymen. London, Allen and Unwin, 1930; New York, Macmillan, 1931.

Unemployment Problems in 1931, with others. Geneva, International Labour Organisation, 1931.

The Bank of England. London, Society for Socialist Inquiry and Propaganda, 1931(?).

How Capitalism Works. London, Society for Socialist Inquiry and Propaganda, 1931(?).

The Crisis: What It Is, How It Arose, What to Do, with Ernest Bevin. London, New Statesman and Nation, 1931.

British Trade and Industry, Past and Future. London, Macmillan, 1932.

Banks and Credit. London, Society for Socialist Inquiry and Propaganda, 1932.

Economic Tracts for the Times. London, Macmillan, 1932.

The Essentials of Socialisation. London, New Fabian Research Bureau, 1932.

Scope and Method in Social and Political Theory (lecture). Oxford, Clarendon Press, 1932.

What to Read on Economic Problems of Today and Tomorrow. Leeds, Leeds Public Libraries, 1932.

War Debts and Reparations: What They Are, Why They Must Be Cancelled, with Richard Seymour Postgate. London, New Statesman and Nation, 1932.

The Intelligent Man's Guide Through World Chaos. London, Gollancz, 1932; as *A Guide Through World Chaos,* New York, Knopf, 1932.

Some Essentials of Socialist Propaganda. London, Fabian Society, 1932.

Modern Theories and Forms of Industrial Organisation. London, Gollancz, 1932.

The Gold Standard. London, Society for Socialist Inquiry and Propaganda, 1932.

Theories and Forms of Political Organisation. London, Gollancz, 1932.

Saving and Spending; or, The Economics of "Economy." London, New Statesman and Nation, 1933.

Socialism in Pictures and Figures, with J.F. Horrabin. London, Socialist League, 1933.

The Intelligent Man's Guide to Europe Today, with Margaret Cole. London, Gollancz, and New York, Knopf, 1933.

A Plan for Britain. London, Clarion Press, 1933.

What Is This Socialism? Letters to a Young Inquirer. London, Gollancz, 1933.

A Study-Guide to Socialist Policy. London, Socialist League, 1934(?).

A Guide to Modern Politics, with Margaret Cole. London, Gollancz, and New York, Knopf, 1934.

Some Relations Between Political and Economic Theory. London, Macmillan, 1934.

Planning International Trade, with *Self-Sufficiency,* by Walter Lippmann. New York, Carnegie Endowment, 1934.

Studies in World Economics. London, Macmillan, 1934; Freeport, New York, Books for Libraries, 1967.

What Marx Really Meant. London, Gollancz, and New York, Knopf, 1934.

Marxism, with others. London, Chapman and Hall, 1935.

The Need for a Socialist Programme; with Dick Mitchison. London, Socialist League, 1935(?).

Principles of Economic Planning. London, Macmillan, 1935; as *Economic Planning,* New York, Knopf, 1935.

The Simple Case for Socialism. London, Gollancz, 1935.

Fifty Propositions about Money and Production. London, Nott, 1936.

The Condition of Britain, with Margaret Cole. London, Gollancz, 1937; New York, Garland, 1985.

The People's Front. London, Gollancz, 1937.

What Is Ahead of Us?, with others. London, Allen and Unwin, 1937.

Practical Economics; or, Studies in Economic Planning. London, Penguin, 1937.

The Common People 1746–1938, with Raymond Postgate. London, Methuen, 1938; revised edition, 1946; as *The British Common People,* New York, Knopf, 1939; revised edition, as *The British People,* Knopf, 1947.

Living Wages: The Case for a New Minimum Wage Act. London, Gollancz, 1938.

The Machinery of Socialist Planning. London, Hogarth Press, 1938.

Economic Prospects: 1938 and After. London, Fact, 1938.

Persons and Periods: Studies. London, Macmillan, 1938; New York, Kelley, 1969.

Etude du Statut de la Production et du Rôle du Capital, with Thomas Nixon Carver and Carl Brinkmann. Paris, Librairie du Recueil Sirey, 1938.

Socialism in Evolution. London, Penguin, 1938.

British Trade-Unionism Today: A Survey, with the Collaboration of Thirty Trade Union Leaders and Other Experts. London, Gollancz, 1939; revised edition, as *An Introduction to Trade Unionism,* London, Allen and Unwin, 1953; New York, Barnes and Noble, 1955.

Plan for Democratic Britain. London, Labour Book Service, 1939.

War Aims. London, New Statesman and Nation, 1939.

British Working Class Politics 1834–1914. London, Routledge, 1941.

James Keir Hardie. London, Gollancz, 1941.

Chartist Portraits. London, Macmillan, 1941; New York, St. Martin's Press, 1965.

A Letter to an Industrial Manager. London, Fabian Publications, 1941.

Europe, Russia and the Future. London, Gollancz, 1941; New York, Macmillan, 1942.

The War on the Home Front. London, Fabian Society, 1941.

Victory or Vested Interest? London, Routledge, 1942.

A Memorandum on the Reorganization of Local Government in England. New York, Committee on Public Administration, 1942.

Great Britain in the Post-War World. London, Gollancz, 1942.

Beveridge Explained: What the Beveridge Report on Social Security Means. London, New Statesman and Nation, 1942.

The Fabian Society, Past and Present. London, Fabian Society, 1942; revised edition with Margaret Cole, London, Fabian Publications, 1952.

Richard Carlile, 1790–1843. London, Gollancz, 1943.

John Burns. London, Gollancz, 1943.

Building Societies and the Housing Problem. London, Dent, 1943.

Fabian Socialism. London, Allen and Unwin, 1943.

Monetary Systems and Theories. London, Rotary International, 1943.

When the Fighting Stops. London, National Peace Council, 1943.

The Means to Full Employment. London, Gollancz, 1943.

How to Obtain Full Employment. London, Odhams Press, 1944.

The Planning of World Trade. London, Odhams Press, 1944.

A Century of Co-Operation (history of the Co-Operative movement). London, Allen and Unwin, 1944.

The British Working-Class Movement: An Outline and Study Guide. London, Fabian Publications, 1944; revised edition, 1949.

Money: Its Present and Future. London, Cassell, 1944; revised edition, 1947; revised edition, as *Money, Trade, and Investment*, 1954.

Reparations and the Future of German Industry. London, Fabian Publications, 1945.

Welfare and Peace, with John Boyd Orr. London, National Peace Council, 1945.

The Co-Ops and Labour. London, London Co-Operative Society, 1945.

Building and Planning. London, Cassell, 1945.

Banks and Credit. London, Society for Socialist Inquiry and Propaganda, 1946(?).

Labour's Foreign Policy. London, New Statesman and Nation, 1946.

The Intelligent Man's Guide to the Post-War World. London, Gollancz, 1947.

A Guide to the Elements of Socialism. London, Labour Party, 1947.

Local and Regional Government. London, Cassell, 1947.

The Rochdale Principles: Their History and Application (lecture). London, London Co-Operative Society, 1947.

Samuel Butler and The Way of All Flesh. London, Home and Van Thal, 1947; as *Samuel Butler*, Denver, Swallow, 1948.

The National Coal Board: Its Tasks, Its Organisation, and Its Prospects. London, Fabian Publications, 1948.

A History of the Labour Party from 1914. London, Routledge, 1948; New York, Kelley, 1969.

British Social Services. London, Longman, 1948.

The Meaning of Marxism. London, Gollancz, 1948; Ann Arbor, University of Michigan Press, 1964.

Europe and the Problem of Democracy. London, National Peace Council, 1948.

Why Nationalise Steel? London, New Statesman and Nation, 1948; revised edition, 1948.

World in Transition: A Guide to the Shifting Political and Economic Forces of Our Time. New York, Oxford University Press, 1949.

Facts for Socialists, revised edition. London, Fabian Publications, 1949.

Labour's Second Term. London, Fabian Publications, 1949.

Consultation or Joint Management? A Contribution to the Discussion of Industrial Democracy, with J.M. Chalmers and Ian Mikardo. London, Fabian Publications, 1949.

Essays in Social Theory. London, Macmillan, 1950.

Socialist Economics. London, Gollancz, 1950.

Weakness Through Strength: The Economics of Re-Armament. London, Union of Democratic Control, 1951.

The British Co-Operative Movement in a Socialist Society: A Report. London, Allen and Unwin, 1951.

British Labour Movement: Retrospect and Prospect (lecture). London, Gollancz, 1951.

Samuel Butler. London, Longman, 1952; revised edition, 1961.

Introduction to Economic History 1750–1950. London, Macmillan, 1952; New York, St. Martin's Press, 1960.

The Development of Socialism During the Past Fifty Years (lecture). London, Athlone Press, 1952.

A History of Socialist Thought. London, Macmillan, 5 vols., and New York, St. Martin's Press, 5 vols., 1953–60.

Attempts at General Union: A Study in British Trade Union History 1818–1834. London, Macmillan, 1953.

Is This Socialism? London, New Statesman and Nation, 1954.

Studies in Class Structure. London, Routledge, 1955.

World Socialism Restated. London, New Statesman and Nation, 1956; revised edition, 1957.

The Post-War Condition of Britain. London, Routledge, and New York, Praeger, 1956.

What Is Wrong with Trade Unions? London, Fabian Society, 1956.

The Case for Industrial Partnership. London, Macmillan, and New York, St. Martin's Press, 1957.

William Morris as a Socialist (lecture). London, William Morris Society, 1960; Folcroft, Pennsylvania, Folcroft Editions, 1973.

The Pluralist Theory of the State: Selected Writings of G.D.H. Cole, J.N. Figgis and H.J. Laski, edited by Paul Q. Hirst. London, Routledge, 1989.

Editor, with G.P. Dennis and Sherard Vines, *Oxford Poetry 1910–13.* Oxford, Blackwell, 1913.

Editor, with Sherard Vines, *Oxford Poetry 1914.* Oxford, Blackwell, 1914.

Editor, with T.W. Earp, *Oxford Poetry 1915.* Oxford, Blackwell, 1915.

Editor, *The Library of Social Studies.* London, Methuen, 4 vols., 1920–21.

Editor, with Margaret Cole, *The Bolo Book* (political songs). London, Allen and Unwin, 1921.

Editor, with Margaret Cole, *The Ormond Poets.* London, Noel Douglas, 16 vols., 1927–28.

Editor, *The Life and Adventures of Peter Porcupine, with Other Records of His Early Career in England and America*, by William Cobbett. London, Nonesuch Press, 1927.

Editor, with Margaret Cole, *Rural Rides in Southern, Western and Eastern Counties of England, Together with Tours in Scotland and the Northern and Midland Counties of England and Letters from Ireland*, by William Cobbett. London, Davies, 3 vols., 1930.

Editor, with William Mellor, *Workers' Control and Self-Government in Industry.* London, Gollancz, 1933.

Editor, *What Everybody Wants to Know about Money: A Planned Outline of Monetary Problems by Nine Economists from Oxford.* London, Gollancz, 1933.

Editor, *Stories in Verse, Stories in Prose, Shorter Poems, Lectures and Essays*, by William Morris. London, Nonesuch Press, and New York, Random House, 1934.

Editor, *Studies in Capital and Investment.* London, Gollancz, 1935.

Editor, *The Rights of Man*, by Thomas Paine. London, Watts, 1937.

Editor, *Letters to Edward Thornton Written in the Years 1797 to 1800*, by William Cobbett. London, Oxford University Press, 1937.
Editor, with Margaret Cole, *The Opinions of William Cobbett*. London, Cobbett Publishing Company, 1944.
Editor, *The Essential Samuel Butler*. London, Cape, and New York, Dutton, 1950.
Editor, with A.W. Filson, *British Working Class Movements: Selected Documents 1789–1875*. London, Macmillan, 1951; New York, St. Martin's Press, 1965.
Editor, with André Philip, *A Report on the Unesco La Bréviére Seminar on Workers' Education*. Paris, Unesco, 1953.

Translator, *The Social Contract and Discourse*, by Rousseau. London, Dent, 1913; New York, Dutton, 1935.
Translator, *Planned Socialism*, by Henri de Man. London, Gollancz, 1935.

OTHER PUBLICATIONS by Margaret Cole

Verse

Bits of Things, with others. Cambridge, Heffer, 1914.
Poems. London, Allen and Unwin, 1918.

Other

A Story of Santa Claus for Little People. London, Bell, 1920.
The Control of Industry. London, Labour Publishing Company, 1921.
Rents, Rings, and Houses, with G.D.H. Cole. London, Labour Publishing Company, 1923.
An Introduction to World History for Classes and Study Circles. London, Labour Research Department, 1923.
Local Government for Beginners. London, Longman, 1927.
A Book List of Local Government. London, Tutors' Association, 1933.
The Intelligent Man's Guide to Europe Today, with G.D.H. Cole. London, Gollancz, and New York, Knopf, 1933.
A Guide to Modern Politics, with G.D.H. Cole. London, Gollancz, and New York, Knopf, 1934.
The Condition of Britain, with G.D.H. Cole. London, Gollancz, 1937.
The New Economic Revolution. London, Fact, 1937.
Books and the People. London, Hogarth Press, 1938.
Women of Today. London, Nelson, 1938.
Marriage, Past and Present. London, Dent, 1938; New York, AMS Press, 1975.
Wartime Billeting. London, Gollancz, 1941.
A Letter to a Student. London, Fabian Society, 1942.
Education for Democracy. London, Allen and Unwin, 1942.
The General Election, 1945, and After. London, Gollancz, 1945.
Beatrice Webb. London, Longman, 1945; New York, Harcourt Brace, 1946.
The Rate for the Job. London, Gollancz, 1946.
The Social Services and the Webb Tradition. London, Fabian Publications, 1946.
Makers of the Labour Movement. London, Longman, 1948.
Growing Up into Revolution (autobiography). London, Longman, 1949.
Miners and the Board. London, Fabian Publications, 1949.
The Fabian Society, Past and Present, revised edition, with G.D.H. Cole. London, Fabian Publications, 1952.
Robert Owen of New Lanark. London, Batchworth Press, and New York, Oxford University Press, 1953.

What Is a Comprehensive School? The London Plan in Practice. London, London Labour Party, 1953.
Beatrice and Sidney Webb. London, Fabian Society, 1955.
Servant of the County (on local government). London, Dobson, 1956.
Plan for Industrial Pensions. London, Fabian Society, 1956.
The Story of Fabian Socialism. London, Heinemann, and Stanford, California, Stanford University Press, 1961.
Robert Owen: Industrialist, Reformer, Visionary: Four Essays, with others. London, Robert Owen Bi-Centenary Association, 1971.
The Life of G.D.H. Cole. London, Macmillan, and New York, St. Martin's Press, 1971.

Editor, with G.D.H. Cole, *The Bolo Book* (political songs). London, Allen and Unwin, 1921.
Editor, with G.D.H. Cole, *The Ormond Poets*. London, Noel Douglas, 16 vols., 1927–28.
Editor, with G.D.H. Cole, *Rural Rides in Southern, Western, and Eastern Counties of England, Together with Tours in Scotland and the Northern and Midland Counties of England and Letters from Ireland*, by William Cobbett. London, Davies, 3 vols., 1930.
Editor, *Twelve Studies in Soviet Russia*. London, Fabian Research Bureau, 1933.
Editor, *The Road to Success: Twenty Essays on the Choice of a Career for Women*. London, Methuen, 1936.
Editor, with Charles Smith, *Democratic Sweden: A Volume of Studies Prepared by Members of the New Fabian Research Bureau*. London, Routledge, 1938; New York, Greystone Press, 1939.
Editor, with Richard Padley, *Evacuation Survey: A Report to the Fabian Society*. London, Routledge, 1940.
Editor, *Our Soviet Ally*. London, Labour Book Service, 1943.
Editor, with G.D.H. Cole, *The Opinions of William Cobbett*. London, Cobbett Publishing Company, 1944.
Editor, with Barbara Drake, *Our Partnership*, by Beatrice Webb. London, Longman, 1948.
Editor, *The Webbs and Their Work*. London, Muller, 1949; New York, Barnes and Noble, 1974.
Editor, *Beatrice Webb: Diaries 1912–1924* and *1924–32*. London, Longman, 2 vols., 1952–56.

*

Critical Studies: *Margaret Cole 1893–1980: A Political Biography* by Betty D. Vernon, Beckenham, Kent, Croom Helm, 1986.

*   *   *

In *The Life of G.D.H. Cole*, Dame Margaret Cole dismisses in two pages the detective fiction she and her husband co-authored. Both viewed the detective stories as a pleasant, undemanding sideline, and Dame Margaret's view that the books are "competent but not more" is accurate. Generally indistinguishable from dozens of other detective novels written during the interwar period, the Coles' work is marred by serious deficiencies in characterization and by slow-moving plots in which details are recapitulated at far-too-frequent intervals. G.D.H. Cole's reputation will, of course, rest upon his studies in social and economic history, especially the classic five-volume *History of Socialist Thought*, while Dame Margaret's is secured by her biography of Beatrice Webb and her edition of Mrs. Webb's journals. The detective stories provide only an interesting footnote to the leisure-time activities of two eminent social historians.

The first Cole novel, *The Brooklyn Murders*, was written by G.D.H. alone. Subsequent novels appeared under a joint by-line, even though one author was usually responsible for an entire volume. In only a handful of books, most notably *Murder at the Munition Works*, is the Coles' socio-economic knowledge used to advantage. Country house and university settings, upper-class characters, and virtual absence of references to contemporary events are typical of the Coles' novels, as they are of others of the period. All the detectives, including Everard Blatchington, James Warrender, and the Coles' principal detective, Superintendent Henry Wilson, lack memorable personalities; Wilson, in fact, is surely one of the most colorless detectives ever created.

Of the country house novels, *The Murder at Crome House* and *Double Blackmail* are perhaps the best. Casual amateur detection, light romantic interest, an unusual alibi, and clever unmasking of identity distinguish the first, while the second is a well-plotted account of blackmail and murder in a wealthy, respectable English family. In Amelia Selvidge, the family matriarch, and her son Brian, Bishop of Silchester, the Coles have created two characters who possess sufficient individuality to make their actions psychologically valid; and they have provided a delightfully satiric account of the political maneuvers by which Brian, a comfort-loving windbag, achieves his bishopric.

The Coles devoted a collection of short stories, *Mrs. Warrender's Profession*, to Warrender's mother. Other collections of short stories feature Wilson, who appears to advantage in the shorter form in which his methods of detection can be viewed without obscuring detail.

Of the Coles' remaining novels, *Counterpoint Murder*, *End of an Ancient Mariner*, and *Murder at the Munition Works* are worthy of attention. *Counterpoint Murder*, one of Wilson's best cases, has a skilfully worked-out plot in which two men exchange victims in order to secure alibis and avoid suspicion. Sound police work eventually links the two apparently unrelated murders through a series of fairly presented clues. *End of an Ancient Mariner*, in which the villain is an appealing confidence man, contains careful reconstruction of past events by Wilson and an appealing character in Philip Blakway. *Murder at the Munition Works* is the one novel in which the Coles make extensive use of their knowledge of trade unionism and the working class. Set in a factory during an industrial dispute, the novel features a large cast of characters drawn from both management and labor. The Coles work out the solution to murder by traditional methods with careful attention to alibis, timetables, and diagrams, while simultaneously offering fresh subject matter and characters unusual to the genre. It is to be regretted that they did not do so more often.

—Jeanne F. Bedell

COLES, Manning. Pseudonym for Cyril Henry Coles and Adelaide Frances Oke Manning; also wrote as Francis Gaite. British. **COLES, Cyril Henry:** Born in London, 11 June 1899. Educated at a school in Petersfield, Hampshire. Served in the Hampshire Regiment and later with British Intelligence during World War I; also served with British Intelligence during World War II. Married Dorothy Cordelia Smith in 1934; two sons. Apprentice at John I. Thornycroft, shipbuilders, Southampton, after World War I; worked in Australia during the 1920's as a railwayman, garage manager, and columnist on a Melbourne newspaper; returned to England, 1928. Lived in East Meon, Hampshire. *Died 9 October 1965.* **MANNING, Adelaide Frances Oke:** Born in London in 1891. Educated at the High School for Girls, Tunbridge Wells, Kent. Worked in a munitions factory and at the War Office, London, during World War I. Lived in East Meon, Hampshire. *Died 25 September 1959.*

CRIME PUBLICATIONS

Novels (series: Tommy Hambledon in all books except *This Fortress*)

Drink to Yesterday. London, Hodder and Stoughton, 1940; New York, Knopf, 1941.
Pray Silence. London, Hodder and Stoughton, 1940; as *A Toast for Tomorrow;* New York, Doubleday, 1941.
They Tell No Tales. London, Hodder and Stoughton, 1941; New York, Doubleday, 1942.
This Fortress. New York, Doubleday, 1942.
Without Lawful Authority. London, Hodder and Stoughton, and New York, Doubleday, 1943.
Green Hazard. London, Hodder and Stoughton, and New York, Doubleday, 1945.
The Fifth Man. London, Hodder and Stoughton, and New York, Doubleday, 1946.
Let the Tiger Die. New York, Doubleday, 1947; London, Hodder and Stoughton, 1948.
A Brother for Hugh. London, Hodder and Stoughton, 1947; as *With Intent to Deceive*, New York, Doubleday, 1947.
Among Those Absent. London, Hodder and Stoughton, and New York, Doubleday, 1948.
Diamonds to Amsterdam. New York, Doubleday, 1949; London, Hodder and Stoughton, 1950.
Not Negotiable. London, Hodder and Stoughton, and New York, Doubleday, 1949.
Dangerous by Nature. London, Hodder and Stoughton, and New York, Doubleday, 1950.
Now or Never. London, Hodder and Stoughton, and New York, Doubleday, 1951.
Alias Uncle Hugo. New York, Doubleday, 1952; London, Hodder and Stoughton, 1953; as *Operation Manhunt*, New York, Spivak, 1954.
Night Train to Paris. London, Hodder and Stoughton, and New York, Doubleday, 1952.
A Knife for the Juggler. London, Hodder and Stoughton, 1953; New York, Doubleday, 1964; as *The Vengeance Man*, New York, Pyramid, 1967.
Not for Export. London, Hodder and Stoughton, 1954; as *All That Glitters*, New York, Doubleday, 1954; as *The Mystery of the Stolen Plans*, New York, Berkley, 1960.
The Man in the Green Hat. London, Hodder and Stoughton, and New York, Doubleday, 1955.
Basle Express. London, Hodder and Stoughton, and New York, Doubleday, 1956.
Birdwatcher's Quarry. New York, Doubleday, 1956; as *The Three Beans*, London, Hodder and Stoughton, 1957.
Death of an Ambassador. London, Hodder and Stoughton, and New York, Doubleday, 1957.
No Entry. London, Hodder and Stoughton, and New York, Doubleday, 1958.
Crime in Concrete. London, Hodder and Stoughton, 1960; as *Concrete Crime*, New York, Doubleday, 1960.
Search for a Sultan, with Tom Hammerton. London, Hodder and Stoughton, and New York, Doubleday, 1961.
The House at Pluck's Gutter, with Tom Hammerton. London, Hodder and Stoughton, 1963; New York, Pyramid, 1968.

Novels as Francis Gaite (series: Charles and James Latimer; published as Manning Coles in US)

Brief Candles (Latimers).   London, Hodder and Stoughton, and New York, Doubleday, 1954.
Happy Returns (Latimers).   New York, Doubleday, 1955; as *A Family Matter*, London, Hodder and Stoughton, 1956.
The Far Traveller.   New York, Doubleday, 1956; London, Hodder and Stoughton, 1957.
Come and Go (Latimers).   London, Hodder and Stoughton, and New York, Doubleday, 1958.
Duty Free.   London, Hodder and Stoughton, and New York, Doubleday, 1959.

Short Stories

Nothing to Declare.   New York, Doubleday, 1960.

Uncollected Short Story

"Death Keeps a Secret," in *The Mystery Bedside Book*, edited by John Creasey.   London, Hodder and Stoughton, 1960.

OTHER PUBLICATIONS

Novel

Half-Valdez (by Manning alone).   London, Hodder and Stoughton, 1939.

Other

Great Caesar's Ghost (for children).   New York, Doubleday, 1943; as *The Emperor's Bracelet*, London, University of London Press, 1947.

*   *   *

The best-known longer works of the Manning Coles writing team are the Tommy Hambledon stories, featuring Thomas Elphinstone Hambledon of the British Intelligence Service. Tommy's adventures were based on Cyril Coles's own war experiences with the Nazis, and his characterization on a much admired professor of Coles's. Tommy, like Coles, has a talent for emerging unscathed from behind enemy lines. And, like the professor, he has an uncanny knack at mastering foreign languages.

Drink to Yesterday and *Pray Silence* cover Tommy's experiences from the end of World War I until shortly before World War II. He is a victim of amnesia, but as the second novel draws to a close he discovers his real identity and looks forward to using his talents in the future to help Scotland Yard. However, as the 1940's ended, the public taste for spy fiction about Nazis declined, and the team attempted to adapt Tommy's adventures to the international scene of the 1950's. It was at this point that their reputation began to slip, with reviewers commenting on the formulaic nature of both settings and plots.

At about the same time, the team turned to a second type of fiction, loosely categorized as "novels." In reality they are thinly disguised ghost stories laced with a good bit of social satire and, like the Tommy Hambledon series, were received at first with high praise.

In the first book in this series, *Brief Candles*, James and Charles Latimer—two cousins, the former English, the latter from Virginia—are killed and buried near each other alongside their pet monkey, Ulysses, who died with them in 1870 in the Franco-Prussian Wars. Later in the book, and in later books, the Latimers come back from the grave, accompanied by Ulysses, and help their descendant Richard Scroby through a number of hair-raising scrapes. *Brief Candles* was highly praised for its whimsical humor and charm; people seemed to enjoy reading about a crook named Pepi the Crocodile (he had a wide smile) and a thief named Finger Dupre. But even as early as the second book, reviewers began complaining that this kind of whimsical satire wears pretty thin.

And so, in 1959, the team tried a kind of fiction that could be termed a satiric romance, *Duty Free*. It did not feature Tommy Hambledon, but had lots of international skullduggery mingled with European urbanity. In short fiction, the team showed a similar pattern of running out of imaginative energy. In the mid-1940's they published a dozen short stories featuring Tommy Hambledon under the title *Nothing to Declare*. Threaded among the intrigue and adventure episodes are farcical characters like Superintendent Bagshott of Scotland Yard, Mr. Heaven, an undertaker, Joseph Joseph, a fence for stolen goods, and Butler Harry, a housebreaker. The stories are also full of ghosts, missing jewels, stolen tombstones and other predictable elements of whimsy.

—Elizabeth F. Duke

———

COLLIER, John (Henry Noyes).   British.   Born in London, 3 May 1901. Educated privately. Married 1) Shirley Lee Palmer in 1936 (divorced 1943); 2) Margaret Elizabeth Eke in 1945. Poetry editor, *Time and Tide*, London, in the 1920's and 1930's. Scriptwriter in the United States. Recipient: Mystery Writers of America Edgar Allan Poe award, 1951; International Fantasy award, 1952. *Died 6 April 1980.*

CRIME PUBLICATIONS

Short Stories

No Traveller Returns.   London, White Owl Press, 1931.
An Epistle to a Friend.   London, Ulysses Bookshop, 1931.
Green Thoughts.   London, Joiner and Steele, 1932.
The Devil and All.   London, Nonesuch Press, 1934.
Variation on a Theme.   London, Grayson, 1935.
Witch's Money.   New York, Viking Press, 1940.
Presenting Moonshine: Stories.   London, Macmillan, and New York, Viking Press, 1941.
The Touch of Nutmeg and More Unlikely Stories.   New York, Readers Club, 1943.
Green Thoughts and Other Strange Tales.   New York, Editions for the Armed Services, 1943.
Fancies and Goodnights.   New York, Doubleday, 1951; abridged version as *Of Demons and Darkness*, London, Corgi, 1965.
Pictures in the Fire.   London, Hart Davis, 1958.

OTHER PUBLICATIONS

Novels

His Monkey Wife; or, Married to a Chimp.   London, Davies, 1930; New York, Appleton, 1931.
Tom's A-Cold.   London, Macmillan, 1933; as *Full Circle*, New York, Appleton Century, 1933.

Defy the Foul Fiend; or, The Misadventures of a Heart.   London, Macmillan, and New York, Knopf, 1934.

Plays

Wet Saturday (produced New York).   New York, One-Act, n.d.
His Monkey Wife, music by Sandy Wilson, adaptation of the novel by Collier (produced London, 1971).
Milton's "Paradise Lost": Screenplay for Cinema of the Mind.   New York, Knopf, 1973.

Screenplays: *Sylvia Scarlett*, with Gladys Unger and Mortimer Offner, 1936; *Elephant Boy*, with Akos Tolnay and Marcia de Sylva, 1937; *Her Cardboard Lover*, with Anthony Veiller and William H. Wright, 1942; *Deception*, with Joseph Than, 1946; *Roseanna McCoy*, 1949; *The Story of Three Loves*, with others, 1953; *I Am a Camera*, 1955; *The War Lord*, with Millard Kaufman, 1965.

Verse

Gemini: Poems.   London, Ulysses Bookshop, 1931.

Other

Just the Other Day: An Informal History of Britain since the War, with Iain Lang.   London, Hamish Hamilton, and New York, Harper, 1932.
The John Collier Reader.   New York, Knopf, 1972; London, Souvenir Press, 1975.

Editor, *The Scandal and Credulities of John Aubrey.*   London, Davies, and New York, Appleton, 1931.

*   *   *

The short stories of John Collier have been favorites of fantasy and mystery anthologists for over 50 years, ever since Dashiell Hammett reprinted *Green Thoughts* (about a sinister orchid) in his 1931 horror anthology *Creeps by Night*. The reason for their popularity with editors and readers is easy to understand. Collier had the knack of writing about the fantastic and the bizarre with a special quality that often approaches whimsy. It's doubtful if any reader was ever terrified or revolted by the horrors of John Collier. A more likely reaction would be a quiet chuckle of satisfaction.

Collier's two novels, *His Monkey Wife* and *Defy the Foul Fiend*, are both fantasies, as are many of his 60 or more short stories. But several stories dealing with murder are of special interest to mystery readers. Two of the most familiar are "De Mortuis" and "Back for Christmas," both included in Collier's mammoth collection *Fancies and Goodnights*. It's safe to say that most stories about a husband killing his wife and burying her body in the basement are variations on one or the other of these definitive tales. Yet another variation on the husband as wife-killer can be found in Collier's uncollected story "Anniversary Gift," in which the husband brings home a poisonous snake, with surprising results.

Other Collier stories deal with poison or the hint of poison, as in "Over Insurance" and "The Chaser." An elixir of youth figures in the non-criminous "Youth from Vienna," which could have been written by O. Henry. Another murder story, "Wet Saturday," was successfully presented on television by Alfred Hitchcock, and Hitchcock expressed regret at not being able to televise Collier's "The Lady on the Grey," a fantasy about a man transformed into a dog by a beautiful woman with whom he has fallen in love. Many of Collier's stories lend themselves quite well to television, and "Evening Primrose"—about people who live by night in a large department store—was even transformed into a television musical.

A recurring theme in Collier's fantasy is a deal with the devil, or with some sort of evil spirit. In "Bottle Party" the traditional jinn in the bottle manages to change places with the man who buys the bottle. In "Pictures in the Fire" the devil is a movie producer, and much of "The Devil George and Rosie" is set in Hell.

Collier's success with the short story owes much to his early days as a poet and his later experience as a screenwriter. His stories combine visual perfection with a perfect choice of words—especially in his endings, where the most shocking denouements are often rendered in a style that brings a smile to the reader's lips.

—Edward D. Hoch

———

COLLINS, Hunt. *See* **McBAIN, Ed.**

———

COLLINS, Max Allan. American. Born in Muscatine, Iowa, 3 March 1948. Educated at Muscatine Community College, 1966–68, Associate of Arts 1968; University of Iowa, Iowa City, 1968–72, B.A. 1970, M.F.A. 1972. Married Barbara Jane Mull in 1968; one son. Musician, with Daybreakers group, 1966–71, and Crusin' group, 1976–79; songwriter, Tree International, Nashville, 1967–71; reporter, Muscatine *Journal*, 1968–70; Instructor in English, Muscatine Community College, 1971–77. Has written the comic strips *Dick Tracy* since 1977, *Mike Mist* since 1979, and *Ms. Tree* since 1981, for newspapers and magazines. Recipient: Inkpot award, for comic strip, 1982. Agent: Dominick Abel, 498 West End Avenue, Apartment 12-C, New York, New York 10024. Address: 117 Lord Avenue, Muscatine, Iowa 52761, U.S.A.

CRIME PUBLICATIONS

Novels (series: Nathan Heller; Mallory; Nolan; Quarry)

Bait Money (Nolan).   New York, Curtis, 1973; London, New English Library, 1976; revised edition, New York, Pinnacle, 1981.
Blood Money (Nolan).   New York, Curtis, 1973; London, New English Library, 1977; revised edition, New York, Pinnacle, 1981.
The Broker (Quarry).   New York, Berkley, 1976.
The Broker's Wife (Quarry).   New York, Berkley, 1976.
The Dealer (Quarry).   New York, Berkley, 1976.
The Slasher (Quarry).   New York, Berkley, 1977.
Fly Paper (Nolan).   New York, Pinnacle, 1981.
Hush Money (Nolan).   New York, Pinnacle, 1981.
Hard Cash (Nolan).   New York, Pinnacle, 1981.
Scratch Fever (Nolan).   New York, Pinnacle, 1982.
The Baby Blue Rip-Off (Mallory).   New York, Walker, 1983; London, Hale, 1984.
No Cure for Death (Mallory).   New York, Walker, 1983; London, Hale, 1985.

True Detective (Heller).   New York, St. Martin's Press, 1983;
   London, Sphere, 1984.
Kill Your Darlings (Mallory).   New York, Walker, 1984;
   London, Hale, 1986.
True Crime (Heller).   New York, St. Martin's Press, 1985.
A Shroud for Aquarius (Mallory).   New York, Walker, 1985.
The Million-Dollar Wound (Heller).   New York, St. Martin's
   Press, 1986; London, Gollancz, 1989.
Quarry's Deal.   Woodstock, Vermont, Countryman Press,
   1986.
Quarry's Cut.   Woodstock, Vermont, Countryman Press, 1986.
A Nice Weekend for a Murder (Mallory).   New York, Walker,
   1986.
Midnight Have I.   Woodstock, Vermont, Countryman Press,
   1986.
Spree (Nolan).   New York, Tor, 1987.
Primary Target (Quarry).   Woodstock, Vermont, Countryman
   Press, 1987.
Butcher's Dozen.   New York, Bantam, 1988.
Neon Mirage (Heller).   New York, St. Martin's Press, 1988;
   London, Gollancz, 1989.
Dick Tracy (novelization of screenplay).   New York, Bantam,
   1990.

Uncollected Short Stories

"The Mike Mist Minute Mist-eries," in *Eclipse*, April 1981.
"The Strawberry Teardrop," in *The Eyes Have It*, edited by
   Robert J. Randisi.   New York; Mysterious Press, 1984;
   London, Severn House, 1988.
"Red Light," in *The Files of Ms. Tree.*   Kitchener, Ontario,
   Aardvark Vanaheim, 1984.

OTHER PUBLICATIONS

Other

Dick Tracy Meets Angeltop, illustrated by R. Fletcher.   New
   York, Ace, 1980.
Dick Tracy Meets the Punks, illustrated by R. Fletcher.   New
   York, Ace, 1980.
Jim Thompson: The Killers Inside Him, with Ed Gorman.   Ce-
   dar Rapids, Iowa, Fedora Press, 1983.
One Lonely Knight: Mickey Spillane's Mike Hammer, with James
   L. Traylor.   Bowling Green, Ohio, Popular Press, 1984.
The Files of Ms. Tree, illustrated by Terry Beatty.   Kitchener,
   Ontario, Aardvark Vanaheim, 1984.
The Best of Crime and Detective Television, with John
   Javna.   New York, Crown, 1988.

Editor, *Mike Hammer: The Comic Strip*, by Mickey Spillane,
   illustrated by Ed Robbins.   Park Forest, Illinois, Pierce, 2
   vols., 1982–84.
Editor, *Tomorrow I Die*, by Mickey Spillane.   New York,
   Mysterious Press, 1984.
Editor, with Dick Locher, *The Dick Tracy Casebook: Favorite
   Adventures 1931–1990.*   New York, St. Martin's Press, 1990.

*

Manuscript Collection: Bowling Green State University, Ohio.

Max Allan Collins comments:
   For many years now I've been in love with the private-eye
novel: the lean prose, the sharp dialogue, the understated
poetry at least as found in the works of those three proponents

of the form, Dashiell Hammett, Raymond Chandler, and
Mickey Spillane. But when I began writing my own suspense
novels in the early 1970's I found myself uncomfortable with
the private eye: my heroes tended to be anti-heroes, perhaps
reflecting the troubled times around me as I worked. (Also, I
was influenced by the non-private-eye novels of such "hard-
boiled" writers as James M. Cain, Horace McCoy, Jim
Thompson, and Richard Stark.)
   So I came up with Nolan, an aging thief, a self-described
"dinosaur" of an earlier, tough-guy era; and Quarry, the quietly
psychotic Vietnam vet who makes his living as a hired killer.
Despite their criminal backgrounds, both Nolan and Quarry
frequently behaved like private eyes, however, and with my
subsequent series about small-town mystery writer Mallory (a
character shamelessly patterned on myself), I drifted ever
closer to the Hammett/Chandler/Spillane tradition.
   Even so, I rejected the private eye, because I could not find a
way to write about him in the 1970's that didn't seem foolish to
me—the private eye in the 1970's (and now 1980's) seemed an
anachronism. Then it occured to me that the private eye now
existed in *history*—that Hammett had created archetypical P.I.
Sam Spade in 1929—making Spade a contemporary of Al
Capone's. From this starting point I developed the historical
private-eye novel *True Detective*—a departure, I think, from
"period" private-eye stories seeking to evoke a sense of
nostalgia and nothing more. It was my hope in *True Detective* to
portray history as accurately as possible—the events, the
characters in the novel, are for the most part real—and yet still
tell a compelling, emotionally involving mystery.
   While I am not abandoning the shorter, traditional mystery
novel (*True Detective* is easily twice as long as any of my other
books), or my other series characters (another Mallory story is
currently in the works, for example), I do hope to concentrate in
the next few years on historical detective novels, taking my
private eye Nate Heller "up through history." A second novel,
True Crime, has just been completed, and research on a third (to
be set in World War Two) is under way.
   I must admit I consider my work in comics to play a
supporting role in my career (and not just financially); still, it
often tends to take center-stage, since *Dick Tracy* is obviously
more famous than anyone who merely writes it. And there is
still a prejudice against writers of comic strips—Raymond
Chandler once dismissed Mickey Spillane by calling him a
"comic book writer." Perhaps Chandler forgot that Hammett
wrote the *Secret Agent X-9* strip.

*   *   *

   An author whose major acknowledged influences are Mickey
Spillane and Richard Stark (Donald E. Westlake), Max Allan
Collins is solidly entrenched in the hard and tough school of
crime fiction. His protagonists have often been professional
criminals. But his sense of humor and underlying humanity,
coupled with a gift for intricate plotting and cinematically
effective action scenes, make his novels palatable even to
readers who normally would eschew the very hardboiled.
   The early books in Collins's Nolan series owe a heavy debt to
Stark's grim Parker novels, even to the chapter numbering
pattern. Though the action and most of the characters are just
as hard and uncompromising, Collins conveys an overt
empathy with his criminal characters not allowed by the
studied objectivity of Stark. As the series goes on, with an eight-
year hiatus between the second and third books, the differences
become more pronounced. Nolan's young sidekick, Jon, a rock
musician and comics collector, becomes a more and more
important character, virtually co-equal with Nolan. *Fly Paper*,
involving a comic convention and a skyjacking, is a particu-

larly good example of Collins's plotting expertise and sympathetically ironic view of his characters. *Hush Money*, more somber than earlier Nolans, looks at the Executioner-type wipe-out-the-Mafia novel from a fresh angle. *Scratch Fever*, though more thinly plotted than earlier entries, employs a knowledgeable rock music background rare in mystery fiction. *Spree*, about a shopping-mall knockover, represents a powerful encore after a five-year hiatus.

Between the earliest and later Nolans, Collins introduced his second series character, Quarry, an embittered Vietnam veteran turned killer-for-hire. His chilling rationalization: "... certain people are going to want certain other people dead, and what are you going to do? ... Anybody I ever hit was set to go anyway. I saw to it that it happened fast and clean. It was something like working in a butcher shop, only my job pays better, the hours are shorter and there isn't the mess" (*The Broker*). In *The Broker*, Quarry becomes possibly the first detective in fiction to commit the murder before trying to solve it. He is among the least admirable characters (I think intentionally so) to be the protagonist of a series of crime novels. That he is acceptable in that role through five books, most recently the decade-later comeback *Primary Target*, is a tribute to Collins's talent.

Mallory, a student mystery writer who delivers hot meals for senior citizens in his small Iowa town, is the first of Collins's surname-only protagonists to operate on the right side of the law. The Mallory novels are softer edged, appropriate to a more conservative hardcover market, but in certain stretches the author's hardboiled roots are apparent. Most notable about the Mallory books is their understanding depiction of the Vietnam generation and their sense of nostalgia for the recent past. In the most memorable chapter of *The Baby Blue Rip-Off*, Mallory looks back on junior high school courtship rites with wonderful humor and insight. The "prequel," *No Cure for Death*, set in 1974, contains some of Collins's best characters, notable a now-elderly Depression-era medical quack. Collins makes his closest approach to classical detective fiction in a pair of enjoyable mystery buff's mysteries, *Kill Your Darlings*, set at Bouchercon (the annual World Mystery Convention), and *A Nice Weekend for Murder*, concerning a mystery game at upstate New York's Mohonk Mountain House. But the best of the Mallory novels is the darker-toned *A Shroud for Aquarius*, with its poignant look back at the 1960's.

With *True Detective*, a long historical mystery illustrated with period photographs, Collins began the series that represents his major contribution to date. Set in the Chicago of the 1930's, it stars the author's first two-name hero, Nate Heller, who quits the corruption-riddled Chicago police force to become a private eye. Paradoxically, it's easier to bring a wholly fictitious creation to life in a novel than to animate real-life guest stars, but Collins does the job amazingly well, making fully realized, multi-faceted characters of Eliot Ness, Barney Ross, General Dawes, George Raft, Al Capone, Frank Nitti, Mayor Cermak, and other personalities of the time. And Collins achieves something else that many best-selling block-buster-writers do not: getting full measure from his thorough research without ever sounding like a history term paper. Subsequent novels in the series have continued in the same effective vein, taking Heller through World War II (*The Million-Dollar Wound*) and in to the post-war world of gang-dominated Las Vegas (*Neon Mirage*).

Recently Collins has introduced as a spin-off of the Heller books, a second historical series about Eliot Ness's work as public safety officer in Cleveland. *Butcher's Dozen*, about the hunt for a serial killer known as the Mad Butcher of Kingsbury Run, ranks with the author's best books. An admirable feature of each of Collins's historical crime novels is a concluding note

spelling out exactly what is fact and what fiction. How much is true is usually surprising.

—Jon L. Breen

—————

COLLINS, Michael. Pseudonym for Dennis Lynds; also writes as William Arden; Nick Carter; John Crowe; Carl Decker; John Douglas; Maxwell Grant; Mark Sadler. American. Born in St. Louis, Missouri, January 15 1924. Educated at Brooklyn Technical High School; Cooper Union, New York, 1942–43; Texas Agricultural and Mechanical College, College Station, 1943–44; Hofstra University, Hempstead, New York, B.A. in Chemistry 1949; Syracuse University, New York, M.A. in journalism, 1951. Served with the United States Army Infantry, 1943–46: Bronze Star, Purple Heart, Combat Infantry Badge, three battle stars. Married 1) Doris Flood in 1949 (divorced 1956); 2) Sheila McErlean in 1961 (divorced 1985), two daughters); 3) Gayle Hallenbeck Stone in 1986. Assistant chemist, Charles Pfizer and Company, Brooklyn, 1942–43 and 1946; assistant editor, *Chemical Week*, New York, 1951–52; editorial director, American Institute of Management, New York, 1952–54; associate editor, then managing editor, *Chemical Engineering Progress*, New York, 1955–61; part-time editor, *Chemical Equipment* and *Laboratory Equipment*, New York, 1962–66; Instructor, Santa Barbara City College Adult Education Division, California, 1966–67; editor, *International Instrumentation*, Great Neck, New York, 1975–82. Since 1960 self-employed writer. President, Private Eye Writers of America, 1985. Recipient: Mystery Writers of America Edgar Allan Poe award, 1968, special award, 1969; Private Eye Writers of America Lifetime Achievement award, 1988. Agent: Agnes Birnbaum, Bleecker Street Associates, 88 Bleecker Street, Suite 6P, New York, New York 10012. Address: 12 St. Anne Drive, Santa Barbara, California 93109, U.S.A.

CRIME PUBLICATIONS

Novels (series: Dan Fortune in all books)

Act of Fear. New York, Dodd Mead, 1967; London, Joseph, 1968.
The Brass Rainbow. New York, Dodd Mead, 1969; London, Joseph, 1970.
Night of the Toads. New York, Dodd Mead, 1970; London, Hale, 1972.
Walk a Black Wind. New York, Dodd Mead, 1971; London, Hale, 1973.
Shadow of a Tiger. New York, Dodd Mead, 1972; London, Hale, 1974.
The Silent Scream. New York, Dodd Mead, 1973; London, Hale, 1975.
Woman in Marble (as Carl Dekker). Indianapolis, Bobbs Merrill, 1973.
Blue Death. New York, Dodd Mead, 1975; London, Hale, 1976.
The Blood-Red Dream. New York, Dodd Mead, 1976; London, Hale, 1977.
The Nightrunners. New York, Dodd Mead, 1978; London, Hale, 1979.
The Slasher. New York, Dodd Mead, 1980; London, Hale, 1981.

Freak. New York, Dodd Mead, and London, Hale, 1983.
Minnesota Strip. New York, Fine, 1987; London, Oldcastle, 1990.
Red Rosa. New York, Fine, 1988; London, Oldcastle, 1990.
Castrato. New York, Fine, 1989.
Chasing Eights. New York, Fine, 1990.

Novels as Maxwell Grant (series: The Shadow in all books)

The Shadow Strikes. New York, Belmont, 1964.
Shadow Beware. New York, Belmont, 1965.
Cry Shadow. New York, Belmont, 1965.
The Shadow's Revenge. New York, Belmont, 1965.
Mark of the Shadow. New York, Belmont, 1966.
Shadow—Go Mad! New York, Belmont, 1966.
The Night of the Shadow. New York, Belmont, 1966.
The Shadow—Destination: Moon. New York, Belmont, 1967.

Novels as William Arden (series: Kane Jackson in all books)

A Dark Power. New York, Dodd Mead, 1968; London, Hale, 1970.
Deal in Violence. New York, Dodd Mead, 1969; London, Hale, 1971.
The Goliath Scheme. New York, Dodd Mead, 1971; London, Hale, 1973.
Die to a Distant Drum. New York, Dodd Mead, 1972; as *Murder Underground*, London, Hale, 1974.
Deadly Legacy. New York, Dodd Mead, 1973; London, Hale, 1974.

Novels as Mark Sadler (series: Paul Shaw in all books)

The Falling Man. New York, Random House, 1970.
Here to Die. New York, Random House, 1971.
Mirror Image. New York, Random House, 1972.
Circle of Fire. New York, Random House, 1973.
Touch of Death. Toronto, Raven House, 1983.
Deadly Innocents. New York, Walker, 1986.

Novels as John Crowe

Another Way to Die. New York, Random House, 1972.
A Touch of Darkness. New York, Random House, 1972.
Bloodwater. New York, Dodd Mead, 1974.
Crooked Shadows. New York, Dodd Mead, 1975.
When They Kill Your Wife. New York, Dodd Mead, 1977.
Close to Death. New York, Dodd Mead, 1979; London, Hale, 1983.

Novels as Nick Carter (series: Nick Carter in all books)

The N3 Conspiracy. New York, Award, 1974.
The Green Wolf Connection. New York, Award 1976.
Triple Cross. New York, Award, 1976.

Novels as Dennis Lynds

Charlie Chan Returns (novelization of television play). New York, Bantam, 1974.
S.W.A.T.—Crossfire (novelization of television play). New York, Pocket Books, 1975.

Uncollected Short Stories

"Death, My Love" (as John Douglas), in *Mink Is for a Minx: The Best from Mike Shayne's Mystery Magazine.* New York, Dell, 1964.

"Murder from Inside," in *Mike Shayne Mystery Magazine* (New York), March 1968.
"Hot Night Homicide," in *Mike Shayne Mystery Magazine* (New York), August 1968.
"Freedom Fighter," in *Crime Without Murder*, edited by Dorothy Salisbury Davis. New York, Scribner, 1970.
"Long Shot," in *Alfred Hitchcock's Mystery Magazine* (North Palm Beach, Florida), July 1972.
"Occupational Hazard" (as John Crowe), in *Alfred Hitchcock's Mystery Magazine* (North Palm Beach, Florida), September 1972.
"The Choice" (as Mark Sadler), in *Alfred Hitchcock's Mystery Magazine* (North Palm Beach, Florida), February 1973.
"No One Likes to Be Played for a Sucker," in *All But Impossible!*, edited by Edward D. Hoch. New Haven, Connecticut, Ticknor and Fields, 1981.
"Scream All the Way," in *Alfred Hitchcock's Tales to Make You Quake and Quiver*, edited by Cathleen Jordan. New York, Dial Press, 1982.
"Who?," in *Alfred Hitchcock's Death-Reach*, edited by Cathleen Jordan. New York, Dial Press, 1982.
"The Woman Who Ruins John Ireland (Dan Fortune and the Hollywood Caper)," in *Alfred Hitchcock's Mystery Magazine* (New York), November 1983.
"The Oldest Killer," in *The Year's Best Mystery and Suspense Stories 1984*, edited by Edward D. Hoch. New York, Walker, 1984.
"Eighty Million Dead," in *The Eyes Have It*, edited by Robert J. Randisi. New York, Mysterious Press, 1984; London, Severn House, 1988.
"A Reason to Die," in *New Black Mask*. San Diego, California. Harcourt Brace Jovanovich, 1985.
"Killer's Mind," in *New Black Mask*. San Diego, California, Harcourt Brace Jovanovich, 1986.
"The Motive," in *A Matter of Crime*. San Diego, Harcourt Brace Jovanovich, 1987.
"Black in the Snow," in *An Eye for Justice*, edited by Robert J. Randisi. New York, Mysterious Press, 1988.
""Crime and Punishment," in *The Year's Best Mystery and Suspense Stories 1989*, edited by Edward D. Hoch. New York, Walker, 1989.
"The Chair," in *Justice for Hire*, edited by Robert J. Randisi. New York, Mysterious Press, 1990.

Uncollected Short Stories as Dennis Lynds

"It's Whisky or Dames," in *Mike Shayne Mystery Magazine* (New York), August 1962.
"The Bodyguard," in *Mike Shayne Mystery Magazine* (New York), October 1962.
"Accidents Will Happen," in *Mike Shayne Mystery Magazine* (New York), November 1962.
"Carrier Pigeon," in *Mike Shayne Mystery Magazine* (New York), February 1963.
"The Blue Hand," in *Mike Shayne Mystery Magazine* (New York), April 1963.
"The Price of a Dollar," in *Mike Shayne Mystery Magazine* (New York), June 1963.
"Harness Bull," in *Mike Shayne Mystery Magazine* (New York), July 1963.
"Even Bartenders Die," in *Mike Shayne Mystery Magazine* (New York), August 1963.
"Death for Dinner," in *Mike Shayne Mystery Magazine* (New York), October 1963.
"Nobody Frames Big Sam," in *Alfred Hitchcock's Mystery Magazine* (North Palm Beach, Florida), October 1963.

"The Heckler," in *Mike Shayne Mystery Magazine* (New York), November 1963.
"A Better Murder," in *Mike Shayne Mystery Magazine* (New York), January 1964.
"No Way Out," in *Mike Shayne Mystery Magazine* (New York), February 1964.
"Silent Partner," in *Alfred Hitchcock's Mystery Magazine* (North Palm Beach, Florida), April 1964.
"The Sinner," in *Alfred Hitchcock's Mystery Magazine* (North Palm Beach, Florida), May 1964.
"Winner Pay Off," in *Mike Shayne Mystery Magazine* (New York), May 1964.
"Hard Cop," in *Mike Shayne Mystery Magazine* (New York), July 1964.
"Homecoming," in *Mike Shayne Mystery Magazine* (New York), September 1964.
"No Loose Ends," in *Mike Shayne Mystery Magazine* (New York), November 1964.
"Man on the Run," in *Mink Is for a Minx: The Best from Mike Shayne's Mystery Magazine.* New York, Dell 1964.
"Full Circle," in *Mike Shayne Mystery Magazine* (New York), January 1965.
"The Hero," in *Mike Shayne Mystery Magazine* (New York), May 1965.
"A Well-Planned Death," in *Mike Shayne Mystery Magazine* (New York), December 1965.
"No Way Out," in *Best Detective Stories of the Year, 19th Annual Collection*, edited by Anthony Boucher. New York, Dutton, and London, Boardman, 1965.
"Viking Blood," in *Manhunt* (New York), April–May 1966.
"The Dirk," in *Man from U.N.C.L.E. Mystery Magazine* (New York), June 1966.
"Climate of Immorality," in *Shell Scott Mystery Magazine* (New York), 1967.

Uncollected Short Stories as William Arden

"Success of a Mission," in *Argosy* (New York), April 1968.
"The Savage," in *Argrosy* (New York), January 1970.
"The Bizarre Case Expert," in *Ellery Queen's Mystery Magazine* (New York), June 1970.
"Clay Pigeon," in *Argosy* (New York), March 1971.

OTHER PUBLICATIONS

Novels

Combat Soldier (as Dennis Lynds). New York, New American Library, 1962.
Uptown Downtown (as Dennis Lynds). New York, New American Library, 1963.
Lukan War. New York, Belmont, 1969.
The Planets of Death. New York, Berkley, 1970.

Short Stories

Why Girls Ride Sidesaddle (as Dennis Lynds). Chicago, December Press, 1980.

Other (for children) as William Arden

The Mystery of the Moaning Cave. New York, Random House, 1968; London, Collins, 1969.
The Mystery of the Laughing Shadow. New York, Random House, 1969; London, Collins, 1970.
The Secret of the Crooked Cat. New York, Random House, 1970; London, Collins, 1971.

The Mystery of the Shrinking House. New York, Random House, 1972; London, Collins, 1973.
The Mystery of the Blue Condor. Lexington, Massachusetts, Ginn, 1973.
The Secret of the Phantom Lake. New York, Random House, 1973; London, Collins, 1974.
The Mystery of the Dead Man's Riddle. New York, Random House, 1974; London, Collins, 1975.
The Mystery of the Dancing Devil. New York, Random House, 1976; London, Collins, 1977.
The Mystery of the Headless Horse. New York, Random House, 1977; London, Collins, 1978.
The Mystery of the Deadly Double. New York, Random House, 1978; London, Collins, 1979.
The Secret of Shark Reef. New York, Random House, 1979; London, Collins, 1980.
The Mystery of the Purple Pirate. New York, Random House, 1982.
The Mystery of the Smashing Glass. New York, Random House, 1984; London, Collins, 1985.
The Mystery of the Wreckers Rock. New York, Random House, 1986; London, Collins, 1987.
Hot Wheels. New York, Random House, 1989.

*

Manuscript Collection: Center for the Study of Popular Culture, Bowling Green State University, Ohio.

Michael Collins comments:

I write about people driven to violent actions by forces from inside and outside. The forces of the world in which they live. A real world. Our world. If anything distinguishes my books particularly from other books, it is that I write what could be called *socio-dramas*. I want to understand and show what made these people as they are, what created the pressures that will explode within them. What made them, then, act in a crisis as they acted, and what made violence their ultimate solution.

A novel is a novel; suspense novels are no less novels than sonnets are poems. The basic mark of a "crime" novel is exactly that—it centers on an overt crime, a specific moment of violence at a particular time and place. I chose to write "crime" novels precisely for this reason—I think a society and its people can be seen in sharp outline at such moments of violence.

I hope my books excite, thrill and entertain, but what I try to give is the excitement of truth, the thrill of understanding our own world as it is, the entertainment of living a real experience with real people. Still, I do not write primarily to thrill or entertain, but to know what makes our world tick—your world and mine—in all its strengths and its weaknesses, its hopes and its horrors, its everyday streets and its hidden corners.

* * *

Michael Collins is the best-known persona of Dennis Lynds who has written under a number of different pseudonyms. The Buena Costa California stories (as John Crowe), the William Arden industrial espionage novels, and the Mark Sadler mysteries are solid work in the hard-boiled tradition, but it is in the Collins series that Lynds manages to write tales distinguished by a strong personal flavor and originality. In these the typical hard-boiled characteristics are enriched, developed in complex and subtle fashion, primarily because of Dan Fortune, the one-armed, essentially passive, compassionate, and philosophical private investigator who is both the narrator and the principal character.

Lynds' novels are densely plotted, with an intricate pattern of events and characters, as many as 20 of the latter, all playing active roles. A minor problem, at least for mysteries—the disappearance of a relative, an apparent mugging, a man struggling for a renewal of his lease—becomes the initial thread that leads to a vast, entangled web of hatred, obsessions, assaults and multiple murders. The minor problem spreads out to involve a host of characters until both the detective and the reader are wandering in a maze of interconnected lives and motivations. Eventually the mystery itself is solved, the murderer or murderers revealed, although the resolution is ambiguous and incomplete. We discover that the events are in reality a web, as in the classic mystery story, where just about every character and event, no matter how seemingly insignificant, has had its place. Our interest may become focused on the murder and mayhem, especially that directed toward Dan Fortune, but Collins keeps his pattern firmly in hand. Following his plots requires close attention to detail and a rather retentive memory; but they reward the effort, for they are precisely crafted, credibly motivated, and ingenious.

Collins does not create these plots primarily as puzzles to be solved but as analogues to the complex interconnections of contemporary American society. Greed, ambition, corruption, and their opposites, idealism, loyalty, integrity are to be found in every level of our culture. They link the corporate boardroom with the seedy bar, the mansion with the barrio shack. The richly diverse areas of New York and Southern California—Collins's favorite locales—provide him with a great variety of types: wealthy ranchers, developers, executive vice-presidents, small businessmen, hippies, hookers, gamblers, hitmen, Hispanics, strong-arm cops, and venal politicians. His lens is both wide-angle and microscopic: we see not only a cross-section of American life but peer deeply into the motivations and attitudes of many people representative of modern culture. Collins is, however, more a philosopher of culture than a sociologist. He does not merely present and observe; he invests his portraits and his situations with values, or more frequently, *dis*values. Wherever he looks he sees deceit, ruthless ambition, and self-aggrandizement, the straight way made crooked, the American dream belly-up in the sun, and violence and murder the result.

The picture is bleak but not totally pessimistic. There are people in Collins's novels who have their values straight, Dan Fortune most particularly. He is unequivocally opposed to everything sleazy and corrupt, to the lies and deceit, even to the violence with which he is inevitably involved. The intricate plotting and social analysis depend for their unique effect on this searcher for the truth. The reader, often the reviewer, who does not see that Dan is essentially different from other private eyes misses an important point. For, although he is a drop-out from conventional society in a beret and duffel coat, a man without family and only fleeting sexual relationships, much like hard-boiled detectives in general, unlike the rest he is far more a thinker, a philosophical contemplator of human frailty drawn into whirlpools of crime because that is his job, the life that has been laid out for him. He is neither out for himself nor for vengeance; he is more often a victim rather than an aggressor; he is tough enough but not hard; he is often afraid but has that two-o'clock courage that makes him go on.

His being one-armed is no gimmick, a diversion like Columbo's raincoat designed to mislead the wicked into underestimating him, although it often has that effect because he is far smarter and cleverer than most of them realize, until too late. He lost the arm as a juvenile delinquent trying to hijack a Dutch freighter, but he fobs off the inevitable questions with talk about tanks or crocodiles. His greatest fear is for his remaining arm, and villains often play on this. But he continues his investigations regardless.

Fortune is incredibly persistent. Hounded, threatened, beaten, shot, baffled at every turn he never surrenders. He is told in story after story that the case is solved, that there is no case, that he had better lay off, but none of this deters him. In *Blue Death*, for example, probably the best of the early Collins novels, he works his way from the death of a parking-lot owner to the offices of a giant corporation that leases the lot, to the scientists who work for IMR, from New York to California and back to New Jersey, on and on. Although at different times he is drugged, kidnapped, stonewalled, even shot at, he bores into the affairs of Franklin Weaver, the powerful and glamorous executive vice-president, until he finally has the answer not only to the death of Jake Carter in his parking-lot, but also to two other deaths for which Weaver was responsible. On the way to solving the case he engages in a running debate with Weaver over the basic values in a corporate society. Weaver's ethics are those of the complete corporate man: what is good for the company is good. To which Dan makes the only just reply: because something is, doesn't make it right. Behind the intricate plot is this theme: that evil grows as naturally as weeds out of such warped values and distorted visions.

This kind of situation typifies Collins's novels up to the early 1980's but recently he has explored different themes, characters, and methods of narrative development. In *The Slasher*, for instance, he expands the arena of crime, which begins with the deaths of a young hooker/model and a liaison man for the modeling agency, spreads out into questions about the involvement of the CIA and FBI, and comes to the eventual revelation of the killer's motive to protect his mother's cover, since she was a former Nazi death-camp mistress who has been given U.S. citizenship in exchange for her knowledge of communist plans and agents. What appears at first merely a sordid murder reaches back in time and up the ladder of society to demonstrate how evil proliferates through time and social space.

In *Freak* Collins explores a different kind of proliferation: how one person's psychic state can result in widespread violence and death. J.J. is the most alienated figure in Collins's novels, perhaps one of the most alienated in modern fiction. Castrated when mauled by a bear in his youth, J.J. is a moral monster, the most chilling murderer in the novels, a man whose only satisfaction in life is listening to Mahler and Sibelius, not for enjoyment, but because their dark strains echo his own inner darkness. Collins has nothing more macabre than the scene at the end where J.J., mortally wounded, holds Dan at gunpoint, making him operate J.J.'s portable stereo for his own grotesque requiem.

Minnesota Strip and *Red Rosa* also make moderate excursions into new perspectives. The plots are of the familiar type, following the thread of a seemingly run-of-the-mail murder and a disappearance as each develops into a complicated pattern of corruption and deceit, but they also show shifts in point of view and explore two different kinds of alienation. Red Rosa herself is the archetypal radical who has finally become a bag lady, killed almost accidentally. She represents one way in which a separation from bourgeois American society can proceed, while Roy Carter, the central figure of *Minnesota Strip*, is psychically alienated because of his loss in the belief in any values and his commitment to eradicating evil as he sees it. He eventually becomes a terrorist.

In *Castrato* Collins again probes into the life of a man in the grip of an illusion, or delusion, but in addition he employs several different fictional strategies to add varying perspectives to the story. The principal character—principal in the metaphoric sense so important in this novel—is Frank Owen, prey to the powerful myth of America, particularly the West, as a land of freedom and individuality, the land of the cowboy. He feels he has been robbed of his heritage, castrated, primarily by women, who seek only security and stability. His way out is through alcohol and snorting coke, a way that, through various convolutions brings death and destruction around him. The plot is not especially original, a scam fueled by greed, but the story is told with interpolations new for Collins and for the hard-boiled genre in particular: shifts in point of view; flashbacks to earlier events that give depth to the present; brief biographies that flesh out the psychology of Frank Owen, his brother Billy, and Elizabeth Martin, Owen's opposite in ideology, a believer in getting what you can, never mind the freedom; bits of history of the West, particularly an account of the real Alamo rather than the legend; and even the erotic dreams of Dianne Owen, Frank's wife. All of which make *Castrato* a "breakout novel," as one commentator has expressed it.

Chasing Eights, the most recent Collins, goes even further. We see characters nearly as bizarre as J. J. in two extremely violent and foul-mouthed hitmen, and the Genius, poker-player extraordinary and a revolutionary who had plans to assassinate the President with homemade ground-to-air missiles, along with a number of other strange personalities. The shifts in point of view are lengthier, while biographies and historical sketches relate symbolically to the principal themes of greed and "making it." The style is more varied, more often breathless and jagged, using italic passages to change tone. The basic plot is another scam by a speculator/developer, but many people are involved, notably Jack Price, the central character whom Dan has been hired to find. The ending is unusually violent, Dan here, as in *Castrato*, breaking from his usual role and shooting the two hitmen with the gun he fondly calls his "old cannon," and which he has practically never used, certainly not in this way, in previous novels.

Win some, lose some. For these varied ways of telling the story, this emphasis on the metaphoric and symbolic, as in the stud-poker game that runs all through *Chasing Eights*, the gambling Nirvana-experience that is the key to much American life nowadays, do shift the focus from Dan Fortune, with all that that gained for Collins. Dan is always in the scene, pursuing the truth, knitting the events together, doing his job. But with his new strategies Collins has moved into another dimension of the mystery/detective story. These last novels are not only more complex, even more violent, they are harsher, more pessimistic. Powerful and memorable, they indicate that Collins has embarked on a new course after some 60 books. Truly he is a writer to be reckoned with.

—Richard C. Carpenter

COLLINS, Tom. *See* **LUTZ, John.**

CONDON, Richard (Thomas). American. Born in New York City, 18 March 1915. Educated in public schools in New York. Served in the United States Merchant Navy. Married Evelyn Hunt in 1938; two daughters. Worked briefly in advertising; publicist in the American film industry for 21 years: worked for Walt Disney Productions, 1936–41, Hal Horne Organization, Twentieth Century Fox, 1941–45, Richard Condon Inc., 1945–48, Paramount, 1948–53, United Artists, 1953–57, and other firms; theatrical producer, New York, 1951–52. Agent: Harold Matson Company Inc., 276 Fifth Avenue, New York, New York 10001, U.S.A.; or, Abner Stein, 10 Roland Gardens, London SW7 3PH, England. Address: 3436 Asbury Avenue, Dallas, Texas 75205, U.S.A.

CRIME PUBLICATIONS

Novels (series: Captain Colin Huntington; The Prizzi Family)

The Oldest Confession.   New York, Appleton Century Crofts, 1958; London, Longman, 1959; as *The Happy Thieves*, New York, Bantam, 1962.
The Manchurian Candidate.   New York, McGraw Hill, 1959; London, Joseph, 1960.
An Infinity of Mirrors.   New York, Random House, 1964; London, Heinemann, 1967.
The Ecstasy Business.   New York, Dial Press, and London, Heinemann, 1967.
Mile High.   New York, Dial Press, and London, Heinemann, 1969.
Arigato (Huntington).   New York, Dial Press, and London, Weidenfeld and Nicolson, 1972.
Winter Kills.   New York, Dial Press, and London, Weidenfeld and Nicolson, 1974.
The Whisper of the Axe.   New York, Dial Press, and London, Weidenfeld and Nicolson, 1976.
Bandicoot (Huntington).   New York, Dial Press, and London, Hutchinson, 1978.
Death of a Politician.   New York, Marek, 1978; London, Hutchinson, 1979.
The Entwining.   New York, Marek, 1980; London, Hutchinson, 1981.
Prizzi's Honor.   New York, Coward McCann, and London, Joseph, 1982.
Prizzi's Family.   New York, Putnam, and London, Joseph, 1986.
Prizzi's Glory.   New York, Dutton, and London, Joseph, 1988.
Emperor of America.   New York, Simon and Schuster, and London, Joseph, 1990.

OTHER PUBLICATIONS

Novels

Some Angry Angel: A Mid-Century Faerie Tale.   New York, McGraw Hill, 1960; London, Joseph, 1961.
A Talent for Loving; or, The Great Cowboy Race.   New York, McGraw Hill, 1961; London, Joseph, 1963.
Any God Will Do.   New York, Random House, 1964; London, Heinemann, 1967.
The Vertical Smile.   New York, Dial Press, 1971; London, Weidenfeld and Nicolson, 1972.
The Star-Spangled Crunch.   New York, Bantam, 1974.
Money Is Love.   New York, Dial Press, and London, Weidenfeld and Nicolson, 1975.
The Abandoned Woman.   New York, Dial Press, 1977; London, Hutchinson, 1978.
A Trembling upon Rome.   New York, Putnam, and London, Joseph, 1983.

Plays

Men of Distinction (produced New York, 1953).

Screenplays: *A Talent for Loving*, 1965; *The Summer Music*, 1969; *The Long Loud Silence*, 1969; *Prizzi's Honor*, with Janet Roach, 1985.

Other

And Then We Moved to Rossenarra; or, The Art of Emigrating. New York, Dial Press, 1973.
The Mexican Stove: A History of Mexican Food, with Wendy Bennett. New York, Doubleday, 1973.
!Olé Mole! Great Recipes in the Classic Mexican Tradition, with Wendy Condon. Dallas, Taylor, 1988.

*

Manuscript Collection: Mugar Memorial Library, Boston University.

*   *   *

No matter what genre Richard Condon chooses for his canvas, he brings to all his work a love for the complexities and dark crannies of motive and circumstance; even his minor characters have something to conceal.

A man of mordant wit, an absolutely fearless penchant for taking on sacred cows, and an immense preoccupation with detail, Condon has for over 25 years perplexed critics who berate him for not being a more conventional writer of thrillers, and who associate him with the term satirist more out of impatience than respect.

Fortunately, Condon's readers know better: they have come to expect a character like Raymond Shaw—the walking time-bomb of Condon's most famous thriller, *The Manchurian Candidate*—in every outing. Readers have also come to anticipate bizarre entanglements, even more Byzantine explanations, unexpected tensions, and denouements that go beyond but do not abuse our wildest expectations. Condon is the literary version of the psychiatrist in the *New Yorker* cartoon who tells his patient, "I'm afraid you're not paranoid. People really *are* out to get you." His novels all take on our worst communal fears and present us with scenarios even more dire than we suspected.

By focusing on such institutions as the U.S Army, the Central Intelligence Agency, the Kennedy family, the Mafia, the motion picture industry, the office of the American presidency, wine connoisseurs, the Papacy, the art world, scientists, and sexuality, Condon, with great moral tantivy, performs the satirist's art without apology or anesthesia. His plots often focus on elaborate capers—such as in *Arigato* or *Winter Kills*—but not in the who-done-it vein of, say, P.D James, or even in the why-it-was-done focus of Ross Macdonald. By giving us engaging characters or the promise of an interesting and new slant on an established institutio, Condon holds our interest, then pays off with a vision that is slightly more askew than his promise held.

Like other full-fledged satirists, Condon often appears to be saying that our values have been held in the balance and found wanting, largely because we are going along with the scheme instead of trying to get it called out.

In more recent books, Condon's sharpness of focus seems to have fallen, suggesting that he might take more time with his work before allowing it in print and turning to travel, cooking, or political review when the money runs short. *A Trembling upon Rome*, which deals with lust, greed, murder, and power, is a splendid example of Condon going at a historical hot potato. He could have done so with greater polish. *Prizzi's Honor* is a noble attempt to make the Mafia seem more interesting than it

really is. *Arigato*, a more conventional caper novel than Condon's usual, is memorable for truly antic and delightful characters, though marred by poor copy editing.

At his strongest, Richard Condon can deliver chilling reality and thoughtfulness to his off-beat, antic descriptions of the labyrinth of human connivance. When he is working on a muddy track, he still gives good value, an entertaining ride, and the hope of a better outing next time.

—Shelly Lowenkopf

———

CONNINGTON, J.J. Pseudonym for Alfred Walter Stewart. British. Born in 1880. Educated at the University of Glasgow; University of Marburg; University College, London, D.Sc. Married Jessie Lily Courts in 1916; one daughter. Mackay-Smith Scholar, 1901, 1851 Exhibition scholar, 1903–05, Carnegie Research Fellow, 1905–08, and Lecturer in Organic Chemistry, 1909–14, Queen's University, Belfast; Lecturer in Physical Chemistry and Radioactivity, University of Glasgow, 1914–19; Professor of Chemistry, 1919–44, and Dean of Faculties, Queen's University, Belfast. *Died 1 July 1947.*

CRIME PUBLICATIONS

Novels (series: Mark Brand; Sir Clinton Driffield; Superintendent Ross)

Death at Swaythling Court. London, Benn, and Boston, Little Brown, 1926.
The Dangerfield Talisman. London, Benn, 1926; Boston, Little Brown, 1927.
Murder in the Maze (Driffield). London, Benn, and Boston, Little Brown, 1927.
Tragedy at Ravensthorpe (Driffield). London, Benn, 1927; Boston, Little Brown, 1928.
The Case with Nine Solutions (Driffield). London, Gollancz, 1928; Boston, Little Brown, 1929.
Mystery at Lynden Sands (Driffield). London, Gollancz, and Boston, Little Brown, 1928.
Nemesis at Raynham Parva (Driffield). London, Gollancz, 1929; as *Grim Vengeance*, Boston, Little Brown, 1929.
The Eye in the Museum (Ross). London, Gollancz, 1929; Boston, Little Brown, 1930.
The Two Tickets Puzzle (Ross). London, Gollancz, 1930; as *The Two Ticket Puzzle*, Boston, Little Brown, 1930.
The Boat-House Riddle (Driffield). London, Gollancz, and Boston, Little Brown, 1931.
The Sweepstake Murders (Driffield). London, Hodder and Stoughton, 1931; Boston, Little Brown, 1932.
The Castleford Conundrum (Driffield). London, Hodder and Stoughton, and Boston, Little Brown, 1932.
Tom Tiddler's Island. London, Hodder and Stoughton, 1933; as *Gold Brick Island*, Boston, Little Brown, 1933.
The Ha-Ha Case (Driffield). London, Hodder and Stoughton, 1934; as *The Brandon Case*, Boston, Little Brown, 1934.
In Whose Dim Shadow (Driffield). London, Hodder and Stoughton, 1935; as *The Tau Cross Mystery*, Boston, Little Brown, 1935.
A Minor Operation (Driffield). London, Hodder and Stoughton, and Boston, Little Brown, 1937.

For Murder Will Speak (Driffield). London, Hodder and Stoughton, 1938; as *Murder Will Speak*, Boston, Little Brown, 1938.
Truth Comes Limping (Driffield). London, Hodder and Stoughton, and Boston, Little Brown, 1938.
The Counsellor (Brand). London, Hodder and Stoughton, and Boston, Little Brown, 1939.
The Four Defences (Brand). London, Hodder and Stoughton, and Boston, Little Brown, 1940.
The Twenty-One Clues (Driffield). London, Hodder and Stoughton, and Boston, Little Brown, 1941.
No Past Is Dead (Driffield). London, Hodder and Stoughton, and Boston, Little Brown, 1942.
Jack-in-the-Box (Driffield). London, Hodder and Stoughton, and Boston, Little Brown, 1944.
Common Sense Is All You Need (Driffield). London, Hodder and Stoughton, 1947.

Uncollected Short Stories

"Before Insulin," in *Fifty Masterpieces of Mystery*. London, Odhams Press, 1935.
"A Criminologist's Bookshelf," in *Detective Medley*, edited by John Rhode. London, Hutchinson, 1939.
"The Thinking Machine," in *My Best Mystery Story*. London, Faber, 1939.

OTHER PUBLICATIONS

Novels

Nordenholt's Millions. London, Constable, 1923.
Almighty Gold. London, Constable, 1924.

Other as A.W Stewart

Stereochemistry. London, Longman, 1907.
Recent Advances in Organic Chemistry. London, Longman, 1908.
Recent Advances in Physical and Inorganic Chemistry. London, Longman, 1909.
A Manual of Practical Chemistry for Public Health Students. London, Bale and Danielsson, 1913.
Chemistry and Its Borderland. London, Longman, 1914.
Some Physico-Chemical Themes. London, Longman, 1922.
Alias J.J. Connington (essays). London, Hollis and Carter, 1947.

*   *   *

J.J. Connington possessed the British flavour of Freeman Wills Crofts and others, the same rather humourless approach, the same pedantic and sometimes stilted use of language, and the same ingenuity of murder methods and alibis. He also displayed certain characteristics of his own—his scientific background was often put to good use, including the medical aspects of crime such as poisons and blood tests, and his occasional whiff of the occult was achieved competently and unsensationally. He was inclined to introduce more physical action than the cerebral exponents of the Crofts school, including some good chases, as in *The Eye in the Museum*.

Like those of Crofts, Connington's first books contained no series detective. *Death at Swaythling Court* was not an auspicious start to his career, but it is possible to muster a certain affection for his second, *The Dangerfield Talisman*. Here Connington managed the difficult task of producing an exciting and intellectually satisfying detective novel without a real detective, and without even a murder. The disappearance of a family heirloom, with its dark history of closely guarded secret, is combined with a chess problem against the well-worn background of a country house-party to present a readable story with little to complain about.

In spite of some competent non-series novels during his career, one tends to associate Connington (like so many other writers) with his series characters. Together, Chief Constable Sir Clinton Driffield and Squire Wendover investigated a considerable number of cases. Although Connington used another series character, Mark Brand ("The Counsellor"), it is for the Driffield/Wendover books that historians of the genre tend to remember him. By giving these two men a somewhat uneasy relationship, Connington hit upon a good idea. It was no Holmes/Watson combination, for it is often unclear as to who is the detective and who is playing second fiddle. The two frequently disagree, but are thrown together time after time by the fact that murders and strange happenings abound in the county of which Wendover is principal landlord and Driffield is top policeman. Of the many Driffield/Wendover cases, it is possible to single out for special commendation *Murder in the Maze*, *The Boat-House Riddle*, *The Sweepstake Murders* (perhaps the best), and *A Minor Operation*. Of the non-series novels, one must particularly mention again *The Eye in the Museum;* the title refers to a camera obscura, and this book was quoted for some time as the only appearance of this type of equipment in detective fiction. (This claim, incidentally, has now been invalidated by at least one book, Janet Caird's *Murder Reflected*.)

It is unaccountable that Connington has not achieved the place in the genre's history afforded to similar writers such as Crofts. He told a good tale, broke many an "unbreakable" alibi, displayed the customary plot-before-characterisation priority of his contemporaries, conveyed the atmosphere of classy county life most acceptably, and laced his crime with ballistics, footprints, maps of the scene, railway timetables in a sometimes ingenious but always meticulous manner. He just didn't have the benefit of Croft's Inspector French.

—Melvyn Barnes

———

CONRAD, Brenda. *See* **FORD, Leslie.**

———

CONROY, Al. *See* **ALBERT, Marvin.**

———

CONROY, Albert. *See* **ALBERT, Marvin.**

———

CONSTANTINE, K.C. (a pseudonym). American. Agent: Bertha Klausner, 71 Park Avenue, New York, New York 10016, U.S.A.

CRIME PUBLICATIONS

Novels (series: Mario Balzic in all books)

The Rocksburg Railroad Murders. New York, Saturday Review Press, 1972; London, Coronet, 1989.
The Man Who Liked to Look at Himself. New York, Saturday Review Press, 1973; London, Hodder and Stoughton, 1986.
The Blank Page. New York, Saturday Review Press, 1974.
A Fix Like This. New York, Saturday Review Press, 1975.
The Man Who Liked Slow Tomatoes. Boston, Godine, 1982.
Always a Body to Trade. Boston, Godine, 1983; London, Hodder and Stoughton, 1985.
Upon Some Midnights Clear. Boston, Godine, 1985; London, Hodder and Stoughton, 1986.
Joey's Case. New York, Mysterious Press, and London, Hodder and Stoughton, 1988.
Sunshine Enemies. New York, Mysterious Press, and London, Hodder and Stoughton, 1990.

* * *

Since 1972, K. C. Constantine has published nine novels featuring Mario Balzic, police chief of Rocksburg, a fictional western Pennsylvania town. The writers of many of the most popular police procedurals (McBain, Wambaugh, and Linington/Shannon) have used urban settings, but some notable work has also been done by writers like Hillary Waugh, John Holbrook (Jack) Vance and now K.C. Constantine, whose protagonists work in rural or small-town settings. Like Simenon's Maigret, Balzic achieves his successes more through his sensitivity to the ways people think and feel than through routine police work and laboratory procedures. Balzic is overweight, drinks too much, and has trouble controlling his temper and his tongue, but this small-town policeman is a match for the state investigators who occasionally intrude into his territory, and his eye for a significant movement or gesture seems to take us into the dark and troubled interior of his world.

The novels have increasingly become novels of place and character. Although *The Man Who Liked Slow Tomatoes* is identified as "A Mario Balzic Mystery," it is, in reality, the study of the effect on the lives of one family of the loss of mining and industrial jobs in the area, and it coincides with one of Balzic's most difficult professional periods. Its deeply pessimistic tone records poignantly the disturbances in the lives of people whose jobs have disappeared and who see little hope of climbing out of the emotional and financial pit into which they have fallen.

Even when, in *Joey's Case*, Constantine appears to be involving Balzic in a tortuous investigation, Balzic's personal problems are also in the foreground. By the end of the novel, the investigation has been resolved off-stage and the final chapter in the case of Joey Castelucci is related by Balzic in a scene where the crucial issue is the long-delayed discussion of the relationship between Balzic and his wife. In the latest book, *Sunshine Enemies*, a brutal murder is subordinate to Balzic's attempt to come to terms with his mother's sudden death.

Almost two decades after the publication of *The Rocksburg Railroad Murders*, Constantine has achieved considerable critical success. A nomination by the Mystery Writers of America for their Edgar Allan Poe award in 1989 is testimony to his recognition by his peers, but as a self-conducted interview reveals (in a new edition of *The Man Who Liked to Look at Himself* [Godine, 1984]), he clearly considers himself to be primarily a writer of novels of character. He is also the creator

of one of the most sustained, accomplished studies of regional America in recent fiction.

—Walter Albert

————

COOK, Robin. *See* **RAYMOND, Derek.**

————

COOKE, M.E. *See* **CREASEY, John.**

————

COOMBS, Murdo. *See* **DAVIS, Frederick C.**

————

COOPER, Brian (Newman). British. Born in Stockport, Cheshire, 15 September 1919. Educated at Jesus College, Cambridge, M.A. 1945, Dip. Ed. 1947. Served in the Bedfordshire and Hertfordshire Regiment, 1940–42, and in the Intelligence Corps, 1942–45. Married Ellen Martin in 1942; one son and one daughter. History assistant, County Grammar School, Bromley, Kent, 1947–48; senior history master, Selective Central School, Shirebrook, Derbyshire, 1948–55, and Bolsover School, Derbyshire, 1955–79. Address: 43 Parkland Close, Southlands, Mansfield, Nottinghamshire NG18 4PP, England.

CRIME PUBLICATIONS

Novels

Where the Fresh Grass Grows. London, Heinemann, 1955; as *Maria*, New York, Vanguard Press, 1956.
A Path to the Bridge. London, Heinemann, 1958; as *Giselle*, New York, Vanguard Press, 1958.
The Van Langeren Girl. London, Heinemann, and New York, Vanguard Press, 1960.
A Touch of Thunder. London, Heinemann, 1961; New York, Vanguard Press, 1962.
A Time to Retreat. London, Heinemann, and New York, Vanguard Press, 1963.
Genesis 38. London, Heinemann, 1965; as *The Murder of Mary Steers*, New York, Vanguard Press, 1966.
A Mission for Betty Smith. London, Heinemann, 1967; as *Monsoon Murder*, New York, Vanguard Press, 1968.
Messiter's Dream. London, Hale, 1990.

OTHER PUBLICATIONS

Other

Transformation of a Valley: The Derbyshire Derwent, photographs by Neville Cooper. London, Heinemann, 1983.

*

Brian Cooper comments:

I am, purely and simply, a teller of stories, and, despite the deeper meanings that reviewers persistently find in my work, I prefer that my novels should be regarded as nothing more than well-told tales. After 15 years of research and writing on historical subjects, I have now returned to novels of suspense. *Messiter's Dream*, the story of a man who cherished a dream that turned into a nightmare, is the first of what I hope will be a new clutch of tales.

*   *   *

Brian Cooper has written novels of suspense that have that special ring of authenticity about them. In fact, some readers might pick up a book such as *Genesis 38* and, without reading the author's note, perceive it to be true fact. Cooper in other cases has based his fiction on fact, but these novels seem limited in scope. The court of inquiry in *A Time to Retreat*, for instance, is in essence the entire book. But this is not to say that Cooper has a tendency to dawdle in his approach. Cooper has a crisp, fast-paced delivery; the details unfold quickly. His forte is in his great talent for dialogue. He has that special ability to have his characters talk in real and believable terms. His descriptive abilities do not quite match up to the dialogue. Also missing in many of his books is the one central character that we can identify with. In solving the puzzle, we must meet all involved and become acquainted with their part in the scheme of things.

Cooper's books are well thought out and excellently written. He finds a puzzle that must be unraveled and then lets the reader join in as he unwinds it from the beginning, through court martial or narrative. First, the facts of what happened, and then the post mortem. Cooper does not write what can be called a fast-paced thriller, but indeed a fictional documentary. He can be very sensitive at times to the subtleties of the circumstances surrounding the basic story line, an effective approach. *The New York Times* Sunday Magazine said: "one thinks of thrillers as rushing like runners doing a hundred yard race. Mr. Cooper is a miler and runs a memorable race." To read Brian Cooper is to be curious: to hear of something happening, and wonder why.

—Don Cole

COPPER, Basil. British. Born in 1924. Educated at a grammar school and a private commercial college. Married to Annie Renée Guerin. Journalist for 30 years, including 14 years as news editor with a Kent county newspaper. Chairman, Crime Writers Association, 1981–82. Address: Stockdoves, South Park, Sevenoaks, Kent TN13 1EN, England.

CRIME PUBLICATIONS

Novels (series: Mike Faraday in all books)

The Dark Mirror. London, Hale, 1966.
Night Frost. London, Hale, 1966.
No Flowers for the General. London, Hale, 1967.
Scratch on the Dark. London, Hale, 1967.
Die Now, Live Later. London, Hale, 1968.
Don't Bleed on Me. London, Hale, 1968.
The Marble Orchard. London, Hale, 1969.

Dead File. London, Hale, 1970.
No Letters from the Grave. London, Hale, 1971.
The Big Chill. London, Hale, 1972.
Strong-Arm. London, Hale, 1972.
A Great Year for Dying. London, Hale, 1973.
Shock-Wave. London, Hale, 1973.
The Breaking Point. London, Hale, 1973.
A Voice from the Dead. London, Hale, 1974.
Feedback. London, Hale, 1974.
Ricochet. London, Hale, 1974.
The High Wall. London, Hale, 1975.
Impact. London, Hale, 1975.
A Good Place to Die. London, Hale, 1975.
The Lonely Place. London, Hale, 1976.
Crack in the Sidewalk. London, Hale, 1976.
Tight Corner. London, Hale, 1976.
The Year of the Dragon. London, Hale, 1977.
Death Squad. London, Hale, 1977.
Murder One. London, Hale, 1978.
A Quiet Room in Hell. London, Hale, 1979.
The Big Rip-Off. London, Hale, 1979.
The Caligari Complex. London, Hale, 1980.
Flip-Side. London, Hale, 1980.
The Long Rest. London, Hale, 1981.
The Empty Silence. London, Hale, 1981.
Dark Entry. London, Hale, 1981.
Hang Loose. London, Hale, 1982.
Shoot-Out. London, Hale, 1982.
The Far Horizon. London, Hale, 1982.
Trigger-Man. London, Hale, 1983.
Pressure-Point. London, Hale, 1983.
Hard Contract. London, Hale, 1983.
The Narrow Corner. London, Hale, 1983.
The Hook. London, Hale, 1984.
You Only Die Once. London, Hale, 1984.
Tuxedo Park. London, Hale, 1985.
The Far Side of Fear. London, Hale, 1985.
Snow-Job. London, Hale, 1986.
Jet-Lag. London, Hale, 1986.
Blood on the Moon. London, Hale, 1986.
Heavy Iron. London, Hale, 1987.
Turn Down an Empty Glass. London, Hale, 1987.
Bad Scene. London, Hale, 1987.
House-Dick. London, Hale, 1988.
Print-Out. London, Hale, 1988.

Short Stories (series: Solar Pons)

The Dossier of Solar Pons. Los Angeles, Pinnacle, 1979.
The Further Adventure of Solar Pons. Los Angeles, Pinnacle, 1979.
The Secret Files of Solar Pons. Los Angeles, Pinnacle, 1979.
Some Uncollected Cases of Solar Pons. Los Angeles, Pinnacle, 1980.

OTHER PUBLICATIONS

Novels

The Phantom. New York, Avon, 1972.
The Phantom and the Scorpia Menace. New York, Avon, 1972.
The Phantom and the Slave Market of Mucar. New York, Avon, 1972.
The Great White Space. London, Hale, 1974; New York, St. Martin's Press, 1975.

The Curse of the Fleers. London, Harwood Smart, 1976; New York, St. Martin's Press, 1977.

Necropolis. Sauk City, Wisconsin, Arkham House, 1980; London, Sphere, 1981.

The House of the Wolf. Sauk City, Wisconsin, Arkham House, 1983.

Into the Silence. London, Sphere, 1983.

Short Stories

Not after Nightfall. London, New English Library, 1967.

From Evil's Pillow. Sauk City, Wisconsin, Arkham House, 1973.

When Footsteps Echo: Tales of Terror and the Unknown. London, Hale, and New York, St. Martin's Press, 1975.

And Afterward, the Dark: Seven Tales. Sauk City, Wisconsin, Arkham House, 1977.

Here Be Daemons: Tales of Horror and the Uneasy. London, Hale, and New York, St. Martin's Press, 1978.

Voices of Doom. London, Hale, and New York, St. Martin's Press, 1980.

Other

The Vampire: In Legend, Fact, and Art. London, Hale 1973; Secaucus, New Jersey, Citadel Press, 1974.

The Werewolf: In Legend, Fact, and Art. London, Hale, and New York, St. Martin's Press, 1977.

*

Basil Copper comments:

My most important work lies in the macabre and fantasy fields, but, so far as crime and mystery are concerned, my Mike Faraday novels, set in Los Angeles, may be considered *an hommage* to Ring Lardner, Dashiell Hammett, Raymond Chandler, and the hard-boiled school of thriller writing.

Among those things that have given me most pleasure in recent years is my editing of the Solar Pons series by the late August Derleth, and in my own series I have combined the traditional detective form pioneered by Poe and Conan Doyle with the atmospheric and macabre themes that lie closest to my heart.

*   *   *

Although best known for writing in the general area of fantasy, occult, and macabre, in which apart from fiction he has produced some serious studies of legends such as Dracula, Basil Copper's contribution to crime and mystery writing is popular and well defined. His series character, the Los Angeles investigator Mike Faraday, is in the private-detective tradition of crime fiction and the style of the Faraday novels reflects what Copper has called the "hard-boiled school of thriller writing" which the cognoscenti will associate with Raymond Chandler, whose creation, the tough, romantic, and honourable Marlowe, might have provided a model for Faraday.

Copper's skilful evocation of place, the city and environs of Los Angeles, is an effective device. Faraday's violent and often sleazy occupation takes him through the burger bars, bistros, hotels, and lush apartments of an urban milieu rich in its own contrasts: here society is colourful, brutal, and indifferent, its violence—apparently incalculable and often anonymous—in stark contrast with the brilliant California sunlight. Beyond all this, as the foil which renders human evil even darker and more vicious, is the magnificent natural scenery: harbour, coastline, and lush hinterland. Through this elemental contrast Copper establishes a constant but unobtrusive moral perspective through which Faraday reports his adventures.

As with many series the Faraday novels tend to have an evenness of quality, style, and action which blurs distinctions between them. In part this reflects Copper's accomplished control of the formula: the common narrator, setting, and violent happenings. At the same time it is this reliability which is part of the appeal the series has for its *habitué.* So, for example, however varied in detail, there will be desirable women who will sway Faraday's romantic disposition and add interest to the development of the story without detraction from its dramatic conclusion. In this too there is consistency: the endings are dramatic, often with a surprise twist to events which reflects the brilliance of Faraday's intuitions. Finally, it is common for the loose ends to be drawn together in a quiet closure back in Faraday's office as emotional calm is once more restored.

The office milieu is important. Its dingy surroundings form a habitat which, as with Faraday's five-year-old powder-blue Buick, is an extension of his personality. The cobwebs and dust remind us that he is dominated neither by avarice nor domestic pride. Stella, his cool, elegant, but elusive secretary, while she gives continuity and assistance, reminds us of Faraday's worth: she does not succumb to his sex appeal but remains as the potential serious romantic attatchment who is in the background, the person to whom he returns at the end of each exploit. In short, the office with its routine, Stella's incomparable coffee and legs, is Faraday's proximate domestic base. It emphasises human rather than material qualities and images Faraday's essential values.

Of course it is Faraday himself who is the central and unifying character through the series. By making him both narrator and protagonist Copper defines his character through his speech habits, perceptions, and general style of reporting. For example Faraday's clichés—his shoes are invariably the "number nines" and the effect of a hitched skirt is consistently to have "shot my morale to hell and back"—define his masculinity, worldliness, and even something of his toughness and cynicism. Yet his wry humour, courage, honesty, and perception of beauty establishes him as a very positive "hero" in his dangerous profession. His perseverance in adversity, irrespective of financial gain and despite a context where most are seen to be corruptible, gives him a superior moral stature in keeping with his physical appearance. There is little evidence of his intellectual talents, but a surprise, which is idiosyncratic enough to be convincing, is Faraday's fondness for Palgrave's Golden Treasury and his penchant for quoting Herrick: a nice touch which cements Faraday as a character and a humanist.

—Trevor James

CORRIS, Peter. Australian. Born in Stanwell, Victoria, 8 May 1942. Educated at Melbourne High School; University of Melbourne, Parkville, Victoria; Monash University, Clayton, Victoria; Australian National University, Canberra; 1964–74. Literary editor, *National Times,* 1978–80. Since 1975 freelance writer and journalist. Agent: Rosemary Creswell Literary Agency, P.O. Box 5, Balmain, New South Wales 2041, Australia.

CRIME PUBLICATIONS

Novels (series: Richard Browning; Ray Crawley; Cliff Hardy)

The Dying Trade (Hardy).   New York, McGraw Hill, 1980; Sydney, Pan, 1982.
White Meat (Hardy).   Sydney, Pan, 1981; New York, Fawcett, 1986.
The Marvellous Boy (Hardy).   Sydney, Pan, 1982; New York, Fawcett, 1986.
The Empty Beach (Hardy).   Sydney, Allen and Unwin, 1983; London, Unwin, 1985; New York, Fawcett, 1986.
Make Me Rich (Hardy).   Sydney, Allen and Unwin, and London, Unwin, 1985; New York, Fawcett, 1987.
Pokerface (Crawley).   London, Penguin, 1985.
Deal Me Out (Hardy).   Sydney, Allen and Unwin, and London, Unwin, 1986; New York, Fawcett, 1988.
The Greenwich Apartments (Hardy).   Sydney, Allen and Unwin, 1986; London, Unwin, and New York, Fawcett, 1988.
The January Zone (Hardy).   Sydney, Allen and Unwin, 1987; London, Unwin Hyman, and New York, Fawcett, 1988.
Box Office Browning.   New York, Viking, 1987; London, Penguin, 1988.
Beverly Hills Browning.   London, Penguin, 1987.
The Baltic Business (Crawley).   London, Penguin, 1988.
The Kimberley Killing.   London, Penguin, 1988.
Browning Takes Off.   London, Penguin, 1989.
O'Fear (Hardy).   Sydney, Transworld, 1990.
The Cargo Club (Crawley).   London, Penguin, 1990.

Short Stories

Heroin Annie and Other Cliff Hardy Stories.   Sydney, Allen and Unwin, 1984; London, Unwin, 1985; New York, Fawcett, 1987.
The Big Drop and Other Cliff Hardy Stories.   Sydney, Allen and Unwin, 1985; London, Unwin, 1986; New York, Fawcett, 1988.
Man in the Shadows.   Sydney, Allen and Unwin, 1988; London, Unwin, 1989.

OTHER PUBLICATIONS

Novels

The Winning Side.   Sydney, Allen and Unwin, and London, Unwin, 1984.
The Gulliver Fortune.   Sydney, Transworld, 1989; New York, Bantam, 1990.

Plays

Radio Plays: *The Empty Beach* (from his own novel), 1983; *The Greenwich Apartments* (from his own novel), 1986; *O'Fear* (from his own novel), 1990.

Television Plays: *Off Mike*, 1981; *Pokerface*, with Bill Garner (from the novel by Corris), 1986.

Other

Aborigines and Europeans in Western Victoria.   Canberra, Australian Institute of Aborigine Studies, 1968.
Passage, Port and Plantation: A History of Solomon Islands Labour Migrations 1870–1914.   Carlton, Melbourne University Press, 1973.

Lords of the Ring (on boxing).   Camperdown, New South Wales, Cassell, 1980.
Lightning Meets the West Wind: The Malaita Massacre 1927, with Roger M. Keesing.   Melbourne, Oxford University Press, 1980.
The Australian Book of Quizzes, with Jean Bedford.   Sydney, Allen and Unwin, 1983.
The Australian Kid's Book of Brainteasers and Puzzles.   North Ryde, New South Wales, Angus and Robertson, 1984.
The Australian Family Quiz Book.   North Ryde, New South Wales, Angus and Robertson, 1985.

Editor, *The South-Sea Islanders and the Queensland Labour Trade*, by William T. Waun.   Canberra, Australian National University Press, 1973.
Editor, with Jim Allen, *The Journal of John Sweatman: A Nineteenth Century Surveying Voyage in North Australia and Torres Strait*.   St. Lucia, University of Queensland Press, 1977.
Editor, *The Cruise of the Helena*, by Joseph Dalgarno Melvin.   Melbourne, Hawthorn Press, 1977.

* * *

Although trained as a historian (and the author of a fine historical saga, *The Gulliver Fortune*, as well as a social history of prizefighting in Australia), Peter Corris stands out amongst his sleuthing contemporaries as one of the finest prose painters of the modern city. Throughout his series of novels featuring private eye for hire Cliff Hardy, the steamy mean streets of Sydney emerge as an unforgettable locale, blowsy, rough, vital, and corrupt, but still sprawling, indolent and beautiful in the way the Los Angeles of yesteryear was in the Lew Archer books of Ross McDonald or Chandler's Philip Marlowe tales.

In his beat-up leather jacket and jeans, with a clientele exclusively gained amongst the rich and the desperate, Corris's Cliff Hardy is an eponymous P.I. in the classic American mould; tight, tough, wise but never in danger of losing his humanity. Corris's other principal characters, Ray Crawley (who only really comes into his own in *The Cargo Club*) and Richard Browning, offer further variations on the theme, their murky adventures primarily highlighted by an assured sense of place that is meticulous and revealing, while also remaining mercifully unobtrusive.

One of the more interesting aspects of Corris's novels is how well he has managed to transplant the archetypal American/ California P.I. genre to a foreign context without undue jarring effect (one easily recalls many embarrassing instances of mean streets scenarios travelling, badly, to, say the north of England). In this respect, Corris and Cliff Hardy can be placed in the more relaxed second-generation noir MacDonald (John D. and Ross) tradition, rather than in the Hammett stream, and with a strong sense of humour to boot, which can sometimes go slightly over the top, as in *O'Fear* with its somewhat caricatural archvillain.

The best of the Cliff Hardy novels possibly remains *The Empty Beach* which was the object of an interesting movie adaptation featuring Australian actor Bryan Brown as the rugged detective whose offices are sited in Sydney's notorious King's Cross district.

The crime novels of Corris are quality entertainment, tight, professional without being slick. Hardy, as well as being tough and wise, is also determined and resilient. Amid the mayhem, the footslogging, the action, and the beatings, the twists and turns of ingenious plots, Corris offers nightmarishly grim social descriptions of modern Australia, and particularly Sydney, with wry asides and the right amount of whimsy. He is one of the more exemplary genre practitioners we have today.

—Maxim Jakubowski

———

CORY, Desmond. Pseudonym for Shaun Lloyd McCarthy; also writes as Theo Callas. British. Born in Lancing, Sussex, 16 February 1928. Educated at Steyning Grammar School, Sussex, 1938–44; St. Peter's College, Oxford, 1948–51, B.A. (honours) in English 1951, M.A. 1960; University of Wales, Cardiff, Ph.D. 1976. Served in the 45 Commando Unit, Royal Marines, 1944–48. Married Blanca Rosa Poyatos in 1956; four sons. Freelance journalist and translator in Europe, 1951–54; language teacher in Spain and Sweden, 1954–60; Lecturer, University of Wales Institute of Science and Technology, Cardiff, 1960–77; Lecturer, University of Qatar, Doha, Arabian Gulf, 1977–80; Associate Professor of English, University of Bahrain, 1980–85; Associate Professor of English, University of Sanaa, 1985–87; Adviser to Ministry of Education, Sultanate of Oman, 1987–90. Since 1990, Associate Professor of English, Eastern Mediterranean University, Famagusta, Cyprus. Agent: Macmillan Ltd., 4 Little Essex Street, London WC2R 3LF, England. Address: c/o Lloyds Bank, Penarth, South Glamorgan, Wales.

CRIME PUBLICATIONS

Novels (series: Mr. Dee; Johnny Fedora; Lindy Grey; Mr. Pilgrim)

Secret Ministry (Fedora). London, Muller, 1951; as *The Nazi Assassins*, New York, Award, 1970.
Begin, Murderer! (Grey). London, Muller, 1951.
This Traitor, Death (Fedora). London, Muller, 1952; as *The Gestapo File*, New York, Award, 1971.
This Is Jezebel (Grey). London, Muller, 1952.
Dead Man Falling (Fedora). London, Muller, 1953; as *The Hitler Diamonds*, New York, Award, 1979.
Lady Lost (Grey). London, Muller, 1953.
Intrigue (Fedora). London, Muller, 1954; as *Trieste*, New York, Award, 1968.
The Shaken Leaf (Grey). London, Muller, 1955.
Height of Day (Fedora). London, Muller, 1955; as *Dead Men Alive*, New York, Award, 1969.
City of Kites (as Theo Callas). London, Muller, 1955; New York, Walker, 1964.
The Phoenix Sings. London, Muller, 1955.
High Requiem (Fedora). London, Muller, 1956; New York, Award, 1969.
Johnny Goes North (Fedora). London, Muller, 1956; as *The Swastika Hunt*, New York, Award, 1969.
Pilgrim at the Gate. London, Muller, 1957; New York, Washburn, 1958.
Johnny Goes East (Fedora). London, Muller, 1958; as *Mountainhead*, London, New English Library, 1966; New York, Award, 1968.
Johnny Goes West (Fedora). London, Muller, 1959; New York, Walker, 1967.
Johnny Goes South (Fedora). London, Muller, 1959; New York, Walker, 1964; as *Overload*, London, New English Library, 1964.

Pilgrim on the Island. London, Muller, 1959; New York, Walker, 1961.
The Head (Fedora). London, Muller, 1960.
Stranglehold (Dee). London, Muller, 1961.
Undertow (Fedora). London, Muller, 1962; New York, Walker, 1963.
Hammerhead (Fedora). London, Muller, 1963; as *Shockwave*, New York, Walker, 1964; London, New English Library, 1966.
The Name of the Game (Dee). London, Muller, 1964.
Deadfall. London, Muller, and New York, Walker, 1965.
Feramontov (Fedora). London, Muller, and New York, Walker, 1966.
Timelock (Fedora). London, Muller, and New York, Walker, 1967.
The Night Hawk. London, Hodder and Stoughton, and New York, Walker, 1969.
Sunburst (Fedora). London, Hodder and Stoughton, and New York, Walker, 1971.
Take My Drum to England. London, Hodder and Stoughton, 1971; as *Even If You Run*, New York, Doubleday, 1972.
A Bit of a Shunt up the River. New York, Doubleday, 1974.
The Circe Complex. London, Macmillan, and New York, Doubleday, 1975.
Bennett. London, Macmillan, and New York, Doubleday, 1977.

Uncollected Short Stories

"Uncontrolled Goods," in *London Mystery Magazine*, October—November 1951.
"The Crime of Prince Milo," in *Winter's Crimes 7*, edited by George Hardinge. London, Macmillan, 1975.
"The Story of Stumblebum, The Wizard," in *Winter's Crimes 8*, edited by George Hardinge. London, Macmillan, 1976.
"The Song of Fariq," in *Mystery Guild Anthology*, edited by John Waite. London, Constable, 1980.

OTHER PUBLICATIONS

Novel

Lucky Ham (as Shaun McCarthy). London, Macmillan, 1977.

Plays

Screenplay: *England Made Me*, with Peter Duffell, 1973.

Radio Play: *Orbit One*, 1961.

Other

Ann and Peter in Southern Spain (for children; as Theo Callas). London, Muller, 1959.
Jones on the Belgrade Express (for children). London, Muller, 1960.

*

Bibliography: *The Cold War File* by Andy East, Metuchen, New Jersey, Scarecrow Press, 1983.

Manuscript Collection: Mugar Memorial Library, Boston University.

Critical Study: "Variations on a Theme by Aeschylus: Desmond Cory and Emyr Humphreys" by Vernon Lloyd, in *Anglo-Welsh Review 73* (Tenby), Spring 1983.

Desmond Cory comments:

I published my first novel in 1951. I was then 23. My earliest ambition was to write the kind of books I most enjoyed reading. I did this for quite a few years, and they were very good years, because other (and better) writers were doing the same thing and I could feel I was taking part in a splendid post-war spree. We spy-writers gave pleasure to millions of people, and while it lasted it was all the greatest of fun. But then Fleming took our small success beyond all reasonable measure and our carnival floats were replaced by the noisy band-wagons of the mass media.

For the past ten years or so the questions for me, as for many others, have been What comes next? Which way should it go? Toward more documentary realism? Or towards more imaginative fantasy? Back to detective-story-style ingenuity? Or maybe comedy? Or political satire? You can find all these things in the vintage-years secret agent story, and it's hard to explain why the problem is so difficult to solve. It is easy enough to convince oneself of the rightness of any particular solution—but good stories aren't written out of that kind of a conviction, and any number of clever bad books exist to prove it.

So since 1970 I've probed this way and that, trying to carry along enough readers with me to make the process worth their while as well as worth mine. It's exciting, but in a different way. In a sense, every experienced writer builds books out of the books that he has written before, moving them effortfully towards the books that he didn't write. In my case it's a slow, slow business.

*   *   *

Shaun McCarthy, whose thrillers are written under the name Desmond Cory, is a prolific and versatile stylist. For over 25 years Cory has experimented with various narrative techniques. His broad range of knowledge and his inventiveness have also led him to write several types of suspense fiction—espionage, detective, and crime novels with an emphasis on psychological portraits of the characters. Skillful at creating atmosphere, he frequently uses Spain, a country he knows well, as a setting for his tales.

In five books called the "Feramontov quintet"—*Undertow, Hammerhead, Feramontov, Timelock,* and *Sunburst*—Cory matches the British agent Johnny Fedora, hero of earlier adventures, against Feramontov, formerly a Soviet agent. Feramontov is now a renegade, and all the more dangerous. A worthy opponent, Fedora's arch-enemy is intellectually gifted, physically powerful and a creative genius who manipulates people and events like moves on a chessboard. Fedora and Laura Alonso, a beautiful Spanish agent, make time for interludes of passionate love-making. Political intrigue and corruption do not bring nuclear annihilation—only horrible deaths, often preceded by all-too-well described scenes of sadism and torture. The action is complicated, but well told.

Another political tale set in Spain is *Take My Drum to England*, in which a young Englishman gets involved with aging Spanish revolutionaries. An author's note at the end of the book, warning readers attempting to detonate gelignite by means of the telephone (because "I don't have all that many readers I can spare"), is disarming. The atmosphere is good, but perhaps the author's talent is wasted on what is rather a sordid little story after all. *Deadfall*, also set in Spain, examines the psychology of a jewel thief, Michael Jeye, an acrobatic burglar working with a Spanish couple. Jeye falls in love with the young wife and learns that her husband, an elderly homosexual, is also her father. True love is as elusive as a fortune in jewels.

Cory has an impressive command of psychiatric theory and jargon. In one of his best novels, *A Bit of a Shunt up the River*, Bony Wright, an escaped killer, is called by the prison psychiatrist an "affective schizoid sociopath," and we are told that "Bony thought that he himself was perfectly normal and that the psychiatrist was a bearded weirdie who couldn't have told him breakfast time from Thursday." Bony is matched against Tracy, a former racing driver, in a superb auto chase. Depth of character and Cory's fine wit set this tale far above the average suspense story. *The Circe Complex* is also excellent, both a thoroughly good tale and a satire of psychology and psychiatry. A hapless prison psychologist, beguiled by the wife of a patient (she also ensnares an Irish terrorist and a policeman), finds himself in prison for the same crimes committed by his former patient. He writes a scientific paper, complete with footnotes, describing the "Circe complex."

Bennett, a book within a book, is sophisticated and clever but may be too much of a literary game to entertain most crime fiction fans. Low-key, amusing, and very *nouveau roman*, it should be compared with the works of Alain Robbe-Grillet. One wonders why *Bennett* was not published under the author's own name, since he published *Lucky Ham* as Shaun McCarthy. *Lucky Ham* is a literary spoof, a brilliant take-off on practically everybody—Shakespeare, Kingsley Amis, Lévi-Strauss, Joyce, Conrad, Beckett, and Sir Thomas Malory, to name a few. The hero Hamilton Biggs, called Hamlet or Ham for short, is called home from his anthropological researches in South America when his father, the president of an Oxford college, is murdered by his uncle who then married his mother. A parody of *Hamlet* which goes on for 217 pages is scarcely to be imagined, but McCarthy interweaves pastiches of the classics with shots at contemporaries, and brings it off.

Shaun McCarthy/Desmond Cory has enormous talent and an especially keen sense of humor. Readers who do not yet know his works will do well to read them.

—Mary Helen Becker

———

COULTER, Stephen. Also writes as James Mayo. British. Born in 1914. Educated in England and France. Served in the Royal Navy Intelligence during World War II. Newspaper reporter in British home counties; joined Reuters as Parliamentary staff correspondent in 1937; staff correspondent for Kemsley Newspapers, Paris, 1945–65. Address: c/o Constable, and Company Ltd., 10 Orange Street, London WC2H 7EG, England.

CRIME PUBLICATIONS

Novels

The Loved Enemy. London, Deutsch, 1962.
Threshold. London, Heinemann, and New York, Morrow, 1964.
Offshore! London, Heinemann, 1965; New York, Morrow, 1966.
A Stranger Called the Blues. London, Heinemann, 1968; as *Players in a Dark Game*, New York, Morrow, 1968; as *Death in the Sun*, London, Pan, 1970.

Embassy. London, Heinemann, and New York, Coward McCann, 1969.
An Account to Render. London, Heinemann, 1970.
The Soyuz Affair. London, Hart Davis, 1977.
Blood-Tie. London, Constable, 1988.

Novels as James Mayo (series: Charles Hood)

The Quickness of the Hand. London, Deutsch, 1952.
Rebound. London, Heinemann, 1961.
A Season of Nerves. London, Heinemann, 1962.
Hammerhead (Hood). London, Heinemann, and New York, Morrow, 1964.
Let Sleeping Girls Lie (Hood). London, Heinemann, 1965; New York, Morrow, 1966.
Shamelady (Hood). London, Heinemann, and New York, Morrow, 1966.
Once in a Lifetime (Hood). London, Heinemann, 1968; as *Sergeant Death*, New York, Morrow, 1968.
The Man above Suspicion (Hood). London, Heinemann, 1969.
Asking for It (Hood). London, Heinemann, 1971.

OTHER PUBLICATIONS

Novels

Damned Shall Be Desire: The Loves of Guy de Maupassant. London, Cape, 1958; New York, Doubleday, 1959.
The Devil Inside: A Novel of Dostoevsky's Life. London, Cape, and New York, Doubleday, 1960.

Other

The Chateau. New York, Simon and Schuster, and London, Heinemann, 1974.

*   *   *

Stephen Coulter, who was in the Royal Navy during World War II and later assigned to special intelligence work in Europe, applies his knowledge to bring his readers realism in several exciting novels. *Threshold* tells of the attempted rescue of the 29 survivors of a British nuclear submarine sunk in Russian territorial waters. *Offshore!* is a suspenseful yarn concerning a monstrous oil rig in the North sea, winter weather, sabotage, and a fanatic boss who cares only about himself—"a notable thriller" says Anthony Boucher. In *A Stranger Called the Blues*, the tough American Ed Murray is unwillingly detailed in Calcutta, smuggles in Nepal, and has a run-in with the Chinese on the Nepalese border, during all of which he is haunted by an English nanny. In *Embassy*, Semyon Gorenko, sweating profusely, seeks political asylum in Paris, promising vital secrets in return. The story deals with the upheaval caused by his presence in the U.S. Embassy. This is a fast-paced novel told by an expert. The author has been compared with Eric Ambler in a review of *An Account to Render* for his excellent characterization in this thriller, which is a study of corruption set in South America. Mr. Coulter writes in a more serious vein under his own name than when he uses his Mayo pseudonym.

As James Mayo, Coulter writes novels often centering on tall, handsome, cosmopolitan Charles Hood, elegantly dressed, a gourmet and connoisseur of beautiful girls. Hood would seem to be just a wealthy dealer in objets d'art, but often as in *Hammerhead*, he works on British Government missions for Special Intelligence. Hood, introduced in this book, is based on Ian Fleming's James Bond, but the violence is accented to the point of sadism, as noted by Anthony Boucher in his review of Hood's second case: "*Let Sleeping Girls Lie* has loads of sex, sadism and snobbery, and no sense at all of plot or structure; and Charles Hood's performance as a secret agent makes James Bond look realistic and intelligent." However, Boucher adds that the vivid action is excellently depicted and the sex scenes are amusingly written. In *Shamelady* a computer programmed not only to torture and kill Hood but to record his dying screams is foiled in a battle of wits. The best Mayo suspense story is *Once in a Lifetime*, in which Hood, investigating some incredibly good art forgeries, follows the trail from London through Paris to Teheran, where, in a final explosive climax, he is matched against dangerous U.S.A.F. Master-Sergeant Lloyd Bannion. James Mayo has a wild imagination; his exciting, fast-paced books are not for the squeamish.

—Betty Donaldson

———

COURTIER, S(idney) H(obson). Australian. Born in Kangaroo Flat, Victoria, 28 January 1904. Educated at the University of Melbourne, Cert. Ed. (honours). Married Audrey Jennie George in 1932; two sons and one daughter. Primary school teacher; later principal in Melbourne schools for teacher training for 12 years: retired in 1969. President, Melbourne branch, International P.E.N., 1954–57, 1958–61. *Died in 1974.*

CRIME PUBLICATIONS

Novels (series: Inspector "Digger" Haig; Ambrose Mahon)

The Glass Spear (Mahon). New York, Wyn, 1950; London, Dakers, 1952.
One Cried Murder (Mahon). New York, Rinehart, 1954; London, Hammond, 1956.
Come Back to Murder (Mahon). London, Hammond, 1957.
Now Seek My Bones (Haig). London, Hammond, 1957.
A Shroud for Unlac (Mahon). London, Hammond, 1958.
Death in Dream Time (Haig). London, Hammond, 1959.
Gently Dust the Corpse. London, Hammond, 1960; as *Softly Dust the Corpse*, London, Corgi, 1961.
Let the Man Die (Mahon). London, Hammond, 1961.
Swing High, Sweet Murder (Haig). London, Hammond, 1962.
Who Dies for Me? London, Hammond, 1962.
A Corpse Won't Sing (Mahon). London, Hammond, 1964.
Mimic a Murderer (Mahon). London, Hammond, 1964.
The Ringnecker (Haig). London, Hammond, 1965.
A Corpse at Least (Mahon). London, Hammond, 1966.
Murder's Burning. London, Hammond, and New York, Random House, 1967.
See Who's Dying. London, Hammond, 1967.
No Obelisk for Emily (Haig). London, Jenkins, 1970.
Ligny's Lake. London, Hale, and New York, Simon and Schuster, 1971.
Some Village Borgia. London, Hale, 1971.
Dead If I Remember. London, Hale, 1972.
Listening to the Mocking Bird. London, Hale, 1974.
A Window in Chungking. London, Hale, 1975.

Uncollected Short Stories

"Run for Your Life," in *Argosy Book of Adventure Stories*, edited by Rogers Terrill. New York, A.S. Barnes, 1952.

"Island of No Escape," in *John Creasey's Mystery Bedside Book*, edited by Herbert Harris. London, Hodder and Stoughton, 1966.

OTHER PUBLICATIONS

Novels

Gold for My Fair Lady. New York, Wyn, 1951.
The Mudflat Million, with R.G. Campbell. Sydney, Angus and Robertson, 1955.
Into the Silence. London, Hale, 1973.
The Smiling Trip. London, Hale, 1975.

* * *

For more than a dozen years before his first book, *The Glass Spear*, was published in 1950, S.H. Courtier supplied articles, stories, and serials to Australian periodicals, and also wrote radio scripts. During this period his work also appeared under the name Rui Chestor in the American magazines *Argosy* and *Short Stories*. All but two of Courtier's novels are mysteries. The two exceptions, both eminently worth reading, are *Gold for My Fair Lady*, a historical novel of the gold diggings at Kangaroo Flat, where the author was born, and *The Mudflat Million*, a wild comic novel written with Ronald G. Campbell.

In the London *Sunday Times* in 1959, Julian Symons wrote, "S.H. Courtier writes as well as the highly-praised Arthur Upfield, and is a good deal more ingenious." The ingenuity of plot is combined with an exceptionally skillful use of physical settings. Much of the action in *Come Back to Murder* takes place in the tunnels of a worked-out gold mine. *Now Seek My Bones* is set in the crocodile- and snake-infested environs of McGorrie's Island on the Queensland coast. Brought to life with vividness and economy, these and other settings are not mere exotic back-drops, but are fully integrated into the plot and action of the books.

Two of the best Courtier novels are *Death in Dream Time* and *Murder's Burning*. The former is an extended set-piece, taking up less than twenty-four hours of time, set in Dream Time Land, an entertainment park built around themes from aboriginal creation myths. The latter novel chronicles the investigation of a mysterious fire that had ravaged a remote valley, killing a friend of the hero. The scenes in the subterranean passages beneath the valley are hair-raising.

Not all of Courtier's novels uphold his usual high standard. *See Who's Dying* is a strained James Bond-ish adventure, filled with unconvincing heroics and unbelievable impersonations. In *Some Village Borgia* the unappealing characters and the author's determination to have a surprise ending at all costs undercut the interest and consistency of the plot.

—R.E. Briney

—————

COX, William R(obert). Also wrote as Willard d'Arcy; Mike Frederic; John Parkhill; Joel Reeve; Wayne Robbins; Roger G. Spellman; Jonas Ward. American. Born in Peapack, New Jersey, 14 April 1901. Educated at public schools, Newark, New Jersey; extension courses at Rutgers University, New Brunswick, and Princeton University, both New Jersey. Married 1) Lee Frederick in 1950, one son; 2) Casey Collins. Worked on Newark newspapers and in family fuel business in the 1930's; then freelance writer. Committee member, Writers Guild of America, 20 years; President, Western Writers of America, 1965, 1971. *Died in 1989*

CRIME PUBLICATIONS

Novels (series: Tom Kincaid)

Make My Coffin Strong. New York, Fawcett, 1954; London, Fawcett, 1955.
The Tycoon and the Tigress. New York, Fawcett, 1958.
Hell to Pay (Kincaid). New York, New American Library, 1958.
Murder in Vegas (Kincaid). New York, New American Library, 1960.
Death Comes Early. New York, Dell, 1961.
Death on Location (Kincaid). New York, New American Library, 1962.
Way to Go, Doll Baby! New York, Banner, 1967.
Hot Times. New York, Fawcett, 1973.

Uncollected Short Stories

"Murder Breeds Murder," in *Detective Ace*, July 1937.
"Murder Is My Business," in *Star Detective* (Chicago), February 1938.
"Mr. Murder Man," in *Detective Short Stories* (Chicago), February 1938.
"Mr. Detective Is Annoyed," in *Captain Satan*, March 1938.
"Half a Crook," in *Black Mask* (New York), May 1938.
"Mr. Detective Goes to Jail," in *Captain Satan*, July 1938.
"Crime Crest," in *10 Detective Aces* (New York), November 1938.
"Mr. Sleuth, B.A.," in *Secret Agent X* (Springfield, Massachusetts), December 1938.
"Monopoly on Murder," in *10 Story Detective* (Springfield, Massachusetts), January 1939.
"For the Love of Money," in *Detective Fiction Weekly* (New York), 11 February 1939.
"Homicide Haul," in *Detective Fiction Weekly* (New York), 18 February 1939.
"The Case of the Reluctant Bullet," in *Detective Fiction Weekly* (New York), 15 April 1939.
"Marked for Murder," in *Detective Tales* (New York), June 1939.
"Two-Way Killer," in *Detective Tales* (New York), July 1939.
"Thanks for the Memory," in *Detective Fiction Weekly* (New York), 8 July 1939.
"Gambling Fool," in *Detective Fiction Weekly* (New York), 23 September 1939.
"Million Dollar Corpses," in *Dime Mystery* (Chicago), October 1939.
"Death Wins at Bank Nite," in *10 Detective Aces* (New York), November 1939.
"Return Engagement with Death," in *Ace G-Man Stories* (Chicago), November–December 1939.
"Accounting in Blood," in *Black Mask* (New York), December 1939.
"John Wade—Corpse Attorney," in *Detective Tales* (New York), December 1939.
"Satan Trades in Debutants" (as Willard d'Arcy), in *Dime Mystery* (Chicago), January 1940.
"Night Club for the Dead," in *Strange Detective Mysteries* (Chicago), January–February 1940.
"The Thing in Search of a Body" (as Wayne Robbins), in *Dime Mystery* (Chicago), February 1940.

"The Munitions Murder Syndicate," in *Detective Tales* (New York), February 1940.

"John Wade, Mob Exterminator," in *Detective Tales* (New York), March 1940.

"The Brass Button Murders," in *Detective Tales* (New York), April 1940.

"The Missing General," in *Detective Fiction Weekly* (New York), 8 June 1940.

"Corpses on the Force," in *Detective Tales* (New York), June 1940.

"Corpses Cast a Ballot," in *Detective Tales* (New York), July 1940.

"Beast of the Fortneys," in *Dime Mystery* (Chicago), August 1940.

"John Wade—Dr. of Murder," in *Detective Tales* (New York), September 1940.

"Coming of the Cat-Men," in *Dime Mystery* (Chicago), October 1940.

"Reinstatement for a Killer," in *Detective Tales* (New York), October 1940.

"The Baseball Murder," in *Detective Tales* (New York), November 1940.

"This Is War," in *Fifth Column Stories* (New York), January 1941.

"Gun Ballad for Americans," in *Detective Tales* (New York), February 1941.

"Mad Morgan's Murder Sanction," in *Detective Tales* (New York), April 1941.

"Jewels for Murder's Crown," in *Detective Tales* (New York), July 1941.

"John Wade and the Hanging Corpses," in *Detective Tales* (New York), September 1941.

"Good Cop," in *New Detective* (New York), November 1941.

"The Disappearing Dead Man," in *Detective Tales* (New York), December 1941.

"The Melancholy Corpses," in *10 Story Mystery Magazine* (Chicago), December 1941.

"Mr. Detective Is Chagrined," in *New Detective* (New York), January 1942.

"The Finger of Death," in *Detective Book Magazine* (New York), Spring 1942.

"The Corpse of John Wade," in *Detective Tales* (New York), December 1942.

"Second-Hand Coffin" (as John Parkhill), in *Dime Mystery* (Chicago), March 1943.

"Model for Manslaughter," in *Detective Tales* (New York), April 1943.

"Murder Walks in the Streets," in *Dime Mystery* (Chicago), May 1943.

"Death Owns a Ration Book," in *Detective Tales* (New York), September 1943.

"Roast Beef Special," in *Blue Book* (Chicago), September 1943.

"The Mulraneys Are Lucky," in *Blue Book* (Chicago), November 1943.

"Ham Hangs High," in *Blue Book* (Chicago), December 1943.

"The Mulraneys Are Vulnerable," in *Blue Book* (Chicago), February 1944.

"Pursuit of Murder," in *Detective Tales* (New York), February 1944.

"A Corpse for Mr. Thomas," in *Detective Tales* (New York), June 1944.

"Murder Steps Out," in *Detective Book* (New York), Fall 1944.

"We'll Make a Killing," in *Detective Tales* (New York), January 1945.

"Dark City," in *Detective Tales* (New York), February 1945.

"Malachi Butts In," in *Dime Detective* (New York), March 1945.

"Cold Decked!," in *Detective Tales* (New York), April 1945.

"Slips That Pass in the Night" as (John Parkhill), in *Dime Mystery* (Chicago), May 1945.

"Malachi Attends a Party," in *Dime Detective* (New York), May 1945.

"Shame on Malachi!," in *Dime Detective* (New York), July 1945.

"The Shooting in Hell," in *Dime Mystery* (Chicago), July 1945.

"Strangers on the Kill," in *Dime Mystery* (Chicago), September 1945.

"John Wade's Better Death Trap," in *Detective Tales* (New York), September 1945.

"Tail End of a Shadow," in *Short Stories*, 25 January 1946.

"How Tough Can You Get?," in *Private Detective* (New York), May 1946.

"The Corpse Drops In," in *Detective Tales* (New York), May 1946.

"Death, Here Is Thy Sting," in *Detective Tales* (New York), June 1946.

"Trouble in the Fight Tent," in *Blue Book* (Chicago), April 1947.

"Bye, Bye Black Sheep," in *Detective Tales* (New York), June 1947.

"Rope Enough for Two," in *Detective Tales* (New York), August 1947.

"The Eye and the Pink Man," in *Detective Tales* (New York), October 1947.

"One for the Jammer," in *Blue Book* (Chicago), October 1948.

"I'll Take Care of Maxie," in *Detective Tales* (New York), May 1949.

"A Good Copy," in *Blue Book* (Chicago), October 1949.

"No Bands Playing," in *Blue Book* (Chicago), November 1949.

"Lights! Action! Murder!," in *New Detective* (New York), March 1950.

"Neighborhood Champion," in *Blue Book* (Chicago), August 1950.

"No Guard at All," in *Blue Book* (Chicago), September 1951.

"A Spot Marked Double X," in *15 Detective Stories*, February 1954.

"No Stars in My Crown," in *The Saint* (New York), March 1954.

"When a Cop Hollers," in *15 Detective Stories*, April 1955.

"Iron Man," in *Justice* (New York), May 1955.

"Las Vegas Trap," in *Justice* (New York), October 1955.

"Blood and Moonlight," in *Manhunt* (New York), October 1956.

"Who Wants You?," in *Mike Shayne Mystery Magazine* (New York), April 1957.

"The Phone Call," in *Mike Shayne Mystery Magazine* (New York), January 1972.

Uncollected Short Stories (series: Tom Kincaid in all stories)

"Death's Black Ace," May 1941, "Carnival of Death," July 1941, "Murder Raises the Ante," September 1941, "Black Queen," January 1942, "Murder Deals the Cards," May 1942, "Murder's Private Playground," July 1942, "Draw One to Death," March 1943, "Bodies for the Black Market," July 1943, "Murder in Cinema City," November 1943, "Hell over Hollywood," January 1944, "Hell Comes in Bottles," November 1944, "Ready Action—Murder," January 1945, and "They'll Kill Me," May 1945, all in *Dime Mystery* (Chicago).

Uncollected Short Stories (series: Dumb Dan Trout in all stories).

"See You at Murder Mansion," March 1945, "Murder—with Teeth," August 1945, "Featured Tonight—Murder," September 1945, "That Kill Crazy Cadaver," November 1945, "What's Cookin' Killer," February 1946, "Dumb Dan and the Black Widow," March 1946, "Trout in the Murder Pool," July 1946, "Dames Are Deadly!," September 1946, "Dumb Dan and the Mains," February 1947, "Don't Be a Body, Baby," April 1947, and "Whose Body Are You?," July 1947, all in *Detective Tales* (New York).

Uncollected Short Stories as Joel Reeve

"Who Fights for Glory?," in *Blue Book* (Chicago), February 1942.
"Copper, Come Home!," in *Detective Tales* (New York), August 1945.
"Laugh Corpse Laugh," in *Detective Tales* (New York), November 1945.
"Neighborhood Feud," in *Blue Book* (Chicago), May 1946.
"Slay Rube," in *Detective Tales* (New York), August 1946.
"The Corpse on the Carousel," in *Detective Tales* (New York), January 1947.
"Juke Box Maestra," in *Argosy* (New York), April 1947.
"It's in the Bag," in *Detective Tales* (New York), August 1947.
"Killers Carnival," in *Detective Tales* (New York), October 1947.
"Go Ahead, Georgia," in *Blue Book* (Chicago), December 1948.

Uncollected Short Stories as Joel Reeve (series: Officer Murphy in all stories)

"A Lady Swings Her Right," August 1944, "In the Bag for Looey," September 1944, "A Great Big Wonderful Occasion," November 1944, "A Shiv in the Gizzard," January 1945, "The Wrong Ones," February 1945, "Tough Guys," March 1945, "Little Gooney," June 1945, "Little Gooney Number Two," December 1945, "Neighborhood Feud," May 1946, "The Last of Little Gooney," December 1946, "Murder in the Old Neighborhood," June 1947, "Two Hundred Grand," September 1947, "Starlet in Jeopardy," February 1948, "Geeks Are Like That," March 1948, "Vacations Are Not for Cops," October 1948, "A Serious Cop," December 1948, "A Frame for the Duke," July 1949, "Murphy Goes Uptown," May 1950, "Neighborhood Genius," May 1951, "The Cramped Left Hand," September 1951, and "Set a Thief," April 1952, all in *Blue Book* (Chicago).

OTHER PUBLICATIONS

Novels

The Lusty Men. New York, Pyramid, 1957.
Comanche Moon: A Novel of the West. New York, McGraw Hill, 1959; London, Corgi, 1962.
The Duke. New York, New American Library, 1962; London, New English Library, 1963.
The Outlawed. New York, New American Library, 1963; as *Navajo Blood*, 1973.
Bigger than Texas. New York, Fawcett, and London, Muller, 1963.
Tall for a Texan (as Roger G. Spellman). New York, Fawcett 1965.

The Gunsharp. New York, Fawcett, 1965.
Black Silver. N.p., Profit Press, 1967.
Day of the Gun. New York, Belmont, 1967.
Firecreek (novelization of screenplay). New York, Bantam, 1968.
Moon of Cobre. New York, Bantam, 1969.
Law Comes to Razor Edge. New York, Popular Library, 1970.
The Sixth Horseman. New York, Ballantine, 1972.
Jack o'Diamonds. New York, Dell, 1972.
The Gunshop. London, Gold Lion, 1973.
The Fourth-of-July Kid. New York, Tower, 1981.
Cemetery Jones. New York, Ballantine, 1985.
Cemetery Jones and the Maverick Kid. New York, Fawcett, 1986.

Novels as Jonas Ward

Buchanan's War. New York, Fawcett, 1970; Bath, Avon, Chivers Press, 1986.
Trap for Buchanan. New York, Fawcett, 1971.
Buchanan's Gamble. New York, Fawcett, 1972.
Buchanan's Siege. New York, Fawcett, 1972.
Buchanan on the Run. New York, Fawcett, 1973.
Get Buchanan. New York, Fawcett, 1973.
Buchanan Takes Over. New York, Fawcett, 1974.
Buchanan Calls the Shots. New York, Fawcett, 1975.
Buchanan's Big Showdown. New York, Fawcett, 1976; London, Coronet, 1978.
Buchanan's Texas Treasure. New York, Fawcett, 1976.
Buchanan's Stolen Railway. New York, Fawcett, 1978; London, Coronet, 1983.
Buchanan's Manhunt. New York, Fawcett, 1978.
Buchanan's Range War. New York, Fawcett, 1979.
Buchanan's Big Fight. New York, Fawcett, 1980.
Buchanan's Black Sheep. New York, Ballantine, 1985; Bath, Avon, Chivers Press, 1987.
Buchanan's Stage Line. New York, Ballantine 1986.
Buchanan's Gun. New York, Fawcett, 1986.

Novels (for children)

Five Were Chosen: A Basketball Story. New York, Dodd Mead, 1956.
Gridiron Duel. New York, Dodd Mead, 1959.
The Wild Pitch. New York, Dodd Mead, 1963.
Tall on the Court. New York, Dodd Mead, 1964.
Third and Eight to Go. New York, Dodd Mead, 1964.
Big League Rookie. New York, Dodd Mead, 1965.
Trouble at Second Base. New York, Dodd Mead, 1966.
The Valley Eleven. New York, Dodd Mead, 1966.
Goal Ahead (as Joel Reeve). New York, Phillips, 1967.
Jump Shot Joe. New York, Dodd Mead, 1968.
Rookie in the Backcourt. New York, Dodd Mead, 1970.
Big League Sandlotters. New York, Dodd Mead, 1971.
Third and Goal. New York, Dodd Mead, 1971.
Playoff. New York, Bantam, 1972.
Gunner on the Court. New York, Dodd Mead, 1972.
The Running Back. New York, Bantam, 1972.
Chicano Cruz. New York, Bantam, 1972.
The Backyard Five. New York, Dodd Mead, 1973.
Game, Set, and Match. New York, Dodd Mead, 1973.
The Unbeatable Five. New York, Dodd Mead, 1974.
Battery Mates. New York, Dodd Mead, 1978.
Home Court Is Where You Find It. New York, Dodd Mead, 1980.

Novels (for children) as Mike Frederic

Frank Merriwell, Freshman Quarterback. New York, Award, 1965.
Frank Merriwell, Freshman Pitcher. New York, Award, 1965.
Frank Merriwell, Sports Car Racer. New York, Award, 1965.

Plays

Screenplays: *The Veils of Bagdad*, 1953; *Tanganyika*, with William Sackheim and Alan Simmons, 1954.

Television Plays: 100 scripts for *Fireside Theatre, Broken Arrow*, 1956–57, *Zane Grey Theatre*, 1956–60, *Wells Fargo*, 1957–61, *Bonanza*, 1959–71, *The Grey Ghost, Route 66*, 1960–63, *Alcoa Theatre, The Virginian*, 1962–69, and other series.

Other

Luke Short and His Era. New York, Doubleday, 1961; as *Luke Short, Famous Gambler of the Old West*, London, Foulsham, 1962.
The Mets Will Win the Pennant. New York, Putnam, 1964.

Editor, *River to Cross.* New York, Dodd Mead, 1966.

*

Manuscript Collections: University of Oregon, Eugene; University of Wyoming, Laramie.

Critical Study: interview with James L. Traylor, in *Armchair Detective* (White Bear Lake, Minnesota), 1982.

* * *

William R. Cox began his writing career as a sports reporter in the early 1920's. His first magazine stories were about tough guys and sports figures; however, he has been active in the western and crime markets.

Cox describes the type of crime stories he writes as tales of "action/adventure." In many ways Cox was the classic pulp writer. He wrote weird mystery, detective, sports, and western stories for all the great pulps—*Black Mask, Dime Detective, Detective Tales, Blue Book, Argosy, Dime Western, Sports Novels*, and many others. He wrote more than 1,000 short stories. His first story appeared in *Dime Sports* in 1934; his last, in *Mike Shayne Mystery Magazine* in 1972. By the 1950's Cox shifted to novels and screenplays. In 1951–53 he spent two years writing stories and scripts for television and Universal-International. He wrote over 150 television scripts. In 1954 he published his first novel, a crime story entitled *Make My Coffin Strong*—another one of those "weird" Fawcett titles he says—and went on to write 75 books, covering many fields (his *Luke Short* is one of the best western biographies).

Cox's style is more representative of character study than of pure plot development. He created numerous pulp characters. Among his best crime story characters are Malachi Manatee (from *Dime Detective*), who broke up "political villains"; John Wade (from *Detective Tales*), who fought "crooked millionaires"; Murphy the Neighborhood Cop who ran for eight years in *Blue Book* under the pen-name Joel Reeve; "Dumb Dan" Trout, a not-quite-hardboiled private investigator (from *Detective Tales*) who resembles Richard Diamond; and Tom Kincaid, a professional gambler and trouble-shooter who first appeared in *Dime Mystery* in the early 1940's when that pulp was changing its image from weird menace to a more

traditional crime magazine. Kincaid later became Cox's only pulp crime character to appear in book form, as the lead character in three paperback originals. (Cox used the name of his pulp character John Wade in *Way to Go, Doll Baby!* but the police inspector of that novel in no way resembles the pulp character once blurbed as "John Wade, Corpse Detective".)

The Kincaid novels are solid examples of the action/adventure subgenre of the crime story. One of the three Kincaid novels, *Hell to Pay* is a fast and violent story of rival mobsters, the fixed-fight racket, and personal vengeance. Kincaid appears in two additional crime novels, *Murder in Vegas* and, the best of the series, *Death on Location*, which blends elements of the mystery, sports, and western story. These final two Kincaid exploits explore the labyrinth of Hollywood, Vegas, and the mob.

Cox's crime stories have fast movement and human interest, stressing character motivation. Although he wrote only eight crime novels, Cox might well have become much more appreciated had he received better support from the packagers of his novels. *Hell to Pay* has an atrocious cover, which in no way reveals the humanitarian nature of Tom Kincaid. Similarly, *Way to Go, Doll Baby!* is such a terrible title that it had little chance of success even though it is an entertaining and thoughtful character study of a middle-aged police inspector. Cox's personal favorite of his non-western novels, *Hot Times*, is not really a crime story but a story of the jazz age, beginning quite appropriately with a discussion of one of his close friends in Hollywood, Buster Keaton, the subject of Cox's most recently completed biography.

In the crime and mystery field, Cox is remembered for his 25 years of writing for the best of the pulps. He was a born storyteller with a gift for light and realistic dialogue. His characters are vivid and within the confines of the genre believable as people instead of cardboard figures.

—James L. Traylor

COXE, George Harmon. American. Born in Olean, New York, 23 April 1901. Educated at Purdue University, West Lafayette, Indiana, 1919–1920; Cornell University, Ithaca, New York, 1920–21. Married Elizabeth Fowler in 1929; one daughter and one son. Reporter Santa Monica *Outlook*, California, Los Angeles *Express*, Utica *Observer Dispatch*, New York, *Commercial & Financial Chronicle*, New York, and Elmira *Star-Gazette*, New York, 1922–27; advertising salesman, Cambridge, Massachusetts, 1927–32. Member of the board of directors, 1946–48, 1969–70, and President, 1952, Mystery Writers of America. Recipient: Mystery Writers of America Grand Master award, 1964. *Died 30 January 1984.*

CRIME PUBLICATIONS

Novels (series: Flash Casey; Sam Crombie; Jack Fenner; Max Hale; Kent Murdock)

Murder with Pictures (Murdock). New York, Knopf, 1935; London, Heinemann, 1937.
The Barotique Mystery (Murdock). New York, Knopf, 1936; London, Heinemann, 1937; as *Murdock's Acid Test*, New York, Dell, 1977.
The Camera Clue (Murdock). New York, Knopf, 1937; London, Heinemann, 1938.

Four Frightened Women (Murdock; Fenner). New York, Knopf, 1939; as *The Frightened Woman*, London, Heinemann, 1939.

Murder for the Asking (Hale). New York, Knopf, 1939; London, Heinemann, 1940.

The Glass Triangle (Murdock). New York, Knopf, 1940.

The Lady Is Afraid (Hale). New York, Knopf, and London, Heinemann, 1940.

Mrs. Murdock Takes a Case (Murdock). New York, Knopf, 1941; London, Swan, 1949.

No Time to Kill. New York, Knopf, 1941.

Assignment in Guiana. New York, Knopf, 1942; London, Macdonald, 1943.

The Charred Witness (Fenner; Murdock). New York, Knopf, 1942; London, Swan, 1949.

Silent Are the Dead (Casey). New York, Knopf, 1942.

Alias the Dead. New York, Knopf, 1943; London, Hammond, 1945.

Murder for Two (Casey). New York, Knopf, 1943; London, Hammond, 1944.

Murder in Havana. New York, Knopf, 1943; London, Hammond, 1945.

The Groom Lay Dead. New York, Knopf, 1944; London, Hammond, 1946.

The Jade Venus (Murdock). New York, Knopf, 1945; London, Hammond, 1947.

Woman at Bay. New York, Knopf, 1945; London, Hammond, 1948.

Dangerous Legacy. New York, Knopf, 1946; London, Hammond, 1949.

Fashioned for Murder. New York, Knopf, 1947; London, Hammond, 1950.

The Fifth Key (Murdock). New York, Knopf, 1947; London, Hammond, 1950.

The Hollow Needle (Murdock). New York, Knopf, 1948; London, Hammond, 1952.

Venturous Lady. New York, Knopf, 1948; London, Hammond, 1951.

Inland Passage. New York, Knopf, 1949; London, Hammond, 1953.

Lady Killer (Murdock). New York, Knopf, 1949; London, Hammond, 1952.

Eye Witness (Murdock). New York, Knopf, 1950; London, Hammond, 1953.

The Frightened Fiancée (Crombie). New York, Knopf, 1950; London, Hammond, 1953.

The Man Who Died Twice. New York, Knopf, 1951; London, Hammond, 1955.

The Widow Had a Gun (Murdock). New York, Knopf, 1951; London, Hammond, 1954.

Never Bet Your Life. New York, Knopf, 1952; London, Hammond, 1955.

The Crimson Clue (Murdock). New York, Knopf, 1953; London, Hammond, 1955.

Uninvited Guest. New York, Knopf, 1953; London, Hammond, 1956.

Death at the Isthmus. New York, Knopf, 1954; London, Hammond, 1956.

Focus on Murder (Murdock). New York, Knopf, 1954; London, Hammond, 1956.

Top Assignment. New York, Knopf, 1955; London, Hammond, 1957.

Man on a Rope. New York, Knopf, 1956; London, Hammond, 1958.

Suddenly a Widow. New York, Knopf, 1956; London, Hammond, 1957.

Murder on Their Minds (Murdock). New York, Knopf, 1957; London, Hammond, 1958.

One Minute Past Eight. New York, Knopf, 1957; London, Hammond, 1959.

The Big Gamble (Murdock). New York, Knopf, 1958; London, Hammond, 1960.

The Impetuous Mistress (Crombie). New York, Knopf, 1958; London, Hammond, 1959.

Slack Tide. New York, Knopf, 1959; London, Hammond, 1960.

Triple Exposure (omnibus). New York, Knopf, 1959.

The Last Commandment (Murdock). New York, Knopf, 1960; London, Hammond, 1961.

One Way Out. New York, Knopf, 1960; London, Hammond, 1961.

Error of Judgement (Casey). New York, Knopf, 1961; London, Hammond, 1962; as *One Murder Too Many*, New York, Pyramid, 1969.

Moment of Violence. New York, Knopf, 1961; London, Hammond, 1962.

The Man Who Died Too Soon (Casey). New York, Knopf, 1962; London, Hammond, 1963.

Mission of Fear. New York, Knopf, 1962; London, Hammond, 1963.

The Hidden Key (Murdock). New York, Knopf, 1963; London, Hammond, 1964.

One Hour to Kill. New York, Knopf, 1963; London, Hammond, 1964.

Deadly Image (Casey). New York, Knopf, and London, Hammond, 1964.

The Reluctant Heiress (Murdock). New York, Knopf, 1965; London, Hammond, 1966.

With Intent to Kill. New York, Knopf, and London, Hammond, 1965.

The Ring of Truth. New York, Knopf, 1966; London, Hammond, 1967.

The Candid Imposter. New York, Knopf, 1968; London, Hale, 1969.

An Easy Way to Go (Murdock). New York, Knopf, and London, Hale, 1969.

Double Identity. New York, Knopf, 1970; London, Hale, 1971.

Fenner (Fenner, Murdock). New York, Knopf, 1971; London, Hale, 1973.

Woman with a Gun. New York, Knopf, 1972; London, Hale, 1974.

The Silent Witness (Fenner; Murdock). New York, Knopf, 1973; London, Hale, 1974.

The Inside Man. New York, Knopf, 1974; London, Hale, 1975.

No Place for Murder (Fenner). New York, Knopf, 1975; London, Hale, 1976.

Short Stories

Flash Casey, Photographer. New York, Avon, 1946.

Uncollected Short Stories

"No Provisions for Picnics," in *Street & Smith's Detective Story Magazine* (New York), 1 April 1922.

"Time to a T," in *Street & Smith's Detective Story Magazine* (New York), 21 April 1923.

"Special Delivery," in *Top Notch* (New York), 15 July 1932.

"No Work, No Pay," in *Top Notch* (New York), 15 August 1932.

"Stop Sign," in *Top Notch* (New York), 1 September 1932.

"Bad Medicine," in *Complete Stories* (New York), 15 December 1932.

"Hot Hunches," in *Clues* (New York), February 1933.

"Mad Masquerade," in *Clues* (New York), April 1933.

"Full Payment," in *Argosy* (New York), 1 April 1933.

"Face Value," in *Complete Stories* (New York), 15 April 1933.

"Murder at Eight," in *Dime Mystery Book* (New York), May 1933.

"Ahead of Death," in *Street & Smith's Detective Story Magazine* (New York), 10 May 1933.

"Fifteen a Week," in *Detective Fiction Weekly* (New York), 10 June 1933.

"Counter-Evidence," in *Detective Fiction Weekly* (New York), 10 June 1933.

"Trustworthy," in *Argosy* (New York), 24 June 1933.

"The Weakest Link," in *Complete Stories* (New York), 1 August 1933.

"Planned Luck," in *Detective Fiction Weekly* (New York), 30 September 1933.

"Cyclops," in *Complete Stories* (New York), 1 October 1933.

"Material Witness," in *Detective Fiction Weekly* (New York), 28 October 1933.

"Slay Ride," in *Dime Detective* (New York), 1 November 1933.

"Special Messenger," in *Complete Stories* (New York), 1 November 1933.

"Testimonial," in *Argosy* (New York), 4 November 1933.

"Alias the Killer," in *Complete Stories* (New York), 15 November 1933.

"The Perfect Frame," in *Thrilling Detective* (New York), December 1933.

"Protection Promised," in *Complete Stories* (New York), 1 December 1933.

"The Last Witness," in *Detective Fiction Weekly* (New York), 9 December 1933.

"The Death Club," in *Complete Stories* (New York), 15 December 1933.

"Touch System," in *Complete Stories* (New York), 1 January 1934.

"Turn About," in *Complete Stories* (New York), 15 January 1934.

"Psychology Stuff," in *Thrilling Detective* (New York), February 1934.

"Return Engagement," in *Black Mask* (New York), March 1934.

"The Missing Man," in *Phantom Detective* (New York), March 1934.

"A Letter of Death," in *Complete Stories* (New York), 15 March 1934.

"Special Assignment," in *Black Mask* (New York), April 1934.

"Blackmail Incorporated," in *Complete Stories* (New York), 1 April 1934.

"Clip Killer," in *Dime Detective* (New York), 1 April 1934.

"Licorice Drops," in *Complete Stories* (New York), 30 April 1934.

"Two-Man Job," in *Black Mask* (New York), May 1934.

"Solo!," in *Clues* (New York), May 1934.

"Jailed," in *Thrilling Detective* (New York), May 1934.

"Push-Over," in *Black Mask* (New York), June 1934.

"The Twelfth Woman," in *Complete Stories* (New York), 11 June 1934.

"Hot Delivery," in *Black Mask* (New York), July 1934.

"Easy Money," in *Complete Stories* (New York), 1 July 1934.

"Final Appeal," in *Detective Fiction Weekly* (New York), 7 July 1934.

"Party Murder," in *Detective Fiction Weekly* (New York), 14 July 1934.

"One-Buck Pay-Off," in *Dime Detective* (New York), 15 July 1934.

"Mixed Drinks," in *Black Mask* (New York), August 1934.

"Pinch-Hitters," in *Black Mask* (New York), September 1934.

"It's Teamwork That Counts," in *Complete Stories* (New York), 24 September 1934.

"The Murder Schedule," in *Clues* (New York), November 1934.

"Stuffed Shirts," in *Complete Stories* (New York), 5 November 1934.

"When a Cop's a Good Cop," in *The Mystery Magazine* (New York), December 1934.

"Murder Picture," in *Black Mask* (New York), January 1935.

"Greed Crazy," in *Detective Fiction Weekly* (New York), 5 January 1935.

"The Murder Bridge," in *Thrilling Detective* (New York), February 1935.

"Earned Reward," in *Black Mask* (New York), March 1935.

"Hot Assignment," in *Clues-Detective* (New York), March 1935.

"Reprisal," in *Complete Stories* (New York), 8 March 1935.

"One-Man Job," in *Complete Stories* (New York), 22 April 1935.

"Murder Date," in *Dime Detective* (New York), 1 May 1935.

"Thirty Tickets to Win," in *Black Mask* (New York), June 1935.

"When a Lady's Involved," in *The Mystery Magazine* (New York), June 1935.

"The Seventy Grand Bullet," in *Detective Fiction Weekly* (New York), 1 June 1935.

"Unfair Bargain," in *Maclean's* (Toronto), 1 June 1935.

"Buried Evidence," in *Black Mask* (New York), July 1935.

"Guiana Gold," in *Blue Book* (Chicago), August 1935.

"Mr. Casey Flashguns Murder," in *Black Mask* (New York), October 1935.

"Murder Set-Up," in *Detective Fiction Weekly* (New York), 9 November 1935.

"Murder Touch," in *Detective Fiction Weekly* (New York), 9 November 1935.

"The Dead Can't Hide," in *Detective Fiction Weekly* (New York), 23 November 1935.

"The Isle of New Fortune," in *Blue Book* (Chicago), December 1935.

"Ungallant Evidence," in *Complete Magazine* (New York), December 1935.

"Portrait of Murder," in *Black Mask* (New York), February 1936.

"You Gotta Be Tough," in *Black Mask* (New York), March 1936.

"Letters Are Poison," in *Black Mask* (New York), April 1936.

"Murder Mix-Up," in *Black Mask* (New York), May 1936.

"Fall Guy," in *Black Mask* (New York), June 1936.

"Trouble for Two," in *Black Mask* (New York), July 1936.

"Head-Work Payoff," in *10 Detective Aces* (New York), August 1936.

"Double or Nothing," in *Black Mask* (New York), November 1936.

"The Camera Clue," in *American Magazine* (Springfield, Ohio), February 1937.

"Peril Afloat," in *Thrilling Detective* (New York), July 1937.

"Death Is a Gamble," in *American Magazine* (Springfield, Ohio), October 1939.

"Casey and the Blonde Wren," in *Black Mask* (New York), August 1940.

"Vigilance," in *Collier's* (Springfield, Ohio), 19 April 1941.

"All Routes Covered," in *Coronet* (Chicago), October 1941.

"Boy, Are You Lucky," in *Liberty* (New York), 29 November 1941.

"Surprise in a Bottle," in *This Week* (New York), 1 February 1942.

"Intelligence from the Reich," in *American Magazine* (Springfield, Ohio), April 1942.

"Murder in Red," in *Black Mask* (New York), June 1942.

"Alias the Killer," in *Collier's* (Springfield, Ohio), 26 August 1944.

"The Unloved Corpse," in *Mystery Book Magazine* (New York), December 1945.

"Three Guesses to Guilt," in *Mystery Book Magazine* (New York), March 1946.

"Murder to Music," in *Liberty* (New York), 7 September 1946.

"Post Mortem," in *Liberty* (New York), 16 November 1946.

"The Fourth Visitor," and "The Canary Sang," in *Murder for the Millions*, edited by Frank Owen. New York, Fell, 1946.

"The Doctor Makes It Murder," in *Murder Cavalcade*, edited by Ken Crossen. New York, Duell, 1946; London, Hammond, 1953.

"The Painted Nail," in *Fourth Mystery Companion*, edited by Abraham Louis Furman. New York, Lantern Press, 1946.

"Cause for Suspicion," in *Liberty* (New York), 1 February 1947.

"Death Certificate," in *Four and Twenty Bloodhounds*, edited by Anthony Boucher. New York, Simon and Schuster, 1950; London, Hammond, 1951.

"One for the Book," in *Giant Detective Annual*. New York, Best Books, 1950.

"Invited Witness," in *As Tough as They Come*, edited by Will Oursler. New York, Doubleday, 1951.

"Black Target," in *American Magazine* (Springfield, Ohio), March 1951.

"The Doctor Takes a Case," in *20 Great Tales of Murder*, edited by Helen McCloy and Brett Halliday. New York, Random House, 1951; London, Hammond, 1952.

"The Fatal Hour," in *American Magazine* (Springfield, Ohio), November 1951.

"Weapon of Fear," in *American Magazine* (Springfield, Ohio), May 1952.

"The Captive-Bride Murders," in *American Magazine* (Springfield, Ohio), July 1953.

"No Loose Ends," in *Eat, Drink, and Be Buried*, edited by Rex Stout. New York, Viking Press, 1956; as *For Tomorrow We Die*, London, Macdonald, 1958.

"Courage Isn't Everything," in *For Love or Money*, edited by Dorothy Gardiner. New York, Doubleday, 1957; London, Macdonald, 1959.

"Two Minute Alibi," in *Ellery Queen's Mystery Magazine* (New York), August 1958.

"There's Still Tomorrow," in *Ellery Queen's 15th Mystery Annual*. New York, Random House, 1960; London, Gollancz, 1961.

"The Barbados Beach House," in *Cosmopolitan* (New York), May 1961.

"The Girl in the Melody Lounge," in *Cosmopolitan* (New York), December 1963.

"Circumstantial Evidence," in *Anthology 1965*, edited by Ellery Queen. New York, Davis, 1964.

"When a Wife Is Murdered," in *Anthology 1965 Mid-Year*, edited by Ellery Queen. New York, Davis, 1965.

"A Routine Night's Work," in *Anthology 1968*, edited by Ellery Queen. New York, Davis, 1967.

"A Neat and Tidy Job," in *Anthology 1969*, edited by Ellery Queen. New York, Davis, 1968.

"The Cop Killer," in *Anthology 1970*, edited by Ellery Queen. New York, Davis, 1969.

"Seed of Suspicion," in *Anthology 1971*, edited by Ellery Queen. New York, Davis, 1970.

OTHER PUBLICATIONS

Plays

Screenplays: *Arsene Lupin Returns*, 1938; *The Hidden Eye*, with Harry Ruskin, 1946.

Radio Plays: *Crime Photographer* series, 1943–52; *The Commandos* series.

Television Plays: *Kraft Television Theatre*, 1957.

Other

Editor, *Butcher, Baker, Murder-Maker*. New York, Knopf, 1954; London, Macdonald, 1956.

*

Bibliography: "Mystery Master: A Survey and Appreciation of the Fiction of George Harmon Coxe" by J. Randolph Cox, in *Armchair Detective* (White Bear Lake, Minnesota), February to November 1973.

Manuscript Collection: Beinecke Rare Book and Manuscript Library, Yale University, New Haven, Connecticut.

*   *   *

George Harmon Coxe has been called "the professional's professional" by Anthony Boucher and "a master of the art of the detective novel" by William Lyon Phelps. Erle Stanley Gardner referred to his books as "uniformly entertaining, gripping, and exciting."

His earliest stories in the pulps were told from the point of view of the crook. He avoided the clichés of the locked room mystery; instead he concentrated on ordinary characters who were killed by gun or knife (whichever was most plausible), and then followed the other characters to see what would happen. He soon shifted to third-person narratives from the point of view of the police or the detective (his private detectives were often men who had been on the police force).

The strictly deductive story in the Sherlock Holmes tradition was not among Coxe's stock of material, as he himself admitted. Since writers were told to write what they know, Coxe concentrated on the newspaper business.

The Coxe hero, self taught in the early years, was often a college educated man who clashed with the rough, self taught street educated character. Sometimes there was a degree of cooperation, opposites definitely attracting. The humor arising from such a situation was never forced. Some of his best work was done for *Black Mask*, where his stories of Flash Casey first appeared. Casey was created to fill a gap in the fictional detective field: in the early 1930's there were plenty of reporters who doubled as sleuths, but there was no photographer. Casey originally worked for the Boston *Globe*, but soon transferred to the *Express*, the paper with which he is commonly associated. Jack (Flashgun, or Flash) Casey is a large, rumpled man with a touch of gray at the temples. He may curse at being dragged out of bed in the morning, but will do anything to help a colleague or anyone in genuine trouble. He has a distaste for people who are too smooth and too clever. His eyes are dark, his fists are big, and he weighs 210 pounds under the sweat-stained felt hat he jams onto his head. A Casey plot can be summed up as a triple conflict: Casey is after a news story in pictures, the opposition (the criminals) don't want him to get those pictures, and the police don't want him to interfere. Casey's interference, of course, delivers the criminals to the police. Casey is a figure from American folklore—the sentimental tough guy—and this may account for much of his appeal. Coxe was never a truly hard-boiled writer, preferring to substitute character for action and violence. He used Casey in several novels after the *Black Mask* days. (Another *Black Mask* character, Paul Baron, did not have the appeal of Casey and appeared in only four stories.)

When Coxe began to write books he replaced Casey with photographer Kent Murdock of the *Courier-Herald*. Murdock is more sophisticated than Casey and is more socially at ease. Murdock knows people on all levels of society and his first case (*Murder with Pictures*) is easily among Coxe's best novels with its multiple conflicts. One of the most interesting characters in the series was Murdock's wife, Joyce, confident, self-reliant, intelligent—just the sort of woman the cynical sentimentalist, Kent Murdock, would have married. She was too strong a character, however, and was dropped before she could take over the series. There is a certain amount of pleasant predictability about the Murdock stories. This familiarity may have helped the reader who expected and wanted a story much like the last one. Murdock was expected to stumble over bodies in closets; it was part of his job and part of his character. Murdock's colleague in some of the novels was Jack Fenner. In 1971 he branched out on his own. Flippant and good-natured, there was something hard and unyielding about his character. He was unafraid and, at times, merciless.

Coxe's third major series centers on the medical examiner Paul Standish. The medical background is as authentic in this series as the newspaper background in the Casey and Murdock series. Coxe also wrote books about Sam Crombie (a large man in a seersucker suit and Panama hat, who plods along and does his job) and Maxfield Chauncey Hale (detective in spite of himself).

Nearly half of Coxe's published novels have not been of any series at all. The heroes and villians resemble ones in his series books, but there is more freedom for the author to develop characters, tell different kinds of stories, and use varying backgrounds. One of the obvious advantages in writing a mystery about a character who does not have to survive unchanged for another book is the way the reader is allowed to get inside his skin. The feelings of Murdock and Casey could not be described in the same way as those of Spence Rankin in *Dangerous Legacy*. The settings vary for the non-series books, but within the group are 16 which take place in the Caribbean, an area their author knew well.

To some readers Coxe may seem dull. There is little explicit violence, just tales of people caught up in webs of their own spinning, told in deceptively simple formal style. For others—that's entertainment.

—J. Randolph Cox

———

CRAIG, Alisa. *See* **MacLEOD, Charlotte.**

———

CRAIG, Jonathan. Pseudonym for Frank E. Smith. American. Born in 1919. Head research analyst for the United

States Navy in the Pentagon and for the Joint Chiefs of Staff during World War II; adviser to President Truman at the Potsdam Conference, 1945. *Died 14 September 1984.*

CRIME PUBLICATIONS

Novels (series: Pete Selby)

Red-Headed Sinner.   Rockville Centre, New York, Croydon, 1953.
Alley Girl.   New York, Lion, 1954; as *Renegade Cop*, New York, Berkley, 1959.
The Dead Darling (Selby).   New York, Fawcett, 1955; London, Miller, 1958.
Morgue for Venus (Selby).   New York, Fawcett, 1956; London, Fawcett, 1957.
Case of the Cold Coquette (Selby).   New York, Fawcett, 1957; London, Fawcett, 1958.
The Case of the Beautiful Body (Selby).   New York, Fawcett, 1957; London, Fawcett, 1958.
Come Night, Come Evil.   New York, Fawcett, 1957; London, Miller, 1959.
So Young, So Wicked.   New York, Fawcett, 1957; London, Fawcett, 1958.
Case of the Petticoat Murder (Selby).   New York, Fawcett, 1958; London, Fawcett, 1960.
Case of the Nervous Nude (Selby).   New York, Fawcett, 1959; London, Muller, 1960.
Case of the Village Tramp (Selby).   New York, Fawcett, 1959; London, Muller, 1961.
Case of the Laughing Virgin (Selby).   New York, Fawcett, 1960; London, Muller, 1962.
Case of the Silent Stranger (Selby).   New York, Fawcett, 1964.
Case of the Brazen Beauty (Selby).   New York, Gold Medal, 1966.

Uncollected Short Stories

"Dirge for a Nude," in *Manhunt* (New York), February 1953.
"Services Rendered," in *Manhunt* (New York), May 1953.
"The Corpse That Came Back," in *Pursuit* (New York), September 1953.
"The Scrapbook," in *Manhunt* (New York), September 1953.
"The Bobby-Soxer," in *Manhunt* (New York), October 1953.
"Kid Stuff," in *Manhunt* (New York), November 1953.
"The Quiet Room," in *Manhunt* (New York), December 1953.
"Too Beautiful to Burn," in *Private Eye* (New York), December 1953.
"The Velvet Vise," in *Pursuit* (New York), March 1954.
"The Right One," in *Manhunt* (New York), May 1954.
"Identity Unknown," in *Manhunt* (New York), August 1954.
"Night Watch," in *Manhunt* (New York), September 1954.
"The Dead Darling," in *Manhunt* (New York), October 1954.
"Man from Yesterday," in *Manhunt* (New York), November 1954.
"In the Shadows," in *Pursuit* (New York), November 1954.
"The Red Tears," in *Manhunt* (New York), December 1954.
"The Floater," in *Manhunt* (New York), January 1955.
"Classification: Homicide," in *Manhunt* (New York), February 1955.
"The Punisher," in *Manhunt* (New York), March 1955.
"The Imposters," in *Manhunt* (New York), April 1955.
"The Lady in Question," in *Manhunt* (New York), May 1955.
"The Baby-Sitter," in *Manhunt* (New York), July 1955.
"Cast Off," in *Manhunt* (New York), September 1955.
"The Spoilers," in *Manhunt* (New York), October 1955.

"The Man Between," in *Manhunt* (New York), November 1955.

"The Cheater," in *Manhunt* (New York), January 1956.

"The Temptress," in *Manhunt* (New York), March 1956.

"A Lady of Talent," in *Accused* (New York), July 1956.

"So Much per Body," in *Manhunt* (New York), December 1956.

"Sunday's Slaughter," in *Mike Shayne Mystery Magazine* (New York), January 1957.

"You'll Have to Kill Me First," in *Guilty* (New York), January 1957.

"Stop Calling Me 'Mister,' " in *Alfred Hitchcock's Mystery Magazine* (New York), January 1957.

"Execution at Eleven," in *Terror* (New York), April 1957.

"Remember Biff Bailey?," in *Manhunt* (New York), July 1957.

"Murder—Maestro Please!," in *Mystery Digest* (New York), September 1957.

"Kitchen Kill," in *Best Detective Stories of the Year*, edited by David C. Cooke. New York, Dutton, 1958.

"Holiday for Homicide," in *Mike Shayne Mystery Magazine* (New York), January 1958.

"The Rolleiflex Murder," in *Mystery Tales* (New York), October 1959.

"The Baby," in *Alfred Hitchcock's Mystery Magazine* (New York), February 1964.

"This Day's Evil," in *Alfred Hitchcock's Mystery Magazine* (New York), March 1964.

"Poor Maude," in *Mike Shayne Mystery Magazine* (New York), January 1965.

"Beholder," in *Mike Shayne Mystery Magazine* (New York), February 1966.

"The Natural Nothing," in *Shell Scott Mystery Magazine* (New York), March 1966.

"Hour of the Cobra," in *Shell Scott Mystery Magazine* (New York), May 1966.

"Tough Chippe," in *Manhunt* (New York), June–July 1966.

"The Prodigy," in *Shell Scott Mystery Magazine* (New York), July 1966.

"The Past Is Dead," in *Manhunt* (New York), August–September 1966.

"The Late Unlamented," in *Alfred Hitchcock's Mystery Magazine* (New York), September 1966.

"All the Loose Women," in *Manhunt* (New York), October–November 1966.

"Top Man," in *Ellery Queen's Mystery Magazine* (New York), November 1966.

"The Coffin Maker," in *Shell Scott Mystery Magazine* (New York), November 1966.

"Last Night's Evil," in *Alfred Hitchcock's Mystery Magazine* (New York), January 1967.

"The Man Must Die," in *Alfred Hitchcock's Mystery Magazine* (New York), March 1967.

"As Long as You Live," in *Mike Shayne Mystery Magazine* (New York), November 1967.

"Call Me Nick," in *Alfred Hitchcock's Mystery Magazine* (New York), October 1968.

"The Guiltstone Dagger," in *Mike Shayne Mystery Magazine* (New York), February 1969.

"Hellbound," in *Mike Shayne Mystery Magazine* (New York), April 1969.

"Just Before Midnight," in *Mike Shayne Mystery Magazine* (New York), May 1969.

"Six Skinny Coffins," in *Alfred Hitchcock's Mystery Magazine* (New York), June 1969.

"Early Sunday Morning," in *Alfred Hitchcock's Mystery Magazine* (New York), December 1969.

"Cold Night on Lake Lenore," in *Alfred Hitchcock's Mystery Magazine* (New York), January 1970.

"The Girl in Gold," in *Alfred Hitchcock's Mystery Magazine* (New York), September 1970.

"Yesterday's Evil," in *Alfred Hitchcock's Mystery Magazine* (New York), June 1971.

"Strange Encounter," in *Mike Shayne Mystery Magazine* (Los Angeles), August 1972.

"A Very Special Gift," in *Mike Shayne Mystery Magazine* (Los Angeles), January 1974.

"A Great Sense of Humor," in *Mike Shayne Mystery Magazine* (Los Angeles), May 1974.

"Bus to Chattanooga," in *Alfred Hitchcock's Tales to Scare You Stiff*, edited by Eleanor Sullivan. New York, Dial Press, 1978.

*   *   *

Jonathan Craig (Frank E. Smith) was one of a number of able paperback crime writers who were part of the Gold Medal "stable" during the 1950's and early 1960's. Among his confreres were John D. MacDonald, Richard S. Prather, Edward S. Aarons, Wade Miller, and Peter Rabe, all of whom specialized in fast-paced mysteries geared to a mostly male audience. They made the paperback original an integral part of the mystery field, and established a thriving new market for ex-pulpsters and new writers.

While most of Gold Medal's writers produced private-eye stories and man-on-the-run thrillers, Craig took a slightly different tack and launched a police procedural series, featuring Detective Pete Selby of Manhattan's Sixth Precinct. The first book in the series, *The Dead Darling*, preceded by a year the better-known and much more successful 87th Precinct procedural series by Ed McBain (which also began as a paperback series). Comparisons with the benchmark for big-city police novels established by McBain are unavoidable. Craig's 10 Selby novels lack the large cast of characters, the variety of story ideas, and the innovative use of documentary evidence that characterize McBain's books. However, working on a smaller scale, Craig produced tightly crafted, thoroughly readable stories.

Selby narrates the cases in the first person. The homicide investigations conducted by Selby and his partner, Stan Rayder—who acts as a sounding board and foil—emphasize patient tracing of leads and questioning of witnesses and suspects. Action—car chases, shootouts, and the like—is, atypically for Gold Medal, virtually absent. Kicking in a door or wrestling with a recalcitrant suspect is about as kinetic as things get. Police routine is an integral part of the background: filling out reports, digging out yellow sheets, working with the crime lab and the medical examiner, quizzing stool pigeons.

This basic structure is familiar; it's quite likely that radio's *Dragnet* served as Craig's model for the series. Craig's expert handling of dialogue is what makes the books work. It's not as stylized as Jack Webb's "Just the facts, Ma'am"; but Selby's insistent, thorough, low-key probing in extended question-and-answer sessions with an assortment of suspects carries the narrative along with nary a dead spot.

Though, as noted, violence and action are downplayed, that other Gold Medal staple, sex, is not, as is obvious from the titles: *Case of the Cold Coquette*, . . . *Laughing Virgin*, . . . *Village Tramp*, . . . *Nervous Nude*. Invariably, the novels begin with the discovery of the body of a beautiful young girl. Selby and Rayder trace the girl's background, quizzing neighbors, boyfriends, ex-husbands, skirt-chasing employers, and the like. Greenwich Village is part of the Sixth's territory, and many of the characters thus encountered are Bohemian types, eccentric artists, and homosexuals. The victim, seemingly innocent, is gradually revealed to be an amoral teenage sexpot, adept at manipulating men, and not averse to a spot or two of blackmail. Halfway through the book, the cops have at least a half-dozen prospective murderers to choose from which they finally succeed in doing by thorough interrogation and dogged adherence to police routine.

Though the sex angle is prominent, the books are not sensationalized or sleazy. They are, in fact, rather low-key for male-oriented paperback originals, and quite believable, with surprisingly frank language for books of the time. Given that Craig worked with one basic story idea in all of the Selby novels, each book seems fresh and imaginative in isolation, though if the books are read in a bunch the victims and suspects do tend to blur together.

Apart from the Sixth Precinct novels, Craig wrote a great deal of short fiction for the hardboiled digest-sized mystery magazines: *Manhunt, Accused, Shell Scott Mystery Magazine*. Some of these stories were a "Police Files" series with detectives Steve Manning and Walt Logan—essentially Selby and Rayder tales with only a name change. Others were typical tough-guy crime stories, usually with a sex angle. Craig's three non-series novels also fall in this category, the most interesting of which is *So Young, So Wicked* in which a syndicate killer is assigned to eliminate a 15-year old nymph who is quite competently blackmailing the mob.

Craig was a journeyman genre writer, working within the limited confines of the paperback crime novel; his work was not original in concept or style. He was a fine craftsman, however, and his books are smoothly readable and thoroughly entertaining.

—Art Scott

CRANE, Frances (née Kirkwood). American. Born in Lawrenceville, Illinois, in 1896. Educated at the University of Illinois, Urbana, B.A. (Phi Beta Kappa). Married Ned Crane (died); one daughter.

CRIME PUBLICATIONS

Novels (series: Pat and Jean Abbott in all books except those without color references in the title)

The Turquoise Shop. Philadelphia, Lippincott, 1941; London, Hammond, 1943.
The Golden Box. Philadelphia, Lippincott, 1942; London, Hammond, 1944.
The Yellow Violet. Philadelphia, Lippincott, 1942; London, Hammond, 1944.
The Applegreen Cat. Philadelphia, Lippincott, 1943; London, Hammond, 1945.
The Pink Umbrella. Philadelphia, Lippincott, 1943; London, Hammond, 1944.
The Amethyst Spectacles. New York, Random House, 1944; London, Hammond, 1946.
The Indigo Necklace. New York, Random House, 1945; London, Hammond, 1947.
The Cinnamon Murder. New York, Random House, 1946; London, Hammond, 1948.
The Shocking Pink Hat. New York, Random House, 1946; London, Hammond, 1948.

Murder on the Purple Water. New York, Random House, 1947; London, Hammond, 1949.
Black Cypress. New York, Random House, 1948; London, Hammond, 1950.
The Flying Red Horse. New York, Random House, and London, Hammond, 1950.
The Daffodil Blonde. New York, Random House, 1950; London, Hammond, 1951.
Murder in Blue Street, New York, Random House, 1951; as *Death in the Blue Hour,* London, Hammond, 1952.
The Polkadot Murder. New York, Random House, 1951; London, Hammond, 1952.
Murder in Bright Red. New York, Random House, 1953; London, Hammond, 1954.
13 White Tulips. New York, Random House, and London, Hammond, 1953.
The Coral Princess Murders. New York, Random House, 1954; London, Hammond, 1955.
Death in Lilac Time. New York, Random House, and London, Hammond, 1955.
Horror on the Ruby X. New York, Random House, and London, Hammond, 1956.
The Ultraviolet Widow. New York, Random House, 1956; London, Hammond, 1957.
The Buttercup Case. New York, Random House, and London, Hammond, 1958.
The Man in Gray. New York, Random House, 1958; as *The Gray Stranger,* London, Hammond, 1958.
Death-Wish Green. New York, Random House, and London, Hammond, 1960.
The Reluctant Sleuth. London, Hammond, 1961.
The Amber Eyes. New York, Random House, and London, Hammond, 1962.
Three Days in Hong Kong. London, Hammond, 1965.
Body Beneath a Mandarin Tree. London, Hammond, 1965.
A Very Quiet Murder. London, Hammond, 1966.
Worse Than a Crime. London, Hale, 1968.

Uncollected Short Stories

"The Blue Hat," in *Queen's Awards 1946*, edited by Ellery Queen. Boston, Little Brown, 1946; London, Gollancz, 1948.
"Death in Guatemala," in *Ellery Queen's Mystery Magazine* (New York), June 1960.

OTHER PUBLICATIONS

Novel

The Tennessee Poppy; or, Which Way Is Westminster Abbey. New York, Farrar and Rinehart, 1932.

* * *

Primarily a formula mystery writer, Frances Crane wrote mysteries for over two decades, moving from the conventions of the late Golden Age "Had-I-But-Known" school to the fringes of modern crime novels. Jean Abbott (Holly in her premarriage books) narrates the stories while her husband, Pat, is the strong silent detective. Though they live in San Francisco, many of the Abbotts' cases occur while they are on vacation: in fact, the books are often travelogues, but only occasionally successful in using local color to create atmosphere.

Crane's work is mostly in the mystery field. As in *The Yellow Violet*, hints of spies or gangsters are usually kept vague. A murder occurs, usually off-stage, and Jean becomes involved;

Pat, in charge of the final scenes, catches the villain and explains how and why the murder occurred. His solution is based largely on points learned or discussed by Jean, but his reasoning process to uncover the murderer's identity is not given. The earlier books used Had-I-But-Known teasers to evoke suspense, but Crane dropped most of those by the late 1950's. And Crane moved with the times in other ways, introducing more naturalistic elements, drugs in *Death-Wish Green* and *The Coral Princess Murders* and a retarded child in *The Amber Eyes*.

Crane tried to achieve characterization by bizarreness. Her books often drop the reader into the middle of a situation and then backtrack to show how the Abbotts got into it. A large eccentric family or close-knit group makes up the list of suspects, often not clearly differentiated. There is often a pair of young lovers toward whom Jean is sympathetic, even though at least one of them acts suspiciously. Pat seems to accept them at face value, forcing Jean to withhold some incriminating information.

As a husband and wife team, the Abbotts don't provide the humor or oddity of the Lockridges' Norths, Roos's Jeff and Haila Troy, or Christie's Tommy and Tuppence Beresford. Because we never know what Pat is really thinking, he never becomes truly alive. In the earlier books Jean is a prominent character. Her style is almost chatty, including detailed reporting of clothes and make-up. Later, she is primarily an observer.

Crane's popularity is based on competent working of familiar themes, taking her readers to exotic places, and presenting a non-taxing, unthreatening tale where all ends as it should.

—Fred Dueren

CRAWFORD, Robert. *See* **RAE, Hugh C.**

CREASEY, John. Also wrote as Gordon Ashe; M.E. Cooke; Margaret Cooke; Henry St. John Cooper; Norman Deane; Elise Fecamps; Robert Caine Frazer; Patrick Gill; Michael Halliday; Charles Hogarth; Brian Hope; Colin Hughes; Kyle Hunt; Abel Mann; Peter Manton; J.J. Marric; James Marsden; Richard Martin; Rodney Mattheson; Anthony Morton; Ken Ranger; William K. Reilly; Tex Riley; Jeremy York. British. Born in Southfields, Surrey, 17 September 1908. Educated at Fulham Elementary School and Sloane School, both in London. Married 1) Margaret Elizabeth Cooke in 1935 (divorced 1939), one son; 2) Evelyn Jean Fudge in 1941 (divorced 1970), two sons; 3) the writer Jeanne Williams in 1970 (divorced 1973); 4) Diana Hamilton Farrer in 1973. Worked in various clerical posts, 1923–35; full-time writer from 1935: editor and publisher, *John Creasey Mystery Magazine*, 1956–65; publisher, Jay Books, 1957–59. Co-founder, Crime Writers Association, 1953; Member of the Board, 1957–60, and President, 1966–67, Mystery Writers of America. Liberal Party Parliamentary Candidate for Bournemouth, 1950; founded All Party Alliance Movement, 1967, and Parliamentary Candidate at Nuneaton, 1967, Brierley Hill, April 1967, Gorton, Manchester, 1967, and Oldham West, 1968. Recipient: Mystery Writers of America Edgar Allan Poe

award, 1962. Mystery Writers of America Grand Master award, 1969. M.B.E. (Member, Order of the British Empire), 1946. *Died 9 June 1973.*

CRIME PUBLICATIONS

Novels (series: Sexton Blake; Department Z; Dr. Palfrey; the Hon. Richard Rollison, "The Toff"; Inspector Roger West)

Seven Times Seven. London, Melrose, 1932.
Men, Maids, and Murder. London, Melrose, 1933; revised edition, London, Long, 1973.
Redhead (Department Z). London, Hurst and Blackett, 1933.
The Death Miser (Department Z). London, Melrose, 1933.
First Came a Murder (Department Z). London, Melrose, 1934; revised edition, London, Long, 1969; New York, Popular Library, 1972.
Death round the Corner (Department Z). London, Melrose, 1935; revised edition, London, Long, 1971; New York, Popular Library, 1972.
The Mark of the Crescent (Department Z). London, Melrose, 1935; revised edition, London, Long, 1970; New York, Popular Library, 1972.
The Dark Shadow (as Rodney Mattheson). London, Fiction House, n.d.
Thunder in Europe (Department Z). London, Melrose, 1936; revised edition, London, Long, 1970; New York, Popular Library, 1972.
The Terror Trap (Department Z). London, Melrose, 1936; revised edition, London, Long, 1970; New York, Popular Library, 1972.
The House of Ferrars (as Rodney Mattheson). London, Fiction House, n.d.
Carriers of Death (Department Z). London, Melrose, 1937; revised edition, London, Arrow, 1968; New York, Popular Library, 1972.
The Case of the Murdered Financier (Blake). London, Amalgamated Press, 1937.
Days of Danger (Department Z). London, Melrose, 1937; revised edition, London, Long, 1970; New York, Popular Library, 1972.
Four Motives for Murder (as Brian Hope). London, Newnes, 1938.
Death Stands By (Department Z). London, Long, 1938; revised edition, London, Arrow, 1966; New York, Popular Library, 1972.
Introducing the Toff. London, Long 1938; revised edition, 1954.
Menace! (Department Z). London, Long, 1938; revised edition, Long, and New York, Popular Library, 1972.
The Great Air Swindle (Blake). London, Amalgamated Press, 1939.
Murder Must Wait (Department Z). London, Melrose, 1939; revised edition, London, Long, 1969; New York, Popular Library, 1972.
Panic! (Department Z). London, Long, 1939; New York, Popular Library, 1972.
The Toff Goes On. London, Long, 1939; revised edition, 1955.
The Toff Steps Out. London, Long, 1939; revised edition, 1955.
Triple Murder (as Colin Hughes). London, Newnes, 1940.
Death by Night (Department Z). London, Long, 1940; revised edition, 1971; New York Popular Library, 1972.
Here Comes the Toff! London, Long, 1940; New York, Walker, 1967.

The Island of Peril (Department Z). London, Long, 1940; revised edition, 1970; New York, Popular Library, 1976.

The Man from Fleet Street (Blake). London, Amalgamated Press, 1940.

The Toff Breaks In. London, Long, 1940; revised edition, 1955.

Sabotage (Department Z). London, Long, 1941; revised edition, 1972; New York, Popular Library, 1976.

Go Away Death (Department Z). London, Long, 1941; New York, Popular Library, 1976.

Salute the Toff. London, Long, 1941; New York, Walker, 1971.

The Toff Proceeds. London, Long, 1941; New York, Walker, 1968.

The Case of the Mad Inventor (Blake). London, Amalgamated Press, 1942.

The Day of Disaster (Department Z). London, Long, 1942.

Inspector West Takes Charge. London, Stanley Paul, 1942; revised edition, London, Pan, 1963; New York, Scribner, 1972.

Prepare for Action (Department Z). London, Stanley Paul, 1942; revised edition, London, Arrow, 1966; New York, Popular Library, 1975.

The Toff Goes to Market. London, Long, 1942; New York, Walker, 1967.

The Toff is Back. London, Long, 1942; New York, Walker, 1974.

Traitors' Doom (Palfrey). London, Long, 1942; New York, Walker, 1970.

Inspector West Leaves Town. London, Stanley Paul, 1943; as *Go Away to Murder*, London, Lancer, 1972.

The Legion of the Lost (Palfrey). London, Long, 1943; New York, Daye, 1944; revised edition, New York, Walker, 1974.

No Darker Crime (Department Z). London, Stanley Paul, 1943; New York, Popular Library, 1976.

Private Carter's Crime (Blake). London, Amalgamated Press, 1943.

The Toff among the Millions. London, Long, 1943; revised edition, London, Panther, 1964; New York, Walker, 1976.

The Valley of Fear (Palfrey). London, Long, 1943; as *The Perilous Country*, 1949; revised edition, London, Arrow, 1966; New York, Walker, 1973.

Accuse the Toff. London, Long, 1943; New York, Walker, 1975.

Murder on Largo Island, with Ian Bowen (as Charles Hogarth). London, Selwyn and Blount, 1944.

Dangerous Quest (Department Z). London, Long, 1944; revised edition, London, Arrow, 1965; New York, Walker, 1974.

Dark Peril (Department Z). London, Stanley Paul, 1944; revised edition, London, Long, 1969; New York, Popular Library, 1975.

Inspector West at Home. London, Stanley Paul, 1944; New York, Scribner, 1973.

The Toff and the Curate. London, Long, 1944; New York, Walker, 1969; as *The Toff and the Deadly Parson*, London, Lancer, 1970.

The Toff and the Great Illusion. London, Long, 1944; New York, Walker, 1967.

Death in the Rising Sun (Palfrey). London, Long, 1945; revised edition, 1970; New York, Walker, 1976.

The Hounds of Vengeance (Palfrey). London, Long, 1945; revised edition, 1969.

Inspector West Regrets—. London, Stanley Paul, 1945; revised edition, Hodder and Stoughton, 1965; New York, Lancer, 1971.

Feathers for the Toff. London, Long, 1945; revised edition, London, Hodder and Stoughton, 1964; New York, Walker, 1970.

Holiday for Inspector West. London, Stanley Paul, 1946.

The Peril Ahead (Department Z). London, Stanley Paul, 1946; revised edition, London, Long, 1969; New York, Popular Library, 1974.

Shadow of Doom (Palfrey). London, Long, 1946; revised edition, 1970.

The Toff and the Lady. London, Long, 1946; New York, Walker, 1975.

The Toff on Ice. London, Long, 1946; as *Poison for the Toff*, New York, Pyramid, 1965; revised edition, London, Corgi, 1976.

The House of the Bears (Palfrey). London, Long, 1946; revised edition, London, Arrow, 1962; New York, Walker, 1975.

Dark Harvest (Palfrey). London, Long, 1947; revised edition, London, Arrow, 1962; New York, Walker, 1977.

Hammer the Toff. London, Long, 1947.

The League of Dark Men (Department Z). London, Stanley Paul, 1947; revised edition, London, Arrow, 1965; New York, Popular Library, 1975.

Keys to Crime (as Richard Martin). Bournemouth, Earl, 1947.

Vote for Murder (as Richard Martin). Bournemouth, Earl, 1948.

Battle for Inspector West. London, Stanley Paul, 1948.

The Toff in Town. London, Long, 1948; revised edition, New York, Walker, 1977.

The Toff Takes Shares. London, Long, 1948; New York, Walker, 1972.

Triumph for Inspector West: London, Stanley Paul, 1948; as *The Case Against Paul Raeburn*, New York, Harper, 1958.

The Wings of Peace (Palfrey). London, Long, 1948; New York, Walker, 1978.

Sons of Satan (Palfrey). London, Long, 1948.

The Dawn of Darkness (Palfrey). London, Long, 1949.

The Department of Death (Department Z). London, Evans, 1949.

Inspector West Kicks Off. London, Stanley Paul, 1949; as *Sport for Inspector West*, London, Lancer, 1971.

The League of Light (Palfrey). London, Evans, 1949.

The Toff and Old Harry. London, Long, 1949; revised edition, London, Hodder and Stoughton, 1964; New York, Walker, 1970.

The Toff on Board. London, Evans, 1949; revised edition, New York, Walker, 1973.

The Enemy Within (Department Z). London, Evans, 1950; New York, Popular Library, 1977.

Fool the Toff. London, Evans, 1950; New York, Walker, 1966.

Inspector West Alone. London, Evans, 1950; New York, Scribner, 1975.

Inspector West Cries Wolf. London, Evans, 1950; as *The Creepers*, New York, Harper, 1952.

Kill the Toff. London, Evans, 1950; New York, Walker, 1966.

The Man Who Shook the World (Palfrey). London, Evans, 1950.

A Case for Inspector West. London, Evans, 1951; as *The Figure in the Dusk*, New York, Harper, 1952.

Dead or Alive (Department Z). London, Evans, 1951; New York, Popular Library, 1974.

A Knife for the Toff. London, Evans, 1951; New York, Pyramid, 1964.

The Prophet of Fire (Palfrey). London, Evans, 1951; New York, Walker, 1978.

Puzzle for Inspector West. London, Evans, 1951; as *The Dissemblers*, New York, Scribner, 1967.

The Toff Goes Gay. London, Evans, 1951; as *A Mask for the Toff*, New York, Walker, 1966.

The Children of Hate (Palfrey). London, Evans, 1952; as *The Children of Despair*, New York, Jay, 1958; revised edition, London, Long, 1970; as *The Killers of Innocence*, New York, Walker, 1971.

Inspector West at Bay. London, Evans, 1952; as *The Blind Spot*, New York, Harper, 1954; as *The Case of the Acid Throwers*, New York, Avon, 1960.

Hunt the Toff. London, Evans, 1952; New York, Walker, 1969.

Call the Toff. London, Hodder and Stoughton, 1953; New York, Walker, 1969.

A Gun for Inspector West. London, Hodder and Stoughton, 1953; as *Give a Man a Gun*, New York, Harper, 1954.

Send Inspector West. London, Hodder and Stoughton, 1953; revised edition, as *Send Superintendent West*, London, Pan, 1965; New York, Scribner, 1976.

The Toff Down Under. London, Hodder and Stoughton, 1953; New York, Walker, 1969; as *Break the Toff*, London, Lancer, 1970.

A Beauty for Inspector West. London, Hodder and Stoughton, 1954; as *The Beauty Queen Killer*, New York, Harper, 1956; as *So Young, So Cold, So Fair*, New York, Dell, 1958.

A Kind of Prisoner (Department Z). London, Hodder and Stoughton, 1954; New York, Popular Library, 1975.

The Toff at Butlin's. London, Hodder and Stoughton, 1954; New York, Walker, 1976.

The Toff at the Fair. London, Hodder and Stoughton, 1954; New York, Walker, 1968.

The Touch of Death (Palfrey). London, Hodder and Stoughton, 1954; New York, Walker, 1969.

Inspector West Makes Haste. London, Hodder and Stoughton, 1955; as *The Gelignite Gang*, New York, Harper, 1956; as *Night of the Watchman*, New York, Berkley, n.d.; as *Murder Makes Haste*, New York, Lancer, n.d.

The Mists of Fear (Palfrey). London, Hodder and Stoughton, 1955; New York, Walker, 1977.

A Six for the Toff. London, Hodder and Stoughton, 1955; New York, Walker, 1969; as *A Score for the Toff*, London, Lancer, 1972.

The Toff and the Deep Blue Sea. London, Hodder and Stoughton, 1955; New York, Walker, 1967.

Two for Inspector West. London, Hodder and Stoughton, 1955; as *Murder: One, Two, Three*, New York, Scribner, 1960; as *Murder Tips the Scales*, New York, Berkley, 1962.

Make-Up for the Toff. London, Hodder and Stoughton, 1956; New York, Walker, 1967; as *Kiss the Toff*, London, Lancer, 1971.

The Flood (Palfrey). London, Hodder and Stoughton, 1956; New York, Walker 1969.

Parcels for Inspector West. London, Hodder and Stoughton, 1956; as *Death of a Postman*, New York, Harper, 1957.

A Prince for Inspector West. London, Hodder and Stoughton, 1956; as *Death of an Assassin*, New York, Scribner, 1960.

The Toff in New York. London, Hodder and Stoughton, 1956; New York, Pyramid, 1964.

Accident for Inspector West. London, Hodder and Stoughton, 1957; as *Hit and Run*, New York, Scribner, 1959.

The Black Spiders (Department Z). London, Hodder and Stoughton, 1957; New York, Popular Library, 1975.

Find Inspector West. London, Hodder and Stoughton, 1957; as *The Trouble at Saxby's*, New York, Harper, 1959; as *Doorway to Death*, New York, Berkley, 1961.

Model for the Toff. London, Hodder and Stoughton, 1957; New York, Pyramid, 1965.

The Toff on Fire. London, Hodder and Stoughton, 1957; New York, Walker, 1966.

Murder, London—New York (West). London, Hodder and Stoughton, 1958; New York, Scribner, 1961.

The Plague of Silence (Palfrey). London, Hodder and Stoughton, 1958; New York, Walker, 1968.

Strike for Death (West). London, Hodder and Stoughton, 1958; as *The Killing Strike*, New York, Scribner, 1961.

The Toff and the Stolen Tresses. London, Hodder and Stoughton, 1958; New York, Walker, 1965.

The Toff on the Farm. London, Hodder and Stoughton, 1958; New York, Walker 1964; as *Terror for the Toff*, New York, Pyramid, 1965.

Death of a Racehorse (West). London, Hodder and Stoughton, 1959; New York, Scribner, 1962.

Double for the Toff. London, Hodder and Stoughton, 1959; New York, Walker, 1965.

The Drought (Palfrey). London, Hodder and Stoughton, 1959; New York, Walker, 1967; as *Dry Spell*, London, New English Library, 1967.

The Toff and the Runaway Bride. London, Hodder and Stoughton, 1959; New York, Walker, 1964.

The Case of the Innocent Victims (West). London, Hodder and Stoughton, 1959; New York, Scribner, 1966.

The Mountain of the Blind. London, Hodder and Stoughton, 1960.

Murder on the Line (West). London, Hodder and Stoughton, 1960; New York, Scribner, 1963.

A Rocket for the Toff. London, Hodder and Stoughton, 1960; New York, Pyramid, 1964.

The Toff and the Kidnapped Child. London, Hodder and Stoughton, 1960; New York, Walker, 1965.

Death in Cold Print (West). London, Hodder and Stoughton, 1961; New York, Scribner, 1962.

Follow the Toff. London, Hodder and Stoughton, 1961; New York, Walker, 1967.

The Foothills of Fear. London, Hodder and Stoughton, 1961; New York, Walker, 1966.

The Scene of the Crime (West). London, Hodder and Stoughton, 1961; New York, Scribner, 1963.

The Toff and the Teds. London, Hodder and Stoughton, 1961; as *The Toff and the Toughs*, New York, Walker, 1968.

Policeman's Dread (West). London, Hodder and Stoughton, 1962; New York, Scribner, 1964.

The Terror: The Return of Dr. Palfrey. London, Hodder and Stoughton, 1962; New York, Walker, 1966.

The Depths (Palfrey). London, Hodder and Stoughton, 1963; New York, Walker, 1966.

A Doll for the Toff. London, Hodder and Stoughton, 1963; New York, Walker 1965.

Hang the Little Man (West). London, Hodder and Stoughton, and New York, Scribner, 1963.

Leave It to the Toff. London, Hodder and Stoughton, 1963; New York, Pyramid, 1965.

Look Three Ways at Murder (West). London, Hodder and Stoughton, 1964; New York, Scribner, 1965.

The Sleep! (Palfrey). London, Hodder and Stoughton, 1964; New York, Walker, 1968.

The Inferno (Palfrey). London, Hodder and Stoughton, 1965; New York, Walker, 1966.

Murder, London—Australia (West). London, Hodder and Stoughton, and New York, Scribner, 1965.

The Toff and the Spider. London, Hodder and Stoughton, 1965; New York, Walker, 1966.

Danger Woman (as Abel Mann). New York, Pocket Books, 1966.

Murder, London—South Africa (West). London, Hodder and Stoughton, and New York, Scribner, 1966.

The Toff in Wax. London, Hodder and Stoughton, and New York, Walker, 1966.

A Bundle for the Toff. London, Hodder and Stoughton, 1967; New York, Walker, 1968.

The Executioners (West). London, Hodder and Stoughton, and New York, Scribner, 1967.

The Famine (Palfrey). London, Hodder and Stoughton, 1967; New York, Walker, 1968.

The Blight (Palfrey). London, Hodder and Stoughton, and New York, Walker, 1968.

So Young to Burn (West). London, Hodder and Stoughton, and New York, Scribner, 1968.

Stars for the Toff. London, Hodder and Stoughton, and New York, Walker, 1968.

Murder, London—Miami (West). London, Hodder and Stoughton, and New York, Scribner, 1969.

The Oasis (Palfrey). London, Hodder and Stoughton, 1969; New York, Walker, 1970.

The Toff and the Golden Boy. London, Hodder and Stoughton, and New York, Walker, 1969.

A Part for a Policeman (West). London, Hodder and Stoughton, and New York, Scribner, 1970.

The Smog (Palfrey). London, Hodder and Stoughton, 1970; New York, Walker, 1971.

The Toff and the Fallen Angels. London, Hodder and Stoughton, and New York, Walker, 1970.

Alibi (West). London, Hodder and Stoughton, and New York, Scribner, 1971.

The Unbegotten (Palfrey). London, Hodder and Stoughton, 1971; New York, Walker, 1972.

Vote for the Toff. London, Hodder and Stoughton, and New York, Walker, 1971.

The Insulators (Palfrey). London, Hodder and Stoughton, 1972; New York, Walker, 1973.

The Masters of Bow Street. London, Hodder and Stoughton, 1972; New York, Simon and Schuster, 1973.

A Splinter of Glass (West). London, Hodder and Stoughton, and New York, Scribner, 1972.

The Toff and the Trip-Trip-Triplets. London, Hodder and Stoughton, and New York, Walker, 1972.

The Toff and the Terrified Taxman. London, Hodder and Stoughton, and New York, Walker, 1973.

The Theft of Magna Carta (West). London, Hodder and Stoughton, and New York, Scribner, 1973.

The Voiceless Ones (Palfrey). London, Hodder and Stoughton, 1973; New York, Walker, 1974.

The Extortioners (West). London, Hodder and Stoughton, 1974; New York, Scribner, 1975.

The Toff and the Sleepy Cowboy. London, Hodder and Stoughton, 1974; New York, Walker, 1975.

The Thunder-Maker (Palfrey). London, Hodder and Stoughton, and New York, Walker, 1976.

The Toff and the Crooked Copper. London, Hodder and Stoughton, 1977.

The Toff and the Dead Man's Finger. London, Hodder and Stoughton, 1978.

A Sharp Rise in Crime (West). London, Hodder and Stoughton, 1978; New York, Scribner, 1979.

The Whirlwind. London, Hodder and Stoughton, 1979.

Novels as M.E. Cooke

Fire of Death. London, Fiction House, 1934.
The Black Heart. London, Gramol, 1935.
The Casino Mystery. London, Mellifont Press, 1935.

The Crime Gang. London, Mellifont Press, 1935.
The Death Drive. London, Mellifont Press, 1935.
Number One's Last Crime. London, Fiction House, 1935.
The Stolen Formula Mystery. London, Mellifont Press, 1935.
The Big Radium Mystery. London, Mellifont Press, 1936.
The Day of Terror. London, Mellifont Press, 1936.
The Dummy Robberies. London, Mellifont Press, 1936.
The Hypnotic Demon. London, Fiction House, 1936.
The Moat Farm Mystery. London, Fiction House, 1936.
The Secret Formula. London, Fiction House, 1936.
The Successful Alibi. London, Mellifont Press, 1936.
The Hadfield Mystery. London, Mellifont Press, 1937.
The Moving Eye. London, Mellifont Press, 1937.
The Raven. London, Fiction House, 1937.
The Mountain Terror. London, Mellifont Press, 1938.
For Her Sister's Sake. London, Fiction House, 1938.
The Verrall Street Affair. London, Newnes, 1940.

Novels as Michael Halliday (series: Dr. Emmanuel Cellini; Martin and Richard Fane; Cellini books published as Kyle Hunt in U.S.)

Four Find Adventure. London, Cassell, 1937.
Three For Adventure. London, Cassell, 1937.
Two Meet Trouble. London, Cassell, 1938.
Murder Comes Home. London, Stanley Paul, 1940.
Heir to Murder. London, Stanley Paul, 1940.
Murder by the Way. London, Stanley Paul, 1941.
Who Saw Him Die? London, Stanley Paul, 1941.
Foul Play Suspected. London, Stanley Paul, 1942.
Who Died at the Grange? London, Stanley Paul, 1942.
Five to Kill. London, Stanley Paul, 1943.
Murder at King's Kitchen. London, Stanley Paul, 1943.
Who Said Murder? London, Stanley Paul, 1944.
No Crime More Cruel. London, Stanley Paul, 1944.
Crime with Many Voices. London, Stanley Paul, 1945.
Murder Makes Murder. London, Stanley Paul, 1946.
Murder Motive. London, Stanley Paul, 1947; New York, McKay, 1974.
Lend a Hand to Murder. London, Stanley Paul, 1947.
First a Murder. London, Stanley Paul, 1948; New York, McKay, 1972.
No End to Danger. London, Stanley Paul, 1948.
Who Killed Rebecca. London, Stanley Paul, 1949.
The Dying Witnesses. London, Evans, 1949.
Dine with Murder. London, Evans, 1950.
Murder Week-End. London, Evans, 1950.
Quarrel with Murder. London, Evans, 1951; revised edition, London, Corgi, 1975.
Take a Body (Fanes). London, Evans, 1951; revised edition, London, Hodder and Stoughton, 1964; Cleveland, World, 1972.
Lame Dog Murder (Fanes). London, Evans, 1952; Cleveland, World, 1972.
Murder in the Stars (Fanes). London, Hodder and Stoughton, 1953.
Murder on the Run (Fanes). London, Hodder and Stoughton, 1953; Cleveland, World, 1972.
Death Out of Darkness. London, Hodder and Stoughton, 1954; Cleveland, World, 1971.
Out of the Shadows. London, Hodder and Stoughton, 1954; Cleveland, World, 1971.
Cat and Mouse. London, Hodder and Stoughton, 1955; as *Hilda, Take Heed,* New York, Scribner, 1957.
Murder at End House. London, Hodder and Stoughton, 1955.
Death of a Stranger. London, Hodder and Stoughton, 1957; as *Come Here and Die,* New York, Scribner, 1959.

Runaway. London, Hodder and Stoughton, 1957; Cleveland, World, 1971.
Murder Assured. London, Hodder and Stoughton, 1958.
Missing from Home. London, Hodder and Stoughton, 1959; as *Missing*, New York, Scribner, 1960.
Thicker Than Water. London, Hodder and Stoughton, 1959; New York, Doubleday, 1962.
Go Ahead with Murder. London, Hodder and Stoughton, 1960; as *Two for the Money*, New York, Doubleday, 1962.
How Many to Kill? London, Hodder and Stoughton, 1960; as *The Girl with the Leopard-Skin Bag*, New York, Scribner, 1961.
The Edge of Terror. London, Hodder and Stoughton, 1961; New York, Macmillan, 1963.
The Man I Killed. London, Hodder and Stoughton, 1961; New York, Macmillan, 1963.
Hate to Kill. London, Hodder and Stoughton, 1962.
The Quiet Fear. London, Hodder and Stoughton, 1963; New York, Macmillan, 1968.
The Guilt of Innocence. London, Hodder and Stoughton, 1964.
Cunning as a Fox (Cellini). London, Hodder and Stoughton, and New York, Macmillan, 1965.
Wicked as the Devil (Cellini). London, Hodder and Stoughton, and New York, Macmillan, 1966.
Sly as a Serpent (Cellini). London, Hodder and Stoughton, and New York, Macmillan, 1967.
Cruel as a Cat (Cellini). London, Hodder and Stoughton, and New York, Macmillan, 1968.
Too Good to Be True (Cellini). London, Hodder and Stoughton, and New York, Macmillan, 1969.
A Period of Evil (Cellini). London, Hodder and Stoughton, 1970; Cleveland, World, 1971.
As Lonely as the Damned (Cellini). London, Hodder and Stoughton, 1971; Cleveland, World, 1972.
As Empty as Hate (Cellini). London, Hodder and Stoughton, and Cleveland, World, 1972.
As Merry as Hell (Cellini). London, Hodder and Stoughton, 1973; New York, Stein and Day, 1974.
This Man Did I Kill? (Cellini). London, Hodder and Stoughton, and New York, Stein and Day, 1974.
The Man Who Was Not Himself (Cellini). London, Hodder and Stoughton, and New York, Stein and Day, 1976.

Novels as Peter Manton

Murder Manor. London, Wright and Brown, 1937.
The Greyvale School Mystery. London, Sampson Low, 1937.
Stand By for Danger. London, Wright and Brown, 1937.
The Circle of Justice. London, Wright and Brown, 1938.
Three Days' Terror. London, Wright and Brown, 1938.
The Crime Syndicate. London, Wright and Brown, 1939.
Death Looks On. London, Wright and Brown, 1939.
Murder in Highlands. London, Wright and Brown, 1939.
The Midget Marvel. London, Mellifont Press, 1940.
Policeman's Triumph. London, Wright and Brown, 1948.
Thief in the Night. London, Wright and Brown, 1950.
No Escape from Murder. London, Wright and Brown, 1953.
The Crooked Killer. London, Wright and Brown, 1954.
The Charity Killers. London, Wright and Brown, 1954.

Novels as Anthony Morton (series: John Mannering, The Baron [Blue Mask])

Meet the Baron. London, Harrap, 1937; as *The Man in the Blue Mask*, Philadelphia, Lippincott, 1937.
The Baron Returns. London, Harrap, 1937; as *The Return of Blue Mask*, Philadelphia, Lippincott, 1937.

The Baron Again. London, Sampson Low, 1938; as *Salute Blue Mask!*, Philadelphia, Lippincott, 1938.
The Baron at Bay. London, Sampson Low, 1938; as *Blue Mask at Bay*, Philadelphia, Lippincott, 1938.
Alias the Baron. London, Sampson Low, 1939; as *Alias Blue Mask*, Philadelphia, Lippincott, 1939.
The Baron at Large. London, Sampson Low, 1939; as *Challenge Blue Mask!*, Philadelphia, Lippincott, 1939.
Versus the Baron. London, Sampson Low, 1940; as *Blue Mask Strikes Again*, Philadelphia, Lippincott, 1940.
Call for the Baron. London, Sampson Low, 1940; as *Blue Mask Victorious*, Philadelphia, Lippincott, 1940.
The Baron Comes Back. London, Sampson Low, 1943.
Mr. Quentin Investigates. London, Sampson Low, 1943.
Introducing Mr. Brandon. London, Sampson Low, 1944.
A Case for the Baron. London, Sampson Low, 1945; New York, Duell, 1949.
Reward for the Baron. London, Sampson Low, 1945.
Career for the Baron. London, Sampson Low, 1946; New York, Duell, 1950.
The Baron and the Beggar. London, Sampson Low, 1947; New York, Duell, 1950.
Blame the Baron. London, Sampson Low, 1948; New York, Duell, 1951.
A Rope for the Baron. London, Sampson Low, 1948; New York, Duell, 1949.
Books for the Baron. London, Sampson Low, 1949; New York, Duell, 1952.
Cry for the Baron. London, Sampson Low, 1950; New York, Walker, 1970.
Trap the Baron. London, Sampson Low, 1950; New York, Walker, 1971.
Attack the Baron. London, Sampson Low, 1951.
Shadow the Baron. London, Sampson Low, 1951.
Warn the Baron. London, Sampson Low, 1952.
The Baron Goes East. London, Sampson Low, 1953.
The Baron in France. London, Hodder and Stoughton, 1953; New York, Walker, 1976.
Danger for the Baron. London, Hodder and Stoughton, 1953; New York, Walker, 1974.
The Baron Goes Fast. London, Hodder and Stoughton, 1954; New York, Walker, 1972.
Nest-Egg for the Baron. London, Hodder and Stoughton, 1954; as *Deaf, Dumb and Blonde*, New York, Doubleday, 1961.
Help from the Baron. London, Hodder and Stoughton, 1955; New York, Walker, 1977.
Hide the Baron. London, Hodder and Stoughton, 1956; New York, Walker, 1978.
Frame the Baron. London, Hodder and Stoughton, 1957; as *The Double Frame*, New York, Doubleday, 1961.
Red Eye for the Baron. London, Hodder and Stoughton, 1958; as *Blood Red*, New York, Doubleday, 1960.
Black for the Baron. London, Hodder and Stoughton, 1959; as *If Anything Happens to Hester*, New York, Doubleday, 1962.
Salute for the Baron. London, Hodder and Stoughton, 1960; New York, Walker, 1973.
A Branch for the Baron. London, Hodder and Stoughton, 1961; as *The Baron Branches Out*, New York, Scribner, 1967.
Bad for the Baron. London, Hodder and Stoughton, 1962; as *The Baron and the Stolen Legacy*, New York, Scribner, 1967.
A Sword for the Baron. London, Hodder and Stoughton, 1963; as *The Baron and the Mogul Swords*, New York, Scribner, 1966.
The Baron on Board. London, Hodder and Stoughton, 1964; New York, Walker, 1968.

The Baron and the Chinese Puzzle. London, Hodder and Stoughton, 1965; New York, Scribner, 1966.

Sport for the Baron. London, Hodder and Stoughton, 1966; New York, Walker, 1969.

Affair for the Baron. London, Hodder and Stoughton, 1967; New York, Walker, 1968.

The Baron and the Missing Old Masters. London, Hodder and Stoughton, 1968; New York, Walker, 1969.

The Baron and the Unfinished Portrait. London, Hodder and Stoughton, 1969; New York, Walker, 1970.

Last Laugh for the Baron. London, Hodder and Stoughton, 1970; New York, Walker, 1971.

The Baron Goes A-Buying. London, Hodder and Stoughton, 1971; New York, Walker, 1972.

The Baron and the Arrogant Artist. London, Hodder and Stoughton, 1972; New York, Walker, 1973.

Burgle the Baron. London, Hodder and Stoughton, 1973; New York, Walker, 1974.

The Baron, King-Maker. London, Hodder and Stoughton, and New York, Walker, 1975.

Love for the Baron. London, Hodder and Stoughton, 1979.

Novels as Gordon Ashe (series: Patrick Dawlish in all books except *The Man Who Stayed Alive* and *No Need to Die*)

Death on Demand. London, Long, 1939.

The Speaker. London, Long, 1939; as *The Croaker*, New York, Holt Rinehart, 1972.

Who Was the Jester? London, Newnes, 1940.

Terror by Day. London, Long, 1940.

Secret Murder. London, Long, 1940.

'Ware Danger! London, Long, 1941.

Murder Most Foul. London, Long, 1942; revised edition, London, Corgi, 1973.

There Goes Death. London, Long, 1942; revised edition, London, Corgi, 1973.

Death in High Places. London, Long, 1942.

Death in Flames. London, Long, 1943.

Two Men Missing. London, Long, 1943; revised edition, London, Corgi, 1971.

Rogues Rampant. London, Long, 1944; revised edition, London, Corgi, 1973.

Death on the Move. London, Long, 1945.

Invitation to Adventure. London, Long, 1945.

Here Is Danger! London, Long, 1946.

Give Me Murder. London, Long, 1947.

Murder Too Late. London, Long, 1947.

Dark Mystery. London, Long, 1948.

Engagement with Death. London, Long, 1948.

A Puzzle in Pearls. London, Long, 1949; revised edition, London, Corgi, 1971.

Kill or Be Killed. London, Evans, 1949.

Murder with Mushrooms. London, Evans, 1950; revised edition, London, Corgi, 1971; New York, Holt Rinehart, 1974.

Death in Diamonds. London, Evans, 1951.

Missing or Dead? London, Evans, 1951.

Death in a Hurry. London, Evans, 1952.

The Long Search. London, Long, 1953; as *Drop Dead*, New York, Ace, 1954.

Sleepy Death. London, Long, 1953.

Double for Death. London, Long, 1954; New York, Holt Rinehart, 1969.

Death in the Trees. London, Long, 1954.

The Kidnapped Child. London, Long, 1955; New York, Holt Rinehart, 1971; as *The Snatch*, London, Corgi, 1965.

The Man Who Stayed Alive. London, Long, 1955.

No Need to Die. London, Long, 1956; New York, Ace, 1957.

Day of Fear. London, Long, 1956; New York, Holt Rinehart, 1978.

Wait for Death. London, Long, 1957; New York, Holt Rinehart, 1972.

Come Home to Death. London, Long, 1958; as *The Pack of Lies*, New York, Doubleday, 1959.

Elope to Death. London, Long, 1959; New York, Holt Rinehart, 1977.

The Crime Haters. New York, Doubleday, 1960; London, Long, 1961.

The Dark Circle. London, Evans, 1960.

Don't Let Him Kill. London, Long, 1960; as *The Man Who Laughed at Murder*, New York, Doubleday, 1960.

Rogues' Ransom. New York, Doubleday, 1961; London, Long, 1962.

Death from Below. London, Long, 1963; New York, Holt Rinehart, 1968.

The Big Call. London, Long, 1964; New York, Holt Rinehart, 1975.

A Promise of Diamonds. New York, Dodd Mead, 1964; London, Long, 1965.

A Taste of Treasure. London, Long, and New York, Holt Rinehart, 1966.

A Clutch of Coppers. London, Long, 1967; New York, Holt Rinehart, 1969.

A Shadow of Death. London, Long, 1968; New York, Holt Rinehart, 1976.

A Scream of Murder. London, Long, 1969; New York, Holt Rinehart, 1970.

A Nest of Traitors. London, Long, 1970; New York, Holt Rinehart, 1971.

A Rabble of Rebels. London, Long, 1971; New York, Holt Rinehart, 1972.

A Life for a Death. London, Long, and New York, Holt Rinehart, 1973.

A Herald of Doom. London, Long, 1974; New York, Holt Rinehart, 1975.

A Blast of Trumpets. London, Long, and New York, Holt Rinehart, 1975.

A Plague of Demons. London, Long, 1976; New York, Holt Rinehart, 1977.

Novels as Norman Deane (series: The Liberator; Bruce Murdoch)

Secret Errand (Murdoch). London, Hurst and Blackett, 1939; New York, McKay, 1974.

Dangerous Journey (Murdoch). London, Hurst and Blackett, 1939; New York, McKay, 1974.

Unknown Mission (Murdoch). London, Hurst and Blackett, 1940; revised edition, London, Arrow, and New York, McKay, 1972.

The Withered Man (Murdoch). London, Hurst and Blackett, 1940; New York, McKay, 1974.

I Am the Withered Man (Murdoch). London, Hurst and Blackett, 1941; revised edition, London, Long, 1972; New York, McKay, 1973.

Where Is the Withered Man? (Murdoch). London, Hurst and Blackett, 1942; revised edition, London, Arrow, and New York, McKay, 1972.

Return to Adventure (Liberator). London, Hurst and Blackett, 1943; revised edition, London, Long, 1974.

Gateway to Escape (Liberator). London, Hurst and Blackett, 1944.

Come Home to Crime (Liberator). London, Hurst and Blackett, 1945; revised edition, London, Long, 1974.

Play for Murder. London, Hurst and Blackett, 1946; revised edition, London, Arrow, 1975.
The Silent House. London, Hurst and Blackett, 1947; revised edition, London, Arrow, 1973.
Why Murder? London, Hurst and Blackett, 1948; revised edition, London, Arrow, 1975.
Intent to Murder. London, Hurst and Blackett, 1948; revised edition, London, Arrow, 1975.
The Man I Didn't Kill. London, Hurst and Blackett, 1950; revised edition, London, Hutchinson, 1973.
No Hurry to Kill. London, Hurst and Blackett, 1950; revised edition, London, Arrow, 1973.
Double for Death. London, Hurst and Blackett, 1951; revised edition, London, Hutchinson, 1973.
Golden Death. London, Hurst and Blackett, 1952.
Look at Murder. London, Hurst and Blackett, 1952.
Murder Ahead. London, Hurst and Blackett, 1953.
Death in the Spanish Sun. London, Hurst and Blackett, 1954.
Incense of Death. London, Hurst and Blackett, 1954.

Novels as Jeremy York (series: in revised versions only: Superintendent Folly)

By Persons Unknown. London, Bles, 1941.
Murder Unseen. London, Bles, 1943.
No Alibi. London, Melrose, 1943.
Murder in the Family. London, Melrose, 1944; New York, McKay, 1976.
Yesterday's Murder. London, Melrose, 1945.
Find the Body (Folly). London, Melrose, 1945; revised edition, New York, Macmillan, 1967.
Murder Came Late (Folly). London, Melrose, 1946; revised edition, New York, Macmillan, 1969.
Wilful Murder. Los Angeles, McNaughton, 1946.
Let's Kill Uncle Lionel. London, Melrose, 1947; revised edition, London, Corgi, 1973; New York, McKay, 1976.
Run Away to Murder. London, Melrose, 1947; New York, Macmillan, 1970.
Close the Door on Murder (Folly). London, Melrose, 1948; revised edition, New York, McKay, 1973.
The Gallows Are Waiting. London, Melrose, 1949; New York, McKay, 1973.
Death to My Killer. London, Melrose, 1950; New York, Macmillan, 1966.
Sentence of Death. London, Melrose, 1950; New York, Macmillan, 1964.
Voyage with Murder. London, Melrose, 1952.
Safari with Fear. London, Melrose, 1953.
So Soon to Die. London, Stanley Paul, 1955; New York, Scribner, 1957.
Seeds of Murder. London, Stanley Paul, 1956; New York, Scribner, 1958.
Sight of Death. London, Stanley Paul, 1956; New York, Scribner, 1958.
My Brother's Killer. London, Long, 1958; New york, Scribner, 1959.
Hide and Kill. London, Long, 1959; New York, Scribner, 1960.
To Kill or to Die. London, Long, 1960; New York, Macmillan, 1965.

Novels as J.J. Marric (series: Commander George Gideon)

Gideon's Day. London, Hodder and Stoughton, and New York, Harper, 1955; as *Gideon of Scotland Yard*, New York, Berkley, 1958.

Gideon's Week. London, Hodder and Stoughton, and New York, Harper, 1956; as *Seven Days to Death*, New York, Pyramid, 1958.
Gideon's Night. London, Hodder and Stoughton, and New York, Harper, 1957.
Gideon's Month. London, Hodder and Stoughton, and New York, Harper, 1958.
Gideon's Staff. London, Hodder and Stoughton, and New York, Harper, 1959.
Gideon's Risk. London, Hodder and Stoughton, and New York, Harper, 1960.
Gideon's Fire. London, Hodder and Stoughton, and New York, Harper, 1961.
Gideon's March. London, Hodder and Stoughton, and New York, Harper, 1962.
Gideon's Ride. London, Hodder and Stoughton, and New York, Harper, 1963.
Gideon's Vote. London, Hodder and Stoughton, and New York, Harper, 1964.
Gideon's Lot. New York, Harper, 1964; London, Hodder and Stoughton, 1965.
Gideon's Badge. London, Hodder and Stoughton, and New York, Harper, 1966.
Gideon's Wrath. London, Hodder and Stoughton, and New York, Harper, 1967.
Gideon's River. London, Hodder and Stoughton, and New York, Harper, 1968.
Gideon's Power. London, Hodder and Stoughton, and New York, Harper, 1969.
Gideon's Sport. London, Hodder and Stoughton, and New York, Harper, 1970.
Gideon's Art. London, Hodder and Stoughton, and New York, Harper, 1971.
Gideon's Men. London, Hodder and Stoughton, and New York, Harper, 1972.
Gideon's Press. London, Hodder and Stoughton, and New York, Harper, 1973.
Gideon's Fog. New York, Harper, 1974; London, Hodder and Stoughton, 1975.
Gideon's Drive. London, Hodder and Stoughton, and New York, Harper, 1976.

Novels as Kyle Hunt

Kill Once, Kill Twice. New York, Simon and Schuster, 1956; London, Barker, 1957.
Kill a Wicked Man. New York, Simon and Schuster, 1957; London, Barker, 1958.
Kill My Love. New York, Simon and Schuster, 1958; London, Barker, 1959.
To Kill a Killer. London, Boardman, and New York, Random House, 1960.

Novels as Robert Caine Frazer (series: Mark Kirby in all books)

Mark Kirby Solves a Murder. New York, Pocket Books, 1959; as *R.I.S.C.*, London, Collins, 1962; as *The Timid Tycoon*, London, Fontana, 1966.
Mark Kirby and the Secret Syndicate. New York, Pocket Books, 1960; London, Collins, 1963.
Mark Kirby and the Miami Mob. New York, Pocket Books, 1960; with *Mark Kirby Stands Alone*, London, Collins, 1965.
The Hollywood Hoax. New York, Pocket Books, 1961; London, Collins, 1964.

Mark Kirby Stands Alone. New York, Pocket Books, 1962; with *The Miami Mob*, London, Collins, 1965; as *Mark Kirby and the Manhattan Murders*, London, Fontana, 1966.
Mark Kirby Takes a Risk. New York, Pocket Books, 1962.

Short Stories

The Toff on the Trail. London, Everybody's Books, n.d.
Murder Out of the Past, and Under-Cover Man (Toff). Leigh-on-Sea, Essex, Barrington Gray, 1953.

Uncollected Short Stories

"Hair of His Head," in *The Evening Standard Detective Book.* London, Gollancz, 1950.
"Piece of Cake," in *Eat, Drink and Be Buried*, edited by Rex Stout. New York, Viking Press, 1956; as *For Tomorrow We Die*, London, Macdonald, 1958.
"Betrayal of the Hopeless," in *Ellery Queen's Mystery Magazine* (New York), February 1957.
"Inspector West Triumphs," in *Ellery Queen's Mystery Magazine* (New York), August 1957.
"The Chief Witness," in *Planned Departures*, edited by Elizabeth Ferrars. London, Hodder and Stoughton, 1958.
"The Book of Honour," in *The Sixth Mystery Bedside Book*, edited by John Creasey. London, Hodder and Stoughton, 1965.
"Shadow of the Noose," in *The Saint* (New York), August 1966.
"The Greyling Crescent Mystery," in *Ellery Queen's All-Star Lineup.* New York, New American Library, 1967.

OTHER PUBLICATIONS

Novels

One-Shot Marriott (as Ken Ranger). London, Sampson Low, 1938.
Roaring Guns (as Ken Ranger). London, Sampson Low, 1939.
Adrian and Jonathan (as Richard Martin). London, Hodder and Stoughton, 1954.

Novels as Margaret Cooke

For Love's Sake. N.p., Northern News Syndicate, 1934.
Troubled Journey. London, Fiction House, 1937.
False Love or True. N.p., Northern News Syndicate, 1937.
Fate's Playthings. London, Fiction House, 1938.
Web of Destiny. London, Fiction House, 1938.
Whose Lover? London, Fiction House, 1938.
A Mannequin's Romance. London, Fiction House, 1938.
Love Calls Twice. London, Fiction House, 1938.
The Road to Happiness. London, Fiction House, 1938.
The Turn of Fate. London, Fiction House, 1939.
Love Triumphant. London, Fiction House, 1939.
Love Comes Back. London, Fiction House, 1939.
Crossroads of Love. London, Mellifont Press, 1939.
Love's Journey. London, Fiction House, 1940.

Novels as Elise Fecamps

Love of Hate. London, Fiction House, 1936.
True Love. London, Fiction House, 1937.
Love's Triumph. London, Fiction House, 1937.

Novels as Henry St. John Cooper

Chains of Love. London, Sampson Low, 1937.
Love's Pilgrimage. London, Sampson Low, 1937.

The Tangled Legacy. London, Sampson Low, 1938.
The Greater Desire. London, Sampson Low, 1938.
Love's Ordeal. London, Sampson Low, 1939.
The Lost Lover. London, Sampson Low, 1940.

Novels as Tex Riley

Two-Gun Girl. London, Wright and Brown, 1938.
Gun-Smoke Range. London, Wright and Brown, 1938.
Gunshot Mesa. London, Wright and Brown, 1939.
The Shootin' Sheriff. London, Wright and Brown, 1940.
Rustler's Range. London, Wright and Brown, 1940.
Masked Riders. London, Wright and Brown, 1940.
Death Canyon. London, Wright and Brown, 1941.
Guns on the Range. London, Wright and Brown, 1942.
Range Justice. London, Wright and Brown, 1943.
Outlaw Hollow. London, Wright and Brown, 1944.
Hidden Range. Bournemouth, Earl, 1946.
Forgotten Range. Bournemouth, Earl, 1947.
Trigger Justice. Bournemouth, Earl, 1948.
Lynch Hollow. Bournemouth, Earl, 1949.

Novels as William K. Reilly

Range War. London, Stanley Paul, 1939.
Two Gun Texan. London, Stanley Paul, 1939.
Gun Feud. London, Stanley Paul, 1940.
Stolen Range. London, Stanley Paul, 1940.
War on Lazy-K. London, Stanley Paul, 1941; New York, Phoenix Press, 1946.
Outlaw's Vengeance. London, Stanley Paul, 1941.
Guns over Blue Lake. London, Jenkins, 1942.
Rivers of Dry Gulch. London, Jenkins, 1943.
Long John Rides the Range. London, Jenkins, 1944.
Miracle Range. London, Jenkins, 1945.
The Secrets of the Range. London, Jenkins, 1946.
Outlaw Guns. Bournemouth, Earl, 1949.
Range Vengeance. London, Ward Lock, 1953.

Plays

Gideon's Fear, adaptation of his novel *Gideon's Week* (produced Salisbury, 1960). London, Evans, 1967.
Strike for Death (produced Salisbury, 1960).
The Toff. London, Evans, 1963.
Hear Nothing, Say All (produced Salisbury, 1964).

Other (for children) as Patrick Gill

The Fighting Footballers. London, Mellifont Press, 1937.
The Laughing Lightweight. London, Mellifont Press, 1937.
The Battle for the Cup. London, Mellifont Press, 1939.
The Fighting Tramp. London, Mellifont Press, 1939.
The Mystery of the Centre-Forward. London, Mellifont Press, 1939.
The £10,000 Trophy Race. London, Melifont Press, 1939
The Secret Super-Charger. London, Melifont Press, 1940.

Other (for children)

Ned Cartwright—Middleweight Champion (as James Marsden). London, Mellifont Press, 1935.
The Men Who Died Laughing. Dundee, Thompson, 1935.
The Killer Squad. London, Newnes, 1936.
Our Glorious Term. London, Sampson Low, n.d.
The Captain of the Fifth. London, Sampson Low, n.d.
Blazing the Air Trail. London, Sampson Low, 1936.
The Jungle Flight Mystery. London, Sampson Low, 1936.

The Mystery 'plane. London, Sampson Low, 1936.
Murder by Magic. London, Amalgamated Press, 1937.
The Mysterious Mr. Rocco. London, Mellifont Press, 1937.
The S.O.S Flight. London, Sampson Low, 1937.
The Secret Aeroplane Mystery. London, Sampson Low, 1937.
The Treasure Flight. London, Sampson Low, 1937.
The Air Marauders. London, Sampson Low, 1937.
The Black Biplane. London, Sampson Low, 1937.
The Mystery Flight. London, Sampson Low, 1937.
The Double Motive. London, Mellifont Press, 1938.
The Doublecross of Death. London, Mellifont Press, 1938.
The Missing Hoard. London, Mellifont Press, 1938.
Mystery at Manby House. N.p., Northern News Syndicate, 1938.
The Fighting Flyers. London, Sampson Low, 1938.
The Flying Stowaways. London, Sampson Low, 1938.
The Miracle 'plane. London, Sampson Low, 1938.
Dixon Hawke, Secret Agent. Dundee, Thompson, 1939.
Documents of Death. London, Mellifont Press, 1939.
The Hidden Hoard. London, Mellifont Press, 1939.
Mottled Death. Dundee, Thompson, 1939.
The Blue Flyer. London, Mellifont Press, 1939.
The Jumper. N.p., Northern News Syndicate, 1939.
The Mystery of Blackmoor Prison. London, Mellifont Press, 1939.
The Sacred Eye. Dundee, Thompson, 1939.
The Ship of Death. Dundee, Thompson, 1939.
Peril by Air. London, Newnes, 1939.
The Flying Turk. London, Sampson Low, 1939.
The Monarch of the Skies. London, Sampson Low, 1939.
The Fear of Felix Corder. London, Fleetway Press, n.d.
John Brand, Fugitive. London, Fleetway Press, n.d.
The Night of Dread. London, Fleetway Press, n.d.
Dazzle—Air Ace No. 1. London, Newnes, 1940.
Dazzle and the Red Bomber. London, Newnes, n.d.
Five Missing Men. London, Newnes, 1940.
The Poison Gas Robberies. London, Mellifont Press, 1940.
The Crimea Crimes. Manchester, Pemberton, 1945.
The Missing Monoplane. London, Sampson Low, 1947.

Other

Fighting Was My Business, by Jimmy Wilde (ghost written by Creasey). London, Joseph, 1938.
Log of a Merchant Airman, with John H. Lock. London, Stanley Paul, 1943.
Heroes of the Air: A Tribute to the Courage, Sacrifice, and Skill of the Men of the R.A.F. Dorchester, Dorset Wings for Victory Committee, 1943.
The Printers' Devil: An Account of the History and Objects of the Printers' Pension, Almshouse, and Orphan Asylum Corporation, edited by Walter Hutchinson. London, Hutchinson, 1943.
Man in Danger. London, Hutchinson, 1949.
Round the World in 465 Days, with Jean Creasey. London, Hale, 1953.
Round Table: The First Twenty-Five Years of the Round Table Movement. London, National Association of Round Tables of Great Britain and Ireland, 1953.
Let's Look at America, with others. London, Hale, 1956.
They Didn't Mean to Kill: The Real Story of Road Accidents. London, Hodder and Stoughton, 1960.
Optimists in Africa, with others. Cape Town, Timmins, 1963.
African Holiday, drawings by Martin Creasey. Cape Town, Timmins, 1963.
Good, God, and Man: An Outline of the Philosophy of Selfism. London, Hodder and Stoughton, 1967; New York, Walker, 1971.

Evolution to Democracy. London, Hodder and Stoughton, 1969.

Editor, *Action Stations! An Account of the H.M.S. Dorsetshire and Her Earlier Namesakes.* London, Long, 1942.
Editor, *The First [Second, Third, Fourth, Fifth, Sixth] Mystery Bedside Book.* London, Hodder and Stoughton, 6 vols., 1960–65.
Editor, *Crimes Across the Sea: The 19th Annual Anthology of the Mystery Writers of America 1964.* New York, Harper and London, Longman, 1964.

*

Bibliography: "A John Creasey Bibliography" by R.E. Briney and John Creasey, in *The Armchair Detective* (White Bear Lake, Minnesota), October 1968.

Critical Study: *John Creasey—Fact or Fiction? A Candid Commentary in Third Person, With a Bibliography by John Creasey and Robert E. Briney,* White Bear Lake, Minnesota, Armchair Detective Press, 1968; revised edition, 1969.

* * *

The phenomenal John Creasey wrote some 560 novels under more than 20 names. Over 60 million copies of his books have been sold throughout the world, and they continue to sell steadily today. Although his early novels gave little evidence of the good standard of his work to come, he was later to show that he possessed a well of ideas which was never to run dry, a facility to keep countless readers enthralled with action as well as mystery, and the ability to improve upon the literary quality of his actual writings as his career progressed.

Of Creasey's series characters, The Hon. Richard Rollison ("The Toff") and Roger West of Scotland Yard present an interesting contrast. Rollison, rich and gentlemanly, is a larger-than-life character who encounters more than his share of damsels in distress and is a stickler for fair play. The stories are fast-moving, with a succession of twists and crises; they are straight thrillers, far from the detective stories of so many of Creasey's contemporaries, although the identity of the master criminal is sometimes well concealed until the finale. The Toff is portrayed as a glamorous adventurer on the lines of Charteris's The Saint, in a series of books entirely unpretentious, typically British, thoroughly readable, apparently seeking only to entertain yet being prepared to wrestle with the occasional social problem. When we turn to the Roger West books, we find something more solid, not only a competent picture of life and relationships at Scotland Yard, but good examples of detection and pursuit. West may be a little too much the romantic figure, and his domestic life may be somewhat intrusive in those books where it has little bearing upon the investigation in hand. Nevertheless Creasey produced some quite excellent West books in structure (*Look Three Ways at Murder*), in topicality (*Strike for Death*), and in variety of background. Although most of West's cases are set in London, those with international connections and titles are particularly good.

Creasey's "Department Z" and Dr. Palfrey books also have a large following. The former are craftsmanlike counter-espionage stories featuring tough Scotsman Gordon Craigie and his agents, which well convey the wartime atmosphere. Dr. Palfrey was similarly active during the hostilities, and the tales of his organisation pitted against spies or those seeking world domination are enjoyable if a little sensational. The later development of the Palfrey series into the science fiction field is most interesting—on the surface they might appear to be thrillers concerning evil attempts to plague the world into submission, but the underlying messages are frightening and prophetic.

Creasey's pseudonymous series are many, and comments must therefore be selective. As Gordon Ashe, his tales of Patrick Dawlish and "The Crime Haters" are brisk and tough thrillers but unmemorable; much the same may be said about Norman Deane's books featuring Bruce Murdoch and "The Liberator," although Murdoch's wartime adventures are further evidence of Creasey's skill in weaving a good spy yarn. There is much confusion surrounding the novels Creasey wrote as Michael Halliday, as they have also been published in the United States variously as by Jeremy York and by Kyle Hunt. Of these, the straight non-series thrillers concerning people enmeshed in murder have a tense and psychological quality which is most satisfying. The Halliday (or Hunt) series featuring Dr. Emmanuel Cellini, with their ingenious uniformity of title—*Cunning as a Fox, Cruel as a Cat*, etc.—are perhaps the author's most successful forays into the realm of psychology, whereas the Superintendent Folly novels by Jeremy York are the nearest he comes to classical detection. In the books by Anthony Morton, central character John Mannering ("The Baron") is a reformed jewel thief and man-about-town who is always ready to turn his expertise to good use on the side of the angels; his relationship with Superintendent Bristow, who is forever suspicious that Mannering is capable of returning to his old trade, is one of the more entertaining aspects of these adventures.

Pride of place must be given to the novels written under the J.J. Marric pseudonym, which are police procedural novels of a considerable standard. Gideon of Scotland Yard was a major breakthrough for Creasey in terms of the critics' approbation, a character of greater credibility than any of Creasey's other heroes. In their almost documentary coverage of Gideon's professional life, the books give the impression that this is the real Scotland Yard, and the police officers surrounding Gideon have a welcome ring of authenticity. In the skilful inter-twining of the strands of various investigations, and in the unobtrusive scenes from Gideon's domestic life, there are both naturalism and suspense. By switching from case to case and back again, the result is not confusion but a satisfying and well-rounded picture of the life of a busy detective. They are the best things Creasey produced, which is intended as no empty compliment—there is little doubt that Gideon *is* the British procedural novel.

No attempt need be made to examine Creasey's huge output for philosophical messages or sociological import, although these can be found if one feels them to be essential attributes before deeming a crime novelist respectable. Suffice it to say that his reported belief, that the crime novel is almost the only novel worth reading today, was amply justified by the tremendous public response to the sheer entertainment value of his books. In spite of his easy style, the historians of the genre will be very stuffy if they choose to ignore him.

—Melvyn Barnes

CRICHTON, (John) Michael. Also writes as Michael Douglas (with Douglas Crichton); Jeffery Hudson; John Lange. American. Born in Chicago, Illinois, 23 October 1942. Educated at Harvard University, Cambridge, Massachusetts, A.B. (summa cum laude) in anthropology 1964 (Phi Beta Kappa); Harvard Medical School, M.D. 1969; Salk Institute, La Jolla, California, 1969–70. Married 1) Joan Radam in 1965 (divorced 1971); 2) Kathleen St. Johns in 1978 (divorced 1980). Recipient: Mystery Writers of America Edgar Allan Poe award, 1968, 1980; Association of American Medical Writers award, 1970. Agent: International Creative Management, 40 West 57th Street, New York, New York 10019. Address: 2049 Century Park East, No. 4000, Los Angeles, California 90067, U.S.A.

CRIME PUBLICATIONS

Novels

A Case of Need (as Jeffery Hudson). Cleveland, World, and London, Heinemann, 1968.
The Andromeda Strain. New York, Knopf, and London, Cape, 1969.
Dealing; or, The Berkeley-to-Boston Forty-Brick Lost-Bag Blues (as Michael Douglas, with Douglas Crichton). New York, Knopf, 1971; London, Talmy Franklin, 1972.
The Terminal Man. New York, Knopf, and London, Cape, 1972.
Westworld. New York, Bantam, 1975.
The Great Train Robbery. New York, Knopf, and London, Cape, 1975.
Eaters of the Dead. New York, Knopf, and London, Cape, 1976.
Congo. New York, Knopf, 1980; London, Allen Lane, 1981.
Sphere. London, Macmillan, 1987.
Travels. New York, Knopf, 1988.

Novels as John Lange

Odds On. New York, New American Library, 1966.
Scratch One. New York, New American Library, 1967.
Easy Go. New York, New American Library, 1968; London, Sphere, 1972; as *The Last Tomb* (as Michael Crichton), New York, Bantam, 1974.
The Venom Business. Cleveland, World, 1969.
Zero Cool. New York, New American Library, 1969; London, Sphere, 1972.
Drug of Choice. New York, New American Library, 1970; as *Overkill*, London, Sphere, 1972.
Grave Descend. New York, New American Library, 1970.
Binary. New York, Knopf, and London, Heinemann, 1972.

OTHER PUBLICATIONS

Plays

Screenplays: *Westworld*, 1973; *Coma*, 1978; *The Great Train Robbery*, 1978; *Looker*, 1981; *Runaway*, 1984.

Other

Five Patients: The Hospital Explained. New York, Knopf, 1970; London, Cape, 1971.
Jasper Johns. New York, Abrams, and London, Thames and Hudson, 1977.
Electronic Life: How to Think about Computers. New York, Knopf, and London, Heinemann, 1983.

*

Theatrical Activities:

Director: **Films**—*Westworld*, 1973; *Coma*, 1978; *The Great Train Robbery*, 1978; *Looker*, 1981. **Television**—*Pursuit*, 1972.

*   *   *

Michael Crichton's goal (and his achievement) seems to have been technical virtuosity. His best work has a stylistic ease and pace that make writers with greater literary reputations, on a technical level, seem like work horses.

He is a complex writer, and not the simplistic "computer" one critic tried to reduce him to. Like many highly intelligent and sophisticated writers who have written to make money, but also to make life more interesting, he seems to have reached a stagnation point in aesthetic and philosophical goals, tending toward both fantasy and the trivialized concrete.

His plots—the hallmark of the mystery-thriller—are weak. His early thrillers written as John Lange, and a weak collaboration with his brother on drug traffic among youth, contain only a modicum of ingenuity, but the John Lange adventures can be above-average entertainment. But, some of his best touches—the snake containers concealing a compartment for double dealing in underground traffic, an exciting chase through the Alhambra in Granada or the bureaucratic entrapments that inspire a skilled crook into near heroic endeavor to loot an Egyption tomb—are largely wasted on conventional plot and characters.

His villains are only a shade more villainous than many of his heroes, but his women, sophisticated with an out-of-the-ordinary intelligence that makes them attractive, are interesting. His best-selling science-documentary thrillers, *The Andromeda Strain* and *The Terminal Man*, achieved wide attention, but are not his most successful literary accomplishments. An under-appreciated strength is his excellent ability to pace the shorter novel; the best example is *Binary*.

His one first-rate mystery is *A Case of Need*, written as Jeffrey Hudson. The appeal is in the focus of hero-pathologist's mind tracking down the evidence of death, making the story engrossing and believable. The plot is somewhat helterskelter, but the angle of approach and the coordination of style and characterization draw it together. The pace is swift, almost unique in such a complex mystery.

The Great Train Robbery is an effort in the Victorian mystery, a hybrid form that took many skillful writers years to evolve into good entertainment. Now, with exceptions like Peter Lovesey's *The False Inspector Dew*, some writers are trying to put the worst conventions of Victorianism back into the historical mystery with bits and pieces of the modern. The form has a particular built-in contradiction to Crichton's forte of fast-paced action, as it substitutes history for plot, the chronicle for invention. Crichton was unable to transfer the pace of *Binary* into film, but, in his one good film effort, he improved upon the pace of the printed version of *The Great Train Robbery* by cutting data and focusing on action in the film.

More recently he has gone back further in history to Burroughs or Rider Haggard-like fabulism or to futurism, trading off ancient, irrational views of existence for equally irrational modern views of man. *Eaters of the Dead* is not a historical mystery but a shallow dip into the puzzle of this kind of mysticism. The promise of Crichton is a unique background from which the values of science (a proper springboard for adventure and romance) might be resolved in the appropriate form of the mystery. The disappointment has nothing to do with his penchant (and success) in marketing, but with his confusion and/or rejection of other than technical values. To integrate the dichotomy of man's mind-body duality and channel creativity into a rational, moral course is a "case of need" of not only Michael Crichton, but an entire culture.

—Newton Baird

CRIDER, Bill. Also writes as Nick Carter; Jack MacLane. American. Born in Mexia, Texas, 28 July 1941. Educated at the University of Texas, Austin, B.A. 1963, PhD. 1972; North Texas State University, Denton, M.A. 1967. Married Judy Stutts Crider in 1965; one daughter and one son. English teacher, Cosicana, Texas, 1963–65; Associate Professor, 1971–74, Chair, Department of English, Howard Payne University, Brownwood, Texas, 1977–83. Since 1983 chair, Department of English, Alvin Community College, Texas. Recipient: Anthony award (for first novel), 1986. Agent: Peekner Literary Agency Inc., P.O. Box 3308, Bethlehem, Pennsylvania 18017. Address: 1606 South Hill, Alvin, Texas 77511, U.S.A.

CRIME PUBLICATIONS

Novels (series: Carl Burns; Dan Rhodes)

The Coyote Connection (with Jack Davis, as Nick Carter). New York, Charter 1981.
Too Late to Die (Rhodes). New York, Walker, 1986.
Shotgun Saturday Night (Rhodes). New York, Walker, 1987.
Cursed to Death (Rhodes). New York, Walker, 1988.
One Dead Dean (Burns). New York, Walker, 1988.
Death on the Move (Rhodes). New York, Walker, 1989.
Dying Voices (Burns). New York, St. Martin's Press, 1989.
Evil at the Root (Rhodes). New York, St. Martin's Press, 1990.

Uncollected Short Stories

"My Heart Cries for You," in *14 Vicious Valentines*, edited by Martin Greenberg and Charles Waugh, New York, Avon, 1988.
"Wolf Night," in *Westeryear*, edited by Ed Gorman, New York, Evans, 1988.
"Franklin and the Can of Whup-Ass," in *Obsessions*, edited by Gary Raizor, Arlington Heights, Illinois, Dark Harvest, 1990.

OTHER PUBLICATIONS

Novels

Ryan Rides Back. New York, Evans, 1988.
Galveston Gunman. New York, Evans, 1988.
A Time for Hanging. New York, Evans, 1989.
Medicine Show. New York, Evans, 1990.

Novels as Jack MacLane

Keepers of the Beast. New York, Zebra, 1988.
Goodnight Momm. New York, Zebra, 1989.
Blood Dreams. New York, Zebra, 1989.
Rest in Peace. New York, Zebra, 1990.
Just Before Dark. New York, Zebra, 1990.

Other

A Vampire Named Fred (for children). Lufkin, Texas, Temple Press, 1990.

Editor, *Mass Market American Papaerbacks*. Boston, G.K. Hall, 1982.

*

Bill Crider comments

I grew up in a small Texas town, and I've lived in similar towns for a large part of my life, so most of my novels are set in small towns and deal with small-town crimes. There are no threats to the fate of the world and no events of cosmic significance—just the things of everyday life. I write about people like the ones I know and talk to, and I try to look at life with a little humor. It works for me, and I hope it works for the reader.

*   *   *

Unlike the science fiction field, crime fiction has had few writers rise to the professional ranks from organized fandom. If not the first of these, Bill Crider is certainly one of the best.

Crider's first novel, *The Coyote Connection*, is a collaborative effort, with Jack Davis, in the Nick Carter series. It was written strictly to formula, though here and there touches of Crider's slightly outré sense of humor do show through. Crider's first novel under his own name is *Too Late to Die* and is also the first book in his continuing series about Sheriff Dan Rhodes of Blacklin County, Texas.

Rhodes is a widower whose wife has been dead a little over a year in *Too Late to Die* and who lives with his 23-year-old daughter in the first book. He's not maudlin about his wife's death and is just beginning to think about other women again, with help from his daughter. Unlike other county sheriffs, Rhodes is not a particularly astute politician. He just wants to do the job the best he can. As *Too Late to Die* begins Rhodes is up for re-election and his opponent *is* a politician. What he does not need is a murder. How Rhodes handles the election, the murder and various other small town problems forms the core of this fine novel.

Other books in the Rhodes series involve the local dentist disappearing after having a curse put on him, a riot at the local nursing home, motorcycle gangs, assorted severed limbs, and the hiring of a woman police officer. All of these plots are rendered with Crider's gentle, though slightly skewed, sense of humor and all the while we get an excellent sense of rural Texas.

As good as the Dan Rhodes series is, Crider's other series featuring Carl Burns, professor of English literature at Hartley Gorman College in Pecan City, Texas is even more satisfactory. Since Crider himself taught at a small Baptist college in a Texas town one might infer that that these books are somewhat autobiographical. Certainly the characters that populate Hartley Gorman are drawn true to life, though I doubt that there were a significant number of murders at Crider's college while he was there.

The first book in this series, *One Dead Dean*, concerns the murder of the college dean who is in the process of trying to turn the college into a diploma mill. Burns, much against his better judgment, gets involved in trying to solve the murder of Dean Elmore and this brings him into conflict with Sheriff "Boss" Napier who is surely one of the more adroitly drawn secondary characters to come down the pike. If Carl Burns is the star of the book, then "Boss" Napier is certainly a worthy co-star.

The second book in the Burns series is *Dying Voices*. It describes the return to Hartley Gorman College of a former teacher and now best-selling author, Edward Street, for a conference in his honor. Shortly after his arrival Burns finds him murdered. Was Street murdered out of jealousy or because he had supposedly written a book about his time at the college? Of course, the alleged manuscript of said book is missing and also, of course, Burns and "Boss" Napier lock horns in trying to find the truth.

Crider has also written five novels under the pseudonym Jack MacLane which, while marketed as horror novels, are for the most part straight suspense. They are quite different from either the Rhodes series or the Burns series but are still worth looking up. He has also written a number of Western novels which contain strong mystery elements. One particular short story also deserves mention. "Wolf Night" takes the werewolf legend and does a totally unexpected twist on it which again shows Crider's singular way of looking at the world.

For those who like their mysteries medium-boiled with a modicum of humor, they could do much worse than to read the work of Bill Crider.

—Steven A. Stilwell

———

CRISPIN, Edmund. Pseudonym for Robert Bruce Montgomery. British. Born in Chesham Bois, Buckinghamshire, 2 October 1921. Educated at the Merchant Taylors' School, London; St. John's College, Oxford, B.A. 1943. Married. Schoolmaster, Shrewsbury School, 1943–45; composer of choral and orchestral works, songs, and film music. *Died 15 September 1978.*

CRIME PUBLICATIONS

Novels (series: Gervase Fen in all books)

The Case of the Gilded Fly. London, Gollancz, 1944; as *Obsequies at Oxford*, Philadelphia, Lippincott, 1945.
Holy Disorders. London, Gollancz, 1945; Philadelphia, Lippincott, 1946.
The Moving Toyshop. London, Gollancz, and Philadelphia, Lippincott, 1946.
Swan Song. London, Gollancz, 1947; New York, Walker, 1980; as *Dead and Dumb*, Philadelphia, Lippincott, 1947.
Love Lies Bleeding. London, Gollancz, and Philadelphia, Lippincott, 1948.
Buried for Pleasure. London, Gollancz, 1948; Philadelphia, Lippincot, 1949.
Frequent Hearses. London, Gollancz, 1950; as *Sudden Vengeance*, New York, Dodd Mead, 1950.
The Long Divorce. London, Gollancz, and New York, Dodd Mead, 1951; as *A Noose for Her*, New York, Spivak, 1952.
The Glimpses of the Moon. London, Gollancz, 1977; New York, Walker, 1978.

Short Stories

Beware of the Trains: Sixteen Stories. London, Gollancz, 1953; New York, Walker, 1962.
Fen Country. London, Gollancz, 1979; New York, Walker, 1980.

Uncollected Short Story

"St. Bartholomew's Day," in *Ellery Queen's Mystery Magazine* (New York), February 1975.

OTHER PUBLICATIONS

Play

Screenplay: *Raising the Wind*, 1961.

Other

Editor, *Best SF: Science Fiction Stories*. London, Faber, 7 vols., 1955–70.
Editor, *Best Detective Stories*. London, Faber, 2 vols., 1959–64.
Editor, *Best Tales of Terror*. London, Faber, 2 vols., 1962–65.
Editor, *The Stars and Under: A Selection of Science Fiction*. London, Faber, 1968.
Editor, *Best Murder Stories 2*. London, Faber, 1973.
Editor, *Outwards from Earth: A Selection of Science Fiction*. London, Faber, 1974.

*

Published music includes *An Ode on the Resurrection of Christ*, 1947; *Mary Ambree*, 1948; *Four Shakespeare Songs*, 1948; *Two Suites for Chorus and Strings: Venus' Praise* (*1952*), *and Christ's Birthday*, 1948; *Concertino for String Orchestra*, 1950; *An Oxford Requiem*, 1950; *Concerto Waltz for Two Pianos*, 1952; *John Barleycorn: An Opera for Children*, 1962. Unpublished work includes music for 38 films.

Edmund Crispin commented (1978):

I have no great liking for spy stories, or, come to that, for the more so-called "realistic" type of crime story. I believe that crime stories in general and detective stories in particular should be essentially imaginative and artificial in order to make their best effect. Another way of putting it would be to say that I make Jacques Barzun's distinction between the novel and the tale, and think that you try to mix the two things at your peril.

*   *   *

Any review of the writings of Edmund Crispin must begin by bemoaning his relatively small output. Once discovered, enormous frustration is felt when, all too quickly, one has tracked down and read these fine examples of traditional English detective fiction. However, one positive outcome of this modest body of work is the consistently high quality of the books. Unlike many of his contemporaries, Crispin did not provide his readers with formulaic reworkings of previous successes.

Each book is set against a different backdrop, enabling Crispin to show off the versatility of his detective, Gervase Fen, Professor of English Language and Literature at the University of Oxford. Fen is cast in the now outmoded mould of amateur detective, jealously guarding his independent status. We find out very little about him, apart from his occupation and appearance—Crispin assiduously mentions in every book his dark unruly hair ineffectually plastered down with water. However, despite this two-dimensional characteri-

zation, Fen has been established as one of the most endearing fictional detectives of his generation. If Fen has one fault, it is shared by his creator—a sometimes irritating habit of over-indulging in literary allusion. Crispin was no doubt aware of this criticism. In typical tongue-in-cheek style in *The Moving Toyshop* he has one character complain to another, "I don't care who it was a quotation from. It's really rather rude to quote when you know I shan't understand. Like talking about someone in a language they don't know."

Crispin always acknowledged his debt to the great detective story writers of his time, in particular to Michael Innes and John Dickson Carr (he dedicates *Love Lies Bleeding* to the Carr Club). With his first book, *The Gilded Fly*, he combines Innes's literary style with an ingenious, if highly improbable, "locked room" mystery that would not have shamed Carr himself. However, Carr's influence is most strongly felt in *Swan Song*, which, although ultimately let down by a weak motive, has a brilliant central puzzle reminiscent of Gideon Fell—Carr's great detective—at his best.

Although no doubt owing much to the classic detective writers of the 1930's and 1940's, Crispin quickly developed a style very much his own—amusing narrative, clever plotting and theatrical set pieces. His works are not literary novels and don't pretend to be. There is no great analysis of character, which in some cases (notably *The Gilded Fly* and *Swan Song*) leads to disappointingly weak motives for the crimes committed. His settings are the traditional (one could argue stereotypical) arenas of the classic detective story—he moves effortlessly through opera, the theatre, academia, and the Church. He uses his own experience to give us plots set in a film studio and a boys' public school, and is equally at home in the small English village.

However, if one accepts the books in the spirit in which they were written, they are splendid examples of the detective story as great entertainment. They amuse, they shock, and they surprise. *Buried for Pleasure*, set against the backdrop of an election campaign (Fen at his most versatile standing for Parliament), does all three. The book introduces Inspector Humbleby (who appears in *Frequent Hearses* and plays an important role in Crispin's short stories), has a wonderful cast of characters, a cleverly interwoven plot of blackmail, poisoning and murder, and has a surprising twist at the end.

There was a gap of 24 years between *Beware of the Trains* and Crispin's final full length mystery, *The Glimpses of the Moon*. A macabre tale of sexual jealousy and gruesome murder, *The Glimpses of the Moon* is Crispin's most satisfying work. Although he tries too hard to bring in contemporary references, (which ultimately only serve to date the book more quickly), Crispin does succeed in bringing his writing and characters up to date. Gervase Fen is now Dean of his college and is writing a book in a Devonshire village, home to a cast of characters of whom one member at least is capable of carrying out the most grotesque and shocking atrocities. The ensuing multi-layered plot is funny and tragic in turn and the book deserved the critical praise it received on publication.

His second volume of short stories completed Crispin's works. As with most short story writers, Crispin ranges from the sublime to the average. As an example of simple perfection, I would recommend "The Evidence for the Crown" in which the clue to the culprit is so blindingly obvious, one misses it totally. Mention should also be made of "We Know You're Busy Writing But We Thought You Wouldn't Mind If We Just Dropped In For a Minute," a heartfelt tale of grisly murder narrated by a minor crime fiction writer.

Crispin was himself an unashamed fan of detective story writers. I have no doubt he deserves his place amongst the best.

—Roda M. Morrison

———

CROFT-COOKE, Rupert. *See* **BRUCE, Leo.**

———

CROFTS, Freeman Wills. British. Born in Dublin, Ireland, 7 June 1879. Educated at Methodist and Campbell colleges, Belfast. Married Mary Bellas Canning in 1912. Apprenticed at 17 to Berkeley D. Wise, Belfast and North Countries Railway: junior assistant engineer, 1899; district engineer, Coleraine, 1900; chief assistant engineer, Belfast, 1923; resigned, 1929, to become full-time writer. Fellow, Royal Society of Arts, 1939. *Died 11 April 1957.*

CRIME PUBLICATIONS (series: Inspector Joseph French)

Novels

The Cask. London, Collins, 1920; New York, Seltzer, 1924.
The Ponson Case. London, Collins, 1921; New York, Boni, 1927.
The Pit-Prop Syndicate. London, Collins, 1922; New York, Seltzer, 1925.
The Groote Park Murder. London, Collins, 1924; New York, Seltzer, 1925.
Inspector French's Greatest Case. London, Collins, and New York, Seltzer, 1925.
Inspector French and the Cheyne Mystery. London, Collins, 1926; as *The Cheyne Mystery*, New York, Boni, 1926.
Inspector French and the Starvel Tragedy. London, Collins, 1927; as *The Starvel Hollow Tragedy*, New York, Harper, 1927.
The Sea Mystery (French). London, Collins, and New York, Harper, 1928.
Double Death, with others. London, Gollancz, 1929.
The Box Office Murders (French). London, Collins, 1929; as *The Purple Sickle Murders*, New York, Harper, 1929.
Sir John Magill's Last Journey (French). London, Collins, and New York, Harper, 1930.
Mystery in the Channel (French). London, Collins, 1931; as *Mystery in the English Channel*, New York, Harper, 1931.
The Floating Admiral, with others. London, Hodder and Stoughton, 1931; New York, Doubleday, 1932.
Sudden Death (French). London, Collins, and New York, Harper, 1932.
Death on the Way (French). London, Collins, 1932; as *Double Death*, New York, Harper, 1932.
The Hog's Back Mystery (French). London, Hodder and Stoughton, 1933; as *The Strange Case of Dr. Earle*, New York, Dodd Mead, 1933.
The 12:30 from Croydon (French). London, Hodder and Stoughton, 1934; as *Wilful and Premeditated*, New York, Dodd Mead, 1934.
Mystery on Southampton Water (French). London, Hodder and Stoughton, 1934; as *Crime on the Solent*, New York, Dodd Mead, 1934.

Crime at Guildford (French). London, Collins, 1935; as *The Crime at Nornes*, New York, Dodd Mead, 1935.
The Loss of the "Jane Vosper" (French). London, Collins, and New York, Dodd Mead, 1936.
Six Against the Yard, with others. London, Selwyn and Blount, 1936; as *Six Against Scotland Yard*, New York, Doubleday, 1936.
Man Overboard! (French). London, Collins, and New York, Dodd Mead, 1936; abridged, as *Cold-Blooded Murder*, New York, Avon, 1947.
Found Floating (French). London, Hodder and Stoughton, and New York, Dodd Mead, 1937.
The End of Andrew Harrison (French). London, Hodder and Stoughton, 1938; as *The Futile Alibi*, New York, Dodd Mead, 1938.
Antidote to Venom (French). London, Hodder and Stoughton, 1938; New York, Dodd Mead, 1939.
Fatal Venture (French). London, Hodder and Stoughton, 1939; as *Tragedy in the Hollow*, New York, Dodd Mead, 1939.
Golden Ashes (French). London, Hodder and Stoughton, and New York, Dodd Mead, 1940.
James Tarrant, Adventurer (French). London, Hodder and Stoughton, 1941; as *Circumstantial Evidence*, New York, Dodd Mead, 1941.
The Losing Game (French). London, Hodder and Stoughton, and New York, Dodd Mead, 1941.
Fear Comes to Chalfont (French). London, Hodder and Stoughton, and New York, Dodd Mead, 1942.
The Affair at Little Wokeham (French). London, Hodder and Stoughton, 1943; as *Double Tragedy*, New York, Dodd Mead, 1943.
Enemy Unseen (French). London, Hodder and Stoughton, and New York, Dodd Mead, 1945.
Death of a Train (French). London, Hodder and Stoughton, 1946; New York, Dodd Mead, 1947.
Silence for the Murderer (French). New York, Dodd Mead, 1948; London, Hodder and Stoughton, 1949.
Dark Journey. New York, Dodd Mead, 1951; as *French Strikes Oil*, London, Hodder and Stoughton, 1952.
Anything to Declare? (French). London, Hodder and Stoughton, 1957.
The Scoop, and Behind the Screen, with others. London, Gollancz, and New York, Harper, 1983.

Short Stories

The Hunt Ball Murder. London, Todd, 1943.
Mr. Sefton, Murderer. London, Vallancey Press, 1944.
Murderers Make Mistakes. London, Hodder and Stoughton, 1947.
Many a Slip. London, Hodder and Stoughton, 1955.
The Mystery of the Sleeping Car Express and Other Stories. London, Hodder and Stoughton, 1956.

Uncollected Short Stories

"Fingerprints," in *The Evening Standard* (London), 20 March 1952.
"The Faulty Stroke," in *The Evening Standard* (London), 30 December 1952.
"The Target," in *The Evening Standard* (London), 14 October 1953.

OTHER PUBLICATIONS

Plays

Radio Plays: *The Nine-Fifty Up Express*, 1942; *Chief Inspector's Cases* (series), 1943; *Mr. Pemberton's Commission*, from his own story, 1952; *The Greuze*, 1953; *East Wind*, 1953.

Other

Bann and Lough Neagh Drainage. Belfast, His Majesty's Stationery Office, 1930.
Young Robin Brand, Detective (for children). London, University of London Press, 1947; New York, Dodd Mead, 1948.
The Four Gospels in One Story. London, Longman, 1949.

*   *   *

Purity of plot construction is the principal feature for which Freeman Wills Crofts will be remembered. In all but a handful of his books the ramifications of the criminal investigation fit together in a most satisfying manner. His ability to break down the supposedly unbreakable alibi is almost legendary. This automatically means that as whodunits, in the Agatha Christie sense, his novels fail; look for the person with the cast-iron alibi, and you have your murderer. For this reason, if one knows his style, one tends not to regard a Crofts novel as the time-honoured duel between author and reader. There is little pleasure in attempting to guess or to deduce the murderer's identity, but every satisfaction in trying to outpace the detective in deciding how the murder was committed and how the murderer covered his tracks.

Crofts's first detective novel, *The Cask*, remained his masterpiece. It has been generally regarded by experts as the finest first novel in the field, and as a significant landmark in the history of the genre, with Anthony Boucher describing it as "the definitive novel" in its use of alibis and timetables. The solid, plodding, logical detective work and almost fanatical attention to detail were to become the hallmark of Crofts. From the moment the cask at the London docks is found to contain gold coins and a woman's hand instead of statuary, an enthralling trail leads to Paris and engages the attention of detectives on both sides of the Channel. Anyone wishing to experience the quintessence of Crofts should turn to *The Cask*.

Of Crofts's highly competent books following *The Cask*, but preceding the introduction of his famous series detective Inspector French, perhaps *The Pit-Prop Syndicate* is the most interesting. Although none of Crofts's plots could be described as racy or fast moving, this one goes close to combining the elements of the thriller and the detective novel; the action alternates between France and England (a favourite device of Crofts), and two amateur detectives find themselves out of their depth (another favourite device), from which point the professionals take over.

Inspector French's Greatest Case was the first in a long line of investigations by French, in which he was consistently meticulous, perhaps a skilful plodder, with the cases as neatly dove-tailed as the railway timetables which were so often his stock-in-trade. The stories were the product of a brilliantly logical mind, a mind with a background of engineering and mathematics. It may well be pedantic, it may well be mechanical, it may well be too ponderous for the reader requiring faster action, but it is tremendously enjoyable to accompany French on the job. We accompany him rather than follow him, for Crofts is the epitome of fair play; the reader is with French each step of the way, sharing his every thought, his disappointing leads and his lucky breaks, and being presented with each clue at the same moment as the detective. Not until late in his career did Crofts become a little wearisome in his technique, stemming either from his pool of ideas running dry or the fact that he was by then competing with far livelier writers.

Although Crofts was at home mainly in the novel, it being the best medium for the systematic development of an investigation, he also wrote some very creditable short stories and radio plays. Of the former, the volume entitled *The Mystery of the Sleeping Car Express* shows him to be adept at the concise detective plot with a quick twist; in *Murderers Make Mistakes* there are examples of the "inverted" type, in which the criminal's actions are first described and then French reveals how he established the truth.

Various devices and stylistic techniques are common to some or all of Crofts's novels. There is never, for example, any attempt to present a murderer whose culpability is in question—quite often the motive is sheer monetary gain, and indeed murder is often connected with either a financial swindle or a robbery. Time and again we find a strong railway interest (*Death of a Train, Sir John Magill's Last Journey*) or shipping interest (*The Loss of the "Jane Vosper," Found Floating*) where Crofts puts his technical knowledge to excellent use. Then again, although Crofts's characters occasionally fall in love, this is treated most clinically and is rarely developed as an integral part of the stories, a facet of a wider criticism often made of him—he seldom attempts to explore character. His books are peopled with ciphers, existing merely as the links in a criminal investigation, and when toward the end of his career he attempted more complex characterisation (*Silence for the Murderer*) he failed at it. One book, *The 12:30 from Croydon*, can be regarded as a successful attempt to go rather deeper, and to show us the workings of a murderer's mind; in most of his other books, crime is seen purely in black and white terms, the mechanics of the investigation being paramount.

In spite of all this, or perhaps because of it, Crofts remains the supreme exponent of his type of detective fiction. He created arguably the greatest police detective, whose solid and tireless work enabled countless readers to identify with his triumphs and frustrations. Even the moral—crime is wrong, and criminals will be caught by the inexorable machinery of the law—was something with which, though not always fashionable today, readers could associate. His method of telling a tale was ordinary and straightforward, and he seldom strayed from the confines of his set pattern. Perhaps, as Julian Symons suggests, he was the best of what may be termed "the Humdrum School"; to be entirely complimentary, he was in Raymond Chandler's words, "the soundest builder of them all."

—Melvyn Barnes

———

CROSS, Amanda. Pseudonym for Carolyn G(old) Heilbrun. American. Born in East Orange, New Jersey, 13 January 1926. Educated at Wellesley College, Massachusetts, B.A. 1947 (Phi Beta Kappa); Columbia University, New York, M.A. 1951, Ph.D. in English 1959. Married James Heilbrun in 1945; two daughters and one son. Instructor, Brooklyn College, 1959–60. Instructor, 1960–62, Assistant Professor, 1962–67, and since 1972, Professor of English, and since 1986 Avalon Foundation Professor of Humanities, Columbia University. Visiting Lecturer, Union Theological Seminary, New York,

1968–70, Swarthmore College, Pennsylvania, 1970, Yale University, New Haven, Connecticut, 1974, University of California, Santa Cruz, 1979, and Princeton University, New Jersey, 1982. President, Modern Language Association, 1984. Since 1985 co-editor, Gender and Culture series, Columbia University Press; Recipient: Guggenheim Fellowship, 1965; Rockefeller Fellowship, 1976; Radcliffe Institute Fellowship, 1976; Nero Wolfe award, 1981; National Endowment for the Humanities Fellowship, 1983; D.H.L.: University of Pennsylvania, 1984; Bucknell University, 1985; Russell Sage College, 1987; Smith College, 1989; D.F.A.: Rivier College, 1986. Agent: Ellen Levine Literary Agency, 432 Park Avenue South, Suite 1205, New York, New York 10016. Address: 615 Philosophy Hall, Columbia University, New York, New York 10027, U.S.A.

CRIME PUBLICATIONS

Novels (series: Professor Kate Fansler in all books)

In the Last Analysis. New York, Macmillan, and London, Gollancz, 1964.
The James Joyce Murder. New York, Macmillan, and London, Gollancz, 1967.
Poetic Justice. New York, Knopf, and London, Gollancz, 1970.
The Theban Mysteries. New York, Knopf, 1971; London, Gollancz, 1972.
The Question of Max. New York, Knopf, and London, Gollancz, 1976.
Death in a Tenured Position. New York, Dutton, 1981; as *A Death in the Faculty*, London, Gollancz, 1981.
Sweet Death, Kind Death. New York, Dutton, and London, Gollancz, 1984.
No Word from Winifred. New York, Dutton, 1986; London, Virago Press, 1987.
A Trap for Fools. New York, Dutton, 1989; London, Virago Press, 1990.

Uncollected Short Stories

"Tania's W X No Where," in *Ellery Queen's Mystery Magazine* (New York), March 1987.
"Once Upon a Time," in *Ellery Queen's Mystery Magazine* (New York), August 1987.
"Arrie and Jaspar," in *Ellery Queen's Mystery Magazine* (New York), December 1987.

OTHER PUBLICATIONS as Carolyn G. Heilbrun

Other

The Garnett Family. New York, Macmillan, and London, Allen and Unwin, 1961.
Christopher Isherwood. New York, Columbia University Press, 1970.
Towards a Recognition of Androgyny: Aspects of Male and Female in Literature. New York, Harper, 1973; as *Towards Androgyny*, London, Gollancz, 1973.
Reinventing Womanhood. New York, Norton, and London, Gollancz, 1979.
Writing a Woman's Life. New York, Norton, 1988; London, Virago Press, 1989.
Hamlet's Mother and Other Women. New York, Columbia University Press, 1990.

Editor, *Lady Ottoline's Album.* New York, Knopf, 1976; London, Joseph, 1977.
Editor, with Margaret R. Higonnet, *The Representation of Women in Fiction*, Baltimore, Johns Hopkins University Press, 1983.

*

Manuscript Collection: Smith College, Northampton, Massachusetts.

Amanda Cross comments:

I began writing the Amanda Cross novels in 1963 because I could not find any detective fiction that I enjoyed reading. Alas, the situation (except for the work of P.D. James) is largely unchanged since then. I expect that I represent an old style of detective fiction, perhaps even anachronistic. From the number of sales, the letters I receive, paperback reprints, and the infrequency with which my out-of-print novels turn up in the second-hand market, I conclude that I have some following. At the same time, I have been largely ignored by those who now dominate the mystery field, and I feel as though I do not rightfully belong, for example, to the MWA.

What was it I wanted in detective fiction and could no longer find? First of all, conversation, and an ambiance in which violence was unexpected and shocking. In short, the exact opposite of what Chandler wanted (or said he wanted) in "The Simple Art of Murder." Second of all, I like literary mysteries, not necessarily with a quotation at the head of every chapter, though I don't mind that, but with a cast of characters comprising those who may not now know much literature only because they have forgotten it. Also, I like fiction in which women figure as more than decoration and appendages, domestic machinery, or sex objects. In short, I like the women in my novels to be people, as they were in Nicholas Blake's early works, and in a novel like Edward Grierson's *The Second Man*.

My sort of detective fiction will always be accused of snobbery. This, I have decided, is inevitable. I myself am that apparently rare anomaly, an individual who likes courtesy and intelligence, but would like to see the end of reaction, stereotyped sex-roles, and convention that arises from the fear of change, and the anxiety change brings. I loathe violence, and do not consider sex a spectator sport. I like humor, but fear unkindness, and the cruelty of power.

One day Kate Fansler, therefore, sprang from my brain to counter these things I loathe, to talk all the time, occasionally with wit, and to offer to those who like it the company of people I consider civilized, and a plot, feeble, perhaps, but reflecting a moral universe.

* * *

Amanda Cross is the pseudonym of an American academic who found herself in possession of more wit than could be gracefully accommodated in the average scholarly monograph, and of a conviction that literature illuminates life, even the apparent chaos of American campus life in the 1960's. Knowing how commodious the genre of detective fiction is, Carolyn Heilbrun began writing novels of manners with strong detective sub-plots. There is a murder, or at least a death that requires concealment, in each of her novels, and each crime is unravelled by the series heroine, Professor Kate Fansler.

Kate is a strong and likeable character—fastidious without being cold, thoughtful without pedantry, and able to appreciate and communicate with a wide variety of people. She is the central consciousness in a picture of American university life that calmly flouts the modern literary fashion for demeaning satires of self-deluded professors. Heilbrun insists on describing the university with charity as well as clarity, and with considerable elegance of style. Some early reviewers of Kate's conversation find it "pompous," "lecture-talky," and "peppered with the kind of erudite quotation that truly academic people would consider show-off." One may also feel that Kate simply has the courage of the syntax that she is capable of, and that she is asking, in her usual straightforward way, whether William F. Buckley, Jr., should have all the fun.

Heilbrun gives us a cross section of the types of *homo academicus*: the great humane scholar, the cliché-ridden administrator with a heart of gold, the hungry graduate student and the brilliant one, the scholar harmlessly crazed by devotion to his minor poet, the teacher who can also do, the facile and the snobbish. All of these characters are believable as types and often as individuals. Heilbrun involves them in situations that range from the farcical to the tragic, and most of them emerge with considerable dignity. Her academic community manages to hold to its ideals while tolerating the inevitable proportion of fools and knaves.

Three of Heilbrun's novels are built around major writers or works of literature, the first around Freud. *In the Last Analysis* is one of her most satisfying puzzles. When a friend of Kate's who is a psychoanalyst becomes a murder suspect, Kate sets to work to clear him. She comes up with a brilliant, nearly unprovable, hypothesis about the murderer's identity. In the process, she demonstrates that the mind of the literary critic can also decipher dreams and piece together apparently unrelated incidents and slips of the tongue, but has less tendency to ignore the obvious than the psychoanalytic mind does. One scene, a conversation between Kate's neophyte assistant detective and a suspect from Madison Avenue, demonstrates Heilbrun's fine talent for social comedy, which she rightly gives rein to in later books.

The James Joyce Murder is one of her less successful mysteries, containing some startling implausibilities in the murderer's actions and one flagrant error in Kate's reasoning. But the book should not be missed for the success of its translation of the paralytic characters from *The Dubliners* to the modern Berkshires and its zestful deflation of certain popular myths about country life.

Heilbrun's next two books, *Poetic Justice* and *The Theban Mysteries*, take their themes from the political disorders of the 1960's as they affect a proud old university and a proud old private girl's school, respectively. The university is found to be a bit stiffer in the knees and its faculty a bit more fragile than that of the girl's school. *Poetic Justice* examines the ways in which some worthwhile people react to a frontal assault on the value of what they have given their lives to. Fatigue, rather than lack of justice or commitment, is found to be the major obstacle to reformation. The book is chock full of Auden's poetry, and if the poet were not Auden, there would be too much of it. *The Theban Mysteries* demonstrates the relevance of the *Antigone* to the moral position of the Vietnam draft resister. Heilbrun's contemporary Creon is entirely convincing, though some elements of the plot are not.

In *The Question of Max*, the plot is tight and plausible as Kate and the reader are presented with an apparent double mystery. Kate first comes up with the wrong solution because she is a feminist as well as a detective, and because research scholars can be over-imaginative. But because scholarship demands thoroughness, Kate arrives at the right answer, and brings a convincing villan to justice.

Kate's feminism and her interest in the progress of that revolution emerge as major themes in *Death in a Tenured Position* and *Sweet Death, Kind Death*. The levels of elegance and astringency in the conversation in these novels remain high, but the authoritative report on academic prejudice gives them a somber tone. In both cases, Kate finds that envy, misunderstanding, and plain old misogyny make life hazardous for the upwardly mobile female professor.

No Word from Winifred finds Kate in search of Winifred Ashby, who disappears after a meeting with her honorary Aunt's biographer. Kate follows her trail from Oxford to New York, and then on to Santa Cruz in an attempt to determine whether Winifred is still alive. The novel plays with the lives of Dorothy L. Sayers, Mary Renault, and Muriel St. Clare Byrne and explores the puzzles of friendship and passion.

In *A Trap for Fools* racial tension becomes the major theme. The body of Canfield Adams is found on the sidewalk below his office. Kate is asked to investigate. The university is hesitant to charge the police's chief suspect—an outspoken black lecturer, since it could lead to an outbreak of racial warfare on the campus.

—Carol Cleveland

CROSSEN, Ken(dell Foster). Also wrote as Bennett Barlay; M.E. Chaber; Richard Foster; Christopher Monig; Clay Richards. American. Born in Albany, Ohio, 25 July 1910. Educated at Rio Grande College, Ohio. Married Lisa Palmieri Magazu (third wife) in 1958; married Marcelia Wild in 1971; four children. Worked as insurance investigator in Cleveland, and on WPA Writers' Project, New York; editor, *Detective Fiction Weekly*, New York, 1936. Self-employed writer. *Died 28 November 1981.*

CRIME PUBLICATIONS

Novels (series: Jason Jones and Necessary Smith; Kim Locke)

The Case of the Curious Heel (Jones and Smith). New York, Vulcan, 1944.
The Case of the Phantom Fingerprints (Jones and Smith). New York, Vulcan, 1945.
Murder Out of Mind. New York, Green, 1945.
Satan Comes Across (as Bennett Barlay). New York, Eerie, 1945.
The Tortured Path (Locke; as Kendell Foster Crossen). New York, Dutton, 1957; London, Eyre and Spottiswoode, 1958.
The Big Dive (Locke; as Kendell Foster Crossen). New York, Dutton, and London, Eyre and Spottiswoode, 1959.

Novels as Richard Foster (series: Pete Draco; Chin Kwang Kham)

The Laughing Buddha Murders (Chin). New York, Vulcan, 1944.
The Invisible Man Murders (Chin). New York, Green, 1945.
The Girl from Easy Street. New York, Popular Library, 1952.
Blonde and Beautiful. New York, Popular Library, 1955.
Bier for a Chaser (Draco). New York, Fawcett, 1959; London, Muller, 1960.
The Rest Must Die. New York, Fawcett, 1959; London, Muller, 1960.
Too Late for Morning (Draco). New York, Fawcett, 1960; London, Muller, 1961.

Novels as M.E. Chaber (series: Milo March in all books)

Hangman's Harvest. New York, Holt, 1952; as *Don't Get Caught*, New York, Popular Library, 1953.

No Grave for March. New York, Holt, 1953; London, Eyre and Spottiswoode, 1954; as *All the Way Down*, New York, Popular Library, 1953.

As Old as Cain. New York, Holt, 1954; as *Take One for Murder*, New York, Spivak, 1955.

The Man Inside. New York, Holt, 1954; London, Eyre and Spottiswoode, 1955; as *Now It's My Turn*, New York, Popular Library, 1954.

The Splintered Man. New York, Holt, 1955; London, Boardman, 1957.

A Lonely Walk. New York, Holt, 1956; London, Boardman, 1957.

The Gallows Garden. New York, Holt, and London, Boardman, 1958; as *The Lady Came to Kill*, New York, Pocket Books, 1959.

A Hearse of Another Color. New York, Holt, 1958; London, Boardman, 1959.

So Dead the Rose. New York, Holt Rinehart, 1959; London, Boardman, 1960.

Jade for a Lady. New York, Holt Rinehart, and London, Boardman, 1962.

Softly in the Night. New York, Holt Rineheart, and London, Boardman, 1963.

Six Who Ran. New York, Holt Rineheart, 1964; London, Boardman, 1965.

Uneasy Lies the Dead. New York, Holt Rinehart, and London, Boardman, 1964.

Wanted: Dead Men. New York, Holt Rinehart, 1965; London, Boardman, 1966.

The Day It Rained Diamonds. New York, Holt Rinehart, 1966; London, Macdonald, 1968.

A Man in the Middle. New York, Holt Rinehart, 1967.

Wild Midnight Falls. New York, Holt Rinehart, 1968.

The Flaming Man. New York, Holt Rinehart, 1969; London, Hale, 1970.

Green Grow the Graves. New York, Holt Rinehart, 1970; London, Hale, 1971.

The Bonded Dead. New York, Holt Rinehart, 1971; London, Hale, 1973.

Born to Be Hanged. New York, Holt Rinehart, 1973.

Novels as Christopher Monig (series: Brian Brett in all books)

The Burned Man. New York, Dutton, 1956; London, Boardman, 1957; as *Don't Count the Corpses*, New York, Dell, 1958.

Abra-Cadaver. New York, Dutton, and London, Boardman, 1958.

Once upon a Crime. New York, Dutton, 1959; London, Boardman, 1960.

The Lonely Graves. New York, Dutton, 1960; London, Boardman, 1961.

Novels as Clay Richards (series: Grant Kirby)

The Marble Jungle (Kirby). New York, Obolensky, 1961; London, Cassell, 1963.

Death of an Angel (Kirby). Indianapolis, Bobbs Merrill, 1963.

The Gentle Assassin. Indianapolis, Bobbs Merrill, 1964; London, Boardman, 1965.

Who Steals My Name. Indianapolis, Bobbs Merrill 1964; London, Boardman, 1965.

Uncollected Short Stories

"The Aaron Burr Murder Case," in *Detective Fiction Weekly* (New York), September 1939.

"John Brown's Body," in *Detective Fiction Weekly* (New York), 16 December 1939.

"The Bowman of Mons," in *Argosy* (New York), 25 January 1940.

"The Red Rooster of Death," in *Detective Fiction Weekly* (New York), 10 August 1940.

"A Vision of Murder," in *Stirring Detective and Western Stories* (New York), October 1940.

"A Shield and a Club," in *Stirring Detective and Western Stories* (New York), November 1940.

"The Cat and the Foil," in *Detective Fiction Weekly* (New York), 14 December 1940.

"The Parson Returns," in *Detective Fiction Weekly* (New York), 22 March 1941.

"Presto-Chango Murder," in *Detective Fiction Weekly* (New York), 12 April 1941.

"The Earl of Loretta," in *Detective Fiction Weekly* (New York), 19 April 1941.

"Fifty to One Is Murder," in *Detective Fiction Weekly* (New York), 26 April 1941.

"The Miniature Murders," in *Detective Fiction Weekly* (New York), 17 May 1941.

"The Crime in the Wastebasket," in *Detective Fiction Weekly* (New York), 31 May 1941.

"Three on a Murder," in *Detective Fiction Weekly* (New York), June 1941.

"Murder Is a Fine Art," in *Detective Fiction Weekly* (New York), June 1941.

"Trouble with Twins," in *Detective Fiction Weekly* (New York), June 1941.

"Ax for the Parson," in *Detective Fiction Weekly* (New York), June 1941.

"And So to Murder," in *Detective Fiction Weekly* (New York), 2 August 1941.

"An Angle to Murder" and "Death's Key Ring," in *Baffling Mysteries* (Mt. Morris, Illinois), May 1943.

"The Crime in the Envelope," in *Murder Cavalcade*, edited by Ken Crossen. New York, Duell, 1946; London, Hammond, 1953.

"Too Late for Murder," in *Four and Twenty Bloodhounds*, edited by Anthony Boucher. New York, Simon and Schuster, 1950; London, Hammond, 1951.

"The Murder Trap," in *Stories Annual*, 1955.

"The Closed Door," in *Space Police*, edited by Andre Norton. Cleveland, World, 1956.

Uncollected Short Stories as Richard Foster

"The Green Lama," in *Double Detective* (New York), April 1940.

"Croesus of Crime," in *Double Detective* (New York), May 1940.

"Babies for Sale," in *Double Detective* (New York), June 1940.

"The Wave of Death," in *Double Detective* (New York), July 1940.

"The Man Who Wasn't There," in *Double Detective* (New York), August 1940.

"The Man with the Death's Head Face," in *Double Detective* (New York), September 1940.

"The Clown Who Laughed," in *Double Detective* (New York), October 1940.

"The Invisible Enemy," in *Double Detective* (New York), December 1940.

"The Case of the Mad Maji," in *Double Detective* (New York), February 1941.
"The Case of the Vanishing Ships," in *Double Detective* (New York), April 1941.
"The Case of the Fugitive Fingerprints," in *Double Detective* (New York), June 1941.
"The Case of the Crooked Cane," in *Double Detective* (New York), August 1941.
"The Case of the Hollywood Ghost," in *Double Detective* (New York), October 1941.
"The Case of the Beardless Corpse," in *Double Detective* (New York), March 1943.

Uncollected Short Stories as M.E. Chaber

"Assignment: Red Berlin," in *Blue Book* (Chicago), December 1952.
"Hair the Color of Blood," in *Blue Book* (Chicago), July 1953.
"The Hot Ice Blues," in *Blue Book* (Chicago), September 1953.
"The Man Inside," in *Blue Book* (Chicago), December 1953.
"Murder on the Inside," in *Blue Book* (Chicago), January 1954.
"The Red, Red Flower," in *Blue Book* (Chicago), February 1961.
"The Twisted Trap," in *Blue Book* (Chicago), June 1961.

OTHER PUBLICATIONS

Novels

Once upon a Star. New York, Holt, 1953.
Year of Consent. New York, Dell, 1954.
The Acid Nightmare (as M.E. Chaber). New York, Holt Rinehart, 1967.
The Green Lama (as M.E. Chaber). Chicago, Pulp Press, 1976.

Other

Comeback: The Story of My Stroke, by Robert E. Van Rosen as told to Ken Crossen. Indianapolis, Bobbs Merrill, 1963.
The Conspiracy of Death, with George Redston. Indianapolis, Bobbs Merrill, 1965.

Editor, *Murder Cavalcade*. New York, Duell, 1946; London, Hammond, 1953.
Editor, *Adventures in Tomorrow*. New York, Greenberg, 1951; London, Lane, 1953.
Editor, *Future Tense: New and Old Tales of Science Fiction*. New York, Greenberg, 1952; London, Lane, 1954.

*

Manuscript Collection: Mugar Memorial Library, Boston University.

*   *   *

Detective fiction is often formula fiction. Writers employ formulas in the creation of their plots to facilitate composition, but the formula can also be applied to the development of characters. Ken Crossen was one such writer. After several decades of writing, he discovered a successful plot and character which he polished to an artful smoothness. Crossen wrote under a variety of aliases which helps to disguise the commonalities in his writing, but he was best known as M.E. Chaber.

It is under that name that Crossen developed his formula as typified by his Milo March novels. March is an unusual character in that he operates as an investigator for the Intercontinenal Insurance Company and as a sometime CIA agent. As such, his adventures are divisible into the separate categories of the tough private detective novel (*Softly in the Night*) and the espionage adventure (*So Dead the Rose*). Regardless of story type, March's adventures follow a formula pattern in which he is employed to locate a missing person or object. He may be in pursuit of stolen jade in Hong Kong (*Jade for a Lady*) or a defector in East Berlin (*The Splintered Man*). The particulars may vary, but the essentials of plot and its development are the same.

There is little suspense to be found in March's CIA assignments and less actual detection present in his insurance investigations. March is a hedonist, albeit a tough hedonist, who dislikes legwork or violence and prefers large expense accounts, fine restaurants, good drink, and at least two women per novel. He spends a great deal of each novel indulging himself, while his presence actuates violent events among his quarry. He sometimes pushes the latter, whom he usually identifies early and with a minimum of effort, until they incriminate themselves, as in *The Bonded Dead*. When he chooses, he will play his suspects against one another (*Six Who Ran*) until attrition reduces his quarry to a manageable number. Through it all, he is wry and philosophical, but as unconcerned with justice as he is uninvolved with the people he meets.

Codified within the March novels are most of the elements of Crossen's fiction. His other characters strongly resemble March in part, but never in totality. Under the name Christopher Monig, Crossen wrote about another insurance investigator, Brian Brett, and a third series, published as Richard Foster, concerned an insurance investigator, of the future, Pete Draco. Another character, Kim Locke, is a virtual twin of March's CIA incarnations. *The Gentle Assassin*, written as Clay Richards, is essentially a Milo March novel in which the lead character is assisted by a trained dog as a gesture to innovation.

Such reliance upon formula is the signature of the pulp-magazine writer. Ken Crossen favored the devices he learned writing for those magazines. (As Richard Foster, he wrote a series of novelettes for *Double Detective* about a character named the Green Lama and a later variation on the character, the Tibetan detective Chin Kwang Kham, appeared in such novels as *The Laughing Buddha Murders* and *The Invisible Man Murders*.) But he mastered those devices and made them work for him. Further, Crossen invested those formulas with the lustre of craft and fine writing, a not inconsiderable accomplishment.

—Will Murray

———

CROWE, John. *See* **COLLINS, Michael.**

———

CROWTHER, Brian. *See* **GRIERSON, Edward.**

———

CRUMLEY, James. American. Born in Three Rivers, Texas 12 October 1939. Educated at Georgia Institute of Technology, Atlanta, 1957–58; Texas Arts and Industries University, Kingsville, B.A. in history 1964; University of Iowa, Iowa City, M.F.A. in English 1966. Served in the United States Army, 1958–61. Married 1) Judith Ann Ramey in 1975; 2) Bronwyn Pughe in 1979; four children. Instructor in English, University of Montana, Missoula, 1966–69; Assistant Professor of English, University of Arkansas, Fayetteville, 1969–70, and Colorado State University, Fort Collins, 1971–74; freelance writer, 1974–76; Visiting Writer, Reed College, Portland, Oregan, 1976–77, and Carnegie-Mellon University, Pittsburgh, 1979–80; Assistant Professor of English, University of Texas, El Paso, 1981–84. Agent: Owen Laster, William Morris Agency, 1350 Avenue of the Americas, New York, New York 10019. Address: Department of English, University of Texas, El Paso, Texas 79968, U.S.A.

CRIME PUBLICATIONS

Novels (series: Milodragovitch)

The Wrong Case (Milodragovitch). New York, Random House, 1975; London, Hart Davis MacGibbon, 1976.
The Last Good Kiss. New York, Random House, 1978; London, Granada, 1979.
Dancing Bear (Milodragovitch). New York, Random House, 1983; London, Penguin, 1987.

OTHER PUBLICATIONS

Novel

One to Count Cadence. New York, Random House, 1969.

*

James Crumley comments:
I always introduce my work by explaining that I am a bastard child of Raymond Chandler—without his books, my books would be completely different. We cover some of the same ground, his dark streets in LA, my twisted highways in the mountain west. But because of the events surrounding the Vietnam War, my detectives are not as comfortable with traditional morality as Philip Marlowe seems to be. I saw my friends in the 1960's and 1970's get criminal records for political protests and for smoking a herb that until the early 1920's was the recommended relief for asthma patients. As a result, my detectives are more comfortable around criminals than in the company of solid, middle-class citizens, so of course, my vision of justice is less clear-cut, perhaps more complex, more confused, closer perhaps to Robert Stone and Harry Crews, than to detective fiction.

* * *

The earliest American private-eye characters were portrayed uniformly as tough-guy professionals, captured definitively in the persona of Humphrey Bogart and totally antithetical to the Sherlock Holmes tradition of gentlemen amateur sleuths. In the 1950's and 1960's Ross Macdonald with his Lew Archer novels reshaped the PI and his setting, replacing the big city's menacing night streets with sunny affluent suburbs, ousting the customary gangster antagonists in favor of well-to-do WASP's with unbearable personal crises. In Macdonald's hands the investigator was no longer a macho but a man sensitive to human feelings and failings, torn by inner pain and slow to use force. It's this new and presently dominant tradition that James Crumley has extended to and perhaps beyond its limits.

Crumley's principal setting is the bleak magnificence of western Montana and his prevailing mood a wacked-out post-Vietnam empathy with all sorts of dopers, dropouts, losers, and loonies, the human wreckage of the institutionalized butchery we call the real world. Nobility resides in the wilderness, animals, and a handful of people who can't cope with the nightmare of living. Crumley refuses to romanticize such characters. Milodragovitch from *The Wrong Case* and *Dancing Bear* is a cocaine addict and boozer, the child of two suicides, a compulsive womanizer like his wealthy Hemingwayesque father, a man literally marking time until he will turn 52 and inherit the family fortune which his pioneer ancestors legally stole from the Indians. Sughrue from *The Last Good Kiss* has a background as a Vietnam war criminal and army spy on domestic dissenters and is drinking himself to death by inches. And yet these men are the purest Jesus figures in the history of detective fiction, and the most reverent towards the earth and its creatures.

Crumley has minimal interest in plot and even less in explanations, but he's so uncannily skillful with character and language and relationship and incident that he can afford to throw structure overboard. What makes his books live in the reader's mind and blood is the accumulation of small crazy encounters, full of confusion and muddle, disorder and despair. What one remembers about them is the graphic violence and sweetly casual sex, the coke-snorting and alcohol guzzling, the endless drives through mountain snowscapes and long pit stops at seedy backwoods bars, the sympathetic outcasts—psycho Viet vets, Indians, gentle hippies, rumdums, and love-seekers—and the moneyed sociopaths. He can send Milodragovitch to interview a rich old client in a plant-filled solarium, or trap Sughrue in the maw of a best-selling novelist's family, and make us forget we ever read the greenhouse scene in Chandler's *The Big Sleep* or the Roger Wade chapters of *The Long Goodbye*. He can punctuate the detective's quest with short bursts of the staples of PI fiction, sex and gore, and make each one fresh and vivid and unforgettable. He can move us to accept the dregs of the race as our brothers and sisters, to feel the rape of the earth; in short, as Chandler said of Dashiell Hammett, he can write scenes that seem never to have been written before.

—Francis M. Nevins, Jr.

———

CULLINGFORD, Guy. Pseudonym for Constance Lindsay Taylor, née Dowdy. British. Born in Dovercourt, Essex, 10 January 1907. Educated at Malvern Girls College, 1920–25. Married Morris Lindsay Taylor in 1930; one daughter and two sons. Agent: (fiction) A.M. Health & Co. Ltd., 79 St. Martin's Lane, London WC2N 4AA.; or (plays) Elspeth Cochrane Agency, 11–13 Orlando Road, London SW4 OLE, England. Address: 64 High Street, Ardersier, Inverness IV1 2QF, Scotland.

CRIME PUBLICATIONS

Novels

Murder with Relish (as C. Lindsay Taylor). London, Skeffington, 1948.

If Wishes Were Hearses. London, Hammond, 1952; Philadelphia, Lippincott, 1953.
Post Mortem. London, Hammond, and Philadelphia, Lippincott, 1953.
Conjurer's Coffin. London, Hammond, and Philadelphia, Lippincott, 1954.
Framed for Hanging. London, Hammond, and Philadelphia, Lippincott, 1956.
The Whipping Boys. London, Hammond, 1958.
A Touch of Drama. London, Hammond, 1960.
Third Party Risk. London, Bles, 1962.
Brink of Disaster. London, Bles, 1964; New York, Roy, 1966.
The Stylist. London, Bles, 1968.

Uncollected Short Stories

"Kill and Cure," in *Planned Departures*, edited by Elizabeth Ferrars. London, Hodder and Stoughton, 1958.
"Change Partners," in *Alfred Hitchcock's Mystery Magazine* (New York), February 1958.
"My Unfair Lady," in *Alfred Hitchcock Presents: My Favorites in Suspense.* New York, Random House, 1959.
"Mr. Mowbray's Predecessor," in *Ellery Queen's Mystery Magazine* (New York), December 1961.
"Something to Get at Quick," in *Ellery Queen's Mystery Magazine* (New York), July 1967.
"Locals Should Know Best," in *Ellery Queen's Mystery Magazine* (New York), October 1968.
"The Incurable Complaint," in *Ellery Queen's Mystery Magazine* (New York), May 1969.

OTHER PUBLICATIONS

Novel

The Bread and Butter Miss. London, Hale, 1979.

Plays

Television Plays: *Sarah*, 1973; *Boy Dave*, 1975; *The Winter Ladies*, 1979.

*   *   *

Guy Cullingford has written a group of interesting, even unusual books, set firmly in what everybody (including the English themselves), consider to be most typically English settings. A London boarding house in a wet summer, or the timelessness of an East Anglian village holding almost feudal attitudes and trying to come to grips, not too successfully, with today and now.

A good start could be made by examining *Post Mortem*, a most unusual novel where an account of the murder is given to us by the victim himself. Gilbert Worth, a writer with an adequate private income, is shot while asleep at his desk. One moment he is sitting comfortably inside his skin and the next he is outside and viewing his own corpse, wondering, along with the police, "whodunit." There are many suspects, as he is generally loathed by family, servants, and neighbours. Not too shocked to find his children hate him (he disliked them heartily), he is not very pleased to learn that after death duties they will go their own ways. His least favourite child is planning to become a clergyman and to marry his own ex-mistress. Worth feels a vague desire for revenge and, feeling the detectives are not particularly interested, he decides to do the investigation himself.

Conjurer's Coffin is about the sudden disappearance of a magician's help with worse to come. A damp Coronation year at the Bellevue Hotel where Madame hopes to put everything in the black with all those foreigners bashing down the door eager for bed and breakfast in Soho. The Gormans are well-used to the grimy and uncomfortable rooms with unwilling service provided. They are not dismayed to see another new face at the desk as they have never seen the same one twice. Miss Jessie Milk, a devoted and dutiful daughter, is now realizing a life's ambition to live and work in London. Travelling salesmen, unstable actors, a fat bad-tempered dog, and nice village-bred old ladies up for a thrill week in The Big City: all enjoying themselves or suffering in their own manner until death spoils the Coronation celebrations for them.

If Wishes Were Hearses is a step back to The Golden Age, although it is set in the 1950's. The scene is an isolated, almost feudal village. George White is the owner of the old-fashioned chemist's where he mixes his own remedies for most things and does not possess a telephone. While short on both culture and entertainment the village does possess two inns, one run by Miss Death who is a strict teetotaller. The young may be leaving hastily for the thrills of Camden Town or Bayswater but the old folk left behind are also having a few thrills when the Major dies suddenly. His wife is amusing herself with the doctor and nobody seems to regret the man's death as he was considered "slightly difficult" or "damned impossible" according to temperament. Much more sad is the fire that destroys the oldest village building.

A speech written by an aggravating and bossy husband blows out of a lady's hand and starts a new political party for the benefit of women in *Third Party Risk*. The benefits are short-lived as deadly disagreements begin between the various organizers. *Framed for Hanging* looks backwards to the days after the Maybrick trial when death was much more respectable than divorce.

If Guy Cullingford has a fault, it is perhaps that all the characterizations are so entertaining that one can lose sight of the crime and the victim.

—Mary Groff

_____

CULVER, Timothy J. *See* **WESTLAKE, Donald E.**

_____

CUNNINGHAM, E.V. Pseudonym for Howard (Melvin) Fast; also writes as Walter Ericson. American. Born in New York City, 11 November 1914. Educated at George Washington High School, New York, graduated 1931; National Academy of Design, New York. Served with the Office of War Information, 1942–43, and the Army Film Project, 1944. Married Bette Cohen in 1937; one daughter and one son, the writer Jonathan Fast. War Correspondent in the Far East for *Esquire* and *Coronet* magazines, 1945. Taught at Indiana University, Bloomington, Summer 1947; imprisoned for contempt of Congress, 1947; owner, Blue Heron Press, New York, 1952–57. Founder, World Peace Movement, and member, World Peace Council, 1950–55. Currently, member of the Fellowship for Reconciliation. American Labor Party candidate for Congress for the 23rd District of New York, 1952. Recipient: Bread Loaf Writers Conference award, 1933;

Schomburg Race Relations award, 1944; Newspaper Guild award, 1947; Jewish Book Council of America award, 1948; Stalin International Peace prize (now Soviet International Peace prize), 1954; Screenwriters award, 1960; National Association of Independent Schools award, 1962; Emmy award, for television play, 1976. Agent: Sterling Lord Literistic Inc., 1 Madison Avenue, New York, New York 10010. Address: 1 Mountain Wood Drive, Greenwich, Connecticut 06830, U.S.A.

CRIME PUBLICATIONS

Novels (series: John Comaday and Larry Cohen; Harvey Krim; Masao Masuto)

Fallen Angel (as Walter Ericson). Boston, Little Brown, 1952; as *The Darkness Within*, New York, Ace, 1953; as *Mirage* (as Howard Fast), New York, Fawcett, 1965.
The Winston Affair (as Howard Fast) New York, Crown, 1959; London, Methuen, 1960.
Sylvia. New York, Doubleday, 1960; London, Deutsch, 1962.
Phyllis. New York, Doubleday, and London, Deutsch, 1962.
Alice. New York, Doubleday, 1963; London, Deutsch, 1965.
Lydia (Krim). New York, Doubleday, 1964; London, Deutsch, 1965.
Shirley. New York, Doubleday, and London, Deutsch, 1964.
Penelope (Comaday and Cohen). New York, Doubleday, 1965; London, Deutsch, 1966.
Helen. New York, Doubleday, 1966; London, Deutsch, 1967.
Margie (Comaday and Cohen). New York, Morrow, 1966; London, Deutsch, 1968.
Sally. New York, Morrow, and London, Deutsch, 1967.
Samantha (Masuto). New York, Morrow, 1967; London, Deutsch, 1968; as *The Case of the Angry Actress*, New York, Dell, 1984.
Cynthia (Krim). New York, Morrow, 1968; London, Deutsch, 1969.
The Assassin Who Gave Up His Gun. New York, Morrow, 1969; London, Deutsch, 1970.
Millie. New York, Morrow, 1973; London, Deutsch, 1975.
The Case of the One-Penny Orange (Masuto). New York, Holt Rinehart, 1977; London, Deutsch, 1978.
The Case of the Russian Diplomat (Masuto). New York, Holt, Rinehart, 1978; London, Deutsch, 1979.
The Case of the Poisoned Eclairs (Masuto). New York, Holt Rinehart, 1979; London, Deutsch, 1980.
The Case of the Sliding Pool (Masuto). New York, Delacorte Press, 1981; London, Gollancz, 1982.
The Case of the Kidnapped Angel (Masuto). New York, Delacorte Press, 1982; London, Gollancz, 1983.
The Case of the Murdered Mackenzie (Masuto). New York, Delacorte Press, 1984; London, Gollancz, 1985.
The Wabush Factor. New York, Delacorte Press, 1986; London, Gollancz, 1987.
The Confession of Joe Cullen (as Howard Fast). Boston, Houghton Mifflin, 1989.

OTHER PUBLICATIONS as Howard Fast

Novels

Two Valleys. New York, Dial Press, 1933; London, Dickson, 1934.
Strange Yesterday. New York, Dodd Mead, 1934.
Place in the City. New York, Harcourt Brace, 1937.

Conceived in Liberty: A Novel of Valley Forge. New York, Simon and Schuster, and London, Joseph, 1939.
The Last Frontier. New York, Duell, 1941; London, Lane, 1948.
The Unvanquished. New York, Duell, 1942; London, Lane, 1947.
The Tall Hunter. New York, Harper, 1942.
Citizen Tom Paine. New York, Duell, 1943; London, Lane, 1946.
Freedom Road. New York, Duell, 1944; London, Lane, 1946.
The American: A Middle Western Legend. New York, Duell, 1946; London, Lane, 1949.
The Children. New York, Duell, 1947.
Clarkton. New York, Duell, 1947.
My Glorious Brothers. Boston, Little Brown, 1948; London, Lane, 1950.
The Proud and the Free. Boston, Little Brown, 1950; London, Lane, 1952.
Spartacus. Privately printed, 1951; London, Lane, 1952.
Silas Timberman. New York, Blue Heron Press, 1954; London, Lane, 1955.
The Story of Lola Gregg. New York, Blue Heron Press, 1956; London, Lane, 1957.
Moses, Prince of Egypt. New York, Crown, 1958; London, Methuen, 1959.
The Golden River, in *The Howard Fast Reader.* New York, Crown, 1960.
April Morning. New York, Crown, and London, Methuen, 1961.
Power. New York, Doubleday, 1962; London, Methuen, 1963.
Agrippa's Daughter. New York, Doubleday, 1964; London, Methuen, 1965.
Torquemada. New York, Doubleday, 1966; London, Methuen, 1967.
The Hunter and the Trap. New York, Dial Press, 1967.
The Crossing. New York, Morrow, 1971; London, Eyre Methuen, 1972.
The Hessian. New York, Morrow, 1972; London, Hodder and Stoughton, 1973.
The Immigrants. Boston, Houghton Mifflin, 1977; London, Hodder and Stoughton, 1978.
Second Generation. Boston, Houghton Mifflin, and London, Hodder and Stoughton, 1978.
The Establishment. Boston, Houghton Mifflin, 1979; London, Hodder and Stoughton, 1980.
The Legacy. Boston, Houghton Mifflin, and London, Hodder and Stoughton, 1981.
Max. Boston, Houghton Mifflin, 1982; London, Hodder and Stoughton, 1983.
The Outsider. Boston, Houghton Mifflin, 1984; London, Hodder and Stoughton, 1985.
The Immigrant's Daughter. Boston, Houghton Mifflin, 1985; London, Hodder and Stoughton, 1986.
The Dinner Party. Boston, Houghton Mifflin, and London, Hodder and Stoughton, 1987.
The Call of the Fife and Drum: Three Novels of the Revolution (includes *The Unvanquished, Conceived in Liberty, The Proud and the Free*). Secaucus, New Jersey, Citadel Press, 1987.
The Pledge. Boston, Houghton Mifflin, 1988; London, Hodder and Stoughton, 1989.

Short Stories

Patrick Henry and the Frigate's Keel and Other Stories of a Young Nation. New York, Duell, 1945.
Departures and Other Stories. Boston, Little Brown, 1949.

The Last Supper and Other Stories. New York, Blue Heron Press, 1955; London, Lane, 1956.

The Edge of Tomorrow. New York, Bantam, 1961; London, Corgi, 1962.

The General Zapped an Angel. New York, Morrow, 1970.

A Touch of Infinity. New York, Morrow, 1973; London, Hodder and Stoughton, 1975.

Time and the Riddle: Thirty-One Zen Stories. Pasadena, California, Ward Ritchie Press, 1975.

Plays

The Hammer (produced New York, 1950).

Thirty Pieces of Silver (produced Melbourne, 1951). New York, Blue Heron Press, and London, Lane, 1954.

General Washington and the Water Witch. London, Lane, 1956.

The Crossing (produced Dallas, 1962).

The Hill (screenplay). New York, Doubleday, 1964.

David and Paula (produced New York, 1982).

Citizen Tom Paine, adaptation of his own novel (produced Williamstown, Massachusetts, 1985). Boston, Houghton Mifflin, 1986.

Screenplay: *The Hessian*, 1971.

Television Plays: *What's a Nice Girl Like You . . .?*, 1971; *21 Hours at Munich*, with Edward Hume, 1976.

Verse

Never to Forget the Battle of the Warsaw Ghetto, with William Gropper. New York, Jewish Peoples Fraternal Order, 1946.

Other

The Romance of a People (for children) New York, Hebrew Publishing Company, 1941.

Lord Baden-Powell of the Boy Scouts. New York, Messner, 1941.

Haym Salomon, Son of Liberty. New York, Messner, 1941.

The Picture-Book History of the Jews, with Bette Fast. New York, Hebrew Publishing Company, 1942.

Goethals and the Panama Canal. New York, Messner, 1942.

The Incredible Tito. New York, Magazine House, 1944.

Intellectuals in the Fight for Peace. New York, Masses and Mainstream, 1949.

Tito and His People. Winnipeg, Contemporary Publishers, 1950.

Literature and Reality. New York, International Publishers, 1950.

Peekskill, U.S.A.: A Personal Experience. New York, Civil Rights Congress, and London, International Publishing Company, 1951.

Korean Lullaby. New York, American Peace Crusade, n.d.

Tony and the Wonderful Door (for children). New York, Blue Heron Press, 1952; as *The Magic Door*, Culver City, California, Peace Press, 1979.

Spain and Peace. New York, Joint Anti-Fascist Refugee Committee, 1952.

The Passion of Sacco and Vanzetti: A New England Legend. New York, Blue Heron Press, 1953; London, Lane, 1954.

The Naked God: The Writer and the Communist Party. New York, Praeger, 1957; London, Bodley Head, 1958.

The Howard Fast Reader. New York, Crown, 1960.

The Jews: Story of a People. New York, Dial Press, 1968; London, Cassell, 1970.

The Art of Zen Meditation. Culver City, California, Peace Press, 1977.

Editor, *The Selected Work of Tom Paine.* New York, Modern Library, 1946; London, Lane, 1948.

Editor, *The Best Short Stories of Theodore Dreiser.* Cleveland, World, 1947.

*

Manuscript Collections: University of Pennsylvania Library, Philadelphia; University of Wisconsin, Madison.

E.V. Cunningham comments:

My involvement as a mystery writer began, I believe, in 1958, when I wrote a book called *Sylvia*. Its content was so very different from the other books I had published up to that point that I decided to use a pseudonym. That was also the period of the great blacklist in America that had grown out of the McCarthy era. My agent, Paul Reynolds, picked the name of E.V. Cunningham, using only the initials so that no one could claim an infringement of privacy. The success of that initial book, which was made into a film, was very pleasant at the time, and I decided to do another. They were far more fun to write than serious novels, and so one following another, I kept at it. That's more or less the story.

* * *

Between 1960 and 1968, E.V. Cunningham produced mystery novels, each with the one-word title of its heroine's first name. These were followed by *The Assassin Who Gave Up His Gun*, then one last woman's mystery, *Millie*, before a new series was begun about Masuto, a Japanese-American attached to the Beverly Hills Police Department. Cunningham's prolific and successful output is particularly impressive because he is actually Howard Fast, who has produced 35 books under his own name.

In the first few of his high-heeled thrillers, Cunningham's style resembled Ian Fleming's in some, and a cross between Dashiell Hammett's and Rex Stout's in others. The "given" conditions strained plausibility: in *Sylvia* a multi-millionaire hires a small-time investigator to find out, almost on the eve of the wedding, who his prospective bride really is; in *Alice* a stranger, just before jumping into the path of a subway train, slips a safe-deposit key into the narrator's pocket; *Phyllis* works the tired atom-bomb theme of guilt-ridden scientists and the desperate crisis of getting to the villain before he can blow up the world. In *Sally* a young woman, mistakenly told she has leukemia, hires a gunman to kill her without warning; when she discovers that she is really well the chain of communication has been snapped and she is the unwilling prey in the "contract" she has purchased.

Cunningham's gimmick of building each novel around an "ordinary" woman violated both the private-eye tradition of male domination and the lesser genre of girl-detective. His women, usually the victims of bizarre situations, are pluckier, cleverer, and more honest than the men they meet; perhaps by discovering deeper resources in themselves than they or others suspected, they foreshadowed the women's liberation novels of the 1960's. In about half of these thrillers (e.g., *Penelope, Margie, Cynthia*) the author's touch is light, with liberal use of "screwball comedy" heroines and situations reminiscent of the 1930's film comedies of Carole Lombard or Claudette Colbert. In others, such as *Helen* and *Samantha*, there is a somber, brooding quality in what are essentially mysteries of character and motivation rather than plot. These latter suggest the allegorical explorations of the "entertainments" of Graham Greene, a writer whom Cunningham has always admired. (Perhaps the most Greene-like of this author's mysteries, however, is *Fallen Angel*, written under the pseudonym of Walter Ericson.)

Nisei detective Masao Masuto first appeared as a character in *Samantha* and has "spun-off" into his own series. He is a Zen Buddhist (as is his creator), aloof in philosophy but socially involved as detective and family man. A karate expert, lover of roses, and possessor of caustic wit, Masuto moves coolly among the richly corrupt of Beverly Hills and Los Angeles. In *The Case of the One-Penny Orange*, he chases down the rare one-penny orange stamp that has occasioned murder, while in *The Case of the Russian Diplomat* an apparent drowning in the Beverly Glen hotel leads to a Russian diplomat, an East German spy, and Masuto's kidnapped daughter. In both, Masuto's personality and his relations with colleagues and family are as appealing as the plot; his Charlie Chan put-on before bigots is especially beguiling.

—Frank Campenni

CURTISS, Ursula (née Reilly). American. Born in Yonkers, New York, 8 April 1923; daughter of Helen Reilly, *q.v.*, and the artist Paul Reilly; sister of Mary McMullen, *q.v.* Educated at Staples High School, Westport, Connecticut. Married John Curtiss, Jr., in 1947; two daughters and three sons. Columnist for Fairfield *News*, Connecticut, 1942–43; fashion copywriter, Gimbels, 1944, Macy's, 1944–45, Bates Fabrics Inc., 1945–47. Self-employed writer. *Died.*

CRIME PUBLICATIONS

Novels

Voice Out of Darkness. New York, Dodd Mead, 1948; London, Evans, 1949.
The Second Sickle. New York, Dodd Mead, 1950; as *The Hollow House*, London, Evans, 1951.
The Noonday Devil. New York, Dodd Mead, 1951; London, Eyre and Spottiswoode, 1953; as *Catch a Killer*, New York, Pocket Books, 1952.
The Iron Cobweb. New York, Dodd Mead, and London, Eyre and Spottiswoode, 1953.
The Deadly Climate. New York, Dodd Mead, 1954; London, Eyre and Spottiswoode, 1955.
Widow's Web. New York, Dodd Mead, and London, Eyre and Spottiswoode, 1956.
The Stairway. New York, Dodd Mead, 1957; London, Eyre and Spottiswoode, 1958.
The Face of the Tiger. New York, Dodd Mead, 1958; London, Eyre and Spottiswoode, 1960.
So Dies the Dreamer. New York, Dodd Mead, and London, Eyre and Spottiswoode, 1960.
Hours to Kill. New York, Dodd Mead, 1961; London, Eyre and Spottiswoode, 1962.
The Forbidden Garden. New York, Dodd Mead, 1962; London, Eyre and Spottiswoode, 1963; as *Whatever Happened to Aunt Alice?*, New York, Ace, 1969.

The Wasp. New York, Dodd Mead, 1963; London, Eyre and Spottiswoode, 1964.
Out of the Dark. New York, Dodd Mead, 1964; as *Child's Play*, London, Eyre and Spottiswoode, 1965.
Danger: Hospital Zone. New York, Dodd Mead, 1966; London, Hodder and Stoughton, 1967.
Don't Open the Door. New York, Dodd Mead, 1968; London, Hodder and Stoughton, 1969.
Letter of Intent. New York, Dodd Mead, 1971; London, Macmillan, 1972.
The Birthday Gift. New York, Dodd Mead, 1975; as *Dig a Little Deeper*, London, Macmillan, 1976.
In Cold Pursuit. New York, Dodd Mead, 1977; London, Macmillan, 1978.
The Menace Within. New York, Dodd Mead, and London, Macmillan, 1979.
The Poisoned Orchard. New York, Dodd Mead, and London, Macmillan, 1980.
Dog in the Manger. New York, Dodd Mead, 1982; as *The Graveyard Shift*, London, Macmillan, 1982.
Death of a Crow. New York, Dodd Mead, and London, Macmillan, 1983.

Short Stories

The House on Plymouth Street and Other Stories. New York, Dodd Mead, 1985.

*

Manuscript Collection: Mugar Memorial Library, Boston University.

* * *

For over 35 years, Ursula Curtiss successfully blended elements of the gothic and the detective genres into popular suspense stories. She was a master at creating intriguing chapter endings and swiftly paced plots, and the portraits of even relatively minor characters—Kate Clemence of *So Dies the Dreamer* or Barney Maynard of *The Wasp*, for example—are sharply and memorably drawn.

In several novels, the protagonist undertakes some seemingly simple task, only to find herself caught up in intrigue. In *The Birthday Gift*, Lydia Peel is put at risk by simply agreeing to deliver a present. A more arduous favor is undertaken by Harriet Crewe, in *The Forbidden Garden*; when she brings her sickly little nephew to the Southwest, she encounters a deadly elderly woman who is perfectly willing to murder to ensure her own comfort. In both books, the contrast between the mundaneness of the errand and the deadliness of the hidden dangers proves very effective. *The Forbidden Garden*, like *Letter of Intent*, is an "inverted" mystery, for the murderer is known from the outset. In *Letter of Intent*, the killer exchanges other people's lives for her own upward mobility. In these novels, Curtiss contrasts utterly selfish, untamed personalities with ordinary people who practice decent self-restraint. The portrayals are among her best.

Another pattern studies young women whose peace and security are threatened by the re-emergence of some old crime. A good measure of the tension arises from the sense that innocence is no protection from calumny or danger for Lou Fabian (*The Face of the Tiger*), or Katy Meredith (*Voice Out of Darkness*). Unable to trust anyone else, each turns amateur sleuth; the results are satisfying to the reader.

Coincidence figures largely in two novels which represent a third pattern. In the splendid *Out of the Dark*, children's random telephone pranks trigger danger and death. When Caroline Emmett (*The Deadly Climate*) accidentally witnesses a murder, she immediately becomes a potential victim. These novels illustrate the old saw that even the most sedate-seeming people have much to hide, and Curtiss makes full use of the irony inherent in each situation. Further, the sense of terrorizing isolation felt by Caroline Emmett, a total stranger in the community and uncertain of the identity of her pursuer, is remarkably well drawn; the reader is wholly convinced that the protagonist is drawing on the deepest reserves of her strength and courage.

Another set of novels depicts protagonists who deliberately seek vengeance. Both Nick Sentry (*The Noonday Devil*) and Torrant (*Widow's Web*) discover evidence which satisfies them that murders have been committed. Because of deep personal loyalties, the men undertake to avenge the victims, only to become entangled in danger and—as always in a Curtiss work—romance. *The Noonday Devil*'s evocation of World War II prison camps is extremely effective, as is the portrayal of the post-war period.

Curtiss is adept at several patterns, each successfully wrought. Refusing to romanticize her characters, she produced works which are a satisfying blend of the expected and the surprising. Often, the surprise arises not only from a variation of a familiar pattern but also from startling and effective endings. *The Wasp* and *Letter of Intent* are good examples of this device. In each instance, the reader is at first shocked and then gratified. The conclusions seem grimly appropriate, and they testify to Curtiss's skill.

—Jane S. Bakerman

* * *

CURZON, Clare. Pseudonym for Eileen-Marie Duell; also writes as Marie Buchanan; Rhona Petrie. British. Born in Hastings, Sussex, in 1922. Educated at the University of London, B.A. (honours) 1944; Associateship of King's College 1944. Married Jimmy Duell; two daughters and one son. Has worked as an interpreter, translator, teacher, probation officer, and social secretary. Lives in Gerrards Cross, Buckinghamshire. Agent: Harvey Klinger Inc., 301 West 53rd Street, New York, New York 10019, U.S.A.; or, David Grossman Literary Agency, 110–114 Clerkenwell Road, London EC1M 5SA, England.

CRIME PUBLICATIONS

Novels (series: Superintendent Mike Yeadings and Sergeant Angus Mott)

A Leaven of Malice. London, Collins, 1979.
Special Occasions. London, Collins, 1981.
I Give You Five Days (Yeadings and Mott). London, Collins, 1983.
Masks and Faces (Yeadings and Mott). London, Collins, 1984.
The Trojan Hearse (Yeadings and Mott). London, Collins, 1985.
The Quest for K (Yeadings and Mott). London, Collins, 1986.
Trail of Fire. London, Collins, 1987.
Shot Bolt. London, Collins, 1988.
Three-Core Lead. London, Collins, 1988; New York, Doubleday, 1990.

The Face in the Stone. London, Collins, 1989.
The Blue-Eyed Boy (Yeadings and Mott). London, Collins, 1990.

Novels as Rhona Petrie (series: Inspector Marcus MacLurg; Dr. Nassim Pride)

Death in Deakins Wood (MacLurg). London, Gollancz, 1963; New York, Dodd Mead, 1964.
Murder by Precedent (MacLurg). London, Gollancz, 1964.
Running Deep (MacLurg). London, Gollancz, 1965.
Dead Loss (MacLurg). London, Gollancz, 1966.
Foreign Bodies (Pride). London, Gollancz, 1967.
MacLurg Goes West. London, Gollancz, 1968.
Despatch of a Dove (Pride). London, Gollancz, 1969.
Thorne in the Flesh. London, Gollancz, 1971.

Short Stories (as Rhona Petrie)

Come Hell and High Water: Eleven Short Stories. London, Gollancz, 1970.

OTHER PUBLICATIONS

Novels as Marie Buchanan

Greenshards. London, Gollancz, 1972; as *Anima*, New York, St. Martin's Press, 1972.
An Unofficial Death. London, Hodder and Stoughton, and New York, St. Martin's Press, 1973.
The Dark Backward. New York, Coward McCann, 1975.
Morgana. New York, Doubleday, 1977.
The Countess of Sedgwick. London, Collins, 1980; New York, Doubleday, 1990.

* * *

As Rhona Petrie, Clare Curzon has written two different series of crime novels; the first of these, featuring Inspector MacLurg, consists of fairly traditional whodunnits. With the creation in her other series of Dr. Nassim Pride, Petrie introduces a most original detective; the canon of crime fiction cannot contain many Anglo-Sudanese forensic scientists of dubious legitimacy. Pride approaches his investigations with relentless logic and a computer-like brain which analyses and reassembles the facts, to disgorge them in the form of the solution on the penultimate page—in the true detective tradition!

In complete contrast, the series detectives created under the name of Clare Curzon are fairly bland examples of the species: Superintendent Mike Yeadings and Sergeant (later Inspector) Angus Mott are pleasant, unexceptional policemen. The reader does not receive any impression of distinctive personalities or of any quirks of character; these men go about their detecting in a fairly unhurried, relaxed fashion, and appear able to concentrate on one case at a time without the pressure of other crimes being committed even as they are trying to solve the current one. They seem to belong to that lucky breed of detectives who just happen to know somebody who just happens to be connected with the case. Within these limitations Curzon has produced several pleasing murder mysteries; it is in fact a welcome change to meet policemen who are not so harassed that one cares more about what happens to them (or their wives or their cats) than about the eventual solution of the crime.

In *The Trojan Hearse* Yeadings and Mott are involved in a murder investigation by virtue of their having been present at the purely social occasion where the crime was committed. Mott's new girlfriend Paula happens to share a flat with the daughter of the supposed victim, and in a blend of detection and burgeoning romance the complex web of both deliberately and accidentally mistaken identities is unravelled. The plot is fairly involved but neither the major characters nor the reader undergoes much strain while the mystery is being solved.

The Quest for K is a tenser novel, which opens with the disappearance of Mott's girlfriend Paula while on holiday in Crete. After the initial few chapters in which Mott instigates a search into her whereabouts, the action of the book recedes to Paula's holiday—seemingly happy and relaxed. The tension builds as the reader, well aware that something drastic must happen, waits for the inevitable climax. The lives of many of Paula's fellow holidaymakers involve odd or tense relationships, and there is much analysis of these as Paula compares her own situation (she is on a semi-pilgrimage to Knossos to honour the memory of her much-loved father) with those of the other parent/child relationships which are integral to the plot. The action is fairly complicated and even when the reader quite justifiably assumes that the next step can be predicted, one of the many sub-plots intervenes and the direction of the events is altered once more. Needless to say Paula is rescued (from shipwreck and near starvation) and after a remarkably speedy recovery resumes her romance with Mott.

In *The Blue-Eyed Boy* the detection of the crime, while operating within the usual Yeadings and Mott framework, is interestingly different. Not only is the actual day-to-day running of the case described in rather more detail than usual, but a third officer, out of those involved in the solving of this particular murder, takes as prominent a role in the novel as does the customary pair of detectives. We see much of the action from the point of view of W.P.C. Rosemary Zyczynski, seconded from the uniformed division for the duration of the case; there is no doubt that as a character she is a welcome addition to the Yeadings/Mott set-up, which might otherwise be in danger of stagnating a little.

Not all of Clare Curzon's novels feature Yeadings and Mott, however. In *Shot Bolt*, newly-wed Sian Vassilakis (previously encountered as Sian Westbury in *Trail of Fire*) accompanies her husband Andreas to Geneva, where she is soon embroiled in a tale of disappearance and murder. She becomes an unwitting accomplice in the arranged defection of a Soviet official, and is unhappily far from sure of her husband's role in this and other international affairs. Fourneval and Gilbert, the two Swiss policemen featured in this novel, are intelligent and articulate and Curzon would do well to feature them in future novels. Particularly effective is a passage in which they discuss in detail all the possible permutations of the crimes which are known to have been committed, as well as some which are only the subject of speculation. The reader knows that some of their conjectures are false, yet it is impossible to fault the logic of the detectives' thinking as they ponder upon the identities both of the murder victims and of the perpetrators. At the same time Sian herself is, with a different set of facts, attempting to solve exactly the same problems. Interestingly different from the books featuring Yeadings and Mott of the Thames Valley Police, the background of this novel draws on Curzon's own knowledge of the international community of Geneva.

Yeadings and Mott do appear (albeit in fairly minor roles) in *Masks and Faces*, told from the point of view of 13-year-old Julian Tawney, who mistakenly believes that he has created an evil magical force which has compelled him to murder his father. This fairly early Yeadings novel has echoes of *A Leaven of Malice*, unusual in that it features no detective either amateur

or professional; instead, this tale of voodoo and supernatural possession is unravelled by an ex-nun with psychic powers of her own. And this novel in turn harks back to Curzon's books written under the name Marie Buchanan, which concern themselves with the subconscious and the supernatural. It is interesting to observe this author's progression through the various sub-genres of mystery writing, and to note her increase in stature as she becomes one of the more noteworthy of today's crime writers.

—Judith Rhodes

CUSSLER, Clive. American. Born in Aurora, Illinois, 15 July 1931. Educated at Pasedena City College, California, 1949–51; Orange Coast College; California State University, Los Angeles. Served in the United States Air Force, 1950–54. Married Barbara Knight in 1955; three children. Owner, Bestgen and Cussler Advertising, Newport Beach, California, 1961–66; copy director, D'Arcy Advertising, Hollywood, 1965–67; advertising director, Newport Beach, 1967–69; Vice President and creative director, Mefford Advertising, Denver, Colorado, 1970–75. Since 1978 founder, National Underwater Marine Agency, Washington, D.C. Agent: Peter Lampack, The Lampack Agency, 551 Fifth Avenue, New York, New York 10017, U.S.A.

CRIME PUBLICATIONS

Novels (series: Dirk Pitt)

The Mediterranean Caper. New York, Pyramid, 1973; as *Mayday!*, London, Sphere, 1977.
Iceberg (Pitt). New York, Dodd Mead, 1975; London, Sphere, 1976.
Raise the Titanic! (Pitt). New York, Viking Press, 1976; London, Joseph, 1977.
Vixen 03 (Pitt). New York, Viking Press, and London, Hodder and Stoughton, 1978; as *Vixen Zero Three*, London, Sphere, 1979.
Night Probe! (Pitt). New York, Bantam, and London, Hodder and Stoughton, 1981.
Pacific Vortex! (Pitt). New York, Bantam, and London, Sphere, 1983.
Deep Six (Pitt). New York, Simon and Schuster, and London, Hamish Hamilton, 1984.
Cyclops. New York, Simon and Schuster, and London, Hamish Hamilton, 1986.
Treasure. London, Grafton, 1988.
Dragon (Pitt). New York, Simon and Schuster, and London, Hamish Hamiton, 1990.

*   *   *

Clive Cussler's thrilling adventure novels are fine escapist fiction for readers who like fast-paced action. The author's background as a leader of marine salvage expeditions, his knowledge of high-technology and marine history, all enable him to provide a refreshing change of scene from other stories of international intrigue and financial schemes. Deep-sea diving, vanished ships, and combat on the land, sea, and air all are common elements of these books. Along with these, one finds a multitude of villains to be confronted, from the usual

Russians and greed-driven financiers, to a plethora of faceless men who ambush the hero at any given time.

The entertainment that these books provide can be attributed to the presence of a hero who is larger-than-life. Cussler writes in the foreword to *Pacific Vortex?* about how he came to creating Dirk Pitt: "... I cast around for a hero who cut a different mold. One who wasn't a secret agent, police detective, or a private investigator. Someone with rough edges, yet a degree of style, who felt equally at ease entertaining a gorgeous woman ... or downing a beer with the boys. ... A congenial kind of guy with a tinge of mystery about him."

Dirk Pitt is the Special Projects Director of the National Underwater and Marine Agency, a congressman's son, and an ex-Air Force pilot. He is a multi-faceted character, physically fit, intelligent, and possessed of common sense. He questions authority, but also is the first to volunteer for dangerous missions. Pitt is both compassionate and vengeful, as he will risk his life to save a friend, but will kill the enemy without thinking twice. He is talented as a swimmer and a fighter, and has vast knowledge of marine and air technology. Add to these traits strong natural instincts and an eye for detail, and Dirk Pitt becomes Cussler's superhero. For, as a character mentions in *Pacific Vortex!*, "With this man, almost anything is possible."

Pacific Vortex! opens with the disappearance of the nuclear submarine *Starbuck* in a remote area of the Pacific Ocean. Dirk Pitt unwittingly gets involved in a decades-old mystery when he comes across a communications capsule apparently sent by the *Starbuck*. Working with the Navy, he goes on a search and salvage mission for the submarine—knowing that 38 ships have disappeared in the same area. An ancient Hawaiian legend of a mythical island, a mysterious fogbank, and a man with golden eyes all combine to add to the suspense. Pitt survives numerous attempts on his life—a beautiful girl with a deadly syringe, a shark, a killer in a truck, and more—as he tries to retrieve the *Starbuck* and rescue a kidnapped woman. The action is non-stop as the story builds to its climax and an undersea explosion.

In *Iceberg*, Pitt is sent on a mission to search for the *Lax*, a ship which has been missing for more than a year with the generous mining magnate Kristan Fyrie on board. Its discovery—burned out and imbedded in an iceberg—leads Pitt on to a dangerous scheme of murder and blackmail. In Iceland, Pitt meets Kirsti Fyrie, the long-lost twin sister of Kristan, and Oskar Rondheim, an unscrupulous fishing fleet owner. In the guise of a gay man, Pitt is able to avoid suspicion and keep death at bay as he uncovers clues to the mystery of the *Lax*. A

poetry reading party at the house of Oskar Rondheim sheds more light on the scheme as an elite group called Hermit Unlimited reveal plans for the take-over of Central and South America. Pitt's physical and mental capabilities are taxed to their limit as he tries to stay alive and rescue his friends. Revenge is finally his, however, as the action moves to its deadly climax in the incongruous location of Disneyland.

Cyclops, a recent Cussler novel, varies in many respects from his earlier books. Whereas the plots of those stories may not seem plausible, this one totally lacks verisimilitude, and its complexity takes away from the suspense that should be building. Some of the other qualities found in the earlier books are lost too, as Dirk becomes only one of a large cast of characters. So many things are happening in this story, and their interconnection is often improbable. There is the mystery of the *Cyclops*, a ship that vanished with treasure on board in 1918; the disappearance of a wealthy man in his blimp while searching for the *Cyclops;* a manned space colony on the moon that must be defended against the Russians; and a bizarre Russian plot for taking control of Cuba.

The scenes change from Pitt's search for the missing millionaire in Cuban waters, to Washington where the President is trying to avoid an international incident, over to Russia where they are scheming to take control of the moon colony and the space data, and onto the moon where the colonists are readying for their return to Earth.

Pitt manages to get involved in much of the climactic action; however, he is not present for the shoot-out on the moon. He does some of the things that readers expect of him—rescues his friends, solves the mystery of the lost ship—, plus he is brutally beaten by a sadistic Russian, slips in and out of Cuba at will, saves Havana from destruction, and is praised by Fidel Castro.

In the Foreword to *Pacific Vortex!*, Cussler says that he was hesitant to publish it because it "was [Dirk Pitt's] first adventure, and because it does not weave the intricate plots of his later exploits." What Cussler feels to be shortcomings of that book also can be viewed as strengths when one looks at *Cyclops*. Cussler's novels are good entertainment when he allows the plots to remain simple. He has created a great hero in Dirk Pitt, and this, combined with the intrigue of the sea, are enough to provide these stories with all the action and suspense they need.

—Karen Hinckley

D

DALE, William. *See* DANIELS, Norman A.

———

DALTON, Priscilla. *See* AVALLONE, Michael.

———

DALY, Carroll John. Also wrote as John D. Carroll. American. Born in Yonkers, New York, 14 September 1889. Educated at Yonkers High School; De La Salle Institute and American Academy of Dramatic Arts, New York. Married Margaret G. Blakley in 1913; one son. Theatre manager: owner/operator of theatres in Atlantic City, Asbury Park, New Jersey; Averne, New York; Yonkers. Writer from 1922. *Died 16 January 1958.*

CRIME PUBLICATIONS

Novels (series: Vee Brown; Satan Hall; Race Williams)

The White Circle. New York, Clode, 1926; London, Hutchinson, 1927.
The Snarl of the Beast (Williams). New York, Clode, 1926; London, Hutchinson, 1928.
The Man in the Shadows. New York, Clode, 1928; London, Hutchinson, 1929.
The Hidden Hand (Williams). New York, Clode, 1929; London, Hutchinson, 1930.
The Tag Murders (Williams). New York, Clode, 1930; London, Hutchinson, 1931.
Tainted Power (Williams). New York, Clode, and London, Hutchinson, 1931.
The Third Murderer (Williams). New York, Farrar and Rinehart, 1931; London, Hutchinson, 1932.
The Amateur Murderer (Williams). New York, Washburn, and London, Hutchinson, 1933.
Murder Won't Wait (Brown). New York, Washburn, 1933; London, Hutchinson, 1934.
Murder from the East (Williams). New York, Stokes, and London, Hutchinson, 1935.
Death's Juggler (Hall). London, Hutchinson, 1935; as *The Mystery of the Smoking Gun,* New York, Stokes, 1936.
Mr. Strang. New York, Stokes, 1936; London, Hale, 1937.
Emperor of Evil (Brown). London, Hutchinson, 1936; New York, Stokes, 1937.
Better Corpses (Williams). London, Hale, 1940.
The Legion of the Living Dead. Toronto, Popular Publications, 1947.
Murder at Our House. London, Museum Press, 1950.
Ready to Burn (Hall). London, Museum Press, 1951.

Short Stories

The Adventures of Race Williams. New York, Mysterious Press, 1987.
The Adventures of Satan Hall. New York, Mysterious Press, 1988.

Uncollected Short Stories

"Dolly," in *Black Mask* (New York), October 1922.
"Roarin' Jack" (as John D. Carroll), in *Black Mask* (New York), December 1922.
"It's All in the Game," in *Black Mask* (New York), 15 April 1923.
"Three Gun Terry," in *Black Mask* (New York), 15 May 1923.
"Three Thousand to the Good," in *Black Mask* (New York), 15 July 1923.
"Action! Action!," in *Black Mask* (New York), 1 January 1924.
"One Night of Frenzy," in *Black Mask* (New York), 15 April 1924.
"The Red Peril," in *Black Mask* (New York), June 1924.
"Them That Lives by Their Guns," in *Black Mask* (New York), August 1924.
"Devil Cat," in *Black Mask* (New York), November 1924.
"The Face Behind the Mask," in *Black Mask* (New York), February 1925.
"Conceited, Maybe," in *Black Mask* (New York), April 1925.
"Say It with Lead," in *Black Mask* (New York), June 1925.
"I'll Tell the World," in *Black Mask* (New York), August 1925.
"Alias, Buttercup," in *Black Mask* (New York), October 1925.
"Under Cover," in *Black Mask* (New York), December 1925–January 1926.
"South Sea Steel," in *Black Mask* (New York), May 1926.
"The False Clara Burkhart," in *Black Mask* (New York), July 1926.
"The Super Devil," in *Black Mask* (New York), August 1926.
"The Code of the House," in *Detective Story* (New York), October 1926.
"Half-Breed," in *Black Mask* (New York), November 1926.
"Twenty Grand," in *Black Mask* (New York), January 1927.
"Blind Alleys," in *Black Mask* (New York), April 1927.
"The Egyptian Lure," in *Black Mask* (New York), March 1928.
"The Law of Silence," in *Black Mask* (New York), April–May 1928.
"The House of Crime," in *Detective Fiction Weekly* (New York), 10 November 1928.
"Gun Law," in *Complete Stories* (New York), February 1929.
"The Silver Eagle," in *Black Mask* (New York), October–November 1929.
"Shooting Out of Turn," in *Black Mask* (New York), October 1930.
"The Crime Machine," in *Dime Detective* (New York), January 1931.
"Murder by Mail," in *Black Mask* (New York), March 1931.
"The Flame and Race Williams," in *Black Mask* (New York), June–August 1931.
"Death for Two," in *Black Mask* (New York), September 1931.

"Satan's Kill," in *Detective Fiction Weekly* (New York), 19 November 1932.

"Merger with Death," in *Black Mask* (New York), December 1932.

"The Death Drop," in *Black Mask* (New York), May 1933.

"If Death Is Respectable," in *Black Mask* (New York), July 1933.

"The Sign of the Rat," in *Detective Fiction Weekly* (New York), 2 September 1933.

"Murder in the Open," in *Black Mask* (New York), October 1933.

"Blood on the Curtain," in *Dime Detective* (New York), 1 December 1933.

"Answered in Blood," in *Dime Detective* (New York), 1 March 1934.

"The Killer in the Hood," in *Detective Fiction Weekly* (New York), 14 April 1934.

"Make Your Own Corpse," in *Dime Detective* (New York), 15 April 1934.

"Six Have Died," in *Black Mask* (New York), May 1934.

"Flaming Death," in *Black Mask* (New York), June 1934.

"Behind the Black Hood," in *Detective Fiction Weekly* (New York), 23 June 1934.

"The Mexican Legion," in *Frontier Stories* (New York), July 1934.

"Death Drops In," in *Dime Detective* (New York), 1 July 1934.

"Murder Book," in *Black Mask* (New York), August 1934.

"Red Friday," in *Dime Detective* (New York), 1 September 1934.

"The Clawed Killer," in *Dime Detective* (New York), 15 October 1934.

"The Eyes Have It," in *Black Mask* (New York), November 1934.

"Excuse to Kill," in *Dime Detective* (New York), 15 December 1934.

"Ready to Burn," in *Detective Fiction Weekly* (New York), 16 February 1935.

"The Bridal Bullet," in *Dime Detective* (New York), 1 May 1935.

"Some Die Hard," in *Dime Detective* (New York), September 1935.

"Dead Hands Reaching," in *Dime Detective* (New York), November 1935.

"The Mark of the Raven," in *Dime Detective* (New York), January 1936.

"Corpse & Company," in *Dime Detective* (New York), February 1936.

"Satan's Vengeance," in *Detective Fiction Weekly* (New York), 7 March–25 April 1936.

"Just Another Stiff," in *Dime Detective* (New York), April 1936.

"Red Dynamite," in *Dime Detective* (New York), July 1936.

"City of Blood," in *Dime Detective* (New York), October 1936.

"The Tongueless Men," with William E. Barrett and others, in *Dime Detective* (New York), November 1936.

"The Morgue's Our Home," in *Dime Detective* (New York), December 1936.

"Monogram in Lead," in *Dime Detective* (New York), February 1937.

"Dead Men Don't Kill," in *Dime Detective* (New York), August 1937.

"Anyone's Corpse!" in *Dime Detective* (New York), October 1937.

"The $1,000,000 Corpse," in *Dime Detective* (New York), December 1937.

"The Book of the Dead," in *Dime Detective* (New York), January 1938.

"I Am the Law," in *Black Mask* (New York), March 1938.

"Wrong Street," in *Black Mask* (New York), May 1938.

"A Corpse for a Corpse," in *Dime Detective* (New York), July 1938.

"Men in Black," in *Dime Detective* (New York), October 1938.

"The Quick and the Dead," in *Dime Detective* (New York), December 1938.

"Hell with the Lid Lifted," in *Dime Detective* (New York), March 1939.

"Murder Made Easy," in *Black Mask* (New York), May 1939.

"A Corpse in the Hand," in *Dime Detective* (New York), June 1939.

"The White-Headed Corpse," in *Dime Detective* (New York), November 1939.

"Mr. Sinister," in *Detective Fiction Weekly* (New York), 11 November–25 November 1939.

"Beauty and the Feast," in *Argosy* (New York), 25 May 1940.

"Victim for Vengeance," in *Clues* (New York), September 1940.

"No Sap for Murder," in *Black Mask* (New York), November 1940.

"The Strange Case of Iva Grey," in *Dime Detective* (New York), December 1940.

"Five Minutes for Murder," in *Black Mask* (New York), January 1941.

"Too Dead to Pay," in *Clues* (New York), March 1941.

"Clay Holt, Detective," in *Detective Story* (New York), February 1942.

"City of the Dead," in *Detective Fiction* (New York), June 1944.

"Murder Theme," in *Black Mask* (New York), July 1944.

"Body, Body—Who's Got the Body?" in *Detective Story* (New York), October 1944.

"A Corpse Loses Its Head," in *Detective Story* (New York), March 1945.

"I'll Be Killing You," in *New Detective* (New York), September 1945.

"The Seventh Murderer," in *Detective Story* (New York), November 1945.

"The Giant Has Fleas," in *Detective Story* (New York), February 1947.

"This Corpse on Me," in *Thrilling Detective* (New York), June 1947.

"Dead Man's Street," in *New Detective* (New York), September 1947.

"I'll Feel Better When You're Dead," in *Thrilling Detective* (New York), December 1947.

"Not My Corpse," in *Thrilling Detective* (New York), June 1948.

"Race Williams' Double Date," in *Dime Detective* (New York), August 1948.

"The Law of the Night," in *New Detective* (New York), September 1948.

"The Wrong Corpse," in *Thrilling Detective* (New York), February 1949.

"Half a Corpse," in *Dime Detective* (New York), May 1949.

"Race Williams Cooks a Goose," in *Dime Detective* (New York), October 1949.

"The $100,000 Corpse," in *Popular Detective* (New York), March 1950.

"Cash for a Killer," in *The Evening Standard Detective Book*. London, Gollancz, 1950.

"The Strange Case of Alta May," in *Thrilling Detective* (New York), April 1950.

"If I Go in a Hearse," in *Phantom Detective* (New York), Spring 1950.

"Little Miss Murder," in *Smashing Detective* (New York), June 1952.

"This Corpse Is Free," in *Smashing Detective* (New York),
   September 1952.
"Gas," in *Smashing Detective* (New York), June 1953.
"The Cops Came at Seven," in *Famous Detective* (New York),
   August 1953.
"Lantern in the Mind" (as John D. Carroll), in *Famous
   Detective* (New York), August 1953.
"Jackpot," in *Thrilling Detective* (New York), Winter 1953.
"Avenging Angel," in *Famous Detective* (New York), February
   1954.
"Manhunter," in *Famous Detective* (New York), August 1954.
"Murder Yet to Come," in *Famous Detective* (New York),
   December 1954.
"With a Bullet in You," in *Smashing Detective* (New York),
   March 1955.
"Head over Homicide," in *Smashing Detective* (New York),
   May 1955.
"The False Burton Combs," in *The Hard-Boiled Detective:
   Stories from Black Mask Magazine (1920–1951)*, edited by
   Herbert Ruhm. New York, Vintage, 1977.
"Knights of the Open Palm," in *The Great American Detective*,
   edited by William Kittredge and Steven M. Krauzer. New
   York, New American Library, 1978.

OTHER PUBLICATIONS

Other

Two-Gun Gerta, with C.C. Waddell. New York, Chelsea
   House, 1926.

*   *   *

It is universally accepted that the hard-boiled school of
detective fiction originated in the American pulp magazine
Black Mask during the early 1920's. An outgrowth of the
lawless prohibition era, this new kind of mystery writing
explored the realism and violence of modern society through
the professional detective, be he private or police. These
stories, which embraced an odd sentimentality and a signature
toughness of characterization and prose, were written in the
first person and always in the vernacular.

Carroll John Daly initiated the movement away from the
traditional tale of ratiocination which had been the staple of the
mystery field and toward the story of urban violence. Daly
accomplished this neither deliberately nor spontaneously in his
1922 *Black Mask* story "The False Burton Combs," which is
considered to be the first hard-boiled detective story. Although
its protagonist is not a detective, his attitudes are those of the
later Daly detectives. The story's narrator is a nameless
adventurer for hire who operates in the shady half-world
between the criminal and the police, and is willing to risk his
life—or to kill—for a fee.

This character prefigures Race Williams, who, like Daly's
other characters—Satan Hall, Vee Brown, Clay Holt, and
others—is a fictional cowboy transferred to the modern streets.
Williams is a pragmatic cynical gunman who lives by his gun
and trades on his reputation as a killer of criminals. He is a
private investigator, often at odds with the law, who describes
himself as "a middleman—just a half-way house between the
cops and the crooks" and who boasts that he "never bumped off
a guy what didn't need it." He is a uncomplicated figure who
believes in a simple code of ethics which demands that he earn
his fee and remain loyal to his client, though he will forego
payment for a friend ("Death for Two") or gun down a
treacherous client if he "deserves it" (*The Amateur Murderer*).

Williams, like Daly's other characters, is an aggressive
investigator who accomplishes his aims through violence. He
espouses a kind of frontier retribution which equates justice
with a bullet in the brain of the malefactor. Aware of public
antagonism toward his pragmatic philosophy, he is unconcerned and unapologetic, though when a woman adopts his
cold-blooded attitude toward criminals he is both sickened and
horrified, indicating lingering moral reservations ("Anyone's
Corpse").

Daly's stories are marked by a curious strain of melodrama
which undermines their illusion of realism. Race Williams uses
the affected speech of the dime-novel hero as much as he does
the hard-boiled idiom. His cases often take him into the
unremitting grimness of underworld life ("Not My Corpse"),
but they also find him in opposition to dime-novel master
criminals (*The Hidden Hand*). Essentially, Daly was a transitional writer who was not above placing one of his hard-boiled
protagonists in a more traditional mystery (*The Man in the
Shadows*), and who did not find his direction until later, more
gifted writers legitimized his ideas, thereby showing him the
way.

—Will Murray

———

DALY, Elizabeth. American. Born in New York City, 15
October 1878. Educated at Miss Baldwin's School; Bryn Mawr
College, Pennsylvania, B.A. 1901; Columbia University, New
York, M.A. 1902. Reader in English, Bryn Mawr College,
1904–06; tutor in French and English; producer of amateur
theatre. Recipient: Mystery Writers of American Edgar Allan
Poe award, 1960. *Died 2 September 1967.*

CRIME PUBLICATIONS

Novels (series: Henry Gamadge in all books)

Unexpected Night. New York, Farrar and Rinehart, and
   London, Gollancz, 1940.
Deadly Nightshade. New York, Farrar and Rinehart, 1940;
   London, Hammond, 1948.
Murders in Volume 2. New York, Farrar and Rinehart, 1941;
   London, Eyre and Spottiswoode, 1943.
The House Without the Door. New York, Farrar and
   Rinehart, 1942; London, Hammond, 1945.
Evidence of Things Seen. New York, Farrar and Rinehart,
   1943; London, Hammond, 1946.
Nothing Can Rescue Me. New York, Farrar and Rinehart,
   1943; London, Hammond, 1945.
Arrow Pointing Nowhere. New York, Farrar and Rinehart,
   1944; London, Hammond, 1946; as *Murder Listens In,* New
   York, Bantam, 1949.
The Book of the Dead. New York, Farrar and Rinehart, 1944;
   London, Hammond, 1946.
Any Shape or Form. New York, Farrar and Rinehart, 1945;
   London, Hammond, 1949.
Somewhere in the House. New York, Rinehart, 1946; London,
   Hammond, 1949.
The Wrong Way Down. New York, Rinehart, 1946; London,
   Hammond, 1950; as *Shroud for a Lady,* New York, Spivak,
   1956.
Night Walk. New York, Rinehart, 1947; London, Hammond,
   1950.

The Book of the Lion. New York, Rinehart, 1948; London, Hammond, 1951.
And Dangerous to Know. New York, Rinehart, 1949; London, Hammond, 1952.
Death and Letters. New York, Rinehart, 1950; London, Hammond, 1953.
The Book of the Crime. New York, Rinehart, 1951; London, Hammond, 1954.

OTHER PUBLICATIONS

Novel

The Street Has Changed. New York, Farrar and Rinehart, 1941.

*   *   *

When asked the name of her favorite American mystery writer, Agatha Christie replied that it was Elizabeth Daly. It isn't too difficult to explain this phenomenon because Daly has transposed most of the apparatus of the cozy British Golden Age detective story, as written by Christie, to a New York setting in the 1940's. Here are crime problems among the well-to-do classes who spend most of their time observing the social conventions in a closed circle that is isolated from much of the reality of World War II, crime, and the struggle for existence among the lower classes.

Daly's series detective, Henry Gamadge, lives in an old but respectable house in the fashionable Murray Hill district of New York City. He doesn't work for a living, but is an author and bibliophile. He accepts commissions as a consultant on old books, manuscripts, inks or autographs—all of which fall within his expertise. On many occasions his bibliographic skills become intertwined with crime problems that include theft, forgery, and murder. Gamadge's blunt features and poor posture rule out a role as the conventionally suave and handsome detective of Golden Age fiction. He has a wife, a son, a cat named Martin, and an assistant, Harold Bantz. He numbers among his hobbies bridge, golf, music, and the conservation of the transitive verb. Anthony Boucher stated that he "is a man so well-bred as to make Lord Peter Wimsey seem a trifle coarse."

Gamadge tries to live a quiet, civilized life and pursue his literary interests, but his tranquility is disrupted by a series of disquieting incidents that often lead to murder investigations. In *Unexpected Night* a million-dollar legacy results in its recipient's demise. *Deadly Nightshade* is set in Maine, and deals with several cases of poisoning caused by a wild flower. *Murders in Volume 2* concerns a girl who claims to be the reincarnation of a missing 19th-century governess, and a volume of Lord Byron's poems that seems to have disappeared. *Nothing Can Rescue Me* presents Gamadge's Aunt Florence's attempt to write a novel, but she finds additional material added to her manuscript during the night. Gamadge is in the army in *Evidence of Things Seen,* but his wife Clara, vacationing in the Berkshires, is troubled when she sees an apparition on a hill at sunset. *Arrow Pointing Nowhere* presents Gamadge with a strangely marked railroad timetable.

The Book of the Dead might be solved by a clue in a copy of Shakespeare's *The Tempest.* This is one of the few Daly works (excluding the non-mystery *The Street Has Changed*) to display her vast theatrical expertise. A far-from-subtle rifle shot explodes the serenity of a rose garden in *Any Shape or Form.* An elderly caretaker uses the wrong door and takes *The Wrong Way Down* to the street with lethal consequences. The local library in the village of Fraser Mills is troubled by a prowler in *Night Walk.* *The Book of the Lion* concerns a lost Chaucer manuscript, and a recently deceased poet-playwright. A young woman leaves her home and vanishes into thin air for no explicable reason in *And Dangerous to Know*—recalling the famous Dorothy Arnold case. A crossroad puzzle contains a message from a widow being held against her will and threatened with institutionalization in *Death and Letters.*

Daly's youthful fondness for games and puzzles led to a lifetime interest in defective fiction which she considered to be a high form of literary art. Her own work is unsensational, and conceived with subtle skill. It is always both civilized and literate.

—Charles Shibuk

———

DANA, Freeman. *See* **TAYLOR, Phoebe Atwood.**

———

DANE, Mark. *See* **AVALLONE, Michael.**

———

DANE, Mary. *See* **MORLAND, Nigel.**

———

DANIELS, Norman A. Pseudonym for Norman A. Danberg; also writes as John L. Benton; William Dale; Peter Grady; Frank Johnson; G. Wayman Jones; Harrison Judd; C.K.M Scanlon; Robert Wallace. American. Educated at Columbia University, New York, and Northwestern University, Evanston, Illinois. Married Dorothy Smith (i.e., the writer Dorothy Daniels) in 1937. Agent: Richard Curtis Associates Inc., 164 East 64th Street, New York, New York 10021. Address: 6107 Village 6, Camarillo, California 93010, U.S.A.

CRIME PUBLICATIONS

Novels (series: Bruce Baron; Kelly Carvel; John Keith)

The Mausoleum Key. New York, Gateway, 1942.
John Doe—Murderer (as William Dale). New York, Gateway, 1942.
Mistress on a Deathbed. New York, Falcon, 1952.
The Captive. New York, Avon, 1959.
The Deadly Game. New York, Avon, 1959.
Lady for Sale. New York, Avon, 1960.
Lover, Let Me Live. New York, Avon, 1960.
Some Die Running. New York, Avon, 1960.
Spy Hunt. New York, Pyramid, 1960.
Suddenly by Shotgun. New York, Fawcett, 1961; London, Muller, 1962.
Shadow of a Doubt (as Harrison Judd). New York, Fawcett, 1961; London, Muller, 1962.

The Detectives (novelization of television series). New York, Lancer, 1962.

Something Burning. New York, Fawcett, and London, Muller, 1963.

Arrest and Trial (novelization of television series). New York, Lancer, 1963.

The Hunt Club (Keith). New York, Pyramid, 1964.

The Missing Witness (novelization of television play). New York, Lancer, 1964.

Overkill (Keith). New York, Pyramid, 1964.

The Secret War. New York, Pyramid, 1964.

Spy Ghost (Keith). New York, Pyramid, 1965.

Murder under the Big Top (as Robert Wallace). San Diego, Regency, 1965.

Operation K (Keith). New York, Pyramid, 1965.

Operation N (Keith). New York, Pyramid, 1965.

The Baron of Hong Kong. New York, Lancer, 1967.

A Killing in the Market. New York, Lancer, 1967.

Operation T (Keith). New York, Pyramid, 1967.

Operation VC (Keith). New York, Pyramid, 1967.

Baron's Mission to Peking. New York, Lancer, 1968.

The Magnetic Man (novelization of television play). New York, Berkley, 1968.

The Kono Diamond. New York, Berkley, 1969.

Moon Express (novelization of television play). New York, Berkley, 1969.

The Rape of a Town (Carvel). New York, Pyramid, 1970.

One Angry Man (Carvel). New York, Pyramid, 1971.

Operation S-L (Keith). New York, Pyramid, 1971.

Meet the Smiths (novelization of television play). New York, Berkley, 1971.

License to Kill (Carvel). New York, Pyramid, 1972.

Chase (novelization of television series). New York, Berkley, 1974.

Uncollected Short Stories

"Twice Dead," in *The Shadow* (New York), December 1943.

"Underground Agent," in *Doc Savage* (New York), January 1944.

"Death—Princess Style," in *Doc Savage* (New York), November 1944.

"The Will to Live," in *The Shadow* (New York), February 1945.

"Training by Hickory," in *Doc Savage* (New York), February 1945.

"The Feminine Touch," in *The Shadow* (New York), March 1945.

"Nothing Will Harm Him," in *The Shadow* (New York), April 1945.

"The Pointing Flowers," in *Doc Savage* (New York), May 1945.

"A Deal in Miniatures," in *Doc Savage* (New York), June 1945.

"Starch on the Rug," in *The Shadow* (New York), June 1945.

"Slightly Perfect," in *Best Detective Stories of the Year,* edited by David C. Cooke. New York, Dutton, 1946.

"Death Reaches Out." in *Black Book Detective 3* (Manchester), 1946.

"Ask for Murder," in *The Shadow* (New York), January 1946.

"Stormy, with Murder," in *The Shadow* (New York), May 1946.

"Exit Laughing," in *The Shadow* (New York), December 1947–January 1948.

"Final Hour," in *The Saint* (New York), September 1955.

"Dead Man's Millions," in *The Saint* (New York), January 1956.

"Laura Rarely takes Chances," in *The Saint* (New York), April 1956.

"Rooftop," in *Mike Shayne Mystery Magazine* (New York), September 1956.

"Mascot for Murder," in *The Saint* (New York), November 1956.

"Mr. Dove Retires," in *The Saint* (New York), December 1958.

"Killer at the Window," in *Suspense* (London), December 1958.

"With His Eyes Shut," in *Mystery Digest* (New York), March 1959.

"Set Up for Dying," in *Suspense* (London), October 1959.

"The Tin Box," in *Ellery Queen's Mystery Magazine* (New York), November 1959.

"Left Hand of Justice," in *Bestseller Mystery Magazine* (New York), March 1960.

"Two Sides to Everything," in *Ellery Queen's Mystery Magazine* (New York), March 1960.

"Act of Friendship," in *Ellery Queen's Mystery Magazine* (New York), May 1960.

"Something Has to Break," in *Ellery Queen's Mystery Magazine* (New York), June 1960.

"The Trap," in *Keyhole* (New York), June 1960.

"Memory Man," in *Bestseller Mystery Magazine* (New York), September 1960.

"Chink in the Armor," in *Ellery Queen's Mystery Magazine* (New York), September 1960.

"Duet," in *Bestseller Mystery Magazine* (New York), November 1960.

"The Town That Will Never Forget," in *Ellery Queen's 16th Mystery Annual*. New York, Random House, 1961.

"The Door Without a Key," in *Ellery Queen's Mystery Magazine* (New York), March 1961.

"The Loophole," in *The Saint* (London), April 1961.

"The Art of Murder," in *The Saint* (London), July 1961.

"Callahan's Hat," in *Ellery Queen's Mystery Magazine* (New York), July 1961.

"The Retirement of Muldoon," in *Ellery Queen's Mystery Magazine* (New York), March 1962.

"Strictly a Neighborhood Problem," in *Ellery Queen's Mystery Magazine* (New York), August 1962.

"Father Keough's Decision," in *Ellery Queen's Mystery Magazine* (New York), November 1962.

"A Funeral for Patrolman Cameron," in *Ellery Queen's Double Dozen*. New York, Random House, 1964; London, Gollancz, 1965.

"Most Beautiful Mannequin in the World," in *Ellery Queen's Mystery Magazine* (New York), November 1964.

"The Beach House," in *The Saint* (London), July 1965.

"A Matter of Patience," in *The Man from U.N.C.L.E.* (New York), October 1966.

"The Red Knife," in *Mike Shayne Mystery Magazine* (New York), January 1967.

"The Tin Sword," in *Mike Shayne Mystery Magazine* (New York), March 1967.

"The Uptown Man," in *Mike Shayne Mystery Magazine* (New York), April 1967.

"Burden of Guilt," in *The Man from U.N.C.L.E.* (New York). April 1967.

"The Petard Hoist," in *The Man from U.N.C.L.E.* (New York), May 1967.

"The Wisdom of the Wicked," in *Mike Shayne Mystery Magazine* (New York), June 1967.

"The Small House," in *Mike Shayne Mystery Magazine* (New York), September 1967.

"The Beelzebub Wish," in *The Man from U.N.C.L.E.* (New York), September 1967.

"The Hour of the Man," in *Mike Shayne Mystery Magazine* (New York), November 1967.

"Well in Hand," in *Mike Shayne Mystery Magazine* (New York), December 1967.

"She wouldn't Go Away," in *Mike Shayne Mystery Magazine* (New York), February 1968.

"Affairs in Order," in *Mike Shayne Mystery Magazine* (New York), September 1969.

"The Unleashed," in *Mike Shayne Mystery Magazine* (New York), December 1969.

Uncollected Short Stories (series: The Phantom in all works)

"Merchant of Murder," "Death on Swift Wings," "Master of the Damned," "Notes of Doom," "The Prince of Murder," "The Pharaoh's Ark," "Master of the World," "Island of Sudden Death," "Murder Empire," "The Diamond Murders," "Chateau of Crime," "The Circus Murders," "Six Prints of Murder," "Specter of Death," "Murder Rides the Skies," "Murder of a Plastic Saint," "The Rubber Knife Murders," "The Hijack Murders," "The Booby-Trap Murders," "Mansions of Despair," "The Fatal Masterpiece," "The Listening Eyes," "The City of Dreadful Night," "The Black Ball of Death" (with C.S. Montayne), "The Tall Tomb," "The Happyland Murders," "The Deadly Diamonds," "Murder Money," "The Video Victims," "Crimson Harvest," "Murder Millions," "The Silent Killer," "The Doomed Millions," "The Murder Machine," "Murder's Agent," October 1934–Summer 1953, all in *The Phantom Detective* (New York).

Uncollected Short Stories as John L. Benton (series: Jerry Wade in all works)

"Murder in Pictures," "Candid Camera Murders," "The Silver Mask Murders," "Negatives of Death," "The Candid Camera Kid Vanishes," "Picture of a Killer," "Focus on Murder," "The Auto Race Murders," "Death at the World's Fair," "The Refugee Murders," "Murder Makes News," "Fur Wrapped Murder," "The Weeping Willow Murders," "The Doomed Five," "Camera Trap," "Picture of a Ghost," "Murder Never Dies," "Murder Montage," "Phantom Evidence," "Gems of Disaster," "Appointment with Murder," "Murder of a Shutterbug," June 1939–June 1944, all in *Detective Novels* magazine (New York).

Uncollected Short Stories as G. Wayman Jones (series: The Black Bat in all works) all works appeared in *Black Book Detective* magazine)

"Brand of the Black Bat," "Murder Calls the Black Bat," "The Black Bat Strikes Again [and the Trojan Horse, and the Red Menace]," "The Black Bat's Challenge [Spy Trail, Crusade, Triumph, Justice, Invisible Enemy]," "The Voice of Doom," "The Eyes of the Blind," "The Blackout Murders," "The Shadow of Evil," "The Faceless Satan," "The Nazi Spy Murders," "The Seventh Column," "Captains of Death," "Guardian in Black," "Markets of Treason," "The White Witch," "Death for Charity," "Murder Deals in Ersatz," "The Skeleton's Secret," "The Marked Man," "Murder on the Loose," "Murder among the Dying," "The Man Behind Murder," "The Survivor Murders," "With Malice Afterthought," "The Crime to Come," "The Lakeside Mystery," "The Murder Prophet," "Dead Man's Plunder," "The Long Ago Murder," "City of Hidden Death," "The Coiled Serpent," "Inheritance of Murder," "The Murder Maker," "The Lying Killer," "City of Hate," "Thirty-One Deadly Guns," "The Riddle of the Dead Man's Bequest," "Murder's Playground," "The Missing Million," "The Dennison Document," "Murder Town," "Blueprint of Crime," "The

Murder Genius," "The Black Bat Fights for Life," "The League of Faceless Men," "The Dangerous Corpse," "The Killer Who Wasn't," July 1939–Winter 1952, all in *Black Book Detective* magazine (Chicago).

Uncollected Short Stories as Frank Johnson (series: the Crimson Mask in all works)

"Enter the Crimson Mask," "The Crimson Mask's Murder Trial [Death Gamble, Scorpion Trail, Ghost Trail]," "Sign of the Crimson Mask," "The Crimson Mask and the Vanishing Men," "The Diamond Death Trail," "The Money Trail," "The Murders at the Black Rose," "Four Men of Murder," "The Dangerous Gamble," "Three Men of Evil," "Five Clues to Murder," "Traffic in Murder," August 1940–April 1944, all in *Detective Novels* magazine (New York).

Uncollected Short Stories as Norman A. Daniels and C.K.M. Scanlon (series: Dan Fowler in all works)

"The Convention Murders," "Specialist in Murder," "G-Men Strike Hard," "The Fire in the Sky," "The Underground," "Men of Treason," "Surrender or Die," "One Thousand Suspects," "The Private Murders," "The Private World of Murder," "Doubled in Death," "The Crown of Murder," "The Kidnap Kills," "Web of Murder," "Murder Guns," "The Big Break," "Slumbering Death," "Cargo of Death," "The Harbor of Death," "Crimson Tomorrows," "The Big Fix," "City of Deception," "The White Rover Murders," "Mistress of Death," "The Brink of Death," "Red, White—and Blood," September 1940–Winter 1952, all in *G-Men Detective* magazine (New York).

Uncollected Short Stories as C.K.M. Scanlon (series: The Masked Detective in all works; all works appeared in *The Masked Detective* magazine)

"Alias the Masked Detective," "The Masked Detective's Warning [Manhunt]," "The League of the Iron Cross," "The Canal Zone Murders," Fall 1940–Summer 1942, all in *The Masked Detective* Magazine (New York).

OTHER PUBLICATIONS

Novels

Colt Law. New York, Avalon, 1956.
Two Trails to Bannack (as Peter Grady). New York, Avalon, 1956.
Back Trails. New York, Avalon, 1962.
The Marshal of Winter Gap (as Peter Grady). New York, Avalon, 1962.
County Hospital. New York, Fawcett, and London, Muller, 1963.
Showdown. New York, Lancer, 1963.
Dr. Kildare's Finest Hour (novelization of television play). New York, Lancer, 1963; London, Fontana, 1964.
Dr. Kildare's Secret Romance (novelization of television play). London, Fontana, 1963; New York, Lancer, 1964.
Jennifer James, R.N. New York, Fawcett, and London, Muller, 1963.
Gun Empire. New York, Avalon, 1963.
The Hunt Club. New York, Pyramid, 1964.
Battalion. New York, Pyramid, 1965.
Moments of Glory. New York, Paperback Library, 1965.
Strike Force. New York, Lancer, 1965.
Dark Desire. New York, Lancer, 1967.

The Tarnished Scalpel. New York, Lancer, 1968.
The Deadly Ride. New York, Lancer, 1968.
Law of the Lash. New York, Warner, 1968.
Master of Wyndward. New York, Warner, 1969.
Jubal. New York, Paperback Library, 1970; London, New English Library, 1973.
Slave Rebellion. New York, Paperback Library, 1970; London, New English Library, 1973.
Voodoo Slave. New York, Paperback Library, 1970; London, New English Library, 1973.
Wyndward Passion (includes *Law of the Lash* and *Master of Wyndward*). New York, Warner, 1978; London, Hamlyn, 1980.
Wyndward Fury. New York, Warner, 1979.
Wyndward Glory. New York, Warner, 1981.
Wyndward Forever. New York, Warner, 1984.

Plays

Radio Plays: for *Nick Carter* series.

Television Plays: for *Ben Casey, The Avengers, Dr. Kildare, Ellery Queen, General Electric Theatre, Ford Theatre, The Web, Restless Gun,* and *Alfred Hitchcock Presents* series.

*

Manuscript Collection: Bowling Green University, Ohio.

*   *   *

Because he was one of the most industrious, versatile, and prolific contributors to the mystery and detective pulp magazines of the 1930's and 1940's, the true extent of Norman A. Daniels's canon is unappreciated by virtue of its being unsuspected. Under his own name, Daniels was so prolific as to be ubiquitous. He wrote for nearly every detective magazine published between 1931, the year he entered the field, and 1953, when the last of those titles ceased publication, from novelettes in *Thrilling Detective* and *Popular Detective* to short stories in *The Shadow, 10 Detective Aces, Crime Busters, Clues,* and others. But the greater portion of his magazine fiction, including most of his novel-length works, were published under an assortment of personal pseudonyms, such as Kirk Rand—his byline in *Spicy Detective Stories* and *Spicy Mystery Stories*—and house names.

Over a 20-year period, he wrote nearly 40 novels featuring the exploits of Richard Curtis Van Loan, alias the manhunting Phantom, a character created by D.L. Champion for *The Phantom Detective* magazine in 1933 and continued by numerous other writers under the house pseudonym of Robert Wallace. For a companion magazine, *Black Book Detective,* he created the Black Bat, a cloaked and masked crime-fighter in the Shadow tradition who was really district attorney Tony Quinn. Daniels wrote nearly all of the 63 Black Bat novels printed between 1939 and 1953 under the name G. Wayman Jones. For *G-Men Detective,* he wrote 26 separate stories featuring F.B.I. agent Dan Fowler, who had been created by George Fielding Eliot in 1936. These were published under Daniels's own name as well as under the byline C.K.M. Scanlon, a house name which also concealed Daniels's authorship of the hero of *The Masked Detective* magazine, another Daniels brainchild. For *Detective Novels,* he juggled two alternating series, one featuring Jerry Wade, the Candid Camera Kid and bylined John L. Benton and the other starring the Crimson Mask and bylined Frank Johnson. All of these characters were published by Standard Magazines, Daniels's chief client.

Although he became adept at turning out thousands of pages of tight formula fiction to satisfy editorial needs, Daniels never lost his edge. During the late 1940's he produced his best short crime fiction for Street and Smith's *Shadow Mystery* and *Doc Savage, Science Detective,* including "Exit Laughing" and "Slightly Perfect," the latter of which was included in E.P. Dutton's *Best Detective Stories of the Year* for 1947, and four stories featuring Rick Trent, private detective and ex-convict, for *Black Mask.* As the pulp magazines declined, he wrote for radio, scripting *Nick Carter,* and later scripted television shows like *Alfred Hitchcock Presents* and *Dr. Kildare.*

With the paperback revolution, Daniels shifted his attention to meeting the shifting demand for softcover novels and wrote in a number of genres. After a time he concentrated on espionage books featuring his characters John Keith, the Man from A.P.E. and Bruce Baron, alias the Baron, and television novelizations of *Arrest and Trail* and *The Avengers.* Not content to remain locked in the genre where he has toiled since the beginning of his career, Daniels has since retired his own name to write gothics and historical novels under the byline of his wife and lifelong collaborator, Dorothy Daniels.

Having written formula fiction for so long, Daniels's work is, in substance, athematic and because much of it seems to have been written in often-uncredited collaboration with his wife, that work eludes evaluation except to remark that a recurring concern seems to be the innocuousness of evil. If anything, Daniels's output speaks most eloquently of a consummate professionalism combined with indefatigable ability to adjust to changing trends in genre fiction.

—Will Murray

————

DANIELS, Philip. *See* **CHAMBERS, Peter.**

————

DANNAY, Frederic. *See* **QUEEN, Ellery.**

————

D'ARCY, Willard. *See* **COX, William R.**

————

DAVEY, Jocelyn. Pseudonym for Chaim Raphael. British. Born in Middlesbrough, Yorkshire, 14 July 1908. Educated at Portsmouth Grammar School, 1921–27; University College, Oxford (history scholar), 1927–30, B.A. in philosophy, politics and economics 1930, M.A. 1933; James Mew Graduate Scholar in Hebrew, 1931; Kennicott Fellow in Hebrew, 1934–36. Married Diana Rose in 1934 (marriage dissolved 1964); one son and one daughter. Cowley Lecturer in Post-Biblical Hebrew, Oxford University, 1932–39; engaged in government work, 1939–70: Liaison officer for Internment Camps, 1939–42; economics adviser, 1942–45, and economics director, 1945–

57, British Information Services, New York; deputy head, 1957–59, and head of the information division, 1959–69, Department of the Treasury; head of the information division, Civil Service Department, 1968–69. Research Fellow in Jewish Social History, University of Sussex, Brighton, 1969–75. Recipient: Wingate prize, 1983. O.B.E. (Officer, Order of the British Empire), 1951; C.B.E. (Commander, Order of the British Empire), 1965. Agent: Elaine Greene Ltd, 37 Goldhawk Road, London W12 8QQ; or, Georges Borchardt Inc., 136 East 57th Street, New York, New York 10022, U.S.A. Address: Flat 1, The Priory, Kingsway, Hove, East Sussex BN3 2RQ

CRIME PUBLICATIONS

Novels (series: Ambrose Usher in all books)

The Undoubted Deed.   London, Chatto and Windus, 1956; as *A Capitol Offense,* New York, Knopf, 1956.
The Naked Villainy.   London, Chatto and Windus, and New York, Knopf, 1958.
A Touch of Stagefright.   London, Chatto and Windus, 1960.
A Killing in Hats.   London, Chatto and Windus, 1965.
A Treasury Alarm.   London, Chatto and Windus, 1976; New York, Walker, 1981.
Murder in Paradise.   London, Chatto and Windus, and New York, Walker, 1982.
A Dangerous Liaison.   New York, Walker, 1988.

OTHER PUBLICATIONS as Chaim Raphael

Other

Memoirs of a Special Case.   London, Chatto and Windus, and Boston, Little Brown, 1962.
The Walls of Jerusalem: An Excursion into Jewish History. London, Chatto and Windus, and New York, Knopf, 1968.
A Feast of History: Passover Through the Ages as a Key to Jewish Experience.   London, Weidenfeld and Nicolson, and New York, Simon and Schuster, 1972.
A Coat of Many Colours: Memoirs of Jewish Experience. London, Chatto and Windus, 1979; as *Encounters with the Jewish People,* New York, Behrman House, 1979.
The Springs of Jewish Life.   New York, Basic Books, 1982; London, Chatto and Windus, 1983.
The Road from Babylon: The Story of Sephardi and Oriental Jews.   London, Weidenfeld and Nicolson, 1985; New York, Harper, 1986.
A Jewish Book of Common Prayer.   London, Weidenfeld and Nicolson, 1986.

*

Jocelyn Davey comments:
My mysteries are adventures in which the central character, Ambrose Usher, an Oxford philosophy don who is intended to be both erudite and entertaining, finds himself in various parts of the world, roped in on some mysterious project by the British Government. Reviewers (and, I hope, the public) have found the books satisfyingly light-hearted. They all echo personal experience in some degree.

*   *   *

Under the pseudonym Jocelyn Davey, Chaim Raphael has written a series of detective novels, which he describes as "entertainments." These feature the cheerfully arcane ratiocinations of Ambrose Usher, the most learned, sophisticated, and literary detective since Dorothy L. Sayers's Lord Peter Wimsey.

A witty and amorous bachelor of middle age, Oxford don Ambrose Usher specializes in philosophy. He is a fluent speaker of several languages, an avid reader of ancient and modern classics, and a connoisseur of music and music manuscripts. His ill-defined foreign embassy assignments involve him often with international intrigue and always with murder. Usher particularly relishes assignments to the United States, the setting for two of the novels in which he appears.

Davey's "entertainments" are complicated: all develop crowds of characters in subplots clustered around one central literary theme. While the discovery of the criminal usually ties the subplots together, the murder itself often seems less important than the people, social events, and scholarly forays between which Usher must dash, cocktail in hand, in order to solve it. Needless to say, a scholarly diplomat-detective operates with brain rather than brawn. In *The Naked Villainy,* the clue appears in Usher's interpretation of the Bible story of Jacob and Esau. In *A Touch of Stagefright,* a series of telephone calls and a spot of research at the New York Public Library solve the criminal puzzle.

While some critics object to the far-fetched murders and bookishly convoluted plots of the Ambrose Usher novels, far more admire Davey's humor; his odd characters flourish in even odder situations. Flat-footed FBI agents, English treasury investigators, svelte Russian emigrés, eccentric aristocrats, antivivisectionists, fashionable ladies, loyal retainers, self-made industrialists, and bookish dons throng through these crowded novels. Davey unifies his tales with theme and allusion, not plot, succeeding more as a novelist than as a detective novelist.

Murder in Paradise and *A Dangerous Liaison* develop plots and central themes unified around more fully developed central characters. As Ambrose Usher ages, his investigative and social pace becomes less frenzied. In *A Dangerous Liaison,* he appears as a supporting character, providing moral and computer support for Victoria McKenzie, an Oxford historian who becomes the central scholarly investigator. Like Sayers's Harriet Vane, Victoria uses her investigation to explore her own identity as a woman and as an author. The novel's central themes of revenge, power, and gamesmanship unify subplots which all lead to both the crime and the recognition of guilt.

The career and interests of Chaim Raphael parallel those of his detective hero. Like Usher, he is amused and intrigued by America, which he describes as his "recreation." He has enjoyed a university teaching career, and has published a number of serious non-fiction works, notably on Judaica. He also served as Intelligence Advisor in the United States and in Canada during World War II and as a Treasury and Civil Service Officer. Raphael's interests, experience, scholarship, and wit all appear in his detective fiction.

—Katherine Staples

DAVIDSON, Lionel. Also writes as David Line. British. Born in Hull, Yorkshire, 31 March 1922. Served in the Royal Naval Submarine Service, 1941–46. Married Fay Jacobs in 1949; two sons. Freelance magazine journalist and editor, 1946–59. Recipient: Crime Writers Association Gold Dagger award, 1961, 1967, 1979. Agent: Curtis Brown, 162–168 Regent Street, London W1R 5TB, England.

CRIME PUBLICATIONS

Novels

The Night of Wenceslas. London, Gollancz, 1960; New York, Harper, 1961.
The Rose of Tibet. London, Gollancz, and New York, Harper, 1962.
A Long Way to Shiloh. London, Gollancz, 1966; as *The Menorah Men,* New York, Harper, 1966.
Making Good Again. London, Cape, and New York, Harper, 1968.
The Sun Chemist. London, Cape, and New York, Knopf, 1976.
The Chelsea Murders. London, Cape, 1978; as *Murder Games,* New York, Coward McCann, 1978.

Uncollected Short Stories

"Note to Survivors," in *Alfred Hitchcock's Mystery Magazine* (New York), May 1958.
"Where Am I Going? Nowhere!," in *Suspense* (London), February 1961.

OTHER PUBLICATIONS

Novel

Smith's Gazelle. London, Cape, and New York, Knopf, 1971.

Fiction (for children) as David Line

Soldier and Me. New York, Harper, 1965.
Run for Your Life. London, Cape, 1966.
Mike and Me. London, Cape, 1974.
Under Plum Lake (as Lionel Davidson). London, Cape, and New York, Knopf, 1980.
Screaming High. London, Cape, and Boston, Little Brown, 1985.

*   *   *

Lionel Davidson is a crime writer whose career has taken a by no means common path. Instead of finding a successful formula and sticking to it with perhaps some gradual expansion he has bounded from sub-genre to sub-genre, each bound taking him usually yet higher.

Beginning with *The Night of Wenceslas,* an espionage thriller that won him deserved prizes for its uncluttered sharpness of tone and its memorable vividness (all the more remarkable since Davidson had never visited Czechoslovakia, where most of the story takes place), he went on at once to write quite a different sort of book, a novel of pure adventure, *The Rose of Tibet.* This perhaps falls outside our brief here, but it is worth nothing that Graham Greene said of its extraordinary evocation of the forbidden, exotic land of Tibet, "I hadn't realised how much I had missed the genuine adventure story," and Daphne du Maurier asked, "Is Lionel Davidson today's Rider Haggard?"

Four years later—he is by no means a prolific author—he gave her her answer. And it was "No." *A Long Way to Shiloh* has stunning adventure in it, as well as excellent jokes and a sophisticated strain of sex, but it is a good deal more than "the genuine adventure story." It is not only ceaselessly gripping with its account of a hunt for the centuries-lost true Menorah from the Temple at Jerusalem, but it has a setting that is not merely an exotic or unusual background, a mere commercial additive. In it the background, Israel in the 1960's, becomes a major character in its own right. This makes the book, whatever your political allegiance and despite the sad events of later days, a joy to devour, a hymn to hopefulness. Not that it is all lyrical. Davidson's gift of vividness and his ability to be immensely funny are not forgotten.

Making Good Again is perhaps not dissimilar in intention, though in method it largely eschews adventure in favour of a complex, gradual unravelling. Set in post-war Germany (with a sombre chapter at the Auschwitz memorial), it tackles head-on one of the great themes of our times, a theme that would have challenged our mightiest novelists, the meaning of the phenomenon of Nazism. And to do this Davidson employs to the full the methods of the novelist, those layers of ever richer meaning. But again he did not abandon humour.

The complex novel *Smith's Gazelle* has about it something of the world-creating myth, which has made it a treasured book among young people. Its story of the chances and determinations that preserve a herd of almost extinct deer take it, again, out of the strict confines of these pages. But it had all the immense vividness that is perhaps Davidson's chief hallmark.

The novel that followed, *The Sun Chemist,* falls, however, squarely into the espionage bracket with its excellent plot-spring, the supposed existence among the forgotten papers of the scientist-statesman Chaim Weizmann of a formula that will free any nation possessing it of dependence on oil. The whole is told with Davidson's characteristic combination of cleverness and warmth, a rare enough blend. But the cleverness is not used just to make good jokes, but to dig with jokes the long needles of the acupuncturist deep into the body politic.

Finally, after another long gap, we have had *The Chelsea Murders,* a book whose title exactly describes it, a mystery story set in the bohemian world of London's art district and a dazzling send-up of the conventional whodunnit. Where Davidson will go after that is anybody's guess, but wherever it is it will be well worth going to.

—H.R.F. Keating

DAVIES, L(eslie) P(urnell). Also writes as Leslie Vardre. British. Born in Crewe, Cheshire, 20 October 1914. Educated at Manchester College of Science and Technology, University of Manchester, qualified as optometrist 1939 (Fellow, British Optical Association). Served in the British Army Medical Corps in France, North Africa, and Italy, 1939–45. Married Winifred Tench in 1940. Dispensing pharmacist, Crewe, Cheshire, 1930–39; freelance artist in Rome, 1945–46; postmaster, West Heath, Birmingham, 1946–56; optician in private practice, and gift shop owner, Deganwy, North Wales, 1956–75. Since 1975, has lived in Tenerife. Agent: Howard Moorepark, 444 East 82nd Street, New York, New York 10028, U.S.A. Address: Apartment K-1, Edificio Alondra, El Botanico, Puerto de la Cruz, Tenerife, Canary Islands, Spain.

CRIME PUBLICATIONS

Novels

The Paper Dolls. London, Jenkins, 1964; New York, Doubleday, 1966.
Man Out of Nowhere. London, Jenkins, 1965; as *Who Is Lewis Pinder?*, New York, Doubleday, 1966.
The Artificial Man. London, Jenkins, 1965; New York, Doubleday, 1967.
The Lampton Dreamers. London, Jenkins, 1966; New York, Doubleday, 1967.
Tell It to the Dead (as Leslie Vardre). London, Long, 1966; as *The Reluctant Medium*, as L.P. Davies, New York, Doubleday, 1967.
The Nameless Ones (as Leslie Vardre). London, Long, 1967; as *A Grave Matter*, as L.P. Davies, New York, Doubleday, 1968.
Stranger to Town. London, Jenkins, and New York, Doubleday, 1969.
The White Room. New York, Doubleday, 1969; London, Barrie and Jenkins, 1970.
The Shadow Before. New York, Doubleday, 1970; London, Barrie and Jenkins, 1971.
Give Me Back Myself. New York, Doubleday, 1971; London, Barrie and Jenkins, 1972.
What Did I Do Tomorrow? London, Barrie and Jenkins, 1972; New York, Doubleday, 1973.
Assignment Abacus. London, Barrie and Jenkins, and New York, Doubleday, 1975.
Possession. London, Hale, and New York, Doubleday, 1976.
The Land of Leys. New York, Doubleday, 1979; London, Hale, 1980.
Morning Walk. London, Hale, 1983.

Uncollected Short Stories

"The Way of the East," in *London Mystery Magazine,* December 1959.
"The Prisoner," in *London Mystery Magazine,* March 1960.
"Oasis Incident," in *London Mystery Magazine,* June 1960.
"Infiltrant," in *London Mystery Magazine,* September 1960.
"The Rainmakers," in *London Mystery Magazine,* December 1960.
"Mirror Boy," in *London Mystery Magazine,* March 1961.
"The Ju-Ju," in *London Mystery Magazine,* May 1961.
"Mr. Always," in *London Mystery Magazine,* September 1961.
"The Addict," in *London Mystery Magazine,* November 1961.
"Dressed to Kill," in *London Mystery Magazine,* March 1962.
"Members Only," in *London Mystery Magazine,* June 1962.
"Gilda," in *London Mystery Magazine,* September 1962.
"The Seventh Man," in *London Mystery Magazine,* December 1962.
"The Gate," in *London Mystery Magazine,* March 1963.
"BT 563," in *London Mystery Magazine,* June 1963.
"Breaking Point," in *London Mystery Magazine,* September 1963.
"The Man Who Liked to Talk," in *London Mystery Magazine,* December 1963.

"The Neighbour," in *London Mystery Magazine,* March 1964.
"The Day of the Dog," in *London Mystery Magazine,* June 1964.
"Poplar Cottage," in *London Mystery Magazine,* September 1964.
"140,000 Red Toadstools," in *London Mystery Magazine,* December 1964.
"The Unknown Factor," in *The Sixth Mystery Bedside Book,* edited by John Creasey. London, Hodder and Stoughton, 1965.
"Think Big," in *London Mystery Magazine,* March 1965.
"Interference," in *London Mystery Magazine,* June 1965.
"The Parasite," in *London Mystery Magazine,* September 1965.
"Spare Part," in *London Mystery Magazine,* June 1966.
"Number Eighteen," in *London Mystery Magazine,* September 1966.
"Jenny," in *London Mystery Magazine,* May 1967.
"End Game," in *The Tenth Ghost Book,* edited by Aidan Chambers. London, Barrie and Jenkins, 1974.

Uncollected Short Stories as Leslie Vardre

"The Sight of Blood," in *London Mystery Magazine,* March 1960.
"The Wall of Time," in *London Mystery Magazine,* June 1960.
"The Messenger," in *London Mystery Magazine,* September 1960.
"Tea-Time," in *London Mystery Magazine,* December 1960.
"The Man with No Face," in *London Mystery Magazine,* March 1961.
"No School on Friday," in *London Mystery Magazine,* May 1961.
"The Dream Pedlar," in *London Mystery Magazine,* November 1961.
"Sleeping Beauty," in *London Mystery Magazine,* September 1962.
"Mermaid Beach," in *London Mystery Magazine,* December 1962.
"Time in Hand," in *London Mystery Magazine,* March 1963.
"Death of a Witch," in *London Mystery Magazine,* June 1963.
"Bait," in *London Mystery Magazine,* September 1963.
"The Sleeping Man," in *London Mystery Magazine,* December 1963.
"Weeds," in *London Mystery Magazine,* March 1964.
"The Alien," in *London Mystery Magazine,* June 1964.
"Sorry, Mr. Hepple," in *London Mystery Magazine,* December 1964.
"To Maidy—a Son," in *London Mystery Magazine,* March 1965.
"The Monsters," in *London Mystery Magazine,* June 1965.

OTHER PUBLICATIONS

Novels

Psychogeist. London, Jenkins, 1966; New York, Doubleday, 1967.
Twilight Journey. London, Jenkins, 1967; New York, Doubleday, 1968.
The Alien. London, Jenkins, 1968; New York, Doubleday, 1971.
Dimension A. London, Jenkins, and New York, Doubleday, 1969.
Genesis Two. London, Jenkins, 1969; New York, Doubleday, 1970.

Adventure Holidays Ltd. New York, Doubleday, 1970.
The Silver Man (in Swedish). Stockholm, Wahlströms Bok-
förlag, 1972.

*

L.P.Davies comments:

Although I think I have written every type of material
available, I have mainly concentrated on what I call "Pyscho
fiction" and my American editor calls "Tomorrow fiction." It
has proved remunerative—this fiction based on the workings
of the human mind—but has had its drawbacks. My first novel,
The Paper Dolls, was rejected by four publishers because it
didn't fit into any of their categories. I try to puzzle my readers;
I have no axes to grind; I think I have always played fair with
my readers when offering them what I hope may seem like an
unsolvable mystery. I try to offer entertainment only.

*   *   *

An author who has written under other names, L.P. Davies
writes science fiction and thrillers in his own name. Fascinated
with psychic phenomena and the supernatural, he has based
most of his suspense novels on these themes. Some of his books
published as mystery or crime fiction have science fiction
elements so that classification is not always clear.

The Paper Dolls, Davies's first thriller, is considered a crime
novel, though it could just as well be shelved with the science
fiction. The story opens and closes in a school with a class of
boys reading from *A Midsummer Night's Dream*. Two young
teachers, Gordon Seacombe and Joan Grey, determined to
discover the truth about some peculiar happenings in their
school which seem to revolve about one boy, learn that, instead
of one boy, brothers are involved. The brothers seem able to
induce terrifying psychic states in other people. Seacombe,
after one such experience, says: "I think that in some way he
reached a mental finger into our minds, pressing the button
labeled 'fear.' The things we saw we each made up ourselves.
The things we have the greatest horror of." The explanation
deals with a condition said to be abnormal, as opposed to
supernatural. The story is out of the ordinary and well executed.
In addition to the romantic interest between two teachers, the
feelings of a grandson are nicely evoked.

The Artificial Man is Davies's earliest tale in which the
protagonist is uncertain of his identity, a situation frequently
exploited by the author, though from different angles. A
political struggle between the army and the Bureau of Counter-
Psycho-conflict underlies the hero's personal difficulties. *Tell It
to the Dead*, perhaps Davies's least interesting yarn, debunks
fraudulent fortune-tellers while managing to suggest that there
is such a thing as a real medium. *Man Out of Nowhere* is a
thriller in which the central character does not know who he is,
although he is "positively" identified, more or less vehemently,
as four different individuals, all of whom are thought to be dead
and buried.

From the late 1960's to the present, L.P. Davies has turned
out some dozen thrillers, each dealing with some aspect of
psychic disturbance—caused by drugs, brain tumor, amnesia,
hypnosis, or deception. The depersonalization or disorientation
of the hero, or the seemingly supernatural goings-on are
satifactorily—sometimes ingeniously—explained. In *Stranger
to Town*, a widow who belongs to the "Return" church is
befriended by a man who appears to be the recipient of thought
transference from her late husband. She, of course, thinks her
husband has somehow come back in another man's body. A
good plot and some successful detection by the "stranger"
enliven this book. The hero of *The White Room*, Axel

Champlee, who suffers from a curious form of depersonalization, believes he is being drugged and subtly driven to murder.
Romance is part of the plot, as it often is in Davies's thrillers.

The Shadow Before, Give Me Back Myself, and *What Did I Do
Tomorrow?*, all very clever narratives, represent Davies at his
best, and also reveal his own obsessive concern with characters
who are disoriented in time or space, victims of their own
delusions as well as of the evil designs of those around them;
each is a variation on the theme. In *Assignment Abacus*, a
businessman is whisked away to an isolated house in Scotland
and subjected to some confusing tests, one of which is to figure
out why he has been brought there. *Possession* contains a weird
cult, an unethical scientist, and a rich old man who wishes to
take over the body of a healthy young person.

L.P. Davies can surely be considered the master of the
suspenseful identity crisis—one character after another must
confront reality (or apparent reality) with a disordered
perception. The author is proficient at sketching English
villages and rural scenes for background, and adroitly
constructs thrillers which are unusual and entertaining.

—Mary Helen Becker

———

DAVIOT, Gordon. *See* **TEY, Josephine.**

———

DAVIS, Dorothy Salisbury. American. Born in Chicago,
Illinois, 26 April 1916. Educated at Holy Child High School,
Waukegan, Illinois; Barat College, Lake Forest, Illinois, A.B.
1938. Married Harry Davis in 1946. Member of the board of
directors, Palisades Free Library, New York, 1967–72; past
president, Mystery Writers of America. Since 1986 honorary
member of the board of directors, Rockland Center for the
Arts, New York. Recipient: Mystery Writers of America
Grand Master award, 1984; Bouchercon Lifetime Achievement award, 1989. Agent: McIntosh and Otis Inc., 310
Madison Avenue New York, New York 10017, U.S.A.

CRIME PUBLICATIONS

Novels (series: Julie Hayes; Mrs. Norris and Jasper Tully)

The Judas Cat. New York, Scribner, 1949; London, Corgi,
1952.
The Clay Hand. New York, Scribner, 1950; London, Corgi,
1952.
A Gentle Murderer. New York, Scribner, 1951; London,
Corgi, 1953.
A Town of Masks. New York, Scribner, 1952.
Death of an Old Sinner (Norris and Tully). New York,
Scribner, 1957; London, Secker and Warburg, 1958.
A Gentleman Called (Norris and Tully). New York, Scribner,
and London, Secker and Warburg, 1958.
Old Sinners Never Die (Norris). New York, Scribner, 1959;
London, Secker and Warburg, 1960.
Black Sheep, White Lamb. New York, Scribner, 1963;
London, Boardman, 1964.
The Pale Betrayer. New York, Scribner, 1965; London,
Hodder and Stoughton, 1967.

Enemy and Brother. New York, Scribner, 1966; London, Hodder and Stoughton, 1967.
God Speed the Night, with Jerome Ross. New York, Scribner, 1968; London, Hodder and Stoughton, 1969.
Where the Dark Streets Go. New York, Scribner, 1969; London, Hodder and Stoughton, 1970.
Shock Wave. New York, Scribner, 1972; London, Hodder and Stoughton, 1974.
The Little Brothers. New York, Scribner, 1973; London, Barker, 1974.
A Death in the Life (Hayes). New York, Scribner, 1976; London, Gollancz, 1977.
Scarlet Night (Hayes). New York, Scribner, 1980; London, Gollancz, 1981.
Lullaby of Murder (Hayes). New York, Scribner, and London, Gollancz, 1984.
The Habit of Fear (Hayes). New York, Scribner, 1987; London, Chivers, 1989.

Short Stories

Tales for a Stormy Night: The Collected Crime Stories. Woodstock, Vermont, Countryman Press, 1984.

Uncollected Short Stories

"Justina," in *Ellery Queen's Mystery Magazine* (New York), November 1989.
"Christopher and Maggie," in *Mistletoe Mysteries* edited by Charlotte MacLeod. New York, Mysterious Press, 1989.

OTHER PUBLICATIONS

Novels

Men of No Property. New York, Scribner, 1956.
The Evening of the Good Samaritan. New York, Scribner, 1961.

Other

Editor, *A Choice of Murders.* New York, Scribner, 1958; London, Macdonald, 1960.
Editor, *Crime Without Murder.* New York, Scribner, 1970.

*

Dorothy Salisbury Davis comments:

I am a restless and sometimes troubled writer. Although I am content at this point in my life, and indeed proud, to be a crime writer, I have often wondered why I am in the field. I have not been able to develop a running character—except perhaps myself and I do not mean to be facetious—I think because my own interest flags after he or she has finished one good job; also because detection, per se, is not my strong point. My detectives always turn out to be straight men to a lot of character actors. I am fonder of my villains, if the truth be told; and I suppose that is it: the pursuit of truth which shines best in the dark excesses of human behavior. I am at my best in *A Gentle Murderer, The Pale Betrayer,* and *God Speed the Night* where the villains are known, and the police less spectacular. But I should dearly love to have been able to create an Inspector Maigret, my all-time favorite among the detectives of fiction. I think I could have lived happily with him through many more books than I have written. And yet, and yet. . .Julie Hayes has appeared in four

novels now, and two short stories. She has grown. I like to think I have too, and now I do have a running character.

*   *   *

That Dorothy Salisbury Davis is equally skilled at writing novels and short stories can be seen by the fact that her seven Edgar nominations include four for novels and three for short stories.

Though her second novel, *The Clay Hand,* drew critical attention for its sympathetic view of the poor in a Kentucky coal mining area, it was Davis's third novel, *A Gentle Murderer,* which established her as a major suspense writer. It remains a novel central to her work, the one which best explains the themes of religious crisis and an opposition to violence which recur in later books. The murderer of the title, truly a gentle man, confesses his crime to a priest, who must then track him down to prevent further violence. The insight into the characters of these two men raises the book far above the level of the usual suspense novel. Davis's dislike of violence, almost unique among modern mystery writers, led her to edit a 1970 anthology called *Crime Without Murder.* In its introduction she attempts to come to grips with the problem of violence in the mystery, and to explain why she and others continue to write of it.

Her fourth novel, *A Town of Masks,* deals with the impact of murder on a small midwestern town, and especially upon the life of a middle-aged spinster who attempts to solve it. *Death of an Old Sinner* is about a retired general whose blackmail activities lead to his murder. The author was so fond of her victim that she revived him two years later in *Old Sinners Never Die,* a "prequel" to the prior book.

Davis again chose a priest as her protagonist in *Where the Dark Streets Go,* a return to the American scene following two novels set in Europe. *Where the Dark Streets Go* is very much a New York story, and Father McMahon's slum parish has all the problems of violence and despair one would expect. But the priest's problems are not merely with his parish but also with himself, and with a girl he meets while investigating a murder case.

Shock Wave deals with murder at a midwestern university during the student unrest of the early 1970's. *The Little Brothers* tells of a murdered shopkeeper in New York's Little Italy, and a group of boys who may be involved in the crime. In each case Davis perfectly captured the atmosphere of the times, and the feelings of people trapped by events around them. In a sense these books were a form of preparation for *A Death in the Life,* the best of her recent novels and one which speaks directly to the problems of city life today. Its tale of young Julie Hayes, who opens a storefront fortune-telling service in the heart of New York's pornography-prostitution district, tells us much about the real lives of the people who exist there—and tells it with an understanding and compassion which are Davis's hallmark.

Among her short stories, "Born Killer," an excellent psychological study of a midwestern farm boy, is most typical. "Backward, Turn Backward," is one of her rare detective short stories, in which Sheriff Willets solves a small town murder involving two families. Again, psychology plays a large part in the outcome. "The Purple Is Everything" deals with a woman who rescues a valuable painting during a museum fire and finds herself becoming a criminal against her will.

Dealing as they do with both small town and big city life, with both male and female protagonists, the novels and stories of Dorothy Salisbury Davis may seem difficult to categorize. But they are all marked by an awareness of the stress of modern living on the individual, and by a deeply felt compassion for both victim and criminal alike which are rare in mystery fiction today.

—Edward D. Hoch

———

DAVIS, Frederick C(lyde). Also wrote as Murdo Coombs; Stephen Ransome; Curtis Steele. American. Born in St. Joseph, Missouri, 2 June 1902. Educated at Dartmouth College, Hanover, New Hampshire, 1924–25. Married. Professional writer from 1924. Wrote 20 to 30 novels as Curtis Steele for *Secret Operator No. 5* in the 1930's. Lived in later life in Pennsylvania. *Died in 1977.*

CRIME PUBLICATIONS

Novels (series: Schyler Cole and Luke Speare; Professor Cyrus Hatch; published as Stephen Ransome in UK)

Coffins for Three (Hatch). New York, Doubleday, 1938; as *One Murder Too Many,* London, Heinemann, 1938.
He Wouldn't Stay Dead (Hatch). New York, Doubleday, and London, Heinemann, 1939.
Poor, Poor Yorick (Hatch). New York, Doubleday, 1939; as *Murder Doesn't Always Out,* London, Heinemann, 1939.
The Graveyard Never Closes (Hatch). New York, Doubleday, 1940.
Deep Lay the Dead. New York, Doubleday, 1942.
Let the Skeletons Rattle (Hatch). New York, Doubleday, 1944.
Detour to Oblivion (Hatch). New York, Doubleday, 1947.
A Moment of Need (as Murdo Coombs). New York, Dutton, 1947.
Thursday's Blade (Hatch). New York, Doubleday, 1947.
Gone Tomorrow (Hatch). New York, Doubleday, 1948.
The Deadly Miss Ashley (Cole and Speare). New York, Doubleday, and London, Gollancz, 1950.
Lilies in Her Garden Grew (Cole and Speare). New York, Doubleday, and London, Gollancz, 1951.
Tread Lightly, Angel (Cole and Speare). New York, Doubleday, and London, Gollancz, 1952.
Drag the Dark (Cole and Speare). New York, Doubleday, 1953; London, Gollancz, 1954.
Another Morgue Heard From (Cole and Speare). New York, Doubleday, 1954; as *Deadly Bedfellows,* London, Gollancz, 1955.
Night Drop (Cole and Speare). New York, Doubleday, 1955; London, Gollancz, 1956.
High Heel Homicide. New York, Ace, 1961.

Novels as Stephen Ransome (series: Lieutenant Lee Barcello; Steve Ransome)

Death Checks In. New York, Doubleday, 1939; as *Whose Corpse?,* London, Davies, 1939.
A Shroud for Shylock. New York, Doubleday, 1939.
Hearses Don't Hurry. New York, Doubleday, 1941.
False Bounty. New York, Doubleday, 1948; London, Gollancz, 1949; as *I, The Executioner,* New York, Ace, 1953.
Hear No Evil (Ransome). New York, Doubleday, 1953; London, Gollancz, 1954.
The Shroud Off Her Back (Ransome). New York, Doubleday, and London, Gollancz, 1953.

The Frazer Acquittal. New York, Doubleday, and London, Gollancz, 1955.
The Men in Her Death. New York, Doubleday, 1956; London, Gollancz, 1957.
So Deadly My Love. New York, Doubleday, 1957; London, Gollancz, 1958.
I'll Die for You. New York, Doubleday, and London, Gollancz, 1959.
The Unspeakable. New York, Doubleday, and London, Gollancz, 1960.
Warning Bell. New York, Doubleday, and London, Gollancz, 1960.
Some Must Watch. New York, Doubleday, and London, Gollancz, 1961.
Without a Trace. New York, Doubleday, and London, Gollancz, 1962.
The Night, The Woman (Barcello). New York, Dodd Mead, and London, Gollancz, 1963.
Meet in Darkness. New York, Dodd Mead, and London, Gollancz, 1964.
One-Man Jury (Barcello). New York, Dodd Mead, 1964; London, Gollancz, 1965.
Alias His Wife (Barcello). New York, Dodd Mead, and London, Gollancz, 1965.
The Sin File (Barcello). New York, Dodd Mead, 1965; London, Gollancz, 1966.
The Hidden Hour (Barcello). New York, Dodd Mead, and London, Gollancz, 1966.
Trap No. 6 (Barcello). New York, Doubleday, 1971; London, Gollancz, 1972.

Novels as Curtis Steele (series: James Christopher, Operator No. 5 in all books)

The Invisible Empire. New York, Corinth, 1966.
The Army of the Dead. New York, Corinth, 1966.
Blood Reign of the Dictator. New York, Corinth, 1966.
Hosts of the Flaming Death. New York, Corinth, 1966.
Invasion of the Yellow Warlords. New York, Corinth, 1966.
Legions of the Death Master. New York, Corinth, 1966.
March of the Flame Marauders. New York, Corinth, 1966.
Master of Broken Men. New York, Corinth, 1966.
The Masked Invasion. N.p., Freeway, 1974.
The Yellow Scourge. N.p., Freeway, 1974.

Uncollected Short Stories

"Blood on the Block," in *Dime Detective* (New York), 15 December 1933.
"Skeleton Without Arms," in *Dime Detective* (New York), 1 February 1934.
"Death Lights the Candle," in *Dime Detective* (New York), 15 June 1934.
"Death on Delivery," in *Dime Detective* (New York), 1 September 1934.
"The Green Ghoul," in *Dime Detective* (New York), 15 June 1935.
"Doorway to Doom," in *Dime Detective* (New York), 1 July 1935.
"Dynamite Friendship," in *Detective Tales* (Chicago), August 1935.
"Death's Flaming Hour," in *Detective Tales* (Chicago), September 1935.
"Guardian Against the Law," in *Detective Tales* (Chicago), December 1935.
"The Smiling Killer," in *Dime Mystery* (Chicago), January 1936.

"The Case of the Smiling Giantess," in *Dime Detective* (New York), March 1936.

"Crime Crusader," in *Detective Tales* (Chicago), May 1936.

"Suicide Sweepstakes," in *Ace G-Man* (New York), May–June 1936.

"Four Alarm Murder," in *Ace Detective* (New York), August 1936.

"Princess of Death's Desire," in *Ace Mystery* (New York), September 1936.

"Poison Plunder," in *Ace Detective* (New York), October 1936.

"The Case of the Terrified Twins," in *Dime Detective* (New York), March 1937.

"The Trail of the Thirteenth Brain," in *Detective Tales* (Chicago), April 1937.

"Murder Made Easy," in *Dime Detective* (New York), May 1937.

"Mistress of Satan's Hounds," in *Terror Tales* (Chicago), May–June 1938.

"Seven Knocks at My Door," in *Black Mask* (New York), August 1938.

"Nameless Brides of Forbidden City," in *Uncanny Tales* (Chicago), April–May 1939.

"The Premature Obituary," in *Ten Detective Aces* (Springfield, Massachusetts), October 1941.

"The Case of the Gambling Corpse," in *New Detective* (New York), January 1942.

"I'm the Corpse," in *Detective Tales* (Chicago), January 1942.

"No Appeal for the Dead," in *Detective Tales* (Chicago), October 1942.

"Pick Your Casket," in *Detective Tales* (Chicago), December 1942.

"More Deadly than the Male," in *Dime Detective* (New York), December 1942.

"Home Sweet Homicide," in *Dime Detective* (New York), May 1943.

"Blood on My Doorstep," in *Detective Tales* (Chicago), July 1943.

"Hostage," in *New Detective* (New York), September 1943.

"Clinic for Corpses," in *Dime Detective* (New York), October 1943.

"I'll See You at the Morgue," in *Detective Tales* (Chicago), April 1944.

"Boomerang Scoop," in *Dime Detective* (New York), June 1944.

"Little Green Door of Doom," in *Dime Mystery* (New York), July 1944.

"Death Wears Red Heels," in *Dime Detective* (New York), December 1944.

"The Killer Waits," in *New Detective* (New York), May 1945.

"The Corpse Takes a Wife," in *Dime Detective* (New York), June 1945.

"Assignment—Death!" in *New Detective* (New York), January 1946.

"Some Like 'em Dead," in *Dime Detective* (New York), March 1946.

"Murder in Two-Time," in *Dime Detective* (New York), July 1947.

"Nine Toes Up," in *Dime Detective* (New York), March 1948.

"Death Is a Dame," in *Shock* (New York), March 1948.

"Dicks Die Hard," in *Dime Detective* (New York), May 1948.

"I'll Marry a Killer," in *Shock* (New York), July 1948.

"Kill-and-Run Blonde," in *Dime Detective* (New York), January 1949.

"Hide Behind Homicide," in *F.B.I. Detective,* February 1949.

"Flaming Angel," in *Black Mask* (New York), March 1949.

"Up in Murder's Room," in *Dime Detective* (New York), June 1949.

"Sinner Take All," in *Dime Detective* (New York), September 1949.

"Swing Low, Sweet Casket," in *Black Mask* (New York), March 1950.

"So Dead the Rogue," in *15 Story Detective* (Kokomo, Indiana), August 1950.

"Kill Me, Kate," in *Dime Detective* (New York), August 1950.

"Guns Across the Table," in *Dime Detective* (New York), June 1951.

"Lenore," in *Manhunt* (New York), May 1956.

"Goddess of Evil Revelry," in *Weird Menace No. 1.* Chicago, Pulp Press, 1977.

OTHER PUBLICATIONS

Other

Making Your Camera Pay. New York, McBride, 1922.

"Why Did She Shoot Him?," in *Writer's Digest* (Cincinnati), March 1942.

"Synopses Without Sorrow," in *Writer's Digest* (Cincinnati), October 1942.

"Mysteries Plus," in *Writing Detective and Mystery Fiction,* edited by A.S. Burack. Boston, The Writer, 1945.

"How to Organize a Book," in *The Mystery Writer's Handbook,* edited by Herbert Brean. New York, Harper, 1956.

*

Critical Study: *America's Secret Service Ace: The Operator 5 Story* by Nick Carr, Mercer Island, Washington, Starmont, 1985.

*   *   *

There were many writers in the heyday of the pulp magazines whose total published wordage reached staggering proportions, writers like Max Brand, Arthur J. Burks, H. Bedford Jones, Walter B. Gibson, Norman Daniels, and Frederick C. Davis. For more than 25 years Davis's byline appeared on at least 1000 pulp stories. Early 1930's issues of *Dime Detective* featured his long-running "casebook" series about Doctor Carter Cole; later issues introduced additional series characters, among them newspaper columnist Bill Brent. Other top-line pulps such as *Black Mask, Detective Tales,* and *Dime Mystery* were also regular showcases for his work.

Under the house name Curtis Steele he was also the author of dozens of Operator No. 5 novels for the *Shadow*-rival "hero pulp" of the same title. While a large percentage of pulp stories seem dated and somewhat juvenile by today's fictional standards, Davis's fiction was among the most literate and entertaining of its day and stands up well to the test of time. The Carter Cole "cases" in *Dime Detective* are of a particularly high quality.

In 1938 Davis began writing novels for Doubleday and he published a total of 16 under his own name. Many of these feature the deductive abilities of Professor Cyrus Hatch and of the semi-hard-boiled detective team of Schyler Cole and Luke Speare. A memorable non-series book is *Deep Lay the Dead,* which is fashioned around the classic mystery situation of murder and intrigue among a group of people trapped in a snowbound country house.

Davis wrote one novel as Murdo Coombs, but it was his mysteries as by Stephen Ransome which were perhaps the most successful of all his longer works, as evidenced by the fact that he continued to write novels with the Ransome byline for ten years after retiring his own name. *The Unspeakable* involves a brutal and heinous crime in a small Pennsylvania town, and is notable for its sensitive handling and excellent characterization.

—Bill Pronzini

DAVIS, Gordon. *See* **HUNT, E. Howard.**

DAVIS, Kenn. American. Born in Salinas, California, 20 February 1932. Educated at San Francisco City College; San Francisco Art Institute. Served in the United States Army, 1952–54. Married Elizabeth Calkins Davis in 1985; one daughter and two stepsons. Artist, San Francisco *Chronicle*, 1959–85; video producer, Transamerica Insurance, Los Angeles, 1987–89. Artist: individual shows—Studio 44, San Francisco, 1956; Sherman Gallery, Chicago, 1959; Gump's Gallery, San Francisco, 1960; Jean Dichter Gallery, Denver, 1966; Zantman Gallery, Carmel, California, 1967; Weeden Gallery, Boston, 1969; Orlando Gallery, Los Angeles, 1970; Braverman Gallery, New York City, 1972; Standiford Gallery, San Francisco, 1975; Torsiello Gallery, Oakland, California, 1987. Agent: Ellen Levine, 432 Park Avenue South, New York, New York 10016. Address: P.O. Box 1736, Colfax, California 95713, U.S.A.

CRIME PUBLICATIONS

Novels (series: Carver Bascombe in all books except *Bogart '48* and *Dead to Rights*)

The Dark Side (Bascombe). New York, Avon, 1976.
The Forza Trap (Bascombe). New York, Avon, 1979.
Bogart '48, with John Stanley. New York, Dell, 1979.
Dead to Rights. New York, Avon, 1981.
Words Can Kill (Bascombe). New York, Fawcett, 1984.
Melting Point (Bascombe). New York, Fawcett, 1984.
Nijinsky Is Dead (Bascombe). New York, Fawcett, 1987.
As October Dies (Bascombe). New York, Fawcett, 1987.
Acts of Homicide (Bascombe). New York, Fawcett, 1989.
Blood of Poets (Bascombe). New York, Fawcett, 1990.

Uncollected Short Story

"Dead Ringer," in *Alfred Hitchcock's Mystery Magazine* (New York), July 1980.

OTHER PUBLICATIONS

Plays

Screenplay: *Nightmare in Blood* with John Stanley, 1975.

*

Kenn Davis comments:

In the series of novels featuring the black private investigator, Carver Bascombe, I want to illustrate that the art world, and the creative people in all of these worlds, can be the levelers of intolerance. Therefore I created plots and characters that weave in and out and around the complex world of the arts (which is what I know best).

I had the idea of also showing that racial cultures in America can (and do) live side by side without the question of racial hatred being the main issue. I believe that a theme of color blind stories (although bigotry does arise) can blend these factors into entertaining novels of crime, art, and suspense.

* * *

It is natural for Kenn Davis, who was brought up in the multiracial environment of central California, to create a series character who is a member of an ethnic minority. That his San Franciscan private eye is not a typical Californian is not. Carver Bascombe, black, suave, and streetwise, is out of the blue collar stratum of Detroit. He is self-motivated and strives to become more educated than his background would normally allow. In the early books, he is working for a law degree with the intent to become an advocate of the people; not in the sense of carrying a banner against "oppression of the masses" but on a more personal basis. Until such times as he can open a legal office, albeit a storefront operation, he practices as a private detective.

Early in his life in his adopted city, San Francisco, he was befriended by an art dealer who became his cultural mentor. From him, Carver learns about paintings and from there moves into artistic fields. Along the way he develops a taste for classical music.

Davis started his fiction writing career as a comic strip artist while still a teenager. A parallel interest in photography and journalism led him to what was to become Carter Bascombe's turf and a position on the San Francisco *Chronicle*. While working for the paper Davis met and collaborated with John Stanley on a series of short film scripts. These led to the joint effort that resulted in the publication of *Bogart '48* in 1979.

The third Bascombe novel, *Words Can Kill*, marked a turning point in Davis's writing methodology. The first two books wrote themselves, more or less, as the action followed the natural course from one scene to another without a great deal of plot justification. That is not to say that they were necessarily simplistic or loose, but just good action private-eye stories. The first, *The Dark Side*, earned a nomination for the Mystery Writers of America Edgar Allan Poe award for the best paperback mystery of 1976. The second found Bascombe involved with a delectable but devious diva with the San Francisco Opera.

With his third novel, Davis found himself embroiled in plot subtlties and changes in the characters' motives as the story progressed. Rewrite followed rewrite as subplots came and went and major protagonists kept redefining their roles. In his own words, Davis says, "I began to get a glimmer of what writing was all about. (I'm learning of course.) By constantly changing characters (especially the villain), the plot, adding and subtracting sub-plots, and altering the clues and the pacing, I fully realized the difficulty of writing. Also I had acquired the initial ability to analyze to some degree what I was doing (and possibly what other writers did or were doing). And I realized I was a re-writer. Also, I aquired the internal desire to succeed as a creative writer. So *Words Can Kill* became a bell-weather, a frame or reference for future endeavors. It's also one hell of a story!"

The persistence paid off. After rejection by three publishers including Davis's original publisher Avon, *Words Can Kill* saw print and was nominated for an Edgar Allan Poe award in 1984.

The other non-series book, *Dead to Rights*, is a Kafka/Sartre-like piece more in keeping with Davis's graphic style. His own comment is terse, accurate and very much in the mood of the story itself, "The crooks are crooked, the cops are crooked, the politicians are crooked, and almost everyone dies at the end." As a "Nore" genre piece, it will stand well with those of Jim Thompson and W.R. Burnett.

No list of ethnic characters that could include Charlie Chan, Masao Masuto, Joe Leaphorn, Mr. Moto, Jim Chee, Virgil Tibbs, and Penny Wanawake would be complete without Carver Bascombe.

—Richard G. La Porte

————

DAVIS, Robert Hart. *See* **POWELL, Talmage; PRONZINI, Bill.**

————

DAY, LEWIS, C. *See* **BLAKE, Nicholas.**

————

DEAN, Spencer. *See* **STERLING, Stewart.**

————

DEAN, S.F.X. Pseudonym for Francis Smith. Address: c/o Atheneum Publishers, 866 Third Avenue, New York, New York 10022, U.S.A.

CRIME PUBLICATIONS

Novels (series: Professor Neil Kelley in all books)

By Frequent Anguish. New York, Walker, and London, Collins, 1982.
Such Pretty Toys. New York, Walker, 1982; London, Collins, 1983.
It Can't Be My Grave. London, Collins, 1983; New York, Walker, 1984.
Ceremony of Innocence. New York, Walker, 1984; London, Gollancz, 1985.
Death and the Mad Heroine. New York, Walker, 1985; London, Gollancz, 1986.
Nantucket Soap Opera. New York, Atheneum, 1987.

*

S. F. X. Dean's widely praised first novel *By Frequent Anguish* introduced Neil Kelly, professor of English at Old Hampton College, to detective fiction. Distinguished by individualized and credible characters, a well developed university setting, and a fairly clued plot, *By Frequent Anguish* features a middle-aged intellectual thrust into detection by the murder of his fiancée. Kelly's catholicism, his strict moral principles, and awareness of his emotional needs set him apart

from most contemporary detectives. Unfortunately, the promise of the first novel has not been borne out in most subsequent volumes in the series. *Death and the Mad Heroine,* also set at Old Hampton, is superior and *It Can't Be My Grave,* which investigates the authorship of *Arden of Feversham* interesting, but other novels rely too heavily on thriller techniques and do not display Kelly at his best. A shift from first to third person narration, successful in *Death and the Mad Heroine,* which emphasizes Welsh professor Dewi Morgan-Evans and his wife, fails in *Nantucket Soap Opera,* where the contrast between Kelly's moral authority and the immoral activities of a film crew is both gratuitous and irritating.

Dean (Francis Smith, Professor of Humanities at Hampshire College in Amherst, Massachusetts) is thoroughly at home with Kelly's academic background and uses his knowlege to good effect in relating Kelly's scholarly activities and professional obligations, although a number of stereotypical academic fantasies appear in the novels. In *By Frequent Anguish* Kelly's advisee and goddaughter, a beautiful 20-year-old woman, falls madly in love with him, and later readers learn that Kelly's biography of John Donne has become a bestseller and been made into a successful television mini-series. However unlikely these events, they are acceptable within Dean's ·fictional context. His academic satire is often both amusing and acute: job-hunting Dewi Morgan-Evans, faced with affirmative action policies, wonders if a "Welshperson" could qualify as "third world," and Dean's portraits of an academic lecher and the English department's "creative writer" are acidic. Outside academe, however, the satire is less satisfying. Attempting to satirize espionage in *Ceremony of Innocence,* he depicts a Chinese spy and boyhood friend (Kelly was brought up in China) as committing murder to gain possession of the meteorological data of Kelly's father, whom he calls a "crank" who could not even predict the weather for the next day. While the seriousness of the crimes committed and the absurdity of the data sought are no doubt meant to emphasize the ludicrous nature of international espionage, the inconsistent tone of the novel defeats Dean's purpose. The inability to fuse successfully satirical exaggeration with moral seriousness (as the best satirists do) is most noticeable in *Nantucket Soap Opera,* where a degenerate film crew whose lives approximate those of soap opera characters, pursue Kelly relentlessly to hire him to work on their film. Two subplots, also intended as satirical commentary on soaps, are not well integrated with the main narrative and the central mystery, the identity of a child molester, is known from the beginning.

Dean calls his novels "interfictions," punning on both the Latin *interficio,* to kill, and the obvious English relationship between types of fiction. *By Frequent Anguish,* subtitled *A Love Story Interrupted by a Murder,* combines the two forms expertly, and *It Can't Be My Grave* meshes literary scholarship, problems in contemporary publishing, and Kelly's developing love for his English editor, Dolly Allen, in believable fashion, but the mingling of Kelly's personal life with satire produces a nonsensical farrago in *Ceremony of Innocence* and *Nantucket Soap Opera* and to a lesser extent in *Such Pretty Toys.*

In the three traditional detective stories Dean writes credibly and well; he understands academic politics and offers accurate portraits of academics. The plot of *Death and the Mad Heroine* is especially well worked out and neatly dovetails investigation of crime in the past with current agitation against pollution, bringing the two together in a highly ingenious manner. Neil Kelly is an intelligently realized and usually sympathetic amateur detective, and although Dean's excursions into the thriller mode are regrettable, his other novels are readable and recommended.

—Jeanne F. Bedell

DeANDREA, William L(ouis). Also writes as Philip DeGrave; Lee Davis Willoughby. American. Born in Port Chester, New York, 1 July 1952. Educated at Syracuse University, New York, B.S. 1974. Married the writer, Orania Papazoglou in 1984; one son. Reporter, Westchester-Rockland Newspapers, New York, 1969–70; factory worker, Electrolux Corporation, Old Greenwich, Connecticut, 1975–76; then freelance writer. Recipient: Mystery Writers of America Edgar Allan Poe award, 1978, 1979. Agent: Meg Ruley, Jane Rotrosen Literary Agency, 318 East 51st Street, New York, New York 10022, U.S.A.

CRIME PUBLICATIONS

Novels (series: Matt Cobb; "Clifford Driscoll")

Killed in the Ratings (Cobb). New York, Harcourt Brace, 1978.
The HOG Murders. New York, Avon, 1979.
The Lunatic Fringe. New York, Evans, 1980.
Killed in the Act (Cobb). New York, Doubleday, 1981.
Five O'Clock Lightning. New York, St. Martin's Press, 1982.
Killed with a Passion (Cobb). New York, Doubleday, 1983.
Killed on the Ice (Cobb). New York, Doubleday, 1984.
Cronus ("Driscoll"). New York, Mysterious Press, 1984.
Unholy Moses (as Philip DeGrave). New York, Doubleday, 1985.
Snark ("Driscoll"). New York, Mysterious Press, 1985.
Keep the Baby, Faith (as Philip DeGrave). New York, Doubleday, 1986.
Azrael ("Driscoll"). New York, Mysterious Press, 1987.
Killed in Paradise (Cobb). New York, Mysterious Press, 1988.
Atropos ("Driscoll"). New York, Mysterious Press, 1990.
Killed on the Rocks (Cobb). New York, Mysterious Press, 1990.

Uncollected Short Stories

"Snowy Reception," in *Alfred Hitchcock's Mystery Magazine* (New York), June 1979.
"Hero's Welcome," in *Mercury News* (San Jose, California), November 1985.
"Killed Top to Bottom," in *Syracuse University Magazine* (New York), Fall 1989.

OTHER PUBLICATIONS

Novel

The Voyageurs (as Lee Davis Willoughby). New York, Dell, 1983.

*

Manuscript Collection: Mugar Memorial Library, Boston University.

William L. DeAndrea comments:
My mother used to say that once you got a reputation, there was no getting rid of it, and boy was she right. I have become identified as a comical or satirical writer. I once submitted a manuscript that contained two gruesome murders in the first paragraph. The rejection letter (a very kind one) began, "Of course, *everything* Bill writes is hilarious. . ."

Not that I'm sure I *want* to get rid of this particular reputation. If only I *could* make everything I write hilarious, I'd be rich enough to be a publisher. And satire, I think, is probably a lot harder to do well than what it is I think I *am* doing—telling entertaining stories about people who feel obligated to clean up after the mess a criminal makes.

To get into detective stories, you have to buy a set of assumptions, all of which are arguable: that Objective Truth exists; that it's desirable to find out what it is; that it's *possible* to find out what it is; that people have an obligation to respect the lives and property of others; that they should be forced to live up to that obligation. I'm not especially interested in criminals—robbing and killing are far less sophisticated impulses than confronting their results and, as far as possible, setting things right.

Humor is a defense, a way of making it tolerable. I told an interviewer that I write "situation tragedy—terrible things happen in funny ways." And that, according to my experience of it, is Life. I am probably the only American alive who ever accidently whacked off his own finger in an attempt to get better reception on a television broadcast of a soccer game between Mexico and Iran.

Detective stories are also about problem-solving, about illusion and reality, and telling one from the other. My series character, Matt Cobb, works for a television network, a world where illusion *is* the reality. His job is expressly to keep the real world from spoiling everybody's fun. If he couldn't laugh at that, it would kill him.

What I confront all my protagonists with—Matt Cobb, "Clifford Driscoll" the real-nameless spy in *Cronus,* who works in a world where everything is deadly and negotiable, even Theodore Roosevelt, when I induced him to star in *The Lunatic Fringe,* and the rest—is what my American history professor used to call the Puritan Dilemma: What is the Good Man or Woman to do in an Evil World? The answer is, he keeps his sense of humor and does his best. Sometimes, he even wins.

* * *

Matt Cobb, the narrator-hero of five of William L. DeAndrea's novels to date, is a sort of company detective for a television network, a position that allows him to become involved in numerous mysteries. In his debut, *Killed in the Ratings,* it's a plot that could hardly be more un-American: to rig the sacred statistics that tell the networks what the public wants to watch. Cobb is smart-aleck on the surface but a true believer deep down, a guy who really *likes* commercial TV, as does his creator. The relatively fresh background is humorously but sympathetically observed, and there is some genuinely witty writing, including much fun with similes and metaphors. ("My secretary keeps a diary on her face.") The time-honored gathering-of-the-suspects at the end of the book reveals DeAndrea's affinity with the Golden Age masters of puzzle-making, and there are some excellent clues and plot gimmicks. The choice of quotes from old TV shows as epigraphs to the chapters is a nice touch that is carried on in subsequent Cobb novels.

Killed in the Act, centering on the Network's fiftieth anniversary show, also offers much technical ingenuity, especially in the matter of the fire and bowling ball. It has, however, the obligatory action scenes of a TV movie, including a car-chase menace and an effective bit of slapstick in the catching-the-killer sequence. It is the rare mystery that has one twist too many: one of the stock Least Suspected Person gimmicks is trotted out once more, and the ending is a touch corny. Cobb wears his heart even more on his sleeve in *Killed with a Passion,* wherein he gets involved with cable-TV skulduggery while attending the wedding of an old friend. The narration is smoother and funnier than ever, and DeAndrea's reliable sense of fair play makes him showcase his clues so audaciously some readers may actually solve the case on the evidence provided. *Killed in Paradise* is one of the best in the recent spate of mystery-game-interrupted-by-real-murder novels, exploiting the comic possibilities of sorting out the real mystery from the manufactured one.

DeAndrea's other series involves an American espionage writer whose real name is never revealed. He is known as Clifford Driscoll in *Cronus,* then as Jeffrey Bellman in *Snark,* most recently as Allan Trotter in *Azrael* and *Atropos.* The latter is an intricately plotted Cold War thriller extrapolating an elaborate conspiracy from thinly disguised players and events in recent history. Though far different from the classical plots of the Cobb novels, the spy books reveal the same skeptical but uncynical world view as well as the same talent for manipulating story elements in surprising ways.

The author's non-series books are also worth seeking out, though generally less rewarding than the Cobb novels. *The HOG Murders* offers one of the most original and deceptive serial-murder plots I've ever come across, though Prof. Niccolo Benedetti, for all his large entourage, doesn't quite make it as a new Great Detective candidate. *The Lunatic Fringe,* set in 1896 New York, has as its detective Police Commissioner Theodore Roosevelt. Though the customary humor is here in abundance, the author relies too much on pure physical action and perpetuates some of the persistent clichés of historical fiction, including reverse-prescience (an Irish cop avers moving pictures are too unsettling to last, and a rich car-owner thinks Ford's mass production the fancy of a dreamer) and trumped-up origins for famous catchphrases (that same Irish cop inspires TR's "Speak softly and carry a big stick"). *Five O'Clock Lightning* is a baseball story set in 1953, wherein former minor-leaguer Russ Garrett acts as detective, solving the murder of red-baiting Congressman Rex Harwood Simmons. Slugger Mickey Mantle makes a guest appearance. The two historicals are more action and suspense thrillers than pure detective stories, but in each DeAndrea displays his reader-bamboozling proclivities. In *Lunatic Fringe* especially, he manages to produce both a surprising murderer *and* an exhaustive catalogue of clues to the killer's identity.

Unholy Moses, the first of DeAndrea's two novels under the punning pseudonym Philip DeGarve, introduces Glenn and Terry Webb, comic strip artist and cop respectively, a pleasant variation on the husband-and-wife detecting team. The tale combines art-world satire with typically ingenious classical detection, and the style is distinctive enough not to fool careful readers about the author's true identity. The Webbs do not reappear in the second DeGarve novel, *Keep the Baby, Faith,* and it is not known if they are destined to remain one-shot elements.

DeAndrea shares some attributes in common with the British writer Robert Barnard, who began writing at about the same time. Both combine humor with old-style puzzle-making. While DeAndrea's humor is considerably gentler and less stinging than Barnard's, his dedication to artful clueing may be even greater. He is one of the best of the new writers to set up

shop on detective fiction's Main Street, long occupied by the departed Queen, Christie, and Carr.

—Jon L. Breen

———

DEANE, Norman. *See* **CREASEY, John.**

———

de BEKKER, Jay. *See* **STERLING, Stewart.**

———

DEBRETT, Hal. *See* **HALLIDAY, Brett.**

———

DECOLTA, Ramon. *See* **WHITFIELD, Raoul.**

———

DeGRAVE, Philip. *See* **DeANDREA, William L.**

———

DEIGHTON, Len (Leonard Cyril Deighton). British. Born in London, 18 February 1929. Educated at Marylebone Grammar School, St. Martin's School of Art, and Royal College of Art, all London. Served in the Royal Air Force. Married Shirley Thompson in 1960. Has worked as a railway lengthman, pastry cook, dress factory manager, waiter, illustrator, teacher, and photographer; art director of advertising agencies in London and New York; steward, British Overseas Airways Corporation, 1956–57; wrote a weekly comic strip on cooking for *The Observer,* London, in the 1960's; founder of Continuum One literary agency, London. Agent: Jonathan Clowes Ltd., 22 Prince Albert Road, London NW1 7ST, England.

CRIME PUBLICATIONS

Novels

The Ipcress File. London, Hodder and Stoughton, 1962; New York, Simon and Schuster, 1963.
Horse under Water. London, Cape, 1963; New York, Putnam, 1968.
Funeral in Berlin. London, Cape, 1964; New York, Putnam, 1965.
Billion-Dollar Brain. London, Cape, and New York, Putnam, 1966.

An Expensive Place to Die. London, Cape, and New York, Putnam, 1967.

Spy Story. London, Cape, and New York, Harcourt Brace, 1974.

Yesterday's Spy. London, Cape, and New York, Harcourt Brace, 1975.

Twinkle, Twinkle, Little Spy. London, Cape, 1976; as *Catch a Falling Spy,* New York, Harcourt Brace, 1976.

SS-GB: Nazi-Occupied Britain 1941. London, Cape, 1978; New York, Knopf, 1979.

XPD. London, Hutchinson, and New York, Knopf, 1981.

Goodbye Mickey Mouse. London, Hutchinson, and New York, Knopf, 1982.

Game, Set and Match. London, Hutchinson, 1985; New York, Knopf, 1989.

   Berlin Game. London, Hutchinson, 1983; New York, Knopf, 1984.

   Mexico Set. London, Hutchinson, 1984; New York, Knopf, 1985.

   London Match. London, Hutchinson, 1985; New York, Knopf, 1986.

Winter: A Berlin Family 1899–1945. London, Century Hutchinson, and New York, Knopf, 1987.

Spy Hook. London, Century Hutchinson, and New York, Knopf, 1988.

Spy Line. London, Century Hutchinson, and New York, Knopf, 1989.

Spy Sinker. New York, Harper, 1990.

OTHER PUBLICATIONS

Novels

Only When I Larf. London, Joseph, 1968.; as *Only When I Laugh,* New York, Mysterious Press, 1987.

Bomber. London, Cape, and New York, Harper, 1970.

Close-Up. London, Cape, and New York, Atheneum, 1972.

Short Stories

Declarations of War. London, Cape, 1971; as *Eleven Declarations of War,* New York, Harcourt Brace, 1975.

Plays

Screenplay: *Oh! What a Lovely War,* 1969.

Television Plays: *Long Past Glory,* 1963; *It Must Have Been Two Other Fellows,* 1977.

Other

Action Cook Book: Len Deighton's Guide to Eating. London, Cape, 1965; as *Cookstrip Cook Book,* New York, Geis, 1966.

Où Est Le Garlic; or, Len Deighton's French Cook Book. London, Penguin, 1965; New York, Harper, 1977; revised edition, as *Basic French Cooking,* London, Cape, 1979; Berkeley, California, Creative Arts, 1987.

Len Deighton's Continental Dossier: A Collection of Cultural, Culinary, Historical, Spooky, Grim and Preposterous Fact, compiled by Victor and Margaret Pettitt. London, Joseph, 1968.

Fighter: The True Story of the Battle of Britain. London, Cape, 1977; New York, Knopf, 1978.

Airshipwreck, with Arnold Schwartzman. London, Cape, 1978; New York, Holt Rinehart, 1979.

Blitzkrieg: From the Rise of Hitler to the Fall of Dunkirk. London, Cape, 1979; New York, Knopf, 1980.

Battle of Britain. London, Cape, and New York, Coward McCann, 1980.

ABC of French Food. London, Century Hutchinson, 1989; New York, Bantam, 1990.

Editor, *London Dossier.* London, Cape, 1967.

Editor, with Michael Rund and Howard Loxton, *The Assassination of President Kennedy.* London, Cape, 1967.

Editor, *Tactical Genius in Battle,* by Simon Goodenough. Oxford, Phaidon Press, and New York, Dutton, 1979.

*

Bibliography: *Len Deighton: An Annotated Bibliography 1954–85* by Edward Milward-Oliver. Maidstone, Kent, Sammler, 1985.

Critical Studies: *Secret Agents in Fiction: Ian Fleming, John le Carré, and Len Deighton* by L.O. Saverberg, London, Macmillan, 1984; *The Len Deighton Companion* by Edward Milward-Oliver. London, Grafton, 1987.

*   *   *

In a succession of stylish, witty, well-crafted novels beginning with *The Ipcress File* in 1962, Len Deighton has established himself as a master of modern spy fiction and one of the most innovative writers in the short but eventful history of the form. He brings to the novel of espionage some highly relevant interests and concerns, most of which had never troubled the minds of previous practitioners; along with his brilliant contemporary, John le Carré, he sketches a convincingly detailed picture of the world of espionage while carefully examining the ethics and morality of that world. The darker aspects of his novels, however seriously intended, are frequently illuminated by understated irony and humor. His prose is bright and breezy, clearly influenced by Raymond Chandler, with a somewhat Chandleresque taste for metaphors and wisecracks. In some ways, in fact, he seems rather a mid-Atlantic writer—he is just about the only English writer who can create credible Americans who speak credible American. Another of his strengths lies in his ability to provide his best works with powerfully elliptical structures; his architecture never seems fully clear until his books end, revealing themselves as solid and intricate creations. Together with their structures, the plots of his novels usually entangle his protagonist in knots of double- and triple-crosses tricky enough to satisfy even the most finicky connoisseur of spy fiction. He has contributed substantially to the genre and, in the process, to the education of a large reading public in the realities of espionage, especially as practiced by a depressingly perfidious Albion.

An air of authenticity permeates his books, making them doubly influential in the canon of espionage. Whether he is describing a sunset in Lebanon, cocktails in a Berlin nightclub, dinner at a Helsinki restaurant, an automobile chase through the Sahara, or a submarine journey under the polar ice cap, Deighton convincingly captures the atmosphere of a real place—he has been there and he takes his reader with him. The authenticity extends to the actual business of espionage; his novels display a thorough and intimate knowledge of spies and spying, demonstrated in their action and in their detailed attention to the particulars of a specialized profession—documents, memos, technical data, learned appendices. The attention to the minutiae of all aspects of spying not only lends considerable realism to his books but also suggests some further truths of espionage. Spies, we see, are real people, a special kind of bureaucrat or civil servant; their activities represent a kind of institutionalized deceit, the normal practice of modern government in the modern world. The intricate puzzles of his novels, full of deceptions and betrayals, are made entirely believable by Deighton's careful and fascinating documentation, and at the same time made aptly symbolic of our time by their apparent universality. Espionage, a battle in the shadows, appropriately symbolizes the crepuscular morality of today's vague alliances and complicated struggles.

In the early novels Deighton's protagonist, significantly, is a man without a name, or rather, a man of many names; although he is the same person throughout the books, he uses a variety of pseudonyms and aliases, as if identity itself were a shifting, unknowable, or simply meaningless concept in the world of espionage. In the two recent trilogies—*Berlin Game, Mexico Set, London Match* and *Spy Hook, Spy Line,* and *Spy Sinker*—he is Bernard Samson, an older and wearier version of the anonymous narrator of the early books, who nevertheless speaks with the same cynicism and encounters the same reasons for that cynicism. In the best traditions of the British espionage novel, the enemies are not only Russians and frequently Germans, but more disturbing, the English themselves, often a traitor within the protagonist's department, sometimes a respected and privileged citizen, and in the trilogies, even his own wife. Deighton's agent is frequently endangered by the incompetence or the malevolence of impassioned ideologues. He often recognizes the state of his nation and service, debilitated by the futility of rank and class, the Old Boy network, the collection of ninnies, dolts, and eccentrics who appear to control his life: "what chance did I stand between the Communists on one side and the Establishment on the other?" (*The Ipcress File*). When he comes to understand the depth of his wife's betrayal, Bernard Samson comes to an even more difficult conclusion about the nature of his position—"treason and infidelity have too much in common" (*London Match*), which nicely suggests the changes in Deighton's work and the world around us. The Angry Young Man of espionage fiction, reacting with humor and outrage to the state of his society, has not abandoned the class struggle, with its wit and tension, but discovers a greater possibility for betrayal in the ordinary and everyday: love, marriage, and children may enrich his life, but they also make him more vulnerable.

Thematically and architecturally, the labyrinthine plots and unusual structures of the spy novels support their ambiguity and intricacy, showing the literary sophistication that has led the author to attempt some ambitious "straight" fiction. *The Ipcress File* shows the hero constantly a jump behind several elaborate schemes while counterpointing his adventures with his daily horoscope; *Horse Under Water* underlines its confusing puzzles with chapter headings that together make up one of those punning crosswords that only the British can solve. Deighton's finest novel, *Funeral in Berlin,* explores the Cold War, neo-Nazism, and complicated treachery, unifying all themes with some repeated phrases, musical references, and epigraphs from a chess book; the agent is a pawn moving among the conflicting spaces of a vast board, his fate determined by the turns and counterturns of competing organizations, the schemes of traitors, the guilt and greed of his antagonists. Under whatever name, Deighton's protagonist succeeds in all the novels through dedication to professionalism and to his own personal integrity.

Deighton's wry and ironic recognition of the realities of espionage and his mature understanding of the personal cost of the profession place him in the first rank of spy novelists. The crackling energy and documentary authenticity of his best books makes them entertaining as well as thoughtful contributions to their form. Together with his straight novels, his thrillers deserve careful reading and rereading; his work rewards study and inspires affection. He is a writer to be cherished and enjoyed, one of the most dependably interesting novelists in England today.

—George Grella

———

DEKKER, Carl. *See* **COLLINS, Michael.**

———

de la TORRE, Lillian. Pseudonym for Lillian McCue, née de la Torre Bueno.   American.   Born in New York City, 15 March 1902. Educated at College of New Rochelle, New York, A.B. 1921; Columbia University, New York, M.A. 1927; University of Munich, 1928; Harvard University, Cambridge, Massachusetts, M.A. 1933; University of Colorado, Boulder, 1934–35. Married George S. McCue in 1932. High school teacher, New York City, 1923–34; Instructor, Colorado College, Colorado Springs, 1937, and University of Colorado (Extension), 1937–41. Technical advisor, Twentieth Century-Fox, 1945. Since 1942, self-employed writer. Agent: Harold Ober Associates, 40 East 49th Street, New York, New York 10017. Address: 2719 North Union Boulevard, #819, Colorado Springs, Colorado 80909, U.S.A.

CRIME PUBLICATIONS

Novels

Elizabeth Is Missing.   New York, Knopf, 1945; London, Joseph, 1947.
The Heir of Douglas.   New York, Knopf, 1952; London, Joseph, 1953.
The Truth about Belle Gunness.   New York, Fawcett, 1955; London, Muller, 1960.

Short Stories (series: Dr. Sam: Johnson)

Dr. Sam: Johnson, Detector.   New York, Knopf, 1946; London, Joseph, 1948.
The Detections of Dr. Sam: Johnson.   New York, Doubleday, 1960; London, Xanadu, 1989.
The Return of Dr. Sam: Johnson, Detector.   New York, International Polygonics, 1985.
The Exploits of Dr. Sam: Johnson, Detector.   New York, International Polygonics, 1985.

OTHER PUBLICATIONS

Plays

Goodbye, Miss Lizzie Borden (produced Colorado Springs, 1948).   Published in *Murder Plain and Fanciful,* edited by James Sandoe, New York, Sheridan House, 1948.
Cheat the Wuddy (produced Colorado Springs, 1948).
Remember Constance Kent (produced Colorado Springs, 1949).

The Sally Cathleen Claim (produced Cripple Creek, Colorado, 1952).

The Coffee Cup (produced Willimantic, Connecticut, 1955). Published in *Butcher, Baker, Murder Maker*, edited by George Harmon Coxe, New York, Knopf, 1954; London, Macdonald, 1956.

The Queen's Choristers, music by J. Julius Baird (for children; produced Colorado Springs, 1961).

The Jester's Apprentice, music by J. Julius Baird (for children; produced Colorado Springs, 1962).

The Bar-Room Floor (produced Central City, Colorado, 1964).

The Stroller's Girl, music by J. Julius Baird (for children; produced Colorado Springs, 1966).

Verse

Stars (as Lillian Bueno McCue).   Privately printed, 1982.

Other

The 60 Minute Chef, with Carol Truax.   New York, Macmillan, 1947.

Villainy Detected.   New York, Appleton Century, 1947.

The White Rose of Stuart (for children).   New York, Nelson, 1954.

The Actress (for children).   New York, Nelson, 1957.

"The Scholar as Sherlock," in *New York Times Book Review,* 9 June 1963.

The New 60 Minute Chef, with Carol Truax.   New York, Bantam, 1975.

"The Pleasures of Histo-Detection," in *Armchair Detective* (San Diego), May 1976.

*

Bibliography: "Blood on the Periwigs" by James Mark Purcell, in *Mystery Readers Newsletter* (Melrose, Massachusetts), July-August 1971.

Manuscript Collection: Harold B. Lee Collection, Brigham Young University, Provo, Utah.

Lillian de la Torre comments:

I call myself a "histo-detector." The name comes from the funny papers, but the calling is a serious one, the craft of solving mysteries of the long-ago. I began "histo-detecting" for fun when in 1942 I was inspired to write mystery fiction featuring as a "detector" Dr. Johnson, the real-life eighteenth-century lexicographer and sage, narrated by his biographer, the facinating rake, James Boswell. The crime scene in their time was rich and raffish, and afforded many an intriguing mystery to be fictiously unravelled. 31 "Dr. Sam: Johnson" mystery short stories have appeared. The mysteries, characters, and settings are real but the solutions only rarely make any pretence of being other than fiction.

Once in a while, it may become apparent to me that I have lit on the truth of one of those old cases in sober earnest. Then a book results, exhaustively researched and definitive. Such are my books on Elizabeth Canning, Belle Gunness, and the disputed Douglas claim. "Sir, I think such a publication does good," said Dr. Johnson of an earlier book on the Douglas Cause, "as it does good to show us the possibilities of human life."

I agree. Thoughtful consideration of such mysterious moments in history, in my opinion, is uniquely fitted to illuminate the human condition, probing as it does man's behavior under stress, brilliantly flood-lighted in the glare of public curiosity. Thus in serious "histo-detection" the humane value will equal or transcend the usual amusement values of sensational narrative and puzzle-solving.

*   *   *

Best known as the creator of the "Dr. Sam: Johnson" stories, Lillian de la Torre is a writer of considerable range. Her contributions to mystery/detective literature include three historical mystery novels, several plays based on historical crimes, and two articles which present convincing arguments in favour of the seriousness of crime literature as a means of probing human motivation.

Goodbye, Miss Lizzie Borden, a one-act play, exemplifies de la Torre's method at its best. She is able to take a well-known historical case and present it in a form which is both viable dramatically and believable in realistic terms. The surprise ending is not contrived, and the play as a whole is infinitely more touching than many historical dramas which attempt simply to recreate known events.

De la Torre calls herself a "histo-detector," and her 29 published stories featuring Dr. Johnson, narrated by the ideal "Watson," James Boswell, are successful examples of histo-detection. Having fastened upon a historical period rich in criminal possibilities, the author concentrates upon the presentation of character, setting, and atmosphere, with little pretence at providing an original or ingenious puzzle. The tone of the stories, which gracefully reflects the style of Dr. Johnson and his period, allows the author to point a moral, explain an historical mystery, or otherwise indulge in a didacticism which might be out of place in a contemporary crime story. Julian Symons has referred to these stories as "pastiches," a description which fails to suggest the author's originality. In such historical novels as *Elizabeth Is Missing* or *The Heir of Douglas,* de la Torre exhibits a combination of careful attention to historical detail and a humane interest in justice as the result of a proper understanding of human behaviour. Like the Dr. Johnson stories, the novels present thoughtful but lively considerations of mysterious moments in history as these reveal universal human traits.

—Joanne Harack Hayne

———————

DEMILLE, Nelson (Richard). Also writes as Ellen Kay; Kurt Ladner; Brad Matthews. American. Born in New York City, 23 August 1943. Educated at Hofstra University, Long Island, New York, B.A. in political science and history 1970. Served in the United States Army Infantry, 1966–69; Bronze Star, Vietnamese Cross of Gallantry. Married 1) Ellen Wasserman in 1971 (divorced 1987), two children; 2) Virginia Sindel Witte in 1988. Has had a variety of jobs including carpenter, electrian's apprentice, house painter, art dealer, insurance investigator, and editorial assistant. Agent: Nick Ellison, Sanford J. Greenburger Associates, Inc., 55 Fifth Avenue, New York, New York 10022, Address: 61 Hilton Avenue, Suite 25, Garden City, New York 11530-2813, U.S.A.

CRIME PUBLICATIONS

Novels (series: Joe Keller; Joe Ryker)

The Sniper (Ryker).   New York, Leisure, 1974.
The Hammer of God (Ryker).   New York, Leisure, 1974.

The Agent of Death (Ryker).   New York, Leisure, 1974.
The Smack Man (Keller).   New York, Manor, 1975.
The Cannibal (Keller).   New York, Manor, 1975.
Night of the Phoenix (Keller).   New York, Manor, 1975.
The Death Squad (Keller).   New York, Manor, 1975.
By the Rivers of Babylon.   New York, Harcourt Brace, and
   London, Hart Davis, 1978.
Cathedral.   New York, Delacorte Press, and London, Gran-
   ada, 1981.
The Talbot Odyssey.   New York, Delacorte Press, and
   London, Granada, 1984.
Word of Honor.   New York, Warner, and London, Granada,
   1985.
The Charm School.   New York, Warner, and London, Graf-
   ton, 1988.
The Gold Coast.   New York, Warner, and London, Grafton,
   1990.

OTHER PUBLICATIONS

Novels

Hitler's Children (as Kurt Ladner).   New York, Manor, 1976.
Mayday with Thomas H. Block.   New York, Marek, 1979.

Other

Killer Sharks: The Real Story (as Brad Matthews).   New York,
   Manor, 1976.
The Five Million Dollar Woman: Barbara Walters (biography;
   as Ellen Kay).   New York, Manor, 1979.

* * *

Nelson DeMille has written two kinds of crime novel so
startlingly different that the reader at first presumes two
synonymous authors. In 1974, DeMille began with action/ad-
venture police novels published as entries in two paperback
series, Ryker and Keller. In 1978, after seven of these series
novels and a few non-crime books, he began to publish
blockbuster thrillers. Although DeMille's two groups of crime
novels differ in plot, theme, tone, character, diction, length,
and sales, what they have in common is basic and rare among
writers. In a word, Demille's books have flow. All of his crime
novels, the strong ones and weaker ones alike, display a well
buffed polish and a galloping readability.

DeMille's police novels are among the very best of that
marketable but oft-snubbed publishing format, the paperback
crime series. By the time of DeMille's first book, the paperback
action category had become a *fait accompli,* and in the film
world, Clint Eastwood had made a hero figure of a violent cop.
But when DeMille's Ryker series began in 1974 with *The
Sniper,* paperback fiction gained a fictional milieu grimmer
than in Richard Stark's Parker novels, and a cop tougher than
Dirty Harry. The harshness of DeMille's world is justly
captured by the opening of *The Sniper's* second chapter: "Of all
the depraved sections of the degenerating city of New York,
certainly the most vile must be the section known as the upper
West side."

DeMille's Joe Ryker, Homicide Detective Sergeant in the
New York Police Department's 21st Precinct, appears in three
novels published in 1974, and Joe Keller appeared in three
published in 1975. Ryker/Keller is a craggy, unrefined,
cheroot-smoking Korean War veteran utterly devoted to
busting bad guys. He's violent, smart, single, and not a
womanizer. He distinguishes between law and justice, and

works outside the system, perpetrating occasional brutalities
that even 1990's movie screens can't show. Though Ryker
doesn't philosophize, he can be pushed into discussing
Dostoevsky, Marx, Caesar, Hitler, and Muhammad.

A Hobbesian war of all against all, Ryker's New York world
is inhabited by an infernal sideshow of characters. In *The
Sniper,* the purest police novel in the series, Ryker chases a
crazed Vietnam vet who indiscriminately shoots passersby. In
The Hammer of God, he stalks a demented cleric who follows
female actresses home from plays like *Faust* and *Macbeth,*
accuses them of witchcraft, and drives stakes through their
hearts. *The Agent of Death* is DeMille's most audacious Ryker
novel. The titular agent is a renegade CIA man on a New York
killing spree, and the book details leech baths, flaying, and
other exotic Asian tortures. In the Joe Keller series, Keller
hunts drug dealers in *The Smack Man,* and a right-wing
vigilante police cabal in *The Death Squad.* Despite the fact that
they often end in showers of blood, bones, and brain, the Ryker
and Keller books generate a compelling sense of drama. This is
due to DeMille's level-headed sense of situation and irony, and
his spare, witty, no-nonsense dialogue. In 1989, Pocket Books
reprinted two books from each series as an integrated set of four
Ryker novels as by Jack Cannon. Carefully updated and
rewritten, the new series towers above other contemporary
action/adventure crime series, and reasserts DeMille's primacy in the field of the roughneck crime novel.

As though written by another person, the blockbusters from
1978 to the present average 250,000 words, about five times as
long as the paperback originals. Written in an elevated,
educated tone, they employ the devices of crosscut narration
and the siege-narrative set piece. These devices take up most of
By the Rivers of Babylon, a Mid-East hijack thriller that
appeared shortly after the provocative Entebbe incident.
Three-quarters of the book describes the passengers' defense
against a Palestinian onslaught after the plane is brought down.
In *Cathedral,* New York's St. Patrick's cathedral is assaulted on
St. Patrick's Day by IRA terrorists fighting for their age-old
cause. In *The Talbot Odyssey,* a talky book and DeMille's
weakest, one of the CIA's preppy, blueblood OSS members has
reportedly been a Soviet agent for decades, and it's up to a
young couple in a CIA-aligned private law firm to investigate.

Word of Honor draws on DeMille's army experiences as an
Infantry Lieutenant. Using a linear plot about a Lieutenant
Calley-type massacre in Vietnam, it chronicles the disintegra-
tion of Ben Tyson's upper-middle class corporate and suburban
existence when a historian publishes an account of war crimes
attributed to Tyson. *The Charm School* is an enjoyable romp
through Russia with an American tourist and his blue Pontiac
Trans Am. While driving from Smolensk to Moscow, Gregory
Fisher picks up a man who claims to be an Air Force major and
a prisoner of war for 20 years in "Mrs. Ivanova's Charm
School," a Russian training camp for total immersion in
Americana. Actually talkier but better than *The Talbot
Odyssey,* DeMille's recent *The Gold Coast* has more sociology
than crime. When mafioso Frank Bellarosa moves to the posh
Gold Coast area of the northwestern Long Island next door to
Wall Street lawyer John Sutter, we're treated to a cultural
juxtaposition of the old-moneyed, silver-spoon, Ivy League
WASP with the crass Italian mobster parvenu. By the time
Sutter defends Bellarosa in a murder case, we see Episcopalian-
ism, yacht clubs, and Sperry Top-Siders clash with Catholi-
cism, plaster saints, and *calamaretti fritti.*

Whether in his paperback police shockers or his more sedate
blockbusters, DeMille always exercises his superb talent for
narrative smoothness. Fluent but rarely glib, he has a word for
everything, and is seldom stumped by a fictional challenge he
poses for himself. In DeMille's books one finds solid

craftsmanship distilled by wartime experience, erudition and media consciousness—all delivered in roller-coaster prose.

—Greg Goode.

———

DEMING, Richard. Also wrote as Halsey Clark; Richard Hale Curtis; Max Franklin; Emily Moor; Nick Marino; Ellery Queen; Lee Davis Willoughby. American. Born in Des Moines, Iowa, 25 April 1915. Educated at Central College, Fayette, Missouri, 1933–35; Washington University, St. Louis, B.A. 1937; University of Iowa, Iowa City, M.A. 1939. Served in the United States Army, 1941–45: Captain. Married Ruth DuBois in 1948; two daughters. Social worker, St. Louis, 1939–41; worked for American Red Cross, Dunkirk, New York, 1945–50; then self-employed writer. Member of the board of directors, Mystery Writers of America, 1976–83. *Died 5 September 1983.*

CRIME PUBLICATIONS

Novels (series: The Mod Squad; Manville "Manny" Moon; Matt Rudd)

The Gallows in My Garden (Moon). New York, Rinehart, 1952; London, Boardman, 1953.
Tweak the Devil's Nose (Moon). New York, Rinehart, and London, Boardman, 1953; as *Hand-Picked to Die,* New York, Spivak, 1956.
Whistle Past the Graveyard (Moon). New York, Rinehart, 1954; London, Boardman, 1955; as *Give the Girl a Gun,* New York, Spivak, 1955.
Juvenile Delinquent (Moon). London, Boardman, 1958.
Dragnet: The Case of the Courteous Killer. New York, Pocket Books, 1958.
City Limits (as Nick Marino). New York, Pyramid, and London, Digit, 1958.
Dragnet: The Case of the Crime King. New York, Pocket Books, 1959.
Fall Girl. Rockville Centre, New York, Zenith, 1959; as *Walk a Crooked Mile,* London, Boardman, 1959.
Kiss and Kill. Rockville Centre, New York, Zenith, 1960; London, Digit, 1961.
Edge of the Law. New York, Berkley, 1960.
Hit and Run. New York, Pocket Books, 1960.
Vice Cop (Rudd). New York, Belmont, 1961.
This Is My Night. Derby, Connecticut, Monarch, 1961.
Body for Sale. New York, Pocket Books, 1962.
The Careful Man. London, W.H. Allen, 1962.
She'll Hate Me Tomorrow. Derby, Connecticut, Monarch, 1963.
Anything But Saintly (Rudd). New York, Pocket Books, 1963.
Death of a Pusher (Rudd). New York, Pocket Books, 1964.
This Game of Murder. Derby, Connecticut, Monarch, 1964.
The Mod Squad: The Greek God Affair (novelization of television series). New York, Pyramid, 1968.
The Mod Squad: A Groovy Way to Die (novelization of television series). New York, Pyramid, 1968.
The Mod Squad: The Sock-It-to-Em Murders (novelization of television series). New York, Pyramid, 1969.
The Mod Squad: Spy-In (novelization of television series). New York, Pyramid, 1969.

The Mod Squad: The Hit (novelization of television series). New York, Pyramid, 1970.
What's the Matter with Helen? (novelization of screenplay). New York, Beagle, 1971.
The Shadowed Porch (as Emily Moor). New York, Beagle, 1972.

Novels as Max Franklin (series: Charlie's Angels; Starsky and Hutch)

Justice Has No Sword. New York, Rinehart, 1953; London, Boardman, 1954; as *Murder Muscles In,* New York, Spivak, 1956.
Hell Street. New York, Rinehart, 1954.
99 44/100% Dead (novelization of screenplay). New York, Award, and London, Tandem, 1974.
The Destructors (novelization of screenplay). New York, Ballantine, 1974.
The 5th of November (novelization of screenplay). New York, Ballantine, 1975; as *Hennessy,* London, Futura, 1975.
Starsky and Hutch (novelization of television play). New York, Ballantine, 1975; London, Futura, 1976.
Starsky and Hutch: Kill Huggy Bear (novelization of television play). New York, Ballantine, 1976; London, Barker, 1977.
Starsky and Hutch: Death Ride (novelization of television play). New York, Ballantine, and London, Futura, 1976.
Starsky and Hutch: Bounty Hunter (novelization of television play). New York, Ballantine, and London, Futura, 1977.
Starsky and Hutch: Terror on the Docks (novelization of television play). New York, Ballantine, 1977.
Starsky and Hutch: The Psychic (novelization of television play). New York, Ballantine, 1977.
Charlie's Angels (novelization of television play). New York, Ballantine, and London, Futura, 1977.
Charlie's Angels: The Killing Kind (novelization of television play). New York, Ballantine, and London, Futura, 1977.
Charlie's Angels: Angels on a String (novelization of television play). New York, Ballantine, 1977.
Charlie's Angels: Angels in Chains (novelization of television play). New York, Ballantine, and London, Futura, 1977.
Starsky and Hutch: The Setup (novelization of television play). New York, Ballantine, and London, Futura, 1978.
Starsky and Hutch: Murder on Playboy Island (novelization of television play). New York, Ballantine, and London, Futura, 1978.
Good Guys Wear Black. New York, New American Library, 1978.
The Dark. New York, New American Library, 1978.
Vega$ (novelization of television play). New York, Ballantine, 1978.
Charlie's Angels: Angels on Ice (novelization of television play). New York, Ballantine, and London, Futura, 1978.

Novels as Ellery Queen (series: Tim Corrigan)

Death Spins the Platter. New York, Pocket Books, 1962; London, Gollancz, 1965.
Wife or Death. New York, Pocket Books, and London, Four Square, 1963.
The Copper Frame. New York, Pocket Books, 1965; London, Four Square, 1968.
Losers. New York, Pocket Books, 1966.
Shoot the Scene. New York, Dell, 1966.
Why So Dead? (Corrigan). New York, Popular Library, and London, Four Square, 1966.
How Goes the Murder? (Corrigan). New York, Popular Library, 1967.

Which Way to Die? New York, Popular Library, 1967.
What's in the Dark? (Corrigan). New York, Popular Library, 1968; as *When Fell the Night,* London, Gollancz, 1970.
The Black Hearts Murder. New York, Lancer, 1970.

Uncollected Short Stories

"No Game for a Poor Man," in *The Shadow* (New York), December 1944.
"A Ram to the Slaughter," in *Detective Fiction* (New York), July 1951.
"For Value Received," in *Best Detective Stories of the Year 1953,* edited by David Coxe Cooke. New York, Dutton, and London, Boardman, 1953.
"The Lesser Evil," in *Manhunt* (New York), February 1953.
"The Loyal One," in *Manhunt* (New York), June 1953.
"Bonus Cop," in *Manhunt* (New York), September 1953.
"Balanced Account," in *Manhunt* (New York), October 1953.
"Open File," in *Ellery Queen's Mystery Magazine* (New York), December 1953.
"The Way It Really Is," in *Private Eye* (New York), December 1953.
"Mugger Murder," in *Best Detective Stories of the Year 1954,* edited by David Coxe Cooke. New York, Dutton, and London, Boardman, 1954.
"Hook Up Murder," in *Double-Action Detective Stories 1* (New York), 1954.
"The Six-Bit Fee," in *Manhunt* (New York), January 1954.
"The Blonde in the Bar," in *Manhunt* (New York), May 1954.
"The Cop-Killer," in *Pursuit* (New York), September 1954.
"Love Affair," in *Manhunt* (New York), October 1954.
"Death Trap," in *Pursuit* (New York), November 1954.
"The Posse," in *Menace* (New York), November 1954.
"Summer Boarder," in *Hunted* (New York), December 1954.
"The Choice," in *Best Detective Stories of the Year 1955,* edited by David Coxe Cooke. New York, Dutton, and London, Boardman, 1955.
"The Competitors," in *Manhunt* (New York), February 1955.
"Heist Artist's Homicide," in *Hunted* (New York), February 1955.
"The Happy Marriage," in *Manhunt* (New York), August 1955.
"The War," in *Manhunt* (New York), September 1955.
"Custody," in *Best Detective Stories of the Year 1956,* edited by David Coxe Cooke. New York, Dutton, and London, Boardman, 1956.
"The Neighbor," in *Double-Action Detective Stories 5* (New York), 1956.
"Scented Clues," in *Justice* (New York), January 1956.
"Stationary Target," in *Accused* (New York), January 1956.
"Sauce for the Gander," in *Manhunt* (New York), February 1956.
"The Better Bargain," in *Manhunt* (New York), April 1956.
"The Squeeze," in *Manhunt* (New York), June 1956.
"Kill for Me, Lover," in *Guilty* (New York), July 1956.
"C Is for Culprit," in *Suspect* (New York), August 1956.
"A Soda for Susan," in *Mantrap* (New York), October 1956.
"Kiss of Death," in *Murder* (New York), December 1956.
"Kill, If You Want Me," in *Alfred Hitchcock's Mystery Magazine* (New York), January 1957.
"Comfort for the Grave," in *Mike Shayne Mystery Magazine* (New York), January 1957.
"Tough Young Punk," in *Guilty* (New York), January 1957.
"The Cesspool," in *Murder* (New York), March 1957.
"Pick-Up," in *Manhunt* (New York), March 1957.
"The Strange Collaboration," in *Mike Shayne Mystery Magazine* (New York), April 1957.

"A Little Sororicide," in *Alfred Hitchcock's Mystery Magazine* (New York), May 1957.
"The Charles Turner Case," in *Manhunt* (New York), May 1957.
"The Amateur," in *Manhunt* (New York), June 1957.
"The Man Who Was Two," in *Manhunt* (New York), July 1957.
"I Want It Foolproof," in *The Saint* (New York), August 1957.
"Secondary Target," in *Manhunt* (New York), October 1957.
"The Doubles," in *Manhunt* (New York), December 1957.
"Trouble in Town," in *Manhunt* (New York), April 1958.
"The Strange Case of Linda Strange," in *Mike Shayne Mystery Magazine* (New York), September 1958.
"The Strangler," in *Manhunt* (New York), December 1958.
"Death Be a Lady," in *Mystery Tales* (New York), February 1959.
"A Hood Is Born," in *Mike Shayne Mystery Magazine* (New York), March 1959.
"The Front," in *The Saint* (New York), May 1959.
"Pay Off or Die," in *Mike Shayne Mystery Magazine* (New York), October 1959.
"Two Kinds of Murder," in *The Saint* (New York), November 1959.
"Ultimate Terror," in *The Saint* (New York), November 1959.
"Optical Illusion," in *Dames, Danger, and Death,* edited by Leo Margulies. New York, Pyramid, 1960.
"Die a Little Longer," in *Mike Shayne Mystery Magazine* (New York), May 1960.
"The Triple Cross," in *Saturn Web* (New York), October 1960.
"Acting Job," in *Mike Shayne Mystery Magazine* (New York), January 1961.
"Blackout," in *Alfred Hitchcock's Mystery Magazine* (New York), March 1961.
"The Hasty Homicides," in *Mike Shayne Mystery Magazine* (New York), August 1961.
"The Hard Man," in *The Saint* (New York), December 1961.
"The Blood Oath," in *The Saint* (New York), March 1962.
"Number One Suspect," in *Alfred Hitchcock's Mystery Magazine* (New York), June 1962.
"A Medal for Don Carlos," in *The Saint* (New York), July 1962.
"Reward," in *Manhunt* (New York), October 1962.
"Homicide, Inc.," in *The Saint* (New York), November 1962.
"Second Honeymoon," in *Best Detective Stories of the Year: 17th Annual Collection,* edited by Brett Halliday. New York, Dutton, 1962.
"No One Said a Word," in *The Saint* (London), January 1963.
"The Men in Aunt Annabel's Life," in *Mike Shayne Mystery Magazine* (New York), March 1963.
"Death at Midnight," in *The Saint* (New York), July 1963.
"The Man Who Chose the Devil," in *The Saint* (New York), October 1963.
"A Girl Must Be Practical," in *Alfred Hitchcock's Mystery Magazine* (New York), November 1963.
"Red Herring," in *Best Detective Stories of the Year,* edited by Anthony Boucher. New York, Dutton, and London, Boardman, 1963.
"The Sensitive Juror," in *Alfred Hitchcock's Mystery Magazine* (New York), February 1964.
"The Price of Fame," in *Alfred Hitchcock's Mystery Magazine* (New York), March 1964.
"Medicine Woman," in *Alfred Hitchcock's Mystery Magazine* (New York), June 1964.
"Uncle Willie," in *The Saint* (New York), July 1964.
"Blood Kin," in *Alfred Hitchcock's Mystery Magazine* (New York), July 1964.
"Escape Route," in *Alfred Hitchcock's Mystery Magazine* (New York), August 1964.

"The Bracelet," in *Alfred Hitchcock's Mystery Magazine* (New York), September 1964.

"System Player," in *Alfred Hitchcock's Mystery Magazine* (New York), November 1964.

"The Lonely Heart," in *Alfred Hitchcock's Mystery Magazine* (New York), December 1964.

"False Alarm," in *Alfred Hitchcock's Mystery Magazine* (New York), February 1965.

"Errand Boy," in *The Saint* (New York), March 1965.

"The Most Ethical Man in the Business," in *Ellery Queen's Mystery Magazine* (New York), April 1965.

"Conscience Money," in *Alfred Hitchcock's Mystery Magazine* (New York), April 1965.

"The Hypothetical Plan," in *Alfred Hitchcock's Mystery Magazine* (New York), May 1965.

"The Promotion," in *Alfred Hitchcock's Mystery Magazine* (New York), June 1965.

"Birthday Present," in *Mike Shayne Mystery Magazine* (New York), June 1965.

"Gentle Bluebeard," in *Alfred Hitchcock's Mystery Magazine* (New York), July 1965.

"A Good Friend," in *Alfred Hitchcock's Mystery Magazine* (New York), August 1965.

"Suicide Clause," in *Alfred Hitchcock's Mystery Magazine* (New York), September 1965.

"The Common Factor," in *Alfred Hitchcock's Mystery Magazine* (New York), October 1965.

"Lily Bell," in *Alfred Hitchcock's Mystery Magazine* (New York), December 1965.

"The Taipei Affair," in *Intrigue* (New York), January 1966.

"In Self Defense," in *Manhunt* (New York), February–March 1966.

"Houseboat," in *The Man from U.N.C.L.E.* (New York), April 1966.

"The Comb of Death," in *Mike Shayne Mystery Magazine* (New York), April 1966.

"Honeymoon Cruise," in *Alfred Hitchcock's Mystery Magazine* (New York), October 1966.

"The Monster Brain," in *Alfred Hitchcock's Mystery Magazine* (New York), November 1966.

"The Organization," in *Alfred Hitchcock's Mystery Magazine* (New York), January 1967.

"The Calculated Alibi," in *Alfred Hitchcock's Mystery Magazine* (New York), March 1967.

"The Jolly Jugglers, Retired," in *Ellery Queen's Mystery Magazine* (New York), March 1967.

"Cheers," in *Alfred Hitchcock's Mystery Magazine* (New York), February 1968.

"The New Hand," in *Mike Shayne Mystery Magazine* (New York), November 1968.

"The Skim," in *Alfred Hitchcock's Mystery Magazine* (New York), January 1969.

"Howdy," in *Mike Shayne Mystery Magazine* (New York), April 1969.

"Positive Print," in *Alfred Hitchcock's Mystery Magazine* (New York), July 1970.

"Mr. Olem's Secrets," in *Alfred Hitchcock's Mystery Magazine* (New York), August 1971.

"Jailbreak," in *Alfred Hitchcock's Mystery Magazine* (New York), November 1971.

"Big Jim's Pocket," in *Mike Shayne Mystery Magazine* (Los Angeles), November 1971.

"Mint Mark," in *Mike Shayne Mystery Magazine* (Los Angeles), December 1971.

"An Element of Risk," in *Alfred Hitchcock's Mystery Magazine* (New York), September 1972.

"Black Belt," in *Alfred Hitchcock's Mystery Magazine* (New York), November 1972.

"Comeback Performance," in *Alfred Hitchcock's Mystery Magazine* (New York), March 1973.

"The Art of Deduction," in *Alfred Hitchcock's Mystery Magazine* (New York), June 1973.

"Premarital Agreement," in *Alfred Hitchcock's Mystery Magazine* (New York), July 1973.

"The Critic," in *Mike Shayne Mystery Magazine* (Los Angeles), August 1973.

"My Face Is My Fortune," in *Alfred Hitchcock's Mystery Magazine* (New York), November 1973.

"A Putting Away of Toys," in *Alfred Hitchcock's Mystery Magazine* (North Palm Beach, Florida), April 1974.

"Say It With Flowers," in *Alfred Hitchcock's Mystery Magazine* (North Palm Beach, Florida), July 1974.

"Doorway to Death," in *Mike Shayne Mystery Magazine* (Los Angeles), October 1974.

"Maggie's Grip," in *Alfred Hitchcock's Mystery Magazine* (North Palm Beach, Florida), March 1975.

"The Coup," in *Executioner* (Los Angeles), August 1975.

"Guardian of the Hearth," in *Mike Shayne Mystery Magazine* (Los Angeles), December 1979.

"Stolen Goods," in *Alfred Hitchcock's Mystery Magazine* (New York), 2 January 1980.

"The Evils of Drink," in *Alfred Hitchcock's Mystery Magazine* (New York), 23 April 1980.

"A Place to Hide," in *Alfred Hitchcock's Tales to Make Your Teeth Chatter,* edited by Eleanor Sullivan. New York, Dial Press, 1980.

"Mother Love," in *Mike Shayne Mystery Magazine* (Los Angeles), April 1981.

"Nice Guy," in *Alfred Hitchcock's Tales to Make You Quake and Quiver,* edited by Cathleen Jordon. New York, Dial Press, 1982.

Uncollected Short Stories as Max Franklin

"Diary of a Devout Man," in *Manhunt* (New York), December 1954.

"Incident in a Barroom," in *Pursuit* (New York), May 1955.

"The Careful Man," in *Manhunt* (New York), June 1955.

"The Joker," in *Hunted* (New York), October 1955.

"Sudden Death," in *Pursuit* (New York), November 1955.

"Dead Giveaway," in *Pursuit* (New York), March 1956.

"Triple Payoff," in *Pursuit* (New York), July 1956.

"The Burden," in *Accused* (New York), July 1956.

"The Geniuses," in *Manhunt* (New York), June 1957.

"Top Dog," in *Manhunt* (New York), October 1957.

"The New Girl," in *Manhunt* (New York), January 1958.

"The Threat," in *Manhunt* (New York), June 1958.

OTHER PUBLICATIONS

Novels

Baby Blue Marine (as Max Franklin). New York, New American Library, 1976.

The Last of the Cowboys (as Max Franklin). New York, New American Library, 1977.

The Barnstormers (as Richard Hale Curtis). New York, Dell, 1982.

The Smugglers (as Lee Davis Willoughby). New York, Dell, 1983.

Grand Finale (as Halsey Clark). New York, Dell, 1983.

The Bounty Hunters (as Lee Davis Willoughby). New York, Dell, 1984.

Other

American Spies.   Racine, Wisconsin, Whitman, 1960.
Famous Investigators.   Racine, Wisconsin, Whitman, 1963.
The Police Lab at Work.   Indianapolis, Bobbs Merrill, 1967.
Heroes of the International Red Cross.   New York, Meredith Press, 1969.
Man and Society: Criminal Law at Work.   New York, Hawthorn, 1970.
Man Against Man: Civil Law at Work.   New York, Hawthorn, 1972.
Sleep, Our Unknown Life.   New York, Nelson, 1972.
Man and the World: International Law at Work.   New York, Hawthorn, 1974.
Metric Power: Why and How We Are Going Metric.   New York, Nelson, 1974; as *Metric Now,* New York, Dell, 1976.
Women: The New Criminals.   New York, Nelson, 1977.
The Paralegal: A New Career.   New York, Lodestar, 1979.

*   *   *

Richard Deming is rather typical of that generation of crime writers who began writing during the latter days of the pulp magazine era. When the pulps expired, he moved to writing short stories for the digest-sized mystery magazine (*Manhunt, Alfred Hitchcock's Mystery Magazine, Mike Shayne Mystery Magazine,* etc.) and original paperback novels. The new post-pulp markets required much the same skills as the pulps: the ability to write crisp, realistic dialogue; to plot competently, without over-elaboration; to know how to blend sex, violence, and sensationalism for maximum sales appeal without getting in trouble with the censors. Drawbacks to this sort of career included generally unspectacular pay, short deadlines, and a fast-changing market, where magazines and paperback houses were formed and dissolved, and a writer frequently did not know who his next publisher would be.

Some writers working in this field eventually achieved notable popular and critical success—John D. MacDonald is the prime example—usually by virtue of having happened on a steady publisher and a series character of broad appeal. Others, like Deming, never quite broke out of the paperback ghetto; nevertheless, his work is interesting, varied, thoroughly professional, and very much worth the attention of those who love good crime writing.

He did try his hand at a series detective, Manville "Manny" Moon, who appeared in three early novels and in many short stories. Manny is tough, honest, quick-witted, fast with the wise-cracks, and equipped with an artificial leg. His home base is the El Patio Cafe; his girlfriend is Fausta Moreni, the proprietress. The plot material is the familiar sort of nastiness that keeps the hard-boiled genre alive: vice, racketeering, blackmail, and casual murder. The Moon books have strong atmosphere, crackling dialogue, and considerable forward momentum, very much in the Hammett-Chandler tradition. That the Moon series never caught on while less appealing and well-crafted private eye series enjoyed great success is one of those baffling mysteries of the paperback market.

Deming's non-series works in the suspense field display the same virtues as the Moon novels. Such books as *Edge of the Law* and *She'll Hate Me Tomorrow* are rousing reworkings of the classic hard-boiled theme of the man on the run from the Syndicate; money, mayhem, and sex are stirred together with considerable skill. *Hit and Run* is noteworthy for Deming's dedication: "For the Bureau of Internal Revenue"—a reminder of the driving force behind the work of the journeyman crime writer.

Deming launched another short-lived series in 1963. *Anything But Saintly* and *Death of a Pusher* are hard-boiled procedural novels featuring Matt Rudd (Mateusz Rudowski), a vice cop in the fictional Southern California town of St. Cecilia—a corrupt and violence-ridden city reminiscent of Chandler's Bay City.

Deming also did many television novelizations, most recently a series of books based on the *Mod Squad* series. The television tie-in has become an increasingly important market for experienced and versatile writers like Deming. In the late 1950's Deming also did two *Dragnet* books, in which he displayed a fine feel for the modern police procedural novel; his personal approach to dialogue, however, was sacrificed to the peculiar style associated with the television series.

—Art Scott

———

DENT, Lester. Also wrote as H.O. Cash; Cliff Howe; Kenneth Roberts; Kenneth Robeson; Tim Ryan; C.K.M. Scanlon; Robert Wallace. American. Born in La Plata, Missouri, 12 October 1904. Studied telegraphy at Chillicothe Business College, Missouri, 1923–24. Married Norma Gerling in 1925. Taught at Chillicothe Business College, 1924; telegrapher, Western Union, Carrolton, Missouri, 1924, and Empire Oil and Gas Company, Ponca City, Oklahoma, 1925; telegrapher, then teletype operator, Associated Press, Tulsa, 1926; house-writer for Dell, publishers, 1930; freelance writer from 1930, and also dairy farmer and aerial photographer. *Died 11 March 1959.*

CRIME PUBLICATIONS

Novels (series: Chance Malloy)

Dead at the Take-Off (Malloy).   New York, Doubleday, 1946; London, Cassell, 1948; as *High Stakes,* New York, Ace, 1953.
Lady to Kill (Malloy).   New York, Doubleday, 1946; London, Cassell, 1949.
Lady Afraid.   New York, Doubleday, 1948; London, Cassell, 1950.
Lady So Silent.   London, Cassell 1951.
Cry at Dusk.   New York, Fawcett, 1952; London, Fawcett, 1959.
Lady in Peril.   New York, Ace, 1959.
Hades and Hocus Pocus, edited by Robert Weinberg. Chicago, Pulp Press, 1979.

Novels as Kenneth Robeson (series: Doc Savage in all books)

The Man of Bronze.   New York, Street and Smith, 1935; London, Corgi, 1975.
The Land of Terror.   New York, Street and Smith, 1935; London, Tandem, 1965.
Quest of the Spider.   New York, Street and Smith, 1935.
The Thousand-Headed Man.   New York, Bantam, 1964; London, Corgi, 1975.
Meteor Menace.   New York, Bantam, 1964; London, Corgi, 1975.
The Polar Treasure.   New York, Bantam, 1965.
Brand of the Werewolf.   New York, Bantam, 1965.
The Lost Oasis.   New York, Bantam, 1965.
The Monsters.   New York, Bantam, 1965.

Quest of Qui. London, Bantam, 1965; New York, Bantam, 1966.

The Mystic Mullah. New York, Bantam, 1965; London, Bantam, 1966.

The Phantom City. New York, Bantam, 1966.

Fear Cay. New York, Bantam, 1966.

Land of Always-Night. New York, Bantam, 1966.

The Fantastic Island. New York, Bantam, 1966; London, Bantam, 1967.

The Spook Legion. New York, Bantam, 1967.

The Red Skull. New York, Bantam, 1967.

The Sargasso Ogre. New York, Bantam, 1967.

Pirate of the Pacific. New York, Bantam, 1967.

The Secret of the Sky. New York, Bantam, 1967; London, Bantam, 1968.

The Czar of Fear. New York, Bantam, 1968.

Fortress of Solitude. New York, Bantam, 1968.

The Green Eagle. New York, Bantam, 1968.

Death in Silver. New York, Bantam, 1968.

The Mystery under the Sea. New York, Bantam, 1968; London Bantam, 1969.

The Deadly Dwarf. New York, Bantam, 1968.

The Other World. New York, Bantam, 1968; London, Bantam, 1969.

The Flaming Falcons. New York, Bantam, 1968; London, Bantam, 1969.

The Annihilist. New York, Bantam, 1968; London, Bantam, 1969.

Hex. London, Bantam, 1968; New York, Bantam, 1969.

The Squeaking Goblin. New York, Bantam, 1969.

Mad Eyes. New York, Bantam, 1969.

The Terror in the Navy. New York, Bantam, 1969.

Dust of Death. New York, Bantam, 1969.

Resurrection Day. New York, Bantam, 1969.

Red Snow. New York, Bantam, 1969.

World's Fair Goblin. New York, Bantam, 1969.

The Dagger in the Sky. New York, Bantam, 1969.

Merchants of Disaster. New York, Bantam, 1969.

The Gold Ogre. New York, Bantam, 1969.

The Man Who Shook the Earth. New York, Bantam, 1969.

The Sea Magician. New York, Bantam, 1970.

The Midas Man. New York, Bantam, 1970.

The Feathered Octopus. New York, Bantam, 1970.

The Sea Angel. New York, Bantam, 1970.

Devil on the Moon. New York, Bantam, 1970.

The Vanisher. New York, Bantam, 1970.

The Mental Wizard. New York, Bantam, 1970.

He Could Stop the World. New York, Bantam, 1970.

The Golden Peril. New York, Bantam, 1970.

The Giggling Ghosts. New York, Bantam, 1971.

Poison Island. New York, Bantam, 1971.

The Munitions Master. New York, Bantam, 1971.

The Yellow Cloud. New York, Bantam, 1971.

The Majii. New York, Bantam, 1971.

The Living Fire Menace. New York, Bantam, 1971.

The Pirate's Ghost. New York, Bantam, 1971.

The Submarine Mystery. New York, Bantam, 1971.

The Motion Menace. New York, Bantam, 1971.

The Green Death. New York, Bantam, 1971.

Mad Mesa. New York, Bantam, 1972.

The Freckled Shark. New York, Bantam, 1972.

The Mystery on the Snow. New York, Bantam, 1972.

Spook Hole. New York, Bantam, 1972.

The Mental Monster. New York, Bantam, 1973.

The Seven Agate Devils. New York, Bantam, 1973.

The Derrick Devil. New York, Bantam, 1973.

Land of Fear. New York, Bantam, 1973.

The South Pole Terror. New York, Bantam, 1974.

The Crimson Serpent. New York, Bantam, 1974.

The Devil Genghis. New York, Bantam, 1974.

The King Maker. New York, Bantam, 1975.

The Stone Man. New York, Bantam, 1976.

The Evil Gnome. New York, Bantam, 1976.

The Red Terrors. New York, Bantam, 1976.

The Mountain Monster. New York, Bantam, 1976.

The Boss of Terror. New York, Bantam, 1976.

The Angry Ghost. New York, Bantam, 1977.

The Spotted Men. New York, Bantam, 1977.

The Roar Devil. New York, Bantam, 1977.

The Magic Island. New York, Bantam, 1977.

The Flying Goblin. New York, Bantam, 1977.

The Purple Dragon. New York, Bantam, 1978.

The Awful Egg. New York, Bantam, 1978.

Tunnel Terror. New York, Bantam, 1979.

The Hate Genius. New York, Bantam, 1979.

The Red Spider. New York, Bantam, 1979.

Mystery on Happy Bones. New York, Bantam, 1979.

Satan Black, Cargo Unknown. New York, Bantam, 1980.

Hell Below, The Lost Giant. New York, Bantam, 1980.

The Pharaoh's Ghost, The Time Terror. New York, Bantam, 1981.

The Whisker of Hercules, The Man Who Was Scared. New York, Bantam, 1981.

They Died Twice, The Screaming Man. New York, Bantam, 1981.

Jiu San; The Black, Black Witch. New York, Bantam, 1981.

The Shape of Terror, Death Had Yellow Eyes. New York, Bantam, 1982.

One-Eyed Mystic, The Man Who Fell Up. New York, Bantam, 1982.

The Talking Devil, The Ten Ton Snake. New York, Bantam, 1982.

Pirate Isle, The Speaking Stone. New York, Bantam, 1983.

The Golden Man, Peril in the North. New York, Bantam, 1984.

The Laugh of Death, The King of Terror. New York, Bantam, 1984.

The Three Wild Men, The Fiery Menace. New York, Bantam, 1984.

Devils of the Deep. New York, Bantam, 1984.

The Goblins, The Secret of the Su. New York, Bantam, 1984.

Doc Savage Omnibus:

1. *The All-White Elf, The Running Skeletons, The Angry Canary, The Swooning Lady.* New York, Bantam, 1986.
2. *King Joe Cay, The Thing That Pursued.* New York, Bantam, 1987.
3. *The Spook of Grandpa Eben, Measures for a Coffin, The Three Devils, Strange Fish.* New York, Bantam, 1987.
4. *Mystery Island, Men of Fear, Rock Sinister, The Pure Evil.* New York, Bantam, 1987.
5. *No Light to Die By, The Monkey Suit, Let's Kill Ames, Once Over Lightly, I Died Yesterday.* New York, Bantam, 1988.
6. *The Awful Dynasty, The Magic Forest.* New York, Bantam, 1988.
7. *The Men Vanished, The Terrible Stork, Five Fathoms Dead, Danger Lies East.* New York, Bantam, 1988.
8. *The Mental Monster, The Pink Lady, Weird Valley, Trouble on Parade.* New York, Bantam, 1989.
9. *The Invisible-Box Murders, Birds of Death, The Wee Ones, Terror Takes 7.* New York, Bantam, 1989.
10. *The Devil's Black Rock, Waves of Death, Terror and the Lonely Widow, The Two-Wise Owl.* New York, Bantam, 1989.

11. *See-Pah-Poo, Colors for Murder, Three Times a Corpse, Death Is a Round Black Spot, The Devil Is Jones.* New York, Bantam, 1990.
12. *The Exploding Lake.* New York, Bantam, 1990.
13. *The Derelict of Skull Shoal, Terror Wears No Shoes, The Green Master, Return from Cormoral, Up from the Earth's Center.* New York, Bantam, 1990.

Short Stories

The Sinister Ray. New York, Gryphon, 1987.

Uncollected Short Stories

"Pirate Cay," in *Top-Notch* (New York), 1 September 1929.
"Death Zone," in *Top-Notch* (New York), 1 April 1930.
"Buccaneers of the Midnight Sun," in *Top-Notch* (New York), 1 May 1930.
"The Thirteen Million Dollar Robbery," in *The Popular Magazine* (New York), 1 May 1930.
"The Devil's Derelict," in *Action Stories* (New York), December 1930.
"Wildcat," in *Scotland Yard* (New York), March 1931.
"Teeth of Revenge," "Out China Way," and "Doom Ship," in *Scotland Yard* (New York), May 1931.
"One Billion Gold," in *Scotland Yard* (New York), June 1931.
"Diamond Death," in *Scotland Yard* (New York), August 1931.
"Terror, Inc.," in *Detective-Dragnet* (Springfield, Massachusetts), May 1932.
"The Devil's Cargo," in *Detective-Dragnet* (Springfield, Massachusetts), July 1932.
"The Invisible Horde," in *Detective-Dragnet* (Springfield, Massachusetts), September 1932.
"The Whistling Death," in *Ten Detective Aces* (Springfield, Massachusetts), March 1933.
"The Hang String," in *The Shadow* (New York), 1 March 1933.
"The Cavern of Heads," in *Ten Detective Aces* (Springfield, Massachusetts), April 1933.
"The Stamp Murders," in *The Shadow* (New York), 1 April 1933.
"Murder Street," in *Ten Detective Aces* (Springfield, Massachusetts), June 1933.
"The Death Blast," in *Ten Detective Aces* (Springfield, Massachusetts), July 1933.
"The Skeleton's Clutch," in *Ten Detective Aces* (Springfield, Massachusetts), August 1933.
"The Diving Dead," in *Ten Detective Aces* (Springfield, Massachusetts), September 1933.
"The Tank of Terror," in *Ten Detective Aces* (Springfield, Massachusetts), October 1933.
"The Flaming Mask," in *Ten Detective Aces* (Springfield, Massachusetts), December 1933.
"Hell in Boxes," in *All-Detective* (New York), February 1934.
"White-Hot Corpses," in *All-Detective* (New York), March 1934.
"Murder by Circles," in *All-Detective* (New York), May 1934.
"Mud Money," in *The Phantom Detective* (New York), August 1934.
"The Red Owl," in *The Phantom Detective* (New York), December 1934.
"The Finger," in *All-Detective* (New York), December 1934.
"Behind the Ears," in *Thrilling Detective* (New York), April 1935.
"Talking Toad," in *Crime Busters* (New York), November 1937.
"Genius Jones," in *Argosy* (New York), 28 November; 4, 11, 18, 25, December 1937; 1 January 1938.

"Death in Boxes," in *Crime Busters* (New York), December 1937.
"Funny Faces," in *Crime Busters* (New York), January 1938.
"The Scared Swamp," in *Crime Busters* (New York), February 1938.
"Windjam," in *Crime Busters* (New York), March 1938.
"The Little Mud Men," in *Crime Busters* (New York), April 1938.
"The Hairless Wonders," in *Crime Busters* (New York), May 1938.
"Run, Actor, Run," in *Crime Busters* (New York), June 1938.
"A Man and a Mess," in *Crime Busters* (New York), July 1938.
"The Wild Indians," in *Crime Busters* (New York), August 1938.
"Ring Around a Rosey," in *Crime Busters* (New York), August 1938.
"The Dancing Dog," in *Crime Busters* (New York), September 1938.
"The Itching Men," in *Crime Busters* (New York), October 1938.
"The Queer Bees," in *Crime Busters* (New York), November 1938.
"The Devils Smelled Nice," in *Crime Busters* (New York), December 1938.
"The Foolish Whales," in *Crime Busters* (New York), January 1939.
"Six White Horses," in *Crime Busters* (New York), February 1939.
"The Poet's Bones," in *Crime Busters* (New York), March 1939.
"The Mysterious Jugs," in *Crime Busters* (New York), April 1939.
"The Horse's Egg," in *Crime Busters* (New York), July 1939.
"The Remarkable Zeke," in *Crime Busters* (New York), August 1939.
"The Frightened Yachtsmen," in *Crime Busters* (New York), September 1939.
"The Green Birds," in *Mystery* (New York), December 1939.
"Death Wore Skis," in *The Star Weekly* (Toronto), 25 October 1941.
"Sail," in *Hard-Boiled Omnibus: Early Stories from Black Mask,* edited by Joseph T. Shaw. New York, Simon and Schuster, 1946.
"Smith Is Dead," in *Shadow Mystery* (New York), February 1947.
"Angelfish," in *The Hardboiled Dicks,* edited by Ron Goulart. Los Angeles, Sherbourne Press, 1965; London, Boardman, 1967.
"Arctic Loot," in *Pulp Vault* (Chicago), September 1988.

OTHER PUBLICATIONS

Plays

The Incredible Radio Exploits of Doc Savage. Melrose, Massachusetts, Odyssey, 1984.

Radio Plays: *Scotland Yard,* 1931; *Doc Savage,* 1934.

Other

"Waves Those Tags," in *Writer's Digest Yearbook* (Cincinnati), 1940.
"The Master Fiction Plot," in *The Mystery Writer's Handbook,* edited by Herbert Brean. New York, Harper, 1956.

*

Bibliography: "The Secret Kenneth Robesons" and "The *Duende* Doc Savage Index" by Will Murray, in *Duende 2* (North Quincy, Massachusetts), 1977.

Manuscript Collection: University of Missouri, Columbia.

Critical Studies: *Doc Savage: His Apocalyptic Life* by Philip José Farmer, New York, Doubleday, 1973, revised edition, London, Panther, 1975; *The Man Behind Doc Savage* edited by Robert Weinberg, Chicago, Weinberg, 1974; *Doc Savage,* 1978, and *Secrets of Doc Savage,* 1981, both by Will Murray, Melrose, Massachusetts, Odyssey.

*   *   *

The contributors to the American pulp magazines were not concerned, by and large, with craft but with production. Except in the rare instance of a *Black Mask,* their editors did not pay well enough to insure quality and, as Raymond Chandler has pointed out elsewhere, they actively discouraged it. As a result, these writers either became word-production drudges or considered the pulps as a training ground for better fields. Despite their talent, many pulp authors were too long writing for these markets ever fully to escape them.

Lester Dent, who enjoys a curious dual reputation in the mystery field, falls into this latter category. Dent is best known for the nearly 200 Doc Savage pulp adventure novels which he wrote under the pseudonym Kenneth Robeson and for his unusual detectives—Click Rush, the Gadget Man; Lee Nace, the Blond Adder; and Foster Fade, the Crime Spectacularist— all of the Craig Kennedy type.

At the same time, Dent is considered to be one of the major exponents of the *Black Mask* school of detective fiction, despite the fact that he contributed only two stories, "Sail" and "Angelfish," to the magazine. While these are fine examples of that school's craftsmanship, they are grounded in the same themes which characterize his *Doc Savage* work. His protagonist, Oscar Sail, is a physically unusual investigator who exists apart from society and whose principal techniques involve violence and deception. The plots are largely treasure hunts in which the characters move at cross-purposes and no one is to be trusted.

Dent's later mystery novels are both extensions of his *Black Mask* work and reactions against the kind of fiction he had previously written, and they represent the by-products of the more sophisticated writing he was applying to *Doc Savage.* These are novels of intrigue and psychological interaction in which realistic characters and emotions dominate. Violence and mystery are subordinated to conflict and tension between individuals and their ambitions.

Dent is partial to protagonists who are larger than life. In his non-pulp work their greatness is bounded by their maturity and moral rectitude as measured against a real world, and not by their *physical* prowess. They are capable men who are drawn into conflict because their lives, friends, or positions in society are imperiled. Chance Malloy (*Dead at the Take-Off*) resorts to unsavory tactics only because his airline company has become the victim of such tactics. Mitchell Loneman (*Lady in Peril*) is a lobbyist for a food co-operative whose need to identify a killer stems from his desire to protect his wife and exonerate his employer. Women are often the focus of the conflict, the catalysts who themselves are transmuted (*Lady to Kill*).

Murder is incidental to Dent's plots and his formula treasure hunt is replaced by the hidden secret which murder conceals. The dead man and his killer are less crucial than the buried complexities of human failings and ambitions which threaten the characters in *Lady So Silent.* While the kidnapped child may be the focus of *Lady Afraid,* the deeper motives of the kidnapper are decidedly more significant. In *Cry at Dusk,* Johnny Marks's search for his uncle's killer is less important than his struggle against an evil which threatens to absorb him spiritually.

In spite of their skill and craft, Dent's novels are marred by a self-conscious stiffness indicative of a writer not fully at ease with his material and one who, in attempting to purge the stylistics of the pulp magazines from his prose, goes too far because their formula has become inextricable from his own style. Yet his less serious Doc Savage novels continue to enjoy a seemingly timeless acceptance, one auguring a kind of literary immortality.

—Will Murray

————

DENTINGER, Stephen. *See* **HOCH, Edward D.**

————

de PRE, Jean-Anne. *See* **AVALLONE, Michael.**

————

DERLETH, August (William). Also wrote as Stephen Grendon; Tally Mason. American. Born in Sauk City, Wisconsin, 24 February 1909. Educated at St. Aloysius School; Sauk City High School; University of Wisconsin, Madison, B.A. 1930. Married Sandra Winters in 1953 (divorced 1959); one daughter and one son. Editor, Fawcett Publications, Minneapolis, 1930–31; editor, *The Midwesterner,* Madison, 1931; Lecturer in American Regional Literature, University of Wisconsin, 1939–43. Owner and co-founder (with Donald Wandrei, 1939–42), Arkham House Publishers (including the imprints Mycroft and Moran, and Stanton and Lee), Sauk City, 1939–71. Editor, *Mind Magic,* 1931; literary editor and columnist, Madison *Capital Times,* 1941–71; editor, *The Arkham Sampler,* 1948–49, *Hawk and Whippoorwill,* 1960–63, and *The Arkham Collector,* 1967–71, all Sauk City. Recipient; Guggenheim fellowship, 1938; *Scholastic* award, 1958; Midland Authors award, for poetry, 1965; Ann Radcliffe award, 1967. *Died 4 July 1971.*

CRIME PUBLICATIONS

Novels (series: Judge Ephraim Peck; Solar Pons)

Murder Stalks the Wakely Family (Peck). New York, Loring and Mussey, 1934; as *Death Stalks the Wakely Family,* London, Newnes, 1937.
The Man on All Fours (Peck). New York, Loring and Mussey, 1934; London, Newnes, 1936.
Three Who Died (Peck). New York, Loring and Mussey, 1935.
Sign of Fear (Peck). New York, Loring and Mussey, 1935; London, Newnes, 1936.
Sentence Deferred (Peck). New York, Scribner, 1939; London, Heinemann, 1940.

The Narracong Riddle (Peck). New York, Scribner, 1940.
The Seven Who Waited (Peck). New York, Scribner, 1943; London, Muller, 1945.
Mischief in the Lane (Peck). New York, Scribner, 1944; London, Muller, 1948.
No Future for Luana (Peck). New York, Scribner, 1945; London, Muller, 1948.
Fell Purpose (Peck). New York, Arcadia House, 1953.
Death by Design. New York, Arcadia House, 1953.
Mr. Fairlie's Final Journey (Pons). Sauk City, Wisconsin, Mycroft and Moran, 1968.

Short Stories (series: Solar Pons)

"In Re: Sherlock Holmes"—The Adventure of Solar Pons. Sauk City, Wisconsin, Mycroft and Moran, 1945; as *Regarding Sherlock Holmes,* New York, Pinnacle, 1974; as *The Adventures of Solar Pons,* London, Robson, 1975.
The Memoirs of Solar Pons. Sauk City, Wisconsin, Mycroft and Moran, 1951.
Three Problems for Solar Pons. Sauk City, Wisconsin, Mycroft and Moran, 1952.
The Return of Solar Pons. Sauk City, Wisconsin, Mycroft and Moran, 1958.
The Reminiscences of Solar Pons. Sauk City, Wisconsin, Mycroft and Moran, 1961.
The Adventure of the Orient Express. New York, Candlelight Press, 1965; London, Panther, 1975.
The Casebook of Solar Pons. Sauk City, Wisconsin, Mycroft and Moran, 1965.
Praed Street Papers. New York, Candlelight Press, 1965.
The Adventure of the Unique Dickensians (Pons). Sauk City, Wisconsin, Mycroft and Moran, 1968.
A Praed Street Dossier. Sauk City, Wisconsin, Mycroft and Moran, 1968.
The Chronicles of Solar Pons. Sauk City, Wisconsin, Mycroft and Moran, 1973; London, Robson, 1975.

OTHER PUBLICATIONS

Novels

Still Is the Summer Night. New York, Scribner, 1937.
Wind over Wisconsin. New York, Scribner, 1938.
Restless Is the River. New York, Scribner, 1939.
Bright Journey. New York, Scribner, 1940.
Evening in Spring. New York, Scribner, 1941.
Sweet Genevieve. New York, Scribner, 1942.
Shadow of Night. New York, Scribner, 1943.
The Shield of the Valiant. New York, Scribner, 1945.
The Lurker at the Threshold, with H.P. Lovecraft. Sauk City, Wisconsin, Arkham House, 1945; London, Gollancz, 1948.
The House on the Mound. New York, Duell, 1958.
The Hills Stand Watch. New York, Duell, 1960.
The Trail of Cthulhu. Sauk City, Wisconsin, Arkham House, 1962; London, Spearman, 1974.
The Shadow in the Glass. New York, Duell, 1963.
The Wind Leans West. New York, Candlelight Press, 1969.

Short Stories

Place of Hawks. New York, Loring and Mussey, 1935.
Any Day Now. Chicago, Normandie House, 1938.
Country Growth. New York, Scribner, 1940.
Someone in the Dark. Sauk City, Wisconsin, Arkham House, 1941.

Something Near. Sauk City, Wisconsin, Arkham House, 1945.
Sac Prairie People. Sauk City, Wisconsin, Stanton and Lee, 1948.
Not Long for This World. Sauk City, Wisconsin, Arkham House, 1948.
The House of Moonlight. Iowa City, Prairie Press, 1953.
The Survivor and Others, with H.P. Lovecraft. Sauk City, Wisconsin, Arkham House, 1957.
The Mask of Cthulhu. Sauk City, Wisconsin, Arkham House, 1958; London, Consul, 1961.
Wisconsin in Their Bones. New York, Duell, 1961.
Lonesome Places. Sauk City, Wisconsin, Arkham House, 1962.
Mr. George and Other Odd Persons (as Stephen Grendon). Sauk City, Wisconsin, Arkham House, 1963; as *When Graveyards Yawn,* London, Tandem, 1965.
Colonel Markesan and Less Pleasant People, with Mark Schorer. Sauk City, Wisconsin, Arkham House, 1966.
The Shadow Out of Time and Other Tales of Horror, with H.P. Lovecraft. London, Gollancz, 1968; abridged edition, as *The Shuttered Room and Other Tales of Horror.* London, Panther, 1970.
A House above Cuzco. New York, Candlelight Press, 1969.
The Watchers Out of Time and Others, with H.P. Lovecraft. Sauk City, Wisconsin, Arkham House, 1974.
Harrigan's File. Sauk City, Wisconsin, Arkham House, 1975.
Dwellers in Darkness. Sauk City, Wisconsin, Arkham House, 1976.

Verse

To Remember, with *Salute Before Dawn,* by Albert Edward Clements. Hartland Four Corners, Vermont, Windsor, 1931.
Hawk on the Wind. Philadelphia, Ritten House, 1938.
Elegy: On a Flake of Snow. Muscatine, Iowa, Prairie Press, 1939.
Man Track Here. Philadelphia, Ritten House, 1939.
Here on a Darkling Plain. Philadelphia, Ritten House, 1941.
Wind in the Elms. Philadelphia, Ritten House, 1941.
Rind of Earth. Prairie City, Illinois, Decker Press, 1942.
Selected Poems. Prairie City, Illinois, Decker Press, 1944.
And You, Thoreau! New York, New Directions, 1944.
The Edge of Night. Prairie City, Illinois, Decker Press, 1945.
Habitant of Dusk: A Garland for Cassandra. Boston, Walden Press, 1946.
Rendezvous in a Landscape. New York, Fine Editions Press, 1952.
Psyche. Iowa City, Prairie Press, 1953.
Country Poems. Iowa City, Prairie Press 1956.
Elegy: On the Umbral Moon. Forest Park, Illinois, Acorn Press, 1957.
West of Morning. Francestown, New Hampshire, Golden Quill Press, 1960.
This Wound. Iowa City, Prairie Press, 1962.
Country Places. Iowa City, Prairie Press, 1965.
The Only Place We Live. Iowa City, Prairie Press, 1966.
By Owl Light. Iowa City, Prairie Press, 1967.
Collected Poems, 1937–1967. New York, Candlelight Press, 1967.
Caitlin. Iowa City, Prairie Press, 1969.
The Landscape of the Heart. Iowa City, Prairie Press, 1970.
Listening to the Wind. New York, Candlelight Press, 1971.
Last Light. New York, Candlelight Press, 1971.

Recordings: *Psyche: A Sequence of Love Lyrics,* Cuca, 1960; *Sugar Bush by Moonlight and Other Poems of Man and Nature,* Cuca, 1962; *Caitlin,* Cuca, 1971.

Other

The Heritage of Sauk City. Sauk City, Wisconsin, Pioneer Press, 1931.
Consider Your Verdict: Ten Coroner's Cases for You to Solve (as Tally Mason). New York, Stackpole, 1937.
Atmosphere of Houses. Muscatine, Iowa, Prairie Press, 1939.
Still Small Voice: The Biography of Zona Gale. New York, Appleton Century, 1940.
Village Year: A Sac Prairie Journal. New York, Coward McCann, 1941.
Wisconsin Regional Literature. Privately printed, 1941; revised edition, 1942.
The Wisconsin: River of a Thousand Isles. New York, Farrar and Rinehart, 1942.
H.P.L.: A Memoir (on H.P. Lovecraft). New York, Abramson, 1945.
Oliver, The Wayward Owl (for children). Sauk City, Wisconsin, Stanton and Lee, 1945.
Writing Fiction. Boston, The Writer, 1946.
Village Daybook: A Sac Prairie Journal. Chicago, Pellegrini and Cudahy, 1947.
A Boy's Way: Poems (for children). Sauk City, Wisconsin, Stanton and Lee, 1947.
Sauk County: A Centennial History. Baraboo, Wisconsin, Sauk County Centennial Committee, 1948.
It's a Boy's World: Poems (for children). Sauk City, Wisconsin, Stanton and Lee, 1948.
Wisconsin Earth: A Sac Prairie Sampler (selection). Sauk City, Wisconsin, Stanton and Lee, 1948.
The Milwaukee Road: Its First 100 Years. New York, Creative Age Press, 1948.
The Country of the Hawk (for children). New York, Aladdin, 1952.
The Captive Island (for children). New York, Aladdin, 1952.
Empire of Fur: Trading in the Lake Superior Region (for children). New York, Aladdin, 1953.
Land of Gray Gold: Lead Mining in Wisconsin (for children). New York, Aladdin, 1954.
Father Marquette and the Great Rivers (for children). New York, Farrar Straus, 1955; London, Burns and Oates, 1956.
Land of Sky-Blue Waters (for children). New York, Aladdin, 1955.
St. Ignatius and the Company of Jesus (for children). New York, Farrar Straus, and London, Burns and Oates, 1956.
Columbus and the New World (for children). New York, Farrar Straus, and London, Burns and Oates, 1957.
The Moon Tenders (for children). New York, Duell, 1958.
The Mill Creek Irregulars (for children). New York, Duell 1959.
Wilbur, The Trusting Whippoorwill (for children). Sauk City, Wisconsin, Stanton and Lee, 1959.
Arkham House: The First Twenty Years—1939–1959. Sauk City, Wisconsin, Arkham House, 1959.
Some Notes on H.P. Lovecraft. Sauk City, Wisconsin, Arkham House, 1959.
The Pinkertons Ride Again (for children). New York, Duell, 1960.
The Ghost of Black Hawk Island (for children). New York, Duell, 1961.
Walden West (autobiography). New York, Duell, 1961.
Sweet Land of Michigan (for children). New York, Duell, 1962.

Concord Rebel: A Life of Henry D. Thoreau. Philadelphia, Chilton, 1962.
Countryman's Journal. New York, Duell, 1963.
The Tent Show Summer (for children). New York, Duell, 1963.
Three Literary Men: A Memoir of Sinclair Lewis, Sherwood Anderson, Edgar Lee Masters. New York, Candlelight Press, 1963.
The Irregulars Strike Again (for children). New York, Duell, 1964.
Forest Orphans (for children). New York, Ernest, 1964; as *Mr. Conservation,* Park Falls, Wisconsin, MacGregor, 1971.
Wisconsin Country: A Sac Prairie Journal. New York, Candlelight Press, 1965.
The House by the River (for children). New York, Duell, 1965.
The Watcher on the Heights (for children). New York, Duell, 1966.
Wisconsin (for children). New York, Coward McCann, 1967.
The Beast in Holger's Woods (for children). New York, Crowell, 1968.
Vincennes: Portal to the West. Englewood Cliffs, New Jersey, Prentice Hall, 1968.
Walden Pond: Homage to Thoreau. Iowa City, Prairie Press, 1968.
Wisconsin Murders. Sauk City, Wisconsin, Mycroft and Moran, 1968.
The Wisconsin Valley New York, Teachers College Press, 1969.
Thirty Years of Arkham House: A History and a Bibliography 1939–1969. Sauk City, Wisconsin, Arkham House, 1970.
The Three Straw Men (for children). New York, Candlelight Press, 1970.
Return to Walden West. New York, Candlelight Press, 1970.
Love Letters to Caitlin. New York, Candlelight Press, 1971.
Emerson, Our Contemporary. New York, Crowell Collier, 1971.

Editor, with R.E. Larsson, *Poetry Out of Wisconsin.* New York, Harrison, 1937.
Editor, with Donald Wandrei, *The Outsider and Others,* by H.P. Lovecraft. Sauk City, Wisconsin, Arkham House, 1939.
Editor, with Donald Wandrei, *Beyond the Wall of Sleep,* by H.P. Lovecraft. Sauk City, Wisconsin, Arkham House, 1943.
Editor, with Donald Wandrei, *Marginalia,* by H.P. Lovecraft. Sauk City, Wisconsin, Arkham House, 1944.
Editor, *Sleep No More: Twenty Masterpieces of Horror for the Connoisseur.* New York, Farrar and Rinehart, 1944; abridged edition, London, Panther, 1964.
Editor, *The Best Supernatural Stories of H.P. Lovecraft.* Cleveland, World, 1945; revised edition, as *The Dunwich Horror and Others,* Sauk City, Wisconsin, Arkham House, 1963.
Editor, *Who Knocks? Twenty Masterpieces of the Spectral for the Connoisseur.* New York, Rinehart, 1946; abridged edition, London, Panther, 1964.
Editor, *The Night Side: Masterpieces of the Strange and Terrible.* New York, Rinehart, 1947; London, New English Library, 1966.
Editor, *The Sleeping and the Dead.* Chicago, Pellegrini and Cudahy, 1947; as *The Sleeping and the Dead* and *The Unquiet Grave,* London, New English Library, 2 vols., 1963–64.
Editor, *Dark of the Moon: Poems of Fantasy and the Macabre.* Sauk City, Wisconsin, Arkham House, 1947.
Editor, *Strange Ports of Call.* New York, Pellegrini and Cudahy, 1948.

Editor, *The Other Side of the Moon.*   New York, Pellegrini and Cudahy, 1949; abridged edition, London, Grayson, 1956.

Editor, *Something about Cats and Other Pieces,* by H.P. Lovecraft.   Sauk City, Wisconsin, Arkham House, 1949.

Editor, *Beyond Time and Space.*   New York, Pellegrini and Cudahy, 1950.

Editor, *Far Boundaries: 20 Science-Fiction Stories.*   New York, Pellegrini and Cudahy, 1951; London, Consul, 1965.

Editor, *The Outer Reaches: Favorite Science-Fiction Tales Chosen by Their Authors.*   New York, Pellegrini and Cudahy, 1951; as *The Outer Reaches* and *The Time of Infinity,* London, Consul, 2 vols., 1963.

Editor, *Beachheads in Space.*   New York, Pellegrini and Cudahy, 1952; London, Weidenfeld and Nicolson, 1954; abridged edition, as *From Other Worlds,* London, New English Library, 1964.

Editor, *Night's Yawning Peal: A Ghostly Company.*   Sauk City, Wisconsin, Arkham House, 1952; London, Consul, 1965.

Editor, *Worlds of Tomorrow: Science Fiction with a Difference.*   New York, Pellegrini and Cudahy, 1953; London, Weidenfeld and Nicolson, 1954; abridged edition as *New Worlds for Old,* London, New English Library, 1963.

Editor, *Time to Come: Science-Fiction Stories of Tomorrow.*   New York, Farrar Straus, 1954; London, Consul, 1963.

Editor, *Portals of Tomorrow: The Best Tales of Science Fiction and Other Fantasy.*   New York, Rinehart, 1954; London, Cassell, 1956.

Editor, *The Shuttered Room and Other Pieces by H.P. Lovecraft and Divers Hands.*   Sauk City, Wisconsin, Arkham House, 1959.

Editor, *Fire and Sleet and Candlelight: New Poems of the Macabre.*   Sauk City, Wisconsin, Arkham House, 1961.

Editor, *Dark Mind, Dark Heart.*   Sauk City, Wisconsin, Arkham House, 1962; London, Mayflower, 1963.

Editor, *When Evil Wakes: A New Anthology of the Macabre.*   London, Souvenir Press, 1963.

Editor, *Over the Edge.*   Sauk City, Wisconsin, Arkham House, 1964; London, Gollancz, 1967.

Editor, *At the Mountains of Madness and Other Novels,* by H.P. Lovecraft.   Sauk City, Wisconsin, Arkham House, 1964; London, Gollancz, 1966.

Editor, *Dagon and Other Macabre Tales,* by H.P. Lovecraft.   Sauk City, Wisconsin, Arkham House, 1965; London, Gollancz, 1967.

Editor, with Donald Wandrei (3 vols.) and James Turner (2 vols), *Selected Letters,* by H.P. Lovecraft.   Sauk City, Wisconsin, Arkham House, 5 vols., 1965–76.

Editor, *The Dark Brotherhood and Other Pieces,* by H.P. Lovecraft and others.   Sauk City, Wisconsin, Arkham House, 1966.

Editor, *A Wisconsin Harvest.*   Sauk City, Wisconsin, Stanton and Lee, 1966.

Editor, *Travellers by Night.*   Sauk City, Wisconsin, Arkham House, 1967.

Editor, *New Poetry Out of Wisconsin.*   Sauk City, Wisconsin, Stanton and Lee, 1969.

Editor, *Tales of the Cthulhu Mythos,* by H.P. Lovecraft and others.   Sauk City, Wisconsin, Arkham House, 1969.

Editor, *The Horror in the Museum and Other Revisions,* by H.P. Lovecraft.   Sauk City, Wisconsin, Arkham House, 1970; abridged edition, London, Panther, 1975.

Editor, *Dark Things.*   Sauk City, Wisconsin, Arkham House, 1971.

*

Bibliography: *100 Books by August Derleth,* Sauk City, Wisconsin, Arkham House, 1962; *August Derleth: A Bibliography* by Alison M. Wilson, Metuchen, New Jersey, Scarecrow Press, 1983.

Manuscript Collection: State Historical Society of Wisconsin Library, Madison.

*   *   *

On the dust jacket of his second novel, *The Man on All Fours,* August Derleth's publishers described him as "this astonishing young author." Throughout his life, Derleth continued to astonish publishers and readers alike with the volume and diversity of his writing. Among his more than 150 books are contemporary novels, historical novels, biographies, personal journals, compilations of nature observations, poetry, mystery fiction, true crime essays, macabre tales, science fiction, regional history, pastiches, and children's books. As an editor and publisher he was an active champion of weird and macabre fiction. He was almost single-handedly responsible for the preservation and popularization of the works by H.P. Lovecraft, and his Arkham House publishing firm issued the first books of such authors as Ray Bradbury, Fritz Leiber, and A.E. Van Vogt.

Derleth sold his first fiction, a weird story called "Bat's Belfry," when he was 15 years old. Weird fiction continued to occupy a large part of his attention. His stories in this vein were eventually collected in eleven volumes, from *Someone in the Dark* to the posthumously issued *Dwellers in Darkness.* The least effective of these stories are the ones written in imitation of Lovecraft; but others such as "Mrs. Manifold" and "The Lonesome Place," have a definite power to chill.

Derleth's contributions to mystery fiction began when he was 19 years old. He had read and re-read the Sherlock Holmes stories, and was finally impelled to write to Sir Arthur Conan Doyle to ask if there would ever be any more of them. Receiving a non-committal reply, he determined to fill the void himself. In the autumn of 1928 he wrote "The Adventure of the Black Narcissus," the first of some 70 stories featuring Solar Pons of 7B Praed Street London, and his companion Dr. Lyndon Parker. In the words of Vincent Starrett, "Solar Pons is—as it were—an ectoplasmic emanation of his great prototype, and his adventures are pure pastiche.. . . He is.. .a clever impersonator, with a twinkle in his eye, which tells us that he is not Sherlock Holmes, and knows that *we* know it, but that he hopes we will like him anyway for what he symbolizes." This hope was certainly fulfilled. The appearance of that first story in the February 1929 issue of *The Dragnet* magazine led eventually to the publication of six volumes of stories (a pastiche not only of the Holmes character but of the Holmesian canon as whole), one novel, and a volume of miscellaneous commentary. It also inspired the formation of an organization called The Praed Street Irregulars, in imitation of The Baker Street Irregulars, and the publication of a journal *The Pontine Dossier.* As might be expected in so extended a series, the Pons stories are variable in quality and in their effectiveness as echoes of the original model; but the average is high, as exemplified in such stories as "The Adventure of the Norcross Riddle," "The Adventure of the Remarkable Worm," and "The Adventure of the Unique Dickensians."

Derleth's most ambitious literary creation was his Sac Prairie Saga, a multivolume project designed to portray life in the fictional Sac Prairie (based on the Sauk City-Prairie du Sac region of Wisconsin where Derleth was born and spent most of his life) from the early nineteenth century up to the present day. In addition to its more serious uses in the furtherance of his

Saga, Derleth employed Sac Prairie as the setting for his series of ten detective novels featuring Judge Ephraim Peabody Peck. The Judge, a shrewd, elderly small-town lawyer, was introduced in *Murder Stalks the Wakely Family,* followed in the same year by *The Man on All Fours.* The latter book is typical of the early Judge Peck novels; it has all the trappings of the formal puzzle novel, with floor plans, an annotated list of characters, a plot centering around multiple murders in an isolated country house, and the John Dickson Carr-like touch of a mysterious bare-footed figure who prowls the house and environs on all fours. Later in the series, Derleth changed from third person to first person narration, telling the stories through the medium of a smart-talking young assistant to the Judge. The change of tone jarred against the leisurely pace and rural setting. And a narrator who could accost a female witness (in *Mischief in the Lane*) with the words "Come on, Mouse eyes, out with it!" wore out his welcome rapidly. By the author's own admission, the Judge Peck books were written in 10 days each. The consequent lack of polish and the internal inconsistencies are regrettable, but the generally clever plots and the well-realized small-town setting and incidental characters make the books worth sampling. Sac Prairie is also the setting for a series of "junior mysteries" featuring a pair of teen-age detectives, Steve Grendon and Sim Jones.

Not part of a series, though similar in its characters and small-town setting to the Judge Peck books, was *Consider Your Verdict: Ten Coroner's Cases for You to Solve.* This was a collection of ten short murder mysteries, each in the form of the transcript of a coroner's inquest. In each case, a particular misstatement by one of the witnesses pointed the way to the solution of the crime, and the reader was invited to identify the crucial bit of testimony. In fact, the book's introduction suggested that it could be used as the basis of a parlor game. The solutions were given in a sealed section at the end of the book.

—R.E. Briney

DEVINE, Dominic. *See* **DEVINE, D.M.**

DEWEY, Thomas B(lanchard). Also wrote as Tom Brandt; Cord Wainer. American. Born in Elkhart, Indiana, 6 March 1915. Educated at Kansas State Teachers College, Emporia, B.S. 1936; University of Iowa, Iowa City, 1937–38; University of California, Los Angeles, Ph.D. 1973. Married Maxine Morley Sorensen (second wife) in 1951; 3) Doris L. Smith in 1972; two children by first marriage. Clerical worker, Harding Market Company, Chicago, 1936–37; editor, Storycraft Inc., correspondence school, Hollywood, 1938–42; administrative and editorial assistant, Department of State, Washington, D.C., 1942–45; worked in advertising, Los Angeles, 1945–52. Self-employed writer, 1952–71, and from 1977. Assistant Professor of English, Arizona State University, Tempe, 1971–77. *Died.*

Crime Publications

Novels (series: Singer Batts; Mac; Pete Schofield)

Hue and Cry (Batts). New York, Jefferson House, 1944; as *The Murder of Marion Mason,* London, Dakers, 1951; as *Room for Murder,* New York, New American Library, 1950.
As Good as Dead (Batts). New York, Jefferson House, 1946; London, Dakers, 1952.
Draw the Curtain Close (Mac). New York, Jefferson House, 1947; London, Dakers, 1951; as *Dame in Danger,* New York, New American Library, 1958.
Mourning After (Batts). New York, Mill, 1950; London, Dakers, 1953.
Handle with Fear (Batts). New York, Mill, 1951; London, Dakers, 1955.
Every Bet's a Sure Thing (Mac). New York, Simon and Schuster, and London, Dakers, 1953.
Kiss Me Hard (as Tom Brandt). New York, Popular Library, 1954.
Run, Brother, Run! (as Tom Brandt). New York, Popular Library, 1954; London, Consul, 1961.
Prey for Me (Mac). New York, Simon and Schuster, and London, Boardman, 1954; as *The Case of the Murdered Model,* New York, Avon, 1955.
The Mean Streets (Mac). New York, Simon and Schuster, and London, Boardman, 1955.
The Brave, Bad Girls (Mac). New York, Simon and Schuster, 1956; London, Boardman, 1957.
My Love Is Violent. New York, Popular Library, 1956; London, Consul, 1961.
And Where She Stops (Schofield). New York, Popular Library, 1957; as *I.O.U. Murder,* London, Boardman, 1958.
You've Got Him Cold (Mac). New York, Simon and Schuster, 1958; London, Boardman, 1959.
The Case of the Chased and the Unchaste (Mac). New York, Random House, 1959; London, Boardman, 1960.
Go to Sleep Jeannie (Schofield). New York, Popular Library, 1959; London, Boardman, 1960.
The Girl Who Wasn't There (Mac). New York, Simon and Schuster, and London, Boardman, 1960; as *The Girl Who Never Was,* New York, Mayflower, 1962.
Too Hot for Hawaii (Schofield). New York, Popular Library, 1960; London, Boardman, 1963.
The Golden Hooligan (Schofield). New York, Dell, 1961; as *Mexican Slayride,* London, Boardman, 1961.
Hunter at Large. New York, Simon and Schuster, 1961; London, Boardman, 1962.
Go, Honeylou (Schofield). New York, Dell, and London, Boardman, 1962.
How Hard to Kill (Mac). New York, Simon and Schuster, 1962; London, Boardman, 1963.
The Girl with the Sweet Plump Knees (Schofield). New York, Dell, and London, Boardman, 1963.
A Sad Song Singing (Mac). New York, Simon and Schuster, 1963; London, Boardman, 1964.
Don't Cry for Long (Mac). New York, Simon and Schuster, 1964; London, Boardman, 1965.
The Girl in the Punchbowl (Schofield). New York, Dell, 1964; and London, Boardman, 1965.
Only on Tuesdays (Schofield). New York, Dell, and London, Boardman, 1964.
Nude in Nevada (Schofield). New York, Dell, 1965; and London, Boardman, 1966.
Can a Mermaid Kill? New York, Tower, 1965.
Portrait of a Dead Heiress (Mac). New York, Simon and Schuster, 1965; London, Boardman, 1966.

Deadline (Mac). New York, Simon and Schuster, 1966; London, Boardman, 1967.
A Season for Violence. New York, Fawcett, 1966.
Death and Taxes (Mac). New York, Putnam, 1967; London, Hale, 1969.
The King-Killers (Mac). New York, Putnam, 1968; as *Death Turns Right,* London, Hale, 1969.
The Love-Death Thing (Mac). New York, Simon and Schuster, 1969.
The Taurus Trip (Mac). New York, Simon and Schuster, 1970.

Uncollected Short Stories

"Thorn in the Flesh," in *Cosmopolitan* (New York), January 1953.
"Never Send to Know," in *Ellery Queen's Mystery Magazine* (New York), January 1965.
"The Prevalence of Monsters," in *Ellery Queen's Mystery Magazine* (New York), April 1965.
"The Big Job," in *Best Detective Stories of the Year,* edited by Anthony Boucher. New York, Dutton, and London, Boardman, 1966.
"Lucien's Nose," in *Ellery Queen's Mystery Magazine* (New York), July 1966.

OTHER PUBLICATIONS

Novel

Mountain Girl (as Cord Wainer). New York, Fawcett, 1953.

Other

What Women Want to Know, with Harold M. Imerman. New York, Crown, 1958; London, Hammond, 1960.

Editor, *Sleuths and Consequences.* New York, Simon and Schuster, 1966.

*

Manuscript Collection: Mugar Memorial Library, Boston University.

* * *

Thomas B. Dewey was a prolific writer of crime fiction. He wrote about a troubled but honest District Attorney (in *A Season for Violence*), an avenging cop whose wife was killed by mistake (*Hunter at Large*), and a Los Angeles private eye named Pete Schofield, whose chief distinction among such characters is that he is married. But Dewey wrote most often and most successfully about a Chicago private detective whose first and last names are a carefully guarded secret; he is known always only as "Mac."

Mac is very much in the Sam Spade/Philip Marlowe/Lew Archer tradition of private eyes. He is always, if sometimes reluctantly, on the side of the underdog; he tells his own stories, and he seems to have no life apart from his activities as a detective; he lives alone, and his existence is spartan; he is tough, but partial to children; gorgeous women throw themselves, or are thrown, into his path, but with rare exceptions he is chaste; and he always solves his cases before the police do. Mac differs from the other famous detectives of his type in a few ways. For one thing, until late in his career, when he goes to Los Angeles, he operates in Chicago, and while the novels in which he appears are not burdened with local color, he is more likely to encounter gangsters of the old school than are the West Coast operatives. For another, Mac almost always works with a veteran police officer named Donovan, who had trained him as a cop and who either helps him with cases or pushes him into situations which policemen are supposed to avoid; Donovan is always a somewhat shadowy, if bulky, figure, since we see him only in his official role. The other variant on the standard pattern is that Mac is ageless; he was still the same robust man in early middle age in 1970 that he had been in his earliest appearances in the early 1950's.

In his typical cases, Mac is approached by an old friend, or a friend of a friend, who has run afoul of the law. There is almost always, early in the novel, a murder; Mac's client is either a suspect, in which case Mac's job is to solve the puzzle and get the client off the hook, or the client becomes the victim, and Mac's job is to ease his conscience by tracking down the killer. At least twice during the course of the action, Mac will find himself isolated with one or two tough opponents, usually gangsters and usually armed when he is not; although he occasionally loses the first fight, Mac usually wins, and he always wins the last fight. Apart from these encounters, Dewey's novels are not particularly gruesome or violent, and there are seldom spectacular death scenes. The cases with which Mac becomes involved often include kidnapped children or adolescent girls; the latter are in some way lost and helpless, but they never prove to be criminals and they almost always find reasonably happy endings. None of the kidnapped children is ever seriously harmed. In the end, Mac sorts out the clues and, with the help of Donovan, apprehends the culprits.

Dewey's novels combine the classic private-eye pattern with the equally classic mystery pattern. During the course of his narration, Mac provides the reader with the clues which, if put together properly, will point to the criminal. Properly, such clues are not highlighted when they are first presented, but they do afford the reader the opportunity to solve the mystery before it is explained to him. Fortunately, the solution is seldom given away early in the novel.

Dewey's novels are interesting and successful, and Mac is a memorable private eye, even if he too often exemplifies the "White Knight" referred to in several of these stories. Dewey is less tough than Hammett, and his stories lack both the pungent local color which makes Chandler's and Ross Macdonald's novels distinctive and the moral ambiguity which tantalizes Philip Marlowe and Lew Archer. But Dewey belongs at the head of the second rank of the hard-boiled writers.

—John M. Muste

DEWHURST, Eileen (Mary). British. Born in Liverpool, Merseyside, 27 May 1929. Educated at Huyton College for Girls, Liverpool, 1937–47; St. Anne's College, Oxford, 1948–51, B.A. (honours) in English, 1951, M.A. 1956. Held various administrative posts in London and Liverpool universities and Liverpool Chamber of Commerce, 1953–64; freelance journalist, 1964–80; official guide to the Lady Lever Art Collection, Port Sunlight, 1976–82. Agent: Gregory and Radice, Riverside Studios, Crisp Road, London W6 9RL. Address: 4 The Garth, Waterford Road, Oxton, Birkenhead, Wirral L43 6US, England.

CRIME PUBLICATIONS

Novels (series: Detective Inspector Neil Carter; Helen Markam/Johnson)

Death Came Smiling. London, Hale, 1975; Boston, G.K. Hall, 1989.
After the Ball. London, Macmillan, 1976; Boston, G.K. Hall, 1989.
Curtain Fall (Carter). London, Macmillan, 1977; New York, Doubleday, 1982.
Drink This (Carter). London, Collins, 1980; New York, Doubleday, 1981.
Trio in Three Flats (Carter). London, Collins, and New York, Doubleday, 1981.
Whoever I Am (Johnson). London, Collins, 1982; New York, Doubleday, 1983.
The House That Jack Built. London, Collins, 1983; New York, Doubleday, 1984.
There Was a Little Girl (Carter). London, Collins, 1984; New York, Doubleday, 1986.
Playing Safe (Johnson). London, Collins, 1985; New York, Doubleday, 1987.
A Private Prosecution. London, Collins, 1986; New York, Doubleday, 1987.
A Nice Little Business (Carter). New York, Doubleday, 1987; London, Piatkus, 1990.
The Sleeper. London, Collins, and New York, Doubleday, 1988.
Dear Mr. Right. New York, Doubleday, 1990; London, Piatkus, 1991.

*

Manuscript Collection: Mugar Memorial Library, Boston University.

Eileen Dewhurst comments:

Most of my books are murder mysteries, but I have written three suspense novels and one (*The Sleeper*) experimentally combining the genres. My prime interest is in reactions and relationships under stress in everyday life—out of which the frightening and the dangerous can arise with peculiar shock.

* * *

Questions of identity lie at the heart of Eileen Dewhurst's work. Impersonation and disguise are recurrent elements in her novels and in both *A Private Prosecution* and *A Nice Little Business* transvestism is essential to the story-line. Given that her characters are seldom as they seem, it is hardly surprising that her two most memorable heroines, Helen Markam/Johnson and Susan Halliday, are actresses and that several of her books are set in the shadowy world of espionage.

Dewhurst's first book, *Death Came Smiling,* gives an early hint at her preoccupation with the nature of personality: it is the story of identical twin sisters, one of whom investigates the murder of the other. In *After The Ball* a naive teenage girl who witnesses a violent killing is persuaded to preserve her own safety by assuming a new identity. There is a puzzle, but it is of secondary importance and easily solved; Dewhurst's main concern is to describe how Angela Canford starts to learn about life while pretending to be Caroline Thompson.

In the later novels, Dewhurst's powerful imagination is more evident. An intriguing idea is the starting point of almost every book. *There Was a Little Girl* begins with the murder of the daughter of the principal of an adult education college, a girl

who has been leading a double life as a prostitute. *The Sleeper* offers a bold combination of spy story and classic closed-circle detective mystery. *Playing Safe* opens brilliantly with an account of the early responses to Helen Johnson's advertisement of her acting skills—she offers to play the part of a wife, girlfriend, mother or aunt to fit all manner of tricky social situations. The early promise of these stories is not, however, always fulfilled, for the plot development is at times implausible. *Playing Safe,* for instance, falters once Helen (who also appears in the earlier, appropriately titled *Whoever I Am* and is now married to an official in British Intelligence) takes up the role of a simple-minded girl who is a patient in an Anglo-Soviet psychiatric hospital for captured Western scientists.

More consistently effective is *The House That Jack Built,* the story of Susan Halliday, who was "born" into a long-running television serial (which Dewhurst cleverly sets 20 years in the past) and who has spent all her 16 years in the cast. A bizarre sequence of parallels between accidents to the soap opera characters and accidents in real life to the people who play them culminates in murder. The strength of the book lies not only in the well-researched television background, but also in Dewhurst's skilful manipulation of a least-likely-culprit plot.

Neil Carter of the Metropolitan Police appears in five novels. He is a subsidiary character in *Curtain Fall,* but thereafter takes centre stage. Carter becomes an increasingly sympathetic character as time goes on and the books chart the progress of his relationship with Cathy McVeigh, whom he marries in *There Was a Little Girl.* In *A Nice Little Business* Cathy, now pregnant, is a possible suspect when she finds the murdered body of her dressmaker. This latest story in the series is well told in Dewhurst's admirably crisp, unfussy style, but Neil's behaviour—he assaults a fellow policeman, interferes with a crucial piece of evidence, and spends much of his time whilst on disciplinary suspension dressed as a woman and covertly conducting his own inquiry into the crime—would have Gideon of the Yard turning in his grave.

Dewhurst's finest novel is *A Private Prosecution,* which introduces Detective Chief Superintendent Maurice Kendrick. His hunt for a serial killer in a quiet seaside town runs in tandem with the unofficial investigation being carried on by his friend Humphrey Barnes, who knows the family of one of the victims. One of the major plot twists anticipates a similar development in P.D. James's celebrated *Devices And Desires.* This book, like much of Dewhurst's uneven but often thought-provoking work, deserves to be better known.

—Martin Edwards

DEXTER, (Norman) Colin. British. Born in Stamford, Lincolnshire, 29 September 1930. Educated at Stamford School, 1940–48; Christ's College, Cambridge, 1950–54, B.A. in classics 1953, M.A. 1958. Served in the Royal Corps of Signals, 1948–50. Married Dorothy Cooper in 1956; one daughter and one son. Assistant classics master, Wyggeston School, Leicester, 1954–57, and Loughborough Grammar School, 1957–59; senior classics master, Corby Grammar School, Northamptonshire, 1959–66. Assistant Secretary, 1966–78, and Senior Assistant Secretary, 1978–87 Oxford Local Examinations Board. Former national champion, Ximenes and Azed crossword competitions. Recipient: Crime Writers Association Silver Dagger award, 1979, 1981; Gold Dagger award, 1989; M.A.: Oxford University, 1966. Address: 456 Banbury Road, Oxford OX2 7RG, England.

CRIME PUBLICATIONS

Novels (series: Inspector Morse in all books)

Last Bus to Woodstock. London, Macmillan, and New York, St. Martin's Press, 1975.
Last Seen Wearing. London, Macmillan, and New York, St. Martin's Press, 1976.
The Silent World of Nicholas Quinn. London, Macmillan, and New York, St. Martin's Press, 1977.
Service of All the Dead. London, Macmillan, 1979; New York, St. Martin's Press, 1980.
The Dead of Jericho. London, Macmillan, and New York, St. Martin's Press, 1981.
The Riddle of the Third Mile. London, Macmillan, 1983.
The Secret of Annexe 3. London, Macmillan, 1986; New York, St. Martin's Press, 1987.
The Wench Is Dead. London, Macmillan, 1989; New York, St. Martin's Press, 1990.

Uncollected Short Stories

"Evans Tries an O Level," in *Winter's Crimes 9,* edited by George Hardinge. London, Macmillan, and New York, St. Martin's Press, 1978.
"At the Lulu Bar Motel," in *Winter's Crimes 13,* edited by George Hardinge. London, Macmillan, 1981; New York, St. Martin's Press, 1982.
"Morse's Greatest Mystery," in *T.V. Times* (London), 19 December 1987.
"A Case of Mis-identity," in *Winter's Crimes 21,* edited by Hilary Hale, London, Macmillan, 1989.

OTHER PUBLICATIONS as N.C. Dexter

Liberal Studies: An Outline Course 1–2, with E.G. Rayner. Oxford, Pergamon Press, and New York, Macmillan, 2 vols., 1964.
Guide to Contemporary Politics, with E.G. Rayner. Oxford, Pergamon Press, 1966.

*

Colin Dexter comments:
  If, like Gaul, the area of Crime Writing can be divided into three parts, we may distinguish the "why-," the "how-," and the "who-dunnit." If the first of these divisions is characterized by the exploration of the criminal mentality, and the second by the faithful description of police procedure—the third is characterized by what may be termed (though it sounds a bit posh) the exploitation of reader-mystification. My books come under this third category, since each of them is a puzzle, with many a twist and many a turn, as well as (I would love to believe this!) one almighty wallop of a surprise at the end. According to friendly reviewers, my plots are (variously) "labyrinthine," "craftily spun as spider-webs," "byzantine" (I like that word); in the eyes of less generous souls, the sequence of events is sometimes improbably convoluted and preternaturally coincidental. My English style *ought* to be adequate, both because in my youth I studied the Classics, and (more importantly) because I have tried so very hard (as one must always do) to make the pages easy reading. The very first review I read (by Edmund Crispin) spoke of my "mandarin" style, and I am still pretending that this fine word was meant to be complimentary.

It was certainly better than the first three words of a review of my third book (from *The Times*): "Alas, the style. . . ." (I read no further.) I am lucky that I live in Oxford, in which city all my books are set. It is place that many know, or at least would like to know; and I take much pleasure in describing it. Would Rotherham (for all I know, a splendid town) have made as suitable a stage for Morse and the murders he is sent to solve? I doubt it. I myself do not measure up to the requisite height for the police force; I am neither mean with money nor too readily irascible; I am not a man of alpha-plus acumen. In most respects, therefore, Inspector Morse is quite unlike his creator, except (and it is a very big except) in his love of crossword puzzles, Wagner, and A.E. Housman.

* * *

Colin Dexter arrived comparatively late at crime writing—his first novel was published when he was in his mid 40's. However he has established himself in the forefront of British writers with some of the cleverest and most complicated plots, delighting a vast and ever growing band of devoted readers.

Dexter has two police detectives, Inspector Morse and Sergeant Lewis, who appear in all the stories and it is the relationship between the two men that is of as much interest as the puzzle element. Morse (we never get to find out his first name) is a Wagnerian, a bachelor, and lover of fine beers. He is every bit as human and prone to the usual frailties as the rest of us and not infrequently can be irascible towards those that deserve it least. Sergeant Lewis, on the other hand, is a perfect foil for Morse, being married with children and the associated responsibilities (and drawbacks for a policeman) of being expected for meals at home at certain times of the day. Whilst Morse can be up and running on a course which will prove to be a dead end, Lewis can be putting in essential hours of background work.

Much of the delight in Dexter's work is the inevitable rug-pulling exercise that the author perpetrates. The reader will have been led by the nose into thinking that one particular character is the culprit; all the facts and clues point to one person, the net closes and hey presto!, the author provides a neat little dog-leg in plotting and away we go again in search of the real murderer.

The characters in the books are all realistically drawn and many of the men are apt to be less than faithful to their wives and partners. The Oxford settings are imbued with the sound of the illicit rustling of bedsheets and whispered love-making in cars down country lanes or pub carparks. Invariably there is one character who needs to maintain an alibi for other reasons than the murder and who tends to muddy the investigative waters.

"Everything fits, you see, once you turn the pattern upside down" is Morse's motto, an adherence to lateral thinking which is essential for the solution of the puzzle. Even so, Morse often finds himself barking up the wrong tree and will have perforce to retreat to his beloved Wagner or a couple of pints of Morrell's bitter to take stock.

Dexter's novels have won Crime Writers awards (Silver Daggers for *Service of All the Dead* and *The Dead of Jericho* and a Gold Dagger for *The Wench Is Dead*) and rightly so. His eight works to date rank among the best in "puzzle" crime novels of the genre, a task that seems to be second nature to an author who takes delight in solving and setting some of the most difficult crosswords in the British Press.

The Wench is Dead finds Morse back in the local hospital with a stomach ulcer, twiddling his thumbs and bored out of his mind. Salvation comes in the form of a booklet produced by a local historian outlining the murder of a young woman on the Oxford canal some 130 years before. Morse is sure that the men apprehended for her murder were innocent and from his hospital bed begins an investigation into the case. This kind of plot has been tackled before, most notably in Josephine Tey's *The Daughter of Time.* While there may be a couple of happenstances and coincidences that facilitate the investigation, Morse's discovery of the real culprit is a *coup de théâtre* and no-one should be allowed to peek at the last page!

The Silent World of Nicholas Quinn is perhaps Dexter's most successful novel for its labyrinthine plot, its sense of fun, and especially for the stunning ending which leaves the reader kicking oneself for not having spotted the fairly placed clues.

—Ralph Spurrier

DIBDIN, Michael. British. Born in Wolverhampton, Staffordshire, 21 March 1947. Educated at Friends' School, Lisburn, County Antrim, Northern Ireland, 1957–65; University of Sussex, Brighton, B.A. in English literature, 1968; University of Alberta Edmonton, M.A. in English literature, 1969. Married 1) Benita Mitbrodt in 1971 (dissolved 1979), one daughter; 2) Sybil Sheringham in 1986, one daughter. Had a variety of jobs in Western Canada, 1969–75; English teacher, International House, Perugia, Italy, 1980–82; language assistant, University of Perugia, 1982–84. Recipient: Crime Writers Association Gold Dagger award, 1988. Agent: Pat Kavanagh, Peters Fraser and Dunlop Group Ltd., 5th Floor. The Chambers, Chelsea Harbour, Lots Road, London SW10 OXF, England.

CRIME PUBLICATIONS

Novels (series: Aurelio Zen)

The Last Sherlock Holmes Story. London, Cape, and New York, Pantheon, 1978.
A Rich Full Death. London, Cape, 1986.
Ratking (Zen). London, Faber, 1988; New York, Bantam, 1989.
The Tryst. London, Faber, 1989; New York, Summit, 1990.
Vendetta (Zen). London, Faber, 1990.

*

Michael Dibdin comments:

My first two novels were Victorian pastiches, the first bringing together the fictional Sherlock Holmes and the factual Jack the Ripper, the second casting Robert Browning, the poet, in the role of amateur detective in Florence. Those were followed by *Ratking,* a police detective story set in contemporary Italy, which has since spawned a series with the character Aurelio Zen in an attempt to illuminate different aspects of Italy and Italian society. Between these I have written more loosely-defined crime-related novels such as *The Tryst* and *Fatalities* (forthcoming) set in modern Britain, in which the crime element is emblematic of large social and historical forces.

*　　*　　*

Michael Dibdin's career as a writer of crime fiction has been short, but the range and diversity of the five novels he has so far produced suggest both substantial achievement and great promise. His first two novels, *The Last Sherlock Holmes Story* and *A Rich Full Death* are highly entertaining and stylish exercises in historical pastiche. The former involves a dramatic showdown between Holmes and Moriarty, heightened by deftly handled Freudian psychological innuendo, and very atmospherically narrated by the dogged, confused Watson. It ends with a splendid twist, and even if it proves not to be the very final appearance by the great sleuth, it is an excellent, knowing postscript to his brilliant career. The ambience of gaslit London is finely evoked in that novel, and in Dibdin's second book, similar attention is given to the atmosphere of Victorian Florence. In this witty and highly readable novel, an awestruck American gets all too willingly involved in shenanigans surrounding multiple murder, spiritualism, Dante's *Inferno* and both Robert and Elizabeth Barrett Browning. His acquaintance with the great poet turns out to be rather more eventful than expected, and once again, there is a startling and provocatively ambiguous twist at the end.

These two novels represent a very promising beginning, but it is Dibdin's third book, *Ratking,* which marks him out as special. Winner of the Crime Writer's Association Golden Dagger for 1988, it is a highly intelligent and elaborate tale, distinguished by real feeling for its Italian location, genuine narrative drive, and the introduction of an excellent new character, Police Commissioner Aurelio Zen. In a complex plot involving civic corruption, kidnapping, and a network of contending ambitions, Zen has to search for the truth through a maze of confusions. With something of the subtlety of Leonardo Sciascia, Dibdin exploits the forensic investigation to construct an ironic vision of a society beset by internal tensions. Without seeming pretentious, the book moves beyond the generic conventions of crime fiction to create a broad and stimulating social analysis, and in the quizzical, all too human figure of Zen, Dibdin has produced an image of both the strengths and weaknesses of the human spirit.

Dibdin's next novel, *The Tryst,* represents yet another impressive departure. In the manner of Patricia Highsmith or Ruth Rendell (especially in her Barbara Vine identity), it is a fable of everyday obsessions and mundane madness, where different stories are inexorably drawn together to an explosive climax. It deals with the entanglement of a female psychiatrist, trapped in an unsatisfactory marriage, with one of her clients, a deeply disturbed boy whose attachment to her is closer than she realises at first. Through a series of intertwining plots, the book takes the powerful themes of betrayal, complicity and delusion, heightens them with the drama of crime fiction, and produces a sinister and menacing narrative which ends with an absorbing sense of mystery and nemesis. Although more a study of character and fate than an orthodox crime novel, *The Tryst* is a most rewarding venture, taking some of the features of the psychological mystery and moving them towards the more enigmatic mainstream novel.

Most recently, Dibdin has returned to the figure of Aurelio Zen, and produced another Italian novel, *Vendetta.* At first, the book offers an intriguing variation on the "locked room" mystery, with a wealthy business man meeting his death in the top-security haven he has built for himself in Sardinia. Zen's investigation takes in terrorism, corruption, and violence, but despite the personal danger and his moments of doubt, he carries on fastidiously towards some vision of the truth. It is to be hoped that Dibdin continues his association with the Italian Police Commissioner, but it is also to be hoped that he maintains his willingness to experiment. He is such a good writer, so careful and precise in his prose, that each new novel from him will remain something to look forward to. Clearly, Dibdin has quickly become a major figure in contemporary British crime writing.

—Ian A. Bell

* * *

DICKINSON, Peter (Malcolm de Brissac). British. Born in Livingstone, Zambia, 16 December 1927. Educated at Eton College (King's Scholar), 1941–46; King's College, Cambridge (exhibitioner), B.A. in English 1951. Served in the British Army, 1946–48. Married Mary Rose Barnard in 1953; two daughters and two sons. Assistant editor and reviewer, *Punch,* London, 1952–69. Chairman of the Management Committee, Society of Authors, 1978–80. Recipient: Crime Writers Association Gold Dagger award, 1968, 1969; *Guardian* award, 1977; Boston *Globe-Horn Book* award, for non-fiction, 1977; Whitbread award, 1979; Library Association Carnegie Medal, 1980, 1981. Agent: A.P. Watt Ltd., 20 John Street, London, WC1N 2DR. Address: Bramdean Lodge, Near Alresford, Hampshire SO24 0JN, England.

CRIME PUBLICATIONS

Novels (series: Superintendent James Pibble)

Skin Deep (Pibble). London, Hodder and Stoughton, 1968; as *The Glass-Sided Ants' Nest,* New York, Harper, 1968.
A Pride of Heroes (Pibble). London, Hodder and Stoughton, 1969; as *The Old English Peep Show,* New York, Harper, 1969.
The Seals (Pibble). London, Hodder and Stoughton, 1970; as *The Sinful Stones,* New York, Harper, 1970.
Sleep and His Brother (Pibble). London, Hodder and Stoughton, and New York, Harper, 1971.
The Lizard in the Cup (Pibble). London, Hodder and Stoughton, and New York, Harper, 1972.
The Green Gene. London, Hodder and Stoughton, and New York, Pantheon, 1973.
The Poison Oracle. London, Hodder and Stoughton, and New York, Pantheon, 1974.
The Lively Dead. London, Hodder and Stoughton, and New York, Pantheon, 1975.
King and Joker. London, Hodder and Stoughton, and New York, Pantheon, 1976.
Walking Dead. London, Hodder and Stoughton, 1977; New York, Pantheon, 1978.
One Foot in the Grave (Pibble). London, Hodder and Stoughton, 1979; New York, Pantheon, 1980.
A Summer in the Twenties. London, Hodder and Stoughton, and New York, Pantheon, 1981.
The Last House-Party. London, Bodley Head, and New York, Pantheon, 1982.
Hindsight. London, Bodley Head, and New York, Pantheon, 1983.
Death of a Unicorn. London, Bodley Head, and New York, Pantheon, 1984.
Tefuga. London, Bodley Head, and New York, Pantheon, 1986.
Perfect Gallows. London, Bodley Head, and New York, Pantheon, 1988.

Skeleton-in-Waiting. London, Bodley Head, 1989; New York, Pantheon, 1990.

Uncollected Short Story

"Who Killed the Cat?" in *Verdict of Thirteen,* edited by Julian Symons. London, Faber, and New York, Harper, 1979.

OTHER PUBLICATIONS (for children)

Fiction

The Changes. London, Gollancz, 1975.
    The Weathermonger. London, Gollancz, 1968; Boston, Little Brown, 1969.
    Heartsease. London, Gollancz, and Boston, Little Brown, 1969.
    The Devil's Children. London, Gollancz, and Boston, Little Brown, 1970.
Emma Tupper's Diary. London, Gollancz, and Boston, Little Brown, 1971.
The Dancing Bear. London, Gollancz, 1972; Boston, Little Brown, 1973.
The Iron Lion. Boston, Little Brown, 1972; London, Allen and Unwin, 1973.
The Gift. London, Gollancz, 1973; Boston, Little Brown, 1974.
The Blue Hawk. London, Gollancz, and Boston, Little Brown, 1976.
Annerton Pit. London, Gollancz, and Boston, Little Brown, 1977.
Hepzibah. Twickenham, Middlesex, Eel Pie, 1978; Boston, Godine, 1980.
Tulku. London, Gollancz, and New York, Dutton, 1979.
The Seventh Raven. London, Gollancz, and New York, Dutton, 1981.
Healer. London, Gollancz, 1983; New York, Delacorte Press, 1985.
Giant Cold. London, Gollancz, and New York, Dutton, 1984.
A Box of Nothing. London, Gollancz, 1985; New York, Delacorte Press, 1987.
Mole Hole. London, Blackie, and New York, Bedrick, 1987.
Eva. London, Gollancz, 1988; New York, Delacorte Press, 1989.
Merlin Dreams. London, Gollancz, and New York, Delacorte Press, 1988.

Plays

Television Series: *Mandog,* 1972.

Other

Chance, Luck, and Destiny (miscellany). London, Gollancz, 1975; Boston, Little Brown, 1976.
The Flight of Dragons. London, Pierrot, and New York, Harper, 1979.
City of Gold and Other Stories from the Old Testament. London, Gollancz, and New York, Pantheon, 1980.
Editor, *Presto! Humorous Bits and Pieces.* London, Hutchinson, 1975.
Editor, *Hundreds and Hundreds.* London, Penguin, 1984.

*

Peter Dickinson comments:

I think of myself as writing science fiction with the science left out. I try to write proper detective stories, with clues and solutions, which work in the traditional way, but also provide something extra by way of ideas, without getting portentous about it. My books have tended to deal with closed worlds—partly because that makes it easier to limit suspects, etc. (as in the good old snowbound country house), and partly because it allows me to give the inhabitants of that closed world a definite twist which sets them apart from the outside world. For my main characters I like competent women and weedy men, and tend to overpopulate my books with grotesques.

*　　*　　*

Peter Dickinson's gift to the crime story has been an imagination of unusual, even extraordinary, forcefulness. Think of the settings of some of his books—a New Guinea tribe living in the attics of a row of London houses, a home for children suffering from a disease which turns them into sleepily charming psychic sensitives, an oil-sheik's palace where a chimpanzee is learning grammar. Each is put before you with such conviction, such vividness, such coherence that you come easily to believe that they actually exist. In his power to create new worlds Dickinson is the Tolkien of the crime novel.

Yet all the while he has, with perhaps only one exception, kept rigidly to the form of the old classical detective story. There is a mystery; there is a detective to solve it (for the first five books a Scotland Yard superintendent, James Pibble, reticent, quiet, very British, almost wanting to be done down, yet an excellent policeman, a getter of his man); there is a murderer; you suspect various people; there are clues to be picked up and seen for what they are, if you are clever enough. Dickinson plainly likes the sub-genre. Not for nothing did he review crime for years in *Punch*.

But each of his classical mysteries has had its extraordinary "background," its small odd world. Note the smallness. If Pibble was typically British, so is Dickinson, an eccentric, a romantic, and nowhere more so than in his careful keeping within limits. Yet inside this smallness he has become increasingly willing to go for the big themes, all the more successfully for not trying to echo them in grandeur of gesture.

He has, however, tackled subjects as formidably large as all that can be summed up in the word ecology. *The Poison Oracle* is the book that deals with this, besides of course having a complex murder plot with a splendidly gripping climactic scene where the murderer, in true classical fashion (Poirot might have gathered the suspects in a library), is exposed. Here the poison of the title is both murder means and the process that is blotting out in the name of civilisation whole tracts of nature. But Dickinson takes no simple stance in this. Like a true novelist, he lets all the implications of the situation percolate through his imagination to emerge as differing characters, as contradictory aspects of the book's setting. And the characters, each vividly presented, range from a sympathetic and entirely likely intelligent chimpanzee, through a formidably clever psycho-linguist who is yet delightfully naive and an Oxford-veneered sheik, truly charming, believably ruthless, to half a dozen differing tribesmen living in almost inaccessible marsh-land, credibly primitive and at the same time recognisably fellow humans to us 20th-century sophisticated readers.

The fantastic background, the sheik's desert castle built upside-down (for the good practical reason that this provides maximum shade), the marshes, even the hobby zoo inside the castle—all not only create a literally marvellous atmosphere but also contribute to the theme that underlies the whole, even

down to the smallest detail like a croaking sound which is heard at a moment of suspense in the marshes, "the ugly noise of the lung-fish adapting themselves over thousands of generations to live in an altered world."

There is perhaps a substratum common to all Dickinson's lively, suspenseful detection tales—and that is a plea for the instincts as opposed to the intellect. *The Poison Oracle* ends with the balance in favour of the slow processes of nature rather than the corner-cutting, though often beneficial, ways of civilising man. *Walking Dead,* set in a Haiti-like tropical island, explores the relationship between id, mind, and soul, and comes down in favour of those mysterious, almost forgotten powers that humans, in the western world at least, have often done their best to suppress. *The Lively Dead,* set in an ordinary London house that is yet as extraordinary as any of the other settings I have mentioned, makes a plea for us to look askance at empty dreams of a future or at a past that is finished in favour of acknowledging and welcoming the life that is, with "its green blade thrusting through."

Finally it should be said that Dickinson writes extremely well. Not only are those characters wonderfully vivid and his settings such that you remember them for years afterwards, but the actual prose is excellent. Phrases leap out, sending sharp images into the distant reader's mind. Yet occasionally, it must be admitted, words do go to Dickinson's head. He has an immense vocabulary and is himself as intelligent as a table quorum of dons. And sometimes the checks that ought to be put on these qualities flick off. Once he described somebody's nose as "less accipitrine than columbaceous." This is a small blemish, but the phrase does signal a quality in Dickinson's work that will not appeal to everyone. He is formidably intelligent, and he feels no need to conceal this. So for the less learned reader he is perhaps at times heavy-going, even too heavy-going. But reach up to his level, and the rewards are far greater than the mere feeling that you too have been bright today.

—H.R.F. Keating

————

DICKSON, Carr. *See* **CARR, John Dickson.**

————

DICKSON, Carter *See* **CARR, John Dickson.**

————

DIETRICH, Robert. *See* **HUNT, E. Howard.**

————

DISNEY, Doris, Miles. American. Born in Glastonbury, Connecticut, 22 December 1907. Educated at schools in Glastonbury. Married George J. Disney in 1936 (died); one daughter. Worked in an insurance office and did publicity for social agencies. *Died 9 March 1976.*

CRIME PUBLICATIONS

Novels (series: Jeff DiMarco; David Madden; Jim O'Neill)

A Compound for Death (O'Neill).   New York, Doubleday, 1943.

Murder on a Tangent (O'Neill).   New York, Doubleday, 1945.

Dark Road (DiMarco).   New York, Doubleday, 1946; London, Nimmo, 1947; as *Dead Stop,* New York, Dell, 1956.

Who Rides a Tiger.   New York, Doubleday, 1946; as *Sow the Wind,* London, Nimmo, 1948.

Appointment at Nine (O'Neill).   New York, Doubleday, 1947.

Enduring Old Charms.   New York, Doubleday, 1947; as *Death for My Beloved,* New York, Spivak, 1949.

Testimony by Silence.   New York, Doubleday, 1948.

That Which Is Crooked.   New York, Doubleday, 1948.

Count the Ways.   New York, Doubleday, 1949.

Family Skeleton (DiMarco).   New York, Doubleday, 1949.

Fire at Will (O'Neill).   New York, Doubleday, 1950.

Look Back on Murder.   New York, Doubleday, 1951.

Straw Man (DiMarco).   New York, Doubleday, 1951; as *The Case of the Straw Man,* London, Foulsham, 1958.

Heavy, Heavy Hangs.   New York, Doubleday, 1952.

Do unto Others.   New York, Doubleday, 1953.

Prescription: Murder.   New York, Doubleday, 1953.

The Last Straw (O'Neill).   New York, Doubleday, 1954; as *Driven to Kill,* London, Foulsham, 1957.

Room for Murder.   New York, Doubleday, 1955; London, Foulsham, 1959.

Trick or Treat (DiMarco).   New York, Doubleday, 1955; as *The Halloween Murder,* London, Foulsham, 1957.

Unappointed Rounds (Madden).   New York, Doubleday, 1956; as *The Post Office Case,* London, Foulsham, 1957.

Method in Madness.   New York, Doubleday, 1957; as *Quiet Violence,* London, Foulsham, 1959; as *Too Innocent to Kill,* London, Avon, 1957.

My Neighbor's Wife.   New York, Doubleday, 1957; London, Foulsham, 1958.

Black Mail (Madden).   New York, Doubleday, 1958; London, Foulsham, 1960.

Did She Fall or Was She Pushed? (DiMarco).   New York, Doubleday, 1959; London, Hale, 1962.

No Next of Kin.   New York, Doubleday, 1959; London, Foulsham, 1961.

Dark Lady.   New York, Doubleday, 1960; as *Sinister Lady,* London, Hale, 1962.

Mrs. Meeker's Money (Madden).   New York, Doubleday, 1961; London, Hale, 1963.

Find the Woman (DiMarco).   New York, Doubleday, 1962; London, Hale, 1964.

Should Auld Acquaintance.   New York, Doubleday, 1962; London, Hale, 1963.

Here Lies.   New York, Doubleday, 1963; London, Hale, 1964.

The Departure of Mr. Gaudette.   New York, Doubleday, 1964; as *Fateful Departure,* London, Hale, 1965.

The Hospitality of the House.   New York, Doubleday, 1964; as *Unsuspected Evil,* London, Hale, 1965.

Shadow of a Man.   New York, Doubleday, 1965; London, Hale, 1966.

At Some Forgotten Door.   New York, Doubleday, 1966; London, Hale, 1967.

The Magic Grandfather.   New York, Doubleday, 1966; as *Mask of Evil,* London, Hale, 1967.

Night of Clear Choice.   New York, Doubleday, 1967; as *Flame of Evil,* London, Hale, 1968.

Money for the Taking.   New York, Doubleday, and London, Hale, 1968.

Voice from the Grave.   New York, Doubleday, 1968; London, Hale, 1969.

Two Little Children and How They Grew.   New York, Doubleday, 1969; as *Fatal Choice,* London, Hale, 1970.

Do Not Fold, Spindle, or Mutilate.   New York, Doubleday, 1970; as *Death by Computer,* London, Hale, 1971.

The Chandler Policy (DiMarco).   New York, Putnam, 1971; London, Hale, 1973.

Three's a Crowd.   New York, Doubleday, 1971; London, Hale, 1972.

The Day Miss Bessie Lewis Disappeared.   New York, Doubleday, 1972; London, Hale, 1973.

Only Couples Need Apply.   New York, Doubleday, 1973; London, Hale, 1974.

Don't Go into the Woods Today.   New York, Doubleday, 1974.

Cry for Help.   New York, Doubleday, 1975; London, Hale, 1976.

Winifred.   New York, Doubleday, 1976.

Uncollected Short Story

"Ghost of a Chance," in *American Magazine* (Springfield, Ohio), October 1954.

*

Manuscript Collection: Mugar Memorial Library, Boston University.

*   *   *

Investigation into fictional murders usually causes the reader to *care* only on an intellectual level. Because Doris Miles Disney so often wrote of crimes involving the most vulnerable members of society, the old and the very young, she created an emotional nexus between writer and reader that was rare in crime fiction. The wealthy elderly, traditional victims in mysteries, are presented in depth and with considerable sympathy—e.g., Mrs. Carroll, placed in a nursing home by greedy relatives in *Method in Madness,* and the title character of *Mrs. Meeker's Money,* subjected to mail fraud and murder. We care when another titular character vanishes mysteriously on the eve of his retirement in *The Departure of Mr. Gaudette.*

Often the young and the old interact in Disney books, as in *The Magic Grandfather,* and her observations are acute, especially of the devices lonely old people use to gain the attention and affection of children.

The impact of murder on the victim's survivors is another neglected area—even among authors who stress characterization. At her best, Disney did a superb job of presenting this. A young mother dies at the start of *Heavy, Heavy Hangs,* possibly by suicide. Disney carefully integrates in her plot the impact of this death on her young son. Convincing scenes about the necessity of notifying next-of-kin are adroitly used to advance the plot and introduce characters. Another small boy and his mother are central to Disney's best book, *No Next of Kin,* and she successfully creates shock and outrage in the reader.

No one has used New England's suburbs and small towns as often and effectively as Disney. She possessed a special knack for weaving the area's past with its present as in one of her earliest, and best works, *Who Rides a Tiger.* The reading of an old lady's will in 1945 discloses roots and conflicts in a northern Connecticut town going back to 1879. She depicted (and probably reflected) middle class values and was at her best when her characters, including her murderers, were "nice" people. She conveyed quite believably the stresses that could lead "the people next door" to commit murder.

Though most of her books were not part of any series, she did use three continuing characters. Each had integrity and dedication to the task of crime-solving: none had unusual idiosyncrasies. Almost forgotten is Jim O'Neill, a policeman in a small Connecticut city who appeared three times in a series of procedural novels about a Postal Inspector.

The best-known Disney character is insurance investigator Jeff DiMarco; he is also the most believable. In his first appearance, *Dark Road,* he falls in love with a murderess. In *Method in Madness* his sympathies are better directed as he becomes convinced that the old lady in the nursing home is the victim of a murderous scheme. DiMarco ages believably during the series, exhibiting understandable concern as his hair grows gray and his waistline thickens.

Unfortunately, there is often a bewildering change of viewpoint or style in her work. For example, the heroine of *Heavy, Heavy Hangs* is initially depicted as having enough intellectual and emotional resources to discover the solution to her sister's death. But the last quarter of the book takes on elements of a standard Gothic novel, and Disney offers a patchwork solution and gratuitous violence to conclude a very promising book. The switch in *Straw Man* was even more disconcerting as, at midpoint, she changes focus from a DiMarco detective puzzle to an inverted mystery, disclosing the identity of the murderer.

If individual books showed changes that did not seem wise, Disney's entire body of work suffered a disappointing shift in her last decade. She abandoned the "decent" people inadvertently involved in crime and changed her viewpoint. *Money for the Taking* is told from the perspective of Donna Jenner, a young bank teller driven by her love for an amoral man to help him in a bank robbery. Unfortunately, the book contains no virtues like careful plotting or depth of characterization to offset the completely unsympathetic protagonist. *Voice from the Grave, Only Couples Need Apply,* and *Cry for Help* suffer from similar defects.

Though occasionally disappointing, especially at the end of a career that spanned more that three decades, Disney's legacy is an impressive one: a body of work with a strong narrative drive, believable characters, and considerable emotional impact, with seldom a descent into bathos.

—Marvin Lachman

DISNEY, Dorothy Cameron. American. Born in the Indian Territory, now Oklahoma, in 1903. Educated at Barnard College, New York, B.A. Married Milton MacKaye. Worked as stenographer, nightclub hostess, copy writer, film extra; marriage editor, *Ladies' Home Journal,* New York.

CRIME PUBLICATIONS

Novels

Death in the Back Seat. New York, Random House, 1936; London, Hale, 1937.
The Golden Swan Murder. New York, Random House, 1939; London, Hale, 1940.
Strawstack. New York, Random House, and London, Hale, 1939; as *Strawstack Murders,* New York, Dell, 1944.
The Balcony. New York, Random House, 1940; London, Hale, 1941.
Thirty Days Hath September, with George Sessions Perry. New York, Random House, 1942; London, Hale, 1950.

Crimson Friday. New York, Random House, 1943; London, Hale, 1945.
The Seventeenth Letter. New York, Random House, 1945; London, Hale, 1948.
Explosion. New York, Random House, 1948.
The Hangman's Tree. New York, Random House, 1949.

OTHER PUBLICATIONS

Other

Guggenheim, with Milton MacKaye. New York, Boni, 1927.
Mary Roberts Rinehart, with Milton MacKaye. New York, Rinehart, 1948.
Can This Marriage Be Saved?, with Paul Popenoe. New York, Macmillan, 1960.

* * *

Dorothy Cameron Disney's novels remain quite fresh and readable, not only because they are fast-paced but also because the major characters are fully drawn and believable. As is appropriate for books by the *Ladies' Home Journal* marriage editor, most of Disney's works feature a tightly knit group, either a family or a small group bound by work or community ties. The members of the group are forced to realize that one of them is a murderer. In several books, the motive for murder is directly related to a family situation. The murderer kills to protect a family, to protect a marriage, or to get out of a marriage. The protagonists are either young married couples or spinsters with strong family ties. The families are often upper-middle-class and afflicted or strengthened by a strong case of ancestor worship. Inherited family money, dissipated or unfairly distributed, figures in several of the novels.

In spite of such beginnings as "it seems to me now. . . I could have prevented the dreadful series of crimes which so hideously involved us all," (*Strawstack*) which sets a tone of horror, the novels are actually realistic. Disney manipulates the episodes so that strategic moments are chilling without being terrifying. In *Strawstack,* Margaret Tilbury allows herself but a "thin scream" upon finding a body in a shower. Immediately she begins to worry about the impression the ugly scene might have upon her approaching niece.

The surprising note for the period, and for the white-collar, upper-middle-class milieu Disney favors, is that the women of the novels, in spite of hats, gloves, dresses, and apparently conventional attitudes, are liberated. Her females are actresses, doctors, successful businesswomen, civil servants—and villains. In fact, the strongest aspect of Disney's novels is her characterization of women. Three distinct types stand out. One type includes strong spinsters, often leading characters and narrators. Although Disney pokes mild fun at their unworldliness and set ways, she draws deft and sympathetic portraits of strong-willed women who move with intelligence, boldness, and fierceness to protect their loved ones. Less prominent but commonly used women characters are the attractive, self-centered, hard-working businesswomen. The third type appears most frequently and in the most varied forms. These are the really wicked women. They are usually young and attractive. If they love, the love is poisonous and all-possessive. Often, they love only themselves. Their strength is in managing to appear something they are not. The author plays fair, planting clues consistently, but they are easy to overlook as the characters steadily build a deceptive facade.

Disney presents interesting characters, lots of action, and cleverly devised plots that will interest readers who cannot themselves make a nickel phone call or ride in a rumble seat. It would be easy to slight Disney as writer of "women's stories." She deserves revisiting as a writer of people stories.

—Neysa Chouteau and Martha Alderson

———

DITTON, James. *See* **CLARK, Douglas.**

———

DOBYNS, Stephen. American. Born in Orange, New Jersey, 19 February 1941. Educated at Shimer College, Mount Carroll, Illinois, 1959–60; Wayne State University, Detroit, B.A. 1964; University of Iowa, Iowa City, M.F.A. 1967. Married; three children. Instructor in English, State University of New York College, Brockport, 1968–69; reporter, Detroit *News,* 1969–71; Visiting Lecturer, University of New Hampshire, Durham, 1973–75, University of Iowa, 1977–78, and Boston University, 1978–79. Member of the Department of creative writing, Goddard College, Plainfield, Vermont, 1978–80, Warren Wilson College, Swannanoa, North Carolina, from 1982. Since 1987 Director, Creative Writing Program, Syracuse University, New York. Recipient: Lamont Poetry Selection award, 1971; MacDowell Colony fellowship, 1972, 1976; Yaddo fellowship, 1972, 1973, 1977, 1981, 1984; National Endowment for the Arts grant, 1974, 1981; Guggenheim fellowship, 1983; National Poetry Series prize, 1984. Agent: Harold Ober Associates, 425 Madison Avenue, New York, New York 10017. Address: 208 Brattle Road, Syracuse, New York 13203, U.S.A.

CRIME PUBLICATIONS

Novels (series: Charlie Bradshaw)

A Man of Little Evils. New York, Atheneum, 1973; London, Davies, 1974.
Saratoga Longshot (Bradshaw). New York, Atheneum, 1976; London, Hale, 1978.
Saratoga Swimmer (Bradshaw). New York, Atheneum, 1983; London, Allison and Busby, 1986.
Dancer with One Leg. New York, Dutton, 1983.
Saratoga Headhunter (Bradshaw). New York, Viking Press, 1985; London, Allison and Busby, 1986.
Cold Dog Soup. New York, Viking Press, 1985; London, Arena, 1988.
Saratoga Snapper (Bradshaw). New York, Viking Press, 1986; London, Century, 1988.
A Boat Off the Coast. New York, Viking, 1987.
The Two Deaths of Señora Puccini. New York, and London, Viking, 1988.
Saratoga Bestiary (Bradshaw). New York, Viking, 1988; London, Mysterious Press, 1989.
The House of Alexandrine. Detroit, Wayne State University Press, 1990.
Saratoga Hexameter (Bradshaw). New York, Viking, and London, Mysterious Press, 1990.

OTHER PUBLICATIONS

Verse

Concurring Beasts. New York, Atheneum, 1972.
Griffon. New York, Atheneum, 1976.
Heat Death. New York, Atheneum, 1980.
The Balthus Poems. New York, Atheneum, 1982.
Black Dog, Red Dog. New York, Holt Rinehart, 1984.
Cemetery Nights. New York, Viking, 1987.
Body Traffic. New York, Viking, 1990.

* * *

A writer of considerable versatility, the prolific and accomplished Stephen Dobyns has worked successfully in a number of areas of literature and earned high praise in all of them. He has written several well received volumes of poetry, some rather derivative and self consciously arty academic fiction, and most important, a series of detective novels featuring Charlie Bradshaw, a private detective in Saratoga, New York. Unlike many academics and writers of "straight" fiction, Dobyns doesn't resort to a pseudonym for the Bradshaw books, which suggests that he regards them as seriously as any of his other work, a commendable attitude.

The Saratoga novels, all of which begin with the town's name, exhibit a pleasantly easy confidence, discernible in his other works, but here decidedly both more original and more firmly controlled than his non-detective fiction. Charlie Bradshaw is a lovable bumbler, a former member of the town police force, a former stable security guard, a former husband—in fact a former number of things—who investigates some rather offbeat crimes in the surprisingly violent environs of scenic, historic Saratoga.

Bradshaw often stumbles into his cases, or is drawn in by circumstance or even by accident. Since private detecting hardly pays the rent in a small town, he finds himself doing odd things to get by, like delivering milk or managing a hotel in the off season, which somehow involve him in some bloody and violent business. In *Saratoga Swimmer,* for example, Bradshaw's boss at the stables is murdered in the YMCA swimming pool, apparently in a mob slaying; in *Saratoga Headhunter* a jockey is decapitated in Charlie's living room. Though he works without any particular flair and certainly without any particular method, Bradshaw also often ends up defeating some rough customers in some melodramatic manner.

The Dobyns books move, however, with a comforting competence through a wealth of subjects and generate some nicely understated humor. We learn a great deal about the long, rich history of Saratoga, from revolutionary days through the Gilded Age, from the times of the gambling casinos to the affluence of the racing season. Charlie enjoys the beauty and serenity of the region in all seasons of the year and shows us some sides of Saratoga that a tourist would never see, including the ordinary life of a resort town.

We follow Bradshaw's various friendships and love affairs, his comically failed relationships with his family, who all regard him as a loser. We get to know a number of the citizens of the town—Bradshaw's best friend, the priapic sexagenarian Victor Plotz, Artemis, the enigmatic equestrian, Chief Peterson, Bradshaw's constant adversary, and a variety of more or less harmless ex-cons and lowlifes who are Bradshaw's version of the Baker Street Irregulars.

Modest, unassuming, and tending toward the spherical in shape, despite his ordinariness Charlie Bradshaw retains some of the characteristic eccentricity of the Great Detectives of fiction. He spends a good deal of his time reading about famous outlaws, from Billy the Kid through Willie Sutton; in fact, he seems something of an expert on the badmen of the Old West. He often quotes significant sayings of the various crooks and robbers he admires and even draws occasional inspiration from their words and deeds in the pursuit of his investigations. He solves his cases by perseverance and intuition, working harder than anyone expects and thinking just a bit better than anyone believes he can. He often takes on a problem because of some personal reason—he liked the victim, he feels sorry for someone, or he believes that people shouldn't treat other people badly. Not especially gifted, he is both smarter and tougher than perhaps even he realizes. Most of all, Bradshaw succeeds because he is simply more decent than anyone else in his novels, a good friend, a sympathetic listener, a kind man who hates to hurt anyone. That unsensational kindness and decency, coupled with the absolutely accurate background and the general charm of the atmosphere, make Dobyns's Charlie Bradshaw novels quite unusual and quite special. From *Saratoga Longshot* through the latest, *Saratoga Hexameter*, Dobyns has written, in addition to several other volumes, six novels, which indicates the potential within Charlie Bradshaw and the Saratoga setting; it also suggests that the series will continue for some time, a most gratifying notion for any reader of detective fiction. Charlie Bradshaw is one of the most original detectives currently practicing, and his investigations are virtually addictive in their appeal.

—George Grella

———

DOCHERTY, James L. *See* **CHASE, James Hadley.**

———

DODGE, David (Francis). American. Born in Berkeley, California, in August 1910. Attended high school in Los Angeles. Served in the United States Naval Reserve, 1941–45. Married Elva Keith in 1936; one child. Bank clerk, ship's fireman, social worker, San Francisco; accountant, 1935–42. Self-employed author. Address: 706 Kingston Road, Princeton, New Jersey 08540, U.S.A.

CRIME PUBLICATIONS

Novels (series: Al Colby; John Abraham Lincoln; Whit Whitney)

Death and Taxes (Whitney). New York, Macmillan, 1941; London, Joseph, 1947.
Shear the Black Sheep (Whitney). New York, Macmillan, 1942; London, Joseph, 1949.
Bullets for the Bridegroom (Whitney). New York, Macmillan, 1944; London, Joseph, 1948.
It Ain't Hay (Whitney). New York, Simon and Schuster, 1946; as *A Drug on the Market*, London, Joseph, 1949.
The Long Escape (Colby). New York, Random House, 1948; London, Joseph, 1950.
Plunder of the Sun (Colby). New York, Random House, 1949; London, Joseph, 1950.
The Red Tassel (Colby). New York, Random House, 1950; London, Joseph, 1951.

To Catch a Thief. New York, Random House, 1952; London, Joseph, 1953.
The Lights of Skaro. New York, Random House, and London, Joseph, 1954.
Angel's Ransom. New York, Random House, 1956; as *Ransom of the Angel,* London, Joseph, 1957.
Loo Loo's Legacy. London, Joseph, 1960; Boston, Little Brown, 1961.
Carambola. Boston, Little Brown, 1961; as *High Corniche,* London, Joseph, 1961.
Hooligan (Lincoln). New York, Macmillan, 1969; as *Hatchetman,* London, Joseph, 1970.
Troubleshooter (Lincoln). New York, Macmillan, 1971; London, Joseph, 1972.

Uncollected Short Story

"Murder Is No Accident," in *Ellery Queen's Mystery Magazine* (New York), September 1953.

OTHER PUBLICATIONS

Other

How Green Was My Father: A Sort of Travel Diary. New York, Simon and Schuster, 1947; London, Home and Van Thal, 1950.
How Lost Was My Weekend: A Greenhorn in Guatemala. New York, Random House, 1948; London, Home and Van Thal, 1949.
The Crazy Glasspecker; or, High Life in the Andes. New York, Random House, 1949; as *High Life in the Andes,* London, Barker, 1951.
20,000 Leagues Behind the 8 Ball. New York, Random House, 1951.
With a Knife and Fork down the Amazon. London, Barker, 1952.
The Poor Man's Guide to Europe. New York, Random House, 1953 (and later editions).
Time Out for Turkey. New York, Random House, 1955; as *Talking Turkey,* London, Barker, 1955.
The Rich Man's Guide to the Riviera. Boston, Little Brown, 1962; London, Cassell, 1963.
The Poor Man's Guide to the Orient. New York, Simon and Schuster, 1965.
Fly Down, Drive Mexico. New York, Macmillan, 1968; revised edition, as *The Best of Mexico by Car,* 1969.

*   *   *

Prior to becoming a writer, David Dodge was an accountant, and he drew on this background in creating his first series character, Whit Whitney, a tax accountant and unwilling investigator of assorted murders. The first Whitney novel, *Death and Taxes,* is very much in the tradition of the screwball comedy mystery style which began with Dashiell Hammett's *The Thin Man* and reached an apex in the Bill Crane novels of Jonathan Latimer. There is a good bit of action and a medium-hard-boiled atmosphere, but the focus is on sharp, witty dialogue, with much attendant consumption of cocktails. Whitney is a likeable, generally bemused hero, not particularly happy with having to solve murders, but not lacking in brains and courage when called for. Kitty MacLeod, Whitney's girlfriend (and later his wife), plays the Nora Charles role to Whit's Nick in fine fashion. The four Whitney books are consistently well-crafted and entertaining examples of the screwball style.

Dodge became a world traveler, and began a second career as writer of humorous travel books. He dropped the Whitney series and thereafter drew on his familiarity with exotic locales for his later books. The Cote d'Azur is the setting for both *Angel's Ransom,* a crackling suspense yarn involving the kidnapping of the kept woman of a rich American wastrel, and *To Catch a Thief,* Dodge's best-known book, which Hitchcock made into a memorable movie with Cary Grant and Grace Kelly.

Central and South America was Dodge's favorite locale, and the scenery figures prominently in the three continent-spanning adventures of Al Colby, a hard-boiled private investigator based in Mexico City. In contrast to Whitney, Colby is a cynical tough-guy detective-adventurer; the light touch of the Whitney novels is consequently absent in the Colby novels, but the crisp dialogue, fast pace, and thoroughly professional plotting are not.

—Art Scott

DOMINIC, R.B. *See* **LATHEN, Emma.**

DONAVAN, John. *See* **MORLAND, Nigel.**

DONOVAN, Dick. Pseudonym for Joyce Emmerson Preston Muddock. British. Born in Southampton, Hampshire, 28 May 1842. Educated at a collegiate school in Cheshire, and in India. Married; two sons. Worked for the British Government in India; employed for a time at a gun foundry at Cossipore, near Calcutta; special correspondent for the *Hour* in Asia and the Pacific for several years; Swiss correspondent for the London *Daily News* for five years; attached to the Special Constabulary, London, during World War I. *Died 23 January 1934.*

CRIME PUBLICATIONS

Novels

From the Bosom of the Deep (as J.E. Muddock). London, Swan Sonnenschein, 1886.
The Man from Manchester. London, Chatto and Windus, 1890; New York, Street and Smith, 1900.
Tracked to Doom. London, Chatto and Windus, 1891.
Eugene Vidocq, Soldier, Thief, Spy, Detective: A Romance Founded on Facts. London, Hutchinson, 1895.
The Mystery of Jamaica Terrace. London, Chatto and Windus, 1896.
Deacon Brodie; or, Behind the Mask. London, Chatto and Windus, 1901.
Jim the Penman: The Life Story of One of the Most Astounding Criminals That Have Ever Lived. London, Newnes, 1901.
Whose Was the Hand? (as J.E. Muddock). London, Digby Long, 1901.

The Scarlet Seal: A Tale of the Borgias. London, Long, 1902.
The Crime of the Century. London, Long, 1904.
The Fatal Ring. London, Hurst and Blackett, 1905.
A Knight of Evil. London, White, 1905.
Thurtell's Crime. London, Laurie, 1906.
The Knutsford Mystery. London, White, 1906.
The Gold-Spinner. London, White, 1907.
The Shadow of Evil. London, Everett, 1907.
In the Queen's Service. London, Long, 1907.
A Gilded Serpent. London, Ward Lock, 1908.
In the Face of the Night. London, Long, 1908.
The Sin of Preaching Jim. London, Everett, 1908; as *Preaching Jim,* London, Aldine Publishing Company, 1919.
Tangled Destinies. London, Laurie, 1908.
A Wild Beauty. London, White, 1909.
Lil of the Slums. London, Laurie, 1909.
For Honour or Death. London, Ward Lock, 1910.
The Naughty Maid of Mitcham. London, White, 1910.
The Fatal Woman. London, White, 1911.
The Trap: A Revelation. London, White, 1911.
The Rich Man's Wife, with E.W. Elkington. London, Ham Smith, 1912.
The Turning Wheel. London, White, 1912.
Out There: A Romance of Australia. London, Everett, 1922.

Short Stories (series: Dick Donovan)

The Man-Hunter: Stories from the Note-Book of a Detective (Donovan). London, Chatto and Windus, 1888; New York, Lovell, 1889.
Caught at Last! Leaves from the Note-Book of a Detective (Donovan). London, Chatto and Windus, and New York, Lovell, 1889.
Who Poisoned Hetty Duncan? and Other Detective Stories (Donovan). London, Chatto and Windus, 1890.
Tracked and Taken: Detective Sketches (Donovan). London, Chatto and Windus, and New York, Lovell, 1890.
A Detective's Triumphs (Donovan). London, Chatto and Windus, 1891.
Wanted! A Detective's Strange Adventures (Donovan). London, Chatto and Windus, 1892.
In the Grip of the Law (Donovan). London, Chatto and Windus, 1892.
From Information Received (Donovan). London, Chatto and Windus, 1893.
Link by Link (Donovan). London, Chatto and Windus, 1893.
From Clue to Capture (Donovan). London, Hutchinson, 1893.
Suspicion Aroused (Donovan). London, Chatto and Windus, 1893.
Found and Fettered (Donovan). London, Hutchinson, 1894.
Dark Deeds (Donovan). London, Chatto and Windus, 1895.
Riddles Read (Donovan). London, Chatto and Windus, 1896.
The Chronicles of Michael Danevitch of the Russian Secret Service. London, Chatto and Windus, 1897.
The Records of Vincent Trill of the Detective Service. London, Chatto and Windus, 1899.
Tales of Terror (Donovan). London, Chatto and Windus, 1899.
The Adventures of Tyler Tatlock, Private Detective. London, Chatto and Windus, 1900.
Startling Crimes and Notorious Criminals. London, Pearson, 1908.
The Great Turf Fraud and Other Notable Crimes. London, Pearson, 1909.
Scarlet Sinners: Stories of Notorious Criminals and Crimes. London, Newnes, 1910.

The Triumphs of Fabian Field, Criminologist. London, White, 1912.

OTHER PUBLICATIONS as J.E. Muddock

Novels

Grace O'Malley. London, People's Pocket Story Books, 1873.
A False Heart. London, Tinsley, 3 vols., 1873.
A Wingless Angel. London, Virtue, 1875.
As the Shadows Fall. London, Tinsley, 3 vols., 1876.
"Doll": A Dream of Haddon Hall, Being the Story of Dorothy Vernon's Wooing and Flight. London, Heywood, 1880.
Snowdrops: A Story of Three Christmas Eves. London, Wyman, 1887.
The Shadow Hunter. London, Unwin, 1887.
Stormlight. London, Ward Lock, 1888.
The Dead Man's Secret; or, The Valley of Gold. London, Chatto and Windus, 1889.
For God and the Czar. London, Newnes, 1892.
Maid Marian and Robin Hood. London, Chatto and Windus, and Philadelphia, Lippincott, 1892.
Only a Woman's Heart. London, Newnes, 1893.
The Star of Fortune. London, Chapman and Hall, 2 vols., 1894.
Stripped of the Tinsel. London, Digby Long, 1896.
Young Lochinvar. London, Chatto and Windus, 1896.
The Great White Hand; or, The Tiger of Cawnpore. London, Hutchinson, 1896.
Without Faith or Fear. London, Digby Long, 1896.
Basile the Jester. London, Chatto and Windus, 1896; New York, New Amsterdam Book Company, 1897.
The Lost Laird. London, Digby Long, 1898.
In the King's Favour. London, Digby Long, 1899.
The Golden Idol. London, Chatto and Windus, 1899.
The Sting of the Scorpion. London, Simpkin Marshall, 1899.
Kate Cameron of Brux; or, The Feud. London, Digby Long, 1900.
Fair Rosalind. London, Long, 1902.
A Woman's Checkmate. London, Long, 1902.
Liz. London, White, 1903.
Sweet "Doll" of Haddon Hall. London, Long, 1903; revised edition, 1905.
In the Red Dawn. London, Long, 1904.
The Sunless City. London, White, 1905.
Jane Shore. London, Long, 1905.
From the Clutch of the Sea: The Story of Some Real Lives. London, Long, 1905.
For the White Cockade. London, Long, 1905.
The Alluring Flame. London, Long, 1906.

Short Stories

Stories Weird and Wonderful. London, Chatto and Windus, 1889.
For Love of Lucille and Other Stories. London, White, 1905.

Other

Did Dorothy Vernon Elope? A Rejoinder. London, Drane, 1907.
Pages from an Adventurous Life (as Dick Donovan). London, Laurie, and New York, Kennerley, 1907.
The Romance and History of the Crystal Palace. London, Gill, 1911.

A Patriotic American (on Harold Shaw; as Dick Donovan). London, Baldwin, 1916.
All Clear: A Brief Record of the Work of the London Special Constabulary 1914–1919. London, Everett, 1920.

Editor, *The "J.E.M." Guide to Davos-Platz.* London, Simpkin Marshall, 1881.
Editor, *The "J.E.M." Guide to Switzerland.* London, Simpkin Marshall, 1882.
Editor, *Pocket Guide to Geneva and Chamounix.* London, Wyman, 1886.
Editor, *For Valour: The V.C.: A Record of the Brave and Noble Deeds for Which Her Majesty Has Bestowed the Victoria Cross.* London, Hutchinson, 1895.
Editor, *The Savage Club Papers.* London, Hutchinson, 1895.

* * *

In the 1880's and 1890's Dick Donovan (Joyce Emmerson Preston Muddock) was one of the most prolific and popular British writers. With well over 200 short stories to his credit in newspapers and periodicals, he was as well-known on the lower reading levels as Sherlock Holmes later became on higher levels.

Dick Donovan appeared as both author and police detective in *The Man-Hunter,* a collection reprinted from earlier newspaper publications. The name Donovan, according to Muddock's memoirs, was that of an 18th-century Bow Street Runner; the stories themselves, however, were all modern in setting. Dick Donovan remained the central figure in succeeding short story collections until *The Chronicles of Michael Danevitch,* in which Muddock wrote about a Czarist police official and Peter Brodie, an English detective. Later volumes are concerned with private detectives Fabian Field, Tyler Tatlock, and Vincent Trill.

Although Donovan is remembered today primarily as a writer of short stories, he also wrote much incidental journalism and many novels. Of his mystery novels, *The Man from Manchester* is generally considered the best. He also worked in the area of fictionalized factual crime. Here *Eugene Vidocq, Jim the Penman,* and *Thurtell's Crime* are best-known.

Muddock's work is marked by a strong conservatism and an archaic quality which seem to have been matched by his political and social views. Just as he retained the mid-Victorian practice of coincident detective and author, his Dick Donovan stories are undramatic, first-person narratives in the manner of "Waters." His subject matter came partly from factual crime and partly from the romantic themes of the day—anarchist plots, Oriental vengeance. *The Man from Manchester,* which attempts a character portrayal as well as a crime, might have been written a generation earlier, while *The Mystery of Jamaica Terrace* often reads like a stage melodrama. In his later fiction Muddock attempted to write a more contemporary story, but without too much success.

—E.F. Bleiler

DOUGLAS, Arthur. *See* HAMMOND, Gerald.

DOUGLAS, John. *See* **COLLINS, Michael.**

DOUGLAS, Michael. *See* **CRICHTON, Michael.**

DOWNES, Quentin. *See* **HARRISON, Michael.**

DOYLE, (Sir) Arthur Conan. British. Born in Edingburgh, Scotland, 22 May 1859. Educated at the Hodder School, Lancashire, 1868–70, Stonyhurst College, Lancashire, 1870–75, and the Jesuit School, Feldkirch, Austria (editor, *Feldkirchian Gazette*), 1875–76; studied medicine at the University of Edinburgh, 1876–81, M.B. 1881, M.D. 1885. Served as senior physician at a field hospital in South Africa during the Boer War, 1899–1902; knighted, 1902. Married 1) Louise Hawkins in 1885 (died 1906), one daughter and one son; 2) Jean Leckie in 1907, two sons and one daughter. Practised medicine in Southsea, Hampshire, 1882–90; full-time writer from 1891; stood for Parliament as Unionist candidate for Central Edinburgh, 1900, and tariff reform candidate for the Hawick Burghs, 1906. Member, Society for Psychical Research, 1893–1930 (resigned). LL.D.: University of Edinburgh, 1905. Knight of Grace of the Order of St. John of Jerusalem. *Died 7 July 1930.*

CRIME PUBLICATIONS

Novels (series: Sherlock Holmes)

A Study in Scarlet (Holmes). London, Ward Lock, 1888; Philadelphia, Lippincott, 1890.
The Mystery of Cloomber. London, Ward and Downey, 1888; New York, Fenno 1895.
The Sign of Four (Holmes). London, Blackett, 1890; New York, Collier, 1891.
The Doings of Raffles Haw. London, Cassell, and New York, Lovell, 1892.
The Hound of the Baskervilles (Holmes). London, Newnes, and New York, McClure, 1902.
The Valley of Fear (Holmes). New York, Doran, 1914; London, Smith Elder, 1915.

Short Stories (series: Sherlock Holmes)

Mysteries and Adventures. London, Scott, 1889; as *The Gully of Bluemansdyke and Other Stories,* 1892.
The Captain of the Polestar and Other Tales. London, Longman, 1890; New York, Munro, 1894.
The Adventures of Sherlock Holmes. London, Newnes, and New York, Harper, 1892.
My Friend the Murderer and Other Mysteries and Adventures. New York, Lovell, 1893.
The Memoirs of Sherlock Holmes. London, Newnes, 1893; New York, Harper, 1894.
The Great Keinplatz Experiment and Other Stories. Chicago, Rand McNally, 1894.

Round the Red Lamp, Being Facts and Fancies of Medical Life. London, Methuen, and New York, Appleton, 1894.
The Green Flag and Other Stories of War and Sport. London, Smith Elder, and New York, McClure, 1900.
Hilda Wade (completion of book by Grant Allen). London, Richards, and New York, Putnam, 1900.
The Return of Sherlock Holmes. London, Newnes, and New York, McClure, 1905.
Round the Fire Stories. London, Smith Elder, and New York, McClure, 1908.
The Last Galley: Impressions and Tales. London, Smith Elder, and New York, Doubleday, 1911.
His Last Bow: Some Reminiscences of Sherlock Holmes. London, Murray, and New York, Doran, 1917.
Danger! and Other Stories. London, Murray, 1918; New York, Doran, 1919.
Tales of Terror and Mystery. London, Murray, 1922; as *The Black Doctor and Other Tales of Terror and Mystery* (selection). New York, Doran, 1925.
The Case-Book of Sherlock Holmes. London, Murray, and New York, Doran, 1927.
Great Stories, edited by John Dickson Carr. London, Murray, and New York, London House and Maxwell, 1959.
The Annotated Sherlock Holmes, edited by William S. Baring-Gould. New York, Potter, 2 vols., 1967; London, Murray, 2 vols., 1968.
The Adventures of Sherlock Holmes (facsimile of magazine stories). New York, Schocken, 1976; as *The Sherlock Holmes Illustrated Omnibus,* London, Murray-Cape, 1978.
Sherlock Holmes: The Published Apocrypha, with others, edited by Jack Tracy. Boston, Houghton Mifflin, 1980.
The Final Adventures of Sherlock Holmes, edited by Peter Haining. London, W.H. Allen, 1981.

OTHER PUBLICATIONS

Novels

Micah Clarke. London, Longman, and New York, Harper, 1889.
The Firm of Girdlestone. London, Chatto and Windus, and New York, Lovell, 1890.
The White Company. London, Smith Elder, 3 vols., 1891; New York, Lovell, 1 vol., 1891.
The Great Shadow. New York, Harper, 1892.
The Great Shadow, and Beyond the City. Bristol, Arrowsmith, 1893; New York, Ogilvie, 1894.
The Refugees. New York, Longman, 3 vols., 1893; New York, Harper, 1 vol., 1893.
The Parasite. London, Constable, 1894; New York, Harper, 1895.
The Stark Munro Letters. London, Longman, and New York, Appleton, 1895.
Rodney Stone. London, Smith Elder, and New York, Appleton, 1896.
Uncle Bernac: A Memory of Empire. London, Smith Elder, and New York, Appleton, 1897.
The Tragedy of Korosko. London, Smith Elder, 1898; as *Desert Drama,* Philadelphia, Lippincott, 1898.
A Duet, with an Occasional Chorus. London, Grant Richards, and New York, Appleton, 1899; revised edition, London, Smith Elder, 1910.
Sir Nigel. London, Smith Elder, and New York, McClure, 1906.
The Lost World. London, Hodder and Stoughton, and New York, Doran, 1912.

The Poison Belt. London, Hodder and Stoughton, and New York, Doran, 1913.

The Land of Mist. London, Hutchinson, and New York, Doran, 1926.

Short Stories

The Exploits of Brigadier Gerard. London, Newnes, and New York, Appleton, 1896.

The Man from Archangel and Other Stories. New York, Street and Smith, 1898.

Adventures of Gerard. London, Newnes, and New York, McClure, 1903.

Tales of the Ring and Camp. London, Murray, 1922; as *The Croxley Master and Other Tales of the Ring and Camp,* New York, Doran, 1925.

Tales of Pirates and Blue Water. London, Murray, 1922; as *The Dealings of Captain Sharkey and Other Tales of Pirates,* New York, Doran, 1925.

Tales of Long Ago. London, Murray, 1922; as *The Last of the Legions and Other Tales of Long Ago,* New York, Doran, 1925.

Tales of Adventure and Medical Life. London, Murray, 1922; as *The Man from Archangel and Other Tales of Adventure,* New York, Doran, 1925.

The Maracot Deep and Other Stories. London, Murray, and New York, Doubleday, 1929.

The Conan Doyle Historical Romances. London, Murray, 2 vols., 1931–32.

The Field Bazaar. Privately printed, 1934; Summit, New Jersey, Pamphlet House, 1947.

The Professor Challenger Stories. London, Murray, 1952.

Strange Studies from Life, Containing Three Hitherto Uncollected Tales, edited by Peter Ruber. New York, Candlelight Press, 1963.

The Best Supernatural Tales of Arthur Conan Doyle, edited by E.F. Bleiler. New York, Dover, 1979.

The Best Science Fiction of Arthur Conan Doyle, edited by Charles G. Waugh and Martin H. Greenberg. Carbondale, Southern Illinois University Press, 1981.

The Edinburgh Stories. Edinburgh, Polygon, 1981.

Uncollected Stories, edited by John Michael Gibson and Roger Lancelyn Green. London, Secker and Warburg, and New York, Doubleday, 1982.

The Best Horror Stories of Arthur Conan Doyle, edited by Martin H. Greenberg and Charles G. Waugh. Chicago, Academy, 1988.

The Supernatural Tales of Sir Arthur Conan Doyle, edited by Peter Haining. Slough, Berkshire, Foulsham, 1988.

Plays

Jane Annie: or, The Good Conduct Prize, with J.M. Barrie, music by Ernest Ford (produced London, 1893). London, Chappell, and New York, Novello Ewer, 1893.

Foreign Policy, adaptation of his story "A Question of Diplomacy" (produced London, 1893).

Waterloo, adaptation of his story "A Straggler of 15" (as *A Story of Waterloo,* produced Bristol, 1894; London, 1895; as *Waterloo,* produced New York, 1899). London, French, 1907; in *One-Act Plays of To-Day,* 2nd series, edited by J.W. Marriott, Boston, Small Maynard, 1926.

Halves, adaptation of the story by James Payne (produced Aberdeen and London, 1899).

Sherlock Holmes, with William Gillette, adaptation of works by Doyle (produced Buffalo and New York, 1899; Liverpool and London, 1901).

A Duet (A Duologue) (produced London, 1902). London, French, 1903.

Brigadier General, adaptation of his stories (produced London and New York, 1906).

The Fires of Fate: A Modern Morality, adaptation of his novel *The Tragedy of Korosko* (produced Liverpool, London, and New York, 1909).

The House of Temperley, adaptation of his novel *Rodney Stone* (produced London, 1910).

The Pot of Caviare, adaptation of his story (produced London, 1910).

The Speckled Band: An Adventure of Sherlock Holmes (produced London and New York, 1910). London, French, 1912.

The Crown Diamond (produced Bristol and London, 1921). Privately printed, 1958.

It's Time Something Happened. New York, Appleton, 1925.

Verse

Songs of Action. London, Smith Elder, and New York, Doubleday, 1898.

Songs of the Road. London, Smith Elder, and New York, Doubleday, 1911.

The Guards Came Through and Other Poems. London, Murray, 1919; New York, Doran, 1920.

The Poems of Arthur Conan Doyle: Collected Edition (includes play *The Journey*). London, Murray, 1922.

Other

The Great Boer War. London, Smith Elder, and New York, McClure, 1900.

The War in South Africa: Its Cause and Conduct. London, Smith Elder, and New York, McClure, 1902.

Works. (Author's Edition). London, Smith Elder, 12 vols., and New York, Appleton, 13 vols., 1903.

The Fiscal Question. Hawick, Roxburgh, Henderson, 1905.

An Incursion into Diplomacy. London, Smith Elder, 1906.

The Story of Mr. George Edalji. London, Daily Telegraph, 1907.

Through the Magic Door (essays). London, Smith Elder, 1907; New York, McClure, 1908.

The Crime of the Congo. London, Hutchinson, and New York, Doubleday, 1909.

Divorce Law Reform: An Essay. London, Divorce Law Reform Union, 1909.

Sir Arthur Conan Doyle: Why He Is Now in Favour of Home Rule. London, Liberal Publication Department, 1911.

The Case of Oscar Slater. London, Hodder and Stoughton, 1912; New York, Doran, 1913.

Divorce and the Church, with Lord Hugh Cecil. London, Divorce Law Reform Union, 1913.

Great Britain and the Next War. Boston, Small Maynard, 1914.

In Quest of Truth, Being Correspondence Between Sir Arthur Conan Doyle and Captain H. Stansbury. London, Watts, 1914.

To Arms! London, Hodder and Stoughton, 1914.

The German War. London, Hodder and Stoughton, 1914; New York, Doran, 1915.

Western Wanderings (travel in Canada). New York, Doran, 1915.

The Outlook on the War. London, Daily Chronicle, 1915.

An Appreciation of Sir John French. London, Daily Chronicle, 1916.

A Petition to the Prime Minister on Behalf of Sir Roger Casement. Privately printed, 1916

A Visit to Three Fronts: Glimpses of British, Italian, and French Lines. London, Hodder and Stoughton, and New York, Doran, 1916.

The British Campaign in France and Flanders. London, Hodder and Stoughton, 6 vols., 1916–20; New York, Doran, 6 vols., 1916–20; revised edition, as *The British Campaigns in Europe 1914–18,* London, Bles, 1 vol., 1928.

The New Revelation; or, What Is Spiritualism? London, Hodder and Stoughton, and New York, Doran, 1918.

The Vital Message (on spiritualism). London, Hodder and Stoughton, and New York, Doran, 1919.

Our Reply to the Cleric. London, Spiritualists' National Union, 1920.

A Public Debate on the Truth of Spiritualism, with Joseph McCabe. London, Watts, 1920; as *Debate on Spiritualism,* Girard, Kansas, Haldeman Julius, 1922.

Spiritualism and Rationalism. London, Hodder and Stoughton, 1920.

The Wanderings of a Spiritualist. London, Hodder and Stoughton, and New York, Doran, 1921.

Spiritualism: Some Straight Questions and Direct Answers. Manchester, Two Worlds, 1922.

The Case for Spirit Photography, with others. London, Hutchinson, 1922; New York, Doran, 1923.

The Coming of the Fairies. London, Hodder and Stoughton, and New York, Doran, 1922.

Three of Them: A Reminiscence. London, Murray, 1923.

Our American Adventure. London, Hodder and Stoughton, and New York, Doran, 1923.

Our Second American Adventure. London, Hodder and Stoughton, and Boston, Little Brown, 1924.

Memories and Adventures. London, Hodder and Stoughton, and Boston, Little Brown, 1924.

Psychic Experiences. London and New York, Putnam, 1925.

The Early Christian Church and Modern Spiritualism. London, Psychic Bookshop, 1925.

The History of Spiritualism. London, Cassell, 2 vols., and New York, Doran, 2 vols., 1926.

Pheneas Speaks: Direct Spirit Communications. London, Psychic Press, and New York, Doran, 1927.

What Does Spiritualism Actually Teach and Stand For? London, Psychic Bookshop, 1928.

A Word of Warning. London, Psychic Press, 1928.

An Open Letter to Those of My Generation. London, Psychic Press, 1929.

Our African Winter. London, Murray, 1929.

The Roman Catholic Church: A Rejoinder. London, Psychic Press, 1929.

The Edge of the Unknown. London, Murray, and New York, Putnam, 1930.

Works (Crowborough Edition). New York, Doubleday, 24 vols., 1930.

Strange Studies from Life, edited by Peter Ruber. New York, Candlelight Press, 1963.

Arthur Conan Doyle on Sherlock Holmes. London, Favil, 1981.

Essays on Photography, edited by John Michael Gibson and Roger Lancelyn Green. London, Secker and Warburg, 1982.

Letters to the Press: The Unknown Conan Doyle, edited by John Michael Gibson and Roger Lancelyn Green. London, Secker and Warburg, and Iowa City, University of Iowa Press, 1986.

The Sherlock Holmes Letters, edited by Richard Lancelyn Green. London, Secker and Warburg, 1986.

Editor, *D.D. Home: His Life and Mission,* by Mrs. Douglas Home. London, Paul Trench Trubner, and New York, Dutton, 1921.

Editor, *The Spiritualist's Reader.* Manchester, Two Worlds Publishing Company, 1924.

Translator, *The Mystery of Joan of Arc,* by Léon Denis. London, Murray, 1924.; New York, Dutton, 1925.

*

Bibliography: *A Bibliographical Catalogue of the Writings of Sir Arthur Conan Doyle* by Harold Locke, Tunbridge Wells, Kent, Webster, 1928; *The World Bibliography of Sherlock Holmes and Dr. Watson* by Ronald Burt De Waal, Boston, New York Graphic Society, 1975; *A Bibliography of A. Conan Doyle* by Richard Lancelyn Green and John Michael Gibson, Oxford, Clarendor Press, 1983.

Manuscript Collection: Humanities Research Center, University of Texas, Austin.

Critical Studies: *The Private Life of Sherlock Holmes* by Vincent Starrett, New York, Macmillan, 1933, London, Nicholson and Watson, 1934, revised edition, Chicago, University of Chicago Press, 1960, London, Allen and Unwin, 1961; *Conan Doyle: His Life and Art* by Hesketh Pearson, London, Methuen, 1943, New York, Walker, 1961; *The Life of Sir Arthur Conan Doyle* by John Dickson Carr, London, Murray, and New York, Harper, 1949; *In the Footsteps of Sherlock Holmes* by Michael Harrison, London, Cassell, 1958, New York, Fell, 1960, revised edition, Newton Abbot, Devon, David and Charles, 1971, New York, Drake, 1972; *The Man Who Was Sherlock Holmes* by Michael and Mollie Hardwick, London, Murray, and New York, Doubleday, 1964; *Conan Doyle: A Biography* by Pierre Nordon, London, Murray, 1966, New York, Holt Rinehart, 1967; *A Sherlock Holmes Commentary* by D. Martin Dakin, Newton Abbot, Devon, David and Charles, 1972; *A Biography of the Creator of Sherlock Holmes* by Ivor Brown, London, Hamish Hamilton, 1972; *Sherlock Holmes in Portrait and Profile* by Walter Klinefelter, New York, Schocken, 1975; *The Sherlock Holmes File* by Michael Pointer, Newton Abbot, Devon, David and Charles, 1976; *Sir Arthur Conan Doyle's Sherlock Holmes: The Short Stories: A Critical Commentary* by Mary P. De Camara and Stephen Hayes, New York, Monarch, 1976; *The Adventures of Conan Doyle: The Life of the Creator of Sherlock Holmes* by Charles Higham, London, Hamish Hamilton, and New York, Norton, 1976; *The Encyclopedia Sherlockiana* by Jack Tracy, New York, Doubleday, 1977, London, New English Library, 1978; *Conan Doyle: A Biographical Solution* by Ronald Pearsall, London, Weidenfeld and Nicolson, 1977; *Sherlock Holmes and His Creator* by Trevor H. Hall, London, Duckworth, 1978, New York, St. Martin's Press, 1983; *Conan Doyle: Portrait of an Artist* by Julian Symons, London, G. Whizzard, 1979; *Sherlock Holmes: The Man and His World* by H.R.F. Keating, London, Thames and Hudson, and New York, Scribner, 1979; *Who's Who in Sherlock Holmes* by Scott R. Bullard and Michael Collins, New York, Taplinger, 1980; *The International Sherlock Holmes* by Ronald Burt De Waal, Hamden, Connecticut, Shoe String Press, and London, Mansell, 1980; *A Sherlock Holmes Compendium* edited by Peter Haining, London, W.H. Allen, 1980; *Sherlock Holmes in America* by Bill Blackbeard, New York, Abrams, 1981; *Sherlock Holmes: A Study in Sources* by Donald A. Redmond, Montreal, McGill-Queen's University Press, 1982; *The Quest for Sherlock Holmes: A Biographical Study of the Early Life of Sir Arthur Conan Doyle* by Owen Dudley Edwards, Edinburgh, Mainstream, 1982, Totowa, New Jersey, Barnes and Noble,

1983; *A Study in Surmise: The Making of Sherlock Holmes* by Michael Harrison, Bloomington, Indiana, Gaslight, 1984; *Arthur Conan Doyle* by Don Richard Cox, New York, Ungar, 1985; *The Complete Guide to Sherlock Holmes* by Michael Hardwick, London, Weidenfeld and Nicolson, 1986; *Sherlock Holmes: A Centenary Celebration* by Allen Eyles, London, Murray, 1986; *Elementary My Dear Watson: Sherlock Holmes Centenary: His Life and Times* by Graham Nown, New York, Ward Lock, 1986; *The Unrevealed Life of Doctor Arthur Conan Doyle: A Study in Southsea* by Geoffrey Stavert, Horndean, Hampshire, Milestone, 1987; *Arthur Conan Doyle* by Jacqueline A. Jaffe, Boston, Twayne, 1987; *The Quest for Sir Arthur Conan Doyle: Thirteen Biographers in Search of a Life* edited by Jon L. Lellenberg, Carbondale, Southern Illinois University Press, 1987.

*   *   *

The young impecunious doctor who invented, without at first much success, Sherlock Holmes may be said to have in doing so brought about crime literature as a distinct entity. Had it not been for the extraordinary eventual triumph of his character, it is quite possible that what we now call crime writing would not be considered as a separate category at all.

What was it that was so right about Holmes that he had this effect? First, that he was a human being, a person, a man, not a mere single walking attribute nor even a cunning collection of attributes. Wherever he came from—a little from Dr. Joseph Bell, remarkable medical diagnostician, more from someone hidden in the stolid body of Arthur Conan Doyle—he was a person whose opposing qualities, extreme mental and physical agility as against drug-induced opting-out, all that is summed up by the phrase "an English gentleman" as against a "decadent" aesthete dreaming over his violin, somehow complemented each other to make one single, extraordinarily believable person. Second, Holmes was a scientist in an age that was just ready to acknowledge a scientist as hero. General education had just reached the point, when the first Holmes stories appeared in the *Strand* magazine, of providing enough readers armed with some idea of the scientific attitude to make this figure, first seen just after discovering a way of testing for minute quantities of blood, set a chord humming in thousands of minds. Third, Doyle made two valuable technical writing discoveries. There was the series character, which he believed he was the first to hit on. And there was the Watson, the person through whom the average reader can see a superman operating and yet feel comfortable, a pair of eyes to see a clue and miss its meaning.

To these major innovations Doyle was able to add other extremely useful qualities. He could create a memorable character with remarkable economy. A page and a half suffices for the evilly menacing Dr. Grimesby Roylott. And indeed often much of his character creation is done by his simple genius for hitting on the right name (Bartholomew Sholto, Mr. Hall Pycroft, even John H. Watson, M.D.). He found, too, plots that are excellent and stories that would intrigue even if Holmes were absent. He had a gift for laying down some initial oddity that hardly a reader can resist, like the whole conception of the Red-headed League, or he could put in, with just the right judgment, some eerily outré touch, like the two severed ears in the story to which he gave (how rightly) the flat title "The Cardboard Box." And, though by no means all the stories are in the pure puzzle pattern, he was enormously skilful with that, as in the whodunit "Silver Blaze," paving the way for all the puzzle stories of the Golden Age of detection.

Doyle was, too, a splendid writer in the sheer writing. He got his dialogue marvellously right, swiftly economical without any feeling of thinness or austerity, illuminating character in a hundred tiny touches, and when called on wonderfully trenchant ("Mr. Holmes, they were the footsteps of a gigantic hound"). He was equally successful in narrative. He tells his readers just what they need to know just when they need to know it. Seldom indeed does he allow the least digression, and when he does, as in Holmes's sudden discussion of the German essayist Jean-Paul Richter in *The Sign of Four,* it is barely noticeable, totally in character, and put to good service with that sudden jump back into the story proper, "You have not a pistol, have you?"

Always his English is simple and direct, though perfectly naturally so and perfectly capable of rising to a polysyllabic word where a polysyllabic word is called for. And every now and again he produces a phrase that is telling indeed without any appearance of striving to be so. This he was able to do right from the beginning with that description (it is only one of scores as good) in *A Study in Scarlet* of the houses in a Brixton street all with vacant windows on which "here and there a To Let card had developed like a cataract upon the bleared pane."

It is from touches like this as well as from more developed evil characters like the blackmailer Charles Augustus Milverton (another splendid name) that Doyle built up the sense of evil which it gives us so much interior satisfaction to watch Holmes vanquishing. And it is from other phrases quietly rising from the general level that he builds up the necessary counterpoise to that streak of evil, the surrounding cushion of pure cosiness, "the hall-light shining through stained glass, the barometer, and the bright stair rods" (*The Sign of Four*).

But the stories and yet more the novels are not without fault. The four novels are really too long for the Holmes formula to work properly, and indeed in all of them Holmes disappears from the action for long (and generally pretty dull) periods. In the stories the logic can sometimes be found wanting; occasionally the end hardly lives up to the beginning; we are not invariably given the clues Holmes has seen. There are, too, feeble repetitions of particularly successful devices. Holmes even was not always as up-to-date scientifically as he might have been (hot though he was on footprints, fingerprints, with the single exception of an unlikely sealing-wax transfer, are ignored). There are unlikelinesses, generally to do with impenetrable disguises.

But none of these matter. Doyle's extraordinary gifts, for story-telling, for the sounding in us of primeval depths that respond to the mystery of the tale, for the creation of characters, sweep away all criticism. Sherlock Holmes lives, and will as long as there are books, or films, or television series, or feelies, or telethinks.

—H.R.F. Keating

———

DRESSER, Davis. *See* **HALLIDAY, Brett.**

———

DRISCOLL, Peter. British. Born in London, 4 February 1942. Educated at St. David's Marist College, Johannesburg, 1955–58; University of the Witwatersrand, Johannesburg, 1964–66, B.A. 1967. Served in the South African Army, intermittently 1961–66. Married Angela Hennessy in 1967; two daughters. Reporter, *Rand Daily Mail*, Johannesburg, 1959–67;

news editor, Post Newspapers, Johannesburg, 1967–68; scriptwriter and sub-editor, Independent Television News, London, 1969–73. Agent: David Higham Associates, 5–8 Lower John Street, London W1R 4HA, England. Address: Castlecrest, Killincarrig, Delgany, County Wicklow, Ireland.

CRIME PUBLICATIONS

Novels

The White Lie Assignment. London, Macdonald, 1971; Philadelphia, Lippincott, 1975.
The Wilby Conspiracy. Philadelphia, Lippincott, 1972; London, Macdonald, 1973.
In Connection with Kilshaw. Philadelphia, Lippincott, and London, Macdonald 1974.
The Barboza Credentials. Philadelphia, Lippincott, and London, Macdonald and Jane's, 1976.
Pangolin. Philadelphia, Lippincott, and London, Macdonald and Jane's, 1979.
Heritage. London, Granada, and New York, Doubleday, 1982.
Spearhead. New York, Bantam, 1988.

OTHER PUBLICATIONS

Play

Television Play: *The Babysitters,* 1981.

*

Manuscript Collection: Mugar Memorial Library, Boston University.

Peter Driscoll comments:

I have always considered a good crime novel/suspense story/thriller to be an achievement at least as solid as a mediocre serious novel. This is truer than ever today, when novelists, in their search for new horizons, have moved into the realms of surrealism; crime writers are increasingly filling the gap to meet the demand for good old-fashioned story-telling, and some have achieved a depth and insight worthy of the best "straight" novelists. So, while I accept the limitations imposed by the genre, I hope one day to be able to extend them.

The starting point for all the books I have written—and perhaps the key by which any one of them might be described—is a setting. Often it is a place with a background of some political or social instability which I like to examine in some detail and which gives an undertone of tension to the narrative. One critic (writing in the St. Louis *Post-Dispatch*) said, "Driscoll weaves a tight drama of suspense and adventure around an existing social-political situation." My first book, *The White Lie Assignment,* was set in the Greek-Albanian border country; the story of *The Wilby Conspiracy* unfolded against the background of apartheid in South Africa; *In Connection with Kilshaw* dealt with the troubles in Northern Ireland; *The Barboza Credentials* was set in newly-independent Mozambique.

Beyond the obvious elements of action, conflict, and suspense, what I try hardest to communicate are authenticity, atmosphere, and—an elusive but essential ingredient—the quality of fear. That, after all, is what every thriller ought to be about.

*   *   *

The Wilby Conspiracy showed Peter Driscoll to be a first-rate practitioner of the type of thriller, developed by Buchan and perfected by Ambler, in which an individual inadvertently becomes enmeshed in a dangerous bit of international intrigue. Driscoll's hero, James Keogh, resembles Richard Hannay more than a little. A mining engineer on holiday in Cape Town, Keogh suddenly finds himself on the run from the South African police, accompanied by a black nationalist fugitive recently escaped from prison. Gradually Keogh discovers that he and his companion are being used by the South African secret police in a complicated plot to kidnap a black revolutionary leader living in exile in Botswana since his escape from South Africa several years earlier. Driscoll successfully individualizes Keogh, in part by creating a romantic sub-plot, and he is particularly effective at creating and sustaining suspense through a well-paced chase sequence that takes up the central portion of the book. *The Wilby Conspiracy,* however, is something more than a well-executed variation of a formula thriller. Driscoll offers a devastating portrait of the South African secret police—cunning, brutal, sadistic—who are the linchpin of apartheid.

In Connection with Kilshaw is equally accomplished in technique and political statement. Harry Finn, the central character, is a burnt-out case, a British army intelligence officer who has barely survived massive radiation treatments for throat cancer. Attached to a high-ranking Home Office civil servant with vaguely defined responsibilities, Finn agrees to go into Northern Ireland, ostensibly to collect damaging information about a Protestant demagogue, James Kilshaw, who is moving openly toward civil war. Gradually Finn realizes that he has been set up to play an unwitting part in a conspiracy to assassinate Kilshaw in such a way as to leave no trace of British complicity. A tough, resourceful, but basically decent man, Finn is appalled to discover that the price of Kilshaw's death, agreed to by Finn's superior, is a shipment of M-16 rifles delivered into the hands of an IRA faction for use in a future revolution in the south of Ireland.

The White Lie Assignment, his first novel, is a merely competent, routine thriller. To the character of Michael Mannis, a naturalized British citizen of Greek ancestry, Driscoll gives perfunctory attention. Mannis, a freelance photographer rather than a trained agent, agrees to go into Albania on a one-shot contract to photograph a secret missile site established by the Chinese. He succeeds in getting the photographs but is double-crossed and spends the second half of the book extricating himself from the erstwhile employer. A workmanlike but hardly stylish effort, *The White Lie Assignment* lacks the originality and the intensity of the later two books. A fourth novel, *The Barboza Credentials,* too, lacks their brilliance. The central character, Joe Hickey, is a former Kenyan police officer turned mining machinery salesman and engaged in evading the United Nation's sanctions against Rhodesia. Vulnerable to blackmail, he finds himself compelled to aid Mozambique officials in their search for the "Barboza credentials," documents that will permit a notorious Portuguese former secret police officer to flee the country. Though Driscoll shows himself adept at contriving a complicated conspiracy, the story lacks the sustained tension of *Wilby* or the skillful evocation of place that enriches *Kilshaw.* And Joe Hickey, while more substantially characterized than Michael Mannis, is not as convincing as Keogh or Finn. Given the quality of his middle two books, *The Barboza Credentials* may represent Driscoll's temporary decline to the level of creditable but not remarkable competency.

—R. Gordon Kelly

DRUMMOND, Charles. *See* **McGirr, Edmund.**

DRUMMOND, Ivor. *See* **PARRISH, Frank.**

DRUMMOND, J. *See* **CHANCE, John Newton.**

DRUMMOND, June. South African. Born in Durban, Natal, 15 November 1923. Educated at the University of Cape Town, B.A. 1944. Journalist, *Woman's Weekly* and *Natal Mercury,* both Durban, 1946–48; secretary in London, 1948–50, and with Durban Civic Orchestra, 1950–53; assistant secretary, Church Adoption Society, London, 1954–60; chair, Durban Adoption Committee, Indian Child Welfare Society, 1963–74. Address: 24 Miller Grove, Durban, 4001 Natal, South Africa.

CRIME PUBLICATIONS

Novels

The Black Unicorn. London, Gollancz, 1959.
Welcome, Proud Lady. London, Gollancz, 1964; New York, Holt Rinehart, 1968.
Cable-Car. London, Gollancz, 1965; New York, Holt Rinehart, 1967.
The Saboteurs. London, Gollancz, 1967; New York, Holt Rinehart, 1969.
The Gantry Episode. London, Gollancz, 1968; as *Murder on a Bad Trip,* New York, Holt Rinehart, 1968.
The People in Glass House. London, Gollancz, 1969; New York, Simon and Schuster, 1970.
Farewell Party. London, Gollancz, 1971; New York, Dodd Mead, 1973.
Bang! Bang! You're Dead. London, Gollancz, 1973.
The Boon Companions. London, Collins, 1974; as *Drop Dead,* New York, Walker, 1976.
Slowly the Poison. London, Gollancz, 1975; New York, Walker, 1976.
Funeral Urn. London, Gollancz, 1976; New York, Walker, 1977.
The Patriots. London, Gollancz, 1979.
I Saw Him Die. London, Gollancz, 1979.
Such a Nice Family. London, Gollancz, 1980.
The Trojan Mule. London, Gollancz, 1982.
The Bluestocking. London, Gollancz, 1985.

Junta. London, Gollancz, 1989.
The Unsuitable Miss Pelham. London, Gollancz, 1990.

OTHER PUBLICATIONS

Novels

Thursday's Child. London, Gollancz, 1961.
A Time to Speak. London, Gollancz, 1962; Cleveland, World, 1963.
A Cage of Humming-Birds. London, Gollancz, 1964.

*

June Drummond comments:
Readers of crime fiction are, I believe, interested in two things. The first is the puzzle to be solved. The second is the nature of the crime itself, what creates and motivates the criminal, and how his actions affect his environment, be it family, city, state or world. In writing crime novels, I try to satisfy readers on these two counts.

*   *   *

June Drummond, a native of South Africa, has written 18 crime and mystery novels. Her two recent novels, *Junta,* a topical thriller set in South Africa, and *The Bluestocking,* a witty mystery set in London and the rural countryside in the world of high society during the Regency period, represent Drummond at her best in two of the strains that have characterized her writings.

Junta benefits richly from the author's South African past. Published shortly before the release of Nelson Mandela and De Klerk's announcement of his platform to dismantle apartheid, the novel offers a timely commentary upon racism, international politics, terrorism, and South Africa while spinning its tale of intrigue. The plot involves events surrounding the decision of the newly elected president of South Africa to release from prison a young black revolutionary leader, Vusi Matlala, whose charismatic personality can either calm or ignite the black community. News of his imminent release stirs unrest within the black townships, and a newly organized group of roaming black gangs threaten to produce the kind of violence for which the white reactionary forces long. We swiftly discover that these gangs are the creations of Mathias, who has hired mercenaries to incite riots. He is also plotting to have Matlala assassinated, which will cause the economic markets to tumble and so bring about the fall of the new president and South Africa's government. It is the task of Ross McCrae, also an employee of the multinational corporation in which Mathias has a strong interest, to come to the assistance of Matlala and expose the corruption in his own company. The success of this novel lies in its topicality, Drummond's journalistic skill in describing the racial tensions in South Africa, and her treatment of characters, particularly the black leaders and the native South Africans of Afrikaner descent.

The Bluestocking represents a change of pace for Drummond, but its cast of characters will be familiar to her fans as will its interest in scandal, rape, contested inheritances, and other material often found in gothic novels. In *The Bluestocking* Drummond attempts a recreation of an earlier period in Britain's history where she can show her skill at recreating the costumes, the spectacle, the masquerades, fashions, and punctilios of an earlier time. Like Erica Jong in *Fanny,* or Joyce Carol Oates in her excursions into American neo-gothic, Drummond shows her wit, high spirits, and fondness of dialect and precise diction in this novel. She certainly lacks the talent of Jane Austen, but there are many moments in this book reminiscent of Austen's treatment of Wickham's elopement in *Pride and Prejudice* or of her humor at Catherine's expense in *Northanger Abbey*. Drummond should make further excursions in this vein of writing.

An examination of Drummond's earlier writings reveals *Cable-Car* to typify her writings. Set in an Alpine village, it spins an admirably contrived tale of several suspenseful days when a famous engineer, Paul Roman, and his daughter, Lisa, are held in a cable car stuck midway in the air to prevent a dam being built. Steve Talbot, Lisa's fiancé and the bodyguard and secretary of Roman, and Anton Dominic, Commissioner of Police, struggle to save their lives in an atmosphere of intrigue and an impending political election. Seeking clues about the identity of the conspirators holding Roman, Talbot and Dominic delve into Roman's past when his beautiful wife, believed dead, and he were partisans. Ultimately, Talbot recalls an illusionist's trick and realizes that Roman's wife is not dead, but is a defector from the West, bent on revenge upon her husband's name and upon the town whose future he was shaping to capitalistic ends. The story reaches its climax when Marthe Roman is captured, and Talbot realizes that an imposter, and not Roman, is in the cable car.

The elements in this novel recur in various forms in all other Drummond tales. In *Cable-Car*, Marthe Roman is the liar, saboteur, and traitor to her country, the beautiful but deadly goddess who bewitches men to destroy them. In *The People in Glass House*, two women shape the tale: Grace Villier, the president of a vast industrial empire, who uses blackmail and putative bastardy to guarantee that her son shall assume her place in the business, and Emma Salt, the mysterious claimant of half this empire, who, too, resorts to blackmail and guerilla tactics to ensure that her story is heard and her identity determined. In *Farewell Party* Drummond creates two women enchantresses: Kate Falconer, a vibrant reckless woman artist whose mysterious disappearance amid rumors of scandal, murder, and suicide must be unravelled if the lives of the inhabitants of Kolumbe and Michael Crescent are to be secure, and a half-mad keeper of a secret garden, Gretha Corbitt, who knows the truth about Kate. *Welcome, Proud Lady* features a brilliant female who fears that the frequent accidents in her family's past are part of a dark design in which her sanity is being tested. In both *The Gantry Episode* and *The Saboteurs* the estranged wife of the powerful protagonist figures prominently in the mystery. Drummond seems fond of weaving tales that distantly descend from gothic horror stories. Half-mad women, mistaken identities, bitter rivalries among kin, men of raffish ways, and women moon-goddesses who destroy those near them, all appear in her pages.

The settings in her novels are of two kinds: the imaginary village in a changing world, fraught by factions, or real cities, London or Durban, populated by powerful, socially elite individuals who struggle to maintain their inheritances, be it an industrial empire or personal legacy such as the rare Rigborough Missal, a medieval illuminated manuscript. Drummond's failure in novels like *Cable-Car* and *The Gantry Episode* to locate her story in real places mars the credibility of her tales. It is as though she asks us to believe there is a convenient Transylvania-Chinese border where her story can be set. Much of the success of *Junta* derives from Drummond's decision to set the action in the country of her birth.

Finally, Drummond's fascination with men of money and power who are rendered helpless by a beautiful, but destructive woman, usually either their mother, mistress, or wife, is a recurring element. Too, there is frequently a hint of love interest. In *Farewell Party*, the first-person narrator, who works to unravel the mystery of her aunt's disappearance, finds herself drawn to a young man who also has inordinate interest in her aunt's history. In *Cable-Car*, Lisa and Steve Talbot are courting one another; in *The People in Glass House*, the heir apparent of the industrial empire is drawn to the mysterious claimant who turns out to be his half-sister. In *The Bluestocking*, Lucas Rowan regains his good name and wins the hand of the heroine, Davina Wakeford. In many of Drummond's more recent novels, especially *Farewell Party* and *Funeral Urn*, the cast of characters and the mode of narration are reminiscent of Mary Roberts Rinehart's. And, like Rinehart, Drummond seems to be unable to resist involving her characters in moral dilemmas and using the suspense tale as a novel of character development. This impulse is strongest in her treatment of the moral redemption of Casper Douglas in *The Saboteurs*.

Many of Drummond's novels have been marred by a lack of inventiveness in her construction of character. Too often the characters are trivial, the situations stock, and the moralizing too obtrusive. She works best telling a tale of the personal past of her protagonists. Generally, these tales are convoluted, full of false identities and moments of discovery. Recently, she has been able to locate these tales in convincingly real settings, or in very cleverly reconstructed settings from the past. More to her credit is the fact that in *The Bluestocking* she manipulated a genre that permits her moments of didactic commentary. In *Junta* her unsparing descriptions of a racist society provide a marked departure from some of the easy moralizing that marred her earlier writings. She is a skillful writer who handles prose well.

—Carol Simpson Stern

DUDLEY-SMITH, T. *See* **HALL, Adam.**

DUKE, Will. *See* **GAULT, William Campbell.**

---

du MAURIER, Daphne. British. Born in London, 13 May 1907; daughter of the actor/manager Sir Gerald du Maurier; granddaughter of the writer George du Maurier. Educated privately and in Paris. Married Lieutenant-General Sir Frederick Browning in 1932 (died 1965); two daughters and one son. Recipient: Mystery Writers of America Grand Master award, 1977. Fellow, Royal Society of Literature, 1952. D.B.E. (Dame Commander, Order of the British Empire), 1969. *Died 19 April 1989.*

CRIME PUBLICATIONS

Novels

Jamaica Inn. London, Gollancz, and New York, Doubleday, 1936.
Rebecca. London, Gollancz, and New York, Doubleday, 1938.
My Cousin Rachel. London, Gollancz, 1951; New York, Doubleday, 1952.

The Scapegoat. London, Gollancz, and New York, Doubleday, 1957.
The Flight of the Falcon. London, Gollancz, and New York, Doubleday, 1965.
The House on the Strand. London, Gollancz, and New York, Doubleday, 1969.

Short Stories

The Apple Tree: A Short Novel, and Some Stories. London, Gollancz, 1952; as *Kiss Me Again, Stranger: A Collection of Eight Stories, Long and Short,* New York, Doubleday, 1953; as *The Birds and Other Stories,* London, Penguin, 1968.
The Breaking Point: Eight Stories. London, Gollancz, and New York, Doubleday, 1959; as *The Blue Lenses and Other Stories,* London, Penguin, 1970.
Not after Midnight and Other Stories. London, Gollancz, 1971; as *Don't Look Now,* New York, Doubleday, 1971.
Echoes from the Macabre: Selected Stories. London, Gollancz, 1976; New York, Doubleday, 1977.
Classics of the Macabre. London, Gollancz, and New York, Doubleday, 1987.

OTHER PUBLICATIONS

Novels

The Loving Spirit. London, Heinemann, and New York, Doubleday, 1931.
I'll Never Be Young Again. London, Heinemann, and New York, Doubleday, 1932.
The Progress of Julius. London, Heinemann, and New York, Doubleday, 1933.
Frenchman's Creek. London, Gollancz, 1941; New York, Doubleday, 1942.
Hungry Hill. London, Gollancz, and New York, Doubleday, 1943.
The King's General. London, Gollancz, and New York, Doubleday, 1946.
The Parasites. London, Gollancz, 1949; New York, Doubleday, 1950.
Mary Anne. London, Gollancz, and New York, Doubleday, 1954.
Castle Dor, by Arthur Quiller-Couch, completed by du Maurier. London, Dent, and New York, Doubleday, 1962.
The Glass-Blowers. London, Gollancz, and New York, Doubleday, 1963.
Rule Britannia. London, Gollancz, 1972; New York, Doubleday, 1973.

Short Stories

Happy Christmas (story). New York, Doubleday, 1940; London, Todd, 1943.
Come Wind, Come Weather. London, Heinemann, 1940; New York, Doubleday, 1941.
Nothing Hurts for Long, and Escort. London, Todd, 1943.
Consider the Lilies (story). London, Todd, 1943.
Spring Picture (story). London, Todd, 1944.
Leading Lady (story). London, Vallancey Press, 1945.
London and Paris (two stories). London, Vallancey Press, 1945.
Early Stories. London, Todd, 1954.
The Treasury of du Maurier Short Stories. London, Gollancz, 1960.
The Lover and Other Stories. London, Ace, 1961.
The Rendezvous and Other Stories. London, Gollancz, 1980.

Plays

Rebecca, adaptation of her own novel (produced Manchester and London, 1940; New York, 1945). London, Gollancz, 1940; New York, Dramatists Play Service, 1943.
The Years Between (produced Manchester, 1944; London, 1945). London, Gollancz, 1945; New York, Doubleday, 1946.
September Tide (produced Oxford and London, 1948). London, Gollancz, 1949; New York, Doubleday, 1950.

Screenplay: *Hungry Hill,* with Terence Young and Francis Crowdry, 1947.

Television Play: *The Breakthrough,* 1976.

Other

Gerald: A Portrait (on Gerald du Maurier). London, Gollancz, 1934; New York, Doubleday, 1935.
The du Mauriers. London, Gollancz, and New York, Doubleday, 1937.
The Infernal World of Branwell Brontë. London, Gollancz, 1960; New York, Doubleday, 1961.
Vanishing Cornwall, photographs by Christian Browning. London, Gollancz, and New York, Doubleday, 1967.
Golden Lads: Sir Francis Bacon, Anthony Bacon, and Their Friends. London, Gollancz, and New York, Doubleday, 1975.
The Winding Stair: Francis Bacon, His Rise and Fall. London, Gollancz, 1976; New York, Doubleday, 1977.
Growing Pains: The Shaping of a Writer (autobiography). London, Gollancz, 1977; as *Myself When Young,* New York, Doubleday, 1977.
The Rebecca Notebook and Other Memories (includes short stories). New York, Doubleday, 1980; London, Gollancz, 1981.
Enchanted Cornwell: Her Pictorial Memoir, edited by Piers Dudgeon, photographs by Nick Wright. London, Joseph, 1989; New York, Viking, 1990.

Editor, *The Young George du Maurier: A Selection of His Letters 1860–1867.* London, Davies, 1951; New York, Doubleday, 1952.
Editor, *Best Stories,* by Phyllis Bottome. London, Faber, 1963.

*   *   *

Among Daphne du Maurier's excellent studies in suspense are four novels which focus upon the beautifully paced delineation of an unusually powerful personality. Also portrayed is a less glamorous but equally fascinating protagonist who recounts a plot complicated by jealousy and misconception. The impact of some criminal act, real or imagined, affects each situation, and the novels end on notes of ironic justice.

The unnamed protagonist of *Rebecca* is kept from full happiness by her lack of self-confidence and because she lives under the ghostly shadow of a brilliant, headstrong first wife. The mounting tension surrounding Rebecca's mysterious death combines with a vividly evoked setting to achieve the novel's remarkable and deserved success. The title character of *My Cousin Rachel* is beloved by two cousins, Ambrose and Philip Ashley. Rachel may be a true gentlewoman or a merciless poisoner, and this mystery is enchanced by Philip's convincingly dramatized search for maturity. *The Scapegoat* makes probable a wild coincidence when the narrator is tricked into temporarily living the life of Jean de Gué whom he strikingly resembles. Much of the impact stems from his developing sense of himself as he learns to wield the power de Gué customarily exercises. *The Flight of the Falcon* contrasts Armino and Aldo Donati in a compelling examination of the hunger for personal and political power of both modern and Renaissance man.

These, like many of du Maurier's works, raise serious questions about the nature of good and of evil—then enticingly leave the answers to the reader's imagination.

—Jane S. Bakerman

———

DUNCAN, Robert L. *See* **ROBERTS, James Hall.**

———

DUNLAP, Susan (D. née Sullivan). Born in Kew Gardens, New York, 20 June 1943. Educated at Bucknell University, Lewisburg, Pennsylvania, B.A. in English 1965; University of North Carolina, MAT in English 1966. Married Newell Dunlap in 1970. Social worker, Department of Social Services, Baltimore, Maryland, 1966–67, New York City, 1967–67, and Contra Costa County, California 1968–84. President, Sisters in Crime 1990–91. Agent: Dominick Abel, 146 West 82nd Street, New York, New York 10024, U.S.A.

CRIME PUBLICATIONS

Novels (series: Vejay Haskell; Jill Smith)

Karma (Smith). New York, Paperjacks, 1984.
As a Favor (Smith). New York, St. Martin's Press, 1984; London, Hale, 1986.
An Equal Opportunity Death (Haskell). New York, St. Martin's Press, 1984; London, Hale, 1986.
Not Exactly a Brahmin (Smith). New York, St. Martin's Press, 1985.
The Bohemian Connection (Haskell). New York, St. Martin's Press, 1985. London, Hale, 1987.
The Last Annual Slugfest (Haskell). New York, St. Martin's Press, 1986.
Too Close to the Edge (Smith). New York, St. Martin's Press, 1987.
A Dinner to Die For (Smith). New York, St. Martin's Press, 1987.
Pious Deception. New York, Villard, 1989.
Diamond in the Buff (Smith). New York, St. Martin's Press, 1990.

Uncollected Short Stories

"Double Jeopardy," in *Ellery Queen's Mystery Magazine* (New York), 1980.
"A Burning Issue," in *Alfred Hitchcock's Mystery Magazine* (New York), April 1981.
"Hit-and-Run," in *Criminal Elements*, edited by Bill Pronzini and Martin H. Greenberg. New York, Ivy Books, 1988.
"Out on a Limb," in *Mistletoe Mysteries,* edited by Charlotte MacLeod. New York, Mysterious Press, 1989.
"No Safety," in *Sisters in Crime*, edited by Marilyn Wallace. New York, Berkley, 1989; London, W.H. Allen, 1990.

"The Celestial Buffet," in *Sisters in Crime 2*, edited by Marilyn Wallace. New York, Berkley, 1990.

*

Susan Dunlap comments:
I write in the three categories of detective: the police detective, the private investigator, and the amateur. All my detectives are women who hold or have had non-traditional jobs. But the unifying factor in all my books is a "sense of place" because I believe where people live has a strong influence on the way they think, live, react, and who and how they choose to kill.

Homicide Detective Jill Smith moved to Berkeley, California, with no clear plan for her life. She passed the test for the police department and was pleasantly surprised at how well she handled the job. In the years she has lived in Berkeley, she has shifted her view from that of an outsider, to someone who has found her place and come to love the peculiarities of her city: the more left-than-thou politics, the passionate interest in the environment, the underdog, California cuisine. "In Berkeley, nothing is too inconsequential to be the center of controversy. . . People in Berkeley love their city and its liberal heritage, and they are prepared to defend it against all comers—and against each other. The battles are fierce, attenuated, bitter, and deep down, enjoyed by all." (*Too Close to the Edge*)

Kiernan O'Shaughnessy, who first appears in *Pious Deception*, runs her own successful agency in which she investigates cases that require her background as a forensic pathologist. As an adolescent she was a competitive gymnast. "I don't take small cases. I have a decadent life style to maintain." She lives in a duplex on the beach in LaJolla (just north of San Diego, California) and has an ex-football player as her houseman, cook, and dog walker.

Vejay Haskell left the rat race in San Francisco to become a utility meter reader in the Russian River Resort area north of there, climbing up "endless staircases" to electric meters that reveal secrets not only about the summer people's electricity usage or the winter people's lack of it, but the conflict between the two groups as the area changes from a woodsy, folksy area to "affordable housing" for San Franciscans.

* * *

Susan Dunlap specializes in creating California atmosphere; in two of her three series, setting is as important as plot. The Vejay Haskell series is set in fictional Russian River resort town in Sonoma County, California. The Russian River is renowned for being flooded out almost annually, for its summer and weekend cottages, and its arts-and-crafts community which is actually more of a hold-over from the flower-power days of the 1960's. Vejay is a newly hired meter reader for P.G. & E, the northern California electric power and natural gas supplier. It is Vejay's access to various homes, her native curiosity, and her status as outsider that gets her started on the detection trail. In *An Equal Opportunity Death,* she investigates the murder of a local bartender because she is suspected of the murder herself. In subsequent novels, she is considered an "expert" in murder investigation and is recruited by suspects to clear them. The atmosphere of a Sonoma County landmark, the all-male Bohemian Club retreat, and all the associated crimes that accompany it (drugs, prostitution, etc.) are featured in *The Bohemian Connection,* while salmon fishing, logging and a festival featuring various ways to serve up slugs (the state mollusc) are the central themes in *The Last Annual Slugfest.*

The "radical" university town of Berkeley, California is the setting for the Jill Smith series and the choice of such a location lends authenticity to the novels. For example, *As a Favor* starts out in the People's Park, and *A Dinner to Die For* is centered around food poisoning and eventual murder in the "Gourmet Ghetto." *Not Exactly a Brahmin* takes the reader on a tour of the fast food joints; the street people of Telegraph Avenue; the high class neighborhoods in the hills overlooking the city and the Bay; and other Berkeley landmarks as the police pursue the perpetrators. Weather is often a key factor in the stories, and Berkeley's radically liberal politics is reflected in the humor of the crimes which start off each book, regardless of the brutality of the ultimate murder. For example, *As a Favor* begins with the systematic theft of radio antennae, hub caps, and tail light reflectors from Seth Howard's patrol car, and *Diamond in the Buff* begins with an assault by eucalyptus branch, on "Has-Bitched" Diamond, a local character and pest who is carrying on a feud, through the courts and police department, with his neighbor.

The Smith series is a police prodecural, with multiple case loads and parallel investigations, some of which intersect. Dunlap is expert in combining the actual ambience of the Berkeley police department with a series of characterizations of beat officers and detectives: Connie Pereira, the beat officer who just happens to be a financial wizard; Murakawa, who wants to be a physical therapist; Raksen, the obsessive ID tech; Sergeant Grayson, who wanted the job in homicide and therefore resents Jill who got it; Inspector Doyle, who isn't convinced that a woman *can* be a homicide detective; Jackson, the veteran homicide detective whose son trades fresh-brewed coffee for swimming lessons from Jill; and Seth Howard, Jill's office mate who works vice. Beginning with *Too Close to the Edge* and continuing through *Diamond in the Buff*, Dunlap's writing shows a trend toward deeper reliance on characterization and less on background scenery. As the series progresses the reader learns more about Jill's background and her relationship with Howard.

Dunlap's third series features former medical examiner turned private eye, Kiernan O'Shaughnessy. Kiernan is hardboiled but still a little vulnerable in *Pious Deception*. In this case she travels from her beach-side San Diego home to a small Phoenix parish to investigate the suicide (or was it murder?) of an ambitious parish priest. Kiernan's antagonism toward the Catholic Church almost makes her turn the job down, and she starts to regret taking it when it begins to look as if she is being set up to take the blame for the potential scandal the Church hopes to avoid. In this novel, the California background is just that—background, not the central theme—while the characterization of Kiernan is critical in the solution to the crime.

Dunlap has employed three different backgrounds with three radically different heroines (amateur detective, police officer, and licensed private detective) to create eminently readable novels which couple authenticity of setting with a bizarre sense of humor.

—Carol M. Harper

DUNNETT, Dorothy (nee Halliday). Has also written as Dorothy Halliday. British. Born in Dunfermline, Fife, 25 August 1923. Educated at James Gillespie's High School, Edinburgh; Edinburgh College of Art; Glasgow School of Art. Married Alistair M. Dunnett in 1946; two sons. Assistant press officer, Scottish government departments, Edinburgh, 1940–46; member of the Board of Trade Scottish Economics Department, Glasgow, 1946–55. Since 1950 professional portrait painter: exhibitions at the Royal Scottish Academy,

Edinburgh; since 1979 director, Scottish Television plc, Edinburgh. Since 1986 trustee, National Library of Scotland. Recipient: Scottish Arts Council award, 1976. Fellow, Royal Society of Arts, 1986. Agent: Curtis Brown, 162–168 Regent Street, London W1R 5TB, England. Address: 87 Colinton Road, Edinburgh EH10 5DF, Scotland.

CRIME PUBLICATIONS

Novels (series: Johnson Johnson in all Dolly books; originally published as Dorothy Halliday in UK)

Dolly and the Singing Bird. London, Cassell, 1968; as *The Photogenic Soprano*, Boston, Houghton Mifflin, 1968.
Dolly and the Cookie Bird. London, Cassell, 1970; as *Murder in the Round*, Boston, Houghton Mifflin, 1970.
Dolly and the Doctor Bird. London, Cassell, 1971; as *Match for a Murderer*, Boston, Houghton Mifflin, 1971.
Dolly and the Starry Bird. London, Cassell, 1973; as *Murder in Focus*, Boston, Houghton Mifflin, 1973.
Dolly and the Nanny Bird. London, Joseph, 1976; New York, Knopf, 1982.
Dolly and the Bird of Paradise. London, Joseph, 1983; New York, Knopf, 1984.
Untitled. London, Chatto and Windus, 1990.

OTHER PUBLICATIONS

Novels

The Game of Kings. New York, Putnam, 1961; London, Cassell, 1962.
Queens' Play. London, Cassell, and New York, Putnam, 1964.
The Disorderly Knights. London, Cassell, and New York, Putnam, 1966.
Pawn in Frankincense. London, Cassell, and New York, Putnam, 1969.
The Ringed Castle. London, Cassell, 1971; New York, Putnam, 1972.
Checkmate. London, Cassell, and New York, Putnam, 1975.
King Hereafter. London, Joseph, and New York, Knopf, 1982.
Niccolò Rising. London, Joseph, and New York, Knopf, 1986.
The Spring of the Ram. London, Joseph, 1987; New York, Knopf, 1988.
Race of Scorpions. London, Joseph, 1989; London, Knopf, 1990.

Other

The Scottish Highlands, with Alistair M. Dunnett, photographs by David Paterson. Edinburgh, Mainstream, 1988.

*

Bibliography: in *Book and Magazine Collector* 53 (London), August 1988.

Dorothy Dunnett comments:
My crime books are fast fun-thrillers about a portrait painter called Johnson Johnson who sails his own yacht, the *Dolly,* to a series of glamorous posts as a cover for a world-wide Intelligence job. The narrator of each is a pretty girl—each one quite different, with a distinctive job of her own. Which of

them gets Johnson in the end will not be apparent until his series finishes.

* * *

Dorothy Dunnett has produced a series of detective/suspense novels loosely united by the presence of their hero, Johnson Johnson, an international portrait painter and spy. Johnson, whose baggy sweaters and bifocals camouflage a first-rate mind, owes a great deal to Allingham's early Albert Campion, including his generous capacity to keep to the background while some remarkable heroines occupy center stage and narrate their adventures. There is little to choose between the heroines for intelligence, competence, or charm, but perhaps the most impressive, in different ways, are Tina Rossi, the coloratura of *Dolly and the Singing Bird,* and Dr. Beltanno Douglas Mac Rannoch of *Dolly and the Doctor Bird.* Tina Rossi is a portrait whose full tragic dimensions are concealed until almost the last page. Dr. Mac Rannoch must be brought to accept her sexuality before she can take charge of her own destiny, and Dunnett handles the theme with as much delicacy as humor.

The basic genre of the novels is the suspense story: each is full of action, including at least one superb chase sequence. In *Dolly and the Doctor Bird,* Johnson's ketch *Dolly* only narrowly escapes an explosive small boat with a homing device. In *Dolly and the Starry Bird,* there is a car chase with explosive balloons along Roman roads in rush-hour traffic that modulates from the chilling to the farcical. All of this is rendered in a sophisticated prose which is elegantly constructed, idiomatic, and thick with detail from the worlds of music, medicine, astronomy, and gastronomy.

—Carol Cleveland

DURBRIDGE, Francis (Henry). Also writes as Paul Temple. British. Born in Hull, Yorkshire, 25 November 1912. Educated at Bradford Grammar School; Wylde Green College; Birmingham University, 1933. Married Norah Elizabeth Lawley in 1940; two sons. Worked briefly in a stockbroker's office before becoming full-time writer. Agent: Lemon, Unna and Durbridge Ltd., 24–32 Pottery Lane, London W11 4LZ, England.

CRIME PUBLICATIONS

Novels (series: Tim Frazer; Paul Temple)

Send for Paul Temple (novelization of radio serial), with John Thewes. London, Long, 1938.
Paul Temple and the Front Page Men (novelization of radio serial), with Charles Hatton. London, Long, 1939.
News of Paul Temple (novelization of radio serial), with Charles Hatton. London, Long, 1940.
Paul Temple Intervenes (novelization of radio serial), with Charles Hatton. London, Long, 1944.
Send for Paul Temple Again! (novelization of radio serial), with Charles Hatton. London, Long, 1948.
The Back Room Girl. London, Long, 1950.
Beware of Johnny Washington. London, Long, 1951.
Design for Murder. London, Long, 1951.

The Tyler Mystery (Temple), with Douglas Rutherford (as Paul Temple). London, Hodder and Stoughton, 1957.
The Other Man. London, Hodder and Stoughton, 1958.
East of Algiers (Temple), with Douglas Rutherford (as Paul Temple). London, Hodder and Stoughton, 1959.
A Time of Day. London, Hodder and Stoughton, 1959.
The Scarf. London, Hodder and Stoughton, 1960; as *The Case of the Twisted Scarf,* New York, Dodd Mead, 1961.
Portrait of Alison. London, Hodder and Stoughton, and New York, Dodd Mead, 1962.
The World of Tim Frazer. London, Hodder and Stoughton, and New York, Dodd Mead, 1962.
My Friend Charles. London, Hodder and Stoughton, 1963.
Tim Frazer Again. London, Hodder and Stoughton, 1964.
Another Woman's Shoes. London, Hodder and Stoughton, 1965.
The Desperate People. London, Hodder and Stoughton, 1966.
Dead to the World. London, Hodder and Stoughton, 1967.
My Wife Melissa. London, Hodder and Stoughton, 1967.
The Pig-Tail Murder. London, Hodder and Stoughton, 1969.
Paul Temple and the Kelby Affair. London, Hodder and Stoughton, 1970.
Paul Temple and the Harkdale Robbery. London, Hodder and Stoughton, 1970.
A Man Called Harry Brent (novelization of television series). London, Hodder and Stoughton, 1970.
The Geneva Mystery (Temple). London, Hodder and Stoughton, 1971.
Bat Out of Hell. London, Hodder and Stoughton, 1972.
The Curzon Case (Temple). London, Coronet, 1972.
A Game of Murder. London, Hodder and Stoughton, 1975.
The Passenger. London, Hodder and Stoughton, 1977.
Tim Frazer Gets the Message. London, Hodder and Stoughton, 1978.
The Breakaway. London, Hodder and Stoughton, 1981.
The Doll. London, Hodder and Stoughton, 1982.
Paul Temple and the Margo Mystery. London, Hodder and Stoughton, 1986.
Paul Temple and the Madison Case. London, Hodder and Stoughton, 1988.

OTHER PUBLICATIONS

Plays

Suddenly at Home (produced London, 1971). London, French, 1973.
The Gentle Hook (produced London, 1974). London, French, 1975.
Murder with Love (produced Windsor, 1976). London, French, 1977.
The Grandma Game (produced Brighton, 1980).
House Guest (produced London, 1981). London, French, 1982.
Nightcap (produced Guildford, 1983). London, French, 1986; as *Deadly Nightcap* (produced London, 1986).
A Touch of Danger, (produced Leatherhead and London, 1988).

Screenplays: *Send for Paul Temple,* with John Argyle, 1946; *Calling Paul Temple,* with A.R. Rawlinson, 1948; *Paul Temple Returns,* 1952; *The Teckman Mystery,* with James Matthews, 1954; *The Vicious Circle (The Circle),* 1957.

Radio Plays: *Promotion,* 1933; *Paul Temple,* 1938; *Information Received,* 1938; *And Anthony Sherwood Laughed,* 1940; *We Were Strangers,* 1941; *Send for Paul Temple,* 1941; *Mr. Hartington Died Tomorrow* (as Lewis Middleton Harvey), 1942;

Paul Temple Intervenes, 1942; *The Essential Heart,* 1943; *Farewell Leicester Square* (as Lewis Middleton Harvey), 1943; *News of Paul Temple,* 1944; *Send for Paul Temple Again,* 1945; *Over My Dead Body,* 1946; *Paul Temple and the Gregory Affair,* 1946; *The Case for Paul Temple,* 1946; *Paul Temple and Steve,* 1947; *Paul Temple and the Sullivan Mystery,* 1947; *Mr. and Mrs. Paul Temple,* 1947; *Paul Temple and the Curzon Case,* 1948; *Paul Temple and the Madison Mystery,* 1949; *Johnny Washington Esquire* (series), 1949; *Paul Temple and the Vandyke Affair,* 1950; *Paul Temple and the Jonathan Mystery,* 1951; *Paul Temple and Steve Again,* 1953; *Paul Temple and the Lawrence Affair,* 1956; *Paul Temple and the Spencer Affair,* 1957; *Paul Temple and the Conrad Case,* 1959; *Paul Temple and the Margot Mystery,* 1961; *What Do You Think?,* 1962; *Paul Temple and the Geneva Mystery,* 1965; *La Boutique,* 1967; *Paul Temple and the Alex Affair,* 1968.

Television Plays (all serials): *The Broken Horseshoe,* 1952; *Operation Diplomat,* 1952; *The Teckman Biography,* 1953; *Portrait of Alison,* 1955; *My Friend Charles,* 1956; *The Other Man,* 1956; *A Time of Day,* 1957; *The Scarf,* 1959; *The World of Tim Frazer,* with others, 1960; *The Desperate People,* 1963; *Melissa,* 1964, 1974; *A Man Called Harry Brent,* 1965; *A Game of Murder,* 1966; *Bat Out of Hell,* 1966; *The Passenger,* 1971; *The Doll,* 1975; *Breakaway,* 1979.

*   *   *

The name of Francis Durbridge will always be associated with the BBC radio serials featuring the novelist-detective Paul Temple and his wife Steve. Durbridge was the master of the cliff-hanger, albeit verbal rather than unpleasantly physical; his radio serials were produced and re-produced from the 1930's onwards. Temple cases also appeared as novels, and Durbridge later brought his character to life by collaborating with Douglas Rutherford in writing two books "by Paul Temple." Today, millions are aware of Durbridge as one of the most successful writers for television. His television serials have been produced sparingly, which has enabled him to maintain a freshness within a type of mystery he has made very much his own. The compulsive viewing of his serials throughout a large part of the world speaks greatly for his power as a storyteller.

Many of the television serials have been transferred by Durbridge to the printed page. They have no series character like Temple—perhaps the inter-linked adventures of Tim Frazer come closest—but this enables Durbridge each time to make his central character a protagonist rather than an onlooker, either an anti-hero or a suspect who is attempting to extricate himself from a web which enmeshes him more securely at every turn. Although he has freed himself from the Temple strait-jacket, Durbridge appears to know precisely what his readers and viewers expect of him, and he works almost exclusively within his own particular niche. The cast is normally drawn from what is popularly termed the gin-and-tonic set—upper-middle-class estate agents, photographers, and antique dealers abound, as do others who appear to have ample time to indulge in deception and criminal intrigue.

Followers of Durbridge must be so well acquainted with his

style that the twists and turns of his plots become somewhat predictable. As a master of his craft, however, he is capable of springing a surprise or two and revealing a totally unexpected murderer—one recalls, for example, *The Other Man.* Transferred to the printed page, his serials tend to betray their origin by a succession of cliff-hangers throughout, and the shortage of descriptive passages and predominance of dialogue indicate that his real skill lies in creating scripts rather than novels. Other areas of predictability may be mentioned, not necessarily as adverse criticism, but as examples of the Durbridge milieu and style. His plots are frequently populated with pals of the hero or hail-fellows who turn out to be something completely different. Then there are his settings—switching from London to Thames-side commuter country, and back again. When the hero is lured to a cottage at Marlow or a houseboat on the river, we can be sure he will find a door ajar and a corpse just beyond. We can also expect, more often than not, that the murder victims will be women and the master criminal will turn out to be a man; a strange point this, but the whole atmosphere surrounding Durbridge's plots tends to be one of male chauvinism.

Durbridge has no special message, no mission to examine the springs of violence or the motivation which leads a man to murder, and seemingly no purpose other than to present to his audience one piece of craftsmanlike escapism after another. Nevertheless, whether in adaptations from the screen or original novels—*The Pig-Tail Murder* is a competent example of the latter—Durbridge's ability as a skillful weaver of webs and a typically British exponent of the guessing-game has maintained his position as one of the most consistently entertaining crime writers.

—Melvyn Barnes

———

DURHAM, David. *See* **VICKERS, Roy.**

———

DURRANT, Theo. *See* **BOUCHER, Anthony.**

———

DWYER, Deanna. *See* **KOONTZ, Dean R.**

———

DWYER, K.R. *See* **KOONTZ, Dean R.**

———

E

EBERHART, Mignon G(ood). American. Born in University Place, Nebraska, 6 July 1899. Educated in local schools; Nebraska Wesleyan University, Lincoln, 1917–20. Married 1) Alanson C. Eberhart in 1923 (divorced); remarried in 1948 (died); 2) John P. Hazen Perry in 1946 (died). Since 1930 full-time writer. Past President, Mystery Writers of America. Recipient: Scotland Yard prize, 1931; Mystery Writers of America Grand Master award, 1970. D.Litt.: Nebraska Wesleyan University 1935. Agent: Brandt and Brandt, 1501 Broadway, New York, New York 10036. Address: c/o Random House, 201 East 50th Street, New York, New York 10022, U.S.A.

CRIME PUBLICATIONS

Novels (series: Sarah Keate and Lance O'Leary)

The Patient in Room 18 (Keate and O'Leary). New York, Doubleday, and London, Heinemann, 1929.
The Mystery of Hunting's End (Keate and O'Leary). New York, Doubleday, 1930; London, Heinemann, 1931.
While the Patient Slept (Keate and O'Leary). New York, Doubleday, and London, Heinemann, 1930.
From This Dark Stairway (Keate and O'Leary). New York, Doubleday, 1931; London, Heinemann, 1932.
Murder by an Aristocrat (Keate and O'Leary). New York, Doubleday, 1932; as *Murder of My Patient,* London, Lane, 1934.
The Dark Garden. New York, Doubleday, 1933; as *Death in the Fog,* London, Lane, 1934.
The White Cockatoo. New York, Doubleday, and London, Falcon, 1933.
The House on the Roof. New York, Doubleday, and London, Collins, 1935.
Fair Warning. New York, Doubleday, and London, Collins, 1936.
Danger in the Dark. New York, Doubleday, 1937; as *Hand in Glove,* London, Collins, 1937.
The Pattern. New York, Doubleday, and London, Collins, 1937; as *Pattern of Murder,* New York, Popular Library, 1948.
The Glass Slipper. New York, Doubleday, and London, Collins, 1938.
Hasty Wedding. New York, Doubleday, 1938; London, Collins, 1939.
Brief Return. London, Collins, 1939.
The Chiffon Scarf. New York, Doubleday, 1939; London, Collins, 1940.
The Hangman's Whip. New York, Doubleday, 1940; London, Collins, 1941.
Strangers in Flight. Los Angeles, Bantam, 1941; revised edition, as *Speak No Evil,* New York, Random House, and London, Collins, 1941.
With This Ring. New York, Random House, 1941; London, Collins, 1942.
Wolf in Man's Clothing (Keate). New York, Random House, 1942; London, Collins, 1943.

The Man Next Door. New York, Random House, 1943; London, Collins, 1944.
Unidentified Woman. New York, Random House, 1943; London, Collins, 1944.
Escape the Night. New York, Random House, 1944; London, Collins, 1945.
Wings of Fear. New York, Random House, 1945; London, Collins, 1946.
Five Passengers from Lisbon. New York, Random House, and London, Collins, 1946.
The White Dress. New York, Random House, 1946; London, Collins, 1947.
Another Woman's House. New York, Random House, 1947; London, Collins, 1948.
House of Storm. New York, Random House, and London, Collins, 1949.
Hunt with the Hounds. New York, Random House, 1950; London, Collins, 1951.
Never Look Back. New York, Random House, and London, Collins, 1951.
Dead Men's Plans. New York, Random House, 1952; London, Collins, 1953.
The Unknown Quantity. New York, Random House, and London, Collins, 1953.
Man Missing (Keate). New York, Random House, and London, Collins, 1954.
Postmark Murder. New York, Random House, and London, Collins, 1956.
Another Man's Murder. New York, Random House, 1957; London, Collins, 1958.
Melora. New York, Random House, 1959; London, Collins, 1960; as *The Promise of Murder,* New York, Dell, 1961.
Jury of One. New York, Random House, 1960; London, Collins, 1961.
The Cup, The Blade, or the Gun. New York, Random House, 1961; as *The Crime at Honotassa,* London, Collins, 1962.
Enemy in the House. New York, Random House, 1962; London, Collins, 1963.
Run Scared. New York, Random House, 1963; London, Collins, 1964.
Call after Midnight. New York, Random House, 1964; London, Collins, 1965.
R.S.V.P. Murder. New York, Random House, 1965; London, Collins, 1966.
Witness at Large. New York, Random House, 1966; London, Collins, 1967.
Woman on the Roof. New York, Random House, and London, Collins, 1968.
Message from Hong Kong. New York, Random House, and London, Collins, 1969.
El Rancho Rio. New York, Random House, 1970; London, Collins, 1971.
Two Little Rich Girls. New York, Random House, and London, Collins, 1972.
The House by the Sea. New York, Pocket Books, 1972.
Murder in Waiting. New York, Random House, 1973; London, Collins, 1974.

Danger Money. New York, Random House, and London, Collins, 1975.

Family Fortune. New York, Random House, 1976; London, Collins, 1977.

Nine O'Clock Tide. New York, Random House, and London, Collins, 1978.

The Bayou Road. New York, Random House, and London, Collins, 1979.

Casa Madrone. New York, Random House, and London, Collins, 1980.

Family Affair. New York, Random House, and London, Collins, 1981.

Next of Kin. New York, Random House, 1982; London, Collins, 1983.

The Patient in Cabin C. New York, Random House, 1983; London, Collins, 1984.

Alpine Condo Cross Fire. New York, Random House, 1984; London, Collins, 1985.

A Fighting Chance. New York, Random House, 1986; London, Collins, 1987.

Three Days for Emeralds. New York, Random House, and London, Collins, 1988.

Short Stories

The Cases of Susan Dare. New York, Doubleday, 1934; London, Lane, 1935.

Five of My Best: Deadly Is the Diamond, Bermuda Grapevine, Murder Goes to Market, Strangers in Flight, Express to Danger. London, Hammond, 1949.

Deadly Is the Diamond. New York, Dell, 1951.

Deadly Is the Diamond and Three Other Novelettes of Murder: Bermuda, Grapevine, The Crimson Paw, Murder in Waltz Time. New York, Random House, 1958; Hornchurch, Essex, Henry, 1981.

The Crimson Paw. London, Hammond, 1959.

Uncollected Short Stories

"Postiche," in *Ellery Queen's Mystery Magazine* (New York), September 1944.

"The Flowering Face," in *Ellery Queen's Mystery Magazine* (New York), November 1946.

"The E-String Murder," in *The Saint* (New York), Spring 1953.

"The Wagstaff Pearls," in *Best Detective Stories of the Year 1953,* edited by David Coxe Cooke. New York, Dutton, and London, Boardman, 1953.

"The Man Who Was Missing," in *The Saint* (New York), March 1954.

"No Cry of Murder," in *Ellery Queen's Mystery Magazine* (New York), August 1955.

"Dangerous Widows," in *Ellery Queen's Mystery Magazine* (New York), April 1956.

"Murder in the Rain," in *Ellery Queen's Mystery Magazine* (New York), June 1956.

"The Hound of the Wellingtons," in *Ellery Queen's Mystery Magazine* (New York), June 1957.

"Mr. Wickwire's 'Gun Moll,'" in *A Choice of Murders,* edited by Dorothy Salisbury Davis. New York, Scribner, 1958; London, Macdonald, 1960.

"When the Clocks Struck Seven," in *Suspense* (London), February 1959.

"Final Entry," in *Suspense* (London), October 1959.

"Mr. Wickwire Adds and Subtracts," in *Ellery Queen's Mystery Magazine* (New York), December 1959.

"Date to Die," in *Anthology 1961,* edited by Ellery Queen. New York, Davis, 1960.

"Murder on St. Valentine's Day," in *Anthology 1966 Mid-Year,* edited by Ellery Queen. New York, Davis, 1966.

"Murder at the Dog Show," in *Anthology 1968,* edited by Ellery Queen. New York, Davis, 1967.

"Mr. Wickwire's Widow," in *With Malice Toward All,* edited by Robert L. Fish. New York, Putnam, 1968; London, Macmillan, 1969.

OTHER PUBLICATIONS

Plays

320 College Avenue, with Fred Ballard. New York, French, 1938.

Eight O'Clock Tuesday, with Robert Wallsten, adaptation of a novel by Eberhart (produced New York, 1941). New York, French, 1941.

*

Manuscript Collection: Mugar Memorial Library, Boston University.

*   *   *

The author of more than 50 mystery novels and numerous short stories, Mignon G. Eberhart is usually associated with the school of suspense fiction founded by Mary Roberts Rinehart. Certainly her early works, particularly those featuring nurse Sarah Keate and detective Lance O'Leary, are reminiscent of Rinehart at her most mediocre, presenting a succession of events experienced by a spinster heroine who combines the pluckiness and stupidity which are characteristic of the worst of the "Had-I-But-Known" narrators. The stories featuring Susan Dare, a writer of mystery fiction, are rather more successful, as are those concerning the baker James Wickwire. However, Eberhart's contribution to mystery fiction does not lie in her creation of serial detectives; to the tradition of the eccentric private eye, she adds little that is noteworthy. Rather, her best works, and the most popular, are those which combine elements of the gothic romance with those of the classic mystery story. She has many imitators, particularly in the field of pure romance, but few of them exhibit the assurance of the Eberhart style.

Typical of the Eberhart mystery/romance is its insistence upon an exotic locale, and its attention to details of local color. Careful presentation of the milieu in which the mystery unfolds is evident in her serial detective stories (it is perhaps this feature which has attracted film makers to Eberhart's works). In the mystery/romances, the exotic locale corresponds to the strange events which must take place before the heroine can be united with her true love. Unlike the novels of Mary Roberts Rinehart, which take place in a cozily normal world, Eberhart's are set in a world replete with mystery at the outset, so that the heroine—together with the reader—is catapulted into an environment which is strange and vaguely threatening.

The presentation of exotic setting is typical of the gothic romance. What distinguishes an Eberhart novel is the presence of a crime—usually murder, often associated with shady financial dealings—for which the heroine is suspect. Typically, she is an orphan (again, emphasizing her relative helplessness) married to a man about whom she knows relatively little. The husband may be an alcoholic (*Strangers in Flight*) or an invalid (*With This Ring*); he is often the first murder victim, making his wife a prime suspect. In the course of her investigations, which are usually undertaken in order to prove her own innocence, the heroine comes to realize that her interest in a family friend is far from innocent. She also begins to suspect that she herself has over-heard or involuntarily discovered a vital clue to the identity of the criminal. She identifies the murderer just at the moment of peril, from which she is rescued by the masterful hero, who reconstructs the crime and claims her for his own.

Eberhart's originality lies in her compelling studies of the psychological processes of her characters, particularly the heroines. Her dialogue, especially in scenes of emotional crisis, is sometimes overwrought ("Elizabeth, the world is wide. And war changes things. So the real things—love and time—are so terribly important. Elizabeth, I want you . . . "—*Strangers in Flight*), but her treatment of sexual motivation is generally free from the coyness associated with the more pedestrian modern romances. The perilous situations are believable precisely because the heroines are depicted in the midst of them, rather than being narrated by them in retrospect. The stories are escape fantasy/adventures, from which the heroines emerge wiser women than they were at the beginning. Within the confines of formula fiction, the novels of Mignon G. Eberhart embody an unusual degree of clarity and intelligence.

—Joanne Harack Hayne

EGAN, Leslie. *See* **LININGTON, Elizabeth.**

EGLETON, Clive. Also writes as Patrick Blake; John Tarrant. British. Born in South Harrow, Middlesex, 25 November 1927. Educated at Haberdashers' Aske's School, London, 1938–44; Army Staff College, Camberley, Surrey, graduated 1957. Married Joan Evelyn Lane in 1949; two sons. Served in the British Army, rising to the rank of Lieutenant Colonel, 1945–75; had many appointments throughout the world dealing with logistics operations and law; did intelligence work in Cyprus, 1955–56, the Persian Gulf, 1958–59, and East Africa, 1964; civil servant, Ministry of Defence, 1981–89. Agent: Anthony Goff, David Higham Associates, 5-8 Lower John Street, London W1R 4HA. Address: Dolphin House, Beach House Lane, Bembridge, Isle of Wight PO35 5TA, England.

CRIME PUBLICATIONS

Novels (series: David Garnett)

A Piece of Resistance (Garnett). London, Hodder and Stoughton, and New York, Coward McCann, 1970.
Last Post for a Partisan (Garnett). London, Hodder and Stoughton, and New York, Coward McCann, 1971.
The Judas Mandate (Garnett). London, Hodder and Stoughton, and New York, Coward McCann, 1972.
Seven Days to a Killing. London, Hodder and Stoughton, and New York, Coward McCann, 1973; as *The Black Windmill*, New York, Fawcett, 1974.
The October Plot. London, Hodder and Stoughton, 1974; as *The Bormann Brief*, New York, Coward McCann, 1974.
Skirmish. London, Hodder and Stoughton, and New York, Coward McCann, 1975.

State Visit. London, Hodder and Stoughton, 1976.
The Mills Bomb. London, Hodder and Stoughton, and New York, Atheneum, 1978.
Backfire. London, Hodder and Stoughton, and New York, Atheneum, 1979.
Escape to Athena (novelization of screenplay; as Patrick Blake). London, Fontana, and New York, Berkley, 1979.
The Winter Touch. London, Hodder and Stoughton, 1981; as *The Eisenhower Deception*, New York, Atheneum, 1981.
Double Griffin (as Patrick Blake). New York, Jove, 1981; London, Macdonald, 1982.
The Russian Enigma. New York, Atheneum, 1982; London, Hodder and Stoughton, 1983.
A Falcon for the Hawk. London, Hodder and Stoughton, 1982; New York, Walker, 1984.
A Conflict of Interests. New York, Atheneum, 1983; London, Hodder and Stoughton, 1984.
Troika. London, Hodder and Stoughton, and New York, Atheneum, 1984.
A Different Drummer. London, Hodder and Stoughton, 1985.
Picture of the Year. London, Hodder and Stoughton, 1987.
Gone Mi$$ing. London, Hodder and Stoughton, 1988; as *Missing from the Record*, New York, St. Martin's Press, 1988.
Death of a Sahib. London, Hodder and Stoughton, 1989.
In the Red. London, Hodder and Stoughton, and New York, St. Martin's Press, 1990.

Novels as John Tarrant

The Rommel Plot. London, Macdonald and Jane's, and Philadelphia, Lippincott, 1977.
The Clauberg Trigger. London, Macdonald and Jane's, 1978; New York, Atheneum, 1979.
China Gold. London, Macdonald, 1982.

*

Manuscript Collection: Mugar Memorial Library, Boston University.

Clive Egleton comments:
My field is the crime and suspense novel. I hope the story I tell is good enough to make the reader want to turn over to the next page to see what happens next.

* * *

Clive Egleton writes tough, realistic espionage tales in which secret agencies thwart local police investigative efforts in order to deal with national and international crises, particularly terrorism and KGB operations. His police stories simply give the other side of the coin: the police detective who is given misinformation and red herrings to keep him from the heart of a murder case and then is framed for misdemeanors when he gets too close to information the agencies want covered up. Egleton's narrative is brisk, his language terse, his plots well-made, and his endings surprising.

These stories are hard-hitting and cynical. Scheming men of power sacrifice the reputations and lives of others, supposedly in the name of national security, but often for personal advancement; good men die for bad reasons, and bad men are rewarded for murder and mayhem. High ranking officials will pay any price to cover up their indiscretions, and agencies live with the constant suspicion that members of the rank and file have sold out. No one can be trusted; model citizens prove sleepers, and agents with years of honest service prove turncoats. For the men at the top the only question is the degree of guilt. Sexual proclivities determine politics, and nothing is ever what it seems. Double-dealing, violence, and treachery are the way of the world. For instance, in *The Winter Touch,* CIA and British intelligence clash as the British try blackmail (Eisenhower's wartime romance with his WAC driver is manipulated and extended) to determine the fate of Egypt and Israel, while in *The October Plot* "allies" on both sides attempt to sabotage a seemingly impossible mission, a plot (contrived by a defecting German General and a British Intelligence agent) to shorten the war by assassinating Martin Bormann. In *A Conflict of Interests* a CID investigation clashes with an SIS cover-up, and political pressure threatens the life and career of Detective Inspector Coghill as he determinedly traces the blackmail victims of a murdered woman.

Place is not as important to Egleton as character and plot. Action moves from London to Paris to Washington, D.C. to Saigon or from a sophisticated metropolis to a sleepy village with little note of differences. Instead, Egleton's focus is on men whose integrity is questioned, men set up, shoved about, used, and abused: put in situations which inevitably initiate a sequence of acts and reprisals that a secret agency can use to its advantage. If one of these men survives and makes the right moves, perhaps he will be used again, but no matter how brave or how loyal he seems, he will never be fully trusted. Even at the end of many of Egleton's novels, when a character seems to have proven his honesty, integrity and patriotism, the top officials (who often carry over from book to book, as does Winter, an officer as cold and calculating as his name suggests) remain doubtful and initiate more deeply-probing investigations. The innocent are tainted and the tainted white-washed. Yet, Egleton's heroes remain men and women of conviction and courage, who act on conscience, even if it means disobeying authority. The intelligence networks play their complicated games, and their pawns are eliminated or endure on the basis of covert stratagems. For example, framed by the KGB, condemned by British intelligence, and imprisoned by a British court, the hard, embittered, violent, and wronged central figure of *The Mills Bomb,* Edward Mills, hunts the mole responsible for his plight, unknowingly directed by intelligence agents who think of him as a grenade, lethal but easily directed, while at the same time uninformed police officers methodically uncover evidence of his innocence. In *Backfire* Army trouble-shooter Major Robert Donaldson, assigned to stop a career officer turned psychotic killer, discovers that that officer's illusions of persecution might well prove true and that his final target might well deserve his fate.

Drawing on his first-hand knowledge of military and intelligence strategy and tactics, Egleton writes with convincing detail about the inner workings of intelligence agencies, particularly in their dealings with the Middle-East. Characters in one book are seen in a new way in later books. There is a cynical, ironic, and bitter edge to these tales that makes them all the more convincing. In *Seven Days to a Killing* only Major John Tarrant stands between his kidnapped son, the top-level defector who uses him, and Tarrant's own intelligence network. Tarrant's estranged wife blames him, and his superiors suspect him as he is forced to choose between duty and fatherhood when his son is made a living bomb to shield a defector. *Troika* reverses the perspective, focusing on machinations within the politburo, the KGB and the Red Army, as each vies to put forward their choice to replace a dying Soviet leader. A Major Kirov, commissioned to eliminate the defected son of the Army's choice, finds himself on a hit list and forced to use the FBI to walk a tightrope to safety. *The Russian Enigma* evokes the Cuban Missile Crisis while Lee Harvey Oswald waits anonymously in the background.

A Piece of Resistance, Last Post for a Partisan, and *The Judas Mandate* envision a Russian-occupied England and a secret guerrilla war between collaborators and the underground resistance (comprised primarily of former English soldiers). Their central figure, the weary but valiant resistance fighter David Garnett plays a deadly game in which even the woman he loves is suspect; as he says, it's "the sort of war in which you cannot afford the luxury of trusting anyone until their loyalty is proved beyond doubt."

Garnett's statement sums up the essence of the Egleton novel, whether police procedural, espionage, or futuristic: mistrust, doubt, and betrayal, and shifting views of events.

—Gina Macdonald

ELDER, Evelyn. *See* **KENNEDY, Milward.**

ELKINS, Aaron, J. American. Born in Brooklyn, New York, 24 July 1935. Educated at Hunter College, New York (now City University of New York), B.A. 1956; University of Wisconsin, 1957–59; University of Arizona, Tucson, M.A. 1959; California State University, Los Angeles, M.A. 1962; University of California, Berkeley, Ed.D 1976. Married 1) Toby Siev in 1959 (divorced 1972), two children; 2) Charlotte Trangmar in 1972. Management analyst and training director, various local and federal government agencies in California, 1960–70, 1971–76, and 1979–83; adjunct Lecturer and Professor, Golden Gate University, California State University, and Santa Ana College, all California, 1963–76, and 1980–82; management consultant, Ernst and Whinney, Chicago, 1970–71; Lecturer, University of Maryland, European Division, Heidelberg, West Germany, 1976–78 and 1984–85. Since 1985 full-time writer. Recipient: Mystery Writers of America Edgar Allan Poe award, 1988. Agent: Karpfinger Agency, 500 Fifth Avenue, Suite 2800, New York, New York 10110, U.S.A.

CRIME PUBLICATIONS

Novels (series: Gideon Oliver in all books except *A Deceptive Clarity* and *A Wicked Slice*)

Fellowship of Fear (Oliver). New York, Walker, 1982.
The Dark Place (Oliver). New York, Walker, 1983; London, Hale, 1986.
Murder in the Queen's Armes (Oliver). New York, Walker, 1985.
A Deceptive Clarity. New York, Walker, 1987.
Old Bones (Oliver). New York, Mysterious Press, 1987.
Curses! (Oliver). New York, Mysterious Press, 1989.
A Wicked Slice, with Charlotte Elkins. New York, St. Martin's Press, 1989.
Icy Clutches (Oliver). New York, Mysterious Press, 1990.

Uncollected Short Story

"Dutch Treat," in *Mistletoe Mysteries,* edited by Charlotte MacLeod. New York, Mysterious Press, 1989.

*

Aaron J. Elkins comments:

The protagonist of most of my books is Gideon Oliver, the "skeleton detective," a professor of physical anthropology who often consults with the police, applying his knowledge of the human skeleton to forensic problems (e.g.: How old was the person whose skull this was? How tall? Which sex? What did this person look like? When did this person die? How? How did he or she live?) My primary aim is to make the stories and characters engrossing and enjoyable, but as a one-time anthropology professor myself, I admit to hoping that readers come away having painlessly learned something about the way forensic scientists work, and something about anthropological lore as well.

I love mysteries myself, and especially enjoy books by authors who teach me something about subjects that they themselves know and obviously love—books for example, by Jonathan Gash, or Dick Francis, or Tony Hillerman. Those are the kinds of books I try and write.

*　　*　　*

Once an author has decided to write a series of books that feature a single character, he or she is faced with the difficult task of achieving a degree of variety and avoiding repetitions. By making Gideon Oliver a physical anthropologist, Aaron J. Elkins has practically guaranteed the required element of diversity, since Gideon must travel to unusual locales throughout the world in order to engage in his professional activities. *Fellowship of Fear* finds him in Germany with side trips to Italy and Spain. In *The Dark Place* he is on a dig in the Ho Rain Forest of the Olympic Peninsula in Washington. *Murder in the Queen's Armes* takes place in England where he is on his honeymoon with Julie, the chief ranger in the Olympic National Park, whom he had met in *The Dark Place*. In *Old Bones,* he is in France with his friend, FBI agent John Lau, to attend a conference on science and detection and to deliver a series of lectures on forensic anthropology. In *Curses!* Gideon and Julie have gone to the Yucatán Peninsula to assist Abe Goldstein, Gideon's old professor and mentor.

As might be expected of an author who is an academic, all of Elkins's books are meticulously researched. This is true not only of the Gideon Oliver books, but also of the two that feature other central characters, *A Deceptive Clarity* and *A Wicked Slice*. In the former, the world of art is portrayed with convincing reality (Elkins acknowledges the assistance of his wife, Charlotte, a former museum staffer). The professional women's golf tour supplies the background for the latter. Co-written with Charlotte Elkins, *A Wicked Slice* provides a vivid behind-the-scenes view of what life is like on the tour and in the negotiating sessions where a successful profession golfer makes real money. There is never any doubt that Elkins has experienced the locales he describes, or that he possesses detailed knowledge of the technical aspects of his protagonists' professions. His minute descriptions of Gideon's work as a "skeleton detective," in particular, are a delight.

In addition to his proficiency with setting and with professional detail, Elkins is a skillful plotter, and all of the events leading up to the solution of the crime follow a logical development. It is never necessary to stretch credulity to accept that Gideon continually finds himself in situations in which the police require his help.

But meticulous research and skillful plotting are not the only characteristics of first-rate detective fiction. Even more important is character development, and Elkins is particularly adroit at this aspect of writing, especially in the case of his central figure, Gideon Oliver. Gideon does not fit the professorial stereotype. Tall and athletically built, he is not

heroic, but is able to defend himself when necessary. He is not a "conventionally handsome man," yet the total effect is one that many women find attractive. Nevertheless, he does not take advantage of the women he meets. He is not on the prowl, and is not the sort of man whose antennae are "always quivering and alert." In *Fellowship of Fear*, his beloved wife Nora has been dead for two years, the victim of an automobile accident. Still struggling to accept Nora's death, it is difficult for him to begin to go out with other women. Janet Feller, whom he meets in *Fellowship of Fear*, is the first woman since his wife's death who inspires him to seek a significant emotional relationship. By the end of the book, there are indications that something serious may develop, yet in the next novel, *The Dark Place,* she is no longer present, apparently having come into his life too soon. But now, three years after Nora's death, Gideon has come to realize that he is not destined to live alone. Never much for one night stands, he is ready for a commitment when he meets Julie Tendler. They soon become lovers, and in *Murder in the Queen's Armes* they have been married for five days when the book opens. Although she is not developed as extensively as Gideon, Julie's intuition and perceptiveness are a perfect complement to her husband's logical, scientific methods, and from the beginning she makes significant contributions to the solving of the crimes, even when it is only by long distance telephone as in *Old Bones.*

Some of the secondary characters are somewhat less successful, although former Army Intelligence investigator and present FBI agent John Lau makes an acceptable Watson to Gideon's Holmes, and the interaction between Gideon and his former professor, Abe Goldstein, recounted with humor and affection, provides a convincing account of male friendship based upon mutual respect, admiration, and understanding. Although the demands of the detective genre require the author to concentrate on his primary character, Elkins manages in *Old Bones* to examine the surviving members of the decadent du Rocher family to excellent psychological effect and with a deft satirical touch. Gideon is scarcely more than mentioned in the first five chapters, and the author uses the space to good advantage in providing background to the plot and introducing the fascinating cast of what is easily the most complex of his novels. It is quite likely that Elkins's success with these characters, along with the finely structured plot, was instrumental in his winning the Mystery Writers of America Edgar Allan Poe award for *Old Bones.*

Although *A Deceptive Clarity* and *A Wicked Slice* are pleasant diversions, and both Cris Norgren, the art curator, and professional golfer Lee Ofsted are engaging characters, Gideon Oliver fans eagerly await the next appearance of "The Skeleton Detective." Not only are we curious to see where his next adventure will take him, but we also want to see if he increases Julie's participation and continues to develop her character along with Gideon's. If *Curses!* is any indication, he is on his way to developing one of the best husband-wife teams since Nick and Nora Charles.

—Dale Carter

———

ELLIN, Stanley (Bernard). American. Born in Brooklyn, New York, 6 October 1916. Educated at Brooklyn College, New York, B.A. 1936. Served in the United States Army, 1944–45. Married Jeanne Michael in 1937; one daughter. Worked as teacher, steelworker, dairy farmer. Full-time writer from 1946. Past President, Mystery Writers of America. Recipient:

Mystery Writers of America Edgar Allan Poe award, for short story, 1954, 1956, for novel, 1958; Le Grand Prix de Littérature Policière, 1975. *Died 31 July 1986.*

CRIME PUBLICATIONS

Novels (series: John Milano)

Dreadful Summit. New York, Simon and Schuster, 1948; London, Boardman, 1958; as *The Big Night,* New York, Lion, 1950.
The Key to Nicholas Street. New York, Simon and Schuster, 1952; London, Boardman, 1953.
The Eighth Circle. New York, Random House, 1958; London, Boardman, 1959.
The Winter after This Summer. New York, Random House, 1960; London, Boardman, 1961.
The Panama Portrait. New York, Random House, 1962; London, Macdonald, 1963.
House of Cards. New York, Random House, and London, Macdonald, 1967.
The Valentine Estate. New York, Random House, and London, Macdonald, 1968.
The Bind. New York, Random House, 1970; as *The Man from Nowhere,* London, Cape, 1970.
Mirror, Mirror on the Wall. New York, Random House, 1972; London, Cape, 1973.
Stronghold. New York, Random House, and London, Cape, 1975.
The Luxembourg Run. New York, Random House, 1977; London, Cape, 1978.
Star Light, Star Bright (Milano). New York, Random House, and London, Cape, 1979.
The Dark Fantastic (Milano). New York, Mysterious Press, and London, Deutsch, 1983.
Very Old Money. New York, Arbor House, 1984; London, Deutsch, 1985.

Short Stories

Mystery Stories. New York, Simon and Schuster, 1956; London, Boardman, 1957; as *Quiet Horror,* New York, Dell, 1959; as *The Speciality of the House and Other Stories,* London, Penguin, 1967.
The Blessington Method and Other Strange Tales. New York, Random House, 1964; London, Macdonald, 1965.
Kindly Dig Your Grave and Other Wicked Stories, edited by Ellery Queen. New York, Davis, 1975.
The Specialty of the House and Other Stories: The Complete Mystery Tales 1948–1978. New York, Mysterious Press, 1979.

Uncollected Short Stories

"Graffiti," in *Ellery Queen's Mystery Magazine* (New York), March 1983.
"Mrs. Mouse," in *Ellery Queen's Mystery Magazine* (New York), October 1983.

OTHER PUBLICATIONS

Play

Screenplay: *The Big Night,* with Joseph Losey, 1951.

*

Manuscript Collection: Mugar Memorial Library, Boston University.

Stanley Ellin commented (1984):
The crime fiction genre offers the writer infinite diversity of theme and treatment. I like to take advantage of that diversity.

*   *   *

Stanley Ellin's career was blessed with a first story that everyone remembers and many consider the finest of the three dozen or so short stories he produced in over 35 years.

But in truth even without "The Specialty of the House" Ellin would be one of the modern masters of the genre, with a reputation built firmly upon novels and some of the most imaginative stories in the mystery-suspense field.

Ellin's second novel, *The Key to Nicholas Street,* is of special interest, with its viewpoint shifting among the five members of the Ayres household. The woman next door has been found dead at the bottom of the cellar stairs, and her death is to affect the members of the Ayres household as much as her life had. It is a book of near-classic stature, curiously overlooked by most critics, and one of Ellin's three best novels.

The Eighth Circle is an attempt at a long, serious novel about a modern private detective. It succeeds admirably. Murray Kirk is far removed from the standard private eye, yet there is a hard-edged sentimentality about him that recalls the best of his predecessors. His case is a good one, and the reader regrets he never made a second appearance in an Ellin novel. The third of Stanley Ellin's top trio is undoubedly *Mirror, Mirror on the Wall,* a breakthrough novel that carries the mystery into psycho-sexual areas where it had previously feared to tread.

Slightly behind these three are a group of mystery-adventure novels in which the protagonist, a young man, somehow becomes involved with wealthy and glamorous people in Miami Beach or Europe. Often an estate or a legacy is involved, and the action is fast and deadly. Fitting generally into this group are *House of Cards, The Valentine Estate, The Bind,* and *The Luxembourg Run. Stronghold* portrays a family of nonviolent Quakers at the mercy of four murderous criminals bent on holding them for ransom.

Despite his achievements in the novel, it is for his short stories that Stanley Ellin is best known. Beginning with the unforgettable "The Specialty of the House" (1948), about a New York restaurant with a special treat for gourmets, Ellin produced a remarkable series of tales collected as *Mystery Stories.* The volume has been hailed by Julian Symons as "the finest collection of stories in the crime form published in the past half century."

Many of these first 10 stories deserve special mention. "The Cat's-Paw" is a neat variation on the situation in Doyle's "The Red-Headed League." "The Orderly World of Mr. Appleby" is about a wife-murderer who seems to have the formula for the perfect crime. "The House Party" (Edgar-winner) is one of Ellin's rare fantasies. "Broker's Special" is his contribution to the subgenre combining crime and trains. And "The Moment of Decision," a stunning riddle story about a magician, comes very close to equaling "The Specialty of the House" in its impact.

"The Blessington Method" (Edgar-winner) became the title story of Ellin's second collection. Again, many of the 10 stories deserve special mention. "You Can't Be a Little Girl All Your Life" is the story of a rape, with the identity of the rapist revealed only at the end. It is one of Ellin's few attempts at a whodunit in the short form, and one of the best stories in the volume. "The Day of the Bullet" tells of the murder of a

Brooklyn rackets boss, with a flashback to an incident in his boyhood. "The Nine-to-Five Man" is a memorable tale of a typical working day in the life of a man who just happens to be a professional arsonist. And "The Question" is also about a professional man—an executioner who must face his son's question about the work he does.

If the stories in Ellin's third collection, *Kindly Dig Your Grave*, seem a bit less remarkable it is only because of the high standards he has set with the previous books. Even so, there are at least two more small masterpieces here. "The Crime of Ezechiele Coen" is set in Rome, with roots going back to World War II. And "The Last Bottle in the World" could easily be one of the half-dozen best short stories about wine. There is more detection in Ellin's later short stories, and more foreign settings as in the later novels. Though some may lack the stunning surprise of the earlier work, they are solid professional jobs.

—Edward D. Hoch

———

ELLIS, Scott. *See* **SCHORR, Mark.**

———

ELLROY, James. American. Born in Los Angeles, California, 4 March 1948. Served in the United States Army, 1965. Married Mary Doherty in 1988. Has had a variety of jobs including country club caddy, 1965–84. Agent: Nat Sobel, 146 East 19 Street, New York, New York 10003. Address: 84 Siwanoy Boulevard, Eastchester, New York 10707, U.S.A.

CRIME PUBLICATIONS

Novels

Brown's Requiem.   New York, Avon, 1981; London, Allison and Busby, 1984.
Clandestine.   New York, Avon, 1982; London, Allison and Busby, 1984.
Blood on the Moon.   New York, Mysterious Press, 1984; London, Allison and Busby, 1985.
Because the Night.   New York, Mysterious Press, 1985; London, Century Hutchinson, 1987.
Suicide Kill.   New York, Mysterious Press, 1986.
Silent Terror.   New York, Avon, 1986.
The Black Dahlia.   New York, Mysterious Press, 1987; London, Century Hutchinson, 1988.
The Big Nowhere.   New York, Mysterious Press, 1988; London, Mysterious Press, 1989.
L.A. Confidential.   New York and London, Mysterious Press, 1990.

*

James Ellroy comments:
Dark, dense, profane, sex obsessed, emotionally complex—I hope I live up to these tags.

*   *   *

All of James Ellroy's books are set in Los Angeles, and most of them in the Los Angeles of the past. Los Angeles of his novels is awash in chaos and corruption, a city of lurid and violent anarchy. The heroes are heroic only in comparison to the villains, who are unspeakably evil. Every character—from the police to the drug dealers and bag men, from the loftiest of politicians to the cheapest of gangsters—is running scared, running on pure adrenaline. Life expectancy is short. Death, when quick, is merciful. Dreadful mutilations are frequent.

Ellroy's books are among the darkest in modern fiction. He plumbs depths unsought by his thematic predecessors James M. Cain, Jim Thompson, and Joseph Wambaugh. The characters' humanity, smothered by twisted passions and obsessions, rarely surfaces. These epic police novels are a demonic Grand Guignol, with only the blackest of humor for relief. Like Thomas Harris, the starker Ellroy bridges the gap between crime and out-and-out horror.

Ellroy's literary ambitions and talents have grown with each new book. He followed his debut novel, the semi-autobiographical private eye work *Brown's Requiem*, with the sprawling *Clandestine*—according to Ellroy, "a thinly veiled, chronologically altered account of my mother's killing." (When Ellroy was 10 years old his divorcee mother was murdered. The body was found, semi-nude, in the bushes near a Los Angeles highschool. No one was ever arrested.) *Clandestine* tells the story of LAPD cop Fred Underhill and his quest for professional glory, criminal thrills by proxy, and cheap sex in early 1950's California.

The three novels featuring Lloyd Hopkins, the Los Angeles Police Department's most brilliant homicide detective, represent Ellroy's rare foray into modern-day Los Angeles. In *Blood on the Moon, Because the Night*, and *Suicide Hill*, Hopkins—fortified with an almost suicidal aggression—does battle against psychotics, sex-obsessed serial killers, his wife, and a corrupt police department. The moral ambiguity inherent in the Hopkins character, who at times appears more fearsomely deranged than the monstrous killers he tracks, leads directly to Ellroy's most impressive achievements to date: the four novels of the Los Angeles Quartet.

Ellroy's fondness for German Romantic composers is evident in the Quartet; in more ways than numerically it's his *Ring of the Nibelung*. The novels comprehensively cover Los Angeles criminality and corruption during the years of the author's youth, beginning with what is still his best-known book, *The Black Dahlia*—which fictionalizes the infamous L.A. murder case of 1947. The second book of the Quartet, *The Big Nowhere*, utilizes film industry union-busting and the Hollywood "red scare" of the early 1950's as its backdrop. Book three, *L.A. Confidential*—the longest and most complex novel of the cycle—centers on dreadful secrets, their exposure in movie gossip magazines, and the building of a Disneyland-like theme park by a tainted Hollywood mogul. Rounding out the series is the 1958–1960 based *White Jazz* (forthcoming), a portrait of the end of an era, a dense and hallucinogenic tale of incest and madness.

Ellroy's ambition is to eventually go beyond his hometown, and to create a panorama of 20th-century America through a sprawling series of epic crime novels. Among the projects awaiting realization are a book about America's Jewish gangsters from the 1920's to the 1940's, a novel about Huey Long and his bag men in the Louisiana of the 1920's, and another about Marilyn Monroe and the Kennedys. The author states: "I want to recreate America to my own specifications—big, broad, sweeping, dark, dense, rich, Tolstoyan novels . . ."

Ellroy's talents have already made an indelible mark on the history of crime fiction; his massive novels will be read for years to come.

—William Malloy

————

EMERSON, Earl W. American. Born in Tacoma, Washington, 8 July 1948. Educated at Principia College, Elsah, Illinois, 1966–67; University of Washington, Seattle, 1967–68. Married Sandra Evans in 1968; one daughter and two sons. Since 1978 lieutenant, Seattle Fire Department, Washington. Recipient: Private Eye Writers of America Shamus award, 1985. Agent: Dominick Abel, 498 West End Avenue, New York, New York 10024, U.S.A.

CRIME PUBLICATIONS

Novels (series: Thomas Black in all novels except *Black Hearts and Slow Dancing*)

The Rainy City.   New York, Avon, 1985.
Poverty Bay.   New York, Avon, 1985.
Nervous Laughter.   New York, Avon, 1986.
Fat Tuesday.   New York, Morrow, 1987.
Deviant Behaviour.   New York, Morrow, 1988.
Black Hearts and Slow Dancing.   New York, Morrow, 1988.

*   *   *

The narrator-protagonist of Earl W. Emerson's first five novels is Thomas Black, a private detective. Black resembles the classic private eye in a number of ways: he lives alone, he is an ex-policeman, he is in business less for profit than to right the wrongs in other peoples' lives; in his 40's, he is old enough to be a skeptic, but is not yet cynical. More specifically, the novels in which he appears resemble those of Ross Macdonald in their emphasis on the things done to children as causes of violent events much later in the lives of the characters.

Black is unusual in a number of specifics. He works in Seattle, Washington, rather than in New York or Los Angeles; all of the Black novels contain copious detail about Seattle and local color about the Pacific Northwest. He quit the police force because he had killed a young law violator to save his own life, and although he still carries a gun on occasion he can no longer bring himself to fire it at a human target. Black's retirement income from his service as a policeman gives him financial independence, so that he can work for nothing when he wants to, and can turn down potentially lucrative cases if he doesn't feel like working. He drives a pickup truck and often rides a bicycle.

A particularly unusual feature of Black's persona is his relationship with the only woman in his life, Kathy Birchfield. Much younger than Black, in the early novels she rents the basement apartment in his house. In the course of the five Black novels, she develops from a law student to an associate in a large Seattle firm to an independent practitioner. She is gorgeous, mercurial, prescient and bright. Many of Black's cases come to him through Kathy.

Their relationship is passionate but celibate. Even after Kathy leaves the basement apartment to rent quarters more suitable for a rising young attorney, she and Black occasionally spend a chaste night together, doggedly resisting their strong mutual attraction. She is less content with the arrangement than Black is, but as he explains to her in one of the novels, they need each other so much as friends that the friendship might suffer if they became lovers.

A typical Black case begins with Kathy Birchfield coming to him with fears about the fate of a friend, or bringing him a client. The novels all contain high levels of violence, and Black himself, although adept at the martial arts, comes in for beatings; like many fictional detectives, he sometimes loses the first fight but he never loses the last one. Early in the case, there is a murder or an apparent murder; in *Poverty Bay,* for example, it seems that a young man has been killed. He reappears, but not much later he is in fact murdered. What lies behind this crime is an old misunderstanding between a father and one of his sons, going back to the eventual victim's childhood. Before Black can sort things out, there are other murders, Black has been exposed to violence, and he has discovered that one of the victim's relatives is heavily involved with drugs. In the end, he bends the law somewhat to satisfy his own sense of justice.

A similar sense of the importance of what is done to children is present in other novels. The plot of *The Rainy City* is resolved when Black discovers that a young woman had, as a child, witnessed her father murdering his business partner. The father had terrorized the daughter all her life, in fear that she would reveal the secret crime. In *Fat Tuesday,* the central mystery has to do with an episode of the sexual abuse of a child. The supposed criminal is cast out by his friends and family, but his evident affection for a retarded son leads Black to investigate the case and, eventually, to clear the man. Several people have, of course, died before the case is solved. It is characteristic of Black that solving the mystery is not enough; he usually arranges matters to restore some semblance of justice to the situations in which he has been involved.

Emerson's sixth novel introduced a new protagonist. *Black Hearts and Slow Dancing* has as its central character Max Fontana, who lives in a small town near Seattle. A refugee from the fire department in a large Eastern city, he is now the head of the town's small fire department and temporary sheriff. Since Emerson is himself an officer in the Seattle Fire Department, he is able to include in this novel considerable technical detail about fires, the ways in which they are caused, and the lives of the men who try to control them. As a character, Fontana closely resembles Thomas Black, although he does not share Black's celibate state.

Emerson's prose is clean and his narratives move well. The plots of these novels are appropriately complicated, but the resolutions are generally clear. Black's relationship with Kathy Birchfield is interesting but unfortunately often too cute; they call each other "Cisco" and "Pancho" a little too often, and the celibate aspect of their relationship becomes improbable by the fourth novel. The invention of Fontana may have been a means of moving away from that relationship without providing it with a definite resolution. As a group, Emerson's novels provide a fresh setting, some relaxed humor and a different perspective for plots that are not entirely original.

—John M. Muste

————

ENGEL, Howard. Also writes as F.X. Woolf. Born in Toronto, 2 April 1931. Educated at St. Catherines, Ontario, collegiate honours graduation diploma, 1950; McMaster University, Hamilton, Ontario, B.A. 1955; Ontario College of Education, secondary school teaching certificate, 1956. Married 1) Marian

Ruth Passmore in 1962 (divorced 1977); 2) Janet Evelyn Hamilton in 1978; two sons and one daughter. Freelance broadcaster, 1956–67, radio producer, 1967–68, executive producer, 1968–80, literary editor, 1980–85, Canadian Broadcasting Corporation, Toronto. Since 1985 full-time novelist. Co-founder, 1982, treasurer, 1982–85, chairman, 1986–7, and editor of *Fingerprints*, 1985–6, *Crime Writers* of Canada. Recipient: Ontario Arts Council grant, 1981; Arthur Ellis award, 1984; Academy of Canadian Film and Television award (for film script), 1988. Agent: Beverly Slopen Literary Agency, Suite 711, 131 Bloor Street West, Toronto, Ontario M5S 1S3. Address: 281 Major Street, Toronto, Ontario M5S 2L5, Canada.

CRIME PUBLICATIONS

Novels (series: Benny Cooperman in all books except *Murder in Space*)

The Suicide Murders.   Toronto, Clarke Irwin, 1980; as *The Suicide Notice*. New York, St. Martin's Press, 1980, London, Gollancz, 1984.
The Ransom Game.   Toronto, Clarke Irwin, 1981; London, Gollancz, 1982; New York, St. Martin's Press, 1984.
Murder on Location.   Toronto, Clarke Irwin, 1982; London, Gollancz, 1983; New York, St. Martin's Press, 1985.
Murder Sees the Light.   Markham, Ontario, Viking, 1984; London, Gollancz, and New York, St. Martin's Press, 1985.
Murder in Space, (with Janet Hamilton as F.X. Woolf; novelization of television script). Markham, Ontario, Viking, 1985.
A City Called July.   Markham, Ontario, Viking, and New York, St. Martin's Press, 1986; London, Gollancz, 1987.
A Victim Must Be Found.   Markham, Ontario, Viking, and London, Gollancz, 1988; New York, St. Martin's Press, 1989.
Dead and Buried.   Markham, Ontario, Viking, 1990.

Uncollected Short Stories

"The Corned Beef Madeleine," in *Jewish Dialog* (Toronto), 1973.
"The First Tuesday of Every Month," in *Canadian Forum* (Toronto), 1976.
"Quiet Chat," in *Canadian Forum* (Toronto), May 1978.
"My Vacation in the Numbers Packet," in *Fingerprints,* Toronto, Irwin, 1984.
"The Three Wise Guys," in *Mistletoe Mysteries,* edited by Charlotte MacLeod, New York, Mysterious Press, 1989.

OTHER PUBLICATIONS

Plays

Radio Plays: *Where is Ambrost Small?,* 1984; *Hangman's Hands,* 1985; *The Wrong Man: The Donald Marshall Jr. Case,* 1985; *The Ransom Game* (from his own novel), 1985.

Screenplays: *The Suicide Murders* (from his own novel), 1984; *Murder Sees the Light* (from his own novel), 1985.

Other

"Mystery Writing Considered as One of the Fine Arts," in *Descant* (Toronto), Winter, 1985–86.

"The Mystery Writer as an Endangered Species," in *American Review of Canadian Studies* (Toronto), Spring, 1988.

*

Howard Engel comments:
   Until recently Canadian identity was a well-hidden light. Our authors, including our crime writers, had to go elsewhere to be published and had to pretend to being part of the publishing country's traditions. Grant Allen (1848–1899) and Robert Barr (1850–1912) tried to pass as Englishmen; Arthur Stinger (1874–1950) and Frank L. Packard (1877–1942) remade themselves into Americans. The first Canadian crime writer to write about a Canadian sleuth in a Canadian setting, was Margaret Miller, whose Inspector Sands worked for the Toronto Police. Another early bird was John Norman Harris, whose *The Weird World of Wes Beattie* was published first in 1963. My intention in creating Benny Cooperman was to turn the tables on what had been already done in crime fiction. I wanted a Canadian detective, instead of American or British; I wanted a small towner, rather than a big-city sleuth; a Jew, rather than a Christian, a soft-boiled rather than a hard-boiled private investigator; someone who was sickened at the sight of blood, who didn't fall into bed with every female in the story, who was not a gourmet cook, who couldn't take a lot of strong drink, who was not a great success, who took the cases Philip Marlowe wouldn't touch with a barge-pole, who had living relations including a visible mother and father. As a Jewish private eye, he is not like most of his fellow Jews in that he is non-observant, badly educated, with a mother who is a terrible cook. As far as the cases he has solved go, he began as a failed divorce investigator. After the success of his first few cases, he began to get a slightly better clientele. Benny is a born tidier of other people's lives, while his own is "on hold." He uses both his reason and his intuition to solve his cases. Although he lacks education, he has excellent equipment for untying troublesome knots. Benny is not a spoof on the American private eye. He is a man of the 1980's and 1990's being as honest as he can afford to be.

*   *   *

   The fictional private eye is such a quintessentially American hero that few attempts to transplant him to foreign soil have been successful. One notable exception is Benny Cooperman, the Canadian private detective created by Howard Engel. Soft-boiled Benny may not be as flashy or as tough as his neighbors to the south, but his dedication, persistence, and believability qualify him for inclusion among their ranks.
   Benny's beat is Grantham, a fictionalized Ontario town located a few miles from Niagara Falls. One of the notable features of the series is the small-town atmosphere Engel evokes. Benny grew up in Grantham, and went to high school with one of the local police detectives he now often works with; his parents still live in town, and like the dutiful son he is he calls often and dines with them every Friday night. His office is even located in his father's former place of business.
   Everything about Benny is, in typical Canadian fashion, unflashy and low-key. He lives in a furnished room at the local hotel. His favorite meal is a chopped-egg sandwich and a glass of milk, followed by a dish of ice cream. He eschews violence and doesn't own a gun. Drinking often gives him a headache and he sometimes gets sick at the sight of a dead body. His best leads come not from brilliant deductions but painstaking library research. Even his similes are uninspired compared with most of his peers.

But he gets the job done. Like Hammett's Continental Op, whom he resembles in many ways, he sticks to a case until he gets an answer. His methods may be hit and miss, but as Benny himself notes, "It's doggedness that pays off in the end."

In his debut appearance, *The Suicide Murders,* he is hired by a woman to find out if her husband is cheating on her. When the man turns up dead, the apparent victim of suicide, Benny has his doubts. Before he's finished, he uncovers a blackmail scheme and a crime rooted in the past.

Murder on Location takes him to nearby Niagara Falls in search of a missing wife; the woman is an aspiring amateur actress and Benny has a hunch she might have been drawn to a Hollywood film being shot there. But what he figured would be a simple missing-wife case turns more deadly when a number of murders occur. Benny's expertise is divorce work and he prefers to leave murder to the police. But thanks to some persistent digging into the past, Benny sorts through all the confusion and comes up with an explanation for all the deaths.

The Ransom Game also begins as a missing-person case. A woman hires Benny to find her boyfriend, an ex-convict recently paroled from prison after serving a sentence for kidnapping. Not only is the boyfriend missing, but also the half-million dollar ransom that was never recovered. Soon, several key figures in the case turn up dead. Benny once again untangles a complicated web of crime and deceit and provides a satisfying conclusion to this puzzling case.

Engel's plots are sometimes as convoluted as those of Ross Macdonald, another mystery writer with a Canadian background. A good example is *Murder Sees the Light.* Benny is dispatched to the north woods to keep an eye on a famous television evangelist. Soon, murder, blackmail, satanism, and assorted other matters complicate things in a not entirely convincing manner.

One element that distinguishes Benny from most of his fellow private eyes is his Jewishness. Engel doesn't overemphasize his detective's ethnic background, but it does play a significant role in *A City Called July.* Benny is asked by the local rabbi and the president of the congregation to look into a delicate matter: a trusted member of the Grantham Jewish community has disappeared with 2.6 million dollars defrauded from fellow members of the community. This time Benny has to solve a crime with the rabbi looking over his shoulders.

Benny lacks Sam Spade's cynical toughness, Philip Marlowe's colorful narrative voice, Lew Archer's poetic sensibility, and Spenser's sense of humor. He's just a "poor working stiff," as he describes himself, steady and dependable. These aren't virtues that produce heart-thumping fiction. However, in his own quiet and plodding way, likeable Benny grows as comfortable on the reader as a pair of old shoes.

—David Geherin

ERDMAN, Paul E(mil). American. Born in Stratford, Ontario, Canada, 19 May 1932. Educated at Concordia College, Fort Wayne, Indiana (later St. Louis), B.A. 1954; Georgetown University School of Foreign Service, Washington, D.C. B.S.F.S.; University of Basel, Switzerland, M.A. 1965, Ph.D. 1958. Married Helly Elizabeth Boeglin in 1954; two daughters. Economist, European Coal and Steel Community, Luxemburg, 1958–59, and Stanford Research Institute, Menlo Park, California, 1959–61; executive vice-president, Electronics International Capital Ltd., Hamilton, Bermuda, 1962–64; President and vice-chairman, United California Bank, Basel, 1965–70; host, Moneytalk Station, KGO, ABC, San Francisco, 1983–80. Since 1987 radio commentator, California. Recipient: Mystery Writers of America Edgar Allan Poe award, 1973. Address: 1817 Lytton Springs Road, Healdsburg, California 95448, U.S.A.

CRIME PUBLICATIONS

Novels

The Billion Dollar Sure Thing. London, Scribner, 1973; as *The Billion Dollar Killing,* London, Hutchinson, 1973.
The Silver Bears. New York, Scribner, and London, Hutchinson, 1975.
The Crash of '79. New York, Simon and Schuster, 1976; London, Secker and Warburg, 1977.
The Last Days of America. New York, Simon and Schuster, and London, Secker and Warburg, 1981.
The Panic of '89. London, Deutsch, 1986; New York, Doubleday, 1987.
The Palace. London, Deutsch, 1987; New York, Viking, 1988.

OTHER PUBLICATIONS

Other

Swiss-American Economic Relations. Tuebingen, Mohr and Siebeck, 1958.
Die Europaeische Wirtschaftsgemeinschaft und die Drittlaender. Tuebingen, Mohr and Siebeck, 1959.
Paul Erdman's Money Book: An Investor's Guide to Economics and Finance. New York, Random House, 1984; as *Paul Erdman's Money Guide,* London, Secker and Warburg, 1984.
What's Next?: How to Prepare Yourself for the Crash of '89 and Profit in the 1990's. New York, Doubleday, and London, Bantam, 1988.

* * *

Entering a new field and becoming an immediate star performer is not a usual pattern, though Paul E. Erdman accomplished it. A onetime baker in California and Switzerland, Erdman was jailed in a Swiss prison, and there he wrote his first novel, the best-selling mystery about banking in Switzerland, *The Billion Dollar Sure Thing.* Even a person who can't add a row of figures could understand Erdman's story, and speak in superlatives about its plot machinations. He followed it the next year with *The Silver Bears,* another story of international banking in Switzerland. Without any hinting by the author, *The Silver Bears* would seem to be the story, somewhat fictionalized, of how Erdman managed to get himself into the Swiss prison, almost inadvertently and certainly with no criminal intent.

His third book repeated the familiar success story. *The Crash of '79* is that paradox, an upbeat story of complete disaster. What it relates is the logical ending to the oil situation of the late 20th century, spelling the end of the civilized world as modern man has known it. One need not accept Erdman's conclusion, but one must admit its logic. *The Panic of '89* deals with the world of international high finance. In a futuristic tale the Swiss, Russians, and Latin Americans conspire to bring the United States economy to its knees. In this fast moving and stylish thriller, political game playing at immense proportions threatens to trigger the greatest economic catastrophe the world has ever known.

Erdman writes with pace and panache. Each of his books is as intellectually amusing as it is instructive.

—Dorothy B. Hughes

———

ERICSON, Walter. *See* **CUNNINGHAM, E.V.**

———

ERSKINE, Margaret. Pseudonym for Margaret Wetherby Williams. British. Born in Kingston, Ontario, Canada; grew up in Devon. Educated privately. *Died in 1984.*

CRIME PUBLICATIONS

Novels (series: Inspector Septimus Finch in all books)

And Being Dead. London, Bles, 1938; as *The Limping Man,* New York, Doubleday, 1939; as *The Painted Mask,* New York, Ace, 1972.
The Whispering House. London, Hammond, 1947; as *The Voice of the House,* New York, Doubleday, 1947.
I Knew MacBean. London, Hammond, and New York, Doubleday 1948; as *Caravan of Night,* New York, Ace, 1972.
Give Up the Ghost. London, Hammond, and New York, Doubleday, 1949.
The Disappearing Bridegroom. London, Hammond, 1950; as *The Silver Ladies,* New York, Doubleday, 1951.
Death of Our Dear One. London, Hammond, 1952; as *Look Behind You, Lady,* New York, Doubleday, 1952; as *Don't Look Behind You,* New York, Ace, 1972.
Dead by Now. London, Hammond, 1953; New York, Doubleday, 1954; revised edition, New York, Ace, 1972.
Fatal Relations. London, Hammond, 1955; as *Old Mrs. Ommanney Is Dead,* New York, Doubleday, 1955; as *The Dead Don't Speak,* Roslyn, New York, Detective Book Club, 1955.
The Voice of Murder. London, Hodder and Stoughton, and New York, Doubleday, 1956.
Sleep No More. London, Hodder and Stoughton, 1958; New York, Ace, 1969.
The House of the Enchantress. London, Hodder and Stoughton, 1959; as *A Graveyard Plot,* New York, Doubleday, 1959.
The Woman at Belguardo. London, Hodder and Stoughton, and New York, Doubleday, 1961.
The House in Belmont Square. London, Hodder and Stoughton, 1963; as *No. 9 Belmont Square,* New York, Doubleday, 1963.
Take a Dark Journey. London, Hodder and Stoughton, 1965; as *The Family at Tammerton,* New York, Doubleday, 1966.
Case with Three Husbands. London, Hodder and Stoughton, and New York, Doubleday, 1967.
The Ewe Lamb. London, Hodder and Stoughton, and New York, Doubleday, 1968.
The Case of Mary Fielding. London, Hodder and Stoughton, and New York, Doubleday, 1970.
The Brood of Folly. London, Hodder and Stoughton, and New York, Doubleday, 1971.

Besides the Wench Is Dead. London, Hodder and Stoughton, and New York, Doubleday, 1973.
Harriet Farewell. London, Hodder and Stoughton, and New York, Doubleday, 1975.
The House in Hook Street. New York, Doubleday, 1977; London, Hale, 1978.

*   *   *

Mysteries by Margaret Erskine began to appear in the late 1930's, and over the years there have been over 20 of them. Erskine's hero is Septimus (a seventh son, of course) Finch of the CID. In *The House of the Enchantress* Finch is described: "... he was large, bland, and solemn-looking. His walk was deceptively lazy. His voice was small and soft as a woman's. From his mother he had inherited a sensitiveness to his surroundings that amounted almost to a sixth sense. With his aunt Lilian he shared an immense but impersonal curiosity. People fascinated him even though, in the course of years, he had lost the capacity to be surprised." When his creator forgets about lending him distinguishing features and idiosyncrasies, he is quite acceptable as the investigator in charge of a case. Finch doesn't always do a lot of detecting, and at times, he seems to relish the problems of other people. Finch's delight mirrors that of his author.

Erskine wrote about creepy old houses with sliding panels and secret rooms, strange art works and curios which conceal information bearing on the crime at hand; she was interested in witchcraft and psychic phenomena; but, most of all, she likes large eccentric families. Several generations of loonies under one roof, with assorted—and ill-assorted—in-laws, relics of past marriages, and odd connections too remote to keep track of fascinated her, and she reveled in bright and breathless descriptions of their antics. *Case with Three Husbands* contains just such a bunch—two elderly brothers, one of whom renounced his military rank and gave back his medals when India got independence, and the twin sister of one of them, who live, along with three younger generations of the same tribe, in a house whose front gates have not been opened since the abdication of Edward VIII. Other books have clans just as unfathomable. One wishes that Erskine would exercise population control in regard to casts of characters, since masses of them, while amusing in the aggregate, confuse the reader and are detrimental to neat plotting. Also, after the initial sketch, the author usually neglects to develop them into separate personalities, leaving the scene strewn with cartoon—if not cardboard—characters.

While certain aspects of Erskine's mystery fiction are predictable, the overall success of any particular book is not. *Give Up the Ghost,* a fairly early novel with a Jack-the-Ripper theme, holds together rather well; although there are too many characters, motivations are clear. *Dead by Now,* a slightly later book, does not come off as well. Set in an old theater, it has ghosts, ancient tragedy, and multiple murder, but the spooky atmosphere shows up as fake. *The Woman at Belguardo,* typically convoluted, is well worked out, and the truth is discovered because a jade figurine is not cracked—a nice touch. *The Ewe Lamb,* set in a 16th-century house filled with musical instruments, is one of Erskine's best. The house, a museum as well as a family home, is satisfactorily described and the situation is suspenseful. *The Case of Mary Fielding,* shorter than most of Erskine's tales, with fewer but better-drawn characters, is a good story, tight and well-written. Other recent books are also entertaining.

Erskine wrote conventional crime fiction. She is perhaps a paradigm of the female English mystery writer. Not really in the first rank, she is nevertheless better than many, and hers is a dependable product. Horrible things happen but they are packaged for polite society. The traditional trappings are all here, and are rearranged to make new but ever familiar puzzles.

—Mary Helen Becker

———

ESMOND, Harriet. *See* **BURKE, John.**

———

ESTLEMAN, Loren D. American. Born in Ann Arbor, Michigan, 15 September 1952. Educated at Dexter community schools, Michigan, 1957–70; Eastern Michigan University, Ypsilanti, 1970–74, B.A. in English and journalism 1974. Married Carole Ann Ashley in 1987. Reporter, Ypsilanti *Press,* 1973; editor, *Community Foto-News,* Pinckney, Michigan, 1975–76; special writer, Ann Arbor *News,* 1976–77; staff writer, Dexter *Leader,* 1977–80. Recipient: Western Writers of America Spur award, 1982. Agent: Ray Puechner, Ray Peekner Literary Agency, 3210 South Seventh Street, Milwaukee, Wisconsin 53215. Address: 5552 Walsh Road, Whitmore Lake, Michigan 48189, U.S.A.

CRIME PUBLICATIONS

Novels (series: Sherlock Holmes; Peter Macklin; Amos Walker)

The Oklahoma Punk. Canoga Park, California, Major, 1976; as *Red Highway,* New York, Paperjacks, 1987.
Sherlock Holmes Versus Dracula; or, The Adventure of the Sanguinary Count. New York, Doubleday, and London, New English Library, 1978.
Dr. Jekyll and Mr. Holmes. New York, Doubleday, 1979; London, Penguin, 1980.
Motor City Blue (Walker). Boston, Houghton Mifflin, 1980; London, Hale, 1982.
Angel Eyes (Walker). Boston, Houghton Mifflin, 1981; London, Hale, 1982.
The Midnight Man (Walker). Boston, Houghton Mifflin, 1982; London, Hale, 1983.
The Glass Highway (Walker). Boston, Houghton Mifflin, 1983; London, Hale, 1984.
Sugartown (Walker). Boston, Houghton Mifflin, 1984; London, Macmillan, 1986.
Kill Zone (Macklin). New York, Mysterious Press, 1984; London, Mysterious Press, 1987.
Roses are Dead (Macklin). New York, Mysterious Press, 1985; London, Century, 1987.
Every Brilliant Eye (Walker). Boston, Houghton Mifflin, and London, Macmillan, 1986.
Any Man's Death (Macklin). New York, Mysterious Press, 1986; London, Mysterious Press, 1989.
Lady Yesterday (Walker). Boston, Houghton Mifflin, and London, Macmillan, 1987.
Downriver (Walker). Boston, Houghton Mifflin, and London, Macmillan, 1988.
General Murders: Ten Amos Walker Mysteries. Boston, Houghton Mifflin, 1988; London, Macmillan, 1989.
Silent Thunder (Walker). Boston, Houghton Mifflin, and London, Macmillan, 1989.

Peeper. New York, Bantam, 1989.
Sweet Women Lie (Walker). Boston, Houghton Mifflin, and London, Macmillan, 1990.

Uncollected Short Stories

"The Tree on Execution Hill," in *Alfred Hitchcock's Mystery Magazine* (New York) August 1977.
"The Pioneer Strain," in *Alfred Hitchcock's Mystery Magazine* (New York), October 1977.
"Robber's Roost," in *Mystery* (Glendale, California), April 1982.
"Lock, Stock, and Casket," in *Pulpsmith* (New York), Summer 1982.
"The Used," in *Alfred Hitchcock's Mystery Magazine* (New York), June 1982.
"Dead Soldier," in *Alfred Hitchcock's Mystery Magazine* (New York), Mid-September 1982.
"Diminished Capacity," in *Alfred Hitchcock's Mystery Magazine* (New York), December 1982.
"A Web of Books," in *Alfred Hitchcock's Mystery Magazine* (New York), February 1983.
"Fast Burn," in *Alfred Hitchcock's Mystery Magazine* (New York), May 1983.
"Greektown," in *Alfred Hitchcock's Mystery Magazine* (New York), December 1983.
"The Prettiest Dead Girl in Detroit," in *The Eyes Have It,* edited by Robert J. Randisi. New York, Mysterious Press, 1984; London, Severn House, 1988.
"Eight Mile and Dequindre," in *The Saint* (New York), 1984.
"Bloody July," *and* "Blond and Blue," both in *New Black Mask,* both edited by Matthew J. Bruccoli and Richard Layman. San Diego, Harcourt Brace Jovanovich, 1985.
"Major Crimes," in *Alfred Hitchcock's Mystery Magazine* (New York), March 1986.
"Bad Blood," in *Alfred Hitchcock's Mystery Magazine* (New York), July 1986.
"I'm in the Book," in *The Mean Streets.* New York, Mysterious Press, 1986.
"Doge," in *Alfred Hitchcock's Mystery Magazine* (New York), May 1987.
"Bodyguards," in *A Matter of Crime,* edited by Matthew J. Bruccoli and Richard Layman. San Diego, Harcourt Brace Jovanovich, 1987.
"State of Grace," in *An Eye for Justice,* edited by Robert J. Randisi. New York, Mysterious Press, 1988.
"The Crooked Way," in *A Matter of Crime,* edited by Matthew J. Bruccoli and Richard Layman. San Diego, Harcourt Brace Jovanovich, 1988.
"Gun Music," in *Raymond Chandler's Philip Marlowe,* edited by Byron Preiss, New York, Knopf, 1988.
"Cabaaa," in *Armchair Detective* (New York), Spring, 1990.

Play

"Dr. and Mrs. Watson at Home, in *The New Adventures of Sherlock Holmes,* edited by Martin H. Greenberg and Carol-Lynn Rössel-Waugh. New York, Carroll and Graf, 1987.

OTHER PUBLICATIONS

Novels

The Hider. New York, Doubleday, 1978.
The High Rocks. New York, Doubleday, 1979; London, Hale, 1983.
Stamping Ground. New York, Doubleday, 1980.

Aces and Eights. New York, Doubleday, 1981; London, Hale, 1983.
The Wolfer. New York, Pocket Books, 1981; London, Hale, 1983.
Murdock's Law. New York, Doubleday, 1982; London, Hale, 1983.
Mister St. John. New York, Doubleday, 1983; London, Hale, 1985.
This Old Bill. New York, Doubleday, 1984.
The Strangers. New York, Doubleday, 1984; London, Hale, 1988.
Gun Man. New York, Doubleday, 1985.
Bloody Season. New York, Bantam, 1988.
Whiskey River. New York, Bantam, 1990.

Short Stories

The Best Western Short Stories of Loren D. Estleman, edited by Bill Pronzini and Martin Greenberg. Ohio, Swallow Press, 1989.

Other

"Plus Expenses: The Private Eye as Great American Hero," in *Alfred Hitchcock's Mystery Magazine* (New York), September 1983.
"No Trap So Deadly: Recurring Devices in the Private Eye Story," in *Alfred Hitchcock's Mystery Magazine* (New York), December 1983.
The Wister Trace: Classic Novels of the American Frontier. Ottawa, Illinois, Jameson, 1987.

*

Loren D. Estleman comments:

The camera is anything but objective in that it reflects the photographer's choice of subjects, angles, and lenses to tell a story with the objects at hand. Yet the instrument's unique power lies in its general acceptance as the medium of honest expression. Similarly, the writer has it within his ability to select those physical points that will establish mood and personality while seeming to stand off and allow the reader to draw conclusions already determined. This is a process I refer to as the subjective objective.

My detective, Detroit private investigator Amos Walker, is especially suited to this purpose. His cynicism and jaundiced eye provide the conscience of the story through observation and description. His co-star is and will continue to be the city of Detroit, that reformed prostitute of a town whose love-hate relationship with its solitary hero is the gritty thread that binds the series. It's the place where the American Dream stalled and sat rusting in the rain.

But the setting is of the moment. I never concern myself with what I'm saying, believing that if I concentrate on my narrative and dialogue it will get said. I write of a society evolving toward nonviolence past a hard knot of conscienceless individuals oiling its weapons and waiting for an exposed back. It's a theme that can be split a hundred ways from the middle and I'm still counting.

*   *   *

The private lives of many authors may seem perfectly serene and uneventful, but time and again this sort of existence has proven to be no hindrance in the pursuit of a literary destiny. The career of Michigandian Loren D. Estleman is a case in point. He has demonstrated that for the traditional first words

of advice to the beginning writer—write what you know—there is a corollary that may even be considered a separate credo—know what you write.

Estleman has parlayed a journalist's training, a passion for research and documentation, and an uncommon gift for vivid description of imagined things into the very model of a writer's apprenticeship: eighteen published novels in the space of a decade. Of these, eight are works of detective fiction. Most of the rest are westerns, based on research into historical moments or personages of the Old American frontier. Our concern here is with the former.

Estleman's first two exercises in the formal crime genre were inspired by the model and success of Nicholas Meyer's *The Seven-Per-Cent Solution.* Encouraged by a band of local Sherlockians (The Arcadia Mixture of Ann Arbor), and drawing on an abiding love of detective fiction, he produced first in 1978 *Sherlock Holmes Versus Dracula,* and the following year *Dr. Jekyll and Mr. Holmes.* The first of these offers a fairly predictable narrative concerning Holmes's efforts to prevent the Sanguinary Count from taking up residence in England. There is a well-intentioned but somewhat unsuccessful attempt to evoke a Victorian prose style appropriate to Dr. Watson, but in general it stands as a competent and readable tale. The high point for Holmes enthusiasts is doubtlessly the scene in which Dracula interrogates Watson on the subject of his unswerving devotion to Holmes—a genuinely touching moment. The Jekyll and Holmes "manuscript" has many good touches, but the pace is slow. Only a much more confident evocation of the Watsonian literary voice distinguishes it from dozen or so other Holmes spin-offs of the seventies.

These experiments with stylized language turned out to be useful credentials when Estleman next blended his admiration of the classical hard-boiled detective tale, speculation on the character it might acquire in our day, and a journalist's fascination with the nearby crucible of crime known as Detroit. *Motor City Blue* was the first of the four novels to date to provide first-person narratives by Amos Walker, Estleman's Motown private eye, and it commanded the attention of the *New York Times,* which cited it as one of the notable mysteries of the year.

The elements of the first Walker case constituted a modern-day amalgam of urban lawlessness: drug dealing, prostitution, Ku Klux Klan activity, venal politics, and pornography. Yet Estleman found his way to a type of protagonist (quiet but strong, street-wise but almost a social introvert) and a narrative viewpoint of weary compassion that was right for his Detroit detective.

In 1981 *Angel Eyes* followed and Estleman began broadening the canvas of the menacing city that he had undertaken to depict. His clients, cops and adversaries were clearly linked to crucial events and at times appeared to be shadow images of prominent figures in the recent experience of the city—a city, moreover, whose history and character he has thoroughly assimilated.

The Midnight Man is the best example of the author's intricate interweaving of disparate conflicts through which Walker makes his way, taking knocks and giving them, offering wise-cracks as his shield against the moral and physical carnage that he must witness. Walker's spiritual home is centered in Hamtramck, the predominantly Polish enclave, where he lives alone with only his TV set for companionship. But his range of activity is the whole city. In *The Glass Highway* his work takes him to the posh up-river suburb of Grosse Pointe, and here the intimate association of corruption and affluence is portrayed in the pages that nostalgically evoke the spectre of Philip Marlowe.

The tenth Amos Walker novel, *Sweet Woman Lie,* was published in 1990, and the author has assembled a collection of

Amos Walker short stories. However, even if the future were not so promising, on the basis of his past performance, Walker's permanence would be assured.

—Donald A. Yates

———

ESTRIDGE, Robin. *See* **LORAINE, Philip.**

———

EUSTIS, Helen (White). American. Born in Cincinnati, Ohio, 31 December 1916. Educated at Hillsdale School, Cincinnati; Smith College, Northampton, Massachusetts, B.A. 1938; Columbia University, New York. Married 1) Alfred Young Fisher, one son; 2) Martin Harris (divorced). Worked briefly as copywriter. Recipient: Mystery Writers of America Edgar Allan Poe award, 1947. Address: c/o Green Tiger Press, 7458 La Jolla Boulevard, La Jolla, California 92037, U.S.A.

CRIME PUBLICATIONS

Novels

The Horizontal Man. New York, Harper, 1946; London, Hamish Hamilton, 1947.
The Fool Killer. New York, Doubleday, 1954; London, Secker and Warburg, 1955.

OTHER PUBLICATIONS

Short Stories

The Captains and the Kings Depart and Other Stories. New York, Harper, 1949.

Other

Mr. Death and the Redheaded Woman (for children). La Jolla, California, Green Tiger, 1983.

Translator, *When I Was Old,* by Georges Simenon. New York, Harcourt Brace, 1971; London, Hamish Hamilton, 1972.

*   *   *

A writer who has attracted considerable critical acclaim as the result of a single work, Helen Eustis owes her permanent place in the history of detective fiction to her first novel, the Edgar award-winning *The Horizontal Man.* In addition, she has published *The Fool Killer,* a mystery novel for both children and adults, somewhat self-consciously imitative of Mark Twain; and numerous short stories, some of which are collected in the volume *The Captains and the Kings Depart.* The stories are not, generically, mysteries, but they are informed by an almost gothic interest in human psychology and motivation.

A similar, though more specifically psychoanalytic, sensibility characterizes *The Horizontal Man.* Connoisseurs of detective fiction praise the unique use of the "least likely person" device, which has been compared, in its originality and impact, to that used by Agatha Christie in *The Murder of Roger Ackroyd.* The novel is set in Hollymount College, an Eastern American girl's school (modelled, perhaps, on Smith College, the author's *alma mater.*) Several "private detectives," including a young newspaper reporter, a homely but witty student, and a beleaguered college president become involved in the murder of handsome English professor Kevin Boyle. It is the staff psychiatrist who finally puts the pieces together.

Unlike many detective stories set in academe, *The Horizontal Man* is not in the least self-conscious in its use of literary allusions or intellectual puns. The story, which contains an element of the bizarre, is told with a charming combination of sophistication and humour, and the author's presentation of both locale and characters is so realistic that what might be regarded as artificial or "symbolic" always arises naturally from the action. It is the essential realism which distinguishes the novel from the category of merely clever pastiches of detective story devices. Its originality lies both in its honest treatment of sexual motivation and in its use of such traditional devices as shifting narrative point of view in an uncompromisingly realistic context.

—Joanne Harack Hayne

———

EVANS, John. *See* **BROWNE, Howard.**

———

EVANS, Jonathan. *See* **FREEMANTLE, Brian.**

———

F

FAIR, A.A. *See* **GARDNER, Erle Stanley.**

———

FAIRBAIRN, Roger. *See* **CARR, John Dickson.**

———

FAIRLEIGH, Runa. *See* **MORSE, L.A.**

———

FAIRLIE, Gerard. British. Born in London, 1 November 1899. Educated in Brussels, 1906–11; Downside School, 1912–17; Royal Military Academy, Sandhurst, 1917–18. Served in the Scots Guards, 1918–24 (Army heavyweight boxer, 1919); Lieutenant-Colonel, Royal Sussex Regiment, 1939–45; Croix de Guerre; Bronze Star. Married Joan Roskell in 1923; two daughters and one son. Assistant to Bernard Darwin, golf correspondent of *The Times,* London, 1924–25; golf correspondent, *Bystander,* 1925–30, and *Britannia,* 1930, both London; screen writer for British and American film companies, 1931–49. Member, British Olympic Bobsleigh Team, Chamonix, France, 1924. *Died in April 1983.*

CRIME PUBLICATIONS

Novels (series: Victor Caryll; Bulldog Drummond; Johnny Macall; Mr. Malcolm)

Scissors Cut Paper (Caryll). London, Hodder and Stoughton, 1927; Boston, Little Brown, 1928.
The Man Who Laughed (Caryll). London, Hodder and Stoughton, and Boston, Little Brown, 1928.
Stone Blunts Scissors (Caryll). London, Hodder and Stoughton, 1928; Boston, Little Brown, 1929.
The Exquisite Lady. London, Hodder and Stoughton, 1929; as *Yellow Munro,* Boston, Little Brown, 1929.
The Reaper. Boston, Little Brown, 1929.
The Muster of Vultures. London, Hodder and Stoughton, 1929; Boston, Little Brown, 1930.
Suspect. London, Hodder and Stoughton, and New York, Doubleday, 1930.
Unfair Lady. London, Hodder and Stoughton, 1931.
The Man with Talent. London, Hodder and Stoughton, 1931.
Shot in the Dark (Malcolm). London, Hodder and Stoughton, and New York, Doubleday, 1932.
The Rope Which Hangs. London, Hodder and Stoughton, 1932.
Mr. Malcolm Presents. London, Hodder and Stoughton, 1932.

Birds of Prey. London, Hodder and Stoughton, 1932.
Men for Counters (Malcolm). London, Hodder and Stoughton, 1933.
The Treasure Nets. London, Hodder and Stoughton, 1933.
That Man Returns (Caryll). London, Hodder and Stoughton, 1934.
Copper at Sea. London, Hodder and Stoughton, 1934.
Bulldog Drummond on Dartmoor. London, Hodder and Stoughton, 1938; New York, Curl, 1939.
The Pianist Shoots First. London, Hodder and Stoughton, 1938.
Bulldog Drummond Attacks. London, Hodder and Stoughton, 1939; New York, Gateway, 1940.
Captain Bulldog Drummond. London, Hodder and Stoughton, 1945.
They Found Each Other. London, Hodder and Stoughton, 1946.
Bulldog Drummond Stands Fast. London, Hodder and Stoughton, 1947.
Hands Off Bulldog Drummond. London, Hodder and Stoughton, 1949.
Calling Bulldog Drummond. London, Hodder and Stoughton, 1951.
Winner Take All (Macall). London, Hodder and Stoughton, and New York, Dodd Mead, 1953.
The Return of the Black Gang (Drummond). London, Hodder and Stoughton, 1954.
No Sleep for Macall. London, Hodder and Stoughton, 1955.
Deadline for Macall. London, Hodder and Stoughton, and New York, Mill, 1956.
Double the Bluff (Macall). London, Hodder and Stoughton, 1957.
Macall Gets Curious. London, Hodder and Stoughton, 1959.
Please Kill My Cousin (Macall). London, Hodder and Stoughton, 1961.

Uncollected Short Story

"The Ghost of a Smile," in *Fifty Masterpieces of Mystery.* London, Odhams Press, 1935.

OTHER PUBLICATIONS

Novels

Moral Holiday. London, Hutchinson, 1936.
Approach to Happiness. London, Hutchinson, 1939.
The Mill of Circumstance: A Novelized History of the Life and Times of General Wolfe. London, Hutchinson, 1941.

Plays

Bulldog Drummond Hits Out, with Sapper (produced Brighton and London, 1937).
Number Six, with Guy Bolton, adaptation of a novel by Edgar Wallace (produced London, 1938).

Screenplays: *Jack Ahoy!*, with others, 1934; *Open All Night*, 1934; *Lazybones*, 1935; *Charlie Chan in Shanghai*, with Edward R. Lowe, 1935; *The Lad*, 1935; *The Ace of Spades*, 1935; *Bulldog Jack (Alias Bulldog Drummond)*, with Sapper and J.O.C. Orton, 1935; *Brown on Resolution (Born for Glory)*, with Michael Hogan and J.O.C. Orton, 1935; *Troubled Waters*, 1936; *The Big Noise*, 1936; *The Lonely Road (Scotland Yard Commands)*, with James Flood and Anthony Kimmins, 1936; *Chick*, with others, 1936; *Conspirator*, with Sally Benson, 1949; *Calling Bulldog Drummond*, with Howard Emmett Rogers and Arthur Wimperis, 1951.

Other

With Prejudice: Almost an Autobiography.   London, Hodder and Stoughton, 1952.
Flight Without Wings: The Biography of Hannes Schneider. London, Hodder and Stoughton, and New York, A.S. Barnes, 1957.
The Reluctant Cop: The Story, and the Cases, of Superintendent Albert Webb.   London, Hodder and Stoughton, 1958.
The Fred Emney Story.   London, Hutchinson, 1960.
The Life of a Genius (biography of Sir George Cayley), with Elizabeth Cayley.   London, Hodder and Stoughton, 1965.

*

Gerard Fairlie commented (1980):
I met Lieutenant-Colonel H.C. McNeile (Sapper) at the end of the First World War. We were soon helping each other—he helping me far more than I was helping him. The relationship was master-pupil except when it came to writing dialogue. His has been the greatest influence on me in my now long and varied career. Both of us wrote to entertain, not to impress.

* * *

Gerard Fairlie's fame is linked to Sapper's: he was, by Sapper's own account, the original for Bulldog Drummond, and on Sapper's death in 1937 he took over the Drummond series. In Fairlie's hands Drummond mellows, becomes a more likeable character, is more at ease with women, who become more believable; even Irma is referred to, in *Bulldog Drummond Stands Fast* (we may allow for irony) as a "peach." Much of the sadism and the jingoistic hostility has gone, but so has much of Sapper's narrative gift, and the sense of Drummond as a figure larger than life. (In Fairlie's autobiography, *With Prejudice*, it is Fairlie himself, not Sapper—though the older writer is treated barely this side of idolatry—who comes across as the more mature and balanced personality, and the difference is felt in the two Drummonds.)
Fairlie wrote more than 20 novels outside Sapper's shadow; he also worked as a screenwriter, both in England and Hollywood. As samples of his fiction, one may take an early novel, *The Muster of Vultures*, and *They Found Each Other*. The first is a thriller, not without relevance for the 1970's, in which high officials are kidnapped and ransomed by a gang of criminals—and takes the view that lives are insignificant when set against the public good. The second presumably draws upon Fairlie's very distinguised service with the French Resistance (for which he was decorated), and is set in occupied Paris at the time of D-Day. Fairlie mixes exciting incident—crime and espionage—with a love story. The ultimate difference between him and Sapper is that Fairlie does not fuse a racial or national belief with an imaginative character creation, and so does not,

as Sapper however disagreeably does, rise to a level of myth and archetype.

—Barrie Hayne

————

FALKIRK, Richard. *See* **LAMBERT, Derek.**

————

FALLON, Martin. *See* **HIGGINS, Jack.**

————

FARR, Caroline. *See* **BROWN, Carter.**

————

FARR, John. *See* **WEBB, Jack.**

————

FARRER, Katharine (Dorothy, neé Newton).   British.   Born in Chippenham, Wiltshire, 27 September 1911. Educated at St. Anne's College, Oxford, diploma in education 1933. Married Austin Farrer in 1937; one daughter. Teacher of Latin and Greek, 1933–37. Agent: David Higham Associates Ltd. 5–8 Lower John Street, London W1R 4HA. England.

CRIME PUBLICATIONS

Novels (series: Inspector Richard Ringwood in all books)

The Missing Link.   London, Collins, 1952.
The Cretan Counterfeit.   London, Collins, 1954.
Gownsman's Gallows.   London, Hodder and Stoughton, 1957.

OTHER PUBLICATIONS

Novel

At Odds with Morning.   London, Hodder and Stoughton, 1960.

Other

Translator, *Being and Having*, by Gabriel Marcel.   London, Dacre Press, 1949.
Translator, *The Church Which Presides in Love* (symposium). London, Faith Press, 1962.

Translator, *The Primacy of Peter*, by Jean Meyendorff and others.   London, Faith Press, 1963.

* * *

Katherine Farrer's three detective novels almost but not quite fit into the sub-genre of the Academic Mystery, Her series detective Richard Ringwood, with his wife and "Watson," Clare, is called in to solve suspicious circumstances in intellectual circles. In *Gownsman's Gallows* and *The Missing Link* we are taken into traditional collegiate settings while *The Cretan Counterfeit* is set amongst archaeologists in Britain and Greece.

Farrer was not the most proficient of plotters; her novels are more remarkable for their wealth of corroborative detail. In *The Missing Link* in particular, we are given a range of information on such diverse topics as modern childrearing, vaguely socialist eugenicist theories, and the Romany dialect. *The Cretan Counterfeit* is full of information about archaeology and is very good on describing the British Museum, its workers and the surrounding area of Bloomsbury. It leads the reader to wonder why so few detective novels have been written with such a theme when the disciplines of archaeology and deductive reasoning would seem to be similarly involved in puzzle-solving.

The endings of Farrer's novels are particularly unwieldy; Ringwood frequently gets involved in physical violence, the writing of which seems to owe more to Sexton Blake than to more contemporary writers. Since in *Gownsman's Gallows* we are also transported to a poorly-drawn France where some more action takes place, it may be that Farrer would have slotted more happily into the adventure story canon.

—Linda Semple

FAST, Howard. *See* **CUNNINGHAM, E.V.**

FEARING, Kenneth (Flexner). Also wrote as Donald F. Bedford. American. Born in Oak Park, Illinois, 28 July 1902. Educated at the University of Wisconsin, Madison, B.A. 1924. Married 1) Rachel Meltzer in 1933, one son; 2) the painter Nan Lurie in 1945 (divorced 1958). Reporter in Chicago; freelance writer in New York from 1925: contributor to poetry magazine, and staff writer, *Time* magazine. Recipient: Guggenheim Fellowship, 1936, 1939; American Academy award, 1945. *Died 26 June 1961.*

CRIME PUBLICATIONS

Novels

Dagger of the Mind. New York, Random House, and London, Lane, 1941; as *Cry Killer!*, New York, Avon, 1958.
The Big Clock. New York, Harcourt Brace, 1946; New York, Lane, 1947; as *No Way Out,* New York, Perennial, 1980.
Loneliest Girl in the World. New York, Harcourt Brace, 1951; London, Lane, 1952; as *The Sound of Murder,* New York, Spivak, 1952.

The Generous Heart. New York, Harcourt Brace, 1954; London, Lane, 1955.
The Crozart Story. New York, Doubleday, 1960.

Uncollected Short Stories

"The Jury," in *Manhunt* (New York), March 1955.
"Shake-Up," in *Manhunt* (New York), May 1955.
"Shadow of Fame," in *Mike Shayne Mystery Magazine* (New York), December 1956.
"Three Wives Too Many," in *Best Detective Stories of the Year 1957,* edited by David Coxe Cooke. New York, Dutton and London, Boardman, 1957.
"Champagne and Bitters," in *Ed McBain's Mystery Book 2* (New York), 1960.

OTHER PUBLICATIONS

Novels

The Hospital. New York, Random House, 1939; London, Thorpe and Porter, 1962.
Clark Gifford's Body. New York, Random House, 1942; London, Lane, 1943.
John Barry (as Donald F. Bedford, with Donald Freide and Henry Bedford-Jones). New York, Creative Age Press, 1947.

Verse

Angel Arms. New York, Coward McCann, 1929.
Poems. New York, Dynamo, 1935.
Dead Reckoning. New York, Random House, 1938.
Collected Poems. New York, Random House, 1940.
Afternoon of a Pawnbroker and Other Poems. New York, Harcourt Brace, 1943.
Stranger at Coney Island and Other Poems. New York, Harcourt Brace, 1948.
New and Selected Poems. Bloomington, University of Indiana Press, 1956.

* * *

Better known as a post-Depression era American poet, Kenneth Fearing also wrote seven novels, between 1939 and 1960, several of them qualifying in the thriller or intrigue categories. They are distinguished by their use of the technique of multiple and recurrent narrators, which Fearing borrowed from Faulkner and which he used brilliantly in at least one novel, *The Big Clock.* He also used the technique effectively in his first novel, *The Hospital;* he was still using it in the interesting though labored *The Crozart Story,* published just a year before his death in 1961. But I agree with Julian Symons that *The Big Clock* is Fearing's principal contribution to crime fiction.

In this novel Fearing excels, not only as the teller of a gripping suspense thriller but also as the creator of a number of convincingly drawn psychological character portraits. The chief of these is the novel's protagonist, George Stoud, who is depicted as an intelligent, sensitive individual chafing under the collar of conformity imposed upon him by life in the big city magazine publishing game, but whose flight from conformity is also perceptively shown by his creator to contain an element of the reckless and self-destructive as well, which makes the plight he ultimately finds himself in perfect. Stroud's boss, the magazine mogul Earl Janoth, commits a murder but is seen leaving the scene of the crime by an unidentified observer. Janoth then puts Stroud at the head of an investigative unit of crime writers to find the unknown witness, whom Janoth has marked for destruction. What Stroud alone knows, the moment that the situation is described to him, is that the man they're all seeking is Stroud himself. Extraordinary suspense follows, as each piece of new information brought in to the command post at the magazine offices tightens the net around Stroud, who must use his wits to keep those working for him from making the connection and realizing *he* is their mystery witness.

But Fearing adds still another element to this novel to elevate it even further above the level of the average crime thriller. In the center of things he places a symbol, The Big Clock. Representing as it does the constantly moving hand of time, the clock is an obviously apt symbol for the plight of Stroud, for whom time must sooner or later run out. But the symbol also operates in a larger sphere; it serves as a constant reminder to Stroud of his mortality, and in doing so becomes sufficiently universalized to speak to us as well. In having his protagonist rebel against the conformity of the rat-race while all the time confronting the Big Clock, Fearing reminds his protagonist—and us—that there is one kind if conformity from which all of us have ultimately no escape.

The Big Clock is, because of its gripping story, a classic of thriller fiction. But because of the masterful way in which he also uses narrative technique, characterization, and symbolism, Kenneth Fearing lays legitimate claim, in at least this one novel, to being a serious and significant writer of fiction without any further qualifying label.

—Frank Occhiogrosso

FENWICK, Elizabeth (Elizabeth Fenwick Way). Also writes as E. P. Fenwick. American. Born in 1920.

CRIME PUBLICATIONS

Novels

The Inconvenient Corpse (as E.P. Fenwick). New York, Farrar and Rinehart, 1943.
Murder in Haste (as E.P. Fenwick). New York, Farrar and Rinehart, 1944.
Two Names for Death (as E.P. Fenwick). New York, Farrar and Rinehart, 1945; London, Wells Gardner, 1949.
Poor Harriet. New York, Harper, 1957; London, Gollancz, 1958.
A Long Way Down. New York, Harper, and London, Gollancz, 1959.
A Friend of Mary Rose. New York, Harper, 1961; London, Gollancz, 1962.
A Night Run. New York, Gollancz, 1961.
The Silent Cousin. New York, Gollancz, 1962; New York, Atheneum, 1966.
The Make-Believe Man. New York, Harper, and London, Gollancz, 1963.
The Passenger. New York, Atheneum, and London, Gollancz, 1967.
Disturbance on Berry Hill. New York, Atheneum, and London, Gollancz, 1968.

Goodbye, Aunt Elva. New York, Atheneum, 1968; London, Gollancz, 1969.
Impeccable People. London, Gollancz, 1971.
The Last of Lysandra. London, Gollancz, 1973.

OTHER PUBLICATIONS

Novels

The Long Wing. New York, Rinehart, 1947.
Afterwords. New York, Rinehart, 1950.
Days of Plenty. New York, Harcourt Brace, 1956.
Cockleberry Castle (for children). New York, Pantheon, 1963.

*

Manuscript Collection: Mugar Memorial Library, Boston University.

* * *

Elizabeth Fenwick's suspense novels are remarkable for the degree of horror they can extract from minimal materials. Each novel deals with a closed or isolated community, or records a collision between families of very different kinds. The psychology of these small groups is exposed with fastidious authority. Fenwick can describe the best and worst of a character in one sentence, and can make a single gesture tell of years of accumulated pain or madness. In *The Passenger*, the destruction of a woman's garden halfway through the book is unexpectedly shocking in itself, and foreshadows the tragedy to come. In *Goodbye, Aunt Elva*, an elderly woman's years of harmless vanity are exposed by her hysteria when it is suggested that a dying woman looks like her.

Fenwick's novels are all beautifully plotted in human intimacy. The depraved families in *Poor Harriet* and *Goodbye, Aunt Elva* draw extra strength for wickedness from their kin. The tragic family in *The Silent Cousin* has seen its great strength deteriorate into madness. The sound families in *Poor Harriet*, *The Make-Believe Man*, and *Disturbance on Berry Hill* are cause for celebration.

Fenwick's characters are highly individual and often memorable. A woman in *A Long Way Down* is a masterpiece of manipulative menace, even though she never appears in person. And the same novel gives us an elderly bachelor college professor whose isolation has not stunted his charity or understanding.

—Carol Cleveland

FERRARS, Elizabeth. Pseudonym for Morna Doris Brown (née MacTaggart); also writes as E.X. Ferrars. British. Born in Rangoon, Burma, 6 September 1907. Educated at Bedales School, Petersfield, Hampshire, 1918–24; University College, London, 1925–28, diploma in journalism 1928. Married Robert Brown in 1940. Founding Member, Crime Writers Association, 1953 chair, 1977–78. Recipient: Crime Writers Association Silver Dagger award, 1981. Agent: David Higham Associates Ltd., 5–8 Lower John Street, London W1R 4HA. Address: 5 Treble House Terrace, London Road, Blewbury, Didcot OX11 9NZ, England.

CRIME PUBLICATIONS

Novels (series: Andrew Basnett; Toby Dyke; Virginia and Felix Freer; published as E.X. Ferrars in US)

Give a Corpse a Bad Name (Dyke). London, Hodder and Stoughton, 1940.
Remove the Bodies (Dyke). London, Hodder and Stoughton, 1940; as *Rehearsals for Murder*, New York, Doubleday, 1941.
Death in Botanist's Bay (Dyke). London, Hodder and Stoughton, 1941; as *Murder of a Suicide*, New York, Doubleday, 1941.
Don't Monkey with Murder (Dyke). London, Hodder and Stoughton, 1942; as *The Shape of a Stain*, New York, Doubleday, 1942.
Your Neck in a Noose (Dyke). London, Hodder and Stoughton, 1942; as *Neck in a Noose*, New York, Doubleday, 1943.
I, Said the Fly. London, Hodder and Stoughton, and New York, Doubleday, 1945.
Murder among Friends. London, Collins, 1946; as *Cheat the Hangman*, New York, Doubleday, 1946.
With Murder in Mind. London, Collins, 1948.
The March Hare Murders. London, Collins, and New York, Doubleday, 1949.
Hunt the Tortoise. London, Collins, and New York, Doubleday, 1950.
Milk of Human Kindness. London, Collins, 1950.
The Clock That Wouldn't Stop. London, Collins, and New York, Doubleday, 1952.
Alibi for a Witch. London, Collins, and New York, Doubleday, 1952.
Murder in Time. London, Collins, 1953.
The Lying Voices. London, Collins, 1954.
Enough to Kill a Horse. London, Collins, and New York, Doubleday, 1955.
Always Say Die. London, Collins, 1956; as *We Haven't Seen Her Lately*, New York, Doubleday, 1956.
Murder Moves In. London, Collins, 1956; as *Kill or Cure*, New York, Doubleday, 1956.
Furnished for Murder. London, Collins, 1957.
Count the Cost. New York, Doubleday, 1957; as *Unreasonable Doubt*, London, Collins, 1958.
Depart This Life. New York, Doubleday, 1958; as *A Tale of Two Murders*, London, Collins, 1959.
Fear the Light. London, Collins, and New York, Doubleday, 1960.
The Sleeping Dogs. London, Collins, and New York, Doubleday, 1960.
The Busy Body. London, Collins, 1962; as *Seeing Double*, New York, Doubleday, 1962.
The Wandering Widows. London, Collins, and New York, Doubleday, 1962.
The Doubly Dead. London, Collins, and New York, Doubleday, 1963.
The Decayed Gentlewoman. New York, Doubleday, 1963; as *A Legal Fiction*, London, Collins, 1964.
Ninth Life. London, Collins, 1965.
No Peace for the Wicked. London, Collins, and New York, Harper, 1966.
Zero at the Bone. London, Collins, 1967; New York, Walker, 1968.
The Swaying Pillars. London, Collins, 1968; New York, Walker, 1969.

Skeleton Staff. London, Collins, and New York, Walker, 1969.
The Seven Sleepers. London, Collins, and New York, Walker, 1970.
A Stranger and Afraid. London, Collins, and New York, Walker, 1971.
Breath of Suspicion. London, Collins, and New York, Doubleday, 1972.
Foot in the Grave. New York, Doubleday, 1972; London, Collins, 1973.
The Small World of Murder. London, Collins, and New York, Doubleday, 1973.
Hanged Man's House. London, Collins, and New York, Doubleday, 1974.
Alive and Dead. London, Collins, 1974; New York, Doubleday, 1975.
Drowned Rat. London, Collins, and New York, Doubleday, 1975.
The Cup and the Lip. London, Collins, 1975; New York, Doubleday, 1976.
Blood Flies Upward. London, Collins, 1976; New York, Doubleday, 1977.
The Pretty Pink Shroud. London, Collins, and New York, Doubleday, 1977.
Murders Anonymous. London, Collins, 1977; New York, Doubleday, 1978.
Last Will and Testament (Freer). London, Collins, and New York, Doubleday, 1978.
In at the Kill. London, Collins, 1978; New York, Doubleday, 1979.
Witness Before the Fact. London, Collins, 1979; New York, Doubleday, 1980.
Frog in the Throat (Freer). London, Collins, and New York, Doubleday, 1980.
Experiment with Death. London, Collins, and New York, Doubleday, 1981.
Thinner Than Water. London, Collins, 1981; New York, Doubleday, 1982.
Skeleton in Search of a Cupboard. London, Collins, 1982; as *Skeleton in Search of a Closet*, New York, Doubleday, 1982.
Death of a Minor Character. London, Collins, and New York, Doubleday, 1983.
Something Wicked (Basnett). London, Collins, 1983; New York, Doubleday, 1984.
Root of All Evil (Basnett). London, Collins, and New York, Doubleday, 1984.
The Crime and the Crystal (Basnett). London, Collins, and New York, Doubleday, 1985.
I Met Murder. London, Collins, 1985; New York, Doubleday, 1986.
The Other Devil's Name (Basnett). London, Collins, 1986; New York, Doubleday, 1987.
Come and Be Killed. London, Collins, and New York, Doubleday, 1987.
A Murder Too Many (Basnett). London, Collins, 1988; New York, Doubleday, 1989.
Trial by Fury. London, Collins, and New York, Doubleday, 1989.
Woman Slaughter (Freer). London, Collins, 1989.
Smoke Without Fire (Basnett). London, Collins, 1990.

Short Stories

Designs on Life. London, Collins, and New York, Doubleday, 1980.

Uncollected Short Stories

"When a Young Girl's Eyes Are Crazy with Worry," in *The Evening Standard* (London), 8 December 1958; as "The Case of the Two Questions," in *Ellery Queen's Mystery Magazine* (New York), August 1959.
"No More Milk for Mrs. Toomes," in *The Evening Standard* (London), 9 December 1958; as "The Case of the Blue Bowl," in *Ellery Queen's Mystery Magazine* (New York), October 1959.
"A Lunch Plate Stopped Bardell's Escape," in *The Evening Standard* (London), 11 December 1958; as "The Cast of the Left Hand," in *Ellery Queen's Mystery Magazine* (New York), December 1960.
"Invitation to Murder—on the Party Line," in *The Evening Standard* (London), 12 December 1958.
"A Lipstick Smear Points to the Killer," in *The Evening Standard* (London), 13 December 1958.
"Playing with Fire," in *Ellery Queen's Mystery Magazine* (New York), January 1960.
"The Collector Who Ran Away from Murder," in *The Evening Standard* (London); as "The Case of the Auction Catalogue," in *Ellery Queen's Mystery Magazine* (New York), January 1960.
"Suicide: In a Car with the Lights on? X," in *The Evening Standard* (London), 19 March 1963; as "Suicide?," in *The Saint* (New York), October 1964.
"When a Girl Has a Grudge, Look for Trouble," in *The Evening Standard* (London), 8 June 1964; as "Look for Trouble," in *The Saint* (New York), May 1965.
"The Long way Round," in *Winter's Crimes 4*, edited by George Hardinge. London, Macmillan, 1972.
"Ashes to Ashes," in *Ellery Queen's Giants of Mystery*. New York, Davis, 1976.
"Sequence of Events," in *Winter's Crimes 9*, edited by George Hardinge. London, Macmillan, 1977.
"Instrument of Justice," in *Winter's Crimes 13*, edited by George Hardinge. London, Macmillan, and New York, St. Martin's Press, 1981.
"Fly, Said the Spy," in *Winter's Crime 15*, edited by Hilary Hale. London, Macmillan, and New York, St. Martin's Press, 1983.

OTHER PUBLICATIONS

Novels as Morna MacTaggart

Turn Simple. London, Nicholson and Watson, 1932.
Broken Music. London, Nicholson and Watson, and New York, Dutton, 1934.

Other

Editor, *Planned Departures*. London, Hodder and Stoughton, 1958.

*   *   *

Morna Brown, whose thrillers appear under the name Elizabeth Ferrars or E.X. Ferrars, is a prolific writer of well-made traditional suspense fiction. Even a nervous reader alone on a dark night may enjoy the tales concocted by this competent British writer. Anything gruesome or horrible is treated in such a way that the reader is spared nightmares or undue distress.

Ferrars writes about nice people who inhabit a world in which good manners predominate. Her educated, upper-middle-class characters, unused to the intrusion of violence or crime into their lives, at times exclaim that murder and things like that simply don't happen to them. The author excels at creating sympathetic and natural types whose personalities are convincingly delineated and whose involvement in murder does not fail to arouse interest.

Her protagonists are often writers or artists, scholars or graduate students. Her female characters are politely feminist, independent young women who do not submerge their work or their professional identity in a quest for romance. Ferrars admirably rejects trite "happily-ever-after" solutions to the love affairs which usually figure in her tales. Even an early book like *I, Said the Fly*, set in wartime London, features a self-reliant heroine whose sentimental difficulties are not neatly resolved on the last page.

Backgrounds for the tales range from Greece to Australia, from Africa to Madeira, but most frequently are English or Scottish locales. In several books the author has developed the town of Helsington with its surrounding villages, creating a fabric of communities that add charm and familiarity to her fictional world. Though they may be played out in exotic places, the plots tends to be domestic intrigues. Murder in a household or among friends, though sometimes a bit claustrophobic, gives the author an occasion to explore the feelings and motivations of ordinary people. *The Small World of Murder*, which contains a kidnapping and a complex conspiracy among intimates, rather ironically unfolds while the participants travel around the world from London to Mexico to Fiji to Australia. The foreign scenery is integrated into the plot and is sketched as seen by one member of the party, a bystander who is, at the same time, inexplicably involved.

The author incorporates enough specialized information into her stories to add dimension but not enough to overwhelm the reader who, it is presumed, has picked up the book to be entertained and not to be treated to a dissertation on falconry or the art market. Although Ferrars is obviously familiar with university and literary milieux, her books are never marred by excessive academic jargon or too many literary allusions. She is sometimes quite witty, and her subtle, gentle humor enhances many passages in her fiction.

Her readers expect good plotting and ingenious situations and are not often disappointed. In *Breath of Suspicion*, a scientist mixed up in espionage reveals his whereabouts to a deadly enemy by writing a successful thriller. In *Ninth Life*, a crime reporter turned gourmet cook unwisely taunts a criminal from his past and gets himself murdered. In *The Decayed Gentlewoman*, the ownership of a painting, long unrecognized as by Rubens, depends upon an obscure point of law. A group of women who enjoy travelling together harbor a swindler and murderer in their midst in *The Wandering Widows*, a cleverly constructed tale set in the Inner Hebrides, on Iona and Mull. A Helsington story, *Alive and Dead*, revolves around an agency for unwed mothers, and contains a pair of Ferrars's best characters, an elderly woman volunteer and her cantakerous male boarder whose gruff exterior hides a kindly nature.

Ferrars combines fine craftsmanship with skillful plotting and likable people to provide first-rate entertainment. She is one of the best contemporary writers of civilized murder mysteries.

—Mary Helen Becker

FIELD, Temple. *See* **WHITFIELD, Raoul.**

FINNEGAN, Robert. Pseudonym for Paul William Ryan; also wrote as Mike Quinn. American. Born in San Francisco, California, in 1906. Left school at age 15. Married Mary King O'Donnell in 1944; one daughter. Worked in shops and offices until becoming a sailor, 1925–29; worked in book store in Hollywood; joined the John Reed Club of Hollywood, and contributed to the club magazine, *Partisan;* returned to San Francisco in 1934, became active in the labor movement writing for the International Longshoreman and Warehouseman's Union's *The Waterfront Worker* and *The Dispatcher,* and *Western Worker* (later *People's World*); employed on WPA Writers' Project; Public Relations Director, Congress of Industrial Organizations in California in the 1940's: "CIO Reporter on the Air," 1943–45, columnist, *Daily People's World,* 1946–47, and produced broadcasts for National Maritime Union and others; active member of the Communist Party. *Died 14 August 1947.*

CRIME PUBLICATIONS

Novels (series: Dan Banion in all books)

The Lying Ladies. New York, Simon and Schuster, 1946; London, Lane, 1949.
The Bandaged Nude. New York, Simon and Schuster, 1946; London, Boardman, 1949.
Many a Monster. New York, Simon and Schuster, 1948; London, Boardman, 1950.

OTHER PUBLICATIONS as Paul W. Ryan

Other

And We Are Millions: The League of Homeless Youth (as Mike Quin). Hollywood, John Reed Club, 1933.
The C.S. Case Against Labor. San Francisco, International Labor Defense, 1936.
Ashcan the M-Plan (as Mike Quin). San Francisco, Yanks Are Not Coming Committee, 1938.
Dangerous Thoughts. San Francisco, People's World, 1940.
The Yanks Are Not Coming. San Francisco, Maritime Federation of the Pacific, 1940.
The Enemy Within. San Francisco, People's World, 1941.
More Dangerous Thoughts. San Francisco, People's World, 1941.
On the Drumhead: A Selection from the Writings of Mike Quin, edited by Henry Carlisle. San Francisco, Pacific Publishing Foundation, 1948.
The Big Strike (as Mike Quin). Olema, California, Olema Publishing Company, 1949.

*   *   *

Robert Finnegan died young, having produced a handful of books demonstrating a very real talent. Of these, perhaps *The Bandaged Nude* has remained the best known. Finnegan painted his backgrounds and characters, whether of low or high life, with a sure touch. The whole post-war atmosphere is there, which journalist Dan Banion feels even within himself as he drifts around following his discharge from the army. In the people he meets, he "could see it in their eyes and sense it in their conversation. Restlessness. Dissatisfaction. An uncertainty about the world and about themselves. The war had left everybody on edge." So Banion ends up in San Francisco, and in a bar learns of the painting of a bandaged nude; the artist, just back from the war, tries to trace it and becomes a corpse in a lorry-load of bad spaghetti. Banion invades artistic circles in his quest for the killer, and Finnegan presents some nice character sketches and a line in wisecracking dialogue worthy of Raymond Chandler. Complex relationships are conveyed clearly and with a standard of writing not always evident in the semi-tough detective field: Finnegan's dry humour is used to good effect. The story twists and turns toward a satisfying climax with more murders en route, and Banion finds both the murderer and himself.

It is a tragedy that Banion, with his streak of social conscience, could not have appeared in a longer series. There have been too few writers as good as Finnegan.

—Melvyn Barnes

FINNEY, Jack (Walter Braden Finney). American. Born in Milwaukee, Wisconsin, in 1911. Educated at Knox College, Galesburg, Illinois. Married Marguerite Guest; one daughter and one son. Full-time writer. Agent: Harold Matson Company, 276 Fifth Avenue, New York, New York 10001, U.S.A.

CRIME PUBLICATIONS

Novels

Five Against the House. New York, Doubleday, and London, Eyre and Spottiswoode, 1954.
The House of Numbers. New York, Dell, and London, Eyre and Spottiswoode, 1957.
Assault on a Queen. New York, Simon and Schuster, 1959; London, Eyre and Spottiswoode, 1960.
The Night People. New York, Doubleday, 1977.

Short Stories

Forgotten News: The Crime of the Century and Other Lost Stories. New York, Doubleday, 1983.

OTHER PUBLICATIONS

Novels

The Body Snatchers. New York, Dell, and London, Eyre and Spottiswoode, 1955; revised edition, as *Invasion of the Body Snatchers,* Dell, 1961; London, Sphere, 1978.
Good Neighbor Sam. New York, Simon and Schuster, and London, Eyre and Spottiswoode, 1963.
The Woodrow Wilson Dime. New York, Simon and Schuster, 1968.
Time and Again. New York, Simon and Schuster, 1970; London, Weidenfeld and Nicholson, 1980.
Marion's Wall. New York, Simon and Schuster, 1973.

Short Stories

The Third Level. New York, Rinehart, 1957; as *The Clock of Time,* London, Eyre and Spottiswoode, 1958.
I Love Galesburg in the Springtime: Fantasy and Time Stories. New York, Simon and Schuster, 1963; London, Eyre and Spottiswoode, 1965.

Play

Telephone Roulette. Chicago, Dramatic Publishing Company, 1956.

*   *   *

Though none of Jack Finney's nine novels is primarily concerned with the investigation and solution of crime, he has a place in the history of American mystery fiction. From *Five Against the House* to *The Night People,* Finney has dealt with bizarre, sensational, and often criminal aspects of American life in a continuing effort to contrast ugly contemporary realities with his romantic vision of the gracious past. In *Assault on a Queen,* a band of adventurers plot to refloat a sunken World War I U-Boat as part of an elaborate plot—fully revealed only at the conclusion—to rob the *Queen Mary.* In *Time and Again,* his best-known work, a young artist becomes involved in a secret government project, in the course of which he literally travels back in time to the New York of the 1880's. In *Marion's Wall,* a young couple who move into an old California house make contact with the spirit of a 1920's starlet who once lived there. In *The Night People,* a group of San Francisco pranksters bedevil the police and amaze fellow Californians by a series of bizzare events culminating in a monster film-showing-cum-traffic-jam on the Golden Gate Bridge. In these and other writings, including the science fiction novel *The Body Snatchers* and two short story collections, Finney creates ingenious, suspenseful narratives, treats regretfully, though sometimes humorously, the tensions and conflicts in mid-20th-century America, and contrasts the latter, though not always explicitly, with a romantic imagined pre-modern age.

Some of Finney's novels have been adapted as films, Don Siegel's *Invasion of the Body Snatchers,* a science-fiction classic, being the most highly regarded among them. Though short stories of his have been included in collections of detective fiction, much of his work lies beyond the bounds of any strict definition of detective or mystery fiction. He continues to use fictional form to create, often with apparent light-heartedness, images of the grim contemporary American scene and to set them—in actuality or by implication—against his sense of the past.

—Seymour Rudin

———

FISCHER, Bruno. Also writes as Russell Gray. American. Born in Berlin, Germany, 29 June 1908; emigrated to the United States in 1913. Educated at Richmond Hill High School, Long Island, New York; Rand School of Social Sciences, New York. Married Ruth Miller in 1934; one daughter and one son. Editor, *Socialist Call,* 1936; executive editor, Collier Books, New York; education editor, Arco Publishing Company, New York, in the 1960's. Address: 19 Twin Pines Road, Putnam Valley, New York 10579, U.S.A.

CRIME PUBLICATIONS

Novels (series: Ben Helm; Rick Train)

So Much Blood. New York, Greystone Press, 1939; as *Stairway to Death,* New York, Pyramid, 1951.
The Hornet's Nest (Train). New York, Morrow, 1944; London, Quality Press, 1947.
Quoth the Raven. New York, Doubleday, 1944; as *Croaked the Raven,* London, Quality Press, 1947; as *The Fingered Man,* New York, Ace, 1953.
The Dead Men Grin (Helm). Philadelphia, McKay, 1945; London, Quality Press, 1947.
Kill to Fit (Train). New York, Green, 1946; London, Instructive Arts, 1951.
The Pigskin Bag. New York, Ziff Davis, 1946; London, Foulsham, 1951.
The Spider Lily. Philadelphia, McKay, 1946; London, Quality Press, 1953.
More Deaths Than One (Helm). New York, Ziff Davis, 1947; London, Foulsham, 1950.
The Bleeding Scissors. New York, Ziff Davis, 1948; as *The Scarlet Scissors,* London, Foulsham, 1950.
The Restless Hands (Helm). New York, Dodd Mead, 1949; London, Foulsham, 1950.
The Lustful Ape (as Russell Gray). New York, Lion, 1950; as Bruno Fischer, New York, Fawcett, and London, Red Seal, 1959.
The Angels Fell. New York, Dodd Mead, 1950; London, Boardman, 1951; as *The Flesh Was Cold,* New York, New American Library, 1951.
House of Flesh. New York, Fawcett, 1950; London, Red Seal, 1958.
The Silent Dust (Helm). New York, Dodd Mead, 1950; London, Boardman, 1951.
Fools Walk In. New York, Fawcett, 1951; London, Red Seal, 1958.
The Lady Kills. New York, Fawcett, 1951.
The Paper Circle (Helm). New York, Dodd Mead, 1951; London, Broadman, 1952; as *Stripped for Murder,* New York, New American Library, 1953.
The Fast Buck. New York, Fawcett, 1952; London, Red Seal, 1959.
Run for Your Life. New York, Fawcett, 1953; London, Fawcett, 1954.
So Wicked My Love. New York, Fawcett, 1954; London, Fawcett, 1957.
Knee-Deep in Death. New York, Fawcett, 1956; London, Fawcett, 1957.
Murder in the Raw. New York, Fawcett, 1957; London, Fawcett, 1959.
Second-Hand Nude. New York, Fawcett, 1959; London, Muller, 1960.
The Girl Between. New York, Fawcett, 1960.
The Evil Days. New York, Random House, 1974; London, Hale, 1976.

Uncollected Short Stories

"The Light That Killed," in *Dime Mystery* (New York), August 1940.
"The Sign of the Skull," in *Dime Mystery* (New York), September 1940.
"Bubbles of Death," in *Dime Mystery* (New York), October 1940.
"The Death Dolls," in *Horror Stories* (Chicago), October 1940.

"The Body I Stole," in *Terror Tales* (Chicago), November 1940.

"Death Has Three Sisters," in *Dime Mystery* (New York), November 1940.

"The Mummy Men," in *Dime Mystery* (New York), November 1940.

"Death Comes Crawling," in *Dime Mystery* (New York), December 1940.

"Beware the Blind Killer," in *Strange Detective* (Chicago), January 1941.

"Inn of Shipwreck Corpses," in *Dime Mystery* (New York), January 1941.

"We Who Are Lost," in *Terror Tales* (Chicago), January 1941.

"Home of the Headless Ones," in *Horror Stories* (Chicago), February 1941.

"Which One of Us?" in *Dime Mystery* (New York), February 1941.

"Death's Old Women," in *Dime Mystery* (New York), March 1941.

"Satan's Theme Song," in *Detective Tales* (Chicago), April 1941.

"Satan's Watch Fob," in *Dime Mystery* (New York), May 1941.

"City under Fire," in *Five Novels* September 1941.

"His Good Angel," in *Dime Mystery* (New York), September 1941.

"They Can't Kill Us," in *Dime Mystery* (New York), September 1941.

"Death Hitch-Hikes South," in *Dime Mystery* (New York), January 1942.

"Murder Is News," in *Big Book Detective* (Chicago), February 1942.

"Homicide Jest," in *10-Story Detective* (Springfield, Massachusetts), March 1942.

"They Knew Dolly," in *10-Story Mystery,* April 1942.

"The Dead Hang High," in *Dime Mystery* (New York), May 1942.

"The Female of the Species," in *The Avenger* (New York), May 1942.

"Waldo Jones and the Killers," in *Big Book Detective* (Chicago), June 1942.

"But I Call It Murder," in *Detective Short Stories* (Chicago), July 1942.

"Homicide Can't Happen Here," in *Detective Short Stories* (Chicago), July 1942.

"Satan's Scandal Sheet," in *10-Story Detective* (Springfield, Massachusetts), July 1942.

"Murder Has Seven Guests," in *10-Story Mystery* (Chicago), August 1942.

"Bring 'em Back Dead," in *New Detective* (New York), September 1942.

"Suicide Circus," in *New Detective* (New York), September 1942.

"Come to My Dying," in *10-Story Mystery* (Chicago), October 1942.

"Daughter of Murder," in *10-Story Mystery* (Chicago), October 1942.

"The Dead Laugh Last," in *10-Story Mystery* (Chicago), October 1942.

"Death Is a Saboteur" in *Detective Short Stories* (Chicago), November 1942.

"Bargain Day for Corpses," in *Strange Detective* (Chicago), November 1942.

"The Caricature Murders," in *Dime Mystery* (New York), November 1942.

"Happy Death Day to You," in *New Detective* (New York), November 1942.

"Call the Cops," in *Detective Short Stories* (Chicago), January 1943.

"Death's Black Bag," in *Strange Detective* (Chicago), January 1943.

"Kill and Run," in *New Detective* (New York), January 1943.

"Murder Begins at Midnight," in *The Spider* (Chicago), January 1943.

"Murder Is Where You Find It," in *New Detective* (New York), January 1943.

"Murder Man," in *Read,* January 1943.

"Murder Mask," in *10-Story Mystery* (Chicago), February 1943.

"Nine Dead Men and a Girl," in *Big Book Detective* (Chicago), February 1943.

"The Riddle House," in *10-Story Mystery* (Chicago), February 1943.

"Death Lives on the Lake," in *Strange Detective* (Chicago), March 1943.

"The Killer Waits," in *Dime Mystery* (New York), March 1943.

"Locket for a Lady," in *Mammoth Detective* (Chicago), March 1943.

"Me, My Coffin, and My Killer," in *Strange Detective,* (Chicago), March 1943.

"Satan's Servant," in *10-Story Mystery* (Chicago), April, 1943.

"Secret Weapons Murders," in *Detective Short Stories* (Chicago), April 1943.

"The Woman in the Case," in *Detective Fiction* (New York), April 1943.

"Cold Is the Grave," in *Strange Detective* (Chicago), May 1943.

"A Friend of Goebbels," in *Detective Fiction* (New York), May 1943.

"One Thousand Ways to Die," in *Dime Mystery* (New York), May 1943.

"Death Is the Wedding Guest," in *Dime Mystery* (New York), July 1943.

"Killers' Tournament," in *Dime Mystery* (New York), July 1943.

"Sing a Song of Death," in *New Detective* (New York), July 1943.

"The Coward," in *Mammoth Detective* (Chicago), August 1943.

"The Night Is for Dying," in *Detective Fiction* (New York), August 1943.

"The Lady Smiles at Fate," in *Crack Detective* (New York), September 1943.

"Murder Is Simple," in *Detective Fiction* (New York), September 1943.

"Murder on Wheels," in *Dime Mystery* (New York), September 1943.

"Ride for Mr. Two-by-Four," in *10-Story Detective* (Chicago), September 1943.

"This Girl, Miss Murder," in *Detective Short Stories* (Chicago), October 1943.

"The Gift," in *Mammoth Detective* (Chicago), November 1943.

"I'll Slay You Later," in *Dime Mystery* (New York), November 1943.

"The League of Little Men," in *Detective Fiction* (New York), November 1943.

"Murder Is Unlucky," in *Detective Fiction* (New York), November 1943.

"Seven Doorways to Death," in *Crack Detective* (New York), November 1943.

"A Female on the Squad," in *Detective Story* (New York), December 1943.

"Case of the Handless Corpse," in *Dime Mystery* (New York), January 1944.

"The House That Wasn't There," in *Crack Detective* (New York), January 1944.

"Kill Without Murder," in *Black Mask* (New York) January 1944.

"The Lady of Death," in *Detective Fiction* (New York), January 1944.

"Death on the Beach," in *Mammoth Detective* (Chicago), February 1944.

"Little Men, What Now?" in *Detective Fiction* (New York), February 1944.

"My Problem Is—Murder," in *10 Detective Aces* (New York), February 1944.

"X Marks the Redhead," in *Crack Detective* (New York), March 1944.

"Fatally Yours," in *New Detective* (New York), May 1944.

"I'll Bury You Deeper," in *Dime Mystery* (New York), May 1944.

"The Man Who Would Be Hitler," in *Dime Mystery* (New York), May 1944.

"The Twelfth Bottle," in *Detective Story* (New York), May 1944.

"Murder Takes No Furlough," in *Crack Detective* (New York), July 1944.

"Anything But the Truth," in *Mammoth Detective* (Chicago), August 1944.

"I Am Thinking of Murder," in *The Shadow* (New York), August 1944.

"The Little Things," in *Detective Fiction* (New York), August 1944.

"The Bride Wore Black," in *Dime Mystery* (New York), September 1944.

"Death's Secret Agent," in *Crack Detective* (New York), September 1944.

"My Friend—The Killer," in *Dime Mystery* (New York), September 1944.

"Come Home to Murder," in *Mammoth Detective* (Chicago), November 1944.

"The Man Who Wasn't Himself," in *New Detective* (New York), November 1944.

"Blood on My Doorstep," in *New Detective* (New York), January 1945.

"Death Paints a Picture," in *Crack Detective* (New York), January 1945.

"Ike Walsh and the Boy Wonder," in *The Shadow* (New York), January 1945.

"Bones Will Tell," in *Mammoth Mystery* (Chicago), February 1945.

"Murder Throws One Stone," in *The Shadow* (New York), February 1945.

"Scream Theme," in *10 Detective Aces* (New York), March 1945.

"Deadlier Than the Male," in *Dime Mystery* (New York), May 1945.

"Smart Guy," in *Mystery Quarterly* May 1945.

"Wrap Up the Corpse," in *Detective Story* (New York), May 1945.

"TNT for Two," in *10-Story Detective* (Springfield, Massachusetts), June 1945.

"Ask a Body," in *New Detective* (New York), July 1945.

"Mind Your Own Murder," in *Mammoth Detective* (Chicago), August 1945.

"Night Race," in *Doc Savage* (New York), September 1945.

"Killing the Goose," in *Detective Story* (New York), October 1945.

"Come to My Funeral," in *Dime Mystery* (New York), November 1945.

"Night Time Is Murder Time," in *New Detective* (New York), November 1945.

"Give a Dog the Name," in *Mammoth Detective* (Chicago), January 1946.

"Murder—My Aunt," in *Dime Mystery* (New York), January 1946.

"Two Mice for a Cat," in *Crack Detective* (New York), January 1946.

"The Enemy," in *Doc Savage* (New York), May 1946.

"A Copy with Wings," in *Mammoth Detective* (Chicago), July 1946.

"Don't Bury Him Deep," in *Doc Savage* (New York), July 1946.

"Two's Company, 22's a Shroud," in *10-Story Detective* (Springfield, Massachusetts), September 1946.

"Case of the Sleeping Doll," in *Detective Story* (New York), October 1946.

"Death's Bright Red Lips," in *Mammoth Mystery* (Chicago), December 1946.

"The Man Who Lost His Head," in *Best Detective Stories of the Year 1945*, edited by David Coxe Cooke. New York, Dutton, 1946.

"Double Deadline," in *Detective Book* (New York), 1946.

"I'll Slay You in My Dreams," in *Rue Morgue No. 1*, edited by Rex Stout and Louis Greenfield. New York, Creative Age Press, 1946.

"A Killer in the Crowd," in *Black Mask* (New York), July 1947.

"Killers Leave Me Cold," in *Dime Mystery* (New York), October 1947.

"The Face of Fear," in *New Detective* (New York), November 1947.

"Homicide Homework," in *Detective Tales* (Chicago), November 1947.

"Middleman for Murder," in *Black Mask* (New York), November 1947.

"Smile, Corpse, Smile," in *Dime Mystery* (New York), February 1948.

"Homicidal Homestead," in *Shock* (New York), March 1948.

"The Trap," in *Detective Tales* (Chicago), March 1948.

"Guest from the Grave," in *10 Detective Aces* (New York), May 1948.

"Silent as a Shiv," in *Detective Tales* (Chicago), May 1948.

"The Mam'selle Means Murder," in *10 Detective Aces* (New York), June 1948.

"I Thought I'd Die," in *New Detective* (New York), September 1948.

"Murder Turns the Curve," in *Popular Detective* (New York), September 1948.

"Terror Had Two Faces," in *New Detective* (New York), September 1948.

"The Green Vest," in *The Shadow* (New York), Fall 1948.

"Strange Man, Strange Murder," in *Crack Detective* (New York), November 1948.

"The Hour of the Rat," in *Dime Mystery* (New York), December 1948.

"Pickup on Nightmare Road," in *10-Story Detective* (Springfield, Massachusetts), December 1948.

"The Hands of Mr. Prescott," in *Popular Detective* (New York), March 1949.

"The Dead Don't Die," in *Popular Detective* (New York), November 1949.

"Lady in Distress," in *Thrilling Detective* (New York), December 1949.

"The Dream," in *Male*, July 1950.

"Hotel Murder," in *Giant Detective Annual*. New York, Best Books, 1950.

"The Dog Died First," in *Best Detective Stories of the Year 1950,* edited by David Coxe Cooke.   New York, Dutton, 1950.

"The Deep, Dark Grave," in *Giant Detective* (New York), Winter 1951.

"No Escape," in *As Tough As They Come,* edited by Will Oursler.   New York, Doubleday, 1951.

"Kiss the Dead Girl," in *Popular Detective* (New York), May 1952.

"Stop Him," in *Manhunt* (New York), March 1953.

"Say Good-Bye to Janie," in *Manhunt* (New York), July 1953.

"Coney Island Incident," in *Manhunt* (New York), November 1953.

"Nobody's Business," in *Crooks' Tour,* edited by Bruno Fischer.   New York, Dodd Mead, 1953; London, Macdonald, 1954.

"Double," in *Manhunt* (New York), April 1954.

"My Aunt Cecilia," in *Butcher, Baker, Murder-Maker,* edited by George Harmon Coxe.   New York, Knopf, 1954; London, Macdonald, 1956.

"The Quiet Woman," in *Dell Mystery Novels* (New York), January–March 1955.

"Hang That Husband High," in *Dangerous Dames,* edited by Brett Halliday.   New York, Dell, 1955.

"The Shallow Grave," in *Suspect,* February 1956.

"They Came with Guns," in *Manhunt* (New York), July 1957.

"Sam Rall's Private Ghost," in *For Love or Money,* edited by Dorothy Gardiner.   New York, Doubleday, 1957; London, Macdonald, 1959.

"The Portraits of Eve," in *Manhunt* (New York), February 1958.

"The Wind Blows Death," in *Murder in Miami,* edited by Brett Halliday.   New York, Dodd Mead, 1959.

"Bugged," in *Manhunt* (New York), August 1961.

"Service Call," in *Best Detective Stories of the Year, 17th Annual Collection,* edited by David Coxe Cooke.   New York, Dutton, 1962.

"Five O'Clock Menace," in *The Hard-Boiled Detective: Stories from Black Mask Magazine 1920–1950,* edited by Herbert Ruhm.   New York, Vintage, 1977.

OTHER PUBLICATIONS

Other

Editor, *Crooks' Tour.*   New York, Dodd Mead, 1953; London, Macdonald, 1954.

*   *   *

Like many other mystery and suspense writers, Bruno Fischer began his career in the pages of the pulp magazines. In the late 1930's, under the pseudonym of Russell Gray, he appeared regularly in most of the mystery-horror (or "shudder") pulps; later, he graduated to the detective magazines and began signing his work with his real name. He is the author of hundreds of short stories, including "The Man Who Lost His Head," considered by some to be a minor classic, "The Dog Died First," and "Service Call."

Fischer's first novel, *So Much Blood,* appeared in 1939; but it was not until 1944 that he turned in earnest to the full-length mystery with two above-average books, *Quoth the Raven* and *The Hornet's Nest.* In 1945 one of his best novels, *The Dead Men Grin,* introduced Ben Helm, a likable private detective who depends more on his wits than on his fists and who stars in several other adventures.

With the rise of the paperback in the early 1950's, Fischer turned to that medium and wrote several books for the house generally considered to have published the best of the early soft-cover originals, Fawcett Gold Medal; among his noteworthy Gold Medal novels are *House of Flesh* and *So Wicked My Love.*

Much of Fischer's work deals with shocking and gruesome crimes, a good percentage of which takes place in small upstate New York communities; but his handling of this material is deft and restrained, with emphasis on detection and characterization rather than on the lurid aspects. One of his recurring themes is the morality play: ordinary people thrust into extraordinary situations in which their moral standards are tested and sometimes corrupted. An example is his last novel, *The Evil Days*—a mordant tale of thievery, kidnapping, murder, and adultery.

—Bill Pronzini

———

FISH, Robert L(loyd). Also wrote as Robert L. Pike; Lawrence Roberts. American. Born in Cleveland, Ohio, 21 August 1912. Educated at Case School of Applied Science (now Case-Western Reserve University), Cleveland, B.S. 1933. Served three years in the National Guard, Ohio 37th Division. Married Mamie Kates in 1935; two daughters. Managerial positions in many companies, including Firestone Tire and Rubber; for 20 years was a consulting engineer on vinyl plastics in Brazil, Argentina, England, Korea, Taiwan, Colombia, Mexico, Venezuela. President, Mystery Writers of America, 1978. Recipient: Mystery Writers of America Edgar Allan Poe award for novel, 1962, short story, 1971. *Died 24 February 1981.*

CRIME PUBLICATIONS

Novels (series: Carruthers, Simpson, and Briggs; Captain José da Silva; Kek Huuygens)

The Fugitive (da Silva).   New York, Simon and Schuster, 1962; London, Boardman, 1963.

The Assassination Bureau Ltd. (completion of Jack London story).   New York, McGraw Hill, and London, Deutsch, 1963.

Isle of the Snakes (da Silva).   New York, Simon and Schuster, 1963; London, Boardman, 1964.

The Shrunken Head (da Silva).   New York, Simon and Schuster, 1963; London, Boardman, 1965.

Brazilian Sleigh Ride. (da Silva).   New York, Simon and Schuster, 1965; London, Boardman, 1966.

The Diamond Bubble (da Silva).   New York, Simon and Schuster, and London, Boardman, 1965.

Trials of O'Brien (novelization of television play).   New York, New American Library, 1965.

Always Kill a Stranger (da Silva).   New York, Putnam, 1967.

The Hochmann Miniatures (Huuygens).   New York, New American Library, 1967.

The Bridge That Went Nowhere (da Silva).   New York, Putnam, 1968; London, Long, 1970.

The Murder League (Carruthers *et al.*).   New York, Simon and Schuster, 1968; London, New English Library, 1970.

The Xavier Affair (da Silva).   New York, Putnam, 1969; London, Hale, 1974.

Whirligig (Huuygens). New York, Putnam, 1970.
The Green Hell Treasure (da Silva). New York, Putnam, 1971.
Rub-a-Dub-Dub (Carruthers *et al.*). New York, Simon and Schuster, 1971; as *Death Cuts the Deck,* New York, Ace, 1972.
The Tricks of the Trade (Huuygens). New York, Putnam, 1972; London, Hale, 1974.
A Handy Death, with Henry Rothblatt. New York, Simon and Schuster, 1973; London, Hale, 1975.
The Wager (Huuygens). New York, Putnam, 1974; London, Hale, 1976.
Trouble in Paradise (da Silva). New York, Doubleday, 1975.
Pursuit. New York, Doubleday, 1978; London, Macdonald and Jane's, 1980.
A Gross Carriage of Justice (Carruthers *et al.*). New York, Doubleday, 1979; London, Hale, 1981.
The Gold of Troy. New York, Doubleday, 1980.
Rough Diamond. New York, Doubleday, 1981; London, Heinemann, 1982.

Novels as Robert L. Pike (series: Lieutenant Clancy; Lieutenant Jim Reardon)

Mute Witness (Clancy). New York, Doubleday, 1963; London, Deutsch, 1965; as *Bullitt,* New York, Avon, 1968.
The Quarry (Clancy). New York, Doubleday, 1964.
Police Blotter (Clancy). New York, Doubleday, 1965; London, Deutsch, 1966.
Reardon. New York, Doubleday, 1970.
The Gremlin's Grampa (Reardon). New York, Doubleday, 1972.
Bank Job (Reardon). New York, Doubleday, 1974; London, Hale, 1975.
Deadline 2 A.M. (Reardon). New York, Doubleday, 1976; London, Hale, 1977.

Short Stories (series: Schlock Homes; Kek Huuygens)

The Incredible Schlock Homes. New York, Simon and Schuster, 1966.
The Memoirs of Schlock Homes. Indianapolis, Bobbs Merrill, 1974.
Kek Huuygens, Smuggler. Yonkers, New York, Mysterious Press, 1976.

Uncollected Short Stories

"One of the Oldest Con Games," in *Ellery Queen's Mystery Magazine* (New York), March 1977.
"Stranger in Town," in *Antaeus* (New York), Spring–Summer 1977.
"The Adventure of the Elite Type," in *Ellery Queen's Mystery Magazine* (New York), July 1977.
"The Adventures of the Odd Lotteries," in *Ellery Queen's Searches and Seizures.* New York, Davis, 1977.
"No Rough Stuff," in *Ellery Queen's Faces of Mystery.* New York, Davis, 1977.
"The Adventure of the Animal Fare," in *Ellery Queen's Scenes of the Crime.* New York, Davis, 1979; London, Hale, 1981.
"The Art of Deduction," in *Ellery Queen's Mystery Magazine* (New York), June 1979.
"The Adventure of the Common Code," in *Ellery Queen's Mystery Magazine* (New York), September 1979.
"In the Bag," in *Ellery Queen's Veils of Mystery.* New York, Davis, 1980.

"The Patsy," in *Ellery Queen's Windows of Mystery.* New York, Davis, 1980.
"Moonlight Gardener," in *The Edgar Winners,* edited by Bill Pronzini. New York, Random House, 1981.
"The Adventures of the Patient Resident," in *Best Detective Stories of the Year 1981,* edited by Edward D. Hoch. New York, Dutton, 1981.
"The Wager," in *The Arbor House Treasury of Mystery and Suspense,* edited by Bill Pronzini, Barry N. Malzberg, and Martin H. Greenberg. New York, Arbor House, 1981.
"Adventure of the Ukrainian Founding Orphans," in *ellery Queen's Mystery Magazine* (New York), 28 January 1981.
"The Adventure of the Pie-Eyed Piper," in *Ellery Queen's Mystery Magazine* (New York), 17 June 1981.
"The Adventure of the Ascot Tie," in *Ellery Queen's Book of First Appearances.* New York, Davis, 1982.
"Muldoon and the Numbers Game," in *Ellery Queen's Eyewitnesses.* New York, Davis, 1982.

OTHER PUBLICATIONS

Novel

Weekend '33, with Bob Thomas. New York, Doubleday. 1972.

Other

The Break In (as Lawrence Roberts). New York, Scholastic, 1974.
Big Wheels (as Lawrence Roberts). New York, Scholastic, 1977.
Pele: My Life and a Wonderful Game, with Pele. New York, Doubleday, 1978.
Alley Fever (as Lawrence Roberts) New York, Scholastic, 1979.

Editor, *With Malice Toward All.* New York, Putnam, 1968; London, Macmillan, 1969.
Editor, *Every Crime in the Book.* New York, Putnam, 1975; London, Macmillan, 1976.

*

Manuscript Collection: Mugar Memorial Library, Boston University.

Robert L. Fish commented (1980):
I write to entertain; if it is possible to inform at the same time, all the better, but entertainment comes first. I like to write using places I have been and enjoyed as the background location for my stories and books. I write the kind of stories and books I like to read, and if I can get a reader to turn the page, I feel I have succeeded in what I started out to do.

*   *   *

Although Robert L. Fish did not begin his writing career until he was in his late forties, he made up for his late start by the quality and versatility of his talents. Ranging from Sherlockian parodies to fascinatingly realistic police procedural novels, Fish's short stories and novels are witty and well-plotted, alternating between expertly crafted humor and breath-taking suspense.

In 1960, *Ellery Queen's Mystery Magazine* published the first of a series of Sherlockian parodies by Robert Fish, "The Adventure of the Ascot Tie," introducing the remarkably inept Schlock Homes and his enthusiastically tolerant assistant, Dr. Watney. Since then, over 25 of the Schlock Homes stories have been published. Although the adventures of Schlock Homes have received disparaging criticism from Barzun and Taylor, who in their *A Catalogue of Crime* describe the parodies as "distressing" and "indifferent attempts at parody," the reception by both Doyle scholars and mystery fans in general has been very favorable. Utilizing hilarious puns, extremely astute misobservations, and outrageously illogical solutions, Fish dares to invade the austere Sherlockian's den with rampant comedy.

The Brazilian climate of Rio de Janeiro where Fish was employed as an engineering consultant to a Brazilian plastics firm must have been particularly conducive to mystery-plotting since not only Schlock Homes, but several other notable characters were conceived there, such as Kek Huuygens, the smuggler, and José da Silva, a liaison officer between the Brazilian police and Interpol. Kek Huuygens, an international smuggler extraordinaire, with tastes in wine, women, and entertainment which match his aesthetic taste in the fine arts, appears in a number of novels and stories.

Fish's best-known character, the swarthy, vibrant, Captain José da Silva, as much at home in the Brazilian jungles as on the streets of Manhattan, first appeared in the Edgar-winning novel *The Fugitive*. Since then, a wealth of adventure has befallen this intuitive, witty, romantic, and extremely courageous character. Da Silva has tangled with swarms of poisonous snakes (*Isle of the Snakes*), bands of head-shrinking Indians, Brazilian revolutionaries (*The Shrunken Head*), and even New York's gambling syndicate (*Brazilian Sleigh Ride*). Usually accompanied by his own faithful Watson in the form of the often amusing, sometimes harrowing, Mr. Wilson of the American Embassy in Rio de Janeiro, da Silva always gets his "man," even when the ultimate culprit turns out to be feminine in nature.

Writing under the name of Robert L. Pike, Fish portrays the demanding, frustrating, and occasionally rewarding life of an American policeman. In *Mute Witness* (the basis of the film *Bullitt*) the astute deductive reasoning of the indefatigable Lieutenant Clancy, whose sidekicks Kaproski and Stanton prowl the streets of Manhattan's 52nd precinct, devises a daring rescue of a famous underworld figure from gang execution. *Police Blotter* finds the same trio in a race against time and professional killers who are determined to assassinate one of the U.N. delegates.

On the other side of the continent, roaming the hilly streets of San Francisco is Pike's amorous and resourceful Lieutenant Jim Reardon.

—Mary Ann Grochowski

FISHER, Steve (Stephen Gould Fisher). Also wrote as Stephen Gould; Grant Lane. American. Born in 1912. Served in the United States Navy, 1928–32. Wrote for Navy publications; settled in New York City to write for pulp magazines; worked in Hollywood as screenwriter and television writer. *Died 27 March 1980.*

CRIME PUBLICATIONS

Novels (series Sheridan Doome)

Spend the Night (as Grant Lane).   New York, Phoenix Press, 1935.
Satan's Angel.   New York, Macaulay, 1935.
Murder of the Admiral (Doome; as Stephen Gould).   New York, Macaulay, 1936.
Murder of the Pigboat Skipper (Doome).   New York, Curl, 1937.
The Night Before Murder.   New York, Curl, 1939.
Homicide Johnny (as Stephen Gould).   New York, Arcadia House, 1940; London, Pemberton, 1946.
I Wake Up Screaming.   New York, Dodd Mead, 1941; London, Hale, 1943; revised edition, New York, Bantam, 1960.
Winter Kill.   New York, Dodd Mead, 1946.
The Sheltering Night.   New York, Fawcett, 1952.
Take All You Can Get.   New York, Random House, 1955.
No House Limit.   New York, Dutton, 1958.
Image of Hell.   New York, Dutton, 1961.
Saxon's Ghost.   Los Angeles, Sherbourne Press, 1969.
The Big Dream.   New York, Doubleday, 1970.
The Hell-Black Night.   Los Angeles, Sherbourne Press, 1970.

Uncollected Short Stories

"Hell's Scoop," in *Sure-Fire Detective Magazine* (Springfield, Massachusetts), March 1934.
"Shanghai Sue," in *Spicy Mystery Stories* (Wilmington, Delaware), July 1934.
"Murder in the Navy," in *Thrilling Detective* (New York), November 1934.
"Louie was Smart," in *Thrilling Detective* (New York), January 1935.
"The Navy Spirit," in *True Gang Life* (New York), February 1935.
"Corpse Number 4," in *Secret Agent X* (Springfield, Massachusetts), March 1935.
"The Light Clue," in *Ten Detective Aces* (Springfield, Massachusetts), March 1935.
"Curios and Corpses," in *The Shadow* (New York), 15 April 1935.
"He Worked Alone," in *Detective Fiction Weekly* (New York), 27 April 1935.
"Mistress Death," in *New Mystery Adventures* (New York), May–June 1935.
"The Tattooed Skipper," in *The Shadow* (New York), 1 May 1935.
"Studio Mystery," in *Underground Detective* (Springfield, Massachusetts), May 1935.
"The Butcher of Hell," in *Thrilling Detective* (New York), May 1935.
"Pigboat Peril," in *The Shadow* (New York), 15 June 1935.
"Battleship Loot," in *The Gang Magazine* (New York), July 1935.
"Murders in Paradise," in *New Mystery Adventures* (New York), July 1935.
"Night Patrol," in *Bill Barnes Air Adventurer* (New York), August 1935.
"Wrecked Wings," in *The Shadow* (New York), 1 September 1935.
"Bloody Portholes," in *New Mystery Adventures* (New York), September 1935.
"Princess of Death," in *The Mysterious Wu Fang* (Chicago), September 1935.

"While the Earth Shook," in *Clues* (New York), September 1935.

"Dollars of Death," in *The Shadow* (New York), 1 October 1935.

"The Death Design," in *The Shadow* (New York), 15 October 1935.

"Demons of Death," in *Prison Life Stories* (Dunellen, New Jersey), October 1935.

"The Jade Cat," in *The Mysterious Wu Fang* (Chicago), October 1935.

"The Mystery of River Street," in *Nick Carter Magazine* (New York), October 1935.

"The Yellow Cat," in *The Shadow* (New York), 1 November 1935.

"Million Dollar Beggar," in *New Mystery Adventures* (New York), November 1935.

"The Blue Coffin," in *The Mysterious Wu Fang* (Chicago), November 1935.

"The Ring," in *Clues* (New York), November 1935.

"Genius of Murder," in *The Shadow* (New York), 15 December 1935.

"Shanghai Murder," in *The Mysterious Wu Fang* (Chicago), December 1935.

"The Sign of Murder," in *Nick Carter Magazine* (New York), December 1935.

"Captain Babyface," in *Dare-Devil Aces* (Chicago), January 1936.

"He Died Smiling," in *Phantom Detective* (New York), January 1936.

"The Sacred Dragon," in *The Mysterious Wu Fang* (Chicago), January 1936.

"The Squadron from Hell," in *Dare-Devil Aces* (Chicago), February 1936.

"An Order For Murder," in *Popular Detective* (New York), March 1936.

"The Dark Angel," in *Dare-Devil Aces* (Chicago), March 1936.

"The Man from Hell," in *The Mysterious Wu Fang* (Chicago), March 1936.

"Death Laughs Last," in *Dare-Devil Aces* (Chicago), April 1936.

"Blonde Baby," in *The Shadow* (New York), 15 May 1936.

"Death in the Dawn," in *Dare-Devil Aces* (Chicago), May 1936.

"Death Rides Alone," in *Dare-Devil Aces* (Chicago), May 1936.

"G is for Girl," in *Saucy Romantic Adventures* (New York), May 1936.

"Satan's Faceless Henchmen," in *Ace Mystery* (Springfield, Massachusetts), May 1936.

"Murderer," in *Mystery Adventure* (New York), June 1936.

"Shoe-Shine Boy," in *The Shadow* (New York), 1 July 1936.

"The Brand of Death," in *Dare-Devil Aces* (Chicago), July 1936.

"The Clue of the Oil Lamp," in *Clues* (New York), July 1936.

"The Crime Reporter," in *Mystery Adventure* (New York), July 1936.

"White Sails Against the Sun," in *Saucy Romantic Adventures* (New York), July 1936.

"Carfare to the Chair," in *The Shadow* (New York), 1 August 1936.

"Alhoa Oe," in *Saucy Romantic Adventures* (New York), August 1936.

"Corpse Keeper," in *Ace Detective* (Springfield, Massachusetts), August 1936.

"Death's Screaming Wings," in *Dare-Devil Aces* (Chicago), August 1936.

"Snatch Racket," in *Mystery Adventure* (New York), August 1936.

"Dash of Death," in *The Shadow* (New York), 1 September 1936.

"Death, Guts and Glory," in *Dare-Devil Aces* (Chicago), September 1936.

"The China-Doll Clue," in *Headquarters Detective* (Springfield, Massachusetts), September 1936.

"What Price Murder?," in *Detective Tales* (Kokomo, Indiana), September 1936.

"Daughter of the Deep," in *Saucy Romantic Adventures* (New York), October 1936.

"Death Maneuvers," in *Feds* (New York), October 1936.

"Horror Over Honolulu," in *Mystery Adventure* (New York), October 1936.

"The Clue of an Old Man," in *The Whisperer* (New York), October 1936.

"The Kid from Hell," in *Dare-Devil Aces* (Chicago), October 1936.

"Blood of the Octopus," in *The Shadow* (New York), 1 November 1936.

"Shine, Mister?," in *The Shadow* (New York), 15 November 1936.

"Man Who Died Twice," in *Ace-High Detective Magazine* (Chicago), November 1936.

"Murder on a Pigboat," in *Feds* (New York), November 1936.

"On the Bottom of the Sea," in *Doc Savage* (New York), November 1936.

"Receipt from Satan," in *Headquarters Detective* (Springfield, Massachusetts), November 1936.

"Scalpel of the Damned," in *Detective Tales* (Kokomo, Indiana), November 1936.

"Shanghai Submarine," in *Mystery Adventure* (New York), November 1936.

"The Girl from Hell's Half Acre," in *Detective Romances* (Springfield, Massachusetts), November 1936.

"Shoe Leather Kid," in *The Shadow* (New York), 15 December 1936.

"The Devil's Squadron," in *Feds* (New York), December 1936.

"Chinatown Kid," in *The Shadow* (New York), 15 January 1937.

"Death High Up," in *The Whisperer* (New York), January 1937.

"Merry Christmas, Killer!," in *Thrilling Detective* (New York), January 1937.

"Night Flame," in *Feds* (New York), January 1937.

"Police Kid," in *The Shadow* (New York), 15 February 1937.

"Catapult," in *Hardboiled* (New York), February 1937.

"Flame in the Wind," in *Doc Savage* (New York), February 1937.

"Murder on the Beef Boat," in *Popular Detective* (New York), February 1937.

"Sabotage," in *Feds* (New York), February 1937.

"Undercover," in *Secret Agent X* (Springfield, Massachusetts), February 1937.

"Voice of the Fire God," in *Skipper* (New York), February 1937.

"A Case for the Kid," in *The Shadow* (New York), 15 March 1937.

"Death on Set 13," in *Detective Fiction Weekly* (New York), 27 March 1937.

"Emperor Blackmail," in *Ten Detective Aces* (Springfield, Massachusetts), March 1937.

"Hospital for Murder," in *Feds* (New York), March 1937.

"Murder Treadmill," in *Headquarters Detective* (Springfield, Massachusetts), March 1937.

"The Kid's Clue," in *The Shadow* (New York), 15 April 1937.

"Claws of the Hell-Cat," in *Sure-Fire Detective* (Springfield, Massachusetts), April 1937.

"Murder Comes to Town," in *The Whisperer* (New York), April 1937.

"Murder Maiden," in *Ten Detective Aces* (Springfield, Massachusetts), April 1937.

"Murder on Ice," in *Doc Savage* (New York), April 1937.

"Peril at Panama," in *Feds* (New York), April 1937.

"Murder Game with Mirrors," in *Detective Fiction Weekly* (New York), 15 May 1937.

"The Kid Faces Death," in *The Shadow* (New York), 15 May 1937.

"Ah Fu Goes to Sea," in *Feds* (New York), May 1937.

"Good with Guns," in *Federal Agent* (New York), May 1937.

"Iron Mike," in *Dare-Devil Aces* (Chicago), May 1937.

"Sailor Boy," in *Don Winslow of the Navy* (St. Louis, Missouri), May 1937.

"The Deacon and the Demon," in *The Spider* (Chicago), May 1937.

"The Night it Rained," in *G-Men* (New York), May 1937.

"Saturday Night Kid," in *The Shadow* (New York), 15 June 1937.

"Batten Down that Killer," in *Detective Fiction Weekly* (New York), 19 June 1937.

"Battle Condition One," in *Feds* (New York), June 1937.

"Riot at Dawn," in *Feds* (New York), July 1937.

"Say It in Chinese," in *Skipper* (New York), July 1937.

"The Kid Comes Along," in *The Shadow* (New York), 1 August 1937.

"The Kid and the Killer," in *The Shadow* (Elizabeth, New Jersey), 15 August 1937.

"Death on the S-13," in *Popular Detective* (New York), August 1937.

"Murder at Eight," in *Black Mask* (Chicago), August 1937.

"The Kid Goes to Jail," in *The Shadow* (Elizabeth, New Jersey), 1 September 1937.

"Fly a Kite," in *Skipper* (New York), September 1937.

"Murder on Paradise," in *Feds* (New York), September 1937.

"The Corpse that Cried," in *The Whisperer* (New York), September 1937.

"Good-bye to Killing," in *Pocket Detective* (New York), September 1937.

"The Kid and the Corpse," in *The Shadow* (Elizabeth, New Jersey), 1 October 1937.

"Corpse at West Point," in *Feds* (New York), October 1937.

"The Keeper of Codes," in *Feds* (New York), October 1937.

"The Valley of Death," in *G-Men* (New York), October 1937.

"Kidnap the Kid," in *The Shadow* (Elizabeth, New Jersey), 1 November 1937.

"Mystery at Malibu," in *Detective Fiction Weekly* (New York), 20 November 1937.

"Murder at Pensacola," in *Feds* (New York), November 1937.

"Odds on Murder," in *Crime Busters* (New York), November 1937.

"The Kid and the Cat," in *The Shadow* (Elizabeth, New Jersey), 1 December 1937.

"If Christmas Comes," in *Detective Fiction Weekly* (New York), 25 December 1937.

"Alias the Captain," in *Feds* (New York), December 1937.

"Espionage, U.S.N.," in *Skipper* (New York), December 1937.

"The Picture Kid," in *The Shadow* (Elizabeth, New Jersey), 1 January 1938.

"Murder in Daylight," in *The Shadow* (Elizabeth, New Jersey), 15 January 1938.

"Me and Mickey Mouse," in *Detective Fiction Weekly* (New York), 22 January 1938.

"No Gentleman Strangles His Wife," in *Black Mask* (Chicago), January 1938.

"Take a Whirl at Murder," in *Crime Busters* (New York), January 1938.

"The Museum Kid," in *The Shadow* (Elizabeth, New Jersey), 1 February 1938.

"Death of a Dummy," in *Black Mask* (Chicago), February 1938.

"Singapore," in *Crime Busters* (New York), February 1938.

"Arson Case Kid," in *The Shadow* (Elizabeth, New Jersey), 1 March 1938.

"Death Goes to Hollywood," in *Detective Fiction Weekly* (New York), 26 March 1938.

"Appointment in Hollywood," in *Crime Busters* (New York), March 1938.

"You'll Always Remember Me," in *Black Mask* (Chicago), March 1938.

"Race Track Kid," in *The Shadow* (Elizabeth, New Jersey), 1 April 1938.

"Powder Puff Kid," in *The Shadow* (Elizabeth, New Jersey), 1 May 1938.

"The Magnificent Mouse," in *Detective Fiction Weekly* (New York), 7 May 1938.

"Murder in Mexico," in *Thrilling Detective* (New York), May 1938.

"Wait for Me," in *Black Mask* (Chicago), May 1938.

"The Subway Kid," in *The Shadow* (Elizabeth, New Jersey), 1 June 1938.

"Hollywood Party," in *Black Mask* (Chicago), June 1938.

"The Kid Gets Cocky," in *The Shadow* (Elizabeth, New Jersey), 1 July 1938.

"Johnny Get Your Gun," in *Detective Fiction Weekly* (New York), 16 July 1938.

"Day Never Came," in *Detective Story Magazine* (New York), July 1938.

"Shanghai Renegade," in *Crime Busters* (New York), July 1938.

"Kid in the Rain," in *The Shadow* (Elizabeth, New Jersey), 1 August 1938.

"Hulu Town," in *Crime Busters* (New York), August 1938.

"Lucky Kid," in *The Shadow* (Elizabeth, New Jersey), 1 September 1938.

"The Glamour and the Glory," in *Detective Fiction Weekly* (New York), 3 September 1938.

"I'll Send You a Card," in *Detective Fiction Weekly* (New York), 24 September 1938.

"The Other Guy's Girl," in *Clues* (New York), September 1938.

"The Kid and the Rat," in *The Shadow* (Elizabeth, New Jersey), 1 October 1938.

"Pennies on Your Eyes," in *Detective Fiction Weekly* (New York), 22 October 1938.

"The Man from Manitoba," in *Detective Fiction Weekly* (New York), 29 October 1938.

"Me and the Kid," in *The Shadow* (Elizabeth, New Jersey), 1 November 1938.

"I Want to Be Like Gable," in *Detective Fiction Weekly* (New York), 26 November 1938.

"Espionage Island," in *Crime Busters* (New York), November 1938.

"Sky-High Kid," in *The Shadow* (Elizabeth, New Jersey), 1 December 1938.

"Goodbye to Hollywood," in *Detective Fiction Weekly* (New York), 10 December 1938.

"Don't Say a Word," in *Crime Busters* (New York), December 1938.

"Kid Gone Crazy," in *The Shadow* (Elizabeth, New Jersey), 1 January 1939.

"Jake and Jill," in *Black Mask* (Chicago), January 1939.

"Slant-Eyed Kid," in *The Shadow* (Elizabeth, New Jersey), 1 February 1939.

"Flight to Paris," in *Black Mask* (Chicago), February 1939.

"Spies for Sale," in *Crime Busters* (New York), February 1939.

"Kid from New York," in *The Shadow* (Elizabeth, New Jersey), 1 March 1939.

"Melody at Midnight," in *Detective Story Magazine* (New York), March 1939.

"Ask the Kid," in *The Shadow* (Elizabeth, New Jersey), 1 April 1939.

"The Affair of the Needless Corpse," in *Detective Fiction Weekly* (New York), 22 April 1939.

"Latitude Unknown," in *Black Mask* (Chicago), April 1939.

"Wave a Flag," in *Crime Busters* (New York), April 1939.

"Storm Kid," in *The Shadow* (Elizabeth, New Jersey), 1 May 1939.

"Thunder in Paradise," in *Crime Busters* (New York), May 1939.

"The Kid's Sweetheart," in *The Shadow* (Elizabeth, New Jersey), 1 June 1939.

"Lucky," in *Detective Fiction Weekly* (New York), 3 June 1939.

"World's Fair Kid," in *The Shadow* (Elizabeth, New Jersey), 1 July 1939.

"The Donovan Kid," in *The Shadow* (Elizabeth, New Jersey), 1 August 1939.

"I'll Never Let You Go," in *Clues* (New York), August 1939.

"Get Out of Town," in *Detective Story Magazine* (New York), September 1939.

"The Kid With a Song," in *The Shadow* (Elizabeth, New Jersey), 1 October 1939.

"Homicide Johnny," in *Clues* (New York), November 1940.

"Gentlemen of the Night," in *Detective Fiction Weekly* (New York), 11 January 1941.

"Goodby at Dawn," in *Detective Fiction Weekly* (New York), 8 February 1941.

"This Girl Ann," in *Detective Fiction Weekly* (New York), 12 April 1941.

"Cinderella Wore Black," in *Detective Fiction Weekly* (New York), 19 April 1941.

"Little Red Book," in *Clues* (New York), May 1941.

"The Last Time I Saw Paris," in *Detective Tales* (Kokomo, Indiana), May 1941.

"Murder Melody," in *Detective Tales* (Kokomo, Indiana), June 1941.

"Rain in Hollywood," in *Detective Fiction Weekly* (New York), 26 July 1941.

"The Monster," in *Detective Story Magazine* (New York), July 1941.

"Three Faces of Death," in *Mystery Magazine* (New York), July 1941.

"No More Medals," in *Doc Savage* (New York), September 1941.

"Goodbye to Hannah," in *To the Queen's Taste*. Boston, Little Brown, 1946; London, Faber, 1949.

"Winter Kill," in *Triple Detective* (New York), Summer 1947.

"The Night Before Murder," in *Triple Detective* (New York), Spring 1948.

"Ambulance at Dawn," in *19 Tales of Intrigue, Mystery and Adventure* 1950.

"Hotel Murder," in *Giant Detective Annual* (New York), 1950.

"The Man in the Window," in *Top Detective Annual* (New York), 1951.

"Blues for a Dead Lady," in *Detective Tales* (Kokomo, Indiana), March 1951.

"The Body Beautiful," in *Detective Tales* (Kokomo, Indiana), June 1952.

"Lucky Cop," in *Ellery Queen's Mystery Magazine* (New York), March 1956.

OTHER PUBLICATIONS

Novels

Forever Glory. New York, Macaulay, 1936.
Destroyer. New York, Appleton Century, 1941.
Destination Tokyo. New York, Appleton Century, 1943.
Giveway. New York, Random House, 1954.

Plays

Susan Slept Here, with Alex Gottlieb (produced New York, 1961). New York, French, 1956.

Screenplays: *Typhoon*, with Allen Rivkin and Leonard Lee, 1940; *To the Shores of Tripoli*, with Lamar Trotti, 1942; *Berlin Correspondent*, with Jack Andrews, 1942; *Destination Tokyo*, with Delmer Daves and Albert Maltz, 1943; *Johnny Angel*, with Frank Gruber, 1945; *Lady in the Lake*, 1946; *Dead Reckoning*, with others, 1946; *That's My Man*, with Bradley King, 1947; *Song of the Thin Man*, with others, 1947; *The Hunted*, 1948; *I Wouldn't Be in Your Shoes*, 1948; *Tokyo Joe*, with others, 1949; *A Lady Without Passport*, with others, 1950; *Roadblock*, with others, 1951; *Battle Zone*, 1952; *Whispering Smith Hits London* (*Whispering Smith Versus Scotland Yard*), with John Gilling, 1952; *The Lost Hours* (*The Big Frame*), with John Gilling, 1952; *Flat Top*, 1952; *San Antone*, 1953; *Woman They Almost Lynched*, 1953; *The Man from the Alamo*, with others, 1953; *City That Never Sleeps*, 1953; *Sea of Lost Ships*, with Norman Reilly Raine, 1953; *Night Freight*, 1953; *Hell's Half Acre*, 1954; *The Shanghai Story*, with Seton I. Miller and Lester Yard, 1954; *Thirty-Six Hours* (*Terror Street*), 1954; *The Big Tip-Off*, 1955; *Las Vegas Shakedown*, 1955; *Top Gun*, with Richard Schayer, 1955; *Silent Fear*, 1955; *Toughest Man Alive*, 1956; *Betrayed Women*, with Paul L. Peil, 1956; *The Restless Breed*, 1957; *Courage of Black Beauty*, 1957; *I, Mobster*, 1959; *Noose for a Gunman*, with Robert B. Gordon, 1960; *September Storm*, with W.R. Burnett, 1961; *Law of the Lawless*, 1964; *The Quick Gun*, with Robert E. Kent, 1964; *Young Fury*, with A.C. Lyles, 1965; *Black Spurs*, 1965; *Johnny Reno*, with Andrew Craddock, 1966; *Waco*, 1966; *Red Tomahawk*, with Andrew Craddock, 1967; *Fort Utah*, with Andrew Craddock, 1967; *Hostile Guns*, with Sloane Nibley and James Edward Grant, 1968; *Arizona Bushwhackers*, with Andrew Craddock, 1968; *Rogue's Gallery*, with A.C. Lyles, 1968; *Savage Red—Outlaw White*, 1974; *The Great Gundown*, 1974.

Television Plays: "*Goodbye Hannah*" episode for the *Dick Powell Show*, 1961. *The Last Day*, with Jim Byrnes and A.C. Lyles, 1975; and some 200 scripts for *McMillan and Wife*, *Starsky and Hutch*, *Barnaby Jones*, and other series.

* * *

Steve Fisher had a long career writing mystery fiction. He wrote for the pulps—*Black Mask*, *Adventure*, and *Argosy*—and for the leading fiction magazines—*Esquire*, *Cosmopolitan*, and *The Saturday Evening Post*. Fisher also wrote more than 30 motion picture screenplays including *Lady in the Lake*, *Johnny Angel*, *The Big Frame*, *I, Mobster*, *Johnny Reno*, and *Rogue's Gallery*.

Fisher's writing style can best be described as hard-boiled laced with sentimentality; his characters are prone to strong emotions; his plots are action-packed and melodramatic. But Fisher's strengths are his professional writing and honest presentation of characters pushed to their limits.

The best of Steve Fisher's 19 novels is the frequently reprinted *Saxon's Ghost.* Joe Saxon, one of the world's best stage magicians, known as "The Great Saxon," finds himself involved in the occult arts when his beautiful, young assistant, Ellen Hayes, disappears. Saxon has to use all his arts of legerdemain to arrive at the chilling truth: the ESP powers he and Ellen fooled audiences into believing in are real. Saxon uses these ESP powers to reach out to Ellen from beyond the grave.

Other recommended Steve Fisher mysteries are *The Night Before Murder,* and his most famous novel, *I Wake Up Screaming* which was also turned into a movie with the same title starring Victor Mature and Betty Grable.

—George Kelley

FITT, Mary. Pseudonym for Kathleen Freeman; also wrote as Caroline Cory; Stuart Mary Wick. British. Born 22 June 1897. Educated at University College of South Wales and Monmouthshire, Cardiff, B.A. 1918, M.A. 1922. Lecturer in Greek, University College of South Wales and Monmouthshire, 1919–46. Lecturer for the Ministry of Information and the National Scheme for Education, 1939–45. D.Litt.: University College of South Wales and Monmouthshire, 1940. *Died 21 February 1959.*

CRIME PUBLICATIONS

Novels (series: Superintendent Mallett)

Murder Mars the Tour. London, Nicholson and Watson, 1936.
Three Sisters Flew Home. London, Nicholson and Watson, and New York, Doubleday, 1936.
The Three Hunting Horns. London, Nicholson and Watson, 1937.
Bulls Like Death. London, Nicholson and Watson, 1937.
Expected Death (Mallett). London, Nicholson and Watson, 1938.
Sky-Rocket (Mallett). London, Nicholson and Watson, 1938.
Death at Dancing Stones (Mallet). London, Nicholson and Watson, 1939.
Murder of a Mouse. London, Nicholson and Watson, 1939.
Death Starts a Rumour (Mallett). London, Nicholson and Watson, 1940.
Death and Mary Dazill (Mallett). London, Joseph, 1941; as *Aftermath of Murder,* New York, Doubleday, 1941.
Death on Herons' Mere (Mallett). London, Joseph, 1941; as *Death Finds a Target,* New York, Doubleday, 1942.
Requiem for Robert (Mallet). London, Joseph, 1942.
Clues for Christabel (Mallett). London, Joseph, and New York, Doubleday, 1944.
Death and the Pleasant Voices (Mallett). London, Joseph, and New York, Putnam, 1946.
A Fine and Private Place (Mallett). London, Macdonald, and New York, Putnam, 1947.
Death and the Bright Day (Mallet). London, Macdonald, 1948.

And Where's Mr. Bellamy? (as Stuart Mary Wick). London, Hutchinson, 1948.
The Banquet Ceases (Mallett). London, Macdonald, 1949.
The Statue and the Lady (as Stuart Mary Wick.) London, Hodder and Stoughton, 1950.
Pity for Pamela. London, Macdonald, 1950; New York, Harper, 1951.
An Ill Wind (Mallet). London, Macdonald, 1951.
Death and the Shortest Day (Mallett). London, Macdonald, 1952.
The Night-Watchman's Friend. London, Macdonald, 1953.
Love from Elizabeth (Mallett). London, Macdonald, 1954.
Sweet Poison (Mallett). London, Macdonald, 1956.
The Late Uncle Max. London, Macdonald, 1957.
Case for the Defence. London, Macdonald, and New York, British Book Centre, 1958.
Mizmaze (Mallett). London, Joseph, 1958; New York, British Book Centre, 1959.
There Are More Ways of Killing. . . . London, Joseph, and New York, British Book Centre, 1960.

Short Stories

The Man Who Shot Birds and Other Tales of Mystery-Detection. London, Macdonald, 1954.

Uncollected Short Stories

"The Box of Coins," in *Detective Stories of Today,* edited by Raymond Postgate. London, Faber, 1940.
"The Amethyst Cross," in *The Second Ghost Book,* edited by Cynthia Asquith. London, Barrie, 1952.
"The Doctor," in *The Third Ghost Book,* edited by Cynthia Asquith. London, Barrie, 1955.
"A Dumb Friend," in *Choice of Weapons.* London, Hodder and Stoughton, 1958.
"Highlight," in *Choice of Weapons.* London, Hodder and Stoughton, 1958.

Uncollected Short Stories as Kathleen Freeman

"Murder in Athens," in *London Mystery Magazine,* October 1950.
"Mystery in Athens," in *London Mystery Magazine,* June 1951.
"Scandal in Athens," in *London Mystery Magazine,* October–November 1951.

Play

A Death in the Blackout (radio play), in *The Butcher's Dozen,* London, Heinemann, 1956.

OTHER PUBLICATIONS as Kathleen Freeman

Novels

Martin Hanner: A Comedy. London, Cape, and New York, Harcourt Brace, 1926.
Quarrelling with Lois. London, Cape, 1928.
This Love. London, Cape, 1929.
The Huge Shipwreck. London, Dent, 1934.
Adventure from the Grave. London, Davies, 1936.
Gown and Shroud. London, Macdonald, 1947.
Doctor Underground (as Caroline Cory). London, Macdonald, 1956.

Short Stories

The Intruder and Other Stories. London, Cape, 1926.

Other

The Work and Life of Solon. Cardiff, University of Wales Press, 1926.; New York, Arno Press, 1976.
Voices of Freedom. London, Muller, 1943.
What They Said at the Time: A Survey of the Causes of the Second World War and the Hopes for a Lasting Peace as Exhibited in the Utterances of the World's Leaders and Some Others from 1917–1944. London, Muller, 1945.
The Pre-Socratic Philosophers: A Companion to Diels, Fragmente der Vorsokratiker. Oxford, Blackwell, 1946; Cambridge, Massachusetts, Harvard University Press, 1948.
The Murder of Herodes and Other Trials from the Athenian Law Courts. London, Macdonald, 1946; New York, Norton, 1963.
Greek City-States. London, Macdonald, and New York, Norton, 1950.
God, Man and State: Greek Concepts. London, Macdonald, and Boston, Beacon Press, 1952.
The Paths of Justice. London, Lutterworth Press, 1954; New York, Roy, 1957(?).
T'other Miss Austen (on Jane Austen). London, Macdonald, 1956.
If Any Man Build: The History of the Save the Children Fund. London, Hodder and Stoughton, 1965.
Parson Mansell's Daughter. London, Hale, 1983.

Editor and Translator, *It Has All Happened Before: What the Greeks Thought of Their Nazis.* London, Muller, 1941.
Editor and Translator, *The Greek Way: An Anthology.* London, Macdonald, 1947.
Editor and Translator, *Fighting Words from the Greeks for Today's Struggle.* Boston, Beacon Press, 1952.
Editor, *Everyday Things in Ancient Greece,* revised edition by Marjorie and C.H.B. Quennell. London, Batsford, 1954.

Translator, *Ancilla to the Pre-Socratic Philosophers: A Complete Translation of the Fragments in Diels, Fragmente der Vorsokratiker.* Oxford, Blackwell, and Cambridge, Massachusetts, Harvard University Press, 1948.
Translator, *The Philoctetes of Sophocles: A Modern Version.* London, Muller, 1948.
Translator, *The Sophists,* by Mario Untersteiner. Oxford, Blackwell, 1954.

Other (for children) as Mary Fitt

The Island Castle. London, Nelson, 1953.
Annabella at the Lighthouse. London, Nelson, 1955.
Annabella Takes a Plunge. London, Nelson, 1955.
Annabella to the Rescue. London, Nelson, 1955.
Pomeroy's Postscript. London, Nelson, 1955.
The Turnip Watch. London, Nelson, 1956.
Annabella and the Smugglers. London, Nelson, 1957.
Man of Justice: The Story of Solon. London, Nelson, 1957.
Vendetta. London, Nelson, 1957.
Alfred the Great. London, Nelson, 1958.
The Shifting Sands. London, Nelson, 1958.
The Great River. London, Nelson, 1959.

*   *   *

As might be expected from a lecturer in Classical Greek, the novels of Mary Fitt are patently the products of a cultivated mind. A character in them is likely to comment on a situation with the words "as in Turgeniev," and the reader is expected to pick up the allusion. But her books were designed for the sort of reader who could, or who could nearly, recognise such a glancing hint and derive satisfaction from it. And to that sort of reader they will still give considerable pleasure.

Although the last of her many novels did not come out till 1960, it is not unfair to say that she was a writer of the 1930's in the intelligent tradition of Dorothy L. Sayers. Indeed, even a book like the fine *Death and the Pleasant Voices* (1946) seems to have been set in pre-1939 Britain where large country houses had immaculate gardens, where servants (though mildly complained about) were taken for granted and performed their duties with silent efficiency, where people could expect not to have to work for their living. And Fitt wrote very much in the style of the best of the 1930's British women novelists, of, say, someone like Elizabeth Bowen, supple, intelligent, quiet.

Perhaps in the crime novel this is, if not a fault, at least a weakness (perhaps it is so even in the mainstream novel). Fitt lacked that touch of bravura, that insistence, which pulls Dorothy L. Sayers out of the ruck. She never created a hero that a large public could identify easily with and come to worship. In many of her books a stolidly efficient Scottish Superintendent Mallett appears, but even when he does so he does not necessarily take the hero's role and brilliantly solve the case. Instead often one detects for oneself, by seeing character slowly revealed. It is a method worth trying.

—H.R.F. Keating

———

FITZALAN, Roger. *See* **HALL, Adam.**

———

FITZGERALD, Eric. *See* **BREWER, Gil.**

———

FLEMING, Ian (Lancaster). British. Born in London, 28 May 1908. Educated at Durnford School, Isle of Purbeck, Eton College; Royal Military Academy, Sandhurst; studied languages at the University of Munich and the University of Geneva. Served in the Royal Naval Volunteer Reserve, as personal assistant to the Director of Naval Intelligence, 1939–45: Lieutenant. Married Anne Geraldine Charteris in 1952; one son. Moscow correspondent, Reuters news agency, London, 1929–33; worked for Cull and Company, merchant bankers, London, 1933–35; stockbroker, Rowe and Pitman, London, 1935–39; Moscow correspondent, *The Times,* London, 1939; foreign manager, Kemsley, later Thomson, Newspapers, 1945–49: publisher, *Book Collector,* London, 1949–64. Order of the Dannebrog, 1945. *Died 12 August 1964.*

CRIME PUBLICATIONS

Novels (series: James Bond in all books)

Casino Royale.   London, Cape, and New York, Macmillan, 1954; as *You Asked for It,* New York, Popular Library, 1955.
Live and Let Die.   London, Cape, 1954; New York, Macmillan, 1955.
Moonraker.   London, Cape, and New York, Macmillan, 1955; as *Too Hot to Handle,* New York, Permabooks, 1957.
Diamonds Are Forever.   London, Cape, and New York, Macmillan, 1956.
From Russia, With Love.   London, Cape, and New York, Macmillan, 1957.
Doctor No.   London, Cape, and New York, Macmillan, 1958.
Goldfinger.   London, Cape, and New York, Macmillan, 1959.
Thunderball.   London, Cape, and New York, Viking Press, 1961.
The Spy Who Loved Me.   London, Cape, and New York, Viking Press, 1962.
On Her Majesty's Secret Service.   London, Cape, and New York, New American Library, 1963.
You Only Live Twice.   London, Cape, and New York, New American Library, 1964.
The Man with the Golden Gun.   London, Cape, and New York, New American Library, 1965.

Short Stories

For Your Eyes Only: Five Secret Occasions in the Life of James Bond.   London, Cape, and New York, Viking Press, 1960.
Octopussy, and The Living Daylights.   London, Cape, and New York, New American Library, 1966.

OTHER PUBLICATIONS

Novel

The Diamond Smugglers.   London, Cape, 1957; New York, Macmillan, 1958.

Play

Screenplay: *Thunderball,* with Kevin McClory and Jack Whittington, 1965.

Other

Thrilling Cities.   London, Cape, 1963; New York, New American Library, 1964.
Chitty-Chitty-Bang-Bang (for children).   London, Cape, 3 vols., 1964–65; New York, Random House, 1 vol., 1964; collected edition, Cape, 1971.
Ian Fleming Introduces Jamaica, edited by Morris Cargill. London, Deutsch, 1965; New York, Hawthorn, 1966.

*

Bibliography: *Ian Fleming: A Catalogue of a Collection: Preliminary to a Bibliography* by Iain Campbell, privately printed, 1978.

Critical Studies: *007 James Bond: A Report* by O.F. Snelling, London, Spearman, 1964, New York, New American Library, 1965; *The James Bond Dossier* by Kingsley Amis, London, Cape, and New York, New American Library, 1965; *The Life of Ian Fleming,* London, Cape, and New York, McGraw Hill, 1966, *007 James Bond,* London, Sidgwick and Jackson, and New York, Morrow, 1973, and *James Bond: The Authorised Biography of 007,* London, Granada, 1985, New York, Grove Press, 1986, all by John Pearson; *The Bond Affair* by Oreste Del Buono and Umberto Eco, London, Macdonald, 1966; *Ian Fleming: The Spy Who Came In with the Gold* by Henry Zieger, New York, Duell, 1966; *You Only Live Once: Memories of Ian Fleming* by Ivar Bryce, London, Weidenfeld and Nicolson, 1975, Frederick, Maryland, University Publications of America, 1985; *The James Bond Films* by Steven Jay Rubin, London, Arlington, 1982; *Murder in the Millions: Erle Stanley Gardner, Mickey Spillane, Ian Fleming* by J. Kenneth Van Dover, New York, Ungar, 1984; *The James Bond Bedside Companion* by Raymond Benson, New York, Dodd Mead, 1984; *Secret Agents in Fiction: Ian Fleming, John Le Carré, and Len Deighton* by L.O. Saverberg, London, Macmillan, 1984; *James Bond: A Celebration* by Peter Haining, London, W.H. Allen, 1987; *Ian Fleming's James Bond* by John E. Gardner, New York, Avenel, 1987.

*   *   *

Whatever his present standing among readers and critics, Ian Fleming accomplished an extraordinary amount in the history of the thriller. Almost singlehandedly, he revived popular interest in the spy novel, spawning legions of imitations, parodies, and critical and fictional reactions, thus indirectly creating an audience for a number of novelists who followed him in the form. Through the immense success of the filmed versions of his books, his character James Bond became the best known fictional personality of his time and Fleming the most famous writer of thrillers since Sir Arthur Conan Doyle. Everybody tried to jump on the Bondwagon—there were Bond-style books, films, comic strips, and television shows; children played with 007 games, toys, dolls, and puzzles; one could munch bread endorsed by Bond or anoint oneself with toiletries that guaranteed the virility and sex appeal of Bond to the user. Whatever Fleming's merit or defects, he created more than novels of action and adventure, sex and violence—he created a phenomenon. Such an achievement is eminently worthy of attention.

Fleming's enormous popularity—which actually came later in his career, after most of his work had been done—and the phenomenon of James Bond have always troubled both his admirers and his detractors, who have great difficulty simply accounting for it. Although it may require the passage of time to evaluate Fleming's achievement fully, the major sources of his appeal are not entirely obscure. For one thing, the James Bond novels are a perfect example of the right thing at the right time, as appropriate an expression and index of their age as, for example, the Sherlock Holmes stories or the novels of Dashiell Hammett. Fleming caught the *Zeitgeist* and grasped it firmly.

The initial reactions to Fleming—especially the negative responses—involved the sex and violence in the novels. Violence, though perhaps not so spectacularly presented, had always appeared prominently in thrillers, but readers had forgotten about the kinds of novels that Fleming's work imitated and were not accustomed to villains so grotesquely presented as Hugo Drax or Blofeld or Doctor No. Sex, especially in an English writer, was something new for the thriller, which had previously concerned itself with juvenile adventures or cerebral puzzles; to a hard-bitten reader of American popular fiction, a non-traditionalist (fans of the genre tend to be very conservative in their literary tastes), or anyone vaguely aware of the facts of life, of course, the sexuality of the James Bond novels was tame, minor, and not at all pornographic. To any sophisticated reader it hardly seemed likely that Fleming's success was based on an erotic appeal.

Like any writer of any level of quality, Fleming burglarized from the past. The closest source for his novels was the sensational thriller of such writers as Erskine Childers, John Buchan, and Sapper, who initiated the notion of espionage as a jolly, healthy, outdoor activity for patriotic public-school graduates. James Bond's world is the world of British gentlemen and the gentlemanly code; despite his ostensibly professional status and his vaunted license to kill, he is amateur in the grand tradition, a jazzed-up Richard Hannay or Bulldog Drummond giving his all for dear old England. His caste-consciousness, his snobbishness, his racism, his unmitigated delight in the perquisites of wealth, class, and privilege place him squarely in the ranks of the gentleman amateurs who dominate a large area of English popular fiction.

In addition to updating the rather motheaten material of the Childers-Buchan-Sapper school, Fleming skillfully combined it with the perennially new forms and patterns of a far more distant past, the folklore, fairy tales, legends, and myths that give his books their often outrageously unreal atmosphere. *Goldfinger,* for example, is built upon the Midas myth; *Moonraker* uses the story of St. George and the dragon; *Doctor No* and *You Only Live Twice* present two versions (or perversions) of the universal fertility myth that lies behind much literature, including *The Waste Land.* Fleming's audacity in placing his rather humdrum hero in situations out of a primordial past is astonishing; even more astonishing, he gets away with it, which is the final key to the puzzle of his success. He supports his essentially implausible works with a special sort of surface authenticity, derived from a minute (though not always accurate) attention to both the ordinary and the extraordinary details of places, objects, and experience. He paints a broad and garish canvas but varnishes it with a glossy layer of glamorous materialism and knowing archness, what Kingsley Amis dubbed the "Fleming effect." Thus we are told more than we could ever want to know about cars, airplanes, weapons, resort hotels, casinos, private clubs, high-stakes card games, skindiving, jewelry, perfume, hairbrushes, shampoos, colognes, luggage. Possessing the talent of a born copywriter, Fleming probably did more for names like Guerlain, Lanvin, Yardley, Rolex, and Cartier than a century of advertising in slick magazines. But the instruction of the reader in the arcana of 20th-century consumer goods and luxuries, the author's own unabashed enjoyment of material reality, and the reader's vicarious participation in the six-page meals, the special Martinis, and the vintage champagne combine to give the novels a glittering superficial reality that was both seductive and convincing. Fleming in his own way mastered one of the most enviable and admirable feats in all of literature—the mingling of the barely credible, the utterly incredible, and the specifically identifiable in an excitingly sustained narrative fiction. In literary circles the product of such a mixture is often referred to as the concrete universal; it is no mean accomplishment, and is shared by writers like Chaucer, Fielding, Dickens, Melville, and Faulkner. Whatever the final quality of Fleming's achievement, his undeniable popularity and financial success, his powerful influence over the writers who follow him, and his union of the fantastic and the absolutely real deserve serious and careful study. It may be a very long time before that study reaches its proper point, but it may eventually establish Ian Fleming as one of the most appropriate writers of his time.

—George Grella

FLEMING, Joan (Margaret). British. Born in Horwich, Lancashire, 27 March 1908. Educated at Brighthelmston School, Southport, Lancashire; Grand Belle Vue, Lausanne; Lausanne University. Married Norman Bell Beattie Fleming in 1932 (died 1968); three daughters and one son. Secretary to a doctor, London, 1928–32. Recipient: Crime Writers Association Gold Dagger award, 1962, 1970. *Died 15 November 1980.*

CRIME PUBLICATIONS

Novels (series Nuri Iskirlak)

Two Lovers Too Many. London, Hutchinson, 1949.
A Daisy-Chain for Satan. London, Hutchinson, and New York, Doubleday, 1950.
The Gallows in My Garden. London, Hutchinson, 1951.
The Man Who Looked Back. London, Hutchinson, 1951; New York, Doubleday, 1952; as *A Cup of Cold Poison,* London, Hamish Hamilton, 1969.
Polly Put the Kettle On. London, Hutchinson, 1952.
The Good and the Bad. London, Hutchinson, and New York, Doubleday, 1953.
He Ought to Be Shot. London, Hutchinson, and New York, Doubleday, 1955.
The Deeds of Dr. Deadcert. London, Hutchinson, 1955; New York, Washburn, 1957; as *The Merry Widower,* London, Hamish Hamilton, 1975.
You Can't Believe Your Eyes. London, Collins, and New York, Washburn, 1957.
Maiden's Prayer. London, Collins, 1957; New York, Washburn, 1958.
Malice Matrimonial. London, Collins, and New York, Washburn, 1959.
Miss Bones. London, Collins, 1959; New York, Washburn, 1960.
The Man from Nowhere. London, Collins, 1960; New York, Washburn, 1961.
In the Red. London, Collins, and New York, Washburn, 1961.
When I Grow Rich (Iskirlak). London, Collins, and New York, Washburn, 1962.
Death of a Sardine. London, Collins, 1963; New York, Washburn, 1964.
The Chill and the Kill. London, Collins, and New York, Washburn, 1964.
Nothing Is the Number When You Die (Iskirlak). London, Collins, and New York, Washburn, 1965.
Midnight Hag. London, Collins, and New York, Washburn, 1966.
No Bones about It. London, Collins, and New York, Washburn, 1967.
Kill or Cure. London, Collins, and New York, Washburn, 1968.
Hell's Belle. London, Collins, 1968; New York, Washburn, 1969.
Young Man, I Think You're Dying. London, Collins, and New York, Putnam, 1970.
Screams from a Penny Dreadful. London, Hamish Hamilton, 1971.
Grim Death and the Barrow Boys. London, Collins, 1971; as *Be a Good Boy,* New York, Putnam, 1972.
Alas, Poor Father. London, Collins, 1972; New York, Putnam, 1973.
Dirty Butter for Servants. London, Hamish Hamilton, 1972.
You Won't Let Me Finish. London, Collins, 1973; as *You Won't Let Me Finnish,* New York, Putnam, 1974.

How to Live Dangerously. London, Collins, 1974; New York, Putnam, 1975.

Too Late! Too Late! the Maiden Cried: A Gothic Novel. London, Hamish Hamilton, and New York, Putnam, 1975.

. . . To Make an Underworld. London, Collins, and New York, Putnam, 1976.

Every Inch a Lady. London, Collins, 1977; New York, Putnam, 1978.

The Day of the Donkey Derby. London, Collins, and New York, Putnam, 1978.

Uncollected Short Stories

"The Graduate," in *London Mystery Magazine,* October–December 1950.

"Writer's Witch," in *London Mystery Magazine,* June–July 1951.

"Boo to a Kiss," in *London Mystery Magazine,* September 1955.

"Cat on the Trail of a Wife Killer," in *The Evening Standard* (London), 12 March 1963.

"Cat on the Trail," in *The Saint* (New York), June 1964.

"Gone Is Gone," in *Tales of Unease,* edited by John Burke. London, Pan, 1966; New York, Doubleday, 1969.

"Still Waters," in *Winter's Crimes 1,* edited by George Hardinge. London, Macmillan, 1969.

"The Bore," in *Winter's Crimes 4,* edited by George Hardinge. London, Macmillan, 1972.

OTHER PUBLICATIONS

Other

Dick Brownie and the Zaga Bog (for children). London, Fairston, 1944.

Mulberry Hall (for children). Bognor Regis, Sussex, Crowther, 1945.

The Riddle in the River (for children). London, Hammond, 1946.

Button Jugs (for children). London, Hammond, 1947.

The Jackdaw's Nest (for children). London, Hammond, 1949.

Quonian Quartet (includes the 4 previous books). London, Hutchinson, 1949.

Shakespeare's Country in Colour. London, Batsford, 1960.

*

Manuscript Collection: Mugar Memorial Library, Boston University.

*   *   *

Often the crime novels of Joan Fleming concentrate on the psychological reactions of her characters rather than the detective's investigation. In this way, they are somewhat less complex versions of the works of Patricia Highsmith. Fleming is less demanding in her consideration of the criminal while nonetheless writing competently. Her interest in the mental and emotional reactions of the crime's victims—either direct or indirect victims—is always in line with contemporary trends.

The Man from Nowhere is one of the best examples of her probing the psychological aspects of crime's victims as she examines the reaction by a small closed community to murder and the presence of a birthmarked stranger. The man Rockambole first disconcerts by his appearance and later by his ideas: he is quiet about his past; he is unconcerned about possessions; he does not overvalue money. Fleming demonstrates how the villagers, including the cleric whose fiancé was attracted to Rock, turn these traits to suspicious motives, despite their difficulty in doing so. Although the novel ends on an ironic note, the conclusion is an unsettling rather than a unifying one. Much the same motif, with an even more tragic consequence, is employed in *Midnight Hag.* Fleming again demonstrates the malice of a small town which can destroy an innocent person while the guilty prosper. As in *The Man from Nowhere,* a quiet love story between two mature people who had never expected to find someone to love adds poignancy to the plot's unfolding.

In other examples of Fleming's work it is possible to see the opposite side of this psychological investigation, as a kind of flippancy comes to the foreground. Miss Maiden (her name bettered only by the implications of her mother's—Mrs. Maiden) is convingly wooed by a Mr. Alladin who hopes to cheat her of her inheritance and finally plots to kill her. The conclusion of *Maiden's Prayer,* so unlike that of *The Man from Nowhere* or *Midnight Hag,* almost denies the possibility of successful villainy in the world. What the *San Francisco Chronicle* calls Fleming's "charming oddities" can be clearly seen here, as well as in the burglar-detective exchanges in *Miss Bones,* an otherwise grim tale of dual identities and a skeleton exhumed from the shop court-yard.

In an unusual pair of detective novels featuring the Turkish philosopher Nuri Iskirlak, Fleming alternates Eastern and Western attitudes even as Nuri Iskirlak frequently crosses the Bosphorus from Europe to Asia. *When I Grow Rich* draws an English girl into a Turkish opium smuggling attempt and *Nothing Is the Number When You Die* takes Iskirlak to Oxford to find a friend's missing son and again be involved in opium smuggling. With the cultural differences accentuated by the outsider in each novel and the contrast between Nuri Iskirlak's contemplative, bookish way of life and the active, criminal world into which he enters, a variety of tensions is produced. Adaptation to the changing demands of time and circumstances is described in the portraits of Mme. Miasma of Turkey and Lady Mercia Mossops of England as well as in the destruction of Nuri Iskirlak's home and library, and the difference between the Oxford of his expectation and of reality. These and the cultural distinctions dominate the novels more than the suspense and detection: the opium selling is never explicitly horrible; killers only menace; the deaths of even Mme. Miasma, Rhonda and Hadji are secondary. Tamara Yenish's destruction of her dead husband's opium field is too easily accomplished in view of the potential danger. Nevertheless, the descriptions of Turkish life in the Sultan's time and Iskirlak's understanding but amusing misconceptions at Oxford make these multi-cultural explorations fascinating.

Fleming's enormous variety in plots and concerns makes it impossible to generalize about her works. She can generally be expected to produce a slightly different approach to the mystery novel with each new book. These unexpected "oddities" are always carefully written and interestingly oriented, although seldom outstanding.

—Kathleen Gregory Klein

————

FLEMING, Oliver. *See* **MacDONALD, Philip.**

————

FLETCHER, David. Pseudonym for Dulan Barber, also wrote as Owen Brookes; Robert Rush. British. Born in Reading, Berkshire, 11 October 1940. Educated at Leamington College for Boys; Leeds University, 1958–59. Married Paddy Kitchen in 1968; one stepson. Editor, Calder and Boyars, London, 1963–68; Charles Skilton, London, 1968–72; executive councillor, Writers Guild of Great Britain, London, in the mid 1970's; Tutor, Morley College, London, 1976–78, City Literature College, 1978–79. Recipient: Thomas R. Coward Memorial award, 1974. *Died 7 October 1988.*

CRIME PUBLICATIONS

Novels

A Lovable Man. London, Macmillan, 1974; New York, Coward McCann, 1975.
A Respectable Woman. London, Macmillan, and New York, Coward McCann, 1975.
Don't Whistle "Macbeth". London, Macmillan, 1976.
Accomplices. London, Macmillan, 1976.
Only Children. London, Macmillan, 1976.
Raffles (novelization of the stories by E.W. Hornung). London, Pan, and New York, Putnam, 1977.
Rainbow in Hell. London, Macmillan, 1983.
Rainbows End in Tears. London, Macmillan, 1984.
On Suspicion. London, Macmillan, 1985.
The Accident of Robert Luman London, Macmillan, 1988.
A Wagon-Load of Monkeys. London, Macmillan, 1988.
Dismal Ravens Crying. London, Macmillan, 1989.

Uncollected Short Stories

"Corabella," in *Winter's Crimes 7,* edited by George Hardinge. London, Macmillan, 1975.
"Mass Murder," in *Winter's Crimes 10,* edited by Hilary Watson. London, Macmillan, 1978; New York, St. Martin's Press, 1979.
"The Scribbler's Tale," in *Winter's Crimes 12,* edited by Hilary Watson. London, Macmillan, and New York, St. Martin's Press, 1980.
"Mother Elder," in *Winter's Crimes 14,* edited by Hilary Watson, London, Macmillan, and New York, St. Martin's Press, 1982.

OTHER PUBLICATIONS

Novels

The Marriage Ring (novelization of television series, with Paddy Kitchen). London, W.H. Allen, 1976.
A Crime for the Family. London, Macmillan, 1978.
Beasts. London, Macmillan, 1980.

Novels as Owen Brookes

The Widow of Ratchets. New York, Holt, 1979; London, Fontana, 1980.
Inheritance. New York, Holt, and London, Hutchinson, 1980.
The Touch. London, Macmillan, 1981.
The Gatherer. New York, Holt, and London, Macdonald, 1982.
Deadly Communion. New York, Holt, and London, Macdonald, 1984.

Forget Me Knots. New York, Holt, and London, Macdonald, 1986.

Novels as Robert Rush

The Birthday Treat. London, Macdonald, 1981.
The Birthday Girl. London, Macdonald, 1983.

Other

Three Canterbury Tales (for children). London, Blackie, 1966.
Pornography and Society. London, Skilton, 1972.
The Horrific World of Monsters (for children). London, Marshall Cavendish, 1974.
Unmarried Fathers (interviews). London, Hutchinson, 1975.

Editor, *Concerning Thomas Hardy: A Composite Portrait from Memory,* by J. Stevens Cox, London, Skilton, 1968.
Editor, *One Parent Families.* London, Davis Poynter, 1975.
Editor, with Giles Gordon, *Members of the Jury,* London, Wildwood House, 1976.

*   *   *

"People are not simply 'good' or 'bad' but a fascinating, truthful mixture of both." This comment appears almost at the end of David Fletcher's first book, *A Lovable Man,* in the context of a discussion about a Monteverdi opera, but it is a conclusion which could be drawn from any of the crime novels which Dulan Barber wrote under the Fletcher name.

Fletcher's preoccupation with the ambiguity of moral standards is not altogether absent even from his one potboiler. *Raffles,* based on scripts written by Philip Mackie for the popular Yorkshire television series about the amateur cracksman created by E.W. Hornung, scarcely compares in quality or depth with the rest of Fletcher's work. Yet the ambivalence of A.J. Raffles's ethical code no doubt added spice to this frankly commercial project so far as Fletcher was concerned.

A Lovable Man is much more typical. The ironic title sets the tone and it is plain that mere mystification is of little interest to Fletcher, although the reader remains unsure until the closing pages whether Roger Kilby will be able to escape the consequences of having murdered his wife Antonia. Detective work is also unimportant, despite the presence in the book of a splendidly realised policeman, Detective Inspector Ruby, an irascible eccentric who is unable to convince his superiors of Kilby's guilt. Fletcher's aim is to highlight the odd, unpredictable way in which people behave and to suggest that bad deeds do not necessarily preclude their perpetrator's finding happiness.

Fletcher's protagonists often commit horrifying crimes. He sets himself the task of getting inside the heads of those whom tabloid newspapers would no doubt describe as monsters and presents them as recognisable, complex human beings. He is playing for high literary stakes and does not succeed with everything he attempts. The impact of *Rainbow in Hell,* for instance, is weakened because Fletcher's account of the horrors which Martin Rainbow saw whilst working as a war correspondent, although powerful so far as it goes, is not presented in the degree of relentless detail necessary to make Rainbow's determination himself to commit murder wholly convincing.

For all that, *Rainbow in Hell* seizes the reader's attention from first page to last. Again in this book the question is not whether the protagonist is guilty, but what will become of him. The emphasis is different in the sequel, *Rainbows End in Tears.* Nestor Rainbow, Martin's son, is obsessed with the need to find out whether his father had in fact killed a young gypsy girl.

CRIME AND MYSTERY WRITERS

Time has passed and no-one to whom he speaks seems sure of the truth. At one point, a character says of another: "She was nice. I could have liked her a lot." The words are conventional, but the unspoken emotions which lie behind the platitude are not: for this is a murderer talking about his victim.

The Accident of Robert Luman sees Fletcher exploring the disjointed mental processes of a brain-damaged young man who may or may not be responsible for the disappearance of a teenager called Leni Mitchell. This is a bold and memorable book. The apparent awkwardness of its construction in fact conceals great art. Only towards the end of the story does the significance of the discovery of a dreadful crime in the prologue become apparent. And the final, quiet sentence is as chilling as any that one could imagine. How sad that Fletcher's career should have been cut short by his early death. He had already achieved considerable success, but promised a great deal more.

—Martin Edwards

FLETCHER, J(oseph) S(mith). British. Born in Halifax, Yorkshire, 7 February 1863. Educated privately and at Silcoates School. Married Rosamond Langbridge; one son. Sub-editor, *Practical Teacher* magazine, London, 1881–83; freelance journalist in London, 1883–90; staff member, Leeds *Mercury,* 1890–1900; columnist ("A Son of the Soil") on rural life for several newspapers. Fellow, Royal Historical Society, 1918. *Died 30 January 1935.*

CRIME PUBLICATIONS

Novels (series: Ronald Camberwell; Sergeant Charlesworth; Richard Goulburn; Inspector Skarratt)

Andrewlina. London, Kegan Paul, 1889.
The Winding Way. London, Kegan Paul, 1890.
Old Lattimer's Legacy. London, Jarrolds, 1892; New York, Clode, 1929.
The Three Days' Terror. London, Long, 1901; New York, Clode, 1927.
The Golden Spur. London, Long, 1901; New York, Dial Press, 1928.
The Investigators. London, Long, 1902; New York, Clode, 1930.
The Secret Way. London, Digby Long, 1903; Boston, Small Maynard, 1925.
The Diamonds. London, Digby Long, 1904; as *The Diamond Murders,* New York, Dodd Mead, 1929.
The Threshing-Floor. London, Unwin, 1905.
The Queen of a Day. London, Unwin, 1907; New York, Doubleday, 1929.
Paradise Court. London, Unwin, 1908; New York, Doubleday, 1929.
The Harvest Moon. London, Nash, 1908; New York, McBride, 1909.
The Mantle of Ishmael (Goulburn). London, Nash, 1909.
Marchester Royal (Skarratt). London, Everett, 1909; New York, Doran, 1926.
Hardican's Hollow. London, Everett, 1910; New York, Doran, 1927.
The Bartenstein Case. London, Long, 1913; as *The Bartenstein Mystery,* New York, Dial Press, 1927.

Perris of the Cherry-Trees. London, Nash, 1913; New York, Doubleday, 1930.
The Secret Cargo. London, Ward Lock, 1913.
The Ransom for London. London, Long, 1914; New York, Dial Press, 1929.
The Shadow of Ravenscliffe. London, Digby Long, 1914; New York, Clode, 1928.
The Marriage Lines. London, Nash, 1914.
The Wolves and the Lamb (Skarratt). London, Ward Lock, 1914; New York, Knopf, 1925.
The King Versus Wargrave. London, Ward Lock, 1915; New York, Knopf, 1924.
The Annexation Society. London, Ward Lock, 1916; New York, Knopf, 1925.
Families Repaired. London, Allen and Unwin, 1916.
The Lynne Court Spinney. London, Ward Lock, 1916; as *The Mystery of Lynne Court,* Baltimore, Norman Remington, 1923; as *And Sudden Death,* New York, Curl, 1938; as *Pedigreed Murder Case,* n.p., Detective Novel Classics, n.d.
Malvery Hold. London, Ward Lock, 1917; as *The Mystery of the Hushing Pool,* New York, Curl, 1938.
The Perilous Crossways. London, Ward Lock, 1917; New York, Curl, 1938.
The Rayner-Slade Amalgamation. London, Allen and Unwin, 1917; New York, Knopf, 1922.
The Amaranth Club. London, Ward Lock, 1918; New York, Knopf, 1926.
The Chestermarke Instinct. London, Allen and Unwin, 1918; New York, Knopf, 1921.
The Borough Treasurer. London, Ward Lock, 1919; New York, Knopf, 1921.
Droonin' Watter. London, Allen and Unwin, 1919; as *Dead Man's Money,* New York, Knopf, 1930.
The Middle Temple Murder. London, Ward Lock, and New York, Knopf, 1919.
The Seven Days' Secret. London, Jarrolds, 1919; New York, Clode, 1930.
The Talleyrand Maxim. London, Ward Lock, 1919; New York, Knopf, 1920.
The Valley of Headstrong Men. London, Hodder and Stoughton, 1919; New York, Doran, 1924.
The Herapath Property. London, Ward Lock, 1920; New York, Knopf, 1921.
The Lost Mr. Linthwaite. London, Hodder and Stoughton, 1920; New York, Knopf, 1923.
The Orange-Yellow Diamond. London, Newnes, 1920; New York, Knopf, 1921.
Scarhaven Keep. London, Ward Lock, 1920; New York, Knopf, 1922.
The Paradise Mystery. New York, Knopf, 1920; as *Wrychester Paradise,* London, Ward Lock, 1921.
The Markenmore Mystery. London, Jenkins, 1921; New York, Knopf, 1923.
The Root of All Evil. London, Hodder and Stoughton, 1921; New York, Doran, 1924.
The Heaven-Kissed Hill. London, Hodder and Stoughton, 1922; New York, Doran, 1924.
In the Mayor's Parlour. London, Lane, 1922; as *The Time-Worn Town,* New York, Knopf, 1924; as *Behind the Panel,* London, Collins, 1931.
The Mazaroff Murder. London, Jenkins, 1922; as *The Mazaroff Mystery,* New York, Knopf, 1924.
The Middle of Things. London, Ward Lock, and New York, Knopf, 1922.
Ravensdene Court. London, Ward Lock, and New York, Knopf, 1922.

The Ambitious Lady. London, Ward Lock, 1923.

The Charing Cross Mystery. London, Jenkins, and New York, Putnam, 1923.

The Copper Box. London, Hodder and Stoughton, and New York, Doran, 1923.

The Million-Dollar Diamond (Goulburn). London, Jenkins, 1923; as *The Black House in Harley Street,* New York, Doubleday, 1923.

The Mysterious Chinaman. London, Jenkins, 1923; as *Rippling Ruby,* New York, Putnam, 1923.

The Cartwright Gardens Murder. London, Collins, 1924; New York, Knopf, 1926.

False Scent. London, Jenkins, 1924; New York, Knopf, 1925.

The Kang-He Vase. London, Collins, 1924; New York, Knopf, 1926.

The Safety Pin. London, Jenkins, and New York, Putnam, 1924.

The Bedford Row Mystery. London, Hodder and Stoughton, 1925; as *The Strange Case of Mr. Henry Marchmont,* New York, Knopf, 1927.

The Great Brighton Mystery. London, Hodder and Stoughton, 1925; New York, Knopf, 1926.

Sea Fog. London, Jenkins, and New York, Knopf, 1925.

The Mill of Many Windows. London, Collins, and New York, Doran, 1925.

The Mortover Grange Mystery. London, Jenkins, 1926; as *The Mortover Grange Affair,* New York, Knopf, 1927.

The Stolen Budget. London, Hodder and Stoughton, 1926; as *The Missing Chancellor,* New York, Knopf, 1927.

The Green Rope. London, Jenkins, and New York, Knopf, 1927.

The Murder in the Pallant. London, Jenkins, 1927; New York, Knopf, 1928.

The Passenger to Folkestone. London, Jenkins, and New York, Knopf, 1927.

Cobweb Castle. London, Jenkins, and New York, Knopf, 1928.

The Double Chance. London, Nash and Grayson, and New York, Dodd Mead, 1928.

The Wrist Mark. New York, Knopf, 1928; London, Jenkins, 1929.

The Box Hill Murder. New York, Knopf, 1929; London, Jenkins, 1931.

The House in Tuesday Market. New York, Knopf, 1929; London, Jenkins, 1930.

The Matheson Formula. New York, Knopf, 1929; London, Jenkins, 1930.

The Secret of Secrets (Skarratt). New York, Clode, 1929.

The Dressing-Room Murder. London, Jenkins, 1930; New York, Knopf, 1931.

The Borgia Cabinet (Charlesworth). New York, Knopf, 1930; London, Jenkins, 1932.

The South Foreland Murder. London, Jenkins, and New York, Knopf, 1930.

The Yorkshire Moorland Murder. London, Jenkins, and New York, Knopf, 1930.

The Guarded Room. London, Long, and New York, Clode, 1931.

Murder at Wrides Park (Camberwell). London, Harrap, and New York, Knopf, 1931.

Murder in Four Degrees (Camberwell). London, Harrap, and New York, Knopf, 1931.

The Burma Ruby (Charlesworth). London, Benn, 1932; New York, Dial Press, 1933.

Murder in the Squire's Pew (Camberwell). London, Harrap, and New York, Knopf, 1932.

Murder of the Ninth Baronet (Camberwell). London, Harrap, and New York, Knopf, 1932.

The Solution of a Mystery. London, Harrap, and New York, Doubleday, 1932.

Murder of the Only Witness (Camberwell). London, Harrap, and New York, Knopf, 1933.

The Mystery of the London Banker (Camberwell). London, Harrap, 1933; as *Murder of a Banker,* New York, Knopf, 1933.

Who Killed Alfred Snowe? (Camberwell). London, Harrap, 1933; as *Murder of the Lawyer's Clerk,* New York, Knopf, 1933.

Murder of the Secret Agent (Camberwell). London, Harrap, and New York, Knopf, 1934.

The Ebony Box (Camberwell). London, Butterworth, and New York, Knopf, 1934.

The Eleventh Hour (Camberwell). London, Butterworth, and New York, Knopf, 1935.

Todmanhawe Grange, completed by Torquemada. London, Butterworth, 1937; as *The Mill House Murder, Being the Last of the Adventures of Ronald Camberwell,* New York, Knopf, 1937.

Short Stories

Pasquinado. London, Ward Lock, 1898.

The Death That Lurks Unseen. London, Ward Lock, 1899.

The Air-Ship and Other Stories. London, Digby Long, 1903.

The Fear of the Night. London, Routledge, 1903.

The Ivory God and Other Stories. London, Murray, 1907.

The Adventures of Archer Dawe, Sleuth-Hound. London, Digby Long, 1909; as *The Contents of the Coffin,* London, London Book Company, 1928.

The Wheatstack and Other Stories. London, Nash, 1909.

Paul Campenhaye, Specialist in Criminology. London, Ward Lock, 1918; as *The Clue of the Artificial Eye,* New York, Curl, 1939.

Exterior to the Evidence. London, Hodder and Stoughton, 1920; New York, Knopf, 1923.

Many Engagements. London, Long, 1923.

The Secret of the Barbican and Other Stories. London, Hodder and Stoughton, 1924; New York, Doran, 1925.

Green Ink and Other Stories. London, Jenkins, and Boston, Small Maynard, 1926.

The Massingham Butterfly and Other Stories. London, Jenkins, and Boston, Small Maynard, 1926.

Behind the Monocle and Other Stories. London, Jarrolds, 1928; New York, Doubleday, 1930.

The Ravenswood Mystery and Other Stories. London, Collins, 1929; as *The Canterbury Mystery,* London, Collins, 1933.

The Heaven-Sent Witness. New York, Doubleday, 1930.

The Malachite Jar and Other Stories. London, Collins, 1930; as *The Flamstock Mystery,* 1932; abridged edition, as *The Manor House Mystery,* 1933.

The Marrendon Mystery and Other Stories of Crime and Detection. London, Collins, 1930.

The Man in No. 3 and Other Stories. London, Collins, 1931.

Safe Number Sixty-Nine and Other Stories. Boston, International Pocket Library, 1931.

The Man in the Fur Coat and Other Stories. London, Collins, 1932.

The Murder in Medora Mansions and Other Stories of Crime and Mystery. London, Collins, 1933.

Find the Woman. London, Collins, 1933.

The Carrismore Ruby and Other Stories. London, Jarrolds, 1935.

Uncollected Short Story

"Bickmore Deals with the Duchess," in *Ellery Queen's Mystery Magazine* (New York), November 1951.

OTHER PUBLICATIONS

Novels

Frank Carisbroke's Stratagem; or, Lost and Won. London, Jarrolds, 1888.
Mr. Spivey's Clerk. London, Ward and Downey, 1890.
Through Storm and Stress. London, Chambers, 1892.
When Charles the First Was King. London, Bentley, 1892; Chicago, McClurg, 1895.
The Remarkable Adventure of Walter Trelawney. London, Chambers, 1893.
The Quarry Farm: A Country Tale. London, Ward and Downey, 1893.
In the Days of Drake. London, Blackie, 1895; Chicago, Rand McNally, 1897.
Where Highways Cross. London and New York, Macmillan, 1895.
At the Gate of the Fold. London, Ward and Downey, and New York, Macmillan, 1896.
Life in Arcadia. London, Lane, and New York, Macmillan, 1896.
Mistress Spitfire. London, Dent, 1896.
The Making of Matthias. London, Lane, 1897.
The Builders. London, Methuen, 1897; New York, Mansfield, 1898; as *The Furnace of Youth,* London, Pearson, 1914.
The Paths of the Prudent. London, Methuen, and New York, Page, 1899.
The Harvesters. London, Long, 1900.
Morrison's Machine. London, Hutchinson, 1900.
Bonds of Steel. London, Digby Long, 1902.
Anthony Everton. London, Chambers, 1903.
The Arcadians: A Whimsicality. London, Long, 1903.
Lucian the Dreamer. London, Methuen, 1903.
David March. London, Methuen, 1904.
The Pigeon's Cave. London, Partridge, 1904.
Grand Relations. London, Unwin, 1905.
Highcroft Farm. London, Cassell, 1906; as *The Harringtons of Highcroft Farm,* 1907.
A Maid and Her Money. London, Digby Long, 1906; New York, Doubleday, 1929.
Daniel Quayne. London, Murray, 1907; New York, Doran, 1926.
Mr. Poskitt. London, Nash, 1907.
Mothers in Israel: A Study in Rustic Amenities. London, Murray, and New York, Moffat, 1908.
The Pinfold. London, Everett, 1911; New York, Doran, 1928.
The Fine Air of Morning: A Pastoral Romance. London, Nash, 1912; Boston, Estes, 1913.
The Golden Venture. London, Nash, 1912.
I'd Venture All for Thee. London, Nash, 1913; New York, Doubleday, 1928.
Both of This Parish. London, Nash, 1914.
Heronshaw Main: The Story of a Yorkshire Colliery. London, Ward Lock, 1918.
The Wild Oat. London, Jarrolds, 1928; New York, Doubleday, 1929.
The Grocer's Wife. London, Hutchinson, 1933.

Short Stories

One of His Little Ones and Other Tales in Prose and Verse. London, Washbourne, 1888.
The Wonderful Wapentake. London, Lane, 1894; Chicago, McClurg, 1895.
God's Failures. London, Lane, 1897.
At the Blue Bell Inn. Chicago, Rand McNally, 1898.
From the Broad Acres: Stories Illustrative of Rural Life in Yorkshire. London, Grant Richards, 1899.
For Those Were Stirring Times and Other Stories. London, Everett, 1904.
Mr. Poskitt's Nightcaps: Stories of a Yorkshire Farmer. London, Nash, 1910.

Play

Hearthstone Corner (produced Leeds, 1926).

Verse

The Bride of Venice. London, Poole, 1879.
The Juvenile Poems of Joseph S. Fletcher. Dartford, Kent, Snowden, 1879.
Songs after Sunset. London, Poole, 1881.
Early Poems. London, Poole, 1882.
Anima Christi. Bradford, Yorkshire, Fletcher, 1884.
Deus Homo. London, Washbourne, 1887.
Poems, Chiefly Against Pessimism. London, Ward and Downey, 1893.
Ballads of Revolt. London, Lane, 1897.
Leet-Livvy: A Verse-Story in the Dialect of Osgoodcross. London, Simpkin Marshall, 1915.
Verses Written in Early Youth. Privately printed, 1931.
Collected Verse 1881–1931. London, Harrap, 1931.

Other

Jesus Calls Thee! Thoughts for One in Indecision. London, Washbourne, 1887.
Our Lady's Month: A Manual of Devotion for the Month of May. London, Washbourne, 1887.
A Short Life of Cardinal Newman. London, Ward and Downey, 1890.
Where Shall We Go for a Holiday? York, Waddington, 1894.
A Picturesque History of Yorkshire. London, Dent, 3 vols., 1899–1900.
Roberts of Pretoria: The Story of His Life. London, Methuen, 1900.
Baden-Powell of Mafeking. London, Methuen, 1900.
The History of the St. Leger Stakes 1776–1901. London, Hutchinson, 1902; revised edition, as *The History of the St. Leger Stakes 1776–1926,* 1927.
Owd Poskitt: His Opinions on Mr. Chamberlain in Particular and on English Trade in General. London and New York, Harper, 1903.
A Book about Yorkshire. London, Methuen, and New York, McClure, 1908.
The Enchanting North. London, Nash, 1908.
Recollections of a Yorkshire Village. London, Digby Long, 1910.
Nooks and Corners of Yorkshire. London, Nash, 1911.
Memories of a Spectator. London, Nash, 1912.
The Adventures of Turco Bullworthy, His Dog Shrimp, and His Friend Dick Wynyard (for children). London, Washbourne, 1912.

The Town of Crooked Ways. London, Nash, and Boston, Estes, 1912.

Memorials of a Yorkshire Parish: A Historical Sketch of the Parish of Darrington. London, Lane, 1917.

The Making of Modern Yorkshire 1750–1914. London, Allen and Unwin, 1918.

The Cistercians of Yorkshire. London, S.P.C.K., and New York, Macmillan, 1919.

Sheffield. London, S.P.C.K., and New York, Macmillan, 1919.

Leeds. London, S.P.C.K., and New York, Macmillan, 1919.

Pontefract. London, S.P.C.K., and New York, Macmillan, 1920.

Harrogate and Knaresborough. London, S.P.C.K., and New York, Macmillan, 1920.

Yorkshiremen of the Restoration. London, Allen and Unwin, 1921.

Halifax. London, S.P.C.K., and New York, Macmillan, 1923.

The Life and Work of St. Wilfrid of Ripon, Apostle of Sussex (lecture). Chichester, Thompson, 1925.

The Reformation in Northern England: Six Lectures. London, Allen and Unwin, 1925; Port Washington, New York, Kennikat Press, 1971.

*   *   *

J.S. Fletcher's works are little known today, yet at the height of his fame he was one of the most popular detective novelists on both sides of the Atlantic. He produced at an incredible rate during the 1920's and early 1930's, at which time his only rival in terms of quantity was Edgar Wallace, and like Wallace his best books were submerged in a torrent of mediocre work.

It is an oft-recorded fact by historians of the genre that Fletcher was "discovered" by President Woodrow Wilson, a compulsive reader of detective fiction. *The Middle Temple Murder* was the book in question, and it still holds together well today; from the moment journalist Frank Spargo is involved in the discovery of a body in Middle Temple Lane, the pace is faster than many detective novels of the period, and the atmosphere of London is well conveyed. Fletcher was adept at London settings, and *The Charing Cross Mystery* deserves to stand with *The Middle Temple Murder* as the best examples. Hetherwick is an eager young barrister, of a type appearing regularly in Fletcher's stories; when he catches the last train at Sloane Square, and is faced with the body of a fellow passenger at Charing Cross, we are treated to a lively tale of some gusto and nicely contrived mystery which bears re-reading.

Fletcher by no means confined his settings to London. Not only do his detectives frequently have to hare about the English countryside in pursuit of leads, but he also excelled in mysteries with rural settings. A Yorkshireman himself, he was able to depict the wide open spaces with some skill. His long list contains many in which the background is the best feature, and such books as *Scarhaven Keep* are sufficiently atmospheric for us to overlook the trivial nature of some of his plots.

It must be said that the largest proportion of Fletcher's work falls outside the field of pure detective fiction. Although there is often a mystery to be solved, his detectives are in many cases young men who are fortuitously involved in the mystery and pursue its solution with little professional dedication. The equivalent of Crofts's Inspector French or Freeman's Dr. Thorndyke is not to be found in Fletcher. On the credit side, the fact that his stories border on the thriller form is inclined to make them more readable and sometimes less pedantic than those of some of his contemporaries. His occasional carelessness over details, his almost total lack of characterisation, and

the melodramatic nature of many of the mysteries were all overlooked by the many readers who found the pace of his narratives completely enthralling. During the 1920's he epitomised for many people all that was best in the field.

In retrospect, it is a pity that a writer so influential in popularising detective fiction throughout two continents, and possessing the innate craftsmanship of a real storyteller, should produce such a mass of hastily conceived second-class work that his genuine contributions to detective fiction are now almost forgotten. His only significant series character, Ronald Camberwell, appeared in some poor novels toward the end of Fletcher's career. It must be recalled, however, that he had the talent to produce some good novels approaching the classic form (*The Middle Temple Murder* and *The Charing Cross Mystery*) and some excellent short stories of detection (*The Adventures of Archer Dawe, Sleuth-Hound* and *Paul Campenhaye, Specialist in Criminology*), all in the early part of his career, presumably before the public's voracious appetite had brought about a parallel rise in output and reduction in quality.

—Melvyn Barnes

⸻

FLETCHER, Lucille. American. Born in Brooklyn, New York, 28 March 1912. Educated in public schools in Brooklyn; Vassar College, Poughkeepsie, New York, B.A. 1933. Married 1) Bernard Herrmann in 1939; 2) John Douglass Wallop, III, in 1949; two daughters. Employed by the Columbia Broadcasting System as music librarian, copyright clerk, and publicity writer, 1934–39. Self-employed writer. Recipient: Mystery Writers of America Edgar Allan Poe award, 1959. Agent: William Morris Agency, 1350 Avenue of the Americas, New York, New York 10019. Address: Avon Light, Oxford, Maryland 21654, U.S.A.

CRIME PUBLICATIONS

Novels

Blindfold. New York, Random House, and London, Eyre and Spottiswoode, 1960.

. . . and Presumed Dead. New York, Random House, and London, Eyre and Spottiswoode, 1963.

The Strange Blue Yawl. New York, Random House, 1964; London, Eyre and Spottiswoode, 1965.

The Girl in Cabin B54. New York, Random House, 1968; London, Hodder and Stoughton, 1969.

Eighty Dollars to Stamford. New York, Random House, 1975; London, Hale, 1977.

Mirror Image. New York, Morrow, 1988; London, Heywood, 1989.

Uncollected Short Story

"The Night Man," in *The Saint's Choice 7* (New York), 1946.

OTHER PUBLICATIONS

Novel

The Daughters of Jasper Clay. New York, Holt Rinehart, 1958.

Plays

My Client Curley, with Norman Corwin (broadcast, 1940). Published in *Best Broadcast of 1939–1940,* edited by Max Wylie, New York, Whittlesey House, 1940.
The Hitch-Hiker (broadcast, 1941). Included in *Sorry, Wrong Number,* 1952.
Sorry, Wrong Number (broadcast, 1944). New York, Dramatists Play Service, 1952.
Night Watch (produced New York and York, 1972). New York, Dramatists Play Service, 1972.

Screenplay: *Sorry, Wrong Number,* 1948.

Radio Plays: *My Client Curley,* 1940; *The Hitch-Hiker,* 1941; *Sorry, Wrong Number,* 1944; *Remodeled Brownstone, The Furnished Floor, The Diary of Sophronia Winters, The Search for Henri Le Fevre,* and other contributions to *Suspense* and *Mercury Theatre on the Air* series; *Bad Dreams Fugue in C Minor; Someone Else; Night Man; Dark Journey; The Intruder.*

*

Lucille Fletcher comments:

I don't think I can be regarded as a writer of crime fiction since I have never written a detective story, but specialize in mysteries. I write stories that deal with baffling situations or events which unravel to a climax involving peril to the protagonist.

*   *   *

The typical suspense novel of Lucille Fletcher is less concerned with the solution of a mystery than with the anticipation and fear which the protagonist and the reader experience. Both are misdirected by the events while even a careful reverse accounting of the clues does not always demonstrate how the solution was reached. Since the police force is uninvolved, the protagonist's apprehensiveness and isolation can be emphasized to control mood, the primary focus of the novels. The hallmark of Fletcher's work is that the solution of the mystery is only the first part of a two-fold conclusion. The second climax of each story provides an unexpected twist—a new murder is committed, a disguise penetrated, a motive revealed. Even with foreknowledge of Fletcher's style, the reader becomes absorbed in the tension of the plot and is unlikely to anticipate the specific ending.

Fletcher's best known work, *Sorry, Wrong Number* (adapted for various media), demonstrates the mounting terror and hysteria of an apparent invalid, alone in her apartment, who hears the details of a murder plot over the telephone when she tries to call her husband's office. Without friends, she calls the police to report her suspicion and her doctor to ask him to make a house call; neither of these societal caretakers gives her story much credence and both refuse to humor her desire for "protection"—actually companionship. The rejection of requests for assistance, the anticipation of a rejection, or the fear of being disbelieved and suspected often traumatizes Fletcher's protagonists. They become increasingly isolated from society, suspicious of others, and easily frightened by their lack of knowledge. As a consequence they often reject safe and trustworthy assistance which could save them from the problems they fear. This reversal is the dramatic twist at the conclusion of *Sorry, Wrong Number* where ironically

every attempt to cope with the terror has contradictory results.

Because of its first person narration, *The Strange Blue Yawl* (involving boats and waterways, as do several other Fletcher novels) is especially fascinating and misleading. The "artist"-narrator relays the information gathered by his wife's investigation while he tries to compose the music which will win him fame and assure their fortune. To discover if an unknown woman whose screams she'd heard from a blue yawl docked near their home had been murdered, the wife investigates every blue-painted boat and every recently repainted yawl in the Maryland-Virginia vicinity. However, it is the narrator who solves the mystery in one instant of inspiration. As in Fletcher's other novels, this is only the apparent climax for, strange as the discovery is, it is followed by a predictable but shocking twist.

Eighty Dollars to Stamford provides a slight departure from the previous suspense novels. The recently widowed protagonist, driving a cab to occupy his mind, is framed for the murder of his wife's alleged hit-and-run killer. To extricate himself, he decides to solve the mystery himself; this independent detective work is a variation for Fletcher but allows the manipulation of suspense by having him avoid the police investigation which would charge him to uncover the real killer and the motives for both the murder and the frame attempt. This case is also different in allowing the suspect-detective a trusted family and a friend who can shield him from the police and assist in the investigation besides offering advice, support, and reassurance. As a result, the sheer terror and fear of the unknown are subordinated here to detection—despite the improbable collection of clues and unlikely conclusion.

In *Mirror Image,* the beautiful Robin Chodoff puts her own life on hold to solace her mother over the childhood kidnapping of her younger sister Marya; in the process, she postpones romance and investigates false claimants. This novel traces the surprisingly effective plot of one claimant and the talented troupe of gypsy actors who support her. Robin's life is threatened in a suspenseful, twisting plot which ultimately reveals the strength of her desire to be persuaded against her own common sense. The reader is misled along with the protagonist although our suspicions are naturally raised earlier than hers.

Fletcher's competently written suspense-mystery novels seldom vary from a predictable pattern: fear of the unknown, followed by relief of the tension, concluded with a destroying revelation which provides a distinctive twist to the plot. Nevertheless, they are generally satisfying examples of this variation of the genre.

—Kathleen Gregory Klein

FLORA, Fletcher. American. Born in Parsons, Kansas, 20 May 1914. Educated at Parsons Junior College, A.A. 1934; Kansas State College, Manhattan, B.S. 1938; University of Kansas, Lawrence, 1938–40. Served in the United States Army Infantry in New Guinea, Leyte, Luzon, 1943–45: Sergeant. Married Betty Ogden in 1940; three children. Teacher in public schools of Golden City, 1939–41, and Fairview High School, Missouri, 1941–42; Education adviser, Department of the Army, Fort Leavenworth, Kansas, 1945–63. *Died in 1968.*

CRIME PUBLICATIONS

Novels

Strange Sisters. New York, Lion, 1954.
Desperate Asylum. New York, Lion, 1955; as *Whisper of Love,* New York, Pyramid, 1959.
The Hot Shot. New York, Avon, 1956.
The Brass Bed. New York, Lion, 1956; London, Miller, 1959.
Let Me Kill You, Sweetheart. New York, Avon, 1958.
Leave Her to Hell. New York, Avon, 1958.
Whispers of the Flesh. New York, New American Library, 1958.
Park Avenue Tramp. New York, Fawcett, 1958; London, Fawcett, 1959.
Take Me Home. Derby, Connecticut, Monarch, 1959.
Wake Up with a Stranger. New York, New American Library, 1959.
Killing Cousins. New York, Macmillan, 1960; London, Cape, 1961.
Most Likely to Love. Derby, Connecticut, Monarch, 1960.
The Seducer. Derby, Connecticut, Monarch, 1961.
The Irrepressible Peccadillo. New York, Macmillan, 1962; London, Boardman, 1963.
Skuldoggery. New York, Belmont, 1967.
Hildegarde Withers Makes the Scene, with Stuart Palmer. New York, Random House, 1969.

Uncollected Short Stories

"The Two-Faced Corpse," in *New Detective* (New York), April 1952.
"Tall Guys Come High," in *Detective Story* (Kokomo, Indiana), November 1952.
"Torrid Zone," in *The Queen's Awards: 7th Series,* edited by Ellery Queen. Boston, Little Brown, 1952.
"So Lovely—and So Dead," in *Detective Tales* (Chicago), December 1952.
"The Heat is Killing Me," in *Dime Detective* (New York), February 1953.
"As I Lie Dead," in *Manhunt* (New York), February 1953.
"Pursued," in *Ellery Queen's Mystery Magazine* (New York), April 1953.
"Death in Waiting," in *Fifteen Detective Stories* (Kokomo, Indiana), December 1953.
"Heels Are for Hating," in *Manhunt* (New York), February 1954.
"Death Lives Here," in *Fifteen Detective Stories* (Kokomo, Indiana), June 1954.
"Points South," in *Manhunt* (New York), June 1954.
"Tough," in *Pursuit* (New York), July 1954.
"The Day It Began Again," in *Manhunt* (New York), April 1955.
"The Silent One," in *Hunted* (New York), December 1955.
"Handy Man," in *Manhunt* (New York), February 1956.
"Late Date with Death," in *Mike Shayne Mystery Magazine* (New York), October 1956.
"Three Gallons of Gas," in *Mike Shayne Mystery Magazine* (New York), August 1957.
"A Husband Is Missing," in *Alfred Hitchcock's Mystery Magazine* (New York), August 1957.
"Setup," in *Manhunt* (New York), November 1957.
"Loose Ends," in *Manhunt* (New York), August 1958.
"Of the Five Who Came," in *Alfred Hitchcock's Mystery Magazine* (New York), March 1959.

"Nine, Ten, and Die," in *Mystery Tales* (New York), June 1959.
"Sounds and Smells," in *Ed McBain's Mystery Book* (New York), 1962.
"The Spent Days," in *To Be Read Before Midnight,* edited by Ellery Queen. New York, Random House, 1962; London, Gollancz, 1963.
"Most Agreeably Poisoned" in *Alfred Hitchcock Presents: Hangman's Dozen.* New York, Dell, 1962.
"Dinner Will Be Cold," in *Alfred Hitchcock's Mystery Magazine* (New York), August 1963.
"Homicide and Gentlemen," in *Alfred Hitchcock Presents: 16 Skeletons from My Closet.* New York, Dell, 1963.
"Mrs. Dearly's Special Day," in *Ellery Queen's Double Dozen.* New York, Random House, 1964; as *19th Mystery Annual,* London, Gollancz, 1965.
"Cool Swim on a Hot Day," in *Alfred Hitchcock's Once upon a Dreadful Time.* New York, Dell, 1964.
"Six Reasons for Murder," in *Ellery Queen's Mystery Magazine,* (New York), March 1964.
"How? When? Who?," in *Ellery Queen's Mystery Magazine,* (New York), September 1964.
"The Satin-Quilted Box," in *Ellery Queen's Mystery Magazine* (New York), December 1964.
"The Tool," in *Alfred Hitchcock's Mystery Magazine* (New York), December 1964.
"The Capsule," in *Mike Shayne Mystery Magazine* (New York), December 1964.
"My Father Died Young," in *Ellery Queen's Mystery Magazine* (New York), July 1965.
"Tune Me In," in *Alfred Hitchcock's Anti-Social Register.* New York, Dell, 1965.
"Hink Dink," in *Mike Shayne Mystery Magazine* (New York), August 1965.
"Something Very Special," in *Alfred Hitchcock's Mystery Magazine* (New York), September 1965.
"Wait and See," in *The Saint* (New York), December 1965.
"Darling, You Deserve Me," in *Shell Scott Mystery Magazine* (New York), March 1966.
"Obituary," in *Man from U.N.C.L.E.* (New York), March 1966.
"Affair of the Gander's Shoes," in *Mike Shayne Mystery Magazine* (New York), April 1966.
"A Lesson in Reciprocity," in *Alfred Hitchcock's Mystery Magazine* (New York), August 1966.
"For Money Received," in *Alfred Hitchcock: Meet Death at Night.* London, New English Library, 1967.
"The Seasons Come, The Seasons Go," in *Ellery Queen's All-Star Lineup.* New York, New American Library, 1967; as *22nd Mystery Annual,* London, Gollancz, 1968.
"I'll Be Loving You," in *Alfred Hitchcock's Mystery Magazine* (New York), December 1967.
"The Scrap of Knowledge," in *Ellery Queen's Mystery Magazine* (New York), May 1968.
"Handle of the Pump," in *Mike Shayne Mystery Magazine* (New York), December 1968.
"A Word for Murder," in *Homicide Department,* edited by Ed McBain. London, New English Library, 1968.
"Where's Milo?" in *Alfred Hitchcock's Mystery Magazine* (New York), May 1969.
"Tutored to Death," in *Mike Shayne Mystery Magazine* (New York), July 1969.
"I'll Race You," in *Alfred Hitchcock's Mystery Magazine* (New York), August 1969.
"Two Bits Worth of Luck," in *Alfred Hitchcock's Mystery Magazine* (New York), May 1970.

"Bach in a Few Minutes," in *Alfred Hitchcock's Get Me to the Wake on Time.* New York, Dell, 1970.
"In the Shade of the Old Apple Tree," in *Crimes and Misfortunes,* edited by J. Francis McComas. New York, Random House, 1970.
"Beside a Flowering Wall," in *Alfred Hitchcock's Death Can Be Beautiful.* New York, Dell, 1972.
"The Invisible Gauntlet," in *Ellery Queen's Window of Mystery.* New York, Davis, 1980.
"The Witness Was a Lady," in *Alfred Hitchcock's Tales to Fill You with Fear and Trembling,* edited by Eleanor Sullivan. New York, Dial Press, 1980.
"Not Exactly Love," in *Alfred Hitchcock's Death-Reach,* edited by Cathleen Jordan. New York, Dial Press, 1982.
"Variations on an Episode," in *Alfred Hitchcock's Tales to Make You Quake and Quiver,* edited by Cathleen Jordan. New York, Dial Press, 1982.

OTHER PUBLICATIONS

Other

"Six Burrs in the Blanket," in *The Writer* (Boston), August 1967.

*　*　*

Fletcher Flora was a talented writer whose work received regrettably little attention during his lifetime. Although his short stories earned him considerable stature among editors, writers, and magazine readers, his novels—with one exception—were unsuccessful. Part of the reason for this was emphasis on style and characterization rather than on intricate plotting; but a much greater part seems to have been disinterested agents and publishers and poor advice. A case in point is *Skuldoggery,* a marvelously witty and clever mystery which was sold to one of the lesser paperback houses and given such poor distribution that few people have read it or even know that it exists. It deserves a far better fate.

Flora began writing for the detective pulps in the early 1950's and soon graduated to *Ellery Queen's Mystery Magazine, Manhunt, Alfred Hitchcock's Mystery Magazine,* and other digest crime periodicals. His only successful novel, *Killing Cousins* (Macmillan Cock Robin award) is a delightful tongue-in-cheek story of a lethal lady named Willie, and a fine example of Flora's literate, urbane, and sometimes lyrical style. Additional books of note are *Strange Sisters, The Hot Shot, The Irrespressible Peccadillo,* and the above-mentioned *Skuldoggery.*

Ironically, since Flora's death in 1968 a small cult following of his work has formed, but the fact that he was never able to realize his full potentiality is a tragic one.

—Bill Pronzini

FOLLETT, Ken(neth Martin). Also writes as Martin Martinsen; Symon Myles; Bernard L. Ross; Zachary Stone. British. Born in Cardiff, Glamorgan, 5 June 1949. Educated at University College, London, B.A. in philosophy 1970. Married 1) Mary Emma Ruth Elson in 1968 (separated 1984); one son and one daughter; 2) Barbara Broer in 1985. Reporter and rock music columnist, *South Wales Echo,* Cardiff, 1970–73; reporter, London *Evening News,* 1973–74; editorial director 1974–76, and deputy managing editor, 1976–77, Everest Books, London. Since 1977, full-time writer. Recipient: Mystery Writers of America Edgar Allan Poe award, 1979. Agent: Albert Zuckerman, Writers House Inc., 21 West 26th Street, New York, New York 10010, U.S.A. Address: P.O. Box 708, London SW10 ODH, England.

CRIME PUBLICATIONS

Novels (series: "Apples" Carstairs in Symon Myles books; Piers Roper)

The Big Black (as Symon Myles). London, Everest, 1974.
The Big Needle (as Simon Myles). London, Everest, 1974; as *The Big Apple,* New York, Zebra, 1975.
The Big Hit (as Symon Myles). London, Everest, 1975.
The Shakeout (Roper). Lewes, Sussex, Harwood Smart, 1975.
The Bear Raid (Roper). London, Harwood Smart, 1976.
The Modigliani Scandal (as Zachary Stone). London, Collins, 1976; as Ken Follett, New York, Morrow, 1985.
Paper Money (as Zachary Stone). London, Collins, 1977; as Ken Follett, New York, Morrow, 1987.
Storm Island. London, Macdonald, 1978; as *Eye of the Needle,* New York, Arbor House, 1978.
Triple. London, Macdonald, and New York, Arbor House, 1979.
The Key to Rebecca. London, Hamish Hamilton, and New York, Morrow, 1980.
The Man from St. Petersburg. London, Hamish Hamilton, and New York, Morrow, 1982.
Lie Down with Lions. London, Hamish Hamilton, 1985; New York, Morrow, 1986.

OTHER PUBLICATIONS

Play

Television Play: *Fringe Banking* (in *Target* series), 1978.

Other

The Secret of Kellerman's Studio (for children). London, Abelard Schuman, 1976; as *The Mystery Hideout,* New York, Morrow, 1990.
The Power Twins and the Worm Puzzle (as Martin Martinsen for children). London, Abelard Schuman, 1976.
Amoki: King of Legend (as Bernard L. Ross). London, Futura, 1976.
Capricorn One (as Bernard L. Ross). London, Futura, 1976; New York, Fawcett, 1978.
The Heist of the Century (as René Louis Maurice, with others). London, Fontana, 1978; as *The Gentlemen of 16 July,* New York, Arbor House, 1980; as *Under the Streets of Nice; The Bank Heist of the Century,* Bethesda, Maryland, National Press, 1986.
On Wings of Eagles. New York, Morrow, and London, Collins, 1983.
The Pillars of the Earth. New York, Morrow, and London, Macmillan, 1989.

*　*　*

Though all of his fiction is generally admired and he has also written non-fiction, Ken Follett's popularity and reputation rests primarily upon four novels—*Eye of the Needle (Storm*

Island), *The Key to Rebecca*, *Triple*, and *The Man from St. Petersburg*—which re-imagine modern history. Follett chooses a moment of international crisis, suggests what forces might have conspired to alter the outcome of that crisis, and spins a tale which sets his fictional history back upon its factual course. As he comments in the preface to *Eye of the Needle*, "one suspects that something like this must have happened."

Follett's plots generally follow a glossy, successful formula which begins by catapulting readers and characters into the moment of crisis. Then, often using flashbacks, he sketches the dramatic, often tragic, backgrounds of most of his major characters fully enough that they absorb readers' attention, and the story is off and running; it never slows until its breathtaking climax where action breaks off abruptly. Follett avoids anticlimatic denouement by simply abandoning falling action; instead, he appends final details in an epilogue, this section being the least persuasive because the tempo has been broken, the strong narrative thrust dismissed. Only *The Key to Rebecca*, a conjectural treatment of Rommel's defeat in Africa, incorporates closure as a legitimate chapter, and even there it has a flavor of afterthought. The pattern works, however, because at the climax of the plot, the heroes have achieved their goals—they have preserved history as we know it; they have defended a just cause; and they have demonstrated that one person can make a difference. The epilogues comfortingly suggest that worth merits happiness.

The formula also amalgamates hefty measures of heroic derring-do, chases, confrontations, historical verisimilitude (including the appearance of real figures such as Churchill, Rommel, Sadat, Andropov, and Pankhurst), patriotism, sex, and violence. These elements combine with the swift pace to solve Follett's chief auctorial problem, the fact that readers already know the ultimate outcome of the adventure. However, this knowledge becomes submerged in the wealth of action and descriptive detail and is replaced by compelling suspense arising from deadly personal conflict between protagonist and antagonist.

Even *Triple*, which initially pinpoints three important characters in its account of how Israel might have acquired nuclear capability, essentially boils down to the confrontation between two dedicated, determined characters: Nat Dickstein, an Israeli spy, and David Rostov, his Soviet counterpart. This pattern pertains in all four novels. As in *The Key to Rebecca*, Follett often employs yet another formulaic device; through their sexual relationship, hero and heroine regain emotional health. Lucy Rose, in *Eye of the Needle* is the only person who can stop Germany's crack agent, a merciless killer called The Needle, from destroying the Allies' invasion strategy. *The Man from St. Petersburg* is set in pre-World War I England where the Earl of Walden must strike a vital treaty with Russia before an assassin can eliminate the Czarist negotiator. Like the other protagonists, Lucy and Walden pass from arid isolation to involvement and fulfillment by meeting extraordinary challenges.

Neither Follett's heroes, his villains, nor the wide range of other effectively drawn characters are superpeople, though many perform superhuman feats; instead, they are flawed, struggling human beings who undergo personal torment, pain, and deprivation. His protagonists, representing the best in the national characters of their countries, become heroes because they must; their exciting stories entertain and reassure—such heroes, after all, *might* actually have existed.

—Jane S. Bakerman

———

FOOTNER, (William) Hulbert. Canadian. Born in Hamilton, Ontario, 2 April 1879. Educated in evening high school in New York City. Married Gladys Marsh in 1916; three daughters and two sons. Journalist: in New York, 1905, and Calgary, 1906; then freelance writer. Lived in Maryland. *Died 25 November 1944.*

CRIME PUBLICATIONS

Novels (series: Amos Lee Mappin; Rosika Storey)

The Fugitive Sleuth. London, Hodder and Stoughton, 1918.
Thieves' Wit. New York, Doran, 1918; London, Hodder and Stoughton, 1919.
The Substitute Millionaire. New York, Doran, 1919; London, Collins, 1921.
The Owl Taxi. New York, Doran, 1921; London, Collins, 1922.
The Deaves Affair. New York, Doran, and London, Collins, 1922.
Ramshackle House. New York, Doran, 1922; London, Collins, 1923; as *Mystery at Ramshackle House*, London, Collins, 1932.
Officer! New York, Doran, and London, Collins, 1924.
The Chase of the "Linda Belle." London, Hodder and Stoughton, 1925.
The Under Dogs (Storey). New York, Doran, and London, Collins, 1925.
Queen of Clubs. New York, Doran, 1927; London, Collins, 1928.
The Doctor Who Held Hands (Storey). London, Doubleday, and London, Collins, 1929; as *The Murderer's Challenge*, London, Collins, 1932.
A Self-Made Thief. New York, Doubleday, and London, Collins, 1929.
Anybody's Pearls. London, Hodder and Stoughton, 1929; New York, Doubleday, 1930.
The Mystery of the Folded Paper (Mappin). New York, Harper, and London, Collins, 1930.
Trial by Water. London, Hodder and Stoughton, 1930; New York, Farrar and Rinehart, 1931.
Easy to Kill (Storey). New York, Harper, and London, Collins, 1931.
Dead Man's Hat. New York, Harper, and London, Collins, 1932.
The Ring of Eyes. New York, Harper, and London, Collins, 1933.
Dangerous Cargo (Storey). New York, Harper, and London, Collins, 1934.
Murder Runs in the Family. New York, Harper, and London, Collins, 1934.
Scarred Jungle. New York, Harper, and London, Cassell, 1935.
The Whip-Poor-Will Mystery. New York, Harper, 1935; as *The New Made Grave*, London, Collins, 1935.
Murder of a Bad Man London, Collins, 1935; New York, Harper, 1936.
The Island of Fear. New York, Harper, and London, Cassell, 1936.
The Dark Ships. New York, Harper, and London, Collins, 1937.
The Obeah Murders. New York, Harper, 1937; as *Murder in the Sun*, London, Collins, 1938.
The Death of a Celebrity (Mappin). New York, Harper, and London, Collins, 1938.

The Murder That Had Everything (Mappin). New York, Harper, and London, Collins, 1939.
The Nation's Missing Guest (Mappin). New York, Harper, and London, Collins, 1939.
Murderer's Vanity (Mappin). New York, Harper, 1940; London, Collins, 1941.
Sinfully Rich. New York, Harper, and London, Collins, 1940.
Who Killed the Husband? (Mappin). New York, Harper, 1941; London, Collins, 1942.
The House with the Blue Door (Mappin). New York, Harper, 1942; London, Collins, 1943.
Death of a Saboteur (Mappin). New York, Harper, 1943; London, Collins, 1944.
Unneutral Murder (Mappin). New York, Harper, and London, Collins, 1944.
Orchids to Murder (Mappin). New York, Harper, and London, Collins, 1945.

Short Stories (series: Rosika Storey)

Madame Storey. New York, Doran, and London, Collins, 1926.
The Velvet Hand: New Madame Storey Mysteries. New York, Doubleday, and London, Collins, 1928.
The Viper London, Collins, 1930.
The Casual Murderer. London, Collins, 1932; Philadelphia, Lippincott, 1937; as *The Kidnapping of Madame Storey and Other Stories,* London, Collins, 1936.
The Almost Perfect Murder: More Madame Storey Mysteries. London, Collins, 1933; Philadelphia, Lippincott, 1937.
Tortuous Trails. London, Collins, 1937.

OTHER PUBLICATIONS

Novels

Two on the Trail: A Story of the Far Northwest. New York, Doubleday, and London, Methuen, 1911.
Jack Chanty: A Story of Athabasca. New York, Doubleday, 1913; London, Hodder and Stoughton, 1917.
The Sealed Valley. New York, Doubleday, 1914; London, Hodder and Stoughton, 1915.
The Fur-Bringers: A Tale of Athabasca. London, Hodder and Stoughton, 1916; New York, Coward McCann, 1920.
The Huntress. London, Hodder and Stoughton, 1917; New York, Coward McCann, 1922.
On Swan River. London, Hodder and Stoughton, 1919; as *The Woman from Outside,* New York, Coward McCann, 1921.
Country Love. London, Hodder and Stoughton, 1921.
The Wild Bird. New York, Doran, and London, Hodder and Stoughton, 1923.
Roger Manion's Girl. London, Hodder and Stoughton, 1925.
The Shanty Sled. London, Hodder and Stoughton, 1925; New York, Doran, 1926.
A Backwoods Princess. New York, Doran, and London, Hodder and Stoughton, 1926.
Antennae. New York, Doran, 1926; as *Rich Man, Poor Man,* London, Faber, 1928.
Cap'n Sue. London, Hodder and Stoughton, 1927; New York, Doubleday, 1928.
A New Girl in Town. London, Hodder and Stoughton, 1927.
More Than Bread. Philadelphia, Lippincott, and London, Faber, 1938.

Plays

Shirley Kaye (produced New York, 1916).

Screenplays: *The Millionaire,* with Wallace Clifton, 1921; *Youth to Youth,* with Edith Kennedy, 1922.

Other

New Rivers of the North. New York, Outing, 1912; London, Unwin, 1913.
New York, City of Cities. Philadelphia, Lippincott, 1937.
Charles Gift: Salute to a Maryland House of 1650. New York, Harper, 1939; London, Faber, 1940.
Sailor of Fortune: The Life and Adventures of Commodore Barney, U.S.N. New York, Harper, 1940.
Maryland Main and the Eastern Shore. New York, Appleton Century, 1942.
Rivers of the Eastern Shore. New York, Farrar and Rinehart, 1944.

* * *

Hulbert Footner, Canadian-born author, actor, playwright, and journalist, had an undistinguished literary style, with characters common to the detective thrillers of the 1920's and 1930's. His first books were adventure novels of the Canadian northwest, but he soon began writing thrillers and detective novels, usually set in New York, but occasionally in London, as in *Anybody's Pearls.*

The sleuths which Footner created were interesting and diversified although not always the hero or heroine of the yarn. The first was the youthful B. Enderby, then Amos Lee Mappin, who resembled Dickens's Mr. Pickwick, and finally the voluptuous but cool-headed Mme. Rosika Storey. Mme. Storey is portrayed in *The Under Dogs* as having deliberately cultivated a faculty of inspiring awe in other people. But, alone, with her assistant Bella she was "keen, human, lovable, and full of laughter." Amos Lee Mappin, wealthy author and criminologist, is the brains behind the solution of many of Footner's mysteries, although he rarely does any of the actual sleuthing himself, leaving the "dirty work" to his many friends and associates. Footner, an admirer and friend of the writer Christopher Morley, featured Morley as one of his main characters in *The Mystery of the Folded Paper.* In return, Christopher Morley wrote a touching biographical tribute to Footner in *Orchids to Murder,* published after Footner's death.

—Mary Ann Grochowski

FORBES, Colin. British. Born in Hampstead, London. Educated at the Lower School of John Lyon, Harrow. Married Jane Robertson. Agent: Elaine Green Ltd., 37 Goldhawk Road, London W12 8QQ, England.

CRIME PUBLICATIONS

Novels (series: Tweed, Paula Grey and Bob Newman)

Tramp in Armour. London, Collins, 1969; New York, Dutton, 1970.

The Heights of Zervos. London, Collins, 1970; New York, Dutton, 1971.

The Palermo Ambush. London, Collins, and New York, Dutton, 1972.

Target Five. London, Collins, and New York, Dutton, 1973.

Year of the Golden Ape. London, Collins, and New York, Dutton, 1974.

The Stone Leopard. London, Collins, 1975; New York, Dutton, 1976.

Avalanche Express. London, Collins, and New York, Dutton, 1976.

The Stockholm Syndicate. London, Collins, 1981; New York, Dutton, 1982.

Double Jeopardy (Tweed, Grey and Newman). London, Collins, 1982.

The Leader and the Damned. London, Collins, 1983; New York, Atheneum, 1984.

Terminal (Tweed, Grey and Newman). London, Collins, 1984; New York, Atheneum, 1985.

Cover Story (Tweed, Grey and Newman). London, Collins, 1985; New York, Atheneum, 1986.

The Janus Man (Tweed, Grey and Newman). London, Collins, and New York, Harcourt, 1988.

Deadlock (Tweed, Grey and Newman). London, Collins, 1988.

The Greek Key (Tweed, Grey and Newman). London, Collins, 1989.

Shockwave (Tweed, Grey and Newman). London, Pan, 1990.

Whirlpool (Tweed, Grey and Newman). London, Pan, 1991.

*

Colin Forbes comments:

My novels are basically thriller books, translated into twenty-two languages. They cover three different categories in each novel. They can be read as whodunnits, as adventure novels and as espionage thrillers. Tweed, Paula Grey and Bob Newman have now become established characters.

* * *

For the last two decades, Colin Forbes has been writing novels in the classic British thriller tradition—war and adventure in the 1970's, and blockbuster suspense in the 1980's.

Common to all of Forbes's books, however, are extensively researched international settings, vigorous plots, and continual movement. A beloved Forbesian narrative device is the roving omniscient point of view, in which the story advances by focussing on the thoughts and actions of one character after another. Forbes's best books display an expertise in maintaining swift-paced suspense while enlightening you in the arcana of foreign affairs, natural phenomena, history, and science. Many of the books are natural for the screen; *Avalanche Express* has been filmed, and five others have been optioned for film rights. A word of caution about the mysteries of names and attribution. According to Forbes himself, the nearly universal claim in reference books that Colin Forbes is a pseudonym of Raymond H. Sawkins is misinformed. Forbes has stated that all his books carry his own byline—which entails that the books usually attributed to the name Sawkins and its pennames Jay Bernard and Richard Raine were written by someone else.

Forbes's novels written in the 1970's sit squarely within the war and high adventure categories popularized by Alistair MacLean, Jack Higgins, and Ken Follett. These are Forbes's best known books. The well trod fields of World War II serve as the background for several of them. In *The Heights of Zervos*, set in 1941 Greece, Germany is preparing to invade. *The Palermo Ambush* is a commando story set in 1943, with four men braving the Gestapo, the SS, and the Carabinieri to sabotage a crucial train-ferry in Sicily. *Tramp in Armour* tells about a lone British tank in Nazi-infested Northern France fighting its way towards Dunkirk. In the little known *Target Five,* one of Forbes's finest, a top Soviet oceanographer wishes to defect to the U.S. across the Arctic icefields to meet an American icebreaker. Forbes does a superb job of fusing the deadly hazards of the Arctic to the more common race and chase motif, and his description of such mysterious Arctic phenomena as black frost and ghost icebergs is so expressive, haunting and magnificent that it approaches the lyrical. In *Avalanche Express,* a Politburo informer escapes to the West on the Atlantic Express, a train rushing through blizzards between Milan and Amsterdam via Zurich. Published before Mid-eastern politics became a wearisome thriller cliché, *Year of the Golden Ape* is a crisp authoritative story of Arab terrorism, as a British oil tanker booby-trapped with a plutonium device is sailed into the San Francisco harbor.

In the 1980's Forbes's books took on the characteristics of blockbuster suspense novels. A bit longer and more contemporary than the novels written in the 1970's, most of the 1980's thrillers feature Tweed, second-in-command in the British SIS, and Bob Newman, freelance foreign correspondent. *Terminal,* with its ambience of mystery and threat of biological warfare, outshines most of the later books. Its plot melds an aggressive and unexpected new nationalism with a fearful and realistic viral menace that seems quite genuine in today's Europe. Forbes's other themes also cluster towards international intrigue—a murder combined with possible defection from the U.S. in *Cover Story,* the risk of war with the Soviets in *Deadlock,* the hunt for an SIS mole in *The Janus Man,* and an international search for Tweed added to the rescue of a McGuffin-like computer in *Shockwave. The Stockholm Syndicate* is probably Forbes's most implausible book, about a super-secret, super-powerful international counterinsurgency squad whose mission is to quash a communist-funded conspiracy that's overtaking Europe. The book lacks Tweed and Newman, and suffers from irrelevant characters, poorly conceived situations, and vapid prose, such as this anticlimactic zonker about one of the villains: "You dared not ask him the wrong question. The penalty was to be instantly crossed off his list of social acquaintances."

Forbes's most serious, smoothly flowing, and accomplished novel is *The Leader and the Damned,* a superlative exemplar of that small but persistent subgenre, the speculative Hitler novel. Not to be dismissed because of its theme or the swastika on the cover, it is a thrilling and plausible historical conjecture about abrupt changes in Adolf Hitler's behavior during his last years. Whereas most authors treating this topic solemnly might entrap you in a thicket of historical detail, Forbes launches you immediately into the midst of a lightning plot. More than the other novels, it brilliantly demonstrates his insight into the psyche of his characters, and epitomizes his gift of weaving several plots seamlessly into one.

—Greg Goode

FORBES, Daniel. *See* **KENYON, Michael.**

FORBES, (Deloris Florine) Stanton. Also writes as De Forbes (D.E. Forbes); Forbes Rydell (with Helen Rydell); Tobias Wells. American. Born in Kansas City, Missouri, 10 July 1923. Educated at Wichita High School North, Kansas; Oklahoma A. and M. (now Oklahoma State University), Stillwater; University of Chicago. Married William J. Forbes, Jr., in 1948; one daughter and two sons. Assistant editor, Wellesley *Townsman,* Massachusetts, 1960–73; broadcaster, De Forbes talk show, Station PJD2, St. Martin, French West Indies, 1974–75. Owner and operator, with husband, of Pierre Lapin clothing shop and workshop, Grand Case, St. Martin. Address: Goetz House, Grand Case, St. Martin, French West Indies.

CRIME PUBLICATIONS

Novels

Grieve for the Past. New York, Doubleday, 1963; London, Gollancz, 1964.
The Terrors of the Earth. New York, Doubleday, 1964; as *The Long Hate,* London, Hale, 1966; as *Melody of Terror,* New York, Pyramid, 1967.
Relative to Death. New York, Doubleday, 1965; London, Hale, 1966.
Terror Touches Me. New York, Doubleday, and London, Hale, 1966.
A Business of Bodies. New York, Doubleday, 1966; London, Hale, 1967.
Encounter Darkness. New York, Doubleday, 1967; London, Hale, 1968.
If Two of Them Are Dead. New York, Doubleday, and London, Hale, 1968.
Go to Thy Death Bed. New York, Doubleday, 1968; London, Hale, 1969.
The Name's Death, Remember Me? New York, Doubleday, 1969; London, Hale, 1970.
She Was Only the Sheriff's Daughter. New York, Doubleday, and London, Hale, 1970.
If Laurel Shot Hardy the World Would End. New York, Doubleday, 1970; as *Murder Runs Riot,* London, Hale, 1971.
The Sad, Sudden Death of My Fair Lady. New York, Doubleday, and London, Hale, 1971.
All for One and One for Death. New York, Doubleday, 1971; London, Hale, 1972.
A Deadly Kind of Lonely. New York, Doubleday, 1971; London, Hale, 1973.
But I Wouldn't Want to Die There. New York, Doubleday, 1972; London, Hale, 1973.
Welcome, My Dear, to Belfrey House. New York, Doubleday, 1973; London, Hale, 1974.
Some Poisoned by Their Wives. New York, Doubleday, 1974; London, Hale, 1975.
Bury Me in Gold Lamé. New York, Doubleday, 1974; London, Hale, 1975.
Buried in So Sweet a Place. New York, Doubleday, 1977; London, Hale, 1978.
The Will and Last Testament of Constance Cobble. New York, Doubleday, and London, Hale, 1980.
Don't Die on Me, Billie Jean. New York, Doubleday, 1987.

Novels as Forbes Rydell (with Helen Rydell)

Annalisa. New York, Dodd Mead, 1959; London, Gollancz, 1960.
If She Should Die. New York, Doubleday, and London, Gollancz, 1961.
They're Not Home Yet (by Forbes alone). New York, Doubleday, and London, Gollancz, 1962.
No Questions Asked. New York, Doubleday, and London, Gollancz, 1963.

Novels as Tobias Wells (series: Knute Severson in all books)

A Matter of Love and Death. New York, Doubleday, and London, Gollancz, 1966.
What Should You Know of Dying? New York, Doubleday, and London, Gollancz, 1967.
Dead by the Light of the Moon. New York, Doubleday, 1967; London, Gollancz, 1968.
Murder Most Fouled Up. New York, Doubleday, 1968; London, Hale, 1969.
Die Quickly, Dear Mother. New York, Doubleday, and London, Hale, 1969.
The Young Can Die Protesting. New York, Doubleday, 1969; London, Hale, 1970.
Dinky Died. New York, Doubleday, and London, Hale, 1970.
The Foo Dog. New York, Doubleday, 1971; as *The Lotus Affair,* London, Hale, 1973.
What to Do Until the Undertaker Comes. New York, Doubleday, 1971; London, Hale, 1973.
How to Kill a Man. New York, Doubleday, 1972; London, Hale, 1973.
A Die in the Country. New York, Doubleday, 1972; London, Hale, 1974.
Brenda's Murder. New York, Doubleday, 1973; London, Hale, 1974.
Have Mercy upon Us. New York, Doubleday, 1974; London, Hale, 1975.
Hark, Hark, The Watchdogs Bark. New York, Doubleday, 1975; London, Hale, 1976.
A Creature Was Stirring. New York, Doubleday, 1977; London, Hale, 1978.

Uncollected Short Stories as De Forbes (D.E. Forbes)

"Suffer Little Children," in *Manhunt* (New York), March 1956.
". . . Puddin' and Pie . . . ," in *Manhunt* (New York), August 1956.
"Lie Down—You're Dead," in *Mike Shayne Mystery Magazine* (New York), November 1956.
"I Dig You, Real Cool," in *Manhunt* (New York), December 1956.
"The Secret Secret Secret," in *Mike Shayne Mystery Magazine* (New York), December 1956.
"Just Watching," in *Alfred Hitchcock's Mystery Magazine* (New York), February 1957.
"New Girl," in *Manhunt* (New York), May 1957.
"So I Can Forget," in *Ellery Queen's Mystery Magazine* (New York), May 1957.
"In a Neat Package," in *Mike Shayne Mystery Magazine* (New York), June 1957.
"Who Screamed?," in *Alfred Hitchcock's Mystery Magazine* (New York), June 1957.
"The Fifth One," in *Mike Shayne Mystery Magazine* (New York), December 1957.
"Speak No Evil," in *The Saint* (New York), March 1958.

"Stage Fright," in *Manhunt* (New York), June 1958.

"The High Cost of Dying," in *Alfred Hitchcock's Mystery Magazine* (New York), June 1958.

"A Mind Burns Slowly," in *Alfred Hitchcock's Mystery Magazine* (New York), August 1960.

"Flora Africana," in *Alfred Hitchcock's Mystery Magazine* (New York), April 1962.

"The Courtship of Jingoe Moon," in *Alfred Hitchcock's Mystery Magazine* (New York), November 1966.

"Quetzelcoatl," in *Murder in Mind,* edited by Lawrence Treat. New York, Dutton, 1967.

"The Day of the Inchworms," in *Alfred Hitchcock's Mystery Magazine* (New York), April 1968.

"My Sister Annabelle," in *Best of the Best Detective Stories,* edited by Allen J. Hubin. New York, Dutton, 1971.

*

Manuscript Collection: Mugar Memorial Library, Boston University.

Stanton Forbes comments:

Writing has been, for me, a distinct pleasure, a privilege, a duty, the Hyde to my Jekyll or vice versa. Often asked when and/or how did you begin to write mysteries I answer, "I didn't *begin,* it was always there" (no answer at all, but the truth). When asked where do you get your ideas, I answer, "From a question, 'What If?'" (again perhaps no answer at all). At any rate, to the powers that be who gave me the desire and the will and a certain natural aptitude with words I say, "Thank you!" That I didn't (so far—who knows?) do a better job with my tools is my fault.

*   *   *

The lady who publishes under the names of Stanton Forbes and Tobias Wells, among others, is one of the most prolific of American women in mystery. It follows that she is also one of the most proficient. She writes of people, everyday people, not rich and not poor, not famous or infamous, just people who find themselves involved in ordinary murders arising out of the troubles in their own neighborhoods. More often than not the narrator is an author who must get on with her fictional problems while helping to discover the cause of the real ones.

For the most part her background is the small town, sometimes in the midwest, sometimes New England, and recently the Caribbean island of St. Martin. Tobias Wells has moved there as has her writer character, Constance Cobble. Although her Massachusetts detective, Knute Severson, is on deck in *Hark, Hark, The Watchdogs Bark,* island customs and its people are the plot movers.

As Stanton Forbes, she wrote one of the finest mysteries of the 1960's, *Grieve for the Past.* It is a beautifully crafted story, told with the quiet simplicity that intensifies impact. The time is the 1930's, an ordinary summer in the "small town city" of Wichita, Kansas. It is the 15th summer of Ramona, the narrator. In the heat which characterizes a Kansas summer, an extraordinary double murder takes place in the neighborhood. How she divines the murderer is written with a gifted hand, moving to a climax wherein one feels that even a breath will topple its perfection.

It is unfortunate that the prolific writer more often than not is taken for granted. That Tobias Wells and Stanton Forbes can write better than many of her less active peers has been evident over and again. There is always an engrossing story in her

books, each with its well-made plot and its characters who are real, not puppets.

—Dorothy B. Hughes

———

FORD, Elbur. *See* **HOLT, Victoria.**

———

FORD, Leslie. Pseudonym for Zenith Brown, née Jones; also wrote as Brenda Conrad; David Frome. American. Born in Smith River, California, 8 December 1898. Educated at the University of Washington, Seattle, 1917–21. Married Ford K. Brown in 1921 (died 1977); one daughter. Assistant, departments of Greek and Philosophy, 1918–21, and Instructor and teaching assistant, Department of English, 1921–23, University of Washington; assistant to editor and circulation manager, *Dial* magazine, New York, 1922–23. After 1927, freelance writer. Correspondent for United States Air Force in the Pacific and England during World War II. *Died 1 September 1983.*

CRIME PUBLICATIONS

Novels (series: Lieutenant Joseph Kelly; Grace Latham; Colonel John Primrose)

The Sound of Footsteps. New York, Doubleday, 1931; as *Footsteps on the Stairs,* London, Gollancz, 1931.

By the Watchman's Clock. New York, Farrar and Rinehart, 1932.

Murder in Maryland (Kelly). New York, Farrar and Rinehart, 1932; London, Hutchinson, 1933.

The Clue of the Judas Tree (Kelly). New York, Farrar and Rinehart, 1933.

The Strangled Witness (Primrose). New York, Farrar and Rinehart, 1934.

Burn Forever. New York, Farrar and Rinehart, 1935; as *Mountain Madness,* London, Hutchinson, 1935.

Ill Met by Moonlight (Latham; Primrose). New York, Farrar and Rinehart, and London, Collins, 1937.

The Simple Way of Poison (Latham; Primrose). New York, Farrar and Rinehart, 1937; London, Collins, 1938.

Three Bright Pebbles (Latham). New York, Farrar and Rinehart, and London, Collins, 1938.

Reno Rendezvous (Latham; Primrose). New York, Farrar and Rinehart, 1939; as *Mr. Cromwell Is Dead,* London, Collins, 1939.

False to Any Man (Latham; Primrose). New York, Scribner, 1939; as *Snow-White Murder,* London, Collins, 1940.

The Town Cried Murder. New York, Scribner, and London, Collins, 1939.

Old Lover's Ghost (Latham; Primrose). New York, Scribner, 1940.

Road to Folly. New York, Scribner, 1940; London, Collins, 1941.

The Murder of a Fifth Columnist (Latham; Primrose). New York, Scribner, 1941; as *The Capital Crime,* London, Collins, 1941.

Murder in the O.P.M. (Latham; Primrose). New York, Scribner, 1942; as *The Priority Murder,* London, Collins, 1943.

Murder with Southern Hospitality. New York, Scribner, 1942; as *Murder Down South,* London, Collins, 1943.

Siren in the Night (Latham; Primrose). New York, Scribner, 1943; London, Collins, 1944.

All for the Love of a Lady (Primrose). New York, Scribner, 1944; as *Crack of Dawn,* London, Collins, 1945.

The Philadelphia Murder Story (Latham; Primrose). New York, Scribner, and London, Collins, 1945.

Honolulu Story (Latham; Primrose). New York, Scribner, 1946; as *Honolulu Murder Story,* London, Collins, 1947; as *Honolulu Murders,* New York, Popular Library, 1967.

The Woman in Black (Latham; Primrose). New York, Scribner, 1947; London, Collins, 1948.

The Devil's Stronghold (Latham; Primrose). New York, Scribner, and London, Collins, 1948.

Date with Death. New York, Scribner, 1949; as *Shot in the Dark,* London, Collins, 1949.

Murder Is the Pay-Off. New York, Scribner, and London, Collins, 1951.

The Bahamas Murder Case. New York, Scribner, and London, Collins, 1952.

Washington Whispers Murder (Latham; Primrose). New York, Scribner, 1953; as *The Lying Jade,* London, Collins, 1953.

Invitation to Murder. New York, Scribner, 1954; London, Collins, 1955.

Murder Comes to Eden. New York, Scribner, 1955; London, Collins, 1956.

The Girl from the Mimosa Club. New York, Scribner, and London, Collins, 1957.

Trial by Ambush. New York, Scribner, 1962; as *Trial from Ambush,* London, Collins, 1962.

Novels as David Frome (series: Major Gregory Lewis; Evan Pinkerton)

The Murder of an Old Man (Lewis). London, Methuen, 1929.

In at the Death. London, Skeffington, 1929; New York, Longman, 1930.

The Hammersmith Murders (Pinkerton). New York, Doubleday, and London, Methuen, 1930.

The Strange Death of Martin Green (Lewis). New York, Doubleday, 1931; as *The Murder on the Sixth Hole,* London, Methuen, 1931.

Two Against Scotland Yard (Pinkerton). New York, Farrar and Rinehart, 1931; as *The By-Pass Murder,* London, Longman, 1932.

The Man from Scotland Yard (Pinkerton). New York, Farrar and Rinehart, 1932; as *Mr. Simpson Finds a Body,* London, Longman, 1933.

The Eel Pie Murders (Pinkerton). New York, Farrar and Rinehart, and London, Longman, 1933.

Scotland Yard Can Wait! New York, Farrar and Rinehart, 1933; as *That's Your Man, Inspector!,* London, Longman, 1934.

Mr. Pinkerton Goes to Scotland Yard. New York, Farrar and Rinehart, 1934; as *Arsenic in Richmond,* London, Longman, 1934.

Mr. Pinkerton Finds a Body. New York, Farrar and Rinehart, 1934; as *The Body in the Turl,* London, Longman, 1935.

Mr. Pinkerton Grows a Beard. New York, Farrar and Rinehart, 1935; as *The Body in Bedford Square,* London, Longman, 1935.

Mr. Pinkerton Has the Clue. New York, Farrar and Rinehart, and London, Longman, 1936.

The Black Envelope: Mr. Pinkerton Again. New York, Farrar and Rinehart, 1937; as *The Guilt Is Plain,* London, Longman, 1938.

Mr. Pinkerton at the Old Angel. New York, Farrar and Rinehart, and London, Longman, 1939.

Homicide House: Mr. Pinkerton Returns. New York, Rinehart, 1950; as *Murder on the Square,* London, Hale, 1951.

Novels as Brenda Conrad

The Stars Give Warning. New York, Scribner, 1941.

Caribbean Conspiracy. New York, Scribner, 1942.

Girl with a Golden Bar. New York, Scribner, 1944.

Short Stories

Passage for One (as David Frome). New York, Royce, 1945.

Uncollected Short Stories

"Visitor in the Night," in *American Magazine* (Springfield, Ohio), July 1939.

"Death Stops at a Tourist Camp," in *The Mystery Book.* New York, Farrar and Rinehart, 1939.

"The Clock Strikes," in *The Second Mystery Book.* New York, Farrar and Rinehart, 1940.

"The Farewell Party," in *The Third Mystery Book.* New York, Farrar and Rinehart, 1941.

"Story of Jenny Wingate" (novel), in *Collier's* (Springfield, Ohio), 17 February-10 March 1945.

"Jealousy" (novel), in *Collier's* (Springfield, Ohio), 6 April-27 April 1946.

"The Collapsing Clues," in *My Favorite True Mystery,* edited by Ernest V. Heyn. New York, Coward McCann, 1954.

"Death of a Quiet Girl," in *American Weekly* (New York), 21 February 1954.

"The Lonely Hearts Case," in *American Weekly* (New York), 14 March 1954.

"The Lively Corpse," in *American Weekly* (New York), 9 May 1954.

Uncollected Short Stories as David Frome

"Mr. Pinkerton Is Present," in *American Magazine* (Springfield, Ohio), October 1936.

"Mr. Pinkerton Lends a Hand," in *The Second Mystery Book.* New York, Farrar and Rinehart, 1940.

"The Policeman's Cape," in *The Third Mystery Book.* New York, Farrar and Rinehart, 1941.

"The Man on the Iron Palings," in *Ellery Queen's Mystery Magazine* (New York), December 1953.

OTHER PUBLICATIONS

Other

"Why Murder Fascinates Me," in *Good Housekeeping* (New York), May 1940.

*

Manuscript Collection: St. John's College Library, Annapolis, Maryland.

*   *   *

The hallmark of Mrs. Zenith Brown (under her Leslie Ford and David Frome pseudonyms) was the use of a variety of interesting places with accurate descriptions of local scenery, manners, and mores. Her earliest mysteries date from a time when her husband was doing research in Oxford, and she had extra time to devote to writing.

Accepting the conventional wisdom of the time that mysteries by men sold better than those of women, she adopted the name David Frome for her first book *The Murder of an Old Man*. She continued to write as Frome, and Ellery Queen wrote, "She soaked in so much local color and acquired so much familiarity with English idiom that . . . no one dreamed she was an American." When the Browns returned to the United States, Mrs. Brown began to write books with American backgrounds, adopting a second, androgynous pseudonym, Leslie Ford, which eventually became far better known than "Frome."

At first Ford described the Maryland scene, basing the college town in *By the Watchman's Clock* on Annapolis, the site of St. John's College. Other early mysteries with Maryland settings include *Murder in Maryland* and *Ill Met by Moonlight*. Roaming only slighter farther afield, she used Washington D.C.'s Georgetown in *The Simple Way of Poison* and the Supreme Court Building in the 1935 novelet "The Clock Strikes."

As Ford became more successful she was able to combine a love of travel with the opportunity to do research at different locations. Frome mysteries like *Mr. Pinkerton Finds a Body* and *Mr. Pinkerton Grows a Beard* reflect visits to Oxford and the British Museum. More often, she travelled in the United States, where she described restored colonial Williamsburg, Virginia, in *The Town Cried Murder*, Yellowstone National Park in *Old Lover's Ghost*, the historic Garden Club Pilgrimage of Natchez, Mississippi, in *Murder with Southern Hospitality*, and Hawaii in *Honolulu Story*. One of her best was *Siren in the Night*, a portrait of an attractive city, San Francisco, as well as a good description of attitudes, especially toward those of Japanese ancestry, shortly after the attack on Pearl Harbor. Washington politics and gossip were often used, most notably in *Murder in the O.P.M.*, *The Woman in Black*, and *Washington Whispers Murder*, the last named one of the few mystery stories about McCarthyism.

Holding a belief contrary to Raymond Chandler's of restricting murder mysteries to "the mean streets," Brown wrote of murder as committed by the wealthy, urbane, and intelligent. She once said she was only interested in "murder done by people I can understand—people I might play bridge with or dine with. That kind of murder is a powerfully compelling, even primitive impulse that lies deep, dormant in every one of us."

Though she created two famous detective teams, the detection in her novels does not measure up to the backgrounds. As Frome she wrote of the rabbity Mr. Pinkerton and his friend Sergeant Bull. Deduction is minimal, with Pinkerton literally stumbling over dead bodies and figuratively stumbling into solutions. As Ford she wrote of middle-aged Colonel Primrose, ex-U.S. Army Intelligence who continues his career as an investigator, assisted by his loyal army aide Sergeant Buck. In *Ill Met by Moonlight* Ford introduced Grace Latham, an attractive Georgetown widow, to the team. Though Latham is a fairly sensible, independent person, Brown apparently felt that the conventions of her era required her to wander

senselessly into danger, and the Colonel shows up to rescue her and solve the case. His solutions are often without air-tight detection and may involve information withheld from the reader. The Primrose-Latham relationship grows warmer, but never beyond the platonic state.

Ford was extremely popular, especially with readers of *The Saturday Evening Post* where much of her work was originally serialized. She received her best reviews for such non-series books as *The Bahamas Murder Case* and her last book, *Trial by Ambush*, which, in anticipation of another era, dealt (albeit discreetly) with rape. Her series books suffered by comparison because she had too many sleuths in each, thus diffusing reader identification.

—Marvin Lachman

————

FOREST, Norman. *See* **MORLAND, Nigel.**

————

FORREST, Katherine V. Canadian. Born in Windsorm Ontario, 29 April 1939. Educated at Cass Technical High School; Detroit, Michigan, Wayne State University, Detroit; University of California, Los Angeles. Address: P.O. Box 25225, Los Angeles, California 90025, U.S.A.

CRIME PUBLICATIONS

Novels (series: Kate Delafield in all books)

Amateur City. Tallahassee, Florida, Naiad Press, 1984; London, Women's Press, 1987.
Murder at the Nightwood Bar. Tallahassee, Florida, Naiad Press, and London, Pandora Press, 1987.
The Beverly Malibu. Tallahassee, Florida, Naiad Press, 1989; London, Pandora Press, 1990.

Short Stories

Dreams and Swords. Tallahassee, Florida, Naiad Press, 1987.

Uncollected Short Story

"Jessie," in *Finale*. Boston, Massachusetts, Alyson, 1989.

OTHER PUBLICATIONS

Novels

Curious Wine. Tallahassee, Florida, Naiad Press, 1983.
Daughters of a Coral Dawn. Tallahassee, Florida, Naiad Press, 1984.
An Emergence of Green. Tallahassee, Florida, Naiad Press, 1986; London, Silver Moon Press, 1990.

*

Katherine V. Forrest comments:
Amateur City, Murder at the Nightwod Bar, The Beverly Malibu, and the short story "Jessie", feature a Los Angeles

Police Department homicide detective named Kate Delafield. She is 38 as the series opens, and a closeted lesbian. My objective in writing this series is not only to create entertaining fiction, but to portray a lesbian life in process—a woman in a high-pressure, high-visibility profession. How she handles her sexuality under the circumstances of a totally homophobic police department, how she maintains her integrity—these issues form the subtext for the Kate Delafield novels.

*   *   *

Among readers of crime fiction, Katherine V. Forrest is known for her three Kate Delafield novels: *Amateur City,* which immediately established her as an exciting new presence on the crime scene, *Murder at the Nightwood Bar,* and *The Beverly Malibu.* Like many of the recent lesbian/femininist practitioners of the crime novel, Forrest has apparently appropriated this popular fiction genre in order to challenge its conservative politics and its often negative or reactionary images of women. Unlike some of her lesbian and/or feminist sisters Forrest also contrives to construct taut and plausible plots that keep the reader eagerly turning the page for the denouement.

Forrest's Kate Delafield is unusual among the new breed of femininist sleuths in that she is a lesbian, who, instead of inhabiting the radical-lesbian world of women's groups, collectives and left-political activism, is a hard working full-time member of the Los Angeles Police Department. The Delafield stories belong to that comparatively rare breed of feminist crime novel—the police procedural. Forrest makes much of Kate's patient detective work, the hard, unglamorous slog of work in the homicide division, as she carefully follows all the correct procedures, and observes all the (to the police) restrictive legislation that slows down the detective process but preserves civil liberties. Kate is a successful professional, who is tough, tenacious, and shrewd. She is a very positive role model of a woman who has made it in an emphatically male, and frequently mysogynistic world. Delafield's career in police work seems to have been chosen partly for its ability to express her self-perceived "butch" identity, but she is not simply the hard *femme* equivalent of the tough guy cop, and is far from impervious to the routine horrors of her daily work.

Delafield's professionalism is tested in cases which raise questions about the boundaries of her professional and personal lives. In *Murder at the Nightwood Bar,* for example, the scene of the crime is a Los Angeles lesbian bar whose habituees, and particularly Maggie Schaeffer its owner, challenge Delafield's own way of living her lesbian life. Delafield has long ago decided that being an "out" lesbian is not an option for someone who wishes to succeed in the Los Angeles police force. However, in this story, which turns on mysteries of sexual exploitation and child abuse, Kate not only solves her case, she also resolves some of her own uncertainties and timidities. When the case is completed she proudly, but discreetly joins her new friends on the Gay Pride March.

The most recent Delafield case, *The Beverly Malibu,* raises similar tensions between the detective's personal and professional lives as she becomes emotionally and sexually involved with two of the potential suspects in the murder case which she and her partner, Ed Taylor, are called out to investigate on Thanksgiving Day. The case in question is a premeditated and particularly ghoulish murder in a Los Angeles apartment block—the Beverly Malibu. Everyone in this building would appear to have a motive for the murder of Owen Sinclair, a superannuated, unsuccessful Hollywood director. The early stages of the novel focus minutely on police procedure, as Kate and Taylor go through the routines of arranging for the autopsy, the bagging-up of the contents of the victim's apartment, and the interviewing of each of the building's residents in turn. These interviews are wonderful vignettes, which set up a series of individual dramas, and also establish a cast of interesting eccentrics, including the building's owner Hazel Turner, who keeps the ashes of her dead husband Jerome in four separate urns so that she always has him on hand for conversation and advice.

As usual Forrest reverses the sexual stereotypes. It is Taylor, Delafield's irascible and bone-headed partner, who goes for the "gut reaction" (the male equivalent of "feminine intuition") and fixes on a suspect despite flaws in the evidence. Both partners miss important clues, not because they are obtuse (Taylor), or emotionally distracted (Delafield), but because the indications in question only becomes clues after the event, when the pattern of the case has been built up. As in the other Delafield mysteries the reader is kept guessing until the end.

Like *Murder at the Nightwood Bar* (whose Maggie Schaeffer also makes a brief and humorous appearance here to provide affectionately cynical advice on Kate's love life), *The Beverly Malibu* involves its detective-heroine in a reassessment of her sexuality. In this respect it engages in the debates about the nature of lesbian desire and the range of lesbian sexualities which preoccupy a number of recent lesbian/feminist crime writers. Forrest has the advantage of being both more sucessful as an erotic writer, and less preachy than some of her contemporaries. Like other feminist crime writers Forrest also engages in wider political questions. The continual challenge that faces Kate of reconciling her marginalised sexual identity with her conformist and potentially oppressive police work is one particularly important political focus in all of the novels. The politics of the family, and problems of social deprivation underlie *Murder at the Nightwood Bar.* In *The Beverly Malibu* the central plot role of Owen Sinclair's involvement in the House un-American Activities Committee, raises again important questions about truth, justice and the American way of life.

Like many of the new breed of lesbian/feminist crime writers Forrest writes with wit and verve, and a great sense of relish in her own revisions and disruptions of the conventions of the police procedural genre.

—Lyn Pykett

FORREST, Richard (Stockton). Also writes as Stockton Woods. American. Born in Orange, New Jersey, 8 May 1932. Attended New York Dramatic Workshop, 1950; University of South Carolina, Columbia, 1953–55. Served in the United States Army Infantry in Korea, 1951–54: Staff Sergeant. Married 1) Frances Anne Reese in 1952 (divorced 1955), one son; 2) Mary Bolan Brumby in 1955, five children. Branch manager, Lawyers Title Insurance Company, Hartford, Connecticut, 1958–68; vice president, Chicago Title Insurance Company, Hartford, 1968–72. Since 1972 full-time writer. Recipient: Mystery Writers of America award, 1975. Agent: Phyllis Westberg, Harold Ober Associates, 40 East 49th Street, New York, New York 10017. Address: Box 724, Old Saybrook, Connecticut 06475, U.S.A.

CRIME PUBLICATIONS

Novels (series: Lyon and Bea Wentworth) in all books except *Who Killed Mr. Garland's Mistress?* and *The Killing Edge*)

Who Killed Mr. Garland's Mistress? New York, Pinnacle, 1974.
A Child's Garden of Death. Indianapolis, Bobbs Merrill, 1975; London, Hale, 1979.
The Wizard of Death. Indianapolis, Bobbs Merrill, 1977; London, Hale, 1978.
Death Through the Looking Glass. Indianapolis, Bobbs Merrill, 1978; London, Hale, 1979.
The Death in the Willows. New York, Holt Rinehart, 1979; London, Hale, 1980.
The Killing Edge. New York, Tower, 1980.
Death at Yew Corner. New York, Holt Rinehart, and London, Hale, 1981.
Death Under the Lilacs. New York, St. Martin's Press, 1985.
Death on the Mississippi. New York, St. Martin's Press, 1989.

Novels as Stockton Woods

The Laughing Man. New York, Fawcett, 1980.
Game Bet. New York, Fawcett, 1981.
The Man Who Heard Too Much. New York, Fawcett, 1983.

Uncollected Short Stories

"Mark of the Beast," in *Mystery Monthly* (New York), August 1976.
"Return of the Beast," in *Mystery Monthly* (New York), December 1976.
"With Forked Tongue," in *Mystery Monthly* (New York), March 1977.
"The Headmaster Helps One of His Boys," in *Ellery Queen's Mystery Magazine* (New York), 27 January 1982.

*

Manuscript Collection: Mugar Memorial Library, Boston University.

Richard Forrest comments:

I believe that my primary work to date is the Lyon and Bea Wentworth series of mystery novels. In these books, the ambience in the Wentworths' milieu is as important as the mysteries they become involved in. Lyon, a children's book writer and basically a gentle man, is deeply in love with his wife, Bea, a feisty state senator and feminist. Other friends, the huge Rocco Herbert, chief of police in the small town where the Wentworths reside, and Kim, Bea's assistant, complete the inner circle.

The mysteries are often locked-room murders, either in the traditional sense or open-air impossible disappearances such as flying airplanes that disappear. There are always traditional clues which when combined with Lyon's unique turn of mind provide interesting denouements.

It is hoped that there is an underlying theme throughout the series which encompasses the main precept by which the Wentworths govern their lives, that is to say, their full commitment to "a reverence for life."

*   *   *

Richard Forrest's novels of crime in Connecticut villages should appeal to many readers. They combine the intricate puzzle plotting of classic murder mysteries with the portrayal of corruption in high places that characterize hard-boiled detective fiction. Moreover, they evoke individual human pain with the heightened immediacy that distinguishes the best recent mystery novels from their more distanced predecessors. Forrest presents this mixture in consistently graceful prose and adds reasonably restrained moments of sex and violence.

Most of the novels feature Lyon Wentworth—former English professor, writer of books for children, and astute, if sometimes reluctant, amateur sleuth. Wentworth works with Rocco Herbert, chief of the Murphysville police. The two men met in Korea, where Wentworth served in Army intelligence, coordinating information Herbert gathered as a ranger captain. Bea Wentworth, Lyon's wife, is a successful politician, holding various public offices in various novels, and her ability to wrest information rapidly from state bureaucracies frequently helps Wentworth and Herbert in their investigations. Kimberly Ward is another recurring character; she came to Nutmeg Hill (the Wentworths' house) to lead welfare mothers in a protest march and stayed to become Bea's trusted aide.

As even these brief descriptions suggest, Forrest is uncomfortable with stereotypical assumptions; more accurately, he alerts his readers to the oversimplifications inherent in such assumptions. For example, the history of Wentworth and Herbert's friendship might lead one to expect a schematic contrast of brains and brawn. But the original relationship of information-gatherer to interpreter is more complicated in civilian than in military life. Herbert often draws intelligent inferences, and Wentworth not only accompanies the police chief on investigations, but also frequently searches on his own—sailing his hot air balloon over the scene of a crime (*A Child's Garden of Death*), consorting with a nasty motorcycle gang (*The Wizard of Death*), or attending a dinner party only Charles Addams could illustrate adequately (*Death at Yew Corner*). Too, Forrest presents one mobster who reads Proust and another who has made his home a haven of Japanese style and serenity. And I must admit that more than once, after the initial description of a character, I have been jolted by the pronoun *she* where I had expected *he*. These are subtle touches, never preachy, but they add up to acute social observations.

Forrest weaves this social commentary into gratifying versions of the mystery genre. In fact, as he describes Lyon Wentworth's books for children, Forrest reveals much about his own purposes in writing and about the emotional appeal of murder mysteries in general. Wentworth wrote his Ph.D. dissertation on violence in Victorian children's literature; not surprisingly, then, he is conscious of the power of literature to exorcise fears, to render private terrors manageable. His children's books present the ultimate victories of benign monsters; similarly, Forrest's own books recount the ultimate defeats of adults made monstrous by greed. And much as the titles of Wentworth's books suggest highly particularized settings (e.g., *The Cat in the Capitol* or *The Monster on the Mantel*), so Forrest carefully delineates the technical and sociological milieu of each novel—whether a toy factory in *Death Through the Looking Glass* or an automobile dealership in *The Killing Edge*.

Forrest's novels are well-written, with thoroughly realized backgrounds and persuasively likeable characters. Occasionally in the earliest books, the machinery of planning creaks a bit too obviously, but the care and craft with which Forrest approaches his writing have led to increasing subtlety. There is nothing slapdash here; above all, Richard Forrest writes *thoughtful* mysteries, socially conscious and emotionally satisfying.

—Susan Baker

FORSYTH, Frederick. British. Born in Ashford, Kent, in 1938. Educated at Tonbridge School, Kent. Served in the Royal Air Force 1956–58. Married; two children. Journalist, *Eastern Daily Press,* Norwich, and in King's Lynn, Norfolk, 1958–61; reporter for Reuters, London, Paris, and East Berlin, 1961–65; reporter, BBC Radio and Television, London, 1965–67; assistant diplomatic correspondent, BBC, 1967–68; freelance journalist in Nigeria, 1968–70; presenter, *Soldiers* television programme, 1985. Recipient: Mystery Writers of America Edgar Allan Poe award, 1971, 1983. Lives in London. Address: c/o Hutchinson, 62-65 Chandos Place, London WC2N 4NW, England.

CRIME PUBLICATIONS

Novels

The Day of the Jackal. London, Hutchinson, and New York, Viking Press, 1971.
The Odessa File. London, Hutchinson, and New York, Viking Press, 1972.
The Dogs of War. London, Hutchinson, and New York, Viking Press, 1974.
The Devil's Alternative. London, Hutchinson, 1979; New York, Viking Press, 1980.
The Fourth Protocol. London, Hutchinson, and New York, Viking Press, 1984.
The Negotiator. London, and New York, Bantam, 1989.

Short Stories

No Comebacks: Collected Short Stories. London, Hutchinson, and New York, Viking Press, 1982.

OTHER PUBLICATIONS

Novel

The Shepherd. London, Hutchinson, 1975; New York, Viking Press, 1976.

Other

The Biafra Story. London, Penguin, 1969; revised edition, as *The Making of an African Legend: The Biafra Story,* 1977.

*   *   *

In Frederick Forsyth's best suspense thrillers a highly professional man of action, in his thirties in the earlier books but forty-ish more recently, is pitted against either an antagonist who also works alone or an establishment bureaucracy or organization. The hero often has difficulties in conforming to the rigid, unimaginative procedures established by politicians and bureaucrats, but nevertheless lives up to his own high professional standards; the established organization, whether a highly respectable police organization or a secret society, attempts to impose its will on others in ways the general populace is unaware of. The novels' scenes shift back and forth from the one character or group to the other; a collision course is set up early and the action gradually quickens to the inevitable confrontation. The main characters travel constantly; if their movements were represented on road maps, the opponents would begin in widely separated locations, zig-zag

with increasing rapidity across the map, sometimes ironically crossing paths, and then finally head inexorably toward one another for the denouement. Forsyth's technique suggests a hidden pattern governing great events, a pattern not always obvious even to the participants, much less to newspaper readers, who receive only a sanitized version of current history. The novels provide the appeal of the inside story, the secret knowledge about how and why things "really" happen, knowledge known only to the perceptive few and the innermost circles. In an age enchanted with conspiracies, their popularity is understandable.

Forsyth comes to suspense fiction from journalism, his other major work being reportage, non-fiction (*The Biafra Story*), and a finely crafted yarn about a modern jet pilot in trouble, guided to safety by a ghost airplane from World War II (*The Shepherd*). Authenticity in his novels comes from journalistic writing at its best: concrete, immediate, and immensely well-informed. A reserved authorial persona confines himself to precise, thorough description about how illegal actions and transactions are managed (the construction of the special rifle in *The Day of the Jackal,* the bomb-making in *The Odessa File* and *The Fourth Protocol,* gun-running in *The Dogs of War* are all marvels of technical description). This journalistic precision is enhanced by the use of real people, places, and events in the immediate background; the ultimate effect is less that of fiction than of a fictional projection into the lives of the real makers of history, not the great leaders but their lieutenants, details about whom never make the front page.

The Day of the Jackal, based on real attempts to assassinate de Gaulle, contrasts the professional and amateur—the professional assassin with the OAS amateur terrorist, the professional gun maker with the amateur forger, the professional detective with political appointees—with only a true professional capable of appreciating the subtlety and thoroughness of a fellow professional, since each pays close attention to trivial details, checks remote angles and contingency plans, and deals with situations intellectually rather than emotionally. In *The Odessa File,* Peter Miller, a highly competent crime reporter, tracks down a former SS concentration camp commandant (a real person, Captain Eduard Roschmann, whose story is historically accurate). Miller's investigative expertise serves him well until he runs up against the professionalism of the Odessa (the organization of former SS) and of the anti-Nazi underground. *The Dogs of War* concerns the efforts of a mercenary leader, Cat Shannon, to topple an Idi Amin-like African tyrant on behalf of Sir James Manson, director of a British mining company, who has discovered a mountain of platinum in the tyrant's country. Shannon and a handful of mercenaries are engaged to install a puppet government which will turn over mining rights to Manson, but change sides out of sympathy for the underdog (again, the plot is based on a true story in which Forsyth may have been involved, at least indirectly).

The Devil's Alternative reflects the hostage-taking and terrorism of the 1970's, focusing on the seizure of an oil-filled supertanker; such an attack had not occurred, but had great credibility then (and now), given the historical events Forsyth calls up as analogues. The vision of this novel is dark—the title means "no choice at all"—and the book was less popular with both readers and critics than its predecessors. *No Comebacks* is a collection of short stories surprising for their humor and light irony, qualities notably absent in the novels. Though replete with the kind of insider's technical expertise one comes to expect from the novels, the stories are more conventionally "literary;" they focus on the domestic and everyday, rather than on world leaders and events in "docudrama" form. *The*

Fourth Protocol follows the efforts of a rogue Soviet group to change the direction of British and Western politics by violating the prohibition summed up in the title, the gentleman's agreement not to introduce portable nuclear weapons onto the territory of the enemy. The situation and the movement of the plot are reminiscent of *The Day of the Jackal* in that a lone wolf assassin who is trying to penetrate anti-espionage defenses is opposed by a nondescript policeman, completely lacking in charisma but long on competence. The novel was received well and a popular film was made from it.

The Negotiator falls prey to a hazard for every writer of fact-based fiction: the accelerated pace of change can date a novel even before it hits print. In this case, the plot follows the attempt of Texas and Soviet conservatives to scuttle an unprecedented disarmament agreement arranged between Gorbachev and U.S. President John Cormack, a treaty which would cut arms and expenditures in half and establish true peace. Both Russian and American established powers have too much invested in the status quo to allow peace to break out, and they arrange for the president's only son, who is studying at Oxford, to be kidnapped. Forsyth's main character, another in the long series of quiet, low-key, but supercompetent technicians, is the hostage negotiator, Quinn, a bit clumsily paired with Sam(antha) Somerville, a beautiful female FBI agent with whom he has a torrid romance. After his negotiations with the kidnapper fail, Quinn and Sam race across Europe to capture the escaped malefactors, finding them too late as the organizers of the plot execute their erstwhile employees. Their search ends in a remote Vermont wilderness cabin in midwinter, with Russian KGB agents ironically on the "right" side.

Forsyth's importance as a writer hinges on his phenomenal popularity (over 30 million copies of his books have been sold, and in addition to *The Fourth Protocol, The Day of the Jackal, The Odessa File,* and *The Dogs of War* have been made into films). His novels have been praised for their plotting and page-turning force but also panned as weak in character and prose. What is undeniable is that Forsyth is the most successful practitioner of a new kind of fiction, the popular thriller combined with journalistically immediate issues of the moment, and told in a spare, cinematic style loaded with convincing technical detail. This "docudrama" genre, interweaving truth and fiction, was not Forsyth's invention—numerous writers have practiced it as well—but he is certainly its most prolific exponent.

—Andrew F. Macdonald

FOSTER, Richard. *See* **CROSSEN, Ken.**

FOX, James M. Pseudonym for Johannes Matthijs Willem Knipscheer; has also written as Grant Holmes. American. Born in The Hague, Netherlands; came to the United States in 1946; naturalized citizen, 1949. Educated at the University of Leiden and the University of Utrecht. Practiced foreign commercial law in the Netherlands and New York; legal adviser to the minister of war in the Netherlands Government-in-Exile during World War II. Lived in Palm Springs, California. *Died*

CRIME PUBLICATIONS

Novels (series: Steve Harvester; Sergeants Jerry Long and Chuck Conley; John and Suzy Marshall)

Journey into Danger (Marshall).   London, Withy Grove Press, 1943.
Don't Try Anything Funny (Marshall).   London, Davies, 1943.
Hell on the Way (Marshall).   London, Davies, 1943.
Cheese from a Mousetrap (Marshall).   London, Davies, 1944.
The Lady Regrets (Marshall).   New York, Coward McCann, and London, Davies, 1947.
Death Commits Bigamy (Marshall).   New York, Coward McCann, 1948; London, Home and Van Thal, 1950.
The Inconvenient Bride (Marshall).   New York, Coward McCann, 1948; London, Home and Van Thal, 1951.
The Gentle Hangman (Marshall).   Boston, Little Brown, 1950; London, Home and Van Thal, 1952.
The Aleutian Blue Mink (Marshall).   Boston, Little Brown, 1951; London, Home and Van Thal, 1952; as *Fatal in Furs,* New York, Dell, 1952.
The Iron Virgin (Marshall).   Boston, Little Brown, 1951; London, Hammond, 1954.
The Wheel Is Fixed.   Boston, Little Brown, 1951; London, Home and Van Thal, 1952.
The Scarlet Slippers (Marshall).   Boston, Little Brown, 1952; London, Hammond, 1955.
A Shroud for Mr. Bundy (Marshall).   Boston, Little Brown, 1952; London, Hammond, 1955.
Bright Serpent (Marshall).   Boston, Little Brown, 1953; London, Hammond, 1956; as *Rites for a Killer,* n.p., Jonathan, 1957.
Code Three (Long and Conley).   Boston, Little Brown, 1953; London, Hammond, 1956; as *Dead Shot,* Canoga Park, California, Major, 1979.
Dark Crusade (Harvester).   Boston, Little Brown, 1954; as Grant Holmes, London, Cassell, 1955.
Surabaya (as Grant Holmes).   London, Cassell, 1956.
Free Ride (Long and Conley).   New York, Popular Library, and London, Cassell, 1957; as *Cell Car 54,* Canoga Park, California, Major, 1977.
Save Them for Violence.   Derby, Connecticut, Monarch, 1959.
Dead Pigeon (Long and Conley).   London, Hammond, 1967; as *The Dead Canary,* Canoga Park, California, Major, 1979.
Operation Dancing Dog (Harvester).   New York, Walker, 1974.

Uncollected Short Stories

"Start from Scratch," in *Four and Twenty Bloodhounds,* edited by Anthony Boucher.   New York, Simon and Schuster, 1950; London, Hammond, 1951.
"Reward," in *Mercury* (New York), February 1957.
"The Candid Corpse," in *The Saint* (New York), May 1958.
"Project: Murder," in *The Saint* (New York), September 1958.
"The Lady Regrets," in *Bestseller Mystery* Magazine (New York), November 1960.
"Reward for Murder," in *The Saint* (New York), May 1962.

OTHER PUBLICATIONS

Novels

A Lover's Blade.   New York, Hillman, 1960.
The Exiles.   New York, Weybright and Talley, and London, Cassell, 1970.

Courier to Marlborough (as Grant Holmes). London, Hale, 1971.

* * *

J.M.W. Knipscheer's best known pseudonym was James M. Fox. The Johnny and Suzy Marshall mystery series published during the late 1940's and early 1950's remain the most enduring part of his work.

The first book in the series, *The Lady Regrets,* introduces the young couple as an up-beat variation of Mr. and Mrs. North. Major John Conger Marshall has just taken an honorable discharge from the Army's Counter-Intelligence Corps and is entitled to a terminal leave. When Johnny and his wife, Suzy, accept a stranger's invitation to spend that leave on a swank California estate, the couple get caught up in an insidious murder plot. *The Lady Regrets* sets the tone for the rest of the Johnny and Suzy Marshall series: each is narrated in the first person by Johnny. The tone is hard-boiled with the conventional glib dialogue so common in books of this era.

As a result of the successful solution of the mystery in *The Lady Regrets,* Johnny applies for and receives a California private investigator's license. In the second book in the series, *Death Commits Bigamy,* Johnny and Suzy find themselves arrested for murder and only some clever plotting by Knipscheer saves them from conviction.

In *The Inconvenient Bride,* Suzy forces Johnny to accept a case of a deserted bride to find the missing groom. The simple search turns into a complicated scheme to gain control of a fortune. The concluding asylum scene is the most chilling of the entire series. *The Gentle Hangman* features a beautiful blonde who disappears from a popular radio program; the sponsors hire Johnny to find her. Johnny finds her dead, hanged from a bedpost in a cheap motor court. From that moment on, Johnny and Suzy find themselves in danger of being the next victims of the gentle hangman.

The Iron Virgin sends Johnny and Suzy on a search for a missing woman that takes them to Hollywood, Las Vegas, and Mexico. Knipscheer shows his skill at creating realistic settings in this book and the next in the series, *The Scarlet Slippers.* Suzy finds herself involved in a case in Los Angeles while Johnny follows a trail of clues in New York City. Both books display Knipscheer's increased control over his characters and plotting.

The best book in the Johnny and Suzy Marshall series is *A Shroud for Mr. Bundy.* Jeremiah Peter Bundy hires Johnny to investigate the burial of someone claiming to be Jeremiah Peter Bundy, diamond merchant with links to the Mafia. When the living Mr. Bundy disappears with a fortune in diamonds Johnny and Suzy, with the help of their great Dane, Khan, race against the clock to solve their most difficult case. Knipscheer's writing is under firm restraint with only a slight hard-boiled flavor: "The Army .45 in his big hairy paw looked like a trinket from the five-and-dime."

Knipscheer's other books lack the vitality of the Johnny and Suzy Marshall books. *The Wheel Is Fixed* gives the chronic gambler Richard Bailey a run for his life as the Mafia sets him up as the fall guy in a murder plot. *Free Ride* turns a train trip from New Orleans to California into a free-for-all for murder. Sergeant Jerry Long's assignment is to escort Leo Maxwell, a Mafia hood facing a manslaughter charge, across the country without being killed. But the Mafia wants Maxwell dead and Long has his hands full fighting a trainload of hitmen. Neither book rises above pulp hackwork.

The Exiles is Knipscheer's attempt to write a bestseller: the setting is World War II London where dozens of small governments-in-exile ready themselves for D-Day. There is a large cast of characters, love affairs, jealousies, and tedious writing. Knipscheer's attempt at a spy novel, *Operation Dancing Dog,* is also unsuccessful. Secret agent Steve Harvester battles against a plot to blackmail the West into submission with the threat of a mutated rabies virus that renders victims insane within a half-hour. The descriptions of the locales— Tangier, Marbella, Cannes, Paris, and New York—are the books's only virtues.

Knipscheer's output is large and varied, but the Johnny and Suzy Marshall mystery series remains the highpoint of his long career.

—George Kelley

———

FOXX, Jack. *See* **PRONZINI, Bill.**

———

FRANCIS, Dick (Richard Stanley Francis). British. Born in Tenby, Pembrokeshire, 31 October 1920. Educated at Maidenhead County Boys' School, Berkshire. Served as a Flying Officer in the Royal Air Force, 1940–45. Married Mary Margaret Brenchley in 1947; two sons. Amateur National Hunt (steeplechase) jockey, 1946–48; professional, 1948–57; National Hunt champion, 1953–54. Racing correspondent, *Sunday Express,* London, 1957–73. Chairman, Crime Writers Association, 1973–74. Recipient: Crime Writers Association Silver Dagger award, 1965, Gold Dagger award, 1980; Diamond Dagger award, 1989. Mystery Writers of America Edgar Allan Poe award, 1969, 1981. O.B.E. (Officer, Order of the British Empire), 1984. Agent: John Johnson, 45-47 Clerkenwell Green, London EC1R 0HT. Address: 5100 North Ocean Boulevard, Apartment 609, Fort Lauderdale, Florida 33308, U.S.A.

CRIME PUBLICATIONS

Novels (series: Sid Halley)

Dead Cert. London, Joseph, and New York, Holt Rinehart, 1962.
Nerve. London, Joseph, and New York, Harper, 1964.
For Kicks. London, Joseph, and New York, Harper, 1965.
Odds Against (Halley). London, Joseph, 1965; New York, Harper, 1966.
Flying Finish. London, Joseph, 1966; New York, Harper, 1967.
Blood Sport. London, Joseph, 1967; New York, Harper, 1968.
Forfeit. London, Joseph, and New York, Harper, 1969.
Enquiry. London, Joseph, and New York, Harper, 1969.
Rat Race. London, Joseph, 1970; New York, Harper, 1971.
Bonecrack. London, Joseph, 1971; New York, Harper, 1972.
Smokescreen. London, Joseph, and New York, Harper, 1972.
Slay-Ride. London, Joseph, and New York, Harper, 1973.
Knock-Down. London, Joseph, 1974; New York, Harper, 1975.
High Stakes. London, Joseph, 1975; New York, Harper, 1976.

In the Frame. London, Joseph, 1976; New York, Harper, 1977.
Risk. London, Joseph, 1977; New York, Harper, 1978.
Trial Run. London, Joseph, 1978; New York, Harper, 1979.
Whip Hand (Halley). London, Joseph, 1979; New York, Harper, 1980.
Reflex. London, Joseph, 1980; New York, Putnam, 1981.
Twice Shy. London, Joseph, 1981; New York, Putnam, 1982.
Banker. London, Joseph, 1982; New York, Putnam, 1983.
The Danger. London, Joseph, 1983; New York, Putnam, 1984.
Proof. London, Joseph, 1984; New York, Putnam, 1985.
Break In. London, Joseph, and New York, Putnam, 1986.
Bolt. London, Joseph, 1986; New York, Putnam, 1987.
Hot Money. London, Joseph, 1987; New York, Putnam, 1988.
The Edge. London, Joseph, 1988; New York, Putnam, 1989.
Straight. London, Joseph, and New York, Putnam, 1989.
Longshot. London, Joseph, 1990.

Uncollected Short Stories

"A Day of Wine and Roses," in *Sports Illustrated* (New York), May 1973.
"The Gift," in *Winter's Crimes 5,* edited by Virginia Whitaker. London, Macmillan, 1973.
"A Carrot for a Chestnut," in *Stories of Crime and Detection,* edited by Joan D. Berbrich. New York, McGraw Hill, 1974.
"The Big Story," in *Ellery Queen's Crime Wave.* New York, Putnam, 1976.
"Nightmare," in *Ellery Queen's Searches and Seizures.* New York, Davis, 1977.
"The Day of the Losers," in *John Creasey's Crime Collection 1980,* edited by Herbert Harris. London, Gollancz, 1980.

OTHER PUBLICATIONS

Play

Screenplay: *Dead Cert,* 1974.

Other

The Sport of Queens: The Autobiography of Dick Francis. London, Joseph, 1957; revised edition, 1968, 1974, 1982, 1988; New York, Harper, 1969.
Lester: The Official Biography. London, Joseph, 1986; as *A Jockey's Life: The Biography of Lester Piggott,* New York, Putnam, 1987.

Editor, with John Welcome, *Best Racing and Chasing Stories 1-2.* London, Faber, 2 vols., 1966–69.
Editor, with John Welcome, *The Racing Man's Bedside Book.* London, Faber, 1969.

*

Critical Studies: *Dick Francis* by Melvyn Barnes, New York, Ungar, 1986; *Dick Francis* by J. Madison Davis, Boston, Twayne, 1989.

*   *   *

It is rare indeed for a writer to win both popular success as well as high critical acclaim. Yet Dick Francis, who until he was approaching 40 had never put pen to paper, has achieved just that. He began with an autobiography, written at the casual suggestion of a friend when he had ended his career as a top jockey in British racing. Then, in need he says of the price of a new carpet, he thought he would try his hand at a thriller and produced, with the active encouragement of his wife, Mary, *Dead Cert,* an immediate success. Each year since then a new adventure tale, often with a turf setting, has appeared. Their standard is always remarkably high, and indeed grew year by year.

His method is to write a first version and then to read it aloud on to tape. I suspect that it is this process that accounts for the first of his virtues, the extreme easiness of his style. But easy reading generally comes from hard work first, and Francis has said that producing a novel is "just as tiring" as race riding. Besides the style, there are solid plots underneath the whole, the way whatever turns out to have happened in the end has its reasonable and likely cause. There is the continuing pull of the story, so that you are all the time wanting to know what will happen next. You get told what you want to know, too, and not something just a little bit different as often with less skilled authors. And at the same time you are made to want to know some new thing.

Then there is the language. Francis never succumbs to the temptation to use a long or complex word where a simple one exists, something that writers with high reputations are often guilty of. Francis chooses straightforward words and never wastes them. This virtue comes perhaps from his sense of timing, a gift he brought with him from racing to writing. The art of judging at just what moment to put a new fact into the reader's head, whether the fact is as important as the discovery of a body (most adroitly done in *Slay-Ride*) or just some necessary detail, is one that Francis shares with the masters of his craft, figures as outwardly different as Agatha Christie or the subtle Simenon.

But more important than the pacing of a book or than its plot, more even than a well-told story, are the people that the writer invents for it. It is through people that the story-teller affects an audience. The people in the Francis books are as real as real-life people. Perhaps the best example of the kind of human being in his pages is the girl the hero either loves or comes to love. There is not one in every book (Francis has succeeded in bringing considerable variety to thrillers that might with their customary Turf settings or references have become formula affairs), but she has featured often enough to be easily identifiable as a certain sort of person. She will have some grave handicap, needing to live in an iron lung or simply being widowed or, as in *The Danger,* having been victim of a cruel kidnapping. Many thriller writers would not dare to use such people because the reality of their situation would show up the tinsel world around them. But Francis is tough enough, and compassionate enough, to be able to write about such things.

His knowledge of the effects of tragedy comes from his own experience. While his wife was expecting their first child she was struck down by poliomyelitis and confined to an iron lung. It is from personal experience, too, that the typically stoic Francis hero comes. One of the few complaints that have been made about the books is that the hero (usually a different one each time, a jockey, a horse-owner, a trainer, a painter, a film star, an accountant, a photographer, a merchant banker) is too tough to be credible. But the fact is that most critics are not used to taking actual physical hard knocks; Francis, the jumps jockey, was. So if you look carefully at what he says happens when one of his heroes gets beaten up (as almost invariably they do) you find that, unlike many a pseudo-Bond or carbon-copy private eye, he gets really hurt and recovers only as fast as a physically fit and resilient man would in real life.

A Francis hero will have another characteristic as well as bodily toughness. He will be a man not scared of judging. He weighs up the people he meets and sees them for what they are, tough men, good men, nasty men, weak men, tough women, greedy women, sensitive women. And, more than this, the Francis books make judgements on a wider scale. Each one is about something. By its particular choice of hero it takes some particular human dilemma. *Slay-Ride,* for instance, though it might seem to be no more than a good story about dirty work on the Norwegian race-courses, is in fact a book about what it is like to be the parent of children, to give these hostages to fortune, to be taking part in the continuing pattern of human existence. Similarly, *Reflex* is about the need to accept inevitable change, and *Twice Shy* is about the acquiring of maturity.

The Edge, though an exciting puzzle set on a Canadian train with a cargo of bloodstock and a posse of actors playing a "murder mystery," is fundamentally about the need (to quote) "to retain order" and all its events reflect this. While in *Straight* Francis takes the metaphor of "the straight," the last yards of a jumps race course, as illustrating a man facing the end of a particular career (a jockey, once again) but he also goes deeper in saying something through his story about that human ideal of being "straight." It is such hidden themes that give the Francis books the weight that lifts them right out of the run of good but ordinary thrillers.

—H.R.F. Keating

FRANKLIN, Max *See* **DEMING, Richard.**

FRASER, Anthea. Also writes as Lorna Cameron; Vanessa Graham. British. Born in Blundellsands, Lancashire. Educated at Cheltenham Ladies' College, Gloucestershire. Married Ian Mackintosh Fraser in 1956; two daughters. Since 1986 secretary, Crime Writers Association, London. Agent: Laurence Pollinger Ltd., 18 Maddox Street, London W1R OEU, England.

CRIME PUBLICATIONS

Novels (series: Detective Chief Inspector David Webb and Detective Sergeant Ken Jackson in all books)

A Shroud for Delilah. London, Collins, 1984; New York, Doubleday, 1986.
A Necessary End. London, Collins, 1985; New York, Walker, 1986.
Pretty Maids all in a Row. London, Collins, 1986; New York, Doubleday, 1987.
Death Speaks Softly. London, Collins, and New York, Doubleday, 1987.
The Nine Bright Shiners. London, Collins, 1987; New York, Doubleday, 1988.
Six Proud Walkers. London, Collins, 1988; New York, Doubleday, 1989.
The April Rainers. London, Collins, 1989; New York, Doubleday, 1990.

Symbols at Your Door. London, Collins, 1990; New York, Doubleday, 1991.

Uncollected Short Story

"Nemesis," in *A Suit of Diamonds.* London, Collins, 1990.

OTHER PUBLICATIONS

Novels

Designs of Annabelle. London, Mills and Boon, 1971.
In the Balance. London, Mills and Boon, 1973.
Laura Possessed. Aylesbury, Buckinghamshire, Milton House, and New York, Dodd Mead, 1974.
Home Through the Dark. Aylesbury, Buckinghamshire, Milton House, and New York, Dodd Mead, 1974.
Whistler's Lane. Aylesbury, Buckinghamshire, Milton House, and New York, Dodd Mead, 1975.
Death of Brimstone. New York, Dodd Mead, 1977; London, Corgi, 1978.
Presence of Mind. London, Corgi, 1978.
Island-in-Waiting. London, Hale, and New York, St. Martin's Press, 1979.
The Stone. London, Hale, and New York, St. Martin's Press, 1980.
Summer in France (as Lorna Cameron). London, Mills and Boon, 1981.

Novels as Vanessa Graham

Time of Trial. London, Hale, 1979.
Second Time Around. New York, Doubleday, 1980.
The Stand-In. London, Hale, 1984.

*

Anthea Fraser comments:
My books tend to be about ordinary people leading normal, uneventful lives, who are suddenly catapulted into danger. It may come without warning from outside, or as a direct result of family stress, relationships pushed to the limit till something snaps. I've a suspicion we could all become murderers under sufficient provocation—threat to a loved one, for instance.

All the books are set in Broadshire, an imaginary county located where the northern part of Wiltshire actually lies. I have copious maps of its towns and villages, and could find my way around blindfold. So although each novel has a new set of characters, the background is familiar, as are my Chief Inspector and Sergeant, who appear in all the books.

More interested in why than who dunnit, my aim is to write about believable people with whom the reader can identify; in short, the type of book I myself most enjoy reading.

*　　*　　*

Firmly established in the English village mystery genre, Anthea Fraser lulls her audience with the comfort, traditions, and surroundings of rural England only to jolt them with sudden murder, boldly revealed family skeletons, and intricately woven plots. With a sharp eye for character, detail, and conversation, she draws an essentially realistic world caught up in the turmoil of murder and its aftermath. Among Fraser's earlier works stand successful attempts at novels combining suspense, the supernatural, and the mildly erotic, but later efforts center on the police procedural mystery.

Indicative of Fraser's early efforts, *Laura Possessed* constructs the isolated stage for a very personal drama. Laura, as the recovering accident victim who "senses" things about a dead woman's house, becomes the mental receptacle for the woman's spirit. Predictable in its melodramatic depiction of a failed love affair and fatal attractions, the novel derives much of its interest from Laura's brush with insanity and death. *The Stone,* in which legends of the ominous Druid Stone test an adolescent girl's sanity, retains similar Gothic elements, but Fraser employs them here with more finesse and less cliché. Persistent foreshadowing, sometimes embodied in objects, like the ancient well, an old diary, and some ritualistic pebbles, emphasizes Vanessa's growing psychological stress. Competent but mostly unremarkable, these novels fall well within the mainstream of the emotional suspense type.

Fraser incorporates the best elements of her earlier efforts in her widely recognized and carefully crafted Inspector Webb series, where Webb, lady friend Hannah, and various Shillingham co-workers appear as welcome, familiar constants. These novels rank much higher in quality and mark Fraser's coming-of-age as a mystery writer. Webb, as central figure, assiduously and devotedly collects and sorts out clues, interrogates suspects, and makes inspired leaps of faith to corner the culprit. Clearly admirable as a series protagonist, Inspector Webb exhibits extensive experience with police procedure, thorough knowledge of his service area, and an acute empathy for people.

Fraser begins *A Necessary End* in typical fashion. The opening scenes introduce a number of interesting characters, hint at various undercurrents in their relationships, delineate a rural setting, and deliver a dead body. After discovery and identification of the well-dressed corpse, Inspector Webb deftly unravels the complicated inter-relationships among the principal characters. Fraser's plot (and Webb's investigation) progresses quite logically, if unexpectedly, to discovery of the murderer.

Webb's relationship with Hannah, of minor importance in *A Necessary End,* takes on added importance in *Death Speaks Softly,* where the two more-or-less repair a rift that occurred in a previous novel. Once again, though, Fraser neatly uses the subplot both to forward the principal one and to increase suspense. While Webb searches for a missing French girl, locates her broken-necked body, and traces the movements of her killer, he also rebuilds his friendship with Hannah, whom he involves in the case as a translator for his interrogation of a French couple. Fraser, in fact, frequently uses dialog or interior monolog to advance her plots. While doubt lingers as to whether someone actually murdered the French girl or not, the dramatic and unexpected conclusion of the work certainly resolves the matter with shocking clarity.

Fraser's knack for ending her mysteries with similar bizarre twists shows itself once more in *The April Rainers,* although revelation of the actual murderer's identity arrives without too much surprise. Webb's investigation, a musician's quest for a biographer, and events in an unfeeling publisher's life coalesce into one unified plot as the author, who maintains strict narrative control throughout, advances Inspector Webb's case with the usual conversation and introspection. Despite peripheral conflicts, tie-ins to murders elsewhere in England, and references to previous mysteries, Fraser ends with a tidily wrapped and very attractive package.

The newest and certainly a prime addition to the Inspector Webb canon, *Symbols at Your Door,* sustains Fraser's reputation as a master of police procedure and plot. As in her other series titles, the author introduces a limited but varied array of characters, establishes their interconnectedness in a small Shillingham community, and proceeds to unveil details and secrets that ultimately prove motive for murder. Webb must determine why someone in "up-and-coming" Beckworth Village drowned pretty Carol Dexter and then slit her neighbor's throat. With Hannah as sounding board, Webb proceeds efficiently to a satisfactory conclusion of both cases.

The Inspector Webb series, then, surpasses Fraser's early works in quality and presents the author at her best. Here, as indicated, Fraser offers realistic vignettes of life in a not-too-rural England, interesting, multilevel characters, and detailed descriptions of Webb's procedural and empathetic abilities. Inspector Webb may prove to be Fraser's crowning achievement.

—Rex E. Klett

FRASER, (Lady) Antonia. British. Born in London, 27 August 1932; daughter of the writer Lord Longford. Educated at the Dragon School, Oxford, 1940–44; Godolphin School, Salisbury, 1944–45; St. Mary's Convent, Ascot, Berkshire, 1946–48; Lady Margaret Hall, Oxford, 1950–53, B.A. in history 1953, M.A. Married 1) Hugh Fraser in 1956 (marriage dissolved 1977), three daughters and three sons; 2) the writer Harold Pinter in 1980. General editor, Kings and Queens of England series, Weidenfeld and Nicolson, publishers, London 1953–55. Chairman, Society of Authors, 1974–75, Crime Writers Association, 1985–86, Writers in Prison Committee, 1985–88, and since 1990; president, PEN, 1989. Recipient: Black Memorial prize, for biography, 1970: Wolfson prize for history, 1984 D. Litt., University of Hull, 1986, and University of Sussex, 1990. Lives in London. Agent: Curtis Brown Ltd., 162–168 Regent Street, London W1R 5TA, England.

CRIME PUBLICATIONS

Novels (series: Jemima Shore in all books)

Quiet as a Nun. London, Weidenfeld and Nicolson, and New York, Viking Press, 1977.
The Wild Island. London, Weidenfeld and Nicolson, and New York, Norton, 1978.
A Splash of Red. London, Weidenfeld and Nicolson, 1981; New York, Norton, 1982.
Cool Repentance. London, Weidenfeld and Nicolson, 1982; New York, Norton, 1983.
Oxford Blood. London, Weidenfeld and Nicolson, and New York, Norton, 1985.
Your Royal Hostage. London, Weidenfeld and Nicolson, 1987; New York, Atheneum, 1988.
The Cavalier Case. London, Bloomsbury, 1990.

Short Stories

Jemima Shore's First Case and Other Stories. London, Weidenfeld and Nicolson, 1986; New York, Norton, 1987.

Uncollected Short Stories

"Jemima Shore and the Cry-By-Night," in *Woman's Realm* (London), 4 and 11 April 1987.
"The Twist," in *London Daily News,* 1 June 1987.
"Dead Leaves," in *Ellery Queen's Mystery Magazine* (New York), August 1987.

"House Poison," in *John Creasey's Crime Collection 1987,* edited by Herbert Harris.   London, Gollancz, 1987.

OTHER PUBLICATIONS

Plays

Radio Plays: *On the Battlements,* 1975; *The Heroine,* 1976; *Penelope,* 1976.

Television Plays: *Charades,* 1977; *Mister Clay, Mister Clay,* 1985; *Have a Nice Death,* 1985.

Other

King Arthur and the Knights of the Round Table (for children). London, Weidenfeld and Nicolson, 1954; New York, Knopf, 1970.
Robin Hood (for children).   London, Weidenfeld and Nicolson, 1957; New York, Knopf, 1971.
Dolls.   London, Weidenfeld and Nicolson, and New York, Putnam, 1963.
A History of Toys.   London, Weidenfeld and Nicolson, and New York, Delacorte Press, 1966.
Mary, Queen of Scots.   London, Weidenfeld and Nicolson, and New York, Delacorte Press, 1969.
Cromwell Our Chief of Men.   London, Weidenfeld and Nicolson, 1973; as *Cromwell, The Lord Protector,* New York, Knopf, 1973.
Mary, Queen of the Scots, and the Historians.   Ilford, Essex, Royal Stuart Society, 1974.
King James: VI of Scotland, I of England.   London, Weidenfeld and Nicolson, 1974; New York, Knopf, 1975.
King Charles II.   London, Weidenfeld and Nicolson, 1979; as *Royal Charles,* New York, Knopf, 1979.
The Weaker Vessel: Woman's Lot in Seventeenth-Century England.   London, Weidenfeld and Nicolson, and New York, Knopf, 1984.
Boadicea's Chariot: The Warrior Queens.   London, Weidenfeld and Nicolson, 1988; as *The Warrior Queens,* New York, Knopf, 1989.

Editor, *The Lives of the Kings and Queens of England.*   London, Weidenfeld and Nicolson, and New York, Knopf, 1975.
Editor, *Scottish Love Poems: A Personal Anthology.*   Edinburgh, Canongate, 1975; New York, Viking Press, 1976.
Editor, *Love Letters: An Anthology.*   London, Weidenfeld and Nicolson, 1976; New York, Knopf, 1977; as *Love Letters: An Illustrated Anthology,* London, Barrie and Jones, and Chicago, Contemporary, 1989.
Editor, *Heroes and Heroines.*   London, Weidenfeld and Nicolson, 1980.
Editor, *Mary, Queen of Scots: An Anthology of Poetry.* London, Eyre Methuen, 1981.
Editor, *Oxford and Oxfordshire in Verse.*   London, Secker and Warburg, 1982.

Translator, *Martyrs in China,* by Jean Monsterleet.   London, Longman, 1956.
Translator, *Dior by Dior: The Autobiography of Christian Dior.* London, Weidenfeld and Nicolson, 1957.

*

Antonia Fraser comments:
I aim to produce a straightforward mystery story (if that is not a contradiction in terms!) in the tradition of those writers I most admire, as it happens principally women. They include Dorothy L. Sayers, Emma Lathen, Ruth Rendell, and P.D. James, as well as the great Patricia Highsmith. I have a horror of blood dripping from the page in the books I read, thinking effects are better achieved with more subtlety; my books are therefore aimed at readers who feel likewise. I am very interested in the possibilities of my amateur sleuth, Jemima Shore, Investigator, the celebrated TV reporter, and hope to explore them further in future books—against a variety of backgrounds other than Catholic convents and the Highlands of Scotland, which I have already considered.

*   *   *

Also a notable contributor to popular history writing, as a crime writer Antonia Fraser is best known for her Jemima Shore novels, and for the television series based upon them— *Jemima Shore Investigates.* The Jemima Shore novels continue the English tradition of the (upper) middle-class, amateur sleuth. Shore is a modern, "liberated" version of the inquisitive spinster detective. Like her predecessors, Shore is propelled into her investigations by her "Eve-like" curiosity (*Quiet as a Nun*), and like theirs her success in detection derives in large measure from her class and gender position. She is usually a privileged insider in the social circles which form the locus of her investigations. She is often on the scene before the crime occurs and the police arrive, and her convent-educated, Cambridge-honed brain, and her social *savoir-faire* take her in directions where flat-footed policemen may not tread. Ultimately she is, perhaps, in the tradition of Dorothy L. Sayers's Harriet Vane, rather than Agatha Christie's Miss Marple. She is a throroughly modern young woman, unconventional and with a natural love of mischief. A smart, sexy, Cambridge-educated media person, she felt "the first stirrings of primitive feminism in her breast" at the age of 15 when faced with the values and assumptions of the aristocratic Italian family of one of her schoolfriends ("Jemima Shore's First Case,") Shore's detective activities are usually an off-shoot of her professional role as an investigative journalist with her own television programme. However, her cool journalistic professionalism is offset by her apparent attraction to dangerous situations, and the fact that she is prone to sudden extremes of sexual attraction, often to rather unsuitable men.

Although a protestant, Shore (like her creator) is convent-educated. Her convent upbringing is an important part of Jemima's make-up. Mother Agnes "the young but increasingly formidable Reverend Mother of that convent," and "the only truly serene person that she knew" features in several of the novels, if only as a kind of inner voice or conscience which beckons Jemima to a rather stern and often conservative duty. The old school provides the setting of "Jemima Shore's First Case" and *Quiet as a Nun.* The Convent of the Blessed Eleanor forms the unlikely setting for this tale of murder and financial machinations which opens with the death of Sister Miriam, a rich nun whose extensive property interests include the convent itself. Jemima is summoned to sort out the mystery surrounding this death and other strange events (such as the mysterious apparition of the Black Nun) which disrupt the calm of conventual life. The plot is complex, and Jemima hurtles from one crisis to another, including one where her life is saved by a pistol-toting Sister. Fraser has a great deal of fun in disrupting her reader's expectations and prejudices about the constraints of nuns' lives and minds before the mystery is solved, the property is restored to the Sisterhood and the convent resumes its orderly life.

The disruption of a closed community is also the focus of *The Wild Island,* in which the supposedly holidaying heroine becomes caught up in gothic family feuds amongst the descendants of the Stuart Pretender on a remote Scottish island. The death of her erstwhile landlord, Charles Beauregard, sets off a chain of intrigue among the anachronistically feudal family and their eccentric crew of servants and dependants. Jemima becomes strongly attracted to the philandering patriarch of this bizarre family, and her involvement with Beauregard *père* leads her to the roots of the murders which have riven the Beauregard clan. Coming perilously close to death herself in the process, Jemima solves the mystery and effects a kind of catharsis in this introverted community. Class, sexual jealousy, and the politics of the family are at the centre of this, as of most of Fraser's crime novels.

In *A Splash of Red*, which was used as the basis for the Jemima Shore television series, Jemima becomes entangled with an odd assortment of Bloomsbury and other types, when her summer researches in the British Library are interrupted by the disappearance of the friend whose flat she has borrowed, and the discovery of a particularly shocking murder. Again Jemima's detachment from rooted relationships and places puts her into positions in which she becomes involved in mystery, crime, and personal danger. Literary London is replaced by literary Larminster in *Cool Repentance*, in which Jemima, who is covering the Larminster Arts Festival for Megalith Television, is caught up in a trial of intrigue and murder surrounding the attempted come-back of a once-famous actress who has sought to put her scandalous past behind her by returning to the bosom of her family and playing the part of the English country lady. Once more Jemima finds herself investigating and confronting the mysteries of a woman's past.

Another bastion of English privilege is exposed in *Oxford Blood*, in which Jemima's journalistic investigation of the university's bright and beautiful youth suddenly takes on more sinister undertones when she discovers that Lord Saffron, the leader of the expensive frivolity of the fast set, is a changeling and not the true heir to his title and fortune. Once more Shore courts danger as her own life becomes entangled with Saffron's and, like his, is threatened.

Oxford, literary London, and the glamorous world of the media are Fraser's stock-in-trade in the Jemima Shore novels. Famous names and designer labels abound. Fraser's novels are always bright and witty, and their denouements are usually surprising. Fraser pokes cool fun at some of the absurdities of British society, but does not seriously challenge them.

—Lyn Pykett

FRASER, James. Pseudonym for Alan White, also writes as Alec Whitney. British. Born in Yorkshire in 1924. Address: c/o Granada, 8 Grafton Street, London W1X 3LA, England.

CRIME PUBLICATIONS

Novels (series: Inspector Superintendent Bill Aveyard in all books)

The Evergreen Death. London, Jenkins, 1968; New York, Harcourt Brace, 1969.
A Cock-Pit of Roses. London, Jenkins, 1969; New York, Harcourt Brace, 1970.
Deadly Nightshade. London, Jenkins, and New York, Harcourt Brace, 1970.

Death in a Pheasant's Eye. London, Barrie and Jenkins, 1971; New York, Walker, 1972.
Blood on a Widow's Cross. London, Barrie and Jenkins, 1972.
The Five-Leafed Clover. London, Barrie and Jenkins, 1973.
A Wreath of Lords and Ladies. London, Barrie and Jenkins, 1974; New York, Doubleday, 1975.
Who Steals My Name? London, Barrie and Jenkins, 1974; New York, Doubleday, 1975.
Hearts Ease in Death. London, Barrie and Jenkins, and New York, Doubleday, 1977.

Novels as Alec Whitney

Every Man Has His Price. London, W.H. Allen, 1968.
The Triple Zero. London, W.H. Allen, 1971.
Armstrong. London, Barrie and Jenkins, 1973; New York, Doubleday, 1977.
Death in Darkness. London, Barrie and Jenkins, 1975; New York, Doubleday, 1977.

OTHER PUBLICATIONS

Novels as Alan White

The Long Day's Dying. London, Hodder and Stoughton, 1965; as *Death Finds the Day.* New York, Harcourt Brace, 1965.
The Wheel. London, Hodder and Stoughton, 1966; New York, Harcourt Brace, 1967.
The Long Night's Walk. London, Hodder and Stoughton, 1968; New York, Harcourt Brace, 1969.
The Long Drop. London, Jenkins, 1969; New York, Harcourt Brace, 1970.
The Long Watch. London, Barrie and Jenkins, and New York, Harcourt Brace, 1971.
Climate of Revolt. London, Barrie and Jenkins, 1971.
The Long Midnight. London, Barrie and Jenkins, 1972; New York, Harcourt Brace, 1974.
The Long Fuse. London, Barrie and Jenkins, 1973; New York, Harcourt Brace, 1974.
The Long Summer. London, Barrie and Jenkins, 1974; New York, Harcourt Brace, 1975.
Death in Darkness. London, Barrie and Jenkins, 1975.
The Long Silence. London, Barrie and Jenkins, 1976; New York, Charter, 1977.
Ravenswycke. London, Hutchinson, and Boston, Houghton Mifflin, 1980.
Cassidy's Yard. London, Granada, 1980.
The Homeward Tide. London, Granada, 1981.
The Vanishing Land. London, Granada, 1982.
The Years of Change. London, Granada, 1983.
Black Alert. London, Granada, 1985.

*   *   *

James Fraser is an undervalued detective novelist, perhaps more widely known for a series of war and adventure novels in his own name, Alan White. The sequence of nine books published under the Fraser pseudonym is unusually distinguished and may reasonably be described as unlike any other. In one sense they are traditional whodunits, with the concealment of the killer's identity as a prime concern; and in another they are police procedurals, detailed and accurate in their presentation of official methods and continually dependent on the minutiae of forensic evidence. In addition, they have a curious charged intensity that gives them a particular distinction, making them interesting beyond the ordinary.

Although they are all village mysteries, these books are a long way from the genteel routines of Mayhem Parva (as Colin Watson named the stock setting for much English mystery fiction). Despite the fantastic events and neurotic personalities with which they deal, they are rooted in reality, with a particular appreciation of erotic tensions and the power and prevalence of the sexual impulse. They lean heavily on the traditional village structure, with a strong line in squires and publicans and respect for the "ritual of simple things a townbred person wouldn't understand." The ancient families who head their rural communities are scrupulously documented and the surviving power of feudalism is strongly evoked, with the force and conviction of truth. Incomers are contemptuously dismissed as "bungaloids," unworthy of the author's attention: even the "strange tolerance in village life" does not extend to them.

The publisher defined "the James Fraser authenticity" as "the fascinating detail of crime detection probing into village life;" and it is precisely this continual play of tension between an efficient police machine and a range of deeply secretive individuals that gives the series its special power. Each book contains free-wheeling passages in which the author surveys his terrain: purple patches, perhaps, but arresting and highly imaginative. He often renders the thoughts of his characters, to similar uninhibited effect. Several novels draw on botanical expertise and a succession of plants contributes to the distinctive texture of the series: cacti and succulents, Sedum Pulchellum and the Monstera Deliciosa. The policeman in all the novels is Bill Aveyard, who moves from Inspector to Superintendent in the course of the sequence. He is young for his rank, ambitious and confident, tough but not insensitive. Though unmarried he is conspicuously heterosexual, with a list of available women and a deep dislike for homosexuals. He is an expert cook, using gourmet meals as an aid to seduction.

Aveyard first appears in *The Evergreen Death,* a potent account of ritual delusion and obsession that sets the tone for the series. However fantastic the revelations, the narrative is so cogent and compelling as to sustain belief and dispel doubt; and the reader is left, like Aveyard's chief, "astounded by the human vagary." In *A Cock-pit of Roses* Aveyard himself is the initial suspect, since appearances suggest that he may have raped and then murdered a young woman during a party. The mystery is complex and absorbing, tracing the links between character and circumstance with assurance and address. The confusions are compounded by a freakish woman leading "a spider's existence . . . at the centre of a web, weaving strands around the lives of other people." *Deadly Nightshade* centres on old bones and a vanished mother and child, and ramifies so provokingly that Aveyard's mind is set "buzzing" by bewilderment. Nothing seems certain and even a name has power to administer a subtle shock. *Death in a Pheasant's Eye* opens with a body on a bonfire and develops with vigorous invention and masterly control. Aveyard is fully occupied with four investigations, two of which converge finally to considerable effect. *Blood on a Widow's Cross* is arguably the most intricate and fantastic of the series, a bravura performance on a high level. Though it defies credibility, it does so grandly, with immense aplomb. Fraser's powers of contrivance and grasp of character and motive are at their most impressive here: even his title contributes to the enigmatic richness of the design. *The Five-Leafed Clover* begins with a stake-out to trap a thief but soon becomes a murder investigation. The victim has returned home after many years away and her past and present life are both in question.

The later books are less flamboyant and inventive, with diminished power to allure and engage the reader. *A Wreath of Lords and Ladies,* indeed, seems spare and undernourished beside the fullness of its predecessors. Though the plant motif recurs agreeably, the familiar cunning is less in evidence and there is little in reserve for the denouement. The victim deserves his death but his viciousness is too narrowly focused to serve as the mainstay of the action. A secondary theme is soon exhausted and a third no more than hinted at; and neither meshes adequately with the main thrust of events. *Who Steals My Name?* puts Aveyard under threat again, when a charge of taking bribes bars him from a murder inquiry. To clear his name he has to solve the case: the dual action is most deftly achieved. The last of the series, *Hearts Ease in Death,* is a subtle inheritance mystery launched with a violent storm, causing havoc and provoking murder. Though adroit and attractive, it is relatively low-keyed and confirms, perhaps, that the end had indeed arrived.

—B.A. Pike

FRAZER, Andrew. *See* **MARLOWE, Stephen.**

FRAZER, Robert Caine. *See* **CREASEY, John.**

FREELING, Nicolas. Also writes as F.R.E. Nicolas. British. Born in London, 3 March 1927. Educated in local primary and secondary schools. Served in the British military forces. Married Cornelia Termes in 1954; four sons and one daughter. Hotel and restaurant cook, throughout Europe, 1945–60. Recipient: Crime Writers Association Gold Dagger award, 1964; Grand Prix de Roman Policier, 1964; Mystery Writers of America Edgar Allan Poe award, 1966. Agent: Curtis Brown Ltd., 162–168 Regent Street, London, W1R 5TB, England. Address: Grandfontaine, 67130 Schrimeck, Bas Rhin, France.

CRIME PUBLICATIONS

Novels (series: Henri Castang; Inspector Piet Van der Valk; Arlette Van der Valk)

Love in Amsterdam (Van der Valk).   London, Gollancz, and New York, Harper, 1962; as *Death in Amsterdam,* New York, Ballantine, 1964.
Because of the Cats (Van der Valk).   London, Gollancz, 1963; New York, Harper, 1964.
Gun Before Butter (Van der Valk).   London, Gollancz, 1963; as *Question of Loyalty,* New York, Harper, 1963.
Valparaiso (as F.R.E. Nicolas).   London, Gollancz, 1964; as Nicolas Freeling, New York, Harper, 1965.
Double-Barrel (Van der Valk).   London, Gollancz, 1964; New York, Harper, 1965.
Criminal Conversation (Van der Valk).   London, Gollancz, 1965; New York, Harper, 1966.
The King of the Rainy Country (Van der Valk).   London, Gollancz, and New York, Harper, 1966.

The Dresden Green (Van der Valk). London, Gollancz, 1966; New York, Harper, 1967.

Strike Out Where Not Applicable (Van der Valk). London, Gollancz, and New York, Harper, 1967.

This Is the Castle. London, Gollancz, and New York, Harper, 1968.

Tsing-Boum (Van der Valk). London, Hamish Hamilton, 1969; as *Tsing-Boum!*, New York, Harper, 1969.

Over the High Side (Van der Valk). London, Hamish Hamilton, 1971; as *The Lovely Ladies*, New York, Harper, 1971.

A Long Silence (Van der Valk; Arlette Van der Valk). London, Hamish Hamilton, 1972; as *Auprès de ma Blonde*, New York, Harper, 1972.

A Dressing of Diamond (Castang). London, Hamish Hamilton, and New York, Harper, 1974.

What Are the Bugles Blowing For? (Castang). London, Heinemann, 1975; as *The Bugles Blowing*, New York, Harper, 1976.

Lake Isle (Castang). London, Heinemann, 1976; as *Sabine*, New York, Harper, 1978.

Gadget. London, Heinemann, and New York, Coward McCann, 1977.

The Night Lords (Castang). London, Heinemann, and New York, Pantheon, 1978.

The Widow (Arlette Van der Valk). London, Heinemann, and New York, Pantheon, 1979.

Castang's City. London, Heinemann, and New York, Pantheon, 1980.

One Damn Thing after Another. London, Heinemann, 1981; as *Arlette*, New York, Pantheon, 1981.

Wolfnight (Castang). London, Heinemann, and New York, Pantheon, 1982.

The Back of the North Wind (Castang). London, Heinemann, and New York, Viking Press, 1983.

No Part in Your Death (Castang). London, Heinemann, and New York, Viking, 1984.

A City Solitary (Castang). London, Heinemann, and New York, Viking, 1985.

Cold Iron (Castang). London, Deutsch, and New York, Viking, 1986.

Lady Macbeth (Castang). London, Deutsch, 1988.

Not as Far as Velma (Castang). London, Deutsch, and New York, Mysterious Press, 1989.

Sand Castles (Van der Valk). London, Deutsch, 1989; New York, Mysterious Press, 1990.

Those in Peril. London, Deutsch, and New York, Mysterious Press, 1990.

Uncollected Short Stories

"The Beach Murder," in *Ellery Queen's Mystery Magazine* (New York), May 1969.

"Van der Valk and the Old Seaman," in *Ellery Queen's Mystery Magazine* (New York), August 1969.

"Van der Valk and the Four Mice," in *Ellery Queen's Mystery Magazine* (New York), November 1969.

"Van der Valk and the Young Man," in *Ellery Queen's Mystery Magazine* (New York), December 1969.

"Van der Valk and the High School Riot," in *Ellery Queen's Mystery Magazine* (New York), March 1970.

"Van der Valk and the Great Pot Problem," in *Ellery Queen's Mystery Magazine* (New York), April 1970.

"Van der Valk and the Wolfpack," in *Ellery Queen's Mystery Magazine* (New York), August 1970.

"Van der Valk and the False Caesar," in *Ellery Queen's Mystery Magazine* (New York), February 1972.

"Van der Valk and the Man from Nowhere," in *Ellery Queen's Mystery Magazine* (New York), May 1972.

"Van der Valk: The Train Watcher," in *Ellery Queen's Mystery Magazine* (New York), April 1973.

"Van der Valk and the Cavalier," in *Ellery Queen's Mystery Magazine* (New York), January 1974.

"Van der Valk and the Spanish Galleon," in *Ellery Queen's Mystery Magazine* (New York), August 1975.

"Van der Valk and the Two Pigeons," in *Ellery Queen's Magicians of Mystery*. New York, Davis, 1976.

OTHER PUBLICATIONS

Other

Kitchen Book. London, Hamish Hamilton, 1970; as *The Kitchen: A Delicious Account of the Author's Years as a Grand Hôtel Cook*, New York, Harper, 1970.

Cook Book. London, Hamish Hamilton, and New York, Harper, 1971.

*

Nicolas Freeling comments:

I believe that fiction should be written to entertain; for the enjoyment of a casual, uncommitted reader. In this context the label "crime" has value as an indication to a potential reader that here is a book he may enjoy.

To be formally classified as "crime-writer" is a distinction I have always found too vague and too narrow, and I protest at it. I can see only one valid distinction between different types of fiction: those designed to be consumed and discarded like a box of cornflakes/those designed to be kept, and hopefully, to be reread. If any book of mine has the luck not to be jettisoned, and yields some reward upon a further occasion, then I am made happy for such is my purpose.

In "series" writing I have tried to avoid the purely mechanical repetition of a formula. If a series seems to me in danger of exhaustion, I bring it to an end.

I think it legitimate to demand of a writer a constant, continuing effort towards renewal.

* * *

Nicolas Freeling rightly relates fact and form in his stories of crime and its common companions, destruction, anxiety, guilt, and cruelty. From the start he has written out of a sharp awareness of the need for reality. *Love in Amsterdam* conveys convincingly the general feeling of the Dutch city and the particular attitudes of its inhabitants, whose actions take place not so much against a backdrop as within a locale. *Because of the Cats* builds upon his achievement in adumbrating the life of the city of Amsterdam; now he has moved his action to a new town, "The pride of Dutch building and planning," half an hour by train from Amsterdam. Here by the peaceful seaside a gang of teenagers behave with brutality, with a cunning ruthlessness. Their actions are probed by Freeling's Dutch detective Van der Valk, who carries Freeling's commentary upon crime unobstrusively; he is compassionate, but skeptical; he has no illusions but he has an intense intellectual curiosity which compels him to the solution of the puzzles which crime presents, the oddities of human behaviour under stress.

Van der Valk is a character who shares his thoughts with Freeling's readers; he is sufficiently unorthodox to be attractively human, sufficiently intuitive to lift these stories above the mechanically commercial. In the initial stages of his investigation Van der Valk gets to know the nature of the new town, and conveys the uneasy relationships between parents and children in it. Then the story speeds up, with a horrifying inevitability, while the policeman, long stripped of illusions, comments skeptically but in the process paradoxically reveals his own humanity.

The atmosphere of place permeates *Valparaiso;* it is a mediterranean novel, set in Porquerolles, where a Parisian film star meets and energises Raymond into attempting his dream of crossing the Atlantic in his boat, the *Olivia*. But money is needed to refit her, and crime seems to promise its quick acquisition. Here the mood shifts from easy timeless drifting into urgent activity, and the story moves faster to its climax, the encounter between Raymond and the French patrol-boat. The action is well and economically described, and the characters are established effectively, rather in the manner of Simenon story.

There is a move away from the genre of the *roman policier* in *This Is the Castle* where Freeling develops his techniques further, where his narrative art encompasses a larger less precise dimension where the imagination can create its own apparent reality. Here the novelist living in Switzerland is neurotic; his menage of adoring wife, secretary-mistress, sons, and teenage daughter is visited by a publisher and an American journalist when a macabre shooting takes place; we see the tensions, the eccentricities through the eyes of the novelist and his wife, and the strange strains of the successful writer's life are explored with sensitive understanding.

Tsing-Boum develops the Van der Valk story to deeper levels, to a balanced view of the human motives behind the machine-gunning of the wife of a Dutch sergeant in her municipal flat while a television gangster serial is proceeding. Van der Valk is led into the after effects of the French surrender at Dien Bien Phu, but the way to violence goes through cowardice and revenge, blackmail and jealousy. The Dutch police Commissionaire is older, wiser—suffering from wounds incurred in an action described in an earlier novel—and more tolerant; he finds himself regarding the best as well as the worst of human behaviour, and the dullness of the surroundings of the crime makes the strange, but universal nature of the human activities unfolded seem completely acceptable in their variety.

Freeling has not wanted to become set in any mould; he killed off Van der Valk as a clear indication of this, but kept his sense of experiment alive and in the process he has become more capable of creating character. Take, for instance, Colette Delavigne, the children's Judge, a French examining magistrate who seems secure in her cosy little world until Rachel, her child, is kidnapped. Through her sufferings we are reminded of the emptiness brought by the disappearance. Freeling's skill in guiding his readers unobtrusively enough with his comments ("flatly," "with sarcastic emphasis," "mildly," "carefully," "thoughtfully") is effective because he largely relies on dialogue or conversation presented without adverbial or other guidance. And the speech presented has the genuineness of ordinary speech, not the strange syntax we hear from a tape recording of ourselves, but speech produced by literary art to seem that of casual or intense conversation.

Whereas the reader is often reminded of Simenon—and Freeling is obviously conscious of his technique; he is mentioned twice in *Tsing-Boum,* for instance—the difference between the novelists is that Freeling is allowing his characters more time for reflection, he is taking pains to provide suggestions, in order to bring home ethical ideas, and to convey them effectively through the form of his writing. He is using pattern, narrative rhythm, counterpointing to give coherence to the human condition he creates and analyses. His art is to leave questions in the reader's mind by showing the disruptive effects of crime upon all those who are involved in the action, as well as upon society as a whole. His policemen may be Dutch or French, his scenes may be in Amsterdam, Paris, Geneva or Cannes; but his policemen are representative of decent, honest policemen anywhere, under stress, like the public he describes, who can stand as the modern Everyman or Everywoman. This generalising ability, this capacity for understanding what it is like to live anywhere, here and now, raises him above mere mechanical practitioners of the form of the crime novel, because, while presenting his stories with increasing subtlety in shape and style, he develops and deepens his view of human nature.

—A. Norman Jeffares

FREEMAN, Kathleen. *See* **FITT, Mary.**

FREEMAN, R(ichard) Austin. Also wrote as Clifford Ashdown (with J.J. Pitcairn). British. Born in London, 11 April 1862. Educated at boarding school in London. Apprenticed as apothecary; studied at Middlesex Hospital, London; qualified as Physician and Surgeon, 1887. Served in Royal Army Medical Corps, 1915–19: Captain. Married Annie Elizabeth Edwards in 1887; two sons. Assistant colonial surgeon, Accra, Gold Coast (now Ghana), 1887–91; appointed boundary commissioner, 1891; invalided home 1891; assistant medical officer, Holloway Prison, 1900; Port of London Authority physician. Settled in Gravesend, 1903; worked as private tutor, then after 1919 as self-employed writer. Member of the Council, Eugenics Society. *Died 28 September 1943.*

CRIME PUBLICATIONS

Novels (series: Dr. John Evelyn Thorndyke)

The Red Thumb Mark (Thorndyke).   London, Collingwood, 1907; New York, Newton, 1911.
The Eye of Osiris: A Detective Romance (Thorndyke). London, Hodder and Stoughton, 1911; as *The Vanishing Man,* New York, Dodd Mead, 1912.
The Mystery of 31, New Inn (Thorndyke).   London, Hodder and Stoughton, 1912; Philadelphia, Winston, 1913.
The Uttermost Farthing: A Savant's Vendetta.   Philadelphia, Winston, 1914; as *A Savant's Vendetta,* London, Pearson, 1920.
A Silent Witness (Thorndyke).   London, Hodder and Stoughton, 1914; Philadelphia, Winston, 1915.
The Exploits of Danby Croker, Being Extracts from a Somewhat Disreputable Autobiography.   London, Duckworth, 1916.
Helen Vardon's Confession (Thorndyke).   London, Hodder and Stoughton, 1922.
The Cat's Eye (Thorndyke).   London, Hodder and Stoughton, 1923; New York, Dodd Mead, 1927.
The Mystery of Angelina Frood (Thorndyke).   London, Hodder and Stoughton, 1924; New York, Dodd Mead, 1925.

The Shadow of the Wolf (Thorndyke). London, Hodder and Stoughton, and New York, Dodd Mead, 1925.

The D'Arblay Mystery (Thorndyke). London, Hodder and Stoughton, and New York, Dodd Mead, 1926.

A Certain Dr. Thorndyke. London, Hodder and Stoughton, 1927; New York, Dodd Mead, 1928.

As a Thief in the Night (Thorndyke). London, Hodder and Stoughton, and New York, Dodd Mead, 1928.

Mr. Pottermack's Oversight (Thorndyke). London, Hodder and Stoughton, and New York, Dodd Mead, 1930.

Pontifex, Son and Thorndyke. London, Hodder and Stoughton, and New York, Dodd Mead, 1931.

When Rogues Fall Out. London, Hodder and Stoughton, 1932; as *Dr. Thorndyke's Discovery,* New York, Dodd Mead, 1932.

Dr. Thorndyke Intervenes. London, Hodder and Stoughton, and New York, Dodd Mead, 1933.

For the Defence: Dr. Thorndyke. London, Hodder and Stoughton, and New York, Dodd Mead, 1934.

The Penrose Mystery (Thorndyke). London, Hodder and Stoughton, and New York, Dodd Mead, 1936.

Felo De Se? (Thorndyke). London, Hodder and Stoughton, 1937; as *Death at the Inn,* New York, Dodd Mead, 1937.

The Stoneware Monkey (Thorndyke). London, Hodder and Stoughton, 1938; New York, Dodd Mead, 1939.

Mr. Polton Explains (Thorndyke). London, Hodder and Stoughton, and New York, Dodd Mead, 1940.

Dr. Thorndyke's Crime File (omnibus). New York, Dodd Mead, 1941.

The Jacob Street Mystery (Thorndyke). London, Hodder and Stoughton, 1942; as *The Unconscious Witness,* New York, Dodd Mead, 1942.

Short Stories

John Thorndyke's Cases. London, Chatto and Windus, 1909; as *Dr. Thorndyke's Cases,* New York, Dodd Mead, 1931.

The Singing Bone. London, Hodder and Stoughton, 1912; New York, Dodd Mead, 1923; as *The Adventures of Dr. Thorndyke,* New York, Popular Library, 1947.

The Great Portrait Mystery. London, Hodder and Stoughton, 1918.

Dr. Thorndyke's Case Book. London, Hodder and Stoughton, 1923; as *The Blue Scarab,* New York, Dodd Mead, 1924.

The Puzzle Lock. London, Hodder and Stoughton, 1925; New York, Dodd Mead, 1926.

The Magic Casket. London, Hodder and Stoughton, and New York, Dodd Mead, 1927.

The Famous Cases of Dr. Thorndyke. London, Hodder and Stoughton, 1929; as *The Dr. Thorndyke Omnibus,* New York, Dodd Mead, 1932.

Dr. Thorndyke Investigates. London, University of London Press, 1930.

Short Stories as Clifford Ashdown (with J.J. Pitcairn; series: Romney Pringle)

The Adventures of Romney Pringle. London, Ward Lock, 1902; Philadelphia, Oswald Train, 1968.

The Further Adventures of Romney Pringle. Philadelphia, Oswald Train, 1970.

The Queen's Treasure. Philadelphia, Oswald Train, 1975.

From a Surgeon's Diary. London, Ferret Fantasy, 1975; Philadelphia, Oswald Train, 1977.

OTHER PUBLICATIONS

Novels

The Golden Pool: A Story of a Forgotten Mine. London, Cassell, 1905.

The Unwilling Adventurer. London, Hodder and Stoughton, 1913.

The Surprising Adventures of Mr. Shuttlebury Cobb. London, Hodder and Stoughton, 1927.

Flighty Phyllis. London, Hodder and Stoughton, 1928.

Other

Travels and Life in Ashanti and Jaman. London, Constable, 1898.

Social Decay and Regeneration. London, Constable, and Boston, Houghton Mifflin, 1921.

*

Manuscript Collection: Occidental College, Los Angeles.

Critical Study: *In Search of Dr. Thorndyke* by Norman Donaldson, Bowling Green, Ohio, Popular Press, 1971.

*   *   *

Dr. John Evelyn Thorndyke remains the only convincing scientific investigator of detective fiction. That is the measure of R. Austin Freeman's achievement, and it rests not particularly on the accuracy of the technical details presented—accurate though they are—but on the impact of "scientific method" as a way of thought brought to bear in convincing fashion on the essentially romantic materials of the detective story. On the one hand, Freeman was a leisurely, old-fashioned writer, tending to platitudes, though Raymond Chandler found his style achieved "an even suspense that is quite unexpected." On the other, whether his materials were drawn from marine zoology or tropical medicine, Thorndyke's impact on non-scientists was always sharp and unequivocal. "Precise measurements don't seem to matter much," said an old lawyer in one story. "On the other hand," retorted Thorndyke, "inexact measurements are of no use at all."

Freeman achieved a second breakthrough. With his fictional investigator's career only just launched—in *The Red Thumb Mark*—he wrote for *Pearson's Magazine* a series of "inverted" stories, in which he forfeited the element of surprise by identifying the criminal and letting us see him at his nefarious work. As he put it himself, "the usual circumstances are reversed; the reader knows everything, the detective knows nothing, and the interest focuses on the unexpected significance of trivial circumstances." As television viewers watch the *Colombo* series and other examples of this form, how many of them know who originated it? John Adams, reviewing the first collection, *The Singing Bone,* admitted them to be "beyond the range of the ordinary devourer of 'sleuth' novels.... A very obvious and natural criticism of the stories is that they are too clever; they ask too much of the reader. But unlike some clever writers, Mr. Freeman is clever enough to carry off his cleverness. His exposition is so clear, his arrangement of events so methodical, that the reader is led along with the minimum amount of effort consistent with a very definite exercise of the reason."

The short stories and novels of the Freeman canon, however, are dominated by the handsome, usually impassive medical jurist of 5A King's Bench Walk in London's Inner Temple, Dr. Thorndyke. In the short tales the narrator is almost always his chief associate, Christopher Jervis, M.D., but several of the novels open with the discovery of a crime by a young physician who subsequently becomes romantically involved in the investigation. *The Red Thumb Mark,* which has to do with forged fingerprints, ends with Jervis's marriage. A finer example is *A Silent Witness,* with its persuasive description of the laboratory upstairs at No. 5A, lighted by the glow of the furnace and alive with workers, including Thorndyke's factotum, the diminutive, crinkly Nathaniel Polton.

The Cat's Eye has perhaps the most complex plot of all the novels, and is entirely successful. In *The Mystery of Angelina Frood* the author takes a scientific fallacy from Dicken's unfinished *Mystery of Edwin Drood* and weaves a lighthearted mystery around it. *The Shadow of the Wolf* is an expanded version of a two-part inverted magazine story published in 1914; the indispensable clue is a marine worm. Only occasionally did Freeman write a classic "whodunit," in which one of the main characters is identified as the criminal; *As a Thief in the Night* is a fine example—a dramatic novel rich in deep-felt emotions. *Mr. Pottermack's Oversight,* a general favorite, is an inverted novel that shows the good Doctor at his most amiable in dealing with the murderer of a blackmailer. *Dr. Thorndyke Intervenes* uses as its basis the real-life Druce-Portland Case of 1907, whereas a fictitious excavation in *The Penrose Mystery* was instrumental in bringing about a real "dig" at the same site a little later.

Although some falling off in quality is evident in Freeman's writing as he approached his eighties, his ability to ring the changes from one Thorndyke case to the next is almost as remarkable a feat as his original conception of the great medical jurist.

—Norman Donaldson

FREEMANTLE, Brian (Harry). Also writes as Jonathan Evans; Richard Grant; John Maxwell; Jack Winchester. British. Born in Southampton, Hampshire, 10 June 1936. Educated at Bitterne Park Secondary Modern School, Southampton. Married Maureen Hazel Tipney in 1956; three daughters. Reporter, New Milton *Advertiser,* Hampshire, 1953–58, Bristol *Evening World,* 1958, and *Evening News,* London, 1958–60; reporter, later assistant foreign editor, *Daily Express,* London, 1960–69; foreign editor, *Daily Sketch,* London, 1969–70, and *Daily Mail,* London, 1970–75; as a foreign correspondent worked in 30 countries. Agent: Jonathan Clowes Ltd., 22 Prince Albert Road, London NW1 7ST, England.

CRIME PUBLICATIONS

Novels (series: Charlie Muffin)

Goodbye to an Old Friend. London, Cape, and New York, Putnam, 1973.
Face Me When You Walk Away. London, Cape, 1974; New York, Putnam, 1975.
The Man Who Wanted Tomorrow. London, Cape, and New York, Stein and Day, 1975.
The November Man. London, Cape, 1976.

Charlie Muffin. London, Cape, 1977; as *Charlie M,* New York, Doubleday, 1977; London, Sphere, 1978.
Clap Hands, Here Comes Charlie. London, Cape, 1978; as *Here Comes Charlie M,* New York, Doubleday, 1978.
The Inscrutable Charlie Muffin. London, Cape, and New York, Doubleday, 1979.
Charlie Muffin's Uncle Sam. London, Cape, 1980; as *Charlie Muffin U.S.A.,* New York, Doubleday, 1980.
The Solitary Man (as Jack Winchester). London, Hamish Hamilton, and New York, Coward McCann, 1980.
Madrigal for Charlie Muffin. London, Hutchinson, 1981.
Deaken's War. London, Hutchinson, 1982 (as Jack Winchester). London, Arrow, 1985.
Vietnam Legacy. New York, Tor, 1984.
The Lost American. New York, Tor, 1984.
Rules of Engagement. London, Century, 1984.
Charlie Muffin and the Russian Rose. London, Century, 1985.
The Kremlin Kiss. London, Century, 1986.
The Choice of Eddie Franks (as Jack Winchester). London, Collins, 1986; New York, Tor, 1987.
The Blind Run. London, and New York, Bantam, 1986.
Charlie Muffin San. London, Century, 1987.
See Charlie Run. New York, Bantam, 1987.
The Runaround (Muffin). London, Century, 1988; New York, Bantam, 1989.
The Bearpit. London, Century, 1988.
Comrade Charlie. London, Century, 1989.
Betrayals. New York, Tor, 1989.
O'Farrell's Law. New York, Tor, 1990.

Novels as Jonathan Evans

Misfire. London, Joseph, and New York, Tor, 1980.
The Midas Men. London, Joseph, 1981; as *Sagomi Gambit,* New York, Tor, 1981.
Chairman of the Board. London, Joseph, 1982; as *Takeover,* New York, Tor, 1982.
Monopoly. London, Joseph, 1984.
The Laundryman. London, Joseph, 1985; as *Dirty White,* New York, Tor, 1986.

Short Stories

The Factory and Other Stories. London, Century, 1990.

OTHER PUBLICATIONS

Novels

The Touchables (novelization of screenplay). London, Hodder and Stoughton, 1969.
H.M.S. Bounty (as John Maxwell). London, Cape, 1977.
The Mary Celeste (as John Maxwell). London, Cape, 1979.

Other

Sean Connery: Gilt-Edged Bond (as Richard Grant). London, Mayflower, 1967.
KGB. London, Joseph, and New York, Holt Rinehart, 1982.
CIA. London, Joseph, and New York, Stein and Day, 1983.
The Fix: Inside the World Drug Trade. London, Joseph, 1985; New York, Tor, 1986.
The Steal: Counterfeiting and Industrial Espionage. London, Joseph, 1986.

*

Brian Freemantle comments:

Although I write spy fiction, I have always tried to make my novels good *as novels,* and I rely heavily upon characterisation. I am happiest with the traditional type of plot line, and, through the use of strong plots and strong characterisation, I try to create a "rooftop" effect in my stories.

* * *

Brian Freemantle's protagonists are weak, fallible human beings, wounded by circumstances and events outside their control, such as a working-class upbringing (Charlie Muffin, Freemantle's series hero), a father's pursuit across Europe by Jew hunters (Eddie Franks in *The Choice of Eddie Franks*), the death of a spouse (Janet Stone in *Betrayals*), or a mother's suicide (Charles O'Farrell in *O'Farrell's Law*). These vulnerable protagonists attempt to act and make choices, to assert their integrity, but they are used as pawns by intelligence services, the business world, and the media.

In the murky, labyrinthine reality of Freemantle's thrillers, the protagonists are betrayed by those organizations and individuals they trust the most. Charlie Muffin is deceived again and again by his British intelligence superiors; Eddie Franks, by his foster brother; Janet Stone, by the men she loves; Charles O'Farrell, by his CIA bosses. The heroes' vital needs for love and physical as well as psychological safety are frustrated, their integrity becomes impaired, and they themselves become betrayers.

The distinction between the betrayed and the betrayer is blurred in this world. Freemantle often gives his characters psychological doubles, emphasizing the similarities between the "good" and the "bad." For example, the Israelis in *The Man Who Wanted Tomorrow* are as vicious as the former Nazis upon whom they seek revenge. And in *O'Farrell's Law,* Rivera, the Cuban ambassador to England who deals in drugs for arms, comes to be as sympathetic a character as the eponymous hero, a CIA assassin whose job it is to kill Rivera in order to save lives.

In Freemantle's world of confusion, doubt, envy, anger, and pain, the protagonists often come to deceive not only others, but also themselves, with this self-deception leading to their self-destruction. Only the scruffy hero in Hush Puppies of the Charlie Muffin series is able to operate successfully in this world. He is betrayed and in turn betrays (his snobbish British intelligence superiors, the CIA, the FBI, the KGB, and the Chinese), but he is never self-deceived. And he is always in the end a survivor.

—Joan M. Saliskas

FREMLIN, Celia (Margaret). British. Born in Ryarsh, Kent, 20 June 1914. Educated at Berkhamsted School for Girls, Hertfordshire; Somerville College, Oxford, B.A. in classics 1936, B. Litt. in philosophy 1937. Served as an air raid warden during World War II. Married Elia Goller in 1942 (died); one son and two daughters. Recipient: Mystery Writers of America Edgar Allan Poe award, 1960. Address: 11 Parkhill Road, London NW3 2YH, England.

CRIME PUBLICATIONS

Novels

The Hours Before Dawn. London, Gollancz, 1958; Philadelphia, Lippincott, 1959.
Uncle Paul. London, Gollancz, 1959; Philadelphia, Lippincott, 1960.
Seven Lean Years. London, Gollancz, 1961; as *Wait for the Wedding,* Philadelphia, Lippincott, 1961.
The Trouble-Makers. London, Gollancz, and Philadelphia, Lippincott, 1963.
The Jealous One. London, Gollancz, and Philadelphia, Lippincott, 1965.
Prisoner's Base. London, Gollancz, and Philadelphia, Lippincott, 1967.
Possession. London, Gollancz, and Philadelphia, Lippincott, 1969.
Appointment with Yesterday. London, Gollancz, and Philadelphia, Lippincott, 1972.
The Long Shadow. London, Gollancz, 1975; New York, Doubleday, 1976.
The Spider-Orchid. London, Gollancz, 1977; New York, Doubleday, 1978.
With No Crying. London, Gollancz, 1980; New York, Doubleday, 1981.
The Parasite Person. London, Gollancz, and New York, Doubleday, 1982.
Listening in the Dusk. London, Gollancz, and New York, Doubleday, 1990.

Short Stories

Don't Go to Sleep in the Dark. London, Gollancz, and Philadelphia, Lippincott, 1970.
By Horror Haunted. London, Gollancz, 1974.
A Lovely Day to Die and Other Stories. London, Gollancz, and New York, Doubleday, 1984.

Uncollected Short Stories

"The Christmas Drop-Outs," in *Woman's Realm* (London), 1973.
"The Coldness of a Thousand Suns," in *Ellery Queen's Crookbook.* New York, Random House, 1974.
"If It's Got Your Number," in *Ellery Queen's Murdercade.* New York, Random House, 1975.
"Accommodation Vacant," in *Winter's Crimes 7,* edited by George Hardinge. London, Macmillan, 1975.
"Don't Be Frightened," in *MS Mysteries,* edited by Arthur Liebman. New York, Washington Square Press, 1976.
"Dangerous Sport," in *Ellery Queen's Mystery Magazine* (New York), September 1976.
"Golden Tuesday," in *Ellery Queen's Champions of Mystery.* New York, Davis, 1977.
"The Woman Who Had Everything," in *John Creasey's Crime Collection,* edited by Herbert Harris. London, Hodder and Stoughton, 1977.
"The Postgraduate Thesis," in *Verdict of Thirteen,* edited by Julian Symons. London, Faber, and New York, Harper, 1979.
"A Case of Maximum Need" and "Etiquette for Dying," in *Ellery Queen's Scenes of the Crime.* New York, Davis, 1979.
"The Magic Carpet," in *Ellery Queen's Veils of Mystery.* New York, Davis, 1980.
"Bluebeard's Key," in *Ellery Queen's Mystery Magazine* (New York), 1984.

"Drown Her of Saturday," in *Ellery Queen's Mystery Magazine* (New York), 1985.
"The Sensory Deprivation Tank," in *Ellery Queen's Mystery Magazine* (New York), 1985.
"In the Clear," in *Ellery Queen's Mystery Magazine* (New York), 1985.
"The Magic Touch," in *Woman's Own* (London), 1986.
"Out of the Blue," *Woman's Own* (London), 1987.

OTHER PUBLICATIONS

Other

The Seven Chars of Chelsea (on domestic service).   London, Methuen, 1940.
War Factory.   London, Gollancz, 1943.
Living Through the Blitz, with Tom Harrisson.   London, Collins, 1976.

*

Manuscript Collection: Mugar Memorial Library, Boston University.

Celia Fremlin comments:
    The kind of crime novels I write are usually listed as "novels of suspense," since there are no policemen, no detectives, and (quite often) no murder: just some sort of mysterious threat hanging over someone and escalating (or so I hope!) chapter by chapter.
    What first launched me on writing this sort of book was simply the fact that this was the sort of book I wanted to read, and there seemed to be terribly few of them. What I aim at, I think, is an exciting or even terrifying plot set against a very ordinary sort of humdrum domestic background, with a hero or heroine beset by day-to-day problems, as well as the mysterious outside threat. I find that by this juxtaposition I can throw across my characters a lurid sort of illumination which enables me to explore them in much greater depth than I could by any other means.

*   *   *

    There is no-one to equal Celia Fremlin in the writing of the modern "woman-in-jeopardy" novel—even Ruth Rendell. But Fremlin's women are not the had-I-but-known heroines of Mary Roberts Rinehart or Mignon G. Eberhart: her women face their peril on the domestic front and it is this which makes her work truly revolutionary.
    Since the late 1950's Fremlin has been exploring the everyday tensions and terrors of ordinary women. In *The Hours Before Dawn,* Louise Henderson, worn ragged by the wakefulness of her new baby, convinces herself that her new woman lodger is a threat to her and her baby. Of course, in her delicate state of nerves no-one believes her and her own home becomes gradually more alien and frightening. In *With No Crying,* Miranda Field is pressured into an unwanted abortion so feigns pregnancy to regain the attention she has enjoyed. In her most recent novel *Listening in the Dusk* a young women in a lodging house is haunted by a dark secret involving a murder.
    Fremlin's understanding of the small tyrannies and unfairnesses of women's lives place her firmly as a precursor of more recent feminist thriller writers; she displays similar concern for issues of interest to women and uses the conventions of the genre to convey these concerns to the reader. She also has a

healthy resistance to the critical assertion that domestic mysteries are somehow inferior to those set in the big, wide world.
    While her novels do sometimes have concealed agendas, they are always immaculately crafted and plotted as befits a writer who is mistress of the difficult art of the short mystery story. Her way with the twists and turns of final chapters and ends of stories serves as a model for any budding practitioners.

—Linda Semple

———

FREYER, Frederic. *See* **BALLINGER, Bill S.**

———

FRIEDMAN, Kinky. American. Singer and Songwriter. Address: c/o William Morrow and Company Inc., 105 Madison Avenue, New York, New York 10016, U.S.A.

CRIME PUBLICATIONS

Novels

When the Cat's Away.   New York, Beach Tree, 1980.
Greenwich Killing Time.   New York, Morrow, 1986.
A Case of Lone Star.   New York, Beach Tree, 1987.
Frequent Flyer.   New York, Morrow, 1989.

*   *   *

    The detective fiction of Kinky Friedman provides an excellent argument for those interested in linking popular literature with reality. Friedman is his own protagonist (a device first used by the mythical Nicholas Carter in 1886, but rarely taken advantage of by actual flesh-and-blood authors) and his books are filled with Friedman acquaintances. Chet Flippo, author of a popular biography of Hank Williams, is featured in *A Case of Lone Star,* a murder mystery in which vital clues are scribblings of Williams's country songs. Friedman's "Watson" is a rather unkempt individual named Ratso who in real life works for National Lampoon Magazine. All this provides interesting background material but might become little more than a tedious gimmick if not for Friedman's masterful weaving of atmosphere. He states that he wants the books to "smell" like New York City, and the uniqueness and beauty of the city provide Friedman with a symbolic landscape on which to philosophize about the "big picture" peppering his soliloquies with wit and humor.
    The Friedman protagonist often reminisces of the years spent on the road with his band "The Texas Jew-Boys," and *Frequent Flyer,* Friedman's fourth book, describes his experiences in the wilds of Borneo while working in the Peace Corps. Few are the authors whose lives are interesting enough from which to create fiction. Friedman has little trouble doing so, and it is his personality which unifies the works and keeps readers reading despite time of day or night.
    Friedman's voice is strong enough to hold the books together despite what might appear to be flimsy plotlines. Friedman has stated that, "plots are for cemeteries. If you get a plot in a

Kinky book, you can consider it gravy." The Friedman persona, however, is an interesting blend of Holmesian melancholy and Continental Op pragmatism. He frequently "mixes things up" to see what will come of it and on occasion brings all the suspects together—sometimes even solving the mystery before the irate characters leave in disgust. Throughout it all the dreary street scenes of New York City cloud the hero's thoughts, provoking such lines as, "In six days the Lord created the heavens and the earth and all the wonders therein. There are some of us who feel that He might have taken just a little more time."

Friedman was prompted into writing fiction and out of writing country music by an incident in Greenwich Village in which he rescued a young woman from a lunatic with a knife. The *New York Post* headline read, "Country Singer Plucks Victim from Mugger," and Friedman's writing career began soon after. Although the actual event does not show up in the first book, *Greenwich Killing Time,* it is discussed at some length by the characters therein.

Because of the newness of the technique, *Greenwich Killing Time* is a good place for any inquisitive reader to begin. As the books continue, however, the humor is reinforced by an almost poetic narration. *A Case of Lone Star* is ideal for country music fans, useful no doubt for uniting Friedman's earlier fans with those of detective fiction. *When the Cat's Away* evolves around a lost cat in Madison Square Garden, weaving into the plot a story of ancient occultism. *Frequent Flyer* begins with the funeral of a close friend of Friedman, although the corpse is not the face Kinky remembers. This precipitates a journey through the jungles of Borneo in and out of the clutches of escaped Nazi criminals. As Friedman continues to publish it is interesting to note that more and more his persona lingers within the confines of his New York apartment contemplating the rain, wind, universe, nature of humankind, and the puppet head above his refrigerator. Such introspection reminds one of the later writings of Mark Twain. Below the surface of these pleasant and humorous writings lies a darker vision of the futile struggle of humankind that everyone must glimpse sooner or later. It is much more entertaining to face such a scene with Friedman close by.

As detective fiction increases in popularity it is all too easy to classify most works as hard-boiled, Golden Age revisited, or spoofs of the above. Friedman attempts to blend these forms together with his own unique voice. The confines of country music were too constricting for Friedman's talent, mystery fiction seems an ideal place for him. He states that, "mysteries offer resolution and life itself rarely does;" for the reader of Friedman's fiction it is the road to resolution which is most rewarding.

—Michael Pettengell

FRIEND, Ed. *See* WORMSER, Richard.

FROME, David. *See* FORD, Leslie.

FULLER, Roy (Broadbent). British. Born in Failsworth, Lancashire, 11 February 1912. Educated at Blackpool High School, Lancashire, qualified as a solicitor, 1934. Served in the Royal Navy, 1941–46; Lieutenant, Royal Naval Volunteer Reserve. Married Kathleen Smith in 1936; one son, the poet John Fuller. Assistant solicitor, 1938–58, solicitor, 1958–69; Director, Woolwich Equitable Building Society, London, 1969–87, Chairman of the Legal Advisory Panel, 1958–69, vice-president, Building Societies Association 1967–87. Professor of Poetry, Oxford University, 1968–73. Chairman, Poetry Book Society, London, 1960–68; Governor, BBC, 1972–79; Member, Arts Council of Great Britain, and chairman of the Literature Panel, 1976–77 (resigned). Recipient: Arts Council Poetry award, 1959; Duff Cooper Memorial prize, for poetry, 1968; Queen's Gold Medal for Poetry, 1970; Cholmondeley award, 1980; Heinemann prize, 1990. M.A.: Oxford University. Fellow, Royal Society of Literature, 1958. C.B.E. (Commander, Order of the British Empire), 1970. Address: 37 Langton Way, Blackheath, London S.E.3, England.

CRIME PUBLICATIONS

Novels

The Second Curtain. London, Verschoyle, 1953; New York, Macmillan, 1956.
Fantasy and Fugue. London, Verschoyle, 1954; New York, Macmillan, 1956; as *Murder in Mind,* Chicago, Academy, 1986.
Image of a Society. London, Deutsch, 1956; New York, Macmillan, 1957.
The Ruined Boys. London, Deutsch, 1959; as *That Distant Afternoon,* New York, Macmillan, 1959.
The Father's Comedy. London, Deutsch, 1961.
The Perfect Fool. London, Deutsch, 1963.
My Child, My Sister. London, Deutsch, 1965.
The Carnal Island. London, Deutsch, 1970.
The Roy Fuller Crime Omnibus (includes *With My Little Eye, The Second Curtain, Fantasy and Fugue*). Manchester, Carcanet, 1988.

OTHER PUBLICATIONS

Verse

Poems. London, Fortune Press, 1940.
The Middle of a War. London, Hogarth Press, 1942.
A Lost Season. London, Hogarth Press, 1944.
Epitaphs and Occasions. London, Lehmann, 1949.
Counterparts. London, Verschoyle, 1954.
Brutus's Orchard. London, Deutsch, 1957; New York, Macmillan, 1958.
Collected Poems 1936–1961. London, Deutsch, 1962.
Buff. London, Deutsch, 1965.
New Poems. London, Deutsch, 1968.
Confrontation Off Korea. Oxford, Sycamore Press, 1968.
Pergamon Poets 1, with R.S. Thomas, edited by Evan Owen. Oxford, Pergamon Press, 1968.
Off Course. London, Turret, 1969.
Penguin Modern Poets 18, with A. Alvarez and Anthony Thwaite. London, Penguin, 1970.
To an Unknown Reader. London, Poem-of-the-Month Club, 1970.
Song Cycle from a Record Sleeve. Oxford, Sycamore Press, 1972.
Tiny Tears. London, Deutsch, 1973.

An Old War. Edinburgh, Tragara Press, 1974.
Waiting for the Barbarians: A Poem. Richmond, Surrey, Keepsake Press, 1974.
From the Joke Shop. London, Deutsch, 1975.
The Joke Shop Annexe. Edinburgh, Tragara Press, 1975.
An Ill-Governed Coast. Sunderland, Ceolfrith Press, 1976.
Re-treads. Edinburgh, Tragara Press, 1979.
The Reign of Sparrows. London, London Magazine Editions, 1980.
The Individual and His Times: A Selection of the Poetry of Roy Fuller, edited by V.J. Lee. London, Athlone Press, 1982.
House and Shop. Edinburgh, Tragara Press, 1982.
As from the Thirties. Edinburgh, Tragara Press, 1983.
Mianserin Sonnets. Edinburgh, Tragara Press, 1984.
New and Collected Poems 1934–84. London, Secker and Warburg, 1985.
Subsequent to Summer. Edinburgh, Salamander Press, 1985.
Outside the Cannon. Edinburgh, Tragara Press, 1986.
Lessons of the Summer. Edinburgh, Tragara Press, 1987.
Consolations. London, Secker and Warburg, 1987.
Available for Dreams. London, Collins Harvill, 1989.
The World Though the Window: Collected Poems for Children. London, Blackie, 1989.

Other

Savage Gold (for children). London, Lehmann, 1946.
With My Little Eye (for children). London, Lehmann, 1948; New York, Macmillan, 1957.
Questions and Answers in Building Society Law and Practice. London, Franey, 1949.
Catspaw (for children). London, Alan Ross, 1966.
Owls and Artificers: Oxford Lectures on Poetry. London, Deutsch, and New York, Library Press, 1971.
Seen Grandpa Lately? (for children). London, Deutsch, 1972.
Professors and Gods: Last Oxford Lectures on Poetry. London, Deutsch, 1973; New York, St. Martin's Press, 1974.
Poor Roy (for children). London, Deutsch, 1977.
The Other Planet and Three Other Fables (for children). Richmond, Surrey, Keepsake Press, 1979.
Souvenirs (memoirs). London, London Magazine Editions, 1980.
More about Tompkins and Other Light Verse (for children). Edinburgh, Tragara Press, 1981.
Vamp Till Ready: Further Memoirs. London, London Magazine Editions, 1982.
Upright, Downfall (for children), with Barbara Giles and Adrian Rumble. London, Oxford University Press, 1983.
Home and Dry: Memoirs 3. London, London Magazine Editions, 1984.
Twelfth Night: A Personal View. Edinburgh, Tragara, 1985.
The Strange and the Good: Collected Memoirs. London, Collins Harvill, 1989.

Editor, *Byron for Today.* London, Porcupine Press, 1948.
Editor, with Clifford Dyment and Montagu Slater, *New Poems 1952.* London, Joseph, 1952.
Editor, *The Building Societies Acts 1874–1960: Great Britain and Northern Ireland,* 5th edition. London, Franey, 1961.
Editor, *Supplement of New Poetry.* London, Poetry Book Society, 1964.
Editor, *Fellow Mortals: An Anthology of Animal Verse.* Plymouth, Macdonald and Evans, 1981.
Editor, with John Lehmann, *The Penguin New Writing 1940–50: An Anthology.* London, Penguin, 1985.

*

Manuscript Collections (Verse): State University of New York, Buffalo; British Library, London; Brotherton Collection, Leeds University.

Critical Study: *Roy Fuller* by Allen E. Austin, Boston, Twayne, 1979.

Roy Fuller comments:
I am afraid my contribution to crime fiction has remained meagre and now looks decidedly historical. I can only say that I love the genre at its best and wish I had done more in that line.

*   *   *

Roy Fuller is best known as a poet who developed in the 1930's and whose work has since retained those concerns with the relationship between the individual and the collectivity that were characteristic of that decade. His novels all belong to later decades, and the difference between them and his poetry of the 1930's lies in the extent to which the collective has assumed a negative and hostile role. The novels are really moral thrillers, in which there is sometimes an actual crime that the central character finds himself forced to attempt to solve, but in which the real mystery lies in how the individual, who cannot command the strength needed to defeat powerful institutions, may still himself retain some shred of undefeated integrity.

It is perhaps in *The Second Curtain* that the two sides are most clearly demarcated, for the Power Industries Protection Corporation is in the most literal sense a criminal organization which operates on behalf of industrial interests generally regarded as pillars of society. Drawn into conflict with it is George Garner, a minor writer who lives largely by the drudgery of reading for publishers, an untidy and no more than ordinarily courageous man unwittingly involved in a web of violence and treachery when a friend mysteriously dies and he sets out, with no detective's training, to find out why and how. What Garner does find, to his consternation, is that the very patrons who propose to make him editor of a new literary magazine, and so liberate him from Grub Street drudgery, are in fact responsible for his friend's death. In the end, faced with naked brutality, the experience of violence, the threat of death, Garner gives up. He has learnt the truth about power. He cannot make his knowledge work effectively.

Individuals overshadowed by yet defying collectivities recur in Fuller's novels. In *Image of a Society* the collectivity is a Building Society like that in which Fuller himself worked for three decades; in *The Ruined Boys* it is a near-bankrupt private school. In *My Child, My Sister* the collectivity does not take institutional form, but an ageing man sexually stirred by his wife's daughter by another marriage finds himself facing and judging the structure of moral convention and its relevance to his own life. None of these books is a "mystery" in the same literal way as *The Second Curtain,* yet in their essential moral flavour, in their central opposition of the individual and the collectivity they belong in the same world.

This particularly applies to Fuller's fifth and perhaps most ambitious novel, *The Father's Comedy,* in which Colmore, an ambitious and successful civil servant employed by the mysterious "Authority," which is really an image for society as a whole, finds himself in a moral dilemma when his son rebels against the repression of the army and faces a court martial from which he can only be saved by the father's revelation of his own left-wing past. Colmore allows the call of human distress to overcome that of duty, and gains his son's acquittal, but when he returns "To show himself to the Authority," we know that what may happen in the future is less significant than the present, in which Colmore is able to accept that his planned career may be ruined when he declares for human love. In so far as in modern thrillers this kind of basic social conflict is one of the imponderable but necessary issues, one of the mysteries, all of Roy Fuller's fiction is essentially mysterious.

—George Woodcock

———

FUREY, Michael. *See* **ROHMER, Sax.**

———

FUTRELLE, Jacques. American. Born in Pike County, Georgia, 9 April 1875. Married the writer L. May Peel in 1895. Theatrical manager; staff member, Boston *American*. *Died on the Titanic 15 April 1912.*

CRIME PUBLICATIONS

Novels (series: Professor Augustus S.F.X. Van Dusen, The Thinking Machine)

The Chase of the Golden Plate (Van Dusen). New York, Dodd Mead, 1906.
The Simple Case of Susan. New York, Appleton, 1908; expanded by May Futrelle as *Lieutenant What's-His-Name,* Indianapolis, Bobbs Merrill, 1915.
Elusive Isabel. Indianapolis, Bobbs Merrill, 1909; as *The Lady in the Case,* London, Nelson, 1910.
The High Hand. Indianapolis, Bobbs Merrill, 1911; as *The Master Hand,* London, Hodder and Stoughton, 1914.
My Lady's Garter. Chicago, Rand McNally, 1912; London, Hodder and Stoughton, 1913.
Blind Man's Buff. London, Hodder and Stoughton, 1914.

Short Stories

The Thinking Machine. New York, Dodd Mead, and London, Chapman, 1907; as *The Problem of Cell 13,* New York, Dodd Mead, 1918.

The Thinking Machine on the Case. New York, Appleton, 1908; as *The Professor on the Case,* London, Nelson, 1909.
The Diamond Master. Indianapolis, Bobbs Merrill, 1909; London, Holden, 1912; collected with *The Haunted Bell,* New York, Burt, 1915.
Best Thinking Machine Detective Stories, edited by E.F. Bleiler. New York, Dover, 1973.
Great Cases of the Thinking Machine. New York, Dover, and London, Constable, 1976.

*   *   *

The most popular story in mystery literature, with the possible exception of certain adventures of Sherlock Holmes, is probably Jacques Futrelle's "The Problem of Cell 13," which first appeared serially as a contest in a Boston newspaper in 1905. It was eventually followed by 42 other short stories about the Thinking Machine (Professor Augustus S.F.X. Van Dusen), in which the Professor continued his joust against the impossible. In the same series is a short novel, *The Haunted Bell,* which contains a note of the supernatural, and a longer work, *The Chase of the Golden Plate,* which is an automobile and society novel with mystery elements.

The essence of The Thinking Machine stories, which first appeared in newspapers, is that they were stories of idea at a time when most detective short stories were concerned with incident or situation. Most of Futrelle's earlier stories were built upon scientific concepts that permitted "impossible" situations; the later stories, on the other hand, were explications of weirdly colorful events in terms of ordinary circumstances.

Excellent characterization, ingenious ideas, fast-moving journalistic prose and amusing small touches make Futrelle's better stories outstanding in their period, but it must be admitted that his work is uneven. Futrelle was prolific in other areas of fiction, and in his later years he concentrated on frothy Edwardian romances. His mystery novels *Elusive Isabel, My Lady's Garter,* and *Blind Man's Buff* are in this vein. Futrelle also wrote a few miscellaneous detective stories which have not been collected; these are on the trivial side. Apart from the better stories about The Thinking Machine, Futrelle's finest work is *The Diamond Master,* a puzzling mystery with a small element of science-fiction.

—E.F. Bleiler

———

G

GADNEY, Reg. British. Born in Cross Hills, Yorkshire, 20 January 1941. Educated at Stowe School, Buckinghamshire; St. Catharine's College, Cambridge, 1962–66, M.A. 1966. Served in the Coldstream Guards, 1959–62: Lieutenant. Married Annette Margot Kobak in 1966; one son and one daughter. Research Fellow and Instructor, School of Architecture and Planning, Massachusetts Institute of Technology, Cambridge, 1966–67; Deputy Controller, National Film Theatre, London, 1967–68; Senior Tutor, 1968–78, and Pro-Rector, 1978–82, Royal College of Art, London. Regular contributor of articles on crime fiction for *London Magazine,* 1964–78. Recipient: Josephine de Karman Trust Scholarship, 1966. Fellow, Royal College of Art, 1978. Agent: Peters Fraser and Dunlop, 5th Floor, The Chambers, Chelsea Harbour, Lots Road, London SW10 0XF

CRIME PUBLICATIONS

Novels

Drawn Blanc. London, Heinemann, 1970; New York, Coward McCann, 1972.
Somewhere in England. London, Heinemann, 1971; New York, St. Martin's Press, 1972.
Seduction of a Tall Man. London, Heinemann, 1972.
Something Worth Fighting For. London, Heinemann, 1974.
The Last Hours Before Dawn. London, Heinemann, 1975; as *Victoria,* New York, Coward McCann, 1975.
The Champagne Marxist. London, Hutchinson, 1977; as *The Cage,* New York, Coward McCann, 1977.
Nightshade. London, Heinemann, 1987; New York, St. Martin's Press, 1988.

Uncollected Short Story

"The Democratic Murder," in *Winter's Crimes 10,* edited by Hilary Watson. London, Macmillan, 1978.

OTHER PUBLICATIONS

Plays

Television Plays: *Forgive Our Foolish Ways,* 1980; *The Bell,* from the novel by Iris Murdoch, 1982; *Last Love,* 1983; *Kennedy,* 1983; *Drummonds* series, 1985; *Goldeneye,* 1989.

Other

Constable and His World. London, Thames and Hudson, and New York, Norton, 1976.
John Constable, R.A.: Catalogue of Drawings and Watercolours. London, Arts Council, 1976.
Kennedy. London, Macdonald, and New York, Holt Rinehart, 1983.
Cry Hungary!: Uprising 1956. London, Weidenfeld and Nicolson, and New York, Atheneum, 1986.

*

Manuscript Collection: Mugar Memorial Library, Boston University.

* * *

Reg Gadney is, or was, a writer who appeared to have risen up like a rocket in the spasmodically starlit night of British crime fiction and to have been extinguished as thoroughly. In the years between 1970 and 1977 six books, and then silence. (Or, semi-silence: other ventures have burst out from time to time, notably a television series on the Kennedys that succeeded in the tightrope difficult task of avoiding equally gooey sensationalism and clumping hagiography.) One can only hope, however, that he was no rocket but a comet due at some undivined date to reappear brilliant as ever because from his very beginnings he struck a unique note. Reviewing only his second book, *Somewhere in England,* for *The Times* of London I was moved already, I find, to refer to "the sad and semen-stained Gadney world."

Perhaps this short flowering arose from the fact that Gadney is not a full-time novelist but a professional art historian. So one can see his first venture into crime fiction, *Drawn Blanc,* as the work of one of those people of mature mind turning to crime through a decently unpretentious desire to embark with modesty on what might seem to be the knowinger-than-thou business of novel writing.

But nevertheless he sprang fully armed into the fiction fray and *Drawn Blanc* is both a considerable comment on homo non sapiens and a highly entertaining thriller. As a novelist he takes that most disoriented of men, the stateless refugee, and places him in that most disoriented situation, that of a secret agent who is committed to no particular nation or philosophy. And like this hero, O.B. Blanc by name (neither initial stands for anything), the reader is placed totally under the logic of "need to know." Almost nothing but Blanc's immediate situation is described, bar perhaps the swiftly evocative London and Wiltshire backdrops. The effect is powerfully to transfer to us a state of mind. One experiences a feeling of curious detachment, as if one was able to communicate with a solitary bubble caught in glass, there but cut-off and pure. As a crime-writer he does not fail to provide both mystery and excitement.

The Gadney atmosphere, it must be admitted, could be caviar to the general, though equally it is caviar to those with a taste for the sophisticated. Gadney can on occasion be eyebrow-raisingly erudite. In an article in the *London Magazine* in 1969 about those odd crime portfolios stuffed with "real" clues that were produced in the late 1930's by Dennis Wheatley and J.G. Links, very much toys for the hoi polloi or at least for the defiantly middle-brow, he contrived to introduce comparisons with the surrealist painter Marcel Duchamp, the "Total Art" painter Edward Kienholz, and concrete poetry.

The unique Gadney atmosphere was fully maintained in the next two books, *Somewhere in England,* a story of an introvert researcher caught up in Nazi beastliness (real-sounding beastliness), and *Seduction of a Tall Man* which took a sharp look at London seamy-side up with a drop-out hero becoming involved with arms dealing, spiritualism, and the face of violence in all its plain unpleasantness. Yet this latter book shows the weakness of Gadney's almost surrealistic way of describing our world in the at times cavalier treatment of the facts of existence. Certainly no writer of proper fiction should feel themselves hidebound by every fact of the real world, but some real facts (2 + 2 = 4) cannot be fictionally transmogrified. Yet this Gadney tended to do.

Perhaps he realized he was going too far. His next book, *Something Worth Fighting For,* in which the hero far from being a non-figure like O.B. Blanc is a sympathetic Mayfair tycoon, is much less surrealistic. Gain. But, alas, too, I think, loss. The book retains something, even a good deal, of Gadney's savouring delight in the dark side of things but it seems to lack his first dizzying impetus. Much the same can be said of his crime-writing swansong, *The Champagne Marxist,* a thriller set in a U.S. secret communications base in the very English countryside of Suffolk. It is full of what seems to be authentic detail of such an establishment. Yet this Deighton-like fidelity to the real world is not what aficionados of those first books look for. And, for all that the story is full of the old fine sharpness of observation and comment, perhaps a feeling that the original fire had shrunk low caused Gadney's subsequent silence.

—H.R.F. Keating

———

GAINHAM, Sarah. Pseudonym for Rachel Ames, née Stainer. British. Born 1 October 1922. Educated at Newbury High School for Girls, Berkshire. Married 1) Antony Terry; 2) Kenneth Ames in 1964 (died 1975). From 1947 travelled in Eastern and Central Europe: Central Europe correspondent for the *Spectator,* London, 1956–66. Fellow, Royal Society of Literature, 1984. Agent: Brian Stone, Aitken and Stone Ltd., 29 Fernshaw Road, London SW10 0TG, England. Address: Forsthaus, Schlosspark, 2404 Petronell, Austria.

CRIME PUBLICATIONS

Novels

Time Right Deadly. London, Barker, 1956; New York, Walker, 1961.
The Cold Dark Night. London, Barker, 1957; New York, Walker, 1961.
The Mythmaker. London, Barker, 1957; as *Appointment in Vienna,* New York, Dutton, 1958.
The Stone Roses. London, Eyre and Spottiswoode, and New York, Dutton, 1959.
The Silent Hostage. London, Eyre and Spottiswoode, and New York, Dutton, 1960.

Uncollected Short Story

"Business Hazard," in *Winter's Crimes 11,* edited by George Hardinge. London, Macmillan, and New York, St. Martin's Press, 1979.

OTHER PUBLICATIONS

Novels

Night Falls on the City. London, Collins, and New York, Holt Rinehart, 1967.

A Place in the Country. London, Weidenfeld and Nicolson, and New York, Holt Rinehart, 1969.
Takeover Bid. London, Weidenfeld and Nicolson, 1970; New York, Holt Rinehart, 1972.
Private Worlds. London, Weidenfeld and Nicolson, and New York, Holt Rinehart, 1971.
Maculan's Daughter. London, Macmillan, 1973; New York, Putnam, 1974.
To the Opera Ball. London, Macmillan, 1975; New York, Doubleday, 1977.
The Tiger, Life. London, Methuen, 1983.

Play

Radio Play: *Night Falls on the City* (from her own novel), 1990.

Other

The Habsburg Twilight: Tales from Vienna. London, Weidenfeld and Nicolson, and New York, Atheneum, 1979.

*   *   *

Sarah Gainham is now a well-known author in the field of the general novel. However, before abandoning the mystery/thriller, she was one of the most important of espionage-suspense writers. The first of her novels to lift her into the upper ranks of suspense was the brilliant *The Mythmaker.* The story unfolded the background of the postwar years, when the once glittering city of Vienna was under the occupation of the four allied powers, Russia, England, France, and the United States. Espionage was indigenous to the time and Gainham handles the material with authority and grace.

Time Right Deadly played against the same background. Its catalyst was the finding of the body of a London news correspondent in the Russian zone. Gainham was married to a London *Sunday Times* correspondent and with him travelled to all the trouble spots of Continental Europe. They were in Hungary for the abortive revolution there. All of her material was personally observed and translated later with invention into her books. One of the most intriguing of her novels is *The Silent Hostage,* which takes place in Yugoslavia in its revolutionary period. Hungarian refugees, an English husband of one of the protagonists, and the partisans are all central to the plot. Whether writing of cities or the countryside, Gainham brings a sensitivity to the scene as well as a special understanding of characters during political upheaval.

—Dorothy B. Hughes

———

GAITE, Francis. *See* **COLES, Manning.**

———

GALWAY, Robert Conington. *See* **McCUTCHAN, Philip.**

———

GARDNER, Erle Stanley. Also wrote as A.A. Fair; Carleton Kendrake; Charles J. Kenny. American. Born in Malden, Massachusetts, 17 July 1889. Educated at Palo Alto High School, California, graduated 1909; Valparaiso University, Indiana, 1909; studied in law offices and admitted to the California Bar, 1911. Married 1) Natalie Talbert in 1912 (separated 1935; died 1968), one daughter; 2) Agnes Jean Bethell in 1968. Lawyer, Oxnard, California, 1911–18; salesman, Consolidated Sales Company, 1918–21; lawyer, Ventura, California, 1921–33. Contributed hundreds of stories, often under pseudonyms, to magazines, 1923–32; self-employed writer after 1933. Founding member, Court of Last Resort (now the Case Review Committee), 1948–60; frequent reporter on criminal trials; founder Paisano Productions, 1957. Honorary Life Member, American Polygraph Association. Recipient: Mystery Writers of America Edgar Allan Poe award, 1952; Grand Master award, 1961. Honorary alumnus: Kansas City University, 1955; D.L.: McGeorge College of Law, Sacramento, California, 1956. *Died 11 March 1970.*

CRIME PUBLICATIONS

Novels (series: Terry Clane; Sheriff Bill Eldon; Perry Mason; Doug Selby; Gramps Wiggins)

The Case of the Velvet Claws (Mason). New York, Morrow, and London, Harrap, 1933.
The Case of the Sulky Girl (Mason). New York, Morrow, 1933; London, Harrap, 1934.
The Case of the Lucky Legs (Mason). New York, Morrow, and London, Harrap, 1934.
The Case of the Howling Dog (Mason). New York, Morrow, 1934; London, Cassell, 1935.
The Case of the Curious Bride (Mason). New York, Morrow, 1934; London, Cassell, 1935.
The Clew of the Forgotten Murder (as Carleton Kendrake). New York, Morrow, and London, Cassell, 1935.
This Is Murder (as Charles J. Kenny). New York, Morrow, 1935; London, Methuen, 1936.
The Case of the Counterfeit Eye (Mason). New York, Morrow, and London, Cassell, 1935.
The Case of the Caretaker's Cat (Mason). New York, Morrow, 1935; London, Cassell, 1936.
The Case of the Sleepwalker's Niece (Mason). New York, Morrow, and London, Cassell, 1936.
The Case of the Stuttering Bishop (Mason). New York, Morrow, 1936; London, Cassell, 1937.
The D.A. Calls It Murder (Selby). New York, Morrow, and London, Cassell, 1937.
The Case of the Dangerous Dowager (Mason). New York, Morrow, and London, Cassell, 1937.
The Case of the Lame Canary (Mason). New York, Morrow, and London, Cassell, 1937.
Murder up My Sleeve (Clane). New York, Morrow, 1937; London, Cassell, 1938.
The Case of the Substitute Face (Mason). New York, Morrow, and London, Cassell, 1938.
The Case of the Shoplifter's Shoe (Mason). New York, Morrow, 1938; London, Cassell, 1939.
The D.A. Holds a Candle (Selby). New York, Morrow, 1938; London, Cassell, 1939.
The Case of the Perjured Parrot (Mason). New York, Morrow, and London, Cassell, 1939.
The Case of the Rolling Bones (Mason). New York, Morrow, 1939; London, Cassell, 1940.

The D.A. Draws a Circle (Selby). New York, Morrow, 1939; London, Cassell, 1940.
The Case of the Baited Hook (Mason). New York, Morrow, and London, Cassell, 1940.
The D.A. Goes to Trial (Selby). New York, Morrow, 1940; London, Cassell, 1941.
The Case of the Silent Partner (Mason). New York, Morrow, 1940; London, Cassell, 1941.
The Case of the Haunted Husband (Mason). New York, Morrow, 1941; London, Cassell, 1942.
The Case of the Turning Tide (Wiggins). New York, Morrow, 1941; London, Cassell, 1942.
The Case of the Empty Tin (Mason). New York, Morrow, 1941; London, Cassell, 1943.
The D.A. Cooks a Goose (Selby). New York, Morrow, 1942; London, Cassell, 1943.
The Case of the Drowning Duck (Mason). New York, Morrow, 1942; London, Cassell, 1944.
The Case of the Careless Kitten (Mason). New York, Morrow, 1942; London, Cassell, 1944.
The Case of the Smoking Chimney (Wiggins). New York, Morrow, 1943; London, Cassell, 1945.
The Case of the Buried Clock (Mason). New York, Morrow, 1943; London, Cassell, 1945.
The Case of the Drowsy Mosquito (Mason). New York, Morrow, 1943; London, Cassell, 1946.
The D.A. Calls a Turn (Selby). New York, Morrow, 1944; London, Cassell, 1947.
The Case of the Crooked Candle (Mason). New York, Morrow, 1944; London, Cassell, 1947.
The Case of the Black-Eyed Blonde (Mason). New York, Morrow, 1944; London, Cassell, 1948.
The Case of the Golddigger's Purse (Mason). New York, Morrow, 1945; London, Cassell, 1948.
The Case of the Half-Wakened Wife (Mason). New York, Morrow, 1945; London, Cassell, 1949.
The D.A. Breaks a Seal (Selby). New York, Morrow, 1946; London, Cassell, 1950.
The Case of the Backward Mule (Clane). New York, Morrow, 1946; London, Heinemann, 1955.
The Case of the Borrowed Brunette (Mason). New York, Morrow, 1946; London, Cassell, 1951.
Two Clues (novelets; Eldon). New York, Morrow, 1947; London, Cassell, 1951.
The Case of the Fan Dancer's Horse (Mason). New York, Morrow, 1947; London, Heinemann, 1952.
The Case of the Lazy Lover (Mason). New York, Morrow, 1947; London, Heinemann, 1954.
The Case of the Lonely Heiress (Mason). New York, Morrow, 1948; London, Heinemann, 1952.
The Case of the Vagabond Virgin (Mason). New York, Morrow, 1948; London, Heinemann, 1952.
The D.A. Takes a Chance (Selby). New York, Morrow, 1948; London, Heinemann, 1956.
The Case of the Dubious Bridegroom (Mason). New York, Morrow, 1949; London, Heinemann, 1954.
The Case of the Cautious Coquette (Mason). New York, Morrow, 1949; London, Heinemann, 1955.
The D.A. Breaks an Egg (Selby). New York, Morrow, 1949; London, Heinemann, 1957.
The Case of the Negligent Nymph (Mason). New York, Morrow, 1950; London, Heinemann, 1956.
The Case of the Musical Cow. New York, Morrow, 1950; London, Heinemann, 1957.
The Case of the One-Eyed Witness (Mason). New York, Morrow, 1950; London, Heinemann, 1956.

The Case of the Fiery Fingers (Mason).   New York, Morrow, 1951; London, Heinemann, 1957.

The Case of the Angry Mourner (Mason).   New York, Morrow, 1951; London, Heinemann, 1958.

The Case of the Moth-Eaten Mink (Mason).   New York, Morrow, 1952; London, Heinemann, 1958.

The Case of the Grinning Gorilla (Mason).   New York, Morrow, 1952; London, Heinemann, 1958.

The Case of the Hesitant Hostess (Mason).   New York, Morrow, 1953; London, Heinemann, 1959.

The Case of the Green-Eyed Sister (Mason).   New York, Morrow, 1953; London, Heinemann, 1959.

The Case of the Fugitive Nurse (Mason).   New York, Morrow, 1954; London, Heinemann, 1959.

The Case of the Runaway Corpse (Mason).   New York, Morrow, 1954; London, Heinemann, 1960.

The Case of the Restless Redhead (Mason).   New York, Morrow, 1954; London, Heinemann, 1960.

The Case of the Glamorous Ghost (Mason).   New York, Morrow, 1955; London, Heinemann, 1960.

The Case of the Sun Bather's Diary (Mason).   New York, Morrow, 1955; London, Heinemann, 1961.

The Case of the Nervous Accomplice (Mason).   New York, Morrow, 1955; London, Heinemann, 1961.

The Case of the Terrified Typist (Mason).   New York, Morrow, 1956; London, Heinemann, 1961.

The Case of the Demure Defendant (Mason).   New York, Morrow, 1956; London, Heinemann, 1962.

The Case of the Gilded Lily (Mason).   New York, Morrow, 1956; London, Heinemann, 1962.

The Case of the Lucky Loser (Mason).   New York, Morrow, 1957; London, Heinemann, 1962.

The Case of the Screaming Woman (Mason).   New York, Morrow, 1957; London, Heinemann, 1963.

The Case of the Daring Decoy (Mason).   New York, Morrow, 1957; London, Heinemann, 1963.

The Case of the Long-Legged Models (Mason).   New York, Morrow, 1958; London, Heinemann, 1963.

The Case of the Foot-Loose Doll (Mason).   New York, Morrow, 1958; London, Heinemann, 1964.

The Case of the Calendar Girl (Mason).   New York, Morrow, 1958; London, Heinemann, 1964.

The Case of the Deadly Toy (Mason).   New York, Morrow, 1959; London, Heinemann, 1964.

The Case of the Mythical Monkeys (Mason).   New York, Morrow, 1959; London, Heinemann, 1965.

The Case of the Singing Skirt (Mason).   New York, Morrow, 1959; London, Heinemann, 1965.

The Case of the Waylaid Wolf (Mason).   New York, Morrow, 1960; London, Heinemann, 1965.

The Case of the Duplicate Daughter (Mason).   New York, Morrow, 1960; London, Heinemann, 1965.

The Case of the Shapely Shadow (Mason).   New York, Morrow, 1960; London, Heinemann, 1966.

The Case of the Spurious Spinster (Mason).   New York, Morrow, 1961; London, Heinemann, 1966.

The Case of the Bigamous Spouse (Mason).   New York, Morrow, 1961; London, Heinemann, 1967.

The Case of the Relucant Model (Mason).   New York, Morrow, 1962; London, Heinemann, 1967.

The Case of the Blonde Bonanza (Mason).   New York, Morrow, 1962; London, Heinemann, 1967.

The Case of the Ice-Cold Hands (Mason).   New York, Morrow, 1962; London, Heinemann, 1968.

The Case of the Mischievous Doll (Mason).   New York, Morrow, 1963; London, Heinemann, 1968.

The Case of the Stepdaughter's Secret (Mason).   New York, Morrow, 1963; London, Heinemann, 1968.

The Case of the Amorous Aunt (Mason).   New York, Morrow, 1963; London, Heinemann, 1969.

The Case of the Daring Divorcee (Mason).   New York, Morrow, 1964; London, Heinemann, 1969.

The Case of the Phantom Fortune (Mason).   New York, Morrow, 1964; London, Heinemann, 1970.

The Case of the Horrified Heirs (Mason).   New York, Morrow, 1964; London, Heinemann, 1971.

The Case of the Troubled Trustee (Mason).   New York, Morrow, 1965; London, Heinemann, 1971.

The Case of the Beautiful Beggar (Mason).   New York, Morrow, 1965; London, Heinemann, 1972.

The Case of the Worried Waitress (Mason).   New York, Morrow, 1966; London, Heinemann, 1972.

The Case of the Queenly Contestant (Mason).   New York, Morrow, 1967; London, Heinemann, 1973.

The Case of the Careless Cupid (Mason).   New York, Morrow, 1968; London, Heinemann, 1972.

The Case of the Fabulous Fake (Mason).   New York, Morrow, 1969; London, Heinemann, 1974.

The Case of the Fenced-In Woman (Mason).   New York, Morrow, 1972; London, Heinemann, 1976.

The Case of the Postponed Murder (Mason).   New York, Morrow, 1973; London, Heinemann, 1977.

The Adventures of Paul Pry.   New York, Mysterious Press, 1989.

Dead Men's Letters.   New York, Carroll and Graf, 1990.

Novels as A.A. Fair (series: Bertha Cool and Donald Lam in all books)

The Bigger They Come.   New York, Morrow, 1939; as *Lam to the Slaughter*, London, Hamish Hamilton, 1939.

Turn On the Heat.   New York, Morrow, and London, Hamish Hamilton, 1940.

Gold Comes in Bricks.   New York, Morrow, 1940; London, Hale, 1942.

Spill the Jackpot.   New York, Morrow, 1941; London, Hale, 1948.

Double or Quits.   New York, Morrow, 1941; London, Hale, 1949.

Owls Don't Blink.   New York, Morrow, 1942; London, Hale, 1951.

Bats Fly at Dusk.   New York, Morrow, 1942; London, Hale, 1951.

Cats Prowl at Night.   New York, Morrow, 1943; London, Hale, 1949.

Give 'em the Ax.   New York, Morrow, 1944; as *An Axe to Grind*, London, Heinemann, 1951.

Crows Can't Count.   New York, Morrow, 1946; London, Heinemann, 1953.

Fools Die on Friday.   New York, Morrow, 1947; London, Heinemann, 1955.

Bedrooms Have Windows.   New York, Morrow, 1949; London, Heinemann, 1956.

Top of the Heap.   New York, Morrow, 1952; London, Heinemann, 1957.

Some Women Won't Wait.   New York, Morrow, 1953; London, Heinemann, 1958.

Beware the Curves.   New York, Morrow, 1956; London, Heinemann, 1957.

You Can Die Laughing.   New York, Morrow, 1957; London, Heinemann, 1958.

Some Slips Don't Show.   New York, Morrow, 1957; London, Heinemann, 1959.

The Count of Nine. New York, Morrow, 1958; London, Heinemann, 1959.
Pass the Gravy. New York, Morrow, 1959; London, Heinemann, 1960.
Kept Women Can't Quit. New York, Morrow, 1960; London, Heinemann, 1961.
Bachelors Get Lonely. New York, Morrow, 1961; London, Heinemann, 1962.
Shills Can't Cash Chips. New York, Morrow, 1961; as *Stop at the Red Light,* London, Heinemann, 1962.
Try Anything Once. New York, Morrow, 1962; London, Heinemann, 1963.
Fish or Cut Bait. New York, Morrow, 1963; London, Heinemann, 1964.
Up for Grabs. New York, Morrow, 1964; London, Heinemann, 1965.
Cut Thin to Win. New York, Morrow, 1965; London, Heinemann, 1966.
Widows Wear Weeds. New York, Morrow, and London, Heinemann, 1966.
Traps Need Fresh Bait. New York, Morrow, 1967; London, Heinemann, 1968.
All Grass Isn't Green. New York, Morrow, and London, Heinemann, 1970.

Short Stories

Over the Hump. London, Martin, 1945.
The Case of the Murderer's Bride and Other Stories, edited by Ellery Queen. New York, Davis, 1969.
The Case of the Crimson Kiss. New York, Morrow, 1971; London, Heinemann, 1975.
The Case of the Crying Swallow. New York, Morrow, 1971; London, Heinemann, 1974.
The Case of the Irate Witness. New York, Morrow, 1972; London, Heinemann, 1975.
The Amazing Adventures of Lester Leith, edited by Ellery Queen. New York, Dial Press, 1981.

OTHER PUBLICATIONS

Short Stories

The Human Zero: The Science Fiction Stories, edited by Martin H. Greenberg and Charles G. Waugh. New York, Morrow, 1981.
Whispering Sands: Stories of Gold Fever and the Western Desert, edited by Charles G. Waugh and Martin H. Greenberg. New York, Morrow, 1981.
Pay Dirt and Other Whispering Sands Stories, edited by Charles G. Waugh and Martin H. Greenberg. New York, Morrow, 1983.

Other

"The Coming Fiction Trend," in *Writer's Digest* (Cincinnati), September 1936.
"Doing It the Hard Way," in *Writer's Digest Year Book* (Cincinnati), 1937.
"Within Quotes," in *Writer's Digest* (Cincinnati), August 1938.
"They Wanted Horror," in *Writer's Digest* (Cincinnati), August 1939.
"The Greatest Detectives I Know," in *McClurg Book News* (Chicago), January–February 1944.
"A Method to Mystery" (as A.A. Fair), in *The Writer* (Boston), August 1944.

"The Case of the Early Beginning," in *The Art of the Mystery Story,* edited by Howard Haycraft. New York, Simon and Schuster, 1946.
"Come Right In, Mr. Doyle," in *Atlantic Monthly* (Boston), September 1947.
"Is Clarence Boggie Innocent?," in *Argosy* (New York), September 1948 (first of the Court of Last Resort series: 75 articles between 1948 and October 1958).
The Land of Shorter Shadows. New York, Morrow, 1948.
The Court of Last Resort. New York, Morrow, 1952.
Neighborhood Frontiers. New York, Morrow, 1954.
"My Casebook of True Crime—Introduction," in *American Weekly* (New York), 4 September 1955 (first of 28 articles between 1955 and 3 November 1957).
The Case of the Boy Who Wrote "The Case of the Missing Clue" with Perry Mason. New York, Morrow, 1959.
Hunting the Desert Whale. New York, Morrow, 1960.
Hovering over Baja. New York, Morrow, 1961.
The Hidden Heart of Baja. New York, Morrow, 1962.
The Desert Is Yours. New York, Morrow, 1963.
The World of Water. New York, Morrow, 1964.
Hunting Lost Mines by Helicopter. New York, Morrow, 1965.
"Getting Away with Murder," in *Atlantic Monthly* (Boston), January 1965.
Off the Beaten Track in Baja. New York, Morrow, 1967.
Gypsy Days on the Delta. New York, Morrow, 1967.
Mexico's Magic Square. New York, Morrow, 1968.
Drifting Down the Delta. New York, Morrow, 1969.
Host with the Big Hat. New York, Morrow, 1970.
Cops on Campus and Crime in the Streets. New York, Morrow, 1970.

*

Bibliography: "Bibliography of Erle Stanley Gardner" by Ruth Moore, in *The Case of the Real Perry Mason: A Biography* by Dorothy B. Hughes, New York, Morrow, 1978.

Manuscript Collection: Humanities Research Center, University of Texas, Austin.

Critical Studies: *The Case of Erle Stanley Gardner* by Alva Johnston, New York, Morrow, 1947; *Erle Stanley Gardner: The Case of the Real Perry Mason* by Dorothy B. Hughes, New York, Morrow, 1978; *Murder in the Millions: Erle Stanley Gardner, Mickey Spillane, Ian Fleming* by J. Kenneth Van Dover, New York, Ungar, 1984.

*   *   *

Erle Stanley Gardner spent much of his childhood traveling with his mining-engineer father through the remote regions of California, Oregon, and the Klondike. In his teens he not only boxed for money but promoted a number of unlicensed matches. Soon after entering college he was, by his own account, expelled for slugging a professor. But in the practice of law he found the form of combat he seemed born to master. He was admitted to the California bar in 1911 and opened an office in Oxnard, where he represented the Chinese community and gained a reputation for flamboyant trial tactics. In one case, for instance, he had dozens of Chinese merchants exchange identities so that he could discredit a policeman's identification of a client. In the early 1920's he began to write western and mystery stories for magazines, and eventually he was turning out and selling the equivalent of a short novel every three nights while still lawyering during the business day. With the sale of his first novel in 1933 he gave up the practice of law and devoted himself to full-time writing, or more precisely to dictating. Thanks to the popularity of his series characters—lawyer-detective Perry Mason, his loyal secretary Della Street, his private detective Paul Drake, and the foxy trio of Sergeant Holcomb, Lieutenant Tragg and District Attorney Hamilton Burger—Gardner became one of the wealthiest mystery writers of all time.

The 82 Mason adventures from *The Case of the Velvet Claws* (1933) to the posthumously published *The Case of the Postponed Murder* (1973) contain few of the literary graces. Characterization and description are perfunctory and often reduced to a few lines that are repeated in similar situations book after book. Indeed virtually every word not within quotation marks could be deleted and little would be lost. For what vivifies these novels is the sheer readability, the breakneck pacing, the involuted plots, the fireworks displays of courtroom tactics (many based on gimmicks Gardner used in his own law practice), and the dialogue, where each line is a jab in a complex form of oral combat.

The first nine Masons are steeped in the hardboiled tradition of *Black Mask* magazine, their taut understated realism leavened with raw wit, sentimentality, and a positive zest for the dog-eat-dog milieu of the free enterprise system during its worst depression. The Mason of these novels is a tiger in the social-Darwinian jungle, totally self-reliant, asking no favors, despising the weaklings who want society to care for them, willing to take any risk for a client no matter how unfairly the client plays the game with him. Asked what he does for a living, he replies: "I fight!" or "I am a paid gladiator." He will bribe policemen for information, loosen a hostile witness's tongue by pretending to frame him for murder, twist the evidence to get a guilty client acquitted and manipulate estate funds to prevent a guilty non-client from obtaining money for his defense. Besides *Velvet Claws,* perhaps the best early Mason novels are *The Case of the Howling Dog* and *The Case of the Curious Bride* (both 1934).

From the late 1930's to the late 1950's the main influence on Gardner was not *Black Mask* but the *Saturday Evening Post,* which serialized most of the Masons before book publication. In these novels the tough-guy notes are muted, "love interest" plays a stronger role, and Mason is less willing to play fast and loose with the law. Still the oral combat remains breathlessly exciting, the pace never slackens and the plots are as labyrinthine as before, most of them centering on various sharp-witted and greedy people battling over control of capital. Mason of course is Gardner's alter ego throughout the series, but in several novels of the second period another author-surrogate arrives on the scene in the person of a philosophical old desert rat or prospector who delights in living alone in the wilderness, discrediting by his example the greed of the urban wealth-and power-hunters. Among the best cases of this period are *Lazy Lover; Hesitant Hostess* which deals with Mason's breaking down a single prosecution witness; and *Lucky Loser* and *Foot-Loose Doll* with their spectacularly complex plots.

Gardner worked without credit as script supervisor for the long-running *Perry Mason* television series (1957–66), starring Raymond Burr, and within a few years television's restrictive influence had infiltrated the new Mason novels. The lawyer evolved into a ponderous bureaucrat mindful of the law's niceties, just as Burr played him, and the plots became chaotic and the courtroom sequences mediocre, as happened all too often in the television scripts. But by the mid 1960's the libertarian decisions of the Supreme Court under Chief Justice Earl Warran had already undermined a basic premise of the Mason novels, namely that defendants menaced by the sneaky tactics of police and prosecutors needed a pyrotechnician like Mason in their corner. Once the Court ruled that such tactics

required reversal of convictions gained thereby, Mason had lost his *raison d'être.*

Several other detective series sprang from Gardner's dictating machine during his peak years. The 29 novels he wrote under the byline of A.A. Fair about diminutive private eye Donald Lam and his huge irascible partner Bertha Cool are often preferred over the Masons because of their fusion of corkscrew plots with fresh writing, characterizations, and humor, the high spots of the series being *The Bigger They Come* and *Beware the Curves.* And in his nine books about small-town district attorney Doug Selby, Gardner reversed the polarities of the Mason series, making the prosecutor his hero and the defense lawyer the oft-confounded trickster. But most of Gardner's reputation stems from Perry Mason, and his best novels in both this and other series offer abundant evidence of his natural storytelling talent, which is likely to retain its appeal as long as people read at all.

—Francis M. Nevins, Jr.

———

GARDNER, John (Edmund). British. Born in Seaton Delaval, Northumberland, 20 November 1926. Educated at Cottham's Preparatory School, Newcastle on Tyne, 1931–34; King Alfred's School, Wantage, Berkshire, 1934–43; St. John's College, Cambridge, 1947–50, B.A. in theology 1950, M.A. 1951; St. Stephen's House, Oxford, 1950–52. Served in the Royal Navy and the Royal Marines, 1943–47: Commando Service in the Far and Middle East. Married Margaret Mercer in 1952; one daughter and one son. Entertainer, American Red Cross Entertainments Department, London, 1943; clerk in Holy Orders, Church of England, 1952–58; spent some time as a Chaplain in the Royal Air Force; theatre and cultural reviewer, Stratford upon Avon *Herald*, 1959–67. Lives in the United States. Agent: Desmond Elliot, Kingsbury House, 15–17 King Street, London SW1Y 6QU, England.

CRIME PUBLICATIONS

Novels (series: James Bond; Herbie Kruger; Professor Moriarty; Boysie Oakes; Derek Torry)

The Liquidator (Oakes). London, Muller, and New York, Viking Press, 1964.
The Understrike (Oakes). London, Muller, and New York, Viking Press, 1965.
Amber Nine (Oakes). London, Muller, and New York, Viking Press, 1966.
Madrigal (Oakes). London, Muller, 1967; New York, Viking Press, 1968.
Founder Member (Oakes). London, Muller, 1969.
A Complete State of Death (Torry). London, Cape, and New York, Viking Press, 1969; as *The Stone Killer,* New York, Award, 1973.
Traitor's Exit (Oakes). London, Muller, 1970.
The Airline Pirates (Oakes). London, Hodder and Stoughton, 1970; as *Air Apparent,* New York, Putnam, 1971.
The Return of Moriarty. London, Weidenfeld and Nicolson, and New York, Putnam, 1974; as *Moriarty,* London, Pan, 1976.
The Corner Men (Torry). London, Joseph, 1974; New York, Doubleday, 1976.

A Killer for a Song (Oakes).   London, Hodder and Stoughton, 1975.

The Revenge of Moriarty.   London, Weidenfeld and Nicolson, and New York, Putnam, 1975.

To Run a Little Faster.   London, Joseph, 1976.

The Werewolf Trace.   London, Hodder and Stoughton, and New York, Doubleday, 1977.

The Dancing Dodo.   London, Hodder and Stoughton, and New York, Doubleday, 1978.

The Nostradamus Traitor (Kruger).   London, Hodder and Stoughton, and New York, Doubleday, 1979.

The Garden of Weapons (Kruger).   London, Hodder and Stoughton, 1980; New York, McGraw Hill, 1981.

Golgotha.   London, W.H. Allen, 1980; as *The Last Trump*, New York, McGraw Hill, 1980.

Licence Renewed (Bond).   London, Cape, and New York, Marek, 1981.

For Special Services (Bond).   London, Cape, and New York, Coward McCann, 1982.

The Quiet Dogs (Kruger).   London, Hodder and Stoughton, 1982; New York, Berkley, 1989.

Icebreaker (Bond).   London, Cape-Hodder and Stoughton, and New York, Putnam, 1983.

Flamingo.   London, Hodder and Stoughton, 1983.

Role of Honour (Bond).   London, Cape-Hodder and Stoughton, and New York, Putnam, 1984.

The Secret Generations.   London, Heinemann, and New York, Putnam, 1985.

Nobody Lives Forever (Bond).   London, Cape, and New York, Putnam, 1986.

No Deals, Mr. Bond.   London, Cape, and New York, Putnam, 1987.

The Secret Houses (Kruger).   New York, Putnam, 1987; London, Bantam, 1988.

Scorpius.   London, Hodder and Stoughton, and New York, Putnam, 1988.

The Secret Families (Kruger).   New York, Putnam, and London, Bantam, 1989.

Win, Lose, or Die (Bond).   London, Hodder and Stoughton, and New York, Putnam, 1989.

Brokenclaw (Bond).   New York, Putnam, and London, Hodder and Stoughton, 1990.

Short Stories

Hideaway.   London, Corgi, 1968.
The Assassination File.   London, Corgi, 1974.

Other Publications

Novels

The Censor.   London, New English Library, 1970.

Every Night's a Bullfight.   London, Joseph, 1971; as *Every Night's a Festival*, New York, Morrow, 1973; as *The Director*, London, W.H. Allen, 1982.

Other

Spin the Bottle: The Autobiography of an Alcoholic.   London, Muller, 1964.

"Smiley at the Circus: Cold War Espionage," in *Murder Ink: The Mystery Reader's Companion*, edited by Dilys Winn. New York, Workman, 1977.

*

John Gardner comments:

To write a personal statement introducing one's work, seems to me to be an act of wanton folly. Everything you say or write about yourself can, in turn, be written down and may be used in evidence—colouring future critical comment and clouding more important issues. I wince because I am still marked down by some people as being politically of the far left because of an interview with the *Morning Star* in the mid-sixties. In fact I am a political observer with no allegiance to any one party or creed. The world, attitudes, economies, and societies change with the rapidity of a scorpion's sting—and sometimes with as much pain and danger. So, naturally, the work, if not the aim, of a suspense writer's fiction changes; relevant one year; passé the next.

For instance, the "Boysie Oakes" series of books was born in the hope of being an amusing counter-irritant to the excesses of the many imitators of 007. They were meant to be irreverent, glossy black comedies, edged with tight plotting, overloaded with belly laughs and vulgar schoolboy humour. This seemed to be the way to provide an antidote to the snobby pseudo-sophistication of the Bond business. Looking back on it, that aim seems pretentious and, happily, Bond changed direction, the books becoming amusing send-ups of themselves when transferred to film. As for the Oakes books, they were a shade naughty at the time they were written. Now they seem tame, though my mail tells me they are still enjoyed. As for Bond, he has again changed direction—and did so when I accepted the invitation from the literary copyright holders to take on Ian Fleming's mantle.

So also, the two Derek Torry books were more of a comment on criminal violence, and the unpleasant side effects of that violence on those who have to deal with it. The Moriarty Journals were a different business: a peep into the past, and an attempt to recreate a fictional character—the arch enemy of the stuffy Sherlock Homes—within the framework of a factual reconstruction of the Victorian underworld. Here, the fun for me (and, one hopes, the reader) came in the creation of a secret criminal world, together with the language and methods of nineteenth-century crime.

In recent years, I have sought to combine the classic suspense story, together with espionage and detection of a different kind. At the time of writing, my last three books have—while grounded in the present—been aimed at the most recent past: World War II and its effect on contemporary characters.

The future? I think that, after one more attempt to recreate a classic suspense style from the past (this time, Shanghai of the early thirties in the style of Hollywood c. 1945) it is probably ripe for the suspense story to take off into the future: not in terms of science fiction, but in political, military, and espionographical content.

The classic, "who-done-it?" detective story does not appeal to me, though there must always be more than a hint of mystery about suspense: certainly a maze to be entered, a puzzle to be solved. My main passions lie in the secret worlds of security services, politics, crime, and police agencies. Above everything else, however, I am convinced that these interests must be harnessed to one purpose as far as suspense fiction is concerned: the purpose of entertainment—in the fullest sense of the word. Through that one word the writer of suspense should bring to his readers both horror and laughter, joy and fear, delight and terror. If there is any merit in my past work—and, I trust, in work to come—then I would wish it to be no more than the merit of being entertaining.

*   *   *

John Gardner is one of those writers (the late Victor Canning was another) far more interested in the story they have to tell than the genre to which it might belong. His fictional debut, *The Liquidator,* is a good example of this: a spy story, clearly; equally clearly a comedy in a farcical (indeed Rabelaisian) vein. Boysie Oakes (anti-hero of the book and the subsequent series) was a risk that paid off handsomely: he embodied the missing ingredient (the belly-laugh) in spy stories up to that date. He was stupid, lecherous, a blunderer and a coward, who only made it to the end of each adventure by the skin of his teeth. The ironical jumping-off point of the series—that Boysie the government-hired hitman became nauseous at the thought of killing and had to hire someone else to do his dirty work—clearly couldn't last too long as a plot-device, but while it did Gardner extracted a good deal of black farce out of the situations into which he plunged his hapless hero. Perhaps most representative is *Amber Nine,* with a nicely complex plot played out on the shores of Lake Maggiore and involving plague-rockets and a splendid cast of bizarre characters, including a demonic Javan killer-dwarf and a lady who might or might not be Hitler's daughter.

Cleverly Gardner soon lifted his oafish hero out of the Intelligence Service and turned him into a freelancer. Then, in 1970, he took five years leave-of-absence from him—which is probably why the final book in the series, *A Killer for a Song,* is so good. The plot was well-worn (shadows from the past reaching out to threaten Boysie) but entertainingly handled, and that special blend of sex, farce, and tension peculiar to a Boysie Oakes book seemed all the more fresh after the lay-off.

Meanwhile Gardner had diversified. There were two straight novels—one of which, the vastly entertaining *Every Night's A Bullfight,* was based on his intimate knowledge of the Royal Shakespeare Company—and two tightly-plotted tough-cop thrillers, *A Complete State of Death* and the superior *The Corner Men,* both featuring the sharply drawn Derek Torry, a Scotland Yard detective with religious problems. Two volumes of short stories, though readable enough, showed that Gardner was perhaps happier using a broader canvas, and this was certainly achieved with his two Moriarty books, superbly researched and written thrillers set in the late 19th century and featuring the arch-criminal of the Sherlock Holmes saga.

After immersing himself in Victorian London for so long, Gardner returned to the straight thriller with the much under-rated Munich-era story *To Run A Little Faster. The Werewolf Trace,* his next book, shows him in cracking form. A compulsively readable thriller with delicately-handled paranormal undertones and a bitter ending (the destruction of an innocent man by the monolithic and ruthless forces of the State), this is his most flawless book to date.

What at first appears to be a fine horror novel, *The Dancing Dodo,* falls apart badly when the supernatural elements are rationalised in a somewhat absurd and definitely long-winded explanation. Happily *The Nostradamus Traitor,* introducing his Herbie Kruger cycle of novels, found him back on form with a vengeance. Kruger, built like a bear and with a disarmingly stupid face, is a masterpiece of characterization, a brilliant but flawed senior Intelligence operative who, during the course of a densely-plotted and wholly satisfying trilogy of novels—*The Garden of Weapons* and *The Quiet Dogs* are the sequels—is caught up in a hideously Byzantine web of treachery and deceit, plumbs the depths of misery and despair, yet emerges at the end with some triumph (intelligently Gardner never allows his best characters total victory).

In 1979 Gardner was chosen from a secret short-list of six to continue Ian Fleming's James Bond saga; he has, since 1981 and *Licence Renewed,* written almost a book a year. Doubtless the financial benefits of such a commission have their cheering

aspects, but writing about another man's character—a character, moreover, so firmly fixed in the public psyche already, through books, films, comic-strips, toys and games—can have a debilitating effect on the imagination. Gardner's Bond is not Fleming's: the pace is swifter, the plotting more intricate, and there is less vulgarity, less drooling over brand-name flummery at the expense of the storyline. Nevertheless, all the trickings-out and trappings of the myth are there, though up-dated. *Scorpius* is perhaps representative: a fast-paced melange of hi-tech hokum, human bombs, killer scorpions, and venomous snakes, and the power-crazed leader of a bizarre religious cult. Bond sails through it all, hardly scathed.

At the same time, during the 1980's, Gardner hit on the ingenious notion of combining the family-saga blockbuster with the spy story. His "Secret" trilogy charts the fortunes and disasters of the Railton family from the birth of the British Intelligence service in 1910 to the present day with the fate of various members of the family (some are heroes, some traitors) inextricably intertwined with many of the watersheds of 20th-century history. It is a vast, complex, almost forbidding canvas (made somehow reader-friendly by the appearance in *The Secret Houses* of a youthful Herbie Kruger, who plays a crucial role in the plot), yet Gardner's matchless narrational skills make it a riveting and impressive achievement.

—Jack Adrian

GARFIELD, Brian (Francis Wynne). Also writes as Bennett Garland; Alex Hawk; John Ives; Drew Mallory; Frank O'Brian; Jonas Ward; Brian Wynne; Frank Wynne. American. Born in New York City, 26 January 1939. Educated at Southern Arizona School, Tucson, graduated 1955; University of Arizona, Tucson, B.A. 1959, M.A. 1963. Served in the United States Army and Army Reserve, 1957–65. Married 1) Virve Sein in 1962 (divorced 1965); 2) Shan Willson Botley in 1969 (divorced 1982); 3) Bina Crossblat in 1985. Musician and bandleader, "The Casuals," 1958–59, "The Palisades," 1959–63; teaching assistant in English, University of Arizona, 1962–63. Since 1963 self-employed writer; since 1975 president, Shan Production Company. Advertising manager, director, and vice-president, 1965–69, and president, 1967–68, Western Writers of America; director, 1974–78, and president, 1983–84, Mystery Writers of America; co-organizer, Second International Congress of Crime Writers, New York, 1978. Recipient: Mystery Writers of America Edgar Allan Poe award, 1976. Agent: Jane C. Cushman, JCA Agency, Suite 4-A, 242 West 27th Street, New York, New York 10001. Address: 11333 Moorpark, Suite 15, Studio City, California 91602, U.S.A.

CRIME PUBLICATIONS

Novels (series: Paul Benjamin; Sam Watchman)

The Rimfire Murders (as Frank O'Brian). New York, Bouregy, 1962.
The Last Bridge. New York, McKay, 1966.
The Villiers Touch. New York, Delacorte Press, 1970.
The Hit. New York, Macmillan, 1970.
What of Terry Coniston? Cleveland, World, 1971; London, Hodder and Stoughton, 1976.

Deep Cover. New York, Delacorte Press, 1971; London, Hodder and Stoughton, 1972.
Relentless (Watchman). Cleveland, World, 1972; London, Hodder and Stoughton, 1973.
Line of Succession. New York, Delacorte Press, 1972; London, Hodder and Stoughton, 1974.
Death Wish (Benjamin). New York, McKay, 1972; London, Hodder and Stoughton, 1973.
Gangway! with Donald E. Westlake. New York, Evans, 1973; London, Barker, 1975.
Tripwire. New York, McKay, 1973; London, Hodder and Stoughton, 1976.
Kolchak's Gold. New York, McKay, and London, Macmillan, 1974.
The Romanov Succession. New York, Evans, and London, Macmillan, 1974.
The Threepersons Hunt (Watchman). New York, Evans, 1974; London, Hodder and Stoughton, 1975.
Hopscotch. New York, Evans, and London, Macmillan, 1975.
Target Manhattan (as Drew Mallory). New York, Putnam, 1975.
Death Sentence (Benjamin). New York, Evans, 1975; London, Macmillan, 1976.
Recoil. New York, Morrow, and London, Macmillan, 1977.
Fear in a Handful of Dust (as John Ives). New York, Dutton, 1977; as *Fear,* London, Macmillan, 1978.
The Marchand Woman (as John Ives). New York, Dutton, 1979; London, Macmillan, 1980.
The Paladin. New York, Simon and Schuster, and London, Macmillan, 1980.
Necessity. New York, St. Martin's Press, and London, Macmillan, 1984.
Manifest Destiny. New York, Mysterious Press, 1989.

Short Stories

Checkpoint Charlie. Yonkers, New York, Mysterious Press, 1981.

Uncollected Short Stories

"The Toll at Yaeger's Ferry," in *Toronto Star Weekly,* July 1965.
"Ends and Means," in *Alfred Hitchcock's Mystery Magazine* (New York), February 1977.
"The Gun Law," in *Alfred Hitchcock's Mystery Magazine* (New York), March 1977.
"Hunting Accident," in *Ellery Queen's Mystery Magazine* (New York), June 1977.
"The Glory Hunter," in *Ellery Queen's Mystery Magazine* (New York), September 1977.
"Jode's Last Hunt," in *Best Detective Stories of the Year 1978,* edited by Edward D. Hoch. New York, Dutton 1978.
"Joe Cutter's Game," in *Alfred Hitchcock's Anthology, Spring–Summer 1978.* New York, Davis, 1978.
"Two-way Street" (as John Ives), in *Ellery Queen's Mystery Magazine* (New York), August 1978.
"Scrimshaw," in *Ellery Queen's Mystery Magazine* (New York), 17 December 1979.
"The Chalk Outline," in *Ellery Queen's Mystery Magazine* (New York), 20 May 1981.
"The Shopping List," in *Ellery Queen's Mystery Magazine* (New York), 2 December 1981.
"The View," in *Ellery Queen's Mystery Magazine* (New York), July 1983.

OTHER PUBLICATIONS

Novels

Range Justice. New York, Bouregy, 1960; as *Justice at Spanish Flat,* New York, Ace, 1961.
The Arizonans. New York, Bouregy, 1961.
The Lawbringers. New York, Macmillan, 1962; London, Long, 1963.
Trail Drive. New York, Bouregy, 1962.
Vultures in the Sun. New York, Macmillan, 1963; London, Long, 1964.
Apache Canyon. New York, Bouregy, 1963.
The Vanquished. New York, Doubleday, 1964.
Buchanan's Gun (as Jonas Ward). New York, Fawcett, and London, Hodder and Stoughton, 1968.
Savage Guns (as Alex Hawk). New York, Paperback Library, 1968.
Valley of the Shadow. New York, Doubleday, 1970; London, White Lion, 1973.
Sliphammer. New York, Dell, 1970.
Gun Down. New York, Dell, 1971; as *The Last Hard Men* (as Frank Wynne), London, Hodder and Stoughton, 1974.
Sweeny's Honor. New York, Dell, 1971; as Frank Wynne, London, Hodder and Stoughton, 1974.
Wild Times. New York, Simon and Schuster, 1978; London, Macmillan, 1979.

Novels as Bennett Garland

Seven Brave Men. Derby, Connecticut, Monarch, 1962.
High Storm, with Theodore V. Olsen. Derby, Connecticut, Monarch, 1963.
The Last Outlaw. Derby, Connecticut, Monarch, 1964.
Rio Chama. New York, Award, 1968.

Novels as Frank O'Brian

Bugle and Spur. New York, Ballantine, 1966; as Brian Garfield, London, Sphere, 1968.
Arizona. New York, Ballantine, 1969.
Act of Piracy. New York, Dell, 1975.

Novels as Brian Wynne

Mr. Sixgun. New York, Ace, 1964.
The Night It Rained Bullets. New York, Ace, 1965.
The Bravos. New York, Ace, 1966.
The Proud Riders. New York, Ace, 1967.
A Badge for a Badman. New York, Ace, 1967.
Brand of the Gun. New York, Ace, 1968.
Gundown. New York, Ace, 1969.
Big Country, Big Men. New York, Ace, 1969.

Novels as Frank Wynne

Massacre Basin. New York, Bouregy, 1961.
The Big Snow. New York, Bouregy, 1962.
Arizona Rider. New York, Bouregy, 1962.
Dragoon Pass. New York, Bouregy, 1963.
Rio Concho. New York, Bouregy, 1964.
Rails West. New York, Bouregy, 1964.
Lynch Law Canyon. New York, Ace, 1965.
The Wolf Pack. New York, Ace, 1966.
Call Me Hazard. New York, Ace, 1966.
The Lusty Breed. New York, Bouregy, 1966; London, Hale, 1974.

Play

Screenplay: *Hopscotch,* with Bryan Forbes, 1981; *Legs,* 1982.

Other

The Thousand-Mile War: World War II in Alaska and the Aleutians. New York, Doubleday, 1969.
"Suspense Is Where the Action Is," in *The Writer* (Boston), December 1976.
"Dear Mr. Garfield: An Author Opens His Mail," in *Murder Ink: The Mystery Reader's Companion,* edited by Dilys Winn. New York, Workman, 1977.
Western Films: A Complete Guide. New York, Rawson Associates, 1982.

Editor, *War Whoop and Battle Cry.* New York, Scholastic, 1968.
Editor, *I, Witness: True Personal Encounters with Crime by Members of the Mystery Writers of America.* New York, Times Books, 1978.
Editor, *The Crime of My Life: Favorite Stories by Presidents of the Mystery Writers of America.* New York, Walker, 1984; London, Severn House, 1986.

*

Manuscript Collection: University of Oregon Library, Eugene.

Brian Garfield comments:

I grew up in Arizona accustomed to having writers about the house, since a number of our neighbors were writers and my mother was the cover-artist for *Satuday Review;* her job entailed painting author's portraits from life. By the time I was 12 or so I had concluded that writing was not only an honorable calling but perhaps the only palatable one. Under the tutelage of a sympathetic high-school English teacher and the late Western writer Frederick D. Glidden ("Luke Short") I wrote dozens of short stories in my teens, but each time I sent one to a pulp magazine the magazine died; this caused a bit of paranoia but finally I managed to write a novel when I was 18 and, after three years' rejections from publishers, it appeared in print in 1960 and after that I did not look back.

For the next ten years I wrote mainly Westerns, most of them for fringe publishers and paperback-originals outfits: it was ephemeral apprenticeship work and I have retired nearly all those books from circulation by repossessing the publication rights. The books don't embarrass me but I'd rather not confuse the present book-buying world with relics.

At the same time, however, I began to make tentative forays into crime fiction, war novels, and historical stories. In my twenties I traveled extensively about the Western world, from Helsinki to Tangier, from Istanbul to Loch Ness, from Berlin to Anchorage, from Montreal to Tijuana; it became apparent there were things of interest in the world other than cowboys. The sort of writing I do is rather a follow-your-nose operation; I become interested in an idea, a place, a character, an event or a question, and proceed to write a book about it. This seems to have induced apoplexy in several of my publishers over the past decade because they find it impossible to type-cast me; I sympathize with their public-relations dilemma but remain impatient with writers who keep writing the same book time and again. (One suspects, sometimes, that they may plan to keep writing until they get it right.) Writers are dreamers; dreamers are children; perhaps I am the sort of child whose attention-span is limited; in any case each book I write tends to be quite different—in kind and in subject-matter—from its predecessor; otherwise I risk boredom—and if the writer is bored how can the reader be enthralled?

As a result I do not particularly think of myself as a mystery writer, a Western-writer, a thriller-writer or any other sort of hyphenate. I'm simply a teller of tales. What they have in common, I suppose, is a sense of dramatic conflict—they tend to be stories of action rather than ratiocination or introspection, but I must hedge the word "action" a bit because usually I tend to eschew extreme violence, both because of an aversion to it (a matter of taste) and because I believe it is improper to confuse violence with suspense (a matter of judgement).

Because of a popular film made from one of my books I seem to be known, if at all, as "the author of *Death Wish,*" and while the popularity and commerical success have been gratifying, I nevertheless dislike the film and tend to resent the distorted public-image of my work that *Death Wish* seems to have caused. That novel is the only modern urban crime thriller I've written, and it is one of the very few books I've attempted in which there is not a heroic protagonist. Unlike *Death Wish,* most of my novels are romances (in the old sense); I'm not at heart a cynic.

My claim to categorization as a "mystery writer" is tenuous. Normally my stories do not emphasize the unraveling of mysteries. Stanley Ellin defined the difference between mysteries and thrillers by pointing out that in the mystery a crime takes place at the beginning; in the thriller if there is a crime at all, it is more likely to take place at the end rather than the beginning. By that definition I suppose I'm a thriller writer. But I prefer to be simply a writer.

*   *   *

A prolific writer skillful in a variety of genres (ranging from westerns and historical tales—generally excluded from this discussion—to spy thrillers), Brian Garfield has produced only a few works, such as *The Hit* and *The Threepersons Hunt,* that fit the description of conventional mysteries. He has created no single sleuth, no Poirot or Maigret, whose continuing adventures fill most of his pages. A few characters, such as CIA operative Charlie Dark, do enjoy serial treatment, but their stories form only a small portion of Garfield's works; most characters play out their roles within a single book. In the few conventional mysteries, the main characters are busy tracking clues to a murder committed before the time of the novel's action: in the thrillers, they are busily trying to avoid becoming the victim of an impending crime. The American southwest is a favorite setting, but Garfield's characters also turn up in such diverse locations as Moscow's GUM, New York's Wall Street, and the bomb-shattered floor of the U.S. Senate.

While the players and places change, the world they define remains generally recognizable from novel to novel. It is a world threatened by such power-greedy organizations as the Mafia, FBI, CIA, and KGB; even the police threaten Garfield's world, although less by their villainy than by their institutional incompetence. Yet it is from the ranks of the agencies that many of Garfield's protagonists spring. By the time of their stories' action, however, they have become alienated and disillusioned. Simon Crane in *The Hit* (as much a thriller as a mystery, since Crane must solve the mystery to save his own life) is an ex-cop retired early, to his superiors' relief, because of an injury from a fellow policeman's gun. After having to battle with both the Mafia and the police to solve the mystery, Crane trusts no official authorities to parcel out either justice or the loot: "the system thinks a lot about the rules of the game but never asks whether the game itself has any meaning." Even Sam Watchman in *Relentless* and *The Threepersons Hunt,* always working within the law as an Arizona State Trooper, is outside the full blessing of his force; he is repeatedly passed over for promotion because of his Navajo blood. In both novels, fellowship with victimized Indians more than blind professional loyalty keeps Watchman on the trail of justice.

Despite the menaces, however, Garfield's world is seldom hopeless. In it, strident but generally principled individualists can succeed in fighting off their foes, sometimes skirting but rarely defying conventional law. Paul Benjamin, the vigilante murderer in *Death Wish* and its sequel *Death Sentence*, is an exception: by far the most defiant of Garfield's characters, he is also the least effective in making peace with his world. In the end, he gives up his private brand of justice, rehabilitated in part by a remedy common in Garfield's novels: love. Never officially punished, Benjamin is nonetheless made to suffer; his penance is to give up the woman whose love brought him to reason and to live out his life imprisoned in loneliness. Love is frequently risky in Garfield's world, but it is just as frequently worth the risk, often swerving evil-doers, as in *Recoil* and *Deep Cover,* from their paths of violence.

Revenge motivates many of Garfield's characters, who spend much of their time pursued or in pursuit: "The hunting way of life is the only one natural to man" (*Hopscotch*). In Garfield's fundamentally moral world, however, the hunt need not climax in the kill. Charlie Dark is emphatic: "I flatly refuse to kill" ("Trust Charlie"). In fact, Fred Mathieson in *Recoil* squirms free of the Mafia without even harming anyone, although he does resort to blackmail and kidnapping. Garfield's world recognizes a difference between moral and written law, tolerating violations of certain written laws for the sake of moral justice. Murder, however, is intolerable, as even Paul Benjamin learns.

Occasionally, as in *Recoil,* the characters themselves take time to debate the moral issues their actions raise. More often, and more successfully, Garfield stops for nothing in the telling of his tales, and with simple and powerful language builds suspense well designed to keep the pages turning.

—Carol Ann Bergman

GARNETT, Roger. *See* **MORLAND, Nigel.**

GARVE, Andrew. Pseudonym for Paul Winterton; also writes as Roger Bax; Paul Somers. British. Born in Leicester, 12 February 1908. Educated at the London School of Economics, B.Sc. 1928. Staff Member, *Economist,* London, 1929–33; reporter, leader writer, and foreign correspondent, London *News Chronicle,* 1933–46: in Moscow, 1942–45. Founding member, and first joint secretary, Crime Writers Association, 1953. Address: c/o William Collins Ltd., 8 Grafton Street, London, W1X 3LA, England.

CRIME PUBLICATIONS

Novels

No Tears for Hilda. London, Collins, and New York, Harper, 1950.

No Mask for Murder. London, Collins, 1950; as *Fontego's Folly,* New York, Harper, 1950.
Murder in Moscow. London, Collins, 1951; as *Murder Through the Looking Glass,* London, Harper, 1952.
A Press of Suspects. London, Collins, 1951; as *By-Line for Murder,* New York, Harper, 1951.
A Hole in the Ground. London, Collins, and New York, Harper, 1952.
The Cuckoo Line Affair. London, Collins, and New York, Harper, 1953.
Death and the Sky Above. London, Collins, 1953; New York, Harper, 1954.
The Riddle of Samson. London, Collins, 1954; New York, Harper, 1955.
The End of the Track. London, Collins, and New York, Harper, 1956.
The Megstone Plot. London, Collins, 1956; New York, Harper, 1957.
The Narrow Search. London, Collins, 1957; New York, Harper, 1958.
The Galloway Case. London, Collins, and New York, Harper, 1958.
A Hero for Leanda. London, Collins, and New York, Harper, 1959.
The Far Sands. New York, Harper, 1960; London, Collins, 1961.
The Golden Deed. London, Collins, and New York, Harper, 1960.
The House of Soldiers. New York, Harper, 1961; London, Collins, 1962.
Prisoner's Friend. London, Collins, and New York, Harper, 1962.
The Sea Monks. London, Collins, and New York, Harper, 1963.
Frame-Up. London, Collins, and New York, Harper, 1964.
The Ashes of Loda. London, Collins, and New York, Harper, 1965.
Murderer's Fen. London, Collins, 1966; as *Hide and Go Seek,* New York, Harper, 1966.
A Very Quiet Place. London, Collins, and New York, Harper, 1967.
The Long Short Cut. London, Collins, and New York, Harper, 1968.
The Ascent of D-13. London, Collins, and New York, Harper, 1969.
Boomerang. London, Collins, 1969; New York, Harper, 1970.
The Late Bill Smith. London, Collins, and New York, Harper, 1971.
The Case of Robert Quarry. London, Collins, and New York, Harper, 1972.
The File on Lester. London, Collins, 1974; as *The Lester Affair,* New York, Harper, 1974.
Home to Roost. London, Collins, and New York, Crowell, 1976.
Counterstroke. London, Collins, and New York, Crowell, 1978.

Novels as Roger Bax (series: Inspector James)

Death Beneath Jerusalem. London, Nelson, 1938.
Red Escapade. London, Skeffington, 1940.
Disposing of Henry. London, Hutchinson, 1946; New York, Harper, 1947.
Blueprint for Murder (James). London, Hutchinson, 1948; as *The Trouble with Murder,* New York, Harper, 1948.
Came the Dawn. London, Hutchinson, 1949; as *Two If by Sea,* New York, Harper, 1949.

A Grave Case of Murder (James). London, Hutchinson, and New York, Harper, 1951.

Novels as Paul Somers (series: Hugh Curtis)

Beginner's Luck (Curtis). London, Collins, and New York, Harper, 1958.
Operation Piracy (Curtis). London, Collins, 1958; New York, Harper, 1959.
The Shivering Mountain (Curtis). London, Collins, and New York, Harper, 1959.
The Broken Jigsaw. London, Collins, and New York, Harper, 1961.

Uncollected Short Stories

"The Downshire Terror," in *Ellery Queen's Mystery Magazine* (New York), June 1957.
"The Man Who Wasn't Scared," in *A Choice of Murders,* edited by Dorothy Salisbury Davis. New York, Scribner, 1958; London, Macdonald, 1960.
"The Man on the Cliff," in *Bestseller Mystery Magazine* (New York), May 1959.
"Revenge," in *The Saint* (New York), September 1963.
"The Last Link," in *Best Detective Stories of the Year,* edited by Anthony Boucher. New York, Dutton, 1963.
"Who Would Steal a Mailbox?," in *John Creasey's Mystery Bedside Book 1969,* edited by Herbert Harris. London, Hodder and Stoughton, 1968.
"Line of Communication," in *Ellery Queen's Mystery Parade.* New York, New American Library, 1968; London, Gollancz, 1969.
"A Case of Blackmail," in *John Creasey's Mystery Bedside Book 1972,* edited by Herbert Harris. London, Hodder and Stoughton, 1971.
"A Glass of Port," in *Winter's Crimes 7,* edited by George Hardinge. London, Macmillan, and New York, St. Martin's Press, 1975.

OTHER PUBLICATIONS as Paul Winterton

Other

A Student in Russia. Manchester, Co-operative Union, 1931.
Russia—with Open Eyes. London, Lawrence and Wishart, 1937.
Mending Minds: The Truth about Our Mental Hospitals. London, Davies, 1938.
Eye-Witness on the Soviet War-Front. London, Russia Today Society, 1943.
Report on Russia. London, Cresset Press, 1945.
Inquest on an Ally (on Soviet foreign policy). London, Cresset Press, 1948.

*

Manuscript Collection: Mugar Memorial Library, Boston University.

*   *   *

Paul Winterton has used the pseudonym Andrew Garve for most of his suspense novels, though he published several books as Roger Bax and Paul Somers. A fine craftsman, he is prolific as well as proficient, having turned out some 40 thrillers over the past four decades. What is most impressive about this

productivity is the amazing variety that distinguishes it. Winterton does not rely on a familiar detective or recurring cast of characters—each new book is separate and discrete, each tale seeming to arise inevitably from the concurrence of personalities and settings. What does carry over from book to book is a straightforward, transparent writing style, and a certain type of hero, to all appearances ordinary, but whose perseverance and courage in crisis prove to be extraordinary. The diversity of the settings—English villages, the Scilly Isles, Ireland, France, Australia, Russia, and the Baltic Sea and the Gulf of Finland, Africa, the Indian Ocean—is equalled by that of the sub-genres of suspense fiction this author handles with ease—detection, mystery, espionage, adventure, romance and combinations thereof. Winterton's Russian experience, including his stint as a newspaper correspondent in Moscow during World War II, has been turned to good advantage in several stories, notably *Came the Dawn* (Bax), *Murder in Moscow, The Ashes of Loda, The Ascent of D-13,* and *The Late Bill Smith.* His knowledge of the Russians and the Soviet government lends these tales an unusual authenticity. His acquaintance with archaeology adds background for *The Riddle of Samson* and *The House of Soldiers.* Themes which reappear most frequently in the Winterton books, however, are small boats and the sea. The author has the knack of providing a wealth of information on these favorite topics in such an appealing way that even the most confirmed landlubber is fascinated. Two splendid sailing yarns, where the heroes overcome apparently insuperable odds, are *Came the Dawn* (Bax) and *A Hero for Leanda.* His sailors find adventure not only on the high seas, but in coastal waters, as in *The Megstone Plot* and *The File on Lester.* Other protagonists ply the waterways of England in canal boats, houseboats, dinghies, and other small craft. Only P.M. Hubbard among contemporary English thriller writers is so preoccupied with seamanship and other nautical matters.

Scotland Yard inspectors and assorted policemen figure in Winterton's stories, and they are not fools. Policemen gone bad make formidable villains: Stratton, for example, in *The Broken Jigsaw* (Somers), or Parker in *The End of the Track.* Some of Winterton's wrongdoers, when they are the central characters, arouse considerable sympathy because of the author's skill in portraying their feelings and motives, making them seem human, not so much worse than other people, exceptional only because of their ingenuity and boldness. In *The Megstone Plot,* the lustful and cynical ex-war hero Clive Easton, whose plotting is indisputably dishonorable, nevertheless retains some scruples, is physically courageous, and is a quite disarming narrator. Still more engaging outlaws are to be found in *The Long Short Cut* and *Boomerang.*

Most often, however, Winterton's heroes are private individuals forced by circumstances to use whatever strengths they have. When confronted by a situation which everybody else, including officialdom, accepts, these heroes achieve their ends—the removal of an intolerable threat, the exoneration of a loved one—by persistence. In Winterton's detective stories this hero becomes the detective, an amateur indefatigably pursuing facts, testing theories, and finally arriving at a solution. *The Cuckoo Line Affair* contains just such a stubborn hero, doggedly determined to clear his father of a ruinous indictment. In *The Narrow Search,* the kidnapping of a baby is solved by clear reasoning and relentless investigation. Sometimes the police do the detecting, as in *Murderer's Fen* and *Frame-Up.*

Winterton excels at domestic murders, especially triangles of husband, wife, and lover. Although critics say that he never writes the same book—as indeed he does not—he explores certain themes such as the triangle from all different angles, each time constructing an absorbing book: *The Case of Robert Quarry,* for instance, or the ingenious *Home to Roost.* His classic

No Tears for Hilda, in which a husband is charged with the murder of a really obnoxious wife, reveals his talent for depicting married couples and lovers in various combinations, connections which result in murder, with a typically satisfactory denouement. Families threatened from without, taking desperate action to survive, are shown in *The End of the Track, The Golden Deed,* and *The House of Soldiers.* The author, though occasionally writing about libertines, in numerous tales creates chivalrous romantic heroes, made more attractive because of their all too human doubts and imperfections. The unfolding of a love story often provides a more gentle suspense as counterpoint to the violent excitement of the adventure.

Winterton, so skilled at detailing domestic drama and familial felony, also concocts first-rate tales of his adventure. *The Sea Monks,* which recounts the confrontation between a group of murderous young hoodlums and a team of lighthouse keepers, is a good example. The evocation of the storm at sea and its devastating effects inside the lighthouse is memorable. A most admirable tale is *The Ascent of D-13,* a compelling account of mountain climbing on the Turkish-Russian frontier. The hazards of blizzard, avalanche, and East-West romance, combined with an eloquent passage in praise of mountaineering in general, and the superiority of freedom over totalitarianism, make a story that is Garve of the first order.

Paul Winterton by any other name would write as well! Not surprisingly, several of his books have been turned into successful films. Some of his earlier tales are more complicated than those of recent years. Simple, even austere, in regard to incident and number of characters, they are nevertheless gripping stories, forceful and fascinating. Winterton's suspense fiction is tasteful, discriminating, intelligent, at times ironic, and often witty. It is hard to praise him too highly, as he is surely one of the finest contemporary practitioners of the art.

—Mary Helen Becker

GASH, Joe. *See* **GRANGER, Bill.**

GASH, Jonathan. Pseudonym for John Grant; also writes as Graham Gaunt. British. Born in Bolton, Lancashire, 30 September 1933. Educated at the University of London, M.B. and B.S. 1958; Royal College of Surgeons and Physicians, London, M.R.C.S. and L.R.C.P. 1958. Served in the British Army Medical Corps: Major. Married Pamela Richard in 1955; three daughters. General practitioner, London, 1958–59; pathologist, London and Essex, 1959–62; clinical pathologist, Hanover and Berlin, 1962–65; Lecturer and Head of the Division of Clinical Pathology, University of Hong Kong, 1965–68; microbiologist, Hong Kong and London, 1968–71, and Faculty of Medicine, University of London, 1970–88. Since 1988 private consultant, infectious diseases. Recipient: Crime Writers Association John Creasey award, 1977. Address: Desmond Elliott Management, 38 Bury Street, London SW1Y 6AV, England.

CRIME PUBLICATIONS

Novels (series: Lovejoy in all books except *The Incomer*)

The Judas Pair.   London, Collins, and New York, Harper, 1977.
Gold from Gemini.   London, Collins, 1978; as *Gold by Gemini,* New York, Harper, 1979.
The Grail Tree.   London, Collins, 1979; New York, Harper, 1980.
Spend Game.   London, Collins, 1980; New Haven, Connecticut, Ticknor and Fields, 1981.
The Vatican Rip.   London, Collins, 1981; New Haven, Connecticut, Ticknor and Fields, 1982.
The Incomer (as Graham Gaunt).   London, Collins, 1981; New York, Doubleday, 1982.
Firefly Gadroon.   London, Collins, 1982; New York, St. Martin's Press, 1984.
The Sleepers of Erin.   London, Collins, and New York, Doubleday, 1983.
The Gondola Scam.   London, Collins, 1983; New York, St. Martin's Press, 1984.
Pearlhanger.   London, Collins, and New York, St. Martin's Press, 1985.
The Tartan Ringers.   London, Collins, 1986; as *The Tartan Sell,* New York, St. Martin's Press, 1986.
Moonspender.   London, Collins, 1986; New York, St. Martin's Press, 1987.
Jade Woman.   London, Collins, 1988; New York, St. Martin's Press, 1989.
The Very Last Gambado.   London, Collins, 1989; New York, St. Martin's Press, 1990.
The Great California Game.   London, Random Century, 1990; New York, St. Martin's Press, 1991.

Uncollected Short Stories

"Eyes for Offa Rex," in *Winter's Crimes 11,* edited by George Hardinge.   London, Macmillan, and New York, St. Martin's Press, 1979.
"The Hours of Angelus," in *The Year's Best Mystery and Suspense Stories 1982,* edited by Edward D. Hoch.   New York, Walker, 1982.
"The Julian Mondays," in *Winter's Crimes 18,* edited by Hilary Hale.   London, Macmillan, 1986.
"The Contras of Bloomsbury Square, in *Winter's Crimes 21,* edited by Hilary Hale.   London, Macmillan, 1989.

OTHER PUBLICATIONS

Play as Jonathan Grant

Terminus (produced Chester, Cheshire, 1976).

*   *   *

Jonathan Gash has used a mix of several ingredients to create a distinctive mystery series built around the antics of his amateur sleuth, Lovejoy, an antiques dealer who lives in East Anglia. The ingredients include a wealth of information about antiques, a seldom varied plot formula, and paradox upon paradox.

The subject of antiques serves Gash well. Each book is chock full of history, detailed suggestions for handling and caring for antiques, and information on everything from where in Britain to find all kinds of antique specialties to methods of making and detecting fakes. If it were not for Lovejoy's first-person chatty style, the story would bog down terribly during these lengthy asides. Instead, though, the antique discussions add to confidence in the absolute knowledge and eventual infallibility of this unlikely hero.

All of the stories are built around antiques and greed. Usually someone desperately wants them, although in *Moonspender* someone desperately wants to keep archeological treasures from being found at all. Lovejoy is a "divvie," a person gifted with powers of divining antiques. Lovejoy's adventures as detective come from his being dragged into unpleasant situations because of his unique talent and his enormous body of knowledge. Unsavory characters may give him offers he cannot refuse as in *The Vatican Rip* and *The Sleepers of Erin*. He may chase hopefully after legendary, priceless antiques as in *The Judas Pair, Gold by Gemini, The Grail Tree,* and *Spend Game.* In several books the climax of the chase finds Lovejoy unarmed, trapped by his enemies in a dreadful environment. He manages to rescue himself through his knowledge of odd mechanical devices, knowledge gained through his studies and faking of antiques.

Violence abounds. Lovejoy is more prone to vengeance than to justice, having little respect for the judicial system of punishment and less for the officers of the law. He prefers to carry out his own punishments, batting around the women in his life when they annoy him and ruthlessly murdering the bad guys. Even the gory passages, however, are filled with Lovejoy's wisecracks, which if they do not exactly make the gore any less gory do provide speedy transition so as to distract the reader from the unpleasantness. Here, too, is a paradox of unchecked violence carried out with humor and speed. The speed also distracts the reader from a number of unexplained or contradictory details that occur within books or from book to book.

Gash's depiction of the world of antiques is as paradoxical as his treatment of violence. Again and again, antiques are linked to stupidity, cupidity, ignorance, and violence. We learn all this from Lovejoy, and yet we also learn Lovejoy's Law of Loving: antiques are things made with love, and it is that love, and that only that makes them precious. A porcelain bowl brings tears to Lovejoy's eyes in *The Grail Tree.* He blows his cover by shouting in anguish as robbers are about to smash a 300-year old lock in *The Sleepers of Erin.*

Lovejoy himself is the most paradoxical element of all. We know nothing of how he looks, only of how he dresses—like the pauper that he is. He has the unique gift of a divvie yet is always broke. He treats women shabbily but cannot leave them alone, nor can they leave him alone. He is a mooch who always pays his debts. He is completely selfish, yet he risks his life for his friends. He is hot-tempered and violent yet tenderhearted toward animals, flowers, and his barker (a "sniffer-out of antiques") Tinker. Lovejoy causes and endures immeasurable physical pain yet he whines and cries and cowers in the face of it. Lovejoy is the character we hate to love but somehow do.

The Gash mysteries are fascinating for their special focus on antique lore. They are also fascinating for their way of being nasty and horrible in a pleasant sort of way.

—Neysa Chouteau and Martha Alderson

———

GAULT, William Campbell. Also writes as Will Duke; Dial Forest; Roney Scott. American. Born in Milwaukee, Wisconsin, 9 March 1910. Educated at the University of Wisconsin, Madison, 1929. Served with the 166th Infantry, 1943–45. Married Virginia Kaprelian in 1942; one daughter and one son. Manager and part-owner, Blatz Hotel, Milwaukee, 1932–39. Since 1939 self-employed writer. Recipient: Mystery Writers of America Edgar Allan Poe award 1953;

Boys Clubs of America Junior Book award, 1957. Agent: Don Congdon Associates, 156 Fifth Avenue, Suite 625, New York, New York 10010. Address: 482 Vaquero Lane, Santa Barbara, California 93111, U.S.A.

CRIME PUBLICATIONS

Novels (series: Brock Callahan; Joe Puma)

Don't Cry for Me. New York, Dutton, and London, Boardman, 1952.
The Bloody Bokhara. New York, Dutton, 1952; as *The Blood-stained Bokhara,* London, Boardman, 1953.
The Canvas Coffin. New York, Dutton, and London, Boardman, 1953.
Blood on the Boards. New York, Dutton, 1953; London, Boardman, 1954.
Shakedown (Puma; as Roney Scott). New York, Ace, 1953.
Run, Killer, Run. New York, Dutton, 1954; London, Boardman, 1955.
Ring Around Rosa (Callahan). New York, Dutton and London, Boardman, 1955; as *Murder in the Raw,* New York, Dell, 1956.
Square in the Middle. New York, Random House, 1956; London, Boardman, 1957.
Day of the Ram (Callahan). New York, Random House, 1956; London, Boardman, 1958.
Fair Prey (as Will Duke). Hasbrouck Heights, New Jersey, Graphic, 1956; London, Boardman, 1958.
The Convertible Hearse (Callahan). New York, Random House, 1957; London, Boardman, 1958.
End of a Call Girl (Puma). New York, Fawcett, 1958; as *Don't Call Tonight,* London, Boardman, 1960.
Night Lady (Puma). New York, Fawcett, 1958; London, Boardman, 1960.
Death Out of Focus. New York, Random House, and London, Boardman, 1959.
Sweet Wild Wench (Puma). New York, Fawcett, 1959; London, Boardman, 1961.
The Wayward Widow (Puma). New York, Fawcett, 1959; London, Boardman, 1960.
Come Die with Me (Callahan). New York, Random House, 1959; London, Boardman, 1961.
The Sweet Blond Trap. New York, Zenith, 1959.
Million Dollar Tramp (Puma). New York, Fawcett, 1960; London, Boardman, 1962.
The Hundred-Dollar Girl (Puma). New York, Dutton, 1961; London, Boardman, 1963.
Vein of Violence (Callahan). New York, Simon and Schuster, 1961; London, Boardman, 1962.
County Kill (Callahan). New York, Simon and Schuster, 1962; London, Boardman, 1963.
Dead Hero (Callahan). New York, Dutton, 1963; London, Boardman, 1964.
The Bad Samaritan (Callahan). Toronto, Raven, 1982.
The Cana Division (Callahan). Toronto, Raven 1982.
Death in Donegal Bay (Callahan). New York, Walker, 1984.
The Dead Seed. New York, Walker, 1985; London, Hale, 1987.
The Chicane War. New York, Walker, 1986.
Cat and Mouse (Callahan). New York, St. Martin's Press, 1988.

Uncollected Short Stories

"Crime Collection," in *Ten Story Detective* (Springfield, Massachusetts), January 1940.

"Agent for Murder," in *10 Detective Aces* (New York), April 1940.

"Picture of Doom," in *10 Detective Aces* (New York), December 1940.

"The Revolt of Widow Murphy," in *Detective Fiction Weekly* (New York), 24 May 1941.

"Killer's Game," in *Detective Book Magazine* (New York), Winter 1941.

"Four Men and a Girl," in *10 Detective Aces* (New York), March 1942.

"The Things You Never See," in *Strange Detective Mysteries* (Chicago), May 1942.

"Murder Comes High," in *Black Book Detective* (Chicago), May 1942.

"Danger, A Head," in *10 Detective Aces* (New York), June 1942.

"Five Steps from Heaven," in *Dime Mystery* (New York), July 1942.

"Beat of His Heart," in *Mystery Magazine* (New York), August 1942.

"Three Men in a Hearse," in *Flynn's Detective* (New York), September 1942.

"You Can't Burn Me," in *Dime Mystery* (New York), September 1942.

"Death Has Yellow Eyes" (as Roney Scott), in *Dime Mystery* (New York), September 1942.

"They Die by Night," in *Detective Tales* (Chicago), September 1942.

"Driver for Death," in *Detective Book Magazine,* (New York), Fall 1942.

"The Golden Web," in *Detective Tales* (Chicago), December 1942.

"Four Kings and a Jack," in *Thrilling Detective* (New York), December 1942.

"The Dead Man's Hand," in *Thrilling Mystery Magazine* (New York), Winter 1942.

"Dark Is the Night," in *Detective Tales* (Chicago), January 1943.

"Death and the Little Daisy," in *Mammoth Detective* (Chicago), January 1943.

"The Corpse Wore Gloves," in *5-Detective Mysteries* (New York), February–March 1943.

"The Man Who Died Too Often," in *Strange Detective Mysteries* (Chicago), March 1943.

"Dead of the Night," in *Mystery Magazine* (New York), March 1943.

"Death Pays the Winner," in *Thrilling Detective* (New York), April 1943.

"The Devil's Agent," in *The Shadow* (New York), May 1943.

"Money Is the Motive," in *Clues* (New York), May 1943.

"Black Market Payoff," in *Detective Book Magazine* (New York), Summer 1943.

"Whistle in the Dark," in *Detective Story* (New York), November 1943.

"The Open Grave," in *Clues* (New York), November 1943.

"Shadows in the Night," in *Detective Story* (New York), December 1945.

"Red Runaround," in *Black Mask* (New York), March 1946.

"They'd Die for Linda," in *Detective Story* (New York), September 1946.

"Hot House Homicide," in *Black Mask* (New York), September 1946.

"Assassin Anonymous," in *Detective Tales* (Chicago), September 1946.

"And Dust to Dust," in *The Shadow* (New York), October 1946.

"Curtain Call for the Corpse," in *Detective Tales* (Chicago), November 1946.

"Tin Pan Alibi" in *Dime Detective* (New York), November 1946.

"The Cold Cold Ground," in *Black Mask* (New York), January 1947.

"No Weeds for the Widow," in *Detective Story* (New York), February 1947.

"A Murder for Mac," in *Black Mask* (New York), March 1947.

"Pick-Up," in *Detective Story* (New York), March 1947.

"Two Biers for Buster," in *Dime Detective* (New York), March 1947.

"Pale Hands I Loathed," in *Detective Story* (New York), April 1947.

"The Walls Are Hard and High," in *Detective Tales* (Chicago), May 1947.

"The Man in the Street," in *Detective Story* (New York), May 1947.

"The Pewter Urn," in *G-Man Detective* (New York), July 1947.

"The Constant Shadow," in *Black Mask* (New York), July 1947.

"The Girl Next Door," in *Detective Story* (New York), October 1947.

"The Case of the Sleeping Beauty," in *Black Mask* (New York), November 1947.

"A Tombstone for Taro," in *Detective Story* (New York), December 1947.

"Dead-End Road," in *Dime Detective* (New York), January 1948.

"Satan's Children," in *Dime Mystery* (New York), February 1948.

"Waikiki Widow," in *Detective Story* (New York), March 1948.

"The Silent Suckers," in *Detective Tales* (Chicago), March 1948.

"Night Fall," in *Detective Story* (New York), May 1948.

"Home to Die," in *Detective Story* (New York), June 1948.

"White Hands I Fear," in *Dime Mystery* (New York), June 1948.

"Don't Bet on Death," in *Black Mask* (New York), July 1948.

"Fallen Star," in *Detective Story* (New York), September 1948.

"The Man Who Couldn't Die," in *Dime Mystery* (New York), October 1948.

"Hot Shot, Big Shot, Dead Shot," in *Detective Tales* (Chicago), February 1949.

"A Bier for Baby," in *New Detective* (New York), March 1949.

"The Last Guest," in *Detective Novel Magazine* (New York), Spring 1949.

"Blood for the Murder Master," in *Dime Mystery* (New York), April 1949.

"The Longest Count," in *Dime Mystery* (New York), June 1949.

"What Do You Want—Blood?," in *Detective Tales* (Chicago), July 1949.

"Some Other Body," in *New Detective* (New York), July 1949.

"Send Me Your Killers," in *Detective Tales* (Chicago), August 1949.

"Return to Terror," in *Dime Mystery* (New York), October 1949.

"All That Murder Can Buy," in *Detective Tales* (Chicago), October 1949.

"Red Head, Stay Dead!," in *Detective Tales* (Chicago), October 1949.

"Slay You in My Dreams," in *Dime Mystery* (New York), December 1949.

"Moment of Flame," in *Fifteen Mystery Stories* (Kokomo, Indiana), February 1950.

"The Corpse and the Cackle Bladder," in *Detective Tales* (Chicago), March 1950.

"This Way to the Morgue," in *Detective Tales* (Chicago), April 1950.
"Keeper of the Cat Bride," in *Fifteen Mystery Stories* (Kokomo, Indiana), April 1950.
"The Last Count," in *Detective Tales* (Chicago), June 1950.
"No Grave So Deep," in *Fifteen Mystery Stories* (Kokomo, Indiana), June 1950.
"Hot Rod Homicide" (as Roney Scott), in *Detective Tales* (Chicago), June 1950.
"Satan's Protege," in *Fifteen Story Detective* (Kokomo, Indiana), August 1950.
"So Dead, My Love," in *Fifteen Mystery Stories* (Kokomo, Indiana), August 1950.
"See No Murder," in *New Detective* (New York), September 1950.
"Creature of Habit," in *Fifteen Mystery Stories* (Kokomo, Indiana), October 1950.
"Death Watch," in *Thrilling Detective* (New York), October 1950.
"The Big Time," in *Detective Tales* (Chicago), November 1950.
"Dead End for Delia," in *Black Mask* (New York), November 1950.
"None But the Lethal Heart," in *Dime Detective* (New York), January 1951.
"Murderer's Way," in *Detective Tales* (Chicago), February 1951.
"And Murder Makes Four," in *Detective Tales* (Chicago), March 1951.
"Blood on the Rocks," in *Popular Detective* (New York), March 1951.
"The Big Fix," in *Detective Tales* (Chicago), June 1951.
"Deadly Cargo," in *Detective Tales* (Chicago), October 1951.
"A Little Murder Music, Professor!," in *Detective Tales,* (Chicago), December 1951.
"Marksman," in *Maiden Murders,* edited by John Dickson Carr. New York, Harper, 1952.
"Father, May I Go Out to Kill?," in *Detective Tales* (Chicago), February 1952.
"There's Gotta Be an Angle," in *Dime Detective* (New York), April 1952.
"The Long Night," in *Five Detective Novels* (Springfield, Massachusetts), Fall 1952.
"The Bleeding Heart," in *Detective Story* (New York), May 1953.
"Sweet Rolls and Murder," in *The Saint* (New York), October–November 1953.
"Night Work," in *The Saint* (New York), July 1954.
"Punk's Widow," in *Fifteen Detective Stories* (Kokomo, Indiana), October 1954.
"The Sacrificial Lamb," in *The Saint* (New York), August 1955.
"Who's Buying Murder?," in *The Saint* (New York), December 1955.
"But the Prophet Died," in *Dell Mystery Novels* (New York), January–March 1955.
"The Unholy Three," in *Manhunt* (New York), May 1956.
"Deadly Beloved," in *Manhunt* (New York), October 1956.
"Kill If You Have To," in *Mike Shayne Mystery Magazine* (New York), October 1956.
"Be Smart, Really Smart," in *The Saint* (New York), December 1956.
"Death of a Big Wheel," in *Manhunt* (New York), April 1957.
"Don't Crowd Your Luck," in *Ellery Queen's Mystery Magazine* (New York), May 1957.
"Blood of the Innocent," in *The Saint* (New York), July 1957.
"Conspiracy," in *Alfred Hitchcock's Mystery Magazine* (New York), August 1957.

"Stolen Star," in *Manhunt* (New York), November 1957.
"Million Dollar Gesture," in *Best Detective Stories of the Year,* edited by David C. Cooke. New York, Dutton, and London, Boardman, 1958.
"Nobody Wants to Kill," in *The Saint* (New York), October 1959.
"Murderous Parlay" (as Dial Forest), in *Saga,* February 1961.
"See No Evil," in *The Arbor House Treasury of Detective and Mystery Stories from the Great Pulps,* edited by Bill Pronzini. New York, Arbor House, 1983.
"The Threatening Three," in *Child's Ploy.* New York, Macmillan, 1984.
"The Kerman Kill," in *Murder in Los Angeles,* edited by Bill Adler and D.C. Fontana. New York, Morrow, 1987.

OTHER PUBLICATIONS

Other (for children)

Thunder Road. New York, Dutton, 1952.
Mr. Fullback. New York, Dutton, 1953.
Gallant Colt. New York, Dutton, 1954.
Mr. Quarterback. New York, Dutton, 1955.
Speedway Challenge. New York, Dutton, 1956.
Bruce Benedict, Halfback. New York, Dutton, 1957.
Dim Thunder. New York, Dutton, 1958.
Rough Road to Glory. New York, Dutton, 1958.
Drag Strip. New York, Dutton, 1959.
Dirt Track Summer. New York, Dutton, 1961.
Through the Line. New York, Dutton, 1961.
Road-Race Rookie. New York, Dutton, 1962.
Two-Wheeled Thunder. New York, Dutton, 1962.
Little Big Foot. New York, Dutton, 1963.
Wheels of Fortune: Four Racing Stories. New York, Dutton, 1963.
The Checkered Flag. New York, Dutton, 1964.
The Karters. New York, Dutton, 1965.
The Long Green. New York, Dutton, 1965.
Sunday's Dust. New York, Dutton, 1966.
Backfield Challange. New York, Dutton, 1967.
The Lonely Mound. New York, Dutton, 1967.
The Oval Playground. New York, Dutton, 1968.
Stubborn Sam. New York, Dutton, 1969.
Quarterback Gamble. New York, Dutton, 1970.
The Last Lap. New York, Dutton, 1972.
Trouble at Second. New York, Dutton, 1973.
Gasoline Cowboy. New York, Dutton, 1974.
Wild Willie, Wide Receiver. New York, Dutton, 1974.
The Big Stick. New York, Dutton, 1975.
Underground Skipper. New York, Dutton, 1975.
Showboat in the Backcourt. New York, Dutton, 1976.
Cut-Rate Quarterback. New York, Dutton, 1977.
Thin Ice. New York, Dutton, 1978.
Sunday Cycles. New York, Dodd Mead, 1979.
Super Bowl Bound. New York, Dodd Mead, 1980.

*

Manuscript Collection: University of Oregon, Eugene, Oregon.

William Campbell Gault comments:
    There isn't much I can say about my mystery novels. I sold all that I wrote through the years I was actively in the field. Ten years after I had left, in 1962, I tried another mystery novel, but

nobody wanted it (though it has recently been accepted for publication). I started to concentrate on the juvenile novels in 1962. Though they weren't as much fun to write, they stayed in print much longer, earning me considerably more money. My Edgar winner—*Don't Cry for Me*—came out in 1952 and was out of print two months later. In 1952, I also wrote a juvenile novel, *Thunder Road*, which is still in print. So, one has to eat. ... My only mystery fame lately has been in someone else's novel—Ross Macdonald dedicated *The Blue Hammer* to me.

*   *   *

William Campbell Gault's detective and suspense novels are representative of the high standard of professionalism that marks the work of many of the genre writers who learned their trade in the pulp magazines and turned to the hardcover and paperback original markets when the pulps folded. All but his very recent work has been undeservedly neglected and long out of print, lost in the mass of mostly mediocre private-eye fiction that flooded the mystery field in the 1950's. His two series private eyes, Brock Callahan and Joe Puma, are memorable, believable characters, notable for their directness, integrity and—atypically for most 1950's private eyes—healthy, non-satyr-like relationship with women.

The usual scene is Southern California, and Gault covers that overworked territory with keen observation, coherent plotting, and fresh, direct writing. The familiar subjects for Los Angeles hardboiled novels are to be found in Gault's work: cars (Callahan versus hot car racketeers in *The Convertible Hearse*), cults ("ButThe Prophet Died," a fascinating novelette, and *Sweet Wild Wench*, with Puma), and the movie industy (*Death Out of Focus*); but the handling of these topics is far from hackneyed.

Gault's other career has been as a writer of juvenile sports fiction, and this interest surfaces in *Day of the Ram*, in which Callahan, an ex-football player himself ("Brock the Rock"), investigates the blackmailing of a pro football star, and in *The Canvas Coffin*, a gritty crime novel about boxing. Gault's one major departure from the California venue is *The Bloody Bokhara*, which involves murder among Armenian rug dealers in Milwaukee.

Anthony Boucher was a consistent champion of Gault's work, calling him "a fresh voice—a writer who sounds like nobody else, who has ideas of his own and his own way of uttering them."

After the publication of *Dead Hero* in 1963, Gault abandoned mystery writing for children; but happily, he (and Callahan) returned with the publication of *The Bad Samaritan*. Callahan is now married, moderately wealthy and comfortably retired, living in the coast city of San Valdesto (Gault's own Santa Barbara, thinly disguised). Callahan, somewhat reluctantly, returns to detective work, investigating the apparent suicide of a local civic activist and friend. Callahan is again compelled to track down a killer in the follow-on novel, *The Cana Diversion*, which also features a cameo appearance—of sorts—by Joe Puma. The pace and tone of these novels are somewhat more subdued than in Gault's earlier work, but his sharp eye for detail and feel for character remain undiminished. The promise of still further novels from this reliable craftsman is pleasant news for readers of private eye fiction.

—Art Scott

GAUNT, Graham. *See* GASH, Jonathan.

———

GEORGE, Elizabeth. American. Born in Warren, Ohio, 26 February 1949. Educated at the University of California, Riverside, B.A. in English; California State University, Fullerton, M.S. in counselling. Married Ira Tobin in 1971. English teacher, Mater Dei High School, Santa Anna, 1974–75, and El Toro High School, 1975–87, both California. Since 1988 creative writing teacher, Coastline College, Costa Mesa, Irvine Valley College, Irvine, 1989, and University of California, Irvine, 1990, all California. Recipient: Anthony award, 1989; Le Grand Prix de Littérature Policière, 1990. Agent: Deborah Schneider, John Farquharson Ltd., 157 West 57th Street, New York, New York 10107; or, Vivienne Schuster, John Farquharson Ltd., 162–168 Regent Street, London W1R 5TB, England. Address: 611 13th Street, Huntington Beach, California 92648, U.S.A.

CRIME PUBLICATIONS

Novels (series: Inspector Thomas Lynley and Sergeant Barbara Havers in all books)

A Great Deliverance. New York, Bantam, 1988; London, Bantam Press, 1989.
Payment in Blood. New York, Bantam, and London, Bantam Press, 1989.
Well-Schooled in Murder. New York, Bantam, and London, Bantam Press, 1990.

Uncollected Short Story

"The Evidence Exposed," in *Sisters in Crime 2*, edited by Marilyn Wallace. New York, Berkeley, 1990.

*

Manuscript Collection: Mugar Memorial Library, Boston University.

Elizabeth George comments:
As an American, I frequently encounter the same question from readers: why do I write British detective novels? I would answer by addressing my basic philosophy that a writer should write about that which he loves. Since I have a great love for England and a great interest in British fiction and since I taught a course based on the great British detective novelists, it seemed logical to try my hand at a setting I love and in a genre I know. My novels tend to hark back to the Golden Age of the detective story in that they attempt to reflect the glamour of Dorothy L. Sayers's type of writing rather than the grim reality of present day dissections of murder. Nonetheless, the issues they revolve around are very much part of contemporary life.

*   *   *

A Great Deliverance, Elizabeth George's first novel, prompted enough critical enthusiasm to warm any writer's heart, and *Payment in Blood*, the second book in her series, was also highly praised. With these works, George has set herself a high standard; fortunately, every indication suggests that she will continue to meet it. A number of factors contribute to the impact of these works: an intriguing range of continuing characters who are interesting individually as well as in their interactions with one another, gripping plots, well-drawn descriptive passages, and plenty of gore. The crimes depicted in these novels are horrific not only in physical detail but also in their psychological impact upon the cast of characters—and upon the readers. Strongly sexual undercurrents color and inform all these factors. With sharp realism but without exploitation, then, George notes and capitalizes upon the human fascination with sex and violence. Crime writers often focus on these subjects, of course, but not many display the control George commands.

Though *A Great Deliverance* and *Payment in Blood* can in no way be considered "message" novels, George presents serious themes conveyed by well-conceived symbols, as the ancient background tale of *A Great Deliverance* demonstrates. Safely hidden from Cromwell's troops, the Roman Catholic inhabitants of the Keldale Valley were almost betrayed by a sobbing baby. To avoid discovery, they smothered the infant whose ghostly cry still pierces the Yorkshire night, reminding hearers of the questions of guilt, responsibility, and forgiveness with which everyone lives. This old story points up other old crimes and misdemeanors which also reverberate throughout the novel, influencing almost every action. As George reveals the secrets—some miserable, some heartbreaking—in various characters' pasts, she also reveals their personalities and motivations which are almost always realistic mixtures of the admirable and the regrettable.

Murder brings Scotland Yard's Inspector Thomas Lynley, eighth earl of Asherton, to Keldale. Their wedding trip brings Simon and Deborah Allcourt-St. James to the same area. When Lynley calls upon St. James's forensic expertise, he interrupts the honeymoon of his best friend and the woman whom Lynley himself deeply loves. Another Scotland Yard officer assists Lynley, and the voltage generated between these investigators is equally great and much more overt than that in the Lynley-St. James triangle. Detective Sergeant Barbara Havers generates a good deal of the tension. Perpetually defensive, often offensive, Havers knows that failure on this case will condemn her to permanent street patrol. This awareness couples with her scorn for Lindley's reputation as a womanizer and her distrust of his social position to complicate an already difficult case.

When the decapitated body of William Teys, prosperous farmer and devoted churchgoer, is discovered, his teenage daughter, Roberta, sitting beside the corpse, declares, "I did it. I'm not sorry" before collapsing into total silence. Though all the villagers hold strong opinions about the girl, her father, and one another, they are generally less than helpful during the investigation being preoccupied with personal secrets and personal problems. Consequently, Lynley and Havers must not only reconstruct the crime but also reconstruct the dark history of the Teys and various other villagers. By the end of the investigation, a number of characters are called to book for a number of failings, thus raising again the question of how much one generation should sacrifice for another, of how individuals are accountable for their actions and for their inaction. Both Lynley and Havers endure some painful soul-searching; both are better and worse for the experience; both have learned a good bit about themselves and about the other—and both have considerable growing yet to do.

Whereas Havers's self-control is almost constantly at risk in George's first novel, in *Payment in Blood,* it is Lynley who wavers, allowing class distinctions and personal animosity to cloud his judgement. By offering him protection and support, however, Havers reveals something of her personal development and of her growing respect for their professional relationship just as Lynley reveals some dangerous flaws in his

code. Here, Lady Helen Clyde, Lynley's close friend and companion, is the most important continuing character other than the police officers themselves, for she is present at the crime scene, and her relationship with a major suspect distracts Lynley, who has fallen in love with her.

This case again takes the detectives far afield, to an isolated Scottish country house where the cast and staff of a new play have gathered to work on the production. When the abrasive playwright is murdered in her bed, suspects abound. As Havers and Lynley evaluate physical evidence, they must also analyze the intricacies of various overlapping relationships. Painfully, they uncover the truth, and if the identity of the murderer seems, finally, a bit contrived, the gritty poignancy of late scenes between Tommy and Helen balance that impression. By such means, George leaves readers satisfied with this tale, eager for the next.

—Jane S. Bakerman

———

GIBBS, Henry. *See* **HARVESTER, Simon.**

———

GIBSON, Walter B. Also wrote as Andy Adams; Ishi Black; Douglas Brown; Maborushi Kineji. American. Born in Philadelphia, Pennsylvania, 12 September 1897. Educated at the Peddie Institute (now Peddie School), 1915–16; Colgate University, Hamilton, New York, 1916–19. Married Pearl Litzka Raymond in 1949. Worked for the Philadelphia *Public Ledger,* 1922–32; freelance writer: wrote The Shadow stories for *The Shadow Magazine* and Norgil stories for *Crime Busters;* wrote *The Shadow comic* books 1941–47; professional magician. *Died 6 December 1985.*

Crime Publications

Novels

A Blonde for Murder. Chicago, Atlas, 1948.
Looks that Kill. Chicago, Atlas, 1948.

Novels as Maxwell Grant (series: The Shadow, in all books; some later volumes as Walter B. Gibson)

The Living Shadow. New York, Street and Smith, 1931; London, New English Library, 1976.
Eyes of the Shadow. New York, Street and Smith, 1931.
The Shadow Laughs. New York, Street and Smith, 1931.
The Shadow and the Voice of Murder. Los Angeles, Bantam, 1945.
Return of the Shadow. New York, Belmont, 1963.
The Weird Adventures of the Shadow: Grove of Doom, Voodoo Death, Murder by Moonlight. New York, Grosset and Dunlap, 1966.
The Death Tower. New York, Bantam, 1969.
Gangdom's Doom. New York, Bantam, 1970.
The Ghost Makers. New York, Bantam, 1970.
Hidden Death. New York, Bantam, 1970.
The Mobsmen on the Spot. New York, Pyramid, 1974; London, New English Library, 1976.
The Black Master. New York, Pyramid, 1974; London, New English Library, 1975.

The Red Menace. New York, Pyramid, 1975.
The Crime Oracle and The Teeth of the Dragon: Two Adventures of the Shadow. New York, Dover, and London, Constable, 1975.
The Shadow: The Mask of Mephisto and Murder by Magic. New York, Doubleday, 1975.
Mox: From the Shadow's Private Annals. New York, Pyramid, 1975.
The Romanoff Jewels. New York, Pyramid, 1975.
The Crime Cult. New York, Pyramid, 1975.
The Silent Seven. New York, Pyramid, 1975.
Double Z. New York, Pyramid, 1975.
Hands in the Dark. New York, Pyramid, 1975; London, New English Library, 1977.
Kings of Crime. New York, Pyramid, 1976.
Shadowed Millions. New York, Pyramid, 1976.
Green Eyes. New York, Pyramid, 1977.
The Creeping Death. New York, Pyramid, 1977.
Gray Fist. New York, Pyramid, 1977.
The Shadow's Shadow. New York, Pyramid, 1977.
Fingers of Death. New York, Jove, 1977.
Murder Trail. New York, Jove, 1977.
Zemba. New York, Jove, 1977.
Charg, Monster. New York, Jove, 1977.
The Wealth Seeker. New York, Jove, 1978.
The Silent Death. New York, Jove, 1978.
The Shadow: A Quarter of Eight and The Freak Show Murders. New York, Doubleday, 1978.
The Death Giver. New York, Jove, 1978.
The Shadow: Crime over Casco and The Mother Goose Murders. New York, Doubleday, 1979.
The Shadow: Jade Dragon, and The House of Ghosts. New York, Doubleday, 1981.
The Shadow and the Golden Master (*includes The Golden Master and Shiwan Khan Returns*). New York, Mysterious Press, 1984.

Short Stories (series: Norgil)

The Twilight Zone. New York, Grosset and Dunlap, 1960.
The Twilight Zone Revisited. New York, Grosset and Dunlap, 1964.
Norgil the Magician. Yonkers, New York, Mysterious Press, 1976.
Norgil: More Tales of Prestidigitection. Yonkers, New York, Mysterious Press, 1979.

Uncollected Novels as Maxwell Grant (series: The Shadow in all works)

"The Blackmail Ring," August 1932; "The Five Chameleons," 1 November 1932; "Dead Men Live," 15 November 1932; "Six Men of Evil," 15 February 1933; "The Shadow's Justice," 15 April 1933; "The Golden Grotto," 1 May 1933; "The Red Blot," 1 June 1933; "The Ghost of the Manor," 15 June 1933; "The Living Joss," 1 July 1933; "The Silver Scourge," 15 July 1933; "The Black Hush," 1 August 1933; "The Isle of Doubt," 15 August 1933; "Master of Death," 15 September 1933; "Road of Crime," 1 October 1933; "The Death Triangle," 15 October 1933; "The Killer," 1 November 1933; "The Crime Clinic," 1 December 1933; "Treasures of Death," 15 December 1933; "The Embassy Murders," 1 January 1934; "The Black Falcon," 1 February 1934; "The Circle of Death," 1 March 1934; "The Green Box," 15 March 1934; "The Cobra," 1 April 1934; "Crime Circus," 15 April 1934; "Tower of Death," 1 May 1934; "Death Clew," 15 May 1934; "The Key," 1 June 1934; "The Crime Crypt,"

15 June 1934; "Chain of Death," 15 July 1934; "The Crime Master," 1 August 1934; "Gypsy Vengeance," 15 August 1934; "Spoils of The Shadow," 1 September 1934; "The Garaucan Swindle," 15 September 1934; "Murder Marsh," 1 October 1934; "The Death Sleep," 15 October 1934; "The Chinese Disks," 1 November 1934; "Doom on the Hill," 15 November 1934; "The Unseen Killer," 1 December 1934; "Cyro," 15 December 1934; "The Four Signets," 1 January 1935; "The Blue Sphinx," 15 January 1935; "The Plot Master," 1 February 1935; "The Dark Death," 15 February 1935; "Crooks Go Straight," 1 March 1935; "Bells of Doom," 15 March 1935; "Lingo," 1 April 1935; "The Triple Trail," 15 April 1935; "The Golden Quest," 1 May 1935; "The Third Skull," 15 May 1935; "Murder Every Hour," 1 June 1935; "The Condor," 15 June 1935; "The Fate Joss," 1 July 1935; "Atoms of Death," 15 July 1935; "The Man from Scotland Yard," 1 August 1935; "The Creeper," 15 August 1935; "The Mardi Gras Mystery," 1 September 1935; "The London Crimes," 15 September 1935; "The Ribbon Clues," 1 October 1935; "The House That Vanished," 15 October 1935; "The Chinese Tapestry," 1 November 1935; "The Python," 15 November 1935; "The Case of Congressman Coyd," 15 December 1935; "The Ghost Murders," 1 January 1936; "Castle of Doom," 15 January 1936; "Death Rides the Skyway," 1 February 1936; "The North Woods Mystery," 15 February 1936; "The Voodoo Master," 1 March 1936; "The Third Shadow," 15 March 1936; "The Salamanders," 1 April 1936; "The Man from Shanghai," 15 April 1936; "The Gray Ghost," 1 May 1936; "The City of Doom," 15 May 1936; "Murder Town," 15 June 1936; "The Yellow Door," 1 July 1936; "The Broken Napoleons," 15 July 1936; "The Sledge Hammer Crimes," 1 August 1936; "Terror Island," 15 August 1936; "The Golden Masks," 1 September 1936; "Jibaro Death," 15 September 1936; "City of Crime," 1 October 1936; "Death by Proxy," 15 October 1936; "The Strange Disappearance of Joe Cardona," 15 November 1936; "The Seven Drops of Blood," 1 December 1936; "Intimidation, Inc.," 15 December 1936; "Vengeance Is Mine," 1 January 1937; "Loot of Death," 1 February 1937; "Quetzal," 15 February 1937; "Death Token," 1 March 1937; "Murder House," 15 March 1937; "Washington Crime," 1 April 1937; "The Masked Headsman," 15 April 1937; "Treasure Trail," 15 May 1937; "Brothers of Doom," 1 June 1937; "The Shadow's Rival," 15 June 1937; "Crime, Insured," 1 July 1937; "House of Silence," 15 July 1937; "The Shadow Unmasks," 1 August 1937; "The Yellow Band," 15 August 1937; "Buried Evidence," 1 September 1937; "The Radium Murders," 15 September 1937; "The Keeper's Gold," 15 October 1937; "Death Turrets," 1 November 1937; "The Sealed Box," 1 December 1937; "Racket Town," 15 December 1937; "The Crystal Buddha," 1 January 1938; "Hills of Death," 15 January 1938; "The Murder Master," 15 February 1938; "The Golden Pagoda," 1 March 1938; "Face of Doom," 15 March 1938; "Serpents of Siva," 15 April 1938; "Cards of Death," 1 May 1938; "The Hand," 15 May 1938; "Voodoo Trail," 1 June 1938; "The Rackets King," 15 June 1938; "Murder for Sale," 1 July 1938; "The Golden Vulture," with Lester Dent, 15 July 1938; "Death Jewels," 1 August 1938; "The Green Hoods," 15 August 1938; "Crime over Boston," 15 September 1938; "The Dead Who Lived," 1 October 1938; "Vanished Treasure," 15 October 1938; "The Voice," 1 November 1938; "Chicago Crime," 15 November 1938; "Shadow over Alcatraz," 1 December 1938; "Silver Skull," 1 January 1939; "Crime Rides the Sea," 15 January 1939; "Realm of Doom," 1 February 1939; "The Lone Tiger," 15 February 1939; "The Vindicator," 15 March 1939; "Death Ship," 1 April 1939;

"Battle of Greed," 15 April 1939; "The Three Brothers," 15 May 1939; "Smugglers of Death," 1 June 1939; "City of Shadows," 15 June 1939; "Death from Nowhere," 15 July 1939; "Isle of Gold," 1 August 1939; "Wizard of Crime," 15 August 1939; "The Crime Ray," 1 September 1939; "Castle of Crime," 1 October 1939; "The Masked Lady," 15 October 1939; "Ships of Doom," 1 November 1939; "City of Ghosts," 15 November 1939; "House of Shadows," 15 December 1939; "Death Premium," 1 January 1940; "The Hooded Circle," 15 January 1940; "The Getaway Ring," 1 February 1940; "Voice of Death," 15 February 1940; "The Invincible Shiwan Khan," 1 March 1940; "The Veiled Prophet," 15 March 1940; "The Spy Ring," 1 April 1940; "Death in the Stars," 1 May 1940; "Masters of Death," 15 May 1940; "The Scent of Death," 1 June 1940; "Q," 15 June 1940; "Gems of Doom," 15 July 1940; "Crime at Seven Oaks," 1 August 1940; "The Fifth Face," 15 August 1940; "Crime County," 1 September 1940; "The Wasp," 1 October 1940; "Crime over Miami," 1 November 1940; "Xitli, God of Fire," 1 December 1940; "The Shadow, The Hawk, and the Skull," 15 December 1940; "Forgotten Gold," 1 January 1941; "The Wasp Returns," 1 February 1941; "The Chinese Primrose," 15 February 1941; "Mansion of Crime," 1 March 1941; "The Time Master," 1 April 1941; "The House on the Ledge," 15 April 1941; "The League of Death," 1 May 1941; "Crime under Cover," 1 June 1941; "The Thunder King," 15 June 1941; "The Star of Delhi," 1 July 1941; "The Blur," 15 July 1941; "The Shadow Meets the Mask," 15 August 1941; "The Devil-Master," 15 September 1941; "Garden of Death," 1 October 1941; "Dictator of Crime," 15 October 1941; "The Blackmail King," 1 November 1941; "Temple of Crime," 15 November 1941; "Murder Mansion," 1 December 1941; "Crime's Stronghold," 15 December 1941; "Alibi Trail," 1 January 1942; "The Book of Death," 15 January 1942; "Death Diamonds," 1 February 1942; "Vengeance Bay," 1 March 1942; "Formula for Crime," 15 March 1942; "Room of Doom," 1 April 1942; "The Northdale Mystery," 1 May 1942; "Twins of Crime," 1 June 1942; "The Devil's Feud," 15 June 1942; "Five Ivory Boxes," 1 July 1942; "Death about Town," 15 July 1942; "Legacy of Death," 1 August 1942; "Judge Lawless," 15 August 1942; "The Vampire Murders," 1 September 1942; "Clue for Clue," 15 October 1942; "Trail of Vengeance," 1 November 1942; "The Murdering Ghost," 15 November 1942; "The Hydra," 1 December 1942; "The Money Master," 15 December 1942; "The Museum Murders," 1 January 1943; "Death's Masquerade," 15 January 1943; "The Devil Monsters," 1 February 1943; "Wizard of Crime," 15 February 1943; "The Black Dragon," 1 March 1943; "The Robot Master," May 1943; "Murder Lake," June 1943; "Messenger of Death," August 1943; "King of the Black Market," October 1943; "The Muggers," November 1943; "The Crystal Skull," January 1944; "Syndicate of Death," February 1944; "The Toll of Death," March 1944; "Crime Caravan," April 1944; "Town of Hate," July 1944; "Death in the Crystal," August 1944; "The Chest of Chu-Chan," September 1944; "Fountain of Death," November 1944; "No Time for Murder," December 1944; "Guardian of Death," January 1945; "Merry Mrs. Macbeth," February 1945; "Five Keys to Crime," March 1945; "Death Has Gray Eyes," April 1945; "Teardrops of Buddha," May 1945; "Three Stamps of Death," June 1945; "The Taiwan Joss," September 1945; "The White Skulls," November 1945; "The Stars Promise Death," December 1945; "The Banshee Murders," January 1946; "Crime Out of Mind," February 1946; "The Curse of Thoth," May 1946; "Alibi Trail," June 1946; "Malmordo," July 1946; "Dead Man's Chest," Fall 1948; "The Magigals

Mystery," Winter 1949; "The Black Circle," Spring 1949; "The Whispering Eyes," Summer 1949, all in *The Shadow* magazine (New York).

Uncollected Short Stories

"The Green Light," in *The Shadow* (New York), April 1931.
"The Florentine Masks," in *The Saint* (New York), March 1955.
"One Night in Paris," in *The Saint* (New York), November 1955.
"The Riddle of the Rangoon Ruby," in *The Shadow Scrapbook*, edited by Gibson. New York, Harcourt Brace, 1979.
"Blackmail Bay," in *The Duende History of The Shadow Magazine* by Will Murray. Melrose, Massachusetts, Odyssey, 1980.
"Gray Face," in *Detective Comics* (New York), March 1981.

Uncollected Short Stories as Maxwell Grant (series: Norgil the Magician in all stories)

"The Mad Magician," July 1938, and "The Chest of Ching Ling Foo," September 1939, both in *Crime Busters* (New York); "The Blue Pearls," December 1939, "The Lady and the Lion," January 1940, "Crime in the Crystal," March 1940, "Too Many Ghosts," May 1940, and "Tank-Town Tour," November 1940, all in *Mystery Magazine* (New York).

OTHER PUBLICATIONS

Novels

The Sin of Roger Diddlebock (as Harry Hershfield, with Harry Hershfield). New York, Bart House, 1947.
Anne Bonny, Pirate Queen (as Douglas Brown). Derby, Connecticut, Monarch, 1962.

Novels (for children) as Andy Adams

Brazilian Gold Mine Mystery. New York, Grosset & Dunlap, 1960.
Mystery of the Mexican Treasure. New York, Grosset & Dunlap, 1961.
Mystery of the Ambush in India. New York, Grosset & Dunlap, 1962.
Egyptian Scarab Mystery. New York, Grosset & Dunlap, 1963.
The Mystery of the Alpine Pass. New York, Grosset & Dunlap, 1965.

Other

After Dinner Tricks. Columbus, Ohio, Magic Publishing Company, 1921.
Practical Card Tricks. Hika, Wisconsin, Mill, 1921.
The Book of Secrets, Miracles Ancient and Modern. Scranton, Pennsylvania, Personal Arts, 1927.
The Bunco Book. Privately printed, 1927.
The Magic Square. New York, Scully, 1927.
The Mystic Fortune Teller. New York, Scully, 1927.
The Science of Numerology. New York, Scully, 1927.
The World's Best Book of Magic. Philadelphia, Penn, 1927.
Popular Card Tricks. New York, E.I., 1928.
Brain Tests: or Your Brains if Any. Boston, Page, 1930.
Houdini's Escapes. New York, Harcourt Brace, 1930.
Houdini's Magic. New York, Harcourt Brace, 1932.

Magic Made Easy; More than 200 Mystifying Feats. Springfield, Massachusetts, McLoughlin, 1932.

Magician's Manual. New York, Magician's League of America, 1933.

The New Magician's Manual. New York, Kemp, 1936.

Secrets of Magic. New York, Popper, 1945.

Professional Magic for Amateurs. New York, Prentice Hall, 1947; London, Kaye, 1948.

Magic Explained. New York, Doubleday, 1949.

The Key to Hypnotism. Baltimore, Oppenheimer, 1956.

What's New in Magic? New York, Hanover House, 1956.

The Key to Astronomy. New York, Key, 1958.

The Key to Judo and Jiujitsu (as Ishi Black). New York, Key, 1958.

The Key to Yoga. New York, Key, 1958.

Magic Explained. New York, Vista House, 1958.

Astrology Explained. New York, Vista House, 1959.

Fell's Official Guide to Knots and How to Tie Them. New York, Fell, 1961; revised edition, as *Fell's Guide to Knots and How to Tie Them.* Hollywood, Florida, Fell, 1988; as *Knots and How to Tie Them,* London, Hutchinson, 1985.

Houdini's Fabulous Magic, with Morris N. Young. Philadelphia, Chilton, 1961.

Hypnotism Through the Ages. New York, Vista House, 1961.

Judo: Attack and Defense (as Maborushi Kineji). New York, Vista House 1961.

Fell's Guide to Papercraft Tricks, Games and Puzzles. New York, Fell, 1963.

Magic Made Simple. New York, Doubleday, 1963; as *Junior Magic,* New York, Sterling, 1977.

Hoyle's Simplified Guide to the Popular Card Games. New York, Doubleday, 1963; revised edition, 1971.

How to Win at Solitaire. New York, Doubleday, 1964.

Hoyle Card Games: Reference Crammer. New York, Ken, 1964.

The Complete Illustrated Book of the Psychic Sciences, with Litzka R. Gibson. New York, Doubleday, 1966; London, Souvenir Press, 1967.

How to Bet the Harness Races. New York, Doubleday, 1966.

The Key to Solitaire (as Douglas Brown). New York, Bell, 1966; as *150 Solitaire Games,* as Walter B. Gibson, New York, Barnes Noble, 1985.

The Master Magicians: Their Lives and Most Famous Tricks. New York, Doubleday, 1966.

Secrets of Magic, Ancient and Modern. New York, Grosset and Dunlap, 1967; as *Secrets of the Great Magicians,* London, Collins, 1976.

Winning the $2 Bet. New York, Doubleday, 1967.

Magic with Science. New York, Grosset and Dunlap, 1968.

How to Develop an Exceptional Memory, with Morris N. Young. Hollywood, Wilshire, 1968.

Dreams. New York, Constellation International, 1969.

The Mystic and Occult Arts, with Litzka R. Gibson. West Nyack, New York, Parker, 1969.

The Complete Illustrated Book of Card Magic. New York, Doubleday, 1969.

Family Games America Plays. New York, Doubleday, 1970.

Hypnotism. New York, Grosset and Dunlap, 1970.

What Are the Odds?, with Melvin Evans. New York, Western, 1972.

Witchcraft. New York, Grosset and Dunlap, 1973.

The Complete Illustrated Book of Divination and Prophecy, with Litzka R. Gibson. New York, Doubleday, 1973; London, Souvenir Press, 1974; as *The Encyclopaedia of Prophecy,* London, Mayflower, 1977.

Fell's Guide to Winning Backgammon. New York, Fell, 1973; as *How to Win at Backgammon,* New York, Grosset and Dunlap, 1978.

Hoyle's Modern Encyclopedia of Card Games. New York, Doubleday, and London, Hale, 1974.

Pinochle Is the Name of the Game. New York, Barnes and Noble, 1974.

Poker Is the Name of the Game. New York, Harper, 1974.

Fell's Beginner's Guide to Magic. New York, Fell, 1976.

Walter Gibson's Encyclopedia of Magic and Conjuring. New York, Drake, 1976.

Mastering Magic. New York, Fell, 1977.

Big Book of Magic for All Ages. New York, Doubleday, 1980; Kingswood, Surrey, Kaye and Ward, 1982.

The Complete Illustrated Book of Close-Up Magic. New York, Doubleday, 1980; London, Hale, 1981.

25 Ways to Beat the Horses. New York, Casino Press, 1984.

Editor, *Houdini on Magic.* New York, Dover, 1953.

Editor, *The Fine Art of Murder* [*Spying, Robbery, Swindling*]. New York, Grosset and Dunlap, 4 vols., 1965–66.

Editor, *Rogue's Gallery: A Variety of Mystery Stories.* New York, Doubleday, 1969.

Editor, *The Original Houdini Scrapbook.* New York, Sterling, 1976; London, Oak Tree Press, 1977.

Editor, *The Shadow Scrapbook.* New York, Harcourt Brace, 1979.

*

Bibliography: *Gangland's Doom* by Frank Eisgruber, Jr., Oaklawn, Illinois, Robert Weinberg, 1974; *The Duende History of the Shadow Magazine* by Will Murray, Melrose, Massachusetts, Odyssey, 1980; *Man of Magic and Mystery: A Guide to the Work of Walter B. Gibson* by J. Randolph Cox, Metuchen, New Jersey, Scarecrow Press, 1988.

*   *   *

The mystery story writer and the professional stage magician share many of the same techniques in the execution of their respective crafts. Whether it be the creation of a successful illusion or the crafting of an intricate mystery, the professional in each case intends to create a precise *effect* while concealing from his audience the mechanisms by which he achieves that effect. Mystery, drama, deception, and misdirection are the essential techniques employed. Unlike the magician who will never reveal his secrets for fear of destroying his illusions, the mystery writer must reveal all for his story to succeed.

Many writers have consciously applied the illusionist's techniques to the mystery story but few have done so with greater ability than has Walter B. Gibson, himself a magician and a confidant of Houdini, Thurston, and Dunninger. Gibson was conversant with all aspects of the Black Arts, having written several books and articles on magic and its modern practitioners, when he was asked to create the lead character for the Street and Smith pulp, *The Shadow Magazine.* Under the pseudonym Maxwell Grant, he wrote nearly 300 Shadow novels.

The Shadow is Gibson's signal contribution to the detective story genre and to popular literature. He is a Machiavellian creation, a crepuscular version of Sherlock Holmes garbed in a magician's cloak. The Shadow, like Holmes, is an analytical, passionless intellect engaged in the pursuit of criminals for reasons which are intrinsic to his nature but extrinsic of the published stories. He appears, however, to regard the processes of suppressing criminal activity as a game, rather like chess, but one in which there are no set rules. Like Leblanc's Arsène Lupin, whom The Shadow also resembles, he flagrantly disregards the law in favor of his own ideal of justice. Unlike his predecessors, The Shadow relies equally upon deduction and gunplay.

Gibson infused his Shadow mysteries with magician's lore. Although few Shadow stories had as their background the world of the professional magician, as do *Murder by Magic* and *The Magigals Mystery*, illusionist's paraphernalia pervade the novels. The basis of The Shadow's "invisibility" is the ancient Black Art Illusion, and he is a master of the Houdiniesque escape (Gibson wrote a book titled *Houdini's Escapes*). The Shadow's antagonists also applied magician's equipment to crime, as they do in *The Unseen Killer, The Blur, Room of Doom,* and others.

Gibson's genius, however, lies in his application of the techniques of misdirection and illusion to his plots. He manipulates his readers with the same deftness that a magician controls his audience. Facts are withheld, or made ambiguous. Characters are presented in false lights which cloud their motives (*The Green Box*). The Shadow himself is enwrapped in a cloak of obfuscation in which his actions are rendered but his thoughts are hidden. Thus, he may have several incarnations in a given story (*Lingo* or *Zemba*) without the other characters or Gibson's audience being aware of it. The Shadow may see through misleading actions and clues, while Gibson leads the reader to believe them valid. Misdirection is employed so freely that one is hard-pressed to accept any character or event at face value.

Such controlled techniques were common to the Golden Age mystery story and, despite their violence, the Shadow novels fall into this category. The plots possess the same artificial ingeniousness, bizarre murder devices, arraying of suspects and occasional costumed villains. Such manipulations of convention, no matter how artful, do have their limitations, however. Whether Gibson is writing about The Shadow, Norgil, Valdor, Ardini or any of his other stage-magician detectives, the reader knows, in the end, that the illusions generated are not those of reality, but of invention.

—Will Murray

———

GIELGUD, Val (Henry). British. Born in Earl's Court, London, 28 April 1900; brother of the actor Sir John Gielgud. Educated at Hillside School, Godalming, Surrey; Rugby School, Warwickshire; Trinity College, Oxford. Married 1) Natalie Mamontoff in 1921 (marriage dissolved 1925); 2) Barbara Druce in 1928 (marriage dissolved), one son; 3) Rita Vale in 1946 (marriage dissolved); 4) Monica Grey in 1955 (marriage dissolved); 5) Vivienne June Bailey in 1960. Worked as a secretary to an M.P., a sub-editor for a comic paper, and an actor, in the 1920's; staff member, *Radio Times,* London, 1928–29; appointed Dramatic Director, BBC, London, 1929, and worked in the Drama Department until 1963: Head of Television Drama, 1950–52; retired as Head of Drama (Sound). O.B.E. (Officer, Order of the British Empire), 1942; C.B.E. (Commander, Order of the British Empire), 1958. *Died 30 November 1981.*

CRIME PUBLICATIONS

Novels (series: Antony Havilland; Inspector Gregory Pellew and Viscount Clymping; Inspector Simon Spears)

Imperial Treasure. London, Constable, and Boston, Houghton Mifflin, 1931.

The Broken Men. London, Constable, 1932; Boston, Houghton Mifflin, 1933.

Under London, with Holt Marvell. London, Rich and Cowan, 1933.

Gravelhanger (Havilland). London, Cassell, 1934; as *The Ruse of the Vanished Women,* New York, Doubleday, 1934.

Death at Broadcasting House (Spears), with Holt Marvell. London, Rich and Cowan, 1934; as *London Calling,* New York, Doubleday, 1934.

Death of an Extra (Spears), with Holt Marvell. London, Rich and Cowan, 1935.

Death in Budapest (Spears), with Holt Marvell. London, Rich and Cowan, 1937.

Outrage in Manchukuo (Havilland). London, Cassell, 1937.

The Red Account. London, Rich and Cowan, 1938.

The First Television Murder, with Eric Maschwitz. London, Hutchinson, 1940.

Confident Morning. London, Collins, 1943.

Fall of a Sparrow (Havilland). London, Collins, 1949; as *Stalking Horse,* New York, Morrow, 1950.

Special Delivery (Havilland). London, Collins, 1950.

The High Jump. London, Collins, 1953; as *Ride for a Fall,* New York, Morrow, 1953.

Cat. London, Collins, 1956; New York, Random House, 1957.

Gallows' Foot (Pellew and Clymping). London, Collins, 1958.

To Bed at Noon (Pellew and Clymping). London, Collins, 1960.

And Died So? (Pellew and Clymping). London, Collins, 1961.

The Goggle-Box Affair (Pellew and Clymping). London, Collins, 1963; as *Through a Glass Darkly,* New York, Scribner, 1963.

Prinvest-London (Pellew and Clymping). London, Collins, 1965.

Conduct of a Member (Pellew and Clymping). London, Collins, 1967.

A Necessary End (Pellew and Clymping). London, Collins, 1969.

The Candle-Holders (Pellew and Clymping). London, Macmillan, 1970.

The Black Sambo Affair (Pellew and Clymping). London, Macmillan, 1972.

In Such a Night... (Pellew and Clymping). London, Macmillan, 1974.

A Fearful Thing (Pellew and Clymping). London, Macmillan, 1975.

Short Stories

Beyond Dover, Announcer's Holiday, Africa Flight. London, Hutchinson, 1940.

Uncollected Short Stories

"Hot Water," in *The Great Book of Thrillers,* edited by H. Douglas Thomson. London, Odhams Press, n.d.

"Life Is Like That," in *Best Stories of the Underworld.* London, Faber, 1942.

"Who Killed the Drama Critic," in *The Evening Standard* (London), 11 March, 1963.

"The Man Who Forgot His Blind Spot," in *The Evening Standard* (London), 9 June 1964.

"To Make a Holiday," in *Winter's Crimes 2,* edited by George Hardinge. London, Macmillan, 1970.

"A Policeman's Lot," in *Winter's Crimes 6,* edited by George Hardinge.   London, Macmillan, 1974.

OTHER PUBLICATIONS

Novels

Black Gallantry.   London, Constable, 1928; as *Old Swords,* Boston, Houghton Mifflin, 1928.
Gathering of Eagles: A Story of 1812.   London, Constable, 1929; as *White Eagles,* Boston, Houghton Mifflin, 1929.

Plays

Self (produced London, 1926).
The Job (produced London, 1928).
Chinese White (produced London, 1929).   Published in *Five Three-Act Plays,* London, Rich and Cowan, 1933.
Red Triangle, adaptation of the novel *Special Providence* by Mary Agnes Hamilton (produced London, 1932).
Red Tabs, Exiles, and *Friday Morning,* in *How to Write Broadcast Plays.*   London, Hurst and Blackett, 1932.
I May Be Old-Fashioned (produced London, 1934).
Fours into Seven—Won't Go, with Stephen King-Hall, in *Twelve One-Act Plays,* edited by Geoffrey Whitworth. London, Sidgwick and Jackson, 1934.
Punch and Judy (also director: produced London, 1937).
Mr. Pratt's Waterloo, with Philip Wade (broadcast, 1937). Included in *Radio Theatre,* edited by Gielgud, London, Macdonald, 1946.
Music at Dusk (broadcast, 1939).   Included in *Radio Theatre,* edited by Gielgud, London, Macdonald, 1946.
Africa Flight (produced Richmond, Surrey, 1939).
Man's Company (produced Northampton, 1942).
Away from It All (produced London, 1946).   Published in *Embassy Successes 3,* London, Sampson Low, 1948.
Party Manners (produced London, 1950).   London, Muller, 1950.
A Shadow of Death, from a translation by Alan Blair of a play by Stig Dagerman (broadcast, 1950; as *Condemned to Live,* produced London, 1952).
Iron Curtain (produced London, 1951).
The Bombshell (produced Croydon, Surrey, and London, 1954).
Mediterranean Blue (produced Northampton, 1956).
Not Enough Tragedy (produced Colchester, Essex, 1959).

Screenplays: *Royal Cavalcade,* with others, 1935; *Cafe Colette* (*Danger in Paris*), with others, 1937; *Inspector Silence Takes the Air,* 1942; *Thirteen to the Gallows,* 1945.

Radio Plays: *Exiles,* 1928; *Red Tabs,* 1930; *Waterloo,* with Norman Edwards, 1932; *Gallipoli,* 1935; *The Sergeant Major,* 1936; *Mr. Pratt's Waterloo,* with Philip Wade, 1937; *Death of a Queen,* from a work by Hilaire Belloc, 1937; *Hassan,* with Dulcima Glasby, from the play by James Elroy Flecker, 1938; *Ending It,* 1938; *Music at Dusk,* 1939; *Scott in the Antarctic,* with Peter Cresswell, 1940; *Valiant for Truth,* with Igar Vinogradoff, 1940; *The Field of Kings,* with Cynthia Pughe, from a work by Thiery Maulnier, 1947; *Roman Holiday,* 1949; *A Shadow of Death,* from a translation by Alan Blair of a work by Stig Dagerman, 1950; *Unhurrying Chase* with Margaret Gore Browne, 1954; *The Lanchester Tradition,* from a work by G.F. Bradley, 1956; *Mr. Justice Raffles,* from works by E.W. Hornung, 1964; *The Goggle-Box Affair,* from his own novel, 1964; *The Crimson Star,* from a novel by Anthony Hope, 1964; *Fog,* 1964; *The Gentleman* (serial), from a work by Aldred

Olivant, 1965; *They Were So Few,* from a work by W.S. Davis, 1966; *The Bad Samaritan,* 1966; *Porto Bello Gold,* from a work by A.D.M. Smith, 1967; *Too Clever by Half,* 1967; *The Tents of Kedar,* from a work by H. Seton Merriman, 1967; *So Easy to Forget,* 1968; *The Hornblower Story,* from works by C.S. Forester, 1968; *The Fall of Edward Barnard, Flotsam and Jetsam, Gigolo and Gigolette, Sanatorium,* and *Dark Eagle,* from stories by W.S. Maugham, 1968–70; *Hornblower and the Crisis,* from a story by C.S. Forester, 1970; *The Time of My Life,* 1970; *The Tumbled House,* from a story by Winston Graham, 1971; *Conscience Doth Make Cowards,* 1971; *Cry Wolf,* from stories by Saki, 1971; *A Necessary End,* from his own novel, 1972; *Broome Stages,* from the novel by Clemence Dane, 1975; *Les Misérables,* with B. Campbell and C. Cox, from the novel by Victor Hugo, 1976; *Mr. Perrin and Mr. Traill,* from the novel by Hugh Walpole, 1978.

Other

How to Write Broadcast Plays (includes *Friday Morning, Red Tabs, Exiles*).   London, Hurst and Blackett, 1932.
Years of the Locust (autobiography).   London, Nicholson and Watson, 1947.
The Right Way to Radio Playwriting.   Kingswood, Surrey, Andrew George Eliot, 1948.
One Year of Grace: A Fragment of Autobiography.   London, Longman, 1950.
British Radio Drama 1922–1956: A Survey.   London, Harrap, 1957.
Years in a Mirror (autobiography).   London, Bodley Head, 1965.
My Cats and Myself: A Fragment of Autobiography.   London, Joseph, 1972.

Editor, *Radio Theatre: Plays Specially Written for Broadcasting.* London, Macdonald, 1946.
Editor, *Cats: A Personal Anthology.*   London, Newnes, 1966.

*

Theatrical Activities:

Director: **Plays**—*Tread Softly* by Peter Traill, London, 1935; *The Road to Ruin* by Thomas Holcroft, London, 1937; *Punch and Judy,* London, 1937; *Home and Beauty* by W.S. Maugham, Wimbledon and London, 1942; *This Land Is Ours* by Lionel Brown, London, 1945; *Autumn Gold* by Lionel Brown, London, 1948.

Actor: **Plays**—Mr. Malakoff in *For First-Class Passengers Only* by Osbert and Sacheverell Sitwell, London, 1927; Ronald Keith in *The Eldest Son* by John Galsworthy, London, 1928; Karl Starck in *Comrades* by Strindberg, London, 1928; Mr. Veal in *The Last Man In* by W.B. Maxwell, London, 1928; Pongo Hodge in *Flies and Treacle* by C. Dudley Ward, London, 1928. **Films**—*Death at Broadcasting House,* 1934; *Men Are Not Gods,* 1936.

*   *   *

Val Gielgud produced a varied group of mystery novels for almost five decades. Two unexceptional novels in the late 1920's were followed by a short (1933–40) but fruitful collaboration with Holt Marvell (pseudonym of Eric Maschwitz). Their detective novels featured the young and ambitious Detective-Inspector Simon Spears of Scotland Yard who is frequently assisted by BBC executive Julian Caird. Their best effort, *Death at Broadcasting House,* concerns the murder of an actor during a radio broadcast. This novel's plot, puzzle, characterizations, and especially its radio background are beautifully combined, and Gielgud's experiences as head of sound drama for the BBC was a special asset in the creation of this minor masterpiece.

A later but minor series featured Inspector Gregory Pellew and Viscount Humphrey Clymping. They eventually become partners in a private enquiry agency called Prinvest, after the former's retirement from the CID, and are aided by the latter's wife and mother. Of more than passing interest is the non-series *Cat,* an acronym for its protagonist Charles Adolphus Trent. The first short chapter deals with the discovery of a murder and the punishment of its perpetrator. The bulk of this inverted novel outlines the life of its central character and details the events leading to the crime. This is a flawed effort that might have been notable if it were more deeply felt by its author. *A Necessary End* has been lavishly praised by Jacques Barzun and Wendell Hertig Taylor as one of the best shipboard stories for its first-class detection and its amusing sidelights cast on the United States by a Londoner.

—Charles Shibuk

GIFFORD, Thomas (Eugene). American. Born in Dubuque, Iowa, 16 May 1937. Educated at Harvard University, Cambridge, Massachusetts, A.B. 1959. Married 1) Kari Sandven (divorced); 2) Camille d'Ambrose; two children. Textbook salesman, Minneapolis, Minnesota, 1960–68; editor-in-chief, *Twin Citian,* Minneapolis, 1968–69; Director of Public Relations, Tyrone Guthrie Theatre, Minneapolis, 1970; editor and columnist, Sun Newspapers, Minneapolis, 1971–75. Since 1975, self-employed writer. Agent: Julian Bach Literary Agency Inc., 747 Third Avenue, New York, New York 10017, U.S.A.

CRIME PUBLICATIONS

Novels

The Wind Chill Factor. New York, Putnam, and London, Hamish Hamilton, 1975.
The Cavanaugh Quest. New York, Putnam, 1976; London, Hamish Hamilton, 1977.
The Man from Lisbon. New York, McGraw Hill, 1977; London, Hamish Hamilton, 1978.
The Glendower Legacy. New York, Putnam, 1978; London, Hamish Hamilton, 1979.
Hollywood Gothic. New York, Putnam, 1979; London, Hamish Hamilton, 1980.

OTHER PUBLICATIONS

Other

Benchwarmer Bob (for children). Blue Earth, Minnesota, Piper, 1974.

* * *

Thomas Gifford's first book, *The Wind Chill Factor,* is, at first glance, yet another tale of resurgent Nazis. It is

distinguised, however, by the quality of the writing, the excellent descriptive passages, the superb sense of place, and the fine characterization. The book takes its hero John Cooper to South America and Europe in an attempt to unravel the Nazi conspiracy, and keeps the reader enthralled.

Gifford's knowledge of Minneapolis and the rest of Minnesota, scene of the early part of *The Wind Chill Factor,* comes through to an even greater extent in his second book, *The Cavanaugh Quest.* A man commits suicide, and Paul Cavanaugh is asked to find out why. Motivated only by curiosity at first, he finds himself drawn deeper into the case by his attraction to the man's ex-wife. The case has roots in a hunting and fishing club of the 1930's, whose members start dying in rapid succession as Cavanaugh gets closer to the answer. The brilliantly realized characters and settings and the fine writing make the book engrossing reading, even though the solution is clear to the reader long before Cavanaugh sees it.

The Man from Lisbon is a departure from Minnesota and the character types of the earlier books. It is an interesting novelization of a true crime of the 1920's, when a man swindled the Bank of Portugal out of five million dollars.

—Jeffrey Meyerson

GIGGAL, Kenneth. *See* ROSS, Angus.

GILBERT, Anthony. Pseudonym for Lucy Beatrice Malleson; also wrote as J. Kilmeny Keith; Anne Meredith. British. Born in Upper Norwood, London, 15 February 1899. Educated at St. Paul's Girls' School, Hammersmith, London. Worked as a secretary for the Red Cross, Ministry of Food, and Coal Association. Founding member, and general secretary, Detection Club. *Died 9 December 1973.*

CRIME PUBLICATIONS

Novels (series: Arthur G. Crook; M. Dupuy; Scott Egerton)

The Man Who Was London (as J. Kilmeny Keith). London, Collins, 1925.
The Sword of Harlequin (as J. Kilmeny Keith). London, Collins, 1927.
The Tragedy at Freyne (Egerton). London, Collins, and New York, Dial Press, 1927.
The Murder of Mrs. Davenport (Egerton). London, Collins, and New York, Dial Press, 1928.
The Mystery of the Open Window (Egerton). London, Gollancz, 1929; New York, Dodd Mead, 1930.
Death at Four Corners (Egerton). London, Collins, and New York, Dial Press, 1929.
The Night of the Fog (Egerton). London, Gollancz, and New York, Dodd Mead, 1930.
The Case Against Andrew Fane. London, Collins, and New York, Dodd Mead, 1931.
The Body on the Beam (Egerton). London, Collins, and New York, Dodd Mead, 1932.
The Long Shadow (Egerton). London, Collins, 1932.
The Musical Comedy Crime (Egerton). London, Collins, 1933.
Death in Fancy Dress. London, Collins, 1933.

Portrait of a Murderer (as Anne Meredith). London, Gollancz, 1933; New York, Reynal, 1934.

The Man in Button Boots (Dupuy). London, Collins, 1934; New York, Holt, 1935.

An Old Lady Dies (Egerton). London, Collins, 1934.

The Man Who Was Too Clever (Egerton). London, Collins, 1935.

Murder by Experts (Crook). London, Collins, 1936; New York, Dial Press, 1937.

Courtier to Death (Dupuy) London, Collins, 1936; as *The Dover Train Mystery,* New York, Dial Press, 1936.

The Man Who Wasn't There (Crook). London, Collins, 1937.

Murder Has No Tongue (Crook). London, Collins, 1937.

Treason in My Breast (Crook). London, Collins, 1938.

The Clock in the Hat Box (Crook). London, Collins, 1939; New York, Arcadia House, 1943.

The Bell of Death (Crook). London, Collins, 1939.

Dear Dead Woman (Crook). London, Collins, 1940; New York, Arcadia House, 1942; as *Death Takes a Redhead,* New York, Arrow Editions, 1944.

The Vanishing Corpse (Crook). London, Collins, 1941; as *She Vanished in the Dawn,* New York, Arcadia House, 1941.

There's Always Tomorrow (as Anne Meredith). London, Faber, 1941; as *Home Is the Heart,* New York, Howell Soskin, 1942.

The Woman in Red (Crook). London, Collins, 1941; New York, Smith and Durell, 1943; as *The Mystery of the Woman in Red,* New York, Quin, 1944.

Something Nasty in the Woodshed (Crook). London, Collins, 1942; as *Mystery in the Woodshed,* New York, Smith and Durrell, 1942.

The Case of the Tea-Cosy's Aunt (Crook). London, Collins, 1942; as *Death in the Blackout,* New York, Smith and Durrell, 1943.

The Mouse Who Wouldn't Play Ball (Crook). London, Collins, 1943; as *Thirty Days to Live,* New York, Smith and Durrell, 1944.

A Spy for Mr. Crook. New York, A.S. Barnes, 1944.

He Came by Night. London, Collins, 1944; as *Death at the Door,* New York, Smith and Durrell, 1945.

The Scarlet Button (Crook). London, Collins, 1944; New York, Smith and Durrell, 1945; as *Murder Is Cheap,* New York, Bantam, 1949.

The Black Stage (Crook). London, Collins, 1945; New York, A.S. Barnes, 1946; as *Murder Cheats the Bride,* New York, Bantam, 1948.

Don't Open the Door (Crook). London, Collins, 1945; as *Death Lifts the Latch,* New York, A.S. Barnes, 1946.

The Spinster's Secret (Crook). London, Collins, 1946; as *By Hook or Crook,* New York, A.S. Barnes, 1947.

Death in the Wrong Room (Crook). London, Collins, and New York, A.S. Barnes, 1947.

Die in the Dark (Crook). London, Collins, 1947; as *The Missing Widow,* New York, A.S. Barnes, 1948.

Lift Up the Lid (Crook). London, Collins, 1948; as *The Innocent Bottle,* New York, A.S. Barnes, 1949.

Death Knocks Three Times (Crook). London, Collins, 1949; New York, Random House, 1950.

Murder Comes Home (Crook). London, Collins, 1950; New York, Random House, 1951.

A Nice Cup of Tea (Crook). London, Collins, 1950; as *The Wrong Body,* New York, Random House, 1951.

Lady-Killer (Crook). London, Collins, 1951.

Miss Pinnegar Disappears. London, Collins, 1952; as *A Case for Mr. Crook,* New York, Random House, 1952.

Footsteps Behind Me (Crook). London, Collins, 1953; as *Black Death,* New York, Random House, 1953; as *Dark Death,* New York, Pyramid, 1963.

Snake in the Grass (Crook). London, Collins, 1954; as *Death Won't Wait,* London, Random House, 1954.

A Question of Murder (Crook). New York, Random House, 1955; as *Is She Dead Too?,* London, Collins, 1956.

Riddle of a Lady (Crook). London, Collins, 1956; New York, Random House, 1957.

And Death Came Too (Crook). London, Collins, and New York, Random House, 1956.

Give Death a Name (Crook). London, Collins, 1957.

Death Against the Clock (Crook). London, Collins, and New York, Random House, 1958.

Death Takes a Wife (Crook). London, Collins, 1959; as *Death Casts a Long Shadow,* New York, Random House, 1959.

Third Crime Lucky (Crook). London, Collins, 1959; as *Prelude to Murder,* New York, Random House, 1959.

Out for the Kill (Crook). London, Collins, and New York, Random House, 1960.

Uncertain Death (Crook). London, Collins, 1961; New York, Random House, 1962.

She Shall Die (Crook). London, Collins, 1961; as *After the Verdict,* New York, Random House, 1961.

No Dust in the Attic (Crook). London, Collins, 1962; New York, Random House, 1963.

Ring for a Noose (Crook). London, Collins, 1963; New York, Random House, 1964.

Knock, Knock, Who's There? (Crook). London, Collins, 1964; as *The Voice,* New York, Random House, 1965.

The Fingerprint (Crook). London, Collins, 1964, New York, Random House, 1965.

Passenger to Nowhere (Crook). London, Collins, 1965; New York, Random House, 1966.

The Looking Glass Murder (Crook). London, Collins, 1966; New York, Random House, 1967.

The Visitor (Crook). London, Collins, and New York, Random House, 1967.

Night Encounter (Crook). London, Collins, 1968; as *Murder Anonymous,* New York, Random House, 1968.

Missing from Her Home (Crook). London, Collins, and New York, Random House, 1969.

Death Wears a Mask. London, Collins, 1970; as *Mr. Crook Lifts the Mask,* New York, Random House, 1970.

Tenant for the Tomb (Crook). London, Collins, and New York, Random House, 1971.

Murder's a Waiting Game (Crook). London, Collins, and New York, Random House, 1972.

A Nice Little Killing (Crook). London, Collins, and New York, Random House, 1974.

Crime on the Coast, and No Flowers by Request, with others. London, Gollancz, 1984.

Uncollected Short Stories

"The Cockroach and the Tortoise" and "Horseshoes for Luck," in *Detection Medley,* edited by John Rhode. London, Hutchinson, 1939; as *Line Up,* New York, Dodd Mead, 1940.

"You Can't Hang Twice," in *To the Queen's Taste,* edited by Ellery Queen. Boston, Little Brown, 1946; London, Faber, 1949.

"Black for Innocence," in *The Evening Standard Detective Book.* London, Gollancz, 1950.

"What Would You Have Done?," in *The Evening Standard Detective Book,* 2nd series. London, Gollancz, 1951.

"Over My Dead Body," in *Ellery Queen's Mystery Magazine* (New York), July 1952.

"Remember Madame Clementine," in *Ellery Queen's Mystery Magazine* (New York), October 1955.

"Give Me a Ring," in *Illustrated London News,* 11 November 1955.

"Once Is Once Too Many," in *Ellery Queen's Mystery Magazine* (New York), December 1955.

"Sequel to Murder," in *Eat, Drink, and Be Buried,* edited Rex Stout. New York, Viking Press, 1956; as *For Tomorrow We Die,* London, Macdonald, 1958.

"Blood Will Tell," in *A Choice of Murders,* edited by Dorothy Salisbury Davis. New York, Scribner, 1958; London, Macdonald, 1960.

"The Goldfish Button," in *Ellery Queen's Mystery Magazine* (New York), February 1958.

"The Blackmailer," in *The Second Mystery Bedside Book,* edited by John Creasey. London, Hodder and Stoughton, 1961.

"A Nice Little Mare Called Murder," in *Crime Writers' Choice,* edited by Roy Vickers. London, Hodder and Stoughton, 1964.

"Even a Woman," in *The Saint* (New York), July 1964.

"He Found Out Too Late," in *The Saint* (New York), May 1966.

"Cat among the Pigeons," in *Ellery Queen's Mystery Magazine* (New York), October 1966.

"The Eternal Chase," in *Ellery Queen's Crime Carousel.* New York, New American Library, 1966.

"Sleep Is the Enemy," in *Ellery Queen's All-Star Lineup.* New York, New American Library, 1967.

"Point of No Return," in *Ellery Queen's Mystery Magazine* (New York), May 1968.

"The Intruders," in *Ellery Queen's Mystery Parade.* New York, New American Library, 1968.

"The Puzzled Heart," in *Ellery Queen's Mystery Magazine* (New York), March 1969.

"The Mills of God," in *Ellery Queen's Mystery Magazine* (New York), April 1969.

"Who Cares about an Old Woman?," in *Ellery Queen's Murder Menu.* Cleveland, World, 1969.

"Tiger on the Premises," in *Ellery Queen's Mystery Magazine* (New York), September 1969.

"The Funeral of Dendy Watt," in *Ellery Queen's Mystery Magazine* (New York), January 1970.

"The Quiet Man," in *Ellery Queen's Grand Slam.* Cleveland, World, 1970.

"Door to a Different World," in *Ellery Queen's Headliners.* Cleveland, World, 1971; London, Gollancz, 1972.

"When Suns Collide," in *Ellery Queen's Mystery Bag.* Cleveland, World, 1972.

"A Day of Encounters," in *Ellery Queen's Crookbook.* New York, Random House, 1974.

"Fifty Years After," in *Ellery Queen's Murdercade.* New York, Random House, 1975.

"The Invisible Witness," in *Ellery Queen's Crime Wave.* New York, Putnam, 1976.

OTHER PUBLICATIONS

Novels as Anne Meredith

The Coward. London, Gollancz, 1934.
The Gambler. London, Gollancz, 1937.
The Showman. London, Faber, 1938.
The Stranger. London, Faber, 1939.
The Adventurer. London, Faber, 1940.
The Family Man. London, Faber, and New York, Howell Soskin, 1942.
Curtain, Mr. Greatheart. London, Faber, 1943.

The Beautiful Miss Burroughes. London, Faber, 1945.
The Rich Woman. London, Faber, and New York, Random House, 1947.
The Sisters. London, Faber, 1948; New York, Random House, 1949.
The Draper of Edgecumbe. London, Faber, 1950; as *The Unknown Path,* New York, Random House, 1950.
A Fig for Virtue. London, Faber, 1951.
Call Back Yesterday. London, Faber, 1952.
The Innocent Bride. London, Hodder and Stoughton, 1954.
The Day of the Miracle. London, Hodder and Stoughton, 1955.
Impetuous Heart. London, Hodder and Stoughton, 1956.
Christine. London, Hodder and Stoughton, 1957.
A Man in the Family. London, Hodder and Stoughton, 1959.
The Wise Child. London, Hodder and Stoughton, 1960.
Up Goes the Donkey. London, Hodder and Stoughton, 1962.

Plays

Mrs. Boot's Legacy (as Anne Meredith). London, French, 1941.

Radio Plays: *The Plain Woman,* 1940; *Death at 6:30,* 1940; *A Cavalier in Love,* 1940; *The Bird of Passage,* 1941; *There's Always Tomorrow,* 1941; *Calling Mr. Brown,* 1941; *He Came by Night,* 1941; *The Adventurer,* 1941; *Footprints,* 1941; *Thirty Years Is a Long Time,* 1941; *A Bird in a Cage,* 1942; *His Professional Conscience,* 1942; *Find the Lady,* 1942; *The Home-Coming,* 1944; *Mystery Man of New York,* 1945; *Of Brides in Baths,* 1945; *Full Circle,* 1946; *Hard Luck Story,* 1947; *The Sympathetic Table,* 1948; *A Nice Cup of Tea,* 1948; *Profitable Death,* 1950; *After the Verdict,* 1952; *Now You Can Sleep,* 1952; *My Guess Would Be Murder,* 1954; *I Love My Love with an "A,"* 1957; *No One Will Ever Know,* 1960; *Black Death,* from her own novel, 1960; *And Death Came Too,* from her own novel, 1962.

Other

Three-a-Penny (autobiography; as Anne Meredith). London, Faber, 1940.

"The British or the American Story," in *The Mystery Writers' Handbook,* edited by Herbert Brean. London, Harper, 1956.

*   *   *

Although Lucy Beatrice Malleson also wrote as J. Kilmeny Keith and Anne Meredith, and though she also created other series characters, it is as Anthony Gilbert, the creator of lawyer-detective Arthur G. Crook, one of the most interesting fictional detectives yet to solve a case, that she enjoyed the greatest success.

From Gilbert's originally rather unattractive creation (*Murder by Experts*), Crook developed into an irrepressible Cockney who earns his living by diligent work, constant watchfulness, and occasional lapses from standard professionalism, for "The Criminals' Hope and The Judges' Despair" frequents pubs, drinking beer and distributing his oversized business cards to chance acquaintances. A colorful, cheeky, confident man of perpetual middle age, Crook is addicted to bright brown, off-the-rack suits which, like his chaotic office at the top of a shabby building in a disreputable part of town, reflect his personality and serve to reassure his clients (usually young women) and to mislead his opponents. Mistaking Crook's cover for foolishness, murderers remain off-guard—until Crook's trap has sprung.

Generally, Crook is not the protagonist of the novels. Rather, Gilbert uses either the frame technique or the rider-to-the-rescue method. *And Death Came Too* is a good example of the frame story, for readers meet Crook when a fellow lawyer confides his fear that trouble is destined to haunt Ruth Appleyard. The plot then shifts to explore Ruth's personality, love affairs, and adventures. But when she becomes involved in a third questionable death, Crook is called in, and, having met him in the frame, the reader is prepared to accept his intervention. Gilbert has suspended disbelief and coincidence becomes destiny.

In *A Question of Murder,* however, Crook arrives on the scene much later in the story. The early chapters focus on the deadly conflict between Edward Poulden and his boarder. Caught up in the struggle is young Margaret Reeve, the protagonist. When Poulden eliminates the boarder and attempts to implicate Margaret, a mutual friend summons Crook to exonerate her. Though here Crook's appearance comes about more naturally than in *And Death Came Too,* both novels, like the others of their types, succeed handily. These books also reveal that Gilbert is adroit at both the conventionally ordered mystery and the "inverted" mystery in which the criminal is known from the outset and the suspense depends on the reader's concern lest the murderer succeed.

Another of Gilbert's strengths is splendid development of supporting characters. Two of the best are headstrong, independent divorcée Margaret Ross, the blackmailed protagonist of *The Visitor,* and her neighbor, Angela Muir, seemingly a stereotypical spinster who emerges as a humorous, determined companion in crisis. And perhaps Gilbert's most charming supporting figure is May Forbes in *Death Wears a Mask,* a brisk, capable, middle-aged woman worthy of Crook's respect. There is no hint of romance between the two, but instead a beautifully depicted friendship.

Though the novels center around murder, Gilbert substitutes Crook's ebullience for violent action, and, using his adoration of his autos (the Scourge and then the Superb) as a trigger, creates some remarkably vivid and gripping car chases.

For skillful plotting, lively characterization, and clever action, then, Gilbert can be highly ranked among mystery writers, and for the creation of Arthur Crook, she cannot be faulted.

—Jane S. Bakerman

GILBERT, Michael (Francis). British. Born in Billinghay, Lincolnshire, 17 July 1912. Educated at St. Peter's School, Seaford, Sussex; Blundell's School, 1926–31; University of London, LL.B. (honours) 1937. Served in the Royal Horse Artillery in North Africa and Europe, 1939–45: mentioned in despatches. Married Roberta Mary Marsden in 1947; five daughters and two sons. Articled clerk, Ellis Bickersteth Aglionby and Hazel, London, 1938–39; solicitor, 1947–51, and since 1952, partner, Trower Still and Keeling, London. Legal Adviser, Government of Bahrain, 1960. Series editor, Classics of Detection and Adventure, Hodder and Stoughton, publishers, London. Founding member, Crime Writers Association, 1953. C.B.E. (Commander, Order of the British Empire), 1980. Recipient: Mystery Writers of America Grand Master award, 1988; Anthony Life Time Achievement award, 1990. Agent: Curtis Brown Ltd., 162-168 Regent Street, London W1R 5TB. Address: The Old Rectory, Luddesdown, Gravesend, Kent DA13 0XE England.

CRIME PUBLICATIONS

Novels (series: Inspector Hazelrigg)

Close Quarters (Hazelrigg).   London, Hodder and Stoughton, 1947; New York, Walker, 1963.
They Never Looked Inside (Hazelrigg).   London, Hodder and Stoughton, 1948; as *He Didn't Mind Danger,* New York, Harper, 1949.
The Doors Open (Hazelrigg).   London, Hodder and Stoughton, 1949; New York, Walker, 1962.
Smallbone Deceased (Hazelrigg).   London, Hodder and Stoughton, and New York, Harper, 1950.
Death Has Deep Roots (Hazelrigg).   London, Hodder and Stoughton, 1951; New York, Harper, 1952.
Death in Captivity.   London, Hodder and Stoughton, 1952; as *The Danger Within,* New York, Harper, 1952.
Fear to Tread (Hazelrigg).   London, Hodder and Stoughton, and New York, Harper, 1953.
Sky High.   London, Hodder and Stoughton, 1955; as *The Country-House Burglar,* New York, Harper, 1955
Be Shot for Sixpence.   London, Hodder and Stoughton, and New York, Harper, 1956.
Blood and Judgement.   London, Hodder and Stoughton, and New York, Harper, 1959.
After the Fine Weather.   London, Hodder and Stoughton, and New York, Harper, 1963.
The Crack in the Teacup.   London, Hodder and Stoughton, and New York, Harper, 1966.
The Dust and the Heat.   London, Hodder and Stoughton, 1967; as *Overdrive,* New York, Harper, 1968.
The Etruscan Net.   London, Hodder and Stoughton, 1969; as *The Family Tomb,* New York, Harper, 1969.
The Body of a Girl.   London, Hodder and Stoughton, and New York, Harper, 1972.
The Ninety-Second Tiger.   London, Hodder and Stoughton, and New York, Harper, 1973.
Flash Point.   London, Hodder and Stoughton, and New York, Harper, 1974.
The Night of the Twelfth.   London, Hodder and Stoughton, and New York, Harper, 1976.
The Empty House.   London, Hodder and Stoughton, 1978; New York, Harper, 1979.
Death of a Favourite Girl.   London, Hodder and Stoughton, 1980; as *The Killing of Katie Steelstock,* New York, Harper, 1980.
The Final Throw.   London, Hodder and Stoughton, 1982; as *End-Game,* New York, Harper, 1982.
The Black Seraphim.   London, Hodder and Stoughton, 1983; New York, Harper, 1984.
The Long Journey Home.   London, Hodder and Stoughton, and New York, Harper, 1985.
Trouble.   London, Hodder and Stoughton, and New York, Harper, 1987.
Paint Gold and Blood.   London, Hodder and Stoughton, and New York, Harper, 1989.

Short Stories (series: Patrick Petrella)

Game Without Rules.   New York, Harper, 1967; London, Hodder and Stoughton, 1968.
Stay of Execution and Other Stories of Legal Practice.   London, Hodder and Stoughton, 1971.
Amateur in Violence.   New York, Davis, 1973.
Petrella at Q.   London, Hodder and Stoughton, and New York, Harper, 1977.

Mr. Calder and Mr. Behrens. New York, Harper, and London, Hodder and Stoughton, 1982.

Young Petrella. London, Hodder and Stoughton, and New York, Harper, 1988.

Anything for a Quiet Life. London, Hodder and Stoughton, and New York, Carroll and Graf, 1990.

Uncollected Short Stories

"Basilio," in *Winter's Crimes 1,* edited by George Hardinge. London, Macmillan, and New York, St. Martin's Press, 1969.

"The Cork in the Bottle," in *Ellery Queen's Mystery Magazine* (New York), October 1969.

"Verdict of Three," in *Verdict of Thirteen,* edited by Julian Symons. London, Faber, and New York, Harper, 1979.

"The Man at the Bottom," in *Ellery Queen's Mystery Magazine* (New York), April 1979.

"The Man in the Middle," in *Ellery Queen's Mystery Magazine* (New York), May 1979.

"The Man at the Top," in *Ellery Queen's Mystery Magazine* (New York), June 1979.

"Audited and Found Correct," in *Winter's Crime 12,* edited by Hilary Watson. London, Macmillan, and New York, St. Martin's Press, 1980.

"Coronation Year," in *Who Done It?,* edited by Alice Laurance and Isaac Asimov. Boston, Houghton Mifflin, 1980.

"Camford Cottage," in *After Midnight Ghost Book.* London, Hutchinson, 1980.

"The Inside Pocket," in *Crime Wave.* London, Collins, 1980.

"Who Killed Carol Carver," in *TV Times* (London), April 1981.

"A Very Special Relationship," in *Winter Crimes 16,* edited by Hilary Hale. London, Macmillan, and New York, St. Martin's Press, 1984.

"The Two Footmen," in *New Adventures of Sherlock Holmes.* New York, Carroll and Graf, 1987.

"The Jackal and the Tiger," in *Winter Crimes 20,* edited by Hilary Hale. London, Macmillan, 1988.

"The Rules of the Game," in *The Rigby File,* edited by Tim Heald. London, Hodder and Stoughton, 1989.

OTHER PUBLICATIONS

Plays

A Clean Kill (produced London, 1959). London, Constable, 1961.

The Bargain (produced London, 1961). London, Constable, 1961.

The Shot in Question (produced Brighton and London, 1963). London, Constable, 1963.

Windfall (produced Liverpool and London, 1963). London, Constable, 1963.

Radio Plays: *Death in Captivity,* 1953; *The Man Who Could Not Sleep,* 1955; *Crime Report,* 1956; *Doctor at Law,* 1956; *The Waterloo Table,* 1957; *You Must Take Things Easy,* 1958; *Stay of Execution,* 1965; *Game Without Rules* series, 1968; *The Last Chapter,* 1970; *Black Light,* 1972; *Flash Point,* 1974; *Petrella* series, 1976; *In the Nick of Time,* 1979; *The Last Tenant,* 1979; *The Oyster Catcher,* 1983.

Television Plays: *The Crime of the Century* (serial), 1956; *Wideawake* (serial), 1957; *The Body of a Girl,* 1958; *Fair Game* (serial), 1958; *Crime Report* (documentary), 1958; *Blackmail Is*

So Difficult, 1959; *Dangerous Ice,* 1959; *A Clean Kill,* 1961; *The Men from Room 13* (serial), from a work by Stanley Firmin, 1961; *Scene of the Accident,* 1961; *The Betrayers,* from a work by Stanley Ellin, 1962; *Trial Run,* 1963; *The Blackmailing of Mr. S.,* 1964; *The Mind of the Enemy* (serial), 1965; *The Man in Room 17* series (1 episode), 1966; *Misleading Cases* series with Christopher Bond, from a work by A.P. Herbert, 1971; *Hadleigh* series (1 episode), 1971; *Money to Burn,* from the novel by Margery Allingham, 1974; *Where There's a Will,* 1975.

Other

Dr. Crippen. London, Odhams Press, 1953.

"Technicalese," in *The Mystery Writers' Handbook,* edited by Herbert Brean. New York, Harper, 1956.

The Claimant. London, Constable, 1957.

The Law. Newton Abbot, Devon, David and Charles, 1977.

"The Invisible Bond," in *Murder Ink: The Mystery Reader's Companion,* edited by Dilys Winn. New York, Workman, 1977.

The Fraudsters: Six Against the Law. London, Constable, 1987.

Editor, *Crime in Good Company: Essays on Criminals and Crime-Writing.* London, Constable, 1959.

Editor, *Best Detective Stories of Cyril Hare.* London, Faber, 1959; New York, Walker, 1961; as *Death Among Friends and Other Detective Stories,* New York, Perennial, 1984.

Editor, *The Oxford Book of Legal Anecdotes.* Oxford, and New York, Oxford University Press, 1986.

*

Manuscript Collections: University of California, Berkeley; Mugar Memorial Library, Boston University.

Michael Gilbert comments:

(1980) It is impossible in a brief space to make any useful summary of an output that spans forty years (my first book was actually written in 1938), and that comprises twenty novels, three collections of short stories, three or four hundred other short stories, four stage plays, and a good number of television and radio plays. I can best introduce my crime writing with two quotations. One is from Julian Symons's compendium *Bloody Murder.* He says (in a section headed "Entertainers"), "In our time there are many writers who put into their books little or nothing of their own personalities. Now that the old rules no longer apply they are able to treat lightly and amusingly many subjects that would not have been touched 30 years age." Under this heading he mentions my name and Emma Lathen's, a coupling I appreciate.

So I am an entertainer? A fact that Harry Keating, in his review of one of my recent books, found "disappointing." In fact he went on to say that he found this book less disappointing, in this respect, than earlier ones. I find the whole thing puzzling. What is a writer to do if he is not allowed to entertain?

(1990) The view expressed 10 years ago has received a good deal of support. The novels which serve as show cases for their authors' personalities, which indulge in fine writing and are loaded with deep analytical studies of their characters ("am I a couch" complained Professor Jacques Barzun) are not, in my opinion members of the true, and honourable line of crime stories. They may be something else. As to what I offer no opinion.

*   *   *

Michael Gilbert, a London solicitor, has written strict intellectual puzzles, romantic thrillers, espionage, and police procedural novels. All are done with skill and a high level of artistic achievement. Gilbert is a master of complex plotting and well-rounded characters. With great detail and a special feel for the places he uses as settings, he delivers stories which are compelling and engage the reader immediately.

Gilbert has also written short stories and plays with equal success. Anthony Boucher, critic for the *New York Times,* called Gilbert's collection of spy stories *Game Without Rules* "the second best volume of spy short stories ever published": he ranked only *Ashenden,* by Somerset Maugham, higher.

While his early novels, beginning in 1947 with *Close Quarters,* are now considered somewhat weak, it is only by comparison. Experience brought maturity of writing. Combining a humor rarely found in the genre with layers of plotting, clues, and suspects, Gilbert can always be depended upon to deliver solid reading entertainment. He has created several exceptional series characters, the chief of whom is Patrick Petrella. Followers have watched Petrella deal with blackmail, arson, theft and murder, while rising steadily from constable to Detective Chief Inspector with the Metropolitan Police. Calder and Behrens are Counter-Intelligence agents featured in short stories, and Inspector Hazelrigg was featured in six early novels. Mercer is a highly individualistic inspector in *The Body of a Girl,* who later quits the force.

Gilbert also writes non-series novels. *Smallbone Deceased* has been called a masterpiece by more than one critic. In *The Etruscan Net* the amateur is an art gallery owner. *Death in Captivity* is a classic of escape of prisoners of war in Italy, and may be partially autobiographical as Gilbert was captured and imprisoned in North Africa during World War II. *The Empty House,* set on Exmoor, is a fine example of Gilbert's knowledge and utilization of place in his novels.

Gilbert's recent books reveal once again his wide-ranging interests. *Death of a Favourite Girl* begins with the murder of a glamorous television singer. The final dramatic courtroom sequence features a formidable woman lawyer. *Mr. Calder and Mr. Behrens* is the second collection of short stories of vigorous adventure which have appeared in *EQMM.* The two are sometimes mild country gentlemen, but also remorseless, extremely clever spies, ruthless against adversaries. *The Final Throw* is a police novel, featuring a drunken but inquisitive Welsh policeman. More thriller than mystery, it centers on a shady tour guide operation, tax evasion, and a young woman in more danger than she suspects. With great wit and urbanity, *The Black Seraphim* explores the murder of an archdeacon who has argued with the Dean about selling cathedral land to crooked developers. The Dean is a suspect, but a visiting pathologist and the Dean's lovely daughter turn detective.

Gilbert's legal background has contributed to excellent novels concerning law firms, young solicitors, courtroom style, technique, procedure, and drama.

Gilbert's novels and short stories mark him as a careful writer rather than a prolific one. Such care has contributed believable plots, characters with whom we can identify, and details of setting and geography. Wit and humor used judiciously add greatly to the reader's enjoyment. Gilbert's novels are not only plausible but of unusual substance.

—Frank Denton

GILES, Kenneth. *See* **McGIRR, Edmund.**

GILL, B.M. Pseudonym for Barbara Margaret Trimble; also writes as Margaret Blake. British. Born in Holyhead, Anglesey, Wales, 15 February 1921. Educated at Le Bon Sauveur Convent, Holyhead; Redland College, Bristol. Divorced. Clerk/typist, Trinity House Service, Holyhead; school teacher, Avon Education Authority, Bristol; chiropodist, National Health Service clinic, Bristol. Currently full-time writer. Lives in Holyhead. Recipient: Crime Writers Association Gold Dagger award, 1984. Agent: Patricia Robertson, 87 Caledonian Road, London, N1 9BT, England.

CRIME PUBLICATIONS

Novels (series: Detective Chief Inspector Tom Maybridge)

Target Westminster.   London, Hale, 1977.
Death Drop.   London, Hodder and Stoughton, 1979; New York, Scribner, 1980.
Victims (Maybridge).   London, Hodder and Stoughton, 1981; as *Suspect,* New York, Scribner, 1981.
The Twelfth Juror.   London, Hodder and Stoughton, and New York, Scribner, 1984.
Seminar for Murder (Maybridge).   London, Hodder and Stoughton, 1985; New York, Scribner, 1986.
Nursery Crimes.   London, Hodder and Stoughton, 1986; New York, Scribner, 1987.
Dying to Meet You.   London, Hodder and Stoughton, 1988; New York, Bantam, 1990.
Time and Time Again.   London, Hodder and Stoughton, 1989; New York, Scribner, 1990.

Uncollected Short Stories

"A Certain Kind of Skill," in *Winter's Crimes 18,* edited by Hilary Hale.   London, Macmillan, 1986.
"Murder Most Kind," in *Good Housekeeping* (London), November 1987.

OTHER PUBLICATIONS

Novels as Margaret Blake

Stranger at the Door.   London, Hale, 1967.
Bright Sun, Dark Shadow.   London, Hale, 1968.
The Rare and the Lovely.   London, Hale, 1969.
The Elusive Exile.   London, Hale, 1971.
Flight from Fear.   London, Hale, 1973.
Courier to Danger.   London, Hale, 1973.
Apple of Discord.   London, Hale, 1975.
Walk Softly and Beware.   London, Hale, 1977.

*

B.M. Gill comments:
My crime stories are concerned with people and their reactions to horrifying situations. I don't make them react in a certain way to fit a preconceived pattern. I know when I start a book that it must go from A to B within a certain structure, but if the characters develop their own unexpected idiosyncrasies and flatly refuse to contemplate certain routes I let them

deviate, and if B is not quite where I thought it was going to be that is all to the good. It means the characters are viable.

The principal character in *Death Drop* is John Fleming whose son has fallen to his death on a school outing. Fleming rightly suspects that it wasn't an accident. The identity of the murderer is obvious early on. The way Fleming deals with him and in so doing discovers his own strengths and weaknesses forms the climax.

Victims has a hospital setting. There are a series of what appear to be revenge killings. Two young nurses and an anaesthetist are murdered. One of the nurses is the daughter of the neuro-surgeon, the other is his theatre sister, the anaesthetist is his mistress. The main suspect is the hospital worker, George Webber, whose wife was unsuccessfully operated on by the surgeon and is now paralysed. Webber's emotional response to the innuendoes and hostility carries the book through to its conclusion.

The Twelfth Juror is set in the Old Bailey. A television personality, Edward Carne, is on trial for the murder of his wife. One of the jurors, Robert Quinn, has inside knowledge of the case. He is breaking the law by being on the jury, but has his own good reason for not opting out. The accent is on him, on the accused, and on the accused's daughter. The other jurors play more minor roles, but are dangerously powerful when debating the verdict. Whether or not the verdict is the right one is only revealed when it is too late to do anything about it.

Physical violence is inevitably part of all crime stories—emotional violence strikes deeper. I am interested in the circumstances leading up to the act, and in the consequences.

*   *   *

B.M. Gill's books have often been likened to those of P.D. James and Ruth Rendell, but they are distinctive enough to be judged on their own merits. At her best, Gill is skilled at building suspense and creating believable people; as a result, she is able to depict the effects of emotional disturbance with both power and sensitivity. Mystification for its own sake appeals to her much less and she has yet to create a major series detective. Tom Maybridge, the Detective Chief Inspector who appears in two novels and one short story, is pleasant but unremarkable. What is most striking about Gill is her versatility. Few of her contemporaries—certainly not Rendell or James—experiment with so many different types of story.

B.M. Gill is the pen-name chosen by Barbara Trimble when she belatedly turned to crime after writing, as Margaret Blake, a string of novels of romantic suspense. In her new incarnation she began with an unexceptional thriller, *Target Westminster,* about a plot to overthrow the government. This book is seldom mentioned in her publicity material nowadays, but a change of publisher and of approach yielded immediate rewards and she began to make up for lost time.

Her next novel, *Death Drop,* describes John Fleming's search for the truth about the death of his 12-year-old son, a boarding school pupil, during an expedition to a maritime museum. The "solution" matters less than Fleming's struggle to come to terms with his bereavement. Eventually he finds himself in a position to determine whether the person responsible for his boy's death should live or die. The outcome of the confrontation convinces and satisfies the reader: Fleming feels "as if he, too, had lost blood and that the wound had been washed clean."

Very different is *Victims,* a chilling novel set within a hospital community. Arguably it remains Gill's finest achievement, offering both a genuine puzzle and mounting tension. Three women are killed—a nurse; the daughter of neurosurgeon Paul McKendrick; and his mistress, a doctor. Maybridge makes his first appearance without ever dominating the action; Gill is more concerned with atmosphere and characterisation than with chronicling police routine.

The Twelfth Juror is a courtroom thriller. Edward Carne, presenter of a popular television show, is on trial at the Old Bailey, accused of murdering his wife. His daughter Frances is a squatter who lives in the same house as one of the members of the jury. Julian Symons has rightly commented in *Bloody Murder* that "stories about juries tend to have a dismal similarity," a criticism from which he excepted Raymond Postgate's classic *Verdict of Twelve*. Gill's Gold Dagger-winning book also offers a rare combination of credibility and originality.

In *Seminar For Murder* Maybridge reappears, this time to play a more central role than in *Victims*. He is asked to lecture to a group of crime writers, the Golden Guillotine Club, at their annual weekend seminar and before long murder follows. This competent updating of the traditional whodunit hardly prepares one for the extraordinary change of direction marked by *Nursery Crimes,* a black comedy about a lovely young girl, Zanny Moncrief, who commits murder repeatedly and without compunction. Unfortunately, much of the humour seems forced.

The uneasy pun in the title of *Dying To Meet You* suggests another attempt at macabre wit. Lowell Marshall, a former concert pianist, seeks escape from his wife and job in a remote Gloucestershire cottage. There he finds a faded sepia photograph of a beautiful girl from Victorian times, with whom he becomes obsessed, with predictably disastrous consequences. There is an ironic epilogue, but the tone throughout is depressingly bleak.

Nor can *Time And Time Again* be counted a complete success. It is an unusual story told in the first person by Maeve Barclay, a young middle-class woman who has served a prison sentence for wounding a policeman during an anti-nuclear demonstration. Following her release she is unable to settle down with her stockbroker husband and hankers for the friendship of a seasoned criminal, Rene, whom she met inside. The idea is interesting, but like Zanny and Lowell, Maeve is in some respects an unsatisfactory and unappealing figure.

By her own high standards, Gill's most recent books are flawed. This is because she is straining too hard after something new. Yet her refusal to be pigeonholed as cosy and conventional deserves admiration. Only if other talented writers are willing to take similar risks will the endless possibilities of crime fiction continue to be revealed.

—Martin Edwards

GILL, Bartholomew. Pseudonym for Mark McGarrity. American. Born in Holyoke, Massachusetts, 22 July 1943. Educated at Brown University, Providence, Rhode Island, B.A. 1966; Trinity College, Dublin, M.Litt. 1971. Married Margaret Wellstood Dull in 1966. Worked as a speech writer, public relations writer, financial reporter, insurance investigator, and teacher. Since 1971, freelance writer; Writer in Residence, Dover Public Schools, New Jersey, 1984–85. Agent: Robin Rue, Anita Diamant Agency, 310 Madison Avenue, New York, New York 10017. Address: 159 North Shore Road, Andover, New Jersey 07821, U.S.A.

CRIME PUBLICATIONS

Novels (series: Inspector Peter McGarr in all books)

McGarr and the Politician's Wife. New York, Scribner, 1977; London, Hale, 1978.
McGarr and the Sienese Conspiracy. New York, Scribner, 1977; London, Hale, 1979.
McGarr on the Cliffs of Moher. New York, Scribner, 1978; London, Hale, 1980.
McGarr at the Dublin Horse Show. New York, Scribner, 1980; London, Hale, 1981.
McGarr and the P.M. of Belgrave Square. New York, Viking Press, 1983; London, Penguin, 1984.
McGarr and the Method of Descartes. New York, Viking, 1984; London, Penguin, 1985.
McGarr and the Legacy of a Woman Scorned. New York, Viking, 1986.
The Death of a Joyce Scholar (McGarr). New York, Morrow, 1989.

OTHER PUBLICATIONS as Mark McGarrity

Novels

Little Augie's Lament. New York, Grossman, 1973.
Lucky Shuffles. New York, Grossman, 1973.
A Passing Advantage. New York, Rawson Wade, 1980.
Neon Caesar. New York, Pocket Books, 1989.

Other

"Maigret's Raincoat" (as Bartholomew Gill), in *Murderess Ink,* edited by Dilys Winn. New York, Workman, 1980.

*   *   *

The hard core of the *roman policier* is still dominated by the British model, in which a pair of police officers, one senior, one junior, deals with crime, most often murder. Of course, one immediately thinks of the variations on this model (including the American); one of these variations is the police-procedural novel in which the workings of foreign police organizations are used as a backdrop to the character and skills of an officer "translated" for English-speaking consumption. Freeling's Van der Valk and Castang are excellent examples of the type. Bartholomew Gill's Peter McGarr, of the Garda Siochána of the Republic of Eire, is one of these translated policeman.

Much of the dramatic tension in Gill's eight (to date) McGarr novels comes from the peculiar relationship of Ireland and its institutions to the British model: as simultaneously like and not-like. McGarr speaks English (and French) but not Gaelic; his organization, though firearms are commonly carried, is apparently based on a familiar British pattern. Of course, the matter of history and the continuing affray in Ulster compounds the difficulty of relating one culture and nation to the other, and it ought to be expected that McGarr will have to deal with the IRA and all its effects and permutations, and with the Cause. This he does, and with admirable finesse: he is able to ask a character, as in *McGarr and the P.M. of Belgrave Square,* "are you political?" and he can accurately read the response. McGarr himself, it is explained early on, successfully conceals his own politics.

As a created character, McGarr is cleverly but sometimes confusingly drawn. A lower-class Dubliner by birth and breeding, he is short, stocky, ordinary-faced, bald, middle-aged, and married to a wife 20 years his junior. An unheroic appearance is the norm for these translated policemen, almost a cliché. The skills that produce his hard-won successes are variously given: he is easy to talk to, has no belief in any psychological theory but "reads" individuals, depends on his eyes and, often, on long silences: McGarr "could tell Dineen was about to lie to him" (*McGarr and the Cliffs of Moher*), a valuable gift for a policeman, if rather naively conferred. McGarr is also capable of playing the hard, even brutal cop, though this posture is usually left to a subordinate. Gill's protagonist is not, in fact, a Great Detective Brain, though he is almost certainly more intelligent than he sometimes appears. He is a plugger, though not a plodder. McGarr has a fairly stable group of assistants, who tend to reveal in a programmatic way a range of personal characteristics, from the introverted to the thuggish. The technical side of police detection is given more respect in the earlier novels than in the later. McGarr is often assisted by his good-looking young wife, Noreen, whose skills as an art historian are elaborately detailed in *McGarr and the P.M. of Belgrave Square,* and Noreen is a congenial addition to the novels, though it is not easy to see how, in real life, the wife of a high-ranking officer would be permitted to go up to the firing line as often as she does.

As the McGarr series has progressed, Gill has expanded some themes and techniques, contracted others, and added a taste for complexity of plot. The early novels tend to be interrupted by improbably arranged violence, are stylistically blunt and even awkward, but always show character, emotional nuance, and personal interplay well. Later McGarr adventures are stylistically more complex and—sometimes self-consciously—better crafted, but the author does not lose his talent for believable characterization: *McGarr and the Method of Descartes* is a political suspense-thriller; *McGarr and the Legacy of a Woman Scorned* puts McGarr in a stew of Irish peasantry, fading Anglo-Irish ascendancy, with the history of the local land for seasoning. "How the past can tyrannize" is a frequent theme.

Since "Bartholomew Gill" is in fact the pen-name of Mark McGarrity, who is Irish-American, one may ask how skillfully or believably the author constructs his Republic and its citizens. The Roman Catholic Church, and religion in Ireland generally, is curiously absent from the novels, except for a priest who is interviewed by McGarr in *McGarr at the Dublin Horse Show*—though the childlessness of McGarr and his wife is frequently commented on. As for politics, and the perpetual aggravation of the Six Counties, McGarrity/Gill is usually as sensible and nimble-footed as his detective and sometimes as oblique, making his observations indirectly and by insinuation. The sentimental Irishness of the typical Irish-American seems to have no particular appeal to the author. In sum, McGarr's adventures are laid out with more character and less caricature; speech and speech-patterns are allowed, usually skillfully, to advance plot and establish atmosphere. Gill is rarely an intrusive or an idiosyncratic writer, as he makes a good case for his conclusion, that "we [the Irish] are a strange, unlikely people." The McGarr novels have a rich, sometimes dense and difficult texture, and provide the challenge of a highly atmospheric, but intellectually satisfying, police procedural technique.

—D.A. Miller

GILMAN, Dorothy. Also writes as Dorothy Gilman Butters. American. Born in New Brunswick, New Jersey, 25 June

1923. Educated at Pennsylvania Academy of Fine Arts, Philadelphia (William Emlen Cresson European Scholarship, 1944); Art Students' League, New York, 1964. Married Edgar A. Butters, Jr., in 1945 (divorced 1965); two sons. Instructor in Drawing, Samuel Fleischer Art Memorial, Philadelphia, 1945–46, and in creative writing, Cherry Lawn School, Darien, Connecticut, 1969–70. Agent: Howard Morhaim Agency, 175 Fifth Avenue, New York, New York 10010. Address: 340 Eastern Promenade, No. 242, Portland, Maine 04101, U.S.A.

CRIME PUBLICATIONS

Novels (series: Mrs. Emily Pollifax)

The Unexpected Mrs. Pollifax. New York, Doubleday, 1966; London, Hale, 1967; as *Mrs. Pollifax, Spy,* London, Tandem, 1971.
Uncertain Voyage. New York, Doubleday, 1967; London, Hale, 1968.
The Amazing Mrs. Pollifax. New York, Doubleday, 1970; London, Hale, 1971.
The Elusive Mrs. Pollifax. New York, Doubleday, 1971; London, Hale, 1973.
A Palm for Mrs. Pollifax. New York, Doubleday, 1973; London, Hale, 1974.
A Nun in the Closet. New York, Doubleday, 1975; as *A Nun in the Cupboard,* London, Hale, 1976.
The Clairvoyant Countess. New York, Doubleday, 1975; London, Prior, 1976.
Mrs. Pollifax on Safari. New York, Doubleday, and London, Hale, 1977.
The Tightrope Walker. New York, Doubleday, 1979; London, Hale, 1980.
Mrs. Pollifax on the China Station. New York, Doubleday, 1983; London, Hale, 1984.
Mrs. Pollifax and the Hong Kong Buddha. New York, Doubleday, 1985; London, Hale, 1986.
Mrs. Pollifax and the Golden Triangle. New York, Doubleday, 1988; London, Piatkus, 1989.
Incident at Badmayâ. New York, Doubleday, 1989.
Mrs. Pollifax and the Whirling Dervish. New York, Doubleday, 1990.

OTHER PUBLICATIONS as Dorothy Gilman Butters

Other (for children)

Enchanted Caravan. Philadelphia, Macrae Smith, 1949.
Carnival Gypsy. Philadelphia, Macrae Smith, 1950.
Ragamuffin Alley. Philadelphia, Macrae Smith, 1951.
The Calico Year. Philadelphia, Macrae Smith, 1953.
Four-Party Line. Philadelphia, Macrae Smith, 1954.
Papa Dolphin's Table. New York, Knopf, 1955.
Girl in Buckskin. Philadelphia, Macrae Smith, 1956.
Heartbreak Street. Philadelphia, Macrae Smith, 1958.
Witch's Silver. Philadelphia, Macrae Smith, 1959.
Masquerade. Philadelphia, Macrae Smith, 1961.
Ten Leagues to Boston Town. Philadelphia, Macrae Smith, 1962.
The Bells of Freedom. Philadelphia, Macrae Smith, 1963.
A New Kind of Country (for adults). New York, Doubleday, 1978.
The Maze in the Heart of the Castle. New York, Doubleday, 1983.

*

Manuscript Collection: Mugar Memorial Library, Boston University.

*   *   *

After more than a decade of writing for magazines and producing books for young readers, Dorothy Gilman began to write suspense fiction for an adult audience in the 1960's. *The Unexpected Mrs. Pollifax* is the first of a series which has wide appeal to young and old alike.

In her first adventure, Mrs. Pollifax is a sweet, elderly widow whose life has settled into a routine of volunteer work, garden club and women's associations, and comfortable monotony. Her children and grandchildren live far away and no longer need her. She feels useless and depressed. Not a personality to succumb in such a crisis, she remembers a childhood dream of becoming a spy, travels to CIA headquarters, and applies for a job. By a series of coincidences that would seem merely absurd were it not for the author's charming and delightful way of telling a tale, Emily Pollifax is taken on as a courier for a single mission. She is hired because she looks and acts so completely unlike an agent, and becomes a part-timer whose brilliant improvisations and stunning successes are nothing short of fantastic.

In her various adventures, Mrs. Pollifax rescues a Chinese scientist from a seemingly impregnable fortress in Albania; joins a gypsy caravan in Turkey to rescue a woman whose career in espionage dates from World War II, at the same time exposing a dangerous double agent; smuggles passports and counterfeit money into Bulgaria; inspires an audacious raid on a maximum security prison; and prevents the assassination of an African leader. In *A Palm for Mrs. Pollifax,* she substitutes canned peaches for cannisters of plutonium and foils Arab terrorists. Dorothy Gilman recounts her heroine's exploits with such liveliness, optimism, and humor that disbelief is willingly suspended. Warmhearted and open minded, Mrs. Pollifax is without prejudice and is always sympathetic to those in trouble. Disarmingly self-mocking, whenever she is in a tight spot, Mrs. Pollifax imagines what would happen in the movies and acts accordingly, all the while regretting her own clichés. After her first triumph, she studies karate, a skill put to good use in subsequent adventures. She makes friends of all ages and even finds romance. A Bulgarian patriot, grown fond of her, exclaims: "If only you were born Bulgarian, Amerikanski, we would change the world!" In Africa, an attractive American widower proposes marriage. In perilous circumstances as she and her companions attempt to escape from Albania, Mrs. Pollifax feels "a stirring in her that was almost mystical; an exhilarating sense of freedom that she had never known before. . . ." At another crucial moment, she considers that she is at "exactly the age . . . when life ought to be spent, not hoarded. There had been enough years of comfortable living, and complacency was nothing but delusion. One could not always change the world, she felt, but one could change oneself."

In Gilman's other suspense novels, the heroines are young women who rise above psychiatric problems and surmount personal danger to become strong individuals; cloistered nuns who take on some of the difficult problems of the modern world; and a psychic who overcomes prejudice against "fortune-tellers" and solves crimes for the police. Two young nuns shelter a gangster with three bullet holes in him, run headlong into the Mafia, the FBI, crooked lawmen, a commune with its own guru, and some oppressed migrant workers. They manage to sort things out and "mend a little of the world" in a comic morality play. *The Tightrope Walker* features an allegorical fairy tale, a lost manuscript, and a young woman recovering from emotional illness who solves a murder committed years earlier.

Gilman creates appealing characters whose "ordinary" lives are changed by their encounters with danger. Naive and innocent to begin with, apparently handicapped by age, poverty, or emotional problems, they pit their courage, perseverance, and resourcefulness (fortified by inner strength discovered in time of need), against the organized powers of evil. Gilman is interested in mysticism, psychic phenomena, and Oriental philosophies, and incorporates them into her fiction. Her readers will enjoy *A New Kind of Country,* an inspirational account of her quest for self-understanding and for harmony in her own nature and with her environment.

Gilman's action-filled plots unfold amidst the upheavals of world events—power politics, cold war struggles, oil shortages, the arms race, and the problems of emerging nations, complicated in the personal sphere by greed, prejudice, dishonesty, and cruelty. The achievements of her heroines are made plausible by the matter-of-fact tone of the narration, by the author's sense of humor and skillful use of topical detail. Goodness and kindness prevail in these tales which show things the way we wish they were. Gilman's suspense fiction is wholesome, up-beat entertainment for readers of all ages.

—Mary Helen Becker

GIROUX, E.X. Pseudonym for Doris Shannon (née Giroux). Canadian. Born in Elmira, New York, 7 August 1924. Educated at Napanee Collegiate Institute, Ontario, 1939–42. Married Frank Owen Shannon in 1942; two daughters. Bank clerk, Royal Bank of Canada, Napanee, Ontario, 1942–47, and Vancouver, British Columbia, 1948–49. Address: c/o St. Martin's Press, 175 Fifth Avenue, New York, New York 10010, U.S.A.

CRIME PUBLICATIONS

Novels (series: Robert Forsythe and Abigail Sanderson in all books)

A Death for Adonis. New York, St. Martin's Press, 1984; London, Hale, 1986.
Death for a Darling. New York, St. Martin's Press, 1985; London, Hale, 1987.
A Death for a Dancer. New York, St. Martin's Press, 1985; as Doris Shannon, London, Severn House, 1987.
A Death for a Doctor. New York, St. Martin's Press, 1986; as Doris Shannon, London, Severn House, 1987.
A Death for a Dilettante. New York, St. Martin's Press, 1987.
A Death for Dietitian. New York, St. Martin's Press, 1988.
A Death for a Dreamer. New York, St. Martin's Press, 1989.
A Death for a Double. New York, St. Martin's Press, 1990.

OTHER PUBLICATIONS

Novels as Doris Shannon

The Whispering Runes. New York, Lenox Hill, 1972.
22 Hallow Field. New York, Fawcett, 1974.
The Seekers. New York, Fawcett, 1975.

Hawthorn Hill. New York, St. Martin's Press, and London, Collins, 1977; as *The Devil's Servant,* London, Fontana, 1978.
The Lodestar Legacy. New York, Popular Library, 1977.
Cain's Daughters. New York, St. Martin's Press, and London, Collins, 1978.
Beyond the Shining Mountains. New York, St. Martin's Press, 1979.
The Punishment. New York, St. Martin's Press, 1980; London, Sphere, 1982.
Little Girls Lost. New York, St. Martin's Press, 1981; London, Sphere, 1983.
Family Money. New York, St. Martin's Press, 1984; London, Severn House, 1986.

* * *

E. X. Giroux has created a pair of detectives who get into the business by accident; who, in the course of amateur detection, make contacts which prove useful in subsequent investigations; and who develop a reputation as redoubtable detectives. Robert (Robby) Forsythe is barrister, first and foremost, although we never see him practice. Abigail (Sandy) Sanderson is his secretary. They have special knowledge, special skills, which make them a fascinating team, respected by the police and lionized by the press.

In *A Death for Adonis,* Robby is drawn out of early retirement to investigate the case of famed sculptor Sebastian Calvert who, 25 years earlier, had been convicted of the murder of his model and lover, and subsequently committed to an asylum. Calvert's adopted daughter wants Forsythe to prove her now-dead father innocent. In the course of his investigation, Robby must face up to his own shady past, allowing him to return to his law practice in succeeding books.

Each book in the series places Forsythe and Sandy in slightly different, but still British, settings, each of which leads to a murder. In *Death for a Darling,* Forsythe is going on a fishing trip, and Sandy is off to visit a friend. She finds a movie in the making, starring Forsythe's favorite actress. Being the thoughtful lady she is, Sandy calls Forsythe before he even finishes packing and invites him for tea and a surprise on his trip north. Unfortunately, the co-star, Mickey Darling, is murdered on that supposedly idyllic weekend, and Forsythe forsakes fishing for detecting.

Winslow Maxwell Penndragon is a not very likeable man, a hedonist who prides himself on never having worked for a living. After two failed attempts on his life, he asks Robby and Sandy to investigate in *A Death for a Dilettante.* Robert, complete with a walking cast from a disastrous ski trip in Switzerland, is bored and needs a diversion. This case might make a suitable diversion but, unfortunately, he and Sandy arrive to late to prevent Penndragon's murder.

A Death for a Double explores the fragile ego of Forsythe. Anthony Funicelli has married Lucie, a child bride, and brought her back to England to live at his family house with his mother, teenage twins from a former marriage, and look-alike cousin. When Anthony begins to get threats on his life, he calls in Forsythe, and then hesitates to tell Robby the real reason for his call. Robby forms an unreasonable dislike for Funicelli and, while he prepares to depart for home, the look-alike cousin is murdered and Robby must solve the crime to salve his own conscience.

Once they have acquired a reputation as detectives, Robby and Sandy deliberately set out to investigate murder. In *A Death for a Dancer,* a solicitor acquaintance brings Forsythe into a case involving the Dancers—an eccentric family who had been robbed by Katherine St. Croix. The solicitor wants

Forsythe, who has now earned the nickname "Mission Impossible" Forsythe from the tabloids, to investigate the subsequent disappearance, murder and discover of St. Croix's body on the Dancer estate.

In some of the series, Sandy acts as principal investigator. Sandy masquerades as a cousin of Gillian Foster—murder victim along with her husband, Doctor Foster, and their two young sons—in her first solo detective roll (*A Death for a Doctor*). She is recruited by the dapper Chief Inspector Adam Kepesake, because of a similarity in names and appearance with the real cousin. Robby sees that Sandy might be in danger, even if Kepesake is blind to the possibility, and Forsythe comes to Sandy's aid near the completion of this dangerous investigation.

In *A Death for a Dietitian,* Sandy is invited to a murder weekend at a fashionable private island resort, to act as the detective. It sounded like fun until a famous chef, and later his homely wife, are found murdered and the guests are stranded. Sandy must act as a real detective, with no help from Robert. It is in this book that the closeness between Robby and Sandy is really made evident.

A Death for a Dreamer also employs Sandy as the initial investigator, although Robert helps out eventually. The donation of pets by a pet food company for use in therapy in a nursing home is what draws Sandy to a northern town, to act as proxy for a client. And that is exactly what Sandy does, until the poisoning of one of the dogs in question, the smothering of one of the patients, and the discovery of a skeleton in the garden cause Sandy to call in Robby.

Forsythe, his reputation damaged by a past indiscretion, has recovered over the span of the series, primarily as a result of his taking up detection to alleviate "boredom." He has learned to face his past mistakes, and with the help of his secretary, regain self esteem. In the course of this series, he has built a reputation as a successful detective who solves "impossible" cases.

—Carol M. Harper

GODEY, John. Pseudonym for Morton Freedgood; also writes as Stanley Morton. American. Born in Brooklyn, New York, in 1912. Educated at City College of New York; New York University. Served in the United States Army, 1943–46. Public Relations Agent for United Artists, Twentieth Century-Fox, Paramount, J. Arthur Rank. Agent: Clyde Taylor, Curtis Brown Ltd., 10 Astor Place, New York, New York 10003, U.S.A.

CRIME PUBLICATIONS

Novels (series: Jack Albany)

The Gun and Mr. Smith. New York, Doubleday, 1947; London, Hodder and Stoughton, 1976.
The Blue Hour. New York, Doubleday, 1948; London, Boardman, 1949; as *Killer at His Back,* New York, Spivak, 1955; as *The Next to Die,* London, Tandem, 1975.
The Man in Question. New York, Doubleday, 1951; London, Boardman, 1953; as *The Blonde Betrayer,* New York, Spivak, 1955.
This Year's Death. New York, Doubleday, and London, Boardman, 1953.

The Clay Assassin. London, Boardman, 1959; New York, Berkley, 1973.
The Fifth House. London, Boardman, 1960; New York, Berkley, 1973.
The Reluctant Assassin (Albany). London, Hale, 1966; as *A Thrill a Minute with Jack Albany,* New York, Simon and Schuster, 1967.
Never Put Off till Tomorrow What You Can Kill Today (Albany). New York, Random House, 1970.
The Three Worlds of Johnny Handsome. New York, Random House, 1972; London, Hodder and Stoughton, 1973.
The Taking of Pelham One Two Three. New York, Putnam, and London, Hodder and Stoughton, 1973.
The Talisman. New York, Putnam, 1976; London, W.H. Allen, 1977.
The Snake. New York, Putnam, and London, New English Library, 1978.
Nella. New York, Delacorte Press, 1981; London, Sphere, 1982.
Fatal Beauty. New York, Atheneum, 1984; London, Methuen, 1985.

Uncollected Short Stories

"The Blue Hour," in *Two Complete Detective Books* (New York), September 1948.
"The Gun and Mr. Smith," in *Two Complete Detective Books* (New York), November 1948.
"This Year's Death," in *Two Complete Detective Books* (New York), Winter 1953–54.
"The Lovers," in *Manhunt* (New York), October 1956.
"It's All Quite Painless," in *Alfred Hitchcock's Mystery Magazine* (New York), August 1957.

OTHER PUBLICATIONS

Novels

Yankee Trader (as Stanley Morton), with Stanley Freedgood. New York, Sheridan House, 1947.
The Wall-to-Wall Trap (as Morton Freedgood). New York, Simon and Schuster, 1957; London, Jarrolds, 1958.

Other

The Crime of the Century and Other Misdemeanors (autobiography). New York, Putnam, 1973.

*   *   *

Although he is the author of numerous short stories, John Godey's most memorable claim to fame is his best-selling novel *The Taking of Pelham One Two Three.* In this alarmingly realistic and breathtakingly tense novel, four armed men hijack a New York subway train containing 16 passengers and hold them for a ransom of one million dollars. Godey's intimate knowledge of New York City, where he has spent most of his life, enables him to bring to life the interworkings of the city's political leaders, news reporters, police force, and subway authorities in a cooperative effort to capture the ruthless kidnappers who have threatened to kill hostages if the money is not delivered.

Godey's characters are vivid, particularly in his later novels. A good example of this is *The Talisman,* the tense, fast-paced story of a revolutionary group which steals the remains of the unknown soldier. The climax is scorchingly ironic. Godey frequently switches the narrative viewpoint from character to character, adding depth to the story in the transition. He is also adept in the wise use of "street language" which adds another dimension of credibility to his characters. Although Godey's novels could not really be classified as typically hard-boiled or gangster stories, they do involve ex-cons, prostitutes, crooked cops, grafting politicians, and crimes methodically planned, motivated primarily by greed rather than by passion.

Somewhat lacking in the credibility of their plotting, Godey's earlier novels rely heavily on characterization, and, in some instances, on humor. The Albany series, *The Reluctant Assassin*. and *Never Put Off till Tomorrow What You Can Kill Today,* for instance are farcical thrillers involving Jack Albany, a bit-part character actor, with intricate plots which allow plenty of room for Albany's blustery bungling. Both novels start off with a case of mistaken identity, since Albany looks much like a crook should look. Of course, when the actor in Albany cannot resist playing the role in which he has been mistakenly cast, the real action starts, and comedic errors are compiled in a witty and amusing romp.

—Mary Ann Grochowski

————

GOINES, Donald. American. Also wrote as Al C. Clark. Born in Detroit, Michigan, 15 December 1937. Attended Catholic elementary school. Served in the United States Air Force, 1952–55. Lived with Shirley Sailor; two daughters. Pimp, numbers runner, bootlegger, and thief; served prison sentences totaling 6½ years; after 1971, self-employed writer. *Died 21 October 1974.*

CRIME PUBLICATIONS

Novels

Dopefiend: The Story of a Black Junkie. Los Angeles, Holloway, 1971.
Whoreson: The Story of the Ghetto Pimp. Los Angeles, Holloway, 1972.
Black Gangster. Los Angeles, Holloway, 1972.
Black Girl Lost. Los Angeles, Holloway, 1973.
Street Players. Los Angeles, Holloway, 1973.
White Man's Justice, Black Man's Grief. Los Angeles, Holloway, 1973
Daddy Cool. Los Angeles, Holloway, 1974.
Eldorado Red. Los Angeles, Holloway, 1974.
Never Die Alone. Los Angeles, Holloway, 1974.
Swamp Man. Los Angeles, Holloway, 1974.
Inner City Hoodlum. Los Angeles, Holloway, 1975.

Novels as Al C. Clark (series: Kenyatta)

Crime Partners (Kenyatta). Los Angeles, Holloway, 1974.
Cry Revenge! Los Angeles, Holloway, 1974.
Death List (Kenyatta). Los Angeles, Holloway, 1974.
Kenyatta's Escape. Los Angeles, Holloway, 1974.
Kenyatta's Last Hit. Los Angeles, Holloway, 1975.

*

Critical Study: *Donald Writes No More: A Biography of Donald Goines* by Eddie Stone, Los Angeles, Holloway, 1974.

*   *   *

Donald Goines is the foremost example of a cultural phenomenon possible no earlier than the 1970's—a successful Black author of mass-market crime fiction who wrote about Blacks and primarily for a Black readership. All of Goines's books are paperback originals and have never been out of print since their original publication approximately two decades ago. They have sold well over five million copies and have been on option to movie studios and independents.

Goines's protagonists are pimps, prostitutes, thieves, hit men, gangsters, dope addicts, and hustlers of all kinds. He certainly wrote what he knew, for he pursued most of these professions himself for over half of his life. Inspired by the work of Iceberg Slim, Goines wrote his first (but second-to-be-published) novel, *Whoreson: The Story of a Ghetto Pimp,* while in jail. Later, perhaps as a tribute to Chester Himes, he penned a crime novel set largely in prison, *White Man's Justice, Black Man's Grief.*

The 16 books, including five published under the "Al C. Clark" pseudonym, are all slice-of-ghetto-life crime novels. All but *Swamp Man* are set in the Black inner city, in Detroit, Los Angeles, or New York. The stories are moral tales of passion, greed, lust, and survival. They are about people who stop at nothing to claw their way to the top of the ghetto ladder. Goines's fictional world is cold and harsh, and the operative moral standard is the Ghetto Golden Rule, "what goes around comes around." So, for example, in *Dopefiend: The Story of a Black Junkie,* a nice respectable Black couple sinks into gruesome degradation for abusing heroin; the pimp Earl the Black Pearl in *Street Players* loses his best woman and finally his life for trampling on associates during his rise to the top; the pusher King David in *Never Die Alone* is brutally stabbed to death for his various killings and heroin deals. But Goines can also write tender, touching moments, such as the almost idyllic love scenes in *Black Girl Lost,* and the over-powering affection felt by the hit man protagonist of *Daddy Cool* for his daughter.

Goines's most bizarre contribution to crime fiction is undoubtedly his series hero, Kenyatta, the first Black revolutionary series hero in fiction. In the four-book series, *Crime Partners, Death List, Kenyatta's Escape* and *Kenyatta's Last Hit,* all written under the "Al C. Clark" pseudonym, Kenyatta's militant organization mushrooms. It grows from 40 members to 2000, with branches from Detroit to Watts, as Kenyatta begins to succeed in his goals of ridding American ghettos of drugs and prostitution, and of eliminating all white policemen. In Goines's novelistic world, the bellicose Kenyatta is clearly a hero, even if his methods do resemble those of gangsters and terrorists. Perhaps as a pessimistic comment on the state of his own society, Goines has Kenyatta killed off in a shootout in the final book of the series, as though acknowledging that even Kenyatta's powerful methods must ultimately fail.

The style of Goines's books is unpolished and often crude. They are written in an uneasy mix of Black English and very poorly edited American Standard English. Plots, transitions, and narrative voice are sandpaper rough. The stories contain obscenity, sex, and violence, both graphic and explicit. Nevertheless the Goines corpus of crime novels is important because it gives perhaps the most sustained and realistic criminous picture ever created by an author of the lives, activities, and frustrations of one segment of the Black ghetto population.

Goines wrote at a furious pace, at times as quickly as a book a month, until his mysterious death by shooting in Detroit at age 37, by persons and for reasons as yet unknown.

—Greg Goode

————

GOLDSTONE, Lawrence A. *See* **TREAT, Lawrence.**

———

GOODIS, David. American. Born in Philadelphia, Pennsylvania, 2 March 1917. Educated at Simon Gratz High School, Philadelphia; Indiana University, Bloomington; Temple University, Philadelphia, B.Sc. in journalism 1938. Worked for an advertising agency, Philadelphia, 1938; freelance writer in New York, 1939–46: wrote pseudonymous stories for *Horror Stories, Terror Tales, Western Tales, Dime Mystery, Flighting Aces, Manhunt,* and other magazines; studio writer for Warner Brothers, Hollywood, from 1946. *Died 7 January 1967.*

CRIME PUBLICATIONS

Novels

Retreat from Oblivion. New York, Dutton, 1939.
Dark Passage. New York, Messner, 1946; London, Heinemann, 1947.
Nightfall. New York, Messner, 1947; London, Heinemann, 1948; as *The Dark Chase,* New York, Lion, 1953.
Behold This Woman. New York, Appleton, 1947.
Of Missing Persons. New York, Morrow, 1950.
Cassidy's Girl. New York, Fawcett, 1951; London, Miller, 1958.
Of Tender Sin. New York, Fawcett, 1952.
Street of the Lost. New York, Fawcett, 1952; London, Fawcett, 1959.
The Burglar. New York, Lion, 1953.
The Moon in the Gutter. New York, Fawcett, 1953.
Black Friday. New York, Lion, 1954.
The Blonde on the Street Corner. New York, Lion, 1954.
Street of No Return. New York, Fawcett, 1954; London, Miller, 1958.
The Wounded and the Slain. New York, Fawcett, 1955; London, Miller, 1959.
Down There. New York, Fawcett, 1956; London, Fawcett, 1958; as *Shoot the Piano Player,* New York, Grove Press, 1962.
Fire in the Flesh. New York, Fawcett, 1957; London, Fawcett, 1958.
Night Squad. New York, Fawcett, 1961; London, Muller, 1962.
Somebody's Done For. N.p., Banner, 1967.
Nightfall, Down There, Dark Passage, The Moon in the Gutter. London, Zomba, 1983.

Uncollected Short Stories

"Bullets for the Brave," in *Battle Birds* (Chicago), February 1940.
"Death's Behind That Door," in *Double-Action Detective* (Holyoke, Massachusetts), February 1940.
"Fresh Blood for the Damned," in *Sinister Stories* (Chicago), May 1940.
"Sky Coffins for Nazis," in *Battle Birds* (Chicago), May 1940.
"Bullets for Nazis," in *Captain Combat* (Chicago), June 1940.
"Things to Worry About," in *Detective Fiction Weekly* (New York), 20 July 1940.
"Three Aces from Hell," in *Battle Birds* (Chicago), July 1940.
"The Blood of Warriors," in *Captain Combat* (Chicago), August 1940.

"No More Brains," in *G-Men* (New York), September 1940.
"The High-Hat Squadron from Hell," in *Battle Birds* (Chicago), September 1940.
"Death Flies the Coffins of Hitler," in *Battle Birds* (Chicago), November 1940.
"Descendant of the Witch," in *Mystery Novels and Short Stories* (New York), November 1940.
"Red Wings for the Doomed," in *Battle Birds* (Chicago), January 1941.
"Killer Ace," in *The Lone Eagle* (New York), February 1941.
"Destination-Death," in *Battle Birds* (Chicago), March 1941.
"Token of Glory," in *Air War* (New York), Spring 1941.
"All Boiled Up," in *Detective Yarns* (Holyoke, Massachusetts), April 1941.
"Death Rides My Cockpit," in *Battle Birds* (Chicago), May 1941.
"Death Waits Below," in *Battle Birds* (Chicago), August 1941.
"Blood on the Eastern Front," in *Battle Birds* (Chicago), December 1941.
"Hot Lead for Heinkels," in *Air War* (New York), Winter 1941.
"Three Guesses," in *Hooded Detective* (Holyoke, Massachusetts), January 1942.
"Wings of the Death Patrol," in *Battle Birds* (Chicago), February 1942.
"Fiats Over Albania," in *Air War* (New York), March 1942.
"Doom for the Hawks of Nippon," in *Battle Birds* (Chicago), April 1942.
"Bombs for the Rising Sun," in *Battle Birds* (Chicago), June 1942.
"Vickers Pay-Off," in *Battle Birds* (Chicago), August 1942.
"A Smile and a Nod," in *Crack Detective* (Holyoke, Massachusetts) September 1942.
"The Professor's Last Dogfight," in *Battle Birds* (Chicago), December 1942.
"Twilight Raid," in *Battle Birds* (Chicago), May 1943.
"Beyond Courage," in *Battle Birds* (Chicago), July 1943.
"Dive Bomber," in *Battle Birds* (Chicago), September 1943.
"Guns of the Sea Raiders," in *Battle Birds* (Chicago), November 1943.
"Grandstand Ace," in *Dare-Devil Aces* (Chicago), December 1943.
"Wings Against the World," in *Battle Birds* (Chicago), January 1944.
"Wings Over Kiska," in *Battle Birds* (Chicago), January 1944.
"East of Chungking," in *Air War* (New York), Spring 1944.
"Wings of the Free," in *Battle Birds* (Chicago), March 1944.
"The Fiftieth Mission," in *Battle Birds* (Chicago), May 1944.
"The Last Dogfight," in *Dare-Devil Aces* (Chicago), February 1946.
"Marauders Never Retreat," in *Dare-Devil Aces* (Chicago), March 1946.
"The Warhawks Are Coming," in *Dare-Devil Aces* (Chicago), May 1946.
"It's a Wise Cadaver," in *New Detective Magazine* (Kokomo, Indiana), July 1946.
"Raiders Fight Alone," in *Dare-Devil Aces* (Chicago), November 1946.
"A Photo and a Voice," in *G-Men* (New York), January 1947.
"The Cop on the Corner," in *Popular Detective* (New York), September 1947.
"Nightfall," in *Two Complete Detective Books* (Stanford, Connecticut), January 1949.
"The Blue Sweetheart," in *Manhunt* (New York), April 1953.
"Professional Man," in *Manhunt* (New York), October 1953.
"Black Pudding," in *Manhunt* (New York), December 1953.

"The Plunge," in *Mike Shayne Mystery Magazine* (New York), October 1958.
"The Sweet Taste," in *Manhunt* (New York), January 1965.

OTHER PUBLICATIONS

Plays

Screenplays: *The Unfaithful*, with James Gunn, 1947; *The Burglar*, 1957.

Radio Plays: scripts for *Hop Harrigan, House of Mystery*, and *Superman* serials.

* * *

David Goodis entered the field shortly after World War II, and his first four crime novels were published in hardcover with huge commercial success, *Dark Passage*, for instance, being not only serialized in the *Saturday Evening Post* but adapted by writer-director Delmer Daves into a fascinating *film noir* starring Humphrey Bogart and Lauren Bacall. Goodis's style was closer to Hemingwayesque naturalism but his initial impact on suspense fiction approximated that of Cornell Woolrich. All his later novels, however, were published as paperback originals, and if stylistically they resembled his work of the 1940's, a vital element had been deliberately left out of their substance.

What makes Woolrich the greatest suspense writer of all time is his uncanny genius for making us feel the terror and uncertainty of his menaced protagonists. But we can't experience true terror or uncertainty unless the outcome is genuinely in doubt, and in fact we can't tell until the climax of a Woolrich novel or story whether it's *allegre* or *noir*, whether the characters whose nightmares we share will be saved or destroyed. In Goodis's paperbacks, however, there is no basis for even a moment's hope and thus no real suspense. His people are born losers and victims who try to cheat their fate by living as zombies, shunning all involvement with others and the world, sustained by booze, cigarettes, and mechanical sex. What they learn is that there's no way out of the trap they're in and that, whatever they do or don't do, life is going to get them.

Many of the character types, settings, and motifs from Goodis's hardcover novel *Behold This Woman* recur with ritualistic frequency in his later paperbacks. A run-down old house in the lower class district of Baltimore during a hellish heat wave. A loud corner tavern, filled at all hours of the night with smoke and sweat, gin fumes and derelicts beyond hope. The docks, with at least one graphically described fistfight every time Goodis takes us there. A frightened, friendless, lonely man, living in the night. A fat sadistic woman, oozing grotesque sexuality. A brilliant creative person defeated by the world so badly that he's reduced to a passive drunken wisp, muttering mournfully of meaninglessness. Bizarre little philosophic conversations between total strangers. Beaten protagonists dully resuming zombie lives as the novels end. It's typical of Goodis's world that in *The Moon in the Gutter* the viewpoint character Kerrigan lets go free the parolee who was hired to beat him to death, gives up hunting for the man who raped his sister and caused her suicide, and goes back to live with the woman who paid for his murder.

Goodis is a powerful but endlessly depressing writer, whose novels provide something like the grim fascination one feels watching the newsfilm of the wirewalker Wallenda's death: you see him crossing between skyscrapers on that wisp of steel, desperate to keep his balance in the high wind, and you know

that in a few seconds he'll fall hundreds of feet and be flattened, and as if in a trance you watch the struggle and, at the last moment, the death written on his face. Although long out of print in the United States, Goodis is recognized in France as a master of *roman noir Américain* second only to Woolrich, and young directors from Truffaut in the early 1960's to Jean-Jacques Beineix in the early 1980's have made films based closely on Goodis novels. Someday perhaps he'll be rediscovered here.

—Francis M. Nevins, Jr.

———

THE GORDONS: Mildred Gordon and Gordon Gordon. Americans. **GORDON, Mildred (née Nixon):** Born in Eureka, Kansas, 24 July 1905. Educated at the University of Arizona, Tucson, B.A. 1930. Married Gordon Gordon in 1932. Teacher, Carrillo School, Tucson, 1931–32; editor, *Arizona* magazine, 1932–34; correspondent, United Press, 1935; self-employed author after 1935. *Died 3 February 1979.* **GORDON, Gordon:** Born in Anderson, Indiana, 12 March 1906. Educated at the University of Arizona, Tucson, B.A. 1929. Married 1) Mildred Nixon in 1932 (died 1979); 2) Mary Dorr in 1981. Reporter, 1930–31, and managing editor, 1931–35, Tucson *Daily Citizen;* publicist, Twentieth Century-Fox, Hollywood, 1935–42; counter-espionage agent, Federal Bureau of Investigation, Washington, D.C., and Chicago, 1942–45. Self-employed author after 1945. Joint Recipients: Book Society of Great Britain award, 1954; Writers Guild of America award, 1965; American Humor Society award, 1965; University of Arizona Achievement award, 1970. Agent: William Morris Agency Inc., 1350 Avenue of the Americas, New York, New York 10019. Address: 22556 Marlin Place, Canoga Park, California 91307, U.S.A.

CRIME PUBLICATIONS

Novels (series: Gail and Mitch; D.C. Randall, The Cat; John Ripley)

The Little Man Who Wasn't There (as Mildred Gordon). New York, Doubleday, 1946.
Make Haste to Live. New York, Doubleday, 1950.
FBI Story (Ripley). New York, Doubleday, 1950; London, Corgi, 1957.
Campaign Train. New York, Doubleday, and London, Wingate, 1952; as *Murder Rides the Campaign Train*, New York, Bantam, 1976.
Case File: FBI (Ripley). New York, Doubleday, 1953; London, Macdonald, 1954.
The Case of the Talking Bug. New York, Doubleday, 1955; as *Playback*, London, Macdonald, 1955.
The Big Frame. New York, Doubleday, and London, Macdonald, 1957.
Captive (Ripley). New York, Doubleday, 1957; London, Macdonald, 1958.
Tiger on My Back. New York, Doubleday, and London, Macdonald, 1960.
Operation Terror (Ripley). New York, Doubleday, and London, Macdonald, 1961; as *Experiment in Terror*, New York, Bantam, 1962.
Menace. New York, Doubleday, 1962; as *Journey with a Stranger*, London, Macdonald, 1963.

Undercover Cat. New York, Doubleday, 1963; London, Macdonald, 1964; as *That Darn Cat,* New York, Bantam, and London, Corgi, 1966.
Power Play. New York, Doubleday, 1965; London, Macdonald, 1966.
Undercover Cat Prowls Again. New York, Doubleday, 1966; London, Macdonald, 1967.
Night Before the Wedding (Gail and Mitch). New York, Doubleday, and London, Macdonald, 1969.
The Informant (Ripley). New York, Doubleday, and London, Macdonald, 1973.
Catnapped: The Further Adventures of Undercover Cat. New York, Doubleday, 1974; London, Macdonald, 1975.
Ordeal. New York, Doubleday, 1976; London, Macdonald, 1977.
Night after the Wedding (Gail and Mitch). New York, Doubleday, 1979; London, Macdonald and Jane's, 1980.
Race for the Golden Tide (by Gordon Gordon and Mary Dorr). New York, Doubleday, 1983.

Uncollected Short Story

"The Terror Racket," in *Ellery Queen's Mystery Magazine* (New York), August 1967.

OTHER PUBLICATIONS

Novel

The Tumult and the Joy. New York, Doubleday, 1971.

Plays

Screenplays: *Down Three Dark Streets,* with Bernard C. Schoenfeld, 1954; *Experiment in Terror,* 1962; *That Darn Cat,* with Bill Walsh, 1965.

Other

With This Ring, with Judge Louis H. Burke. New York, McGraw Hill, 1958.
"A Marriage of Minds," in *Murder Ink: The Mystery Reader's Companion,* edited by Dilys Winn. New York, Workman, 1977.

Editor, *A Pride of Felons.* New York, Macmillan, 1963; London, Dobson, 1964.

*

Manuscript Collection: Mugar Memorial Library, Boston University.

Gordon Gordon comments:
In novels we tried to write the kind of stories that we ourselves enjoyed reading. Fast moving ones with excitement and surprises, flashes of humor, and about very ordinary people, much like ourselves.
Usually the tales were about an innocent person—someone struggling to make a living—who was caught up unexpectedly in a kidnapping, extortion, or blackmail. He was caught up because he just happened to be standing in a certain spot at a certain time, a facet of everyday living that keeps increasing with terrifying regularity. During our newspaper and FBI days we encountered much of this and marveled at the innate courage and jaw-setting of even the quietest victims.

We liked characters who never gave up, no matter the odds, who struggled to live decent lives, who knew there is a God and tomorrow will be better, who loved deeply and who rose above the sordid world in which many of them lived. We have been told by critics that there are no such people, that we were romanticists hiding in the suspense and excitement of very real situations and settings. We admit that our violence was brief, our sex never explicit, and our bad people often had signs of being redeemable. We thank the critics for granting that the stories possessed realism. Because we enjoyed backgrounds in the novels we read, we worked long and hard over the ones in our own books.
Since our third or fourth novel, we have used a "continuous suspense situation," a single crime that unfolds in its creation and detection quickly with many logical tangents and twists. Most of our books were morality plays, in that good triumphed over evil. Not a squashy kind of good but that of courage, strength, and high intentions.

*   *   *

The Gordons write first-rate escapist suspense fiction. Their best books adhere to a definite formula, but it is a good one and skillfully handled. This formula can be summed up as *the girl, the crook, the cop, and the clock.* Take one spunky, not-beautiful-but-pertly-attractive heroine, and place her in acute danger; bring to her aid a determined, not-handsome-but-ruggedly-attractive cop who is conscientious and competent; create a deadline before which the crook must be caught or the girl will be killed, and delay the resolution to the last possible moment before time runs out. Although capturing the criminal depends on the hero's accurate deductions, the emphasis is not on a process of detection, but rather on the steadily ticking clock. The formula is standard, but the Gordons exploit to the fullest its emotional potential.
This formula works because it sharply excites but ultimately assuages feelings of helplessness and vulnerability. The Gordons use several techniques to intensify both halves of his response. First of all, a Gordons heroine rarely brings her trouble on herself; rather, the threat to her safety intrudes suddenly, apparently out of nowhere: in *Operation Terror* Kelly is thrust into a nightmare simply because she works in a bank; *Menace* is half over before we discover why Sheri is being persecuted. The reader's sense of the heroine's vulnerability is compounded by an ever-present possibility of sexual violence. Furthermore, the heroine is often responsible for a younger person who is also in danger, thus limiting her freedom to deal with her tormentor. The Gordons emphasize the psychological pressures on the heroine of terror, vulnerability, and the tension of waiting. With a feral viciousness, the criminal threatens not just her life but also her sanity. Thus the reader's question becomes not just "Will she survive?" but "Will she survive psychically intact?" The psychological battle of the heroine parallels the hero's battle of wits with the criminal. The hero commands the tools of modern scientific detection, but finally he must outwit the crook. And to do so he is willing to act independently of the procedural rules he should officially follow. When the criminal is foiled, then, the reader is reassured that the forces of good have the psychic strength, the intellectual resources, and the flexibility necessary to defeat a threatened evil.
The formula outlined above can be varied considerably without destroying its impact. In *The Informant* and *Power Play,* not just a single girl but our whole society is in jeopardy. *Undercover Cat* successfully presents a humorous version of the formula by displacing the danger onto someone we know less well than the attractive heroine. Tension is thus diffused, and

the audience freed to laugh. (The sequels to *Undercover Cat*, particularly *Catnapped*, suffer from being too obviously constructed as sequences of cute scenes suitable for filming.)

Within their narrow genre, the Gordons write effectively and responsibly. As is appropriate to escapist fiction, they do not dwell on their material's implicit moral issues—such as the ethics of wiretapping or the ambiguous morality of using or being an informant—but neither do they evade or oversimplify them. (Indeed, *The Case of the Talking Bug* reveals a surprisingly early concern with wiretapping.) Mr. Gordon's background as an ex-FBI agent lends authenticity to portrayals of investigative procedures, and the settings for all the Gordons's books are drawn with care. In general, a novel by the Gordons can be relied upon to provide an evening of suspenseful entertainment.

—Susan Baker

GORES, Joe (Joseph Nicholas Gores). American. Born in Rochester, Minnesota, 25 December 1931. Educated at the University of Notre Dame, Indiana, A.B. 1953; Stanford University, California, M.A. 1961. Served in the United States Army, 1958–59. Married Dori Corfitzen in 1976; one son and one daughter. Worked as laborer, logger, clerk, driver, carnival helper, assistant motel manager; Instructor, Floyd Page's Gymnasium, Palo Alto, 1953–55; private investigator, L.A. Walker Company, 1955–57, and David Kikkert and Associates, 1959–62, 1965–67, both San Francisco; English teacher, Kakamega Boys Secondary School, Kenya, 1963–64; manager and auctioneer, Automobile Auction Company, San Francisco, 1968–76. Self-employed writer. Secretary, 1966, 1968, vice-president, 1967, 1969–70, member of the board of directors, 1967–70, 1975–76, General awards chair, 1976–77, and President, 1987, Mystery Writers of America. Recipient: Mystery Writers of America Edgar Allan Poe award, for novel, 1969, for short story, 1969, for television series, 1975. Agent: Henry Morrison Inc., P.O. Box 235, Belford Hills, New York 10507. Address: P.O. Box 446, Fairfax, California 94930, U.S.A.

CRIME PUBLICATIONS

Novels (series: DKA [Dan Kearney Associates])

A Time of Predators. New York, Random House, 1969; London, W.H. Allen, 1970.
Dead Skip (DKA). New York, Random House, 1972; London, Gollancz, 1973.
Final Notice (DKA). New York, Random House, 1973; London, Gollancz, 1974.
Interface. New York, Evans, 1974; London, Futura, 1977.
Hammett: A Novel. New York, Putnam, 1975; London, Macdonald, 1976.
Gone, No Forwarding (DKA). New York, Random House, 1978; London, Gollancz, 1979.
Come Morning. New York, Mysterious Press, 1986; London, Century, 1988.
Wolf Time. New York, Putnam, 1989.

Uncollected Short Stories

"Chain Gang," in *Manhunt* (New York), December 1957.
"Pro," in *Manhunt* (New York), June 1958.

"Down and Out," in *Manhunt* (New York), June 1959.
"You Aren't Yellow," in *Mike Shayne Mystery Magazine* (New York), January 1960.
"Sailor's Girl," in *Man's World* (New York), August 1961.
"John Henry on the Mountain," in *Negro Digest* (Chicago), August 1961.
"Night Out," in *Manhunt* (New York), October 1961.
"The Mob," in *Negro Digest* (Chicago), December 1961.
"Muscle Beach," in *Rogue* (Chicago), March 1962.
"The Main Chance," in *Gent* (Chicago), April 1962.
"Trouble in Papeete," in *Rake* (Chicago), April 1962.
"Darl I Luv U," in *Ellery Queen's Mystery Mix,* New York, Random House, 1963; London, Gollancz, 1964.
"The Price of Lust," in *Manhunt* (New York), April 1963.
"The One Upstairs," in *Negro Digest* (Chicago), April 1963.
"Sweet Vengeance," in *Manhunt* (New York), July 1964.
"A Sad and Bloody House," in *Ellery Queen's Mystery Magazine* (New York), April 1965.
"The Catalyst," in *Rogue* (Chicago), April 1965.
"The Seeker of Ultimates," in *Ellery Queen's Mystery Magazine* (New York), November 1965.
"The Writing on the Wall," in *Topper* (Chicago), February 1966.
"Kanaka," in *Adam 10* (Los Angeles), no. 11, 1966.
"The Second Coming," in *Murder in Mind,* edited by Lawrence Treat. New York, Dutton, 1967.
"File No. 1: The Mayfield Case," in *Best Detective Stories of the Year,* edited by Anthony Boucher. New York, Dutton, 1968.
"Oldmurani," in *Argosy* (New York), February 1968.
"The Golden Tiki," in *Argosy* (New York), June 1968.
"File No. 3: The Pedretti Case," in *Ellery Queen's Mystery Magazine* (New York), July 1968.
"South of Market," in *Alfred Hitchcock Presents: A Month of Mystery.* New York, Random House, 1969.
"File No. 2: Stakeout on Page Street," in *Ellery Queen's Murder Menu.* Cleveland, World, and London, Gollancz, 1969.
"Talking of Michaelangelo," in *Adam 13* (Los Angeles), no. 7, 1969.
"South of the Moon," in *Argosy* (New York), January 1969.
"File No. 5: The Maria Navarro Case," in *Ellery Queen's Mystery Magazine* (New York), June 1969.
"Gunman in Town," in *Zane Grey's Western Magazine* (Los Angeles), October 1969.
"Quit Screaming," in *Adam's Reader 41* (Los Angeles), November 1969.
"The House of God," in *Adam 14* (Los Angeles), no. 9, 1970.
"The Criminal," in *Adam 14* (Los Angeles), no. 12, 1970.
"File No. 4: Lincoln Sedan Deadline," in *Crimes and Misfortunes,* edited by J. Francis McComas. New York, Random House, 1970.
"O Black and Unknown Bard," in *Best Detective Stories of the Year 1970,* edited by Allen J. Hubin. New York, Dutton, 1970.
"The Bear's Paw," in *Argosy* (New York), April 1970.
"Odendahl," in *Murder Most Foul,* edited by Harold Q. Masur. New York, Walker, 1971.
"The Andrech Samples," in *Best Detective Stories of the Year 1971,* edited by Allen J. Hubin. New York, Dutton, 1971.
"Force Twelve," in *Argosy* (New York), January 1971.
"Trouble at 81 Fathoms," in *Argosy* (New York), June 1971.
"The War Club," in *Argosy* (New York), May 1972.
"Faulty Register," in *Two Views of Wonder,* edited by Thomas N. Scortia and Chelsea Quinn Yarbro. New York, Ballantine, 1973.
"The O'Bannon Blarney File," in *Men and Malice,* edited by Dean Dickensheet. New York, Doubleday, 1973.

"Watch for It," in *Mirror, Mirror, Fatal Mirror*, edited by Hans S. Santesson. New York, Doubleday, 1973.

"You're Putting Me On—Aren't You?" in *Killers of the Mind*, edited by Lucy Freeman. New York, Random House, 1974.

"Goodbye, Pops," in *Every Crime in the Book*, edited by Robert L. Fish. New York, Putnam, 1975.

"Kirintaga," in *Ellery Queen's Mystery Magazine* (New York), March 1975.

"Black Man's Burden," in *Swank* (New York), September 1975.

"File No. 10: The Maimed and the Halt," in *Ellery Queen's Mystery Magazine* (New York), January 1976.

"File No. 6: Beyond the Shadow," in *Ellery Queen's Magicians of Mystery*. New York, Davis, 1976.

"Rope Enough," in *Tricks and Treats*, edited by Joe Gores and Bill Pronzini. New York, Doubleday, 1976; as *Mystery Writers' Choice*, London, Gollancz, 1977.

"The Three Halves," in *When Last Seen*, edited by Arthur Maling. New York, Harper, 1977.

"Raptor," in *Ellery Queen's Mystery Magazine* (New York), October 1983.

"File No. 9: Full Moon Madness," in *Ellery Queen's Mystery Magazine* (New York), February 1984.

"File No. 11: Jump Her Lively, Boys!" in *Ellery Queen's Mystery Magazine* (New York), July 1984.

"Smart Guys Don't Snore," in *A Matter of Crime 2*, edited by Mathew J. Bruccoli and Richard Layman. San Diego, Harcourt Brace Jovanovich, 1987.

"Detectivitis, Anyone?" in *Ellery Queen's Mystery Magazine* (New York), January 1988.

"File No. 12: Do Not Go Gentle," in *Ellery Queen's Mystery Magazine* (New York), March 1989.

OTHER PUBLICATIONS

Plays

Screenplays: *Deadfall*, 1976; *Hammett*, 1978; *Paper Crimes*, 1978; *Paradise Road*, 1978; *A Wayward Angel*, 1981; *Interface*, 1982.; *Cover Story*, 1985; *Run Cunning*, 1986; *Gangbusters*, 1990.

Television Plays: *No Immunity for Murder, Bad Dude, Sad Sunday, Was It Worth It, Lady?*, and *Case Without a File* (Kojak series), 1975–77; *Golden Gate Memorial*, 1978; *In the Finest Tradition* (Eischied, series), 1979; *Love on Instant Replay* (Kate Loves a Mystery series), 1979; *On His Last Legs* and *This, My Firstborn Son* (The Gangster Chronicles series), 1981; *Fallen Angel* (Strike Force series), 1982; *Animal Crackers*, and *a Pretty Good Dancing Chicken* (Magnum P.I. series), 1983–84; *Seven Dead Eyes* and *Nightmare* (Mickey Spillane's Mike Hammer series), 1983–86; *A Piece of Cake* (Eye to Eye series), 1984; *To Kill a Lawyer* (Scene of the Crime series), 1984; *To Steele a Plot* (Remington Steele series), 1984; *Beyond the Grave* (Helltown series), 1985; *Death Trip* (T.J. Hooker series), 1985; *Quicker Than the Eye* (Blacke's Magic series), 1985; *Blind Chess* (B.L. Stryker series), 1989; *The Stuff Dreams Are Made of* (Colombo series), 1990.

Other

Marine Salvage. New York, Doubleday, 1971; Newton Abbot, Devon, David and Charles, 1972.

"Writing the Mystery Short Story," in *The Writer* (Boston), August 1971.

"Hammett the Writer," in *Xenophile 12* (St. Louis), 1978.

Editor, *Honolulu: Port of Call*. New York, Ballantine, 1974.

Editor, with Bill Pronzini, *Tricks and Treats*. New York, Doubleday, 1976; as *Mystery Writers' Choice*, London, Gollancz, 1977.

*

Joe Gores comments:

I started out thinking I wanted to write and draw comic strips, and entered Notre Dame University with that in mind. But I quickly realized that I was at best a derivative artist, and that writing the stories was what interested me the most. Unfortunately, the only thing that teaches you how to write is writing—constantly. But I did have one teacher at Notre Dame who contributed materially to my being a writer. Professor Richard Sullivan taught creative writing and had once been a radio soap opera writer. As I was graduating, I asked him the burning question: "Mr. Sullivan, should I be a writer?" I never forgot his answer. "Joe," he said, "it is very simple. Go to a big city and rent a little room with a chair and a table in it. Put your typewriter on the table and your behind on the chair. Start typing. When you stand up ten years later, you'll be a writer."

It was closer to 15 years before I was able to devote myself full-time to writing. In between I had done and been many things, including private investigator for 12 years. Writing thousands of reports taught me to get in the who, what, where, when, and why that made the client willing to shell out all those hard-earned bucks to the agency. I learned there has to be a beginning, a middle and an end. In short, I learned how to *tell a story*.

I started out on short stories, and this was all I did until 1968—all the time swearing I was too scared to try a novel. But I finally did. Then I said I would never write screenplays or television plays—I was too scared. But I was invited to write the screenplay for one of my novels which had sold to an independent movie producer, so I did. And then I was invited to write a teleplay for *Kojak*—a producer named Jack Laird had read some of my detective novels and liked the way I handled dialogue. Thus one thing led to another, and now I do everything in the writing field I can—short stories, articles, photo journalism, book reviews, critical essays, novels, fact books, television and movie scripts.

The only thing I have never written is a legitimate stage drama. I doubt that I ever will. I am too scared to try. Still, I have this idea for a Broadway musical . . .

*   *   *

The San Francisco author Joe Gores is the only writer to have won the Mystery Writers of America Edgars in three categories: short story, television drama, and novel. He has written more than 100 short stories, a number of television and movie scripts, and eight quite varied crime novels.

The first, *A Time of Predators*, concerns a sociology professor, Curt Halstead, who abandons his academic theories about violence when his wife, the only witness to a vicious assault, commits suicide after having been gang-raped by the four young thugs she can identify. Halstead gradually reverts to the "bloody-mindedness" he had learned as a young man in a British Commando unit, and seeks his own vengeance on the rapists when the law fails. The book is flawed (particularly in characterization), but its strong, well-paced narrative showed a promise that has been realized in subsequent novels.

Three of them are procedural novels involving a team of auto repossessors, Dan Kearney Associates, in the San Francisco area. Gores, himself a private detective for a dozen years, uses that experience well: this is perhaps the best procedural series written, as far as attention to actual detective practices is concerned. The first "DKA File" novel, *Dead Skip,* involves the efforts of Dan Kearney and Larry Ballard to track down the man who attempted to kill their colleague, Bart Heslip, and disguise it as an accident. Heslip had discovered something odd in one of the repossessions he had been working on: the DKA men, while Heslip is in a coma, work through his current cases to discover the guilty person. In the process, the reader is introduced to a sad spectrum of broken and damaged lives in a vividly-described variety of squalid circumstances before the DKA men catch a kinky killer. In *Final Notice,* the DKA men are drawn into an investigation which uncovers the attempted blackmail of a Mafia boss, power struggle within that organization, and two murders. They unravel the complicated plot but are unable to provide enough hard evidence to turn the clever killer over to the police. Kearney, acting on his own, tips the mob off to the fact that the killer murdered the top Mafia boss to gain power himself, and it is intimated that he won't escape syndicate punishment.

Early in *Gone, No Forwarding,* we see that punishment enacted. Most of the book, however, concerns someone's efforts to get Kearney's license revoked. The harassment, it turns out, is to provide an alibi for a mob assassin. In breaking the case against Kearney and uncovering a murderer, the DKA men range over the country tracking down witnesses. The same vivid portrayal of the underbelly of humanity enlivens this DKA novel also, as is true of a different kind of book, *Interface.* Here a mysterious killer known only as Docker weaves a complicated plot against several mob figures. Docker has been hired by Neil Fargo, a tough, shady private investigator, to import heroin for the mobsters, but Docker runs amok for his own unfathomable reasons. Revolving around a cleverly concealed false identity, the book is a fast-paced, violent, sordid tale of chase and revenge as Fargo and the gangsters try to catch and destroy the elusive Docker before he destroys them.

Different from all the above is *Hammett,* Gores's most ambitious and successful book to date. Gores combines Hammett the writer and Hammett the detective, recreates San Francisco in 1928, and invents a plausible, action-filled plot in which Hammett, to avenge the murder of a detective-friend, leads a reform committee investigation of corruption. It is a difficult task to reconstruct a city and an era and to dramatize such a well-known figure at work as writer-detective; Gores, as San Franciscan, scholar, writer, and ex-detective, is uniquely suited for this demanding job and carries it off superbly.

Gores has established himself securely as one of the best and most versatile authors of crime novels.

—Donald C. Wall

GORMAN, Ed(ward). American. Born in Cedar Rapids, Iowa, 29 November 1941. Educated at Coe College, Iowa, 1962–65. Married Carol Gorman in 1982; one son and one stepson. Worked in advertising as a writer and freelance writer, 20 years. Since 1989 full-time writer. Agent: Dominick Abel, 146 West 82nd Street, New York, New York 10024. Address: 3840 Clark Road South East, Cedar Rapids, Iowa 52403, U.S.A.

CRIME PUBLICATIONS

Novels (series: Jack Dwyer; Tobin)

Rough Cut (Dwyer). New York, St. Martin's Press, 1985; London, Hale, 1987.
New, Improved Murder (Dwyer). New York, St. Martin's Press, 1986.
Murder Straight Up (Dwyer). New York, St. Martin's Press, 1986.
Murder in the Wings (Dwyer). New York, St. Martin's Press, 1986.
Murder on the Aisle (Tobin). New York, St. Martin's Press, 1987.
The Autumn Dead (Dwyer). New York, St. Martin's Press, 1987; London, Allison and Busby, 1989.
Several Deaths Later (Tobin). New York, St. Martin's Press, 1988.
Grave's Retreat. New York, Doubleday, 1989.
A Cry of Shadows (Dwyer). New York, St. Martin's Press, 1990.
Night of Shadows. New York, Doubleday, 1990.

Uncollected Short Stories

"Turn Away," in *Black Lizard Anthology of Crime Fiction.* New York, Black Lizard Press, 1987.
"The Reason Why," in *Criminal Elements,* edited by Bill Pronzini and Martin H. Greenberg. New York, Fawcett, 1988.
"Failed Prayers," in *Felonious Assaults,* edited by Bill Pronzini and Martin H. Greenberg. New York, Fawcett, 1989.
"Prisoners," in *New Crimes,* edited by Maxim Jakubowski. London, Robinson, 1990.

OTHER PUBLICATIONS

Novels

Guild. New York, Evans, 1987.
Death Ground. New York, Evans, 1988.
Blood Game. New York, Evans, 1989.
Night Kills. New York, Ballantine, 1990.

Other

Editor, *Westeryear.* New York, Evans, 1988.

*　　*　　*

Ed Gorman is among the best of the American writers to enter the crime-fiction field in the 1980's, bringing fresh ideas, characters, and approaches. He writes with wit and real feeling, in an often lean, deliberately rough-edged style that deepens the impact of his narratives. His mysteries are an amalgam of pure entertainment, social commentary, symbolic statement, and in-depth studies of what he terms "outsiders trying to make their peace with the world."

In the few short years since his first novel, *Rough Cut,* appeared, he has created a number of series characters—outsiders and misfits, all. The first and most prominent, Jack Dwyer, is an ex-cop, part-time actor and security guard who has been featured in six novels. In *Murder Straight Up,* Dwyer solves the on-camera slaying of a television anchorman—and Gorman provides a knowledgeable, mordant look at what goes on behind the public facade of a television news program; in *The Autumn Dead,* Dwyer is drawn to a former lover and, through her, into violence and a confrontation with his past that profoundly changes him; in *A Cry of Shadows,* he wanders the mean streets with his city's homeless and disaffected, and is forced to deal with other types of alienation as well. If any criticism can be leveled against the Dwyer novels, it is that the city and state in which they take place are unnamed (although by implication they are Gorman's home town and state of Cedar Rapids, Iowa). This amorphousness of locale robs them of an extra measure of reality that they might otherwise have had.

Partly for this reason, Gorman's second private detective protagonist, the man known only as Walsh, may well become his most important series character. In his fifties, scarred by the death of his partner, Walsh operates out of the fully realized Cedar Rapids milieu that Dwyer does not. And, too, he is an even more complex individual, with ties to the past that color his dealings in the present and his attitude toward the future. *The Night Remembers,* the only Walsh novel to date (more are planned), is the most emotionally charged of the author's works—so much so that the mystery, even though it focuses on a major topical theme, is secondary throughout to Walsh's agonized involvement with his young woman friend's probable cancer and the fate of her (and perhaps his) infant son.

A third series character, Tobin, a five-foot-five-inch movie critic with an explosive temper, appears in two novels. *Murder on the Aisle* takes place during the Christmas season and follows Tobin through the events surrounding the stabbing death of his syndicated television show partner and his affair with the partner's wife. *Several Deaths Later* has a shipboard setting, and concerns murder among the members of a popular game show called "Celebrity Circle" that is filming a week's worth of broadcasts at sea. These books contain much that is insightful and thought-provoking, and are excellent detective stories, but they do not represent the cutting edge of Gorman's work.

Closer to that edge is his Western/mystery series about 1890's bounty hunter Leo Guild, in particular *Blood Game* with its sharply delineated boxing background. The Guild novels have a haunting, almost mystical quality that lifts them to the brink of allegory. Two non-series books, *Graves' Retreat* and *Night of Shadows,* although packaged as Westerns (as are the Guilds), are also crime stories with historical settings. The former title, which takes place in Cedar Rapids in 1884, mixes early baseball lore with homicide and bank robbery; the latter, even better, is a fact-based portrait of Anna Tolan, Cedar Rapids' first uniformed policewoman. *Night Kills,* a contemporary suspense novel, is likewise memorable. It combines advertising—a field Gorman, a former advertising executive, knows well—and the dark and deadly teenage-runaway underground.

An increasingly impressive body of fiction is not Gorman's only contribution to the genre. He is also the editor and publisher of *Mystery Scene,* an important magazine devoted to news, features, and commentary about crime fiction (and horror and Western fiction). And he is an accomplished anthologist as well.

—Bill Pronzini

GOSLING, Paula. Also writes as Ainslie Skinner. American. Born in Detroit, Michigan, 12 October 1939. Educated at Mackenzie High School, Detroit, 1953–57; Wayne State University, Detroit, 1958–62, B.A. in English 1962. Married 1) Christopher Gosling in 1968 (marriage dissolved 1978), two daughters; 2) John A. Hare in 1981. Trainee copywriter, Campbell-Ewald Advertising, Detroit, 1962–64; copywriter, Mitchell's Advertising, 1964–67, Pritchard-Wood Advertising, 1967–68, and David Williams Advertising, 1968–69, all London; copy consultant, Mitchell's Advertising, 1969–70, and ATA Advertising, Bristol, 1977–79. Recipient: Crime Writers Association John Creasey Memorial award, 1978; Gold Dagger award, 1985. Chair, Crime Writers Association, 1988–89. Lives in Bath, Avon. Agent: Elaine Greene Ltd., 37 Goldhawk Road, London W12 8QQ, England.

CRIME PUBLICATIONS

Novels (series: Lieutenant Jack Stryker)

A Running Duck. London, Macmillan, 1978; revised edition, as *Fair Game,* New York, Coward McCann, 1978.
The Zero Trap. London, Macmillan, 1979; New York, Coward McCann, 1980.
Loser's Blues. London, Macmillan, 1980; as *Solo Blues,* New York, Coward McCann, 1981.
Mind's Eye (as Ainslie Skinner). London, Secker and Warburg, 1980; as *The Harrowing,* New York, Rawson Wade, 1981.
The Woman in Red. London, Macmillan, 1983; New York, Doubleday, 1984.
Monkey Puzzle (Stryker). London, Macmillan, and New York, Doubleday, 1985.
The Wychford Murders. London, Macmillan, and New York, Doubleday, 1986.
Hoodwink. London, Macmillan, and New York, Doubleday, 1988.
Backlash (Stryker). London, Macmillan, and New York, Doubleday, 1989.

Uncollected Short Stories

"The Man in the Bicycle Shop" (serial), in *Woman* (London), 1980.
"The Poacher Code" (serial), in *Woman* (London), 1983.
"I Wonder If She's Changed?," in *Woman's Realm* (London), 1983.
"Dark Inheritance" (serial), in *Woman's Weekly* (London), 1985.
"Mr. Felix," in *Fiction Magazine* (London), 1986.
"The Foxglove Murder" (serial), in *Woman's Realm* (London), 1987.
"The Perfect Alibi," in *Winter's Crimes 17,* edited by Hilary Hale. London, Macmillan, 1987.
"A Little Learning, in *The Rigby File,* edited by Tim Heald. London, Hodder and Stoughton, 1989.
"Killer," in *Winter's Crimes 21,* edited by Hilary Hale. London, Macmillan, 1989.
"The Mikado Mystery" (serial), in *Woman's Realm* (London), 1989.

*

Manuscript Collection: Mugar Memorial Library, Boston University.

Paula Gosling comments:
I am more a writer of suspense than of detective fiction. My "detectives" are ordinary people caught up in extraordinary situations, doing their best to survive and make sense of their various dilemmas. This interests me more than the concept of the super-hero or super-sleuth. I believe there is a bit of "hero"

in most people, and, given circumstances similar to those in my books, I think the average person might do pretty well. What's more, I feel the average person thinks so, too. Suspense fiction is often read in bed, when we're safe under the covers, because we *like* the game of going disquiet into that dark night. The suspense writer must play that game as fairly as possible with the reader, giving him a landscape and a map, a start and a goal. The game is called "What if. . . . "

* * *

The skill with which she constructs her action-thrillers places Paula Gosling well forward among practitioners of this subgenre once considered primarily a male preserve. In keeping with the conventions of the form, Gosling depicts characters in transition, people who, under enormous stress, redefine their lives. Originally the passive victim of fate or circumstance, each becomes a person who attempts to control his or her destiny, and each, to one degree or another, succeeds.

This pattern always includes her male protagonist's progression from relative, usually elected, isolation to involvement, and the change is made more urgent and more believable because he acts not only to save himself but also to protect the woman he is beginning to love. Thus, conflict occurs both within himself and between him and some criminal antagonist who invariably represents evil as well as blind, destructive fate.

As they are initially portrayed, Gosling's protagonists might well be termed deliberately withdrawn, inconspicuous specialists: Mike Malcheck (*A Running Duck*) once a crack army sniper, is now a police officer, tracking criminal snipers and bringing them to justice; John Owen Cosatelli (*Loser's Blues*) is a brilliant pianist who has abandoned his concert career for what he considers "minor" levels of performance; David Skinner (*The Zero Trap*) is an astronomer apparently devoid of warmth and passion, and Charles Lewellyn (*The Woman in Red*) is drifting in the backwaters of the diplomatic corps. Under threat, these men abandon their detachment; they become heroic, discovering within themselves enormously strong will, great courage—and considerable propensity for violence. This final revelation is, perhaps, more than a little disquieting, for it suggests that if Everyman can become a hero, Everyman can fight and even kill.

Because readers of crime fiction generally expect restoration of social order once the mystery has been solved and the criminal punished, Gosling, like many of her peers, uses romantic subplots to affirm that order. Her heroes and heroines are always survivors of earlier, damaging sexual relationships, and this new, sustaining alliance represents healing and a second chance at happiness. Emotional commitment (and usually marriage) underscores the heroes' permanent abandonment of isolation and also indicates that they will sublimate their capacity for violence. By the assumption of familial responsibility, the protagonists will continue to discharge their duties of loving protectiveness and thus preserve their sense of masculine power.

This use of the love subplot as symbol of the reconciliation between the protagonists' ordinary and heroic personae clearly indicates the subordinate role played by most of Gosling's conventional heroines. Though Clare Randall precipitates the action of *A Running Duck* by an act of simple courtesy which makes her the target for a hit man, she remains essentially passive. Holly Partridge (*The Woman in Red*) is vibrant and assertive, but her headstrong behavior tends to cause more problems than it solves. Mere coincidence involves Laura Ainslie (*The Zero Trap*) and Elizabeth Fisher (*Loser's Blues*) in deadly situations, and though, like their suitor-protectors, they move from self-imposed isolation toward involvement, their

chief functions are symbolic. They demonstrate that Everywoman can be loved and that she can thus ratify not only her own but also her man's worth.

The traditionalism of Gosling's stylish plots and of the roles filled by her major characters satisfies readers' desire for the expected even as the chilling complications, vivid settings—California's redwood forests, the Arctic, the world of the London musician, Spain and the intricacies of art forgery—and swift, compelling action feed their desire for the unusual; it's a very successful combination.

—Jane S. Bakerman

———

GOULART, Ron(ald Joseph). Also writes as Josephine Kains; Jullian Kearny; Howard Lee; Kenneth Robeson; Frank S. Shawn; Con Steffanson. American. Born in Berkeley, California, 13 January 1933. Educated at the University of California, Berkeley, B.A. 1955. Married Frances Sheridan in 1964; two sons. Advertising copywriter, Guild Bascom and Bonfigci, San Francisco, 1955–57, 1958–60, Alan Alch Inc., Hollywood, 1960–63, and Hoefer Dietrich and Brown, San Francisco, 1966–68. Author of science-fiction comic strip *Star Hawks,* with Gil Kane, 1977–79. Member, board of directors, Mystery Writers of America, 1979–83, 1984–88, 1989–91. Recipient: Mystery Writers of America Edgar Allan Poe award, 1971. Address: 30 Farrell Road, Weston, Connecticut 06883, U.S.A.

CRIME PUBLICATIONS

Novels (series: John Easy)

The Sword Swallower. New York, Doubleday, 1968.
After Things Fell Apart. New York, Ace, 1970; London, Arrow, 1975.
If Dying Was All (Easy). New York, Ace, 1971.
Hawkshaw. New York, Doubleday, 1972; London, Hale, 1973.
Too Sweet to Die (Easy). New York, Ace, 1972.
The Same Lie Twice (Easy). New York, Ace, 1973.
Cleopatra Jones (novelization of screenplay). New York, Warner, 1973.
One Grave Too Many (Easy). New York, Ace, 1974.
Spacehawk, Inc. New York, DAW, 1974.
Cleopatra Jones and the Casino of Gold (novelization of screenplay). New York, Warner, 1975.
The Enormous Hour Glass. New York, Award, 1976.
Calling Dr. Patchwork. New York, DAW, 1978.
Capricorn One. New York, Fawcett, 1978.
Skyrocket Steele. New York, Pocket Books, 1980.
Ghosting. Toronto, Raven, 1980.
A Graveyard of My Own. New York, Walker, 1985.
The Wisemann Originals. New York, Walker, 1989.
The Tijuana Bible. New York, St. Martin's Press, 1990.

Novels as Kenneth Robeson (series: the Avenger in all books)

The Man from Atlantis. New York, Warner, 1974.
Red Moon. New York, Warner, 1974.
The Purple Zombie. New York, Warner, 1974.
Dr. Time. New York, Warner, 1974.
The Nightwitch Devil. New York, Warner, 1974.
The Black Chariots. New York, Warner, 1974.

The Cartoon Crimes. New York, Warner, 1974.
The Iron Skull. New York, Warner, 1974.
The Death Machine. New York, Warner, 1975.
The Blood Countess. New York, Warner, 1975.
The Glass Man. New York, Warner, 1975.
Demon Island. New York, Warner, 1975.

Short Stories

What's Become of Screwloose? and Other Inquiries. New York, Scribner, and London, Sidgwick and Jackson, 1971.
Clockwork's Pirates, Ghost Breaker. New York, Ace, 1971.
Odd Job No. 101 and Other Future Crimes and Intrigues. New York, Scribner, 1975; London, Hale, 1976.

Uncollected Short Stories

"You Have to Stay Dead So Long," in *Mystery Monthly* (New York), September 1976.
"They're Gonna Kill You after Awhile," in *Mystery Monthly* (New York), January 1977.
"Please Don't Help the Bear," in *Ellery Queen's Mystery Magazine* (New York), January 1977.
"Now He Thinks He's Dead," in *Ellery Queen's Mystery Magazine* (New York), November 1977.
"The Laughing Chef," in *Ellery Queen's Who's Who of Whodunits.* New York, Davis, 1977.
"And the Winner Is," in *Ellery Queen's Mystery Magazine* (New York), April 1978.
"The Story of My Life," in *Alfred Hitchcock's Mystery Magazine* (New York), August 1978.
"Out of the Inkwell," in *Alfred Hitchcock's Mystery Magazine* (New York), September 1978.
"How Come My Dog Don't Bark," in *Ellery Queen's Mystery Magazine* (New York), September 1978.
"Running," in *Alfred Hitchcock's Mystery Magazine* (New York), November 1978.
"Why the Funnies Museum Never Opened," in *Alfred Hitchcock's Mystery Magazine* (New York), December 1978.
"News from Nowhere," in *Alfred Hitchcock's Tales to Scare You Stiff,* edited by Eleanor Sullivan. New York, Davis, 1978.
"Ninety-Nine Clop Clop," in *Ellery Queen's Mystery Magazine* (New York), January 1979.
"Nervous Laughter," in *Alfred Hitchcock's Mystery Magazine* (New York), November 1979.
"Big Bang," in *Alfred Hitchcock's Mystery Magazine* (New York), 2 January 1980.
"The Decline and Fall of Norbert Tuffy," in *Ellery Queen's Mystery Magazine* (New York), 17 June 1981.
"Never," in *Alfred Hitchcock's Mystery Magazine* (New York), September 1981.
"Wooing Chips Tortuga," in *Alfred Hitchcock's Mystery Magazine* (New York), October 1981.
"Christmastime in Prison," in *Alfred Hitchcock's Mystery Magazine* (New York), November 1981.
"Tales of the Tomb," in *Alfred Hitchcock's Mystery Magazine* (New York), December 1981.
"Private Nose," in *Alfred Hitchcock's Mystery Magazine* (New York), January 1982.
"Funny Stuff," in *Alfred Hitchcock's Mystery Magazine* (New York), November 1982.
"Suspense," in *The Year's Best Mystery and Suspense Stories 1982,* edited by Edward D. Hoch. New York, Walker, 1982.
"Adam and Eve on a Raft," in *Ellery Queen's Mystery Magazine* (New York), 1984.

OTHER PUBLICATIONS

Novels

The Fire Eater. New York, Ace, 1970.
Gadget Man. New York, Doubleday, 1971; London, New English Library, 1977.
Death Cell. New York, Beagle, 1971.
Plunder. New York, Beagle, 1972.
Wildsmith. New York, Ace, 1972.
Shaggy Planet. New York, Lancer, 1973.
A Talent for the Invisible. New York, DAW, 1973.
The Tin Angel. New York, DAW, 1973.
Superstition (novelization of television play; as Howard Lee). New York, Warner, 1973.
Flux. New York, DAW, 1974.
When the Waker Sleeps. New York, DAW, 1975.
Bloodstalk (novelization of comic strip; Vampirella). New York, Warner, 1975; London, Sphere, 1976.
On Alien Wings (novelization of comic strip; Vampirella). New York, Warner, 1975; London, Sphere, 1977.
The Hellhound Project. New York, Doubleday, 1975; London, Hale, 1976.
The Tremendous Adventures of Bernie Wine. New York, Warner, 1975.
A Whiff of Madness. New York, DAW, 1976.
Quest of the Gypsy. New York, DAW, 1976.
Deadwalk (novelization of comic strip; Vampirella). New York, Warner, 1976; London, Sphere, 1977.
Blood Wedding (novelization of comic strip; Vampirella). New York, Warner, 1976.
Deathgame (novelization of comic strip; Vampirella). New York, Warner, 1976.
Snakegod (novelization of comic strip; Vampirella). New York, Warner, 1976.
Crackpot. New York, Doubleday, and London, Hale, 1977.
The Emperor of the Last Days. New York, Popular Library, 1977.
The Panchronicon Plot. New York, DAW, 1977.
Nemo. New York, Berkley, 1977; London, Hale, 1980.
Eye of the Vulture. New York, Pyramid, 1977.
The Wicked Cyborg. New York, DAW, 1978.
Flux, and The Tin Angel. London, Millington, 1978.
Agent of Love (as Jullian Kearny). New York, Warner, 1979.
Cowboy Heaven. New York, Doubleday, 1979; London, Hale, 1980.
Dr. Scofflaw, in *Binary Star 3.* New York, Dell, 1979.
Hello, Lemuria, Hello. New York, DAW, 1979.
Star Hawks: Empire 99, illustrated by Gil Kane. Chicago, Playboy Press, 1980.
Hail Hibbler. New York, DAW, 1980.
Brinkman. New York, Doubleday, 1981.
Star Hawks: The Cyborg King. Chicago, Playboy Press, 1981.
The Robot in the Closet. New York, DAW, 1981.
Upside Downside. New York, DAW, 1982.
Big Bang. New York, DAW, 1982.
Greetings from Earth, with Glen A. Larson. New York, Berkley, 1983.
Experiment in Terra, with Glen A. Larson. New York, Berkley, 1984.
The Long Patrol, with Glen A. Larson. New York, Berkley, 1984.
Hellsquad. New York, DAW, 1984.
The Prisoner of Blackwood Castle. New York, Avon, 1984.
Brainz, Inc. New York, DAW, 1985.
Galaxy Jane. New York, Berkley, 1986.
Daredevils, Ltd. New York, St. Martin's Press, 1987.

The Curse of the Obelisk. New York, Avon, 1987.
Starpirate's Brain. New York, St. Martin's Press, 1987.
Everybody Come to Cosmo's. New York, St. Martin's Press, 1988.

Novels as Frank S. Shawn

The Veiled Lady. New York, Avon, 1973.
The Golden Circle. New York, Avon, 1973.
The Mystery of the Sea Horse. New York, Avon, 1973.
The Hydra Monster. New York, Avon, 1974.
The Goggle-Eyed Pirates. New York, Avon, 1974.
The Swamp Rats. New York, Avon, 1974.

Novels as Con Steffanson

The Lion Men of Mongo. New York, Avon, 1974.
The Plague of Sound. New York, Avon, 1974.
The Space Circus. New York, Avon, 1974.
Laverne and Shirley: Teamwork (novelization of television play). New York, Warner, 1976.
Laverne and Shirley: Easy Money (novelization of television play). New York, Warner, 1976.
Laverne and Shirley: Gold Rush (novelization of television play). New York, Warner, 1976.

Novels as Josephine Kains

The Devil Mask Mystery. New York, Zebra, 1978.
The Curse of the Golden Skull. New York, Zebra, 1978.
The Green Lama Mystery. New York, Zebra, 1979.
The Whispering Cat Mystery. New York, Zebra, 1979.
The Witch's Tower Mystery. New York, Zebra, 1979.
The Laughing Dragon Mystery. New York, Zebra, 1980.

Short Stories

Broke Down Engine and Other Troubles with Machines. New York, Macmillan, 1971.
The Chameleon Corps and Other Shape Changers. New York, Macmillan, 1972; London, Collier Macmillan, 1973.
Nutzenbolts and More Troubles with Machines. New York, Macmillan, 1975; London, Hale, 1976.

Other

The Assault on Childhood. Los Angeles, Sherbourne Press, 1969; London, Gollancz, 1970.
Cheap Thrills: An Informal History of the Pulp Magazines. New Rochelle, New York, Arlington House, 1972.
An American Family. New York, Warner, 1973.
The Adventurous Decade: Comic Strips in the Thirties. New Rochelle, New York, Arlington House, 1975.
Focus on Jack Cole. Agoura, California, Fantographics, 1986.
The Great Comic Book Artists. New York, St. Martin's Press, 1986.
The Dime Detectives. New York, Mysterious Press, 1988.

Editor, *The Hardboiled Dicks: An Anthology and Study of Pulp Detective Fiction.* Los Angeles, Sherbourne Press, 1965; London, Boardman, 1967.
Editor, *Lineup Tough Guys.* Los Angeles, Sherbourne Press, 1966.
Editor, *The Great British Detective.* New York, New American Library, 1982.

*

Ron Goulart comments:

The fact that I am, to the best of my knowledge, the only writer ever to win a Mystery Writers of America award for a science fiction novel indicates my dual fascination with both detective stories and fantasies. I had the good fortune to study with Anthony Boucher in my youth, and he also practiced in both genres and sometimes mixed them. It isn't only the opportunity to construct puzzles and extrapolations which drew me to these two areas. I also discovered quite early that both fields allowed you to be funny. This is important to me and I plan to keep mixing murder, bugeyed monsters and satire for as long as I can get away with it.

* * *

Ron Goulart's fictional world bears only a superficial resemblance to our own. His science-fiction is usually set in the Barnum System which exists far beyond our own Solar System and contains as many planets as the current story may call for. To anyone's knowledge, no one has ever charted or mapped the Barnum System. His mysteries are often set in Southern California, a state which exists far beyond mortal imagination and contains whatever the current story may call for. Sometimes, reading one genre example next to another, there is a sudden feeling of time warp *déjà vu*: his science-fiction often has a mystery in its basic plot, and his mysteries have a touch of fantasy. Even in his straightest, most deadpan, serious mysteries there is a glimpse of glee.

Some of his earliest contributions to the genre were parodies of well known crime writers: Ross Macdonald, Raymond Chandler, John D. MacDonald, Richard Stark, and Ed McBain. His first John Easy story, "The Tin Ear," was a subtle spoof on parts of *The Maltese Falcon*.

The stories of Max Kearny, amateur occult detective, in *Ghost Breaker* are concerned more with fantasy than detection though some might consider them a border-line category. *The Enormous Hour Glass* is a science-fiction novel about a "time-detective" named Sam Brimmer, while "Monte Cristo Complex" (in *What's Become of Screwloose*) features a psychiatric detective named Vincent Hawthorn.

He has used only a few series characters. Hilda and Jake Pace of Odd Jobs, Inc. investigate cases no sane detective would touch. The stories are also set in the future. His short stories narrated by an anonymous account executive for an advertising agency present a satiric commentary on the jealousies between actors, writers, directors, and other artists in the motion picture and television industry. Since Goulart has never given his narrator a name, it is tempting to think of him as a sort of Hollywood Op, although he merely observes and does not really participate in the action. Perhaps he should just be called the Hollywood Ad Man. Goulart's most solid contribution to the literature of the private eye is his Hollywood Dick, John Easy, who seems to specialize in missing-persons cases, especially women. The minor characters in the Easy novels are even more wildly unconventional than the usual Hollywood detective story calls for. Hagopian, the writer for *TV Look* who opens his files to Easy, has choice criticism for the city and its inhabitants, but he is as cockeyed as any of them. John Easy is the one sane man in an insane world. His story is his attempt to restore sanity, while maintaining his own. (Easy was named after Roy Crane's newspaper cartoon strip hero.)

There is an air of the unreal in much of Goulart, as though the story were being told at a party where the reader's attention was being constantly diverted. The story is carried largely by the dialogue; the physical background and characters are sketched in lightly. Much of his style and content can be traced to his experience as an advertising copywriter; his stories often begin with a sentence designed to hold the reader's interest. He is probably not breaking new ground in the detective field, but he is holding up the Hollywood scene for a fresh and not completely cynical scrutiny.

Ever the quintessential Professional Writer who accepts and delivers a wide variety of assignments, Goulart can be found in all categories on the bookshelves. Easily shifting from crime shorts for the leading genre fiction magazines to the guise of a female writer of puzzlers and semi-gothics (about television-reporter-detective, Terry Spring) to the role of anthologist, historian, and critic of popular culture, he continues to defy classification.

—J. Randolph Cox

———

GOULD, Stephen. *See* **FISHER, Steve.**

———

GRAEME, Bruce. Pseudonym for Graham Montague Jeffries; also wrote as Peter Bourne; David Graeme; Roderic Hastings. British. Born in London, 23 May 1900. Educated privately. Served in the Queen's Westminster Rifles, 1918. Married Lorna Hélène Louch in 1925; one son, Roderic Jeffries, *q.v.,* and one daughter. Film producer in 1919 and in the 1940's; reporter, *Middlesex County Times,* Ealing, in the 1920's; entered Gray's Inn, London, 1930. Founding member, Crime Writers Association, 1953. *Died 14 May 1982.*

Crime Publications

Novels (series: Auguste Jantry; Detective Sergeant Robert Mather; Superintendent William Stevens and Inspector Pierre Allain; Theodore I. Terhune)

La Belle Laurine. London, Unwin, 1926; revised edition, as *Laurine,* London, Philip Allan, 1935.
The Trail of the White Knight. London, Harrap, 1926; New York, Doran, 1927.
Hate Ship. London, Hutchinson, and New York, Dodd Mead, 1928.
Trouble! London, Harrap, and Philadelphia, Lippincott, 1929.
Through the Eyes of the Judge. London, Hutchinson, and Philadelphia, Lippincott, 1930.
The Penance of Brother Alaric. London, Hutchinson, 1930.
A Murder of Some Importance (Stevens and Allain). London, Hutchinson, and Philadelphia, Lippincott, 1931.
Unsolved. London, Hutchinson, 1931; Philadelphia, Lippincott, 1932.
Gigins Court. London, Hutchinson, 1932.
The Imperfect Crime (Stevens and Allain). London, Hutchinson, 1932; Philadelphia, Lippincott, 1933.
Impeached! London, Hutchinson, 1933.
Epilogue (Stevens and Allain). London, Hutchinson, 1933; Philadelphia, Lippincott, 1934.
An International Affair (Stevens and Allain). London, Hutchinson, 1934.

Public Enemy—No. 1. London, Hutchinson, 1934; as *John Jenkin, Public Enemy,* Philadelphia, Lippincott, 1935.
Madame Spy. London, Philip Allan, 1935.
Satan's Mistress (Stevens and Allain). London, Hutchinson, 1935.
Not Proven (Stevens and Allain). London, Hutchinson, 1935.
Cardyce for the Defence. London, Hutchinson, 1936.
Mystery on the Queen Mary (Stevens and Allain). London, Hutchinson, 1937; Philadelphia, Lippincott, 1938.
Disappearance of Roger Tremayne. London, Hutchinson, 1937.
Racing Yacht Mystery. London, Hutchinson, 1938.
The Man from Michigan (Stevens and Allain). London, Hutchinson, 1938; as *The Mystery of the Stolen Hats,* Philadelphia, Lippincott, 1939.
Body Unknown (Stevens and Allain). London, Hutchinson, 1939.
Poisoned Sleep (Stevens and Allain). London, Hutchinson, 1939.
Thirteen in a Fog. London, Hutchinson, 1940.
The Corporal Died in Bed, Being the Swan-Song of Pierre Allain (Stevens and Allain). London, Hutchinson, 1940.
Seven Clues in Search of a Crime (Terhune). London, Hutchinson, 1941.
Encore Allain! (Stevens and Allain). London, Hutchinson, 1941.
House with Crooked Walls (Terhune). London, Hutchinson, 1942.
News Travels by Night (Stevens and Allain). London, Hutchinson, 1943.
A Case for Solomon (Terhune). London, Hutchinson, 1943.
Work for the Hangman (Terhune). London, Hutchinson, 1944.
Ten Trails to Tyburn (Terhune). London, Hutchinson, 1944.
The Coming of Carew. London, Hutchinson, 1945.
A Case of Books (Jantry). London, Hutchinson, 1946.
Without Malice. London, Hutchinson, 1946.
No Clues for Dexter. London, Hutchinson, 1948.
And a Bottle of Rum (Terhune). London, Hutchinson, 1949.
Tigers Have Claws. London, Hutchinson, 1949.
Cherchez la Femme (Jantry). London, Hutchinson, 1951.
Dead Pigs at Hungry Farm (Terhune). London, Hutchinson, 1951.
Lady in Black (Jantry). London, Hutchinson, 1952.
Mr. Whimset Buys a Gun. London, Hutchinson, 1953.
Suspense. London, Hutchinson, 1953.
The Way Out. London, Hutchinson, 1954.
So Sharp the Razor. London, Hutchinson, 1955.
Just an Ordinary Case. London, Hutchinson, 1956.
The Accidental Clue. London, Hutchinson, 1957.
Naked Tide (as Roderic Hastings). New York, Avon, 1958.
The Long Night. London, Hutchinson, 1958.
Boomerang. London, Hutchinson, 1959.
Fog for a Killer. London, Hutchinson, 1960.
The Undetective. London, Hutchinson, 1962; New York, London House and Maxwell, 1963.
Almost Without Murder. London, Hutchinson, 1963.
Holiday for a Spy. London, Hutchinson, 1963.
Always Expect the Unexpected. London, Hutchinson, 1965.
The Devil Was a Woman. London, Hutchinson, 1966.
Much Ado about Something. London, Hutchinson, 1967.
Never Mix Business with Pleasure. London, Hutchinson, 1968.
Some Geese Lay Golden Eggs. London, Hutchinson, 1968.
Blind Date for a Private Eye. London, Hutchinson, 1969.
The Quiet Ones (Mather). London, Hutchinson, 1970.
The Lady Doth Protest. London, Hutchinson, 1971.
Tomorrow's Yesterday. London, Hutchinson, 1972.

Two and Two Make Five (Mather).   London, Hutchinson, 1973.
The D Notice (Mather).   London, Hutchinson, 1974.
The Snatch (Mather).   London, Hutchinson, 1976.
Two-Faced (Mather).   London, Hutchinson, 1977.
Double Trouble (Mather).   London, Hutchinson, 1978.
Mather Again.   London, Hutchinson, 1979.
Invitation to Mather.   London, Hale, 1980.
Mather Investigates.   London, Hale, 1980.

Novels as David Graeme (series: Monsieur Blackshirt)

Monsieur Blackshirt.   London, Harrap, and Philadelphia, Lippincott, 1933.
The Vengeance of Monsieur Blackshirt.   London, Harrap, 1934; Philadelphia, Lippincott, 1935.
The Sword of Monsieur Blackshirt.   London, Harrap, and Philadelphia, Lippincott, 1936.
The Inn of Thirteen Swords (Monsieur Blackshirt).   London, Harrap, 1938.
The Drums Beat Red.   London, Harrap, 1963.

Short Stories (series: Blackshirt; Lord Blackshirt)

Blackshirt.   London, Unwin, and New York, Dodd Mead, 1925; revised edition, London, Benn, 1930.
The Return of Blackshirt.   London, Unwin, and New York, Dodd Mead, 1927; revised edition, London, Benn, 1927.
Blackshirt Again.   London, Hutchinson, 1929; as *Adventures of Blackshirt,* New York, Dodd Mead, 1929.
Alias Blackshirt.   London, Harrap, and New York, Dodd Mead, 1932.
Blackshirt the Audacious.   London, Hutchinson, 1935; Philadelphia, Lippincott, 1936.
Blackshirt the Adventurer.   London, Hutchinson, 1936.
Blackshirt Takes a Hand.   London, Hutchinson, 1937.
Blackshirt, Counter-Spy.   London, Hutchinson, 1938.
Blackshirt Interferes.   London, Hutchinson, 1939.
Blackshirt Strikes Back.   London, Hutchinson, 1940.
Son of Blackshirt (Lord Blackshirt).   London, Hutchinson, 1941.
Lord Blackshirt: The Son of Blackshirt Carries On.   London, Hutchinson, 1942.
Calling Lord Blackshirt.   London, Hutchinson, 1943.
A Brief for O'Leary and Two Other Episodes in His Career.   London, Hutchinson, 1947.

Uncollected Short Stories

"Hand of Steele," in *My Best Thriller.*   London, Faber, 1933.
"Miss Mystery," in *A Century of Spy Stories,* edited by Dennis Wheatley.   London, Hutchinson, 1938.
"The Empty House," in *My Best Mystery Story.*   London, Faber, 1939.
"Chequemate," in *The Saint* (New York), May 1958.
"Unseen Alibi," in *Murder in Mind,* edited by Lawrence Treat.   New York, Dutton, 1967.

OTHER PUBLICATIONS

Novels as Peter Bourne

When the Bells Ring (as Bruce Graeme), with Anthony Armstrong.   London, Harrap, 1943.
Black Saga.   London, Hutchinson, 1947; as *Drums of Destiny,* New York, Putnam, 1947.

Flames of Empire.   New York, Putnam, 1949; as *Dupe of Destiny,* London, Hutchinson, 1950.
Ten Thousand Shall Die.   London, Hutchinson, 1951; as *The Golden Road,* New York, Putnam, 1951.
Gateway to Fortune.   London, Hutchinson, and New York, Putnam, 1952.
Twilight of the Dragon.   London, Hutchinson, and New York, Putnam, 1954.
When Gods Slept.   London, Hutchinson, and New York, Putnam, 1956.
The Court of Love.   London, Hutchinson, and New York, Putnam, 1958.
Soldiers of Fortune.   London, Hutchinson, 1962; New York, Putnam, 1963.
Black Gold.   London, Hutchinson, 1964.
Fall of the Eagle.   London, Hutchinson, 1967.
And Bay the Moon.   London, Hutchinson, 1975.

Other

Passion, Murder and Mystery.   London, Hutchinson, and New York, Doubleday, 1928.
The Story of Buckingham Palace.   London, Hutchinson, 1928; revised edition, London, Howard Baker, 1970.
The Story of St. James's Palace.   London, Hutchinson, 1929.
A Century of Buckingham Palace 1837–1937.   London, Hutchinson, 1937.
The Story of Windsor Castle.   London, Hutchinson, 1937.
Danger in the Channel (for children).   London, Kaye and Ward, 1973.

*   *   *

Bruce Graeme (pseudonym of Graham Montague Jeffries) was noted for his literary longevity, his production (averaging almost two books per year), and his series characters. Graeme was an extremely competent professional storyteller whose best work is worth revival today.

Graeme's first attempt to write a novel ended in fiasco, but he hit the jackpot on his next try with a series of short stories that were later published in book form as *Blackshirt.* This volume and its successor, *The Return of Blackshirt,* went on to sell a million copies. Blackshirt is a well-known and respected mystery writer named Richard Verrell. By night he becomes a gentleman thief who disguises himself by dressing completely in black. He commits his thefts for the sheer love and excitement of the game. Blackshirt went on to become, in William Vivian Butler's words, "the most durable desperado of them all." The length of Blackshirt's career (1923–69) has been exceeded only by that of Charteris's the Saint. Graeme provided a successor in 1941; *Son of Blackshirt* was the first of these novels detailing the adventures of Verrell's son Anthony, who eventually becomes Lord Blackshirt. Graeme had also created a series of four novels about a Monsieur Blackshirt, a 17th-century ancestor of Verrell, whose adventures were set in France; these books were published under the pseudonym David Graeme. (But that wasn't all. Graeme's son, Roderic Graeme Jeffries, continued the original Blackshirt series with some 20 novels published as Roderic Graeme.)

Bruce Graeme's best series started in 1931 with *A Murder of Some Importance,* which introduced the conservative and very British Superintendent William Stevens of Scotland Yard, and the fiery Inspector Pierre Allain of the Sûreté who is noted for his prowess in detection as well as love. This series of some dozen novels featured some of Graeme's best writing and detective puzzles. Among the best is *The Imperfect Crime* with its deceptive clues and its neat (though not unprecedented) variation of the least-likely suspect gambit that is only solved by a slip of the murderer's tongue. Not as effective is *Not Proven,* a partially inverted tale that starts with a murder by a policeman who is subsequently placed in charge of the investigation, anticipating Kenneth Fearing's *The Big Clock.* Stevens and Allain finally discover the murderer's identity— but can't prove it.

Another series centers on Theodore I. Terhune, a young bookseller in a small British town whose desire to live a quiet life is often interrupted by murder problems. Graeme's most recent character, Detective-Sergeant Robert Mather of the Bretton Police, was introduced in *The Quiet Ones;* his investigations are more concerned with adventure than detection.

Graeme also wrote many non-series novels. *The Undetective* has a mystery writer as its protagonist. He seeks material that will expose police methods, but finds trouble instead. An early and lucid section on the economic perils of mystery writing is of interest.

Graeme's voyage on the *Queen Mary*'s initial outing provided the inspiration for *Mystery on the Queen Mary.* It's one of the best shipboard mysteries ever written, intensely entertaining, and a thorough delight. In *Epilogue* Superintendent Stevens goes back through time and finds himself obliged to solve the mystery of Edwin Drood, which Dickens left unfinished. Several of Graeme's efforts contain legal problems. His masterpiece, *Through the Eyes of the Judge,* is a long, detailed courtroom novel whose ironic ending is a challenge to the British legal system. It had some influence on one of Richard Hull's novels, and the work of his son.

—Charles Shibuk

GRAEME, David. *See* **GRAEME, Bruce.**

GRAEME, Roderic. *See* **JEFFRIES, Roderic.**

GRAFTON, C(ornelius) W(arren). American. Born in China, of missionary parents, in 1909. University degrees in journalism and law. One daughter, the writer Sue Grafton *q.v.* Practised law in Louisville, Kentucky. Recipient: Mary Roberts Rinehart award, 1943. *Died in 1982.*

CRIME PUBLICATIONS

Novels (series: Gil Henry)

The Rat Began to Gnaw the Rope (Henry). New York, Farrar and Rinehart, 1943; London, Gollancz, 1944.
The Rope Began to Hang the Butcher (Henry). New York, Farrar and Rinehart, 1944; London, Gollancz, 1945.
Beyond a Reasonable Doubt. New York, Rinehart, 1950; London, Heinemann, 1951.

OTHER PUBLICATIONS

Novel

My Name Is Christopher Nagel. New York, Rinehart, 1947.

*   *   *

With *The Rat Began to Gnaw the Rope,* lawyer C.W. Grafton embarked on one of detective fiction's most original title patterns. Following the lines of the old nursery rhyme, he could have completed a ten-volume series about lawyer Gilmore Henry of Calhoun County, Kentucky. That he stopped the skein at two is regrettable not so much because such tantalizing tags as *The Water Began to Quench the Fire* and *The Stick Began to Beat the Dog* were never published over his name as because Henry was one of the most promising new sleuths of the 1940's.

Though he has a voice of his own, Grafton displays some of the key attributes of his best contemporaries. The rapid plot movement and legal background recall Erle Stanley Gardner, while the vivid, breezy style seems to be inspired by Raymond Chandler and Rex Stout. His solid understanding of the business world and his invention of crimes with their roots in events decades in the past foreshadow some of the techniques of John D. MacDonald and Ross Macdonald. More determined than some writers to root his fiction in a specific time, Grafton conveys a strong sense of immediate pre-World War II America with war clouds conspicuous on the horizon. At times, he throws in as many topical references (prices and products; song titles; names of radio and movie stars, politicians, and sports heroes) as would someone writing a historical novel about the time.

The Rat Began to Gnaw the Rope employs many of the whodunit clichés (movie-type as well as book-type), and the extremely complicated plot, involving stock manipulation, requires too much final-chapter exposition. But the novel has a freshness about it that overcomes its defects. Narrator Henry is short and chubby, thoroughly likeable but far from the traditional hero mold, at least superficially. He goes through most of the tough-hero paces, however, including a tendency to wise-crack and to get hit over the head with painful frequency. But he suffers more from his wounds than the average hardboiled hero.

In *The Rope Began to Hang the Butcher,* one of the very best Gardner-style novels not by Gardner himself, Grafton really hits his stride. Henry's fancy footwork would do Perry Mason credit, and the courtroom scenes, absent from the first book, serve to focus interest better than additional action scenes would. The portrait of a backwoodsy Kentucky court where the judge wanders around the room during the trial, challenging out-of-towners to tell him from advocates or spectators, is unique. The stylistic touches and period observations are even sharper than those in the first Henry case. The plot, involving real estate and insurance finagling, is equally complex but worked out more efficiently.

Beyond a Reasonable Doubt, Grafton's return to the field without his series character, is his best-known book and probably his finest achievement, one of the most unusual and suspenseful of courtroom novels. The reader knows lawyer Jess London is guilty of the not-unjustified murder of his brother-in-law, Mitchell Sothern, and the novel draws its suspense from the question of whether (and how) he will manage to escape punishment. Tried for the crime after recanting an earlier confession, Jess acts as his own attorney, surviving some of the narrowest escapes in trial fiction. The only problem is that Jess leads somewhat too charmed a life in the courtroom, but few readers outside of lawyers will think about that, at least until the book is laid aside.

If Grafton had chosen to continue in the field, he might have become one of the major names in American crime fiction. As it is, his three contributions to the genre should continue to attract new readers for many years to come.

—Jon L. Breen

GRAFTON, Sue. American. Born in Louisville, Kentucky, 24 April 1940; daughter of the writer C.W. Grafton, *q.v.* Educated at the University of Louisville, Kentucky, B.A. in English 1961. Married Steven Frederick Humphrey in 1978; three children from previous marriages. Recipient: Private Eye Writers of America Shamus award, 1986; Mystery Readers of America Macavity award, for short story, 1986; Anthony award, for novel, 1986, 1987, and for short story, 1987. Agent: Molly Friedrich, The Aaron Priest Agency, 122 West 42nd Street, No. 3902, New York, New York 10168, U.S.A.

CRIME PUBLICATIONS

Novels (series: Kinsey Millhone in all books except *Keziah Dane* and *The Lolly-Madonna War*)

Keziah Dane. New York, Macmillan, 1967; London, Owen, 1968.
The Lolly-Madonna War. London, Owen, 1969.
"A" Is for Alibi. New York, Holt, 1982; London, Macmillan, 1986.
"B" Is for Burglar. New York, Holt, 1985; London, Macmillan, 1986.
"C" Is for Corpse. New York, Holt, 1986; London, Macmillan, 1987.
"D" Is for Deadbeat. New York, Holt, and London, Macmillan, 1987.
"E" Is for Evidence. New York, Holt, and London, Macmillan, 1988.
"F" Is for Fugitive. New York, Holt, and London, Macmillan, 1989.
"G" Is for Gumshoe. New York, Holt, and London, Macmillan, 1990.

Uncollected Short Stories

"She Didn't Come Home," in *Redbook Magazine* (New York), April 1986.
"Murder Between the Sheets," in *Redbook Magazine* (New York), October 1986.
"The Parker Shotgun," in *Mean Streets,* edited by Robert J. Randisi. New York, Mysterious Press, 1986.
"Falling Off the Roof," in *Sisters in Crime,* edited by Marilyn Wallace. New York, Berkley, 1989; London, Robinson, 1990.
"A Poison That Leaves No Trace," in *Sisters in Crime 2,* edited by Marilyn Wallace. New York, Berkley, 1990.

OTHER PUBLICATIONS

Plays

Screenplay: *Lolly-Madonna XXX,* with Rodney Carr-Smith, 1973.

Television Plays: *With Friends Like These* (*Rhoda* series), 1975; *Walking Through the Fire,* from the book by Laurel Lee, 1979; *Sex and the Single Parent,* from the book by Jane Adams, 1979; *Nurse,* from the book by Peggy Anderson, 1980; *Mark, I Love You,* from the book by Hal Painter, 1980; *Seven Brides for Seven Brothers, I Love You, Molly McGraw,* and *A House Divided,* with Steven Humphrey (*Seven Brides for Seven Brothers* series), 1982–83; *A Caribbean Mystery,* with Steven Humphrey, from the novel by Agatha Christie, 1983; *A Killer in the Family,* with Steven Humphrey and Robert Aller, 1983; *Sparkling Cyanide,* with Steven Humphrey and Robert Malcolm Young, from the novel by Agatha Christie, 1983; *Love on the Run,* with Steven Humphrey, 1985; *Tonight's the Night,* with Steven Humphrey, 1987.

* * *

The most exciting development in the private-eye novel during the 1980's was the emergence of several creditable female private eyes. One of the best of the lot is Kinsey Millhone, a twice-divorced 32-year-old California private detective created by Sue Grafton.

Kinsey is more than a Philip Marlowe in skirts. She is tough and brainy, independent and confident of her ability to do what has long been viewed largely as a man's job. She is both credible as a private detective and fully convincing as a self-reliant contemporary woman.

In the first of her alphabetical cases, *"A" Is for Alibi,* Kinsey is hired by a woman just released from prison to prove her innocence of the crime (poisoning her husband) for which she has just served eight years. Thanks to persistence, determination, and an ability to get people to talk to her, she tracks down every lead and untangles relationships to solve the eight-year-old murder.

In *"B" Is for Burglar,* Kinsey is hired by a woman to locate her sister, whose signature she needs on a legal document. An apparently routine missing-person case leads to the discovery of another murder along the way. But with the assistance of such memorable characters as a spunky 88-year-old woman and a 17-year-old punk with a pink Mohawk haircut, Kinsey pieces everything together to expose a complicated murder plot.

In several ways, Grafton's books call to mind Ross Macdonald's Lew Archer series. Kinsey lives and works in Santa Teresa, the fictionalized California coastal town that Macdonald himself used in several of the Archer books. (Santa Teresa is modeled on Santa Barbara, home to both Macdonald and Grafton.) Like Archer, Kinsey is as much an investigator into other people's lives as she is a crime-solver. Like Archer, she often also forges an emotional bond with her clients; for example in *"C" Is for Corpse,* her commitment to a young crippled client extends beyond his death.

Many of the cases she pursues also turn up family secrets hidden deep in the past, another notable characteristic of the Archer series. In *"F" Is for Fugitive,* Kinsey is hired to investigate a murder that occurred 17 years earlier; in *"G" Is for Gumshoe,* she uncovers evidence of several murders that were committed 50 years earlier.

As a character, however, Kinsey is much more developed than Archer ever was. She has an active private life, including some romantic involvements. Sometimes she herself becomes the focus of the book. In *"E" Is for Evidence* she must become her own client in order to discover who is trying to frame her on a fraud charge; she also has to deal with the unexpected (and unwelcome) return of her ex-husband, whom she has not seen in eight years. In *"G" Is for Gumshoe,* her search for a woman's elderly missing mother is complicated by a threat to her own life, as she must elude a hitman hired to kill her by a man she helped send to prison.

Sassy and irreverant, Kinsey is a very appealing character. She has an engaging sense of humor, an eye alertly poised to expose the phony, and a scathing tongue she isn't afraid to use. She's emotionally tough, yet refreshingly candid about her own vulnerabilities. She isn't often called upon to prove herself in physically threatening situations, but when she does find herself in a tight spot, as for example at the end of *"A" Is for Alibi,* she isn't afraid to use her gun to shoot the man who is stalking her.

Grafton (the daughter of mystery writer C.W. Grafton) writes in a breezy, entertaining style and has a gift for vivid description and sharp characterization. Each of her characters, no matter how secondary to the plot, springs to life on the page. Grafton also understands well how the distinctive voice of first-person narration can be used for more than mere storytelling purposes. Through her colorful descriptions, offhand remarks, and self-deprecating admissions, Kinsey reveals herself to be earthy, unpretentious, and wholly engaging.

Readers looking for a well-plotted mystery won't be disappointed in any of Grafton's books. They will also be treated to much more than a mystery, for Kinsey Millhone, like Philip Marlowe and Spenser, is the sort of person whose company one would enjoy keeping even if she weren't describing a mystery investigation.

—David Geherin

GRAHAM, Caroline. British. Born in Nuneaton, Warwickshire, 17 July, 1931. Educated at Nuneaton High School for Girls, 1943–46; Salle Wacker Ballet School Paris, 1954–55; Open University, 1976–82, B.A. 1982. Served in the Women's Royal Navy Service. Married Michael Graham-Cameron in 1953 (divorced 1966); one son. Has had a variety of jobs including dancer, actress, stage manager, freelance radio journalist. Recipient: Mystery Readers of America Macavity award, 1989. Agent: David Higham, 6–8 Lower John Street, London WC1 4AR.

CRIME PUBLICATIONS

Novels (series: Detective Chief Inspector Tom Barnaby)

The Envy of the Stranger. London, Century, 1984.
The Killings at Badger's Drift (Barnaby). London, Century Hutchinson, 1987; Bethesda, Maryland, Adler and Adler, 1988.
Death of a Hollow Man (Barnaby). London, Century Hutchinson, 1989.
Murder at Madingley Grange. London, Century Hutchinson, 1990.

OTHER PUBLICATIONS

Novels

Fire Dance. London, Collins, 1982.
BMX Star Rider. London, Beaver Books, 1985.
BMX'ers Battle It Out! London, Beaver Books, 1985.

Plays

Radio Plays: *High Spirits and Low Cunning,* 1971; *The Cotswold Connubials,* 1978; *The Sea Shell,* 1979; *Adonis in Dark Glasses,* 1981; *The Envy of the Stranger* (from her own novel), 1983.

Television Plays: *The Common Lot* series, 1977; *Crossroads* series, 1978.

* * *

Caroline Graham's crime fiction pays considerable homage to the classic English detective novel, using stock enclosed locations such as the village, the country-house, and the theatre, and dramatis personae who are reassuringly familiar.

Her first two novels, *Fire Dance* and *The Envy of the Stranger,* appeared in 1982 and 1984, and despite a radio dramatisation of the latter, they attracted little notice, and are now largely forgotten. Much better received was her third work, *The Killings at Badger's Drift,* published in 1987, which established Graham as a member of the late 20th-century Mayhem Parva school of writing alongside Colin Dexter, Martha Grimes, Robert Barnard, and many others. Announced as "An English Village Whodunnit," this novel is an amalgam of idyllic "Golden Age" fiction and neo-gothic tale. A genteel old lady cannot believe her eyes when she goes down to the woods one day, and is later found dead in her cottage in the Home Counties' village of Badger's Drift. Detective Chief Inspector Tom Barnaby (who becomes Graham's recurrent character) is called in to investigate, with his bumptious assistant, Detective Sergeant Troy. Together they discover a village full of carefully described suspects, including a womanising farm-manager, an effete "Mummy's Boy," a struggling genius of an artist and a seedy family doctor.

The Killings at Badger's Drift is a little uneven in tone, mixing cosy realism with heightened sensationalism. However, it does contain some splendidly baroque moments in its resolution, and more particularly in its creation of the monstrous Mrs Rainbird, a grossly over-weight and financially grasping Peeping Tom. Within Graham's fairly clear moral scheme of the elect and the damned in this novel, the ghastly creature's life and Grand Guignol murder can be relished.

Death of a Hollow Man is more successful. Here Graham exploits the closed setting of the amateur theatre. The milieu is well delineated, presumably drawing on Graham's previous professional experience of theatrical endeavours, and she produces a cast of sympathetically drawn types. The novel is a "clue-puzzle" complete with all the paraphernalia of misunderstood dying words, deadly stage-props and mysterious parcels. Tom Barnaby, who is witness to the murder on stage of the preciously-named Esslyn Carmichael, and the ever-irritant Troy unravel a web of grand and sordid passions. The raw emotions and complicated lives of most of the amateur players are contrasted with the comfortable domesticity of the Barnaby menage. Having the whole proceedings acted out against the backdrop of an amateur production of Peter Schaffer's *Amadeus* allows Graham room for great glee in describing this "hollow" world of personal vanity, melodrama, and farcical pomposity.

Graham's most recent novel continues her development along slightly different lines, whilst still placing her well within British traditions of crime writing. *Murder at Madingley Grange* exploits her wit and humour more forcefully than the Barnaby stories. Set in the elaborately described late Victorian pile of Madingley Grange, the book concerns the attempts by its owner's relatives to set up country-house murder holidays. Unfortunately, there may or may not have been a real murder of one of the Anglo-Saxon types Graham is so good at portraying. The highly mannered farce is well-conducted, and in its elaborate artifice resembles, and is as true to life as, a game of *Cluedo*. Graham is now planning a third Barnaby novel, taking one of the most conventional forms of British detective writing late into the 20th Century.

—Anna-Marie Taylor

GRAHAM, James. *See* **HIGGINS, Jack.**

GRAHAM, Winston (Mawdsley). British. Born in Victoria Park, Manchester, Lancashire, 30 June 1910. Married Jean Mary Williamson in 1939; one son and one daughter. Chairman, Society of Authors, London, 1967–69. Recipient: Crime Writers Association award, 1956. Fellow, Royal Society of Literature, 1968. O.B.E. (Officer, Order of the British Empire), 1983. Agent: A.M. Heath and Company Ltd., 79 St. Martin's Lane, London WC2N 4AA. Address: Abbotswood House, Buxted, East Sussex, TN22 4PB, England.

CRIME PUBLICATIONS

Novels

The House with the Stained-Glass Windows. London, Ward Lock, 1934.
Into the Fog. London, Ward Lock, 1935.
The Riddle of John Rowe. London, Ward Lock, 1935.
Without Motive. London, Ward Lock, 1936.
The Dangerous Pawn. London, Ward Lock, 1937.
The Giant's Chair. London, Ward Lock, 1938.
Strangers Meeting. London, Ward Lock, 1939.
Keys of Chance. London, Ward Lock, 1939.
No Exit: An Adventure. London, Ward Lock, 1940.
Night Journey. London, Ward Lock, 1941; New York, Doubleday, 1968.
My Turn Next. London, Ward Lock, 1942.
The Merciless Ladies. London, Ward Lock, 1944; revised edition, London, Bodley Head, 1979; New York, Doubleday, 1980.
The Forgotten Story. London, Ward Lock, 1945; as *The Wreck of The Grey Cat,* New York, Doubleday, 1958.
Take My Life. London, Ward Lock, 1947; New York, Doubleday, 1967.
Night Without Stars. London, Hodder and Stoughton, and New York, Doubleday, 1950.
Fortune Is a Woman. London, Hodder and Stoughton, and New York, Doubleday, 1953.
The Little Walls. London, Hodder and Stoughton, and New York, Doubleday, 1955; abridged edition, as *Bridge to Vengeance,* New York, Spivak, 1957.
The Sleeping Partner. London, Hodder and Stoughton, and New York, Doubleday, 1956.
Greek Fire. London, Hodder and Stoughton, and New York, Doubleday, 1958.
The Tumbled House. London, Hodder and Stoughton, 1959; New York, Doubleday, 1960.

Marnie. London, Hodder and Stoughton, and New York, Doubleday, 1961.
After the Act. London, Hodder and Stoughton, 1965; New York, Doubleday, 1966.
The Walking Stick. London, Collins, and New York, Doubleday, 1967.
Angell, Pearl and Little God. London, Collins, and New York, Doubleday, 1970.
Woman in the Mirror. London, Bodley Head, and New York, Doubleday, 1975.

Short Stories

The Japanese Girl and Other Stories. London, Collins, 1971; New York, Doubleday, 1972.

Uncollected Short Stories

"The Circus," in *Winter's Crimes 6,* edited by George Hardinge. London, Macmillan, and New York, St. Martin's Press, 1974.
"Nothing in the Library," in *Winter's Crimes 19,* edited by Hilary Hale. London, Macmillan, 1987.

OTHER PUBLICATIONS

Novels

Ross Poldark: A Novel of Cornwall 1783–1787. London, Ward Lock, 1945; as *The Renegade,* New York, Doubleday, 1951.
Demelza: A Novel of Cornwall 1788–1790. London, Ward Lock, 1946; New York, Doubleday, 1953.
Cordelia. London, Ward Lock, 1949; New York, Doubleday, 1950.
Jeremy Poldark: A Novel of Cornwall 1790–1791. London, Ward Lock, 1950; as *Venture Once More,* New York, Doubleday, 1954.
Warleggan: A Novel of Cornwall 1792–1793. London, Ward Lock, 1953; New York, Ballantine, 1977, as *The Last Gamble,* New York, Doubleday, 1955.
The Grove of Eagles. London, Hodder and Stoughton, 1963; New York, Doubleday, 1964.
The Black Moon: A Novel of Cornwall 1794–1795. London, Collins, 1973; New York, Doubleday, 1974.
The Four Swans: A Novel of Cornwall 1795–1797. London, Collins, 1976; New York, Doubleday, 1977.
The Angry Tide: A Novel of Cornwall 1798–1799. London, Collins, 1977; New York, Doubleday, 1978.
The Stranger from the Sea: A Novel of Cornwall 1810–1811. London, Collins, 1981; New York, Doubleday, 1982.
The Miller's Dance: A Novel of Cornwall 1812–1813. London, Collins, 1982; New York, Doubleday, 1983.
The Loving Cup: A Novel of Cornwall 1813–1815. London, Collins, 1984; New York, Doubleday, 1985.
The Green Flash. London, Collins, 1986; New York, Random House, 1987.
Cameo. London, Collins, 1988.
The Twisted Sword: A Novel of Cornwall 1815–1816. London, Chapman, 1990.

Plays

Shadow Play (produced Salisbury, 1978).
Circumstantial Evidence (produced Guildford, Surrey, 1979).

Screenplays: *Take My Life,* with Valerie Taylor and Margaret Kennedy, 1948; *Night Without Stars,* 1951.

Other

The Spanish Armadas. London, Collins, and New York, Doubleday, 1972.
Poldark's Cornwall, photographs by Simon McBride. London, Bodley Head, 1983.

*   *   *

The novels of Winston Graham cover a wide generic range, including the spy story *Night Journey,* the psychological thriller *Marnie,* several historical novels, and a number of detective stories. In his mysteries, the influence of the other genres is apparent, and this versatility helps to insure against the formulaic and the merely conventional.

In Graham's novels the detective is usually an amateur: a lawyer or a young boy (*The Forgotten Story*); an insurance claims adjuster (*Fortune Is a Woman*); and even an opera singer (*Take My Life*). The amateur status of these sleuths lends itself to an emotional atmosphere which is characteristic of Graham's work. The "detective" is personally involved with the suspected party or is himself the suspect; his motives are seldom unmixed. The result is that Graham's stories place less emphasis upon methods of detection than they do upon the interplay of suspicion and guilt, of love and revenge, within his cast of characters.

In the "Prologue" to *The Forgotten Story,* a historical mystery, Graham raises an issue which may be considered a primary theme of his work, the relation of the past to the present. Speaking of the difficulty of reconstructing real events from newspaper accounts, he observes that we are "like palaeontologists trying to reconstruct an extinct animal." Graham's characters are frequently beset by the difficulties of extrapolating the truth from mere remnants of fact or from the often deceptive surfaces of things.

The discovery of and response to the past is a theme central to what is probably Graham's finest novel, *Marnie.* In it, the protagonist, like Oedipus, is at once the core of the mystery, a criminal, and the detective. Marnie's reluctant journey into the secret of her past is a fascinating example of the fusion of the psychological novel with the mystery genre.

Graham's interest in human psychology is observable throughout his career and is reflected in his preference for first-person narration. He gives his readers access to the thought processes of his protagonists, their delusions, fears, and moral struggles. In doing so, he avoids mere riddle-making and produces intriguing character studies. These serious concerns in Graham's work, along with the finesse of his style and his careful handling of description and atmosphere, place him among the best of contemporary mystery writers.

—Jeanne Carter Emmons

———

GRANDOWER, Elissa. *See* **WAUGH, Hilary.**

———

GRANGE, John. *See* **BALLARD, Willis Todhunter; BELLEM, Robert Leslie.**

———

GRANGER, Bill. Also writes as Joe Gash; Bill Griffith. American. Born in Chicago, Illinois, 1 June 1941. Educated at De Paul University, Chicago, 1959–63. Served with the United States Army 1963–65. Married Lori Meschke in 1967; one son. Reporter, Chicago *Tribune,* 1966–69; reporter and columnist, Chicago *Sun Times* 1969–78. Since 1980 freelance columnist. Address: Box 1214 Oak Park, Illinois 60304, U.S.A.

CRIME PUBLICATIONS

Novels (series: Devereaux)

The November Man (Devereaux). New York, Fawcett, 1979; London, New English Library, 1981.
Sweeps. New York, Fawcett, 1980.
Public Murders. New York, Jove, 1980; London, New English Library, 1981.
Schism (Devereaux). New York, Crown, 1981; London, New English Library, 1982.
Queen's Crossing. New York, Fawcett, 1982.
The Shattered Eye (Devereaux). New York, Crown, 1982; London, New English Library, 1984.
Time for Frankie Coolin (as Bill Griffith). New York, Random House, 1982.
The British Cross (Devereaux). New York, Crown, 1983; London, Sphere, 1985.
The Zurich Numbers (Devereaux). New York, Crown, 1984; London, Sphere, 1986.
Priestly Murders (as Joe Gash). New York, Holt Rinehart, 1984.
Newspaper Murders (as Joe Gash). New York, Holt Rinehart, 1985.
Hemingway's Notebook (Devereaux). New York, Crown, 1986.
There Are No Spies (Devereaux). New York, Warner, 1986.
The El Murders. New York, Holt, 1987.
The Infant of Prague (Devereaux). New York, Warner, 1987.
Lords of the Last Machine. New York, Random House, 1987.
Henry MaGee Is Not Dead (Devereaux). New York, Warner, 1988.
The Man Who Heard Too Much (Devereaux). New York, Warner, 1989.

OTHER PUBLICATIONS

Other

Fighting Jane: Mayor Jane Byrne and the Chicago Machine, with Lori Granger. New York, Dial Press, 1980.
The Magic Feather: The Truth about Special Education, with Lori Granger. New York, Dutton, 1986.

*   *   *

Bill Granger's November Man novels are the most critically acclaimed American spy series currently published. These outstanding espionage novels feature a middle-aged spy named

Devereaux—code name November Man—and his shadowy organization: R Section. R Section was formed by John F. Kennedy after the Bay of Pigs disaster to provide an independent audit of intelligence: "Who will watch the watchers? Who will spy upon the spies?" Kennedy demanded, and answered his own question by establishing R Section, hidden in the Department of Agriculture.

Granger's first novel, *The November Man,* introduces Devereaux as he investigates an IRA plot to kill one of England's most powerful men, Lord Slough. Complicating the plot is the involvement of a Russian agent and CIA treachery. Granger presents Devereaux as a loner, a professional spy who doesn't even trust his own agency—with good reason.

The November Man gained national publicity when the IRA assassinated Lord Louis Mountbatten by planting a bomb aboard Mountbatten's converted fishing boat on 27 August 1979. The novel's plot comes very close to predicting the motives and methods the IRA actually used in the Mountbatten assassination even though the book was finished in 1978.

The second November Man book, *Schism,* opens with an intriguing mystery: why would a priest—missing and presumed dead in Cambodia's jungles for over 20 years—reappear and suddenly be taken into CIA custody? Devereaux is assigned the job to discover the priest's secrets before the CIA does. But before he can, a woman reporter named Rita Macklin makes contact with the priest, and the Russians get involved. Before the book's end, Devereaux and Rita fall in love and risk death to tell the priest's secrets in order to avert a world war.

In *The Shattered Eye,* R Section's computer detects misinformation in the intelligence system; at the same time, the Russian's war game computer is manipulated to forecast a victory if they attack Europe. Devereaux is thrown into the middle of a plot to start World War II. *The Shattered Eye* is the most controlled of the November Man series.

The British Cross reunites Devereaux and Rita Macklin. A Russian defector promises to deliver a secret potent enough to threaten the superpower's governments. At the same time, Devereaux attempts to "retire" from R Section to live with Rita. But the rules of the espionage game require Devereaux to carry out this one last mission. Devereaux goes outside the system to deal with the secret, but the cost is a Russian assassination attempt on Rita and Devereaux at the book's conclusion.

The Zurich Numbers is the most revealing of the series. Devereaux's past, growing up in Chicago and being raised by his great-aunt Melvina, is revealed for the first time as he investigates the tangled web of immigrants who lead him to a broker in Zurich. Devereaux stumbles on a plot that threatens him and Rita.

Hemingway's Notebook features Devereaux's nemesis—Colonel Ready—in a plot to terminate both Devereaux and Rita. Events are set in motion to draw Devereaux and Rita out of hiding into a search for the secrets in the lost Hemingway notebook. Devereaux manages to turn the tables on Ready at the book's conclusion and convince KGB hunters that Ready is really the November Man they are ordered to terminate.

There Are No Spies begins with Devereaux's control in R Section—Hanley—having a "nervous breakdown" and being hospitalized in a government asylum. Hanley manages to get a cryptic message to Devereaux while a plot is unleashed to destroy both November Men—Colonel Ready and Devereaux. Plot and counterplot twist together in this most devious volume in the November Man series.

The Infant of Prague features Devereaux escorting a Czech defector through Belgium. But Colonel Ready captures both of them and sells them to the Czech secret police. But surprisingly, the buyer makes Devereaux a deal: his daughter has defected to America. If Devereaux returns her, then Rita Macklin—held hostage—will be released. Devereaux returns to the States but finds the plot involves more than the child: arms-smuggling and money-laundering between the CIA and a powerful television network executive are also involved. Only Devereaux's talent at sifting truth from fiction resolves the tangled plot.

Henry McGee Is Not Dead leads Devereaux to Alaska where he must discover whether former Agent Henry McGee is dead or alive. McGee's secrets could lead to a complete breakdown of American intelligence operations unless Devereaux discovers the truth about McGee and his stories. Subplots involve an Eskimo terrorist group which plans to attach an atomic bomb to the Alaskan pipeline and a corrupt woman politician whose only interests are sex and money.

Granger's latest November Man novel is *The Man Who Heard Too Much.* A Soviet defector brings some interesting information with him: the Russians have a computer program that is immune to computer viruses. The Russians plan to share this technology with the U.S. in return for a scaled down Star Wars program. But Henry McGee escapes from prison with the help of the Mafia and a secret tape of a treaty conference between the U.S. and the Russians ends up in the hands of a translator who sometimes works for the intelligence section of the Vatican. Devereaux has to find the missing tape, capture Henry McGee, and decide the truth of the stories of *The Man Who Heard Too Much.* This book also introduces the most bizarre character in the November Man series: a violent, disturbed woman named Rat who lives in the sewers under Berlin. Readers will want to see more of her in future November Man novels.

The best of Granger's other novels is the superb *Time for Frankie Coolin* written under the pseudonym "Bill Griffith." *Time for Frankie Coolin* is written in a tough, George V. Higgins style, that presents a small-time operator in Chicago in naturalistic detail. The portrait of the underside of the law and lawlessness Granger presents is utterly convincing.

Also notable are Granger's police procedurals—*Public Murders, Priestly Murders* and *Newspaper Murders* written under the pseudonym of "Joe Gash," and the best of the series, *The El Murders.* Police Detectives Terry Flynn and Karen Kovac investigate a series of crimes on the Chicago public transport system, chiefly a rape and the murder of a homosexual stockbroker. The bleakness of the underside of Chicago is captured in riveting detail and the scenes of the criminal justice system at work ring true.

Granger's early novels are flawed. *Sweeps* is a vicious attack on the way television news and the people who deliver it are manipulated by the pressure of television ratings. A psychopath is thrown into the muddled plot to keep the action moving, but the book never gels. *Queen's Crossing* could have been subtitled *Nazis on the Love Boat.* The *Queen Elizabeth II* leaves New York for England. Among the passengers is a former Nazi prison camp commander, a New York City homicide cop, an Israeli spy, a Russian assassin, and a wealthy Arab prince. The cardboard characters move through a silly plot that never really holds together.

Granger's best work is the long-running November Man series and the excellent, but little known, *Time for Frankie Coolin.* Granger does his best work when he spins off plots dealing with actual events and then extrapolates their consequences.

—George Kelley

GRANT-ADAMSON, Lesley (née Heycock). British. Born in London, 26 November 1942. Educated in London and Wales. Married Andrew Duncan Grant-Adamson in 1968. Editorial assistant, Leonard Hill Publishing, London, 1960; sub-editor, Thomson Publications, London, 1961–63; reporter, Palmers Green and Southgate *Gazette,* London, 1963–66; *The Citizen,* Gloucester, 1966–68; Rugby *Advertiser,* Warwickshire, 1968; Coventry *Telegraph,* Warwickshire, 1969–71; news editor, Herts *Advertiser,* Hertfordshire, 1971–73; feature writer, *The Guardian,* London, 1973–80; since 1980 freelance writer. Agent: Caroline Dawnay, Peters Fraser and Dunlop, 5th Floor, The Chambers, Chelsea Harbour, Lots Road, London SW10 OXF. Address: 30 Bewdley Street, London N1 1HB, England.

CRIME PUBLICATIONS

Novels (series: Rain Morgan)

Patterns in the Dust (Morgan). London, Faber, 1985; as *Death on Widows Walk,* New York, Scribner, 1985.
The Face of Death (Morgan). London, Faber, 1985; New York, Scribner, 1986.
Guilty Knowledge (Morgan). London, Faber, 1986; New York, St. Martin's Press, 1988.
Wild Justice (Morgan). London, Faber, 1987; New York, St. Martin's Press, 1988.
Threatening Eye. London, Faber, 1988; New York, St. Martin's Press, 1989.
Curse the Darkness (Morgan). London, Faber, and New York, St. Martin's Press, 1990.

Uncollected Short Stories

"Members of the Jury," in *New Welsh Review,* 1989.
"Ex Voto," in *Prima* (London), 1990.

OTHER PUBLICATIONS

Play

Radio Play: *A Reasonable Woman,* 1984.

*

Lesley Grant-Adamson comments:

Although several of my novels feature Fleet Street gossip columnist Rain Morgan they are very varied in form. For instance, *Patterns in the Dust,* which introduced her, is a classic English whodunnit whereas *The Face of Death,* which came next, is a psychological thriller. Actually I'm uneasy about the "crime" or "detective" label. "Suspense fiction" is more apt. When Faber and Faber bought my first book they asked for more stories about Rain Morgan and her black colleague, Holly Chase. I agreed, with the proviso that I should experiment with the crime genre. *Cursed the Darkness* is the most experimental, a long book in which I marry the whodunnit and the psychological thriller to make a wide-ranging contemporary novel about greed and social inequality. This is the most political of the novels, others, (such as *The Face of Death* and *Guilty Knowledge*) have taken overtly feminist themes.

Through them all I find certain themes recurring: characters are trapped, sometimes physically as in *Patterns in the Dust,* but more often in situations, as in *Curse the Darkness,* where a disguise that has become a danger cannot be dropped because of a greater risk un-disguised; social mobility and restlessness; the way people use beauty (music, paintings usually) to insulate themselves from the unpleasant things in their own and others' lives.

I'm very much a writer of realism and so I've been sceptical about the use of the professional private detective in English crime fiction. The detectives here haven't the scope of American private eyes, and neither do their authors. Despite this I've written *Flynn* (forthcoming), introducing a sparky London-Irish feminist Laura Flynn, who has her own private detective agency in Islington!

*   *   *

The five novels featuring Rain Morgan, an attractive and inquisitive gossip columnist with a taste for sleuthing, lends a degree of unity to Lesley Grant-Adamson's varied crime fiction. Rain has a habit of getting mixed up with murder to rival Miss Marple's, but although an element of mystery sparks Grant-Adamson's imagination, concocting elaborate puzzles has little appeal for her. She is not afraid to use the crime form as a medium for exploring contemporary social issues, although her stories are by no means didactic. In a short space of time she has progressed from the competent orthodoxy of *Patterns in the Dust* to the complexity of *Curse the Darkness,* which combines elements of the detective story, psychological suspense novel, and action thriller with a compassionate study of the effects of homelessness in modern London.

Rain is a celebrity whose photograph appears beside her column in the *Daily Post.* Her fame is often an asset, since in the course of her investigations she finds many people who are willing to talk frankly to a media personality. But there are drawbacks: she cannot choose anonymity and towards the end of *Curse the Darkness* she is taken hostage by two desperate killers who see in her a chance to escape the police net which has been closing in on them. This is not the only time Rain finds herself in danger as a result of being too curious. In *Patterns in the Dust,* having identified a double killer (not, in this case, too onerous a task), she has to confront and conquer her childhood fear of the dark when in the penultimate chapter the villain pursues her into an unlit village church. Someone tries to garrotte her in *Guilty Knowledge,* a story notable for an unusual murder motive—although it must be added that the killer is inadequately characterized and the story-line, involving art fraud and drug dealing, lacks sustained suspense despite a series of cliffhanging chapter endings.

Grant-Adamson excels at evoking place. Nether Hampton, the Somerset village in which Rain holidays during *Patterns in the Dust,* is splendidly real and so too are such contrasting locales as the housing estate where much of the action in *The Face of Death* occurs, an artistic community on the French Riviera in *Guilty Knowledge* and the bustling London scene of *Wild Justice.* Grant-Adamson achieves her effects not by piling on the descriptive detail but through short sharp sentences in which every word has to earn its keep. Sometimes she overdoes it. The bald opening paragraph of *Wild Justice* ("The proprietor of the *Daily Post* was found dead at his desk. He had owned the paper barely a month. He had been stabbed.") teeters on the brink of self-parody and the book as a whole is disappointing, save for its vivid realization of life on a daily newspaper.

As Grant-Adamson has gained in confidence, her books have become more ambitious. *The Face of Death* is an early attempt to blend a whydunnit with detection in which Rain plays only a subordinate part. Rain does not appear at all in *Threatening Eye,* a crisp story which, had the main characters been drawn in a little more depth, would have ranked high amongst modern novels of suspense. *Curse the Darkness* is much longer, but this time the page-turning pull never slackens. Rain's search for the truth about the death of a once-famous television writer is integrated without strain into an account of a novelist's stage-managed disappearance. Near the end of the book the novelist reflects: "Nobody set out in life with the aim of being a criminal, they had ends and adopted fatal means." Grant-Adamson has the ability unsentimentally to understand those ends, and to describe the fatal means with chilling but elegant economy.

—Martin Edwards

————

GRANT, Ambrose. *See* **CHASE, James Hadley.**

————

GRANT, Maxwell. *See* **COLLINS, Michael.**

————

GRAY, Dulcie. Pseudonym for Dulcie Winifred Catherine Denison, née Bailey. British. Born in Kuala Lumpur, Malaya, 20 November 1920. Educated at schools in England and Malaya, and at the Academy des Beaux Arts, London, and the Webber-Douglas Dramatic School, London. Married the actor Michael Denison in 1939. Actress from 1939. Recipient: Queen's Silver Jubilee Medal, 1977; *Times Educational Supplement* award, for non-fiction, 1978. C.B.E. (Commander, Order of the British Empire), 1983. Fellow, Royal Society of Arts, 1984. Agent: Douglas Rae, 28 Charing Cross Road, London WC2H 0DB. Address: Shardeloes, Amersham, Buckinghamshire, England.

CRIME PUBLICATIONS

Novels (series: Inspector Cardiff)

Murder on the Stairs.   London, Barker, 1957; New York, British Book Centre, 1958.
Murder in Melbourne.   London, Barker, 1958.
Baby Face.   London, Barker, 1959.
Epitaph for a Dead Actor (Cardiff).   London, Barker, 1960.
Murder on a Saturday.   London, Barker, 1961.
Murder in Mind.   London, Macdonald, 1963.
The Devil Wore Scarlet.   London, Macdonald, 1964.
No Quarter for a Star.   London, Macdonald, 1964.
The Murder of Love.   London, Macdonald, 1967.
Died in the Red (Cardiff).   London, Macdonald, 1968.
Murder on Honeymoon.   London, Macdonald, 1969.
For Richer for Richer.   London, Macdonald, 1970.
Deadly Lampshade.   London, Macdonald, 1971.
Understudy to Murder.   London, Macdonald, 1972.
Dead Give Away.   London, Macdonald, 1974.
Ride on a Tiger.   London, Macdonald and Jane's, 1975.
Dark Calypso.   London, Macdonald and Jane's, 1979.

Short Stories

Stage Door Fright.   London, Macdonald and Jane's, 1977.

OTHER PUBLICATIONS

Novels

The Glanville Women.   London, Joseph, 1982.
Anna Starr.   London, Joseph, 1984.
Mirror Image.   London, Joseph, 1987.

Plays

Love Affair (produced Birmingham, 1955; London, 1956).

Radio Plays (from her own novels): *Murder in Melbourne,* 1961; *The Devil Wore Scarlet,* 1964; *No Quarter for a Star,* 1965; *The Happy Honeymoon,* 1966; *Self-Defence,* 1970.

Other

The Actor and His World: A Young Person's Guide, with Michael Denison.   London, Gollancz, 1964.
Death in Denims (for children).   London, Everest, 1977.
Butterflies on My Mind: Their Life and Conservation in Britain Today.   Brighton, Angus and Robertson, 1978.

*

Theatrical Activities:

Actress: **Plays**—Sorrel Bliss in *Hay Fever* by Noël Coward, Aberdeen, 1939; in repertory with H.M. Tennent company, Edinburgh and Glasgow, 1940, and with Harrogate Repertory Company, 1940–41; Maria in *Twelfth Night,* Hermia in *A Midsummer Night's Dream,* and Bianca in *The Taming of the Shrew,* London, 1942; Alexandra Giddens in *The Little Foxes* by Lillian Hellman, London, 1942; Rose Wilson in *Brighton Rock* by Frank Harvey, London, 1943; Vivien in *Landslide* by Dorothy Albertyn and David Peel, London, 1943; Greta in *Lady from Edinburgh* by Aimée Stuart and L. Arthur Rose, London, 1945; Ruth Wilkins in *Dear Ruth* by Norman Krasna, London, 1946; Jean Ritchie in *The Wind Is Ninety* by Ralph Nelson, London, 1946; in *Fools Rush In* by Kenneth Horne, toured, 1946; Nurse Ransome in *Rain on the Just* by Peter Watling, London, 1948; Norah Fuller in *Queen Elizabeth Slept Here* by Talbot Rothwell, London, 1949; Agnes in *The Four-Poster* by Jan de Hartog, London, 1950, and toured South Africa, 1954–55; in *See You Later* (revue) by Sandy Wilson, London, 1951; Nina in *Dragon's Mouth* by J.B. Priestley and Jacquetta Hawkes, London, 1952; Robina Jevons in *Sweet Peril* by Mary Orr and Reginald Denham, London, 1952; Anna Lutcar in *The Distant Hill* by James Parish, tour, 1953; Toni Oberon in *We Must Kill Toni* by Ian Stuart Black, London, 1954; Mrs. Pooter in *The Diary of a Nobody* by Basil Dean and Richard Blake, London, 1954; the White Queen in *Alice Through the Looking-Glass* by Felicity Douglas, London, 1955, and Croydon, Surrey, 1972; Marion Field in *Love Affair,* Birmingham, 1955, and London, 1956; Lady Shotter in *South Sea Bubble* by Noël Coward, and Laura Reynolds in *Tea and Sympathy* by Robert Anderson, toured South Africa and Australia, 1956–57; Sarah Banning in *Double Cross* by John O'Hare, Richmond, Surrey, and London, 1958; title role in *Candida* by G.B. Shaw, Oxford, 1958, and Bath and London, 1960; Duchess of Hampshire in *Let Them Eat Cake* by

Frederick Lonsdale, London, 1959; Mary in *The Bald Prima Donna,* and Old Woman in *The Chairs,* both by Eugène Ionesco, Oxford, 1961; Lady Utterword in *Heartbreak House* by Shaw, Oxford and London, 1961; Z in *A Village Wooing* by G.B. Shaw (also London, 1970, and tour, 1971), and Lady Aline in *A Marriage Has Been Arranged* by Alfred Sutro, Hong Kong, 1962; in a Shakespeare Recital, Berlin, 1962; Katerina of Aragon in *Royal Gambit* by Hermann Gressieker, Croydon, Surrey, 1962; Caroline Abbott in *Where Angels Fear to Tread* by Elizabeth Hart, London, 1963; in *Merely Players* Shakespeare programme, toured, 1964; Madame Arkadina in *The Seagull* by Chekhov, Birmingham, 1964; Lady Chiltern in *An Ideal Husband* by Oscar Wilde, London, 1965; Maria Wislack in *On Approval* by Frederick Lonsdale, London, 1966; and in repertory with role of Susan in *Happy Family* by Giles Cooper, London, 1967; Julia Pyrton in *Number Ten* by Ronald Millar, London, 1967; May in *Vacant Possession* by Maisie Mosco and Yulya Glebova in *Confession at Night,* by Alexei Arbuzov, Nottingham, 1968; Celia Pilgrim in *Out of the Question* by Ira Wallach, London, 1968; Mrs. Banger in *Press Cuttings* by G.B. Shaw, London, 1970; Gina Ekdal in *The Wild Duck* by Ibsen, London, 1970; Mrs. Heidelberg in *The Clandestine Marriage* by George Colman the Elder and David Garrick, toured, 1971; Mrs. Alving in *Ghosts* by Ibsen, York, 1972; Ellen Blake in *The Dragon Variation* by Robert King, Windsor, 1972, and tour, 1973; Mabel Jackson in *At the End of the Day* by William Douglas Home, London, 1973; Grace Bishop in *The Sack Race* by George Ross and Campbell Singer, London, 1974; Olivia Cameron in *The Pay-Off* by William Fairchild, London, 1974 and 1975; Mrs. Conway in *Time and the Conways* by J.B. Priestley, toured 1976; Ellen Creed in *Ladies in Retirement* by Reginald Denham and Edward Percy, toured, 1976; Lady Twombley in *The Cabinet Minister* by A.W. Pinero, toured, 1977; Miss Marple in *A Murder Is Announced* by Agatha Christie, London, 1977; Delia in *Bedroom Farce* by Alan Ayckbourn, London, 1979; Evelyn in *The Kingfisher* by William Douglas Home, Windsor, 1980, and tour, 1981; Madame Ranevsky in *The Cherry Orchard* by Chekhov, Exeter, 1980; Lady Boothroyd in *Lloyd George Knew My Father* by William Douglas Home, tour, 1980; Sheila in *Relatively Speaking* by Alan Ayckbourn, Far Eastern tour, 1981; Lady Ashbrook in *Coat of Varnish* by Ronald Millar, London, 1982; Mrs. Cavell in *Cavell* by Keith Baxter, Chichester, 1982; Lady Sneerwell in *The School for Scandal* by R.B. Sheridan, London, 1983; Carlotta Gray in *A Song at Twilight* by Noël Coward, tour, 1983; Mrs. Candour in *The School for Scandal* by R.B. Sheridan, London, 1984, and European tour, 1984; Daphne in *There Goes the Bride* by Ray Cooney and John Chapman, Far Eastern tour, 1985; Miss Skillon in *See How They Run* by Philip King Windsor, 1986; Teresa Browne in *The Living Room* by Graham Greene, London, 1987; **Films**—*Victory Wedding,* 1944; *2,000 Women,* 1944; *Madonna of the Seven Moons,* 1944; *A Place of One's Own,* 1945; *They Were Sisters,* 1945; *Wanted for Murder* (*A Voice in the Night*), 1946; *The Years Between,* 1946; *A Man about the House,* 1947; *Mine Own Executioner,* 1947; *My Brother Jonathan,* 1948; *The Glass Mountain,* 1949; *The Franchise Affair,* 1951; *Angels One Five,* 1952; *There Was a Young Lady,* 1953; *A Man Could Get Killed,* 1965. **Radio**—*Front Line Family* serial, 1941, and other plays. **Television**—Kate Harvey in *Howard's Way* series, since 1985.

Manuscript Collection: Mugar Memorial Library, Boston University.

Dulcie Gray comments:
I started writing detective stories because I enjoyed reading them, and also because I admired Agatha Christie (as who does

not?). I started by writing "whodunits." By my third book, *Baby Face,* however, I found I was becoming less interested in providing a puzzle to be solved than in attempting to delve into the mind of my "criminal," and so began writing what might be called "whydunits." Of my 17 crime books, 11 are whodunits, one an adventure story, and five are crime novels (the last group involving careful character analysis). These five books—*Baby Face, Murder in Mind, The Murder of Love, For Richer for Richer,* and *Ride on a Tiger*—are all violent and perhaps horrifying. I find sick minds, whatever compassion I feel toward their owners, alarming when they destroy the innocent. Of the more conventional books, *Murder on a Saturday* is a horror story and the rest are fairly straightforward puzzles. *Butterflies on My Mind,* a carefully researched study of British butterflies and their conservation, was the book I most wanted to write.

* * *

Even if you did not know that Dulcie Gray is a star of the London stage (Agatha Christie's Miss Marple is among her many leading roles) you might perhaps guess it from her crime books. Some, of course, reflect that background, like *No Quarter for a Star* and *Epitaph for a Dead Actor.* But, first, her extraordinarily speakable dialogue indicates that it has been written by someone used to putting over words aloud. Yet this might be no more than a small-part actress writing. It is another quality that indicates the star: her zest and energy. Sometimes this is a little larger than life and careless even of everyday rules, so that in her pages it is no surprise to find a bank manager happily telling the police all about a client's affairs, though a real British bank manager finding himself doing that would be surprised indeed. She will, too, on occasion pile up necessary information, and sometimes more information than is strictly necessary, with a fine disregard for the proper methods of fiction.

But the zest is the main thing. It has enabled her to produce as many books as some full-time writers while simultaneously having a busy and successful theatrical career. And the books have not been throwaway efforts. They are in principle murder puzzles, but generally they are more. *The Murder of Love,* for instance, tackles the decidedly difficult theme of the relation between violence and sexual attraction. *Dead Give Away* probes the greed and jealousies of a family, and even shows the characters coming to see themselves for what they are.

—H.R.F. Keating

GRAY, Jonathan. *See* **ADAMS, Herbert.**

GRAY, Malcolm. *See* **STUART, Ian.**

GRAY, Russell. *See* **FISCHER, Bruno.**

GREELEY, Andrew M(oran). American. Born in Oak Park, Illinois, 5 February 1928. Educated at St. Mary of the Lake Seminary, A.B. 1950, S.T.B. 1952, S.T.L. 1954; University of Chicago, M.A. 1961, Ph.D. 1962. Ordained priest, Roman Catholic Church, 1954; assistant pastor, Church of Christ the King, Chicago, 1954–64; Program Director, National Opinion Research Center, Chicago, 1961–68; Lecturer of Sociology, 1963–72; Director, Center for the Study of American Pluralism, 1973, all University of Chicago; since 1978 Professor of Sociology, University of Arizona, Tucson. Since 1985 columnist, Chicago *Sun Times.* Recipient: Catholic Press Association award, 1965; Thomas Alva Edison award, for radio broadcast, 1963; National Catholic Education Association C. Albert Kobb award, 1977. LL.D St. Joseph's College, Rensselaer, Indiana, 1967; Litt.D. St. Mary's College, Winona, Minnesota, 1967. Address, c/o Warner Publishing Company, 666 Fifth Avenue, New York, New York 10103, U.S.A.

CRIME PUBLICATIONS

Novels (series: Monsignor John Blackwood Ryan)

Death in April. New York, McGraw Hill, 1980; London, Macdonald, 1987.
The Cardinal Sins. New York, Warner, and London, W.H. Allen, 1981.
Thy Brother's Wife. New York, Warner, and London, W.H. Allen, 1982.
Ascent Into Hell. New York, Warner, and London, W.H. Allen, 1983.
Lord of the Dance. New York, Warner, 1984; Bath, Chivers Press, 1985.
Virgin and Martyr: A Christmas Legend. New York, Warner, and London, Macdonald, 1985.
Happy Are the Meek (Ryan). New York, Warner, 1985; London, Macdonald, 1986.
Happy Are the Clean of Heart (Ryan). New York, Warner, 1986; London, Macdonald, 1987.
Angels of September. New York, Warner, and, London, Macdonald, 1986.
Patience of a Saint. New York, Warner, and London, Macdonald, 1987.
The Final Planet. New York, Warner, 1987; London, Century Hutchinson, 1988.
Rite of Spring. New York, Warner, 1987; London, Macdonald, 1988.
Happy Are Those Who Thirst for Justice (Ryan). New York, Mysterious Press, 1987; London, Severn House, 1988.
Angel Fire. New York, Warner, 1988.
Love Song. New York, Warner, 1989.
The Cardinal Virtues. New York, Warner, 1990.

Short Stories

All About Women. New York, Tor, 1990.

OTHER PUBLICATIONS

Novel

God Game. New York, Walker, and London, Century Hutchinson, 1986.

Other

The Church and the Suburbs. New York, Sheed and Ward, 1959; revised edition, New York, Paulist Press, 1963.
Strangers in the House: Catholic Youth in America. New York, Sheed and Ward, 1961; revised edition, New York, Image, 1967.
The Influence of Religion on the Career Plans and Occupational Values of June, 1961 College Graduates. n.p. 1962.
Religion and Career: A Study of College Graduates. New York, Sheed and Ward, 1963.
Priests for Tomorrow. Notre Dame, Indiana, Ave Maria Press, 1964.
And Young Men Shall See Visions: Letters from Andrew M. Greeley. New York, Sheed and Ward, 1964.
Letters to Nancy from Andrew M. Greeley. New York, Sheed and Ward, 1964; revised edition, New York, Image, 1967.
The Social Effects of Catholic Education, with Peter H. Rossi and Leonard J. Pinto. Chicago, National Opinion Research Center, 1964.
The Education of Catholic Americans, with Peter H. Rossi. Chicago, Aldine, 1966.
The Hesitant Pilgrim: American Catholicism After the Council. New York, Sheed and Ward, 1966.
Stratification and Social Conflict in American White Ethnic Groups, with Joe Spaeth. Chicago, National Opinion Research Center, 1967.
The Changing Catholic College, with William Van Cleve and Grace Ann Carroll. Chicago, Aldine, 1967.
The Catholic Experience: An Interpretation of the History of American Catholicism. New York, Doubleday, 1967.
The Crucible of Change: The Social Dynamics of Pastoral Practice. New York, Sheed and Ward, 1968.
Uncertain Trumpet: The Priest in Modern America. New York, Sheed and Ward, 1968.
What Do We Believe?, with Martin E. Marty. New York, Meredith Press, 1968.
The Future of the Christian Church in the 1970's, with Martin E. Marty. Fort George, Maryland, U.S. Army Chaplain Board, 1969.
Religion in the Year 2000. New York, Sheed and Ward, 1969.
Life for a Wanderer. New York, Doubleday, 1969.
A Future to Hope In: Socio-Religious Speculations. New York, Doubleday, 1969.
From Backwater to Mainstream: A Profile of Catholic Higher Education. New York, McGraw Hill, 1969.
Why Can't They Be Like Us?: Facts and Fallacies about Ethnic Differences and Group Conflicts in America. New York, Institute of Human Relations Press, 1969; revised edition as *Why Can't They Be Like Us?: America's White Ethnic Groups,* New York, Dutton, 1971.
Recent Alumni and Higher Education: A Survey of College Graduates, with Joe H. Spaeth. New York, McGraw Hill, 1970.
The Life of the Spirit Mind (also the Heart, the Libido) ... Kansas City, Missouri, National Catholic Reporter, 1970.
Can Catholic Schools Survive?. New York, Sheed and Ward, 1970.
Youth Asks, Does God Still Speak? Camden, New Jersey, Nelson, 1970.
New Horizons for the Priesthood. New York, Sheed and Ward, 1970.
The Friendship Game. New York, Doubleday, 1970.
Come Blow Your Mind with Me. New York, Doubleday, 1971.
The Jesus Myth. New York, Doubleday, 1971.

The Touch of the Spirit. New York, Herder, 1971.

Attitudes Towards Racial Integration, with Paul B. Sheatsley. San Francisco, Freeman, 1971.

A Fresh Look at Vocations. Chicago, Claretian, 197(?)

What a Modern Catholic Believes About God. Chicago, Thomas More Press, 1971.

That Most Distressful Nation: The Taming of the American Irish. Chicago, Quadrangle, 1972.

The Denominational Society: A Sociological Approach to Religion in America. Glenview, Illinois, Scott Foresman, 1972.

Priests in the United States: Reflections on a Survey. New York, Doubleday, 1972.

The Sinai Myth. New York, Doubleday, 1972.

The Church, the National Parish and Immigration: Same Old Mistakes. Staten Island, New York, Center for Migration Studies, 1972.

Teenage World: Its Crises and Anxieties. Techny, Illinois, Divine World, n.d.

Unsecular Man: The Persistence of Religion. New York, Schocken, 1972; London, SCM Press, 1973.

What a Modern Catholic Believes About the Church. Chicago, Thomas More Press, 1972.

The New Agenda. New York, Doubleday, 1973.

The Persistence of Religion. New York, Herder, and London, SCM Press, 1973.

Sexual Intimacy. Chicago, Thomas More Press, 1973.

Ecstasy: A Way of Knowing. Englewood Cliffs, New Jersey, Prentice Hall, 1974.

Ethnicity in the United States: A Preliminary Reconnaissance. New York, Wiley, 1974.

Building Coalitions: American Politics of the 1970's. New York, Viewpoint, 1974.

The Devil, You Say!: Man and His Personal Devil and Angels. New York, Doubleday, 1974.

Church as an Institution, with Gregory Baum. New York, Herder, 1974.

Media: Ethnic Media in the United States, with Douglas J. Zeman. Hanover, New Hampshire. Project Impress, 1974.

Love and Play. Chicago, Thomas More Press, 1975.

May the Wind Be at Your Back: The Prayer of St. Patrick. New York, Seabury Press, 1975.

The Sociology of the Paranormal: A Reconnaissance. Beverly Hills, California, Sage, 1975.

Ethnicity, Denomination and Inequality. Beverly Hills, California, Sage, 1976.

The Ultimate Values of the American Population, with William C. McCready. Beverly Hills, California, Sage, 1976.

Catholic Schools in a Declining Church, with William C. McCready and Kathleen McCourt. Kansas City, Missouri, Sheed and Ward, 1976.

The Communal Catholic: A Personal Manifesto. New York, Seabury Press, 1976.

Death and Beyond. Chicago, Thomas More Press, 1976.

The Great Mysteries: An Essential Catechism. New York, Seabury, 1976.

Nor, Maeve and Sebi (for children; with Diane Dawson). New York, Paulist Press, 1976.

The American Catholic: A Social Portrait. New York, Basic, 1977.

No Bigger Than Necessary: An Alternative to Socialism, Capitalism, and Anarchy. New York, New American Library, and London, New English Library, 1977.

The Mary Myth: On the Feminity of God. New York, Seabury Press, 1977.

Neighborhood. New York, Seabury Press, 1977.

An Ugly Litle Secret: Anti-Catholicism in North America. Kansas City, Missouri, Sheed Andrews and McMeel, 1977.

Christ for All Seasons, with Nancy McCready. Chicago, Thomas More Press, 1977.

Communication in the Church. New York, Seabury Press, 1978.

Everything You Wanted to Know About the Catholic Church But Were Too Pious to Ask. Chicago, Thomas More Press, 1978.

The Making of the Popes 1978: The Politics of Intrigue in the Vatican. Kansas City, Missouri, Andrews and McMeel, and London, Futura, 1979.

Crisis in the Church: A Study of Religion in America. Chicago, Thomas More Press, 1979.

The Family in Crisis or in Transition. New York, Seabury Press, 1979.

The Magic Cup: An Irish Legend. New York, McGraw Hill, 1979; London, Futura, 1984.

Ethnic Drinking Subcultures, with William C. McCready and Gary Theisen. New York, Praeger, 1980.

The Young Catholic Family. Chicago, Thomas More Press, 1980.

The Irish Americans: The Rise to Money and Power. New York, Harper, 1981.

The Religious Imagination. Los Angeles, Sadlier, 1981.

Religion: A Secular Theory. New York, Free Press, and London, Macmillan, 1982.

The Bottom Line Catechism for Contemporary Catholics. Chicago, Thomas More Press, 1982; London, W.H. Allen, 1983.

A Church to Come Home To, with Mary G. Durkin. Chicago, Thomas More Press, 1982.

Catholic High Schools and Minority Students. New Brunswick, New Jersey, Transaction, 1982.

A Piece of My Mind—On Just About Everything. New York, Doubleday, 1983.

Angry Catholic Women, with Mary G. Durkin. Chicago, Thomas More Press, 1984.

How to Save the Catholic Church. New York, Viking, 1984.

American Catholics Since the Council. Chicago, Thomas More Press, 1985.

Confessions of a Parish Priest. New York, Simon and Schuster, 1986.

Catholic Contributions. Chicago, Thomas More Press, 1987.

The Incarnate Imagination. Bowling Green, Ohio, Popular Press, 1988.

When Life Hurts. Chicago, Thomas More Press, 1988.

Conversations with Andrew M. Greeley. Boston, Quinlan Press, 1988.

God in Popular Culture. Chicago, Thomas More Press, 1988.

Religious Change in America. Cambridge, Massachusetts, Harvard University Press, 1989.

Myths of Religion. New York, Warner, 1989.

The Bible and Us: A Priest and a Rabbi Read Scripture Together, with Jacob Neusner. New York, Warner, 1990.

The Catholic Myth: The Behaviour and Beliefs of American Catholics. New York, Scribner, 1990.

* * *

Father Andrew M. Greeley—the "writer-priest"—a natural storyteller trained as a sociologist—defies classification as a priest, as a sociologist, as a writer. Is he a writer who by vocation is a priest, or a priest who happens to be a writer? A prolific author, Father Greeley has conducted countless surveys on issues related to American Catholicism, e.g. birth control, the role of the Church in the lives of American

Catholics, ethnicity, etc. His findings are written not only for the scholars but, more importantly, for the general audience, and they reappear in a slightly different form in his novels.

It is not possible to separate the writer, the priest, the sociologist when one reads a Greeley novel. All the strands come together in a well-written, compelling, and usually sensational story. Father Greeley's best-selling novels (*The Cardinal Sins, Thy Brother's Wife, Ascent into Hell, Lord of the Dance, Virgin and Martyr*) are impossible to set aside for many reasons. He writes about people he knows well: Irish Catholics, usually of successful middle-class backgrounds in Chicago— who even if they have left their neighborhoods and are lax about Church attendance—cannot forget the forces which shaped them. Sex is a pivotal factor in Father Greeley's novels; in fact, there have been many references to the "steamy sex" of his fiction. For those who are familiar with Father Greeley's work as a priest and a sociologist, the sexual passages of *Thy Brother's Wife, The Cardinal Sins,* etc. may be seen as the fictional representation of his thesis that sexual intimacy is a major problem facing most married couples who need the sustenance of a vigorous physical relationship without guilt.

Finally, Father Greeley's novels highlight the tensions in the Church caused by Vatican II. The "old" and the "new" Catholicism, in simplistic terms, created crises for priests, parishioners, entire religious orders, as well as for the older and younger generations.

For mystery aficionados who like series characters, Father Greeley's priest-detective, the Reverend Monsignor John Blackwood Ryan, S.T.L., Ph.D., better known as Blackie Ryan, is a colorful addition to the genre. Initially, comparisons may be made with television's Father Dowling or William X. Kienzle's Father Bob Koesler. Blackie Ryan is not the cherubic Colombo-like Dowling or the more action oriented Koesler. Ryan is reflective and more removed from the action throughout most of his cases. Greeley uses the confessional mode as the means of laying out the story, analyzing the clues, and identifying the murderer. The story is told many times from varying points of view by the different suspects, in accounts interspersed with Blackie's own chapters of reflection and analysis. If one word could be used to describe the content of these revelations beyond the events themselves, it would be "secret." Through these confessions, the secrets of the victim, the sins of the suspects, their doubts about marriage, sex, raising children, belonging to the Church, the essence of their Irishness, and their feelings about their families surface. *Happy Are the Meek* introduces the family of Wolfe Quinlan who is found murdered in a locked room which houses a miniature museum of medieval artifacts. Unpleasant stories are revealed about infidelity, incest, a battered wife, and membership in a religious cult with an aberrant sexual orientation. In *Happy Are the Clean of Heart,* the attempted murder of Blackie's first girlfriend, Lisa Malone, a successful entertainer and film star, promotes an unburdening of sexual secrets and draws out the feelings of jealousy, envy, and resentment harbored by people from her old Chicago neighborhood. In *Happy Are Those Who Thirst for Justice,* the murder of Violet Enright, matriarch of a Chicago Irish family, serves as the occasion for the revelation of secrets about family rivalry, sexual inadequacy, and the games people play to avoid becoming the target of a malicious woman whose power over her children ruins their lives. In all three novels, Blackie Ryan is the priest who helps people work out the penitential rite or the sacrament of reconciliation. Greeley's approach is the same technique used by Robert Browning in *The Ring and the Book* which may be described as a murder mystery in poetic form. Although Greeley does not allude to Browning's structure in the preface of any of the

novels, he does quote from the poem in the first novel in the series, *Happy Are the Meek.*

Unity is achieved in the series through the characters, the locale, and the thematic use of the Beatitudes from the Sermon on the Mount. The main character, of course, is Father Blackie Ryan, rector of Holy Name Cathedral, who completed his Ph.D. in philosophy by writing a thesis on William James. Blackie is very close to his family, and his parents, brothers and sisters who are frequent and active participants in the series as is Sean Cronin, the archbishop of Chicago. Blackie is known as a staunch supporter of Chicago's football and baseball teams; his ties to his old Irish-American neighborhood in Chicago are usually the reason for his becoming involved in the crimes he has to unravel. Greeley's portrayal of the characters and the locale are drawn with feeling because he writes about what he knows best.

In a preface to each of the novels, Greeley explains the beatitudes, the eight blessings pronounced by Christ in the Sermon on the Mount, and recorded by Saint Matthew (whose version Greeley uses) and Saint Luke. The beatitudes used thus far by Greeley are the second ("Blessed are the meek, for they shall possess the earth"); the sixth ("Blessed are the clean of heart, for they shall see God"); and the fourth ("Blessed are they who hunger and thirst for justice, for they shall be satisfied.") Greeley works out the paradigm of each beatitude through the development of the plot line and the resolution of the crime. His intention is to demonstrate the beatitudes as "descriptive, not normative" ways of living a moral life. The preface to each novel as well as Blackie's reflections on and explanations of the beatitudes within the context of the plot lines constitute sermons or homilies. With this in mind, Father Greeley's comment in his latest book, *The Catholic Myth: The Behavior and Beliefs of American Catholics* brings us full-circle to the writer-priest: "Note the ironic paradox: The parish is the church of the people, and the priest is the parish, and the homily is the priest (the most important contact the priest has with his people), yet the people rank the quality of the homily very low." Blackie Ryan's homilies are of excellent quality, and he owes readers at least five more.

—Katherine M. Restaino

GREEN, Anna Katharine. American. Born in Brooklyn, New York, 11 November 1846. Educated in public schools in New York City and Buffalo; Ripley Female College, Poultney, Vermont, B.A. 1867. Married Charles Rohlfs in 1884; one daughter and two sons. Lived most of her life in Buffalo. *Died 11 April 1935.*

CRIME PUBLICATIONS

Novels (series: Ebenezer Gryce; Caleb Sweetwater)

The Leavenworth Case: A Lawyer's Story (Gryce). New York, Putnam, 1878; London, Routledge, 1884.
A Strange Disappearance (Gryce). New York, Putnam, 1880; London, Routledge, 1884.
The Sword of Damocles: A Story of New York. New York, Putnam, 1881; London, Ward Lock, 1884.
XYZ. New York, Putnam, and London, Ward Lock, 1883.
Hand and Ring (Gryce). New York, Putnam, 1883; London, Ward Lock, 1884.
The Mill Mystery. New York, Putnam, and London, Routledge, 1886.

7 to 12. New York, Putnam, and London, Routledge, 1887.

Behind Closed Doors (Gryce). New York, Putnam, and London, Routledge, 1888.

The Forsaken Inn. New York, Bonner, and London, Routledge, 1890.

A Matter of Millions (Gryce). New York, Bonner, and London, Routledge, 1890.

Cynthia Wakeham's Money. New York, Putnam, 1892; London, Ward Lock, 1904.

Marked "Personal." New York, Putnam, 1893; London, Ward Lock, 1904.

Miss Hurd: An Enigma. New York, Putnam, 1894.

The Doctor, His Wife, and the Clock (Gryce). New York, Putnam, and London, Allen and Unwin, 1895.

Doctor Izard. New York, Putnam, and London, Cassell, 1895.

That Affair Next Door (Gryce). New York, Putnam, 1897; London, Nash, 1903.

Lost Man's Lane: A Second Episode in the Life of Amelia Butterworth (Gryce). New York, Putnam, 1898.

Agatha Webb (Sweetwater). New York, Putnam, 1899; London, Ward Lock, 1900.

The Circular Study (Gryce). New York, McClure, 1900; London, Ward Lock, 1902.

One of My Sons (Gryce). New York, Putnam, 1901; London, Ward Lock, 1904.

Three Women and a Mystery. New York, Lovell, 1902.

The Filigree Ball. Indianapolis, Bobbs Merrill, 1903; London, Allen and Unwin, 1904.

The Millionaire Baby. Indianapolis, Bobbs Merrill, and London, Chatto and Windus, 1905.

The Amethyst Box. Indianapolis, Bobbs Merrill, and London, Chatto and Windus, 1905.

The Woman in the Alcove (Sweetwater). Indianapolis, Bobbs Merrill, and London, Chatto and Windus, 1906.

The Chief Legatee. New York, Authors and Newspapers Association, 1906; as *A Woman of Mystery,* London, Collier, 1909.

The Mayor's Wife. Indianapolis, Bobbs Merrill, 1907; London, Daily Mail, 1909.

The House of the Whispering Pines (Sweetwater). New York, Putnam, and London, Nash, 1910.

Three Thousand Dollars. Boston, Badger Gorham Press, 1910.

Initials Only (Gryce; Sweetwater). New York, Dodd Mead, 1911; London, Nash, 1912.

Dark Hollow. New York, Dodd Mead, and London, Nash, 1914.

The Mystery of the Hasty Arrow (Gryce; Sweetwater). New York, Dodd Mead, 1917.

The Step on the Stair. New York, Dodd Mead, and London, Lane, 1923.

Short Stories

The Old Stone House and Other Stories. New York, Putnam, 1891.

A Difficult Problem and Other Stories. New York, Lupton, 1900; London, Ward Lock, 1903.

The House in the Mist. Indianapolis, Bobbs Merrill, 1905.

Masterpieces of Mystery. New York, Dodd Mead, 1913; as *Room Number 3 and Other Stories,* 1919.

The Golden Slipper and Other Problems for Violet Strange. New York, Putnam, 1915.

To the Minute and Scarlet and Black: Two Tales of Life's Perplexities. New York, Putnam, 1916.

OTHER PUBLICATIONS

Play

Risifi's Daughter. New York, Putnam, 1887.

Verse

The Defense of the Bride and Other Poems. New York, Putnam, 1882.

*

Manuscript Collection: Humanities Research Center, University of Texas, Austin.

* * *

A contemporary British review said of Anna Katharine Green that she had "proved herself able to write an interesting story of mysterious crime as well as any man living." However, tastes change, and Green's books no longer appeal to many modern readers. She is a prime example of the author who for much of her career, was a household word; now, her name is known only by scholars of popular fiction and by superannuated library-goers. When Green published her first book, *The Leavenworth Case,* the New York papers assumed the author was a man. This was 1878 and Wilkie Collins, for one, was still producing novels. She published simultaneously with Doyle, Bailey, Rohmer, Freeman, Rinehart, and the early Christie. Yet we read Collins and Doyle and Rohmer today and Green is forgotten. For one thing, Green, for all her mechanical skills, lacked both divine genius and the genius of immutable schlock. Her books reveal a talent that is *too* hardworking, *too* earnest, *too* grounded in the tradition of heavy-breathing melodramas in which orphans and wills and madness are the primary ingredients, and in which pale, beautiful women are always giving low, thrilling laughs from beneath dark veils. There *are* crimes and clues aplenty, as well as a respectable amount of deduction, but, by modern standards, these elements are tainted and slowed down by pathos and sentimentality.

Nonetheless, the genteel woman is a significant figure in the history of the genre. Odd as it may seem, *The Leavenworth Case* brought middle-class respectability and a wider readership to the mystery novel. For this achievement—perhaps more of a social than a strictly professional one—Green is often referred to as the "mother of the detective story." *The Leavenworth Case* introduces Green's best-known detective, Ebenezer Gryce, of the New York police force. It makes use of a number of devices that were to become staples of the genre: a map of the scene of the crime, lists of deductions and possibilities, headlines to show the developments of the case. The young lawyer-narrator, in a foreshadowing of the amorous susceptibilities of Watson and Hastings, falls in love with one of the comely suspects. With its treatment of murder amid polite Manhattan society (the same milieu which provides the background of a novelist to whom Anthony Boucher has compared Green—Edith Wharton), its refined luridness caused it to become a bestseller and launched Green as a writer to be imitated.

In addition to the "portly comfortable" Gryce, Green created two other sleuths worthy of note. Both are women: one, the elderly and excessively nosy Miss Amelia Butterworth, first appears in *That Affair Next Door,* joining Gryce in his investigation; the other, Violet Strange, is a dainty girl detective whose cases are chronicled in *The Golden Slipper and Other Problems for Violet Strange.* Moreover, both can be seen as prototypes, Miss Butterworth for the Jane Marples and

Maud Silvers, and Violet Strange for the Nancy Drews.

With regard to Mr. Gryce, it is interesting to pay attention to the changing manner in which Green presents him as the years pass. In *The Circular Study,* 22 years after his debut, he is said to be needing fresh challenges to keep him from retiring to a farm. By 1917, in *The Mystery of the Hasty Arrow,* he arrives on the scene in an automobile, being physically weak but with his mental powers undimmed. Like Green's own, Mr. Gryce's was a long and honorable career. (Here, the similarities to Christie and to Poirot must be noted.)

For all of her longevity and productivity, Green left behind a legacy that is now dimmed in the light of her many successors. But one evocative sentence, uttered by Miss Butterworth, is an inheritance for which all mystery fans should be grateful: "For though I have had no adventures, I feel capable of them."

—Michele Slung

GREENE, Graham. British. Born in Berkhamsted, Hertfordshire, 2 October 1904. Educated at Berkhamsted School; Balliol College, Oxford. Served in the Foreign Office, London, 1941–44. Married Vivien Dayrell-Browning in 1927; one son and one daughter. Staff Member, *The Times,* London 1926–30; film critic, 1937–40, and literary editor, 1940–41, *Spectator,* London. Director, Eyre and Spottiswoode, publishers, London, 1944–48, and The Bodley Head, publishers, London, 1958–68. Member, Panamanian Canal Treaty Delegation to Washington, 1977. Recipient: Hawthornden prize, 1941; James Tait Black Memorial prize, 1949; Shakespeare prize (Hamburg), 1968; Thomas More Medal, 1973; Dos Passos prize, 1980; City of Madrid Medal, 1980; Jerusalem prize, 1981; Litt.D.: Cambridge University, 1962; D.Litt.: Edinburgh University, 1967; Oxford University, 1979. Honorary Fellow, Balliol College, 1963. Honorary Citizen, Anacapri, 1978. Companion of Honour, 1966. Chevalier, Legion of Honour (France), 1967; Grand Cross, Order of Balboa (Panama), 1983; Commandant, Order of Arts and Letters (France), 1984; Companion of Literature, Royal Society of Literature, 1984; O.M. (Order of Merit), 1986; Order of Ruben Dario (Nicaragua), 1987. Address: c/o Reinhardt Books Ltd., 27 Wrights Lane, London W8 5TZ, England.

CRIME PUBLICATIONS

Novels

The Man Within. London, Heinemann, and New York, Doubleday, 1929.
The Name of Action. London, Heinemann, 1930; New York, Doubleday, 1931.
Rumour at Nightfall. London, Heinemann, 1931; New York, Doubleday, 1932.
Stamboul Train. London, Heinemann, 1932; as *Orient Express,* New York, Doubleday, 1933.
It's a Battlefield. London, Heinemann, and New York, Doubleday, 1934; revised edition, Heinemann, 1948; New York, Viking Press, 1962.
England Made Me. London, Heinemann, and New York, Doubleday, 1935; as *The Shipwrecked,* New York, Viking Press, 1953.
A Gun for Sale: An Entertainment. London, Heinemann, 1936; as *This Gun for Hire,* New York, Doubleday, 1936.

Brighton Rock. London, Heinemann, 1938; as *Brighton Rock: An Entertainment,* New York, Viking Press, 1938.
The Confidential Agent: An Entertainment. London, Heinemann, and New York, Viking Press, 1939.
The Power and the Glory. London, Heinemann, 1940; as *The Labyrinthine Ways,* New York, Viking Press, 1940.
The Ministry of Fear: An Entertainment. London, Heinemann, and New York, Viking Press, 1943.
The Heart of the Matter. London, Heinemann, and New York, Viking Press, 1948.
The Third Man. New York, Viking Press, 1950.
The Third Man, and The Fallen Idol. London, Heinemann, 1950.
The End of the Affair. London, Heinemann, and New York, Viking Press, 1951.
Loser Takes All. London, Heinemann, 1955; New York, Viking Press, 1957.
The Quiet American. London, Heinemann, 1955; New York, Viking Press, 1956.
Our Man in Havana: An Entertainment. London, Heinemann, and New York, Viking Press, 1958.
A Burnt-Out Case. London, Heinemann, and New York, Viking Press, 1961.
The Comedians. London, Bodley Head, and New York, Viking Press, 1966.
Travels with My Aunt. London, Bodley Head, 1969; New York, Viking Press, 1970.
The Honorary Consul. London, Bodley Head, and New York, Simon and Schuster, 1973.
The Human Factor. London, Bodley Head, and New York, Simon and Schuster, 1978.
Doctor Fischer of Geneva; or, The Bomb Party. London, Bodley Head, and New York, Simon and Schuster, 1980.
Monsignor Quixote. London, Bodley Head, and New York, Simon and Schuster, 1982.
The Tenth Man. London, Bodley Head, and New York, Simon and Schuster, 1985.
The Captain and the Enemy. London, Reinhardt, 1988.

Short Stories

The Basement Room and Other Stories. London, Cresset Press, 1935.
Nineteen Stories. London, Heinemann, 1947; New York, Viking Press, 1949; augmented edition, as *Twenty-One Stories,* Heinemann, 1954; Viking Press, 1962; selection, as *Across the Bridge and Other Stories,* Bath, Chivers, 1981.
A Sense of Reality. London, Bodley Head, and New York, Viking Press, 1963.

OTHER PUBLICATIONS

Short Stories

The Bear Fell Free. London, Grayson, 1935.
24 Short Stories, with James Laver and Sylvia Townsend Warner. London, Cresset Press, 1939.
A Visit to Morin. London, Heinemann, 1959.
May We Borrow Your Husband? and Other Comedies of the Sexual Life. London, Bodley Head, and New York, Viking Press, 1967.
The Collected Stories of Graham Greene. London, Bodley Head-Heinemann, 1972; New York, Viking Press, 1973.
How Father Quixote Became a Monsignor. Los Angeles, Sylvester and Orphanos, 1980.
The Last Word. London, Reinhardt, 1990.

Plays

The Living Room (produced London, 1953; New York, 1954). London, Heinemann, 1953; New York, Viking Press, 1954.
The Potting Shed (produced New York, 1957). New York, Viking Press, 1957; revised version (produced London, 1958), London, Heinemann, 1958.
The Complaisant Lover (produced London, 1959; New York, 1961). London, Heinemann, 1959; New York, Viking Press, 1961.
Carving a Statue (produced London, 1964; New York 1968). London, Bodley Head, 1964.
The Third Man: A Film, with Carol Reed. London, Lorrimer Films, 1968; New York, Simon and Schuster, 1969.
Alas, Poor Maling, adaptation of his own story (televised, 1975). Published in *Shades of Greene,* London, Bodley Head-Heinemann, 1975.
The Return of A.J. Raffles: An Edwardian Comedy Based Somewhat Loosely on E.W. Hornung's Characters in "The Amateur Cracksman" (produced London, 1975). London, Bodley Head, 1975; New York, Simon and Schuster, 1976.
Yes and No, and For Whom the Bell Chimes (produced Leicester, 1980). London, Bodley Head, 1983.
The Great Jowett (broadcast, 1980). London, Bodley Head, 1981.

Screenplays: *The First and the Last* (*21 Days*), 1937; *The New Britain,* 1940; *Brighton Rock* (*Young Scarface*), with Terence Rattigan, 1947; *The Fallen Idol,* with Lesley Storm and William Templeton, 1948; *The Third Man,* with Carol Reed, 1950; *The Stranger's Hand,* with Guy Elmes and Giorgio Bassani, 1954; *Loser Takes All,* 1956; *Saint Joan,* 1957; *Our Man in Havana,* 1960; *The Comedians,* 1967.

Radio Play: *The Great Jowett,* 1980.

Television Play: *Alas, Poor Maling,* 1975.

Verse

Babbling April. Oxford, Blackwell, 1925.
For Christmas. Privately printed, 1951.

Other

Journey Without Maps. London, Heinemann, and New York, Doubleday, 1936.
The Lawless Roads: A Mexican Journey. London, Longman, 1939; as *Another Mexico,* New York, Viking Press, 1939.
British Dramatists. London, Collins, 1942; included in *The Romance of English Literature,* New York, Hastings House, 1944.
The Little Train (for children; published anonymously). London, Eyre and Spottiswoode, 1946; as Graham Greene, New York, Lothrop, 1958.
Why Do I Write? An Exchange of Views Between Elizabeth Bowen, Graham Greene, and V.S. Pritchett. London, Marshall, and New York, British Book Centre, 1948.
After Two Years. Privately printed, 1949.
The Little Fire Engine, (for children). London, Parrish, 1950; as *The Little Red Fire Engine,* New York, Lothrop, 1953.
The Lost Childhood and Other Essays. London, Eyre and Spottiswoode, 1951; New York, Viking Press, 1952.
The Little Horse Bus (for children). London, Parrish, 1952; New York, Lothrop, 1954.
The Little Steamroller: A Story of Adventure, Mystery, and Detection (for children). London, Parrish, 1953; New York, Lothrop, 1955.

Essais Catholiques, translated by Marcelle Sibon. Paris, Seuil, 1953.
In Search of a Character: Two African Journals. London, Bodley Head, 1961; New York, Viking Press, 1962.
The Revenge: An Autobiographical Fragment. Privately printed, 1963.
Victorian Detective Fiction: A Catalogue of the Collection Made by Dorothy Glover and Graham Greene. London, Bodley Head, 1966.
Collected Essays. London, Bodley Head, and New York, Viking Press, 1969.
A Sort of Life (autobiography). London, Bodley Head, and New York, Simon and Schuster, 1971.
The Virtue of Disloyalty. Privately printed, 1972.
The Pleasure-Dome: The Collected Film Criticism 1935–40, edited by John Russell Taylor. London, Secker and Warburg, 1972; as *Graham Greene on Film: Collected Film Criticism 1935–1940,* New York, Simon and Schuster, 1972.
The Portable Graham Greene, edited by Philip Stratford. New York, Viking Press, 1973; London, Penguin, 1977.
Lord Rochester's Monkey, Being the Life of John Wilmot, Second Earl of Rochester. London, Bodley Head, and New York, Viking Press, 1974.
Ways of Escape. London, Bodley Head, 1980; New York, Simon and Schuster, 1981.
J'Accuse: The Dark Side of Nice (bilingual edition). London, Bodley Head, 1982.
A Quick Look Behind: Footnotes to an Autobiography. Los Angeles, Sylvester and Orphanos, 1983.
Getting to Know the General: The Story of an Involvement. London, Bodley Head, and New York, Simon and Schuster, 1984.
Graham Greene Country, paintings by Paul Hogarth. London, Pavilion-Joseph, 1986.
Why the Epigraph? London, Reinhardt, 1989.
Yours Etc.: Letters to the Press, edited by Christopher Haetree. London, Reinhardt, 1989; New York, Viking-Reinhardt, 1990.
Graham Greene: Reflections 1923–88, edited by Judith Adamson. London, Reinhardt, 1990.

Editor, *The Old School: Essays by Divers Hands.* London, Cape, 1934.
Editor, *The Best of Saki.* London, Lane, 1950; New York, Viking Press, 1961.
Editor, with Hugh Greene, *The Spy's Bedside Book: An Anthology.* London, Hart Davis, 1957.
Editor, *The Bodley Head Ford Madox Ford.* London, Bodley Head, 4 vols., 1962, 1963.
Editor, *An Impossible Woman: The Memories of Dottoressa Moor of Capri.* London, Bodley Head, 1975; New York, Viking Press, 1976.
Editor, with Hugh Greene, *Victorian Villainies: Four Classic Victorian Tales.* London, Viking, 1984; New York, Viking, 1985.

*

Bibliography: *Graham Greene: A Checklist of Criticism* by J.D. Vann, Kent, Ohio, Kent State University Press, 1970; *Graham Greene: A Descriptive Catalog* by Robert H. Miller, Lexington, University Press of Kentucky, 1978; *Graham Greene: A Bibliography and Guide to Research* by R.A. Wobbe, New York, Garland, 1979; *Graham Greene: An Annotated Bibliography of Criticism* by A.F. Cassis, Metuchen, New Jersey, Scarecrow Press, 1981.

Manuscript Collection: Humanities Research Center, University of Texas, Austin.

Critical Studies (selection): *Graham Greene and the Heart of the Matter* by Marie Mesnet, London, Cresset Press, 1954; *Graham Greene* by Francis Wyndham, London, Longman, 1955, revised edition, 1958; *Graham Greene* by John Atkins, London, Calder, and New York, Roy, 1957, revised edition, London, Calder and Boyars, 1966, New York, Humanities Press, 1967; *The Labyrinthine Ways of Graham Greene* by Francis Leo Kunkel, New York, Sheed and Ward, 1960, revised edition, Mamaroneck, New York, Appel, 1973; *Graham Greene* by David Pryce-Jones, Edinburgh, Oliver and Boyd, 1963, New York, Barnes and Noble, 1968; *Graham Greene: Some Critical Considerations* (includes bibliography by N. Brennan) edited by Robert O. Evans, Lexington, University of Kentucky Press, 1963; *Graham Greene* by A.A. DeVitis, New York, Twayne, 1964; *Graham Greene* by David Lodge, New York, Columbia University Press, 1966; *Graham Greene: A Critical Essay* by Martin Turnell, Grand Rapids, Michigan, Eerdmans, 1967; *Graham Greene: The Aesthetics of Exploration* by Gwenn R. Boardman, Gainesville, University of Florida Press, 1971; *Graham Greene the Entertainer* by Peter Wolfe, Carbondale, Southern Illinois University Press, 1972; *Graham Greene: A Collection of Critical Essays* edited by Samuel Hynes, Englewood Cliffs, New Jersey, Prentice Hall, 1973; *Graham Greene the Novelist* by J.P. Kulshrestha, Delhi, Macmillan, and Atlantic Highlands, New Jersey, Humanities Press, 1977; *The Other Man: Conversations with Graham Greene* by Marie Françoise Allain, London, Bodley Head, and New York, Simon and Schuster, 1983; *Graham Greene* by John Spurling, London, Methuen, 1983; *Saints, Sinners, and Comedians: The Novels of Graham Greene* by Roger Sharrock, Tunbridge Wells, Kent, Burns and Oates, 1984; *Graham Greene* by Richard Kelley, New York, Ungar, 1985; *The Achievement of Graham Greene* by Grahame Smith, Brighton, Sussex, Harvester Press, 1985, New York, Barnes and Noble, 1986; *Graham Greene: His Mind and Art* by B.P. Lambo, New Delhi, Sterling, 1987; *A Reader's Guide to Graham Greene* by Paul O'Prey, London, Thames and Hudson, 1988; *Graham Greene: On the Frontier: Politics and Religion in the Novels* by Maria Cuoto, London, Macmillan, 1988; *Graham Greene* by Neil MacEwan, London, Macmillan, 1988; *An Underground Fate: The Idiom of Romance in the Later Novels of Graham Greene* by Brian Thomas, Athens, University of Georgia Press, 1988; *The Life of Graham Greene: Vol. 1 1904–1939* by Vincent Sherry, London, Cape, and New York, Viking, 1989; *Graham Greene: A Reevaluation* edited by Jeffrey Meyers, London, Macmillan, 1990; *Graham Greene: The Dangerous Edge* by Judith Adamson, London, Macmillan, 1990.

Theatrical Activities:

Actor: **Film**—*La Nuit americaine* (*Day for Night*), 1973.

*   *   *

Crime is a dominant element in most of Graham Greene's fictions, whether he calls them "entertainments" or "novels." In fact, the boundary between the two kinds of books is as ambiguous as the real frontiers that figure in so many of them. For Greene in all his books is a superb storyteller, which is one of the reasons why he has a considerable popular appeal as well as being regarded as one of the most important serious writers of his period. Adventure and suspense are constant elements in his novels as well as his entertainments, and in both of them his characters usually find their way into difficult physical predicaments that parallel moral crises. In everything he writes Greene is a master at creating memorable backgrounds drawn from the memories of a life of restless travel; the Cuba of *Our Man in Havana*, the Mexico of *The Power and the Glory*, the Vietnam of *The Quiet American*, the Argentina-Paraguay frontier of *The Honorary Consul*, and no less striking is the exotic feeling Greene can give with his unerring eye for the seedy and the eccentric to the strange places he makes out of familiar ones, like the Brighton of *Brighton Rock* and the London of *The Ministry of Fear*. Always, whether it is manifest in action or merely thickens the air, one is aware of evil as a constant presence in Greene's worlds: "Hell lay about them in their infancy," he remarked in his travel book on Mexico, *The Lawless Roads*, and his writings lead one to assume that for his characters its presence is lifelong.

Perhaps the main difference between the novels and the entertainments, of which *Stamboul Train, A Gun for Sale,* and *The Confidential Agent* are typical, is that in these books action is dominant and constant. They are authentic thrillers in the sense that in them we become involved in the plights of hunted men who in one way or another are social outcasts, whether they are criminals in the literal sense of being professional killers, like the gunman in *A Gun for Sale,* or in the legalistic sense of being leaders of revolutionary groups or of wrong sides in civil wars, like Dr. Czinner in *Stamboul Train* and D. in *The Confidential Agent.* The moral issue is there, as it always is in Graham Greene's books; he was a typical man of the Thirties in the way he symbolized political or ethical conflicts in terms of frontiers and police, of gun-battles and no less lethal betrayals, of life on the run, and his entertainments can indeed be read for their excitement alone.

It is a different matter with the books he calls novels. They too involve one in action, often in pursuit, and usually with crime and criminals, though the latter are not always the main characters. In *Brighton Rock* a stool pigeon is murdered by a petty race-track gang dominated by a teenage boy driven by evil. In *The Power and the Glory* a drunken priest continues to pursue his vocation in a Mexican state where practicing Christianity is forbidden under penalty of death, and he is eventually caught and shot. In *The Heart of the Matter* a British police chief in a wartime West African town, tempted by bribing smugglers, connives at a murder, commits adultery, and finally kills himself. In *England Made Me* a group of English semi-innocents in Sweden find themselves pitted against a ruthless gang of criminal capitalists. Very few of Greene's novels lack these elements of pervading violence and looming evil, and often they are emphasized to the verge of melodrama.

But what cannot be ignored in the novels, as it can in the entertainments, is that behind the melodramatic facade a genuine moral drama is always being enacted, and not merely a moral drama but a religious one, for Greene is perpetually concerned with the problem of grace, with the shape of God's mercy. It is at this point that crime shades off into sin, the burden which the practicing Christian bears in order that by the exercise of his free will he may rise above it. In this context it is impossible to forget that Greene is a Catholic; he was converted two years before he published his first novel, *The Man Within*, in 1929. But he has never been a Catholic apologist in the dogmatic manner of writers like G.K. Chesterton and Hilaire Belloc. Given his dark view of the human condition, he sees Catholicism not as a creed for the triumphant, but rather for the desperate, and he shares with his atheist contemporaries, the existentialists, the tendency to lead his characters to self-knowledge by driving them into life-and-death situations where they learn of God's mercy, as it were, "between the saddle and the ground." And perhaps, if we are to consider

Graham Greene a mystery writer, the central mystery lies precisely there. As the priest in *The Heart of the Matter,* Father Rank, says to the dead police chief's widow, "For goodness sake, Mrs. Scobie, don't imagine you—or I—know a thing about God's mercy." In this sense, of acknowledging that the central mystery of Christianity is unknowable, Greene has been justified in calling himself "a Catholic agnostic."

In the more technical sense that they involve plots or betrayals or criminal conspiracies that are gradually revealed to us through a good deal of thrilling action, Greene's books—both entertainments and novels—can be classed as mysteries. Detection is also an element in them, particularly when, like *The Third Man, Our Man in Havana,* or *The Human Factor,* they involve the kind of intelligence operations in which Greene was himself employed as a British secret agent during World War II. But the solution of a problem by a detective is never a dominant element; the interest is likely to lie in the pursuit rather than in the detection itself, as in *The Human Factor,* in which we learn very quickly that an apparently impeccable employee of British Intelligence has been corrupted by a sense of gratitude into becoming a double agent. The drama lies not in the reader's being eventually enlightened about the facts, but in the suspenseful time when the investigators are sorting out the clues relating to the leak they have discovered, while the reader enters the guilty man's mind and sees how love led him into a situation that, even if he escapes physically—as he does—must morally destroy him. The criminal rather than the crime, the sinner rather than the sin, are Greene's ultimate concerns.

—George Woodcock

———

GREENE, Steven. *See* **LUTZ, John.**

———

GREENLEAF, Stephen (Howell). American. Born in Washington, D.C. 17 July 1942. Educated at Carleton College, Northfield, Minnesota, B.A. 1964; University of California, Berkeley, J.D. 1967; University of Iowa, Iowa City, 1978–79. Served in the United States Army, 1967–69. Married Ann Garrison in 1968; one son. Admitted to Bar of California, 1968, and Iowa, 1977; researcher, Multnomah County Legal Aid, Portland, Oregon, 1969–70; associate attorney, Thompson and Hubbard, Monterey, California, 1970–71, and Sullivan Jones and Archer, San Francisco, 1972–76; adjunct professor of Trial Advocacy, University of Iowa, 1979–81. Agent: Esther Newberg, International Creative Management, Inc., 40 West 57th Street, New York, New York, 10019, U.S.A.

CRIME PUBLICATIONS

Novels (series: John Marshall Tanner in all books)

Grave Error (Tanner). New York, Dial Press, 1979; London, New English Library, 1981.
Death Bed. New York, Dial Press, 1980; London, New English Library, 1982.
State's Evidence. New York, Dial Press, 1982; London, New English Library, 1983.

Fatal Obsession. New York, Dial Press, 1983; London, Hale, 1984.
Beyond Blame. New York, Villard, 1986; London, Bodley Head, 1987.
Toll Call. New York, Villard, 1987.

OTHER PUBLICATIONS

Novels

The Ditto List. New York, Villard, 1985.
Impact. New York, Morrow, 1989; London, Century, 1990.

*   *   *

The detective-protagonist of Stephen Greenleaf's series, John Marshall Tanner, is a former lawyer from San Francisco, like his creator. Like Ross Macdonald's Lew Archer, Tanner is a hard-boiled loner, his wisecracking cynicism masking old-fashioned idealism. Greenleaf's early plots begin with Tanner's search for a missing person, and, like Macdonald's, Greenleaf's plots hinge on his detective's search through the characters' pasts, his uncovering of the complex interrelationships those characters have concealed, the complicated lies upon which they have built their present identities.

A man of indeterminate years but old enough to have served in the Korean conflict, Tanner views with scorn the blighted urban California landscape in which the novels are set. Often in each novel he will retire for a period of contemplation either in his apartment, where he drinks Scotch and listens to Mozart or Beethoven, or to his office, where he drinks Scotch and where his two prized possessions—his grandfather's desk and a painting by Klee—remind him, respectively, of the values of the past so clearly lacking in the present and of the way people's lives, like the lines in Klee's painting, intersect so unexpectedly.

Greenleaf's plots always revolve around family. *Grave Error* opens when Tanner is hired by Mrs. Jacqueline Nelson to discover if her husband, Roland, a Naderian consumer activist, is being blackmailed. Tanner learns that the Nelson's adopted daughter has hired his fellow detective and best friend, Harry Spring, to uncover the identity of her true parents. When his friend is murdered, Tanner is true to the code made famous by Hammett: he drops the Nelson case to pursue Harry Spring's murderer. But, of course, his case, Spring's case, and Spring's murder are all intertwined, here in unlikely ways: Roland Nelson is indeed being blackmailed, but by his wife; the Nelsons have adopted their own daughter, after having abandoned her 20 years earlier; and Spring has been murdered by Nelson's former girlfriend who now works for him as secretary and fellow activist. The plot requires considerable suspension of reader disbelief and lengthy disquisition among the many principals at the novel's close before it becomes relatively clear. *Grave Error* is very much a first novel, one which adheres to the hard-boiled formula, particularly in its talky, explanatory last chapters. Roland Nelson's dialogue is so stilted that even Greenleaf feels the need for an explanation, having Nelson claim that he consciously models his speech on Trollope's characters; why other characters—waitresses, toughs, and whores—talk similarly is not explained. And Greenleaf disposes of inconvenient plot ends and characters here by killing them off; here, too, his hero handles his fists and his gun surprisingly well for a mature adult who neither works out nor practices at the pistol range. Still, Tanner's account of the case is filled with amusing observations and crackling similes, and, as a character, Tanner is altogether well-delineated and appealing.

The plots of the later novels also revolve around family problems. In *Death Bed* Tanner is hired to find the lost and politically radical son of an oil billionaire, and, in *State's Evidence*, the wife of an accountant, a woman who has apparently witnessed a mob-connected hit-and-run. Both plots become more complicated as Tanner delves into the principals' pasts, uncovering the truth about both his prey and his clients. Greenleaf's plots in these later novels are more probable, and he relies less on violence to unravel their threads. He also relies less on the formulaic conclusion, leaving the reader of *State's Evidence*, intriguingly, to tie up many of those threads for himself.

In *Fatal Obsession,* perhaps his best novel, Tanner returns to his Midwestern hometown to confer with his sister and two brothers about the fate of the family farm. While there, his nephew, a Vietnam veteran tormented by his part in that conflict, angry with the town fathers, and dying from the effects of Agent Orange, is murdered. Tanner's investigation into that crime leads to a series of revelations about his own past—about his mother and father, his high-school classmates and former sweetheart, and his brothers and sister—and about the townspeople. Greenleaf effectively portrays a wide range of desperate people unable to stop the economic collapse of their town, middle-aged people struggling to deal with the collapse of their youthful dreams, young people trapped by their hormones and the vast horizon. Greenleaf's juxtaposition in the final chapters of the novel's two mysteries—the nephew's murder and the fate of the farm—provides a subtle comment on the American Heartland's economic values and their costs.

In *Beyond Blame* Tanner is hired by the parents of a murdered woman to prove that her husband, a brilliant law professor specializing in insanity defenses, a man who has confessed to the murder, was not insane when he killed his wife. The novel contains interesting discussions of the vagaries of such defenses and depictions of and poignant commentary on the changes in Berkeley, California, in the past 20 years—from the center of American student radicalism in the 1960's (when Tanner was a law student) into a "gourmet ghetto," center of Western yuppiedom. Greenleaf's ear for speech has improved markedly; indeed his handling of teenagers' jargon here is both perfectly accurate and finely comic. His exposure of the real murderer's identity seems somewhat unlikely and the exposure scene reliant on the grotesque, but otherwise the novel is a strong one.

Tanner's attempt to help his secretary, Peggy Nettleton, in the series' most recent effort, *Toll Call,* leads to an investigation of not only her late-night caller but also to the psychological effects of victimization and to the ways some victims are driven to strike back. Tanner enlists in his investigation the hilariously foulmouthed Ruthie Spring, widow of his former mentor Harry, who provides an earthy contrast to Tanner's frustratingly civilized and ineffectual efforts here. Indeed, in an intriguing reversal of sex roles, Ruthie and Peggy combine to kill one of the novel's villains while Tanner lies trussed and helpless, and it is Tanner who provides psychological nurturing after the killing, the most protracted and bloodiest of the series.

Throughout the series, Tanner has remained an interesting and thoughtful character, a decent and ethical man who succeeds through persistence and native wit and who confronts villainy with scorn and a kind of skeptical wonder. Greenleaf's development as a writer since the series began has been remarkable: his plotting, his character portrayals, and his ear for dialogue now are sure; he has relied less and less on cynical one-liners and violent solutions, more and more on intelligent probing of the law, human behaviour, and psychology. In sum, Greenleaf's series represents a significant variation on the Hammett-Chandler-Macdonald pattern.

—David K. Jeffrey

————

GREENWOOD, John. *See* **HILTON, John Buxton.**

————

GREW, William. *See* **O'FARRELL, William.**

————

GREX, Leo. *See* **GRIBBLE, Leonard.**

————

GREY, Louis. *See* **GRIBBLE, Leonard.**

————

GRIBBLE, Leonard (Reginald). Also writes as Sterry Browning; Lee Denver; London Grant; Leo Grex; Louis Grey; Dexter Muir. British. Born in London, 1 February 1908. Educated at schools in England. Served in the Press and Censorship Division of the Ministry of Information, London, 1940–45. Married Nancy Mason in 1932; one daughter. Has worked as a literary adviser to several publishers; started the Empire Bookshelf series, BBC Radio, London. Founding member, Crime Writers Association, 1953. Address: Chandons, Firsdown Close, High Salvington, Worthing, West Sussex, England.

Crime Publications

Novels (series: Superintendent Anthony Slade)

The Case of the Marsden Rubies (Slade). London, Harrap, 1929; New York, Doubleday, 1930.
The Gillespie Suicide Mystery (Slade). London, Harrap, 1929; as *The Terrace Suicide Mystery,* New York, Doubleday, 1929.
The Grand Modena Murder (Slade). London, Harrap, 1930; New York, Doubleday, 1931.
Is This Revenge? (Slade). London, Harrap, 1931; as *The Serpentine Murder,* New York, Dodd Mead, 1932.
The Stolen Home Secretary (Slade). London, Harrap, 1932; as *The Stolen Statesman,* New York, Dodd Mead, 1932.
The Secret of Tangles (Slade). London, Harrap, 1933; Philadelphia, Lippincott, 1934.
The Yellow Bungalow Mystery (Slade). London, Harrap, 1933.
The Death Chime. London, Harrap, 1934.
The Riddle of the Ravens (Slade). London, Harrap, 1934.
The Signet of Death (as Louis Grey). London, Nicholson and Watson, 1934.

Mystery at Tudor Arches (Slade). London, Harrap, 1935.
The Case of the Malverne Diamonds (Slade). London, Harrap, 1936; New York, Greenberg, 1937.
Riley of the Special Branch (Slade). London, Harrap, 1936.
Who Killed Oliver Cromwell? (Slade). London, Harrap, 1937; New York, Greenberg, 1938.
Tragedy in E Flat (Slade). London, Harrap, 1938; New York, Curl, 1939.
The Arsenal Stadium Mystery (Slade). London, Harrap, 1939; revised edition, London, Jenkins, 1950.
Atomic Murder (Slade). London, Harrap, and Chicago, Ziff Davis, 1947.
Hangman's Moon (Slade). London, W.H. Allen, 1950.
They Kidnapped Stanley Matthews (Slade). London, Jenkins, 1950.
The Frightened Chameleon (Slade). London, Jenkins, 1951; New York, Roy, 1957.
Mystery Manor. London, Goulden, 1951.
Crime at Cape Folly (as Sterry Browning). London, Clerke and Cockeran, 1951.
The Glass Alibi (Slade). London, Jenkins, 1952; New York, Roy, 1956.
Murder Out of Season (Slade). London, Jenkins, 1952.
She Died Laughing (Slade). London, Jenkins, 1953.
Murder Mistaken, with Janet Green. London, W.H. Allen, 1953.
Sex Marks the Spot (as Sterry Browning). London, Long, 1954.
The Inverted Crime (Slade). London, Jenkins, 1954.
Sally of Scotland Yard, with Geraldine Laws. London, W.H. Allen, 1954.
Death Pays the Piper (Slade). London, Jenkins, 1956; New York, Roy, 1958.
Stand-In for Murder (Slade). London, Jenkins, 1957; New York, Roy, 1958.
Don't Argue with Death (Slade). London, Jenkins, and New York, Roy, 1959.
Wantons Die Hard (Slade). London, Jenkins, 1961; New York, Roy, 1962.
Heads You Die (Slade). London, Jenkins, 1964.
The Violent Dark (Slade). London, Jenkins, 1965.
Strip-Tease Macabre (Slade). London, Jenkins, 1967.
A Diplomat Dies (Slade). London, Jenkins, 1969.
Alias the Victim (Slade). London, Hale, 1971.
Programmed for Death. London, Hale, 1973.
You Can't Die Tomorrow. London, Hale, 1975.
Midsummer Slay Ride. London, Hale, 1976.
Crime on Her Hands. London, Hale, 1977.
Death Needs No Alibi. London, Hale, 1979.
Dead End in Mayfair. London, Hale, 1981.
The Dead Don't Scream. London, Hale, 1983.
Violent Midnight. London, Hale, 1986.

Novels as Leo Grex (series: Paul Irving; Phil Sanderson)

The Tragedy at Draythorpe (Irving). London, Hutchinson, 1931.
The Nightborn. London, Hutchinson, 1931.
The Lonely Inn Mystery (Irving). London, Hutchinson, 1933.
The Madison Murder (Irving). London, Hutchinson, 1933.
The Man from Manhattan. London, Hutchinson, 1934; New York, Doubleday, 1935.
Murder in the Sanctuary (Irving). London, Hutchinson, 1934.
Crooner's Swan Song. London, Hutchinson, 1935.
Stolen Death (Irving). London, Hutchinson, 1936.
Transatlantic Trouble. London, Hutchinson, 1937.

The Carlent Manor Crime (Irving). London, Hutchinson, 1939.
The Black-Out Murders. London, Harrap, 1940.
The Stalag Mites. London, Harrap, 1947.
King Spiv. London, Harrap, 1948.
Crooked Sixpence. London, Harrap, 1949.
Ace of Danger (Irving). London, Hutchinson, 1952.
Thanks for the Felony. London, Long, 1958.
Larceny in Her Heart. London, Long, 1959.
Terror Wears a Smile. London, Long, 1962.
The Brass Knuckle. London, Long, 1964.
Violent Keepsake (Sanderson). London, Long, 1967.
The Hard Kill (Sanderson). London, Long, 1969.
Kill Now—Pay Later. London, Long, 1971.
Die—as in Murder. London, Hale, 1974.
Death Throws No Shadow. London, Hale, 1976.
Mix Me a Murder. London, Hale, 1978.
Hot Ice. London, Hale, 1983.

Novels as Dexter Muir

The Pilgrims Meet Murder. London, Jenkins, 1948.
The Speckled Swan. London, Jenkins, 1949.
Rosemary for Death. London, Jenkins, 1953.

Short Stories

The Case-Book of Anthony Slade. London, Quality Press, 1937.
The Velvet Mask and Other Stories. London, W.H. Allen, 1952.
Superintendent Slade Investigates. London, Jenkins, 1956; New York, Roy, 1957.

OTHER PUBLICATIONS

Novels

Coastal Commandoes (as Sterry Browning). London, Nicholson and Watson, 1946.
Santa Fé Gunslick (as Sterry Browning). London, Clerke and Cockeran, 1951.
Dangerous Mission. London, Brown and Watson, 1957.

Novels as Landon Grant

Rustlers' Gulch. London, Rich and Cowan, 1935.
Wyoming Deadline. London, Rich and Cowan, 1939.
Texas Buckaroo. London, Sampson Low, 1948.
Ramrod of the Bar X. London, Sampson Low, 1949.
Scar Valley Bandit. London, Sampson Low, 1951.
The Rawhide Kid. London, Burke, 1951.
Gunsmoke Canyon. London, Sampson Low, 1952.
Outlaws of Silver Spur. London, Stanley Paul, 1953.
Marshal of Mustang. London, Macdonald, 1954.
Thunder Valley Deadline. London, Stanley Paul, 1956.

Novels as Lee Denver

Cheyenne Jones, Maverick Marshal. London, Hale, 1977.
Cheyenne's Sixgun Justice. London, Hale, 1980.
Cheyenne's Trail to Perdition. London, Hale, 1982.
Cheyenne's Two—Gun Shoot—Out. London, Hale, 1983.
Cheyenne at Dull Knife Pass. London, Hale, 1984.

Play

Screenplay: *Death by Design*, 1943.

Verse

Toy Folk and Nursery People. London, Jenkins, 1945.

Other

Queens of Crime. London, Hurst and Blackett, 1932.
Famous Feats of Detection and Deduction. London, Harrap, 1933; New York, Doubleday, 1934.
All the Year Round Stories, with Nancy Gribble. London, Hutchinson, 1935.
Heroes of the Fighting R.A.F. London, Harrap, 1941.
Epics of the Fighting R.A.F. London, Harrap, 1943.
Heroes of the Merchant Navy. London, Harrap, 1944.
Battle Stories of the R.A.F. London, Burke, 1945.
Great Detective Feats. London, Burke, 1946.
Murder First Class. London, Burke, 1946.
On Secret Service. London, Burke, 1946.
The Secret of the Red Mill (for children). London, Burke, 1948.
The Missing Speed Ace (for children). London, Burke, 1950.
The Riddle of the Blue Moon (for children). London, Burke, 1950.
Speed Dermot, Junior Reporter (for children). London, Burke, 1951.
Famous Manhunts: A Century of Crime. London, Long, 1953; New York, Roy, 1955.
Adventures in Murder Undertaken by Some Notorious Killers in Love. London, Long, 1954; New York, Roy, 1955.
Triumphs of Scotland Yard: A Century of Detection. London, Long, 1955.
Famous Judges and Their Trials: A Century of Justice. London, Long, 1957.
The True Book about Scotland Yard (for children). London, Muller, 1957.
Great Detective Exploits. London, Long, 1958.
Murders Most Strange. London, Long, 1959.
The True Book about the Old Bailey. London, Muller, 1959; New Rochelle, New York, Sportshelf, 1960.
Hands of Terror: Notable Assassinations of the Twentieth Century. London, Muller, 1960.
The True Book about the Mounties. London, Muller, 1960; New Rochelle, New York, Sportshelf, 1961.
Clues That Spelled Guilty. London, Long, 1961.
The True Book about Great Escapes. London, Muller, 1962.
When Killers Err. London, Long, 1962.
Stories of Famous Detectives. London, Barker, and New York, Hill and Wang, 1963.
They Challenged the Yard. London, Long, 1963.
The True Book about Smugglers and Smuggling. London, Muller, 1963.
The True Book about the Spanish Main. London, Muller, 1963.
Stories of Famous Spies. London, Barker, 1964.
Such Women Are Deadly. London, Long, 1965; New York, Arco, 1969.
Great Manhunters of the Yard. London, Long, and New York, Roy, 1966.
Stories of Famous Explorers. London, Barker, 1966.
Famous Stories of the Wild West (for children). London, Barker, 1967.
They Had a Way with Women. London, Long, 1967; New York, Roy, 1968.

Stories of Famous Conspirators. London, Barker, 1968.
Famous Stories of Police and Crime. London, Barker, 1968.
Famous Historical Mysteries. London, Muller, 1969.
Famous Stories of Scientific Detection. London, Barker, 1969.
Stories of Famous Modern Trials. London, Barker, 1970; as *Justice?*, New York, Abelard Schuman, 1971.
Strange Crimes of Passion. London, Long, 1970.
Famous Detective Feats. London, Barker, 1971.
They Got Away with Murder. London, Long, 1971.
More Famous Historical Mysteries. London, Muller, 1972.
Sisters of Cain. London, Long, 1972.
Famous Feats of Espionage. London, Barker, 1972.
The Hallmark of Horror. London, Long, 1973.
Stories of Famous Master Criminals. London, Barker, 1973.
Such Was Their Guilt. London, Long, 1974.
Famous Stories of the Murder Squad. London, Barker, 1974.
They Conspired to Kill. London, Long, 1975.
Murder Stranger than Fiction (as Leo Grex). London, Hale, 1975.
Famous Mysteries of Detection. London, Barker, 1976.
Famous Mysteries of Modern Times. London, Muller, 1976.
The Cardinal's Diamonds. London, Hale, 1976.
The Deadly Professionals. London, Long, 1976.
Compelled to Kill. London, Long, 1977.
Detection Stranger than Fiction (as Leo Grex). London, Hale, 1977.
They Came to Kill. London, Long, 1979.
Mystery Stranger Than Fiction (as Leo Grex). New York, St. Martin's Press, and London, Hale, 1979.
These Crimes Made Headlines (as Leo Grex). London, Hale, 1980.
Crime Stranger Than Fiction. London, Hale, 1981.
Notorious Killers in the Night. London, Hale, 1983.
Mysteries Behind Notorious Crimes. London, Hale, 1984.
Notorious Crimes. London, Hale, 1985.
Such Lethal Ladies. London, Hale, 1985.
They Shot to Slay. London, Hale, 1986.

Editor, *A Christmas Treasury in Prose and Verse.* London, SPCK, and New York, Macmillan, 1929.
Editor, *The Jesus of the Poets: An Anthology.* London, Student Christian Movement Press, and New York, R.R. Smith, 1930.
Editor, *Best Children's Stories of the Year.* London, Burke, 4 vols., 1946–49.
Editor, *Fifty Famous Stories for Boys.* London, Burke, 1948.
Editor, *Fifty Famous Stories for Girls.* London, Burke, 1949.
Editor, *Fifty Famous Animal Stories* (for children). London, Burke, 1949.
Editor, *The Story Trove: A Collection of the Best Stories of Today for Boys and Girls.* London, Burke, 1950.
Editor, *Stories for Boys.* London, Spring Books, 1961.
Editor, *Stories for Girls.* London, Spring Books, 1961.
Editor, *Famous Stories of High Adventure* (for children). London, Barker, 1962; New York, Hill and Wang, 1964.
Editor, *Famous Stories of the Sea and Ships* (for children). London, Barker, 1962; New York, Hill and Wang, 1964.
Editor, *Great War Adventures.* London, Barker, 1966.

* * *

One of the most prolific writers of detective fiction under at least six names, Leonard Gribble is probably best known for his long series of cases featuring Anthony Slade of Scotland Yard, and for his factual studies of detection and crime.

Slade followed in the footsteps of such investigators as Crofts's Inspector French by pursuing his cases in a solid and dependable manner. There is little of the hero-worship surrounding such figures as Creasey's Inspector West, and there is none of the way-out unconventionality displayed by many of Edgar Wallace's Scotland Yard men. Nevertheless it is possible to draw parallels between Gribble and Wallace; one detects occasional similarities of style, frequent touches of London background, and over all an impression that for most of the time the police are pitted against professional criminals and organised crime rather than the cosy drawing-room murderers depicted in so many detective novels. Gribble does not ignore the domestic murder, but it seems not to play a significant part in his work, although it must be emphasised that throughout his career he has shown a versatility of subject and a stamina in his output that few detective novelists have equalled.

His sometimes stilted manner of writing, and the almost total lack of characterisation, combine to make Gribble's books a little less readable than one would wish. This is a pity, for many of them are well-constructed stories and in some the suspense is well built up. He has a good knowledge of police procedures, and gives an impression of authenticity which contrasts with the heavily fictionalised and sensational exploits of the police in many other author's books. His settings, too, are often original as are his plot ideas—one recalls, for example, *The Arsenal Stadium Mystery* and *They Kidnapped Stanley Matthews*. He has also shown a deft hand at the short story form in *Superintendent Slade Investigates,* and his story "The Case of Jacob Heylyn" has appeared in several anthologies.

Gribble's detective novels are pieces of escapism rather than police procedural stories as such, although it is understood that his accurately described police techniques are the product of a lifetime's association with friends at Scotland Yard. One wishes, however, that he had managed to inject a little more personality into Slade, that he had sometimes conveyed a more ambitious message than that Crime Does Not Pay, and that he had made the occasional attempt to paint more complex relationships between his police officers in the manner of the best J.J. Marric and John Wainwright novels.

His books of true criminal cases are clearly aimed at the general reader rather than those with a deep interest in criminology. The latter would do better to turn to Lustgarten, Furneaux, Jesse, or a host of others. The most appropriate description of Gribble's non-fiction would be that it is enthralling and entertaining; concentrating as he often does upon the stranger aspects of crime and the more bizarre cases of murder, they certainly hold the imagination. Written in a non-intellectual and straightforward style, with many of the volumes reflecting police and judicial procedures throughout the world, they make a welcome change from detailed examination of every nuance of criminal behaviour and provide ample evidence that detective fact is often more incredible than detective fiction.

—Melvyn Barnes

GRIERSON, Edward (Dobbyn). Also wrote as Brian Crowther; John P. Stevenson. British. Born in Bedford, 9 March 1914. Educated at St. Paul's School, London, 1927–32; Exeter College, Oxford, 1932–35, B.A. (honours) in jurisprudence 1935; Inner Temple, London: called to the Bar, 1937. Served in the British Army Infantry, 1939–46: Lieutenant Colonel. Married Helen D. Henderson in 1938; one daughter. Barrister,

Bradford, Yorkshire, 1938–39; Announcer, Australian Broadcasting Commision Sydney, 1948–49; justice of the peace, Northumberland, 1957–75; chairman of petty sessions, Bellingham, Northumberland, 1960–75; deputy-chairman, Northumberland Quarter Sessions, 1960–71; deputy traffic commissioner, Northern Traffic Area, 1974–75. Recipient: Crime Writers Association award, 1956. *Died 24 May 1975.*

CRIME PUBLICATIONS

Novels

Reputation for a Song. London, Chatto and Windus, and New York, Knopf, 1952.
The Second Man. London, Chatto and Windus, and New York, Knopf, 1956.
The Massingham Affair. London, Chatto and Windus, 1962; New York, Doubleday, 1963.
A Crime of One's Own. London, Chatto and Windus, and New York, Putnam, 1967.

OTHER PUBLICATIONS

Novels

Shall Perish with the Sword (as Brian Crowther). London, Quality Press, 1949.
The Lilies and the Bees. London, Chatto and Windus, 1953; as *The Hastening Wind,* New York, Knopf, 1953; as *The Royalist,* New York, Bantam, 1956.
Far Morning. London, Chatto and Windus, and New York, Knopf, 1955.
The Captain General (as John P. Stevenson). New York, Doubleday, 1956; as Edward Grierson, London, Chatto and Windus, 1958.
Dark Torrent of Glencoe. New York, Doubleday, 1960; London, Chatto and Windus, 1961.

Plays

His Mother's Son, with Raymond Lulham (produced Harrogate, Yorkshire, 1953).

Radio Plays: *The Ninth Legion,* 1956; *The Second Man,* 1956; *Mr. Curtis's Chambers,* 1959.

Other

Storm Bird: The Strange Life of Georgina Weldon. London, Chatto and Windus, 1959.
The Fatal Inheritance: Philip II and the Spanish Netherlands. London, Gollancz, and New York, Doubleday, 1969.
The Imperial Dream: The British Commonwealth and the Empire 1775–1969. London, Collins, 1972; as *The Death of the Imperial Dream,* New York, Doubleday, 1972.
Confessions of a Country Magistrate. London, Gollancz, 1972.
King of Two Worlds: Philip II of Spain. London, Collins, and New York, Putnam, 1974.
The Companion Guide to Northumbria. London, Collins, 1976.

*   *   *

The books of Edward Grierson are not detective fiction but crime fiction. To claim that he is a descendant of the realistic school of Francis Iles would be to deny him his individuality, yet the development of crime fiction appears to be obligatorily segmented into this or that school by historians of the genre. To compare him too closely with Iles would also be to overlook the fact that with Grierson we are outsiders observing the relationships between his characters, whereas with Iles we identify with the protagonist and follow his or her every thought.

It is really Grierson's novel *Reputation for a Song* which caused him to be categorised with the movement towards modern crime fiction as a novel of character. The book is so good that it can stand on its own. Far removed from classic detective fiction, it is at once a supremely competent study of domestic murder and a perfect example of courtroom drama. The tempestuous family relationships at the home of the stolid and respectable small-town solicitor are skillfully conveyed. Gradually, with apparent ease, Grierson shows us resentment building to hatred, and eventually to murder. By detective fiction standards, it is a simple case. The murderer is soon arrested. The point of the book then becomes apparent, as we are left in little doubt that the simplest case is open to distortion by those inside and outside the legal system. It would be wrong to reveal why the title of the book, from Omar Khayyam, is so apt. Suffice it to say that many readers might unfortunately fail to observe the deftness of Grierson's touch in presenting his characters, and the power of his dialogue throughout some of the best courtroom scenes in modern fiction, in their eager pursuit of the answer to one question—not the identity of the murderer, but whether he will hang. That answer is given at the climax, but we are left with more worrying questions still unanswered after closing the book.

With *The Second Man,* Grierson gives an authentic study of a woman barrister. In this novel he also makes good use of his own legal background so that the atmosphere of the courts can be positively felt. Marion Kerrison fights two battles—to assert her position as a woman in a predominantly male profession, and to clear a man accused of murder who appears to be his own worst enemy—and the two are knitted together so adroitly that the book fully justifies the award made to it as the best British crime novel of 1956.

The Massingham Affair presented further evidence of his talent. Concerning the ceaseless efforts of two men to reconstruct a Victorian *Cause célèbre,* and to question the evidence against those convicted, it has the combined qualities of the historical thriller and the perfectly constructed detective story. *A Crime of One's Own,* with the young and romantic bookseller who suspects that a spy ring is mis-using his establishment, does not attain the standard of Grierson's earlier work, although it suggests that he could produce a spirited and witty romp which will keep many readers entertained.

In short, although Grierson produced other books, *Reputation for a Song, The Second Man,* and *The Massingham Affair* are the quintessence of his very real contribution to the field of crime fiction.

—Melvyn Barnes

———

GRIFFITH, Bill. *See* **GRANGER, Bill.**

———

GRIMES, Martha. American. Born in Pittsburgh, Pennsylvania. Educated at the University of Maryland, B.A., M.A. Divorced; one son. English Instructor, University of Iowa, Iowa City; Assistant Professor of English, Frostburg State College, Maryland; Professor of English, Montgomery College, Takoma Park, Maryland. Recipient: Nero Wolfe award, 1983. Lives in Silver Spring, Maryland. Address: c/o Little Brown and Company, 34 Beacon Street, Boston, Massachusetts 02108, U.S.A.

CRIME PUBLICATIONS

Novels (series: Inspector Richard Jury in all books)

The Man with a Load of Mischief.   Boston, Little Brown, 1981.
The Old Fox Deceiv'd.   Boston, Little Brown 1982.
The Anodyne Necklace.   Boston, Little Brown, 1983; London, O'Mara, 1989.
The Dirty Duck. Boston, Little Brown, 1984; London, O'Mara, 1986.
Jerusalem Inn.   Boston, Little Brown, 1984; London, O'Mara, 1987.
Help the Poor Struggler.   Boston, Little Brown, 1985; London, O'Mara, 1988.
The Deer Leap.   Boston, Little Brown, 1985; London, Headline, 1989.
I Am the Only Running Footman.   Boston, Little Brown, and London, O'Mara, 1986.
The Five Bells and Bladebone.   Boston, Little Brown, 1987; London, O'Mara, 1988.
The Old Silent.   Boston, Little Brown, 1989.

*   *   *

Martha Grimes's trademark is her fanciful titles, taken from the English country inns and pubs which are the setting for much of the action, and frequently the venue for the murders in her stories. Many other pubs besides the titular ones are used as settings also—they are convenient gathering places for groups of people—but the pubs that Grimes most enjoys are apparently those with names like The Man with a Load of Mischief, I Am the Only Running Footman, and The Five Bells and Bladebone. They are part and parcel of the very English ambience that characterizes her work, all the more remarkable for her being an American. To read Grimes with full appreciation it is helpful to have a grasp of English topography, customs, modes of expression, the class system, cuisine—if that is not too eleevated a term for much pub food—and, of course, that center of a great deal of English life, the pub itself.

Grimes also writes for a culturally literate audience, attuned to the arts and literature, and especially for readers familiar with the classic English mystery story. A more than passing acquaintance with antiques, painting, architecture, *objets d'art* in general, and literature in particular adds to the reader's enjoyment of the Grimes novels. *I Am the Only Running Footman,* for example, uses as a basic metaphor for the *modus operandi* of the murders "Porphyria's Lover," a poem by Browning in which a girl is strangled with her own flaxen hair. The particular circumstances surrounding the death of Christopher Marlowe play an important role in *The Dirty Duck,* even to the point of one of the murders seeming to be an imitation of Marlowe's. Literary references abound in *The Five Bells and Bladebone*—to Trollope's method of writing his novels, Coleridge's "Kubla Khan" and the man from Porlock who interrupted its composition, to Henry James's *The Golden Bowl.*

The significance of all of these, and more, would certainly slip by the reader unfamiliar with the canon of English literature.

Additionally, Grimes alludes frequently to the masters of the classic mystery, to Sayers, Christie (not always favorably), Tey and others. And her plots, characters and situations often echo in one way or another those of her distinguished predecessors. Her central character, Superintendent Richard Jury of Scotland Yard, reminds one in certain ways of such figures as P. D. James's Adam Dalgleish and Ngaio Marsh's Roderick Alleyn—tall, good-looking, quiet, cultured, determined, thoughtful, and sensitive. Melrose Plant, Grimes's aristocratic and wealthy amateur sleuth, shows traces of Lord Peter Wimsey and Albert Campion: behind his dilettantish appearance is an exceptionally keen mind, and a logical, that can solve the *Times* crossword in 15 minutes. Her plots are exceedingly convoluted and clever, with adroitly placed red herrings, delicate problems of time and place, and most unexpected conclusions. She often employs the popular device of mistaken identity. Her picture postcard English villages look much like St. Mary Mead, and she even has the nerve to create a *tour de force* using a Christmas party in a great house in Yorkshire, snowed in whilst murders occur.

Although Grimes does not suffer from the anxiety of influence, she is far from a thing of shreds and patches taken from other writers' cloth. She is *using* both her literary allusions and her echoes of the classic mystery to her own ends. She is saying in effect, "I know I am working in a tradition and accept it. Now just watch what I can do with it." She puts a spin on the tradition and makes it her own thing.

The most striking evidence of this Grimsian spin is the comedy that counterpoints the murder mystery in every novel. This comedy has two orientations; the social comedy oriented around Melrose Plant, especially in the village of Long Piddleton, and a kind of domestic comedy concerned with Jury and his relationships with his associates and neighbors. Plant's Aunt Agatha, with her rapacious appetite for fairy-cakes and whatever bibelots she can purloin from Plant's estate of Ardry End, is one of Grimes's best comic creations, supplemented by other Long Pidd types such as Marshall Trueblood, gay dealer in antiques; Mrs. Withersby, village drunk and oracle; and Ruthven (pronounced Ri'vn), Plant's archetypal butler. Jury's comic coterie includes Chief Superintendent Racer, Jury's superior in rank and inferior in brains, who tries unsuccesfully to browbeat Jury at every opportunity but is in turn tormented by Cyril, the cat, who sneaks into Racer's office equally at every opportunity. Jury's Sergeant Wiggins brings comedy into the murder investigation with his hypochondriacal chugging of nostrums in great variety; while at Jury's apartment house Mrs. Wasserman, fearful of a non-existent pursuer, and Carole-anne, a teenage beauty, continually call on his help and concern. Moreover, in most the stories Jury's empathy with children elicits a quiet comedy that adds still another dimension to his character as he jokes and plays with them.

The movement of Grimes's novels is essentially contrapuntal, rather fugue-like, as she takes up first the murder, say, then switches to Long Pidd and its comic interplay, then goes back to the murder investigation, then perhaps to Racer or Mrs. Wasserman, then again returns to the main theme of the murder, which by this time has probably become several more murders. The murders are grizly, bizarre, the investigation plodding with innumerable interviews and speculations, the comedy light and sparkling, or amusingly outrageous. She works these elements back and forth, gradually weaving them all together as Jury and Plant, and in later novels, Chief Superintendent Macalvie of the Devon Constabulary, a most feisty and tough cop who contrasts effectively with Jury, bring the plot to its conclusion.

Grimes is not, however, stuck with this pattern. Throughout her 10 novels she varies her approach, the settings, and the supplementary characters with great skill and flexibility. Which of these novels can be considered the "best" or "most effective" is a matter of taste, but for this writer at least, *The Man with a Load of Mischief, The Old Fox Deceived,* and *The Anodyne Necklace,* her first three stories, and the recent *The Five Bells and Bladebone* are among the most interesting for rather different reasons. *The Man with a Load of Mischief* creates a most detailed picture of Long Piddleton, even to the extent of a map, so that the village takes on depth and verisimilitude to a greater degree than in the other novels. The comic characters, especially Aunt Agatha, are also introduced in depth, so that when we meet them in later stories they are familiar friends. The murders are exceptionally ingenious and bizarre, one victim garotted and thrust into a butt of ale, reminiscent of the Duke of Clarence, as we are reminded, while the other is placed atop the beam that holds the "Jack" that strikes the hours at the Jack and Hammer pub. Two more murders occur at or near pubs, thus establishing a landmark practice of Grimes. The climax, a confrontation between the murderer and Jury in a darkened church, is a real thriller, with a marvelous feeling of danger unusual in Grimes. This first book shows the perfect control that has characterized the rest; Grimes has always known what she was doing.

The Old Fox Deceived and *The Anodyne Necklace* are admirable in their creation of setting, too, especially the former, where the village of Rackmoor, tilted on the edge of the North Sea, has wonderfully convoluted streets and byways important to the plot, as is the mistaken identification which puzzles the reader as it puzzles Jury, a most satisfying conundrum. *The Anodyne Necklace* is distinctive in the way it alternates between the village of Littlebourne and London's East End, where the Dickensian family of the Cripps are a superbly vulgar and comic bunch that shows still another side of Grimes's flair for comedy. And, although children often are important to Jury in his investigations, Emily Louise Perk, age 10, is really central to this mystery, while her escape on horseback from the murderer is just about as thrilling as Jury's earlier meeting in the darkened church. Here also is an inconclusive romantic attachment begun for Jury and Lady Kennington. Jury has long felt drawn to Vivian Rivington, a poet who lives in Long Pidd, but here is drawn in another direction which adds another aspect to his nature, since both women seem lost and subdued, calling on the intense sympathy and deep melancholy which occasionally comes to the surface in Jury.

The Five Bells and Bladebone might be called a "late" Grimes, despite the fact that she has been writing mysteries for only 10 years, because it at once shows her trying out a more formal fugue-like approach, with the serious and comic presented for much of the novel in separate sections, and also presents the reader with a fundamental ambiguity at the end. Either Sadie Diver and Simon Lean were killed by Hannah Lean, who stabbed Sadie on Wapping Old Stairs in London's East End, and, after stabbing her husband, stuffed him in a valuable antique desk in Long Piddleton, *or* Sadie killed Hannah with Simon's connivance, then did him in, and took Hannah's place, and money, relying on her resemblance to Hannah and various other strategems to support the charade. Which woman is Jury pursuing? One never knows for sure, because the woman's last words as she is dying after slashing her wrists are, "I'm not her." Probably she is Hannah, but for this story Grimes leaves us with a genuine mystery. It seems to be her *Turn of the Screw* or *Benito Cereno,* a radically ambiguous fiction.

The Old Silent, longest and most complex of her works, shows her venturing into yet another territory, since its sub-theme is the world of popular music and several of the characters musicians. Throughout the story there are phrases from popular songs, and the movement of the novel resembles that of jazz, with shifts of perspective, more "riffs." The plot is as complex as ever, and the problem of identity crucial as it often is, but the music motif makes this novel unique among her works. Grimes is a writer of infinite resource and great skill; *The Old Silent* shows that there are undoubtedly still more intriguing mystery stories to come.

—Richard C. Carpenter

GRUBER, Frank. Also wrote as Stephen Acre; Charles K. Boston; John K. Vedder. American. Born in Elmer, Minnesota, 2 February 1904. Attended high school. Served in the United States Army, 1920–21. Married Lois Mahood in 1931; one son. Editor of trade journals; teacher in correspondence schools; self-employed writer from 1934. *Died 9 December 1969.*

CRIME PUBLICATIONS

Novels (series: Otis Beagle; Johnny Fletcher and Sam Cragg; Simon Lash)

The French Key (Fletcher and Cragg). New York, Farrar and Rinehart, 1940; London, Hale, 1941; as *The French Key Mystery,* New York, Avon, 1942; as *Once Over Deadly,* New York, Spivak, 1956.
The Laughing Fox (Fletcher and Cragg). New York, Farrar and Rinehart, 1940; London, Nicholson and Watson, 1942.
The Hungry Dog (Fletcher and Cragg). New York, Farrar and Rinehart, 1941; London, Nicholson and Watson, 1950; as *The Hungry Dog Murders,* New York, Avon, 1943; as *Die Like a Dog,* New York, Spivak, 1957.
The Navy Colt (Fletcher and Cragg). New York, Farrar and Rinehart, 1941; London, Nicholson and Watson, 1942.
Simon Lash, Private Detective. New York, Farrar and Rinehart, 1941; as *Simon Lash, Detective,* London, Nicholson and Watson, 1943.
The Silver Jackass (Beagle; as Charles K. Boston). New York, Reynal, 1941; London, Cherry Tree, 1952.
The Talking Clock (Fletcher and Cragg). New York, Farrar and Rinehart, 1941; London, Nicholson and Watson, 1942.
The Last Doorbell (as John K. Vedder). New York, Holt, 1941; as *Kiss the Boss Goodbye* (as Frank Gruber), New York, Spivak, 1954.
The Buffalo Box (Lash). New York, Farrar and Rinehart, 1942; London, Nicholson and Watson, 1944.
The Gift Horse (Fletcher and Cragg). New York, Farrar and Rinehart, 1942; London, Nicholson and Watson, 1943.
The Yellow Overcoat (as Stephen Acre). New York, Dodd Mead, 1942; London, Boardman, 1945; as *Fall Guy for a Killer* (as Frank Gruber), New York, Spivak, 1955.
The Mighty Blockhead (Fletcher and Cragg). New York, Farrar and Rinehart, 1942; London, Nicholson and Watson, 1948; as *The Corpse Moved Upstairs,* New York, Belmont, 1964.
The Silver Tombstone (Fletcher and Cragg). New York, Farrar and Rinehart, 1945; London, Nicholson and Watson, 1949; as *The Silver Tombstone Mystery,* New York, New American Library, 1959.

Beagle Scented Murder. New York, Rinehart, 1946; as *Market for Murder,* New York, New American Library, 1947.
The Fourth Letter. New York, Rinehart, 1947.
The Honest Dealer (Fletcher and Cragg). New York, Rinehart, 1947.
The Whispering Master (Fletcher and Cragg). New York, Rinehart, 1947.
The Lock and the Key. New York, Rinehart, 1948; Kingswood, Surrey, World's Work, 1950; as *Too Tough to Die,* New York, Spivak, 1954; as *Run Thief Run,* New York, Fawcett, 1955.
Murder 97 (Lash). New York, Rinehart, 1948; London, Barker, 1956; as *The Long Arm of Murder,* New York, Spivak, 1956.
The Scarlet Feather (Fletcher and Cragg). New York, Rinehart, 1948; London, Cherry Tree, 1951; as *The Gamecock Murders,* New York, New American Library, 1949.
The Leather Duke (Fletcher and Cragg). New York, Rinehart, 1949; Manchester, Pemberton, 1950; as *A Job of Murder,* New York, New American Library, 1950.
The Limping Goose (Fletcher and Cragg). New York, Rinehart, 1954; London, Barker, 1955; as *Murder One,* New York, Belmont, 1973.
The Lonesome Badger (Beagle). New York, Rinehart, 1954; as *Mood for Murder,* Hasbrouck Heights, New Jersey, Graphic, 1956.
Twenty Plus Two. New York, Dutton, and London, Boardman, 1961.
Brothers of Silence. New York, Dutton, and London, Boardman, 1962.
Bridge of Sand. New York, Dutton, 1963; London, Boardman, 1964.
The Greek Affair. New York, Dutton, 1964; London, Boardman, 1965.
Swing Low Swing Dead (Fletcher and Cragg). New York, Belmont, 1964.
Little Hercules. New York, Dutton, 1965; London, Boardman, 1966.
Run, Fool, Run. New York, Dutton, 1966; London, Hale, 1967.
The Twilight Man. New York, Dutton, and London, Hale, 1967.
The Gold Gap. New York, Dutton, and London, Hale, 1968.
The Etruscan Bull. New York, Dutton, 1969; London, Hale, 1970.
The Spanish Prisoner. New York, Dutton, 1969; London, Hale, 1970.

Short Stories

Brass Knuckles. Los Angeles, Sherbourne Press, 1966.

Uncollected Short Stories

"Strangler's Clue," in *Underworld Magazine* (Springfield, Massachusetts), August 1933.
"Wooden Nails," in *Phantom Detective* (New York), December 1933.
"House of Death," in *Underworld Magazine* (Springfield, Massachusetts), February 1934.
"Master of Fear," in *Secret Agent X* (Springfield, Massachusetts), March 1934.
"The Hundred Grand Snatch," in *Underworld Detective* (Springfield, Massachusetts), September 1934.

"Three Dead Merchants," in *Underworld Detective* (Springfield, Massachusetts), November 1934.

"Death in Disguise," in *Secret Detective Operator* (Chicago), April 1935.

"A Toast to Death," in *Secret Detective Operator* (Chicago), August 1935.

"The Murder Chest," in *The Whisperer* (New York), September 1935.

"The Coffin That Went to Sea," in *Secret Detective Operator* (Chicago), October, 1935.

"The Devil's Coin," in *The Whisperer* (New York), October 1935.

"Fugitive for Honor," in *Detective Tales* (Kokomo, Indiana), November 1935.

"Witch's Curse," in *The Shadow* (New York), 1 December 1935.

"Dust of Doom," in *Secret Detective Operator* (Chicago), December 1935.

"Empire at Auction," in *Secret Detective Operator* (Chicago), January 1936.

"Red Hands Reaching," in *Detective Tales* (Kokomo, Indiana), January 1936.

"Formula for Death," in *Secret Detective Operator* (Chicago), February 1936.

"Slant-Eyed Satan," in *Dr. Yen Sin* (Chicago), May–June 1936.

"Murder Invitation," in *G-Men* (New York), May 1936.

"Red Dust of Death," in *Secret Detective Operator* (Chicago), June–July 1936.

"Road Through Hell," in *Detective Tales* (Kokomo, Indiana), June 1936.

"Satan's Talisman," in *Dime Mystery Magazine* (Kokomo, Indiana), June 1936.

"Traitor's Legacy," in *Secret Detective Operator* (Chicago), August–September 1936.

"Shackled Doom," in *Ace Mystery* (Springfield, Massachusetts), September 1936.

"The Choking Chalice," in *Dr. Yen Sin* (Chicago), September–October 1936.

"Doom's Lottery," in *Ten Detective Aces* (Springfield, Massachusetts), October 1936.

"Brass Knuckles," in *Thrilling Detective* (New York), November 1936.

'Dime-a-Dance Murder," in *Detective Romances* (Springfield, Massachusetts), November 1936.

"Racket Buster," in *The Spider* (Chicago), November 1936.

"Rough Diamonds," in *Popular Detective* (New York), November 1936.

"Death at the Main," in *Thrilling Detective* (New York), December 1936.

"Death, Incorporated," in *Detective & Murder Mysteries* (Philadelphia), December 1936.

"Death Rides the Rails," in *G-Men* (New York), December 1936.

"Murder in the Want Ads," in *The Spider* (Chicago), December 1936.

"Clip-Joint Adventuress," in *Detective Romances* (Springfield, Massachusetts), January 1937.

"Death at Thirty Below," in *G-Men* (New York), January 1937.

"Murder on the Midway," in *Thrilling Detective* (New York), January 1937.

"Salesman of Doom," in *Secret Detective Operator* (Chicago), January 1937.

"Second-Hand Death," in *The Spider* (Chicago), January 1937.

"Too Smart to Live," in *Ace-High Detective Magazine* (Chicago), February–March 1937.

"Assignment to Hell," in *Secret Agent X* (Springfield, Massachusetts), February 1937.

"Doubling in Death," in *Secret Detective Operator* (Chicago), February 1937.

"Fur-Coated Murder," in *The Spider* (Chicago), February 1937.

"Pictures of Death," in *Thrilling Detective* (New York), February 1937.

"Death by Appointment," in *Federal Agent* (New York), March 1937.

"Death Subscribes," in *Pocket Detective* (New York), March 1937.

"Dogs of Death," in *Crime Busters* (New York), March 1937.

"Fat Man," in *The Whisperer* (New York), March 1937.

"Murder on the Mat," in *Popular Detective* (New York), March 1937.

"The Devil's Checkroom," in *Secret Agent X* (Springfield, Massachusetts), April 1937.

"The Arrow of Doom," in *Secret Detective Operator* (Chicago), May–June 1937.

"Death From the Blue," in *Popular Detective* (New York), May 1937.

"The Human Camera," in *Pocket Detective* (New York), May 1937.

"Fox Trap," in *The Shadow* (New York), 1 June 1937.

"The Flying Skull," in *The Shadow* (New York), 15 June 1937.

"Bullet Biography," in *Detective Fiction Weekly* (New York), 26 June 1937.

"Ask Me Another," in *Black Mask* (Chicago), June 1937.

"No Peddlers Wanted," in *Pocket Detective Magazine* (New York), June 1937.

"The Stars Foretell," in *The Shadow* (New York), 15 July 1937.

"Candid Witness," in *Black Mask* (Chicago), July 1937.

"Inventions of Death," in *The Whisperer* (New York), July 1937.

"Death Makes a Bid," in *The Shadow* (Elizabeth, New Jersey), 15 August 1937.

"Death Signs the Payroll," in *The Spider* (Chicago), August, 1937.

"Wire-House Kill," in *The Shadow* (Elizabeth, New Jersey), 15 September 1937.

"Educated Eyes," in *Clues* (New York), September 1937.

"Rain, the Killer," in *Black Mask* (Chicago), September 1937.

"Detour to Murder," in *Secret Agent X* (Springfield, Massachusetts), October 1937.

"Ozark Outlaws," in *Feds* (New York), October 1937.

"Suits for the Dead," in *The Whisperer* (New York), October 1937.

"The Raw Deal," in *Pocket Detective* (New York), October 1937.

"Without Benefit," in *The Whisperer* (New York), November 1937.

"Hen House Homicide," in *Detective Fiction Weekly* (New York), 4 December 1937.

"Antidote for Hell," in *Ten Detective Aces* (Springfield, Massachusetts), December 1937.

"Death on Eagle's Crag," in *Black Mask* (Chicago), December 1937.

"Too Many Browns," in *The Whisperer* (New York), December 1937.

"The Red Meal Ticket," in *Crime Busters* (New York), January 1938.

"Racket Toll," in *Crime Busters* (New York), February 1938.

"Dog Show Murder," in *Black Mask* (Chicago), March 1938.

"Seeds of Death," in *The Shadow* (Elizabeth, New Jersey), 1 April 1938.

"If I Can Ever Forget," in *Detective Fiction Weekly* (New York), 30 April 1938.

"Goose Island Kill," in *Crime Busters* (New York), April 1938.

"No Motive," in *Black Mask* (Chicago), April 1938.

"Magenta Murders," in *The Shadow* (Elizabeth, New Jersey), 15 May 1938.

"Innocent Bystander," in *Detective Fiction Weekly* (New York), 28 May 1938.

"Death Sits Down," in *Black Mask* (Chicago), May 1938.

"Silk Stocking Death," in *Crime Busters* (New York), May 1938.

"Death is Lonesome," in *Crime Busters* (New York), June 1938.

"Fur Coat Murder," in *Crime Busters* (New York), July 1938.

"Patented Death," in *The Shadow* (Elizabeth, New Jersey), 1 August 1938.

"A Swede Called Johnson," in *Detective Fiction Weekly* (New York), 13 August 1938.

"The Ring and the Finger," in *Black Mask* (Chicago), August 1938.

"The Cat Creeps," in *The Shadow* (Elizabeth, New Jersey), 15 September 1938.

"Camera Kill," in *Crime Busters* (New York), September 1938.

"Stamps of Doom," in *G-Men* (New York), September 1938.

"Forced Landing," in *Black Mask* (Chicago), October 1938.

"Death Comes Home." in *Crime Busters* (New York), 15 December 1938.

"Tough Guy," in *Clues* (New York), November 1938.

"Coins of Death," in *The Shadow* (Elizabeth, New Jersey), 15 December 1938.

"Murder for a Laugh," in *The Shadow* (Elizabeth, New Jersey), 15 January 1939.

"Roof Over Murder," in *Crime Busters* (New York), January 1939.

"Skip Murder," in *Clues* (New York), February 1939.

"State Fair Murder," in *Black Mask* (Chicago), February 1939.

"The Sad Serbian," in *Black Mask* (Chicago), March 1939.

"Minneapolis Death, " in *The Shadow Mask* (Elizabeth, New Jersey), 15 April 1939.

"No Bullets Today," in *Popular Detective* (New York), April 1939.

"Duplicate Death," in *Clues* (New York), May 1939.

"Funny Man," in *Black Mask* (Chicago), May 1939.

"Song of Death," in *Crime Busters* (New York), May 1939.

"Jim Strong in Hollywood," in *Crime Busters* (New York), June 1939.

"Sweet Charity," in *Crime Busters* (New York), September 1939.

"Death Goes Psychic," in *Mystery Magazine* (New York), November 1939.

"Oliver Quade at the Races," in *Black Mask* (Chicago), November 1939.

"Backflash to Murder," in *Mystery Magazine* (New York), December 1939.

"Death's Understudy," in *Clues* (New York), January 1940.

"Jobs of Jeopardy," in *Mystery Magazine* (New York), February 1940.

"The Dead Don't Sue," in *Clues* (New York), February 1940.

"Words and Music," in *Black Mask* (Chicago), March 1940.

"Free Lots," in *Mystery Magazine* (New York), April 1940.

"The Murder Book," in *Clues* (New York), May 1940.

"Death Going Up," in *Mystery Magazine* (New York), June 1940.

"Death Elects a Governor," in *Detective Fiction Weekly* (New York), 21 September 1940.

"The Old Mink Game," in *Mystery Magazine* (New York), September 1940.

"The Talking Clock," (Pt.1) in *Detective Fiction Weekly* (New York), 12 October 1940.

"Death is Vain," in *Mystery Magazine* (New York), January 1941.

"Movie Murder," in *Detective Fiction Weekly* (New York), 26 April 1941.

"Death on Post No. 7," in *Detective Story Magazine* (New York), April and May 1941.

"The Box from Burma," in *Clues* (New York), May 1941.

"The Silver Owl," in *Avenger* (New York), May 1941.

"The Old Tin Box," in *Clues* (New York), September 1941.

"The Murder Gun," in *All Fiction Detective Stories* (New York), 1942.

"The Man from Manitoba," in *Detective Tales* (Kokomo, Indiana), February 1942.

"The Honest Dealer," in *Mammoth Detective* (Chicago), December 1946.

"Whispering Master," in *Mammoth Detective* (Chicago), July 1947.

"The Fourth Letter," in *Shadow Mystery* (New York), October–November 1947.

"The Lock and Key," in *Shadow Mystery* (New York), June–July 1948.

"Cat and Mouse," in *Ellery Queen's Mystery Magazine* (New York), September 1949.

"Trailer Town," in *Giant Detective Annual* (New York), 1950.

"The Gold Cup," in *Ellery Queen's Mystery Magazine* (New York), February 1952.

"The Dragon Pistol," in *Ellery Queen's Mystery Magazine* (New York), August 1952.

"Murder at the Race Track," in *The Saint* (New York), September 1955.

"Falcon City Frame-Up," in *Mercury* (New York), October 1955.

"You Can't Crack a Modern Safe," in *Ellery Queen's Mystery Maagazine* (New York), November 1955.

"Honesty Is My Motto," in *Ellery Queen's Mystery Magazine* (New York), December 1960.

"1000-to-1 for Your Money," in *Ellery Queen's Anthology 1965 Mid-Year*. New York, Davis, 1965.

"Eagle in His Mouth," in *Ellery Queen's Mystery Magazine* (New York), September 1967.

"The Booty Hunters," in *Mike Shayne Mystery Magazine* (New York), September 1968.

"The Gun," in *Mike Shayne Mystery Magazine* (Los Angeles), March 1970.

OTHER PUBLICATIONS

Novels

Peace Marshal. New York, Morrow, 1939; London, Barker, 1957.

Outlaw. New York, Farrar and Rinehart, 1941; London, Wright and Brown, 1942.

Gunsight. New York, Dodd Mead, 1942; London, Wright and Brown, 1943.

Fighting Man. New York, Rinehart, 1948; London, Wright and Brown, 1951.

Broken Lance. New York, Rinehart, 1949; London, Wright and Brown, 1952.

Smoky Road. New York, Rinehart, 1949; London, Wright and Brown, 1952; as *The Lone Gunhawk*, New York, Lion, 1953.

Fort Starvation. New York, Rinehart, 1953.

Quantrell's Raiders. New York, Ace, 1954.

Bitter Sage. New York, Rinehart, 1954; London, Wright and Brown, 1955.

Bugles West. New York, Rinehart, 1954; London, Barker, 1956.

Johnny Vengeance. New York, Rinehart, 1954; London, Wright and Brown, 1956.

Rebel Road. New York, Ace, 1954.

The Highwayman. New York, Rinehart, 1955; London, Barker, 1957; as *Ride to Hell,* New York, New American Library, 1955.

The Man from Missouri, New York, Popular Library, 1956.

Buffalo Grass. New York, Rinehart, 1956; London, Barker, 1957.

The Big Land. New York, Bantam, 1957.

Lonesome River. New York, Rinehart, 1957; London, Barker, 1958.

The Marshal. New York, Rinehart, 1958; London, Barker, 1959.

Town Tamer. New York, Rinehart, and London, Barker, 1958.

The Bushwhackers. New York, Rinehart, 1959; London, New English Library, 1960.

This Gun Is Still. New York, Bantam, 1967.

The Dawn Riders. New York, Bantam, 1968.

The Curly Wolf. New York, Bantam, 1969; London, Bantam, 1979.

Wanted! New York, Bantam, 1971; London, Bantam, 1979.

Short Stories

Tales of Wells Fargo. New York, Bantam, and London, Corgi, 1958.

Plays

Screenplays: *Northern Pursuit,* with Alvah Bessie, 1943; *The Mask of Dimitrios,* 1944; *Johnny Angel,* with Steve Fisher, 1945; *The French Key,* 1946; *Terror by Night,* 1946; *Accomplice,* with Irving Elman, 1946; *In Old Sacramento,* with Frances Hyland and Jerome Odlum, 1946; *Dressed to Kill,* with Leonard Lee, 1946; *Bulldog Drummond at Bay,* 1947; *The Challenge,* with Irving Elman, 1948; *Fighting Man of the Plains,* 1949; *The Cariboo Trail,* with John Rhodes Sturdy, 1950; *Dakota Lil,* with Maurice Geraghty, 1950; *The Texas Rangers,* with Richard Schayer, 1950; *The Great Missouri Raid,* 1951; *Warpath,* 1951; *Silver City,* 1951; *Flaming Feather,* with Gerald Drayson Adams, 1952; *The Denver and Rio Grande,* 1952; *Hurricane Smith,* 1952; *Pony Express,* with Charles Marquis Warren, 1953; *Rage at Dawn,* with Horace McCoy, 1955; *Twenty Plus Two,* 1961; *Town Tamer,* 1965; *Arizona Raiders,* with others, 1965.

Television Plays: creator of *Tales of Wells Fargo, The Texan,* and *Shotgun Slade* series; author of some 200 scripts.

Other

Horatio Alger, Jr.: A Biography and Bibliography. Privately printed, 1961.

The Pulp Jungle (autobiography). Los Angeles, Sherbourne Press, 1967.

Zane Grey: A Biography. Cleveland, World, 1970.

*　　*　　*

Frank Gruber's production of popular fiction has been immense. About half of his many short stories, novels, and film and television scripts are concerned with detectives and crime. In the 1930's his Oliver Quade stories, along with a variety of others appeared regularly in the pulp magazines. During the 1940's and 1950's his detective novels appeared sometimes at the rate of three or four a year, interspersed with more short stories, and westerns. The Quade stories emphasized the encyclopedic knowledge of the hero and his exploits with his partner, Charlie Boston. Beginning with *The French Key,* the Johnny Fletcher novels are produced at a furious pace and signalled a shift from the classic detective hero to Gruber's version of the representative man—an adventurer, however reluctantly, who lives by his wits in an often topsy-turvy world. Johnny Fletcher is mildly hard-boiled and street-wise, often without money except for the sale of books promoting the great strength of his sidekick, Sam Cragg. The brief Otis Beagle series features a detective with the opposite tendencies: flashy clothes and imitation diamonds in his rings and stickpin. In addition to the short Simon Lash series, more than a dozen further novels feature central characters who are caught in circumstances that force them into detection. The odyssey of Gruber's detectives takes them from the relatively mannered world of the classical detective in the early stories, through the witty decencies of the 1940's and early 1950's, into the hard picaresque intrigues of the late 1960's. In *The Gold Gap* the genteel assumptions of the earliest stories have become polished deceptions that mask the successful psychopath at the center of an international plot.

Anthony Boucher credits Gruber's success to the fast pace of his fiction and his incredibly fertile imagination. Certainly he could be compared in this respect with such prolific pulp writers as Frederick Faust, with whom he also shared an astute market sense and an instinct for light, entertaining plots. In *The Pulp Jungle,* however, Gruber traced his success with mystery stories to his discovery in the 1930's of an 11-point plot formula. The successful story, Gruber argued, had to have a colorful hero, a theme that contains information the reader is not likely to have, a villain more powerful than the hero, a colorful background for the action, an unusual murder method or unusual circumstances surrounding the murder, unusual variations on the motives of hate and greed, a concealed clue, the trick that extricates the hero from certain defeat, moving and carefully paced action, a smashing climax, and a hero who is personally involved. In practice Gruber also relied on another element that might be traced to his fondness for Horatio Alger: the play of chance lends a juvenile innocence to many of his stories. On their way through Death Valley in *The Honest Dealer,* Fletcher and Cragg happen across a dying man who gives them a deck of cards that proves to be the key to the mystery; as they approach Las Vegas they give a ride to the key woman; a colorful policeman finds them a room next to hers when a bribe has failed to turn one up in the entire city; and Fletcher parlays his last dollar into 20 thousand at the gambling tables. Yet after the formula, or in the midst of it, comes the story-teller who has been able to hold his reader's attention regardless of the mechanical thinness of his plots and characters. Few writers have been so consistently successful.

—Larry N. Landrum

H

HADDON, Christopher. *See* **BEEDING, Francis.**

———

HADLEY, Joan. *See* **HESS, Joan.**

———

HAGGARD, William. Pseudonym for Richard Henry Michael Clayton. British. Born in Croydon, Surrey, 11 August 1907. Educated at Lancing College, Sussex; Christ Church, Oxford, B.A. 1929. Served in the Indian Army, 1939–46: Lieutenant Colonel, General Staff. Married Barbara Myfanwy Sant in 1936; one son and one daughter. Served in the Indian Civil Service, 1931–39; worked for the Board of Trade, 1947–69; controller of enemy property, 1965–69. M.A.: Oxford University, 1947. Agent: John Farquharson Ltd., 162-168 Regent Street, London WIR 5TB; or, 250 West 57th Street, New York, New York 10107, U.S.A. Address: 3 Linkside, Frinton-on-Sea, Essex CO13 9EN, England.

CRIME PUBLICATIONS

Novels (series: Paul Martiny; Colonel Charles Russell; William Wilbeforce Smith)

Slow Burner (Russell). London, Cassell, and Boston, Little Brown, 1958.
The Telemann Touch. London, Cassell, and Boston, Little Brown, 1958.
Venetian Blind (Russell). London, Cassell, and New York, Washburn, 1959.
Closed Circuit. London, Cassell, and New York, Washburn, 1960.
The Arena (Russell). London, Cassell, and New York, Washburn, 1961.
The Unquiet Sleep (Russell). London, Cassell, and New York, Washburn, 1962.
The High Wire (Russell). London, Cassell, and New York, Washburn, 1963.
The Antagonists (Russell). London, Cassell, and New York, Washburn, 1964.
The Powder Barrel (Russell). London, Cassell, and New York, Washburn, 1965.
The Hard Sell (Russell). London, Cassell, 1965; New York, Washburn, 1966.
The Power House (Russell). London, Cassell, 1966; New York, Washburn, 1967.
The Conspirators (Russell). London, Cassell, 1967; New York, Walker, 1968.

A Cool Day for Killing (Russell). London, Cassell, and New York, Walker, 1968.
The Doubtful Disciple (Russell). London, Cassell, 1969.
The Hardliners (Russell). London, Cassell, and New York, Walker, 1970.
The Bitter Harvest (Russell). London, Cassell, 1971; as *Too Many Enemies,* New York, Walker, 1972.
The Protectors (Martiny). London, Cassell, and New York, Walker, 1972.
The Old Masters (Russell). London, Cassell, 1973; as *The Notch on the Knife,* New York, Walker, 1973.
The Kinsmen (Martiny). London, Cassell, and New York, Walker, 1974.
The Scorpion's Tail (Russell). London, Cassell, and New York, Walker, 1975.
Yesterday's Enemy (Russell). London, Cassell, and New York, Walker, 1976.
The Poison People (Russell). London, Cassell, 1978; New York, Walker, 1979.
Visa to Limbo (Russell). London, Cassell, 1978; New York, Walker, 1979.
The Median Line (Russell). London, Cassell, 1979; New York, Walker, 1981.
The Money Men. London, Hodder and Stoughton, and New York, Walker, 1981.
The Mischief-Makers. London, Hodder and Stoughton, and New York, Walker, 1982.
The Heirloom. London, Hodder and Stoughton, 1983.
The Need to Know. London, Hodder and Stoughton, 1984.
The Meritocrats. (Russell). London, Hodder and Stoughton, 1985.
The Martello Tower (Smith). London, Hodder and Stoughton, 1986.
The Diplomatist (Smith). London, Hodder and Stoughton, 1987.
The Expatriates (Russell). London, Hodder and Stoughton, 1989.
The Vendettists (Russell). London, Hodder and Stoughton, 1990.

Uncollected Short Stories

"Night Train to Milan," in *Best Secret Service Stories 2,* edited by John Welcome. London, Faber, 1965.
"Why Beckett Died," in *Blood on My Mind.* London, Macmillan, 1972.
"The Hirelings," in *Winter's Crimes 4,* edited by George Hardinge. London, Macmillan, and New York, St. Martin's Press, 1972.
"Timeo Danaos," in *Winter's Crimes 8,* edited by Hilary Watson. London, Macmillan, and New York, St. Martin's Press, 1976.
"The Great Divide," in *The Rigby File,* edited by Tim Heald. London, Hodder and Stoughton, 1989.

OTHER PUBLICATIONS

Other

The Little Rug Book. London, Cassell, 1972.

* * *

The flavour of William Haggard: it is one of the pleasures left in life. Bread today is made of bouncy plastic; beer is fizzed-up by chemicals; but the taste of a Haggard book is unique, inimitable (though not too hard to parody, I hazard), and delightful. His view of the world, his tone of voice, enter almost all his characters' heads and certainly permeate every phrase he writes as narrator or describer. He cannot put pen to paper without showing in every word an unchippable top-level view of the world. Even when he chances to reflect on the Almighty this view comes banging across. Listen to a typical Haggard character (from *The Doubtful Disciple*) musing: he "hadn't expected his God would be a fool. He'd be a senior administrator. . . . He wouldn't hold it against a colleague that he'd simply done his duty." Even the use of that "He'd" is typical, indicating a brusque disregard for the conventional usage of the middle classes, a *droit de seigneur* of grammar.

Whatever story Haggard embarks on he takes you with superb unconcern straight into the highest of high places in the stacked hierarchy of British life (and occasionally into what he sees as the equally hierarchic life of Soviet Russia). It is an entrancing process, because the highest places are of their nature very small places. There is not room at the very top for all of us. But in Haggard we have a proxy in the seats of power. And, note, these highest places are not your mere Cabinet Rooms or Prime Minister's studies. They are the rooms behind these, the rooms occupied by the people who view prime ministers as simply the awkward and temporary holders of an office. They are the less grandiloquent rooms of those who have acquired, or semi-inherited, the duty of protecting the children of Demos from themselves. I do not know whether in drab real life they actually exist, but while I am reading the pages of a book by Haggard they certainly do.

To descend to details: William Haggard writes what might be called action novels of international power politics. Generally, but not invariably, their hero is Colonel Russell of the Security Executive (a fictitious body). The books work in terms of real-politik, that is to say their plots are designed to show that it is the realities of any situation that dictate its final outcome. But, though the flavour is always (and savoursomely) the same, the books themselves have been admirably varied. Russell in the course of them retired as Head of the Security Executive and there have been books in which he did not appear at all, or only briefly. Once (in *The Protectors*) he was replaced by a sort of gentleman master-criminal, an investor in the directly criminal activities of others, a man motivated to a large extent by a desire to kick the pompous part of the Establishment, the prating Ministers and others, on the backside.

This desire to tumble tin gods is a strong strain in all the books. Haggard is no mean iconoclast. He it was who had the temerity to draw a portrait (in *The Power House*) of an actual Prime Minister then in office, easily recognisable and cast in vigorously contemptuous terms. Another book had to be withdrawn on the eve of publication while a portrait of a well-known extreme leftist was hurriedly disguised.

Of course, this attitude, full of flavour though it be, is not necessarily to everybody's taste. The conventional are apt to be shocked. To many readers, unable to put themselves in the shoes of Haggard Sahib, his books will be disquieting, or even occasionally downright repulsive. This may be so especially with women readers confronting his treatment of sex. Increasingly (as it has become more and more possible, or even desirable, to put explicit sex into fiction), he has introduced sexual events into his pages, always certainly illuminating character if not advancing the action. He has eschewed those minutely descriptive passages that other, and generally younger, writers have come to use, but he has written of sexual acts with a direct, if generalised, brutality. It was the realpolitik of the bedsheets, and as such certainly offensive to the romantic.

A Haggard novel is, as I have indicated, always politically firmly oriented to the right, though he is not so slavishly attached to current dogma as to make all his villains soft lefties and all his heroes straight-thinking men (and women) of the right. He is quite capable of bestowing his praise—and that is how it comes across—on a socialist, provided he is a socialist who in power will exercise that power with a feeling for its reality rather than by idealistic criteria. So the books were front-runners in a trend that was noticeable in both British and American crime writing from the late 1960's onwards, a turning of the tide to flow to the right. After the revolution carried out in the late 1930's by Eric Ambler in the espionage field and, less markedly, by writers such as Nicholas Blake in detection—a revolution which swung crime writing generally to the left (something to be seen in a host of tiny judgements in any text)— there had been little change. With the Haggard books the first signs of a silent swing began to show.

—H.R.F. Keating

––––––––

HALL, Adam. Also writes as Mansell Black; Trevor Burgess; T. Dudley-Smith; Roger Fitzalan; Howard North; Simon Rattray; Warwick Scott; Caesar Smith; Elleston Trevor. British. Born Trevor Dudley Smith in Bromley, Kent, 17 February 1920. Educated at Yardley Court Preparatory School, Kent, 1928–32; Sevenoaks School, Kent, 1932–38. Served in the Royal Air Force, 1939–45: Flight Engineer. Married 1) Jonquil Burgess in 1947 (died 1986), one son; 2) Chaille Anne Groom in 1987. Lived in France, 1958–73, and in the United States since 1973. Recipient: Mystery Writers of America Edgar Allan Poe award, 1965; Grand Prix Littérature Policière, 1965. Agent: Morton Janklow Associates, 598 Madison Avenue, New York, New York 10022. Address: Star Route 2, Box 821, Cave Creek, Arizona 85331, U.S.A.

CRIME PUBLICATIONS

Novels (series: Quiller)

The Mystery of the Missing Book (as Trevor Burgess). London, Hutchinson, 1950.
Heat Wave (as Caesar Smith). London, Wingate, 1957; New York, Ballantine, 1958.
The Volcanoes of San Domingo. London, Collins, 1963; New York, Simon and Schuster, 1964.
The Berlin Memorandum (Quiller). London, Collins, 1965; as *The Quiller Memorandum,* New York, Simon and Schuster, 1965; London, Collins, 1967.
The 9th Directive (Quiller). London, Heinemann, and New York, Simon and Schuster, 1966.
A Blaze of Arms (as Roger Fitzalan). London, Davies, 1967.

The Striker Portfolio (Quiller). London, Heinemann, and New York, Simon and Schuster, 1969.
The Warsaw Document (Quiller). New York, Doubleday, and London, Heinemann, 1970.
The Tango Briefing (Quiller). London, Collins, and New York, Doubleday, 1973.
Expressway (as Howard North). London, Collins, and New York, Simon and Schuster, 1973.
The Mandarin Cypher. (Quiller). London, Collins, and New York, Doubleday, 1975.
The Kobra Manifesto (Quiller). London, Collins, and New York, Doubleday, 1976.
The Sinkiang Executive (Quiller). London, Collins, and New York, Doubleday, 1978.
The Scorpion Signal (Quiller). London, Collins, 1979; New York, Doubleday, 1980.
The Sibling (Quiller). New York, Playboy Press, 1979; London, New English Library, 1980.
Pekin Target (Quiller). London, Collins, 1981; as *The Peking Target,* New York, Playboy Press, 1982.
Northlight (Quiller). New York, Berkley, and London, W.H. Allen, 1985)
Quiller. New York, Jove, 1985.
Siren Song (as Lesley Stone). London, W.H. Allen, 1985.
Riviera Story (as Lesley Stone). London, W.H. Allen, 1987.
Quiller's Run. London, W.H. Allen, and New York, Jove, 1988.
Quiller K.G.B. New York, Charter, 1989.
Quiller Barracuda. New York, Morrow, and London, W.H. Allen, 1990.

Novels as T. Dudley-Smith

Over the Wall. London, Swan, 1943.
Double Who Double Crossed. London, Swan, 1944.
Escape to Fear. London, Swan, 1948.
Now Try the Morgue. London, Swan, 1948.

Novels as Elleston Trevor

The Immortal Error. London, Swan, 1946.
Chorus of Echoes. London and New York, Boardman, 1950.
Redfern's Miracle. London and New York, Boardman, 1951.
Tiger Street. London, Boardman, 1951; New York, Lion, 1954.
A Blaze of Roses. London, Heinemann, and New York, Harper, 1952; as *The Fire-Raiser,* London, New English Library, 1970.
The Passion and the Pity. London, Heinemann, 1953.
The Big Pick-Up. London, Heinemann, and New York, Macmillan, 1955.
Squadron Airborne. London, Heinemann, 1955; New York, Macmillan, 1956.
The Killing Ground. London, Heinemann, 1956; New York, Macmillan, 1957.
Gale Force. London, Heinemann, 1956; New York, Macmillan, 1957.
The Pillars of Midnight. London, Heinemann, 1957; New York, Morrow, 1958.
Dream of Death. London, Brown and Watson, 1958.
Silhouette. London, Swan, 1959.
The V.I.P. London, Heinemann, 1959; New York, Morrow, 1960.
The Billboard Madonna. London, Heinemann, 1960; New York, Morrow, 1961.
The Mind of Max Duvine. London, Swan, 1960.

The Burning Shore. London, Heinemann, 1961; as *The Pasang Run,* New York, Harper, 1962.
The Flight of the Phoenix. London, Heinemann, and New York, Harper, 1964.
The Second Chance. London, Consul, 1965.
Weave a Rope of Sand. London, Consul, 1965.
The Shoot. London, Heinemann, and New York, Doubleday, 1966.
The Freebooters. London, Heinemann, and New York, Doubleday, 1967.
A Place for the Wicked. London, Heinemann, and New York, Doubleday, 1968.
Bury Him among Kings. London, Heinemann, and New York, Doubleday, 1970.
The Paragon. London, New English Library, 1975; as *Night Stop,* New York, Doubleday, 1975.
The Theta Syndrome. London, New English Library, and New York, Doubleday, 1977.
Blue Jay Summer. London, New English Library, and New York, Dell, 1977.
Seven Witnesses. London, Remploy, 1977.
The Damocles Sword. London, Collins, 1981; New York, Playboy Press, 1982.
The Penthouse. London, Collins, and New York, New American Library, 1983.
Death Watch. New York, Beaufort, 1984; London, W.H. Allen, 1985.

Novels as Mansell Black

Dead on Course. London, Hodder and Stoughton, 1951.
Sinister Cargo. London, Hodder and Stoughton, 1951.
Shadow of Evil. London, Hodder and Stoughton, 1953.
Steps in the Dark. London, Hodder and Stoughton, 1954.

Novels as Warwick Scott

Image in the Dust. London, Davies, 1951; as *Cockpit,* New York, Lion, 1953.
The Domesday Story. London, Davies, 1952; as *Doomsday,* New York, Lion, 1953.
Naked Canvas. London, Davies, 1954; New York, Popular Library, 1955.

Novels as Simon Rattray (series: Hugo Bishop in all books; published as Adam Hall in US)

Knight Sinister. London, Boardman, 1951; New York, Pyramid, 1971.
Queen in Danger. London, Boardman, 1952; New York, Pyramid, 1971.
Bishop in Check. London, Boardman, 1953; New York, Pyramid, 1971.
Dead Silence. London, Boardman, 1954; as *Pawn in Jeopardy,* New York, Pyramid, 1971.
Dead Circuit. London, Boardman, 1955; as *Rook's Gambit,* New York, Pyramid, 1972.
Dead Sequence. London, Boardman, 1957.

OTHER PUBLICATONS

Novels (for children).

Into the Happy Glade (as T. Dudley-Smith). London, Swan, 1943.
By a Silver Stream (as T. Dudley-Smith). London, Swan, 1944.

Wumpus. London, Swan, 1945.

Deep Wood. London, Swan, 1945; New York, Longman, 1947.

Heather Hill. London, Swan, 1946; New York, Longman, 1948.

More about Wumpus. London, Swan, 1947.

The Island of the Pines. London, Swan, 1948.

The Secret Travellers. London, Swan, 1948.

Where's Wumpus? London, Swan, 1948.

Badger's Beech. London, Falcon Press, 1948; Nashville, Aurora, 1970.

The Wizard of the Wood. London, Falcon Press, 1948.

Badger's Moon. London, Falcon Press, 1949.

A Spy at Monk's Court (as Trevor Burgess). London, Hutchinson, 1949.

Ants' Castle. London, Falcon Press, 1949.

Mole's Castle. London, Falcon Press, 1951.

Sweethallow Valley. London, Falcon Press, 1951.

Challenge of the Firebrand. London, Jenkins, 1951.

Secret Arena. London, Jenkins, 1951.

The Racing Wraith (as Trevor Burgess). London, Hutchinson, 1953.

Forbidden Kingdom. London, Lutterworth Press, 1955.

Badger's Wood. London, Heinemann, 1958; New York, Criterion, 1959.

The Crystal City. London, Swan, 1959.

Green Glades. London, Swan, 1959.

Squirrel's Island. London, Swan, 1963.

Short Stories

Elleston Trevor Miscellany. London, Swan, 1944.

Plays

The Last of the Daylight (produced Bromley, Kent, 1959).

Murder by All Means (produced Madrid, 1960; Farnham, Surrey, and London, 1961).

A Pinch of Purple (produced Bradford, 1971).

A Touch of Purple (produced Leatherhead, Surrey, and London, 1972). London, French, 1973.

Just Before Dawn (produced London, 1972).

Screenplay: *Wings of Danger,* with John Gilling and Packham Webb, 1952.

Other

Animal Life Stories: Rippleswim the Otter, Scamper-Foot the Pine Marten, Shadow the Fox. London, Swan, 3 vols., 1943–45.

*

Manuscript Collection: Mugar Memorial Library, Boston University.

* * *

With *The Berlin Memorandum* (1965), for which he won an Edgar, Adam Hall introduced the character of Quiller (no given name), a British intelligence agent, a "shadow executive" employed by "the Bureau." So sensitive are its tasks, the Bureau doesn't exist—officially. Quiller, its top operative, learned his trade infiltrating Nazi concentration camps during World War II to arrange escapes. Quiller's expertise comes into

play when the stakes are highest and then only at the authorization of the Prime Minister. In *The Quiller Memorandum,* he exposes an extensive, well-organized neo-Nazi conspiracy based in Berlin. *The Striker Portfolio* finds him back in Germany, this time to investigate a series of fighter crashes, the result of sabotage despite elaborate precautions to protect the aircraft. In *The Warsaw Document,* Quiller wrecks a Soviet plot to invade Warsaw on the pretext of fabricated evidence alleging a Western conspiracy to support Polish dissidents. He rescues a member of the Royal family from kidnappers in Bangkok in *The 9th Directive,* and parachutes into the Libyan desert (*The Tango Briefing*) with a tactical nuclear device to destroy British-manufactured nerve gas aboard a crashed plane before Arab agents can reach the site. When an American submarine is sunk while monitoring Russian naval activity at Murmansk, Quiller discovers the truth of the incident and insures that a super power summit will be held as scheduled (*Quiller*). In *Quiller KGB.,* he temporarily joins forces with his opposite number in the K.G.B. to foil the plans of a Kremlin faction to assassinate Mikhail Gorbachev.

Hall's conception of Quiller, established in *The Berlin Memorandum* and unchanged in its essentials throughout the series, offers little scope for development, even in comparison with James Bond and Matt Helm—the fictional agents that he most resembles. It is this narrowness of concept that presumably led one reviewer to call for Quiller to be pensioned off after *The Kobra Manifesto* (1976). Hall defines Quiller exclusively in terms of the knowledge and skills required for his exacting, dangerous work. Living only for the challenge of the mission, Quiller has no emotional or intellectual life independent of his work. Indeed, he apparently needs the pressures and dangers of the mission to sustain and periodically confirm his very identity. Quiller's considerable, if specialized, knowledge of psychology, neurophysiology, and such arcana as the processes of sleep and memory enhances his capacity for rational self-control under the extreme stress of the mission. In the final phases of his missions, Quiller finds himself isolated, his life apparently forfeit. On these occasions, struggling to maintain rational control of himself, he observes with clinical, detached contempt his body's instinctual responses that threaten the success of his mission: "the organism had started panicking because some of the brain-think had filtered through and it was squealing to know what I intended to do about its survival and there wasn't an answer." This "I"—to the disciplined perfection of which Quiller single-mindedly devotes himself—is as chilling a voice of disembodied rationality as contemporary espionage fiction affords. Irascible, humorless, suspicious of everyone, especially his superiors, Quiller, like fictional agents in general, is Hall's answer to the question of survival in a world of trickery and deceit, where betrayal is the norm and trust in any other person an unacceptable risk. It is a bleaker answer than is given by Len Deighton, Brian Freemantle, John le Carré, or Anthony Price, none of whom can be said to reckon the costs of intelligence work lightly.

—R. Gordon Kelley

HALLAHAN, William H(enry). American. Born in Brooklyn, New York. Educated at Temple University, Philadelphia, degrees in journalism and English. Recipient: Mystery Writers of America Edgar Allan Poe award, 1978. Address: c/o William Morrow Inc., 105 Madison Avenue, New York, New York 10016, U.S.A.

CRIME PUBLICATIONS

Novels (series: Charley Brewer)

The Dead of Winter. Indianapolis, Bobbs Merrill, 1972; London, Sphere, 1979.
The Ross Forgery. Indianapolis, Bobbs Merrill, 1973; London, Gollancz, 1977.
The Search for Joseph Tully. Indianapolis, Bobbs Merrill, 1974; London, Macmillan, 1975.
Catch Me, Kill Me. Indianapolis, Bobbs Merrill, 1977; London, Gollancz, 1979.
Keeper of the Children. New York, Morrow, 1978; London, Gollancz, 1979.
The Trade. New York, Morrow, and London, Gollancz, 1981.
The Monk. New York, Morrow, and London, Gollancz, 1983.
Foxcatcher (Brewer). New York, Morrow and London, Gollancz, 1986.
Tripletrap. New York, Morrow, 1989.

*   *   *

William H. Hallahan's writing can best be described as unique. Because of the genius of his fertile imagination, the result can either be very successful or detrimental to his career. Some shy away from Hallahan because he has written lately in very metaphysical terms. But no one doubts his splendid creativity and his almost perfect writing style. He is a polished and prolific writer who has made his name with a series of quite different books on the marginal figures of society.

The name Hallahan seemed to leap out of nowhere in 1972 with a book named *The Dead of Winter*. The scene was New York where four good poker buddies of varying backgrounds encounter dark violence. One of the four is fatally beaten. Amateurishly, the other three decide to strike back and find the friend's murderer. But soon they discover they are not the hunters but the hunted. They also find that though they played poker as a foursome once a week, they really knew very little about each other. The heart-thudding conclusion leaves the reader weak. The ending, however, is not a simple wrap-up, but a gigantic moral dilemma, with a particularly good and exciting finale. Other books came then in quick succession. But none reminded one of the other. *The Search for Joseph Tully* was a minor success, almost a cult book, that sold well. It is a strange and brooding book reeking with revenge. It is sad, a little hard to understand, and very, very moody. But what stirred the public's interest was the writing. Hallahan has a masterful way of creating an aura of horror.

Hallahan had written an espionage thriller in the early 1970's, *The Ross Forgery*. Then in the late 1970's, he decided seriously to invade the world of le Carré with *Catch Me, Kill Me*. This won him an Edgar. *Time* magazine called it a "masterpiece of bamboozlement, a kind of *Catch-22* between rival and riven U.S. agencies, written in a style that ranges from hardest-boiled egg to soufflé, with nothing poached." The plot is intricate but believable. But it too had a strange thread weaving through its fabric. As in Graham Greene's entertainments, Hallahan's featured players are really strangers to the reader. They are very elusive. You are never allowed to know them intimately. Hallahan was certainly not writing with a motion picture in mind but in his own, sometimes infuriating style. Then, for at least one book, he seemed to conform with a big spy thriller called *The Trade*. This was by far his most commercial novel. Reviewers compared him to Robert Ludlum; some said he was even better. A good adventure with real people and a well-thought-out plot made *The Trade* a model for future stories of this type.

But for those who have followed the career of this man, you will know that he cannot and will not be categorized. *Keeper of the Children* and *The Monk* led him in yet another direction, that of the occult. Both very well written but far from mysteries. Then in 1986 it was back to the spy novel, this time a lightly moving and rather humorous novel titled *Foxcatcher*. This was the first of the Charley Brewer series and sees agent Brewer wind up in a not quite happy situation. This one, though of a serious subject is written almost with a tongue in cheek style. And finally in 1989 *Tripletrap*, the second in the Brewer series and Hallahan's effort to bring criminal deduction into his list of plots and sub-plots. Again, very well written with winter weather playing a big part in the background but again with a hands off approach to really "knowing" the characters.

Hallahan is a very complex author and his works will be remembered, though not always admired. He may not be our top mystery writer of the day, but part of that could be that perhaps he doesn't *want* to be. But he certainly is one of the most interesting and enticing writers today, and one wonders where his career will lead him next.

—Don Cole

———

HALLIDAY, Brett. Pseudonym for Davis Dresser; also wrote as Asa Baker; Matthew Blood; Kathryn Culver; Don Davis; Hal Debrett; Anthony Scott; Anderson Wayne. American. Born in Chicago, Illinois, 31 July 1904. Raised in Texas; joined the United States Army Cavalry at 14; returned to Texas to finish high school; educated at Tri-State College, Angola, Indiana, Certificate in Civil Engineering. Married 1) Helen McCloy, *q.v.,* in 1946 (divorced 1961), one daughter; 2) Kathleen Rollins; 3) Mary Savage. Writer from 1927, contributing stories under many pseudonyms to mystery, western and adventure pulps; novels by-lined Brett Halliday after 1958 were ghostwritten by others; co-founder, with Helen McCloy, Torquil Publishing Company, and Halliday and McCloy, Literary Agency, 1953–64; founding editor, *Mike Shayne Mystery Magazine*, 1956 (magazine still carries works by-lined Brett Halliday). Recipient: Mystery Writers of America Edgar Allan Poe award, for criticism, 1953. *Died 4 February 1977.*

CRIME PUBLICATIONS

Novels (series: Jerry Burke in both books as Asa Baker; Michael Shayne in all books as Halliday; Morgan Wayne in both books as Matthew Blood)

Mum's the Word for Murder (as Asa Baker). New York, Stokes, 1938; London, Gollancz, 1939.
The Kissed Corpse (as Asa Baker). New York, Carlyle, 1939.
Dividend on Death. New York, Holt, 1939; London, Jarrolds, 1941.
The Private Practice of Michael Shayne. New York, Holt, 1940; London, Jarrolds, 1941.
The Uncomplaining Corpses. New York, Holt, 1940; London, Jarrolds, 1942.
Tickets for Death. New York, Holt, 1941; London, Jarrolds, 1942.
Bodies Are Where You Find Them. New York, Holt, 1941; in *Michael Shayne Investigates*, 1943.
Michael Shayne Takes Over (omnibus). New York, Holt, 1941.

The Corpse Came Calling. New York, Dodd Mead, 1942; in *Michael Shayne Investigates,* 1943; as *The Case of the Walking Corpse,* Kingston, New York, Quin, 1943.

Murder Wears a Mummer's Mask. New York, Dodd Mead, 1943; in *Michael Shayne Takes a Hand,* 1944; as *In a Deadly Vein,* New York, Dell, 1956.

Blood on the Black Market. New York, Dodd Mead, 1943; in *Michael Shayne Takes a Hand,* 1944; revised edition, as *Heads You Lose,* New York, Dell, 1958.

Michael Shayne Investigates (omnibus). London, Jarrolds, 1943.

Michael Shayne Takes a Hand (omnibus). London, Jarrolds, 1944.

Michael Shayne's Long Chance. New York, Dodd Mead, 1944; London, Jarrolds, 1945.

Murder and the Married Virgin. New York, Dodd Mead, 1944, London, Jarrolds, 1946.

Murder Is My Business. New York, Dodd Mead, and London, Jarrolds, 1945.

Marked for Murder. New York, Dodd Mead, 1945; London, Jarrolds, 1950.

Dead Man's Diary, and Dinner at Dupre's. New York, Dell, 1945.

Blood on Biscayne Bay. Chicago, Ziff Davis, 1946; London, Jarrolds, 1950.

Counterfeit Wife. Chicago, Ziff Davis; 1947; London, Jarrolds, 1950.

Blood on the Stars. New York, Dodd Mead, 1948; as *Murder Is a Habit,* London, Jarrolds, 1951.

Michael Shayne's Triple Mystery (*Dead Man's Diary, A Taste for Cognac, Dinner at Dupre's*). New York, Ziff Davis, 1948.

A Taste for Violence. New York, Dodd Mead, 1949; London, Jarrolds, 1952.

Call for Michael Shayne. New York, Dodd Mead, 1949; London, Jarrolds, 1951.

Before I Wake (as Hal Debrett, with Kathleen Rollins). New York, Dodd Mead, 1949; London, Jarrolds, 1953.

A Lonely Way to Die (as Hal Debrett, with Kathleen Rollins). New York, Dodd Mead, 1950; London, Jarrolds, 1954.

This Is It, Michael Shayne. New York, Dodd Mead, 1950; London, Jarrolds, 1952.

Framed in Blood. New York, Dodd Mead, 1951; London, Jarrolds, 1953.

When Dorinda Dances. New York, Dodd Mead, 1951; London, Jarrolds, 1953.

What Really Happened. New York, Dodd Mead, 1952; London, Jarrolds, 1953.

The Avenger (as Matthew Blood, with Ryerson Johnson). New York, Fawcett, 1952.

One Night with Nora. New York, Torquil, 1953; as *The Lady Came by Night,* London, Jarrolds, 1954.

She Woke to Darkness. New York, Torquil, 1954; London, Jarrolds, 1955.

Death Is a Lovely Dame (as Matthew Blood, with Ryerson Johnson). New York, Fawcett, 1954.

Death Has Three Lives. New York, Torquil, and London, Jarrolds, 1955.

Stranger in Town. New York, Torquil, 1955; London, Jarrolds, 1956.

The Blonde Cried Murder. New York, Torquil, 1956; London, Jarrolds, 1957.

Weep for a Blonde. New York, Torquil, 1957; London, Long, 1958.

Shoot the Works. New York, Torquil, 1957; London, Long, 1958.

Murder and the Wanton Bride. New York, Torquil, 1958; London, Long, 1959.

Uncollected Short Stories

"The Million-dollar Motive," in *Murder Cavalcade,* edited by Ken Crossen. New York, Duell, 1946; London, Hammond, 1953.

"Human Interest Stuff," in *Ellery Queen's Murder by Experts.* Chicago, Ziff Davis, 1947; London, Sampson Low, 1950.

"Big Shot," in *Ellery Queen's Mystery Magazine* (New York), August 1947.

"Extradition," in *Queen's Awards,* edited by Ellery Queen. Boston, Little Brown, 1948; London, Gollancz, 1950.

"Murder Before Midnight," in *Popular Detective* (New York), March 1950.

"Women Are Poison," in *The Saint* (New York), November 1954.

"The Reluctant Client," in *Manhunt* (New York), June 1955.

"Dead Man's Code," in *Crime for Two,* edited by Frances and Richard Lockridge. Philadelphia, Lippincott, 1955.

"Not Tonight—Danger," in *Ellery Queen's Mystery Magazine* (New York), September 1957.

"Second Honeymoon," in *Ellery Queen's Mystery Magazine* (New York), July 1959.

"Death Goes to the Post," in *Dames, Danger, and Death,* edited by Leo Margulies. New York, Pyramid, 1960.

"Pieces of Silver," in *Alfred Hitchcock Presents: Stories for Late at Night.* New York, Random House, 1961.

"I'm Tough," in *Best Detective Stories of the Year,* edited by Brett Halliday. New York, Dutton, 1962.

"Death of a Dead Man," in *Mink Is for Minx,* edited by Leo Margulies. New York, Dell, 1964.

"Murder in Miami," in *Ellery Queen's Mystery Magazine* (New York), May 1970.

OTHER PUBLICATIONS

Novels as Anthony Scott

Mardi Gras Madness. New York, Godwin, 1934.
Test of Virtue. New York, Godwin, 1934.
Ten Toes Up. New York, Godwin, 1935.
Virgin's Holiday. New York, Godwin, 1935.
Stolen Sins. New York, Godwin, 1936.
Ladies of Chance. New York, Godwin, 1936.
Satan Rides the Night. New York, Godwin, 1938.
Temptation. New York, Godwin, 1938.

Novels as Kathryn Culver

Love Is a Masquerade. New York, Phoenix Press, 1935.
Too Smart for Love. New York, Curl, 1937.
Million Dollar Madness. New York, Curl, 1937.
Green Path to the Moon. New York, Curl, 1938.
Once to Every Woman. New York, Godwin, 1938.
Girl Alone. New York, Gramercy, 1939.

Novels as Davis Dresser

Let's Laugh at Love. New York, Curl, 1937.
Romance for Julie. New York, Curl, 1938.
Death Rides the Pecos. New York, Morrow, and London, Ward Lock, 1940.
The Hangmen of Sleepy Valley. New York, Morrow, 1940; as *The Masked Riders of Sleepy Valley,* London, Ward Lock, 1941.

Gunsmoke on the Mesa. New York, Carlton, and London, Ward Lock, 1941.

Lynch-Rope Law. New York, Morrow, 1941; London, Ward Lock, 1942.

Charlie Dell (as Anderson Wayne). New York, Coward McCann, 1952; London, Hale, 1953; as *A Time to Remember*, New York, Popular Library, 1959.

Murder on the Mesa. London, Ward Lock, 1953.

Novels as Don Davis

Return of the Rio Kid. New York, Morrow, 1940; London, Ward Lock, 1950.

Death on Treasure Trail. London, Hutchinson, 1940; New York, Morrow, 1941.

Rio Kid Justice. New York, Morrow, 1941.

Two-Gun Rio Kid. New York, Morrow, 1941.

Other

Editor, with Helen McCloy, *20 Great Tales of Murder.* New York, Random House, 1951; London, Hammond, 1952.

Editor, *Dangerous Dames.* New York, Dell, 1955.

Editor, *Big Time Mysteries.* New York, Dodd Mead, 1958.

Editor, *Murder in Miami.* New York, Dodd Mead, 1959.

Editor, *Best Detective Stories of the Year* (*16th* [and *17th*] *Annual Collection*). New York, Dutton, 2 vols., 1961–62.

*   *   *

Beginning in 1939 with a book no publisher wanted, and ending in 1976 with a book that would be sure to sell in the hundreds of thousands, Brett Halliday wrote more than 60 mystery novels that featured private detective Mike Shayne. In the intervening years those books sold in the millions, were translated into seven languages and published all across the world, were made into motion pictures and a television series, placed their hero into a magazine of his own that is still being published every month, and established the big, rawboned, redhead Michael Shayne as one of the few really immortal fictional detectives.

In a long and often stormy career, Davis Dresser wrote many books under many names, but it is on the Mike Shayne novels he wrote as Brett Halliday that his fame and reputation will rest. The fame is probably secure, but the reputation has sometimes been tarnished by critics. It is true that Halliday was not a literary stylist, a penetrating psychologist, or a keen analyzer of current society. But he was a writer who knew a good story when he found one, and who knew how to tell that story. He knew how to catch the reader's interest from the opening page. He knew how people act with each other both day to day and at violent moments. He knew that a good suspense novel is not an abstract puzzle, but is people acting one way or another. Above all he knew something more important than everything else—he knew that his audience did not want literary style, or unique plot, or dazzling psychology—they wanted to see their hero in action. It is Mike Shayne the audience wants to read about: Mike, and his crony Tim Rourke, his good friend Chief Will Gentry, his faithful secretary/girlfriend Lucy Hamilton, and, yes, his archantagonist Miami Beach Chief of Detectives Peter Painter. The writing and the plot don't really matter any more than they do in a successful television series; the hero is the book—Mike Shayne in action, with the crime there only for Mike to solve, the criminal there for Mike to defeat.

Halliday was also an honest writer, and Mike Shayne is a real person—complete, accurate, uniquely American, and the personification of one facet of the American dream. He shapes and dominates each book. We see and understand each adventure through his eyes and his eyes only. We do not see people objectively, or as they see themselves, but as Mike sees them, and he is a man with a firm, steady, totally confident view of everything. He knows what he is, what he wants, and why he acts. He knows right from wrong, morality from immorality, justice from law, and has no hesitation in either action or judgement if his principles conflict with others'. He has no qualms about breaking either law or custom in the name of justice, and he will die for the truth as he sees it. In a time of chaos and confusion he is a man with his own code and no doubts at all. Halliday may not have delved too deeply into the psychology of the other characters in his books, but he knew Mike Shayne's psychology completely, and never wrote a line or scene that wasn't totally accurate and honest to Shayne.

Davis Dresser grew up in the early years of this century in the rugged, vast, barren deserts and mountains of West Texas. He lost an eye to barbed wire as a boy. He rode with Pershing after Pancho Villa. He was one of the last of a generation that grew up on the closing frontier, and it shaped him into a man who knew who and what he was, with a definite view on just about everything, a man like Mike Shayne. Both men stood for a simpler, more confident, less confused time in America. They are loners because they rely on no one but themselves in either action or thought. Wrong they may be, from time to time, but it will never be because of anyone but themselves, because of any code but their own. And that code is in essence the code of the old frontier, of a rugged individualist populism. If they are wrong, as another folk hero used to say, they'll apologize, but they will never hesitate to follow their own code and judgement wherever it takes them, and they will judge harshly any man who fails either their code or his own.

—Michael Collins

————

HALLIDAY, Brett. *See* **PRONZINI, Bill.**

————

HALLIDAY, Dorothy. *See* **DUNNETT, Dorothy.**

————

HALLIDAY, Michael. *See* **CREASEY, John.**

————

HALLS, Geraldine. *See* **JAY, Charlotte.**

————

HAMILTON, Donald (Bengtsson). American. Born in Uppsala, Sweden, 24 March 1916; emigrated to the United States in 1924. Educated at the University of Chicago, B.S.

1938. Served in the United States Naval Reserve: Lieutenant. Married Kathleen Stick in 1941; two daughters and two sons. Since 1946, self-employed writer and photographer. Agent: Brandt and Brandt, 1501 Broadway, New York, New York, 10017. Address: P.O. Box 1045, Santa Fe, New Mexico 87504, U.S.A.

CRIME PUBLICATIONS

Novels (series: Matt Helm)

Date with Darkness. New York, Rinehart, 1947; London, Wingate, 1951.
The Steel Mirror. New York, Rinehart, 1948; London, Wingate, 1950.
Murder Twice Told. New York, Rinehart, 1950; London, Wingate, 1952.
Night Walker. New York, Dell, 1954; as *Rough Company,* London, Wingate, 1954.
Line of Fire. New York, Dell, 1955; London, Wingate, 1956.
Assignment: Murder. New York, Dell, 1956; as *Assassins Have Starry Eyes,* New York, Fawcett, 1966.
Death of a Citizen (Helm). New York, Fawcett, and London, Muller, 1960.
The Wrecking Crew (Helm). New York, Fawcett, 1960; London, Muller, 1961.
The Removers (Helm). New York, Fawcett, 1961; London, Muller, 1962.
Murderer's Row (Helm). New York, Fawcett, 1962; London, Muller, 1963.
The Silencers (Helm). New York, Fawcett, 1962; London, Hodder and Stoughton, 1966.
The Ambushers (Helm). New York, Fawcett, 1963; London, Hodder and Stoughton, 1967.
The Shadowers (Helm). New York, Fawcett, and London, Muller, 1964.
The Ravagers (Helm). New York, Fawcett, 1964.
The Devastators (Helm). New York, Fawcett, 1965; London, Hodder and Stoughton, 1967.
The Betrayers (Helm). New York, Fawcett, 1966; London, Hodder and Stoughton, 1968.
The Menacers (Helm). New York, Fawcett, and London, Hodder and Stoughton, 1968.
The Interlopers (Helm). New York, Fawcett, and London, Hodder and Stoughton, 1969.
The Poisoners (Helm). New York, Fawcett, and London, Hodder and Stoughton, 1971.
The Intriguers (Helm). New York, Fawcett, 1972; London, Hodder and Stoughton, 1973.
The Intimidators (Helm). New York, Fawcett, and London, Hodder and Stoughton, 1974.
The Terminators (Helm). New York, Fawcett, 1975; London, Hodder and Stoughton, 1976.
The Retaliators (Helm). New York, Fawcett, 1976; London, Coronet, 1979.
The Terrorizers (Helm). New York, Fawcett, 1977.
The Mona Intercept. New York, Fawcett, 1980.
The Revengers (Helm). New York, Fawcett, 1982.
The Annihilators (Helm). New York, Fawcett, 1983.
The Infiltrators (Helm). New York, Fawcett, 1984.
The Detonators (Helm). New York, Fawcett, 1985.
The Vanishers (Helm). New York, Fawcett, 1986.
The Demolishers (Helm). New York, Fawcett, 1987.
The Frighteners (Helm). New York, Fawcett, 1989.

Uncollected Short Story

"Throwback," in *Manhunt* (New York), August 1953.

OTHER PUBLICATIONS

Novels

Smoky Valley. New York, Dell, 1954.
Mad River. New York, Dell, 1956; London, Wingate, 1957.
The Big Country. New York, Dell, 1957; London, Panther, 1958.
The Man from Santa Clara. New York, Dell, 1960; as *The Two-Shoot Gun,* New York, Fawcett, 1971.
Texas Fever. New York, Fawcett, 1960; London, Muller, 1961.

Play

Screenplay: *Five Steps to Danger,* with Henry S. Kesler and Turnley Walker, 1957.

Other

On Guns and Hunting. New York, Fawcett, 1970.
Cruises with Kathleen. New York, McKay, 1980.

Editor, *Iron Men and Silver Stars.* New York, Fawcett, 1967.

*

Manuscript Collection: University of California, Los Angeles.

Donald Hamilton comments:
Crime/mystery fiction and the kind of suspense/action novels in which I specialize really need no introduction. They've been around since the invention of language. Is Jason going to make it home with the Golden Fleece? Is Achilles going to get revenge for the death of Patroclus? Is Matt Helm going to get revenge for the death of Eleanor Brand, meanwhile saving Latin America for the forces of good, as opposed to the forces of evil? The themes are universal; only the presentation varies. It is not my place to say where, in the scale of literary quality, my own presentations stand, or fall.

*   *   *

Donald Hamilton created Matt Helm at a time when secret agents were very much in vogue thanks to the incredible popularity of Ian Fleming's James Bond. It was perhaps natural that Helm would be identified as "the American James Bond" and this confusion was intensified by a series of silly motion picture parodies which completely miscast Dean Martin (giving his patented performance as a lecherous, inebriated buffoon) in the role of Helm. Like Bond, Helm is a professional assassin who works for an ultra-secret government agency. There the resemblance ends.
Hamilton, in one of the rare occasions in which he has discussed his hero, once characterized Helm as "A) He's actually a pretty good guy. B) He kills." This typically understated description does not begin to suggest the complexity of Helm's character or the importance of his place in genre fiction.

Although Helm often claims that he is no detective, it is interesting to note that Hamilton's work holds more comparisons to Hammett's work than Fleming's. In many of the best Helm stories, particularly those written during the 1960's and 1970's, Helm usually must solve a rather complex mystery before he can "make the touch" (i.e. kill his target). In these early stories other parallels often present themselves as well. Like Hammett's Continental Op, Helm makes it clear that he cannot be bought at any price. Neither money nor power will give him the satisfaction he achieves from doing his job.

While he will engage in sex with female opponents (something Hammett's Op could never do) Helm tells us that what happens in bed has no effect on anything that may happen later. To Helm the worst sin is not failure of a mission, but failure to behave in a professional manner. This strict adherence to a code of professional conduct is probably Helm's single most important character trait.

Another similarity between Hamilton and Hammett is seen in Helm's relationship with his boss. The Op answered to a shadowy figure he referred to as "the Old Man." Helm takes his orders from a man known only as Mac, a gray-haired man in a gray suit who seems never to have aged a day in all the years Helm has known him. Like "the Old Man," Mac is punctilious in both speech and manner, something that belies his essential ruthlessness and his willingness to send his agents out on "suicide missions." Hamilton eventually reveals a great deal about Mac's personal life and the origins of his mysterious agency, a gambit that unfortunately removes the tantalizing aura of mystery that has been built around Helm's boss.

One of the things that made the Helm stories truly unique was the fact that Helm, himself, was a proletarian hero who drew from the mystique of the American frontier. Many of Helm's most exciting confrontations occur in a wilderness setting, something that he prefers. Helm idealizes the frontier hero and his own rigid personal code is a curious mixture of medieval chivalry and the Code of the West. He draws strength from it and a sense of justification as well. Often he calls up the names of western heroes in his explanations of his sometimes sentimental, sometimes ruthless behavior.

With women Helm is something of a rustic romantic, although he harbors a deep contempt for women whom he considers prissy or overly concerned with their personal appearances. A standard fixture in many of the Helm stories is the sexual tension that develops between Helm and a prim, proper woman before she finally surrenders to his peculiar charms.

It is with his enemies that the aggressive, frontiersman's side of his nature usually asserts itself. Although we know from his earliest appearance that his primary expertise is that of a long-range sniper, most of his kills are dealt out *mano-a-mano* in stand-up pistol duels or knife fights. Helm enjoys these contests and, as is typical of naturalistic heroes from Natty Bumppo on down, he can give a full measure of respect to a fellow professional regardless of his politics.

He can be most eloquent on this subject. At the end of one story he ventures the opinion that a single assassin pitting himself against massed security to kill a lone target is someone to be respected. Modern terrorists, who will destroy a building full of people simply to create fear are "destroying the same human values they claim they're trying to save." In so doing, claims Helm, they are worse than cowards; they're amateurs. To Helm, of course, there is nothing worse.

Unlike many pulp heroes, Matt Helm has endured for more than 30 years. Hamilton has tried, albeit semi-successfully, to have his hero grow emotionally and engage in adventures that were timely. At the end of *The Terrorizers* (1977), Helm is nearly killed exterminating a band of leftist American terrorists. For the first time in his career, he seems not only sickened by the killing but by the person he has become. He ends the story unsure of his future and at least entertaining the notion of taking a high-level desk job that Mac (by now almost a paternal figure) has offered him.

This marks a watershed in the Helm canon because he does not appear in another story for five years. When he reappears in *The Revengers* (1982), it is as more of a company troubleshooter than as an active field agent. He has changed emotionally, as well, because while the ruthlessness and single-minded devotion to duty remain in his character, he is less callous and more susceptible to emotional involvement with women. These newer stories which appeared throughout the 1980's are twice as long as the earlier ones and often show Helm pitted against terrorists, Latin American revolutionaries, and sinister forces growing within the American system. It is tempting to believe that Hamilton realized some time ago that America's future enemies would not be Russian or Chinese communists, but would spring from ideologies not yet recognized.

On the negative side, Helm seems out of place in these later stories and his speeches and attitudes have taken on a right-wing and at times jingoistic tone. Since his creator began writing at the tail-end of the pulp era and at the beginning of the era of paperback originals, it is probably not surprising that a man of Helm's character and morals might seem anachronistic and out of touch with his times. These later stories have their moments but overall are not up to the standards Hamilton set during the first 15 years of this series.

In both of Helm's incarnations, Hamilton has adhered to a strict formula which, while often predictable, is unfailingly entertaining. His ability to create a fully realized protagonist, crisp, tough dialog, and skillfully choreographed fight scenes make the Matt Helm series not only one of the most enduring but certainly one of the all-time best series of original paperback thrillers.

—Robert E. Skinner

HAMILTON, Patrick. British. Born in Hassocks, Sussex, 17 March 1904. Educated at Holland House School, Hove, Sussex; Colet Court, London; Westminster School, London (Vincent Prize, 1918), 1918–19. Married 1)Lois Martin in 1930 (divorced 1953); 2) Ursula Stewart in 1953. Actor and assistant stage manager to Andrew Melville in the 1920's. *Died 23 September 1962.*

CRIME PUBLICATIONS

Novels (series: Ernest Ralph Gorse)

Hangover Square; or, The Man with Two Minds: A Story of Darkest Earl's Court in the Year 1939. London, Constable, 1941; New York, Random House, 1942.
The West Pier (Gorse). London, Constable, 1951; New York, Doubleday, 1952.
Mr. Stimpson and Mr. Gorse. London, Constable, 1953.
Unknown Assailant (Gorse). London, Constable, 1955.

OTHER PUBLICATIONS

Novels

Monday Morning. London, Constable, and Boston, Houghton Mifflin, 1925.
Craven House. London, Constable, 1926; Boston, Houghton Mifflin, 1927; revised edition, Constable, 1943.
Twopence Coloured. London, Constable, and Boston, Houghton Mifflin, 1928.
The Midnight Bell: A Love Story. London, Constable, 1929; Boston, Little Brown, 1930.
The Siege of Pleasure. London, Constable, and Boston, Little Brown, 1932.
The Plains of Cement. London, Constable, 1934; Boston, Little Brown, 1935.
Twenty Thousand Streets Under the Sky: A London Trilogy (includes *The Midnight Bell, The Siege of Pleasure,* and *The Plains of Cement*). London, Constable, 1935.
Impromptu in Moribundia. London, Constable, 1939.
The Slaves of Solitude. London, Constable, 1947; as *Riverside,* New York, Random House, 1947.

Plays

Rope: A Play with a Preface on Thrillers (produced London, 1929). London, Constable, 1929; as *Rope's End* (produced New York, 1929), New York, R.R. Smith, 1930.
The Procurator of Judea, adaptation of a work by Anatole France (produced London, 1930).
John Brown's Body (produced London, 1930).
Gas Light: A Victorian Thriller (produced Richmond, Surrey, 1938; London, 1939). London, Constable, 1939; as *Angel Street* (produced New York, 1941), New York, French, 1942.
Money with Menaces and To the Public Danger: Two Radio Plays. London, Constable, 1939.
This Is Impossible (broadcast, 1941). London, French, 1942.
The Duke in Darkness (produced Edinburgh and London, 1942; New York, 1944). London, Constable, 1943.
The Governess (produced London, 1946).
The Man Upstairs (produced Blackpool, 1953). London, Constable, 1954.

Radio Plays: *Money with Menaces,* 1937; *To the Public Danger,* 1939; *This Is Impossible,* 1941; *Caller Anonymous,* 1952; *Miss Roach,* from his novel *The Slaves of Solitude,* 1958; *Hangover Square,* from his own novel, 1965.

* * *

Patrick Hamilton's novels have been compared to Dickens's, and he has been described as a true delineator of the "defeated classes" and praised by Doris Lessing for his descriptions of London Streets, comparable to Thomas Burke's concentration on the streets and denizens of the East End of London and in particular Chinatown. Within the genre of crime fiction, Hamilton wrote novels, radio and stage plays, although even his non-crime novels have the intrinsic taint of latent criminality. Much of Hamilton's work has been successfully transferred to the cinema or television screen.

Hamilton's outstanding crime novel is *Hangover Square,* the title being a cross between Hanover Square in the Mayfair area of London and his own heavy drinking ruefully known as a "little stroll round Hangover Square." It is a powerful study of George Harvey Bone, a schizophrenic, and his hopeless passion for a wanton who continually deceives him with tragic results. The novel was adapted to become an outstanding film in 1945 in a version that strayed from Hamilton's original.

Hamilton's most famous play *Rope* was based on the Chicago teenagers Leopold and Loeb and their Nietzschean murder which is discovered by some exceedingly elementary mistakes, like dropping one of the killer's prescription spectacles. The battle of wits and the mounting tension between logic and ruthless pride reach a shattering denouement. It was made into a Hollywood film by Alfred Hitchcock in 1948, with James Stewart as the investigating professor and is well-known for the use of a single set of a New York flat and by what appears to be one complete take. *Gas Light* was an even greater artistic and financial success in which a sinister, charming husband endeavours to drive his young wife mad as he tries to recover the jewels he has hidden in her house.

Hamilton wrote two plays for BBC radio in the 1930's. *Money with Menaces* tells of a bullied schoolboy Steven seeking revenge as an adult on his tormentor by telephoning to tell him that his child has been kidnapped: another crisp delineation of a warped criminal mind. *To the Public Danger,* a reference to careless driving followed. Hamilton had himself been knocked down and injured by a car, and he used this idea twice, the other occasion back in 1932, in *The Siege of Pleasure,* the second volume in a trilogy of life in suburban London. This is not without a crime element as it depicts the demise of a maid servant, Jenny, descending into prostitution through drink on the night the speeding car hits a cyclist without stopping.

Hamilton also wrote three books featuring a ruthless, amoral, lady-killer, Ernest Ralph Gorse. The novels are set in Brighton with its west pier and environs, and the character of Gorse is based on the English murderer Neville George Clevely Heath.

Hamilton's letters to his brother reveal much of his personal unhappiness; financial problems, and heavy drinking. He is a sad example of a talent that could have produced so much more without diluting the output he did achieve.

—John Kennedy Melling

HAMMETT, (Samuel) Dashiell. American. Born in St. Mary's County, Maryland, 27 May 1894. Educated at Baltimore Polytechnic Institute to age 13. Served in the Motor Ambulance Corps of the United States Army, 1918–19: Sergeant; also served in the United States Army Signal Corps in the Aleutian Islands, 1942–45. Married Josephine Annas Dolan in 1920 (divorced 1937); two daughters. Worked as a clerk, stevedore, and advertising manager; private detective, Pinkerton Agency, 1908–22; full-time writer from 1922: book reviewer, *Saturday Review of Literature,* 1927–29, and New York *Evening Post,* 1930; lived in Hollywood, 1930–42; began long relationship with Lillian Hellman in 1930; teacher of creative writing, Jefferson School of Social Science, New York, 1946–56. Convicted of contempt of Congress and sentenced to six months in prison, 1951. President, League of American Writers, 1942 and Civil Rights Congress of New York, 1946–47; member of the Advisory Board, *Soviet Russia Today. Died 10 January 1961.*

Novels (series: The Continental Op)

Red Harvest (Op).   New York and London, Knopf, 1929.
The Dain Curse (Op).   New York and London, Knopf, 1929.
The Maltese Falcon.   New York and London, Knopf, 1930.
The Glass Key.   New York and London, Knopf, 1931.
The Thin Man.   New York, Knopf, and London, Barker, 1934.
$106,000 Blood Money (Op).   New York, Spivak, 1943; as *Blood Money,* Cleveland, World, 1943; as *The Big Knock-Over,* New York, Spivak, 1948.

Short Stories (series: Sam Spade)

The Adventures of Sam Spade and Other Stories, edited by Ellery Queen.   New York, Spivak, 1944; as *They Can Only Hang You Once,* 1949; as *A Man Called Spade,* New York, Dell, 1945.
The Continental Op, edited by Ellery Queen.   New York, Spivak, 1945.
The Return of the Continental Op, edited by Ellery Queen.   New York, Spivak, 1945.
Hammett Homicides, edited by Ellery Queen.   New York, Spivak, 1946.
Dead Yellow Women, edited by Ellery Queen.   New York, Spivak, 1947.
Nightmare Town, edited by Ellery Queen.   New York, Spivak, 1948.
The Creeping Siamese, edited by Ellery Queen.   New York, Spivak, 1950.
Woman in the Dark, edited by Ellery Queen.   New York, Spivak, 1951; London, Headline, 1988.
A Man Named Thin and Other Stories, edited by Ellery Queen.   New York, Ferman, 1962.
The Big Knockover: Selected Stories and Short Novels, edited by Lillian Hellman.   New York, Random House, 1966; as *The Hammett Story Omnibus,* London, Cassell, 1966; as *The Big Knockover and The Continental Op,* New York, Dell, 2 vols., 1967.
The Continental Op, edited by Steven Marcus.   New York, Random House, 1974; London, Macmillan, 1975.

Uncollected Short Story

"The Road Home," in *The Hard-Boiled Detective: Stories from Black Mask Magazine,* edited by Herbert Ruhm.   New York, Random House, 1977.

OTHER PUBLICATIONS

Plays

Watch on the Rhine (screenplay), with Lillian Hellman, in *Best Film Plays of 1943–44,* edited by John Gassner and Dudley Nichols.   New York, Crown, 1945.

Screenplays: *City Streets,* with Oliver H.P. Garrett and Max Marcin, 1931; *Mister Dynamite,* with Doris Malloy and Harry Clork, 1935; *After the Thin Man,* with Frances Goodrich and Albert Hackett, 1936; *Another Thin Man,* with Frances Goodrich and Albert Hackett, 1939; *Watch on the Rhine,* with Lillian Hellman, 1943.

Other

"From the Memoirs of a Private Detective," in *The Smart Set Anthology,* edited by Burton Rascoe and Groff Conklin. New York, Reynal, 1934.
Secret Agent X-9 (cartoon strip), with Alex Raymond.   Philadelphia, McKay, 2 vols., 1934.
"Tempo in the Novel," in *Fighting Words,* edited by Donald Ogden Stewart.   New York, Harcourt Brace, 1940.
The Battle of the Aleutians, with Robert Colodny.   Privately printed, 1944.

Editor, *Creeps by Night.*   New York, Day, 1931; as *Modern Tales of Horror,* London, Gollancz, 1932; as *The Red Brain,* New York, Belmont, 1961; as *Breakdown,* London, New English Library, 1968.

*

Bibliography: *Dashiell Hammett: A Casebook* by William F. Nolan, Santa Barbara, California, McNally and Loftin, 1969; *Dashiell Hammett: A Descriptive Bibliography* by Richard Layman, Pittsburgh, University of Pittsburgh Press, and London, Fetter and Simons, 1979.

Manuscript Collection: Humanities Research Center, University of Texas, Austin.

Critical Studies: *Beams Falling: The Art of Dashiell Hammett* by Peter Wolfe, Bowling Green, Ohio, Popular Press, 1980; *Shadow Man: The Life of Dashiell Hammett* by Richard Layman, New York, Harcourt Brace, and London, Junction, 1981; *Dashiell Hammett* by Dennis Dooley, New York, Ungar, 1983; *Hammett: A Life at the Edge* by William F. Nolan, New York, Congdon and Weed, and London, Barker 1983; *Dashiell Hammett: A Life* by Diane Johnson, New York, Random House, 1983, as *The Life of Dashiell Hammett,* London, Chatto and Windus, 1984; *Dashiell Hammett* by William Marling, Boston, Twayne, 1983; *Private Investigations: The Novels of Dashiell Hammett* by Sinda Gregory, Carbondale, Illinois, Southern Illinois University Press, 1984; *Dashiell Hammett* by Julian Symons, San Diego, Harcourt Brace, 1985.

*   *   *

What is there in Dashiell Hammett's work that makes it a standard for judging the work of other writers? His output was surprisingly small. He wrote some short stories for the pulps, and between 1929 and 1934 wrote all the novels he was ever to write: *Red Harvest, The Dain Curse, The Maltese Falcon, The Glass Key,* and *The Thin Man.* He left the fragment of another novel, *Tulip,* but there's enough to show that he was trying to go in another direction.

Some of the short stories are very good ("The Gutting of Couffignal"), some are not ("Corkscrew"), but none benefits from comparison to, say, Hemingway's; and, despite the arguments of Steven Marcus, they do not form the basis of Hammett's reputation. The novels do.

And what are the novels about? They are about men who persist in the face of adversity until they do what they set out to do. They are about men who have few friends and no permanent social context. Except for Ned Beaumont in *The Glass Key* these men are detectives. Except for Nick Charles in *The Thin Man* they are alone. They have no family. Their allegiance is not to law but to something else, call it order, a sense of the way things ought to be. They are not of the police any more than they are of the mob. They are of the people. But they are immune to the things that compel the people. They do not succumb to the temptations of money or sex. They are not hostage to the fear of death. They are beset with no illusions. In these ways they are larger than we are; they are supermen, giants of autonomy. Despite the hard-edged vernacular in which the stories are told, and the mean streets in which they take place, Hammett is not writing realistic fiction, he is writing romance. He is writing of heroes who are superior in degree to ordinary men.

Taken as a whole, and chronologically, the novels may be seen to speculate on the way a man should deal with disorder, on the things to which he should give allegiance. In *Red Harvest,* the Continental Op is motivated by what appears to be a work ethic. He finds Personville corrupt and he cleans it up for no better reason than that it's his job (though not his assignment). In *The Dain Curse* the work ethic may be muted by compassion. The Op finds a young woman beset by neurosis, drugs, and lineage. He saves her. In *The Maltese Falcon* Sam Spade's partner is killed. A valuable statue is sought. Spade solves the murder, turns in the seekers. In *The Glass Key* Ned Beaumont endures great pain on behalf of a friend. At the end of the novel he severs the friendship. *The Thin Man* is unfortunate. Let us not speak of it.

The motivation for the behavior of these men is always murky. But in *The Maltese Falcon,* Spade tells Brigid O'Shaughnessy a story while they wait, in Spade's apartment, for Joel Cairo. It is the story of a man named Flitcraft (Hammett was always fond of suggestive names) who was nearly killed by a beam falling from a half-built building as Flitcraft was going to lunch. The beam missed, but "he felt like somebody had taken the lid off life and let him look at the works." Flitcraft discovered that "life could be ended for him at random by a falling beam: he would change his life at random by simply going away." The story is casually told and Brigid pays it little heed. It appears to her a time-killer. But it is not. It is a parable, and it is the code that Spade lives by. In fact, the vision of life embodied in Flitcraft's story is the central spring in Hammett's work. It gives motion to his protagonists. The novels suggest a random universe in which a man may impose his own order if he is tough enough (and has seen under life's lid). The cost of that is probably isolation. But the alternative is chaos.

All of this is, of course, very much in the American grain, and very much of Hammett's time (*Red Harvest* was published in the same year as *A Farewell to Arms*). For Hammett the matters of crime and detection served simply as metaphor for life (for Hemingway it was hunting and war that served). "The essential American soul," D.H. Lawrence wrote, "is hard, isolate, almost selfless, stoic, and a killer. . . . A man who keeps his moral integrity hard and intact. An isolate, almost selfless, stoic enduring man who lives by death, by killing. . . . This is the very intrinsic-most American."

—Robert B. Parker

HAMMOND, Gerald (Arthur Douglas). Also writes as Dalby Holden; has also written as Arthur Douglas. Born in Bournemouth, Hampshire, 7 March 1926. Educated at St. Edmund's School, Hindhead, 1933–39; Wellington College, 1939–43; Aberdeen School of Architecture, 1946–52, diploma in architecture 1952. Served in the Queen's Royal Regiment. Married Gilda Isobel Watt in 1952; three sons. Architect, Navy, Army, Airforce Institute, Claygate, Surrey, 1952–54, and County Council, Aberdeen, 1954–59; assistant resident architect, St. Andrews University, Fife, 1959–69; depute chief architect and planning officer, Livingston Development Corporation, Lothian, 1969–83. Since 1983 full-time writer. Agent: Michael Thomas, A.M. Heath and Company Ltd., 79 St. Martin's Lane, London WC2N 4AA, England. Address: Corrienearn Cottage, Aboyne, Aberdeenshire AB3 5HY, Scotland.

CRIME PUBLICATIONS

Novels (series: Keith Calder; Captain John Cunningham)

Fred in Situ. London, Hodder and Stoughton, 1965.
The Loose Screw. London, Hodder and Stoughton, 1966.
Mud in His Eye. London, Hodder and Stoughton, 1967.
Dead Game (Calder). London, Macmillan, 1979.
The Reward Game (Calder). London, Macmillan, and New York, St. Martin's Press, 1980.
The Revenge Game (Calder). London, Macmillan, and New York, St. Martin's Press, 1981.
Fair Game (Calder). London, Macmillan, and New York, St. Martin's Press, 1982.
The Game (Calder). London, Macmillan, and New York, St. Martin's Press, 1982.
Cousin Once Removed (Calder). London, Macmillan, and New York, St. Martin's Press, 1984.
Sauce for the Pigeon (Calder). London, Macmillan, and New York, St. Martin's Press, 1984.
Pursuit of Arms (Calder). London, Macmillan, and New York, St. Martin's Press, 1985.
Silver City Scandal (Calder). London, Macmillan, and New York, St. Martin's Press, 1986.
The Executor (Calder). London, Macmillan, and New York, St. Martin's Press, 1986.
The Worried Widow (Calder). London, Macmillan, 1987; New York, St. Martin's Press, 1988.
Adverse Report (Calder). London, Macmillan, 1987.
Doldrum (as Dalby Holden). London, Hale, 1987.
Stray Shot (Calder). London, Macmillan, 1988.
Dog in the Dark (Cunningham). London, Macmillan, 1989.
Doghouse (Cunningham). London, Macmillan, 1989.
A Brace of Skeet (Calder). London, Macmillan, 1989.
Whose Dog Are You? (Cunningham). London, Macmillan, 1990.
Let Us Prey (Calder). London, Macmillan, 1990.

Novels as Arthur Douglas

The Gods. London, Macmillan, 1985.
Last Rights. London, Macmillan, 1986; New York, St. Martin's Press, 1987.
A Very Wrong Number. London, Macmillan, 1987.
A Worm Turns. London, Macmillan, 1988; New York, St. Martin's Press, 1989.

*

Gerald Hammond comments:
My work and hobbies have been very largely technical so, turning to writing (my first love), I suppose it was inevitable that I should write mysteries. I would have enjoyed writing humour, but my preferred format is the novel and publishers

believe that humour never sells in book form, notwithstanding all the contrary evidence.

After the first three books there was a gap while I changed jobs and built a house. I then looked for characters and a background for, as I thought, one more book. I was (and am) deeply involved with gundogs and shooting generally and was irritated by the stereotypes of the shooting fraternity which seemed to be universal. I set out to depict the shooting scene (particularly in Scotland) as I knew it, most of them centered around the character of Keith Calder, a gunsmith of unreliable habits and an enquiring mind. Keith has now featured in 16 novels.

I try very hard to be technically accurate, and this may be why my novels bring me correspondence from all over the world. Americans, in particular, send me supporting material which I wish I had while writing that particular book. A fictional incident in one of my novels recently suggested to a detective in San Francisco the solution to a real crime, and convictions followed.

*   *   *

The hero of Gerald Hammond's first, brief series of murder mysteries is the somewhat nauseatingly nicknamed 'Beau' Pepys, architect and amateur racing driver. In the first book, *Fred in Situ,* Pepys (the narrator) becomes the first patient in the hospital he himself has designed; he sets about trying to solve the disappearance of a workman from the building site more than a year before. Light-hearted, fairly implausible (not least when Pepys and his sole fellow-patient decide to make wine from the unwanted grapes brought by their visitors), this nevertheless pleasant tale seemed to set the style for a series. However the next book, *The Loose Screw,* proves to be set prior to *Fred In Situ* and is told in the first person by Beau's cousin Jacqueline, a model and, unusually, expert motor rally navigator. As well as being an interesting and entertainingly related murder mystery, this novel imparts much fascinating information about the art (or is it a science?) of rally navigation.

Technical information is a feature of Hammond's books, for when his next series detective, Keith Calder, bursts upon the scene in *Dead Game* it is to bombard the reader, and any character in the book who will pay him any attention, with intricate details of firearms and firearm history. Calder, in his capacity as gunsmith, shooting instructor, and poacher, is in his younger days none too choosey about which side of the law he operates on. As the series progresses through over a dozen books he marries, sets up a gunshop, and as the years pass becomes a relatively respectable figure, upon whom his former adversary Chief Inspector Munro comes unwillingly to rely. A counterpoint to this developing maturing of character is the incredible speed with which his daughter Deborah ages (unlike the majority of children in series novels). A baby (happily sitting in her playpen chewing on Keith's powder flask) in *Cousin Once Removed,* a mere four books later she is taking her 'O' levels and engraving guns; in the next book, *Adverse Report,* she is viewing dead bodies and in *A Brace of Skeet* she becomes acting steward of a gun club and a sleuth in her own right (her father being away in America). As Hammond takes on average only a year to produce two books, this is startling progress indeed.

Most of the Keith Calder novels are set in Newton Lauder, a small town in Lowland Scotland. Here various local worthies (and unworthies, notably Keith's brother-in-law Ronnie) form fixed points against which Calder conducts both his investigations and his more nefarious activities. In *Sauce for the Pigeon* Keith, called in to assist the police when they discover a body in

a burnt-out Landrover, expertly interprets the forensic evidence in a *tour de force* that almost rivals the legendary Sherlock Holmes, much to the dismay of Chief Inspector Munro, whom Keith looks upon as a latter day Lestrade. Legal help from local solicitor Mr. Enterkin and illegal help from a variety of local poachers enable this engaging reprobate to solve the crime, thereby preventing the wrongful conviction of a friend.

As Calder starts to work more and more on the side of the law his reputation as a firearms expert grows, and in *Silver City Scandal* he is employed by an Aberdeen-based oil firm to prove the innocence of one of their employees who has been accused of murder. Tireless in his quest for evidence, Keith selflessly allows himself to be seduced by the murder victim's companion, in between fighting his way through the various echelons of the criminal underworld.

Keith Calder takes something of a back seat in *Adverse Report* and *Stray Shot,* two novels narrated in the first person by detective writer Simon Parbitter. A town-bred Englishman, Simon comes to Newton Lauder to claim his inheritance consisting of a house left to him by his uncle—and ultimately to claim the housekeeper too. It transpires that the uncle has been murdered, and in his investigations Simon is aided by both Keith and Deborah, who in the course of solving the crime introduce him to their world of guns and dogs. To see the familiar background through the eyes of a stranger, and moreover one who is not totally sympathetic to their way of life, adds an interesting dimension to these novels.

We depart from Newton Lauder, but not from firearms and sporting dogs, in a third series of books; these novels feature John Cunningham, an ex-soldier. Invalided out of the army when he contracted a mysterious and debilitating tropical disease, Cunningham is still far from well when he starts his second career as a professional breeder and trainer of springer spaniels. His partners in business and detection are introduced in the first book *Dog in the Dark;* they are Isobel Kitts, a vet with an unfortunate tendency to overindulge in both drink and sex whenever there is cause for celebration, and kennelmaid Beth Cattrell. Beth progresses from this initial position to become John's mistress, fiancée and by the third book, *Whose Dog Are You?,* his wife. In all these books the joint expertise of the three partners (Cunningham's in guns, Isobel's in dog-breeding and Beth's in sheer commonsense) helps in solving murders and associated canine and ballistic puzzles.

Hammond uses both the John Cunningham and the Keith Calder novels to promote the validity of shooting and bloodsports and he makes some very scathing comments about their opponents, and about well-meaning but in his view ignorant conservationists. This proselytising has appeared in his more recent books and introduces a serious element which does not necessarily enhance these otherwise racingly entertaining novels.

—Judith Rhodes

———

HAMMOND INNES, Ralph. *See* **INNES, Hammond.**

———

HANSEN, Joseph. Also writes as Rose Brock; James Colton. American.   Born in Aberdeen, South Dakota, 19 July 1923. Educated at public schools in Aberdeen, South Dakota, and

Minneapolis, Pasedena, 1929–42. Married Jane Bancroft in 1943; one daughter. Self-employed writer. Teacher of mystery and other fiction writing, University of California Extension Programs. Recipient: National Endowment for the Arts Fellowship, 1974; British Arts Council Grant, 1975. Agent: Stuart Krichevsky, Sterling Lord Literistic Inc., 1 Madison Avenue, New York, New York, 10010. Address: 2638 Cullen Street, Los Angeles, California 90034, U.S.A.

CRIME PUBLICATIONS

Novels (series: Dave Brandstetter in all books except *Backtrack* and *Steps Going Down*)

Fadeout. New York, Harper, 1970; London, Harrap, 1972.
Death Claims. New York, Harper, and London, Harrap, 1973.
Troublemaker. New York, Harper, and London, Harrap, 1975.
The Man Everybody Was Afraid Of. New York, Holt Rinehart, and London, Faber, 1978.
Skinflick. New York, Holt Rinehart, 1979; London, Faber, 1980.
Gravedigger. New York, Holt Rinehart, and London, Owen, 1982.
Backtrack. Woodstock, Vermont, Countryman Press, 1982; London, Gay Men's Press, 1987.
Nightwork. New York, Holt Rinehart, and London, Owen, 1984.
Steps Going Down. Woodstock, Countryman Press, 1985; London, Arlington, 1986.
The Little Dog Laughed. New York, Holt, 1986.
Early Graves. New York, Mysterious Press, 1987.
Obedience. New York, Mysterious Press, 1988.

Short Stories

The Dog and Other Stories. Los Angeles, Momentum Press, 1979.
Brandstetter and Others: Five Fictions. Woodstock, Vermont, Foul Play Press, 1984
Bohannon's Book: Five Mysteries. Woodstock, Vermont, Countryman Press, 1988.

Uncollected Short Stories

"Murder on the Surf," in *Mystery Monthly* (New York), December 1976
"The Olcott Nostrum," in *Alfred Hitchcock's Mystery Magazine* (New York), December 1987.
"The Owl in the Oak," in *Alfred Hitchcock's Mystery Magazine* (New York), March 1988.
"Molly's Aim," in *Ellery Queen's Mystery Magazine* (New York), June 1989.

OTHER PUBLICATIONS

Novels

Tarn House (as Rose Brock). New York, Avon, 1971; London, Harrap, 1975.
Longleaf (as Rose Brock). New York, Harper, and London, Harrap, 1974.
Pretty Boy Dead. New York, Major, 1977.
A Smile in His Lifetime. New York, Holt Rinehart, 1981; London, Owen, 1982.

Job's Year. New York, Holt Rinehart, 1983; London, Arlington, 1988.

Novels as James Colton

Lost on Twilight Road. Fresno, California, National Library, 1964.
Strange Marriage. Los Angeles, Argyle Books, 1965.
Known Homosexual. Los Angeles, Brandon House, 1968; as *Stranger to Himself*, Los Angeles, Major Books, 1978.
Cocksure. San Diego, Greenleaf, 1969.
Hang-Up. Los Angeles, Brandon House, 1969.
Gard. New York, Award, 1969.
The Outward Side. New York, Olympia Press, 1971.
Todd. New York, Olympia Press, 1971.

Short Stories as James Colton

The Corrupter and Other Stories. San Diego, Greenleaf, 1968.

Verse

One Foot in the Boat. Los Angeles, Momentum Press, 1977.

Other

"The New Mystery," in *The Writer* (Boston), September 1973.
"The Fag as Pop Art Target," in *New Review* (London), March 1975.
"What's Wrong with Your Story?," in *The Writer* (Boston), October 1976.
"Plotting a Murder," in *The Writer* (Boston), October 1979.

*

Joseph Hansen comments:

Homosexuals have commonly been treated shabbily in detective fiction—vilified, pitied, at best patronized. This was neither fair nor honest. When I sat down to write *Fadeout* in 1967 I wanted to write a good, compelling whodunit, but I also wanted to right some wrongs. Almost all the folksay about homosexuals is false. So I had some fun turning clichés and stereotypes on their heads in that book. It was easy. I gather from the reviews that it worked. But before there were reviews there had to be a published book. And that took some doing. It also took three years. Publishers were leery of my matter-of-fact, non-apologetic approach to a subject that the rule book said had to be treated sensationally or not at all. At last a brave lady named Joan Kahn, mystery editor at Harper and Row, took a chance on me. Brandstetter, shrewd, cool, tough-minded, and, in spite of this(!), a homosexual, now has readers in Britain, Denmark, France, Germany, Holland, Italy, and Japan as well. Peter Preston of the London *Guardian* asked me once if it was right for Dave always to be mixed up in mystery plots involving homosexuals and homosexuality. I said it seemed to me there were plenty of mystery plots involving heterosexuals and heterosexuality, weren't there? And Julian Symons has been kind enough to remark somewhere that Dave's special bent gives him insights into areas of everyday life the common reader ordinarily wouldn't see, or if he did see, wouldn't understand. The message that homosexuals are no different from other people hardly seems earth shaking—at least not to men and women of goodwill and commonsense. Alas, such men and women make up a breed small in numbers. I hope the Dave Brandstetter novels can add to them.

*   *   *

Early Graves, in which a young man appears to be the victim of a racist cult, is the tenth of Joseph Hansen's Dave Brandstetter mysteries and the second, including *Obedience,* in which the investigator comes out of retirement to take a case. Dave began in *Fadeout* as a middle-aged, increasingly world-weary investigator of insurance claims. He is homosexual and his problems include keeping a lover. Many of the people he runs into in his work are homosexual, but by this time one almost fails to notice the difference. By means of the mystery and detective problems in his best work, Hansen universalized the fact of homosexuality, a commendable achievement.

Many of the Brandstetter books are strong in Southern California, particularly Los Angeles, atmosphere. Avid readers can enjoy the details regarding houses, cars, beverages, cooking, friends, enemies and out-of-the-ordinary people and events. And find them, like all of Hansen's beautifully styled description and dialogue, a purposeful and meaningful part of characterization. At this, he is not James M. Cain or John O'Hara, but he knows the technique that makes their work readable because of the way in which it is written, but he has his own cleverness and devices. Hansen is often compared to his predecessors, Chandler and Millar, but in style and plotting he is more entertaining than either.

In "The Mystery Novel as Serious Business," a 1984 article, one can get insights into the inspiration for several of his plots and characters, as well as his goals in writing and views on the mystery. But, these can be deceptive. He writes, "The task of a fiction writer is to be a faithful observer of things as they are." He admires Gertrude Stein. He disparages Mickey Spillane as a writer on the level of Bugs Bunny and Spider Man, "all action." He calls the mysteries of Christie and Sayers "parlor games" and says the "serious mystery" is never that. He especially describes his "serious" belief in the mystery. To some readers these ideas may not always match his performance.

In Hansen's best Brandstetter mysteries, antagonisms and love-relationships are parallel. In *Fadeout,* his lover is dead of cancer. Dave clears a young man of murder and the young man becomes his new lover. Lover fades out, and another fades in. Victim fades out by way of investigation; motive for murder fades in. The title fits the radio *mise en scene* and plot, and is an indication of the use of language that makes up an important factor in Hansen's style.

Death Claims, memorable and readable repeatedly, has Dave and his new lover "coming apart." Each has a dead lover in his memory. Dave investigates the death of a bookseller who fought to stay alive through tortuous skin-graft surgery, sustained by the love of a younger girl. Finding the murderer, Dave restores the girl's faith in herself and her ability to be happy. Dave and his lover bury the past and their relationship is restored in a sophisticated, subtly humorous interplay. Title doubles plot and theme. Integrated throughout, the work shows how a mystery can be purposeful and entertaining at the same time.

Troublemaker deals with interlopers. One is the murderer of a gay-bar operator. Sorting out the victim's associates, Dave finds the killer. A parasite who attempts to break up Dave's relationship, meanwhile, is kicked out. The interlopers get what they deserve in the parallel and the entire plot works.

The series from then on becomes increasingly conventional with format replacing invention. *Skinflick's* porno scene is actually interesting, as well-styled as any Hansen has done, in a few well-chosen essentials integrated into the action. But, *The Man Everybody Was Afraid Of* is not a fearsome ghost, but a frightfully dull stereotype. Starting with *Gravedigger,* and in *Nightwork, The Little Dog Laughed,* and, to some extent, *Obedience,* there is a trendiness with social and political

concerns substituting for better plot ideas, with some books hurried and unbelievable.

This might have seemed true of *Early Graves,* but this mystery stands next to *Death Claims* as a novel that will gradually build its audience and be reread and enjoyed for both writing and content. This is especially surprising, and all the more difficult to have accomplished, because the subject that ties the work together is the Aids epedemic. Unlike most treatments of this subject, however, again Hansen had the ability to universalize his material. Brandstetter is preparing for retirement from investigation when he finds a man's body that was placed on his patio with his investigator's business card fallen to the ground below. Thus intrigued, almost forced into investigation, Dave pursues the devious path of "knifings in the dark" and the many victims of "early" deaths, all victims of Aids, but claimed by death early by the knife wound of a serial killer, or so it seems. As the jeopardy Brandstetter places himself in increases, so do suspense and intrigue. Almost like an explosion, a climax occurs that seems in Dostoevskian overtones to solve everything. But unreason and disease are not that simple (nor were they in Dostoevsky). With the final solution yet to come, a cunning victim and a cunning killer use other people's lives and money for their own purposes, to conceal or dredge-up, one upon the other, the past. Parallel lives of sub-plot and plot, lovers and victims, motives and murders, are intricately woven in what seems an unanswerable web of circumstance. Unfortunately, serious faults develop in Hansen's story. The circumstances, characters and solution regarding the concealed killer seem contrived in the end. And, Dave's grousing relationship with Cecil, the black lover acquired a few books back, is tiresome, despite reconciliation. The book is not the balanced, conceptualized whole that *Death Claims* is, but it is more ambitious and a work of great effort and results.

Obedience comes as rather a let-down then, and its ending is even more contrived. But the Vietnamese sub-culture, harbor intrigue, and dark restaurant humor are entertaining, but it is hard to believe Dave would have got into this one. *Brandstetter and Others* is several stories featuring the series character. But the "others" are the best: "The Anderson Boy" his closest effort to the twists of the 1940's plot, and "Willow's Money" with two classic portraits of women you will both love and hate as fictional treats. *Bohannon's Book* collects five stories about Hansen's straight detective who practices his private trade by tracking back-country roads and trails, mostly in the hills. More often than not he arrives accidentally on plots and solutions. Hansen's best story remains "Getting Rid of Mr. Granger" in *The Dog and Other Stories.*

Backtrack, a book Hansen struggled to get published and takes very seriously, and *Steps Going Down* are two non-series mysteries, serious in technique, but seriously or not, unattractive to this reader. *Backtrack* features a character-staple for Hansen. In *Lost on Twilight Road,* for example, an attractive youth overcomes poverty, matures and defeats his enemies. *Backtrack's* Alan is a cute, "wise" kid. Abandoned and a ready pickup, he trots on to find his father's killer with planted knowledge, with environment and behavior strictly sleaze. *Steps Going Down,* were the detection and crime removed, would stumble down to trash.

Hansen may write in the manner of the California private eye genre, but in his best efforts he is a unique individual with a style you can't wait to find again. He is not just a reporter of things as they are—thank heavens, but an inventor, especially of classic types and settings. When his plots depend on conventional situations and issues, style and sensibility cannot salvage the artificiality, and his effort shows it. However, even in a sea of mediocrity, at his best, Hansen would stand, somewhat obscure at times, above it.

—Newton Baird

———————

HANSHEW, Thomas W. Also wrote as Charlotte Mary Kingsley. American. Born in 1857. Married Mary E. Hanshew. An actor for some years. *Died 3 March 1914.*

CRIME PUBLICATIONS

Novels (series: Hamilton Cleek)

Beautiful But Dangerous; or, The Heir of Shadowdene. New York, Street and Smith, 1891.
The World's Finger. London, Ward Lock, and New York, Irwin, 1901; as *The Horton Mystery,* New York, Ogilvie, 1905.
The Mallison Mystery. London, Ward Lock, 1903.
The Great Ruby. London, Ward Lock, 1905.
The Shadow of a Dead Man. London, Ward Lock, 1906.
Fate and the Man. London, Cassell, 1910.
Cleek of Scotland Yard. London, Cassell, and New York, Doubleday, 1914.
Cleek's Greatest Riddles. London, Simpkin Marshall, 1916; as *Cleek's Government Cases,* New York, Doubleday, 1917 (possibly not by Hanshew).

Short Stories

The Man of the Forty Faces. London, Cassell, 1910; revised (novel) version, as *Cleek, The Man of the Forty Faces,* Cassell, 1913; short story version as *Cleek, The Master Detective,* New York, Doubleday, 1918.

OTHER PUBLICATIONS

Novels

Young Mrs. Charnleigh. New York, Carleton, 1883.
Leonie; or, The Sweet Street Singer of New York. New York, Munro, 1884.
A Wedded Widow; or, The Love That Lived. New York, Street and Smith, 1887.
Arrol's Engagement (as Charlotte Mary Kingsley). London, Ward Lock, 1903.

Plays

The Forty-Niners; or, The Pioneer's Daughter, adaptation of his own story (also director: produced). Clyde, Ohio, Ames, n.d.
Oath Bound; or, Faithful unto Death (produced Chicago). Clyde, Ohio, Ames, n.d.
Will-o'-the-Wisp; or, The Shot in the Dark. Clyde, Ohio, Ames, n.d.

*   *   *

The reader who is unprepared or unable to suspend disbelief will never be able to read Thomas W. Hanshew with pleasure.

Some have called him an obscure writer who deserves obscurity. Admittedly, he is a "period author" who must be read in the context of his times and the tradition from which he came. Hanshew was an American dime novelist who found his niche in detective history with a long series of stories about Hamilton Cleek, the man of the forty faces. According to tradition he was one of the writers of the Nick Carter stories, but this has never been proved. His use of the pseudonym Bertha M. Clay is also in doubt; both his family and his publishers denied the attribution.

Some three dozen of the more than 80 Cleek stories had been published when their author died; the remaining stories, after an initial magazine appearance, were edited by Hanshew's daughter, Hazel, into collections disguised as novels. The books were published as by Hanshew and his widow, Mary. The Cleek stories have many weaknesses, not the least of which are the melodramatic style and improbable situations. Read with the right approach, though, they can be enjoyed in spite of themselves. At the core of most are some ingenious ideas which tantalize and mystify and disappoint only for the reason many mysteries disappoint: the solution is never as ingenious as the mystery itself. A magician's trick is only as good as his art of misdirection. There are a nine-fingered skeleton, a death on the tenth of each month, inexplicable footprints, a tell-tale tattoo that can be removed only at the expense of an arm, a person who vanishes in plain view, and other mysteries.

Behind the individual stories of detection is the mystery of Cleek himself, which is used to bind episodes into longer stories. Once he was known to the police as the Vanishing Cracksman, his main attribute being the ability to disguise himself. He didn't need putty or false whiskers, for he possessed the talent to alter his features by sheer will power. Because of his love for Ailsa Lorne, Cleek resolved to go straight and become Scotland Yard's chief riddle solver. Cleek had forty faces and reserved his real one for the people close to him: Superintendent Maverick Narkom, Dollops (his cockney associate), and Ailsa Lorne. His real identity was that of the true king of Maurevania (bounded, no doubt, on the North by Ruritania and on the South by Graustark), and for Ailsa he renounced the throne. Cleek is continually pursued through the stories by the ghosts of his past, both criminal and regal. This creates a tension which can be enjoyed along with the puzzles.

It is argued that Hanshew knew little of Scotland Yard and less of the mysterious East, both of which play major roles in the chronicles of Cleek. But Cleek is not a real person and his world is not the real one. This is the world of romance and high adventure. With tongue in cheek and child-like acceptance of fantasy, the reader of Hanshew can truly escape the mundane. On one level the books may even be read as a burlesque of Edwardian detective stories and all the works of romance which their author once spun for his American publishers. Hanshew's significance may lie in the influence he had on some later writers, like John Dickson Carr, who also had an interest in ingenious situations and intricate plots. Cleek's method of disguise was adapted by Paul Ernst for his novels about Richard Benson in *The Avenger* magazine (1939–42).

—J. Randolph Cox

———————

HARBAGE, Alfred B. *See* **KYD, Thomas.**

———————

HARE, Cyril. Pseudonym for Alfred Alexander Gordon Clark. British. Born in Mickleham, Surrey, 4 September 1900. Educated at Rugby School, Warwickshire; New College, Oxford, B.A. (honours) in history; Inner Temple, London: called to the Bar, 1924. Married Mary Barbara Lawrence in 1933; one son and two daughters. Joined firm of Ronald Oliver and practiced in civil and criminal courts; temporary officer, Ministry of Economic Warfare, 1940, and temporary legal assistant, Director of Public Prosecutions Department, 1940–45; County Court Judge, Surrey, 1950–58. *Died 25 August 1958.*

CRIME PUBLICATIONS

Novels (series: Inspector Mallett; Francis Pettigrew)

Tenant for Death (Mallett). London, Faber, and New York, Dodd Mead, 1937.
Death Is No Sportsman (Mallett). London, Faber, 1938.
Suicide Excepted (Mallett). London, Faber, 1939; New York, Macmillan, 1954.
Tragedy at Law (Mallett; Pettigrew). London, Faber, 1942; New York, Harcourt Brace, 1943.
With a Bare Bodkin (Mallett; Pettigrew). London, Faber, 1946; New York, Harper, 1980.
When the Wind Blows (Pettigrew). London, Faber, 1949; New York, Garland, 1976; as *The Wind Blows Death,* Boston, Little Brown, 1950.
An English Murder. London, Faber, and Boston, Little Brown, 1951; as *The Christmas Murder,* New York, Spivak, 1953.
That Yew Tree's Shade (Pettigrew). London, Faber, 1954; as *Death Walks the Woods,* Boston, Little Brown, 1954.
He Should Have Died Hereafter (Mallett; Pettigrew). London, Faber, 1958; as *Untimely Death,* New York, Macmillan, 1958; London, Hogarth Press, 1987.

Short Stories

Best Detective Stories of Cyril Hare, edited by Michael Gilbert. London, Faber, 1959; New York, Walker, 1961; as *Death Among Friends and Other Detective Stories,* New York, Perennial, 1984.

Uncollected Short Stories

"Spare the Rod and Spoil the Crime," in *The Evening Standard* (London), 24 January 1951.
"The Will," in *The Evening Standard* (London), 6 December 1951.
"Accident," in *The Evening Standard* (London), 21 June 1952.
"This Side Up with Care," in *The Evening Standard* (London), 8 July 1954.
"The Man from Pannonia," in *The Evening Standard* (London), 30 September 1955.
"The Magnifying Glass," in *The Evening Standard* (London), 10 March 1956.
"The Euthanasia of Hilary's Aunt," in *Some Like Them Dead.* London, Hodder and Stoughton, 1960.
"The Boldest Course," in *Ellery Queen's Mystery Magazine* (New York), November 1960.
"The Homing Wasp," in *Ellery Queen's Mystery Magazine* (New York), March 1961.

"Blenkinsop's Biggest Boner," in *Ellery Queen's Mystery Magazine* (New York), September 1961.
"I Never Forget a Face," in *The Saint* (New York), June 1966.

OTHER PUBLICATIONS

Play

The House of Warbeck (produced Margate, Kent, 1955).

Other

The Magic Bottle (for children). London, Faber, 1946.

Editor (as A.A. Gordon Clark), with Alan Garfitt, *Roscoe's Criminal Evidence,* 16th edition, by Henry Roscoe. London, Stevens, 1952.
Editor (as A.A. Gordon Clark), *Leith Hill Musical Festival 1905–1955: A Record of Fifty Years of Music-Making in Surrey.* Epsom, Surrey, Pullingers, 1955.

*   *   *

The legal profession has attracted some highly talented writers of crime fiction. One of the first and most noteworthy examples is Melville Davisson Post (his lawyer-protagonist is Randolph Mason). Other prominent lawyer-authors with legal sleuths include Erle Stanley Gardner (Perry Mason), and Harold Q. Masur (Scott Jordon). Several authors without legal training such as H.C. Bailey and Anthony Gilbert created, respectively, shyster-lawyer Joshua Clunk and Arthur Crook—a lawyer who is much more honest than his name would indicate, and whose clients are never guilty anyway. There are also Dr. R. Austin Freeman's Dr. Thorndyke who qualified as both doctor and lawyer, and specialized in forensic science, and Francis M. Nevins, Jr., who graduated (as did his creation Loren Mensing) from practice to theory and became professor of law.

And there is Cyril Hare, the pseudonym of Alfred Alexander Gordon Clark, who became county court judge in Surrey in 1950. His series detective Francis Pettigrew, however, is an aging and unsuccessful lawyer who is barely making a living. He originally showed great promise and aptitude for the law, but a series of misfortunes prevented his career from reaching fruition, and left him a bitter and unhappy person.

Neither Pettigrew nor his creator is well-known, especially in America, and Hare's reputation as a mystery writer lapsed into obscurity for a decade after his death in 1958, but recent critical revaluation has established him as a master with at least four major novels and a notable collection of short stories to his credit. *Tenant for Death* introduced Inspector Mallett, a Scotland Yard detective who is tall and stout, and not unlike Freeman Wills Croft's Inspector Joseph French. This novel and its successor, *Death Is No Sportsman,* are good, solid detective stories, very typical of the work being turned out during the 1930's, but neither of them drew to any great extent on Hare's legal expertise. *Suicide Excepted* is about three amateurs who play detective in order to change a verdict of suicide to murder. It showed an advance over previous work, was lighter in tone, more entertaining, had more detailed characterizations, and an unexpected ending.

Hare's own favorite novel, *Tragedy at Law,* is completely unorthodox, brilliantly characterized, and a masterpiece. It is a lovingly detailed story of a judge on a second-rate circuit who falls on the wrong side of the law when, while he is far from sober, his car hits a pedestrian. Very near the end of the novel, a murder problem arises, and Pettigrew (in his debut) matches wits with Inspector Mallett and bests him.

Tragedy at Law, which was based on Hare's tour as a judge's marshal, received rave reviews. Henry Cecil, a jurist whose legal farces fall within the mystery genre, later stated, "This book is acknowledged by many lawyers to be the classic detective story with a legal background. It has stood the test of time. . . . [It was] written with a master's hand and wit of a very high order, and I have no reason to doubt the correctness of the opinion . . . that in detective fiction it is a work of the highest class." *Tragedy at Law* and Hare's three subsequent major novels placed him at the top of his literary profession.

Hare's service with the Ministry of Economic Warfare during World War II provided the inspiration for *With a Bare Bodkin,* which detailed a murder, committed with a spiked paper holder, in a government office. The collaboration between Mallett and Pettigrew is more conventional than in *Tragedy at Law;* it bears comparison to Nicholas Blake's *Minute for Murder* (1947). Even better is *When the Wind Blows* which begins with the death of England's foremost violinist before he can perform with a local music society. This solo investigation by Pettigrew was highly praised by Anthony Boucher, and Barzun and Taylor consider it to be Hare's masterpiece. Hare's great interest in music lent authenticity to this novel's vivid background.

Hare's last major work, *An English Murder,* involves a typical English Christmas house party in a castle that becomes snowbound. Czech refugee Dr. Bottwink does the honors here in solving three murders. Much more entertaining than the earlier books, this is a completely unexpected and absolutely delightful work. *An English Murder* is my favorite Hare novel, a model of the British fair-play school, and a "must" item for anyone who likes Agatha Christie. I have encountered very few mysteries that are as sheerly likable as *An English Murder.* Its only flaw is the absence of Frank Pettigrew. Hare's subsequent work declined, but found Pettigrew happily married to a girl half his age. The last novel, *He Should Have Died Hereafter,* is short and fragmentary.

Hare's great friend Michael Gilbert edited the posthumous *Best Detective Stories of Cyril Hare*—an excellent collection of 30 crime stories. Gilbert's introduction to Hare's life and work is illuminating, and serves as an excellent memorial tribute by a fellow lawyer and mystery writer.

—Charles Shibuk

———

HARLING, Robert. Also writes as Nicholas Drew. British. Born in 1910. Editor, *Image: A Quarterly of the Visual Arts,* London, in the 1950's; former design consultant, *Times Literary Supplement* and *Sunday Times,* both London. Since 1957, editor, *House and Garden* magazine, London. Address: c/o Chatto and Windus, Ltd., 30 Bedford Square, London WC1B 3RP, England.

CRIME PUBLICATIONS

Novels

The Paper Palace. London, Chatto and Windus, and New York, Harper, 1951.

The Dark Saviour. London, Chatto and Windus, 1952; New York, Harper, 1953.
The Enormous Shadow. London, Chatto and Windus, 1955; New York, Harper, 1956.
The Endless Colonnade. London, Chatto and Windus, 1958; New York, Putnam, 1959.
The Hollow Sunday. London, Chatto and Windus, 1967.

OTHER PUBLICATIONS

Novels

The Athenian Widow. London, Chatto and Windus, 1974.
The Summer Portrait. London, Chatto and Windus, 1979.

Other

The London Miscellany: A Nineteenth-Century Scrapbook. London, Heinemann, 1937; New York, Oxford University Press, 1938.
Home: A Victorian Vignette. London, Constable, 1938; New York, Appleton Century, 1939.
Amateur Sailor (as Nicholas Drew). London, Constable, 1944.
Notes on the Wood-Engravings of Eric Ravilious. London, Faber, 1946.
The Steep Atlantick Stream (wartime autobiography). London, Chatto and Windus, 1946.
Edward Bawden. London, Art and Technics, 1950.
The Letter Forms and Type Designs of Eric Gill. Westerham, Kent, Svensson, 1976.
British Gardeners: A Biographical Dictionary, with Miles Hadfield and Leonie Highton. London, Zwemmer-Condé Nast, 1980.

Editor, *House and Garden's Interiors and Colour.* London, Condé Nast, 1959.
Editor, with others, *Small Houses.* London, Condé Nast, 1961.
Editor, *House and Garden Book of Interiors.* London and New York, Condé Nast, 1962.
Editor, *House and Garden Book of Cottages.* London, Condé Nast, 1963; New York, Condé Nast, 1964.
Editor, *The Modern Interior.* London, Condé Nast, 1964; New York, St. Martin's Press, 1965.
Editor, *House and Garden Garden Book.* London, Condé Nast, 1965; New York, St. Martin's Press, 1966.
Editor, *House and Garden First Cook Book.* London, Condé Nast, 1965.
Editor, *House and Garden Book of Modern Houses and Conversions.* London, Condé Nast, 1966.
Editor, *House and Garden Guide to Interior Decoration.* London, Condé Nast, and New York, St. Martin's Press, 1967.
Editor, *House and Garden Book of Holiday and Weekend Houses.* London, Condé Nast, and New York, St. Martin's Press, 1968.
Editor, *Historical Houses: Conversations in Stately Homes.* London, Condé Nast-Collins, 1969; as *The Great Houses and Finest Rooms in England,* New York, Viking Press, 1969.
Editor, *House and Garden Modern Furniture and Decoration.* London, Condé Nast-Collins, 1971; as *Modern Furniture and Decoration,* New York, Viking Press, 1971.

Editor, *House and Garden Dictionary of Design and Decoration.* London, Condé Nast-Collins, 1973; as *Studio Dictionary of Design and Decoration,* New York, Viking Press, 1973.

Editor, with Leonie Highton and John Bridges. *The House and Garden Book of Romantic Rooms.* Salem, New Hampshire, Salem House, and London, Collins, 1985.

Editor, with Leonie Highton and John Bridges. *The House and Garden Book of Classic Rooms.* London, Chatto and Windus, 1989.

*   *   *

Robert Harling has used his long experience in journalism and advertising to produce novels memorable for their accurate, lively details about newsmaking, their interest in the moral ambiguities of reporting, and their focus on grudging admiration between men whose different ideologies compel them to conflict. Harling humanizes his villains by their dreams, weaknesses, and unexpected strengths, but suggests that surface changes never touch the unchanging core. His first-person narrator is usually an established, worldly-wise newspaperman, often divorced, susceptible to feminine allure but obsessed by the lone pursuit of "a story." Always his editor's placid facade hides a tough, cynical inner core, a sharp nose for a story, a dual commitment to making money from news and to seeking truth and justice. Harling explores the reporter/editor relationship, the differences between the finished article and the writer's total views, the potentially destructive power of rhetorically manipulated news.

The Hollow Sunday traces a cautious investigation of scandal involving an M.P.'s wife. *The Athenian Widow* portrays the painful, vacillating process a newspaper goes through to decide whether to publish a controversial exposé. *The Dark Saviour* raises the question of moral responsibility, as a journalist discovers his paper's Caribbean man-on-the-spot providing communist support for a black take-over and, despite his sympathy for the "dark saviour," prints a misleading picture that results in death and violence and the end of a potential revolution. In *The Enormous Shadow* a journalist discovers a conservative British M.P.'s strong communist attachments, and, despite his understanding of the man's idealistic commitment, precipitates an exciting midnight chase down the Thames. In the heavily ironic *The Endless Colonnade,* a British psychiatrist on holiday in Italy (detailed sightseeing) fails to take seriously a traitorous young physicist's misplaced idealism, and by procrastinating causes the death of his closest friend. *The Paper Palace,* Harling's first book and perhaps his most ingenious, dramatizes the slow, tedious investigative techniques of a journalist who seeks patterns in obscure details about what a dead man did and why, until they add up to a horrifying story of a wealthy English communist's atrocities and the ironic twist of blackmail producing blackmail.

—Gina Macdonald

———

HARRINGTON, Joyce. American. Born in Jersey City, New Jersey. Studied at Pasadena Playhouse, California. Has two sons. Director of Public Relations, Foote Cone and Belding, advertising agency, New York. Recipient: Mystery Writers of America Edgar Allan Poe award, for short story, 1973. Agent: Scott Meredith Literary Agency Inc., 845 Third Avenue, New York, New York 10022, U.S.A.

CRIME PUBLICATIONS

Novels

No One Knows My Name. New York, St.Martin's Press, 1980; London, Macmillan, 1981.
Family Reunion. New York, St. Martin's Press, 1982; London, Severn House, 1983.
Dreemz of the Night. New York, St. Martin's Press, 1987.

Uncollected Short Stories

"Things Change," in *Ellery Queen's Mystery Magazine* (New York), July 1974.
"The Purple Shroud," in *Ellery Queen's Crookbook.* New York, Random House, and London, Gollancz, 1974.
"The Green Patch," in *Ellery Queen's Mystery Magazine* (New York), June 1975.
"The Garage Apartment," in *Alfred Hitchcock's Mystery Magazine* (North Palm Beach, Florida), September 1975.
"Death of a Princess," in *Ellery Queen's Mystery Magazine* (New York), November 1975.
"What My Left Hand Does," in *Alfred Hitchcock's Mystery Magazine* (North Palm Beach, Florida), December 1975.
"The Plastic Jungle," in *Every Crime in the Book,* edited by Robert L. Fish. New York, Putnam, 1975.
"The Pretty Lady Passes By," in *Ellery Queen's Mystery Magazine* (New York), January 1976.
"The Season Ticket Holder," in *Ellery Queen's Mystery Magazine* (New York), March 1976.
"Gemini and the Missing Mother," in *Alfred Hitchcock's Mystery Magazine* (New York), June 1976.
"My Neighbor, Ay" and "The Cabin in the Hollow," in *Ellery Queen's Crime Wave.* New York, Putnam, and London, Gollancz, 1976.
"Don't Wait for Me," in *Alfred Hitchcock's Mystery Magazine* (New York), December 1976.
"August Is a Good Time for Killing," in *Alfred Hitchcock's Mystery Magazine* (New York), April 1977.
"Night Crawlers," in *Ellery Queen's Searches and Seizures.* New York, Davis, 1977.
"The Thirteenth Victim," in *Antaeus* (New York), Spring–Summer 1977.
"When Push Comes to Shove," in *Alfred Hitchcock's Mystery Magazine* (New York), November 1977.
"Looking for Milliken Street," in *Alfred Hitchcock's Anthology, Spring–Summer 1978.* New York, Davis, 1978.
"Blue Monday," in *Ellery Queen's A Multitude of Sins.* New York, Davis, 1978.
"The Old Gray Cat," in *Best Detective Stories of the Year 1978,* edited by Edward D. Hoch. New York, Dutton, 1978.
"The Two Sisters," in *Women's Wiles,* edited by Michele Slung. New York, Harcourt Brace, 1979.
"Grass," in *Ellery Queen's Scenes of the Crimes.* New York, Davis, 1979.
"Happy Birthday Darling," in *Ellery Queen's Mystery Magazine* (New York), February 1979.
"Vienna Sausage," in *Alfred Hitchcock's Tales to Make Your Teeth Chatter,* edited by Eleanor Sullivan. New York, Dial Press, 1980.
"It Never Happened," in *Ellery Queen's Windows of Mystery.* New York, Davis, 1980.
"My Friend, Mr. Cunningham," in *Ellery Queen's Mystery Magazine* (New York), July 1980.

"The Couple Next Door," in *Ellery Queen's Doors to Mystery*. New York, Davis, 1981.

"A Place of Her Own," in *Ellery Queen's Crime Cruise round the World*. New York, Davis, 1981.

"Dispatching Bootsie," in *Ellery Queen's Mystery Magazine* (New York), January 1981.

"Honeymoon Home," in *Ellery Queen's Mystery Magazine* (New York), December 1981.

"Sweet Baby Jenny," in *The Year's Best Mystery and Suspense Stories 1982,* edited by Edward D. Hoch. New York, Walker, 1982.

"The Tomato Man's Daughter," in *Ellery Queen's Lost Ladies*. New York, Davis, 1983.

"Address Unknown," in *The Year's Best Mystery and Suspense Stories 1983*, edited by Edward D. Hoch. New York, Walker, 1983.

"Why Don't I Drink Lemonade," in *Ellery Queen's Mystery Magazine* (New York), August 1984.

"Bird Brain," in *Murder in Manhattan*, edited by Bill Adler and D.C. Fontana. New York, Morrow, 1986.

*   *   *

Even before publication of her two novels in 1980 and 1982, Joyce Harrington had already established herself as one of the past decade's brightest discoveries in the crime-suspense field. Her first story, the Edgar-winning "The Purple Shroud," is a quiet tale of a summer art instructor and the wife he has betrayed, building into a murder story of understated terror. Harrington's second story, "The Plastic Jungle," is even better—a macabre tale of a girl and her mother living in today's plastic society.

Two of her 1974 stories, "My Neighbor, Ay" and "The Cabin in the Hollow," offer settings as different as Brooklyn and rural West Virginia. "Night Crawlers" presents a memorable portrait of a woman worm-farmer and a hidden treasure. "Blue Monday" offers a gripping study of a murderer and his victim. Three Harrington stories published during 1977 best illustrate her many moods. "Grass" is a domestic drama of conflict between a husband and wife. "The Old Gray Cat" is a tantalizing mood piece full of deft surprises for the unwary reader. And "The Thirteenth Victim" is a horror story about a man who constructs art works around the bodies of the dead.

No doubt as a result of the time devoted to her novels, Joyce Harrington's short stories became less frequent after 1978. However, special attention should be called to "A Place of Her Own," a penetrating study of a New York bag lady, "Sweet Baby Jenny," and "Address Unknown." All reflect her fascinating, and sometimes bizarre, examination of the human condition.

Harrington's first novel, *No One Knows My Name,* was in some ways a more conventional murder mystery than one might have expected from her. The psychotic killer stalking cast members of a summer theater at the Duck Creek Playhouse made for first-rate suspense and a fine debut in the novel length, but it was not until her second novel, *Family Reunion,* that all of Harrington's skill with plots and characters came together in a perfect blend. When Jenny Holland returns from New York City to the reunion at River House the result is a major treat for mystery readers, combining the best elements of the gothic novel with the psychological suspense tale she has always done so well. And while the question in *No One Knows My Name* is basically one of whodunit, *Family Reunion* goes much deeper, asking the reader also to discover what it was they did so long ago. The answer, when it comes, is as shocking as it is believable.

At her best, Joyce Harrington has perfected two of the most important rules of good fiction—her characters are always interesting, and her endings never disappoint the reader.

—Edward D. Hoch

————

HARRINGTON, William. American. Born in Marietta, Ohio 21 November 1931. Educated at Marietta College, A.B. 1953; Duke University, Durham, North Carolina, M.A. 1955; Ohio State University, Columbus J.D. 1958. Married Diana C. Fitch in 1972. Lawyer, Marietta, 1958–62; Columbus, 1971–78; elections counsel, Office of Ohio Secretary of State, Columbus, 1962–65; senior attorney, Mead Data Central, 1978–80. Address: c/o Donald I. Fine Inc., 19 West 21st Street, New York, New York 10010, U.S.A.

CRIME PUBLICATIONS

Novels

Which the Justice, Which the Thief. Indianapolis, Bobbs Merrill, 1963; London, Joseph, 1965.

The Power. Indianapolis, Bobbs Merrill, 1964; as *The Gospel of Death,* London, Joseph, 1966.

Yoshar the Soldier. New York, Dial Press, 1966; London, Eyre and Spottiswoode, 1967.

The Search for Elizabeth Brandt. New York, McKay, 1969.

Trial. New York, McKay, and London, Barrie and Jenkins, 1970.

The Jupiter Crisis. New York, McKay, 1971.

Mister Target. New York, Delacorte Press, 1973; London, Joseph, 1974.

Scorpio 5. New York, Coward McCann, 1975.

Partners. New York, Seaview, 1980.

The English Lady. New York, Seaview, 1982; London, Severn House, 1984.

Skin Deep. New York, Seaview, 1983.

The Cromwell File. New York, St. Martin's Press, and London, Severn House, 1986.

Oberst. New York, Fine, 1987.

For the Defense. New York, Fine, 1988.

*   *   *

William Harrington began his unusually varied novel-writing career using his legal expertise as a specialist in courtroom fiction. *Which the Justice, Which the Thief,* designed as a corrective to inaccurate media depictions of courtroom procedure, concerns the trial of a man and a woman for an armed jewelry store robbery in a small Ohio town. The unhurried narrator is William H.H. Applegate, a nonagenarian retired judge. Despite the lack of the customary Big Trial glitz, the clarity of the writing and the keen observation of people and institutions make this a classic of legal fiction.

The Power, less well known, is nearly as good. When a farm woman with diabetes and a heart condition stops taking her medication and dies after a faith healer has assured her she is cured, an Ohio prosecutor brings a charge of manslaughter against the evangelist. As in the best "issue" novels, the author gives a fair representation of both men's points of view and eschews pat solutions.

Trial, moving the action from small-town courts to the city of Cleveland, begins with a relatively routine crime: a shooting death in the course of a grocery-store robbery. Despite the title, the novel is more police procedural than courtroom book, the trial occupying only a dozen or so pages. The presence of detective Clement Yacobucci, who has a media reputation as a local Sherlock Holmes, moves the book closer to detective fiction than Harrington's earlier crime novels, but the real subject is the politics of capital punishment.

Harrington returns to the courtroom in another impressive novel, *Partners,* about the interlocking lives of three female lawyers in Texas, none of them (refreshingly) either wholly laudable or villainous. Like all the author's courtroom novels, it is rich in the ambiguity of law and morality and refuses to arrive at any easy answers. One continuing theme is that the truth and the appropriate verdict on the evidence do not always coincide.

If Harrington's legal novels are often characterized by an ability to make relatively routine crimes effective fictional subjects, his thrillers tend to be more "high concept." *The English Lady,* for example, is a large-canvas espionage novel about a British aviatrix who spies for Churchill as a member of Hitler's inner circle. The fictional Lady Nancy Brookeford emerges as a complex and fascinating character, and the real-life Nazis surrounding Hitler, especially Reinhard Heydrich, are brought to life in surprising ways. The segment leading up to the failed assassination attempt on the Fuehrer is especially suspenseful, and there is some excellent (and highly cinematic) aviation action. The novel is a natural for film adaptation, and such a project has been in the works for several years.

The Jupiter Crisis, another thriller of notable ambition and execution, is blurbed as a Cold War melodrama in the vein of *Fail-Safe* and *Seven Days in May,* but the titular crisis, the Soviet capture of a U.S. spy satellite, is more of a framing device for the real story: young counter-culture reporter Gib Hubbard's investigation of Erich Traver, object of a 1950's Communist witch-hunt that made the reputation of current President Warren Bradley. The inspiration of Richard Nixon and the Alger Hiss case is clear, though there is no reason to think the plot reflects a serious theory of the affair. The novel contains some memorable characters and scenes, including the kind of sequence that today would draw justifiable feminist outrage: a painfully detailed and extended account of the torture (with the good guys in reluctant collabortion) of a female Soviet agent.

The sweeping scope, tantalizing plot concepts, and explicit (sometimes bordering on exploitative) sex scenes of many of Harrington's novels make it easy to typecast him as another seeker after blockbuster bestsellerdom, but any implication he is a schlockmeister is unfair. His books would have a better chance at the bestseller lists if he really were as conventional in his writing and plotting as the dustjacket blurbs sometimes suggest. His novels constantly ring surprising changes on standard situations and reflect an individual and thoughtful viewpoint.

Harrington's work rarely resembles conventional detective fiction. The first part of *Scorpio 5* includes some slick sleuthing, though, including a neat solution to the seemingly impossible theft of a computer tape.

In the acknowledgements to several of the Eleanor Roosevelt detective novels signed by Elliott Roosevelt, Harrington is credited with assistance to the author. The exact extent of his contribution is unclear. The enjoyable series casts the first lady as sleuth in formal mystery puzzles with many historical figures included as characters.

—Jon L. Breen

HARRIS, Herbert. British. Born in London, 25 August 1911. Educated at Clapham College, London. Married Bonney Genn in 1944. Has published more than 3000 short stories in newspapers and magazines under his own name and a number of pseudonyms including Michael Moore, Frank Bury, Peter Friday, and Jerry Regan. Founding editor, *Red Herrings,* bulletin of the Crime Writers Association, London, 1956–65, and chairman of the association, 1969–70. Recipient: Crime Writers Association award, 1965. Address: 20 Castle Court, Ventnor, Isle of Wight PO38 1UE, England.

CRIME PUBLICATIONS

Novels

Who Kill to Live.   London, Jenkins, 1962.
Painted in Blood.   New York, King Features, 1972.
Serpents in Paradise.   London, W.H. Allen, 1975.
The Angry Battalion.   London, W.H. Allen, 1976.

Uncollected Short Stories (selection)

"The Big Teddy Bears," in *Choice of Weapons,* edited by Michael Gilbert.   London, Hodder and Stoughton, 1958.
"Detective's Wife," in *The First Mystery Bedside Book,* edited by John Creasey.   London, Hodder and Stoughton, 1960.
"Budding Sleuth," in *The Second Mystery Bedside Book,* edited by John Creasey.   London, Hodder and Stoughton, 1961.
"Death of a Tramp," in *The Third Mystery Bedside Book,* edited by John Creasey.   London, Hodder and Stoughton, 1962.
"Link with the Locals," in *The Fifth Mystery Bedside Book,* edited by John Creasey.   London, Hodder and Stoughton, 1964.
"Hate-in-the-Mist," in *Crime Writers' Choice,* edited by Roy Vickers.   London, Hodder and Stoughton, 1964.
"Danny's Real Talent," in *The Sixth Mystery Bedside Book,* edited by John Creasey.   London, Hodder and Stoughton, 1965.
"A Long Rest for Rosie," in *John Creasey's Mystery Bedside Book,* edited by Herbert Harris.   London, Hodder and Stoughton, 1966.
"A Nice Cup of Tea," in *John Creasey's Mystery Bedside Book,* edited by Herbert Harris.   London, Hodder and Stoughton, 1967.
"Saviour of San Fernando," in *John Creasey's Mystery Bedside Book,* edited by Herbert Harris.   London, Hodder and Stoughton, 1968.
"The Dumb Friend," in *Best Underworld Stories,* edited by Douglas Rutherford.   London, Faber, 1969.
"The Escort," in *More Tales of Unease,* edited by John Burke. London, Pan, 1969.
"The Chee Min Vase," in *John Creasey's Mystery Bedside Book 1970,* edited by Herbert Harris.   London, Hodder and Stoughton, 1969.
"Revenge Is Sweet," in *John Creasey's Mystery Bedside Book 1971,* edited by Herbert Harris.   London, Hodder and Stoughton, 1970.
"The Wall Game," in *John Creasey's Mystery Bedside Book 1972,* edited by Herbert Harris.   London, Hodder and Stoughton, 1971.
"Low Marks for Murder," in *John Creasey's Mystery Bedside Book 1973,* edited by Herbert Harris.   London, Hodder and Stoughton, 1972.
"The Athlete and the Necktie," in *John Creasey's Mystery Bedside Book 1974,* edited by Herbert Harris.   London, Hodder and Stoughton, 1973.

"Dogs of Peace," in *John Creasey's Mystery Bedside Book 1975,* edited by Herbert Harris. London, Hodder and Stoughton, 1974.

"Reprieve," in *John Creasey's Mystery Bedside Book 1976,* edited by Herbert Harris. London, Hodder and Stoughton, 1975.

"A Nice Cup of Tea," in *The Gourmet Crook Book,* edited by Tony Wilmot. London, Everest, 1976.

"Mind over Blackmail," in *John Creasey's Crime Collection 1977,* edited by Herbert Harris. London, Gollancz, 1977.

"The Big Fix," in *John Creasey's Crime Collection 1978,* edited by Herbert Harris. London, Gollancz, 1978.

"The Way of Release," in *John Creasey's Crime Collection 1979,* edited by Herbert Harris. London, Gollancz, 1979.

"Picture of Guilt," in *John Creasey's Crime Collection 1980,* edited by Herbert Harris. London, Gollancz, 1980.

"A Swig of Strychnine," in *John Creasey's Crime Collection 1981,* edited by Herbert Harris. London, Gollancz, 1981; New York, St. Martin's Press, 1982.

"The Death of Mr. X," in *John Creasey's Crime Collection 1982,* edited by Herbert Harris. London, Gollancz, and New York, St. Martin's Press, 1982.

"Hooch, Mon!," in *John Creasey's Crime Collection 1983,* edited by Herbert Harris. London, Gollancz, and New York, St. Martin's Press, 1983.

"Give Him an Inch," in *John Creasey's Crime Collection 1984,* edited by Herbert Harris. London, Gollancz, and New York, St. Martin's Press, 1984.

"Detective's Wife," in *John Creasey's Crime Collection 1985,* edited by Herbert Harris. London, Gollancz, and New York, St. Martin's Press, 1985.

"The Doctor Afraid of Blood," in *John Creasey's Crime Collection 1986,* edited by Herbert Harris. London, Gollancz, 1986; New York, St. Martin's Press, 1987.

"Death at the Barbecue," in *John Creasey's Crime Collection 1987,* edited by Herbert Harris. London, Gollancz, 1987; New York, St. Martin's Press, 1988.

"Gin and Murder," in *John Creasey's Crime Collection 1988,* edited by Herbert Harris. London, Gollancz, 1988.

"Bird of Paradise," in *John Creasey's Crime Collection 1989,* edited by Herbert Harris. London, Gollancz, 1989.

"Two of a Kind," in *John Creasey's Crime Collection 1990,* edited by Herbert Harris, London, Gollancz, 1990.

OTHER PUBLICATIONS

Play

Radio Play: *Detective's Wife,* from his own story, 1961.

Other

Editor, *John Creasey's Mystery Bedside Book.* London, Hodder and Stoughton, 11 vols., 1966–76.

Editor, *John Creasey's Crime Collection.* London, Gollancz, 14 vols., 1977–90; 7 vols. published New York, St. Martin's Press, 1981–88.

Editor, *Great Short Stories of Scotland Yard.* London, Reader's Digest, 1978; as *Great Cases of Scotland Yard,* New York, Norton, 1978.

Editor, *A Handful of Heroes: Five Short Stories.* London, Reader's Digest, 1978.

*

Herbert Harris comments:

My speciality has been the short-short story of 1000–2000 words aimed principally at magazines and newspapers, and nearly always containing a surprise sting in the tail. Through writing such a very large number of short-shorts, with their taut economy of words, I have always found writing full-length novels difficult and have thus produced only a few, three of them specially commissioned.

*   *   *

Herbert Harris is very unusual as a crime writer of the post-1945 period in that his work has been almost exclusively in the short story. Even in the short story field he has kept his best efforts for the short-short. Perhaps for this reason there is not even a collection of his work: a volume consisting entirely of the sort of story which lives by making a quick, snappy impression would be like a meal of plate after plate of cocktail snacks. To a fair extent, however, it may be said that to read one Harris story is to have read them all, though naturally when an author has written more stories—it is believed—than anyone else living there are bound to be so many exceptions to any one rule that they will perhaps form a considerable body of writing on their own.

That being said, let us look at what would seem to be the typical Harris story. First, it is a crime story. Crime seems particularly to suit a writer who depends for his effects on actions, on things being done and being seen (sometimes only in the outcome) to have been done. So not for Harris the sort of story that depends on some subtle change in relations between people, something that might be expressed by a handshake, or the raising of an eyebrow or even the omission of a handshake, an eyebrow not raised. With Harris it is much more likely that someone will have been murdered, though by no means all his stories depend on murder.

Second, the Harris story is, as we have said, short. Characters do not change in them, except from alive to dead, from free to arrested. So within the very short length that particularly suits his talent he cannot put over as fiction all the facts necessary to a particular tale. He cannot afford to devote perhaps two or three pages to describing some incident that simply reflects character. He has brutally to tell you that such-and-such a person is as he is. "The English detective-sergeant from the Hong Kong police was an old-stager with sour cynicism written all over his face." That and no more.

The quotation—it is the first sentence of a story called "The Chee Min Vase"—tells us one other thing about the Harris story: it can be set anywhere in the world, and probably in some exotic place. Harris is adept at seizing on some flavoursome setting and using it to give an "extra" to his tale. And he is skillful, given any particular setting, in flicking in just one or two details that give to the reader the impression that the author is writing from that particular location itself. "In gutter Cantonese," the narrator says casually in "The Chee Min Vase" and, at the other extreme of the world almost, in a second-rank British boarding school a master goes up to his room to fetch (ostensibly) a volume of Racine for his class.

Finally, and rather surprisingly, the Harris story is not markedly ingenious, though it may, as in his Sicily-set Mafia tale "Reprieve," have a neat final reversal. But he does not, as does a short-story writer like Edmund Crispin, go in for the dazzling piece of legerdemain. Instead he gives you a quick series of hard-thought clicking into place, of turns as opposed to twists. And the result provides the casual reader with just what he is looking for.

—H.R.F. Keating

HARRIS, John. *See* **HEBDEN, Mark**

HARRIS, Thomas. American. Born in Mississippi, Missouri, in 1940. Has worked as a news reporter and reporter and editor for the Associated Press, New York City. Lives in New York. Address: c/o St. Martin's Press, 175 Fifth Avenue, New York, New York 10010, U.S.A.

CRIME PUBLICATIONS

Novels

Black Sunday. New York, Putnam, and London, Hodder and Stoughton, 1975.
Red Dragon. New York, Putnam, 1981; London, Bodley Head, 1982; as *Manhunter,* New York, Bantam, 1986.
The Silence of the Lambs. New York, St. Martin's Press, and London, Heinemann, 1988.

*   *   *

In three stunning novels Thomas Harris has established a reputation for excellence that few of his more prolific peers in crime writing can approach. All of his books have sold widely and all three have been made into motion pictures. His work, which confronts some of the most disturbing and relevant crimes of our time, apparently strikes a responsive chord in the contemporary imagination.

Harris writes simultaneously of crime and detection. His crimes touch our deepest fears and fascinations; his detection proceeds through a technological and psychological labyrinth that aptly represents the human condition in these times. Building upon a history we all dwell in, he has written about the threat to ordinary citizens from Middle Eastern terrorism in *Black Sunday* and about elusive serial murderers in *Red Dragon* and *The Silence of the Lambs.* In both sorts of book he deals with the ways in which anyone, anywhere, at any time can be vulnerable, chosen to suffer by a random fate incarnated in a person of a highly motivated malignity.

Black Sunday balances its detailed depiction of the painstaking plans to explode an enormous bomb at the Super Bowl with the equally painstaking efforts of the Israeli intelligence forces to frustrate those plans. The book displays the insider knowledge that distinguishes so many techno-thrillers in our time, showing what it's like to survive in a North Vietnamese prison camp, how to fly a blimp and a helicopter, how to construct a bomb, how terrorists and counterterrorists operate. Unlike the usual authors of research thrillers, Harris doesn't borrow his literary methods from some training manual, but constructs his sentences with energy and strength and, more important, creates characters on all stages of the moral spectrum who behave like real human beings. In the book the profoundly disturbed Vietnam veteran, the female Palestinian terrorist, and the Israeli Secret Service operative do not merely serve the author's exciting plot, but take on a three-dimensional life of their own.

His methods serve him well in the two related studies of serial murder, *Red Dragon* and *The Silence of the Lambs.* In the first he very carefully shows the cleverness and brutality of a killer motivated by a horrible childhood and his own disfigurement; to balance that, he also makes credible the investigation of Will Graham, an FBI agent who specializes in catching psychotic criminals. More important, he shows that Graham's success does not come only from his perception and intelligence, but also from his special sensitivity to the personality of the murderer he seeks. Graham also understands, horribly, that he can solve the crimes because of the possibility of murderous psychosis within himself.

In *The Silence of the Lambs* Harris returns to the subject of mass murder, this time using a female detective, FBI trainee Clarice Starling, and basing some of his subject roughly on the exploits of the notorious Ed Gein, whose exploits inspired *Psycho, Texas Chainsaw Massacre,* and dozens of imitations. Harris links *The Silence of the Lambs* to *Red Dragon* through the allusions to Will Graham, the approximate similarity of the subjects of serial murderer, and the continuing presence of his most intriguing character, Dr. Hannibal "The Cannibal" Lecter. Lecter, a brilliant psychiatrist captured by Will Graham after he murdered several people, apparently for the sheer fun of it, agrees to assist Graham in his investigation and understands both the detective's fear of him—he almost killed Graham—and his adversary's character. He knows that Graham is horrified by his own recognition of their sympathetic relationship. For his own reasons Lecter also helps Clarice Starling in the second book and despite his confinement under the most stringent conditions, may be the best detective of them all. He is also clearly the embodiment of evil, an identification made explicitly toward the end of *The Silence of the Lambs,* when he has managed to escape his incarceration and is described in terms that echo the Book of Job. Obviously, the sequel to that novel will bring back Dr. Lecter for what many readers will expect to be the greatest of the author's efforts.

Harris's work stands out from the rest of the research thrillers through its literary achievements. The prose moves powerfully, the characters are entirely human, the contexts are carefully drawn, and the narration is remarkably compelling. If the author continues to write his long, powerful books in the same way, he will carve out a special place for himself in crime literature. In the wake of a number of notorious American cases, many writers have dealt with the now fashionable subjects of terrorism and mass murder, and a few even demonstrate the appeal of assiduous research, but none writes with the intelligence, imagination, and understanding of Harris, a very special novelist who entirely deserves his success.

—George Grella

HARRIS, Timothy, (Hyde). American. Born in Los Angeles, California, 21 July 1946. Educated at Peterhouse College, Cambridge, B.A. (honours) 1969, M.A. 1974. Married Mary Bess Walker in 1980. Has had a variety of jobs including, sailor, carpenter, painter. Address: c/o Delacorte Press, 666 Fifth Avenue New York, New York 10103, U.S.A.

CRIME PUBLICATIONS

Novels (series: as Thomas Kyd)

Steelyard Blues (novelization of screenplay). New York, Bantam, 1972.
Kyd for Hire. London, Gollancz, 1977; New York, Dell, 1978.
Heat Wave (novelization of screenplay). New York, Dell, 1979.
Good Night and Good-Bye (Kyd). New York, Delacorte Press, 1979; London, Pan, 1981.

OTHER PUBLICATIONS

Novels

Kronski/McSmash. London, Joseph, 1969; New York, Doubleday, 1970.
American Gigolo (novelization of screenplay). New York, Delacorte Press, and London, Hamlyn, 1979.

Plays

Screenplays: *Cheaper to Keep Her,* 1980; *French Kiss,* 1980.

* * *

Since 1979, Timothy Harris has concentrated on writing screenplays but the two novels of his brief Thomas Kyd saga, *Kyd for Hire* and *Good Night and Good-Bye,* are among the few recent novels that merit inclusion in the private eye canon initiated by Dashiell Hammett and developed by Raymond Chandler and Ross Macdonald.

Harris has said that he has little respect for the hard-boiled school with its "inflated" treatment of the private eye, but he has also admitted his debt to Chandler for his sense of humor and "deadpan poetics" and to Patricia Highsmith "for her insight and misanthropy." With his feeling (in *Kyd for Hire*) that there may not be a "hell of a lot" to his life, Kyd's motive for staying with this first case is his dislike for the "psychopath for hire" he seems to be tracking. The plotting derives from Chandler and Ross Macdonald territory, with its roots in a family's murky past. The structure, curiously, is reminiscent of the classical mystery with the final wrap-up conducted in a highly charged gathering of the surviving principal suspects. This apparently conventional climax to an odyssey that begins in the "seamier section of Hollywood" where Kyd has his unglamorous office is, however, characteristic of Harris's manipulation of an intricate story line. The final ironic turn that develops outside this traditional closure is both appropriate and unexpected and owes nothing to its predecessors except, perhaps, to Chandler's poetics.

It is not difficult to see *Good Night and Good-Bye* as the "big" Kyd novel since *Kyd for Hire* was published in this country only in a paperback edition. The motives are, on the surface of it, more complex than those of *Kyd for Hire* and involve Kyd's self-destructive infatuation with Laura Cassiday, a beautiful, contradictory inhabitant of the world of movie game-playing, with its fast-changing patterns of mob, drugs and sexual violence. But in both novels there is a purity in Kyd's actions that rises from recognized but uncontrolled feelings that put him constantly in jeopardy. *Good Night and Good-Bye,* as well as being an unusually powerful Hollywood private-eye novel, also draws on unresolved tensions of the Vietnam conflict in ways that were not to be examined in the crime novel for several years. This plot thread connects with Kyd's perception that his own motives had become "tarnished" and "unclear" to him, "which [was]was another way of saying I'd lost my luck."

Both *Good Night and Good-Bye* and *Heat Wave* end with loss and some suggestion of narrowing opportunities. The best way, perhaps, to summarize Harris's contribution to the private eye novel is to say that it is an exploration of essential human gestures within a structurally tight environment where the apparently conventional elements seem somehow fresh and newly minted. The Thomas Kyd saga bears comparison with the classic novels of Chandler and Ross Macdonald and, a

decade after its first publication, seems—unlike Kyd's motives—untarnished by time.

—Walter Albert

————

HARRISON, Chip. *See* **BLOCK, Lawrence.**

————

HARRISON, Michael. Also writes as Quentin Downes. Irish. Born in Milton, Kent, England, 25 April 1907. Educated at King's College, and the School of Oriental and African Studies, University of London, Married Maryvonne Aubertin in 1950 (died 1977); two step daughters. Editor (founding editor, *The British Ink Maker* and others), market research executive, and industrial and technical consultant; creative director of advertising agency, now retired. Agent: Jonathan Clowes Ltd., 22 Prince Albert Road, London NW1 7ST. Address: 5A Palmeira Court, 31-33 Palmeira Square, Hove, Sussex BN3 2JP, England.

CRIME PUBLICATIONS

Novels as Quentin Downes (series character: Detective Inspector Abraham Kozminski in all books by Downes)

The Darkened Room (as Michael Harrison). London, Home and Van Thal, 1952.
No Smoke, No Flame. London, Wingate, 1952; New York, Roy, 1956.
Heads I Win. London, Wingate, 1953; New York, Roy, 1955.
They Hadn't a Clue. London, Arco, 1954.

Short Stories

The Exploits of the Chevalier Dupin. Sauk City, Wisconsin, Mycroft and Moran, 1968; expanded version, as *Murder in the Rue Royale,* London, Stacey, 1972.

Uncollected Short Stories

"The Vanished Treasure," in *Ellery Queen's Crime Carousel.* New York, New American Library, 1966.
"Wit's End," in *Best Detective Stories of the Year 1971,* edited by Allen J. Hubin. New York, Dutton, 1971.
"Whatever Happened to Young Russell?," in *Ellery Queen's Headliners.* Cleveland, World, 1971; London, Gollancz, 1972.
"The Facts in the Case of the Missing Diplomat," in *Ellery Queen's Mystery Anthology.* New York, Davis, 1973.
"The Jewel of Childeric," in *Ellery Queen's Faces of Mystery.* New York, Davis, 1977.
"The Murder in the Rue St. André des Arts," in *50 Classics of Crime Fiction 1950–75: Classic Short Stories of Crime Detection,* edited by Jacques Barzun and Wendell Hertig Taylor. New York, Garland, 1983.
"Sherlock Holmes and the Woman," in *The New Adventures of Sherlock Holmes.* New York, Carroll and Graf, 1987.
"Some Very Odd Happenings at Kibblesham Manor House," in *Eternal City,* edited by David Drake. New York, Baen, 1990.

OTHER PUBLICATIONS

Novels

Weep for Lycidas. London, Barker, 1934.
Spring in Tartarus: An Arabesque. London, Barker, 1935.
All the Trees Were Green. London, Barker, 1936.
What Are We Waiting For? London, Rich and Cowan, 1939.
Vernal Equinox. London, Collins, 1939.
Battered Caravanserai. London, Rich and Cowan, 1942.
Reported Safe Arrival: The Journal of a Voyage to Port X. London, Rich and Cowan, 1943.
So Linked Together. London, Macdonald, 1944.
Higher Things. London, Macdonald, 1945.
The House in Fishergate. London, Macdonald, 1946.
Treadmill. London, Langdon Press, 1947.
Sinecure. London, Laurie, 1948.
There's Glory for You! London, Laurie, 1949.
Thing Less Noble: A Modern Love Story. London, Laurie, 1950.
Long Vacation. London, Laurie, 1951.
The Brain. London, Cassell, 1953.
The Dividing Stone. London, Cassell, 1954.
A Hansom to St. James's. London, Cassell, 1954.

Short Stories

Transit of Venus. London, Fortune Press, 1936.

Other

Dawn Express: There and Back. London, Collins, 1938.
Gambler's Glory: The Story of John Law of Lauriston. London, Rich and Cowan, 1940.
Count Cagliostro, Nature's Unfortunate Child. London, Rich and Cowan, 1942.
They Would be King. London, Somers, 1947.
Post Office, Mauritius 1847: The Tale of Two Stamps. London, Stamp Collecting, 1947.
The Story of Christmas: Its Growth and Development from Earliest Times. London, Odhams Press, 1951; revised edition as *Saturnalia,* London, Skoob Books, 1990.
Airborne at Kitty Hawk: The Story of the First Heavier-than-Air Flight Made by the Wright Brothers. London, Cassell, 1953.
Charles Dickens: A Sentimental Journey in Search of an Unvarnished Portrait. London, Cassell, 1953; New York, Haskell House, 1976.
A New Approach to Stamp Collecting, with Douglas Armstrong. London, Batsford, 1953; New York, Hanover Press, 1954.
Beer Cookery: 101 Traditional Recipes. London, Spearman Calder, 1954.
Peter Cheyney, Prince of Hokum: A Biography. London, Spearman, 1954.
In the Footsteps of Sherlock Holmes. London, Cassell, 1958; New York, Fell, 1960; revised edition, Newton Abbot, Devon, David and Charles, 1971; New York, Drake, 1972.
The History of the Hat. London, Jenkins, 1960; New York, Berkeley, 1974.
London Beneath the Pavement. London, Davies, 1961; revised edition, 1971.
Rosa (biography of Rosa Lewis). London, Davies, 1962.
Painful Details: Twelve Victorian Scandals. London, Parrish, 1962.
London by Gaslight 1861–1911. London, Davies, 1963.
London Growing: The Development of a Metropolis. London, Hutchinson, 1965.
Mulberry: The Return in Triumph. London, W.H. Allen, 1965.

Lord of London: A Biography of the Second Duke of Westminster. London, W.H. Allen, 1966.
Technical and Industrial Publicity. London, Business Publications, 1968.
The London That Was Rome: The Imperial City Recreated by the New Archaeology. London, Allen and Unwin, 1971.
Fanfare of Strumpets. London, W.H. Allen, 1971.
Clarence: The Life of H.R.H. the Duke of Clarence and Avondale 1864–1892. London, W.H. Allen, 1972; as *Clarence: Was He Jack the Ripper?,* New York, Drake, 1974.
The London of Sherlock Holmes. Newton Abbot, Devon, David and Charles, and New York, Drake, 1972.
The Roots of Witchcraft. London, Muller, 1973; Secaucus, New Jersey, Citadel Press, 1974; revised edition, London, Skoob Books, 1990.
The World of Sherlock Holmes. London, Muller, 1973; New York, Dutton, 1975.
Theatrical Mr. Holmes: The World's Greatest Consulting Detective, Considered Against the Background of the Contemporary Theatre. London, Convent Garden Press, 1974.
Fire from Heaven; or, How Safe Are You from Burning? (on spontaneous combustion). London, Sidgwick and Jackson, 1976; revised edition, London, Pan, 1977; London, Skoob Books, 1990. New York, Methuen, 1978.
I, Sherlock Holmes. New York, Dutton, 1977.
Vanishings. London, New English Library, 1981.
Immortal Sleuth: Sherlockian Musings and Memories. Dubuque, Iowa, Gasogene Press, 1983.
A Study in Surmise: The Making of Sherlock Holmes. Bloomington, Indiana, Gaslight, 1984.
A Sheaf of Sherlock. Dubuque, Iowa, Gasogene Press, 1990.

Editor, *Under Thirty* (anthology of short stories). London, Rich and Cowan, 1939.
Editor, *Beyond Baker Street: A Sherlockian Anthology.* Indianapolia, Bobbs Merrill, 1976.

*

Manuscript Collection: Mugar Memorial Library, Boston University.

Michael Harrison comments:

The preference for—indeed, perhaps, the real need for—violence in thriller fiction, has greatly influenced the novel of pure detection, and has almost obscured the essential difference which ought to exist between the novel of detection (what Poe called "of ratiocination") and the novel in which violence is more important than the solving of those problems arising from that violence. That there is every excuse for this confusion between the two forms is understandable; indeed, it seems to have been inevitable, since the tendency to confuse exists at the very beginning of the detective story, as in the four stories of the writer, Poe, who invented the detective story, violence—and very violent violence it is—occurs to originate the problem that the "ratiocinator" has to solve. (In three cases it is Dupin; in the fourth, the solver is unnamed.)

But no matter how much blood-and-thunder is now regarded as an essential ingredient of even the "novel of pure detection," the difference between the thriller and the novel of detection ought rigidly to be maintained—as I have tried to maintain it. There isn't much violence in my novels or stories of detection—there isn't even much blood. But each begins with the clear statement of a problem that intentional crime or unintentional misadventure has left to be solved, and, to the best of my ability, I explain to the reader how the solver arrived at his solution. Such "surprises" as I use are reserved for the criminal, rather than for the detective, though in my many pastiches of Poe's Dupin tales, I am forced to retain for Dupin those characteristics that his brilliant and immortal creator gave him when inventing the detective story.

* * *

Michael Harrison's contributions to mystery and crime writing fall into several areas. His nonfiction books about Holmes and Watson, starting with *In the Footsteps of Sherlock Holmes,* recreate the London of Victorian times. Another work of nonfiction, *Clarence,* offers speculation on the identity of Jack the Ripper. Harrison has also published ghost stories and, under the pseudonym of Quentin Downes, three minor mystery novels.

But Harrison's major contribution has been his short stories, with a series of excellent pastiches of Edgar Allan Poe's detective C. Auguste Dupin. Mystery readers who have long bemoaned the fact that Poe wrote only three Dupin tales can take heart from the work of Michael Harrison, who created 12 new adventures, collected in *Murder in the Rue Royale* (*The Exploits of the Chevalier Dupin* contains only seven). Of the stories themselves at least six deserve special mention. "The Vanished Treasure" finds Dupin solving a 50-year-old mystery involving missing Spanish gold. The discovery of some old Roman ruins masks a crime in "The Man in the Blue Spectacles." "The Fires in the Rue Honoré" reveals an ingenious method of arson. A diplomat who vanishes in an empty street provides the mystery in "The Facts in the Case of the Missing Diplomat." Another type of seemingly impossible crime is presented in "The Assassination of Sir Ponsonby Brown." "The Clew of the Single Word" is a clever spy tale. Mention should also be made of a non-Dupin detective story, "Wit's End," a clever tale in the classic tradition.

—Edward D. Hoch

HARRISON, Ray(mond). British. Born in Chorley, Lancashire, 26 October 1928. Educated at Ormskirk Grammar School, 1939–47; Magdalene College, Cambridge, 1949–52, B.A. (honours) 1952, M.A. 1954. Served in the British Army, 1947–49. Married Gwyneth Margaret Hughes in 1977. Inspector of Taxes, 1952–62, fraud investigator, 1962–68; and principal inspector of taxes, 1968–77, Inland Revenue; managing director, Howden Group, London, 1977–80; managing director, Lloyd's Underwriting Company, London, 1980–82. Agent: Curtis Brown Ltd., 162–168 Regent Street, London, W1R 5TB, England. Address: Forthill, Kinsale, County Cork, Eire.

CRIME PUBLICATIONS

Novels (series: Sergeant Joseph Bragg and Constable James Morton in all books)

French Ordinary Murder. London, Quartet, 1983; as *Why Kill Arthur Potter,* New York, Scribner, 1984.
Death of an Honourable Member. London, Quartet, 1984; New York, Scribner, 1985.
Deathwatch. London, Quartet, 1985; New York, Scribner, 1986.
Death of a Dancing Lady. London, Quartet, 1985; New York, Scribner, 1986.

Counterfeit of Murder. London, Quartet, 1986; New York, St. Martin's Press, 1987.
A Season for Death. London, Quartet, and New York, St. Martin's Press, 1987.
Harvest of Death. London, Quartet, and New York, St. Martin's Press, 1988.
Tincture of Death. London, Quartet, 1989; New York, St. Martin's Press, 1990.

*

Ray Harrison comments:

My novels are Victorian, but not Dickensian. They are set in the 1890's, a time of rapid technological progress. Electric underground trains were running in London, the telephone, telegraph, and automobile were in use; radio and airplanes were just around the corner. In high society, the Prince of Wales's set flouted conventional propriety; but in the wider population, sanctimonious morality still underpinned rigid social structures. But women had begun to challenge men's monopoly of the professions and to campaign for the vote. One of my main characters is a young woman journalist.

The City of London was the commercial capital of the world. Its teeming millions encompassed all the criminal problems we have today—drugs, prostitution, violence, child abuse. As down-to-earth Sergeant Bragg and upper-crust constable Morton investigate their cases, I am able to comment obliquely on modern society.

* * *

The 1980's brought a spate of historical mystery novels set in the Victorian era, and one of the most prolific writers in this subgenre is Ray Harrison. In his series Harrison follows the career of Detective-Sergeant Joseph Bragg and Constable James Morton, ensuring through these two characters entree into the full range of social classes and life styles of the time. Bragg is lower middle class and in some ways innocently devoted to his calling as upholder of the Queen's law. He is assigned as an aide in most instances Constable James Morton, who has chosen a career in the police over the enforced idleness expected of the second son of an aristocratic family. Making a fairly regular appearance is Catherine Marsden, a young gentlewoman who has chosen to pursue the career of a journalist, much to her family's discomfort and concern. James pursues Catherine off and on throughout the series.

In the first book in the series, *French Ordinary Murder,* set in 1890, Bragg and Morton investigate the murder of Arthur Potter, a clerk at a London shipping company, who is beaten and killed by a gang of toughs on his way home one evening. Potter was no more than a steady, ordinary clerk, but his death hints at professional killers. The police investigation leads to the upper levels of finance in the City and to France and Monte Carlo, with Constable Morton moving easily where Sergeant Bragg cannot. With this story Harrison establishes the pattern he will follow: the crime involves members of several distinct social classes, Morton and Bragg share for the other's benefit an insider's view of a particular class, and the investigation reveals the inner workings of an institution of Victorian England.

In *Death of an Honourable Member,* set in 1891, Sir Walter Greville, one of two members of Parliament for the City of London, falls to his death. An anonymous note suggests murder and the police duly look into Sir Walter's life and connections, including Tory party politics and banking. In *Deathwatch,* set a month later in 1891, Bragg is investigating the grisly murder of a policeman when he is told to step aside and let it rest. He refuses and soon faces another problem: he is charged and arrested for rape. Bragg must now rely on his young colleague, Morton, to investigate the death of the policeman and the charge against Bragg himself. Harrison opens up the world of Lloyds of London in 1892 in *Death of a Dancing Lady*. When Lloyds of London suspects sabotage on a ship sunk off Texas, Bragg investigates in England and Morton, who happens to be visiting relatives in Boston, travels to Louisiana.

In the fifth novel, *Counterfeit of Murder,* Bragg and Morton are in London investigating a ring of counterfeiters, giving us a close look at the Bank of England and its currency in the 1890's. In *A Season for Death,* Morton pursues a blackmailer who has driven the dean of St.Paul's Cathedral to his death and later turns his or her attention to Catherine Marsden. To catch the culprit, Morton returns to his former life and enters the whirl of the London Season. In the seventh book, *Harvest of Death,* Harrison leaves what he seems to know best, moving from London to the rustic world of a village in Dorset, where Bragg grew up, and gives the reader one of his richer collections of characters. When a tradesman is found murdered, the local police want no help from Bragg, freeing him to investigate as best he can with the help of Ernie Toop, the village cripple, and Fanny Hildred, who has romantic plans for the sergeant.

Tincture of Death is Harrison's least successful mystery but most illuminating in its mirroring of 20th-century problems and social issues. Bragg and Morton are called in to investigate the deaths of three men who have just returned from India after investigating the effects of opium and the opium trade on the natives and the trade of the Empire; at the same time Morton must view at close hand the effects of opium on the life of an artist and those who care for him. Despite its occasional weaknesses in plot, this is a powerful tale of drugs and the respectable powers of society.

Harrison knows well the period and institutions he writes about, and uses historical detail effectively to enhance his tale; his purpose remains always the story, and any parallels, lessons, or insights to be found between the 1890's and 1990's are in most cases gracefully suggested. It is no small feat to have maintained in one series such a high level of historical accuracy and narrative interest over so many books.

—Susan Oleskiw

HARRISON, Whit. *See* **WHITTINGTON, Harry.**

HART, Carolyn G. (née Gimpel). American. Born in Oklahoma City, 25 August 1936. Educated at the University of Oklahoma, Norman, B.A. (Phi Beta Kappa) in journalism 1958. Married Philip D. Hart in 1958; one son and one daughter. Reporter, *The Norman Transcript,* 1958–59; editor, *Sooner Newsmakers alumni newspaper*), University of Oklahoma, 1959–60; freelance writer, 1961–82; Assistant Professor of journalism, School of Journalism and Mass Communications, University of Oklahoma, 1982–85. Since 1986 full-time writer. Agent: Deborah C. Schneider, John Farquharson Ltd., 250 West 57th Street, New York, New York 10107. Address: 1705 Drakestone Avenue, Oklahoma City, Oklahoma 73120, U.S.A.

CRIME PUBLICATIONS

Novels (series: Annie Laurance and Max Darling)

Flee From the Past.   New York, Bantam, 1975.
A Settling of Accounts.   New York, Doubleday, 1976; London, Hale, 1978.
The Rich Die Young.   London, Hale, 1983.
Death By Surprise.   London, Hale, 1983.
Castle Rock.   London, Hale, 1983.
Skulduggery.   London, Hale, 1984.
Death on Demand (Laurance and Darling).   New York, Bantam, 1987.
Design for Murder (Laurance and Darling).   New York, Bantam, 1988.
Something Wicked (Laurance and Darling).   New York, Bantam, 1988.
Honeymoon with Murder (Laurance and Darling).   New York, Bantam, 1989.
A Little Class on Murder (Laurance and Darling).   New York, Doubleday, 1989.
Deadly Valentine (Laurance and Darling).   New York, Doubleday, 1990.

Uncollected Short Stories

"Life-Interest," in *Mystery Scene* (Cedar Rapids, Iowa), December 1989.
"Upstaging Murder," in *Sisters in Crime 2* edited by Marilyn Wallace.   New York, Berkley, 1990.

OTHER PUBLICATIONS

Novels

Escape from Paris.   London, Hale, 1982; New York, St. Martin's Press, 1983.
The Devereaux Legacy.   Toronto, Harlequin, 1986.
Brave Hearts.   New York, Pocket Books, 1987.

Other

The Secret of the Cellars (for children).   New York, Dodd Mead, 1964.
Dangerous Summer (for children).   New York, Four Winds Press, 1968.
No Easy Answers.   New York, Evans, 1970.
Rendezvous in Veracruz.   New York, Evans, 1972.
Danger, High Explosives!   New York, Evans, 1972.
The Sooner Story, 1890–1980, with Charles F. Long.   Norman, University of Oklahoma Foundation, 1980.
"In Celebration of the Cozy," in *Malice Domestic Program* (Bethesda, Maryland), April 1989.
"And That's the Truth," in *Mystery Readers Journal* (Berkeley, California), Spring, 1989.
"On Writing Mysteries," in *Mystery Writers of America Annual,* (New York), May 1989.
"Cozies, Face Front and Fire!" in *Mystery Scene* (Cedar Rapids, Iowa), May–June 1989.
"Anybody out There?" in *Mystery Scene* (Cedar Rapids, Iowa), July–August, 1989.
"Professionalism," in *Mystery Scene* (Cedar Rapids, Iowa), September–October, 1989.
"Writing Bibliomysteries," in *Mystery Readers Journal* (Berkeley, California), Winter, 1989.

"The New (?) Woman Sleuth," in *American Crime Writers League Bulletin* (Lisbon Falls, Maine), Winter, 1989.

*

Carolyn G. Hart comments

I spent a good many years writing a variety of mystery, suspense, and romantic suspense before I wrote *Death on Demand*, the first in the Annie Laurance-Max Darling series and the book which launched me on a more successful career and a much more challenging and interesting path as a writer. I have always loved the traditional mystery and I am especially indebted to Agatha Christie, Mary Roberts Rinehart, and Phoebe Atwood Taylor. Although (much to my delight) some critics have compared my work to Christie's, I feel that I am much closer in tone to Phoebe Atwood Taylor. I try to provide readers lighthearted entertainment, a complex plot with clues fairly offered, and information about the mystery itself. I find the mystery intellectually fascinating. The mystery, as a character states in *A Little Class on Murders*, "provides moral judgements. Damn near the only place in the world we find 'em anymore." That makes mysteries worth the writing and worth writing about.

*   *   *

A bookstore is an ideal place for a mystery series to be set. It provides the author with an opportunity to indulge in a little name-dropping—favorite authors and titles may be prominently shelved, purchased by customers, or read by the store owner, while friends and acquaintances in the mystery business may be mentioned in an aside. If the setting is a store that specializes in mysteries, like Carolyn Hart's Death on Demand bookstore in Broward's Rock Island, South Carolina, the amateur sleuth has a pattern around which to model her own investigations. And that is exactly how Annie Laurance, Hart's heroine, gets involved in the detection business.

In *Death on Demand*, we meet Annie, her boyfriend Max Darling, her assistant and various of her regular customers, many of whom appear in subsequent books and develop as the series progresses. A star of the series is the bookstore itself. In a perfect location—a coastal resort—Death on Demand has all the features that the mystery bibliophile would like to see in a bookstore, including the special few that Hart introduces. Illustrated by floor plans in several of the books, the store has a children's corner; a coffee bar with fresh-ground coffee and mugs printed with the titles and authors of classic mysteries; a reading area furnished with ferns, lamps, easy chairs and tables; a stuffed raven named Edgar; and a bookstore cat (black, of course) named Agatha. Annie holds regular book signing parties, readers' groups and a regular meeting of resident authors in the store. Perhaps the premiere attraction is a monthly display of watercolors done by local artists, depicting a scene in a classic mystery. If a customer can identify title and author, he or she will win a free book of his/her choice! The reader gets to play along, as the solutions to these puzzles within puzzles are revealed in the last pages of the book.

Later books in the series take Annie out of the bookstore, although its operation, the paintings and mugs, and the references to popular titles and authors continue as background. In *Design for Murder*, Annie stages a "mystery night" for a local festival, a mystery that becomes real as one of the participants is murdered. *Something Wicked* involves Annie, Max and the other residents of Broward's Rock in the production of "Arsenic and Old Lace," a production starring a washed-up beach-blanket hunk who is ultimately marked for murder. *Honeymoon with Murder* finds Annie defending her

long-time employee Ingrid Jones in the murder of a peeping Tom. In this book, Max's spacey mother Laurel, Annie's most irritating customer Henny, and Dora, a dotty local matriarch, team up to help in the investigation. In *A Little Class on Murder*, Annie, invited to teach a course on mystery fiction at the local community college, instead finds herself investigating a scandal involving the school newspaper, the journalism department and a subsequent suicide. Annie's preparation for the course—"The Three Grande Dames of Mystery Fiction"— is as enlightening to the reader as it is to her class—Laurel, Henny and Dora!

Hart's Annie Laurance series is as "cozy" as American fiction gets, with as much humor as blood scattered through the pages.

—Carol M. Harper

———

HART, Frances (Newbold) Noyes. American. Born in Silver Springs, Maryland, 10 August 1890. Educated in private schools, and in Italy; the Sorbonne and Collège de France, Paris; Columbia University, New York. Married Edward Henry Hart in 1921; two daughters. Translator for Naval Intelligence, 1917–18; YMCA canteen worker in France, 1918–19. *Died 25 October 1943.*

CRIME PUBLICATIONS

Novels

The Bellamy Trial. New York, Doubleday, and London, Heinemann, 1927.
Hide in the Dark. New York, Doubleday, and London, Heinemann, 1929.
The Crooked Lane. New York, Doubleday, and London, Heinemann, 1934.

Short Stories

Contact and Other Stories. New York, Doubleday, 1923.

OTHER PUBLICATIONS

Novel

Mark. New York, Clode, 1913.

Play

The Bellamy Trial, with Frank E. Carstarphen, adaptation of the novel by Hart (produced New York, 1931). New York, French, 1932.

Other

My A.E.F.: A Hail and Farewell. New York, Stokes, 1920.
Pigs in Clover (travel). New York, Doubleday, 1931; as *Holiday*, London, Heinemann, 1931.

*   *   *

Frances Noyes Hart's mother was a Newbold, as was Edith Wharton's, and Hart writes of the same classes, by now more in decline. Her *Hide in the Dark* presents a group of bright young things who meet at Hallowe'en for a game party which rapidly degenerates into an accusing match as an old suicide is recalled, a number of bitter truths are exchanged, and a further murder takes place. Rather more agreeable, though darker in its detailing of twisted emotions and family insanity, is *The Crooked Lane,* told from the point of view of a young Viennese police official who renews a childhood acquaintance in Washington, informally investigates a murder, and finds himself at the end of a very dark alley indeed. Both these novels create effectively an atmosphere of leisured, if certainly decadent, social life in and around the Washington of 1930, within a class yet untouched by the Depression.

But Hart's fame is primarily attached to *The Bellamy Trial.* Here the locale is the courtroom throughout, and the novel derives much of its immediacy and conviction from being told through the consciousnesses of a young woman on her first reporting assignment and a more cynical and experienced reporter, who fall in love over the eight days of the trial. Based on the famous Hall-Mills case, *The Bellamy Trial* unfolds the totally absorbing story of the misalliances and crossed lives of two couples from the gentry of upstate New York: one wife has been murdered, and her husband and the other wife are the accused. During the trial sensations occur—a key witness commits suicide; a dilatory witness, in compromising circumstances, appears at the last moment; the solution is finally revealed only in a letter the judge receives in his chambers. But these sensational elements in no way detract from the verisimilitude of what is the best of all crime novels told within the format of a court procedure.

—Barrie Hayne

HARVESTER, Simon. Pseudonym for Henry St. John Clair Rumbold-Gibbs; also wrote as Henry Gibbs. British. Born in 1910. Educated at Marlborough College, Wiltshire; studied painting in London, Paris, and Venice. Served in the Royal Corps of Signals, 1941. Married three times, lastly to Mary Elizabeth Hutchings; one son from first marriage. Worked as a journalist, publisher's reader, and farmer. Recipient: Anisfield-Wolf award, 1950. *Died in April 1975.*

CRIME PUBLICATIONS

Novels (series: Roger Fleming; Malcolm Kenton; Heron Murmur; Dorian Silk)

Let Them Prey (Fleming). London, Rich and Cowan, 1942.
Epitaphs for Lemmings (Fleming). London, Rich and Cowan, 1943; New York, Macmillan, 1944.
Maybe a Trumpet (Fleming). London, Rich and Cowan, 1945.
A Lantern for Diogenes. London, Rich and Cowan, 1946.
Whatsoever Things Are True. London, Rich and Cowan, 1947.
The Sequins Lost Their Lustre. London, Rich and Cowan, 1948.
A Breastplate for Aaron (Fleming). London, Rich and Cowan, 1949.
Good Men and True. London, Rich and Cowan, 1949.
Sheep May Safely Graze (Fleming). London, Rich and Cowan, 1950.
Obols for Charon (Fleming). London, Jarrolds, 1951.

The Vessel May Carry Explosives (Fleming). London, Jarrolds, 1951.
Witch Hunt. London, Jarrolds, 1951.
Cat's Cradle. London, Jarrolds, 1952.
Traitor's Gate. London, Jarrolds, 1952.
Lucifer at Sunset. London, Jarrolds, 1953.
Spiders' Web. London, Jarrolds, 1953.
Arrival in Suspicion. London, Jarrolds, 1953.
Delay in Danger. London, Jarrolds, 1954.
The Bamboo Screen (Kenton). London, Jarrolds, 1955; New York, Walker, 1968.
Tiger in the North. London, Jarrolds, 1955; New York, Walker, 1963.
Dragon Road (Silk). London, Jarrolds, 1956; New York, Walker, 1969.
The Paradise Men (Kenton). London, Jarrolds, 1956.
The Copper Butterfly (Kenton). London, Jarrolds, 1957; New York, Walker, 1962.
The Golden Fear (Kenton). London, Jarrolds, 1957.
The Yesterday Walkers. London, Jarrolds, 1958.
An Hour Before Zero. London, Jarrolds, 1959.
Unsung Road (Silk). London, Jarrolds, 1960; New York, Walker, 1961.
The Chinese Hammer (Murmur). London, Jarrolds, 1960; New York, Walker, 1961.
The Moonstone Jungle. London, Jarrolds, 1961.
Silk Road (Silk). London, Jarrolds, 1962; New York, Walker, 1963.
Troika (Murmur). London, Jarrolds, 1962; as *The Flying Horse,* New York, Walker, 1964.
Red Road (Silk). London, Jarrolds, 1963; New York, Walker, 1964.
Flight in Darkness. London, Jarrolds, 1964; New York, Walker, 1965.
Assassins Road (Silk). London, Jarrolds, and New York, Walker, 1965.
Shadows in a Hidden Land. London, Jarrolds, and New York, Walker, 1966.
Treacherous Road (Silk). London, Jarrolds, 1966; New York, Walker, 1967.
Battle Road (Silk). London, Jarrolds, and New York, Walker, 1967.
Zion Road (Silk). London, Jarrolds, and New York, Walker, 1968.
Nameless Road (Silk). London, Jarrolds, 1969; New York, Walker, 1970.
Moscow Road (Silk). London, Jarrolds, 1970; New York, Walker, 1971.
Sahara Road (Silk). London, Jarrolds, and New York, Walker, 1972.
A Corner of the Playground. London, Jarrolds, 1973.
Forgotten Road (Silk). London, Hutchinson, and New York, Walker, 1974.
Siberian Road (Silk). London, Hutchinson, and New York, Walker, 1976.

Novels as Henry Gibbs

At a Farthing's Rate. London, Jarrolds, 1943.
Not to the Swift. London, Jarrolds, 1944.
From All Blindness. London, Jarrolds, 1944.
Blue Days and Fair. London, Jarrolds, 1946.
Know Then Thyself. London, Jarrolds, 1947.
Children's Overture: A Study of Juvenile Delinquency in London Slums. London, Jarrolds, 1948.
Ten-Thirty Sharp. London, Jarrolds, 1949.
Withered Garland. London, Jarrolds, 1950.

Taps, Colonel Roberts. London, Jarrolds, 1951.
Cream and Cider. London, Jarrolds, 1952.
The Six-Mile Face. London, Jarrolds, 1952.
Disputed Barricade. London, Jarrolds, 1952.
Cape of Shadows. London, Jarrolds, 1954.
The Splendour and the Dust. London, Jarrolds, 1955.
The Winds of Time. London, Jarrolds, 1956.
Thunder at Dawn. London, Jarrolds, 1957.
The Tumult and the Shouting. London, Jarrolds, 1958.
The Bamboo Prison. London, Jarrolds, 1961.
The Mortal Fire. London, Jarrolds, 1963.

OTHER PUBLICATIONS as Henry Gibbs

Novels

Pawns in Ice. London, Jarrolds, 1948.
Man about Town (as Simon Harvester), with Cyril Campion.
  London, Rich and Cowan, 1948.
The Crimson Gate. New York, Walker, 1963.

Other

Affectionately Yours, Fanny: Fanny Kemble and the Theatre.
  London, Jarrolds, 1947.
Theatre Tapestry. London, Jarrolds, 1949.
Twilight in South Africa. London, Jarrolds, and New York,
  Philosophical Library, 1950.
Crescent in Shadow (on the Middle East). London, Jarrolds,
  1952.
Italy on Borrowed Time. London, Jarrolds, 1953.
Background to Bitterness: The Story of South Africa 1652–1954.
  London, Muller, and New York, Philosophical Library,
  1954.
Africa on a Tightrope. London, Jarrolds, 1954.
The Masks of Spain. London, Muller, 1955.
The Hills of India. London, Jarrolds, 1961.

*   *   *

If you are pining for an adventure in an exotic setting but
don't want to plow through the red tape of obtaining a passport,
or are squeamish about the required immunizations, Simon
Harvester can effortlessly transport you to the country of your
dreams. Adventure, romance, suspense, and intrigue can all be
yours, and all you have to do is turn the pages. Harvester has
sampled the hospitality of even the most remote areas about
which he writes. The authenticity of descriptions, the insightful
analysis of political structures, and the portrayal of idiosyncratic characters make each novel a journey well worth making.
His knowledge of six languages, his wealth of experience as a
war reporter, and his background as a portrait painter all
contribute to the richness of his literary style and his ability to
portray realistically the political and aesthetical intrigue of the
countries visited by his daring espionage agents.

Dorian Silk, Harvester's most popular spy, a ruggedly human
character, has appeared in some dozen novels traveling from
his native London to Moscow, China, Japan, North Africa,
Egypt, and Israel. Like a chameleon, Silk has the ability to
assume an unpretentious local identity complete with native
coloring and dialect, no matter where he finds himself. His
knowledge of regional customs is undeniably complete. Silk's
women also leave little to be desired. They are wily, seductive,
sometimes petulant, flamboyant, and, above all, cunning.
Their shapes and nationalities, and, certainly, their political
loyalties, may change from adventure to adventure, but never
their essential importance in Silk's mission. Silk's enemies are
varied depending upon his assignment—communists, renegades, revolutionists, or, occasionally, counterspies.

The series of novels about Dorian Silk is recognizable by the
appearance of the word Road in each title. *Red Road,* set in the
bleak Russian hills along the Soviet frontier, finds Silk, having
completed his mission, disguised as an old Turkoman,
complete with lice, spouting communist doctrine to Arab
peasant children and trying vainly to cross the last few miles to
freedom. *Zion Road* varies from the usual Silk adventure since
he has a personal interest involved. Fathiya, Silk's glamorous
Egyptian girlfriend, is kidnapped. A Russian agent comments
to Silk, "I figure you imagine yourself a John Buchan hero
maybe. Was it Richard Hanoi and the thirty-eight steps?"
Harvester's sense of humor and dry wit are frequently apparent
in Silk's sardonic philosophy when he is placed in difficult
circumstances. In *Sahara Road* Silk, in the interests of his
mission, is forced to submit to the amorous designs of a Saharan
female informant. After some delaying tactics, Silk succumbs,
"He saw no future in treating her like an Agatha Christie
heroine or one of the neurotic females dreamed up by the
Brontës. Her hand stayed on him. The Prisoner of Zenda was
nothing like this."

Those novels not featuring Dorian Silk are also inviting
excursions to exotic lands. Dorian Silk's co-worker, Giles
Priest, is featured in *Shadows in a Hidden Land* which is set in
the bitter Sinkiang terrain, the site of China's nuclear tests. *The
Bamboo Screen* is a tense, action-packed story of a nuclear
engineer plagued by murderous "accidents" in Hong Kong.

Harvester is sometimes compared to other superior espionage writers, such as Graham Greene, Eric Ambler, Victor
Canning, and Alistair MacLean. He is, indeed, a master of the
trade and a superb storyteller.

—Mary Ann Grochowski

————

HASTINGS, Graham. *See* **JEFFRIES, Roderic.**

————

HASTINGS, Roderic. *See* **GRAEME, Bruce.**

————

HAYES, Joseph (Arnold). Also writes as Joseph H. Arnold.
American. Born in Indianapolis, Indiana, 2 August 1918.
Educated at Indiana University, Bloomington, 1938–41.
Married Marrijane Johnston in 1938; three children. Assistant
editor, Samuel French, publishers, New York, 1941–43. Since
1954, Partner, Erskine and Hayes, theatrical producers, New
York. Chairman, Sarasota Community Theatre for the
Performing Arts, Florida, and Sarasota Chapter, American
Civil Liberties Union. Recipient: Sergel Drama prize, Univer-
sity of Chicago, 1948; Grand Prix de Littérature Policière;
Tony award, for drama, 1956; Mystery Writers of America
Edgar Allan Poe award, for screenplay, 1956. D.H.L.: Indiana
University, 1970. Agent: James Oliver Brown, Curtis Brown
Associates Ltd., 575 Madison Avenue, New York, New York
10022. Address: 1168 Westway Drive, Sarasota, Florida 33577,
U.S.A.

CRIME PUBLICATIONS

Novels

The Desperate Hours. New York, Random House, and London, Deutsch, 1954.
The Hours after Midnight. New York, Random House, 1958; London, Deutsch, 1959.
Don't Go Away Mad. New York, Random House, 1962; London, W.H. Allen, 1964.
The Third Day. New York, McGraw Hill, 1964; London, W.H. Allen, 1965.
The Deep End. New York, Viking Press, and London, W.H. Allen, 1967.
Like Any Other Fugitive. New York, Dial Press, 1971; London, Deutsch, 1972.
The Long Dark Night. New York, Putnam, and London, Deutsch, 1974.
Missing . . . and Presumed Dead. New York, New American Library, 1975; London, Deutsch, 1977.
Winner's Circle. New York, Delacorte Press, 1980; London, Deutsch, 1981.
No Escape. New York, Delacorte Press, and London, Deutsch, 1982.
The Ways of Darkness. New York, Morrow, 1985.
Act of Rage. New York, St. Martin's Press, 1989.

OTHER PUBLICATIONS

Novels

Bon Voyage, with Marrijane Hayes. New York, Random House, and London, Deutsch, 1957.
Island on Fire. New York, Grosset and Dunlap, and London, Deutsch, 1979.

Plays

And Came the Spring, with Marrijane Hayes. New York, French, 1942.
Christmas at Home. New York, French, 1943.
The Thompsons. New York, French, 1943.
The Bridegroom Waits. New York, French, 1943.
Kidnapped, in *On the Air,* edited by Garrett H. Leverton. New York, French, 1944.
Sneak Date (as Joseph H. Arnold). New York, Peterson, 1944.
Come Rain or Shine, with Marrijane Hayes. New York, French, 1944.
Life of the Party, with Marrijane Hayes. New York, French, 1945.
Ask for Me Tomorrow, with Marrijane Hayes. New York, French, 1946.
Where's Laurie (as Joseph H. Arnold). New York, French, 1946.
Come Over to Our House, with Marrijane Hayes. New York, French, 1946.
Home for Christmas. New York, French, 1946.
A Woman's Privilege. New York, French, 1947.
Quiet Summer, with Marrijane Hayes. New York, French, 1947.
Change of Heart, with Marrijane Hayes. New York, French, 1948.
Leaf and Bough (produced New York, 1949).
Too Many Dates, with Marrijane Hayes. New York, French, 1950.

Curtain Going Up, with Marrijane Hayes. New York, French, 1950.
Turn Back the Clock, with Marrijane Hayes. New York, French, 1950.
June Wedding, with Marrijane Hayes. New York, French, 1951.
Once in Every Family, with Marrijane Hayes. New York, French, 1951.
Penny, with Marrijane Hayes. New York, French, 1951.
Too Young, Too Old. Boston, Baker, 1952.
Mister Peepers, with Marrijane Hayes. New York, French, 1952.
Head in the Clouds, with Marrijane Hayes. New York, French, 1952.
The Desperate Hours, adaptation of his own novel (produced New York and London, 1955). New York, Random House, 1955.
The Midnight Sun (produced New Haven, Connecticut, 1959).
Calculated Risk (produced New York, 1962). New York, French, 1963.
The Deep End, adaptation of his own novel (produced New York, 1969).
Is Anyone Listening? (produced Tallahassee, Florida, 1970).
Impolite Comedy. New York, French, 1977.
Come Into My Parlor (produced Palm Beach, Florida, 1985).

Screenplays: *The Desperate Hours,* 1955; *The Young Doctors,* 1962.

Radio Play: *Kidnapped.*

*

Manuscript Collection: Lilly Library, Indiana University, Bloomington.

*   *   *

Joseph Hayes has enjoyed a varied career as a novelist, playwright, and theatrical producer. He was born in Indianapolis, a locale he used in *The Desperate Hours,* his first and best-known novel. *The Desperate Hours* was an immediate best-seller; it was adapted as a Broadway play and a screenplay in 1955. The story of *The Desperate Hours,* based on factual circumstances, is a gripping one. Readers of the novel become fully involved in the nightmare of suspense in which Dan Hilliard, his wife, and children find themselves enmeshed. Hayes uses the plot of three escaped convicts holding a family hostage to demonstrate various levels of tension: the tension of a family who must function under such extraordinary circumstances, the tension among the three escapees, the tension as well as the bonds of mutual respect developed during the ordeal between the Hilliards and the convicts.

The three convicts, Glenn Griffin, his younger brother Hank, and their companion Robish, represent very different personalities. Glenn, the leader of the group, demonstrates operational reason to the degree possible under such circumstances. Hank has followed his brother's lead, from the commission of crime to imprisonment; he differs from Hank in having a faint sense of humanity. Robish, on the other hand, symbolizes the criminal pushed beyond the bounds; he is happiest when he is able to kill. The conflict among the three, the urgency with which Glenn Griffin must control Robish, and the doubt facing Hank about his brother escalate the tension that develops once they take over the Hilliard home.

Hayes poses the questions we all would ask: How does the ordinary man protect his family? How does he deal with minds so alien to his? How does he choose between heroic impulsive action and what might appear to be cowardly but more thoughtful and safer alternatives? Much of the drama of *The Desperate Hours* derives from the familiarity of the scene for the principals. Glenn Griffin returns to the Indianapolis area for revenge against the sheriff, Jesse Webb, who made the arrest leading to his imprisonment. Through a series of hunches, which Webb describes as the essence of police work, Webb is able to free the Hilliard family of their nightmare.

Of Hayes's other novels, two bear close analysis—*Like Any Other Fugitive* and *The Long Dark Night*. *Like Any Other Fugitive,* a sharply drawn psychological portrait of two young people on the run, is a picaresque novel whose comedy is erased by the burden placed on the protagonists by society and paranoid parents. Written in a quasi-stream-of-consciousness manner, the novel deals with a young couple, one a Vietnam veteran, placed at odds with the law by those close to them—a sister and a right-wing father. A cross-country pursuit brings the two youngsters, B.C. Chadwicke and Laurel Taggart, into the lives of ordinary people—old men from the Midwest who run motels, rancher couples, ladies who own general stores. Hayes draws unforgettable portraits of the American Gothic in these characters. Through their actions they reveal their trust, or suspicion, of the strange young couple touching their lives. Throughout the novel, B.C. and Laurel also confront the same questions of trust, suspicion, and betrayal. Each time they are betrayed, they experience genuine shock and hurt because at heart they are innocents.

In *The Long Dark Night* Hayes tells a gruesome, violent story of revenge. The protagonist, a criminal psychopath, Boyd Ritchie, revisits a New England town and avenges the wrongful conviction and eight-year imprisonment he endured. Systematically Ritchie visits the home of each person who affected his life eight years before. Upon each one he inflicts extreme physical torture (eye gouging, sodomy, etc.), and causes some of his victims to murder others. The physical horrors are graphic and unrelieved, and the novel is paced on a strict timetable—from victim to victim and horror to horror. Hayes creates a tapestry of characters ranging from an innocent teenager to a nymphomaniac and a slightly off-kilter retired Texas Ranger. As in *The Desperate Hours,* Hayes aptly contrasts normality with manic behavior. The race against the clock in *The Long Dark Night* is reminiscent of the pace of *Night of the Juggler* by William P. McGivern.

—Katherine M. Restaino

HAYMON, S(ylvia). T. British. Born in Norwich, Norfolk, in 1918. Married; two daughters. Has had a variety of jobs including in public relations, broadcasting, journalism, and farming. Recipient: Crime Writers Association Silver Dagger award, 1983. Lives in London. Address: c/o Constable and Company Ltd., 10 Orange Street, London WC2H 7EG, England.

CRIME PUBLICATIONS

Novels (series: Inspector Ben Jurnet in all books)

Death and the Pregnant Virgin. London, Constable, and New York, St. Martin's Press, 1980.

Ritual Murder. London, Constable, and New York, St. Martin's Press, 1982.
Stately Homicide. London, Constable, and New York, St. Martin's Press, 1984.
Death of a God. London, Constable, and New York, St. Martin's Press, 1987.
A Very Particular Murder. London, Constable, and New York, St. Martin's Press, 1989.

OTHER PUBLICATIONS

Novel

The Loyal Traitor. London, Chatto and Windus, 1965.

Other

Television and Radio as a Career. London, Batsford, 1963.
Bonnie Prince Charlie. London, Macdonald, 1969.
King Monmouth. London, Macdonald, 1970.
Norwich. London, Longman, 1973.
Opposite the Cross Keys (memoirs). London, Constable, and New York, St. Martin's Press, 1988.
The Quivering Tree (memoirs). London, Constable, and New York, St. Martin's Press, 1990.

* * *

S.T. Haymon writes one of the more literate, well written series now being published, a series most highly recommended to those readers who like the British "cozy" procedural. Her series stars Detective Inspector Benjamin Jurnet, who strongly resembles a portrait of George Bullen, the Viscount Rochford, who was the brother of Anne Boleyn. They both have black hair, a long lean face, smoldering eyes, and a prominent nose which impart an air of moody disdain to their appearances. These dark, exotic, almost-Mediterranean good looks, however English they might in fact be, earn Jurnet a nickname from his fellow police—Valentino—a nickname of which he is well aware and which embarrasses him somewhat. In actual fact, Jurnet "never [sets] out consciously to charm underlings, who consequently, once they [get] over his foreign appearance, [get] on well with him."

Ben Jurnet is with the Norfolk CID. At the start of a case, he acts like "a bear with a sore head" due to a delicacy, a reluctance to intrude upon the privacy of others, an uncharitable shying away from other people's troubles. The living always trouble him more than the dead during the investigation, and at a case's conclusion, he " . . . always [needs] a little time to recover from the backwash of other people's emotions." His partner, Detective Sergeant Jack Ellers, seems to understand this quirk of Jurnet's, and Ellers's talents compliment Jurnet's on the cases they work together.

Jurnet's personal religious conflict is apparent throughout the series. In the course of his investigations in *Ritual Murder,* he discovers that there was a medieval Jurnet: Jurnet of Norwich, the Rothschild of the Middle Ages, a Jewish man whose money built abbeys and cathedrals and financed crusades in the 12th Century. A witness in the case asks him if he is, indeed, related to this Jurnet. This becomes of particular interest to him since Miriam, who is Jewish, wants him to convert before she will marry him.

He was raised Unitarian, but does not consider himself a religious man. While he approves of religion as a whole, since, "if practiced in moderation, . . . [it tends] to make people behave better than worse," he distrusts it when it is carried to an extreme. In *Ritual Murder,* and in the later books, he is studying at the synagogue under Rabbi Leo Schnellman; but he had thought conversion would be faster than this! The Rabbi will not pass Jurnet on his studies without a sign of true commitment on Jurnet's part, and Jurnet is having difficulty finding this commitment. In fact, he is sorely tested when, in *A Very Particular Murder,* he has to go to Israel to talk to a witness. He finds that that place, and Jerusalem in particular, do not affect him as he was told it should. He keeps wishing he were back home in comfortable Norfolk. When he sees the change in Miriam, who has been working on a kibbutz for the handicapped, he begins to have doubts, not only about conversion. Perhaps *she* doesn't want him any more. . . .

Death and the Pregnant Virgin concerns the murder of a young girl in a shrine to a medieval saint. In *Ritual Murder,* Jurnet investigates the murder of a choirboy in a Norfolk cathedral. In *Stately Homicide,* the corpse of a Hungarian hero is found in the moat of a stately home and estate, which has been made up like a pre-Industrial Revolution village to attract tourists; it is this attraction which has drawn Jurnet there initially—he is buying a piece of hand-made jewelry for Miriam. In *Death of a God,* the lead singer of the rock group, The Second Coming, is found dead, tied to a cross in the market place of a village. Jurnet actually witnesses the death, by poisoning, of a Nobel prize winner, a survivor of the death camps of World War II, at a conference of renowned physicists in *A Very Particular Murder;* he had been assigned to security and ended up at the dead man's table.

The series is, basically, a British police procedural series, but the charm of the books is in the character study of Benjamin Jurnet. As the series progresses, it is enlightening to compare the Jurnet of *Ritual Murder* with the Jurnet of *A Very Particular Murder.* In *Ritual Murder,* he is a man of unquestioning love and dedication; in *A Very Particular Murder,* he is afraid to announce his presence to Miriam when he sees her in Jerusalem. His intellectual and emotional conflicts regarding his love for Miriam and his as-of-yet unsuccessful conversion to Judaism provide a picture of a policeman with very human problems.

—Carol M. Harper

———

HAYWARD, Richard. *See* **KENDRICK, Baynard H.**

———

HEAD, Matthew. Pseudonym for John (Edwin) Canaday. American. Born in Fort Scott, Kansas, 1 February 1907. Educated at the University of Texas, Austin, B.A. 1925; Yale University, New Haven, Connecticut, M.A. 1932. Served in the United States Marine Corps, 1943–45; First Lieutenant. Married Katherine Hoover in 1935; two children. Teacher of art history, University of Virginia, Charlottesville, 1938–50; Head, School of Art at Newcomb College of Tulane University, New Orleans, Louisiana, 1950–52; chief, Division of Education, Philadelphia Museum of Art, 1952–59; art critic, 1959–77, and restaurant critic, 1974–77, New York *Times;* Visiting Professor, University of Texas, Austin, 1978; State Department Lecturer in Latin America, 1979. Recipient: Athenaeum Library award, 1959. Honorary doctorate: University of Rochester, New York, 1973; Tulane University, New Orleans, 1983. *Died in 1985.*

CRIME PUBLICATIONS

Novels (series: Dr. Mary Finney)

The Smell of Money.   New York, Simon and Schuster, 1943.
The Devil in the Bush (Finney).   New York, Simon and Schuster, 1945.
The Accomplice.   New York, Simon and Schuster, 1947.
The Cabinda Affair (Finney).   New York, Simon and Schuster, 1949; London, Heinemann, 1950.
The Congo Venus (Finney).   New York, Simon and Schuster, 1950; London, Garland, 1976.
Another Man's Life.   New York, Simon and Schuster, 1953.
Murder at the Flea Club (Finney).   New York, Simon and Schuster, 1955; London, Heinemann, 1957.

Uncollected Short Story

"Three Strips of Flesh," in *Four and Twenty Bloodhounds,* edited by Anthony Boucher.   New York, Simon and Schuster, 1950; London, Hammond, 1951.

OTHER PUBLICATIONS as John Canaday

Other

Metropolitan Seminars in Art.   New York, Metropolitan Museum of Art, 12 vols., 1958; 2nd series, 12 vols., 1959.
Mainstreams of Modern Art: David to Picasso.   New York, Simon and Schuster, and London, Thames and Hudson, 1959; revised edition, New York, Holt Rinehart, 1981.
Embattled Critic: Views on Modern Art.   New York, Farrar Straus, 1962.
Keys to Art, with Katherine H. Canaday.   New York, Tudor, 1963; as *Look; or, The Keys to Art.* London, Methuen, 1964.
The Lives of the Painters.   New York, Norton, and London, Thames and Hudson, 4 vols., 1969.
Culture Gulch: Notes on Art and Its Public in the 1960's.   New York, Farrar Straus, 1969.
Baroque Painters.   New York, Norton, 1972.
Late Gothic to Renaissance Painters.   New York, Norton, 1972.
Neoclassic to Post-Impressionist Painters.   New York, Norton, 1972.
The New York Guide to Dining Out in New York.   New York, Atheneum, 1972; revised edition, 1976.
The Artful Avocado.   New York, Doubleday, 1973.
Richard Estes: The Urban Landscape.   Boston, New York, Graphic Society, 1979.
What Is Art?   New York, Knopf, and London, Hutchinson, 1980.
Michelangelo.   New York, Abbeville, 1980.

Editor, *Western Painting Illustrated: Giotto to Cézanne.*   New York, Norton, 1972.

*

Manuscript Collection: Alderman Library, University of Virginia, Charlottesville.

*   *   *

In 1943 Matthew Head published his first mystery, *The Smell of Money.* Particularly interesting were the descriptive passages of the great house and estate which "smelled of money." But it was with his second book that Head made his name as a mystery writer—since then he has never been overlooked by connoisseurs.

The Devil in the Bush was published in 1945, predating by a good many years Nicholas Monsarrat's *The Tribe That Lost Its Head*. It was perhaps the first modern view in fiction of emerging Africa. There is autobiographical background to the story, which relates the experiences of a young man sent to the Congo on a government mission. Head wrote two more African books, *The Cabinda Affair* and *The Congo Venus*, both as engaging and as revealing as his first African book. With subtlety he foreshadowed a time of change on the African continent. Head also wrote several mysteries with a European background, using his artist's eye to convey the enchantment of Paris and Venice.

—Dorothy B. Hughes

HEALD, Tim(othy Villiers). Also writes as David Lancaster. British. Born in Dorchester, Dorset, 28 January 1944. Educated at Connaught House School, Bishops Lydeard, Somerset, 1952–57; Sherborne School, Dorset, 1957–62; Balliol College, Oxford (Galpin Scholar), 1962–65, B.A. (honours) in modern history 1965. Married Alison Martina Leslie in 1968; two daughters and two sons. Reporter, "Atticus" column, *Sunday Times,* London, 1965–67; feature editor, *Town* magazine, London, 1967; feature writer, *Daily Express,* London, 1967–72; freelance writer and journalist, London, 1972–77; associate editor, *Weekend Magazine,* Toronto, 1977–78. Chairman, Crime Writers Association, 1987–88. Agent: Aitken and Stone Ltd., 29 Fernshaw Road, London SW10 0TG, England.

CRIME PUBLICATIONS

Novels (series: Simon Bognor in all books)

Unbecoming Habits. London, Hutchinson, and New York, Stein and Day, 1973.
Blue Blood Will Out. London, Hutchinson, and New York, Stein and Day, 1974.
Deadline. London, Hutchinson, and New York, Stein and Day, 1975.
Let Sleeping Dogs Die. London, Hutchinson, and New York, Stein and Day, 1976.
Just Desserts. London, Hutchinson, 1977; New York, Scribner, 1979.
Murder at Moose Jaw. London, Hutchinson, and New York, Doubleday, 1981.
Masterstroke. London, Hutchinson, 1982; as *A Small Masterpiece,* New York, Doubleday, 1982.
Red Herrings. London, Macmillan, 1985; New York, Doubleday, 1986.
Brought to Book. London, Macmillan, and New York, Doubleday, 1988.
Business Unusual. London, Macmillan, 1989.

Uncollected Short Stories

"The Case of the Frozen Diplomat," in *Weekend Magazine* (Toronto), 17 June 1978.
"Simon Bognor and the Case of the Ridiculous Hat," in *Ellery Queen's Mystery Magazine* (New York), August 1983.
"Simon Bognor and the Apocrypha Tie," in *Ellery Queen's Mystery Magazine* (New York), April 1984.

"Simon Bognor and the Man Overboard," in *Ellery Queen's Mystery Magazine* (New York), October 1984.
"The Butler Dunnit," in *Ellery Queen's Mystery Magazine* (New York), Mid-December 1984.
"Simon Bognor and the Sudden Death," in *Ellery Queen's Mystery Magazine* (New York), Mid-December 1986.
"We Are Not Amused," in *The Rigby File,* edited by Tim Heald. London, Hodder and Stoughton, 1989.

OTHER PUBLICATIONS

Novel

Caroline R. New York, Arbor House, 1980; as David Lancaster, London, Hutchinson, 1981.
Class Distinctions. London, Hutchinson, 1984.

Other

It's a Dog's Life. London, Elm Tree Books, 1971.
The Making of Space 1999. New York, Ballantine 1976.
John Steed: An Authorized Biography. London, Weidenfeld and Nicolson, 1977.
H.R.H.: The Man Who Will Be King, with Mayo Mohs. New York, Arbor House, 1979; London, Sphere, 1980.
Networks: Who We Know and How We Use Them. London, Hodder and Stoughton, 1983; as *Old Boy Networks,* New Haven, Connecticut, Ticknor and Fields, 1984.
The Character of Cricket. London, Pavilion, 1986.
By Appointment. London, Macdonald, 1989.

Editor, *The Newest London Spy.* London, Muller, Blond and White, 1987.
Editor, *The Rigby File* (short story anthology). London, Hodder and Stoughton, 1989.

*

Tim Heald comments:
All the mysteries are meant to be light (not to say comic) and, as mysteries go, not as mysterious as they might be. They star Simon Bognor who is a special investigator from the Board of Trade, and silly with it. He moves from an Anglican friary to the English stately home business. Fleet Street, dogbreeding, and, Food, Toronto, Oxford village life, and middle England. I know about all of these from personal experience. Bognor always gets his man but is not entirely faithful to Monica who is plain but long-suffering. He smokes, drinks, and takes no exercise.

* * *

Tim Heald's detective Simon Bognor must be one of the few characters in crime (or indeed any) fiction to make a real virtue out of sheer mediocrity. Physically unprepossessing (his complexion blotchy, "his hair was going fast and his waist, never a dominant feature, had finally disappeared"), he eats and drinks far too much, and the reader is treated to detailed descriptions of his physical symptoms on the occasions of his overindulgence. As with many fictional detectives, both amateur and professional, Bognor suffers frequent blows to the cranium from both blunt and sharp instruments and his condition is almost invariably exacerbated (and his recovery impeded) by a hangover! Simon Bognor is an unusual detective in that he does not write poetry, collect incunabula or grow orchids—his only passions (and that is really too strong a word for them) are for his wife Monica and for food and drink. One redeeming and rather endearing feature is Bognor's awareness of his own inadequacy in—*Masterstroke* (set at a college reunion) he thinks to himself "the trouble with this reunion was that it was making him feel a failure. He *was* a failure—he knew that—but this reminded him of the fact all too forcibly."

Bognor is a Special Investigator for the Board of Trade—one questions the likelihood but appreciates the convenience of this profession—and as such is called upon by his boss Parkinson to investigate various suspicious deaths (of which the most suspicious feature as far as the reader is concerned is that Bognor is always on the spot already—albeit in all innocence). Parkinson, the possessor of a dry sense of humour, finds Bognor exasperating in the extreme—one can only sympathise: the thought of having Bognor on one's staff is enough to make one apply for early retirement. Bognor's wife Monica, while possessing a great deal of affection (even love) for her incompetent spouse, is frequently in complete accord with Parkinson. After living together for several years she and Bognor decide to marry for various negative reasons, one of which is a vague desire on both their parts to be unfaithful and a realisation that this would be easier if they were in fact married. Incredibly, at least one female in each book finds Bognor attractive but his somewhat half-hearted lust is rarely if ever consummated.

His Board of Trade work does not confine Bognor to the shores of Britain—in *Murder at Moose Jaw* he co-operates with the Royal Canadian Mounted Police (whose officers, to his growing irritation, call him "Si") to solve the murder of a highly unpopular industrialist by the unusual, not to say unique, weapon of poisoned bath oil. Amazingly, the R.C.M.P. hold Bognor in very high esteem owing to his assistance in a previous case—all the more amazing since in that instance his solution was not the correct one. The humour in this and all the novels lies in the understated reaction of the protagonists to the events. The reader is privy to Bognor's thoughts and they are always low-key, self-deprecating, and wryly realistic—he is not a man of action nor even of tremendously active thought-processes. Almost an anti-hero, this detective is refreshingly different from those supermen who people the pages of other authors' novels; whereas they seem capable of bouncing back from daunting encounters (which ought to have resulted in serious physical injury) to present a correct solution arrived at by intensive ratiocination, Bognor stumbles upon his solutions almost by accident.

This implausibly successful detective frequently functions in settings which are themselves a little surreal, and whose characters sometimes rival Bognor in their improbability. *Business Unusual* is set in Scarpington, which is a fictional "middle England" town run by the Artisans, an organization seemingly combining the worst features of the Freemasons with the best ones of the Mafia. An important Artisan drops dead at an official dinner at which Simon (to no-one's surprise) is present, and as one learns of the organization's stranglehold on the town one is prepared for some real villainy and double-dealing. But even the baddies can be quite amiable in these novels and the reader is almost prepared to believe that both the Freemasons and the Mafia are really rather charitable organisations. All the novels are raised from the purely comic by pleasing literary allusions and quotations, and by a certain amount of political and social comment. Here Bognor reveals his (and presumably Heald's) politics as being leftish of centre, and in commenting upon the dealings of the Scarpington business community he has some fairly scathing comments to make on Thatcherism.

Chapter Five of *Business Unusual* is entitled "Not a tremendously good show", and this seems to encapsulate Bognor, his methods and his general view of life. But the

seemingly incompetent investigator, helped by his forthright and astute Monica, invariably shines through his own inadequacy to provide light and amusing entertainment in which the actual solution of the crime is secondary to the interplay of characters and situations.

—Judith Rhodes

———

HEALEY, Ben. *See* **STURROCK, Jeremy.**

———

HEALY, Jeremiah. American. Born in Teaneck, New Jersey, 15 May 1948. Educated at Rutgers University, New Brunswick, A. B. (phi beta kappa) 1970; Harvard University, Cambridge, Massachusetts, J.D. 1973. Served in the United States Army Military Police; Captain. Married Bonnie M. Tisler in 1978. Litigation associate, Withington, Cross, Park and Groden, Boston, Massachusetts, 1973–78; member of faculty 1978–83, and since 1983 Professor, New England School of Law, Boston. Member, Executive Council of the International Association of Crime Writers. Recipient: Private Eye Writers of America Shamus award, 1986. Agent: Jed Mattes, Inc., 175 West 73rd Street, New York, New York 10023. Address: 186 Commonwealth Avenue, Boston, Massachusetts 02116, U.S.A.

CRIME PUBLICATIONS

Novels (series: John Francis Cuddy in all books)

Blunt Darts.   New York, Walker, 1984; London, Macmillan, 1986.
The Staked Goat.   New York, Harper, 1986; as *The Tethered Goat,* London, Macmillan, 1986.
So Like Sleep.   New York, Harper, and London, Macmillan, 1987.
Swan Dive.   New York, Harper, and London, Macmillan, 1988.
Yesterday's News,   New York, Harper, and London, Macmillan, 1989.

Uncollected Short Stories

"Till Tuesday," in *Alfred Hitchcock's Mystery Magazine* (New York), April 1988.
"In the Line of Duty," in *Raymond Chandler's Philip Marlowe,* New York, Knopf, 1988.
"One Eye Open," in *Ellery Queen's Mystery Magazine* (New York), July 1989.
"Bertie's Mom," in *Ellery Queen's Mystery Magazine* (New York), September 1989.
"Someone to Turn out the Lights," in *Justice for Hire* edited by Robert J. Randisi, New York, Mysterious Press, 1990.
"The Three Musketeers," in *Ellery Queen's Mystery Magazine* (New York), April 1990.

*

Jeremiah Healy comments:
Through my experiences in law enforcement and law

practice, I realized that some matters simply fell between the cracks in the system. Given the opportunity to teach, leaving my summers free, I decided to explore those cracks in novels, using a Boston-based private investigator, John Francis Cuddy. As a Vietnam veteran and a widower, he is no stranger to the anguish shared by many of the people with whom he comes in contact. I think he therefore has been, and with luck will continue to be, a credible series character.

* * *

Jeremiah Healy has given his fictional private investigator John Francis Cuddy—featured thusfar in five novels and a handful of short stories—the requisite inquisitiveness and macho tendencies, but has tempered the last with a rare sensitivity.

When we are introduced to Cuddy in *Blunt Darts,* he has been terminated by mutual agreement as chief claims investigator for Empire Insurance in Boston after refusing to endorse a false report. His options are few. He served in the military police during the Vietnam War. He lost his wife Beth who died of a brain tumor after eight all-too-short years of marriage. He's on the brink of alcoholism. He opens a one-man detective agency.

That first novel has one of the more twisted puzzles of the series and a gut-punch of an ending. Judge Kinnington apparently doesn't want his 14-year-old son Stephen found, but the grandmother Eleanor Kinnington does—without telling Cuddy all the family's sordid past. Cuddy knocks on doors, tangles with corrupt cops, visits the bottle, commiserates with Beth at her grave, and barely survives a trek into the Berkshire wilderness to piece things together.

The Staked Goat intertwines two plots: Marco D'Amico's relentless quest for vengeance after his brother Joey is sent to prison for arson based on Cuddy's testimony; and the violent death of Cuddy's war buddy Al Sachs, the apparent victim of a homosexual attack. Two recurring characters show up. They are assistant district attorney Nancy Meagher, who tried the D'Amico case and has fallen for her key witness, and black Boston Detective Lieutenant Robert Murphy, Cuddy's lone friend on the force.

Cuddy is frequently in physical peril in the books, and never more so than here. The author emphasizes this duality—of a Vietnam-trained killing machine and an ultra-loving man. The tales are well-paced, the prose tense but leaving breathing room for character development. The books have a fine sense of place. Boston and its environs ring true, if some place names are occasionally transposed.

Cuddy's third case, *So Like Sleep,* involves a black college student who, apparently over his head in leaving the ghetto to live on an upper middle-class campus, confesses at a hypnosis-therapy group to having killed his white girlfriend. As he probes and questions, Cuddy meets a number of well-drawn characters, from a 35-year-old divorcée who is into the singles scene to a 74-year-old jogger and weight lifter.

Swan Dive, as with all the novels in the series, picks up virtually without time lapse from the previous entry. Cuddy helps Chris Christedes, an old friend who is now a lawyer, with a divorce case. Cuddy usually shuns divorce work, but he feels sorry for Christedes, whose wife is suffering from debilitating multiple sclerosis. The client is Hanna Marsh, who because of Christedes's inept handling likely won't get a cent from her vile soon-to-be-ex Ray. Marsh skins their young daughter's cat alive in a fit of pique. Cuddy confronts him, and becomes the leading suspect the next day when Marsh is found pushed from a high-rise window. To complicate things, a satchel of drugs is missing. Again there are interested characters, from the

repulsive thugs J.J. and Terdell to the streetwise gang leader Nino.

There are nice moments of humor in the book. Cuddy, jogging along the Charles River, almost collides with actor Robert Ullrich who is filming a scene from "Spencer for Hire" (you know, the other Boston PI). His relationship with Nancy threatens to get too cutesy; still pining for Beth, he's afraid to lose his chastity. But Beth is an understanding sort, and the Cuddy-Meagher relationship becomes a strong one as we fade into *Yesterday's News.*

In this latest book, the hero is hired by a southeast Massachusetts newspaper reporter to look into the death of one of her confidential sources. Cuddy is not too keen to handle the case—until the reporter also turns up dead. By now, booze has faded into Cuddy's background, though he doesn't mind sharing a bottle of Killian Irish Red with a curmudgeonly Emil Jones, proprietor of the Crestview Motel and a likeable throw-away character of the type which has become the Healy hallmark.

Healy's Cuddy short stories, in *Ellery Queen's Mystery Magazine* and *Alfred Hitchcock's Mystery Magazine,* shear away the extraneous characters, the humor and the personal relationships to leave simply plot. They're well done whodunits but are not representative.

Healy has a few-frills writing style, brisk pace, eye for characterization, devious plotting mind and a willingness to let his characters progress.

—Bernard A. Drew

————

HEARD, Gerald. *See* **HEARD, H.F.**

————

HEARD, H(enry) F(itzgerald). Also wrote as Gerald Heard. British. Born in London, 6 October 1889. Educated at Gonville and Caius College, Cambridge, B.A. (honours) in history 1911, graduate work 1911–12. Worked with the Agricultural Co-operative Movement in Ireland, 1919–23, and in England, 1923–27; editor, *Realist,* London, 1929; Lecturer, Oxford University, 1929–31; science commentator, BBC Radio, London, 1930–34; settled in the United States, 1937; Visiting Lecturer, Washington University, St. Louis, 1951–52, 1955–56; Haskell Foundation Lecturer, Oberlin College, Ohio, 1958. Recipient: Bollingen grant, 1955; British Academy Hertz award. *Died 14 August 1971.*

CRIME PUBLICATIONS

Novels (series: Mr. Mycroft in all books except *Murder by Reflection* and *The Black Fox*)

A Taste for Honey. New York, Vanguard Press, 1941; London, Cassell, 1942; as *A Taste for Murder,* New York, Avon, 1955.
Reply Paid. New York, Vanguard Press, 1942; London, Cassell, 1943.
Murder by Reflection. New York, Vanguard Press, 1942; London, Cassell, 1945.

Doppelgangers: An Episode of the Fourth, the Psychological Revolution, 1997. New York, Vanguard Press, 1947; London, Cassell, 1948.
The Notched Hairpin. New York, Vanguard Press, 1949; London, Cassell, 1952.
The Black Fox. London, Cassell, 1950; New York, Harper, 1951.

Short Stories

The Great Fog and Other Weird Tales. New York, Vanguard Press, 1944; London, Cassell, 1947; as *Weird Tales of Terror and Detection,* New York, Sun Dial Press, 1946.
The Lost Cavern and Other Tales of the Fantastic. New York, Vanguard Press, 1948; London, Cassell, 1949.

Uncollected Short Stories

"The President of the U.S., Detective," in *The Queen's Awards 1946,* edited by Ellery Queen. Boston, Little Brown, 1946.
"Mr. Montalba, Obsequist," in *To the Queen's Taste,* edited by Ellery Queen. Boston, Little Brown, 1946; London, Faber, 1949.

OTHER PUBLICATIONS

Other as Gerald Heard

Narcissus: An Anatomy of Clothes. London, Kegan Paul, and New York, Dutton, 1924.
The Ascent of Humanity: An Essay on the Evolution of Civilization. London, Cape, and New York, Harcourt Brace, 1929.
The Emergence of Man. London, Cape, 1931; New York, Harcourt Brace, 1932.
Social Substance of Religion: An Essay on the Evolution of Religion. London, Allen and Unwin, and New York, Harcourt Brace, 1931.
This Surprising World: A Journalist Looks at Science. London, Cobden Sanderson, 1932.
These Hurrying Years: An Historical Outline 1900–1933. London, Chatto and Windus, and New York, Oxford University Press, 1934.
Science in the Making. London, Faber, 1935.
The Source of Civilisation. London, Cape, 1935; New York, Harper, 1937.
The Significance of the New Pacifism, with *Pacifism and Philosophy,* by Aldous Huxley. London, Headley, 1935.
Exploring the Stratosphere. London, Nelson, 1936.
Science Front 1936. London, Cassell, 1937.
The Third Morality. London, Cassell, and New York, Morrow, 1937.
Pain, Sex and Time: A New Hypothesis of Evolution. New York, Harper, and London, Cassell, 1939.
The Creed of Christ: An Interpretation of the Lord's Prayer. New York, Harper, 1940; London, Cassell, 1941.
A Quaker Meditation. Wallingford, Pennsylvania, Pendle Hill, 1940 (?).
The Code of Christ: An Interpretation of the Beatitudes. New York, Harper, 1941; London, Cassell, 1943.
Training for the Life of the Spirit. London, Cassell, 2 vols., 1941–44; New York, Harper, 1 vol, n.d.
Man the Master. New York, Harper, 1941; London, Faber, 1942.
A Dialogue in the Desert. London, Cassell, and New York, Harper, 1942.

A Preface to Prayer. New York, Harper, 1944; London, Cassell, 1945.
The Recollection. Stanford, California, Delkin, 1944.
The Gospel According to Gamaliel. New York, Harper, 1945; London, Cassell, 1946.
Militarism's Post-Mortem. London, P.P.U., 1946.
The Eternal Gospel. New York, Harper, 1946; London, Cassell, 1948.
Is God Evident? An Essay Toward a Natural Theology. New York, Harper, 1948; London, Faber, 1950.
Is God in History? An Inquiry into Human and Pre-Human History in Terms of the Doctrine of Creation, Fall, and Redemption. New York, Harper, 1950; London, Faber, 1951.
Morals since 1900. London, Dakers, and New York, Harper, 1950.
The Riddle of the Flying Saucers. London, Carroll and Nicholson, 1950; as *Is Another World Watching?,* New York, Harper, 1951; revised edition, New York, Bantam, 1953.
Ten Questions on Prayer. Wallingford, Pennsylvania, Pendle Hill, 1951.
Gabriel and the Creatures. New York, Harper, 1952; as *Wishing Well: An Outline of the Evolution of the Mammals Told as a Series of Stories about How Animals Got Their Wishes,* London, Faber, 1953.
The Human Venture. New York, Harper, 1955.
Kingdom Without God: Road's End for the Social Gospel, with others. Los Angeles, Foundation for Social Research, 1956.
Training for a Life of Growth. Santa Monica, California, Wayfarer Press, 1959.
The Five Ages of Man: The Psychology of Human History. New York, Julian Press, 1964.

Editor, *Prayers and Meditations.* New York, Harper, 1949.

*   *   *

H.F. Heard (Gerald Heard), despite his many serious books on social thought and his later works on mysticism, occultism, and pseudoscience, is now remembered mostly for his delightful novel *A Taste for Honey.* It tells of the experiences of Mr. Mycroft (detective) and Mr. Silchester (narrator) against a criminal who "sends" bees with hypertrophied stinging apparatus. Set in the British countryside, ably characterized, with a leisurely pace, it is perhaps the finest novel-length pastiche of Sherlock Holmes—even though Holmes is not mentioned by name.

In *Reply Paid* Mycroft and Silchester are relocated in California, where they are now concerned with a mystery involving a cryptogram, supernatural phenomena, bacterial murder, and a radioactive meteorite. A third novel, *The Notched Hairpin,* and two short stories, "Mr. Montalba, Obsequist" and "The Enchanted Garden," complete the Mycroft canon. The consensus is that none of these stories matches the first novel.

Heard's other mystery material includes *Murder by Reflection,* a fairly routine mystery; *Doppelgangers,* about crime and politico-mystical intrigue in 1997; and several of the stories in the mixed collections *The Great Fog* and *The Lost Cavern.* In all of these, good, original ideas are likely to be overturned by meandering development and garrulity.

—E.F. Bleiler

HEBDEN, Mark. Pseudonym for John Harris; also writes as Max Hennessy. British. Born in Rotherham, Yorkshire, 18 October 1916. Educated at Rotherham Grammar School 1924–32. Served in the Royal Air Force 1939–45. Married Betty Wragg in 1947; one son and one daughter. Worked as merchant seaman, 1938–39, history teacher, 1963–64, journalist, and cartoonist; full-time writer from the mid-1950's. Agent: Curtis Brown Ltd., 162-168 Regent Street, London W1R 5TB. Address: Beaumont, Rookwood Road, West Wittering, Sussex PO20 8LT, England.

CRIME PUBLICATIONS

Novels (series: Colonel Mostyn; Inspector Clovis Pel)

What Changed Charley Farthing. London, Harrap, 1965.
Eyewitness. London, Harrap, 1966; as *The Eyewitness,* New York, Harcourt Brace, 1967.
The Errant Knights. London, Harrap, and New York, Harcourt Brace, 1968.
Portrait in a Dusty Frame. London, Harrap, 1969; as *Grave Journey,* New York, Harcourt Brace, 1970.
Mask of Violence (Mostyn). New York, Harcourt Brace, 1970; London, Joseph, 1971.
A Killer for the Chairman. London, Joseph, and New York, Harcourt Brace, 1972.
The Dark Side of the Island. London, Joseph, and New York, Harcourt Brace, 1973.
A Pride of Dolphins (Mostyn). London, Joseph, 1974; New York, Harcourt Brace, 1975.
The League of 89 (Mostyn). London, Hamish Hamilton, 1977.
Death Set to Music (Pel). London, Hamish Hamilton, 1979; New York, Walker, 1983.
Pel and the Faceless Corpse. London, Hamish Hamilton, 1979; New York, Walker, 1982.·
Pel under Pressure. London, Hamish Hamilton, 1980; New York, Walker, 1983.
Pel Is Puzzled. London, Hamish Hamilton, 1981.
Pel and the Staghound. London, Hamish Hamilton, 1982; New York, Walker, 1984.
Pel and the Bombers. London, Hamish Hamilton, 1982; New York, Walker, 1985.
Pel and the Predators. London, Hamish Hamilton, 1984.; New York, Walker, 1985.
Pel and the Pirates. London, Hamish Hamilton, 1984; New York, Walker, 1987.
Pel and the Prowler. London, Hamish Hamilton, 1985; New York, Walker, 1986.
Pel and the Paris Mob. London, Hamish Hamilton, 1986.
Pel Among the Pueblos. London, Constable, 1987; New York, Walker, 1988.
Pel and the Touch of Pitch. London, Constable, 1987; New York, Walker, 1988.
Pel and the Picture of Innocence. London, Constable, 1988; New York, St. Martin's Press, 1989.
Pel and the Party Spirit. London, Constable, 1989.

Novels as John Harris

The Lonely Voyage. London, Hurst and Blackett, 1951.
Hallelujah Corner. London, Hurst and Blackett, 1952.
The Sea Shall Not Have Them. London, Hurst and Blackett, 1953; as *The Undaunted,* New York, Sloane, 1953.
The Claws of Mercy. London, Hurst and Blackett, 1955.
Getaway. London, Hurst and Blackett, 1956; as *Close to the Wind,* New York, Sloane, 1956.

The Sleeping Mountain. London, Hutchinson, and New York, Sloane, 1958.
Road to the Coast. London, Hutchinson, 1959; as *Adventure's End,* New York, Sloane, 1959.
Sunset at Sheba. London, Hutchinson, and New York, Sloane, 1960.
Covenant with Death. London, Hutchinson, and New York, Sloane, 1961.
The Spring of Malice. London, Hutchinson, and New York, Sloane, 1962.
The Unforgiving Wind. London, Hutchinson, 1963; New York, Sloane, 1964.
Vardy. London, Hutchinson, 1964; New York, Sloane, 1965.
The Cross of Lazzaro. London, Hutchinson, and New York, Morrow, 1965.
The Old Trade of Killing. London, Hutchinson, and New York, Morrow, 1966.
Light Cavalry Action. London, Hutchinson, and New York, Morrow, 1967.
Right of Reply. London, Hutchinson, and New York, Coward McCann, 1968.
The Mercenaries. London, Hutchinson, 1969; as *The Jade Wind,* New York, Doubleday, 1969.
The Courtney Entry. New York, Doubleday, 1970; London, Hutchinson, 1971.
The Mustering of the Hawks. London, Hutchinson, 1972.
A Kind of Courage. London, Hutchinson, 1972.
Smiling Willie and the Tiger. London, Hutchinson, 1974.
Ride Out the Storm. London, Hutchinson, and New York, Mason Charter, 1975.
The Thirty Days' War. London, Century Hutchinson, 1986.
China Seas. London, Century Hutchinson, 1987.

Uncollected Short Stories as John Harris

"Sleepless Nightmare," in *Suspense* (London), June 1959.
"Below the Surface," in *Suspense* (London), January 1960.

OTHER PUBLICATIONS as John Harris

Novels

Take or Destroy! London, Hutchinson, 1976.
Army of Shadows. London, Hutchinson, 1977.
The Fox from His Lair. London, Hutchinson, 1978.
Corporal Cotton's Little War. London, Hutchinson, 1979; as *Cotton's War,* London, Arrow, 1980.
Swordpoint. London, Hutchinson, 1980.
North Strike. London, Hutchinson, 1981.
Live Free or Die! London, Hutchinson, 1982.
Harkaway's Sixth Column. London, Hutchinson, 1983; New York, Walker, 1985.
A Funny Place to Hold a War. London, Hutchinson, 1984.
Up for Grabs. London, Hutchinson, 1985.
Picture of Defeat. London, Hutchinson, 1988.
So Far From God. London, Hutchinson, 1989.

Novels as Max Hennessy

The Lion at Sea:
   The Lion at Sea. London, Hamish Hamilton, 1977; New York, Atheneum, 1978.
   The Dangerous Years. London, Hamish Hamilton, 1978; New York, Atheneum, 1979.
   Back to Battle. London, Hamish Hamilton, 1979; New York, Atheneum, 1980.

Soldier of the Queen. London, Hamish Hamilton, and New York, Atheneum, 1980.

Blunted Lance. London, Hamish Hamilton, and New York, Atheneum, 1981.

The Iron Stallions. London, Hamish Hamilton, and New York, Atheneum, 1982.

The Bright Blue Sky. London, Hamish Hamilton, 1982; New York, Atheneum, 1983.

The Challenging Heights. London, Hamish Hamilton, and New York, Atheneum, 1983.

The Crimson Wind. London, Hamish Hamilton, 1984; New York, Atheneum, 1985.

Once More the Hawks. London, Hamish Hamilton, and New York, Atheneum, 1984.

Plays

The Sword of General Frapp (for children), from his own story. London, French, 1972.

Television Play: *Hallelujah Corner,* from his own novel.

Other

The Charge of the Light Brigade (for children). London, Parrish, 1965.

The Wonderful Ice Cream (for children), illustrated by the author. London, Hutchinson, 1966.

The Somme: Death of a Generation. London, Hodder and Stoughton, 1966.

The Sword of General Frapp (for children). London, Hutchinson, 1967.

The Big Slump. London, Hodder and Stoughton, 1967.

Sir Sam and the Dragon (for children). London, Hutchinson, 1968.

Sam and the Kite (for children). London, Hutchinson, 1968.

The Fledglings (for children). London, Hutchinson, 1971.

A Matter of Luck (for children). London, Hutchinson, 1971.

The Gallant Six Hundred: A Tragedy of Obsession. London, Hutchinson, and New York, Mason and Lipscomb, 1973.

The Indian Mutiny. London, Hart Davis MacGibbon, 1973.

The Professionals (for children). London, Hutchinson, 1973.

The Victors (for children). London, Hutchinson, 1975.

Much Sounding of Bugles: The Siege of Chitral 1895. London, Hutchinson, 1975.

A Tale of a Tail (for children). London, Hutchinson, 1975.

The Interceptors (for children). London, Hutchinson, 1977.

The Revolutionaries (for children). London, Hutchinson, 1978.

Dunkirk: The Storm of War. Newton Abbot, Devon, David and Charles, 1980.

Without Trace: The Last Voyages of Eight Ships. London, Eyre Methuen, 1981.

The Court Martial of Lord Lucan. London, Severn House, 1987.

Scapegoat: Famous Court Martials. London, Severn House, 1988.

Editor, *Farewell to the Don: The Journal of Brigadier H.N.H. Williamson.* London, Collins, 1970; New York, Day, 1971.

*

Manuscript Collection: Mugar Memorial Library, Boston University.

Mark Hebden comments:

I just enjoy writing, and perhaps it shows. I don't claim to write deathless prose—just stories with strong plots.

*   *   *

John Harris, the author of World War II espionage novels such as *The Fox from His Lair*, and, under the pseudonym of Max Hennessy, of adventure novels such as the series about Anglo-Irish sailor Kelly Maguire which span both World Wars (*The Lion at Sea, The Dangerous Years* and *Back to Battle*), also writes under the pseudonym Mark Hebden. As Hebden, he has written suspense novels, such as *The Dark Side of the Island*, set in the Scottish islands and featuring a teenaged girl and a painter of birds as the heroes. However, Hebden's Chief Inspector Pel series is of primary interest to mystery readers.

Evariste Clovis Desiré Pel of the Brigade Criminelle of the Police Judiciare of the Republic of France is no Maigret (he says that often enough in the first book, *Death Set to Music,* for it to become a litany). However, like Simenon's Maigret series and others written about French policemen, the reader gets a good sense of place. In this case, Burgundian place.

Pel himself lives in an unidentified city in Burgundy in a run-down house with a horrible garden. His housekeeper, Madame Routy, must be the only woman in Burgundy, if not all of France, who can't cook. What is more, she is addicted to television at top volume and prevents Pel from using the only comfortable chair in the house so that *she* can view at all hours. She hates him and he hates her and he is unable to rid himself of her!

Pel is a hypochondriac who is always trying, unsuccessfully, to quit smoking, or at least cut down from 1 million to 500,000 per day. He dislikes just about everything and everyone he is in contact with but is considered to be an excellent cop by his superiors, by his staff, who have great regard for him, and even, to his surprise, by his "enemies." However, until he is on his honeymoon with Madame Pel (*Pel and the Pirates*), he is unaware of his excellent reputation in Burgundy, let alone in all of France.

Pel hates his name even though his parents had all the best intentions by bestowing it upon him. Girls have laughed at it all his life and, even though he sometimes feels that he is the epitome of French masculine appearance, it isn't enough to overcome that name.

He is cheap, not poor, and is saving every penny for his retirement, which, if he lives that long, he is convinced will be impoverished and miserable, just like his working days. When, in the course of an investigation (*Pel and the Faceless Corpse*), he meets Madame Genviève Faivre-Perret, wealthy and an heiress with a large family all over France, he is intrigued, but of course, she wouldn't be interested in him! He can't believe his luck as he timidly pursues her through several books, until he finally proposes in *Pel and the Predators* and she accepts!

Like most police procedurals, while Pel is the lead character, there is a continuing cast who people the pages of these stories. The policemen include Inspector Daniel Darcy, Pel's second in command and ladies' man who is also an excellent investigator; Sergeant Jean-Luc Nosjean, inspector material who is always unsuccessfully courting girls who look like Cathérine Deneuve or Charlotte Rampling; Misset, a laggard who is always asking for the night off and whom Pel would dearly love to demote to traffic patrol; Lagé, overeager but with no imagination who does Misset's work; Du Troc', a penniless baron and art expert who transfers in from another district in *Pell Is Puzzled;* and

Kraus, who is counting the days until he can retire to his country cottage. We also meet several cadets, including Didier Darras, Madame Routy's nephew, who, as a boy, meets Pel in *Death Set to Music* and hits it off with him right away. Each has a skill or talent which supplements Pel, and each grows in the series, aging, being promoted, retiring, and being replaced.

Pel is biased against anything not Burgundian. Luckily, most of his cases are set in Burgundy, but Pel has made reluctant trips to Innsbruck (which caused him to stand up Madame Faivre-Perret on their first date), Paris ("It was too busy and too noisy, smelled too much of hot oil and petrol fumes, and there were so many Americans it looked like the fifty-first state of the Union."), and London (where he finds, to his surprise, that the *rosbifs* don't all fit his stereotype of Englishmen).

Each book centers on one or two major crimes directly under Pel's control, while each of his team pursues peripheral, or satellite cases. Many of the leads tie one or more of the seemingly unrelated cases together, as is common in many police procedural novels, but not so many are tied together that the reader gets a feeling of overwhelming coincidence. Crimes often involve invasion of the Marseilles underworld into Pel's peaceful corner of France and major themes range from art theft, smuggling, and drugs to kidnapping and murder.

—Carol M. Harper

HEILBRUN, Carolyn G. *See* **CROSS, Amanda.**

HELD, Peter. *See* **VANCE, John Holbrook.**

HENRY, Robert. *See* **POWELL, Talmage.**

HENSLEY, Joe L. (Joseph Louis Hensley). American. Born in Bloomington, Indiana, 19 March 1926. Educated at Indiana University, Bloomington, B.A. 1950, LL.B. 1955; called to the Indiana Bar, 1955. Served as a hospital corpsman in the United States Navy, 1944–46; recalled as journalist, 1951–52. Married Charlotte Ruth Bettinger in 1950; one son. Partner, Metford and Hensley, 1955–72, and Hensley Todd and Castor, 1972–75, Madison, Indiana; Judge Pro-Tempore, 80th Judicial Circuit, Versailles, Indiana, 1975–76. Since 1977 Judge, 5th Judicial Circuit, Madison. Member, Indiana General Assembly, 1961–62; Prosecuting Attorney, 5th Judicial Indiana Circuit, 1963–66. President, Indiana Judges Association, 1983–84. Agent: Virginia Kidd, Box 278, Milford, Pennsylvania 18337. Address: 2315 Blackmore, Madison, Indiana 47250, U.S.A.

CRIME PUBLICATIONS

Novels (series: Donald Robak)

The Color of Hate.   New York, Ace, 1960; as *Color Him Guilty,* New York, Walker, 1987.
Deliver Us to Evil (Robak).   New York, Doubleday, 1971.
Legislative Body (Robak).   New York, Doubleday, 1972.
The Poison Summer.   New York, Doubleday, 1974.
Song of Corpus Juris (Robak).   New York, Doubleday, 1974.
Rivertown Risk.   New York, Doubleday, 1977.
A Killing in Gold (Robak).   New York, Doubleday, 1978; London, Gollancz, 1979.
Minor Murders (Robak).   New York, Doubleday, 1979.
Outcasts (Robak).   New York, Doubleday, 1981.
Robak's Cross.   New York, Doubleday, 1985.
Robak's Fire.   New York, Doubleday, 1986.
Fort's Law.   New York, Doubleday, 1987.

Short Stories

Final Doors (includes essay).   New York, Doubleday, 1981.
Robak's Firm (includes essay).   New York, Doubleday, 1987.

OTHER PUBLICATIONS

Novel

The Black Roads.   Toronto, Laser, 1976.

*

Manuscript Collection: Lilly Library, Indiana University, Bloomington.

Joe L. Hensley comments:
  I write mostly about the law and about people who become involved in it. I retired from the bench in 1989, but that has not ended my fascination with courtrooms, trials and lawyers. So I continue to write my novels about such things.

*   *   *

  Throughout his legal career—as a private attorney, county prosecutor, one-term state legislator and, until his recent retirement, as a trial judge with Indiana's Fifth Judicial Circuit—Joe L. Hensley has kept up a second career as a mystery writer. Most of his novels are set in the riverside city of Bington, which is clearly modeled on the southern Indiana community of Madison where he lives. The majority of his books deal with crusading criminal lawyer Donald Robak and three others—*The Color of Hate, The Poison Summer* and *Fort's Law*—are about small-city attorneys who resemble Robak in everything but name. Hensley, however, has little interest in fireworks displays of legal ingenuity in the Erle Stanley Gardner tradition, and his novels tend to avoid the courtroom. Typically his fighting liberal protagonist is called on to defend some out-group person accused of murder—a black ex-convict in *The Color of Hate,* a female juvenile offender in *Minor Murders,* a disgraced former cop in *Outcasts*—and has to cope with harassment from police, corrupt politicians and suspects with secrets as he probes the layers of local graft and hypocrisy and tries to clear his clients prior to trial. Hensley's tone is quiet and low-key, his pace unhurried and unfrenetic, his plots rather loose and not terribly involuted. He has a nice talent for character-drawing and for describing how mid-America functions and much empathy with blacks, Jews, rebellious young people, and others outside the corn-fed mainstream. Most of his books are solidly satisfying and he's at his best in *Robak's Cross,* which has more courtroom action than all the other Robaks put together.

—Francis M. Nevins, Jr.

————

HESS, Joan. Also writes as Joan Hadley. American. Educated at high school in Fayetteville, Arkansas 1967; University of Arkansas, Fayetteville, B.A. in art 1972; Long Island University, C.W. Post Center, Greenvale, New York, M.S. in education 1974. Has two children. Has had a variety of jobs including, in real estate, insurance, and teaching. Lives in Fayetteville. Agent: Dominick Abel, 146 West 82nd Street, Suite 1B, New York, New York 10024. Address: c/o St. Martin's Press, 175 Fifth Avenue, New York, New York 10010, U.S.A.

CRIME PUBLICATIONS

Novels (series: Theo Bloomer; Claire Malloy; Ozark)

Strangled Prose (Malloy). New York, St. Martin's Press, 1986.
The Night-Blooming Cereus (Bloomer; as Joan Hadley). New York, St. Martin's Press, 1986.
The Murder at the Murder at the Mimosa Inn (Malloy). New York, St. Martin's Press, 1986.
Malice in Maggody (Ozark). New York, St. Martin's Press, 1987.
Dear Miss Demeanor (Malloy). New York, St. Martin's Press, 1987.
Mischief in Maggody (Ozark). New York, St. Martin's Press, 1988.
A Really Cute Corpse (Malloy). New York, St. Martin's Press, 1988.
The Deadly Ackee (Bloomer; as Joan Hadley). New York, St. Martin's Press, 1988.
Much Ado in Maggody (Ozark). New York, St. Martin's Press, 1989.
A Diet to Die For (Malloy). New York, St. Martin's Press, 1989.
Madness in Maggody (Ozark). New York, St. Martin's Press, 1990.

Uncollected Short Stories

"Death of a Romance Writer," in *Alfred Hitchcock's Mystery Magazine* (New York), March 1988.
"Too Much to Bare," in *Sisters in Crime 2* edited by Marilyn Wallace. New York, Berkley, 1990.

OTHER PUBLICATIONS

Novels

Future Tense. New York, Silhouette, 1987.
Red Rover, Red Rover. New York, Crosswinds, 1988.

*

Joan Hess comments:
I've always loved traditional mystery fiction's fine balance between the complexity of the plot and the simplicity of the solution. The writers whom I most admire are those who focus on ordinary characters driven to take extraordinary actions in order to protect themselves or their perceived assets. In my work, I struggle to share with the reader the sense of possibility—that this *could* happen to either of us. I also enjoy the opportunity to make sardonic observations about the vagaries of society, and to be able to do so from the relative sanctuary of my office.

*   *   *

A prolific and remarkably even writer, Joan Hess has published 11 mystery novels in three series and two novels for young adults in the first four years of her career as a writer. Her mysteries are marked by sharp wit and a satiric eye as well as by perceptive delineation of character, especially of young poeple.

Hess carefully distinguishes between her three mystery series, although all are marked by deft use of irony and humor and by plots which are full of unexpected twists. Major distinguishing characteristics are setting, use of continuing characters, and point of view. Additionally, one series is set apart by being published under a pseudonym.

Hess's two best-known series, both published under her own name, are set in Arkansas. Most popular thus far is the series centering around Claire Malloy, set in "Farberville" and told in the first person by Claire. The young widow of an English professor, she supports herself and her teenaged daughter Caron by operating a bookstore called the Book Depot (it is in a refurbished train station). The relationship between mother and daughter is an important continuing motif in these novels; Claire views Caron with an amusing mixture of detachment, love, and dismay, and Caron's antics and enthusiasms are comically but sympathetically depicted. The other major continuing characters are Inez, Caron's best friend, and Lieutenant Peter Rosen of the Farberville CID, whom Claire meets in *Strangled Prose;* their relationship varies between frustrated rivalry and passion as it grows from novel to novel.

The Claire Malloy novels vary in theme. *Strangled Prose* is an academic mystery which turns on secrets in the background of English professors at Farber College and on the identity of a writer of steamy romance novels. *The Murder at the Murder at the Mimosa Inn* is based on the fad for "murder weekends" in which participants are challenged to solve a fictitious mystery; the fake mystery becomes real, and Claire must solve not only the staged mystery but also Peter's real mystery involving drug dealing. *Dear Miss Demeanor* takes Claire into a public school as she substitutes for a journalism teacher accused of embezzling school funds; the homecoming festivities particularly bemuse Claire, and her description of the game and of the half-time events is one of Hess's best comic set-pieces.

A Really Cute Corpse and *A Diet to Die For,* take satiric views of provincial beauty pageants and of fad diets.

Hess's Ozarks series is set in and around the village of Maggody (population 755) and is related to the "mainstream" comic tradition of Caldwell's *Tobacco Road* and Faulkner's Snopes novels. The setting is backwoods Arkansas, with a larger than usual number of continuing characters and much more attention to specific and recurring settings, devices which succeed in making Maggody itself thematically central to the novels. The protagonist is police chief Arly Hanks, who brings detachment and relatively broad experience to her work, since she lived for some years in New York City.

The Ozarks mysteries have a harsher tone and somewhat

more farcical plotting than the Claire Malloy novels. Particularly interesting is their mixed point of view, in which segments narrated by Arly alternate with segments told in third-person perspective which allow readers to have information not available to Arly. This device permits Hess to enter the consciousness of a prospective murder victim as the trap is about to be sprung or even, in a hilarious instance in *Malice in Maggody*, to observe a skunk in the moment before it is startled into attacking an unsuspecting victim. The comedy is often broad and the view of rural life anything but romantic.

The third series, centered around Theo Bloomer, retired florist, is published under the pseudonym of Joan Hadley; it is distinguished from the other two series by using in its titles the names of exotic plants which are either important symbols or plot devices, by using a male protagonist, by being written entirely in third-person narration, and by being set outside Arkansas. The pattern is for Theo's sister to call him to rescue his niece, Dorrie, a spoiled Wellesley student, from an escapade she has gotten herself into in Israel (*The Night-Blooming Cereus*) or to chaperone Dorrie and her insufferable friends on a holiday in Jamaica (*The Deadly Ackee*). Dorrie and her friends are amusingly portrayed, and their preppie language is nicely captured.

Hess achieves variety of theme, tone, and approach while maintaining a remarkable evenness of quality. Her female detectives are believable and likable protagonists and investigators, and readers will follow with interest their relationships with their families and lovers. So far, each new Hess novel has been a well crafted mystery as well as an amusing examination of a particular setting and social milieu.

—Mary Jean DeMarr

HEXT, Harrington. *See* **PHILLPOTTS, Eden.**

HEYER, Georgette. Also wrote as Stella Martin. British. Born in Wimbledon, Surrey, 16 August 1902. Educated at seminary schools and Westminster College, London. Married George Ronald Rougier in 1925; one son. Lived in Tanganyika (now Tanzania), 1927–28, Yugoslavia, 1928–29, Sussex 1930–42, and London after 1942. *Died 5 July 1974.*

CRIME PUBLICATIONS

Novels (series: Superintendent Hannasyde; Inspector Hemingway)

Footsteps in the Dark. London, Longman, 1932.
Why Shoot a Butler? London, Longman, 1933; New York, Doubleday, 1936.
The Unfinished Clue. London, Longman, 1934; New York, Doubleday, 1937.
Death in the Stocks (Hannasyde). London, Longman, 1935; as *Merely Murder,* New York, Doubleday, 1935.
Behold, Here's Poison! (Hannasyde). London, Hodder and Stoughton, and New York, Doubleday, 1936.
They Found Him Dead (Hannasyde). London, Hodder and Stoughton, and New York, Doubleday, 1937.

A Blunt Instrument (Hannasyde). London, Hodder and Stoughton, and New York, Doubleday, 1938.
No Wind of Blame (Hemingway). London, Hodder and Stoughton, and New York, Doubleday, 1939.
Envious Casca (Hemingway). London, Hodder and Stoughton, and New York, Doubleday, 1941.
Penhallow. London, Heinemann, 1942; New York, Doubleday, 1943.
Duplicate Death (Hemingway). London, Heinemann, 1951; New York, Dutton, 1969.
Detection Unlimited (Hemingway). London, Heinemann, 1953; New York, Dutton, 1969.

OTHER PUBLICATIONS

Novels

The Black Moth. London, Constable, and Boston, Houghton Mifflin, 1921.
The Great Roxhythe. London, Hutchinson, 1922; Boston, Small Maynard, 1923.
The Transformation of Philip Jettan (as Stella Martin). London, Mills and Boon, 1923; as *Powder and Patch* (as Georgette Heyer), London, Heinemann, 1930; New York, Dutton, 1968.
Instead of the Thorn. London, Hutchinson, 1923; Boston, Small Maynard, 1924.
Simon the Coldheart. London, Heinemann, and Boston, Small Maynard, 1925.
These Old Shades. London, Heinemann, and Boston, Small Maynard, 1926.
Helen. London and New York, Longman, 1928.
The Masqueraders. London, Heinemann, 1928; New York, Longman, 1929.
Beauvallet. London, Heinemann, 1929; New York, Longman, 1930.
Pastel. London, and New York, Longman, 1929.
Barren Corn. London and New York, Longman, 1930.
The Conqueror. London, Heinemann, 1931; New York, Dutton, 1966.
The Convenient Marriage. London, Heinemann, 1934; New York, Dutton, 1966.
Devil's Cub. London, Heinemann, 1934; New York, Dutton, 1966.
Regency Buck. London, Heinemann, 1935; New York, Dutton, 1966.
The Talisman Ring. London, Heinemann, 1936; New York, Doubleday, 1937.
An Infamous Army. London, Heinemann, 1937; New York, Doubleday, 1938.
Royal Escape. London, Heinemann, 1938; New York, Doubleday, 1939.
The Spanish Bride. London, Heinemann, and New York, Doubleday, 1940.
The Corinthian. London, Heinemann, 1940; as *Beau Wyndham,* New York, Doubleday, 1941.
Faro's Daughter. London, Heinemann, 1941; New York, Doubleday, 1942.
Friday's Child. London, Heinemann, 1944; New York, Putnam, 1946.
The Reluctant Widow. London, Heinemann, and New York, Putnam, 1946.
The Foundling. London, Heinemann, and New York, Putnam, 1948.
Arabella. London, Heinemann, and New York, Putnam, 1949.

The Grand Sophy. London, Heinemann, and New York, Putnam, 1950.
The Quiet Gentleman. London, Heinemann, 1951; New York, Putnam, 1952.
Cotillion. London, Heinemann, and New York, Putnam, 1953.
The Toll-Gate. London, Heinemann, and New York, Putnam, 1954.
Bath Tangle. London, Heinemann, and New York, Putnam, 1955.
Sprig Muslin. London, Heinemann, and New York, Putnam, 1956.
April Lady. London, Heinemann, and New York, Putnam, 1957.
Sylvester; or, The Wicked Uncle. London, Heinemann, and New York, Putnam, 1957.
Venetia. London, Heinemann, 1958; New York, Putnam, 1959.
The Unknown Ajax. London, Heinemann, 1959; New York, Putnam, 1960.
A Civil Contract. London, Heinemann, 1961; New York, Putnam, 1962.
The Nonesuch. London, Heinemann, 1962; New York, Dutton, 1963.
False Colours. London, Bodley Head, 1963; New York, Dutton, 1964.
Frederica. London, Bodley Head, and New York, Dutton, 1965.
Black Sheep. London, Bodley Head, 1966; New York, Dutton, 1967.
Cousin Kate. London, Bodley Head, 1968; New York, Dutton, 1969.
Charity Girl. London, Bodley Head, and New York, Dutton, 1970.
Lady of Quality. London, Bodley Head, and New York, Dutton, 1972.
My Lord John. London, Bodley Head, and New York, Dutton, 1975.

Short Stories

Pistols for Two and Other Stories. London, Heinemann, 1960; New York, Dutton, 1964.

Play

Radio Play: *The Toll-Gate,* from her own novel, 1974.

*

Critical Study: *The Private World of Georgette Heyer* by Jane Aiken Hodge, London, Bodley Head, 1984.

*   *   *

The dozen detective novels of Georgette Heyer illustrate perfectly the development of the mystery genre in the Golden Age of the 1920's and 1930's. Usually operating within the closed world of a country house or a London party with the addition of extended family groups as major suspects and inheritance eventually revealed as the primary motive for murder, the novels rely on stock plots and characters so deftly handled and so cleverly written as to seem unique.

Although the plotting is successful in individual novels, when all of them are read in close succession their similarities become apparent. Shootings, hair-trigger devices, poisons, and daggers are repeated; identical methods for second murders are used several times in the novels, although each use is different. Heyer's unusual plot accessories include an ancient pair of stocks and a police truncheon.

The Scotland Yard detectives called in to solve several of the crimes are the unremarkable Superintendent Hannasyde and his subordinate Inspector Hemingway. In later novels the principal detective, Hemingway, is distinguished by his penchant for psychology and the theatre, his good-natured ribbing of subordinates, his claim to "flair," and a firm conviction that, when a case seems impossibly confused, he is close to a solution.

Among a plethora of suspects, Heyer creates a remarkable group of comic characters whose eccentric behavior often thwarts the serious investigation. Kenneth and Antonia Verker, who will inherit their step-brother's estate, cheerfully calculate for Hannasyde the many ways they might easily have murdered Arnold and still established their alibis (*Death in the Stocks*). Rosemary Kane, whose limited Russian ancestry provides her with a "tortured soul," is mocked by the characters in the novel and by Heyer in *They Found Him Dead,* but even more improbable is the self-centered, flamboyant, practical cabaret dancer Lola de Silva who arrives at Sir Arthur Billington-Smythe's proper house party as his son's fiancée (*The Unfinished Clue*). The most delightful figure is Vicky Fanshawe who costumes herself for various roles played out hourly for any audience in *No Wind of Blame;* as "Innocent Girl Suspected of Murder," "Mystery Woman," or "Tragic Muse," she annoys and amuses Hemingway whose psychological and theatrical interests are strongly tested.

In a regular subplot, Heyer includes a romance quite clearly patterned on her Regency love stories. The man, hero and sometimes also rake, is arrogant, intelligent, handsome, and often able to control the investigation despite being under suspicion himself. The heroine, generally spunky, is astonished by his declaration and proposal, having believed herself disliked and overlooked.

Heyer's most unusual mystery is *Penhallow* in which the wife of a bullying tyrant is shown plotting and executing his murder with ease. Suspicion falls on almost everyone else in the family and she begins to wish she could undo the murder. Eventually Penhallow's eldest son commits suicide for reasons known only to the reader, but the local police and the family assume that guilt for patricide was responsible. Unable to effect any change by a confession, the murderer keeps silent and remains undiscovered. The novel is rare in removing all internal suspicion from the wife and allowing only the reader to know the whole truth; the convention of "justice done" is forcefully challenged.

Although not so popular as her Regency romances Heyer's detective novels are better crafted and more enduring. They illustrate the style of mystery writing in her time while being sufficiently original to carry her unmistakable signature.

—Kathleen Gregory Klein

HIAASEN, Carl. American. Born in Fort Lauderdale, Florida, 12 March 1953. Educated at Emory University, Atlanta, Georgia 1970–72; University of Florida, Gainesville, 1972–74, B.A. in journalism 1974. Married Constance Lyford in 1970; one son. Reporter, Cocoa *Today,* Florida, 1974–76; since 1976, journalist, Miami *Herald,* Florida. Agent: Esther Newberg, International Creative Management, 40 West 57th Street, New York, New York 10019, U.S.A.

CRIME PUBLICATIONS

Novels

Powder Burn, with William D. Montalbano. New York, Atheneum, 1981.
Trap Line, with William D. Montalbano. New York, Atheneum, 1982.
A Death in China, with William D. Montalbano, New York, Atheneum, 1984; London, Sidgwick and Jackson, 1985.
Tourist Season. New York, Putnam, 1986; London, Futura, 1987.
Double Whammy. New York, Putnam, 1987; London, Century, 1988.
Skin Tight. New York, Putnam, 1989.

*

Manuscript Collection: Mugar Memorial Library, Boston University.

Carl Hiaasen comments:
My novels, especially the last three, exhibit a black humor peculiar to the newspaper business. Each of them also benefits from their location in South Florida, one of the most perverse and exciting places in America. As extreme as some of my scenes and characters may appear to many readers, they are easily recognised and appreciated by anyone who has spent a little time in Miami. Nothing that happens in my novels could not happen here in real life; much of it already has.

*   *   *

Carl Hiaasen's characters basically want to be left alone. But once roused, they are more than capable of striking back. They know their way around, they're good in a fight, and they know how to turn an enemy's weakness to their advantage. What makes Hiaasen's novels stand out is the unusual nature of the intrusions, the weird inventiveness of the situations, and the satirical edge in his writing. Hiaasen's imagination is completely unique, yet his writing is so matter-of-fact that the extraordinary seems reasonable. As Hiaasen notes in Double Whammy, "Living in Miami tended to recalibrate one's view of society."

A reporter and columnist for the Miami Herald, Hiaasen began his fiction writing career with three thrillers written in collaboration with William D. Montalbano. Powder Burn is a well-executed and quite readable version of a standard revenge story, in which an architect witnesses the incidental killing of an old girlfriend and her daughter by drug dealers. The details of Florida's drug world might have been sensational when the book was first published in 1981, but the television series Miami Vice has made it commonplace. The book is also naive and melodramatic in a way that Hiaasen's solo efforts never are, with portentous talk of justice, vigilantes and judicial restraint on cops. But Powder Burn also establishes the parameters for the Hiaasen hero and his plots. Architect Chris Meadows dislikes what newcomers are doing to his native state. He would not be involved but for the actions of others who intrude into his life. When he's mugged, he first accepts it "as a form of taxation people who walk at night must be prepared to pay," but when the mugger threatens his female companion, Meadows quickly disarms him and "methodically stripped the man of his clothes, mugging the mugger." When Meadows plans his retribution against the drug kingpins, he concocts an elaborate plan that takes advantage of their own weaknesses; he's too cool to do anything too direct.

Trap Line, the second and best of the three Hiaasen and Montalbano collaborations, explores the Conch-fishing community of Key West. It's also a revenge story. Drug dealers pressure Breeze Albury, a fisherman with a criminal record, into transporting a group of Colombians from the Bahamas into Florida. The pressure includes injuring Breeze's son, and the deal turns out to be a set-up when the Colombians try to kill Breeze and his crew. Breeze's retribution is typically clever and expertly managed, and the book is a satisfying page-turner. A Death in China doesn't fit the mold, with its setting and unsurprising plot; though the authors' view of China is not without interest, the novel lacks distinction.

Hiaasen's first novel on his own was Tourist Season and, like each of his subsequent books, it's a wildly original creation, even in light of the three thrillers that preceded it. It opens with the disappearance of a Shriner, who's in Miami for a convention. At the same time, the president of the Greater Miami Chamber of Commerce is found murdered: he was dressed in a garish tropical outfit, covered with suntan oil, choked by a toy alligator lodged in his throat and finally stuffed in a suitcase and tossed into the ocean. Reporter turned private investigator Brian Keyes is hired to clear the man driving the Chamber president's car after the murder. The case takes him back to the Miami Sun and to columnist Skip Wiley, who once listed his occupation on his tax form as "prophet, redeemer, and sage," and who recently suggested that what Florida really needed was a killer hurricane to clear the state out.

Tourist Season is consistently inventive, but what's more surprising is that Skip Wiley's outlandish point of view—and the lengths to which he goes to further it—develops its own peculiar logic; by the end we're as much on his side as anyone else's. What really makes the novel work, however, is Hiaasen's calm, sensible prose; it goes a long way towards making even his most outrageous ideas and situations make sense. Hiaasen scores his points and skewers his targets, but the tone is never bitter; he writes passionately but never turns us off with anger. Early on, we learn about the Allen Mutilation Theorem, which posits that Miami's high rate of mutilation homicides is attributable to its "terrific climate. In warm weather, Allen noted, there were no outdoor elements to deter a lunatic from spending six, seven, eight hours hacking away on a victim." Later, he explains how a terrorist is singled out for the position of defense minister due to his "Ivy League typing skills . . . one of the most vital roles in any terrorist group was the composing of letters to take credit for the violence. The letters had to be ominous, oblique, and neatly typed." The cheerful reasonableness of these explanations is vintage Hiaasen.

In Double Whammy, private detective R.J. Decker investigates cheating on the professional bass-fishing circuit. The story is certainly unusual and the characters are wonderfully colorful, but the book suffers from an inconsistent pace and shades of melodrama. Much more successful is Skin Tight, which opens with Mick Stranahan surviving an inexplicable assassination attempt. Stranahan, a retired investigator for the Florida State Attorney's Office, backtracks to figure out which of the cases he investigated has come back to haunt him. He finally lands on the disappearance of a woman who had just had her nose fixed by a plastic surgeon.

The machinations of the large cast are bizarre and convoluted, but Hiaasen manages every twist perfectly, achieving a new level of control over his material without sacrificing the humor or the originality. Skin Tight revels in

Florida's "climate of unabashed corruption." With Hiaasen's wit and imagination, there isn't a better place to be.

—Jim Huang

————

HIGGINS, George V(incent). American. Born in Brockton, Massachusetts, 13 November 1939. Educated at Rockland High School, Massachusetts; Boston College, A.B. in English 1961; Stanford University, California, 1961–62, M.A. 1965; Boston College Law School, Brighton, Massachusetts, J.D. 1967; admitted to the Massachusetts Bar, 1967. Married 1) Elizabeth Mulkerin in 1965 (divorced 1979), one daughter and one son; 2) Loretta Lucas Cubberley in 1979. Reporter, *Journal* and *Evening Bulletin,* Providence, Rhode Island, 1962–63; bureau correspondent, Springfield, Massachusetts, 1963–64, and journalist, Boston, 1964–66, Associated Press; researcher, Guterman Horvitz and Rubin, attorneys, Boston, 1966–67; legal assistant, Administrative Division and Organized Crime Section, 1967, Deputy Assistant Attorney General, 1967–69, and Assistant Attorney General, 1969–70, Commonwealth of Massachusetts; Assistant U.S. Attorney for the District of Massachusetts, 1970–73, and Special Assistant U.S. Attorney, 1973–74; President, George V. Higgins, Inc., Boston, 1973–78; Partner, Griffin and Higgins, Boston, 1978–82. Consultant, National Institute of Law Enforcement and Criminal Law, Washington, D.C., 1970–71; Instructor in Trial Practice, Boston College Law School, 1973–74 and 1978–79; columnist, Boston *Herald American,* 1977–79, Boston *Globe* 1979–85, and *Wall Street Journal,* 1984–87. Visiting Professor, SUNY, Buffalo, 1988. DHL, Westfield State College, Massachusetts, 1986. Address: 15 Brush Hill Lane, Milton, Massachusetts 02186, U.S.A.

CRIME PUBLICATIONS

Novels (series: Kennedy)

The Friends of Eddie Coyle. New York, Knopf, and London, Secker and Warburg, 1972.
The Digger's Game. New York, Knopf, and London, Secker and Warburg, 1973.
Cogan's Trade. New York, Knopf, and London, Secker and Warburg, 1974.
The Judgment of Deke Hunter. Boston, Little Brown, and London, Secker and Warburg, 1976.
A Year or So with Edgar. New York, Harper, and London, Secker and Warburg, 1979.
Kennedy for the Defense. New York, Knopf, and London, Secker and Warburg, 1980.
The Rat on Fire. New York, Knopf, and London, Secker and Warburg, 1981.
The Patriot Game. New York, Knopf, and London, Secker and Warburg, 1982.
A Choice of Enemies. New York, Knopf, and London, Secker and Warburg, 1984.
Penance for Jerry Kennedy. New York, Holt, and London, Deutsch, 1985.
Imposters. New York, Holt, and London, Deutsch, 1986.
Outlaws. New York, Holt, and London, Deutsch, 1987.
The Sins of Their Father. London, Deutsch, and New York, Holt, 1988.

Wonderful Years, Wonderful Years. New York, Holt, and London, Deutsch, 1988.
Trust. New York, Holt, and London, Deutsch, 1989.

Uncollected Short Stories

"All Day Was All There Was," in *Arizona Quarterly* (Tucson), Spring 1963.
"Something of a Memoir," in *Massachusetts Review* (Amherst), Summer 1969.
"Mass in Time of War," in *Cimarron Review* (Stillwater, Oklahoma), September 1969.
"Something Dirty You Could Keep," in *Massachusetts Review* (Amherst), Autumn 1969.
"Dillon Explained That He Was Frightened," in *North American Review* (Cedar Falls, Iowa), Fall 1970.
"The Habits of Animals, The Progress of the Seasons," in *The Best American Short Stories 1973,* edited by Martha Foley. Boston, Houghton Mifflin, 1973.
"Two Cautionary Tales: Donnelly's Uncle and The Original Watercourse," in *North American Review* (Cedar Falls, Iowa), Winter 1974.
"Warm for September" and "A Place of Comfort, Light, and Hope," in *North American Review* (Cedar Falls, Iowa), Spring 1977.
"Dublin Coat," in *Harper's* (New York), August 1980.
"Adults," in *Playboy* (Chicago), December 1982.
"Devlin's Wake," in *Playboy* (Chicago), December 1983.
"Ducks and Other Citizens," in *Hudson Review* (New York), Winter 1983–84.

OTHER PUBLICATIONS

Novels

A City on a Hill. New York, Knopf, and London, Secker and Warburg, 1975.
Dreamland. Boston, Little Brown, and London, Secker and Warburg, 1977.

Other

The Friends of Richard Nixon. Boston, Little Brown, 1975.
Style Versus Substance: Boston, Kevin White, and the Politics of Illusion. New York, Macmillan, 1984.
Progress of the Seasons: Forty Years of Baseball in Our Town. New York, Holt, 1989.
On Writing: Advice to Those Who Write to Publish (or Would Like to). New York, Holt, 1990.

*   *   *

George V. Higgins has been associated with realistic dialog, intricate plotting, and a persistent digging into the political, social, and criminal landscapes of Greater Boston since the publication in 1972 of *The Friends of Eddie Coyle.* In one deft performance, Higgins had landed a first-rate publisher, established a large following, and inspired imitators.

A year later came *The Digger's Game,* and more of the same: dialog as polished as a gem-collector's specimens, a labyrinthine plot, and, above all, understated sympathy for the little people of the world who are forced by circumstances to elbow their way to the trough before the sustenance therein is all gone, slurped up by the bigger guys. Words like promising, unrelenting, and authentic were intoned over his works, and he was clearly someone to watch.

By profession a lawyer and with considerable background in writing, Higgins speaks in a voice that rings with social conscience and aspires to the timbre of Dickens; his targets are the legal proceedings and finessing of Massachusetts politics. He is especially forceful at detailing the trickle-down from the political deals at their inceptions to their lower points, where they become the day-to-day payoffs and petty crime of those less fortunate than the king makers.

When Higgins turned over the rock in the fecund garden of the small-time hood, the cop on the pad, and the corrupt politico, it was neither to point a reproving finger or offer the homily that boys will be boys; it was to let the characters scramble, connive, and reveal themselves. What they revealed is that some of them stole, looked the other way, perjured themselves, and conspired on such mean levels because they were taking the only opportunity at the trough that they were likely to get.

Higgins's language sounded so real that we believed it was Boston Irish whether we knew better or not: we believe it because Higgins so deftly made it so, and we waited for more, thinking that here was the authentic stuff, because didn't Higgins know the language of crime, corruption, and plea-bargaining, too.

In the subsequent years, Higgins has published *Cogan's Trade, The Judgment of Deke Hunter, Kennedy for the Defense,* and *A Choice of Enemies, Penance for Jerry Kennedy,* and others which fall within the purview of this volume, plus material that lies outside it, although it is certainly arguable that *The Friends of Richard Nixon* is aptly included among Higgins's mystery and crime writing. The jury that was out after Eddie Coyle and the Digger came shambling in with Cogan; they couldn't look us in the eye when they pronounced it a solid work. Deke Hunter had some of the old magic, but by now we could see that the veneer was wearing thin. Kennedy brought a hope of new gloss, but *A Choice of Enemies* leads the reader to the uneasy conviction that Higgins now believes his own voice and feels no need to show us how his people became the way they are. Change the names, locales, and ethnicity, and Higgins's people can be moved to Albuquerque, Seattle, or St. Paul, a fact that effectively demonstrates the paradox of his work to date: he can be brilliantly universal, but he remains to be convincingly specific.

It would be patronizing and unfair to write him off as promising; he is properly ranked with such polished and original stylists as Wambaugh and Leonard. It will be instructive and entertaining to watch him peel more of the onion that is the Commonwealth of Massachusetts, with its rich assortment of individuals who perform for reasons Higgins has yet to divulge.

—Shelly Lowenkopf

HIGGINS, Jack. Pseudonym for Henry Patterson; also writes as Martin Fallon; James Graham; Hugh Marlowe. British and Irish (dual citizenship). Born in Newcastle on Tyne, 27 July 1929. Educated at Leeds Training College for Teachers, Cert. Ed. 1958; University of London, B.Sc. (honours) in sociology 1962. Served in the Royal Horse Guards, British Army, 1947–49. Married 1) Amy Margaret Hewitt in 1958 (dissolved 1984), three daughters and one son. 2) Denise Lesley Anne Palmer in 1985. Worked in commercial and civil service posts, 1950–55; History Teacher, Allerton Grange Comprehensive School, Leeds, 1958–64; Lecturer in Liberal Studies, Leeds College of Commerce, 1964–68; Senior Lecturer in Education, James Graham College, New Farnley, Yorkshire, 1968–70; Tutor, Leeds University, 1971–73. Fellow, Royal Society of Arts. Agent: Ed Victor, 162 Wardour Street, London W1V 3AT, England.

CRIME PUBLICATIONS

Novels (series: Liam Devlin; Brigadier Dougal Munro and Captain Jack Carter)

East of Desolation. London, Hodder and Stoughton, 1968; New York, Doubleday, 1969.
In the Hour Before Midnight. London, Hodder and Stoughton, 1969; as *The Sicilian Heritage,* New York, Lancer, 1970.
Night Judgment at Sinos. London, Hodder and Stoughton, 1970; New York, Doubleday, 1971.
The Last Place God Made. London, Collins, 1971; New York, Holt Rinehart, 1972.
The Savage Day. London, Collins, and New York, Holt Rinehart, 1972.
A Prayer for the Dying. London, Collins, 1973; New York, Holt Rinehart, 1974.
The Eagle Has Landed (Devlin). London, Collins, and New York, Holt Rinehart, 1975; revised edition, London, Pan, 1982.
Storm Warning. London, Collins, and New York, Holt Rinehart, 1976.
Day of Judgement. London, Collins, 1978; New York, Holt Rinehart, 1979.
Solo. London, Collins, and New York, Stein and Day, 1980.
Luciano's Luck. London, Collins, and New York, Stein and Day, 1981.
Touch the Devil (Devlin). London, Collins, and New York, Stein and Day, 1982.
Exocet. London, Collins, and New York, Stein and Day, 1983.
Confessional (Devlin). London, Collins, and New York, Stein and Day, 1985.
Night of the Fox (Munro and Carter). London, Collins, 1986; New York, Simon and Schuster, 1987.
A Season in Hell. London, Collins, and New York, Simon and Schuster, 1989.
Memoirs of a Dance Hall Romeo. London, Collins, and New York, Simon and Schuster, 1989.
Cold Harbour (Munro and Carter). London, Heinemann, and New York, Simon and Schuster, 1990.

Novels as Harry Patterson (series: Nick Miller; published as Jack Higgins in US)

Sad Wind from the Sea. London, Long, 1959.
Cry of the Hunter. London, Long, 1960.
The Thousand Faces of Night. London, Long, 1961.
Comes the Dark Stranger. London, Long, 1962.
Hell Is Too Crowded. London, Long, 1962; New York, Fawcett, 1976.
Pay the Devil. London, Barrie and Rockliff, 1963.
The Dark Side of the Island. London, Long, 1963; New York, Fawcett, 1977.
A Phoenix in the Blood. London, Barrie and Rockliff, 1964.
Thunder at Noon. London, Long, 1964.
Wrath of the Lion. London, Long, 1964; New York, Fawcett, 1977.
The Graveyard Shift (Miller). London, Long, 1965.
The Iron Tiger. London, Long, 1966; New York, Fawcett, 1974.

Brought in Dead (Miller).   London, Long, 1967.

Hell Is Always Today.   London, Long, 1968; New York, Fawcett, 1979.

Toll for the Brave.   London, Long, 1971; New York, Fawcett, 1976.

The Valhalla Exchange.   New York, Stein and Day, 1976; London, Hutchinson, 1977.

To Catch a King.   New York, Stein and Day, and London, Hutchinson, 1979.

Dillinger.   London, Hutchinson, and New York, Stein and Day, 1983.

Novels as Martin Fallon (series: Paul Chavasse in all books)

The Testament of Caspar Schultz.   London and New York, Abelard Schuman, 1962.

Year of the Tiger.   London and New York, Abelard Schuman, 1963.

The Keys of Hell.   London and New York, Abelard Schuman, 1965.

Midnight Never Comes.   London, Long, 1966; New York, Fawcett, 1975.

Dark Side of the Street.   London, Long, 1967; New York, Fawcett, 1974.

A Fine Night for Dying.   London, Long, 1969.

Novels as Hugh Marlowe

Seven Pillars to Hell.   London and New York, Abelard Schuman, 1963.

Passage by Night.   London and New York, Abelard Schuman, 1964.

A Candle for the Dead.   London and New York, Abelard Schuman, 1966; as *The Violent Enemy,* London, Hodder and Stoughton, 1969.

Novels as James Graham

A Game for Heroes.   London, Macmillan, and New York, Doubleday, 1970.

The Wrath of God.   London, Macmillan, and New York, Doubleday, 1971.

The Khufra Run.   London, Macmillan, 1972; New York, Doubleday, 1973.

Bloody Passage.   London, Macmillan, 1974; as *The Run to Morning,* New York, Stein and Day, 1974.

OTHER PUBLICATIONS

Play

Radio Script: *The Island City,* 1987; *Dead of Night,* (1 episode), 1990.

*

Jack Higgins comments:

The change in style of writing after many books which led to international fame and translation into as many as 42 languages came with *The Savage Day,* a thriller dealing with the early years of the Irish Troubles which contained an underlying quite serious political theme. From *The Eagle Has Landed* onwards, a string of international best sellers has contained, within the format of the successful thriller, an underlying theme of importance to do with either politics, morality, religion, or the human condition. This and a gift for characterisation not normally found on the thriller shelf have helped create a very recognisable "Higgins" style.

*   *   *

Of all the pseudonyms Harry Patterson writes under, Jack Higgins is by far the best known. A Higgins book features adventure, action, strong characters, and breathless excitement. The best Higgins books take a plausible plotline and add a mix of real and fictional characters. The most successful and well known Jack Higgins novel is *The Eagle Has Landed,* the story of a secret Nazi operation to kidnap Winston Churchill in 1943. A small group of German paratroopers attempt to change the balance of the war, while the English and Americans race against the clock to stop them. The suspense is generated by the novel's realism in depicting World War II and historical events.

The latest Higgins bestseller, *Cold Harbour,* contains all of these elements. The setting is France, May 1944—just a month from D-Day. The Allies know that if they can discover the gun placements of the Nazis' Atlantic Wall, thousands of lives could be saved during the invasion and success would be assured. The Germans plan a conference at an elegant French chateau where Rommel will be in attendance. Brigadier Dougal Munro and his top agent Craig Osbourne, plan to use a beautiful amateur, Anne-Marie Trevaunce to spy on the conference, but when she is disabled, they turn to Anne-Marie's twin sister, Genevieve Trevaunce. Racing with the clock, they prepare Genevieve to take on Anne-Marie's identity for a mission that could control the success or failure of D-Day. *Cold Harbour* is Higgins at his best.

A Season in Hell blends other of Higgins's themes together in a satisfying thriller. A young widow, Sarah Talbot, tries to discover why her stepson was brutally murdered in Paris. But officials are unable to explain the cause of the death or bring his killers to justice. Sarah finds help in the form of a SAS sergeant, Sean Egan, and together they follow the trail of death from London to Paris, to the Sicilian fortress of a Mafia don to the estate of a powerful Ulster politician. *A Season in Hell* is top-notch entertainment.

In *Night of the Fox,* Higgins further develops his preoccupation with D-Day. Colonel Kelso is one of the few members of the Allied high command who know the full details of D-Day. But when he is captured and held on German-occupied Jersey, agent Harry Martineau is called upon to rescue Kelso before he's forced to tell his secrets to the Nazis. The plot is exciting and the action is furious. *Night of the Fox* is one of Higgins's best World War II thrillers.

Considered the best of Higgins's novel, *Storm Warning,* opens with a small band of Germans and five nuns attempting to cross the storm-racked Atlantic aboard an old sailing ship. Germany is losing World War II but these characters want to leave Brazil to join their families 5,000 miles away. Many Higgins books are set during World War II, but in *Storm Warning,* the war is only a backdrop to the real action to the struggle of the characters against the sea. In the powerful conclusion, allegiances are forgotten as the English and Germans join forces to battle the sea. *Storm Warning* is a classic tale of epic proportions.

Another best-selling Higgins novel, *Exocet,* deals with a Russian plot to assist Argentina's effort to obtain more Exocet missiles to use against the British in the Falklands war. The secret British intelligence agency D15 fights against long odds to foil the hijack of the French missiles. In *Exocet,* Patterson proves he can write a Jack Higgins novel with a contemporary setting as realistic and exciting as his best-selling World War II books.

Patterson writes successful novels under his own name. The best known is *To Catch a King*. After the Duke of Windsor has abandoned the throne of England to marry the woman he loved, he lives in semi-exile in Portugal, slowly becoming bitter toward his brother, the king of England. Hitler believes the Duke would accept an offer to rule England after Germany triumphs. From this premise, Patterson builds an overpowering plot to convince the Duke—and if that fails, to kidnap the Royal couple for propaganda purposes. Only a young Jewish singer, Hannah Winter, stands between the Nazis' success or failure.

Other successful Patterson novels include *Dillinger*, a gangster *tour de force*, and *The Valhalla Exchange*, the story of Martin Bormann's plot to escape to South America. All the novels published under the Harry Patterson byline share the virtues of the Jack Higgins books: realistic plotting, strong characters, and plenty of action.

As popular as the Jack Higgins/Harry Patterson novels are, Patterson's best work was written under the James Graham pseudonym. This series of high adventure novels feature daring and energy ranking with the best of Alistair MacLean. *A Game for Heroes* involves a commando raid on a Nazi-held island in the English Channel. *The Wrath of God* presents three criminals a choice: take the police offer of an impossible mission to hunt down Mexico's most vicious bandit—or be hanged. They take the mission and the result is Roaring Twenties non-stop action. In *The Khufra Run*, Jack Nelson, a freelance pilot and soldier of fortune, gets into more hairbreadth escapes and cliff-hanging situations than Indiana Jones. *Bloody Passage*, the story of an attempt to break a prisoner out of an impenetrable Libyan prison, is the most exciting of the James Graham books.

Patterson's books written under the Martin Fallon pseudonym are his weakest; essentially these books are Patterson's apprenticeship as a suspense writer. The Martin Fallon books all star special agent Paul Chavasse in a variety of locales, giving Patterson a chance to stretch his writing skills with each book. The best of the Fallon books is *Dark Side of the Street* where Chavasse's mission is to stop a criminal group specializing in prison breakouts.

The Hugh Marlowe books are a step up in quality from the Martin Fallon novels, but *Seven Pillars to Hell*, *Passage By Night*, and *Candle for the Dead* all show flaws of a writer learning his craft. The best of these is *Passage By Night*, a powerful vengeance novel marred only by shallow characterizations.

Harry Patterson has produced a steady stream of suspense novels for the past 30 years. Although prolific, Patterson maintains a standard of quality that keeps his work—both under his name and the Jack Higgins pseudonym—constantly on the best-seller lists.

—George Kelley

————

HIGHLAND, Dora. *See* **AVALLONE, Michael.**

————

HIGHSMITH, Patricia. Has also written as Claire Morgan. American. Born Mary Patricia Plangman in Fort Worth, Texas, 19 January 1921; took stepfather's name. Educated at Julia Richmond, High School, New York; Barnard College, New York, B.A. 1942. Has lived in Europe since 1963. Recipient: Grand Prix de Littérature Policière, 1957; Crime Writers Association Silver Dagger award, 1964. Agent: Marianne Ligginstofer, Diogenes Verlag, Sprecherstrasse 8, CH-8032 Zurich, Switzerland.

CRIME PUBLICATIONS

Novels (series: Tom Ripley)

Strangers on a Train. New York, Harper, and London, Cresset Press, 1950.
The Blunderer. New York, Coward McCann, 1954; London, Cresset Press, 1956; as *Lament for a Lover*, New York, Popular Library, 1956.
The Talented Mr. Ripley. New York, Coward McCann, 1955; London, Cresset Press, 1957.
Deep Water. New York, Harper, 1957; London, Heinemann, 1958.
A Game for the Living. New York, Harper, 1958; London, Heinemann, 1959.
This Sweet Sickness. New York, Harper, 1960; London, Heinemann, 1961.
The Cry of the Owl. New York, Harper, 1962; London, Heinemann, 1963.
The Two Faces of January. New York, Doubleday, and London, Heinemann, 1964.
The Glass Cell. New York, Doubleday, 1964; London, Heinemann, 1965.
The Story-Teller. New York, Doubleday, 1965; as *A Suspension of Mercy*, London, Heinemann, 1965.
Those Who Walk Away. New York, Doubleday, and London, Heinemann, 1967.
The Tremor of Forgery. New York, Doubleday, and London, Heinemann, 1969.
Ripley under Ground. New York, Doubleday, 1970; London, Heinemann, 1971.
A Dog's Ransom. New York, Knopf, and London, Heinemann, 1972.
Ripley's Game. New York, Knopf, and London, Heinemann, 1974.
Edith's Diary. New York, Simon and Schuster, and London, Heinemann, 1977.
The Boy Who Followed Ripley. New York, Lippincott, and London, Heinemann, 1980.
People Who Knock on the Door. London, Heinemann, 1983; New York, Mysterious Press, 1985.
Found in the Street. London, Heinemann, 1986; New York, Atlantic Monthly Press, 1987.

Short Stories

The Snail-Watcher and Other Stories. New York, Doubleday, 1970; as *Eleven*, London, Heinemann, 1970.
Kleine Geschichten für Weiberfeinde. Zurich, Diogenes, 1974; as *Little Tales of Misogyny*, London, Heinemann, 1977; New York, Mysterious Press, 1986.
The Animal-Lover's Book of Beastly Murder. London, Heinemann, 1975; New York, Mysterious Press, 1986.
Slowly, Slowly in the Wind. London, Heinemann, 1979; New York, Mysterious Press, 1987.
The Black House. London, Heinemann, 1981.
Mermaids on the Golf Course and Other Stories. London, Heinemann, 1985; New York, Mysterious Press, 1988.
Tales of Natural and Unnatural Catastrophes. London, Bloomsbury, 1987; New York, Atlantic Monthly Press, 1989.

OTHER PUBLICATIONS

Novel

The Price of Salt (as Claire Morgan). New York, Coward McCann, 1952; as *Carol* (as Patricia Highsmith), London, Bloomsbury, 1990.

Other

Miranda the Panda Is on the Veranda (for children), with Doris Sanders. New York, Coward McCann, 1958.
Plotting and Writing Suspense Fiction. Boston, The Writer, 1966; London, Poplar Press, 1983.

*

Critical Study: *Über Patricia Highsmith* edited by Franz Cavigelli and Fritz Senn, Zurich, Diogenes, 1980.

*   *   *

In a writing career spanning 40 years, Patricia Highsmith has dignified and complicated the forms of crime fiction. Her remarkable output is highly distinctive in its austerity of mood and in its dark brooding qualities. Her characterisation and her construction of setting are more subtle and deft than that of any of her contemporaries, and she has attracted praise and admiration from such authorities as Graham Greene and Julian Symons. Although she has never achieved the popularity of Christie or Chandler, her writing is treated with immense respect, particularly in France and Germany.

Highsmith's crime novels resist easy categorisation as either "whodunnits" or thrillers, and there are complex issues and provocative tensions lying beneath the surface of even her raciest stories. In her first (and still her best-known) novel, *Strangers on a Train,* she introduced an elaborate plot in which two men, previously unconnected, apparently agree to dispose of the encumbrance in each other's lives. Guy Haines, a respectable architect, has an unhappy marriage, and Bruno, the man he falls into casual conversation with on a train journey, has a domineering mother. The most obvious solution, as proposed by the chillingly friendly Bruno, is that he murders Guy's wife, and Guy murders Bruno's mother. Since there would be no real connection between murderer and victim in either case, the crimes would be untraceable. From this simple beginning, Highsmith spins an enthralling suspense plot involving all her recurrent themes of coincidence, guilt, complicity, rationality, and neurosis. In many of her subsequent novels, she takes these basic elements, and reformulates them to powerful effect, without her books ever seeming merely formulaic. In *The Blunderer*, for instance, she shows how the central character, Walter Stackhouse, inadvertently incriminates himself in his wife's accidental death by repeatedly visiting a man who murdered his own wife in a suspiciously similar fashion. In the brilliant *Deep Water*, we are shown how madness and obsession co-exist with the humdrum and orderly life of the psychopathic killer Walter Van Allen. Further examinations of the difference between being guilty and feeling guilty and of the role of obsession and fantasy in "ordinary" life are worked out with austere fascination in her cosmopolitan novels of the 1960's, the best of which include *The Cry of the Owl, The Glass Cell, The Story-Teller, A Suspension of Mercy,* and *The Tremor of Forgery*.

In all of these books, set throughout Europe, North Africa and the United States, Highsmith seems very dismissive of the emotional possibilities of innocence. Her characters are all surrounded by circumstantial evidence of their own guilt and complicity in crime, which the truly innocent haplessly internalise and which the truly guilty ignore. Highsmith's writing is thus profoundly ironic in its refusal to recognise the possibilities of justice, and it is appropriately aloof and distanced in its treatment of the moral issues raised. As she puts it herself, in her fascinating book *Plotting and Writing Suspense Fiction,* "creative people do not pass moral judgements—at least not at once—on what meets their eye. There is time for that later in what they create, if they are so inclined, but art has nothing to do with morality, convention or moralizing."

This reluctance to judge or to help readers easily allocate sympathy or animosity to characters makes her writing approach the condition of black comedy at times. This is particularly obvious in the series of novels featuring the agreeable and urbane psychopath, Tom Ripley, namely *The Talented Mr. Ripley, Ripley under Ground, Ripley's Game,* and *The Boy Who Followed Ripley*. Although some critics have found Highsmith's laconic and cerebral presentation of her fraudulent and murderous hero lacking in perspective, it is her very disinterest which makes her work remarkable. In many ways, particularly in her scrupulous avoidance of emotional rhetoric, she is one of the most faithful progeny of the naturalist novel. She may restrict the emotional subjects of her writing to those bounded by obsession, fear, and distrust, but within that range she is fastidious and unremitting in her dissections.

With the publication of *Edith's Diary* in 1977, Highsmith's writing took on greater strength of purpose. This very disconcerting book reveals a woman collapsing into madness through her invention of an alternative fantasy world. To replace her own unsatisfactory domestic life (unfaithful husband, wastrel son, incontinent and ill-tempered live-in relative), she constructs a more soothing and therapeutic version in her diary (loving husband, successful son, charming old relative). Her strategy works for a while, but eventually the stress of having to avoid confrontation with reality proves impossible to sustain. This book was followed by another critique of the alleged security of middle-class American family life, *People Who Knock on the Door,* in which the fundamentalist religious revival wreaks havoc in an intense and representatively awkward household. There are scenes in this book—the embarrassing family Thanksgiving meal, the meetings between the adolescent male and his ex-girlfriend—which are the most accomplished things Highsmith has written to date. Her most recent novel, *Found in the Street,* is an even more discomforting analysis of urban alienation and the dislocation of values, worked out through an inspection of contemporary New York life. In its unpretentious way, it is a much more provocative and caustic novel than many more lauded productions, like Tom Wolfe's *Bonfire of the Vanities*.

With these three novels, which represent the fruition of everything that her work has attempted, Highsmith has taken the suspense story to new heights. She has developed a form which is subtle enough to contain shrewd political and social analysis, without sacrificing compulsiveness or the simple responsibilities of story-telling. She may still be, as Julian Symons believed an "acquired taste," and her bleakness of vision may not be attractive to everyone, but her work demands to be read by anyone interested in the potential of crime fiction to carry more important themes, or to represent all the tensions and complexities of modern life.

Highsmith has also been a prolific writer of anecdotal short stories, and her most recent collection, *Tales of Natural and Unnatural Catastrophes,* sees her taking on wider ecological themes. The suspense in these tales is created by the feeling that time is running out, not just for one character within a novel, but for all of us.

—Ian A. Bell

* * *

HILL, Reginald. Also writes as Dick Morland; Patrick Ruell; Charles Underhill. British. Born in Hartlepool, County Durham, 3 April 1936. Educated at the Grammar School, Carlisle, Cumberland, 1947–55; St. Catherine's College, Oxford, 1957–60, B.A. (honours) in English 1960. Served in the Border Regiment, British Army, 1955–57. Married Patricia Ruell in 1960. Student officer, British Council, Edinburgh, 1960–61; schoolmaster, Essex, 1962–67; Lecturer, Doncaster College of Education, Yorkshire 1967–81. Since 1981 full-time writer. Agent: Caradoc King. A.P. Watt Ltd., 20 John Street, London WC1N 2DR. Address: "Oakbank," Broad Oak, Ravenglass, Cumbria CA18 1RN, England.

CRIME PUBLICATIONS

Novels (series: Superintendent Andrew Dalziel and Sergeant Pascoe)

A Clubbable Woman (Dalziel and Pascoe). London, Collins, 1970; Woodstock, Vermont, Countryman Press, 1984.
Fell of Dark. London, Collins, 1971; New York, New American Library, 1986.
An Advancement of Learning (Dalziel and Pascoe). London, Collins, 1971; Woodstock, Vermont, Countryman Press, 1985.
A Fairly Dangerous Thing. London, Collins, 1972; Woodstock, Vermont, Countryman Press, 1983.
Ruling Passion (Dalziel and Pascoe). London, Collins, 1973; New York, Harper, 1977.
A Very Good Hater. London, Collins, 1974; Woodstock, Vermont, Countryman Press, 1982.
An April Shroud (Dalziel and Pascoe). London, Collins, 1975; Woodstock, Vermont, Countryman Press, 1986.
Another Death in Venice. London, Collins, 1976; New York, New American Library, 1987.
A Pinch of Snuff (Dalziel and Pascoe). London, Collins, and New York, Harper, 1978.
The Spy's Wife. London, Collins, and New York, Pantheon, 1980.
A Killing Kindness (Dalziel and Pascoe). London, Collins, 1980; New York, Pantheon, 1981.
Who Guards a Prince? London, Collins, 1982; as *Who Guards the Prince?*, New York, Pantheon, 1982; as *Guardians of the Prince,* London, Fontana, 1983.
Traitor's Blood. London, Collins, 1983; Woodstock, Vermont, Countryman Press, 1986.
Deadheads (Dalziel and Pascoe). London, Collins, 1983; New York, Macmillan, 1984.
Exit Lines (Dalziel and Pascoe). London, Collins, 1984; New York, Macmillan, 1985.
No Man's Land. London, Collins, and New York, St. Martin's Press, 1985.
Child's Play (Dalziel and Pascoe). London, Collins, and New York, Macmillan, 1987.
The Collaborators. London, Collins, 1987; Woodstock, Vermont, Countryman Press, 1989.

Under World (Dalziel and Pascoe). London, Collins, and New York, Scribner, 1988.
Bones and Silence (Dalziel and Pascoe). London, Collins, and New York, Delacorte Press, 1990.

Novels as Patrick Ruell

The Castle of the Demon. London, Long, 1971; New York, Hawthorn, 1973.
Red Christmas. London, Long, 1972; New York, Hawthorn, 1974.
Death Takes the Low Road. London, Hutchinson, 1974; New York, Mysterious Press, 1987.
Urn Burial. London, Hutchinson, 1975; Woodstock, Vermont, Countryman Press, 1987.
The Long Kill. London, Methuen, 1986; Woodstock, Vermont, Countryman Press, 1988.
Death of a Dormouse. London, Methuen, and New York, Mysterious Press, 1987.
Dream of Darkness. London, Methuen, 1989.

Short Stories

Pascoe's Ghost. London, Collins, 1979; New York, New American Library, 1989.
There Are No Ghosts in the Soviet Union. London, Collins, 1987; Woodstock, Vermont, Countryman Press, 1988.

Uncollected Short Stories

"The Thaw," in *Winter's Crimes 5,* edited by Virginia Whitaker. London, Macmillan, 1973.
"The Worst Crime Known to Man," in *Sunday Express* (London), 28 July 1984.
"Urban Legend," in *Ellery Queen's Mystery Magazine* (New York), March 1989.

Novels

Heart Clock (as Dick Morland). London, Faber, 1973.
Albion! Albion! (as Dick Morland). London, Faber, 1974.
Captain Fantom (as Charles Underhill). London, Hutchinson, 1978; New York, St. Martin's Press, 1980.
The Forging of Fantom (as Charles Underhill). London, Hutchinson, 1979.

Plays

Radio Play: *Ordinary Levels,* 1982.

Television Play: *An Affair of Honour,* 1972.

Other

"The Educator: The Case of the Screaming Spires," in *Murder Ink: The Mystery Reader's Companion,* edited by Dilys Winn. New York, Workman, 1977.
"Sherlock Holmes: The Hamlet of Crime Fiction," in *Crime Writers,* edited by H.R.F. Keating. London, BBC Publications, 1978.
"A Pre-History: Crime Fiction Before the 19th Century," in *Whodunit?,* edited by H.R.F. Keating. London, Windward, and New York, Van Nostrand, 1982.
"A Little Talent, Lots of Practice," in *The Writer* (Boston), November 1985.
"Serial Rites," in *The Writer* (Boston), December 1988.

*

Manuscript Collection: Mugar Memorial Library, Boston University.

Reginald Hill comments:

The crime fiction I write under my own name divides easily into two categories. First there are those books that feature my two police detectives Superintendent Dalziel (pronounced Dee-ell) and Sergeant (later Inspector) Pascoe. They are set mainly in Yorkshire and are concerned with the official investigations of crimes by two men who are absolutely contrasted in background, attitudes, and approach, but are forced to admit grudging respect for each other.

The second category covers the rest: individual novels with no connection. They all contain crime but not all contain detection. They are about characters into whose lives crime comes, sometimes tragically, sometimes comically, often both.

Both categories, I hope, share one thing—well-shaped plots. Plot is the basis of narrative interest, that force that drives a reader along paths which ahead seem totally mysterious, but behind appear clear as day. It is easy to mystify. The good mystery writer's real skill lies in clarification which must be done without evasion, without dishonesty, and above all without the tedium of long-windedness. So here I'll stop!

*   *   *

Over 20 years Reginald Hill has developed into a master craftsman. The hallmarks of his work are shrewd, often witty characterization, authentic settings, and well-constructed plots. During his apprenticeship in the crime writing trade he turned out several light thrillers, including *Fell of Dark* (his first-written but second-published book) and, under the name Patrick Ruell, *Red Christmas* and *Death Takes the Low Road.* For a reader willing to suspend disbelief, they remain fun to read. As Hill's professional skills have matured, his novels have become longer, more complex, darker and more powerful. Yet he continues to avoid pretentiousness and to remember that his first duty to an ever-growing readership is to entertain.

The 11 novels about the mid-Yorkshire policemen Andrew Dalziel and Peter Pascoe reflect Hill's literary progress. The stories are best read in chronological sequence, for Dalziel and Pascoe defy the law of diminishing returns which applies to most series detectives. Hill keeps them fresh in two ways. First, he never writes two successive books featuring the same characters. Second, he keeps pushing out the frontiers of the police story. From a competent if orthodox beginning with *A Clubbable Woman,* which is set in the North of England's rugby world, he has advanced to ambitious books like *Under World* and *Bones and Silence,* which end with justice done, but not in the simple and-he-was-duly-hanged way popular with writers of the Golden Age.

Superintendent Dalziel is fat and coarse, but indestructible. From the outset he is contrasted with Pascoe, "a Detective Sergeant who was 20 years younger, had a degree in social sciences and read works of criminology." Through the series, Pascoe rises to the rank of Detective Chief Inspector and acquires a wife and child; he also learns never to underestimate Dalziel. For his part, Dalziel develops into something much more than a foil or a caricature. It becomes clear that his gross habits conceal sensitivity as well as shrewdness. The two men respect each other but nothing can reconcile their differing outlooks. Pascoe argues in *A Killing Kindness* that life is "a sorrow and a mystery." Dalziel earlier voiced his own philosophy in *Ruling Passion:* "Life's a series of wrecks. Make sure you get washed up with the survivors."

In *An April Shroud,* the holidaying Dalziel becomes embroiled in a mystery, although for a long time it is unclear whether any serious crime has been committed. For the most part he acts unofficially and at the end of the book some important questions are left unanswered—but the effect is one of uncertainty that is pleasing, not irksome. The same is true of *Deadheads,* which poses the question: is likeable, rose-growing Patrick Aldermann a multiple murderer? The final twist is ironic and tantalising.

A Killing Kindness is a story of serial murders committed by the Shakespeare-quoting Yorkshire Choker and is notable not only for the Choker's unusual motive but also for a piece of ledgerdemain worthy of Agatha Christie: Hill gives a clear but adroitly concealed clue to the culprit's identity at a remarkably early stage of the narrative. *Exit Lines* begins with the deaths of three old men on the same November night. The plot is cleverly devised, but most memorable is what Hill has to say about the ageing process and the inevitability of death itself.

Hill knows his Yorkshire and his Yorkshiremen. *Under World,* which deals with the consequences of a young girl's murder, derives much strength from its setting in a mining community still coming to terms with the defeat of the miners' union in the national strike of the mid-1980's. The pride, stubbornness and insularity of the locals is depicted superbly, yet without sentiment. In *Bones and Silence,* the medieval Yorkshire mystery plays are neatly woven into the fabric of the plot.

Hill has published non-series crime fiction under his own name as well as that of Ruell. *Another Death in Venice* (half of which is actually set in Rimini) offers an intriguing, if not wholly convincing, study in psychology. *A Very Good Hater* is an ingenious story which begins in London in 1963 when two ex-servicemen think they have spotted a former Nazi war criminal. The more recent Patrick Ruell novels have not been as lighthearted as their predecessors from the 1970's. Perhaps the best of them is *Death of a Dormouse,* which like the Hill book *The Spy's Wife* begins with a woman suffering a double blow: not only the loss of a husband, but the realisation that he had a secret life apart from her.

Although Dalziel and Pascoe are not seen to best advantage in the short story, Hill is adept at the form and uses it to experiment freely and with much success. "Poor Emma" is an enjoyable mystery featuring Jane Austen's heroine; "The Rio De Janeiro Paper" is highly original; and "Bring Back The Cat!" introduces a black private detective, Joe Sixsmith, about whom it would be good to read more.

—Martin Edwards

———

HILLERMAN, Tony. American. Born in Sacred Heart, Oklahoma, 27 May 1925. Raised among Pottawatomie and Seminole Indians; attended Indian boarding school for eight years; Oklahoma State University, Stillwater; University of Oklahoma, Norman, B.A. in journalism 1948; University of New Mexico, Albuquerque, M.A. in English 1965. Served in the United States Army Infantry during World War II: Silver Star, Bronze Star, Purple Heart. Married Marie E. Unzner in 1948; three daughters and three sons. Reporter, *News Herald,* Borger, Texas, 1948; news editor, *Morning Press,* 1949, and city editor, *Constitution,* 1950, Lawton, Oklahoma; political reporter, United Press, Oklahoma City, 1952; bureau manager, United Press, Santa Fe, New Mexico, 1953; executive editor, *The New Mexican,* Santa Fe, 1954. Associate Professor 1965–66, since 1966 Professor of Journalism and Chairman of Department, and since 1975 Assistant to the President,

University of New Mexico. Recipient: Burrows award, for journalism; Shaffer award, for reporting, 1952; Mystery Writers of America Edgar Allan Poe award, 1974. Agent: Curtis Brown Ltd., 10 Astor Place, New York, New York 10003. Address: 2729 Texas N.E., Albuquerque, New Mexico 87110, U.S.A.

CRIME PUBLICATIONS

Novels (series: Sergeant Jim Chee; Lieutenant Joe Leaphorn)

The Blessing Way (Leaphorn). New York, Harper, and London, Macmillan, 1970.
The Fly on the Wall. New York, Harper, 1971.
Dance Hall of the Dead (Leaphorn). New York, Harper, 1973.
Listening Woman (Leaphorn). New York, Harper, 1978; London, Macmillan, 1979.
People of Darkness (Chee). New York, Harper, 1980; London, Gollancz, 1982.
The Dark Wind (Chee). New York, Harper, 1982; London, Gollancz, 1983.
The Ghostway (Chee). New York, Harper, and London, Gollancz, 1985.
Skinwalkers (Chee and Leaphorn). New York, Harper, 1987; London, Joseph, 1988.
A Thief of Time (Chee and Leaphorn). New York, Harper, 1988; London, Joseph, 1989.
Talking God (Chee and Leaphorn). New York, Harper, 1989; London, Joseph, 1990.
The Joe Leaphorn Mysteries (omnibus). New York, Harper, 1989.
Coyote Waits (Chee and Leaphorn). New York, Harper, 1990.

OTHER PUBLICATIONS

Other

The Boy Who Made Dragonfly: A Zuni Myth. New York, Harper, 1972.
The Great Taos Bank Robbery and Other Indian Country Affairs. Albuquerque, University of New Mexico Press, 1973.
New Mexico, photographs by David Muench. Portland, Oregon, Belding, 1974.
Rio Grande, photographs by Robert Reynolds. Portland, Oregon, Graphic Arts Center, 1975.
Indian Country: America's Sacred Land, photographs by Béla Kalman. Flagstaff, Arizona, Northland Press, 1987.

Editor, *The Spell of New Mexico.* Albuquerque, University of New Mexico Press, 1977.

*

Manuscript Collection: Zimmerman Library, University of New Mexico.

Tony Hillerman comments:
Novels of mystery and suspense seem to be an ideal way to engage readers in a subject of life-long interest to me—the religions, cultures, and value systems of Navajo and Pueblo Indians. To play the game as it should be played, I think the setting must be genuine—the reader must be shown the Indian reservation as it is today. More important, my Navajo tribal policeman's knowledge of his people, their customs, and their values must be germane to the plot. More than that, the details

must be exactly accurate—from the way a hogan is built, to the way a sweat bath is taken, to the way it looks, and sounds, and smells at an Enemy Way Ceremonial at 2:00 A.M. on a wintry morning.

It has been a great source of pleasure to me that both Navajos and Zuñis have recognized themselves and their society in my books. They are heavily used in schools on both reservations and—for that matter—throughout the Indian world by other tribes. In fact, the authenticity of ceremonial details in *Dance Hall of the Dead* caused Zuñi elders to cross-examine me about whether members of their kiva societies had revealed secrets to me.

The background must be authentic. *But,* the name of the game is mystery and suspense. What's really important is the narration which moves against the authentic background. I feel strongly that in our genre, the reader must be caught up quickly and moved rapidly along. I like to keep my novels in a very tight time frame.

*   *   *

As we all know, Dashiell Hammett, according to Raymond Chandler, took Murder out of the Venetian Vase and put it in the alley. If he had lived to see it, Chandler no doubt would have said of Tony Hillerman that he took murder out of the alley and put in the desert.

And "the desert" in this case is the Navajo reservation in Arizona and the surrounding areas of Arizona, Utah, and New Mexico. Hillerman's leading characters Lieutenant Joe Leaphorn and Sergeant Jim Chee are both members of the Navajo Tribal Police.

Hillerman was brought up among Indians, went to an Indian boarding school, and has spent almost all his life among Indians. His knowledge of the customs, religions, and folklore of different tribes is extensive. All his novels—apart from *The Fly on the Wall,* a story of political corruption with a journalist as the leading character—have a folkloristic or religious *leitmotif.*

In his first novel, *The Blessing Way,* the motive for murder is witchcraft in the shape of a Navajo Wolf—a sort of werewolf; the sinister *Skinwalkers* also features some kind of witch as the main threat. The Shalako ceremony plays an integral part in *Dance Hall of the Dead,* and in *Talking God,* the Yeibichai, a healing ceremony, and the mask used by the leading character in one of the ritual dances of the ceremony, is the focal point of the novel.

In *A Thief of Time,* Hillerman's so far most successful (and probably best) novel, archaeology is the background, and the novel is as much a search for the lost Anasazi tribe as for the killer. History and tradition play integral parts in all Hillerman's novels and especially in this one, where the ruins and artefacts of this once flourishing but now extinct civilization are central to the murder mystery. The Hunch-backed God Kokopelli, the Watersprinkler, with his flute is almost as fully realized a character as Leaphorn and Chee.

The main theme of Hillerman's novels though is the clash between the Navajo Way and the so called American Way of Life, between tradition and the emptiness of modern society, between life in the Navajo reservation and the surrounding world and sometimes between the Navajo Tribal police and the F.B.I.

This conflict is expressed in different ways. In *A Thief of Time* the theme has a powerful metaphor in the concept of the "time-thief," the pothunter who steals Indian artefacts to sell for profit. In *Talking God* "old bones" is a metaphor: when the Smithsonian Museum in Washington is full of thousands of Native Indians' bones, why is there such a fuss when Henry

Highhawk digs up a few white persons' bones to make a point? In the later novels the conflict of life-styles is crystalized in the almost hopeless love affair between Jim Chee and the *belagaana* (non-Navajo) girl Mary Landon: they love each other, but Mary doesn't want to live in the Navajo reservation, and Jim can't think of living elsewhere.

This pattern is more clearly expressed in the later novels where Joe Leaphorn and Jim Chee are brought together: Leaphorn the disillusioned Agnostic (if there is such a thing as a Navajo Agnostic), and Chee, the Believer, who studies to be a *hathaali;* a shaman. Hillerman expresses the interconnectedness of the two ways of life in the plots of his novels. Each detective starts with a mystery of his own to solve, but it is soon revealed that they are intricately interwoven.

The police procedural of course gets a rather special flavour in Hillerman's novels. The diligent police work is blended with a strong element of Navajo customs: the circumspect way of approaching the problems, the patience in taking on the mystery, so unthinkable for a city-dweller, the "lobbying" through old family ties, the way traditional thought patterns are visible behind the thin veil of modern civilization.

Crime fiction is often better than other kinds of literature—fact or fiction—in depicting social, political, and moral problems; because the crime—especially a murder—highlights the problem. Apart from offering the reader thrilling entertainment, Hillerman's novels probably better than most other sources of information discuss important questions of racial relations and moral values in modern society.

—Karl G. and Lilian Fredriksson

———

HILTON, John Buxton. Also writes as John Greenwood. British. Born in Buxton, Derbyshire, 8 June 1921. Educated at The College, Buxton, 1931–39; Pembroke College, Cambridge, 1939–41, 1946, B.A. in modern and medieval languages 1943, M.A. and Cert. Ed. 1946. Served in the Royal Artillery, 1941–43, and the Intelligence Corps, 1943–46: mentioned in despatches. Married 1) Mary Skitmore in 1943 (died 1968), three daughters; 2) Rebecca Adams in 1969. Language teacher, Royds Hall School, Huddersfield, Yorkshire, 1946–47; language teacher, Chatham House School, Ramsgate, Kent, 1947–53; Head of the Languages Department, King Edward VI School, Chelmsford, Essex, 1953–57; headmaster, Chorley Grammar School, Lancashire, 1957–64; Inspector of Schools, Department of Education and Science, London, 1964–70; part-time Tutor-Counsellor, Open University, Milton Keynes, Buckinghamshire, 1971–78. *Died 19 June 1986.*

CRIME PUBLICATIONS

Novels (series: Inspector Thomas Brunt; Superintendent Simon Kenworthy)

Death of an Alderman (Kenworthy). London, Cassell, and New York, Walker, 1968.
Death in Midwinter (Kenworthy). London, Cassell, and New York, Walker, 1969.
Hangman's Tide (Kenworthy). London, Macmillan, and New York, St. Martin's Press, 1975.
No Birds Sang (Kenworthy). London, Macmillan, 1975; New York, St. Martin's Press, 1976.

Rescue from the Rose (Brunt). London, Macmillan, and New York, St. Martin's Press, 1976.
Gamekeeper's Gallows (Brunt). London, Macmillan, 1976; New York, St. Martin's Press, 1977.
Dead-Nettle (Brunt). London, Macmillan, and New York, St. Martin's Press, 1977.
Some Run Crooked (Kenworthy). London, Macmillan, and New York, St. Martin's Press, 1978.
The Anathema Stone (Kenworthy). London, Collins, and New York, St. Martin's Press, 1980.
Playground of Death. London, Collins, 1981; New York, St. Martin's Press, 1983.
Surrender Value (Kenworthy). London, Collins, and New York, St. Martin's Press, 1981.
The Green Frontier (Kenworthy). London, Collins, 1981; New York, St. Martin's Press, 1982.
The Sunset Law (Kenworthy). New York, St. Martin's Press, 1982.
Mr. Fred (Brunt). London, Collins, and New York, St. Martin's Press, 1983.
The Asking Price (Kenworthy). London, Collins, and New York, St. Martin's Press, 1983.
Corridors of Guilt (Kenworthy). London, Collins, and New York, St. Martin's Press, 1984.
The Hobbema Prospect (Kenworthy). London, Collins, and New York, St. Martin's Press, 1984.
The Quiet Stranger (Brunt). London, Collins, and New York, St. Martin's Press, 1985.
Passion in the Park (Kenworthy). London, Collins, and New York, St. Martin's Press, 1986.
Moondrop to Murder (Kenworthy). London, Collins, and New York, St. Martin's Press, 1986.
The Innocents at Home (Kenworthy). London, Collins, 1986; New York, St. Martin's Press, 1987.
Slickensides (Brunt). London, Collins, and New York, St. Martin's Press, 1987.
Displaced Persons (Kenworthy). London, Collins, 1987; New York, St. Martin's Press, 1988.

Novels as John Greenwood (series: Inspector Mosley in all books)

Murder, Mr. Mosley. London, Quartet, and New York, Walker, 1983.
Mosley by Moonlight. London, Quartet, 1984; New York, Walker, 1985.
Mosley Went to Mow. London, Quartet, 1985; as *The Missing Mr. Mosley,* New York, Walker, 1985.
Mists Over Mosley. London, Quartet, and New York, Walker, 1986.
The Mind of Mr. Mosley. London, Quartet, and New York, Walker, 1987.
What, Me, Mr. Mosley?. London, Quartet, 1987; New York, Walker, 1988.

Uncollected Short Stories

"Taken at the Ebb," in *Winter's Crimes 7,* edited by George Hardinge. London, Macmillan, 1975.
"Bellany's Bus," in *Winter's Crimes 8,* edited by Hilary Watson. London, Macmillan, and New York, St. Martin's Press, 1976.
"Saskja," in *Winter's Crimes 10,* edited by Hilary Watson. London, Macmillan, 1978.
"The Wedding Party," in *Alfred Hitchcock's Mystery Magazine* (New York), 27 October 1980.

OTHER PUBLICATIONS

Other

The Language Laboratory in School. London, Methuen, 1964.
Language Teaching: A Systems Approach. London, Methuen, 1973.

*

Manuscript Collection: Mugar Memorial Library, Boston University.

John Buxton Hilton commented (1984):

I suppose I am less interested in puzzles—and certainly less in violence—than in character, local colour, folk-lore, social history, and historical influences, most of which loom large in most of my books. With these ingredients I try to write the sort of books that I wish I could find to read. I believe that the distinction between suspense fiction and the "literary" novel is an unreal one and my effort is to bridge the gap. Consequently I believe that my books should appeal to readers of some literary sensitivity who do not normally read "thrillers."

* * *

When John Buxton Hilton died in 1986, he left mystery readers a legacy of 29 novels written under his own name and that of John Greenwood. Not a bad legacy when you consider writing crime novels was his second career. He published his first, *Death of an Alderman,* in 1968, two years before he retired from his job as Inspector of Schools.

The novels feature three police detectives operating in vastly different settings. Under his own name, he wrote the Superintendent Simon Kenworthy and Inspector Thomas Brunt series and, as John Greenwood, the Inspector Mosley series. As the books appeared, they moved from seriousness to increasing amounts of satire, until one of the last Kenworthy novels, *Passion in the Park,* is entirely satiric. The Mosley books were satire from the first.

In a way, it's a pity the majority of Buxton Hilton's novels are in the Kenworthy series. Not that they are poor novels; they are very competent contemporary police procedurals, and I wouldn't have missed one. Kenworthy was a hard working, straight arrow detective whose imagination fueled standard police procedures and moved him through the ranks of Scotland Yard to his retirement as Chief Superintendent and into the ranks of PI's.

However, many writers can and do write books of this type, but no one else could have written either the Brunt or Mosley books. In these you hear a voice that is unmistakably and uniquely his. It comes from Buxton Hilton's intimate knowledge of the hill country in the North of England, with its scattered villages and farms and the people peculiar to them. He spent his early years as a school master there, and the impressions went deep.

He brings this area to life, first, seriously through CID Inspector Thomas Brunt; dogged and relentless, toiling up and down the hills in the late 19th-early 20th century; then light-heartedly in present time through, the inimitable Inspector Mosley, one of those eccentrics who light up the pages of English novels.

In the Inspector Brunt series, Hilton recreates turn-of-the-century mountain villages where a few families have lived in isolation for generations, some on the same farms, fighting the same feuds, loving the same loves, living and working according to the same ignorances. These people feel with an intensity nurtured by their isolation in unrelenting, comfortless, and usually unrewarding toil on barren land. Their emotions survive unchanged for several lifetimes, passed with the farms from generation to generation, retaining the full force of their arrogant ignorance, twisted intolerance, and convoluted loyalties.

Mr. Fred, for example, moves back and forth through time to show the effects of passions, stimulated 40–50 years ago, that lived on with the same intensity until they brought disaster into the novel's present—the World War II era.

This book, more than *Gamekeeper's Gallows, Dead-Nettle, Rescue from the Rose, Slickensides,* etc., illustrates with chilling effect the slavery in which parents kept their children working the farm. Although the boys had a little freedom, their sisters were practically chained to the house: cleaning, cooking, scrubbing, milking, churning, 18–20 hours a day, in the cold and the heat, seeing only their families from one year's end to the next.

One can never know with accuracy what the language of another era might have been, but Hilton's imaginative transcription gives it not only direction, but also dignity and rhythm. *Dead-Nettle* is the one that achieves distinction, but all the Brunt books are strong as well in local lore, the effects of the weather (particularly winter), social customs, and detection.

In the Inspector Mosley books, the locale is the same, the Lancashire-Yorkshire border country with the same scattered villages and farms and the people peculiar to them, but transformed into a pleasant land full of amusing incidents. The intolerance, hatred, and convoluted loyalties that in Brunt's time produced agony, dispair, and acts of brutality become, in Inspector Mosley's time, fun and games among a population of eccentrics. Their disastrous ignorance became " . . . Mosley's people . . . were a sensitive race, their lives constantly in fee to such imponderables as whether the changes in the county border might affect the climate."

In the first book, *Murder, Mr. Mosley,* his superiors reluctantly allow him, after 34 years on the force, to handle a homicide only because "He's good at talking to people—especially hill-folk. He *knows* everybody. They all like him—even when he's clapping his horny old hand on their shoulders. And we've got one here that has its roots well and truly in Mosley soil," Detective-Superintendent Grimshaw tells the Assistant Chief Constable.

Described as "A solid little man with his greatcoat flapping open, a black homburg jammed tightly and evenly on his head . . ." and " . . . a cheerful-looking gentleman, who cultivated a shabby appearance and tried to seem older than his fifty-five years . . . ," Mr. Mosley knows everyone and everyone knows him. He solves the crimes, but metes out justice in his own way, much to his superior's despair but the people's satisfaction. When he turns up at a murder scene, " . . . there was general local relief that the murder in their midst had been left in the hands of a man so unlikely to create anything unpleasant out of it as Jack Mosley."

On his patch, Mosley is a one-man police force, and prefers it that way, outwitting and out-manipulating the forces of orthodoxy in the forms of Grimshaw, et al. They hate it, but there are times when they *have* to call on him. Once, " . . . due to some atypical unpreparedness on his part, [he] was located within less than half a day." *In Mosley Went to Mow/ The Missing Mr. Mosley,* he eluded Grimshaw for almost two weeks, appearing when he chose with the murder solved.

What, Me, Mr. Mosley?, Buxton Hilton's last book, was

published posthumously and is a fitting conclusion to a noteworthy career.

—Pearl G. Aldrich

———

HIMES, Chester (Bomar). American. Born in Jefferson City, Missouri, 19 July 1909. Educated at Glenville High School, Cleveland, graduated 1926; Ohio State University, 1926–28. Married 1) Jean Lucinda Johnson in 1937; 2) Lesley Packard. Imprisoned for armed robbery, Ohio State Penitentiary, 1928–36; worked for the Works Progress Administration (WPA) Writers Project in Ohio, 1938–41 and on Cleveland *Daily News;* from 1941 worked in shipyards in California. After 1953, lived in Paris and Spain. Recipient: Rosenwald Fellowship, 1944; Grand Prix de Littérature Policière, 1958; Before Columbus Foundation award, 1982. *Died 12 November 1984.*

CRIME PUBLICATIONS

Novels (series: Coffin Ed Johnson and Grave Digger Jones in all books except *Run Man Run* and *Une Affaire de Viol;* all books except *Blind Man with a Pistol* originally published in French by Gallimard, Paris)

For Love of Imabelle. New York, Fawcett, 1957; as *A Rage in Harlem,* New York, Avon, 1965; London, Panther, 1969.
The Crazy Kill. New York, Avon, 1959; London, Panther, 1968.
The Real Cool Killers. New York, Avon, 1959; London, Panther, 1969.
All Shot Up. New York, Avon, 1960; London, Panther, 1969.
The Big Gold Dream. New York, Avon, 1960; London, Panther, 1968.
Cotton Comes to Harlem. New York, Putnam, and London, Muller, 1965.
The Heat's On. New York, Putnam, and London, Muller 1966; as *Come Back Charleston Blue,* New York, Berkley, 1970.
Run Man Run. New York, Putnam, 1966; London, Muller, 1967.
Une Affaire de Viol. Paris, Les Yeux Ouverts, 1968.
Blind Man with a Pistol. New York, Morrow, and London, Hodder and Stoughton, 1969; as *Hot Day, Hot Night,* New York, Dell, 1970.
Plan B. Paris, Lieu Commun, 1983.

Short Stories

Un Manteau du reve? Paris, Lieu Commun, 1982.

OTHER PUBLICATIONS

Novels

If He Hollers Let Him Go. New York, Doubleday, 1945; London, Falcon Press, 1947.
Lonely Crusade. New York, Knopf, 1947; London, Grey Walls Press, 1950.
Cast the First Stone. New York, Coward McCann, 1952.
The Third Generation. Cleveland, World, 1954.
The Primitive. New York, New American Library, 1956.

Pinktoes. Paris, Olympia Press, 1961; New York, Putnam, and London, Barker, 1965.

Other

The Quality of Hurt (autobiography). New York, Doubleday, 1972; London, Joseph, 1973.
Black on Black: Baby Sister and Selected Writings. New York, Doubleday, 1973; London, Joseph, 1975.
My Life of Absurdity (autobiography). New York, Doubleday, 1976.
A Case of Rape. New York, Targ Editions, 1980.

*

Critical Studies: "Chester Himes Issue" of *Black World* (Chicago), March 1972; *Chester Himes,* by James Lundquist, New York, Ungar, 1976; *Chester Himes: A Critical Appraisal* by Stephen F. Milliken, Columbia, University of Missouri Press, 1976; *Too Close to the Truth: The American Fiction of Chester Himes* by Melvin Troy Peters, unpublished dissertation, East Lansing, Michigan State University, 1978.

*   *   *

Like Raymond Chandler, Chester Himes was nearly 50 when he began to write detective novels. But the careers of those two leading American writers of crime fiction were quite different: Chandler, with his English gentleman's upbringing, was a director of oil companies, whereas Himes, after seven years in the Ohio State Penitentiary, became an aggressive Negro novelist and after his first success was down and out in Paris. Himes once claimed some connection with the hard-boiled school in an interview: "When I could see the end of my time inside I bought myself a typewriter and taught myself touch typing. I'd been reading stories by Dashiell Hammett in *Black Mask* and I thought I could do them just as well. When my stories finally appeared, the other convicts thought exactly the same thing. There was nothing to it. All you had to do was tell it like it is."

Yet he became a writer of detective novels purely by chance. He accepted the proposal of Marcel Duhamel—editor of the famous *Série Noire* of Gallimard—to write a detective novel in the American style, for the French in the 1950's were very impressed by the American hard-boiled school. His first book, *La Reine des pommes* (later called *For Love of Imabelle* and *A Rage in Harlem*) was an instant success. It secured the "Grand Prix de Littérature Policière" of 1958 for Himes. With the exception of *Run Man Run* Himes kept to his successful formula, creating a violent and funny microcosm in nine novels which he later ironically named "Harlem domestic detective stories." In France (and later in Germany) Himes was accepted as a serious novelist who wrote sociological crime novels (Chandler once protested against this labelling), but America was wary. After the success of the sex satire *Pinktoes* his novels were sold in the "sex and soul" category, promising the reader "lush sex and stark violence, colored Black and served up raw by a great Negro writer." Once again, as so often in America, commercialism was taking over, selling literature under an incorrect label. Of course, there are sex and violence in Himes's novels, but this doesn't make him a disciple of Mickey Spillane. In discussing the merits of Himes it would be too easy to state that he has augmented the world of fictional detectives by creating two unforgettable characters: Grave Digger Jones and Coffin Ed Johnson. They are tough and violent, and (though they are not private eyes, but official Harlem policemen) they are still in some ways "the cowboys adapted to life on the city streets," as Leslie Fiedler once phrased it. But Jones and Johnson are no flat characters like so many fictional detectives; they are in some ways tragic heroes; fighting for the law against their corrupt soul brothers, becoming more cynical and disillusioned with every successive novel, their compassion gradually turning into emptiness and cynicism. At the end of *Blind Man with a Pistol* there is a scene where in a world of chaos they are shooting rats with their famous nickel-plated 38's. Himes once stated that "the only way the American Negro will ever be able to participate in the American way of life is by a series of acts of violence. It's tragic, but it's true," and he wanted to end this series with "a final book" in which his heroes get killed, trying to prevent a black revolution: "But I had to stop. The violence shocks even me."

Violence as an American experience becomes an artistic form in the novels of Chester Himes. Like Hammett and Chandler (or Hemingway) he presents violence without any emotional attachment, acting as a sort of camera eye. But he adds a special finesse to this technique, the qualities of the grotesque and absurd. The moral element, the clear division of the fictional world into goodies and baddies, is missing. People die by chance, walking through Harlem with knives in their backs, knives in their heads, burning to death in a church, driving along on a motorcycle and beheaded by a truck carrying steel blades. As one critic has stated, this is nearer to the world of Hieronymous Bosch than to any conventional treatment of violence. Though Himes always maintained that he stayed within the tradition—"I haven't created anything whatsoever; I just made the faces black, that's all"—he clearly gave a new quality to the American detective novel. Superficially he stayed within the limits of the detective novel by employing clearly defined heroes, elements of detection, fast moving action, and the denouement at the end. But even with the loving description of his soul brothers, his gentle humour is deceptive: like his heroes, Himes becomes more and more bitter and cynical. Even if he claims that he is telling it as it is, he transcends the genre (as Hammett and Chandler did in their best novels), writing no longer formula stories but sociological crime novels. "To tell it like it is," to have a message, means the end of the orthodox detective novel.

"To accept a mediocre form and make something like literature out of it": Raymond Chandler wrote in a letter two years before his death, the very year Himes published his first detective novel. And here Himes is a true follower of Chandler, for he made literature out of a mediocre form, or as Raymond Nelson phrased it in his essay on Himes (*Virginia Quarterly Review 48*, 1972):

we may be grateful for the substantial achievement he has already wrung from an improbable genre, and salute both the integrity and the force of the imagination that conceived it. If the vehicle itself is small, Himes's accomplishments within it are not, and the residual portrait left by these books—of Coffin Ed and Grave Digger outlined against the dull, lurid light of a criminal city—is one of the compelling images of our time.

—Jens Peter Becker

———

HITCHENS, Bert. *See* **OLSEN, D.B.**

———

HITCHENS, Dolores. *See* **OLSEN, D.B.**

———

HOCH, Edward D(entinger). Also writes as Irwin Booth; Anthony Circus; Stephen Dentinger; Pat McMahon; Ellery Queen; R.L. Stevens; Mr.X. American. Born in Rochester, New York, 22 February 1930. Educated at the University of Rochester, New York, 1947–49. Served in the United States Army, 1950–52. Married Patricia A. McMahon in 1957. Research assistant, Rochester Public Library, 1949–50; circulation assistant, Pocket Books, New York City, 1952–54; public relations writer, Hutchins Advertising Company, Rochester, 1954–68. Since 1968, self-employed writer. Columnist, as R.E. Porter, *Ellery Queen's Mystery Magazine*, 1980–85, and as Edward D. Hoch, *The Armchair Detective*, 1982–89, both New York. President, 1982, and member, board of directors, Mystery Writers of America. Recipient: Mystery Writers of America Edgar Allan Poe award, for short story, 1968. Agent: Larry Sternig, 742 Robertson Street, Milwaukee, Wisconsin 53213. Address: 2941 Lake Avenue, Rochester, New York 14612, U.S.A.

CRIME PUBLICATIONS

Novels (series: Carl Crader and Earl Jazine)

The Shattered Raven. New York, Lancer, 1969; London, Hale, 1970.
The Transvection Machine (Crader and Jazine). New York, Walker, 1971; London, Hale, 1974.
The Blue Movie Murders (as Ellery Queen). New York, Lancer, 1972; London, Gollancz, 1973.
The Fellowship of the Hand (Crader and Jazine). New York, Walker, 1973; London, Hale, 1976.
The Frankenstein Factory (Crader and Jazine). New York, Warner, 1975; London, Hale, 1976.

Short Stories (series: Simon Ark)

The Judges of Hades and Other Simon Ark Stories. North Hollywood, California, Leisure Books, 1971.
City of Brass and Other Simon Ark Stories. North Hollywood, California, Leisure Books, 1971.
The Spy and the Thief. New York, Davis, 1971.
The Thefts of Nick Velvet. Yonkers, New York, Mysterious Press, 1978.
The Quests of Simon Ark. New York, Mysterious Press, 1984.
Leopold's Way, edited by Francis M. Nevins and Martin H. Greenberg. Carbondale, Southern Illinois University Press, 1985.
Tales of Espionage, with Robert Edward Eckels and Brian Garfield. Secaucus, New Jersey, Castle, 1989.

Uncollected Short Stories

"Getaway," in *Murder!* (New York), September 1956.
"The Wolves of Werclaw," in *Famous Detective* (New York), October 1956.
"The Chippy" (as Irwin Booth, in *Guilty Detective* (New York), November 1956.
"Inspector Fleming's Last Case," in *Crime and Justice* (New York), January 1957.
"Blood in the Stands," in *Terror Detective* (New York), February 1957.

"Jealous Lover," in *Crime and Justice* (New York), March 1957.

"The Naked Corpse," in *Killers Mystery Story* (New York), March 1957.

"Execution on Clover Street," in *Murder!* (New York), March 1957.

"Serpent in Paradise," in *Crack Detective* (New York), April 1957.

"Killer Cop" (as Irwin Booth), in *Terror Detective* (New York), April 1957.

"Versus," in *Fantastic Universe* (New York), June 1957.

"Twelve for Eternity," in *Crack Detective* (New York), July 1957.

"The Last Darkness," in *Fast Action Detective* (New York), August 1957.

"Darkness for Dawn Stevens," in *Fast Action Detective* (New York), February 1958.

"Desert of Sin," in *Double-Action Detective* (New York), May 1958.

"Traynor's Cipher," in *The Saint* (New York), July 1958.

"The Dragon Murders," in *Double-Action Detective* (New York), September 1958.

"Street of Screams," in *Double-Action Detective* (New York), January 1959.

"Journey to Death," in *Mystery Digest* (New York), February 1959.

"The Case of the Sexy Smugglers," in *Double-Action Detective* (New York), July 1959.

"The Case of the Naked Niece," in *Double-Action Detective* (New York), September 1959.

"The Case of the Vanished Virgin," in *Double-Action Detective* (New York), November 1959.

"The Case of the Ragged Rapist," in *Double-Action Detective* (New York), January 1960.

"The Long Count," in *The Saint* (New York), January 1960.

"Flame at Twilight," in *The Saint Mystery Library* (New York), January 1960.

"The Case of the Mystic Mistress," in *Double-Action Detective* (New York), May 1960.

"The Passionate Phantom," in *Off Beat Detective* (New York), May 1960.

"The Clouded Venus," in *Tightrope Detective* (New York), June 1960.

"Sisters of Slaughter," in *Web Detective* (New York), June 1960.

"A Blade for the Chicken," in *Two-Fisted Detective* (New York), August 1960.

"Murder Is Eternal!" in *Web Detective* (New York), August 1960.

"The Man Who Knew Everything," in *Shock* (New York), September 1960.

"Don't Laugh at Murder," in *Off Beat Detective* (New York), January 1961.

"Drive My Hearse, Darling," in *Two-Fisted Detective* (New York), January 1961.

"The Night People," in *Web Detective* (New York), May 1961.

"Lust Loves the Dark," in *Off Beat Detective* (New York), July 1961.

"Hell's Handmaiden," in *Off Beat Detective* (New York), September 1961.

"The Valley of Arrows," in *The Saint* (New York), September 1961.

"To Serve the Dead," in *Web Detective* (New York), September 1961.

"Frontier Street," in *The Saint* (New York), February 1962.

"Dial 120 for Survival," in *Alfred Hitchcock's Mystery Magazine* (New York), March 1962.

"Lovely Lady of Lust," in *Keyhole Detective* (New York), April 1962.

"Setup for Murder," in *Off Beat Detective* (New York), May 1962.

"Layout for Murder," in *Off Beat Detective* (New York), July 1962.

"The Flying Man," in *The Saint* (New York), July 1962.

"A Corpse Can Love," in *Off Beat Detective* (New York), September 1962.

"Madman's Hotel," in *Off Beat Detective* (New York), November 1962.

"Ghost Town," in *The Saint* (New York), January 1963.

"The Man in the Alley," in *The Saint* (New York), June 1963.

"The Man Who Was Everywhere," in *Alfred Hitchcock Presents: Stories My Mother Never Told Me*. New York, Random House, 1963.

"Where There's Smoke," in *Manhunt* (New York), March 1964.

"The Patient Waiter," in *Alfred Hitchcock's Mystery Magazine* (New York), May 1964.

"Walk with a Wizard," in *Alfred Hitchcock's Mystery Magazine* (New York), July 1964.

"I'd Know You Anywhere," in *Ellery Queen's Double Dozen*. New York, Random House, 1964; London, Gollancz, 1965.

"The Crime of Avery Mann," in *Ellery Queen's Mystery Magazine* (New York), October 1964.

"Secret Ballot," in *Alfred Hitchcock's Mystery Magazine* (New York), November 1964.

"The Clever Mr. Carton," in *Ellery Queen's Mystery Magazine* (New York), January 1965.

"Snow in Yucatan," in *The Saint* (New York), January 1965.

"In Some Secret Place," in *The Saint* (New York), August 1965.

"The Way of Justice," in *Alfred Hitchcock's Mystery Magazine* (New York), September 1965.

"The Empty Zoo," in *Magazine of Horror* (New York), November 1965.

"They Never Came Back," in *Alfred Hitchcock's Mystery Magazine* (New York), February 1966.

"The Only Girl in His Life," in *Signature* (New York), February 1966.

"Game of Skill," in *Sleuths and Consequences*, edited by Thomas B. Dewey. New York, Simon and Schuster, 1966.

"The Long Way Down," in *Best Detective Stories of the Year*, edited by Anthony Boucher. New York, Dutton, 1966.

"The Wolfram Hunters," in *The Saint Magazine Reader*, edited by Leslie Charteris and Hans Stefan Santesson. New York, Doubleday, 1966; as *The Saint's Choice*, London, Hodder and Stoughton, 1967.

"The Fifth Victim," in *Signature* (New York), May 1966.

"Children of Judas," in *The Saint* (New York), October 1966.

"A Girl Like Cathy," in *Signature* (New York), October 1966.

"The Spy Who Walked Through Walls," in *Ellery Queen's Mystery Magazine* (New York), November 1966.

"The Spy Who Did Nothing," in *Spies and More Spies*, edited by Robert Arthur. New York, Random House, 1967.

"The People of the Peacock," in *Spies and More Spies*, edited by Robert Arthur. New York, Random House, 1967.

"A Gift of Myrrh," in *Alfred Hitchcock's Mystery Magazine* (New York), January 1967.

"Fall of Zoo," in *The Saint* (New York), January 1967.

"After the Verdict," in *Alfred Hitchcock's Mystery Magazine* (New York), April 1967.

"The Spy Who Came Out of the Night," in *Ellery Queen's Mystery Magazine* (New York), April 1967.

"Stop at Nothing," in *Alfred Hitchcock's Mystery Magazine* (New York), May 1967.

"The Dying Knight," in *Signature* (New York), June 1967.

"It Could Get Warmer," in *Alfred Hitchcock's Mystery Magazine* (New York), July 1967.

"The Times We Had," in *Famous Science Fiction* (New York), Fall 1967.

"The Spy Who Didn't Exist," in *Ellery Queen's Mystery Magazine* (New York), December 1967.

"The Spy Who Clutched a Playing Card," in *Ellery Queen's Mystery Magazine* (New York), February 1968.

"After the Fact," in *Alfred Hitchcock's Mystery Magazine* (New York), March 1968.

"Cold Cognisance," in *Alfred Hitchcock's Mystery Magazine* (New York), May 1968.

"Hawk in the Valley," in *Alfred Hitchcock's Mystery Magazine* (New York), August 1968.

"The Spy Who Read Latin," in *Ellery Queen's Mystery Magazine* (New York), August 1968.

"No Good at Riddles," in *Alfred Hitchcock's Mystery Magazine* (New York), December 1968.

"Cassidy's Saucer," in *Flying Saucers in Fact and Fiction,* edited by Hans S. Santesson. New York, Lancer, 1968.

"The Ring with the Velvet Ropes," in *With Malice Toward All,* edited by Robert L. Fish. New York, Putnam, 1968.

"The Spy Who Worked for Peace," in *Rogues' Gallery,* edited by Walter B. Gibson. New York, Doubleday, 1969.

"Poor Sport," in *Alfred Hitchcock's Mystery Magazine* (New York), February 1969.

"Homecoming," in *Alfred Hitchcock's Mystery Magazine* (New York), April 1969.

"Emergency," in *Alfred Hitchcock's Mystery Magazine* (New York), May 1969.

"The Tomb at the Top of the Tree," in *Mike Shayne Mystery Magazine* (New York), June 1969.

"The Dictator's Double," in *Alfred Hitchcock's Mystery Magazine* (New York), July 1969.

"The Spy and the Shopping List Code," in *Ellery Queen's Mystery Magazine* (New York), July 1969.

"Dead Man's Song," in *Mike Shayne Mystery Magazine* (New York), September 1969.

"The Impossible 'Impossible' Crime," in *Ellery Queen's Murder Menu.* Cleveland, World, 1969.

"The Secret Savant," in *Alfred Hitchcock's Mystery Magazine* (New York), October 1969.

"Picnic at Midnight," in *Mike Shayne Mystery Magazine* (New York), October 1969.

"The Murder Parade," in *Mike Shayne Mystery Magazine* (New York), November 1969.

"Unnatural Act," in *Gentle Invaders,* edited by Hans S. Santesson. New York, Belmont, 1969.

"Computer Cops," in *Crime Prevention in the 30th Century,* edited by Hans S. Santesson. New York, Walker, 1969.

"The Magic Bullet," in *Best Detective Stories of the Year,* edited by Allen J. Hubin. New York, Dutton, 1970.

"The Theft of the Laughing Lions," in *Ellery Queen's Mystery Magazine* (New York), February 1970.

"The Uttering Man," in *Alfred Hitchcock's Mystery Magazine* (New York), March 1970.

"The Seventh Assassin," in *Ellery Queen's Mystery Magazine* (New York), March 1970.

"The Seventieth Number," in *Ellery Queen's Mystery Magazine* (New York), March 1970.

"Flapdragon," in *Alfred Hitchcock's Mystery Magazine* (New York), April 1970.

"A Place to See the Dark," in *Alfred Hitchcock's Mystery Magazine* (New York), May 1970.

"Zone," in *Mike Shayne Mystery Magazine* (Los Angeles), June 1970.

"Murder Offstage," in *Ellery Queen's Grand Slam.* Cleveland, World, 1970.

"Every Fifth Man," in *Ellery Queen's Grand Slam.* Cleveland, World, 1970.

"The Nile Cat," in *Ellery Queen's Grand Slam.* Cleveland, World, 1970.

"The Afternoon Ear," in *Mike Shayne Mystery Magazine* (Los Angeles), September 1970.

"Verdict of One," in *Alfred Hitchcock's Mystery Magazine* (New York), October 1970.

"Bag of Tricks," in *Alfred Hitchcock's Mystery Magazine* (New York), November 1970.

"Twist of the Knife," in *Mike Shayne Mystery Magazine* (Los Angeles), December 1970.

"The Spy and the Diplomat's Daughter," in *Ellery Queen's Mystery Magazine* (New York), January 1971.

"Die Hard," in *Mike Shayne Mystery Magazine* (Los Angeles), February 1971.

"A Little More Rope," in *Alfred Hitchcock's Mystery Magazine* (New York), March 1971.

"The Poison Man," in *Mike Shayne Mystery Magazine* (Los Angeles), March 1971.

"The Way Out," in *Ellery Queen's Mystery Magazine* (New York), April 1971.

"Blow-Up!" in *Adventure* (Glendale, California), April 1971.

"Siege Perilous," in *Mike Shayne Mystery Magazine* (Los Angeles), April 1971.

"Climax Alley," in *Alfred Hitchcock's Mystery Magazine* (New York), May 1971.

"The Spy and the Nile Mermaid," in *Ellery Queen's Mystery Magazine* (New York), May 1971.

"The Sugar Man," in *Mike Shayne Mystery Magazine* (Los Angeles), June 1971.

"Dead on the Pavement," in *Alfred Hitchcock's Mystery Magazine* (New York), July 1971.

"The Thing in Lovers' Lane," in *Mike Shayne Mystery Magazine* (Los Angeles), July 1971.

"The Spy Who Knew Too Much," in *Ellery Queen's Mystery Magazine* (New York), August 1971.

"The League of Arthur," in *Argosy* (New York), September 1971.

"Blood Money," in *Mike Shayne Mystery Magazine* (Los Angeles), September 1971.

"Lady with a Cat," in *Alfred Hitchcock's Mystery Magazine* (New York), November 1971.

"The Theft of the Leather Coffin," in *Ellery Queen's Mystery Magazine* (New York), November 1971.

"Twilight Thunder," in *Alfred Hitchcock's I Am Curious Bloody.* New York, Dell, 1971.

"The Rusty Rose," in *Alfred Hitchcock's Rolling Gravestones.* New York, Dell 1971.

"The Sound of Screaming," in *Mike Shayne Mystery Magazine* (Los Angeles), November 1971.

"Rubber Bullets," in *Alfred Hitchcock's Mystery Magazine* (New York), December 1971.

"Captain Leopold Does His Job," in *Ellery Queen's Mystery Magazine* (New York), December 1971.

"The Zap Effect," in *Mike Shayne Mystery Magazine* (Los Angeles), December 1971.

"The Man at the Top," in *Alfred Hitchcock's Mystery Magazine* (New York), February 1972.

"The Spy Without a Country," in *Ellery Queen's Mystery Magazine* (New York), February 1972.

"The Lost Pilgrim," in *Mike Shayne Mystery Magazine* (Los Angeles), February 1972.

"A Country Like the Sun," in *Mike Shayne Mystery Magazine* (Los Angeles), March 1972.

"End of the Day," in *Best Detective Stories of the Year,* edited by Allen J. Hubin. New York, Dutton, 1972.

"The Spy and the Reluctant Courier," in *Ellery Queen's Mystery Magazine* (New York), June 1972.

"The Soft Asylum," in *Alfred Hitchcock's Mystery Magazine* (New York), July 1972.

"The Ripper of Storyville," in *Dear Dead Days,* edited by Edward D. Hoch. New York, Walker, 1972; London, Gollancz, 1974.

"Suicide," in *Mike Shayne Mystery Magazine* (Los Angeles), August 1972.

"Leopold at Rest," in *Alfred Hitchcock's Mystery Magazine* (New York), September 1972.

"The Holy Witch," in *Mike Shayne Mystery Magazine* (Los Angeles), September 1972.

"The Theft of the Foggy Film," in *Ellery Queen's Mystery Magazine* (New York), November 1972.

"The Spy Who Was Expected," in *Ellery Queen's Mystery Magazine* (New York), December 1972.

"Bullets for Two," in *Mike Shayne Annual* (Los Angeles), 1972.

"Leopold on Edge," in *Alfred Hitchcock's Mystery Magazine* (New York), January 1973.

"The Million-Dollar Jewel Caper," in *Ellery Queen's Mystery Magazine* (New York), January 1973.

"Burial Monuments Three," in *Best Detective Stories of the Year,* edited by Allen J. Hubin. New York, Dutton, 1973.

"The Man Who Came Back," in *Alfred Hitchcock's Mystery Magazine* (New York), May 1973.

"Captain Leopold Saves a Life," in *Ellery Queen's Anthology: Spring–Summer.* New York, Davis, 1973.

"The Plastic Man," in *Alfred Hitchcock's Mystery Magazine* (New York), June 1973.

"The Case of the November Club," in *Ellery Queen's Mystery Magazine* (New York), June 1973.

"Home Movies," in *Mike Shayne Mystery Magazine* (Los Angeles), June 1973.

"The Theft of the Cuckoo Clock," in *Ellery Queen's Mystery Magazine* (New York), September 1973.

"Captain Leopold Swings a Bat," in *Ellery Queen's Mystery Magazine* (New York), October 1973.

"Snowsuit," in *Alfred Hitchcock's Mystery Magazine* (New York), November 1973.

"The Serpent in the Sky," in *Ellery Queen's Anthology: Fall–Winter.* New York, Davis, 1973.

"The Gold Buddha Caper," in *Ellery Queen's Mystery Magazine* (New York), December 1973.

"Night of the Millennium," in *The Other Side of Tomorrow,* edited by Roger Elwood. New York, Random House, 1973.

"The Witch of Westwood," in *Alfred Hitchcock's Mystery Magazine* (New York), January 1974.

"The Spy and the Intercepted Letters," in *Ellery Queen's Mystery Magazine* (New York), January 1974.

"The Infernal Machine," in *Mike Shayne Mystery Magazine* (Los Angeles), January 1974.

"Dinner with the Boss," in *Charlie Chan Mystery Magazine* (Los Angeles), February 1974.

"The Lollipop Cop," in *Ellery Queen's Mystery Magazine* (New York), June 1974.

"The Theft of the Legal Eagle," in *Ellery Queen's Mystery Magazine* (New York), July 1974.

"The Perfect Time for the Perfect Crime," in *Killers of the Mind,* edited by Lucy Freeman. New York, Random House, 1974.

"Story for an October Issue," in *Alfred Hitchcock's Mystery Magazine* (North Palm Beach, Florida), October 1974.

"The Credit Card Caper," in *Ellery Queen's Mystery Magazine* (New York), October 1974.

"The Spy and the Talking House," in *Ellery Queen's Mystery Magazine* (New York), November 1974.

"The Boy Who Bought Love," in *Crisis,* edited by Roger Elwood. New York, Nelson, 1974.

"Captain Leopold Drops a Bomb," in *Alfred Hitchcock's Mystery Magazine* (North Palm Beach, Florida), January 1975.

"The Kindergarten Witch," in *Ellery Queen's Mystery Magazine* (New York), January 1975.

"The Neptune Fund," in *Mike Shayne Mystery Magazine* (Los Angeles), January 1975.

"The Case of the Broken Wings," in *Ellery Queen's Mystery Magazine* (New York), February 1975.

"The Problem of the Old Gristmill," in *Ellery Queen's Mystery Magazine* (New York), March 1975.

"Bodyguard," in *Executioner* (Los Angeles), April 1975.

"The Spy Who Took a Vacation," in *Ellery Queen's Mystery Magazine* (New York), April 1975.

"The Enchanted Tooth," in *Ellery Queen's Mystery Magazine* (New York), May 1975.

"One Eden Too Many," in *87th Precinct* (Los Angeles), August 1975.

"Twine," in *Mike Shayne Mystery Magazine* (Los Angeles), August 1975.

"The Odor of Melting," in *Alfred Hitchcock Presents: Stories to Be Read with the Door Locked.* New York, Random House, 1975.

"The Problem of the Lobster Shack," in *Ellery Queen's Mystery Magazine* (New York), September 1975.

"Arbiter of Uncertainties," in *Alfred Hitchcock's Murderer's Row.* New York, Dell, 1975.

"Man in Hiding," in *Nugget* (Coral Gables, Florida), October 1975.

"Two Days in Organville," in *Alfred Hitchcock's Speak of the Devil.* New York, Dell, 1975.

"The Death of Lame Jack Lincoln," in *Alfred Hitchcock's Mystery Magazine* (North Palm Beach, Florida), December 1975.

"Winter Run," in *Alfred Hitchcock Presents Tales To Keep You Spellbound,* edited by Eleanor Sullivan. New York, Dial Press, 1976.

"The Theft of the Dinosaur's Tale," in *Magicians of Mystery,* edited by Ellery Queen. New York, Dial Press, 1976.

"The Case of the Lapidated Man," in *Ellery Queen's Crime Wave.* New York, Putnam, 1976.

"The Reindeer Clue" (as Ellery Queen), in *Best Detective Stories of the Year 1976,* edited by Edward D. Hoch. New York, Dutton, 1976.

"The Basilisk Hunt," in *Alfred Hitchcock's Mystery Magazine* (New York), January 1976.

"The Problem of the Haunted Bandstand," in *Ellery Queen's Mystery Magazine* (New York), January 1976.

"The Man Who Knew the Method," in *Nugget* (Coral Gables, Florida), February 1976.

"The Spy Who Collected Lapel Pins," in *Ellery Queen's Mystery Magazine* (New York), March 1976.

"The Theft of the Admiral's Snow," in *Ellery Queen's Mystery Magazine* (New York), April 1976.

"The Diamond Frog," in *Alfred Hitchcock's Mystery Magazine* (New York), May 1976.

"Captain Leopold Tries Again," in *Ellery Queen's Mystery Magazine* (New York), June 1976.

"The Bank Job," in *Mystery Monthly* (New York), June 1976.

"The Theft of the Wooden Egg," in *Ellery Queen's Mystery Magazine* (New York), July 1976.

"Plastique," in *Alfred Hitchcock's Mystery Magazine* (New York), August 1976.

"The Quest for Jason Stannis," in *Alfred Hitchcock's Mystery Magazine* (New York), September 1976.

"The Scorpion Girl," in *Alfred Hitchcock's Mystery Magazine* (New York), October 1976.

"The Murder of Captain Leopold," in *Ellery Queen's Mystery Magazine* (New York), October 1976.

"Day of Judgement," in *Mike Shayne Mystery Magazine* (Los Angeles), December 1976.

"Something for the Dark," in *Stories that Go Bump in the Night,* edited by Alfred Hitchcock. New York, Random House, 1977.

"The Theft of the Satin Jury," in *Champions of Mystery,* edited by Ellery Queen. New York, Dial Press, 1977.

"The Spy and the Mysterious Card," in *Ellery Queen's Searches and Seizures.* New York, Dial Press, 1977.

"The Theft of the Venetian Window," in *Ellery Queen's Searches and Seizures.* New York, Dial Press, 1977.

"The Problem of the Locked Caboose," in *Midnight Specials,* edited by Bill Pronzini. Indianapolis, Bobbs Merrill, 1977.

"The Centennial Assassin," in *Best Detective Stories of the Year 1977,* edited by Edward D. Hoch. New York, Dutton, 1977.

"End of the Line," in *Alfred Hitchcock Presents Tales to Take Your Breath Away,* edited by Eleanor Sullivan. New York, Dial Press, 1977.

"Anniversary Gift," in *Alfred Hitchcock's Mystery Magazine* (New York), February 1977.

"The Theft of the Sherlockian Slipper," in *Ellery Queen's Mystery Magazine* (New York), February 1977.

"A Touch of Red," in *Mike Shayne Mystery Magazine* (Los Angeles), February 1977.

"The Problem of Cell 16," in *Ellery Queen's Mystery Magazine* (New York), March 1977.

"Web," in *Dude* (Coral Gables, Florida), March 1977.

"The Wooden Dove," in *Mike Shayne Mystery Magazine* (Los Angeles), March 1977.

"A Simple Little Thing," in *Alfred Hitchcock's Mystery Magazine* (New York), May 1977.

"The Case of the Battered Wives," in *Ellery Queen's Mystery Magazine* (New York), June 1977.

"The Spy Who Died Twice," in *Ellery Queen's Mystery Magazine* (New York), July 1977.

"Money on the Skull," in *Antaeus* (New York), Spring–Summer 1977.

"All Knives Are Sharp," in *Alfred Hitchcock's Mystery Magazine* (New York), August 1977.

"No Holiday for Captain Leopold," in *Ellery Queen's Mystery Magazine* (New York), August 1977.

"The Problem of the Country Inn," in *Ellery Queen's Mystery Magazine* (New York), September 1977.

"The Theft of the Child's Drawing," in *Ellery Queen's Mystery Magazine* (New York), October 1977.

"The Problem of the Voting Booth," in *Ellery Queen's Mystery Magazine* (New York), December 1977.

"Zoo," in *100 Great Science Fiction Short-Short Stories,* edited by Isaac Asimov, Martin H. Greenberg and Joseph D. Olander. New York, Doubleday, 1978.

"The Last Paradox," in *100 Great Science Fiction Short-Short Stories,* edited by Isaac Asimov, Martin H. Greenberg and Joseph D. Olander. New York, Doubleday, 1978.

"The Picnic People," in *Alfred Hitchcock Presents Tales to Make Your Blood Run Cold,* edited by Eleanor Sullivan. New York Dial Press, 1978.

"The Spy Who Didn't Remember," in *Napoleon's of Mystery,* edited by Ellery Queen. New York, Dial Press, 1978.

"Captain Leopold Finds a Tiger," in *Rogue's Gallery,* edited by Alfred Hitchcock. New York, Dell, 1978.

"The Electric Girl Caper," in *Murder-Go-Round,* edited by Alfred Hitchcock. New York, Dell, 1978.

"Captain Leopold and the Impossible Murder," in *Ellery Queen's A Multitude of Sins.* New York, Dial Press, 1978.

"The Theft of the Family Portrait," in *Ellery Queen's Mystery Magazine* (New York), March 1978.

"The Nameless Crime," in *Mike Shayne Mystery Magazine* (Los Angeles), May 1978.

"Home Is the Hunter," in *Alfred Hitchcock's Mystery Magazine* (New York), June 1978.

"Warrior's Farewell," in *Alfred Hitchcock's Tales to Scare You Stiff,* edited by Eleanor Sullivan. New York, Davis, 1978.

"The Problem of the Old Oak Tree," in *Ellery Queen's Mystery Magazine* (New York), July 1978.

"The Theft of the Turquoise Elephant," in *Ellery Queen's Mystery Magazine* (New York), August 1978.

"The Pact of the Five," in *Alfred Hitchcock's Mystery Magazine* (New York), August 1978.

"Captain Leopold and the Three Hostages," in *Ellery Queen's Mystery Magazine* (New York), September 1978.

"A Man Could Get Killed," in *Mike Shayne Mystery Magazine* (Los Angeles), September 1978.

"Memory in the Dark," in *Alfred Hitchcock's Mystery Magazine* (New York), October 1978.

"The Obsession of Officer O'Rourke," in *Alfred Hitchcock's Mystery Magazine* (New York), November 1978.

"After Class," in *Mike Shayne Mystery Magazine* (Los Angeles), November 1978.

"The Problem of the Revival Tent," in *Ellery Queen's Mystery Magazine* (New York), November 1978.

"Three Weeks in a Spanish Town," in *Alfred Hitchcock's Mystery Magazine* (New York), December 1978.

"Another War," in *Alfred Hitchcock's Presents Tales to Send Chills Down Your Spine,* edited by Eleanor Sullivan. New York, Dial Press, 1979.

"A Melee of Diamonds," in *Alfred Hitchcock Presents Tales to Be Read with Caution,* edited by Eleanor Sullivan. New York, Dial Press, 1979.

"Captain Leopold Gets Angry," in *Secrets of Mystery,* edited by Ellery Queen. New York, Dial Press, 1979.

"Bread Upon the Waters," in *John Creasey's Crime Collection 1979,* edited by Herbert Harris, London, Gollancz, 1979.

"Second Chance," in *Women's Wiles,* edited by Michele B. Slung. New York, Harcourt Brace, 1979.

"Captain Leopold and the Ghost-Killer," in *Ellery Queen's Wings of Mystery.* New York, Dial Press, 1979.

"The Theft of Nothing at All," in *Ellery Queen's Scenes of the Crime.* New York, Davis, 1979.

"Captain Leopold on the Spot," in *Ellery Queen's Mystery Magazine* (New York), January 1979.

"In a Foreign City," in *Mike Shayne Mystery Magazine* (Los Angeles), January 1979.

"The Man Who Shot the Werewolf," in *Ellery Queen's Mystery Magazine* (New York), February 1979.

"The Thing in the Lake," in *Child Life Mystery and Science Fiction Magazine* (Indianapolis), February–March 1979.

"The Gun," in *Mike Shayne Mystery Magazine* (Los Angeles), March 1979.

"Three Hot Days," in *Mike Shayne Mystery Magazine* (Los Angeles), April 1979.

"Captain Leopold and the Murderer's Son," in *Alfred Hitchcock's Mystery Magazine* (New York), May 1979.

"The Spy Who Had a List," in *Ellery Queen's Mystery Magazine* (New York), May 1979.

"Tough Cop's Girl," in *Mike Shayne Mystery Magazine* (Los Angeles), June 1979.

"Captain Leopold Incognito," in *Best Detective Stories of the Year*, edited by Edward D. Hoch. New York, Dutton, 1979.

"The Rattlesnake Man," in *Alfred Hitchcock's Mystery Magazine* (New York), July 1979.

"The Paris Strangler," in *Alfred Hitchcock's Mystery Magazine* (New York), August 1979.

"The Golden Lady," in *Mike Shayne Mystery Magazine* (Los Angeles), August 1979.

"The Spy Who Was Alone," in *Ellery Queen's Mystery Magazine* (New York), September 1979.

"Where Is Danny Storm?" in *Mike Shane Mystery Magazine* (New York), September 1979.

"The Avenger from Outer Space," in *Ellery Queen's Mystery Magazine* (New York), October 1979.

"The Dog That Barked All Day," in *Hers* (Englewood, New Jersey), 1 October 1979.

"Stairway to Nowhere," in *Mike Shayne Mystery Magazine* (Los Angeles), November 1979.

"The Problem of the General Store," in *Ellery Queen's Mystery Magazine* (New York), November 1979.

"The Theft of Sahara's Water," in *Ellery Queen's Mystery Magazine* (New York), December 1979.

"Code of Honor," in *Alfred Hitchcock's Mystery Magazine* (New York), December 1979.

"The Spy Who Wasn't Needed," in *Ellery Queen's Mystery Magazine* (New York), 17 December 1979.

"The Eye of the Pigeon," in *Alive and Screaming*, edited by Alfred Hitchcock, New York, Dell, 1980.

"The Lady or the Lion?" in *John Creasey's Crime Collection 1980*, edited by Herbert Harris. London, Gollancz, 1980.

"The Weekend Magus," in *Mummy!*, edited by Bill Pronzini. New York, Arbor House, 1980.

"The Faceless Thing," in *Bug-Eyed Monsters*, edited by Bill Pronzini and Barry N. Malzberg. New York, Harcourt Brace, 1980.

"The Choker," in *Alfred Hitchcock's Tales to Make Your Teeth Chatter*, edited by Eleanor Sullivan. New York, Dial Press, 1980.

"The Spy with the Knockout Punch," in *Ellery Queen's Windows of Mystery*. New York, Davis, 1980.

"The Theft of the Firefighter's Hat," in *Best Detective Stories of the Year 1980*, edited by Edward D. Hoch. New York, Dutton, 1980.

"Exu," in *Voodoo!*, edited by Bill Pronzini. New York, Arbor House, 1980.

"The Locked Room Cipher," in *Who Done It?*, edited by Alice Laurance and Isaac Asimov. Boston, Houghton Mifflin, 1980.

"Just Like the Old Days," in *Mike Shayne Mystery Magazine* (Los Angeles), January 1980.

"The Case of the Straw Serpent," in *Ellery Queen's Mystery Magazine* (New York), 14 January 1980.

"High Bid," in *Mike Shayne Mystery Magazine* (Los Angeles), February 1980.

"The Theft of the Banker's Ashtray," in *Ellery Queen's Mystery Magazine* (New York), 11 February 1980.

"Vulcan's Widow," in *Mike Shayne Mystery Magazine* (Los Angeles), March 1980.

"The Case of the Chloroformed Clerics," in *Ellery Queen's Mystery Magazine* (New York), 10 March 1980.

"Midsummer Night's Scream," in *Mike Shayne Mystery Magazine* (Los Angeles), April 1980.

"The Weapon Out of the Past," in *Ellery Queen's Mystery Magazine* (New York), 7 April 1980.

"The Ides of April," in *Mike Shayne Mystery Magazine* (Los Angeles), May 1980.

"The Traveling Man," in *Mike Shayne Mystery Magazine* (Los Angeles), June 1980.

"The Spy Who Came Back from the Dead," in *Ellery Queen's Mystery Magazine* (New York), 2 June 1980.

"The Problem of the Courthouse Gargoyle," in *Ellery Queen's Mystery Magazine* (New York), 30 June 1980.

"A Passing Stranger," in *Mike Shayne Mystery Magazine* (Los Angeles), July 1980.

"The Sorceress of the Sea," in *Ellery Queen's Mystery Magazine* (New York), 18 August 1980.

"Cop Killer," in *Mike Shayne Mystery Magazine* (Los Angeles), September 1980.

"Assignment: Enigma" (as Anthony Circus), in *Ellery Queen's Mystery Magazine* (New York), 10 September 1980.

"The Problem of the Pilgrims Windmill," in *Ellery Queen's Mystery Magazine* (New York), 10 September 1980.

"The Daltonic Fireman," in *Mike Shayne Mystery Magazine* (Los Angeles), October 1980.

"The Theft of the Four of Spades," in *Ellery Queen's Mystery Magazine* (New York), 6 October 1980.

"High School Reunion," in *Woman's World* (Englewood, New Jersey), 14 October 1980.

"Common Factor," in *Woman's World* (Englewood, New Jersey), 14 October 1980.

"Fiction," in *Alfred Hitchcock's Mystery Magazine* (New York), 27 October 1980.

"Captain Leopold's Gamble," in *Alfred Hitchcock's Mystery Magazine* (New York), 19 November 1980.

"The Theft of the Thanksgiving Turkey," in *Ellery Queen's Mystery Magazine* (New York), 1 December 1980.

"Assignment: Labyrinth," in *Alfred Hitchcock's Mystery Magazine* (New York), 15 December 1980.

"In the Straw," in *Creature!*, edited by Bill Pronzini. New York, Arbor House, 1981.

"The Man Who Came Back," in *Alfred Hitchcock's Tales to Make Your Hair Stand on End*, edited by Eleanor Sullivan. New York, Dial Press, 1981.

"The Problem of the Christmas Steeple," in *The Twelve Crimes of Christmas*, edited by Carol-Lynn Rössel Waugh, Martin H. Greenberg, and Isaac Asimov. New York, Avon, 1981.

"The Problem of the Covered Bridge," in *All But Impossible!*, edited by Edward D. Hoch. New Haven, Connecticut, Ticknor and Fields, 1981.

"The Spy at the Crime Writers Congress," in *Ellery Queen's Doors to Mystery*. New York, Davis, 1981.

"The Theft of Yesterday's Newspaper," in *Ellery Queen's Crime Cruise round the World*. New York, Davis, 1981.

"Who Rides with Santa Anna?," in *Ghosts*, edited by Marvin and Saralee Kaye. New York, Doubleday, 1981.

"The Other Eye," in *Crime Wave*. London, Collins, 1981.

"Co-Incidence," "Thirteen," "A Deal in Diamonds," all in *Miniature Mysteries*, edited by Isaac Asimov, Martin H. Greenberg and Joseph D. Olander. New York, Taplinger, 1981.

"Shattered Rainbow" in *Alfred Hitchcock's Tales to Make You Weak at the Knees*, edited by Eleanor Sullivan. New York, Dial Press, 1981.

"Captain Leopold and the Silver Foxes," in *Ellery Queen's Mystery Magazine* (New York), 1 January 1981.

"The Problem of the Gingerbread Houseboat," in *Ellery Queen's Mystery Magazine* (New York), 28 January 1981.

"When the War Is Over," in *Mike Shayne Mystery Magazine* (Los Angeles), February 1981.

"The Dying Marabout," in *Alfred Hitchcock's Mystery Magazine* (New York), 4 February 1981.

"The Theft of the Lopsided Cobweb," in *Ellery Queen's Mystery Magazine* (New York), 25 February 1981.

"The Vorpal Blade," in *Mystery* (Los Angeles), March 1981.

"The Spy and the Walrus Cipher," in *Ellery Queen's Mystery Magazine* (New York), 25 March 1981.

"Rubbish," in *Mike Shayne Mystery Magazine* (Los Angeles), April 1981.

"The Woman Without a Past," in *Ellery Queen's Mystery Magazine* (New York), 22 April 1981.

"The Carnival Caper," in *Woman's World* (Englewood, New Jersey), 5 May 1981.

"Lady of the Impossible," in *Ellery Queen's Mystery Magazine* (New York), 20 May 1981.

"The Problem of the Pink Post Office," in *Ellery Queen's Mystery Magazine* (New York), 17 June 1981.

"Captain Leopold Goes Fishing," in *Ellery Queen's Mystery Magazine* (New York), 15 July 1981.

"The Theft of the Red Balloon," in *Ellery Queen's Mystery Magazine* (New York), 12 August 1981.

"Seven Billion Day," in *Alfred Hitchcock's Mystery Magazine* (New York), 19 August 1981.

"The Spy Who Didn't Defect," in *Ellery Queen's Mystery Magazine* (New York), 9 September 1981.

"The Killer and the Clown," in *Alfred Hitchcock's Mystery Magazine* (New York), 14 October 1981.

"Damsel With a Derringer," in *Black Cat* (Toronto), Halloween 1981.

"The Spy Who Stayed Up All Night," in *Ellery Queen's Mystery Magazine* (New York), 4 November 1981.

"The Theft of the Picture Postcards," in *Ellery Queen's Mystery Magazine* (New York), 2 December 1981.

"The Girl with the Dragon Kite," in *Ellery Queen's Death-Reach.* New York, Davis, 1982.

"The Nine Eels of Madame Wu," in *A Special Kind of Crime,* edited by Lawrence Treat. New York, Doubleday, 1982.

"The Problem of the Octagon Room," in *The Year's Best Mystery and Suspense Stories 1982,* edited by Edward D. Hoch. New York, Walker, 1982.

"The Theft of the Four of Spades," in *The Big Apple Mysteries,* edited by Carol-Lynn Rössel Waugh, Martin H. Greenberg and Isaac Asimov. New York, Avon, 1982.

"The Problem of the Gypsy Camp," in *Ellery Queen's Mystery Magazine* (New York), 1 January 1982.

"The Man With Five Faces," in *Ellery Queen's Mystery Magazine* (New York), 27 January 1982.

"Murder at Tomorrow City," in *Ellery Queen's Mystery Magazine* (New York), 24 March 1982.

"The Theft of the Sliver of Soap," in *Ellery Queen's Mystery Magazine* (New York), May 1982.

"Behind Closed Doors," in *Woman's World* (Englewood, New Jersey), 18 May 1982.

"The Spy at the Film Festival," in *Ellery Queen's Mystery Magazine* (New York), June 1982.

"The Sunken Car," in *Mike Shayne Mystery Magazine* (New York), June 1982.

"The Problem of the Bootlegger's Car," in *Ellery Queen's Mystery Magazine* (New York), July 1982.

"The Flying Fiend," in *Ellery Queen's Mystery Magazine* (New York), Mid-July 1982.

"One Moment of Madness," in *Ellery Queen's Mystery Magazine* (New York), September 1982.

"The Spy and the Village Murder," in *Ellery Queen's Mystery Magazine* (New York), October 1982.

"Terrorist," in *Mike Shayne Mystery Magazine* (Los Angeles), November 1982.

"The Problem of the Tin Goose," in *Ellery Queen's Mystery Magazine* (New York), December 1982.

"Five-Day Forecast," in *Ellery Queen's Prime Crimes,* edited by Eleanor Sullivan. New York, Davis, 1983.

"Dreaming Is a Lonely Thing," in *Alfred Hitchcock Presents Mortal Errors,* edited by Cathleen Jordan. New York, Dial Press, 1983.

"A Certain Power," in *A Choice of Evils,* edited by Elana Lore. New York, Davis, 1983.

"Day of the Vampire," in *13 Horrors of Halloween,* edited by Carol-Lynn Rössel Waugh, Martin H. Greenberg and Isaac Asimov. New York, Avon, 1983.

"The Vultures of Malabar," in *Alfred Hitchcock's Fatal Attractions,* edited by Elana Lore. New York, Dial Press, 1983.

"Just Passing Through," in *The Year's Best Mystery and Suspense Stories 1983,* edited by Edward D. Hoch. New York, Walker, 1983.

"The Cat and Fiddle Murders," in *Ellery Queen's Mystery Magazine* (New York), January 1983.

"The Second Captain Leopold," in *Ellery Queen's Mystery Magazine* (New York), February 1983.

"Violet Crime," in *Woman's World* (Englewood, New Jersey), 22 February 1983.

"The Theft of the White Queen's Menu," in *Ellery Queen's Mystery Magazine* (New York), March 1983.

"The Street with No Houses," in *Mike Shayne Mystery Magazine* (Los Angeles), March 1983.

"The Spy Who Sat in Judgment," in *Ellery Queen's Mystery Magazine* (New York), April 1983.

"Captain Leopold Beats the Machine," in *Ellery Queen's Mystery Magazine* (New York), June 1983.

"The Doom Balloons," in *Mike Shayne Mystery Magazine* (Los Angeles), June 1983.

"The Theft of the Unsold Manuscript," in *Ellery Queen's Mystery Magazine* (New York), July 1983.

"The Spy Who Stepped Back in Time," in *Ellery Queen's Mystery Magazine* (New York), Mid-July 1983.

"The Problem of the Body in the Haystack," in *Ellery Queen's Mystery Magazine* (New York), August 1983.

"Line of Succession," in *Mike Shayne Mystery Magazine* (Los Angeles), August 1983.

"Suddenly in September," in *Ellery Queen's Mystery Magazine* (New York), September 1983.

"The Theft of the Halloween Pumpkin," in *Ellery Queen's Mystery Magazine* (New York), October 1983.

"The Graveyard on the Hill," in *The Lawmen,* edited by Bill Pronzini and Martin H. Greenberg. New York, Fawcett, 1984.

"The Last Unicorns," "The Maiden's Sacrifice," "Just One More," all in *100 Great Fantasy Short-Short Stories,* edited by Isaac Asimov, Terry Carr and Martin H. Greenberg. New York, Doubleday, 1984.

"Captain Leopold Looks for the Cause," in *Ellery Queen's Crimes and Punishments,* edited by Eleanor Sullivan and Karen A. Prince. New York, Dial Press, 1984.

"The Theft of the Used Teabag," in *Murder on the Menu,* edited by Carol-Lynn Rössel Waugh, Martin H. Greenberg and Isaac Asimov. New York, Avon, 1984.

"Deceptions," in *The Year's Best Mystery and Suspense Stories 1984,* edited by Edward D. Hoch. New York, Walker, 1984.

"The Case of the Drowned Coroner," in *Ellery Queen's Mystery Magazine* (New York), January 1984.

"Taxi!," in *Woman's World* (Englewood, New Jersey), 24 January 1984.

"Finding Joe Finch," in *Ellery Queen's Mystery Magazine* (New York), February 1984.

"Lottery," in *Mike Shayne Mystery Magazine* (Los Angeles), February 1984.

"Last Year's Murder," in *Ellery Queen's Prime Crimes 2,* edited by Eleanor Sullivan and Karen A. Prince, New York, Davis, 1984.

"The Problem of the Graveyard Picnic," in *Ellery Queen's Mystery Magazine* (New York), June 1984.

"The Spy at the Top of the List," in *Ellery Queen's Mystery Magazine* (New York), July 1984.

"The Rented Scar," in *The Eyes Have It,* edited by Robert J. Randisi. New York, Mysterious Press, 1984.

"Prison Bus," "Who Killed Lenore," both in *The Saint Magazine* (Van Nuys, California), August 1984.

"The Woman from Yesterday," in *Woman's World* (Englewood, New Jersey), 14 August 1984.

"Captain Leopold and the Mystery Woman," in *Ellery Queen's Mystery Magazine* (New York), September 1984.

"The Theft of the Dead Houseplant," in *Ellery Queen's Mystery Magazine* (New York), October 1984.

"The Problem of the Crying Room," in *Ellery Queen's Mystery Magazine* (New York), November 1984.

"The 500 Hours of Dr. Wisdom," in *Ellery Queen's Mystery Magazine* (New York), December 1984.

"Ark in the Desert," in *Alfred Hitchcock's Mystery Magazine* (New York), December 1984.

"The Hatchtree Assignment," in *Espionage* (Teaneck, New Jersey), December 1984.

"Too Long at the Fair," in *The Wickedest Show on Earth,* edited by Marcia Muller and Bill Pronzini. New York, Morrow, 1985.

"The Melting Man," in *The Deadly Arts,* edited by Bill Pronzini and Marcia Muller. New York, Arbor House, 1985.

"Murder at the Bouchercon," in *Chapter and Hearse,* edited by Marcia Muller and Bill Pronzini, New York, Morrow, 1985.

"The Spy Who Went to the Opera," and "The Problem of the Little Red Schoolhouse," in *The Deadly Arts,* edited by Bill Pronzini and Marcia Muller. New York, Arbor House, 1985.

"The Vanished Steamboat," in *The Year's Best Mystery and Suspense Stories 1985,* edited by Edward D. Hoch. New York, Walker, 1985.

"The Spy and the Suicide Club," in *Ellery Queen's Mystery Magazine* (New York), January 1985.

"Leopold in New York," in *Ellery Queen's Mystery Magazine* (New York), February 1985.

"The Spy on the Seaway," in *Espionage* (Teaneck, New Jersey), February 1985.

"The Theft of the Ball of Twine," in *Ellery Queen's Mystery Magazine* (New York), March 1985.

"The Trail of the Bells," in *Ellery Queen's Mystery Magazine* (New York), April 1985.

"Cover Story," in *Espionage* (Teaneck, New Jersey), May 1985.

"Smothered Mate," in *Mike Shayne Mystery Magazine* (Los Angeles), May 1985.

"The Luck of a Gypsy," in *The Ethnic Detectives,* edited by Bill Pronzini and Martin H. Greenberg. New York, Dodd Mead, 1985.

"Odds on a Gypsy," in *Ellery Queen's Mystery Magazine* (New York), July 1985.

"Bigfish," in *A Treasury of American Horror Stories,* edited by Frank D. McSherry, Jr., Charles G. Waugh and Martin H. Greenberg. New York, Bonanza 1985.

"The Spy Who Looked Back," in *Ellery Queen's Mystery Magazine* (New York), August 1985.

"The Phantom Stallion," in *Ellery Queen's Mystery Magazine* (New York), October 1985.

"Captain Leopold and the Arrow Murders," "The Sweating Statue," both in *Detectives A to Z,* edited by Frank D. McSherry, Jr., Martin H. Greenberg and Charles G. Waugh. New York, Bonanza 1985.

"The Theft of the Cardboard Castle," in *Ellery Queen's Mystery Magazine* (New York), November 1985.

"Wait Until Morning," in *Ellery Queen's Mystery Magazine* (New York), December 1985.

"Prisoner of Zerfall," in *Espionage* (Teaneck, New Jersey), November 1985.

"The Spy at the Spa," in *Ellery Queen's Mystery Magazine* (New York), Mid-December 1985.

"The Teddy Bear Mystery," in *Upstate* (Rochester, New York), 22 December 1985.

"Day of the Wizard," in *Locked Room Puzzles,* edited by Martin H. Greenberg and Bill Pronzini. Chicago, Academy, 1986.

"The Homesick Chicken," in *101 Science Fiction Stories,* edited by Martin H. Greenberg, Charles G. Waugh and Jenny-Lynn Waugh. New York, Avenel, 1986.

"The Problem of the Whispering House," in *Ellery Queen's Blighted Dwellings,* edited by Eleanor Sullivan. New York, Davis, 1986.

"Captain Leopold Goes to the Dogs," in *Great Modern Police Stories,* edited by Bill Pronzini and Martin H. Greenberg. New York, Walker, 1986.

"The Problem of the Fatal Fireworks," in *Tales from Ellery Queen's Mystery Magazine,* edited by Eleanor Sullivan and Cynthia Manson. San Diego, Harcourt Brace Jovanovich, 1986.

"Captain Leopold's Secret," in *The Year's Best Mystery and Suspense Stories 1986,* edited by Edward D. Hoch. New York, Walker, 1986.

"Blood of a Gypsy," in *Ellery Queen's Mystery Magazine* (New York), January 1986.

"Centaur Fielder for the Yankees," in *Mythical Beasties,* edited by Isaac Asimov, Martin H. Greenberg and Charles G. Waugh. New York, Signet, 1986.

"The Problem of the Unfinished Painting," in *Ellery Queen's Mystery Magazine* (New York), February 1986.

"The Sacramento Waxworks," in *Ellery Queen's Mystery Magazine* (New York), March 1986.

"Captain Leopold Views a Crime Scene," in *Ellery Queen's Mystery Magazine* (New York), April 1986.

"Day of the Dead," in *Espionage* (Teaneck, New Jersey), April 1986.

"The Gypsy Treasure," in *Ellery Queen's Mystery Magazine* (New York), May 1986.

"Mystery at Wimbledon," in *Women's Sports and Fitness* (Palo Alto, California), May–June 1986.

"The Theft of the Author's Eraser," in *Ellery Queen's Mystery Magazine* (New York), June 1986.

"The Spy Who Knew the Future," in *Ellery Queen's Mystery Magazine* (New York), July 1986.

"Leopold and the Thunderer," in *Ellery Queen's Mystery Magazine* (New York), August 1986.

"The Sleeper Assignment," in *Espionage* (Teaneck, New Jersey), August 1986.

"Murder at Rose Cottage," in *The Agatha Christie Mystery Collection.* New York, Bantam, 1986.

"The Problem of the Sealed Bottle," in *Ellery Queen's Mystery Magazine* (New York), September 1986.

"The Only Tree in Tasco," in *Ellery Queen's Mystery Magazine* (New York), October 1986.

"The Theft of McGregor's Skunk," in *Ellery Queen's Mystery Magazine* (New York), November 1986.

"The S.S.S.," in *Mystery Scene* (Cedar Rapids, Iowa), November 1986.

"The Film Festival Assignment," in *Ellery Queen's Prime Crimes 4*, edited by Eleanor Sullivan. New York, Davis, 1986.

"The Problem of the Invisible Acrobat," in *Ellery Queen's Mystery Magazine* (New York), Mid-December 1986.

"The Terrier Recognition," (jigsaw puzzle story). New York, International Polygonics, 1986.

"The Maze and the Monster," in *Devils and Demons*, edited by Marvin Kaye. New York, Doubleday, 1987.

"The Problem of the County Fair," in *Uncollected Crimes*, edited by Bill Pronzini and Martin H. Greenberg. New York, Walker, 1987.

"The Vanishing Men," in *Prime Suspects*, edited by Bill Pronzini and Martin H. Greenberg. New York, Ivy, 1987.

"The Problem of the Boston Common," in *Murder and Mystery in Boston*, edited by Carol-Lynn Rössel Waugh, Martin H. Greenberg and Frank D. McSherry, Jr. New York, Dembner, 1987.

"The Spy's Story," in *The Year's Best Mystery and Suspense Stories 1987*, edited by Edward D. Hoch. New York, Walker, 1987.

"Punishment for a Gypsy," in *Ellery Queen's Mystery Magazine* (New York), January 1987.

"Leopold and the Four O'Clock Felon," in *Ellery Queen's Mystery Magazine* (New York), February 1987.

"Poker Game at the Golden Nugget," in *Ellery Queen's Mystery Magazine* (New York), March 1987.

"The Theft of the Lost Slipper," in *Ellery Queen's Mystery Magazine* (New York), April 1987.

"Spy For Sale," in *The New Black Mask 8*, edited by Matthew J. Bruccoli and Richard Layman. San Diego, Harcourt Brace Jovanovich, 1987.

"A Flash of Red," in *A Matter of Crime 1*, edited by Matthew J. Bruccoli and Richard Layman. San Diego, Harcourt Brace Jovanovich, 1987.

"The Gypsy Wizard," in *Ellery Queen's Mystery Magazine* (New York), May 1987.

"The Spy and the Short-Order Cipher," in *Ellery Queen's Mystery Magazine,* (New York), June 1987.

"The Problem of the Curing Barn," in *Ellery Queen's Mystery Magazine* (New York), August 1987.

"The Theft of the Matador's Cape," in *Ellery Queen's Mystery Magazine* (New York), September 1987.

"The Return of the Speckled Band," in *The New Adventures of Sherlock Holmes*, edited by Martin H. Greenberg and Carol-Lynn Rössel Waugh. New York, Carroll and Graf, 1987.

"The Murder in Room 1010," in *Ellery Queen's Mystery Magazine* (New York), November 1987.

"The Hostage Gypsies," in *Ellery Queen's Mystery Magazine* (New York), Mid-December 1987.

"Funeral in the Fog," in *Weird Tales*, edited by Marvin Kaye. New York, Doubleday, 1988.

"The Day We Killed the Madman," in *Alfred Hitchcock's Shrouds and Pockets*, edited by Cathleen Jordan. New York, Davis, 1988.

"The Three Travellers," in *Crime at Christmas*, edited by Jack Adrian. Wellingborough, Northamptonshire, Equation, 1988.

"The Theft of the Overdue Library Book," in *Murder and Mystery in Chicago*, edited by Carol-Lynn Rössel Waugh, Martin H. Greenberg and Frank D. McSherry, Jr. New York, Dembner, 1988.

"The Invisible Intruder," in *Lady on the Case*, edited by Marcia Muller, Bill Pronzini and Martin H. Greenberg. New York, Bonanza, 1988.

"Leopold and the Broken Bride," in *The Year's Best Mystery and Suspense Stories 1988*, edited by Edward D. Hoch. New York, Walker, 1988.

"The Spy and the Embassy Murders," in *Ellery Queen's Mystery Magazine* (New York), January 1988.

"The Way Up to Hades," in *Alfred Hitchcock's Mystery Magazine* (New York), January 1988.

"The Virgins of Valentine," in *14 Vicious Valentines*, edited by Rosalind M. Greenberg, Martin H. Greenberg and Charles G. Waugh. New York, Avon 1988.

"The Nude Over the Bar," in *Ellery Queen's Mystery Magazine* (New York), February 1988.

"Leopold and the Cemetary Bandits," in *Ellery Queen's Mystery Magazine* (New York), March 1988.

"The Problem of the Thunder Room," in *Ellery Queen's Mystery Magazine* (New York), April 1988.

"The Theft of the Birthday Cake," in *Ellery Queen's Mystery Magazine* (New York), May 1988.

"The River of Doubt," and "The Tragedy of 1799," in *Mr. President, Private Eye*, edited by Martin H. Greenberg and Francis M. Nevins, Jr. New York, Ballantine, 1988.

"A Game for Spies," in *Ellery Queen's Mystery Magazine* (New York), June 1988.

"Murder of a Gypsy King," in *Ellery Queen's Mystery Magazine* (New York), July 1988.

"The Theft of the Faded Flag," in *Ellery Queen's Mystery Magazine* (New York), September 1988.

"The Crime in Heaven," in *Ellery Queen's Mystery Magazine* (New York), October 1988.

"The Problem of the Black Roadster," in *Ellery Queen's Mystery Magazine* (New York), November 1988.

"Essence D'Orient," in *Raymond Chandler's Philip Marlowe*, edited by Byron Preiss. New York, Knopf, 1988.

"Gypsy at Sea," in *Ellery Queen's Mystery Magazine* (New York), Mid-December 1988.

"Something Green," in *Special Reports: Fiction* (Knoxville, Tennessee), November 1988–January 1989.

"The Bad Samaritan," in *John Creasey's Crime Collection 1989*, edited by Herbert Harris. London, Gollancz, 1989.

"The House of a Hundred Birds," in *Senior Sleuths*, edited by Isaac Asimov, Martin H. Greenberg and Carol-Lynn Rössel Waugh. Boston, Hall, 1989.

"The Problem of the Hunting Lodge," in *Beastly Tales*, edited by Sara Paretsky. New York, Wynwood, 1989.

"The Problem of Santa's Lighthouse," in *Murder in New England*, edited by Eleanor Sullivan and Chris Dorbandt. Secaucus, New Jersey, Castle, 1989.

"Brothers on the Beach," in *A Treasury of American Mystery Stories*, edited by Frank D. McSherry Jr., Charles G. Waugh and Martin H. Greenberg. New York, Bonanza, 1989.

"Kansas in August," in *A Treasury of American Mystery Stories*, edited by Frank D. McSherry Jr., Charles G. Waugh and Martin H. Greenberg. New York, Bonanza, 1989.

"The Tombstone Hearse," in *The Arizonans*, edited by Bill Pronzini and Martin H. Greenberg. New York, Fawcett, 1989.

"The Problem of the Snowbound Cabin," in *Murder and Mystery in Maine*, edited by Carol-Lynn Rössel Waugh, Frank D. McSherry Jr., and Martin H. Greenberg. New York, Dembner, 1989.

"The Spy and the Guy Fawkes Bombing," in *The Year's Best Mystery and Suspense Stories 1989*, edited by Edward D. Hoch. New York, Walker, 1989.

"Sacajawea's Gold," in *Ellery Queen's Mystery Magazine* (New York), January 1989.

"The Theft of the Doctor's Chopsticks," in *Ellery Queen's Mystery Magazine* (New York), February 1989.

"The Killer Everyone Knew," in *Ellery Queen's Mystery Magazine* (New York), March 1989.

"The Underground Spy," in *Ellery Queen's Mystery Magazine* (New York), April 1989.

"The Problem of the Two Birthmarks," in *Ellery Queen's Mystery Magazine* (New York), May 1989.

"The Other Phantom," in *Phantoms*, edited by Martin H. Greenberg and Rosalind M. Greenberg. New York, DAW, 1989.

"The Gypsy and the Pilgrims," in *Ellery Queen's Mystery Magazine* (New York), June 1989.

"The Theft of the Empty Birdcage," in *Ellery Queen's Mystery Magazine* (New York), July 1989.

"The Circus Murders," in *Ellery Queen's Mystery Magazine* (New York), August 1989.

"The Pirate of Millionaires' Cove," in *The Further Adventures of Batman*, edited by Martin H. Greenberg. New York, Bantam, 1989.

"The Urgent Message," in *Ellery Queen's Mystery Magazine* (New York), September 1989.

"The Spy and the Geomancers," in *Ellery Queen's Mystery Magazine* (New York), October 1989.

"The Overheard Conversation," in *Foundation's Friends*, edited by Martin H. Greenberg. New York, Tor, 1989.

"The Gypsy Bear," in *Ellery Queen's Mystery Magazine* (New York), November 1989.

"The Problem of the Dying Patient," in *Ellery Queen's Mystery Magazine* (New York), December 1989.

"The Touch of Kolyada," in *Mistletoe Mysteries*, edited by Charlotte MacLeod. New York, Mysterious Press, 1989.

"The Theft of the Christmas Stocking," in *Ellery Queen's Mystery Magazine* (New York), Mid-December 1989.

"The Stalker of Souls," in *Stalkers*, edited by Ed Gorman and Martin H. Greenberg. Arlington Heights, Illinois, Dark Harvest, 1989.

"The Victorian Hangman," in *Under the Gun*, edited by Ed Gorman, Robert J. Randisi and Martin H. Greenberg. New York, Plume, 1990.

"The Trial of Ben Snow," in *Ellery Queen's Mystery Magazine* (New York), January 1990.

"Captain Leopold's Birthday," in *Ellery Queen's Mystery Magazine* (New York), February 1990.

"The Joker is Mild," in *The Further Adventures of the Joker*, edited by Martin H. Greenberg. New York, Bantam 1990.

"The Spy Who Went to Camelot," in *Ellery Queen's Mystery Magazine* (New York), March 1990.

"The Crypt of the Gypsy Saint," in *Ellery Queen's Mystery Magazine* (New York), April 1990.

"The Problem of the Protected Farmhouse," in *Ellery Queen's Mystery Magazine*, May 1990.

Uncollected Short Stories as Stephen Dentinger

"Dark Campus," in *Smashing Detective* (New York), March 1956.

"The Late Sports," in *Crack Detective* (New York), December 1956.

"Circus," in *The Saint* (New York), January 1962.

"The Night My Friend," in *The Saint* (London), July 1962.

"Festival in Black," in *The Saint* (London), August 1962.

"The Tattooed Priest," in *The Saint* (New York), February 1963.

"The Demon at Noon," in *The Saint* (New York), February 1963.

"The Freech Case," in *The Saint* (New York), May 1964.

"A Stranger Came to Reap," in *The Saint* (New York), September 1964.

"A Question of Punishment," in *The Saint* (New York), September 1965.

"To Slay an Eagle," in *The Award Espionage Reader*, edited by Hans S. Santesson. New York, Award, 1965.

"It Happens, Sometimes," in *The Saint* (New York), April 1966.

"Ring the Bell Softly," in *The Saint* (New York), July 1966.

"What's It All About," in *The Saint* (New York), January 1967.

"Recruitment," in *The Saint* (New York), October 1967.

"God of the Playback," in *Gods for Tomorrow*, edited by Hans S. Santesson. New York, Award, 1967.

"First Offense," in *Ellery Queen's Mystery Magazine* (New York), January 1968.

"The Future Is Ours," in *Crime Prevention in the 30th Century*, edited by Hans S. Santesson. New York, Walker, 1969.

"Fifty Bucks by Monday," in *Mike Shayne Mystery Magazine* (Los Angeles), November 1971.

"The Judas Kiss," in *Alfred Hitchcock's Mystery Magazine* (New York), July 1976.

Uncollected Short Stories as Pat McMahon

"The Suitcase," in *The Saint* (New York), September 1962.

"The Authentic Death of Cotton Clark," in *The Saint* (New York), May 1966.

"Uncle Max," in *Child's Ploy*, edited by Marcia Muller and Bill Pronzini. New York, Macmillan, 1984.

Uncollected Short Stories as Mr. X

The Will-o'-the-Wisp Mystery ("The Pawn," "The Rook," "The Knight," "The Bishop," "The Queen," "The King"), in *Ellery Queen's Mystery Magazine* (New York), April–September 1971; as Edward D. Hoch, in *Ellery Queen's Maze of Mysteries*, New York, Dial Press, 1982.

Uncollected Short Stories as R.L. Stevens

"The Physician and the Opium Fiend," in *Ellery Queen's Mystery Bag*. Cleveland, World, 1972.

"Just Something That Happened," in *Ellery Queen's Mystery Magazine* (New York), February 1972.

"The Legacy," in *Ellery Queen's Mystery Magazine* (New York), August 1972.

"The Lot's Wife Caper," in *Ellery Queen's Anthology, Spring–Summer*. New York, Davis, 1973.

"King's Knight's Gambit Declined," in *Ellery Queen's Mystery Magazine* (New York), July 1973.

"Nothing to Chance," in *Ellery Queen's Mystery Magazine* (New York), January 1974.

"The Most Dangerous Man," in *Ellery Queen's Murdercade*. New York, Random House, 1975.

"Here Be Dragons," in *Alfred Hitchcock's Mystery Magazine* (New York), May 1976.

"EQMM Number 400," in *Ellery Queen's Mystery Magazine* (New York), March 1977.

"Innocent Victim," in *Ellery Queen's Mystery Magazine* (New York), January 1978.

"The Missing Money," in *Ellery Queen's Mystery Magazine* (New York), July 1978.

"Five Rings in Reno," in *A Multitude of Sins*, edited by Ellery Queen. New York, Davis, 1978.

"The Price of Wisdom," in *Best Detective Stories of the Year,* edited by Edward D. Hoch. New York, Dutton, 1978.

"The Forbidden Word," in *Mysterious Visions.* New York, St. Martin's Press, 1979.

"Deduction, 1996," in *Ellery Queen's Mystery Magazine* (New York), 6 October 1980.

"Lot 721/XT258," in *Miniature Mysteries,* edited by Isaac Asimov, Martin H. Greenberg and Joseph D. Olander, New York, Taplinger, 1981.

"The Crime of the Century," in *The Big Apple Mysteries,* edited by Carol-Lynn Rössel Waugh, Martin H. Greenberg and Isaac Asimov. New York, Avon, 1982.

"The Chicken Soup Kid," in *Murder on the Menu,* edited by Carol-Lynn Rössel Waugh, Martin H. Greenberg and Isaac Asimov. New York, Avon, 1984.

"The Great American Novel," in *Chapter and Hearse,* edited by Marcia Muller and Bill Pronzini, New York, Morrow, 1985.

"Bull and Bear," in *A Treasury of American Mystery Stories,* edited by Frank D. McSherry Jr., Charles G. Waugh and Martin H. Greenberg, New York, Bonanza, 1989.

OTHER PUBLICATIONS

Other

"Writing the Mystery Short Story," in *The Writer's Handbook,* edited by A.S. Burack. Boston, The Writer, 1975.

"The Cryptography Bureau: How to Tell a Vigenère from a Pigpen," in *Murder Ink: The Mystery Reader's Companion,* edited by Dilys Winn. New York, Workman, 1977.

The Monkey's Clue, and *The Stolen Sapphire* (for children). New York, Grosset and Dunlap, 1978.

Editor, *Dear Dead Days.* New York, Walker, 1972; London, Gollancz, 1974.

Editor, *Best Detective Stories of the Year.* New York, Dutton, 6 volumes, 1976–81.

Editor, *All But Impossible! An Anthology of Locked Room and Impossible Crime Stories.* New Haven, Connecticut, Ticknor and Fields, 1981; London, Hale, 1983.

Editor, *The Year's Best Mystery and Suspense Stories.* New York, Walker, 9 volumes, 1982–90.

Editor, with Martin H. Greenberg, *Great British Detectives.* Chicago, Academy, 1987.

Editor, with Martin H. Greenberg, *Women Write Murder,* Chicago, Academy, 1987.

Editor, with Martin H. Greenberg, *Murder Most Sacred: Great Catholic Tales of Mystery and Suspense,* New York, Dember, 1989.

*

Bibliography: "Edward D. Hoch: A Checklist," by William J. Clark, Edward D. Hoch, and Francis M. Nevins, Jr., in *Armchair Detective* (White Bear Lake, Minnesota), February 1976; revised edition, by Nevins and Hoch, privately printed, 1979.

Edward D. Hoch comments:

I work mainly in the short story because I find that form most satisfying to me, and amenable to the type of formal detective story I like to do best. Series characters work especially well for me within the framework of a short story. Writing a novel has always been, to me, a task to be finished as quickly as possible.

Writing a short story is a pleasure one can linger over, with delight in the concept and surprise at the finished product.

*   *   *

If ever there was a member of an endangered species it's Ed Hoch, the sole surviving professional writer of short mysteries. Since his debut in 1955, in addition to five novels, he has published more than 650 such tales, including numerous non-series stories and a total of 22 separate series. Among his recurring characters are an occult detective who claims to be two thousand years old, a private eye, a Western drifter who may be a reincarnation of Billy the Kid, a priest, a British cryptographer-sleuth, a science-fictional Computer Investigation Bureau, a con man, two Interpol agents reminiscent of the stars of TV's *The Avengers,* a Lollipop Cop, and a New England physician-detective of the 1920's. His longest-running and perhaps best series are those dealing with Nick Velvet, the thief who steals only valueless objects and often has to detect while thieving, and Captain Leopold, the tough but sensitive violent-crime specialist on the force of a large north-eastern city.

In the stories of Hoch's pre-1960 apprenticeship the ideas are occasionally quite original (e.g., the murder of one of a sect of Penitentes while the cult members are hanging on crucifixes in a dark cellar), but the execution tends to be crude and naive and the Roman Catholic viewpoint somewhat obtrusive. As his work matured it came to reflect the influence of several of his own favorite writers, including Graham Greene, Jorge Luis Borges, and especially John Dickson Carr and Ellery Queen. Such Hoch stories as "The Long Way Down," in which a man leaps from a skyscraper window but doesn't hit the ground until hours later, and "The Vanishing of Velma," in which a woman disappears without trace from a moving ferris wheel, are among the finest works in the tradition of Carr's impossible-crime tales.

Some of Hoch's most vividly written stories appeared in the *Alfred Hitchcock* and *Saint* mystery magazines during the 1960's, among them his Edgar-winning "The Oblong Room," in which Captain Leopold investigates a college campus murder with bizarre religious overtones. But from 1965 to the present his most consistent market has been *Ellery Queen's Mystery Magazine* which, with very few exceptions, has featured at least one Hoch story per issue since the early 1970's. Although his EQMM output is usually written in the plainest nuts-and-bolts style, the story concepts are generally stimulating, and his best efforts for the magazine are lovely miniaturizations of the classical fair-play detective novels for which Queen himself is famous.

—Francis M. Nevins, Jr.

———

HOCKING, (Mona Naomi) Anne (Messer). Also wrote as Mona Messer. British. Born in the 1890's; daughter of the writer Joseph Hocking.

CRIME PUBLICATIONS

Novels (series: Inspector/Superintendent William Austen)

A Castle for Sale. London, Methuen, and New York, Dial Press, 1930.

Mouse Trap (as Mona Messer). London, Jarrolds, and New York, Putnam, 1931.
Cat's Paw. London, Stanley Paul, 1933.
Death Duel. London, Stanley Paul, 1933.
Walk into My Parlour. London, Stanley Paul, 1934.
The Hunt Is Up. London, Stanley Paul, 1934.
Without the Option. London, Stanley Paul, 1935.
Stranglehold. London, Stanley Paul, 1936.
The House of En-Dor. London, Stanley Paul, 1936.
As I Was Going to St. Ives. London, Stanley Paul, 1937.
What a Tangled Web. London, Stanley Paul, 1937.
Ill Deeds Done. London, Bles, 1938.
The Little Victims Play. London, Bles, 1938.
So Many Doors. London, Bles, 1939.
Old Mrs. Fitzgerald (Austen). London, Bles, 1939; as *Deadly Is the Evil Tongue,* New York, Doubleday, 1940.
The Wicked Flee. London, Bles, 1940.
Miss Milverton (Austen). London, Bles, 1941; as *Poison Is a Bitter Brew,* New York, Doubleday, 1942.
Night's Candles. London, Bles, 1941.
One Shall Be Taken (Austen). London, Bles, 1942.
Death Loves a Shining Mark (Austen). New York, Doubleday, 1943.
Nile Green (Austen). London, Bles, 1943.
Six Green Bottles (Austen). London, Bles, 1943.
The Vultures Gather (Austen). London, Bles, 1945.
Death at the Wedding (Austen). London, Bles, 1946.
Prussian Blue (Austen). London, Bles, 1947; as *The Finishing Touch,* New York, Doubleday, 1948.
At the Cedars (Austen). London, Bles, 1949.
Death Disturbs Mr. Jefferson (Austen). New York, Doubleday, 1950; London, Bles, 1951.
The Best Laid Plans (Austen). New York, Doubleday, 1950; London, Bles, 1952.
Mediterranean Murder (Austen). London, Evans, 1951; as *Killing Kin,* New York, Doubleday, 1951.
There's Death in the Cup. London, Evans, 1952.
Death among the Tulips (Austen). London, W.H. Allen, 1953.
The Evil That Men Do (Austen). London, W.H. Allen, 1953.
And No One Wept (Austen). London, W.H. Allen, 1954.
Poison in Paradise (Austen). London, W.H. Allen, and New York, Doubleday, 1955.
A Reason for Murder (Austen). London, W.H. Allen, 1955.
Murder at Mid-Day (Austen). London, W.H. Allen, 1956.
Relative Murder (Austen). London, W.H. Allen, 1957.
The Simple Way of Poison (Austen). London, W.H. Allen, and New York, Washburn, 1957.
Epitaph for a Nurse (Austen). London, W.H. Allen, 1958; as *A Victim Must Be Found,* New York, Doubleday, 1959.
Poisoned Chalice (Austen). London, Long, 1959.
To Cease upon the Midnight (Austen). London, Long, 1959.
The Thin-Spun Life (Austen). London, Long, 1960.
Candidates for Murder (Austen). London, Long, 1961.
He Had to Die (Austen). London, Long, 1962.
Murder Cries Out (Austen), completed by Evelyn Healey. London, Long, 1968.

OTHER PUBLICATIONS as Mona Messer

Novels

Eternal Compromise. London, Stanley Paul, and New York, Putnam, 1932.
A Dinner of Herbs. London, Stanley Paul, 1933.
The End of the Lane. London, Stanley Paul, 1933.
Playing Providence. London, Stanley Paul, 1934.

Wife of Richard. London, Stanley Paul, 1934.
Cuckoo's Brood. London, Stanley Paul, 1935.
Life Owes Me Something. London, Stanley Paul, 1936.
Tomorrow Also. London, Stanley Paul, 1937.
Marriage Is Like That. London, Stanley Paul, 1938.
Stranger's Vineyard. London, Stanley Paul, 1939.
The Gift of a Daughter. London, Stanley Paul, 1940.

*   *   *

That Mona Messer supplemented her career as a "straight" novelist with over 40 mysteries written as Anne Hocking should surprise no one. Her father, Joseph Hocking, although a religious novelist, was well versed in the use of suspense. And her sister, Elizabeth Nisot, also wrote thrillers—first under the pseudonym William Penmare, and later under her own name. Anne Hocking's own career began in the early 1930's with a series of mysteries containing little detection, but a great many arch-villains, cultured innocents, and obligatory brave-and-beautiful career-girl heroines. Her evolution toward classic detection culminated in the creation, in the late 1930's, of Chief Inspector (later Superintendent) William Austen of Scotland Yard. Thereafter, virtually all of Hocking's mysteries feature Austen. One notable, and appealing, exception is *Night's Candles* in which the co-sleuths are the commandant of the Famagusta Police and his wife, a detective novelist.

Austen is a policeman of the Roderick Alleyn school. He is tall, impeccably dressed, and possessed of a vague military air. He is Oxford educated, "with a charming voice and delightful manners." Suspects often admit that he shatters their stereotyped image of a policeman. Unlike Alleyn, Austen ("a lonely man") never marries. But he does eventually acquire two Watsons: Inspector Curtis and Sergeant Flyte. Neither is highly developed as a character. They do, however, fulfill their major function—as sounding boards for Austen's theories.

Scotland Yard notwithstanding, Austen detects very little in London. Instead, he pursues murderers in such exotic locales as Cyprus, Egypt, South Africa, and the Costa Brava of Spain. And some of Hocking's most effective novels are set in Cornwall.

Like many prolific mystery writers, Hocking displays a certain repetitiousness in her novels. Murder victims tend to be either sadistic older husbands or blackmailers. As to murder methods, a great many barbiturate poisonings are punctuated by an occasional fall or bashing. And murderers tend to be so sympathetic that, if they are not saved from the gallows by madness, Austen (always the gent) allows a suicide exit. Suspects often drop a suitable quotation. Unfortunately, the same source may be quoted by different characters in different novels.

This is not to say that Hocking is all cardboard and contrivance. She will often produce a highly satisfying murder method—as in *Prussian Blue*—or a compelling character—as in *Old Mrs. Fitzgerald* and *Miss Milverton*. And she always produces a quiet, amiable mystery, of a type now classic.

—Kathleen L. Maio

HODGSON, William Hope. British. Born in Blackmore End, Essex, 15 November 1877. Apprentice seaman, 1891–95; officer in the Mercantile Marine: Lieutenant; founder and teacher, W.H. Hodgson's school of Physical Culture, Blackburn, Lancashire, 1899–1901. Joined University of London

Officer Training Corps, 1914; commissioned in Royal Field Artillery, 1915; left service because of injury, 1916; recommissioned, 1917, and died at Ypres. Recipient: Royal Humane Society Medal, 1898. *Died 17 April 1918.*

CRIME PUBLICATIONS

Short Stories (series: Carnacki)

Carnacki, The Ghost Finder, and a Poem. New York, Reynolds, 1910.
Carnacki, The Ghost Finder (collection). London, Nash, 1913; augmented edition, Sauk City, Wisconsin, Mycroft and Moran, 1947.
Captain Gault, Being the Exceedingly Private Log of a Sea-Captain. London, Nash, 1917; New York, McBride, 1918.

OTHER PUBLICATIONS

Novels

The Boats of the "Glen Carrig". London, Chapman and Hall, 1907; New York, Ballantine, 1971.
The House on the Borderland. London, Chapman and Hall, 1908.
The Ghost Pirates. London, Stanley Paul, 1909; Westport, Connecticut, Hyperion Press, 1976.
The Night Land. London, Nash, 1912; Westport, Connecticut, Hyperion Press, 1976.

Short Stories

The Ghost Pirates, A Chaunty, and Another Story. New York, Reynolds, 1909.
Men of the Deep Waters. London, Nash, 1914.
The Luck of the Strong. London, Nash, 1916.
Deep Waters. Sauk City, Wisconsin, Arkham House, 1967.
Out of the Storm: Uncollected Fantasies, edited by Sam Moskowitz. West Kingston, Rhode Island, Grant, 1975.

Verse

Poems and The Dream of X. London, Watt, and New York, Paget, 1912.
Cargunka and Poems and Anecdotes. London, Watt, and New York, Paget, 1914.
The Calling of the Sea. London, Selwyn and Blount, 1920.
The Voice of the Ocean. London, Selwyn and Blount, 1921.
Poems of the Sea. London, Ferret Fantasy, 1977.

*

Bibliography: by A.L. Searles, in *The House on the Borderland and Other Novels,* Sauk City, Wisconsin, Arkham House, 1946.

Critical Study: *William Hope Hodgson: Voyages and Visions,* edited by Ian Bell. Privately printed 1987.

* * *

William Hope Hodgson was a frequent contributor to the British variety magazines of the early 20th century. He worked in many areas of fiction and non-fiction, and much of his material (including stories with crime elements) is still uncollected.

Captain Gault contains 10 adventures of a merchant marine captain who is modelled after C.J. Cutcliffe Hyne's then-popular Captain Kettle. These stories are concerned mostly with outwitting customs authorities in various criminal ways. Much more important are Hodgson's excursions into supernatural fiction, where he is a major figure. His novels *The House on the Borderland, The Ghost Pirates,* and *The Night Land* are visionary accounts that have no real parallels in English literature. Related to them are the adventures of Carnacki, an occult detective.

Carnacki, The Ghost-Finder contains six cases set among the haunts of England and Ireland. While some of these cases are rationalized, others are truly supernatural. These stories embody a mythology which they share with the novels mentioned above: that humanity lives in a state of spiritual and physical peril, surrounded by supernatural forces of utmost malignancy. To futher Carnacki's accomplishments Hodgson invented a body of suppositious literature and lore to deal with his hostile universe. In this the influence of Arthur Machen (*The Great God Pan,* "The White People") is probable. The 1947 edition of *Carnacki, The Ghost-Finder* adds three hitherto uncollected stories, two supernatural, and one a rational detective story. Carnacki's adventures, along with those of Le Fanu's Dr. Hesselius and Algernon Blackwood's John Silence, constitute three great classics in this interesting subdivision of the detective story, where the detective really amounts to a white magician.

—E.F. Bleiler

HOGARTH, Charles. *See* CREASEY, John.

HOLDEN, Dalby. *See* HAMMOND, Gerald.

HOLDING, Elisabeth Sanxay. American. Born in Brooklyn, New York, 8 June 1889. Educated at Miss Whitcombe's School; Packer Institute; Miss Botsford's School; Staten Island Academy. Married George E. Holding in 1913 (died 1943); one daughter and one son. Traveled widely in South America and lived in Bermuda where her husband was a British government officer. *Died 7 February 1955.*

CRIME PUBLICATIONS

Novels (series: Lieutenant Levy)

Miasma. New York, Dutton, 1929.
Dark Power. New York, Vanguard Press, 1930.
The Death Wish. New York, Dodd Mead, 1934; London, Nicholson and Watson, 1935.
The Unfinished Crime. New York, Dodd Mead, 1935; London, Newnes, 1936.
The Strange Crime in Bermuda. New York, Dodd Mead, 1937; London, Lane, 1938.

The Obstinate Murderer. New York, Dodd Mead, 1938; as *No Harm Intended,* London, Lane, 1939.
The Girl Who Had to Die. New York, Dodd Mead, 1940.
Who's Afraid? New York, Duell, 1940; as *Trial by Murder,* New York, Novel Selections, n.d.
Speak of the Devil. New York, Duell, 1941; as *Hostess to Murder,* n.p., Mystery Novel Classics, 1943.
Kill Joy. New York, Duell, 1942; as *Murder Is a Kill-Joy,* New York, Dell, 1946.
Lady Killer. New York, Duell, 1942.
The Old Battle Ax. New York, Simon and Schuster, 1943.
Net of Cobwebs. New York, Simon and Schuster, 1945; London, Corgi, 1952.
The Innocent Mrs. Duff. New York, Simon and Schuster 1946.
The Blank Wall (Levy). New York, Simon and Schuster, 1947.
Too Many Bottles (Levy). New York, Simon and Schuster, 1951; London, Muller, 1953; as *The Party Was the Pay-Off,* New York, Spivak, 1952.
The Virgin Huntress. New York, Simon and Schuster, 1951.
Widow's Mite (Levy). New York, Simon and Schuster, 1953; London, Muller, 1954.

Uncollected Short Stories

"Kiskadee Bird," in *Third Mystery Companion,* edited by Abraham Louis Furman. New York, Gold Label Books, 1945.
"The Blue Envelope," in *Murder for the Millions,* edited by Frank Owen. New York, Frederick Fell, 1946.
"Unbelievable Baroness," in *Fourth Mystery Companion,* edited by Abraham Louis Furman. New York, Lantern Press, 1946.
"Farewell to a Corpse," in *Mystery Book Magazine* (New York), October 1946.
"People Do Fall Downstairs," in *Queen's Awards 1947,* edited by Ellery Queen. Boston, Little Brown, and London, Gollancz, 1947.
"The Stranger in the Car," in *American Magazine* (Springfield, Ohio), July 1949.
"Farewell, Big Sister," in *Ellery Queen's Mystery Magazine* (New York), July 1952.
"Most Audacious Crime," in *Nero Wolfe Mystery Magazine* (New York), January 1954.
"Glitter of Diamonds," in *Ellery Queen's Mystery Magazine* (New York), March 1955.
"Very, Very Dark Mink," in *The Saint* (New York), December 1956.
"The Darling Doctor," in *Alfred Hitchcock's Mystery Magazine* (New York), March 1957.
"Game for Four Players," in *Alfred Hitchcock's Mystery Magazine* (New York), June 1958.
"The Blank Wall," in *Alfred Hitchcock Presents: My Favorites in Suspense.* New York, Random House, 1959.
"Bait for a Killer," in *The Saint* (New York), March 1959.

OTHER PUBLICATIONS

Novels

Invincible Minnie. New York, Doran, and London, Hodder and Stoughton, 1920.
Rosaleen among the Artists. New York, Doran, 1921.
Angelica. New York, Doran, 1921.
The Unlit Lamp. New York, Dutton, 1922.

The Shoals of Honor. New York, Dutton, 1926.
The Silk Purse. New York, Dutton, 1928.

Other

Miss Kelly. New York, Morrow, 1947.

* * *

Best known as a mystery writer, Elisabeth Sanxay Holding also wrote romantic novels and short stories. All reveal deep interest in psychology and are personality studies flavored with social criticism or murder. Holding was especially intrigued by middle-aged people under stress, and she was more concerned with justice than with the letter of the law. Her continuing character, Lieutenant Levy, is an experienced, clever policeman, unfailingly decent, courteous, and thoughtful—but not infallible. Levy is never the protagonist; instead, he symbolizes social order as opposed to the chaos generated by violence.

This pattern is especially effective in two of Holding's best works. In *The Old Battle Ax,* Charlotte Herriott allows others to control her life until murder forces her to reevaluate herself and her extended family circle. In *The Blank Wall,* Lucia Holley's preoccupation with ration stamps and supportive letters to her serviceman husband is interrupted by murder and the unsought affection of a criminal. Both women's portraits are clear and realistic; the symbolism is sound, and the treatment of the generation gap is vivid.

Lady Killer and *Too Many Bottles* study unwise marriages; *Net of Cobwebs* examines a damaged personality under extreme pressure. For these protagonists, murder triggers honest appraisals of midlife situations which are ultimately set right. *The Virgin Huntress* is a compelling portrait of a cowardly, vain, self-indulgent, and deadly man. Less realistic, *Dark Power* and *Miasma* are essentially gothics.

A careful, able writer, Holding experimented with many forms within the genre; the works are good, stimulating reading.

—Jane S. Bakerman

———

HOLDING, James. Also writes as Clark Carlisle; Jay Freeman; Ellery Queen, Jr. American. Born in Pittsburgh, Pennsylvania, 27 April 1907. Educated at Yale University, New Haven, Connecticut (editor, *Yale Record*; John Masefield Poetry prize; John Hubbard Curtis Poetry prize—twice), B.A. 1928. Married Janet Spice in 1931; two sons. Firebrick salesman, Harbison-Walker, Pittsburgh, 1929–30; copywriter, 1930–45, copy chief, 1945–49, vice-president, 1949–57, and consultant, 1958–68, Batten Barten Durstine and Osborn Advertising Agency, Pittsburgh. Agent: Scott Meredith Literary Agency Inc., 845 Third Avenue, New York, New York 10022. Address: 1251 Southport Drive, Sarasota, Florida 33581, U.S.A.

CRIME PUBLICATIONS

Uncollected Short Stories

"The Treasure of Pachacamac," in *Ellery Queen's Mystery Magazine* (New York), June 1960.
"An Accident at Honiara," in *Alfred Hitchcock's Mystery Magazine* (New York), June 1960.

"Go to Sleep, Darling," in *Alfred Hitchcock's Mystery Magazine* (New York), August 1960.

"The Most Surprised Man in the World" (as Clark Carlisle), in *Alfred Hitchcock's Mystery Magazine* (New York), September 1960.

"The Lipstick Explosion," in *Alfred Hitchcock's Mystery Magazine* (New York), November 1960.

"The Norwegian Apple Mystery," in *Ellery Queen's Mystery Magazine* (New York), November 1960.

"A Question of Ethics," in *Best Detective Stories of the Year,* edited by Brett Halliday. New York, Dutton, 1961.

"Silent Partner," in *Mike Shayne Mystery Magazine* (New York), March 1961.

"You Can't Be Too Careful," in *Alfred Hitchcock's Mystery Magazine* (New York), March 1961.

"Fair Warning," in *Manhunt* (New York), April 1961.

"The Lost Sapphire," in *Alfred Hitchcock's Mystery Magazine* (New York), April 1961.

"The African Fish Mystery," in *Ellery Queen's Mystery Magazine* (New York), April 1961.

"Murder's No Bargain," in *The Web,* May 1961.

"The Stolen Masterpiece," in *Mike Shayne Mystery Magazine* (New York), June 1961.

"Cotton Cloak, Wood Dagger," in *Alfred Hitchcock's Mystery Magazine* (New York), June 1961.

"No Whitewash for the Doctor," in *Guilty* (New York), June 1961.

"Where Is Thy Sting," in *Alfred Hitchcock's Mystery Magazine* (New York), August 1961.

"The Italian Tile Mystery," in *Ellery Queen's Mystery Magazine* (New York), September 1961.

"Death in New Zealand," in *Mike Shayne Mystery Magazine* (New York), December 1961.

"The Vapor Club," in *Alfred Hitchcock's Mystery Magazine* (New York), December 1961.

"Mexico with Money," in *Alfred Hitchcock's Mystery Magazine* (New York), March 1962.

"Do-It-Yourself Escape Kit," in *Ellery Queen's Mystery Magazine* (New York), March 1962.

"Those Cunning Florentines," in *Alfred Hitchcock's Mystery Magazine* (New York), June 1962.

"Diagnosis: Death," in *The Saint* (New York), July 1962.

"The Lost Leopard," in *Mike Shayne Mystery Magazine* (New York), October 1962.

"Cop Killer," in *Alfred Hitchcock's Mystery Magazine* (New York), November 1962.

"The Photographer and the Undertaker," in *Ellery Queen's Mystery Magazine* (New York), November 1962.

"Variations on a Theme," in *Alfred Hitchcock's Mystery Magazine* (New York), June 1963.

"A Mishap in Venice," in *Mike Shayne Mystery Magazine* (New York), June 1963.

"Murder of an Unknown Man," in *Mike Shayne Mystery Magazine* (New York), August 1963.

"The Hong Kong Jewel Mystery," in *Ellery Queen's Mystery Magazine* (New York), November 1963.

"The Zanzibar Shirt Mystery," in *Ellery Queen's Mystery Magazine* (New York), December 1963.

"Set 'em Up in the Other Alley," in *Mike Shayne Mystery Magazine* (New York), December 1963.

"The Queen's Jewel," in *Crimes Across the Sea,* edited by John Creasey. New York, Harper, 1964.

"The Photographer and the Policeman," in *Ellery Queen's Mystery Magazine* (New York), April 1964.

"Miranda's Lucky Punch," in *Alfred Hitchcock's Mystery Magazine* (New York), July 1964.

"The Sunburned Fisherman," in *Alfred Hitchcock's Mystery Magazine* (New York), October 1964.

"The Tahitian Powder Box Mystery," in *Ellery Queen's Mystery Magazine* (New York), October 1964.

"The Spook Goes West," in *Mike Shayne Mystery Magazine* (New York), November 1964.

"Contraband," in *Alfred Hitchcock's Mystery Magazine* (New York), December 1964.

"An Exercise in Insurance," in *Masters of Mayhem,* edited by Edward D. Radin. New York, Morrow, 1965.

"Live and Let Live," in *Ellery Queen's Mystery Magazine* (New York), January 1965.

"The Japanese Card Mystery," in *Ellery Queen's Mystery Magazine* (New York), October 1965.

"Career Man," in *Alfred Hitchcock's Mystery Magazine* (New York), October 1965.

"Let the Credit Go," in *Mike Shayne Mystery Magazine* (New York), November 1965.

"Who Steals My Purse," in *Alfred Hitchcock's Mystery Magazine* (New York), November 1965.

"A Turn to the Right," in *Alfred Hitchcock's Mystery Magazine* (New York), December 1965.

"The Monkey King," in *Alfred Hitchcock's Mystery Magazine* (New York), February 1966.

"Death of a King," in *Shell Scott Mystery Magazine* (New York), February 1966.

"Suicide Clause," in *The Man from U.N.C.L.E.* (New York), March 1966.

"Grounds for Divorce," in *Ellery Queen's Mystery Magazine* (New York), March 1966.

"A Felony in the Family," in *Mike Shayne Mystery Magazine* (New York), April 1966.

"The Photographer and the Jeweler," in *Ellery Queen's Mystery Magazine* (New York), May 1966.

"No Hiding Place," in *Shell Scott Mystery Magazine* (New York), June 1966.

"Fly Away Home," in *The Man from U.N.C.L.E.* (New York), June 1966.

"The Woman Who Loved Children," in *Shell Scott Mystery Magazine* (New York), July 1966.

"The Toothpick Murder," in *Ellery Queen's Mystery Magazine* (New York), July 1966.

"The Photographer and the Professor," in *Ellery Queen's Mystery Magazine* (New York), September 1966.

"The Moonlighter," in *Alfred Hitchcock's Mystery Magazine* (New York), November 1966.

"The New Zealand Bird Mystery," in *Ellery Queen's Mystery Magazine* (New York), January 1967.

"The Photographer and the Columnist," in *Ellery Queen's Mystery Magazine* (New York), June 1967.

"A Padlock for Charlie Draper," in *Alfred Hitchcock's Mystery Magazine* (New York), July 1967.

"The Inquisitive Butcher of Nice," in *With Malice Toward All,* edited by Robert L. Fish. New York, Putnam, 1968; London, Macmillan, 1969.

"The Misopedist," in *Alfred Hitchcock's Mystery Magazine* (New York), April 1968.

"Lesson One," in *Alfred Hitchcock's Mystery Magazine* (New York), August 1968.

"The Dream-Destruction Syndrome," in *Alfred Hitchcock's Mystery Magazine* (New York), October 1968.

"A Steal at the Price," in *Alfred Hitchcock's Mystery Magazine* (New York), September 1969.

"The Dutiful Rookie," in *Alfred Hitchcock's Mystery Magazine* (New York), November 1969.

"A Case of Brotherly Love," in *Alfred Hitchcock's Mystery Magazine* (New York), January 1970.

"Cause for Alarm," in *Ellery Queen's Mystery Magazine* (New York), April 1970.

"Just What the Doctor Ordered," in *Alfred Hitchcock's Mystery Magazine* (New York), May 1970.

"Test Run," in *Ellery Queen's Mystery Magazine* (New York), July 1970.

"Wild Mink," in *Alfred Hitchcock's Mystery Magazine* (New York), July 1970.

"The Photographer and the Servant Problem," in *Ellery Queen's Mystery Magazine* (New York), October 1970.

"The Consultant," in *Alfred Hitchcock's Mystery Magazine* (New York), November 1970.

"Second Talent," in *Alfred Hitchcock Presents: Stories to Stay Awake By.* New York, Random House, 1971.

"A Good Kid," in *Alfred Hitchcock's Mystery Magazine* (New York), March 1971.

"A Funny Place to Park," in *Alfred Hitchcock's Mystery Magazine* (New York), May 1971.

"Mystery Fan," in *Ellery Queen's Mystery Magazine* (New York), May 1971.

"Conflict of Interest," in *Alfred Hitchcock's Mystery Magazine* (New York), July 1971.

"T'ang of the Suffering Dragon," in *Alfred Hitchcock's Mystery Magazine* (New York), September 1971.

"The Borneo Snapshot Mystery," in *Ellery Queen's Mystery Magazine* (New York), January 1972.

"A Man of His Age," in *Mike Shayne Mystery Magazine* (Los Angeles), June 1972.

"The Gambler," in *Mike Shayne Mystery Magazine* (Los Angeles), July 1972.

"A Homemade Dress," in *Alfred Hitchcock's Mystery Magazine* (New York), October 1972.

"Listen to the Dial Tone," in *Mike Shayne Mystery Magazine* (Los Angeles), October 1972.

"A Message from Marsha," in *Alfred Hitchcock's Mystery Magazine* (New York), November 1972.

"Conversation Piece," in *Alfred Hitchcock's Mystery Magazine* (New York), December 1972.

"Hell in a Basket," in *Mike Shayne Mystery Magazine* (Los Angeles), December 1972.

"Weak in the Head," in *Alfred Hitchcock's Mystery Magazine* (New York), January 1973.

"More Than a Mere Story Book," in *Ellery Queen's Mystery Magazine* (New York), February 1973.

"The 1861 Twelve," in *Alfred Hitchcock's Mystery Magazine* (New York), April 1973.

"The Photographer and the Artist," in *Ellery Queen's Mystery Magazine* (New York), May 1973.

"The Duty of Every Citizen," in *Alfred Hitchcock's Mystery Magazine* (New York), May 1973.

"The Photographer and the Butcher," in *Ellery Queen's Mystery Magazine* (New York), July 1973.

"The Montevideo Squeeze," in *Alfred Hitchcock's Mystery Magazine* (New York), November 1973.

"Recipe for Murder," in *Alfred Hitchcock's Mystery Magazine* (New York), December 1973.

"Cornerback," in *Killers of the Mind,* edited by Lucy Freeman. New York, Random House, 1974.

"The Bookmark," in *Ellery Queen's Mystery Magazine* (New York), January 1974.

"Busman's Holiday," in *Alfred Hitchcock's Mystery Magazine* (New York), January 1974.

"Triple Play," in *Alfred Hitchcock's Mystery Magazine* (New York), February 1974.

"A Visitor to Mombasa," in *Alfred Hitchcock's Mystery Magazine* (New York), March 1974.

"The Elusive Mrs. Stout," in *Ellery Queen's Mystery Magazine* (New York), April 1974.

"Special Delivery," in *Alfred Hitchcock's Mystery Magazine* (North Palm Beach, Florida), April 1974.

"Your Money for Your Life," in *Charlie Chan Mystery Magazine* (Los Angeles), May 1974.

"The Zamboango Shuttle," in *Alfred Hitchcock's Mystery Magazine* (North Palm Beach, Florida), June 1974.

"Passport to Paradise," in *Alfred Hitchcock's Mystery Magazine* (North Palm Beach, Florida), July 1974.

"The Photographer and the Jockey," in *Ellery Queen's Mystery Magazine* (New York), August 1974.

"Border Crossing," in *Alfred Hitchcock's Mystery Magazine* (North Palm Beach, Florida), February 1975.

"One Plus One Makes Three," in *Mike Shayne Mystery Magazine* (Los Angeles), April 1975.

"A Rope Through His Ear," in *Mike Shayne Mystery Magazine* (Los Angeles), August 1975.

"Christian Charity," in *87th Precinct* (Los Angeles), August 1975.

"Still a Cop," in *Ellery Queen's Mystery Magazine* (New York), December 1975.

"The Mutilated Scholar," in *Ellery Queen's Doors to Mystery.* New York, Davis, 1976.

"Library Fuzz," in *Ellery Queen's Magicians of Mystery.* New York, Davis, 1976.

"Hand in Glove," in *Tricks and Treats,* edited by Joe Gores and Bill Pronzini. New York, Doubleday, 1976; London, Gollancz, 1977.

"The Fund-Raisers," in *Best Detective Stories of the Year 1976,* edited by Edward D. Hoch. New York, Dutton, 1976.

"Break-In," in *Alfred Hitchcock's Mystery Magazine* (North Palm Beach, Florida), January 1976.

"The Photographer: Lisbon Assignment," in *Ellery Queen's Mystery Magazine* (New York), February 1976.

"Is There a Doctor in the House?," in *Mike Shayne Mystery Magazine* (Los Angeles), April 1976.

"In the Soup," in *Mike Shayne Mystery Magazine* (Los Angeles), September 1976.

"The Savonarola Syndrome," in *Mike Shayne Mystery Magazine* (Los Angeles), October 1976.

"The Packing Case," in *Mike Shayne Mystery Magazine* (Los Angeles), November 1976.

"Hero with a Headache," in *Mike Shayne Mystery Magazine* (Los Angeles), December 1976.

"The Philippine Key Mystery," in *When Last Seen,* edited by Arthur Maling. New York, Harper, 1977.

"Rediscovery," in *Best Detective Stories of the Year 1977,* edited by Edward D. Hoch. New York, Dutton, 1977.

"The Blood Tests," in *Alfred Hitchcock's Mystery Magazine* (New York), January 1977.

"The Photographer and the Unknown Victim," in *Ellery Queen's Mystery Magazine* (New York), April 1977.

"The Henchman Case," in *Alfred Hitchcock's Mystery Magazine* (New York), May 1977.

"The Contract," in *Alfred Hitchcock's Mystery Magazine* (New York), August 1977.

"Reason Enough," in *Alfred Hitchcock's Mystery Magazine* (New York), September 1977.

"Once Upon a Bank Floor," in *Alfred Hitchcock's Tales to Scare You Stiff,* edited by Eleanor Sullivan. New York, Davis, 1978.

"Open till Nine," in *Alfred Hitchcock's Mystery Magazine* (New York), January 1978.

"The Swap Shop," in *Alfred Hitchcock's Mystery Magazine* (New York), February 1978.

"One for the Road," in *Mike Shayne Mystery Magazine* (Los Angeles), February 1978.

"The Photographer and the B.L.P.," in *Ellery Queen's Mystery Magazine* (New York), March 1978.

"The Baby Bit," in *Ellery Queen's Mystery Magazine* (New York), June 1978.

"The Young Runners," in *Ellery Queen's Mystery Magazine* (New York), July 1978.

"The Honeycomb of Silence," in *Alfred Hitchcock's Mystery Magazine* (New York), August 1978.

"Paper Caper," in *Alfred Hitchcock's Mystery Magazine* (New York), February 1979.

"The Hummelmyer Operation," in *Alfred Hitchcock's Mystery Magazine* (New York), March 1979.

"The Jack O'Neal Affair," in *Alfred Hitchcock's Mystery Magazine* (New York), May 1979.

"In the Presence of Death," in *Ellery Queen's Mystery Magazine* (New York), June 1979.

"Card Sense," in *Ellery Queen's Mystery Magazine* (New York), December 1979.

"Half a Loaf," in *Ellery Queen's Mystery Magazine* (New York), 5 May 1980.

"The Photographer and the Arsonist," in *Ellery Queen's Mystery Magazine* (New York), 19 November 1980.

"The Reward," in *Best Detective Stories of the Year 1981,* edited by Edward D. Hoch. New York, Dutton, 1981.

"Shima Maru," in *Alfred Hitchcock's Mystery Magazine* (New York), 7 January 1981.

"Work of Art," in *Alfred Hitchcock's Mystery Magazine* (New York), 4 February 1981.

"The Only One of Its Kind," in *Ellery Queen's Mystery Magazine* (New York), 25 February 1981.

"By Person or Persons Unknown," in *Ellery Queen's Mystery Magazine* (New York), 22 April 1981.

"The Search for Tamerlane," in *Ellery Queen's Mystery Magazine* (New York), 20 May 1981.

"Portrait in Yellow," in *Alfred Hitchcock's Mystery Magazine* (New York), 9 December 1981.

"The Photographer and the Letter," in *Ellery Queen's Mystery Magazine* (New York), 24 February 1982.

"China Trader," in *Alfred Hitchcock's Mystery Magazine* (New York), 3 March 1982.

"A Deal in Rubies," in *Ellery Queen's Mystery Magazine* (New York), 24 March 1982.

"Sideswipe," in *Ellery Queen's Mystery Magazine* (New York), June 1982.

"A Decent Price for a Painting," in *Ellery Queen's Mystery Magazine* (New York), August 1982.

"The Photographer and the Final Payment," in *Ellery Queen's Mystery Magazine* (New York), December 1982.

"First Class All the Way," in *Alfred Hitchcock's Mystery Magazine* (New York), Mid-September 1983.

"A Temporary Bind," in *Ellery Queen's Mystery Magazine* (New York), January 1984.

"The Book Clue," in *Ellery Queen's Mystery Magazine* (New York), February 1984.

"The Photographer and the Sailor," in *Ellery Queen's Mystery Magazine* (New York), March 1984.

"The Grave Robber," in *Ellery Queen's Prime Crimes 2,* edited by Eleanor Sullivan and Karen A. Prince. New York, Davis, 1984.

OTHER PUBLICATIONS

Other (for children)

The Lazy Little Zulu. New York, Morrow, 1962; Kingswood, Surrey, World's Work, 1963.

Cato the Kiwi Bird. New York, Putnam, 1963.

Mr. Moonlight and Omar. New York, Morrow, 1963; Kingswood, Surrey, World's Work, 1964.

The King's Contest and Other North African Tales. London, Abelard Schuman, 1964.

The Mystery of the False Fingertips. New York, Harper, 1964.

Sherlock on the Trail. New York, Morrow, 1964.

The Country Cousins (as Jay Freeman). Racine, Wisconsin, Whitman, 1964.

The Purple Bird Mystery (as Ellery Queen, Jr.). New York, Putnam, 1965.

The Three Wishes of Hu. New York, Putnam, 1965.

The Sky-Eater and Other South Sea Tales. London, Abelard Schuman, 1966.

Poko and the Golden Demon. London, Abelard Schuman, 1968.

The Robber of Featherbed Lane. New York, Putnam, 1968.

The Mystery of the Dolphin Inlet. New York, Macmillan, 1968.

Bugs Bunny's Carrot Machine (as Clark Carlisle). Racine, Wisconsin, Western, 1971.

A Bottle of Pop. New York, Putnam, 1972.

The Watchcat. Middletown, Connecticut, Xerox, 1975.

The Ugliest Dog in the World. Middletown, Connecticut, Xerox, 1979.

*

Manuscript Collection: University of Minnesota Library, Minneapolis.

* * *

Retiring from a successful career in advertising, James Holding launched a second career, as a mystery writer, in 1960 with "The Treasure of Pachacamac," a short story about ancient archaeology and modern Peru. He next wrote a series of pastiches about Ellery Queen, the author, rather than the detective, using King Danforth and Martin Leroy (names based on Frederic Dannay and Manfred Lee), creators of detective Leroy King. They are on a round-the-world cruise and encounter murder at sea and in almost every port. This permits Holding to present and solve some fine problems involving time-tested Queenian devices like the dying message and the locked room. His titles add to the charm of the series, evoking the early Queen with "The Norwegian Apple Mystery," "The Hong Kong Jewel Mystery," and "The Tahitian Powder Box Mystery," best in the series.

In a second Holding series, entirely different but equally clever, Manuel Andradas is a Brazilian who uses photography to hide his main occupation: professional assassin for "The Big Ones," Brazil's organized crime group. The stories are well plotted, with unexpected complications invariably arising. "The Photographer and the Final Payment" is the most intriguing entry because in it Holding accepted Editor Queen's challenge to give Andradas an assignment in which the photographer, himself, is the intended victim.

In addition to some good (albeit not very deep) views of life in Rio, Holding provides some humorous touches which offset the depressing amorality of the stories. Andradas uses the euphemism "nullification" to refer to his work. His discussion of fees with his employers is a parody of labor-management negotiations, as a professional killer talks about base pay and his lack of a retirement plan and fringe benefits.

A third series by Holding is less exotic but still depicts an unusual detective. Hal Johnson, the "Library Fuzz," has the job of recovering stolen and long overdue books for the public library. Inevitably, he comes across more serious crimes, like murder, which he solves by using his prior experience as a homicide detective. Though Holding never makes it clear how (or why) a capable detective could be transferred from homicide to library work, his idea is interesting and appealing to mystery fans and book lovers. Rare book lore is used convincingly in "The Search for Tamerlane" about a book apparently written by Poe under the pseudonym "A Bostonian." "The Book Clue" is one of the most satisfying Johnson stories, once the reader can accept the idea of a bank robber leaving an overdue library book at the scene of the crime.

When unencumbered by a series character, Holding gives his imagination even freer rein. A delightful tale of blackmail and murder, "The Inquisitive Butcher of Nice," begins with the finding of a corpse in a refrigerated display case. "Miranda's Lucky Punch," published in 1964, predates the current wave of stories about using computers to steal. "A Temporary Bind" presents a car insurance scam built around the premise that one can have a car "stolen," collect from the insurance company, and still keep the car. Critics nominated "A Decent Price for a Painting" for an MWA Edgar, obviously taken by one of the more ingenious art forgery stories of recent years.

—Marvin Lachman

HOLME, Timothy.   British.   Worked as an actor for several years and as a journalist for the Windsor, Slough, and Eton *Express.* Married Bianca Ghirardelli; two adopted children. *Died 31 May 1987.*

CRIME PUBLICATIONS

Novels (series: Commissario Achille Peroni in all books)

The Neapolitan Streak.   London, Macmillan, and New York, Coward McCann, 1980.
A Funeral of Gondolas.   London, Macmillan, 1981; New York, Coward McCann, 1982.
The Devil and the Dolce Vita.   London, Macmillan, 1982; New York, Walker, 1988.
The Assissi Murders.   London, Macmillan, 1985; New York, Walker, 1988.
At the Lake of Sudden Death.   London, Macmillan, 1987; New York, Walker, 1988.

OTHER PUBLICATIONS

Novel

Mamma Mia! London, Joseph, 1968.

Other

Sardinia, with B. Ghirardelli.   London, Cape, 1967; revised edition, 1977.
Gondola, Gondolier. London, Gentry, 1971.

Viaggio a Roma, with Bianca Ghirardelli.   London, Longman, 1975.
A Servant of Many Masters: The Life and Times of Carlo Goldini.   London, Jupiter, 1976.
One Europe: Italy, with Bianca Ghirardelli.   London, Longman, 1978.
Trip to Rome, with Philippa Whitbread.   London, Longman, 1980.
Vile Florentines: The Florence of Dante, Giotto, and Boccaccio.   London, Cassell, and New York, St. Martin's Press, 1980.
Survive in Italian, with L.G. Alexander and Bianca Holme.   London, Longman, 1980.
Longman Italian Pocket Traveller, with L.G. Alexander and Bianca Holme.   London, Longman, 1983.

Editor, *The Penguin Italian Reader.*   London, Penguin, 1974.

* * *

Timothy Holme's stories are fine escapist fiction that will appeal in particular to those readers who have had the good fortune to spend their holidays in the beautiful scenery and amidst the cultural riches of the cities of northern Italy, in Venice (*A Funeral of Gondolas* and *The Devil and the Dolce Vita*), Verona (*The Neapolitan Streak*) and Assisi (*The Assisi Murders*) and on the shores of Lake Garda (*At the Lake of Sudden Death*). There is always just the right amount of description of the setting and of local customs, not to mention the wine of the region, to bring back pleasant memories and, hardly less important, to create that flattering sense of being in the know. The occasional Italian word adds to the atmosphere too in tales whose attitude to Italian life and politics, especially in *The Neapolitan Streak,* is an oddly British mixture of amusement, disapproval, and fascination. History also often adds a dimension to tales set in the present day, for instance in *The Assisi Murders* where the past is shown as particularly relevant to the crime under investigation.

The hero of the tales, which do not have to be read in sequence, though it is interesting to see the gradual development of Holme's techniques, is a stranger to the region too. Commissario Achille Peroni did spend six months at Scotland Yard, which gave him a smattering of English, a liking for English women and a taste for Chivas Regal and English cigarettes, of which he generally has a smuggled packet in his pocket. But essentially he is a Neapolitan, and his character is an attractive bundle of contradictions. He is a Southerner, and a guttersnipe at that, which leads to conflicts with his present duties as a respected senior detective in the Veneto who, on occasion, can even be tempted by the prospect of using influence to start his way up the greasy pole of Italian politics. He is a free-thinker too, yet in a scrape—and he is always getting into them—a prayer to Saint Januarius, patron of Naples, comes unbidden to his lips, and, surprisingly enough, that generally seems to do the trick. Achille sometimes pretends to be disconcerted when people recall an article in the press that called him the "Rudolf Valentino of the Italian police," a description in which he apparently never discerned the least hint of irony, but it seems that his great exploits as a lover are in the past. Now he certainly responds to a beautiful woman, but he rarely gets beyond admiring glances or a delicious embrace before death intervenes.

Murder is the basis of Holme's plots. But it is never too messy or upsetting, just mysterious, and the reader is always confident that Achille will make sense of it all in due course. There is little in the way of complicated forensic procedures or technical detective work, and the police force as such has little part to play, unless brought in for some specific purpose by the

Commissario, who generally prefers to seek solutions on his own. At first he is simply confused, but he doggedly follows up clues and hunches, taking risks where necessary so that he can eavesdrop and observe. Gradually a rich panorama of vivid character types is unveiled, and the truth emerges. It could be argued that Achille is no more than an expert detective than he is an accomplished lover, yet few would complain about this because the object of the tales is more to convey atmosphere through a character and spin a more or less improbable yarn in a plausible setting than to grip the attention through the plot.

At the Lake of Sudden Death shows Holme at his best. The Italian-English connection is brought out by the fact that Achille is first attracted by the beautiful Cordelia, an enigmatic English girl. She has hardly had time to teach him the delights of midnight sailing on Lake Garda, a picturesque setting where, of course, storms can blow up unexpectedly, when she is murdered. Before the truth emerges we have been taken back to the exciting last days of Mussolini, Churchill makes a brief appearance, and there is a mixture of Fascism and hi-tec in an account of the recovery of something mysterious that had been hidden away in those seemingly bottomless waters.

Holme's narrative manner is attractive, though it could be argued that some of his flashbacks to events that took place before the time of Achille's investigation smack rather too much of a television detective series. Generally, though, he is content to let things unfold chronologically, and some pattern is imposed by his practice of grouping his short chapters into rather larger sections to which he gives titles indicating the nature of the episode in question. A fluent prose style also plays its part in making the Achille Peroni stories eminently enjoyable reading.

—Christopher Smith

HOLMES, Gordon. *See* SHIEL, M.P.

HOLMES, Grant. *See* FOX, James M.

HOLMES, H.H. *See* BOUCHER, Anthony.

HOLT, Victoria. Pseudonym for Eleanor Alice Hibbert, née Burford; also writes as Philippa Carr; Jean Plaidy; has also written as Eleanor Burford; Elbur Ford; Kathleen Kellow; Ellalice Tate. British. Born in London, in 1906. Educated privately. Married G.P. Hibbert. Agent: A.M. Heath and Company Ltd., 79 St. Martin's Lane, London WC2N 4AA, England.

CRIME PUBLICATIONS

Novels

Mistress of Mellyn. New York, Doubleday, 1960; London, Collins, 1961.
Kirkland Revels. New York, Doubleday, and London, Collins, 1962.
Bride of Pendorric. New York, Doubleday, and London, Collins, 1963.
The Legend of the Seventh Virgin. New York, Doubleday, and London, Collins, 1965.
Menfreya in the Morning. New York, Doubleday, 1966; as *Menfreya,* London, Collins, 1966.
The King of the Castle. New York, Doubleday, and London, Collins, 1967.
The Shivering Sands. New York, Doubleday, and London, Collins, 1969.
The Secret Woman. New York, Doubleday, 1970; London, Collins, 1971.
The Shadow of the Lynx. New York, Doubleday, 1971; London, Collins, 1972.
On the Night of the Seventh Moon. New York, Doubleday, 1972; London, Collins, 1973.
The Curse of the Kings. New York, Doubleday, and London, Collins, 1973.
The House of a Thousand Lanterns. New York, Doubleday, and London, Collins, 1974.
Lord of the Far Island. New York, Doubleday, and London, Collins, 1975.
The Pride of the Peacock. New York, Doubleday, and London, Collins, 1976.
The Mask of the Enchantress. New York, Doubleday, and London, Collins, 1980.
The Judas Kiss. New York, Doubleday, and London, Collins, 1981.
The Demon Lover. New York, Doubleday, and London, Collins, 1982.
The Time of the Hunter's Moon. New York, Doubleday, and London, Collins, 1983.
The Landower Legacy. London, Collins, and New York, Doubleday, 1984.
The Road to Paradise Island. London, Collins, and New York, Doubleday, 1985.
Secret for a Nightingale. London, Collins, and New York, Doubleday, 1986.
The Silk Vendetta. London, Collins, and New York, Doubleday, 1987.
The Indian Fan. London, Collins, and New York, Doubleday, 1988.
The Captive. London, Collins, and New York, Doubleday, 1989.
The Snare of Serpents. London, Collins, and New York, Doubleday, 1990.

Novels as Elbur Ford

Poison in Pimlico. London, Laurie, 1950.
Flesh and the Devil. London, Laurie, 1950.
The Bed Disturbed. London, Laurie, 1952.
Such Bitter Business. London, Heinemann, 1953; as *Evil in the House,* New York, Morrow, 1954.

Novels as Philippa Carr

The Miracle at St. Bruno's. London, Collins, and New York, Putnam, 1972.

The Lion Triumphant. London, Collins, and New York, Putnam, 1974.

The Witch from the Sea. London, Collins, and New York, Putnam, 1975.

OTHER PUBLICATIONS

Novels

The Queen's Confession. New York, Doubleday, and London, Collins, 1968.

The Devil on Horseback. New York, Doubleday, and London, Collins, 1977.

My Enemy the Queen. New York, Doubleday, and London, Collins, 1978.

The Spring of the Tiger. New York, Doubleday, and London, Collins, 1979.

Novels as Eleanor Burford

Daughter of Anna. London, Jenkins, 1941.
Passionate Witness. London, Jenkins, 1941.
The Married Lover. London, Jenkins, 1942.
When All the World Is Young. London, Jenkins, 1943.
So the Dreams Depart. London, Jenkins, 1944.
Not in Our Stars. London, Jenkins, 1945.
Dear Chance. London, Jenkins, 1947.
Alexa. London, Jenkins, 1948.
The House at Cupid's Cross. London, Jenkins, 1949.
Believe the Heart. London, Jenkins, 1950.
The Love Child. London, Jenkins, 1950.
Saint or Sinner? London, Jenkins, 1951.
Dear Delusion. London, Jenkins, 1952.
Bright Tomorrow. London, Jenkins, 1952.
Leave Me My Love. London, Jenkins, 1953.
When We Are Married. London, Jenkins, 1953.
Castles in Spain. London, Jenkins, 1954.
Heart's Afire. London, Jenkins, 1954.
When Other Hearts. London, Jenkins, 1955.
Two Loves in Her Life. London, Jenkins, 1955.
Begin to Live. London, Mills and Boon, 1956.
Married in Haste. London, Mills and Boon, 1956.
To Meet a Stranger. London, Mills and Boon, 1957.
Pride of the Morning. London, Mills and Boon, 1958.
Blaze of Noon. London, Mills and Boon, 1958.
The Dawn Chorus. London, Mills and Boon, 1959.
Red Sky at Night. London, Mills and Boon, 1959.
Night of Stars. London, Mills and Boon, 1960.
Now That April's Gone. London, Mills and Boon, 1961.
Who's Calling. London, Mills and Boon, 1962.

Novels as Jean Plaidy

Together They Ride. London, Swan, 1945.
Beyond the Blue Mountains. New York, Appleton Century, 1947; London, Hale, 1948.
Murder Most Royal. London, Hale, 1949; New York, Putnam, 1972; as *The King's Pleasure,* New York, Appleton Century Crofts, 1949.
The Goldsmith's Wife. London, Hale, and New York, Appleton Century Crofts, 1950; as *The King's Mistress,* New York, Pyramid, 1952.
Catherine de' Medici. London, Hale, 1969.
  Madame Serpent. London, Hale, and New York, Appleton Century Crofts, 1951.

The Italian Woman. London, Hale, 1952; New York, Putnam, 1975.
Queen Jezebel. London, Hale, and New York, Appleton Century Crofts, 1953.
Daughter of Satan. London, Hale, 1952; New York, Putnam, 1973; as *The Unholy Woman,* Toronto, Harlequin, 1954.
The Sixth Wife. London, Hale, 1953; New York, Putnam, 1969.
The Spanish Bridegroom. London, Hale, 1954; Philadelphia, Macrae Smith, 1956.
St. Thomas's Eve. London, Hale, 1954; New York, Putnam, 1970.
Gay Lord Robert. London, Hale, 1955; New York, Putnam, 1972.
Royal Road to Fotheringay. London, Hale, 1955; New York, Putnam, 1968.
Charles II. London, Hale, 1972.
  The Wandering Prince. London, Hale, 1956; New York, Putnam, 1971.
  A Health unto His Majesty. London, Hale, 1956; New York, Putnam, 1972.
  Here Lies Our Sovereign Lord. London, Hale, 1957; New York, Putnam, 1973.
Flaunting Extravagant Queen (Marie Antoinette). London, Hale, 1957.
Lucrezia Borgia. London, Hale, 1976.
  Madonna of the Seven Hills. London, Hale, 1958; New York, Putnam, 1974.
  Light on Lucrezia. London, Hale, 1958; New York, Putnam, 1976.
Louis, The Well-Beloved. London, Hale, 1959.
The Road to Compiègne. London, Hale, 1959.
Isabella and Ferdinand. London, Hale, 1970.
  Castile for Isabella. London, Hale, 1960.
  Spain for the Sovereigns. London, Hale, 1960.
  Daughters of Spain. London, Hale, 1961.
Katharine of Aragon. London, Hale, 1968.
  Katharine, The Virgin Widow. London, Hale, 1961.
  The Shadow of the Pomegranate. London, Hale, 1962.
  The King's Secret Matter. London, Hale, 1962.
The Captive Queen of Scots. London, Hale, 1963; New York, Putnam, 1970.
The Thistle and the Rose. London, Hale, 1963; New York, Putnam, 1973.
Mary, Queen of France. London, Hale, 1964.
The Murder in the Tower. London, Hale, 1964; New York, Putnam, 1974.
Evergreen Gallant. London, Hale, 1965; New York, Putnam, 1973.
The Last of the Stuarts. London, Hale, 1977.
  The Three Crowns. London, Hale, 1965; New York, Putnam, 1977.
  The Haunted Sisters. London, Hale, 1966; New York, Putnam, 1977.
  The Queen's Favourites. London, Hale, 1966; New York, Putnam, 1978.

Georgian Saga:

1. *Queen in Waiting.* London, Hale, 1967; New York, Putnam, 1985.
2. *The Princess of Celle.* London, Hale, 1967; New York, Putnam, 1985.
3. *The Prince and the Quakeress.* London, Hale, 1968; New York, Putnam, 1986.
4. *Caroline, The Queen.* London, Hale, 1968; New York, Putnam, 1986.

5. *The Third George.* London, Hale, 1969; New York, Putnam, 1987.
6. *Perdita's Prince.* London, Hale, 1969; New York, Putnam, 1987.
7. *Sweet Lass of Richmond Hill.* London, Hale, 1970; New York, Putnam, 1988.
8. *Indiscretions of the Queen.* London, Hale, 1970.
9. *The Regent's Daughter.* London, Hale, 1971; New York, Putnam, 1989.
10. *Goddess of the Green Room.* London, Hale, 1971; New York, Putnam, 1989.

Victorian Saga:

1. *The Captive of Kensington Palace.* London, Hale, 1972; New York, Putnam, 1976.
2. *Victoria in the Wings.* London, Hale, 1972; New York, Putnam, 1990.
3. *The Queen and Lord M.* London, Hale, 1973; New York, Putnam, 1977.
4. *The Queen's Husband.* London, Hale, 1973; New York, Putnam, 1978.
5. *The Widow of Windsor.* London, Hale, 1974; New York, Putnam, 1978.

Norman Trilogy:

1. *The Bastard King.* London, Hale, 1974; New York, Putnam, 1979.
2. *The Lion of Justice.* London, Hale, 1975; New York, Putnam, 1979.
3. *The Passionate Enemies.* London, Hale, 1976; New York, Putnam, 1979.

Plantagenet Saga:

1. *The Plantagenet Prelude.* London, Hale, 1976; New York, Putnam, 1980.
2. *The Revolt of the Eaglets.* London, Hale, 1977; New York, Putnam, 1980.
3. *The Heart of the Lion.* London, Hale, 1977; New York, Putnam, 1980.
4. *The Prince of Darkness.* London, Hale, 1978; New York, Putnam, 1980.
5. *The Battle of the Queens.* London, Hale, 1978; New York, Putnam, 1981.
6. *The Queen from Provence.* London, Hale, 1979; New York, Putnam, 1981.
7. *Edward Longshanks.* London, Hale, 1979; as *Hammer of the Scots,* New York, Putnam, 1981.
8. *The Follies of the King.* London, Hale, 1980; New York, Putnam, 1982.
9. *The Vow on the Heron.* London, Hale, 1980; New York, Putnam, 1982.
10. *Passage to Pontefract.* London, Hale, 1981; New York, Putnam, 1982.
11. *The Star of Lancaster.* London, Hale, 1981; New York, Putnam, 1982.
12. *Epitaph for Three Women.* London, Hale, 1981; New York, Putnam, 1983.
13. *Red Rose of Anjou.* London, Hale, 1982; New York, Putnam, 1983.
14. *The Sun in Splendour.* London, Hale, 1982; New York, Putnam, 1983.

15. *Uneasy Lies the Head.* London, Hale, 1982; New York, Putnam, 1984.

Queens of England series:

1. *My Self, My Enemy.* London, Hale, 1983; New York, Putnam, 1984.
2. *Queen of This Realm: The Story of Queen Elizabeth I.* London, Hale, 1984; New York, Putnam, 1985.
3. *Victoria Victorious.* London, Hale, 1985; New York, Putnam, 1986.
4. *The Lady in the Tower.* London, Hale, and New York, Putnam, 1986.
5. *The Courts of Love.* London, Hale, 1987; New York, Putnam, 1988.
6. *In the Shadow of the Crown.* London, Hale, 1988; New York, Putnam, 1989.
7. *The Queen's Secret.* London, Hale, 1989; New York, Putnam, 1990.
8. *The Reluctant Queen.* London, Hale, 1990.

Novels as Kathleen Kellow

Danse Macabre. London, Hale, 1952.
Rooms at Mrs. Oliver's. London, Hale, 1953.
Lilith. London, Hale, 1954.
It Began in Vauxhall Gardens. London, Hale, 1955.
Call of the Blood. London, Hale, 1956.
Rochester, The Mad Earl. London, Hale, 1957.
Milady Charlotte. London, Hale, 1959.
The World's a Stage. London, Hale, 1960.

Novels as Ellalice Tate

Defenders of the Faith. London, Hodder and Stoughton, 1956.
The Scarlet Cloak. London, Hodder and Stoughton, 1957.
The Queen of Diamonds. London, Hodder and Stoughton, 1958.
Madame du Barry. London, Hodder and Stoughton, 1959.
This Was a Man. London, Hodder and Stoughton, 1961.

Novels as Philippa Carr

Saraband for Two Sisters. London, Collins, and New York, Putnam, 1976.
Lament for a Lost Lover. London, Collins, and New York, Putnam, 1977.
The Love-Child. London, Collins, and New York, Putnam, 1978.
The Song of the Siren. London, Collins, and New York, Putnam, 1980.
The Drop of the Dice. London, Collins, and New York, Putnam, 1981.
Will You Love Me in September. New York, Putnam, 1981.
The Adulteress. London, Collins, and New York, Putnam, 1982.
Zipporah's Daughter. London, Collins, 1983; as *Knave of Hearts.* New York, Putnam, 1983.
Voices in a Haunted Room. London, Collins, and New York, Putnam, 1984.
The Return of the Gypsy. London, Collins, and New York, Putnam, 1985.
Midsummer's Eve. London, Collins, and New York, Putnam, 1986.
The Pool of St. Branok. London, Collins, and New York, Putnam, 1987.
The Changeling. London, Collins, and New York, Putnam, 1989.

The Black Swan. London, Collins, and New York, Putnam, 1990.

Other as Jean Plaidy

A Triptych of Poisoners. London, Hale, 1958.
The Rise [Growth, End] of the Spanish Inquisition. London, Hale, 3 vols., 1959–61; as *The Spanish Inquisition: Its Rise, Growth, and End,* New York, Citadel Press, 1 vol., 1967.
The Young Elizabeth (for children). London, Parrish, and New York, Roy, 1961.
Meg Roper, Daughter of Sir Thomas More (for children). London, Constable, 1961; New York, Roy, 1964.
The Young Mary Queen of Scots (for children). London, Parrish, 1962; New York, Roy, 1963.
Mary, Queen of Scots, The Fair Devil of Scotland. London, Hale, and New York, Putnam, 1975.

*

Victoria Holt comments:
I don't write crime stories, The only ones I did are those by Elbur Ford in the 1950's—reconstructions of real life crimes.

*   *   *

Victoria Holt is a prolific writer of romantic suspense novels. Her vivid descriptions and well-rounded characters absorb the reader into the stories' intricate plots. These plots are various; yet, death, love, blackmail, and secrets are often found. The setting of her stories is usually England of the 19th century, but her characters at times embark on journeys to distant places such as Australia, India, or Hong Kong.

The main character is typically a young woman of above average intelligence, and fair—but not beautiful—looks. She is commonly from an unconventional household, without a complete family, or has been brought up in a home to learn about art. From this background the heroine may go away to school, work as a governess, or run a business. There is rarely any prospect of wealth in her future. Many elements combine to work against her, and she often finds herself a victim of deceit; however, her common-sense and intelligence are her weapons of defense.

The other characters in these novels are also interesting and diverse. There may be a rich woman who tries to run everyone's lives, servants who do all they can to help the heroine, a friend who hides many secrets, and, of course, men with varying amounts of integrity. Although there are similarities in Holt's stories, each character and plot line is still unique.

In *The Legend of the Seventh Virgin,* the main character is Kerensa Carlee, a servant girl. She has been brought up by her grandmother to be proud and to go after what she wants. Yet, she betrays a friend, and ultimately is betrayed herself.

The Queen's Confession tells a sympathetic story of Marie Antoinette, from her arranged marriage to the French dauphin, to the violence that she finally faces. This story is told from her memoirs, which makes it feel like a first-hand account. Holt provides details of court life and the feelings of the time in France.

Dallas Lawson is the heroine of *The King of the Castle.* She is a brave and independent young woman who continues her father's work as a restorer of paintings in a French chateau. She finds much intrigue in her new position, from a mystery surrounding a count, a lost fortune, to an unexpected romance.

The Secret Woman tells the story of Anna Brett, a young woman brought up by her aunt to learn about antiques. Yet, it is also a story about Chantel Loman, a nurse who befriends Anna and leads her on exciting, but dangerous, adventures. At the heart of the story are the Creditons, a wealthy family who own a shipping line, and a history of scandals that keep on multiplying. People die mysterious deaths while Chantel leads Anna through one crisis to another.

In *The House of a Thousand Lanterns,* Jane Lindsay has grown up to learn about Chinese art. Her knowledge leads her to Hong Kong, where its beauty and intrigue shrouds the evils in those around her. Superstitions flourish in this strange land and Jane almost falls victim to them. She finds herself a unique woman in a place dominated by men, where she must use her intelligence to take charge of her life.

Drusilla Delany is a rational and intelligent daughter of a rector in *The India Fan.* Her village is dominated by the wealthy Framling family who are important in the East India Company. Drusilla is seen to be an appropriate companion to Lavinia Framling, a beautiful but rich young lady. Drusilla is supposed to make sure that Lavinia does not get herself into trouble. However, Lavinia has a mind of her own, without a conscience, and soon finds herself in a great predicament. Scandals abound in this story, and blackmail and murder are closely linked. Drusilla is found useful to the Framlings again when she joins Lavinia in India. But when the bloody Sepoy Mutiny takes place among them, she is unable to help. Throughout the story many characters make unfortunate decisions for themselves, yet Drusilla finds that her actions eventually pay off, and also finds love where she never expected it.

The countless stories that Holt has written all have the ability to grip the readers and make them feel as if they are there. Her knowledge and descriptions of English social life, exotic places, and works of art give her books a fullness that makes them favorites for many readers worldwide.

—Karen Hinckley

———

HOLTON, Leonard. Pseudonym for Leonard (Patrick O'Connor) Wibberley; also wrote as Patrick O'Connor; Christopher Webb. Irish. Born in Dublin, 9 April 1915. Educated at Ring College, Ireland; Abbey House, Romsey, Hampshire; Cardinal Vaughan's School, London, 1925–30; El Camino College, Torrance, California. Served in the Trinidad Artillery Volunteers, 1938–40: Lance Bombardier. Married Katherine Hazel Holton in 1948; two daughters and four sons. Reporter, *Sunday Dispatch,* 1931–32, *Sunday Express,* 1932–34, and *Daily Mirror,* 1935–36, all London; editor, Trinidad *Evening News,* 1936; oilfield worker, Trinidad, 1936–43; cable editor, Associated Press, New York, 1943–44; New York correspondent and bureau chief, London *Evening News,* 1944–46; editor, *Independent Journal,* San Rafael, California, 1947–49; reporter and copy editor, Los Angeles *Times,* 1950–54; columnist, San Francisco *Chronicle. Died 22 November 1983.*

CRIME PUBLICATIONS

Novels (series: Father Joseph Bredder in all books)

The Saint Maker. New York, Dodd Mead, 1959; London, Hale, 1960.
A Pact with Satan. New York, Dodd Mead, 1960; London, Hale, 1961.
Secret of the Doubting Saint. New York, Dodd Mead, 1961.

Deliver Us from Wolves. New York, Dodd Mead, 1963.
Flowers by Request. New York, Dodd Mead, 1964.
Out of the Depths. New York, Dodd Mead, 1966; London, Hammond, 1967.
A Touch of Jonah. New York, Dodd Mead, 1968.
A Problem in Angels. New York, Dodd Mead, 1970.
The Mirror of Hell. New York, Dodd Mead, 1972.
The Devil to Play. New York, Dodd Mead, 1974.
A Corner of Paradise. New York, St. Martin's Press, 1977.

OTHER PUBLICATIONS as Leonard Wibberley

Novels

Mrs. Searwood's Secret Weapon. Boston, Little Brown, 1954; London, Hale, 1955.
The Mouse That Roared. Boston, Little Brown, 1955; London, Corgi, 1959; as *The Wrath of Grapes,* London, Hale, 1955.
McGillicuddy McGotham. Boston, Little Brown, 1956; London, Hale 1958.
Take Me to Your President. New York, Putnam, 1957.
Beware of the Mouse. New York, Putnam, 1958.
The Quest for Excalibur. New York, Putnam, 1959.
The Hands of Cormac Joyce. New York, Putnam, 1960; London, Muller, 1962.
Stranger at Killknock. New York, Putnam, 1961; London, Muller, 1963.
The Mouse on the Moon. New York, Morrow, 1962; London, Muller, 1964.
A Feast of Freedom. New York, Morrow, 1964.
The Island of the Angels. New York, Morrow, 1965.
The Centurion. New York, Morrow, 1966.
The Road from Toomi. New York, Morrow, 1967.
Adventures of an Elephant Boy. New York, Morrow, 1968.
The Mouse on Wall Street. New York, Morrow, 1969.
Meeting with a Great Beast. New York, Morrow, 1971; London, Chatto and Windus, 1972.
The Testament of Theophilus. New York, Morrow, 1973; as *Merchant of Rome,* London, Cassell, 1974.
The Last Stand of Father Felix. New York, Morrow, 1974.
1776—and All That. New York, Morrow, 1975.
One in Four. New York, Morrow, 1976.
Homeward to Ithaka. New York, Morrow, 1978.
The Mouse That Saved the West. New York, Morrow, 1981.

Fiction (for children)

The King's Beard. New York, Farrar Straus, 1952; London, Faber, 1954.
The Secret of the Hawk. New York, Farrar Straus, 1953; London, Faber, 1956.
Deadmen's Cave. New York, Farrar Straus, and London, Faber, 1954.
The Wound of Peter Wayne. New York, Farrar Straus, 1955; London, Faber, 1957.
Kevin O'Connor and the Light Brigade. New York, Farrar Straus, 1957; London, Harrap, 1959.
John Treegate's Musket. New York, Farrar Straus, 1959.
Peter Treegate's War. New York, Farrar Straus, 1960.
Sea Captain from Salem. New York, Farrar Straus, 1961.
The Time of the Lamb. New York, Washburn, 1961.
Treegate's Raiders. New York, Farrar Straus, 1962.
Encounter near Venus. New York, Farrar Straus, 1967; London, Macdonald, 1968.
Attar of the Ice Valley. New York, Farrar Straus, 1968; London, Macdonald, 1969.

Journey to Untor. New York, Farrar Straus, 1970; London, Macdonald, 1971.
Leopard's Prey. New York, Farrar Straus, 1971.
Flint's Island. New York, Farrar Straus, 1972; London, Macdonald, 1973.
Red Pawns. New York, Farrar Straus, 1973.
The Last Battle. New York, Farrar Straus, 1976.
Perilous Gold. New York, Farrar Straus, 1978.
Little League Family. New York, Doubleday, 1978.
The Crime of Martin Coverly. New York, Farrar Straus, 1980.

Fiction (for children) as Patrick O'Connor

The Lost Harpooner. New York, Washburn, 1947; London, Harrap, 1959.
Flight of the Peacock. New York, Washburn, 1954.
The Society of Foxes. New York, Washburn, 1954.
The Watermelon Mystery. New York, Washburn, 1955.
Gunpowder for Washington. New York, Washburn, 1956.
The Black Tiger. New York, Washburn, 1956.
Mexican Road Race. New York, Washburn, 1957.
Black Tiger at Le Mans. New York, Washburn, 1958.
The Five-Dollar Watch Mystery. New York, Washburn, 1959.
Black Tiger at Bonneville. New York, Washburn, 1960.
Treasure at Twenty Fathoms. New York, Washburn, 1961.
Black Tiger at Indianapolis. New York, Washburn, 1962.
The Raising of the Dubhe. New York, Washburn, 1964.
Seawind from Hawaii. New York, Washburn, 1965.
South Swell. New York, Washburn, 1967; London, Macdonald, 1968.
Beyond Hawaii. New York, Washburn, 1969; as Leonard Wibberley, London, Macdonald, 1970.
A Car Called Camellia. New York, Washburn, 1970.

Fiction (for children) as Christopher Webb

Matt Tyler's Chronicle. New York, Funk and Wagnalls, 1958; London, Macdonald, 1966.
Mark Toyman's Inheritance. New York, Funk and Wagnalls, 1960.
The River of Pee Dee Jack. New York, Funk and Wagnalls, 1962.
The Quest of the Otter. New York, Funk and Wagnalls, 1963; London, Macdonald, 1965.
The "Ann and Hope" Mutiny. New York, Funk and Wagnalls, 1966; London, Macdonald, 1967.
Eusebius, The Phoenician. New York, Funk and Wagnalls, 1969; London, Macdonald, 1970.

Plays

The Heavenly Quarterback. Chicago, Dramatic Publishing Company, 1968.
Gift of a Star. Chicago, Dramatic Publishing Company, 1969.
The Vicar of Wakefield, adaptation of the novel by Oliver Goldsmith. Chicago, Dramatic Publishing Company, n.d.
Black Jack Rides Again. Chicago, Dramatic Publishing Company, 1971.
1776—and All That. Chicago, Dramatic Publishing Company, 1973.
Once, In a Garden. Chicago, Dramatic Publishing Company, 1975.

Ballet Scenario: *Encounter near Venus*, 1978.

Verse (for children)

The Ballad of the Pilgrim Cat. New York, Washburn, 1962.
The Shepherd's Reward. New York, Washburn, 1963.

Other

The Trouble with the Irish (or the English, Depending on Your Point of View). New York, Holt, 1956; London, Muller, 1958.
The Coming of the Green. New York, Holt, 1958.
No Garlic in the Soup (on Portugal). New York, Washburn, 1959; London, Faber, 1960.
The Land That Isn't There: An Irish Adventure. New York, Washburn, 1960.
Yesterday's Land: A Baja California Adventure. New York, Washburn, 1961.
Ventures into the Deep: The Thrill of Scuba Diving. New York, Washburn, 1962.
Ah Julian! A Memoir of Julian Brodetsky. New York, Washburn, 1963.
Fiji: Islands of the Dawn. New York, Washburn, 1964.
Toward a Distant Island: A Sailor's Odyssey. New York, Washburn, 1966.
Something to Read. New York, Washburn, 1967.
Hound of the Sea. New York, Washburn, 1969.
Voyage by Bus. New York, Morrow, 1971.
The Shannon Sailors: A Voyage to the Heart of Ireland. New York, Morrow, 1972.
The Good-Natured Man: A Portrait of Oliver Goldsmith. New York, Morrow, 1979.

Other (for children)

The Coronation Book: The Dramatic Story in History and Legend. New York, Farrar Straus, 1953.
The Epics of Everest. New York, Farrar Straus, 1954; London, Faber, 1955.
The Life of Winston Churchill. New York, Farrar Straus, 1956; revised edition, 1965.
John Barry, Father of the Navy. New York, Farrar Straus, 1957.
Wes Powell, Conqueror of the Grand Canyon. New York, Farrar Straus, 1958.
Zebulon Pike, Soldier and Explorer. New York, Funk and Wagnalls, 1961.
Man of Liberty: A Life of Thomas Jefferson. New York, Farrar Straus, 1968.
  1. *Young Man from the Piedmont: The Youth of Thomas Jefferson*. New York, Farrar Straus, 1963.
  2. *A Dawn in the Trees: Thomas Jefferson, The Years 1776 to 1789*. New York, Farrar Straus, 1964.
  3. *The Gales of Spring: Thomas Jefferson, The Years 1789 to 1801*. New York, Farrar Straus, 1965.
  4. *Time of the Harvest: Thomas Jefferson, The Years 1801 to 1826*. New York, Farrar Straus, 1966.
Guarneri: Story of a Genius. New York, Farrar Straus, 1974; as *Guarneri: Violin Maker of Genius*, London, Macdonald and Jane's, 1976.

*

Manuscript Collection: University of Southern California, Los Angeles.

*   *   *

Leonard Wibberley, probably best known as the author of *The Mouse That Roared,* used the pseudonym Leonard Holton for publishing his series of mystery novels featuring a detective-priest, Father Joseph Bredder, OFM. Father Bredder, ex-marine, skilled boxer, and chaplain for the Convent of Holy Innocents, solves mysteries with well-drawn backgrounds as diverse as the worlds of scuba-diving, professional baseball, and rare violins. He most often works with his friend Lieutenant Minardi of the police, and the novels include a cast of recurring colorful characters from the seamy section of east Los Angeles.

Holton handles well the technical problems of classic puzzle mystery stories. Father Bredder's status as a priest eliminates the mildly distasteful undercurrent of officious meddling that often taints fiction's amateur detectives. His vocation inherently demands a real concern with sin and sinners, and his interest in identifying criminals is an extension of his commitment to save souls and combat evil. Holton's priest has other advantages as a plausible series detective: his work naturally involves him with people of all classes and backgrounds; his clerkly poverty explains his odd bits of out-of-the-way knowledge, since he can afford only those randomly assorted books sold two-for-a-quarter at bookstalls; people readily confide in and trust him, and years of hearing confessions have honed his sense of human motives. Moreover, since Father Bredder and Lieutenant Minardi frequently solve a case almost simultaneously—one relying on "spiritual fingerprints," the other on more conventional methods of detection—the requisite exposition of the puzzle's solution is gracefully motivated by their mutual explanations of how they reached the same conclusion by different routes. This double chain of evidence also reinforces the reader's sense of the appropriateness of the offered solution.

While each of the Holton books presents a perfectly adequate puzzle in detection, the books are equally enjoyable for the delineation of Father Bredder's personality and his approach to the problems he encounters. Bredder's chief characteristic, as both priest and detective, is his spiritually derived sense of the deep connectedness of superficially disparate things. Sometimes this quality leads him to perceive relationships between a current mystery and events of long ago. In *Flowers by Request,* for example, he solves the puzzle of a mobster's murder by comparing him with the killing of William Rufus, son of William the Conqueror, in 1100. Similarly, in *Deliver Us from Wolves,* his investigation of apparent outbreaks of lycanthropy in a rural Portuguese village reveals the answers to two mysteries, one highly contemporary, one unsolved since the early 18th century. Father Bredder more than once intuits a connection between present-day crimes the police are treating as unrelated (e.g., in *Out of the Depths* and *A Problem in Angels*).

Characteristically, the Bredder books contain two corollary plots, one involving criminal detection, the other Father Bredder's clerical activities. This strategy of double plotting is successful largely because each of the novels is informed by a single spiritual concern. *Secret of the Doubting Saint,* for example, turns on the importance of doubt as a path to truth; the solution of the mystery through active doubting on the part of Bredder and Minardi thus becomes emblematic of this larger principle. Similarly, *A Corner of Paradise* involves multiple instances of racial prejudice; indeed, prejudice, in a surprising variation, turns out to have motivated the novel's murder. This technique of pervading each novel with a single informing theme gives Holton's books a structural coherence both rare in detective fiction and persuasively suited to the nature of their protagonist.

—Susan Baker

———

HOME, Michael. *See* **BUSH, Christopher.**

———

HOMES, Geoffrey. Pseudonym for Daniel Mainwaring. American. Born in Dunlap, California in 1902. Educated at Fresno State College, California. Office boy, itinerant fruit picker, salesman, private detective, teacher, and reporter for 10 years on San Francisco *Chronicle*. Self-employed writer, later employed as screenwriter and publicist for Warner Brothers and scenarist for Paramount; produced and recorded unusual sound effects for rental to film studios in the 1930's and 1940's. *Died in 1978.*

CRIME PUBLICATIONS

Novels (series: Robin Bishop; Humphrey Campbell; Jose Manuel Madero)

One Against the Earth (as Daniel Mainwaring). New York, Long and Smith, 1933.
The Doctor Died at Dusk (Bishop). New York, Morrow, 1936.
The Man Who Murdered Himself (Bishop). New York, Morrow, and London, Lane, 1936.
The Man Who Didn't Exist (Bishop). New York, Morrow, 1937; London, Eyre and Spottiswoode, 1939.
The Man Who Murdered Goliath (Bishop). New York, Morrow, 1938; London, Eyre and Spottiswoode, 1940.
Then There Were Three (Bishop and Campbell). New York, Morrow, 1938; London, Cherry Tree, 1945.
No Hands on the Clock (Campbell). New York, Morrow, 1939.
Finders Keepers (Campbell). New York, Morrow, 1940.
Forty Whacks (Campbell). New York, Morrow, 1941; as *Stiffs Don't Vote*, New York, Bantam, 1947.
The Street of the Crying Woman (Madero). New York, Morrow, 1942; as *Seven Died*, London, Cherry Tree, 1943; as *The Case of the Mexican Knife*, New York, Bantam, 1948.
The Hill of the Terrified Monk (Madero). New York, Morrow, 1943; as *Dead as a Dummy*, New York, Bantam, 1949.
Six Silver Handles (Campbell). New York, Morrow, 1944; London, Cherry Tree, 1946; as *The Case of the Unhappy Angels*, New York, Bantam, 1950.
Build My Gallows High. New York, Morrow, 1946.

Uncollected Short Story

"The Judge Finds the Body," in *The Mystery Companion*, edited by Abraham Louis Furman. New York, Gold Label, 1943.

OTHER PUBLICATIONS

Plays

Screenplays: *Secrets of the Underworld*, with Robert Tasker, 1943; *Dangerous Passage*, 1945; *Scared Stiff*, with Maxwell Shane, 1945; *Swamp Fire*, 1946; *Tokyo Rose*, with Maxwell Shane and Whitman Chambers, 1946; *Hot Cargo*, 1946; *They Made Me a Killer*, with others, 1946; *Big Town*, with Maxwell Shane, 1947; *Out of the Past*, with Frank Fenton, 1947; *Roughshod*, with Hugo Butler and Peter Viertel, 1949; *The Big Steal*, with Gerald Drayson Adams, 1949; *The Eagle and the Hawk*, with Lewis R. Foster and Jess Arnold, 1950; *The Lawless*, 1950; *The Last Outpost*, with others, 1950; *Roadblock*, with others, 1951; *The Tall Target*, with others, 1951; *This Woman Is Dangerous*, with George Worthing Yates and Bernard Girard, 1952; *Bugles in the Afternoon*, with Harry Brown, 1952; *Powder River*, with Sam Hellman, 1953; *Those Redheads from Seattle*, with Lewis R. Foster and George Worthing Yates, 1953; *Alaska Seas*, with Walter Doniger, 1954; *Black Horse Canyon*, with David Lang, 1954; *Southwest Passage*, with Harry Essex, 1954; *The Desperado*, 1954; *The Annapolis Story*, with Daniel Ullman, 1955; *A Bullet for Joey*, with A.I. Bezzerides and James Benson Nablo, 1955; *The Phenix City Story*, with Crane Wilbur, 1955; *Invasion of the Body Snatchers*, 1956; *Thunderstorm*, with George St. George, 1956; *Baby Face Nelson*, with Robert Adler and Irving Shulman, 1957; *Cole Younger, Gunfighter*, 1957; *Space Master X-7*, with George Worthing Yates, 1958; *The Gun Runners*, with Paul Monash, 1958; *Walk Like a Dragon*, with James Clavell, 1960; *Atlantis, The Lost Continent*, 1961; *The Minotaur*, with S. Continenza and G.P. Calligari, 1961; *Revolt of the Slaves* (English dialogue), with Duccio Tessaria and Stefano Strucchi, 1961; *East of Kilimanjaro*, with Arnold Belgard and Richard Goldstone, 1962; *Convict Stage*, with Donald Barry, 1966; *The Woman Who Wouldn't Die*, 1966.

* * *

There is a body of mystery writers whose work is of consistently high quality, but who, for unexplainable reasons, have received little attention among students and aficionados of the genre. Geoffrey Homes is one of these writers. Between 1936 and 1946, Homes published 12 detective and suspense novels set primarily in the valleys and foothills of north-central California. Each is distinguished by clever plotting, semi-hard-boiled realism, fast-paced action, witty and remarkably good dialogue, and some of the finest and most vivid descriptive passages in mystery fiction. Each also offers an excellent portrait of rural and smalltown life in California during the Depression and World War II years.

His first five books feature the adventures of newspaperman Robin Bishop; the best of these are *The Doctor Died at Dusk* and *The Man Who Didn't Exist*. His most memorable series character, however, is his second: Humphrey Campbell, an unconventional private detective who, with his fat, lazy, and corrupt partner Oscar Morgan, appears in one of the Robin Bishop novels and four of his own. *Finders Keepers* is perhaps the most effective of the Campbell sagas, although *No Hands on the Clock* and *Forty Whacks* rank as close seconds. The best of the other novels—and his best book overall—in his last, *Build My Gallows High*. This is a powerful suspense tale, strong on mood and characterization, which tells the story of a man named Red Bailey who is haunted and ultimately destroyed by events in his past. It was transferred to the screen as *Out of the Past*, starring Robert Mitchum and Kirk Douglas—a film which is considered by many to be a crime classic.

Homes began to write "B" pictures in Hollywood in 1942,

and abandoned novels in 1946 to become a full-time scriptwriter.

—Bill Pronzini

* * *

HONE, Joseph. Irish. Born in London, 25 February 1937. Educated at the University of London, extra mural film course 1953–54. Married Jacqueline Mary Yeend in 1963; one daughter and one son. English teacher in a grammar school, Drogheda, Louth, Ireland, 1956; third assistant director to John Ford, Mark Robson, John Gilling Denys de la Patellière, and Joseph Losey, 1956–57; English teacher, Eygptian Ministry of Education, Heliopolis and Suez, 1957–58; editorial assistant, Rupert Hart-Davis, publishers, London, 1958–59; co-founding producer, Envoy Productions, theatrical producers, Dublin, 1960–62; producer, Talks and Current Affairs Department, BBC Radio, London, 1963–66; radio and television officer, Office of Public Information, United Nations, New York, 1967–68; producer of radio programs, World Bank, Washington, D.C., 1968–69. Since 1969, freelance writer and broadcaster: has presented more than 100 radio features, most recently *Flasback,* 1987 and *Ottoman Adventure,* 1990. Agent: Deborah Rogers, Rogers, Coleridge and White Ltd, 20 Powis Mews, London W11 1JN, England.

CRIME PUBLICATIONS

Novels (series: Peter Marlow in all books except *The Paris Trap*)

The Private Sector. London, Hamish Hamilton, 1971; New York, Dutton, 1972.
The Sixth Directorate. London, Secker and Warburg, and New York, Dutton, 1975.
The Paris Trap. London, Secker and Warburg, 1977.
The Flowers of the Forest. London, Secker and Warburg, 1980; as *The Oxford Gambit,* New York, Random House, 1980.
The Valley of the Fox. London, Secker and Warburg, 1982; New York, St. Martin's Press, 1984.

OTHER PUBLICATIONS

Novel

Summer Hill. London, Sinclair Stevenson, 1990.

Plays

Screenplays: *King and Country,* with Evan Jones and Joseph Losey, 1964; *The Sixth Directorate,* 1976.

Other

The Dancing Waiters: Some Collected Travels. London, Hamish Hamilton, 1975.
Gone Tomorrow: Some More Collected Travels. London, Secker and Warburg, 1981.
Children of the Country: Coast to Coast Across Africa. London, Hamish Hamilton, 1986; as *Africa of the Heart: A Personal Journey,* New York, Beech Tree-Morrow, 1986.

Duck Soup in the Black Sea: Further Collected Travels. London, Hamish Hamilton, 1988.

* * *

Like any other contemporary British espionage novelist with a modicum of literacy, Joseph Hone must experience the inevitable parallels with John le Carré; unlike most other writers, however, he does not suffer too severely from the comparison. His books are generally quiet, thoughtful, written with some elegance, and distinguished by their authentic presentation of foreign places. They tend to stress character and atmosphere over action and excitement, interior rather than exterior events, and may be even more introspective than the works of le Carré. If his novels lack the taut grace and structural strength of le Carré's, they share a concern for the moral condition of today's England and a profound disillusionment with its government, from elected officials to civil servants.

With the exception of *The Paris Trap,* all of Hone's novels are narrated by Peter Marlow, a protagonist who might justly be called the continuing victim of the books. Outside of those innumerable unfunny spoofs of espionage fiction, Marlow must be the most feckless and passive spy in the literature. He is manipulated, deceived, and betrayed by just about everyone who inhabits his world—colleagues and superiors, friends and enemies, wives and lovers. Although he manages, just barely, to survive the numerous deceptions and doublecrosses he encounters, virtually all of his ventures end in personal disaster and professional failure.

Perhaps more than any other British espionage novelist, Hone seems to have been largely inspired by contemporary history; a substantial amount of his fiction is based on recognizable people and events, and he is one of those writers for whom the Philby affair remains a vital and significant matter. His first novel, *The Private Sector,* is located primarily in Egypt, with references to the Suez crisis of 1956, the Six-Day War of 1967, and the disappearance of Kim Philby, ending with Peter Marlow's intelligence service framing him for treason. In the second, *The Sixth Directorate,* he is released in order to impersonate a British diplomat at the United Nations; in that book, Hone may be the first writer to employ Yuri Andropov, then head of the KGB, as a character. In both novels he is very good on locale and atmosphere, capturing with the ring of authenticity the tropical languor of Egypt, the confusing bustle of New York, the austere chill of contemporary Russia. He is even better on the manners of particularly unusual societies—the faded grandeur and seedy Anglophilia of post-Suez Egypt, the rituals of diplomatic life, the Byzantine intricacy of the Soviet pecking order, and of course the complicated and suicidal internal conflicts of the British bureaucracy.

In his later work Hone has further indulged his almost masochistic interest in the victimization of Peter Marlow. His taste for complication leads him into deceptions and betrayals that leave the mere doublecross far behind, moving into the quadruple or even octuple version of that peculiar practice of modern espionage. The plots and counterplots, the mysteries and their solutions, the manifold confusions sometimes become impossible to unravel. Sometimes they are simply preposterous, even if grounded in fact, as in the impersonation in *The Sixth Directorate* or the disappearance of an important English intelligence officer in *The Oxford Gambit,* later found mummified in his own attic.

His more recent books also show the fatality of scenic charm, indulging in a kind of Lawrentian love of landscape and hymning the glories of England's green and pleasant land. *The*

Valley of the Fox turns into another version of a work by Geoffrey Household, a pure pursuit thriller that sends the (once again) deceived and hunted Peter Marlow into a primitive Robinson Crusoe survival fiction. It is further weakened by the presence of an apparently autistic child, an African tribe bent on revenge, and a mad American heiress, combining Edgar Rice Burroughs, H. Rider Haggard, and Henry James; the result, though often lyrically written and engaging, remains something of an incredible mess.

Hone certainly deserves high ranking among the contemporary practitioners of espionage, however, and deserves to be much better known than he now seems to be: the beauty of his prose and the intelligence of his vision qualify him for that inevitable comparison with John le Carré. At the moment he seems a writer in transition, drawing from his own experience certain background strengths and moving toward a more imaginative if perhaps too inventive sort of thriller. He will prove to be a writer well worth knowing whose career may be fascinating to observe; he shows a real sense of change and growth, which may turn out to be a continuing and distinguished progress to excellence.

—George Grella

HOPLEY, George. *See* **WOOLRICH, Cornell.**

HORLER, Sydney. Also wrote as Peter Cavendish; Martin Heritage. British. Born in Leytonstone, Essex, 18 July 1888. Educated at Redcliffe and Colston schools, Bristol. Served in the Propaganda Section of Air Intelligence, 1918. Married. Journalist: reporter, *Western Daily Press,* Bristol, 1905–11; special writer, E. Hulton Ltd., Manchester, and on staffs of *Daily Mail* and *Daily Citizen,* both London, before 1918; worked for Newnes publications, London, and sub-editor, *John O'London's Weekly,* 1919. *Died 27 October 1954.*

CRIME PUBLICATIONS

Novels (series characters: The Ace; Sir Harker Bellamy; Brett Carstairs; Bunny Chipstead; H. Emp; Sir Brian Fordingh-ame; Gerald Lissendale; Chief Constable Meatyard; Night-hawk [Gerald Frost]; Sebastian Quin; Peter Scarlett; Tiger Standish; Baron Veseloffsky; Paul Vivanti; Robert Wynnton)

The Breed of the Beverleys. London, Odhams Press, 1921.
Love, The Sportsman. London, Hodder and Stoughton, 1923; as *The Man with Two Faces,* London, Collins, 1934.
The Mystery of No. 1 (Vivanti). London, Hodder and Stoughton, 1925; as *The Order of the Octopus,* New York, Doran, 1926.
False-Face (Veseloffsky; Fordinghame). London, Hodder and Stoughton, and New York, Doran, 1926.
The House of Secrets. London, Hodder and Stoughton, 1926; New York, Doran, 1927.
The Black Heart. London, Hodder and Stoughton, 1927; New York, Doubleday, 1928.
In the Dark (Chipstead). London, Hodder and Stoughton, 1927; as *A Life for Sale,* New York, Doubleday, 1928.

Vivanti. London, Hodder and Stoughton, and New York, Doran, 1927.
Chipstead of the Lone Hand. London, Hodder and Stoughton, 1928; New York, Holt, 1929.
The 13th Hour. London, Readers' Library, 1928.
The Curse of Doone. London, Hodder and Stoughton, 1928; New York, Mystery League, 1930.
Miss Mystery (Veseloffsky). London, Hodder and Stoughton, 1928; Boston, Little Brown, 1935.
The Secret Service Man (Lissendale). London, Hodder and Stoughton, 1929; New York, Knopf, 1930.
Heart Cut Diamond. London, Hodder and Stoughton, 1929.
Lady of the Night. London, Hodder and Stoughton, 1929; New York, Knopf, 1930.
Peril! New York, Mystery League, 1930; as *Cavalier of Chance,* London, Hodder and Stoughton, 1931.
Checkmate. London, Hodder and Stoughton, 1930.
Danger's Bright Eyes. London, Hodder and Stoughton, 1930; New York, Harper, 1932.
The Evil Chateau. London, Hodder and Stoughton, 1930; New York, Knopf, 1931.
The Murder Mask (Fordinghame). London, Readers' Library, 1930.
Adventure Calling! London, Hodder and Stoughton, 1931.
The Man Who Walked with Death (Carstairs). New York, Knopf, 1931; London, Hodder and Stoughton, 1942.
Princess after Dark. London, Hodder and Stoughton, 1931; as *The False Purple,* New York, Mystery League, 1932.
The Spy (Carstairs). London, Hodder and Stoughton, 1931.
The Temptation of Mary Gordon. London, Newnes, 1931.
Wolves of the Night. London, Readers' Library, 1931.
Vivanti Returns. London, Hodder and Stoughton, 1931.
Gentleman-in-Waiting. London, Benn, 1932.
High Stakes (Fordinghame). London, Collins, 1932; Boston, Little Brown, 1935.
Horror's Head (Emp). London, Hodder and Stoughton, 1932.
My Lady Dangerous (Bellamy). London, Collins, 1932; New York, Harper, 1933.
Tiger Standish (Bellamy). London, Long, 1932; New York, Doubleday, 1933.
The Formula. London, Long, 1933; as *The Charlatan,* Boston, Little Brown, 1934; London, Marshall, 1949.
Harlequin of Death. London, Long, and Boston, Little Brown, 1933.
Huntress of Death. London, Hodder and Stoughton, 1933.
The Menace. London, Collins, and Boston, Little Brown, 1933.
The Man from Scotland Yard. London, Hutchinson, 1934.
The Secret Agent (Chipstead). London, Collins, and Boston, Little Brown, 1934.
S.O.S. London, Hutchinson, 1934.
The Prince of Plunder (Fordinghame). London, Hodder and Stoughton, and Boston, Little Brown, 1934.
Tiger Standish Comes Back (Bellamy). London, Hutchinson, 1934.
The Lessing Murder Case. London, Collins, 1935.
Lord of Terror (Vivanti). London, Collins, 1935; New York, Curl, 1937.
The Mystery of the Seven Cafés: The Novel of the Famous Wireless Play (Standish; Bellamy). London, Hodder and Stoughton, 1935.
The Vampire. London, Hutchinson, 1935; New York, Bookfinger, 1974.
Death at Court Lady. London, Collins, 1936.
The Grim Game (Standish; Bellamy). London, Collins, and Boston, Little Brown, 1936.
The Traitor. London, Collins, and Boston, Little Brown, 1936.

The Hidden Hand. London, Collins, 1937.
Instruments of Darkness. London, Hodder and Stoughton, 1937.
They Called Him Nighthawk. London, Hodder and Stoughton, 1937.
The Destroyer, and The Red-Haired Death (Bellamy). London, Hodder and Stoughton, 1938.
The Evil Messenger (Quin). London, Hodder and Stoughton, 1938.
Dark Journey. London, Hodder and Stoughton, 1938.
A Gentleman for the Gallows. London, Hodder and Stoughton, and New York, Curl, 1938.
The Phantom Forward. London, Hodder and Stoughton, 1939.
Terror on Tip-Toe. London, Hodder and Stoughton, 1939.
Tiger Standish Takes the Field (Bellamy). London, Hodder and Stoughton, 1939.
Here Is an S.O.S. (Meatyard). London, Hodder and Stoughton, 1939.
The Man Who Died Twice. London, Hodder and Stoughton, 1939.
The Enemy Within the Gates (Chipstead). London, Hodder and Stoughton, 1940.
The Return of Nighthawk. London, Hodder and Stoughton, 1940.
Tiger Standish Steps on It (Bellamy). London, Hodder and Stoughton, 1940.
Enter the Ace. London, Hodder and Stoughton, 1941.
Nighthawk Strikes to Kill. London, Hodder and Stoughton, 1941.
Tiger Standish Does His Stuff (2 novelets). London, Hodder and Stoughton, 1941.
Danger Preferred. London, Hodder and Stoughton, 1942.
Fear Walked Behind (Quin). London, Hale, 1942.
The Man in White. London, Staples Press, 1942.
The Night of Reckoning. London, Eyre and Spottiswoode, 1942.
The Hostage. London, Quality Press, 1943.
High Hazard. London, Hodder and Stoughton, 1943.
The Man Who Preferred Cocktails. London, Crowther, 1943.
Murder Is So Simple. London, Eyre and Spottiswoode, 1943.
The Lady with the Limp (Standish; Bellamy). London, Hodder and Stoughton, 1944.
The Man with Dry Hands. London, Eyre and Spottiswoode, 1944.
Nighthawk Mops Up. London, Hodder and Stoughton, 1944.
A Bullet for the Countess. London, Quality Press, 1945.
Virus X (Vivanti). London, Quality Press, 1945.
Dark Danger. New York, Mystery House, 1945.
Terror Comes to Twelvetrees. London, Eyre and Spottiswoode, 1945.
Great Adventure, and Out of a Dark Sky (2 novelets). London, Hale, 1946.
Corridors of Fear. London, Quality Press, 1947.
Ring Up Nighthawk. London, Hodder and Stoughton, 1947.
The Closed Door (Lissendale). London, Pilot Press, 1948.
Exit the Disguiser (Standish). London, Hodder and Stoughton, 1948.
The House with the Light. London, Hodder and Stoughton, 1948.
The Man Who Did Not Hang. London, Quality Press, 1948.
The Man Who Loved Spiders (Meatyard). London, Barker, 1949.
They Thought He Was Dead (Standish). London, Hodder and Stoughton, 1949.
Whilst the Crowd Roared. Stoke on Trent, Archer Press, 1949.
A Man of Affairs. London, Pilot Press, 1949.

Master of Venom (Emp). London, Hodder and Stoughton, 1949.
The Blanco Case. London, Quality Press, 1950.
The High Game. London, Redman, 1950.
The House of the Uneasy Dead. London, Barker, 1950.
Nap on Nighthawk. London, Hodder and Stoughton, 1950.
Scarlett—Special Branch. London, Foulsham, 1950.
The Devil Comes to Bolobyn. London, Marshall, 1951.
The Man in the Cloak (Wynnton). London, Eyre and Spottiswoode, 1951.
The House of Jackals (Standish). London, Hodder and Stoughton, 1951.
The Man of Evil. London, Barker, 1951.
Murderer at Large (Emp). London, Hodder and Stoughton, 1951.
The Mystery of Mr. X. London, Foulsham, 1951.
Scarlett Gets the Kidnapper. London, Foulsham, 1951.
These Men and Women. London, Museum Press, 1951.
The Blade Is Bright (Lissendale). London, Eyre and Spottiswoode, 1952.
The Face of Stone. London, Barker, 1952.
Hell's Brew (Ace). London, Hodder and Stoughton, 1952.
The Man Who Used Perfume (Wynnton). London, Wingate, 1952.
The Mocking Face of Murder. London, Hale, 1952.
The Web. London, Redman, 1952.
The Cage. London, Hale, 1953.
The Dark Night (Ace). London, Hodder and Stoughton, 1953.
Death of a Spy. London, Museum Press, 1953.
The Secret Hand. London, Barker, 1954.
Nighthawk Swears Vengeance. London, Hodder and Stoughton, 1954.
The Man in the Hood. London, Redman, 1955.
The Man in the Shadows. London, Hale, 1955.
The Dark Hostess. London, Eyre and Spottiswoode, 1955.

Short Stories

The Worst Man in the World. London, Hodder and Stoughton, 1929.
The Screaming Skull and Other Stories. London, Hodder and Stoughton, 1930.
The Mystery Mission and Other Stories. London, Hodder and Stoughton, 1931.
The Man Who Shook the Earth. London, Hutchinson, 1933.
Beauty and the Policeman. London, Hutchinson, 1933.
Dying to Live and Other Stories. London, Hutchinson, 1935.
The House in Greek Street. London, Hodder and Stoughton, 1935; revised edition, London, Crowther, 1946.
The Stroke Sinister and Other Stories. London, Hutchinson, 1935.
Knaves & Co. London, Collins, 1938.
Tiger Standish Has a Party. London, Todd, 1943.
Murder for Sale. London, Vallancey Press, 1945.

OTHER PUBLICATIONS

Novels

Standish of the Rangeland: A Story of Cowboy Pluck and Daring. London, Newnes, 1916.
Goal! A Romance of the English Cup Ties. London, Odhams Press, 1920.
A Legend of the League. London, Hodder and Stoughton, 1922.
McPhee. London, Jenkins, 1922; as *The Great Game,* London, Collins, 1935.

The Ball of Fortune. London, Aldine Press, 1925.
School! School! London, Partridge, 1925.
On the Ball! London, Blackie, 1926.
The Man Who Saved the Club. London, Aldine Press, 1926.
The Fellow Hagan! London, Cassell, 1927.
The House of Wingate (as Martin Heritage). London, Hurst and Blackett, 1928; as *A House Divided,* New York, Macaulay, 1929.
Romeo and Julia (as Peter Cavendish). London, Hodder and Stoughton, 1928.
A Pro's Romance. London, Newnes, 1930.
The Exploits of Peter. London, Collins, 1930.
Song of the Scrum. London, Hutchinson, 1934.
The Man Who Stayed to Supper: A Comedy. London, Jenkins, 1941.
Now Let Us Hate. London, Quality Press, 1942.
Springtime Comes to William. London, Jenkins, 1943.
Marry the Girl. London, Jenkins, 1945.
High Pressure. London, Jenkins, 1946.
Oh, Professor! London, Jenkins, 1946.
The Man with Three Wives. London, Jenkins, 1947.
Man Alive. London, Jenkins, 1948.
Haloes for Hire. London, Jenkins, 1949.
The Beacon Light. London, Jenkins, 1949.
Wedding Bells. London, Jenkins, 1950.
Dr. Cupid. London, Jenkins, 1951.
Girl Trouble. London, Jenkins, 1951.

Plays

The House of Secrets, adaptation of his own novel (produced London, 1927).
Oh! My Aunt (produced Birmingham, 1928).
Midnight Love (produced London, 1931). London, Jenkins, 1931.
Death at Court Lady (produced London, 1934).
The Man Who Died Twice. London, Nelson, 1941.
The Man Who Mislaid the War. London, Muller, 1943.

Other

Black Soul. London, Jarrolds, 1931.
Writing for Money. London, Nicholson and Watson, 1932.
Excitement: An Impudent Autobiography. London, Hutchinson, 1933.
Strictly Personal: An Indiscreet Diary. London, Hutchinson, 1934.
London's Underworld: The Record of a Month's Sojourn in the Crime Centres of the Metropolis. London, Hutchinson, 1934.
More Strictly Personal: Six Months of My Life. London, Rich and Cowan, 1935.
Malefactor's Row: A Book of Crime Studies. London, Hale, 1940.
I Accuse the Doctors, Being a Candid Commentary on the Hostility Shown by the Leaders of the Medical Profession Towards the Healing Art of Osteopathy, and How the Public Suffers in Consequence. London, Redman, 1949.

*   *   *

Sydney Horler competed for the same audience as Edgar Wallace, though the latter, an equally prolific writer, had the advantage of having appeared much earlier. Each specialized in the thriller; Horler's publisher advertised his books with the phrase "Horler for Excitement." After Wallace's untimely death in 1932, Horler acquired many of his readers. Never

reticent, Horler ignored few opportunities for self-advertisement, even stressing the number of words (25,000) he dictated weekly. Once Horler announced that, having purchased the machine Edgar Wallace had used, he was shocked to discover the late owner's voice appearing on a *new* cylinder he had dictated. Though many were skeptical, no one was able to prove or disprove Horler's allegations.

A man of strong likes and dislikes, Horler wrote five books in which he combined autobiography, personal opinion, and advice to the reader. His fiction does an equally good job of conveying his tastes. Horler greatly respected British royalty, and his most famous series character is an aristocrat, the Honourable Timothy Overbury "Tiger" Standish. Horler invested Standish with some of his own prejudices against non-Anglo-Saxons. Thus, we find Standish referring to Jews in a derogatory manner and using expressions such as "stinking Italianos."

A self-proclaimed moralist, Horler was critical of much of the post-World War I behavior in Europe. He especially abhorred the French Riviera, an implied criticism of another competitor, E. Phillips Oppenheim, whose high living there was well-known. Horler probably let his own moral code influence him most in his series about Gerald Frost, better known as Nighthawk. In such books as *They Called Him Nighthawk* and *The Return of Nighthawk,* Frost is a cracksman who steals jewelry only from society women he feels are of loose morality. He writes "wanton" on their pillowslips, with their own lipsticks, at the conclusions of his burglaries.

Horler was repelled by homosexuality, taking care to describe his heroes in terms that would leave no doubts in the reader's mind. Thus, of the hero of the non-crime book *The House of Wingate* Horler says, "no one could have mistaken him for being anything but a virile man." He described Standish as possessing "all the attributes of a thoroughly likable fellow ... he likes his glass of beer, he is a confirmed pipe smoker, he is always ready to smile back into the face of danger."

Creator of larger-than-life heroes, Horler himself is recognizable in some of his supporting characters. In *The Curse of Doone* secret agent Ian Heath is aided by Jerry Hartsell, a farmer with poor eyesight, who enjoys writing. Horler's own visual impairment prevented him from achieving his ambition to become an RAF pilot, limiting his wartime service to propaganda writing. The hero's best friend in *The House of Wingate,* the brave and loyal Selby Fowne, is described as a "stout comfortable tub of a man," an accurate picture of the author, according to available photographs.

Horler's considerable narrative skill gained him enormous popularity with a relatively undemanding public. This storytelling ability was able to overcome his recurring tendency to, in his own words, "give old man coincidence's arm a frightful twist." Characters constantly meet, disappear, and reappear in his books, with little thought of credibility. As a result of these coincidences and Horler's lack of subtlety in plotting and characterization, time has not treated his work very well. At present hardly anyone reads Horler, while his contemporaries such as Christie, Sayers, Blake, Allingham, and even Edgar Wallace, remain popular.

—Marvin Lachman

HORNIG, Doug. Also writes as Peter Caine. American. Born in New York City, 19 November 1943. Educated at

George Washington University, Washington, D.C., B.A. 1965. One son. Has had a variety of jobs including factory worker, journalist, computer programmer, taxi driver, and census taker. Agent: Philip Spitzer, 788 Ninth Avenue, New York, New York 10019. Address: Route 3, Box 482, Afton, Virginia 22920, U.S.A.

CRIME PUBLICATIONS

Novels (series: Steven Kirk; Loren Swift)

Foul Shot (Swift).   New York, Scribner, 1984.
Hardball (Swift).   New York, Scribner, 1985; London, Macmillan, 1986.
The Dark Side (Swift).   New York, Mysterious Press, 1986; London, Macmillan, 1987.
Waterman (Kirk).   New York, Mysterious Press, 1987.
Deep Dive (Swift).   New York, Mysterious Press, 1988.
Virus (as Peter Caine).   New York, New American Library, 1989.
Stinger (Kirk).   New York, New American Library, 1990.

Uncollected Short Stories

"Acess to Power," in *Ellery Queen's Mystery Magazine* (New York), May 1986.
"The Game of Magical Death," in *Fantasy and Science Fiction*, March 1987.
"Entropy," in *Fantasy and Science Fiction*, July 1988.

*

Doug Hornig comments:

I am a writer, as opposed to a particular *kind* of writer. I've published novels, short stories, poetry, non-fiction, have written two screenplays and had a song commercially recorded. Within the category of novel, I've published four mysteries, two political suspense thrillers and a police procedural/suspense horror thriller. My mysteries all include the private investigator Loren Swift, who has been critically described as, at best, medium-boiled. The two political thrillers feature lapsed CIA agent Steven Kirk and his ongoing antagonist, the enigmatic Smith, of the agency's Operations Directorate, a would-be jazz saxophonist who manipulates geopolitical events for his own pleasure. I have a very broad span of interests and have no idea where they will lead me from one piece of work to the next.

*   *   *

Doug Hornig is a relative newcomer to the world of the private eye story and he brings to it a mixture of pluses and minuses. The bulk of his work has been about Loren Swift, a laid-back Vietnam veteran who has set himself up as a private investigator in the college town of Charlottesville, Virginia. The most readily noticeable aspect of his personality is his continuing connection to the culture of the 1960's and 1970's. His narration is peppered with references to rock groups and other pop culture icons from that period. His idea of a good time is playing old records and admiring his collection of rock posters.

It should come as no surprise that, with this background, Swift is a political liberal. Hornig emphasizes that by having

his creation draw parallels between the things he sees currently on the national scene and those he remembers from his earlier life. References to the dirty deeds of Nixon, Haldeman, and Ehrlichman are common.

Hornig's liberal and humanitarian interests also show up in the backdrops against which his heroes operate. In *Deep Dive,* for example, the Aids controversy and its effect on Charlottesville constantly intrude on Swift's thoughts as he investigates. He remains undecided about how he feels until he finds his personal life touched by it.

In *The Dark Side,* the story is played out against the backdrop of a group of environmentalists who have attempted to create a utopian community in the mountains. In *Waterman,* Hornig's only non-series title to date, the hero's preoccupation with government duplicity in the Grenada invasion causes him to divorce himself from the world he has known.

Hornig tells a passable tale and he has no trouble inventing a credible mystery. His telling of the story is also enhanced by his ability to bring the Virginia countryside vibrantly to life. It is, in fact, his choice of rural Virginia as the backdrop to all his work thus far that makes his mysteries unique. His evocation of the little Chesapeake Bay community of Brawlton in *Waterman* is particularly effective.

Hornig's major weakness is characterization. Loren Swift and Scott Craik, in *Waterman,* are far too idealistic and naive to be participating in the dangerous work that each pursues. Swift is a particularly "soft-boiled" private eye and Hornig's attempts to have him assume the tough, wise-cracking habits of his predecessors clash badly with his mellow personality. Hornig has also attempted to endow Swift with a sixth sense, something which seems curiously out of place in a private-eye novel.

Hornig is especially weak in his attempts to characterize sympathetic female characters. They seem rather juvenile and, indeed, all of his attempts to depict adult romantic and sexual relationships are ultimately defeated by his adolescent approach.

Waterman is an ambitious book but it is derivative and is certainly Hornig's weakest effort so far. The plot seems to have been lifted from *Shane,* although the hero, Scott Craik, has far more in common with the character David Carradine played in *Kung-Fu.* This might have succeeded on a purely superficial level had not Hornig decided to throw in a few Columbian drug dealers to give the story a currency and an additional urgency that it didn't really need.

In spite of his inability to create fully fleshed-out adult characters, Hornig has proven himself to be a reliable writer of private-eye stories. His choice of rural Virginia as the setting for his stories, coupled with his ability to work timely political and social concerns into the fabric of his work, provides the reader with both an unusual and creative approach to the mystery.

—Robert E. Skinner

———

HORNUNG, E(rnest) W(illiam).   British.   Born in Middlesbrough, Yorkshire, 7 June 1866. Educated at Uppingham School. Married Constance Doyle, sister of Arthur Conan Doyle, *q.v.*, in 1893; one son. Tutor at Mossgiel Station, Riverina, Australia, 1884–86; worked for the YMCA in France during World War I. *Died 22 March 1921.*

CRIME PUBLICATIONS

Novels

A Bride from the Bush. London, Smith Elder, and New York, United States Book Company, 1890.
Tiny Luttrell. London and New York, Cassell, 2 vols., 1893.
The Boss of Taroomba. London, Bliss, 1894; New York, Scribner, 1900.
The Rogue's March. London, Cassell, and New York, Scribner, 1896.
Irralie's Bushranger. London, Beeman, and New York, Scribner, 1896.
My Lord Duke. London, Cassell, and New York, Scribner, 1897.
Young Blood. London, Cassell, and New York, Scribner, 1898.
Dead Men Tell No Tales. London, Methuen, and New York, Scribner, 1899.
The Belle of Toorak. London, Richards, 1900; as *The Shadow of a Man,* New York, Scribner, 1901.
Peccavi. London, Richards, and New York, Scribner, 1900.
At Large. London, Scribner, 1902.
Denis Dent. London, Isbister, 1903; New York, Stokes, 1904.
Mr. Justice Raffles. London, Smith Elder, and New York, Scribner, 1909.
The Camera Fiend. London, Unwin, and New York, Scribner, 1911.
The Thousandth Woman. London, Nash, and Indianapolis, Bobbs Merrill, 1913.

Short Stories (series: A.J. Raffles)

Under Two Skies. London, A. and C. Black, 1892; New York, Macmillan, 1895.
Some Persons Unknown. London, Cassell, and New York, Scribner, 1898.
The Amateur Cracksman. London, Methuen, and New York, Scribner, 1899; as *Raffles, The Amateur Cracksman,* London, Nash, 1906.
The Black Mask. London, Richards, 1901; as *Raffles: Further Adventures of the Amateur Cracksman,* New York, Scribner, 1901.
The Shadow of the Rope. London, Chatto and Windus, and New York, Scribner, 1902.
Stingaree. London, Chatto and Windus, and New York, Scribner, 1905.
A Thief in the Night (Raffles). London, Chatto and Windus, and New York, Scribner, 1905.
Witching Hill. London, Hodder and Stoughton, and New York, Scribner, 1913.
The Crime Doctor. London, Nash, and Indianapolis, Bobbs Merrill, 1914.
Old Offenders and a Few Old Scores. London, Murray, 1923.
The Complete Short Stories of Raffles, The Amateur Cracksman. London, Souvenir Press, and New York, St. Martin's Press, 1984.
The Collected Raffles. London, Dent, 1985.

OTHER PUBLICATIONS

Novels

The Unbidden Guest. London and New York, Longman, 1894.
No Hero. London, Smith Elder, and New York, Scribner, 1903.

Fathers of Men. London, Smith Elder, and New York, Scribner, 1912.

Plays

Raffles, The Amateur Cracksman, with Eugene W. Presbrey, adaptation of stories by Hornung (produced New York, 1903; London, 1906).
Stingaree, The Bushranger, adaptation of his own stories (produced London, 1908).
A Visit from Raffles, with Charles Sansom, adaptation of stories by Hornung (produced London, 1909).

Verse

The Ballad of Ensign Joy. New York, Dutton, 1917.
Wooden Crosses. London, Nisbet, 1918.
The Young Guard. London, Constable, 1919.

Other

Trusty and Well Beloved: The Little Record of Arthur Oscar Hornung (as E.W.H.). Colchester, Essex, privately printed, 1915.
Notes of a Camp-Follower on the Western Front. London, Constable, and New York, Dutton, 1919.
E.W. Hornung and His Young Guard, 1914 (poems and addresses), edited by Shane R. Chichester. Crowthorne, Berkshire, Wellington College Press, 1941.

*   *   *

I put E.W. Hornung's linked stories about A.J. Raffles, gentleman cracksman, squarely beside the Holmes tales of Conan Doyle (curiously, Hornung's brother-in-law). Both sets of stories seem to me to have that feeling of absolute rightness, perhaps the surest way of distinguishing that hard to define thing "the classic." There are blemishes in the Raffles stories, as there are (whisper it not) in the Holmes tales. But the faults in the end seem no more than flakes of rust on engines that work with smooth perfection.

There is certainly no need to make more allowances than that for Hornung's stories. Although they date from the turn of the century, they can be read today with shining pleasure. And this comes not simply from their period atmosphere, strong and delightful though that is. Unless you remember them exceptionally well, they can be re-read and still provide genuine surprises. Hornung had grasped the secret of the adventure tale, which is not only to make your reader ask "What next? What next?" but also to make him cry out "How on earth will he wriggle out of it this time?"

For Hornung was a fine craftsman, and craftsmanship is a quality more necessary within the tight limits of the short story than it is in the novel where there is room for diversions to conceal basic machinery inclined to clank. Look, however, at the way in which Hornung adroitly varies a basic formula (a gentleman who is a thief and who gets away with it despite the odds) which on the face of it one would think could hardly bear repetition more than two times or three times. Sometimes he takes Raffles out of the snug, snobby private flats of the Albany to a different location; sometimes he gives him a tinge of being a righter of wrongs; sometimes he makes a story a duel with the formidable Inspector Mackenzie; sometimes he shows Raffles as a master of disguise. Finally, he showed his craftsmanship to the utmost in killing Raffles off and, bar writing a few "posthumous" tales, refusing more firmly than his brother-in-law to bring an immensely popular figure back to life.

But what ingenuity he showed in working the formula while

there was still life in it. I quote only one instance—but it must stand for many. In the story "Out of Paradise" Raffles's friend Bunny, artless as ever, tells him about a goodies-crammed house owned by one Hector Carruthers with whose niece Bunny is in love. Of course, it is taboo to burgle a place Bunny has got to know in these circumstances. Ah, but, says Raffles, the present owner is not Mr. Carruthers but Lord Lochmaben. Oh, replies Bunny, reader of nothing in the papers but the cricket and the racing news, that's all right then. And, whether we know in advance or not that Mr. Carruthers has recently been made Lord Lochmaben, the trick delights us.

Yet Hornung was more than merely clever. He had all the sensitivity of the good writer. It was George Orwell who pointed out that a lesser writer would have crudely made his gentleman-burglar a lord or a baronet to get the maximum showy contrast. Hornung made Raffles no more than a gentleman pure and simple. Time and again in the stories one comes across not the brutally obvious (and dull), but the next-to-obvious and truth-stamped.

The reason, ultimately, why Raffles has lived when other creations using much the same contrast formula have vanished is that Raffles is far more than a walking formula. He is a person. I have already said that instead of being a stuffed aristocrat he is no more than a gentleman. But note how precisely Hornung placed him in society: a gentleman, yes, but one always strapped for money. And what other attributes he gives him. Yes, he is a cricketer of renown (an easy, but not too easy way of giving him heroic qualities) but he is no sporting hearty. On the walls of the Albany apartment are pre-Raphaelite etchings, the arty okay painters of that day.

Compare him here to Sherlock Holmes who also had a strain of the art-lover in him under the outer shell of the scientific, emotionless detective. There is yet more, in fact, to this comparison. Both Holmes and Raffles were apt to act from motives that brought them not great rewards but rather the satisfaction of exercising their arts. And both too had a similar relationship with the fictitious person who presented them to the public. For Doyle's stolid, mildly obtuse Watson, Hornung gave us Bunny, not the brightest of intellects but brave and all too loyal, a puppy to the bulldog Watson. Add, too, that to redeem anti-social traits (Holmes's cocaine) both heroes were ardent patriots in the days when this was a natural feeling among the great body of the public. Holmes has a pock-marked "VR" in honour of Queen Victoria on his walls; Raffles sent the Queen a (stolen) gold cup for her Jubilee declaring, "For sixty years, Bunny, we've been ruled over by absolutely the finest sovereign the world has ever seen." Like Doyle, one might add, Hornung could capture to a T the right way for his hero to speak.

Finally, if Sherlock Holmes went from rough conception in his creator's mind to become first a recognisable human being and then a figure of myth, exactly the same process happened with A.J. Raffles. It happened perhaps on a lesser scale, but it happened securely nevertheless. Raffles is an abiding hero.

—H.R.F. Keating

HOUGH, S(tanley) B(ennett). Also writes as Rex Gordon; Bennett Stanley. British. Born in Preston, Lancashire, 25 February 1917. Educated at Preston Grammar School; Radio Officers College, Preston; attended classes of the Workers Educational Association. Married Justa E.C. Wodschow in 1938. Radio operator, Marconi Radio Company, 1936–38;

radio officer, International Marine Radio Company, 1939–45; ran a yachting firm, 1946–51; since the 1970's teacher of creative writing, Workers Educational Association, and local authorities, Cornwall. Recipient: Infinity award, for science fiction, 1957. Agent: A.M. Heath and Company Ltd., 79 St. Martin's Lane, London WC2N 4AA. Address: 21 St. Michael's Road, Ponsanooth, Truro, Cornwall, England.

CRIME PUBLICATIONS

Novels (series: Inspector Brentford)

Frontier Incident. London, Hodder and Stoughton, 1951; New York, Crowell, 1952.
Moment of Decision. London, Hodder and Stroughton, 1952.
Mission in Guemo. London, Hodder and Stoughton, 1953; New York, Walker, 1964.
The Alscott Experiment (as Bennett Stanley). London, Hodder and Stoughton, 1954.
Government Contract (as Bennett Stanley). London, Hodder and Stoughton, 1956.
Extinction Bomber. London, Lane, 1956.
The Bronze Perseus (Brentford). London, Secker and Warburg, 1959; New York, Walker, 1962; as *The Tender Killer,* New York, Avon, 1963.
Dear Daughter Dead (Brentford). London, Gollancz, 1965; New York, Walker, 1966.
Sweet Sister Seduced (Brentford). London, Gollancz, 1968; New York, Harper, 1983.
Fear Fortune, Father (Brentford). London, Gollancz, 1974; New York, Harper, 1984.

OTHER PUBLICATIONS

Novels

Sea Struck (as Bennett Stanley). New York, Crowell, 1953; as *Sea to Eden,* London, Hodder and Stoughton, 1954.
The Seas South. London, Hodder and Stoughton, 1953.
The Primitives. London, Hodder and Stoughton, 1954.
Beyond the Eleventh Hour. London, Hodder and Stoughton, 1961.

Novels as Rex Gordon

Utopia 239. London, Heinemann, 1955.
No Man Friday. London, Heinemann, 1956; as *First on Mars,* New York, Ace, 1957.
First to the Stars. New York, Ace, 1959; as *The Worlds of Eclos,* London, Consul, 1961.
First Through Time. New York, Ace, 1962; as *The Time Factor,* London, Tandem, 1964.
Utopia minus X. New York, Ace, 1966; as *The Paw of God,* London, Tandem, 1967.
The Yellow Fraction. New York, Ace, 1969; London, Dobson, 1972.

Other

A Pound a Day Inclusive: The Modern Way to Holiday Travel. London, Hodder and Stoughton, 1957.
Expedition Everyman: Your Way on Your Income to All the Desirable Places of Europe. London, Hodder and Stoughton, 1959.
Expedition Everyman 1964. London, Hodder and Stoughton, 1964.

Where? An Independent Report on Holiday Resorts in Britain and the Continent. London, Hodder and Stoughton, 1964.
Creative Writing: A Handbook for Students, Tutors, and Education Authorities. Plymouth, Workers Education Association, 1983.

*

Manuscript Collection: Archive of Contemporary History, University of Wyoming, Laramie.

S.B. Hough comments:

Much of the literature of our time is formless and shapeless; the detective story on the other hand can and frequently does have a form as demanding as that of a Mozart symphony, while, at the same time, offering the literary artist a medium of inquiry into human folly and psychology and the life of his times. I am honoured to have made a small contribution to this major artform which, in other hands than mine, uses the simplest of literary devices to explore the depths of human motivation; but I would rather that readers approached my work anticipating what they have a right to expect—an entertaining story.

* * *

Readers of S.B. Hough's fiction quickly become aware that Hough is a crime writer with a purpose. His purpose is twofold and clearly set forth in the fiction itself. First, Hough uses crime writing to chart the "human character as a whole." He does this because, as a surgeon says in *Dear Daughter Dead*, "you can't throw up surgery and take to the study of the brain. . . . We know nothing about the subject. Who studies the human character as a whole? We leave it to novelists and playwrights." Second, Hough puts crime fiction to the task of exploring the "modern predicament," modern meaning existential. Morality in such a world is personal and situational. Hence, as Hough himself suggests in an author's apology to *Sweet Sister Seduced*, his works are more appropriately called "did-he-do-its" than "whodunits." Even when we know that a Hough character "did it" (literally), we are not sure he "did it" morally. The converse is also true.

Hough pursues the task of studying the human character as a whole and exploring the modern predicament through two distinct types of crime writing. On the one hand, he writes novels of the criminal mind in the tradition of Dostoevsky, Patricia Highsmith, and Julian Symons. Two of the better novels in this mode are *The Bronze Perseus* and *Fear Fortune, Father*. On the other hand, he presents a more reflective, distanced view of the human character in police procedural novels, featuring Chief Detective Inspector Brentford. Brentford serves as both a filter and a focus for further studies of the criminal mind.

Hough is at his best when he makes the reader sympathetic with the criminal's moral world. This is done boldly in *Fear Fortune, Father*. There Hough presents a criminal mind *sans* filter. Told in first-person, the whole of the novel is a chronicle of Dalby Pearson's journey from unemployed technical manager to master criminal. Since the reader is locked into the narrative perspective of Dalby, Dalby's moral world becomes the reader's own. That moral world is cynical and existential. And it is the subject of the novel. Dalby's world is almost convincing, almost acceptable. His anger toward the established business order is made understandable. His compassion for a crippled girl, Delicia, is admirable. And his activity as a criminal is non-violent, victimless. Nevertheless, the story refuses to resolve itself into the happy ending Dalby's move to

Penfolds (an exclusive seaside retreat) betokens. In the final pages, Dalby comes to realize that his inventions now have a history and a will of their own. His nicely created world is threatened by his own history as a thief, his wife's unpunished crimes, and the emergence of Delicia as his "Lolita." The web he has spun may become his own death trap, or at least spell the end of his good fortune. Then we discover that the tale he has told is both his novel (for money's sake) and his last testament (for conscience's sake). The book is Dalby's hedge against a future he now doubts he can either posit or control.

The world presented in Hough's procedural novels is but a step from his psychological, existential crime novels. Inspector Brentford is a likeable detective—dedicated, plodding, right-headed, middle-class. At his best, Brentford is both foil to and investigator of the criminal mind. In *Sweet Sister Seduced*, Brentford's own happy marriage and middle-class success clash with the failed middle-class world of one Mr. Milham. Like Dalby in *Fear Fortune, Father*, Milham lives in a fragile world spun from his own mind. Milham's family, in a fit of Victorian rage, disowns Elizabeth (his sister) because she is pregnant out of wedlock. Milham resolves to help her. And through a series of strange, unforeseeable events he finds it necessary to pose as her husband. Once struck, the pose lasts for decades, ending only with his sister/wife's death. Elizabeth's death is investigated by Brentford. During the investigation, Brentford, his wife, and the reader are forced to contemplate the relativity and fragility of the morality and reality as they are understood by the "average person." The entire investigation takes place under a shadow cast by the works of Freud and Kafka. And the final solution does little to erase the terror inherent in the case.

Hough is a crime writer who places the crime story into the philosophical and moral web Dostoevsky wove for it and which existentialism stretched into "truth." At bottom, though, Hough is a stern critic of the existentialist world-view—but he can make it perform a dazzling death dance across the surface of his narratives.

—Larry E. Grimes

———

HOUSEHOLD, Geoffrey (Edward West). British. Born in Bristol, 30 November 1900. Educated at Clifton College, Bristol, 1914–19; Magdalen College, Oxford, 1919–22, B.A. (honours) in English 1922. Served in the Intelligence Corps, 1939–45: Lieutenant Colonel; Territorial Decoration; mentioned in despatches. Married Ilona M.J. Zsoldos-Gutmán in 1942; one son and two daughters. Engaged in commerce abroad, 1922–35; worked for Bank of Romania, Bucharest, 4 years; Elders and Fyffes, importers in Spain; 1926–29; writer for encyclopedias in the U.S.A; composer of children's radio plays, Columbia Broadcasting System; salesman, John Kidd in Europe, Middle East and South America, 1933–39. *Died 4 October 1988.*

Crime Publications

Novels (series: Roger Taine)

The Third Hour. London, Chatto and Windus, 1937; Boston, Little Brown, 1938.
Rogue Male. London, Chatto and Windus, and Boston, Little Brown, 1939; as *Man Hunt*, New York, Triangle, 1942.

Arabesque. London, Chatto and Windus, and Boston, Little Brown, 1948.

The High Place. London, Joseph, and Boston, Little Brown, 1950.

A Rough Shoot (Taine). London, Joseph, and Boston, Little Brown, 1951.

A Time to Kill (Taine). Boston, Little Brown, 1951; London, Joseph, 1952.

Fellow Passenger. London, Joseph, and Boston, Little Brown, 1955; as *Hang the Man High,* New York, Spivak, 1957.

Watcher in the Shadows. London, Joseph, and Boston, Little Brown, 1960.

Thing to Love. London, Joseph, and Boston, Little Brown, 1963.

Olura. London, Joseph, and Boston, Little Brown, 1965.

The Courtesy of Death. London, Joseph, and Boston, Little Brown, 1967.

Dance of the Dwarfs. London, Joseph, and Boston, Little Brown, 1968; as *The Adversary,* New York, Dell, 1970.

Doom's Caravan. London, Joseph, and Boston, Little Brown, 1971.

The Three Sentinels. London, Joseph, and Boston, Little Brown, 1972.

The Lives and Times of Bernardo Brown. London, Joseph, 1973; Boston, Little Brown, 1974.

Red Anger. London, Joseph, and Boston, Little Brown, 1975.

Hostage—London: The Diary of Julian Despard. London, Joseph, and Boston, Little Brown, 1977.

The Last Two Weeks of Georges Rivac. London, Joseph, and Boston, Little Brown, 1978.

The Sending. London, Joseph, and Boston, Little Brown, 1980.

Summon the Bright Water. London, Joseph, and Boston, Little Brown, 1981.

Rogue Justice. London, Joseph, 1982; Boston, Little Brown, 1983.

Arrows of Desire. London, Joseph, 1985; Boston, Atlantic Monthly Press, 1986.

Face to the Sun. London, Joseph, 1988.

Short Stories

The Salvation of Pisco Gabar and Other Stories. London, Chatto and Windus, 1938; augmented editions, Boston, Little Brown, 1940.

Tales of Adventurers. London, Joseph, and Boston, Little Brown, 1952.

The Brides of Solomon and Other Stories. London, Joseph, and Boston, Little Brown, 1958.

Sabres on the Sand and Other Stories. London, Joseph, and Boston, Little Brown, 1966.

Capricorn and Cancer. London, Joseph, 1981.

The Days of Your Fathers. London, Joseph, 1987.

OTHER PUBLICATIONS

Short Stories

The Cats to Come. London, Joseph, 1975.

The Europe That Was. Newton Abbot, Devon, David and Charles, and New York, St. Martin's Press, 1979.

Other

The Terror of Villadonga (for children). London, Hutchinson, 1936; revised edition, as *The Spanish Cave,* Boston, Little Brown, 1936; London, Chatto and Windus, 1940.

The Exploits of Xenophon (for children). New York, Random House, 1955; as *Xenophon's Adventure,* London, Bodley Head, 1961.

Against the Wind (autobiography). London, Joseph, 1958; Boston, Little Brown, 1959.

Prisoner of the Indies (for children). London, Bodley Head, and Boston, Little Brown, 1967.

Escape into Daylight (for children). London, Bodley Head, and Boston, Little Brown, 1976.

*

Manuscript Collection: Lilly Library, Indiana University, Bloomington.

Critical Study: "The Lives and Times of Geoffrey Household" by Michael Barber, in *Books and Bookmen* (London), January 1974.

*   *   *

The long list of Geoffrey Household's books is varied in both nature and quality, but it includes at least three thrillers of the first order: *Rogue Male, Watcher in the Shadows,* and *Dance of the Dwarfs.* The subject and sustaining interest of these three works is the same: the human hunt or chase. As a chase novelist Household deserves to rank with Buchan, Greene, and the wartime Michael Innes; he occupies an especially interesting place in the history of the genre because of his knack of combining the atmosphere of open-air virility that distinguishes Buchan's work with the interest in political anxiety and private terrors that characterize more recent contributions to the form.

All of Household's heroes are to some degree descendants of Buchan's Richard Hannay. They are slightly raffish gentleman-adventurers, deeply involved in the world of English blood sports and imbued with a public-school code of honour, chivalry, and sportsmanship. Their adventures are frequently conducted against the background of the English counties; in *Rogue Male,* for example, the hero finally confronts his enemy on the territory of the Cattistock Hunt in Dorset. Yet at the same time the stories are impregnated with modern political turmoil. *Rogue Male* begins with the hero's attempt to assassinate an unnamed European dictator (presumably Hitler), continues with his torture by Gestapo-like interrogators, and ends with his return to the task of assassination, promising, "I shall not miss." In *Watcher in the Shadows* the hero is pursued by a man who mistakenly believes him to have participated in Nazi atrocities. The hero of *Dance of the Dwarfs* is a research scientist living in the South American jungle on terms of uneasy truce with the local Marxist guerillas.

Although both genteel sportsmanship and modern politics are part of the essential background of Household's stories, they rarely predominate. His main interest is in the psychology of his heroes, their reactions to accumulating fears and dangers. His favourite story-telling device (and he handles it like a master) is the first-person narrative, the confessional diary in which the writer attempts to understand and order the experiences he is undergoing. "I have recently noted a tendency to talk to myself," begins Dr. Owen Dawnay in *Dance of the Dwarfs.* "I start on this exercise book again, for I dare not leave my thoughts uncontrolled," explains the nameless narrator of *Rogue Male.*

Viewed in thriller terms, the stories that these men tell are a series of artfully contrived shocks and reversals in which hunter and hunted stalk each other, lay elaborate false scents and exchange roles, before eventually confronting each other in a life-and-death struggle. In psychological terms, the stories show the heroes shedding, first, the appurtenances of civilized life and, finally, some of the attributes of human identity itself. Their narratives have the isolated and desperate quality of Poe's "MS Found in a Bottle" or William Godwin's *Caleb Williams*. Toward the end of *Rogue Male* the hero has himself become a hunted animal, quite literally going to earth in a hole in the ground. Dr. Dawnay of *Dance of the Dwarfs* is drawn into a complex intimacy with the sinister jungle animals whom he hunted and who now hunt him. Such books are sophisticated and gripping revelations of the animal beneath the veneer of civilized life. And Household clearly sees that animal state to which his heroes are reduced not as a form of debasement but as a condition of stubborn courage and integrity—a final manifestation of grace under pressure.

—Ian Ousby

HOUSTON, R.B. *See* **RAE, Hugh C.**

HOWARD, Clark. American. Born in Tennessee, in 1934. Educated at schools in Chicago. Served in the United States Marine Corps. Recipient: Mystery Writers of America Edgar Allan Poe award, for short story, 1980. Address: c/o Marek, St. Martin's Press, 175 Fifth Avenue, New York, New York, 10010, U.S.A.

CRIME PUBLICATIONS

Novels

A Movement Toward Eden. Durham, North Carolina, Moore, 1969.
The Doomsday Squad. New York, Weybright and Talley, 1970; London, W.H. Allen, 1971.
The Killings. New York, Dial Press, 1973; London, Souvenir Press, 1974.
Last Contract. New York, Pinnacle, 1973.
Summit Kill. New York, Pinnacle, 1975.
Mark the Sparrow. New York, Dial Press, 1975; London, Souvenir Press, 1976.
The Hunters. New York, Dial Press, 1976.
The Last Great Death Stunt. New York, Berkley, 1977.
The Wardens. New York, Marek, 1979.
Traces of Mercury. New York, Jove, 1980.
Dirt Rich. New York, St. Martin's Press, 1986.
Quick Silver. New York, Dutton, 1988.

Uncollected Short Stories

"Handcuffed," in *Crime and Justice* (New York), January 1957.
"Enough Rope for Two," in *Manhunt* (New York), February 1957.
"Put Yourself in My Place," in *Alfred Hitchcock's Mystery Magazine* (New York), April 1962.
"Money to Burn," in *Alfred Hitchcock's Mystery Magazine* (New York), September 1962.
"Night Work," in *Alfred Hitchcock's Mystery Magazine* (New York), November 1962.

"The Losers," in *Manhunt* (New York), June 1963.
"It Could Be Fatal," in *Alfred Hitchcock's Mystery Magazine* (New York), June 1963.
"The Little Things," in *Alfred Hitchcock's Mystery Magazine* (New York), August 1963.
"Four and Twenty Blackbirds," in *Alfred Hitchcock's Mystery Magazine* (New York), February 1964.
"The Junkie Trap," in *Manhunt* (New York), March 1964.
"Prisoners," in *Alfred Hitchcock's Mystery Magazine* (New York), April 1964.
"Recommendation," in *Alfred Hitchcock's Mystery Magazine* (New York), November 1964.
"Line of Duty," in *Alfred Hitchcock's Mystery Magazine* (New York), December 1964.
"One Way Out," in *Alfred Hitchcock's Mystery Magazine* (New York), February 1965.
"The Target," in *Alfred Hitchcock's Mystery Magazine* (New York), March 1965.
"The First of April," in *Alfred Hitchcock's Mystery Magazine* (New York), April 1965.
"From the Bard, With Love," in *Alfred Hitchcock's Mystery Magazine* (New York), May 1965.
"A Small Dose of Salvation," in *Alfred Hitchcock's Mystery Magazine* (New York), June 1965.
"The Peregrine," in *Alfred Hitchcock's Mystery Magazine* (New York), July 1965.
"The Apprentice," in *Alfred Hitchcock's Mystery Magazine* (New York), September 1965.
"Keeper of the Crypt," in *Alfred Hitchcock's Mystery Magazine* (New York), December 1965.
"The Suspect," in *Alfred Hitchcock's Mystery Magazine* (New York), July 1966.
"Attorney of Choice," in *Alfred Hitchcock's Mystery Magazine* (New York), August 1966.
"Sycophant," in *Alfred Hitchcock's Mystery Magazine* (New York), September 1966.
"Eyes of the Beholder," in *Alfred Hitchcock's Mystery Magazine* (New York), February 1967.
"The Marksman," in *Alfred Hitchcock's Mystery Magazine* (New York), March 1967.
"Time Element," in *Alfred Hitchcock's Mystery Magazine* (New York), April 1967.
"Flight Plan," in *Alfred Hitchcock's Mystery Magazine* (New York), February 1968.
"Goodbye, Mr. Madison," in *Alfred Hitchcock's Mystery Magazine* (New York), August 1968.
"Memory of a Murder," in *Alfred Hitchcock's Mystery Magazine* (New York), October 1969.
"The Deal," in *Alfred Hitchcock's Mystery Magazine* (New York), September 1970.
"We Spy," in *Best Detective Stories of the Year 1971,* edited by Allen J. Hubin. New York, Dutton, 1971.
"The Protectors," in *Alfred Hitchcock's Mystery Magazine* (New York), July 1971.
"The Juror," in *Mike Shayne Mystery Magazine* (Los Angeles), August 1971.
"The Keeper," in *Alfred Hitchcock's Mystery Magazine* (New York), October 1971.
"The Diver," in *Alfred Hitchcock's Mystery Magazine* (New York), December 1971.
"Christmas Plans," in *Alfred Hitchcock's Mystery Magazine* (New York), January 1972.
"Road Gang," in *Alfred Hitchcock's Mystery Magazine* (New York), February 1972.
"A Few Extra Pounds," in *Alfred Hitchcock's Mystery Magazine* (New York), March 1972.

"The Escapee," in *Alfred Hitchcock's Mystery Magazine* (New York), April 1972.
"The Hostages," in *Alfred Hitchcock's Mystery Magazine* (New York), May 1972.
"Cameron's Kill," in *Alfred Hitchcock's Mystery Magazine* (New York), June 1972.
"The Masterpiece," in *Alfred Hitchcock's Mystery Magazine* (New York), July 1972.
"The Last Revival," in *Alfred Hitchcock's Mystery Magazine* (New York), August 1972.
"The Best Hideout," in *Alfred Hitchcock's Mystery Magazine* (New York), March 1973.
"The Last Bullet," in *Alfred Hitchcock's Mystery Magazine* (New York), April 1973.
"Next in Line," in *Alfred Hitchcock's Mystery Magazine* (New York), June 1973.
"Deadly August," in *Alfred Hitchcock's Mystery Magazine* (New York), August 1973.
"The Inside Man," in *Mike Shayne Mystery Magazine* (Los Angeles), September 1973.
"Mother of Pearl," in *Mike Shayne Mystery Magazine* (Los Angeles), October 1973.
"The Seven Strangers," in *Mike Shayne Mystery Magazine* (Los Angeles), November 1973.
"A Place to Hide," in *Alfred Hitchcock's Mystery Magazine* (North Palm Beach, Florida), July 1974.
"Spook House," in *Alfred Hitchcock's Tales to Keep You Spellbound*, edited by Eleanor Sullivan. New York, Dial Press, 1976.
"Logan's Cross," in *Alfred Hitchcock's Mystery Magazine* (North Palm Beach, Florida), January 1976.
"A Price on His Life," in *Ellery Queen's Mystery Magazine* (New York), 6 October 1980.
"Horn Man," in *Best Detective Stories of the Year 1981*, edited by Edward D. Hoch. New York, Dutton, 1981.
"Payoff Time," in *Alfred Hitchcock's Tales to Make Your Hair Stand on End*, edited by Eleanor Sullivan. New York, Dial Press, 1981.
"Top Con," in *Ellery Queen's Mystery Magazine* (New York), 25 March 1981.
"Hit and Run," in *Alfred Hitchcock's Mystery Magazine* (New York), 16 September 1981.
"Mexican Triangle," in *Ellery Queen's Mystery Magazine* (New York), 7 October 1981.
"The Specialist," in *Twilight Zone*, November 1981.
"Second Jeopardy," in *Ellery Queen's Mystery Magazine* (New York), 2 December 1981.
"Termination Point," in *Alfred Hitchcock's Mystery Magazine* (New York), 21 March 1982.
"The Last Downhill," in *Alfred Hitchcock's Mystery Magazine* (New York), May 1982.
"Death Snow," in *Ellery Queen's Mystery Magazine* (New York), Mid-July 1982.
"Old Soldiers," in *Ellery Queen's Mystery Magazine* (New York), September 1982.
"All the Heroes Are Dead," in *Ellery Queen's Mystery Magazine* (New York), December 1982.
"Puerto Rican Blues," in *Ellery Queen's Mystery Magazine* (New York), April 1983.
"Custer's Ghost," in *Ellery Queen's Mystery Magazine* (New York), May 1983.
"Run from the Hunter," in *Ellery Queen's Mystery Magazine* (New York), July 1983.
"New Orleans Getaway," in *Ellery Queen's Mystery Magazine* (New York), August 1983.
"Return to the OK Corral," in *Ellery Queen's Mystery Magazine* (New York), November 1983.

"Wild Things," in *Ellery Queen's Mystery Magazine* (New York), December 1983.
"The Last Private Eye," in *Ellery Queen's Mystery Magazine* (New York), April 1984.
"The Plateau," in *Ellery Queen's Mystery Magazine* (New York), July 1984.

OTHER PUBLICATIONS

Novel

The Arm. Los Angeles, Sherbourne Press, 1967.

Other

Six Against the Rock. New York, Dial Press, 1977; London, Hart Davis MacGibbon, 1978.
The Wardens. New York, Marek, and London, New English Library, 1979.
Zebra: The True Account of the 179 Days of Terror in San Francisco. New York, Marek, 1979; as *The Zebra Killings*, London, New English Library, 1980.
American Saturday. New York, Marek, 1981.
Brothers in Blood. New York, Marek, 1983.

*　　*　　*

Although Clark Howard has published a dozen crime-suspense novels to date his growing popularity today rests mainly upon the fact-crime books and frequent short stories which have earned him five nominations and an Edgar award from the Mystery Writers of America.

The first of Howard's Edgar-nominated fact-crime books, *Six Against the Rock,* dealt with events at Alcatraz before that prison was closed. It was followed in 1979 by *Zebra,* his Edgar-nominated account of San Francisco's infamous Zebra killings in 1973 and 1974. Next came *American Saturday,* about the killing of black militant George Jackson and others at San Quentin prison in 1971. And more recently *Brothers in Blood* dealt with multiple murders in Georgia in 1973.

The themes that run through Howard's fact-crime books—and some of his novels as well—are the reasons why men kill, and the effects of prison life upon such men. Howard is careful never to offer his personal judgements, and his writing shows great compassion for criminal and victim alike, as can be clearly seen from a book like *Brothers in Blood*.

Clark Howard began publishing short stories at least as early as 1957, while still in his early twenties. He averaged a few stories a year for the next two decades, mainly in *Alfred Hitchcock's Mystery Magazine*. An especially good example is "We Spy," a neat little crime story with a surprise ending.

In 1980 he published his first story in *Ellery Queen's Mystery Magazine,* and "Horn Man" went on to win MWA's Edgar as best story of the year. "Horn Man," telling of a great jazz trumpet player who returns home to New Orleans after serving a prison sentence, again shows Howard's deep interest in convicts and ex-convicts, a theme that runs through much of his writing. The Edgar Award spurred him on to greater productivity in the short story and he quickly became an *EQMM* regular while still appearing in *AHMM* as well.

The next three years saw more than a dozen stories of remarkably high quality, including "Mexican Triangle," set in the Mexican oil fields where convicts work as laborers; "Death Snow," a detective story with an ending one would never find in Christie or Queen; the Edgar-nominated "All the Heroes Are Dead," an anti-detective story about Georgia bootlegging; another Edgar nominee, "Puerto Rican Blues," the story of two brothers and heroin smuggling; "Custer's Ghost," a moving tale of an aging American Indian bent on revenge; and "Run from the Hunter," a story of futuristic violence.

Clark Howard's concerns are for the outcast, the minority, the prisoner. He has woven these concerns into some of the most exciting short fiction of the 1980's.

—Edward D. Hoch

HOWARD, Hartley. *See* **CARMICHAEL, Harry.**

HOYT, Richard. American. Born in Hermiston, Oregon, 28 January 1941. Educated at Umatilla High School, Oregon, 1955–59; Columbia Basin College, Pasco, Washington, 1960–61; University of Oregon, Eugene, 1961–63, 1966–67, B.S. in journalism 1963, M.S. in journalism 1967; Washington Journalism Center, Washington, D.C. (Fellow), 1967; University of Hawaii, Honolulu, 1968–72, Ph.D. in American Studies 1972. Served in the United States Army 1963–66: Special Agent, Army Intelligence. Married 1) Carole Hoyt in 1967 (divorced 1978), one daughter; 2) Sheila Hoyt in 1980 (divorced 1981). Reporter, Honolulu *Star-Bulletin,* 1968–69; reporter, later assistant city editor, Honolulu *Advertiser,* 1969–72; correspondent, *Newsweek* magazine, 1969–72; Assistant Professor of Journalism, University of Maryland, College Park, 1972–76; Assistant Professor, later Associate Professor of Communications, Lewis and Clark College, Portland, Oregon, 1976–83. Since 1983, freelance writer. Agent: Jacques de Spoelberch, Shagbark Road, Wilson Point, South Norwalk, Connecticut 06854. Address: 13120 Southwest Cavalier Court, Beaverton, Oregon 97005, U.S.A.

CRIME PUBLICATIONS

Novels (series: James Burlane; John Denson)

Decoys (Denson). New York, Evans, 1980; London, Hale, 1982.
30 for a Harry (Denson). New York, Evans, 1981; London, Hale, 1982.
The Manna Enzyme. New York, Morrow, 1982.
Trotsky's Run (Burlane). New York, Morrow, 1982; London, Severn House, 1987.
The Siskiyou Two-Step (Denson). New York, Morrow, 1983; London, Hale, 1986; revised edition, as *Siskiyou,* New York, Tor, 1984.
Cool Runnings. New York, Viking, 1984.
Fish Story (Denson). New York, Viking, 1985; London, Hale, 1987.
Head of State (Burlane). New York, Tor, 1985; London, Severn House, 1986.
The Dragon Portfolio. New York, Tor, 1986; London, Grafton, 1988.
Seige. New York, Tor and London, Grafton, 1987.
Darwin's Secret. New York, Doubleday, 1989.

*

Manuscript Collection: Mugar Memorial Library, Boston University.

*　　*　　*

Since 1980 the young American writer Richard Hoyt has produced a number of suspense and mystery novels which bode well for both genres. Of the former, particularly good is *Trotsky's Run,* a political espionage thriller which is reminiscent—but not derivative—of Richard Condon's *The Manchurian Candidate.* A Soviet mole (to borrow le Carré's now standard nomenclature) recruited during the so-called free speech movement in Berkeley becomes the leading candidate for the presidency of the United States, an interesting premise which is enhanced by the candidate's psychotic conviction that he is the avenging reincarnation of Leon Trotsky. The plot and its resolution pivot on Hoyt's splendid evocation of Kim Philby and the machinations of the KGB in removing their potentially explosive "sleeper."

Better still, however, and more suited to Hoyt's talents, are his mysteries, which feature a series gumshoe by the name of John Denson. A thoroughly contemporary westerner that one reviewer has described, aptly, as "soft-boiled," Denson is a self-admitted "flake" who works the more unsavory corridors of the Pacific Northwest. Apparently insouciant rather than cynical, Denson is in fact a romantic whose working knowledge of the human condition saves him from the sort of garrulous idealism that the previous generation of American mystery writers sometimes saddled their own heroes with.

Hoyt's stories to date are painstakingly plotted and tightly written, and his attention to detail and atmosphere lends a seductive verisimilitude to the various proceedings. The economical, not to say overly spare, prose unobtrusively conveys the narratives along and rarely intrudes on the business at hand or the reader's sensibilities. Hoyt has a considerable gift for comic writing but indulges it only where appropriate, that is to say, in the dialogue, which is generally trenchant and frequently hilarious. Denson, of course, gets the best lines.

Especially enjoyable of the Denson cases are *Decoys,* which pits the detective against a vicious pimp-turned-smuggler in a milieu of drug traffic and prostitution, and *30 for a Harry,* a complicated but credible tale of murder and corporate cannibalism in the newspaper business. While both of these cases are slightly flawed by convenient gunplay in the denouements, they are also unusually intricate exercises which avoid the fanciful and surreal, and Hoyt's control of these ambitious forays is surehanded and artistically mature. If mysteries, like Olympic dives, were rated by both degree of difficulty and execution, the Denson stories would merit high marks on both counts. While the body of his work is as yet relatively small, one hopes that Hoyt will be prolific. Like his contemporary Gregory Mcdonald (creator of the Fletch series) he may prove instrumental in revivifying the American private eye for a new generation of readers.

—Curtis S. Gibson

HUBBARD, P(hilip) M(aitland). British. Born in Reading, Berkshire, 9 November 1910. Educated at Elizabeth College, Guernsey, 1919–29; Jesus College, Oxford (Newdigate Prize, 1933), 1929–34. Had three children. Worked in the Indian Civil Service in the Punjab 1934–47; worked for the British Council,

1948–51; freelance writer, 1951–55; worked for the National Union of Manufacturers, 1955–60. *Died 17 March 1980.*

CRIME PUBLICATIONS

Novels

Flush as May.   London, Joseph, and New York, British Book Centre, 1963.
Picture of Millie.   London, Joseph, and New York, British Book Centre, 1964.
A Hive of Glass.   London, Joseph, and New York, Atheneum, 1965.
The Holm Oaks.   London, Joseph, 1965; New York, Atheneum, 1966.
The Tower.   New York, Atheneum, 1967; London, Bles, 1968.
The Country of Again.   New York, Atheneum, 1968; as *The Custom of the Country,* London, Bles, 1969.
Cold Waters.   New York, Atheneum, 1969; London, Bles, 1970.
High Tide.   New York, Atheneum, 1970; London, Macmillan, 1971.
The Dancing Man.   New York, Atheneum, and London, Macmillan, 1971.
The Whisper of the Glen.   New York, Atheneum, and London, Macmillan, 1972.
A Rooted Sorrow.   New York, Atheneum, and London, Macmillan, 1973.
A Thirsty Evil.   New York, Atheneum, and London, Macmillan, 1974.
The Graveyard.   New York, Atheneum, and London, Macmillan, 1975.
The Causeway.   London, Macmillan, 1976; New York, Doubleday, 1978.
The Quiet River.   London, Macmillan, and New York, Doubleday, 1978.
Kill Claudio.   London, Macmillan, and New York, Doubleday, 1979.

Uncollected Short Stories

"The Running of the Deer," in *Winter's Crimes 6,* edited by George Hardinge.   London, Macmillan, 1974.
"The Altar Tomb," in *Scottish Short Stories 1977.*   London, Collins, 1977.
"Leave It to the River," in *Scottish Short Stories 1978.*   London, Collins, 1978.

OTHER PUBLICATIONS

Play

Radio Play: *Dead Man's Bay,* 1966.

Verse

Ovid among the Goths.   Oxford, Blackwell, 1933.

Other (for children)

Anna Highbury.   London, Cassell, 1963.
Rat-Trap Island.   London, Cassell, 1964.

*   *   *

After 1963 P.M. Hubbard produced a fine suspense novel almost every year. His writing is singular in its simplicity and elegance. A survey of his crime fiction reveals that there is, in fact, quite a variety of settings and situations, but an impression remains of almost mythic conflict between few characters, of elemental struggle acted out in a lonely world of brooding landscapes and cold waters. Protagonists, some merely odd or whimsical, others clearly abnormal, are driven by their compulsions.

Hubbard's first two novels, *Flush as May* and *Picture of Millie,* are decidedly different from those that follow. The former is a traditional mystery in which two Oxford undergraduates discover why a body found by the heroine early one May morning disappears. The Old Religion is alive and well in some remote villages. Perhaps less successful, and certainly unrepresentative, is *Picture of Millie,* a tale with numerous characters and an unexpected ending which does not quite hold together.

The central character in *A Hive of Glass,* more rogue than hero, is a passionate collector of old glass. His collecting mania drives him to extraordinary action when a peculiar household on an isolated tidal island seems to invite violence. In a sense, *The Holm Oaks* sets the pattern for what is to evolve as the Hubbard model: a solitary hero is compelled by circumstances or his own needs to commit acts which, once begun, must continue to a climax, either satisfactory or disastrous. A menacing atmosphere overshadows eroticism and violence, the more powerful for being understated. A matter-of-fact recital of information about seemingly ordinary people, as it accumulates, turns into a very threatening narrative. Occasionally Hubbard misses his mark, as in, some may think *A Rooted Sorrow* or *The Graveyard.* When he succeeds the results are memorable.

In *The Holm Oaks* the stark setting and dark deeds are lightened by humor. Jake Haddon, the narrator, meets Dennis Wainwright, a sinister type, and muses: "He was a very tall, stiff man, and curiously neat. In a place and weather which sent me naturally to superimposed jerseys, he wore a solid dark suit with a collar and tie. I wondered whether he had been somebody's butler." Wainwright seeks obliquely to learn Haddon's interests, and Haddon notes: "I hesitated between necromancy and numismatics." Ironically, Elizabeth, Jake's unloved wife, is delighted with the dismal woods. A fanatic bird-watcher, she hopes to identify a night heron which her husband calls a "queer tern."

The Country of Again, a fine and original novel set in Pakistan, charts the resolution of a crime which took place 20 years earlier when the protagonist was a magistrate in the Indian Civil Service. In *The Dancing Man,* Hubbard portrays a remote place in Wales where the ruins of a Cistercian abbey rest uneasily atop a prehistoric site similar to the one at Avebury. Centuries ago, vandals destroyed the abbey and changed the image of a cross, incised on the only stone left standing, into a cavorting ithyphallic figure, mocking the intrusion of the monks. An archeologist who comes to visit the owner of the site, a medievalist with an excessive pride of possession, disappears. *A Thirsty Evil,* one of Hubbard's best, concerns an artificial lake, deep and always cold, a peculiar stone pillar which sticks up from the bottom of the lake, and an odd family. The hero arrives in search of Julia, a woman he loves almost at first sight. Her brother and sister, beautiful and golden, seem like sea creatures in the water, but the brother is insane and the sister is a nymphomaniac whom the hero likens to Cressida. The text is sprinkled with Shakespearean allusions and the hero is, in Julia's words, intent on "his proper bane."

P.M. Hubbard is easily one of the best contemporary writers of suspense fiction. His "thrillers" are, in psychological complexity and literary quality, comparable to the novels of Patricia Highsmith. His fascination with water, sailing, and adventure invites comparison with Andrew Garve's, but while

Garve is basically optimistic and upbeat, Hubbard deals with darker aspects of these subjects. Most crime novels are quickly read and as quickly forgotten but P.M. Hubbard's books linger in the memory and in the imagination.

—Mary Helen Becker

———

HUDSON, Jeffrey. *See* CRICHTON, Michael.

———

HUGHES, Dorothy B(elle, née Flanagan). American. Born in Kansas City, Missouri, 10 August 1904. Educated at the University of Missouri, Columbia, B.J. 1924; University of New Mexico, Albuquerque; Columbia University, New York. Married Levi Allen Hughes, Jr., in 1932 (died 1975); two daughters and one son. Teaching Fellow, University of New Mexico; reporter and woman's editor in the 1920's. Crime reviewer since the 1930's: for the Albuquerque *Tribune,* Los Angeles *News* and *Mirror,* New York *Herald-Tribune,* and since 1961, Los Angeles *Times.* Recipient: Mystery Writers of America Edgar Allan Poe award, for criticism, 1950, Grand Master award, 1978. Agent: Blanche Gregory, 2 Tudor City Place, New York, New York 10017. Address: 2107 Arbutus Street, Newport Beach, California 92660, U.S.A.

CRIME PUBLICATIONS

Novels (series: Inspector Tobin)

The So Blue Marble (Tobin). New York, Duell, 1940; London, Bantam, 1979.
The Cross-Eyed Bear (Tobin). New York, Duell, 1940; London, Nicholson and Watson, 1943.
The Bamboo Blonde. New York, Duell, 1941.
The Fallen Sparrow (Tobin). New York, Duell, 1942; London, Nicholson and Watson, 1943.
The Blackbirder. New York, Duell, 1943; London, Nicholson and Watson, 1948.
The Delicate Ape. New York, Duell, 1944.
Johnnie. New York, Duell, 1944; London, Nicholson and Watson, 1946.
Dread Journey. New York, Duell, 1945; London, Nicholson and Watson, 1948.
Ride the Pink Horse. New York, Duell, 1946; London, Bantam, 1979.
The Scarlet Imperial. New York, Mystery Book Club, 1946; as *Kiss for a Killer,* New York, Spivak, 1954.
In a Lonely Place. New York, Duell, 1947; London, Nicholson and Watson, 1950.
The Candy Kid. New York, Duell, 1950.
The Davidian Report. New York, Duell, 1952; as *The Body on the Bench,* New York, Dell, 1955.
The Expendable Man. New York, Random House, 1963; London, Deutsch, 1964.

Uncollected Short Stories

"The Spitting Tongue," in *Mystery Book Magazine* (New York), July 1945.

"The Spotted Pup," in *Mystery Book Magazine* (New York), October 1945.
"The Homecoming," in *Rex Stout Mystery Quarterly 9* (New York), 1947.
"You Killed Miranda," in *The Saint* (New York), August 1958.
"The Granny Woman," in *Gamma* (North Hollywood), 1963.
"The Black and White Blues," in *Chase* (New York), January 1963.
"Danger at Deerfawn," in *Ellery Queen's Mystery Magazine* (New York), August 1964.
"Everybody Needs a Mink," in *The Saint* (New York), July 1965.

OTHER PUBLICATIONS

Novel

The Big Barbecue. New York, Random House, 1949.

Verse

Dark Certainty. New Haven, Connecticut, Yale University Press, 1931.

Other

Pueblo on the Mesa: The First Fifty Years of the University of New Mexico. Albuquerque, University of New Mexico Press, 1939.
Erle Stanley Gardner: The Case of the Real Perry Mason. New York, Morrow, 1978.

*

Dorothy B. Hughes comments:
I always intended to write books from when I was six years old and learned to write words. I wrote poetry, then short stories, before writing novels. It is true indeed that one learns to write by writing, and it takes time to learn to handle your material.

*   *   *

Dorothy B. Hughes has distinguished herself as a critic and historian of the mystery genre as well as an author of mystery fiction. For her reviews she received an Edgar in 1950 and has gained the approbation of Julian Symons, who names her in *Mortal Consequences* as one of the three contemporary Americans who review detective fiction as competently as he does himself. The decade of the 1940's was her most prolific period as a novelist: 11 of her 14 novels appeared then. Three of them, *The Fallen Sparrow, Ride the Pink Horse,* and *In a Lonely Place,* have been made into major films.

Her first novel, *The So Blue Marble,* concerns a fashion designer who discovers that she is the principal agent through which a ruthless pair of European outlaws are attempting to gain possession of a mysterious priceless treasure. Complications arise when she tries to protect her sisters and her estranged husband from the wrath of the outlaws and the rigors of the law. Most of Hughes's other novels are felicitous variations on this single, unusual formula: domestic thrillers in which the accomplished and upper-class protagonist becomes innocently involved in a situation of evil intrigue, finally resolved through the hero's cunning, character, and sheer luck. The reviewer Will Cuppy called *The Cross-Eyed Bear* "glittering, but not hard-boiled."

The Expendable Man is not a domestic spy thriller but a novel of detection, although it resembles her earlier formula in that the protagonist is both innocent of the crimes he is charged with and a member of the upper class. In this case, however, the crimes are abortion as well as murder, and the hero, Hugh Densmore, is a black intern from UCLA. The theme here is bigotry and the disadvantages of coping with the prejudices of law enforcement officers when one is both black and a stranger.

One of Hughes's most significant contributions to the genre is her masterful re-creation of setting. Streets are named, hotels are placed precisely, descriptions of transit from one place to another are so carefully written that the reader feels he has received directions to join the group. While she employs a variety of locales, such as New York and other cities on the East coast, her novels are most typically set in the Southwest. For instance, detailed descriptions of Juarez, Mexico, and Los Alamos, New Mexico, are featured in *The Candy Kid*. Action in *The Expendable Man* is centered in the Phoenix-Scottsdale area of Arizona. Through this attention to place, Hughes gives to her tales of romantic adventure an impressive verisimilitude.

—Nancy C. Joyner

HULL, Richard. Pseudonym for Richard Henry Sampson. British. Born in London, 6 September 1896. Educated at Rugby School, Warwickshire. Served as an officer in an infantry battalion and in the Machine Gun Corps in World War I; on active list until 1929; also served 1939–40. Worked for a firm of chartered accountants in the early 1920's, then set up his own practice; chartered accountant with the Admiralty, London, during World War II and until the mid-1950's. Fellow, Institute of Chartered Accountants. *Died in 1973.*

CRIME PUBLICATIONS

Novels (series: Inspector Fenby)

The Murder of My Aunt. London, Faber, and New York, Minton Balch, 1934.
Keep It Quiet. London, Faber, and New York, Putnam, 1935.
Murder Isn't Easy. London, Faber, and New York, Putnam, 1936.
The Ghost It Was. London, Faber, 1936; New York, Putnam, 1937.
The Murderers of Monty (Fenby). London, Faber, and New York, Putnam, 1937.
Excellent Intentions (Fenby). London, Faber, 1938; as *Beyond Reasonable Doubt,* New York, Messner, 1941.
And Death Came Too. London, Collins, 1939; New York, Messner, 1942.
My Own Murderer. London, Collins, and New York, Messner, 1940.
The Unfortunate Murderer. London, Collins, 1941; New York, Messner, 1942.
Left-Handed Death. London, Collins, 1946.
Last First. London, Collins, 1947.
Until She Was Dead. London, Collins, 1949.
A Matter of Nerves. London, Collins, 1950.

Invitation to an Inquest. London, Collins, 1950.
The Martineau Murders. London, Collins, 1953.

Uncollected Short Story

"Mrs. Brierley Supplies the Evidence," in *Evening Standard Detective Book,* 2nd series. London, Gollancz, 1951.

*   *   *

Richard Hull was one of the most notable and inventive crime novelists of the 1930's, and a major practitioner of the inverted school. Hull was deeply influenced by the work of Francis Iles—especially the inverted *Malice Aforethought* (1931) which told its story from the murderer's point of view. Iles's work was infused with mordant wit, and his important characters were less than admirable. The Hull narratives contain an acid bite ("brilliantly vicious" one critic stated), and many of his characters are extremely unpleasant because Hull thought he had a great deal more to say about such characters, and found them very amusing. Hull, himself, was noted for his kind-hearted qualities.

Hull's debut and masterpiece, *The Murder of My Aunt,* is told by a worthless and unpleasant young man who wishes to kill his equally detestable aunt in order to inherit her fortune. His first two attempts fail resoundingly, but he finally thinks he has discovered the perfect method. This classic inverted tale is an accomplishment of a high order, and deserves comparison with the best of Iles, Vulliamy, and Bruce Hamilton. Christopher Morley called it "Really brilliant savage comedy with the coldest and most deliberate cruelty beneath the highly amusing surface."

Hull had a great deal more to contribute to the mystery novel. *Keep It Quiet* details the efforts of a club secretary to hide a poisoning incident, while a blackmailer tries to take advantage of his difficulties. Closer to the detective novel is *Murder Isn't Easy* which tells of the murder of a company director from the points of view of several of the people involved—anticipating the narrative structure of Vera Caspary's *Laura* (1943). *The Murderers of Monty* concerns a group of people who form a company to kill Monty as part of an elaborate practical joke, but the joke turns sour when Monty is found murdered. *Excellent Intentions* is a long courtroom novel with more detection than usual. The victim is utterly worthless, and the murderer has acted from the most unselfish of motives. How can the judge temper justice with mercy? *My Own Murderer* details an elaborate conspiracy in which an unwitting substitute is supposed to take the place of a murderer, and die in his place. One of the most unpleasant characters in this story is named Richard Henry Sampson (after his creator) in order to underline a "but for the grace of God" message. Jacques Barzun thought it the most gripping and best written of the Hull's novels. *The Unfortunate Murderer* is a straightforward detective story about the murder of an executive in a munitions factory.

Literary inactivity during most of World War II was followed by a group of six novels that were published only in England. The creative spark was gone. The acid bite had turned sour and corrosive. The police interrogation of witnesses in *Invitation to an Inquest* makes similar material in Julian Symons's *The Progress of a Crime* or the more powerful *My Name Is Michael Sibley* by John Bingham seem warm and pleasant by comparison. But some of the old inventiveness remained. The otherwise dull *Last First* places its final chapter at the start of this book which is dedicated to "those who habitually read the last chapter first." Possibly Hull's best post-war novel is *A Matter of Nerves* which purports to be the diary of a murderer that relates how he committed his crime, and the events of its aftermath, but conceals the murderer's identity.

—Charles Shibuk

HUME, Fergus(on Wright). British. Born in England, 8 July 1859. Educated at Dunedin High School, and University of Otago, both New Zealand. Admitted to the New Zealand Bar in 1885, and worked as a barrister's clerk; lived in Melbourne, Australia, 1885–88; moved to England in 1888 and settled in Thundersley, Essex. *Died 13 July 1932.*

CRIME PUBLICATIONS

Novels (series: Octavius Fanks)

The Mystery of a Hansom Cab. Melbourne, Kemp and Boyce, 1886; London, Hansom Cab Company, and New York, Munro, 1888; revised edition. London, Jarrolds, 1896.
Madame Midas. London, Hansom Cab Company, and New York, Munro, 1888.
The Girl from Malta. London, Hansom Cab Company, and New York, Lovell, 1889.
The Gentleman Who Vanished: A Psychological Phantasy. London, White, 1890; as *The Man Who Vanished,* New York, Liberty Book Company, 1892.
The Man with a Secret. London, White, 3 vols., 1890.
Miss Mephistopheles. London, White, and New York, Lovell, 1890.
Whom God Hath Joined. London, White, 3 vols., 1891.
A Creature of the Night: An Italian Enigma. London, Sampson Low, and New York, Lovell, 1891.
The Fever of Life. New York, Lovell, 1891; London, Sampson Low, 2 vols., 1892.
Monsieur Judas (Fanks). London, Blackett, and New York, Waverly, 1891.
The Black Carnation. London, Gale and Polden, and New York, United States Book Company, 1892.
Aladdin in London. London, A. and C. Black, and Boston, Houghton Mifflin, 1892.
Dowker—Detective. New York, Seaside, 1892.
A Speck of the Motley. London, Innes, 1893.
The Harlequin Opal. London, W.H. Allen, 3 vols., 1893; Chicago, Rand McNally, 1893.
The Chinese Jar (Fanks). London, Sampson Low, 1893.
The Best of Her Sex. London, W.H. Allen, 2 vols., 1894.
The Gates of Dawn. London, Sampson Low, and New York, Neely, 1894.
The Lone Inn. London, Jarrolds, 1894; New York, Cassell, 1895.
A Midnight Mystery. London, Gale and Polden, 1894.
The Mystery at Landy Court. London, Jarrolds, 1894.
The Cruise of the Liza Jane. London, Ward Lock, 1895.
The Masquerade Mystery. London, Digby Long, 1895.
The Third Volume. New York, Cassell, 1895.
The Unwilling Bride. New York, Ogilvie, 1895.
The White Prior. London, Warne, 1895.
The Carbuncle Clue (Fanks). London, Warne, 1896.
A Marriage Mystery, Told from Three Points of View. London, Digby Long, 1896.
Tracked by a Tattoo. London, Warne, 1896.

Claude Duval of Ninety-Five: A Romance of the Road. London, Digby Long, and New York, Dillingham, 1897.
The Tombstone Treasure. London, Jarrolds, 1897.
The Clock Struck One. London, Warne, 1898.
The Devil-Stick. London, Downey, 1898.
For the Defense. Chicago, Rand McNally, 1898.
Lady Jezebel. London, Pearson and New York, Mansfield, 1898.
The Rainbow Feather. London, Digby Long, and New York, Dillingham, 1898.
The Indian Bangle. London, Sampson Low, 1899.
The Red-Headed Man. London, Digby Long, 1899.
The Silent House in Pimlico. London, Long, 1899; as *The Silent House,* New York, Doscher, 1907; London, Long, 1912.
The Bishop's Secret. London, Long, 1900; as *Bishop Pendle,* Chicago, Rand McNally, 1900.
The Crimson Cryptogram. London, Long, 1900; New York, New Amsterdam Book Company, 1901.
Shylock of the River. London, Digby Long, 1900.
A Traitor in London. London, Long, and New York, Buckles, 1900.
The Lady from Nowhere. London, Chatto and Windus, and New York, Brentano's, 1900.
The Vanishing of Tera. London, White, 1900.
The Crime of the Crystal. London, Digby Long, 1901.
The Golden Wang-Ho. London, Long, 1901; as *The Secret of the Chinese Jar,* Cleveland, Westbrook, 1928.
The Millionaire Mystery. London, Chatto and Windus, and New York, Buckles, 1901.
A Woman's Burden. London, Jarrolds, 1901.
The Pagan's Cup. London, Digby Long, and New York, Dillingham, 1902.
The Turnpike House. London, Long, 1902.
Woman: The Sphinx. London, Long, 1902.
The Jade Eye. London, Long, 1903.
The Miser's Will. London, Treherne, 1903.
The Silver Bullet. London, Long, 1903.
The Guilty House. London, White, 1903.
The Yellow Holly. London, Digby Long, and New York, Dillingham, 1903.
The Coin of Edward VII. London, Digby Long, and New York, Dillingham, 1903.
The Mandarin's Fan. London, Digby Long, 1904; New York, Dillingham, 1905.
The Lonely Church. London, Long, 1904.
The Red Window. London, Digby Long, and New York, Dillingham, 1904.
The Wheeling Light. London, Chatto and Windus, 1904.
The Wooden Hand. London, White, 1904.
The Fatal Song. London, White, 1905.
Lady Jim of Curzon Street. London, Laurie, 1905; New York, Dillingham, 1906.
The Opal Serpent. London, Long, and New York, Dillingham, 1905.
The Scarlet Bat. London, White, 1905.
The Secret Passage. London, Long, and New York, Dillingham, 1905.
The Black Patch. London, Long, 1906.
Jonah's Luck. London, White, 1906.
The Mystery of the Shadow. London, Cassell, and New York, Dodge, 1906.
Flies in the Web. London, White, 1907.
The Purple Fern. London, Everett, 1907.
The Sealed Message. New York, Dillingham, 1907; London, Digby Long, 1908.
The Yellow Hunchback. London, White, 1907.
The Amethyst Cross. London, Cassell, 1908.

The Crowned Skull. London, Laurie, 1908; as *The Red Skull,* New York, Dodge, 1908.

The Green Mummy. London, Long, and New York, Dillingham, 1908.

The Mystery of a Motor Cab. London, Everett, 1908.

The Sacred Herb. London, Long, and New York, Dillingham, 1908.

The Devil's Ace. London, Everett, 1909.

The Disappearing Eye. London, Digby Long, and New York, Dillingham, 1909.

The Top Dog. London, White, 1909.

The Solitary Farm. London, Ward Lock, and New York, Dillingham, 1909.

The Lonely Subaltern. London, C.H. White, 1910.

The Mikado Jewel. London, Everett, 1910.

The Peacock of Jewels. London, Digby Long, and New York, Dillingham, 1910.

The Spider. London, Ward Lock, 1910.

High Water Mark. London, White, 1910.

The Jew's House. London, Ward Lock, 1911.

The Pink Shop. London, White, 1911.

The Rectory Governess. London, White, 1911.

Red Money. New York, Dillingham, 1911; London, Ward Lock, 1912.

The Steel Crown. London, Digby Long, and New York, Dillingham, 1911.

Across the Footlights. London, White, 1912.

The Blue Talisman. London, Laurie, 1912; New York, Clode, 1925.

Mother Mandarin. London, White, 1912.

The Mystery Queen. London, Ward Lock, and New York, Dillingham, 1912.

The Curse. London, Laurie, 1913.

In Queer Street. London, White, 1913.

The Thirteenth Guest. London, Ward Lock, 1913.

Seen in the Shadow. London, White, 1913.

The 4 P.M. Express. London, White, 1914.

Not Wanted. London, White, 1914.

The Lost Parchment. London, Ward Lock, and New York, Dillingham, 1914.

Answered: A Spy Story. London, White, 1915.

The Caretaker. London, Ward Lock, 1915.

The Red Bicycle. London, Ward Lock, 1916.

The Silent Signal. London, Ward Lock, 1917.

The Grey Doctor. London, Ward Lock, 1917.

The Black Image. London, Ward Lock, 1918.

Heart of Ice. London, Hurst and Blackett, 1918.

Next Door. London, Ward Lock, 1918.

Crazy-Quilt. London, Ward Lock, 1919.

The Master-Mind. London, Hurst and Blackett, 1919.

The Dark Avenue. London, Ward Lock, 1920.

The Other Person. London, White, 1920.

The Singing Head. London, Hurst and Blackett, 1920.

The Woman Who Held On. London, Ward Lock, 1920.

Three. London, Ward Lock, 1921.

The Unexpected. London, Odhams Press, 1921.

A Trick of Time. London, Hurst and Blackett, 1922.

The Moth-Woman. London, Hurst and Blackett, 1923.

The Whispering Lane. London, Hurst and Blackett, 1924; Boston, Small Maynard, 1925.

The Caravan Mystery. London, Hurst and Blackett, 1926.

The Last Straw. London, Hutchinson, 1932.

The Hurton Treasure Mystery. London, Mellifont Press, 1937.

Short Stories as Humes

The Piccadilly Puzzle. London, White, and New York, Lovell, 1889.

The Dwarf's Chamber and Other Stories. London, Ward Lock, 1896.

Hagar of the Pawn-Shop. London, Skeffington, 1898; New York, Buckles, 1899.

The Dancer in Red and Other Stories. London, Digby Long, 1906.

OTHER PUBLICATIONS

Novels

Professor Brankel's Secret. Melbourne, Baird's Railway Bookstall, 1886.

The Year of Miracle: A Tale of the Year One Thousand Nine Hundred. London, Routledge, and New York, Lovell, 1891.

The Island of Fantasy. London, Griffith Farran, 3 vols., 1892; New York, Lovell, 1892.

When I Lived in Bohemia: Papers Selected from the Portfolio of Peter—, Esq. Bristol, Arrowsmith, and New York, Tait, 1892.

The Expedition of Captain Flick. London, Jarrolds, 1895; New York, New Amsterdam Book Company, 1899.

The Mother of Emeralds. London, Hurst and Blackett, 1901.

The White Room. London, White, 1905.

A Son of Perdition. London, Rider, 1912.

Short Stories

The Chronicles of Faeryland. London, Griffith Farran, 1892; Philadelphia, Lippincott, 1893.

Plays

The Mystery of a Hansom Cab, with Arthur Law (produced London, 1888).

Indiscretion (produced Folkestone, Kent, 1888).

Madame Midas, The Gold Queen, with P. Beck (produced Exeter, Devon, 1888).

The Fool of the Family (produced London, 1896).

Teddy's Wives (produced Eastbourne, Sussex, and London, 1896).

Honours Divided (produced Margate, Kent, 1902).

A Scotch Marriage (produced London, 1907).

The Mystery of the Red Web, with Newman Harding (produced Liverpool and London, 1908).

*   *   *

Fergus Hume, so the conventional wisdom has it, is a one-book author, the book being his first, *The Mystery of a Hansom Cab,* the other nearly 150 of his novels being "unreadable." This is far from the truth. Certainly none of his other novels achieved the circulation of his first, which is one of the great bestsellers of history. But there are at least 20 of Hume's novels, mostly written before 1910, which are eminently readable, more readable than the melodramatic Victorian romances of, say, Mary Elizabeth Braddon.

Hume, indeed, aims at realism. One of the characters in his famous novel describes the events in which he finds himself as "a romance in real life, which beats Miss Braddon hollow." "Truth is stranger than fiction" is an adage repeatedly stated in Hume's novels, as though to justify his breaches of *vraisemblance*. But as the scene moves from high society to the mean streets of the great Victorian metropolis (usually London, but in the first novel Melbourne) one sees Hume's sure grasp of a documentary realism. The stories are scarcely realistic, however, and Hume's novels suffer from the overplotting of late Victorian fiction. The last half of a typical novel is frequently a gradual disclosure of familial and marital relationships hitherto unguessed at. In *The Piccadilly Puzzle* there are two women who look alike (they turn out to be sisters); one elopes with the murder suspect, the other is murdered. But there has been a substitution, and Hume keeps us guessing until the end as to which is which. In *The Bishop's Secret,* the children of A, after much suspense, turn out to be legitimate, because though A's former husband proves to have been still alive at the time of her second marriage, he had been previously married, and so her marriage to him was invalid! In *A Coin of Edward VII,* the central character, in the midst of the *éclaircissement* which forms one of the climaxes in any novel of Hume's, finds his brain "in a whirl," and later has to ask his interlocutor to repeat the intricate account of marriages, remarriages, and changes of identity she has just provided.

Though it was Gaboriau who is supposed to have given Hume the impetus to write, it is Wilkie Collins who is his principal master; wills (Hume was trained as a lawyer) are often important, especially eccentrically drawn wills; there are occasional inset narratives; and many of the criminals confess in written documents duly reproduced by the author. Moreover again after Collins, several of Hume's novels deal with stolen precious stones; as late as *The Blue Talisman* (1912) he wrote a novel about a man who steals a gem from an idol in Africa, and is pursued by the curse of its custodians. Hume is as concerned as Collins in seeing fate as the embodiment of the victim's past crimes, now catching up with him, as in *The Red Skull.* The scenes of Hume's characters' pasts are often exotic—Australia, South Africa, Mexico—and yet are realistically evoked.

Hume's method of initial exposition is often contrived, given in a colloquy between characters otherwise of no importance (though in one notable case the character who receives the opening information turns out to be the murderer). Hume's detectives, in so large a body of novels, are legion, often merely interested parties seeking to clear themselves or these dear to them. One detective, Octavius Fanks, appears several times, and may be seen to best advantage in *Monsieur Judas* or *The Carbuncle Clue.* He is an "idler" in the salon, but a brilliant detective in the streets. In this ingenious way he overcomes the disabilities of such "lower-class" detectives as Cuff or Ebenezer Gryce.

The Mystery of a Hansom Cab, finally: for on its fame Hume's reputation will continue to stand or fall. The plot is as complicated as those which come later; the murdered man's mistress turns out to be the former wife of his prospective father-in-law. The sense of the metropolis is omnipresent, and in the scene of the murder, the apprehension of the criminal, and the weight of the past upon the present the book (though the question of influence does not arise) anticipates *A Study in Scarlet.* That, for better or worse, may be the lasting epitaph for this fluent, readable, and literate novelist.

—Barrie Hayne

HUNT, E(verette) Howard. Also writes as John Baxter; Gordon Davis; Robert Dietrich; David St. John. American. Born in Hamburg, New York, 9 October 1918. Educated at Brown University, Providence, Rhode Island, A.B. 1940. Served in the United States Naval Reserve, 1940–42, and the United States Army Air Force, 1943–46: First Lieutenant. Married 1) Dorothy L. Wetzel in 1949 (died 1972), two daughters and two sons; 2) Laura E. Martin in 1977, one son and one daughter. Scriptwriter and editor, *March of Time* newsreel series, 1942–43; war correspondent, *Life* magazine, 1943; screenwriter, 1947–48; American Embassy Attaché, Paris, 1948–49, Vienna, 1949–50, and Mexico City, 1950–53; political officer, Far East Command, Tokyo, 1954–56; First Secretary, American Embassy, Montevideo, 1957–60; consultant, Department of Defense, Washington, D.C., 1960–65; with Department of State, Washington, D.C., 1965–70; Vice President and Creative Director, Robert R. Mullen, public relations firm, 1970–72; consultant to President Richard M. Nixon, 1971–72. Served terms in federal prison for his role in Watergate scandal, 1973–74 and 1975–77. Recipient: Guggenheim Fellowship, 1946. Address: 1245 Northeast 85th Street, Miami, Florida `33138, U.S.A.

CRIME PUBLICATIONS

Novels (series: Jack Novak)

Maelstrom. New York, Farrar Straus, 1948; as *Cruel Is the Night,* New York, Berkley, 1955.
Bimini Run. New York, Farrar Straus, 1949.
The Violent Ones. New York, Fawcett, 1950; London, Fawcett, 1958.
Dark Encounter. New York, Fawcett, 1950.
The Judas Hour. New York, Fawcett, 1951; London, Fawcett, 1953.
Whisper Her Name. New York, Fawcett, 1952; London, Fawcett, 1958.
Lovers Are Losers. New York, Fawcett, 1953.
The Berlin Ending. New York, Putnam, 1973.
The Hargrave Deception. New York, Stein and Day, 1980.
The Gaza Intercept. New York, Stein and Day, 1981.
The Kremlin Conspiracy. New York, Stein and Day, 1985.
Cozumel (Novak). New York, Stein and Day, 1985.
Guadalajara (Novak). New York, Stein and Day, 1986.
Mazatlan (Novak). New York, Stein and Day, 1987.
Murder in State. New York, St. Martin's Press, 1990.

Novels as Gordon Davis

I Came to Kill. New York, Fawcett, 1953; London, Fawcett, 1955.
House Dick. New York, Fawcett, 1961; London, Muller, 1962; as *Washington Payoff* (as E. Howard Hunt), New York, Pinnacle, 1975.
Counterfeit Kill. New York, Fawcett, 1963; London, Muller, 1964.
Ring Around Rosy. New York, Fawcett, 1964.
Where Murder Waits. New York, Fawcett, 1965.

Novels as Robert Dietrich (series: Steve Bentley)

One for the Road. New York, Pyramid, 1954.
The Cheat. New York, Pyramid, 1954.
Be My Victim. New York, Dell, 1956.
Murder on the Rocks (Bentley). New York, Dell, 1957; London, Ward Lock, 1958.
The House on Q Street (Bentley). New York, Dell, 1959.

End of a Stripper (Bentley).   New York, Dell, 1959.
Mistress to Murder (Bentley).   New York, Dell, 1960.
Murder on Her Mind (Bentley).   New York, Dell, 1960.
Angel Eyes (Bentley).   New York, Dell, 1961.
Steve Bentley's Calypso Caper.   New York, Dell, 1961.
Curtains for a Lover (Bentley).   New York, Lancer, 1961.
My Body (Bentley).   New York, Lancer, 1962.

Novels as David St. John (series Peter Ward in all books)

On Hazardous Duty.   New York, New American Library,
    1965; as *Hazardous Duty,* London, Muller, 1966.
Return from Vorkuta.   New York, New American Library,
    1965; London, Muller, 1967.
The Towers of Silence.   New York, New American Library,
    1966.
Festival for Spies.   New York, New American Library, 1966.
The Venus Probe.   New York, New American Library, 1966.
One of Our Agents Is Missing.   New York, New American
    Library, 1967.
The Mongol Mask.   New York, Weybright and Talley, 1968;
    London, Hale, 1969.
The Sorcerers.   New York, Weybright and Talley, 1969.
Diabolus.   New York, Weybright and Talley, 1971.
The Coven.   New York, Weybright and Talley, 1972.

OTHER PUBLICATIONS

Novels

East of Farewell.   New York, Knopf, 1942; London, Hutchin-
    son, 1944.
Limit of Darkness.   New York, Random House, 1944.
Stranger in Town.   New York, Random House, 1947.

Novels as John Baxter

A Foreign Affair.   New York, Avon, 1954.
Unfaithful.   New York, Avon, 1955.
A Gift for Gomala.   Philadelphia, Lippincott, 1962.

Other

Give Us This Day.   New Rochelle, New York, Arlington
    House, 1973.
Undercover: Memoirs of an American Secret Agent.   New York,
    Putnam, 1974; London, W.H. Allen, 1975.

*   *   *

There is much in E. Howard Hunt's fiction that, with
hindsight, enables us to say this was a man likely to get involved
in the Bay of Pigs, the break-in at the office of Daniel Ellsberg's
psychiatrist, and at Watergate. The series about C.I.A. agent
Peter Ward, written under his pseudonym of David St. John
(the first names of his two sons) is especially full of personal
references.

Both Ward and Hunt are graduates of Brown and active in
Washington social circles. Described as "the secret agent with
the taste and the talent for fine living," Ward is a snob but not
offensive. Hunt's own background as a C.I.A. agent causes him
to have Ward utter paeans to that organization, but they are not
intrusive. Hunt also includes such accurate touches to the series
as realistic terminology, plausible descriptions of the mechanics of spying, and authentic locations. He often sets his Ward
novels in the countries to which he had been assigned in his
own career.

Hunt showed considerable imagination in the plots he
concocted for Peter Ward. *The Venus Probe* requires his
investigation into the disappearances of seven Western
scientists who, together, have the knowledge to send a rocket to
the moon. *Return from Vorkuta,* the best of the series,
compellingly meshes Spanish and Russian history. A Royalist
who may be a Russian spy is returned to Spain from Siberia,
where he has been a prisoner since the Spanish Civil War. He
claims the throne, and the C.I.A. is worried about the U.S.
NATO bases in Spain.

When Hunt's heroes are not travelling the world, they, like
he, are in Washington, D.C., the city he most often described.
As Gordon Davis he wrote about Pete Novak, a none-too-
bright Washington hotel detective. In *House Dick* Novak hides
the corpse he finds at his hotel and investigates without ever
notifying the police. Of not much better quality is the Davis
book *Where Murder Waits,* about Washington attorney Pat
Conroy. Conroy, who was involved in the Bay of Pigs, is
recruited to recover funds which had been collected to
overthrow Castro. The plot is confusing, and the writing cliché-
ridden.

Writing as Robert Dietrich, Hunt wrote nine popular
paperback novels about a Washington accountant, Steve
Bentley, who acts more like a member of the C.I.A. or a private
eye than a C.P.A. Bentley likes Washington, but he describes it
as a "great city. All you need is money, endurance, and
powerful friends." These lines in *Angel Eyes* are prophetic, as is
the plot involving tapes which can destroy a Washington
political figure. One reads things into Hunt's books, and it is
amusing, in a book published in 1961, to have Hunt's hero say,
"Don't think I can't smell a cover-up."

The Bentley series contains some of Hunt's best writing. It is
fast moving, and Bentley's wise-cracking narration fits nicely
into the private eye tradition. *Angel Eyes* has an exciting climax
at the Jefferson Memorial. *Murder on Her Mind* makes good use
of Washington and Maryland locales and also deals with Latin
American politics as Bentley's client is an exile, apparently
from Cuba, who is gathering funds to support a revolution at
home.

Originally of limited fame or reputation as a mystery writer,
Hunt became prominent because of his arrest and conviction.
Many of the books he had written under pseudonyms were
quickly reprinted under his own name. Mystery readers and
others who followed Watergate were encouraged to read the
books of a man whose name appeared in the newspapers almost
daily. They found, often to their surprise, that, with occasional
misses, Howard Hunt had written some of more readable spy
and hardboiled detective fiction to come out in paperback
originals during the 1960's.

—Marvin Lachman

———

HUNT, Harrison. *See* **BALLARD, Willis Todhunter.**

———

HUNT, Kyle. *See* **CREASEY, John.**

———

HUNTER, Alan (James Herbert). British. Born in Hoveton, Norfolk, 25 June 1922. Educated at Wroxham School, Norfolk, 1927–36; studied advertising, B.Ins. 1939. Served as an aircraft electrician in the Royal Air Force Volunteer Reserve, 1940–46. Married Adelaide Cubitt in 1944; one daughter. Poultry farmer, Norfolk, 1936–40; manager of antiquarian books department, Charles Cubitt, booksellers, Norwich, 1946–49; owner, Maddermarket Bookshop, Norwich, 1950–57. Regular contributor since 1955, and crime fiction reviewer, 1955–71, *Eastern Daily Press,* Norwich. Address: 3 St. Laurence Avenue, Brundall, Norwich, Norfolk NR13 5QH, England.

CRIME PUBLICATIONS

Novels (series: Inspector/Chief Superintendent George Gently in all books)

Gently Does It. London, Cassell, and New York, Rinehart, 1955.
Gently by the Shore. London, Cassell, and New York, Rinehart, 1956.
Gently down the Stream. London, Cassell, 1957; New York, Roy, 1960.
Landed Gently. London, Cassell, and New York, British Book Centre, 1957.
Gently Through the Mill. London, Cassell, 1958; included in *Gently in an Omnibus,* New York, St. Martin's Press, 1971.
Gently in the Sun. London, Cassell, 1959; New York, Berkley, 1964.
Gently with the Painters. London, Cassell, 1960; New York, Macmillan, 1976.
Gently to the Summit. London, Cassell, 1961; New York, Berkley, 1964.
Gently Go Man. London, Cassell, 1961; New York, Berkley, 1964.
Gently Where the Roads Go. London, Cassell, 1962; included in *Gently in Another Omnibus,* New York, St. Martin's Press, 1972.
Gently Floating. London, Cassell, 1963; New York, Berkley, 1964.
Gently Sahib. London, Cassell, 1964.
Gently with the Ladies. London, Cassell, 1965; New York, Macmillan, 1974.
Gently North-West. London, Cassell, 1967; as *Gently in the Highlands,* New York, Macmillan, 1975.
Gently Continental. London, Cassell, 1967.
Gently Coloured. London, Cassell, 1969.
Gently with the Innocents. London, Cassell, 1970; New York, Macmillan, 1974.
Gently at a Gallop. London, Cassell, 1971.
Vivienne: Gently Where She Lay. London, Cassell, 1972.
Gently French. London, Cassell, 1973.
Gently in Trees. London, Cassell, 1974; as *Gently Through the Woods,* New York, Macmillan, 1975.
Gently with Love. London, Cassell, 1975.
Gently Where the Birds Are. London, Cassell, 1976.
Gently Instrumental. London, Cassell, 1977.
Gently to a Sleep. London, Cassell, 1978.
The Honfleur Decision. London, Constable, 1980; New York, Walker, 1981.
Gabrielle's Way. London, Constable, 1981; as *The Scottish Decision,* New York, Walker, 1981.
Fields of Heather. London, Constable, 1981; as *Death on the Heath,* New York, Walker, 1982.

Gently Between Tides. London, Constable, 1982; New York, Walker, 1983.
Amorous Leander. London, Constable, 1983; as *Death on the Broadlands,* New York, Walker, 1984.
The Unhung Man. London, Constable, 1984; as *The Unhanged Man,* New York, Walker, 1984.
Once a Prostitute. London, Constable, 1984.
The Chelsea Ghost. London, Constable, 1985.
Goodnight Sweet Prince. London, Constable, 1986.
Strangling Man. London, Constable, 1987.
Traitor's End. London, Constable, 1988.
Gently with the Millions. London, Constable, 1989.

OTHER PUBLICATIONS

Plays

The Wolf, adaptation of a play by Terence (produced Norwich, 1952).
The Thunderbird (produced Norwich, 1953).
Don't Make Passes at Theo (produced Norwich, 1953?).

Verse

The Norwich Poems 1943–44. Norwich, Soman Wherry Press, 1945.

*

Alan Hunter comments:
My instincts are those of a playwright, and in consequence I tend to arrange my books so that the time covered is kept to the minimum, and the narrative proceeds in a succession of taut confrontations.

In effect my investigator, Chief Superintendent Gently, comes into a situation which has arisen over months, perhaps years, at its moment of crisis, and acts as a catalyst to bring it to a climax. To understand what is happening he must understand those involved and their relations during the previous development of the situation. Only then can he make a correct interpretation of circumstance and evidence. Needless to say, the enquiry proceeds without flashback, a device artistically suspect. The past is to be understood through the present, and by moment to moment response.

I find the environment of a dramatic situation a critical factor in its evocation: this time, this place, belong to these characters, this mystery. And so I choose a location which is directly familiar to me, usually one I have known for many years. As a result my books are set mostly in East Anglia, though three have Scottish backgrounds, three London, one Normandy, and one Wales.

I have experimented a little with narrative method. The three books *Go Man, Where the Roads Go,* and *Floating* are successive attempts to write a completely objective style. Conversely, with *Continental,* I chose a strongly subjective style, a serious matter in these post-Hemingway times. A few critics liked it very much, most did not. Now I tend to an objective style with subjective overtones. In three books I have switched from third to first-person narrative. They are not the worst.

A note on Gently's genealogy. At the time I was planning my first crime novel, Anthony Martienssen's *Crime and the Police* had just appeared in paperback. In it he gives thumb-nail sketches of four top-ranking detectives; I amalgamated traits from these and built them into my own concept. Some were phased out later. The character was not, as some people assume, based on myself. Or not entirely.

*   *   *

Alan Hunter's Gently series, set mainly in East Anglia, though occasionally in London, Wales, Scotland, and even France, follows the career of Chief Inspector (and later Superintendent) Gently of the C.I.D. as he is called in on homicide cases which puzzle local authorities. These books demonstrate the need for homicide specialists whose training and experience produce an instinct for murder that ordinary policemen lack. Most of Hunter's works are written in the third-person, and depend on question-answer exchanges and brusque dialogue interspersed with poetic description and reflection.

The series focuses on police procedure and, most particularly, carefully controlled interrogation that requires a sixth-sense about human frailty and response. Bodies show up in grain hoppers, gardens and boats, on beaches, heaths, and mountain roads, or in offices, yachts, and Elizabethan mansions, and are strangled, stabbed, riddled with bullets, pushed down stairs, gassed in caravans, or even mauled by tigers (as in *Gently Sahib*). Where the local police look for easy solutions and quick convictions, Gently slowly and methodically weighs the physical evidence, explores the scene of the crime, interrogates all involved, and contemplates mood and milieu. His unorthodox approaches get results. For example, in *The Unhung Man*, when a "hanging judge" dies from a gunshot wound, local police suspect a poacher, but fingerprints lead Gently to a man the judge sentenced to hang 18 years before. For Gently detection is more an art than a science. At first he finds the situation "like a picture out of focus," but gradually it takes shape, the blurred outlines become sharper, each new fact adds a dash of color, and the whole eventually seems inescapably clear. Often both Gently and the reader know what happened and who did it halfway through the investigation, but the rest of Gently's effort is spent slowly gathering conclusive evidence that will allow the police to make a convincing court case. As he constructs his case, Gently must deal with the incredulity of the local police, the interference of the local citizens, the secrecy of a closed rural community, the obstructions of the press and of those fearful of having their private lives exposed, and the assaults of the guilty who fear his knowledge and skill. He continually reminds his associates: "It's our job to make a case, not to break it. Justice belongs to the court. It's nothing to do with the police" (*Gently Does It*). Only when he can undermine an alibi, prove motive and opportunity, and produce a foolproof case is he ready to act on his suspicions.

As he munches peppermint creams or fiddles with his pipe, the self-deprecating Gently modestly attributes to luck his instinctive guesses. Generally, the villains he exposes often prove to have had a carefully hidden but predictable history of criminal behavior, as does the bank robber turned mayor in *Gently Through the Mill* or the publican/bookie spy in *Gently by the Shore*. Sometimes, however, madness turns guesses on end. Gently feels particularly guilty about a second murder at the end of *Gently Between Tides*, wherein the discovery of a woman's body in an abandoned dinghy points first to a romantic intrigue and then an emotionally distraught father.

Gently himself is in his fifties in Hunter's first book, but ages little over the years. He remains romantically accessible, half-in-love with the provocative and enigmatic murder victim in *Gently in the Sun*, vamped by a truck driver's delight in *Gently Where the Roads Go*, romantically involved with Brenda Marryn (half-sister to the murder victim) in *Gently with the Ladies* and in *Gently North-West*. In *Gently with the Ladies* all of the suspects are women (as is the bisexual murder victim) and their cattiness and wiles must be dealt with adroitly. Gently first meets the woman he later marries, Gabrielle Orbec, in *The Honfleur Decision*, while on holiday in France; as he plays decoy and is shot at time and again while helping capture a vicious killer, her beauty and intelligence win his love despite his doubting heart. In *Gabrielle's Way*, he finds himself disturbingly intrigued by her again. Gently must make painful choices as he savagely races cross alien moors, trying to restrain an aggressive underling, to correctly interpret Gabrielle's disturbingly ambiguous acts, to eliminate armed thugs, to figure out Scottish road signs, and to rescue a kidnapped French industrialist.

Hunter's works reveal a dislike for newspaper reporters but a sympathy for the inarticulate working man. Hunter deals with tapestry weaving in *Landed Gently*, artists in *Gently with the Painters*, the world of motorcycling and the beat generation in *Gently Go Man*, mountain climbing in *Gently to the Summit*, antiques in *Gently with the Innocents*, acting and directing in *Gently in Trees*, music in *Gently Instrumental*, Scottish clans, a Scottish Nationalist Action Group, and guerrilla warfare in *Gently North-West*, writers in *Amorous Leander*, and boats and seagoing in *Gently in the Sun*, *Gently down the Stream* and *Gently Floating*. He includes offbeat characters—half-wits, recluses, eccentrics, and the occasional Eastern European spy. Hunter's Zen-Buddhist philosophy forms a philosophical base throughout his canon, but especially in *Gently with Love*, in which a policeman's daughter seeks refuge in Scotland. His later books include more cases of international crime, with Superintendent Gently, beset by the pressures of seniority, behaving more and more like an English Maigret, coaching up-and-coming younger inspectors in calm detachment, psychoanalysis, and intuitive guesswork.

Overall, Hunter's books regularly include a number of suspects, clues that point in several directions, and silence, evasion, and lies. They depend on the presence of Gently (amiable, imperturbable, and unrelentingly logical) to sift out the chaff and find the kernel of truth.

—Gina Macdonald

———

HUNTER, Evan. *See* **McBAIN, Ed.**

———

HUXLEY, Elspeth (Josceline, née Grant). British. Born in London, 23 July 1907; lived in Kenya, 1912–25. Educated at the European School, Nairobi; Reading University, Berkshire, Diploma in Agriculture 1927–28; Cornell University, Ithaca, New York. Married Gervas Huxley in 1931 (died 1971); one son. Assistant press officer, Empire Marketing Board, London, 1929–32; News Talks assistant, 1941–43, and Colonial Office liaison, 1943–44, BBC, London; farmer in Wiltshire, 1950–65. Member of the BBC Advisory Council 1954–60; Independent Member, Monckton Advisory Commission on Central Africa, 1959–61. Justice of the Peace for Wiltshire, 1947–77. C.B.E. (Commander, Order of the British Empire), 1962. Agent: Heather Jeeves, 15 Campden Hill Square, London W8 7JY. Address: Green End, Oaksey, near Malmesbury, Wiltshire SN16 9TL, England.

CRIME PUBLICATIONS

Novels (series: Superintendent Vachell)

Murder at Government House (Vachell).   London, Methuen, and New York, Harper, 1937.
Murder on Safari (Vachell).   London, Methuen, and New York, Harper, 1938.
Death of an Aryan (Vachell).   London, Methuen, 1939; as *The African Poison Murders*, New York, Harper, 1940.
The Merry Hippo.   London, Chatto and Windus, 1963; as *The Incident at the Merry Hippo*, New York, Morrow, 1964.

OTHER PUBLICATIONS

Novels

Red Strangers.   London, Chatto and Windus, and New York, Harper, 1939.
The Walled City.   London, Chatto and Windus, 1948; Philadelphia, Lippincott, 1949.
I Don't Mind If I Do.   London, Chatto and Windus, 1950.
A Thing to Love.   London, Chatto and Windus, 1954.
The Red Rock Wilderness.   London, Chatto and Windus, and New York, Morrow, 1957.
A Man from Nowhere.   London, Chatto and Windus, and New York, Morrow, 1964.

Other

White Man's Country: Lord Delamere and the Making of Kenya. London, Macmillan, 2 vols., 1935; New York, Praeger, 1968.
Atlantic Ordeal: The Story of Mary Cornish.   London, Chatto and Windus, 1941; New York, Harper, 1942.
East Africa.   London, Collins, 1941.
The Story of Five English Farmers.   London, Sheldon Press, 1941.
English Woman.   London, Sheldon Press, 1942.
Brave Deeds of the War.   London, Sheldon Press, 1943.
Race and Politics in Kenya: A Correspondence Between Elspeth Huxley and Margery Perham.   London, Faber, 1944; revised edition, 1956; Westport, Connecticut, Greenwood Press, 1975.
Colonies: A Reader's Guide.   Cambridge, University Press, 1947.
Settlers of Kenya.   Nairobi, Highway Press, and London, Longman, 1948; Westport, Connecticut, Greenwood Press, 1975.
The Sorcerer's Apprentice: A Journey Through East Africa. London, Chatto and Windus, 1948; Westport, Connecticut, Greenwood Press, 1975.
African Dilemmas.   London, Longman, 1948.
Four Guineas: A Journey Through West Africa.   London, Chatto and Windus, 1954; Westport, Connecticut, Greenwood Press, 1974.
Kenya Today.   London, Lutterworth Press, 1954.
What Are Trustee Nations?   London, Batchworth Press, 1955.
No Easy Way: A History of the Kenya Farmers' Association and Unga Limited.   Nairobi, East African Standard, 1957.
The Flame Trees of Thika: Memories of an African Childhood. London, Chatto and Windus, and New York, Morrow, 1959.
A New Earth: An Experiment in Colonialism.   London, Chatto and Windus, and New York, Morrow, 1960.
The Mottled Lizard.   London, Chatto and Windus, 1962; as *On the Edge of the Rift: Memories of Kenya*, New York, Morrow, 1962.

Forks and Hope: An African Notebook.   London, Chatto and Windus, 1964; as *With Forks and Hope*, New York, Morrow, 1964.
Back Street New Worlds: A Look at Immigrants in Britain. London, Chatto and Windus, 1964; New York, Morrow, 1965.
Suki: A Little Tiger, photographs by Laelia Goehr.   London, Chatto and Windus, and New York, Morrow, 1964.
Brave New Victuals: An Inquiry into Modern Food Production. London, Chatto and Windus, 1965.
Their Shining Eldorado: A Journey Through Australia. London, Chatto and Windus, and New York, Morrow, 1967.
Love among the Daughters: Memories of the Twenties in England and America.   London, Chatto and Windus, and New York, Morrow, 1968.
The Challenge of Africa.   London, Aldus, 1971.
Livingstone and His African Journeys.   London, Weidenfeld and Nicolson, and New York, Saturday Review Press, 1974.
Florence Nightingale.   London, Weidenfeld and Nicolson, 1975.
Gallipot Eyes: A Wiltshire Diary.   London, Weidenfeld and Nicolson, 1976.
Scott of the Antarctic.   London, Weidenfeld and Nicolson, 1977; New York, Atheneum, 1978.
Nellie: Letters from Africa.   London, Weidenfeld and Nicolson, 1980.
Whipsnade: Captive Breeding for Survival.   London, Collins, 1981.
The Prince Buys the Manor: An Extravaganza.   London, Chatto and Windus, 1982.
Last Days in Eden, photographs by Hugo van Lawick. London, Harvill Press, 1984.
Out in the Midday Sun: My Kenya.   London, Chatto and Windus, 1985; New York, Viking, 1987.

Editor, *The Kingsleys: A Biographical Anthology*.   London, Allen and Unwin, 1973.
Editor, *Travels in West Africa*, by Mary Kingsley.   London, Folio Society, 1976.
Editor, with Arnold Curtis, *Pioneer's Scrapbook: Reminiscences of Kenya 1890 to 1968*.   London, Evans, 1980.
Editor, *Nine Faces of Kenya*.   London, Collins Harvill, 1990.

*

Elspeth Huxley comments:
   In the 1930's my husband's job took us both on many journeys, in those days mainly by sea, and I took to writing crime stories to pass the time on shipboard and avoid playing bridge. After the 1939–45 War I specialized on African subjects, and abandoned crime fiction, but returned to it again after serving on the Monckton Commission in central Africa, which provided a background for *The Merry Hippo*. In fact all my crime stories have an African setting. Despite Africa's immensity, diversity, and richness in crime, I don't know of any specifically African detective story writers.

*   *   *

   Elspeth Huxley's whodunits are set in mythical and not so mythical parts of British Africa. A cross between P.G. Wodehouse and Evelyn Waugh, Huxley is gifted in portraying, with a mixture of comedy and satire, the reality and the mentality of Whitehall, Africa, and the criminal. Her gift is well demonstrated in *The Merry Hippo*, in which a Royal Commission is sent to Hapana to take advice on constitutional arrangements for the independence of that colony. A number of vested interests—tapioca growers, the sterilisation lobby, the copper barons—offer evidence and threats to the Commission; and Huxley's skill is such that it is almost impossible to guess which member of the Commission is leaking information to the press and who is killing off members of the Commission. Two engaging policemen add much to this novel—John Jacey, the British Colonial, and his mercurial assistant and pending replacement, Chisango. The two have quite different, and ethnically distinct, methods of interrogation and detection. Equally comic and serious are two murder victims, Lord and Lady Bagpus, pig-breeders named to the Commission in error.

Where it serves to thicken her plot, Huxley is adept at using the whole range of African detail from politics to big-game hunting. She strews her novels with red herrings; she achieves disconcerting endings; and she does not shrink from brutal physical detail. *Death of an Aryan* is as memorable for its mutilated animals as for another appearance by Huxley's attractive Canadian detective, Vachell, head of the Chanian CID.

—Ann Massa

I

ILES, Francis. *See* BERKELEY, Anthony.

————

INNES, (Ralph) Hammond. Has also written as Ralph Hammond. British. Born in Horsham, Sussex, 15 July 1913. Educated at Cranbrook School, Kent, 1927–31. Served in the British Army Artillery, 1940–46; Major. Married Dorothy Mary Lang in 1937 (died 1989). Staff member, *Financial News,* London, 1934–40. C.B.E. (Commander, Order of the British Empire), 1978. D.Litt.: Bristol University, 1985. Agent: Curtis Brown Ltd., 162–168 Regent Street, London WIR 5TB. Address: Ayres End, Kersey, Ipswich, Suffolk IP7 6EB, England.

CRIME PUBLICATIONS

Novels

The Doppelganger. London, Jenkins, 1937.
Air Disaster. London, Jenkins, 1937.
Sabotage Broadcast. London, Jenkins, 1938.
All Roads Lead to Friday. London, Jenkins, 1939.
Wreckers Must Breathe. London, Collins, 1940; as *Trapped,* New York, Putnam, 1940.
The Trojan Horse. London, Collins, 1940.
Attack Alarm. London, Collins, 1941; New York, Macmillan, 1942.
Dead and Alive. London, Collins, 1946.
The Killer Mine. London, Collins, and New York, Harper, 1947; as *Run by Night,* New York, Bantam, 1951.
The Lonely Skier. London, Collins, 1947; as *Fire in the Snow,* New York, Harper, 1947.
Maddon's Rock. London, Collins, 1948; as *Gale Warning,* New York, Harper, 1948.
The Blue Ice. London, Collins, and New York, Harper, 1948.
The White South. London, Collins, 1949; as *The Survivors,* New York, Harper, 1950.
The Angry Mountain. London, Collins, 1950; New York, Harper, 1951.
Air Bridge. London, Collins, 1951; New York, Knopf, 1952.
Campbell's Kingdom. London, Collins, and New York, Knopf, 1952.
The Strange Land. London, Collins, 1954; as *The Naked Land,* New York, Knopf, 1954.
The Mary Deare. London, Collins, 1956; as *The Wreck of the Mary Deare,* New York, Knopf, 1956.
The Land God Gave to Cain. London, Collins, and New York, Knopf, 1958.
The Doomed Oasis. London, Collins, and New York, Knopf, 1960.
Atlantic Fury. London, Collins, and New York, Knopf, 1962.
The Strode Venturer. London, Collins, and New York, Knopf, 1965.
Levkas Man. London, Collins, and New York, Knopf, 1971.

Golden Soak. London, Collins, and New York, Knopf, 1973.
North Star. London, Collins, 1974; New York, Knopf, 1975.
The Big Footprints. London, Collins, and New York, Knopf, 1977.
Solomons Seal. London, Collins, and New York, Knopf, 1980.
The Black Tide. London, Collins, 1982; New York, Doubleday, 1983.
High Stand. London, Collins, 1985; New York, Atheneum, 1986.
Medusa. London, Collins, and New York, Atheneum, 1988.

OTHER PUBLICATIONS

Plays

Screenplay: *Campbell's Kingdom,* with Robin Estridge, 1957.

Television Play: *The Story of Captain James Cook,* 1975.

Other

Cocos Gold (for children; as Ralph Hammond). London, Collins, and New York, Harper, 1950.
Isle of Strangers (for children; as Ralph Hammond). London, Collins, 1951; as *Island of Peril,* Philadelphia, Westminster Press, 1953.
Saracen's Tower (for children; as Ralph Hammond). London, Collins, 1952; as *Cruise of Danger,* Philadelphia, Westminster Press, 1954.
Black Gold on the Double Diamond (for children; as Ralph Hammond). London, Collins, 1953.
Harvest of Journeys. London, Collins, and New York, Knopf, 1960.
Scandinavia, with editors of Life. New York, Time, 1963.
Sea and Islands. London, Collins, and New York, Knopf, 1967.
The Conquistadors. London, Collins, and New York, Knopf, 1969.
Hammond Innes Introduces Australia, edited by Clive Turnbull. London, Deutsch, and New York, McGraw Hill, 1971.
The Last Voyage: Captain Cook's Lost Diary. London, Collins, 1978; New York, Knopf, 1979.
Hammond Innes' East Anglia. London, Hodder and Stoughton, 1986.

Editor, *Tales of Old Inns,* by Richard Keverne, revised edition. London, Collins, 1947.

*

Manuscript Collection: Mugar Memorial Library, Boston University.

*   *   *

Hammond Innes has long been an important author of suspense novels. His tales are unique in the genre. He writes of the conflict of man against man, good against evil, but this is no more than an undercurrent to his main theme, that of man against the overpowering force of implacable nature. The initial Innes books pitted his protagonists against varied natural disasters, volcanic eruptions, mine explosions, mountain avalanches, but since *The Mary Deare*, he has repeatedly used the sea as a force in his stories.

Innes himself is a seaman. After his first success as a writer he bought a boat and took to ocean racing: "I ploughed my earnings back into travel." For some 20 years he maintained a pattern of "six months travelling, six months writing," and he used his travels to provide settings for his books. He sailed to Antarctica for *The White South*, to the islands of Greece for *Levkas Man*, and to the Indian ocean for *The Strode Venturer*. On land he has traveled the wastes of Labrador for *The Land God Gave to Cain*, the emptiness of the Arabian sands for *The Doomed Oasis*, and the deserts of Australia for *Golden Soak*.

As have most of the best writers, Innes served an apprenticeship before becoming a novelist; he was in newspaper work before World War II. He knew he would in time be a novelist and worked at his writing mornings and nights, before and after work. His early novels caused little stir, but the ones he wrote after the war were instantly successful. He writes strong, clear prose and instils it with an excitement that makes for compulsive reading.

There is no one comparable to Hammond Innes. No one had the material he has gathered, and the craftsmanship to transport his readers to the far-flung places of the earth. In a Hammond Innes book, you do not read of the adventures, you experience them. As a reader who has followed Hammond Innes with heart and mind for many years, my personal opinion is that his stature as a novelist has not yet been fully recognized. There is a greatness in his work which should lead to the books becoming classics, to be rediscovered by future generations.

—Dorothy B. Hughes

INNES, Michael. Pseudonym for J(ohn) I(nnes) M(ackintosh) Stewart. British. Born in Edinburgh, Scotland, 30 September 1906. Educated at Edinburgh Academy; Oriel College, Oxford (Matthew Arnold Memorial prize, 1929; Bishop Fraser's Scholar, 1930), B.A. (honours) in English 1928. Married Margaret Hardwick in 1932 (died 1979); three sons and two daughters. Lecturer in English, University of Leeds, Yorkshire, 1930–35; Jury Professor of English, University of Adelaide, South Australia, 1935–45; Lecturer, Queen's University, Belfast, 1946–48; Student (i.e., Fellow) of Christ Church, Oxford, 1949–73, now Emeritus; Reader in English Literature, Oxford University, 1969–73. Walker-Ames Professor, University of Washington, Seattle, 1961. D. Litt.: University of New Brunswick, Fredericton, 1962; University of Leicester 1979; University of St. Andrews, Scotland, 1980. Address: Lower Park House, Occupation Road, Lindley, Huddersfield HD3 3EE, England.

CRIME PUBLICATIONS

Novels (series: John Appleby; Charles Honeybath)

Death at the President's Lodging (Appleby). London, Gollancz, 1936; as *Seven Suspects*, New York, Dodd Mead, 1937.

Hamlet, Revenge! (Appleby). London, Gollancz, and New York, Dodd Mead, 1937.
Lament for a Maker (Appleby). London, Gollancz, and New York, Dodd Mead, 1938.
Stop Press (Appleby). London, Gollancz, 1939; as *The Spider Strikes*, New York, Dodd Mead, 1939.
The Secret Vanguard (Appleby). London, Gollancz, 1940; New York, Dodd Mead, 1941.
There Came Both Mist and Snow (Appleby). London, Gollancz, 1940; as *A Comedy of Terrors*, New York, Dodd Mead, 1940.
Appleby on Ararat. London, Gollancz, and New York, Dodd Mead, 1941.
The Daffodil Affair (Appleby). London, Gollancz, and New York, Dodd Mead, 1942.
The Weight of the Evidence (Appleby). New York, Dodd Mead, 1943; London, Gollancz, 1944.
Appleby's End. London, Gollancz, and New York, Dodd Mead, 1945.
From London Far. London, Gollancz, 1946; as *The Unsuspected Chasm*, New York, Dodd Mead, 1946.
What Happened at Hazelwood? London, Gollancz, and New York, Dodd Mead, 1946.
A Night of Errors (Appleby). New York, Dodd Mead, 1947; London, Gollancz, 1948.
The Journeying Boy. London, Gollancz, 1949; as *The Case of the Journeying Boy*, New York, Dodd Mead, 1949.
Operation Pax (Appleby). London, Gollancz, 1951; as *The Paper Thunderbolt*, New York, Dodd Mead, 1951.
A Private View (Appleby). London, Gollancz, 1952; as *One-Man Show*, New York, Dodd Mead, 1952; as *Murder Is an Art*, New York, Avon, 1959.
Christmas at Candleshoe. London, Gollancz, and New York, Dodd Mead, 1953; as *Candleshoe*, London, Penguin, 1978.
The Man from the Sea. London, Gollancz, and New York, Dodd Mead, 1955; as *Death by Moonlight*, New York, Avon, 1957.
Old Hall, New Hall. London, Gollancz, 1956; as *A Question of Queens*, New York, Dodd Mead, 1956.
Appleby Plays Chicken. London, Gollancz, 1957; as *Death on a Quiet Day*, New York, Dodd Mead, 1957.
The Long Farewell (Appleby). London, Gollancz, and New York, Dodd Mead, 1958.
Hare Sitting Up (Appleby). London, Gollancz, and New York, Dodd Mead, 1959.
The New Sonia Wayward. London, Gollancz, 1960; as *The Case of Sonia Wayward*, New York, Dodd Mead, 1960.
Silence Observed (Appleby). London, Gollancz, and New York, Dodd Mead, 1961.
A Connoisseur's Case (Appleby). London, Gollancz, 1962; as *The Crabtree Affair*, New York, Dodd Mead, 1962.
Money from Holme. London, Gollancz, 1964; New York, Dodd Mead, 1965.
The Bloody Wood (Appleby). London, Gollancz, and New York, Dodd Mead, 1966.
A Change of Heir. London, Gollancz, and New York, Dodd Mead, 1966.
Appleby at Allington. London, Gollancz, 1968; as *Death by Water,*, New York, Dodd Mead, 1968.
A Family Affair (Appleby). London, Gollancz, 1969; as *Picture of Guilt*, New York, Dodd Mead, 1969.
Death at the Chase (Appleby). London, Gollancz, and New York, Dodd Mead, 1970.
An Awkward Lie (Appleby). London, Gollancz, and New York, Dodd Mead, 1971.
The Open House (Appleby). London, Gollancz, and New York, Dodd Mead, 1972.

Appleby's Answer. London, Gollancz, and New York, Dodd Mead, 1973.

Appleby's Other Story. London, Gollancz, and New York, Dodd Mead, 1974.

The Mysterious Commission (Honeybath). London, Gollancz, 1974; New York, Dodd Mead, 1975.

The "Gay Phoenix" (Appleby). London, Gollancz, 1976; New York, Dodd Mead, 1977.

Honeybath's Haven. London, Gollancz, 1977; New York, Dodd Mead, 1978.

The Ampersand Papers (Appleby). London, Gollancz, 1978; New York, Dodd Mead, 1979.

Going It Alone. London, Gollancz, and New York, Dodd Mead, 1980.

Lord Mullion's Secret. London, Gollancz, and New York, Dodd Mead, 1981.

Sheiks and Adders (Appleby). London, Gollancz, and New York, Dodd Mead, 1982.

Appleby and Honeybath. London, Gollancz, and New York, Dodd Mead, 1983.

Carson's Conspiracy. (Appleby). London, Gollancz, and Dodd Mead, 1984.

Appleby and the Ospreys. London, Gollancz, 1986; New York, Dodd Mead, 1987.

Short Stories

Appleby Talking: Twenty-Three Detective Stories. London, Gollancz, 1954; as *Dead Man's Shoes,* New York, Dodd Mead, 1954.

Appleby Talks Again: Eighteen Detective Stories. London, Gollancz, 1956; New York, Dodd Mead, 1957.

The Appleby File. London, Gollancz, 1975; New York, Dodd Mead, 1976.

Uncollected Short Stories

"The Scattergood Emeralds," in *The Evening Standard* (London), 10 August 1954; as "True or False?," in *Ellery Queen's Mystery Magazine* (New York), May 1955.

"A Small Peter Pry," in *The Evening Standard* (London), 12 August 1954.

"The Impressionist," in *The Evening Standard* (London), 23 July 1955.

"The Perfect Murder," in *The Evening Standard* (London), 5 August 1955.

"The General's Wife Is Blackmailed," in *The Evening Standard* (London), 22 April 1957.

"The Left-Handed Barber," in *The Evening Standard* (London), 23 April 1957.

"A Change of Face," in *The Evening Standard* (London), 24 April 1957.

"The Theft of the Downing Street Letter," in *The Evening Standard* (London), 24 April 1957.

"The Man Who Collected Satchels," in *The Evening Standard* (London), 26 April 1957.

"The Tinted Diamonds," in *The Evening Standard* (London), 27 April 1957.

"Jerry Does a Good Turn for the DJAM," in *The Evening Standard* (London), 7 April 1958.

"The Mystery of Paul's 'Posthumus' Portrait," in *The Evening Standard* (London), 8 April 1958.

"Who Suspects the Postman?," in *The Evening Standard* (London), 9 April 1958; as "In the Bag," in *The Saint* (London), July 1960.

"The Inspector Feels the Draught," in *The Evening Standard* (London), 10 April 1958.

"The Author Changes His Style," in *The Evening Standard* (London), 10 April 1958; as "News Out of Persia," in *The Saint* (London), July 1960.

"The Party That Never Got Going," in *The Evening Standard* (London), 19 February 1959.

"The Secret in the Woodpile," in *Ellery Queen's Mystery Magazine* (New York), October 1975.

"Pelly and Cullis," in *Verdict of Thirteen,* edited by Julian Symons. London, Faber, and New York, Harper, 1979.

OTHER PUBLICATIONS as J.I.M. Stewart

Novels

Mark Lambert's Supper. London, Gollancz, 1954.

The Guardians. London, Gollancz, 1955; New York, Norton, 1957.

A Use of Riches. London, Gollancz, and New York, Norton, 1957.

The Man Who Won the Pools. London, Gollancz, and New York, Norton, 1961.

The Last Tresilians. London, Gollancz, and New York, Norton, 1963.

An Acre of Grass. London, Gollancz, 1965; New York, Norton, 1966.

The Aylwins. London, Gollancz, 1966; New York, Norton, 1967.

Vanderlyn's Kingdom. London, Gollancz, 1967; New York, Norton, 1968.

Avery's Mission. London, Gollancz, and New York, Norton, 1971.

A Palace of Art. London, Gollancz, and New York, Norton, 1972.

Mungo's Dream. London, Gollancz, and New York, Norton, 1973.

The Gaudy. London, Gollancz, 1974; New York, Norton, 1975.

Young Pattullo. London, Gollancz, 1975; New York, Norton, 1976.

A Memorial Service. London, Gollancz, and New York, Norton, 1976.

The Madonna of the Astrolabe. London, Gollancz, and New York, Norton, 1977.

Full Term. London, Gollancz, 1978; New York, Norton, 1979.

Andrew and Tobias. New York, Norton, 1980; London, Gollancz, 1981.

A Villa in France. London, Gollancz, 1982; New York, Norton, 1983.

An Open Prison. London, Gollancz, and New York, Norton, 1984.

The Naylors. London, Gollancz, and New York, Norton, 1985.

Short Stories

Three Tales of Hamlet (as Michael Innes), with Rayner Heppenstall. London, Gollancz, 1950.

The Man Who Wrote Detective Stories and Other Stories. London, Gollancz, and New York, Norton, 1959.

Cucumber Sandwiches and Other Stories. London, Gollancz, and New York, Norton, 1969.

Our England Is a Garden and Other Stories. London, Gollancz, 1979; New York, Norton, 1980.

The Bridge at Arta and Other Stories. London, Gollancz, 1981; New York, Norton, 1982.

My Aunt Christina and Other Stories. London, Gollancz, and New York, Norton, 1983.

Parlour 4 and Other Stories. London, Gollancz, and New York, Norton, 1986.

Play as Michael Innes

Strange Intelligence (broadcast, 1947). Published in *Imaginary Conversations,* edited by Rayner Heppenstall, London, Secker and Warburg, 1948.

Radio Play: *Strange Intelligence,* 1947.

Other

Educating the Emotions. Adelaide, New Education Fellowship, 1944.

Character and Motive in Shakespeare: Some Recent Appraisals Examined. London, Longman, 1949; New York, Barnes and Noble, 1966.

James Joyce. London, Longman, 1957; revised edition, 1960.

Thomas Love Peacock. London, Longman, 1963.

Eight Modern Writers. London and New York, Oxford University Press, 1963.

"Death as a Game" (as Michael Innes), in *Ellery Queen's Mystery Magazine* (New York), November 1965.

Rudyard Kipling. London, Gollancz, and New York, Dodd Mead, 1966.

Joseph Conrad. London, Longman, and New York, Dodd Mead, 1968.

Thomas Hardy: A Critical Biography. London, Longman, and New York, Dodd Mead, 1971.

Shakespeare's Lofty Scene (lecture). London, Oxford University Press, 1971.

Myself and Michael Innes: A Memoir. London, Gollancz, 1987; New York, Norton, 1988.

Editor, *Montaigne's Essays: John Florio's Translation.* London, Nonesuch Press, and New York, Random House, 1931.

Editor, *The Moonstone,* by Wilkie Collins. London, Penguin, 1966.

Editor, *Vanity Fair,* by Thackeray. London, Penguin, 1968.

*

Critical Study: *Michael Innes* by George L. Scheper. New York, Ungar, 1985.

*   *   *

In one Michael Innes novel a character says of a painting that "the Englishness is unchallengeable . . . and the whole effect a landscape in the fullest sense of the word." This statement can be applied equally well to the entire body of Innes's fiction. And it is hard to resist, in describing the persona of Innes himself as he comes through in his books, a portrayal of the title figure in the novella *The Man Who Wrote Detective Stories* (by Stewart): "He loved tumbling out scraps of poetry from a ragbag collection in his mind—and particularly in absurd and extravagant contexts. There was a strong vein of fantasy in him." What could be more mischievously autobiographical than that, from a man whose own thrillers are landmined with literary allusions and quotations, practical jokes, and elaborate hoaxes?

Thus, the flavor of Innes is very strong and very idiosyncratic: English, bookish, jokey, and bizarre. (In fact, it could be said that certain Innes stories are the ones in the genre best

suited for light opera, in the manner of Gilbert and Sullivan.) Over the years there has come to be a word appended to just this sort of mystery, and that word is *donnish*. Not surprisingly, J.I.M. Stewart was an Oxford don, and though not all of his books have university settings, the piquant spirit of an enlightened pedantry hovers over each one.

Hardly a colorful figure, Appleby is of the breed of "noble" policemen; with his good manners, empathy, and erudition, he is a gentleman not by birth but by consensus. He is introduced casually in *Death at the President Lodging* as a man of "contemplative habit and a tentative mind, poise as well as force, reserve rather than wariness." He is that rare being (in the mid-1930's, anyway)—a policeman with a liberal education. And, as he rises over the years at Scotland Yard, from inspector to detective inspector to commissioner of the metropolitan police, the qualities that serve him the best are his curiosity, his irony, and his love of books, with patience, good nature, and egalitarianism following close behind. Appleby, who along the way acquires a charming wife and eventually a not-so-charming son, does finally retire but continues detecting as he "stumbles" into cases. He accepts a knighthood but refuses to be impressed with himself.

There are basically four sorts of Innes/Appleby tales, each of which is overlaid with the donnish sensibility. One type involves "pursuit and flight"; these tales follow the best John Buchan tradition. In these stories, which include *The Secret Vanguard, Operation Pax, From London Far, The Journeying Boy,* and *The Man from the Sea,* Appleby is not always a primary figure; when he does appear, he performs as an avuncular rescuer representing sanity and authority. Innes is quite skilled at presenting the traumas of the fugitive who, like Richard Hannay in *The Thirty-Nine Steps,* finds that there is a darker side to the everyday world and that not every good samaritan is to be trusted.

The second type contains the novels and stories which deal satirically with the world of art. Many of these are marked by the presence of the egregious Hildebert Braunkopf, an art dealer who labels his old masters in "an orgy of scepticism." *Private View* and *A Family Affair* are in this category, in which Appleby is seen to treat the proprietor of the DaVinci Gallery with affectionate disrespect.

The third kind of Innes plot has as its milieu the university itself, with dons and tutors and undergraduates moving sedately amid mayhem and madness. *The Weight of the Evidence* is one of these, presenting a wicked look at high table and the senior common-room.

The last variety, to which Innes has returned again and again, can only be called pure farce. He has favored this approach especially in his most recent books, although his delightful *Appleby's End,* in which villages are named Drool, Sneak, and Snarl, is an earlier example of his comic talents at their most ditheringly droll. His early novel *Stop Press* is somewhat manically humorous, showing more of the playfulness and whimsy that were to come than did his very first books. But the elements of farce and mystery, more balanced in the middle years, are now weighted in favor of the former and the books are beginning to seem exasperatingly self-indulgent.

Still, Innes devotees have had their rewards, not the least of which has been Innes's productivity. As the progenitor and popularizer of the donnish school, he has given quantity as well as quality to those readers who have become addicted to such fare.

—Michele Slung

IRISH, William. *See* **WOOLRICH, Cornell.**

IRVINE, Robert. American. Born in Salt Lake City, Utah, 16 March 1936. Educated at the University of Utah, Salt Lake City, 1954–55; University of California, Berkeley, 1955–59, B.A. in anthropology and art history 1959. Served in the United States Army Counterintelligence, 1959–61. Married Angela P. Irvine in 1959. Reporter, *Daily Signal,* Huntington Park, California, 1962–63; reporter and Los Angeles City Hall bureau chief, *Citizen News,* Hollywood, California, 1963–64; newswriter, producer, and assistant assignment editor, KTLA Television, 1964–65; writer, producer, and news director, CBS Radio, 1965–68; news director, KABC Television, 1968–71; freelance writer for KCBS Television, 1979–82, all Los Angeles. Agent: Dominick Abel, 146 West 82nd Street, New York, New York 10024, U.S.A.

CRIME PUBLICATIONS

Novels (series: Robert Christopher; Moroni Traveler)

Jump Cut (Christopher). New York, Popular Library, 1974.
Freeze Frame (Christopher). New York, Popular Library, 1976.
The Face Out Front. New York, Popular Library, 1977.
Horizontal Hold (Christopher). New York, Popular Library, 1978.
Ratings Are Murder (Christopher). New York, Walker, 1985.
Baptism for the Dead (Traveler). New York, Dodd Mead, 1988.
The Angel's Share (Traveler). New York, St. Martin's Press, 1989.
Gone to Glory (Traveler). New York, St. Martin's Press, 1990.

Uncollected Short Stories

"Another Case of Identity," in *Best Detective Stories of the Year 1975,* edited by Allen J. Hubin. New York, Dutton, 1976.
"Lobster Shift," in *Ellery Queen's Faces of Mystery,* New York, Davis, 1977.
"A Hard Way to Die," in *The Deadly Arts,* edited by Bill Pronzini and Marcia Muller. New York, Arbor House, 1985.
"In the Dead Hours," in *Murder California Style,* edited by Jon L. Breen and John Ball, New York, St. Martin's Press, 1987.

OTHER PUBLICATIONS

Novels

The Devil's Breath. New York, Pinnacle, 1982.
Footsteps. New York, Pinnacle, 1982.

*

Robert Irvine comments:
I grew up in Utah, with its stark mountains and salt deserts and Mormon theocracy. My Ancestors were pioneers. My great grandfather, also a Robert R. Irvine, was a surveyor for the Union Pacific Railroad before he joined Brigham Young and the Mormons in Salt Lake City. My great grandmother pulled a handcart across the Great Plains and the Rocky Mountains to join him there. My father was an antique dealer for sixty years in Salt Lake, Utah is in my blood. I am haunted by it. It's an experience—an obsession—I want to share with my readers.

* * *

Robert Irvine came to fiction writing from a career in television news, and his short stories and earliest novels, written as R.R. Irvine, make optimum use of that background. *Jump Cut* introduces Vietnam veteran Bob Christopher, field reporter for Los Angeles' Channel 3, an animal lover with a persistent weight problem whose bleeding heart is ill-concealed by a wisecracking front. *Jump Cut* is an effective debut in the Ross Macdonald vein, but *Freeze Frame* is even better, spinning a complex plot of corporate shenanigans from an Apache woman's claim her house has been precipitously bulldozed. *Horizontal Hold,* about the blowing up of a much-hated anchorman, is the weakest of the four Christopher novels, but *Ratings Are Murder,* switching from first to third person narration and putting added emphasis on comedy and satire, is probably the best. The only one of Irvine's television novels that is unsuccessful on balance is *The Face Out Front,* in which mystery is unwisely sacrificed for pure suspense in the story of a menaced anchorman. The television books are characterized by frenetic plot action, insider details, strong compassion for human and animal underdogs, and well-executed action climaxes, often topped off with a satisfying dose of irony. Their main weakness is the cartoonish quality of some of the characters, particularly anchor people who seem as exaggerated in their vain stupidity as *The Mary Tyler Moore Show's* Ted Baxter, though the author claims he has to tone down the ludicrousness of real-life anchor people to make them acceptable for fiction.

The Christopher novels are fine entertainment, and one hopes the television reporter will someday return. However, Irvine draws on another area of specialized knowledge for his major contribution to detective fiction. Two horror novels with a Utah setting were precursors of the novels about Salt Lake City private eye Moroni Traveler, beginning with *Baptism for the Dead.* Traveler is like a number of other fictional private eyes in coming from a professional football career, unlike them in most other ways. Despite being named for the L.D.S. church's founding angel, Traveler is not himself a Mormon, but like his creator, he grew up among them and understands them well. Irvine is not the only author to set mystery novels in Salt Lake, but he is the best at capturing the essence of the city and its people, the pervasive influence of the church and the compromises its adherents sometimes make in the interest of commerce.

Baptism for the Dead refers to the Mormon practice of insuring salvation for one's ancestors by retroactively baptizing them, one reason for the Church's concern with genealogy. Client Penny Varney wants her mother, who disappeared several years before, to enjoy the benefit of such a baptism but must first know if she is really dead. Irvine gets maximum value from a couple of irresistible plot elements for a novel with a Mormon background: an outlaw fundamentalist (i.e. polygamous) cult and an inflammatory church document. He also introduces a case of vividly drawn characters who will recur throughout the series, most notably a non-Mormon street preacher known as Mad Bill, Traveler's father and detecting partner Martin, his boyhood friend now high church official Willis Tanner, and his wolf-crying ex-girlfriend Claire Benyon.

The second Traveler book, *The Angel's Share,* is the best of the series to date. The title refers to Brigham Young's concept of paying one's tithe in converts if too poor to do it in money, and the double-pronged plot concerns a church missionary who supposedly disappeared in England and a Ripper-like Salt Lake serial killer who sends a video message (ending with the words "Jack's back!") instead of writing notes to the police and press. The plot is well-managed, the various characters and Traveler's relationship with them even more so.

Gone to Glory, in which Traveler investigates on behalf of a boyhood baseball hero accused of murder, employs a tricky but effective fictional technique: one of the major characters is talked about throughout the book but doesn't appear until near the end, leaving the reader to ponder what he will be like based on the conflicting evidence offered by other characters.

The Moroni Traveler series is one of the best examples of the recent regional trend in private eye fiction.

—Jon L. Breen

J

JACKS, Oliver. *See* **ROYCE, Kenneth.**

JAMES, P(hyllis) D(orothy). British. Born in Oxford, 3 August 1920. Educated at Cambridge Girls' High School, 1931–37. During World War II worked as a Red Cross nurse and at the Ministry of Food. Married Ernest Connor Bantry White in 1941 (died 1964); two daughters. Prior to World War II, assistant stage manager, Festival Theatre, Cambridge; principal administrative assistant, North West Regional Hospital Board, London, 1949–68; principal, Home Office, in police department, 1968–72, and criminal policy department, 1972–79. Justice of the Peace, Willesden, London, 1979. Fellow, Institute of Hospital Administrators; chairman, Society of Authors, 1985–87; member, Arts Council, and chairman of Literary Advisory Panel, 1988. Since 1988 governor, BBC. Recipient: Crime Writers Association award, 1967, Silver Dagger award, 1971, 1975, 1986, Diamond Dagger award, 1987. Fellow, Royal Society of Authors, 1987. O.B.E. (Officer, Order of the British Empire), 1983. Agent: Elaine Greene Ltd., 31 Newington Green, London N16 9PU, England.

CRIME PUBLICATIONS

Novels (series: Commander Adam Dalgliesh; Cordelia Gray)

Cover Her Face (Dalgliesh). London, Faber, 1962; New York, Scribner, 1966.
A Mind to Murder (Dalgliesh). London, Faber, 1963; New York, Scribner, 1967.
Unnatural Causes (Dalgliesh). London, Faber, and New York, Scribner, 1967.
Shroud for a Nightingale (Dalgliesh). London, Faber, and New York, Scribner, 1971.
An Unsuitable Job for a Woman (Gray). London, Faber, 1972; New York, Scribner, 1973.
The Black Tower (Dalgliesh). London, Faber, and New York, Scribner, 1975.
Death of an Expert Witness (Dalgliesh). London, Faber, and New York, Scribner, 1977.
Innocent Blood. London, Faber, and New York, Scribner, 1980.
The Skull Beneath the Skin (Gray). London, Faber, and New York, Scribner, 1982.
A Taste for Death (Dalgliesh). London, Faber and Faber, and New York, Knopf, 1986.
Devices and Desires (Dalgliesh). London, Faber and Faber, 1989; New York, Knopf, 1990.

Uncollected Short Stories

"Moment of Power," in *Ellery Queen's Murder Menu*. Cleveland, World, 1969.

"The Victim," in *Winter's Crimes 5*, edited by Virginia Whitaker. London, Macmillan, 1973.
"Murder, 1986," in *Ellery Queen's Masters of Mystery*. New York, Davis, 1975.
"A Very Desirable Residence," in *Winter's Crimes 8*, edited by Hilary Watson. London, Macmillan, and New York, St. Martin's Press, 1976.
"Great-Aunt Ellie's Flypapers," in *Verdict of Thirteen*, edited by Julian Symons. London, Faber, and New York, Harper, 1979.
"The Girl Who Loved Graveyards," in *Winter's Crimes 15*, edited by George Hardinge. London, Macmillan, and New York, St. Martin's Press, 1983.

OTHER PUBLICATIONS

Play

A Private Treason (produced Watford, Hertfordshire, 1985).

Other

The Maul and the Pear Tree: The Ratcliffe Highway Murders, 1811, with Thomas A. Critchley. London, Constable, 1971; New York, Mysterious Press, 1986.
"Ought Adam to Marry Cordelia?" and "A Fictional Prognosis," in *Murder Ink: The Mystery Reader's Companion*, edited by Dilys Winn. New York, Workman, 1977.
"Dorothy L. Sayers: From Puzzle to Novel," in *Crime Writers*, edited by H.R.F. Keating. London, BBC Publications, 1978.
"One Clue at a Time," in *The Writer* (Boston), February 1984.

*

Critical Study: *P.D. James* by Norma Siebenheller, New York, Ungar, 1981; *P.D. James* by Richard B. Gidez, Boston, Hall, 1986.

* * *

Starting from a conventional first detective story, *Cover Her Face*, P. D. James has moved toward fiction in which criminal investigation provides merely a loose structure for characterization, atmosphere, and theme, which now seem most important to her. In this assault on generic boundaries, she resembles, but is more determined than, Dorothy L. Sayers, Josephine Tey, and Ngaio Marsh. Consequently, James's detectives—Cordelia Gray (private and young) and Adam Dalgliesh (professional and middle-aging)—have been absent from or muted in recent works.

Commander Dalgliesh resembles other detectives created by women writers: tall, dark, attractive, and frangible (he is ill, bashed, or burned in half his novels). "When the Met . . . want to show that the police know . . . what bottle to order with the *canard à l'orange* . . . , they wheel out Dalgliesh," a hostile chief inspector says. Sensitive under seeming coldness, Dalgliesh sometimes fears failure or considers resignation. Like Sayers's Lord Peter, he is quotatious, but where the former delights in or hides behind literary quotations, James uses them to establish her detective's *bona fides,* for Dalgliesh is a published poet.

Before his first appearance in *Cover Her Face,* Dalgliesh's wife and son have died in childbirth, but in successive novels her image becomes fainter and her presence dies away. At one time readers hoped that Cordelia Gray would take her place, and recently James has introduced Inspector Kate Miskin, but romantic notes are now struck faintly. In fact, few James characters are happily married, and there are no juvenile leads to assert the normality of love. There are, however, close, psychologically incestuous brother-sister relationships.

As a detective, Dalgliesh combines inexorably meticulous routine with abstract intelligence, although these have become less apparent in *A Taste for Death* and *Devices and Desires.* His devotion to truth is equalled only by Cordelia Gray's clear honesty, she was conditioned by a revolutionary father and a convent education, he by a rectory childhood.

Blunt instruments and hanging are James's preferred but not exclusive methods of murder, although *Shroud for a Nightingale* contains a harrowing account of corrosive poisoning during a teaching demonstration. James once told an interviewer that she believes detective fiction can lessen our fear of death. Yet her details of what happens after death—the doctor's fingers penetrating the orifices of the female body, the first long opening cut of an autopsy—are scarcely reassuring to readers and sometimes affect even her supposedly inured detectives. Other shocks of mortality include the skulls of plague victims packed cheekbone to cheekbone in the crypt of Courcy Castle in *The Skull Beneath the Skin.* This is James's most gothic novel, featuring a "Black Museum," tales of sexual outrage and murder, a dead face smashed to pulp, and a Eugène Sue situation in which Cordelia is caught between a bolted trap-door and the rising tide in the Devil's Kettle.

Although few of James's settings are as conventional as the house party on an island, her action generally takes place in closed, often bureaucratic communities: a writer's colony (*Unnatural Causes*); a teaching hospital (*Shroud for a Nightingale*); a quasi-religious home for the disabled (*The Black Tower*); a psychiatric clinic (*A Mind to Murder*); a forensic laboratory (*Death of an Expert Witness*), or a nuclear power station (*Devices and Desires*). These organizations draw upon the author's own experience in health service administration and forensic science.

In terms of plot, James is most successful when dealing with the processes of investigation and is weakest in motivation. She thinks in terms of film sequences, and the long "panning" shots and close-ups in which she relentlessly describes interiors have become an intrusive mannerism. Paradoxically, she approves morally of uncluttered space. Like the intensely private persons they are, Cordelia and Adam both live in austere flats above the Thames. Perhaps James's best, most controlled use of domestic detail occurs in *Innocent Blood,* where Phillipa furnishes a flat to greet her just-released murderess mother. Indeed, this novel with its plot of discoveries, its ambiguities and psychological images is James's best claim to consideration as a "serious" novelist. Neither Dalgliesh nor Gray appears in it, however.

James's characters have always thought and talked about truth, faith, responsibility, and justice, even if not profoundly. But in the books which follow *Innocent Blood,* plot is almost lost amid talkiness and theme. The nature of Sir Paul Berowne's religious experience in *A Taste for Death* is, for instance, more important and less explicable than the identity of his blood-happy killer. In *Devices and Desires* (title drawn from the Common Book of Prayer) a nuclear power station and a ruined abbey confront each other in one of James's bleak coastal landscapes, perhaps adversarily, perhaps not. They are surrounded by serial murder, terrorism, anti-nuclear and pro-animal protesters, cancer, drowning, anti-racism, a libel suit—all pretexts and conveniences for a plot which the novel is not about. Or perhaps, having discarded the neatness and process of classic detective fiction, James felt that she, like one of her characters, owes us a death. Lacking the psychological interest of *Innocent Blood, Devices and Desires* remains an ambitious, controversial book, not for its ideas but for its ambivalence of genre.

—Jane W. Stedman

———

JASON, Stuart. *See* **AVALLONE, Michael.**

———

JASON, Veronica. *See* **JOHNSTON, Velda.**

———

JAY, Charlotte. Pseudonym for Geraldine Mary Jay; also writes as Geraldine Halls. Australian. Born in Adelaide, South Australia, 17 December 1919. Educated at Girton School, Adelaide, 1926–37; University of Adelaide, 1939–41. Married to Albert James Halls. Worked as a secretary in Adelaide, Sydney, Melbourne, and London during the 1940's; court stenographer, Court of Papua New Guinea, 1949; lived in Pakistan, Thailand, Lebanon, India, and France, 1950–58. With her husband operated an oriental antique business in Somerset, 1958–71, and since 1971, in Adelaide. Recipient: Mystery Writers of America Edgar Allan Poe award, for novel, 1953. Agent: Richard Scott Simon Ltd., 32 College Cross, London N1 1PR, England. Address: 21 Commercial Road, Hyde Park, South Australia 5061, Australia.

CRIME PUBLICATIONS

Novels

The Knife Is Feminine.   London, Collins, 1951.
Beat Not the Bones.   London, Collins, 1952; New York, Harper, 1953.
The Fugitive Eye.   London, Collins, 1953; New York, Harper, 1954.
The Yellow Turban.   London, Collins, and New York, Harper, 1955.
The Feast of the Dead (as G.M. Jay).   London, Hale, 1956; as *The Brink of Silence,* as Charlotte Jay, New York, Harper, 1957.
The Man Who Walked Away.   London, Collins, 1958; as *The Stepfather,* New York, Harper, 1958.
Arms for Adonis.   London, Collins, 1960; New York, Harper, 1961.

A Hank of Hair. London, Heinemann, and New York, Harper, 1964.
The Voice of the Crab (as Geraldine Halls). London, Constable, and New York, Harper, 1974.

OTHER PUBLICATIONS

Novels as Geraldine Halls

The Silk Project. London, Heinemann, 1956.
The Cats of Benares. London, Heinemann, and New York, Harper, 1967.
The Cobra Kite. London, Constable, 1971.
The Last Summer of the Men Shortage. London, Constable, 1976.
The Felling of Thawle. London, Constable, 1979; as *The Last Inheritor,* New York, St. Martin's Press, 1980.
Talking to Strangers. London, Constable, 1982.

*

Charlotte Jay comments:

I began writing mystery stories largely because of my delight in the novels of Wilkie Collins and Le Fanu and the stories of Poe. I read these books with terror and fascination when I was quite young and their influence can be seen in several of my early novels. When my first books were published most of the crime stories at that time were written by skilled writers of Crime and Detection, usually with a well-born ex-Oxford or Cambridge amateur detective as the central character, appearing, in the manner of the Scarlet Pimpernel, something of a fool, but omniscient and strides ahead of the reader. In America the same fashion prevailed along with crime stories following in the tradition of Dashiell Hammett and Raymond Chandler. I knew I could not compete with the excellent exponents of these various trends. Many had had direct experience of police procedure which I did not feel competent of learning anything much about. And indeed I felt no interest in doing so. I set out to frighten and mystify my readers by asking them to identify themselves with a character battling for survival in a lonely, claustrophobic situation. My publishers on several occasions demanded that, in the interests of logicality, my threatened character should call the Police. I always contested their suggestions and sometimes rewrote whole chapters to accommodate my conviction that my characters must stumble on alone and unaided through their private nightmares.

*   *   *

In the early 1950's there was a unique and powerful experience in mystery/suspense writing engendered by a new writer who signed herself Charlotte Jay. Jay was an Australian girl who worked in the most primitive parts of the island of Papua New Guinea. From her experiences, and with a writer's inspiration, she composed the story *Beat Not the Bones.* It was received with superlatives by critics; Charlotte Armstrong wrote that the book "works you up to the revelation of a horrible secret, and the secret turns out to be the horrible susprise you hoped it would." Constant readers of mysteries are aware that fewer than one in a thousand books live up to the promise of their threats.

For her next novel Jay wrote of a superb suspense chase across the English countryside. She lived for a time in Pakistan whence came *The Yellow Turban.* From her years in Lebanon came *Arms for Adonis,* published in 1960 and even more potent

today with its Arab, Syrian, Lebanese, and English characters interwoven in mid-Eastern intrigue. Jay returned to Papua New Guinea for the setting of *The Voice of the Crab.* It was another of her probing ethnological studies of the conflict of the stone age and the 20th century.

If she were not strongly identified as one of the most important writers of far-off places and their mysterious qualities, Jay might be more well known as one of the classic writers of the horror story. Certainly *A Hank of Hair* is one of the small number of horror books that contain scenes to set the reader screaming.

Jay is a gifted writer; one wishes that her output were larger.

—Dorothy B. Hughes

————

JAY, G.M. *See* **JAY, Charlotte.**

————

JEFFREY, William. *See* **PRONZINI, Bill.**

————

JEFFREYS, J.G. *See* **STURROCK, Jeremy.**

————

JEFFRIES, Roderic. Also writes as Peter Alding; Jeffrey Ashford; Hastings Draper; Roderic Graeme; Graham Hastings. British. Born in London, 21 October 1926; son of Graham Montague Jeffries, i.e. Bruce Graeme, *q.v.* Educated at Harrow View Preparatory School; University of Southampton School of Navigation, 1942–43; Gray's Inn, London: called to the Bar, 1952. Married Rosemary Powys Woodhouse in 1958; one daughter and one son. Served in the Merchant Navy, 1943–49, rising to the rank of 3rd Officer in the New Zealand Shipping Company and the Union Castle Shipping Company; practised law, 1952–54. Agent: William Collins Ltd., 8 Grafton Street, London W1X 3LA; or, Jennifer Luithlen Agency, The Rowans, 88 Holmfield Road, Leicester LE2 15B, England. Address: Ca Na Paiaia, Pollensa, Mallorca, Spain.

CRIME PUBLICATIONS

Novels (series: Enrique Alvarez)

Twice Checked (as Graham Hastings). London, Hale, 1959.
Deadly Game (as Graham Hastings). London, Hale, 1961.
Evidence of the Accused. London, Collins, 1961; New York, British Book Centre, 1963.
Exhibit No. Thirteen. London, Collins, 1962.
The Benefits of Death. London, Collins, 1963; New York, Dodd Mead, 1964.
An Embarrassing Death. London, Collins, 1964; New York, Dodd Mead, 1965.

Dead Against the Lawyers. London, Collins, 1965; New York, Dodd Mead, 1966.

Death in the Coverts. London, Collins, 1966.

A Deadly Marriage. London, Collins, 1967.

A Traitor's Crime. London, Collins, 1968.

Dead Man's Bluff. London, Collins, 1970.

Mistakenly in Mallorca (Alvarez). London, Collins, 1974.

Two-Faced Death (Alvarez). London, Collins, 1976.

Troubled Deaths (Alvarez). London, Collins, 1977; New York, St. Martin's Press, 1978.

Murder Begets Murder (Alvarez). London, Collins, and New York, St. Martin's Press, 1979.

Just Desserts (Alvarez). London, Collins, 1980; New York, St. Martin's Press, 1981.

Unseemly End (Alvarez). London, Collins, and New York, St. Martin's Press, 1981.

Deadly Petard (Alvarez). London, Collins, and New York, St. Martin's Press, 1983.

Three and One Make Five (Alvarez). London, Collins, and New York, St. Martin's Press, 1984.

Layers of Deceit (Alvarez). London, Collins, and New York, St. Martin's Press, 1985.

Almost Murder (Alvarez). London, Collins, and New York, St. Martin's Press, 1986.

Relatively Dangerous (Alvarez). London, Collins, and New York, St. Martin's Press, 1987.

Death Trick (Alvarez). London, Collins, and New York, St. Martin's Press, 1988.

Dead Clever (Alvarez). London, Collins, and New York, St. Martin's Press, 1989.

Too Clever by Half (Alvarez). London, Collins, 1990.

Novels as Roderic Graeme (series: Blackshirt in all books)

Concerning Blackshirt. London, Hutchinson, 1952.

Blackshirt Wins the Trick. London, Hutchinson, 1953.

Blackshirt Passes By. London, Hutchinson, 1953.

Salute to Blackshirt. London, Hutchinson, 1954.

The Amazing Mr. Blackshirt. London, Hutchinson, 1955.

Blackshirt Meets the Lady. London, Hutchinson, 1956.

Paging Blackshirt. London, Long, 1957.

Blackshirt Helps Himself. London, Long, 1958.

Double for Blackshirt. London, Long, 1958.

Blackshirt Sets the Pace. London, Long, 1959.

Blackshirt Sees It Through. London, Long, 1960.

Blackshirt Finds Trouble. London, Long, 1961.

Blackshirt Takes the Trail. London, Long, 1962.

Blackshirt on the Spot. London, Long, 1963.

Call for Blackshirt. London, Long, 1963.

Blackshirt Saves the Day. London, Long, 1964.

Danger for Blackshirt. London, Long, 1965.

Blackshirt at Large. London, Long, 1966.

Blackshirt in Peril. London, Long, 1967.

Blackshirt Stirs Things Up. London, Long, 1969.

Novels as Jeffrey Ashford (series: Detective Inspector Don Kerry)

Counsel for the Defence. London, Long, 1960; New York, Harper, 1961.

Investigations Are Proceeding (Kerry). London, Long, 1961; as *The D.I.,* New York, Harper, 1962.

The Burden of Proof. London, Long, and New York, Harper, 1962.

Will Anyone Who Saw the Accident . . . London, Long, 1963; New York, Harper, 1964; as *Hit and Run,* London, Arrow, 1966.

Enquiries Are Continuing (Kerry). London, Long, 1964; as *The Superintendent's Room,* New York, Harper, 1965.

The Hands of Innocence. London, Long, 1965; New York, Walker, 1966.

Consider the Evidence. London, Long, and New York, Walker, 1966.

Forget What You Saw. London, Long, and New York, Walker, 1967.

Prisoner at the Bar. London, Long, and New York, Walker, 1969.

To Protect the Guilty. London, Long, and New York, Walker, 1970.

Bent Copper. London, Long, and New York, Walker, 1971.

A Man Will Be Kidnapped Tomorrow. London, Long, and New York, Walker, 1972.

The Double Run. London, Long, and New York, Walker, 1973.

The Colour of Violence. London, Long, and New York, Walker, 1974.

Three Layers of Guilt. London, Long, 1975; New York, Walker, 1976.

Slow Down the World. London, Long, and New York, Walker, 1976.

Hostage to Death. London, Long, and New York, Walker, 1977.

The Anger of Fear. London, Long, 1978; New York, Walker, 1979.

A Recipe for Murder. London, Long, and New York, Walker, 1980.

The Loss of the Culion. London, Collins, and New York, Walker, 1981.

Guilt with Honour. London, Collins, and New York, Walker, 1982.

A Sense of Loyalty. London, Collins, 1983; New York, Walker, 1984.

Presumption of Guilt. London, Collins, and New York, Walker, 1984.

An Ideal Crime. London, Collins, 1985; New York, Walker, 1986.

A Question of Principle. London, Collins, 1986; New York, St. Martin's Press, 1987.

A Crime Remembered. London, Collins, 1987; New York, St. Martin's Press, 1988.

The Honourable Detective. London, Collins, 1988; New York, St. Martin's Press, 1989.

A Conflict of Interests. London, Collins, 1989; New York, St. Martin's Press, 1990.

Novels as Peter Alding (series: Constable Kerr and Inspector Fusil in all books)

The C.I.D. Room. London, Long, 1967; as *All Leads Negative,* New York, Harper, 1967.

Circle of Danger. London, Long, 1968.

Murder among Thieves. London, Long, 1969; New York, McCall, 1970.

Guilt Without Proof. London, Long, 1970; New York, McCall, 1971.

Despite the Evidence. London, Long, 1971; New York, Saturday Review Press, 1972.

Call Back to Crime. London, Long, 1972.

Field of Fire. London, Long, 1973.

The Murder Line. London, Long, 1974.

Six Days to Death. London, Long, 1975.

Murder Is Suspected. London, Long, and New York, Walker, 1977.

Ransom Town. London, Long, and New York, Walker, 1979.

A Man Condemned. London, Hale, and New York, Walker, 1981.

Betrayed by Death. London, Hale, and New York, Walker, 1982.

One Man's Justice. London, Hale, 1983.

OTHER PUBLICATIONS

Novels as Hastings Draper

Wiggery Pokery. London, W.H. Allen, 1956.
Wigged and Gowned. London, W.H. Allen, 1958.
Brief Help. London, W.H. Allen, 1961.

Other (for children)

Brandy Ahoy! (as Roderic Graeme). London, Hutchinson, 1951.
Where's Brandy? (as Roderic Graeme). London, Hutchinson, 1953.
Brandy Goes a Cruising (as Roderic Graeme). London, Hutchinson, 1954.
Police and Detection. Leicester, Brockhampton Press, 1962; as *Against Time!,* New York, Harper, 1964.
Police Dog. Leicester, Brockhampton Press, and New York, Harper, 1965.
Police Car. Leicester, Brockhampton Press, 1967; as *Patrol Car,* New York, Harper, 1967.
Grand Prix Monaco (as Jeffrey Ashford). New York, Putnam, 1968.
River Patrol. New York, Harper, 1969.
Grand Prix United States (as Jeffrey Ashford). New York, Putnam, 1971.
Police Patrol Boat. Leicester, Brockhampton Press, 1971.
Trapped. New York, Harper, 1972.
Grand Prix Britain (as Jeffrey Ashford). New York, Putnam, 1973.
Dick Knox at Le Mans (as Jeffrey Ashford). New York, Putnam, 1974.
The Riddle of the Parchment. London, Hodder and Stoughton, 1976.
The Boy Who Knew Too Much. London, Hodder and Stoughton, 1977.
Eighteen Desperate Hours. London, Hodder and Stoughton, 1979.
The Missing Man. London, Hodder and Stoughton, 1980.
Voyage into Danger. London, Hodder and Stoughton, 1981.
Peril at Sea. London, Hodder and Stoughton, 1983.
Sunken Danger. London, Hodder and Stoughton, 1985.
Meeting Trouble. London, Hodder and Stoughton, 1986.
The Man Who Couldn't Be. London, Hodder and Stoughton, 1987.

*

Manuscript Collection, Mugar Memorial Library, Boston University.

Roderic Jeffries comments:

My earlier books were straight detective with no series character. Then in 1972 I moved to Mallorca, for health reasons, and introduced a Spanish detective, Enrique Alvarez. In these Mallorquin books I try to add to the mystery and detection a background which sketches in an island people who have known poverty and are now adapting to a sudden prosperity brought about by tourism.

*　　*　　*

Roderic Jeffries, a prolific British writer with almost 90 mysteries to his credit, specializes in whodunits, many set in the English countryside, the more recent ones moved to sunny Mallorca and its British tourist colony. Writing under a number of pseudonyms, he often produces three or more books a year, each devoted to a different series. Starting in 1952, he assumed the name of Roderic Graeme and added another two dozen books to the Blackshirt detective series originated by his father. During the 1960's, he spun a number of murder tales that hinge upon clever courtroom antics and often require the accused to undertake his own defense. In 1972 he embarked upon a series of mysteries featuring his Spanish detective, Enrique Alvarez, whose oral vices of eating and drinking are true to the genre—weaknesses that make our detective aesthetically interesting, while not "of the kind which outrage ethics," as W.H. Auden reminds us in his essay, "The Guilty Vicarage." Under the name of Peter Alding, he created his series based on Constable Kerr and Inspector Fusil, living in the English seatown of Fortrow. These are engrossing novels of police procedures which also probe the psyche of the police force.

Almost all his novels meet the formula of the whodunit—a murder occurs, there are many suspects, one of whom is the murderer, and the murderer is arrested, dies, or in certain cases, is left free, the knowledge of his crime being its own kind of punishment. What he varies is the point of view of the telling, the country in which the crime is set, the particular motive for the crime, the strategies which lead to its detection and its resolution, and in some cases, the end to which the murderer comes. True to the form when well-practiced, Jeffries's novels embellish the natural and human milieu and make the detective a bungling, but lovable, good man even though most are also professional policemen. His detective fiction descends from Agatha Christie and G.K. Chesterton; his detectives are poetic figures; crime is a complicated matter often resolved not by an appeal to the law, but to a higher morality which provides a suitable redress for those affected by the crime as well as its perpetuators. Jeffries's sympathies often lie with the criminal who committed a dastardly deed for reasons we come to understand. Very often it is only the trappings that are modern in his tales, some derived from "hard-boiled" fiction to give a little more appearance of reality to the crimes. Basically his detectives are romantics.

Evidence of the Accused, An Embarrassing Death, and *Dead Against the Lawyers* are typical of Jeffries's tales of courtroom antics. In *Evidence of the Accused,* skillfully narrated in the first person, two men, a husband and a lover, are tried consecutively for the murder of a wealthy socialite. Each confesses to the crime when the other is being tried. The ending is a *tour de force* which produces the true murderer and leaves him free, outside the reach of the law. This, surely, is one of Jeffries's most ingenious tales. Like Agatha Christie's *Witness for the Prosecution,* the book has the reader guessing right to the end, and leaves him or her startled by its amorality. In *An Embarrassing Death* circumstantial evidence points to Bill Stemple, an executive, as the murderer of a social-climbing stenographer who has been earning money on the side by posing for pornographic pictures. Stemple is tried and found guilty, but a new trial is ordered in which he is advised to undertake his own defense. He extracts an incriminating admission from the stenographer's boyfriend and his lawyer steps in to win his acquittal. In *Dead Against the Lawyers* Jeffries gives his formulaic plot a novel twist: the hero, though acquitted of murder, returns to his young, weak, opportunistic wife, a captive of her sexual lures.

Jeffries's Inspector Alvarez series derives from the British country-house detective fiction, where the society is a closed one, the suspect must be selected from a small group of guests or occupants of a quaint town, and the detective is slightly eccentric, but doggedly logical. In this series, Inspector Enrique Alvarez, a heavy-set, easy-going Spaniard, sets about solving a number of murders. In *Just Desserts* the death of a woman who has fallen from her balcony appears to be an accident until Alvarez, at the prompting of Brenda, a friend of the pretty, young, dead woman, discovers it is actually a murder. Before the tale is over, he discovers two murders which have been made to appear as accidents and stumbles into the midst of a third. Jeffries, a master at tricky endings, gives the plot another twist. The third murder is no fake, and it is perpetrated by Brenda, with whom Alvarez has fallen in love. Its victim is the murderer who killed twice and caused the suicide of Brenda's husband. It is a case of just desserts and Alvarez permits Brenda to return to England, unapprehended, never even to be suspected. Jeffries conceals the denouement just as ingeniously in *Unseemly End*. In this novel, too, the knight-errant, Inspector Alvarez, takes justice into his own hands. Knowing that too often the law, by demanding justice, makes the innocent suffer, Alvarez extends his deep compassion to a married couple and permits their acts of murder to go unreported so that an innocent daughter of the murdered Dolly Lunt can benefit from the estate. *Murder Begets Murder* finds Alvarez again confronting a seemingly accidental death, through poison, and finding instead a murder and numerous suspects. As in *Just Desserts,* Alvarez knows that a wronged woman will kill and he knows he will not prevent it.

Jeffries has published 14 novels in the Inspector Alvarez series. All adhere to the same formula, but he is sufficiently good at contriving his devious plots that his readers do not tire of his coñac-swilling detective and his stubborn ways of seemingly complicating the apparently most simple of crimes. In *Three and One Make Five* Alvarez finally concludes that the five deaths he has worked with cannot be explained unless he assumes that one of the supposedly dead men is in fact the murderer he seeks. In this tale Jeffries cleverly complicates the same formula he established in *Just Desserts,* namely the woman seductress Alvarez finds himself involved with is herself implicated in the crime, and it is his relationship with her that leads to his discovery of the murderer and the prevention of further crime, while at the same time he is left with the bitter knowledge that the woman used him. In *Layers of Deceit* Alvarez conceals a murder from Superior Chief Salas and allows the murderer to go free, only requiring that the murderer distribute some of his new found wealth to two individuals who had been most hurt by the murdered man. In *Almost Murder,* Alvarez again misleads his superior, allowing a series of murders to be reported as accidents rather than revealing a more sordid tale of corruption of a British member of Parliament whose death opens the novel. In *Relatively Dangerous* Alvarez allows a swindler to go free, but this choice on his part also permits him not to have to apprehend a woman who had attempted to poison the swindler, but has been thwarted due to his change of identity which saved his life and left an unknown hitch-hiker dead. *Death Trick* is plotted with extreme cunning, with the criminal faking death, coming back to life, and faking another death before Alvarez discovers his duplicities, confronts him with them, but again, lets him go free.

As Ashford, Jeffries writes suspense tales in which ordinary, likable people are placed at the center of an action over which they have little control. They find they must depend upon cunning and a survival instinct they never knew they possessed. Generally, a member of the British CID combines tedious discipline with savvy and solves the mystery and arrests the criminal. It is always the psychology of the criminal and the detective that interests Ashford. His plots, like Andrew Garve's, are fascinated with police procedures. Coshings occur in almost every book and usually the assaults upon women are practiced by sadists and homosexuals who delight in torturing women in unmentionable ways.

Ashford is interested in what forces turn a law-abiding citizen into a criminal, or political idealist into a psychopath. *Investigations Are Proceeding* concludes with order restored. Later books end on a grimmer note. In *A Man Will Be Kidnapped Tomorrow,* the hostage is ultimately freed, but not before she has undergone acts of sadistic perversion. In *Three Layers of Guilt* an innocent man is the unknowing pawn in a plot to defraud an insurance company. He has to employ extralegal and violent means before he can be reabsorbed into the fabric of society. In *Hostage to Death* another law-abiding citizen turns criminal, then has to battle the law and the criminals to extricate himself. In *The loss of the Culion* a seasoned sailor finds himself caught in the middle of an insurance swindle. The early chapters of the tale are reminiscent of the early portions of Joseph Conrad's *Lord Jim.* Ashford draws on Jeffries's own experiences in the Merchant Navy in this book. It is a superb suspense tale. In *A Crime Remembered* Ashford weaves another yarn of the sea. This time a man has wrongfully come to believe he is responsible for murder and cannibalism in an event at sea which occurred in his youth during World War II. A murder of an elderly homosexual leads the police to Tourkville and his long repressed memory of the crime in his past. True to the Ashford formula, this crime is solved in such a way that the accused is exonerated.

In *The Anger of Fear* Detective Constable Athana is assigned to prevent any harm coming to the son of an Arab Sheik who plans to attend a British school. The boy is kidnapped by a plot master-minded by a policeman gone bad. Another policeman on the force, and the father of a woman Athana is dating, is subtly drawn into the conspiracy, and to cover himself, he plants evidence to incriminate Athana. It is a tautly plotted novel of police procedures. In *Guilt with Honour* Ashford tracks the course of one man's right to pursue the truth against the denials of high ranking CID officials who are involved in covering up the crime and the pleas of his wife who is certain that both her life and his are endangered by his acts. The protagonist, Bob Howe, a race-car driver, is not entirely likable: at times he seems willing to sacrifice everything for his code of beliefs, for his sense of truth. His insistence on his own rightness nearly costs him and his wife their lives, but in a superbly narrated story, he vindicates himself. He also kills the killer in what appears to be an automobile accident and the police cannot bring him to justice.

An Ideal Crime is another novel in which the falsely accused murderer clears his own name and also permits the real culprit, a former policeman, to go free, punished only by his knowledge that his crime cost the life of a security guard and employee. Again it is Ashford's conviction that many acts cannot be handled by the law and cannot be mended by resorting to the courts which leaves him to mete out his own brand of justice. Most of the books written by Ashford mix the same ingredients: a law-abiding citizen compelled by circumstance to criminal action; a heist or kidnapping of some sort designed by a gang of ex-convicts who are greedy for loot, influence, and power in a world of crime; and a doggedly determined police force with an inspector who uses his intelligence and knowledge of people to ferret out the bizarre elements of the crime and discover the motives of the criminal. Usually, the detective is caught between the illegal code of the criminal and the dispassionate code of law, both of which conspire against the individual and justice.

The Honourable Detective offers another variant of the tale in which crime pays. The police are fettered by laws too protective of criminals so they cannot prevent a brutal, sado-masochistic attack upon an innocent man and his wife. They finally take the law into their own hands. Although their peculiar brand of justice ultimately serves to protect one set of witnesses of the hit-and-run accident which opens the novel, the real witness who recognizes the terrorist who drove the car gets off completely free, even though his unwillingness to give testimony unleashes further murders. At the close of the book he is reaping vast monetary profits from an assassination attempt upon an oil minister.

The books written under the pseudonym of Peter Alding have much in common with the suspense tales of Ashford, but all involve Constable Kerr and Inspector Fusil. Kerr is a young, likable, lusty detective, engaged to a proper young woman. Fusil, Kerr's superior, works long hours, is hard to please, despises criminals—perhaps because he is too much like them—and is mothered by an over-protective wife. Together, Kerr and Fusil work on cases where the evidence is misleading, the public unreliable as witnesses, and the criminals brilliant in their cunning. In *Despite the Evidence* they are pitted against the wit of a wealthy club owner with a past record who is in the midst of planning a $2.5 million jewel theft. In *Murder Is Suspected* Fusil stands against his peers and insists on investigating a hit-and-run accident. In *Murder among Thieves* Kerr and Fusil resist the obvious explanation of the heist of a pay-truck and what appears to be the murder of two security guards and finally identify the thief who has been murdering his own co-conspirators. *Guilt Without Proof* and *The C.I.D Room* treat a similar theme. In *Betrayed by Death* a community is terrorized by a murderer who has killed eight young boys. Fusil, who has a young son, is obsessed by the murders. Cleverly, he recognizes a connection between the murders of the young boys and a spate of petty thefts. He and Kerr pursue every clue, ultimately cracking the fake alibis of the gang of thieves and discovering the identity of the sex-offender. Alding spins a good tale, recounts the myriad details the police must put in order if they are to find the criminal, fleshes out his characters, and offers good descriptions of the seaside locale.

Jeffries in all his guises can be depended upon to tell a good whodunit. His detectives believe in duty and honor, but this is a fallen world, and they usually have to tamper with evidence, inflict pain and go outside the law before they can bring criminals to justice, or, as in most cases, leave the criminal unapprehended. In his detective tales, often it is poetic, not legal, justice that reigns. And his criminals are always motivated by greed and hunger for power.

—Carol Simpson Stern

———

JEPSON, Selwyn. British. Born in 1899; son of the writer Edgar Jepson. Educated at St. Paul's School, London; the Sorbonne, Paris. Served in the Royal Tank Corps, 1918, and in Military Intelligence and the Special Operations Executive during World War II: Major. Married twice; one son and two daughters. Worked for Associated Press publishers in the early 1920's. *Died 10 March 1989.*

CRIME PUBLICATIONS

Novels (series: Eve Gill; Ian MacArthur)

The Qualified Adventurer (MacArthur). London, Hutchinson, and New York, Harcourt Brace, 1922; as *Manchu Jade,* London, Mellifont Press, 1935.
Puppets of Fate. London, Hutchinson, 1922.
That Fellow MacArthur. London, Hutchinson, 1923.
The King's Red-Haired Girl. London, Hutchinson, 1923.
Golden-Eyes. London, Harrap, 1924; as *The Sutton Papers,* New York, Dial Press, 1924.
Rogues and Diamonds. London, Harrap, and New York, Dial Press, 1925.
Snaggletooth. London, Harrap, 1926.
The Death Gong. London, Harrap, and New York, Watt, 1927.
Love—and Helen. London, Harrap, and New York, Watt, 1928.
Tiger Dawn. London, Hodder and Stoughton, 1929.
I Met Murder. London, Hodder and Stoughton, and New York, Harper, 1930.
The Floating Admiral, with others. London, Hodder and Stoughton, 1931; New York, Doubleday, 1932.
Rabbit's Paw. London, Hodder and Stoughton, 1932; as *The Mystery of the Rabbit's Paw,* New York, Harper, 1932.
Love in Peril. London, Mellifont Press, 1934.
The Wise Fool. London, Mellifont Press, 1934.
Keep Murder Quiet. London, Joseph, 1940; New York, Doubleday, 1941.
Man Running (Gill). London, Macdonald, 1948; as *Outrun the Constable,* New York, Doubleday, 1948; as *Killer by Proxy,* New York, Bantam, 1950.
Riviera Love Story. London, Mellifont Press, 1948.
Tempering Steel. London, Mellifont Press, 1949.
The Golden Dart (Gill). London, Macdonald, and New York, Doubleday, 1949.
The Hungry Spider (Gill). New York, Doubleday, 1950; London, Macdonald, 1951.
Man Dead. London, Collins, and New York, Doubleday, 1951.
The Black Italian (Gill). London, Collins, and New York, Doubleday, 1954.
The Assassin. London, Collins, and Philadelphia, Lippincott, 1956.
A Noise in the Night. London, Hart Davis, and Philadelphia, Lippincott, 1957.
The Laughing Fish (Gill). London, Hart Davis, 1960; as *Verdict in Question,* New York, Doubleday, 1960.
Fear in the Wind (Gill). London, W.H. Allen, 1964.
The Third Possibility. London, W.H. Allen, 1965.
The Angry Millionaire. New York, Harper, 1968; London, Macmillan, 1969.
Letter to a Dead Girl. London, Macmillan, 1971.

Short Stories

Heads and Tails, with Michael Joseph. London, Jarrolds, 1933.

Uncollected Short Stories

"By the Sword," in *A Century of Detective Stories,* edited by G.K. Chesterton. London, Hutchinson, 1935.
"The Tea Leaf," with Robert Eustace, in *Tales of Detection.* London, Dent, 1936.
"The Case of the Absconding Financier," in *Creeps, Crimes, and Thrills.* London, Samuel, 1936.

"Nor the Jury," in *Ellery Queen's Mystery Magazine* (New York), February 1947.
"Letter of the Law," in *Ellery Queen's Mystery Magazine* (New York), July 1952.

OTHER PUBLICATIONS

Plays

Dark Horizon, with Lesley Storm (produced London, 1935).

Screenplays: *Going Gay* (*Kiss Me Goodbye*), with John Marks and K.R.G. Browne, 1933; *For Love of You*, 1933; *Money Mad*, 1934; *The Love Test*, with Jack Celestin, 1935; *The Riverside Murder*, with Leslie Landau, 1935; *Dark World*, with Leslie Landau, 1935; *Wedding Group* (*Wrath of Jealousy*), with Hugh Brooke, 1936; *The Scarab Murder Case*, 1936; *Toilers of the Sea*, 1936; *Well Done, Henry*, with Wilfred Noy and A. Barr-Smith, 1937; *Carnet de bal*, with others, 1937; *Sailing Along*, with Lesser Samuels and Sonnie Hale, 1938.

Radio Plays: *The Hungry Spider* (serial), 1958; *The Bath That Sang*, 1958; *Friend of the Man Smith*, 1958; *The Commodore's Ruby*, 1958; *Tears for the Bride*, 1959; *A Noise in the Night*, 1959; *Art for Art's Sake*, 1959; *Small Brother*, 1960; *Uncle Murderer*, 1960; *Call It Greymail*, 1963; *The Golden Dart*, 1968.

Television Plays: *Scheherazade*, with Irving Rubine, 1956; *The Face of the Law*, with Lance Sieveking, 1957.

*

Theatrical Activities:

Director: **Film**—*Toilers of the Sea*, with Ted Fox, 1936.
Selwyn Jepson commented (1984):
   I have never pretended to write anything more serious than fairy stories for grownups.

*   *   *

Selwyn Jepson had a long career of writing thrillers—most of which feature a chase or quest of some sort. The early and uncharacteristic fairy tale for adults, *The Death Gong*, tells of Sir John Perrin's search for his beloved who has been kidnapped from Italy and is on a ship bound for Tunis. His American millionaire friend Carfew Northcote, a collector of antiquities, has triggered this situation because he urgently seeks the ancient gong whose vibrations are powerful enough to kill.

   Jepson's most impressive performance, *Keep Murder Quiet*, a variation of the *Hamlet* story, has often been compared to Philip MacDonald's 1938 book, *The Nursemaid Who Disappeared*, which it resembles in technique. It tells the story of Roger Spain who swears vengeance on the man who brutally murdered his father, but has next to nothing to help him identify and locate the man whom he would destroy.

   Jepson's series character, the attractive Eve Gill, was featured in six thrillers written between 1948 and 1964. Although she narrates her own peripatetic adventures, her mode of story-telling is never overly-feminine, and the constant physical movement and suspenseful situations have a strong appeal to all readers, men or women. Most of Eve's problems are caused by her father Commodore Rupert Gill's constant desire to smuggle goods—usually drinkable—into England in spite of confinement to a wheelchair. The first Eve Gill title is

indicative of the plots of the series: *Man Running*, changed to *Outrun the Constable* in America.

—Charles Shibuk

———

JESSE, F(ryniwyd) Tennyson. Also wrote as Beamish Tinker. British. Born Wynifried Tennyson Jesse in 1888. Studied painting with Stanhope Forbes in Newlyn, Cornwall. Married Harold Marsh Harwood in 1918. Journalist from age 20: reporter for the *Times* and *Daily Mail*, and reviewer for the *Times Literary Supplement* and the *English Review*, all London; staff member, *Metropolitan Magazine*, New York, 1914; war correspondent (unaccredited), 1914–18; during World War I worked for the Ministry of Information and as a French Red Cross visitor to frontline hospitals. Fellow, Royal Society of Literature. *Died 6 August 1958.*

CRIME PUBLICATIONS

Novels

The Man Who Stayed at Home (as Beamish Tinker).   London, Mills and Boon, 1915.
A Pin to See the Peepshow.   London, Heinemann, and New York, Doubleday, 1934.
Double Death, with others.   London, Gollancz, 1939.

Short Stories

The Solange Stories.   London, Heinemann, and New York, Macmillan, 1931.

Uncollected Short Stories

"Last Times," in *Many Mysteries*, edited by E. Phillips Oppenheim.   London, Rich and Cowan, 1933.
"Treasure Trove," in *My Best Thriller*.   London, Faber, 1933.
"The Mask," in *And the Darkness Falls*, edited by Boris Karloff.   Cleveland, World, 1946.
"In Death They Were Divided," in *Ellery Queen's Mystery Magazine* (New York), August 1948.
"The Railway Carriage," in *Fantasy and Science Fiction* (New York), February 1951.
"Lord of the Moment," in *Ellery Queen's Mystery Magazine* (New York), February 1951.

OTHER PUBLICATIONS

Novels

The Milky Way.   London, Heinemann, 1913; New York, Doran, 1914.
Secret Bread.   London, Heinemann, and New York, Doran, 1917.
The White Riband; or, A Young Female's Folly.   London, Heinemann, 1921; New York, Doran, 1922.
Tom Fool.   London, Heinemann, and New York, Knopf, 1926.
Moonraker; or, The Female Pirate and Her Friends.   London, Heinemann, and New York, Knopf, 1927.
The Lacquer Lady.   London, Heinemann, 1929; New York, Macmillan, 1930.

Act of God. London, Heinemann, and New York, Greystone Press, 1937.
The Alabaster Cup. London, Evans, 1950.
The Dragon in the Heart. London, Constable, 1956.

Short Stories

Beggars on Horseback. London, Heinemann, and New York, Doran, 1915.
Many Latitudes. London, Heinemann, and New York, Knopf, 1928.

Plays

The Mask, with H.M. Harwood, adaptation of a story by Jesse (as *The Black Mask,* produced New York, 1913; as *The Mask,* produced London, 1915). Published in *Three One-Act Plays,* by Harwood, London, Benn, 1926.
Billeted, with H.M. Harwood (as *The Lonely Soldiers,* produced Pittsburgh, 1917; as *Billeted,* produced New York and London, 1917). London, French, 1920.
The Hotel Mouse, with H.M. Harwood, adaptation of a play by Paul Armont and Marcel Gerbidon (produced London, 1921).
Quarantine (produced Brighton and London, 1922; New York, 1924).
The Pelican, with H.M. Harwood (produced London, 1924; New York, 1925). London, Benn, 1926.
Anyhouse (produced London, 1925). London, Heinemann, 1925.
How to Be Healthy Though Married, with H.M. Harwood (produced London, 1930). London, Heinemann, 1930.
Birdcage, with Harold Dearden (produced London, 1950).
A Pin to See the Peepshow, with H.M. Harwood, adaptation of the novel by Jesse (produced London, 1951; New York, 1953).

Screenplay: *San Demetrio—London,* with Robert Hamer and Charles Frend, 1943.

Verse

The Happy Bride. London, Heinemann, and New York, Doran, 1920.
The Compass and Other Poems. London, Hodge, 1951.

Other

The Sword of Deborah: First-Hand Impressions of the British Women's Army in France. London, Heinemann, and New York, Doran, 1919.
Murder and Its Motives. London, Heinemann, and New York, Knopf, 1924; revised edition, London, Harrap, 1952.
Sabi Pas; or, I Don't Know. London, Heinemann, 1935.
The London Front: Letters Written to America, August 1939–July 1940, with H.M. Harwood. London, Constable, 1940; New York, Doubleday, 1941.
While London Burns: Letters Written to America, July 1940–June 1941, with H.M. Harwood. London, Constable, 1942.
The Saga of San Demetrio. London, HMSO, and New York, Knopf, 1942.
The Story of Burma. London, Macmillan, 1946.
Comments on Cain (on murder trials). London, Heinemann, 1948.

Editor, *The Trial of Madeleine Smith.* London, Hodge, 1927; revised edition, 1950.

Editor, *The Trial of Samuel Herbert Dougal.* London, Hodge, 1928.
Editor, *The Baffle Book,* by Lassiter Wren and Randle Mac Kay. London, Heinemann, 1930.
Editor, *The Trial of Sidney Harry Fox.* London, Hodge, 1934.
Editor, *The Trial of Alma Victoria Rattenbury and George Percy Stoner.* London, Hodge, 1935.
Editor, *The Trial of Thomas John Ley and Lawrence John Smith.* London, Hodge, 1947.
Editor, *The Trial of Timothy John Evans and John Reginald Halliday Christie.* London, Hodge, 1957.

Translator, *The City Curious,* by Jean de Bosschère. London, Heinemann, and New York, Dodd Mead, 1920.

*

Critical Study: *A Portrait of Fryn: A Biography of F. Tennyson Jesse* by Joanna Colenbrander, London, Deutsch, 1984.

* * *

Although one of Sinclair Lewis's characters admired F. Tennyson Jesse's play *The Black Mask* ("Glorious ending, where this woman looks at the man with his face all blown away, and she just gives one horrible scream"), Jesse has survived best as the author of the realistic novel *A Pin to See the Peepshow.*

Closely based on the 1922 Bywaters-Thompson case, this long narrative describes the life and death of Julia Almond, an Emma Bovary of World War I, of Herbert Starling, her nagging older husband, and of Leonard Carr, her much younger lover, who unexpectedly attacks and kills Starling. Julia is charged with inciting him to murder, and both are executed. Jesse devoted many pages to the trial of Julia and Leonard; in her account of the trial and in her interpretation of Julia's character, she followed the Bywaters-Thompson volume edited by Filson Young in the "Notable British Trials" series, several volumes of which Jesse herself edited. Like Edith Thompson, Julia is hanged, partly because of bad luck in her defense and her judge, but chiefly because she wrote her lover many letters describing her imaginary attempts to poison her husband, fictive letters which were intended to assure him of her devotion even unto murder and which were part of Julia's continuous secret reverie. She murders in dreams and wakes to find it taken as true.

Jesse's novel begins when Julia is a school-girl, vital, vivid, already living in imagination. The author fills in much detail, physical, social, and psychological: the background of the war and its new freedoms; the early 1920's; Julia's dull, intrusive family; her first physical attraction, to Alfie, who dies in France; her satisfying, competent work for a superior dress shop; her heavy husband, demanding his "rights" in her bedroom with Chinese-patterned chintzes; her pleasure in the theatre; her brief episodes of utter delight with Leonard when flesh and fantasy unite; her sordid abortion of Herbert's child; Leonard's gift of an Italian officer's cape, which Julia's mother sells to "the waxwork people" for 50 pounds. For the murder itself Jesse drew heavily on testimony at the trial, and, like Young, she pointed out that had Edith/Julia belonged to a class in which divorce was easily affordable and socially acceptable, she would not have been destroyed.

Jesse's style is sometimes rather heavy and her ironies rather too emphatic, as when the prison doctor thinks that Julia has "evaded the womb's responsibilities, while partaking of its pleasures" and that nature has had its "last ironic revenge in the body of the man who had killed for what he had called love, making a final gesture, lewd as a sneer." Yet the description of Julia's consciousness of her dwindling life as she waits for execution and of the prison routine which delivers her, collapsed and drugged, through the door to the gallows, produces in the reader a cold realization of the helplessness of mortality and is far more effective than its sentimental prototype, "The Ballad of Reading Gaol."

—Jane W. Stedman

JESSUP, Richard. Also wrote as Richard Telfair. American. Born in 1925. Merchant sailor for 11 years. *Died 22 October 1982.*

CRIME PUBLICATIONS

Novels

The Cunning and the Haunted. New York, Fawcett, 1954.
A Rage to Die. New York, Fawcett, 1955.
Cry Passion. New York, Dell, 1956.
Night Boat to Paris. New York, Dell, 1956; London, Consul, 1960.
The Young Don't Cry. New York, Fawcett, 1957; London, Miller, 1959.
The Man in Charge. London, Secker and Warburg, 1957.
Lowdown. New York, Dell, and London, Secker and Warburg, 1958.
The Deadly Duo. New York, Dell, 1959; London, Boardman, 1961.
Port Angelique. New York, Fawcett, 1961.
Wolf Cop. New York, Fawcett, 1961; London, Muller, 1963.
Threat. New York, Viking Press, and London, Gollancz, 1981.

Novels as Richard Telfair (series: Monty Nash in all books except *Target for Tonight*)

The Bloody Medallion. New York, Fawcett, 1959; London, Muller, 1960.
The Corpse That Talked. New York, Fawcett, 1959; London, Muller, 1960.
Scream Bloody Murder. New York, Fawcett, 1960; London, Muller, 1961.
Good Luck, Sucker. New York, Fawcett, 1961; London, Muller, 1962.
The Slavers. New York, Fawcett, 1961; London, Muller, 1962.
Target for Tonight (novelization of television series). New York, Dell, 1962.

OTHER PUBLICATIONS

Novels

Cheyenne Saturday. New York, Fawcett, 1957; London, Fawcett, 1958.
Comanche Vengeance. New York, Fawcett, 1957; London, Fawcett, 1959.
Long Ride West. New York, Fawcett, 1957; London, Fawcett, 1958.
Texas Outlaw. New York, Fawcett, 1958; London, Fawcett, 1959.

Sabadilla. New York, Fawcett, 1960; London, Muller, 1961.
Chuka. New York, Fawcett, 1961; London, Muller, 1962.
The Cincinnati Kid. Boston, Little Brown, 1963; London, Gollancz, 1964.
The Recreation Hall. Boston, Little Brown, 1967.
Sailor. Boston, Little Brown, 1969.
A Quiet Voyage Home. Boston, Little Brown, and London, Hutchinson, 1970.
Foxway. Boston, Little Brown, 1971.
The Hot Blue Sea. New York, Doubleday, 1974; London, W.H. Allen, 1975.

Novels as Richard Telfair

Wyoming Jones. New York, Fawcett, 1958; London, Fawcett, 1959.
Day of the Gun. New York, Fawcett, 1958; London, Fawcett, 1960.
The Secret of Apache Canyon. New York, Fawcett, 1959; London, Muller, 1960.
Wyoming Jones for Hire. New York, Fawcett, 1959; London, Muller, 1960.
Sundance. New York, Fawcett, 1960; London, Muller, 1961.

Plays

Screenplays: *The Young Don't Cry,* 1957; *Chuka,* 1967.

* * *

Richard Jessup attained his greatest fame in 1963 with the publication of his first hardcover novel, *The Cincinnati Kid,* and its subsequent movie version. But before writing that book, Jessup had served a lengthy apprenticeship, writing a number of paperback novels. Several of these books, despite their appearance in bibliographies devoted to crime fiction, are related to criminous topics only peripherally. *The Cunning and the Haunted,* for example, is basically the story of a boy's coming of age in a Georgia orphanage, though a sub-plot does involve a well-planned escape from a chain gang. *A Rage to Die* features crooked politicians and prostitutes, but its major concern is the fate of a man driven by inner forces he scarcely understands. It hardly touches on crime at all.

Night Boat to Paris is Jessup's first real genre novel, a story of stolen microfilm and its recovery. The story's protagonist is so cold-blooded that the book is generally unconvincing, however, and *Cry Passion* published the same year, is much better. It is a police procedural in which the ambitions of everyone involved in a murder investigation, with the exception of one honest cop, seem to count for more than justice. Jessup returns to this theme in *Wolf Cop,* in which a policeman accused of being a "compulsive law enforcement officer" becomes the focal point of the story. The question of his character comes to overshadow the crimes he is investigating.

The Deadly Duo, Jessup's attempt at a "clever" mystery with a twist ending, doesn't quite work. The plot seems too incredible, and the characters, usually Jessup's strong point, are not entirely convincing. *Port Angelique,* on the other hand, works very well, despite the use of a *deus ex machina* to resolve the various plot threads. The Caribbean setting is carefully detailed, and there are more plots, sub-plots, and counter-plots than anyone would expect to find in a book of fewer than 175 pages.

According to Allen J. Hubin's *Bibliography,* Jessup also wrote a number of novels as Richard Telfair. The books in Telfair's Monty Nash series are outrageously entertaining, tongue-in-cheek spy novels. Nash works for the Department of

Counter Intelligence, the only lone operative in an organization whose members usually work in two-man teams. The action in the Nash stories is literally non-stop, and Nash is perhaps the toughest spy in literature, a sort of latter-day Race Williams. Though he is also clearly related to the narrator of *Night Boat to Paris*, Nash is not to be taken too seriously as he pursues "the Reds" ("There is only one enemy," he says). In *The Slavers*, readers discover just how tough and single-minded Nash can be: "It takes a lot of man to shoot someone down in cold blood, especially a woman," he says after having done exactly that. "I'm a lot of man."

After the success of *The Cincinnati Kid*, Jessup published fewer books, and few of these were related to crime or mystery. *A Quiet Voyage Home* is interesting for its depiction of the violent takeover of an ocean liner by college students, but the best of the later novels is *Threat*, an excellent thriller. The story deals with a Viet Nam veteran and his desire to obtain the freedom of his twin brother, still being held captive in Southeast Asia. When he learns that he can buy his brother's freedom for four million dollars, the veteran, a demolitions expert, decides to hold a gun (figuratively speaking) to the head of the owner of a luxury apartment hotel, and to reach others through him. The caper is exciting and meticulously worked out, the resolution is satisfactory, and the result is one of Jessup's best books, a worthy close to a notable career.

—Bill Crider

JOHNS, Veronica Parker. American. Born in New York City, 28 December 1907. Attended Columbia School of Journalism, 1925–26. Married Richard Johns in 1935 (died). From 1964, Owner, Seashells Unltd. Inc., New York. President, New York Shell Club, 1975. *Died*

CRIME PUBLICATIONS

Novels (series: Webster Flagg; Agatha Welch)

Hush, Gabriel! (Welch).   New York, Duell, 1941.
Shady Doings (Welch).   New York, Duell, 1941.
The Singing Widow.   New York, Duell, 1941.
Murder by the Day (Flagg).   New York, Doubleday, 1953.
Servant's Problem (Flagg).   New York, Doubleday, 1958.

Uncollected Short Stories

"Bezique of Death," in *Maiden Murders*.   New York, Harper, 1946.
"Homecoming," in *The Queen's Awards 7*, edited by Ellery Queen.   Boston, Little Brown, 1952; London, Gollancz, 1954.
"The Gentleman Caller," in *The Queen's Awards 10*, edited by Ellery Queen.   Boston, Little Brown, 1955; London, Collins, 1957.
"Mr. Hyde-de-Ho," in *The Queen's Awards 11*, edited by Ellery Queen.   New York, Simon and Schuster, 1956; London, Collins, 1958.
"The Bushy-Haired Stranger," in *Mercury* (New York), February 1956.
"The Cannibal Queen," in *Mike Shayne Mystery Magazine* (New York), February 1957.
"The Cannibal Oxen," in *Mike Shayne Mystery Magazine* (London), October 1957.

"Kold Komfort," in *The Saint* (London), December 1961.
"Green Goose Chase," in *Ellery Queen's Mystery Magazine* (New York), October 1962.
"No Trace," in *Murder Mixture*, edited by Elizabeth Lee. London, Elek, 1963.
"Webster and the Wienerwalz," in *The Saint Magazine Reader*, edited by Leslie Charteris and Hans Santesson.   New York, Doubleday, 1966; as *The Saint's Choice*, London, Hodder and Stoughton, 1967.

OTHER PUBLICATIONS

Other

She Sells Sea Shells.   New York, Funk and Wagnalls, 1968.

*   *   *

Veronica Parker Johns was an active member of the Mystery Writers of America during its formative years. She held offices in the newly formed organization and contributed by writing and performing the skits presented during the annual awards dinner. She wrote short stories for such magazines as *Ellery Queen's Mystery Magazine* and *The Saint*.

Her best known character is Webster Flagg, houseman, landlord, and former actor and singer. *Murder by the Day* introduced him to the reading public in 1953; *Servant's Problem* was published in 1958, and he also appears in the short story "Webster and the Wienerwalz."

Webster learned how to serve when Belasco set a fashion for negro butlers, and was taught about fine Italian cooking by Caruso when they were both in *Aida*. Experience taught him to save his money, but even with it invested in securities and real estate, he has found it necessary to work on a semiregular basis. He is houseman for the disagreeable Mr. Rutherford, an art collector, who is found burned to death in a fireproof chair. Webster's key to the flat comes up missing from his key chain, and to avert suspicion he begins investigating the rest of the occupants of the building, finding that all the other residents were either related to the dead man or employed by him in some capacity or other. The police are willing to take all the help they can get in the baffling case. Through eavesdropping during a lobster thermidor dinner party he has prepared and served to the apparent beneficiaries of the Rutherford estate, Webster finds the method, motive, and solution, although not in time to prevent another murder. An unusual will provides an adroit, double-twist ending.

Servant's Problem has the same setting—a single building full of assorted residents who are up to something, but, in this case, a young woman whose father is a friend of Webster's asks him to find out what is going on. The building has been sublet by the owner with the proviso that Stella (the young woman) be retained as the maid. She is attacked in an apparent mugging while wearing a coat given to her by one of the building's occupants. Webster takes her place on the job to investigate from within. Another party provides Webster with the necessary clues about what is going on and about what might be buried in the garden.

Webster is much given to soliloquies, and it is through this device that the reader gets to know what he is thinking, and how his logical mind works. The atmosphere of New York is well done in both books with attention paid to the transportation system, current slang, and fashion. The characters, many from out of town, are realistic and memorable.

Two of her earlier books chronicle the criminological and romantic adventures of Agatha Prentiss (née Welch) in the

Virgin Islands and Connecticut. In *Hush, Gabriel!* Agatha, well on her way to becoming a professional spinster, is invited by her much younger sister, Clotilda, to visit her and her husband on a Caribbean island. When a house guest is found murdered and suspicion seems to be settling on Clotilda, Agatha gets fully involved with the assistance of Judge Prentiss, also an island resident. *Shady Doings* has Agatha back in suburban Connecticut, where murder intrudes. Johns's familiarity with the area is evident in her careful, colorful descriptions of places and atmosphere.

The Singing Widow is best remembered for its dialogue and the dire predicament of Mona Fenton, bride of two weeks and now, suddenly, a widow. The Brooklyn-born singer finds herself in a Virginia town named after her late husband's family, and hires a detective to get details of her bridegroom's death. It is a bright and fast-moving story with entangling family relationships exposed, at last, by the young hero, after he has set Mona up as a mysterious night club singer who wears only black.

John's talents were equally divided between the spatial limitations of the short story and the novel; however her best work was in the two-book Webster Flagg series where character development was an integral part of the plot.

Johns gave up mystery writing to run a shop in New York City which she tells about in her autobiographical, *She Shells Sea Shells*.

—Ellen A. Nehr

JOHNSON, E(mil) Richard. American. Born in Printice, Wisconsin, 23 April 1937. Served in the United States Army Intelligence, 1956–60: Sergeant. Married 1) Joan Balie in 1959 (divorced 1961); 2) Kathy Heldt in 1979; one daughter. Logger, forester for Department of Agriculture, 1962–64, ranch hand, and well-driller. Since 1964 inmate in Stillwater State Prison, Wisconsin, serving a third sentence. Recipient: Mystery Writers of America Edgar Allan Poe award, 1968. Address: Box 55 Stillwater, Minnesota, U.S.A.

CRIME PUBLICATIONS

Novels (series: Tony Lonto)

Silver Street (Lonto). New York, Harper, 1968; as *The Silver Street Killer*, London, Hale, 1969.
The Inside Man (Lonto). New York, Harper, 1969; London, Macmillan, 1970.
Mongo's Back in Town. New York, Harper, 1969; London, Macmillan, 1970.
Cage Five Is Going to Break. New York, Harper, 1970; London, Macmillan, 1971.
The God Keepers. New York, Harper, 1970; London, Macmillan, 1971.
Case Load—Maximum. New York, Harper, 1971.
The Judas. New York, Harper, 1971.
The Cardinalli Contract. New York, Pyramid, 1975.
Blind Man's Bluff. New York, St. Martin's Press, 1987.
The Hands of Eddy Loyd. New York, St. Martin's Press, 1988.
Dead Flowers. New York, International Polygonics, 1990.

OTHER PUBLICATIONS

Other

Fur, Food and Survival. Miami, Florida, Flores, 1988.

*

Manuscript Collection: Mugar Memorial Library, Boston University.

E. Richard Johnson comments:
After more than 20 years of writing from prison I look forward to writing outside where research material is available. With the story notes I've collected on the prison yard over the years, I have enough mystery ideas to last more than my lifetime. Here, my problem isn't finding story ideas—it's which stories to write and what research material is available.

*   *   *

The publication of E. Richard Johnson's *Silver Street* in 1968 heralded the addition of a major new talent to the ranks of the established crime novelists. In this and the 10 novels which followed, Johnson, writing from his cell in Minnesota's Stillwater State Prison, presented his uncompromising insider's view of the dark underbelly of American life—the neon-spangled world of crime, "where cruelty of man to man was a matter of fact." Urban cesspools of depravity with names like The Strip and Pimp's Row "are a cop's nightmare, a festering gash on the city's face that stinks of evil when you walk it on dark nights" and "you know the evil is real, and the hate is there."

In Johnson's urban nightmare two basic themes provide the connecting link. First, everyone is driven by compulsive needs, desires, and social pressures into ways of life, character, and behavior from which there is no escape. All are trapped—the winos, pimps, and whores, the narcotics suppliers, pushers, and addicts, the gangsters, hit-men, and killers, even the policemen, good or bad, honest or dishonest, compassionate or brutal—all alike must function according to the dictates of their own immutable natures. They have no choice. Second, everyone betrays or is betrayed by his own or others' needs. Johnson's best two novels—*Silver Street* and *Case Load—Maximum*—demonstrate both these themes superlatively. In the former, the policeman-hero discovers that the woman he loves is a prostitute, his experience thus paralleling that of the psychopathic killer of pimps he has been assigned to apprehend and forcing him to face the seeds of the killer's madness—their common bond, as it were—within himself. In *Case Load—Maximum*—a novel which shows the impossibility of any genuine relationship or communication between the truly criminal and the truly decent—an idealistic young parole officer trusts one of his charges to such a degree that he almost loses his job, but, though he learns that his faith was misplaced, he nevertheless overcomes his disillusionment by hanging on to his idealism. Johnson, working in the tradition of the hard-boiled genre, but adding his own unique insights to it, is undoubtedly one of the best talents that appeared during the 1960's and 1970's.

—Kenneth D. Alley

JOHNSTON, Frank. *See* **DANIELS, Norman A.**

JOHNSTON, Velda. Also writes as Veronica Jason. American. Attended schools in California. Address: c/o Dodd Mead, 79 Madison Avenue, New York, New York 10016, U.S.A.

CRIME PUBLICATIONS

Novels

Along a Dark Path.   New York, Dodd Mead, 1967; Aylesbury, Buckinghamshire, Milton House, 1974.
House above Hollywood.   New York, Dodd Mead, 1968; Aylesbury, Buckinghamshire, Milton House, 1974.
A Howling in the Woods.   New York, Dodd Mead, 1968; London, Hale, 1969.
I Came to the Castle.   New York, Dodd Mead, 1969; as *Castle Perilous,* London, Hale, 1971.
The Light in the Swamp.   New York, Dodd Mead, 1970; London, Hale, 1972.
The Phantom Cottage.   New York, Dodd Mead, 1970; London, Hale, 1971.
The Face in the Shadows.   New York, Dodd Mead, 1971; London, Hale, 1973.
The People on the Hill.   New York, Dodd Mead, 1971; as *Circle of Evil,* London, Hale, 1972.
The Mourning Trees.   New York, Dodd Mead, 1972; Aylesbury, Buckinghamshire, Milton House, 1974.
The Late Mrs. Fonsell.   New York, Dodd Mead, 1972; Aylesbury, Buckinghamshire, Milton House, 1974.
The White Pavilion.   New York, Dodd Mead, 1973; Aylesbury, Buckinghamshire, Milton House, 1974.
Masquerade in Venice.   New York, Dodd Mead, 1973; Aylesbury, Buckinghamshire, Milton House, 1974.
I Came to the Highlands.   New York, Dodd Mead, 1974; Aylesbury, Buckinghamshire, Milton House, 1975.
The House on the Left Bank.   New York, Dodd Mead, 1975.
A Room with Dark Mirrors.   New York, Dodd Mead, 1975; London, Prior, 1976.
Deveron Hall.   New York, Dodd Mead, 1976; London, Prior, 1977.
The Frenchman.   New York, Dodd Mead, and London, Prior, 1976.
The Etruscan Smile.   New York, Dodd Mead, 1977; London, W.H. Allen, 1980.
The Hour Before Midnight.   New York, Dodd Mead, 1978; London, W.H. Allen, 1981.
The Silver Dolphin.   New York, Dodd Mead, 1979; London, Prior, 1981.
The People from the Sea.   New York, Dodd Mead, 1979; London, Prior, 1981.
A Presence in an Empty Room.   New York, Dodd Mead, 1980; London, W.H. Allen, 1982.
The Stone Maiden.   New York, Dodd Mead, 1980; Bath, Chivers, 1983.
The Fateful Summer.   New York, Dodd Mead, 1981; Bath, Chivers, 1983.
So Wild a Heart (as Veronica Jason).   New York, New American Library, 1981.
The Other Karen.   New York, Dodd Mead, 1983; Bath, Chivers, 1985.

Voices in the Night.   New York, Dodd Mead, 1984; Bath, Chivers, 1985.
Shadow Behind the Curtain.   New York, Dodd Mead, 1985; London, Severn House, 1986.
The Crystal Cat.   New York, Dodd Mead, 1985; London, Severn House, 1987.
Fatal Affair.   New York, Dodd Mead, 1986; Bath, Firecrest, 1988.
The House on Bostwick Square.   New York, Dodd Mead, 1987; Bath, Firecrest, 1989.
The Girl on the Beach.   New York, Dodd Mead, 1987.
The Man at Windermere.   New York, Dodd Mead, 1988.
Flight to Yesterday.   New York, St. Martin's Press, 1990.

*   *   *

Velda Johnston's romantic suspense novels contain important elements of detection and center around narrator-protagonists who are self-sufficient, intelligent women in their early or middle twenties and who themselves discover the solutions to their mysteries. Although Johnston uses such staple ingredients of the gothic as the marriage of convenience which becomes a passionate love match (as in *The Late Mrs. Fonsell* and *House above Hollywood*), her characters and plots avoid had-I-but-knownism, and her psychological examinations of her self-aware female heroes avoid stereotypical characterizations.

Although Sag Harbor, Long Island (where Johnston maintains a home), appears frequently, Johnston's novels vary widely in setting, in both time and place. One major type is that set in the present, sometimes in exotic places. *House above Hollywood,* for example, takes its protagonist into the opulent home of a former silent film star who is surrounded by apparently threatening figures, and *The White Pavilion* uses a suitably named Dolor Island, Florida, for its tale of modern drug running which is paralleled with historical illegal importation of slaves for which the island had been a way-station. A tone of evil and impending doom pervades the island and the house where the protagonist has come to visit her cruel, malicious aunt.

In several novels, notably *Voices in the Night* and *Flight to Yesterday,* young women investigate mysteries from their own or their families' pasts in order to set their present lives in order. Novels set entirely in the past tend to be period pieces rather than true historical novels. Thus *The Late Mrs. Fonsell,* set in Sag Harbor in the 1870's, is primarily a story of family intrigue, although some attention is given to economic changes occurring in the period. Similarly, *Masquerade in Venice,* occurring in the 1880's, contains many descriptive passages with much local color but is basically a tale of greed and deception, again based on family relationships. The historical setting, however, is more crucial to *The Man at Windmere,* set in Yorkshire in 1857; her observations of appalling conditions in the mines, including brutal treatment of children and rank injustice toward women, motivate a crucial instigating action by the protagonist.

A true historical novel in which time and place are integrated into plot is *The House on the Left Bank.* Set in Paris during the Franco-Prussian War, the siege of Paris, and the Commune, this novel traces external events, shows their impact on the protagonist, and relates those events to motivations for murder. The protagonist, typically for Johnston's central female characters, insists she wants "to be a *person* as well as a woman" and she deeply needs "to have control of my own life . . . to be able to choose."

Johnston's protagonists usually tell their own stories. *The Man at Windermere,* however, is told in third person, although the point of view is limited to the protagonist. More exceptional is *The Stone Maiden,* presented in an omniscient third-person method, containing flashbacks and using the points of view of three central characters. Although detective elements are important in most of the novels, *The Silver Dolphin* is mainly a story of love thwarted by misunderstandings and pride and accidents of timing. Only in the last eighth of this novel do suspense and the solution and apprehension of the criminal become central.

Though Johnston's plotting tends to be rather simple and straightforward, her novels are tautly crafted and suspenseful. An interesting experiment is *A Presence in an Empty Room,* which combines the central plot motifs of Du Maurier's *Rebecca* and Poe's "Ligeia." The basic situation parallels Du Maurier: a plain and insecure young woman suddenly and unexpectedly marries a wealthy man, owner of an unusual home (here, on the Maine coast); his first wife had appeared to be beautiful, accomplished and good. Like Du Maurier's Rebecca, however, the first wife is gradually revealed to have been faithless and evil. Like Ligeia, she was a powerful personality, and her spirit struggles to conquer her successor's body, briefly succeeding on several occasions. However, Susan, who corresponds to Du Maurier's unnamed narrator and to Poe's Rowena, is one of Johnston's typically resourceful and determined young women, and she seeks out the truth about her predecessor even as she manages to fight off the spiritual onslaught upon her.

Johnston's novels are notable for their portraits of assertive women caught up in intrigues that affect their futures and test their intelligence and courage. These female heroes are equal to the challenges facing them, and, in conquering obstacles, they present to the reader stories filled with suspense and mystery. Though the plot lines of Johnston's novels tend to be rather simple, the depiction of character, the evocation of scene, and the creation of suspense make them effective exemplars of the genre of romantic suspense.

—Mary Jean De Marr

———

JONES, G. Wayman. *See* **DANIELS, Norman A.**

———

JORDAN, Robert Furneaux. *See* **PLAYER, Robert.**

———

JUDD, Harrison. *See* **DANIELS, Norman A.**

———

K

KALLEN, Lucille (née Chernos). American. Born in Los Angeles, California, in 1926. Attended Harbord Collegiate, Toronto. Married Herbert W. Engel in 1952; one son and one daughter. Writer, *Your Show of Shows* television program, N.B.C., New York 1949–54. Since 1954, freelance writer. Agent: Arnold Goodman Associates, 500 West End Avenue, New York, New York 10024. Address: c/o Random House Inc., 201 E. 50th Street, New York, New York 10022, U.S.A.

CRIME PUBLICATIONS

Novels (series: C.B. Greenfield in all books)

Introducing C.B. Greenfield. New York, Crown, and London, Collins, 1979.
The Tanglewood Murder. New York, Wyndham, and London, Collins, 1980.
No Lady in the House. New York, Wyndham, and London, Collins, 1982.
The Piano Bird. New York, Random House, and London, Collins, 1984.
A Little Madness. New York, Random House, and London, Collins, 1986.

OTHER PUBLICATIONS

Novel

Outside There, Somewhere! New York, Macmillan, 1964; as *Gentlemen Prefer Slaves,* London, Cassell, 1973.

Plays

Maybe Tuesday, with Mel Tolkin (produced New York, 1958). New York, French, 1958.
State Fair (book only), adaptation of film version, lyrics by Oscar Hammerstein, music by Richard Rodgers (produced St. Louis, 1969).

Television Writing: scripts for *Bell Telephone Hour; U.S. Steel Hour; David Frost Revue.*

*   *   *

The battle of the sexes rages on in Sloan's Ford, Connecticut, the primary setting for Lucille Kallen's novels featuring newspaper editor C.B. Greenfield and his part-time reporter, Maggie Rome. The battle against crime also continues in Sloan's Ford as Greenfield, an avid amateur detective, dragoons Maggie into reluctantly assisting in his murder investigations. Participation, voluntary or conscripted, in both campaigns stems directly from the carefully delineated personalities of Greenfield and Rome. Consequently, characterization and plot are firmly united.

Despite Maggie's protests, for example, it is impossible to imagine her refusing to investigate the hit-and-run accident which injures a very young employee (*Introducing C.B. Greenfield*), the murder of a musician (*The Tanglewood Murder*), or the murder of Greenfield's cleaning woman (*No Lady in the House*). As reporters, responsible citizens, and very inquisitive individuals, she and Greenfield must act, and they must act redemptively. They do not, however, act harmoniously.

Firmly based on mutual trust and essential respect, their relationship is nevertheless marked by tension and bickering fostered by divergent attitudes and life styles. Greenfield is a curmudgeonly male chauvinist who browbeats any handy female into whatever household or office services he requires, taking her aid as his due—he's the boss, and he's a man. In return for the benefits he expects simply because he is male, Greenfield is perfectly willing to protect the defenseless and to defend his traditional values. He gladly assumes and discharges responsibility, albeit in a very paternalistic fashion.

Except that she must always be on guard against Greenfield's determined exploitation, Maggie Rome's situation is, by her standards, nearly ideal: she enjoys all the fruits of genuine equality with her husband and relishes their mutual capacity for seeing other people, including their grown sons, as individuals who deserve respect. Though she is also willing to assume and to fulfill responsibilities, Maggie is far less apt than Greenfield to infringe on others' rights under the guise of behaving responsibly. Yet, infringe she does, for he insists upon it, saddling her with the most guileful (sometimes frankly deceitful) phases of each investigation.

Maggie's subordinate role in these investigations does not, however, obviate her independence or her individuality. Kallen avoids that pitfall because Maggie is the more active character. She also narrates each story; therefore, her point of view dominates every plot, the readers identify with her rather than with Greenfield. Furthermore, all of his attitudes, actions, heroics, and foibles are subjected to Maggie's tart, stringent evaluations. Though she cheers his strengths, Maggie, the "weaker" partner, also enthusiastically jeers at Greenfield's childish pettiness (he hates change, for instance, and pouts for days over the unavailability of his favorite insect repellant). She thus uses one of exploited people's oldest, cruelest, most effective weapons against him.

Yet Maggie's regard for C.B. Greenfield's essential decency and for their many shared values wards off shrewishness just as her sensitivity and introspection protect her from reader's scorn at allowing herself to be exploited. Maggie Rome understands herself very well, and she is struggling to understand her society. She knows that without her consent he could not impress her into service. She compares and contrasts the roles demanded by her home, her job, and her sleuthing, and to readers' delight, she elects to fight on in Sloan's Ford battles.

For Maggie, the Greenfield-Rome war is always stimulating though often annoying; for readers, it's an enjoyable subplot to the mysteries; for Kallen, it's a clever device which deepens her plots and adds humor to her excellent novels.

—Jane S. Bakerman.

KAMINSKY, Stuart M(elvin). American. Born in Chicago, Illinois, 29 September 1934. Educated at the University of Illinois, Urbana, B.S. in journalism 1957, M.A. in English 1959; Northwestern University, Evanston, Illinois, Ph.D. in speech 1972. Served in the United States Army, 1957–59. Married 1) Merle Gordon in 1959, two sons and one daughter; 2) Enid Lisa Perll in 1988, one daughter. Director, office of Public Information, University of Chicago, 1968–71. Assistant Professor, 1973–75, Associate Professor of Speech, 1975–79, and since 1979, Professor of Radio, Television, and Film, and Head of the Film Division, Northwestern University. Chairman, 1972–74; since 1978, consultant, National Endowment for the Humanities; since 1989 Professor and Director of Florida State University Conservatory of Motion Picture, Television and Recording Arts, Sarasota. Recipient: Mystery Writers of America Edgar Allan Poe award, 1989; Prix du Roman d'adventures, 1990. Agent: Dominick Abel, 146 West 82nd Street, 1B, New York, New York 16024. Address: Florida State University Conservatory of Motion Picture, Television and Recording Arts at the Asolo Center, 5555 North Tamiani Trail, Sarasota, Florida 34243, U.S.A.

CRIME PUBLICATIONS

Novels (series: Toby Peters; Porfiry Petrovich Rostnikov)

Bullet for a Star (Peters). New York, St. Martin's Press, 1977; London, Severn House, 1981.
Murder on the Yellow Brick Road (Peters). New York, St. Martin's Press, 1978; London, Severn House, 1981.
You Bet Your Life (Peters). New York, St. Martin's Press, 1979.
The Howard Hughes Affair (Peters). New York, St. Martin's Press, 1979; London, Severn House, 1980.
Never Cross a Vampire (Peters). New York, St. Martin's Press, 1980.
Rostnikov's Corpse. London, Macmillan, 1981; as *Death of a Dissident*, New York, Ace, 1981.
High Midnight (Peters). New York, St. Martin's Press, 1981; London, Severn House, 1982.
Catch a Falling Clown. New York, St. Martin's Press, 1982.
He Done Her Wrong (Peters). New York, St. Martin's Press, 1983.
When the Dark Man Calls. New York, St. Martin's Press, 1983.
Black Night in Red Square. New York, Berkley, 1983, London, Macdonald, 1988.
The Fala Factor (Peters). New York, St. Martin's Press, 1984.
Down for the Count (Peters). New York, St. Martin's Press, 1985; Bath, Chivers, 1987.
Red Chameleon (Rostnikov). New York, Scribner, 1985.
Exercise in Terror. New York, St. Martin's Press, 1985.
The Man Who Shot Lewis Vance (Peters). New York, St. Martin's Press, 1986.
Smart Moves. New York, St. Martin's Press, 1987.
A Fine Red Rain (Rostnikov). New York, Scribner, 1987.
Think Fast, Mr. Peters. New York, St. Martin's Press, 1988.
A Cold Red Sunrise (Rostnikov). New York, Scribner, 1988.
Buried Caesars (Peters). New York, Mysterious Press, 1989.
Poor Butterfly (Peters). New York, Mysterious Press, 1990.
The Man Who Walked Like a Bear (Rostnikov). New York, Scribner, 1990.

Uncollected Short Stories

"Drup Number One," in *New Mexico Quarterly*, Winter, 1966.
"A Child Shall Lead Them, in *The Man from U.N.C.L.E.* (New York), April 1966.
"It Takes a Child," in *The Man from U.N.C.L.E.* (New York), 1967.
"It Comes with the Badge," in *The Wooster Review*, March 1984.
"The Man Who Shot Lewis Vance," in *The Eyes Have It*, edited by Robert J. Randisi. New York, Mysterious Press, 1985.
"Busted Blossoms," in *Mean Streets*, edited by Robert J. Randisi. New York, Mysterious Press, 1986.
"The Final Toast," in *The New Adventures of Sherlock Holmes* edited by Martin H. Greenberg and Carol-Lynn Rössel Waugh. New York, Mysterious Press, 1986.
"Bitter Lemons," in *The New Adventures of Philip Marlowe.* New York, Knopf, 1988.
"The Batman Memoes," in *The New Adventures of Batman.* New York, Bantam, 1989.
"The Man Who Laughs," in *The New Adventures of the Joker.* New York, Bantam, 1989.

OTHER PUBLICATIONS

Plays

Here Comes the Interesting Part (produced New York, 1968).

Screenplays: *More Pampered than Pets*, 1965; *A Last Minute Marriage*, with Steve Fagin, 1974; *A Black and White Film in Sound and Color*, 1976; *Once upon a Time in America*, with others, 1984; *Enemy Territory*, 1986; *A Woman in the Wind*, 1987.

Other

Don Siegel, Director. New York, Curtis, 1974.
Clint Eastwood. New York, New American Library, 1974.
American Film Genres: Approaches to a Critical Theory of Popular Film. Dayton, Ohio, Pflaum, 1974.
John Huston, Maker of Magic. Boston, Houghton Mifflin, and London, Angus and Robertson, 1978.
Coop: The Life and Legend of Gary Cooper. New York, St. Martin's Press, 1980.
Basic Filmmaking, with Dana Hodgdon. New York, Arco, 1981.
American Film Genres (textbook). Chicago, Nelson Hall, 1984.
American Television Genres, with Jeffrey Mahan. Chicago, Nelson Hall, 1985.
Writing for Television, with Mark Walker. New York, Dell, 1988.

Editor, with Joseph F. Hill, *Ingmar Bergman: Essays in Criticism.* London and New York, Oxford University Press, 1975.

*

Theatrical Activities:

Director: Film—*A Last Minute Marriage*, with Steve Fagin, 1974; *A Black and White Film in Sound and Color*, 1976.

Stuart M. Kaminsky comments:

To date my fiction has been somewhat intentionally eclectic. My Toby Peters novels and short stories have been and continue to be first-person trips into a comic and nostalgic world of the hard-boiled private eye. My Porfiry Petrovich novels set in Moscow are slightly sardonic excursions into the police procedural tale heavily laced with (I hope) hints of Russian literature. My "thrillers" are essentially humorless tales of self-reliant women who must turn and face the dark shadows of their past. Regardless of the formula, however, I want my novels to be entertaining. If there is Meaning in my tales, and I have no doubt that there is as there is in any mythic story, then let it be absorbed rather than academized. My goal is to be a storyteller, a storyteller who transports the reader into the tale, to lose himself or herself for the duration of the reading. It is the power of popular writers ranging from Herman Melville to Raymond Chandler to Stephen King. The process of writing my tales is, I hope, akin to the reader's process in reading them. On my first draft at least, I laugh, am frightened, can't stop going till I find out what will happen. I am, I freely admit, one of my favorite authors. Pity the author who doesn't feel the same about his or her work.

My strengths: an ability to empathize with my characters, all of them, to hear them speak. My weaknesses: a tendency to feel too strongly about them, not to want them to go away. My hopes: to continue to exercise my strengths and weaknesses.

*   *   *

In a recent article in *Mysterious News* (Summer, 1989) Stuart M. Kaminsky alludes to the fantasy behind his fiction, especially in the Toby Peters's series: "I am less interested in exploring the "real" historical figure than in bringing back to life the fantasy we have about those historical figures. Nostalgia is, I guess, the key word . . . Nostalgia, however, is essential to our belief that the life we have lived is poignant." This is not a surprising statment from a writer whose career includes a distinguished record as a professor of film. Kaminsky has written a number of critical studies on major film figures such as Don Siegel, Clint Eastwood, John Huston, and Gary Cooper, books on film theory (*American Film Genres*), books on film-making (*Basic Filmmaking,* with Dana Hodgdon; *Writing for Television,* with Mark Walker), and has a screenplay credit for *Once Upon a Time in America.* The decision to write *Bullet for a Star,* featuring Errol Flynn and introducing Toby Peters, an impoverished private investigator, seems a natural outgrowth of Kaminsky's academic interests.

Toby Peters, hero of some 14 adventures, is a memorable series character. He fits the mold peculiar to the down-and-out private eye in L.A., only he's poorer than most and operates out of quarters shared with an eccentric dentist, Sheldon Minck. Like most P.I.'s, he's divorced, but is always finding an excuse to see his ex-wife Ann. Peters's connection with the police force is through his own brother, Phil Pevsner, a captain in the Wilshire District. Throughout the series, Toby Peters (whose name is derived from Kaminsky's children, Peter Michael and Toby Arthur) operates in a grey area: he knows the law, uses it or evades it according to the circumstances and usually has to account to Phil for his transgressions. Toby is not only without clients much of the time, but frequently without the rent for his landlady, Mrs. Plaut, or money for food. The motivation for taking on impossible cases is the real need for money to live on as well as the sense of honor he feels for doing slightly dubious jobs for famous people such as Howard Hughes (*The Howard Hughes Affair*), Errol Flynn (*Bullet for a Star*), Judy Garland (*Murder on the Yellow Brick Road*), Eleanor Roosevelt (*The Fala Factor*), Gary Cooper (*High Midnight*), the Marx Brothers (*You Bet Your Life*), and Mae West (*He Done Her Wrong*). Toby is fascinated by celebrities, and Kaminsky's unlikely pairing of Toby and his famous clients is part of the fun of reading this series. Kaminsky uses the 1930's and 1940's in a loving, respectful fashion but provides the humor and a spoofish quality through the characters of Toby and his friends. Although the series is formulaic, it is never boring. *Buried Caesars* is a fine illustration of Kaminsky's ability to tell a fast-moving, intricately-plotted story in which the famous and not-so famous mingle. The client in this case is General Douglas MacArthur; the issue is one of national security. Toby's assistant on this caper is none other than Dashiell Hammett, one of the victims of Dr. Minck's "painless dentistry." Kaminsky has managed to avoid the pitfalls of a series character who appears in a number of books. There is always the danger that a series detective can become predictable or repetitive, but this does not happen in the Toby Peters's books because of the famous and near-famous figures who people them.

Kaminsky's other series character, Inspector Porfiry Rostnikov of the MVD, is the complete opposite of Toby Peters, L.A. private investigator. This series of police procedurals presents a very human portrait of a Moscow policeman who is regarded suspiciously by his superiors in the MVD and is not trusted by the KBG. Rostnikov is a talented policeman who breaks the rules, works around bureaucracy, employs clandestine methods, and simply does not fit into the general scheme of themes. He is an outsider because of his marriage to Sarah, a Jewess, and because of his love for her, he agrees to apply for an exit visa which is denied. For this reason, as the series progresses, Rostnikov loses stature and is transferred to offices where his superiors are always giving him impossible cases. They use the threat of sending the couple's only child, Josef, a soldier in the Soviet Army, to an undesirable post, and the young man is assigned to the front in Afghanistan. Rostnikov's cases involve the murder of a dissident, Aleksander Granovsky, whose death must be shown not to have been instigated by the KGB (*Rostnikov's Corpse*), the murder of a journalist and terrorist incidents at the Moscow Film Festival (*Black Night on Red Square*), the murders of circus clowns in connection with an immigration smuggling scheme (*A Fine Red Rain*); the killings of a child, a police commissar, and an elaborate conspiracy against the government (*A Cold Red Sunrise*), and the tracking of a lady sniper (*Red Chameleon*).

Kaminsky's Russian policeman is a man of suffering and forebearance. The reader is aware of the constant pain Rostnikov experiences because of a war wound to his leg. Unless a case is special and warrants use of a police car, he travels by public transport. An avid reader, Rostnikov's favorite authors include the classic Russians (Dostoevsky, Tolstoi, Gorki) and forbidden American detective stories, with Ed McBain's Steve Carella as his hero. Rostnikov's hobbies include weightlifting and fixing toilets. With rare humor, Kaminsky illustrates how the inspector, referred to as Washtub by his colleagues, circumvents the rules in order to repair leaky plumbing and then uses this newly gained expertise to obtain valuable information from witnesses. These qualities and eccentricities almost make the dreary Moscow landscape seem jolly at times.

Similar personal details about Rostnikov's assistants, Sasha and Karpo also add to the humanity of these procedurals. Sasha, a relatively young man, lives in a small apartment with his wife and deaf mother and much of the humor in the novels comes from vignettes of their family life. Karpo, known as the Tatar and frightening in aspect and demeanor, is a persistent policeman who never gives up on a case. Like Rostnikov, he endures chronic pain because of a wound which almost resulted in the amputation of his arm. Sasha and Karpo represent various aspects of Rostnikov (Sasha's family orientation and sense of humanity, Karpo's intensive, thorough, and intuitive approach to cases). Rostnikov is the ideal, the father figure, the one Sasha and Karpo wish to emulate.

Kaminsky has written other types of mystery fiction, the most notable of which is *Exercise in Terror,* a suspense thriller with an unusual ending. The premise rather than the plot is the major interest, buttressed by an increasing intensity in the pace of the suspense. In many ways the book reinforces Kaminsky's talents as a writer of screenplays and television scripts.

In conclusion, Kaminsky is a gifted writer who has created a host of entertaining characters and good stories within two genres, hard-boiled stories and police procedurals. While observing the conventions of the genres, he has avoided their stereotypical qualities, largely through humor and a quiet sense of humanity.

—Katherine M. Restaino

———

KANE, Frank. Also wrote as Frank Boyd. American. Born in Brooklyn, New York, 19 July 1912. Educated at City College of New York, B.S.S.; night law student, St. John's University, Jamaica, New York, 1939–41. Married Ann Herlehy in 1939; three children. Columnist, New York *Press,* 1935–37; editor-in-chief, Trade Newspapers Corporation, New York, 1937–40; associate editor, New York *Journal of Commerce,* 1940–42; public relations director, Conference of Alcoholic Beverage Industries, 1942–46; after 1946 freelance writer, radio and television producer, and President, Frank Kane Corporation, National Liquor Review Company, Frank Kane Associates, and Report to Writers Company. *Died 29 November 1968.*

CRIME PUBLICATIONS

Novels (series: Mickey Denton; Johnny Liddell)

About Face (Liddell). New York, Curl, 1947; as *Death About Face,* Kingston, New York, Quin, 1948; as *The Fatal Foursome,* New York, Dell, 1958.
Green Light for Death (Liddell). New York, Washburn, 1949; London, Mayflower, 1966.
Slay Ride (Liddell). New York, Washburn, 1950.
Bullet Proof (Liddell). New York, Washburn, 1951; London, Mayflower, 1969.
Dead Weight (Liddell). New York, Washburn, 1951.
Bare Trap (Liddell). New York, Washburn, 1952.
Poisons Unknown (Liddell). New York, Washburn, 1953.
Grave Danger (Liddell). New York, Washburn, 1954.
Red Hot Ice (Liddell). New York, Washburn, 1955; London, Boardman, 1956.
Key Witness. New York, Dell, 1956.
A Real Gone Guy (Liddell). New York, Rinehart, 1956; London, Boardman, 1957.
The Living End (Liddell). New York, Dell, 1957.
Liz. Beacon, New York, Beacon Signal, 1958.
Syndicate Girl. New York, Dell, 1958.
Trigger Mortis (Liddell). New York, Rinehart, 1958.
Juke Box King (Denton). New York, Dell, 1959.
The Line-Up (novelization of television play). New York, Dell, 1959; London, Consul, 1960.
The Flesh Peddlers (as Frank Boyd). Derby, Connecticut, Monarch, 1959.
Johnny Staccato (novelization of television play; as Frank Boyd). New York, Fawcett, 1960; London, Consul, 1964.
A Short Bier (Liddell). New York, Dell, 1960; London, Mayflower, 1964.
Time to Prey (Liddell). New York, Dell, 1960; London, Mayflower, 1964.
Due or Die (Liddell). New York, Dell, 1961; London, Mayflower, 1963.
The Mourning After (Liddell). New York, Dell, 1961.
The Conspirators. New York, Dell, 1962.
Crime of Their Life (Liddell). New York, Dell, 1962; London, Mayflower, 1964.
Dead Rite (Denton; Liddell). New York, Dell, 1962; London, Mayflower, 1968.
Ring-a-Ding-Ding (Liddell). New York, Dell, 1963; London, Mayflower, 1964.
Johnny Come Lately (Liddell). New York, Dell, 1963; London, Mayflower, 1964.
Hearse Class Male (Liddell). New York, Dell, 1963; London, Mayflower, 1969.
Barely Seen (Liddell). New York, Dell, and London, Mayflower, 1964.
Final Curtain (Liddell). New York, Dell, and London, Mayflower, 1964.
Fatal Undertaking (Liddell). New York, Dell, 1964; London, Mayflower, 1965.
The Guilt-Edged Frame (Liddell). New York, Dell, 1964.
Esprit de Corpse (Liddell). New York, Dell, 1965.
Two to Tangle (Liddell). New York, Dell, 1965.
Maid in Paris (Liddell). New York, Dell, 1966.
Margin for Terror (Liddell). New York, Dell, 1967.

Short Stories

Johnny Liddell's Morgue. New York, Dell, 1956; London, Consul, 1958.
Stacked Deck. New York, Dell, 1961; London, Mayflower, 1964.

Uncollected Short Stories

"Suicide," in *Rue Morgue 1,* edited by Rex Stout and Louis Greenfield. New York, Creative Age Press, 1946.
"Slay upon Delivery," in *Four-and-Twenty Bloodhounds,* edited by Anthony Boucher. New York, Simon and Schuster, 1950; London, Hammond, 1951.
"The Uncertain Corpse," in *Scarab* (Chicago), November 1950.
"The Frozen Grin," in *Manhunt* (New York), January 1953.
"Payoff," in *Manhunt* (New York), March 1953.
"Evidence," in *Manhunt* (New York), July 1953.
"Slay Belle," in *Manhunt* (New York), August 1953.
"Keeper of the Killed," in *Verdict* (New York), September 1953.
"It's Murder," in *Pursuit* (New York), November 1953.
"The Icepick Artists," in *Manhunt* (New York), December 1953.
"Play-and-Slay Girl," in *Double-Action Detective Stories 1* (New York), 1954.
"Finish the Job," in *Manhunt* (New York), January 1954.
"Bullets, Back to Back," in *The Saint* (New York), March 1954.
"A Package for Mr. Big," in *The Saint* (New York), September 1954.
"Make It Neat," in *Manhunt* (New York), August 1955.
"The Dead Stand-In," in *Manhunt* (New York), January 1956.

"Insurance," in *Accused* (New York), March 1956.

"The Rumble," in *Mike Shayne Mystery Magazine* (New York), February 1957.

"Dead Pigeon," in *Manhunt* (New York), July 1957.

"The Patsy," in *Mike Shayne Mystery Magazine* (New York), August 1957.

"Sleep Without Dreams," in *Dames, Danger, and Death,* edited by Leo Margulies. New York, Pyramid, 1960.

"Pass the Word Along," in *Manhunt* (New York), April 1960.

"The Great Pretender," in *Mike Shayne Mystery Magazine* (New York), July 1960.

"Big Steal," in *The Saint* (New York), May 1962.

"With Frame to Match," in *Come Seven, Come Death,* edited by Henry Morrison. New York, Pocket Books, 1965.

"Play Tough," in *Manhunt* (New York), March 1965.

"Clean-Up," in *Manhunt* (New York), May 1965.

OTHER PUBLICATIONS

Plays

Radio Plays: *The Shadow, The Fat Man, Gangbusters, Claims Agent,* and *Lawless Twenties* series.

Television Plays: *Mike Hammer, S.A. 7,* and *The Investigators* series.

Other

Anatomy of the Whiskey Business. Manhasset, New York, Lake House Press, 1965.
Travel Is for the Birds. Manhasset, New York, Lake House Press, 1966.
Lewis S. Rosenstiel: Industry Statesman. Manhasset, New York, Lake House Press, 2 vols., 1966.

*   *   *

Frank Kane's most popular work was his Johnny Liddell private eye series. Liddell first appeared in the pulps (primarily *Crack Detective*) in 1944. During this time Kane was also working as a script writer for such radio suspense shows as *The Shadow, The Fat Man* and *Gangbusters.* The first Liddell novel was also Kane's first novel, *About Face.* By the time of Kane's death, the 29 books in the series had sold over five million copies. Kane never claimed to be anything but a pulp writer, and his limitations and the high speed at which he wrote are evident in much of his work. He often plagiarized himself, recycling entire scenes and descriptive passages from his previous books and stories. There were little detection and generally far too much killing in the Liddell novels. Yet the writing was always lean and powerful, almost cinematic (during the early 1960's Kane wrote scripts for the *Mike Hammer* television show, among others), and the books are classic examples of the hard-boiled private eye formula, stripped bare of any frills.

In the early books of the series Liddell is an operative for the Acme Detective Agency, working out of New York. By the time of *Dead Weight,* however, he has branched out on his own with an office in Manhattan and a sexy red-haired secretary named Pinky. Though Kane rarely deviated from the basic ingredients of the private eye formula, the books were often distinguished by a gritty, authentic portrayal of New York cops and their methods. Kane's brother was a New York policeman, credited as technical advisor on the series. Kane never again matched the pace and raw storytelling drive that he achieved in

Bullet Proof, probably the best of the Liddell books. His backgrounds were always well researched and vividly realistic, as evidenced by his colorful depiction of New York's Chinatown in *Dead Weight. Fatal Undertaking,* a fine late entry in the series, scores high points for both characterization and a tightly woven plot concerning dirty tricks in UN diplomatic circles.

In addition to the Liddell novels Kane produced a number of non-series suspense paperbacks. The best of these is *Key Witness,* a tersely written story about white precinct cops in Harlem dealing with a teenage gang murder. A claustrophobic air of fear and urban frustration permeates the book, and it is this that lifts *Key Witness* several notches above the better-known Liddell tales.

—Stephen Mertz

––––––––

KANE, Henry. Also writes as Anthony McCall; Kenneth R. McKay; Mario J. Sagola; Katherine Stapleton. American. Born in New York City in 1918. Attorney, then self-employed writer. Address: c/o Arbor House, 235 East 45th Street, New York, New York 10017, U.S.A.

CRIME PUBLICATIONS

Novels (series: Peter Chambers; Inspector McGregor; Marla Trent)

A Halo for Nobody (Chambers). New York, Simon and Schuster, 1947; London, Boardman, 1950; as *Martinis and Murder,* New York, Avon, 1956.
Armchair in Hell (Chambers). New York, Simon and Schuster, 1948; London, Boardman, 1949.
Hang by Your Neck (Chambers). New York, Simon and Schuster, 1949; London, Boardman, 1950.
Edge of Panic. New York, Simon and Schuster, 1950; London, Boardman, 1951.
A Corpse for Christmas (Chambers). Philadelphia, Lippincott, 1951; London, Boardman, 1952; as *The Deadly Doll,* Rockville Centre, New York, Zenith, 1959; as *Homicide at Yuletide,* New York, New American Library, 1966.
Until You Are Dead (Chambers). New York, Simon and Schuster, 1951; London, Boardman, 1952.
Laughter Came Screaming. London, Boardman, 1953; New York, Avon, 1954; as *Mask for Murder,* New York, Avon, 1957.
My Business Is Murder (Chambers; novelets). New York, Avon, 1954.
Trinity in Violence (Chambers; novelets). London, Boardman, 1954; (different contents) New York, Avon, 1955.
Trilogy in Jeopardy (Chambers; novelets). London, Boardman, 1955.
Too French and Too Deadly (Chambers). New York, Avon, 1955; as *The Narrowing Lust,* London, Boardman, 1956.
Who Killed Sweet Sue? (Chambers). New York, Avon, 1956; as *Sweet Charlie,* London, Boardman, 1957.
The Deadly Finger. New York, Popular Library, 1957; as *The Finger,* London, Boardman, 1957.
Death on the Double (Chambers; novelets). New York, Avon, 1957; London, Boardman, 1958.
Death for Sale. New York, Dell, 1957; as *Sleep Without Dreams,* London, Boardman, 1958; New York, Lancer, 1970.

Fistful of Death (Chambers). New York, Avon, 1958; as *The Dangling Man,* London, Boardman, 1959.

Death Is the Last Lover (Chambers). New York, Avon, 1959; as *Nirvana Can Also Mean Death,* London, Boardman, 1959.

The Private Eyeful (Trent). New York, Pyramid, 1959; London, Boardman, 1960.

Peter Gunn (novelization of television play). New York, Dell, 1960.

Run for Doom. London, Boardman, 1960; New York, New American Library, 1962.

The Crumpled Cup. London, Boardman, 1961; New York, New American Library, 1963.

Death of a Flack (Chambers). New York, New American Library, and London, Boardman, 1961.

My Darlin' Evangeline. New York, Dell, 1961; as *Perfect Crime,* London, Boardman, 1961; New York, Belmont, 1967.

Dead in Bed (Chambers). New York, Lancer, 1961; London, Boardman, 1963.

Death of a Hooker (Chambers). London, Boardman, 1961; New York, Avon, 1963.

Kisses of Death (Chambers; Trent). New York, Belmont, 1962; as *Killer's Kiss,* London, Boardman, 1962.

Death of a Dastard (Chambers). London, Boardman, 1962; New York, New American Library, 1963.

Never Give a Millionaire an Even Break (Chambers). New York, Lancer, 1963; as *Murder for the Millions,* London, Boardman, 1964.

Nobody Loves a Loser (Chambers). New York, Belmont, 1963; London, Boardman, 1964; as *Who Dies There?,* New York, Lancer, 1969.

Snatch an Eye (Chambers). London, Boardman, 1963; New York, Permabooks, 1964.

Two Must Die. New York, Tower, 1963; as *Prey by Dawn,* London, Boardman, 1965.

Dirty Gertie. London, Boardman, 1963; New York, Belmont, 1965; as *To Die or Not to Die,* Belmont, 1964.

Frenzy of Evil. London, Boardman, 1963; New York, Dell, 1966.

The Midnight Man (McGregor). New York, Macmillan, 1965; as *Other Sins Only Speak,* London, Boardman, 1965.

Conceal and Disguise (McGregor). New York, Macmillan, and London, Boardman, 1966.

The Devil to Pay (Chambers). London, Boardman, 1966; as *Unholy Trio,* New York, Pocket Books, 1967; as *Better Wed Than Dead,* New York, Lancer, 1970.

Operation Delta (as Anthony McCall). New York, Trident Press, 1966; London, Joseph, 1967.

Holocaust (as Anthony McCall). New York, Trident Press, 1967.

Laughter in the Alehouse (McGregor). New York, Macmillan, 1968; London, Penguin, 1978.

Don't Call Me Madame (Chambers). New York, Lancer, 1969.

The Schack Job (Chambers). New York, Lancer, 1969.

The Bomb Job (Chambers). New York, Lancer, 1970.

Don't Go Away Dead (Chambers). New York, Lancer, 1970.

The Virility Factor. New York, McKay, 1971.

The Glow Job (Chambers). New York, Lancer, 1971.

The Moonlighter. New York, Geis, 1971; London, Hale, 1972.

The Tail Job (Chambers). New York, Lancer, 1971.

Come Kill with Me (Chambers). New York, Lancer, 1972.

The Escort Job (Chambers). New York, Lancer, 1972.

Kill for the Millions (Chambers). New York, Lancer, 1972.

Decision. New York, Dial Press, 1973.

A Kind of Rape. New York, Atheneum, 1974.

The Violator. New York, Warner, 1974.

The Avenger. New York, Atheneum, 1975.

Lust of Power. New York, Atheneum, 1975.

The Tripoli Documents. New York, Simon and Schuster, 1976; London, Hamlyn, 1979.

The Manacle (as Mario J. Sagola). New York, Macmillan, 1978.

Shadow of the Knife (as Kenneth R. McKay). New York, Playboy, 1978.

Without Sin among You (as Katherine Stapleton). New York, Zebra, 1979.

The Naked Bishop (as Mario J. Sagola). New York, Coward McCann, 1980.

Indecent Relations (as Kenneth R. McKay). New York, Playboy, 1982.

The Little Red Phone. New York, Arbor House, 1982.

Short Stories

Report for a Corpse. New York, Simon and Schuster, 1948; London, Boardman, 1950; as *Murder of the Park Avenue Playgirl,* New York, Avon, 1957.

The Case of the Murdered Madame. New York, Avon, 1955; as *Triple Terror,* London, Boardman, 1958.

The Name Is Chambers. New York, Pyramid, 1957.

Kiss! Kiss! Kill! Kill! New York, Lancer, 1970.

Uncollected Short Stories

"The Deadly Sins," in *Manhunt* (New York), May 1957.

"Please Forgive Me," in *Alfred Hitchcock's Mystery Magazine* (New York), January 1959.

"A Corpse That Didn't Die," in *Manhunt* (New York), June 1959.

"Sweet Charlie," in *Dames, Danger, and Death,* edited by Leo Margulies. New York, Pyramid, 1960.

"Death in Bell," in *Ed McBain's Mystery Book 2* (New York), 1960.

"I'm No Hero," in *Suspense* (London), March 1960.

"Ghost Story," in *Alfred Hitchcock's Mystery Magazine* (New York), October 1960.

"Death of a Flack," in *Mike Shayne Mystery Magazine* (New York), November 1960.

"The Gorgeous Murderer," in *Mike Shayne Mystery Magazine* (New York), May 1961.

"The Death of the Golden Trumpet," in *Mike Shayne Mystery Magazine* (New York), November 1962.

"Circle of Jeopardy," in *Manhunt* (New York), July 1964.

"The Memory Guy," in *Come Seven, Come Death,* edited by Henry Morrison. New York, Pocket Books, 1965.

"Graveyard Shift," in *Manhunt* (New York), June–July 1966.

OTHER PUBLICATIONS

Other

How to Write a Song. New York, Macmillan, 1962.

*

Manuscript Collection: Mugar Memorial Library, Boston University.

* * *

Henry Kane's career is rather typical of that of the post-pulp era hard-boiled writer. Most of his works have appeared in paperback only, and he has attempted to follow changing trends in the paperback market, producing—in addition to the long-running series of Peter Chambers private eye novels— "suspense" novels of the man-on-the-run variety (*Edge of Panic*), television novelizations (*Peter Gunn*), and hardcore sex novels (the "X-Rated" Chambers series, beginning in 1969). He later turned to would-be "blockbuster" books like *The Tripoli Documents,* a thriller involving Israeli spies and Arab assassins.

It is the Peter Chambers private dick (Kane prefers "private Richard") series which has been Kane's mainstay, and it contains his best work. Chambers relates his cases in the usual first-person fashion, but though the tough-guy attitudes, generous supply of sexy women, and sleazy-decadent milieu (New York rather than Los Angeles, for a change) are typical hard-boiled stuff, the prose style is not. Kane writes in a distinctively eccentric prose; his characters tend to speak in a strangely stilted circumlocutionary fashion ("And what please, in hell, does she want?"); he delights in elaborately wacky descriptive passages ("with mammary proportions of such prodigious insouciance as to have Brigette look warily to her breastworks . . . "). Chambers is a thoroughly likeable private eye, with a tendency to indulge in much wry self-deprecation, rendered in this florid "Kanese." As might be expected in so lengthy a series the quality and variety of the plotting are variable, but at his best Kane is a first-rate plotter, capable of constructing sensible, logical mysteries. It is Kane's unique approach to the hard-boiled writing style, however, that sets the Chambers series apart from the ordinary.

—Art Scott

KAVANAGH, Dan. Pseudonym for Julian Barnes. British. Born in Leicester, 19 January 1946. Educated at City of London School, 1957–64; Magdalen College, Oxford, 1964–68, B.A. (honours) in modern languages 1968. Studied law, qualified as a barrister. Married the literary agent Pat Kavanagh in 1987. Editorial assistant, *Oxford English Dictionary* supplement, 1969–72; assistant literary editor, 1977–79, and television critic, 1977–81, *New Statesman,* London; deputy literary editor, *Sunday Times,* London, 1980–82; television critic, *The Observer,* London 1982–86. Contributing editor, *New Review,* London, 1977–78. Since 1986 full-time writer. Recipient: Maugham award, 1981; Faber Memorial prize, 1985; Mediciq Essai prize in 1986; Gutenburg prize, 1987. Agent: A.D. Peters, 10 Buckingham Street, London WC2N 6BU, England.

CRIME PUBLICATIONS

Novels (series: Nick Duffy in all books)

Duffy. London, Cape, 1980.
Fiddle City. London, Cape, 1981.
Putting the Boot In. London, Cape, 1985.
Going to the Dogs. London, Viking, and New York, Pantheon, 1987.

Uncollected Short Story

"The 50p Santa," in *Time Out* (London), 19 December 1985–1 January 1986.

OTHER PUBLICATIONS

Novels

Metroland. London, Cape, 1980; New York, McGraw Hill, 1987.
Before She Met Me. London, Cape, 1982; New York, McGraw Hill, 1986
Flaubert's Parrot. London, Cape, 1984; New York, Knopf, 1985.
Staring at the Sun. London, Cape, 1986; New York, Knopf, 1987.
A History of the World in 10½ Chapters. London, Cape, and New York, Knopf, 1989.

Other

Translator, *The Truth About Dogs,* by Volker Kriegel. London, Bloomsbury, 1988.

*   *   *

It was hardly ever the literary world's best-kept secret that Dan Kavanagh was a pseudonym. The autobiographical blurb on the dust-jacket of his first book *Duffy,* although at first glance apparently striking precisely the right self-promotional note (a pre-authorial life spent in the kind of colourful, not to say mildly gamey, jobs one would expect from someone who has written a colourful, not to say mildly—or no, extremely gamey thriller), at second glance a finger of doubt crept in. At third glance occupations such as "steer-wrestling" and "waiter-on-roller-skates at a drive-in eaterie," while conventional enough in the school-of-hard-knocks university-of-life sense, all at once had a pranky air to them. The blurb for his second novel *Fiddle City* ("pianist in a waterfront bar in Macao . . . has flown light planes on the Colombian cocaine route") resolved all doubts.

In fact Dan Kavanagh is the British novelist Julian Barnes, a writer who can be both larky and profound; an uneasy combination, and one especially frowned on by critics, who invariably—indeed, with all the stubbornness of a herd of dead mules—equate larkiness with superficiality. Matters are not helped by Barnes's penchant, on occasion, for dressing up for the role. For at least one interview as Kavanagh he appeared with gelled-back hair, garish shirt, and a stick-on moustache not quite as unspeakable as that once worn (or not quite worn) by W.C. Fields.

Barnes, as Barnes, has so far written three more or less straight novels as well as two dazzling exercises—*Flaubert's Parrot* and *A History of the World in 10½ Chapters*—in what he himself terms "fabulation:" an audacious melange of not-quite-fiction (although each contains stories), literary analysis, art critique, intellectual pyrotechnics, fact and fancy; in short, an imaginative, and highly original, attempt to create patterns out of the cruel derangement of existence.

Perhaos too imaginative, too original. In the literary establishment he is viewed with some suspicion, especially as a writer of pseudonymous thrillers (not to mention the translator of a book of German dog cartoons), as being rather too clever by three-quarters, in much the same way that Graham Greene is regarded by many as a lightweight because of his "entertainments."

Like Greene, Barnes, in his Kavanagh persona (come to think of it, as Barnes too), effortlessly combines the entertaining with the pessimistic; unlike Greene (a distinctly unfunny writer), jokes and high-jinks with moral uncertainties. And just as Barnes plays fast-and-loose with the novel form, so

Barnes/Kavanagh writes thrillers that, while by no means plotless, are not over-strong on neat and tidy resolution. But then he is not particularly concerned with the normal paraphernalia of the mystery novel. What fascinates him is the careless, dispassionate, utterly chilling amorality of people who bully and terrorise and torture and murder simply because they've been told to or (worse) it's just occurred to them.

Duffy, his (for want of a better word) detective, is a classic hero of the 1980's: a bi-sexual ex-cop whose main stamping-ground is the back-street midden of massage parlours and tacky drinking-clubs that constitutes most of London's West End. *Duffy* itself concerns extortion, violence, prostitution, pornography, villains on the make, coppers on the take. With *Fiddle City* Duffy moves to Heathrow (Thiefrow) Airport, where things have a habit of going missing and, more to the point, things (like drugs) a habit of turning up. In *Putting the Boot In* Barnes's well known partiality for soccer is put to good use in portraying convincingly the seamier side of third-rate club football (boardroom shenanigans, shady property deals, neo-Nazi whackos). *Going to the Dogs* is the kind of country-house mystery country-house-mystery writers of the old school would blanch on reading.

Barnes writes thrillers because, clearly, he likes writing thrillers. They do not constitute French leave from the (so called) serious business of novel-writing; more like a busman's holiday. In both much the same authorial tone (quizzical, buttonholing, serious, ironic) and a colloquial, even slangy, no-nonsense style is used. The thrillers are rather more violent (although his "straight" novel *Before She Met Me* ends in a positive frenzy of blood-letting), and a good deal more creatively—well, raunchy: it's doubtful that readers will ever be able to think of squeegee mops (*Duffy*) or billiard-table pockets (*Going to the Dogs*) in quite the same way again.

The Duffy books are hugely entertaining, appallingly realistic (few mainstream novelists, surely, can boast an encomium from *Police World* on the grounds of authenticity), and reasonably moral. Duffy himself represents the forces of order (not the forces of good, or law); while he may revenge himself on those in the books who humiliate him, fit him up, or stick one on him, in the final analysis (to use a footballing metaphor Barnes himself would doubtless approve of) he ends up with, if not a result, at least a draw. Which, in real life too, is all one can really hope for.

—Jack Adrian

———

KAVANAGH, Paul. *See* **BLOCK, Lawrence.**

———

KEATING, H(enry) R(eymond) F(itzwalter). Also writes as Evelyn Hervey. British. Born in St. Leonards-on-Sea, Sussex, 31 October 1926. Educated at Merchant Taylors' School, London, 1940–44; Trinity College, Dublin (Vice-Chancellor's prose prize), 1948–52, B.A. 1952. Served in the British Army, 1945–48. Married Sheila Mary Mitchell in 1953; three sons and one daughter. Sub-editor, *Wiltshire Herald,* Swindon, 1953–56; *Daily Telegraph,* London, 1956–58; and *Times,* London, 1958–60; crime books reviewer, *Times,* 1967–83. Chairman, Crime Writers Association, 1970–71, and Society of Authors, 1983–84; President, Detection Club, 1985. Recipient: Crime Writers Association Gold Dagger award, 1964; Mystery Writers of America Edgar Allan Poe award, 1965, 1980; *Ellery Queen's Mystery Magazine* prize, for short story, 1970. Agent: Peters Fraser and Dunlop, 5th Floor, The Chambers, Chelsea Harbour, Lots Road, London SW10 0XF. Address: 35 Northumberland Place, London W2 5AS, England.

CRIME PUBLICATIONS

Novels (series: Inspector Ganesh Ghote)

Death and the Visiting Firemen. London, Gollancz, 1959; New York, Doubleday, 1973.
Zen There Was Murder. London, Gollancz, 1960.
A Rush on the Ultimate. London, Gollancz, 1961; New York, Doubleday, 1982.
The Dog It Was That Died. London, Gollancz, 1962.
Death of a Fat God. London, Collins, 1963; New York, Dutton, 1966.
The Perfect Murder (Ghote). London, Collins, 1964; New York, Dutton, 1965.
Is Skin-Deep, Is Fatal. London, Collins, and New York, Dutton, 1965.
Inspector Ghote's Good Crusade. London, Collins, and New York, Dutton, 1966.
Inspector Ghote Caught in Meshes. London, Collins, 1967; New York, Dutton, 1968.
Inspector Ghote Hunts the Peacock. London, Collins, and New York, Dutton, 1968.
Inspector Ghote Plays a Joker. London, Collins, and New York, Dutton, 1969.
Inspector Ghote Breaks an Egg. London, Collins, 1970; New York, Doubleday, 1971.
Inspector Ghote Goes by Train. London, Collins, 1971; New York, Doubleday, 1972.
Inspector Ghote Trusts the Heart. London, Collins, 1972; New York, Doubleday, 1973.
Bats Fly Up for Inspector Ghote. London, Collins, and New York, Doubleday, 1974.
A Remarkable Case of Burglary. London, Collins, 1975; New York, Doubleday, 1976.
Filmi, Filmi, Inspector Ghote. London, Collins, 1976; New York, Doubleday, 1977.
Inspector Ghote Draws a Line. London, Collins, and New York, Doubleday, 1979.
The Murder of the Maharajah. London, Collins, and New York, Doubleday, 1980.
Go West, Inspector Ghote. London, Collins, and New York, Doubleday, 1981.
The Sheriff of Bombay (Ghote). London, Collins, and New York, Doubleday, 1984.
Under a Monsoon Cloud (Ghote). London, Century Hutchinson, and New York, Viking, 1986.
The Body in the Billiard Room. London, Century Hutchinson, and New York, Viking, 1987.
Dead on Time (Ghote). London, Century Hutchinson, 1988; New York, Mysterious Press, 1989.
Inspector Ghote, His Life and Crimes. London, Century Hutchinson, 1989.
The Iciest Sin (Ghote). London, Century Hutchinson, 1990.

Novels as Evelyn Hervey (series: Harriet Unwin in all books)

The Governess. London, Weidenfeld and Nicolson, and New York, Doubleday, 1984.

The Man of Gold. London, Weidenfeld and Nicolson, and New York, Doubleday, 1985.
Into the Valley of Death. London, Weidenfeld and Nicolson, and New York, Doubleday, 1986.

Short Stories

Mrs. Craggs: Crimes Cleaned Up. London, Buchan and Enright, 1985; New York, St. Martin's Press, 1986.

Uncollected Short Stories

"The Justice Boy," in *Ellery Queen's Mystery Parade.* New York, New American Library, 1968.
"An Upright Woman," in *Winter's Crimes 2,* edited by George Hardinge. London, Macmillan, 1970.
"The Old Shell Collector," in *Ellery Queen's Headliners.* Cleveland, World, 1971; London, Gollancz, 1972.
"The Old Haddock," in *Ellery Queen's Mystery Magazine* (New York), June 1971.
"A Little Rain in a Few Places," in *Ellery Queen's Mystery Magazine* (New York), September 1972.
"Memorial to Speke," in *Ellery Queen's Mystery Magazine* (New York), November 1972.
"The Butler Did It," in *Ellery Queen's Mystery Magazine* (New York), May 1973.
"Torture Chamber," in *Ellery Queen's Mystery Magazine* (New York), September 1974.
"Liar, Liar, Pants on Fire," in *Ellery Queen's Mystery Magazine* (New York), April 1976.
"Gup," in *Verdict of Thirteen,* edited by Julian Symons. London, Faber, and New York, Harper, 1979.
"The Adventure of the Suffering Ruler," in *Blackwood's* (Edinburgh), May 1979.
"A Dose of Physic," in *Blackwood's* (Edinburgh), October 1979.
"A Trifling Affair," in *John Creasey's Crime Collection 1980,* edited by Herbert Harris. London, Gollancz, 1980.
"The Locked Bathroom," in *Ellery Queen's Mystery Magazine* (New York), June 1980.
"Miss Unwin Goes A-Hunting," in *Ellery Queen's Mystery Magazine* (New York), March 1982.
"A Hell of a Story," in *Ellery Queen's Mystery Magazine* (New York), June 1982.
"Dead-Letter Drop," in *Ellery Queen's Mystery Magazine* (New York), Mid-July 1982.
"And We in Dreams," in *Winter's Crimes 15,* edited by George Hardinge. London, Macmillan, and New York, St Martin's Press, 1983.
"A Crime Child," in *Ellery Queen's Mystery Magazine* (New York), Mid-July 1983.
"The Evidence I Shall Give," in *Winter's Crimes 21,* edited by Hilary Hale. London, Macmillan, 1989.
"A Snaking Suspicion," in *Ellery Queen's Mystery Magazine* (New York), Mid-December 1989.
"In Disgrace," in *The Rigby File,* edited by Tim Heald. London, Hodder and Stoughton, 1989.

OTHER PUBLICATIONS

Novels

The Strong Man. London, Heinemann, 1971.
The Underside. London, Macmillan, 1974.
A Long Walk to Wimbledon. London, Macmillan, 1978.
The Lucky Alphonse. London, Enigma, 1982.

Plays

Radio Plays: *The Dog It Was That Died,* from his own novel, 1971; *The Affair at No. 35,* 1972; *Inspector Ghote and the All-Bad Man,* 1972; *Inspector Ghote Makes a Journey,* 1973; *Inspector Ghote and the River Man,* 1974.

Other

Understanding Pierre Teilhard de Chardin: A Guide to "The Phenomenon of Man," with Maurice Keating. London, Lutterworth Press, 1969.
Murder Must Appetize (on detective stories of the 1930's). London, Lemon Tree Press, 1975; New York, Mysterious Press, 1981.
"I.N.I.T.I.A.L.S.," in *Murder Ink: The Mystery Reader's Companion,* edited by Dilys Winn. New York, Workman, 1977.
"New Patents Pending," in *Crime Writers,* edited by H.R.F. Keating. London, BBC Publications, 1978.
Sherlock Holmes: The Man and His World. London, Thames and Hudson, and New York, Scribner, 1979.
Great Crimes. London, St. Michael, and New York, Crown, 1982.
Writing Crime Fiction. London, A. & C. Black, 1986; New York, St. Martin's Press, 1987.
Crime and Mystery: The 100 Best Books. London, Xanadu, and New York, Carroll and Graff, 1987.
The Bedside Companion to Crime. London, O'Mara, 1989; New York, Mysterious Press, 1990.

Editor, *Blood on My Mind.* London, Macmillan, 1972.
Editor, *Agatha Christie: First Lady of Crime.* London, Weidenfeld and Nicolson, and New York, Holt Rinehart, 1977.
Editor, *Crime Writers: Reflections on Crime Fiction.* London, BBC Publications, 1978.
Editor, *Whodunit? A Guide to Crime, Suspense, and Spy Fiction.* London, Windward, and New York, Van Nostrand, 1982.
Editor, *Last Will and Testament, Dr. Benjamin Tancred Investigates* by G.D.H. and Margaret Cole. London, Collins, 1985.
Editor, *The Best of Father Brown* by G. K. Chesterton. London, Dent, 1987.

*

H.R.F. Keating comments:
Most of my crime novels are set in India and feature Inspector Ghote (pronounced Go-tay) of the Bombay CID, though Ghote has had one trip to London and one to California, and on television he has spent some time as a visiting officer (apt to be caught up in crimes) at Scotland Yard. While the books do provide a reasonably accurate picture of today's India—a picture conditioned, I admit, by the fact that for the first ten years I wrote about Ghote I had not actually visited his country—I like to think they chiefly put a recognizable human being into broad general situations likely to happen to any one of us. Ghote has had to decide how far he should try to be perfect, just where his loyalties should lie, etc. And while this is my main driving-force in writing the books, I like to think too that they conform well to the canons of crime-writing, with a good mystery to solve where they promise one or with a high ration of suspense where this is what's on the menu.

*   *   *

Many readers of crime fiction will know H.R.F. Keating solely or principally as the creator of Inspector Ganesh Ghote of the Bombay Police, but any implication that the rest of his writing is peripheral must be strongly resisted. Indeed it is possible to argue that, as with many another running-character series, the Ghote canon has imposed more limits than it has offered opportunities and that we should look elsewhere for the most interesting and revealing demonstrations of this author's creative powers. But the voice of the people is loud and may not be ignored.

At first glance the Ghote mix of "weak" hero and "odd" background does not seem a likely formula for popular success. Of course, India holds a special place in the British colonial memory, but the world-wide appeal of the novels needs an explanation less parochial than mere collective nostalgia for the Raj. There can, however, be no doubt that the Indian setting so vividly evoked is one of the books' many attractions. Perhaps the pleasure given derives from the perception of similitude in dissimilitude. India's climate, culture, and condition are completely alien to most of Keating's audience, yet many of its institutions, not least those of law and order, still bear the unmistakable stamp of colonial rule. The same principle applies to many of the characters and, most importantly, to Ganesh Ghote himself. Here we have a fascinating portrait of a non-western mind at work. He rarely astounds like the Great Detectives by educing hidden truths from disparate facts, but he constantly delights by the simple *otherness* of his response to people and places, success and disappointment, pain and comfort. It is a major triumph for Keating that he persuades us that his hero's reaction to, say, the long train journey in *Inspector Ghote Goes by Train* or the Indian film industry in *Filmi, Filmi, Inspector Ghote* is not simply a modified version of a western tourist's reaction, but that which is proper to a Hindu policeman.

Yet at the same time in the midst of all this *otherness*, we find a comfortable and attractive familiarity, whose source lies in Ghote's humanity. Doubts and fears and errors and awkwardnesses are so universal that nearly every culture has a place in it for the Holy Fool whose very simplicity can open up the way to truth and understanding, or, perhaps more to the point (for Ghote is no fool and not very holy), some fable or parable in which a quiet, self-effacing, and disregardable man is forced out of his diffidence by duty, or a sense of grievance, or simple humanity. Nearly all the Ghote books have as their dynamic the placing of the Bombay detective in relation to situations or people that are potentially overwhelming. He must overcome his own doubts and inhibitions to get to the truth. Interestingly when Keating transports his hero to be tested, Candide-like, by the outside world (to London in *Inspector Ghote Hunts the Peacock* and California in *Go West, Inspector Ghote*) the effect is less happy. These encounters are predictably amusing, but the comedy is broader, the emphasis has shifted. Ghote's qualities shine best in their proper setting.

There are, of course, other pleasure-giving elements besides the hero and the backgrounds. The plots are ingenious enough to satisfy the basic puzzler's appetite, the other characters are fleshed out to fit more than their functions, there is action, there is suspense. But these are all subsidiary; the books rest predominantly upon their hero. If the best crime novels, and indeed the best novels, are those where plot, setting, and theme are perfectly integrated with the protagonist's essential self, then, without doubt, *Inspector Ghote Trusts the Heart* is the most considerable work of the series so far. But the danger in any consistently good series is that the truly excellent will pass unremarked, and it is fortunate that Keating has not neglected to develop the wide range of his talents in other directions.

Still on the Indian theme, but completely different in all other respects, in *The Murder of the Maharajah*, he breathes new life into the classical detective story. Set in 1930 with the Raj in full swing, the book has the style and manner of those of the Golden Age of detective fiction. It is basically a country house murder except that the country house is a Maharajah's palace. With lots of suspects, an ingenious mode of killing and a denouement both startling and impeccably logical, the pastiche is so successful that when one of the minor characters is revealed as Inspector Ghote's father-to-be, there is a slight sense of dislocation, as though two worlds, the mythic and the real, have bumped into each other.

Another world altogether is recreated with equal success in *A Remarkable Case of Burglary*, the world of the Victorians which, with its fascinating duality of upstairs/downstairs, private vice and public morality, is further explored in his powerful straight novel *The Underside*. Another straight, *A Long Walk to Wimbledon*, set in a post-catastrophic future, illustrates Keating's power of imaginative fantasy so strongly signposted in a group of early crime novels, all delightfully original in style and theme. One of the best 10 titles of all time must be *A Rush on the Ultimate*, ingeniously derived from the murder with a croquet mallet at its centre, while *The Dog It Was That Died* is an introverted spy thriller, with a chase that stands still, as an errant psycho-linguistic expert flees from his own side and finds asylum in almost every sense in Dublin.

To complete the picture of Keating as a crime writer, reference must be made to his work as a critic and reviewer. From 1967 to 1983 he was the chief mystery reviewer for the London *Times*, where his column was noted for its keen perceptions, generous judgments, and friendly encouragement of new talent. His study, *Sherlock Holmes: The Man and His World*, draws upon his Victorian expertise to set the great detective in his historical context. As an editor of volumes like *Crime Writers: Reflections on Crime Fiction* and *Whodunit?*, an engagingly accessible reference book, and as the contributor of many learned articles to these and similar volumes, he has been in the forefront of the movement to place crime-writing in a proper literary critical context. Above all, of course, he has led by example as well as explication and has practised in the wide variety of his own work the virtues he has praised in others'.

—Reginald Hill

KEELER, Harry Stephen. American. Born in Chicago, Illinois, 3 November 1890. Educated at Armour Institute (now Illinois Institute of Technology), degree in electrical engineering 1912. Married 1) Hazel Goodwin in 1919 (died 1960); 2) Thelma Rinoldo in 1963. Electrician in steel mill; editor, *10-Story Book* magazine, 1919—40. *Died 22 January 1967.*

CRIME PUBLICATIONS

Novels (series: Angus MacWhorter; Tuddleton Trotter)

The Voice of the Seven Sparrows. London, Hutchinson, 1924; New York, Dutton, 1928.
Find the Clock. London, Hutchinson, 1925; New York, Dutton, 1927.
The Spectacles of Mr. Cagliostro. London, Hutchinson, 1926; New York, Dutton, 1929; as *The Blue Spectacles*, London, Ward Lock, 1931.
Sing Sing Nights. London, Hutchinson, 1927; New York, Dutton, 1928.

The Amazing Web. London, Ward Lock, 1929; New York, Dutton, 1930.

The Fourth King. London, Ward Lock, 1929; New York, Dutton, 1930.

Thieves' Nights. New York, Dutton, 1929; London, Ward Lock, 1930.

The Green Jade Hand. New York, Dutton, and London, Ward Lock, 1930.

The Riddle of the Yellow Zuri. New York, Dutton, 1930; as *The Tiger Snake,* London, Ward Lock, 1931.

The Matilda Hunter Murder (Trotter). New York, Dutton, 1931; as *The Black Satchel,* London, Ward Lock, 1931.

The Box from Japan. New York, Dutton, 1932; London, Ward Lock, 1933.

Behind That Mask. London, Ward Lock, 1933; expanded version, as *Behind That Mask* and *Finger! Finger!,* New York, Dutton, 2 vols., 1938.

The Face of the Man from Saturn. New York, Dutton, 1933; as *The Crilly Court Mystery,* London, Ward Lock, 1933.

The Washington Square Enigma. New York, Dutton, 1933; as *Under Twelve Stars,* London, Ward Lock, 1933.

The Mystery of the Fiddling Cracksman. New York, Dutton, and London, Ward Lock, 1934.

The Riddle of the Traveling Skull. New York, Dutton, and London, Ward Lock, 1934.

Ten Hours. London, Ward Lock, 1934; expanded version, as *The Skull of the Waltzing Clown. Ten Hours, The Defrauded Yeggman,* New York, Dutton, 3 vols., 1935–37.

The Five Silver Buddhas. New York, Dutton, and London, Ward Lock, 1935.

The Marceau Case. New York, Dutton, and London, Ward Lock, 1936.

X. Jones of Scotland Yard. New York, Dutton, 1936; as *X. Jones,* London, Ward Lock, 1936.

The Mysterious Mr. I. Ward Lock, 1937; expanded version as *The Mysterious Mr. I.* and *The Chameleon,* New York, Dutton, 2 vols., 1938–39.

The Wonderful Scheme of Mr. Christopher Thorne. New York, Dutton, 1937; as *The Wonderful Scheme,* London, Ward Lock, 1937.

When Thief Meets Thief. London, Ward Lock, 1938.

Cheung, Detective. London, Ward Lock, 1938; as *Y. Cheung, Business Detective,* New York, Dutton, 1939.

The Man with the Magic Eardrums. New York, Dutton, 1939; as *The Magic Eardrums,* London, Ward Lock, 1939.

Find Actor Hart. London, Ward Lock, 1939; as *The Portrait of Jirjohn Cobb,* New York, Dutton, 1940.

Cleopatra's Tears. New York, Dutton, and London, Ward Lock, 1940.

The Man with the Crimson Box. New York, Dutton, 1940; as *The Crimson Box,* London, Ward Lock, 1940.

The Man with the Wooden Spectacles. New York, Dutton, 1941; as *The Wooden Spectacles,* London, Ward Lock, 1941.

The Peacock Fan. New York, Dutton, 1941; London, Ward Lock, 1942.

The Sharkskin Book. New York, Dutton, 1941; as *By Third Degree,* London, Ward Lock, 1948.

The Vanishing Gold Truck (MacWhorter). New York, Dutton, 1941; London, Ward Lock, 1942.

The Lavender Gripsack. London, Ward Lock, 1941; New York, Phoenix Press, 1944.

The Book with the Orange Leaves, New York, Dutton, 1942; London, Ward Lock, 1943.

The Bottle with the Green Wax Seal. New York, Dutton, 1942.

The Case of the Two Strange Ladies. New York, Phoenix Press, 1943; London, Ward Lock, 1945.

The Search for X-Y-Z. London, Ward Lock, 1943; as *The Case of the Ivory Arrow,* New York, Phoenix Press, 1945.

The Case of the 16 Beans. New York, Phoenix Press, 1944; London, Ward Lock, 1945.

The Iron Ring. London, Ward Lock, 1944; as *The Case of the Mysterious Moll,* New York, Phoenix Press, 1945.

The Case of the Canny Killer. New York, Phoenix Press, 1946; as *Murder in the Mills,* London, Ward Lock, 1946.

The Monocled Monster. London, Ward Lock, 1947.

The Case of the Barking Clock (Trotter), with Hazel Goodwin. New York, Phoenix Press, 1947; London, Ward Lock, 1951.

The Case of the Jeweled Ragpicker (MacWhorter). New York, Phoenix Press, 1948; as *The Ace of Spades Murder,* London, Ward Lock, 1948.

The Case of the Transposed Legs, with Hazel Goodwin. New York, Phoenix Press, 1948; London, Ward Lock, 1951.

The Murdered Mathematician. London, Ward Lock, 1949.

The Strange Will, with Hazel Goodwin. London, Ward Lock, 1949.

The Steeltown Strangler. London, Ward Lock, 1950.

The Murder of London Lew. London, Ward Lock, 1952.

Stand By—London Calling (MacWhorter), with Hazel Goodwin. London, Ward Lock, 1953.

Uncollected Short Stories

"John Jones' Dollar," in *Strange Ports of Call,* edited by August Derleth. New York, Pellegrini and Cudahy, 1948.

"The Hand of God," in *20 Great Tales of Murder,* edited by Helen McCloy and Brett Halliday. New York, Random House, 1951; London, Hammond, 1952.

"Victim No. 5," in *Maiden Murders,* edited by John Dickson Carr. New York, Harper, 1952.

*   *   *

Harry Stephen Keeler's more than 70 novels form a self-contained universe of monstrously complicated intrigues, blending elements of farce, Grand Guignol, and radical social criticism while also serving as a labyrinth in which he hid himself. He was the inventor of the "webwork novel," in which literally hundreds of bizarre events explode like cigars in the white-knight hero's face but ultimately prove to be mathematically interrelated, with every absurd incident making blissfully perfect sense within Keeler's zany frame of reference. His favorite devices for tying story elements together were the loony law, the nutty religious tenet, the wacky will, the crackpot contract, and—commonest of all—the interlocking network of backbreaking coincidence. He loved to have his characters converse in outrageous ethnic dialects and to toss them into quasi-science-fictional situations. He loved to attack the social evils he saw: racism, police brutality, the military, corrupt politicians, capital punishment, the maltreatment of the mentally ill, all the dark underside of an America where "Money was Emperor, and Might was Right." And most of all he loved cats, even dedicating some novels to favorite felines.

Keeler grew up among thespians of Victorian melodrama in his widowed mother's theatrical boardinghouse. Between 1914 and 1924 he published dozens of magazine serials and novelettes, then switched to novels, many expanded from earlier magazine tales. His first books, like *The Spectacles of Mr. Cagliostro* and *Thieves' Nights,* are usually set in his beloved Chicago, constructed on the Arabian Nights model and packed with grotesque characters and events, coincidence, bitter social comment, and Victorian dialogue. In the early 1930's he wrote some of the longest mystery novels of all time, like *The Box from Japan* with its 765 closely printed pages, and some of the shortest and swiftest, like *The Washington Square Enigma*. By the mid-1930's his books had become longer, wilder, wackier, and less constrained by conventional discipline than ever, including several multi-volume meganovels like *The Mysterious Mr. I* and its sequel *The Chameleon*. During the 1940's and 1950's he alternated between single titles, of standard length and brain-boggling contents, and several series of novels dealing respectively with the adventures of a book, a circus, a house, an industrial plant, and a skull. But the wilder Keeler's flights of fancy became, the fewer readers flew with him. After 1953 his books appeared only in Spanish or Portuguese translations, if at all. Nevertheless he continued to turn out novels as well as a weekly mimeographed newsletter full of theosophical and literary and cat lore. He died in 1967, leaving a dozen books unfinished, confident that one day he would be read again.

Certainly he should be. For close to half a century he spun an alternate universe totally and uniquely his own from its metaphysical underpinnings to the speech and costumes of its inhabitants. Committed humanist-radical and exuberant clown, he was the true original of Kesey's R.P. MacMurphy and Vonnegut's Kilgore Trout, the sublime nutty genius of the mystery genre, who deserves to be remembered as long as boundless creativity is cherished.

—Francis M. Nevins, Jr.

———

KEENE, Day. American. Married. Wrote radio soap operas in 1930's and 1940's. Lived in Chicago, Florida, and California. *Died c. 1969.*

CRIME PUBLICATIONS

Novels (series: Johnny Aloha)

This Is Murder, Mr. Herbert, and Other Stories (novelets). New York, Avon, 1948.
Framed in Guilt. New York, Mill, 1949; as *Evidence Most Blind,* London, Hennel Locke, 1950.
Farewell to Passion. New York, Hanro, 1951; as *The Passion Murders,* New York, Avon, 1955.
My Flesh Is Sweet. New York, Lion, 1951.
Love Me and Die. New York, Phantom, 1951.
To Kiss or Kill. New York, Fawcett, 1951; London, Fawcett, 1953.
Hunt the Killer. New York, Phantom, 1952.
About Doctor Ferrel. New York, Fawcett, 1952; London, Fawcett, 1958.
Home Is the Sailor. New York, Fawcett, 1952.
If the Coffin Fits. Hasbrouck Heights, New Jersey, Graphic, 1952.
Naked Fury. New York, Phantom, 1952.
Wake Up to Murder. New York, Phantom, 1952.
Mrs. Homicide. New York, Ace, 1953.
Strange Witness. Hasbrouck Heights, New Jersey, Graphic, 1953.
The Big Kiss-Off. Hasbrouck Heights, New Jersey, Graphic, 1954.
Death House Doll. New York, Ace, 1954.
Homicidal Lady. Hasbrouck Heights, New Jersey, Graphic, 1954.
Joy House. New York, Lion, 1954; London, Consul, 1964.
Notorious. New York, Fawcett, 1954; London, Fawcett, 1956.
Sleep with the Devil. New York, Lion, 1954.
There Was a Crooked Man. New York, Fawcett, 1954; London, Fawcett, 1955.
Who Has Wilma Lathrop? New York, Fawcett, 1955; London, Jenkins, 1966.
The Dangling Carrot. New York, Ace, 1955.
Murder on the Side. New York and London, Fawcett, 1956.
Bring Him Back Dead. New York, Fawcett, 1956.
Flight by Night. New York, Ace, 1956; London, Red Seal, 1960.
It's a Sin to Kill. New York, Avon, 1958.
Passage to Samoa. New York, Fawcett, 1958; London, Fawcett, 1960.
Dead Dolls Don't Talk. New York, Fawcett, 1959; London, Muller, 1963.
Dead in Bed (Aloha). New York, Pyramid, 1959.
Moran's Woman. Rockville Centre, New York, Zenith, 1959.
Miami 59. New York Dell, 1959; London, Mayflower, 1966.
So Dead My Lovely. New York, Pyramid, 1959.
Take a Step to Murder. New York, Fawcett, 1959; London, Muller, 1960.
Too Black for Heaven. Rockville Centre, New York, Zenith, 1959.
Too Hot to Hold. New York, Fawcett, 1959; London, Muller, 1960.
The Brimstone Bed. New York, Avon, 1960.
Payola (Aloha). New York, Pyramid, 1960.
Seed of Doubt. New York, Simon and Schuster, 1961; London, W.H. Allen, 1962.
Bye, Baby Bunting. New York, Holt Rinehart, and London, W.H. Allen, 1963.
Carnival of Death. New York, Macfadden, 1965.

Uncollected Short Stories

"The Stars Say Die," in *Detective Tales* (New York), November 1941.
"The Corpse That Ran Away," in *Dime Mystery* (New York), March 1942.
"Murder Is My Sponsor," in *Detective Tales* (New York), April 1942.
"A Slight Mistake in Corpses," in *Detective Tales* (New York), May 1942.
"Til the Day You Die," in *Ten Detective Aces* (New York), June 1942.
"The Mystery of Tarpon Key," in *Detective Tales* (New York), August 1942.
"Blaze of Glory," in *Detective Tales* (New York), November 1942.
"Hearse of Another Color," in *Dime Mystery* (New York), November 1942.
"He Who Dies Last, Dies Hardest," in *Detective Tales* (New York), May 1943.
"The Female Is More Deadly," in *Dime Detective* (New York), December 1943.
"Corpses Come in Pairs," in *Detective Tales* (New York), April 1944.
"Brother, Can You Spare a Grave?" in *Dime Mystery* (New York), July 1944.
"Make Mine Murder," in *New Detective* (New York), September 1944.
"Murder on My Mind," in *Detective Tales* (New York), July 1945.
"The Night I Died," in *Detective Story Magazine* (New York), August 1945.
"A Corpse Walks in Brooklyn," in *Detective Tales* (New York), October 1945.

"As Deep as the Grave," in *Detective Tales* (New York), January 1946.

"Claws of the Hell-Cat," in *Dime Mystery* (New York), January 1946.

"Doc Egg's Graveyard Reunion," in *Dime Mystery* (New York), February 1946.

"Little Miss Murder," in *Detective Tales* (New York), November 1946.

"The Case of the Sobbing Girl," in *Best Detective Stories of the Year 1946,* edited by David Coxe Cooke. New York, Dutton, 1946.

"So Dead the Rogue," in *New Detective* (New York), January 1947.

"Married to Murder," in *Dime Mystery* (New York), January 1947.

"No Grave Could Hold Him," in *Dime Mystery* (New York), February 1948.

"Marry the Sixth for Murder," in *Detective Tales* (New York), May 1948.

"Some Die Easy," in *New Detective* (New York), May 1948.

"Knock Twice for Murder," in *Detective Tales* (New York), June 1949.

"Wait for the Dead Man's Tide," in *Dime Mystery* (New York), August 1949.

"Murder—Do Not Disturb," in *New Detective* (New York), March 1950.

"Old Homicide Week," in *Detective Tales* (New York), April 1950.

"The Bloody Tide," in *Dime Mystery* (New York), June 1950.

"Remember the Night," in *Best Detective Stories of the Year 1950,* edited by David Coxe Cooke. New York, Dutton, 1950.

"Murder Stop," in *Famous Detective* (Dunellen, New Jersey), November 1950.

"Blonde and Bad," in *Smashing Detective* (New York), March 1951.

"The Passing of Johnny Maguire," in *15 Story Detective* (New York), May 1951.

"Mighty Like a Rogue," in *As Tough As They Come,* edited by Will Oursler. New York, Doubleday, 1951.

"How Deep My Grave?," in *Famous Detective* (Dunellen, New Jersey), November 1952.

"A Great Whirring of Wings," in *Maiden Murders,* edited by John Dickson Carr. New York, Harper, 1952.

"Homicide House," in *Crook's Tour,* edited by Bruno Fischer. New York, Dodd Mead, 1953.

"Booty and the Beast," in *Private Eye* (New York), July 1953.

"A Better Mantrap," in *Dangerous Dames,* edited by Brett Halliday. New York, Dell, 1955.

"I'll Die for You," in *Crime and Justice* (New York), September 1956.

"Dead Dreams for Sale," in *Terror* (New York), February 1957.

"The Ghost of Cock Robin," in *Detective Tales* (New York), August 1958.

"Mr. Smith's Flying Corpses," in *Detective Tales* (New York), November 1961.

"For Old Crimes Sake," in *Mike Shayne Mystery Magazine* (New York), December 1964.

OTHER PUBLICATIONS

Novels

His Father's Wife. New York, Pyramid, 1954.
Chautauqua, with Dwight Vincent. New York, Putnam, 1960; London, W.H. Allen, 1963.

World Without Women, with Leonard Pruyn. New York, Fawcett, 1960.
Chicago 11. New York, Dell, 1966.
Southern Daughter. New York, Macfadden, 1967.
Live Again, Love Again. New York, New American Library, 1970.
Wild Girl. New York, Macfadden, 1970.

*   *   *

During his long career, Day Keene was one of the most popular, readable, and prolific of the writers who specialized first in pulp fiction and then in the paperback original. In the 1940's his name appeared with amazing regularity on the covers and contents pages of such top crime pulps as *Black Mask, Dime Detective,* and *Detective Tales.* When the pulp market collapsed in the early 1950's, Keene found a ready home for his work in the burgeoning paperback field. He wrote dozens of original novels for Fawcett Gold Medal, Graphic, Ace, and others; noteworthy are *Home Is the Sailor* and *Murder on the Side.* Probably his best crime novel, however, is his first—a hardcover entitled *Framed in Guilt;* it is a nicely plotted story of blackmail, treachery, and murder involving a Hollywood screenwriter. Keene abandoned the paperback novel in the late 1950's to do more ambitious (but less crime-oriented) fiction. Keene's primary virtue as a writer was a strong sense of pace and narrative drive: he knew how to tell a story that gripped the reader immediately and held him to the end. If the quality of some of his early work suffers from the speed with which it was written, it is nonetheless entertaining and thoroughly professional.

—Bill Pronzini

———

KEITH, J. Kilmeny. *See* **GILBERT, Anthony.**

———

KELLERMAN, Faye (née Marder). American. Born in St. Louis, Missouri, 31 July 1952. Educated at the University of California, Los Angeles, A.B. in Mathematics 1974; doctor of dental surgery, 1978; Regents Research Fellow, oral biology, 1977–78. Married Jonathan Kellerman, *q.v.* in 1972; one son and two daughters. Independent investor and real estate manager, Los Angeles, 1974. Recipient: Mystery Readers of America Macavity award, 1986. Agent: Barney Karpfinger, 500 Fifth Avenue, New York, New York 10110, U.S.A.

CRIME PUBLICATIONS

Novels (series: Sergeant Peter Decker in all books)

The Ritual Bath. New York, Arbor House, 1985; London, Collins, 1987.
Sacred and Profane. New York, Arbor House, 1987; London, Coronet, 1989.
Milk and Honey. New York, Morrow, and London, Headline, 1990.

Uncollected Short Stories

"Bonding," in *Sisters in Crime,* edited by Marilyn Wallace. New York, Berkley, 1989; London, Robinson, 1990.
"Malibu," in *Sisters in Crime 2,* edited by Marilyn Wallace. New York, Berkley, 1990.

OTHER PUBLICATIONS

Novel

The Quality of Mercy.   New York, Morrow, 1988; London, W.H. Allen, 1989.

*

Faye Kellerman comments:

My novels always start with just a germ of an idea and *characters.* Incorporated into the plots are themes I choose to explore. The *characters* are used to further the theme and all its variations. *Sacred and Profane* deals with religious beliefs in a venal world. *Milk and Honey* deals with the destructive forces inherent in the family. *Day of Atonement* (forthcoming), is an exploration into the expiation of guilt. Plot is my last device to be designed and constructed.

*   *   *

Three of Faye Kellerman's four novels are classic police procedurals featuring Sergeant Peter Decker of the LAPD (Los Angeles Police Department). Decker is a typical American cop, hard-boiled with a soft centre, who loves his work but hates the tragedy and misery it brings him into contact with.

In Kellerman's first novel, *The Ritual Bath,* he is called with his partner Marge Dunn to investigate a rape at an orthodox Jewish yeshiva. There he meets Rina Lazarus, a young widow who is involved in the incident as a witness and he eventually falls in love with her. As the story of their attraction unfolds, it is played out against the background of the rape investigation and the conflicts it causes for the religious community. There is conflict in Rina and Peter's relationship as well, since he was raised a Baptist, but this is solved somewhat by the revelation that he was adopted as a child, and is actually Jewish.

The story is absorbing on a number of levels, both as a romance and as a mystery. Kellerman obviously understands orthodox Judaism well and portrays the close community with affection and sometimes humour. The casual mention of various rituals and expressions adds colour and makes for fascinating, informative reading for those who are not familiar with this religious tradition.

Unfortunately there are scenes of extreme violence in this book and in Kellerman's other novels. The murder of Florence Marley, the security guard hired to protect the yeshiva women from the rapist, is gory and horrible and an anti-Semitic physical attack on Rina is also graphically described. Kellerman is writing about life in America as it is played out in the evening news and it is not a pretty sight.

Her third novel *Milk and Honey* also features Peter and Rina, by now passionate lovers with plans to marry. Decker has reverted to Judaism and is doing his best to maintain a level of orthodoxy Rina would approve of. The character of Rabbi Schulman, spiritual leader of the yeshiva, returns in this book as Peter's teacher, giving advice on the conflicts he finds in his new life.

There is another ugly rape in this book as well as a truly gruesome quadruple murder, again with graphic descriptions of the bodies. If you can stomach the violence, the plot is intriguing and this book also explores further the relationship between Decker and his tough, but insecure partner Marge Dunn.

The Peter Decker and Rina Lazarus books explore the importance of religious culture to people in a nation where Church and State are separate, and look at what it can mean to be an outsider in your own country. It is refreshing to encounter characters whose moral sense is based on something rather than a reaction against something. These gripping books are a far cry from the gentlemanly police cases of Roderick Alleyn. In Kellerman's work, the blood and guts and pain are real and the victims aren't the only ones who suffer.

In between *Sacred and Profane,* and *Milk and Honey,* Kellerman tried her hand with great success at a historical mystery and romance. *The Quality of Mercy* is the epic (605 pages) story of Rebecca Lopez, daughter of Queen Elizabeth I's personal physician. Dr. Roderigo Lopez was a historical figure who was hung and quartered at Tyburn in 1594, accused of plotting to poison the queen. In a note at the end of the book, Kellerman suggests that he could have been the inspiration for Shylock in Shakespeare's *Merchant of Venice.* The fictional Shakespeare in the book is passionately in love with Rebecca who is involved with her family in smuggling Jews out of Spain to escape the Inquisition. As in her modern works, Kellerman's Jewish characters have a deep faith and she brings to vibrant life the customs and practices of the crypto-Jewish community in 16th-century England.

The Quality of Mercy also contains fairly graphic scenes of violence. The prologue is an account of death by garotting and burning during an auto-da-fe of the Inquisition. It is ghastly and upsetting to read, but Kellerman's descriptions of death are not gratuitous. It is crucial for readers to understand the horrors that motivate the characters' sometimes ruthless deeds. In contrast to the scenes of violence the doomed romance between Shakespeare and Rebecca is touching and lovely. At the end of the book when he sits down to begin to write: "In sooth I know not why I am so sad . . . ", it is for her.

Kellerman also contributed an odd short story called "Bonding" to the anthology *Sisters in Crime,* edited by Marilyn Wallace. In this bleak, but strangely entertaining tale of modern American suburbia, a teenager murders her mother because she is "bored." Unusually for Kellerman, there's no messy physical violence in this one, but her command of the dialect of the shopping mall and the neon strip make it interesting and even amusing in a weird way. This story is a departure for Kellerman in that she is not writing about people who are motivated by faith. The family in "Bonding" have nothing to hold them together except inertia.

Kellerman is a powerful, inventive writer whose plots and characters hold the reader's attention from beginning to end. She truly understands modern America and the prejudices and pressures that lurk behind its façade of flag-waving family values.

—Gillian Rodgerson

———

KELLERMAN, Jonathan. American. Born in New York City, 9 August 1949. Educated at the University of California, Los Angeles, A.B. in psychology 1971; University of Southern California, Los Angeles, A.M. in psychology 1973, Ph.D. 1974; Fellowship in clinical psychology, University of Southern California Medical School, 1975. Married Faye Marder, *q.v.,* in

1972; one son and two daughters. Freelance illustrator, 1966–72; staff psychologist, Children's Hospital of Los Angeles, 1975–81; Assistant Clinical Professor, pediatrics, 1978–79, Since 1979 Associate Clinical Professor, University of Southern California School of Medicine; head, Jonathan Kellerman Ph.D and Associates, Los Angeles, 1981–85; Director, Psychosocial Program, Children's Hospitals of Los Angeles, 1970–81. Since 1989, member of the Board of Directors, Mystery Writers of America Southern Chapter, California. Recipient: Mystery Writers of America Edgar Allan Poe award, 1985; Anthony Boucher award, 1986. Agent. Barney Karpfinger, 500 Fifth Avenue, New York, New York 10110, U.S.A.

CRIME PUBLICATIONS

Novels (series: Alex Delaware in all books except *The Butcher's Theatre*)

When the Bough Breaks. New York, Atheneum, 1985; as *Shrunken Heads,* London, Macdonald, 1985.
Blood Test. New York, Atheneum, and London, Macdonald, 1986.
Over the Edge. New York, Atheneum, and London, Macdonald, 1987.
The Butcher's Theatre. New York, Bantam, and London, Macdonald, 1988.
Silent Partner. New York, Bantam, and London, Macdonald, 1989.
Time Bomb. New York, Bantam, and London, Macdonald, 1990.

Uncollected Short Story

"The Questioner," in *Alfred Hitchcock's Mystery Magazine* (New York), December 1977.

OTHER PUBLICATIONS

Other

Psychological Aspects of Childhood Cancer. Springfield, Illinois, C.C. Thomas, 1980.
Helping the Fearful Child: A Parent's Guide to Everyday and Problem Anxieties. New York, Norton, 1981.

*

Jonathan Kellerman comments:

My curiosity about the human condition and the nature of good and evil helped direct me towards both of my careers: clinical psychologist and crime novelist.

I write about family psychopathology taken to the extreme. I'm motivated by the exploration of character and motivation—the characters always come first, then the story. I strive to construct a story with a very strong plot so as never to cheat the readers. Utilizing a building-construction analogy, plot is the framing, the skillful, graceful use of language, the interior decorating. Both are necessary in order to create something of value. Though my books have been described as dealing with social issues, this is not intentional. I am a coward and follow the old saying that recommends writing what one knows. Because of my years as a psychologist and other life experiences, I seem to gravitate toward "socially relevant" topics. But my primary goal is to create an exciting story that

will keep the reader turning pages. I love writing, love the fact that so many people seem to be getting pleasure from my novels.

*   *   *

Since 1985, Jonathan Kellerman has created, in the five Alex Delaware novels, one of the most successful detective series of recent times. Like his creator, Alex is a clinical psychologist who specializes in children's problems, yet the books cannot rightfully be called autobiographical. Kellerman has simply adhered to the ancient admonishment to authors to "write about what you know." And Kellerman does, indeed, know what he is writing about, from the psychological basis of each case to the nearly flawless evocation of Los Angeles that is reminiscent of Raymond Chandler in his portrayal of the city's glitter and gloss, as well as its seamier side.

As in the work of Andrew Vachss, Kellerman's novels often involve child sexual abuse. Unlike Vachss, however, Kellerman rarely exacts a violent punishment from his molesters. They are always punished, and they often die, but no one shoots them in the kneecaps or breaks their fingers one by one. Also unlike Vachss, who is nearly obsessive about the subject, child abuse (psychological as well as sexual) is not the major element in Kellerman's carefully-plotted, often emotionally-draining novels. Instead, as he, himself, has pointed out, they deal with "family disturbance and with class struggle—the inevitable tension between the haves and the have-nots—and the violence that sometimes results."

Alex Delaware makes his first appearance in *When the Bough Breaks* (winner of both the Edgar Allan Poe and Anthony Boucher awards for best first novel), a complex tale involving a ring of child molesters. Delaware is 32, handsome, brilliant (Ph.D. at 24), and financially independent, having been able to retire as the result of his shrewd real estate investments. He now works only when he chooses, accepting only patients that interest him or who have been referred by the courts, an attorney friend, or the police, usually in the person of Milo Sturgis. Milo is big (6'2", 220 pounds), intelligent, tough, and homosexual. Kellerman deals with his character's homosexuality with much sensitivity, particularly in his depiction of the relationship between Milo and his lover, surgeon Rick Silverman, which reflects, without being a parody of, that of Alex and his girlfriend, Robin Castagna, beset as it is with separations, doubts, and fears of loving too much and of not being loved enough.

Although it is unusual, as Robin observes in *Over the Edge,* "for a straight guy and a gay guy to be as close as you two," Alex and Milo are true friends, and their relationship is one of the strong points of the series. There is never any question of a romantic interest between them, yet they are able to share their most intimate personal problems, as in *When the Bough Breaks* when Milo confesses that he has murdered a judge who was deeply involved in child molestation, or in *Over the Edge* when he confides that "down deep I'm a closet homophobe myself." Alex is no less forthcoming as he discusses his burn-out, the demons that pursue him, the guilt that he feels for his rare failures with his patients, or his problems with Robin.

Alex is a model of integrity. In *Over the Edge,* he agonizes over having failed to help young Jamey Cadmus five years previously when the boy was his patient. Alex decides to return the $10,000 retainer given him by Jamey's attorney as soon as he realizes that he is being used to create a diminished capacity defense for the boy, who has been accused of a particularly grisly series of homosexual murders. He does not hesitate to place himself in danger for the sake of his patients or his friends, nor is he able to avoid feeling guilty for even an imagined infidelity. In *Blood Test,* for instance, he is called in as a consultant by a former colleague, an eminent oncologist who is treating a gravely ill boy whose parents are threatening to remove him from treatment. The parents are murdered, the boy disappears, and Alex is led to the headquarters of a cocaine ring masquerading as a religious cult. He risks his life to save the boy, and discovers a dark tale of incest along with the parents' killer. In *Silent Partner,* he is called upon to aid an old lover who is killed before she can reveal the nature of her difficulty. As he investigates her murder, he recalls the intimate details of their love affair. Although nothing happens between them in the present, he still feels compelled to confess to Robin that he feels that he has betrayed her, even though "she captured my head, not my cock. Now she's gone forever. But it changed me."

Alex and Robin attempt another reunion, after another of their separations, separations not born out of anger, or distrust, or lack of love, but out of uneasiness with their relationship, an inability to make the final commitment, an ambivalence they feel toward one another. As Robin reminds Alex, he is "Dr. Perfect, Ph.D., problem-solver. Looks, brains, charm, money, all those patients who think you're God. Dammit, Alex, when I first met you, you had problems—the burn-out, all those self-doubts. You were a *mortal* and I could care for you." In *Blood Test,* Alex still retained some of this self-doubt. Robin, a talented luthier who is becoming increasingly successful, has gone to Japan to investigate an offer to mass-produce a guitar she is to design. When she returns, Alex admits that he is "just another selfish, sexist bastard, threatened by your success, and worried that it won't be the same." He needs for *her* to feel dependent upon *him,* just as she needs for *him* to feel dependent on *her.* They want to be together, but each is afraid of relinquishing too much freedom. That each is growing is the source of their discomfort.

Although the Delaware novels are Kellerman's major achievement within the mystery *genre,* it would be an injustice not to comment, however briefly, on *The Butcher's Theater.* Kellerman once again draws heavily upon his psychological training and professional experience to create one of the most chilling portraits of a psychopathic killer that I have ever read. Set in Jerusalem, the "butcher's theater" of the title, the novel is carefully researched and graced by Kellerman's usual skill at plotting and sharp, witty dialogue. Yet I was never able really to identify with Daniel Sharavi, the novel's protagonist, nor with any of the other characters.

—Dale Carter

KELLY, Mary (Theresa, née Coolican). British. Born in London, 28 December 1927. Educated at the University of Edinburgh, M.A. 1951. Married Denis Charles Kelly in 1950. Teacher in a private school and in Surrey County Council schools, 1952–54. Recipient: Crime Writers Association Gold Dagger award, 1961. Agent: Curtis Brown Ltd., 162–168 Regent Street, London WIR 5TB, England.

CRIME PUBLICATIONS

Novels (series Nicholson; Inspector Brett Nightingale)

A Cold Coming (Nightingale). London, Secker and Warburg, 1956; New York, Walker, 1968.

Dead Man's Riddle (Nightingale). London, Secker and Warburg, 1957; New York, Walker, 1967.
The Christmas Egg (Nightingale). London, Secker and Warburg, 1958; New York, Holt Rinehart, 1966.
The Spoilt Kill (Nicholson). London, Joseph, 1961; New York, Walker, 1968.
Due to a Death (Nicholson). London, Joseph, 1962; as *The Dead of Summer,* New York, Mill, 1963.
March to the Gallows. London, Joseph, 1964; New York, Holt Rinehart, 1965.
Dead Corse. London, Joseph, 1966; New York, Holt Rinehart, 1967.
Write on Both Sides of the Paper. London, Joseph, 1969; Elmsford, New York, London House and Maxwell, 1970.
The Twenty-Fifth Hour. London, Macmillan, 1971; New York, Walker, 1972.
That Girl in the Alley. London, Macmillan, and New York, Walker, 1974.

Uncollected Short Stories

"A Bit Out of Place," in *Winter's Crimes 1,* edited by George Hardinge. London, Macmillan, 1969.
"Life the Shadow of Death, " in *Winter's Crimes 8,* edited by Hilary Watson. London, Macmillan, and New York, St. Martin's Press, 1976.

*

Manuscript Collection: Mugar Memorial Library, Boston University.

*   *   *

One of the best contemporary British crime writers, *but*: such must be the verdict on Mary Kelly. The "but" has two aspects, perhaps linked. She was too apt, as are some other fine writers, to skimp on the basic plot. And, more serious, she brought herself to write less and less frequently, producing nothing after 1974. That being said, however, there is enormous pleasure to be got from her books.

The essential quality of her art is perhaps obscured by the manner in which she began. It plainly occurred to her when she first thought of writing a crime story that the important element of "background" in the late classical whodunit (the advertising agency or the bellringing lore of Dorothy L. Sayers) could be given a more up-to-date treatment. So she found various industrial settings, papermaking, steel making, pottery manufacture, that were at least as interesting as the fields conventionally adopted by detective-story writers and which for the alert reader had extra interest as descriptions of neglected aspects of modern society.

It was a device which had its own success, but eventually Mary Kelly understandably tired of it, and in subsequent books the true nature of what she was able to do was revealed. This is the giving of pure pleasure, the taking of readers out of themselves and deeply into another world. To achieve it she patently experiences the process herself. Her writing is moment by moment intense, and is successful as such. Whatever she had to describe, whether scene or action (or sexual behaviour, in the description of which—a difficult task—she did particularly good), she did so in a way that puts the reader there. Unusually for crime novels, therefore, what propels the reader through the pages is not the tug of "who done it" nor the excitements of men with guns coming in through doors, but the sheer excellence of the writing.

Take a book like *The Twenty-Fifth Hour.* It tells of an

Englishwoman holidaying in Normandy with a small barely illegal task to perform on the side. A story so mild as hardly to exist. The woman does later become involved in a plot concerned with an extreme Rightist organisation, but again this is pretty conventional and even tame. Yet one reads almost as eagerly as if the story had been put together by Alistair MacLean and the plot devised by Ira Levin because from her very first sentence Mary Kelly observed so meticulously, described so exactly and economically. Hers was a never-blinking eye.

This exactness brings with it, of course, another valuable constituent for any work of fiction: a respect for human beings as they are, as individuals not figures from a mould. It is something that Kelly herself, in the person of one of her characters, once called "human incorrigibility." And it marked out the best books from the merely good. A crime book can reach the status of "good" on sheer plot, on sheer storytelling, on sheer ingenuity, on sheer suspense. But to go higher real human beings are needed in its pages. They are there in plenty in Mary Kelly's work.

But. And the "but" must be re-emphasised, alas. But a novel that is all acute description, and especially a crime novel that is largely such, must be accounted to some extent a failure. A dimension of the novel is story, and a dimension of the crime novel is plot. Mary Kelly's books, even at their most perverse (*That Girl in the Alley*), do not totally lack either of these two dimensions, but they got dangerously thin.

—H.R.F. Keating

KELLY, Patrick. *See* **ALLBEURY, Ted.**

KEMELMAN, Harry. American. Born in Boston, Massachusetts, 24 November 1908. Educated at Boston Latin School, 1920–26; Boston University, A.B. in English Literature 1930; Harvard University, Cambridge, Massachusetts, M.A. in English Philology 1931, further study 1932–33. Married Anne Kessin in 1936; two daughters and one son. Teacher in Boston high schools, 1935–41, and Manter Hall School, Cambridge, 1936–40; Northeastern University Evening Division, 1938–41; Chief Wage Administrator, United States Army Transportation Corps, Boston, 1942–46; chief job analyst and wage administrator, War Assets Administration, New England Division, 1948–49; freelance writer and private businessman, 1949–63; Assistant Professor of English, Franklin Technical Institute, Boston, 1963, and Boston State College, in the 1960's. Recipient: Mystery Writers of America Edgar Allan Poe award, 1964. Address: P.O. Box 674, Marblehead, Massachusetts 01945, U.S.A.

CRIME PUBLICATIONS

Novels (series: Rabbi David Small in all books)

Friday the Rabbi Slept Late. New York, Crown, 1964; London, Hutchinson, 1965.
Saturday the Rabbi Went Hungry. New York, Crown, 1966; London, Hutchinson, 1967.

Sunday the Rabbi Stayed Home. New York, Putnam, and London, Hutchinson, 1969.
Monday the Rabbi Took Off. New York, Putnam, and London, Hutchinson, 1972.
Tuesday the Rabbi Saw Red. New York, Fields, 1973; London, Hutchinson, 1974.
Wednesday the Rabbi Got Wet. New York, Morrow, and London, Hutchinson, 1976.
Thursday the Rabbi Walked Out. New York, Morrow, 1978; London, Hutchinson, 1979.
Someday the Rabbi Will Leave. New York, Morrow, and London, Hutchinson, 1985.
One Fine Day the Rabbi Bought a Cross. New York, Morrow, 1987; London, Century Hutchinson, 1988.

Short Stories

The Nine Mile Walk. New York, Putnam, 1967; London, Hutchinson, 1968.

OTHER PUBLICATIONS

Other

Commonsense in Education. New York, Crown, 1970.
Conversations with Rabbi Small. New York, Morrow, 1981.

* * *

Harry Kemelman's hero, Rabbi David Small, follows a long tradition of religious detectives, including G.K. Chesterton's Father Brown, Margaret Scherf's Sister Mary Ursula, and H. H. Holmes's Reverend Buell. Small is drawn into the events of a murder when he tries to help a parishioner in trouble. He then applies his own kind of deductive logic to find the real culprit. Along the way, Kemelman, himself a rabbi as well as a skilled narrative writer, gives the reader a picture of the rabbi's life and moral code and his troubles with his congregation.

The books can be instantly recognized by their titles: each shows the rabbi on one day of the week. He sleeps late on Friday, gets wet on Wednesday, and takes off on Thursday, and on through book number seven. The structure of the stories is also similar. Typically, the first half of the book shows the personalities and politics of the rabbi's congregation. In one book, a group of his parishioners attempt to fire him. In another, he opposes the idea of having religious retreats. A death occurs around the middle of the story and as the net tightens around someone he is close to, the rabbi begins his detecting close to the end. In *Wednesday the Rabbi Got Wet,* he becomes fully involved on page 257 of a 288 page book. These stories, therefore, are not typical detective novels in that not much detecting is done. They are more precisely accounts of Jewish life in an American small town (Barnard's Crossing, Massachusetts), during which time some detecting occurs.

While these features remain the same across the years, Kemelman keeps the situations and characters up to date. *Sunday the Rabbi Stayed Home,* published in 1969, involves marijuana, race, and young people who question adult values. *Wednesday the Rabbi Got Wet* (1976) features mystical religious sects and malpractice suits. By *One Fine Day the Rabbi Bought a Cross* (1987), the characters are caught up in Middle Eastern intrigue and contraband weapon sales. The rabbi also ages slightly, from his thirties to his forties, throughout these books.

David Small is a very likeable hero, and an unusual one. He is described as young-looking though he walks with a scholarly stoop; he is mild, although strong in defense of his principles. He possesses a kind of practical commonsense, which he applies to mysteries as well as to moral advising. In *Wednesday the Rabbi Got Wet,* a young man tells Small how he followed the instructions of another rabbi, who can see so much farther than others can. It is as if he had a telescope, the youth explains:

> I would probably ask if I might take a peek through the telescope, the rabbi said drily.
> All right, say he didn't have a telescope, but he just had keener vision?
> I'd want proof of it before I started walking, said the rabbi with a smile.

The same commonsense is used in unraveling the means and motives of murder suspects. Small simply arrays more facts and carries them further in logic than others can. The rabbi uses *pilpul* (a Talmudic form of logical reasoning using very fine distinctions), according to his friend the Irish chief of police. But the rabbi's logical reasoning as it is set forth at the end of each of these novels is less *pilpul* than a combination of cold logic and Yankee commonsense.

Small's role in these stories becomes clearer by comparison with another amateur detective, Agatha Christie's Miss Marple. Both live in small towns and often visit other members of the community. Indeed, this continual close contact, along with their keen understanding of human nature, helps them solve the mysteries that occur. While both have formidable powers of deduction, they also have an eye for the concrete and trivial detail. Small learns something from a broken strand of pearls, a clue Miss Marple would have recognized too. Both are unlikely detectives—the elderly lady and the mild scholarly man. But whereas Christie's heroine devotes all her efforts to solving the murder, a task that takes much of the novel, Small's work of detection is only a brief forced interruption in the course of his work.

Kemelman's books, therefore, will not appeal to all murder mystery lovers, since the mystery itself is only one of several themes. Nor will they appeal to those who dislike commentaries on religion and ethics: the author teaches his readers as he entertains them through the books. *Sunday the Rabbi Stayed Home* gives extensive details about the Passover celebration, while *Wednesday the Rabbi Got Wet* lays out the different role of mysticism in the Jewish and Christian faiths. Nevertheless, these well-crafted stories have a wide appeal. Non-Jewish readers can learn much about Judaism, while Jewish readers can enjoy the familiar portraits. *Someday the Rabbi will Leave,* Kemelman announces in a recent book title. But with the titles now moving beyond the seven days of the week, there is promise of more of these stories to come.

—Barbara Hinckley

KENDRAKE, Carleton. *See* **GARDNER, Erle Stanley.**

KENDRICK, Baynard H(ardwick). Also wrote as Richard Hayward. American. Born in Philadelphia, Pennsylvania, 8 April 1894. Educated at Tome School, Port Deposit, Maryland; Episcopal Academy, Philadelphia, graduated 1912. Served with the Canadian Infantry in England, France, and Salonica, 1914–18: Segeant; instructor for blind veterans in

World War II. Married 1) Edythe Stevens in 1919 (died), two daughters and one son; 2) Jean Morris in 1971. Secretary, Selden Cypress Door Company, Patalka, Florida, 1919–27; president, Trades Publishing Company, Philadelphia, 1928; general manager, Peter Clark Inc., New York, 1929, and Bing and Bing's Hotels, New York, 1930–32. Freelance writer after 1932. Member, editorial board, *Florida Historical Quarterly* and Director, Florida Historical Society; Columnist, "Florida's Fabulous Past," Tampa *Sunday Tribune,* 1961–64. First President, Mystery Writers of America, 1945. Recipient: Screen Writers Guild Robert Meltzer award, 1951; Mystery Writers of America Grand Master award, 1967. *Died 22 March 1977.*

CRIME PUBLICATIONS

Novels (series: Captain Duncan Maclain; Miles Standish Rice)

Blood on Lake Louisa.   New York, Greenberg, 1934; London, Methuen, 1937.
The Iron Spiders (Rice).   New York, Greenberg, 1936; London, Methuen, 1938.
The Eleven of Diamonds (Rice).   New York, Greenberg, 1936; London, Methuen, 1937.
The Last Express (Maclain).   New York, Doubleday, 1937; London, Methuen, 1938.
The Whistling Hangman (Maclain).   New York, Doubleday, 1937; London, Hale, 1959.
Death Beyond the Go-Thru (Rice).   New York, Doubleday, 1938.
The Odor of Violets (Maclain).   Boston, Little Brown, and London, Methuen, 1941; as *Eyes in the Night,* New York, Grossett and Dunlap, 1942.
Blind Man's Bluff (Maclain).   Boston, Little Brown, 1943; London, Methuen, 1944.
Out of Control (Maclain).   New York, Morrow, 1945; London, Methuen, 1947.
Death Knell (Maclain).   New York, Morrow, 1945; London, Methuen, 1946.
Make Mine Maclain (omnibus).   New York, Morrow, 1947; reprinted in part as *The Murderer Who Wanted More,* New York, Dell, 1951.
The Tunnel.   New York, Scribner, 1949.
You Die Today (Maclain).   New York, Morrow, 1952; London, Hale, 1958.
Trapped (as Richard Hayward).   New York, Fawcett, 1952.
Blind Allies (Maclain).   New York, Morrow, 1954.
The Soft Arms of Death (as Richard Hayward).   New York, and London, Fawcett, 1955.
Reservations for Death (Maclain).   New York, Morrow, 1957; London, Hale, 1958.
Clear and Present Danger (Maclain).   New York, Doubleday, 1958; London, Hale, 1959.
Hot Red Money.   New York, Dodd Mead, 1959; London, Hale, 1962.
The Aluminum Turtle (Maclain).   New York, Dodd Mead, 1960; as *The Spear Gun Murders,* London, Hale, 1961.
Frankincense and Murder (Maclain).   New York, Dodd Mead, 1961; London, Hale, 1962.
Flight from a Firing Wall.   New York, Simon and Schuster, 1966; London, Hale, 1968.

Uncollected Short Stories

"The Eye," in *Ellery Queen's Mystery Magazine* (New York), November 1945.

"Death at the Porthole," in *Murder Cavalcade,* edited by Ken Crossen. New York, Duell, 1946; London, Hammond, 1953.

"The Case of the Stuttering Sextant," in *Ellery Queen's Mystery Magazine* (New York), March 1947.

"Room for Murder," in *American Magazine* (Springfield, Ohio), September 1951.

"Melody of Death," in *The Saint* (New York), January 1956.

"The Cloth-of-Gold Murders," in *American Magazine* (Springfield, Ohio), February 1956.

"Headless Angel," in *The Saint* (New York), December 1957.

"Whipsaw," in *The Saint* (New York), November 1959.

"A Clue from Bing Crosby," in *Ellery Queen's Mystery Magazine* (New York), January 1963.

"Jose Gaspar and the Princess," in *The Saint* (New York), August 1963.

"Silent Night," in *Three Times Three,* edited by Howard Haycraft and John Beecroft. New York, Doubleday, 1964.

"5 − 4 = Murderer," in *Anthology* 1965, edited by Ellery Queen. New York, Davis, 1964.

"$10,000 Reward," in *Mike Shayne Mystery Magazine* (New York), October 1964.

"Murder Made in Moscow," in *The Award Espionage Reader,* edited by Hans Santefan Santesson. New York, Award, 1965.

"Mary—Mary—," in *Murder in Mind,* edited by Lawrence Treat. New York, Dutton, 1967.

OTHER PUBLICATIONS

Novels

Lights Out. New York, Morrow, 1945; London, W.H. Allen, 1948.
The Flames of Time. New York, Scribner, 1948.

Other

They Never Talk Back, with Henry Trefflick. New York, Appleton Century Crofts, 1954.
Florida Trails to Turnpikes. Gainesville, University of Florida Press, 1964.
Orlando: A Century Plus. Orlando, Florida, Sentinel Star, 1976.

*   *   *

Baynard Kendrick is in danger of being forgotten. One of the founders of the Mystery Writers of America—his membership card was Number One—and the MWA's first president, all of Kendrick's work is currently out-of-print in the United States.

Kendrick will best be remembered for his Captain Duncan Maclain series of mysteries. Captain Maclain, totally blind in most of the books, is aided by his two dogs, Schnucke and Dreist, and his best friend and partner, Spud Savage. Maclain operates a successful private detective business.

Captain Maclain's first case, *The Last Express,* involves a murder in a nightclub. The book concludes with a thrilling chase in New York City's abandoned subways. *The Whistling Hangman* displays even more clever plotting as Captain Maclain investigates the apparent suicide of a millionaire who supposedly jumped to his death from a hotel balcony. Yet, Maclain discovers the man actually died of hanging.

The Odor of Violets is a product of pre-World War II writing. Maclain investigates the death of a government agent which leads him to a gruesome murder of a witness by decapitation and the kidnapping of a young girl. The murderer is part of a spy ring that hopes to steal the plans to a new bomber sight and only Captain Maclain stands in their way. The climax where Maclain takes on the ax-wielding murderer is particularly memorable.

Blind Man's Bluff is one of the strongest novels in the series as Captain Maclain investigates a series of impossible murders. *Death Knell,* however, is one of the weaker entries in the series; a simple murder at a cocktail party isn't enough to engage Captain Maclain or the reader.

Out of Control is Captain Maclain's most exciting novel; most of the book centers on Maclain's chase and capture of a psychopathic woman in the Tennessee mountains. *Out of Control* generates edge-of-your-seat suspense as Maclain closes in on the murderer.

The remaining books in the series declined in quality and popularity until Kendrick ended the series with the lame *Frankincense and Murder.* Clearly, Kendrick was at the height of his powers in the 1930's and 1940's. The quality and quantity of his work diminished after 1950. However, Kendrick was awarded the Mystery Writers of America special distinction of Grand Master in 1967. Kendrick's early work, especially the first half dozen Captain Maclain novels, merit this recognition and honor.

—George Kelley

———

KENNEDY, Milward. Pseudonym for Milward Rodon Kennedy Burge; also wrote as Evelyn Elder; Robert Milward Kennedy. British. Born 21 June 1894. Educated at Winchester College; New College, Oxford. Served in the Military Intelligence Directorate of the War Office during World War I: Croix de Guerre; Director of the U.K. Information Office, Dominions Office, Ottawa, 1943–44. Married 1) Georgina Lee in 1921 (died 1924); 2) Eveline Schreiber Billiat in 1926; one son. Worked for the Ministry of Finance, Cairo, 1919–20; staff member, Geneva Office, 1920–24, and Director, London Office, 1924–45, International Labour Office: London editor, *Empire Digest,* 1945–49. Crime fiction reviewer, *Sunday Times,* London, for many years. *Died 20 January 1968.*

CRIME PUBLICATIONS

Novels (series: Sir George Bull; Inspector Cornford)

The Bleston Mystery (as Robert Milward Kennedy), with A. Gordon MacDonnell. London, Gollancz, 1928; New York, Doubleday, 1929.
The Corpse on the Mat (Cornford). London, Gollancz, 1929; as *The Man Who Rang the Bell,* New York, Doubleday, 1929.
Corpse Guard Parade (Cornford). London, Gollancz, 1929; New York, Doubleday, 1930.
Half-Mast Murder. London, Gollancz, and New York, Doubleday, 1930.
Death in a Deck-Chair. London, Gollancz, 1930; New York, Doubleday, 1931.
Murder in Black and White (as Evelyn Elder). London, Methuen, 1931.
Death to the Rescue. London, Gollancz, 1931.
The Floating Admiral, with others. London, Hodder and Stoughton, 1931; New York, Doubleday, 1932.
Angel in the Case (as Evelyn Elder). London, Methuen, 1932.

The Murderer of Sleep. London, Gollancz, 1932; New York, Kinsey, 1933.

Bull's Eye (Bull). London, Gollancz, and New York, Kinsey, 1933.

Ask a Policeman, with others. London, Barker, and New York, Morrow, 1933.

Corpse in Cold Storage (Bull). London, Gollancz, and New York, Kinsey, 1934.

Poison in the Parish. London, Gollancz, 1935.

Sic Transit Gloria. London, Gollancz, 1936; as *The Scornful Corpse,* New York, Dodd Mead, 1936.

I'll Be Judge, I'll Be Jury. London, Gollancz, 1937.

It Began in New York. London, Gollancz, 1943.

Escape to Quebec. London, Gollancz, 1946.

The Top Boot. London, Hale, 1950.

Two's Company. London, Hale, 1952.

Uncollected Short Stories

"Death in the Kitchen," and "Mr. Truefitt Detects," in *Great Short Stories of Detection, Mystery, and Horror 2,* edited by Dorothy L. Sayers. London, Gollancz, 1931; as *The Second Omnibus of Crime,* New York, Coward McCann, 1932.

"The Superfluous Murder," in *A Century of Detective Stories.* London, Hutchinson, 1935.

"End of a Judge," in *Detective Stories of Today,* edited by Raymond Postgate. London, Faber, 1940.

"The Accident," in *Evening Standard Detective Book,* 2nd series. London, Gollancz, 1951.

"The Fool," in *The Saint* (New York), January 1954.

"You've Been Warned," in *The Saint* (New York), February 1955.

"The Lost Ambassador," in *The Second Mystery Bedside Book,* edited by John Creasey. London, Hodder and Stoughton, 1961.

OTHER PUBLICATIONS

Novel

Who Was Old Willy? London, Hutchinson, 1940.

Other

"Are Murders Meant?" and "Murderers in Fiction," in *Detective Medley,* edited by John Rhode. London, Hutchinson, 1939.

* * *

Milward Kennedy was one of those crime writers, like Ellery Queen, Anthony Boucher, Julian Symons, and H. R. F. Keating, who combined fiction with criticism. Indeed, none other than Howard Haycraft in his influential work *Murder for Pleasure: The Life and Times of the Detective Story* singled him out as one of the most worthy writers. Well educated with a distinquished international Civil Service career, followed by an equally prestigious newspaper and literary life, he wrote a score of detective stories, reflecting the social mores of those times.

Kennedy could write equally of police investigations or of private sleuths, his main creation being Sir George Bull, the eponymous hero of *Bull's Eye,* and other books. There is a certain element of ironic humour in some stories; *The Murderer of Sleep* tells of a serial killer in a village in Wales.

Poison in the Parish is told in the first person, subjectively, by an ex-officer in his forties; the style seems older, the narrator is

himself tedious, although to do him justice, he seems to know this, and it is not long before the reader senses this is an "inverted" type of tale, of the genus Keating has described as "acroidal." Equally pompous, but much more unpleasant, is the narrator of *Death to the Rescue,* in which a wealthy estate-owner starts spying on a neighbour he suspects of being a murderer some years earlier, flirts ponderously with a young woman staying nearby, scares off her possible admirer, is violently accused by a village girl of interfering in her romance, is warned off unsubtly by the neighbour's staff—and finally reaches a bitter denoument, necessarily objectively. A cross between an unpleasant old man and an interfering old woman, he rates almost as HIBK—Ogden Nash's "Had I But Known" school, as his blunderings trap him whichever way he might hope to turn. The literary style of these two books is certainly right for the respective narrators, the rythms precise and precious, but the effect is not only to make the narrators unlovable but to slow down the action. This latter novel contains a dedicatory letter to Anthony Berkely Kennedy which stresses the niceness and nastiness of Kennedy's characters, and pleads for the novel of pure detection. Other books have different milieus, for example the high seas for *Half-Mast Murder,* and *Death in a Deck-Chair.*

Kennedy was a member of the famous Detection Club, which brought out at intervals group efforts, similar to the American *The President's Mystery Story,* suggested by President F. D. Roosevelt to Fulton Oursler, who in turn enlisted six others, including his own *alter ego* Anthony Abbot (of whom he truthfully says only one knew of the idea!) to write a chapter each. The Detection Club published *The Floating Admiral* and *Ask a Policeman,* and Kennedy contributed to both volumes. The title of *Ask a Policeman* is taken from a satirical music-hall song, really implying corruption in that if you want to know the time, ask a policeman as he will "of course" have "a watch and chain." In this story newspaper peer Lord Comstock is killed at Hursley Lodge, his visitors, and therefore suspects, including the Government Chief Whip, an Archbishop, and an Assistant Commissioner of Scotland Yard. Part 1 starts with letters from Kennedy to John Rhode, as does Part III, and each contributor, Dorothy L. Sayers, Anthony Berkley, Helen Simpson, or Gladys Mitchell, write their chapters about a sleuth not of their own creation, a somewhat complicated example of parody causing muddle to the publisher who had suggested the title, and to Kennedy who agrees Sayers's slip in her Roger Sheringham chapter. The book is good fun, and good reading for all that. Most of the best writers of the time took part in these group efforts, solving this predecessors' puzzle and creating new ones for these sucessors.

It is obviously right for crime writers, whose books may have been unobtainable for some years, to be re-issued so that some readers may return refreshed, and fresh readers turn to an author previously unknown to them; if the style seems too outré on its own, perhaps the omnibus should make its reappearance with Milward Kennedy as one of its passengers.

—John Kennedy Melling

———

KENRICK, Tony. British. Born in Sydney, New South Wales, Australia, 23 August 1935. Educated at Sydney High School. National service in the Royal Australian Navy, 1953. Married Joan Wells in 1960; one daughter and one son. Advertising copywriter for Farmer's, Sydney, 1953–56, Notley's, London, 1956–57, McClaren's, Toronto, 1957–60, Doyle

Dane Bernbach, New York, 1960–62, Johnson and Lewis, San Francisco, 1962–65, Manhoff, New York, 1965–68, and C.D.P., London, 1968–72. Agent: Jean Naggar, 216 East 75th Street, New York, New York 10021; or, William Morris Agency, Inc., 151 El Camino Drive, Beverly Hills, California 90212, U.S.A. Address: 175 Cumberland Street, No. 1910, Toronto, Ontario M5R 3M9, Canada.

CRIME PUBLICATIONS

Novels

The Only Good Body's a Dead One. London, Cape, 1970; New York, Simon and Schuster, 1971.
A Tough One to Lose. London, Joseph, and Indianapolis, Bobbs Merrill, 1972.
Two for the Price of One. London, Joseph, and Indianapolis, Bobbs Merrill, 1974.
The Kidnap Kid. London, Joseph, 1975; as *Stealing Lillian,* New York, McKay, 1975.
The Seven Day Soldiers. London, Joseph, and Chicago, Regnery, 1976.
The Chicago Girl. New York, Putnam, 1976; London, Joseph, 1977.
Two Lucky People. London, Joseph, and New York, New American Library, 1978.
The Nighttime Guy. London, Granada, and New York, Morrow, 1979.
The 81st Site. New York, New American Library, and London, Granada, 1980.
Faraday's Flowers. New York, Doubleday, 1984; London, Coronet, 1986; as *China White.* Boston, Little Brown, 1986; London, Hodder and Stoughton, 1987.
Shanghai Surprise, New York, Penguin, and London, Hodder and Stoughton, 1986.
Neon Tough. New York, Putnam, and London, Joseph, 1988.

OTHER PUBLICATIONS

Play

Screenplay: *Nobody's Perfect,* 1981.

* * *

Tony Kenrick is best known for his cleverly plotted crime novels in the Donald E. Westlake tradition. *A Tough One to Lose* features a gang of professional thieves who skyjack a Boeing 747—including the 360 passengers. They demand $25 million in ransom with a foolproof method of making the exchange. But the most interesting part of the caper is that they manage to make the plane and passengers disappear. Kenrick practices some first-class trickery here.

In *Two for the Price of One,* another gang of professional thieves take control of a Navy destroyer in the waters just off New York City. They point the five-inch guns at the Chase Manhattan Bank and demand five million dollars or they'll reduce the building to rubble. To show they're not making idle threats, the gang fires an incendiary shell at the bank and wipes out a floor. The surprising conclusion is a classic.

The Kidnap Kid is a caper in reverse. The CIA knows that a band of terrorists plan to kidnap a millionaire's child. So they secretly replace the entire millionaire's family with look-a-likes who happen to be a small-time con man, the con man's latest victim, and a nine-year old orphan who talks like a Marine drill sergeant with a bad hangover. The plan works: the terrorists

kidnap Lillian thinking she's the millionaire's daughter. Kenrick's plot has more dazzling twists than his earlier books.

The Seven Day Soldiers starts out as a caper but changes into a survival novel. Three small business men find they need more money. One of them comes up with a foolproof method of robbing a Swiss bank—by mail. They carry out their plan and it works: they split a cool 20 thousand dollars. Then they get the idea of transferring *all* the funds into an account, not just part of the funds like they did the first time. That works, too. Only too well. The businessmen find they transferred all the funds ($167 million) into a secret account of an exiled South American dictator: and this vicious dictator wants his money back. The three businessmen hide their families and then isolate themselves in a mountain retreat with a drill sergeant they hire. His job is to turn them into soldiers in seven days: that's when the dictator and his 24 body guards are coming after the money. Kenrick again twists the conclusion in an unexpected fashion.

The Chicago Girl begins in 1964 when a hooker with an English accent and lots of class becomes the lover of gangland leader, Ziggy Kurtz. When Ziggy died, he left one request with his partner and best friend, George Devine: give his lover a stolen emerald necklace worth $800,000. Devine's problem is that the hooker has disappeared. Years pass and Henry Redding, hotshot New York reporter, learns of Kurtz's last request and Devine's intention to carry it out. He devises a scheme to con Devine into handing the stolen emerald necklace over—Redding knows the insurance company will pay $400,000 to get it back. Redding thinks he has the perfect scam, but in Kenrick's novels perfect plans always have a flaw and the plot of *The Chicago Girl* is no different.

The Nighttime Guy is a medical thriller. Max Ellis is invited by the CIA to take part in an experiment of a new, top secret drug. Max agrees and finds that he can see in total darkness. Unfortunately, the experiment has an unforeseen side effect: Max can *only* see in total darkness: he can't see in the light of day. Enemy agents try to capture Max and he finds himself despairing that he will ever see normally again. *The Nighttime Guy* is a fast-paced thriller.

The 81st Site is Kenrick writing and plotting at his best. By the end of World War II, the Nazis had built 81 concealed missile sites to launch V1-flying bombs against England. After the war, 80 of the sites were found and destroyed. For 30 years, Willie Lauter, a loyal Nazi, and his secret group have been searching for the 81st site. Now they've found it and they plan to launch a V1 rocket at London. Only this time, instead of carrying high explosives, the V1 will be carrying a homemade atomic bomb. Jimmy Pelham, an insurance investigator, stumbles on the scheme but no one will believe him—no one but a dizzy and beautiful Swiss woman named Rossi. Together they race to stop Lauter and his band of Nazis from nuking London in a story of non-stop suspense.

Faraday's Flowers features an out-of-luck businessman who's got nothing to lose and a beautiful missionary who needs his help. Together they take on Chinese secret societies and secret police over a fortune in drugs. The Oriental setting is an interesting change-of-pace for Kenrick fans.

China White opens with the killing of Atlanta vice detective Billy Marcus' partner's death. Marcus seeks to avenge his partner's murder by assuming a dead drug smuggler's identity. Marcus joins a heroin smuggling ring which leads to its leader, London millionaire Charles Bendroit. When a $50 million deal appears, Marcus arranges for his own deal that includes destroying the heroin ring and its leader while extracting his own personal vengeance. *China White* features a nifty assassin called Jay Jay whose weapon of choice is a coat hanger.

Kenrick returns to an Oriental setting for his latest book,

Neon Tough. U.S. drug enforcement agent Hugh Decker is given one last chance to save his career by investigating the vicious murder of a beautiful DEA agent, Angela Waters. Decker battles against Hong Kong's underworld with an unlikely team of agents: a sexy woman agent called Miriam the Mouth, a computer genius called Bumpy Landing, and a gourmet named Johnny Risotto. Together they take on a multinational conspiracy headed by Arthur Murdoch and his murderous assassin, Major Reggie Slemp.

Kenrick's best works blend comic caper plots with furious action.

—George Kelley

KENYON, Michael. Has also written as Daniel Forbes. British. Born in Huddersfield, Yorkshire, 26 June 1931. Educated at Leighton Park School, Reading, Berkshire; Wadham College, Oxford, 1951–54, M.A. in history; Duke University, Durham, North Carolina, 1954–55. Served in the Royal Air Force, 1949–51 (national service). Married Catherine Bury in 1961 (divorced 1988); three daughters. Reporter, Bristol *Evening Post*, 1955–58; *News Chronicle*, London, 1958–60; and *Guardian*, London, 1960–64. Visiting Lecturer in Journalism, University of Illinois, Urbana, 1964–66; Visiting Lecturer in Journalism and Crime Fiction, Southampton College, Long Island University, New York, 1977–78, 1982–83; 1985–86, 1988, 1990. Since 1971, regular contributor to *Gourmet* magazine, New York. Agent: Richard Scott Simon Ltd., 43 Doughty Street, London WCIN 2LF, England. Address: 164 Halsey Street, Southampton, New York 11968, U.S.A.

CRIME PUBLICATIONS

Novels (series: Superintendent O'Malley; Inspector Henry Peckover)

May You Die in Ireland. London, Collins, and New York, Morrow, 1965.
The Whole Hog. London, Collins, 1967; as *The Trouble with Series Three,* New York, Morrow, 1967.
Out of Season. London, Collins, 1968.
The 100,000 Welcomes (O'Malley). London, Collins, and New York, Coward McCann, 1970.
The Shooting of Dan McGrew (O'Malley). London, Collins, 1972; New York, McKay, 1975.
A Sorry State (O'Malley). London, Collins, and New York, McKay, 1974.
Mr. Big. London, Collins, 1975; (as Daniel Forbes), New York, Coward McCann, 1975.
The Rapist. London, Collins, 1977; (as Daniel Forbes), New York, Coward McCann, 1977.
Deep Pocket. London, Collins, 1978; as *The Molehill File,* New York, Coward McCann, 1978.
Zigzag (O'Malley; Peckover). London, Collins, 1981.
The Elgar Variations (Peckover). New York, Putnam, 1981.
The God Squad Bod (Peckover). London, Collins, 1982; as *The Man at the Wheel,* New York, Doubleday, 1982.
A Free-Range Wife (Peckover). London, Collins, and New York, Doubleday, 1983.
A Healthy Way to Die. London, Hodder and Stoughton, and New York, Doubleday, 1986.

Peckover Holds the Baby. London, Severn House, and New York, Doubleday, 1988.

OTHER PUBLICATIONS

Novel

Green Grass. London, Macmillan, 1969.

Other

Brainbox and Bull (for children). London, Angus and Robertson, 1976.

*

Michael Kenyon comments:

Asking a writer to introduce his work seems reasonable but I have this fairly desperate feeling the result will be pretentious or over-diffident, and certainly misleading. My stories are light-thrillerish rather than mysterious or puzzling. When I fell into crime writing I had read nothing in the genre and was slightly contemptuous of it, which no doubt shows, at least in the earlier books. I wanted to write not suspense fiction but "Childe Harold," and "The Night the Bed Fell" and *Lucky Jim,* and hoped to do so once a dashed-off thriller or two had brought me the time and money. Now that I have read, late in the day, a fair amount of crime fiction, I have only admiration and increasing enthusiasm for it—for the best of it—and an ambition to do as well. I like to think my more recent stories are more serious, plottier, and not necessarily duller than the earlier, jokey ones. My personal best, the really excellent crime novel, is the one about to be written, always. I have not managed it yet, but I will, I will, I will . . .

*   *   *

Michael Kenyon is a thriller writer with a genuine comic (as opposed to farcical) gift. He gave himself a head start by setting most of his early books in Ireland where, to the rest of the English-speaking world, gaiety and sorrow, tragedy and mirth, have long overlapped. Where else could the investigation of rape and murder (*The Rapist*) be made funny and frightening at the same time? In this book as in several others he uses the American visitor to Ireland as the catalyst for both comedy and violence when the new world comes into confrontation with the old. Refereeing the resulting clash we find the *garda* or Irish police, most notably the sympathetic, percipient and on occasions comically lugubrious Superintendent O'Malley. Kenyon's humour and skills of characterization and narrative are beautifully illustrated in the opening sequence of *A Sorry State* which shows O'Malley on a plane journey to the Philippines during which he demonstrates a typically Irish antidote to jet-lag. It's a richly amusing account, but the journey also provides the reader with essential background information in a single easy-to-swallow dose.

But Kenyon is in no way restricted to Irish settings and jokes. In *Mr. Big* he takes us to the centre of things English, Buckingham Palace, where his villain/hero is planning to rob the Queen, *A Free-Range Wife* is set in France, and *The God Squad Bod* ends up in Little Rock, Arkansas. These last two star Kenyon's other police creation, Chief Inspector Henry Peckover, Scotland Yard's Cockney poet who has a hilarious encounter with O'Malley in *Zigzag*. The dangers of Kenyon's writing are that the fast-moving plots can sometimes seem to be free-wheeling out of control, and the quirky humour can sometimes bubble over into mere facetiousness. But these are risks well worth running for the vast amount of honest pleasure and criminal excitement these books have to offer.

—Reginald Hill

* * *

KEPPEL, Charlotte. See **BLACKSTOCK, Charity.**

* * *

KERR, Ben. See **ARD, William.**

* * *

KERSEY, John. See **WARRINER, Thurman.**

* * *

KERSH, Gerald. American. Born in Teddington-on-Thames, Middlesex, England, 6 August 1911; naturalized United States citizen, 1959. Educated at Regent Street Polytechnic, London. Served in the Coldstream Guards, 1940–41; transferred to special duties, 1942; scriptwriter, Army Film Unit, 1943; specialist in the Films Division, Ministry of Information, 1943–44; accredited to SHAEF, 1944. Married 1) Alice Thompson Rostron in 1938 (marriage dissolved 1943); 2) Claire Alyne Pacaud in 1943 (marriage dissolved 1955); 3) Florence Sochis in 1955. Worked as a baker, nightclub bouncer, fish and chips cook, and wrestler in the 1930's; chief feature writer (as Piers England), 1941–45, and war correspondent, 1943, *The People,* London; settled in the United States after World War II. Recipient: Mystery Writers of America Edgar Allan Poe award, 1957. *Died 5 November 1968.*

CRIME PUBLICATIONS

Novels

Jews Without Jehovah. London, Wishart, 1934.
Men Are So Ardent. London, Wishart, 1935; New York, Morrow, 1936.
Night and the City. London, Joseph, 1938; New York, Simon and Schuster, 1946.
They Die with Their Boots Clean. London, Heinemann, 1941; in *Sergeant Nelson of the Guards,* 1945.
The Nine Lives of Bill Nelson. London, Heinemann, 1942; in *Sergeant Nelson of the Guards,* 1945.
The Dead Look On. London, Heinemann, and New York, Reynal, 1943.
Brain and Ten Fingers. London, Heinemann, 1943.
Faces in a Dusty Picture. London, Heinemann, 1944; New York, McGraw Hill, 1945.
An Ape, A Dog, and a Serpent. London, Heinemann, 1945.
Sergeant Nelson of the Guards. Philadelphia, Winston, 1945.
The Weak and the Strong. London, Heinemann, 1945; New York, Simon and Schuster, 1946.

Prelude to a Certain Midnight. New York, Doubleday, and London, Heinemann, 1947.
The Song of the Flea. New York, Doubleday, and London, Heinemann, 1948.
Clock Without Hands. London, Heinemann, 1949.
The Thousand Deaths of Mr. Small. New York, Doubleday, 1950; London, Heinemann, 1951.
The Great Wash. London, Heinemann, 1953; as *The Secret Masters,* New York, Ballantine, 1953.
Fowler's End. New York, Simon and Schuster, 1957; London, Heinemann, 1958.
The Implacable Hunter. London, Heinemann, 1961.
A Long Cool Day in Hell. London, Heinemann, 1965.
The Angel and the Cuckoo. New York, New American Library, 1966; London, Heinemann, 1967.
Brock. London, Heinemann, 1969.

Short Stories

Selected Stories. London, Staples Press, 1943.
The Battle of the Singing Men. London, Everybody's Books, 1944.
The Horrible Dummy and Other Stories. London, Heinemann, 1944.
Neither Man nor Dog. London, Heinemann, 1946.
Clean, Bright, and Slightly Oiled. London, Heinemann, 1946.
Sad Road to the Sea. London, Heinemann, 1947.
The Brazen Bull. London, Heinemann, 1952.
The Brighton Monster and Others. London, Heinemann, 1953.
Guttersnipe: Little Novels. London, Heinemann, 1954.
Men Without Bones and Other Stories. London, Heinemann, 1955; abridged edition, New York, Paperback Library, 1962.
On an Odd Note. New York, Ballantine, 1958.
The Ugly Face of Love and Other Stories. London, Heinemann, 1960.
The Terribly Wild Flowers: Nine Stories. London, Heinemann, 1962.
More Than Once upon a Time. London, Heinemann, 1964.
The Hospitality of Miss Tolliver and Other Stories. London, Heinemann, 1965.
Nightshade and Damnations, edited by Harlan Ellison. New York, Fawcett, 1968; London, Coronet, 1969.

Uncollected Short Stories

"The Ambiguities of Lo Yeing Pai," in *Ellery Queen's Mystery Magazine* (New York), June 1968.
"Karmesin and the Trismagistus Formula," in *Ellery Queen's Mystery Magazine* (New York), March 1969.
"The Pettifur Collection," in *Ellery Queen's Murder Menu.* Cleveland, World, 1969.
"Karmesin the Fixer," in *Ellery Queen's Mystery Magazine* (New York), January 1970.
"Gambling Fever," in *Ellery Queen's Mystery Magazine* (New York), January 1971.
"Mr. Tomorrow," in *Ellery Queen's Headliners.* Cleveland, World, 1971; London, Gollancz, 1972.
"Dr. Ox Will Die at Midnight," in *Best Detective Stories of the Year 1971,* edited by Allen J. Hubin. New York, Dutton, 1971.
"One Case in a Million," in *Ellery Queen's Giants of Mystery.* New York, Davis, 1971.
"The Scar," in *Ellery Queen's Magicians of Mystery.* New York, Davis, 1976.

Plays

Screenplays: *Nine Men,* with Harry Watt, 1943; *The True Glory* (documentary), with others, 1945.

Other

I Got References.   London, Joseph, 1939.
The Best of Gerald Kersh, edited by Simon Raven.   London, Heinemann, 1960.

*   *   *

Gerald Kersh wrote about a man pursued by men without bones, about the Devil, about insane, strange, unforgettable people. Kersh's flair for the bizarre makes him hard to categorize. He was more than a mystery writer, though he wrote hundreds of suspenseful short stories. Gerald Kersh was an original.

Perhaps Kersh's talent for the bizarre stemmed from his bizarre life. When he was four years old, Kersh was declared dead of lung congestion. During the funeral, he sat up in his coffin, very much alive. In World War II, while Kersh served as a war correspondent during the London blitz, he was buried alive three times, and survived. Kersh was once a professional wrestler, and survived.

During his life Kersh produced 5000 magazine articles, 3000 short stories, and almost 40 books. His best-selling novel *Night and the City* was made into a movie. Unfortunately, Kersh's best novel, *Fowler's End,* has never been reprinted. It is a sprawling, Dickensian novel of London populated by Kersh's own brand of memorable characters.

But Kersh will be remembered chiefly for his brilliant short stories. "The Queen of Pig Island" is a love story of a beautiful girl without arms or legs who rules an island where a grim giant and a pair of midgets battle for her love. "What Ever Happened to Corporal Cuckoo?" tells of a soldier who lived for hundreds of years by accidentally becoming immortal. His story of centuries of slaughter and death is both sad and chilling. The best of Kersh's short stories can be found in *Nightshade and Damnations* (with an introduction by Harlan Ellison), and *On an Odd Note.*

Finally, Kersh will be remembered as an outstanding stylist capable of producing startling images like this one: "We hang about the necks of our tomorrows like hungry harlots about the necks of penniless sailors." Kersh's work remains superb, important, and original.

—George Kelley

———————

KIENZLE, William X(avier).   American.   Born in Detroit, Michigan, 11 September 1928. Educated at Sacred Heart Seminary College, Detroit, 1946–50; B.A. 1950; St. John's Seminary, Plymouth, Michigan, 1950–54: ordained priest, Roman Catholic Church, 1954; University of Detroit, 1968. Married Javan Herman Andrews in 1974. Archdiocesan priest in five parishes, Detroit, 1954–74; editor-in-chief, *Michigan Catholic,* Detroit, 1962–74, and *MPLS* magazine, Minneapolis, 1974–77; associate director, Center for Contemplative Studies, Western Michigan University, Kalamazoo, 1977–78; director, Center for Contemplative Studies, University of Dallas, Irving,

Texas, 1978–79. Address: 2465 Middlebelt, West Bloomfield, Michigan 48033-1685, U.S.A.

Novels (series: Father Robert Koesler in all books)

The Rosary Murders.   Mission, Kansas, Andrews and McMeel, and London, Hodder and Stoughton, 1979.
Death Wears a Red Hat.   Mission, Kansas, Andrews and McMeel, 1980; London, Hodder and Stoughton, 1981.
Mind over Murder.   Fairway, Kansas, Andrews and McMeel, and London, Hodder and Stoughton, 1981.
Assault with Intent.   Fairway, Kansas, Andrews and McMeel, 1982.
Shadow of Death.   Fairway, Kansas, Andrews and McMeel, 1983; London, Severn House, 1984.
Kill and Tell.   Fairway, Kansas, Andrews McMeel and Parker, 1984.
Sudden Death.   Fairway, Kansas, Andrews McMeel and Parker, 1985; London, Hale, 1986.
Deathbed.   Kansas City, Missouri, Andrews McMeel and Parker, 1986.
Deadline for a Critic.   Kansas City, Missouri, Andrews McMeel and Parker, 1987; London, Hale, 1988.
Marked for Murder.   Kansas City, Missouri, Andrews and McMeel, 1988; London, Hale, 1990.
Eminence.   Kansas City, Missouri, Andrews and McMeel, 1989.
Masquerade.   Kansas City, Missouri, Andrews and McMeel, 1990.

Play

Campaign Capers (produced Detroit, 1960).

*

Manuscript Collection: University of Detroit Library, Michigan.

William X. Kienzle comments:
The fictional sleuth of my murder mystery series is a Father Robert Koesler. He is—as I was—a Detroit diocesan Catholic priest, past editor of a weekly Catholic paper, and pastor of St. Anselm's, a suburban parish. We are the same age, height, and build. We have a similar philosophy of life. I know him well. Because my sleuth is a Catholic priest, there is a strong religious thread running throughout the series. There is a strong—one might say almost unrelenting—tendency today to depict fictional Catholic priests as troubled, insecure people who doubt their faith and/or vocation, and whose commitment to the celibate life is foundering or has disappeared. None of my priests will have that problem. My fictional priests are human but they are strong in their calling. This is a reflection of the respect I still have for the vocation I once was privileged to exercise. My approach to the mystery genre is, I would hope, in the traditional British style, in that, among a plethora of red herrings, there are the genuine clues needed to solve the mystery. I believe a mystery novel essentially should be a game between author and reader. The game, I think, is the element that adds the ingredient of fun to a mystery.

*   *   *

G.K. Chesterton, in 1901, wrote in defense of the detective story, stating that modern man needed romance and adventure which could be found in an ordinary London street; later, he created Father Brown. The detective story no longer needs defense, and William X. Kienzle must have concluded that contemporary persons also need laughter. With wit and humor, he created Father Robert Koesler for the streets of Detroit. Very unlike Father Brown, Father Koesler is six-foot-three, a mystery buff, and given to reflection. Kienzle's novels are contemporary, Catholic, catholic, urban and urbane.

As editor of the Detroit weekly diocesan paper, Father Koesler becomes interested in and then involved when he discovers the second victim in a series of murders of priests and nuns in *The Rosary Murders*. He is asked for help by Lt. Walter Koznicki who works with black Sgt. Ned Harris. With live-in-lovers, reporters Joe Cox and Pat(ricia) Lennon, a kind of detective triumvirate is formed, but it is Father Koesler who ponders mystery stories for clues, motive, and resolution. In addition to the mystery, this and subsequent novels reveal changes within the Roman Catholic church since Vatican II and reactions to them. They also expose human eccentricities and foibles in vignettes, in anecdotes, and in characterizations, often satiric or comic. They are not restricted to Catholics but are catholic.

Death Wears a Red Hat has a somewhat changed triumvirate. Koznicki is an Inspector, Harris a lieutenant, and Cox has won a Pulitzer for his coverage of the first case. Father Koesler is pastor of a church. Koznicki again comes to him for help because the heads of victims—criminals and malefactors—are found in churches, the first under the Cardinal's hat. Father Koesler has become a friend of Koznicki and of Ramon Toussaint, a married black deacon from Haiti who appears in another novel as do other minor characters. Pat Lennon contributes a great deal here.

Mind over Murder, a tricky title to entrap readers, has a jape for the reader who recognizes a clue to a Poe story before Father Koesler does—and both end with egg on face. But Father Koesler uses ratiocination for the conclusion. *Assault with Intent* zeroes in on diocesan seminaries, where Father Koesler is part-time faculty. There are fewer references to detective fiction, some hilarious satire, and some lengthy "stand" discussions. The tendency toward longer explanations and more anecdotes continues in *Shadow of Death* wherein they travel to Rome for the Archbishop's becoming a cardinal, and then to London and Ireland. *Kill and Tell* is back in Detroit where the most-likely is not the victim at a party attended by Father Koesler. Detroit is a microcosm for contemporary urban society of ethnic and racial mix.

Kienzle's novels are longer and more leisurely than most mysteries, more discursive, and with shorter episodic scenes than in tightly plotted action stories of confrontation and violence. But the bizarre plots, the sharp delineation of even the most minor characters (with more warts than beauty spots), and the sophisticated urbanity of the telling make them first-rate literate reading. One also suspects private jokes. Kienzle acknowledges his indebtedness to Robert Ankeny, staff writer of the Detroit *News*: Pat Lennon's sympathetic editor at the *News* is Bob Ankenazy. Ralph McInerny writes the Father Dowling mystery series, and in *Death Wears a Red Hat* a Father McInerny discovers a derelict in a confessional box who had given a woman two thousand rosaries as a penance. Here is high entertainment with ideas. Even Father Brown dispensed social commentary—but without humor.

—Jane Gottschalk

—————

KING, Rufus (Frederick). American. Born in New York City, 3 January 1893. Educated at Dodsworth School; Yale University, New Haven, Connecticut. Served in the United States Army Cavalry on the Mexican border and in the Field Artillery in France during World War I: First Lieutenant; conspicuous service cross. Wireless operator in the Merchant Marine, and traveled in South America before beginning to write: created the detective Reginald De Puyster in magazine stories in the 1920's. *Died in 1966.*

CRIME PUBLICATIONS

Novels (series: Lieutenant Valcour)

Mystery De Luxe. New York, Doran, 1927; as *Murder De Luxe,* London, Leonard Parsons, 1927.
The Fatal Kiss Mystery. New York, Doubleday, 1928.
Murder by the Clock (Valcour). New York, Doubleday, and London, Chapman and Hall, 1929.
A Woman Is Dead (Valcour). London, Chapman and Hall, 1929; as *Somewhere in This House,* New York, Doubleday, 1930; as *A Murderer in This House,* New York, Novel Selections, 1945.
Murder by Latitude (Valcour). New York, Doubleday, 1930; London, Heinemann, 1931.
Murder in the Willett Family (Valcour). New York, Doubleday, 1931.
Murder on the Yacht (Valcour). New York, Doubleday, and London, Hamish Hamilton, 1932.
Valcour Meets Murder. New York, Doubleday, 1932.
The Lesser Antilles Case. New York, Doubleday, 1934; as *Murder Challenges Valcour,* New York, Dell, 1944.
Profile of a Murder (Valcour). New York, Harcourt Brace, 1935.
The Case of the Constant God (Valcour). New York, Doubleday, 1936; London, Methuen, 1938.
Crime of Violence (Valcour). New York, Doubleday, 1937; London, Methuen, 1938.
Murder Masks Miami (Valcour). New York, Doubleday, and London, Methuen, 1939.
Holiday Homicide. New York, Doubleday, 1940; London, Methuen, 1941.
Design in Evil. New York, Doubleday, 1942.
A Variety of Weapons. New York, Doubleday, 1943.
The Case of the Dowager's Etchings. New York, Doubleday, 1944; London, Methuen, 1946; as *Never Walk Alone,* New York, Popular Library, 1951.
The Deadly Dove. New York, Doubleday, 1945.
Museum Piece No. 13. New York, Doubleday, 1946; as *Secret Beyond the Door,* New York, Triangle, 1947.
Lethal Lady. New York, Doubleday, 1947.
The Case of the Redoubled-Cross. New York, Doubleday, 1949.
Duenna to a Murder. New York, Doubleday, and London, Methuen, 1951.

Short Stories

Diagnosis: Murder. New York, Doubleday, 1941; London, Methuen, 1942.
Malice in Wonderland. New York, Doubleday, 1958.
The Steps to Murder. New York, Doubleday, 1960.
The Faces of Danger. New York, Doubleday, 1964.

Uncollected Short Stories

"A Lonely, Lovely Lady," in *The Saint* (New York), April 1965.
"The Patron Saint of the Impossible," in *Anthology 1967,* edited by Ellery Queen.   New York, Davis, 1966.
"Anatomy of a Crime," in *Ellery Queen's Mystery Magazine* (New York), December 1966.

OTHER PUBLICATIONS

Novels

North Star: A Dog Story of the Canadian Northwest. New York, Watt, 1925.
Whelp of the Winds: A Dog Story.   New York, Doran, and London, Cassell, 1926.

Plays

Murder at the Vanities, with Earl Carroll, music and lyrics by John Green and others (produced New York, 1933).
Invitation to a Murder (produced New York, 1934).   New York, French, 1934.
I Want a Policeman, with Milton Lazarus (produced New York, 1936).   New York, Dramatists Play Service, 1937.

* * *

Rufus King had only one series detective, Lieutenant Valcour, a French-Canadian serving in the New York Police Department. Valcour is courteous, calm, and efficient. In several cases, because the crime has occurred in isolated circumstances, Valcour must work without the back-up of New York colleagues. *Murder on the Yacht* and *Murder by Latitude* take place at sea, and the criminal has prevented radio communication; King also placed Valcour in other remote places, including Canada. But Valcour was equally competent when the crime was urban. His best-known case, *Murder by the Clock,* is set in New York, and provides—typically for the period—many suspects and false trails. It has, moreover, a very nice twist at the end, the kind that makes one sorry the story must finish.

Touches of gentle humour are often lurking in King's novels and stories. One of his finest in this regard is *The Case of the Dowager's Etchings,* a light trifle, with the necessary ingredients of the War period. This is not a Valcour story, nor does he appear in any of the short stories. The best of King's short stories are collected in *Malice in Wonderland;* these are tightly constructed works from his late period, and often end with a malicious twist.

—Neville W. Wood

———

KIRK, Michael. *See* **KNOX, Bill.**

———

KITCHIN, C(lifford) H(enry) B(enn).   British.   Born in Harrogate, Yorkshire, 17 October 1895. Educated at Clifton College, Bristol; Exeter College, Oxford (scholar); Lincoln's Inn, London: called to the Bar, 1924. Served in the British Army in France, 1916–18. Lawyer and member of the Stock Exchange, London. *Died 2 April 1967.*

CRIME PUBLICATIONS

Novels (series: Malcolm Warren in all books)

Death of My Aunt.   London, Hogarth Press, 1929; New York, Harcourt Brace, 1930.
Crime at Christmas.   London, Hogarth Press, 1934; New York, Harcourt Brace, 1935.
Death of His Uncle.   London, Constable, 1939; New York, Harper, 1984.
The Cornish Fox.   London, Secker and Warburg, 1949.

OTHER PULICATIONS

Novels

Streamers Waving.   London, Hogarth Press, 1925.
Mr. Balcony.   London, Hogarth Press, 1927.
The Sensitive One.   London, Hogarth Press, 1931.
Olive E.   London, Constable, 1937.
Birthday Party.   London, Constable, 1938.
The Auction Sale.   London, Secker and Warburg, 1949.
The Secret River.   London, Secker and Warburg, 1956.
Ten Politt Place.   London, Secker and Warburg, 1957.
The Book of Life.   London, Davies, 1960; New York, Appleton Century Crofts, 1961.
A Short Walk in Williams Park.   London, Chatto and Windus, 1971.

Short Stories

Jumping Joan and Other Stories.   London, Secker and Warburg, 1954.

Verse

Curtains.   Oxford, Blackwell, 1919.
Winged Victory.   Oxford, Blackwell, 1921.

Other

Editor, with Vera M. Britain and Alan Porter, *Oxford Poetry 1920.*   Oxford, Blackwell, 1920.

* * *

A lawyer and mainstream novelist, C.H.B. Kitchin turned to the detective story in 1929, and produced his most famous work, *Death of My Aunt,* but mistakenly chose to stress characterization at the expense of puzzle and plot. This novel features the detective Malcolm Warren, a young stockbroker, who is summoned by his rich aunt to her country home to give advice about possible investments. She dies under mysterious circumstances, and Warren (who is the narrator) is suspected. His only recourse is to discover the guilty party.

Death of My Aunt has gathered a small but vocal band of admirers, including Jacques Barzun and Wendell Hertig Taylor who find that "the clues, the ratiocination, and the interplay of feeling among the members of the large family are as effective as the terse, bare prose and the headlong drive of the narrative." I dissent. The narrator seems to be so concerned with his own esthetic sensibilities, and the reactions of the others, that the reader's interest and attention are too often diverted from the novel's narrative flow and crime problem.

Warren gets involved in another mysterious death in *Crime at Christmas*, and is forced to play detective once again. This book moves less rapidly than its predecessor, and is of less interest. *Death of His Uncle* is twice as long and much better than *Death of My Aunt*, although it's easily guessable. Warren is now much more concerned with investigating a crime problem than with himself. Warren's last investigation, *The Cornish Fox*, starts with anonymous letters, continues with burglary, and proceeds to murder. This is a charming and clever mystery.

Julian Symons summed up Kitchin by stating, "There is a great deal of pleasure to be obtained from the always urbane and at times elegant writing." Kitchin himself once wrote, "A historian of the future will probably turn, not to blue books or statistics, but to detective stories if he wishes to study the manners of our age."

—Charles Shibuk

KNIGHT, Clifford (Reynolds). Also wrote as Reynolds Knight. American. Born in Fulton, Kansas, 7 December 1886. Educated at schools in Kansas, and the University of Michigan, Ann Arbor. Newspaper editor in Kansas City, then freelance writer in California. *Died*.

CRIME PUBLICATIONS

Novels (series: Huntoon Rogers in all "Affair" books)

The Affair of the Scarlet Crab. New York, Dodd Mead, and London, Gollancz, 1937.
The Affair of the Heavenly Voice. New York, Dodd Mead, 1937; London, Hale, 1938.
The Affair at Palm Springs. New York, Dodd Mead, 1938.
The Affair of the Ginger Lei. New York, Dodd Mead, 1938.
The Affair of the Black Sombrero. New York, Dodd Mead, 1939.
The Affair on the Painted Desert. New York, Dodd Mead, 1939.
The Affair in Death Valley. New York, Dodd Mead, 1940.
The Affair of the Circus Queen. New York, Dodd Mead, 1940.
The Affair of the Skiing Clown. New York, Dodd Mead, 1941.
The Affair of the Crimson Gull. New York, Dodd Mead, 1941.
The Affair of the Limping Sailor. New York, Dodd Mead, 1942.
The Affair of the Splintered Heart. New York, Dodd Mead, 1942.
The Affair of the Fainting Butler. New York, Dodd Mead, 1943.
The Affair of the Jade Monkey. New York, Dodd Mead, 1943.
The Affair of the Dead Stranger. New York, Dodd Mead, 1944.
The Affair of the Corpse Escort. Philadelphia, McKay, 1946.
The Affair of the Golden Buzzard. Philadelphia, McKay, 1946.
The Affair of the Sixth Button. Philadelphia, McKay, 1947.
Dark Abyss. New York, Dutton, 1949.
Hangman's Choice. New York, Dutton, 1949.
The Yellow Cat. New York, Dutton, 1950.

The Dark Road. New York, Dutton, 1951.
Death of a Big Shot. New York, Dutton, 1951.
Death and Little Brother. New York, Dutton, 1952.

Uncollected Short Stories

"The Affair on the Circle T," in *The Queen's Awards 1946*, edited by Ellery Queen. Boston, Little Brown, 1946; London, Gollancz, 1948.
"Death in the Valley," in *The Saint* (New York), January 1957.
"Never Kill a Cop," in *Ellery Queen's Mystery Magazine* (New York), June 1957.
"The Sergeant and the Skunks," in *The Saint* (New York), September 1959.
"In an Evil Time," in *The Saint* (New York), March 1960.

OTHER PUBLICATIONS

Novel as Reynolds Knight

Tommy of the Voices. Chicago, McClurg, 1918.

*   *   *

Clifford Knight was a reliable if unspectacular creator of classical detective novels with a special knack for eloquently described outdoor backgrounds, most often the natural wonders of the American West. The amiable but colorless amateur sleuth of most of Knight's books is Huntoon Rogers, a Professor of English seemingly on perpetual sabbatical. *The Affair of the Scarlet Crab*, winner of Dodd Mead's first Red Badge mystery award, is an orthodox 1930's entry about a scientific cruise to the Galapagos Islands. Knight plays fair with the reader, but as will often be the case, the setting is more interesting than the mystery plot. *The Affair of the Heavenly Voice*, concerning a school for mystery writers operated by a burnt-out novelist in her palatial home on the California coast, includes much discussion of detective-story construction as practiced by Knight and his contemporaries, including the role of the second murder: to prop up a story's "sagging middle," a problem to which Knight was especially prone. *The Affair of the Ginger Lei*, concerning a vividly described Los Angeles-to-Hawaii yacht race, offers a much stronger puzzle than its two predecessors. These early books include a Clue Index in the back, a device earlier used by C. Daly King, somewhat disappointing in that it mostly consists of facts in the text that are not inconsistent with the killer's identity rather than ones that specifically point to it.

Knight returns to a Hawaiian setting in *The Affair of the Splintered Heart*, less notable for its mystery plot than for its account of life in the Islands in the months after the attack on Pearl Harbor. Among the other colorful backgrounds in the Rogers series are Death Valley, Palm Springs, the Painted Desert, Yosemite National Park (*The Affair of the Jade Monkey*), Lake Tahoe (*The Affair of the Crimson Gull*), a circus ship in the Pacific (*The Affair of the Circus Queen*), the California snow country (*The Affair of the Skiing Clown*), a Mexican village (*The Affair of the Dead Stranger*), and a Nevada dude ranch ("The Affair on the Circle T"). *The Affair of the Fainting Butler*, probably one of the first mysteries to include an unrationalized paranormal element as part of the plot, and *The Affair of the Corpse Escort* offer some lively Hollywood-film-colony humor.

Critically praised in its early entries, the Rogers series declined in favor through the 1940's as mystery fashions changed. *Corpse Escort,* involving a highly unlikely studio publicity stunt, drew a telling description from Anthony Boucher of Huntoon Roger's function as a detective: "sitting around for 70,000 words and then bluntly accusing a man who kindly confesses" (San Francisco *Chronicle,* July 21, 1946).

Seeming determined to move with the times, Knight dropped Rogers and his *Affair* title pattern to experiment with other types of suspense novels. The results were mixed, but *The Yellow Cat,* hailed by Boucher as his best book, is a triumph. Hard and tough, almost entering James M. Cain territory, it has a greed-motivated and amoral murderess as its central character and a strong narrative movement that the Rogers novels sometimes lacked. *Death of a Big Shot* features as protagonist (and hero) a professional hitman, highly unusual at that time, but Knight's reach exceeds his grasp. The reader is never quite made to believe the chivalrous and sentimental Junior is really a hardened killer.

After the last of his novels had been published, Knight kept his hand in with occasional short stories. Exemplifying his continual stretching as a writer, the last two, "The Sergeant and the Skunks," about an LAPD bunco cop investigating the pigeon-drop swindle of Preachin' Annie while trying to combat the raids of skunks on his bee-hives, and "In an Evil Time," in which a college professor's dreams come true in the next morning's papers, are by far the best of them.

—Jon L. Breen

———

KNIGHT, David. *See* **PRATHER, Richard S.**

———

KNIGHT, Kathleen Moore. Also writes as Alan Amos. American.

CRIME PUBLICATIONS

Novels (series: Margot Blair; Elisha Macomber)

Death Blew Out the Match (Macomber). New York, Doubleday, and London, Heinemann, 1935.
The Clue of the Poor Man's Shilling (Macomber). New York, Doubleday, 1936; as *The Poor Man's Shilling,* London, Hammond, 1947.
The Wheel That Turned (Macomber). New York, Doubleday, 1936; as *Murder Greets Jean Holton,* n.p., Thriller Novel Classic, n.d.
Seven Were Veiled (Macomber). New York, Doubleday, 1937; as *Seven Were Suspect,* London, Withy Grove Press, 1942; as *Death Wears a Veil,* n.p., Novel Books, n.d.
The Tainted Token (Macomber). New York, Doubleday, 1938; London, Withy Grove Press, 1942; as *The Case of the Tainted Token,* n.p., Mystery Novel Classic, 1943.
Acts of Black Night (Macomber). New York, Doubleday, 1938.
Death Came Dancing (Macomber). New York, Doubleday, 1940; London, Withy Grove Press, 1946.
Rendezvous with the Past (Blair). New York, Doubleday, 1940; London, Withy Grove Press, 1941.

Exit a Star (Blair). New York, Doubleday, 1941; London, Withy Grove Press, 1943.
Bells for the Dead. New York, Doubleday, 1942; London, Withy Grove Press, 1943.
Terror by Twilight (Blair). New York, Doubleday, 1942; London, Withy Grove Press, 1943.
Trademark of a Traitor. New York, Doubleday, 1943; London, Hammond, 1945.
Design in Diamonds (Blair). New York, Doubleday, 1944; London, Hammond, 1945.
Intrigue for Empire. New York, Doubleday, 1944; London, Hammond, 1946; abridged edition, as *Murder for Empire,* n.p., Thriller Novel Classic, n.d.
Port of Seven Strangers. New York, Doubleday, 1945; London, Hammond, 1948.
Stream Sinister. New York, Doubleday, 1945; London, Hammond, 1948.
The Trouble at Turkey Hill (Macomber). New York, Doubleday, 1946; London, Hammond, 1949.
The Blue Horse of Taxco. New York, Doubleday, 1947; London, Hammond, 1950.
Footbridge to Death (Macomber). New York, Doubleday, 1947; London, Hammond, 1949.
Bait for Murder (Macomber). New York, Doubleday, 1948; London, Hammond, 1951.
Birds of Ill Omen. New York, Doubleday, 1948; London, Hammond, 1951.
The Bass Derby Murder (Macomber). New York, Doubleday, 1949; London, Hammond, 1953.
Dying Echo. New York, Doubleday, 1949; London, Hammond, 1952.
The Silent Partner. New York, Doubleday, 1950; London, Hammond, 1953.
Death Goes to a Reunion (Macomber). New York, Doubleday, 1952; London, Hammond, 1954.
Valse Macabre (Macomber). New York, Doubleday, 1952; London, Hammond, 1954.
Akin to Murder (Macomber). New York, Doubleday, 1953; London, Hammond, 1955.
Three of Diamonds (Macomber). New York, Doubleday, 1953; London, Hammond, 1955.
High Rendezvous. New York, Doubleday, 1954; London, Hammond, 1956.
The Robineau Look. New York, Doubleday, 1955; as *The Robineau Murders,* London, Hammond, 1956.
They're Going to Kill Me. New York, Doubleday, 1955; London, Hammond, 1957.
A Cry in the Jungle. London, Hammond, 1958.
Beauty Is a Beast (Macomber). New York, Doubleday, 1959; London, Hammond, 1960.
Invitation to Vengeance. New York, Doubleday, 1960; London, Hammond, 1961.

Novels as Alan Amos

Pray for a Miracle. New York, Duell, 1941; as *Jungle Murder,* n.p., Adventure Novel Classic, n.d.
Borderline Murder. New York, Doubleday, 1947.
Panic in Paradise. New York, Doubleday, 1951.
Fatal Harvest. New York, Doubleday, 1957; as Kathleen Moore Knight, London, Hammond, 1958.

*   *   *

More than half of the novels of Kathleen Moore Knight take place in areas other than New England, but she is mainly known for her 16 books featuring the adventures of Elisha Macomber. Macomber is the chairman of the Board of Selectmen of Penberthy Township (Penberthy Island), variously identified as Cape Cod or Martha's Vineyard. His similarities to Taylor's Asey Mayo can't be overlooked; however, the two characters differ in many ways. Elisha has a full-time job running a fish market and has more education than Asey ever did. He is also much more of a lone investigator, often trying to solve the cases before the more formal team of police and district attorneys arrive on the scene. In almost all of the Penberthy novels, Elisha's knowledge of the family history of those involved in the frequently gruesome killings provides the essential clue to the final solution. Knight was fond of letting the murderer, after making a final all-encompassing confession, cheat the properly constituted officials of an arrest, conviction, and execution. In one particular case, *Bait for Murder*, Knight doesn't play fair with the reader, by using the Christie ploy that made *The Mysterious Affair at Styles* so memorable. Macomber is softspoken with a genial sense of humor and, sometimes, an accent that almost defies transcription. Although the books were written over a period of 24 years, Elisha stays the same age (early seventies) and never seems to be afflicted with any physical ailments that might curtail his activities.

Three of his adventures take place in Panama during a visit in fulfillment of his lifetime ambition. In each instance the crimes involve young American women, their families, and romantic involvements. Elisha uses his collection of badges and letters of appreciation from governors and mayors to convince the American Consul that he be allowed to assist the local police.

Almost overlooked in the various travel/mysteries and Macomber books are the four adventures of Margot Blair, partner in the public relations firm of Norman and Blair. She is a woman in her middle thirties, with 10 years experience in public relations, and she seems to attract female clients who involve her in cases of murder, blackmail, and spy infiltration. Three cases directly involve the complications of daily life during World War II. One case, *Design in Diamonds*, takes Margot to Mexico City when the daughter of a dead client who had entrusted a fortune to the agency, writes that she wants her legacy sent to her there. Margot's partner is in the Army, stationed near New York when she needs to consult him, but Margot is not the had-I-but-known type of heroine who wanders around in the dark. Her helpers seem to bear most of the brunt of the physical damage inflicted in her books. Some of her more dithery debutante clients can become a bit wearisome.

As Alan Amos, and under her own name, Knight set many of her non-series books in Mexico and Panama, using American heroes, heroines, and a variety of artistic expatriates as characters. In many instances an item as in *The Blue Horse of Taxco* is the focal point of the story, its ownership being the motive behind the crime.

Geographical variety is one of Knight's strengths, with other stories set in Switzerland, Italy, and several states other than Massachusetts. Her heroines are almost always unattached and temporarily buffeted by depressing events in unfamilar towns. Her villains are divided equally between the sexes, but in nearly every instance the victim is well-deserving of elimination. Family relationships involving step-children, adopted children who don't realize that they are adopted, wills with clauses that affect several generations, and family reunions with one or two outsiders who stir up smouldering feuds are used frequently, but always with a different slant and texture.

The jacket designs of the earlier books with their skeleton fingers were an artistic delight and surely helped establish, for the reading public, an appreciation of Knight and her works.

—Ellen A. Nehr

KNOX, Bill (William Knox). Also writes as Michael Kirk; Robert MacLeod; Noah Webster. British. Born in Glasgow, 20 February 1928. Educated at local schools in Scotland. Served in the Royal Naval Auxiliary. Married Myra Ann McKill in 1950; two daughters and one son. Copy boy, Glasgow *Evening Citizen,* 1944–45; reporter, later deputy news editor, Glasgow *Evening News,* 1945–57; news editor, later Scottish editor, *Scottish Empire News,* Glasgow and London, 1957–60; news editor, Scottish Television, Glasgow, 1960–62. Since 1962, freelance author and broadcaster; writer and presenter, "Crime Desk" programme, Scottish Television, 1976–88. Recipient: Crime Writers Association Police Review award, 1986. Paul Harris Fellow, 1989. Agent: Century Hutchinson Ltd., Brookmount House, 62-65 Chandos Place, London WC2N 4NW, England. Address: 55 Newtonlea Avenue, Newton Mearns, Glasgow G77 5QF, Scotland.

CRIME PUBLICATIONS

Novels (series: Chief Officer Webb Carrick; Detective Chief Inspector Colin Thane and Phil Moss)

Deadline for a Dream (Thane and Moss). London, Long, 1957; as *In at the Kill,* New York, Doubleday, 1961.
The Cockatoo Crime. London, Long, 1958.
Death Department (Thane and Moss). London, Long, 1959.
Leave It to the Hangman (Thane and Moss). London, Long, and New York, Doubleday, 1960.
Death Calls the Shots. London, Long, 1961.
Die for Big Betsy. London, Long, 1961.
Little Drops of Blood (Thane and Moss). London, Long, and New York, Doubleday, 1962.
Sanctuary Isle (Thane and Moss). London, Long, 1962; as *The Grey Sentinels,* New York, Doubleday, 1963.
The Man in the Bottle (Thane and Moss). London, Long, 1963; as *The Killing Game,* New York, Doubleday, 1963.
The Drum of Ungara. New York, Doubleday, 1963; as *Drum of Power,* London, Long, 1964.
The Scavengers (Carrick). London, Long, and New York, Doubleday, 1964.
The Taste of Proof (Thane and Moss). London, Long, and New York, Doubleday, 1965.
Devilweed (Carrick). London, Long, and New York, Doubleday, 1966.
The Deep Fall (Thane and Moss). London, Long, 1966; as *The Ghost Car,* New York, Doubleday, 1966.
Blacklight (Carrick). London, Long, and New York, Doubleday, 1967.
Justice on the Rocks (Thane and Moss). London, Long, and New York, Doubleday, 1967.
The Klondyker (Carrick). London, Long, 1968; a *Figurehead,* New York, Doubleday, 1968.
The Tallyman (Thane and Moss). London, Long, and New York, Doubleday, 1969.
Blueback (Carrick). London, Long, and New York, Doubleday, 1969.

Children of the Mist (Thane and Moss).   London, Long, 1970; as *Who Shot the Bull?*, New York, Doubleday, 1970.

Seafire (Carrick).   London, Long, 1970; New York, Doubleday, 1971.

To Kill a Witch (Thane and Moss).   London, Long, 1971; New York, Doubleday, 1972.

Stormtide (Carrick).   London, Long, 1972; New York, Doubleday, 1973.

Draw Batons! (Thane and Moss).   London, Long, and New York, Doubleday, 1973.

Whitewater (Carrick).   London, Long, and New York, Doubleday, 1974.

Rally to Kill (Thane and Moss).   London, Long, and New York, Doubleday, 1975.

Hellspout (Carrick).   London, Long, and New York, Doubleday, 1976.

Pilot Error (Thane and Moss).   London, Long, and New York, Doubleday, 1977.

Witchrock (Carrick).   London, Long, 1977; New York, Doubleday, 1978.

Live Bait (Thane and Moss).   London, Long, 1978; New York, Doubleday, 1979.

Bombship (Carrick).   London, Hutchinson, and New York, Doubleday, 1980.

A Killing in Antiques (Thane and Moss).   London, Hutchinson, and New York, Doubleday, 1981.

Bloodtide (Carrick).   London, Hutchinson, 1982; New York, Doubleday, 1983.

The Hanging Tree (Thane and Moss).   London, Hutchinson, 1983; New York, Doubleday, 1984.

Wavecrest (Carrick).   London, Hutchinson, and New York, Doubleday, 1985.

The Crossfire Killings (Thane and Moss).   London, Century Hutchinson, and New York, Doubleday, 1986.

Dead Man's Mooring. (Carrick).   London, Century Hutchinson, 1987; New York, Doubleday, 1988.

The Interface Man. (Thane and Moss).   London, Century Hutchinson, 1989; New York, Doubleday, 1990.

Novels as Robert MacLeod (series: Talos Cord; Jonathan Gaunt; Andrew Laird; Gaunt books published as Noah Webster and Laird books as Michael Kirk in US)

Cave of Bats (Cord).   London, Long, 1964; New York, Holt Rinehart, 1966.

Lake of Fury (Cord).   London, Long, 1966; as *The Iron Sanctuary*, New York, Holt Rinehart, 1968.

Isle of Dragons (Cord).   London, Long, 1967.

Place of Mists (Cord).   London, Long, 1969; New York, McCall, 1970.

A Property in Cyprus (Gaunt).   London, Long, 1970; as *Flickering Death*, New York, Doubleday, 1971.

Path of Ghosts (Cord).   London, Long, and New York, McCall, 1971.

A Killing in Malta (Gaunt).   London, Long, and New York, Doubleday, 1972.

Nest of Vultures (Cord).   London, Long, 1973.

A Burial in Portugal (Gaunt).   London, Long, and New York, Doubleday, 1973.

All Other Perils (Laird).   London, Long, 1974; New York, Doubleday, 1975.

A Witchdance in Bavaria (Gaunt).   London, Long, 1975; New York, Doubleday, 1976.

Dragonship (Laird).   London, Long, 1976; New York, Doubleday, 1977.

A Pay-Off in Switzerland (Gaunt).   London, Long, and New York, Doubleday, 1977.

Salvage Job (Laird).   London, Long, 1978; New York, Doubleday, 1979.

An Incident in Iceland (Gaunt).   London, Long, and New York, Doubleday, 1979.

Cargo Risk (Laird).   London, Hutchinson, and New York, Doubleday, 1980.

A Problem in Prague (Gaunt).   London, Hutchinson, 1981; New York, Doubleday, 1982.

Mayday from Malaga (Laird).   London, Hutchinson, and New York, Doubleday, 1983.

A Legacy from Tenerife (Gaunt).   London, Hutchinson, and New York, Doubleday, 1984.

The Money Mountain (Gaunt).   London, Century Hutchinson, 1987; as *A Flight from Paris*, New York, Doubleday, 1987.

Witchline (Laird).   London, Century Hutchinson, and New York, Doubleday, 1988.

Short Stories

The View from Daniel Pike, with Edward Boyd.   London, Hutchinson, and New York, St. Martin's Press, 1974.

Uncollected Short Stories

"The Frightened American," in *Crimes Across the Sea,* edited by John Creasey.   New York, Harper, 1964; London, Harrap, 1965.

"The Service Flat," in *John Creasey's Mystery Bedside Book,* edited by Herbert Harris.   London, Hodder and Stoughton, 1966.

"Deerglen Queen," in *Crime Without Murder,* edited by Dorothy Salisbury Davis.   New York, Scribner, 1970.

"The Man Who Died Twice," in *John Creasey's Mystery Bedside Book 1972,* edited by Herbert Harris.   London, Hodder and Stoughton, 1971.

"The Case of the Myra-Ann," in *Cop Cade,* edited by John Ball.   New York, Doubleday, 1978.

"The Reluctant Dueller," in *John Creasey's Crime Collection 1980,* edited by Herbert Harris.   London, Gollancz, 1980.

"A Matter of Honor," in *Women's World* (Englewood, New Jersey), 3 August 1982.

"Don't Open Till Christmas," in *Women's World* (Englewood, New Jersey), 21 December 1983.

"Death at Black Light," in *Espionage* (Teaneck, New Jersey), March 1985.

"The Suspect Soldier," in *Espionage* (Teaneck, New Jersey), January 1986.

OTHER PUBLICATIONS

Plays

Radio Plays: *Leave It to the Hangman,* from his own novel, 1964; *Sanctuary Isle,* from his own novel, 1964; *To Kill a Witch,* from his own novel, 1972; *Death of a Marquis,* 1972; *The Tallyman,* from his own novel, 1973; *Draw Batons,* from his own novel, 1974; *The Taste of Proof,* 1974; *The Service Flat,* from his own story, 1976.

Television Play: *Little Drops of Blood,* from his own novel, 1965.

Other

Life Begins at Midnight, with R. Colquhoun.   London, Long, 1961.

Ecurie Ecosse: The Story of Scotland's International Racing Team, with David Murray.   London, Paul, 1962.

Final Diagnosis, with John Glaister. London, Hutchinson, 1964.
Court of Murder (trials in Glasgow). London, Long, 1968.

Editor, *The Thin Blue Line: The Story of the City of Glasgow Police,* by Douglas Grant. London, Long, 1973.

*

Manuscript Collection: Mugar Memorial Library, Boston University.

Bill Knox comments:

I consider my main strength in writing is my training and experience as a journalist, particularly as a crime reporter in the 1950's. This has given me, with present TV involvement, a close and continually up-dated knowledge of Scottish police and criminals. In the same way later journalism and broadcasting work called for much travel abroad (and still does), producing background material for those novels written under my pen-names Robert MacLeod, Michael Kirk, and Noah Webster.

My main writing output revolves around four series characters. In the Bill Knox books these are Glasgow policeman Colin Thane (procedural stories) and Scottish Fishery Protection Officer Webb Carrick (sea-going detection off the Scottish west coast). In the pseudonymous books these are Jonathan Gaunt, an external auditor with the Queen's and Lord Treasurer's Remembrancer in Edinburgh (overseas settings), and, most recently, Andrew Laird, a marine insurance claims investigator (again travel abroad).

* * *

Under his own name Bill Knox has written a series of police procedurals featuring Colin Thane and Phil Moss of the Glasgow CID and another detailing the action-filled career of Chief Officer Webb Carrick of the Scottish Fishery Protection Service. As Robert MacLeod (Noah Webster in the U.S.), he is the author of two more series, one about Jonathan Gaunt, agent for the Scottish Remembrancer's Office, the other about marine insurance investigator Andrew Laird. Although all the novels are flawed by repetitious introduction of character, the superior Thane-Moss series is distinguished by knowledgeable use of contemporary settings and events and a sure eye for social change. All Knox's novels are formulaic but competently written and plausibly plotted. Settings are smoothly integrated with plot and action, characters given sufficient individualilty for credibility, and humorous touches added to provide pleasant light entertainment.

The Thane-Moss novels, of which *The Taste of Proof* and *The Interface Man* are typical, combine necessary information about CID activities with emphasis upon the personalities of the two policemen. Inspectors in the early novels of the series, the men make a good team: Thane is married, impetuous, and intuitive; Moss, who suffers from chronic indigestion, is a diligent researcher. The fusion of fact and flair emables them to solve successfully a variety of cases, each presented in a separate book. In his most recent novels, *The Hanging Tree, The Crossfire Killings,* and *The Interface Man,* Knox has updated his cast of characters. Thane has been promoted superintendent and deputy chief of the Scottish Crime Squad, Moss sidelined to permanent desk duty, and new officers added. Detective Sergeant Francy Dunbar, motorcycle enthusiast and girl-chaser, provides youthful vigor, dog handler Jock Dawson offers a new area of expertise, and Constable Sandra Laing, both beautiful and intelligent, represents the female sex with

competent professionalism. The new characters modernize Knox's approach to police work without altering the basic formula of the novels. Concentration upon one major case continues, and allows Knox to provide realistic and thorough background for both characters and events and to include pertinent comment on changing aspects of Scottish life. In *The Taste of Proof* he fuses detailed knowledge of illicit whisky manufacture with commentary upon the effectiveness of slum clearance projects, an interest continued in *The Hanging Tree* where it meshes with the very up-to-date subject of video piracy. A financial scam using automated teller machines in *The Crossfire Killings* and computer fraud in *The Interface Man* indicate Knox's skillful use of the contemporary crime scene.

In the Webb Carrick novels, all set at sea or on remote islands in the Hebrides, Knox shows detailed knowledge of ships, deep-sea diving, fishing, and island life. Closer to the thriller than to traditional whodunits, these books follow the career of Chief Officer Webb Carrick of H.M.S. *Marlin,* his crusty captain James Shannon, and Chief Petty Officer William "Clapper" Bell through encounters with smugglers, spies, gun-runners, saboteurs, and hostile islanders. Espionage and oceanographic research are staples in many of the novels, and Carrick's ability to find a girl in every port adds perfunctory romantic interest. In the latest novel *Dead Man's Mooring* Carrick has been given command of his own ship, a promotion that does not really alter the formula although it introduces new characters.

Similar to the Carrick novels, although the exotic foreign locales are less interesting and convincing than Scottish seas and landscape, are those featuring Jonathan Gaunt and Andrew Laird. Gaunt and Laird are given different backgrounds, but are actually indistinguishable. Both young men, they pursue their occupations in such places as Copenhagen, Portugal, Cyprus, and Morocco. The novels are filled with action, but the plots in both series are as alike as the heroes and the denouements repetitious: the protagonist, usually with his current love interest, is captured and his life endangered; he escapes, often in a surge of violence, to ensure capture or elimination of the criminals. These novels are typical thrillers, and while Knox constructs ingenious fraud schemes and displays his usual knowledge of things maritime, they lack the sustained characterization and varied plotting of the Thane-Moss series.

—Jeanne F. Bedell

―――――

KNOX, James. *See* **BRITTAIN, William.**

―――――

KNOX, Ronald A(rbuthnott). British. Born in Knibworth, Leicestershire, 17 February 1888; son of the Bishop of Manchester; brother of the writer E.V. Knox. Educated at Summer Fields School, Oxford, 1896–1900; Eton College (co-editor, *The Outsider,* 1906), 1900–06; Balliol College, Oxford (Davies Scholar; Hertford Scholar, 1907; Ireland and Craven Scholar, 1908; Chancellor's Prize for Latin Verse, 1910), B.A. 1910. Worked at the War Office in military intelligence, summer 1916, 1917–18. Ordained deacon, 1911, and priest, 1912, Church of England; Fellow and Lecturer, 1910–17, and chaplain, 1912–17, Trinity College, Oxford: resigned on being converted to Roman Catholicism, 1917; ordained, 1919: taught at St. Edmund's College, Hertfordshire, 1919–26; Catholic chaplain, Oxford University, 1926–39; retired in 1939 to translate the Bible. D.Litt: National University of Ireland, Dublin, 1954. Honorary Fellow, Trinity College, Oxford, 1941, and Balliol College, Oxford, 1953. Fellow, Royal Society of Literature, 1950. Protonotary Apostolic, 1951; Member, Pontifical Academy, 1956. *Died 24 August 1957.*

CRIME PUBLICATIONS

Novels (series: Miles Bredon)

The Viaduct Murder. London, Methuen, 1925; New York, Simon and Schuster, 1926.
The Three Taps: A Detective Story Without a Moral (Bredon). London, Methuen, and New York, Simon and Schuster, 1927.
The Footsteps at the Lock (Bredon). London, Methuen, 1928; New York, Dover, 1983.
The Floating Admiral, with others. London, Hodder and Stoughton, 1931; New York, Doubleday, 1932.
The Body in the Silo (Bredon). London, Hodder and Stoughton, 1934; as *Settled Out of Court,* New York, Dutton, 1934.
Still Dead (Bredon). London, Hodder and Stoughton, and New York, Dutton, 1934.
Six Against the Yard, with others. London, Selwyn and Blount, 1936; as *Six Against Scotland Yard,* New York, Doubleday, 1936.
Double Cross Purposes (Bredon). London, Hodder and Stoughton, 1937; New York, Dover, 1986.
The Scoop, and Behind the Screen, with others. London, Gollancz, 1983.

Uncollected Short Stories

"Solved by Inspection," in *My Best Detective Story.* London, Faber, 1931.
"The Motive," in *The Second Century of Detective Stories.* London, Hutchinson, 1938(?).
"The Adventure of the First-Class Carriage," in *Strand Magazine* (London), February 1947.

OTHER PUBLICATIONS

Novels

Memories of the Future, Being Memories of the Years 1915–72, Written in 1988 by Opal, Lady Porstock. London, Methuen, and New York, Doran, 1923.
Sanctions: A Frivolity. London, Methuen, 1924.
Other Eyes Than Ours. London, Methuen, 1926.

Plays

Londinium Defensum (in Latin). Ware, Hertfordshire, Edmundian, 1925.
Thesauropolemopompus (in Latin), with Albert B. Purdie. Ware, Hertfordshire, Edmundian, 1925.

Verse

Signa Severa. Privately printed, 1906.
Remigium Alarum. Oxford, Blackwell, 1910.

Absolute and Abitofhel. London, Society of SS. Peter and Paul, 1915.
Q. Horati Carminum Liber Quintus, with others. Oxford, Blackwell, 1920.
In Three Tongues, edited by Laurence Eyres. London, Chapman and Hall, 1959.

Other

Juxta Salices. Privately printed, 1910.
A Still More Sporting Adventure!, with Charles R.L. Fletcher. Oxford, Blackwell, 1911.
Naboth's Vineyard in Pawn (sermons). London, Society of SS. Peter and Paul, 1913.
Some Loose Stones, Being a Consideration of Certain Tendencies in Modern Theology. London and New York, Longman, 1913.
The Church in Bondage (sermons). London, Society of SS. Peter and Paul, 1914.
An Hour at the Front (prayers). London, Society of SS. Peter and Paul, 1914; abridgement as *Ten Minutes at the Front,* 1916.
Reunion All Round; or, Jael's Hammer Laid Aside. London, Society of SS. Peter and Paul, 1914.
Bread or Stone: Four Conferences on Impetrative Prayer. London, Society of SS. Peter and Paul, 1915.
An Apologia. Privately printed, 1917.
The Essentials of Spiritual Unity. London, Catholic Truth Society, 1918.
A Spiritual Aeneid. London and New York, Longman, 1918.
Meditations on the Psalms. London, Longman, 1919.
Patrick Shaw-Stewart. London, Collins, 1920.
A Book of Acrostics. London, Methuen, 1924.
An Open-Air Pulpit. London, Constable, 1926.
The Belief of Catholics. London, Benn, and New York, Harper, 1927.
Anglican Cobwebs (sermons). London, Sheed and Ward, 1928.
Essays in Satire. London, Sheed and Ward, 1928; New York, Dutton, 1930.
Miracles. New York, Paulist Press, 1928.
The Mystery of the Kingdom and Other Sermons. London, Sheed and Ward, 1928.
The Rich Young Man: A Fantasy. London, Sheed and Ward, 1928.
The Church on Earth. London, Burns Oates, and New York, Macmillan, 1929.
On Getting There. London, Methuen, 1929.
Caliban in Grub Street. London, Sheed and Ward, and New York, Dutton, 1930.
Broadcast Minds. London, Sheed and Ward, 1932; New York, Sheed and Ward, 1933.
Difficulties, Being a Correspondence about the Catholic Religion Between Ronald Knox and Arnold Lunn. London, Eyre and Spottiswoode, 1932; revised edition, 1952.
Barchester Pilgrimage. London, Sheed and Ward, 1935; New York, Sheed and Ward, 1936.
Heaven and Charing Cross: Sermons on the Holy Eucharist. London, Burns Oates, 1935; New York, Dutton, 1936.
Let Dons Delight, Being Variations on a Theme in an Oxford Common-Room. London and New York, Sheed and Ward, 1939.
Captive Flames: A Collection of Panegyrics. London, Burns Oates, 1940; New York, Spiritual Book Associates, 1941.
Nazi and Nazarene. London, Macmillan, 1940.
In Soft Garments: A Collection of Oxford Conferences. London, Burns Oates, and New York, Sheed and Ward, 1942.

I Believe: The Religion of the Apostles' Creed. Reading, The Tablet, 1944.

God and the Atom. London and New York, Sheed and Ward, 1945.

A Retreat for Priests. London and New York, Sheed and Ward, 1946.

The Mass in Slow Motion (sermons). London and New York, Sheed and Ward, 1948.

The Creed in Slow Motion (sermons). London and New York, Sheed and Ward, 1949.

A Selection from the Occasional Sermons, edited by Evelyn Waugh. London, Dropmore Press, 1949.

The Trials of a Translator. New York, Sheed and Ward, and London, Burns Oates, 1949.

Enthusiam: A Chapter in the History of Religion, with Special Reference to the XVII and XVIII Centuries. Oxford, Clarendon Press, and New York, Oxford University Press, 1950.

The Gospel in Slow Motion (sermons). London and New York, Sheed and Ward, 1950.

St. Paul's Gospel. London, Catholic Truth Society, 1950; New York, Sheed and Ward, 1951.

Stimuli (sermons). London and New York, Sheed and Ward, 1951.

The Hidden Stream: A Further Collection of Oxford Conferences. London, Burns Oates, 1952; New York, Sheed and Ward, 1953.

A New Testament Commentary for English Readers. New York, Sheed and Ward, 3 vols., 1952–56; London, Burns Oates, 3 vols., 1953–56.

Off the Record. London, Sheed and Ward, 1953; New York, Sheed and Ward, 1954.

A Retreat for Lay Pelple. London and New York, Sheed and Ward, 1955.

The Window in the Wall and Other Sermons on the Holy Eucharist. London, Burns Oates, and New York, Sheed and Ward, 1956.

Bridegroom and Bride. London and New York, Sheed and Ward, 1957.

On English Translation (lecture). Oxford, Clarendon Press, 1957.

Literary Distractions. London and New York, Sheed and Ward, 1958.

The Priestly Life: A Retreat. New York, Sheed and Ward, 1958; London, Sheed and Ward, 1959.

Lightning Meditations. New York and London, Sheed and Ward, 1959.

Proving God: A New Apologetic. London, The Month, 1959.

Retreat for Beginners. New York, Sheed and Ward, 1960; as *Retreat in Slow Motion,* London, Sheed and Ward, 1961.

Occasional Sermons, The Pastoral Sermons, University and Anglican Sermons, edited by Phillip Caraman: London, Burns Oates, 3 vols., 1960–63; New York, Sheed and Ward, 3 vols., 1960–64.

The Layman and His Conscience: A Retreat. New York, Sheed and Ward, 1961; London, Sheed and Ward, 1962.

Editor and translator, *The Miracles of King Henry VI.* Cambridge, University Press, 1923.

Editor and translator, *Virgil: Aeneid, Books vii to ix.* Oxford, Clarendon Press, 1924.

Editor, with Henry Harrington, *The Best Detective Stories of the Year 1928.* London, Faber, 1929; as *The Best English Detective Stories of 1928,* New York, Liveright, 1929.

Editor, with Henry Harrington, *The Best Detective Stories of the Year 1929.* London, Faber, 1930; as *The Best English Detective Stories of the Year,* New York, Liveright, 1930.

Editor, *The Holy Bible: An Abridgement and Rearrangement.* London and New York, Sheed and Ward, 1936.

Editor and translator, with others, *Manual of Prayers.* London, Burns Oates, 1942.

Editor, *Father Brown: Selected Stories,* by G.K. Chesterton. London, Oxford University Press, 1955.

Translator, (*Selected Poems*) (translated into Theocritan hexameters), by Robert Browning. Privately printed, 1908.

Translator, *The Holy Gospel of Jesus Christ According to Matthew.* Privately printed, 1941.

Translator, *The New Testament of Our Lord and Saviour Jesus Christ.* London, Burns Oates, and New York, Sheed and Ward, 1944.

Translator, *The Epistles and Gospels for Sundays and Holidays.* London, Burns Oates, and New York, Sheed and Ward, 1946.

Translator, *The Book of Psalms in Latin and English, with the Canticles Used in the Divine Office,* edited by H. Richards. London, Burns Oates, 1947; New York, Sheed and Ward, 1948.

Translator, *The Old Testament.* New York, Sheed and Ward, 2 vols., 1948–50; London, Burns Oates, 2 vols., 1949.

Translator, with J. O'Connell and H.P.R. Finberg, *The Missal in Latin and English.* London, Burns Oates, 1949; Westminster, Maryland, Newman Press, 1958.

Translator, *Encyclical Letter—Humani Genesis—of his Holiness Pius XII.* London, Catholic Truth Society, 1950.

Translator, *Holy Week: The Text of the Holy Week Offices.* London, Burns Oates, and New York, Sheed and Ward, 1951.

Translator, *The Holy Bible* (complete version). London, Burns Oates, 1955; New York, Sheed and Ward, 1956.

Translator, *Autobiography of a Saint: Thérèse of Lisieux.* London, Harvill Press, and New York, Kenedy, 1958.

Translator, with M. Oakley, *The Imitation of Christ,* by Thomas à Kempis. London, Burns Oates, 1959; New York, Sheed and Ward, 1960.

*

Critical Studies: *The Life of the Right Reverend Ronald Knox* by Evelyn Waugh, London, Chapman and Hall, 1959, as *Monsignor Ronald Knox,* Boston, Little Brown, 1959; *Ronald Knox the Writer* by Robert Speaight, London, Sheed and Ward, 1966.

*   *   *

Father Ronald Knox was one of the first practitioners of Sherlockian scholarship; his "Studies in the Literature of Sherlock Holmes" first appeared in the *Blue Book 1912* and was reprinted in his *Essays in Satire* (1928). Conan Doyle, in a long letter to the author, expressed himself amused by the studies, and also amazed that "anyone should spend such pains on such material."

In a lecture on detective stories, Knox characterized them as "a highly specialized art-form which deserves, as such, its own literature," and differentiated them from thrillers in that "the action takes place before the story begins." His most notable contribution to the genre, however, is a Decalogue for detective-story writers reproduced in his introduction to *The Best Detective Stories of the Year 1928.* His 10 commandments forbid the use of supernatural agencies, poisons unknown to science, Chinamen, fortuitous accidents, unaccountable intuitions, unidentified clues, and identical twins, and place strict limits on secret rooms and passages and the choice of the criminal (who must be "someone mentioned in the early part of the story"—but not the detective). Knox was a prominent member of the Detection Club presided over by his friend G. K. Chesterton.

A comparison of the two Catholic detective-story authors is instructive. Chesterton entered the Church in 1922 in search, he said, of greater freedom in an age of doubt. His genius overflowed every literary form he essayed; into his Father Brown stories he packed an entire philosophy of life, and the dumpy priest holding the rolled umbrella blinks out at us almost tangibly from the printed page. Knox was an Anglican priest seeking authority and discipline when, to the dismay of his father, the low-church Bishop of Manchester, he embraced the Roman faith in 1917. Though his works range widely from poetry to sermons, from acrostics to an able translation of the Bible, each of them keeps within traditional bounds. In particular, his six detective novels, considering his deep knowledge of the field, are disappointing, and his detective Miles Bredon is a faceless nonentity.

The Viaduct Murder was written towards the end of the author's seven-year stint as a master at St. Edmund's preparatory school and seminary in Hertfordshire. The body of the local atheist is found on a golf course below a railway viaduct. The amateur sleuths are the local parson and his three garrulous friends. Robert Speaight in his *Ronald Knox the Writer* (1966) defends the story as "an amiable skit on the Higher Criticism, on the mentality which insists on rejecting *a priori* any explanation which seems likely to be true." But most readers though they praise the writing, damn the plot, with its unlikely clues, secret passages, and stupid criminal.

By the time he wrote *The Three Taps,* Knox was installed as Chaplain to Oxford's Catholic undergraduates. In his study in the ramshackle Old Palace he would type his various books between eight-o'clock Mass and lunch, after which his time was seldom his own. Bredon now makes his appearance; he resembles his creator only in smoking a pipe and playing Patience as an aid to thought (Knox favoured a difficult form of Canfield that "comes out" only once in a thousand games). Miles and his wife, the convent-bred Angela, chatter agreeably and quite unmemorably. "To be frank," writes Speaight, "Bredon is a bore." He is employed by the Indescribable Insurance Company, which will insure almost anyone against almost anything. In his first recorded case the detective investigates the death, by gas poisoning, of a manufacturer in a country pub. The taps of the title are the valves controlling the flow of gas, the chief question being whether they were open or shut. One critic complained of the novel that "its pointlessness and incoherence are almost startling." The best that can be said of it is that one or two minor characters are well done; Mr. Pulteney, an old schoolmaster on a fishing holiday, and an Anglican priest in the Catholic bishop's household, "unfrocked by his own conscience."

The Footsteps at the Lock concerns an empty canoe on the Thames near Oxford. The mystery of the missing occupant is probed in lackadaisical fashion. "You know that Bredon will read the riddle," writes Speaight, "but you do not feel it."

Undoubtedly the best of Knox's mysteries is *The Body in the Silo* (*Settled Out of Court*). Particularly in its concluding scenes, in which the devilry of the murderer is revealed, does the story, set on the beautiful banks of the Wye, attain some of the glow of a fairly good Christie novel.

Still Dead is a Scottish mystery set in a part of the Highlands familiar to the author through his visits to Lady Lovat's home at Beaufort Castle near Inverness. Colin Reiver, driving his new sports car, runs over a little boy and is sent away until local feeling subsides. His dead body is seen early one morning near the family home; a few minutes later it is gone, only to reappear at exactly the same place 48 hours later. The clues are presented fairly, but Knox's style hardly makes for an exciting story. *Double Cross Purposes* begins with a fine description of the Highland countryside, but the mystery is implausible. The Indescribable insures a treasure-hunter against the risk of his shady partner absconding with their find, if any, and Bredon goes up to Scotland to watch the pair. Mr. Pulteney makes a welcome reappearance, but generally the book is a final disappointment. During a cruise, young Lady Acton cast her copy of the book into the Mediterranean, along with her lipstick, of which Father Knox had expressed disapproval. We applaud her judgment.

—Norman Donaldson

KOONTZ, Dean R(ay). Has also written as David Axton; Brian Coffey; Deanna Dwyer; K.R. Dwyer; John Hill; Leigh Nichols; Anthony North; Richard Paige; Owen West. American. Born in Everett, Pennsylvania, 9 July 1945. Educated at Shippensburg State College, Pennsylvania, B. A. in English 1966. Married Gerda Ann Cerra in 1966. Worked in a federal government poverty-alleviation program, 1966–67; high school English teacher, 1967–69. Since 1969 fulltime writer. Lives in Orange, California. Agent: Harold Ober Associates, 40 East 49th Street, New York, New York 10017, U.S.A.

CRIME PUBLICATIONS

Novels

Strike Deep (as Anthony North).   New York, Dial Press, 1974.
After the Last Race.   New York, Atheneum, 1974.
Prison of Ice (as David Axton).   Philadelphia, Lippincott, and London, W.H. Allen, 1976.
Night Chills.   New York, Atheneum, 1976; London, W.H. Allen, 1977.
The Vision.   New York, Putnam, 1977; London, Corgi, 1980.
Whispers.   New York, Putnam, 1980; London, W.H. Allen, 1981.
Strangers.   New York, Putnam, and London, W.H. Allen, 1986.
Watchers.   New York, Putnam, and London, Headline, 1987.
Lightning.   New York, Putnam, and London, Headline, 1988.
Oddkins.   New York, Warner, and London, Headline, 1988.
Midnight.   New York, Putnam, and London, Headline, 1989.

Novels as Deanna Dwyer

The Demon Child.   New York, Lancer, 1971.
Legacy of Terror.   New York, Lancer, 1971.
Children of the Storm.   New York, Lancer, 1972.
The Dark of Summer.   New York, Lancer, 1972.
Dance with the Devil.   New York, Lancer, 1973.

Novels as K.R. Dwyer

Chase.   New York, Random House, 1972; London, Barker, 1974.
Shattered.   New York, Random House, 1973; London, Barker, 1974.

Dragonfly. New York, Random House, 1975; London, Davies, 1977.

Novels as Brian Coffey (series: Michael Tucker)

Blood Risk (Tucker). Indianapolis, Bobbs Merrill, 1973; London, Barker, 1974.
Surrounded (Tucker). Indianapolis, Bobbs Merrill, 1974; London, Barker, 1975.
The Wall of Masks (Tucker). Indianapolis, Bobbs Merrill, 1975.
The Face of Fear. Indianapolis, Bobbs Merrill, 1977; as K.R. Dwyer, London, Davies, 1978.
The Voice of the Night. New York, Doubleday, 1980; London, Hale, 1981.

OTHER PUBLICATIONS

Novels

Star Quest. New York, Ace, 1968.
Fear That Man. New York, Ace, 1969.
The Fall of the Dream Machine. New York, Ace, 1969.
The Dark Symphony. New York, Lancer, 1970.
Hell's Gate. New York, Lancer, 1970.
Dark of the Woods. New York, Ace, 1970.
Beastchild. New York, Lancer 1970.
Anti-Man. New York, Paperback Library, 1970.
The Crimson Witch. New York, Curtis, 1971.
The Flesh in the Furnace. New York, Bantam, 1972.
A Darkness in My Soul. New York, DAW, 1972; London, Dobson, 1979.
Time Thieves. New York, Ace, 1972; London, Dobson, 1977.
Warlock. New York, Lancer, 1972.
Starblood. New York, Lancer, 1972.
Demon Seed. New York, Bantam, 1973; London, Corgi, 1977.
A Werewolf among Us. New York, Ballantine, 1973.
Hanging On. New York, Evans, 1973; London, Barrie and Jenkins, 1974.
The Haunted Earth. New York, Lancer, 1973.
Nightmare Journey. New York, Berkley, 1975.
The Long Sleep (as John Hill). New York, Popular Library, 1975.
The Funhouse (novelization of screenplay; as Owen West). New York, Jove, 1980; London, Sphere, 1981.
The Mask (as Owen West). New York, Jove, 1981; London, Coronet, 1983.
Phantoms. New York, Putnam, and London, W.H. Allen, 1983.
Darkfall, New York, Berkley, 1984, as *Darkness Comes,* London, W.H. Allen, 1984.
Twilight Eyes. Plymouth, Michigan, Land of Enchantment, 1985; London, W.H. Allen, 1987.
The Door to December (as Richard Paige). London, Fontana, 1987.

Novels as Leigh Nichols

The Key to Midnight. New York, Pocket Books, 1979; London, Magnum, 1980.
The Eyes of Darkness. New York, Pocket Books, 1981; London, Fontana, 1982.
The House of Thunder. New York, Pocket Books, 1982; London, Fontana, 1983.

Twilight. New York, Pocket Books, and London, Fontana, 1984; as *The Servants of Twilight* (as Dean R. Koontz), New York, Dark Harvest, 1988.
Shadowfires. London, Fontana, 1987.

Short Stories

Soft Come the Dragons. New York, Ace, 1970.

Other

The Pig Society, with Gerda Koontz. Los Angeles, Aware Press, 1970.
The Underground Lifestyles Handbook, with Gerda Koontz. Los Angeles, Aware Press, 1970.
Writing Popular Fiction. Cincinnati, Writer's Digest, 1973.
How to Write Best-Selling Fiction. Cincinnati, Writer's Digest, and London, Poplar Press, 1981.

*

Dean R. Koontz commented (1984):

When a writer begins publishing as young as I did, and when he has as many enthusiasms as I do, his career is almost certain to include books in a variety of styles, in a number of genres, written at different levels of competence, and he is likely to produce a large body of work before he knows what most interests him and in what area he would most like to build a reputation. I sold my first short story while in college; during the year following graduation (1967), I sold another half dozen short stories and three novels. Those initial efforts were all science fiction, for that had been my primary reading material through college, and I continued working exclusively within that genre until 1971, at which time I began to write crime-suspense novels under two pen names—K. R. Dwyer and Brian Coffey. I found crime fiction more personally rewarding than science fiction, and I decided to concentrate my efforts in that form. However, by 1973, at the age of 27, when I wrote my nineteenth and final science fiction novel, I experienced another change of heart; I decided I did not want to work within the limitations of *any* genre, and I turned my attention toward the establishment of a career in that form of fiction somewhat loosely defined as "mainstream."

My first mainstream effort, *Hanging On,* was a comic novel set in World War II. My second, *After the Last Race,* was in essence a crime novel, the story of a very complex robbery, but it was written using multiple points of view and a style that permitted publication without the category label. That book was followed by *Night Chills,* a story about mind-control and the dangers to individual liberty in a high-technology world. *The Vision,* with a touch of the occult, was the first novel of mine to be selected by major book clubs, but my real breakthrough came at last in 1980, with *Whispers,* a very long psychological-suspense novel dealing with the unknowable and often unrecognized—sometimes positive, sometimes tragic—effects that we have on one another's lives. *Phantoms,* a long novel that attempts to stretch the horror novel to encompass a rational world-view, was published in 1983, and was something of a sidestep in my career, for at this time I do not intend to do any more straight horror novels in the future, although it, too, has sold well.

Whispers is more or less the exemplar to which I will refer while working on new books in the future. More than any other novel of mine, it relies on deeply drawn background and characters for much of its impact. Without doubt, it has a strong suspense plot, and I intend to incorporate suspense in all of my books, but the older I get the more I find that well-drawn *characters* are what make fiction compelling. In 1985, I will publish my most recently completed book, *Twilight Eyes,* an unusual story about bizarre events in a carnival. I am currently at work on a very long and untitled novel about a group of people who endure an incredible ordeal and undergo an astonishing transformation.

It seems pretentious and pompous to have a philosophy of fiction, and I do not have any such dogma to which I subscribe. However, I do believe that the first duty of fiction is to entertain. In addition, it should make us see—and accept!—the world through different eyes, in order that we can perhaps grow more aware and tolerant of the diversity that exists within our xenophobic and belligerent species and, by our acceptance, be less xenophobic and less belligerent. Furthermore, although I do not see it as something in which every writer has to be interested, I am fascinated by technological developments in all the sciences and medicines, and I believe that many of my upcoming books will deal with one aspect or another of the radical changes taking place in our world; fiction can be a valuable tool with which we learn to adapt to those changes and make better lives for ourselves, and it can have admonitory value, as well, revealing the pitfalls sometimes concealed by the attractive gloss and glow of high technology.

*   *   *

Horatio Alger had nothing on Dean R. Koontz. In a career spanning two and a half decades, Koontz has gone from lowly paperback writer to a true international superstar, certainly one of the two or three dominant names in fiction worldwide. More importantly to his readers and admirers, he's also gone from journeyman to genuine artist.

Beginning in 1986, Koontz published five extraordinary bestsellers—each more successful than the last—that redefined the way popular fiction is judged. Despite all the publishing "wisdom" against combining genres, Koontz offered his ever-increasing audience the treat of watching science fiction, mystery, suspense, romance and horror-like elements mixed into the same novel. *Strangers* concerns alien beings; *Watchers* involves a new form of intelligence and its incredible "monster" known as The Outsider; *Lightning* uses the effects of time-travel as one of its themes; *Midnight* demonstrates how a community can be destroyed by indifference, subterfugue and science used against humanity rather than for it; and *Oddkins* posits a "Mr. Blue" who, among many other things, redefines our entire perception of psychopathology.

Always a social critic—very early paperback novels such as *Hell's Gate* tartly and shrewdly observe the society they function in—Koontz's five bestsellers show us the process through which a very good writer becomes a real artist in theme, characterization and sheer exuberant skill. Of course, long-time Koontz-watchers could certainly see this coming in such novels as *Whispers,* a complicated, harrowing and aggressively sexual 1980 novel in which Koontz—in addition to writing a riveting thriller—took on the mantle of Nathanael West in examining Los Angeles and its mores. Even though his subsequent novels have been less explicitly sexual, each has looked without pity (and often with great tart humor) at our evolving society.

There is one particular difficulty in recommending Koontz to a friend—he's done so many good novels you don't know where to start (or stop). In no particular order, the following Koontz novels are well worth reading: *Shattered, The Face of Fear, The Vision, Phantoms,* and *Darkfall. Chase,* an early novel and perhaps his first consciously "serious" work, holds up particularly well as a look at the times and tensions of the

"Flower Power" era. It is a far better novel about the 1960's than many more famous ones.

As yet, we haven't even mentioned the "Leigh Nichols" novels that Koontz wrote in the late 1970's and into the 1980's, novels so ambitious and skilled that most writers would be happy to claim them as entire careers. *The Key to Midnight, The Eyes of Darkness, The House of Thunder, Twilight* and *Shadowfires* are very good examples of Koontz's ability to fuse genres while telling breathtaking stories of real people facing incredible dilemmas. Among these books, *Twilight* is a particularly notable book, combining as it does an ominous present-day witch with the hi-tech criminological techniques of the FBI. If you want to learn how to write a thriller, here's your textbook.

One other pen-name book should be mentioned here, "Richard Paige" 's *The Door to December.* Koontz has always been especially good at creating everyday people but the heroine here must have been especially difficult to portray—a woman almost weary of searching for her lost child but a woman who continues to search despite her occasional exhaustion and despair. The book is chilling, relentless and virtually without flaw. It also demonstrates one of Koontz's other skills—he's one of the few writers around who truly understands how to put a long novel together. His "Richard Paige" is a masterpiece.

Several other Koontz novels beg for inclusion here but since I must limit myself to one, I'll make it *The Funhouse.* This should have been the worst kind of for-hire work—Koontz was to "novelize" a very bad horror script. But man of honor that he is, he told his publishers that he'd rather make something good of it. In other words, he wanted to change it, transmute it from rather incoherent junk (see the movie yourself if you think I'm kidding) into something at least intelligent and entertaining. Koontz ended up doing much more. His version of *The Funhouse* is a small, resonant masterpiece about alcoholism, shattered families, filial love and filial hate, and the effects of Catholicism on children (Koontz is surprisingly benign on the subject). It is dark, scary, and as atmospheric as something by Lovecraft. It sold in excess of a million copies so you can still readily find it in used bookstores under his short-lived "Owen West" pen-name.

Sitting here at the beginning of the 1990's, it safe to predict that Koontz will be one of the dominant voices—if not the dominant voice—of this decade. Instead of getting sloppy with all the success—the penchant of too many bestsellers—Koontz seems to thrive, with each successive novel more daring and more breathtakingly rendered.

—Ed Gorman

———

KURNITZ, Harry. *See* **PAGE, Marco.**

———

KYD, Thomas. Pseudonym for Alfred B(ennett) Harbage. American. Born in Philadelphia, Pennsylvania, 18 July 1901. Educated at the University of Pennsylvania, Philadelphia, A.B. 1924; A.M. 1924; Ph.D. 1929. Married Eliza Price Finnesey in 1926; two daughters and two sons. Member of the English Department from 1924, and Professor, 1942–47,

University of Pennsylvania; Professor of English and Comparative Literature, Columbia University, New York, 1947–52; Professor of English, 1952–60, and Cabot Professor, 1960–70, then Professor Emeritus, Harvard University, Cambridge, Massachusetts. Alexander Lecturer, Toronto University, 1954–55. Trustee, American Shakespeare Festival, Stratford, Connecticut; member of the editorial board, *Studies in English Literature, Studies in Renaissance Drama, Shakespeare Studies, Shakespeare Quarterly.* General editor, Pelican Shakespeare series. Recipient: Guggenheim Fellowship, 1952, 1965; Modern Language Association Macmillan Book award. M.A.: Harvard University, 1952; D.Litt.: University of Pennsylvania, 1954. *Died 2 May 1976.*

CRIME PUBLICATIONS

Novels (series: Sam Phelan)

Blood Is a Beggar (Phelan).   Philadelphia, Lippincott, 1946; London, Hammond, 1949.
Blood of Vintage (Phelan).   Philadelphia, Lippincott, 1947. London, Hammond, 1950.
Blood on the Bosom Devine (Phelan).   Philadelphia, Lippincot, 1948.
Cover His Face.   Philadelphia, Lippincott, 1949.

Uncollected Short Stories

"High Court," in *Ellery Queen's Awards, 8th Series.*   Boston, Little Brown, 1953; London, Gollancz, 1955.
"The Letter," in *Ellery Queen's Mystery Magazine* (New York), February 1956.
"Cottage for August," in *Ellery Queen's Awards, 12th Series.* New York, Simon and Schuster, 1957; London, Collins, 1959.

OTHER PUBLICATIONS as Alfred B. Harbage

Other

Thomas Killigrew: Cavalier Dramatist.   Philadelphia, University of Pennsylvania Press, and London, Oxford University Press, 1930.
Sir William Davenant, Poet-Venturer.   Philadelphia, University of Pennsylvania Press, and London, Oxford University Press, 1935.
Cavalier Drama.   New York, Modern Language Association, and London, Oxford University Press, 1936.
Annals of English Drama, 975–1700.   Philadelphia, University of Pennsylvania Press, 1940.
Shakespeare's Audience.   New York, Columbia University Press, 1941.
As They Liked It: An Essay on Shakespeare and Morality.   New York, Macmillan, 1947.
Shakespeare and the Rival Traditions.   New York, Macmillan, 1952.
Theater for Shakespeare.   Toronto, University of Toronto Press, 1955.
William Shakespeare: A Reader's Guide.   New York, Farrar Straus, 1963.
Conceptions of Shakespeare.   Cambridge, Massachusetts, Harvard University Press, 1966.
Shakespeare Without Words and Other Essays.   Cambridge, Massachusetts, Harvard University Press, 1972.

Editor, *The Tempest,* by Shakespeare.   New York, Crofts, 1946.
Editor, *As You Like It,* by Shakespeare.   New York, Crofts, 1948.
Editor, *The Tragedy of Macbeth,* by Shakespeare.   London, Penguin, 1956.
Editor, *The Tragedy of King Lear,* by Shakespeare.   London, Penguin, 1958.
Editor, with Douglas Bush, *Shakespeare's Sonnets.*   London, Penguin, 1961.
Editor, *Love's Labour's Lost,* by Shakespeare.   London, Penguin, 1963.
Editor, *Shakespeare: The Tragedies: A Collection of Critical Essays.*   Englewood Cliffs, New Jersey, Prentice Hall, 1964.
Editor, *Henry V.* by Shakespeare.   London, Penguin, 1965.
Editor, with Richard Wilbur, *Poems,* by Shakespeare.   London, Penguin, 1966.
Editor, *Complete Pelican Shakespeare.*   London, Penguin, 3 vols, 1969.

*   *   *

Alfred B. Harbage was an eminent Shakespearean scholar. Under the name of Thomas Kyd, which is both a donnish disclaimer and a generic pioneer's self-assertion, he wrote in the last four years of the 1940's four rather bloody murder mysteries, which combine in a unique way the essence of the hard-boiled school with a tone of academic persiflage. The first and best of the four, *Blood Is a Beggar,* is actually set in the university, dramatically setting the two styles, in the police and the dons, side by side. The last, and the least successful, *Cover His Face,* moves away from the Philadelphia of the first three to rural England, where an incredibly bumbling academic hot on Dr. Johnson's trail stumbles into a murder. In this novel Harbage is plainly the farceur, a trifle sophomoric in his depiction of academic ineptitude. Barzun and Taylor's description of the novel as a "Crispinesque entertainment" is accurate, and may be read as either invitation or admonition.

The first three novels, however, create and enlarge upon a police world, a comic chain-of-being of law officers: J. Roth Newbold, the aristocratic district attorney, college graduate, all tidy pinstripes and gold-rimmed pince-nez, is in fairly constant conflict with both Chief of Police Cleveland Jones, a literate man who has walked a beat, and the Chief's most able subordinate, the principal detective in these novels, Sam Phelan, former boxer, more thick-headed in the third than in the first novel, yet practical, adaptable, and, under the hand of the Chief, not averse to some literary reading; he also plays chess.

The three novels are fomulaic; the murder is committed in the first chapter (though in the third novel it comes in chapter two). The police are called in, a little self-enclosed world is scrutinized by a somewhat mystified but never overawed Phelan—the university, the landed gentry, the burlesque theatre. Phelan arrives at the wrong conclusion; then, with some help from his associates, especially the Chief, the right conclusion. He places himself at risk to flush the murderer out of hiding. Each novel ends with an attempt by the Chief to pair the unmarried Phelan with a heroine who is unsuitable to him for various reasons—the English departmental secretary (she is the murderess), the mainline aristocrat (she is too little of the earth), the striptease artiste (she is too much of the earth).

What sets Kyd off from the Inneses and the Crispins is not so much his treatment (in the first novel) of the university as a real place; Amanda Cross and, in *Deadly Meeting,* Robert Barnard would subsequently do as well or better. What stands out is his skillful depiction of the interplay between educated and cultivated people on the one hand, and practical self-educated detectives on the other. But *inter*play: The D.A. is not as cultivated as he thinks he is, and Phelan is not as much the boor as he seems to be. Harbage's particular role, as a pioneer of the realistic crime novels of academe, was to bridge the gap between the snobbish Newbolds and the philistine Phelans. Though the second and third novels, representing a diminution of quality, show him moving further from the university, he remains the hard-boiled academic, his professional tone addressed to both gallery and groundlings, writing the detective novel as they *both* liked it.

—Barrie Hayne

KYLE, Duncan. Pseudonym for John Franklin Broxholme; also writes as James Meldrum. British. Born in Bradford, Yorkshire, 11 June 1930. Educated at Bradford Grammar School. Served in the British Army, 1948–50. Married Alison Millar Hair in 1956; three children. Reporter, Bradford *Telegraph and Argus,* 1946–48, 1950–53; sub-editor, Leicester *Mercury,* 1953–56; picture editor, *Yorkshire Post,* Leeds, 1955–57; assistant editor, *John Bull* and *Today* magazines, London, 1957–68; Editorial Director, Odhams Magazines, London, 1968–69. Since 1970, freelance writer. Chairman, Crime Writers Association, 1976–77. Agent: A.P. Watt Ltd., 20 John Street, London WCIN 2DR. Address: Oak Lodge, Valley Farm Road, Newton, Sudbury, Suffolk, England.

CRIME PUBLICATIONS

Novels

A Cage of Ice. London, Collins, 1970; New York, St. Martin's Press, 1971.
Flight into Fear. London, Collins, and New York, St. Martin's Press, 1972.
A Raft of Swords. London, Collins, 1974; as *The Suvarov Adventure,* New York, St. Martin's Press, 1974.
Terror's Cradle. New York, St. Martin's Press, 1974; London, Collins, 1975.
The Semonov Impulse (as James Meldrum). London, Weidenfeld and Nicolson, 1975; New York, St. Martin's Press, 1976.
In Deep. London, Collins, 1976; as *Whiteout!,* New York, St. Martin's Press, 1976.
Black Camelot. London, Collins, and New York, St. Martin's Press, 1978.
Green River High. London, Collins, 1979; New York, St. Martin's Press, 1980.
Stalking Point. London, Collins, 1981; New York, St. Martin's Press, 1982.
The King's Commissar. London, Collins, 1983; New York, St. Martin's Press, 1984.
The Dancing Men. London, Collins, 1985; New York, Holt, 1986.
The Honey Ant. London, Collins, 1988.

Uncollected Short Story

"The Breathless Hush," in *The Rigby File,* edited by Tim Heald. London, Hodder and Stoughton, 1989.

OTHER PUBLICATIONS

Novel as J.F. Broxholme

The War Queen. London, Frewin, 1967.

*   *   *

Once hailed as "the most exciting thriller-writer discovery of the seventies" by the London *Evening News,* John Franklin Broxholme has written a series of increasingly well-received thrillers under the pseudonym of Duncan Kyle. Broxholme's work falls into two clearly distinguishable categories.

The first five Kyle books establish Kyle as the master of high-adventure suspense. The books are all crime stories set against fascinating, often malevolent natural backgrounds. Not even Alistair MacLean, Hammond Innes, or Desmond Bagley, the recognized experts in the man-versus-nature school of crime adventure, convey as does Kyle the harsh logic, the minute details, and the unbearable tension of man's dependence on nature's hostility to man. In the early Kyle thrillers, mere crime is just not enough. Kyle also makes his heroes survive by wits and brawn in the midst of their environment's vastness and obduracy. Lovingly and accurately, Kyle provides a veritable *Baedeker* of potential disaster, including chases in sub-zero Arctic wastelands (*A Cage of Ice, In Deep*), underwater fight scenes in a flowing logjam (*A Raft of Swords*), tinkering with an airplane's external fuel tank while in flight (*Flight into Fear*), and the perilous climb with a thin rope up a rocky Shetland Island cliff while under gunfire (*Terror's Cradle*). Kyle has a splendid feel for physical situations and a stunning gift for their ultra-close-focus description. To further escalate our anxiety for the hero's precarious survival, Kyle employs odd forms of transport, such as one-man subs, tractors, Ski Doo's, electric winches, elevators, hovercraft, ropes and pulleys. The total effect of Kyle's sense of place and timing rivets you to the book, and you're treated to a breathtaking, white-knuckled, thrill-a-minute roller coaster ride. But as might be expected of a writer who excels in one narrative aspect, others are weaker. These first books have sketchy character development and hurried plots that seem like levers for the scenes of action. *The Semonov Impulse* was published as by James Meldrum, a single-book penname that is usually erroneously attributed to James Mitchell. It is a kidnap and ransom story set largely on an Aeroflot jet and lacks the kinetic energy of the Kyle thrillers.

Starting with *Black Camelot,* the novels by Kyle fall into the category of mainstream thrillers. Longer, with more emphasis on character and a sense of history than on action and a sense of place, the later books often make the present mystery dependent upon the unravelling of a mystery buried in the past. Indeed, Kyle has proved to be as innovative and diversified with the "history mystery" as he is with the straight high adventure. He varies the setting and plot pattern, as well as the key that opens the narrative door to the past.

Black Camelot is a World War II intrigue novel whose Nazi hero is manipulated into smuggling a list of British Nazi sympathizers out of Germany and into Russian hands. *Green River High,* the weakest of the books, tells of a curiously unexciting treasure hunt for a 40-year-old plane downed in Borneo. *Stalking Point* is another World War II intrigue story, with an F.D. Roosevelt/Churchill assassination plot. One of the best of the latter books is *The Dancing Men,* a genealogical mystery about a Kennedyish U.S. presidential candidate with a politically disastrous fact possibly shrouded in his family's past. In his recent *The Honey Ant,* Kyle moves the story to the

Australian outback with a decades-old property deed verification. And in the inimitable Kyle style, the setting is just as fascinating as the plot. The best of all the historical thrillers is *The King's Commissar*. It combines a contemporary British financial plot with the deftly chronicled story of Tsar Nicholas II's downfall with the Russian revolution of 1917—all in an ingenious Rube Goldberg-like manner that's as convincing as it is spellbinding.

Perhaps it is Broxholme's journalistic experience that gives the Kyle thrillers the confident, assured style. All of his books contain well-researched details and are written in a lean, readable style resembling Eric Ambler's or the later Deight-on's. But no other novelist combines Kyle's swift pacing and superbly developed sense of physical threat or historical drama.

—Greg Goode

———

KYLE, Sefton. *See* **VICKERS, Roy.**

———

L

LACY, Ed. Pseudonym for Len Zinberg (Leonard S. Zinberg); also wrote as Steve April. American. Born in New York City in 1911. Married; one child. Magazine writer; correspondent for *Yank* during World War II. Recipient: Twentieth Century-Fox Literary Fellowship; Mystery Writers of America Edgar Allan Poe award, 1958. *Died 7 January 1968.*

CRIME PUBLICATIONS

Novels (series: Lee Hayes; Toussaint Moore; Dave Wintino)

The Woman Aroused. New York, Avon, 1951; London, Hale, 1969.
Sin in Their Blood. New York, Eton, 1952; as *Death in Passing*, London, Boardman 1959.
Strip for Violence. New York, Eton, 1953;
Enter Without Desire. New York, Avon, 1954.
Go for the Body. New York, Avon, 1954; London, Boardman, 1959.
The Best That Ever Did It. New York, Harper, 1955; London, Hutchinson, 1957; as *Visa to Death*, New York, Permabooks, 1956.
The Men from the Boys. New York, Harper, 1956; London, Boardman, 1960.
Lead with Your Left (Wintino). New York, Harper, and London, Boardman, 1957.
Room to Swing (Moore). New York, Harper, 1957; London, Boardman, 1958.
Breathe No More, My Lady. New York, Avon, 1958.
Devil for the Witch. London, Boardman, 1958.
Be Careful How You Live. New York, Harper, and London, Boardman, 1958; as *Dead End*, New York, Pyramid, 1960.
Shakedown for Murder. New York, Avon, 1958.
Blonde Bait. Rockville Centre, New York, Zenith, 1959.
The Big Fix. New York, Pyramid, 1960; London, Boardman, 1961.
A Deadly Affair. New York, Hillman, 1960.
Bugged for Murder. New York, Avon, 1961.
The Freeloaders. New York, Berkley, 1961; London, Boardman, 1962.
South Pacific Affair. New York, Belmont, 1961.
The Sex Castle. New York, Paperback Library, 1963; London, Digit, 1965; as *Shoot It Again*, New York, Paperback Library, 1969.
Two Hot to Handle. New York, Paperback Library, 1963; London, Digit, 1966.
Moment of Untruth (Moore). New York, Lancer, 1964; London, Boardman, 1965.
Pity the Honest. London, Boardman, 1964; New York, Macfadden, 1965.
Harlem Underground (Hayes). New York, Pyramid, 1965.
Double Trouble (Wintino). London, Boardman, 1965; New York, Lancer, 1967.
In Black and Whitey (Hayes). New York, Lancer, 1967.
The Napalm Bugle. New York, Pyramid, 1968.
The Big Bust. New York, Pyramid, 1969; London, New English Library, 1970.

Uncollected Short Stories

"The Smell of Murder," in *Suspect* (New York), August 1956.
"G-String Alibi," in *London Mystery Magazine*, September 1956.
"Keep an Eye on the Body," in *Mercury* (New York), November 1956.
"Finders-Killers," in *Alfred Hitchcock's Mystery Magazine* (New York), March 1957.
"Death in a Squared Ring" (as Leonard S. Zinberg), in *John Creasey Mystery Magazine* (London), June 1957.
"The Devil in Black Lace," in *Mystery Digest* (New York), July 1957.
"The Real Sugar," in *Ellery Queen's Mystery Magazine* (New York), November 1957.
"A Kid Like That," in *London Mystery Magazine*, June 1958.
"Listen to the Night," in *Mercury* (New York), August 1958.
"Life Sentence," in *Alfred Hitchcock's Mystery Magazine* (New York), October 1958.
"As Cockeyed as Truth," in *Sleuth* (New York), October 1958.
"How Heavy Is Green?," in *Alfred Hitchcock's Mystery Magazine* (New York), November 1958.
"We Are All Suspect," in *Sleuth* (New York), December 1958.
"Time Wounds All Heels," in *Mercury* (New York), December 1958.
"Pick-Up," in *Mystery Digest* (New York), January 1959.
"The Liar and the Loot," in *Mystery Digest* (New York), February 1959.
"Killer Nymph," in *Mystery Tales* (New York), August 1959.
"The Reality of Unreality," in *Bestseller Mystery Magazine* (New York), November 1959.
"You're My Knife," in *Off Beat* (New York), May 1960.
"Crime Doesn't Pay—Enough," in *Alfred Hitchcock's Mystery Magazine* (New York), August 1960.
"Burn for Me, Darling," in *Off Beat* (New York), September 1960.
"Mask of Terror," in *Two-Fisted Detective Stories* (New York), December 1960.
"An Estimate of Rita," in *Alfred Hitchcock's Mystery Magazine* (New York), February 1961.
"The Death of El Indio," in *Manhunt* (New York), October 1961.
"Home Free," in *Alfred Hitchcock's Mystery Magazine* (New York), November 1961.
"And Steal No More," in *Keyhole* (New York), January 1962.
"Curtain Speech," in *Alfred Hitchcock's Mystery Magazine* (New York), February 1962.
"The Lonely Beach," in *Mike Shayne Mystery Magazine* (New York), March 1962.
"As Red as Blood," in *Off Beat* (New York), April 1962.
"Lucky Catch," in *Alfred Hitchcock's Mystery Magazine* (New York), May 1962.
"Hard-Nose Bull," in *Off Beat* (New York), July 1962.
"The Smell of Roses," in *Mike Shayne Mystery Magazine* (New York), August 1962.

"No Luck for a Sucker," in *Off Beat* (New York), September 1962.

"The Rich Get Rich," in *Alfred Hitchcock's Mystery Magazine* (New York), September 1962.

"I Did It for—Me," in *The Saint* (New York), September 1962.

"The Passion to Kill," in *Off Beat* (New York), November 1962.

"Stickler for Details," in *A Pride of Felons*, edited by The Gordons. New York, Macmillan, 1963.

"The Frozen Custard Caper," in *Ellery Queen's Mystery Magazine* (New York), January 1963.

"The Devil You Know," in *The Saint* (New York), April 1963.

"The Swinging Sheriff," in *Alfred Hitchcock's Mystery Magazine* (New York), April 1963.

"Death, The Black-Eyed Denominator," in *Alfred Hitchcock's Mystery Magazine* (New York), September 1963.

"Tuxedo Junction," in *Alfred Hitchcock's Mystery Magazine* (New York), October 1963.

"Hollow Hero," in *Mike Shayne Mystery Magazine* (New York), July 1964.

"A Cruise to Hell," in *Manhunt* (New York), July 1964.

"Say, Cheese," in *Alfred Hitchcock's Mystery Magazine* (New York), August 1964.

"My Lady's Malady," in *Chase* (New York), September 1964.

"The Square Root of Death," in *The Saint* (New York), October 1964.

"Red Light," in *Alfred Hitchcock's Mystery Magazine* (New York), December 1964.

"The Specialists," in *Manhunt* (New York), January 1965.

"Saint Coincidence," in *London Mystery Magazine*, March 1965.

"Amen!," in *Alfred Hitchcock's Mystery Magazine* (New York), December 1965.

"The Judges," in *London Mystery Magazine*, December 1965.

"The Dull Snap," in *Mike Shayne Mystery Magazine* (New York), December 1965.

"The Juicy Mango Caper," in *Ellery Queen's Mystery Magazine* (New York), February 1966.

"Sic Transit . . . ," in *The Saint* (New York), March 1966.

"The Missing Link," in *London Mystery Magazine*, March 1966.

"The Straight Line," in *Edgar Wallace Mystery Magazine* (Oxford), April 1966.

"Who Married Dead Old Dad!," in *The Man from U.N.C.L.E.* (New York), April 1966.

"The Listening Cone," in *Alfred Hitchcock's Mystery Magazine* (New York), April 1966.

"Five Minutes Ago," in *Alfred Hitchcock's Mystery Magazine* (New York), May 1966.

"How the Cookie Crumbled," in *The Man from U.N.C.L.E.* (New York), May 1966.

"Break in the Routine," in *Ellery Queen's Mystery Magazine* (New York), June 1966.

"Easy Dough," in *The Man from U.N.C.L.E.* (New York), June 1966.

"The Pussycat Caper," in *Edgar Wallace Mystery Magazine* (Oxford), July 1966.

"You Send Me," in *Mike Shayne Mystery Magazine* (New York), July 1966.

"The Eunuch," in *The Saint* (New York), August 1966.

"Paradise Nightmare," in *Mike Shayne Mystery Magazine* (New York), August 1966.

"Ancestral Muscle" in *Mike Shayne Mystery Magazine* (New York), November 1966.

"My Finger's on the Scales," in *Edgar Wallace Mystery Magazine* (Oxford), November 1966.

"Store Cop," in *Alfred Hitchcock's Mystery Magazine* (New York), January 1967.

"Heir to Murder," in *Alfred Hitchcock's Mystery Magazine* (New York), March 1967.

"The Undertaker's Assistant," in *The Man from U.N.C.L.E.* (New York), May 1967.

"Fade Out—Fade In," in *The Man from U.N.C.L.E.* (New York), June 1967.

"The Can Opener," in *The Girl from U.N.C.L.E.* (New York), June 1967.

"You Can't Win 'em (at) All," in *Alfred Hitchcock's Mystery Magazine* (New York), August 1967.

"The 'Method' Sheriff," in *Alfred Hitchcock's Mystery Magazine* (New York), September 1967.

"The Greatest Snatch in History" (as Steve April), in *Ellery Queen's Mystery Magazine* (New York), September 1967.

"Who Will Miss Arthur?" in *Alfred Hitchcock's Mystery Magazine* (New York) October 1967.

"Murder, He Says?," in *The Girl from U.N.C.L.E.* (New York), October 1967.

"The Gun Ladies," in *Mike Shayne Mystery Magazine* (New York), November 1967.

"The Conch Horse Caper," in *Mike Shayne Mystery Magazine* (New York), December 1967.

"The Fear Salesman," in *London Mystery Magazine*, March 1968.

"Doll of Death," in *London Mystery Magazine*, June 1968.

"The Taut Alibi," in *Mike Shayne Mystery Magazine* (New York), June 1968.

"More Than One Way to Skin a Cat," in *Ellery Queen's Mystery Magazine* (New York), July 1968.

"The Clean-Cut Murder," in *Mike Shayne Mystery Magazine* (New York), October 1968.

"Night Games," in *Mike Shayne Mystery Magazine* (New York), November 1968.

"Making the Murder Scene," in *Mike Shayne Mystery Magazine* (New York), January 1969.

"Don't Make It a Federal Case," in *Mike Shayne Mystery Magazine* (New York), March 1969.

"A Singular Quarry," in *Alfred Hitchcock's Mystery Magazine* (New York), June 1969.

"Time to Kill," in *Mike Shayne Mystery Magazine* (New York), August 1969.

OTHER PUBLICATIONS as Len Zinberg

Novels

Walk Hard—Talk Loud. Indianapolis, Bobbs Merrill, 1940.

What D'ya Know for Sure. New York, Doubleday, 1947; as *Strange Desires*, New York, Avon, 1948.

Hold with the Hares. New York, Doubleday, 1948.

Route 13 (as Steve April). New York, Funk and Wagnalls, 1954.

Sleep in Thunder (as Ed Lacy). New York, Grosset and Dunlap, 1964.

The Hotel Dwellers (as Ed Lacy). New York, Harper, 1966; London, Hale, 1968.

*

Manuscript Collection: Mugar Memorial Library, Boston University.

*   *   *

Before the civil rights movement made it fashionable, Ed Lacy made blacks a part of mystery fiction. Though himself a white man, Lacy had many friends in communities such as Harlem, and he wrote with considerable understanding about blacks. Two of his books are about Toussaint Moore, a black postal worker turned private detective. A sensitive man, Moore is torn between the security of his government job and the chance of greater riches in detective work which, though it repels him, he is good at. The first Moore book, *Room to Swing*, won an Edgar. The second, *Moment of Untruth*, in addition to being a good mystery with a bullfighting background tells much about tourism in Mexico from the viewpoint of a black.

Lacy also created a black police detective, Lee Hayes, who, like Moore, is conscious of his color but does not practice reverse discrimination. He is featured in *Harlem Underground* and *In Black and Whitey*, both of which deal with urban violence.

When the race of Lacy's detectives was not distinctive, their stature was. Barney Harris, the private detective in *The Best That Ever Did It*, weighs 248 pounds. Hal Darling, the private detective in *Strip for Violence*, is only 5′ 1″ tall but a judo expert and a former flyweight boxer; Lee Hayes had also been a fighter.

Lacy's interest in boxing was a long-standing one. His non-mystery novel *Walk Hard—Talk Loud* is about boxing and became a Broadway play. Boxers are important in his mystery short stories such as "The Real Sugar," with a welterweight who constantly overeats yet never has trouble meeting the weight limit, and "The Juicy Mango Caper," about a West Indian robbery planned by Big Gabe, a former heavyweight boxer. The dialogue is excellent, reflecting Lacy's ear for Caribbean speech. Under the pseudonym Steve April he also wrote of extravagantly planned crimes, one of which, "The Greatest Snatch in History" (1967), is about a plot to kidnap the President of the United States.

Most of Lacy's novels sold only to the paperback original market and give evidence of having been rushed in their writing. Yet they were certainly better and more subtle than the titles under which they were published—*The Woman Aroused, Sin in Their Blood, Strip for Violence, The Sex Castle,* and *The Big Bust.* Lacy's work was entertaining and remarkably consistent, and it frequently carried a great deal of meaning. He died before a new race consciousness might have found him the very large audience he deserved.

—Marvin Lachman

———

LAMB, Milton T. *See* **POWELL, Talmage.**

———

LAMBERT, Derek (William). Also writes as Richard Falkirk. British. Born in London, 10 October 1929. Educated at Epsom College, Surrey. Served in the Royal Air Force, 1947–49. Married Diane Joan Brunet in 1970 (second marriage); one son, and three sons from first marriage. Journalist, 1950–68: reporter, Dartmouth *Chronicle*, Devon, *Eastern Daily Press*, Norwich, Norfolk, Sheffield *Star*, Yorkshire, *Daily Mirror*, London, 5 years, and correspondent in Africa and Moscow, *Daily Express*, London, 6 years. Agent: Blake Friedmann Literary Agency, 37–41 Gower Street, London WC1E 6HH, England.

CRIME PUBLICATIONS

Novels

Angels in the Snow. London, Joseph, and New York, Coward McCann, 1969.
The Red House. London, Joseph, and New York, Coward McCann, 1972.
The Yermakov Transfer. London, Arlington, and New York, Saturday Review Press, 1974.
Touch the Lion's Paw. London, Arlington, and New York, Saturday Review Press, 1975; as *Rough Cut*, New York, Bantam, 1980.
The Saint Peter's Plot. London, Arlington, 1978; New York, Bantam, 1979.
The Memory Man. London, Arlington, 1979.
I, Said the Spy. London, Arlington, 1980.
Trance. London, Arlington, 1981.
The Red Dove. London, Hamish Hamilton, 1982; New York, Stein and Day, 1983.
The Judas Code. London, Hamish Hamilton, 1983; New York, Stein and Day, 1984.
The Golden Express. London, Hamish Hamilton, and New York, Stein and Day, 1984.
The Man Who Was Saturday. London, Hamish Hamilton, and New York, Stein and Day, 1985.
Vendetta. London, Hamish Hamilton, 1986.
Chase. London, Hamish Hamilton, 1987.
Triad. London, Hamish Hamilton, 1987.

Novels as Richard Falkirk (series: Edmund Blackstone)

The Chill Factor. London, Joseph, and New York, Doubleday, 1971.
The Twisted Wire. New York, Doubleday, 1971; London, Corgi, 1972.
Blackstone. London, Eyre Methuen, 1972; New York, Stein and Day, 1973.
Beau Blackstone. London, Eyre Methuen, 1973; New York, Stein and Day, 1974.
Blackstone's Fancy. London, Eyre Methuen, and New York, Stein and Day, 1973.
Blackstone and the Scourge of Europe. London, Eyre Methuen, and New York, Stein and Day, 1974.
Blackstone Underground. London, Eyre Methuen, 1976.
Blackstone on Broadway. London, Eyre Methuen, 1977.

OTHER PUBLICATIONS

Novels

The Kites of War. London, Joseph, and New York, Coward McCann, 1969.
For Infamous Conduct. London, Joseph, and New York, Coward McCann, 1970.
Grand Slam. London, Joseph, 1971.
The Great Land. London, Arlington, 1977.
The Lottery. Loughton, Essex, Piatkus, 1983.
The Night and the City. London, Hamish Hamilton, 1988.
The Gate of the Sun. London, Hamish Hamilton, 1990.

Other (autobiographical)

The Sheltered Days: Growing Up in the War. London, Deutsch, 1965.
Don't Quote Me—But. London, Arlington, 1979.
And I Quote. London, Arlington, 1980.
Unquote. London, Arlington, 1981.
Just Like the Blitz: A Reporter's Notebook. London, Hamish Hamilton, 1987.

*

Manuscript Collection: Boston University.

Derek Lambert comments:

I have always tried for realism, hoping at the same time to impart literary value to adventure/thriller novels without being self-indulgent. I use backgrounds that I covered as a journalist, in particular Moscow, and I try to equate the merits and deficiencies of both East and West: neither are necessarily the goodies or the baddies. I believe that the first three quarters of *Gorky Park* is the finest thriller writing in the past decade; the last quarter serves as a lesson to all of us not to lapse into anti-climax and not to terminate abruptly a location and a mood. I cannot resist World War II; nor, mercifully, can readers. Why? I think it is because good and evil were then so unequivocally defined and patriotism was clear-cut. If we thriller writers can assert such qualities in novels set in the 1990's then we can develop creatively without swastikas and iron crosses as crutches.

*   *   *

Most of Derek Lambert's stories are in the thriller-spy mode with fast-moving narrative, broadly drawn characters, varied international settings, and dramatic, if not always surprising, endings. While the ingredients are familiar the reader's interest does not slacken. Lambert relies upon action rather than depth or subtlety, and embeds his stories in a contemporary background with some proximity to historical and political fact. This context, with its sometimes thinly veiled allusions to political identities, enables Lambert to exploit extreme and unusual situations for the stories without undue strain on a reader's credulity. Some extreme examples are the use of the Trans-Siberia railway as the setting for the kidnapping of the Soviet Premier in *The Yermakov Transfer*, and a space shuttle as the vehicle for the defection of a Soviet cosmonaut in *The Red Dove*. Evidence of detailed knowledge increases the plausibility of a bizarre situation as in the thriller *Trance* where hypnosis is used in a courtroom drama to identify a murderer and, while it produces conflicting accounts, ultimately provides the truth.

By comparison with some practitioners of the art, Lambert's characters and settings may appear sketchy but the method reflects his emphasis upon action. He balances those details essential to flesh out the story with those details which, however alluring, might clog the narrative. So the varied settings, mainly in European cities, are lightly painted with bare outlines and incidentals but little to suggest atmosphere, emotions, or a complex social and cultural life. Similarly with his characters: while most achieve some fullness of realisation there is little of their inner life, the springs of motivation and subtleties of awareness. In fact, Lambert seldom concentrates upon a single character but instead deploys a wide focus through a cluster of key characters who provide different perspectives and add complexity and interest to the plot. Among these certain recurrent types prevail, in particular, a mix of cultivated taste, intellect, and physical daring, for

example, Rhodes (*Touch the Lion's Paw*), or, more obviously, the dissident Jewish mathematician-turned-guerilla, Viktor Pavlov (*The Yermakov Transfer*), or, perhaps most clearly, the donnish spy George Prentice (*I, Said the Spy*).

Under the pseudonym of Richard Falkirk, Lambert has drawn upon the tradition of "historical" detective fiction and created a quite different effect using a central series character, Edmund Blackstone, the Bow Street Runner, and a generally concentrated setting, early 19th-century London. Again there is some proximity to historical fact but at the centre is a highly credible personality in Edmund Blackstone, whose intellectual and physical endowments, while they recall Lambert's other protagonists, complement a more fully established inner life for which pre-Victorian London is a crucial setting. The gin shops, dolly-mops, piemen, taverns, stews, cockpits, whores, the violent colourful life of a society in flux, are an almost perfect foil to Blackstone's troubled self.

London is the prime arena where Blackstone wages his battle against a fate which nearly consigned him to the gallows at an early age, and, while he escaped by luck and effort, it images a disaster which may still overwhelm him. Caught between worlds, high and low, Blackstone belongs neither to the comfortable Paddington where he has his chambers, nor to the miserable slums of St. Giles Rookery where he was born. Vocation and origins shape his morality and his administration of the law in a brutal society. His fast-moving adventures reflect both the detection of bizarre crimes—for example, the kidnapping of Princess Victoria (*Blackstone*) or the penetration of the Bank of England (*Blackstone Underground*)—in which failure will mean his ruin, and his pursuit of personal integrity and security. Other characters are less established though frequently well drawn, particularly the dour Birnie, the magistrate in charge of the Runners, with his obsession to protect his charge from Sir Robert Peel's plans to establish a Metropolitan Police Force.

—Trevor James

———

LAND, Milton. *See* **POWELL, Talmage.**

———

LANE, Grant. *See* **FISHER, Steve.**

———

LANGE, John. *See* **CRICHTON, Michael.**

———

LANGTON, Jane (née Gillson). American. Born in Boston, Massachusetts, 30 December 1922. Educated at Wellesley College, Massachusetts, 1940–42; University of Michigan, Ann Arbor, 1942–45, B.S. (Phi Beta Kappa) 1944, M.A. 1945; Radcliffe College, Cambridge, Massachusetts, 1945–46, 1947–48, M.A. 1948; Boston Museum School of Art, 1958–59. Married William Langton in 1943; three sons. Artist, *Discovery* program, WGBH Television, Boston, 1955–56; taught children's literature, Simmons College, Boston, 1979–80, and suspense novel writing at the Radcliffe Seminars, 1981. Recipient: Nero Wolfe award, 1984. Agent: Dorothy Markinko, McIntosh and Otis Inc., 310 Madison Avenue, New York, New York 10017, or Jed Mattes Inc., 175 West 13 Street, New York, New York 10023. Address: 9 Baker Farm Road, Lincoln, Massachusetts 01773, U.S.A.

CRIME PUBLICATIONS

Novels (series: Homer Kelly in all books)

The Transcendental Murder.   New York, Harper, 1964; as *The Minute Man Murder*, New York, Dell, 1976.
Dark Nantucket Noon. New York, Harper, 1975.
The Memorial Hall Murder. New York, Harper, 1978; London, Gollancz, 1990.
Natural Enemy. New Haven, Connecticut, Ticknor and Fields, 1982.
Emily Dickinson Is Dead. New York, St. Martin's Press, 1984; London, Gollancz, 1989.
Good and Dead. New York, St. Martin's Press, 1986; London, Penguin, 1987.
Murder at the Gardner. New York, St. Martin's Press, 1988.

OTHER PUBLICATIONS

Fiction (for children)

The Majesty of Grace. New York, Harper, 1961; as *Her Majesty, Grace Jones*, 1974.
The Diamond in the Window. New York, Harper, 1962; London, Hamish Hamilton, 1969.
The Swing in the Summerhouse. New York, Harper, 1967; London, Hamish Hamilton, 1970.
The Astonishing Stereoscope. New York, Harper, 1971.
The Boyhood of Grace Jones. New York, Harper, 1972.
Paper Chains. New York, Harper, 1977.
The Fledgling. New York, Harper, 1980.
The Fragile Flag. New York, Harper, 1984.

Other

The Hedgehog Boy: A Latvian Folktale. New York, Harper, 1985.

*

Manuscript Collections: Boston University (novels); Kerlan Collection, University of Minnesota, Minneapolis (children's books).

Jane Langton comments:

I began writing suspense novels under the spell of Dorothy L. Sayers, and went on to admire the work of John D. MacDonald. Since I was never closer to Oxford than the Pierre S. DuPont High School in Wilmington, Delaware, and since my experience with the seamy side of life comes from teaching Sunday School, my books lack something their books have. If mine possess anything that is not derivative, it is my flabbergasted astonishment at the world and my delight in the way people go right on being themselves.

When I first read the work of Thoreau and Emerson I recognized a similar thunderstruck stupefaction, and instantly

became a transcendentalist of the Concord stripe. My detective, Homer Kelly, is afflicted in the same way. He has pursued evildoers in Thoreau's back yard in Concord, Massachusetts, on the island of Nantucket during an eclipse of the sun, in Memorial Hall at Harvard during rehearsals for a performance of Handel's *Messiah*, in my own old house in Lincoln, Massachusetts, with the help of a barn spider, and in Emily Dickinson's home town of Amherst on the hundredth anniversary of her death. Homer is given to quoting long extracts from dead literary worthies, bits and pieces he knows by heart after I have diligently grubbed them up from books.

*   *   *

Among mystery writers who combine intelligence, widely ranging interests, wit, and cleverness, it's hard to beat Jane Langton whose novels featuring Homer Kelly, attorney, scholar, and sometime detective, are not only entertaining but also instructive and thoughtful. Homer Kelly himself, tall, ungainly, ill-dressed, and brilliant, fits readily into the ranks of eccentric fictional detectives. He is Langton's primary continuing character, and other characters reappear as well: Homer's wife, Mary, also tall, also a scholar; members of her extended family; and various acquaintances. The rich history of Concord, Massachusetts (and of Nantucket and Harvard-area Boston, also useful Langton settings), the citizens' ongoing efforts to preserve their heritage while meeting contemporary needs, and the abundance of on-site eccentrics all embellish the mysteries, all serve, at one time or another, as red herrings, as legitimate clues, as the basis of subplots.

In keeping with custom, the Langton novels include romantic subplots; in *The Transcendental Murder*, for instance, Homer Kelly meets and courts Mary Morgan while investigating the murders of local amateur experts on the Transcendentalists. *Dark Nantucket Noon* traces the tangled relationship between former lovers Kitty Clark and Joe Green, poet and novelist respectively, which provides both plausible motive and complication when Kitty is accused of killing Joe's wife. A May-September romance deepens the plot of *The Memorial Hall Murder* as the visiting Kellys fight crime among the Harvard faculty, and a May-August love story, the attraction between Mary's young nephew John Hand and Virginia Heron, is one factor which draws Homer into the investigation following the death of Virginia's father.

These subplots also handily serve other purposes which enrich the novels. They help, for instance, to keep the focus off Homer Kelly whose exuberance and eccentricity could cloy if he dominated every plot. Instead, Langton uses other characters—Mary Morgan Kelly, Kitty Clark, Hamilton Dow, and John Hand—as the central consciousnesses of these four novels, and because they are lively, fully developed characters, they readily capture readers' interest and empathy. Further, these major characters are intelligent and gifted, and their special interests add another valuable dimension to each book.

The Langton novels, usually illustrated by the author herself, are mines of information about fascinating topics: the lives and times of Emerson, Thoreau, Dickinson, and the Alcotts, for instance, are crucial to the mystery (and to the courtships) in *The Transcendental Murders*. The murder which sets *Dark Nantucket Noon* in motion occurs during an eclipse of the sun, and knowledge of the island's natural history is important to the solution of the crime. *The Memorial Hall Murder* covers the period of intensive rehearsal for a performance of Handel's *Messiah*, and Langton uses portions of the score as epigraphs. John Hand's preoccupation with entomology not only enriches his characterization but also creates a second subplot, the story of a barn spider, current object of his studies.

These factors do not overshadow the puzzles in Langton's novels, but they do affect their impact, not so much slowing the pace as framing the mysteries, setting them into a context of art, historical fact, or natural history. This perspective emphasizes the terrible disruption imposed by violent crime even as it affirms the human will to overcome problems. Furthermore, it pays readers the compliment of assuming their lively interest in nature and American culture. Her polished combination of mayhem and erudition makes Jane Langton's novels *very* satisfying reading.

—Jane S. Bakerman

———

LANSDALE, Joe R(ichard). American. Born in Gladewater, Texas, 28 October 1951. Educated at Tyler Junior College for one year; University of Texas, Austin; Stephen F. Austin State University, Nacogdoches, Texas for two years. Married 1) Cassie Ellis in 1970 (divorced 1972); 2) Karen Ann Morton in 1973, two children. Has had a variety of jobs including factory worker, ditch digger, carpenter's and plumber's helper, farmer, and custodial supervisor. Since 1981 full-time writer. Vice-president, Horror Writers of America, 1987–88. Agent: Barbara Puechner, 3418 Shelton Avenue, Bethlehem, Pennsylvania 18017. Address: 113 Timber Ridge, Nacogdoches, Texas 75961, U.S.A.

CRIME PUBLICATIONS

Novels

Act of Love. New York, Zebra, 1981; London, Kinnel, 1989.
The Nightrunners. Niles, Illinois, Dark Harvest, 1987.
Cold in July. New York, Bantam, 1989.
Savage Season. New York, Bantam, 1990.

Short Stories

By Bizarre Hands. Shingletown, California, Ziesing, 1989.

OTHER PUBLICATIONS

Novels

Dead in the West. New York, Space and Time, 1986; London, Kinnel, 1990.
The Magic Wagon. New York, Doubleday, 1986.
The Drive-In: A B-Movie with Blood and Popcorn. New York, Bantam, 1988; London, Kinnel, 1990.
The Drive-In 2: Not Just One of Them Sequels. New York, Bantam, and London, Kinnel, 1990.

Other

Editor, *Best of the West* (short story anthology). New York, Doubleday, 1986.
Editor, *New Frontiers.* New York, Doubleday, 1989.
Editor, *Razored Sadles*, with Pat LoBrutto. New York, Dark Harvest, 1989.

*

Joe R. Lansdale comments:

I write what interests me, and it's as simple as that. As a reader I read everything. Literary, genre, comics, plays, screenplays, and I'm influenced by it all. No matter what I write, I do my best to put something of myself and a literary sensibility into it. I hope to be both entertaining and interesting enough that someone might want to read one of my books or stories more than once.

My work often combines my interests, so that a novel or story might be as much horror as crime as suspense as S.F. as western as literary, and perhaps all of these. And maybe it's cat box material. What do I know?

*   *   *

In the late 1970's and early 1980's, Texan Joe R. Lansdale published scores of short stories in a variety of genres including mystery, suspense, horror, western, and science fiction. This may explain why his later and more important work reflects so many disparate influences while relentlessly remaining Lansdale's own.

During the 1980's, Lansdale published four suspense novels beginning with the raw but stunning *Act of Love* and continuing with the dark and somewhat parodistic *The Nightrunners*, which fuses elements of Sam Peckinpahian horror with straightforward suspense. *Cold in July* came at the end of the decade and demonstrated Lansdale's maturing powers, particularly in his control of tone, which veers from belly laughs to genuine tragedy.

Lansdale began the 1990's with *Savage Season*, his best novel to date. *Savage Season* looks back at the virtues and vices of the generation that came of age during the 1960's; and it also looks at what became of that generation in modern day Texas. It accomplishes all this within the confines of a suspense novel of the sort Gold Medal books would have been proud to publish.

Lansdale's fiction is, by turns, gentle and violent, poetic and vulgar, heartwarming and sinister. He writes with grace and dignity of the struggles common people face every day. And he writes with chilling dispassion of what a few uncommon people—monsters, really—also face.

Lansdale's admirers grow in number and passion every day. Read one of his novels (or his short story collection, *By Bizarre Hands*) and you'll see why.

—Ed Gorman

———

LATHEN, Emma. Pseudonym for Mary J. Latsis and Martha Henissart; also write as R.B. Dominic. Americans. **LATSIS, Mary J.:** grew up in Forest Park, Illinois. Educated at Wellesley College, Massachusetts, and Harvard University, Cambridge, Massachusetts. Worked for the United Nations Food and Agricultural Organization, Rome; economist until 1969. **HENISSART, Martha:** born in New York City. Worked in corporate finance and banking until 1973. Recipients: Crime Writers Association Gold Dagger award 1967; Mystery Writers of America Ellery Queen award, 1983. Address: c/o Simon and Schuster, 1230 Avenue of the Americas, New York, New York 10020, U.S.A.

CRIME PUBLICATIONS

Novels (series: John Putnam Thatcher in all books)

Banking on Death. New York, Macmillan, 1961; London, Gollancz, 1962.
A Place for Murder. New York, Macmillan, and London, Gollancz, 1963.
Accounting for Murder. New York, Macmillan, 1964; London, Gollancz, 1965.
Death Shall Overcome. New York, Macmillan, 1966; London, Gollancz, 1967.
Murder Makes the Wheels Go Round. New York, Macmillan, and London, Gollancz, 1966.
Murder Against the Grain. New York, Macmillan, and London, Gollancz, 1967.
A Stitch in Time. New York, Macmillan, and London, Gollancz, 1968.
Come to Dust. New York, Simon and Schuster, 1968; London, Gollancz, 1969.
When in Greece. New York, Simon and Schuster, and London, Gollancz, 1969.
Murder to Go. New York, Simon and Schuster, 1969; London, Gollancz, 1970.
Pick Up Sticks. New York, Simon and Schuster, 1970; London, Gollancz, 1971.
Ashes to Ashes. New York, Simon and Schuster, and London, Gollancz, 1971.
The Longer the Thread. New York, Simon and Schuster, 1971; London, Gollancz, 1972.
Murder Without Icing. New York, Simon and Schuster, 1972; London, Gollancz, 1973.
Sweet and Low. New York, Simon and Schuster, and London, Gollancz, 1974.
By Hook or by Crook. New York, Simon and Schuster, and London, Gollancz, 1975.
Double, Double, Oil and Trouble. New York, Simon and Schuster, 1978; London, Gollancz, 1979.
Going for the Gold. New York, Simon and Schuster, and London, Gollancz, 1981.
Green Grow the Dollars. New York, Simon and Schuster, and London, Gollancz, 1982.
Something in the Air. New York, Simon and Schuster, 1988; London, Simon and Schuster, 1989.

Novels as R.B. Dominic (series: Ben Safford in all books)

Murder Sunny Side Up. New York and London, Abelard Schuman, 1968.
Murder in High Place. London, Macmillan, 1969; New York, Doubleday, 1970.
There Is No Justice. New York Doubleday, 1971; as *Murder Out of Court*, London, Macmillan, 1971.
Epitaph for a Lobbyist. New York, Doubleday, and London, Macmillan, 1974.
Murder Out of Commission. New York, Doubleday, and London, Macmillan, 1976.
The Attending Physician. New York, Harper, and London, Macmillan, 1980.
A Flaw in the System. London, Macmillan, 1983; as *Unexpected Developments*, New York, St. Martin's Press, 1984.

*   *   *

Writing as Emma Lathen and R.B. Dominic, Martha Henissart and Mary J. Latsis have created two series of novels.

Each group is well done; each has attracted many fans, but the Lathen books, featuring Wall Street banker John Putnam Thatcher as amateur detective, were established earlier and are the better known.

The writing team's skillful characterization is evident in almost every portrayal, major or minor. Most of the Lathen characters offer readers a singular pleasure—that of observing the excitement and relish which capable, energetic people derive from their skills. In *Green Grow the Dollars*, for example, an expert amateur gardener, Mary Larabee, is played off against professional plant-developers. Blessed with a green thumb, Mary also has a sharp eye for the main chance and undertakes a career in the glitzy world of television commercials with cheerful pragmatism and a *lot* of savvy. The effect is both charming and brilliant, for such memorable characters rivet the readers' interest and simplify what could have proved an almost impossible task.

Each of the Thatcher books hinges upon some facet of the financial world. The authors must make each business deal quickly and readily clear to the readers, most of whom lack detailed knowledge of finance. The range of businesses examined is generous: chicanery at the National Calculating Company (*Accounting for Murder*), trickery during a Russian wheat deal (*Murder Against the Grain*), and duplicity in the garment industry (*The Longer the Thread*), for instance. Lathen makes the business manipulations palatable and apprehendable in two ways. First, Thatcher and his colleagues lay the situation out in simple, direct terms during staff huddles at the Sloan. Secondly, the books' other sharply drawn characters are themselves fascinated by the deals. They too discuss them freely and informatively, and their grasp is passed along to the reader who is patient and remains interested because of his involvement with the characters. *By Hook or by Crook* is an excellent example of this method.

This device also ensures that the novels fall into the closed-circle-of-suspects school which not only demands full characterization but also limits the field of inquiry to areas where the banker's special knowledge and habits of mind, honed by long service to the Sloan, give him an advantage over the investigating police. No animosity ensues, however, and Thatcher often works closely with professional detectives.

The authors avoid overexposure for Thatcher by releasing details of his personal life very slowly. This practice is acceptable because he is a reserved, distinguished widower whose chief interest in life is his work at the Sloan. Thatcher is human enough to be intriguing, private enough not to be overwhelming. Humanizing touches are carefully provided. While some are fairly commonplace—gifts must be purchased for grandchildren, obligatory family dinners must be endured—others are surprising—the urbane Thatcher is also a long-distance hiker, and in *Pick Up Sticks* he is happily tackling the Appalachian Trail when murder interrupts.

The ultimate result of these devices is that Thatcher joins the ranks of amateur sleuths whose expertise, whose well-developed powers of observation, and whose entree into special interest groups serve his powers of deduction. Wall Street may not be one of the mean streets, but the worldly Thatcher realizes that avarice and murder occur on boulevards and in mansions as well as in less posh neighborhoods.

Traditionally, the banker is seconded by one of his fellow officers at the Sloan, most frequently by an unlikely but useful companion at detection, Everett Gabler, elderly and given to peculiar, soothing diets. Fussy and particular, Gabler is yet human, for when he helps unravel a case involving dog shows and kennel owners (*A Place for Murder*), he is captivated by a Welsh terrier and is as precise in describing bloodlines as he is in handling accounts. It is again Gabler's fixation upon detail which generates the best scenes in *Going for the Gold*, a tale of crime at the Lake Placid Winter Olympics.

The Lathen team's understanding of human nature is never more apparent than when they delineate non-continuing characters central to each plot. In *Murder to Go* Iris Young's intense jealousy of the superior ability and position of her husband's partner triggers an important subplot: her ambition is credible and honestly portrayed. Careful attention is also given to the motivations of the killers. The writers never excuse misdeeds but do ensure that the rationale for criminal behavior is clearly drawn. Thus, heroes and villains alike contribute to the realism of this series.

Humor is consistently used to underscore the penetrating glimpses of human nature. At times, the comedy is gently rueful as when the team examines the generation gap, a social phenomenon treated repeatedly, such as in *Pick Up Sticks*, where grown children are satirized for trying to parent their own parents. Humor is rarely disassociated from irony, and in the hands of these writers irony is a pointed and point-making tool.

The Dominic series, featuring Ohio Congressman Ben Safford and a continuing cast of his legislative colleagues, naturally takes Washington as its locale and government as its source of mystery and murder, and the plots are organized as in the Lathen series. Again, the portraits of non-continuing personalities are remarkably vivid, for instance, Pauline Ives, a successful capital attorney is neatly contrasted with Neva Torrance, a beautiful social climber (*There Is No Justice*). Safford's trips to his constituency introduce other settings for mayhem (*Murder Out of Commission*) and his sister-political-adviser, Janet. In *Unexpected Developments* the demands of a constituent focus attention on the potential for corruption in the alliance between big business and big government, and though crime puzzles are solved, the underlying, dangerous temptations are, of course, ongoing as Safford knows only too well. The perennially rumpled Safford is astute though unassuming and shrewd though comfortable, like Thatcher only in his ability to apply special knowledge to amateur detection.

Both series incorporate serious social commentary, usually informed by irony. *Epitaph for a Lobbyist* treats political bribery, and *A Stitch in Time* finds Thatcher unmasking physicians who prescribe and dispense expensive drugs under their own labels. Occasionally, as in *Death Shall Overcome*, the seriousness of the subject, here racial bigotry, produces straight criticism rather than ironic treatment. The resulting characterizations are weaker than usual, though good points are made.

Generally speaking, however, the books are very well crafted, and the devices brilliantly handled. In many ways, Thatcher and Safford represent numbers of staid Americans who, despite their own restraint and law-abiding natures, cannot help but be touched by either less admirable citizens or by the central social questions of the day, and the novels prove that social comment, humor, clever detection, and splendid plotting can go happily hand in hand.

—Jane S. Bakerman

———

LATIMER, Jonathan (Wyatt). Also wrote as Peter Coffin. American. Born in Chicago, Illinois, 23 October 1906. Educated at Mesa Ranch School, Arizona, 1922–25; Knox College, Galesburg, Illinois, A.B. 1929 (Phi Beta Kappa). Served in the United States Navy, 1942–45. Married 1) Ellen

Baxter Peabody in 1937, one daughter and two sons; 2) Jo Ann Hanzlik in 1954. Reporter, *Herald-Examiner* (later Chicago *Tribune*), 1930–33; ghostwriter for Secretary of the Interior Harold Ickes; screenwriter after 1940. *Died 23 June 1983.*

CRIME PUBLICATIONS

Novels (series: Bill Crane)

Murder in the Madhouse (Crane). New York, Doubleday, and London, Hurst and Blackett, 1935.
Headed for a Hearse (Crane). New York, Doubleday, 1935; London, Methuen, 1936; as *The Westland Case*, New York, Sun Dial Press, 1938.
The Lady in the Morgue (Crane). New York, Doubleday, 1936; London, Methuen, 1937.
The Search for My Great Uncle's Head (as Peter Coffin). New York, Doubleday, 1937.
The Dead Don't Care (Crane). New York, Doubleday, and London, Methuen, 1938.
Red Gardenias (Crane). New York, Doubleday, and London, Methuen, 1939; as *Some Dames Are Deadly*, New York, Spivak, 1955.
Solomon's Vineyard. London, Methuen, 1941; as *The Fifth Grave*, New York, Popular Library, 1950.
Sinners and Shrouds. New York, Simon and Schuster, 1955; London, Methuen, 1956.
Black Is the Fashion for Dying. New York, Random House, 1959; as *The Mink-Lined Coffin*, London, Methuen, 1960.

OTHER PUBLICATIONS

Novel

Dark Memory. New York, Doubleday, and London, Methuen, 1940.

Plays

Screenplays: *The Lone Wolf Spy Hunt*, 1939; *Phantom Raiders*, with William R. Lipman, 1940; *Topper Returns*, with Gordon Douglas and Paul Gerard Smith, 1941; *A Night in New Orleans*, 1941; *The Glass Key*, 1942; *Whistling in Dixie*, with others, 1942; *They Won't Believe Me*, with Gordon McDonell, 1946; *Nocturne*, with Frank Fenton and Rowland Brown, 1946; *The Big Clock*, with Harold Goldman, 1947; *Sealed Verdict*, 1948; *Beyond Glory*, with Charles Marquis Warren and William Wister Haines, 1948; *The Night Has a Thousand Eyes*, with Barré Lyndon, 1948; *Alias Nick Beal*, with Mindret Lord, 1949; *Copper Canyon*, with Richard English, 1950; *The Redhead and the Cowboy*, with Liam O'Brien and Charles Marquis Warren, 1951; *Submarine Command*, 1951; *Botany Bay*, 1953; *Plunder of the Sun*, 1953; *Back from Eternity*, with Richard Carroll, 1956; *The Unholy Wife*, with William Durkee, 1957; *The Whole Truth*, 1958.

Television Plays: *Perry Mason* series, 1960–65.

*   *   *

At the start of the 1935 novel *Murder in the Madhouse*, one William Crane is committed to an asylum for the mentally disturbed. Some three murders and 250 pages later the reader is informed that William Crane is a private detective. The more astute and prescient among the book's original readers might well have concluded that they had been present at the debut of one of the most memorable and original detective series in modern mystery fiction. Jonathan Latimer's Bill Crane series represents the very best of the "screwball comedy" school of 1930's mystery fiction. Dashiell Hammett's *The Thin Man* (published in 1934) is considered the archetype of the school, but Latimer's Crane mysteries, particularly *The Lady in the Morgue*, may well be considered the apotheosis. In addition, they clearly foreshadowed the tongue-in-cheek hard-boiled romps of the 1950's and 1960's: Richard S. Prather's Shell Scott series is a good example.

Some blurb writers have described Bill Crane as an "alcoholic private detective"; technically correct perhaps, but, in truth, Crane's consumption of booze is no more prodigious than that of most detectives of the hard-boiled fraternity. Crane differs from his brethren in that the stuff goes to his head; consequently, he does most of his detecting, if one can call it that, in a giddy, stuporous fog. Much the rest of the time he's hung over, in varying degrees of severity. The liquor doesn't impair his deductive abilities, nor his talent for cracking wise; but it does slow his motor reflexes—Crane is not the most reliable private eye to have handy in a brawl.

The third Crane novel, *The Lady in the Morgue*, is a genuine mystery classic. Latimer moves Crane and his drinking buddies, Doc Williams and Tom O'Malley, through a bizarre series of events at breakneck pace, beginning with a corpsenapping and ending with Crane under a sheet on a morgue slab. In between there are murders and shooting scrapes, a riot in a taxi dance hall, a midnight grave-robbing expedition, plenty of boozing, and the snappiest, wittiest dialogue to be found anywhere. *The Lady in the Morgue* is grotesque and hilarious at the same time, a masterpiece of black comedy. The murder mystery proper is slight, Crane's approach to "detection" might outrage purists, and the final unmasking is unsurprising; but the trip is so wonderfully entertaining that one can readily forgive Latimer's failure to attend to Holmesian rigor.

The final Crane novel, *Red Gardenias*, is rather more sedate, but no less entertaining. Crane is teamed with Ann Fortune, the daughter of his agency's boss, and they pose as husband and wife in an undercover investigation. Their witty exchanges are very much in the manner of Nick and Nora Charles; and one is moved to speculate that, had Hammett chosen to chronicle the cases of bachelor detective Nick Charles, they might closely resemble the investigations of Bill Crane.

Latimer moved to Hollywood shortly before the war to become a screenwriter; most noteworthy is his fine script for Hammett's *The Glass Key*. The Crane series was terminated, and Latimer did not return to the mystery novel until 1955. The two postwar novels, while excellent, lack the bawdy humor and extraordinary vigor of the Crane books. In *Sinners and Shrouds*, Latimer tackles the familiar theme of the man who wakes up to find a corpse (young, female, nude) in his room. *Black Is the Fashion for Dying* involves the murder of an unpleasant Hollywood prima donna, and Latimer makes good use of his movie studio experiences.

—Art Scott

———

LAWLESS, Anthony. *See* **MacDONALD, Philip.**

———

LAWRENCE, Hilda (Hildegarde Lawrence, née Kronmiller). American. Born in Baltimore, Maryland, c. 1906. Educated at Columbia School, Rochester, New York. Married Reginald Lawrence in 1924 (divorced). Worked as reader to the blind; in clippings department of Macmillan, publishers, New York; staff member, *Publishers Weekly*; radio writer.

CRIME PUBLICATIONS

Novels (series: Mark East)

Blood upon the Snow (East).   New York, Simon and Schuster, 1944; London, Chapman and Hall, 1946.
A Time to Die (East).   New York, Simon and Schuster, 1945; London, Chapman and Hall, 1947.
The Pavilion.   New York, Simon and Schuster, 1946; London, Chapman and Hall, 1948; as *The Deadly Pavilion*, New York, Pocket Books, 1948.
Death of a Doll (East).   New York, Simon and Schuster, 1947; London, Chapman and Hall, 1948.
Duet of Death (two novelets).   New York, Simon and Schuster, and London, Chapman and Hall, 1949; published separately as *Death Has Four Hands* and *The Bleeding House*, New York, Spivak, 2 vols., 1950.

Uncollected Short Story

"A Roof in Manhattan," in *For Love or Money*, edited by Dorothy Gardiner.   New York, Doubleday, 1957; London, Macdonald, 1959.

*   *   *

Hilda Lawrence once explained that, as an addict of mystery fiction, she took to writing it herself because she couldn't find enough satisfactory titles to feed her habit. In the mid-1940's, after a varied career (grading papers at Johns Hopkins, working at *Publishers Weekly*, churning out radio scripts for *The Rudy Vallee Show*), she settled down to producing a first novel that was immediately accepted for Simon and Shuster's "Inner Sanctum" imprint. This was *Blood upon the Snow* and it introduced the cast of characters which was to appear in her three most important books.

She once said to an interviewer that "everything you see can be turned into something and almost everything that happens can be used." Such a dictum is appropriate for guiding us to what it is that sets Lawrence's books apart from the other naturalistic *romans noirs* of that decade. For with the characters of Mark East, Beulah Pond, and Bessy Petty, she sets up a cooperative contrast between the ways men and women perceive normality: a complete picture is not available without both points of view.

The facts that East is a private investigator from Manhattan—hardly a typical male—and that Miss Beulah and Miss Bessy, as they are known locally in their New England village, are two spinsters, one slightly scatty—also untypical of their sex—set up the opposing viewpoints quite neatly; in addition to the sexual one, there are also insider/outsider, urban/rural, ingenuous/disingenuous dichotomies which contribute to the sleuthing success of this bizarre *ménage à trois*. It is to East's credit that, within a few hours of his having set foot in Crestwood, uncertain of the case he has been called upon to handle, he recognizes the naive genius of the "two old maids up the lane" when it comes to observation.

The notion that curious elderly women make excellent Sherlocks (or Watsons) is a time-honoured one in the genre, beginning in the late 19th century with Anna Katharine Green's Miss Amelia Butterworth and reaching its apotheosis with Christie's Miss Jane Marple. However, in her use of it, Lawrence takes the interesting chance of combining this softer tradition with the hard-boiled.

Lawrence's masterpiece is *Death of a Doll*. For its claustrophobic, inexorable quality, it would be difficult to find an equal. Set in a New York boarding house for women only, it deals with a young woman whose friends are her enemies. Miss Beulah and Miss Bessy have journeyed down to the big city at the invitation of a rich young matron whom the reader had met in Crestwood in *A Time to Die*. They plan to go out on the town with Mark East and find they have a mystery to offer him when it turns out that their hostess's favorite sales clerk inexplicably committed suicide on the day of moving into the ironically named Hope House, a Home for Girls. Hanging out at Hope House, the two women again become the insiders and, aided and abetted by East, they solve the crime. One unusual touch, but not an unlikely one given the dormitory atmosphere of the novel, is the covert lesbian relationship between the murderer and her benefactor.

Lawrence's plotting is far from flawless but her eye for setting and character make up for it. Her other three books are less appealing, being a trio of suspense melodramas which each resemble a cross between Mary Roberts Rinehart and Margaret Millar. Yet Lawrence has been praised by Boucher and Haycraft, and her reputation is guaranteed, particularly because of the haunting resonances of *Death of a Doll*.

—Michele Slung

———

LEASOR, (Thomas) James. British. Born in Erith, Kent, 20 December 1923. Educated at City of London School, 1935–40; Oriel College, Oxford (Editor, *Isis*), 1946–48, B.A. (honours) in English 1948, M.A. 1952. Served in the Royal Berkshire Regiment, in Burma, India, and Malaya, 1942–46: Captain. Married Joan Margaret Bevan in 1951; three sons. Reporter, *Kentish Times*, Sidcup, 1941–42; reporter, columnist (as William Hickey), feature writer, and foreign correspondent, London *Daily Express*, 1948–55; editorial advisor and consultant, George Newnes and C. Arthur Pearson Ltd., London, 1955–69; director, Elm Tree Books Ltd., London, 1970–73. Underwriting member, Lloyds of London. Since 1959, director, Pagoda Films Ltd.; since 1964, director, Jason Love Ltd. Member of the Order of St. John of Jerusalem; Fellow, Royal Society of Arts. Agent: Aitkew and Stone Ltd., 29 Fernshaw Road, London SW10 OTG. Address: Swallowcliffe Manor, Salisbury, Wiltshire, England.

CRIME PUBLICATIONS

Novels (series: Dr. Jason Love; the owner of Aristo Autos)

Passport to Oblivion (Love). London, Heinemann, 1964; Philadelphia, Lippincott, 1965; as *Where the Spies Are*, London, Pan, 1965.
Passport to Peril (Love). London, Heinemann, 1966; as *Spylight*, Philadelphia, Lippincott, 1966.
Passport in Suspense (Love). London, Heinemann, 1967; as *The Yang Meridian*, New York, Putnam, 1968.
Passport for a Pilgrim (Love). London, Heinemann, 1968; New York, Doubleday, 1969.

They Don't Make Them Like That Any More (Aristo). London, Heinemann, 1969; New York, Doubleday, 1970.
Never Had a Spanner on Her (Aristo). London, Heinemann, 1970.
Love-All. London, Heinemann, 1971:
Host of Extras (Love). London, Heinemann, 1973.
The Chinese Widow. London, Heinemann, 1975.
Love and the Land Beyond. London, Heinemann, 1979.
Open Secret. London, Collins, 1982.
Ship of Gold. London, Collins, 1984.
Tank of Serpents. London, Collins, 1986.
Frozen Assets (Love). London, Grafton, and New York, St. Martin's Press, 1989.

Short Stories

A Week of Love, Being Seven Adventures of Jason Love. London, Heinemann, 1969.

OTHER PUBLICATIONS

Novels

Not Such a Bad Day. Leicester, Blackfriars Press, 1946.
The Strong Delusion. London, Harrap, 1951.
NTR: Nothing to Report. London, Laurie, 1955.
Follow the Drum. London, Heinemann, and New York, Morrow, 1972.
Mandarin-Gold. London, Heinemann, 1973; New York, Morrow, 1974.
Jade Gate. London, Heinemann, 1976.
The Unknown Warrior. London, Heinemann, 1980; as *Code Name Nimrod*, Boston, Houghton Mifflin, 1981.

Plays

Look Where I'm At!, music by Jordan Ramin, lyrics by Frank H. Stanton and Murray Semos, adaptation of the novel *Rain in the Doorway* by Thorne Smith (produced New York, 1971).

Screenplay: *Where the Spies Are*, with Wolf Mankowitz and Val Guest, 1965.

Television Series: *The Michaels in Africa*.

Other

The Monday Story. London, Oxford University Press, 1951.
Author by Profession. London, Cleaver Hume Press, 1952.
Wheels of Fortune: A Brief Account of the Life and Times of William Morris, Viscount Nuffield. London, Lane, 1954.
The Sergeant Major: A Biography of R. S. M. Ronald Brittain, M.B.E., Coldstream Guards. London, Harrap, 1955.
The Red Fort: An Account of the Siege of Delhi in 1857. London, Laurie, 1956; New York, Reynal, 1957; as *Mutiny at the Red Fort*, London, Corgi, 1959.
The One That Got Away, with Kendal Burt. London, Joseph, 1956; New York, Random House, 1957.
The Millionth Chance: The Story of the R. 101. London, Hamish Hamilton, and New York, Reynal, 1957.
War at the Top (based on the experiences of General Sir Leslie Hollis). London, Joseph, 1959; as *The Clock with Four Hands*, New York, Reynal, 1959.
Conspiracy of Silence, with Peter Eton. London, Angus and Robertson, 1960; as *Wall of Silence*, Indianapolis, Bobbs Merrill, 1960.

The Plague and the Fire.   New York, McGraw Hill, 1961;
London, Allen and Unwin, 1962.

Rudolf Hess, The Uninvited Envoy. London, Allen and Unwin,
1962; as *The Uninvited Envoy,* New York, McGraw Hill,
1962.

Singapore: The Battle That Changed the World. London,
Hodder and Stoughton, and New York, Doubleday, 1968.

Green Beach (on the Dieppe raid).   London, Heinemann, and
New York, Morrow, 1975.

Boarding Party.   London, Heinemann, and Boston, Houghton
Mifflin, 1978; as *The Sea Wolves,* London, Corgi, 1980.

X-Troop.   London, Heinemann, 1980.

Who Killed Sir Henry Oakes? London, Heinemann, and
Boston, Houghton Mifflin, 1983.

The Marine from Mandalay.   London, Heinemann, 1988.

*

James Leasor comments:

I grew up a John Buchan enthusiast, and although I started
my writing career with non-fiction books, I always intended to
write thrillers. After several false starts and 14 rewrites I sold
my first, *Passport to Oblivion,* in 1964.

When I left school I became a medical student but
abandoned my intention of qualifying as a doctor to join the
army in the Second World War. My elder sister qualified,
however, and for many years practised in Somerset. Since I
knew the background there well, I made my character, Jason
Love, a Somerset physician. The name Jason is an anagram of
my own Christian name, James, my wife's, Joan, and my eldest
son's, Jeremy; my middle son, Andrew, provides the *a* and my
youngest son, Stuart, the *s.* The surname Love was chosen
because it appears continually in newspaper headlines, and I
felt it might have some subliminal advertising value.

All my thrillers are based on fact and before I write them I
visit the countries and places where I intend to set the action so
that I can research the backgrounds thoroughly. I have long
been attracted by the American Cord car and own one of the
few open Cords in Britain—so I gave my fictitious character
this car to drive.

I write these stories because I enjoy writing them.

*   *   *

The spy fiction phenomenon of the 1960's generated many
interesting variations in both escapist and realist camps. James
Leasor conceived one that is, in some respects, representative
of both disciplines. His series protagonist, Dr. Jason Love, is a
confident country doctor—with a respectable World War II
background—who is persuaded, by British Intelligence mogul
Douglas MacGillivray, out of complacency and into shaded
intrigue in the most alien of locales.

Leasor achieves a consistent level of suspense in the series by
accenting conflicting elements to maximum effect. The
character of Dr. Love, depicted as a world-weary outsider to the
spy craft, is typified by Leasor with the designation of
"Passport" in several of the series' titles. This serves to convey a
sense of passage from Love's placid existence into the dark,
haunting landscape of espionage.

Besieged with the disappearance of Agent K in Teheran in
Passport to Oblivion, MacGillivray recalls Dr. Love from the
ravages of World War II as the agent to locate K. Love is
dispatched to Teheran where British Intelligence has developed a cover organization, The Oil Exploration Centre, a
genuine oil research network, which affords Whitehall freedom
of action on foreign soil.

Leasor has been praised for the authenticity of detail in his
spy fiction, and nowhere is this more expertly exhibited than in
Passport to Oblivion. The author depicts the Middle East of the
1960's as a kingdom in conflict: confident in its control of the
global oil market, and yet curiously divided in its relationship
to the non-Islamic world. The critical significance of oil treaties
in Kuwait (where K was assigned) is a focus of the storyline of
this novel.

From this point, Leasor intensifies his plot with the
incorporation of one Dr. André Simmias (revealed as the Soviet
Control for Persia), as Dr. Love's chief antagonist. This facet
developed from the book's principal Arabic settings to an
electrifying confrontation aboard a Soviet Illyushin Aeroflot
craft enroute to the North that emerges as one of the most
provocative in espionage fiction.

Leasor is no less effective in exhibiting the realistic arena of
the spy genre through the characterization of Axel Lukacs, a
Soviet agent-in-place in Churchill-Manitoba, Canada. The
chapters which detail his function in the book's intricate ploys
are uncompromisingly grim, invoking along the way a past at
Vorkuta.

Leasor achieved a total sense of balance with *Passport to
Oblivion,* acknowledging the entire spectrum of espionage
fiction without being imitative, and fusing the elements of
characterization, plotting, and locales into a cohesive whole.
The tumultuous changes evidenced on the global scene in
recent months has nullified much of the identification value of
postwar spy fiction. *Passport to Oblivion* proves to be an
exception to this development. Leasor's depiction of the Arab
world and its relationship to the world market remains much
the same as when the book was published. This embodies
Soviet involvement in the region, which has not diminished,
unlike the massive reshaping of the Communist ideology in
Europe. In this respect, the Arabic complexion established in
Passport to Oblivion signifies the book as a timeless espionage
classic, darkly haunting and chillingly topical with equal
conviction.

Passport to Peril is more typical of the era's spy fiction but no
less effective in its overall effect of conveying an alien-world of
mystery and discovery.

The principal setting of *Passport to Peril* is the Himalayas,
which Leasor depicts with a foreboding, often nightmarish tone.
Leasor is merely utilizing this as a landscape for The
International Committee for the Preservation of Big Game,
which attempts to blackmail the Nawab. The Pakistani Khan's
son was blinded by a piercing light projected from the hills near
his home in Shahnagar. Love's contact, Ibrahim Khan, whom
he encounters on holiday in Switzerland, is later assassinated
after relating the Shahnagar situation to Love.

Leasor invests a more insidious conspiratorial tone to
Passport to Peril than was exhibited in the previous novel. This
departure is effective, given the plot segment involving a
Peking cover in Geneva to finance an espionage consortium
spanning across the Far East. The Jason Love character is more
seasoned and jaded than was apparent in *Passport to Oblivion,*
which conveys that Leasor defined the style of the series with
the first book and was advancing Love's development.

Although not as enduring as *Passport to Oblivion, Passport to
Peril* utilizes the Red Chinese enigma of the era in a spy thriller
of undeniable intrigue and global menace.

Passport for a Pilgrim is a reversion to the Arab mystique of
Passport to Oblivion, coupled with the technological magnetism
of *Passport to Peril.* Dr. Love is off to Damascus in this mission,
which encompasses a medical convention in the city the Arabs
revere as "The Gateway to God," the disappearance of two
British neurologists, and a scientific technique to program
thought processes as a medium of political anarchy.

While not as hypnotically prophetic as *Passport to Oblivion, Passport for a Pilgrim* is a worthy addition to this inventive series, especially in Leasor's portrayal of Damascus as a comparatively desolate background to the more mystical settings in the original.

Four other books are deserving of note, as they relate to areas covered by Leasor in the Love series. *They Don't Make Them Like That Anymore* and *Never Had a Spanner on Her* both concern the proprietor of Aristo Autos, and reflect Leasor's and Dr. Love's passion for vintage motor cars.

Cast in the authentic mold of *A Man Called Intrepid, The Unknown Warrior* meticulously details the Allied master spy of X-Troop, known as Nimrod, who deployed an ingenious deception to prevent the Nazis from assaulting Normandy. One finds much of the dispassionate professionalism exhibited in Leasor's characterization of Jason Love in the anatomy of Nimrod.

Leasor's mastery with intricate motives and exotic locales is nicely manifested in *Who Killed Sir Henry Oakes?* in which he speculates that Sir Henry was liquidated on his Bahamian estate in 1943 by Mafia associates who opposed his objections to the establishment of a casino in Nassau.

Apart from signifying a 25-year landmark for Dr. Love, *Frozen Assets* is the culmination of Leasor's classic spy series, achieving an aesthetic sense of balance among the canon's diverse designs. Essentially, it strikes a contemporary chord while retaining the darkly mystical sensation of cryptic discovery that made *Passport to Oblivion* so distinctive in its time.

Frozen Assets begins on a dramatically historical note, in a segment detailing an expedition in the Afghan mountains in the 1670's in which a British adventurer, Ralph Ballantyne, falls into an ice-crowned crevasse.

Leasor offers an intriguing account of the Honourable East India Company and the discovery of rare and exotic spices in the East. This development embodies the establishment of Indian warehouses to store the spices, the incursion upon this high-stakes market by the French and Portugese and the documents that granted Ballantyne's group the exclusive right to trade with other parties by the overland route.

The narrative advances to the present when Dr. Jason Love accepts an invitation to journey to Pakistan to estimate the value of a vintage 1935 Cord roadster, as an agent for the Midland Widows Insurance Company. Love is approached by Parkington, the British contact he encountered in Teheran back in *Passport to Oblivion*. The Cord is owned by a Pakistani, Dr. S. Khan, an association which will recall *Passport to Peril*.

Leasor balances this deceptively understated storyline with the explosively authentic Soviet involvement in Afghanistan. Leasor depicts each group judiciously and portrays the Soviets in the thick of an incendiary crisis. This facet is a conspicuous point of contrast to the more unified depiction of the Kremlin moguls in the Cold War trappings of *Passport to Oblivion*.

During an audacious Soviet expedition for minerals in the Afghan mountain passages, a haunting and hypnotic discovery is made—the immaculately chilled corpse of Ralph Ballantyne. The elements of the discovery and the cryptic history behind the vintage Cord provide the missing links of an apocalyptic scheme extending from the desolate limits of Afghanistan to Moscow.

In *Frozen Assets*, Leasor manages to unify the best elements of the classic early Love books, notably *Passport to Oblivion* and *Passport to Peril*, spice them with a topical touch, and blend them into a haunting espionage novel.

The effective series concept has not diminished in the slightest with the passage of time, and the advancement of Dr.

Love, who was presented in a mature light in *Passport to Oblivion*, here leads to a characterization of provocative resourcefulness and daring. In this respect, Leasor has aged Dr. Love engagingly with the times, engraving him as a survivor of the ravaged spy phenomenon.

Dr. Love is heard several times quoting Sir Thomas Browne throughout *Frozen Assets* and this passage magnificently captures the essence of the series concept in its advanced state: "Life is a pure flame—and we live by an invisible sun within us."

—Andy East

---

le CARRÉ, John. Pseudonym for David John Moore Cornwell. British. Born in Poole, Dorset, 19 October 1931. Educated at Sherborne School, Dorset; St. Andrew's Preparatory School; Berne University, Switzerland, 1948–49; Lincoln College, Oxford, B.A. (honours) in modern languages 1956. Married 1) Alison Ann Veronica Sharp in 1954 (divorced 1971), three sons; 2) Valerie Jane Eustace in 1972, one son. Tutor at Eton College, 1956–58; member of the British Foreign Service, 1959–64: second secretary, Bonn Embassy, 1961–64; consul, Hamburg, 1963–64. Recipient: British Crime Novel award, 1963; Somerset Maugham award, 1964; Mystery Writers of America Edgar Allan Poe award, 1965, and Grand Master award, 1984; Crime Writers Association Gold Dagger award, 1978, 1980; Diamond Dagger award, 1988. James Tait Black Memorial award, 1977; Agent: David Higham Associates, 5–8 Lower John Street, London W1R 4HA, England.

CRIME PUBLICATIONS

Novels (series: George Smiley)

Call for the Dead (Smiley). London, Gollancz, 1961; New York, Walker, 1962; as *The Deadly Affair*, London, Penguin, 1966.
A Murder of Quality (Smiley). London, Gollancz, 1962; New York, Walker, 1963.
The Spy Who Came In from the Cold (Smiley). London, Gollancz, 1963; New York, Coward McCann, 1964.
The Looking-Glass War. London, Heinemann, and New York, Coward McCann, 1965.
A Small Town in Germany. London, Heinemann, and New York, Coward McCann, 1968.
Tinker, Tailor, Soldier, Spy (Smiley). London, Hodder and Stoughton, and New York, Knopf, 1974.
The Honourable Schoolboy (Smiley). London, Hodder and Stoughton, and New York, Knopf, 1977.
Smiley's People. London, Hodder and Stoughton, and New York, Knopf, 1980.
The Little Drummer Girl. London, Hodder and Stoughton, and New York, Knopf, 1983.
A Perfect Spy. London, Hodder and Stoughton, and New York, Knopf, 1986.
The Russia House. London, Hodder and Stoughton, and New York, Knopf, 1989.

Uncollected Short Stories

"Dare I Weep, Dare I Mourn," in *Saturday Evening Post* (Philadelphia), 28 January 1967.
"What Ritual Is Being Observed Tonight?," in *Saturday Evening Post* (Philadelphia), 2 November 1968.

OTHER PUBLICATIONS

Novel

The Naive and Sentimental Lover. London, Hodder and Stoughton, 1971; New York, Knopf, 1972.

Play

Television Play: *Smiley's People*, with John Hopkins, from the novel by le Carré, 1982.

Other

Vanishing England, with Gareth H. Davies. Topsfield, Massachusetts, Salem House, 1987.

*

Critical Studies: *Secret Agents in Fiction: Ian Fleming, John le Carré, and Len Deighton* by L.O. Saverberg, London, Macmillan, 1984; *The Novels of John le Carré: The Art of Survival*, Blackwell, 1985, and *Smiley's Circus: A Guide to the Secret World of John le Carré*, London, Orbis, 1986, both by David Monaghan; *John le Carré* by Peter Elfred Lewis, New York, Ungar, 1985; *John le Carré* by Eric Homberger, London, Methuen, 1986; *Taking Sides: The Fiction of John le Carré* by Tony Barley, Milton Keynes, Buckinghamshire, and Philadelphia, Open University Press, 1986; *Corridors of Deceit: The World of John le Carré* by Peter Wolfe, Bowling Green, Ohio, Bowling Green University Popular Press, 1987; *The Quest for John le Carré* edited by Alan Bold, London, Vision Press, and New York, St. Martin's Press, 1988.

*   *   *

Tragedy used to be John le Carré's form, and it is again, with *The Little Drummer Girl*. The *telos* of justice, both canceled and negatively fulfilled, accounts for the chilly power of *The Spy Who Came In from the Cold*, which made le Carré the premier Cold War novelist. In *The Little Drummer Girl* which probes the awful intimacies of Arab-Israeli terror, the ironies of political justice are final.

In between lies the Smiley/Karla antithesis. In *Tinker, Tailor, Soldier, Spy* and *The Honourable Schoolboy* the character of Smiley fills the vacancy left by the old Control of *The Spy Who Came In from the Cold*. But the Circus Smiley inherits is made anachronistic by 1970's détente and morally paralyzed by the betrayal wrought by his immediate predecessor, a "Kim Philby" mole.

All that is left by *Smiley's People*, thus the title, is the man himself, George Smiley. Called once more out of retirement by a service secretly serving none but itself, Smiley puts the screws on his Russian Moriarty: "As with his marriage, so with his sense of public service. I invested my life in institutions—he thought without rancour—and all I am left with is myself. And with Karla, he thought. . . . "

Karla is forced to relinquish his grasp on his British counterpart: emblematically, the cigarette lighter, a present from Smiley's promiscuous wife that Karla has purloined from Smiley (a past incident briefly cited in *The Honourable Schoolboy*), lies unretrieved on the tarmac beneath the Wall. This key to Smiley's heart which Karla had exploited in his earlier *konspiratsia* now represents a balance of betrayals, for the austere Karla is snared by an equal exploitation of the heart. Presumably, then, there will be no more "quest for Karla" from le Carré.

The literary point of this finale, however, is that le Carré had himself "come over," a defector from the anti-politics of tragedy. The true action of le Carré's tragedy goes unrealized in the Smiley/Karla series. For it depends, utterly, on the infernal machine of East-West politics grinding out the condemnation of it all originally articulated by Leamas, the winning loser-losing winner of *The Spy Who Came In from the Cold*. By contrast le Carré's long-arching counter-*konspiratsia* in *Smiley's People* is defaulting proof of Aristotle's quizzical dictum that tragedy comes not from character but from action through plot.

For in opting for the spy novel of character, le Carré naturally has the good spy Smiley win, the bad spy Karla lose. Ruined, then, is the symmetrically tragic architecture of the good/bad vs. bad/good of Leamas/Fiedler. By having Smiley succeed le Carré refurbishes the tarnished trade of intrigue, instead of making it serve as political scaffolding for the larger meanings which are harder to take: "George, you won" . . . "Yes, well I suppose I did." The fastidiously humane Westerner thus eclipses the "absolutist fanatic"; Karla, after all, at heart—to our comfort—is just a very vulnerable Westerner himself, "flawed" by bourgeois love of a daughter driven insane by the revolutionary *ananke* of his role.

Le Carré betrays awareness of this diminution of scale he perpetrates in the Smiley/Karla trilogy, when he considers Smiley reading Karla's file for one last time: "He tried but, as so often before, failed to resist his own fascination at the sheer scale of the Russian suffering, its careless savagery, its flights of heroism. He felt small in the face of it, and soft by comparison, even though he did not consider his own life wanting in its pains." Smiley *is* too "small"; any mere character, complete as personality but lacking as tragic *persona*, would be. Karla is the man we really need to know. Rather, it is the "sheer scale" of the *history* in Karla's *story* we must comprehend.

With *The Little Drummer Girl* le Carré finally tells a big story, one that traces with pain the exactions of history on ordinary lives. No longer is it the irony, merely glimpsed by a winningly "soft" Englishman, of Karla's revolution killing the best in itself, but the full-scale good/bad vs. good/bad of post-Holocaust Israeli and post-Israel Palestinian exterminating the best in themselves. Character, at least cast heroically in *Smiley's People* if not fulfilled, is no longer possible, as the novel's worthiest Israelis and Palestinians acknowledge, they have "no choice"; and authorial irony relentlessly, no exceptions made, recoils on the characters' rationality and professionalism.

Yet to lead us through this historical action/tragic plot, le Carré this time wisely chooses to lock us inside the unmediated experience of his best character to date: Charlie, a defiant English actress whose very profession is to "choose" how to be a character, and at the same time a courageous counter-terrorist horribly manipulated and manipulating, in her best nature as woman, "to save life . . . to take part. To be something." To *act* a part in an Israeli scheme, she hopes, will enable her to *be*, to become valued for a better self, by herself as well as by the man she loves.

The only way open to her hope, however, is to will herself into playing "theatre of the real." And that way lie betrayal, violence, madness: the betrayal of self which is the end of acting out a deception against a man she cannot help but try to save even as she traps him for the sake of saving others; the violence of self-violation that inevitably attends political violence; the madness of having to freeze one's heart in the name of love.

History can tie us in knots like these, especially if we want, as Charlie wants, to feel the truth by doing right. Le Carré shows in *The Little Drummer Girl* that he knows the task of plotting the denouement of his tragedy is to see in world politics our fate writ so large that there is no mistaking it: we forfeit our humanity in the acts of preserving it.

He has also learned the big secret of the tragic novel of international intrigue: that the clearest gauge for such misery is a woman. What held for Euripides still holds for *The Little Drummer Girl*: history may brutalize men, but it desecrates women. Charlie, both the woman, with her impulse to be true, and the actress, with her wit and instinct "to be" others, demands and deserves respect but is forced by her very goodness to succumb to a kind of deceit that eventually savages her self-respect.

Like Lizzie in *The Honourable Schoolboy* and Alexandra/ Tatiana in *Smiley's People*, both early drafts for the heroine properly claiming center-stage in *The Little Drummer Girl*, Charlie serves as a whorish agent of secular grace. Commitment to her elicits the calamitous best from all the men who use her, whether for political good or evil: Joseph, her Israeli runner and romantic exemplar, ends up her "pimp"; Kahlil, the Palestinian terrorist she must betray, becomes as genuine a lover as Joseph—both killers she can love just as she has become a lover who can kill.

Such moral exchanges compose le Carré's most exacting formula for a fiction which is no longer simply "spy" (*Call for the Dead*) or even, more complexly, "political" (*A Small Town in Germany*)—or the unsatisfying hybrid of "spy-political-tragic" genre represented by the Smiley/Karla series. *The Little Drummer Girl*, instead, fully extends the spy genre, all the while maintaining its format, to the dimensions of tragic historical novel.

—John Snyder

LEE, Manfred B. *See* **QUEEN, Ellery.**

LEEK, Margaret. *See* **WOODS, Sara.**

LEJEUNE, Anthony. Pseudonym for Edward Anthony Thompson. British. Born in London, 7 August 1928. Educated at Merchant Taylors' School, London; Balliol College, Oxford, 1949–53. Served in the Royal Navy, 1947–49. Deputy editor, 1955–57, and editor, 1957–58, *Time and Tide*, London; special writer, *Daily Express*, London, 1958–61, and *Sunday Times*, London, 1961–63. Regular broadcaster, and contributor to various British and American journals; since 1954 crime reviewer, *The Tablet*, London. Former editorial director, Tom Stacey Ltd., publishers, London. Address: Lane End, Hillside Road, Pinner Hill, Middlesex, England.

CRIME PUBLICATIONS

Novels (series: Adam Gifford; Glowrey)

Crowded and Dangerous. London, Macdonald, 1959.
Mr. Diabolo. London, Macdonald, 1960.
News of Murder (Gifford). London, Macdonald, 1961.
Duel in the Shadows (Gifford). London, Macdonald, 1962.
Glint of Spears. London, Macdonald, 1963.
The Dark Trade (Gifford). London, Macdonald, 1965; New York, Doubleday, 1966; as *Death of a Pornographer*, New York, Lancer, 1967.
Strange and Private War. London, Macmillan, 1986; New York, Doubleday, 1987.
Professor in Peril (Glowrey). London, Macmillan, 1987; New York, Doubleday, 1988.
Key Without a Door (Glowrey). London, Macmillan, 1988; New York, Doubleday, 1989.

Uncollected Short Stories

"The Interrupted Journey of James Fairbrother," in *Winter's Crimes 6*, edited by George Hardinge. London, Macmillan, and New York, St. Martin's Press, 1974.
"Something on Everyone," in *Winter's Crimes 11*, edited by George Hardinge. London, Macmillan, and New York, St. Martin's Press, 1979.
"The Defector," in *Winter's Crimes 14*, edited by Hilary Watson. London, Macmillan, and New York, St. Martin's Press, 1982.

OTHER PUBLICATIONS

Play

Television Play: *Vicky's First Ball*, with Caroline Alice Lejeune.

Other

Freedom and the Politicians. London, Joseph, 1964.
Enoch Powell's "Income Tax at 4s. 3d. in the £." London, Stacey, 1970.
The Gentlemen's Clubs of London. London, Macdonald and Jane's, and New York, Mayflower, 1979.

Editor, *Time and Tide Anthology.* London, Deutsch, 1956.
Editor, *The Case for South West Africa.* London, Stacey, 1971.
Editor, *Drink and Ink 1919–1977*, by Dennis Wheatley. London, Hutchinson, 1979.
Editor, *The Deception Planners*, by Dennis Wheatley. London, Hutchinson, 1980.

*

Anthony Lejeune comments:
20 years, during which I was relatively busy with work, elapsed between the writing of my first six novels and the more recent group. I should like to think that I had learned something about technique, if not about the world, in the meanwhile, but I can't bring myself to read the early books again to discover if this is true. I can at least claim for *News of Murder* that it gives an authentic picture of London newspaper life—old Fleet Street, now gone like lost Atlantis—as it was in the 1950's. The other things about which I feel modest

satisfaction are the central idea of the short story "Something on Everyone," the Charleston scenes in *Professor in Peril*, and the clue structure in *Key Without a Door*. If a mystery writer can't boast about his clues, what should he boast about?

*   *   *

Anthony Lejeune is an able but undistinguished writer of suspense fiction one of whose books, *Glint of Spears*, deserves accolades.

Several of his books spin tales around Adam Gifford, a crime reporter for a London newspaper who also answers to the call of Arthur Blaise, a highranking official in the British War Office. A bright, eager young woman generally figures in the story, engaging Adam's attentions and complicating the plot. In *News of Murder* two murders lead Gifford to a ring of international drug smugglers; in *The Dark Trade* Gifford's work on a feature article on industrial espionage involves him in the investigation of the murder of a pornographer, which in turn reveals a complicated Russian plot to use blackmail to compel the wealthy owner of an industrial plant to sell atomic secrets to the Russians. Typically, the books contain a scene where Gifford and his female companion are set upon by a gang of thugs. The woman companion is generally depicted as a spirited lady, meant to be Gifford's match, but doomed predictably to be rejected by him when he recognizes that his true mistress is no woman but his job. She invariably commits some foolish act out of the finest motives, and Gifford is left to contrive elaborate plans to guarantee her safety.

Arthur Blaise, a hush-hush figure in Whitehall whose business it is to protect Britain's security, is usually introduced early in the story and left to lurk behind the scenes manipulating the action.

The plot in all these books is quite predictable. Gifford and Blaise are fleshed out by their author but the other characters are mere sterotypes. A journalistic description of the network of crime that governs the story is included in every book, be it drug-abuse, pornography, or industrial espionage. A scene or two in the newspaper office, an urgent cable calling for a rush of "the fullest colorfullest story," and Gifford's fingers tripping over his typewriter keys, producing fresh copy, are all part of the ordinary fare in Lejeune's fiction. Only in *Glint of Spears* does Lejeune offer an interesting departure from his too-formulaic suspense books.

Glint of Spears finds its literary ancestors in Joseph Conrad's *Heart of Darkness* and in some of Alan Paton's books about Africa, but it succeeds because it finds action and setting that are real and frightful. Set in post-independence Congo, it charts, hour by hour and day by day, Andrew Marsden's journey into the Congo where he attempts to locate and rescue Paul Buckley, a missionary whose station has been destroyed. Most of the tale recounts the terrifying journey of Buckley and a small tightly-knit tribe of Africans led by Lobendola to escape from almost certain death at the hands of the Bakona who are murdering any white men or friends of white men they overtake. In a tautly told first-person narrative, Marsden describes the jungle; the stealthy march towards Marieville where help is; the furtive attempts to avoid an encounter with Johnny Mtala, a Bakona "king" who once was the follower of Buckley, but now leads cannibalistic Africans; and, finally, the battle between the two groups which culminates in a duel between Buckley and Mtala which is to settle the fates of the two peoples. In this book, Lejeune's journalistic flair for naturalistic detail and his skill as a story-teller have found a fit subject. The tale is gripping; the landscape, hot, wooded, fly-infested; the people cunning and desperate; and the solution

problematic, befitting the precarious nature of the Congo's independence.

—Carol Simpson Stern

LEMARCHAND, Elizabeth (Wharton). British. Born in Barnstaple, Devon, 27 October 1906. Educated at the Ursuline Convent, Bideford, Devon, 1918–26; University of Exeter, 1926–29, London External B.A. (honours) 1927, M.A. (London) 1929; Geneva School of International Studies (scholar), 1929. Assistant mistress, Clifton High School, Bristol, 1929–35, and Sutton High School, 1935–40; deputy headmistress, Godolphin School, Salisbury, 1940–60; headmistress, Lowther College, Abergele, Wales, 1960–61. Agent: Watson Little Ltd., Suite 8, 26 Charing Cross Road, London WC2H 0DG. Address: Flat 11, Grove House, Fore Street, Topsham, Exeter, Devon EX3 OHF, England.

CRIME PUBLICATIONS

Novels (series: Detective Superintendent Tom Pollard in all books)

Death of an Old Girl. London, Hart Davis, 1967; New York, Award, 1970.
The Affacombe Affair. London, Hart Davis, 1968.
Alibi for a Corpse. London, Hart Davis, 1969; New York, Walker, 1986.
Death on Doomsday. London, Hart Davis, 1971; New York, Walker, 1975.
Cyanide with Compliments. London, MacGibbon and Kee, 1972; New York, Walker, 1973.
Let or Hindrance. London, Hart Davis MacGibbon, 1973; as *No Vacation from Murder*, New York, Walker, 1974.
Buried in the Past. London, Hart Davis MacGibbon, 1974; New York, Walker, 1975.
Step in the Dark. London, Hart Davis MacGibbon, 1976; New York, Walker, 1977.
Unhappy Returns. London, Hart Davis MacGibbon, 1977; New York, Walker, 1978.
Suddenly While Gardening. London, Hart Davis MacGibbon, 1978; New York, Walker, 1979.
Change for the Worse. Loughton, Essex, Piatkus, 1980; New York, Walker, 1981.
Nothing to Do with the Case. Loughton, Essex, Piatkus, and New York, Walker, 1981.
Troubled Waters. Loughton, Essex, Piatkus, and New York, Walker, 1982.
The Wheel Turns. Loughton, Essex, Piatkus, 1983; New York, Walker, 1984.
Light Through Glass. London, Piatkus, 1984; New York, Walker, 1986.
Who Goes Home? London, Piatkus, 1986; New York, Walker, 1987.
The Glade Manor Murder. London, Piatkus, 1988; New York, Walker, 1989.

Uncollected Short Stories

"Pussycats and Owls," in *Argosy* (New York), January 1964.
"The Quiet Pupil," in *Argosy* (New York), March 1964.
"Comfort from Capricorn," in *Argosy* (New York), July 1964.
"The Long House," in *Argosy* (New York), December 1964.

"The Beckoning Beeches," in *John Creasey's Mystery Bedside Book 1969*, edited by Herbert Harris. London, Hodder and Stoughton, 1968.

"The Stone of Witness," in *John Creasey's Mystery Bedside Book 1970*, edited by Herbert Harris. London, Hodder and Stoughton, 1969.

"Time to Be Going," in *More Tales of Unease*, edited by John Burke. London, Pan, 1969.

"Black Bartholomew," in *John Creasey's Mystery Bedside Book 1974*, edited by Herbert Harris. London, Hodder and Stoughton, 1973.

"The Comeback," in *John Creasey's Mystery Bedside Book 1976*, edited by Herbert Harris. London, Hodder and Stoughton, 1975.

*

Elizabeth Lemarchand comments:

I had to retire early because of a serious illness and began to write as a hobby in convalescence. After a modest success with short stories I felt I wanted more elbow room and decided to try my hand at a detective novel. I had always enjoyed detective fiction and it seemed the obvious choice for a late starter. It is, after all, basically the application of a formula, and one is free to concentrate on interesting settings and characterisation. I use only settings of which I have some personal knowledge, and I take a lot of trouble over them. My books are not thrillers (which are sexy and deal with sensational and violent crime), but novels with a "detective" theme of the sort normally described as "classical." Old hat, some would say, but there are still a surprising number of old hatters around.

*   *   *

For more than two decades Elizabeth Lemarchand has been writing detective stories of the classic English variety. Fans of the Golden Age writers such as Christie, Sayers, and Allingham have, if they have not yet encountered Lemarchand's works, a happy surprise in store. She employs such nostalgic niceties as timetables, floor-plans, maps, and casts of characters, and has created a pair of detectives, Scotland Yard officers Tom Pollard and Gregory Toye, who appear in each tale and advance in rank as new books succeed each other in the series. This is not to say that her books are period pieces—they are not; they are worthy entries in the lists of genteel crime fiction and polite problem solving.

Pollard and Toye have no idiosyncrasies of the type that distinguish Nero Wolfe or Lord Peter Wimsey; they are simply thoroughly nice fellows who work well together, who apply considerable ingenuity to solving the crimes that are assigned to them, and who relentlessly pursue that evidence that allows them to eliminate fallacious conclusions. Both are family men, and Toye is shown to be a bit sentimental when he deals with attractive young women. Pollard and his wife Jane, a red-haired artist, are the parents of twins, whose birth is awaited in *The Affacombe Affair*. Subsequent books offer glimpses of the children as they grow, and when they start school Jane takes a job in an art college. Cat hair on clothing is important evidence in *Step in the Dark*, and the cat in question, rejected by its original owners, is adopted by the Pollard family, despite the fact that it tripped Pollard on a staircase, causing him to break a leg.

The author's interest in English history and archaeology is used to good advantage. While not central to the plots, as they would be in the works of Anthony Price, history and archaeology provide interest in the settings and structure of her tales: Bronze Age barrows are part of the scenery, and quaint customs dating back to Saxon times make vivid background material. Olivia Strode, an engaging older woman who appears in *The Affacombe Affair* and again in *Cyanide with Compliments*, is writing a parish history and brings in many fascinating details as well as vital information which her curiosity leads her to uncover. A medievalist seeking to debunk the charters of his home town and thereby make a mockery of its millenary celebration, as well as a 20th-century corpse unearthed in an excavated Roman villa, figure in *Buried in the Past*.

In *Unhappy Returns* a married couple—both writers and both unedifying examples of that species—receive their due, and a medieval chalice is lost for the second time in its elusive history and found again by Pollard. A medieval pilgrimage route and a Bronze Age tomb containing a modern skeleton become part of Pollard's vacation in *Suddenly While Gardening*.

An intricate plot with a real art theft and a simulated one, the actual death of a ne'er-do-well who had faked his own death years before, and the clever juxtaposition of Pollard's professional involvement in a case and the preliminary presentation of the mystery in his personal life—all unfolded in *Change for the Worse*. *Nothing to Do with the Case* contains two separate stories which converge at Marleigh Manor with murder and arson. Detective Inspector Toye, ever the romantic, encourages a pair of young lovers.

The passionate pursuit of privacy, of family history, and of social status motivate various characters in *Troubled Waters* set in the village of Woodcombe, where symbols of ancient superstition survive and continue to incite violence. In *The Wheel Turns* a young historian's research is the background for a crime committed by a politician whose egoism and ambition consume him.

Lemarchand is skilful at portraying the daily life of small communities—whether village, school, or vacation colony. Her characters, even minor ones who are quickly sketched, are lifelike and invite the reader's sympathy; in short, they are people one enjoys reading about whose motivations and reactions are plausible.

A retired headmistress, the author often chooses school settings to the extent that the Commissioner remarks to Pollard in one book that if he keeps on handling school cases he'll wind up teaching. Other settings include a stately home, a private literary and scientific society's headquarters, a cruise ship, and a house on a lonely moor. To take such conventional settings and bring them to life with fresh and entertaining stories is no small accomplishment. The crimes—blackmail, arson, theft, all leading to murder—are also conventional, but the inventive past histories of the characters and the clever twists of the plots are absorbing.

If the fictional England of Lemarchand does not really exist, it is a pleasant and comfortable place to escape to in imagination. Its inhabitants, even those who commit murder, are literate and civilized, and crimes which evoke outrage in the abstract never impinge offensively upon one's sensibilities. Charming vignettes, warmth, wit, and solid detection mark these tasteful tales of violence.

—Mary Helen Becker

———

LEONARD, Elmore. American. Born in New Orleans, Louisiana, 11 October 1925. Educated at the University of Detroit, 1946–50, Ph.B. in English 1950. Served in the United States Naval Reserve, 1943–46. Married 1) Beverly Cline in 1949 (divorced 1977); 2) Joan Shepard in 1979; two daughters and three sons. Copywriter, Campbell Ewald advertising agency, Detroit, 1950–61; writer of industrial and educational films, 1961–63; Director, Elmore Leonard Advertising Company, 1963–66. Since 1967, full-time writer. Recipient: Mystery Writers of America Edgar Allan Poe award, 1984. Agent: H.N. Swanson, 8523 Sunset Boulevard, Los Angeles, California 90069.

CRIME PUBLICATIONS

Novels

The Big Bounce. New York, Fawcett, and London, Hale, 1969.
The Moonshine War. New York, Doubleday, 1969; London, Hale, 1970.
Mr. Majestyk (novelization of screenplay). New York, Dell, 1974; London, Penguin, 1986.
Fifty-Two Pickup. New York, Delacorte Press, and London, Secker and Warburg, 1974.
Swag. New York, Delacorte Press, 1976; London, Penguin 1986; as *Ryan's Rules*, New York, Dell, 1976.
The Hunted. New York, Delacorte Press, 1977; London, Secker and Warburg, 1978.
Unknown Man No. 89. New York, Delacorte Press, and London, Secker and Warburg, 1977.
The Switch. New York, Bantam, 1978; London, Secker and Warburg, 1979.
City Primeval. New York, Arbor House, 1980; London, W.H. Allen, 1981.
Gold Coast. New York, Bantam, 1980; London, W.H. Allen, 1982.
Split Images. New York, Arbor House, 1982; London, W.H. Allen, 1983.
Cat Chaser. New York, Arbor House, 1982; London, Viking, 1986.
Stick. New York, Arbor House, 1983; London, Allen Lane, 1984.
LaBrava. New York, Arbor House, 1983; London, Viking Press, 1984.
Glitz. New York, Arbor House, and London, Viking, 1985.
Bandits. New York, Arbor House, and London, Viking, 1987.
Touch. New York, Arbor House, 1987; London, Viking, 1988.
Freaky Deaky. New York, Arbor House, and London, Viking, 1988.
Killshot. New York, Arbor House, and London, Viking, 1989.
Get Shorty. New York, Delacorte Press, and London, Viking, 1990.

OTHER PUBLICATIONS

Novels

The Bounty Hunters. Boston, Houghton Mifflin, 1953; London, Hale, 1956.
The Law at Randado. Boston, Houghton Mifflin, 1955; London, Hale, 1957.
Escape from Five Shadows. Boston, Houghton Mifflin, 1956; London, Hale, 1957.
Last Stand at Saber River. New York, Dell, 1959; as *Lawless River*, London, Hale, 1959; as *Stand on the Saber*, London, Corgi, 1960.
Hombre. New York, Ballantine, and London, Hale, 1961.

Valdez Is Coming. London, Hale, 1969; New York, Fawcett, 1970.
Forty Lashes Less One. New York, Bantam, 1972.
Gunsights. New York, Bantam, 1979.

Plays

Screenplays: *The Moonshine War*, 1970; *Joe Kidd*, 1972; *Mr. Majestyk*, 1974; *Stick*, with Joseph C. Stinson, 1985.

Television Play: *High Noon, Part II: The Return of Will Kane*, 1980.

*

Manuscript Collection: University of Detroit Library.

* * *

An extremely prolific and versatile novelist who has worked successfully in several areas of popular fiction, Elmore Leonard is also one of those special writers who can comprehend the spirit of his time and place. Few practitioners of crime fiction are so acutely sensitive to the peculiar tensions of American urban life in the last decades of the 20th century. Beyond their recognition of the constant puzzle of human behavior, his books don't provide mysteries in the usual sense; although they deal regularly with the work of policemen, they certainly cannot be called procedurals; instead, they are swiftly paced, accurately reported, pungently flavored stories of armed robbery and murder, stock swindles and drug deals, of cops and crooks and courts of law—in short, of authentic crime committed by and against credible people. His work is distinguished above all by its understated sophistication, its assumption of the reader's awareness of the world, and the kind of apparent effortlessness that marks the true professional.

There's a great difference between talking tough and being tough, and Leonard clearly knows it. His books suggest a firsthand experience and a thorough knowledge of his subject—particular places and backgrounds, methods of crime and detection, and people from just about every stratum of contemporary society. His two major locales are Florida and, especially, the troubled city of Detroit and its region, from urban ghetto to affluent suburb, which he captures with the power and zest of a contemporary Dickens. He seems as much at home in a squadroom as a penthouse, as familiar with criminal trials as with the operation of a small motel, as knowledgeable about the eccentricities of millionaires as about the leisure habits of used-car salesmen. His thugs and pimps, convicts and con men, stockbrokers and coke dealers, his ex-Marines, retired cops, and reformed rummies act and, especially, speak as we know (or think we know) they should.

Leonard belongs to the Hemingway-Hammett-Cain rather than the Faulkner-Chandler-Macdonald school of prose style, which also implies a particular approach to character and action. Although without any particular eloquence, even of the hard-boiled variety, Leonard's language is terse and utilitarian; although he likes to shift it around, he maintains a mostly objective third-person point of view; his dialogue is colloquial, wised-up, and perfectly appropriate to its speaker, who may be a washed-up movie star, a psychotic killer, a dizzy cocktail waitress, an aged hippie, or a Cuban hit man. He handles speech as well as George V. Higgins, without Higgins's reliance on long, digressive anecdotes and self-conscious mannerisms; his people speak sharply and efficiently, without impeding narrative momentum or stalling the flow of action. He reports on the way business works in America—brokers' transactions, tax shelters, legal maneuvers, cocaine deals—at least as instructively as John D. MacDonald, without that author's tedious and melancholy little sermons on modern morality and the decline of the West. He is equally good on another American literary specialty, mechanical process and operation—the kind of gun the ex-cop uses in *Cat Chaser*, the way the Secret Service guards a President's widow in *LaBrava*, how to make and defuse a bomb in *Freaky Deaky*.

Although he occasionally works too hard for a pat irony in his endings, his books generally exhibit a strong sense of structure and a sure control of their subjects. If *City Primeval*, *Swag*, and *Stick*, for example, seem too firmly committed to the author's blueprint, they abound in energy and understated violence. If his protagonists are too often neutral and even pallid—the cops and ex-cops of *City Primeval*, *Split Images*, and *Glitz*, the former Secret Service agent of *LaBrava*—they are men who practice a kind of professional noncommitment anyway. His women tend, especially in his later novels, to undergo a passage through violence which instructs them in their own identity— the gangster's widow in *Gold Coast*, the ex-nun of *Bandits*, the actress in *Freaky Deaky*, the housewife in *Killshot*. Many of his secondary characters, however, are little short of wonderful— the hyperkinetic drug dealer of *Stick*, the corrupt ex-cop of *Split Images*, the kill-crazy country boy in *City Primeval*, the sodden millionaire in *Freaky Deaky*, the prison dietitian in *Killshot* and numerous others almost make the books worthwhile all by themselves.

Leonard has been writing for many years but has only very recently been "discovered" by the influential reviews and magazines, receiving the critical recognition and financial rewards he has long deserved. He is currently just about the hottest crime writer in America, which also means that the critical superlatives now balance the years of neglect. To his credit, despite his recent success, he continues to write the kind of book he has always written, maintaining a remarkable productivity and an admirable level of quality; at the same time, he continues to grow and change, moving to New Orleans for *Bandits*, using a new sort of villain in *Freaky Deaky*, attempting a religious dimension in the resurrected *Touch* to match the political concern of *Bandits*, creating stronger female characters in most of his latest books. Leonard's skill at language, character, action, milieu, and the general sociology of his novels should guarantee him a permanent place among the writers of his time. He knows his world intimately and writes about it with verve and vividness. Like all crime writers he's on the side of the angels, but like the best of them he finds the other side more compelling, and nobody writes about that better than he.

—George Grella

LE QUEUX, William (Tufnell). British. Born in London, 2 July 1864. Educated privately in London and at Pegli, Italy; studied art in Paris. Reporter, Eastbourne *Gazette*, editor, Middlesex *Chronicle*, 1883–88; parliamentary reporter, 1888– 91; foreign editor, London *Globe*, 1891–93; from 1893 freelance journalist and travel writer; Balkan Correspondent, *Daily Mail*, London, during Balkan War, 1912–13; served as Consul to the Republic of San Marino. Popularly supposed to have been a British Secret Service agent. Lived in Switzerland in later life. *Died 13 October 1927.*

CRIME PUBLICATIONS

Novels

Guilty Bonds. London, Routledge, 1891; New York, Fenno, 1895.
The Temptress. London, Tower, and New York, Stokes, 1895.
Zoraida: A Romance of the Harem and the Great Sahara. London, Tower, and New York, Stokes, 1895.
Devil's Dice. London, White, 1896; Chicago, Rand McNally, 1897.
The Great White Queen. London, White, 1896; New York, Arno Press, 1975.
Whoso Findeth a Wife. London, White, 1897; Chicago, Rand McNally, 1898.
A Madonna of the Music Halls. London, White, 1897; as *A Secret Sin*, London, Gardner, 1913.
The Eye of Istar. London, White, and New York, Stokes, 1897.
If Sinners Entice Thee. London, White, 1898; New York, Dillingham, 1899.
Scribes and Pharisees: A Story of Literary London. London, White, and New York, Dodd Mead, 1898.
The Veiled Man. London, White, 1899.
The Bond of Black. London, White, and New York, Dillingham, 1899.
Wiles of the Wicked. London, Bell, 1899.
The Day of Temptation. London, White, and New York, Dillingham, 1899.
England's Peril. London, White, 1899.
An Eye for an Eye. London, White, 1900.
In White Raiment. London, White, 1900.
Of Royal Blood: A Story of the Secret Service. London, Hutchinson, 1900.
The Gamblers. London, Hutchinson, 1901.
The Sign of the Seven Sins. Philadelphia, Lippincott, 1901.
Her Majesty's Minister. London, Hodder and Stoughton, and New York, Dodd Mead, 1901.
The Court of Honour. London, White, 1901.
The Under-Secretary. London, Hutchinson, 1902.
The Unnamed: A Romance of Modern Italy. London, Hodder and Stoughton, 1902.
The Tickencote Treasure. London, Newnes, 1903.
The Three Glass Eyes. London, Treherne, 1903.
The Seven Secrets. London, Hutchinson, 1903.
As We Forgive Them. London, White, 1904.
The Closed Book. London, Methuen, and New York, Smart Set, 1904.
The Hunchback of Westminister. London, Methuen, 1904.
The Man from Downing Street. London, Hurst and Blackett, 1904.
The Red Hat. London, Daily Mail, 1904.
The Sign of the Stranger. London, White, 1904.
The Idol of the Town. London, White, 1905.
The Valley of the Shadow. London, Methuen, 1905.
Who Giveth This Woman? London, Hodder and Stoughton, 1905.
The Spider's Eye. London, Cassell, 1905.
Sins of the City. London, White, 1905.
The Mask. London, Long, 1905.
Behind the Throne. London, Methuen, 1905.
The Czar's Spy. London, Hodder and Stoughton, and New York, Smart Set, 1905.
The Great Court Scandal. London, White, 1906.
The House of the Wicked. London, Hurst and Blackett, 1906.
The Mysterious Mr. Miller. London, Hodder and Stoughton, 1906.

The Mystery of a Motor-Car. London, Hodder and Stoughton, 1906.

Whatsoever a Man Soweth. London, White, 1906.

The Woman at Kensington. London, Cassell, 1906.

The Secret of the Square. London, White, 1907.

The Great Plot. London, Hodder and Stoughton, 1907.

Whatsoever Loveth. London, Hutchinson, 1907.

The Crooked Way. London, Methuen, 1908.

The Looker-On. London, White, 1908.

The Pauper of Park Lane. London, Cassell, and New York, Cupples and Leon, 1908.

Stolen Sweets. London, Nash, 1908.

The Woman in the Way. London, Nash, 1908.

The Red Room. London, Cassell, 1909; Boston, Little Brown, 1911.

The House of Whispers. London, Nash, 1909; New York, Brentano's, 1910.

Fatal Thirteen. London, Stanley Paul, 1909.

Treasure of Israel. London, Nash, 1910; as *The Great God Gold*, Boston, Badger, 1910.

Lying Lips. London, Stanley Paul, 1910.

The Unknown Tomorrow. London, White, 1910.

Hushed Up! London, Nash, 1911.

The Money-Spider. London, Cassell, and Boston, Badger, 1911.

The Death-Doctor. London, Hurst and Blackett, 1912.

Fatal Fingers. London, Cassell, 1912.

The Mystery of Nine. London, Nash, 1912.

Without Trace. London, Nash, 1912.

The Price of Power, Being Chapters from the Secret History of the Imperial Court of Russia. London, Hurst and Blackett, 1913.

The Room of Secrets. London, Ward Lock, 1913.

The Lost Million. London, Nash, 1913.

The White Lie. London, Ward Lock, 1914.

Sons of Satan. London, White, 1914.

The Hand of Allah. London, Cassell, 1914; as *The Riddle of the Ring*, London, Federation Press, 1927.

Her Royal Highness. London, Hodder and Stoughton, 1914.

The Maker of Secrets. London, Ward Lock, 1914.

The Four Faces. London, Stanley Paul, and New York, Brentano's, 1914.

The Double Shadow. London, Hodder and Stoughton, 1915.

At the Sign of the Sword. London, Jack, and New York, Scully and Kleinteich, 1915.

The Mysterious Three. London, Ward Lock, 1915.

The Mystery of the Green Ray. London, Hodder and Stoughton, 1915; as *The Green Ray*, London, Mellifont Press, 1934.

The Sign of Silence. London, Ward Lock, 1915.

The White Glove. London, Nash, 1915.

The Zeppelin Destroyer. London, Hodder and Stoughton, 1916.

Number 70, Berlin. London, Hodder and Stoughton, 1916.

The Place of Dragons. London, Ward Lock, 1916.

The Spy Hunter. London, Pearson, 1916.

The Man about Town. London, Long, 1916.

Annette of the Argonne. London, Hurst and Blackett, 1916.

The Broken Thread. London, Ward Lock, 1916.

Behind the German Lines. London, London Mail, 1917.

The Breath of Suspicion. London, Long, 1917.

The Devil's Carnival. London, Hurst and Blackett, 1917.

No Greater Love. London, Ward Lock, 1917.

Two in a Tangle. London, Hodder and Stoughton, 1917.

Rasputin, The Rascal Monk. London, Hurst and Blackett, 1917.

The Yellow Ribbon. London, Hodder and Stoughton, 1918.

The Secret Life of the Ex-Tsaritza. London, Odhams Press, 1918.

The Sister Disciple. London, Hurst and Blackett, 1918.

The Stolen Statesman. London, Skeffington, 1918.

The Little Blue Goddess. London, Ward Lock, 1918.

The Minister of Evil: The Secret History of Rasputin's Betrayal of Russia. London, Cassell, 1918.

Bolo, The Super-Spy. London, Odhams Press, 1918.

The Catspaw. London, Lloyd's, 1918.

Cipher Six. London, Hodder and Stoughton, 1919.

The Doctor of Pimlico. London, Cassell, 1919; New York, Macaulay, 1920.

The Forbidden Word. London, Odhams Press, 1919.

The King's Incognito. London, Odhams Press, 1919.

The Lure of Love. London, Ward Lock, 1919.

Rasputinism in London. London, Cassell, 1919.

The Secret Shame of the Kaiser. London, Hurst and Blackett, 1919.

Secrets of the White Tsar. London, Odhams Press, 1919.

The Heart of a Princess. London, Ward Lock, 1920.

The Intriguers. London, Hodder and Stoughton, 1920; New York, Macaulay, 1921.

No. 7, Saville Square. London, Ward Lock, 1920.

The Red Widow; or, The Death-Dealers of London. London, Cassell, 1920.

The Terror of the Air. London, Lloyd's, 1920.

Whither Thou Goest. London, Lloyd's, 1920.

This House to Let. London, Hodder and Stoughton, 1921.

The Lady-in-Waiting. London, Ward Lock, 1921.

The Open Verdict. London, Hodder and Stoughton, 1921.

The Power of the Borgias: The Story of the Great Film. London, Odhams Press, 1921.

Mademoiselle of Monte Carlo. London, Cassell, and New York, Macaulay, 1921.

The Fifth Finger. London, Stanley Paul, and New York, Moffat, 1921.

The Golden Face. London, Cassell, and New York, Macaulay, 1922.

The Stretton Street Affair. New York, Macaulay, 1922; London, Cassell, 1924.

Three Knots. London, Ward Lock, 1922.

The Voice from the Void. London, Cassell, 1922; New York, Macaulay, 1923.

The Young Archduchess. London, Ward Lock, and New York, Moffat, 1922.

Where the Desert Ends. London, Cassell, 1923.

The Bronze Face. London, Ward Lock, 1923; as *Behind the Bronze Door*, New York, Macaulay, 1923.

The Crystal Claw. London, Hodder and Stoughton, and New York, Macaulay, 1924.

Fine Feathers. London, Stanley Paul, 1924.

A Woman's Debt. London, Ward Lock, 1924.

The Valrose Mystery. London, Ward Lock, 1925.

The Marked Man. London, Ward Lock, 1925.

The Blue Bungalow. London, Hurst and Blackett, 1925.

The Broadcast Mystery. London, Holden, 1925.

The Fatal Face. London, Hurst and Blackett, 1926.

Hidden Hands. London, Hodder and Stoughton, 1926; as *The Dangerous Game*, New York, Macaulay, 1926.

The Letter E. London, Cassell, 1926; as *The Tattoo Mystery*, New York, Macaulay, 1927.

The Mystery of Mademoiselle. London, Hodder and Stoughton, 1926.

The Scarlet Sign. London, Ward Lock, 1926.

The Black Owl. London, Ward Lock, 1926.

The Office Secret. London, Ward Lock, 1927.

The House of Evil. London, Ward Lock, 1927.

The Lawless Hand. London, Hurst and Blackett, 1927; New York, Macaulay, 1928.
Blackmailed. London, Nash and Grayson, 1927.
The Chameleon. London, Hodder and Stoughton, 1927; as *Poison Shadows*, New York, Macaulay, 1927.
Double Nought. London, Hodder and Stoughton, 1927; as *The Crime Code*, New York, Macaulay, 1928.
Concerning This Woman. London, Newnes, 1928.
The Rat Trap. London, Ward Lock, 1928; New York, Macaulay, 1930.
The Secret Formula. London, Ward Lock, 1928.
The Sting. London, Hodder and Stoughton, and New York, Macaulay, 1928.
Twice Tried. London, Hurst and Blackett, 1928.
The Amazing Count. London, Ward Lock, 1929.
The Crinkled Crown. London, Ward Lock, and New York, Macaulay, 1929.
The Golden Three. London, Ward Lock, 1930; New York, Fiction House, 1931.

Short Stories

Strange Tales of a Nihilist. London, Ward Lock, and New York, Cassell, 1892; as *A Secret Service*, Ward Lock, 1896.
Stolen Souls. London, Tower, and New York, Stokes, 1895.
Secrets of Monte Carlo. London, White, 1899; New York, Dillingham, 1900.
Secrets of the Foriegn Office. London, Hutchinson, 1903.
Confessions of a Ladies' Man, Being the Adventures of Cuthbert Croom, of His Majesty's Diplomatic Service. London, Hutchinson, 1905.
The Count's Chauffeur. London, Nash, 1907.
The Lady in the Car, in Which the Amours of a Mysterious Motorist Are Related. London, Nash, and Philadelphia, Lippincott, 1908.
Spies of the Kaiser: Plotting the Downfall of England. London, Hurst and Blackett, 1909.
Revelations of the Secret Service. London, White, 1911.
The Indiscretions of a Lady's Maid. London, Nash, 1911.
Mysteries. London, Ward Lock, 1913.
The German Spy: A Present Day Story. London, Newnes, 1914.
"Cinders of Harley Street. London, Ward Lock, 1916.
The Bomb-Makers. London, Jarrolds, 1917.
Beryl of the Biplane. London, Pearson, 1917.
Hushed Up at German Headquarters. London, London Mail, 1917.
The Rainbow Mystery: Chronicles of a Colour-Criminologist. London, Hodder and Stoughton, 1917.
The Scandal-Monger. London, Ward Lock, 1917.
The Secrets of Potsdam. London, Daily Mail, 1917.
More Secrets of Potsdam. London, London, Mail, 1917.
Further Secrets of Potsdam. London, London, Mail, 1917.
Donovan of Whitehall. London, Pearson, 1917.
Sant of the Secret Service. London, Odhams Press, 1918.
The Hotel X. London, Ward Lock, 1919.
Mysteries of the Great City. London, Hodder and Stoughton, 1919.
The Secret Telephone. New York, McCann, 1920; London, Jarrolds, 1921.
Society Intrigues I Have Known. London, Odhams Press, 1920.
In Secret. London, Odhams Press, 1921.
The Luck of the Secret Service. London, Pearson, 1921.
The Elusive Four: The Exciting Exploits of Four Thieves. London, Cassell, 1921.
Tracked by Wireless. London, Stanley Paul, and New York, Moffat, 1922.

The Gay Triangle: The Romance of the First Air Adventurers. London, Jarrolds, 1922.
Bleke, The Butler, Being the Exciting Adventures of Robert Bleke During Certain Years of His Service in Various Families. London, Jarrolds, 1924.
The Crimes Club: A Record of Secret Investigations into Some Amazing Crimes, Mostly Withheld from the Public. London, Nash and Grayson, 1927.
The Peril of Helen Marklove and Other Stories. London, Jarrolds, 1928.
The Factotum and Other Stories. London, Ward Lock, 1931.

Uncollected Short Story

"The Secret of the Fox Hunter," in *The Rivals of Sherlock Holmes*, edited by Hugh Greene. London, Bodley Head, 1970.

OTHER PUBLICATIONS

Play

The Proof (produced Birmingham, 1924; as *Vendetta* produced London, 1924).

Other

The Great War in England in 1897. London, Tower, 1894.
The Invasion of 1910, with a Full Account of the Siege of London. London, Nash, 1906.
An Observer in the Near East (published anonymously). London, Nash, 1907; as *The Near East*, New York, Doubleday, 1907; as *The Balkan Trouble; or, An Observer in the Near East*, London, Nash, 1912.
The War of the Nations, vol. 1. London, Newnes, 1914.
German Atrocities: A Record of Shameless Deeds. London, Newnes, 1914.
German Spies in England: An Exposure. London, Stanley Paul, 1915.
Britain's Deadly Peril: Are We Told the Truth? London, Stanley Paul, 1915.
The Devil's Spawn: How Italy Will Defeat Them. London, Stanley Paul, 1915.
The Way to Win. London, Simpkin Marshall, 1916.
Love Intrigues of the Kaiser's Sons. London, Long, and New York, Lane, 1918.
Landru: His Secret Love Affairs. London, Stanley Paul, 1922.
Things I Know about Kings, Celebrities, and Crooks. London, Nash and Grayson, 1923; New York, Stokes, 1924.
Engelberg: The Crown Jewel of the Alps. London, Swiss Observer, 1927.
Interlaken: The Alpine Wonderland: A Novelist's Jottings. Interlaken, Official Information Bureau, n.d.

Translator, *On the "Polar Star" in the Arctic Sea*, by Luigi Amedeo. London, Hutchinson, 1903.

*

Critical Study: *The Real Le Queux* by N. St. Barbe Sladen, London, Nicholson and Watson, 1938.

*   *   *

Artist, journalist, novelist, William Le Queux was one of the earliest spy-fiction writers and set the pattern for this genre for nearly a quarter century. Of his hundred-odd books which deal primarily with political intrigue, about half are about spies. His first novel, *Guilty Bonds*, dramatizes the revolutionary movement in Czarist Russia and was banned in that country. Le Queux gathered much of his background material during his foreign editorship of the *Globe* newspaper (1891–93) from which he resigned in order to devote his time to writing books. Le Queux had a lively imagination and it is difficult to separate his factual from his fictional works. He often extravagantly embellished situations and presented fiction as fact; he is a perplexing author to assess. He seems to have been involved in the British Secret Service both before and after World War I and claimed in one of his books to have had an "intimate knowledge of the secret service of continental powers."

His early novels warned of the unpreparedness of Britain to face a European invasion, and while they lacked literary quality, the stories made potent propaganda because of their topicality and sensationalism.

In *The Great War in England in 1897*, a work of non-fiction, Le Queux dramatized a Russo-Franco plot for the invasion of England. Anti-Jewish pogroms in Russia served as a background for *Strange Tales of a Nihilist*. Many of his spy novels emphasized the German threat to Britain. His first anti-German book was *The Invasion of 1910* and this was followed by a novel, *The Mystery of a Motor-Car*. In this story a country doctor who is called upon to treat the victim of an auto accident finds himself involved in a German plot. It is one of the best examples of Le Queux's detection-intrigue novels; though a stiff, period piece, it maintains a sense of suspense throughout.

The Great War foretold the 1914–18 holocaust, and *Spies of the Kaiser* warned that Britain was "in grave danger of invasion by Germany at a date not far distant," and that thousands of German agents were present in England. Le Queux continued this theme in *Number 70, Berlin, and The Mystery of the Green Ray*. A post-war novel, *Cipher Six*, supposedly was based on "actual events which occurred in the West End of London during the peace negotiations in the Autumn of 1918" during which time he was said to have been "engaged in assisting the police to unravel one of the most extraordinary mysteries of the past decade."

Le Queux had a sense of melodrama and was aware of the virtues of self-publicity. He said during World War I that he habitually carried a revolver on his person since his life was in constant danger from "enemies of the State." He continued writing and lecturing on spies and spying and retired to Switzerland; many of his later books (e.g., *Hidden Hands*) had a Swiss background. The dust-jacket of *Hidden Hands* provides a vivid description of the flavor of these later spy stories: "Seton Darville, elderly novelist and secret service agent, can make love 'for business reasons' with excellent and thrillingly successful results. But between him and Edris Temperley it is a different matter altogether. She loves him—but she is young and so is Carl Weiss, ex-spy, and Darville is not. He nearly loses her, and she nearly loses both him and her unworthy Swiss lover, but comes to her senses in the nick of time."

—Daniel P. King

LESSER, Milton. *See* **MARLOWE, Stephen.**

LESTER, Mark. *See* **RUSSELL, Martin.**

LEVIN, Ira.   American.   Born in New York City, 27 August 1929. Educated at Drake University, Des Moines, Iowa, 1946–48; New York University, 1948–50, A.B. in English 1950. Served in the United States Army Signal Corps, 1953–55. Married 1) Gabrielle Aronsohn in 1960 (divorced 1968), three sons; 2) Phyllis Finkel in 1979 (divorced 1982). Recipient: Mystery Writers of America Edgar Allan Poe award, 1954, and Special award, 1980. Agent: Harold Ober Associates, 40 East 49th Street, New York, New York 10017, U.S.A.

CRIME PUBLICATIONS

Novels

A Kiss Before Dying.   New York, Simon and Schuster, 1953; London, Joseph, 1954.
Rosemary's Baby   New York, Random House, and London, Joseph, 1967.
The Stepford Wives.   New York, Random House, and London, Joseph, 1972.
The Boys from Brazil.   New York, Random House, and London, Joseph, 1976.

OTHER PUBLICATIONS

Novel

This Perfect Day.   New York, Random House, and London, Joseph, 1970.

Plays

No Time for Sergeants, adaptation of the novel by Mac Hyman (produced New York, 1955; London, 1956).   New York, Random House, 1956.
Interlock (produced New York, 1958).   New York, Dramatists Play Service, 1958.
Critic's Choice (produced New York, 1960; London, 1961).   New York, Random House, 1961; London, Evans, 1963.
General Seeger (produced New York, 1962).   New York, Dramatists Play Service, 1962.
Drat! The Cat!, music by Milton Schafer (produced New York, 1965).
Dr. Cook's Garden (also director; produced New York, 1967).   New York, Dramatists Play Service, 1968.
Veronica's Room (produced New York, 1973; Watford, Hertfordshire, 1982).   New York, Random House, 1974; London, Joseph, 1975.
Deathtrap (produced New York and London, 1978).   New York, Random House, 1979; London, French, 1980.
Break a Leg (produced New York, 1979).   New York, French, 1981.
Cantorial (produced Stamford, Connecticut, 1984, New York, 1989).   New York, French, 1990.

*

Critical Study: *Ira Levin* by Douglas Fowler, Mercer Island, Washington, Starmont, 1988.

Theatrical Activities:

Director: **Play**—*Dr. Cook's Garden*, New York, 1967.

* * *

Ira Levin's masterpiece, and the only one of his five novels without at least a touch of fantasy, is *A Kiss Before Dying*. The beauty of this book is that it is really three books in one, each of which could almost represent a separate sub-genre of the mystery novel. Part One is told from the viewpoint of the murderer, and is something of a modern variation on *An American Tragedy*. The young man, attempting to marry into a wealthy family, is thwarted when his girl becomes pregnant and refuses to have an abortion. Knowing this will lose him her family's fortune, he kills her in a highly ingenious manner which the reader follows each step of the way. Her death is ruled a suicide.

It is not until Part Two of the novel that the reader realizes he does not know the identity of the killer. The viewpoint shifts to the dead girl's sister and the genre shifts to the detective story. The sister establishes that the apparent suicide was really murder and tracks down the killer. Unfortunately her deductions are wrong and she becomes the second victim. In Part Three, which has now become a game of wits between the two sides, a third sister and her boyfriend bring the killer to a sort of justice.

Following the clever intricacies of *A Kiss Before Dying*, Levin waited 14 years before publishing his second novel, *Rosemary's Baby*. The best known of his works, it launched a revival of the contemporary occult-horror story in books and films. There are strong elements of mystery in the plot development of *Rosemary's Baby*, as there are in the science-fiction novel *This Perfect Day* and the contemporary fantasy *The Stepford Wives*. In each there is a problem to be solved, and there are murders along the way. *The Boys from Brazil* is an excellent contemporary neo-Nazi tale with only a single plot element—cloning—to shift it toward fantasy. In all other respects it is a suspense-intrigue story of the highest order.

Levin has written no short stories, but notice must be taken of his plays. He is a playwright by preference, and one of the few successful ones working in the mystery field. After establishing himself on Broadway with an adaptation of the non-criminous hit *No Time for Sergeants*, he wrote a trio of interesting but unsuccessful plays—a psychological melodrama, *Interlock*, a musical about a thief, *Drat! The Cat!*, and a murder melodrama, *Dr. Cook's Garden*.

Until 1973 Levin seemed to have had better success with a number of straight plays, but in that year *Veronica's Room* turned the tide and enjoyed a mild success as a mystery chiller. In 1978 Levin's long years of trying for a mystery hit on Broadway finally paid off with the success of *Deathtrap*, the best of his plays and a mystery comedy that manages even more plot twists than Anthony Shaffer's *Sleuth*.

—Edward D. Hoch

———

LEWIN, Michael Z(inn). American. Born in Springfield, Massachusetts, 21 July 1942. Educated at North Central High School, Indianapolis, graduated 1960; Harvard University, Cambridge, Massachusetts (National Merit Scholar), A.B. 1964; Churchill College, Cambridge, 1964–65; University of Bridgeport, Connecticut. Married Marianne Ruth Grewe in 1965; one daughter and one son. Physics teacher, Central High School, Bridgeport, Connecticut, 1966–68; science teacher, George Washington High School, New York, 1968–69. Moved to Britain in 1971. Since 1972 basketball columnist for *Somerset Standard*, Frome; has also written sketches and lyrics for revues. Agent: Wallace and Sheil Agency, 177 East 70th Street, New York, New York 10021, U.S.A.; or, Anthony Sheil Associates Ltd., 43 Doughty Street, London WC1N 2LF. Address: 5 Welshmill Road, Frome, Somerset BA11 2LA, England.

CRIME PUBLICATIONS

Novels (series: Lieutenant Leroy Powder; Albert Samson)

Ask the Right Question (Samson). New York, Putnam, 1971; London, Hamish Hamilton, 1972.
The Way We Die Now (Samson). New York, Putnam, and London, Hamish Hamilton, 1973.
The Enemies Within (Samson). New York, Knopf, and London, Hamish Hamilton, 1974.
The Next Man (novelization). New York, Warner, 1976.
Night Cover (Powder). New York, Knopf, and London, Hamish Hamilton, 1976.
The Silent Salesman (Samson). New York, Knopf, and London, Hamish Hamilton, 1978.
Outside In. New York, Knopf, 1980; London, Magnum, 1981.
Missing Woman (Samson). New York, Knopf, 1981; London, Hale, 1982.
Hard Line (Powder). New York, Morrow, 1982; London, Macmillan, 1983.
Out of Season (Samson). New York, Morrow, 1984; as *Out of Time*, London, Macmillan, 1984.
Late Payments (Powder). New York, Morrow, and London, Macmillan, 1986.
And Baby Will Fall. New York, Morrow, 1988; as *Child Proof*, London, Macmillan, 1988.

Uncollected Short Stories

"The Loss Factor," in *Penthouse* (London), Spring 1975.
"Wrong Number," in *Crime Wave*. London, Collins, 1981.
"Silent Testimony," in *Alfred Hitchcock's Mystery Magazine* (New York), 3 March 1982.
"The Reluctant Detective," in *Winter's Crimes* 16, edited by Hilary Hale. London, Macmillan, and New York, St. Martin's Press, 1984.
"Family Business," in *Winter's Crimes* 20, edited by Hilary Hale, London, Macmillan, 1988.
"At Home," in *New Crimes*, edited by Maxim Jakubowski. London, Robinson, 1989; New York, Carroll and Graf, 1990.
"Students of Disaster," in *Match Me Sidney*. London, No Exit Press, 1989.

OTHER PUBLICATIONS

Plays

The Magnificent Seven (produced, Frome, Dorset, 1987).
Detectives (produced Stroud, Gloucestershire, 1990).

Radio Plays (from his own fiction): *The Way We Die Now*, 1974; *The Loss Factor*, 1975; *The Enemies Within*, 1976; *Arrest Is as Good as a Change*, 1982; *A Place of Safety*, 1985;

Missing Woman, 1987; *Rainey Shines*, 1987; *The Interests of the Child*, 1988; *Ask the Right Question*, from his own novel, 1989; *Wrong Number*, 1989 *The Eyes of Habit*, 1989.

Other

How to Beat College Tests: A Practical Guide to Ease the Burden of Useless Courses. New York, Dial Press, 1970.
"Soft-Boiled But Still an Egg" (on Albert Samson), in *Murder Ink: The Mystery Reader's Companion*, edited by Dilys Winn. New York, Workman, 1977.

*

Michael Z. Lewin comments:

My detective novels, which form the core of my work, are all set in Indianapolis, Indiana. Six (with a seventh due for publication in 1991) are first-person stories about private detective Albert Samson. Three others focus on Indianapolis police lieutenant Leroy Powder. The most recent introduced social worker Adele Buffington. But Buffington has appeared in eight previous books as a minor character. She is Samson's unnamed woman friend and she also knows Powder. Similarly, Samson and Powder appear in a number of each other's books. This means that I am building up a larger fictional world in Indianapolis than is included in any one book. In a sense the city is my real series character.

Samson and Powder appear at first to be typical of their sub-genres, hard-boiled and police procedural respectively. But they are not. Samson does not own a gun, for instance, and neither of them beat up on people. I seek in both series to write books where the people are real and human (and humorous) although the things that happen to them need not necessarily be probable: only possible. Adele Buffington expands this company. An amateur detective in one sense, she has atypical access to professionals and it is the people who count for her.

*   *   *

The Albert Samson books of Michael Z. Lewin began as a lark. Lewin created Samson to entertain himself and his family during an extended stay in Los Angeles. It is quite fitting that Samson was "conceived" in Los Angeles for his cases often revolve around crimes against the family, crimes which threaten both individual indentity and the social order in the manner of the Southern California novels of Raymond Chandler and Ross Macdonald.

Though conceived in Los Angeles, Samson does not work there. His place of operation is Lewin's hometown, Indianapolis. Indianapolis, an ordinary place where ordinary people go about ordinary non-heroic lives. Lewin's shift of hard-boiled geography is both physical and philosophical. The hard-boiled world of Chandler and Macdonald reflects the lonely heroism of existential philosophy. Their literature is set on that border where the tragic and ironic modes touch. Humor there is difficult and tight-lipped.

Samson is not cut from the black cloth of existentialism. He was conceived in a comic mood and operates in the comic mode. By comic mode, I mean a vision and a style which accentuates human potential, life in community, and life in balance. Lewin's world vision is fundamentally comic and this is what sets his work apart from most who write out of the Hammet-Chandler tradition. His Albert Samson, and later protagonists Leroy Powder and Adele Buffington, are "mean" only in the sense of average. In the final analysis, the same can be said of the streets down which they go.

Lewin's importance as a writer in the tradition of Hammett, Chandler, and Macdonald lies in his ability to stay in the tradition while bending it away from existential philosophy into the harmonious world of comedy of manners. His movement from existential crime fiction to comedy is gradual. The early Alfred Samson novels, *Ask the Right Question* and *The Way We Die Now*, are only incidentally comic, though often quite funny, and reflect existential philosophy. Lewin's third Samson novel, *The Enemies Within*, marks his shift toward the comic mode. It ranks with *Missing Woman* as the best in the series and not only signals his shift to the comic mode but confirms his deep concern over the treatment of women in American society. *The Enemies Within* is full of deceit, disguise, and greed. Its plot twists again and again as Samson uncovers the true parentage of Melanie ("Mel") Baer. What Samson uncovers in this novel is a nest totally befouled by human selfishness, deceit, and lust. Nothing is as it seems. Yet Samson plods forward and eventually gets together all the facts needed to explain who is really who. As a result, in a feminist twist, Mel, like Ibsen's Nora, slams the door on the protective world of men and steps into a future both uncertain and open to possibility. With Samson's help she moves from the tragic to the comic mode.

Missing Woman continues the central theme of *Enemies Within:* that it is very difficult for a woman by herself to maintain humanity and dignity in today's society. In this novel Eden goes sour. Terrible things happen in a small Indiana town where a mindless playboy and a genteel lawyer ruin women's lives. There among the shattered panes Samson has agreed to protect for "Glass" Albert, he tries to put together again the pieces of a shattered world. Educated and assisted by a wonderfully strong woman, Sheriff Jeanna Dunlap, Samson brings to a close his missing person case. At the end of the novel he says: "I was suddenly willing to settle for two out of three. Not a bad percentage in most things life has to offer." For all its horrible power in the novel, the cynicism and corruption of this world do not diminish Samson's inherently comic vision of the world.

With *Night Cover* Lewin broke from the Albert Samson series to a new one featuring Lieutenant Leroy Powder. The Powder novels are police procedurals, and true to formula, they follow several cases through to the end. Though in *Night Cover* the cases are independent in many ways, they nevertheless merge. As they do so, Lewin brings together the worlds of Powder, Albert Samson, and Indianapolis social worker Adele Buffington, the investigators he has featured in his novels. Samson, who takes on the case of missing person, Cherry Cable, pushes Powder to expand his by-the-book definition of law and justice. Adele Buffington, Cherry's social worker, also challenges Powder's closed-down world. Finally, Cherry's pony-tailed Maoist friend, Rex Fuckenhouser, offers fresh ways for Powder to see the world he has dismissed as incurable and corrupt. At the novel's end, what matters is not that Cherry has been found or that the murder case has been solved. What matters is that Powder has changed and that he has been changed by the rub and touch of others who care. That is the way of comedy.

In *The Silent Salesman* Lewin continues to expand his comic vision, only this time it is Samson who is the focus of change and growth as he works through issues from the dark night of his own past and reconciles himself with his estranged daughter. In *Hard Line* and *Late Payments* Lewin returns to Powder and the police procedural format, but, as in *The Silent Salesman*, he digs deep into the personal life of his protagonist, focusing on the dysfunctional relationship of Powder and his son. Together these novels form a powerful narrative of professional and personal crisis in Powder's life, a narrative which stands out from the multiplicity of cases which constitute its formula and from which it arises. At the center of the Leroy Powder series there is a comic action which moves him from professional, emotional, and moral paralysis symbolized by his "night cover," contrasts his bitter, cynical life in paralysis against that of the rapid professional rise of crippled police officer, Carolee Fleetwood, and follows him into a world of possibility, hope, and tough, but healing, love.

It is this subtext of hope and reconciliation, mixed with strong feminist concerns which propels *And Baby will Fall*, the only Lewin novel yet to feature social worker Adele Buffington. Buffington's profession is metaphorically significant for it makes clear Lewin's transformation of the investigator from a "private," existential hero into a "public" self who works in close connection with others for the welfare of us all, rather than for the tough, lonely integrity of the individual. Through his work, Lewin has employed comic vision to pry open the existential shell of the Hammett/Chandler hero, proving again and again that criminal investigators, male and female, private and public, can be soft-boiled but still an egg.

—Larry E. Grimes

———

LEWIS, C. Day. *See* **BLAKE, Nicholas.**

———

LEWIS, (John) Roy(ston). Also writes as David Springfield. British. Born in Rhondda, Glamorganshire, 17 January 1933. Educated at Pentre Grammar School, 1944–51; University of Bristol, 1951–54, LL. B. 1954; University of Exeter, 1956–57, Dip. Ed. 1957; Inner Temple, London: called to the Bar, 1965; University of Durham, 1976–78, M.A. 1978. Served in the Royal Artillery, 1954–56. Married Gwendoline Hutchings in 1955 (divorced 1984); one son and two daughters. Teacher, Okehampton Secondary School, Devon, 1957–59; Lecturer, Cannock Chase Secondary School, Staffordshire, 1959–61, Cornwall Technical College, Redruth, 1961–63, and Plymouth College of Technology, Devon, 1963–67; Inspector of Schools, Newcastle on Tyne, 1967–75; deputy principal, New College, Durham, 1975–81; principal, Wigan College of Technology, 1981–90; editor, corporate administrator, managing director, Templar North Ltd., educational publishers, Newcastle on Tyne. Associate, 1962, Fellow, 1983, and President, 1988 Chartered Institute of Secretaries and Administrators. Address Old Park, South Stainmore, Westmorland.

CRIME PUBLICATIONS

Novels (series: Inspector Crow; Eric Ward)

A Lover Too Many (Crow). London, Collins, 1969; Cleveland, World, 1971.
A Wolf by the Ears. London, Collins, 1970; Cleveland, World, 1972.
Error of Judgement (Crow). London, Collins, 1971.
The Fenokee Project. London, Collins, 1971.
A Fool for a Client. London, Collins, 1972.
A Secret Singing (Crow). London, Collins, 1972.
Blood Money (Crow). London, Collins, 1973.

Of Singular Purpose. London, Collins, 1973.
A Question of Degree (Crow). London, Collins, 1974.
Double Take. London, Collins, 1975.
A Part of Virtue (Crow). London, Collins, 1975.
Witness My Death. London, Collins, 1976.
A Distant Banner. London, Collins, 1976.
Nothing but Foxes (Crow). London, Collins, 1977; New York, St. Martin's Press, 1979.
An Uncertain Sound. London, Collins, 1978; New York, St. Martin's Press, 1980.
An Inevitable Fatality. London, Collins, 1978.
A Violent Death. London, Collins, 1979.
A Certain Blindness (Ward). London, Collins, 1980; New York, St. Martin's Press, 1981.
A Relative Distance (Crow). London, Collins, 1981.
Seek for Justice. London, Collins, 1981.
Dwell in Danger (Ward). London, Collins, and New York, St. Martin's Press, 1982.
A Gathering of Ghosts. London, Collins, 1982; New York, St. Martin's Press, 1983.
A Limited Vision (Ward). London, Collins, 1983; New York, St. Martin's Press, 1984.
Once Dying, Twice Dead. London, Collins, and New York, St. Martin's Press, 1984.
Most Cunning Workmen. London, Collins, 1984; New York, St. Martin's Press, 1985.
A Blurred Reality. London, Collins, and New York, St. Martin's Press, 1985.
A Trout in the Milk. London, Collins, and New York, St. Martin's Press, 1986.
Premium on Death. London, Collins, 1986; New York, St. Martin's Press, 1987.
Men of Subtle Craft. London, Collins, 1987; New York, St. Martin's Press, 1988.
The Salamander Chill. London, Collins, 1988; New York, St. Martin's Press, 1989.
The Devil Is Dead. London, Collins, and New York, St. Martin's Press, 1989.
A Necessary Dealing (Ward). London, Collins, 1989.

OTHER PUBLICATIONS

Other as J.R. Lewis

Law of the Retailer: An Outline for Students and Business Men. London, Allman, 1964; as *Law for the Retailer*, 1974.
Cases for Discussion. Oxford, Pergamon Press, 1965.
An Introduction to Business Law. London, Allman, 1965.
Law in Action. London, Allman, 1965.
Questions and Answers on Civil Procedure. London, Sweet and Maxwell, 1966.
Building Law. London, Allman, 1966.
Democracy: The Theory and the Practice. London, Allman, 1966.
Managing Within the Law. London, Allman, 1967.
Principles of Registered Land Conveyancing, with John A. Holland. London, Butterworth, 1967.
Company Law. London, Allman, 1967.
Revision Notes for Ordinary Level British Constitution. London, Allman, 1967.
Civil and Criminal Procedure. London, Sweet and Maxwell, 1968.
Landlord and Tenant. London, Sweet and Maxwell, 1968.
Outlines of Equity. London, Butterworth, 1968.
Mercantile and Commercial Law, with Anne Redish. London, Heinemann, 1969.

The Company Executive and the Law (as David Springfield).
London, Heinemann, 1970.
Law for the Construction Industry. London, Macmillan, 1976.
Administrative Law for the Construction Industry. London,
Macmillan, 1976.
*The Teaching of Public Administration in Further and Higher
Education.* London, Joint Universities Council, 1979.
Certain Private Incidents. Wigan, Templar North, 1980.
The Victorian Bar. London, Hale, 1982.
The Maypole. Wigan, Wigantech, 1983.

*

Roy Lewis comments:
My detective fiction began with an attempt to use my legal
knowledge in a crime/fictional setting and most of my books
continue to have a certain legal flavour. To some extent the
development of a central detective character (John Crow) has
emerged, but more recently I have placed greater emphasis
upon background and location and introduced two new series
detectives (Eric Ward and Arnold London). Thus one novel (*Of
Singular Purpose*) is set on an actual farm location in Scotland;
several novels have been located in the area where I was born
and lived until I was 18—South Wales; and more recently I
have been using locations in the north east of England.

* * *

With Inspector Crow Roy Lewis has created a likeable,
laconic protagonist, useful if not particularly original. The
author seems to employ Crow for his more traditional, if never
quite conventional, novels (e.g., *Nothing but Foxes*); in the
Crow-less novels, Lewis displays a bolder range, both geo-
graphically and emotionally. Some of the best works are set in
Wales, like *Witness My Death*, notable for the deeply felt
descriptions of landscape and the cogent characterization of
the remote valley folk. Even more impressive is *A Distant
Banner*, again with a Welsh locale; here the actual murder and
its solution are far less important than the people themselves,
sympathetically and incisively portrayed. Lewis's strongest
virtues are his grasp of character—his people are seldom
eccentric, but lively, unexpected, even quirkish—and his
unfailing sense of place, of atmosphere, whether he is writing
about a Welsh building site (*A Distant Banner*), the legal world
(*A Fool for a Client*), or the well-to-do bourgeoisie of Durham
(*An Uncertain Sound*).

—William Weaver

LININGTON, (Barbara) Elizabeth. Also wrote as Anne
Blaisdell; Lesley Egan; Egan O'Neill; Dell Shannon.
American. Born in Aurora, Illinois, 11 March 1921. Educat-
ed in public schools in Aurora and Hollywood, California;
graduated from Herbert Hoover High School; educated at
Glendale College, California, A.B. 1942. Self-employed writer.
Died 5 April 1988.

CRIME PUBLICATIONS

Novels (series: Sergeant Ivor Maddox in all books except
Nightmare; published as Anne Blaisdell in UK)

Nightmare (as Anne Blaisdell). New York, Harper, 1961;
London, Gollancz, 1962.
Greenmask! New York, Harper, 1964; London, Gollancz,
1965.
No Evil Angel. New York, Harper, 1964; London, Gollancz,
1965.
Date with Death. New York, Harper, and London, Gollancz,
1966.
Something Wrong. New York, Harper, 1967; London, Gol-
lancz, 1968.
Policeman's Lot. New York, Harper, 1968; London, Gol-
lancz, 1969.
Practice to Deceive. New York, Harper, and London, Gol-
lancz, 1971.
Crime by Chance. Philadelphia, Lippincott, 1973; London,
Gollancz, 1974.
Perchance of Death. New York, Doubleday, 1977; London,
Gollancz, 1978.
No Villain Need Be. New York, Doubleday, and London,
Gollancz, 1979.
Consequence of Crime. New York, Doubleday, 1980; London,
Gollancz, 1981.
Skeletons in the Closet. New York, Doubleday, 1982; London,
Gollancz, 1983.
Felony Report. New York, Doubleday, 1984; London, Gol-
lancz, 1985.
Strange Felony. New York, Doubleday, and London, Gol-
lancz, 1986.
Alter Ego. New York, Mystery Guild, 1987.

Novels as Dell Shannon (series: Lieutenant/Detective Luis
Mendoza in all books)

Case Pending. New York, Harper, and London, Gollancz,
1960.
The Ace of Spades. New York, Morrow, 1961; London,
Oldbourne, 1963.
Extra Kill. New York, Morrow, and London, Oldbourne,
1962.
Knave of Hearts. New York, Morrow, 1962; London, Old-
bourne, 1963.
Death of a Busybody. New York, Morrow, and London,
Oldbourne, 1963.
Double Bluff. New York, Morrow, 1963; London, Oldbourne,
1964.
Mark of Murder. New York, Morrow, 1964; London,
Gollancz, 1965.
Root of All Evil. New York, Morrow, 1964; London,
Gollancz, 1966.
The Death-Bringers. New York, Morrow, 1965; London,
Gollancz, 1966.
Death by Inches. New York, Morrow, 1965; London, Gol-
lancz, 1967.
Coffin Corner. New York, Morrow, 1966; London, Gollancz,
1967.
With a Vengeance. New York, Morrow, 1966; London,
Gollancz, 1968.
Chance to Kill. New York, Morrow, 1967; London, Gollancz,
1968.
Rain with Violence. New York, Morrow, 1967; London,
Gollancz, 1969.
Kill with Kindness. New York, Morrow, 1968; London,
Gollancz, 1969.
Schooled to Kill. New York, Morrow, 1969; London, Gol-
lancz, 1970.
Crime on Their Hands. New York, Morrow, 1969; London,
Gollancz, 1970.

Unexpected Death. New York, Morrow, 1970; London, Gollancz, 1971.

Whim to Kill. New York, Morrow, and London, Gollancz, 1971.

The Ringer. New York, Morrow, 1971; London, Gollancz, 1972.

Murder with Love. New York, Morrow, and London, Gollancz, 1972.

With Intent to Kill. New York, Morrow, 1972; London, Gollancz, 1973.

No Holiday for Crime. New York, Morrow, 1973; London, Gollancz, 1974.

Spring of Violence. New York, Morrow, 1973; London, Gollancz, 1974.

Crime File. New York, Morrow, 1974; London, Gollancz, 1975.

Deuces Wild. New York, Morrow, and London, Gollancz, 1975.

Streets of Death. New York, Morrow, 1976; London, Gollancz, 1977.

Appearances of Death. New York, Morrow, 1977; London, Gollancz, 1978.

Cold Trail. New York, Morrow, 1978; London, Gollancz, 1979.

Felony at Random. New York, Morrow, and London, Gollancz, 1979.

Felony File. New York, Morrow, and London, Gollancz, 1980.

Murder Most Strange. New York, Morrow, and London, Gollancz, 1981.

The Motive on Record. New York, Morrow, and London, Gollancz, 1982.

Exploits of Death. New York, Morrow, and London, Gollancz, 1983.

Destiny of Death. New York, Morrow, 1984; London, Gollancz, 1985.

Chaos of Crime. New York, Morrow, 1985; London, Gollancz, 1986.

Blood Count. New York, Morrow, 1986; London, Gollancz, 1987.

The Dispossessed. New York, Morrow, 1988.

Novels as Lesley Egan (series: Jesse Falkenstein; Vic Varallo)

A Case for Appeal (Falkenstein; Varallo). New York, Harper, and London, Gollancz, 1961.

Against the Evidence (Falkenstein). New York, Harper, 1962; London, Gollancz, 1963.

The Borrowed Alibi (Varallo). New York, Harper, and London, Gollancz, 1962.

Run to Evil (Varallo). New York, Harper, and London, Gollancz, 1963.

My Name Is Death (Falkenstein). New York, Harper, and London, Gollancz, 1965.

Detective's Due (Varallo). New York, Harper, 1965; London, Gollancz, 1966.

Some Avenger, Rise! (Falkenstein). New York, Harper, 1966; London, Gollancz, 1967.

The Nameless Ones (Varallo). New York, Harper, 1967; London, Gollancz, 1968.

A Serious Investigation (Falkenstein). New York, Harper, 1968; London, Gollancz, 1969.

The Wine of Violence (Varallo). New York, Harper, 1969; London, Gollancz, 1970.

In the Death of a Man (Falkenstein). New York, Harper, and London, Gollancz, 1970.

Malicious Mischief (Varallo). New York, Harper, 1971; London, Gollancz, 1972.

Paper Chase (Falkenstein). New York, Harper, 1972; London, Gollancz, 1973.

Scenes of Crime (Varallo). New York, Doubleday, and London, Gollancz, 1976.

The Blind Search (Falkenstein). New York, Doubleday, and London, Gollancz, 1977.

A Dream Apart (Varallo). New York, Doubleday, and London, Gollancz, 1978.

Look Back on Death (Falkenstein). New York, Doubleday, 1978; London, Gollancz, 1979.

The Hunter and the Hunted (Varallo). New York, Doubleday, 1979; London, Gollancz, 1980.

Motive in Shadow (Falkenstein). New York, Doubleday, and London, Gollancz, 1980.

A Choice of Crimes (Varallo). New York, Doubleday, 1980; London, Gollancz, 1981.

The Miser (Falkenstein). New York, Doubleday, 1981; London, Gollancz, 1982.

Random Death (Varallo). New York, Doubleday, and London, Gollancz, 1982.

Little Boy Lost (Falkenstein). New York, Doubleday, 1983; London, Gollancz, 1984.

Crime for Christmas (Varallo). New York, Doubleday, 1983; London, Gollancz, 1984.

Chain of Violence. New York, Doubleday, and London, Gollancz, 1985.

The Wine of Life. New York, Doubleday, 1985; London, Gollancz, 1986.

Short Stories as Dell Shannon

Murder by the Tale. New York, Morrow, 1987.

Uncollected Short Stories

"Flash Attachment," in *Tales for a Rainy Night*, edited by David Alexander. New York, Holt Rinehart, 1961; London, Dobson, 1967.

"The Practical Joke," in *Tales of Unease*, edited by John Burke. London, Pan, 1966; New York, Doubleday, 1969.

OTHER PUBLICATIONS

Novels

The Proud Man. New York, Viking Press, 1955.
The Long Watch. New York, Viking Press, 1956.
Monsieur Janvier. New York, Doubleday, 1957.
The Anglophile (as Egan O'Neill). New York, Messner, 1957; as *The Pretender*, London, W.H. Allen, 1957.
The Kingbreaker. New York, Doubleday, 1958.
The Scalpel and the Sword (as Dell Shannon). New York, Morrow, 1987.

Other

Forging an Empire: Elizabeth I (for children). Chicago, Kingston House, 1961.
Come to Think of It. Boston, Western Islands, 1965.

*

Manuscript Collection: Mugar Memorial Library, Boston University.

Elizabeth Linington commented (1984):

I don't know what to say about the crime fiction, which seems to be very popular, except that three of the series are police procedural stories and I do try to keep them authentic as far as police techniques are concerned. The various cases wandering through these books are not of primary interest to the reader—many are the usual sordid, monotonous cases any Robbery-Homicide office deals with; readers get interested in the men and their families, their pets, homes, and so on. Since the Mendoza series has been going, several of the men have had romances, married, started families, and it seems to be this interest with the police officers' private lives which constitutes the interest on the part of the readers. I do, however, frequently use real crime cases in all these series and try to keep the cases interesting too.

* * *

Elizabeth Linington wrote books of several types: historical novels, gothic/romantic/suspense novel, and detective fiction. *The Proud Man*, her first novel, is set in 16th-century Ireland, where Shane O'Neill, Prince of Ulster, almost succeeds in overthrowing English rule and making himself king of a united Ireland. The second historical novel, *The Long Watch*, appeared the following year. It is set in New York during the American Revolution; the hero, an orphan of 16, runs away from Virginia to begin a new life in New York working as clerk to the editor of the New York *Courier*. *Monsieur Janvier* is set in 18th-century Scotland, Paris, and London, and *The Kingbreaker* deals with Revolution and Civil War in England in the middle of the 17th century. The protagonist is a young Welsh gentleman, Ivor ap-Maddox, who is loyal to the king and who acts as a spy in the household of Oliver Cromwell. Linington has also written one gothic/romantic/suspense novel, *Nightmare*, about an American girl whose holiday ramble leads her into the clutches of a female religious fanatic.

In 1960 Linington, as Dell Shannon, began one of her three series of police stories. *Case Pending* introduced a lieutenant of Mexican heritage named Luis Mendoza, a bookish, scholarly, gentlemanly policeman who inherited a lot of money and began collecting expensive sports cars and exotic cats. He drives a Ferrari, an Aston Martin, and a Facel Vega; at home are several Siamese, Burmese, and Abyssinian cats, the eldest of which loves rye whisky and is named El Señor. Mendoza's first appearance drew warm reviews. Then came *The Ace of Spades*, and it was becoming obvious that it was Mendoza that readers were responding to rather than the book as a whole. The Dell Shannon books continue to attract praise, particularly in the accuracy of police procedure, and because they treat the theme of the stupidity of violence and support the idea of using reason to solve crimes.

In 1961 Linington began a second detectives series, this time as Lesley Egan. This series stars Detective Vic Varallo, and is also set in the Los Angeles metropolitan area, this time in the suburb of Glendale. Also starring are Jesse Falkenstein, a Jewish lawyer, and his wife Nell, and readers seem to like the dramatization of the relationship between Falkenstein and his wife, and the domestic complications of Varallo. One of the best books in this series is *Some Avenger, Rise!* where Falkenstein takes time from his law practice to rescue his friend, Sergeant Andy Clock of the LAPD, from the serious accusation of accepting a bribe. With *A Dream Apart*, Linington was compared positively by readers to John Creasey for her solid, diligent accounts of professional police work, with several cases to each book. In her case, however, she has just a touch too much "suburban domesticity" behind her policeman, and some reviewers pointed out that, in contrast to, say, the

McBain 87th precinct novels, the Egan police procedural novels force characterization onto a conceived plot.

Linington began yet a third series of detective stories, under her own name, with *Greenmask!* This series features Sergeant Ivor Maddox of the Hollywood Police Department, with Detective D'Arcy and Rodriguez and policewoman Sue Carstairs. *Greenmask!* has been highly praised as "a mystery reader's mystery novel." In the story the Hollywood police use tips from old crime novels of the 1920's to solve a series of contemporary murders.

—Elizabeth F. Duke

———

LITTELL, Robert. American. Born in 1935. Served in the United States Naval Reserve: Lieutenant. Married; two children. Formerly an editor with *Newsweek* magazine, based in Eastern Europe and the Soviet Union. Recipient: Crime Writers Association Gold Dagger award, 1974; Mystery Writers of America Edgar Allan Poe award, 1974. Address c/o Simon and Schuster, 1230 Avenue of the Americas, New York, New York 10020, U. S. A.

Crime Publications

Novels

The Defection of A. J. Lewinter. Boston, Houghton Mifflin, and London, Hodder and Stoughton, 1973.
Sweet Reason. Boston, Houghton Mifflin, and London, Hodder and Stoughton, 1974.
The October Circle. Boston, Houghton Mifflin, and London, Hodder and Stoughton, 1976.
Mother Russia. New York, Harcourt Brace, and London, Hutchinson, 1978.
The Debriefing. New York, Harper, and London, Hutchinson, 1979.
The Amateur. New York, Simon and Schuster, and London, Cape, 1981.
The Sisters. New York, Bantam, and London, Cape, 1986.
The Revolutionist. New York, and London, Bantam, 1988.
The Once and Future Spy. New York, Bantam, and London, Faber, 1990.

Other Publications

Other

If Israel Lost the War, with Richard Z. Chesnoff and Edward Klein. New York, Coward McCann, 1969.

Editor, *The Czech Black Book*. New York, Praeger, and London, Pall Mall Press, 1969.

* * *

The culmination of Robert Littell's writing is *The Revolutionist*. This massive story of the Russian Revolution brings back characters and incidents from Littell's previous works and develops them into a historical novel of sadness and triumph.

Alexander "Zander" Til leaves the United States in 1917 with his friend Atticus Tuohy to take part in the Bolshevik Revolution. But the revolution blunders into brutality as Russia is thrust into a civil war that kills millions. Zander meets Lili, and after he saves her life in the fighting, they become lovers. Zander serves the Party, meeting Trotsky, Lenin, and works for Stalin. Tuohy, less principled than Zander, becomes a Party enforcer, dealing out "revolutionary justice" to opponents of the Revolution.

But the revolution goes wrong. Lili is denounced and executed. State institutionalized terrorism and frequent purges kill thousands each week. Still, Zander tries to hold his idealism for the revolution together. Touhy—who isn't burdened with Zander's idealism—becomes a Party boss; he learns the bureaucratic arts of survival: blame someone else and be quick to execute accused "spies" and "enemies of the state." Stalin rules with brutal caprice a population cowed with fear and preoccupied with daily survival.

Littell captures the vast movement of the Russian Revolution with the tragic turn into Stalinism as the country is turned into a police state. But most of all, Littell captures the senseless brutality of the system where any failure becomes proof of anti-Soviet behavior and millions of innocent Russians die at the hands of government thugs. After years of loyal service to the Party, Zander refuses to denounce a friend who reads an anti-Stalin poem. For this offense, Zander is beaten, tortured, and sent to prison. The poet is executed. Through a twist of fate, Zander is released from prison and becomes a movie translator for the Party elite when they watch Hollywood films. This places Zander in the perfect setting to commit a revolutionary act . . . if he still has the will to be a revolutionist. *The Revolutionist* is an eloquent testament to the real heroes of the Russian Revolution: the Russian people.

Littell's first novel, *The Defection of A. J. Lewinter* is a competent novel of how U.S. intelligence handles defections. Lewinter was an M.I.T. professor who memorized the trajectories for American MIRV missiles. He turns this over to the Russians when he defects. But, do the Russians believe that Lewinter can be trusted? Is the information he brings genuine? Or is this some elaborate American scheme to get the Russians to believe false information? Littell handles the complexities of the espionage novel while creating vivid American and Russian characters within the spiderweb framework of political defection.

Sweet Reason is the weakest of Littell's books. It takes place on a reconditioned destroyer, *Eugene F. Ebersole*, off the coast of Vietnam. Most of the characters are eccentric: the Captain collects barbed wire and yearns for action to promote his career, the executive officer has a sign, MAKE WAR NOT LOVE, over his bed. The bizarre crew is puzzled by leaflets posted around the ship advocating resistance to the Vietnam War. The leaflets are signed "Sweet Reason." The Captain sets Proper, a former Chicago policeman, on the trail of uncovering Sweet Reason's identity. Much fun is made of the muddle the Navy was in during the Vietnam War but too much of the book lacks narrative power.

The October Circle returns to Littell's preoccupation with Soviet life. The setting is Communist Bulgaria in 1968. A group of characters called the October Circle are Littell's lens into the nightmarish world of the Bulgarian Communist state. Through his characters, Littell reveals the terror of daily life. The Russian invasion of Czechoslovakia proves to be the catalyst for the October Circle to move against the hated authorities. Much of the mood and tone of *The October Circle* reappears in *The Revolutionist*.

Mother Russia is almost a rough draft of *The Revolutionist*: the character of Mother Russia appears in both books, so does the terrible interrogator Melor, and the constriction of Soviet life graces both books. Robespierre Pravdin, a black marketeer and hustler, is seduced into a dangerous political game by Mother Russia—an old revolutionist—and his mute lover, Nadezhda. Mother Russia has documents which prove that Nobel prize winner Ivan Frolov is a fraud, that he published a dead man's book—the masterpiece *The Deep Don*—under his own name. Mother Russia wants Frolov exposed. But Pravdin's attempts to get the documents to the right government officials run into a counter movement of government officials who don't want their Nobel prize winner exposed as a thief and a fraud thus discrediting the Soviet system. Pravdin finds himself hunted by both groups. Littell's descriptions of the shabby life in contemporary Moscow are hauntingly realistic.

The Debriefing is the telling of *The Defection of A. J. Lewinter* in reverse. In *The Debriefing*, a Soviet courier named Kulakov defects and an American agent named Stone is assigned the task of deciding whether the defection is real or a trick. Eventually, Stone is forced to go behind the Iron Curtain to discover the truth about Kulakov. *The Debriefing's* cynical conclusion rings frighteningly true.

The Amateur features a CIA cryptographer, Charlie Heller, whose fiancée is murdered by terrorists. When the CIA displays its reluctance to punish the terrorists, Charlie blackmails the Agency into training *him* to go after the terrorists. In typical Littell fashion, Charlie's adventure is filled with cross and doublecross as both the terrorists and the CIA are out to stop him. *The Amateur* is Littell's most entertaining novel.

The Sisters is Littell's best novel. The Sisters are Francis and Carroll—two CIA veterans who spend their days and nights plotting and counterplotting. When they discover a KGB sleeper—a spy put in place and allowed to live in the U.S. normally until "awakened" for a mission—they decide to use the agent to commit a crime for which the Russians will be blamed. At the same time, the Russians realize their sleeper is out of their control and they race to avoid disaster. Both forces meet in the novel's explosive conclusion in Dallas on November 22, 1963. *The Sisters* is a classic spy novel.

Littell's latest novel, *The Once and Future Spy*, shifts from scenes of an American Revolutionary War spy and a contemporary setting where a historian working for a supersecret intelligence agency gets involved in counterespionage. This unusual narrative device proves important as the search for the leak of information leads to extreme measures to find the leak and to plug it. Littell shows the amoral and paranoid decision making endemic in intelligence agencies.

Littell's *The Revolutionist* and *The Sisters* make him one of the best writers of spycraft and intrigue now practicing.

—George Kelley

———

LIVINGSTON, Nancy. British. Born in Stockton-on-Tees, County Durham, 18 November 1935. Educated at Whalley Range High School, Manchester; London Academy of Music and Dramatic Art, ALAM (honours); Miss Wilkinson's Academy for Gentlewomen 1954. Married David Edward Foster in 1975. Actress, Harry Hanson's Court Players, and television, 1952–54; secretary, Manchester *Guardian*, and F. Smith's Copper Wire Factory, Salford, 1954–60; airline stewardess, BOAC, 1960–66; television production assistant, Tyne Tees Television, Newcastle, 1966–68; and ATV, Elstree, Hertfordshire, 1968–83, and freelance, London, 1983–89; since 1989 full-time writer. Recipient: Crime Writers Association Poisoned Chalice award, 1985; Punch award, 1988. Lives near

Ipswich, Suffolk. Agent: Mark Lucas, Peters Fraser and Dunlop, Fifth Floor, The Chambers, Chelsea Harbour, Lots Road, London SW10 OXF, England.

CRIME PUBLICATIONS

Novels (series: Mr. G. D. H. Pringle in all books)

The Trouble at Aquitaine. London, Gollancz, 1985; New York, St. Martin's Press, 1986.
Fatality at Bath and Wells. London, Gollancz, 1986; New York, St. Martin's Press, 1987.
Incident at Parga. London, Gollancz, 1987; New York, St. Martin's Press, 1988.
Death in a Distant Land. London, Gollancz, 1988; New York, St. Martin's Press, 1989.
Death in Close-Up. London, Gollancz, 1989; New York, St. Martin's Press, 1990.
Mayhem in Parva. London, Gollancz, 1990.

OTHER PUBLICATIONS

Novels

The Far Side of the Hill. London, Macdonald, 1987; New York, St. Martin's Press, 1988.
The Land of Our Dreams. London, Macdonald, 1988; New York, St. Martin's Press, 1989.
Never Were Such Times. London, Macdonald, 1990.

Plays

Radio Plays: *Alice's Ashes*, 1979; *Slimming Down*, 1984.

Television Script: *The Work of Giants*, 1968.

*

Nancy Livingston comments:

I began by writing radio and television documentary scripts and became a mystery writer by accident, following a lunch with one of the 17 editors who rejected my first saga, *The Far Side of the Hill.* She suggested I "try crime." I shall always be grateful. So far I've written six.

In 1988, the saga was finally published and to date has sold over 40,000 copies: similar books followed. These family histories illustrate the reality of Victorian and Edwardian values rather than as seen at present through sentimental rose-coloured spectacles. All the novels celebrate the triumph of small lives.

The mysteries are much more frivolous and feature Mr. G.D.H. Pringle, again not a superman but a retired income tax inspector, accustomed to prizing out grains of truth from a welter of lies. His friend, Mrs. Mavis Bignell, provides consolation and cheerfulness.

*   *   *

Nancy Livingston's series character Mr. G.D.H. Pringle (H.M. Tax Inspector, retired) makes his sedate way into the annals of crime fiction half-way through *The Trouble at Aquitaine.* Accustomed to supplementing his pension by investigating fraud, Mr Pringle is here called in to detect a murder at Aquitaine, a 12th-century castle now turned into a health farm; the tools of his investigative trade are buff

envelopes, quantities of home-made forms and a calligrapher's pen. But readers should not be deceived by this prim, old-fashioned figure for Mr. Pringle (as we shall see) has hidden depths. Resented by police and suspects alike, he nevertheless perseveres with his enquiries, and when the Detective Inspector in charge of the case is removed (to be charged with accepting bribes in another case), Mr. Pringle receives a more sympathetic hearing from the policeman's successor. Mr. Pringle solves the case and is then able, with his fee, to buy a painting to add to his art collection. The novel is enlivened by the crisply-drawn cast of suspects, some of them sympathetic and some of them downright obnoxious—and including an I.R.A. terrorist with psoriasis.

By far the most endearing character in Livingston's novels appears only briefly in this first book—we see much more of her in the subsequent novels. Mavis Bignell is G.D.H. Pringle's lady-friend, whom he first met when she stepped in at the last minute as a nude model at the art class he was attending. They make an incongruous couple—both are widowed, but there, apparently, the similarity ends. Mr. Pringle is "a man over medium height but stooping slightly, of spare build, with a soft grey moustache, a worried look on his face, and National Health spectacles." A self-deprecating man, when he follows a group of people into a lift, "no-one asked which floor he wanted because G.D.H. Pringle wasn't a man whom anyone thought to ask. He accepted this as he always did and effaced himself at the back." Mavis Bignell, on the other hand, is physically well-endowed and given to wearing bright colours and floral designs (she is referred to as "the seed packet" on one occasion). Their relationship is summed up in *Fatality at Bath and Wells*—"both of them valued their independence, so Mr. Pringle made weekly visits to the Bricklayers where Mavis worked part-time behind the bar because she enjoyed a bit of company. After closing-time he accompanied her home for what she described as 'a bit of supper and what have you.'" And indeed G.D.H. Pringle is rather partial to "what have you." His physical relationship with Mavis is always dealt with very tastefully, and it is left to the reader to imagine his participation in the pleasures of the flesh—although we are left in no doubt as to the quality and quantity of Mrs. Bignell's flesh. A never-failing source of comfort and sound commonsense, and yet possessed of an endearing naivety, Mavis Bignell is the perfect foil to Mr. Pringle—whose first name we never do learn. Even his nephew, who appears in *Incident at Parga* refers to him simply as "uncle," and Mr. Pringle himself somewhat bizarrely introduces himself to the nephew's girlfriend as "G.D.H. Pringle."

As a detective, Mr. Pringle approaches his cases methodically, and takes a modest, low-key approach. His status is never more than semi-official, and yet suspects are usually surprisingly willing to answer his questions. It is sometimes hard to maintain one's belief in this fictional investigator, and yet had he a more flamboyant personality the other character in the books would not be shown up in such sharp relief. For as well as the redoubtable Mavis, Livingston's books are peopled with other larger-than-life characters, a couple of whom appear in more than one novel. Jonathan P. Powers (an obnoxious and self-opinionated television producer) and Ashley Fallowfield (an extremely camp television "personality" and programme controller) both appear in *Fatality at Bath and Wells*, the former having already featured in *The Trouble at Aquitaine*, and the latter surfacing again in *Death in Close-Up*—the first and third of these both being set in television studios.

Not all these novels follow the same "whodunnit" formula. In *The Trouble at Aquitaine*, Mr. Pringle is called in specifically to solve the crime, whereas in two others he happens to be on the spot already. In *Death in Close-Up*, Mr. Pringle plays a smaller part than usual in the work of detection, and for the first time we see the crime-solving from the point of view of the participating policeman. A somewhat formulaic policeman, to be sure—Detective Inspector Newton has a troublesome sergeant, and the customary (almost mandatory) problems at home—he is nevertheless a pleasing character, and one fairly sympathetic to Mr. Pringle's amateur detection.

Two of the novels are set abroad: in the first of these, *Incident at Parga*, Mr. Pringle accompanies his nephew on a sailing tour of the Greek islands. Although this is as light-hearted in detail and minor characters as the other mysteries, Mr. Pringle's close personal involvement in this case adds a new and disturbing dimension. He has been invited on the tour in order to act as a dupe and an alibi for the murder, and has become fond of the victim before she is killed. Luckily Mrs. Bignell is on hand to provide verbal and physical comfort and support when Mr. Pringle returns home, and the novel ends light-heartedly with the speculation that the nude female to whom our hero waved while he was (unbelievably) parascending may well have been a member of the Royal Family, sunbathing aboard *Britannia*.

Death in a Distant Lane, set mainly in Australia, is in rather a different mould. In it, there is no simple murder mystery to unravel; the plot has two strands—firstly, the search for a missing boy (who does in fact turn out to have been killed, but this was a mercy-killing), and secondly, the unwitting involvement of Mrs. Bignell and Mr. Pringle in drug-smuggling. The gradual discovery of the story of the missing child is most poignant, and the doings of the drug-traffickers are sinister and extremely unpleasant, but these are counterbalanced by the hilarious misunderstandings of representatives of the British Foreign Office and the Australian Police as they tail Mavis and Mr. Pringle (in the company of a group of Friends Of Nuclear Energy) across Australia.

In *Mayhem in Parva* Mr Pringle returns to the village of Wuffinge Parva, where he spent part of his boyhood; here the eccentric minor characters include "little Elsie," who used to sell her favours to the village boys for half a crown—G.D.H. Pringle, alas, received only two shillings pocket-money. The elements of farce which hover in the background of the novels here erupt in full force as Mrs. Bignell (loather of the countryside and of all its winged or four-footed inhabitants) undertakes to rid her hosts' garden of moles with the aid of an ancient blunderbuss. Yet in this, as in all Livingston's other mysteries, there is sadness and poignancy in the murder and its causes and effects.

Livingston has also written several non-crime novels. These are competent family sagas, but they contain little to lift them from the normal run of such novels—they certainly have nothing of the wit and charm of the G.D.H. Pringle mysteries. Mr. Pringle and Mavis make an unusual and formidable couple, and each brings a freshness to the sometimes tired array of more conventional detectives and their consorts, which are often encountered in crime fiction.

—Judith Rhodes

LOCHTE, Dick (Richard S. Lochte). American. Born in New Orleans, Louisiana, 19 October 1944. Educated at Tulane University, Louisiana, B.A. in English 1965. Married Jane Bryson in 1989. Served in United States Coast Guard, New London, Connecticut, and New Orleans, 1965–66; promotional copywriter, *Playboy* Enterprises, Chicago, Illinois, 1966–70; West Coast promotional manager, *Playboy* Enterprises, 1970–71; freelance writer, 1971; film critic, Los Angeles *Free Press*, 1971–74; book columnist, Los Angeles *Times*, 1974–85. Since 1975, theater critic, *Los Angeles* magazine and since 1989 audio-taped fiction reviewer, Los Angeles *Daily News* and *The Armchair Detective*, New York. Recipient: Rex Stout Society Nero Wolfe award, 1985. Agent: William Morris Agency, 1350 Avenue of the Americas, New York, New York 10019. Address: P.O. Box 5413, Santa Monica, California 90405, U.S.A.

CRIME PUBLICATIONS

Novels (series: Leo Bloodworth and Serendipity Dahlquist in both books)

Sleeping Dog. New York, Arbor House, 1985; London, Macmillan, 1986.
Laughing Dog. New York, Arbor House, and London, Macmillan, 1988.

Uncollected Short Stories

"Medford and Son," in *Ellery Queen's Mystery Magazine* (New York), October 1972.
"Sad-Eyed Blonde," in *Raymond Chandler's Philip Marlowe* edited by Byron Priess. New York, Knopf, 1988.

OTHER PUBLICATIONS

Novel

Death Mask. New York, Shelbourne Press, 1971.

Plays

Screenplays: *Escape to Athena*, 1979; *Philip Strange*, 1985.

Other

The Playboy Writer. Chicago, HMH Publications, 1968.

*

Dick Lochte comments:
In 1984, I spent several months traveling with a film producer and his family while working on a script. His step-daughter was a bright, funny 13-year-old with the strangely adult attitude of a young person who has spent more of her life with grown-ups than with children her own age. Later, when I decided to write a mystery novel, it seemed like a good idea to saddle my curmudgeonly private eye with a very similar teenage girl. Not only did she take over half the book, narrating it herself (the other narrator is the detective), but she insinuated herself into the detective's series. They're teamed and neither he nor I can do anything about it.

*   *   *

Dick Lochte's two mysteries combine interesting technical innovations in the genre with a careful exploration of some of its more traditional elements. Both *Sleeping Dog* and *Laughing Dog* claim to reproduce alternating chapters of two novels about the same series of events. While Lochte uses this form to comment on and expand the genre, he does it with a style that acknowledges the past. At the same time he develops his own voice, combining wit and insight in his depiction of the present.

The alternating points of view first encountered in *Sleeping Dog* belong to two unlikely associates, Leo G. Bloodworth, a private investigator, and Serendipity Renn Dahlquist, the 14-year-old granddaughter of a soap opera star. While Bloodworth is a private detective who admires the literary tradition of the genre, Sarah, as Bloodworth calls her, wants to become a detective. She too has read the classics of detective fiction, concentrating on female authors. But Sarah is also fully involved in the present; she is a guide to all aspects of contemporary Los Angeles. In the first novel Bloodworth's version of events is called *Die Like a Dog* while Sarah calls hers *Dog Days*. These two presentations overcome one of the limitations of the first person novel: the reader can learn of events occuring in more than one place at the same time, and the reader's information is not limited to that presented by a single character. But if this technical examination of narrative in the mystery were the only value of this technique, *Sleeping Dog* and its successor, *Laughing Dog* would remain minor curiosities. Bloodworth is, in fact, the bloodhound he is nicknamed by his friend and former partner on the police force, Lieutenant Rudy Cugat. He embodies the traits of the traditional private detective, but it is a self-conscious portrayal. He makes constant references to his literary models and imitates Bogart on his answering machine. Sarah furthers Lochte's fascination with what was and what will be. She is the future of the genre, an intuitive, bright, adaptable, young feminist. In *Sleeping Dog* the relationship between this odd couple is convincingly developed. Bloodworth resists and Sarah persists, yet each helps the other in critical moments. In the tradition of the genre the search for Sarah's lost dog, Groucho, becomes an investigation of her past.

The conflicts in Lochte's second novel, *Laughing Dog*, are less personal, but he continues to develop his combination of serious detection and humor. A confrontation between the principle characters takes place during a hare and hounds gala where all are costumed either as dogs or rabbits. Sarah is now 15 and establishes herself in Bloodworth's office by taking a summer job, to explore her career goal of becoming a private investigator. Sarah's presence in the office also gives Lochte the opportunity to play with the genre's tradition of the secretary/assistant. The device of dual narration is continued with even greater facility as the two detectives pursue separate investigations. In this novel Sarah calls her version *Man from the South*, while Bloodworth titles his *Power Play*. However they are joined by a new author, Lieutenant Cugat. Only two paragraphs of his sexy potboiler, *Bay City Heat*, are included in *Laughing Dog*, but Cugat receives a bigger check, Lochte's comment on the relationship between quality and money.

The first novel's locations are confined to the California coast, but in *Laughing Dog* Bloodworth travels to Italy, and Sarah goes with her grandmother on location to England. The clashing perspectives of the two detectives still provide much of the humor. Lochte delicately handles the attraction between two central characters of such disparate ages, avoiding placing his hero in an avuncular or paternal relationship to his heroine. Bloodworth's more realistic love interest reappears in this novel. In *Sleeping Dog* Gwen Nolte, a San Francisco private investigator, earns Bloodworth's respect while she tricks him. This time she arrives at his request, and their sexual attraction increases the tension of the novel's climax. The addition of other characters from *Sleeping Dog* strengthens the sense of continuity in the novels and seems to indicate a pattern for the future. It will be interesting to see how Sarah's character progresses as she grows older.

While Lochte has not written many mysteries he clearly understands the genre's past. And, in his own work, he continues the tradition while he expands its possibilities through his use of attractive yet humorous characters and his presentation of a complex plot. Lochte's first two novels are already the work of a mature author, and he has developed a form and a style that shows great promise for the future.

—Sharon A. Russell

LOCKRIDGE, Richard and Frances. Also wrote as Francis Richards. Americans. **LOCKRIDGE, Richard (Orson):** Born in St. Joseph, Missouri, 25 September 1898. Educated at Kansas City Junior College; University of Missouri, Columbia. Served in the United States Navy, 1918. Married 1) Frances Davis in 1922 (died 1963); 2) Hildegarde Dolson in 1965 (died 1981). Reporter, Kansas City *Kansan*, 1921–22, and Kansas City *Star*, 1922; reporter, 1922–28, and drama critic, 1928 to the 1940's, New York *Sun;* also associated with *The New Yorker. Died 19 June 1982.* **LOCKRIDGE, Frances (Louise, née Davis):** Born in Kansas City, Missouri, 10 January 1896. Educated in public schools in Kansas City; University of Kansas, Lawrence and extension courses. Married Richard Lockridge in 1922. Reporter and music critic, Kansas City *Post*, 1918–22; assistant secretary to adoption and placement committee, State Charities Aid Association, 1922–42. *Died 17 February 1963.* The Lockridges: Co-Presidents, Mystery Writers of America, 1960. Recipient: Mystery Writers of America Edgar Allan Poe award, for radio play, 1945, Special award, 1962.

CRIME PUBLICATIONS

Novels as Frances and Richard Lockridge (series: Paul Lane; Mr. and Mrs. North with Bill Wiegand; Nathan Shapiro; Bernard Simmons; Long editions published as Francis Richards)

The Norths Meet Murder. New York, Stokes, and London, Joseph, 1940.
Murder Out of Turn (Norths). New York, Stokes, and London, Joseph, 1941.
A Pinch of Poison (Norths). New York, Stokes, 1941; London, Joseph, 1948.
Death on the Aisle (Norths). Philadelphia, Lippincott, 1942; London, Hutchinson, 1948.
Hanged for a Sheep (Norths). Philadelphia, Lippincott, 1942; London, Hutchinson, 1944.
Death Takes a Bow (Norths). Philadelphia, Lippincott, 1943; London, Hutchinson, 1945.
Killing the Goose (Norths). Philadelphia, Lippincott, 1944; London, Hutchinson, 1947.
Payoff for the Banker (Norths). Philadelphia, Lippincott, 1945; London, Hutchinson, 1948.
Death of a Tall Man (Norths). Philadelphia, Lippincott, 1946; London, Hutchinson, 1949.
Murder Within Murder (Norths). Philadelphia, Lippincott, 1946; London, Hutchinson, 1949.
Untidy Murder (Norths). Philadelphia, Lippincott, 1947.
Murder Is Served (Norths). Philadelphia, Lippincott, 1948; London, Hutchinson, 1950.

The Dishonest Murderer (Norths). Philadelphia, Lippincott, 1949; London, Hutchinson, 1951.

Murder in a Hurry (Norths). Philadelphia, Lippincott, 1950; London, Hutchinson, 1952.

Murder Comes First (Norths). Philadelphia, Lippincott, 1951.

Dead as a Dinosaur (Norths). Philadelphia, Lippincott, 1952; London, Hutchinson, 1956.

Death Has a Small Voice (Norths). Philadelphia, Lippincott, 1953; London, Hutchinson, 1954.

Curtain for a Jester (Norths). Philadelphia, Lippincott, 1953.

A Key to Death (Norths). Philadelphia, Lippincott, 1954.

Death of an Angel. Philadelphia, Lippincott, 1955; London, Hutchinson, 1957; as *Mr. and Mrs. North and the Poisoned Playboy*, New York, Avon, 1957.

Murder! Murder! Murder! (omnibus). Philadelphia, Lippincott, 1956.

The Faceless Adversary (Shapiro). Philadelphia, Lippincott, 1956; as *Case of the Murdered Redhead*, New York, Avon, 1957.

Voyage into Violence (Norths). Philadelphia, Lippincott, 1956; London, Hutchinson, 1959.

The Tangled Cord (Wiegand). Philadelphia, Lippincott, 1957; London, Hutchinson, 1959.

Catch as Catch Can. Philadelphia, Lippincott, 1958; London, Long, 1960.

The Long Skeleton (Norths). Philadelphia, Lippincott, 1958; London, Hutchinson, 1960.

The Innocent House. Philadelphia, Lippincott, 1959; London, Long, 1961.

Murder and Blueberry Pie (Shapiro). Philadelphia, Lippincott, 1959; as *Call It Coincidence*, London, Long, 1962.

Murder Is Suggested (Norths). Philadelphia, Lippincott, 1959; London, Hutchinson, 1961.

The Golden Man. Philadelphia, Lippincott, 1960; London, Hutchinson, 1961.

The Judge Is Reversed (Norths). Philadelphia, Lippincott, 1960; London, Hutchinson, 1961.

The Drill Is Death (Shapiro). Philadelphia, Lippincott, 1961; London, Long, 1963.

Murder Has Its Points (Norths). Philadelphia, Lippincott, 1961; London, Hutchinson, 1962.

And Left for Dead (Simmons). Philadelphia, Lippincott, and London, Hutchinson, 1962.

Night of Shadows (Lane). Philadelphia, Lippincott, 1962; London, Long, 1964.

The Ticking Clock. Philadelphia, Lippincott, 1962; London, Hutchinson, 1964.

Murder by the Book (Norths). Philadelphia, Lippincott, 1963; London, Hutchinson, 1964.

The Devious Ones (Simmons). Philadelphia, Lippincott, 1964; as *Four Hours to Fear*, London, Long, 1965.

Quest for the Bogeyman (Lane). Philadelphia, Lippincott, 1964; London, Hutchinson, 1965.

Novels as Richard and Frances Lockridge (series: Captain/ Inspector Merton Heimrich in all books; Long editions published as Francis Richards)

Think of Death. Philadelphia, Lippincott, 1947.

I Want to Go Home. Philadelphia, Lippincott, 1948.

Spin Your Web, Lady! Philadelphia, Lippincott, 1949; London, Hutchinson, 1952.

Foggy, Foggy Death. Philadelphia, Lippincott, 1950; London, Hutchinson, 1953.

A Client Is Cancelled. Philadelphia, Lippincott, 1951; London, Hutchinson, 1955.

Death by Association. Philadelphia, Lippincott, 1952; London, Hutchinson, 1957; as *Trial by Terror*, New York, Spivak, 1954.

Stand Up and Die. Philadelphia, Lippincott, 1953; London, Hutchinson, 1955.

Death and the Gentle Bull. Philadelphia, Lippincott, 1954; London, Hutchinson, 1956; as *Killer in the Straw*, New York, Spivak, 1955.

Burnt Offering. Philadelphia, Lippincott, 1955; London, Hutchinson, 1957.

Let Dead Enough Alone. Philadelphia, Lippincott, 1956; London, Hutchinson, 1958.

Practice to Deceive. Philadelphia, Lippincott, 1957; London, Hutchinson, 1959.

Accent on Murder. Philadelphia, Lippincott, 1958; London, Long, 1960.

Show Red for Danger. Philadelphia, Lippincott, 1960; London, Long, 1961.

With One Stone. Philadelphia, Lippincott, 1961; as *No Dignity in Death*, London, Long, 1962.

First Come, First Kill. Philadelphia, Lippincott, 1962; London, Long, 1963.

The Distant Clue. Philadelphia, Lippincott, 1963; London, Long, 1964.

Novels as Richard Lockridge (series: Captain/Inspector Merton Heimrich; Nathan Shapiro; Bernard Simmons; Long editions published as Francis Richards)

Death in the Mind, with G.H. Estabrooks. New York, Dutton, 1945.

A Matter of Taste. Philadelphia, Lippincott, 1949; London, Hutchinson, 1951.

Murder Can't Wait (Heimrich; Shapiro). Philadelphia, Lippincott, 1964; London, Long, 1965.

Squire of Death (Simmons). Philadelphia, Lippincott, 1965; London, Long, 1966.

Murder Roundabout (Heimrich). Philadelphia, Lippincott, 1966; London, Long, 1967.

Murder for Art's Sake (Shapiro). Philadelphia, Lippincott, 1967; London, Long, 1968.

With Option to Die (Heimrich). Philadelphia, Lippincott, 1967; London, Long, 1968.

Murder in False-Face. Philadelphia, Lippincott, 1968; London, Hutchinson, 1969.

A Plate of Red Herrings (Simmons). Philadelphia, Lippincott, 1968; London, Long, 1969.

Die Laughing (Shapiro). Philadelphia, Lippincott, 1969; London, Long, 1970.

A Risky Way to Kill (Heimrich). Philadelphia, Lippincott, 1969; London, Long, 1970.

Troubled Journey. Philadelphia, Lippincott, 1970; London, Hutchinson, 1971.

Twice Retired (Simmons). Philadelphia, Lippincott, 1970; London, Long, 1971.

Inspector's Holiday (Heimrich). Philadelphia, Lippincott, 1971; London, Long, 1972.

Preach No More (Shapiro). Philadelphia, Lippincott, 1971; London, Long, 1972.

Death in a Sunny Place. Philadelphia, Lippincott, 1972; London, Long, 1973.

Something up a Sleeve (Simmons). Philadelphia, Lippincott, 1972; London, Long, 1973.

Write Murder Down (Shapiro). Philadelphia, Lippincott, 1972; London, Long, 1974.

Not I, Said the Sparrow (Heimrich). Philadelphia, Lippincott, 1973; London, Long, 1974.

Death on the Hour (Simmons).   Philadelphia, Lippincott, 1974; London, Long, 1975.
Or Was He Pushed? (Shapiro).   Philadelphia, Lippincott, 1975; London, Long, 1976.
Dead Run (Heimrich).   Philadelphia, Lippincott, 1976; London, Long, 1977.
A Streak of Light (Shapiro).   Philadelphia, Lippincott, 1976; London, Long, 1978.
The Tenth Life (Heimrich).   Philadelphia, Lippincott, 1977; London, Long, 1979.
The Old Die Young (Shapiro).   New York, Harper, 1980; London, Hale, 1981.

Uncollected Short Stories

"Nice Judge Trowbridge," in *Short Stories from the New Yorker*.   New York, Simon and Schuster, 1940.
"Death on a Foggy Morning," in *"This Week's" Stories of Mystery and Suspense*, edited by Stewart Beach.   New York, Random House, 1957.
"All Men Make Mistakes," in *Ellery Queen's 14th Annual*.   New York, Random House, 1959; London, Gollancz, 1961.
"Hit and Run" in *Ellery Queen's Mystery Magazine* (New York), July 1959.
"Cat of Dreams," in *Ellery Queen's Mystery Magazine* (New York), May 1960.
"Captain Heimrich Stumbles," in *Ellery Queen's 15th Mystery Annual*.   New York, Random House, 1960; London, Gollancz, 1961.
"Pattern for Murder," in *Anthology 1961*, edited by Ellery Queen.   New York, Davis, 1960.
"The Accusing Smoke," in *Ellery Queen's Mystery Magazine* (New York), August 1961.
"The Scent of Murder," in *Ellery Queen's 16th Mystery Annual*.   New York, Random House, 1961.
"Nobody Can Ask That," in *Anthology 1962*, edited by Ellery Queen.   New York, Davis, 1961.
"The Searching Cats," in *Anthology 1965*, edited by Ellery Queen.   New York, Davis, 1964.
"Dead Boys Don't Remember," in *Anthology 1966 Mid-Year*, edited by Ellery Queen.   New York, Davis, 1966.
"Flair for Murder," in *Ellery Queen's Crime Carousel*.   New York, New American Library, 1966.
"A Winter's Tale," in *Anthology 1967 Mid-Year*, edited by Ellery Queen.   New York, Davis, 1967.
"If They Give Him Time," in *Anthology 1970 Mid-Year*, edited by Ellery Queen.   New York, Davis, 1970.

OTHER PUBLICATIONS

Novels by Richard Lockridge

Mr. and Mrs. North.   New York, Stokes, 1936; London, Joseph, 1937.
The Empty Day.   Philadelphia, Lippincott, 1965.
Encounter in Key West.   Philadelphia, Lippincott, 1966.

Play

Radio Play: *Mr. and Mrs. North*, 1945.

Other

How to Adopt a Child, by Frances Lockridge.   New York, New York Children, 1928; revised edition, as *Adopting a Child*, New York, Greenberg, 1948.

Darling of Misfortune: Edwin Booth, by Richard Lockridge.   New York, Century, 1932.
Cats and People.   Philadelphia, Lippincott, 1950.
The Proud Cat (for children).   Philadelphia, Lippincott, 1951.
The Lucky Cat (for children).   Philadelphia, Lippincott, 1953.
The Nameless Cat (for children).   Philadelphia, Lippincott, 1954.
The Cat Who Rode Cows (for children).   Philadelphia, Lippincott, 1955.
One Lady, Two Cats (for children), by Richard Lockridge.   Philadelphia, Lippincott, 1967.

Editors, *Crime for Two*.   Philadelphia, Lippincott, 1955; London, Macdonald, 1957.

*   *   *

Richard Lockridge, with Frances until her death, and alone from then, was among the most prolific of mystery writers. Beginning in the 1940's, the Lockridges produced mystery after mystery with gratifying regularity, quickly establishing themselves with their books; movies and television series based on their books spread their fame even beyond their considerable reading public. This popularity is well deserved, though as devisers of mystery plots they have never been in the front rank. Their strength lies in the characters they created, in their descriptive ability, in their remarkable capacity for evoking a mood in a few words and depicting an aura in a couple of sentences, and, to a lesser degree, in their deft handling of witty, amusing dialogue.

Nearly all of the Lockridge novels can be considered as part of an extended series involving quite a number of interconnected sub-series, the principal characters of which often pop up in each other's novels. Indeed, the Lockridges have created an entire world of characters, centered about New York and the surrounding countryside; they handle metropolitan crime and its bucolic cousin with equal aplomb. In the city, the hamlet, or on the farm, the Lockridges are equally at home.

Mr. and Mrs. North—Jerry and Pam—were their first series characters, created in the early 1940's, and in the early 1940's, and in the early days of their writing career the Lockridges confined their writing to the North series (which also included Bill Wiegand and Sergeant Mullins of the New York Police Department). Though the best known of the Lockridge series, the North novels possess characteristics which have put off a number of readers. Pam's intuition is often, perhaps even usually, a bit extreme, the North cats are overly obtrusive, and the practice of ending each novel with a terror-filled chase in which the mysterious murderer is in hot pursuit of Mrs. North soon becomes tiresome. Nevertheless, the novels have a certain charm about them and, taken in moderation, are capable of producing a pleasant glow of well-being in the reader.

Less well known, though of much higher quality in terms of plotting and characterization, is the series centered on Merton Heimrich of the New York State Police. When the Lockridges first began this series, several years after the North series had become well established, Heimrich was single, and the only other regular character in the series was his good friend and colleague, Charlie Forniss. Heimrich's character developed rapidly, and as the series progressed the Putnam County hamlet of The Corners became pleasantly familiar to the reader, especially the Old Stone Inn, featured in a number of the novels. Heimrich eventually marries a young widow, Susan Faye, who has a young son. The Lockridges' treatment of their loving marriage is warming without being cloying, and watching the young boy Michael grow up from novel to novel is just one of the many pleasant features of the series. Though not without humor, the Heimrich series is much more serious than the flighty North novels, and its characters, being better developed, are more human, likeable and believable than the North bunch.

There is also the series featuring Nathan Shapiro, a Jewish cop who usually works in homicide under Bill Wiegand—an example of the overlapping of series characters typical of the Lockridge works. In *Murder Can't Wait*, another combination, Shapiro and Heimrich, teams up to solve the murder of the sportsman Stuart Fleming, who is killed just as he is about to blow the whistle on crooked gambling in collegiate sports. Shapiro harbors considerable doubts about his competence as a policeman. Since he is in fact highly competent, this self-doubt is an endearing foible, as is Heimrich's similarly mistaken belief that he moves like a hippopotamus.

Another Lockridge series features assistant New York City D.A. Bernie Simmons, and one of the most appealing of the recurring characters is retired professor Walter Brinkley, late of Dyckman University (who has an equally likeable black majordomo named Harry Washington), who appears from time to time in the various series without having an extended series of his own.

The Lockridge regulars are all people one would like to know, and getting to know them through the numerous novels is much like acquiring real friends. The Lockridges were never ones to duck social and political issues, and having their characters encounter and react to prejudice, intolerance, and demagogy lends real substance to their books, increasing their vitality and believability.

—Guy M. Townsend

———

LONGRIGG, Roger. *See* **PARRISH, Frank.**

———

LORAC, E.C.R. *See* **CARNAC, CAROL.**

———

LORAINE, Philip. Pseudonym for Robin Estridge; also writes as Robert York. British. Served in the Royal Navy. Has worked as a journalist in London and a dishwasher in Paris. Lives in France and California. Address: c/o Rochelle Stevens, 2 Terretts Place, Upper Street, London N1 1Q2, England.

CRIME PUBLICATIONS

Novels

White Lie the Dead. London, Hodder and Stoughton, 1950; as *And to My Beloved Husband—*, New York, Mill, 1950.
Exit with Intent: The Story of a Missing Comedian. London, Hodder and Stoughton, 1950.
The Break in the Circle. London, Hodder and Stoughton, and New York, Mill, 1951; as *Outside the Law*, New York, Pocket Books, 1953.

The Dublin Nightmare. London, Hodder and Stoughton, 1952; as *Nightmare in Dublin*, New York, Mill, 1952.
The Angel of Death. London, Hodder and Stoughton, and New York, Mill, 1961.
Day of the Arrow. London, Collins, and New York, Mill, 1964; as *The Eye of the Devil*, London, Fontana, 1966; as *13*, New York, Lancer, 1966.
W.I.L. One to Curtis. London, Collins, and New York, Random House, 1967.
The Dead Men of Sestos. London, Collins, and New York, Random House, 1968.
A Mafia Kiss. London, Collins, and New York, Random House, 1969.
Photographs Have Been Sent to Your Wife. London, Collins, and New York, Random House, 1971.
Voices in an Empty Room. London, Collins, 1973; New York, Random House, 1974.
Ask the Rattlesnake. London, Collins, 1975; as *Wrong Man in the Mirror*, New York, Random House, 1975.
Lions' Ransom. London, Collins, 1980.
Sea-Change. London, Collins, 1982; New York, St. Martin's Press, 1983.
Death Wishes. London, Collins, and New York, St. Martin's Press, 1983.
Loaded Questions. London, Collins, 1985; New York, St. Martin's Press, 1986.
Last Shot. London, Collins, and New York, St. Martin's Press, 1986.

OTHER PUBLICATIONS as Robin Estridge

Novels

The Future Is Tomorrow. London, Davies, 1947.
The Publican's Wife. London, Davies, 1948.
Meeting on the Shore. London, Davies, 1949.
Return of a Hero. London, Davies, 1950; as *Sword Without Scabbard*, New York, Morrow, 1950.
The Olive Tree. London, Davies, and New York, Morrow, 1953.
A Cuckoo's Child. London, Davies, 1969.
The Swords of December (as Robert York). London, Constable, and New York, Scribner, 1978.
My Lord the Fox (as Robert York). London, Constable, 1984.

Plays

Screenplays: *House of Darkness*, with John Gilling, 1948; *A Day to Remember*, 1953; *The Young Lovers* (*Chance Meeting*), with George Tabori, 1954; *Simba*, with John Baines, 1955; *Above Us the Waves*, 1955; *Checkpoint*, 1956; *Campbell's Kingdom*, with Hammond Innes, 1957; *Dangerous Exile*, 1957; *North West Frontier* (*Flame over India*), 1959; *Escape from Zahrain*, 1962; *Drums of Africa*, with Arthur Hoerl, 1963; *Eye of the Devil*, with Denis Murphy, 1966; *The Boy Cried Murder*, 1966; *Permission to Kill*, 1975.

*　　*　　*

Philip Loraine is particularly interesting as a crime novelist as much perhaps for where he does not wholly succeed as for where he does. One thing is always perfectly clear in his books: that he is a writer of many talents and considerable skill.

He knows how to tell a good story, leaving the reader always wanting to know what's going to happen next (that simple art that is not so simple). *Lions' Ransom* is an excellent example: its opening pages are as an intriguing a come-on as could be wished. He is an extremely skilled plot creator and confectioner, bringing the same deftness to very different sorts of crime novels. Thus he has written with solid confidence an excursion into the occult, *Voices in an Empty Room*, a hailed success, and a book as different as *Sea-Change*, a spy novel in the central tradition of espionage writing and a notable example of intricate plotting.

His characters, too, are always flesh-and-blood, recognisable as human beings and behaving in a credible manner. He knows as well how to achieve the sort of suspense that requires subsequent recourse to the nail-file, something in which he is aided by that credibility in character portrayal. He sets his books in a wide variety of interesting backgrounds, from California to Vienna via various parts of Africa, from San Francisco to Sicily, and he shows a painter's delight in making his settings come vividly into view. And lastly, but not at all leastly, he is an admirably lucid writer.

With all these virtues it might seem that he should succeed to the fullest extent in whatever he undertakes. Yet he does not always do so. And this, I believe, is because of these very virtues. They tempt him to higher things, and, perhaps because he bears too strongly in mind the crime novelist's implied promise firstly to entertain, he does not hit the highest targets. Thus, although his central characters are never less than well-drawn, he is apt to decline to go to the core of them, to say something striking and memorable about a certain type of person. But with his skills one feels that such a deep dive might not be beyond him.

Essentially what goes wrong when he is—a paradox—at his best is that he chooses a subject, an underlying theme such as that deviousness in human beings is not only a vice but also a cherishable virtue (*Lions' Ransom*), which perhaps demands writing of a very high order and that he then declines to reach up to this height. It is sad. But the books that fail in this way succeed in others. They are exciting. They do create suspense. They certainly give the reader fine tastes of the exotic. They repay reading—at all but the most demanding level.

—H.R.F. Keating

LOVELL, Marc. *See* **McSHANE, Mark.**

LOVESEY, Peter (Harmer). Also writes as Peter Lear. British. Born in Whitton, Middlesex, 10 September 1936. Educated at Hampton Grammar School, 1947–55; University of Reading, Berkshire, 1955–58, B.A. (honours) in English 1958. Served as an Education Officer in the Royal Air Force, 1958–61. Married Jacqueline Ruth Lewis in 1959; one daughter and one son. Lecturer in English, Thurrock Technical College, Essex, 1961–69; Head of General Education Department, Hammersmith College for Further Education, London, 1969–75. Recipient: Crime Writers Association Silver Dagger award, 1978, Gold Dagger award, 1983, award, for short story, 1985; Grand Prix de Littérature Policière, 1985; Prix du Roman d'Aventures, 1987. Agent: Vanessa Holt Associates Ltd., 59 Crescent Road, Leigh-on-Sea, Essex SS9 2PF, England.

CRIME PUBLICATIONS

Novels (series: Sergeant Cribb and Constable Thackeray in first 8 books; Bertie [Albert, Prince of Wales])

Wobble to Death. London, Macmillan, and New York, Dodd Mead, 1970.
The Detective Wore Silk Drawers. London, Macmillan, and New York, Dodd Mead, 1971.
Abracadaver. London, Macmillan, and New York, Dodd Mead, 1972.
Mad Hatter's Holiday: A Novel of Murder in Victorian Brighton. London, Macmillan, and New York, Dodd Mead, 1973.
Invitation to a Dynamite Party. London, Macmillan, 1974; as *The Tick of Death*, New York, Dodd Mead, 1974.
A Case of Spirits. London, Macmillan, and New York, Dodd Mead, 1975.
Swing, Swing Together. London, Macmillan, and New York, Dodd Mead, 1976.
Waxwork. London, Macmillan, and New York, Pantheon, 1978.
The False Inspector Dew: A Murder Mystery Aboard the S.S. Mauretania, 1921. London, Macmillan, and New York, Pantheon, 1982.
Keystone. London, Macmillan, and New York, Pantheon, 1983.
Rough Cider. London, Bodley Head, 1986; New York, Mysterious Press, 1987.
Bertie and the Tinman: From the Detective Memoirs of King Edward VII. London, Bodley Head, 1987; New York, Mysterious Press, 1988.
On the Edge. London, Century Hutchinson, and New York, Mysterious Press, 1989.
Bertie and the Seven Bodies. London, Century Hutchinson, and New York and London, Mysterious Press, 1990.

Short Stories

Butchers and Other Stories of Crime. London, Macmillan, 1985; New York, Mysterious Press, 1987.
The Staring Man and Other Stories. Helsinki, Eurographica, 1989.

Uncollected Short Stories

"Murder in Store," in *Woman's Own* (London), 21 December 1985.
"Friendly Yachtsman, 39," in *Woman's Own* (London), 18 July 1987.
"Curl Up and Dye" in *John Creasey's Crime Collection 1987*, edited by Herbert Harris. London, Gollancz, 1987; New York, St. Martin's Press, 1988.
"The Pomeranian Poisoning," in *Winter's Crimes 19*, edited by Hilary Hale. London, Macmillan, 1987.
"The Curious Computer," in *The New Adventures of Sherlock Holmes*, edited by Martin H. Greenberg and Carol-Lynn Rössel-Waugh. New York, Carroll and Graf, 1987.
"Where Is Thy Sting?," in *Winter's Crimes 20*, edited by Hilary Hale. London, Macmillan, 1988.
"The Munich Posture," in *The Rigby File*, edited by Tim Heald. London, Hodder and Stoughton, 1989.
"A Case of Butterflies," in *Winter's Crimes 21*, edited by Hilary Hale. London, Macmillan, 1989.
"Youdunnit," in *New Crimes*, edited by Maxim Jakubowski. London, Robinson, 1989; New York, Carroll and Graf, 1990.

"The Haunted Crescent," in *Mistletoe Mysteries*, edited by Charlotte MacLeod.   New York, Mysterious Press, 1989.

OTHER PUBLICATIONS

Novels as Peter Lear

Goldengirl.   London, Cassell, 1977; New York, Doubleday, 1978.
Spider Girl.   London, Cassell, and New York, Viking Press, 1980.
The Secret of Spandau.   London, Joseph, 1986.

Plays

Television Plays: *The Detective Wore Silk Drawers*, from his own novel, 1980; *The Horizontal Witness; Something Old, Something New; The Last Trumpet; The Hand That Rocks the Cradle; The Choir that Wouldn't Sing; Murder Old Boy*; with Jacqueline Lovesey (*Cribb* series), 1980–81; *Butchers*, from his own short story, 1988.

Other

The Kings of Distance: A Study of Five Great Runners. London, Eyre and Spottiswoode, 1968; as *Five Kings of Distance*, New York, St. Martin's Press, 1981.
The Guide to British Track and Field Literature 1275–1968, with Tom McNab.   London, Athletics Arena, 1969.
"The Historian: Once upon a Crime," in *Murder Ink: The Mystery Reader's Companion*, edited by Dilys Winn.   New York, Workman, 1977.
The Official Centenary History of the Amateur Athletic Association.   London, Guinness Superlatives, 1979.

Editor, *The Black Cabinet: Stories Based on True Crime.* London, Xanadu, and New York, Carroll and Graf, 1989.

*

Peter Lovesey comments:

Although I am usually identified as a writer of crime novels set in the Victorian age, I have occasionally escaped that particular timewarp, to find myself, for instance, on an ocean-going liner in 1921; with the Keystone Cops in Hollywood in 1916; in the cider orchards of Somerset in 1941; and in "civvy street" in London in 1946. The past has a strong pull, yet I regularly venture into the here and now in short stories, which I regard as my best work. I enjoy the challenge of writing in a variety of voices, forms and styles. The aim of all my writing is to entertain and involve the reader; if successful, then I can be subversive, suggesting ironies, springing surprises, and now and then, chilling the blood.

*   *   *

Peter Lovesey came to writing quite by chance, responding primarily to the lure of a £1000 prize offered by a publisher for the best crime novel by a new author. At the time he was a young teacher, struggling as all of his profession do, to pay the monthly bills and the opportunity to give himself a little breathing space by possibly winning was to prove the spur that eventually led him into full-time writing. It brought to the reading public Sergeant Cribb and Constable Thackeray, steadfast upholders of the law in Victorian England.

His first novel, and the one that won him that prize, was *Wobble to Death*, a clever, catchy title that depicts one of the more bizarre Victorian sporting events—the "Wobble." Like the non-stop dancing contests of the 1930's depicted in Horace McCoy's *They Shoot Horses, Don't They?*, "wobbles" were continuous walking contests set over a period of six days. With this authentic background Lovesey then weaves a murder plot with his two policeman, Cribb and Thackeray, set to solve the puzzle and apprehend the culprit.

A further seven Cribb and Thackeray novels were to follow, all painted with authentic Victorian colours and depicting various facets of that elegant but cruel time. *Abracadaver* portrays the music hall, *Mad Hatter's Holiday* the Victorian obsession for seaside holidays, *Invitation to a Dynamite Party* the Irish dynamiters of 1884 and *Swing, Swing Together* in which the publication of Jerome K. Jerome's *Three Men in a Boat* spurs on a host of copy-cat travellers, three of whom have murderous intent.

Having exhausted, as the author felt, his Victorian creation, Lovesey then moved on a few years to 1921 and arguably his best book to date and the one that won him the Gold Dagger award, *The False Inspector Dew*. The result was a veritable *tour de force* with real characters mixing with the imaginary, showing once again that Lovesey has a good eye for period detail.

Apart from the novels under his Peter Lear byline, Lovesey has always written period crime fiction and the nearest he comes to contemporaneous times is *Rough Cider*, primarily set in 1964 but harking back to 1945. *On the Edge* is also set during World War II and features Rose and Antonia, two ex-WAAF plotters and their metamorphosis into two unlikely murderesses. The setting, style, and feel of the writing is richly authentic and the old cliché "page-turning" is perfectly apt. The will-they won't-they get away with it question hangs over the book right to the very last page. Both these novels have a much tougher centre to them than anything the author produced before and show that he can produce effective period pieces without inserting that humorous touch which runs through his "Victorian" novels.

Notwithstanding the undeniable strength of these two books Lovesey chose to move back to his starting point, namely the Victorian era, but this time with a new detective, none other than King Edward VII or Bertie as he was known. *Bertie and The Tinman* and *Bertie and the Seven Bodies* are the two latest titles, the latter being by far the strongest. Those readers who enjoyed his Cribb and Thackeray books will undoubtedly revel in the author's obvious love for the etiquette, finery, and hypocrisy of the Victorian times, whilst others may hope that he may return to the less whimsical, "tougher" settings of *Rough Cider* and *On The Edge*.

—Ralph Spurrier

———

LOWNDES, Marie (Adelaide) Belloc. Also wrote as Philip Curtin.   British.   Born in London in 1868; sister of the writer Hilaire Belloc. Married the writer Frederic Sawrey Lowndes in 1896 (died 1940); one son and two daughters. Staff member, *Review of Reviews*, London. *Died 14 November 1947.*

CRIME PUBLICATIONS

Novels

The Heart of Penelope.   London, Heinemann, 1904; New York, Dutton, 1915.

The Uttermost Farthing. London, Heinemann, 1908; New York, Kennerley, 1909.
When No Man Pursueth. London, Heinemann, 1910; New York, Kennerley, 1911.
The Chink in the Armour. London, Methuen, and New York, Scribner, 1912; as *The House of Peril*, London, Readers Library, 1935.
The Lodger. London, Methuen, and New York, Scribner, 1913.
The End of Her Honeymoon. New York, Scribner, 1913; London, Methuen, 1914.
Good Old Anna. London, Hutchinson, 1915; New York, Doran, 1916.
The Price of Admiralty. London, Newnes, 1915.
Love and Hatred. London, Chapman and Hall, and New York, Doran, 1917.
Out of the War? London, Chapman and Hall, 1918; as *The Gentleman Anonymous*, London, Philip Allan, 1934.
The Lonely House. London, Hutchinson, and New York, Doran, 1920.
The Terriford Mystery. London, Hutchinson, and New York, Doubleday, 1924.
What Really Happened. London, Hutchinson, and New York, Doubleday, 1926.
The Story of Ivy. London, Heinemann, 1927; New York, Doubleday, 1928.
Thou Shalt Not Kill. London, Hutchinson, 1927.
Cressida: No Mystery. London, Heinemann, 1928; New York, Knopf, 1930.
Love's Revenge. London, Readers Library, 1929.
One of Those Ways. London, Heinemann, and New York, Knopf, 1929.
Letty Lynton. London, Heinemann, and New York, Cape and Smith, 1931.
Vanderlyn's Adventure. New York, Cape and Smith, 1931; as *The House by the Sea*, London, Heinemann, 1937.
Jenny Newstead. London, Heinemann, and New York, Putnam, 1932.
Love Is a Flame. London, Benn, 1932.
The Reason Why. London, Benn, 1932.
Another Man's Wife. London, Heinemann, and New York, Longman, 1934.
The Chianti Flask. New York, Longman, 1934; London, Heinemann, 1935.
Who Rides on a Tiger. New York, Longman, 1935; London, Heinemann, 1936.
And Call It Accident. New York, Longman, 1936; London, Hutchinson, 1939.
The Second Key. New York, Longman, 1936; as *The Injured Lover*, London, Hutchinson, 1939.
The Marriage-Broker. London, Heinemann, 1937; as *The Fortune of Bridget Malone*, New York, Longman, 1937.
Motive. London, Hutchinson, 1938; as *Why It Happened*, New York, Longman, 1938.
Lizzie Borden: A Study in Conjecture. New York, Longman, 1939; London, Hutchinson, 1940.
Reckless Angel. New York, Longman, 1939.
The Christine Diamond. London, Hutchinson, and New York, Longman, 1940.
Before the Storm. New York, Longman, 1941.

Short Stories

Why They Married. London, Heinemann, 1923.
Bread of Deceit. London, Hutchinson, 1925; as *Afterwards*, New York, Doubleday, 1925.

Some Men and Women. London, Hutchinson, 1925; New York, Doubleday, 1928.
A Labour of Hercules. London, Todd, 1943.

OTHER PUBLICATIONS

Novels

Barbara Rebell. London, Heinemann, 1905; New York, Dodge, 1907.
The Pulse of Life. London, Heinemann, 1908; New York, Dodd Mead, 1909.
Jane Oglander. London, Heinemann, and New York, Scribner, 1911.
Mary Pechell. London, Methuen, and New York, Scribner, 1912.
The Red Cross Barge. London, Smith Elder, 1916; New York, Doran, 1918.
Lilla: A Part of Her Life. London, Hutchinson, 1916; New York, Doran, 1917.
From the Vasty Deep. London, Hutchinson, 1920; as *From Out the Vasty Deep*, New York, Doran, 1921.
What Timmy Did. London, Hutchinson, 1921; New York, Doran, 1922.
Duchess Laura: Certain Days of Her Life. London, Ward Lock, 1929; as *The Duchess Intervenes*, New York, Putnam, 1933.
Duchess Laura: Further Days of Her Life. New York. Longman, 1933.
She Dwelt with Beauty. London, Macmillan, 1949.

Short Stories

Studies in Wives. London, Heinemann, 1909; New York, Kennerley, 1910.
Studies in Love and Terror. London, Methuen, and New York, Scribner, 1913.
What of the Night? New York, Dodd Mead, 1943.

Plays

The Lonely House, with Charles Randolph, adaptation of the novel by Lowndes (produced Eastbourne, Sussex, 1924).
The Key: A Love Drama (as *The Second Key*, produced London, 1935). London, Benn, 1930.
With All John's Love. London, Benn, 1930.
Why Be Lonely?, with F.S.A. Lowndes. London, Benn, 1931.
What Really Happened, adaptation of her own novel (produced London, 1936). London, Benn, 1932.
Her Last Avenue (produced London, 1936).
The Empress Eugenie. New York, Longman, 1938.

Other

H.R.H. the Prince of Wales: An Account of His Career (published anonymously). London, Richards, and New York, Appleton, 1898; revised edition, as *His Most Gracious Majesty King Edward VII*, as Mrs. Belloc Lowndes, Richards. 1901.
The Philosophy of the Marquise (sketches and dialogues). London, Richards, 1899.
T.R.H. the Prince and Princess of Wales (published anonymously). London, Newnes, 1902.
Noted Murder Mysteries (as Philip Curtin). London, Simpkin Marshall, 1914.
Told in Gallant Deeds: A Child's History of the War. London, Nisbet, 1914.

"I, Too, Have Lived in Arcadia": A Record of Love and of Childhood (autobiography). London, Macmillan, 1941; New York, Dodd Mead, 1942.
Where Love and Friendship Dwelt (autobiography). London, Macmillan, and New York, Dodd Mead, 1943.
The Merry Wives of Westminster (autobiography). London, Macmillan, 1946.
A Passing World (autobiography). London, Macmillan, 1948.
The Young Hilaire Belloc. London, Kenedy, 1956.

Editor and Translator, with M. Shedlock, *Edmund and Jules de Goncourt, with Letters and Leaves from Their Journals.* London, Heinemann, and New York, Dodd Mead, 2 vols., 1895.

*   *   *

Marie Belloc Lowndes, descendant of Joseph Priestly, protégée of Robert Browning, and sister of Hilaire Belloc, drew on her knowledge of courts and lawyers, of recent crime cases, and of human psychology based on personal observation of such diverse friends as Oscar Wilde, Prime Minister Asquith, and Henry James, to produce a series of carefully plotted crime and suspense novels and short stories. These significant contributions to the genre share a sensitive understanding of women's problems, a modern sensibility, a concern with the psychology of crime, especially motive. They focus on ordinary persons involved in sudden violence, people "enmeshed in a web of tragic circumstances" involving jealousy, greed, sudden love or sexual entanglements, and failure to communicate. They explore questions of loyalty, or childless marriages, between engaged couples, or in doctor/patient, lawyer/client, servant/master relationships.

Lizzie Borden explores the way passionate love causes an intelligent, quiet girl to commit a double murder. This theme of transformation runs throughout Marie Lowndes's novels: "this was an Agatha Cheale she did not know—a violent, unrestrained human being." Part of the horror of her books comes from this stripping away the façade of seemingly respectable women to show how greed or passion could lead them to murder, particularly by poisoning (*Letty Lynton, The Story of Ivy, The Chianti Flask, Motive, The Chink in the Armour*). The most sympathetic of these women are victims of ruined finances, domineering parents, and marriage laws whereby a sensitive woman becomes the slave of a cruel, cantankerous older husband who abuses her; the least sympathetic are totally amoral bits of fluff who seize the main chance to improve their position and who abuse the love and affection of trusting males. Often the openly suspect prove basically sound, and the solidly respectable prove capable of murder or deception. "Strange," "unnatural," "cold," "beastly," "amazing," "extraordinary," and "very clever" resound in her novels. Dreams are portentous, fortune-tellers accurate, and presentiments confirmed. Her characters turn unnaturally pale in true Victorian style, "as does a white camelia seen in a dim light." There are secret trysts, eavesdroppers, anonymous letters, and plenty of arsenic available in common household products. Often the evidence is as trivial as a missing chianti bottle, a bowl of strawberries, a passing motorist, a chance conversation. Gold-diggers dupe innocents, and the "Goddess of play attracts reptiles." Lowndes's one recurring character is a defence lawyer, Sir Joseph Molloy, "the murderer's savior," a wily, competent lawyer with a deep understanding of human nature.

Her novels reproduce court scenes effectively, realistically, and accurately. *The Chianti Flask, Motive, The Terriford Mystery, Lizzie Borden,* and *Letty Lynton* all involve lengthy inquests or trials, the latter two factual and critical résumés of actual court scenes. All depict yellow journalism, prejudging and curious crowds anxious for horror and scandal, and innocents tainted by contact with murderer or victim. *The Terriford Mystery* is typical in its cynical treatment of law and justice; a scandalmongering press, gossiping villagers, a rich, womanizing lawyer, and unimaginative police condemn an innocent man. The experienced and the amateur detectives are ineffective, and only an accidental meeting with a dying man prevents a miscarriage of justice.

Unexpected but reasonable reversals like that in *The Terriford Mystery* make Lowndes's plots continually fascinating. In *Letty Lynton*, the young, amoral murderess escapes one legal trap only to be enmeshed in a more terrifying one. In *The Chink in the Armour* and *One of Those Ways* the reversal derives from the point of view of naive, unsuspecting victims in gambling and murder conspiracies. *The End of Her Honeymoon* contrasts apparent police concern with their real willingness to cover up a plague death. In *The Lodger*, Marie Lowndes's finest work, highly praised by critics and readers (including Gertrude Stein and Ernest Hemingway), a servant couple discover that their lodger is a Jack-the-Ripper-type mass murderer, but are loath to turn him in because of self-interest and self-protection, loyalty to upper-class "gentlefolk," and "decent" values shared by murderers and landlords. The novel is a masterful analysis of inertia caused by divided loyalties; the horror, like that of all Marie Lowndes's best work, is psychological and familiar, never theatrical or stylized.

—Gina Macdonald

———

LUARD, Nicholas. Also writes as James McVean. British. Born in London, 26 June 1937. Educated at Winchester College, Hampshire, 1951–54; the Sorbonne, Paris, 1954–55; Cambridge University, M.A. 1960; University of Pennsylvania, Philadelphia, M.A. 1961. Served in the Coldstream Guards, 1955–57: Lieutenant. Married Elisabeth Baron Longmore in 1963; one son and three daughters. Worked for NATO and in theatre and publishing. Agent: Jonathan Clowes Ltd., 22 Prince Albert Road, London NW1 7ST. Address: 6 Fernshaw Road, London SW10 0TF, England

CRIME PUBLICATIONS

Novels

The Warm and Golden War. London, Secker and Warburg, 1967; New York, Pantheon, 1968.
The Robespierre Serial. London, Weidenfeld and Nicolson, and New York, Harcourt Brace, 1975.
Travelling Horseman. London, Weidenfeld and Nicolson, 1975.
The Orion Line. London, Secker and Warburg, 1976; as *Double Assignment*, New York, Harcourt Brace, 1977.
The Dirty Area. London, Hamish Hamilton, 1979; as *The Shadow Spy*, New York, Harcourt Brace, 1979.
Gondar. London, Century Hutchinson, and New York, Simon and Schuster, 1988.

Novels as James McVean

Bloodspoor. London, Macdonald, 1977; New York, Dial Press, 1979.

Seabird Nine. London, Macdonald, 1981.
Titan. London, Macdonald, 1984.

OTHER PUBLICATIONS

Other

Refer to Drawer, with Dominick Elwes. London, Barker, 1964.
The Last Wilderness: A Journey Across the Great Kalahari Desert. London, Elm Tree, 1981.
Andalucia: A Portrait of Southern Spain. London, Century, 1984.
Wild Life Parks of Africa. London, Joseph, 1985.
Landscape in Spain, photographs by Michael Busselle. London, Pavilion, 1988.

* * *

A major feature of the novels of Nicholas Luard is the extraordinary attention to detail he places in their locales, which are frequently places well off the beaten track in rural Spain and France and in north Africa. As befits a writer who was once a Coldstream Guards officer attached to a NATO forward intelligence unit, Luard allows little to escape his notice. Nothing, whether it be physical oddity or topographical feature, is introduced without it having some significance to the structure of the plot, such as the moment in *The Robespierre Serial* when intelligence controller Handley-Reid studies the map of Spain in an airline in-flight magazine and thereby gets his first clue. This first novel follows the main conventions of a typical spy-thriller plot. Carswell, a solitary operator, has spent most of his career in a quiet backwater of British intelligence in Madrid, before being ordered to involve himself in a bizarre assassination attempt. Inevitably things start to go awry and as he becomes increasingly cut off from his back-up in British intelligence and in the CIA the logic of his orders blurs into insignificance. Drawn into a world of violence and double-dealing intrigue, Carswell finds an unlikely sheet-anchor in Minette, a French prostitute, as the novel takes on its final shape and the pieces are drawn together.

A similar sense of period accuracy permeates *The Orion Line* which also involves a British agent who is dragged out of official obscurity into a hectic adventure. Gareth Owen, an unlikely hero with a quiet Foreign Office intelligence gathering background is plummeted into a wartime mystery surrounding "The Orion Line," a famous French underground escape route. Consigned safely to the indexes of the history of World War II, the Orion Line bursts into dramatic life when two British agents are killed investigating the enigma still surrounding it. As with the previous novel, the ambience is well-nigh perfect from the flashback to the Foreign Office recruitment of Owen, through the steady calm of Whitehall's intelligence mandarins, to the intricate re-working of Allied rivalries and friendships during World War II. The result is an ingenious and sensitive novel with two related plots which take Owen from simply finding out who killed his colleagues to a 30-year-old secret that surrounds a deadly traitor. Luard's knowledge of intelligence work in the field and of the frequently obscurantist policies of government servants make *The Orion Line* as impressive in atmosphere as anything written by John le Carré.

Several of his main characters continue in *The Dirty Area*, a novel with a contemporary setting in the underworld of intelligence networks in Europe and north Africa where relationships have to be taken on trust. There is a seriousness to its telling that was absent from the previous novels, and

throughout Luard maintains the highest standards of characterisation and attention to detail. He is also not afraid occasionally to use his inside knowledge to allow his protagonists to cock a snook at authority.

Under the pseudonym of James McVean he has married his interests in wild-life conservation with thriller writing to produce two memorable novels dealing with natural disasters and government cover-ups, *Bloodspoor*, set in the Kalahari, and *Seabird Nine*, set largely in the Arctic regions.

—Trevor Royle

———

LUDLUM, Robert. Also writes as Jonathan Ryder; Michael Shepherd. American. Born in New York City, 25 May 1927. Educated at Rectory School, Pomfret, Connecticut; Kent School, Connecticut; Cheshire Academy, Connecticut; Wesleyan University, Middletown, Connecticut, B.A. in Fine Arts 1951. Served in the United States Marine Corps, 1945–47. Married Mary Ryducha in 1951; two sons and one daughter. Stage and television actor from 1952; producer, North Jersey Playhouse, Fort Lee, 1957–60, and Playhouse-on-the-Mall, Paramus, New Jersey, 1960–69. Since 1969 freelance writer. Agent: Henry Morrison Inc., 58 West 10th Street, New York, New York 10011, U.S.A.

CRIME PUBLICATIONS

Novels (Series: Bourne)

The Scarlatti Inheritance. Cleveland, World, and London, Hart Davis, 1971.
The Osterman Weekend. Cleveland, World, and London, Hart Davis, 1972.
The Matlock Paper. New York, Dial Press, and London, Hart Davis MacGibbon, 1973.
Trevayne (as Jonathan Ryder). New York, Delacorte Press, 1973; London, Weidenfeld and Nicolson, 1974, as Robert Ludlum, London, Grafton, 1989.
The Cry of the Halidon (as Jonathan Ryder). New York, Delacorte Press, and London, Weidenfeld and Nicolson, 1974.
The Rhinemann Exchange. New York, Dial Press, 1974; London, Hart Davis MacGibbon, 1975.
The Road to Gandolfo (as Michael Shepherd). New York, Dial Press, 1975; London, Hart Davis MacGibbon, 1976.
The Gemini Contenders. New York, Dial Press, and London, Hart Davis MacGibbon, 1976.
The Chancellor Manuscript. New York, Dial Press, and London, Hart Davis MacGibbon, 1977.
The Holcroft Covenant. New York, Marek, and London, Hart Davis, 1978.
The Matarese Circle. New York, Marek, and London, Granada, 1979.
The Bourne Identity. New York, Marek, and London, Granada, 1980.
The Parsifal Mosaic. New York, Random House, and London, Granada, 1982.
The Aquitaine Progression. New York, Random House, and London, Granada, 1984.
The Bourne Supremacy. New York, Random House, and London, Grafton, 1986.

The Icarus Agenda. New York, Random House, and London, Collins, 1988.
The Bourne Ultimatum. New York, Random House, and London, Grafton, 1990.

*

Theatrical Activities:

Actor: **Plays**—Sterling Brown in *Junior Miss* by Jerome Chodorov and Joseph Fields, New York, 1941, and Haskell Cummings on tour, 1943–44; in stock, Canton Show Shop, Connecticut, summer 1952; Soldier in *The Strong Are Lonely* by Fritz Hochwalder, New York, 1952; in stock, Ivorytown Playhouse, Connecticut, summer 1953; Third Messenger in *Richard III*, New York, 1953; Spartacus, in *The Gladiator*, New York, 1954; in stock, Cragsmoor Playhouse, New York, summer 1954; Policeman and, later, Cashel Byron in *The Admirable Bashville* by G.B. Shaw, New York, 1956; D'Estivel in *Saint Joan* by G.B. Shaw, New York, 1956; in stock, Olney Theatre, Maryland, summer 1957.

*   *   *

The motivation behind Robert Ludlum's novels can best be explained by the end note that is found in many of his bestsellers—"I write primarily as an entertainer. But ... you write from a point of view of something that disturbs or outrages you. And that's what I do. I admit to being outraged—mostly by the abuse of power by the fanatics." So, in his books of suspense and international intrigue, he creates a world where groups and governments do such things as try to bring about the financial ruin of the United States, begin and escalate wars, and tear apart bonds of friendship and love. His books often have complex plots with much action, from secret conferences to daring escapes and plenty of murders.

Ludlum chooses somewhat ordinary men as his heroes to fight against these evils. They are often in their forties, of upper-middle class backgrounds, and with strong ideas of what is morally right. This hero usually meets a government man seeking his help in saving the world or at least a significant part of it. He is faced with various difficult tasks, from exposing the evil in his friends, to playing the role of a hardened criminal, or rescuing hostages. Although he may be promised help and protection by those he is working for, inevitably he finds himself alone with only his wits to save him.

The hero of *The Osterman Weekend* is John Tanner, a news director who lives with his wife and children in New Jersey. He is approached by a man named Fasset from the C.I.A. and is told that his help is needed to undermine Operation Omega. It is explained that this is a Soviet scheme to bring about economic disaster to the United States by threatening powerful business executives with blackmail if they do not follow orders. Tanner then is informed that the C.I.A. thinks that one or more of his good friends—the Tremaynes, Cardones, and Ostermans—may be part of Omega. His instructions are to watch and listen to them when they all get together during the coming weekend, but he also must act normally.

In the days leading up to the reunion weekend, the other couples get calls warning them that their friends cannot be trusted, and strange messages with vague meanings. Tanner tries to go about his business as usual, yet begins to have doubts about the whole affair when his family is abducted and left gassed along the roadside, and when he finds a dead government man in the woods behind his house.

The dialogue and action the characters engage in during the weekend increases the suspense of this story. No one trusts any-

one, and arguments ensue over innocent comments. After several more scary incidents, Tanner finds he must work alone to end the terror. This is perhaps one of Ludlum's better novels, as it has an easier plot line and more rounded characters than most of his other books.

In *The Matlock Paper* the hero is James Matlock, a professor at Carlyle University in Connecticut. The Justice Department has chosen him for a task that he may not live through, and they send a man named Loring to see if Matlock will help them. Loring explains that they are after a man called Nimrod who runs a large network of narcotics, prostitution, and gambling through East coast campuses. Matlock is given a paper that has been taken from a narcotics courier, and told that if he can find another paper that matches it they can expose Nimrod. He is supposed to accomplish this task by socializing with other faculty and students to see who may be involved with drugs.

As Matlock carries out his mission, he witnesses the effects that Nimrod has had—and continues to have—on many people's lives. He sees a young professor who is eager to gain his place in the academic world, and an old professor who just wants to ease his pain from a war injury. Matlock finds young college girls who are prostituting themselves by choice, and sees the results of torture on his own girlfriend. He infiltrates gambling operations and witnesses many murders. Then, after he is almost killed himself, he must accept help from another group of people with questionable integrity. Ultimately, Nimrod is exposed, but the book does not come to a tidy conclusion.

The Icarus Agenda is one of Ludlum's more recent novels. It has a complex plot with subplots and many characters, all connected in some way with the hero Congressman Evan Kendrick. Ludlum utilizes much of the world in this book, from the West coast of the United States to southwest Asia, with references to many places in between. One distinction that this novel has from his others is the presence of a heroine who is instrumental in helping Kendrick to accomplish his goals.

The plot of the book ranges from a hostage situation in Oman to an elite group of people who are trying to manipulate the political scene in the United States. Entwined in this are arms sales, assassinations, and a love story. Some interesting characters emerge, including the heroine Khalehla Rashad and the Jewish Emanuel Weingrass, plus an unusual combination of Israelis, Palestinians, Americans, and other Arabs who work together to aid world peace. The action never stops in this story; however, it is a complex plot to follow and difficult to keep tracks of some of the characters.

Ludlum's suspense novels are fine entertainment for people who like fast-paced and action-packed books. They give the reader a chance to experience a different world, where deception is a common occurrence and bullets fly out of unsuspected places. The author writes of evils that may become tomorrow's headlines, but where hope can still be found in the hero's integrity.

—Karen Hinckley

————

LUSTGARTEN, Edgar (Marcus). British. Born in Manchester, Lancashire, 3 May 1907. Educated at Manchester Grammar School; St. John's College, Oxford (President, Oxford Union, 1930), B.A. 1930. Married Joyce Goldstone in 1932 (died 1972). Practising Barrister, 1930–40; counter-propaganda broadcaster, 1940–45, and staff producer, 1945–48, BBC Radio, London; organizer, "In the News" program,

1950–54, and narrator, "Focus" program, 1965–68, BBC Television, London; organizer, "Free Speech" program, 1955–61, and chairman, "Fair Play" program, 1962–65, Associated Television, London. From 1952 presenter of several series of "Famous Trials," BBC Radio and TV. *Died 15 December 1978.*

CRIME PUBLICATIONS

Novels

A Case to Answer. London, Eyre and Spottiswoode, 1947; as *One More Unfortunate,* New York, Scribner, 1947.
Blondie Iscariot. New York, Scribner, 1948; London, Museum Press, 1949.
Game for Three Losers. London, Museum Press, and New York, Scribner, 1952.
I'll Never Leave You. London, Hart Davis, 1971.
Turn the Light Out as You Go. London, Elek, 1978.

Uncollected Short Story

"Forbidden Fruit," in *Ellery Queen's Mystery Magazine* (New York), January 1963.

OTHER PUBLICATIONS

Plays

Screenplay: *The Man Who Wouldn't Talk,* 1958.

Radio Plays: *In the Shade of the Crabapple Tree,* 1966; *The Burden Mystery Case,* 1966; *Trial of John White Webster,* 1967; *Murder at the Follies,* 1967; *The Traitors* series, 1970.

Other

Prisoner at the Bar: The Famous B.B.C. Series. London, Deutsch, 1952.
The Woman in the Case. London, Deutsch, and New York, Scribner, 1955.
The Murder and the Trial, edited by Anthony Boucher. New York, Scribner, 1958; London, Odhams Press, 1960.
The Judges and the Judged. London, Odhams Press, 1961.
The Business of Murder. London, Harrap, and New York, Scribner, 1968.
The Chalk Pit Murder. London, Hart Davis MacGibbon, 1974.
A Century of Murderers. London, Eyre Methuen, 1975.
The Illustrated Story of Crime. London, Weidenfeld and Nicolson, and Chicago, Follett, 1976.

*

Theatrical Activities:

Actor (Narrator): **Films**—*The Drayton Case,* 1953; *The Missing Man,* 1953; *The Candlelight Murder,* 1953; *The Blazing Caravan,* 1954; *The Dark Stairway,* 1954; *Late Night Final,* 1954; *The Strange Case of Blondie,* 1954; *The Silent Witness,* 1954; *Passenger in Tokyo,* 1954; *Night Plane to Amsterdam,* 1955; *Murder Anonymous,* 1955; *Wall of Death,* 1956; *The Case of the River Morgue,* 1956; *Destination Death,* 1956; *Person Unknown,* 1956; *The Lonely House,* 1957; *Bullet from the Past,* 1957; *Inside Information,* 1957; *The Case of the Smiling Widow,* 1957; *The Mail Van Murder,* 1957; *The Tyburn Case,* 1957; *The White Cliffs Mystery,* 1957; *Night Crossing,* 1957; *Print of*

Death, 1958; *Crime of Honour,* 1958; *The Crossroad Gallows,* 1958; *The Unseeing Eye,* 1959; *The Ghost Train Murder,* 1959; *The Dover Road Mystery,* 1960; *The Last Train,* 1960; *Evidence in Concrete,* 1960; *The Silent Weapon,* 1961; *The Grand Junction Case,* 1961; *The Never Never Murder,* 1961; *Wings of Death,* 1961; *The Square Mile Murder,* 1961; *The Guilty Party,* 1962; *A Woman's Privilege,* 1962; *Moment of Decision,* 1962; *The Undesirable Neighbour,* 1963; *The Invisible Asset,* 1963; *Company of Fools,* 1966; *The Haunted Man,* 1966; *Infamous Conduct,* 1966; *Payment in Kind,* 1967.

*   *   *

A British lawyer, criminologist, and novelist, Edgar Lustgarten began his writing career in the early 1930's while he was practicing law. As a busy advocate, he had little time for any major writing, but limited himself to short radio plays, feature articles, and pseudonymous song lyrics. He worked in radio and television for many years and is especially remembered for the famous series, *Prisoner at the Bar.* In his novels he demonstrated an ability to tell a good story and a sympathetic interest in the human condition.

His first novel, *A Case to Answer,* is a masterfully written narrative of the trial of a young man for the murder of a Soho prostitute. Lustgarten realistically portrays lawyers, witnesses, and judges while maintaining suspense to the end. Its realism contrasts with most legal mysteries, American and English, and its powerful climax suggests not only that the verdict is unfair but that the British system of justice is far from perfect. *Blondie Iscariot,* in contrast, is his worst book—a sordid and shoddy melodrama lacking the sensitivity and promise of his earlier tale. *Game for Three Losers* deals with an elaborate plot of blackmail involving a highly regarded member of parliament with bright prospects for a successful political career. Again Lustgarten indicts a legal system that fails to protect the innocent, and, worse, punishes them along with the guilty.

Lustgarten admitted a livelong interest in crime; in his introduction to *The Illustrated Story of Crime,* he wrote: "crime is composed mostly of the vices and the passions; seldom mixed with reason, with virtue hardly ever. Nevertheless it forms a massive part of human nature, and can no more be ignored in a review of our own species than can disease, injury, war, pestilence or death." Lustgarten emphasized that he did not write "detective stories"; his stories of crime—both factual and fictional—are perceptive and illuminating essays into the tragicomedy of crime and the failure of the legal system. He was a profound and talented writer whose best works reflect his incisive wit and probing criticism of the law.

—Daniel P. King

LUTZ, John (Thomas). Also writes as John Bennett; Tom Collins; Steven Greene; Van McCloud; Paul Shepparton; Elwin Strange; John Barry Williams. American. Born in Dallas, Texas, 11 September 1939. Educated at Meramec Community College, St. Louis 1965. Married Barbara Jean Bradley in 1958; two daughters and one son. Worked as construction worker; theater usher; warehouseman; truck driver; switchboard operator, St. Louis Metropolitan Police. Since 1975 self-employed writer. Recipient: Private Eye Writers of America Shamus award, for short story, 1982, for novel, 1988; Mystery Writers of America Edgar Allan Poe award, for short story, 1986. Agent: Dominick Abel, 498 West

End Avenue, New York, New York 10024. Address: 880 Providence Avenue, Webster Groves, Missouri 63119, U.S.A.

CRIME PUBLICATIONS

Novels (series: Fred Carver; Alo Nudger)

The Truth of the Matter. New York, Pocket Books, 1971.
Buyer Beware (Nudger). New York, Putnam, 1976; London, Hale, 1977.
Bonegrinder. New York, Putnam, 1977; London, Hale, 1978.
Lazarus Man. New York, Morrow, 1979; London, New English Library, 1980.
Jericho Man. New York, Morrow, 1980.
The Shadow Man. New York, Morrow, 1981.
Exiled (as Steven Greene), with Steven Greene. New York, Fawcett, 1982.
The Eye, with Bill Pronzini. New York, Mysterious Press, 1984.
Nightlines (Nudger). New York, St. Martin's Press, 1985; London, Macmillan, 1986.
The Right to Sing the Blues (Nudger). New York, St. Martin's Press, 1986.
Tropical Heat (Carver). New York, Holt, and London, Macmillan, 1986.
Ride the Lightning (Nudger). New York, St. Martin's Press, 1987.
Scorcher (Carver). New York, Holt, and London, Macmillan, 1987.
Dancer's Debt (Nudger). New York, St. Martin's Press, 1988.
Shadowtown. New York, Mysterious Press, 1988.
Kiss (Carver). New York, Holt, 1988; London, Macmillan, 1989.
Time Exposure (Nudger). New York, St. Martin's Press, 1989.
Flame (Carver). New York, Holt, 1990.

Short Stories

Better Mousetraps, edited by Francis M. Nevins Jr. New York, St. Martin's Press, 1988.

Uncollected Short Stories

"Quid Pro Quo," in *Ellery Queen's Mystery Magazine* (New York), August 1967.
"Dead, You Know," in *Alfred Hitchcock's Mystery Magazine* (New York), January 1968.
"Death on the Silver Screen," in *Mike Shayne Mystery Magazine* (New York), April 1968.
"The Creator of Spud Moran," in *Alfred Hitchcock's Mystery Magazine* (New York), July 1968.
"Abridged," in *Mike Shayne Mystery Magazine* (New York), October 1968.
"King of the Kennel," in *Mike Shayne Mystery Magazine* (New York), November 1968.
"The Weapon," in *Alfred Hitchcock's Mystery Magazine* (New York), May 1969.
"Thieves' Manor," in *Alfred Hitchcock's Coffin Corner.* New York, Dell, 1969.
"Two by Two," in *Alfred Hitchcock's Mystery Magazine* (New York), November 1970.
"Garden of Dreams," in *Alfred Hitchcock's Mystery Magazine* (New York), June 1971.
"Prospectus on Death," in *Alfred Hitchcock's Mystery Magazine* (New York), July 1971.
"Fair Shake," in *Alfred Hitchcock's This One Will Kill You.* New York, Dell, 1971.

"Murder Malignant," in *Alfred Hitchcock's Mystery Magazine* (New York), August 1971.
"Theft Is My Profession," in *Alfred Hitchcock's Mystery Magazine* (New York), September 1971.
"Case of the Dead Gossip" (as Tom Collins), in *TV Fact*, 26 September–17 October 1971.
"One Way," in *Alfred Hitchcock's I Am Curious Bloody.* New York, Dell, 1971.
"Friendly Hal," in *Alfred Hitchcock's Mystery Magazine* (New York), November 1971.
"The Very Best," in *Alfred Hitchcock's Mystery Magazine* (New York), March 1972.
"Within the Law," in *Alfred Hitchcock's Mystery Magazine* (New York), April 1972.
"Obedience School," in *Alfred Hitchcock's Happy Deathday!* New York, Dell, 1972.
"Living All Alone," in *Alfred Hitchcock's Mystery Magazine* (New York), May 1972.
"A Killer Foiled," in *Mike Shayne Mystery Magazine* (Los Angeles), November 1972.
"So Young, So Fair, So Dead," in *Mike Shayne Mystery Magazine* (Los Angeles), March 1973.
"Shadows Everywhere," in *Alfred Hitchcock's Mystery Magazine* (New York), June 1973.
"Objective Mirror," in *Alfred Hitchcock's Mystery Magazine* (New York), July 1973.
"A Rare Bird," in *Alfred Hitchcock's Let It All Bleed Out.* New York, Dell, 1973.
"The Basement Room," in *Mike Shayne Mystery Magazine* (Los Angeles), October 1973.
"The Lemon Drink Queen," in *Alfred Hitchcock's Mystery Magazine* (New York), February 1974.
"Figure in Flight," in *Charlie Chan Mystery Magazine* (Los Angeles), February 1974.
"Green Death," in *Alfred Hitchcock's Mystery Magazine* (North Palm Beach, Florida), May 1974.
"A Private, Restful Place," in *Mike Shayne Mystery Magazine* (Los Angeles), May 1974.
"A Verdict of Death," in *Charlie Chan Mystery Magazine* (Los Angeles), May 1974.
"Day Shift," in *Mike Shayne Mystery Magazine* (Los Angeles), June 1974.
"The Midnight Train," in *Alfred Hitchcock's Coffin Break.* New York, Dell, 1974.
"A Handgun for Protection," in *Mike Shayne Mystery Magazine* (Los Angeles), September 1974.
"Doom Signal," in *Alfred Hitchcock's Behind the Death Ball.* New York, Dell, 1974.
"Arm of the Law," in *Alfred Hitchcock's Mystery Magazine* (North Palm Beach, Florida), October 1974.
"The Other Side of Reason," in *Mike Shayne Mystery Magazine* (Los Angeles), December 1974.
"The Final Reel," in *Alfred Hitchcock's Bleeding Hearts.* New York, Dell, 1974.
"Rest Assured," in *Mike Shayne Mystery Magazine* (Los Angeles), February 1975.
"It Could Happen to You," in *Alfred Hitchcock's Mystery Magazine* (North Palm Beach, Florida), March 1975.
"Going, Going," in *Executioner* (Los Angeles), April 1975.
"Moon Children" in *87th Precinct* (New York), May 1975.
"The Ledge Walker," in *Executioner* (Los Angeles), June 1975.
"Next to the Woman from Des Moines" (as Paul Shepparton), in *Executioner* (Los Angeles), June 1975.
"The Organization Man" (as Elwin Strange), in *Executioner* (Los Angeles), June 1975.
"Room 33" (as Van McCloud), in *Executioner* (Los Angeles), June 1975.

"Day of Evil" (as John Bennett), in *Executioner* (Los Angeles), June 1975.

"You and the Music," in *Alfred Hitchcock's Mystery Magazine* (North Palm Beach, Florida), June 1975.

"Lease on Life," in *87th Precinct* (New York), June 1975.

"Personalized Copy" (as Elwin Strange), in *87th Precinct* (New York), June 1975.

"The Clarion Call," in *Mike Shayne Mystery Magazine* (Los Angeles), July 1975.

"His Honor the Mayor," in *Executioner* (Los Angeles), August 1975.

"Life Sentence," in *87th Precinct* (New York), August 1975.

"Men with Motives," in *87th Precinct* (New York), August 1975.

"Wonder World," in *Alfred Hitchcock's Mystery Magazine* (New York), January 1976.

"Not Just a Number," in *Mike Shayne Mystery Magazine* (Los Angeles), July 1976.

"Not a Home," in *Alfred Hitchcock's Mystery Magazine* (New York), September 1976.

"The Crooked Picture," in *Tricks and Treats*, edited by Joe Gores and Bill Pronzini.   New York, Doubleday, 1976; as *Mystery Writers Choice*, London Gollancz, 1977.

"Missing Personnel," in *Alfred Hitchcock's Mystery Magazine* (New York), June 1977.

"Explosive Cargo," in *Alfred Hitchcock's Mystery Magazine* (New York), October 1977.

"Death by the Numbers," in *Mike Shayne Mystery Magazine* (Los Angeles), November–December 1977.

"The Man in the Morgue," in *Alfred Hitchcock's Mystery Magazine* (New York), February 1978.

"Where Is, As Is," in *Alfred Hitchcock's Mystery Magazine* (New York), April 1978.

"In by the Tenth," in *Ellery Queen's Mystery Magazine* (New York), May 1978.

"Marked Down," in *Alfred Hitchcock's Mystery Magazine* (New York), July, 1978.

"Cheeseburger" (as John Barry Williams) with Barry N. Malzberg and Bill Pronzini, in *Alfred Hitchcock's Mystery Magazine* (New York), October 1978.

"Have You Ever Seen This Woman?," in *Alfred Hitchcock's Anthology, Spring-Summer*. New York, Davis, 1978.

"Booth 13," in *Dark Sins, Dark Dreams*, edited by Bill Pronzini and Barry N. Malzberg. New York, Doubleday, 1978.

"Past Perfect," in *Alfred Hitchcock's Mystery Magazine* (New York), December 1978.

"Dangerous Game," in *Alfred Hitchcock's Mystery Magazine* (New York), February 1979.

"Where Is Harry Beal?," in *Alfred Hitchcock's Mystery Magazine* (New York), August 1979.

"Franticman," in *Alfred Hitchcock's Mystery Magazine* (New York), October 1979.

"All of a Sudden," in *Alfred Hitchcock's Tales to Make Your Teeth Chatter*, edited by Eleanor Sullivan.   New York, Dial Press, 1980.

"A Glimpse of Evil," in *Alfred Hitchcock's Mystery Magazine* (New York), March 1980.

"That Kind of World," in *Alfred Hitchcock's Mystery Magazine* (New York), July 1980.

"Tough," in *Mike Shayne Mystery Magazine* (Los Angeles), November 1980.

"When Opportunity Knocks," in *Alfred Hitchcock's Mystery Magazine* (New York), December 1980.

"King of the World," in *Alfred Hitchcock's Tales to Make Your Hair Stand on End*, edited by Eleanor Sullivan.   New York, Dial Press, 1981.

"Wriggle," in *Creature!*, edited by Bill Pronzini.   New York, Arbor House, 1981.

"Double Murder," in *Alfred Hitchock's Mystery Magazine* (New York), January 1981.

"The Bear Cottage," in *Mike Shayne Mystery Magazine* (Los Angeles), July 1981.

"Tiger, Tiger," with Bill Pronzini, in *Mystery* (Los Angeles), September 1981.

"The Case of the Canine Accomplice," in *Alfred Hitchcock's Mystery Magazine* (New York), March 1982.

"Time Exposure," in *Alfred Hitchcock's Mystery Magazine* (New York), June 1982.

"What You Don't Know Can Hurt You," in *Alfred Hitchcock's Mystery Magazine* (New York), November 1982.

"The Return of D.B. Cooper," in *Mike Shayne Mystery Magazine* (Los Angeles), December 1982.

"The Right to Sing the Blues," in *Alfred Hitchcock's Mystery Magazine* (New York), May 1983.

"Only One Way to Land," in *Alfred Hitchcock's Mystery Magazine* (New York), October 1983.

"Head over Heart," in *Ellery Queen's Prime Crimes*, edited by Eleanor Sullivan.   New York, Dial Press, 1984.

"Typographical Error," in *The Eyes Have It*, edited by Robert J. Randisi.   New York, Mysterious Press, 1984.

"Split Personalities," in *Mike Shayne Mystery Magazine* (Los Angeles), February 1984.

"Winds of Change," in *Espionage* (Teaneck, New Jersey), December 1984.

"Ride the Lightning," in *Alfred Hitchcock's Mystery Magazine* (New York), January 1985.

"Twice Removed," in *Espionage* (Teaneck, New Jersey), February 1985.

"On Judgement Day," in *Espionage* (Teaneck, New Jersey), August 1985.

"Hector Gomez Provides," in *Mike Shayne Mystery Magazine* (Los Angeles), August 1985.

"Heat," in *Ellery Queen's Mystery Magazine* (New York), September 1985.

"Short Shrift," in *Woman's World* (Englewood, New Jersey), October 1986.

"The Thunder of Guilt," in *Mean Streets*, edited by Robert J. Randisi.   New York, Mysterious Press, 1986.

"The Infernal Machine," in *The New Adventures of Sherlock Holmes*, edited by Martin H. Greenberg and Carol-Lynn Rössel Waugh.   New York, Carroll and Graf, 1987.

"Flotsam and Jetsam," in *The New Black Mask*, edited by Matthew J. Bruccoli and Richard Layman. San Diego, Harcourt Brace, 1987.

"DDS 10752 Libra" with Josh Pachter, in *An Eye for Justice*, edited by Robert J. Randisi.   New York, Mysterious Press, 1987.

"Star Bright," in *Raymond Chandler's Philip Marlowe*, edited by Byron Preiss. New York, Knopf, 1988.

"Sneak Pitch," in *Special Report* (Knoxville, Tennessee), November 1988–January 1989.

"The Live Tree," in *Mistletoe Mysteries*, edited by Charlotte MacLeod.   New York, Mysterious Press, 1989.

OTHER PUBLICATIONS

Other

"Setting for Suspense," in *The Writer* (Boston), July 1974.

"Using Technology in Mysteries," in *The Writer* (Boston), July 1978.

"The Long and the Short of It," in *The Writer* (Boston), December 1987.

*

John Lutz comments:

I hope above all that those reading my work will be compelled to continue reading. Then, if they derive nothing else from what I've written, they will have been entertained. "Entertainment" by my definition can be anything from the diversion of twiddling one's thumbs to the profound illumination of being reached by a classic work of art. I strive for craftsmanship which I hope will occasionally rise to the level of that flash of revelation which many people consider to be art. Mark Twain said, "The difference between the adequate word and the precise word is the difference between the lightning bug and the lightning." Who wants to be a lightning bug?

*   *   *

During John Lutz's first 10 years as a writer he concentrated on short crime stories, selling more than a hundred to *Alfred Hitchcock's Mystery Magazine* and other periodicals. These tales had no series characters and varied widely in quality and content. Some of the best took off from the wildest premises: a lunatic trying to solve a murder in the asylum, the last hours of a tycoon accidentally locked into his walk-in vault by a watchdog, a man who claims he's being hounded by midgets. Several, like "Mail Order" and "Understanding Electricity," combine a strong anti-business viewpoint with imaginative bizarrerie, as if Kafka had come back from the grave to collaborate on fiction with Ralph Nader. Cropping up regularly in Lutz's tales are husbands seeking to dispose of their wives and off-the-wall business organizations, and at times both elements are worked into a single story, like the one about the company that manipulates clients' unwanted spouses into committing adultery. These little gems have become less frequent since Lutz turned to novels, but "Pure Rotten" and "Dear Dorie" and a few others rank among his craziest efforts. His finest short work is collected in *Better Mousetraps*.

That first decade of activity produced only two Lutz novels. *The Truth of the Matter* is an episodic psychological chase ranging across the Midwest, and *Buyer Beware* pits cowardly St. Louis private eye Alo Nudger against a cartel of criminal businessmen. Next came four "breakthrough" books that established Lutz as a contender. The best of the quartet are *Bonegrinder*, an atmosphere-drenched suspense novel about a Bigfoot-like monster terrorizing a small town in the Ozarks, and *Lazarus Man*, a Watergate-era political thriller in which the G. Gordon Liddy figure gets out of prison determined to kill the Nixon figure and his cronies one by one, only to find that they're just as bent on killing him.

The strongest Lutz novels are the latest. In *Nightlines* he revived the St. Louis private eye Nudger and reworked him into one of the most fascinating protagonists in recent detective fiction, a near-total loser plagued by overdue bills, deadbeat clients, and a bloodsucking ex-wife but most of all by his near-paralyzing unaggressiveness and compassion. Nudger shares the world with Charlie Chaplin's tramp: whatever can go wrong for him, will. *Nightlines* and *Ride the Lightning* portray this world in its purest and most devastating form. For those who prefer a more aggressive brand of sleuth, Lutz began a new series set in central Florida and featuring Fred Carver, an ex-cop forced out of the department after being kneecapped by a Latino street punk. This series began with *Tropical Heat* and reached its peak in *Kiss*, one of the most disturbing and downbeat PI novels in the genre and certainly Lutz's best book yet.

—Francis M. Nevins, Jr.

———

LYALL, Gavin (Tudor). British. Born in Birmingham, Warwickshire, 9 May 1932. Educated at King Edward VI School, Birmingham, 1943–51; Pembroke College, Cambridge, 1953–56, B.A. (honours) in English 1956. Served as a Pilot Officer in the Royal Air Force, 1951–53. Married the writer Katharine Whitehorn in 1958; two sons. Reporter, *Picture Post*, London, 1956–57; film director, BBC Television, London, 1958–59; reporter and air correspondent, *Sunday Times*, London, 1959–62. Chairman, Crime Writers Association, 1967–68. Recipient: Crime Writers Association Silver Dagger award, 1964, 1965. Agent: Peters Fraser and Dunlop, 5th Floor, The Chambers, Chelsea Harbour, Lots Road, London SW10 0XF. Address: 14 Provost Road, London NW3 4ST, England.

CRIME PUBLICATIONS

Novels (series: Harry Maxim)

The Wrong Side of the Sky. London, Hodder and Stoughton, and New York, Scribner, 1961.
The Most Dangerous Game. New York, Scribner, 1963; London, Hodder and Stoughton, 1964.
Midnight Plus One. London, Hodder and Stoughton, and New York, Scribner, 1965.
Shooting Script. London, Hodder and Stoughton, and New York, Scribner, 1966.
Venus with Pistol. London, Hodder and Stoughton, and New York, Scribner, 1969.
Blame the Dead. London, Hodder and Stoughton, 1972; New York, Viking Press, 1973.
Judas Country. London, Hodder and Stoughton, and New York, Viking Press, 1975.
The Secret Servant (Maxim). London, Hodder and Stoughton, and New York, Viking Press, 1980.
The Conduct of Major Maxim. London, Hodder and Stoughton, 1982; New York, Viking Press, 1983.
The Crocus List (Maxim). London, Hodder and Stoughton, 1985; New York, Viking, 1986.
Uncle Target (Maxim). London, Hodder and Stoughton, and New York, Viking, 1988.

OTHER PUBLICATIONS

Play

Screenplay: *Moon Zero Two*, with Frank Hardman and Martin Davison, 1969.

Other

Operation Warboard (rules for war games), with Bernard Lyall. London, A. and C. Black, and New York, McKay, 1976.

Editor, *The War in the Air 1939–1945: An Anthology of Personal Experiences*. London, Hutchinson, 1968; New York, Morrow, 1969.

*

Gavin Lyall comments:

I dislike analysing my own books for a purely practical reason: if I identify a trend or common denominator, I subconsciously turn it into an unbreakable rule. Trying to sort out a plot, I once discarded an idea because "You can't do that in a Gavin Lyall book"—then realised with horror that I was type-casting myself. It was probably this sort of feeling that made me change direction somewhat in the late 1970's, although coincidence helped. Somebody asked me to create "a thriller set in Whitehall" for TV. Researching the background, I found that I was already interested in the wheels-within-wheels of government and that a number of my friends had grown not just older but more important. I did the work, redid it, didn't get paid, and ended up with files of material and a handful of characters already better developed than they would ever have been if I had intended them for a book. The Maxim books started from there. I had a lot of trouble finding a "voice" (the word "style" seems a bit pompous in thrillers) in the third person, since it turned out to involve rather more than fighting the temptation to lecture in purple prose. I needed more flexibility in the story and more background detail: writing from God's-eye view, one must assume that He would recognise a Chippendale chair and a Balliol tie whereas a gunrunning pilot might well not. The compensations, however, of both the third person and using characters which continue from book to book (something I am glad I avoided until I had a bit of experience) are many. The biggest is the greater freedom to explore a wider range of characters, and let them develop more slowly: I can put off a development until the next book if I feel like it. I am frankly enjoying myself, although I don't seem to have speeded up much.

*   *   *

The Buchan tradition of thriller writing involves taking dissimilar characters and unlikely situations and then linking them together in a convincing manner. Gavin Lyall's literate novels appear to be firmly within this tradition. He can make the improbable appear not only believable, but inevitable.

Until recently, there are no recurring characters in his novels, but his heroes bear a strong resemblance to one another. They walk a shadowy path between both sides of the law and often need to make moral decisions to attain their objectives. His best stories tell of clear-cut desperate situations in which his hero has to reach a goal while the reader decides who can be trusted among the other characters. The relationships between characters are often as important to the story as the plot itself. Lyall works with traditions, not clichés. His first-person viewpoint allows humor to lighten the grim path of high adventure. His heroes may adopt the flip Chandler style, but they don't overdo it. Like their creator they have a knowledge of guns and many of them are pilots. The research behind each novel is integrated into the plot and not set out as undigested fact.

In *The Wrong Side of the Sky*, Jack Clay is flying cargoes from Athens to the Libyan desert to Tripoli when he meets a wartime buddy, his sometime girlfriend, the Nawab of Tungabhadra, and several millions in stolen jewels. Integral to plot and to his moral decisions is the friendship between Clay and Ken Kitson who fly opposite sides of the sky. Northern Finland is the setting for *The Most Dangerous Game* in which freelance pilot Bill Cary meets an American hunter and learns for himself what it feels like to be tracked for murder. High marks have to be given *Midnight Plus One* with its race against time by Lewis Cane to deliver a millionaire to Liechtenstein. The journey by Rolls-Royce is a slice of Dornford Yates, but the grim duel between gunmen is authentic Lyall. Keith Carr flies a camera plane for a film company on location in the Caribbean in *Shooting Script*. Murder tears the fabric of the world Lyall weaves, and there is some insight into the risk of running someone else's war like a Hollywood western. Art smuggling is the situation in *Venus with Pistol* as Bert Kemp leaves his antique gun shop in London to play the professional among amateurs who want to build an art collection the fast way. In *Blame the Dead*, bodyguard James Card, searching for the killer of a man he just met, follows a vengeance trail from Arras to Norway, and in *Judas Country*, the pilot Roy Case becomes involved in smuggling, blackmail, espionage, and murder in the Middle East.

With the creation of Harry Maxim, a special services major assigned to 10 Downing Street, Lyall joined the series character tradition. While *The Secret Servant* and *The Conduct of Major Maxim* lean toward the le Carré school, there is a lighter touch at work. Suicides and defectors, guilty secrets and the old school tie: these are serious situations with believable and complex characters and a blessed absence of clichés.

Though the plots of these books build slowly, by the time the first bullet thuds home the reader knows the characters well enough to recognize them and, more importantly, to care about their fate on the downward plunge.

—J. Randolph Cox

———

LYNDS, Dennis. *See* **COLLINS, Michael.**

———

LYONS, Arthur. American. Born in Los Angeles, California, 5 January 1946. Educated at the University of California, Santa Barbara, B.A. in political science 1967. Since 1967 owner of a gift shop and restaurant, Palm Springs, California. Address: c/o Holt Rinehart and Winston, 521 Fifth Avenue, New York, New York 10175, U.S.A.

CRIME PUBLICATIONS

Novels (series: Jacob Asch in all books)

The Dead Are Discreet. New York, Mason and Lipscomb, 1974; London, Robson, 1977.
All God's Children. New York, Mason Charter, 1975; London, Robson, 1977.
The Killing Floor. New York, Mason Charter, 1976; London, Hale, 1983.
Dead Ringer. New York, Mason Charter, 1977; London, Hale, 1983.
Castles Burning New York, Holt Rinehart, 1980; London, Hale, 1983.
Hard Trade. New York, Holt Rinehart, 1982; London, Hale, 1984.
At the Hands of Another. New York, Holt Rinehart, 1983.
Three with a Bullet. New York, Holt Rinehart, 1985; London, Macmillan, 1987.
Fast Fade. New York, Mysterious Press, 1987.
Unnatural Causes, with Thomas T. Noguchi. New York, Putnam, 1988.
Other People's Money. New York, Mysterious Press, 1989; London, Macmillan, 1990.

OTHER PUBLICATIONS

Other

The Second Coming: Satanism in America. New York, Dodd Mead, 1970; as *Satan Wants You: The Cult of Devil Worship*, London, Hart Davis, 1971; as *Satan Wants You: The Cult of Devil Worship in America;* New York, Mysterious Press, 1988.
Physical Evidence, with Thomas T. Noguchi. New York, Putnam, 1990.

* * *

Although each of his 10 novels about private detective Jacob Asch remains well within the Hammett-Chandler-Macdonald tradition, Arthur Lyons has consistently striven for variety in his series. Based in Los Angeles, Asch frequently travels to other Southern California urban wastelands, ranging from Vernon with its stinking slaughterhouses to Palm Springs with its sanctuaries for the super-rich. As the locale changes, so does the social level, profession, and basic concerns of the people Asch encounters. For example, *All God's Children* focuses on both a Jesus-flaunting religious group and a morality-flouting motorcycle gang; *Dead Ringer* on pimps, prostitutes, and pugilists; *Castles Burning* on boyish artists, immature businessmen and over-ripe rebellious youths; and *At the Hands of Another* on lawyers, doctors, and manufacturers of inflated rubber sex dolls. As this list implies, Lyons comments on a wide range of social issues, including religious fanaticism, legalized prostitution, pornographic art, exploitation of minorities and the homeless, sadism, masochism, abortion, drug abuse, punk rock stage violence, and political wheeling and dealing. Throughout, he is seeking a dynamic, flexible, and complex conception of integrity that avoids both an excessive concern with purity and a surrender to corruption.

Lyons also achieves variety by highlighting different aspects of Asch's background and personality in different books. *The Dead Are Discreet* emphasizes Asch's past as a newspaperman fired for choosing to go to jail rather than reveal his source for a story. This obviously establishes his integrity, courage, and concern for others. However, in *Dead Ringer* he almost abandons a case because he has been framed for drunken driving and can't bear to spend more time in jail. Moreover, *All God's Children* reveals his capacity for nearly berserk behavior when he knocks an offensive motocycle punk onto the hood of his car and carries him there at top speed until he nearly falls off. His religious attitudes emerge in *The Killing Floor* when a Jewish accountant asks him to find a missing Jewish slaughterhouse owner. Asch notes then that his father was Jewish, his mother Episcopalian, and that his "own Jewishness was a loose, distorted tangle of feelings" since he felt "a strong cultural bond to Judaism, but the faith part of it had never really taken hold." His flexible morality perhaps comes most to the fore in *Three with a Bullet* when, after uncovering his employer's involvement in a record scam, he offers to keep silent if the man will take a lie detector test to establish his innocence in the murder Asch is investigating for him. As Asch explains, "I've taken money from people who have done a hell of a lot worse things than counterfeiting records, and taken it gladly. But the idea of working for a murderer would upset my sensibilities, not to mention make me an accessory."

Several books mention Asch's divorce and explore his temporary relationships with women, the most interesting of which occurs in *At the Hands of Another* when he meets a former lover for whom he had arranged an abortion because he was afraid to try another marriage. The resolution of this affair hangs in doubt until the end and provides as much suspense as the mystery. Suspense of another sort occurs in *Fast Fade* when Asch, as part of his investigation, breaks into the apartment of an actress with whom he has been having an affair, and discovers her medicine for herpes. He naturally worries about getting it himself and wonders whether to ask her about the medicine, revealing his invasion of her privacy, or simply to break off the affair without explanation.

Although Asch began as an imitation of Philip Marlowe, he has grown in individuality and complexity and the series has gained a lot from this. Moreover, the later books, particularly *Castles Burning, Hard Trade*, and *Other People's Money*, are not only superior in characterization but also in style and theme. Lyons's work has always been competent, readable, and well-researched (his first novel, *The Dead Are Discreet*, drew on his non-fiction book on Satanism, and his later novels show the same underpinning of fact), but at first he offered little new in form or content. *Castles Burning*, however, is an intriguing character study with a devastating commentary on the distortion in values in today's society; *Hard Trade* is the best political study in detective fiction since Hammett's *The Glass Key;* and *Three with a Bullet*, though telegraphing the killer's identity, offers a gritty, complex and even at times ambiguous picture of both music business morality and Asch's own professional ethics. Moreover, *At the Hands of Another and Other People's Money* demonstrate Lyons's highly sophisticated appreciation of the genre (and particularly of Hammett's seminal role in shaping it) and his ability to create new characters and plots that consciously echo and comment on those of classic works but with enough differences from them to keep knowledgeable readers off-balance. The former is a witty, suspenseful, and very effective mixture of classic and hard-boiled detective fiction with an elaborate set of references to both and with Asch and his former lover consciously enacting the roles of Nick and Nora Charles in *The Thin Man*, and the latter is a continuously fascinating tribute to *The Maltese Falcon* with a plot involving untrustworthy clients, the disappearance and possible killing of a fellow detective, numerous double and triple crosses, an art treasure that may or may not be real, and a final confrontation with a betraying woman yet somehow it is all made new and rivetingly suspenseful. Paradoxically, with *Other People's Money* and another writer's mysteries, Lyons has become a master in his own right—and a model for others.

Lyons's one detective novel outside the Asch series, *Unnatural Causes*, is a collaboration with the famous chief medical examiner of Los Angeles County, Thomas Noguchi, and, as with any collaboration, it is hard to be certain what Lyons contributed to it. The central figure, not surprisingly, is a coroner and the book abounds in authentic medical examinations of bodies as well as seemingly realistic descriptions of political intrigues surrounding the coroner's office, but the detective's character, his mixture of professional competence, flexible but not throwaway ethics, and problems with women all seem reminiscent of Jacob Asch. Also, the picture of Hollywood life (or insecure half-life), while probably containing some coded inside information by Noguchi who investigated the deaths of Marilyn Monroe, John Belushi, Robert Kennedy and others, is not radically different from the picture of this life in *Fast Fade*. The novel is, in any case, a welcome addition to the works of both Lyons and Noguchi, and well worth reading for its own sake.

—Steven R. Carter

M

MacALISTER, Ian. *See* ALBERT, Marvin.

———

MacDONALD, John D(ann). American. Born in Sharon, Pennsylvania, 24 July 1916. Educated at the University of Pennsylvania, Philadelphia, 1934–35; Syracuse University, New York, B.S. 1938; Harvard University, Cambridge, Massachusetts, M.B.A. 1939. Served with the United States Army, Office of Strategic Services, 1940–46: Lieutenant Colonel. Married Dorothy Mary Prentiss in 1937; one son. Writer in several genres and under a number of pseudonyms for the pulps and other magazines. President, Mystery Writers of America, 1962. Recipient: Benjamin Franklin award, for short story, 1955; Grand Prix de Littérature Policière, 1964; Mystery Writers of America Grand Master award, 1972; American Book award, 1980. D.H.L.: Hobart and William Smith Colleges, Geneva, New York, 1978; University of South Florida, Tampa, 1980. *Died 28 December 1986.*

CRIME PUBLICATIONS

Novels (series: Travis McGee)

The Brass Cupcake. New York, Fawcett, 1950; London, Muller, 1955.
Judge Me Not. New York, Fawcett, 1951; London, Muller, 1964.
Murder for the Bride. New York, Fawcett, 1951; London, Fawcett, 1954.
Weep for Me. New York, Fawcett, 1951; London, Muller, 1964.
The Damned. New York, Fawcett, 1952; London, Muller, 1964.
Dead Low Tide. New York, Fawcett, 1953; London, Fawcett, 1955.
The Neon Jungle. New York, Fawcett, 1953; London, Fawcett, 1954.
All These Condemned. New York, Fawcett, 1954.
Area of Suspicion. New York, Dell, 1954; London, Hale, 1956; revised edition, New York, Fawcett, 1961.
A Bullet for Cinderella. New York, Dell, 1955; London, Hale, 1960; as *On the Make*, New York, Dell, 1960.
Cry Hard, Cry Fast. New York, Popular Library, 1955; London, Hale, 1969.
April Evil. New York, Dell, 1956; London, Hale, 1957.
Border Town Girl (novelets). New York, Popular Library, 1956; as *Five Star Fugitive*, London, Hale, 1970.
Murder in the Wind. New York, Dell, 1956; as *Hurricane*, London, Hale, 1957.
You Live Once. New York, Popular Library, 1956; London, Hale, 1976; as *You Kill Me*, New York, Fawcett, 1961.
Death Trap. New York, Dell, 1957; London, Hale, 1958.
The Empty Trap. New York, Popular Library, 1957; London, Magnum, 1980.

The Price of Murder. New York, Dell, 1957; London, Hale, 1958.
A Man of Affairs. New York, Dell, 1957; London, Hale, 1959.
Clemmie. New York, Fawcett, 1958.
The Executioners. New York, Simon and Schuster, 1958; London, Hale, 1959; as *Cape Fear*, New York, Fawcett, 1962.
Soft Touch. New York, Dell, 1958; London, Hale, 1960; as *Man-Trap*, London, Pan, 1961.
The Deceivers. New York, Dell, 1958; London, Hale, 1968.
The Beach Girls. New York, Fawcett, 1959; London, Muller, 1964.
The Crossroads. New York, Simon and Schuster, 1959; London, Hale, 1961.
Deadly Welcome. New York, Dell, 1959; London, Hale, 1961.
The End of the Night. New York, Simon and Schuster, 1960; London, Hale, 1964.
The Only Girl in the Game. New York, Fawcett, 1960; London, Hale, 1962.
Slam the Big Door. New York, Fawcett, 1960; London, Hale, 1961.
One Monday We Killed Them All. New York, Fawcett, 1961; London, Hale, 1963.
Where Is Janice Gantry? New York, Fawcett, 1961; London, Hale, 1963.
A Flash of Green. New York, Simon and Schuster, 1962; London, Hale, 1971.
The Girl, The Gold Watch, and Everything. New York, Fawcett, 1962; London, Hodder and Stoughton, 1968.
A Key to the Suite. New York, Fawcett, 1962; London, Hale, 1968.
The Drowner. New York, Fawcett, 1963; London, Hale, 1964.
On the Run. New York, Fawcett, 1963; London, Hale, 1965.
The Deep Blue Goodby (McGee). New York, Fawcett, 1964; London, Hale, 1965.
Nightmare in Pink (McGee). New York, Fawcett, 1964; London, Hale, 1966.
A Purple Place for Dying (McGee). New York, Fawcett, 1964; London, Hale, 1966.
The Quick Red Fox (McGee). New York, Fawcett, 1964; London, Hale, 1966.
A Deadly Shade of Gold (McGee). New York, Fawcett, 1965; London, Hale, 1967.
Bright Orange for the Shroud (McGee). New York, Fawcett, 1965; London, Hale, 1967.
Darker Than Amber (McGee). New York, Fawcett, 1966; London, Hale, 1968.
One Fearful Yellow Eye (McGee). New York, Fawcett, 1966; London, Hale, 1968.
The Last One Left. New York, Doubleday, 1967; London, Hale, 1968.
Three for McGee (omnibus). New York, Doubleday, 1967.
Pale Gray for Guilt (McGee). New York, Fawcett, 1968; London, Hale, 1969.
The Girl in the Plain Brown Wrapper (McGee). New York, Fawcett, 1968; London, Hale, 1969.

Dress Her in Indigo (McGee). New York, Fawcett, 1969; London, Hale, 1971.
The Long Lavender Look (McGee). New York, Fawcett, and London, Fawcett, 1970.
A Tan and Sandy Silence (McGee). New York, Fawcett, 1972; London, Hale, 1973.
The Scarlet Ruse (McGee). New York, Fawcett, 1973; London, Hale, 1975.
The Turquoise Lament (McGee). Philadelphia, Lippincott, 1973; London, Hale, 1975.
McGee (omnibus). London, Hale, 1975.
The Dreadful Lemon Sky (McGee). Philadelphia, Lippincott, 1975; London, Hale, 1976.
The Empty Copper Sea (McGee). Philadelphia, Lippincott, 1978; London, Hale, 1979.
The Green Ripper (McGee). Philadelphia, Lippincott, 1979; London, Hale, 1980.
Free Fall in Crimson (McGee). New York, Harper, and London, Collins, 1981.
Cinnamon Skin (McGee). New York, Harper, and London, Collins, 1982.
One More Sunday. New York, Knopf, and London, Hodder and Stoughton, 1984.
The Lonely Silver Rain (McGee). New York, Knopf, and London, Macdonald, 1985.
Barrier Island. New York, Knopf, 1986; London, Hodder and Stoughton, 1987.

Short Stories

End of the Tiger and Other Stories. New York, Fawcett, 1966; London, Hale, 1967.
Seven. New York, Fawcett, 1971; London, Hale, 1974.
The Good Old Stuff: 13 Early Stories, edited by Martin H. Greenberg and others. New York, Harper, 1982; London, Collins, 1984.

Uncollected Short Stories

"Double Hannenframmis," in *Just My Luck*. Chicago, Playboy Press, 1976.
"He Was Always a Nice Boy," in *Ellery Queen's Giants of Mystery*. New York, Davis, 1976.
"Wedding Present," in *Antaeus* (New York), Spring–Summer 1977.
"Blurred View," in *A Special Kind of Crime*, edited by Lawrence Treat. New York, Doubleday, 1982.

OTHER PUBLICATIONS

Novels

Wine of the Dreamers. New York, Greenberg, 1951; as *Planet of the Dreamers*, New York, Pocket Books, 1953; London, Hale, 1955.
Ballroom of the Skies. New York, Greenberg, 1952.
Cancel All Our Vows. New York, Appleton Century Crofts, 1953; London, Hale, 1955.
Contrary Pleasure. New York, Appleton Century Crofts, 1954; London, Hale, 1955.
Please Write for Details. New York, Simon and Schuster, 1959.
I Could Go On Singing (novelization of screenplay). New York, Fawcett, 1963; London, Hale, 1964.

Condominium. Philadelphia, Lippincott, and London, Hale, 1977.

Short Stories

Other Times, Other Worlds. New York, Fawcett, 1978.

Other

The House Guests. New York, Doubleday, 1965; London, Hale, 1966.
No Deadly Drug. New York, Doubleday, 1968.
Nothing Can Go Wrong, with John H. Kilpack. New York, Harper, 1981.
A Friendship: The Letters of Dan Roawan and John D. MacDonald 1967–74. New York, Knopf, 1986.
Reading for Survival. Washington, D.C., Library of Congress, 1987.

Editor, *The Lethal Sex*. New York, Dell, 1959; London, Collins, 1962.

*

Bibliography: *A Bibliography of the Published Works of John D. MacDonald* by Jean and Walter Shine, Gainesville, University of Florida Libraries, 1981.

Manuscript Collection: University of Florida Library, Gainesville.

Critical Study: *John D. MacDonald* by David Geherin, New York, Ungar, 1982.

* * *

For more than 35 years, John D. MacDonald wrote 69 novels published as paperback originals. Like *Condominium*, about corporations grabbing land in Florida, or *One More Sunday*, about an evangelical church raising funds through television and computers, many of the paperback originals deal with corporate swindles and involve greed and violence. Other novels concentrate on the corruptions of local politics or, like *Cancel All Our Vows*, on the fragility and irresponsibility of suburban marriages. MacDonald is, however, best known for the series of novels begun in 1964 with *The Deep Blue Goodby*, all with colors in the title and told through the persona of Travis McGee. Some of the non-McGee novels, like *The Only Girl in the Game*, about an innocent girl blackmailed into working for a criminal syndicate operating a Las Vegas hotel and finally killed, or *Please Write for Details*, about a collection of stray Americans drawn by advertising to a semi-spurious summer art course in Cuernavaca, are too full of stereotypes, outraged innocence, banal writing, and generalized protests against "system". The figure of McGee, however, is sufficiently attractive and complex to hold together pointed commentary on contemporary America, an articulate moral perspective, and a sense of experience. Handsome, strong, a former minor professional football player, six feet four, and omnicompetent, McGee lives independently on his secure and comfortable boat, the *Busted Flush*, which he won by bluffing in a poker game, moored at Bahia Mar in Fort Lauderdale, and, when he needs a car, drives his 1936 Rolls Royce that has been converted into a pick-up truck. He earns the funds to sustain his "retirement" through what he frequently describes as "salvage operations." MacDonald himself, in a 1984 television interview, called him a "tattered knight on a spavined steed." Typically, McGee is drawn into a situation through some obligation from his past, learning that a wife or daughter of some old close friend, now dead, or some helplessly virtuous traditional figure is being destroyed by a corrupt force. He pursues these legacies with fervor, and total involvement, relying on his physical strength, his intelligence, and, sometimes, his contacts with those in authority who owe him favors. McGee's "salvage" is emotional as well as protective and financial, for he frequently restores his female legacies by taking them, alone, for long cruises in the *Busted Flush*. He is the skillful contemporary knight-errant, as well as the therapist building strong individual virtues to survive the corporate corruptions of the modern world.

Inserted essays often underline McGee's moral attitudes. The ecological dangers of industrial pollution, forwarded by corporations interested only in making money, are frequently both the subject of essays and the themes of individual novels. McGee sees the once paradisical Florida world of birds and marshes destroyed by a surplus population, becoming "flashy and cheap, tacky and noisy," gradually paved over by asphalt and suffused with violence. The "locust population" of large cities is drifting down to Florida in "these last remaining years of choice." Dedicated to order, care, and cleanliness on his own boat (a sloppy or ill-kept boat indicates an emotionally irresponsible owner), McGee objects to commercial packaging, "manufactured air" (although he will occasionally use his air-conditioning in the tropical Florida summers), the surfeit of information available through computers, the university circuit supported by federal grants, the proliferation of government-supported boards and agencies that employ most of the people in decaying areas like upstate New York, and most forms of "system" and social organization. In all the novels, MacDonald also forcefully and effectively satirizes the drug culture, the motorbike culture, all forms of conspicuous consumption, hunting and hand-guns, sex without emotion, and attempts to alter human consciousness. In the novels of the 1960's like *One Fearful Yellow Eye*, the evil in the modern world is likely to be connected to social and external causes, to the racist southern culture, a Nazi past, or the requirements, deprivations, and dislocations of World War II; in the more recent novels, the origin of corruption is more likely to be seen in individual psychological terms or in a generalized sense of human evil that overwhelms its cause. Sometimes McGee enjoys particular forms of corruption. In *Pale Gray for Guilt* he and friend Meyer (the brilliant, hairy, chess-playing retired economist who is often his sidekick) cleverly float a large and false stock issue which enables them, simultaneously, to gain a considerable sum themselves, help the widow of their murdered friend, and trap the corporate criminals. All the novels are knowledgeable and interesting about process, about the way the stock market works, about the processes of tattooing, sending up a flotilla of hot air ballons, and making pornographic films in *Free Fall in Crimson*, about how to trace a person through business transaction in *The Empty Copper Sea*, and about how to escape the ocean's undertow or to arrange for elegant call girls in a large city. McGee is far from a primitive moralist, or the voice of outrage that mars some of the pre-McGee novels. He is knowledgeable about travel, food and drink, women, and literature. He can quote, appropriately, Rilke and the Second Law of Thermodynamics as well as Sinclair Lewis; he derides the machismo of Hemingway, General Patton, and Mickey Spillane, yet also satirizes the irrelevance of the "snail darter, the Snow goose, and the ACLU." In *Cinnamon Skin*, Meyer's disastrously exploded boat, the *John Maynard Keynes*, is eventually replaced by the *Thorstein Veblen*.

The supreme sexual stud on the surface, McGee nevertheless has a code of sexual behavior carefully worked out. He will never touch a friend's woman, no matter how closely he helps her. On his therapeutics cruises, he often waits weeks or months, until the woman is healthy, active, and able to talk out her recent trauma, before he makes love to her. McGee's sexuality is a relationship, an appreciation of women, a respect for old-fashioned "sexual mystery," a human and restorative force, never a simple or mechanical exercise. He also humanizes the stereotyped figure of the hard-boiled detective in ways other than sexual, for he calls the human brain a "random computer," talks of pieces that do not fit the puzzle at all, and satirizes those fables in which the detective displays extraordinary feats of either deduction or physical bravery.

The world around McGee is violent as well as corrupt. He confronts the evil with skill, knowledge, and integrity, MacDonald creating him with a terse, biting, yet sometimes metaphorical, sensitive, and humorous prose (a dishonest middle-aged lawyer calls the boat, on which he tries to swing with the younger generation, the *Strawberry Tort*). In some of the earlier novels of the series, McGee is more simply the defender of past American values, loyal to war buddies, seeing the corporation as alien, the criminal as escaped Nazi or racist. Starting in the 1970's, however, in novels like *A Tan and Sandy Silence*, *The Turquoise Lament*, and *Free Fall in Crimson*, McGee recognizes that he himself has the capacity to kill unjustifiably, can sometimes enjoy violence, and can experience greed and indifference to others. The sense of evil is more complicated, some of it more likely to be internalized as McGee becomes more self-questioning and complex, even more vulnerable. Although always finally loyal to his principles and his sensitivity, McGee gradually, through the novels, sees his world and himself in less stridently moralistic terms. In the earlier novels McGee's status as perfect lover is also never likely to be questioned, as in the conventional plot he sends the girls away after the restorative cruise, preserving his sexual independence (in one early novel, *Pale Gray for Guilt*, the girl does leave McGee but only because she is bravely dying of a rare disease). In more recent novels, like *The Turquoise Lament* and *Cinnamon Skin*, grateful legacies, after the therapy, initiate leaving McGee for other jobs or other men, recognizing that gratitude, allegiance to the past, and strong attraction are not the same as love or self-definition. Later novels, too, focus more on Meyer, no longer just the highly knowledgeable sidekick, for he, with McGee's help, must wrestle with his shame at his own cowardice in *Free Fall in Crimson*, finally redeemed in *Cinnamon Skin*. As McGee, gradually aging and becoming more sensitive, recognizes, "salvage" operations are necessary not only for sexually attractive victims, but for discerning friends and for the self as well.

—James Gindin

———

MACDONALD, John Ross. *See* **MACDONALD, Ross.**

———

MacDONALD, Philip. Also wrote as Oliver Fleming; Anthony Lawless; Martin Porlock. British. Born in London, 5 November 1899; grandson of the writer George MacDonald. Served in a cavalry regiment in Mesopotamia during World War I. Married the writer F. Ruth Howard. After World War I, trained horses for the army, and was a show jumper; moved to

Hollywood in 1931 and worked as a scriptwriter and Great Dane breeder. Recipient: Mystery Writers of America Edgar Allan Poe award, 1953, 1956. *Died 10 December 1981.*

CRIME PUBLICATIONS

Novels (series: Colonel Anthony Ruthven Gethryn)

Ambrotox and Limping Dick (as Oliver Fleming), with Ronald MacDonald.   London, Ward Lock, 1920.
The Spandau Quid (as Oliver Fleming), with Ronald MacDonald.   London, Palmer, 1923.
The Rasp (Gethryn).   London, Collins, 1924; New York, Dial Press, 1925.
The White Crow (Gethryn).   New York, Dial Press, and London, Collins, 1928.
The Link (Gethryn).   London, Collins, and New York, Doubleday, 1930.
The Noose (Gethryn).   London, Collins, and New York, Dial Press, 1930.
Rynox.   London, Collins, 1930; as *The Rynox Murder Mystery*, New York, Doubleday, 1931; as *The Rynox Mystery*, Collins, 1933; as *The Rynox Murder*, New York, Avon, 1965.
The Choice (Gethryn).   London, Collins, 1931; as *The Polferry Riddle*, New York, Doubleday, 1931; as *The Polferry Mystery*, Collins, 1932.
Harbour (as Anthony Lawless).   London, Collins, and New York, Doubleday, 1931.
Persons Unknown (Gethryn).   New York, Doubleday, 1931; as *The Maze*, London, Collins, and New York, 1932.
Murder Gone Mad.   London, Collins, and New York, Doubleday, 1931.
The Wraith (Gethryn).   London, Collins, and New York, Doubleday, 1931.
The Crime Conductor (Gethryn).   New York, Doubleday, 1931; London, Collins, 1932.
Rope to Spare (Gethryn).   London, Collins, and New York, Doubleday, 1932.
Death on My Left.   London, Collins, and New York, Doubleday, 1933.
R.I.P.   London, Collins, 1933; as *Menace*, New York, Doubleday 1933.
The Nursemaid Who Disappeared (Gethryn).   London, Collins, 1938; as *Warrant for X*, New York, Doubleday, 1938.
The Dark Wheel, with A. Boyd Correll.   London, Collins, and New York, Morrow, 1948; as *Sweet and Deadly*, Rockville Centre, New York, Zenith, 1959.
Guest in the House.   New York, Doubleday, 1955; London, Jenkins, 1956; as *No Time for Terror*, New York, Spivak, 1956.
The List of Adrian Messenger (Gethryn).   New York, Doubleday, 1959; London, Jenkins, 1960.

Novels as Martin Porlock (published as Philip MacDonald in U.S.)

Mystery at Friar's Pardon.   London, Collins, 1931; New York, Doubleday, 1932.
Mystery in Kensington Gore.   London, Collins, 1932; as *Escape*, New York, Doubleday, 1932.
X v. Rex.   London, Collins, 1933; as *Mystery of the Dead Police*, New York, Doubleday, 1933; as *The Mystery of Mr. X*, London, Literary Press, 1934.

Short Stories

Something to Hide.   New York, Doubleday, 1952; as *Fingers of Fear and Other Stories*, London, Collins, 1953.
The Man Out of the Rain and Other Stories.   New York, Doubleday, 1955; London, Jenkins, 1957.
Death and Chicanery.   New York, Doubleday, 1962; London, Jenkins, 1963.

Uncollected Short Story

"The Star of Starz," in *Ellery Queen's Murdercade.*   New York, Random House, 1975; London, Gollancz, 1976.

OTHER PUBLICATIONS

Novels

Gentleman Bill: A Boxing Story.   London, Jenkins, 1922.
Queen's Mate.   London, Collins, 1926; New York, Dial Press, 1927.
Patrol.   London, Collins, and New York, Harper, 1927; as *The Last Patrol*, London, Novel Library, 1934.
Likeness of Exe.   London, Collins, 1929.
Moonfisher.   London, Gollancz, 1931; (as Anthony Lawless), New York, Doubleday, 1932.

Plays

Rebecca, with others, in *Twenty Best Film Plays*, edited by John Gassner and Dudley Nichols.   New York, Crown, 1943.

Screenplays: *The Star Reporter*, with Ralph Smart, 1931; *Rynox* (from his own novel), with Jerome Jackson and Michael Powell, 1931; *The Rasp* (from his own novel), 1931; *Hotel Splendide*, with Ralph Smart, 1932; *C.O.D.*, with Ralph Smart, 1932; *Charlie Chan in London*, 1934; *Charlie Chan in Paris*, with Edward T. Lowe and Stuart Anthony, 1935; *The Last Outpost*, 1935; *The Mystery Woman*, 1935; *Yours for the Asking*, with others, 1936; *Ourselves (River of Unrest)*, with others, 1936; *The Princess Comes Across*, with others, 1936; *The Mysterious Mr. Moto*, with Norman Foster, 1938; *Mr. Moto's Last Warning*, with Norman Foster, 1938; *Mr. Moto Takes a Vacation*, with Norman Foster, 1938; *Blind Alley*, with Michael Blankfort and Albert Duffy, 1939; *Charlie McCarthy, Detective*, with others, 1939; *Rebecca*, with others, 1940; *Whispering Ghosts*, with Lou Breslow, 1942; *Street of Chance*, with Garrett Fort, 1942; *Sahara*, with others, 1943; *Action in Arabia*, with Herbert Biberman, 1944; *The Body Snatcher*, with Carlos Keith, 1945; *Strangers in the Night*, with Bryant Ford and Paul Gangelin, 1945; *Dangerous Intruder*, with Martin Goldsmith and F. Ruth Howard, 1945; *Love from a Stranger*, 1947; *The Dark Past*, with others, 1949; *The Man Who Cheated Himself*, with Seton I. Miller, 1951; *Mask of the Avenger*, with others, 1951; *Circle of Danger*, 1951; *Ring of Fear*, with Paul Fix and James Edward Grant, 1954; *Tobor the Great*, with Richard Goldstone and Carl Dudley, 1954.

Radio Play: *Glitter*, 1978.

Television Plays: *Thin Ice* (Five Fingers series), 1959–60; *The Impulse* (Thriller series), 1960–61.

*   *   *

The works of Philip MacDonald appear to have fallen into obscurity to some extent, which is a great pity. He could demonstrate with ease the classic features of detective fiction, sometimes adding touches of the macabre, while on other occasions injecting passages little short of farce. His writing had a typically English flavour, although he moved to the United States comparatively early in his life and embarked on a script-writing career in Hollywood.

His first detective novel, *The Rasp*, introduced a series character who was to become an important part of the genre's Golden Age—Colonel Anthony Ruthven Gethryn, very much the attractive and stiff-upper-lipped hero but one who, for a change, does not resort to violence or unnecessary dramatics. *The Rasp* uses the well-worn theme of an eminent body in the study of a country residence, but MacDonald handled his situation rather better than most. By a process of logical deduction, carried out while he was acting as father-confessor to more than one lady in distress, Gethryn arrives at the solution to a seemingly impossible problem. MacDonald adds his own special touches of humour, with here and there a dash of the bizarre. Unlike many of his contemporaries, he was skilled at characterisation; very few of his characters are merely pasteboard puppets. Each of these points, plus his innate desire to play fair with the reader in the revelation of clues, was to set the tone for a long series of Gethryn novels.

Two other excellent early books are *The Link*, a Gethryn mystery set in a country village with a veterinary surgeon as the principal character, and undoubtedly one of the most ingeniously contrived crimes in detection fiction; and *Rynox*, recounting the fate of a large sum of money delivered to an insurance company, in which the author takes the reader into his confidence to an even greater degree than usual. On this latter point, MacDonald made his views clear before writing *Persons Unknown*, stating that he proposed "a due and proper unfolding to the reader of the tale and of the relevant pieces, however small, of the puzzle . . . the ideal detective story is a sort of competition between author and reader." His techniques are more clearly to be seen in *The Noose*, highly praised by Arnold Bennett for its startling yet convincing relevation of the criminal's identity; suspense is guaranteed by the fact that Gethryn has to prove the innocence of a condemned man, with just five days in hand before the execution.

It is virtually impossible, with an author of MacDonald's quality, to label his most outstanding books. There are three, however, which will always epitomise his art. *Murder Gone Mad* is a tour de force, selected by John Dickson Carr as one of the 10 best detective novels, with MacDonald's penchant for the macabre in full flight as an unknown person carries out a daring series of killings and gives the police prior warning of each. Detective novels with too many murders are likely to become monotonous and lose the reader's interest by their very artificiality, but MacDonald showed that he could pull it off without making this sacrifice. What is more, he repeated the exercise in an even better book—*X v. Rex*, originally published under the pseudonym Martin Porlock—this time with the maniac murdering police officers in series. The third of MacDonald's key contributions, and considered by many critics to be his best, was *The Nursemaid Who Disappeared*. This Gethryn novel begins with a conversation overheard by a young American in a London teashop and evolves into one of Gethryn's most enthralling cases. This book features a considerable amount of action, as well as a prime example of MacDonald's delight in hingeing his plots upon small clues; it is also probably the best instance in the field of the positively wraith-like criminal.

MacDonald's literary output thinned in the 1940's and 1950's presumably as his film work increased, but his late period produced some excellent short stories and at least one interesting novel. The latter, *The List of Adrian Messenger*, saw the return of Anthony Gethryn in a very strange and elaborate plot concerning a list of people who appear to have died accidentally. Gethryn is somewhat superfluous, but it is a lively thriller with that touch of sensationalism with which MacDonald's experience in the movies seems to have endowed his last novels. This influence is also noticeable in his short stories, but is to their benefit. Two volumes in particular, *The Man Out of the Rain* and *Something to Hide*, contain clear evidence of MacDonald's abilities in the short form. Some feature Gethryn, others introduce the prophetic Dr. Alcazar, but most are gems of the situation crime story. In these, MacDonald's well-established talent for suspense, twist climaxes, and the combination of farce with horror is seen again. Towering over these attributes, however, is an almost Hitchcockian facility for squeezing something completely terrifying out of a situation which is otherwise normal; the commonplace instantly becomes the bizarre.

MacDonald was given to experimentation; he was very much a part of mainstream detective fiction in the 1920's and 1930's yet rebelled against those devices that made classic detective fiction frankly boring. Anthony Boucher, whose opinion cannot be gainsaid, wrote: "MacDonald is at once a craftsman of writing, whose prose, characterisation and evocation of mood (comic or terrible) might be envied by the most serious literary practitioner, and a craftsman of plot technique, whose construction and misdirection should delight (and startle) Carr or Christie." Although Boucher was referring specifically to the short stories, the comment may be appropriately applied to MacDonald's entire output.

—Melvyn Barnes

MACDONALD, Ross. Pseudonym for Kenneth Millar; also wrote as John Macdonald; John Ross Macdonald. American. Born in Los Gatos, California, 13 December 1915; brought up in Canada. Educated at the Kitchener-Waterloo Collegiate Institute, Ontario, graduated 1932; University of Western Ontario, London, 1933–38, B.A. (honors) 1938; University of Toronto, 1938–39; University of Michigan, Ann Arbor, 1941–44, 1948–49 (Graduate Fellow, 1941–42; Rackham Fellow, 1942–43), M.A. 1942, Ph.D. in English 1951. Served in the United States Naval Reserve, in the Pacific, 1944–46: Lieutenant Junior Grade. Married Margaret Sturm, i.e., Margaret Millar, *q.v.*, in 1938; one daughter (deceased). Teacher of English and History, Kitchener-Waterloo Collegiate Institute, 1939–41; Teaching Fellow, University of Michigan, 1942–44, 1948–49. Book reviewer, San Francisco *Chronicle*, 1957–60. Member, Board of Directors, 1960–61, 1964–65, and President, 1965, Mystery Writers of America. Recipient: Crime Writers Association Gold Dagger award, 1965; University of Michigan Outstanding Achievement award, 1972; Mystery Writers of America Grand Master award, 1973; Popular Culture Association Award of Excellence, 1973; Private Eye Writers of America Life Achievement award, 1981; Los Angeles *Times* Kirsch award, 1982. *Died 11 July 1983.*

CRIME PUBLICATIONS

Novels (series: Lew Archer in all books except *The Ferguson Affair* and *The Wycherly Woman*)

The Moving Target (as John Macdonald).   New York, Knopf, 1949; London, Cassell, 1951; as *Harper*, New York, Pocket Books, 1966.
The Barbarous Coast.   New York, Knopf, 1956; as John Ross Macdonald, London, Cassell, 1957.
The Doomsters.   New York, Knopf, 1958; as John Ross Macdonald, London, Cassell, 1958.
The Galton Case.   New York, Knopf, 1959; as John Ross Macdonald, London, Cassell, 1960.
The Ferguson Affair.   New York, Knopf, 1960; London, Collins, 1961.
The Wycherly Woman.   New York, Knopf, 1961; London, Collins, 1962.
The Zebra-Striped Hearse.   New York, Knopf, 1962; London, Collins, 1963.
The Chill.   New York, Knopf, and London, Collins, 1964.
The Far Side of the Dollar.   New York, Knopf, and London, Collins, 1965.
Black Money.   New York, Knopf, and London, Collins, 1966.
The Instant Enemy.   New York, Knopf, and London, Collins, 1968.
The Goodbye Look.   New York, Knopf, and London, Collins, 1969.
The Underground Man.   New York, Knopf, and London, Collins, 1971.
Sleeping Beauty.   New York, Knopf, and London, Collins, 1973.
The Blue Hammer.   New York, Knopf, and London, Collins, 1976.

Novels as Kenneth Millar (series: Chet Gordon)

The Dark Tunnel (Gordon).   New York, Dodd Mead, 1944; as *I Die Slowly*, London, Lion, 1955.
Trouble Follows Me (Gordon).   New York, Dodd Mead, 1946; as *Night Train*, London, Lion, 1955.
Blue City.   New York, Knopf, 1947; London, Cassell, 1949.
The Three Roads.   New York, Knopf, 1948; London, Cassell, 1950.

Novels as John Ross Macdonald (series: Lew Archer in all books except *Meet Me at the Morgue*)

The Drowning Pool.   New York, Knopf, 1950; as John Macdonald, London, Cassell, 1952.
The Way Some People Die.   New York, Knopf, 1951; London, Cassell, 1953.
The Ivory Grin.   New York, Knopf, 1952; London, Cassell, 1953; as *Marked for Murder*, New York, Pocket Books, 1953.
Meet Me at the Morgue.   New York, Knopf, 1953; as *Experience with Evil*, London, Cassell, 1954.
Find a Victim.   New York, Knopf, 1954; London, Cassell, 1955.

Short Stories

The Name Is Archer (as John Ross Macdonald).   New York, Bantam, 1955.
Lew Archer, Private Investigator.   Yonkers, New York, Mysterious Press, 1977.

Uncollected Short Stories

"Shock Treatment," (as Kenneth Millar), in *Manhunt* (New York), January 1953.
"Murder Is a Public Matter," in *Ellery Queen's Mystery Magazine* (New York), September 1959.
"Bring the Killer to Justice," in *Ellery Queen's Mystery Magazine* (New York), February 1962.
"The Singing Pigeon," in *Alfred Hitchcock Presents: A Month of Mystery*.   New York, Random House, 1969.
"The Missing Sister Case," in *Ellery Queen's Champions of Mystery*.   New York, Davis, 1977; London, Gollancz, 1978.

Uncollected Short Stories as John Ross Macdonald

"The Imaginary Blonde," February 1953, "The Guilty One," May 1953, and "The Beat-Up Sister," October 1953, and "Bad Blood," April–May 1967, all in *Manhunt* (New York).

OTHER PUBLICATIONS

Other

On Crime Writing.   Santa Barbara, California, Capra Press, 1973.
"Down These Streets a Mean Man Must Go," in *Antaeus* (New York), Spring–Summer 1977.
A Collection of Reviews.   Northridge, California, Lord John Press, 1980.
Self-Portrait: Ceaselessly into the Past, edited by Ralph Sipper.   Santa Barbara, California, Capra Press, 1981.

Editor, *Great Stories of Suspense*.   New York, Knopf, 1974.

*

Bibliography: *Kenneth Millar/Ross Macdonald: A Descriptive Bibliography* by Matthew J. Bruccoli, Pittsburgh, University of Pittsburgh Press, and London, Feller and Simons, 1983.

Manuscript Collection: University of California Library, Irvine.

Critical Studies: *Dreamers Who Live Their Dreams: The World of Ross Macdonald's Novels* by Peter Wolfe, Bowling Green, Ohio, Popular Press, 1976; *Ross Macdonald* by Jerry Speir, New York, Ungar, 1978; *Ross Macdonald/Kenneth Millar* by Matthew J. Bruccoli, New York, Harcourt Brace, 1984.

*   *   *

Ross Macdonald ranks among the finest of modern crime novelists. His Lew Archer series is a monumental contribution to detective literature. The sustained excellence of his work over 35 years and the innovations he brought to the genre have led to various honors, and the rare distinction of being represented both on the best-seller lists and in college literature courses. This brief assessment will not attempt to survey the scope of his work or identify his best novels, but will simply suggest some of the tendencies his fiction has shown.

Some of the patterns in Macdonald's early work can be found in his third novel, *Blue City*. The texture of the world in this novel is reminiscent of Dashiell Hammett's fiction, though its sensibility and imagery show the influence of Raymond

Chandler as well. The central figure is an angry young man who returns to his home town after cutting himself adrift five years earlier and serving a hitch in the army. John Weather arrives through the kindness of a trucker, stops at a tavern for a beer, and finds himself a stranger defending an old derelict from two thugs who had lingered on after having been brought in as strike-breakers. When Weather discovers that his father had been the victim of an unsolved murder after marrying a much younger woman, he battles his way toward the solution of the crime and comes to understand his father's contribution to the general corruption of the town. Weather is familiar with Veblen, Marx, Engels, and other social critics. The early part of the novel would appear to be headed toward direct social criticism, as it contrasts Sanford, who owns most of the town, with Kaufman, a radical thinker whose meagre income derives from a secondhand store. But the story shifts to Weather's stepmother and the mobster who is found to have manipulated her and killed Weather's father. The mixture of Hammett's harsh world of political corruption and Chandler's sensual decadence are both apparent here.

Nearly two decades later Macdonald would compare *Blue City* to the last scene of Chandler's *The Long Goodbye:* "this scene was written by a man of tender and romantic sensibility who had been injured. Chandler used Marlowe to shield himself while half-expressing his sensibility and its private hurts." Macdonald sees this tendency in his own work prior to *The Doomsters*, which he feels marks "a fairly clean break with the Chandler tradition." In the decades following *Blue City*, Macdonald's angry young man appears often, but he finds himself in more trouble than he alone can handle. The implicit class struggle is gradually blunted in favor of a psychological view of crime where the "mentally sick people and the criminal" belong to "the same group," so that criticism of the social structure operates on the acausal level of metaphor. The leaking offshore oil platform in *Sleeping Beauty* that protrudes "like the metal handle of a dagger that had stabbed the world and made it spill black blood," has a "psychological connection" to other crimes, but no direct connection to corporate practices or the ambivalent ideals embodied in modern technology. Although Macdonald is clearly concerned about these matters, his emphasis on familial and psychological history leading to crime in effect moves his fiction back toward the class assumptions of British detective fiction that Hammett and Chandler had rejected.

With *The Doomsters* the moral center of the novels moves out of detection into those with whom he comes in contact, so that the detective has become a kind of psychologist who prompts people to reveal their interpretations of events and, ultimately, the illusions surrounding them. One of the characters in this novel is actually a psychologist and it is not surprising that all the characters tend to talk too much. It is not until *The Galton Case*, about which Macdonald has written candidly and affectionately, that the implications of his aesthetic perspective begin to become clear. In it Archer bests the angry young man convincingly, and the novel as a whole is better balanced than the earlier works. What Macdonald had discovered was his own contribution to the genre. His detective would become more clearly "the mind of the novel, . . . a consciousness in which the meanings of other lives emerge." As other lives become the substance of this consciousness, their various forms of brokenness and partial fulfillment yield in the conclusion a final understanding that reverberates back through the work.

Macdonald's sensitivity to people who are caught in the conflicts of social change is apparent throughout his fiction. Husbands and wives fail to learn to work together and their children run away from them or are torn asunder by the dissension. Young women and men break the patterns of their lives to circle warily and uncomprehendingly around the secret tragedies of their elders. Throughout Macdonald's fiction people live illusions in order to conceal from themselves and others their own inadequacies and carry with them petty grievances that they have steadfastly refused to place in perspective. Archer is often spectator to arguments that have been worn down through repetition, but which are repeated once more for a new audience. The guilt that emerges in the novels is rarely traced to one person, but usually involves the full or partial commitments of several people at one stage or another. In many of the novels the identities of characters are interchanged, unexpected parenthood is revealed, or new identities have been assumed.

The plots resulting from these complexities are intricate, the dialogue is a studied vernacular, and the imagery is "intended to have deep psychological and social meanings." Macdonald placed his reader between the innocence of the very young and murder, his objective correlative of guilt, so that Lew Archer is intended finally as a window into ourselves. The process of demystification that occurs as Archer conducts his investigations creates resonances within the reader that urge him toward self-recognition. The critical questions that Macdonald had early posed had been how he could achieve a greater truth and a higher art. A reading of his fiction will leave little doubt that he has achieved both.

—Larry N. Landrum

———

MacHARG, William. *See* **BALMER, Edwin.**

———

MacINNES, Helen (Clark). American. Born in Glasgow, Scotland, 7 October 1907; emigrated to the United States in 1937; naturalized, 1951. Educated at Hermitage School, Helensburgh; High School for Girls, Glasgow; Glasgow University, M.A. 1928; University College, London, Diploma in Librarianship 1931. Married the writer Gilbert Highet in 1932 (died 1978); one son. Special cataloguer, Ferguson Collection, University of Glasgow, 1928–29; employed by the Dunbartonshire Education Authority to select books for county libraries, 1929–30; acted with the Oxford University Dramatic Society and with the Oxford Experimental Theatre, 1934–37. Recipient: Columbia prize in Literature, Iona College, New Rochelle, New York, 1966. *Died 30 September 1985.*

Crime Publications

Novels

Above Suspicion. Boston, Little Brown, and London, Harrap, 1941.
Assignment in Brittany. Boston, Little Brown, and London, Harrap, 1942.
While Still We Live. Boston, Little Brown, 1944; as *The Unconquerable*, London, Harrap, 1944.
Horizon. London, Harrap, 1945; Boston, Little Brown, 1946.
Neither Five Nor Three. New York, Harcourt Brace, and London, Collins, 1951.

I and My True Love. New York, Harcourt Brace, and London, Collins, 1953.

Pray for a Brave Heart. New York, Harcourt Brace, and London, Collins, 1955.

North from Rome. New York, Harcourt Brace, and London, Collins, 1958.

Decision at Delphi. New York, Harcourt Brace, and London, Collins, 1961.

The Venetian Affair. New York, Harcourt Brace, 1963; London, Collins, 1964.

The Double Image. New York, Harcourt Brace, and London, Collins, 1966.

The Salzburg Connection. New York, Harcourt Brace, 1968; London, Collins, 1969.

Message from Málaga. New York, Harcourt Brace, and London, Collins, 1972.

Snare of the Hunter. New York, Harcourt Brace, and London, Collins, 1974.

Agent in Place. New York, Harcourt Brace, and London, Collins, 1976.

Prelude to Terror. New York, Harcourt Brace, and London, Collins, 1978.

The Hidden Target. New York, Harcourt Brace, and London, Collins, 1980.

Cloak of Darkness. New York, Harcourt Brace, and London, Collins, 1982.

Ride a Pale Horse. New York, Harcourt Brace, and London, Collins, 1984.

OTHER PUBLICATIONS

Novels

Friends and Lovers. Boston, Little Brown, 1947; London, Harrap, 1948.

Rest and Be Thankful. Boston, Little Brown, and London, Harrap, 1949.

Play

Home Is the Hunter. New York, Harcourt Brace, 1964.

Other

Translator, with Gilbert Highet, *Sexual Life in Ancient Rome*, by Otto Kiefer. London, Routledge, 1934; New York, Dutton, 1935.

Translator, with Gilbert Highet, *Friedrich Engels: A Biography*, by Gustav Mayer. London, Chapman and Hall, and New York, Knopf, 1936.

*

Manuscript Collection: Princeton University Library, New Jersey.

Helen MacInnes commented: (1984):

Exact category of my novels is difficult to place. They are not really crime stories. They deal with international situations and threats—in the political field. There is more suspense than mystery in their plots. Readers know what is at stake, and the characters in the novels find ways of dealing with that threat.

*   *   *

The appearance of a Helen MacInnes novel was often the appearance of a bestseller which become a movie (*Above Suspicion* and *Assignment in Brittany*) or a Book-of-the-Month Club Selection (*Prelude to Terror*). Early academic training gave MacInnes skill and patience for research; extensive travel provided convincing backgrounds for settings that range from Switzerland to Granada, from Paris to East Hampton, from Venice to Vienna. If reviews in the *Times Literary Supplement* charge that "Miss MacInnes is not interested in achieving even a semblance of authenticity in her novels," reviews in the New York *Times* cite the carefully researched locales as part of the attraction of her books.

In a 1965 interview MacInnes said of her work: "Underlying everything is the fact that I'm interested in international politics, in analyzing news, to read newspapers both on and between the lines, to deduct and add, to utilize memory." Her adventure-suspense novels reflect this persistent concern about contemporary affairs. Plots center on World War II—*Above Suspicion, Assignment in Brittany, While Still We Live*, and *Horizon*; adventures involve World War II secrets, still explosive after the war—*Pray for a Brave Heart* and *The Salzburg Connection*; and political intrigues focus on Communist threats to the West—*I and My True Love, Neither Five Nor Three, North from Rome, Decision at Delphi, The Venetian Affair, Message from Málaga, Snare of the Hunter, Agent in Place*, and *Prelude to Terror*. Her two non-suspenseful novels, *Rest and Be Thankful* and *Friends and Lovers*, were not especially successful and she abandoned this vein when, as she said, "I realized that our international world had gone terribly wrong again."

Her later novels are typical of her skill and appeal. *Snare of the Hunter* plunges an amateur agent (music critic David Mennery) into the dangerous rescue of Irina Kusak from Czechoslovakia to the West. Further plot complications involve danger to Irnia's famous father (a writer who has escaped from behind the Iron Curtain and whose explosives notebooks the daughter carries); threats from Irina's ex-husband, Jiri Kradek, a Communist official; and a romance between David and Irina rekindled after 16 years. Narrow escapes, violent deaths, exciting chases, and betrayals combine to make the danger and potential destruction hair raising.

Agent in Place involves double and triple agents, a secret NATO memorandum, and occasional heavy-handed propaganda. Published before newspaper reporters' confidential sources were seriously threatened, this novel centers on an amateur, Tom Kelso (whose brother gave Part I of the memorandum to a New York *Times* reporter), and a professional, Tony Lawton. Enemy agents are a bit too sinister; Tom and Dorothea Kelso act too bravely; Chuck Kelso dies for being too idealistic. Coded messages, frequent disguises, minute plans for meetings and escapes abound; in short, familiar characteristics of a MacInnes novel to please her faithful readers. In *Prelude to Terror*, Colin Grant, a New York art expert, arrives in Vienna to bid at auction for a Ruysdael painting on behalf of a wealthy industrialist-collector. Predictably, MacInnes's amateur is embroiled in the frightening world of conspiracy, murder, kidnapping, and international intrigue; and he must himself perform a bit of derring-do.

Ralph Harper in *The World of the Thriller* points out that suspense writers like Graham Greene and John le Carré are "able to force the reader into self-examination and self-judgment." MacInnes's novels fail to reach such a philosophical level: characters are good or bad; poetic justice often comes neatly; readers are entertained, not tested. Nevertheless, to the pro-Western lover of adventure and suspense, MacInnes deserved the epithets her critics bestowed: "Queen of suspense" and "Master teller of spy stories."

—Elizabeth Evans

—————

MacKENZIE, Donald. Canadian. Born in Toronto, Ontario, 11 August 1918. Educated at schools in England, Canada, and Switzerland. Divorced; one daughter. Describes his life's stages as: full-time playboy, 1938–41; professional thief, 1930–48; since 1948 self-employed author. Agent: Russell and Volkening Inc., 60 West 29th Street, New York, New York 10001, U.S.A.; or, A.M. Heath and Company Ltd., 40–42 William IV Street, London WC2N 4DD, England.

CRIME PUBLICATIONS

Novels (series: John Raven)

Nowhere to Go. London, Elek, 1956; as *Manhunt*, Boston, Houghton Mifflin, 1957.
The Juryman. London, Elek, 1957; Boston, Houghton Mifflin, 1958.
Scent of Danger. London, Collins, and Boston, Houghton Mifflin, 1958; as *Moment of Danger*, London, Pan, 1959.
Dangerous Silence. London, Collins, and Boston, Houghton Mifflin, 1960.
Knife Edge. Boston, Houghton Mifflin, 1961; London, Pan, 1962.
The Genial Stranger. London, Collins, and Boston, Houghton Mifflin, 1962.
Double Exposure. London, Collins, and Boston, Houghton Mifflin, 1963; as *I Spy*, New York, Avon, 1964.
Cool Sleeps Balaban. London, Collins, and Boston, Houghton Mifflin, 1964.
The Lonely Side of the River. London, Hodder and Stoughton, and Boston, Houghton Mifflin, 1965.
Salute from a Dead Man. London, Hodder and Stoughton, and Boston, Houghton Mifflin, 1966.
Death Is a Friend. London, Hodder and Stoughton, and Boston, Houghton Mifflin, 1967.
Three Minus Two. London, Hodder and Stoughton, 1968; as *The Quiet Killer*, Boston, Houghton Mifflin, 1968.
Dead Straight. London, Hodder and Stoughton, and Boston, Houghton Mifflin, 1969.
Night Boat from Puerto Vedra. London, Hodder and Stoughton, and Boston, Houghton Mifflin, 1970.
The Kyle Contract. Boston, Houghton Mifflin, 1970; London, Hodder and Stoughton, 1971.
Sleep Is for the Rich. London, Macmillan, and Boston, Houghton Mifflin, 1971; as *The Chalice Caper*, London, Mayflower, 1974.
Postscript to a Dead Letter. London, Macmillan, and Boston, Houghton Mifflin, 1973.
Zaleski's Percentage (Raven). London, Macmillan, and Boston, Houghton Mifflin, 1974.
The Spreewald Collection. London, Macmillan, and Boston, Houghton Mifflin, 1975.
Raven in Flight. London, Macmillan, and Boston, Houghton Mifflin, 1976.
Raven and the Ratcatcher. London, Macmillan, and Boston, Houghton Mifflin, 1977.

Raven and the Kamikaze. London, Macmillan, and Boston, Houghton Mifflin, 1977.
Raven Settles a Score. Boston, Houghton Mifflin, 1978; London, Macmillan, 1979.
Deep, Dark and Dead. London, Macmillan, 1978.
Raven after Dark. Boston, Houghton Mifflin, 1979; as *Raven Feathers His Nest*, London, Macmillan, 1979.
Raven and the Paperhangers. London, Macmillan, and Boston, Houghton Mifflin, 1980.
Raven's Revenge. London, Macmillan, and Boston, Houghton Mifflin, 1982.
Raven's Longest Night. New York, Doubleday, 1983; London, Macmillan, 1984.
Raven's Shadow. London, Macmillan, and New York, Doubleday, 1984.
Nobody Here by That Name. London, Macmillan, and New York, Doubleday, 1986.
A Savage State of Grace. London, Macmillan, and New York, Doubleday, 1988.
By Any Illegal Means. London, Macmillan, and New York, Doubleday, 1989.

OTHER PUBLICATIONS

Other

Occupation: Thief (autobiography). Indianapolis, Bobbs Merrill, 1955; as *Fugitives*, London, Elek, 1955.
Gentleman at Crime (autobiography). London, Elek, 1956.

*

Manuscript Collection: Mugar Memorial Library, Boston University.

*   *   *

For author Donald MacKenzie, life and letters are deceptively easy to connect: a convicted thief, he has a perspective on the system of justice (and the system in prison) that gives his work a special bite. His only remaining illusion seems to be a residual belief in the Raffles tradition or, as one of his autobiographic works is entitled, in the *Gentleman at Crime*. Yet little of this romanticism is visible in his earlier books, which tend to feature what we would have to call losers, small men who are pressed hard by fate and circumstance, and who meet a final, often deadly, challenge that lifts them out of the ordinary. Suspense (which is the genre MacKenzie prefers) depends, for him, on simple confrontation: a test, a chase, a resolution. For example (*Dead Straight*, 1968) has an ex-jewel thief and gaolbird who is used as a catspaw in an elaborate conspiracy involving murder; suspected himself, naturally, the protagonist must evade capture and solve the mystery. The author sometimes varies his scheme by shifting the location to the Continent, particularly to Spain, which he describes offhandedly and without romantic flourishes.

In 1974 MacKenzie developed what would become a series character, John Raven, an unorthodox London detective inspector with a penchant for breaking the rules. Raven leaves the force, but he maintains a close emotional relationship with his old job and colleagues, a love-hate tie; his favorite kind of policeman continues to be one who is "straight but hungry," willing to bend the rules to get the job done, but *not* corrupt. Variations on the theme of corruption are common in MacKenzie's work: he has an old-fashioned hatred of it. More than once the author has his character, Raven, remark on the close affinity between cop and criminal, so that experienced officers even grow to look and act like the (respectable) villains they pursue, for in some way their "codes" are similar. Raven keeps his police connections in play, and is kept in play himself; three novels (*Raven and the Ratcatcher, Raven Settles a Score, Raven's Revenge*) involve that most terrifying of adversaries, the bent senior policeman (Commander Drake) with a grudge and the power to sate it. When he was a police officer, Raven is credited with "the nose and instincts of a weasel" (*Raven in Flight*) which he interprets as a recognition of his obsession with the chase; now he is forced to be as skillful in avoiding the hunt, as in himself acting the hunter.

Raven's character owes something to John D. MacDonald's Travis McGee: he lives on a houseboat, appreciates the good things in life, and is by nature a loner. He has a spiritual affinity to MacDonald's creation as well, in his essential elitism and his belief in some sort of loner's code. However, Raven has a more profound view into the depths; bad things can and do happen to good *or* bad people, and the system almost certainly wins in the end. Raven's Quixotish tendencies are underpinned by a stoic, survivor's commonsense.

MacKenzie has a rapid, terse, relatively hard-boiled style, which is fitting to the suspense themes he favors. His plotting is straightforward, with few tricky turns or irrational leaps. As would be expected, the author has a taste and a talent for louche, emotionally dark-hued, or outright villainous characters; his bent and vengeful copper, Drake, is drawn with fullbore scope and psychologically convincing depth, as Drake is himself eventually made a victim of the corruption he commanded (*Raven's Revenge*). The novels depict violence in plenty but not gratuitously; rapid movement rather than percussive excitement is the norm in MacKenzie's prose, and a saturnine and offhand humor is often present.

MacKenzie can be a careless and facile writer, freely using clichés (especially in the earlier novels), but he should be credited with possessing a professional's energy and skills, and a gift for storytelling. This is especially prevalent in his explanation of the darker corners of the suspense genre, where, when he is on his best form, outsize and naive heroism is wryly dismissed, and simple survival, with or without honor (though preferably with it), becomes the desired end.

—D.A. Miller

MacLEAN, Alistair (Stuart). Also writes as Ian Stuart. British. Born in Daviot, Invernesshire, Scotland, 28 April 1922. Educated at Glasgow University, B.A. (honours) in English. Served in the Royal Navy, 1941–45. Married 1) Gisela MacLean, three sons; 2) Marcelle Georgeus in 1972 (died). Teacher, Gallowfleet Secondary School, near Glasgow in the early 1950's; lived in Geneva, 1957–63; owned Jamaica Inn, Bodmin Moor, Cornwall; ran hotels in England for four years in the 1960's. *Died 2 February 1987.*

CRIME PUBLICATIONS

Novels (series: Captain Mallory)

The Guns of Navarone (Mallory). London, Collins, and New York, Doubleday, 1957.
South by Java Head. London, Collins, and New York, Doubleday, 1958.

The Last Frontier. London, Collins, 1959; as *The Secret Ways*, New York, Doubleday, 1959.
Night Without End. London, Collins, and New York, Doubleday, 1960.
Fear Is the Key. London, Collins, and New York, Doubleday, 1961.
The Dark Crusader (as Ian Stuart). London, Collins, 1961; as *The Black Shrike*, New York, Scribner, 1961.
The Satan Bug (as Ian Stuart). London, Collins, and New York, Scribner, 1962.
The Golden Rendezvous. London, Collins, and New York, Doubleday, 1962.
Ice Station Zebra. London, Collins, and New York, Doubleday, 1963.
When Eight Bells Toll. London, Collins, and New York, Doubleday, 1966.
Where Eagles Dare. London, Collins, and New York, Doubleday, 1967.
Force 10 from Navarone (Mallory). London, Collins, and New York, Doubleday, 1968.
Puppet on a Chain. London, Collins, and New York, Doubleday, 1969.
Caravan to Vaccarès. London, Collins, and New York, Doubleday, 1970.
Bear Island. London, Collins, and New York, Doubleday, 1971.
The Way to Dusty Death. London, Collins, and New York, Doubleday, 1973.
Breakheart Pass. London, Collins, and New York, Doubleday, 1974.
Circus. London, Collins, and New York, Doubleday, 1975.
The Golden Gate. London, Collins, and New York, Doubleday, 1976.
Seawitch. London, Collins, and New York, Doubleday, 1977.
Goodbye California. London, Collins, 1977; New York, Doubleday, 1978.
Athabasca. London, Collins, and New York, Doubleday, 1980.
River of Death. London, Collins, 1981; New York, Doubleday, 1982.
Partisans. London, Collins, 1982; New York, Doubleday, 1983.
Floodgate. London, Collins, 1983; New York, Doubleday, 1984.
San Andreas. London, Collins, 1984; New York, Doubleday, 1985.
Santorini. London, Collins, 1986; New York, Doubleday, 1987.

OTHER PUBLICATIONS

Novel

H.M.S. Ulysses. London, Collins, 1955; New York, Doubleday, 1956.

Short Stories

The Lonely Sea: Collected Sea Stories. London, Collins, 1985; New York, Doubleday, 1986.

Plays

Screenplays: *Where Eagles Dare*, 1968; *Puppet on a Chain*, with Don Sharp and Paul Wheeler, 1970; *When Eight Bells Toll*, 1971; *Breakheart Pass*, 1975.

Other

All about Lawrence of Arabia (for children). London, W.H. Allen, 1962; as *Lawrence of Arabia*, New York, Random House, 1962.
Captain Cook. London, Collins, and New York, Doubleday, 1972.

*   *   *

In Alistair MacLean's action-packed adventure stories the hero is plunged into danger in the opening chapter and moves rapidly from crisis to crisis until the final wrap-up. Several books contain mystery. In these books, at the final climactic moments, killers are unmasked, motives are revealed, or major characters switch loyalty. In other books the suspense comes not from who did it or why, but from how—how will the hero stave off catastrophe? In *The Golden Gate* and *Seawitch* the reader knows immediately who the villains are and what they are trying to accomplish. In *Breakheart Pass* mysterious murders are explained at mid-book because the mystery is only incidental to the question of how the hero will get the train through.

MacLean's heroes are men of incredible endurance. Some modestly claim to be human (Carpenter in *Ice Station Zebra*); some immodestly announce that they are infallible (Harlow in *The Way to Dusty Death*). But all have unlimited reserves of energy and quick enough reflexes to foil the strongest villains. Sometimes the heroes possess uncanny skill that is crucial in the contexts of the stories. Mitchell's cat-like night vision in *Seawitch*, Andrea's unusual strength in *The Guns of Navarone* and *Force 10 from Navarone*, and Bruno's excellent high wire walking in *Circus* are all essential to the happy endings. In addition to being shrewd psychologists and karate experts, the heroes are equipped with photographic memories and are witty and charming. In other words, they tend to be interchangeable cardboard figures. In earlier novels, the women are worse: noble, beautiful, long-suffering, and not very bright. However, MacLean's portrayal of women improves in later books. In *Goodbye California* and *Athabasca* the women are spunky, bright, and cheerful. In *Partisans* and *River of Death* they are full participants in the expeditions, although the hero patronizes them insufferably in the process of falling in love with them.

An offensive note in some novels is a moralistic dialogue on the need for violence. Later novels use a set conversation in which the hero defends his killing to the heroine with words such as, "All I do is exterminate vermin. To me, all crooks, armed or not, are vermin" (*Seawitch*). In the good guy-bad guy world of breakneck adventure, such conversations slow down the action as well as force the reader to see the hero as a murderer and the heroine as a fool.

In many books the real stars are the elements. MacLean uses locations and machinery very effectively. In his several novels set north of the Arctic Circle, he makes the noise, the stinging wind-blown ice particles, and the frigid sea real and terrifying. In the many ship stories, the perils relating directly to the ship have a metallic clang of reality. MacLean also uses cable cars, trains, and helicopters for great cling-to, dangle-from, and fight-atop scenes. Another zestful ingredient of MacLean's stories is that the characters play for such big stakes. The President of the United States and two Arab leaders are taken hostage in the middle of the Golden Gate Bridge for a half-billion-dollar ransom. A master criminal plots to rob all the banks in London in one night in *The Satan Bug*. California may be blown off the map in *Goodbye California* and the Netherlands sent back under the sea in *Floodgate*. In *Santorini*, a plane carrying 15 hydrogen bombs and three atom bombs is knocked out of the air into the sea in one of the few areas of the world that is subject to both earthquakes and volcanic eruptions—and one of the bombs is ticking.

Each MacLean novel delivers adventure that is fast and physical. Through war, crime, and espionage plots MacLean uses vivid descriptions of technology, environment, and actions which involve the reader quickly and totally.

—Neysa Chouteau and Martha Alderson

———

MacLEOD, Charlotte (Matilda). Also writes as Alisa Craig; has also written as Matilda Hughes. American. Born in Bath, New Brunswick, Canada, 12 November 1922. Educated at public schools in Weymouth, Massachusetts; Art Institute of Boston. Staff member, later vice-president, N.H. Miller, advertising agency, Boston, 1952–82. Co-founder and President, American Crime Writers League. Lives in Durham, Maine. Agent: Jed Mattes, 175 West 73rd Street, New York, New York 10023, U.S.A.

CRIME PUBLICATIONS

Novels (series: Sarah Kelling; Peter Shandy)

Mystery of the White Knight. New York, Avalon, 1964.
Next Door to Danger. New York, Avalon, 1965.
Rest You Merry (Shandy). New York, Doubleday, 1978; London, Collins, 1979.
The Family Vault (Kelling). New York, Doubleday, 1979; London, Collins, 1980.
The Luck Runs Out (Shandy). New York, Doubleday, 1979; London, Collins, 1981.
The Withdrawing Room (Kelling). New York, Doubleday, 1980; London, Collins, 1981.
The Palace Guard (Kelling). New York, Doubleday, 1981; London, Collins, 1982.
Wrack and Rune (Shandy). New York, Doubleday, and London, Collins, 1982.
The Bilbao Looking Glass (Kelling). New York, Doubleday, and London, Collins, 1983.
Something the Cat Dragged In (Shandy). New York, Doubleday, 1983; London, Collins, 1984.
The Convivial Codfish (Kelling). New York, Doubleday, and London, Collins, 1984.
The Curse of the Giant Hogweed (Shandy). New York, Doubleday, 1985.
The Plain Old Man (Kelling). New York, Doubleday, and London, Collins, 1985.
The Corpse in Oozak's Pond (Shandy). London, Collins, 1986; New York, Mysterious Press, 1987.
The Recycled Citizen (Kelling). London, Collins, 1987; New York, Mysterious Press, 1988.
The Silver Ghost (Kelling). London, Collins, 1987; New York, Mysterious Press, 1988.

Vane Pursuit (Shandy). New York, Mysterious Press, and London, Collins, 1989.

The Gladstone Bag (Kelling). London, Collins, 1989; New York, Mysterious Press, 1990.

Novels as Alisa Craig (series: Grub-and-Stakers; Madoc Rhys)

A Pint of Murder (Rhys). New York, Doubleday, 1980.

The Grub-and-Stakers Move a Mountain. New York, Doubleday, 1981.

Murder Goes Mumming (Rhys). New York, Doubleday, 1981.

The Terrible Tide. New York, Doubleday, 1983; London, Hale, 1985.

The Grub-and-Stakers Quilt a Bee. New York, Doubleday, 1985.

A Dismal Thing to Do (Rhys). New York, Doubleday, 1986.

The Grub-and-Stakers Pinch a Poke. New York, Doubleday, 1988.

Trouble in the Brasses (Rhys). New York, Avon, 1989.

The Grub-and-Stakers Spin a Yarn. New York, Avon, 1990.

Short Stories

Grab Bag. New York, Avon, 1987.

Uncollected Short Story

"A Cozy for Christmas," in *Mistletoe Mysteries*, edited by Charlotte MacLeod. New York, Mysterious Press, 1989.

OTHER PUBLICATIONS

Novels

The Food of Love (as Matilda Hughes). New York, Avalon, 1965.

Headlines for Caroline (as Matilda Hughes). New York, Avalon, 1967.

The Fat Lady's Ghost. New York, Weybright and Talley, 1968.

Ask Me No Questions. Philadelphia, Macrae Smith, 1971.

King Devil. New York, Atheneum, 1978.

We Dare Not Go a-Hunting. New York, Atheneum, 1980.

Other

Mouse's Vineyard (for children). New York, Weybright and Talley, 1968.

Brass Pounder (for children). Boston, Little Brown, 1971.

Astrology for Sceptics. New York, Macmillan, 1972; London, Turnstone, 1973.

Cirak's Daughter (for children). New York, Atheneum, 1982.

Maid of Honor (for children). New York, Atheneum, 1984.

Editor, *Mistletoe Mysteries*. New York, Mysterious Press, 1989.

*

Manuscript Collection: Mugar Memorial Library, Boston University.

*   *   *

Charlotte MacLeod's best-known fiction emphasizes the orderly world vital to cozy mysteries. Moreover, her stories reveal that sweet dispositions, good food, and loyalty are the basic necessities for a happy marriage. Coupling this philosophy with clever plots and plenty of humor has netted her a host of fans and a sound reputation.

One of MacLeod's most popular characters is Sarah Kelling, whose first adventure, *The Family Vault* (in which she is widowed, impoverished, and imperiled), introduces the Kelling clan to whom Boston's Beacon Hill is practically a family enclave. The Kellings' numbers are legion; many of their fortunes are vast, and while their eccentricities are pronounced, those who aren't out-and-out villains constitute a likable crowd prone to discovering corpses and falling in love—intensely, vocally, joyously in love. The Kelling novels trace Sarah's courtship by Max Bittersohn (a specialist in solving art thefts), their marriage, and the birth of their child. Amid all this satisfying romance, Sarah and Max sometimes sleuth separately; in *Mistletoe Mysteries* (stories by various hands collected by MacLeod), "A Cozy for Christmas," details the case which preoccupies Sarah while Max, on his own, handles *The Convivial Codfish*, tracing a valuable artefact stolen from a social club. Working together in *The Palace Guard*, they disguise themselves as East Indians to facilitate their investigation. Disguises, derring-do, and doing good are all important in *The Recycled Citizen*. When murder invades the Senior Citizens Recycling Center, which aids the impoverished elderly, Sarah and Max enlist the skills of Mr. and Mrs. Brooks Kelling (Mrs. Brooks, cousin Theonia, having been reared a gypsy, has particularly helpful talents). Cousin Theonia also rushes to help Sarah's Aunt Emma, who, overseeing a summer artists' colony, finds herself caught up in murder and mystery (*The Gladstone Bag*).

Balaclava Agricultural College is the main setting of another cheerful series featuring Professor Peter Shandy, co-developer of the Balaclava Buster rutabaga, which has brought him fame (especially in Europe where rutabagas are more properly appreciated) and considerable good fortune. During Peter's rebellion against the annual Christmas Illumination, a prickly faculty wife is killed in his home. *Rest You Merry* details his successful pursuit of the murderer and introduces pretty Helen Marsh, soon destined to be Helen Shandy, for, as in the Kelling series, the Balaclava saga is as crowded with love stories as it is with fun. In *The Luck Runs Out*, Helen is kidnapped briefly; terrible as her plight is, that of Belinda of Balaclava, prize hog and the hope of future breeders, seems worse; Belinda is missing for days, and ominous parcels of pork turn up on college doorsteps. The Shandys are surrounded by a fairly wide range of characters, most, like publicly blustery, privately biddable President Thorkjeld Svenson, easily recognized types. Peter and Helen are also, however, blessed with some wonderful old friends such as Catriona McBogle, a writer whose 200-year-old (but comfortably modernized) Maine home is very like MacLeod's own. Catriona appears in *Vane Pursuit*, a tale of theft and shipwreck, which also features Winifred Brinks, an impoverished gentlewoman whose survival skills rival those of the most accomplished mountain man.

Writing as Alisa Craig, MacLeod created the Grub-and-Stake Gardening and Roving Club of Lobelia Falls, Ontario. These novels cover town events pretty thoroughly, especially efforts to sustain a local museum which all too often involve murder. Even the locals' tribute to Robert W. Service, a drama based on "The Shooting of Dan McGrew," turns dangerous (*The Grub-and-Stakers Pinch a Poke*). Royal Canadian Mounted Policeman Madoc Rhys and his wife, Janet Wadman Rhys, star in other Alisa Craig works. The opening scenes of *A Dismal Thing to Do*, a dandy combination of fear, zest, and setting, are typical of incidents which prove the Craig novels as sprightly as the MacLeod books.

Though the supporting figures MacLeod/Craig introduces sometimes tend to be reminiscent of one another and though humor and action dominate characterization, all of her characters are memorable; all are interesting, and their expected foibles, actions, and reactions provide ample amusement and escape. Their peculiarities distance readers so that the emotional cost of eavesdropping on these murderous adventures is very low whereas the profit—entertainment—is very high.

—Jane S. Bakerman

————

MacLEOD, Robert. *See* **KNOX, Bill.**

————

MacNEIL, Duncan. *See* **McCUTCHAN, Philip.**

————

MacNEIL, Neil. *See* **BALLARD, Willis Todhunter.**

————

MAINWARING, Daniel. *See* **HOMES, Geoffrey.**

————

MALCOLM, John. British. Born John Malcolm Andrews in Manchester, Lancashire, 21 August 1936. Educated at British School, Montevideo, Uraquay; Bedford Modern School, Bedford; St. John's College, Cambridge, 1955–58, M.A. in engineering 1958. Married Geraldine Lacey in 1961; one son. Design engineer, London, 1958–63; export manager, Weybridge, Surrey, 1963–70; management consultant, Pyrford, Surrey 1970–76; international marketing manager, Northiam, Sussex 1976. Agent: A.M. Heath and Company, 79 St. Martin's Lane, London WC2N 4AA. Address: Carriers Oast, Northiam, Sussex TN31 6NH, England.

CRIME PUBLICATIONS

Novels (series: Tim Simpson in all books)

A Back Room in Somers Town. London, Collins, 1984; New York, Scribner, 1985.
The Godwin Sideboard. London, Collins, 1984; New York, Scribner, 1985.
The Gwen John Sculpture. London, Collins, 1985; New York, Scribner, 1986.
Whistler in the Dark. London, Collins, 1986; New York, Scribner, 1987.
Gothic Pursuit. London, Collins, and New York, Scribner, 1987.

Mortal Ruin. London, Collins, and New York, Scribner, 1988.
The Wrong Impression. London, Collins, and New York, Scribner, 1990.

Uncollected Short Stories

"The Cisterna," in *A Suit of Diamonds.* London, Collins, 1990.
"Dinah, Reading," in *Winters Tales 22*, edited by Hilary Hale. London, Macmillan, 1990.

OTHER PUBLICATIONS

Other as John Andrews

The Price Guide to Antique Furniture. London, Antique Collectors Club, 1969; revised edition, 1970.
The Price Guide to Victorian, Edwardian and 1920s Furniture. London, Antiques Collectors Club, 1980.
British Antique Furniture. London, Antique Collectors Club, 1989.

*

John Malcolm comments:
My crime novels are art fraud or art crime novels in which events or artefacts from the past affect the present. The basis of all the art history in them is factually correct.

* * *

John Malcolm is one of a growing number of crime-writers who use as the background to their mysteries the world of antiques and fine art—others who write in this genre include Jonathan Gash, Michael Delahaye, Michael Delving, and Anthony Oliver. All these authors successfully combine the seemingly diverse (but actually contiguous) spheres of art and crime, but Malcolm's have the added dimension of dealing with the world of finance and banking.

The narrator/hero/sleuth/expert of these interesting and entertaining tales is Tim Simpson, ex-rugby player and financial consultant turned investment specialist; the general field of interest is British art and antiques of the late 19th and early 20th centuries. Narrow as this field may sound, Simpson strays as far afield as Chicago, Brazil, France, and the seedier stretches of Brighton. Many of the more successful passages, however, are set among the Gothic piles and Victorian terraces of London.

The pattern for the series is set in the first book, *A Back Room in Somers Town*, in which Tim (at the beginning of the book still a business consultant) becomes embroiled in a complex melange of forgery, theft, and murder. On the trail of a missing painting by Mary Godwin (a follower of Sickert), he is forced to break off from this investigation in order to travel to Brazil in the course of a business deal; in fact, owing to the wide-ranging interests and connections of his new employer, a family-run merchant bank, this visit actually aids his investigations rather than impeding them. Most useful, in this particular book, is the Brazilian upbringing of this otherwise fairly conventional product of public school and Cambridge. Even more of an advantage is Tim's background as a Rugby Blue—in this and all the other books he suffers more physical punishment from altercations with criminals than the average boxer would expect to encounter in a lifelong career.

This susceptibility to violence is a constant source of concern and irritation to Tim's girlfriend Sue Westerman and his employer Jeremy White. Jeremy is one of the less conventional scions of White's Bank, and originator of the Art Investment Fund for which Tim seeks out works of art. In these searches he is aided, albeit reluctantly, by Sue in her capacity as an administrative assistant at the Tate Gallery. Tim's ex-rugby-playing friend, policeman Nobby Roberts, feels little of their concern but much irritation at Tim's habit of amateur sleuthing. Of rather more concern to any art-dealer acquaintances of Tim's should be the propensity of such people to get murdered. In seven books, over a dozen dealers personally known to Tim have the unique privilege of having their dead bodies discovered by him. In *Whistler in the Dark* (the punning titles of this and others in the series are indicative of the vein of humour running through the books) no fewer than two dealers and two innocent participants in the story die as a result of the violence which follows upon a visit from Tim Simpson!

But violence, although endemic in these books, is in fact a lesser feature than the wealth of information on antiques and fine art. Malcolm's obvious love of, and expertise in, the art and artefacts of his chosen period permeate the stories. In many of the books the geographical setting (the Victorian terraces of Camden Town in London are affectionately described), together with descriptions of the paintings and the furniture of the period, combine to provide a genuine atmosphere of that era. As various artists are featured or mentioned in more than one book of the series, and their multifarious relationships with each other thus become apparent, one is made aware of the closely interrelated nature of artistic society in the last decades of the 19th and the early decades of the 20th centuries.

Against this background we observe the modern characters and their relationships with each other; although Tim's personality does not show any great development as the series progresses, his perceptions of the other characters do alter slightly. For example, the appearance of his girlfriend Sue remains fairly constant, but Tim's own descriptions of her pass from the somewhat disparaging "like a lady librarian" to the more sympathetically feminist "looking like a female executive." More interestingly, in each of the first few books we find a scathing reference to "poofters" but in the fifth, *Gothic Pursuit*, we meet Toby Prescott, a longstanding and close friend of Tim's who is in fact bisexual (although Tim hastily dispels any suspicions about the nature of their friendship). One is led to wonder if the macho image of Tim as rugby player and womaniser created in the early books is deliberately formed to counteract the traditionally effete fine arts background.

In *The Wrong Impression*, not only do the usual run of dealers receive the by now customary Simpson-induced deathblow, but policeman Nobby Roberts lies close to death and Tim himself is more seriously injured than ever before—this latter being quite an achievement as his injuries in the previous six books would have been enough to deter a lesser man. Despite this Tim, as ever, ends up with a new acquisition for the Art Fund, and in this case with a fiancée too. Sue, who from the beginning has wisely resisted marriage to this none too solid insurance risk, and early in the series (in *The Godwin Sideboard*) even spent a year in Australia, has finally agreed to formalise their longstanding relationship. It is doubtful, however, whether being a family man will prevent Tim from seeking out trouble in future books.

—Judith Rhodes

MALING, Arthur (Gordon). American. Born in Chicago, Illinois, 11 June 1923. Educated at the Francis W. Parker School, Chicago, graduated 1940; Harvard University, Cambridge, Massachusetts (Bliss prize, 1941), B.A. (cum laude) 1944. Served in the United States Navy, 1944–45: Ensign. Married Beatrice Goldberg in 1949 (divorced 1958); one son and one daughter. Reporter, San Diego *Journal*, California, 1945–46; executive, Maling Brothers Inc., retail shoe chain, Chicago, 1946–72. Recipient: Mystery Writers of America Edgar Allan Poe award, 1980. Address: 111 East Chestnut Street, Chicago, Illinois 60611, U.S.A.

CRIME PUBLICATIONS

Novels (series: Brock Potter)

Decoy. New York, Harper, 1969; London, Joseph, 1971.
Go-Between. New York, Harper, 1970; as *Lambert's Son*, London, Joseph, 1972.
Loophole. New York, Harper, 1971.
The Snowman. New York, Harper, 1973.
Dingdong. New York, Harper, 1974.
Bent Man. New York, Harper, 1975; London, Prior, 1976.
Ripoff (Potter). New York, Harper, 1976; London, Hale, 1977.
Schroeder's Game (Potter). New York, Harper, and London, Gollancz, 1977.
Lucky Devil (Potter). New York, Harper, 1978; London, Gollancz, 1979.
The Rheingold Route. New York, Harper, and London, Gollancz, 1979.
The Koberg Link (Potter). New York, Harper, 1979; London, Gollancz, 1980.
From Thunder Bay. New York, Harper, 1981.
A Taste of Treason (Potter). New York, Harper, and London, Gollancz, 1983.
Lover and Thief. New York, Harper, 1988.

Uncollected Short Story

"The Attack," in *Alfred Hitchcock's Mystery Magazine* (New York), April 1977.

OTHER PUBLICATIONS

Other

Editor, *When Last Seen*. New York, Harper, 1977.
Editor, *Mystery Writers' Choice*. London, Gollancz, 1978.

*

Manuscript Collection: Mugar Memorial Library, Boston University.

Arthur Maling comments:

All of the novels I've written fall into the suspense category of crime fiction rather than into the puzzle or classical mystery genre. My aim has been to keep the reader wondering what happens next rather than which of the suspects has committed the crime. Money has always been the catalyst of the crimes my books deal with—often large amounts of money—and Brock Potter, the series character I created, is definitely a big-money type; he is a securities analyst.

*   *   *

With his first book, *Decoy*, Arthur Maling established himself as an author of the crime novel as opposed to the novel of detection. He concentrates on an average man, usually defeated or down-in-his-luck, who is drawn into a situation that takes him outside the bounds of the law. Maling is similar to Ambler in that he shows a common man fighting stronger evil forces without intentionally meaning to get involved. Unlike the motives in Ambler's books, the motives behind Maling's crimes are greed and money, not duty or state secrets. In *Decoy* and *Go-Between* the narrator-hero is nameless; characteristically, he is based in Chicago, but the problem may take him anywhere in the USA or to Mexico or Switzerland. One other common theme, delineated most forcefully in *The Snowman*, is the unique relationship of a father and his son. Frequently protection of a son is the motivating force in the hero's life; the son is the reason to endure the beating that Maling's hero is sure to get before the end of any book.

Maling's books are all first-person narratives, with the narrators well-characterized. We're privy to their thoughts, actions, prejudices, and we experience the problems of their every day lives, complicated by the immediate problem or danger. Most of the other characters are less well developed. One notable exception to that is Dingdong—the violent amoral thug of the novel that bears his name. The terror of his meaningless, unmindful willingness to inflict pain becomes agonizingly real.

In recent books Maling has broken slightly with his pattern by introducing a series hero, Brock Potter, a research analyst for a Wall Street brokerage firm. Potter is more attuned to the affluent life that the other heroes saw only from the outside; but he is still a loner, unsure of close emotional relationships. His interest in the problems posed in each book begins as business, making him more of a private investigator than Maling's amateurs. In all the books the story line is brisk and direct and provides a white knight, easily identifiable, who overcomes the evil, disruptive forces of the world.

—Fred Dueren

———

MALONE, Ruth. *See* **RICE, Craig.**

———

MALZBERG, Barry N(athaniel). Also writes as Mike Barry; Claudine Dumas; Mel Johnson; Lee W. Mason; Francine de Natale; K.M. O'Donnell; Gerrold Watkins; John Barry Williams. American. Born in New York City, 24 July 1939. Educated at Syracuse University, New York (Schubert Fellow, 1964–65), A.B. 1960. Married Joyce Nadine Zelnick in 1964; two daughters. Investigator, New York City Department of Welfare, and Reimbursement Agent, New York State Department of Mental Hygiene; editor, Scott Meredith Literary Agency, New York; editor, *Amazing* and *Fantastic*, 1968; managing editor, *Escapade*, 1968. Freelance writer: author of many novels under various pseudonyms for Midwood, Oracle, Soft Cover Library, and Traveler's Companion Series. Recipient: Campbell Memorial award, 1973; Locus Award, 1983. Address: Box 61, Teaneck, New Jersey 07666, U.S.A.

CRIME PUBLICATIONS

Novels

The Running of Beasts, with Bill Pronzini. New York, Putnam, 1976.
Lady of a Thousand Sorrows (as Lee W. Mason). Chicago, Playboy Press, 1977.
Acts of Mercy, with Bill Pronzini. New York, Putnam, 1977.
Night Screams, with Bill Pronzini. Chicago, Playboy Press, 1979.

Novels as Mike Barry (series: Burton Wulff [The Lone Wolf] in all books)

Night Raider. New York, Berkley, 1973.
Bay Prowler. New York, Berkley, 1973.
Boston Avenger. New York, Berkley, 1973.
Desert Stalker. New York, Berkley, 1974.
Havana Hit. New York, Berkley, 1974.
Chicago Slaughter. New York, Berkley, 1974.
Peruvian Nightmare. New York, Berkley, 1974.
Los Angeles Holocaust. New York, Berkley, 1974.
Miami Marauder. New York, Berkley, 1974.
Harlem Showdown. New York, Berkley, 1975.
Detroit Massacre. New York, Berkley, 1975.
Phoenix Inferno. New York, Berkley, 1975.
The Killing Run. New York, Berkley, 1975.
Philadelphia Blowup. New York, Berkley, 1975.

Uncollected Short Stories

"No Grace Period" in *The Man from U.N.C.L.E.* (New York), November 1967.
"Disorderly," in *The Man from U.N.C.L.E.* (New York), January 1968.
"A Small Respectful Gesture," in *Mike Shayne Mystery Magazine* (Los Angeles), October 1970.
"Beyond Sleep," in *Ellery Queen's Mystery Magazine* (New York), November 1970.
"Backing and Filling," in *Mike Shayne Mystery Magazine* (Los Angeles), February 1972.
"Cornell," in *Ellery Queen's Mystery Magazine* (New York), April 1972.
"Agony Column," in *Alfred Hitchcock Presents: Stories to Be Read with the Lights On.* New York, Random House, 1973.
"The Interceptor," in *Best Detective Stories of the Year 1973*, edited by Allen J. Hubin. New York, Dutton, 1973.
"A Matter of Life and Death," with Bill Pronzini, in *Mike Shayne Mystery Magazine* (Los Angeles), July 1974.
"I Ought to Kill You," with Bill Pronzini, in *Every Crime in the Book*, edited by Robert L. Fish. New York, Putnam, 1975.
"Multiples," with Bill Pronzini, in *Tricks and Treats*, edited by Joe Gores and Pronzini. New York, Doubleday, 1976.
"A Matter of Survival," with Bill Pronzini, in *Alfred Hitchcock's Mystery Magazine* (North Palm Beach, Florida), December 1976.
"Getting In," in *Alfred Hitchcock's Mystery Magazine* (New York), March 1977.
"What Kind of Person Are You?," with Bill Pronzini, in *Alfred Hitchcock's Mystery Magazine* (New York), April 1977.
"The Last Plagiarism," with Bill Pronzini, in *Alfred Hitchcock's Mystery Magazine* (New York), May 1977.
"Night Rider," with Bill Pronzini, in *Alfred Hitchcock's Mystery Magazine* (New York), June 1977.
"Clocks," with Bill Pronzini, in *Shadows 2*, edited by Charles L. Grant. New York, Doubleday, 1978.

"Birds of a Feather," with Bill Pronzini, in *Alfred Hitchcock's Mystery Magazine* (New York), April 1978.

"Inside Out," in *Alfred Hitchcock's Mystery Magazine* (New York), May 1978.

"Getting Out," in *Alfred Hitchcock's Mystery Magazine* (New York), June 1978.

"Cheeseburger" (as John Barry Williams, with John Lutz and Bill Pronzini), in *Alfred Hitchcock's Mystery Magazine* (New York), October 1978.

"Line of Succession," in *Alfred Hitchcock's Mystery Magazine* (New York), October 1978.

"Backing Up," in *Alfred Hitchcock's Mystery Magazine* (New York), November 1978.

"Nightshades," in *Werewolf!*, edited by Bill Pronzini. New York, Arbor House, 1979.

"Murder Is My Business," with Bill Pronzini, in *Mike Shayne Mystery Magazine* (Los Angeles), January 1979.

"Every Day in Every Way," in *Alfred Hitchcock's Mystery Magazine* (New York), January 1979.

"Final Exam," with Bill Pronzini, in *Alfred Hitchcock's Mystery Magazine* (New York), February 1979.

"The Appeal," in *Alfred Hitchcock's Mystery Magazine* (New York), March 1979.

"The Senator," in *Alfred Hitchcock's Mystery Magazine* (New York), April 1979.

"Million-to-One Shot," with Bill Pronzini, in *Ellery Queen's Mystery Magazine* (New York), July 1979.

"After the Unfortunate Accident," in *Alfred Hitchcock's Tales to Fill You with Fear and Trembling*, edited by Eleanor Sullivan. New York, Dial Press, 1980.

"The Last One Left," with Bill Pronzini, in *Bug-Eyed Monsters*, edited by Malzberg and Pronzini. New York, Harcourt Brace, 1980.

"Opening a Vein," with Bill Pronzini, in *Shadows 3*, edited by Charles L. Grant. New York, Doubleday, 1980.

"Problems Solved," with Bill Pronzini, in *Ellery Queen's Veils of Mystery*. New York, Davis, 1980.

"Rebound," with Bill Pronzini, in *Best Detective Stories of the Year 1980*, edited by Edward D. Hoch. New York, Dutton, 1980.

"Running Around," in *Alfred Hitchcock's Mystery Magazine* (New York), 2 January 1980.

"Blazing Guns of the Rio Rangers," with Bill Pronzini, in *Alfred Hitchcock's Mystery Magazine* (New York), 27 February 1980.

"The Lyran Case," with Bill Pronzini, in *Analog* (New York), March 1980.

"Notes Leading Down to the Events at Bedlam," in *Creature!*, edited by Bill Pronzini. New York, Arbor House, 1981.

"Transfer," in *The Arbor House Treasury of Horror and the Supernatural*, edited by Malzberg, Bill Pronzini, and Martin H. Greenberg. New York, Arbor House, 1981.

"The Twentieth Century Murder Case," in *Best Detective Stories of the Years 1981*, edited by Edward D. Hoch. New York, Dutton, 1981.

"Vanishing Point," with Bill Pronzini, in *Analog* (New York), 1 February 1982.

OTHER PUBLICATIONS

Novels

Oracle of the Thousand Hands. New York, Olympia Press, 1968.

Screen. New York, Olympia Press, 1968; London, Olympia Press, 1972.

Diary of a Parisian Chambermaid (as Claudine Dumas). New York, Midwood, 1969.

In My Parents' Bedroom. New York, Olympia Press, 1970.

Confessions of Westchester County. New York, Olympia Press, 1971; London, Olympia Press, 1972.

The Spread. New York, Belmont, 1971.

The Falling Astronauts. New York, Ace, 1971; London, Arrow, 1975.

Overlay. New York, Lancer, 1972; London, New English Library, 1975.

Beyond Apollo. New York, Random House, 1972; London, Faber, 1974.

Revelations. New York, Warner, 1972.

Horizontal Woman. New York, Nordon, 1972; as *The Social Worker*, 1977.

The Case for Elizabeth Moore. New York, Belmont, 1972.

The Masochist. New York, Belmont, 1972; as *Everything Happened to Susan*, 1978.

The Way of the Tiger, The Sign of the Dragon. New York, Warner, 1973.

The Men Inside. New York, Lancer, 1973; London, Arrow, 1976.

Phase IV. New York, Pocket Books, and London, Pan, 1973.

In the Enclosure. New York, Avon, 1973; London, Hale, 1976.

Herovit's World. New York, Random House, 1973; London, Arrow, 1976.

Guernica Night. Indianapolis, Bobbs Merrill, 1974; London, New English Library, 1978.

On an Alien Planet. New York, Pocket Books, 1974.

The Day of the Burning. New York, Ace, 1974.

Tactics of Conquest. New York, Pyramid, 1974.

The Sodom and Gomorrah Business. New York, Pocket Books, 1974; London, Arrow, 1979.

Underlay. New York, Avon, 1974.

The Destruction of the Temple. New York, Pocket Books, 1974; London, New English Library, 1975.

The Gamesman. New York, Pocket Books, 1975.

Conversations. Indianapolis, Bobbs Merrill, 1975.

Galaxies. New York, Pyramid, 1975.

Scop. New York, Pyramid, 1976.

The Last Transaction. New York, Pinnacle, 1977.

Chorale. New York, Doubleday, 1978.

Prose Bowl, with Bill Pronzini. New York, St. Martin's Press, 1980.

The Cross of Fire. New York, Ace, 1982.

The Remaking of Sigmund Freud. New York, Ballantine, 1985.

Novels as K.M. O'Donnell

The Empty Rooms. New York, Lancer, 1969.

Dwellers of the Deep. New York, Ace, 1970.

Universe Day. New York, Avon, 1971.

Gather in the Hall of the Planets. New York, Ace, 1971.

Short Stories

Final War and Other Fantasies (as K.M. O'Donnell). New York, Ace, 1969.

In the Pocket and Other S-F Stories. New York, Ace, 1971.

Out from Ganymede. New York, Warner, 1974.

The Many Worlds of Barry Malzberg. New York, Popular Library, 1975.

Down Here in the Dream Quarter. New York, Doubleday, 1976.

The Best of Barry Malzberg. New York, Pocket Books, 1976.

The Man Who Loved the Midnight Lady. New York, Doubleday, 1980.

Other

The Engines of the Night: Science Fiction in the Eighties. New York, Doubleday, 1982.

Editor, with Edward L. Ferman, *Final Stage*. New York, Charter House, 1974; London, Penguin, 1975.
Editor, with Edward L. Ferman, *Arena: Sports SF*. New York, Doubleday, and London, Robson, 1976.
Editor, with Edward L. Ferman, *Graven Images*. New York, Doubleday, 1976.
Editor, with Bill Pronzini, *Dark Sins, Dark Dreams: Crimes in SF*. New York, Doubleday, 1977.
Editor, with Bill Pronzini, *The End of Summer: Science Fiction in the Fifties*. New York, Ace, 1979.
Editor, with Bill Pronzini, *Shared Tomorrows: Collaboration in SF*. New York, St. Martin's Press, 1979.
Editor, with Martin H. Greenberg, *Neglected Vision*. New York, Doubleday, 1980.
Editor, with Martin H. Greenberg, *The Science Fiction of Mark Clifton*. Carbondale, Southern Illinois University Press, 1980.
Editor, with Bill Pronzini, *Bug-Eyed Monsters*. New York, Harcourt Brace, 1980.
Editor, with Bill Pronzini and Martin H. Greenberg, *The Arbor House Treasury of Horror and the Supernatural* [*Mystery and Suspense*]. New York, Arbor House, 2 vols., 1981.
Editor, with Martin H. Greenberg, *The Science Fiction of Kris Neville*. Carbondale, Southern Illinois University Press, 1984.
Editor, with Bill Pronzini and Martin H. Greenberg, *Mystery in the Mainstream*. New York, Morrow, 1986.

*

Barry N. Malzberg comments:

Although I've never considered myself to be a major writer in the field of mystery-suspense, I did wake up in 1980 or thereabouts to discover that I had published some 18 novels in this field, as well as many short stories—which quantitatively probably puts me in the 90th percentile of those listed in this volume. Ironically, that work which I consider to be my most original and significant contribution in the short story format to the genre, "The Twentieth Century Murder Case," was rejected by the mystery markets and published originally in *Fantasy and Science Fiction* magazine, thus being paradigmatic of my career. Finding more latitude in science fiction when I was trying to become a writer in the mid-1960's, I went gratefully in that direction: if I had found the mystery genre equally accepting, the bulk of my work might have been there. Same difference, as my father would have said.

*   *   *

In the mid-1960's, while marking time as a manuscript reader for a New York literary agency and trying vainly to place his own stories with *Hudson Review* and similar magazines, Barry N. Malzberg was assigned to represent an agency client named Cornell Woolrich. By then Woolrich was a wretched, wasted old man, dying by inches; but he had written the most powerful and terrifying suspense fiction ever, and Malzberg became haunted by his nightworld. Within a few years Woolrich was dead and Malzberg had begun to sell his own fiction in which the spirit of the poet of the shadows lived on. Not that their styles are at all similar: Malzberg writes plotless, characterless stream-of-consciousness interior monologues in the "serious" literary tradition, but the minds into which he plunges us invariably belong to the crazed, and from their word-screams we catch hints of the outer world that drove them mad. Usually it's a world of the future, and much of Malzberg's work is a sort of science-fiction *noir*. But the same dark forces live in his mysteries, which break down into three categories.

Over a 15-year period he has published about 30 very short crime stories, half solo work and half in tandem with Bill Pronzini. Some, like "Agony Column" and "Problems Solved," take the form of letters or documents and end with a grotesque or black-humorous plot twist; many are nightmare streams-of-consciousness in which the narrative voice is insane and, as in Woolrich, murder is the fruit of love's dying. The themes and styles are indistinguishable from those of Malzberg's science-fiction, and several of them are included in his science fiction collection *The Man Who Loved the Midnight Lady*.

In a burst of white heat during the first nine months of 1973, Malzberg wrote most of a cycle of 14 novels, published as paperback originals under the byline of Mike Barry and dealing with The Lone Wolf, a renegade ex-cop on a mad quest to wipe out the drug trade singlehanded after his girlfriend is murdered by an overdose of heroin. The series pattern of course was lifted from Don Pendleton's hugely successful Executioner books, but Malzberg characteristically subverted the format by portraying his Burt Wulff not as a patriotic hero like Pendleton's Mack Bolan but rather as a lunatic, whose paranoia progressively worsens as he tears around the country blasting druglords, until in *Philadelphia Blowup* he starts killing people indiscriminately and is at last shot down by his NYPD ex-partner.

Third and most notable of Malzberg's contributions to the genre is the trio of novels he and Bill Pronzini wrote in the later 1970's. *The Running of Beasts* may well be the finest suspense book since the death of Woolrich, a spine-freezer about a schizoid Ripper whose everyday identity is totally unaware of the night persona that has slashed several women to death. Combining Pronzini's gifts for plotting and tight structure with Malzberg's obsessional style and motifs, the novel is divided into more than 150 brief segments, presented from the alternating viewpoints of six characters: five people in the terrorized Adirondack resort town and the Ripper. We know that one of the five is the Ripper's daylight personality, but the book is so magnificently structured that at the end of each segment we are convinced beyond doubt that *that* viewpoint character is the killer. The frenzy of oscillating suspicion and mounting suspense is sustained over more than 300 pages that challenge us to guess which shell the P (for psychosis) is under. The second Pronzini Malzberg novel, *Acts of Mercy*, is a disappointing political thriller, all too conventionally written but climaxing in the typically Malzbergian revelation that the President of the United States has become, unknown to anyone around him, a raving paranoid. And their final collaboration, *Night Screams*, once again blends the authors' disparate and one would have thought incompatible talents into a superb suspenser about a maniac systematically killing off members of a group of psychics—one of whom comes to believe (although she can't convince outsiders) that the murderer is part of the group. Like *The Running of Beasts* and the best of Woolrich, it's a sharply written tour de force of terror that defies the reader to lay it down unfinished.

—Francis M. Nevins, Jr.

MANN, Abel. *See* **CREASEY, John.**

———

MANN, Jessica. British. Born in London in 1937. Educated at St. Paul's Girls' School, London; Newnham College, Cambridge, B.A. in archaeology and Anglo-Saxon, M.A.; University of Leicester, LL.B. Married, Charles Thomas; two sons and two daughters. Agent: Sheila Watson, Gregory and Radice, Riverside Studios, Crisp Road, Hammersmith, London W6 9RL. Address: Lambessow, St. Clement, Truro, Cornwall, England.

CRIME PUBLICATIONS

Novels (series: Thea Crawford)

A Charitable End. London, Collins, and New York, McKay, 1971.
Mrs. Knox's Profession. London, Macmillan, and New York, McKay, 1972.
The Only Security (Crawford). London, Macmillan, 1973; as *Troublecross*, New York, McKay, 1973.
The Sticking Place. London, Macmillan, and New York, McKay, 1974.
Captive Audience (Crawford). London, Macmillan, and New York, McKay, 1975.
The Eighth Deadly Sin. London, Macmillan, 1976.
The Sting of Death. London, Macmillan, 1978; New York, Doubleday, 1983.
Funeral Sites. London, Macmillan, 1981; New York, Doubleday, 1982.
No Man's Island. London, Macmillan, and New York, Doubleday, 1983.
Grave Goods. London, Macmillan, 1984; New York, Doubleday, 1985.
A Kind of Healthy Grave. London, Macmillan, and New York, St. Martin's Press, 1986.
Death Beyond the Nile. London, Macmillan, 1988; New York, St. Martin's Press, 1989.

OTHER PUBLICATIONS

Other

Deadlier Than the Male: An Investigation into Feminine Crime Writing. Newton Abbot, Devon, David and Charles, and New York, Macmillan, 1981.

* * *

Qualities that distinguish Jessica Mann's slim, ironic novels include literacy, an uneasy feeling that sinister things are constantly happening behind the most ordinary doors, and, above all, a sense of locale so vivid that a reader feels as if he were revisiting a familiar place even when the author's setting is imaginary, like bleak Forway in *No Man's Island.*

There isn't much external violence. Mostly, when it occurs, one senses the author's distaste for it. (An exception is at the end of *No Man's Island,* when the bereaved heroine throws herself into a hand-to-hand showdown with obvious relish.) But violence does exist by inference inside the heads of Mann's characters. With understatement the author conveys a pervasive sense of menace that seeps from the characters and gradually permeates the stories, giving small details and observations an aura of uncertainty and uncomfortable ambiguity. A reader isn't sure: are the Jewish wife's suspicions in *The Sticking Place* grounded in fact or just aspects of her own insecurity? is the heroine of *Funeral Sites* imagining some of the things that cause her mounting panic?

Whether they are the conventional tweedy ladies of an Edinburgh do-good group (*A Charitable End*), the Leicester housewife compensating for humdrumness by acting out her more colorful fantasies (*Mrs. Knox's Profession*), or the Cornish academics bickering among themselves (*The Only Security, Captive Audience*), Mann's protagonists find both their external and their internal lives jarred by something that happens. Characters recur in the books, sometimes shifting from subsidiary to leading roles, as though the author had discovered new facets of their personalities. Sometimes the characters trigger the suspense with their own bizarre behavior (*The English Deadly Sin*), but in the more recent novels, plot dominates and characters are subservient.

Deadlier Than the Male, a non-fiction work, is a tightly researched, entertainingly written study of some acclaimed women mystery writers. Analyzing the work of Christie, Sayers, and others, Mann speculates how the author's life and personality have influenced her work, and what unique trait in each writer continues to appeal to generations of readers.

—Ellen H. Bleiler

———

MANTON, Peter. *See* **CREASEY, John.**

———

MARCH, Maxwell. *See* **ALLINGHAM, Margery.**

———

MARINO, Nick. *See* **DEMING, Richard.**

———

MARLOWE, Dan J(ames). Also wrote as Albert Avellano. American. Born in Lowell, Massachusetts, 10 July 1914. Attended Bentley School of Accounting and Finance. Worked in accounting, insurance, and public relations until 1957. Self-employed writer. Served on City Council and as Mayor pro tem of Harbor Beach, Michigan. Wrote a weekly column for Michigan newspapers and reviews for the Detroit *Free Press.* Died.

CRIME PUBLICATIONS

Novels (series: Earl Drake; Johnny Killain)

Doorway to Death (Killain). New York, Avon, and London, Digit, 1959.
Killer with a Key (Killain). New York, Avon, 1959.

Doom Service (Killain). New York, Avon, 1960.
The Fatal Frails (Killain). New York, Avon, 1960.
Shake a Crooked Town (Killain). New York, Avon, 1961.
Backfire. New York, Berkley, 1961.
The Name of the Game Is Death (Drake). New York, Fawcett, 1962; London, Muller, 1963; as *Operation Overkill*, London, Hodder and Stoughton, 1973.
Strongarm. New York, Fawcett, 1963.
Never Live Twice. New York, Fawcett, 1964.
Death Deep Down. New York, Fawcett, 1965.
Four for the Money. New York, Fawcett, 1966.
The Vengeance Man. New York, Fawcett, 1966.
The Raven Is a Blood Red Bird, with William Odell. New York, Fawcett, 1967.
Route of the Red Gold. New York, Fawcett, 1967.
One Endless Hour (Drake). New York, Fawcett, 1969; London, Gold Lion, 1973; as *Operation Endless Hour*, London, Hodder and Stoughton, 1975.
Operation Fireball (Drake). New York, Fawcett, 1969; London, Hodder and Stoughton, 1972.
Flashpoint (Drake). New York, Fawcett, 1970; as *Operation Flashpoint*, New York, Fawcett, and London, Hodder and Stoughton, 1972.
Operation Breakthrough (Drake). New York, Fawcett, 1971; London, Hodder and Stoughton, 1972.
Operation Drumfire (Drake). New York, Fawcett, and London, Hodder and Stoughton, 1972.
Operation Checkmate (Drake). New York, Fawcett, 1972; London, Hodder and Stoughton, 1973.
Operation Stranglehold (Drake). New York, Fawcett, 1973; London, Hodder and Stoughton, 1974.
Operation Whiplash (Drake). New York, Fawcett, 1973; London, Hodder and Stoughton, 1974.
Operation Hammerlock (Drake). New York, Fawcett, 1974; London, Hodder and Stoughton, 1975.
Operation Deathmaker (Drake). New York, Fawcett, 1975; London, Hodder and Stoughton, 1977.
Operation Counterpunch (Drake). New York, Fawcett, 1976.

Uncollected Short Stories

"Scratch One Mark," in *Mike Shayne Mystery Magazine* (New York), July 1959.
"The Short and Simple Annals," in *Best Detective Stories of the Year*, edited by Anthony Boucher. New York, Dutton, 1965.
"The Live One," in *Alfred Hitchcock's Mystery Magazine* (New York), October 1966.
"The Name of the Game Is Tape," in *The Man from U.N.C.L.E.* (New York), October 1966.
"The Annuity," in *Alfred Hitchcock's Mystery Magazine* (New York), December 1966.
"Center of Attention," in *Alfred Hitchcock's Mystery Magazine* (New York), April 1968.
"Off-Key Payoff," in *Alfred Hitchcock's Mystery Magazine* (New York), June 1968.
"Infinite License," in *Alfred Hitchcock's Mystery Magazine* (New York), September 1968.
"The Second Time Around," in *Alfred Hitchcock's Mystery Magazine* (New York), March 1972.
"Give-and-Take," in *Alfred Hitchcock's Mystery Magazine* (New York), December 1972.
"Grounded," in *Alfred Hitchcock's Mystery Magazine* (New York), February 1973.
"The Donor," in *Tricks and Treats*, edited by Joe Gores and Bill Pronzini. New York, Doubleday, 1976; as *Mystery Writers Choice*, London, Gollancz, 1977.

"All the Way Home," in *When Last Seen*, edited by Arthur Maling. New York, Harper, 1977.
"The Man in Charge," in *Ellery Queen's Mystery Magazine* (New York), November 1977.
"Don't Lose Your Cool," in *Alfred Hitchcock's Tales to Scare You Stiff*, edited by Eleanor Sullivan. New York, Davis, 1978.
"A Casual Crime," in *Alfred Hitchcock's Mystery Magazine* (New York), 26 March 1980.
"The Girl Who Sold Money," in *Alfred Hitchcock's Mystery Magazine* (New York), 2 June 1980.
"Patterns," in *Mike Shayne Mystery Magazine* (Los Angeles), August 1980.
"Operation Good Samaritan," in *Mike Shayne Mystery Magazine* (Los Angeles), March 1981.
"Double Jeopardy," in *Skullduggery*, Summer 1981.
"Pressure," in *Mike Shayne Mystery Magazine* (Los Angeles), February 1982.
"Two Birds with One Stone," in *Ellery Queen's Mystery Magazine* (New York), July 1982.
"Such Gorgeous Legs," in *Woman's World*, 28 September 1982.
"Stakeout," in *Mike Shayne Mystery Magazine* (Los Angeles), November 1982.
"The Playwright," in *Spiderweb*, Winter 1982.
"The Time of Her Life," in *Mike Shayne Mystery Magazine* (Los Angeles), August 1983.
"Dead Giveaway," in *Mike Shayne Mystery Magazine* (Los Angeles), November 1983.

Uncollected Short Stories as Albert Avellano

"The Lion's Share," in *Alfred Hitchcock's Mystery Magazine* (New York), May 1971.
"Nothing Personal," in *Mike Shayne Mystery Magazine* (Los Angeles), September 1972.
"When the Captain Died," in *Alfred Hitchcock's Mystery Magazine* (North Palm Beach, Florida), July 1974.
"Blue Devil," in *Alfred Hitchcock's Mystery Magazine* (North Palm Beach, Florida), March 1975.
"Like Any Other Wild Animal," in *Alfred Hitchcock's Mystery Magazine* (North Palm Beach, Florida), June 1975.
"Crime by Accident," in *Alfred Hitchcock's Mystery Magazine* (North Palm Beach, Florida), July 1975.
"Funeral Talent," in *Mike Shayne Mystery Magazine* (North Palm Beach, Florida), July 1975.
"Open Sights," in *Alfred Hitchcock's Mystery Magazine* (North Palm Beach, Florida), December 1975.
"Routine Investigation," in *Alfred Hitchcock's Mystery Magazine* (North Palm Beach, Florida), March 1976.
"Great Spot," in *Alfred Hitchcock's Mystery Magazine* (North Palm Beach, Florida), April 1976.

*   *   *

Dan J. Marlowe's masterpiece is *The Name of the Game Is Death*, the first of the Earl Drake series. It's a chilling story of how Drake becomes a professional thief, pulling off well-executed robberies and capers. Along with Marlowe's expertise, his humanity is evident in his best-drawn, toughest characters, Johnny Killain and Earl Drake. Marlowe's first five books feature Killain, a semi-detective who is violent with mild flashes of sensitivity. The Earl Drake books, especially *The Name of the Game Is Death*, display an intelligent, sensitive character who turns to crime because of the brutality of middle-class life. Although Marlowe's editors at Fawcett eventually sanitized Drake by changing him from a professional thief to a secret agent, the theme of justice and retribution for wrongs pervades most of the Drake books.

But the post-1962 books Marlowe wrote improved for several reasons. Chief among them is Marlowe's relationship with Al Nussbaum, a bank robber whom Marlowe had helped get paroled. Nussbaum shared his intimate knowledge about weapons, ballistics, locks, safes, vaults, and alarm systems with Marlowe; that detail lent realism to Marlowe's books, so much so Marlowe found himself leaving out one important detail of a process so he wouldn't be accused of writing caper manuals for professional thieves. Two of Marlowe's best novels, *One Endless Hour* and *Four for the Money*, benefited directly from Nussbaum's information. Two other books explore Marlowe's major theme of justice and retribution: *Never Live Twice*, with an ingenious amnesia plot, and *The Vengeance Man*, a powerful thriller with a shattering conclusion.

—George Kelley

MARLOWE, Derek. British. Born in London, 21 May 1938. Educated at Cardinal Vaughan School, London, 1949–57; University of London, 1957–60. Married Sukie Phipps in 1968; two daughters and three sons. Recipient: Writers Guild award, 1972, and Emmy award, 1972, both for television writing. Agent: Tim Corrie, Peters, Fraser and Dunlop, 5th Floor, The Chambers, Chelsea Harbour, Lots Road, London SW10, 0XF, England.

CRIME PUBLICATIONS

Novels

A Dandy in Aspic. London, Gollancz, and New York, Putnam, 1966.
Echoes of Celandine. London, Cape, and New York, Viking Press, 1970; as *The Disappearance*, London, Penguin, 1977.
Do You Remember England? London, Cape, and New York, Viking Press, 1972.
Somebody's Sister. New York, Viking Press, and London, Cape, 1974.
Nightshade. London, Weidenfeld and Nicolson, 1975; New York, Viking Press, 1976.

OTHER PUBLICATIONS

Novels

The Memories of Venus Lackey. London, Cape, and New York, Viking Press, 1968.
A Single Summer with L.B.: The Summer of 1816. London, Cape, 1969; as *A Single Summer with Lord B.*, New York, Viking Press, 1970.
The Rich Boy from Chicago. New York, St. Martin's Press, 1979; London, Weidenfeld and Nicolson, 1980.
Nancy Astor, The Lady from Virginia (novelization of television play). London, Weidenfeld and Nicolson, 1982; New York, Dell, 1984.

Plays

The Seven Who Were Hanged, adaptation of a novel by Andreyev (produced Edinburgh, 1961; as *The Scarecrow*, produced London, 1964).

The Lower Depths, adaptation of a translation by Moura Budberg of a play by Gorki (produced London, 1962).
How Disaster Struck the Harvest (produced London, 1964).
How I Assumed the Role of a Popular Dandy for Purposes of Seduction and Other Base Matters (produced London, 1965).

Screenplays: *A Dandy in Aspic*, 1968; *Universal Soldier*, with Joseph Massot, 1972; *A Single Summer*, 1979; *The Knight*, 1979.

Television Films: *Requiem for Modigliani*, 1970; *The Search for the Nile* series, with Michael Hastings, 1971; *The Knight* series, 1978; *Nancy Astor*, 1982; *A Married Man*, from the novel by Piers Paul Read, 1983; *Jamaica Inn*, from the novel by Daphne du Maurier, 1983; *A Married Man*, 1984; *First Among Equals*, from the novel by Jeffrey Archer, 1986.

*

Derek Marlowe comments:
I have written to date (1978) eight novels, only four of which could be considered thrillers. There is no premeditated purpose to this on my part: I do not choose in advance to write an "entertainment" as opposed to a "novel." Locations influence me very much and usually provoke the story—Berlin for *A Dandy in Aspic*, Haiti for *Nightshade* and, more especially, San Francisco for *Somebody's Sister* which is probably the purest detective story of them all.

I like to intrigue the reader; perhaps this may happen more in a romantic novel (*A Single Summer with L.B.*) than in a straight thriller. I have no answers to *why* I write the particular book at the particular time except that my own state of mind (very mercurial) dictates it. I am Ford Madox Ford wanting to be Chandler or Woolrich, and vice versa.

*   *   *

Derek Marlowe has published a number of mysteries, each using a rather different formula in an interesting but not wholly satisfactory way. His first novel, *A Dandy in Aspic*, is a spy novel somewhat in the manner of John le Carré and based on the excellent, intriguing notion that a double agent is assigned to kill himself. As with Marlowe's other work the result is highly literate (and literary), stylistically most elegant, and with a well-researched, totally credible background (in this case, Berlin). Like le Carré and unlike, say, Ian Fleming, Marlowe depicts the world of espionage as infinitely cold, grey, and maze-like. His range of literary and cultural reference suggests that there is an abiding world of beauty which espionage and all it stands for attempts to negate. The central character, Eberlin, feels that he is "merely marking time" until death, and the world of this novel might easily evoke Eliot's "I had not thought death had undone so many." Despite some moments of pretentiousness the novel is an impressive debut, not least in the adroitness with which Marlowe keeps the reader, along with Eberlin, guessing.

Echoes of Celandine is something of a let-down. Again, the basic idea—that a professional assassin, trying to find his estranged wife, should end by killing her when he believes he is fulfilling an assignment—is reasonably original, but here Marlowe's ability to enmesh the reader in the hero's bewilderment and growing fear is countered by an arch first-person narrator and an intrusive Grail Quest motif (the hero is called Jay Mallory and, like Gatsby, searches for the Grail in the figure of a lost love), coupled with an uneasy use of the isolated locale and remote mastermind figure.

When one reads through Marlowe's books one after the other it seems as though he is never quite sure whether or not he is writing pastiche (albeit serious pastiche). If the first novel owes much to le Carré and *Echoes of Celandine* reminds the reader of Graham Greene, then *Somebody's Sister* undoubtedly represents a move to the world of Hammett and Chandler. Its hero, Walter Brackett, is a middle-aged, unsuccessful British-born private eye who entered the profession with dreams of being like Spade and Marlowe only to discover that he "hadn't just stepped out of the pages of *Dime Detective*. That was simply what [he was] worth." Marlowe rarely puts a foot wrong in depicting the American scene, characters, and dialogue, but Brackett remains a rather shadowy figure and the plot is so mystifying that the world outside the hero, though accurately rendered, is insubstantial. The novel is not, as one reviewer suggested, "a valentine to a romantic legend" so much as rather shaky tangent to that legend. The mean streets are not mean enough.

Nightshade takes place mostly in a Haiti seen as a nightmarish testing-ground for the inadequate married couple, Edward and Amy Lytton, who are on holiday there. Part psychological novel, part occult thriller, *Nightshade*, as the title suggests, uses an exotic island as a vision of what happens when civilized man steps outside the controls of civilization and finds himself face to face with his deepest fears and desires. The novel is often gripping but is flawed by having an unnamed narrator whose intrusions into the novels are fussy and pretentious: "within hours Daniel Azevedo had stepped from the periphery and entered their lives, both Edward's and Amy's, and from that moment the tragedy—for that surely was what it was—took hold of them all. One by one."

Derek Marlowe's talent has now declared itself beyond doubt. Yet since he has written in several thriller formulae, as well as in the genres of romance and historical novel, a doubt remains as to whether he has yet made any of these modes truly his own.

—John S. Whitley

MARLOWE, Hugh. *See* **HIGGINS, Jack.**

MARLOWE, Stephen. Also writes as Adam Chase; Andrew Frazer; Ellery Queen; Jason Ridgway; C. H. Thames. American. Born Milton Lesser in New York City, 7 August 1928; Educated at the College of William and Mary, Williamsburg, Virginia, B.A. 1949. Served in the United States Army, 1952–54. Married 1) Leigh Lang in 1950 (divorced 1962); 2) Ann Humbert; two daughters. Editor, Scott Meredith, New York, 1949–50; now a full-time writer. Writer-in-Residence, College of William and Mary, 1974–75, 1980–81. Member, board of directors, Mystery Writers of America. Agent: Scott Meredith Literary Agency, 845 Third Avenue, New York, New York 10022, U.S.A.

CRIME PUBLICATIONS

Novels (series: Chester Drum)

Catch the Brass Ring. New York, Ace, 1954.
Turn Left for Murder. New York, Ace, 1955.
Model for Murder. Hasbrouck Heights, New Jersey, Graphic, 1955.
The Second Longest Night (Drum). New York, Fawcett, 1955; London, Fawcett, 1958.
Dead on Arrival. New York, Ace, 1956.
Mecca for Murder (Drum). New York, Fawcett, 1956; London, Fawcett, 1957.
Violence Is Golden (as C.H. Thames). New York, Bouregy, 1956.
Killers Are My Meat (Drum). New York, Fawcett, 1957; London, Fawcett, 1958.
Murder Is My Dish (Drum). New York, Fawcett, 1957.
Trouble Is My Name (Drum). New York, Fawcett, 1957; London, Fawcett, 1958.
Violence Is My Business (Drum). New York, Fawcett, 1958; London, Fawcett, 1959.
Terror Is My Trade (Drum). New York, Fawcett, 1958; London, Muller, 1960.
Blonde Bait. New York, Avon, 1959.
Double in Trouble (Drum), with Richard S. Prather. New York, Fawcett, 1959.
Find Eileen Hardin—Alive! (as Andrew Frazer). New York, Avon, 1959.
Passport to Peril. New York, Fawcett, 1959.
Homicide Is My Game (Drum). New York, Fawcett, 1959; London, Muller, 1960.
Danger Is My Line (Drum). New York, Fawcett, 1960; London, Muller, 1961.
Death Is My Comrade (Drum). New York, Fawcett, 1960; London, Muller, 1961.
The Fall of Marty Moon (as Andrew Frazer). New York, Avon, 1960.
Peril Is My Pay (Drum). New York, Fawcett, 1960; London, Muller, 1961.
Dead Man's Tale (as Ellery Queen). New York, Pocket Books, 1961; London, New English Library, 1967.
Manhunt Is My Mission (Drum). New York, Fawcett, 1961; London, Muller, 1962.
Jeopardy Is My Job (Drum). New York, Fawcett, 1962; London, Muller, 1963.
Blood of My Brother (as C. H. Thames). New York, Permabooks, 1963.
Francesca (Drum). New York, Fawcett, and London, Muller, 1963.
Drum Beat—Berlin. New York, Fawcett, 1964.
Drum Beat—Dominique. New York, Fawcett, 1965.
Drum Beat—Madrid. New York, Fawcett, 1966.
The Search for Bruno Heidler. New York, Macmillan, 1966; London, Boardman, 1967.
Drum Beat—Erica. New York, Fawcett, 1967.
Come Over, Red Rover. New York, Macmillan, 1968.
Drum Beat—Marianne. New York, Fawcett, 1968.
The Summit. New York, Geis, 1970.
Colossus. New York, Macmillan, 1972; London, W. H. Allen, 1973.
The Man with No Shadow. Englewood Cliffs, New Jersey, Prentice Hall, and London, W. H. Allen, 1974.
The Cawthorn Journals. Englewood Cliffs, New Jersey, Prentice Hall, 1975; London, W. H. Allen, 1976; as *Too Many Chiefs*, London, New English Library, 1977.
Translation. Englewood Cliffs, New Jersey, Prentice Hall, 1976; London, W. H. Allen, 1977.
The Valkyrie Encounter. New York, Putnam, and London, New English Library, 1978.

1956. New York, Arbor House, 1981; London, New English Library, 1982.
Deborah's Legacy. New York, Zebra, 1983.

Novels as Jason Ridgway (series: Brian Guy)

West Side Jungle. New York, New American Library, 1958.
Adam's Fall (Guy). New York, Permabooks, 1960.
People in Glass Houses (Guy). New York, Permabooks, 1961.
Hardly a Man Is Now Alive (Guy). New York, Permabooks, 1962.
The Treasure of the Cosa Nostra (Guy). New York, Pocket Books, 1966.

Uncollected Short Stories

"The Shill," in *A Choice of Murders*, edited by Dorothy Salisbury Davis. New York, Scribner, 1958; London, Macdonald, 1960.
"Drum Beat," in *Best Detective Stories of the Year*, edited by Brett Halliday. New York, Dutton, 1962.
"Wanted, Dead or Alive," in *Best Detective Stories of the Year*, edited by Anthony Boucher. New York, Dutton, 1964.
"Baby Sitter," in *Come Seven, Come Death*, edited by Henry Morrison. New York, Pocket Books, 1965.
"Wait for a New Lover," in *Nightline 4*, no. 2, 1970.

OTHER PUBLICATIONS

Novels

The Golden Ape (as Adam Chase, with Paul W. Fairman). New York, Avalon, 1959.
Recruit for Andromeda (as Milton Lesser). New York, Ace, 1959.
The Shining. New York, Trident Press, 1963.

Short Stories as Milton Lesser

Secret of the Black Planet. New York, Belmont, 1965.

Other (for children) as Milton Lesser

Earthbound. Philadelphia, Winston, 1952; London, Hutchinson, 1955.
The Star Seekers. Philadelphia, Winston, 1953.
Stadium Beyond the Stars. Philadelphia, Winston, 1960.
Spacemen, Go Home. New York, Holt Rinehart, 1962.
Lost Worlds and the Men Who Found Them. Racine, Wisconsin, Whitman, 1962.
Walt Disney's Strange Animals of Australia. Racine, Wisconsin, Whitman, 1963.

Editor, *Looking Forward: An Anthology of Science Fiction* (for adults). New York, Beechhurst Press, 1953; London, Cassell, 1955.

*   *   *

Stephen Marlowe was already an established science fiction writer under his real name, Milton Lesser, when he began publishing his paperback original mystery novels in the mid-1950's. He has also published mysteries under three other pseudonyms, Andrew Frazer (including the very successful *The Fall of Marty Moon*), Jason Ridgway (a short series about Brian Guy), and C.H. Thames (two of his weaker novels).

Most of the books published by Marlowe are Chester Drum private eye titles. The Marlowe name is an obvious homage to Raymond Chandler, but Drum, at least in his early adventures, was more of a Spillane-type hero. Like Mike Hammer's, Drum's jobs were often as much espionage/counterespionage as they were sleuthing. The carefully established Drum background, including valuable service as an FBI fieldman which yielded invaluable connections in high places, and the location of his office in Washington, D.C., made his frequent involvement in intelligence affairs all the more convincing. His adventures were paced a bit slower than the models Spillane provided and had less spectacular comeuppances for the villains, but they remain among the best of the many imitations of Spillane that appeared in the 1950's. On occasion, as in *Death Is My Comrade*, Marlowe outdid his mentor in his audacious demands for "suspension of disbelief." That book began with a rather conventional murder and an assault on the hero, then moved rapidly through an outlandish CIA plot to spirit a would-be defector out of Russia by exchanging his fabulously successful industrialist brother for him, encounters with impressive Russian security officers who had penetrated Drum's cover before his arrival in Moscow, an escape overland to Finland, and the kidnapping of the female villain by Russian gypsies.

Most of the early books had patterned titles, resembling *Murder Is My Dish* and *Trouble Is My Name*, which were two of the best. Especially in the last five Drum books (the "Drum Beat" series) and in *Francesca*, Marlowe managed a very mature series of international detective adventures combining the exotic locales and furious action more typically seen in the most adventurous spy fiction (yet rarely involving espionage) with quite satisfactory detective puzzles of the hard-boiled variety. The earlier tour de force collaboration with Richard S. Prather, *Double in Trouble*, had Drum and Prather's usually more light-hearted detective hero Shell Scott working at very interesting cross-purposes.

Marlowe's later books, almost all involving espionage, are much more interesting than those which preceded the Drum series. *The Search for Bruno Heidler*, about the tracing of a still dangerous war criminal, *The Summit*, with international intrigue at the highest levels, and *Come Over, Red Rover* are all highly recommended. Among the early non-series books, those involving espionage now seem badly dated, as do early Drum novels with similar content. However, two tough early mysteries, *Model for Murder* and *Catch the Brass Ring*, though not the equals of much of Marlowe's most recent work, remain brilliant early pieces.

—Jeff Banks

————

MARQUAND, John P(hillips). American. Born in Wilmington, Delaware, 10 November 1893. Educated at Newburyport High School, Massachusetts; Harvard University, Cambridge, Massachusetts, 1912–15, A.B. 1915. Served with the Massachusetts National Guard in the Mexican Border Service, 1916; student, Camp Plattsburg, 1917; commissioned 1st Lieutenant in the Field Artillery, and served with the 4th Brigade in France, 1917–18; Special Consultant to the Secretary of War, Washington, D.C., 1944–45; War Correspondent for the United States Navy, 1945. Married 1) Christina Davenport Sedgwick in 1922 (divorced 1935), one son and one daughter; 2) Adelaide Hooker in 1937 (divorced 1958), two sons and one daughter. Assistant magazine editor,

Boston *Transcript*, 1915–17; with the Sunday Magazine Department, New York *Tribune*, 1919–20; advertising copywriter, J. Walter Thompson Company, New York, 1920–21. Member, board of overseers, Harvard University; Member, editorial board, Book-of-the-Month Club, New York. Recipient: Pulitzer prize, 1938; Sarah Josepha Hale award, 1957. Litt. D.: University of Maine, Orono, 1941; University of Rochester, New York, 1944; Yale University, New Haven, Connecticut, 1950; D.H.L.: Bates College, Lewiston, Maine, 1954. Member, American Academy. *Died 16 July 1960.*

CRIME PUBLICATIONS

Novels (series: Mr. Moto)

Ming Yellow. Boston, Little Brown, and London, Lovat Dickson, 1935.
No Hero. Boston, Little Brown, 1935; as *Mr. Moto Takes a Hand*, London, Hale, 1940; as *Your Turn, Mr. Moto*, New York, Berkley, 1963.
Thank You, Mr. Moto. Boston, Little Brown, 1936; London, Jenkins, 1937.
Think Fast, Mr. Moto. Boston, Little Brown, 1937; London, Hale, 1938.
Mr. Moto Is So Sorry. Boston, Little Brown, 1938; London, Hale, 1939.
Don't Ask Questions. London, Hale, 1941.
Last Laugh, Mr. Moto. Boston, Little Brown, 1942; London, Hale, 1943.
It's Loaded, Mr. Bauer. London, Hale, 1949.
Stopover: Tokyo. Boston, Little Brown, and London, Collins, 1957; as *The Last of Mr. Moto*, New York, Berkley, 1963; as *Right You Are, Mr. Moto*, New York, Popular Library, 1977.

OTHER PUBLICATIONS

Novels

The Unspeakable Gentleman. New York, Scribner, and London, Hodder and Stoughton, 1922.
The Black Cargo. New York, Scribner, and London, Hodder and Stoughton, 1925.
Do Tell Me, Doctor Johnson. Privately printed, 1928.
Warning Hill. Boston, Little Brown, 1930.
Haven's End. Boston, Little Brown, 1933; London, Hale, 1938.
The Late George Apley: A Novel in the Form of a Memoir. Boston, Little Brown, and London, Hale, 1937.
Wickford Point. Boston, Little Brown, and London, Hale, 1939.
H.M. Pulham, Esquire. Boston, Little Brown, and London, Hale, 1942.
So Little Time. Boston, Little Brown, 1943; London, Hale, 1944.
Repent in Haste. Boston, Little Brown, 1945; London, Hale, 1949.
B.F.'s Daughter. Boston, Little Brown, 1946; as *Polly Fulton*, London, Hale, 1947.
Point of No Return. Boston, Little Brown, and London, Hale, 1949.
Melville Goodwin, USA. Boston, Little Brown, 1951; London, Hale, 1952.
Sincerely, Willis Wayde. Boston, Little Brown, and London, Hale, 1955.
Women and Thomas Harrow. Boston, Little Brown, 1958; London, Collins, 1959.

Short Stories

Four of a Kind. New York, Scribner, 1923.
Sun, Sea, and Sand. New York, Dell, 1950.
Life at Happy Knoll. Boston, Little Brown, 1957; London, Collins, 1958.

Play

The Late George Apley, with George S. Kaufman, adaptation of the novel by Marquand (produced New York, 1944). New York, Dramatists Play Service, 1946.

Other

Prince and Boatswain: Sea Tales from the Recollections of Rear-Admiral Charles E. Clark, with James Morris Morgan. Greenfield, Massachusetts, E.A. Hall, 1915.
Lord Timothy Dexter of Newburyport, Mass. New York, Minton Balch, and London, Unwin, 1926.
Federalist Newburyport; or, Can Historical Fiction Remove a Fly from Amber? New York, Newcomer Society, 1952.
Thirty Years (miscellany). Boston, Little Brown, 1954; London, Hale, 1955.
Timothy Dexter Revisited. Boston, Little Brown, 1960.

*

Bibliography: "A John P. Marquand Checklist Based on Bibliography of William White," in *The Late John Marquand: A Biography* by Stephen Birmingham, Philadelphia, Lippincott, 1972.

Critical Studies: *Marquand* by John J. Gross, Boston, Twayne, 1963; *Marquand: An American Life* by Millicent Bell, Boston, Little Brown, 1979.

*   *   *

The Pulitzer prize-winning author John P. Marquand won critical acclaim for his fictional analyses of men, manners, and money in a conservative New England setting. Marquand was less proud of his popular mystery fiction. In a 1959 interview, he said of his slight but sinister Japanese secret agent, "Mr. Moto was my literary disgrace. I wrote about him to get shoes for the baby. I can't say why people still remember him." Today's readers disagree. They still find Marquand's six Mr. Moto novels memorable.

Mr. Moto first appeared, fully developed, in *No Hero*. A Japanese aristocrat of many talents and devious ways, university-educated Mr. Moto speaks an impressive number of languages. He can navigate, wait on tables, mix drinks, and act as a competent valet and careful chauffeur. Short, slim, gold-toothed Mr. Moto is agile, an acute judge of character, and an excellent shot proud to risk his life for his Emperor. Although he is a formidable enemy, strong on liquidation, he respects courage, loyalty, patriotism, and professionalism in other agents he meets. His appearance is always impeccable; his English is always flawless, although very Japanese.

The Mr. Moto novels fall into a memorably workable formula. They are set in an exotic foreign locale, and their hero is always a weak, untried, sometimes rather disreputable young American who meets and falls in love with an attractive girl involved directly or indirectly in international espionage. In the course of their adventures this couple will encounter Mr. Moto, sometimes as adversary, sometimes as ally, sometimes as both. After much intrigue and some violence, the American hero will resolve the conflict and end the intrigue, winning both the girl's heart and Mr. Moto's commendation.

In *No Hero*, Casey Lee, a down-and-out flier in Tokyo, is sent to Singapore by a beautiful Russian to search for a secret aviation fuel formula. Lee destroys the formula to prevent it from falling into the hands of America's enemies. In Peking, Tom Nelson, the expatriate hero of *Thank You, Mr. Moto*, blunders into a plot to steal priceless Chinese scroll paintings and to create an anti-American incident. With the help of Mr. Moto and a pretty buyer for an American museum, the rebels are liquidated and the paintings rescued. In *Think Fast, Mr. Moto*, Willian Hitchings, a member of a prominent Singapore banking firm, travels to Honolulu to close a disreputable gambling house. He finds that the house's profits are funding Chinese rebels, but that its owner is young and beautiful. With Mr. Moto's help he ends the scandal and marries the girl. As Calvin Gates (*Mr. Moto Is So Sorry*) drifts towards an archeological dig in North China, he meets a pretty young archeologist, her sinister Russian guide, and Mr. Moto. A coded cigarette case resolves the Russian-Japanese struggle for power in Mongolia and Calvin's personal problems. *Last Laugh, Mr. Moto* pits Bob Bolles, a hard-drinking ex-Navy pilot, against a Nazi, a lovely Vichy French agent, and Mr. Moto in a search for a secret American aviation device lost on an obscure Caribbean Island. *Stopover: Tokyo*, Marquand's most successful mystery, is a sensitive depiction of Jack Rhyce and Ruth Bogart, two American agents who must live out their cover roles as do-gooders in a suspicious Tokyo organization which masks a Soviet plot against the United States. Mr. Moto is able to prevent the international incident, but only at the cost of Ruth's life. In this last novel Marquand brilliantly describes the constant tension, danger, and responsibility a professional secret agent must endure on a mission.

Most memorably, the Mr. Moto novels evoke the atmosphere and mystery of far-off places. Marquand loved travel; he visited Europe, Africa, the Middle East, the Amazon Valley, the Caribbean, Japan, and China. The Mr. Moto novels always use detail to suggest the spectacular and the mundane; to develop a feeling for time, place and custom; to create the beautiful and alien world in which Mr. Moto lives, lurks, and operates.

—Katherine Staples

———

MARRIC, J. J. *See* **CREASEY, John.**

———

MARSH, (Edith) Ngaio. New Zealander. Born in Christchurch, 23 April 1895. Educated at St. Margaret's College, Christchurch, 1910–14; Canterbury University College School of Art, Christchurch, 1915–20. Actress in New Zealand, 1920–23; theatrical producer, New Zealand, 1923–27; interior decorator, in partnership with Mrs. Tahu Rhodes, London, 1928–32. Served in a New Zealand Red Cross transport unit during World War II. Producer for D.D. O'Connor Theatre Management, New Zealand, 1944–52; artistic director, British Commonwealth Theatre Company, 1951–52. Honorary Lecturer in Drama, Canterbury University. Ngaio Marsh Theatre founded at Canterbury University, 1967. Recipient: Mystery Writers of America Grand Master award, 1977. D. Litt.:

Canterbury University, 1962. Fellow, Royal Society of Arts. O.B.E. (Officer, Order of the British Empire), 1948; D.B.E. (Dame Commander, Order of the British Empire), 1966. *Died 18 February 1982.*

CRIME PUBLICATIONS

Novels (series: Inspector/Superintendent Roderick Alleyn in all books)

A Man Lay Dead.   London, Bles, 1934; New York, Sheridan, 1942.
Enter a Murderer.   London, Bles, 1935; New York, Pocket Books, 1941.
The Nursing-Home Murder, with Henry Jellett.   London, Bles, 1935; New York, Sheridan, 1941.
Death in Ecstasy.   London, Bles, 1936; New York, Sheridan, 1941.
Vintage Murder.   London, Bles, 1937; New York, Sheridan, 1940.
Artists in Crime.   London, Bles, and New York, Furman, 1938.
Death in a White Tie.   London, Bles, and New York, Furman, 1938.
Overture to Death.   London, Collins, and New York, Furman, 1939.
Death at the Bar.   London, Collins, and Boston, Little Brown, 1940.
Death of a Peer.   Boston, Little Brown, 1940; as *Surfeit of Lampreys*, London, Collins, 1941.
Death and the Dancing Footman.   Boston, Little Brown, 1941; London, Collins, 1942.
Colour Scheme.   London, Collins, and Boston, Little Brown, 1943.
Died in the Wool.   London, Collins, and Boston, Little Brown, 1945.
Final Curtain.   London, Collins, and Boston, Little Brown, 1947.
Swing, Brother, Swing.   London, Collins, 1949; as *A Wreath for Rivera*, Boston, Little Brown, 1949.
Opening Night.   London, Collins, 1951; as *Night at the Vulcan*, Boston, Little Brown, 1951.
Spinsters in Jeopardy.   Boston, Little Brown, 1953; London, Collins, 1954; as *The Bride of Death*, New York, Spivak, 1955.
Scales of Justice.   London, Collins, and Boston, Little Brown, 1955.
Death of a Fool.   Boston, Little Brown, 1956; as *Off with His Head*, London, Collins, 1957.
Singing in the Shrouds.   Boston, Little Brown, 1958; London, Collins, 1959.
False Scent.   Boston, Little Brown, and London, Collins, 1960.
Hand in Glove.   Boston, Little Brown, and London, Collins, 1962.
Dead Water.   Boston, Little Brown, 1963; London, Collins, 1964.
Killer Dolphin.   Boston, Little Brown, 1966; as *Death at the Dolphin*, London, Collins, 1967.
Clutch of Constables.   London, Collins, 1968; Boston, Little Brown, 1969.
When in Rome.   London, Collins, 1970; Boston, Little Brown, 1971.
Tied Up in Tinsel.   London, Collins, and Boston, Little Brown, 1972.
Black as He's Painted.   London, Collins, and Boston, Little Brown, 1974.
Last Ditch.   Boston, Little Brown, and London, Collins, 1977.

Grave Mistake. Boston, Little Brown, and London, Collins, 1978.

Photo-Finish. London, Collins, and Boston, Little Brown, 1980.

Light Thickens. London, Collins, and Boston, Little Brown, 1982.

Short Stories

The Collected Short Fiction of Ngaio Marsh, edited by Douglas G. Greene. New York, International Polygonics, 1989.

OTHER PUBLICATIONS

Plays

The Nursing-Home Murder, with Henry Jellett, adaptation of their own novel (produced Christchurch, 1935).

False Scent, with Eileen Mackay, adaptation of her own novel (produced Worthing, Sussex, 1961).

The Christmas Tree (for children). London, S.P.C.K., 1962.

A Unicorn for Christmas, music by David Farquhar (produced Wellington, 1962).

Murder Sails at Midnight (produced Auckland, 1963; Bournemouth, Hampshire, 1972).

Television Play: *Evil Liver* (Crown Court series), 1975.

Other

New Zealand, with Randal Matthew Burdon. London, Collins, 1942.

A Play Toward: A Note on Play Production. Christchurch, Caxton Press, 1946.

Perspectives: The New Zealander and the Visual Arts. Auckland, Auckland Gallery Associates, 1960.

New Zealand (for children). New York, Macmillan, 1964; London, Collier Macmillan, 1965.

Black Beech and Honeydew: An Autobiography. Boston, Little Brown, 1965; London, Collins, 1966; revised edition, Collins, 1981.

*

Manuscript Collections: Mugar Memorial Library, Boston University; Alexander Turnbull Library, Wellington.

Theatrical Activities:

Director: **Play**—*Six Characters in Search of an Author* by Pirandello, London, 1950.

* * *

When Ngaio Marsh laid down her pen at the end of *Light Thickens* in 1982, she had completed her thirty-second novel and had spent half a century writing detective fiction. Her first novel, *A Man Lay Dead*, was written 50 years earlier in 1932 (published in 1934) and opened a career which brought her international recognition as one of the "Queens of Crime."

Marsh did not always see herself as a writer. After leaving school, she was convinced that her future lay as a painter. The landscape of her native New Zealand was her inspiration and she painted many canvases in the Southern Alps, whose soaring peaks and high, mysterious lakes form an important backdrop to two later novels, *Died in the Wool* and *Photo-Finish*. But gradually she realized that for her, words were more malleable than paint, and when she embarked on her first trip to England in 1928 at the age of 33 she was earning her way by writing travel articles for the Christchurch *Press* newspaper, and carried with her an unfinished manuscript of a novel set in New Zealand. Two of her own plays had been performed and she had acquired considerable experience as an actress and producer. From this raw material, "a little cellar of experiences which would one day be served up as the table wines of detective cookery," came the first of a long and distinguished series of novels which, although sometimes varying in the quality of plot, can always be relied on for elegance of style and humour in the telling.

Roderick Alleyn made his urbane way into the first novel with a surname taken from the actor Edward Alleyn, founder of Dulwich School in London, where Marsh's father had been educated. Although Ngaio did not fall into the same trap as Dorothy L. Sayers by becoming infatuated with her detective, she did admit to being very fond of him. It is perhaps not surprising that Alleyn falls in love with a painter, Agatha Troy, whom he first encounters in *Artists in Crime* and eventually marries three novels later. Readers first meet Troy on the upper deck of an ocean liner pulling out of Fiji harbour; her description as tall, thin, trouser-clad, "absent-minded, shy and funny" could well be applied to the author herself in the 1930's.

Much of the material for Marsh's novels emerges from intimate knowledge of upper-class English life. As the daughter of a New Zealand bank clerk this world would not normally have been open to her, but friendship with an aristocratic English family whom she met in Christchurch gave her the entree to many country-house weekends and society functions that were to become the breeding grounds for some unfortunate and complicated crimes. Well-connected socially, the handsome and polished Roderick Alleyn has a way of setting the gentry at their ease while methodically uncovering their hypocrisies and pretensions. He is assisted by the large and reliable figure of Inspector Fox, who is more of a stock character than Alleyn, yet is still highly astute and given to unexpected quotations from Shakespeare to match Alleyn's own fondness for the Bard. Another figure in the early novels is journalist Nigel Bathgate who is happy to run around at Alleyn's beck and call but tends to retreat when difficult situations arise. This provides Alleyn with the opportunity to point out that justice inevitably has its consequences; the death penalty causes him, like Lord Peter Wimsey, a severe moral dilemma.

Marsh's reputation was firmly established in the United States and Britain with the eight books written in the 1930's and in the following decade her fiction, attractively blending character study, humour and ingenuity of plot, struck out into new territory. She spent World War II in New Zealand, using up plot material gleaned from her last trip to Europe in 1937, but a profound sense of New Zealand patriotism emerged during this time and she wrote two novels with a New Zealand setting, *Colour Scheme* and *Died in the Wool*. Roderick Alleyn is usefully posted to New Zealand to investigate enemy sympathisers in the South Pacific; not surprisingly, he finds them. But the fascinating aspect of these novels (and of the other two set in New Zealand, *Vintage Murder* and *Photo-Finish*, is how effectively Marsh transposes the classic detective formula from an English country village to a ramshackle hotel beside boiling mud pools, or to a high country sheep station in the Southern Alps. These restricted communities provide Alleyn with an interesting supply of suspects and the New Zealand background emerges vividly from the painterly eye of someone who had often depicted it on canvas.

In 1941, Marsh began an association with the Student Drama Society of Canterbury University College in Christchurch that was to endure for the next 30 years and would bring her great personal satisfaction. Marsh developed a writing pattern that allowed her to spend about nine months writing a book (about the same time as a pregnancy, she used to say) and three months to mount a production of Shakespeare with her student players. She took them on tour in New Zealand and in Australia and, as a result of her abilities as a producer, she was invited to form a professional company, the British Commonwealth Theatre Company, to tour these countries in 1951–52. This unwieldy and over-ambitious project was not successful and from then on Ngaio devoted her talents to working with the Christchurch students. Here she provided a charismatic focus for many young people who wanted to make literary or theatrical careers. For an unmarried only child, now in her late forties, with both parents dead, the students brought her much-needed energy and inspiration. Her novels show how important the immediate experience of theatre was for her. Several novels actually deal with murders in theatres (*Enter a Murderer*, *Vintage Murder*, *Opening Night*, *Killer Dolphin*, *Light Thickens*) and others have actors as important characters.

During the next 30 years, Marsh made several visits back to England and one to the United States, always enjoying long voyages by sea where she had the opportunity to study the passengers and work out ideas for plots. Although admirably equipped to do so, she never felt sufficiently confident to leave the detective fiction genre where she had found such success, and embark on a different kind of fiction. She preferred, instead, to work within the mode, while extending the boundaries in a number of directions. Several novels do in fact give the impression that she was reluctant to abandon her development of character and wrench the narrative back to investigation; this was always a problem for a writer who began with people rather than plot, musing about the tensions within small groups of people and how such tensions could ultimately lead to murder.

The form of the novel was always important; she deplored literature without a shape, and indeed this was one aspect of her chosen genre that she found aesthetically pleasing. A well-plotted detective novel could be compared to a metaphysical poem in its exacting structure, she often maintained.

Marsh revealed a remarkably robust attitude to violence in her books. Her victims seldom meet death by humdrum methods such as knife, gun, or poison. Instead, a jeroboam of champagne descends upon a defenceless head; an elderly morris dancer is decapitated with a sword during bonfire-lit festivities for the winter solstice; a woman M.P. is knocked unconscious and pressed neatly into a bale of wool. In English villages, ladies of the manor dispatch their husbands by impaling them on shooting sticks, and in fashionable London an unwanted politician is executed by a spear flung during a formal reception in an Embassy garden.

Dramatizations of the Marsh novels have been disappointing. In adapting her own novels for the stage, Ngaio lost her sense of theatre and sought to preserve the general shape of the novel, with all the interviews, questions and answers. *Murder Sails at Midnight* was more successful than *False Scent*, but neither play reached the West End at a time when public appetite for "whodunits" on stage was strong. The four novels filmed by New Zealand television in 1978 suffered from the same faults.

Scrupulous though she always was about the detail and plotting of her crimes, Marsh became increasingly out of touch with the nature of modern British police work, and Alleyn and Fox remain trapped in a kind of time warp of the 1950's. This does not detract in any way from the charm of the novels, which have acquired the kind of patina that goes with well-polished brogues or a vintage car.

Marsh made her last trip back to England in 1974 and returned to New Zealand the following year. Then aged eighty, she had no desire to stop writing and her mental powers were as acute as ever. Increasing frailty made writing an effort but many readers felt that her return to a New Zealand setting for *Photo-Finish* provided the kind of creative stimulus that she needed to produce one of her best novels. *Light Thickens*, which was published after her death, blends the two main interests of her life, theatre and the investigation of a gruesome crime.

Although Marsh steadfastly maintained that the theatre was her first love and writing mysteries a source of income that had to be maintained, there is no doubt that all three strands of her life, painting, theatre, and writing nourished each other with great fruitfulness. Her love of England and English life was balanced by her deep response to the landscape of her native land, and to her cherished house and garden in Christchurch, where she died in 1982. She was the last of the 1930's Queens of Crime, predeceased by Dorothy L. Sayers, Margery Allingham, and Agatha Christie; all of whom made their own contribution to the mystery as it has since developed.

—Margaret Lewis

MARSHALL, William (Leonard). Australian. Born in Sydney, in 1944. Educated at Fort Street Boys' High School; Australian National University, Canberra. Married to Mary Fahy; one daughter. Lives in Australia. Address: c/o Secker and Warburg Ltd., Michelin House, 81 Fulham Road, London SW3 6RB, England.

CRIME PUBLICATIONS

Novels (series: Harry Feiffer)

The Fire Circle. London, Macmillan, 1969.
The Age of Death. London, Macmillan, 1970; New York, Viking Press, 1971.
The Middle Kingdom. London, Macmillan, 1971.
Yellowthread Street (Feiffer). London, Hamish Hamilton, 1975; New York, Holt Rinehart, 1976.
Gelignite (Feiffer). London, Hamish Hamilton, 1976; New York, Holt Rinehart, 1977.
The Hatchet Man (Feiffer). London, Hamish Hamilton, 1976; New York, Holt Rinehart, 1977.
Thin Air (Feiffer). London, Hamish Hamilton, 1977; New York, Holt Rinehart, 1978.
Shanghai. London, Hamish Hamilton, and New York, Holt Rinehart, 1979.
Skulduggery (Feiffer). London, Hamish Hamilton, 1979; New York, Holt Rinehart, 1980.
Sci Fi (Feiffer). London, Hamish Hamilton, and New York, Holt Rinehart, 1981.
Perfect End (Feiffer). London, Hamish Hamilton, 1981; New York, Holt Rinehart, 1983.
War Machine (Feiffer). London, Hamish Hamilton, 1982; New York, Mysterious Press, 1988.
The Far Away Man (Feiffer). London, Secker and Warburg, 1984; New York, Holt Rinehart, 1985.
Roadshow (Feiffer). London, Secker and Warburg, and New York, Holt Rinehart, 1985.

Head First (Feiffer).   London, Secker and Warburg, and New York, Holt Rinehart, 1986.
Manila Bay.   London, Secker and Warburg, and New York, Viking, 1986.
Frogmouth (Feiffer).   London, Secker and Warburg, and New York, Mysterious Press, 1987.
Whisper.   London, Century, and New York, Mysterious Press, 1988.
Out of Nowhere (Feiffer).   New York, Mysterious Press, 1988; London, Chatto and Windus, 1989.
The New York Detective.   New York, Mysterious Press, 1989.

*   *   *

"An audacious mixing of near-slapstick comedy with mass murder, realism with pulp-style fantasy." Audacious William Marshall's books certainly are. They defy categorisation. Police procedural perhaps, but like no other police procedural. A reviewer once compared the mixture of crime and comedy, tragedy and bathos with Ed McBain's *Fuzz.* Marshall, however, makes no attempt to soften the contrasts in style. His Hong Kong is a crowded island growing only more crowded, a chaos with its own distinct rules, a bizarre combination of Western society and Chinese values. In this pressure-cooker world, it seems inevitable that the most disparate and contradictory events must be intimately connected. Mass murder mingles with screwball comedy, mundane muggings with the furthest bizarre reaches of criminal mastermind plots. It is the extraordinary, claustrophobic world of Hong Kong itself that allows Marshall to convince us that this is how the world is—tragic, frantic, farcical.

Simply titled *Yellowthread Street,* the first book of the series sets the pattern for the rest: O'Yee is waiting for a sailor who robs cinemas on shore leave, Feiffer is looking for the husband who has halved his wife and quartered his brother, American tourists are looking for one another, everyone is looking for the laconic Mongolian with the kukri who is cutting a profitable swathe through the gangster-owned goldsmiths' shops of Camphorwood Lane, and the Communists on the mainland have just turned off the water.

Yellowthread Street was immediately distinctive for its blend of styles, its energy, its breakneck speed. Indeed all the books seem to start at full speed and then accelerate. The action switches without warning from subplot to subplot, character to character. Apparently inexorably, the initially disparate threads begin to come together. The speed gives the action a kind of hysteria, a sense of the frenzied claustrophobia of Hong Kong. Crime is seen both as part of life and simultaneously a destroyer of it. This is a society on the edge. Everyone is operating by their own rules. The police are no less confused than anyone else. There are no detached, ratiocinating detectives here. Misunderstanding abounds. At times it seems that communication itself has broken down.

What is impressive above all, however, is Marshall's ability to capture the sense of Hong Kong, to note its contradictions, its bizarreness, its exoticism, its comedy, while avoiding any suggestion of racist stereotyping. Everything, Marshall seems to suggest, about the place is extraordinary, unusual, tragic, and comic. Indeed, Marshall has a keen eye for the racist attitudes that linger in the corners of the ramshackle colonial bureaucracy. Perhaps the greatest disservice done to the Yellowthread books by the imbecilic television series based on them was the crass reduction of everything to a series of faceless European hunks with guns surrounded by the inscrutable yellow hordes. You suddenly appreciate how clever Marshall is.

If Marshall's style is distinctive, his plots are hardly less so. In *Yellowthread Street* the free-spirited Mongolian takes on Camphorwood Lane; in *Gelignite* a letter-bomber moves on to larger explosions; in *Thin Air* airliners begin landing with full complements of passengers, all dead. As the series develops, the plots get stranger still. In *Skulduggery* an old skeleton is washed ashore on a raft with a drainpipe, a set of false teeth, a mound of sweet potatoes and a hole in its head, while the Deaf and Dumb gang strikes at will, and a lift stops at a floor that doesn't exist, its occupants mugged by a mugger they never see. In *Sci Fi* a man in a spacesuit opens the science fiction conference with a flamethrower. *War Machine* begins with nothing less than a full-scale attack on the police station by what appears to be a complete unit of the defunct Imperial Japanese Army. As one critic observed, it's hard not to feel that Marshall deliberately gives himself impossible situations. His escapes become increasingly Houdini-esque. Why in *Head First* is Auden disguised as a Sikh policeman, waiting for someone to blow him up, why is O'Yee swapping quotes from Thoreau with a mystery caller, and why is someone digging up dead bodies from China? With the later books, sometimes you get the feeling that maybe even Marshall isn't one hundred per cent certain.

Perhaps it was a feeling that the plots had gone about as far as they could, that prompted Marshall to try a change of scene. With *Manila Bay* Marshall moves to the Philippines. The style, the distinctive blend of farce and tragedy, the complex plotting—this time centring around a champion fighting cock, the Battling Mendez—remains familiar, the new characters finely drawn. Something, however, is lost. Maybe it is just that the series (*Manila Bay* has been followed by *Whisper*) is still young; maybe it is the comparative size of the Philippines, which loses the frantic claustrophobia of Hong Kong; possibly it is just that in the face of poverty and injustice on such a scale Marshall finds it hard to find much to laugh about. Undoubtedly, however, the Manila Bay series promises a new development in Marshall's writing, while for Yellowthread Street fans the recent *Frogmouth* is a heartening indication that the series is far from finished. Marshall remains wholly original and utterly addictive. Whatever he does will be worth reading.

—Philip Plowden

———

MARSHALL, Raymond, *See* **CHASE, James Hadley.**

———

MARSTEN, Richard. *See* **McBAIN, Ed.**

———

MARTIN, Richard, *See* **CREASEY, John.**

———

MASON, A(lfred) E(dward) W(oodley). British. Born in Camberwell, London, 7 May 1865. Educated at Dulwich College, London, 1878–84; Trinity College, Oxford (exhibitioner in classics, 1887), 1884–87, degrees in classics 1886, 1888.

Served in the Royal Marine Light Infantry in World War I, and involved in Naval Intelligence Division secret service missions in Spain, Morocco, and Mexico. Editor, *El Progresso*, Mexico; actor, in provincial touring companies, 1888–94 (appeared in first performance of *Arms and the Man*, 1894); Liberal Member of Parliament for Coventry, 1906–10. Honorary Fellow, Trinity College, 1943. *Died 22 November 1948.*

CRIME PUBLICATIONS

Novels (series: Inspector Hanaud)

The Watchers. Bristol, Arrowsmith, and New York, Stokes, 1899.
Running Water. London, Hodder and Stoughton, and New York, Century, 1907.
At the Villa Rose (Hanaud). London, Hodder and Stoughton, and New York, Scribner, 1910.
The Witness for the Defence. London, Hodder and Stoughton, 1913; New York, Scribner, 1914.
The Summons. London, Hodder and Stoughton, and New York, Doran, 1920.
The Winding Stair. London, Hodder and Stoughton, and New York, Doran, 1923.
The House of the Arrow (Hanaud). London, Hodder and Stoughton, and New York, Doran, 1924.
No Other Tiger. London, Hodder and Stoughton, and New York, Doran, 1927.
The Prisoner in the Opal (Hanaud). London, Hodder and Stoughton, and New York, Doubleday, 1928.
The Sapphire. London, Hodder and Stoughton, and New York, Doubleday, 1933.
They Wouldn't Be Chessmen (Hanaud). London, Hodder and Stoughton, and New York, Doubleday, 1935.
The House in Lordship Lane (Hanaud). London, Hodder and Stoughton, and New York, Dodd Mead, 1946.

Short Stories

Ensign Knightley and Other Stories. London, Constable, and New York, Stokes, 1901.
The Clock. New York, Paget, 1910.
The Four Corners of the World. London, Hodder and Stoughton, and New York, Scribner, 1917.
Dilemmas. London, Hodder and Stoughton, 1934; New York, Doubleday, 1935.
The Secret Fear. New York, Doubleday, 1940.

Uncollected Short Stories

"The Vicar's Conversion," in *Strand* (London), December 1900.
"The Trouble at Beaulieu," in *Lippincott's* (Philadelphia), 19 January 1901.
"The Schoolmaster and Felicia," in *Punch's Holiday Book*, edited by E.T. Reed. London, Punch Office, 1901.
"The Picture in the Bath," in *Illustrated London News*, Christmas, 1901.
"The Man from Socotra," in *Illustrated London News*, 22 November 1902.
"The Guide," in *Daily Mail* (London), 1904.
"Dimoussi and the Pistol," in *London Magazine*, September 1905.
"The Silver Flask," in *Metropolitan Magazine* (New York), July 1907.

"Making Good," in *Cornhill* (London), January 1910.
"The Silver Ship," in *Metropolitan Magazine* (New York), January 1917.
"The Ear," in *Strand* (London), June 1937.
"The Conjuror," in *The Queen's Book of the Red Cross.* London, Hodder and Stoughton, 1939.
"The Watch," in *Homes and Gardens* (London), June 1945.
"Not in the Log," in *Strand* (London), May 1948.
"The Ginger King," in *Great Stories of Detection*, edited by R.C. Bull. London, Barker, 1960.

OTHER PUBLICATIONS

Novels

A Romance of Wastdale. London, Mathews, and New York, Stokes, 1985.
The Courtship of Morrice Buckler. London, Macmillan, 1896; New York, Macmillan, 1903.
Lawrence Clavering. London, Innes, and New York, Dodd Mead, 1897.
The Philanderers. London and New York, Macmillan, 1897.
Miranda of the Balcony. London and New York, Macmillan, 1899.
Parson Kelly, with Andrew Long. New York, Longman, 1899; London, Longman, 1900.
Clementina. London, Methuen, and New York, Stokes, 1901.
The Four Feathers. London, Smith Elder, and New York, Macmillan, 1902.
The Truants. London, Smith Elder, and New York, Harper, 1904.
The Broken Road. London, Smith Elder, and New York, Scribner, 1907.
The Turnstile. London, Hodder and Stoughton, and New York, Scribner, 1912.
The Dean's Elbow. London, Hodder and Stoughton, 1930; New York, Doubleday, 1931.
The Three Gentlemen. London, Hodder and Stoughton, and New York, Doubleday, 1932.
Fire over England. London, Hodder and Stoughton, and New York, Doubleday, 1936.
The Drum. London, Hodder and Stoughton, and New York, Doubleday, 1937.
Königsmark. London, Hodder and Stoughton, 1938; New York, Doubleday, 1939.
Musk and Amber. London, Hodder and Stoughton, and New York, Doubleday, 1942.

Short Stories

Making Good. New York, Paget, 1910.
The Episode of the Thermometer. New York, Paget, 1918.

Plays

Blanche de Malètroit, adaptation of the story "The Sire de Malètroit's Door" by Robert Louis Stevenson (produced London, 1894). London, Capper and Newton, 1894.

The Courtship of Morrice Buckler, with Isabel Bateman, adaptation of the novel by Mason (produced London, 1897).
Marjory Strode (produced London, 1908).
Colonel Smith (produced London, 1909). London, privately printed, 1909; revised version, as *Green Stockings* (produced New York, 1911), New York and London, French, 1914.
The Princess Clementina, with George Pleydell Bancroft, adaptation of the novel *Clementina* by Mason (produced Cardiff and London, 1910).
The Witness for the Defence, adaptation of his own novel (produced London and New York, 1911). Privately printed, 1911.
Open Windows (produced London, 1913).
At the Villa Rose, adaptation of his own novel (produced London, 1920). London, Hodder and Stoughton, 1928.
Running Water (produced London, 1922).
The House of the Arrow, adaptation of his own novel (produced London, 1928).
No Other Tiger, adaptation of his own novel (produced Leicester and London, 1928).
A Present from Margate, with Ian Hay (produced London, 1933). London, French, 1934.

Other

The Royal Exchange. London, Royal Exchange, 1920.
"Detective Novels," in *Nation and Athenaeum* (London), 7 February 1925.
Sir George Alexander and the St. James' Theatre. London, Macmillan, 1935.
The Life of Francis Drake. London, Hodder and Stoughton, 1941; New York, Doubleday, 1942.

*

Critical Study: *A.E.W. Mason: The Adventures of a Story Teller* by Roger Lancelyn Green, London, Parrish, 1952.

*   *   *

An accomplished novelist, A.E.W. Mason wrote several mystery novels in which he tried to "combine the crime story which produces a shiver with the detective story which aims at a surprise." His detective, M. Hanaud of the French Sûreté, is a literary descendent of Lecoq—a stout, broad-shouldered bourgeois with a gift of humor. Although conscious of his reputation, Hanaud has no illusions as to his own infallibilities: he describes detectives as "servants of chance." Their skill, he says, is "to seize quickly the hem of her skirt when it flashes for the fraction of a second" before their eyes.

The first Hanaud novel was *At the Villa Rose* which brought a needed freshness to the detective story of its period. Hanaud and his very distinctive Watson, the wine-loving bachelor Ricardo, work to defend the reputation of a young Englishwoman accused of murder when her wealthy companion is found dead and robbed. The reader, following Hanaud's adroitness and inventiveness, engages in the interesting process of putting two and two together. The puzzle is quickly solved when Mason begins to throw light upon it and the story loses its hold before the concluding chapter.

Mason's second Hanaud novel came 14 years later. *The House of the Arrow* is regarded as almost perfect in its conception and plot. Mason shows his immense skill in narrative and characterization; all of the attributes of a first-rate novel are there: compelling atmosphere, remarkable

conception of character, devastating sense of evil and magnificent satire. The story concerns the murder of the widow of a wealthy English art connoisseur in the old provincial town of Dijon. Her niece, Betty Harlowe, is the center of suspicion since it is she who is to inherit the estate. The local police, plagued by a score of anonymous letters, enlist the aid of the great Parisian detective. The reader is kept guessing until the final chapter in this tense and sinister tale.

Hanaud and Ricardo return in *The Prisoner in the Opal*, the title referring to Ricardo's view of the world "as a vast opal inside which I stood." Devil-worship and the celebration of a Black Mass play a prominent role in this morbid story set in the Bordeaux region of France. Devil-worship is not the usual concern of the police, but when a murder is involved, it becomes Hanaud's duty to investigate. Ricardo is in a constant state of mystification since he is not taken completely into Hanaud's confidence.

They Wouldn't Be Chessmen is set in Trouville and involves murder, theft, a tidal wave, and a confusion of personalities and motives. Mason's last Hanaud novel, *The House in Lordship Lane*, is set in Brittany. Written when Mason was over 80, it suffers from period faults, although it is certainly readable.

Mason was a prolific writer who was at his best in the historical novel. His cloak and dagger stories paralleled his own exploits as the civilian head of British Naval Intelligence during World War I. His substantial earnings from his books enabled him to travel widely which he did with a schoolboy zest for adventure and with an eye for local color. In the mystery genre, he made ample use of the psychological element—and in doing so, was in advance of his time.

—Daniel P. King

———

MASON, F(rancis) Van Wyck. Also wrote as Geoffrey Coffin (with Helen Brawner); Frank W. Mason; Ward Weaver. American. Born in Boston, Massachusetts, 11 November 1901. Educated at Berkshire School, 1919–20; Harvard University, Cambridge, Massachusetts, B.S. 1924. Served in the Allied Expeditionary Forces in France, 1918–19: Second Lieutenant; New York National Guard Cavalry, 1924–29: Sergeant; Maryland National Guard Field Artillery, 1930–33: First Lieutenant; General Staff Corps Officer and Chief Historian, Civil and Military Government Section, 1942–45; Supreme Headquarters, Allied Expeditionary Force, 1943–45: Colonel; Medaille de Sauvetage, Croix de Guerre with two palms, French Legion of Honour. Married 1) Dorothy Louise Macready in 1927 (died 1958), two children; 2) Jeanne-Louise Hand in 1958. Importer and after 1928 self-employed writer; lived in Bermuda, 1956–78. Recipient: Valley Forge Foundation Medal, 1953; Society of Colonial Wars Citation of Honour, 1960. *Died 29 August 1978.*

CRIME PUBLICATIONS

Novels (series: Hugh North in all Mason books except *Spider House*; Inspector Scott Stuart)

Seeds of Murder. New York, Doubleday, 1930; London, Eldon Press, 1937.

The Vesper Service Murders. New York, Doubleday, 1931; London, Eldon Press, 1935.

The Fort Terror Murders. New York, Doubleday, 1931; London, Eldon Press, 1936.

The Yellow Arrow Murders. New York, Doubleday, 1932; London, Eldon Press, 1935.

The Branded Spy Murders. New York, Doubleday, 1932; London, Eldon Press, 1936.

Spider House. New York, Mystery League, 1932; London, Hale, 1959.

The Shanghai Bund Murders. New York, Doubleday, 1933; London, Eldon Press, 1934; revised edition, as *The China Sea Murders*, New York, Pocket Books, 1959; London, Consul, 1961.

The Sulu Sea Murders. New York, Doubleday, 1933; London, Eldon Press, 1936.

Oriental Division G-2 (omnibus). New York, Reynal, n.d.

The Budapest Parade Murders. New York, Doubleday, and London, Eldon Press, 1935.

Murder in the Senate (Stuart; as Geoffrey Coffin, with Helen Brawner). New York, Dodge, 1935; London, Hurst and Blackett, 1936.

The Washington Legation Murders. New York, Doubleday, 1935; London, Eldon Press, 1937.

The Forgotten Fleet Mystery (Stuart; as Geoffrey Coffin, with Helen Brawner). New York, Dodge, 1936; London, Jarrolds, 1943.

The Seven Seas Murders (novelets). New York, Doubleday, 1936; London, Eldon Press, 1937.

The Castle Island Case. New York, Reynal, 1937; London, Jarrolds, 1938; revised edition, as *The Multi-Million Dollar Murders*, New York, Pocket Books, 1960; London, Hale, 1961.

The Hong Kong Airbase Murders. New York, Doubleday, 1937; London, Jarrolds, 1940.

The Cairo Garter Murders. New York, Doubleday, and London, Jarrolds, 1938.

The Singapore Exile Murders. New York, Doubleday, and London, Jarrolds, 1939.

The Bucharest Ballerina Murders. New York, Stokes, 1940; London, Jarrolds, 1941.

Military Intelligence—8 (omnibus). New York, Stokes, 1941.

The Rio Casino Intrigue. New York, Reynal, 1941; London, Jarrolds, 1942.

The Man from G-2 (omnibus). New York, Reynal, n.d. *Saigon Singer.* New York, Doubleday, 1946; London, Barker, 1948.

Dardanelles Derelict. New York, Doubleday, 1949; London, Barker, 1950.

Himalayan Assignment. New York, Doubleday, 1952; London, Hale, 1953.

Two Tickets to Tangier. New York, Doubleday, 1955; London, Hale, 1956.

The Gracious Lily Affair. New York, Doubleday, 1957; London, Hale, 1958.

Secret Mission to Bangkok. New York, Doubleday, 1960; London, Hale, 1961.

Trouble in Burma. New York, Doubleday, 1962; London, Hale, 1963.

Zanzibar Intrigue. New York, Doubleday, 1963; London, Hale, 1964.

Maracaibo Mission. New York, Doubleday, 1965; London, Hale, 1966.

The Deadly Orbit Mission. New York, Doubleday, and London, Hale, 1968.

Uncollected Short Stories

"The Repeater," in *Ellery Queen's Mystery Magazine* (New York), February 1947.

"The Port of Peril," in *The Saint* (New York), August 1955.

"The Plum-Colored Corpse," in *The Saint* (New York), September 1956.

"Port of Intrigue," in *The Saint* (New York), January 1957.

"An Enemy at the Dinner Table," in *Mike Shayne Mystery Magazine* (New York), February 1965.

OTHER PUBLICATIONS

Novels

Captain Nemesis. New York, Putnam, 1931; London, Hale, 1959.

Three Harbours. Philadelphia, Lippincott, 1938; London, Jarrolds, 1939.

Stars on the Sea. Philadelphia, Lippincott, and London, Jarolds, 1940.

Hang My Wreath (as Ward Weaver). New York, Funk and Wagnalls, 1941; London, Jarrolds, 1942.

Rivers of Glory. Philadelphia, Lippincott, 1942; London, Jarrolds, 1944.

End of Track (as Ward Weaver). New York, Reynal, 1943.

Eagle in the Sky. Philadelphia, Lippincott, 1948; London, Jarrolds, 1949.

Cutlass Empire. New York, Doubleday, 1949; London, Jarrolds, 1950.

Valley Forge: 24 December 1777. New York, Doubleday, 1950.

Proud New Flags. Philadelphia, Lippincott, 1951; London, Jarrolds, 1952.

Golden Admiral: A Novel of Sir Francis Drake and the Armada. New York, Doubleday, 1953; London, Jarrolds, 1954.

Wild Drum Beat. New York, Pocket Books, 1953.

The Barbarians. New York, Pocket Books, 1954; London, Hale, 1956.

Blue Hurricane. Philadelphia, Lippincott, 1954; London, Jarrolds, 1955.

Silver Leopard. New York, Doubleday, 1955; London, Jarrolds, 1956.

Captain Judas. New York, Pocket Books, 1955; London, Hale, 1957.

Our Valiant Few. Boston, Little Brown, 1956; as *To Whom Be Glory*, London, Jarrolds, 1957.

Lysander. New York, Pocket Books, 1956; London, Hale, 1958.

The Young Titan. New York, Doubleday, 1959; London, Hutchinson, 1960.

Return of the Eagles. New York, Pocket Books, 1959.

Manila Galleon. Boston, Little Brown, and London, Hutchinson, 1961.

The Sea 'venture. New York, Doubleday, 1961; London, Hutchinson, 1962.

Rascals' Heaven. New York, Doubleday, and London, Hutchinson, 1965.

Wild Horizon. Boston, Little Brown, 1966.

Harpoons in Eden. New York, Doubleday, 1969.

Brimstone Club. Boston, Little Brown, 1971.

Roads to Liberty. Boston, Little Brown, 1972.

Armored Giants. Boston, Little Brown, 1980; London, Hutchinson, 1981.

Novels as Frank W. Mason

Q-Boat. Philadelphia, Lippincott, 1943.
Pilots, Man Your Planes! Philadelphia, Lippincott, 1944.
Flight into Danger. Philadelphia, Lippincott, 1946.

Other

The Winter at Valley Forge (for children). New York, Random House, 1953; as *Washington at Valley Forge,* Eau Claire, Wisconsin, E.M. Hale, 1953.
The Battle of Lake Erie (for children). Boston, Houghton Mifflin, 1960.
The Battle for New Orleans (for children). Boston, Houghton Mifflin, 1962.
The Battle for Quebec (for children). Boston, Houghton Mifflin, 1965.
The Maryland Colony (for children). New York, Macmillan, 1969.

Editor, *The Fighting American.* New York, Reynal, 1943; London, Jarrolds, 1945.
Editor, *American Men at Arms.* Boston, Little Brown, 1964.

* * *

While F. Van Wyck Mason wrote a few mysteries without a series hero it is for the 26 books about Army Intelligence officer Hugh North that he will be remembered.

Some critics have classed Mason's stories in the Oppenheim tradition of international intrigue. The early North novels are fairly straightforward detection, the first two narrated, in the Watson tradition, by a Dr. Walter Allan. Mason apparently felt hampered by this format and dropped the character in *The Fort Terror Murders.* North investigates these early cases mostly because he happens to be on the scene and not because he is a member of Army Intelligence. In *The Vesper Service Murders* his only logical excuse for supervising the investigation comes when another army officer is murdered. These early novels may be called unsophisticated melodrama. They are delightfully dated by a few over-written passages of suspense, a heritage of Mason's pulp training. By the fourth novel, *The Yellow Arrow Murders,* with North assigned by G-2 to get the secret of the Doelger torpedo and solve the murder of a Navy Intelligence agent, the series becomes *sophisticated* melodrama.

Stripped to their essential detective structure, the novels involve a problem for North to solve which includes a series of murders and a puzzle to unravel. This may be a message to be deciphered, the true meaning of a word or phrase, or the location of a treasure, all of which become keys to the larger mystery. The vivid background based on careful research and Mason's own travels is part of the appeal of the stories.

Hugh North is an older version of his creator, according to dust jacket blurbs and the brief biographical sketch in some of the early novels. A Captain in the first dozen novels, he was promoted to Major in *The Singapore Exile Murders* because his mission demanded a higher rank. North, himself, would have been happy to remain a Captain. He became a Colonel in *Himalayan Assignment* and retained that rank for the remainder of his adventures. He is tall, bronzed, with high cheek-bones suggesting a possible American Indian ancestry and a neatly trimmed mustache, and only the patch of gray hair above his ears shows his age. The long career of Hugh North takes him to Cuba, the Middle East, the Balkans, Africa, and most often to the Orient. In the novels may be found a popular capsule history of the changing pattern of U.S. foreign affairs. From Long Island (*Seeds of Murder*) to Tangier (*The Deadly Orbit*

Mission), munitions in Budapest, trouble in Palestine, coming to the rescue of the CIA, Mason keeps his man from G-2 in topical and typical hot water. His own development as a writer may be charted in the North books: from pulp thrillers to smooth, professional entertainment.

—J. Randolph Cox

————

MASON, Lee W. *See* **MALZBERG, Barry N.**

————

MASTERMAN, John (Cecil). British. Born in Kingston Hill, Surrey, 12 January 1891. Educated at Royal Navy College, Osborne, Isle of Wight, and Dartmouth, Devon; Worcester College, Oxford, 1909–1913, M.A. 1913, M.A. 1914. Served in the British Navy during World War I, prisoner of war in Germany; British Army Intelligence Corps, 1940–45; directed British and Allied Counter Intelligence Units: Major. Lecturer, Christ Church College, Oxford, 1913–47; provost, Worcester College, Oxford, 1947–61; Vice-Chancellor, Oxford University, 1957–58. Chairman, Committee on the Political Activities of Civil Servants, and Army Education Advisory Board; member, General Advisory Board, BBC. Recipient: O.B.E. (Officer, Order of the British Empire), 1944; Knight Bachelor, 1959; LL.D. University of Toronto, *Died 6 June, 1977.*

CRIME PUBLICATIONS

Novels (series: Ernst Brendel in both books)

An Oxford Tragedy. London, Gollancz, 1933; New York, DeMer, 1981.
The Case of the Four Friends: Diversion in Pre-Detection. London, Hodder and Stoughton, 1957; New York, British Book Centre, 1959.

Short Stories

Bits and Pieces (includes essay). London, Hodder and Stoughton, 1961.

Uncollected Short Story

"The Case of the Gifted Amateur," in *MacKills Mystery Magazine.* (London), December 1952.

OTHER PUBLICATIONS

Novel

Fate Cannot Harm Me. London, Gollancz, 1935; New York, Penguin, 1940.

Play

Marshall Ney. London, Cobden Sanderson, 1937.

Other

An Oxford Guide-Book. London, Hodder and Stoughton, and New York, Oxford University Press, 1952.
The Double-Cross System in the War of 1939–45. New Haven, Connecticut, Yale University Press, 1971, London, Sphere 1973.
On the Chariot Wheel (autobiography). Oxford, Oxford University Press, 1975.

*   *   *

John Masterman wrote one full-length mystery novel, which is now considered a classic, and a few other short pieces of detective fiction, which have been mostly forgotten. *An Oxford Tragedy*, long considered a classic and one of the earliest of its type, features as detective a Viennese lawyer of international reputation, Ernst Brendel, who arrives at St. Thomas's College in Oxford to give a series of lectures. On his first evening at the college, he dines with the fellows, and engages in a lively discussion of the nature of crime and detection. Brendel dwells at length on what he calls "the drama behind a murder," and he distinguishes murder from crimes of brute force, which are more typical of Americans. Murders in the newer countries lack, to his mind, "the aristocratic touch." Soon after the evening's discussion comes to an end, the least-liked tutor is found shot to death in the dean's rooms, and Brendel begins his investigation.

Masterman, a history tutor at the time of writing the novel, knew Oxford well and draws accurately and in a kindly manner the fellows, staff, and students of a college in 1930. The victim, Mr. Shirley, is repeatedly described as a man of caustic tongue who has only one friend left. Indeed, most of the fellows have few if any deep feelings at the discovery of his death until they realize the effect it will have on his wife, a woman widely regarded with respect and affection. Brendel quickly examines the alibis of the 11 dons, the butler Callendar, who is himself an institution, and four students peripherally involved. The plot follows a fairly predictable path, but the novel is nonetheless interesting. Brendel's discussions of crime in England and elsewhere are not strictly light conversation. He mentions in passing Theodore Dreiser's *An American Tragedy*, and Masterman has named his novel to underscore the comparison and contrast between the two stories.

Masterman did not follow up his initial success with a second mystery. Instead he wrote a straight novel, which did not do well. Finally, in 1956, he published *The Case of the Four Friends*, which he subtitled "A Diversion in Pre-Detection." Ernst Brendel is back at St. Thomas's College, visiting once again and discoursing on the detection of crime. While playing bridge with friends he admits that the skills he uses to win at bridge are the same he uses in the detection of crime. Nevertheless, in this instance, he makes a point of stating that the detection of crime and "the fixing of guilt on the criminal is the work of professionals; there is no short-cut to success and no sort of likelihood that the amateur will succeed where the official or the professional has failed." Thereafter he explains his observing of people in order to determine their manner of conducting their affairs, which reveals to him whether or not the person in question will commit a crime. Brendel narrates a story in which his goal was to "work out the crime before it is committed, to foresee how it will be arranged, and then to prevent it!" Four friends go away every year over New Year. In this year, Charles Sandham, a solicitor, has severe money worries; his junior, Toby Barrick, has both money and legal worries; their friend Evelyn Bannister, a businessman, has a secret that is troubling him but only slightly so far; and Piers Gradon, the hot-headed son of an Irish peer and nephew of Bannister, is smarting over having lost out in his courtship of the heiress Dahlia Constant, who has switched her attentions to Toby. When the four go away together, to stay at the same hotel as Dahlia, the men are fretting over impending disasters. The purpose of Brendel's narration is to illustrate the technique of identifying who will murder whom, and his bridge companions occasionally interrupt the narration with their guesses. In the end no murder is committed, but it is not for want of trying. Masterman's characters in this tale are well drawn if conventional, and the fate of the four men holds the reader's attention. It is, however, talky, giving too much to the frame story of Brendel and his bridge-playing friends. Without the frame story, Masterman might have produced another classic.

Ernst Brendel also appears in two short stories. "The Counter-Alibi" is a simple narration to Brendel in Switzerland in 1937–1938 by a man who was concerned with constructing a successful alibi for murder. "Wine and Silver" again finds Brendel at St. Thomas's, tracking down the Trefusis cup, which was being used as a prop in a painting of the fellows in the Common Room. In "The Case of the Gifted Amateur," Inspector Lestrade shows up Sherlock Holmes and Dr. Watson in the investigation and recovery of the Dark Diamond of Dungbura, which was stolen from the bedside table of the ailing Mr. Wimpfheimer. In this spoof, Holmes is petulant, Watson is an incompetent physician (among other things), and Lestrade parries and puns his way to the end.

It is a loss that Masterman turned so infrequently to Ernst Brendel, for he was an erudite, sophisticated and compassionate detective. When other donnish detectives were slipping into farce, cynicism, or caricature, Brendel was deepening as a man. In *The Case of the Four Friends* Brendel meditates briefly on his memories of the concentration camp as he slips into a corner to wait and watch for a murderer. Masterman moves through the passage so gracefully that the spell cast by the mystery never trembles but the promise of what Brendel might have become is a whisper not missed.

—Susan Oleskiw

————

MASTERTON, Whit. *See* **MILLER, Wade.**

————

MASUR, Harold Q. American. Born 29 January 1909. Educated at Bordentown Military Institute, 1926–28; New York University, B.A. 1932; New York University School of Law, J.D. 1934. Served in the United States Air Force. Engaged in the private practice of law, 1935–42; began writing for pulp magazines in 1940's; has taught detective story writing at New York University, the Cape Cod Writers' Conference, and Iona College Writers' Conference. Past President and currently General Counsel, Mystery Writers of America. Recipient: Mutual Broadcasting System Story Teller's award. Address: 520 East 20th Street, New York, New York 10009, U.S.A.

CRIME PUBLICATIONS

Novels (series: Scott Jordan in all books except *The Broker* and *The Attorney*)

Bury Me Deep. New York, Simon and Schuster, 1947; London, Boardman, 1948.
Suddenly a Corpse. New York, Simon and Schuster, 1949; London, Boardman, 1950.
You Can't Live Forever. New York, Simon and Schuster, 1950; London, Boardman, 1951.
The Metropolitan Opera Murders (ghostwritten for Helen Traubel). New York, Simon and Schuster, 1951.
So Rich, So Lovely, and So Dead. New York, Simon and Schuster, 1952; London, Boardman, 1953.
The Big Money. New York, Simon and Schuster, 1954; London, Boardman, 1955.
Tall, Dark, and Deadly. New York, Simon and Schuster, 1956; London, Boardman, 1957.
The Last Gamble. New York, Simon and Schuster, 1958; as *The Last Breath*, London, Boardman, 1958; as *Murder on Broadway*, New York, Dell, 1959.
Send Another Hearse. New York, Simon and Schuster, and London, Boardman, 1960.
Make a Killing. New York, Random House, and London, Boardman, 1964.
The Legacy Lenders. New York, Random House, and London, Boardman, 1967.
The Attorney. New York, Random House, 1973; London, Souvenir Press, 1974.
The Broker. New York, St. Martin's Press, and London, Souvenir Press, 1981.
The Mourning After. London, Gollancz, 1983.

Short Stories

The Name Is Jordan. New York, Pyramid, 1962.

Uncollected Short Stories

"Dig My Grave," in *Private Eye* (New York), July 1953.
"The Counterfeit Body," in *Mystery Digest* (New York), September 1957.
"Double or Nothing," in *Mystery Digest* (New York), March 1958.
"The $2,000,000 Defense," in *Ellery Queen's Mystery Magazine* (New York), May 1958.
"A Town Called Hades," in *Mystery Digest* (New York), November–December 1959.
"Build Another Coffin," in *Bloodhound* (London), August 1961.
"The Corpse Maker," in *Come Seven, Come Death*, edited by Henry Morrison. New York, Pocket Books, 1965.
"After the Fact," in *Manhunt* (New York), September 1965.
"Wilful Murder," in *Manhunt* (New York), October–November 1966.
"Indian Giver,"in *Manhunt* (New York), February–March 1967.
"Murder Matinee," in *Alfred Hitchcock Presents: A Month of Mystery*. New York, Random House, 1969; London, Reinhardt, 1970.
"Squealer's Reward," in *Killers of the Mind*, edited by Lucy Freeman. New York, Random House, 1974.
"The Graft Is Green," in *Alfred Hitchcock Presents: Stories to Be Read with the Door Locked*. New York, Random House, 1975.

"Pocket Evidence," in *Alfred Hitchcock's Mystery Magazine* (North Palm Beach, Florida), January 1975.
"Doctor's Dilemma," in *Alfred Hitchcock's Mystery Magazine* (North Palm Beach, Florida), June 1975.
"The $1,000,000 Disappearing Act," in *Ellery Queen's Crime Wave*. New York, Putnam, and London, Gollancz, 1976.
"Framed for Murder," in *Ellery Queen's Mystery Magazine* (New York), June 1976.
"Murder Never Solves Anything," in *Ellery Queen's Mystery Magazine* (New York), August 1976.
"Dead Game," in *Alfred Hitchcock Presents: Stories That Go Bump in the Night*. New York, Random House, 1977.
"One Thing Leads to Another," in *Ellery Queen's Mystery Magazine* (New York), April 1978.
"Lawyer's Holiday," in *Ellery Queen's Napoleons of Mystery*. New York, Davis, 1978.
"Trial and Terror," in *Ellery Queen's Mystery Magazine* (New York), May 1979.
"The Opinion," in *Ellery Queen's Mystery Magazine* (New York), May 1989.

OTHER PUBLICATIONS

Other

Editor, *Dolls Are Murder*. New York, Lion, 1957.
Editor, *Murder Most Foul*. New York, Walker, 1971.

*

Harold Q. Masur comments:
The series character, Scott Jordan, a New York attorney, was first conceived to fall somewhere between Perry Mason and Archie Goodwin. It was the author's hope to invent plots as ingenious as Gardner's, featuring a protagonist with the dash and insouciance of Rex Stout's Archie. With one additional ingredient: instead of being approached for help by prospective clients, Jordan would himself be personally involved in each case. And the reader, hopefully indentifying with the hero, would thus be drawn into the simmering kettle, intensifying interest and suspense.

*   *   *

Because Harold Q. Masur is a lawyer, writing about lawyer-detective Scott Jordan, comparisons with Erle Stanley Gardner's Perry Mason are perhaps inevitable. There are more points of difference than similarity however. The Jordan tales generally eschew the elaborately staged courtroom scenes, replete with legalistic fireworks, that are the hallmark of the Perry Mason series. Masur, rather, draws on his legal background to provide plot springboards which turn on some interesting aspect of law which Jordan encounters in his practice. The legal problem generally gives rise to the murder problem (in the Mason novels the murder usually *is* the legal problem). Jordan functions more as a conventional private detective, active away from the office and courtroom, and things are usually wrapped up before the legal proceedings are too far along. The Jordan books are tightly plotted, well clued and frequently surprising in denouement, but they are not the elaborate (and frequently farfetched) Chinese puzzle box affairs that Gardner was so adept at devising.
Jordan, who narrates his cases in the first person, is a relaxed, non-cynical sort of character, who often seems both distressed and bemused to find himself at the center of a web of greedy scheming and murder. Despite his low-key personality,

though, Jordan is capable of fast action and quick thinking. He has a good working relationship with his police contact, homicide detective John Nola, though they are occasionally at odds when Jordan is forced to indulge in a bit of thin ice skating of the Mason variety. Jordan also relates well to the attractive women inevitably involved in his cases, in a not overly wolfish manner. The Jordan novels are compact and fast-paced, the dialogue is crisp and convincing, the supporting characters are free of the taint of cardboard. Murder motives are well-developed and credible.

In *The Legacy Lenders* Jordan investigates a case involving a firm which lends money to prospective heirs on their "expectations." The point at issue: do the lenders hurry things along a bit? *Make a Killing* finds Jordan in the midst of an involved proxy fight for control of a movie studio. In *Tall, Dark, and Deadly* Jordan's career is at stake as he is accused of having faked evidence in a divorce case. *Send Another Hearse* concerns embezzlement at a literary agency and police corruption. This novel is particularly noteworthy for a shock plot twist seldom seen in series books—the murder of one of the continuing supporting characters.

Masur has also written a number of short stories involving Jordan for the mystery magazines. His skill at maintaining a fast pace and tight plot serve him well in the short form. 10 of these tales were collected in the paperback anthology, *The Name Is Jordan.*

Six years after publication of *The Legacy Lenders*, Masur resumed writing with an ambitious 1973 novel, *The Attorney*, an elaborate account of a sensational sex murder trial. The book focuses on the complexities of the criminal trial system, and on matters of legal ethics. The 1981 novel, *The Broker*, is less of a departure from Masur's usual storytelling approach, though Jordan is again absent. The central story idea is a reworking of the theme of *Make a Killing*—financial plots and counterplots surrounding a proxy fight for control of a film studio—this time with greater emphasis on the intricacies of boardroom strategy, though murder is still very much present.

—Art Scott

MATHER, Berkely. Pseudonym for John Evan Weston Davies. British. Soldier in the British Army for 30 years: Lieutenant Colonel. Chairman, Crime Writers Association, 1966. Recipient: Crime Writers Association award, for television plays, 1962. Agent: Curtis Brown Ltd., 162–168 Regent Street, London, W1R 5TA, England.

CRIME PUBLICATIONS

Novels (series: Peter Feltham; Idwal Rees; Stafford family; James Wainwright)

The Achilles Affair (Feltham). London, Collins, and New York, Scribner, 1959.
The Pass Beyond Kashmir (Rees). London, Collins, and New York, Scribner, 1960.
The Road and the Star. London, Collins, and New York, Scribner, 1965.
The Gold of Malabar. London, Collins, and New York, Scribner, 1967.
The Springers (Wainwright). London, Collins, 1968; as *A Spy for a Spy*, New York, Scribner, 1968.

The Break in the Line (Wainwright). London, Collins, 1970; as *The Break*, New York, Scribner, 1970.
The Terminators (Rees). London, Collins, and New York, Scribner, 1971.
Snowline (Rees). London, Collins, and New York, Scribner, 1973.
The White Dacoit. London, Collins, and New York, Scribner, 1974.
With Extreme Prejudice (Feltham). London, Collins, 1975; New York, Scribner, 1976.
The Memsahib. London, Collins, and New York, Scribner, 1977.
The Pagoda Tree (Stafford). London, Collins, 1979; New York, Scribner, 1980.
The Midnight Gun (Stafford). London, Collins, 1981; New York, St. Martin's Press, 1984.
Hour of the Dog (Stafford). London, Collins, and New York, St. Martin's Press, 1982.

Short Stories

Geth Straker and Other Stories (from television series). London, Collins, 1962.

Uncollected Short Stories

"Red for Danger," in *Suspense* (London), August 1958.
"A Duck in Bombay," in *Suspense* (London), November 1960.
"Cri de Coeur," in *Ellery Queen's Mystery Magazine* (New York), August 1961.
"The Fish of My Uncle's Cat," in *Ellery Queen's Mystery Magazine* (New York), November 1961.
"So Deep to the Sky," in *Edgar Wallace Mystery Magazine* (Oxford), August 1966.
"Blood Feud," in *John Creasey's Mystery Bedside Book*, edited by Herbert Harris. London, Hodder and Stoughton, 1967.
"The Diamond Watch," in *Saturday Evening Post* (Philadelphia), 8 April 1967.
"The Troubled Lady," in *Edgar Wallace Mystery Magazine* (Oxford), June 1967.
"The Man in the Well," in *The Playboy Book of Crime and Suspense.* Chicago, Playboy Press, 1968.
"Ma Tante Always Done Her Best," in *Ellery Queen's Mystery Magazine* (New York), December 1968.
"Moon of the Cat," in *John Creasey's Mystery Bedside Book 1969*, edited by Herbert Harris. London, Hodder and Stoughton, 1968.
"Apprentice to Danger," in *John Creasey's Mystery Bedside Book 1970*, edited by Herbert Harris. London, Hodder and Stoughton, 1969.
"Contraband," in *John Creasey's Mystery Bedside Book 1971*, edited by Herbert Harris. London, Hodder and Stoughton, 1970.
"For Want of a Nail," in *Ellery Queen's Grand Slam.* Cleveland, World, 1970.
"The Rajah's Emeralds," in *Ellery Queen's Mystery Magazine* (New York), April 1971.
"There's a Moral in It Somewhere," in *John Creasey's Mystery Bedside Book 1972*, edited by Herbert Harris. London, Hodder and Stoughton, 1971.
"No Questions Asked," in *Ellery Queen's Mystery Magazine* (New York), April 1972.
"Bed and Breakfast," in *John Creasey's Mystery Bedside Book 1974*, edited by Herbert Harris. London, Hodder and Stoughton, 1973.
"Terror Ride," in *Ellery Queen's Aces of Mystery.* New York, Davis, 1975.

"The Big Bite," in *Ellery Queen's Giants of Mystery*. New York, Davis, 1976.

"Treasure Trove," in *Ellery Queen's Doors to Mystery*. New York, Davis, 1981.

OTHER PUBLICATIONS

Novel

Genghis Khan (novelization of screenplay). London, Collins, and New York, Dell, 1965.

Plays

Screenplays: *Information Received*, with Paul Ryder, 1961; *Dr. No*, with Richard Maibaum and Johanna Harwood, 1962; *The Long Ships*, with Beverley Cross, 1964; *Genghis Khan*, with Beverley Cross and Clarke Reynolds, 1965.

Radio Plays: *Southern Channel*, 1953; *The Sand Leopard* series, 1961; *You Can't Win* series, 1961; *The Consolation Prize*, 1961; *Apprentice to Danger*, 1962; *A Necklace for the Warriors*, 1963; *Touch of an Angel*, 1963; *Letter from a Lady*, 1964; *The Maresciallo*, with Victor Francis, 1964; *The Blue Ox*, 1965; *The Bounce Back*, 1967; *The Hard Buy*, 1968; *Tales from the Poona Club*, 1970.

Television Plays: *The Fast Buck*, 1953; *Mid Level*; *Bamboo Bars*; *Old Man of the Air*; *Tales from Soho* series, 1958; *As I Was Saying* series, 1958; *I Spy* (USA); *Charlesworth* series (53 episodes), 1959–64; *Needle Point*, 1962; *To Bury Caesar*, 1963 (USA).

Other

"Establishing a Cover," in *Murder Ink: The Mystery Reader's Companion*, edited by Dilys Winn. New York, Workman, 1977.

*

Berkely Mather comments:

I admire professionalism. I was a professional soldier—and amateur writer—for 30 years. I found I preferred writing, so I stopped being a soldier and became—horrible term—a professional author, crowding into some 12 years that which I would no doubt have done much better had I taken longer.

*   *   *

Berkely Mather's thrillers have the two main ingredients necessary for success, something old that works and something new that works. The old is the well-tried and well-loved agent/boss relationship in which a ruthless unfeeling spy-master manipulates a reluctant agent. This reluctance may be caused by either private emotion or public distaste, and Mather manages both, offering those who read his books in sequence the intriguing spectacle of one hero, the pleasant, reliable, concerned James Wainwright, being superseded by another, the cynical, aggressive Idwal Rees. All they have in common is being in the hands of the same ruthless master, the ghastly Gaffer.

The new in Mather's books is the setting, basically India with forays into various neighbouring territories. For the most part it is modern India that Mather shows us, still with centuries-old problems and some—like the hippie influx of the 1960's—not so old. All the background, from the teeming streets of Bombay and Calcutta to the vast empty mountain wilderness of the north, is portrayed with tremendous realism of colour and detail. In settings as beautifully realized as these, fast-moving action-packed tales of espionage and drug smuggling cannot but grip.

There is, however, another important dimension to Mather's work. Perhaps because of the very timelessness of these eastern settings he has always shown a strong facility for recreating the past, both immediate as in the excellent *The White Dacoit*, set in the 1920's, and more distant as in his historical adventure, *The Road and the Star*. It is this aspect of his work which he has concentrated on in his later novels, the trilogy comprising *The Pagoda Tree*, *The Midnight Gun*, and *Hour of the Dog*, in which he traces the fortunes of the Stafford family from the mid-19th century to the end of World War II. These are adventure romances in the great tradition, ripping yarns packed full of colour and excitement and ranging wide across Australia, Asia, and Africa with Hong Kong at their centre. While they are not strictly crime or mystery stories, nor perhaps even thrillers, they are rich in thrills and mysteries and crimes, and if the protagonists tend to be a little stereotyped, the settings are always vibrant with life.

—Reginald Hill

———

MATTHEWS, Anthony. *See* **BLACK, Lionel.**

———

MAUGHAM, W(illiam) Somerset. British. Born in Paris, 25 January 1874, of English parents. Educated at King's School, Canterbury, Kent, 1885–89; University of Heidelberg, 1891–92; studied medicine at St. Thomas's Hospital, London, 1892–97; interned in Lambeth, London; qualified as a surgeon, L.R.C.P., M.R.C.S., 1897, but never practised. Served with the Red Cross Ambulance Unit, later with the British Intelligence Corps, in World War I. Married Syrie Barnardo Wellcome in 1917 (divorced 1927); one daughter. Writer from 1896; lived abroad, mainly in Paris, 1897–1907; travelled widely during the 1920's, in the South Seas, Malaya, and China; lived at Villa Mauresque, Cap Ferrat in the south of France from 1928; lived in the United States during World War II; instituted annual prize for promising young British writer, 1947. D.Litt.: Oxford University, 1952; University of Toulouse. Fellow, and Companion of Literature, 1961, Royal Society of Literature. Chevalier, 1929, Commander, 1939, Legion of Honour; Honorary Senator, University of Heidelberg, 1961; Honorary Fellow, Library of Congress, Washington, D.C.; Honorary Member, American Academy of Arts and Letters. Companion of Honour, 1954. *Died 15 December 1965.*

CRIME PUBLICATIONS

Short Stories

The Casuarina Tree: Six Stories. London, Heinemann, and New York, Doran, 1926; as *The Letter: Stories of Crime*, London, Collins, 1930.

Ashenden; or, The British Agent. London, Heinemann, and New York, Doubleday 1928.

Ah King: Six Stories. London, Heinemann, and New York, Doubleday, 1933.

OTHER PUBLICATIONS

Novels

Liza of Lambeth. London, Unwin, 1897; revised edition, 1904; New York, Doran, 1921.
The Making of a Saint. Boston, Page, and London, Unwin, 1898.
The Hero. London, Hutchinson, 1901.
Mrs. Craddock. London, Heinemann, 1902; New York, Doran, 1920.
The Merry-Go-Round. London, Heinemann, 1904.
The Bishop's Apron: A Study in the Origins of a Great Family. London, Chapman and Hall, 1906.
The Explorer. London, Heinemann, 1907; New York, Baker and Taylor, 1909.
The Magician. London, Heinemann, 1908; New York, Duffield, 1909; with *A Fragment of Autobiography*, Heinemann, 1956; New York, Doubleday, 1957.
Of Human Bondage. New York, Doran, and London, Heinemann, 1915.
The Moon and Sixpence. London, Heinemann, and New York, Doran, 1919.
The Painted Veil. New York, Doran, and London, Heinemann, 1925.
Cakes and Ale; or, The Skeleton in the Cupboard. London, Heinemann, and New York, Doubleday, 1930.
The Book-Bag. Florence, G. Orioli, 1932.
The Narrow Corner. London, Heinemann, and New York, Doubleday, 1932.
Theatre. New York, Doubleday, and London, Heinemann, 1937.
Christmas Holiday. London, Heinemann, and New York, Doubleday, 1939.
Up at the Villa. New York, Doubleday, and London, Heinemann, 1941.
The Hour Before the Dawn. New York, Doubleday, 1942.
The Razor's Edge. New York, Doubleday, and London, Heinemann, 1944.
Then and Now. London, Heinemann, and New York, Doubleday, 1946.
Catalina: A Romance. London, Heinemann, 1948; New York, Doubleday, 1949.

Short Stories

Orientations. London, Unwin, 1899.
The Trembling of the Leaf: Little Stories of the South Sea Islands. New York, Doran, and London, Heinemann, 1921; as *Sadie Thompson and Other Stories of the South Seas*, London, Readers Library, 1928; as *Rain and Other Stories*, Readers Library, 1933.
Six Stories Written in the First Person Singular. New York, Doubleday, and London, Heinemann, 1931.
The Judgement Seat. London, Centaur Press, 1934.
East and West: Collected Short Stories. New York, Doubleday, 1934; as *Altogether*, London, Heinemann, 1934.
Cosmopolitans. New York, Doubleday, 1936; as *Cosmopolitans: Very Short Stories*, London, Heinemann, 1936.
The Favorite Short Stories of W. Somerset Maugham. New York, Doubleday, 1937.
The Mixture as Before. London, Heinemann, and New York, Doubleday, 1940.
The Unconquered. New York, House of Books, 1944.

Creatures of Circumstance. London, Heinemann, and New York, Doubleday, 1947.
East of Suez: Great Stories of the Tropics. New York, Avon, 1948.
Here and There: Short Stories. London, Heinemann, 1948.
Complete Short Stories. London, Heinemann, 3 vols., 1951.
The World Over: Stories of Manifold Places and People. New York, Doubleday, 1952.
The Best Short Stories, edited by John Beecroft. New York, Modern Library, 1957.
A Maugham Twelve: Stories, edited by Angus Wilson. London, Heinemann, 1966; with *Cakes and Ale*, New York, Doubleday, 1967.
Malaysian Stories, edited by Anthony Burgess. Singapore, Heinemann, 1969.
Seventeen Lost Stories, edited by Craig V. Showalter. New York, Doubleday, 1969.

Plays

Marriages Are Made in Heaven (as *Schiffbrüchig*, produced Berlin, 1902). Published in *The Venture Annual*, edited by Maugham and Laurence Housman, London, Baillie, 1903.
A Man of Honour (produced London, 1903). London, Chapman and Hall, 1903; Chicago, Dramatic Publishing Company, 1912.
Mademoiselle Zampa (produced London, 1904).
Lady Frederick (produced London, 1907). London, Heinemann, 1911; Chicago, Dramatic Publishing Company, 1912.
Jack Straw (produced London, 1908). London, Heinemann, 1911; Chicago, Dramatic Publishing Company, 1912.
Mrs. Dot (produced London, 1908). London, Heinemann, and Chicago, Dramatic Publishing Company, 1912.
The Explorer: A Melodrama (produced London, 1908). London, Heinemann, and Chicago, Dramatic Publishing Company, 1912.
Penelope (produced London, 1909). London, Heinemann, and Chicago, Dramatic Publishing Company, 1912.
The Noble Spaniard, adaptation of a work by Ernest Grenet-Dancourt (produced London, 1909). London, Evans, 1953.
Smith (produced London, 1909). London, Heinemann, and Chicago, Dramatic Publishing Company, 1913.
The Tenth Man: A Tragic Comedy (produced London, 1910). London, Heinemann, and Chicago, Dramatic Publishing Company, 1913.
Landed Gentry (as *Grace*, produced London, 1910). London, Heinemann, and Chicago, Dramatic Publishing Company, 1913.
Loaves and Fishes (produced London, 1911). London, Heinemann, 1924.
A Trip to Brighton, adaptation of a play by Abel Tarride (produced London, 1911).
The Perfect Gentleman, adaptation of a play by Molière (produced London, 1913). Published in *Theatre Arts* (New York), November 1955.
The Land of Promise (produced New Haven, Connecticut, 1913; London 1914). London, Bickers, 1913; New York, Doran, 1923.
The Unattainable (as *Caroline*, produced London, 1916). London, Heinemann, 1923; included in *Six Comedies*, 1937.
Our Betters (produced New York, 1917; London, 1923). London, Heinemann, 1923; New York, Doran, 1924.
Love in a Cottage (produced London, 1918).
Caesar's Wife (produced London, 1919). London, Heinemann, 1922; New York, Doran, 1923.
Home and Beauty (produced Atlantic City, New Jersey, and London, 1919; as *Too Many Husbands*, produced New York,

1919). London, Heinemann, 1923; included in *Six Comedies*, 1937.

The Unknown (produced London, 1920). London, Heinemann, and New York, Doran, 1920.

The Circle (produced London, 1921). London, Heinemann, and New York, Doran, 1921.

East of Suez (produced London, 1922). London, Heinemann, and New York, Doran, 1922.

The Camel's Back (produced Worcester, Massachusetts, 1923; London, 1924).

The Constant Wife (produced New York, 1926; London, 1927). New York, Doran, and London, Heinemann, 1927.

The Letter, adaptation of his own story (produced London, 1927). London, Heinemann, and New York, Doran, 1927.

The Sacred Flame (produced New York, 1928; London, 1929). New York, Doubleday, 1928, London, Heinemann, 1929.

The Bread-Winner (produced London, 1930). London, Heinemann, 1930; New York, Doubleday, 1931.

Dramatic Works. London, Heinemann, 6 vols., 1931–34; as *Collected Plays*, 3 vols., 1952.

For Services Rendered (produced London, 1932). London, Heinemann, 1932; New York, Doubleday, 1933.

The Mask and the Face, adaptation of a play by Luigi Chiarelli (produced Boston, 1933).

Sheppey (produced London, 1933). London, Heinemann, 1933; Boston, Baker, 1949.

Six Comedies. New York, Garden City Publishing Company, 1937.

Trio: Stories and Screen Adaptations, with R.C. Sherriff and Noel Langley. London, Heinemann, and New York, Doubleday, 1950.

Screenplay: *The Verger* (in *Trio*), 1950.

Other

The Land of the Blessed Virgin: Sketches and Impressions of Andalusia. London, Heinemann, 1905; New York, Knopf, 1920.

On a Chinese Screen. New York, Doran, and London, Heinemann, 1922.

The Gentleman in the Parlour: A Record of a Journey from Rangoon to Haiphong. London, Heinemann, and New York, Doubleday, 1930.

The Non-Dramatic Works. London, Heinemann, 28 vols., 1934–69.

Don Fernando; or, Variations on Some Spanish Themes. London, Heinemann, and New York, Doubleday, 1935.

My South Sea Island. Chicago, privately printed, 1936.

The Summing Up. London, Heinemann, and New York, Doubleday, 1938.

Books and You. London, Heinemann, and New York, Doubleday, 1940.

France at War. London, Heinemann, and New York, Doubleday, 1940.

Strictly Personal. New York, Doubleday, 1941; London, Heinemann, 1942.

The Somerset Maugham Sampler, edited by Jerome Weidman. New York, Garden City Publishing Company, 1943; as *The Somerset Maugham Pocket Book*, New York, Pocket Books, 1944.

Of Human Bondage, with a Digression on the Art of Fiction (address). Washington, D.C., Library of Congress, 1946.

Great Novelists and Their Novels: Essays on the Ten Greatest Novels of the World and the Men and Women Who Wrote Them. Philadelphia, Winston, 1948; revised edition, as *Ten Novels and Their Authors*, London, Heinemann, 1954; as *The*

Art of Fiction: An Introduction to Ten Novels and Their Authors, New York, Doubleday, 1955.

A Writer's Notebook. London, Heinemann, and New York, Doubleday, 1949.

A Maugham Reader, edited by Glenway Wescott. New York, Doubleday, 1950.

The Writer's Point of View (lecture). London, Cambridge University Press, 1951; Folcroft, Pennsylvania, Folcroft Editions, 1973.

The Vagrant Mood: Six Essays. London, Heinemann, 1952 New York, Doubleday, 1953.

Mr. Maugham Himself, edited by John Beecroft. New York, Doubleday, 1954.

The Partial View (includes *The Summing Up* and *A Writer's Notebook*). London, Heinemann, 1954.

Points of View. London, Heinemann, 1958; as *Points of View: Five Essays*, New York, Doubleday, 1959.

Purely for My Pleasure. London, Heinemann, and New York, Doubleday, 1962.

Selected Prefaces and Introductions. New York, Doubleday, 1963; London, Heinemann, 1964.

Wit and Wisdom, edited by Cecil Hewetson. London, Duckworth, 1966.

Essays on Literature. New York, New American Library, and London, New English Library, 1967.

The Letters of W. Somerset Maughan to Lady Juliette Duff, edited by Loren D. Rothschild. Pacific Palisades, California, Rasselas Press, 1982.

A Traveller in Romance: Uncollected Writings 1901–1964, edited by John Whitehead. London, Blond, and New York, Crown, 1984.

Editor, with Laurence Housman, *The Venture Annual of Art and Literature*. London, Baillie, 1903.

Editor, with Laurence Housman, *The Venture Annual of Art and Literature 1905*. London, Simpkin Marshall, 1904.

Editor, *The Truth at Last*, by Charles Hawtrey. London, Butterworth, 1924.

Editor, *The Travellers' Library*. New York, Doubleday, 1933; as *Fifty Modern English Writers*, New York, Doubleday, 1933.

Editor, *Tellers of Tales: 100 Short Stories from the United States, England, France, Russia, and Germany*. New York, Doubleday, 1939; as *The Greatest Stories of All Times*, New York, Garden City Publishing Company, 1943.

Editor, *A Choice of Kipling's Prose*. London, Macmillan, 1952; as *Maugham's Choice of Kipling's Best*, New York, Doubleday, 1953.

*

Bibliography: *A Bibliography of the Works of Maugham* by Raymond Toole Scott, London, Nicholas Vane, 1956; revised edition, London, Kaye and Ward, 1973.

Manuscript Collections: Humanities Research Center, University of Texas, Austin; Berg Collection, New York Public Library; Lilly Library, Stanford University, California; Houghton Library, Harvard University, Cambridge, Massachusetts; Fales Collection, New York University; Butler Library, Columbia University, New York; Olin Library, University of Arkansas, Fayetteville; Cornell University, Ithaca, New York.

Critical Studies: *W. Somerset Maugham: A Guide* by Laurence Brander, Edinburgh, Oliver and Boyd, 1963; *Remembering Mr. Maugham* by Garson Kanin, London, Hamish Hamilton, 1966;

Somerset and All the Maughams, London, Heinemann, 1966 and *Conversations with Willie: Recollections of Maugham*, London, W.H. Allen, 1978, both by Robin Maugham; *W. Somerset Maugham and the Quest for Freedom*, London, Heinemann, 1972, and *Willie: The Life of W. Somerset Maugham*, London, Heinemann, 1989, New York, St. Martin's Press, 1990, both by Robert Lorin Calder; *The Pattern of W. Somerset Maugham*, London, Hamish Hamilton, 1974, and *W. Somerset Maugham and His World*, London, Weidenfeld and Nicholson, 1977, both by Anthony Curtis; *W. Somerset Maugham and His World* by Frederic Raphael, London, Thames and Hudson, 1976, revised edition, London, Cardinal Sphere, 1990: *Somerset Maugham* by Ted Morgan, London, Cape, 1980; *W. Somerset Maugham: The Critical Heritage*, edited by Anthony Curtis and John Whitehead, London, Routledge, 1987; *Maugham: A Reappraisal*, edited by John Whitehead, London, Barnes and Noble, 1987.

* * *

Secure in its niche in literary history, *Ashenden* is accepted as the prototype of realistic spy fiction and, after the manner of treatment of such venerable works, quoted and deferred to, but not read. This is unfortunate. Though W. Somerset Maugham's only significant contribution to mystery fiction consists of this one work, it is sufficiently innovative and good—comparing favorably with his best fiction—to deserve the place accorded it. Maugham's comments in the preface on his experience in the Intelligence Corps establish both tone and authorial intent: "The work of an agent ... is on the whole extremely monotonous. A lot of it is uncommonly useless.... In 1917 I went to Russia. I was sent to prevent the Bolshevik Revolution and to keep Russia in the war. The reader will know that my efforts did not meet with success."

Growing out of such experiences, *Ashenden* was unlikely to become either a paean to the glories of Britain or a description of the glamorous life of a spy. A cross between a collection of stories and a novel, narrated in a cool, often epigrammatic style, the work describes the rather minor role played in a series of encounters and catastrophes by the writer Ashenden (no other name is ever given), who has been recruited to the spying trade in the quiet and unexpected circumstances typical of the developed tradition of such fiction. Ashenden has been described as a kind of litmus paper, registering but not participating in the events of the work in which he appears. This is only partly true. What is true is that the central figure is never allowed to take himself with the seriousness characteristic of so many of his contemporaries and that he is not cast in the mold of "The Great Detective." His greatest joy is a hot bath, his worst fear missing a train, and his view of firearms that they are "apt to go off at the wrong time and make a noise." His hired-assassin acquaintance, the Hairless Mexican, advises him never to play cards with strangers. He takes his Russian lover to Paris on a pre-marriage honeymoon, to avoid embarrassing her husband, only to give her up after concluding that not to do so would mean eating scrambled eggs every morning for the rest of his life.

The effects of love on spies and diplomats is a unifying theme in the series of incidents which make up the work. As a powerful, irrational and even transfiguring force, it diverts from their apparently destined paths—or dooms—a number of figures. Neither the French peasant woman, nor the Hairless Mexican, nor the fanatic Indian rebel, Chandra Lal, nor the British traitor, nor his German wife is immune. Love tempts the brilliant young diplomat, Byring, and a famous courtesan into a marriage which will end both their promising careers. Even the British Ambassador finds his present success negated by the memory of a lost love. Implicit in the final chapter are assessments of both love and spying. Ashenden's own experience suggests that the destructive forces of love can only be countered by an ironic view which precludes such abandonment of normal reason as commonly accompanies that emotion. As for the turbulent world of the spy, effectively represented by Russia in 1917, death in it is something absurd and rude, as dreadful as hitting a child, almost farce—nothing approaching high tragedy.

In *Ashenden* there is little profound but nothing foolish. If the work does not entirely anticipate the atmosphere of the "cold war," it achieves an effect of thoroughgoing practicality in its presentation of the work of a spy.

—Nancy Ellen Talburt

———

MAYO, James. *See* **COULTER, Stephen.**

———

McAULIFFE, Frank (Malachi). Also writes as Frank Malachy. American. Born in New York City, 3 December 1926. Served in the United States Army Air Force, 1945. Married Rita May Gibbons in 1951; five daughters and two sons. Recipient: Mystery Writers of America Edgar Allan Poe award, 1972. Address: 1828 Swift Boulevard, Ventura, California 93003, U.S.A.

CRIME PUBLICATIONS

Novel

The Bag Man. New York, Zebra, 1979.

Short Stories (series: Augustus Mandrell in all books)

Of All the Bloody Cheek. New York, Ballantine, 1965; London, New English Library, 1971.
Rather a Vicious Gentleman. New York, Ballantine, 1968.
For Murder I Charge More. New York, Ballantine, 1971.

Uncollected Short Stories

"The Dr. Sherrock Commission," in *Best Detective Stories of the Year 1966*, edited by Anthony Boucher. New York, Dutton, and London, Boardman, 1966.
"The Iranian Farmer Commission," in *Crimes and Misfortunes*, edited by J. Frank McComas. New York, Random House, 1970.
"The Maltese Falcon Commission," in *Men and Malice*, edited by Dean Dickensheet. New York, Doubleday, 1973.

OTHER PUBLICATIONS

Novel

Hot Town (as Frank Malachy). New York, Permabooks, 1956.

* * *

Few authors in the genre are as undeservingly neglected as is Frank McAuliffe. His entire output to date is admittedly meagre, consisting of only five books, of which his first, *Hot Town*, is a first-person western and his most recent, *The Bag Man*, an unexceptional man-on-the-run crime novel.

But his three books recounting the "commissions" of the urbane but whimsically vicious Augustus Mandrell, a professional murderer described variously as possessing the dominant qualities of Don Quixote, Sherlock Holmes, the Scarlet Pimpernel, Raffles, James Bond, and Dr. Strangelove, are decidedly exceptional. No mere killer-for-hire, the very British Mandrell is a freelance assassin who delights in disposing of usually deserving individuals in highly imaginative ways and always in disguise.

The first book, *Of All the Bloody Cheek*, is a collection of short stories and novelettes, as are the other two, each detailing a separate commission undertaken by the firm of Mandrell, Limited—as Mandrell himself styles his one-man operation. Mandrell narrates his own exploits with delicious black humor, frequent knowing asides to the reader, and constant references to other commissions, past and present, published and not, much in the manner of Conan Doyle's signature citing of Sherlock Holmes adventures. Throughout the books, Mandrell continually and accidentally runs into his nemesis, Louis Proferra, who first appears in "The Iranian Farmer Commission" as a Lieutenant with the O.S.S. (Proferra loses his left arm in that encounter), and who last appears in the third book, *For Murder I Charge More*, where, now a C.I.A. agent, he loses his life during a final brush with Mandrell in the course of "The American Apple Pie Commission." During the intervening stories, Proferra loses other portions of his anatomy to Mandrell's machinations.

Despite the short-story structure of the Mandrell books, their interconnectedness of character and time—Mandrell's adventures are for some reason limited to the years during and immediately following World War II—demand that all three books be read in close succession in order that they be fully appreciated, although each book can stand alone. But in this, McAuliffe, with an arch sense of humor worthy of his own character, defeats the reader in the arrangement of stories in the second book, *Rather a Vicious Gentleman*. Flying in the face of their crucial chronological arrangement, the stories are presented in reverse order, but are told with such technical brilliance and wry humor that the reader's appreciation for the recurring characters and allusions is actually heightened. *Rather a Vicious Gentleman* is a tour de force.

McAuliffe's genius is of a two-fold nature. He is able to transform a derivative and distasteful protagonist into one who is not only original but admirable, and weaves a web of outrageous coincidences through all three Mandrell books, yet orchestrates them so skillfully that the reader does not perceive them as a string of artificial incidents, but rather as the logical if not inevitable synchronicities associated with the life of a professional assassin. In a genre in which criminality is confined to the printed page, it is a crime that the Augustus Mandrell books are limited to three volumes and an unpublished novelette, "The General Kincaid Commission," and that Frank McAuliffe's reputation in the field falls so short of what his gift should command.

—Will Murray

McBAIN, Ed. Pseudonym for Evan Hunter; also writes as Curt Cannon; Hunt Collins; Ezra Hannon; Richard Marsten. American. Born Salvatore A. Lombino in New York City, 15 October 1926. Educated at Cooper Union, New York, 1943–44; Hunter College, New York, B.A. 1950 (Phi Beta Kappa). Served in the United States Navy, 1944–46. Married 1) Anita Melnick in 1949 (divorced), three sons; 2) Mary Vann Finley in 1973, one step-daughter. In the early 1950's taught in vocational high schools, and worked for Scott Meredith Literary Agency, in New York. Recipient: Mystery Writers of America Edgar Allan Poe award, 1957; Grand Master award, 1985. Lives in Norwalk, Connecticut. Agent: John Farquharson Ltd., 250 West 57th Street, New York, New York 10019, U.S.A., or, 162–168 Regent Street, London W1R 5TB, England.

CRIME PUBLICATIONS

Novels (series: Officers of the 87th Precinct; Matthew Hope)

Cut Me In (as Hunt Collins). New York, Abelard Schuman, 1954; London, Boardman, 1960; as *The Proposition*, New York, Pyramid, 1955.
Cop Hater (87th Precinct). New York, Permabooks, 1956; London, Boardman, 1958.
The Mugger (87th Precinct). New York, Simon and Schuster, 1956; London, Boardman, 1959.
The Pusher (87th Precinct). New York, Simon and Schuster, 1956; London, Boardman, 1959.
The Con Man (87th Precinct). New York, Permabooks, 1957; London, Boardman, 1960.
Killer's Choice (87th Precinct). New York, Simon and Schuster, 1957; London, Boardman, 1960.
Killer's Payoff (87th Precinct). New York, Simon and Schuster, 1958; London, Boardman, 1960.
April Robin Murders, with Craig Rice (completed by McBain). New York, Random House, 1958; London, Hammond, 1959.
Lady Killer (87th Precinct). New York, Simon and Schuster, 1958; London, Boardman, 1961.
I'm Cannon—For Hire (as Curt Cannon). New York, Fawcett, 1958; London, Fawcett, 1959.
Killer's Wedge (87th Precinct). New York, Simon and Schuster, 1959; London, Boardman, 1961.
'Til Death (87th Precinct). New York, Simon and Schuster, 1959; London, Boardman, 1961.
King's Ransom (87th Precinct). New York, Simon and Schuster, 1959; London, Boardman, 1961.
Give the Boys a Great Big Hand (87th Precinct). New York, Simon and Schuster, 1960; London, Boardman, 1962.
The Heckler (87th Precinct). New York, Simon and Schuster, 1960; London, Boardman, 1962.
See Them Die (87th Precinct). New York, Simon and Schuster, 1960; London, Boardman, 1963.
Lady, Lady, I Did It! (87th Precinct). New York, Simon and Schuster, 1961; London, Boardman, 1963.
Like Love (87th Precinct). New York, Simon and Schuster, 1962; London, Boardman, 1964.
Ten Plus One (87th Precinct). New York, Simon and Schuster, 1963; London, Hamish Hamilton, 1964.
Ax (87th Precinct). New York, Simon and Schuster, and London, Hamish Hamilton, 1964.
The Sentries. New York, Simon and Schuster, and London, Hamish Hamilton, 1965.
He Who Hesitates (87th Precinct). New York, Delacorte Press, and London, Hamish Hamilton, 1965.

Doll (87th Precinct). New York, Delacorte Press, 1965; London, Hamish Hamilton, 1966.

Eighty Million Eyes (87th Precinct). New York, Delacorte Press, and London, Hamish Hamilton, 1966.

Fuzz (87th Precinct). New York, Doubleday, and London, Hamish Hamilton, 1968.

Shotgun (87th Precinct). New York, Doubleday, and London, Hamish Hamilton, 1969.

Jigsaw (87th Precinct). New York, Doubleday, and London, Hamish Hamilton, 1970.

Hail, Hail, The Gang's All Here! (87th Precinct). New York, Doubleday, and London, Hamish Hamilton, 1971.

Sadie When She Died (87th Precinct). New York, Doubleday, and London, Hamish Hamilton, 1972.

Let's Hear It for the Deaf Man (87th Precinct). New York, Doubleday, and London, Hamish Hamilton, 1973.

Hail to the Chief (87th Precinct). New York, Random House, and London, Hamish Hamilton, 1973.

Bread (87th Precinct). New York, Random House, and London, Hamish Hamilton, 1974.

Where There's Smoke. New York, Random House, and London, Hamish Hamilton, 1975.

Blood Relatives (87th Precinct). New York, Random House, 1975; London, Hamish Hamilton, 1976.

Doors (as Ezra Hannon). New York, Stein and Day, 1975; London, Macmillan, 1976.

Guns. New York, Random House, 1976; London, Hamish Hamilton, 1977.

So Long as You Both Shall Live (87th Precinct). New York, Random House, and London, Hamish Hamilton, 1976.

Long Time No See (87th Precinct). New York, Random House, and London, Hamish Hamilton, 1977.

Goldilocks (Hope). New York, Arbor House, 1977; London, Hamish Hamilton, 1978.

Calypso (87th Precinct). New York, Viking Press, and London, Hamish Hamilton, 1979.

Ghosts (87th Precinct). New York, Viking Press, and London, Hamish Hamilton, 1980.

Rumpelstiltskin (Hope). New York, Viking Press, and London, Hamish Hamilton, 1981.

Heat (87th Precinct). New York, Viking Press, and London, Hamish Hamilton, 1981.

Beauty and the Beast (Hope). London, Hamish Hamilton, 1982; New York, Holt Rinehart, 1983.

Ice (87th Precinct). New York, Arbor House, and London, Hamish Hamilton, 1983.

Jack and the Beanstalk (Hope). New York, Holt Rinehart, and London, Hamish Hamilton, 1984.

Lightning (87th Precinct). New York, Arbor House, and London, Hamish Hamilton, 1984.

Snow White and Rose Red (Hope). New York, Random House, and London, Hamish Hamilton, 1985.

Eight Black Horses (87th Precinct). New York, Arbor House, and London, Hamish Hamilton, 1985.

Another Part of the City (87th Precinct). New York, Mysterious Press, 1985; London, Hamish Hamilton, 1986.

Cinderella (Hope). New York, Holt, and London, Hamish Hamilton, 1986.

Poison (87th Precinct). New York, Arbor House, and London, Hamish Hamilton, 1987.

Puss in Boots (Hope). New York, Holt, and London, Arbor House, 1987.

Tricks (87th Precinct). New York, Arbor House, and London, Hamish Hamilton, 1987.

The House That Jack Built (Hope). New York, Holt, and London, Hamish Hamilton, 1988.

Lullaby. New York, Morrow, and London, Hamish Hamilton, 1989.

Downtown. New York, Morrow, and London, Heinemann, 1989.

Three Blind Mice (Hope). New York, Arcade, 1990.

Vespers. New York, Morrow, 1990.

Novels as Evan Hunter

The Evil Sleep! N.p., Falcon, 1952.

The Big Fix. N.p., Falcon, 1952; as *So Nude, So Dead* (as Richard Marsten), New York, Fawcett, 1956.

Don't Crowd Me. New York, Popular Library, 1953; London, Consul, 1960; as *The Paradise Party*, London, New English Library, 1968.

The Blackboard Jungle. New York, Simon and Schuster, 1954; London, Constable, 1955.

A Matter of Conviction. New York, Simon and Schuster, and London, Constable, 1959; as *The Young Savages*, New York, Pocket Books, 1966.

A Horse's Head. New York, Delacorte Press, 1967; London, Constable, 1968.

Nobody Knew They Were There. New York, Doubleday, and London, Constable, 1971.

Every Little Crook and Nanny. New York, Doubleday, and London, Constable, 1972.

Lizzie. New York, Arbor House, and London, Hamish Hamilton, 1984.

Novels as Richard Marsten

Runaway Black. New York, Fawcett, 1954; London, Red Seal, 1957.

Murder in the Navy. New York, Fawcett, 1955; as *Death of a Nurse* (as Ed McBain), New York, Pocket Books, 1968; London, Hodder and Stoughton, 1972.

The Spiked Heel. New York, Holt, 1956; London, Constable, 1957.

Vanishing Ladies. New York, Permabooks, 1957; London, Boardman, 1961.

Even the Wicked. New York, Permabooks, 1958; as Ed McBain, London, Severn House, 1979.

Big Man. New York, Pocket Books, 1959; as Ed McBain, London, Penguin, 1978.

Short Stories

I Like 'em Tough (as Curt Cannon). New York, Fawcett, 1958.

The Empty Hours (87th Precinct). New York, Simon and Schuster, 1962; London, Boardman, 1963.

The McBain Brief. London, Hamish Hamilton, 1982; New York, Arbor House, 1983.

McBain's Ladies: The Women of the 87th Precint. New York, Mysterious Press, and London, Hamish Hamilton, 1988.

McBain's Ladies Too. New York, Mysterious Press, 1989.

Short Stories as Evan Hunter

The Jungle Kids. New York, Pocket Books, 1956.

The Last Spin and Other Stories. London, Constable, 1960.

Happy New Year, Herbie, and Other Stories. New York, Simon and Schuster, 1963; London, Constable, 1965.

Uncollected Short Stories as Evan Hunter

"Ticket to Death," in *Best Detective Stories of the Year 1955*, edited by David Coxe Cooke. New York, Dutton, 1955.

"Classification: Dead" (as Richard Marsten), in *Dames, Danger, and Death*, edited by Leo Margulies. New York, Pyramid, 1960.
"Easy Money," in *Ellery Queen's Mystery Magazine* (New York), September 1960.
"Nightshade" (as Ed McBain), in *Ellery Queen's Mystery Magazine* (New York), August 1970.
"Someone at the Door," in *Ellery Queen's Mystery Magazine* (New York), October 1971.
"What Happened to Annie Barnes?," in *Ellery Queen's Mystery Magazine* (New York), June 1976.

OTHER PUBLICATIONS as Evan Hunter

Novels

Tomorrow's World (as Hunt Collins). New York, Avalon, 1956; as *Tomorrow and Tomorrow*, New York, Pyramid, 1956; as Ed McBain, London, Sphere, 1979.
Second Ending. New York, Simon and Schuster, and London, Constable, 1956; as *Quartet in H*, New York, Pocket Books, 1957.
Strangers When We Meet. New York, Simon and Schuster, and London, Constable, 1958.
Mothers and Daughters. New York, Simon and Schuster, and London, Constable, 1961.
Buddwing. New York, Simon and Schuster, and London, Constable, 1964.
The Paper Dragon. New York, Delacorte Press, 1966; London, Constable, 1967.
Last Summer. New York, Doubleday, 1968; London, Constable, 1969.
Sons. New York, Doubleday, 1969; London, Constable, 1970.
Come Winter. New York, Doubleday, and London, Constable, 1973.
Streets of Gold. New York, Harper, 1974; London, Macmillan, 1975.
The Chisholms: A Novel of the Journey West. New York, Harper, and London, Hamish Hamilton, 1976.
Walk Proud. New York, Bantam, 1979.
Love, Dad. New York, Crown, and London, Joseph, 1981.
Far from the Sea. New York, Atheneum, and London, Hamish Hamilton, 1983.

Short Stories

The Beheading and Other Stories. London, Constable, 1971.
The Easter Man (a Play) and Six Stories. New York, Doubleday, 1972; as *Seven*, London, Constable, 1972.

Plays

The Easter Man (produced Birmingham and London, 1964; as *A Race of Hairy Men*, produced New York, 1965). Included in *The Easter Man (a Play) and Six Stories*, 1972.
The Conjuror (produced Ann Arbor, Michigan, 1969).

Screenplays: *Strangers When We Meet*, 1960; *The Birds*, 1963; *Fuzz*, 1972; *Walk Proud*, 1979.

Television Plays: *Appointment at Eleven* (*Alfred Hitchcock Presents* series), 1955–61; *The Chisholms* series, from his own novel, 1978–79.

Other

Find the Feathered Serpent (for children). Philadelphia, Winston, 1952.
Rocket to Luna (for children; as Richard Marsten). Philadelphia, Winston, 1952; London, Hutchinson, 1954.
Danger: Dinosaurs! (for children; as Richard Marsten). Philadelphia, Winston, 1953.
The Remarkable Harry. New York and London, Abelard Schuman, 1961.
The Wonderful Button. New York, Abelard Schuman, 1961; London, Abelard Schuman, 1962.
Me and Mr. Stenner. Philadelphia, Lippincott, 1976; London, Hamish Hamilton, 1977.

Editor (as Ed McBain), *Crime Squad*. London, New English Library, 1968.
Editor (as Ed McBain), *Homicide Department*. London, New English Library, 1968.
Editor (as Ed McBain), *Downpour*. London, New English Library, 1969.
Editor (as Ed McBain), *Ticket to Death*. London, New English Library, 1969.

*

Manuscript Collection: Mugar Memorial Library, Boston University.

*   *   *

Evan Hunter has written an imposing body of popular fiction under his own name, but mystery fans know him best as Ed McBain, the author of the 87th Precinct stories, which is the longest, the most varied, and by all odds the most popular police procedural series in the world.

According to the disclaimer page at the front of each volume, the 87th Precinct is located in an "imaginary city," but most readers will quickly catch on that the setting is New York with names of areas and localities changed. The "city," for example, is composed of five boroughs: Isola (Manhattan), where the 87th is located; Riverhead (the Bronx); Majesta (Queens); Calm's Point (Brooklyn); and Bethtown (Staten Island). The reader may be puzzled by the fact that the two big rivers, the Harb and the Dix (the Hudson and East River) flow in a westerly direction although the "city" is located on the east coast, until he realizes that the "city" is New York rolled over on its side, so that north becomes east, east becomes south, and so on around the compass.

The 87th Precinct is particularly well situated for the commission of upper-, middle-, and lower-class crimes. Within its borders are located at least one expensive high-rise apartment area, an affluent suburb, several large middle-income neighborhoods, blocks upon blocks of festering slums, a red-light district, and even a convenient number of old gothic mansions.

McBain's stories fit the pattern of the police procedural better than most series because most of the work of crime detection is carried on by groups of detectives working in teams. If there is a "hero" it would be Steve Carella, who is featured in most of the stories, but Carella usually shares the stage with some of the other detectives. There is Lieutenant Byrnes, the competent and respected chief of the detective squad; Meyer Meyer, who learned patience as a Jew growing up in a gentile neighborhood; Bert Kling, who learns both police work and life as a result of mistakes and sorrows; Cotton Hawes, the son of a Protestant minister, who has an almost incredible attraction for women; and a number of other regulars.

Generally the main characters change and mature as the series proceeds. Steve Carella, always a conscientious cop who gives everything he has to his profession, develops a growing sympathy with all kinds of people as a result of his happy marriage and the mutual affection between himself and his children. Meyer Meyer, who has not seen the inside of a synagogue in a quarter century, faces an identity crisis in the novelette "J" that forces him to question the position of a Jew in modern America. Bert Kling, appearing as a green rookie patrolman at the beginning of the series, matures somewhat with experience, is shattered by the murder of his first fiancée, recovers and lives through two more successive engagements, a marriage, and a divorce. Some of the characters remain static, however: Andy Parker continues to be a sadist; Arthur Brown, the only black cop on the squad, remains impatient; Dick Genero, surely the stupidest detective in fiction, never learns anything.

Most series writers, once they have hit upon a successful formula, will use it over and over until it wears out, but McBain likes to experiment with new patterns. In *Killer's Wedge* he keeps two apparently disparate plots going side by side, one a grisly naturalistic cliffhanger in which a disturbed woman threatens to blow up the 87th Squad with a bottle of nitroglycerine, and the other an old-fashioned locked-room story, the two strands neatly unified by the thematic image stated in the title. *He Who Hesitates* is an experiment in point of view, the story of a "perfect crime" seen entirely through the eyes of the murderer, with the police as only minor figures on the stage, but in *Hail, Hail, The Gang's All Here!* McBain manages 14 distinct story-lines and a cast of characters almost as big as the whole precinct. *Fuzz* is a farce in which the police seem incapable of doing anything right.

The one experimental failure in the series is *Hail to the Chief*, obviously designed as political satire but failing as crime fiction because the Nixon parallel is too labored and too obvious, and serves only to obstruct the movement of the narrative.

On the other hand, McBain has markedly succeeded with the device of an apparently indestructible series villain, the Deaf Man, who escapes capture at the end of *The Heckler*, re-appears in *Fuzz* and later in *Let's Hear It for the Deaf Man*, and appears to be immortal. Each of his episodes involves some fantastic caper which the police (or luck) manage to foil, but the Deaf Man is always left alive with the prospect of a future re-entry.

McBain is a master of irony, never subtle but always appropriate. It is most obvious in the case of Roger Broome in *He Who Hesitates*, who, having murdered a young woman and successfully disposed of her body, never comes under the suspicion of the police, but in a later story gets drunk and makes a public confession of his crime. It is also heavy in the promotion of patrolman Genero, who quite by accident blunders upon a pair of hoodlums and manages to capture them and who in the next story has been promoted to detective third grade for "cracking" the case. The ironic tone is strong in "J", where there is an anti-semitic theme growing out of the murder of a rabbi: the date of the crime is the second day of the Passover *seder* and Easter eve, but it is also April Fool.

The comic spirit is seldom absent from the 87th Precinct stories and has contributed to their success. This spirit makes itself felt in the heavy ironies like those just described, and it is also kept alive in such bizarre characters as Monoghan and Monroe, the almost indistinguishable Tweedledum and Tweedledee of Homicide, who usually make a perfunctory appearance at the scene of a crime, tell a few ribald jokes, suggest a few ways of sweeping the dirt under the rug, and then disappear to more comfortable quarters. There is, of course, an abundance

of pathos and even tragedy in the stories, but the comic spirit serves as a leaven and gives the series a balanced tone that is unique in crime fiction.

In 1978 McBain started a new mystery series featuring Matthew Hope, an attorney in "Calusa," Florida. In each of the stories (which have the titles of children's fairy tales, *Goldilocks*, *Rumpelstiltskin*, *Puss in Boots*, *Three Blind Mice*), Hope is drawn into a murder case as a result of the involvement of one of his clients. These novels are quite different from the 87th Precinct accounts, in both the nature of the detection employed and in a heavy reliance upon the erotic element.

—George N. Dove

———

McCALL, Anthony. *See* KANE, Henry.

———

McCALL, Vincent. *See* MORLAND, Nigel.

———

McCARRY, Charles. American. Born in Pittsfield, Massachusetts, 14 June 1930. Editor and reporter, Lisbon *Evening Journal*, Ohio, 1952–55; reporter and columnist, Youngstown *Vindicator*, Ohio, 1955–56; assistant to Secretary of Labor, Washington, D.C. 1956–57; worked for Central Intelligence Agency, 1958–67. Since 1967, freelance writer. Agent: Owen Laster, William Morris Agency, 1350 Avenue of the Americas, New York, New York, 10019, U.S.A.

CRIME PUBLICATIONS

Novels (series: Paul Christopher in all books except *The Better Angels*)

The Miernik Dossier. New York, Saturday Review Press, 1973; London, Hutchinson, 1974.
The Tears of Autumn. New York, Saturday Review Press, and London, Hutchinson, 1975.
The Secret Lovers. New York, Dutton, and London, Hutchinson, 1977.
The Better Angels. New York, Dutton, and London, Hutchinson, 1979.
The Last Supper. New York, Dutton, and London, Hutchinson, 1983.
The Bride of the Wilderness. New York, New American Library, and London, Century Hutchinson, 1988.

OTHER PUBLICATIONS

Other

Citizen Nader. New York, Saturday Review Press, 1972.
Double Eagle, with others. Boston, Little Brown, 1979; London, W.H. Allen, 1980.
Isles of the Caribbean, with others. Washington, D.C., National Geographic, 1979.

The Great Southwest, with others.   Washington, D.C., National Geographic, 1980.

* * *

One of the new generation of writers who may yet make the American spy novel as accomplished a form as its British cousin, Charles McCarry consistently displays sensitive writing, versatile plotting and characterization, and masterful command of background and detail. In all of his novels he examines the lives, work, and relationships of a continuing set of characters involved in the business of espionage and counterespionage, focusing chiefly on two related families, the Hubbards and the Christophers, and the people around them. Inheritors of the iron rectitude and dedication of the great WASP tradition, these families seem an odd but not implausible intermarriage of the Dulles brothers with the Cabots and Lodges, with all of them speaking only to God.

The continuing protagonist of all but one of McCarry's books is Paul Christopher, spy, lover, and poet; most of the novels demonstrate his immense skills in all three vocations, although we have to take his poetic competence on faith. Endowed with great intelligence, sensitivity, and an uncanny emotional control, Christopher solves the most famous contemporary political assassination in *The Tears of Autumn*, one of the best examples of a peculiarly American sub-genre, the post-Kennedy thriller, and pursues traitors over a global landscape in all the other novels. Sometimes degenerating into elegantly written travelogues, the novels are extremely sophisticated in their presentation of a great variety of exotic places, including most of Europe, parts of Africa, and a good deal of the Far East. They are all beautifully written, however, with the special authenticity of a loving expatriate writing of an adopted foreign land and an equally Jamesian flair for the complications of personal relationships.

McCarry's two most memorable performances are an early work, *The Miernik Dossier*, and his recent espionage novel, *The Last Supper*, very different books connected only by the presence of Paul Christopher. *The Miernik Dossier* is something of a masterpiece, a novel of espionage that succeeds at every ambitious level the author attempts and reverberates with possibility. The narrative is carried solely by documents—the reports of various agents, their debriefings, letters, bugged telephone conversations, comments, diaries—and concerns a group of disparate people of several nationalities, all of whom are in one way or another involved in espionage. They accompany a gigantic African prince on a journey from Switzerland to his native land, reporting on his activities, on the work of an apparent revolutionary group, on each other, and on one Tadeusz Miernik, who may or may not be a spy. The characters are all wonderfully believable, the suspense is deftly handled, and the question of the tragicomic Miernik's guilt remains a puzzle even to the end, when his death appears to transfigure him in an immolation that is as moving and ambiguous as it is utterly credible. *The Miernik Dossier* is indeed a dossier, but demonstrates an artfulness and meaning that its documentary authenticity suggests without belaboring; it is truly a remarkable book, one of the finest novels of espionage in recent years.

An equally unusual book, *The Last Supper*, marries the spy novel with a favorite American form, the family saga. Ranging with skill and confidence over a considerable span of time and space, the novel moves from the 1920's to the present, from prewar Germany to post-Mao China, convincingly describing situations as unfamiliar as aristocratic life under Hitler, the war against the Japanese in Burma, and life in a Chinese prison. In relating the life and fortunes of Paul Christopher and his family, the book encompasses the history of our time, suggesting that espionage and treason are the great actions shaping international life. Its lengthy story of complicated betrayals and its apparent admiration for the icy self control of the Christophers reflect a terribly bleak view of the contemporary world—all the traitors are people of passion, while those who defeat treason possess a glacial imperviousness to emotion. The novel's title, its resurrection of a host of characters from previous books, its sense of the completion of relationships, its general air of finality all indicate that it may be the last of McCarry's works dealing with its particular subjects and people. In 1988 McCarry published *The Bride of the Wilderness*, a very fine historical novel about the 17th-century background of the Christopher family in England and France and their settling in America; the book suggests that McCarry may have abandoned the spy novel in order to write the history of the Christophers. That history may also describe the paths of power in the United States and may of course bring him back to the arena where he has performed so impressively in the past—the novel of espionage.

—George Grella

McCLOUD, Van. *See* LUTZ, John.

McCLOY, Helen (Worrell Clarkson). Also writes as Helen Clarkson. American. Born in New York City, 6 June 1904. Educated at Brooklyn Friends School, 1908–19; the Sorbonne, Paris, 1923–24. Married Davis Dresser, i.e., Brett Halliday, q.v., in 1946 (divorced 1961), one daughter. Lived abroad, 1923–32: staff correspondent, Universal Service (Hearst), Paris, 1927–32; Paris art critic for *International Studio*, 1930–31, and London art critic for *New York Times*, 1930–32; freelance contributor to London *Morning Post* and *Parnassus*; co-founder, with Davis Dresser, Torquil Publishing Company, and Halliday and McCloy Literary Agency, 1953–64; co-author of review column for Connecticut newspapers in 1950's and 1960's. Past President, Mystery Writers of America. Recipient: Mystery Writers of America Edgar Allan Poe award, for criticism, 1953. Lives in Boston. Agent: Robert P. Mills Ltd., 333 Fifth Avenue, New York, New York 10016, U.S.A.

CRIME PUBLICATIONS

Novels (series: Dr. Basil Willing)

Dance of Death (Willing).   New York, Morrow, 1938; as *Design for Dying*, London, Heinemann, 1938.
The Man in the Moonlight (Willing).   New York, Morrow, and London, Hamish Hamilton, 1940.
The Deadly Truth (Willing).   New York, Morrow, 1941; London, Hamish Hamilton, 1942.
Who's Calling (Willing).   New York, Morrow, 1942; London, Nicholson and Watson, 1948.
Cue for Murder (Willing).   New York, Morrow, 1942.
Do Not Disturb.   New York, Morrow, 1943.
The Goblin Market (Willing).   New York, Morrow, 1943; London, Hale, 1951.

Panic. New York, Morrow, 1944; London, Gollancz, 1972.

The One That Got Away (Willing). New York, Morrow, 1945; London, Gollancz, 1954.

She Walks Alone. New York, Random House, 1948; London, Coker, 1950; as *Wish You Were Dead*, New York, Spivak, 1958.

Through a Glass, Darkly (Willing). New York, Random House, 1950; New York, Gollancz, 1951.

Better Off Dead. New York, Dell, 1951.

Alias Basil Willing. New York, Random House, and London, Gollancz, 1951.

Unfinshed Crime. New York, Random House, 1954; as *He Never Came Back*, London, Gollancz, 1954.

The Long Body (Willing). New York, Random House, 1955; London, Gollancz, 1956.

Two-Thirds of a Ghost (Willing). New York, Random House, 1956; London, Gollancz, 1957.

The Slayer and the Slain. New York, Random House, 1957; London, Gollancz, 1958.

Before I Die. New York, Torquil, and London, Gollancz, 1963.

The Further Side of Fear. New York, Dodd Mead, and London, Gollancz, 1967.

Mr. Splitfoot (Willing). New York, Dodd Mead, 1968; London, Gollancz, 1969.

A Question of Time. New York, Dodd Mead, and London, Gollancz, 1971.

A Change of Heart. New York, Dodd Mead, and London, Gollancz, 1973.

The Sleepwalker. New York, Dodd Mead, and London, Gollancz, 1974.

Minotaur Country. New York, Dodd Mead, and London, Gollancz, 1975.

The Changeling Conspiracy. New York, Dodd Mead, 1976; as *Cruel as the Grave*, London, Gollancz, 1977.

The Imposter. New York, Dodd Mead, 1977; London, Gollancz, 1978.

The Smoking Mirror. New York, Dodd Mead, and London, Gollancz, 1979.

Burn This (Willing). New York, Dodd Mead, and London, Gollancz, 1980.

Short Stories

The Singing Diamonds and Other Stories. New York, Dodd Mead, 1965; as *Surprise, Surprise*, London, Gollancz, 1965.

Uncollected Short Stories

"The Pleasant Assassin," in *Ellery Queen's Mystery Magazine* (New York), December 1970.

"A Case of Innocent Eavesdropping," in *Ellery Queen's Mystery Magazine* (New York), March 1978.

"Murphy's Law," in *Ellery Queen's Mystery Magazine* (New York), May 1979.

"That Bug That's Going Around," in *Ellery Queen's Mystery Magazine* (New York), August 1979.

OTHER PUBLICATIONS

Novel

The Last Day (as Helen Clarkson). New York, Torquil, 1959.

Other

Editor, with Brett Halliday, *20 Great Tales of Murder.* New York, Random House, 1951; London, Hammond, 1952.

*

Manuscript Collection: Mugar Memorial Library, Boston University.

Helen McCloy comments:

Self-criticism is as difficult an art as autobiography, both being forms of fiction. How can any writer be detached enough to see himself or his work objectively? I cannot say what I have done. I can only say what I have tried to do.

I began in 1938 trying to write the classic detective story with a detective who appears in each book, a startling or puzzling beginning followed by twists and turns in the plot, including hidden clues to the murderer, and a surprise ending in which those clues are shown to lead rationally to one guilty person.

It is a form as rigid as the sonnet or the haiku, and novels of killing, torture, and sex in which crime and detection are incidental have nothing to do with it. The true detective story is fun to write and fun to read. Perhaps that is why a society still unconsciously puritanical in some things frowns upon it. "A good read" is a critic's term of reproach. Readers are not supposed to get pleasure out of reading. It is supposed to be a painful duty and therefore an act of virtue. To this some people state with unmistakable pride that they read only a curiously negative form of literature known as "non-fiction." The pride seems to stem from the fact that so much non-fiction is so inexorably tedious that only an heroic reader can struggle through it. When the novel itself first developed it was scorned for the same reason. It gave pleasure and who wants pleasure?

I hope that my own detective, Dr. Basil Willing, gave pleasure to the readers of the books and stories in which he appeared. I liked him myself. He was, I believe, the first American psychiatrist detective and I am pretty sure he was the first psychiatrist detective to use psychiatry in detecting clues as well as in analyzing the criminal mind. He came from Baltimore, but he had a Russian mother. This made it plausible for him to be a fluent linguist, who could study psychiatry in Paris and Vienna after beginning at Johns Hopkins.

When we first meet him in *Dance of Death*, he is a forensic psychiatric assistant to the District Attorney of New York County, and he lives on Murray Hill, where there were still more brownstones than skyscrapers in 1938. Two books, *The Goblin Market* and *The One That Got Away*, tell us a good deal about his war career in Naval Intelligence, but the war haunts all the early books. When they are re-issued, references to the war are sometimes deleted. I now think that was a mistake. Those war references have real historical interest today. In the tenth book, *Through a Glass, Darkly*, Willing marries an Austrian refugee, Gisela von Hohenems, who first appeared in *The Man in the Moonlight*. In later short stories we find him a widower, removed to Boston, writing books and lecturing at Harvard, with a daughter named Gisela after her mother.

Anyone reading my books in series will notice that they get further and further away from the classic detective patterns as they go along. Apparently I was responding to a trend which came after the war demanding more suspense and less detection. I think that was another mistake, one I hope to rectify in future. I have a feeling that we are now on the verge of a return to the classic detective story. The only thing about fashion that is certain is that it will change. These changes are brought about periodically in all the arts by satiety. When any school of writing or painting or music is run into the ground, the public turns to something new which is usually something old in disguise.

Mystery writers are often asked why the detective story is popular. Could this popularity come from the fact that the detective story is one of the few surviving forms of story-telling? Love of the story is older than any folk-lore we know, as old as human language itself. In the 19th century someone said that a picture must never tell a story. In the 20th century a great many writers seem to believe that a story should never tell a story, so the readers turn to the painful prestige of non-fiction or the detective story.

* * *

Helen McCloy's 40-year career as a writer, critic, and editor of mystery stories has enabled her to produce an imposing body of work, impressive in its quality as well as its quantity. Her cosmopolitan schooling in the United States and France and her work as a newspaper correspondent in Paris have furnished her with a rich background, often featured in her fiction. McCloy's versatility is manifest in the structure, setting, and theme of her works. She has employed both the classic plot of detection as well as the more loosely structured psychological thriller. For her settings she writes convincingly about New York City, Boston, rural New England, Scotland, Latin America, and, in at least one short story, China. That she frequently ties her stories to some document of literary or historical interest is evidence of her wide reading.

Dr. Basil Willing is the detective she uses most often in her early novels, which, like those of Ellery Queen, are most dependably modeled on the classic pattern. In his development over the years he bears a particularly strong resemblance to Ngaio Marsh's Roderick Alleyn: through the course of the novels he meets, marries, and is widowed by the exotic Gisela von Hohenems. Also like many fictional detectives during World War II, Willing saw military service. However, Willing is not merely a pale copy of earlier detectives. As McCloy points out, he is unusual in that he is the first American psychiatrist detective and the first to use psychiatry in discovering clues, as well as in understanding the criminal personality. Dr. Willing appears in 12 of McCloy's novels, and in several short stories.

Novels that do not have the benefit of Willing's expertise tend to be psychological thrillers which focus on an innocent relative of the criminal suspect. An example of this sort of plot is *A Change of Heart*, in which the protagonist's father suffers from the fear that he has accidentally murdered a man. Similarly, *Before I Die* is told from the point of view of a wronged wife, who eventually manages to clear her husband from the suspicion of the murder of the wronged husband. McCloy is as adept at writing the psychological thriller as she is the standard "whodunit," although she has indicated a personal preference for the earlier form.

One of the most impressive characteristics of McCloy's work is her use of literary sources both as a thematic and structural device. Thus the title of *The Goblin Market* is a borrowing from Christina Rossetti and *The Long Body* refers to a philosophical concept in the Upanishads. *Cue for Murder* is a celebrated early novel not only because it captures the flavor of war-time New York so well, but also because it revolves around a revival of Sardou's *Fédora*. *Two-Thirds of a Ghost*, her spoof on publishing practices, contains several comments on the current literary scene and compares serious literature to popular writing. For example, one of the professional critics in the novel concludes a brief discourse on literary fashion with "Today a plot is indecent anywhere outside a mystery, the last refuge of the conservative writer."

In good Holmesian tradition, McCloy has her detectives solve problems by keen observation and application of arcane scientific truths. The use of poisons, the unravelling of codes, optical illusions of various sorts, and other physiological and psychological clues are typical ploys. For instance, in "A Case of Innocent Eavesdropping" the crime is solved through Willing's ability to test eye dominance.

Running counter to traditional practice, McCloy also includes in her mysteries such non-scientific phenomena as flying saucers, poltergeists, and pre-vision. Both the short story and novel entitled *Through a Glass, Darkly* deal skillfully with the *doppelgänger*, an element of plot that flies in the face of Ronald Knox's prohibition against doubles in his ten commandments for the detective story writer.

Surprisingly and regrettably, critics have tended to neglect McCloy's work, perhaps because it sometimes is unfashionably solemn. Yet the variety and the urbane erudition demonstrated in her short stories and novels make them an undisputed and valuable contribution to American detective fiction.

—Nancy C. Joyner

McCLURE, James (Howe). British. Born in Johannesburg, South Africa, 9 October 1939. Educated at Scottsville School, 1947–51, Cowan House, 1952–54, and Maritzburg College, 1955–58, all in Pietermaritzburg, Natal. Married Lorelee Ellis in 1962; two sons and one daughter. Commercial photographer, 1958–59; taught English and art at Cowan House, 1959–63; reporter, *Natal Witness*, 1963–64, *Natal Mercury*, 1964–65, and *Daily News*, 1965, all Pietermaritzburg; sub-editor, *Daily Mail*, Edinburgh, 1965–66, and *Oxford Mail* and *Oxford Times*, 1966–73; deputy editor, Oxford Times Group, 1973–74. Since 1975, Managing Director, Sabensa Gakulu Ltd., Oxford. Recipient: Crime Writers Association Gold Dagger award, 1971, and Silver Dagger award 1976. Agent: Peters Fraser and Dunlop, 5th Floor, The Chambers, Chelsea Harbour, Lots Road, London SW10 0XF. Address: Sabensa Gakulu Ltd., 14 York Road, Headington, Oxford OX3 8NW, England.

CRIME PUBLICATIONS

Novels (series: Lieutenant Kramer and Sergeant Zondi in all books except *Four and Twenty Virgins* and *Rogue Eagle*)

The Steam Pig. London, Gollancz, 1971; New York, Harper, 1972.
The Caterpillar Cop. London, Gollancz, 1972; New York, Harper, 1973.
Four and Twenty Virgins. London, Gollancz, 1973.
The Gooseberry Fool. London, Gollancz, and New York, Harper, 1974.
Snake. London, Gollancz, 1975; New York, Harper, 1976.
Rogue Eagle. London, Macmillan, and New York, Harper, 1976.
The Sunday Hangman. London, Macmillan, and New York, Harper, 1977.
The Blood of an Englishman. London, Macmillan, 1980; New York, Harper, 1981.
The Artful Egg. London, Macmillan, 1984; New York, Pantheon, 1985.
Imago: A Modern Comedy of Manners. New York, Mysterious Press, 1988.

Uncollected Short Stories

"Scandal at Sandkop," in *Winter's Crimes 7*, edited by George Hardinge. London, Macmillan, and New York, St. Martin's Press, 1975.
"Daddy's Turn," in *Winter's Crimes 9*, edited by George Hardinge. London, Macmillan, and New York, St. Martin's Press, 1977.
"Privacy for Bernadette," in *Winter's Crimes 13*, edited by George Hardinge. London, Macmillan, and New York, St. Martin's Press, 1981.
"To the Letter, Harry," in *The Year's Best Mystery and Suspense Stories 1983*, edited by Edward D. Hoch. New York, Walker, 1983.

OTHER PUBLICATIONS

Other

Killers. London, Fontana, 1976.
"Book One: To Be Continued" and "Corella of the 87th," in *Murder Ink: The Mystery Reader's Companion*, edited by Dilys Winn. New York, Workman, 1977.
Spike Island: Portrait of a Police Division. London, Macmillan, and New York, Pantheon, 1980.
Copworld: Policing on the Streets of San Diego, California. London, Macmillan, and New York, Pantheon, 1985.

* * *

James McClure is no doubt one of the most interesting crime writers to have appeared during the last decade. There are many reasons for this judgment.

McClure's novels are set in South Africa, mostly in the town of Trekkersburg, which seems to be a fairly accurate picture of Pietermaritzburg, where the author lived for many years. The most astonishing fact concerning these crime novels, which feature the police team of Lieutenant Kramer and his Zulu assistant Sergeant Zondi, is that McClure succeeds in making them into very acrimonious and unveiled reports on the current South African system without raising his voice and above all without being demagogic. The facts he reveals about the racial situation are sufficient to get his readers to think and to draw their own conclusions. In my opinion McClure's novels become as important in this respect as the works of Alan Paton, Nadine Gordimer, and André Brink. McClure's choice of genre was a very conscious one. He felt that while young people may read books and essays critical of the South African regime, older people were not likely to be as interested. By writing detective fiction, a favourite reading for many elderly people, McClure thought he could influence that generation.

In an interview McClure told me that he had taken a great interest in the 87th Precinct novels by Ed McBain. In a way his own books belong to the procedural school, for in a very convincing, realistic way they show the hard work done by the police force. This is especially true of *The Sunday Hangman*, one of his best novels. John D. MacDonald is also among his favourites in the genre. Although he isn't fond of the puzzle stories of the Golden Thirties, his plots are very cleverly constructed, particularly that of *The Caterpillar Cop*. Among McClure's works outside the Kramer-Zondi cycle the most ambitious is *Rogue Eagle*, a thriller set in the present-day Lesotho. This is one of the best political thrillers for a long time, and in some ways is even better than the Kramer-Zondi novels which run the risk of being somewhat alike.

Among McClure's later works *Spike Island* is of special interest. This is an extremely fascinating but almost too exhaustive fact-book about the police in a specific area of Liverpool, England. It deals with the attitudes and opinions of British policemen and gives a vivid picture of their day-to-day routine work and of English society.

McClure has lately written some short stories, of which one reflects his experience with the San Diego Police, the skillfully written "To the Letter, Harry."

—Jan Broberg

———

McCOY, Horace. American. Born in Pegram, Tennessee, 14 April 1897. Educated in schools in Nashville. Served in the United States Army Air Corps during World War I. Sports editor, Dallas *Journal*, 1919–30; co-founder of Dallas Little Theatre; scriptwriter in Hollywood after 1931. *Died 15 December 1955.*

CRIME PUBLICATIONS

Novels

They Shoot Horses, Don't They? New York, Simon and Schuster, and London, Barker, 1935.
No Pockets in a Shroud. London, Barker, 1937; New York, New American Library, 1948.
I Should Have Stayed Home. New York, Knopf, and London, Barker, 1938.
Kiss Tomorrow Goodbye. New York, Random House, 1948; London, Barker, 1949.
Scalpel. New York, Appleton Century Crofts, 1952; London, Barker, 1953.
Corruption City. New York, Dell, 1959; London, Consul, 1961.

Uncollected Short Stories (series: Jerry Frost in all stories)

"Dirty Work," September 1929, "Hell's Stepsons," October 1929, "Renegades of the Rio," December 1929, "The Little Black Book," January 1930, "Frost Rides Alone," March 1930, "Somewhere in Mexico," July 1930, "The Gun-Runners," August 1930, "The Mailed Fist," December 1930, "Headfirst into Hell," May 1931, "The Trail to the Tropics," March 1932, "The Golden Rule," June 1932, "Wings over Texas," October 1932, "Flight at Sunrise," May 1934, and "Somebody Must Die," October 1934, all in *Black Mask* (New York).

Uncollected Short Stories

"The Devil Man," in *Best Short Stories from the Southwest*, edited by Hilton R. Greer. Dallas, Southwest Press, 1928.
"Killer's Killer," in *Detective-Dragnet*, December 1930.
"Orders to Die," in *Battle Aces* (Chicago), December 1930.
"Night Club," in *Detective Action Stories*, February 1931.
"Death Alley," in *Detective-Dragnet*, March 1931.
"The Sky Hellion," in *Battle Aces* (Chicago), May 1931.
"Juggernaut of Justice," in *Detective-Dragnet*, August 1931.
"Two Smart Guys," in *All Star Detective* (Chicago), November 1931.
"Trapped by Silver," in *Nickel Detective* (Chicago), August 1933.
"Murder in Error," in *Black Mask* (New York), August 1932.

"Death in Hollywood," in *Mystery and Detection Annual 1973*, edited by Donald Adams. Hollywood, Adams, 1973.

"The Mopper-Up," in *The Arbor House Treasury of Detective and Mystery Stories from the Great Pulps*, edited by Bill Pronzini. New York, Arbor House, 1983.

OTHER PUBLICATIONS

Plays

I Should Have Stayed Home (screenplay), edited by Bruce S. Kupelnick. New York, Garland, 1978.

Screenplays: *Postal Inspector*, with Robert Presnell, Sr., 1936; *The Trail of the Lonesome Pine*, with Grover Jones and Harvey Thew, 1936; *Parole!*, with others, 1936; *Dangerous to Know*, with William R. Lipman, 1938; *Hunted Men*, with William R. Lipman, 1938; *King of the Newsboys*, with others, 1938; *Persons in Hiding*, with William R. Lipman, 1939; *Parole Fixer*, with William R. Lipman, 1939; *Television Spy*, with others, 1939; *Island of Lost Men*, with William R. Lipman, 1939; *Undercover Doctor*, with others, 1939; *Women Without Names*, with William R. Lipman, 1940; *Texas Rangers Ride Again*, with William R. Lipman, 1940; *Queen of the Mob*, with William R. Lipman, 1940; *Wild Geese Calling*, 1941; *Texas*, with Lewis Meltzer and Michael Blankfort, 1941; *Valley of the Sun*, 1942; *Gentleman Jim*, with Vincent Lawrence, 1942; *You're Telling Me*, with others, 1942; *Flight for Freedom*, with others, 1943; *Appointment in Berlin*, with Michael Hogan and B.P. Fineman, 1943; *There's Something about a Soldier*, with Barry Trivers, 1943; *The Fabulous Texan*, with Lawrence Hazard and Hal Long, 1947; *Montana Belle*, with others, 1949; *The Fireball*, with Tay Garnett, 1950; *Bronco Buster*, with Lillie Hayward and Peter B. Kyne, 1952; *The Lusty Men*, with David Dortort and Claude Stanush, 1952; *The World in His Arms*, with Borden Chase, 1952; *The Turning Point*, with Warren Duff, 1953; *Bad for Each Other*, with Irving Wallace, 1954; *Dangerous Mission*, with others, 1954; *Rage at Dawn*, with Frank Gruber, 1955; *The Road to Denver*, with Allen Rivkin, 1955; *Texas Lady*, 1955.

*

Bibliography: in "The Life and Writings of Horace McCoy" by John Thomas Sturak, unpublished dissertation, Los Angeles, University of California, 1976.

Manuscript Collection: University of California, Los Angeles.

*   *   *

Four of Horace McCoy's novels deal with violent death, but in two of them, *They Shoot Horses, Don't They?* and *I Should Have Stayed Home*, the deaths result from circumstances inherent in McCoy's firm, deterministic Southern California (which the marathon dance contest of his first novel captures with a brilliant intensity never repeated in his later work) rather than from mystery or thriller formulas. Two of his novels, *No Pockets in a Shroud* and *Kiss Tomorrow Goodbye*, however, show clearly why he is generally regarded as a leading member of the "hard-boiled" school of fiction. Both novels, like Hammett's *Red Harvest*, vividly depict the American city of the 1930's as almost totally corrupt, with violence and depravity as the casual by-products of everyday existence, and both novels have central characters who are individualistic, tough, and doomed. In the earlier novel Mike Dolan, a crusading reporter, is destroyed through a mixture of his own impetuosity and the forces of evil in his city; in the later novel,

Ralph Cotter, a Dolan turned criminal psychopath, falls foul of the same two forces. At his best McCoy has a vigorous style, a keen ear for dialogue, and a robust sense of the dark underside of the American dream. These virtues are, however, sometimes vitiated by inconsistency of characterization deriving from repetitive and hurried plotting and a penchant for including "topical" material, such as the fascist group in *No Pockets in a Shroud* or the Oedipal complexities of Cotter's memory in *Kiss Tomorrow Goodbye*, with too little attempt to relate these aspects either to the requirements of the plot or to a coherent social/psychological view of man.

—John S. Whitley

————

McCREADY, Jack. *See* **POWELL, Talmage.**

————

McCUTCHAN, Philip (Donald). Also writes as Robert Conington Galway; Duncan MacNeil; T.I.G. Wigg. British. Born in Cambridge, 13 October 1920. Educated at St. Helens' College, Southsea, Hampshire, 1926–34; studied for H.M. Forces entry examination, 1934–38; Royal Military College, Sandhurst, 1938. Served in the Royal Naval Volunteer Reserve, 1939–46: Lieutenant. Married Elizabeth May Ryan in 1951; one son and one daughter. Assistant purser, Orient Steam Navigation Company, London, 1946–49; accounts assistant, Anglo-Iranian Oil Company, London, 1949–52; assistant master, in preparatory schools, 1952–54; owner of a teashop, 1953–60. Full-time writer since 1960. Chairman, Crime Writers Association, 1965–66. Address: Myrtle Cottage, 107 Portland Road, Worthing, West Sussex BN1 1QA, England.

CRIME PUBLICATIONS

Novels (series: Detective Chief Superintendent Simon Shard; Commander Esmonde Shaw)

Whistle and I'll Come. London, Harrap, 1957.
The Kid. London, Harrap, 1958.
Storm South. London, Harrap, 1959.
Gibraltar Road (Shaw). London, Harrap, 1960; New York, Berkley, 1965.
Redcap (Shaw). London, Harrap, 1961; New York, Berkley, 1965.
Hopkinson and the Devil of Hate. London, Harrap, 1961.
Bluebolt One (Shaw). London, Harrap, 1962; New York, Berkley, 1965.
Leave the Dead Behind Us. London, Harrap, 1962.
Marley's Empire. London, Harrap, 1963.
The Man from Moscow (Shaw). London, Harrap, 1963; New York, Day, 1965.
Warmaster (Shaw). London, Harrap, 1963; New York, Day, 1964.
Moscow Coach (Shaw). London, Harrap, 1964; New York, Day, 1966.
Bowering's Breakwater. London, Harrap, 1964.
Sladd's Evil. London, Harrap, 1965; New York, Day, 1967.
A Time for Survival. London, Harrap, 1966.

The Dead Line (Shaw).   London, Harrap, and New York, Berkley, 1966.

Skyprobe (Shaw).   London, Harrap, 1966; New York, Day, 1967.

Poulter's Passage.   London, Harrap, 1967.

The Day of the Coastwatch.   London, Harrap, 1968.

The Screaming Dead Balloons (Shaw).   London, Harrap, and New York, Day, 1968.

The Bright Red Businessmen (Shaw).   London, Harrap, and New York, Day, 1969.

The All-Purpose Bodies (Shaw).   London, Harrap, and New York, Day, 1969.

Hartinger's Mouse (Shaw).   London, Harrap, 1970.

Man, Let's Go On.   London, Harrap, 1970.

Half a Bag of Stringer.   London, Harrap, 1970.

This Drakotny (Shaw).   London, Harrap, 1971.

The German Helmet.   London, Harrap, 1972.

The Oil Bastards.   London, Harrap, 1972.

Pull My String.   London, Harrap, 1973.

Coach North.   London, Harrap, 1974; New York, Walker, 1975.

Call for Simon Shard.   London, Harrap, 1974.

A Very Big Bang (Shard).   London, Hodder and Stoughton, 1975.

Blood Run East (Shard).   London, Hodder and Stoughton, 1976.

The Eros Affair (Shard).   London, Hodder and Stoughton, 1977.

Blackmail North (Shard).   London, Hodder and Stoughton, 1978.

Sunstrike (Shaw).   London, Hodder and Stoughton, 1979.

Corpse (Shaw).   London, Hodder and Stoughton, 1980.

Shard Calls the Tune.   London, Hodder and Stoughton, 1981.

Werewolf (Shaw).   London, Hodder and Stoughton, 1982.

The Hoof (Shard).   London, Hodder and Stoughton, 1983.

Rollerball (Shaw).   London, Hodder and Stoughton, 1984.

Shard at Bay.   London, Hodder and Stoughton, 1985.

The Executioners (Shard).   London, Hodder and Stoughton, 1986.

Greenfly (Shaw).   London, Hodder and Stoughton, 1987.

The Boy Who Liked Monsters (Shaw).   London, Hodder and Stoughton, 1989.

The Spatchcock Plan (Shaw).   London, Hodder and Stoughton, 1990.

Novels as Robert Conington Galway (series: James Packard in all books)

Assignment New York.   London, Hale, 1963.

Assignment London.   London, Hale, 1963.

Assignment Andalusia.   London, Hale, 1965.

Assignment Malta.   London, Hale, 1966.

Assignment Gaolbreak.   London, Hale, 1968.

Assignment Argentina.   London, Hale, 1969.

Assignment Fenland.   London, Hale, 1969.

Assignment Seabed.   London, Hale, 1969.

Assignment Sydney.   London, Hale, 1970.

Assignment Death Squad.   London, Hale, 1970.

The Negative Man.   London, Hale, 1971.

OTHER PUBLICATIONS

Novels

Beware, Beware the Bight of Benin.   London, Barker, 1974; as *Beware the Bight of Benin*, New York, St. Martin's Press, 1975.

Halfhyde's Island.   London, Weidenfeld and Nicolson, 1975; New York, St. Martin's Press, 1976.

The Guns of Arrest.   London, Weidenfeld and Nicolson, and New York, St. Martin's Press, 1976.

Halfhyde to the Narrows.   London, Weidenfeld and Nicolson, and New York, St. Martin's Press, 1977.

Halfhyde for the Queen.   London, Weidenfeld and Nicolson, and New York, St. Martin's Press, 1978.

Halfhyde Ordered South.   London, Weidenfeld and Nicolson, 1979; New York, St. Martin's Press, 1980.

Halfhyde and the Flag Captain.   London, Weidenfeld and Nicolson, 1980; New York, St. Martin's Press, 1981.

Cameron, Ordinary Seaman.   London, Barker, 1980.

Cameron Comes Through.   London, Barker, 1980; New York, St. Martin's Press, 1986.

Cameron of the Castle Bay.   London, Barker, 1981.

Lieutenant Cameron RNVR.   London, Barker, 1981; New York, St. Martin's Press, 1985.

Halfhyde on the Yangtze.   London, Weidenfeld and Nicolson, 1981.

Halfyde on Zanatu.   London, Weidenfeld and Nicolson, and New York, St. Martin's Press, 1982.

Cameron's Convoy.   London, Barker, 1982.

Cameron in the Gap.   London, Barker, 1982; New York, St. Martin's Press, 1983.

Orders for Cameron.   London, Barker, and New York, St. Martin's Press, 1983.

Cameron in Command.   London, Barker, 1983; New York, St. Martin's Press, 1984.

Halfhyde Outward Bound.   London, Weidenfeld and Nicolson, 1983; New York, St. Martin's Press, 1984.

Cameron and the Kaiserhof.   London, Barker, and New York, St. Martin's Press, 1984.

The Halfhyde Line.   London, Weidenfeld and Nicolson, 1984; New York, St. Martin's Press, 1985.

Cameron's Raid.   London, Weidenfeld and Nicolson, and New York, St. Martin's Press, 1985.

Halfhyde and the Chain Gangs.   London, Weidenfeld and Nicolson, 1985; New York, St. Martin's Press, 1986.

Cameron's Chase.   London, Weidenfeld and Nicolson, and New York, St. Martin's Press, 1986.

The Convoy Commodore.   London, Weidenfeld and Nicolson, 1986; New York, St. Martin's Press, 1987.

Halfhyde Goes to War.   London, Weidenfeld and Nicolson, 1986; New York, St. Martin's Press, 1987.

Cameron's Troop Lift.   London, Weidenfeld and Nicolson, and New York, St. Martin's Press, 1987.

Convoy North.   London, Weidenfeld and Nicolson, 1987; New York, St. Martin's Press, 1988.

Halfhyde on the Amazon.   London, Weidenfeld and Nicolson, and New York, St. Martin's Press, 1988.

Overnight Express.   London, Hodder and Stoughton, 1988.

Convoy South.   London, Weidenfeld and Nicolson, and New York, St. Martin's Press, 1988.

Cameron's Commitment.   London, Weidenfeld and Nicolson, and New York, St. Martin's Press, 1989.

Convoy East.   London, Weidenfeld and Nicolson, and New York, St. Martin's Press, 1989.

Halfhyde and the Admiral.   London, Weidenfeld and Nicolson, 1990.

Convoy of Fear.   London, Weidenfeld and Nicolson, 1990.

Novels as T.I.G. Wigg

A Job with the Boys.   London, Dobson, 1958.

For the Sons of Gentlemen.   London, Dobson, 1960.

A Rum for the Captain.   London, Dobson, 1961.

Novels as Duncan MacNeil

Drums along the Khyber. London, Hodder and Stoughton, 1969; New York, St. Martin's Press, 1973.
Lieutenant of the Line. London, Hodder and Stoughton, 1970; New York, St. Martin's Press, 1973.
Sadhu on the Mountain Peak. London, Hodder and Stoughton, 1971; New York, St. Martin's Press, 1974.
The Gates of Kunarja. London, Hodder and Stoughton, 1972; New York, St. Martin's Press, 1974.
The Red Daniel. London, Hodder and Stoughton, 1973; New York, St. Martin's Press, 1974.
Subaltern's Choice. London, Hodder and Stoughton, and New York, St. Martin's Press, 1974.
By Command of the Viceroy. London, Hodder and Stoughton, and New York, St. Martin's Press, 1975.
The Mullah from Kashmir. London, Hodder and Stoughton, 1976; New York, St. Martin's Press, 1977.
Wolf in the Fold. London, Hodder and Stoughton, and New York, St. Martin's Press, 1977.
Charge of Cowardice. London, Hodder and Stoughton, and New York, St. Martin's Press, 1978.
The Restless Frontier. London, Hodder and Stoughton, and New York, St. Martin's Press, 1979.
Cunningham's Revenge. London, Hodder and Stoughton, 1980; New York, Walker, 1985.
The Train at Bundarbar. London, Hodder and Stoughton, 1981; New York, Walker, 1986.
A Matter for the Regiment. London, Hodder and Stoughton, 1982.

Plays

Radio Plays and Features: *The Proper Service Manner*, 1954; *Unlawful Occasions*, 1954; *First Command*, 1954; *The Feast of Lanterns* (for children) 1955; *Thirty-Four for Tea*, 1955; *A Run Ashore*, 1956; *Flash Point*, 1956; *The Great Siege*, 1956; *In Partnership*, 1958; *O'Flynn of UBI* (for children), 1963.

Other

On Course for Danger (for children). London, Macmillan, and New York, St. Martin's Press, 1959.
Tall Ships: The Golden Age of Sail. London, Weidenfeld and Nicolson, and New York, Crown, 1976.
Great Yachts. London, Weidenfeld and Nicolson, and New York, Crown, 1979.

*

Philip McCutchan comments:

My main work falls into six groups: "individual" novels using different characters each time; a series featuring Commander Shaw, initially of Naval Intelligence but later of the semi-official organization known as 6D2; another series featuring Detective Chief Superintendent Simon Shard, seconded to the Foreign Office from Scotland Yard; a naval series set during World War II featuring Donald Cameron RNVR; another war series featuring Commodore John Mason Kemp RNR, a Commodore of convoys; and yet another series set in the Royal Navy of the 1890's, when steam had not long replaced sail, featuring Lieutenant St. Vincent Halfhyde, R.N., descendant of a gunner's mate who had fought at Trafalgar under Lord Nelson. In addition, under the pseudonym Duncan MacNeil, I have written a series of military novels, set on the North-West Frontier of India in the 1890's and featuring

Captain James Ogilvie of the 114th Highlanders, The Queen's Own Royal Strathspeys. I have a consuming interest in the armed services as may perhaps be judged, but also very much enjoy writing the kind of book in which Shaw and Simon Shard appear. As to the "individual" books, I find that I have been taken over by my series characters to such an extent that I find no time in which to write anything else these days—and, in any case, I have grown fond of all my series characters and can't wait to get on to the next one as I finish (regretfully) the one before!

* * *

Philip McCutchan's novel *Gibraltar Road* established Commander Esmonde Shaw as one of the most inventive cloak-and-dagger conceptions to emerge from Britain in the 1960's.

In the early books, Shaw is engaged with the Special Services of the Naval Intelligence Division (N.I.D.); later books find him with an intelligence-probe agency known as 6D2. The narrative constant of the series depicts Shaw contending with insidious power blueprints on a global scale.

McCutchan conceived the series with a consistent line of logically developed plots and adversaries while delineating an apocalyptic technological menace in each novel that reflected authenticity, precision, and the darkest dimensions of the Cold War.

Gibraltar Road establishes the general format and tone for the rest of the series. In this novel, McCutchan explores the (then) untested arena of nuclear proliferation. G.E.D. Latymer (the elusive head of Special Services), outlines the development of Project Sinker to Commander Shaw in which Gibraltar would serve as the initiation of an atomic submarine network. Ackroyd, a British physicist, is delineated as the talent responsible for the genesis of the production unit that processed ALG-SIX, the critical fuel for the atomic submarine nucleus. Shaw is sanctioned by Special Services to seek out Ackroyd.

The novel features the obligatory sensuous *femme fatale*, inventively typified by Karina, a seductively lethal Soviet agent who is also on the trail of Ackroyd. McCutchan generates a strong line of suspense with her characterization when it is revealed that she was allied with Shaw during World War II. McCutchan is no less effective in his depiction of the villains in the series. Andres, a double-agent figure in *Gibraltar Road*, is conveyed as capable, resourceful, and the very equal in dedication to his professional pursuits to Commander Shaw.

Having established the constants in his series with *Gibraltar Road*, McCutchan intensified these elements with the advancement of the Shaw canon. *Redcap* finds Shaw on the trail of Lubin, a top electronics trust, who emerges as the crucial liaison for an apocalyptic nuclear project—Radio Regulator Equipment for Defense Coordination Atom Powers, or *Redcap*. McCutchan sketches a more treacherous landscape in *Redcap* than was manifested in the previous novel, with the deceptive ploys of Peking played out during the term in which *Redcap* was being transported to its base in the Central Australian Desert.

The basic Shaw premise is honored for the most part in *Bluebolt One* in which the titular nuclear control system, controlled by an Anglo-American radio network in Nogolia, West Africa, is designated perilous territory by Special Services. McCutchan penetrates new terrain in this novel, with the detailed, albeit mystical, development of Edo, the magnetic master of an African Voodoo coven, which is determined as the cause for the danger engulfing the *Bluebolt One* complex. The occult segments are handled with a credible eye and it imparts an unconventional slant to the series.

Warmaster marked a provocative turning point for the Shaw series, as McCutchan deploys his protagonist, whom he fully established in the first three books, in plots that were marked with the ideology of the advanced Cold War. *Warmaster* is accented by a stock McCutchan plot, namely the liquidation of a critical agent-in-place (as typified by *Bluebolt One*); in this instance, a U.S. Naval Intelligence operative who serves as Latymer's justification to dispatch Shaw to New York in order to pursue a lead linked to a Brooklyn-based packaging complex.

McCutcham also dexterously fuses the elements of a German firm involved in the design of the dock and Otto Keller, the jaded German physicist credited with the development of *Warmaster*. A suspected defection attempt and the intricate moves of two (then) hi-tech crafts, *The Dakota* and *The Moehne*, figured in McCutchan's intrigues. *Warmaster*, by any espionage period genre standard, is a complex spy novel, cutting across genre lines. The McCutchan mastery of precise technological detail is ever present in this novel, as the author meticulously sketches the global powers' latest nuclear toys. And yet, in the segments which follow the New York links, McCutchan shifts gears and executes the narrative in the groove of a traditional mystery. McCutchan is so proficient with this alternating technique throughout *Warmaster* that one current does not intrude upon the other.

If *Warmaster* is the Shaw series' turning point, *Skyprobe* is a transitional, almost transcendental achievement, which signified Shaw's final mission for Special Services before advancing to 6D2 in 1968. McCutchan adroitly shadows both the escapist and realistic dimensions of espionage fiction to intensify the definition of the spy novel.

Special Services perceive a threat to *Skyprobe IV*, a U.S. spacecraft committed to ultra-dimensional space exploration and summon Shaw to ally with select U.S. intelligence networks. On this level, McCutchan ventured into the novel (for its time) alliance of outer space and espionage themes, which previously had been combined in Ian Fleming's *Moonraker* and more audaciously, the same year in which *Skyprobe* initially appeared, in John Creasey's *The Terror*. This narrative area would become conventional in the escapist sky arena by 1968 to the point of overexposure. McCutchan achieved the spectacular effect of *Skyprobe IV* in flight while molding it into a suspenseful event.

McCutchan's insertion of one Colonel Stefan Spalinski, engaged by an anticommunist agency known as the N.I.S., endowed *Skyprobe* with a hauntingly realistic dimension that provided a sense of conflict with the book's science-fiction trappings. Spalinski was savagely liquidated in the thick of the *Skyprobe IV* crisis.

The Shaw-Renke segment of the plot provided the basis for a personal crisis for Shaw which eventually led to his crossover to 6D2 in 1968. This development shaped *Skyprobe* with all the more complexity than suggested earlier, typifying this advanced Shaw novel as an espionage-science fiction epic accented with the dimensions of the escapist school and the darkly crafted cynicism of the realistic arena. *Skyprobe* is also the most personal exploit for McCutchan's secret service creation. In addition to qualifying as the best Commander Shaw novel, *Skyprobe* emerged as a portentous document of the fictional secret agent's future beyond the dictates of the era's boundaries.

Two of the last Shaw entries of the 1960's, *The Screaming Dead Balloons* and *The All-Purpose Bodies*, progress further into science fiction while retaining the best elements of the early books. *The Screaming Dead Balloons* presents Shaw in his new role with 6D2, a global investigative network. In this novel, Shaw is ordered to liquidate a megalomaniacal Maltese scientist, John Zan, who developed a venomous fungus with mass reproduction potential. The only facet reminiscent of the old cloak-and-dagger espionage school is McCutchan's G.R.A.S.P. consortium, which is indicative of the genre in general and not the author as a specific case.

The All-Purpose Bodies emerges as the most cryptic Shaw thriller in which the 6D2 agent is sanctioned to investigate the disappearance of Jake Dunwoodie, a renowned Australian scientist who is the valued talent behind the conception of *Lifeforce*, a critical nuclear complex. Allying with the scientist's wayward wife, Flair, Shaw unmasks Dunwoodie on an island off the Great Barrier Reef—in the cataclysmic kingdom of R. High, a malevolent master of brain transplant surgery, agent for the mysterious W.U.S.W.I.P.P. network and architect of a blueprint to obliterate *Lifeforce* through anatomical techniques.

The Shaw series advanced beyond the 1960's as represented by *Hartinger's Mouse*, *This Drakotny*, and *Sunstrike*. More recent additions to this vintage series include *Werewolf*, *Rollerball*, and *The Boy Who Liked Monsters*. As the 1970's advanced, McCutchan ventured into new terrain. The exploits of Security Service agent Simon Shard tend to be more stylized than the Shaw thrillers, as typified by *Call for Simon Shard*, *A Very Big Bang*, *Blood Run East*, *Blackmail North*, *The Eros Affair*, and *Shard at Bay*.

McCutchan comes full circle with *The Spatchcock Plan*. In this novel, Shaw—still engaged with 6D2—is on the trail of his tested espionage associate, Felicity Mandrake, who has mysteriously vanished.

Shaw's quest draws him into darkly contemporary territory, as McCutchan dramatically encompasses the I.R.A., an insidious Japanese arms merchant named Kyoshiro Ka, and imprisoned Libyan master terrorist, and the designs of a Whitehall mogul, Hubert Spatchcock, who has devised an elaborate blueprint which unifies and intensifies the book's diverse elements.

The Spatchcock Plan signifies an era of 30 years for McCutchan's Commander Shaw character, no mean feat in the elusive espionage market. This provocative novel represents the advancement of the times since the series began in the 1960, the maturation of the Shaw character through these dynamic changes and the effective alliance of the best elements from both the Special Services and 6D2 facets of the series. Symbolically and progressively, *The Spatchcock Plan* is a culmination of McCutchan's classic Commander Shaw series.

—Andy East

MCDONALD, Gregory (Christopher). American. Born in Shrewsbury, Massachusetts, 15 February 1937. Educated at Chauncy Hall School; Harvard University, Cambridge, Massachusetts, B.A. 1958. Married Susan Aiken in 1963; two sons. Marine insurance underwriter, 1959–61; Peace Corps volunteer, 1962; teacher, 1963–64; journalist: Arts and Humanities Editor and Critic-at-Large, Boston *Globe*, 1966–73. Self-employed writer. Director, 1977, and President 1985–86, Mystery Writers of America. Recipient: U.P.I. award, for journalism; Mystery Writers of America Edgar Allan Poe award, 1975, 1977. Agent: William Morris Agency, 1350 Avenue of the Americas, New York, New York 10019. Address: Camaldon Farm, 175 The Rose Hill Road, Pulaski, Tennessee 38478, U.S.A.

CRIME PUBLICATIONS

Novels (series: Irwin "Fletch" Fletcher; Francis Xavier Flynn)

Fletch.   Indianapolis, Bobbs Merrill, 1974; London, Gollancz, 1976.
Confess, Fletch.   New York, Avon, 1976; London, Gollancz, 1977.
Flynn.   New York, Avon, 1977; London, Gollancz, 1978.
Fletch's Fortune.   New York, Avon, and London, Gollancz, 1978.
Who Took Toby Rinaldi?   New York, Putnam, 1980; as *Snatched*, London, Gollancz, 1980.
Fletch and the Widow Bradley.   New York, Warner, and London, Gollancz, 1981.
The Buck Passes Flynn.   New York, Ballantine, 1981; London, Gollancz, 1982.
Fletch's Moxie.   New York, Warner, 1982; London, Gollancz, 1983.
Fletch and the Man Who.   New York, Warner, and London, Gollancz, 1983.
Carioca Fletch.   New York, Warner, and London, Gollancz, 1984.
Flynn's In.   New York, Mysterious Press, 1984; London, Gollancz, 1985.
Safekeeping.   New York, Mysterious Press, 1985; London, Gollancz, 1986.
Fletch Won.   New York, Warner, and London, Gollancz, 1985.
Fletch Too.   New York, Warner, 1986; London, Gollancz, 1987.

OTHER PUBLICATIONS

Novels

Running Scared.   New York, Obolensky, 1964; London, Gollancz, 1977.
Love among the Mashed Potatoes.   New York, Dutton, 1978.
A World Too Wide.   Boston, Hill, 1987.

Other

The Education of Gregory Mcdonald: Writings about America 1966–73, Sketches from the Sixties (articles).   New York, Warner, 1985.
Exits and Entrances.   Boston, Hill, 1988.
Merely Players.   Boston, Hill, 1988.

Editor, *Last Laughs: The 1986 Mystery Writers of America Anthology*.   New York, Mysterious Press, 1986.

*

Gregory Mcdonald comments:
I offer two quotes from the works themselves: "Police Control Crime," and, from Fletch's own mouth, "We are all mysteries awaiting solution."

*   *   *

Running Scared is the first and least generic of Gregory Mcdonald's thrillers, and it is interesting how close he gets even here to the template from which he has built his career. We have the obsession with impersonation closely allied to the inability of the mildly sociopathic to understand why people find their lack of conventional affect so disturbing. His student hero allows his best friend to commit suicide out of respect for his free will, and then woos his sister in disguise, dying in a car crash when she discovers his identity and rejects him. If the book is less than compelling, it is partly because its emotional complexities are established in some depth and then resolved in an almost entirely arbitrary catastrophe, but partly too because Mcdonald's obsession with the trappings of great wealth is something that only F. Scott Fitzgerald could make attractively the stuff of tragedy.

In *Fletch*, the first in the series which Mcdonald has concentrated on, these themes are transmuted by being rendered with a more jaundiced eye, and placed into a farcical rather than a tragic mode. Where the first novel tried for a fine writing that laid every aspect of its hero's feelings sensitively on the line, here Mcdonald exploits deliberate obscurity. Where the first book made impersonation and deceit the subject of the plot, here Mcdonald makes it his novelistic method. We witness a beach bum, signalled as protagonist by the title, and watch him being asked by a rich man to kill him; it is only in the second chapter that we learn that the beach bum is an investigative reporter, and not until the end that the question of what he intends to do is even partly resolved.

This is a plot in which the hero's sociopathy and his professionalism alike have placed him in opposition to a variety of enemies. The book is a classic dream revenge in the way in which I.M. Fletcher, by a variety of deceits and evasions, sets all of his opponents up to collide with each other. He sets off for Brazil with a fortune, secure in the knowledge that one of his intending murderers will be arrested for the killing of the other, that he is free forever of the internal politics of his paper and that his two ex-wives are lumbered with sharing his apartment. This is a book which both describes, and is an example of, fast pacing and good timing.

The second Fletch thriller sets him up against a variety of opponents of more impressive calibre, notably the villainous art dealer Horan, and the eccentric cop and international spy Flynn. Horan is what Fletch would be like if he had no standards of niceness or polite behaviour; Flynn is what he would be like if his sociopathy was countered by an intellectual belief in the necessity of morality. It is perhaps significant that where Fletch and Horan are engaged with the visual arts, Flynn is an amateur musician; there are some arts where you need more rules.

By this stage in his career, Mcdonald had found his hero and found his metier; if the subsequent Fletch thrillers are less startlingly good, and in a few cases rather banal, it is because the fascination of what's difficult gets less interesting each time you succeed in doing it. Mcdonald has tried to counter this by returning to earlier stages in Fletch's career, when he was less good at what he does, and rather more prone to being deceived by others; *Fletch Won*, chronologically the first, is perhaps the best of these, simply because Mcdonald is faced with the task of choreographing the blunders of this more naive Fletch into a hard-won victory.

Flynn became the subject of a progressively rather less interesting series, that contains a couple of minor characters—also present in the Fletch books—Walter March is one of the few survivors of the sequence of killings in *Flynn's In* simply because he has to be to get killed in *Fletch's Fortune*. The problem with this series is that Fletch is always finding things out and improvising accordingly, whereas Flynn gives the impression of knowing everything important to begin with and of sitting back until he feels like intervening; even his minor discomfitures seem part of his plan.

It is perhaps significant that the two protagonists of Mcdonald's two later non-series thrillers are both young kidnapped pre-pubescent boys. His heroes always have an innocence about them that can become rather cloying—which is why Fletch's bouncy promiscuity never becomes either credible or prurient—and always have the air of being lost in a world of threatening larger people. Mcdonald does a few things very well and has made a career out of them, but he has sometimes ridden his formulas into the ground.

—Roz Kaveney

McGERR, Patricia. American. Born in Falls City, Nebraska, 26 December 1917. Educated at Trinity College, Washington, D.C., 1933–34; University of Nebraska, Lincoln, B.A. 1936; Columbia University, New York, M.S. in journalism 1937. Director of public relations, American Road Builders Association, Washington, D.C., 1937–43; assistant editor, *Construction Methods* magazine, New York, 1943–48. Self-employed writer. Recipient: Catholic Press Association prize, 1950; Grand Prix de Littérature Policière, 1952; *Ellery Queen's Mystery Magazine* prize, 1967. *Died 11 May 1985.*

CRIME PUBLICATIONS

Novels (series: Selena Mead)

Pick Your Victim. New York, Doubleday, 1946; London, Collins, 1947.
The Seven Deadly Sisters. New York, Doubleday, 1947; London, Collins, 1948.
Catch Me If You Can. New York, Doubleday, 1948; London, Collins, 1949.
Save the Witness. New York, Doubleday, 1949; London, Collins, 1950.
. . . Follow, As the Night. . . . New York, Doubleday, 1950; as *Your Loving Victim,* London, Collins, 1951.
Death in a Million Living Rooms. New York, Doubleday, 1951; as *Die Laughing,* London, Collins, 1952.
Fatal in My Fashion. New York, Doubleday, 1954; London, Collins, 1955.
Is There a Traitor in the House? (Mead). New York, Doubleday, 1964; London, Collins, 1965.
Murder Is Absurd. London, Doubleday, and London, Gollancz, 1967.
Stranger with My Face. Washington, Luce, 1968; London, Hale, 1970.
For Richer, For Poorer, Till Death. Washington, Luce, 1969; London, Hale, 1971.
Legacy of Danger (Mead). Washington, Luce, 1970.
Daughter of Darkness. New York, Popular Library, 1974.
Dangerous Landing. New York, Dell, 1975.

Uncollected Short Stories

"Murder to the Twist," in *Ellery Queen's Mystery Magazine* (New York), October 1962.
"The Washington D.C. Murders," in *Ellery Queen's Mystery Magazine* (New York), September 1963.
"Justice Has a High Price," in *Ellery Queen's Mystery Mix.* New York, Random House, 1963; London, Gollancz, 1964.
"The King Will Die Tonight," in *This Week* (New York), 27 October 1963.
"Question, Mr. President," in *This Week* (New York), 8 December 1963.

"Grand Prize for Selena," in *This Week* (New York), 23 February 1964.
"Holiday for a Lady Spy," in *This Week* (New York), 5 April 1964.
"Latin Lesson," in *This Week* (New York), 21 June 1964.
"Easy Conquest," in *This Week* (New York), 5 July 1964.
"Secret of Carthage," in *This Week* (New York), 27 September 1964.
"Murder in Red," in *This Week* (New York), 4 October 1964.
"Fox Hunt for Selena," in *This Week* (New York), 12 December 1964.
"Fellow Traveler," in *This Week* (New York), 14 March 1965.
"Ballad for a Spy," in *This Week* (New York), 18 April 1965.
"Truth or Consequences," in *This Week* (New York), 27 June 1965.
"Selena's Black Sheep," in *This Week* (New York), 15 August 1965.
"Good Loser," in *This Week* (New York), 5 September 1965.
"Prophet Without Honor," in *This Week* (New York), 17 October 1965.
"Legacy of Danger," in *Alfred Hitchcock Presents: Sinister Spies.* New York, Random House, 1966; London, Reinhardt, 1967.
"A Time to Die," in *This Week* (New York), 16 January 1966.
"Palace Spy," in *This Week* (New York), 6 March 1966.
"Silent Night, Frantic Night," in *This Week* (New York), 25 December 1966.
"Ladies with a Past" and "Selena in Atlantic City," in *Spies and More Spies,* edited by Robert Arthur. New York, Random House, 1967.
"Match Point in Berlin," in *Ellery Queen's Murder Menu.* Cleveland, World, and London, Gollancz, 1969.
"Selena Robs the White House," in *Murder Most Foul,* edited by Harold Q. Masur. New York, Walker, 1971.
"Campaign Fever," in *Alfred Hitchcock Presents: Stories to Stay Awake By.* New York, Random House, 1971.
"This One's a Beauty," in *Ellery Queen's Mystery Bag.* Cleveland, World, 1972; London, Gollancz, 1973.
"The Last Check," in *Ellery Queen's Mystery Magazine* (New York), March 1972.
"Winner Takes All," in *Ellery Queen's Crookbook.* New York, Random House, and London, Gollancz, 1974.
"View by Moonlight," in *Alfred Hitchcock Presents: Stories to Be Read with the Door Locked.* New York, Random House, 1975.
"Nothing But the Truth," in *Ellery Queen's Masks of Mystery.* New York, Davis, 1978.
"In the Clear," in *Ellery Queen's Mystery Magazine* (New York), April 1978.
"A Choice of Murders," in *Ellery Queen's Napoleons of Mystery.* New York, Davis, 1978.
"The Day of the Bookmobile," in *Ellery Queen's Mystery Magazine* (New York), January 1979.
"Hide and Seek—Russian Style," in *Ellery Queen's Veils of Mystery.* New York, Davis, 1980.
"The Writing on the Wall," in *Ellery Queen's Circumstantial Evidence.* New York, Davis, 1980.
"State Visit," in *Ellery Queen's Mystery Magazine* (New York), 30 November 1980.
"Every Litter Bit Helps," in *Ellery Queen's Mystery Magazine* (New York), 9 September 1981.
"Chain of Terror," in *Ellery Queen's Maze of Mysteries.* New York, Davis, 1982.
"The Bloody Moustache," in *Ellery Queen's Mystery Magazine* (New York), 1 January 1982.
"A Test of Love," *Good Housekeeping* (London), February, 1982.

"Where's Your Sense of Humor?" in *Ellery Queen's Mystery Magazine* (New York), 21 April 1982.
"A Date in Helsinki," in *The Year's Best Mystery and Suspense Stories 1983*, edited by Edward D. Hoch. New York, Walker, 1983.
"We Have Your Wife," in *Ellery Queen's Mystery Magazine* (New York), April 1983.
"Caribbean Clues," in *Ellery Queen's Mystery Magazine* (New York), January 1984.
"Fatal Corner," in *Ellery Queen's Mystery Magazine* (New York), June 1984.

OTHER PUBLICATIONS

Novels

The Missing Years. New York, Doubleday, 1953; London, W.H. Allen, 1954.
Martha, Martha. New York, Kenedy, 1960; London, Hodder and Stoughton, 1961.
My Brothers, Remember Monica. New York, Kenedy, 1964.

*

Manuscript Collections: Institute of Popular Culture, Bowling Green University, Ohio; (non-mystery) Trinity College, Washington, D.C.

Patricia McGerr commented (1984):

I was first inspired to write a mystery novel by the announcement of a contest (which I didn't win). From my reading I knew that a classic mystery included a murderer, a victim, and several suspects. So I began by assembling the cast of characters. But when I began to assign roles, it was obvious that only one of them could commit the murder, whereas any of the other ten might be his victim. So, reversing the formula, I named the murderer on page one and centered the mystery around the identity of the victim. In my next book I carried that idea a little farther by asking the reader to discover both murderer and victim and then, in the third, presented a murderer whose problem was to pierce the disguise of the detective. A witness to the crime was the unknown element in the fourth book and in the fifth, having exhausted the possibilities, I returned to the design of my first crime with the question mark again beside the name of the corpse. Since then I've been writing more conventional mysteries, but in all of them I've tried to make the development of character as interesting as the puzzle.

* * *

Patricia McGerr is perhaps best known for her creative genius and technical skill in producing what Barzun and Taylor have aptly call the "*whodunin?*" wherein the victim of the crime, rather than the culprit, is unknown. Her forte, indeed, her major contribution to the genre, is the mystery with this completely new twist. In her first and most widely acclaimed tour de force, *Pick Your Victim*, a group of Marines in the Aleutians passes the time by attempting to solve a murder committed in Washington, D.C., at the supposedly philanthropic organization SUDS (Society for the Uplift of Domestic Service). A torn clipping from a hometown newspaper informs them of the murderer's name and confession, but a missing segment prompts them to initiate their far-off investigation into the identity of the corpse, which could have been any of some ten persons.

Another large cast is assembled in Patricia McGerr's second work, *The Seven Deadly Sisters*, in which Sally Bowen discovers through a letter that one of her seven aunts has murdered her husband. In many respects superior to its predecessor, this novel entails the unmasking of victim and culprit alike. The very nature of these early puzzlers demands close character studies, a skill at which Miss McGerr excels—indeed, she is at her very best with a large and assorted cast of characters, all of whom she manages to define and individualize with the utmost ease and care. Pacing, however, is consequently much slower than in her later works in which she reverts to the more conventional "whodunit" such as *Fatal in My Fashion* where murder visits the world of *haute couture* in Paris. If some of the characters in her later works appear somewhat less than believable, the high degree of originality in plotting in each case easily permits suspension of any disbelief. *Death in a Million Living Rooms* with its television setting, and *Murder Is Absurd* with its theatrical background are both especially well executed, as are . . . *Follow, As the Night . . .*, *Stranger with My Face*, and *For Richer, For Poorer, Till Death*.

There is little or no use of the customary detective or police investigator in McGerr's works, which are primarily novels of suspense and intrigue, often displaying a rich vein of humor. But McGerr has also created one memorable series character in Selena Mead—a Washington, D.C., socialite, magazine writer, and counter-espionage agent with a top-secret security branch known as Section Q. Ex-widow Selena is now remarried to her immediate superior, Hugh Pierce. Her first published appearance was in *This Week* magazine in October, 1963, which described the knifing death of her first agent-husband, Simon Mead. Since then Selena Mead has appeared in some twenty-five short stories, two novelets, and two novels, *Is There a Traitor in the House?* and *Legacy of Danger*, the latter of which incorporates several short story exploits.

—James R. McCahery

McGIRR, Edmund. Pseudonym for Kenneth Giles; also wrote as Charles Drummond. British. Born in 1922. *Died in 1972.*

CRIME PUBLICATIONS

Novels (series: Piron in all books)

The Funeral Was in Spain. London, Gollancz, 1966.
The Hearse with Horses. London, Gollancz, 1967.
Here Lies My Wife. London, Gollancz, 1967.
The Lead-Lined Coffin. London, Gollancz, 1968.
An Entry of Death. London, Gollancz, and New York, Walker, 1969.
Death Pays the Wages. London, Gollancz, 1970.
No Better Fiend. London, Gollancz, and New York, Walker, 1971.
Bardel's Murder. London, Gollancz, 1973; New York, Walker, 1974.
A Murderous Journey. London, Gollancz, 1974; New York, Walker, 1975.

Novels as Kenneth Giles (series: Inspector Harry James)

Some Beasts No More (James). London, Gollancz, 1965; New York, Walker, 1968.

A Provenance of Death (James). London, Gollancz, 1966; New York, Simon and Schuster, 1967; as *A Picture of Death*, St. Albans, Hertfordshire, Granada, 1970.

The Big Greed. London, Gollancz, 1966.

Death and Mr. Prettyman (James). London, Gollancz, 1967; New York, Walker, 1969.

Death in Diamonds (James). London, Gollancz, 1967; New York, Simon and Schuster, 1968.

Death among the Stars (James). London, Gollancz, and New York, Walker, 1968.

Death Cracks a Bottle (James). London, Gollancz, 1969; New York, Walker, 1970.

Death in the Church (James). London, Gollancz, 1970.

Murder Pluperfect (James). London, Gollancz, and New York, Walker, 1970.

A File on Death (James). London, Gollancz, and New York, Walker, 1973.

Novels as Charles Drummond (series: Sergeant Reed in all books)

Death at the Furlong Post. London, Gollancz, 1967; New York, Walker, 1968.

Death and the Leaping Ladies. London, Gollancz, 1968; New York, Walker, 1969.

The Odds on Death. London, Gollancz, 1969; New York, Walker, 1970.

Stab in the Back. London, Gollancz, and New York, Walker, 1970.

A Death at the Bar. London, Gollancz, 1972; New York, Walker, 1973.

*   *   *

Kenneth Giles, writing under his own name and the pseudonyms Edmund McGirr and Charles Drummond, wrote some two dozen mysteries between 1965 and his death in 1972. The series by Giles introduced a bright young Sergeant, Harry James of Scotland Yard, who rises through the ranks and takes on a wife and children as the series progresses. Drummond's protagonist is Sergeant Reed of Scotland Yard, a brilliant but bibulous man whose name has been removed from the Recommended for Inspectorship list as a result of two charges brought against him, one for violence, the other for accepting the favors of a prostitute, neither of which was proven, but both of which contributed to the decision to use Reed for odd jobs in the Department. McGirr's series features a New York-based Detective Agency run by the Old Man and employing a private investigator, Piron. Some of the books in this last series are set in New York, but most return to England, a more familiar landscape for Giles, where Piron handles work for both the American Embassy and the British government. All the mysteries introduce a lively cast of eccentrics, pub-crawlers, petty crooks, and garrulous landladies, and all display ingenious plots

In *Some Beasts No More*, Giles's first mystery, Superintendent Hawker, presiding over the statistics kept in the government files, given to racy speech and surprisingly right hunches, and wise to the foibles and ambitions of the members of the Yard, assigns young Detective-Sergeant Harry James to investigate a murder. The murder has caught Hawker's attention because it involves a woman who is the only link between four murderers who have themselves been murdered. Elizabeth Holland, also known as Rhonda Gentry, is a beautiful redhead, with a full figure and an intelligent face, and she excites more than the detective in Harry James. James, a bright young man with a knowledge of accountancy and

experience in investigative work, is eager for advancement and a comfortable niche in life. Typical of Giles's story-telling strategy, this story unwinds as James pounds the pavements and frequents pubs and hotels, questioning the local people and following their leads. The characters he encounters are also representative. There are a landlady who was a music-hall star, a distinguished ex-commando, and a member of the British peerage. Giles's gift for dialect and love of convoluted sentences amply sprinkled with British colloquialisms are also evident. Only Giles's fixation with food is missing from this work. It is not until *A Provenance of Death*, that Giles creates Sergeant Honeybody, and revels in baroque extravagances while describing the eating habits of James, Elizabeth Holland, who has now become James's fiancée, and Honeybody.

The other books in the series take a more mature James, assisted by Elizabeth and Honeybody, who daily grows more satisfied with pubs and more discontented with his dour Scots wife, through even bloodier murders. Each murder solved advances James through the ranks until he is finally promoted to Chief Inspector. Whether Giles is depicting the world of diamond or art smugglers, or the world of solicitors, wine importers, or newspaper men, he always knows the world he describes and describes it with an accuracy and a sense of its unique flavor. His literary tastes are always evident in his books: his love for the 18th century is particularly clear. His stories are always fair: their endings, like Agatha Christie's, can generally be guessed by a reader who is wary of jumping at his false clues and accustomed to his sudden denouements. And his flair for extravagant characters and culinary arts gives his detective stories a texture more commonly found in a good novel.

The range of plots of the James series is repeated in the two series by Drummond and McGirr. International art smuggling, faking antique silver and banknotes, diamond smuggling, and fixed horse-racing run through a number of the books in the Drummond series, and are incidental to the plot in a number of McGirr's mysteries. Plots that hinge upon mistaken identity and imposters are common to all the books. What distinguishes the books of Giles is the character of the protagonist. Otherwise the plot, the method of investigation, the sets, and the other characters are much the same.

Drummond's Sergeant Reed, unlike Inspector Harry James, often finds himself suspected of an involvement in the crimes he investigates. In *The Odds on Death*, Reed has the reputation among the racing underworld of being a "bad copper," but he matches his wits against those of the Marquis of Sous-Jouarre, the mastermind of a ring of international criminals, and solves the mystery of the death of a small, failed jockey, breaks the ring of international swindlers in London, and quietly sets a snare for the Marquis when the Yard itself had determined that the man, although criminal, is untouchable. In *A Death at the Bar*, Harry Alwyn, the crooked owner of a bar, is found with his head bashed in by a bottle (reminiscent of the murder committed in Giles's *Death Cracks a Bottle*) and Reed's cunning leads him to the murderer and the loot. He does not arrest the killer who had killed in self-defense, but had not admitted his role in the crime because he saw a quick way to seize the loot. Rather, Reed walks away, saying "arresting you would get me no promotion, just a lot of blooming paper-work," and warning the barman not to touch the money and to get himself a good lawyer. This stance is typical of the bright but disappointed Sergeant whose own code of law and justice is the one he satisfies.

The mysteries written under the name McGirr are of a piece with Giles's other writings: the English peerage, quaint and esoteric encylopaedists, racketeers, and drug-traffickers are still the people of his plots; he still captures the colloquial speech patterns of his crooks and landladies, and he still describes his landscapes with an eye for detail. Only now his protagonist is a private eye who often serves the government, but only in cases which for reasons of decorum or policy the government is loath to touch. And Piron has his own sleuths and his own style of investigation. Like Reed and Honeybody, he is quick to cheat on his expenses and pocket a little cash. Like Reed, he often uses his own cunning and violence to trap the criminal, and he is likely to step outside the law in these endeavors. *A Murderous Journey* is probably the best book in this series, with the most ingenious plot and the most exciting and unexpected denouement.

Giles, writing under any name, is a skilled stylist and a writer gifted with an uncanny sense of the eccentric. His mysteries tease and entertain.

—Carol Simpson Stern

McGIVERN, William P(eter). Also wrote as Bill Peters. American. Born in Chicago, Illinois, 6 December 1922. Educated at the University of Birmingham, 1945–46. Served in the United States Army, 1943–46: Line Sergeant; Soldiers Medal, 1944. Married the writer Maureen Daly in 1948; two children. Reporter and reviewer, Philadelphia *Evening Bulletin*, 1949–51. Co-Owner, KOWN station, Escondido, California. President, Mystery Writers of America, 1980. Self-employed writer. Recipient: Mystery Writers of America Edgar Allan Poe award, 1952. *Died 18 November 1982.*

CRIME PUBLICATIONS

Novels

But Death Runs Faster. New York, Dodd Mead, 1948; London, Boardman, 1949; as *The Whispering Corpse*, New York, Pocket Books, 1950.
Heaven Ran Last. New York, Dodd Mead, 1949; London, Digit, 1958.
Very Cold for May. New York, Dodd Mead, 1950.
Shield for Murder. New York, Dodd Mead, 1951.
Blondes Die Young (as Bill Peters). New York, Dodd Mead, 1952; London, Foulsham, 1956.
The Crooked Frame. New York, Dodd Mead, 1952.
The Big Heat. New York, Dodd Mead, and London, Hamish Hamilton, 1953.
Margin of Terror. New York, Dodd Mead, 1953; London, Collins, 1955.
Rogue Cop. New York, Dodd Mead, 1954; London, Collins, 1955.
The Darkest Hour. New York, Dodd Mead, 1955; London, Collins, 1956; as *Waterfront Cop*, New York, Pocket Books, 1956.
The Seven File. New York, Dodd Mead, 1956; London, Collins, 1957; as *Chicago-7*, London, Sphere, 1970.
Night Extra. New York, Dodd Mead, 1957; London, Collins, 1958.
Odds Against Tomorrow. New York, Dodd Mead, 1957; London, Collins, 1958.
Savage Streets. New York, Dodd Mead, 1959; London, Collins, 1960.
Seven Lies South. New York, Dodd Mead, 1960; London, Collins, 1961.

The Road to the Snail. New York, Dodd Mead, 1961.
A Pride of Place. New York, Dodd Mead, 1962.
Police Special (omnibus). New York, Dodd Mead, 1962.
A Choice of Assassins. New York, Dodd Mead, 1963; London, Collins, 1964.
The Caper of the Golden Bulls. New York, Dodd Mead, 1966; London, Collins, 1967.
Lie Down, I Want to Talk to You. New York, Dodd Mead, 1967; London, Collins, 1968.
Caprifoil. New York, Dodd Mead, 1972; London, Collins, 1973.
Reprisal. New York, Dodd Mead, 1973; London, Collins, 1974.
Night of the Juggler. New York, Putnam, and London, Collins, 1975.
Summitt. New York, Arbor House, 1982; London, Collins, 1983.
A Matter of Honor, completed by Maureen Daly. New York, Arbor House, 1984.

Short Stories

Killer on the Turnpike. New York, Pocket Books, 1961.

Uncollected Short Story

"Graveyard Shift," in *Alfred Hitchcock's Tales to Scare You Stiff*, edited by Eleanor Sullivan. New York, Davis, 1978.

OTHER PUBLICATIONS

Novels

Soldiers of '44. New York, Arbor House, and London, Collins, 1979.
War Games. New York, Arbor House, 1984.

Plays

Screenplays: *I Saw What You Did*, 1965; *The Wrecking Crew*, 1969; *Caprifoil*, 1973; *Brannigan*, with others, 1975; *Night of the Juggler*, 1975.

Television Plays: *San Francisco International Airport* series, 1970; *The Young Lawyers* series, 1970; *Banyon* series, 1972; *Kojak* series, 1973–77.

Other

Mention My Name in Mombasa: The Unscheduled Adventures of an American Family Abroad, with Maureen Daly. New York, Dodd Mead, 1958.
The Seeing, with Maureen McGivern. Norwalk, Connecticut, Tower, 1980.

*

Manuscript Collection: Mugar Memorial Library, Boston University.

* * *

William P. McGivern wrote more than 20 novels covering the gamut of crime—homicide detection, espionage, political corruption, the world of the psychopath, the crooked cop. A number of his novels deal with the metaphor of the jungle—the jungle of crime. In some cases the "good guy" battles the forces of spreading crime and corruption in the big city. Dave Bannion, the detective who refuses to compromise, a big man physically and morally ("always the out-sized one, in high school and college, even on football teams"), feels the big heat of racketeers and corrupt politicians and law enforcers. They, in turn, feel the pressure of the big heat he creates as he seeks the reasons behind the suicide of a colleague, Tom Deery, and the men responsible for the death of his own wife, Kate. Bannion, a man of the streets, has an intellectual fervor unmatched by his colleagues; he reads St. John's *Ascent of Mount Carmel* as a means of self-restoration. But books are abandoned when he sets out on his personal revenge— reflection could distort his mission. St. John does not enter Bannion's meditations again until the close of *The Big Heat*— "My house being now at rest—."

Throughout *The Big Heat*, Dave Bannion stalks through the jungle of crime—city streets, bars, highways, hotel rooms. He does not rest until his work is done. The intense pressure, the constant tracking of suspects, the delaying tactics to avoid being caught in a trap, reappear in *Rogue Cop* where McGivern unfolds a classic story of two brothers—one an honest cop; the other, a sergeant on the take, a man who has given up the principles of two fathers—one his own, now deceased father, a former policeman; the other, God the Father. Sgt. Mike Carmody has allowed himself to succumb to the good life afforded him by racketeers. He falls into the trap of trying to save himself and his brother; he loses his brother, but regains himself and ultimately returns to the memory of his father and the forgiveness of God the Father.

The snare of entrapment moves to a smaller town in *Odds Against Tomorrow* where two men involved in a bank job operate in a jungle of fear. Earl Slater, a white ex-con, highly prejudiced, has as his partner a black, John Ingram. Slater fears betrayal by blacks; Ingram fears because he is black. The distrust and fears of the two men are the real focus of *Odds Against Tomorrow*; survival depends on physical strength and mental capacity. Ingram is dehumanized and treated as an animal by Slater; ironically, Ingram's own fear of betrayal prevents him from betraying Slater. The characterizations are savage portrayals of two beasts in a Pennsylvania jungle of rural life.

The jungle metaphor is most precisely drawn in *Night of the Juggler*, an engrossing study of a psychopathic killer, Gus Soltik, a demented inhabitant of the South Bronx who cannot read or write but who instinctively knows when the anniversary of his mother's death arrives. As the anniversary nears, Gus prepares for his commemoration of his mother. For the fifth time he is about to kill a young girl. The fifth anniversary brings him to Central Park where he will encounter the stalking techniques of the professional law officers Max Prima and Gypsy Tonnelli and a retired military man, Luther Boyd. The map of the jungle-battlefield, Central Park, precedes McGivern's text, and the reader is drawn into a number of arenas simultaneously—the park as the battleground, the instinctive and animal-like reactions of Gus Soltik (an appropriately transparent name), and the strategic thought-processes of the other principals, the searchers.

The characters in all of McGivern's novels are developed precisely. The reader participates in the twistings of the psychopathic mind in *Night of the Juggler* and *A Choice of Assassins* where a man agrees to kill for the price of a drink. The tightrope mentality of McGivern's rogue cops is not merely understood, but actually experienced by the reader. McGivern is not given to excesses in characterization or action. Consequently, his work does not lend itself to stereotypes. A good example of his work is *Killer on the Turnpike*, a collection of short stories which includes the title story, about a psychopath; "Without a Prayer," a variant of the priest-police conflict over a hoodlum; "Old Willie," a city news reporter who becomes involved with mobsters; "The Record of M. Duval," a tale of a man who tries to get away with his wife's murder; and "Missing in Berlin," a precursor of McGivern's works in the espionage story, later realized in his novel, *Caprifoil*.

—Katherine M. Restaino

McGOWN, Jill. British. Born in Campbeltown, Argyll, Scotland, 9 August 1947. Educated at Corby Grammar School and Kettering Technical College, Northamptonshire, 1959–64. Secretary, Corby Development Corporation, 1964–66, and Toller Hales and Collcutt, Corby, 1966–71; administrative assistant, British Steel Corporation, Corby, 1971–80. Address: 29 Rodney Drive, Corby, Northamptonshire NN17 2RL, England.

CRIME PUBLICATIONS

Novels (series: Chief-Inspector Lloyd and Sergeant Judy Hill)

A Perfect Match (Lloyd and Judy). London, Macmillan, and New York, St. Martin's Press, 1983.
Record of Sin. London, Macmillan, 1985; Boston, Massachusetts, Curley, 1987.
An Evil Hour. London, Macmillan, 1986; New York, St. Martin's Press, 1987.
The Stalking Horse. London, Macmillan, 1987; New York, St. Martin's Press, 1988.
Redemption (Lloyd and Judy). London, Macmillan, 1988; as *Murder at the Old Vicarage*, New York, St. Martin's Press, 1989.
Death of a Dancer (Lloyd and Judy). London, Macmillan, 1989; as *Gone to Her Death*, New York, St. Martin's Press, 1990.
Murder Movie. London, Macmillan, and New York, St. Martin's Press, 1990.

Uncollected Short Story

"A Fine Art," in *Winter Crimes 20*, edited by Hilary Hale, London, Macmillan, 1988; New York, Doubleday, 1989.

*

Jill McGown comments:
My novels so far are whodunnits in the traditional mould, sometimes with very traditional settings, but peopled with contemporary characters. Human nature is what fascinates me, and I hope I write about real people with real relationships. I feel that the whodunnit structure satisfies the desire for loose ends to be tied up, and that I can therefore paint a truer picture of my characters' lives, which (assuming they don't lose them before the end) can remain as unresolved and ragged round the edges as my own or anyone else's. The wonderful thing about writing whodunnits is that you know when to stop!

* * *

Jill McGown is a quite exceptional writer whose work entitles her to far greater acclaim than she has so far received.

She has not been hailed as a new "Queen of Crime" nor have her books won any awards; and yet she makes much of the competition look feeble. She is a very confident writer who satisfies both mind and heart. Her novels have depth and substance and a heartening complexity: her gift for contrivance is altogether remarkable and it allows her absolute control over what she is doing. She meets every criterion for both the classic form and the modern crime novel of character, with logic and wit, vigour and perception. She tends to avoid terminal violence, preferring to resolve a situation with intellectual confrontation; and even when she does resort to melodrama she handles it so deftly as to render it plausible and even inevitable in the context.

She began with *A Perfect Match*, an astonishing performance with the thrust and finish of precision engineering and a skill and daring reminiscent of the old masters of detective fiction. She nudges us scrupulously towards the truth without ever lowering her guard to the point where we guess her secret. The action is founded on a most cunning deception and involves an affluent couple whose marriage is about to disintegrate. The narrative unfolds with disciplined elegance and the completion of the pattern casts a dazzling new light on all that has gone before.

Record of Sin makes a less decided impact, despite a more searching scrutiny of character and a tense, brooding atmosphere. The action lacks edge and urgency and pivots on an enigmatic central figure intended to be more endearing than, in fact, she is. Because she is defined largely in emotional terms she appears ill-suited to a novel of detection, and unless she engages the reader's sympathies the whole enterprise is undermined. The victim's death is officially ruled a suicide so that there is no police investigation and the "malevolence" attributed to him does not effectively emerge: he seems more brute than Machiavellian.

An Evil Hour marks a reassuring return to form: it is sharper and brisker, more taut and involving than *Record of Sin*. The setting is a smart sea-side hotel run by an attractive widow, shaken but not beaten by her experience of life. The murder of an M.P. brings her into the line of fire: he was her lover and his wife employs a cynical ex-policeman to assess her possible relevance to his death. The course of his investigation runs in tandem with the progress of their association, which moves from edgy mistrust to attraction and commitment. The action requires that three other murder victims be plausibly linked with the dead M.P. and the gradual accumulation of the necessary evidence is most artfully achieved. The process is not only absorbing but exciting and it culminates grandly in a vivid extended denouement.

The Stalking Horse is even more of a *tour de force*, a daring and intricate work entailing shifts in time which might be confusing were the author less securely in control. The central character has served 16 years in prison for two murders he did not commit. The narrative advances on two fronts, reconstructing the events leading up to the murders and charting the progress of the vengeful innocent as he edges ever closer to the truth. It encompasses aspects of his trial and term in prison and allows him to harass his past associates, unnerving them individually and confounding them collectively.

Redemption has a dark, obsessive quality that sets it rather apart and its setting, a vicarage at Christmas, is anything but cosy. The victim is a young accountant given to battering his wife, the vicar's daughter. She and her parents are the obvious suspects but a neighbour widens the focus with a powerful motive of her own. The investigation is complicated by insistent emotional ties among the suspects and the continual lies and evasions that ensue, as much from loyalty as from self-protection. So closely defined are the limits of the problem that

it seems impossible for any of them to be guilty: yet, since one of them must be, all four remain teasingly in question.

Death of a Dancer is fine indeed, a classic performance with some masterly sleight of hand. The routines of a minor public school are disrupted by the murder of a master's wife. The school setting makes its traditional appeal, enhanced by arresting characters presented in depth: a bibulous head, a railing assistant, an enigmatic head-boy. The personality of the victim adds a subtle dimension to a rich and engrossing narrative.

In *Murder Movie* we are not invited to mourn the victims, since they play with fire and deserve to burn. They are members of an artificial company, assembled in a Scottish coastal town to film a period melodrama. The film's director is a sadistic egomaniac of the kind familiar from the glossier soap operas: he is known by his initials and is so detestable that his destruction becomes a matter of major concern for the reader. The lines between the just and the unjust are clearly and continually drawn and the resolution of a complex action neatly preserves the distinction.

Three of the novels feature Chief-Inspector Lloyd and Sergeant Judy Hill, who are teamed in private as well as public life. The earlier titles deal as much with the frustrations as the satisfactions of their liaison, but in *Death of a Dancer* their situation improves. Lloyd is astute and assiduous but Judy has flair: like her creator, she has an answer for everything.

—B.A. Pike

McGUIRE, (Dominic) Paul. Australian. Born in South Australia, 3 April 1903. Educated at the Christian Brothers' College, Adelaide; University of Adelaide (Tinline Scholar in Australian History). Served in the Royal Australian Naval Volunteer Reserve, 1939–45. Married Frances Margaret Cheadle in 1927. Lecturer, Workers' Educational Association, and University Extension of the University of Adelaide for several years; lectured in the United States, 1936–40, 1946; diplomat: Australian Delegate, United Nations Assembly, New York, 1953; Australian Minister to Italy, 1954–58, and Ambassador to Italy, 1958–59; Envoy Extraordinary to the Holy See at Coronation of Pope John XXIII, 1958. C.B.E. (Commander, Order of the British Empire), 1951. Knight Grand Cross, Order of St. Sylvester, 1959. Commendatore, Order of Merit, Italy, 1967. *Died 15 June 1978.*

CRIME PUBLICATIONS

Novels (series: Chief Inspector Cummings; Inspector/Superintendent Fillinger)

Murder in Bostall (Cummings). London, Skeffington, 1931; as *The Black Rose Murder*, New York, Brentano's, 1932.
Three Dead Men (Cummings). London, Skeffington, 1931; New York, Brentano's, 1932.
The Tower Mystery (Fillinger). London, Skeffington, 1932; as *Death Tolls the Bell*, New York, Coward McCann, 1933.
Murder by the Law (Fillinger). London, Skeffington, 1932.
Death Fugue (Fillinger). London, Skeffington, 1933.
There Sits Death (Fillinger). London, Skeffington, 1933.
Daylight Murder (Cummings; Fillinger). London, Skeffington, 1934; as *Murder at High Noon*, New York, Doubleday, 1935.

Murder in Haste (Cummings; Fillinger). London, Skeffington, 1934.
7.30 Victoria (Cummings). London, Skeffington, 1935.
Born to Be Hanged. London, Skeffington, 1935.
Prologue to the Gallows. London, Skeffington, 1936.
Threepence to Marble Arch. London, Skeffington, 1936.
Cry Aloud for Murder. London, Heinemann, 1937.
W.I. London, Heinemann, 1937.
Burial Service. London, Heinemann, 1938; as *A Funeral in Eden*, New York, Morrow, 1938.
The Spanish Steps. London, Heinemann, 1940; as *Enter Three Witches*, New York, Morrow, 1940.

OTHER PUBLICATIONS

Verse

The Two Men and Other Poems. Adelaide, Preece, 1932.
Selected Poems. Warrendale, South Australia, Pioneer, 1980.

Other

The Poetry of Gerard Manley Hopkins: A Lecture. Adelaide, Preece, 1934.
Australian Journey. London, Heinemann, 1939; revised edition, 1947; as *Australia: Her Heritage, Her Future*, New York, Stokes, 1939.
Westward the Course: The New World of Oceania. London, Oxford University Press, and New York, Morrow, 1942.
The Price of Admiralty, with Frances Margaret McGuire. Melbourne, Oxford University Press, 1944.
The Three Corners of the World: An Essay in the Interpretation of Modern Politics. London, Heinemann, 1948; as *Experiment in World Order*, New York, Morrow, 1948.
The Australian Theatre, with Betty Arnott and Frances Margaret McGuire. London, Oxford University Press, 1948.
There's Freedom for the Brave: An Approach to World Order. London, Heinemann, and New York, Morrow, 1949.
Inns of Australia. Melbourne, Heinemann, 1952; London, Heinemann, 1953.

Editor, with John Fitzsimons, *Restoring All Things: A Guide to Catholic Action.* New York, Sheed and Ward, 1938; London, Sheed and Ward, 1939.

*   *   *

Although born in Australia, Paul McGuire, unlike S.H. Courtier or the transplanted Englishman Arthur W. Upfield, never chose to set his mystery novels there. Much of McGuire's early work is of interest, though not for its detection which is often weak. Some of his later work is classic.

Murder in Bostall introduces Inspector Cummings and Sergeant Wittler who reappear (with promotions) in later books. Their problem is to solve the murder of Edward Steyne who worked for his uncle's detective agency in London. The uncle, Jacob Modstone, gives what help he can to the police, but launches out on an investigation of his own which hinders them. Modstone eventually joins forces with the police, and together they bring the case to a satisfactory conclusion—but not through fair-play detection! This novel is not only notable for its sympathetic treatment of a Jew—uncommon in British mystery fiction of the period—but it also presents the only Jewish detective to function during the Golden Age.

A murder victim is found on the beach in *Murder by the Law;* the blunt instrument in this case is a cannon ball. McGuire's most widely-used series detective, Superintendent Fillinger, a huge man who easily outweighs Nero Wolfe, is introduced. *There Sits Death* is about a murderer who slashes jugulars, and is one of the best of the early McGuire novels. *7.30 Victoria* is more of a thriller than a detective story, and does not quite come off, but its attractive blend of plot, humor, and appealing characters manages to linger in the mind.

McGuire's reputation is assured by *Burial Service*—an absolute masterpiece by any standard. *Burial Service* takes place on the out-of-the-way and idyllic island of Kaitai whose serenity is abruptly shattered when an unpopular and worrisome stranger is found lying dead on the beach with a fractured skull. A tempest of suspicion reveals the hitherto shrouded pasts of many of the inhabitants, and fear and unhappiness reign supreme until the murderer can be found. The many excellences of plot, character, atmosphere, setting, wit, and detection are exceeded only by McGuire's brilliant use of dialogue that tells much about the characters and their relationships, sets the tone of the story, and gives the reader a great deal of exposition in an enjoyable manner.

McGuire's last novel, *The Spanish Steps*, received rave reviews and is considered by many to be the equal of *Burial Service*. It is written with distinction but, except for a chase scene in and about an Italian estate, absolutely nothing happens until one of the characters is murdered almost at the end of the novel. The hero is another newspaper man, and detection is minimal. Unfortunately, nothing, to my mind, can compensate for the static qualities of this novel.

—Charles Shibuk

———

McILVANNEY, William. British. Born in Kilmarnock, Ayrshire, 25 November 1936. Educated at the University of Glasgow, M.A. (honours) 1959. Married Moira Watson in 1961 (divorced 1982); one daughter and one son. Housemaster, Ravenspark Academy, Irvine, Ayrshire, from 1960; Tutor in English, University of Grenoble, France, 1970–71; English teacher, Irvine Royal Academy, 1971–72; Fellow in Creative Writing, University of Strathclyde, Glasgow, 1972–73; assistant rector, Greenwood Academy, Irvine, 1973–75. Recipient: Faber Memorial prize, 1967; Scottish Arts Council award, 1968, 1976; Whitbread award, 1975; Crime Writers Association Silver Dagger award, 1984. Agent: George Greenfield, John Farquharson Ltd., 162–168 Regent Street, London W1R 5TB, England. Address: c/o Mainstream Publishing, 7 Albany Street, Edinburgh EH1 3UG, Scotland.

CRIME PUBLICATIONS

Novels (series: Detective Inspector Jack Laidlaw in all books)

Laidlaw. London, Hodder and Stoughton, and New York, Pantheon, 1977.
The Papers of Tony Veitch. London, Hodder and Stoughton, and New York, Pantheon, 1983.
The Big Man. London, Hodder and Stoughton, and New York, Morrow, 1985.

OTHER PUBLICATIONS

Novels

Remedy Is None. London, Eyre and Spottiswoode, 1966.
A Gift from Nessus. London, Eyre and Spottiswoode, 1968.
Docherty. London, Allen and Unwin, 1975.

Short Stories

Walking Wounded. London, Hodder and Stoughton, 1989.

Verse

The Longships in Harbour. London, Eyre and Spottiswoode, 1970.
Landscapes and Figures, illustrated by Norman Ackroyd. Guildford, Surrey, Circle Press, 1973.
Weddings and After. Edinburgh, Mainstream, 1984.
In Through the Head. Edinburgh, Mainstream, 1988.

Play

Screenplay: *Dreaming*, 1990.

Other

Glasgow 1956–1989: Shades of Grey . . . and Some Light Too, photographs by Oscar Marzaroli. Edinburgh, Mainstream, 1987.

*

Critical Study: "This Shitty Urban Machine Humanised: The Urban Crime Novel and the Novels of William McIlvanney" by Simon Dentith, in *Watching the Detectives: Essays on Crime Fiction*, edited by Ian A. Bell and Graham Daldry, London, Macmillan, 1990.

* * *

Scottish novelist and poet William McIlvanney came to the genre of crime fiction after writing more deliberately serious work, and his attitude to the popular form is unusually complex. His highly-regarded detective stories, *Laidlaw* and *The Papers of Tony Veitch*, recount specific murder mysteries, but in each case the author surrounds a particular enquiry with elaborate probings into wider concerns of truth, integrity and justice, and he situates the narrative in a meticulously realized and evocative urban setting. In neither novel does the actual uncovering of the culprit carry much weight: more emphasis is put on the creation of mood and atmosphere, and on the analysis of human motivation.

In *Laidlaw*, for instance, the identity of the murderer is never in doubt, and the novel concentrates on the philosophical and moral issues which arise in the course of the murder hunt. Although the novel portrays the process of detection, it is by no means a "procedural," with much more space being given over to the meaning and significance of the inquiry than to the forensic practices of the police. McIlvanney's fictional world is much messier than the orderly world of more conventional crime writing, and although the cases in both novels are in one obvious sense solved, the more fundamental mysteries concerning the human capacity for evil remain.

The main focus of the narrative in each of these two books is the figure of the investigating detective. The troubled and self-examining character of Jack Laidlaw is framed between his cynical colleague Milligan and the more impressionable sidekick Harkness. Against these diverse seekers after truth are ranged tough and ruthless underworld figures, Cam Colvin and John Rhodes, who rule their own territories, sometimes coming in contact with, or even overlapping with, the world of more law-abiding citizens. Just as the policemen have recognizable weaknesses and imperfections, so too the criminals have commensurate strengths and skills, and both groups seem to live unorthodox, disfigured lives. And in the tradition of Chandler and Hammett, McIlvanney's lonely men are the battered custodians of integrity in a sordid world.

The first novel involves the murder of a young girl by a youth unsure of his sexual identity, and there are those who find a taint of mysogyny and homophobia beneath the surface of the book. We know who the murderer is early on, and we watch the race to see which group will find him first. Will it be the professional killers, provoked to avenge the girl's death in the most primitive fashion by her aggrieved father? Or will it be the flawed but earnest representatives of justice? There are innocent bystanders caught up in this conflict, and the whole drama is worked out against a stylized city-space, a version of post-industrial Glasgow in which meaningful life has been made difficult. In *The Papers of Tony Veitch*, Laidlaw searches for the elusive central character, finding him too late. The dying words of a wino have raised the possibility of crime. Only Laidlaw seems to care about the possible murder of this wretched character, and once again the book compares his doggedness and insistence with the more physical toughness of the criminal underworld. Through the convoluted plot, the respectable and the criminal, the innocent and the guilty, are brought into discomforting proximity, and Laidlaw's own personal problems lend substance to his apparently involuntary quest after truth.

Both books are inventive in characterization and rich in detail, perhaps more persuasive in individual scenes than as a whole, and their ornate, heavily decorated prose style gives them a plenteous source of incidental felicities. The dialogue is frequently witty and crisp, although the Scots spoken by the characters never figures in the voice of the narrator.

McIlvanney's crime novels show a contested infatuation with "hardness" or "toughness." Although he can subtly illuminate the small, dignified gestures of people trying to live decent lives in grim circumstances, his writing reaches after grander gestures, and he frequently glamorizes the intensities of his characters rather than their sensitivies. In *The Big Man*, this problem is confronted directly. Dan Scoular is a tough but directionless man, with a local reputation for effective violence. He is hired by a powerful underworld figure to fight an equally tough man representing rival interests. Although his combat is meaningless to him, and although he is more like his adversary than his employer, Scoular goes through a strict training programme to become the hardest of men, and the fight takes place. The main plot seems to reproduce elements of the other crime novels, following a man's quest for self-knowledge and the painful triumph of certainty over doubt. The cast of characters contains figures from the earlier books. However, in a parallel plot about the failure of Scoular's marriage, the machismo of McIlvanney's heroes is dismantled. Contrary to expectations, Scoular refuses to enact retribution on his wife's lover, and the book ends ironically. In a much more sophisticated way than in the earlier presentation of Laidlaw's private life, this laconic ending seems to offer a critique of toughness, and a sense of alternative possibilities. It may be that such a perception has made it difficult for McIlvanney to produce further "hard" crime fiction.

—Ian A. Bell

———

McINERNY, Ralph (Matthew). Also writes as Monica Quill. American. Born in Minneapolis, Minnesota, 24 February 1929. Educated at St. Paul Seminary, Minnesota, B.A. 1951; University of Minnesota, Minneapolis, M.A. 1952; Laval University, Quebec, Ph.D. in philosophy 1954. Served in the United States Marine Corps, 1946–47. Married Constance Terrill Kunert in 1953; four daughters and two sons. Instructor in Philosophy, Creighton University, Omaha, Nebraska, 1954–55; Member of the Philosophy Department, 1955–78, and since 1978, Michael P. Grace Professor of Medieval Studies, University of Notre Dame, Indiana. Editor, *New Scholasticism*, Washington, D.C., from 1966; since 1978, Director, Medieval Institute, and since 1979, Director, Jacques Maritain Center, both Notre Dame. Recipient: Fulbright Fellowship, 1959; National Endowment for the Humanities Fellowship, 1977; National Endowment for the Arts Fellowship, 1982. Agent: Ellen Levine Literary Agency, 432 Park Avenue, No. 1205, New York, New York 10016. Address: Box 495, Notre Dame, Indiana 46556, U.S.A.

CRIME PUBLICATIONS

Novels (series: Andrew Broom; Father Roger Dowling)

Her Death of Cold (Dowling).   New York, Vanguard Press, 1977; London, Hale, 1979.
The Seventh Station (Dowling).   New York, Vanguard Press, 1977; London, Hale, 1979.
Romanesque.   New York, Harper, 1978; London, Hale, 1979.
Bishop as Pawn (Dowling).   New York, Vanguard Press, 1978; London, Hale, 1980.
Lying Three (Dowling).   New York, Vanguard Press, 1979; London, Hale, 1980.
Second Vespers (Dowling).   New York, Vanguard Press, 1980; London, Hale, 1981.
Thicker Than Water (Dowling).   New York, Vanguard Press, 1981; London, Hale, 1982.
A Loss of Patients (Dowling).   New York, Vanguard Press, 1982.
The Grass Widow (Dowling).   New York, Vanguard Press, 1983.
Getting a Way with Murder.   New York, Vanguard Press, 1984; London, Hale, 1987.
Rest in Pieces (Dowling).   New York, Vanguard, 1985.
The Basket Case (Dowling).   New York, St. Martin's Press, 1987.
Cause and Effect (Broom).   New York, Atheneum, 1987.
Body and Soul (Broom).   New York, Atheneum, 1989.
Abracadaver.   New York, St. Martin's Press, 1989; as *Sleight of Body*, London, Macmillan, 1989.
Frigor Mortis (Broom).   New York, Atheneum, 1989.
Savings and Loan (Broom).   New York, Atheneum, 1990.

Novels as Monica Quill (series: Sister Mary Teresa in all books)

Not a Blessed Thing!   New York, Vanguard Press, 1981.
Let Us Prey.   New York, Vanguard Press, 1982.
And Then There Was Nun.   New York, Vanguard Press, 1984.

Nun of the Above.   New York, Vanguard Press, 1985.
Sine Qua Nun.   New York, Vanguard Press, 1986.
Veil of Ignorance.   New York, St. Martin's Press, 1988.

Short Stories

Four on the Floor.   New York, St. Martin's Press, 1989.

OTHER PUBLICATIONS

Novels

Jolly Rogerson.   New York, Doubleday, 1967.
A Narrow Time.   New York, Doubleday, 1969.
The Priest.   New York, Harper, 1973; London, Souvenir Press, 1974.
Gate of Heaven.   New York, Harper, 1975.
Rogerson at Bay.   New York, Harper, 1976.
Spinnaker.   South Bend, Indiana, Gateway, 1977.
Quick as a Dodo.   New York, Vanguard Press, 1978.
Abecedary.   Notre Dame, Indiana, Juniper, 1979.
Connolly's Life.   New York, Atheneum, 1983.
The Noonday Devil.   New York, Atheneum, 1985.
Leave of Absence.   New York, Atheneum, 1986.

Play

The Chinese Pedant and Other Plays.   New York, and London, French, 1983.

Other

The Logic of Analogy: An Interpretation of St. Thomas.   The Hague, Nijhoff, 1961.
History of Western Philosophy:
   1. *From the Beginnings of Philosophy to Plotinus.*   Chicago, Regnery, 1963.
   2. *Philosophy from St. Augustine to Ockham.*   Notre Dame, Indiana, University of Notre Dame Press, 1970.
Thomism in an Age of Renewal.   New York, Doubleday, 1966.
Studies in Analogy.   The Hague, Nijhoff, 1968.
St. Thomas Aquinas.   Boston, Twayne, 1977.
Rhyme and Reason: St. Thomas and Modes of Discourse (lecture).   Milwaukee, Marquette University Press, 1981.
Ethica Thomistica: The Moral Philosophy of Thomas Aquinas.   Washington, D.C., Catholic University Press, 1982.
The Frozen Maiden of Calpurnia.   Notre Dame, Indiana, Juniper Press, 1982.
Being and Predication: Thomistic Interpretations.   Washington, D.C., Catholic University of America Press, 1986.
Art and Prudence.   Notre Dame, Indiana, University of Notre Dame Press, 1988.
A First Glance at St. Thomas Aquinas: A Handbook for Peeping Thomists.   Notre Dame, Indiana, University of Notre Dame Press, 1989.

Editor, *New Themes in Christian Philosophy.*   Notre Dame, Indiana, University of Notre Dame Press, 1968.

Translator, with Leo Turcotte, *Kierkegaard: The Difficulty of Being Christian.*   Notre Dame, Indiana, University of Notre Dame Press, 1968.
Translator, with Constance McInerny, *A History of the Ambrosiana.*   Notre Dame, Indiana, University of Notre Dame Press, 1983.

*

Manuscript Collection: University of Notre Dame Library, Indiana.

Ralph McInerny comments:

The attraction of the mystery or thriller for the novelist is that it permits, indeed demands, emphasis on the "soul" of fiction, namely the plot. My mystery fiction has concentrated on two series, the Father Dowling and the Mother Mary Teresa series. To have one's cast of characters awaiting one, to have the sense of returning to familiar scenes, takes away some of the terrors of starting a new book. My Roger Dowling series turns on the conflict between mercy and justice, and Dowling may seem soft on crime but he is hard on sin. By contrast, Captain Keegan is a cop to the soles of his shoes. I think they make a good team. Emtee Dempsey, my nun, is an aged female curmudgeon, what Nero Wolfe might have been if he had taken the veil. I am planning a new series that will enable me to avoid religion on occasion.

* * *

Ralph McInerny's earliest contribution to the mystery genre is the creation of Catholic clergyman Father Roger Dowling, a secular priest, who first appears in *Her Death of Cold*, when he is assigned as sole priest and pastor of St. Hilary's in the fictional town of Fox River some 40 miles west of Chicago. The tall, stooped, thinning-haired, pipe-smoking detective first appears at the age of 49 on the eve of the silver anniversary of his ordination to the priesthood.

Father Dowling is a recuperating alcoholic whose disease has been arrested after some 15 painful years as a Canon lawyer with the Archdiocesan Marriage Court in Chicago where he had the onerous task of examining the "cause for annulment" presented by married Catholics seeking to have their marriages dissolved. While Dowling is clearly a conservative in his religious views and not greatly pleased by the changes in the Church brought about since Vatican II, he is nonetheless an uncomfortable one in certain areas, the most outstanding being the paradoxical relationship between justice and mercy.

Like G.K. Chesterton and Leonard Holton before him, McInerny has created a priest detective whose secular interest in crime is merely a mask for his deeper concern for the spiritual welfare of the victims and criminals involved. And, as with Chesterton, paradox plays an important role in the novels: "Apprehension? Punishment? That was not the essential thing. Far more important was the spiritual condition of the one who had killed. ... He—or she—must recognize the sinfulness of what had been done, ask God's pardon for the deed, repent" (*Her Death of Cold*).

The discussion of Catholic doctrine, which in the earliest novels often appears intrusive, becomes much more closely woven into the fabric of the plot of *Second Vespers*, the fifth in the series, which, together with *Thicker Than Water* and *The Grass Widow*, are probably the most outstanding in the series to date.

Besides the likable Dowling, a number of other series regulars keep the reader looking forward to each new title: Marie Murkin, St. Hilary's housekeeper, "presides" over the rectory, and Fox River's chief of detectives, Captain Phil Keegan, like McInerny himself, is a former seminarian. To the widower policeman, the law is a vocation, not just a job; to Dowling he is the other side of the coin, so to speak: "If Keegan was the representative of justice, Dowling could feel that he represented mercy. It made them—old friends of a sort—antagonists" (*Her Death of Cold*). Other regulars are Lt. Cy Horvath, one of the series' best and most likable characters,

and the later introduced black police officer, Agnes Lamb (*Thicker Than Water*). The series has aged like vintage wine, yet McInerny manages to retain his original freshness and vigor in characters and plot situations, with varied and subtle characterizations, down-to-earth psychology, and darn good stories well told.

In another vein are his novels written under the clever, easily translatable "pen name" of Monica Quill, all revolving around the delightful character of Sister Mary Teresa Dempsey, a five-foot-two, nearly 200 pound, cane-carrying ancient, the "last of a breed," affectionately known as Attila the Nun and Emptee (for M.T.) Dempsey, a stickler for tradition and the old ways of the church. She lives with her now defunct order's two other remaining sisters, her younger associates, Sister Kim and Sister Joyce, in a Frank Lloyd Wright house in Chicago's Walton Street, where she spends her time between writing her opus on early monasticism in France and solving mysteries, much to the chagrin of Sister Kim's brother Richard of the Chicago police force. In the grand Nero Wolfe tradition, she remains at home directing the production, with Sister Kim her eternal Archie Goodwin. The series starts off strong (*Not a Blessed Thing!*), and continues to get better, with the third, *And Then There Was Nun*, the best to date. This revolves around the interesting background of women's soccer. Sister Mary Teresa, with her nearly half a century as a historian, considers herself far better equipped than the police to get to the bottom of man's nefarious deeds by employing "practical reason" and "common sense" as opposed to routine and scientific procedure.

McInerny has written two other non-series novels in the genre as well: *Romanesque*, a Vatican caper novel involving stolen manuscripts, and *Connolly's Life*, a witty ironic novel concerned with the return from the dead of a young priest killed in a plane accident.

McInerny's greatest contribution to the genre, besides sheer entertainment, is the enthralling background use of the Catholic Church in contemporary society and the effects of the modern upheaval in the Church on its members. Both Father Dowling and Sister Mary Teresa are religious first, and detectives only unwittingly, and that only in service to their vocations.

—James R. McCahery

―――――

McKAY, Kenneth R. *See* **KANE, Henry.**

―――――

McMAHON, Pat. *See* **HOCH, Edward, D.**

―――――

McMULLEN, Mary. American. Born in Yonkers, New York, in 1920; daughter of Helen Reilly, *q.v.*, and the artist Paul Reilly; sister of Ursula Curtiss, *q.v.* Studied art, and worked in fashion design and advertising. Recipient: Mystery Writers of America Edgar Allan Poe award, 1952. *Died 4 October 1986.*

CRIME PUBLICATIONS

Novels

Stranglehold. New York, Harper, 1951; as *Death of Miss X*,
  London, Collins, 1952.
The Doom Campaign. New York, Doubleday, 1974; London,
  Hale, 1976.
A Country Kind of Death. New York, Doubleday, 1975;
  London, Hale, 1977.
The Pimlico Plot. New York, Doubleday, 1975; London,
  Hale, 1977.
Funny, Jonas, You Don't Look Dead. New York, Doubleday,
  1976; London, Hale, 1978.
A Dangerous Funeral. New York, Doubleday, 1977; London,
  Hale, 1978.
Death by Bequest. New York, Doubleday, 1977; London,
  Penguin, 1978.
Prudence Be Damned. New York, Doubleday, 1978; London,
  Hale, 1979.
The Man with Fifty Complaints. New York, Doubleday, 1978;
  London, Hale, 1980.
Welcome to the Grave. New York, Doubleday, 1979; London,
  Collins, 1980.
But Nellie Was So Nice. New York, Doubleday, 1979;
  London, Collins, 1981.
My Cousin Death. New York, Doubleday, 1980; London,
  Collins, 1981.
Something of the Night. New York, Doubleday, 1980;
  London, Collins, 1982.
The Other Shoe. New York, Doubleday, 1981; London,
  Collins, 1982.
Better Off Dead. New York, Doubleday, 1982; London,
  Macmillan, 1983.
Until Death Do Us Part. New York, Doubleday, 1982;
  London, Macmillan, 1983.
A Grave Without Flowers. New York, Doubleday, 1983;
  London, Macmillan, 1984.
The Gift Horse. New York, Doubleday, and London, Macmil-
  lan, 1985.
Bad-News Man. New York, Doubleday, and London, Mac-
  millan, 1986.

Uncollected Short Story

"Her Heart's Home," in *Ellery Queen's Eyewitnesses.* New
  York, Davis, 1982.

*   *   *

Mary McMullen's novels, some suspense stories, some crime
fiction, generally involve fairly small groups of relatives,
business associates, or neighbors who, it turns out, have much
more in common than an onlooker might first suspect. The
author pays close attention to characters' preferences in
clothing, food, and drink; these evidences of taste, along with
the literate, rather brittle dialogue, serve as her primary means
of characterization. Weather imagery is very important to the
novels' moods, and McMullen provides detailed settings, be
they the English country gardens of *A Grave Without Flowers*,
the Irish locales of *My Cousin Death*, or the large Maryland
farm-turned-country-house of *The Other Shoe*. This attention to
detail, enjoyable in itself, also lends realism to fairly sensational
plots.

McMullen's heroines are often stunningly lovely, conceal
considerable strength beneath surface gentleness, and frequently are successful career women. These protagonists
engage in intense love affairs, and the heroes, whether suitor or
husband, are tall, attractive, and expert at their professions.
Some villains, like Desmond Byrne of *The Pimlico Plot*, are
addicted to danger; others, like Bernard Caldwell, in *Death by
Bequest*, are simply greedy, and many are very attractive to
women. *A Grave Without Flowers* depicts several villains, as
criminal bilks criminal even as they exploit innocent citizens,
and these various felons are good examples of standard—and
always intriguing—McMullen types. This novel also rings a
small change on the romance motif, for the lovers were
formerly married to one another. *Until Death Do Us Part* also
capitalizes upon the repercussions which can follow the
dissolution of a marriage; here, however, the partners are
linked by hatred, jealousy, and ambition.

Stranglehold employs the convention of the murdered
stranger and is set against the office politics of a New York
advertising firm. Some interesting insights into the role of
women in advertising in the 1950's as well as the characterization of the heroine, Eve Fitzsimmons, strengthen the book. An
interest in free publicity, creative genius, illicit but inventive
merchandising techniques, and avarice complicate the plot of
Better Off Dead, just as they complicate the life of Johanna
Landis, who, only recently reunited with the artist-father who
abandoned her 23 years before, loses him again.

Indeed, complex family relationships inform many of
McMullen's plots, and in *Prudence Be Damned*, perhaps her
best novel, Madeline Devore is kidnapped and held for ransom
by her son and his current lover. The motivations and emotions
of these unlikely abductors, of their victim, and of the other
family members are particularly well delineated. A plea for
help from his young son, Markie, involves Kells Cavenaugh in
an investigation of his ex-wife's fiancé; of considerable interest
are the relationship between father and son and the question of
how much validity Kells can attribute to a fragmentary note
written by a six-year-old. As is often the case in these novels,
trusting one's instincts proves far wiser than ratiocination.

Intriguing contributions to the genre, McMullen's novels are
swift-moving, tightly knit stories of polished, capable people
forced by crime, danger—and romance—to reassess their lives,
reexamine their values, revise their attitudes toward old
associates and habits.

—Jane S. Bakerman

———

McNEILE, H.C. *See* **SAPPER.**

———

McSHANE, Mark. Also writes as Marc Lovell. British.
Born in Sydney, Australia, 28 November 1929. Educated in
Blackpool, Lancashire, 1935–45. Married Pamela Rosemary
Armstrong in 1963; one daughter and three sons (one
deceased). Agent: Collier Associates, 2000 Flat Run Road,
Seaman, Ohio 45679, U.S.A.; or, Diana Avebury, Strathmore
Agency, Park Road, London, N.W.8, England. Address: Can
Tumi, La Cabaneta, Mallorca, Spain.

CRIME PUBLICATIONS

Novels (series: Myra Savage; ex-Detective Sergeant Norman
    Pink)

The Straight and the Crooked.   London, Long, 1960.
Séance on a Wet Afternoon (Savage).   London, Cassell, 1961;
    as *Séance*, New York, Doubleday, 1962.
The Passing of Evil.   London, Cassell, 1961.
Untimely Ripped.   London, Cassell, 1962; New York, Double-
    day, 1963.
The Girl Nobody Knows (Pink).   New York, Doubleday, 1965;
    London, Hale, 1966.
Night's Evil (Pink).   New York, Doubleday, and London,
    Hale, 1966.
The Crimson Madness of Little Doom.   New York, Doubleday,
    1966; London, Hale, 1967.
The Way to Nowhere (Pink).   London, Hale, 1967.
Ill Met by a Fish Shop on George Street.   New York,
    Doubleday, 1968; London, Hodder and Stoughton, 1969.
The Singular Case of the Multiple Dead.   New York, Putnam,
    1969; London, Hodder and Stoughton, 1970.
The Man Who Left Well Enough.   New York, McCall, 1971.
Séance for Two (Savage).   New York, Doubleday, 1972;
    London, Hale, 1974.
The Othello Complex.   Paris, Gallimard, 1974.
The Headless Snowman.   Paris, Gallimard, 1974.
Lashed But Not Leashed.   New York, Doubleday, 1976;
    London, Hale, 1978.
Lifetime.   New York, Manor, 1977.
The Hostage Game.   New York, Zebra, 1979.
The Halcyon Way.   New York, Manor, 1979; London, Hale,
    1982.
Just a Face in the Dark.   New York, Doubleday, 1987.
Once Upon a Fairy Tale.   New York, Doubleday, 1990.

Novels as Marc Lovell (series: Jason Galt; Appleton "Apple"
    Porter)

The Ghost of Megan.   New York, Doubleday, 1968; as *Memory
    of Megan*, New York, Ace, 1970.
The Imitation Thieves.   New York, Doubleday, 1971.
A Presence in the House.   New York, Doubleday, 1972.
An Enquiry into the Existence of Vampires.   New York,
    Doubleday, 1974; as *Vampires in the Shadows*, London, Hale,
    1976.
Dreamers in a Haunted House.   New York, Doubleday, 1975;
    London, Hale, 1976.
The Blind Hypnotist (Galt).   New York, Doubleday, 1976.
The Second Vanetti Affair (Galt).   New York, Doubleday,
    1977.
The Guardian Spectre.   New York, Manor, 1977.
Fog Sinister.   New York, Manor, 1977.
A Voice from the Living.   New York, Doubleday, 1978.
And They Say You Can't Buy Happiness.   London, Hale, 1979.
Hand over Mind.   New York, Doubleday, 1979; London,
    Hale, 1980.
Shadows and Dark Places.   London, Hale, 1980.
The Spy Game (Apple).   New York, Doubleday, 1980;
    London, Hale, 1981.
The Spy with His Head in the Clouds (Apple).   New York,
    Doubleday, and London, Hale, 1982.
Spy on the Run (Apple).   New York, Doubleday, 1982.
The Last Seance.   London, Hale, 1982.
Apple Spy in the Sky.   New York, Doubleday, 1983.

Apple to the Core.   New York, Doubleday, 1983.
Looking for Kingford.   Berlin, Rowohlt, 1983.
How Green Was My Apple.   New York, Doubleday, 1984.
The Only Good Apple in a Barrel of Spies.   New York,
    Doubleday, 1984.
The Spy Who Got His Feet Wet.   New York, Doubleday, 1985.
The Spy Who Barked in the Night.   New York, Doubleday,
    1986.
Good Spies Don't Grow on Trees (Apple).   New York,
    Doubleday, 1986.
That Great Big Trench Coat in the Sky.   New York, Doubleday,
    1988.
The Spy Who Fell Off the Back of a Bus.   New York,
    Doubleday, 1988.
Ethel and the Naked Spy.   New York, Doubleday, 1989.
Comfort Me with Spies.   New York, Doubleday, 1990.

*

Manuscript Collections: Mugar Memorial Library, Boston
University; University of Wyoming, Laramie; Sydney
University.

Mark McShane comments:
    In my teens I read Gerald Kersh's *Prelude to a Certain
Midnight*. To me it was a minor revelation. Up until then my
reading in crime-suspense-mystery had been in the category in
which all turns out well in the end, and the relationship to
reality is a tenth cousin forcibly removed. So I'd been little
interested in this field, except as a time-passer. When I started
writing, over ten years later, it was that book's influence that
made me do what, in most of my work, I'm still doing: trying to
see how far I can take the crime novel away from the cardboard
goodies-baddies scene and into a third world not straight, not
bent; at the same time pressing whenever possible my brief that
the so-called occult is as real and natural as memory; being a
didactic nuisance on the values of liberalism; never writing the
same book twice; earning a living.

*   *   *

    Given his obsession with man's variability and quirkiness, it
is not surprising that Mark McShane (both as himself and Marc
Lovell) has written odd crime novels, each greatly differing
from the others. The strangeness and singularity of his works
are evident in such titles as *The Crimson Madness of Little
Doom*, *Hand over Mind*, and *Lashed But Not Leashed*. They are
evident as well in his plots, which range from a medium seeking
to establish her spiritualistic powers by predicting a kidnapping that will be done by her husband and herself (*Séance on a
Wet Afternoon*) to an ex-policeman trying to identify a nine-
year-old girl accidentally killed in a train wreck (*The Girl
Nobody Knows*) to a group of artistically misinclined social
misfits planning to assassinate the Chancellor of the Exchequer
for imposing a one-cent tax on theater seats (*The Singular Case
of the Multiple Dead*). McShane's writing is also remarkable in
its range; he has produced suspense novels tinged with the
supernatural (*Séance on a Wet Afternoon* and *The Ghost of
Megan*), straight crime novels that are a little bent (*The Girl
Nobody Knows*, *The Blind Hypnotist*, and *The Second Vanetti
Affair*), psychological crime novels that are bent almost to the
breaking point (*Ill Met by a Fish Shop on George Street* and
Lashed But Not Leashed), and bizarre, intriguing mixtures of
the whodunit and the crime novel that additionally combine
tragedy and comedy (*The Singular Case of the Multiple Dead*
and *The Crimson Madness of Little Doom*).

Used effectively, McShane's penchant for the offbeat has enabled him to invent plots that are fascinating because the oddity of his characters makes their behaviour and its outcome nearly unpredictable. It has also led him to explore seldom observed corners of the mind and hence discover new angles of vision (it should be noted that he likes punning). In addition, it has inspired him to enrich the mystery genre with both mordant and extravagant humor. The novels that best demonstrate these virtues are *Séance on a Wet Afternoon, The Crimson Madness of Little Doom, The Singular Case of the Multiple Dead, The Blind Hypnotist, The Second Vanetti Affair,* and *Ill Met by a Fish Shop on George Street.* Used irresponsibly, however, this penchant has resulted in the lifeless grotesques, Krafft-Ebbing kinkiness, and superabundance of Inspector Clouseau-esque pratfalls of *The Man Who Left Well Enough* (McShane didn't) and the disheartening mixture of plot ingenuity and soft-core pornography of *Lifetime.* Also a grotesque, but for a different reason, is *Just a Face in the Dark.* Set in an odd little art colony in the southern United States, it concerns a stranger, John Brown, who has been responsible for the suicide of 11 women and four cold-blooded murders committed by jealous husbands, and relies on a fantastic, mythological explanation for these and other bizarre events.

Throughout his work, McShane has emphasized man's vulnerability to chance, the role of circumstance in creating criminals, the nuttiness of the seemingly normal, and the dangers of excessive idealism. Again and again, he has shown the madness behind too strong a drive for psychological, social, political, or moral purity. In *The Man Who Left Well Enough,* for example, he focuses on the Hitler-like founder of a bricklayer's society who inspired his followers to kill some plasterers for scoffing at the purity of bricklaying. Similarly, in *The Crimson Madness of Little Doom* he sardonically depicts a woman who wrote poison pen letters to people who failed to meet her standard of sexual purity, and, in *The Hostage Game,* he skewers a political opportunist who gained prominence through his campaign to clean up England by throwing out all the foreign workers. An early work, *Untimely Ripped,* shows just how thin the line between a passion for morality and madness is for him since he portrays a policeman who was an insane killer and a lunatic who discovered this through detective work. McShane's philosophy seems to be: human beings are screwed-up enough as they are; tamper with them and they become worse. He also notes that a man's own hatred can hurt him more than anyone else's can.

Recently, as Lovell, McShane has finally created a long running series hero who is—predictably—quirky. A 6'7" spy who blushes and whose nickname "Apple" provides McShane with the opportunity for a multitude of unblushingly punning titles, Appleton Porter can only be used on the most extraordinary assignments, such as finding out which of a group of Russian mind readers can really read minds and which wants to defect and are they the same (*The Spy Game*), taking part in an international track meet to get information before and after the run from a Russian Olympic gold medalist (*Spy on the Run*), and uncovering the identity of a Russian agent who is even more bumbling than he is (*Apple Spy in the Sky*), tangling with a freelance spy and master of disguise known as Clever Freddy in the Scottish Highlands (*The Spy Who Barked in the Night,* perhaps the funniest of the Apple books), and attending a book convention in Cannes to buy a manuscript purported to be an attack on Sherlock Holmes by Conan Doyle (*The Spy Who Fell Off the Back of a Bus*). The series plays off Apple's idealism, decency (leavened a bit by horniness), and highly romanticized view of spying against the cynicism, calculativeness, and coldhearted "realism" of his boss, Angus Watkin. Apple is always ruthlessly manipulated by Watkin throughout,

though his decency always manages a small triumph in the end. In the most interesting book in the series, *Apple to the Core,* Apple moves several steps toward a transformation into the hardened, shrewd operative he would like to be, not realizing that to become better as an agent means to become worse as a human being, but his core of concern for others saves him from this. On the other hand, his perpetually thwarted longing to become hardened and ruthless is probably what helps him to preserve a balance and to avoid the trap of an excessive purity. The only disappointing Apple book, and that only mildly so, is the sixth, *How Green Was My Apple,* since McShane again surrenders to his bent for soft-core pornography, devising several scenes in which a female agent must undress in front of Apple or seduce him to prevent a Russian from discovering that they are tailing him. Otherwise, the series can stand with the best of McShane's other work.

—Steven R. Carter

McVEAN, James. *See* **LUARD, Nicholas.**

MEADE, L.T. (Elizabeth Thomasina Meade). Irish. Born in Bandon, County Cork, in 1854. Married Alfred Toulmin Smith in 1879; one son and two daughters. Worked in the British Museum, London; editor, with A.A. Leith, *Atalanta* girl's magazine for six years. *Died 26 October 1914.*

CRIME PUBLICATIONS

Novels

A Ring of Rubies. London, Innes, and New York, Cassell, 1892.
This Troublesome World, with Clifford Halifax. London, Chatto and Windus, 1893.
The Voice of the Charmer. London, Chatto and Windus, 3 vols., 1895.
Dr. Rumsey's Patient: A Very Strange Story, with Clifford Halifax. London, Chatto and Windus, 1896.
A Son of Ishmael. London, White, and New York, New Amsterdam Book Company, 1896.
On the Brink of a Chasm. London, Chatto and Windus, and New York, Buckles, 1899.
The Blue Diamond. London, Chatto and Windus, 1901.
The Secret of the Dead. London, White, 1901.
Confessions of a Court Milner. London, Long, 1902.
A Double Revenge. London, Digby Long, 1902.
The Lost Square, with Robert Eustace. London, Ward Lock, 1902.
The Adventures of Miranda. London, Long, 1904.
From the Hand of the Hunter. London, Long, 1906.
The Golden Shadow. London, Ward Lock, 1906.
The Chateau of Mystery. London, Everett, 1907.
The Home of Silence. London, Sisley's, 1907.
The Red Ruth. London, Laurie, 1907.
The Necklace of Parmona. London, Ward Lock, 1909.
Twenty-Four Hours. London, White, 1911.
The House of the Black Magic. London, White, 1912.

Short Stories

Stories from the Diary of a Doctor, with Clifford Halifax. London, Newnes, 1894; Philadelphia, Lippincott, 1895; *Second Series*, London, Bliss, 1896.
Under the Dragon Throne, with Robert Kennaway Douglas. London, Wells Gardner, 1897.
A Master of Mysteries, with Robert Eustace. London, Ward Lock, 1898.
The Gold Star Line, with Robert Eustace. London, Ward Lock, 1899; New York, New Amsterdam Book Company, n.d.
The Brotherhood of the Seven Kings, with Robert Eustace. London, Ward Lock, 1899.
Where the Shoe Pinches, with Clifford Halifax. London, Chambers, 1900.
The Sanctuary Club, with Robert Eustace. London, Ward Lock, 1900.
A Race with the Sun, with Clifford Halifax. London, Ward Lock, 1901.
The Sorceress of the Strand. London, Ward Lock, 1903.
Silenced. London, Ward Lock, 1904.
The Oracle of Maddox Street. London, Ward Lock, 1904.
Micah Faraday, Adventurer. London, Ward Lock, 1910.

Uncollected Short Story

"The Face in the Dark," with Robert Eustace, in *Great Short Stories of Detection, Mystery, and Horror*, vol., 1, edited by Dorothy L. Sayers. London, Gollancz, 1928; as *The Omnibus of Crime*, New York, Payson and Clarke, 1929.

OTHER PUBLICATIONS

Novels

Lotty's Last Home. London, Shaw, 1875.
David's Little Lad. London, Shaw, 1877; New York, Harper, 1878.
A Knight of Today. London, Shaw, 1877.
Scamp and I: A Story of City By-Ways. London, Shaw, 1877; New York, Carter, 1878.
Bel Marjory. London, Shaw, 1878.
The Children's Kingdom. London, Shaw, 1878; New York, Burt, n.d.
Your Brother and Mine: A Cry from the Great City. London, Shaw, 1878.
Dot and Her Treasures. London, Shaw, 1879.
Water Gipsies: A Story of Canal Life in England. New York, Carter, 1879; London, Shaw, 1883.
Andrew Harvey's Wife. London, Isbister, 1880.
A Dweller in Tents. London, Isbister, 1880.
Mou-Setsé: A Negro Hero. London, Isbister, 1880.
The Floating Light of Ringfinnan, and Guardian Angels. Edinburgh, Macniven and Wallace, 1880.
Mother Herring's Chicken. London, Isbister, and New York, Carter, 1881.
A London Baby: The Story of King Roy. London, Nisbet, 1882.
The Children's Pilgrimage. London, Nisbet, 1883.
How It All Came Round. London, Hodder and Stoughton, and New York, Lovell, 1883.
The Autocrat of the Nursery. London, Hodder and Stoughton, 1884; New York, Armstrong, 1886.
A Band of Three. London, Isbister, 1884; New York, Seaside Library, n.d.
Scarlet Anemones. London, Hodder and Stoughton, 1884.
The Two Sisters. London, Hodder and Stoughton, 1884.

The Angel of Love. London, Hodder and Stoughton, 1885; Boston, Earle, 1887.
A Little Silver Trumpet. London, Hodder and Stoughton, 1885.
A World of Girls: The Story of a School. London, Cassell, 1886; New York, Mershon, n.d.
Daddy's Boy. London, Hatchards, 1887; New York, White and Allen, 1889.
The O'Donnells of Inchfawn. London, Hatchards, and New York, Harper, 1887.
The Palace Beautiful. London, Cassell, 1887; New York, Grosset and Dunlap, n.d.
Sweet Nancy. London, Partridge, 1887.
Deb and the Duchess. London, Hatchards, 1888; New York, White and Allen, 1889.
Nobody's Neighbours. London, Isbister, 1888.
A Farthingful. London, Chambers, 1889.
The Golden Lady. London, Chambers, 1889; New York, Whittaker, n.d.
The Lady of the Forest. London, Partridge, and New York, Warne, 1889.
The Little Princess of Tower Hill. London, Partridge, 1889.
Polly, A New-Fashioned Girl. London, Cassell, 1889; New York, Hurst, n.d.
Poor Miss Carolina. London, Chambers, 1889.
The Beresford Prize. London, Longman, 1890.
Dickory Dock. London, Chambers, 1890.
Engaged to Be Married. London, Simpkin Marshall, 1890.
Frances Kane's Fortune. London, Warne, and New York, Lovell, 1890.
Heart of Gold. London, Warne, and New York, United States Book Company, 1890.
Just a Love Story. London, Blackett, 1890.
Marigold. London, Partridge, 1890.
The Honourable Miss. New York, United States Book Company, 1890; London, Methuen, 2 vols., 1891.
A Girl of the People. London, Methuen, and New York, Lovell, 1890.
Hepsy Gipsy. London, Methuen, 1891.
A Life for a Love. New York, United States Book Company, 1891; London, Digby Long, 1894.
The Children of Wilton Chase. London, Chambers, and New York, Cassell, 1891.
A Sweet Girl-Graduate. London, Cassell, 1891; New York, Allison, n.d.
Bashful Fifteen. London and New York, Cassell, 1892.
Four on an Island. London, Chambers, and New York, Cassell, 1892.
Jill, A Flower Girl. New York, United States Book Company, 1892; London, Isbister, 1893.
The Medicine Lady. London and New York, Cassell, 3 vols., 1892.
Out of the Fashion. London, Methuen, and New York, Cassell, 1892.
Beyond the Blue Mountains. London, Cassell, 1893.
A Young Mutineer. London, Wells Gardner, and New York, Hurst, 1893.
Betty, A School Girl. London, Chambers, 1894; New York, Cassell, n.d.
In an Iron Grip. London, Chatto and Windus, 2 vols., 1894.
Red Rose and Tiger Lily. London and New York, Cassell, 1894.
A Soldier of Fortune. London, Chatto and Windus, 3 vols., 1894; New York, Fenno, 1 vol., 1894.
Girls, New and Old. London, Chambers, and New York, Cassell, 1895.

A Princess of the Gutter. London, Wells Gardner, 1895; New York, Putnam, 1896.

Catalina, Art Student. London, Chambers, 1896; Philadelphia, Lippincott, 1897.

A Girl in Ten Thousand. Edinburgh, Oliphant, 1896; New York, Whittaker, 1897.

Good Luck. London, Nisbet, 1896; New York, Grosset and Dunlap, n.d.

A Little Mother to the Others. London, White, 1896.

Merry Girls of England. London, Cassell, 1896; Boston, Bradley, 1897.

Playmates. London, Chambers, 1896.

The White Tzar. London, Marshall Russell, 1896.

The House of Surprises. London, Longman, 1896.

Bad Little Hannah. London, White, 1897; New York, Mershon, n.d.

A Handful of Silver. Edinburgh, Oliphant, 1897; New York, Dutton, 1898.

The Way of a Woman. London, White, 1897.

Wild Kitty. London, Chambers, 1897; New York, Burt, n.d.

Cave Perilous. London, Religious Tract Society, 1898.

A Bunch of Cherries. London, Nister, and New York, Dutton, 1898.

The Cleverest Woman in England. London, Nisbet, 1898; Boston, Bradley, 1899.

The Girls of St. Wode's. London, Chambers, 1898; New York, Mershon, n.d.

Mary Gifford, M.B. London, Wells Gardner, 1898.

The Rebellion of Lil Carrington. London, Cassell, 1898.

The Siren. London, White, 1898.

Adventuress. London, Chatto and Windus, 1899.

All Sorts. London, Nisbet, 1899.

The Temptation of Olive Latimer. New York, Mershon, 1899; London, Hutchinson, 1900.

The Desire of Man: An Impossibility. London, Digby Long, 1899.

Light o' the Morning: The Story of an Irish Girl. London, Chambers, 1899; New York, Dutton, n.d.

The Odds and the Evens. London, Chambers, 1899; New York, Burt, n.d.

Wages. London, Nisbet, 1900.

A Plucky Girl. Philadelphia, Jacobs, 1900.

The Beauforts. London, Griffith and Farran, 1900.

A Brave Poor Thing. London, Isbister, 1900.

Daddy's Girl. London, Newnes, 1900; Philadelphia, Lippincott, 1901.

Miss Nonentity. London, Chambers, 1900; New York, Grosset and Dunlap, n.d.

Seven Maids. London, Chambers, 1900.

A Sister of the Red Cross: A Tale of the South African War. London, Nelson, 1900.

The Time of Roses. London, Nister, 1900; New York, Hurst, n.d.

Wheels of Iron. London, Nisbet, 1901.

Cosey Corner; or, How They Kept a Farm. London, Chambers, 1901.

Girls of the True Blue. London, Chambers, and New York, Dutton, 1901.

The New Mrs. Lascelles. London, Clarke, 1901.

A Stumble by the Way. London, Chatto and Windus, 1901.

A Very Naughty Girl. London, Chambers, 1901; New York, Hurst, n.d.

Drift. London, Methuen, 1902.

Girls of the Forest. London, Chambers, 1902; New York, Dutton, n.d.

Margaret. London, White, 1902.

The Pursuit of Penelope. London, Digby, 1902.

Queen Rose. London, Chambers, 1902.

The Rebel of the School. London, Chambers, 1902; New York, Burt, n.d.

The Squire's Little Girl. London, Chambers, 1902.

Through Peril for a Wife. London, Digby, 1902.

The Witch Maid. London, Nisbet, 1903.

The Burden of Her Youth. London, Long, 1903.

By Mutual Consent. London, Digby Long, 1903.

A Gay Charmer. London, Chambers, 1903.

The Manor School. London, Chambers, and New York, Mershon, 1903.

Peter the Pilgrim. London, Chambers, 1903.

Resurgam. London, Methuen, 1903.

Rosebury. London, Chatto and Windus, 1903.

That Brilliant Peggy. London, Hodder and Stoughton, 1903.

A Maid of Mystery. London, White, 1904.

At the Back of the World. London, Hurst and Blackett, 1904.

Castle Poverty. London, Nisbet, 1904.

The Girls of Mrs. Pritchard's School. London, Chambers, 1904; New York, Burt, n.d.

Love Triumphant. London, T. Fisher Unwin, 1904.

A Madcap. London, Cassell, and New York, Mershon, 1904.

A Modern Tomboy. London, Chambers, 1904; New York, Dutton, n.d.

Nurse Charlotte. London, Long, 1904.

Petronella, and The Coming of Polly. London, Chambers, 1904.

Wilful Cousin Kate. London, Chambers, 1905.

Bess of Delaney's. London, Digby Long, 1905.

A Bevy of Girls. London, Chambers, and New York, Still, 1905.

Dumps: A Plain Girl. London, Chambers, and New York, Dutton, 1905.

His Mascot. London, Long, 1905.

Little Wife Hester. London, Long, 1905.

Loveday: The Story of an Heiress. London, Hodder and Stoughton, 1905.

Old Readymoney's Daughter. London, Partridge, 1905.

The Other Woman. London, Walter Scott Publishing Company, 1905.

Virginia. London, Digby, 1905.

The Colonel and the Boy. London, Hodder and Stoughton, 1906.

The Face of Juliet. London, Long, 1906.

The Girl and Her Fortune. London, Hodder and Stoughton, 1906.

The Heart of Helen. London, Long, 1906.

The Hill-Top Girl. London, Chambers, 1906; New York, Burt, n.d.

The Home of Sweet Content. London, White, 1906.

In the Flower of Her Youth. London, Nisbet, 1906.

The Maid with the Goggles. London, Digby, 1906.

Sue. London, Chambers, 1906.

Turquoise and Ruby. London, Chambers, and New York, Chatterton Peck, 1906.

Victory. London, Methuen, 1906.

The Colonel's Conquest. Philadelphia, Jacobs, 1907.

The Curse of the Feverals. London, Long, 1907.

A Girl from America. London, Chambers, 1907.

Kindred Spirits. London, Long, 1907.

The Lady of Delight. London, Hodder and Stoughton, 1907.

Little Josephine. London, Long, 1907.

The Little School-Mothers. London, Cassell, and Philadelphia, McKay, 1907.

The Love of Susan Cardigan. London, Digby Long, 1907.

The Red Cap of Liberty. London, Nisbet, 1907.

The Scamp Family. London, Chambers, 1907; New York, Burt, n.d.

Three Girls from School. London, Chambers, 1907; New York, Burt, n.d.

The Aim of Her Life. London, Long, 1908.

Betty of the Rectory. London, Cassell, 1908; New York, Grosset and Dunlap, n.d.

The Court-Harman Girls. London, Chambers, 1908.

The Courtship of Sybil. London, Long, 1908.

Hetty Beresford. London, Hodder and Stoughton, 1908.

Sarah's Mother. London, Hodder and Stoughton, 1908.

The School Favourite. London, Chambers, 1908.

The School Queens. London, Chambers, 1908; New York, New York Book Company, 1910.

Wild Heather. London, Cassell, 1909.

Oceana's Girlhood. New York, Hurst, 1909.

Aylwyn's Friends. London, Chambers, 1909.

Betty Vivian: A Story of Haddo Court School. London, Chambers, 1909.

Blue of the Sea. London, Nisbet, 1909.

Brother or Husband. London, White, 1909.

The Fountain of Beauty. London, Long, 1909.

I Will Sing a New Song. London, Hodder and Stoughton, 1909.

The Princess of the Revels. London, Chambers, 1909; New York, New York Book Company, 1910.

The Stormy Petrel. London, Hurst and Blackett, 1909.

The A.B.C. Girl. London, White, 1910.

Belinda Treherne. London, Long, 1910.

A Girl of Today. London, Long, 1910.

Lady Anne. London, Nisbet, 1910.

Miss Gwendoline. London, Long, 1910.

Nance Kennedy. London, Partridge, 1910.

Pretty-Girl and the Others. London, Chambers, 1910.

Rose Regina. London, Chambers, 1910.

A Wild Irish Girl. London, Chambers, and New York, Hurst, 1910.

A Bunch of Cousins, and The Barn "Boys." London, Chambers, 1911.

Desborough's Wife. London, Digby Long, 1911.

The Doctor's Children. London, Chambers, and Philadelphia, Lippincott, 1911.

For Dead Dad. London, Chambers, 1911.

The Girl from Spain. London, Digby Long, 1911.

The Girls of Merton College. New York, Hurst, 1911.

Mother and Son. London, Ward Lock, 1911.

Ruffles. London, Stanley Paul, 1911.

The Soul of Margaret Rand. London, Ward Lock, 1911.

Daddy's Girl and Consuelo's Quest of Happiness. New York, New York Book Company, 1911.

Corporal Violet. London, Hodder and Stoughton, 1912.

A Girl of the People. London, Everett, 1912.

Kitty O'Donovan. London, Chambers, and New York, Hurst, 1912.

Lord and Lady Kitty. London, White, 1912.

Love's Cross Roads. London, Stanley Paul, 1912.

Peggy from Kerry. London, Chambers, and New York, Hurst, 1912.

The Chesterton Girl Graduates. New York, Hurst, 1913.

The Girls of Abinger Close. London, Chambers, 1913.

The Girls of King's Royal. New York, Hurst, 1913.

The Passion of Kathleen Duveen. London, Stanley Paul, 1913.

A Band of Mirth. London, Chambers, 1914.

Col. Tracy's Wife. London, Aldine, 1914.

Elizabeth's Prisoner. London, Stanley Paul, 1914.

A Girl of High Adventure. London, Chambers, 1914.

Her Happy Face. London, Ward Lock, 1914.

The Queen of Joy. London, Chambers, and New York, Hurst, 1914.

The Wooing of Monica. London, Long, 1914.

The Darling of the School. London, Chambers, 1915.

The Daughter of a Soldier: A Colleen of South Ireland. New York, Hurst, 1915.

Greater Than Gold. London, Ward Lock, 1915.

Jill the Irresistible. New York, Hurst, 1915.

Hollyhock. London, Chambers, 1916.

Madge Mostyn's Nieces. London, Chambers, 1916.

The Maid Indomitable. London, Ward Lock, 1916.

Mother Mary. London, Chambers, 1916.

Daughters of Today. London, Hodder and Stoughton, 1916.

Better Than Riches. London, Chambers, 1917.

The Fairy Godmother. London, Chambers, 1917.

Miss Patricia. London, Long, 1925.

Roses and Thorns. London, Long, 1928.

In Time of Roses. New York, Grosset and Dunlap, n.d.

Short Stories

Water Lilies and Other Tales. London, Shaw, 1878.

Hermie's Rose-Buds and Other Stories. London, Hodder and Stoughton, 1883.

Little Mary and Other Stories. London, Chambers, 1891.

The Least of These and Other Stories. Cincinnati, Cranston and Curts, 1895.

The Princess Who Gave Away All, and The Naughty One of the Family. London, Nister, 1902.

The Lady Cake-Maker. London, Hodder and Stoughton, 1904.

A Lovely Fiend and Other Stories. London, Digby, 1908.

Play

The Brotherhood of the Seven Kings, with Robert Eustace and Max Elgin, adaptation of the story by Meade and Eustace (produced South Shields, County Durham, 1900).

Other

A Public School Boy (on H.S. Wristbridge). London, Nisbet, 1899.

Stories from the Old, Old Bible. London, Newnes, 1903.

*   *   *

L.T. Meade probably wrote more girls' books than any other author of her day, yet today she is remembered almost solely for her mystery story-chains: *Stories from the Diary of a Doctor*, *A Master of Mysteries*, *The Brotherhood of the Seven Kings*, *The Gold Star Line*, *The Sanctuary Club*, *A Race with the Sun*, and *The Sorceress of the Strand*.

First published as instalments in *The Strand Magazine* and other periodicals, these were usually mystery-adventure stories told in the first person, often based upon some (slightly fantastic) scientific or medical snippet. It is assumed that Meade's collaborators provided such ideas and that she did the actual writing. Unifying factors within each chain could include criminal secret societies, femmes fatales, female masterminds of crime, and similar elements. Meade's fiction often embodied a strange dichotomy between sensational subject matter and a very stuffy *Weltanschauung*.

Meade wrote many other works dealing with crime and mystery, but her exact bibliography is not clear. Her books are now exceedingly rare, and sometimes misleading in title. In the opinion of this reviewer, her best work is not among the famous titles listed above, but is the series, written with Robert Eustace, about Miss Cusack, a female detective.

—E.F. Bleiler

———

MEEK, M(argaret) R(eid) D(uncan). British. Born in Greenock, Renfrewshire, Scotland, 19 March 1918. Educated at Birkenhead Girls' School, 1928–36, College of Law, Lancaster Gate, London, 1963–67; University of London, 1962–66, LL.B. (honours) 1966. Married 1) Donald Gregory in 1942 (died 1959), one son and one daughter; 2) Colin Meek in 1978. Shorthand typist, various companies, Glasgow, 1937–39, and Rolls Royce, Glasgow, 1939–44; clerical assistant, Civil Services, Waltham Abbey, Essex, 1960–62; articled clerk, Smith and Harrison, Waltham Cross, Hertfordshire, 1962–70; solicitor, Macmillans, Wadebridge, Cornwall, 1970–78. Lived in Germany, 1946–50. Address: Waltham Lodge, Trevanion Road, Wadebridge, Cornwall PL27 7NZ, England.

CRIME PUBLICATIONS

Novels (series: Lennox Kemp in all books)

With Flowers that Fell.   London, Hale, 1983.
The Sitting Ducks.   London, Collins, 1984.
Hang the Consequences.   London, Collins, 1984; New York, Scribner, 1985.
The Split Second.   London, Collins, 1985; New York, Scribner, 1987.
In Remembrance of Rose.   London, Collins, 1987; New York, Scribner, 1988.
A Worm of Doubt.   London, Collins, 1987; New York, Scribner, 1988.
A Mouthful of Sand.   London, Collins, 1988; New York, Scribner, 1989.
The Loose Connection.   London, Collins, and New York, Scribner, 1989.

*

M.R.D. Meek comments:

The late start, both in law and in writing, will have been noted. Too busy a life to write until retirement but I've been a voracious reader of crime fiction since finding *A Study in Scarlet* at the age of eight. I write out of my experience of people so true characterisation is essential. I lean—but only lightly— towards the psychological. I am not a careful plotter, nor do I have any structured plan for my novels; things happen but, I hope, not too implausibly . . .

My central protagonist, Lennox Kemp, is a lawyer because practising lawyers tend to see people at their most vulnerable.

I am astonished at my success—particularly with American critics who liken me to P.D. James and Ruth Rendell.

I admire style, and good English, so strive for both in the interests of my publishers and my readers—and because I think crime fiction deserves to be taken seriously.

* * *

There's a quiet precision to M.R.D. Meek's gently witty, calmly worded, sharply insightful, and exceptionally skillful prose. The simple and economical style is quite compatible

with its subject, Lennox Kemp, a superficially laconic "teddy bear" of a man. Kemp's sometime companion, Penelope Marsden, observes that "words had always come so easily to Kemp, he made his living by the correct use of words, the accuracy of their place in a document, their careful hidden strength in cross-examination." It's a description that's all the more appropriate when applied to Meek herself. There isn't a word out of place in her novels. Marsden's observation comes at a rare moment of anger for Kemp; he's as even-tempered as Meek's prose, yet the books are anything but cold. It's a testament to Meek's skill that she's able to evoke a full range of situations and emotions without resorting to histrionics. Meek is compared to P.D. James and Ruth Rendell, and she is their superior in several important respects, most notably her admirable restraint. Her tightly-knit stories are short and to the point.

At the outset of *Hang the Consequences*, Kemp is a shadowy figure. An employee of McCready's Detective Agency of Walthamstow, Kemp prepares to meet a client, thinking "wearily that here was yet another piece of flotsam to be salvaged." McCready "liked to identify his operatives with the late Philip Marlowe or Lew Archer." The comparison is apt as far as the case goes. A woman wants Kemp to find her husband who has run off with another woman; the trail leads to the kind of twisted family history which would not be out of place in a Ross Macdonald novel. The familial discord in Meek's novels is more often between husband and wife; most of the stories are built around strikingly original variations on and solutions to traditional marital problems.

The comparison of Kemp to Archer as individuals fails, however. Meek gives us precious few hints of Kemp's appearance and never challenges him with physical danger, but it's unlikely that he'd be good in a fight. Kemp reminds someone of Hammett's Continental Op: "short, fat and forty." Later, "his thick set figure, the square look of his shoulders, even the slightly comical aspect of the small bald patch on top of his head" bring a smile to a woman's face. Like his hard-boiled American counterparts, Kemp "had long given up the youthful hope that there is in life some earthly paradise just around the next bend."

But Kemp isn't your ordinary private detective. Six years before the opening of *Hang the Consequences*, Lennox Kemp was a married solicitor and enjoyed a comfortable suburban life. He was struck off the Law Society for an action as foolish as it was honourable. Indeed, he doesn't remain a private detective for long: at the beginning the fifth book, Kemp is once again practicing law. The novels represent stages in Kemp's return to respectability; by the time of *The Loose Connection*, he is in charge of the Newtown office of Gillorns, Solicitors. The years at McCready's are later referred to as "sleazy days" and "six years in the wilderness." Yet Kemp retains his connection to that period of his life; Elvira, his secretary at McCready's, made the move with him to Gillorns. And as Marsden realizes, "those years on the underside of the law had left their mark. They had given him an insight into the way people live, an unorthodox perception rare in the legal field, and it tended to make him impatient with the status quo."

Certainly there's little difference in the nature of Kemp's cases between his work as a private inquiry agent and as a lawyer. *Hang the Consequences* and *The Split Second*, both of which take place while Kemp is still in McCready's employ, are missing persons cases. *In Remembrance of Rose* finds Kemp resuming his career as a lawyer, but he's consulted because of his investigative background; the elderly woman who asks Kemp to draft her will believes attempts are being made on her life. In *A Worm of Doubt*, Kemp's client ostensibly asks him for information on having her husband killed because of his affair with a co-worker; when the co-worker dies, Kemp investigates. The difficulty in *The Loose Connection* arises from discord in the law office Kemp manages, but the trail quickly leads to a 20-year-old case of bribery.

Another way in which Kemp's cases resemble American detective novels is his attraction to the striking women Meek creates. Kemp doesn't tumble into bed with any of them, but it's not for lack of interest. Meek is self-conscious enough to acknowledge a pattern which had escaped even Kemp; when Marsden points it out to him in *A Mouthful of Sand*, Kemp is appalled, "struck dumb." *A Mouthful of Sand* skillfully plays on this tendency by contrasting the mysterious and lovely Mirabel Snape against the more conservative Marsden at a point when Kemp and Marsden are evaluating their relationship in order to decide whether to get married. This is Meek's most complex novel and while it's easy to be impatient with the disparate elements of the plot, the conclusion is a stunner.

The consistent excellence of M.R.D. Meek's Lennox Kemp series is a wonder. All of her books can be recommended without reservation.

—Jim Huang

MELDRUM, James. *See* **KYLE, Duncan.**

MELVILLE, James. Pseudonym for (Roy) Peter Martin. British. Born in London, 5 January 1931. Educated at Highbury Grammar School, London, 1942–48; Birkbeck College, University of London, 1948–49, 1951–56, B.A. (honours) in philosophy 1953, M.A. in political philosophy 1956; Tübingen University, 1958–59. Served in the Royal Air Force Education Branch, 1949–51. Married 1) Marjorie Peacock in 1951 (marriage dissolved 1960); 2) Joan Drumwright in 1960 (marriage dissolved 1977), two sons; 3) Catherine Sydee in 1978. Local government officer, London County Council, 1948–49, 1951–54; schoolteacher, London, 1954–56; deputy publicity officer, Royal Festival Hall, London, 1956–60; British Council officer, in Indonesia, Japan, Hungary, and London, 1960–83; posts included cultural attaché, British Embassy, Budapest, and cultural counsellor, British Embassy, Tokyo, from 1979. M.B.E. (Member, Order of the British Empire), 1970. Agent: Curtis Brown, Ltd., 162–168 Regent Street, London W1R 5TB.

CRIME PUBLICATIONS

Novels (series: Superintendent Tetsuo Otani in all books)

The Wages of Zen. London, Secker and Warburg, 1979.
The Chrysanthemum Chain. London, Secker and Warburg, 1980; New York, St. Martin's Press, 1982.
A Sort of Samurai. London, Secker and Warburg, 1981; New York, St. Martin's Press, 1982.
The Ninth Netsuke. London, Secker and Warburg, and New York, St. Martin's Press, 1982.
Sayonara, Sweet Amaryllis. London, Secker and Warburg, 1983; New York, St. Martin's Press, 1984.
Death of a Daimyo. London, Secker and Warburg, 1984.

The Death Ceremony. London, Secker and Warburg, 1985.
Go Gently, Gaijin. London, Secker and Warburg, and New York, St. Martin's Press, 1986.
Kimono for a Corpse. London, Secker and Warburg, 1987; New York, St. Martin's Press, 1988.
The Reluctant Ronin. London, Headline, and New York, Scribner, 1988.
A Haiku for Hanae. London, Headline, and New York, Scribner, 1989.
The Bogus Buddha. London, Headline, 1990.

Uncollected Short Story

"Santa-san Solves It," in *Crime at Christmas*, edited by Jack Adrian. Wellingborough, Northamptonshire, Equation, 1988.

OTHER PUBLICATIONS

Novels

The Imperial Way. London, Deutsch, 1986.
A Tarnished Phoenix. London, Barrie and Jenkins, 1990.

Other as Peter Martin

Japanese Cooking, with Joan Martin. London, Deutsch, 1970; Indianapolis, Bobbs Merrill, 1972.

*

Manuscript Collection: Mugar Memorial Library, Boston University.

James Melville comments:
The primary purpose of my crime writing is to entertain. A subsidiary aim is to communicate to readers in the West a reasonably accurate impression of daily life in urban Japan as experienced by ordinary people, and to highlight some of the areas of misunderstanding resulting from the differing attitudes and cultural conditioning of Japanese and Westerners. Although the format is that of the police procedural, the books are in no sense intended as documentary accounts of Japanese law-enforcement. Characterisation and dialogue are to me more important than plot, and lovers of hard-boiled "realism" will not enjoy my work, from which violence is almost absent, at least overtly. My central character is Superintendent Tetsuo Otani who appears in all my books, with his wife Hanae and his principal lieutenants, Inspectors Jiro Kimura and "Ninja" Noguchi. The murder victim is generally a foreigner resident in Japan, and the action is set in and around the city of Kobe and the Kansai area of western Japan.

* * *

The James Melville mystery novels are a mature and felicitous offshoot of a career in cultural diplomacy. Until recently, their author was Head of the British Council in Tokyo, and his books derive their primary distinction from their unfailing illumination of life in modern Japan. He writes about Japanese mores with authority and affection, with the insight of an intimate and the relish of an enthusiast. The fortunate reader is continually informed as well as entertained.

Much of the appeal of Melville's novels arises from his Japanese policemen: a superintendent, Tetsuo Otani, and two inspectors, Jiro Kimura and "Ninja" Noguchi. Otani heads the third largest force in Japan, in decisive command of nearly nine thousand men. Though properly formidable, with a personal authority to make constables tremble, he is a far cry from the "hateful old-style police" who linger in his memory. He is endearingly human, with curiosity and humour and genial good manners: a sensitive, fallible man with a deep reserve of tenderness for his cherished wife, Hanae.

If the debonair Kimura is his right-hand man, the sinister Noguchi is inescapably his left. Each has a special responsibility: Kimura for foreign residents, Noguchi for drug control. Kimura is an attractive lecher with a liking for Western secretaries and frequent recourse to meticulous disguise. Noguchi needs no such aids: his disreputable appearance is a permanent disguise, and he merges with the background of his accustomed underworld.

The Wages of Zen gives a graceful account of an alien Zen community led by a nest-feathering priest with dubious associates and too much money in the bank. A drugs alert is quickly followed by a murder, and the Japanese detectives confront their assorted foreign suspects. An explosive denouement resolves the larger, political action, and an intimate coda deals gently with a naive and well-intentioned murderer.

The Chrysanthemum Chain involves a young British vice-consul in the complex aftermath of a compatriot's murder, a tangle of blackmail, politics, organised crime, and deviant sex. It's a subtle, alluring book, absorbing as a mystery and deeply fascinating for its insights into Japanese manners and fledgling diplomacy.

In *A Sort of Samurai* Otani himself finds the body, alerted by the howls of the victim's dog. Two old friends of his deceased father participate, one correctly predicting an earthquake, the other earning from Otani the tribute contained in the title. The incidentals include the "odd magic" of the Bunraku puppet theatre and a brave impression of the streamers of Boys' Day.

The Ninth Netsuke puts Hanae in danger and Otani in a limbo of doubt and despair. Anxiety and anger play havoc with his mind: Noguchi loses his trust and Kimura fears for his reason. The crisis evolves from Hanae's discovery of the eighth netsuke in a series of nine: the appearance of the ninth completes the set and agreeably crowns the action.

Sayonara, Sweet Amaryllis links murder by fugu fish with a lucrative drugs trade and attempts to improve the status of Koreans in Japan. The victim is founder of the volatile madrigal group from which the title derives: Kimura sees her collapse and Otani himself confronts her killer. Noguchi appears in an unfamiliar light, as the vulnerable father of a dangerous rebel son.

Death of a Daimyo advances on two fronts: in Japan, where Kimura is in charge, and in England, where Otani and Hanae are on holiday. When the daimyo dies, his heir is not immediately apparent: the gangs muster on the Inland Sea, and the darkest horse dies suddenly on a visit to Cambridge. A resourceful policewoman hoodwinks the succession, while Otani copes with English institutions and the earlier death's outlandish sequel.

—B.A. Pike

———

MELVILLE, Jennie. *See* **BUTLER, Gwendoline.**

———

MEREDITH, Anne. *See* **GILBERT, Anthony.**

———

MERLINI, The Great. *See* **RAWSON, Clayton.**

———

MERRILL, P.J. *See* **ROTH, Holly.**

———

MERTZ, Barbara G. *See* **PETERS, Elizabeth.**

———

MESSER, Mona. *See* **HOCKING, Anne.**

———

MEYER, Nicholas. American. Born in New York City, 24 December 1945. Educated at Fieldston High School, Riverdale, New York; University of Iowa, Iowa City, B.A. in film 1968. Associate publicist, Paramount Pictures, New York, 1968–70; story editor, Warner Brothers, New York, 1970–71. Recipient: Crime Writers Association Gold Dagger award 1975. Agent: C.A.A., 9830 Wilshire Boulevard, Beverly Hills, California 90212, U.S.A.

CRIME PUBLICATIONS

Novels

Target Practice. New York, Harcourt Brace, 1974; London, Hodder and Stoughton, 1975.
The Seven-Per-Cent Solution, Being a Reprint from the Reminiscences of John H. Watson, M.D. New York, Dutton, 1974; London, Hodder and Stoughton, 1975.
The West End Horror: A Posthumous Memoir of John H. Watson, M.D. New York, Dutton and London, Hodder and Stoughton, 1976.
Black Orchid, with Barry J. Kaplan. New York, Dial Press, 1977; London, Corgi, 1978.

OTHER PUBLICATIONS

Novels

The Love Story Story. New York, Avon, 1970.
Confessions of a Homing Pigeon. New York, Doubleday, 1981; London, Hodder and Stoughton, 1982.

Plays

Screenplays: *Invasion of the Bee Girls*, 1973; *The Seven-Per-Cent Solution*, 1976; *Time after Time*, 1979.

Television Plays: *Judge Dee*, from the novel by Robert Gulick, 1974; *The Night That Panicked America*, with Anthony Wilson, 1975; *The Day After*, 1983.

*

Theatrical Activities:

Director: **Play**—*Hamlet*, Beverly Hills, 1984. **Films**—*Time after Time*, 1979; *Star Trek: The Wrath of Khan*, 1982; *Volunteers*, 1985; *The Deceivers*, 1988. **Television**—*The Day After*, 1983; *The Pied Piper*, 1984.

Nicholas Meyer comments:

I try my best to be a story-teller. I do not originate material (as a rule); I stumble onto something that interests me and try to build on it. In this practice I do not know that I differ greatly from other writers of fiction. As to what interests me, I suppose my range is catholic. I read where my nose takes me, not really looking for anything in particular, comic or tragic will do. I am entertained by stories and trust that others may be as well; by entertained, I am not implying superficial or mindless recreation. Good entertainment is supposed to move the reader or audience. *King Lear* is the best entertainment I have ever seen. Sensation in story-telling is all well and good, but shock does not move. It stuns and is not a substitute for the tales that make us laugh or cry. I am not afraid of making demands on an audience. I like to challenge audiences to keep up. By this I do not mean the puerile process of guessing "whodunit." My meaning encompasses rather larger questions and social or moral issues.

*   *   *

Michael Harrison, the noted Sherlock Holmes authority, has commented that Nicholas Meyer "is the brilliant young author of the most successful Sherlockian book of recent years, *The Seven-Per-Cent Solution*"; and in fact not since 1944, when three Sherlockian books were published, has there been generated such an interest in Sherlockiana, and Meyer must be given the credit.

Obviously, there have been a few Sherlockian pastiches published since *The Seven-Per-Cent Solution* and Meyer's sequel, *The West End Horror*, but none has matched the ingenious talent displayed by the young writer from New York. As Harrison further noted, Meyer is a newcomer to the Sherlockian scene, and "it is precisely this quality which enables him to see certain trends in Sherlockian scholarship with a fresh and discerning eye."

Although Meyer received his fair share of criticism from many of the purists, due to the nature of Sherlock Holmes's infatuation with cocaine, Meyer obviously admires Sir Arthur Conan Doyle: "The man didn't know how to write a boring sentence." Meyer further notes that "it is in fact a tribute to Doyle's magnetism and the narcotic appeal of the Sherlock Holmes stories that even today . . . readers both new and old to the Holmes canon come upon them with an enormous sense of relief [that] Holmes did not die." Meyer has contributed significantly to this premise, and, because of him (and some others), Sherlock Holmes continues to live.

—Larry L. French

MEYNELL, Laurence (Walter). Also wrote as Valerie Baxter; Robert Eton; Geoffrey Ludlow; A. Stephen Tring. British. Born in Wolverhampton, Staffordshire, 9 August 1899. Educated at St. Edmund's College, Ware, Hertfordshire. Served in the Honourable Artillery Company during World War I; Royal Air Force, 1939–45: mentioned in despatches. Married 1) Shirley Ruth Darbyshire in 1932 (died 1955), one daughter; 2) Joan Belfrage in 1956 (died 1986). Articled pupil in a land agency, 1920's; worked as a schoolteacher and an estate agent. General editor, Men of the Counties series, Bodley Head, publishers, London, 1955–57; literary editor, *Time and Tide*, London, 1958–60. *Died 14 April 1989.*

CRIME PUBLICATIONS

Novels (series: George Stanhope Berkley; Hooky Hefferman)

Bluefeather (Berkley). London, Harrap, and New York, Appleton, 1928.
Death's Eye. London, Harrap, 1929; as *The Shadow and the Stone*, New York, Appleton, 1929.
Camouflage. London, Harrap, 1930; as *Mystery at Newton Ferry*, Philadelphia, Lippincott, 1930.
Asking for Trouble. London, Ward Lock, 1931.
Consummate Rose. London, Hutchinson, 1931.
Storm Against the Wall. London, Hutchinson, and Philadelphia, Lippincott, 1931.
The House on the Cliff. London, Hutchinson, and Philadelphia, Lippincott, 1932.
Paid in Full. London, Harrap, 1933; as *So Many Doors*, Philadelphia, Lippincott, 1933.
Watch the Wall. London, Harrap, 1933; as *The Gentlemen Go By*, Philadelphia, Lippincott, 1934.
Odds on Bluefeather (Berkley). London, Harrap, 1934; Philadelphia, Lippincott, 1935.
Third Time Unlucky! London, Harrap, 1935.
On the Night of the 18th . . . London, Nicholson and Watson, and New York, Harper, 1936.
The Door in the Wall. London, Nicholson and Watson, and New York, Harper, 1937.
The House in the Hills. London, Nicholson and Watson, 1937; New York, Harper, 1938.
The Dandy. London, Nicholson and Watson, 1938.
The Hut. London, Nicholson and Watson, 1938.
His Aunt Came Late. London, Nicholson and Watson, 1939.
And Be a Villain. London, Nicholson and Watson, 1939.
The Creaking Chair. London, Collins, 1941.
The Dark Square. London, Collins, 1941.
Strange Landing. London, Collins, 1946.
The Evil Hour. London, Collins, 1947.
The Bright Face of Danger. London, Collins, 1948.
The Echo in the Cave. London, Collins, 1949.
The Lady on Platform One. London, Collins, 1950.
Party of Eight. London, Collins, 1950.
The Man No One Knew. London, Collins, 1951.
The Frightened Man (Hefferman). London, Collins, 1952.
Danger round the Corner (Hefferman). London, Collins, 1952.
Too Clever by Half (Hefferman). London, Collins, 1953.
Give Me the Knife. London, Collins, 1954.
Where Is She Now? London, Collins, 1955.
Saturday Out. London, Collins, 1956; New York, Walker, 1962.
The Breaking Point. London, Collins, 1957.
One Step from Murder. London, Collins, 1958.

The Abandoned Doll. London, Collins, 1960.
The House in Marsh Road. London, Collins, 1960.
The Pit in the Garden. London, Collins, 1961.
Virgin Luck. London, Collins, 1963; New York, Simon and Schuster, 1964.
Sleep of the Unjust. London, Collins, 1963.
More Deadly Than the Male. London, Collins, 1964.
Double Fault. London, Collins, 1965.
Die by the Book. London, Collins, 1966.
The Mauve Front Door. London, Collins, 1967.
Death of a Philanderer. London, Collins, 1968; New York, Doubleday, 1969.
Of Malicious Intent. London, Collins, 1969.
The Shelter. London, Hale, 1970.
The Curious Crime of Miss Julia Blossom. London, Macmillan, 1970.
The End of the Long Hot Summer. London, Hale, 1972.
Death by Arrangement (Hefferman). London, Macmillan, and New York, McKay, 1972.
A Little Matter of Arson (Hefferman). London, Macmillan, 1972.
A View from the Terrace. London, Hale, 1972.
The Fatal Flaw (Hefferman). London, Macmillan, 1973; New York, Stein and Day, 1978.
The Thirteen Trumpeters (Hefferman). London, Macmillan, 1973; New York, Stein and Day, 1978.
The Fortunate Miss East. London, Hale, 1973; New York, Coward McCann, 1974.
The Woman in Number Five. London, Hale, 1974; as *Burlington Square*, New York, Coward McCann, 1975.
The Fairly Innocent Little Man (Hefferman). London, Macmillan, 1974; New York, Stein and Day, 1977.
The Footpath. London, Hale, 1975.
Don't Stop for Hooky Hefferman. London, Macmillan, 1975; New York, Stein and Day, 1977.
Hooky and the Crock of Gold. London, Macmillan, 1975.
The Lost Half Hour (Hefferman). London, Macmillan, 1976; New York, Stein and Day, 1977.
Hooky Gets the Wooden Spoon. London, Macmillan, and New York, Stein and Day, 1977.
Papersnake (Hefferman). London, Macmillan, 1978.
Hooky and the Villainous Chauffeur. London, Macmillan, 1979.
Hooky and the Prancing Horse. London, Macmillan, 1980.
Hooky Goes to Blazes. London, Macmillan, 1981.
The Secret of the Pit. London, Macmillan, 1982.
Silver Guilt (Hefferman). London, Macmillan, 1983.
The Open Door (Hefferman). London, Macmillan, 1984.
Hooky Catches a Tartar. London, Macmillan, 1986.
The Abiding Thing. London, Hale, 1986.
Hooky on Loan. London, Macmillan, 1987.
Hooky Hooked. London, Macmillan, 1988.

Uncollected Short Stories

"38," in *My Best Spy Story*. London, Faber, 1938.
"The Cleverest Clue," in *My Best Mystery Story*. London, Faber, 1939.
"Death in My Dreams," in *The Saint* (New York), December 1964.
"Advice to the Cobbler," in *Winter's Crimes 2*, edited by George Hardinge. London, Macmillan, 1970.
"The Winning Trick," in *Winter's Crimes 12*, edited by Hilary Watson. London, Macmillan, 1980.

OTHER PUBLICATIONS

Novels

Mockbeggar. London, Harrap, 1924; New York, Appleton, 1925.
Lois. London, Harrap, and New York, Appleton, 1927.
Inside Out! or, Mad as a Hatter (as Geoffrey Ludlow). London, Harrap, 1934.
Women Had to Do It! (as Geoffrey Ludlow). London, Nicholson and Watson, 1936.
The Sun Will Shine. London, Transworld, 1956.
Moon over Ebury Square. London, Hale, 1962.
The Imperfect Aunt. London, Hale, 1966.
Week-end in the Scampi Belt. London, Hale, 1967.
The Vision Splendid. London, Hale, 1976.
The Folly of Henrietta Dale. London, Hale, 1976.
The Little Kingdom. London, Hale, 1977.
Folly to Be Wise. London, Hale, 1977.
The Dangerous Year. London, Hale, 1978.
The Sisters. London, Hale, 1979.
The Lady Who Wasn't. London, Hale, 1980.
Parasol in the Park. London, Hale, 1981.
The Blue Door. London, Hale, 1982.
The Visitor. London, Hale, 1983.
False Gods. London, Hale, 1984.
Quenells. London, Hale, 1985.
Affair at Barwold. London, Macmillan, 1985.
The Rivals. London, Hale, 1987.

Novels as Robert Eton

The Pattern. London, Harrap, 1934.
The Dividing Air. London, Harrap, 1935.
The Bus Leaves for the Village. London, Nicholson and Watson, 1936.
Not in Our Stars. London, Nicholson and Watson, 1937.
The Journey. London, Nicholson and Watson, 1938.
Palace Pier. London, Nicholson and Watson, 1938.
The Legacy. London, Nicholson and Watson, 1939.
The Faithful Years. London, Nicholson and Watson, 1939.
The Corner of Paradise Place. London, Nicholson and Watson, 1940.
St. Lynn's Advertiser. London, Nicholson and Watson, 1947.
The Dragon at the Gate. London, Nicholson and Watson, 1949.

Fiction (for children)

Smoky Joe. London, Lane, 1952.
Smoky Joe in Trouble. London, Lane, 1953.
Policeman in the Family. London, Oxford University Press, 1953.
Under the Hollies. London, Oxford University Press, 1954.
Bridge under the Water. London, Phoenix House, 1954; New York, Roy, 1957.
Animal Doctor. London, Oxford University Press, 1956.
Smoky Joe Goes to School. London, Lane, 1956.
Sonia Back Stage. London, Chatto and Windus, 1957.
The Young Architect. London, Oxford University Press, 1958.
District Nurse Carter. London, Chatto and Windus, 1958.
Nurse Ross Takes Over. London, Hamish Hamilton, 1958.
The Hunted King. London, Bodley Head, 1959.
Nurse Ross Shows the Way. London, Hamish Hamilton, 1959.
Monica Anson, Travel Agent. London, Chatto and Windus, 1959.
Nurse Ross Saves the Day. London, Hamish Hamilton, 1960.
Bandaberry. London, Bodley Head, 1960.

Nurse Ross and the Doctor.   London, Hamish Hamilton, 1962.
The Dancers in the Reeds.   London, Hamish Hamilton, 1963.
Good Luck, Nurse Ross.   London, Hamish Hamilton, 1963.
Scoop.   London, Hamish Hamilton, 1964.
The Empty Saddle.   London, Hamish Hamilton, 1965.
Break for Summer.   London, Hamish Hamilton, 1965.
Shadow in the Sun.   London, Hamish Hamilton, 1966.
The Suspect Scientist.   London, Hamish Hamilton, 1966.
The Man in the Hut.   London, Kaye and Ward, 1967.
Peter and the Picture Thief.   London, Kaye and Ward, 1969.
Jimmy and the Election.   London, Kaye and Ward, 1970.
Tony Trotter and the Kitten.   London, Kaye and Ward, 1971.
The Great Cup Tie.   London, Kaye and Ward, 1974.

Fiction (for children) as A. Stephen Tring

The Old Gang.   London, Oxford University Press, 1947.
Penny Dreadful.   London, Oxford University Press, 1949.
The Cave by the Sea.   London, Oxford University Press, 1950.
Barry's Exciting Year.   London, Oxford University Press, 1951.
Barry Gets His Wish.   London, Oxford University Press, 1952.
Young Master Carver: A Boy in the Reign of Edward III.   London, Phoenix House, 1952; New York, Roy, 1957.
Penny Triumphant.   London, Oxford University Press, 1953.
Penny Penitent.   London, Oxford University Press, 1953.
Barry's Great Day.   London, Oxford University Press, 1954.
Penny Puzzled.   London, Oxford University Press, 1955.
The Kite Man.   Oxford, Blackwell, 1955.
Penny Dramatic.   London, Oxford University Press, 1956.
Penny in Italy.   London, Oxford University Press, 1957.
Frankie and the Green Umbrella.   London, Hamish Hamilton, 1957.
Pictures for Sale.   London, Hamish Hamilton, 1958.
Penny and the Pageant.   London, Oxford University Press, 1959.
Peter's Busy Day.   London, Hamish Hamilton, 1959.
Ted's Lucky Ball.   London, Hamish Hamilton, 1961.
Penny Says Good-bye.   London, Oxford University Press, 1961.
The Man with the Sack.   London, Hamish Hamilton, 1963.
Chad.   London, Hamish Hamilton, 1966.

Fiction (for children) as Valerie Baxter

Jane: Young Author.   London, Lane, 1954.
Elizabeth: Young Policewoman.   London, Lane, 1955.
Shirley: Young Bookseller.   London, Lane, 1956.
Hester: Ship's Officer.   London, Hamish Hamilton, 1957.

Play

Screenplay: *The Umbrella*, with H. Fowler Mear, 1933.

Verse

The Ballad of Pen Fields, with a Plan of the Battlefield.   Privately printed, 1927.

Other

Bedfordshire.   London, Hale, 1950.
Famous Cricket Grounds.   London, Phoenix House, 1951.
"Plum" Warner.   London, Phoenix House, 1951.
Exmoor.   London, Hale, 1953.

Other (for children)

Builder and Dreamer: A Life of Isambard Kingdom Brunel.   London, Lane, 1952; revised version, as *Isambard Kingdom Brunel*, London, Newnes, 1955.
Rolls, Man of Speed: A Life of Charles Stewart Rolls.   London, Lane, 1953; revised version, as *The Hon. C.S. Rolls*, London, Newnes, 1955.
Great Men of Staffordshire.   London, Lane, 1955.
The First Men to Fly: A Short History of Wilbur and Orville Wright.   London, Laurie, 1955.
James Brindley: The Pioneer of Canals.   London, Laurie, 1956.
Our Patron Saints.   London, Acorn Press, 1957.
Thomas Telford: The Life Story of a Great Engineer.   London, Lane, 1957.
Farm Animals.   London, Ward, 1958.
Airmen on the Run: True Stories of Evasion and Escape by British Airmen of World War II.   London, Odhams Press, 1963.
The Beginning of Words: How English Grew, with Colin Pickles.   London, Blond, 1970; New York, Putnam, 1971.

*

Manuscript Collection: Mugar Memorial Library, Boston University.

*   *   *

Laurence Meynell, a prolific writer in many fields of fiction and non-fiction, may be said to have emerged properly as a crime writer only late in his career with *A View from the Terrace* (1972). In the years following he produced a regular flow of books which may be divided into two distinct sorts. There are the books that have no running hero but generally have some somewhat outré circumstance as their mainspring, and there is the series of charming and salty books that feature "Hooky" Hefferman, a character so well conceived that he lifts the works in which he appears into a class of their own.

It is in these books that the typical Meynell tone of voice, which shows intermittently elsewhere when it is appropriate, comes into its own. Hooky is a man of the bars, and the Meynell voice is a voice heard in bars. But it must be understood what "a man of the bars" is. He is not a bar-fly, someone who can scarcely leave a bar, who cadges drinks and company. He is not, by a long chalk, a drunk. Though he likes drink and is somewhat of a connoisseur of it—Hooky usually drinks a Pimm's No. 1 himself—it is not for the drink alone that he finds bars attractive. It is for the conversation, that special brand of conversation confined to bars. Conversation in clubs and commonrooms may sometimes be as worldly and sometimes more witty, but bar conversation is unique.

So Hooky is most at home in the right sort of bar, and Meynell's characteristic voice is much the voice of bar talk, salty, man-of-the-world, sexy but not dirty, tolerant, with its standards. As to the time that Hooky does not spend in bars, he makes a living, rather a precarious one, as a classy private inquiry agent, having worked once on the edges of journalism. He is often to be found in attractive young ladies' beds (or they may be found in his), but women plainly take only second place in his life. He is sometimes to be found, unwilling and willing, in the flat in sedate Hove, Sussex, where lives his aunt, the formidable, the rich, the Hon. Mrs. Theresa Page-Foley, one of the aunts of literature. Quite often it is this dragon lady who somehow sets Hooky off on some adventure. These are neatly worked out (they might almost be good stage comedies) and show the Hooky virtues—amiability, forcefulness when necessary, and a sort of direct cunning—at their best.

The books outside the Hooky canon are rather more variable. Depending as they generally do on a curious situation or an intriguing set of circumstances, they are apt to be either better or worse according to the effectiveness of their initial premise. Sometimes they will contain, rather unexpectedly, a passage or a character written at a more serious level than the rest of the book. The portrait of a headmistress in *Death of a Philanderer*, an otherwise jaunty whodunit set in a girls' school, is a case in point.

—H.R.F. Keating

————

MICHAELS, Barbara. *See* **PETERS, Elizabeth.**

————

MICHAELS, Steve. *See* **AVALLONE, Michael.**

————

MILLAR, Kenneth. *See* **MACDONALD, Ross.**

————

MILLAR, Margaret (Ellis, née Sturm). American. Born in Kitchener, Ontario, Canada, 5 February 1915. Educated at Kitchener-Waterloo Collegiate Institute, 1929–33; University of Toronto, 1933–36. Married Kenneth Millar, i.e., Ross Macdonald, *q.v.*, in 1938 (died 1983); one daughter (deceased). Screenwriter, Warner Brothers, Hollywood, 1945–46. President, Mystery Writers of America, 1957–58. Recipient: Mystery Writers of America Edgar Allan Poe award, 1956, and Grand Master award, 1982; Los Angeles *Times* Woman of the Year award, 1965. Agent: Harold Ober Associates, 40 East 49th Street, New York, New York 10017.

CRIME PUBLICATIONS

Novels (series: Tom Aragon; Dr. Paul Prye; Inspector Sands)

The Invisible Worm (Prye). New York, Doubleday, 1941; London, Long, 1943.
The Weak-Eyed Bat (Prye). New York, Doubleday, 1942.
The Devil Loves Me (Prye; Sands). New York, Doubleday, 1942.
Wall of Eyes (Sands). New York, Random House, 1943; London, Lancer, 1966.
Fire Will Freeze. New York, Random House, 1944.
The Iron Gates (Sands). New York, Random House, 1945; as *Taste of Fears*, London, Hale, 1950.
Do Evil in Return. New York, Random House, 1950; London, Museum Press, 1952.
Rose's Last Summer. New York, Random House, 1952; London, Museum Press, 1954; as *The Lively Corpse*, New York, Dell, 1956.

Vanish in an Instant. New York, Random House, 1952; London, Museum Press, 1953.
Beast in View. New York, Random House, and London, Gollancz, 1955.
An Air That Kills. New York, Random House, 1957; as *The Soft Talkers*, London, Gollancz, 1957.
The Listening Walls. New York, Random House, and London, Gollancz, 1959.
A Stranger in My Grave. New York, Random House, and London, Gollancz, 1960.
How Like an Angel. New York, Random House, and London, Gollancz, 1962.
The Fiend. New York, Random House, and London, Gollancz, 1964.
Beyond This Point Are Monsters. New York, Random House, 1970; London, Gollancz, 1971.
Ask for Me Tomorrow (Aragon). New York, Random House, 1976; London, Gollancz, 1977.
The Murder of Miranda (Aragon). New York, Random House, 1979; London, Gollancz, 1980.
Mermaid (Aragon). New York, Morrow, and London, Gollancz, 1982.
Banshee. New York, Morrow, and London, Gollancz, 1983.
Spider Webs. New York, Morrow, 1986; London, Gollancz, 1987.

Uncollected Short Stories

"The Couple Next Door," in *Ellery Queen's Awards: Ninth Series*. Boston, Little Brown, 1954; London, Collins, 1956.
"The People Across the Canyon," in *Ellery Queen's Mystery Magazine* (New York), October 1962.
"McGowney's Miracle," in *Every Crime in the Book*. New York, Putnam, 1975.

OTHER PUBLICATIONS

Novels

Experiment in Springtime. New York, Random House, 1947.
It's All in the Family. New York, Random House, 1948.
The Cannibal Heart. New York, Random House, 1949; London, Hamish Hamilton, 1950.
Wives and Lovers. New York, Random House, 1954.

Other

The Birds and Beasts Were There (autobiography). New York, Random House, 1968.

* * *

Following three humorous mystery novels about a somewhat whimsical psychiatrist detective named Paul Prye, Margaret Millar decided to put psychiatry to more serious uses. She took Inspector Sands of the Toronto Police Department, a major secondary character in the last Prye novel, *The Devil Loves Me*, and used him as her lead detective in *Wall of Eyes*. The book was not an immediate success, however, and it wasn't until the second Sands novel, *The Iron Gates*, that she began to attract the critical acclaim she deserved. The bizarre plot elements—a severed finger, an escape from a mental hospital—complemented a solid psychological puzzle that kept the reader guessing till the end. Sadly, these are the only novels about lonely Inspector Sands, though the reader is pleased to encounter him retired to California in a single short story, "The Couple Next Door."

After writing three non-criminous novels, Millar returned to the mystery with *Do Evil in Return* and the more light-hearted *Rose's Last Summer*. *Vanish in an Instant*, set in a Michigan college town during a murderous winter, paved the way for Millar's best novel up to that time, *Beast in View*. Unfortunately, the shock of this book's central plot device has been weakened by repeated use in later books by other authors but rarely has it been done as effectively as here. *Beast in View* was the beginning of a string of exceptional mystery novels. *An Air That Kills* offered a bit of satire along with the mystery, and the next three novels offered something even more special. They are, in a special sense, the peak of the mystery writer's art in that each of them withholds the key element of its solution until the very end of the book.

The first of this special trio was *The Listening Walls*, about an overheard conversation, murder, and a tangled web of trickery that leads to Mexico. The twist, or double twist, is saved until the book's very last words. *A Stranger in My Grave* introduces Steve Pinata, the first private investigator to appear in Millar's novels. Just as the success of her early novels helped launch her husband, Kenneth Millar (Ross Macdonald), on his career as a mystery writer, there is some evidence in *A Stranger in My Grave* and her following novel that she has been influenced by the California tradition of sleuths like Lew Archer. The plot concerns a young woman who dreams she sees her own grave. One day while awake she actually does see it. Like the best of Ross Macdonald's novels the solution lies in the past, in tangled family relationships that are not made completely clear until the last two words of the novel.

The third of this group, and Millar's finest novel, is *How Like an Angel*. Joe Quinn, formerly a Reno casino cop, comes in contact with a California religious cult called the True Believers. Sister Blessing persuades him to investigate the disappearance and possible death of a man named Patrick O'Gorman. Again there is crime in the past, and tangled relationships. But best of all there is a moving and very real portrait of this strange religious community.

Since the mid-1960's, Millar's novels have become less frequent. Their quality has remained high, however. *The Fiend* deals with a possible mental case who may or may not be guilty of child abuse. *Beyond This Point Are Monsters*, set in the San Diego area, offers a moving portrait of Chicanos in the region. And *Ask for Me Tomorrow* follows a young lawyer to Mexico on the trail of a wealthy woman's missing first husband. After scenes in Baja California and a Mexican prison, with murder along the way, the lawyer Tom Aragon reaches the end of his quest—and uncovers a surprising trick of identity worthy of Millar's best novels.

The young Hispanic lawyer Tom Aragon returns in the next two Millar novels, becoming the third of her infrequent series characters. *The Murder of Miranda* has more humor than most of her books, centering around the rich widow of the title and the head lifeguard at a California beach club. In typical Millar fashion, the full meaning of the book's title does not become clear until the final sentence. In *Mermaid*, Tom Aragon is hired to find a retarded young woman, and for its first half the novel reads like some of the better plots of Ross Macdonald. If the ending disappoints, it is only because we have come to expect so much of Millar endings. Aragon is missing from her more recent novel *Banshee*, which deals with the mysterious death of an eight-year-old child. But Millar is back in fine form, with a solution that will surprise most readers. It was fitting the book appeared the same month she received the Grand Master award from the Mystery Writers of America.

Defense attorneys have always held a special fascination for Millar. Before Tom Aragon there was Eric Meecham, the protagonist of *Vanish in an Instant*, and in her most recent novel,

Spider Webs, there is Charles Donnelly, defending the black captain of a private yacht who is accused of murdering a woman passenger for her jewelry. The first words of the book are "All rise," as the trial begins, and the reader follows the case through to the verdict, when a sort of justice is done. It is one of those rare mystery novels that takes place almost entirely in a courtroom, though we also glimpse views of the characters' private lives. If the ending is not as surprising as some of Millar's, it is still a fascinating and rewarding book.

Millar has produced only a handful of short stories. In addition to the Inspector Sands story mentioned above there is a suspense tale entitled "The People Across the Canyon" and a short story, "Notions." She has also written a gem of a story called "McGowney's Miracle," about an undertaker's strange new wife.

Best of all in Millar's novels has been her ability to conjure up what Julian Symons rightly describes as "an atmosphere of uneasiness." Things are never quite right in the worlds she so vividly portrays, and we keep reading to find out why.

—Edward D. Hoch

MILLER, Wade. Pseudonym for Robert Wade and Bill Miller; also wrote as Will Daemer; Whit Masterson; Dale Wilmer. Americans. **MILLER, Bill:** Born in Garrett, Indiana, in 1920. Educated at Woodrow Wilson Junior High School, San Diego; San Diego State College, 1938–42. Served in the United States Air Force in the Pacific 1942–46 during World War II: Sergeant. Married Enid Elena Edwards; one daughter and one son. *Died 21 August 1961.* **WADE, Robert:** Born in San Diego, California, in 1920. Educated at Woodrow Wilson Junior High School, San Diego; San Diego State College. Served in the United States Air Force in Europe during World War II: Sergeant. Married; two daughters and two sons. Wade and Miller began their collaboration while still in school; they edited the East San Diego *Press*, and also wrote radio plays. Since 1977, Wade is columnist ("Spade Work"), San Diego *Union*.

CRIME PUBLICATIONS

Novels (series: Max Thursday)

Deadly Weapon. New York, Farrar Straus, 1946; London, Sampson Low, 1947.
Guilty Bystander (Thursday). New York, Farrar Straus, 1947; London, Sampson Low, 1948.
Pop Goes the Queen (as Bob Wade and Bill Miller). New York, Farrar Straus, 1947; as *Murder—Queen High*, London, W.H. Allen, 1958.
Fatal Step (Thursday). New York, Farrar Straus, 1948; London, Sampson Low, 1949.
Uneasy Street (Thursday). New York, Farrar Straus, 1948; London, Sampson Low, 1949.
Devil on Two Sticks. New York, Farrar Straus, 1949; as *Killer's Choice*, New York, New American Library, 1950.
Calamity Fair (Thursday). New York, Farrar Straus, 1950.
Devil May Care. New York, Fawcett, 1950; London, Fawcett, 1957.
Murder Charge (Thursday). New York, Farrar Straus, 1950.
Stolen Woman. New York, Fawcett, 1950; London, Fawcett, 1958.

The Case of the Lonely Lovers (as Will Daemer). New York, Farrell, 1951.

The Killer. New York, Fawcett, 1951; London, Fawcett, 1957.

Shoot to Kill (Thursday). New York, Farrar Straus, 1951; London, W.H. Allen, 1953.

The Tiger's Wife. New York, Fawcett, 1951; London, Red Seal, 1958.

Branded Woman. New York, Fawcett, 1952; London, Fawcett, 1954.

The Big Guy. New York, Fawcett, 1953; London, Red Seal, 1958.

South of the Sun. New York, Fawcett, and London, Red Seal, 1953.

Mad Baxter. New York, Fawcett, 1955; London, Fawcett, 1956.

Kiss Her Goodbye. New York, Lion, 1956; London, W.H. Allen, 1957.

Kitten with a Whip. New York, Fawcett, 1959; London, Muller, 1960.

Sinner Take All. New York, Fawcett, 1960; London, Muller, 1961.

Nightmare Cruise. New York, Ace, 1961; as *The Sargasso People*, London, W.H. Allen, 1961.

The Girl from Midnight. New York, Fawcett, 1962.

Novels as Dale Wilmer

Memo for Murder. Hasbrouck Heights, New Jersey, Graphic, 1951.

Dead Fall. New York, Bouregy, 1954.

Jungle Heat. New York, Pyramid, 1954; London, Panther, 1962.

Novels as Whit Masterson (continued by Robert Wade alone after 1961)

All Through the Night. New York, Dodd Mead, 1955; London, W.H. Allen, 1956; as *A Cry in the Night*, New York, Bantam, 1956.

Dead, She Was Beautiful. New York, Dodd Mead, and London, W.H. Allen, 1955.

Badge of Evil. New York, Dodd Mead, and London, W.H. Allen, 1956; as *Touch of Evil*, New York, Bantam, 1958.

A Shadow in the Wild. New York, Dodd Mead, and London, W.H. Allen, 1957.

The Dark Fantastic. New York, Dodd Mead, 1959; London, W.H. Allen, 1960.

A Hammer in His Hand. New York, Dodd Mead, and London, W.H. Allen, 1960.

Evil Come, Evil Go. New York, Dodd Mead, and London, W.H. Allen, 1961.

Man on a Nylon String. New York, Dodd Mead, and London, W.H. Allen, 1963.

711—Officer Needs Help. New York, Dodd Mead, 1965; as *Killer with a Badge*, London, W.H. Allen, 1966; as *Warning Shot*, New York, Popular Library, 1967.

Play Like You're Dead. New York, Dodd Mead, 1967; London, Hale, 1969.

The Last One Kills. New York, Dodd Mead, 1969; London, Hale, 1972.

The Death of Me Yet. New York, Dodd Mead, 1970; London, Hale, 1972.

The Gravy Train. New York, Dodd Mead, 1971; London, Hale, 1972; as *The Great Train HiJack*, New York, Pinnacle, 1976.

Why She Cries, I Do Not Know. New York, Dodd Mead, 1972; London, Hale, 1974.

The Undertaker Wind. New York, Dodd Mead, 1973; London, Hale, 1974.

The Man with Two Clocks. New York, Dodd Mead, 1974; London, Hale, 1975.

Hunter of the Blood. New York, Dodd Mead, 1977; London, Hale, 1978.

The Slow Gallows. New York, Dodd Mead, and London, Hale, 1979.

Novels by Robert Wade

The Stroke of Seven. New York, Morrow, 1965; London, Heinemann, 1966.

Knave of Eagles. New York, Random House, 1969; London, Hale, 1970.

Uncollected Short Stories

"Invitation to an Accident," in *Ellery Queen's Awards, 10th Series.* Boston, Little Brown, 1955; London, Collins, 1957.

"A Bad Time of Day," in *Ellery Queen's Awards, 11th Series.* New York, Simon and Schuster, 1956; London, Collins, 1958.

"Midnight Caller," in *Manhunt* (New York), January 1958.

"We Were Picked as the Odd Ones," in *The Saint* (New York), July 1960.

"The Memorial Hour," in *Ellery Queen's 15th Annual.* New York, Random House, 1960; London, Gollancz, 1961.

"The Morning After," in *The Playboy Book of Crime and Suspense.* Chicago, Playboy Press, 1966.

Uncollected Short Stories as Whit Masterson

"The Women in His Life," in *Ellery Queen's 13th Annual.* New York, Random House, 1958; London, Collins, 1960.

"Dark Fantastic," in *Cosmopolitan* (New York), February 1959.

"Suddenly It's Midnight," in *Anthology 1970 Mid-Year*, edited by Ellery Queen. New York, Davis, 1970.

"Seek Him in Shadows," in *Ellery Queen's Mystery Magazine* (New York), 10 March 1980.

*   *   *

In an era when the private-eye novels of Hammett, Chandler, and Macdonald are the subject of serious literary discussion it's odd that virtually no attention is given to the early works of Wade Miller. Certainly Miller's private eye, Max Thursday, is not in the same class as Spade, Marlowe, and Archer, but he is still someone worth knowing, and his six cases, written during a five-year period (1947–1951), are still a pleasure to read.

Even before he created Thursday, Miller wrote an excellent first novel, *Deadly Weapon*. The private eye here is named Walter James, and the novel opens with a murder at a San Diego burlesque house. Also prominent in the proceedings is Lieutenant Austin Clapp of the San Diego police. There is something of the pace and violence of Hammett here, together with an ending unique in the private-eye genre. Though praised at the time of its publication, the book is too little known today.

Miller's next novel, *Guilty Bystander*, introduced the San Diego private detective Max Thursday and brought back Lieutenant Austin Clapp as well. Clapp figures in all of the Thursday novels, occasionally serving as a commentator on violence and the human condition. Thursday's career begins as a house detective in a cheap hotel. He is divorced and drinking too much. He is drawn into a case when his child is kidnapped. The solving of it rehabilitates him and he becomes a successful private eye—though one with a hair-trigger temper that often flares into violence. The first few books end in a burst of violence, until finally he becomes reluctant to carry a gun.

During the late 1940's Miller produced two other fine novels. *Pop Goes the Queen* was published originally as by Bob Wade and Bill Miller, apparently because its amusing plot, involving a young couple in the California desert, was far from the grim realism of the Miller books, but it has a solid mystery plot with a spectacular ending. *Devil on Two Sticks* also offered something new. The "detective" is a member of a criminal gang, chosen by the boss to discover and kill a police informer in their midst. The complete reversal of the usual detective story works quite well; the novel deserves rediscovery.

Shoot to Kill was, unfortunately, the last Wade Miller novel to appear in hardcover. That byline was used during the 1950's on a string of paperback originals like *Kitten with a Whip*, while the authors turned their attention to a new hardcover pseudonym, Whit Masterson. The best of these were probably *All Through the Night*, about a kidnapping; *Badge of Evil*, the basis for the memorable Orson Welles film *Touch of Evil*; and *A Hammer in His Hand*, with a policewoman protagonist.

The authors also wrote three books as Dale Wilmer; the best of these was *Dead Fall*, about murder and espionage in a California aircraft plant.

—Edward D. Hoch

MILNE, A(lan) A(lexander). British. Born in London, 18 January 1882. Educated at Westminster School, London (Queen's Scholar), 1893–1900; Trinity College, Cambridge (Editor, *Granta*, 1902), 1900–03, B.A. (honours) in mathematics 1903. Served in the Royal Warwickshire Regiment, 1914–18. Married Dorothy de Sélincourt in 1913; one son, Christopher Robin Milne. Freelance journalist, 1903–06; assistant editor, *Punch*, London, 1906–14. *Died 31 January 1956.*

CRIME PUBLICATIONS

Novels

The Red House Mystery. London, Methuen, and New York, Dutton, 1922.
Four Days' Wonder. London, Methuen, and New York, Dutton, 1933.

Short Stories

A Table near the Band and Other Stories. London Methuen, and New York, Dutton, 1950.

Uncollected Short Stories

"A Savage Game," and "Bread upon the Waters," in *The Evening Standard Detective Book.* London, Gollancz, 1950.
"It Was a Long Time Ago," in *Ellery Queen's Mystery Magazine* (New York), July 1950.
"It Could Have Happened That Way," in *Ellery Queen's Mystery Magazine* (New York), May 1951.
"Nearly Perfect," in *Best Detective Stories of the Year 1951*, edited by David Coxe Cooke. New York, Dutton, 1951.

"A Perfectly Ordinary Case of Blackmail," in *Ellery Queen's Mystery Magazine* (New York), November 1952.

OTHER PUBLICATIONS

Novels

Lovers in London. London, Alston Rivers, 1905.
Mr. Pim. London, Hodder and Stoughton, 1921; New York, Doran, 1922; as *Mr. Pim Passes By*, London, Methuen, 1929.
Two People. London, Methuen, and New York, Dutton, 1931.
One Year's Time. London, Methuen, 1942.
Chloe Marr. London, Methuen, and New York, Dutton, 1946.

Short Stories

The Secret and Other Stories. London, Methuen, and New York, Fountain Press, 1929.
Birthday Party and Other Stories. New York, Dutton, 1948; London, Methuen, 1949.

Fiction (for children)

Once on a Time. London, Hodder and Stoughton, 1917; New York, Putnam, 1922.
A Gallery of Children. London, Stanley Paul, and Philadelphia, McKay, 1925.
Winnie-the-Pooh. London, Methuen, and New York, Dutton, 1926.
The House at Pooh Corner. London, Methuen, and New York, Dutton, 1928.
Prince Rabbit, and The Princess Who Could Not Laugh. London, Ward, and New York, Dutton, 1966.

Plays

Wurzel-Flummery (produced London, 1917). London and New York, French, 1921; revised version, in *First Plays*, 1919.
Belinda: An April Folly (produced London and New York, 1918). Included in *First Plays*, 1919.
The Boy Comes Home (produced London, 1918). Included in *First Plays*, 1919.
Make-Believe (for children; includes *The Princess and the Woodcutter, Oliver's Island, Father Christmas and the Hubbard Family*), music by George Dorlay, lyrics by C.E. Burton (produced London, 1918). Included in *Second Plays*, 1921.
First Plays (includes *Wurzel-Flummery, The Lucky One, The Boy Comes Home, Belinda, The Red Feathers*). London, Chatto and Windus, and New York, Knopf, 1919.
The Red Feathers (produced Leeds, 1920; London, 1921). Included in *First Plays*, 1919.
The Lucky One (produced New York, 1922; Cambridge, 1923; London, 1924). Included in *First Plays*, 1919; as *Let's All Talk about Gerald* (produced London, 1928).
The Camberley Triangle (produced London, 1919). Included in *Second Plays*, 1921.
Mr. Pim Passes By (produced Manchester, 1919; London, 1920; New York, 1921). Included in *Second Plays*, 1921.
The Romantic Age (produced London, 1920; New York, 1922). Included in *Second Plays*, 1921.
The Stepmother (produced London, 1920). Included in *Second Plays*, 1921.
Second Plays (includes *Make-Believe, Mr. Pim Passes By, The Camberley Triangle, The Romantic Age, The Stepmother*). London, Chatto and Windus, 1921; New York, Knopf, 1922.

The Great Broxopp: Four Chapters in Her Life (produced New York, 1921; London, 1923). Included in *Three Plays*, 1922.

The Truth about Blayds (produced London, 1921; New York, 1922). Included in *Three Plays*, 1922.

The Dover Road (produced New York, 1921; London, 1922). Included in *Three Plays*, 1922.

Three Plays (includes *The Dover Road, The Truth about Blayds, The Great Broxopp*). New York, Putnam, 1922; London, Chatto and Windus, 1923.

Berlud, Unlimited (produced London and New York, 1922).

Success (produced London, 1923; as *Give Me Yesterday*, produced New York, 1931). London, Chatto and Windus, 1923; New York, French, 1924.

The Artist: A Duologue. London and New York, French, 1923.

The Man in the Bowler Hat: A Terribly Exciting Affair (for children; produced New York, 1924; London, 1925). London and New York, French, 1923.

To Have the Honour (produced London, 1924; as *To Meet the Prince*, produced New York, 1929). London and New York, French, 1925.

Ariadne; or, Business First (produced New York and London, 1925). London and New York, French, 1925.

Portrait of a Gentleman in Slippers: A Fairy Tale (produced Liverpool, 1926; London, 1927). London and New York, French, 1926.

King Hilary and the Beggarman (for children; produced London, 1926).

Four Plays (includes *To Have the Honour, Ariadne, Portrait of a Gentleman in Slippers, Success*). London, Chatto and Windus, 1926.

Miss Marlow at Play (produced London, 1927; New York, 1940). London and New York, French, 1936.

The Ivory Door: A Legend (produced New York, 1927; London, 1929). New York, Putnam, 1928; London, Chatto and Windus, 1929.

Gentleman Unknown (produced London, 1928).

The Fourth Wall: A Detective Story (produced London, 1928; as *The Perfect Alibi*, produced New York, 1928). New York, French, 1929; London, French, 1930.

Michael and Mary (produced New York, 1929; London, 1930). London, Chatto and Windus, 1930; New York, French, 1932.

Toad of Toad Hall (for children), music by H. Fraser-Simson, adaptation of the story *The Wind in the Willows* by Kenneth Grahame (produced Liverpool, 1929; London, 1930). London, Methuen, and New York, Scribner, 1929.

They Don't Mean Any Harm (produced London and New York, 1932).

Four Plays (includes *Michael and Mary, To Meet the Prince, The Perfect Alibi, Portrait of a Gentleman in Slippers*). New York, Putnam, 1932.

Other People's Lives (produced London, 1933). London and New York, French, 1935.

More Plays (includes *The Ivory Door, The Fourth Wall, Other People's Lives*). London, Chatto and Windus, 1935.

Miss Elizabeth Bennet, adaptation of the novel *Pride and Prejudice* by Jane Austen (produced London, 1938). London, Chatto and Windus, 1936.

Sarah Simple (produced London, 1937; New York, 1940). London, French, 1939.

The Ugly Duckling (for children). London, French, 1941; in *Twenty-Four Favorite One-Act Plays*, edited by Bennett Cerf and Van H. Cartmell, New York, Doubleday, 1958.

Before the Flood. London and New York, French, 1951.

Screenplays: *The Bump*, 1920; *Five Pounds Reward*, 1920; *Bookworms*, 1920; *Twice Two*, 1920; *Birds of Prey* (*The Perfect Alibi*), with Basil Dean, 1930.

Verse

When We Were Very Young (for children). London, Methuen, and New York, Dutton, 1924.

For the Luncheon Interval: Cricket and Other Verses. London, Methuen, and New York, Dutton, 1925.

Now We Are Six (for children). London, Methuen, and New York, Dutton, 1927.

Behind the Lines. London, Methuen, and New York, Dutton, 1940.

The Norman Church. London, Methuen, 1948.

Other

The Day's Play (*Punch* sketches). London, Methuen, 1910; New York, Dutton, 1925.

The Holiday Round (*Punch* sketches). London, Methuen, 1912; New York, Dutton, 1925.

Once a Week (*Punch* sketches). London, Methuen, 1914; New York, Dutton, 1925.

Happy Days (*Punch* sketches). New York, Doran, 1915.

Not That It Matters. London, Methuen, 1919; New York, Dutton, 1920.

If I May. London, Methuen, 1920; New York, Dutton, 1921.

The Sunny Side. London, Methuen, 1921; New York, Dutton, 1922.

(Selected Works). London, Library Press, 7 vols., 1926.

The Ascent of Man. London, Benn, and New York, Dutton, 1928.

By Way of Introduction. London, Methuen, and New York, Dutton, 1929.

Those Were the Days: The Day's Play, The Holiday Round, Once a Week, The Sunny Side. London, Methuen, and New York, Dutton, 1929.

When I Was Very Young (autobiography). London, Methuen, and New York, Fountain Press, 1930.

A.A. Milne (selections). London, Methuen, 1933.

Peace with Honour: An Enquiry into the War Convention. London, Methuen, and New York, Dutton, 1934; revised edition, 1935.

It's Too Late Now: The Autobiography of a Writer. London, Methuen, 1939; as *Autobiography*, New York, Dutton, 1939.

War with Honour. London, Macmillan, 1940.

War Aims Unlimited. London, Methuen, 1941.

Going Abroad? London, Council for Education in World Citizenship, 1947.

Books for Children: A Reader's Guide. London, Cambridge University Press, 1948.

Year In, Year Out. London, Methuen, and New York, Dutton, 1952.

*

Bibliography: *A.A. Milne: A Handlist of His Writings for Children* by Brian Sibley, Chislehurst Common, Kent, Henry Pootle Press, 1976; *A.A. Milne: A Critical Bibliography* by Tori Haring-Smith, New York, Garland, 1982.

Manuscript Collection: Humanities Research Center, University of Texas, Austin.

Critical Studies: *A.A. Milne* by Thomas Burnett Swann, New York, Twayne, 1971; *The Enchanted Places* by Christopher Milne, London, Eyre Methuen, 1974, New York, Dutton, 1975; *A.A. Milne: His Life* by Ann Thwaite, London, Faber and New York, Random House, 1990.

* * *

Connoisseurs of detective stories differ widely in their assessment of the merits of *The Red House Mystery*. For some—and they must be very numerous, for new editions have been called for repeatedly over a period of more than sixty years—it is almost a masterpiece, a classic of the traditional form which displays the greatest ingenuity, presents an array of memorable and varied characters within the ideal setting for an English murder, and is written with wit and style. The alternative view is that Milne's only detective story is rather irritating. It is not that it is incompetent, but rather the reverse. The trouble is that the book appears rather too obviously to be an exercise in the exploitation of all the conventions of detective fiction popular in the early 1920's. Worse still, the author makes it only too clear that he is amusing himself at the expense of the reader as he doles out fact and opinion in carefully calculated portions. Thus, the reader's appetite is always whetted but never satisfied until the very end, and even then there is a slight feeling of being cheated.

Because A.A. Milne was a humorist working for *Punch*, and the author of some of the best-loved children's literature in the English language, it should not be supposed for one instant that he was ever anything other than a professional writer who enjoyed setting himself very high standards. His attitude was indeed that of the Classicists, for whom it was axiomatic that great art emerged only when authors were prepared to study the rules or conventions of the branch of literature with which they were engaged, took account at every turn of the expectations of their readers (who were themselves supposed to be fully conversant with the tradition to which the new work would belong,) and submitted imagination, observation, and invention to the firm control of the intellect. Drama appealed to Milne precisely because of the technical challenges it threw up, and it was in much the same spirit that he embarked on *The Red House Mystery*.

In his autobiography, *It's Too Late Now*, he records how he came to write it soon after his demobilisation after service in World War I. He had always liked detective stories, and claimed that he "had read most of those that had been written." He added that though he admired their ingenuity he objected to their pompous, unnatural style and to the "anaemic" characters. His ambition was to write "a detective story about real people in real English." As Milne makes plain in a preface to *The Red House Mystery*, he had, moreover, strong views about the correct way to devise a good murder story. Not for him the trained policeman with formidable expertise in forensic science or even the amateur with an exceptional capacity for analysing powders, potions, and drops of blood. He argues that, on the contrary, the sleuth should be like us, with "no more special knowledge than the average reader," and that the means of solving the riddle should be nothing more than acute powers of observation and a talent for "cool inductive reasoning." In other words, the readers should always feel that they ought to be able to do as well as the detective, though, of course, they never can, even if they go back over the pages for a second time, because they are never allowed to realise until too late the significance of the evidence that the author has planted before their very eyes. Milne also firmly believed that his sleuth should "watsonise," by which term he meant that his detective, like Sherlock Holmes, should, at key-points in the narrative, be

prepared to explain patiently to a somewhat slow-witted friend what has been going on and how his thoughts about the case are developing. The result is an increase in what might be called bogus clarity, and the readers' curiosity grows as they realise that for all this assistance they are not really getting any closer to the truth. It is all part of the gentle teasing which Milne holds to be characteristic of good detective fiction. He also deplores any tendency to bring in love interest.

Set in a country house where a cast of interestingly varied characters is assembled at the time of the murder, *The Red House Mystery* exemplifies Milne's principles exactly. The result is a beautifully crafted tale which holds the attention like a well-constructed chess problem. Whether, for all its wealth of closely observed detail and its insights into personalities, it also has that ring of truth which alone make it imperative to solve the mystery, is another question.

—Christopher Smith

———

MILNE, John. British. Born in London, 20 September 1952. Educated at St. Joseph's Academy, Chelsea School of Art, Ravensbourne School of Art, B.A. (honours) in fine art painting, 1980, all London. Married Sarah Letitia Beresford Verity; two sons. Has worked as a policeman, delivery driver, and factory worker. Since 1980 full-time writer. Recipient: Arts Council Creative Writing fellowship, 1983–85; John Llewelyn Rhys prize, 1985. Address: La Poultière, Roz-sur-Covesnon 35610, France.

CRIME PUBLICATIONS

Novels (series: James Jenner)

Tyro. London, Hamish Hamilton, 1982.
London Fields. London, Hamish Hamilton, 1983.
Out of the Blue. London, Hamish Hamilton, 1985.
Dead Birds (Jenner). London, Hamish Hamilton, 1986; New York, Viking, 1987.
Shadow Play (Jenner). London, Heinemann, 1987.
Daddy's Girl (Jenner). London, Heinemann, 1988.
The Moody Man (Jenner). New York, Viking, 1988.

OTHER PUBLICATIONS

Plays

Television Plays: episodes for *The Bill* series, *Bergerac* series, *Boon* series, *Perfect Scoundrels* series, *East Enders* series.

* * *

With the creation of his thoroughly enjoyable and convincing character of the detective James Jenner, John Milne has made his mark as one of the most interesting of the younger English crime writers around. He is a skilled performer in what has recently become known as the new sub-genre of the "London Novel" that has attained a near cult status in some circles.

His three earlier novels were not crime fiction in the usually accepted sense. *Tyro* tells the story of a young squaddy called Joe who is initiated into life in the army, into sexual adulthood and by consequence into the rather brittle literary set in which his girlfriend moves. The action (the search in Northern Ireland, for instance) and the sex scenes have a crisp and authentic feel but most of all the innocence and ordinariness of the central character promises something beyond the ordinary. The London locations ("Sloane Square is a con") work too and the experience of daily life in the capital, immediately recognisable to anybody who has lived there, formed the backbone of the next book, *London Fields*, which tells the story of a young West Indian and his gradual slide into criminal life. This is a more ambitious book, written in the kind of Cockney dialect one can imagine being spoken by Bob Hoskins and divided into sections named after districts of London. Quotations from philosophy (the sceptic Hume) and a sense of the proletarian autobiography suggest a writer with bags of potential, not yet disciplined to a clear goal. *Out of the Blue* is still more ambitious and serious as a novel. It nominally concerns an elusive character, Paul Brown, who tells untrue stories about himself though seems also to be a vehicle to allow the author to ask questions about the reliablity of witnesses and indeed to provoke those self-conscious kinds of questions about the art of writing fiction that University students love to discuss.

In theory my own prejudices are for this kind of intellectual debate over the supposedly less-demanding pleasures of the crime writing genre. However Milne's next three books present a cogent case for the alternative view. In *Dead Birds* he uses his new formula based on the character James Jenner for the first time. "I never dreamed how I'd become a detective" says Jenner, introducing himself, in an instantly recognisable sardonic voice. With a few twists Jenner is the American detectives of Chandler and Hammett translated into an English voice and an English scene. The Inner London suburb of Stoke Newington, experiencing the processes of urban "gentrification" as Milne writes, provides a suitably seedy locale for the action and Milne has a gift for chosing some very English spots (like Audley End) that humanise and localise the genre. Jenner is a shambling Shoestring or Columbo rather than a super smooth or manically vengeful detective. His trademarks are a sense of being on the outside of the social groups he services: he's been pensioned off from the police force with a wooden leg that gives the opportunity for countless situation gags and for continual references to his disabled driver's badge. He doesn't swear in court but affirms. He dislikes the French. His personal life is in a shambles and the torments of his ex-wife add to the complications of the plots. He is always making wry observations to himself, fluently orders "two fingers of Scotch" at the bar, and communicates with the rest of the world largely by means of his telephone answering machine.

In *Shadow Play* the formula is repeated and strengthened. Finding a corpse in the mews flat of a friend, Jenner sets off on a quest for the missing man and the identity of the corpse, which takes him from London to Paris and back. The story becomes an mystery of who is bluffing and who is framing whom, during which he wrestles with a series of distractions, including hostile policemen, his ex-wife and the alluring bombshell Esmerelda Potts.

Daddy's Girl also begins with a corpse and allows the play with the Anglo-French locations to continue. Milne likes a literary joke too, using the associations between Jenner's Stoke Newington and the writer Daniel Defoe to gain some effective authenticating distance from the classical writers of English fiction and to make some subtle comparisons with them too. The missing girl, the search for whom provides the main plot strand of *Daddy's Girl* doesn't appear until well into the book. This is typical of the way in which the experience of Jenner's personality and life and the local settings provide most of the

reading pleasure in these books, almost to the extent that their plots sit in the background and it may be that in more original and more tightly plotted action Milne's best direction for development can be found.

—Richard Brown

MITCHELL, Gladys (Maude Winifred). Also wrote as Stephen Hockaby; Malcolm Torrie. British. Born in Cowley, Oxfordshire, 19 April 1901. Educated at Rothschild School, Brentford, Middlesex; the Green School, Isleworth, Middlesex; Goldsmiths' College, University of London, 1919–21; University College, London, external diploma in history 1926. Taught English and history at St. Paul's School, Brentford, Middlesex, 1921–25, St. Ann's Senior Girls' School, Ealing, London, 1925–39, Senior Girls' School, Brentford, 1941–50, and Matthew Arnold School, Staines, Middlesex, 1953–61. Recipient: Crime Writers Association special award, 1975. *Died 27 July 1983.*

CRIME PUBLICATIONS

Novels (series: Mrs. Beatrice Lestrange Bradley in all books)

Speedy Death. London, Gollancz, and New York, Dial Press, 1929.
The Mystery of a Butcher's Shop. London, Gollancz, 1929; New York, Dial Press, 1930.
The Longer Bodies. London, Gollancz, 1930.
The Saltmarsh Murders. London, Gollancz, 1932; Philadelphia, Macrae Smith, 1933.
Ask a Policeman, with others. London, Barker, and New York, Morrow, 1933.
Death at the Opera. London, Grayson, 1934; as *Death in the Wet,* Philadelphia, Macrae Smith, 1934.
The Devil at Saxon Wall. London, Grayson, 1935.
Dead Men's Morris. London, Joseph, 1936.
Come Away, Death. London, Joseph, 1937.
St. Peter's Finger. London, Joseph, 1938; New York, St. Martin's Press, 1987.
Printer's Error. London, Joseph, 1939.
Brazen Tongue. London, Joseph, 1940.
Hangman's Curfew. London, Joseph, 1941.
When Last I Died. London, Joseph, 1941; New York, Knopf, 1942.
Laurels Are Poison. London, Joseph, 1942.
The Worsted Viper. London, Joseph, 1943.
Sunset over Soho. London, Joseph, 1943.
My Father Sleeps. London, Joseph, 1944.
The Rising of the Moon. London, Joseph, 1945; New York, St. Martin's Press, 1984.
Here Comes a Chopper. London, Joseph, 1946.
Death and the Maiden. London, Joseph, 1947.
The Dancing Druids. London, Joseph, 1948.
Tom Brown's Body. London, Joseph, 1949.
Groaning Spinney. London, Joseph, 1950.
The Devil's Elbow. London, Joseph, 1951.
The Echoing Strangers. London, Joseph, 1952.
Merlin's Furlong. London, Joseph, 1953.
Faintley Speaking. London, Joseph, 1954; New York, St. Martin's Press, 1986.

Watson's Choice. London, Joseph, 1955; New York, McKay, 1976.

Twelve Horses and the Hangman's Noose. London, Joseph, 1956; New York, British Book Centre, 1958; as *Hangman's Noose*, London, Severn House, 1983.

The Twenty-Third Man. London, Joseph, 1957.

Spotted Hemlock. London, Joseph, 1958; New York, St. Martin's Press, 1985.

The Man Who Grew Tomatoes. London, Joseph, and New York, British Book Centre, 1959.

Say It with Flowers. London, Joseph, and New York, London House, 1960.

The Nodding Canaries. London, Joseph, 1961.

My Bones Will Keep. London, Joseph, and New York, British Book Centre, 1962.

Adders on the Heath. London, Joseph, and New York, British Book Centre, 1963.

Death of a Delft Blue. London, Joseph, 1964; New York, British Book Centre, 1965.

Pageant of Murder. London, Joseph, and New York, British Book Centre, 1965.

The Croaking Raven. London, Joseph, 1966.

Skeleton Island. London, Joseph, 1967.

Three Quick and Five Dead. London, Joseph, 1968.

Dance to Your Daddy. London, Joseph, 1969.

Gory Dew. London, Joseph, 1970.

Lament for Leto. London, Joseph, 1971.

A Hearse on May-Day. London, Joseph, 1972.

The Murder of Busy Lizzie. London, Joseph, 1973.

A Javelin for Jonah. London, Joseph, 1974.

Winking at the Brim. London, Joseph, 1974; New York, McKay, 1977.

Convent on Styx. London, Joseph, 1975.

Late, Late in the Evening. London, Joseph, 1976.

Noonday and Night. London, Joseph, 1977.

Fault in the Structure. London, Joseph, 1977.

Wraiths and Changelings. London, Joseph, 1978.

Mingled with Venom. London, Joseph, 1978.

Nest of Vipers. London, Joseph, 1979.

The Mudflats of the Dead. London, Joseph, 1979.

Uncoffin'd Clay. London, Joseph, 1980; New York, St. Martin's Press, 1982.

The Whispering Knights. London, Joseph, 1980.

The Death-Cap Dancers. London, Joseph, and New York, St. Martin's Press, 1981.

Lovers, Make Moan. London, Joseph, 1982.

Here Lies Gloria Mundy. London, Joseph, 1982; New York, St. Martin's Press, 1983.

Death of a Burrowing Mole. London, Joseph, 1982.

The Greenstone Griffins. London, Joseph, 1983.

Cold, Lone, and Still. London, Joseph, 1983.

Crime on the Coast, and No Flowers by Request, with others. London, Gollancz, 1984.

No Winding Sheet. London, Joseph, 1984.

The Crozier Pharaohs. London, Joseph, 1984.

Novels as Malcolm Torrie (series: Timothy Herring in all books)

Heavy as Lead. London, Joseph, 1966.

Late and Cold. London, Joseph, 1967.

Your Secret Friend. London, Joseph, 1968.

Churchyard Salad. London, Joseph, 1969.

Shades of Darkness. London, Joseph, 1970.

Bismarck Herrings. London, Joseph, 1971.

Uncollected Short Stories

"The Case of the 100 Cats," in *Fifty Famous Detectives of Fiction.* London, Odhams Press, 1938.

"Daisy Bell," in *Detective Stories of Today*, edited by Raymond Postgate. London, Faber, 1940.

"Stranger's Hall," and "A Light on Murder," in *The Evening Standard Detective Book.* London, Gollancz, 1950.

"Rushy Glen," in *The Evening Standard* (London), 5 June 1950.

"Juniper Gammon," in *The Evening Standard* (London), 5 June 1950.

"The Jar of Ginger," and "Manor Park," in *The Evening Standard Detective Book*, 2nd series. London, Gollancz, 1951.

"The Knife," in *The Evening Standard* (London), 11 January 1951.

"Practical Joke," in *The Evening Standard* (London), 19 January 1951.

"Our Pageant," in *The Evening Standard* (London), 19 September 1951.

"Sammy," in *The Evening Standard* (London), 19 September 1951.

"The Tree," in *The Evening Standard* (London), 21 September 1951.

"Peach Jam," in *The Evening Standard* (London), 6 November 1951.

"The Plumb-Line," in *The Evening Standard* (London), 13 November 1951.

"Haunted House," in *The Evening Standard* (London), 9 February 1952.

"The Falling Petals," in *The Evening Standard* (London), 6 March 1952.

"The Price of Lead," in *The Evening Standard* (London), 6 June 1952.

"The Spell," in *The Evening Standard* (London), 14 June 1952.

"A Bit of Garden," in *The Evening Standard* (London), 18 June 1952.

"The Swimming Gala," in *The Evening Standard* (London), 25 July 1952.

"The Tooth-Pick," in *The Evening Standard* (London), 3 October 1952.

"The Bodkin," in *The Evening Standard* (London), 11 October 1952.

"The Boxer," in *The Evening Standard* (London), 17 January 1953.

"The Visitor," in *The Evening Standard* (London), 4 February 1953.

"Oversight," in *The Evening Standard* (London), 13 February 1953.

"The Manuscript," in *The Evening Standard* (London), 11 May 1953.

"The Fish Pond," in *The Evening Standard* (London), 19 May 1953.

"Alibi," in *The Evening Standard* (London), 23 May 1953.

"The Vacuum Cleaner," in *The Evening Standard* (London), 2 July 1953.

"Arsenic in the House," in *The Evening Standard* (London), 6 June 1956.

OTHER PUBLICATIONS

Novels as Stephen Hockaby

Marsh Hay. London, Grayson, 1933.

Seven Stars and Orion. London, Grayson, 1934.

Gabriel's Hold. London, Grayson, 1935.

Shallow Brown. London, Joseph, 1936.
Grand Master. London, Joseph, 1939.

Other

Outlaws of the Border (for children). London, Pitman, 1936.
The Three Fingerprints (for children). London, Heinemann, 1940.
Holiday River (for children). London, Evans, 1948.
The Seven Stones Mystery (for children). London, Evans, 1949.
The Malory Secret (for children). London, Evans, 1950.
Pam at Storne Castle (for children). London, Evans, 1951.
Caravan Creek. London, Blackie, 1954.
On Your Marks (for children). London, Heinemann, 1954; revised edition, London, Parrish, 1964.
The Light-Blue Hills (for children). London, Bodley Head, 1959.
"Why Do People Read Detective Stories?," in *Murder Ink: The Mystery Reader's Companion*, edited by Dilys Winn. New York, Workman, 1977.

* * *

There is no doubt that Gladys Mitchell is a special taste and that, even among her admirers, a careful reading of her large *oeuvre* will reinforce affectionately held ambivalences. She has been little published in the United States since the beginning of her career. Yet to mystery readers in England who have followed the classic school she is practically an institution. What is more, from her "retirement" (after many years as a schoolteacher and games-mistress) in a tiny village in Dorset, this *grande dame* of the genre produced a book a year. It is worth remembering too, that Mitchell was an early member of the justly famous Detection Club, whose active participants included such luminaries as Chesterton, Sayers, and Christie.

With the release of *Speedy Death* in 1929, Mitchell unleashed upon the proverbially unsuspecting public that repellently delightful, now immortal, sleuth, Beatrice Adela Lestrange Bradley. It can be said that Mrs. Bradley, later Dame Beatrice, makes in *Speedy Death* a debut which no other detective of such longevity can match. To wit, she *commits* the novel's second murder, is put on trial for it, is pronounced not guilty by a jury, and then blithely admits her culpability to her defense lawyer (who just happens to be her son by her first marriage). And, on top of all this, the reader has to swallow the fact that the first corpse is a well-known, virile explorer who, when found drowned and naked in the bath, turns out to be a woman!

To put it mildly, eccentric goings-on are Mitchell's hallmark. And although some critics have felt that her plots suffered from too much attention paid to witchcraft, the supernatural, and folklore esoterica, this proclivity is what gives her work a consistent flavor, fine for those who like it and to be avoided by those who don't.

A secondary consideration, meshing with the above tendencies, is Mitchell's special feeling for the mystical nature of things British. Barrows and earthworks and Arthurian relics, morris dancing and May-day rituals: all of these are carefully and intricately dealt into the stories illustrating Mitchell's lifelong fascination with the antiquities of the British Isles and their accompanying superstitions. The "green man" of legend figures in one book, and, Mitchell being an unregenerate believer in the Loch Ness monster, a cousin of "Nessie" surfaces to wink a wet eye at Mrs. Bradley's niece in another.

Mrs. Bradley, it seems likely, is a partial stand-in for her creator, for their interests are identical. However, the former is already of an advanced age when first we meet her, in *Speedy Death*, and remains pretty much the same in the years and titles thereafter. Her official profession is that of psychologist, and she runs a clinic and is also a consultant to the Home Office. She is the author of *A Small Handbook of Psychoanalysis*, and her detecting methods combine hocus-pocus and Freud, seasoned with sarcasm and the patience of a predator toying with its intended victim. Those familiar with the many books featuring Mrs. Bradley are aware that her physical appearance is singular, for she is said to look like a sinister pterodactyl with a Cheshire Cat smile. Yet, though she is shrivelled and crone-like, she has a wonderful, treacle-smooth speaking voice, and, in the manner of the best village witches, she is mesmerizing to, and adored by, children and animals.

In addition to writing the Bradley adventures, Mitchell also wrote under two pseudonyms, Stephen Hockaby and Malcolm Torrie. There seems to be no particular reason why these are masculine, although the Torrie books have a hero (eventually joined by a wife), Timothy Herring, who runs a society for the Preservation of Buildings of Historic Interest. It is really not possible to single out Mitchell's most important book or her greatest achievement; at different times *The Rising of the Moon*, *Sunset over Soho*, *The Saltmarsh Murders*, and *Watson's Choice* have been highly acclaimed. A survivor of the Golden Age, Mitchell was significant, most of all, because she was *sui generis*.

—Michele Slung

———

MITCHELL, James (William). Also writes as James Munro. British. Born in South Shields, County Durham, 12 March 1926. Educated at St. Edmund Hall, Oxford, B.A. 1948, M.A. 1950; University of Durham, diploma in education 1950. Married; two sons. Actor and travel agent in Britain and Paris, 1948–50; Lecturer in English, South Shields Technical College, 1950–59; television writer, London, 1959–63; Lecturer in Liberal Studies, Sunderland College of Art, County Durham, 1963–64. Agent: Blake Friedmann Literary Agency Ltd., 37–41 Gower Street, London WC1E 6HH, England.

CRIME PUBLICATIONS

Novels (series: David Callan; Ron Hogget)

Here's a Villain! London, Davies, 1957; as *The Lady Is Waiting*, New York, Morrow, 1958.
A Way Back. London, Davies, 1959; as *The Way Back*, New York, Morrow, 1960.
Steady Boys, Steady. London, Davies, 1960.
Among Arabian Sands. London, Davies, 1962.
A Magnum for Schneider. London, Jenkins, 1969; as *A Red File for Callan*, New York, Simon and Schuster, 1971; as *Callan*, London, Corgi, 1974.
Ilion Like a Mist. London, Cassell, 1969; as *Venus in Plastic*, London, Corgi, 1970.
The Winners. London, Cassell, 1970.
Russian Roulette (Callan). London, Hamish Hamilton, and New York, Morrow, 1973.
Death and Bright Water (Callan). London, Hamish Hamilton, and New York, Morrow, 1974.
Smear Job (Callan). London, Hamish Hamilton, 1975; New York, Putnam, 1977.
The Evil Ones. London, Hamish Hamilton, 1982.

Sometimes You Could Die (Hogget).   London, Hamish Hamilton, 1985.
Dead Ernest (Hogget).   London, Hamish Hamilton, 1986; New York, Holt, 1987.
KGB Kill.   London, Hamish Hamilton, 1987.
Dying Day (Hogget).   London, Hamish Hamilton, 1988; New York, Holt, 1989.
A Woman to Be Loved.   London, Sinclair Stevenson, 1990.

Novels as James Munro (series: James Craig in all books)

The Man Who Sold Death.   London, Hammond, 1964; New York, Knopf, 1965.
Die Rich, Die Happy.   London, Hammond, 1965; New York, Knopf, 1966.
The Money That Money Can't Buy.   London, Hammond, 1967; New York, Knopf, 1968.
The Innocent Bystanders.   London, Jenkins, 1969; New York, Knopf, 1970.

OTHER PUBLICATIONS

Novels (novelizations of television series)

When the Boat Comes In.   London, Hamish Hamilton, 1976.
The Hungry Years.   London, Hamish Hamilton, 1976.
Upwards and Onwards.   London, Hamish Hamilton, 1977.
Goodbye Darling.   London, Hamish Hamilton, 1980.

Plays

Soldier in the Snow, with John Hearne (televised, 1960).
      Published in *New Granada Plays*, London, Faber, 1960.
The Wreckers (produced Newcastle upon Tyne, 1969).

Screenplays: *Innocent Bystanders*, 1972; *Callan*, 1974.

Television Plays: *Soldier in the Snow*, with John Hearne, 1960; *Flight from Treason*, 1960; *Omega Mystery*, 1961; *Immortal Clay*, 1963; *The Lovely Crime*, 1964; *Fresh Off the Boat*, 1966; *Live Like a Man*, 1966; *Magnum for Schneider*, 1967; *Callan*, 1967; *Charlie Says It's Goodbye*, 1974; *Maude*, 1981; *Goodbye Darling*, 1981; *Lina*, 1981; *Janet*, 1981; *Barbara*, 1981; *Daisy*, 1981; *Callan Wet Job*, 1981; *Spyship*, 1983; *Anzac*, 1988; *Confessional*, from the novel by Jack Higgins, 1989.

                              *

James Mitchell comments:
    The writing of thrillers is a craft, and to be acknowledged as a craftsman would for me be more than adequate praise.
    The thriller writer's skills are construction, characterization, and the adroit use of language. This is obvious; it is also extremely difficult to achieve. I have been trying to achieve it in novels and television plays for more than 20 years.
    Thrillers—at least the ones I write—deal with men who live in isolation, and who are subject to the pressures of pursuit, the risks of capture and ultimately death. Certainly the men are remarkable, but then so are the pressures and the risks. They survive because they too are craftsmen, with guns, knives, their bare hands—and with their brains too. They are heroes not because they kill—their opponents do that as well as they—but because, despite the things they must do, they believe in goodness to the point where they will die for it.

                       *   *   *

James Mitchell is best known for his series featuring spy David Callan—and as "James Munro" he gained popularity in the 1960's with the creation of the British agent James Craig.
    Mitchell's agents lack the glitz and glamor of James Bond. He creates a world of espionage where no one can be trusted and in which most agents and their controllers operate unethically. It's a gray, shabby world like the one described in le Carré's *The Spy Who Came in from the Cold.*
    In the Munro books, Mitchell depicts James Craig as a violent but ethical agent. In *The Man Who Sold Death* Craig is a shipping line executive who discovers one of his ships was destroyed by a man wanted by British Intelligence. Craig's success on this mission leads him to search for a missing Greek millionaire named Harry Naxos in *Die Rich, Die Happy.* Yet Craig finds working for Department K and his superior, Loomis, increasingly loathsome, especially in *The Innocent Bystanders* where Loomis uses Craig as a decoy in a plot to kidnap a Russian scientist. In *The Money That Money Can't Buy*, Craig is brutalized and tortured; he vows never to work for Department K and the duplicitious Loomis again. But Mitchell leaves the reader with the knowledge that Loomis has so limited Craig's options that Craig will be forced to work for Department K and Loomis again.
    The David Callan books are similar to the James Craig books. In both series characters, Mitchell explores the implications of agents being more ethical than the espionage organizations and controllers they serve.
    Callan is used by his superior Hunter on especially dangerous missions. In *A Magnum for Schneider*, Callan is ordered to kill an importer named Schneider. But Callan discovers that his mission is more complex than Hunter led him to believe. Hunter emerges as amoral when he manipulates Callan's life secretly in order to use Callan in a trade with the KGB for another British agent. Callan uses all his resourcefulness to avoid the trap and vows never to work for Hunter and his secret department again. But Hunter knows he can manipulate Callan into returning to work.
    Hunter has Callan back to work in *Death and Bright Water*, one of Mitchell's best plotted novels. Then Hunter orders Callan to search for Marx's *Das Kapital* in *Smear Job*, a perfect study in misinformation. The Callan series is one of the best in British spy fiction.
    Mitchell's latest series features London private eye Ron Hogget whose expertise is finding lost items. In *Sometimes You Could Die*, Hogget finds an Athenian deodrachm from 470 BC worth a quarter of a million dollars. Hogget's client, American millionaire Martin Donner, is so impressed by Hogget's success in finding the coin, he hires Hogget and his partner Dave Baxter to find his wife's murderers. Hogget finds the murderers, but finds himself on the list of their next victims. In *Dead Ernest*, Hogget is hired by the incredibly wealthy Imogen Courtenay-Lithgoe to find her horse, Finn MacCool, and her fiancé, Ernest Fluck. Hogget and his violent partner Dave travel to Ireland, Spain, and Australia before Hogget solves the case.
    In *Dying Day*, Hogget is hired to find an airplane that's been missing for 40 years. Hogget's methods are unique and the action is swift and furious as Hogget and Dave solve the mystery behind the missing plane. The Ron Hogget books are as bright and breezy as the Callan and Craig books are dark and serious. This is a refreshing change of style for Mitchell.
    However, Mitchell is still capable of writing a riveting, gritty spy novel: *KGB Kill.* British agents Joe Cave and Sandy Keith are hunted by KGB executioners through France, Spain, Hong Kong, Australia, and Switzerland. The action and suspense of

KGB Kill rank with the best novels of the Callan and Craig series.

—George Kelley

MOFFAT, Gwen. British. Born in Brighton, Sussex, 3 July 1924. Educated at Hove County Grammar School, Sussex 1935–41. Served in the Auxiliary Territorial Service, 1943–47. Married 1) Gordon Moffat in 1948, one daughter; 2) John Lees in 1956. Has worked as a mountain guide; frequent broadcaster and contributor to newspapers on mountain climbing, travel, camping, and related subjects. Recipient: Welsh Arts Council bursary, 1973; Agent: A.M. Heath and Company Ltd., 79 St. Martin's Lane, London WC2N 4AA. Address: c/o Macmillan Publishers Ltd., 4 Little Essex Street, London WC2R 3LF, England.

CRIME PUBLICATIONS

Novels (series: Melinda Pink in all books except *Deviant Death* and *The Corpse Road*)

Lady with a Cool Eye. London, Gollancz, 1973.
Deviant Death. London, Gollancz, 1973.
The Corpse Road. London, Gollancz, 1974.
Hard Pink at the Edge of the World. London, Gollancz, and New York, Scribner, 1975.
Over the Sea to Death. London, Gollancz, and New York, Scribner, 1976.
A Short Time to Live. London, Gollancz, 1976.
Persons Unknown. London, Gollancz, 1978.
Die Like a Dog. London, Gollancz, 1982.
Last Chance Country. London, Gollancz, 1983.
Grizzly Trail. London, Gollancz, 1984.
Snare. London, Macmillan, and New York, St. Martin's Press, 1987.
The Stone Hawk. London, Macmillan, and New York, St. Martin's Press, 1989.
Rage. London, Macmillan, and New York, St. Martin's Press, 1990.
The Raptor Zone. London, Macmillan, 1990.

OTHER PUBLICATIONS

Novels

Hard Option. London, Gollancz, 1975.
The Buckskin Girl. London, Gollancz, 1982.

Other

Space Below My Feet (autobiography). London, Hodder and Stoughton, and Boston, Houghton Mifflin, 1961.
Two Star Red: A Book about R.A.F. Mountain Rescue. London, Hodder and Stoughton, 1964.
On My Home Ground (on climbing). London, Hodder and Stoughton, 1968.
Survival Count (on conservation). London, Gollancz, 1972.
Hard Road West: Alone on the California Trail. London, Gollancz, and New York, Viking Press, 1981.

The Storm Seekers: A Journey in the Footsteps of Charles Frémont (travel). London, Secker and Warburg, 1989.

*

Gwen Moffat comments:

I came to writing by way of my autobiography, *Space Below My Feet*, which described the thrills of my life and work as a climber in Britain and the Alps.

In the 1970's I switched from hard rock to crime. At first my mysteries were set in the wilder parts of the United Kingdom but after Gollancz and Viking commissioned *Hard Road West* (on the trail to California) I fell in love with the American West.

My special interest lies in seeking out remote corners in romantic places, whether in Death Valley or the Rockies, the Colorado canyons or the coast of Oregon. Here, in isolated places it pleases me to inject murder.

For my research I travel rough, by jeep where possible, on horseback or on foot in the wilderness. The books are written close to their subject; adobe houses in the desert and the Rio Grande valley, a log cabin in Montana, on a ranch where I learned to work cattle in bear country for *Grizzly Trail*. In 12 of the novels Miss Pink (hard-riding, tweedy, a pillar of the Women's Institute back home, is the investigator) endearing but implacable in the face of murder in the first degree.

Currently I live in Cumbria, within sight of the Lakeland fells, a region that was the location for *The Corpse Road* and *A Short Time to Live*, and which forms the background for the mystery I am working on, based in the Vale of Eden.

*   *   *

Among women writing mysteries, Gwen Moffat may well be unique, for she has created a woman detective who has the character and resources to face physical danger, yet never becomes a caricature or literary device. Miss Melinda Pink is a Justice of the Peace in England, a mountaineer, and a novelist. She is not afraid of the risks of a hostile and rugged environment, be it the Scottish Highlands in bad weather or the North American Rockies with their wild animals, and her adventures resonate with the experiences of her creator. Unlike her female counterparts in other series, however, Pink never teams up with a man and never appears to have greater intellectual powers than those around her. What she does have is a breadth of experience and the kind of judgment and perception that can only come from an uncompromising look at life. Like other people who grow up in a harsh environment, be it mountain or desert, she is capable of deep compassion where deserved and hard practicality when necessary.

All of the Pink stories are set in mountain regions, in Great Britain or the United States, and the landscape often plays an integral role in the plot. In *Miss Pink at the Edge of the World*, the placid life in a Highland village is interrupted by a group of rock climbers making a movie. The signs of danger are obvious: the lead climber, a man named Stark, enjoys baiting people, including his own climbing partner. Although it is not an obvious theme, Moffat's tales inevitably serve as glosses on people who are so arrogant as to underestimate the cost of carelessness in an unforgiving land. Other novels set in Scotland are *Over the Sea to Death* and *Snare*.

In *Persons Unknown*, the setting is a village near the coast of Wales and the background theme is nuclear power. Roderick Brown has just defeated the effort of the Atomic Energy Authority to build a fast-breeder reactor on his property. Just before he is to celebrate that and his 85th birthday, he falls down a flight of steps. He insists he was pushed, but no one believes him. In this and the next book, *Die Like a Dog*, Moffat offers an intimate view of the Welsh landscape and what it is that the local residents are trying to preserve.

In the 1980's Pink discovered the mountains and deserts of the American West and Moffat turns her clear eye on both the people and the landscape of the western United States. In *Last Chance Country*, Pink visits Sweetwater Ranch in Arizona, the home of a millionaire and isolated from everyone and everything except for a small gas station and motel on the highway. In *Grizzly Trail*, Miss Pink visits Prosper, Montana, where she explores the Rocky Mountains and learns about grizzly bears. In both stories, Moffat depicts the lives of young people who are born and raised in desolate and isolated circumstances, and their interaction with outsiders who find solitude a novelty. In her most recent work, *The Stone Hawk*, Pink travels to Salvation Canyon, Utah, where she rents a small house in a canyon with eight other families. The layout of the landscape—its buttes, trails, canyons, creeks—is a large part of the story, and the characters are truly of their land. The role of the land in shaping character is most readily seen in the children, who are alert and watchful and without sentiment, qualities necessary for survival in the hard landscape they live in. Moffat also deals here with the permutations of child abuse and neglect in a forthright manner devoid of sentimentality, but not without understanding and compassion.

Moffat has written mysteries without her series character. In *Deviant Death*, for example, Ruth Stanton, a novelist, investigates the disappearance of Olive Lynch, who caught her husband with a young woman, Judy Scroop, who also disappears, leaving behind six illegitimate children. Here again, Moffat looks at how children cope in a setting that affords them little of the life professionals think necessary for healthy growth.

Moffat's strengths are her series character and the settings. Pink is a woman who faces the physical danger of mountaineering with forethought and deceptive calm, "deceptive" in that her attitude masks at times from the reader the seriousness of the danger she sometimes finds herself in. In the same way, calmly and matter of factly, she presents her (or Moffat's) views on such issues as nuclear power, the death penalty, conservation, and environmentalism, but never allows the topic at hand to overwhelm the story. It is an understatement to say that any discussion is low key, but every comment is precise and every view justified in the context. For readers who are tired of heroes and heroines who must swagger to show their strength or brag to prove their toughness, Melinda Pink is the breeze of sanity, an example of a woman detective who is honest, realistic, and competent without compromise.

—Susan Oleskiw

* * *

MONAHAN, John. *See* **BURNETT, W.R.**

* * *

MONIG, Christopher. *See* **CROSSEN, Ken.**

* * *

MOODY, Susan (Elizabeth, née Horwood). Has also written as Susannah James. British. Born in Oxford. Educated at Oxford High School for Girls, 1951–59; Open University, 1973–78, B.A. Married 1) Walter F. Bertsch in 1961 (died), two sons; 2) John Moody in 1973, one son. Creative writing tutor, H.M. Prison, Bedford, 1983–85. Vice-chair, 1988–89, and chair, 1989–90, Crime Writers Association, London; executive council member, International Association of Crime Writers (AIEP), 1989. Agent: June Hall Literary Agency, 5th Floor, The Chambers, Chelsea Harbour, Lots Road, London, SW10 0XF, England.

CRIME PUBLICATIONS

Novels (series: Penny Wanawake in all books except *Playing With Fire*)

Penny Black.   London, Macmillan, and New York, Fawcett, 1984.
Penny Dreadful.   London, Macmillan, 1984; New York, Ballantine, 1986.
Penny Post.   London, Macmillan, 1985; New York, Ballantine, 1986.
Penny Royal.   London, Macmillan, 1986; New York, Ballantine, 1987.
Penny Wise.   London, Joseph, 1988; New York, Ballantine, 1989.
Penny Pinching.   London, Joseph, and New York, Ballantine, 1989.
Playing with Fire.   London, Macdonald, 1989.

Uncollected Short Stories

"Penny and the Greenwydd Bard," in *She* (London), April 1985.
"Poisoned Tongues," in *Ellery Queen's Mystery Magazine* (New York), June 1990.
"Freedom," in *New Crimes 2*, edited by Maxim Jakubowski. London, Robinson, 1990.
"All's Fair in Love," in *A Classic English Crime*, edited by Tim Heald.   London, Pavilion, 1990.

OTHER PUBLICATIONS

Novels as Susannah James

A Distant Shore.   New York, New American Library, 1981.
Lucia's Legacy.   New York, New American Library, 1984.

*

Susan Moody comments

Having spent ten years in Tennessee in the turbulent 1960's, I have long been interested in the relationship between black people and white. Penny Wanawake—tall, black, rich—is an attempt to look at this from a quirky angle—my main aim, however is to tell a story which entertains.

Playing with Fire is a move away from straight detective fiction into the bigger more amorphous world of suspense: it is a novel with a mystery at its heart.

*   *   *

Susan Moody's amateur detective must be one of the most unusual ones to reach the printed page. Penny Wanawake (pronounced Wa-na-wa-ke, with each syllable given equal emphasis) is the daughter of Lady Helena Hurley and Dr. Benjamin Wanawake, Permanent Ambassador to the United Nations for the tiny republic of Senangaland. Penny herself is six feet tall, is variously described within the books as "black as your hat," "bovril-black," "black and shiny as a licorice-stick," and wears her hair in beaded corn-row braids. Undeniably a striking appearance, yet one feels that she is likely to be at rather a disadvantage if called upon to embark on any undercover work such as tailing a suspect!

Penny was educated in England, Switzerland, France, and America—"the result was a polished beauty with an impeccable accent, a transatlantic idiom and an entree into high society any time, anywhere." While her jet-set lifestyle persists, she uses it mainly as an instrument to channel resources to the people of the Third World: as a freelance photographer she is able to bring their plight to the attention of the moneyed section of society in which she moves. Even more finance is raised, however, by the nefarious dealings of her lover, jewel-thief and con-man Barnaby Midas, who is aided and abetted by Miss Antonia Ivory, "the sitting tenant" of Penny's London town house, and director of the R.H. Domestic Agency. Miss Ivory takes girls from the very best backgrounds onto her books and places them in the homes of the very rich: she is totally unaware of the break-ins which always follow and of the small and exceedingly valuable objects which are stolen. As the daughter of an upper-class racehorse trainer, this extraordinary spinster is well placed to use an expertise acquired in her youth, in order to maximise the profits of these burglaries—still in all innocence.

This, then, is the background against which Penny Wanawake functions as an amateur sleuth. Her friends and relations seem peculiarly prone to murder and kidnapping, and it is these crimes which she sets out to solve, not those of the kind which her partner and lover is himself committing. Although the morality of the latter may seem dubious, the reader is bound to sympathise with the resulting redistribution of wealth, and Barnaby's crimes never form the foreground to the plot. Penny's very first case precedes the first novel: in each of the books we are given tantalising hints (but no more than hints), regarding the solution of the death of Monsignor Capet at Hurley Court, Penny being the only person to suspect murder in this and some of the subsequent cases.

In *Penny Black*, the first book in which we are privileged to know the details of Penny's investigations, the standard ingredients of her adventures are laid before us: a murder, Penny's own natural curiosity and her desire to avenge a friend's death, a great deal of action and above all the wonderfully racy, wisecracking style in which all these stories are written. Marfa Lund, a beautiful but not very bright blonde model, is murdered shortly after speaking to Penny (with whom she went to school): when she does not turn up for their joint holiday, Penny's involvement in the investigation begins. Political skulduggery, soft and not so soft porn, child molesting and the cutthroat world of orchid breeding all intermingle to form the background to Penny's inquiries. These she conducts with inimitable breeziness, aided and abetted by Aaron Kimbell, a private investigator retained by Marfa's father: although in love with Barnaby, Penny is not averse to the odd brief affair, and Kimbell is glad to oblige—his appearances in some of the subsequent books are rather more chaste.

In this and other respects, Penny Wanawake is a very liberated woman—she assumes the more traditionally masculine role of the sexually free partner, while Barnaby, in the fourth book *Penny Royal* and in subsequent novels, tries to persuade her into marriage. She encounters a certain amount of hostility on account of her sex and rather more on account of her colour, but these issues are not properly addressed in the

books. Rather, they are sidestepped by virtue of Penny's background, intelligence, appearance and lifestyle.

In a complete departure from this series, Moody has written an extremely ambitious thriller in *Playing with Fire;* the complicated plots in the Penny Wanawake books are as nothing compared with this tangle of half-guessed relationships and identities. Tense, taut, fraught with emotions, the complexities of this novel are impossible to describe with brevity: suffice it to say that the plot can be likened to a jigsaw whose final piece is produced only on the last page. Flaws do exist: the heroine, Frances Brett, can be extraordinarily slow on the uptake—but perhaps she has not read as many thrillers as the average Moody reader! She fails to perceive inconsistencies of character and behaviour and overlooks some glaringly obvious facts, yet when she does decide to undertake the investigation she is therefore far more believable than the super-human Penny. Both Frances and the novel lack the witty racy style of Moody's previous books, but although the reader may miss this it would have been totally inappropriate in the context of such a novel; here Moody is dealing with ill-treatment of children (in one case sexual exploitation and in another emotional neglect), with misplaced confidence and reliance, with the dreadful consequences of mistaken identity when revenge is being sought.

With this novel Moody has demonstrated her considerable versatility—it is a far cry from the confident, ebullient Penny Wanawake to the emotionally bruised Frances Brett. And the totally differing style and pace of writing well reflect the disparate characters of the two heroines and the situations in which they respectively find themselves.

—Judith Rhodes

————

MOOR, Emily. *See* **DEMING, Richard.**

————

MORAN, Mike. *See* **ARD, William**

————

MORGAN, Bailey. *See* **BREWER, Gil.**

————

MORICE, Anne. Pseudonym for Felicity Shaw, née Worthington. British. Born in Kent in 1918. Educated privately and at Francis Holland School, London, and in Paris and Munich. Married Alexander Shaw in 1939; two daughters and one son. *Died.*

CRIME PUBLICATIONS

Novels (series: Tessa Crichton Price in all books)

Death in the Grand Manor. London, Macmillan, 1970.
Murder in Married Life. London, Macmillan, 1971.

Death of a Gay Dog. London, Macmillan, 1971.
Murder on French Leave. London, Macmillan, 1972.
Death and the Dutiful Daughter. London, Macmillan, 1973; New York, St. Martin's Press, 1974.
Death of a Heavenly Twin. London, Macmillan, and New York, St. Martin's Press, 1974.
Killing with Kindness. London, Macmillan, 1974; New York, St. Martin's Press, 1975.
Nursery Tea and Poison. London, Macmillan, and New York, St. Martin's Press, 1975.
Death of a Wedding Guest. London, Macmillan, and New York, St. Martin's Press, 1976.
Murder in Mimicry. London, Macmillan, and New York, St. Martin's Press, 1977.
Scared to Death. London, Macmillan, 1977; New York, St. Martin's Press, 1978.
Murder by Proxy. London, Macmillan, and New York, St. Martin's Press, 1978.
Murder in Outline. London, Macmillan, and New York, St. Martin's Press, 1979.
Death in the Round. London, Macmillan, and New York, St. Martin's Press, 1980.
The Men in Her Death. London, Macmillan, and New York, St. Martin's Press, 1981.
Hollow Vengeance. London, Macmillan, and New York, St. Martin's Press, 1982.
Sleep of Death. London, Macmillan, 1982; New York, St. Martin's Press, 1983.
Getting Away with Murder? London, Macmillan, 1984; Boston, G.K. Hall, 1985; as *Murder Post-Dated*, New York, St. Martin's Press, 1984.
Dead on Cue. London, Macmillan, 1985.
Publish and Be Killed. London, Macmillan, 1986; New York, St. Martin's Press, 1987.
Treble Exposure. London, Macmillan, 1987; New York, St. Martin's Press, 1988.
Design for Dying. London, Macmillan, and New York, St. Martin's Press, 1988.
Planning for Murder. London, Macmillan, 1990.

OTHER PUBLICATIONS

Novels as Felicity Shaw

The Happy Exiles. London, Hamish Hamilton, and New York, Harper, 1956.
Sun Trap. London, Blond, 1958.

Play

Dummy Run (produced Henley-on-Thames, Oxfordshire, 1977).

*

Manuscript Collection: Mugar Memorial Library, Boston University.

Anne Morice commented (1984):

Since numerous members of my family (including my father, sister, two daughters, and three nephews) are or were closely connected with the theatre and cinema, in one capacity or another, and I married a film director, this was the background I was most familiar with, and so created Tessa Crichton for the foreground. She has so far appeared in every book.

*   *   *

The considerable charm of Anne Morice's mystery novels comes from the character of their heroine, Tessa Crichton Price, and the relaxed authority of the prose in which she narrates her adventures. Morice can be compared with America's Emma Lathen team for her lightness of touch, acute observation of manners and understanding of psychology, and her constant flow of wit, if wit so dry can be said to flow. Tessa is an actress, currently in her twenties, around whom murders keep happening. Her sharp eyes, keen mind, and unobtrusive nosiness inevitably lead her to the murderer. Her husband, Robin Price, is a self-effacing policeman who amiably plays several supporting roles: he serves as sounding board for Tessa's preliminary theories, and is available to rescue her from the occasional murderer at bay.

The form of the novels is straight from the tradition of Christie and Marsh. A cast of characters is introduced and placed in a situation that simmers with incipient violence. The exposition is sometimes so leisurely that murder is not committed until halfway through the book, but the characters are so lively and Tessa's commentary so entertaining that the pace is not noticeably slowed. In the classic detective tradition, all the necessary clues are faithfully laid out, attention is masterfully misdirected from them, and Tessa explains all in a final conversation, often with Robin and her cousin Toby Crichton, a reclusive and crotchety playwright. Although the form is classic, the flavor of the social world that Morice explores is much sharper than Christie's or Marsh's. Ordinary society as Tessa describes it consists of a thin film of civility floating on a thick stew of folly, passion, vice, and warped development.

Both in Tessa's life and in Morice's philosophy, all the world's a stage, on which professional and amateur actors intermingle, often playing out private dramas with murderous plots. The villain in *Killing with Kindness* is renowned for his perfect manners and general thoughtfulness. What piques Tessa's curiosity is the fact that his wife seems to be an alcoholic wreck. In *Murder in Married Life*, the portrait of "Sandy" Sanderson apparently begins as a gentle exercise in social comedy: the denouement reveals an ungentle exercise in fraud, and puts Tessa in convincing peril. An aging actor in *Sleep of Death* proves to have given his most convincing performance off stage, and one of the plotters in *Hollow Vengeance* is a young girl whose goodness is both pretentious and manipulative. In *Murder Post-Dated*, a young woman who is forced by family pressures of a particularly nasty kind into playing several social roles turns out to be a very untalented actress, and so helps Tessa to unravel the truth.

The highly individual texture of Morice's work comes from the contrast between the dry urbanity of Tessa's mind and the messy realism of the social world she observes. An extremely high percentage of the characters are convincing, and not all of them are as nasty as her villains. A three-year-old protégé and a charming adolescent in *Death of a Wedding Guest*, an American friend in *Murder in Mimicry*, and an African exchange student in *Death of a Heavenly Twin* are all free-standing figures, no matter how brief their appearances. The most dependable relief from the depressing social realism in these books is the continuing characterization of Tessa herself. Despite her premature skepticism about human motives, she retains a measure of youthful enthusiasm. And when her tendency to self-dramatization gets out of hand and is briskly deflated by her husband or cousin, she usually responds by seeing the joke.

If tact and clear sight are the marks of Morice's handling of characterization, tight economy is the chief virtue of her plots. She never drops an obvious clue and never belabors a clue's significance. Morice provides a high quality of entertainment for adults: a realistic imitation of the social world and vigorous exercise for any reader's wits.

—Carol Cleveland

MORLAND, Nigel. Also wrote as Mary Dane; John Donavan; Norman Forrest; Roger Garnett; Vincent McCall; Neal Shepherd. British. Born in London, 24 June 1905. Educated privately. Married 1) Peggy Barwell (divorced); 2) Pamela Hunnex (divorced); 3) Jill Harvey (divorced), one daughter and two sons; 4) Faith Percival; one son and two step-daughters. From the age of 14 had numerous jobs in journalism and publishing in England and the East: editor, *Shanghai Sports, Doctor, Edgar Wallace Mystery Magazine*; on editorial staff of *Shanghai Mercury, China Press, Covers, Fiction Monthly, Movie Day*, New York *Post*, Hearst newspapers, Odhams Press, London, Lettercraft Publishers and Covers Ltd., both in China, Nicholson and Watson Ltd., London, Street and Massey Ltd.; proprietor, The Book Guild and Mystery Book Club. Founding editor, *The Criminologist*, from 1966, *Forensic and Medico-Legal Photography*, from 1972, and *The International Journal of Forensic Dentistry* and *Current Crime*, both from 1973. Co-Founder, Crime Writers Association, 1953. *Died 3 April 1986.*

CRIME PUBLICATIONS

Novels (series: John Finnegan; Detective Inspector Rory Luccan; Steven Malone; Chief Inspector Andy McMurdo; Mrs. Palmyra Pym)

The Phantom Gunman (Pym). London, Cassell, 1935.
The Moon Murders (Pym). London, Cassell, 1935.
The Street of the Leopard (Pym). London, Cassell, 1936.
The Clue of the Bricklayer's Aunt (Pym). London, Cassell, 1936; New York, Farrar and Rinehart, 1937.
Death Took a Publisher (Finnegan; as Norman Forrest). London, Harrap, 1936; New York, Curl, 1938.
Death Took a Greek God (Finnegan; as Norman Forrest). London, Harrap, 1937; New York, Curl, 1938.
The Clue in the Mirror (Pym). London, Cassell, 1937; New York, Farrar and Rinehart, 1938.
The Case Without a Clue (Pym). London, Cassell, and New York, Farrar and Rinehart, 1938.
Death Traps the Killer (as Mary Dane). London, Wright and Brown, 1938.
A Rope for the Hanging (Pym). London, Cassell, 1938; New York, Farrar and Rinehart, 1939.
A Knife for the Killer (Pym). London, Cassell, 1939; as *Murder at Radio City*, New York, Farrar and Rinehart, 1939.
A Gun for a God (Pym). London, Cassell, 1940; as *Murder in Wardour Street*, New York, Farrar and Rinehart, 1940.
The Clue of the Careless Hangman (Pym). London, Cassell, 1940; as *The Careless Hangman*, New York, Farrar and Rinehart, 1941.
Dumb Alibi. New York, MB Books, 1941.
The Corpse on the Flying Trapeze (Pym). London, Cassell, and New York, Farrar and Rinehart, 1941.
A Coffin for the Body (Pym). London, Cassell, 1943.
Murder Runs Wild. London, Halle, 1946.
Strangely She Died (Malone). London, Jenkins, 1946.
Smash and Grab (as Vincent McCall). London, Arrow, 1946.

Dressed to Kill (Pym). London, Cassell, 1947.
The Hatchet Murders. London, Arrow, 1947.
She Didn't Like Dying (McMurdo). London, Sampson Low, 1948.
Fish Are So Trusting. London, Century Press, 1948.
No Coupons for a Shroud (McMurdo). London, Sampson Low, 1949.
Two Dead Charwomen (McMurdo). London, Sampson Low, 1949.
Death Takes an Editor (Malone). London, Aldus, 1949.
The Corpse Was No Lady (McMurdo). London, Sampson Low, 1950.
Blood on the Stars (McMurdo). London, Sampson Low, 1951.
Death When She Wakes (Luccan). London, Evans, 1951.
He Hanged His Mother on Monday (McMurdo). London, Sampson Low, 1951.
The Lady Had a Gun (Pym). London, Cassell, 1951.
Call Him Early for the Murder (Pym). London, Cassell, 1952.
A Girl Died Singing (Luccan). London, Evans, 1952.
The Moon Was Made for Murder (McMurdo). London, Sampson Low, 1953.
Sing a Song of Cyanide (Pym). London, Cassell, 1953.
Death for Sale (McMurdo). London, Hale, 1957.
Look in Any Doorway (Pym). London, Cassell, 1957.
A Bullet for Midas (Pym). London, Cassell, 1958.
Death and the Golden Boy (Pym). London, Cassell, 1958.
Death to the Ladies (McMurdo). London, Hale, 1959.
The Concrete Maze (Pym). London, Cassell, 1960.
So Quiet a Death (Pym). London, Cassell, 1960.
The Dear, Dead Girls (Pym). London, Cassell, 1961.

Novels as John Donavan (series: Sergeant Johnny Lamb in all books except *The Dead Have No Friends*)

The Case of the Rusted Room. London, Hale, and New York, Curl, 1937.
The Case of the Beckoning Dead. London, Hale, and New York, Curl, 1938.
The Case of the Talking Dust. London, Hale, 1938; New York, Arcadia House, 1941.
The Case of the Coloured Wind. London, Hodder and Stoughton, 1939; as *The Case of the Violet Smoke*, New York, Arcadia House, 1940.
The Case of the Plastic Man. London, Hodder and Stoughton, 1940; as *The Case of the Plastic Mask*, New York, Arcadia House, 1941.
The Dead Have No Friends. London, Home and Van Thal, 1952.

Novels as Roger Garnett (series: Chief Inspector Jonathan Black; R.I. Perkins)

Death in Piccadilly (Black). London, Wright and Brown, 1937.
Starr Bedford Dies (Perkins). London, Wright and Brown, 1937.
The Killing of Paris Norton (Perkins). London, Wright and Brown, 1938.
The Croaker (Black). London, Wright and Brown, 1938.
Danger—Death at Work (Black). London, Wright and Brown, 1939.
A Man Died Talking (Black). London, Wright and Brown, 1943.
Death Spoke Sweetly. London, Wright and Brown, 1946.
Dusky Death. London, Wright and Brown, 1948.

Novels as Neal Shepherd (series: Chief Inspector Michael "Napper" Tandy in all books)

Death Flies Low. London, Constable, 1938.
Death Walks Softly. London, Constable, 1938.
Death Rides Swiftly. London, Constable, 1939.
Exit to Music: A Problem in Detection. London, Constable, 1940.

Short Stories

Death Takes a Star. London, Todd, 1943.
The Sooper's Cases. London, Todd, 1943.
The Laboratory Murder and Other Stories. London, Vallancey Press, 1944.
Corpse in the Circus. London, Vallancey Press, 1945.
Eleven Thrilling Mysteries (as Vincent McCall). London, Arrow, 1945.
The Corpse in the Circus and Other Stories. London, Vallancey Press, 1946.
The Big Killing. Hounslow, Middlesex, Foster, 1946.
Mrs. Pym of Scotland Yard. London, Hodgson, 1946.
How Many Coupons for a Shroud? London, Morgan Laird, 1946.
26 Three Minute Thrillers: A Collection of Ingenious Puzzle Yarns. London, Arrow, 1947.
Eve Finds the Killer (as Roger Garnett). London, Arrow, 1947.
The Case of the Innocent Wife. London, Arrow, 1947.
Exit to Music and Other Stories. London, Bonde, 1947; abridged edition, as *Death's Sweet Music*, London, Century Press, 1947.
Mrs. Pym and Other Stories. Henley-on-Thames, Oxfordshire, Aidan Ellis, 1976.

OTHER PUBLICATIONS

Short Story

"Mary!" A Story of the Magdalene, with Peggy Barwell. Paris, Felix Barbier, 1932.

Plays

The Goofus Man: A Fantasy for Children. London, Eric Partridge, 1930.
Dawn Was Theirs, with Peggy Barwell. Paris, Felix Barbier, 1931.

Screenplay: *Mrs. Pym of Scotland Yard*, with Fred Elles and Peggy Barwell, 1939.

Verse

Cachexia: A Collection of Prose Poems, with Peggy Barwell. Paris, Felix Barbier, 1930; revised edition, 1931.
Abrakadabra! Verse for Modern Children, with Peggy Barwell. Paris, Felix Barbier, 1932.

Other

People We Have Never Met: A Book of Superficial Cameos, with Peggy Barwell. Paris, Felix Barbier, 1931.
Finger Prints: An Introduction to Scientific Criminology. London, Street and Massey, 1936.

How to Write Detective Novels. London, Allen and Unwin, 1936.
The Conquest of Crime. London, Cassell, 1937.
Crime Against Children: An Aspect of Sexual Criminology. London, Cassell, 1939.
An Outline of Scientific Criminology. London, Cassell, and New York, Philosophical Library, 1950; revised edition, Cassell, 1971.
Hangman's Clutch. London, Laurie, 1954.
Background to Murder. London, Laurie, 1955.
This Friendless Lady. London, Muller, 1957.
That Nice Miss Smith. London, Muller, 1958; New York, St. Martin's Press, 1989.
Science in Crime Detection. London, Hale, 1958; New York, Emerson, 1960.
An Outline of Sexual Criminology. Oxford, Tallis, 1966; New York, Hart, 1967.
Pattern of Murder. London, Elek, 1966.
An International Pattern of Murder. Hornchurch, Essex, Ian Henry, 1977.
Who's Who in Crime Fiction. London, Elm Tree Books, 1980.

Editor, *Papers from the "Criminologist."* London, Wolfe, 1971; New York, Library Press, 1972.
Editor, *Victorian Crime Stories.* Hornchurch, Essex, Ian Henry, 1978.

*

Nigel Morland commented (1984):
Between 1927 and 1934, Nigel Morland was a hard-working pulp-writer for U.S. and U.K. publishers, turning out a steady average of 30,000 to 50,000 words a week which he (unwisely!) sold outright under pseudonyms for cash; this includes several non-fiction popular volumes and several ghosted works for top screen and notoriety names. Morland kept few records, and such material or notes as he had on his work were destroyed during the London Blitz. Dozens of these crude pulps Morland has completely forgotten, but he does recall that his first hardback was *The Sibilant Whisper* published in Shanghai in 1923, followed by several more locally published works before he returned to England, plus many short stories. His second book, he recalls, was a study of English people for a Chinese publisher, translated directly into Chinese and never issued in English.

*   *   *

Nigel Morland was at one time secretary to Edgar Wallace, and on Wallace's death, the mantle of the old master seemed to fall upon his shoulders. A founder of the Crime Writers Association in 1953 (along with John Creasey), Morland wrote a great many books on crime, most of them detective novels. He gave up fiction in 1965, saying that writing it bored him to tears. Until his death he kept busy editing *The Criminologist* (a journal surveying forensic science, criminology, police, and the law) and *Current Crime* (a review of new crime fiction) and turning out non-fiction books on all aspects of crime.

Mrs. Palmyra Pym is Morland's best-known character. She is an employee of the British War Department, but has been assigned to Scotland Yard for "special investigations." Straight from the hard-bitten school of detectives, Mrs. Pym is determined and resourceful and once she begins investigating, there is no stopping her. She is a terror to evil-doers and unconventional in the eyes of her superiors. She often packs a gun, but usually relies on her fists in tight situations. She is oblivious to regulations and traditions of the Yard and is permitted a freer hand than are her male colleagues. When Mrs. Pym made her appearance in 1935, she was considered too rough and unconventional for a British detective; her clothes were jaunty and eccentric and her language perhaps a bit too blunt. She was brave, skillful, outrageous—an awesome sight when she went into battle. As the years wore on, she became something of a bore, but her clothes changed for the better and her manners became more agreeable. She continued, however, to use her third-degree methods and interpreted Scotland Yard regulations to suit herself. The stories themselves are often fantastic and unashamedly in imitation of Edgar Wallace.

The Clue of the Bricklayer's Aunt opens with the strange behavior of a bedridden paralytic—the bricklayer's aunt— whose wild dancing and throwing of furniture about attract the attention of neighbors. Mrs. Pym finds the connection between this curious behavior and the robberies and murders that follow. The next Pym book, *The Clue in the Mirror*, finds her uncovering a long and involved trail of crime which leads her from a warehouse in Wapping to respectable financial circles. *The Case Without a Clue* deals with Mrs. Pym's efforts to discover why the galley proof of a suppressed book was stolen from a publisher's safe and why a murder followed. The plot is well-conceived, but Mrs. Pym is now engagingly proper—and boring. *A Rope for the Hanging* concerns a street brawl in which a drunken laborer is killed—at first a seemingly common case in which a deputy assistant commissioner of Scotland Yard would scarcely be interested. But once Mrs. Pym begins investigating, the mystery is penetratingly illuminated. Mrs. Pym uses her unconventional third degree methods in *A Knife for the Killer* to solve the mystery of a parachutist who alights on the "Rockefeller Building" and is found by police to be dying of a gunshot wound. *The Corpse on the Flying Trapeze* has her investigating how and why an acrobat was beheaded while swinging from a trapeze in full view of a crowded theatre. The bloody beginning is only a prelude to more murders later on— all seemingly without a motive until Mrs. Pym comes on the scene. The Mrs. Pym stories continued through the 1940's and the plots grew better as the lady's eccentricities became less pronounced.

Morland wrote under several pseudonyms: Mary Dane, John Donavan, Norman Forrest, Roger Garnett, and Neal Shepherd. The best, I think, were the books as Shepherd; *Death Walks Softly* is representative of his style at its best. It is a tale of industrial spying and is characteristic of the Shepherd novels with its brisk writing and clever detection.

—Daniel P. King

MORRISON, Arthur. British. Born in Poplar, London, 1 November 1863. Married Elizabeth Adelaide Thatcher in 1892; one son. Clerk, People's Palace, London, 1886–90, and sub-editor, *Palace Journal*, 1889–90; freelance journalist, 1890–1913; collector of Chinese and Japanese paintings which were acquired by the British Museum in 1913; chief inspector of the Special Constabulary of Epping Forest, Essex, during World War I. Fellow, 1924, and member of the council, 1935, Royal Society of Literature. *Died 4 December 1945.*

CRIME PUBLICATIONS

Novels

The Hole in the Wall. London, Methuen, and New York, McClure Phillips, 1902.
The Red Triangle, Being Some Further Chronicles of Martin Hewitt, Investigator. London, Nash, and Boston, Page, 1903.

Short Stories (series character: Martin Hewitt)

Martin Hewitt, Investigator. London, Ward Lock, and New York, Harper, 1894.
Chronicles of Martin Hewitt. London, Ward Lock, 1895; New York, Appleton, 1896.
Adventures of Martin Hewitt. London, Ward Lock, 1896.
The Dorrington Deed-Box. London, Ward Lock, 1897.
The Green Eye of Goona: Stories of a Case of Tokay. London, Nash, 1904; as *The Green Diamond*, Boston, Page, 1904.

OTHER PUBLICATIONS

Novels

A Child of the Jago. London, Methuen, and Chicago, Stone, 1896.
To London Town. London, Methuen, and Chicago, Stone, 1899.
Cunning Murrell. London, Methuen, and New York, Doubleday, 1900.

Short Stories

The Shadows Around Us: Authentic Tales of the Supernatural. London, Simpkin Marshall, 1891.
Tales of Mean Streets. London, Methuen, 1894; Boston, Roberts, 1895.
Zig-Zags at the Zoo. London, Newnes, 1895.
Divers Vanities. London, Methuen, 1905.
Green Ginger. London, Hutchinson, and New York, Stokes, 1909.
(Stories). London, Harrap, 1929.
Fiddle O'Dreams. London, Hutchinson, 1933.

Plays

That Brute Simmons, with Herbert C. Sargent, adaptation of the story by Morrison (produced London, 1904). London, French, 1904.
The Dumb-Cake, with Richard Pryce, adaptation of a story by Morrison (produced London, 1907). London, French, 1907.
A Stroke of Business, with Horace Newte (produced London, 1907).

Other

The Painters of Japan. London, Jack, 2 vols., and New York, Stokes, 2 vols., 1911.

*   *   *

Arthur Morrison was highly regarded by his contemporaries as one of the pioneers of the New Realism. His collection *Tales of Mean Streets* and his novel *A Child of the Jago* set the pattern for a new hard, factual, unsentimental recording of life and crime in the slums of London. It came, therefore, as an unwelcome surprise when the Martin Hewitt stories began to appear in *The Strand Magazine*. They were skilled commercial work, but without the power of Morrison's serious fiction.

The Martin Hewitt stories adhere closely to the pattern of the Sherlock Holmes stories—consultation, investigation, strange circumstances, and a resolution which clears away difficulties. Hewitt is himself patterned after Holmes, with certain superficial distinctions to conceal the likeness. The stories, however, are ingenious in concept, well-written, and entertaining. If they lack the idiosyncratic snap of Doyle's works, they are smoother and more relaxed. Altogether there are 18 short stories about Hewitt. The first series of six stories appeared in *The Strand Magazine*, while the second and third appeared in *The Windsor Magazine*. An episodic novel, *The Red Triangle*, also centers upon Hewitt, but it is more sensational than the short stories. It deals with a West Indian master criminal who uses hypnosis to control his henchmen. While *The Red Triangle* is not to be taken seriously, the other Hewitt stories still remain second only to Doyle's work in the period 1890–1905.

Morrison wrote two other books in the same commercial vein as the Martin Hewitt stories. *The Dorrington Deed-Box* described the adventures of a criminal who occasionally performs feats of detection when it is to his own interest. The last adventure in the book is noteworthy as Morrison's sole attempt to link slum naturalism with the commercially patterned detective story. *The Green Eye of Goona*, on the other hand, is a light detective fantasy about a gem which is smuggled out of India in a magnum of wine, and the various attempts to gain possession of it. The novel is successful in combining topical humor and mystery. There are also occasional short stories with minor elements of crime in *Divers Vanities* and *Green Ginger*, but these are not significant.

Although few details are available about Morrison's early life, since he was an extremely reticent man, it is known that he grew up in the slums of East London, and that a childhood amid poverty, squalor, and crime left a heavy mark on him. Much of his fiction seems to have been written (probably unconsciously) to break the hold which this past held on him. Indeed, the single theme of his serious fiction is Escape. In his later life, too, Morrison experienced the underworld in his search for material for *A Child of the Jago*. As a result of this background Morrison was the only significant author of his day who had both the literary genius and the personal experience to broaden the scope of the detective story or, as it has been put, to take the detective story out of 221B Baker Street. Unfortunately, Morrison wrote only a single work in this direction. This was *The Hole in the Wall*, which in the opinion of most critics is Morrison's finest work. Told from several points of view, it is the story of a boy who lives with his grandfather in a disreputable water-front pub and becomes embroiled in theft and murder. It is brilliantly imagined and vividly told.

—E.F. Bleiler

MORSE, L(arry) A(lan). Also writes as Runa Fairleigh. American. Born in Fort Wayne, Indiana, 30 July 1945. Educated at the University of California, Berkeley, B.A. in English Literature 1967; San Francisco State University, M.A. in English Literature 1968. Production assistant, educational television station, Toronto, Ontario, 1970; program co-ordinator of adult education, University of Toronto, 1970–75;

since 1975, full-time writer. Lives in Toronto, Ontario. Recipient: Mystery Writers of America Edgar Allan Poe award, 1981. Address: c/o Russell and Volkening, 50 West 29th Street, New York, New York 10001, U.S.A.

CRIME PUBLICATIONS

Novels (series: Sam Hunter)

The Old Dick. New York, Avon, 1981.
The Big Enchilada (Hunter). New York, Avon, 1982.
An Old-Fashioned Mystery (as Runa Fairleigh). Toronto, Lester and Orpen Dennys, 1983; New York, Avon, 1984.
Sleaze (Hunter). New York, Avon, 1985.

OTHER PUBLICATIONS

Novel

The Flesh-Eaters. New York, Warner, 1979.

Other

Who Did It?, with Carlos A. Yorio. Englewood Cliffs, New Jersey, Prentice Hall, 1980.

*

L.A. Morse comments:
My goal was to deliver good value, a few laughs and a couple of hours of entertainment.

*   *   *

Popular fiction is littered with the names of writers who flame like a comet across the literary empyrean, then vanish. Reading old publishers' catalogues—from the 1920's, or the 1930's—is a lowering experience. Who are all these people? Why is it that if their novels were selling 20,000 copies in hardback in 1928 (phenomenal by today's standards), their names are now unknown, not a wrack of their reputations left behind?

An even more melancholy question is: Why do some writers, seemingly at the height of their powers, suddenly cease production and simply . . . disappear? Why (if death is not the answer, and it doesn't seem to have been) did Clifford Witting stop writing when he did? Why did Thurman Warriner? Why is it that Eric Norden appears to have written nothing since *The Ultimate Solution*, one of the most riveting pulp-thrillers of the 1970's, brilliantly, and chillingly, combining the spy story, police procedural and Alternate World genres (gritty police lieutenant tries to track down the last Jew in a nightmarish New York in 1973, in a time-stream in which Hitler won)? Whatever happened to Stephen Robinett?

In the case of L.A. Morse there may well be reasons for his protracted silence, perhaps not unconnected with what are said to have been his activities, or non-activities, during the Vietnam War. Such questions, whether inspired by mere curiosity or outright political malice, ought to have no relevance to a writer's work, yet for some years during the 1980's the editor of a well-known American mystery fanzine refused to allow Morse's name to be mentioned in his columns, thus, somewhat sinisterly, non-personing the author.

To be sure, Morse seems to have a knack for setting critics' teeth on edge: his first Sam Hunter mystery, *The Big Enchilada*, was comprehensively savaged in the Baker/Nietzel survey of

American detective fiction *Private Eyes: 101 Knights* as "the modern nadir of private eye literature ... a classic of bad writing." Yet he has a singular, and impressive, talent, in which pastiche plays no small part: his second book, *Who Did It?* is a volume of short stories, each written in a different mystery-genre style.

However, it is clear that Morse is immensely attracted to pulp themes, pulp characterization—his Sam Hunter books are thoroughly pulp-oriented, and his first book, *The Flesh-Eaters* (based on the old Scottish legend of Sawney Bean, the outlaw who robbed, murdered, then ate his victims) is pure genre exploitation. Though none the worse for that—as Roger Corman proved in another medium there is always room for well-crafted and absorbing trash.

Which is precisely what the Sam Hunter books are. Both *The Big Enchilada* and *Sleaze*, its sequel, are a triumphant mix (perhaps stew is the better word) of outrageous parody, Neanderthalic ethics, insane violence, superb one-liners, appalling amorality and excellent, labyrinthine plotting. It is difficult to believe that Morse was not, at one and the same time, cocking a snook at humourless critics and grinning all the way to the bank.

The Old Dick, his first private eye novel, concerns the 78-year-old ex-gumshoe Jake Spanner who, continually trying to fend off sickeningly jaunty do-gooders from the local senior citizens community centre, and aided, briefly, by a gang of senile delinquents, is dragged back into a world of violence and danger through the bad offices of an elderly (though by no means 'ex') mobster he put away 40 years before. The book (which also features a wonderfully rabid psychopath) is a delight; the writing sharp and at times wickedly funny. Deservedly it won the 1981 Edgar award for best original paperback.

The final book in Morse's known canon is a genuine *tour-de-force*, possibly (to paraphrase Morse himself) the detective story to end all detective stories. It is difficult to discuss *An Old-Fashioned Mystery* without sabotaging it utterly, but briefly it purports to be the work of one Runa Fairleigh, an elderly lady who mysteriously disappeared leaving only the manuscript (288 carefully typed pages) which Morse then edited. Written in the style of a Golden Age mystery, its setting is an isolated house on an isolated island in which is gathered a large cast of disparate characters (some more than mildly unhinged) all of whom, during the course of the book, are bumped off under increasingly bizarre circumstances. One other character is featured, in the epilogue: an eminent English cleric (real not fictional) whose devotion to the classic detective novel and passion for whimsical codification are probably what provided Morse with the jumping-off point for his fantastic, hilarious (one chapter ends with the priceless line, "It's the footprints of a gigantic duck!") and altogether extraordinary book.

Since 1985 Morse appears to have produced nothing. It is hard to believe that he has written himself out; rather more likely that he is still publishing under a pseudonym, or even pseudonyms—a mouth-watering thought. If only one knew what they were.

—Jack Adrian

MORTIMER, John (Clifford). Has also written as Geoffrey Lincoln. British. Born in Hampstead, London, 21 April 1923. Educated at Harrow School, Middlesex, 1937–40; Brasenose College, Oxford, 1940–42, B.A. 1947; called to the Bar, 1948; Queen's Counsel, 1966; Master of the Bench, Inner Temple, 1975. Served with the Crown Film Units as scriptwriter during World War II. Married 1) Penelope Dimont (i.e., the writer Penelope Mortimer) in 1949 (divorced 1971), one son and one daughter; 2) Penny Gollop in 1972; one daughter. Drama critic, *New Statesman, Evening Standard,* and *Observer,* 1972, all in London. Since 1968 member of the National Theatre board, chairman, League of Dramatists, and Royal Society of Literature. Recipient: Italia prize, for radio play, 1958; Screenwriters Guild award, for television play, 1970; British Academy award, for television series, 1980; *Yorkshire Post* award, 1983. D. Litt.: Susquehanna University, Selinsgrove, Pennsylvania, 1985; University of St. Andrews, Fife, 1987; University of Nottingham, 1989; LL.D.: Exeter University, 1986. C.B.E. (Commander, Order of the British Empire), 1986. Agent: Peters Fraser and Dunlop, 5th Floor, The Chambers, Chelsea Harbour, Lots Road, London SW10 OXF, England.

Crime Publications

Short Stories (series: Rumpole)

Rumpole. London, Allen Lane, 1980.
    Rumpole of the Bailey. London, Penguin, 1978; New York, Penguin, 1980.
    The Trials of Rumpole. London, Penguin, 1979; New York, Penguin, 1981.
Regina v. Rumpole. London, Allen Lane, 1981.
    Rumpole's Return. London, Penguin, 1980; New York, Penguin, 1982.
    Rumpole for the Defence. London, Penguin, 1982.
Rumpole and the Golden Thread. New York, Penguin, 1983.
The First Rumpole Omnibus (includes *Rumpole of the Bailey, The Trials of Rumpole, Rumpole's Return*). London, Penguin, 1983.
Rumpole's Last Case. London, Penguin, 1987; New York, Penguin, 1988.
The Second Rumpole Omnibus (includes *Rumpole for the Defence, Rumpole and the Golden Thread, Rumpole's Last Case*). London, Viking, 1987; New York, Penguin, 1988.
Rumpole and the Age of Miracles. London, Penguin, 1988; New York, Penguin, 1989.

Other Publications

Novels

Charade. London, Lane, 1947.
Rumming Park. London, Lane, 1948.
Answer Yes or No. London, Lane, 1950; as *The Silver Hook,* New York, Morrow, 1950.
Like Men Betrayed. London, Collins, 1953; Philadelphia, Lippincott, 1954.
The Narrowing Stream. London, Collins, 1954; New York, Viking, 1989.
Three Winters. London, Collins, 1956.
Will Shakespeare: The Untold Story. London, Hodder and Stoughton, 1977; New York, Delacorte Press, 1978.
Paradise Postponed. London, and New York, Viking, 1985.
Summer's Lease. London, and New York, Viking, 1988.
Titmus Regained. London, Viking, 1990.

Plays

The Dock Brief (broadcast, 1957; produced London, 1958; New York, 1961). Included in *Three Plays,* 1958.

I Spy (broadcast, 1957; produced Salisbury, Wiltshire, and Palm Beach, Florida, 1959). Included in *Three Plays*, 1958.

What Shall We Tell Caroline? (produced London, 1958; New York, 1961). Included in *Three Plays*, 1958.

Three Plays: The Dock Brief, What Shall We Tell Caroline?, I Spy. London, Elek, 1958; New York, Grove Press, 1962.

Call Me a Liar (televised, 1958; produced London, 1968). Included in *Lunch Hour and Other Plays*, 1960; in *The Television Playwright: Ten Plays for B.B.C. Television*, edited by Michael Barry, New York, Hill and Wang, 1960.

Sketches in *One to Another* (produced London, 1959). London, French, 1960.

The Wrong Side of the Park (produced London, 1960). London, Heinemann, 1960.

Lunch Hour (broadcast, 1960; produced Salisbury, Wiltshire, 1960; London, 1961; New York, 1977). Included in *Lunch Hour and Other Plays*, 1960; published separately, New York, French, 1961.

David and Broccoli (televised, 1960). Included in *Lunch Hour and Other Plays*, 1960.

Lunch Hour and Other Plays (includes *Collect Your Hand Baggage, David and Broccoli, Call Me a Liar*). London, Methuen, 1960.

Collect Your Hand Baggage (produced Wuppertal, Germany, 1963). Included in *Lunch Hour and Other Plays*, 1960.

Sketches in *One Over the Eight* (produced London, 1961).

Two Stars for Comfort (produced London, 1962). London, Methuen, 1962.

A Voyage round My Father (broadcast, 1963; produced London, 1970). London, Methuen, 1971.

Sketches in *Changing Gear* (produced Nottingham, 1965).

A Flea in Her Ear, adaptation of a play by Feydeau (produced London, 1966; Tucson, Arizona, 1979). London and New York, French, 1967.

A Choice of Kings (televised, 1966). Published in *Playbill Three*, edited by Alan Durband, London, Hutchinson, 1969.

The Judge (produced London, 1967). London, Methuen, 1967.

Desmond (televised, 1968). Published in *The Best Short Plays 1971*, edited by Stanley Richards, Philadelphia, Chilton, 1971.

Cat among the Pigeons, adaptation of a play by Feydeau (produced London, 1969; Milwaukee, 1971). New York, French, 1970.

Come As You Are: Four Short Plays (includes *Mill Hill, Bermondsey, Gloucester Road, Marble Arch*) (produced London, 1970). London, Methuen, 1971.

Five Plays (includes *The Dock Brief, What Shall We Tell Caroline?, I Spy, Lunch Hour, Collect Your Hand Baggage*). London, Methuen, 1970.

The Captain of Köpenick, adaptation of a play by Carl Zuckmayer (produced London, 1971). London, Methuen, 1971.

Conflicts, with others (produced London, 1971).

I, Claudius, adaptation of the novels *I, Claudius* and *Claudius the God* by Robert Graves (produced London, 1972).

Knightsbridge (televised, 1972). London, French, 1973.

Collaborators (produced London, 1973). London, Eyre Methuen, 1973.

The Fear of Heaven (as *Mr. Luby's Fear of Heaven*, broadcast, 1976; as *The Fear of Heaven*, produced with *The Prince of Darkness* as *Heaven and Hell*, London, 1976). London, French, 1978.

Heaven and Hell (includes *The Fear of Heaven* and *The Prince of Darkness*) (produced London, 1976); revised version of *The Prince of Darkness*, as *The Bells of Hell* (produced Richmond, Surrey, and London, 1977). London, French, 1978.

The Lady from Maxim's, adaptation of a play by Feydeau (produced London, 1977). London, Heinemann, 1977.

John Mortimer's Casebook (includes *The Dock Brief, The Prince of Darkness, Interlude*) (produced London, 1982).

When That I Was (produced Ottawa, 1982).

Edwin (broadcast 1982). Included in *Edwin and Other Plays*, 1984.

A Little Hotel on the Side, adaptation of a play by Feydeau and Maurice Desvalliers (produced London, 1984). Included in *Three Boulevard Farces*, 1985.

Edwin and Other Plays (includes *Bermondsey, Marble Arch, The Fear of Heaven, The Prince of Darkness*). London, Penguin, 1984.

Three Boulevard Farces (includes *A Little Hotel on the Side, A Flea in Her Ear, The Lady from Maxim's*). London, Penguin, 1985.

Die Fledermaus, adaptation of the libretto by Henri Meilhac and Ludovic Halévy, music by Johann Strauss (produced London, 1989). London, Viking, 1989.

Screenplays: *Ferry to Hong Kong*, with Lewis Gilbert and Vernon Harris, 1959; *The Innocents*, with Truman Capote and William Archibald, 1961; *Guns of Darkness*, 1962; *I Thank a Fool*, with others, 1962; *Lunch Hour*, 1962; *The Running Man*, 1963; *Bunny Lake Is Missing*, with Penelope Mortimer, 1964; *A Flea in Her Ear*, 1967; *John and Mary*, 1969.

Radio Plays: *Like Men Betrayed*, 1955; *No Hero*, 1955; *The Dock Brief*, 1957; *I Spy*, 1957; *Three Winters*, 1958; *Lunch Hour*, 1960; *The Encyclopedist*, 1961; *A Voyage round My Father*, 1963; *Personality Split*, 1964; *Education of an Englishman*, 1964; *A Rare Device*, 1965; *Mr. Luby's Fear of Heaven*, 1976; *Edwin*, 1982; *Rumpole*, from his own stories, 1988; *Glasnost*, 1988.

Television Plays: *Call Me a Liar*, 1958; *David and Broccoli*, 1960; *A Choice of Kings*, 1966; *The Exploding Azalea*, 1966; *The Head Waiter*, 1966; *Hughie*, 1967; *The Other Side*, 1967; *Desmond*, 1968; *Infidelity Took Place*, 1968; *Married Alive*, 1970; *Swiss Cottage*, 1972; *Knightsbridge*, 1972; *Rumpole of the Bailey*, 1975, and series, 1978, 1979, 1987, 1988; *A Little Place off the Edgware Road, The Blue Film, The Destructors, The Case for the Defence, Chagrin in Three Parts, The Invisible Japanese Gentlemen, Special Duties*, and *Mortmain*, all from stories by Graham Greene, 1975–76; *Will Shakespeare*, 1978; *Rumpole's Return*, 1980; *Unity*, from the book by David Pryce-Jones, 1981; *Brideshead Revisited*, from the novel by Evelyn Waugh, 1981; *Edwin*, 1984; *The Ebony Tower*, from the story by John Fowles, 1984; *Paradise Postponed*, from his own novel, 1986; *Summer's Lease*, from his own novel, 1989; *The Waiting Room*, 1989.

Ballet Scenario: *Home*, 1968.

Son et Lumière scripts: *Hampton Court*, 1964; *Brighton Pavilion*, 1965.

Other

No Moaning of the Bar (as Geoffrey Lincoln). London, Bles, 1957.

With Love and Lizards (travel), with Penelope Mortimer. London, Joseph, 1957.

Clinging to the Wreckage: A Part of Life. London, Weidenfeld and Nicolson, and New Haven, Connecticut, Ticknor and Fields, 1982.

In Character (interviews). London, Allen Lane, 1983.

The Liberty of the Citizen (lecture), with Franklin Thomas and Lord Hunt of Tanworth. London, Granada, 1983.
Character Parts (interviews). London, Viking, 1986.

Editor, *Famous Trials*, edited by Harry Hodge and James H. Hodge. London, Viking, and New York, Penguin, 1984.

*

Manuscript Collections: Boston University; University of California, Los Angeles.

* * *

John Mortimer, Queen's Counsel, a barrister since 1948, knows his subject well. As a man who has always preferred to think of himself as a writer who "does barristering" rather than as a barrister who writes, he augmented his early lean years by his pen. In his first great success, *The Dock Brief*, he wrote a poignant drama about an aged unsuccessful barrister, one out of "a line of wigged wallflowers," who was chosen at random to defend a murderer for the customary one-guinea fee. Morgenhall, the chief character, is a pale precursor of the ebullient, boisterous Rumpole who was to emerge 15 years later.

Horace Rumpole, barrister-at-law and Old Bailey Hack, is in his late sixties and as podgy and rumpled as his name suggests. When he rises in court (like his creator, *always* for the defense) the judge frowns. Rumpole's wig, purchased many years ago, he claims, from an ex-Chief Justice of Tonga, is more than a little askew. Traces of cigar ash and breakfast egg are evident on his waistcoat; his bands have lost their crispness and sag to reveal a brass collar-stud. Not a pretty sight! But when Rumpole's mellifluous voice caresses the jury's ears and every ruse is taken on behalf of his client with a hasty "As your Lordship pleases" to excuse the most outrageous ploys, at least the client and Rumpole are happy. Everyone is addressed as "Old Darling" or "Old Sweetheart" and no opportunity is lost to spout yards of poetry.

If Morgenhall was a failure in his profession, it would be wrong to regard Rumpole as a success: he eagerly accepts any brief, and to this end regularly treats the clerk in Chambers to a glass of cheap "plonk" in Pommeroy's Wine Bar. His home life is incredibly dreary; his wife Hilda ("She Who Must Be Obeyed") constantly and unfavorably compares him with "Daddy," once Rumpole's Head of Chambers, and so ashamed of him is his beloved son Nicky that he goes off to America to teach sociology. No wonder Rumpole "only [feels] truly alive and happy in the law courts," or in the cells below, where in an atmosphere redolent of smells from the kitchen he interviews his unfortunate clients.

The Rumpole short stories cover every situation from common theft and the receiving of stolen goods to murder and rape. Mortimer paints a wicked picture of the British legal practitioners: the ambitious, indifferent prosecutor; the biased judge who repeatedly interrupts Rumpole in full flow as he reaches his most telling point. The author is adept at the subtle gesture, as when he demonstrates his contempt for law-school academics by having Rumpole light his small cigar with a page torn from the *Criminal Law Review*.

In *Rumpole's Return* the old barrister is tricked into retirement. In a low moment after losing 10 cases in a row he quits Chambers and, with Hilda and his presentation clock, flies to join his son in Florida. Like an old war horse put out to pasture he is restless and unhappy until a friendly letter from England gives him the pretext to leave Hilda behind and steal back to his dismal, beloved Old Bailey. This long story is one of Mortimer's best.

These tales were first devised as one-hour television plays, in which Rumpole is excellently portrayed by Australian-born Leo McKern. But the print versions are more than "Spin-offs"; the dialogue is thoroughly fleshed out with descriptive passages and earthy characterizations, always in Rumpole's own words, for all the stories are told in the first person.

In the five stories that make up *Rumpole and the Golden Thread* we see Hilda's hopes of her husband becoming Head of Chambers disappointed yet again. Rumpole's elation at being summoned to Africa to defend an old pupil is dashed when he realises that, for complex political reasons, he is expected to fail. So forlorn are his chances in the final story that he is reduced to desperate measures; indeed, when the narration is taken over by Fiona Allways, a junior barrister, his very survival is in doubt.

Though a hero of sorts, Rumpole is less than admirable. His courtroom dodges strain the law to the limit and beyond. His views of human nature, especially of female human nature, seldom rise above the deplorable. Nevertheless, a buoyancy and determination shine through that make him one of life's survivors. It is this, together with the conviction that we have been shown something genuine about the English courts and their denizens, that remains after reading these excellent stories.

—Betty Donaldson

———

MORTON, Anthony. *See* **CREASEY, John.**

———

MOYES, Patricia. British. Born in Bray, County Wicklow, Ireland, 19 January 1923. Educated at Overstone School, Northampton, 1934–39, Cambridge School Certificate 1939. Served in the radar section of the Women's Auxiliary Air Force, 1940–45: Flight Officer. Married 1) John Moyes in 1951 (divorced 1959); 2) John S. Haszard in 1962. Company secretary, Peter Ustinov Productions Ltd., London, 1945–53; assistant editor, *Vogue*, London, 1953–58. Lived in Switzerland, 1958–62, Holland, 1962–72, and Washington, D.C., 1972–77. Recipient: Mystery Writers of America Edgar Allan Poe award, 1971. Agent: Curtis Brown Ltd., 162–168 Regent Street, London WIR 5TB, England. Address: P.O. Box 1, Virgin Gorda, British Virgin Islands, West Indies.

CRIME PUBLICATIONS

Novels (series: Henry and Emmy Tibbett in all books)

Dead Men Don't Ski. London, Collins, 1959; New York, Rinehart, 1960.
The Sunken Sailor. London, Collins, 1961; as *Down among the Dead Men*, New York, Holt Rinehart, 1961.
Death on the Agenda. London, Collins, and New York, Holt Rinehart, 1962.
Murder à la Mode. London, Collins, and New York, Holt Rinehart, 1963.
Falling Star. London, Collins, and New York, Holt Rinehart, 1964.

Johnny under Ground. London, Collins, 1965; New York, Holt Rinehart, 1966.
Murder Fantastical. London, Collins, and New York, Holt Rinehart, 1967.
Death and the Dutch Uncle. London, Collins, and New York, Holt Rinehart, 1968.
Who Saw Her Die? London, Collins, 1970; as *Many Deadly Returns*, New York, Holt Rinehart, 1970.
Season of Snows and Sins. London, Collins, and New York, Holt Rinehart, 1971.
The Curious Affair of the Third Dog. London, Collins, and New York, Holt Rinehart, 1973.
Black Widower. London, Collins, and New York, Holt Rinehart, 1975.
To Kill a Coconut. London, Collins, 1977; as *The Coconut Killings*, New York, Holt Rinehart, 1977.
Who Is Simon Warwick? London, Collins, 1978; New York, Holt Rinehart, 1979.
Angel Death. London, Collins, 1980; New York, Holt Rinehart, 1981.
A Six-Letter Word for Death. London, Collins, and New York, Holt Rinehart, 1983.
Night Ferry to Death. London, Collins, and New York, Holt Rinehart, 1985.
Black Girl, White Girl. New York, Holt, 1989; London, Collins, 1990.

Uncollected Short Stories

"The Representative," "The Revenge," "The Judgment of Solomon," "A Question of Timing," "The Treasure," "A Dream of a Girl," and "Fairy God-Daughter," in *Evening News* (London, 1961).
"The Holly Wreath," in *Women's Mirror* (London), 1965.
"Who Killed Father Christmas?," in *Who Done It?*, edited by Alice Laurance and Isaac Asimov. Boston, Houghton Mifflin, 1980.
"Beyond the Reef," in *Ellery Queen's Mystery Magazine* (New York), February 1982.
"A Whispering in the Reeds," in *Ellery Queen's Mystery Magazine* (New York), March 1982.
"A Matter of Succession," in *Ellery Queen's Mystery Magazine* (New York), May 1982.
"Hit and Run," in *Ellery Queen's Mystery Magazine* (New York), July 1982.
"The Honest Blackmailer," in *Ellery Queen's Mystery Magazine* (New York), September 1982.
"The Small Train Robbery," in *Ellery Queen's Mystery Magazine* (New York), November 1982.
"A Lonely Profession," in *Ellery Queen's Mystery Magazine* (New York), March 1983.
"Faces of Betrayal," in *Ellery Queen's Mystery Magazine* (New York), June 1983.
"The Faithful Cat," in *Ellery Queen's Mystery Magazine* (New York), July 1983.
"Flower of the Dead," in *Ellery Queen's Mystery Magazine* (New York), April 1984.
"The Extra Mile," in *Ellery Queen's Mystery Magazine* (New York), March 1989.

OTHER PUBLICATION

Plays

Time Remembered, adaptation of a play by Jean Anouilh (broadcast, 1954; produced London, 1954; New York, 1957). London, Meuthuen, 1955.

Screenplay: *School for Scoundrels*, with Peter Ustinov and Hal E. Chester, 1960.

Radio Play: *Time Remembered*, 1954.

Other

Helter-Skelter (for children). New York, Holt Rinehart, 1968; London Macdonald, 1969.
"Making a Mystery," in *Techniques of Novel Writing.* Boston, The Writer, 1973.
After All, They're Only Cats. New York, Curtis, 1973.
"The Joys of Inexperience," in *The Writer* (Boston), 1973.
"Mysteries Within Mysteries," in *The Writer* (Boston), 1975.
How to Talk to Your Cat. London, Barker, and New York, Holt Rinehart, 1978.

*

Patricia Moyes comments:

Really, all I can say about my work is that I try to write the sort of books that I enjoy reading—that is, I write for my own pleasure and never try to appeal to a particular market. My preference is for mystery stories that are well-plotted (and never cheat the reader), that are ingenious and amusing rather than vicious, and that are placed in a setting which the author clearly knows well, and peopled with characters who are more than dummies to be pushed around by the exigencies of the plot. I know that this sets a high standard, and I can't honestly pretend that I always achieve it—but I do try.

Apart from *Helter-Skelter* (written for teenagers), all my mystery stories feature Henry and Emmy Tibbett, and it has been one of my amusements over the years to round out their lives: Emmy's sister Jane, brother-in-law Bill, and niece Veronica feature in several books; we know where the Tibbetts live, what they like to eat and drink, what their hobbies are, and so on. I am delighted to know that there are readers who can document the Tibbetts almost as throughly as I can talk about Lady Constance Keeble (née Threepwood), now Lady Constance Schoonmaker of New York City (I need hardly add that the late and great P.G. Wodehouse is my favourite author). Talking of Wodehouse, I do not feel that what Noël Coward called "a talent to amuse" is something to be despised. Frankly, I would sooner divert people than put their souls through an emotional meat-grinder, and I have long ago stopped apologizing for not being a "serious" writer.

*   *   *

The advent of World War II appears, to many historians of the genre, to mark the exodus of the great Golden Age of the formal detective stroy. There is much evidence to justify this viewpoint. Several major authors such as Biggers, Freeman, and Van Dine died. Others, including Abbot, Berkeley, Hammett, and Sayers, abandoned the form for different pursuits. A few writers tried to extend the range of the detective story into that of the mainstream novel—often with disastrous results. An appreciable group concentrated on characterization and psychology to the detriment of puzzle and plot. Others emphasized action or suspense. Some eschewed ratiocination in favor of the crime novel. Prominent authors including Hull, Upfield, and Wade produced little or no work during the wartime years. Finally, the skills of too many writers simply fell into decline during this period. Yet a fair number of authors, including a handful of exceptionally talented newcomers, have stubbornly persisted in mining the vein of classic detection; one of the brightest of these luminaries is Patricia Moyes.

This author retains the Golden Age skill of evolving unusually well-constructed plots and puzzles. Her settings, based on travel and personal observation, are vivid, but never obtrusive. Her people, even the minor ones, are characterized with more skill and depth than are commonly found in Golden Age narratives. Almost all her novels are attractive and charming. Her series character, Henry Tibbett, is a slight and unmemorable person—a perfectly ordinary human being. He starts as a Chief Inspector at Scotland Yard, and eventually achieves the rank of Detective Chief Superintendent. His wife Emmy is frequently involved in his investigations, and is usually described as "nice" by most critics. Obviously a model of her sex.

Dead Men Don't Ski, a notable first novel, is set in the Italian Tyrol, and starts with the discovery of a corpse in a ski lift. An excellent follow-up novel, *The Sunken Sailor*, concerns an investigation into the year-old death of a yachtsman. Sailing, another Moyes enthusiasm, is well integrated into the fabric of the novel. *Death on the Agenda* has Tibbett in his official capacity attending an international conference on narcotics in Geneva. Somehow, the customary Moyes magic seems to be missing in this minor effort, but a strong recovery is evident in *Murder à la Mode*. Set in the editorial offices of a fashion magazine, and concerned with the murder of an employee, this novel received rave reviews—especially from Anthony Boucher who was remined of the golden days when Allingham, Blake, and Marsh were reshaping the detective novel.

Moyes's most impressive achievement is *Falling Star*, whose victim dies while acting in a film production. The author's work as a secretary to Peter Ustinov, as well as her work as a screenwriter, provided insight into the film-making process, and ensured an authentic background. *Falling Star* has a lighter, more easily flowing narrative style, and seems to be the beginning of Moyes's tendency to stress characterization over plot and puzzle. The usual third-person narration is here changed to the viewpoint of one of the film executives. *Johnny under Ground* details a murder problem with its roots in Emmy's wartime past while she was serving (as Moyes herself did) in the WAAF; it is not a major effort, but is interesting for its biographical details about Emmy. More conventional is *Murder Fantastical* with two murders, a little espionage, and an eccentric—to put it mildly—family living in the English countryside.

Death and the Dutch Uncle starts with the murder of a minor crook in a dreary London pub, escalates into a problem between two newly-created African nations, and evolves into a stiutation where Tibbett is forced to play nurse-maid to a short-tempered Dutch diplomat in his native land. A birthday for an eccentric old lady ends with her demise in *Who Saw Her Die?* Tibbett suspects foul play, but the medical authorities say natural causes. This is an engaging combination of the weekend house party and the perfect crime, and is one of Moyes's most sucessful books. Even better is *Season of Snows and Sins* which starts with an unfaithful husband's murder by his pregnant wife, and continues with enough ramifications to threaten the security of the French government. This novel is set in a Swiss skiing resort, and is narrated by Emmy and two other women. *The Curious Affair of the Third Dog* includes exciting greyhound racing, a missing hound, and the inevitable murder problem. *Black Widower*, a minor effort, is set in Washington and the Caribbean republic of Tampica—whose ambassador's wife has been murdered. The authorities summon Tibbett from Scotland Yard, and hope that his investigation will be discreet and effective. *To Kill a Coconut* is about the murder of an American senator while he is visiting the British Seaward Islands. This hook is not a major effort, but it has been unfairly maligned by many critics; it contains all the virtues (including detection) one can always expect from a story by Moyes.

The tricky legal problem of finding the long-lost heir to a considerable fortune begs the question *Who Is Simon Warwick?* Two contenders appear claiming to be the titular inheritor, but one is murdered and the other becomes the obvious and logical suspect. This is a warm, civilized, and attractive detective novel firmly investigated and resolved by Tibbett.

Angel Death is uncharacteristic for Moyes, who has here eschewed detection for the thriller form. It's also set in the well-realized British Seaward Islands, and concerns a missing and eccentric elderly lady, the drug traffic, two horrendous storms, and several characters who are not what they appear to be. All-in-all an intelligent and engaging entertainment.

A Six-Letter Word for Death starts with Chief Superintendent Tibbett's reception of an exceedingly difficult crossword puzzle, and continues with a weekend houseparty among a group of pseudonymous mystery writers on the Isle of Wight. Although neglected by many reviewers, this is Moyes's best performance in recent years, and a faultless reminder of the great golden age of the classic detective novel.

—Charles Shibuk

MUIR, Dexter. *See* **GRIBBLE, Leonard.**

MULLER, Marcia. American. Born in Detroit, Michigan, 28 September 1944. Educated at the University of Michigan, Ann Arbor, B.A. in English 1966, M.A. in journalism 1971. Married Frederick T. Gilson in 1967 (divorced 1981). Merchandising supervisor, *Sunset* magazine, Menlo Park, California, 1967–69; interviewer in San Francisco for University of Michigan Institute of Social Research, 1971–73, and other part-time jobs, including proposal writer, freight forwarder, and secretary, until 1979; partner, Invisible Ink, San Francisco, 1979–83. Since 1983 full-time writer. Agent: Molly Friedrich, Aaron Priest Literary Agency Inc., 122 East 42nd Street, Suite 3902, New York, New York 10168. Address: Box 1349, Sonoma, California 95476, U.S.A.

CRIME PUBLICATIONS

Novels (series: Sharon McCone; Elena Oliverez; Joanna Stark)

Edwin of the Iron Shoes (McCone). New York, McKay, 1977; London, Penguin, 1978.
Ask the Cards a Question (McCone) New York, St. Martin's Press, 1982; London, Hale, 1983.
The Cheshire Cat's Eye (McCone). New York, St. Martin's Press, and London, Hale, 1983.
The Tree of Death. (Oliverez). New York, Walker, 1983; London, Hale, 1986.
Games to Keep the Dark Away (McCone). New York, St. Martin's Press, 1984; London, Severn House, 1985.
Leave a Message for Willie (McCone). New York, St. Martin's Press, 1984.

Double (McCone), with Bill Pronzini.   New York, St. Martin's Press, 1984; London, Hale, 1986.

The Legend of the Slain Soldiers (Oliverez).   New York, Walker, 1985; London, Hale, 1986.

There's Nothing to Be Afraid Of (McCone).   New York, St. Martin's Press, 1985.

The Cavalier in White (Stark).   New York, St. Martin's Press, 1986.

Beyond the Grave (Oliverez), with Bill Pronzini.   New York, Walker, 1986.

The Lighthouse, with Bill Pronzini.   New York, St. Martin's Press, 1987; London, Hale, 1988.

Eye of the Storm (McCone), with Bill Pronzini.   New York, Mysterious Press, 1988.

There Hangs the Knife (Stark).   New York, St. Martin's Press, 1988.

Dark Star (Stark).   New York, St. Martin's Press, 1989.

There's Something in a Sunday (McCone).   New York, Mysterious Press, 1989.

The Shape of Dread (McCone).   New York, Mysterious Press, 1989.

Uncollected Short Stories

"Merrill-Go-Round," in *The Arbor House Treasury of Mystery and Suspense*, edited by Bill Pronzini, Barry N. Malzberg, and Martin H. Greenberg.   New York, Arbor House, 1982.

"Dust to Dust," in *Specter!*, edited by Bill Pronzini.   New York, Arbor House, 1982.

"Cattails," in *The Web She Weaves*, edited by Marcia Muller and Bill Pronzini.   New York, Morrow, 1983.

"Kindling Point," in *Witches' Brew*, edited by Marcia Muller and Bill Pronzini.   New York, Macmillan, 1984.

"Wild Mustard," in *The Eyes Have It*, edited by Robert J. Randisi.   New York, Mysterious Press, 1984.

"The Sanchez Sacraments," in *The Ethnic Detectives*, edited by Bill Pronzini and Martin H. Greenberg.   New York, Dodd Mead, 1985.

"The Broken Men," in *Women Sleuths*, edited by Bill Pronzini and Martin H. Greenberg. Chicago, Academy, 1985.

"Deceptions," in *A Matter of Crime*, edited by Matthew J. Bruccoli and Richard Layman. San Diego, Harcourt Brace, 1987.

"Cache and Carry" with Bill Pronzini, in *Small Felonies*, edited by Bill Pronzini.   New York, St. Martin's Press, 1988.

"All the Lonely People," in *Sisters in Crime*, edited by Marilyn Wallace.   New York, Berkley, 1989; London, Robinson, 1990.

"Silent Night," in *Mistletoe Mysteries*, edited by Charlotte MacLeod.   New York, Mysterious Press, 1989.

"Deadly Fantasies," in *Alfred Hitchcock's Mystery Magazine* (New York), April 1989.

"The Place That Time Forgot," in *Sisters in Crime 2*, edited by Marilyn Wallace.   New York, Berkley, 1990.

"Somewhere in the City," in *The Armchair Detective* (New York), Winter 1990.

OTHER PUBLICATIONS

Other

"Creating the Female Sleuth," in *The Writer* (Boston), October 1978.

"The Inner Suspense Story," in *The Writer* (Boston), December 1983.

"Should You Collaborate?" with Bill Pronzini, in *The Writer* (Boston), March 1985.

"Plotting the Realistic Detective Novel," in *The Writer* (Boston), June 1987.

"Free-Form Plotting in the Mystery," in *The Writer* (Boston), September 1989.

Editor, with Bill Pronzini, *The Web She Weaves: An Anthology of Mysteries and Suspicious Stories by Women*.   New York, Morrow, 1983.

Editor, with Bill Pronzini, *Child's Ploy*.   New York, Macmillan, 1984.

Editor, with Bill Pronzini, *Witches' Brew: Horror and Supernatural Stories by Women*.   New York, Macmillan, 1984.

Editor, with Bill Pronzini, *Dark Lessons: Crime and Detection on Campus*.   New York, Macmillan, 1985.

Editor, with Bill Pronzini, *She Won the West: An Anthology of Western and Frontier Stories by Women*.   New York, Morrow, 1985.

Editor, with Bill Pronzini, *Chapter and Hearse: Suspense Stories about the World of Books*.   New York, Morrow, 1985.

Editor, with Bill Pronzini, *Kill or Cure: Suspense Stories about the World of Medicine*.   New York, Macmillan, 1985.

Editor, with Bill Pronzini, *The Wickedest Show on Earth: A Carnival of Circus Suspense*. New York, Arbor House, 1985.

Editor, with Bill Pronzini, *The Deadly Arts: A Collection of Artful Suspense*. New York, Arbor House, 1985.

Editor, with Bill Pronzini, *1001 Midnights: The Aficionado's Guide to Mystery and Detective Fiction*.   New York, Arbor House, 1986.

Editor, with Bill Pronzini and Martin H. Greenberg, *Lady on the Case*.   New York, Bonanza, 1988.

*

Marcia Muller comments:

In my detective fiction I am attempting to explore various problems of contemporary American society through the eyes of women who become involved in situations which compel them to seek the solutions to various crimes. In the cases of amateur detectives Elena Oliverez and Joanna Stark, these circumstances are more or less thrust upon them, and the women have a strong personal stake in seeing the perpetrators of the crimes brought to justice. Private investigator Sharon McCone's involvement is professional, but more often than not she becomes deeply involved with her clients and/or crimes' victims. These characters are people with day-to-day problems and personal lives, who must deal with the increasingly complex pressures and issues posed by modern society. While not superwomen, when forced to confront extraordinary situations, they reach beyond their normal capabilities, and grow and change accordingly.

*   *   *

With the introduction of Sharon McCone, private investigator, licensed by the State of California and operating in San Francisco, we have the first independent woman private investigator character. Unlike other female investigators, Sharon hasn't inherited an office from a relative or partner nor did she develop her job as a sideline with a male accomplice doing the leg work and running around getting beaten up in dark alleys. She is a full time investigator for All Souls Legal Cooperative, now a few years over 30, and she reflects her one-eighth Shoshone Indian heritage with her black hair and dark, flashing eyes.

The first book, *Edwin of The Iron Shoes*, sets the pace for her calm, reasonable style of investigation when she investigates the murder of one of the law firm's clients who was found dead in her antique shop. While completing an inventory of the shop's contents for probate purposes, Sharon uncovers several leads that eventually disclose the motive and the murderer. Lt. Greg Marcus of San Francisco's Homicide Division heads the investigative team and much to Sharon's dismay she is attracted to him.

As the series progresses Sharon finds herself becoming more secure and with a stronger professional attitude toward her clients and their problems, but she still devotes much of her strength and intellect to finding out why a crime has been committed and how the person who committed it thinks and is likely to act. By using the All Souls Legal Cooperative office as a firm base for assignments Muller has given McCone diverse cases that, in some instances, take her out of the city to a fresh new geographical area.

Joanna Stark is a women in her mid-forties who had been an active partner in a firm that provided security systems for art museums and galleries. Now a recent widow, she has moved out of San Francisco to the wine country north of the city but her partner calls on her for help when the titular painting *The Cavalier in White* is stolen from a museum they had wired. Art thief Antony Parducci, who played a large part in her younger years, is someone that we find in all three books as Joanna searches for him in Britain in *There Hangs the Knife* and in the culminating book *Dark Star*. This series is less successful as a mystery but Muller cleverly depicts the results of long held enmity and of generational relationships. The freshness of the wine growing area of Northern California is highlighted by the activities of Joanna's stepson Eliot who is occasionally so busy "finding himself" as to lose track of his goals.

Muller's deft touch is shown by her dialogue that is bright without being brittle and through her presentation of believable settings. Her women characters are strong yet vulnerable as reflected by their professional and personal activities and her meticulous attention to character motivation is subtle and compelling. Sharon McCone continues to mature as a woman and as a professional and it is a measure of Muller's skill that we care that this is so.

Double, a book written with Bill Pronzini, has alternate chapters that feature Sharon and "Nameless" and introduce several members of her family. Later, in *Eye of the Storm*, Sharon works to solve a case of murder that involves one of her sisters who was establishing a bed-and-breakfast hotel in the Sacramento Delta.

The various locales where Sharon's cases take place make this series a delightful change from the back alley, whiskey-bottle-in-the-bottom-drawer, clobbered-on-the-back-of-the-head motifs that permeate other efforts in this field.

In addition to McCone, Muller created another women character who also breaks new ground. Elena Oliverez, a Chicana, is featured in three books that start with *The Tree of Death* in which she is the assistant to the director of a Mexican arts museum in a town that could well be Santa Barbara. Elena's relationship with her slightly eccentric mother, Gabriella, is more focused in the succeeding books when Elena solves a murder the affects residents at the senior citizens' trailer park where her mother lives. Elena's recognition of her Hispanic heritage is strongly focused as she solves *The Legend of the Slain Soldiers*. *Beyond the Grave* highlights a part of California history that will be fresh and new to most readers. She is a fetching amateur sleuth with intuitive deductive skills and commonsense.

—Ellen Nehr

MUNRO, James. *See* MITCHELL, James.

MURPHY, Warren and SAPIR, Richard. Americans. Murphy, Warren B.: Born in Jersey City, New Jersey, 13 September 1933. Educated at St. Peter's College, Jersey City, 1968–60. Served in the United States Air Force Alaskan Air Command, 1952–56: Sergeant. Married 1) Dawn Walters in 1955 (divorced 1973), four children; 2) Molly Cochran in 1984, one son. Worked as reporter and editor, and political consultant; commissioner, New Jersey State Meadowlands, 1978–81. Founding director, Private Eye Writers of America, and American Crime Writers League; member of the board of directors, Mystery Writers of America. Recipient: Private Eye Writers of America special award, 1983, 1984, 1985, 1986, 1987, and Shamus award, 1985; Mystery Writers of America Edgar Allan Poe award, 1985, 1986. Agent: McBride Agency, 7077 Neptune Place, La Jolla, California 92037. Address: RD 3, Box 99, Bethlehem, Pennsylvania 18015, U.S.A. SAPIR, Richard (Ben): Born in New York City, 27 July 1936. Educated at Columbia University, New York, B.S. 1960. Married Patricia Chute in 1980. Worked as a newspaper reporter and editor, and in public relations. *Died 27 January 1987.*

CRIME PUBLICATIONS

Novels (series: Remo Williams, The Destroyer)

The Destroyer (books from no. 35 by Warren Murphy only)
  1. *Created: The Destroyer.* New York, Pinnacle, 1971; London, Corgi, 1973.
  2. *Death Check.* New York, Pinnacle, 1971; London, Corgi, 1973.
  3. *The Chinese Puzzle.* New York, Pinnacle, 1972; London, Corgi, 1973.
  4. *Mafia Fix.* New York, Pinnacle, 1972; London, Corgi, 1974.
  5. *Dr. Quake.* New York, Pinnacle, 1972; London, Corgi, 1974.
  6. *Death Therapy.* New York, Pinnacle, 1972; London, Corgi, 1974.
  7. *Union Bust.* New York, Pinnacle, 1973; London, Corgi, 1974.
  8. *Summit Chase.* New York, Pinnacle, 1973; London, Corgi, 1975.
  9. *Murder's Shield.* New York, Pinnacle, 1973; London, Corgi, 1975.
  10. *Terror Squad.* New York, Pinnacle, 1973; London, Corgi, 1975.
  11. *Kill or Cure.* New York, Pinnacle, 1973; London, Corgi, 1975.
  12. *Slave Safari.* New York, Pinnacle, 1973; London, Corgi, 1976.
  13. *Acid Rock.* New York, Pinnacle, 1973; London, Corgi, 1975.
  14. *Judgment Day.* New York, Pinnacle, 1974; London, Corgi, 1976.
  15. *Murder Ward.* New York, Pinnacle, 1974; London, Corgi, 1976.
  16. *Oil Slick.* New York, Pinnacle, 1974; London, Corgi, 1977.
  17. *Last War Dance.* New York, Pinnacle, 1974; London, Corgi, 1977.

18. *Funny Money.* New York, Pinnacle, 1975; London, Corgi, 1977.
19. *Holy Terror.* New York, Pinnacle, 1975; London, Corgi, 1978.
20. *Assassins Play-Off.* New York, Pinnacle, 1975; London, Corgi, 1978.
21. *Deadly Seeds.* New York, Pinnacle, 1975; London, Corgi, 1978.
22. *Brain Drain.* New York, Pinnacle, 1976; London, Corgi, 1978.
23. *Child's Play.* New York, Pinnacle, 1976; London, Corgi, 1978.
24. *King's Curse.* New York, Pinnacle, 1976; London, Corgi, 1978.
25. *Sweet Dreams* (by Murphy and Richard S. Meyers). New York, Pinnacle, 1976; London, Corgi, 1978.
26. *In Enemy Hands.* New York, Pinnacle, 1977; London, Corgi, 1978.
27. *The Last Temple* (by Murphy and Richard S. Meyers). New York, Pinnacle, 1977; London, Corgi, 1978.
28. *Ship of Death.* New York, Pinnacle, 1977; London, Corgi, 1979.
29. *The Final Death* (by Murphy and Richard S. Meyers). New York, Pinnacle, 1977; London, Corgi, 1979.
30. *Mugger Blood.* Los Angeles, Pinnacle, 1977; London, Corgi, 1979.
31. *The Head Men.* Los Angeles, Pinnacle, 1977; London, Corgi, 1979.
32. *Killer Chromosomes.* Los Angeles, Pinnacle, 1978; London, Corgi, 1979.
33. *Voodoo Die.* Los Angeles, Pinnacle, 1978; London, Corgi, 1980.
34. *Chained Reaction.* Los Angeles, Pinnacle, 1978; London, Corgi, 1980.
35. *Last Call.* Los Angeles, Pinnacle, 1978; London, Corgi, 1981.
36. *Power Play.* Los Angeles, Pinnacle, 1979; London, Corgi, 1981.
37. *Bottom Line.* Los Angeles, Pinnacle, 1979; London, Corgi, 1981.
38. *Bay City Blast.* Los Angeles, Pinnacle, 1979; London, Corgi, 1981.
39. *Missing Link.* Los Angeles, Pinnacle, 1980.
40. *Dangerous Games,* with Robert J. Randisi. Los Angeles, Pinnacle, 1980.
41. *Firing Line.* Los Angeles, Pinnacle, 1980.
42. *Timber Line.* Los Angeles, Pinnacle, 1980.
43. *Midnight Man,* with Robert J. Randisi. Los Angeles, Pinnacle, 1981.
44. *Balance of Power.* Los Angeles, Pinnacle, 1981.
45. *Spoils of War.* New York, Pinnacle, 1981.
46. *Next of Kin.* New York, Pinnacle, 1981.
47. *Dying Space.* New York, Pinnacle, 1982.
48. *Profit Motive,* with Sapir. New York, Pinnacle, 1982.
49. *Skin Deep.* New York, Pinnacle, 1982.
50. *Killing Time.* New York, Pinnacle, 1982.
51. *Shock Value.* New York, Pinnacle, 1983.
52. *Fool's Gold,* with Sapir. New York, Pinnacle, 1983.
53. *Time Trial.* New York, Pinnacle, 1983.
54. *Last Drop.* New York, Pinnacle, 1983.
55. *Master's Challenge.* New York, Pinnacle, 1984.
56. *Encounter Group.* New York, Pinnacle, 1984.
57. *Date with Death.* New York, Pinnacle, 1984.
58. *Total Recall,* with Robert J. Randisi. New York, Pinnacle, 1984.
59. *The Arms of Kali.* New York, New American Library, 1985.
60. *The End of the Game.* New York, New American Library, 1985.
61. *The Lords of the Earth.* New York, New American Library, 1985.
62. *The Seventh Stone.* New York, New American Library, 1985.
63. *The Sky Is Falling* (by Sapir). New York, New American Library, 1986.
64. *The Last Alchemist* (by Sapir). New York, New American Library, 1986.
65. *Lost Yesterday* (by Sapir). New York, New American Library, 1986.
66. *Sue Me* (by Sapir). New York, New American Library, 1986.
67. *Look Into My Eyes* (by Sapir). New York, New American Library, 1987.
68. *An Old-Fashioned War* (by Sapir). New York, New American Library, 1987.
69. *Blood Ties.* New York, New American Library, 1987.
70. *The Eleventh Hour.* New York, New American Library, 1987.
71. *Return Engagement.* New York, New American Library, 1988.
72. *Sole Survivor.* New York, New American Library, 1988.
73. *Line of Succession.* New York, New American Library, 1988.
74. *Walking Wounded.* New York, New American Library, 1988.
75. *Rain of Terror.* New York, New American Library, 1988.
76. *The Final Crusade.* New York, New American Library, 1989.
77. *Coin of the Realm.* New York, New American Library, 1989.
78. *Blue Smoke and Mirrors.* New York, New American Library, 1989.
79. *Shooting Schedule.* New York, New American Library, 1989.
80. *Death Sentence.* New York, New American Library, 1990.

Remo : The First Adventure (novelization of screenplay). New York, New American Library, 1985.

Novels by Warren Murphy (series: Julian "Digger" Burroughs; Grandmaster; Detectives Edward Razoni and William Jackson; Devlin "Trace" Tracy)

One Night Stand (Razoni and Jackson). New York, Pinnacle, 1973.
Dead End Street (Razoni and Jackson). New York, Pinnacle, 1973.
City in Heat (Razoni and Jackson). New York, Pinnacle, 1973.
Down and Dirty (Razoni and Jackson). New York, Pinnacle, 1974.
Lynch Town (Razoni and Jackson). New York, Pinnacle, 1974.
Leonardo's Law. New York, Carlyle, 1978.
Atlantic City, with Frank Stevens. Los Angeles, Pinnacle, 1979; London, Sphere, 1980.
The Red Moon. New York, Fawcett, 1982.
Smoked Out (Digger). New York, Pocket Books, 1982.
Fool's Flight (Digger). New York, Pocket Books, 1982.
Dead Letter (Digger). New York, Pocket Books, 1982.
Lucifer's Weekend (Digger; with Robert J. Randisi). New York, Pinnacle, 1982.
Trace. New York, New American Library, 1983.
And 47 Miles of Rope (Trace). New York, New American Library, 1984.

Grandmaster, with Molly Cochran. New York, Pinnacle, 1984. London, Macdonald, 1985.
When Elephants Forget (Trace). New York, New American Library, 1984.
The Ceiling of Hell. New York, Fawcett, 1984.
Pigs Get Fat (Trace). New York, New American Library, 1985.
Once a Mutt (Trace). New York, New American Library, 1986.
Too Old a Cat. New York, New American Library, 1987.
High Priest (Grandmaster), with Molly Cochran. New York, New American Library, 1987.
Getting Up with Fleas (Trace) New York, New American Library, 1988.
The Hand of Lazarus, with Molly Cochran. New York, Pinnacle, 1988.
The Sure Thing. New York, Pinnacle, 1988.
The Temple Dogs, with Cochran. New York, New American Library, 1989.
Jericho Day. Texas, Diamond, 1989.
Scorpion's Dance. New York, Pinnacle, 1990.

Uncollected Short Stories

"An Element of Surprise," in *Murder in Manhattan*, edited by Bill Adler and D.C. Fontana. New York, Morrow, 1986.

Novels by Richard Sapir

Bressio. New York, Random House, 1975.
Spies. New York, Doubleday, 1984; London, W.H. Allen, 1985.
Quest. New York, Dutton, 1987; London, Macdonald, 1988.

OTHER PUBLICATIONS

Novels by Richard Sapir

The Far Arena. New York, Seaview, 1978; London, Secker and Warburg, 1979.
The Body. New York, Doubleday, 1983; London, W.H. Allen, 1984.

Plays by Warren Murphy

Screenplays: *The Eiger Sanction*, with Hal Dresner and Rod Whitaker, 1975; *Lethal Weapon II*, with Shane Black, 1989.

Other

The Assassins Handbook (by Richard Sapir, and Will Murray). New York, Pinnacle, 1982.

*

Bibliography: "The Destroyer Series," by Will Murray, in *Paperback Quarterly*, Winter 1981.

*   *   *

In 1963 Warren Murphy, then a secretary to the Mayor of Jersey City, New Jersey, and a reporter on the City Hall beat, Richard (Ben) Sapir, decided to collaborate on an adventure novel featuring a brash young Westerner trained in the martial arts by an inscrutable Oriental Master. While it took some time

for the idea to catch on (the first *Destroyer* novel was published in 1971), the theme quickly became a cherished part of popular fiction (e.g. *The Karate Kid* movies). There are now over 30 million copies of the *Destroyer* novels in print, in 11 languages.

80 *Destroyer* books have now been written, together with a novelization of the movie *Remo Williams: The Adventure Begins*, and the characters are as real as ever. Remo Williams, an ex-cop named after the Indiana town in which his hospital bed pan was manufactured, learns Sinanju, a fictional Korean martial art, at the hands of its venerable last Master, Chiun. Together they take on problems of a troubled world that make *The Labors of Hercules* look like mumblety-peg.

Originally conceived as a parody of "Super Spy" novels, the series owes its success to the fact that its heros are real people, their problems and emotions common ones, and the social and political basis for its plots mirrored in everyday reality.

The consistent high quality of the prose stems from the fact that Murphy finished and fine tuned every script, usually from an outline and 95-page start by Sapir. But in 1978, after the first 34 books, Sapir opted to raise his literary sights and disassociated himself from the series. He later recanted this decision and returned to co-author No. 48, *Profit Motive*, and No. 52 *Fool's Gold*, and wrote Numbers 63 through 68 on his own.

Murphy says of him "He had the most amazing talent for coming up with great story 'McGuffins,' plot twists; reading his work was like going to writing school. At his untimely death, he had barely touched how great he was going to be."

The breadth of Murphy's talent staggers the imagination. Comic detectives, caper novels, large suspense novels, sword and sorcery spy novels, and locked-room mysteries, together with short stories, comic books, movies and countless collaborations do not even begin to mark the parameters of his creative genius.

The Ceiling of Hell, winner of the Private Eye Writers of America Shamus award in 1985, is a prime example of Murphy's wide range. The story of disabled Secret Service Agent Steve Hooks's struggle to cope with the collapse of both his personal and professional lives captured the imaginations of millions of readers.

Similarly, *Murphy's Law*, starring George Segal and Maggie Han and based loosely on Murphy's characters "Trace" and "Chico", harvested a huge television following throughout the world.

A mystical event takes place in books co-authored by Murphy and Cochran. For a moment, the suspension of disbelief becomes so profound that readers are transmigrated to lands that never were with such vivid detail that they experience a sense of loss when the books end. *Grandmaster*, an Edgar winner, *High Priest* and *The Temple Dogs* are books like this. Hopefully, they mark only the beginnings of an endless collaboration that will continue to enrich the reading public for countless years.

Because of a glitch in the printing order of the *The Temple Dogs*, the hardcover of this book has become a collector's item in its own time.

Sapir eventually succeeded in achieving judgment on his own terms. The New York *Times* review of his final work, *Quest*, an ambitious project concerning the Holy Grail, ended with the statement "Mr. Sapir is a brilliant professional." Unfortunately, he never got to read it, as it was published after his death.

Murphy, however, is the professional's professional, the hallmark of work of consistently high quality produced in spite of the mercenary peccadilloes of a constantly changing publishing scene. A warm, generous man, he is often the victim of "ricochet discrimination." The sharp, snide, cutting one-line retorts and highly prejudiced viewpoints of some of his characters are wrongfully taken to reflect the author's personal feelings. Nothing could be further from the truth, but such phenomena characteristically fail to bother Murphy. He simply philosophizes "It goes with the territory."

—Robert H. Meier.

MURRAY, Max(well). Born in Australia, in 1901. Married the writer Maysie Greig in 1937. Reporter in Australia, the United States, and England; screenwriter and editor for the BBC, London, during World War II. *Died in 1956.*

CRIME PUBLICATIONS

Novels

The Voice of the Corpse. New York, Farrar Straus, 1947; London, Joseph, 1948.
The King and the Corpse. New York, Farrar Straus, 1948; London, Joseph, 1949.
The Queen and the Corpse. New York, Farrar Straus, 1949; as *No Duty on a Corpse*, London, Joseph, 1950.
The Neat Little Corpse. New York, Farrar Straus, 1950; London, Joseph, 1951.
Good Luck to the Corpse. New York, Farrar Straus, 1951; London, Joseph, 1953.
The Right Honorable Corpse. New York, Farrar Straus, 1951; London, Joseph, 1952.
The Doctor and the Corpse. New York, Farrar Straus, 1952; London, Joseph, 1953.
The Sunshine Corpse. London, Joseph, 1954.
Royal Bed for a Corpse. London, Joseph, and New York, Washburn, 1955.
Breakfast with a Corpse. London, Joseph, 1956; as *A Corpse for Breakfast*, New York, Washburn, 1957.
Twilight at Dawn. London, Joseph, 1957.
Wait for a Corpse. London, Joseph, and New York, Washburn, 1957.

OTHER PUBLICATIONS

Play

The Admiral's Chair (produced London, 1931).

Other

The World's Back Doors. London, Cape, 1927; New York, Cape and Smith, 1929.
Long Way to London. London, Cape, 1931.

* * *

Max Murray worked his way around the world from Australia to London on tramp steamers and even served a season on a Mississippi River tug boat but the ships he used in a number of his books were much smaller but still sea-going yachts. A frequent theme that he used effectively in his novels was that of a young boy in some kind of danger that occasionally included kidnapping. Most of his heroes bear uncompromising British names; Patrick, Peter, Brian, Julian, and Martin and are more or less interchangeable characters with the places of their education unmentioned but the quality taken for granted. They do have highly diverse occupations that range from pianist to boat builder, to farmer, military pilot, junior diplomat, physician, and lawyer. Their clean good looks, hints of past military service and wholesome personalities make them ideal protagonists for these mystery-plus-adventure novels. The romantic angles are not blatantly presented and there is always some sort of misunderstanding, arising usually from lack of communication that also complicates the mystery. In mysteries that involve a little boy the final clinch between the hero and heroine always provides him with a complete family.

Locations range from the stately home of Prior's Cross in *Royal Bed for a Corpse*, where a traitor is found murdered in the Queen's Bed. A typical English village is a target of poison pen notes in *The Voice of the Corpse* and the murder of their writer, Angela Pewsey, who sang while knitting dog hair into sweaters, would have been gratefully covered up were it not for the hero who becomes involved after the fact. Using the clear waters of Jamaica, where a search for documents in a watertight casket hidden in a wrecked ship for 150 years might change the ownership of a plantation, Murray wrote his most colorful novel in *The Neat Little Corpse*. Florida is as much a part of the story as the characters and crime in *The Sunshine Corpse*. Three books take place on and near the coast of the French Riviera in Nice: *The King and the Corpse*, *Good Luck to the Corpse* and *Breakfast with a Corpse*.

Murray was never at a loss when he ascribed motives to his villains. They are uncompromising, uncouth, and unpleasant people who are often involved in drug trafficking, blackmail, treason, treasure acquisition, and land grabbing. His heroines are evenly divided between British young women, and American women. This upper-class milieu often has a black sheep member of the family who plays a small but meaningful part, while the role of the colorful older women is to protect their men at all costs from the follies of their own actions.

Murray was particularly good at providing well-hidden clues to all of the motives for murder but he, more often than not, allowed the killer to be his or her own executioner.

All the stories are set in their own times and might be considered dated by modern standards; however, the morals, motives, and reactions are still fresh and interesting while the geography can never change.

—Ellen Nehr

MYLES, Symon. *See* **FOLLETT, Ken.**

N

NABB, Magdalen. British. Born in Lancashire, 16 January 1947. Moved to Italy in 1977. Freelance writer. Address: c/o William Collins Sons and Company Ltd., 8 Grafton Street, London W1X 3LA, England.

CRIME PUBLICATIONS

Novels (series: Marshal Guarnaccia in all books except *The Prosecutor*)

Death of an Englishman. London, Collins, 1981; New York, Scribner, 1982.
Death of a Dutchman, London, Collins, 1982; New York, Scribner, 1983.
Death in Springtime. London, Collins, 1983; New York, Scribner, 1984.
Death in Autumn. London, Collins, and New York, Scribner, 1985.
The Prosecutor, with Paolo Vagheggi. London, Collins, 1986; New York, Scribner, 1987.
The Marshal and the Murderer. London, Collins, and New York, Scribner, 1987.
The Marshal and the Madwoman. London, Collins, and New York, Scribner, 1988.
The Marshal's Own Case. London, Collins, and New York, Scribner, 1990.

OTHER PUBLICATIONS

Novels (for children)

Josie Smith [*at the Seaside, At School*]. London, Collins, 3 vols., 1988–90; New York, McElderry, first 2 vols., 1989–90.

Play

Florence of the North (produced Croydon, 1978).

* * *

A series of rather prosaic titles such as *The Marshal's Own Case* and *Death in Autumn* gives no clue as to how well-plotted and inventive Magdalen Nabb's crime novels can be.

Assured and humane, Nabb's fiction draws heavily on European precedents, particularly Simenon. Characterised by their meticulously indicated location (Florence and the Tuscan countryside), Nabb's novels offer an all too human police investigator in the likeable, slow-moving and on occasion taciturn Sicilian, Marshal Guarnaccia of the Carabinieri. Like the Belgian writer, who praised her work in no uncertain terms, she also creates gripping and plausible studies of little people caught up in murder as both victims and guilt-torn criminals.

Nabb's debut, *Death of an Englishman,* reveals not only her talent as a writer of detective fiction, but also an outsider's view of Florence. Set physically in a beautiful but also seedy city of much toured palaces and smog-shrouded piazzas, her first novel, however, takes place for the large part in an ex-patriate community of English eccentrics and worthies.

As the Guarnaccia novels proceed, though, Nabb's own understanding of Florentine life and assimilation into Italian culture become prominent, and she concentrates more and more on issues within the indigenous community.

However, she still retains non-Italian characters in the majority of her novels. Tuscany's position as a centre for tourism, and as a favoured place for foreign investment of both a legal and an illegal nature, allows Nabb to introduce outsiders into her Italian settings, very often as victims of crimes.

In *Death in Springtime* a poor little American rich girl is involved in a botched kidnapping. Nabb admirably delineates the terrain of the exiled Sardinian shepherds on the barren Tuscan foothills and their equally displaced children's involvement in Florentine low-life. *Death in Autumn* depicts the reclusive life and lonely death of a German woman of a certain age, and with a mysterious past, in central Florence. Here as in all her novels, Nabb poignantly describes lives of quiet desperation.

Death of a Dutchman, the most obvious clue-puzzle of the Marshal books, uses the central device of the death of a foreigner, setting off the police investigation. A jeweller of Anglo-Italian background, now domiciled in Holland, is found dead in an empty flat, a presumed suicide. Memorable in this novel is Signora Giusti, an over-bearing and over-poweringly vital 91-year-old, who bosses the Marshal into action. *The Marshal and the Murderer* deals with the disappearance of a young Swiss woman, and leads Guarnaccia to a depressed and tight-lipped small town near Florence where a wartime crime still haunts the inhabitants.

In her more recent novels such as *The Marshal and the Madwoman* and *The Marshal's Own Case,* Nabb has had the confidence to shed this pattern of murdered outsiders and investigating insiders, preferring to concentrate on the relationship between the dispossessed and the socially comfortable. The first title produces a pitiful creation in the figure of the taunted madwoman, Clementina, whose earlier happy life was tragically brought to an end by natural catastrophe, and whose unhappy second existence is terminated by human greed. *The Marshal's Own Case* deals with the death of Lulu, a transsexual prostitute. The novel deals sensitively with the lives of social and sexual outcasts, whose trade on the margins of Florence does not, however, prevent contact with and violence from seemingly respectable and securely prosperous citizens.

Many crime writers have felt obliged to individuate and domesticate their detectives by surrounding them with sundry family complications, sometimes without real regard to the central narrative. A salient feature of Nabb's writing is the seemingly effortless way she incorporates the Marshal's extended family affairs into her novels.

—Anna-Marie Taylor

NEBEL, (Louis) Frederick. Also wrote as Grimes Hill. American. Born in Staten Island, New York, 3 November 1903. Married Dorothy Blank in 1930; one son. Worked as car checker on New York docks, on his grandfather's homestead in northern Canada, and on a tramp steamer. Lived in Ridgefield, Connecticut, 1934–59, and in Laguna Beach, California, after 1959. *Died 3 May 1967.*

Crime Publications

Novels

Sleepers East. Boston, Little Brown, 1933; London, Gollancz, 1934.
Fifty Roads to Town. Boston, Little Brown, and London, Cape, 1936.

Short Stories

Six Deadly Dames. New York, Avon, 1950.
The Adventures of Cardigan, New York, Mysterious Press, 1988.

Uncollected Short Stories (series character: Buck Jason; all stories appeared in *Black Mask*, New York)

"China Silk," March 1927; "Hounds of Darkness," April 1927; "Emeralds of Shade," August 1927.

Uncollected Short Stories (series: Captain Steve MacBride and reporter Kennedy)

"The Crimes of Richmond City," September 1928; "Dog Eat Dog," October 1928; "The Law Laughs Last," November 1928; "Law Without Law," April 1929; "Graft," April 1929; "New Guns for Old," September 1929; "Hell-Smoke," November 1929; "Tough Treatment," January 1930; "Alley Rat," February 1930; "Ten Men from Chicago," August 1930; "Shake-Down" September 1930; "Junk," March 1931; "Beat the Rap," May 1931; "Death for a Dago," July 1931; "Some Die Young," December 1931; "The Quick or the Dead," March 1932; "Backwash," May 1932; "Doors in the Dark," February 1933; "Rough Reform," March 1933; "Farewell to Crime," April 1933; "Guns Down," September 1933; "Lay Down the Law," November 1933; "Too Young to Die," February 1934; "Bad News," March 1934; "Take It and Like It," June 1934 (reprinted in *The Hard-Boiled Detective* edited by Herbert Ruhm, New York, Vintage, 1977); "Be Your Age," August 1934; "He Was a Swell Guy," January 1935; "It's a Gag," February 1935; "That's Kennedy," May 1935; "Die-Hard," August 1935; "Winter Kill" November 1935 (reprinted in *The Hardboiled Dicks,* edited by Ron Goulart, Los Angeles, Sherbourne Press, 1966, London, Boardman, 1967); "Fan Dance," January 1936; "No Hard Feelings," February 1936; "Crack Down," April 1936; "Hard to Take," June 1936; "Deep Red," August 1936; all in *Black Mask* (New York).

Uncollected Short Stories (series: Donny Donahue)

"Rough Justice," November 1930; "Gun Thunder," January 1931; "Shake-Up," August 1932 (reprinted as "Dead Date," in *Ellery Queen's Mystery Magazine,* New York, April 1946); "He Could Take It," September 1932; "Red Web," October 1932; "Red Pavement," December 1932; "Song and Dance," July 1933; "Champions Also Die," August 1933;

"Ghost of a Chance," March 1935; all in *Black Mask* (New York); 6 stories reprinted in *Six Deadly Dames.*

Uncollected Short Stories (series: Cardigan)

"Death Alley," November 1931; "Hell's Pay Check," December 1931; "Six Diamonds and a Dick," January 1932; "Phantom Fingers," March 1932; "Murder on the Loose," April 1932; "Rogue's Ransom," August 1932; "Lead Pearls," September 1932; "The Dead Don't Die," October 1932; "The Candy Killer," November 1932; "A Truck-Load of Diamonds," December 1932; "Murder Cure," January 1933; "Me—Cardigan," February 1933; "Doorway to Danger," 1 March 1933; "Heir to Murder," 1 April 1933; "Dead Man's Folly," 1 May 1933; "Murder Won't Wait," 15 May 1933; "Chains of Darkness," 15 June 1933; "Scrambled Murder," 15 June 1933; "Death after Murder," 15 August 1933; "Murder & Co.," 15 September 1933; "Read 'em and Weep," 1 May 1934; "Red Hot," 1 July 1934; "Not So Tough," 15 August 1934; "Too Hot to Handle," 15 September 1934; "Pardon My Murder," 15 November 1934; "Leave It to Cardigan," 15 December 1934; "Hell on Wheels," 1 February 1935; "A Couple of Quick Ones," 1 June 1935; "Death in the Raw," October 1935; "The Curse of Cardigan," December 1935; "Blood in the Dark," January 1936; "The Sign of Murder," March 1936; "Lead Poison," April 1936; "Murder by Mail," June 1936; "Make Mine Murder," November 1936; "Behind the Eight Ball," March 1937; "No Time to Kill," May 1937; all in *Dime Detective* (Kokomo, Indiana).

Uncollected Short Stories (series: Sergeant Brinkhaus)

"The Mystery at Pier 7," September 1931, "The Crooked Spot," October 1931, "Whispers of Death," December 1931, "The X-Circle," January 1932, "The Crimson Fist," March 1932, and "Murder by Ballot," April 1932, all in *Detective Action;* "The Tailormade Clue," in *Dime Detective,* June 1932; "The Devil's Slouch," 10 December 1932, "The Green Widow," 11 February 1933, "The Lemon," 6 May 1933, and "Strangle Hold," 29 July 1933, all in *Detective Fiction Weekly* (New York).

Uncollected Short Stories

"The Breaks of the Game," March 1926, "Grain to Grain," November 1926, "Dumb Luck," January 1927, "A Man with Sand," July 1927, "A Grudge Is a Grudge," September 1927, "With Benefit of Law," November 1927, "The Penalty of the Code," January 1928, "A Gun in the Dark," June 1928, "Hell to Pay," August 1928, "Street Wolf," May 1930, "The Kill," March 1931, "The Spot and the Lady" (as Grimes Hill), March 1931, and "It's the Live Ones That Talk," November 1931, all in *Black Mask* (New York).
"Call It Justice," 15 February 1930, "Muscle Man," 20 June 1931, "Nobody's Fall Guy," 8 August 1931, and "The Pinch," 17 September 1932, all in *Detective Fiction Weekly.*
"The Missing Car," in *Black Bat,* October 1933.
"Mask of Murder," in *Saturday Evening Post* (Philadelphia), 8 October 1955.
"Chance Is Sometimes an Enemy," April 1956, "You Can Take So Much," October 1956, "The Man Who Knew," December 1956, "That's Just Too Bad," May 1957, "No Kid Stuff," April 1958, "Wanted: An Accomplice," July 1958, "Pity the Poor Underdog," August 1958, "The Fifth Question," January 1959; "Killer at Large," September 1961, and "Needle in a Haystack," August 1962, all in *Ellery Queen's Mystery Magazine* (New York).

"Reprieve at Eleven," in *The Saint* (New York), April 1956.
"Try It My Way," in *Ellery Queen's Awards, 11th Series.* New York, Simon and Schuster, 1956; London, Collins, 1958.
"Sudden Life," in *Mike Shayne Mystery Magazine* (New York), August 1958.

OTHER PUBLICATIONS

Novel

But Not the End. Boston, Little Brown, 1934.

*

Manuscript Collection: University of Oregon Library, Eugene.

*   *   *

The hard-boiled detective is an improbable creation. He is a Galahadian hero in an unglamorous profession who is bound by a moral code that embraces a sense of duty and a streak of sentimentality. He is often a wise-cracking humorist and always violent. But above all, he must be tough, for he exists in a hard world and must be equal to that world and the worst of its inhabitants. The challenge of the hard-boiled detective story is to create a believable character out of these traits who will not conflict with the realistic milieu. The best of the hard-boiled writers temper toughness with humor, but this is difficult to manage and, as there exists little room for improvement in the story type, the genre has become particularly vulnerable to excess and parody, as the writings of Mickey Spillane and Richard S. Prather show.

One of the few writers to portray the tough detective realistically was Frederick Nebel, who wrote for *Black Mask* and its early rival, *Dime Detective,* for most of his short career. For these two magazines, Nebel created several characters, Donny "tough dick" Donahue, Cardigan of the Cosmos Detective Agency, and the team of Homicide Captain Steve MacBride and *Free Press* reporter Kennedy. Nebel's characters are genuinely hard-boiled, and his stories realistic. He employs a wry, wise-cracking kind of humor that is acceptable within the contexts of his stories. In the MacBride and Kennedy stories, the humor borders on burlesque when Kennedy's whimsical presence dominates (as it does in "Take It and Like It"), but Nebel never loses his control over the mood.

Nebel's stories are set in the grim world of Depression America in which survival is the guiding imperative. This is a world of greed, political corruption, and inter-familial violence, and his detectives, as a result, are insular, pragmatic men who live by stern moral codes. They are survivors who pride themselves on their toughness and their ability to "take it," i.e. to endure the repercussions when their morality brings them into conflict with a corrupt society, as Donahue demonstrates in "He Could Take It."

To Donahue, Cardigan, and MacBride, duty is an everyday affair. When they are compelled to step beyond the limits of duty, as most hard-boiled detectives are, they are never motivated by sentiment, but rather by pride or responsibility. Donahue is Nebel's quintessential hard-boiled character. He is as tough as tendon in "Pearls Are Tears" when he guns down a cop-killer, not for his crime—Donahue believes that the cop "deserved it"—but to protect himself and his client from complicity in a blackmail cover-up. He endures a savage beating in "He Could Take It" rather than relinquish the evidence that will convict his attackers, only because he wants them to pay for the beating.

Captain Steve MacBride is equally hard, though his hardness is offset by his foil, Kennedy. He feels fear in "Take It and Like It" when it appears that Kennedy is a murderer. In "Some Die Young," his hunt for the killer of a young girl takes on added meaning by his comparison of the dead girl to his own daughter. Though he is a less insular person than Donahue, it is pride, not sentiment, that governs his actions. He goes beyond duty in "Doors in the Dark" to prove that his close friend was murdered, though the evidence indicates suicide, because his pride won't allow him to be wrong. Similarly, Donahue refuses to let the daughter of a notorious vice queen follow in her mother's footsteps in "Red Web" because he was hired to prevent that and as he tells her, "I hate like hell to lose. I'm the world's sorest loser."

Such attitudes are understandable in the contexts. Toughness is a strategy for survival and, as Nebel seems to indicate in *Sleepers East,* perhaps the only way to survive.

—Will Murray

NEELY, Richard. American. Formerly an advertising executive; now a full-time writer. Address: c/o Delacorte Press, 1 Dag Hammarskjold Plaza, 245 East 47th Street, New York, New York 10017, U.S.A.

CRIME PUBLICATIONS

Novels

Death to My Beloved. New York, New American Library, 1969.
The Plastic Nightmare. New York, Ace, 1969; London, Hale, 1971.
While Love Lay Sleeping. New York, Ace, 1969; London, Hale, 1970.
The Walter Syndrome. New York, McCall, 1970; London, Souvenir Press, 1971.
The Damned Innocents. New York, Ace, 1971; as *Dirty Hands,* New York, New American Library, 1976.
The Japanese Mistress. New York, Saturday Review Press, 1972.
The Sexton Women. New York, Putnam, 1972; London, Barker, 1974.
The Smith Conspiracy. New York, New American Library, 1972.
The Ridgway Women. New York, Crowell, 1975, London, Constable, 1976.
A Madness of the Heart. New York, Crowell, 1976; London, Constable, 1978.
Lies. New York, Putnam, 1978.
No Certain Life. New York, Jove, 1978.
The Obligation. New York, Dell, 1979.
An Accidental Woman. New York, Holt Rinehart, 1981; London, Sphere, 1983.
Shadows from the Past. New York, Delacorte Press, 1983.

*   *   *

Richard Neely approaches the suspense novel like a stage conjurer challenging the audience to outguess him. He is determined to separate reader from chair with a thunderous surprise ending, and more often than not he succeeds. His interest in abnormal psychology is reflected in his otherwise dissimilar Edgar-nominated novels, *The Smith Conspiracy* and *A Madness of the Heart,* both of which concern seemingly happy marriages imperiled by mental problems, with psychiatrists in important secondary roles. At times his novels recall the work of Cornell Woolrich in their sense of an everyday world turned into a nightmare and in their use of somewhat incredible plot twists rendered acceptable by stylistic brute force. The difference is that Neely's effects seem somewhat more calculated than Woolrich's and he achieves somewhat less real emotional impact. Other recurring features are backgrounds of journalism and advertising, fields Neely knows well, and nostalgia for the recent past, with stories either set in earlier decades or recalled from a present-day perspective.

From the first novel of his paperback apprenticeship, *While Love Lay Sleeping,* Neely displays the smooth style of an accomplished storyteller. In the flashbacks to the days of World War II, he reveals his ability to capture a time and a mood with well-chosen period details. He also tries the same kind of devious plotting that will become his trademark and does surprise the reader, though at some expense of credibility. The plot would have been resolved a hundred pages sooner given logical behavior by the main character.

By the publication of *The Walter Syndrome,* his best-known novel and quite likely his finest achievement, Neely's strengths are solidly in evidence. The background of New York journalism in 1938 is evocatively established. The multiple-narrator format is adroitly managed. The hunt for a serial killer, inevitably compared with Jack the Ripper, creates much reader tension. And the shock ending is beautifully done. *The Japanese Mistress,* about the bludgeon murder of a Sausalito wife who fears her husband may be resuming relations with the love of his service years, is even more intricate in its plot structure and offers a similarly effective surprise. The novel-within-a-novel approach (a technique later used less extensively in *A Madness of the Heart*) is appropriate to the author's puzzle-box plotting style. *The Smith Conspiracy,* an efficient novel-of-paranoia concerning a right-wing assassination plot engineered by hypnosis and mind control, does not have the usual finishing jolt and is the rare Neely novel that "dates" in a pejorative sense.

Neely occasionally wagers too much on the effect of the final surprise, too little on the creation of characters the reader can identify with. Thus, the reader's opinion of the book sometimes hinges on whether the explosive finale works or not. In *A Madness of the Heart,* involving the search for a New York rapist, the main shock will no doubt be predictable to many readers, especially those primed by other Neely novels, but he has an additional surprise in the closing page that fewer readers will see coming. Still, there is an irritating scent of over-manipulation in the air. *No Certain Life* had me convinced at the halfway mark that I knew what was coming at the end. That Neely fooled me once again left me much more impressed than I would have been if my guess had been right. In *Lies,* a book bereft of sympathetic characters, only previous knowledge of Neely's way with trick endings kept me reading to the end, where he delivered as usual. In *Shadows from the Past,* which returns to the period and journalistic background of *The Walter Syndrome,* the detective story and saga are unsuccessfully combined: the echoes of *The Front Page* and *Citizen Kane* are too pervasive, and for once the finishing surprise seems limp and shopworn.

Occasional defects aside, Neely is one of the most intriguing and challenging of the crop of crime writers to develop in the 1960's and 1970's.

—Jon L. Breen

NEVILLE, Margot. Pseudonym for Margot Goyder and Anne Neville Goyder Joske. Australians. **GOYDER, Margot:** Born in Melbourne in 1903. **JOSKE, Anne Neville, née Goyder:** Born in Melbourne in 1893.

CRIME PUBLICATIONS

Novels (series: Inspector Grogan in all books except *Come, Thick Night* and *The Hateful Voyage*).

Lena Hates Men.   New York, Arcadia House, 1943; as *Murder in Rockwater,* London, Bles, 1944.
Murder and Gardenias.   London, Bles, 1946.
Murder in a Blue Moon.   London, Bles, 1948; New York, Doubleday, 1949.
Murder of a Nymph.   London, Bles, 1949; New York, Doubleday, 1950.
Come, Thick Night.   London, Bles, 1951; as *Divining Rod for Murder,* New York, Doubleday, 1952.
Murder Before Marriage.   London, Bles, and New York, Doubleday, 1951.
The Seagull Said Murder.   London, Bles, 1952.
Murder of the Well-Beloved.   London, Bles, and New York, Doubleday, 1953.
Murder and Poor Jenny.   London, Bles, 1954.
The Hateful Voyage.   London, Bles, 1956.
Murder of Olympia.   London, Bles, 1956.
Murder to Welcome Her.   London, Bles, 1957.
The Flame of Murder.   London, Bles, 1958.
Sweet Night for Murder.   London, Bles, 1959.
Confession of Murder.   London, Bles, 1960.
Murder Beyond the Pale.   London, Bles, 1961.
Drop Dead.   London, Bles, 1962.
Come See Me Die.   London, Bles, 1963.
My Bad Boy.   London, Bles, 1964.
Ladies in the Dark.   London, Bles, 1965.
Head on the Sill.   London, Bles, 1966.

OTHER PUBLICATIONS

Novels

Marietta Is Stolen.   London, Parsons, 1922.
This Can't Be I.   London, Parsons, 1923.
Safety First.   London, Hodder and Stoughton, and Boston, Houghton Mifflin, 1924.
Kiss Proof.   London, Chapman and Hall, 1928; New York, McBride, 1929.
Giving the Bride Away.   London, Chapman and Hall, and New York, McBride, 1930.

Plays

Once a Husband, with Brett Hay (produced London, 1932).
Heroes Don't Care (produced London, 1936). London, French, 1936.

Giving the Bride Away, with Gerald Kirby (produced London, 1939).

*   *   *

The two Australian women who wrote under the pseudonym of Margot Neville began their successful collaboration in crime fiction in the 1940's and wrote prolifically for 20 years. Success came with their first books, *Lena Hates Men* and *Murder and Gardenias*. Most of their books are distinguishable by the fact that the word "murder" occurs in the title. Many of these murder stories have an Australian background, generally with a sophisticated Sydney setting, and feature a highly skilled detective named Grogan, who tracks down the killers with all the finesse associated with the best Scotland Yard practitioners.

—Herbert Harris

––––––

NEVINS, Francis M(ichael), Jr. American. Born in Bayonne, New Jersey, 6 January 1943. Educated at St. Peter's College, Jersey City, A.B. (magna cum laude) 1964; New York University School of Law, J.D. (cum laude) 1967, admitted to New Jersey Bar, 1967. Served in the United States Army Reserve: Instructor, Fort Sill, Oklahoma, 1968–69: Captain. Married 1) Muriel Ann Walter in 1966 (divorced 1978); 2) Patricia Brooks in 1982. Assistant to editor-in-chief, Clark Boardman Co., Law Publishers, New York City, 1967; Adjunct Instructor, St. Peter's College, 1967; staff attorney, Middlesex County Legal Services Corp., New Brunswick, New Jersey, 1970–71. Assistant Professor, 1971–75, Associate Professor, 1975–78, and since 1978 Professor, St. Louis University School of Law, Missouri. Recipient: Mystery Writers of America Edgar Allan Poe award, for criticism, 1975, 1989. Agent: Curtis Brown Ltd., 10 Astor Place, New York, New York 10003. Address: 7045 Cornell, University City, Missouri 63130, U.S.A.

CRIME PUBLICATIONS

Novels (series: Loren Mensing in all books)

Publish and Perish. New York, Putnam, 1975; London, Hale, 1977.
Corrupt and Ensnare. New York, Putnam, 1978; London, Hale, 1979.
The 120-Hour Clock. New York, Walker, 1986.
The Ninety-Million Dollar Mouse. New York, Walker, 1987.

Uncollected Short Stories

"After the Twelfth Chapter," in *Ellery Queen's Mystery Magazine* (New York), September 1972.
"Murder of a Male Chauvinist," in *Ellery Queen's Mystery Magazine* (New York), May 1973.
"Six Thousand Little Bonapartes," in *Ellery Queen's Mystery Magazine* (New York), December 1973.
"The Possibility of Termites," in *Ellery Queen's Mystery Magazine* (New York), May 1974.
"Open Letter to Survivors," in *Ellery Queen's Crookbook*, edited by Ellery Queen. New York, Random House, and London, Gollancz, 1974.

"The Ironclad Alibi," in *Ellery Queen's Mystery Magazine* (New York), November 1974.
"An Ear for the Language," in *Alfred Hitchcock's Mystery Magazine* (North Palm Beach, Florida), March 1975.
"Because the Constable Blundered," in *Best Detective Stories of the Year 1974*, edited by Allen J. Hubin. New York, Dutton, 1975.
"The Benteen Millions," in *Ellery Queen's Mystery Magazine* (New York), May 1975.
"The Matchwit Club," in *Ellery Queen's Mystery Magazine* (New York), July 1976.
"Superscam," in *Alfred Hitchcock's Tales to Take Your Breath Away*, edited by Eleanor Sullivan. New York, Davis, 1977.
"A Picture in the Mind," in *Alfred Hitchcock's Mystery Magazine* (New York), February 1977.
"To Catch a Con Man," in *Ellery Queen's Mystery Magazine* (New York), October 1977.
"Fair Game," in *Cop Cade*, edited by John Ball. New York, Doubleday, 1978.
"Doomchild," in *Alfred Hitchcock's Mystery Magazine* (New York), September 1978.
"Evensong," in *Ellery Queen's Mystery Magazine* (New York), March 1979.
"The Scrabble Clue," in *Ellery Queen's: Wings of Mystery*, edited by Ellery Queen. New York, Davis, 1979.
"Film Flam," in *Best Detective Stories of the Year*, edited by Edward D. Hoch. New York, Dutton, 1979.
"The Last Passenger," in *Mike Shane Mystery Magazine* (Los Angeles), January 1980.
"The Other Man in the Pinstripe," in *Ellery Queen's Mystery Magazine* (New York), May 1980.
"Funeral Music," in *Miniature Mysteries*, edited by Isaac Asimov, Martin H. Greenberg, and Joseph D. Olander. New York, Taplinger, 1981.
"The Kumquat Affair," in *Ellery Queen's Doors to Mystery*, edited by Ellery Queen. New York, Davis, 1981.
"Bad Bargain," in *Alfred Hitchcock's Mystery Magazine* (New York), January 1981.
"The Lobsenz Intrusion," in *Alfred Hitchcock's Mystery Magazine* (New York), May 1982.
"Black Spider," in *Top Crime*, edited by Josh Pachter. London, Dent, 1983; New York, St. Martin's Press, 1984.
"The Shape of the Nightmare," in *The Year's Best Mystery and Suspense Stories 1983*, edited by Edward D. Hoch. New York, Walker, 1983.
"Cop to Cop," in *The Saint* (New York), June 1984.
"Judgement Reversed," in *The Saint* (New York), July 1984.
"A Question of Interpretation," in *Woman's World* (Englewood, New Jersey), 17 July 1984.
"Dogsbody," in *Murder on the Menu*, edited by Carol-Lynn Rössel Waugh, Martin H. Greenberg, and Isaac Asimov. New York, Avon, 1984.
"Counterplot," in *101 Mystery Stories*, edited by Bill Pronzini and Martin H. Greenberg. New York, Avenel, 1986.
"Leap Day," in *Ellery Queen Masters of Mystery*. New York, Galahad, 1987.
"The Garrulous Garrity Grand Scam," in *Manhattan Mysteries*, edited by Bill Pronzini, Carol-Lynn Rössel Waugh and Martin H. Greenberg. New York, Avenel, 1987.
"All the Bagworms on the Block," in *Criminal Elements*, edited by Bill Pronzini and Martin H. Greenberg. New York, Ivy, 1988.
"Consultation in the Dark," in *Raymond Chandler's Philip Marlowe*, edited by Byron Preiss. New York, Knopf, 1988.

Other

Detectionary, with others. Lock Haven, Pennsylvania, Hammermill Paper, 1971; revised edition, New York, Overlook Press, 1977.

Royal Bloodline: Ellery Queen, Author and Detective. Bowling Green, Ohio, Popular Press, 1974.

"The Law of the Mystery Writer v. the Law of the Courts," in *Popular Culture Scholar* (Frostburg, Maryland), 1976.

"The Marquis of Unremembered Manhunters," in *Xenophile* (St. Louis), 1976.

"Name Games: Mystery Writers and Their Pseudonyms," in *The Mystery Story,* edited by John Ball. San Diego, University of California Extension, 1976.

"The World of Milton Propper," in *Armchair Detective* (Del Mar, California), July 1977.

"Murder Like Crazy: Harry Stephen Keeler," in *New Republic* (Washington, D.C.), 30 July 1977.

"Private Eye in an Evil Time: Mark Sadler's Paul Shaw," in *Xenophile* (St. Louis), March–April 1978.

"Murder at Noon: Michael Avallone," in *New Republic* (Washington, D.C.), 22 July 1978.

"The Sound of Suspense: John Dickson Carr as a Radio Writer," in *Armchair Detective* (Del Mar, California), October 1978.

The Sound of Detection: Ellery Queen's Adventures in Radio, with Ray Stanich. Madison, Illinois, Brownstone, 1983.

Missouri Probate: Intestacy, Wills and Basic Administration. Norcross, Georgia, Harrison, 1983.

Cornell Woolrich: First You Dream, Then You Die. New York, Mysterious Press, 1988.

Editor, *The Mystery Writer's Art.* Bowling Green, Ohio, Popular Press, 1971.

Editor, *Nightwebs: A Collection of Stories by Cornell Woolrich.* New York, Harper, 1971; London, Gollancz, 1973.

Co-editor, *Multiplying Villainies: Selected Mystery Criticism of Anthony Boucher.* Privately printed, 1973.

Editor, with others, *The Good Old Stuff* by John D. MacDonald. New York, Harper, 1982.

Editor, with Martin H. Greenberg, *Exeunt Murderers: The Best Mystery Stories of Anthony Boucher.* Carbondale, Southern Illinois University Press, 1983.

Editor, with Martin H. Greenberg, *Buffet for Unwelcome Guests: The Best Short Stories of Christianna Brand.* Carbondale, Southern Illinois University Press, 1983.

Editor, with others, *More Good Old Stuff* by John D. MacDonald. New York, Knopf, 1984.

Editor, with Martin H. Greenberg, *The Best of Ellery Queen.* New York, Beaufort, 1985.

Editor, with Martin H. Greenberg, *Hitchcock in Prime Time.* New York, Avon, 1985.

Editor, *Carnival of Crime* by Frederic Brown. Carbondale, Southern Illinois University Press, 1985.

Editor, with Martin H. Greenberg, *Darkness at Dawn: Early Suspense Classics* by Cornell Woolrich. Carbondale, Southern Illinois University Press, 1985.

Editor, with Martin H. Greenberg, *Leopold's Way* by Edward D. Hoch. Carbondale, Southern Illinois University Press, 1985.

Editor, with Martin H. Greenberg, *The Adventures of Henry Turnbuckle: Detective Comedies by Jack Ritchie.* Carbondale, Southern Illinois University Press, 1987.

Editor, *Better Mousetraps* by John Lutz. New York, St. Martin's Press, 1988.

Editor, *Mr. President—Private Eye.* New York, Ballantine, 1988.

Editor, with Martin H. Greenberg, *Death on Television: The Best of Henry Slesar's Alfred Hitchcock Stories.* Carbondale, Southern Illinois University Press, 1989.

Editor, *Little Boxes of Bewilderment* by Jack Ritchie. New York, St. Martin's Press, 1989.

*

Bibliography: in *St. Louis University Law Faculty Bibliography,* St. Louis, St. Louis University School of Law, 1982.

Francis M. Nevins, Jr. comments:

My concept of the ideal mystery novel is one that combines Erle Stanley Gardner's crackling pace and legal ingenuity, Ellery Queen's labyrinthine plot structure and deductive fair play, and Cornell Woolrich's feel for suspense and the anguish of living and compellingly visual style. If I ever come close to writing that ideal book, most of the credit will go to those three masters.

*   *   *

Even a cursory glance at the writings of Francis M. Nevins, Jr. reveals his depth and range of interest in the mystery crime field. The completion of *The Mystery Writer's Art, Nightwebs,* and *Royal Bloodline* are testaments to his scholarly commitment to the non-fictional areas of the field. With the publication of his first two stories, "Open Letter to Survivors," and "After the Twelfth Chapter," Nevins demonstrated an equal range and skill in the area of mystery fiction. The first story is a pastiche of the traditional and the unusual in detective fiction, a blend of old and new that becomes a Nevins trademark. The second story introduces a Professor of Law detective, Loren Mensing, who becomes the central Nevins character in six other stories and two novels.

A critical assessment of Nevins's work shows him to be a consummate storyteller. Whether working in short fiction, with all of its restrictions and demand for economy and telling detail, or in the novel, with its demands for complex plot structure and sustained character development, he consistently produces entertaining and skillful work. His major fictional detectives, Loren Mensing and Milo Turner, are deftly drawn, complex characters who capture a reader's imagination and challenge his intellect.

Though there is no Nevins "formula," there is a Nevins intention. In most of his works, short or long, Nevins attempts to balance four elements: clues and deductions, visual and suspenseful elements, legal gimmicks, and human relationships. In his best works, and particularly in his novels, Nevins strives for a synthesis of the best of Doyle, Gardner, Woolrich, and Queen. *Publish and Perish* is notable for its complex denouement, with its ironic reversals and red-herring endings. *Corrupt and Ensnare* combines an interesting story with strong character development.

In short, a reader can expect intelligent and skillful plotting, good drama, and quality writing in Nevins's fictional world. His mind is agile, his pen sure—a combination that provides many pleasurable hours of good reading.

—George J. Thompson

NEWMAN, Bernard (Charles). Also wrote as Don Betteridge. British. Born in Ibstock, Leicestershire, 8 May 1897. Educated at Bosworth School. Served in the British Expeditionary Forces in France, 1915–19; Staff Lecturer, Ministry of Information, 1940–45. Married 1) Marjorie Edith Donald in 1928; three daughters; 2) Helen Johnston in 1966. Joined the Civil Service in 1920; lectured for the Ministry of Information and the Department of Army Education in the 1940's and 1950's. Fellow, Royal Society of Arts. Chevalier, Legion of Honour. *Died 19 February 1968.*

CRIME PUBLICATIONS

Novels (series: Sergeant/Inspector Marshall; Papa Pontivy)

Death of a Harlot. London, Laurie, 1934; New York, Godwin, 1935.
Secret Servant (Marshall). London, Gollancz, 1935; New York, Curl, 1936.
Spy (Marshall). London, Gollancz, and New York, Appleton Century, 1935.
German Spy (Marshall). London, Gollancz, and New York, Curl, 1936.
Lady Doctor—Woman Spy. London, Hutchinson, 1937.
Death under Gibraltar. London, Gollancz, 1938.
Death to the Spy (Pontivy). London, Gollancz, 1939.
The Mussolini Murder Plot (Marshall). London, Hutchinson, and New York, Curl, 1939.
Maginot Line Murder. London, Gollancz, 1939; as *Papa Pontivy and the Maginot Murder,* New York, Holt, 1940.
Siegfried Spy (Pontivy). London, Gollancz, 1940.
Secret Weapon (Pontivy). London, Gollancz, 1941.
Death to the Fifth Column (Pontivy). London, Gollancz, 1941.
Black Market (Pontivy). London, Gollancz, 1942.
Second Front—First Spy (Pontivy). London, Gollancz, 1944.
The Spy in the Brown Derby (Pontivy). London, Gollancz, 1945.
Dead Man Murder (Pontivy). London, Gollancz, 1946.
Moscow Murder (Pontivy). London, Gollancz, 1948.
The Flying Saucer. London, Gollancz, 1948; New York, Macmillan, 1950.
Shoot! London, Gollancz, 1949.
Cup Final Murder. London, Gollancz, 1950.
Centre Court Murder. London, Gollancz, 1951.
Death at Lord's. London, Gollancz, 1952.
The Wishful Think. London, Hale, 1954.
The Double Menace (Pontivy). London, Hale, 1955; New York, Viking Press, 1956.
Operation Barbarossa (Pontivy). London, Hale, 1956.
The Otan Plot (Pontivy). London, Hale, 1957.
Taken at the Flood. London, Hale, 1958.
Silver Greyhound. London, Hale, 1960.
This Is Your Life (Pontivy). London, Hale, 1963.
The Travelling Executioners. London, Hale, 1964.
The Spy at Number 10 (Pontivy). London, Hale, 1965.
Evil Phoenix. London, Hale, 1966.
Draw the Dragon's Teeth. London, Hale, 1967.
The Jail-Breakers. London, Hale, 1968.

Novels as Don Betteridge (series: Tiger Lester in all books except *Scotland Yard Alibi* and *Cast Iron Alibi*)

Scotland Yard Alibi. London, Gollancz, 1938.
Cast Iron Alibi. London, Jenkins, 1939.
Balkan Spy. London, Jenkins, 1942.

The Escape of General Gerard. London, Jenkins, 1943.
Dictator's Destiny. London, Jenkins, 1945.
The Potsdam Murder Plot. London, Jenkins, 1947.
Spies Left! London, Hale, 1950.
Not Single Spies. London, Hale, 1951.
Spy—Counter Spy. London, Hale, 1953.
The Case of the Berlin Spy. London, Hale, 1954.
The Gibraltar Conspiracy. London, Hale, 1955.
The Spies of Peenemünde. London, Hale, 1958.
Contact Man. London, Hale, 1960.
The Package Holiday Spy Case. London, Hale, 1962.

Short Stories

Spy Catchers. London, Gollancz, 1945.

Uncollected Short Stories

"Death at the Wicket," in *Butcher's Dozen.* London, Heinemann, 1956.
"Squinting Death," in *John Creasey Mystery Magazine* (London), November 1961.
"Element of Doubt," in *John Creasey's Mystery Bedside Book 1969,* edited by Herbert Harris. London, Hodder and Stoughton, 1968.

OTHER PUBLICATIONS

Novels

The Cavalry Went Through. London, Gollancz, 1930; as *The Cavalry Goes Through,* New York, Holt, 1930.
Hosanna! London, Archer, 1933.
Death in the Valley: A Tale Based on the Origin of the Oberammergau Passion Play. London, Archer, 1934.
Flowers for the Living, with Guy Bolton. London, Jenkins, 1958.
The Dangerous Age. London, Hale, 1967.

Plays

One Silk Stocking. London, Reynolds, 1926.
Burlesque Orations and Comedy Lectures. London, McGlennon, 1929.
Cross-Talk Arguments. London, McGlennon, 1929.
The Dunmow Flitch: A Humorous Mock Trial. London, McGlennon, 1929.
Humorous Monologues for Ladies. London, McGlennon, 1929.
Humorous Monologues on Sport. London, McGlennon, 1929.
The Phantom Voice. London, McGlennon, 1929.
The Second Book of Monologues, Humorous and Dramatic. London, McGlennon, 1929.
Back-Chat for Cross-Talk Comedians, with Charles Hickman. London, McGlennon, 1929.
Appearances and Deceptions: A Comedy Sketch. London, McGlennon, 1930; with *Musical Interruptions,* McGlennon, 1930.
Cupid's Agent. London, McGlennon, 1930.
Farcical Sketches for Male Characters. London, McGlennon, 1930.
Half-Hour Comedies. London, McGlennon, 1930.
Model Artists. London, McGlennon, 1930.
No Followers Allowed. London, McGlennon, 1930.
Poets Made to Order. London, McGlennon, 1930.

Other

How to Run an Amateur Concert Party. London, Reynolds, 1925.

Character Monologues and How to Perform Them. London, Pearson, 1926.

Round about Andorra. London, Allen and Unwin, and Boston, Houghton Mifflin, 1928.

Mock Trials and How to Run Them. London, McGlennon, 1929.

Modern Parody Monologues and How to Recite Them. London, McGlennon, 1929.

Armoured Doves: A Peace Book. London, Jarrolds, 1931.

In the Trail of the Three Musketeers. London, Jenkins, 1934.

Pedalling Poland. London, Jenkins, 1935.

The Blue Danube. London, Jenkins, 1935.

Tunnellers: The Story of the Tunnelling Companies, with W.G. Grieve. London, Jenkins, 1936.

Albanian Back-Door. London, Jenkins, 1936.

Cycling in France—Northern. London, Jenkins, 1936.

I Saw Spain. London, Jenkins, 1937.

Albanian Journey. London, Pitman, 1938.

Danger Spots of Europe. London, Hale, 1938; revised edition, 1939.

Ride to Russia. London, Jenkins, 1938.

Baltic Roundabout. London, Jenkins, 1939; revised edition, 1940.

Secrets of German Espionage. London, Hale, 1940; as *German Secret Service at Work,* New York, McBride, 1940.

The Story of Poland. London, Hutchinson, 1940.

Savoy! Corsica! Tunis! Mussolini's Dream Lands. London, Jenkins, 1940.

One Man's Year. London, Gollancz, 1941.

The New Europe. London, Hale, 1942; New York, Macmillan, 1943.

American Journey. London, Hale, 1943.

The People of Poland. Birkenhead, Cheshire, Polish Publications Committee, 1943.

The Face of Poland. Birkenhead, Cheshire, Polish Publications Committee, 1944.

Balkan Background. London, Hale, 1944; New York, Macmillan, 1945.

British Journey. London, Hale, 1945.

Russia's Neighbour—The New Poland. London, Gollancz, 1946.

Middle Eastern Journey. London, Gollancz, 1947.

The Red Spider Web: The Story of Russian Spying in Canada. London, Latimer House, 1947.

News from the East. London, Gollancz, 1948.

The Captured Archives: The Story of the Nazi-Soviet Documents. London, Latimer House, 1948.

Mediterranean Background. London, Hale, 1949.

The Lazy House. London, Jenkins, 1949.

Come Adventuring with Me. London, Latimer House, 1949.

The Sisters Alsace-Lorraine. London, Jenkins, 1950.

Epics of Espionage. London, Laurie, and New York, Philosophical Library, 1950.

Turkish Cross-Roads. London, Hale, 1951; New York, Philosophical Library, 1952.

Oberammergau Journey. London, Jenkins, 1952.

They Saved London. London, Warner, 1952.

Soviet Atomic Spies. London, Hale, 1952.

Both Sides of the Pyrenees. London, Jenkins, 1952.

Tito's Yugoslavia. London, Hale, 1952.

Morocco Today. London, Hale, 1953.

Ride to Rome. London, Jenkins, 1953.

Yours for Action. London, Jenkins, 1953.

Report on Indo-China. London, Hale, 1953; New York, Praeger, 1954.

Berlin and Back. London, Jenkins, 1954.

The Sosnowski Affair: Inquest on a Spy. London, Laurie, 1954.

North African Journey. London, Hale, 1955.

Still Flows the Danube. London, Jenkins, 1955.

Inquest on Mata Hari. London, Hale, 1956.

Real Life Spies. London, Hutchinson, 1956.

The Three Germanies. London, Hale, 1957.

Spain on a Shoestring. London, Jenkins, 1957.

One Hundred Years of Good Company. Lincoln, Ruston and Hornsby, 1957.

Unknown Germany. London, Jenkins, 1958; New York, McBride, 1959.

Portrait of Poland. London, Hale, 1959.

Danger Spots of the World. London, Hale, 1959.

Visa to Russia. London, Jenkins, 1959.

Speaking from Memory (autobiography). London, Jenkins, 1960.

Unknown Yugoslavia. London, Jenkins, 1960.

Bulgarian Background. London, Hale, 1961.

Far Eastern Journey: Across India and Pakistan to Formosa. London, Jenkins, 1961.

Let's Look at Germany. London, Museum Press, and New York, Pitman, 1961.

The Blue Ants: The First Authentic Account of the Russian-Chinese War of 1907. London, Hale, 1962.

The World of Espionage. London, Souvenir Press, 1962; New York, British Book Centre, 1963.

Mr. Kennedy's America. London, Jenkins, 1962.

Unknown France. London, Jenkins, 1963.

Round the World in Seventy Days. London, Jenkins, 1964.

Behind the Berlin Wall. London, Hale, 1964.

Spies in Britain. London, Hale, 1964.

Background to Viet-Nam. London, Hale, 1965; New York, Roy, 1966.

Let's Visit France (for children). London, Burke, 1965; New York, Roy, 1967.

South African Journey. London, Jenkins, 1965.

Let's Visit Malaysia and Her Neighbours (for children). London, Burke, 1965.

Spain Revisited. London, Jenkins, 1966.

Let's Visit Vietnam (for children). London, Burke, 1967.

To Russia and Back. London, Jenkins, 1967.

Let's Visit South Africa (for children). London, Burke, 1967; New York, Day, 1968.

The Bosworth Story. London, Jenkins, 1967.

Portrait of the Shires. London, Hale, 1968.

Turkey and the Turks. London, Jenkins, 1968.

The New Poland. London, Hale, 1968.

Spy and Counter-Spy: Bernard Newman's Story of the British Secret Service, edited by I.O. Evans. London, Hale, 1970.

Editor, with I.O. Evans, *Anthology of Armageddon.* London, Archer, 1935.

Editor, *Presenting People Living Dangerously.* London, Hamlyn, 1961.

*   *   *

Bernard Newman, throughout a long and prolific career, wrote a great many novels, many under the pseudonym of Don Betteridge. Most were spy thrillers linked to current events, adventure stories with a taste of detection but no crime, or murder mysteries.

The spy thrillers of the 1930's and 1940's are set in wartime, while those of the 1950's and 1960's are cast against a backdrop of international events and civil strife. Much of the historical detail in these novels is accurate, but Newman's perception of espionage is highly romanticized. Characters like Henry and Pontivy, from *Black Market, Second Front—First Spy, The Spy in the Brown Derby,* and *Death to the Fifth Column,* perceive themselves as the vital cogs in the German Secret Service in Britain. *German Spy,* a fictionalized account of the life of the German spy Grein, is filled with intrigue and acts of courage. Grein is Newman's folk hero, an example for all his subsequent heroes of the political and moral supremacy of a nation's spy.

The 1950's marked the beginning of Newman's murder mysteries. The adventure and suspense evident in the war novels emerges in mystery stories like *Centre Court Murder* and *Cup Final Murder.* The latter book chronicles Nicholas Prince's relentless search for a murderer. Prince excels in police work but his resistance to corruption has kept him from securing a position in the field. Prince's investigation is admirably detailed and Newman's characterizations are impeccable. The investigation unearths, not surprisingly, some political intrigue.

A study of Newman's works reveals a fine line between what he considers truth and what he considers fiction. Life for Newman is adventure. His spy thrillers and murder mysteries, though based on fact, reveal a bent for the romantic. Even his travel/adventure accounts and history books share this quality. Newman's perception of the suspense genre is perhaps best illustrated in his analysis of the book by Grein that led him to write *German Spy.* Grein, he says, "would scarcely be human if he did not romanticize a little."

—Donna Casella-Kern

NEWMAN, G(ordon) F. British. Born in London in 1945. Agent: Elaine Steel, 25–27 Oxford Street, London W1R 1RF. Address: Wassingtom Court, Woolhope, Hereford HR1 4QN, England.

CRIME PUBLICATIONS

Novels (series: Inspector Terry Sneed)

Sir, You Bastard (Sneed). London, W.H. Allen, 1970; New York, Simon and Schuster, 1971; as *Rogue Cop,* New York, Lancer, 1973.
The Abduction. London, New English Library, 1972.
You Nice Bastard (Sneed). London, New English Library, 1972.
The Split. London, New English Library, 1973.
The Price (Sneed). London, New English Library, 1974.
A Detective's Tale. London, Sphere, 1977.
The Guvnor. London, Hart Davis MacGibbon, 1977; as *Trade-Off,* New York, Dell, 1979.
A Prisoner's Tale. London, Sphere, 1977.
A Villain's Tale. London, Sphere, 1977.
The List. London, Secker and Warburg, 1979.
The Men with the Guns. London, Secker and Warburg, 1982.

Law and Order (omnibus). London Granada, 1983.
Set a Thief. London, Joseph, 1986.
The Testing Ground. London, Joseph, 1987.

OTHER PUBLICATIONS

Novels

Billy: A Family Tragedy. London, New English Library, 1972.
The Player and the Guest. London, New English Library, 1972.
3 Professional Ladies. London, New English Library, 1973.
The Streetfighter. London, Star, 1975.
The Obsession. London, Granada, 1980.
Charlie and Joanna. London, Granada, 1981.

Plays

Operation Bad Apple (produced London, 1982). London, Methuen, 1982.
An Honourable Trade (produced London, 1986).
The Testing Ground, from his own novel (produced London, 1989).

Screenplay: *Number One,* 1984.

Television Plays: *Law and Order* series, 1978; *Billy,* 1979; *The Nation's Health,* 1983; *Here Is the News,* 1989.

* * *

Gordon F. Newman is one of the most versatile and unpredictable of crime writers. His work is difficult to classify, however, because his range of subjects and themes is unusually broad.

A number of his novels have been devoted to chronicling the world of crooked (or "bent") cops by detailing the career of Terry Sneed. In the aptly-titled *Sir, You Bastard,* we are introduced to Sneed and follow his rise during his first seven years as a cop. His education in the corrupt use of police techniques and powers enables him to fatten hidden bank accounts, convict crooks whether guilty or not, and advance in rank by blackmailing superiors or getting colleagues fired to create openings. Despite his corruptness (and sometimes because of it), the power-hungry Sneed is an excellent detective. He manages, for example, to put away an important crook who had been hitherto untouchable and destroy the man's entire organization. One book in the Sneed series covers the same ground in the case but from the crook's point of view. In *The Price,* Sneed's precarious career encounters its most dangerous threat when he runs afoul of Rosi, an American accountant with Mafia connections who had been paying Sneed off. The series offers a good bit of suspense as to whether Sneed will be able to wriggle out of the next potential exposé.

While these novels depict widespread police corruption, they are a complex treatment of the subject. As Sneed advances, he realizes that the "elite" of society—important businessmen, lawyers, judges, prominent politicians—are as corrupt and venial as the worst felons. Thus a major theme is the pervasive moral decay of society.

Another police novel, *The Guvnor,* introduces us to Detective Chief Inspector John Fordham who, like Sneed, lives in a world of corruption that stretches to the highest levels of society. Unlike Sneed, however, Fordham uses corrupt means only to effect justice, not to consolidate or add to his own power. In a complicated murder investigation, Fordham dodges political influences skillfully to expose the members of The Establishment who are ultimately responsible.

In addition to police novels, Newman has also written thrillers. In *The List* he deals with the antagonism between the Kennedys and J. Edgar Hoover, exposes F.B.I. corruption, and suggests that a shadowy group of extreme right wingers is really responsible for J.F.K.'s assassination, an idea he develops more fully in *The Men with the Guns*. As the tough New York, skip-tracer Jimmy Vanesco tracks down six missing men, the details of C.I.A. involvement emerge, but the C.I.A. turns out to be only an enforcement arm for this California-based group, which in turn is controlled by foreign millionaires. The whole plot is made frighteningly plausible.

A number of Newman's books are not so much mysteries as sympathetic and insightful accounts of people living criminal lives: people who are the raw material of crime. *The Split* is the story of a rich young playboy dominated by an invalid mother, and a fascinating glimpse into the mind and making of a schizophrenic murderer. *The Player and the Guest* takes us into the world of snooker and introduces us to its cheats and hustlers. *3 Professional Ladies* explores the lives of three prostitutes of different social standing and at different stages of their careers. *The Obsession* is a sympathetically-told story of paedophilic love, and *Charlie and Joanna* is a moving account of child abuse which exposes society's inability to understand and deal with the problem.

Thus Newman's canvas is a broad one. He seems to have taken all society to be his subject, particularly its fringes, nor does he ever shy away from the sordid truths he encounters. His talent coupled with his uncompromising honesty mark him as a serious novelist who deserves to be widely read.

—Donald C. Wall

NICHOLS, (John) Beverley. British. Born in Bristol, 9 September 1898. Educated at Marlborough College; Balliol College, Oxford (editor, *Isis;* founding editor, *The Oxford Outlook;* President, Oxford Union), B.A. 1921. Drama critic, *The Weekly Dispatch,* 1926; editor, *The American Sketch,* New York, 1928–29; gossip columnist, *Sunday Chronicle,* London for 14 years; press correspondent, India, 1939–45. *Died 15 September 1983.*

CRIME PUBLICATIONS

Novels (series: Horatio Green in all books)

No Man's Street. London, Hutchinson, and New York, Dutton, 1954.
The Moonflower. London, Hutchinson, 1955; as *The Moonflower Murder,* New York, Dutton, 1955.
Death to Slow Music. London, Hutchinson, and New York, Dutton, 1956.
The Rich Die Hard. London, Hutchinson, 1957; New York, Dutton, 1958.

Murder by Request. London, Hutchinson, and New York, Dutton, 1960.

OTHER PUBLICATIONS

Novels

Prelude. London, Chatto and Windus, 1920.
Patchwork. London, Chatto and Windus, 1921; New York, Holt, 1922.
Self. London, Chatto and Windus, 1922.
Crazy Pavements. London, Cape, and New York, Doran, 1927.
Evensong. London, Cape, and New York, Doubleday, 1932.
Revue. London, Cape, and New York, Doubleday, 1939.
Laughter on the Stairs. London, Cape, 1953; New York, Dutton, 1954.
Sunlight on the Lawn. London, Cape, and New York, Dutton, 1956.

Short Stories

Men Do Not Weep. London, Cape, 1941; New York, Harcourt Brace, 1942.

Plays

Picnic (revue; composer only) (produced London, 1927).
Many Happy Returns (revue; composer only) by Herbert Farjeon (produced London, 1928).
The Stag (produced London, 1929). Included in *Failures,* 1933.
Cochran's 1930 Revue, music by Nichols and Vivian Ellis (produced London, 1930).
Avalanche (produced Edinburgh, 1931; London, 1932). Included in *Failures,* 1933.
Evensong, with Edward Knoblock, adaptation of the novel by Nichols (produced London, 1932; New York, 1933). London and New York, French, 1933.
When the Crash Comes (produced Birmingham, 1933). Included in *Failures,* 1933.
Failures: Three Plays (includes *The Stag, Avalanche, When the Crash Comes*). London, Cape, and New York, Peter Smith, 1933.
Mesmer (produced London, 1938). London, Cape, 1935.
Floodlight, music by Nichols (revue; produced London, 1937).
Shadow of the Vine (produced London, 1954). London, Cape, 1949.
La Plume de Ma Tante (produced Bromley, Kent, 1953).

Other Plays: *Song on the Wind* (operetta), 1948; *Lady's Guide,* 1950.

Screenplay: *Nine till Six,* with Alma Reveille and John Paddy Carstairs, 1932.

Radio Play: *You Bet Your Life,* with Rupert Croft-Cooke, 1938.

Verse

Twilight: First and Probably Last Poems. Maidstone, Kent, Bachman and Turner, 1982.

Other

25, Being a Young Man's Candid Recollections of His Elders and Betters. London, Cape, and New York, Doran, 1926.

Are They the Same at Home? Being a Series of Bouquets Diffidently Distributed. London, Cape, and New York, Doran, 1927.

The Star-Spangled Manner. London, Cape, and New York, Doubleday, 1928.

Women and Children Last. London, Cape, and New York, Doubleday, 1931.

Down the Garden Path. London, Cape, and New York, Doubleday, 1932.

For Adults Only. London, Cape, 1932; New York, Doubleday, 1933.

In the Next War I Shall Be a Conscientious Objector. London, Friends' Peace Committee, 1932.

Cry Havoc! London, Cape, and New York, Doubleday, 1933.

Puck at Brighton: The Offical Handbook of the Corporation of Brighton. Brighton, Corporation of Brighton, 1933.

A Thatched Roof. London, Cape, and New York, Doubleday, 1933.

The Valet as Historian. London, Forsyth, 1934.

A Village in a Valley. London, Cape, and New York, Doubleday, 1934.

How Does Your Garden Grow? (broadcast talks), with others. London, Allen and Unwin, and New York, Doubleday, 1935.

The Fool Hath Said. London, Cape, and New York, Doubleday, 1936.

No Place Like Home (travel). London, Cape, and New York, Doubleday, 1936.

News of England; or, A Country Without a Hero. London, Cape, and New York, Doubleday, 1938.

Green Grows the City: The Story of a London Garden. London, Cape, and New York, Harcourt Brace, 1939.

Verdict on India. London, Cape, and New York, Harcourt Brace, 1944.

The Tree That Sat Down (for children). London, Cape, 1945.

The Stream That Stood Still (for children). London, Cape, 1948; abridged version, with abridged version of *The Tree That Sat Down,* London, Cape, 1960; New York, St. Martin's Press, 1966.

All I Could Never Be: Some Recollections. London, Cape, 1949; New York, Dutton, 1952.

Your Sincerely (*Woman's Own* articles), with Monica Dickens. London, Newnes, 1949.

The Mountain of Magic (for children). London, Cape, 1950.

Uncle Samson (on America). London, Evans, 1950.

Merry Hall. London, Cape, 1951; New York, Dutton, 1953.

A Pilgrim's Progress. London, Cape, 1952.

The Queen's Coronation Day: The Pictorial Record of the Great Occasion. London, Pitkin, 1953.

Cat Book. London, Nelson, 1955.

The Sweet and Twenties. London, Weidenfeld and Nicolson, 1958.

Cat's ABC. London, Cape, and New York, Dutton, 1960.

Cat's XYZ. London, Cape, and New York, Dutton, 1961.

Garden Open Today. London, Cape, and New York, Dutton, 1963.

Forty Favourite Flowers. London, Studio Vista, 1964; New York, St. Martin's Press, 1965.

Powers That Be. London, Cape, and New York, St. Martin's Press, 1966.

A Case of Human Bondage (on Somerset Maugham). London, Secker and Warburg, and New York, Award Books, 1966.

The Art of Flower Arrangement. London, Collins, and New York, Viking Press, 1967.

Garden Open Tomorrow. London, Heinemann, 1968; New York, Dodd Mead, 1969.

The Sun in My Eyes; or, How Not to Go Around the World. London, Heinemann, 1969.

The Wickedest Witch in the World (for children) London, W.H. Allen, 1971.

Father Figure. London, Heinemann, and New York, Simon and Schuster, 1972.

Down the Kitchen Sink (autobiography). London, W.H. Allen, 1974.

Cats' A-Z (includes *Cats' ABC* and *Cats' XYZ*). London, W.H. Allen, 1977.

The Unforgiving Minute: Some Confessions from Childhood to the Outbreak of the Second World War. London, W.H. Allen, 1978.

The Romantic Garden. New York, Gordon Cremonesi, 1980.

Editor, *A Book of Old Ballads.* London, Hutchinson, and New York, Loring and Mussey, 1934.

*

Manuscript Collection: Humanities Research Center, University of Texas, Austin.

*   *   *

Beverley Nichols had been a successful writer for 30 years when his first detective novel was published in 1954. Four more appeared in the next few years, before he abandoned the form, discouraged by hostile criticism. It is hard to see why the books were ill-received, since they were accomplished and alluring mysteries in the classic mode, intricate, ingenious, shapely, and continually absorbing: alibis seem impregnable, suspicion spreads impartially, red herrings proliferate, and the great detective sums up at the end. They are remarkably elegant novels, meticulously contrived and controlled, and stylishly written, with a relative austerity unexpected in a writer so avowedly romantic.

No Man's Street features an opulent retired diva and an eminent conductor in a search for a unique record that has strangely disappeared. The victim is a blackmailing music critic, hated by his lesbian sister and her alcoholic lover. The anonymity of the street where he lives is a key feature of the case. *The Moonflower* is a more exotic confection of greater complexity. What seems a simple case of an old woman murdered for her jewels by an escaped convict ramifies enticingly into a much richer pattern. The flower plays an essential role, blooming too soon and beginning to die even as it reaches perfection. *Death to Slow Music* is a rather sinister story set by the sea and revolving round a star actor in the throes of rehearsal for his new musical show. His unstable accompanist is accused of murder but himself becomes a murder victim. The narrative combines a febrile theatrical gaiety with a darker, more menacing quality. *The Rich Die Hard* centres on a Queen Anne mansion and the great private art collection housed in it. The action links the murder of a tycoon's mistress with the destruction of a great painting and a savage bonfire of schoolboy relics. *Murder by Request* is a mischievous coda to the other novels, set at a health farm called Harmony Hall, and deploying to ironic effect the improbable trappings of a traditional detective story: not for nothing is the first victim an ardent reader of mystery fiction.

The investigator throughout is Horatio Green, a famous detective, now retired but unable to resist a mystery. He is a plump, mild little man known to the Yard as the Human Bloodhound, from an exceptional "olfactory sense" that enables him to determine ethnic origin from body odour. He conducts himself in the time-honoured manner of the great fictional detectives, uttering "cryptic remarks," indulging in "unaccountable behaviour," blinking furiously at moments of "cerebral activity," and outstripping the police with prodigies of perception and deduction. His insights are invariably subtle, deriving from "scraps of dialogue—shadows on faces—fleeting gestures"; a murdered woman's expression seems inappropriate to the way she died; a bust described by a blind man points to a daring musical fraud; a strident record played by a woman of refined taste suggests a guilty secret. There is much to enjoy in Green's career.

—B.A. Pike

NICOLAS, F.R.E. *See* **FREELING, Nicolas.**

NICOLE, Christopher. *See* **YORK, Andrew.**

NIELSEN, Helen (Berniece) American. Born in Roseville, Illinois, 23 October 1918. Educated at Kelvyn Park High School, Chicago; Chicago Art Institute; United States Defense Engineering Program, rated Aero-Layout Engineer, 1942. Freelance commercial artist, Chicago, 1938–42; draftsman and loftsman, Aero-Engineering, Los Angeles, 1942–46; apartment house owner and manager, 1942–78. Agent: Ann Elmo Agency Inc., 60 East 42nd Street, New York, New York 10017. Address: 2622 Victoria Drive, Laguna Beach, California 92651, U.S.A.

CRIME PUBLICATIONS

Novels (series: Simon Drake)

The Kind Man. New York, Washburn, and London, Gollancz, 1951.
Gold Coast Nocturne (Drake). New York, Washburn, 1951; as *Murder by Proxy,* London, Gollancz, 1952; as *Dead on the Level,* New York, Dell, 1954.
Obit Delayed. New York, Washburn, 1952; London, Gollancz, 1953.
Detour. New York, Washburn, 1953; as *Detour to Death,* New York, Dell, 1955.
The Woman on the Roof. New York, Washburn, 1954; London, Gollancz, 1955.
Stranger in the Dark. New York, Washburn, 1955; London, Gollancz, 1956.
The Crime Is Murder. New York, Morrow, 1956; London, Gollancz, 1957.
Borrow the Night. New York, Morrow, and London, Gollancz, 1957; as *Seven Days Before Dying,* New York, Dell, 1958.

The Fifth Caller. New York, Morrow, and London, Gollancz, 1959.
False Witness. New York, Ballantine, 1959.
Sing Me a Murder. New York, Morrow, 1960; London, Gollancz, 1961.
Verdict Suspended. New York, Morrow, 1964; London, Gollancz, 1965.
After Midnight (Drake). New York, Morrow, 1966; London, Gollancz, 1967.
A Killer in the Street. New York, Morrow, and London, Gollancz, 1967.
Darkest Hour (Drake). New York, Morrow, and London, Gollancz, 1969.
Shot on Location. New York, Morrow, and London, Gollancz, 1971.
The Severed Key (Drake). London, Gollancz, 1973.
The Brink of Murder (Drake). London, Gollancz, 1976.

Short Stories

Woman Missing and Other Stories. New York, Ace, 1961.

Uncollected Short Stories

"The Murder Everybody Saw," in *The Saint* (New York), October 1954.
"You Can't Trust a Man," in *Best Detective Stories of the Year 1955,* edited by David C. Cooke. New York, Dutton, 1955.
"Hunch," in *Manhunt* (New York), March 1956.
"First Kill," in *Manhunt* (New York), April 1956.
"A Bad Night for Murder," in *Mantrap* (New York), July 1956.
"The Three-Ball Combination," in *The Saint* (New York), July 1956.
"Death in the Mirror," in *Mantrap* (New York), October 1956.
"Decision," in *Manhunt* (New York), June 1957.
"The Long Walk to Death," in *Mike Shayne Mystery Magazine* (New York), June 1957.
"A Piece of Ground," in *Manhunt* (New York), July 1957.
"The Deadly Mrs. Havershim," in *Alfred Hitchcock's Mystery Magazine* (New York), October 1957.
"Compensation," in *Manhunt* (New York), November 1957.
"Never Trust a Woman," in *Alfred Hitchcock's Mystery Magazine* (New York), December 1957.
"A Degree of Innocence," in *Alfred Hitchcock's Mystery Magazine* (New York), March 1958.
"You're Dead," in *Manhunt* (New York), April 1958.
"Murder and Lonely Hearts," in *Alfred Hitchcock's Mystery Magazine* (New York), May 1958.
"This Man Is Dangerous," in *Ellery Queen's Mystery Magazine* (New York), June 1958.
"Pattern of Guilt," in *Alfred Hitchcock's Mystery Magazine* (New York), July 1958.
"The Deadly Guest," in *Alfred Hitchcock's Mystery Magazine* (New York), October 1958.
"Your Witness," in *Best Detective Stories of the Year* 1959, edited by David C. Cooke. New York, Dutton, 1959.
"The Too Healthy Witness" and "13 Avenida Muerte," in *Toronto Star,* 1959.
"Won't Somebody Help Me," in *Ellery Queen's Mystery Magazine* (New York), January 1959.
"Angry Weather," in *Alfred Hitchcock's Mystery Magazine* (New York), March 1959.
"Obituary," in *Alfred Hitchcock's Mystery Magazine* (New York), April 1959.
"The Very Hard Sell," in *Alfred Hitchcock's Mystery Magazine* (New York), May 1959.

"To the Edge of Murder," in *Alfred Hitchcock's Mystery Magazine* (New York), July 1959.

"Don't Sit under the Apple Tree," in *Alfred Hitchcock's Mystery Magazine* (New York), October 1959.

"Confession," in *Ed McBain's Mystery Book 1* (New York), 1960.

"Who Has Been Sitting in My Chair?," in *Alfred Hitchcock's Mystery Magazine* (New York), February 1960.

"Don't Live in a Coffin," in *Alfred Hitchcock's Mystery Magazine* (New York), March 1960.

"Woman Missing," in *Alfred Hitchcock's Mystery Magazine* (New York), May 1960.

"The Affair Upstairs," in *Alfred Hitchcock's Mystery Magazine* (New York), July 1961.

"The Hopeless Case," in *Ellery Queen's Mystery Magazine* (New York), June 1962.

"Witness for the Defense," in *Ellery Queen's Mystery Magazine* (New York), September 1963.

"Death Scene," in *Ellery Queen's Double Dozen.* New York, Random House, 1964.

"The Breaking Point," in *Ellery Queen's Mystery Magazine* (New York), August 1965.

"The Master's Touch," in *Alfred Hitchcock's Mystery Magazine* (New York), April 1966.

"The Chicken Feed Mine," in *Ellery Queen's Mystery Magazine* (New York), December 1966.

"The Seventh Man," in *Alfred Hitchcock's Mystery Magazine* (New York), September 1967.

"The Perfectionist," in *Alfred Hitchcock's Mystery Magazine* (New York), November 1967.

"No Legal Evidence," in *Ellery Queen's Mystery Magazine* (New York), March 1969.

"The Perfect Servant," in *Ellery Queen's Mystery Bag.* Cleveland, World, 1972.

"The Room at the End of the Hall," in *Alfred Hitchcock's Mystery Magazine* (New York), October 1973.

"What Shall We Do about Angela?," in *Alfred Hitchcock's Mystery Magazine* (New York), December 1973.

"Henry Lowden Alias Henry Taylor," in *Alfred Hitchcock's Death-Reach,* edited by Cathleen Jordan. New York, Dial Press, 1982.

OTHER PUBLICATIONS

Plays

Television Plays: *Alfred Hitchcock Presents, Perry Mason, Markham, Alcoa Theatre, 87th Precinct, Four Star Theatre,* and *Checkmate* series.

*

Manuscript Collection: Mugar Memorial Library, Boston University.

Helen Nielsen comments:

I am old-fashioned enough to believe that characters still make a story, and that every story, especially a mystery, must have a beginning, a middle and an ending. Although the trend today is for more violence, the mystery is still the most demanding form of fiction. No matter how deep the gore flows or how high the bodies are stacked, there must be logic in each crime and no loose ends dangling after the last page.

A critic's comment: "plays fair" is the disciplined mystery writer's reward.

*   *   *

Born in Illinois, Helen Nielsen moved to Southern California in her youth, and her best mysteries are set here in what must surely be an earthly Paradise for novelists with the endlessly strange realities, the overheated emotions, and unconventional professions of this part of the world. Although the weather is often charming (ignoring the occasional earthquake) Nielsen often prefers to stress the worst of winter weather, with the chilling rains or the thick, yellow, and dripping fogs. In *The Fifth Caller* the weather is not the problem but the murder victim and her assistant. Dr. Whitehall specializes in mental problems while equipped with a mail-order degree and an additional one from her own metaphysical college. Her assistant is a Hungarian refugee who actually has an M.D. which makes her uncomfortable in the face of Whitehall's activities; when the doctor is found dead, she is forced to make a suicide attempt on a Santa Monica beach—a little more romantic than Detroit or Liverpool. Most of the story is set in the hospital room where she is recovering from a slashed wrist.

Like every area in the world, even Southern California has its scenic failures with Enchanto-by-the-Sea being one of the most disappointing. Built to become a successful resort, the place has failed miserably and is regularly by-passed by tourist as well as the characters in *Darkest Hour* as they rush up and down the highway outside the town. Most of the latter are has-been actors and even the lawyer in the story is providing a home for a former actress who is now performing as a hostess/house-keeper. *Sing Me a Murder* is another Show Biz story where the pain of the rootless and dispossessed is somewhat ameliorated by money. The widower of a famous singer becomes involved in the murder of her look-alike who is a waitress, perhaps proving how equal democracy can be. When Ty Leander thinks about this case, he feels sure that the arrested man is not guilty, and he seems to sense messages from his dead wife that keep him rushing around and searching out clues. This helps his grief but other people have to do their work by plain slogging without supernatural help.

A Killer in the Street begins horrifyingly in New York City, where crime seems almost natural. Kyle Walker is unlucky enough to witness the attendent in his apartment house garage being murdered and while he gazes in horror at the bound and gagged boy, he knows he will have to flee across country for his own safety. *Detour* goes in another direction, neither country nor town and far from the sea. Danny Ross, not a local man, arrives in a desert community only to be accused of killing a local doctor and is in the position of being in an unfriendly, isolated place that must jog the nightmare memories of many readers. Helpless and surrounded by enemies, Ross is not allowed to speak in his own defence, but miracles can happen even in Hell when one of the locals decides to rescue him.

Many of the Nielsen books feature water in some way, whether lashing rain, dripping fogs, sea, or lake, and damp never cools the raging emotions of the human soul. One lakeside community has a festival in *The Crime Is Murder* where an undistinguished place grabs eagerly at anyone to become a celebrity at their fair, and the amusements cannot stop the crime occurring.

The unsuccessful sister of a rich brother becomes involved in a murder in the bungalow court that belongs to her brother in *The Woman on the Roof,* and the tension and excitement seem to improve the poor mental state that had previously kept her in an asylum, but she, like so many in these mysteries, is isolated and at odds with the world.

The more interesting jobs and professions are well represented in these books with a threatened Judge in *Borrow the Night* proving that even the law is not immune from crime and fear, while *Obit Delayed* shows a reporter coming closer to crime than is really comfortable. Jobs that are quite ordinary elsewhere are bathed with a sunlit strangeness that is more unpleasant than Arctic snow. While some of her mysteries are set in Scandinavia and Central or Southern America, Nielsen is at her best on the West Coast with fog and alienation or sunlight and fear.

—Mary Groff

NILE, Dorothea. *See* **AVALLONE, Michael.**

NOLAN, William F(rancis). Also writes as Frank Anmar; Terance Duncan; F.E. Edwards. American. Born in Kansas City, Missouri, 6 March 1928. Educated at Kansas City Art Institute, 1946–47; San Diego State College, California, 1947–48; Los Angeles City College, 1953. Married Marilyn Seal in 1970. Greeting card designer and cartoonist, Hall Brothers, Kansas City, 1945; mural painter, San Diego, 1940–50; aircraft inspector, Convair, San Diego, 1950–52; credit assistant, Blake Moffit and Towne Paper Company, Los Angeles, 1953–54; interviewer, California State Department of Employment, 1954–56. Since 1956, freelance writer. Contributing editor, *Chase;* managing editor, *Gamma;* West Coast editor, *Auto;* associate editor, *Motor Sport Illustrated;* editor, *You and Your Eyes, In Sight;* reviewer, Los Angeles *Times,* 1964–70. Recipient: American Library Association citation, 1960; Mystery Writers of American Award, 1970, 1972; Academy of Science Fiction and Fantasy award, for fiction, and film, 1976; Maltese Falcon award, 1977. Honorary Doctorate: American River College, Sacramento, California, 1975. Agent: Barbara Puechner, Peekner Agency, 3121 Pontage Road, Bethlehem, Pennsylvania 18017, U.S.A.

CRIME PUBLICATIONS

Novels (series: Bart Challis; Sam Space)

Death Is for Losers (Challis). Los Angeles, Sherbourne Press, 1968.
The White Cad Cross-Up (Challis). Los Angeles, Sherbourne Press, 1969.
Space for Hire. New York, Lancer, 1971.
Look Out for Space. New York, International Polygonics, 1985.
Helltracks. New York, Avon, 1990.

Short Stories

Impact-20. New York, Paperback Library, 1963; London, Corgi, 1966.
Things Beyond Midnight. Santa Cruz, California, Scream Press, 1984.
Blood Sky. San Jose, California, Deadline, 1990.

Uncollected Short Stories

"Dig Me a Home" in *The Saint* (New York), December 1963.
"Death Drag" (as Frank Anmar), in *Chase* (Los Angeles), May 1964.
"Strippers Have to Die" (as F.E. Edwards), in *Chase* (Los Angeles), May 1964.
"The Pop-Op Caper," in *The Best from Playboy 5.* Chicago, Playboy Press, 1971.
"Down the Long Night," in *Men and Malice,* edited by Dean Dickensheet. New York, Doubleday, 1973.
"Sungrab," in *After the Fall,* edited by Robert Sheckley. New York, Ace, and London, Sphere, 1980.
"A Long Time Dying," in *The Eyes Have It,* edited by Robert J. Randisi. New York, Mysterious Press, 1984.
"The Pulpcon Kill," in *New Black Mask Quarterly* (New York), 1985.
"Pirate's Moon," in *Murder in Los Angeles,* edited by Thomas Chastain. New York, Morrow, 1987.
"Die, Clown, Die!" in *14 Vicious Valentines,* edited by Martin H. Greenberg. New York, Avon, 1988.
"The Cure," in *The Horrow Show* (Oak Run, California), Summer 1988.
"Daddy's Girl," in *The Further Adventures of Batman,* edited by Martin H. Greenberg. New York, Bantam, 1989.

OTHER PUBLICATIONS

Novels

Logan's Run, with G.C. Johnson. New York, Dial Press, 1967; London, Gollancz, 1968.
Logan's World. New York, Bantam, 1977; London, Corgi, 1978.
Logan's Search. New York, Bantam, 1980; London, Corgi, 1981.
Logan: A Trilogy. Baltimore, Maclay, 1986.
Rio Renegades (as Terance Duncan). New York, Zebra, 1989.

Short Stories

Alien Horizons. New York, Pocket Books, 1974.
Wonderworlds. London, Gollancz, 1977.

Plays

Screenplays: *The Legend of Machine-Gun Kelly,* 1975; *Logan's Run,* 1976; *Burnt Offerings,* with Dan Curtis, 1976.

Television Plays: *The Joy of Living,* 1971; *The Norliss Tapes,* 1973; *Melvin Purvis, G-Man,* with John Milius, 1974; *The Turn of the Screw,* 1974; *The Kansas City Massacre,* with Bronson Howitzer, 1975; *Sky Heist,* with Rick Rosner 1975; *Julie* and *Millicent and Therese* (in *Trilogy of Terror*), 1975; *Logan's Run* series, 1977; *First Loss,* 1981; *The Partnership,* 1981; *Bridge Across Time* (*Terror of London Bridge*), 1985; *Trilogy of Terror II,* 1990.

Verse

Dark Encounters. Madison, Wisconsin, Dream House, 1986.

Other

Adventure on Wheels: The Autobiography of a Road Racing Champion, with John Fitch. New York, Putnam, 1959.

Barney Oldfield. New York, Putnam, 1961.
Phil Hill, Yankee Champion. New York, Putnam, 1962.
Men of Thunder: Fabled Daredevils of Motor Sport. New York, Putnam, 1964.
Sinners and Supermen. North Hollywood, All Star, 1965.
John Huston, King Rebel. Los Angeles, Sherbourne Press, 1965.
Dashiell Hammett: A Casebook. Santa Barbara, California, McNally and Loftin, 1969.
Steve McQueen: Star on Wheels. New York, Putnam, 1972.
Carnival of Speed. New York, Putnam, 1973.
Hemingway: Last Days of the Lion. Santa Barbara, California, Capra Press, 1974.
The Ray Bradbury Companion. Detroit, Gale, 1975.
Hammett: A Life at the Edge. New York, Congdon and Weed, and London, Barker, 1983.
McQueen (biography of Steve McQueen). New York, Congdon and Weed, and London, Barker, 1984.
The Black Mask Boys. New York, Morrow, 1985.
Max Brand: Western Giant. Bowling Green, Ohio, Popular Press, 1986.
The Work of Charles Beaumont (bibliography). San Bernardino, California, Borgo Press, 1986.
How to Write Horror. Cincinnati, Ohio, Writer's Digest, 1990.

Editor, with Charles Beaumont, *Omnibus of Speed.* New York, Putnam, 1958; London, Paul, 1961.
Editor, with Charles Beaumont, *When Engines Roar.* New York, Bantam, 1964.
Editor, *Man Against Tomorrow.* New York, Avon, 1965.
Editor, *The Pseudo People: Androids in Science Fiction.* Los Angeles, Sherbourne Press, 1965; as *Almost Human,* London, Souvenir Press, 1966.
Editor, *3 to the Highest Power.* New York, Avon, 1968; London, Corgi, 1971.
Editor, *A Wilderness of Stars.* Los Angeles, Sherbourne Press, 1969; London, Gollancz, 1970.
Editor, *A Sea of Space.* New York, Bantam, 1970.
Editor, *The Future Is Now.* Los Angeles, Sherbourne Press, 1970.
Editor, *The Human Equation.* Los Angeles, Sherbourne Press, 1971.
Editor, *The Edge of Forever,* by Chad Oliver. Los Angeles, Sherbourne Press, 1971.
Editor, with Martin H. Greenberg, *Science Fiction Origins.* New York, Fawcett-Popular Library, 1980.
Editor, *Max Brand's Best Western Stories.* New York, Dodd Mead, 3 vols., 1981–87; London, Hale, 2 vols., 1983–86.
Editor, with Martin H. Greenberg. *Urban Horrors.* Arlington Heights, Illinois, n.p., 1990.

*

Bibliography: *The Work of William F. Nolan* by Boden Clark and James Hopkins, San Bernardino, California, Borgo Press, 1988.

Manuscript Collection: Bowling Green State University, Ohio.

Theatrical Activities:

Actor: **Films**—*The Intruder,* 1962; *The Legend of Machine-Gun Kelly,* 1973.

William F. Nolan comments:
    Having been active as a professional for nearly four decades, with 50 published books and more than 700 magazine pieces in some half-a-dozen genres (from sf to show business), I am not an easily categorized writer. It is, therefore, appropriate to define my variegated role in the crime-mystery field.
    Nearly all of my published novels are related, either directly or indirectly, to the crime genre. My two "Bart Challis" novels, written in the hard-boiled tradition, feature a private detective working the Greater Los Angeles area of the 1960's. My two "Sam Space" novels (the first of which was honored by the Mystery Writers of America), are a bizarre cross-mix of mystery and science fiction, with my ultra-tough private eye working out of an office on Mars. (He's a literal descendant of Bart Challis.) My three "Logan" books are basically science fiction, but they may also be considered future-crime novels since they deal with a futuristic policeman in Los Angeles (Logan) hunting lawbreakers (citizens who refuse to turn themselves in for a state-imposed death at 21) and my "horror novel," *Helltracks,* involves a serial killer.
    Several of my crime-suspense short stories have been collected in *Impact 20, Things Beyond Midnight,* and *Nightshapes* and I have had my work selected for many crime-related anthologies. I have contributed genre fiction to *Mike Shayne, The Saint, Chase,* and *Terror Detective.*
    In the non-fiction category of crime-mystery I have been a frequent contributor to *The Armchair Detective* (with essays, checklists, reviews, and profiles), and was the first biographer of Dashiell Hammett (having published two books about him). Also, I've profiled several genre writers such as Raymond Chandler and Ian Fleming (in *Sinners and Supermen*), and have provided the first full history of *Black Mask* magazine, along with its major writers: Hammett, Chandler, Gardner, Daly, Nebel, Whitfield, McCoy and Paul Cain (in *The Black Mask Boys*). Additionally for television, I have several major crime dramas to my credit as well as a European film, *The Legend of Machine-Gun Kelly.*
    All of which clearly demonstrates that I have been continually involved in the crime-mystery field since the mid-1950's as novelist, short story writer, biographer, historian, book reviewer and script writer. The end is not yet in sight.

*   *   *

    William F. Nolan, twice recipient of the Mystery Writers of America's prestigious Edgar Allan Poe Special award, brings to his mystery writing a variegated background stemming from multiple genre interests. Based on an early admiration for the story-telling talent of Max Brand (Frederick Faust), Nolan has developed a fast-paced narrative style in which the plot line is, as it should be, the force that drives his characters to their personal growth or destruction. It is hardly possible to place Nolan in any one field since he is as highly respected for his horror stories and science fiction novels as he is for his mysteries. And then there is the wealth of non-fiction including biographies and criticism. Even in his fiction there is a blending that is most apparent in the Logan trilogy. Set in the 22nd Century, *Logan's Run, Logan's World,* and *Logan's Search* are actually mystery/thrillers in the tradition of *The Thirty-Nine Steps* and *Rogue Male.*
    The versatility of Nolan's work is illustrated by some of the chapter headings in his compiled bibliography. They include short fiction (Nolan has had a hundred stories printed), personality profiles, comics, artwork, reviews, verse, and screenplays in addition to his novels.
    William F. Nolan's first mystery novel was published in 1968 after 12 years as a full-time writer. It is a hard-boiled Los Angeles private-eye story titled *Death Is for Losers.* The detective is Bart Challis and he appeared again in *The*

White Cad Cross-Up. These two books were followed by two that represent a wild blend of science-fiction and mystery about a seedy private detective wryly named Sam Space on the planet Mars in the 21st Century; *Space for Hire* and *Look Out for Space.* Nolan has also written two shorter tales about Sam Space, one of which, "Sungrab," was chosen for the 1988 Mystery Writers of American anthology *Distant Danger.*

Nolan declares, "Whatever excites me, I write about it;" thus his books on motor racing, Steve McQueen and other drivers, and bibliographies of Ray Bradbury and Charles Beaumont, a booklet on Ernest Hemingway, a western (under a pseudonym), a book on *How To Write Horror,* anthologies of fantasy and science fiction, collections of his verse and a book of essays on his early favorite, Max Brand.

Nolan has received particular acclaim for his critical volume *Dashiell Hammett: A Casebook* and his definitive biography *Hammett: A Life at the Edge.* The latter, a result of more than 15 years of research, remains the fundamental book on Hammett, his times and his writing.

No commentary on Nolan, especially in the context of mystery writing, would be complete without mentioning *The Black Mask Boys.* Nolan here provides a full history of *Black Mask* magazine, the most renowned of the pulps, from its concept by H.L. Mencken and George Jean Nathan in 1920 to its demise in 1951. The book features biographical sketches and bibliographies of each of the eight authors selected for inclusion in this anthology. Both Hammett and Raymond Chandler are there, of course, along with such critically neglected hard-boiled pioneers as Carroll John Daly, Horace McCoy, Frderick Nebel, Raoul Whitfield, and Paul Cain. Nolan's enthusiasm is apparent in his biographical personality studies. He admits that he develops an empathic relationship with his subject and that "I *become* that person while writing about him." Nolan's drive is contagious and his dedication to his craft may be best exemplified by his work schedule. This is based on at least four hours of writing each day, Sundays and holidays included. This does not include the time spent on reading and research. The result is more than a thousand published works in a half-a-dozen genres. Nolan is indeed a "multimedia man."

—Richard G. La Porte

NOONE, Edwina. *See* **AVALLONE, Michael.**

NORTH, Anthony. *See* **KOONTZ,** Dean R.

NORTH, Gil. Pseudonym for Geoffrey Horne. British. Born in Skipton, Yorkshire, 12 July 1916. Educated at Ermysted's Grammar School, Skipton, 1925–35; Christ's College, Cambridge (exhibitioner; scholar), 1935–38, 1951–52,

B.A. (honours) 1938, M.A. 1942, diploma in social anthropology 1952. Married Betty Duthie in 1949; one son and one daughter. Administrative officer, Colonial Service, South-East Nigeria and Cameroons, 1938–55.

CRIME PUBLICATIONS

Novels (series: Sergeant Caleb Cluff)

Sergeant Cluff Stands Firm. London, Chapman and Hall, 1960.
The Methods of Sergeant Cluff. London, Chapman and Hall, 1961.
Sergeant Cluff Goes Fishing. London, Chapman and Hall, 1962.
More Deaths for Sergeant Cluff. London, Chapman and Hall, 1963.
Sergeant Cluff and the Madmen (includes *The Blindness of Sergeant Cluff* and *Sergeant Cluff Laughs Last*). London, Chapman and Hall, 1964.
Sergeant Cluff and the Price of Pity. London, Chapman and Hall, 1965.
The Confounding of Sergeant Cluff. London, Chapman and Hall, 1966.
Sergeant Cluff and the Day of Reckoning. London, Chapman and Hall, 1967.
The Procrastination of Sergeant Cluff. London, Eyre Methuen, and Spottiswoode, 1969.
No Choice for Sergeant Cluff. London, Eyre and Spottiswoode, 1971.
Sergeant Cluff Rings True. London, Eyre Methuen, 1972.
A Corpse for Kofi Katt. London, Hale, 1978.

OTHER PUBLICATIONS

Novels as Geoffrey Horne

Winter. London, Hutchinson, 1957.
Land of No Escape. London, Hutchinson, 1958.
Quest for Gold (for children). London, Hutchinson, 1959.
The Man Who Was Chief. London, Chapman and Hall, 1960.
The Portuguese Diamonds. London, Chapman and Hall, 1961.

Plays

Television Plays: *Cluff* series (20 episodes), 1964.

*   *   *

Gil North's books are of no outstanding merit in terms of plot or literary quality, and not complex as detective stories, but similar remarks could be levelled at the Maigret novels of Simenon, who is widely regarded as the world's foremost crime novelist. Intentionally or otherwise, North has succeeded in presenting Sergeant Caleb Cluff as a sort of Yorkshire version of Maigret. Throughout the small town of Gunnarshaw and the surrounding area this obstinate but likable countryman is known and respected by young and old, including the tearaways and those with something to hide. His love of the fells is matched by love of his fellow men, and Cluff exudes compassion rather than sentimentality. There is no clear dividing line between his private and official life, and in the latter capacity Cluff is motivated to right wrongs rather than to seek retribution.

One recalls Cluff's love/hate relationship with his housethe gruff Yorkshire dialect which has proved almost incomprehensible to American critics, and the author's profound approach to such themes as the clash between parents and children (*No Choice for Sergeant Cluff*) or the mental state of men long past their prime (*Sergeant Cluff and the Madmen*). Cluff's methods are unorthodox and even lethargic at times. Often it is a case of waiting and watching the world go by, with the occasional noncommittal nod in the suspect's direction, and there is an over-riding assumption that the murderer (particularly in a domestic situation) will eventually bare his soul.

—Melvyn Barnes

———

NORTH, Howard. *See* **HALL, Adam.**

———

O

O'DONNELL, Lillian (née Udvardy). American. Born in Trieste, Italy, in 1926. Educated at the American Academy of Dramatic Arts, New York. Married J. Leonard O'Donnell in 1954. Actress in Broadway and television productions, and stage manager and director, Schubert Organization, New York, 1940–54. Agent: Roberta Kent, 211 South Beverly Drive, Beverly Hills, California. Address: 200 East 66th Street, New York, New York 10021, U.S.A.

CRIME PUBLICATIONS

Novels (series: Mici Anhalt; Norah Mulcahaney)

Death on the Grass. New York, Arcadia House, 1960.
Death Blanks the Screen. New York, Arcadia House, 1961.
Death Schuss. New York and London, Abelard Schuman, 1963.
Murder under the Sun. New York and London, Abelard Schuman, 1964.
Death of a Player. New York and London, Abelard Schuman, 1964.
Babes in the Woods. New York and London, Abelard Schuman, 1965.
The Sleeping Beauty Murders. New York and London, Abelard Schuman, 1967.
The Face of the Crime. New York and London, Abelard Schuman, 1968.
The Tachi Tree. New York and London, Abelard Schuman, 1968.
Dive into Darkness. New York, Abelard Schuman, 1971; London, Abelard Schuman, 1972.
The Phone Calls (Mulcahaney). New York, Putnam, and London, Hodder and Stoughton, 1972.
Don't Wear Your Wedding Ring (Mulcahaney). New York, Putnam, 1973; London, Barker, 1974.
Dial 577 R-A-P-E (Mulcahaney). New York, Putnam, and London, Barker, 1974.
The Baby Merchants (Mulcahaney). New York, Putnam, 1975; London, Bantam, 1976.
Leisure Dying (Mulcahaney). New York, Putnam, 1976.
Aftershock (Anhalt). New York, Putnam, 1977; London, Hale, 1979.
No Business Being a Cop (Mulcahaney). New York, Putnam, 1979; London, Hale, 1980.
Falling Star (Anhalt). New York, Putnam, 1979; London, Hale, 1981.
Wicked Designs (Anhalt). New York, Putnam, 1980; London, Hale, 1983.
The Children's Zoo (Mulcahaney). New York, Putnam, 1981; London, Hale, 1982.
Cop Without a Shield (Mulcahaney). New York, Putnam, 1983.
Ladykiller (Mulcahaney). New York, Putnam, 1984.
Casual Affairs (Mulcahaney). New York, Putnam, 1985.
The Other Side of the Door (Mulcahaney). New York, Putnam, 1987.
A Good Night to Kill. New York, Putnam, 1989.
A Wreath for the Bride. New York, Putnam, 1990.

OTHER PUBLICATIONS

Other

"Rules and Routines of the Police Procedural," in *The Writer* (Boston), February 1978.
"Fact or Fiction," in *Murderess Ink,* edited by Dilys Winn. New York, Workman, 1979.
"Plot vs. Character in Mystery Fiction," in *The Writer* (Boston), January 1982.

*

Manuscript Collection: Mugar Memorial Library, Boston University.

* * *

The mystery suspense novels of Lillian O'Donnell can be divided into two distinct categories: those featuring the amateur detectives, and the Norah Mulcahaney police procedural series. O'Donnell's first mystery novels primarily featured suspense; the amateur detecting is subordinated to considerable anxiety by the characters about their safety, the unlikely death of one of their number, and the lack of motive or serious clue to solve the mystery. The confusion which surrounds the cases is never really penetrated by the detective, and the police seldom appear with recognizable success. Generally the detective turns up a great deal of indiscriminate evidence which is not put in place during the denouement or, frequently, withholds information from the reader. The three Mici Anhalt mysteries, written after a number of Mulcahaney novels, show a surer command of plotting and character development. This impulsive amateur who works for the Crime Victims' Compensation Board often jumps to conclusions but O'Donnell's development of her milieu is interesting.

The police procedural novels featuring Nora Mulcahaney involve insights into not only professional and technical aspects of her detection but also the private lives of Mulcahaney and her family. The novels do not resemble the best-known police procedural novels. Unlike the Gideon series of J.J. Marric, the novels' investigations center around a single case, with other apparently unrelated crimes eventually discovered to be subplots of the major investigation; unlike the procedural novels of Ed McBain's 87th precinct, O'Donnell's New York based detective novels focus on the relationship between Nora's professional and private lives. They are a combination of the efficient and team-oriented police novel and the traditional domestic mystery with its emphasis on personal relationships.

In this course of the novels, which begin the year after her graduation from the police academy, Norah Mulcahaney is promoted, marries, and adopts a child; later, the adoption is voided, she is widowed and promoted again. In the early novels, her extended family of Irish politico father and domineering Italian mother-in-law becomes involved in the solution of crimes where O'Donnell tends to overdo the blending of stories: several of the investigations are necessary because Pat Mulcahaney, interfering in his daughter's private life, involves her. In other cases, her assumptions about professional rivalry that her husband, Lieutenant Joe Capretto, might feel lead Norah to unwise and dangerous independent investigation. Even her unsuccessful attempts to become pregnant involve the entire family in a series of Mafia vendettas, some 15 years old. After Joe Capretto's hit-and-run death in *Cop Without a Shield*, the strong focus on family becomes muted: Norah's attempts to date show only limited success and her mentoring friendship with rookie cop Audrey Jordan is not sustained. However, the independent spirit and personal appeal of Norah Mulcahaney Capretto are still evident throughout the novels. Her tendency to conceal her concerns gives the reader a unique insight into a believable professional's concern for the successful integration of all aspects of her personality; and her measured adjustment to promotion and supervisory responsibilities reflect contemporary women's problems.

Competently plotted, these novels now suffer from comparison with the range of excellent fiction about women detectives which has emerged during the 1980's. In O'Donnell's work, the technical demands of police work are neither over-emphasized nor overlooked; the development of a series character is consistent and progressive; the interplay between a demanding professional life and a desired private one is realistically presented. In the early years of fiction about women detectives, O'Donnell made a unique contribution to the genre although her later novels do not have the same kind of presence.

—Kathleen Gregory Klein

O'DONNELL, Peter. British. Born in London, 11 April 1920. Educated at Catford Central School, London. Served in the Royal Corps of Signals, 1938–46. Married Constance Doris Green in 1940; two daughters. Associated with Amalgamated Press, London, 1937–39; editor, Clerke and Cochran, 1946–51; author of strip cartoons: *Garth*, 1953–66, *Tug Transom*, 1954–66, *Romeo Brown*, 1956–62, and since 1963, *Modesty Blaise*. Address: 49 Sussex Square, Brighton, Sussex BN2 1GE, England.

CRIME PUBLICATIONS

Novels (series: Modesty Blaise in all books)

Modesty Blaise. London, Souvenir Press, and New York, Doubleday, 1965.
Sabre-Tooth. London, Souvenir Press, and New York, Doubleday, 1966.
I, Lucifer. London, Souvenir Press, and New York, Doubleday, 1967.
A Taste for Death. London, Souvenir Press, and New York, Doubleday, 1969.
The Impossible Virgin. London, Souvenir Press, and New York, Doubleday, 1971.
The Silver Mistress. London, Souvenir Press, 1973; Cambridge, Massachusetts, Archival, 1982.
Last Day in Limbo. London, Souvenir Press, 1976; New York, Mysterious Press, 1985.

Dragon's Claw. London, Souvenir Press, 1978; New York, Mysterious Press, 1985.
The Xanadu Talisman. London, Souvenir Press, 1981; New York, Mysterious Press, 1984.
The Night of Morningstar. London, Souvenir Press, 1982; New York, Mysterious Press, 1987.
Dead Man's Handle. London, Souvenir Press, 1985; New York, Mysterious Press, 1986.

Short Stories

Pieces of Modesty. London, Pan, 1972; New York, Mysterious Press, 1986.

OTHER PUBLICATIONS

Plays

Murder Most Logical (produced Windsor, 1974; as *Mr. Fothergill's Murder*, produced London, 1982).

Screenplays: *Modesty Blaise*, with Stanley Dubens and Evan Jones, 1966; *The Vengeance of She*, 1968.

Television Play: *Take a Pair of Private Eyes* serial, 1966.

Other

"Becoming Modesty," in *Murder Ink: The Mystery Reader's Companion*, edited by Dilys Winn. New York, Workman, 1977.
The Black Pearl, and The Vikings (comic strips). London, Star, 1978.
In the Beginning (comic strip). London, Star, 1978.
The Gabriel Set-Up (graphic novel). London, Titan, 1984.
Mister Sun (graphic novel). London, Titan, 1985.
The Hell-Makers (graphic novel). London, Titan, 1986.
The Warlords of Phoenix (graphic novel). London, Titan, 1986.
Death of a Jester (graphic novel). London, Titan, 1987.
The Puppet Master (graphic novel). London, Titan, 1987.
The Iron God (graphic novel). London, Titan, 1989.

* * *

The 11 novels and one short story collection about the beautiful and deadly ex-criminal Modesty Blaise and her knife-throwing sidekick Willie Garvin are a spin-off from a newspaper strip and a film. Peter O'Donnell created Blaise as a strip character in 1962 (he still likes his villains to be of the larger-than-life-variety preferred by the medium) and wrote the first screenplay for Joseph Losey's film *Modesty Blaise*, but he and it had very little to do with the final film version.

O'Donnell used his screenplay as a basis for the first Blaise novel and still doubles as a script writer for the newspaper strip and as an author of a very successful series of novels about Modesty and Willie: the strips concentrate on action, in the books he gives himself more room to round out characters and settings.

Few thriller writers care about explaining how, where, and when their heroes have got their expertise in all the necessary fields like gun handling, skin diving and love making. O'Donnell is an exception. In frequent flashbacks we are told about Blaise's orphan childhood in refugee camps, her learn-it-or-die education in unarmed combat, her teenage wanderings through deserts and over mountains to Tangiers, where she—aided by her adoring right hand Willie Garvin, picked up in a Saigon gaol—transformed a small-time gang of crooks to the international crime ring The Network. Now Blaise and Garvin are rich and retired, but need the thrills of danger like an addict needs a fix. Enter Sir Gerald Tarrant from a very Secret Service.

More often than not Blaise and Garvin are captured by the villains halfway through the novel, often in the desert or jungle, and have to make their escape, burdened down by a couple of fellow prisoners. In nearly all the stories the climax is a face-to-face fight between Blaise and an expert from the opposition; *A Taste for Death* doubles the formula and first sets her against a master swordsman, then Garvin against an seemingly invincible giant.

O'Donnell builds up these fight scenes as unscrupulously fair as Agatha Christie builds her puzzles: Wenczel *is* a better fencer, the gun slinger in *Dragon's Claw is* that tenth of a second faster, the unarmed combat expert in *The Silver Mistress is* stronger than Blaise. She wins by being creative and choosing her own ground and O'Donnell often lets us see the fight through the eyes of another expert—most often Garvin or Tarrant—who can appreciate the moves and counter moves as well as feel anxious about Modesty's welfare.

Blaise and Garvin are a couple in the combat grounds, but not in bed. O'Donnell provides her with a series of lovers, him with a picturesque string of mistresses past and present and often uses them as a mild comic relief: she has a soft spot for wise-cracking intellectuals with desperate courage when needed but no experience in skulduggery, he surprisingly often finds himself in company with handicapped girls—the blind Dinah Pilgrim first appears in *A Taste for Death* (and later on is married off to Modesty's lover from *I, Lucifer*), one-legged Lady Janet Gillam is introduced in the short story volume and plays an important part in *The Silver Mistress*.

There will perhaps be another short story collection, but no more novels about Blaise, according to interviews with O'Donnell. Perhaps it is just as well; the last two or three of the novels have leaned heavily on stock situations and characters and lacked the pace, the humour, and the happy extravagance of the rest of the series.

The newspaper strip artistically died in 1970 with its first artist, Jim Holdaway: none of his followers, certainly not the present artist, Romero from Spain, has succeeded in capturing the very special mix of wit, easygoing professionalism, and an almost tangible aura of danger that makes Blaise and Garvin quite an exceptional pair.

—Bo Lundin

O'FARRELL, William. Also wrote as William Grew. American. Born in 1904. Recipient: Mystery Writers of America Edgar Allan Poe award, 1959. *Died in 1962.*

CRIME PUBLICATIONS

Novels

Repeat Performance. Boston, Houghton Mifflin, 1942; London, W.H. Allen, 1948; revised edition, n.p., Pennant, 1954.
Brandy for a Hero. New York, Duell, 1948.
The Ugly Woman. New York, Duell, 1948; London, Collier Macmillan, 1966.
Thin Edge of Violence. New York, Duell, 1949.

Causeway to the Past. New York, Duell, 1950; London, Corgi, 1954.
The Snakes of St. Cyr. New York, Duell, 1951; as *Harpoon of Death,* London, Dakers, 1953; abridged edition, as *Lovely in Death,* n.p., Bestseller, 1955.
These Arrows Point to Death. New York, Duell, 1951; London, Foulsham, 1952.
Walk the Dark Bridge. New York, Doubleday, 1952; as *The Secret Fear,* London, Corgi, 1954.
Grow Young and Die. New York, Doubleday, 1952; London, Dakers, 1954.
Doubles in Death (as William Grew). New York, Doubleday, 1953.
The Devil His Due. New York, Doubleday, and London, Hale, 1955.
Murder Has Many Faces (as William Grew). Hasbrouck Heights, New Jersey, Graphic, 1955.
Wetback. New York, Dell, 1956.
Gypsy, Go Home. New York, Fawcett, 1961.
The Golden Key. London, Lancer, 1963.

Uncollected Short Stories

"Exhibit A," in *Ellery Queen's Mystery Magazine* (New York), January 1955.
"The High, Warm Place," in *Ellery Queen's Mystery Magazine* (New York), October 1957.
"The Girl on the Beach," in *Ellery Queen's Mystery Annual 13.* New York, Random House, 1958; London, Collins, 1960.
"It Never Happened," in *Manhunt* (New York), June 1958.
"Over There—Darkness," in *Best Detective Stories of the Year 14,* edited by David C. Cooke. New York, Dutton, 1959.
"Hi, Killer," in *Mercury* (New York), April 1959.
"One Hour Late," in *Manhunt* (New York), April 1959.
"Long Drop," in *Alfred Hitchcock's Mystery Magazine* (New York), June 1959.
"In a Tranquil House," in *Alfred Hitchcock's Mystery Magazine* (New York), October 1959.
"The Girl in White," in *The Saint* (New York), December 1959.
"Lady of the Old School," in *Ellery Queen's Mystery Magazine* (New York), September 1960.
"Death and the Blue Rose," in *Manhunt* (New York), December 1960.
"The Hood Is a Bonnet," in *The Saint* (New York), December 1961.
"Death among the Geraniums," in *The Saint* (New York), April 1962.
"A Plague of Pigeons," in *The Saint* (New York), August 1962.
"A Paper for Mr. Wurley," in *Ellery Queen's Double Dozen.* New York, Random House, 1964; London, Gollancz, 1965.
"Philosophy and the Dutchman," in *The Saint* (New York), January 1965.
"With Blue Ribbons on It," in *Ellery Queen's Mystery Magazine* (New York), October 1966.

*   *   *

Beginning with his nightmare-ridden actor in *Repeat Performance,* William O'Farrell was adept at portraying the minds of a variety of people. Dr. Granville, a researcher nearing a cure for malaria in *Brandy for a Hero,* finds all his notes have been stolen. He must overcome a strong guilt complex and a fear of heights in a breakneck chase against shadowy forces of evil. The title is based on Samuel Johnson: ". . . he who aspires to be a hero must drink brandy."

A political group, almost subliminally shown in *Brandy*, becomes reality in *Thin Edge of Violence*. Moresby, the archetypal O'Farrell hero, is a decent man trying to break off an extramarital affair. His indiscretion involves him with a psychopathic murderer and a fascist organization. Murder also occurs in the novel *Doubles in Death* (published as by William Grew) and the short stories "Long Drop" and "One Hour Late" as men try to discourage unstable women who threaten their marriages.

The more O'Farrell strayed from formula, the more interesting (if not always successful) he was. *Causeway to the Past* involves a young widower in an almost Gothic situation as he visits his wife's family on an isolated island. He annoys the reader by wandering into dangerous situations, but the book, like most, is fast-paced and exciting. *Grow Young and Die* was an atypical attempt to write classic detective story. However, O'Farrell's hero turns out to be more a catalyst than a detective because "I'm inclined to see things in flashes instead of logically reasoning them out . . . my instinct is simply to barge ahead and stir things up . . . " He is kin to the hero of another Grew book, *Murder Has Many Faces*, who admits, "I was neither thinking nor acting normally. That's my only excuse for the stupid thing I did next." The emotional approach to detection is redeemed by that book's narrative drive and well-described Mexican setting.

By the late 1950's O'Farrell's reputation was increasingly that of a hardboiled writer as he wrote tough paperback originals like *Wetback* and *Gypsy, Go Home* and appeared regularly in *Manhunt*. Yet, it was at this time that he did his best work, five short stories in each of which there was an in-depth portrayal of a female character. "Over There—Darkness" won him the 1959 Mystery Writers of America Edgar award for his picture of a complacent middle-aged woman suddenly faced with urban terror. He was successful at depicting women of many different ages. In "The Girl on the Beach" it was a horrifying 11-year-old. Miss Alice Murchison, the superbly described "Lady of the Old School," is 72 and trying to preserve her dignity in a crime story which makes the reader care about her. When a successful writer returns to his boyhood home in "The High, Warm Place," his psyche is upset by the strangely antagonistic woman who now owns the house. Mildred, the plain, shy heroine of "Death and the Blue Rose," is hypnotized to gain courage. She needs it when she accidentally becomes involved with a handsome bank robber running from the mob he has double crossed.

When O'Farrell died in 1962 he was not active as a novelist, having published only three books in the previous six years. However, he had become one of the most popular contributors to the digest-sized magazines then being published. He had found the length that suited him and his readers.

—Marvin Lachman

OFFORD, Lenore Glen. Also writes as Theo Durrant. American. Born in Spokane, Washington, 24 October 1905. Educated at Mills College, Oakland, California, B.A. 1925. Married Harold R. Offord in 1929; one daughter. Mystery book critic, San Francisco *Chronicle*, 1950–82. Address: 641 Euclid Avenue, Berkeley, California 94708, U.S.A.

CRIME PUBLICATIONS

Novels (series: Bill and Coco Hasting; Todd McKinnon)

Murder on Russian Hill (Hastings). Philadelphia, Macrae Smith, 1938; as *Murder Before Breakfast*, London, Jarrolds, 1938.
The 9 Dark Hours. New York, Duell, and London, Eldon Press, 1941.
Clues to Burn (Hastings). New York, Duell, 1942; London, Grayson, 1943.
Skeleton Key (McKinnon). New York, Duell, 1943; London, Eldon Press, 1944.
The Glass Mask (McKinnon). New York, Duell, 1944; London, Jarrolds, 1946.
. . . My True Love Lies. New York, Duell, 1947; as *And Turned to Clay*, London, Jarrolds, 1950.
The Smiling Tiger (McKinnon). New York, Duell, 1949; London, Jarrolds, 1951.
The Marble Forest (as Theo Durrant, with others). New York, Knopf, 1951; as *The Big Fear*, New York, Popular Library, 1953.
The Girl in the Belfry, with Joseph Henry Jackson. New York, Fawcett, 1957.
Walking Shadow (McKinnon). New York, Simon and Schuster, 1959; London, Ward Lock, 1961.

Uncollected Short Stories

"Memoirs of a Mystery Critic," in *Ellery Queen's Mystery Magazine* (New York), April 1967.
"The Old Lady Shows Her Prejudices," in *Ellery Queen's Mystery Magazine* (New York), March 1968.

OTHER PUBLICATIONS

Novels

Cloth of Silver. Philadelphia, Macrae Smith, 1939.
Angels Unaware. Philadelphia, Macrae Smith, 1940; as *Distinguished Visitors*, London, Eldon Press, 1942.

Other

Enchanted August (for children). Indianapolis, Bobbs Merrill, 1956.

*

Manuscript Collections: Bancroft Library, University of California, Berkeley; University of Oregon Library, Eugene.

*   *   *

Appearing late in the classical age of detection, Lenore Glen Offord's handful of mysteries concentrated on romantic entanglements of the heroines and the unpleasant realities of a murder investigation. Suspicion among friends is frequently referred to in *Clues to Burn* and *. . . My True Love Lies*. The fluctuations of love affairs, however, are as important to the heroines, Georgine Wyeth, Noel Bruce, and, later, Georgine's daughter Barbie, as the uncovering of the criminal.

Primarily focussing on the women, Offord blends the everyday chores of cooking, housekeeping, and worrying about raising children with the more sinister elements. The result is a burying of clues among apparently immaterial events. *Walking Shadow* particularly concentrates so much on the work of producing a Shakespeare festival that the mystery takes a secondary position. What is lost in tautness and suspense is compensated for by believability, likable characters, and the appearance of San Francisco and the northwest coast area as an alluring locale.

Todd McKinnon's work as a detective in *Skeleton Key, Walking Shadow,* and *The Smiling Tiger* is representative of Offord's books. The villain has the upper hand through most of the book but is trapped in the chase or flurry of excitement at the end. Until that time, Todd has been merely an observer. Finally, a short explanation tells who did what and why, but the steps of deduction and how the detective knew the answer are missing. Although she broke no new ground, Offord produced high quality examples of the 1940's and 1950's mystery.

—Fred Dueren

O'HAGAN, Joan. Australian. Born in Canberra. Married. Has lived in New Zealand, the South Pacific, America, and Italy. Lives in London. Address: c/o Macmillan Ltd., 4 Little Essex Street, London WC2 3LF, England.

CRIME PUBLICATIONS

Novels

Death and a Madonna. London, Macmillan, 1986.
Against the Grain. London, Macmillan, 1987.
A Roman Death. London, Macmillan, 1988.

OTHER PUBLICATIONS

Novel

Incline and Fall: The Death of Geoffrey Stretton. Sydney and London, Angus and Robertson, 1976.

* * *

Joan O'Hagan's traditionalist approach to the basic formula of the classic murder mystery is nowhere better demonstrated than in her novel *Death and a Madonna*. Here, the author assembles a cast of characters from the ranks of Rome's rich wives and aspring or established intellectuals, posits a genuine motive among them, despatches the action to a remote country setting and allows the process of death, detection and discovery to run its course. Whilst the plotting is creative, and, in the manner of most good murder stories, there are several candidates for the mantle of culpability until reasonably late in the day, it is primarily the embellishments with which O'Hagan enriches her narrative that make *Death and a Madonna* worthwhile.

Dr. Mowbray, the expert art historian around whom the tale revolves, is characterized by the way in which he perceives his surroundings and more specifically, the bodies orbiting about him. Thus, we find him imagining a member of his all-female lecture group in the following terms: "She was full of colour, in warm autumn tones, and it was probable that undressed she might be very like a Giulio Romano nymph. Or Rubens? Yes, one of the Three Graces." Nor can Mowbray's beautiful Latin wife, Rafaella, escape this overwhelming brand of art-related image projection and at the core of the book is her fierce rejection of his impersonality—"You. . . . your art, your paintings. You care for nothing else on earth. I once thought you capable of human relationships. But you are not human! You are cold, callous!" Eventually, it is Mowbray's devotion to art and one piece in particular that proves to be both his and his wife's undoing.

O'Hagan fashions an intriguing web of adulterous deception with sensitivity and poise, developing an emblematic line concerning the perishability of human beauty (both of spirit and physical form) which resurfaces in her later work. The contrast between elevated thought and base motive is as well achieved as the depth of descriptive colour with which the writer renders the Italian landscape although occasionally, the deliberate, highly informed style can seem a little intrusive.

Against the Grain follows an altogether more rugged route, being more in the line of an intercontinental adventure thriller than the traipse up the country house conundrum path which *Death and a Madonna* represents. In it, we find another doctor, this time named Duquesne whose field is not art history, but agriculture. Thankfully, Duquesne is a more sympathetic character than his similarly qualified counterpart in *Death and a Madonna* and there is not one instance of his comparing anyone at all to, say, a species of grass. His business is, however, with a species of wheat, which he has found growing near a uranium mine in Australia's Northern Territory. This mutated genus is exceptional in its tenacity in the face of adverse climatic conditions, its resistance to rust and its dizzyingly high yield. The portents for global farming and the possibilities for reducing famine and poverty are multi-fold and yet, in spite (or because) of its potential Duquesne's efforts to publicise his findings continually meet with obstruction and prevarication.

As various international government agencies intervene to alternatively stifle or exploit Duquesne and his discovery, the scientist concludes that in order to earn the recognition they deserve, he will have to independently announce his results at a U.N. conference in Rome. The subsequent chase from Australia to Italy, via Hong Kong, pursued by American, Australian, and Soviet functionaries is fast and traught with complications. O'Hagan's grasp of large scale bureaucratic plotting and manoeuvre is as convincing as might be expected from the wife of a retired international civil servant and there are odd moments when one wonders just how much of the book is complete fiction.

Against the Grain triumphs over its predecessors in the scope of its concern—O'Hagan makes an issue of the environment rather than being content just to describe it—and the greater quantity and quality of dramatic tension. Despite this increase though, the more sensual dimension of her writing survives the rougher handling intact to remind us that O'Hagan's is one of the calmer voices in contemporary crime fiction and certainly one worth hearing.

—Ian McMechan

OLIVER, Anthony. British. Born in Abersychan, Wales, 4 July 1922. Educated at Monmouth and West Monmouth School. Air-raid warden in London until 1940. Served in the Royal Air Force, 1940–46. Actor, London, 1946–67; owner of an antique shop in London. Agent: A.P. Watt Ltd., 20 John Street, London WC1N 2DL, England.

CRIME PUBLICATIONS

Novels (series: Mrs. Thomas and ex-Detective Inspector John Webber in all books)

The Pew Group. London, Heinemann, 1980; New York, Doubleday, 1981.
The Property of a Lady. London, Heinemann, and New York, Doubleday, 1983.
The Elberg Collection. London, Heinemann, and New York, Doubleday, 1985.
Cover-Up. London, Heinemann, and New York, Doubleday, 1987.

OTHER PUBLICATIONS

The Victorian Staffordshire Figure: A Guide for Collectors. London, Heinemann, 1971; New York, St. Martin's Press, 1972.
Staffordshire Pottery: The Tribal Art of England. London, Heinemann, 1981.

*

Theatrical Activities:

Actor: **Plays**—Sandy Tyrell in *Hay Fever* by Noël Coward, London, 1946; Paul Brant in *Mother of Men,* London, 1947; Plato Cartwright in *Boys in Brown,* London, 1947; Digby in *The Hidden Years,* London, 1948; Peter Gilbert in *The Browning Version,* and Fred Ingram in *A Harlequinade,* both by Terence Rattigan, London, 1949; Kit Neilan in *French Without Tears* by Terence Rattigan, London, 1950; Albert in *Accolade* by Emlyn Williams, London, 1952; Peter in *The Gay Dog,* London, 1953; Ken Wilson in *Red-Headed Blonde;* Edward Bare in *Gently Does It,* New York, 1953; Donald Gresham in *The Moon Is Blue,* London, 1954; Tim Riley in *A Month of Sundays,* London, 1958; Denis Lester in *A Touch of the Sun,* London, 1959; Detective Sergeant Trotter in *The Mousetrap* by Agatha Christie, London, 1962–63, and 1965; Malcolm Rockhart in *The Lizard on the Rocks,* London, 1963; Bill Smith in *Heirs and Graces,* London, 1965; the doctor in *Too True to Be Good* by George Bernard Shaw, London, 1966; Captain Hunter in *After the Rain* by John Bowden, London, 1967, and New York, 1967.

Anthony Oliver comments:
My long friendship with Emlyn Williams over many years first stimulated my interest in crime which was furthered by knowing Agatha Christie and playing the lead role in *The Mousetrap* for two years. I like people more than plots. Crossword puzzles and clues are nothing like as fascinating as people and the unbelievable things they do.

*   *   *

Anthony Oliver began to write crime fiction after some years as an actor, including a stint as Detective-Sergeant Trotter in *The Mousetrap.* With such a background he might well have written theatrical mysteries, but in fact his books draw heavily on a detailed knowledge of the antiques trade. He is an authority on Staffordshire pottery, which figures prominently in the third of his four novels to date. All four books exploit the power of antiques as charismatic objects provoking extremes of desire and greed.

The setting throughout the series is the Suffolk town of Flaxfield, a tranquil enough place in ordinary circumstances, but exceptionally lively on Midsummer Eve. It has been invaded on four occasions in its history—"by Vikings, Normans, Cromwell's men and Mrs. Thomas." The newest invader is a mettlesome Welsh widow, who leaves her dark little house in Cardiff when her son-in-law trips over her daughter's foot and fails to get up again. She has a vivid taste in clothes and wears elastic stockings over legs that will "never again get her to the semi-finals in the Latin American section." Her zest for life is nourished by an awesome curiosity, demanding action and enquiry; and since she is also shrewd and determined she takes to detection like a duck to water. She raises gossip to a fine art and makes good use of her field glasses.

She collaborates with a former policeman named John Webber, newly retired to Flaxfield, his home town. Intending to settle to a quiet life, he is nonetheless easily stirred to action and cheerfully abandons "the old man's garden chores he pretended to enjoy." Though he is overweight and arthritic, his mind is in excellent shape and he continually justifies his partner's faith in him. She woos him through his stomach and they share a succession of marvellous meals. Together they are formidable, a well-matched team with complementary gifts and methods.

They meet in *The Pew Group,* which revolves around "a small piece of white pottery . . . crudely but endearingly fashioned with three little figures sitting stiffly on a high backed settle." It turns up among the jumble at the church fête and immediately arouses the acquisitive instincts of opportunists for miles around. The jostling for possession is abruptly curtailed by its sudden disappearance and the action develops into a diverting quest for the lost treasure. The book is made memorable, however, by its incidentals: the man-to-man tone of the Vicar's prayers; the funeral ham that induces communal diarrhoea; the buttocks adorned with tattooed butterflies; "a cat of morbid pursuits" named Bunter; and the Glockemara Hotel in Notting Hall Gate. Best of all is Jimmie Trottwood, no incidental but a full-scale comic portrait, drawn with accuracy, affection, and wit. As an ageing gay antique dealer he could easily have been the usual comic stereotype, but the author's insight and judgment make him an individual, hopeful and kind, secure in his identity and irresistibly funny. After the violent death of his lover he confounds expectation by marrying Mrs. Thomas's newly-widowed daughter. Their marriage works surprisingly well and reports on its progress are a welcome feature of the series. With *The Property of a Lady* the author gets down to serious business. The humour is less ebullient, more subject to the design, and there is more at stake than a pottery group. The central figure is a likely psychopath and the main concern of the narrative is to establish the pattern of his earlier life. As more of the past is revealed, we become increasingly aware of present dangers: to his mother, to a local girl and to his recently-acquired wife. The action moves from Flaxfield to France and comes to a bold and brilliant climax in the sale-room.

The Elberg Collection is even more ambitious and accomplished, with a more varied and intricate action and a darker tone at times. The narrative is enticingly oblique and insinuating, luring the reader forward with all the familiar wit and elegance, but also with a potent edge of menace. Both Webber and Mrs. Thomas run into danger in the course of their investigation, which centres on the eponymous collection of Staffordshire figures and its more remarkable pieces. The potter who advised in its assembly has died with his wife in circumstances that appear to defy explanation and Webber is as much concerned to find the method of their murder as to identify their killer. He receives invaluable help from the youngest member of his team and comes to realise that even his own selection for the task in hand is a factor in a daring total design.

Cover-Up begins with the death of a dealer on the verge of a significant new acquisition and the aborted transaction ramifies into something altogether more devious and macabre. The action pivots on a painting and a young man, both enigmatic and both unusually desirable. The painting is putative only, an early Stanley Spencer, which retains its mystery to the end; the young man is demonstrably real and his course proves even more astonishing. The Vicar of Flaxfield and his unquiet wife recur more prominently than in *The Pew Group* and are subjected to a much more searching scrutiny. The novel carries a sharp reproof to those who allow dangerous and destructive criminals to delude and exploit them.

—B.A. Pike

———

OLSEN, D.B. Pseudonym for (Julia Clara Catharine) Dolores (Birk Olsen) Hitchens; also wrote as Dolan Birkley; Noel Burke. American. Born in 1907. *Died in 1973.*

CRIME PUBLICATIONS

Novels (series: Lieutenant Stephen Mayhew; Rachel and Jennifer Murdock; Professor A. Pennyfeather)

The Clue in the Clay (Mayhew). New York, Phoenix Press, 1938.
The Cat Saw Murder (Murdock; Mayhew). New York, Doubleday, 1939; London, Heinemann, 1940.
Death Cuts a Silhouette. New York, Doubleday, 1939.
The Ticking Heart (Mayhew). New York, Doubleday, 1940.
The Blue Geranium (as Dolan Birkley). New York, Simon and Schuster, 1941.
The Alarm of the Black Cat (Murdock). New York, Doubleday, 1942.
The Shivering Bough (as Noel Burke). New York, Dutton, 1942.
Cat's Claw (Murdock; Mayhew). New York, Doubleday, 1943.
Catspaw for Murder (Murdock; Mayhew). New York, Doubleday, 1943.
The Cat Wears a Noose (Murdock; Mayhew). New York, Doubleday, 1944.
Bring the Bride a Shroud (Pennyfeather). New York, Doubleday, and London, Aldor, 1945.
Cats Don't Smile (Murdock). New York, Doubleday, 1945; London, Aldor, 1948.
Cats Don't Need Coffins (Murdock; Mayhew). New York, Doubleday, and London, Aldor, 1946.
Gallows for the Groom (Pennyfeather). New York, Doubleday, 1947.
Widows Ought to Weep. Chicago, Ziff Davis, 1947.
Cats Have Tall Shadows (Murdock). Chicago, Ziff Davis, 1948.
Devious Design (Pennyfeather). New York, Doubleday, 1948.
The Cat Wears a Mask (Murdock). New York, Doubleday, 1949.
Death Wears Cat's Eyes (Murdock). New York, Doubleday, 1950.
Something about Midnight (Pennyfeather). New York, Doubleday, 1950.

The Cat and Capricorn (Murdock). New York, Doubleday, 1951.
Love Me in Death (Pennyfeather). New York, Doubleday, 1951.
Enrollment Cancelled (Pennyfeather). New York, Doubleday, 1952; as *Dead Babes in the Wood,* New York, Dell, 1954.
The Cat Walk (Murdock). New York, Doubleday, 1953.
Death Walks on Cat Feet (Murdock). New York, Doubleday, 1956.
Night of the Bowstring. London, Hale, 1963.
The Unloved (as Dolan Birkley). New York, Doubleday, 1965; London, Hale, 1967.

Novels as Dolores Hitchens (series: Jim Sader)

Stairway to an Empty Room. New York, Doubleday, 1951.
Nets to Catch the Wind. New York, Doubleday, 1952; as *Windows Won't Wait,* New York, Dell, 1954.
Terror Lurks in Darkness. New York, Doubleday, 1953.
Beat Back the Tide. New York, Doubleday, 1954; London, Macdonald, 1955; as *The Fatal Flirt,* New York, Spivak, 1956.
Sleep with Strangers (Sader). New York, Doubleday, 1955; London, Macdonald, 1956.
Fools' Gold. New York, Doubleday, and London, Boardman, 1958.
The Watcher. New York, Doubleday, and London, Boardman, 1959.
Sleep with Slander (Sader). New York, Doubleday, 1960; London, Boardman, 1961.
Footsteps in the Night. New York, Doubleday, and London, Boardman, 1961.
The Abductor. New York, Simon and Schuster, and London, Boardman, 1962.
The Bank with the Bamboo Door. New York, Simon and Schuster, and London, Boardman, 1965.
The Man Who Cried All the Way Home. New York, Simon and Schuster, 1966; London, Hale, 1967.
Postscript to Nightmare. New York, Putnam, 1967; as *Cabin of Fear,* London, Joseph, 1968.
A Collection of Strangers. New York, Putnam, 1969; London, Macdonald, 1971.
The Baxter Letters. New York, Putnam, 1971; London, Hale, 1973.
In a House Unknown. New York, Doubleday, 1973; London, Hale, 1974.

Novels by Bert Hitchens and Dolores Hitchens (series: Collins and McKechnie; John Farrel)

F.O.B. Murder (Collins and McKechnie). New York, Doubleday, 1955; London, Boardman, 1957.
One-Way Ticket. New York, Doubleday, 1956; London, Boardman, 1958.
End of the Line (Farrel). New York, Doubleday, and London, Boardman, 1957.
The Man Who Followed Women (Collins and McKechnie). New York, Doubleday, 1959; London, Boardman, 1960.
The Grudge (Farrel). New York, Doubleday, 1963; London, Boardman, 1964.

Uncollected Short Stories

"Miss Rachel on Vacation," in *Detective Story Magazine* (New York), September 1947.
"Murder Walks a Strange Path," in *Detective Story Magazine* (New York), March 1948.

"The Snake Dance," in *Detective Story Magazine* (New York), May 1948.

"Alibi in Ice," in *Detective Story Magazine* (New York), Spring 1949.

"The Fuzzy Things," in *Four and Twenty Bloodhounds,* edited by Anthony Boucher. New York, Simon and Schuster, 1950; London, Hammond, 1951.

"The Absent Hat Pin," in *20 Great Tales of Murder,* edited by Helen McCloy and Brett Halliday. New York, Random House, 1951; London, Hammond, 1952.

OTHER PUBLICATIONS as Dolores Hitchens

Plays

A Cookie for Henry. New York, French, 1941.
To Tommy with Love. New York, French, 1941.

*

Manuscript Collection: Mugar Memorial Library, Boston University.

*   *   *

D.B. Olsen wrote a standardized formula novel that followed the rules of mystery fiction for the 1940's, usually light and breezy, lots of characters to spread suspicion among, and a touch of humor to keep out the brutality of murder. Toward the end of her career in the mid-1950's she used more serious themes and allowed reality to creep in, but enjoyment and diversion remained the prime objective. Most of the allure of her highly popular books lies in the characters of her two series detectives, Rachel Murdock and Professor A. Pennyfeather.

Elderly spinsters, Rachel and Jennifer Murdock achieve their interest and humor through contrast. Jennifer, two years older, is the thin, rigid, conventional epitome of an old lady: a battleaxe incarnate. Rachel (always accompanied by Samantha, her coal-black cat), conscientiously refusing to conform to expectations, belies her slim, tiny figure, snow white hair, and cheery blue eyes, and is determined to experience any excitement she can: whether it is a surreptitious drink, an afternoon at the movies, or meddling in a murder. Jennifer vociferously objects to Rachel's antics but is always there, once even witnessing a murder in *The Cat Wears a Noose,* and then admitting she found a night in jail interesting. Jennifer adds humor and a few diversions, but Rachel is the detective. An inquisitive nature and a tendency to stir things up account for much of her investigation. She watches for the nuances of character or emotion (things that friendly rival Lieutenant Stephen Mayhew would never catch) in order to arrive at her intuitive solution. Clues or oddities that she had noted along the way are used to support her conclusions, but the killer often gives himself away at some trap she had either set up or been caught in herself.

Professor Pennyfeather is similar in his methods but uses the logic and methods derived from a classical education to impart respectability to his detection. While Rachel gets involved in a case through chance or nosiness, Pennyfeather is asked by a friend or relative to help them out of trouble. His first cases, *Bring the Bride a Shroud, Gallows for the Groom,* and *Devious Design,* occur away from the college environment, often in the southwest desert that Olsen also used for *The Cat Wears a Mask* and *The Cat and Capricorn.* Later books, *Love Me in Death* and *Enrollment Cancelled,* are set on the Clarendon campus and involve more than vague hints at the passions behind murder.

Both use sex as underlying problems of the characters. *Enrollment Cancelled* includes a suspect who is almost banished from the college because he has a shoe fetish. Although the handling of these elements is bland by today's standards, it was rather surprising in the 1950's.

The Clue in the Clay and *The Ticking Heart* are first efforts involving Mayhew only. With *The Cat Saw Murder* Olsen developed Rachel and Jennifer to establish the pattern for almost all the rest of her work. One exception was *Widows Ought to Weep,* featuring Mr. Puckett as the detective. This book relies on mood and atmosphere more than most of Olsen's work and builds suspense by involving characters in dangerous situations, then shifting the scene. Both *Widows Ought to Weep* and *The Cat Wears a Noose* use monsters or werewolves to induce an artificial chill, but human monsters are the only real danger in all Olsen's enjoyable output.

—Fred Dueren

———

O'MARIE, Carol Anne. American.

CRIME PUBLICATIONS

Novels (series: Sister Mary Helen)

A Novena for Murder. New York, Scribner, 1984.
Advent of Dying. New York, Delacorte Press, 1986.
The Missing Madonna. New York, Delacorte Press, 1989.

*   *   *

Sister Carol Anne O'Marie successfully merges elements of several crime fiction traditions. Her detective, an elderly nun, combines characteristics of Father Brown and Miss Marple, and her vocation and age, along with her penchant for reading murder mysteries, are her primary distinguishing qualities.

When the series opens, Sister Mary Helen is in her seventies and has been a nun for 50 years. Retiring after a lifetime of teaching, she is sent to Mount St. Francis College for Women in San Francisco where, in *A Novena for Murder,* she expects to undertake historical research. However, she stumbles upon the murder of a professor, and her research is promptly forgotten. In the following novels, the college remains her home and she takes over the operation of the alumnae affairs office, but the settings broaden within San Francisco and even, in *The Missing Madonna,* encompass a trip to New York City. The San Francisco settings are well conveyed, with especial attention being paid to the weather: the bone-chilling fogs and the occasional welcome warm, sunny days are nicely evoked.

Sister Mary Helen is a practical and assertive woman with an uncanny ability to read character through observing people's eyes, a skill learned through her years as a teacher. Often referred to as "the old nun," she is both modern and traditional: she has adopted modern dress but refused the opportunity to return to her baptismal name. Her involvement in murder usually becomes a kind of personal crusade to which she feels God has led her, and her obligation to the victims overcomes her awareness that both her superiors and the police view her as a meddler and busybody.

Other nuns who appear as continuing characters represent varied personality types. Closest to Mary Helen is Sister Eileen, a friend of 50 years who speaks with a bit of an Irish brogue when excited and who has an Irish saying for any situation. She is head librarian at the college and her expertise sometimes is helpful in detecting, but generally she serves primarily as support and companion for Sister Mary Helen. In contrast is Sister Anne, a young and very modern nun, who is college chaplain. She wears jeans and, in *A Novena for Murder,* Paiute moccasins, and she meditates while sitting in the lotus position and burning incense. Other nuns serve to emphasize the presence of a full community; appearing in all three novels are Sister Cecilia, the president of the college, and Sister Therese, whose prayers for the apprehension of the murderer give *A Novena for Murder* its title.

Other continuing characters are police officers. Kate Murphy and Dennis Gallagher work in Homicide and are summoned to investigate in *A Novena for Murder;* later, when Sister Mary Helen becomes involved in other mysteries, she calls on Kate, who is an alumna of the college and of whom she has become particularly fond. A middle-aged husband and father, Gallagher has an avuncular relationship with Kate but is intimidated by the elderly nuns. The mysteries tend to move back and forth between the nuns and the police officers, so that there are elements of both the amateur detective genre and of the police procedural.

Running alongside the mystery in each novel is a subplot depicting a personal problem of Kate's which is always resolved as the perpetrator of the crime is revealed. In *A Novena for Murder,* the mystery concerns the exploitation of illegal Portuguese immigrants by a Portuguese history professor, and Kate's dilemma is whether she should marry Jake Bassetti, a detective with whom she has lived for some time—he wants to marry but she resists. In *Advent of Dying,* Sister Marie Helen's mysterious secretary is murdered, and her background as a former nun, along with the relationships that led to her death, is gradually revealed; at the same time, Kate, now married to Jack, struggles with the pressure on her to behave as a traditional wife and to start a family. In *The Missing Madonna,* the nuns search for a friend, a member with Mary Helen and Eileen of the Older Women's League (OWL) who has unaccountably disappeared, while Kate and Jack try to start their family; in the novel's last lines, Kate's pregnancy is disclosed.

O'Marie's novels present their San Francisco locale effectively. The Roman Catholic post-Vatican II world and customs form an important part of the backdrop to the mysteries; Mary Helen's prayers, her special feelings for Mass at a nearby Carmelite monastery, her affection for Father Adams (who has the ability to complete a full Mass in 25 minutes), even her sheepish use of a plastic prayer-book cover to conceal her beloved murder mysteries, all characterize her effectively. Plotting is sometimes clumsy and transparent, but the novels are appealing for their setting, their characterizations, and especially their use of their religious background, presented with authenticity and with good humor.

—Mary Jean DeMarr

OPPENHEIM, E(dward) Phillips. Also wrote as Anthony Partridge. British. Born in London, 22 October 1866. Educated at Wyggeston Grammar School, Leicester. Served in the Ministry of Information during World War I. Married Elsie Clara Hopkins in 1891; one daughter. Worked in his father's leather business in Leicester until 1906; lived in Norfolk until 1922, then in France and Guernsey. *Died 3 February 1946.*

CRIME PUBLICATIONS

Novels

Expiation. London, Maxwell, 1887.
The Peer and the Woman. New York, Taylor, 1892; London, Ward Lock, 1895.
A Monk of Cruta. London, Ward Lock, and New York, Neely, 1894; as *The Tragedy of Andrea,* New York, Ogilvie, 1906.
A Daughter of the Marionis. London, Ward and Downey, 1895; as *To Win the Love He Sought,* New York, Collier, 1915.
False Evidence. London, Ward Lock, 1896; New York, Ward Lock 1897.
The Postmaster of Market Deignton. London, Routledge, 1896(?).
A Modern Prometheus. London, Unwin, 1896; New York, Neely, 1897.
The Mystery of Mr. Bernard Brown. London, Bentley, 1896; Boston, Little Brown, 1910; as *The New Tenant,* New York, Collier, 1912; as *His Father's Crime,* New York, Street and Smith, 1929.
The Wooing of Fortune. London, Ward and Downey, 1896.
The World's Great Snare. London, Ward and Downey, and Philadelphia, Lippincott, 1896.
The Amazing Judgment. London, Downey, 1897.
As a Man Lives. London, Ward Lock, 1898; Boston, Little Brown, 1908; as *The Yellow House,* New York, Doscher, 1908.
A Daughter of Astrea. Bristol, Arrowsmith, 1898; New York, Doscher, 1909.
Mysterious Mr. Sabin. London, Ward Lock, 1898; Boston, Little Brown, 1905.
The Man and His Kingdom. London, Ward Lock, and Philadelphia, Lippincott, 1899.
Mr. Marx's Secret. London, Simpkin Marshall, 1899; New York, Street and Smith, 1899(?).
A Millionaire of Yesterday. London, Ward Lock, and Philadelphia, Lippincott, 1900.
Master of Men. London, Methuen, 1901; as *Enoch Strone,* New York, Dillingham, 1902.
The Survivor. London, Ward Lock, and New York, Brentano's, 1901.
The Traitors. London, Ward Lock, 1902; New York, Dodd Mead, 1903.
The Great Awakening. London, Ward Lock, 1902; as *A Sleeping Memory,* New York, Dillingham, 1902.
A Prince of Sinners. London, Ward Lock, and Boston, Little Brown, 1903.
The Yellow Crayon. London, Ward Lock, and New York, Dodd Mead, 1903.
The Master Mummer. Boston, Little Brown, 1904; London, Ward Lock, 1905.
The Betrayal. London, Ward Lock, and New York, Dodd Mead, 1904.
Anna the Adventuress. London, Ward Lock, and Boston, Little Brown, 1904.
A Maker of History. London, Ward Lock, and Boston, Little Brown, 1905.
Mr. Wingrave, Millionaire. London, Ward Lock, 1906; as *The Malefactor,* Boston, Little Brown, 1906.
A Lost Leader. London, Ward Lock, and Boston, Little Brown, 1906.
The Vindicator. Boston, Little Brown, 1907.
The Missioner. Boston, Little Brown, 1907; London, Ward Lock, 1908.

The Secret. London, Ward Lock, 1907; as *The Great Secret,* Boston, Little Brown, 1907.

Conspirators. London, Ward Lock, 1907; as *The Avenger,* Boston, Little Brown, 1908.

Berenice. Boston, Little Brown, 1907; London, Ward Lock, 1910.

Jeanne of the Marshes. Boston, Little Brown, 1908; London, Ward Lock, 1909.

The Governors. London, Ward Lock, 1908; Boston, Little Brown, 1909.

The Moving Finger. Boston, Little Brown, 1910; as *The Falling Star,* London, Hodder and Stoughton, 1911.

The Illustrious Prince. London, Hodder and Stoughton, and Boston, Little Brown, 1910.

The Missing Delora. London, Methuen, 1910; as *The Lost Ambassador,* Boston, Little Brown, 1910.

Havoc. Boston, Little Brown, 1911; London, Hodder and Stoughton, 1912.

The Tempting of Tavernake. Boston, Little Brown, 1911; as *The Temptation of Tavernake,* London, Hodder and Stoughton, 1913.

The Lighted Way. London, Hodder and Stoughton, and Boston, Little Brown, 1912.

The Mischief-Maker. Boston, Little Brown, 1912; London, Hodder and Stoughton, 1913.

The Double Life of Mr. Alfred Burton. Boston, Little Brown, 1913; London, Methuen, 1914.

The Way of These Women. Boston, Little Brown, 1913; London, Methuen, 1914.

A People's Man. Boston, Little Brown, 1914; London, Methuen, 1915.

The Vanished Messenger. Boston, Little Brown, 1914; London, Methuen, 1916.

The Black Box (novelization of screenplay). New York, Grosset and Dunlap, 1915; London, Hodder and Stoughton, 1917.

The Double Traitor. Boston, Little Brown, 1915; London, Hodder and Stoughton, 1918.

Mr. Grex of Monte Carlo. London, Methuen, and Boston, Little Brown, 1915.

The Kingdom of the Blind. Boston, Little Brown, 1916; London, Hodder and Stoughton, 1917.

The Hillman. London, Methuen, and Boston, Little Brown, 1917.

The Cinema Murder. Boston, Little Brown, 1917; as *The Other Romilly,* London, Hodder and Stoughton, 1918.

The Zeppelin's Passenger. Boston, Little Brown, 1918; as *Mr. Lessingham Goes Home,* London, Hodder and Stoughton, 1919.

The Pawns Count. London, Hodder and Stoughton, and Boston, Little Brown, 1918.

The Curious Quest. Boston, Little Brown, 1919; as *The Amazing Quest of Mr. Ernest Bliss,* London, Hodder and Stoughton, 1922.

The Strange Case of Mr. Jocelyn Thew. London, Hodder and Stoughton, 1919; as *The Box with Broken Seals,* Boston, Little Brown, 1919.

The Wicked Marquis. London, Hodder and Stoughton, and Boston, Little Brown, 1919.

The Devil's Paw. Boston, Little Brown, 1920; London, Hodder and Stoughton, 1921.

The Great Impersonation. London, Hodder and Stoughton, and Boston, Little Brown, 1920.

Jacob's Ladder. London, Hodder and Stoughton, and Boston, Little Brown, 1921.

Nobody's Man. Boston, Little Brown, 1921; London, Hodder and Stoughton, 1922.

The Profiteers. London, Hodder and Stoughton, and Boston, Little Brown, 1921.

The Evil Shepherd. Boston, Little Brown, 1922; London, Hodder and Stoughton, 1923.

The Great Prince Shan. London, Hodder and Stoughton, and Boston, Little Brown, 1922.

The Mystery Road. Boston, Little Brown, 1923; London, Hodder and Stoughton, 1924.

The Inevitable Millionaires. London, Hodder and Stoughton, 1923; Boston, Little Brown, 1925.

The Passionate Quest. London, Hodder and Stoughton, and Boston, Little Brown, 1924.

The Wrath to Come. Boston, Little Brown, 1924; London, Hodder and Stoughton, 1925.

Gabriel Samara. London, Hodder and Stoughton, 1925; as *Gabriel Samara, Peacemaker,* Boston, Little Brown, 1925.

Stolen Idols. London, Hodder and Stoughton, and Boston, Little Brown, 1925.

The Interloper. Boston, Little Brown, 1926; as *The Ex-Duke,* London, Hodder and Stoughton, 1927.

The Golden Beast. London, Hodder and Stoughton, and Boston, Little Brown, 1926.

Harvey Garrard's Crime. Boston, Little Brown, 1926; London, Hodder and Stoughton, 1927.

Prodigals of Monte Carlo. London, Hodder and Stoughton, and Boston, Little Brown, 1926.

Miss Brown of X.Y.O. London, Hodder and Stoughton, and Boston, Little Brown, 1927.

The Fortunate Wayfarer. London, Hodder and Stoughton, and Boston, Little Brown, 1928.

Matorni's Vineyard. Boston, Little Brown, 1928; London, Hodder and Stoughton, 1929.

The Light Beyond. London, Hodder and Stoughton, and Boston, Little Brown, 1928.

Blackman's Wood, with *The Under Dog,* by Agatha Christie. London, Readers Library, 1929.

The Glenlitten Murder. London, Hodder and Stoughton, and Boston, Little Brown, 1929.

The Treasure House of Martin Hews. London, Hodder and Stoughton, and Boston, Little Brown, 1929.

The Lion and the Lamb. London, Hodder and Stoughton, and Boston, Little Brown, 1930.

The Million Pound Deposit. London, Hodder and Stoughton, and Boston, Little Brown, 1930.

Up the Ladder of Gold. London, Hodder and Stoughton, and Boston, Little Brown, 1931.

Simple Peter Cradd. London, Hodder and Stoughton, and Boston, Little Brown, 1931.

Moran Chambers Smiled. London, Hodder and Stoughton, 1932; as *The Man from Sing Sing,* Boston, Little Brown, 1932.

The Ostrekoff Jewels. London, Hodder and Stoughton, and Boston, Little Brown, 1932.

Jeremiah and the Princess. London, Hodder and Stoughton, and Boston, Little Brown, 1933.

Murder at Monte Carlo. London, Hodder and Stoughton, and Boston, Little Brown, 1933.

The Strange Boarders of Palace Crescent. Boston, Little Brown, 1934; London, Hodder and Stoughton, 1935.

The Bank Manager. London, Hodder and Stoughton, 1934; as *The Man Without Nerves,* Boston, Little Brown, 1934.

The Gallows of Chance. London, Hodder and Stoughton, and Boston, Little Brown, 1934.

The Battle of Basinghall Street. London, Hodder and Stoughton, and Boston, Little Brown, 1935.

The Spy Paramount. London, Hodder and Stoughton, and Boston, Little Brown, 1935.

The Bird of Paradise. London, Hodder and Stoughton, 1936;
as *Floating Peril,* Boston, Little Brown, 1936.
Judy of Bunter's Buildings. London, Hodder and Stoughton,
1936; as *The Magnificent Hoax,* Boston, Little Brown, 1936.
The Dumb Gods Speak. London, Hodder and Stoughton, and
Boston, Little Brown, 1937.
Envoy Extraordinary. London, Hodder and Stoughton, and
Boston, Little Brown, 1937.
The Mayor on Horseback. Boston, Little Brown, 1937.
The Colossus of Arcadia. London, Hodder and Stoughton, and
Boston, Little Brown, 1938.
The Spymaster. London, Hodder and Stoughton, and Boston,
Little Brown, 1938.
Exit a Dictator. London, Hodder and Stoughton, and Boston,
Little Brown, 1939.
Sir Adam Disappeared. London, Hodder and Stoughton, and
Boston, Little Brown, 1939.
The Strangers' Gate. Boston, Little Brown, 1939; London,
Hodder and Stoughton, 1940.
The Grassleyes Mystery. London, Hodder and Stoughton, and
Boston, Little Brown, 1940.
Last Train Out. Boston, Little Brown, 1940; London, Hodder
and Stoughton, 1941.
The Shy Plutocrat. London, Hodder and Stoughton, and
Boston, Little Brown, 1941.
The Man Who Changed His Plea. London, Hodder and
Stoughton, and Boston, Little Brown, 1942.
Mr. Mirakel. London, Hodder and Stoughton, and Boston,
Little Brown, 1943.

Novels as Anthony Partridge

The Ghosts of Society. London, Hodder and Stoughton, 1908;
as *The Distributors,* New York, McClure, 1908.
The Kingdom of Earth. London, Mills and Boon, and Boston,
Little Brown, 1909; as *The Black Watcher,* as E. Phillips
Oppenheim, London, Hodder and Stoughton, 1912.
Passers-By. Boston, Little Brown, 1910; London, Ward Lock,
1911.
The Golden Web. Boston, Little Brown, 1910; as *The
Plunderers,* as E. Phillips Oppenheim, London, Hodder and
Stoughton, 1916.
The Court of St. Simon. Boston, Little Brown, 1912; as *Seeing
Life,* as E. Phillips Oppenheim, London, Lloyds, 1919.

Short Stories (series: General Besserley; Peter Ruff)

The Long Arm of Mannister. Boston, Little Brown, 1908; as
The Long Arm, London, Ward Lock, 1909.
The Double Four. London, Cassell, 1911; as *Peter Ruff and the
Double Four,* Boston, Little Brown, 1912.
Peter Ruff. Boston, Little Brown, 1912.
Those Other Days. London, Ward Lock, 1912; Boston, Little
Brown, 1913.
For the Queen. London, Ward Lock, 1912; Boston, Little
Brown, 1913.
Mr. Laxworthy's Adventures. London, Cassell, 1913.
The Amazing Partnership. London, Cassell, 1914; included in
Shudders and Thrills, 1932.
The Game of Liberty. London, Cassell, 1915; as *The Amiable
Charlatan,* Boston, Little Brown, 1916.
Mysteries of the Riviera. London, Cassell, 1916.
Ambrose Lavendale, Diplomat. London, Hodder and
Stoughton, 1920.
Aaron Rod, Diviner. London, Hodder and Stoughton, 1920;
Boston, Little Brown, 1927.

The Honourable Algernon Knox, Detective. London, Hodder
and Stoughton, 1920.
Michael's Evil Deeds. Boston, Little Brown, 1923; London,
Hodder and Stoughton, 1924.
The Seven Conundrums. Boston, Little Brown, 1923; London,
Hodder and Stoughton, 1924.
The Terrible Hobby of Sir Joseph Londe, Bt. London, Hodder
and Stoughton, 1924; Boston, Little Brown, 1927.
The Adventures of Mr. Joseph P. Cray. London, Hodder and
Stoughton, 1925; Boston, Little Brown, 1927.
The Little Gentleman from Okehampstead. London, Hodder
and Stoughton, 1926.
The Channay Syndicate. London, Hodder and Stoughton, and
Boston, Little Brown, 1927.
Madame. London, Hodder and Stoughton, 1927; as *Madame
and Her Twelve Virgins,* Boston, Little Brown, 1927.
Mr. Billingham, The Marquis and Madelon. London, Hodder
and Stoughton, 1927; Boston, Little Brown, 1929.
Nicholas Goade, Detective. London, Hodder and Stoughton,
1927; Boston, Little Brown, 1929.
Chronicles of Melhampton. London, Hodder and Stoughton,
1928.
The Exploits of Pudgy Pete & Co. London, Hodder and
Stoughton, 1928.
The Human Chase. London, Hodder and Stoughton, 1929;
included in *Shudders and Thrills,* 1932.
Jennerton & Co. London, Hodder and Stoughton, 1929;
included in *Clowns and Criminals,* 1931.
What Happened to Forester. London, Hodder and Stoughton,
1929; Boston, Little Brown, 1930.
Slane's Long Shots. London, Hodder and Stoughton, and
Boston, Little Brown, 1930.
Sinners Beware. London, Hodder and Stoughton, 1931;
Boston, Little Brown, 1932.
Inspector Dickins Retires. London, Hodder and Stoughton,
1931; as *Gangster's Glory,* Boston, Little Brown,
1931.
Clowns and Criminals (omnibus). Boston, Little Brown, 1931.
Shudders and Thrills (omnibus). Boston, Little Brown, 1932.
Crooks in the Sunshine. London, Hodder and Stoughton, 1932;
Boston, Little Brown, 1933.
The Ex-Detective. London, Hodder and Stoughton, and
Boston, Little Brown, 1933.
General Besserley's Puzzle Box. London, Hodder and
Stoughton, and Boston, Little Brown, 1935.
Advice Limited. London, Hodder and Stoughton, 1935;
Boston, Little Brown, 1936.
Ask Miss Mott. London, Hodder and Stoughton, 1936;
Boston, Little Brown, 1937.
Curious Happenings to the Rooke Legatees. London, Hodder
and Stoughton, 1937; Boston, Little Brown, 1938.
And Still I Cheat the Gallows: A Series of Stories. London,
Hodder and Stoughton, 1938.
A Pulpit in the Grill Room. London, Hodder and Stoughton,
1938; Boston, Little Brown, 1939.
General Besserley's Second Puzzle Box. London, Hodder and
Stoughton, 1939; Boston, Little Brown, 1940.
*The Milan Grill Room: Further Adventures of Louis, the
Manager, and Major Lyson, the Raconteur.* London, Hodder
and Stoughton, 1940; Boston, Little Brown, 1941.
The Great Bear. London, Todd, 1943.
The Man Who Thought He Was a Pauper. London, Todd,
1943.
The Hour of Reckoning, and The Mayor of Ballydaghan.
London, Todd, 1944.

OTHER PUBLICATIONS

Plays

The Money-Spider (produced London, 1908).
The King's Cup, with H.D. Bradley (produced London, 1909).
London, French, 1913.
The Gilded Key (produced Blackpool, Lancashire, 1910;
London, 1911).
The Eclipse, with Fred Thompson, music by H. Darewski and
M. Gideon (produced London, 1919).

Other

My Books and Myself. Boston, Little Brown, 1922.
The Quest for Winter Sunshine. London, Methuen, 1926;
Boston, Little Brown, 1927.
The Pool of Memory: Memoirs. London, Hodder and
Stoughton, 1941; Boston, Little Brown, 1942.

Editor, *Many Mysteries.* London, Rich and Cowan, 1933.

*

Critical Study: *The Prince of Story-Tellers* by Robert
Standish, London, Davies, 1957.

* * *

"The Prince of Storytellers" deserves his title. E. Phillips
Oppenheim, who by his own account began each new novel
with only a sense of "the first chapter, and an inkling of
something to follow," spun 150 novels out of one of the most
fertile imaginations ever to apply itself to the thriller; and less
than a tenth of that number can be written off as dull reading.

Oppenheim made an immense amount of money from his
writing, and lived the opulent life of so many of his heroes
(though he never gave them the kind of sultanic existence he
seems to have had himself). He lived much of his life on the
Riviera, where many of his fictions are set. When the setting is
London, it is the West End, around the Savoy and Milan
Hotels; the mean streets do not often appear.

Oppenheim's novels include the Graustarkian mode (*Jeremiah and the Princess, The Stranger's Gate*), but most are set in the
present. Typically there are killings, often by villains of exotic
race; the hero is often outwardly one who lives idly for pleasure,
but is in fact working to save his country; there is usually a love
interest; and Oppenheim has as much sense as Alfred
Hitchcock of how terror may impinge upon the commonplace.
A representative novel is *Miss Brown of X.Y.O.:* Miss Brown, a
secretary, bored with "the starvation of her simple life," sits to
rest (with her typewriter) on the steps of a London mansion.
She is summoned within to take the dying dictation of a famous
explorer who is actually a secret agent—his deposition in the
hands of the enemy, the Bolshevists, would cause "an instant
European war." Miss Brown is badgered, threatened, attacked
by those seeking the document, but she stands firm, and works
with the agent, who has not died but gone under cover, to save
England. The novel fades out on their first kiss.

Oppenheim did write a number of mystery novels (*The
Cinema Murder, The Grassleyes Mystery*), as well as a number of
detective stories, with a variety of detectives. In *Curious
Happenings to the Rooke Legatees,* five beneficiaries to a will
join forces to detect the murder of the testator. But Oppenheim's talent for plotting is primarily a talent for building
suspense rather than for unravelling a mysterious chain of
events, at least at great length; his best detective stories are
short stories. *Advice Limited* traces 11 adventures of Clara,

Baroness Linz and her secret service agency. The title character
of *Nicholas Goade, Detective* is a traveller, with dog, motoring
through rural Devon. *General Besserley's Puzzle Box* (and its
sequel) introduces the retired secret service official from
Washington, now a very popular member of Monaco society,
where he is innocuously providing financial advice at the
tables, but actually solving crimes. Another detective is Sir
Jasper Slane, gentleman and amateur, who solves crimes the
police cannot, in *Slane's Long Shots* (though in one of the best of
these stories it is the police who are triumphant). Perhaps
Oppenheim's most interesting detective is Louis, the *Maitre d'*
of the Milan Hotel, crippled in the war, who solves crimes from
his table in the grill room in collaboration with his friend
Lyson, a retired Army officer now a journalist (*A Pulpit in the
Grill Room* and *The Milan Grill Room*). The common
denominator of these detectives is their outward innocence or
ineptitude: the Zorro figure is very nearly ubiquitous in
Oppenheim's fiction.

The genre Oppenheim made his own (for even about his
detective stories there is frequently the whiff of the secret
service) is the novel of international intrigue, again with the
apparent milksop or ne'er-do-well as hero. While Oppenheim
always had the greatest respect for the aristocratic classes,
especially the English, many of his supermen act on behalf of
the little men; it is a case of *noblesse oblige.* In *The Profiteers* an
American millionaire, to lower the exorbitant price of wheat,
breaks the power of the controlling business syndicate by
kidnapping and starving its principals. In *Prodigals of Monte
Carlo* a wealthy baronet, told by his doctor that he is shortly to
die, provides a holiday on the Riviera for a young woman and
her chosen companion. In *Up the Ladder of Gold,* the most
remarkable of these fantasies of the great power of money, "the
richest man in the world" buys up most of the world's gold
bullion and bribes the great powers, through a legal trustee
device, not to go to war for 40 years. While the ending of *Up the
Ladder of Gold* is unusually pessimistic for Oppenheim, the
novel embodies his favorite theme of world domination for
good purpose, especially pacifism, his admiration for the
superman of wealth, and his fascination with the game of world
politics played as on a chess board. These themes and concerns
appear in various forms from *Mysterious Mr. Sabin* (1898) to his
last novel, *Mr. Mirakel* (1943), where the character of the title
transports a group of people from a world torn by war, and
eventually by earthquake ("the revolt of Nature against
mankind") to his own private Shangri-La, where they pair off
and project the future of the race.

Some of Oppenheim's best books, however, find not
supermen controlling international events, but ordinary diplomats and aristocrats caught up in them before they control
them. An early novel, *A Maker of History,* sets the tone: an
English youth witnesses a meeting between the Kaiser and the
Czar and comes away with a sheet of the secret treaty in which
they have agreed to launch war against England. In *The Double
Traitor,* on the eve of World War I a young diplomat gets
possession of a list of German spies in England; he plays a good
part in England's preparedness when the war comes. *The
Kingdom of the Blind,* in which a prominent member of English
society is shown to be a German spy, is to be set against the best
of this group, and probably Oppenheim's best and most famous
novel, *The Great Impersonation.* Here an English aristocrat,
fallen down the human scale through drink and dissipation,
thwarts the attempt of a German, his physical double, to
replace him, and so introduce a Trojan horse into the very
citadel of the British ruling class. This is one of the few novels
of Oppenheim's which depends upon surprise, and the secret is
well kept to the end.

A final group of Oppenheim's novels are not content with

playing the game of world politics—they project it into the future. *The Great Prince Shan* (1922) is set in 1934; *The Wrath to Come* (1924) in 1950; and *The Dumb Gods Speak* (1937) in 1947. Germany, Russia, and Japan are the usual antagonists of England and the United States, and the happy ending of *The Dumb Gods Speak* is signalled with the restoration of the Czarist regime, now benevolent and democratically based.

No one will contest the readability of Oppenheim's novels, which Grant Overton long ago attributed to the author's own infectious enthusiasm for his story. Oppenheim's novels are written without Buchan's subtlety of intellect, but not without his moral concern; they are free—except for some reserve towards Oriental villains—of Sapper's exclusive Anglo-Saxonism. As a *New York Times* reviewer sniffed in 1927, Oppenheim "has long been accustomed to analyze with a butcher knife and depict with a fence rail." But for readers looking for diversion with a shudder or a thrill one can still repeat Will Cuppy's 1934 axiom: "When in doubt, grab an Oppenheim."

—Barrie Hayne

ORCZY, Baroness (Emma Magdalena Rosalia Maria Josefa Barbara Orczy). British. Born in Tarna-Ors, Hungary, 23 September 1865. Educated in Brussels and Paris; West London School of Art; Heatherley School of Art, London. Married Montagu Barstow in 1894 (died 1943); one son. Artist: exhibited work at the Royal Academy, London. *Died 12 November 1967.*

CRIME PUBICATIONS.

Novel

The Celestial City. London, Hodder and Stoughton, and New York, Doran 1962.

Short Stories (series: Bill Owen, the Old Man in the Corner)

The Case of Miss Elliott (Old Man). London, Unwin, 1905.
The Old Man in the Corner. London, Greening, 1909; as *The Man in the Corner,* New York, Dodd Mead, 1909; augmented edition, edited by E.F. Bleiler, New York, Dover, 1980.
Lady Molly of Scotland Yard. London, Cassell, 1910; New York, Arno, 1976.
The Man in Grey, Being Episodes of the Chouan Conspiracies in Normandy During the First Empire. London, Cassell, and New York, Doran, 1918.
Castles in the Air. London, Cassell, 1921; New York, Doran, 1922.
The Old Man in the Corner Unravels the Mystery of the Khaki Tunic. New York, Doran, 1923.
The Old Man in the Corner Unravels the Mystery of the Pearl Necklace, and The Tragedy in Bishop's Road. New York, Doran 1924.
The Old Man in the Corner Unravels the Mystery of the Russian Prince and of Dog's Tooth Cliff. New York, Doran, 1924.
The Old Man in the Corner Unravels the Mystery of the White Carnation, and The Montmartre Hat. New York, Doran, 1925.
The Old Man in the Corner Unravels the Mystery of the Fulton Gardens Mystery, and The Moorland Tragedy. New York, Doran, 1925.
The Miser of Maida Vale. New York, Doran, 1925.

Unravelled Knots (Old Man). London, Hutchinson, 1925; New York, Doran, 1926.
Skin o' My Tooth. London, Hodder and Stoughton, and New Yord, Doubleday, 1928.

OTHER PUBLICATIONS

Novels

The Emperor's Candlesticks. London, Pearson 1899; New York, Doscher, 1908.
The Scarlet Pimpernel. London, Greening, and New York, Putnam, 1905.
By the Gods Beloved. London, Greening, 1905; as *Beloved of the Gods,* New York, Knickerbocker Press, 1905; as *The Gates of Kamt,* New York, Dodd Mead, 1907.
A Son of the People. London, Greening, and New York, Putman, 1906.
I Will Repay. London, Greening, and Philadelphia, Lippincott, 1906.
In Mary's Reign. New York, Cupples and Leon, 1907.
The Tangled Skein. London, Greening, 1907.
Beau Brocade. Philadelphia, Lippincott, 1907; London, Greening, 1908.
The Elusive Pimpernel. London, Hutchinson, and New York, Dodd Mead, 1908.
The Nest of the Sparrowhawk. London, Greening, and New York, Stokes, 1909.
Petticoat Government. London, Hutchinson, 1910; as *Petticoat Rule,* New York, Doran, 1910.
A True Woman. London, Hutchinson, 1911; as *The Heart of a Woman,* New York, Doran, 1911.
Meadowsweet. London, Hutchinson, and New York, Doran, 1912.
Fire in the Stubble, London, Methuen, 1912; as *The Noble Rogue,* New York, Doran, 1912.
Eldorado: A Story of the Scarlet Pimpernel. London, Hodder and Stoughton, and New York, Doran 1913.
Unto Caesar. London, Hodder and Stoughton, and New York, Doran, 1914.
The Laughing Cavalier. London, Hodder and Stoughton, and New York, Doran, 1914.
A Bride of the Plains. London, Hutchinson, and New York, Doran, 1915.
The Bronze Eagle. London, Hodder and Stoughton, and New York, Doran, 1915.
Leatherface: A Tale of Old Flanders. London, Hodder and Stoughton, and New York, Doran, 1916.
A Sheaf of Bluebells. London, Hutchinson, and New York, Doran, 1917.
Lord Tony's Wife: An Adventure of the Scarlet Pimpernel. London, Hodder and Stoughton, and New York, Doran, 1917.
Flower o' the Lily. London, Hodder and Stoughton, 1918; New York, Doran, 1919.
The League of the Scarlet Pimpernel. London, Cassell, and New York, Doran, 1919.
His Majesty's Well-Beloved. London, Hodder and Stoughton. and New York, Doran, 1919.
The First Sir Percy: An Adventure of the Laughing Cavalier. London, Hodder and Stoughton, 1920; New York, Doran, 1921.
Nicolette. London, Hodder and Stoughton, and New York, Doran, 1922.
The Triumph of the Scarlet Pimpernel. London, Hodder and Stoughton, and New York, Doran 1922.

The Honourable Jim. London, Hodder and Stoughton, and New York, Doran, 1924.

Pimpernel and Rosemary. London, Cassell, 1924; New York, Doran, 1925.

Sir Percy Hits Back: An Adventure of the Scarlet Pimpernel. London, Hodder and Stoughton, and New York, Doran, 1927.

Blues Eyes and Grey. London, Hodder and Stoughton, 1928; New York, Doubleday, 1929.

Marivosa. London, Cassell, 1930; New York, Doubleday, 1932.

A Child of the Revolution. London, Cassell, and New York, Doubleday, 1932.

A Joyous Adventure. London, Hodder Stoughton, and New York, Doubleday, 1932.

The Way of the Scarlet Pimpernel. London, Hodder and Stoughton, 1933; New York, Putnam, 1934.

A Spy of Napoleon. London, Hodder and Stoughton, and New York, Putnam, 1934.

The Uncrowned King. London, Hodder and Stoughton, and New York, Putnam, 1935.

Sir Percy Leads the Band. London, Hodder and Stoughton, 1936.

The Divine Folly. London, Hodder and Stoughton, 1937.

The Greater Love. London, Hodder and Stoughton, 1938.

Mam'zelle Guillotine: An Adventure of the Scarlet Pimpernel. London, Hodder and Stoughton, 1940.

Pride of Race. London, Hodder and Stoughton, 1942.

Will-o'-the-Wisp. London, Hutchinson, 1947.

Short Stories

The Traitor. New York, Paget, 1912.

Two Good Patriots. New York, Paget, 1912.

The Old Scarecrow. New York, Paget, 1916.

A Question of Temptation. New York, Doran, 1925.

Adventures of the Scarlet Pimpernel. London, Hutchinson, and New York, Doubleday.1929.

In the Rue Monge. New York, Doubleday, 1931.

Plays

The Scarlet Pimpernel, with Montagu Barstow (produced Nottingham, 1903; London, 1905; New York, 1910).

The Sin of William Jackson, with Montagu Barstow (produced London, 1906).

Beau Brocade, with Montagu Barstow, adaptation of the novel by Orczy (produced Eastbourn, Sussex, and London, 1908).

The Duke's Wager (produced Manchester, 1911).

The Legion of Honour, adaptation of her novel *A Sheaf of Bluebells* (produced Bradford, 1918; London, 1921).

Leatherface, with Caryl Fiennes, adaptation of the novel by Orczy (produced Portsmouth and London, 1922).

Other

Les Beaux et les Dandys de Grands Siècles en Angleterre. Monaco, Société des Conférences, 1924.

The Scarlet Pimpernel Looks at the World (essays). London, John Heritage, 1933.

The Turbulent Duchess; H.R.H. Madame la Duchesse de Berri, London, Hodder and Stoughton, 1935; New York, Putman,1936.

Links in the Chain of Life (autobiography). London, Hutchinson, 1947.

Editor and Translator, with Montagu Barstow, *Old Hungarian Fairy Tales.* London, Dean, and Philadelphia, Wolf, 1895.

Editor and Translator, *The Enchanted Cat* (fairy tales). London, Dean, 1895.

Editor and Translator, *Fairyland's Beauty* (*The Suitors of Princess Fire-fly*). London, Dean 1895.

Editor and Translator, *Uletka and the White Lizard* (fairy tales). London, Dean, 1895.

*   *   *

When Baroness Orczy was a struggling young author in London, before the success of *The Scarlet Pimpernel* in play and novel form, the editor of the Pearson magazines suggested that she profit from the popularity of Sherlock Holmes by writing a series of detective stories. The result was the Old Man in the Corner, one of the great figures in the early detective story. The Old Man (Bill Owen) sits in a cheap restaurant frequented by jornalists and plays with a bit of string, which he ties into elaborate knots as he talks. Addressing himself to Polly Burton, a young newspaperwoman with whom he has struck up a slight acquaintance, he focuses upon crimes mentioned in the newspapers. He summarizes the circumstances, describes the personalities, and then sneeringly provides the correct solution, which has evaded the police.

38 stories are devoted to the Old Man and Polly Burton. The first three series of stories appeared in *The Royal Magazine* between 1901 and 1904. The third series was published in book form as *The Case of Miss Elliott,* while the first and second were combined into *The Old Man in the Corner.* A fourth series, *Unravelled Knots,* was an unsuccessful attempt to capture the mood of the earlier stories. Typologically the stories are quite important. They are the first significant modern stories about an armchair detective, and structurally they take an extreme position: the explanation-denouement has been enlarged to such an extent that it swallows the antecedents, the crime, and the investigation, which are presented only in retrospective summary.

Four other books of short stories are much less significant. In *Lady Molly of Scotland Yard* a female detective solves 12 cases, some of which are true detective stories and some mystery adventures. Narrated by a female assistant, they are mildly feminist in attitude, but overwritten and sentimental. An unusual formal feature is that the narrator offers a précis of the crime before the entrance of the detective. *Skin o' My Tooth* contains 12 stories about Patrick Mulligan, an Irish lawyer practicing in England. His cases resemble those of Lady Molly de Mazareen, but are superior in execution. Two minor collections, *The Man in Grey* and *Castle in the Air,* combine historical adventure with elements of crime and mystery. *The Man in Grey* chronicles the triumph of the Napoleonic secret agent Fernand against members of the Chouans in 1809, while *Castles in the Air* contains seven cases of M. Hector Ratichon, a highly unscrupulous "volunteer police agent" in the Paris of 1813. They both reflect the attitudes of *The Scarlet Pimpernel.*

—E.F. Bleiler

ORMEROD, Roger. British. Born in Wolverhampton, Staffordshire, 17 April 1920. Married Barbara Joyce Wright in 1952. Country court officer, Wolverhampton, 1937–48; executive officer, Department of Social Security, 1948–72; has worked as a postman, and shop loader in an engineering factory. Agent: Laurence Pollinger Ltd., 18 Maddox Street, London WIR OEV. Address: 3 The Crescent, Tettenhall Wood, Wolverhampton, Staffordshire WV6 8LA, England.

CRIME PUBLICATIONS

Novels (series: David Mallin; Richard Patton)

Time to Kill (Mallin).   London, Hale, 1974.
The Silence of the Night (Mallin).   London, Hale, 1974.
Full Fury (Mallin).   London, Hale, 1975.
A Spoonful of Luger (Mallin).   London, Hale, 1975.
Sealed with a Loving Kill (Mallin).   London, Hale, 1976.
The Colour of Fear (Mallin).   London, Hale, 1976.
A Glimpse of Death (Mallin).   London, Hale, 1976.
Too Late for the Funeral (Mallin).   London, Hale, 1977.
This Murder Come to Mind.   London, Hale, 1977.
A Dip into Murder (Mallin).   London, Hale, 1978.
The Weight of Evidence (Mallin).   London, Hale, 1978.
The Bright Face of Danger (Mallin).   London, Hale, 1979.
The Amnesia Trap (Mallin).   London, Hale, 1979.
Cart Before the Hearse (Mallin).   London, Hale, 1979.
More Dead Than Alive.   London, Hale, 1980.
Double Take.   London, Hale, 1980.
One Deathless Hour (Mallin).   London, Hale, 1981.
Face Value.   London, Constable, 1983; as *The Hanging Doll Murder*, New York, Scribner, 1984.
Seeing Red.   London, Constable, 1984; New York, Scribner, 1985.
Dead Ringer.   London, Constable, 1985; New York, Scribner, 1986.
Still Life with Pistol (Patton).   London, Constable, and New York, Scribner, 1986.
A Death to Remember.   London, Constable, 1986; New York, Scribner, 1987.
An Alibi Too Soon (Patton).   London, Constable, 1987; New York, Scribner, 1988.
The Second Jeopardy.   London, Constable, 1987; New York, Doubleday, 1988.
An Open Window (Patton).   London, Constable, 1988.
By Death Possessed.   London, Constable, 1988; New York, Doubleday, 1988.
Guilt on the Lily (Patton).   London, Constable, 1989; New York, St. Martin's Press, 1990.
Death of an Innocent (Patton).   London, Constable, 1989.
No Sign of Life.   London, Constable, 1990.

OTHER PUBLICATIONS

Plays

Television Plays: *I'll Go Along with That*, 1971; *All Too Tidy*, 1973.

*   *   *

Roger Ormerod's steady and consistent output of detective fiction has confirmed him as one of Britain's best traditional crime writers. Careful always to provide his readers with a goodly selection of clues, both accurate and misleading, he does not sell them short when it comes to solving the mystery. Two private detectives people the greater part of his fictional output: David Mallin and George Coe. They are sometimes employed together as in *Cart Before the Hearse*, or singly as in *The Silence of the Night*—a David Mallin novel—and the combinations bring to Ormerod's writing a freshness of approach that is frequently absent from the work of writers who use a regular pairing of detectives. In each case, the narrative is always first person and a feature of Ormerod's style is his nonchalance which is reminiscent at times of Raymond Chandler and which provides his readers with an easy ambience. As is the case with writers who have turned from other trades or professions to authorship Ormerod uses his knowledge of work in which he has been employed to furnish his novels with authentic backgrounds such as factories or local government offices. As well as realism of background, Ormerod's writing is notable for its terse and natural dialogue and for an ability to switch the direction of the narrative. In *Cart Before the Hearse* Mallin and Coe are suddenly presented with a murder where they know the identity of the killer but cannot find his victim. Until the novel's end they are never quite certain whose murder they are investigating.

An exception to Ormerod's rule of using Mallin and Coe as the principal characters occurs in *A Dip into Murder*, in which he tells the story from the point of view of Mallin's wife, Elsie. Partly the change of emphasis is due to the fact that the story is told from a woman's point of view; but this is no mere stylistic innovation. Elsie Mallin is a rounded character in her own right, one well able to deal with the attentions of an aging, though complex, Lothario who sees her as his next victim.

In *Face Value*, Ormerod introduces a new hero, Detective Inspector Richard Patton, a policeman within three days of retirement when the novel begins. Looking for an easy way in which to spend his remaining days of service in peace and quiet, he is thrown into a missing person case which turns into a murder hunt. As he cautiously builds up the evidence—and in this novel Ormerod reveals himself as a master of professional police procedures in a murder investigation—everything begins to point to the missing man's wife being the principal suspect. It is at this point that Ormerod introduces a new facet into the plot, a triangular relationship into which Patton is drawn, greatly to his discomfort. From starting out as a relatively simple police procedural novel *Face Value* somersaults into a tale where passion plays a major part and the dignity and integrity of the main characters are put at risk. It also presents Ormerod as a novelist of power and imagination whose insight into the complexities of human relationships is one of his major strengths.

—Trevor Royle

————

OWEN, Philip. *See* **PENTECOST, Hugh.**

————

P

PACKARD, Frank L(ucius). Canadian. Born in Montreal of American parents, 2 February 1877. Educated at McGill University, Montreal, B.Sc. 1897; L'Institut Montefiore, Université de Liège, Belgium, 1897–98. Married Marguerite Pearl Macintyre in 1910; one daughter and three sons. Engineer from 1898; worked in Canadian Pacific Railroad shops. *Died 17 February 1942.*

CRIME PUBLICATIONS

Novels (series: Jimmie Dale)

The Miracle Man. New York, Doran, and London, Hodder and Stoughton, 1914.
The Adventures of Jimmie Dale. New York, Doran, 1917; London, Cassell, 1918.
The Sin That Was His. New York, Doran, 1917; London, Hodder and Stoughton, 1926.
The Further Adventures of Jimmie Dale. London, Hodder and Stoughton, 1917; New York, Doran, 1919.
The Wire Devils. New York, Doran, 1918.
From Now On. New York, Doran, 1919.
The White Moll. New York, Doran, and London, Hodder and Stoughton, 1920.
Pawned. New York, Doran, and London, Hodder and Stoughton, 1921.
Doors of the Night. New York, Doran, and London, Hodder and Stoughton, 1922.
Jimmie Dale and the Phantom Clue. New York, Doran, 1922; London, Hodder and Stoughton, 1923.
The Four Stragglers. New York, Doran, and London, Hodder and Stoughton, 1923.
The Locked Book. New York, Doran, and London, Hodder and Stoughton, 1924.
Broken Waters. New York, Doran, 1925; London, Hodder and Stoughton, 1927.
The Red Ledger. New York, Doran, and London, Hodder and Stoughton, 1926.
The Devil's Mantle. New York, Doran, 1927; London, Hodder and Stoughton, 1928.
Two Stolen Idols. New York, Doran, 1927; as *The Slave Junk*, London, Hodder and Stoughton, 1927.
Tiger Claws. New York, Doubleday, 1928; London, Hodder and Stoughton, 1929.
The Big Shot. New York, Doubleday, and London, Hodder and Stoughton, 1929.
Jimmie Dale and the Blue Envelope Murder. New York, Doubleday, and London, Hodder and Stoughton, 1930.
The Gold Skull Murders. New York, Doubleday, and London, Hodder and Stoughton, 1931.
The Hidden Door. New York, Doubleday, and London, Hodder and Stoughton, 1933.
The Purple Ball. New York, Doubleday, 1933; London, Hodder and Stoughton, 1934.
Jimmie Dale and the Missing Hour. New York, Doubleday, and London, Hodder and Stoughton, 1935.

The Dragon's Jaws. New York, Doubleday, and London, Hodder and Stoughton, 1937.

Short Stories

Shanghai Jim. New York, Doubleday, and London, Hodder and Stoughton, 1928.
More Knaves Than One. New York, Doubleday, and London, Hodder and Stoughton, 1938.

OTHER PUBLICATIONS

Novels

Greater Love Hath No Man. New York, Doran, and London, Hodder and Stoughton, 1913.
The Beloved Traitor. New York, Doran, 1915; London, Hodder and Stoughton, 1916.

Short Stories

On the Iron at Big Cloud. New York, Crowell, 1911.
The Night Operator. New York, Doran, 1919.
Running Special. New York, Doran, 1925; London, Hodder and Stoughton, 1926.

*   *   *

Frank L. Packard's crime novels are romances, set in New York's pre-organized crime underworld, that concern the moral dilemmas of those who come into contact with the criminal element. Products of a less egalitarian time, they are predicated upon the gap between the poor and potentially criminal and the upper level of society. Packard's protagonists, like the self-appointed benefactor of the downtrodden, Rhoda Gray (*The White Moll*), are people of the "better class" who are forced to operate within the underworld and to adopt its rules and, as a result, become the victims of a moral erosion that will inevitably result in their assimilation into criminal society.

This problem is central to Packard's novels about Jimmie Dale, the wealthy dilettante clubman who cracks safes by night as the Gray Seal. Jimmie Dale is a modern Robin Hood who preys on other criminals in the tradition of E. W. Hornung's Raffles and Leslie Charteris's Simon Templar. Jimmie Dale is not averse to stealing from thieves, or to being hunted by the police and the underworld, but he is horrified when he becomes involved with murder, or when he is blackmailed into committing criminal acts by a woman who may be a criminal herself. Unlike some of his more hardened counterparts, Jimmie Dale does not easily move through the sordid world of crime, and his deepest fear is not of death, but of bringing disgrace to his name and position in society.

—Will Murray

PAGE, Marco. Pseudonym for Harry Kurnitz. American. Born in Philadelphia, Pennsylvania, 5 January 1909. Educated in public schools; the University of Pennsylvania, Philadelphia. Book and music reviewer for the Philadelphia *Record*; screen writer for Metro-Goldwyn-Mayer after 1938. *Died 18 March 1968.*

CRIME PUBLICATIONS

Novels

Fast Company. New York, Dodd Mead, and London, Heinemann, 1938.
The Shadowy Third. New York, Dodd Mead, 1946; as *Suspects All,* London, Cherry Tree, 1948.
Reclining Figure. New York, Random House, and London, Eyre and Spottiswoode, 1952.
Invasion of Privacy (as Harry Kurnitz). New York, Random House, 1955; London, Eyre and Spottiswoode, 1956.

OTHER PUBLICATIONS as Harry Kurnitz

Plays

Reclining Figure, adaptation of his own novel (produced New York, 1954). New York, Dramatists Play Service, 1955.
Once More, with Feeling (produced New York, 1958; London, 1959). New York, Random House, 1959.
A Shot in the Dark, adaptation of a play by Marcel Achard (produced New York, 1961; London, 1963). New York, Random House, 1962.
The Girl Who Came to Supper, music and lyrics by Noël Coward, adaptation of the play *The Sleeping Prince* by Terence Rattigan (produced New York, 1963).

Screenplays: *Fast Company* (as Marco Page), with Harold Tarshis, 1938; *Fast and Furious,* 1939; *Fast and Loose,* 1939; *I Love You Again,* with Charles Lederer and George Oppenheimer, 1940; *Shadow of the Thin Man,* with Irvine Brecher, 1941; *Ship Ahoy,* with others, 1942; *They Got Me Covered,* with others, 1942; *Pacific Rendezvous,* with P.J. Wolfson and George Oppenheimer, 1942; *The Heavenly Body,* with others, 1943; *See Here, Private Hargrove,* 1944; *The Thin Man Goes Home,* with Robert Riskin and Dwight Taylor, 1945; *What Next, Private Hargrove,* 1945; *The Web,* with William Bowers and Bertram Millhauser, 1947; *Something in the Wind,* with others, 1947; *A Kiss in the Dark,* with Everett Freeman and Devery Freeman, 1948; *One Touch of Venus,* with Frank Tashlin, 1948; *The Adventures of Don Juan,* with George Oppenheimer and Herbert Dalmas, 1949; *My Dream Is Yours,* with others, 1949; *The Inspector General,* with Philip Rapp, 1949; *Pretty Baby,* with others, 1950; *Of Men and Music,* with others, 1951; *Tonight We Sing,* with George Oppenheimer, 1953; *Melba,* 1953; *The Man Between,* with Walter Ebert, 1953; *The Love Lottery,* with Monja Danischewsky, 1954; *Land of the Pharaohs,* with William Faulkner and Harold Jack Bloom, 1955; *The Happy Road,* with Arthur Julian and Joseph Morhain, 1957; *Witness for the Prosecution,* with Billy Wilder and Larry Marcus, 1957; *Once More, with Feeling,* 1960; *Surprise Package,* 1960; *Hatari!,* with Leigh Brackett, 1962; *Goodbye Charlie,* 1964; *How to Steal a Million,* 1966.

*   *   *

The delight of the regrettably few Marco Page novels lies in Page's remarkably adroit use of sprightly and highly amusing dialogue and in his selection of gripping situations around which to construct his stories.

His first mystery, *Fast Company,* involves bookman Joel Glass in a search for some rare books whose disappearance eventually leads to murder. In *The Shadowy Third* lawyer David Calder scrambles after a Stradivarius violin whose theft has similar consequences. Page really hit his stride in *Reclining Figure,* in which a New York art dealer, Ellis Blaise, journeys to California to investigate possible forgeries in a fabulously valuable collection of modern art. Murder, of course, ensues, and the reader is treated to a brief but fascinating glimpse into the world of art forgery in addition to a fast-paced, tightly knit detective tale whose dialogue positively sparkles. Running a very close second to *Reclining Figure* is *Invasion of Privacy* which involves the efforts of Mike Zorn, New York representative of Hollywood's Continental Films, to extricate himself and his company from the consequences arising from the fact that the events portrayed in a just completed movie about an unsolved murder turn out to be real rather than fictional.

Page wrote entertainingly about interesting subjects. He had more than a smidgen of knowledge about rare books, violins, and paintings, and about the workings of the Hollywood film industry, and he used his knowledge to construct convincing backdrops for his novels.

—Guy M. Townsend

———

PALMER, (Charles) Stuart. Also wrote as Jay Stewart. American. Born in Baraboo, Wisconsin, 21 June 1905. Educated at the Chicago Art Institute, 1922–24; University of Wisconsin, Madison, 1924–26; University of California, Los Angeles, 1961. Served in the United States Army as liaison chief for official Army film making, 1943–48: Major. Married 1) Melina Racioppi in 1928 (divorced 1937); 2) Margaret Greppin in 1939 (divorced 1945), one daughter and one son; 3) Ann Higgins in 1947 (divorced 1950), one son; 4) Winifred Graham in 1952 (divorced 1963); 5) Jennifer Elaine Venala in 1966. Screenwriter from 1932. President, Mystery Writers of America, 1954–55. *Died 4 February 1968.*

CRIME PUBLICATIONS

Novels (series: Howie Rook; Hildegarde Withers)

Ace of Jades. New York, Mohawk Press, 1931.
The Penguin Pool Murder (Withers). New York, Brentano's, 1931; London, Long, 1932.
Murder on Wheels (Withers). New York, Brentano's, and London, Long, 1932.
Murder on the Blackboard (Withers). New York, Brentano's, 1932; London, Eldon Press, 1934.
The Puzzle of the Pepper Tree (Withers). New York, Doubleday, 1933; London, Jarrolds, 1934.
The Puzzle of the Silver Persian (Withers). New York, Doubleday, 1934; London, Collins, 1935.
The Puzzle of the Red Stallion (Withers). New York, Doubleday, 1936; as *The Puzzle of the Briar Pipe,* London, Collins 1936.
Omit Flowers. New York, Doubleday, 1937; as *No Flowers by Request,* London, Collins, 1937.

The Puzzle of the Blue Banderilla (Withers). New York, Doubleday, and London, Collins, 1937.

The Puzzle of the Happy Hooligan (Withers). New York, Doubleday, and London, Collins, 1941.

Miss Withers Regrets. New York, Doubleday, 1947; London, Collins, 1948.

Four Lost Ladies (Withers). New York, Mill, 1949; London, Collins, 1950.

Before It's Too Late (as Jay Stewart). New York, Mill, 1950.

The Green Ace (Withers). New York, Mill, 1950; as *At One Fell Swoop,* London, Collins, 1951.

Nipped in the Bud (Withers). New York, Mill, 1951; London, Collins, 1952; as *Trap for a Redhead,* New York, Spivak, 1955.

Cold Poison (Withers). New York, Mill, 1954; as *Exit Laughing,* London, Collins, 1954.

Unhappy Hooligan (Rook). New York, Harper, 1956; as *Death in Grease Paint,* London, Collins, 1956.

Rook Takes Knight. New York, Random House, 1968.

Hildegarde Withers Makes the Scene, with Fletcher Flora. New York, Random House, 1969.

Short Stories

The Riddles of Hildegarde Withers, edited by Ellery Queen. New York, Spivak, 1947.

The Monkey Murder and Other Hildegarde Withers Stories, edited by Ellery Queen. New York, Spivak, 1950.

People vs. Withers and Malone, with Craig Rice. New York, Simon and Schuster, 1963.

The Adventure of the Marked Man and One Other. Boulder, Colorado, Aspen Press, 1973.

Once upon a Train and Other Stories, with Craig Rice, edited by Harold Straubing. Canoga Park, California, Gold Penny Press, 1981.

OTHER PUBLICATIONS

Plays

Screenplays: *Yellowstone,* with others, 1936; *Hollywood Stadium Mystery,* with Dorrell and Stuart McGowan, 1938; *Bulldog Drummond's Peril,* 1938; *Arrest Bulldog Drummond,* 1939; *Bulldog Drummond's Bride,* with Weston Garnett, 1939; *Death of a Champion,* with Cortland Fitzsimmons, 1939; *Seventeen,* with Agnes Christine Johnston, 1940; *Emergency Squad,* with others, 1940; *Opened by Mistake,* with others, 1940; *Who Killed Aunt Maggie?,* with Frank Gill, Jr. and Hal Fimberg, 1940; *Secrets of the Lone Wolf,* 1941; *The Smiling Ghost,* with Kenneth Gamet, 1941; *Pardon My Stripes,* with others, 1942; *X Marks the Spot,* with others, 1942; *Half Way to Shanghai,* 1942; *Home in Wyoming,* with Robert Tasker and M. Coates Webster, 1942; *The Falcon's Brother,* with Craig Rice, 1942; *Murder in Times Square,* with Paul Gangelin, 1943; *Petticoat Larceny,* with Jack Townley, 1943; *The Falcon Strikes Back,* with Edward Dein and Gerald Geraghty, 1943; *Step by Step,* with George Callahan, 1946; *Mrs. O'Malley and Mr. Malone,* with Craig Rice and William Bowers, 1951.

Other

"Some of My Best Friends," in *Ellery Queen's Mystery Magazine* (New York), June 1950.

"Profile of a Bloodhound," in *The Saint* (New York), October 1964.

* * *

Stuart Palmer made his debut as a mystery novelist with *Ace of Jades* in 1931, but it was his next book, *The Penguin Pool Murder,* that established his reputation and provided him with a series character to whom he would be closely wedded thereafter. His creation was Hildegarde Withers, a snoopy old maid sleuth extraordinaire. Withers's personality is quite unlike that of the most famous spinster detective, Agatha Christie's quiet, unassuming Miss Marple. Withers is a schoolteacher, of the sharp-tongued, knuckle-rapping variety, with a take-charge attitude and a tendency to treat suspects and police alike as if they were little boys caught cheating in class. She is lean and horsefaced, and given to wearing ghastly hats. It is perhaps unnecessary to note that beneath the formidable exterior there is a great deal of kindness and sentimentality. She is clearly a caricature, uncomfortably broad at times; but she is difficult to dislike, even if Palmer himself was wont to refer to her as "that meddlesome old battleaxe."

In *The Penguin Pool Murder,* Withers is escorting her class on a tour of an aquarium when she discovers a body amongst the penguins. Her curiosity, and her impatience with stupidity (which she finds the police exhibiting), lead her to see to the solution of the mystery. In this and later investigations her perennial foil (and an excellent one) is New York homicide Inspector Oscar Piper, a harried, cigar-chomping vulgarian— very much the opposite in character to the abstemious schoolteacher.

Though the chief appeal of the Withers novels is the character of "Hildy," and the interplay between her and Piper, Palmer can be credited with an ear for bright and clever dialogue, and he was a fine crafter of puzzle plots. The major weakness of the books is the slight characterization given to the supporting players. The Withers novels were transferred to the screen in a series of six films. Palmer moved to Hollywood to work as a screenwriter, and Withers moved to Los Angeles along with him. Perhaps the best of the later Withers novels is *Cold Poison,* in which Palmer makes an excellent use of background, setting the mystery in a Hollywood animation studio.

Ellery Queen was a great fan of Withers, and Palmer produced a number of short stories for *Ellery Queen's Mystery Magazine.* These were collected in *The Riddles of Hildegarde Withers* and *The Monkey Murder.* Palmer's skill at puzzle plot construction was put to good use in the short form. Withers also appeared in another unique series of short stories, in which she was teamed with Craig Rice's character John J. Malone. This represents one of the very few collaborative pairings of detective characters. Palmer wrote the stories and Rice provided plot springboards and bits of dialogue. Withers and Malone proved a natural yin-yang pairing—boozy, skirt-chasing lawyer versus prim spinster—and the tales are great fun. The stories were collected in *People vs. Withers and Malone.*

Late in his career, Palmer introduced another appealing series character, Howie Rook, a middle-aged, overweight ex-newsman with a streak of misogyny. The first of the two Rook novels, *Unhappy Hooligan,* takes place in a circus setting, Palmer drawing on his own experience as a clown for Ringling Brothers. The light approach to murderous doings that marked the Withers books is also much in evidence in the Rook novels.

—Art Scott

PALMER, John Leslie. *See* **BEEDING, Francis.**

———

PARETSKY, Sara. American. Born in Ames, Iowa, 8 June 1947. Educated at the University of Kansas, Lawrence, B. A. in political science, (summa cum laude) 1967; University of Chicago, Ph.D. in history 1977. Married Courtenay Wright in 1976; three children. Publications and conference manager, Urban Research Corporation, Chicago, 1971–74; freelance business writer, 1974–77; manager of direct mail marketing programs, CNA Insurance, Chicago, 1977–86. Since 1986 full-time writer. Co-founder, and president, Sisters in Crime. Recipient: Crime Writers Association Silver Dagger award, 1988. Agent: Dominick Abel, 146 West 82nd Street, New York, New York 10024. Address: 5831 South Blackstone, Chicago, Illinois 60637, U.S.A.

CRIME PUBLICATIONS

Novels (series: V. I. Warshawski in all books)

Indemnity Only. New York, Dial Press, and London, Gollancz, 1982.
Deadlock. New York, Dial Press, and London, Gollancz, 1984.
Killing Orders. New York, Morrow, 1985; London, Gollancz, 1986.
Bitter Medicine. New York, Morrow, and London, Gollancz, 1987.
Blood Shot. New York, Delacorte Press, 1988; as *Toxic Shock,* London, Gollancz, 1988.
Burn Marks. New York, Delacorte Press, and London, Chatto and Windus, 1990.

Uncollected Short Stories

"This Is for You, Jeannie," in *Women: Journal of Liberation,* February 1972.
"The Takamoku Joseki," in *Alfred Hitchcock's Mystery Magazine* (New York), November 1983.
"Three-Dot Do," in *The Eyes Have It,* edited by Robert J. Randisi. New York, Mysterious Press, 1984; London, Seven House, 1988.
"At the Old Swimming Hole," in *Mean Streets,* edited by Robert J. Randisi. New York, Mysterious Press, 1986.
"Skin Deep," in *Black Mask Quarterly* (New York), October 1986.
"The Pietro Andromache," in *Alfred Hitchcock's Mystery Magazine* (New York), December 1988.

OTHER PUBLICATIONS

Other

Case Studies in Alternative Education. Chicago Center for New Schools, 1975.

Editor, *Eye of a Woman* (short stories). New York, Delacorte Press, 1990.

*

Sara Paretsky comments:
V.I. Warshawski is the protagonist of my first six novels. She is a private investigator who lives and works in Chicago. Like Lew Archer before her she looks beyond the surface to "the far side of the dollar," the side where power and money corrupt people into making criminal decisions to preserve their positions. All of her cases explore some aspect of white collar crime where senior executives preserve position or bolster their companies without regard for the ordinary people who work for them.

*   *   *

In V. I. Warshawski, Sara Paretsky has created one of the best developed and most convincing female private eyes in contemporary mystery fiction. Although the novels are closer to hard-boiled crime fiction than classical detective novels, Paretsky has adjusted the formula to create a new version of the genre with important feminist overtones. Warshawski is a feminist, her view of the world honed by experiences with an underground abortion referral service, civil rights freedom marches, and a stint in the public defender's office; as a private investigator she continues her work for women, for equality, and for fairness. Her targets in each of the novels are entrenched social institutions, secure in their power and privilege.

Paretsky's first novel, *Indemnity Only,* is unusual because the client, union leader Andrew McGrath, is neither a family member nor a friend. But he is still connected to Warshawski slightly from having known her father, a police officer; McGrath erroneously thinks he is hiring the policeman's son. The conclusion of this novel sets the pattern for subsequent ones as Warshawski shifts the focus of her allegiance to the client's daughter when she tells Anita McGrath of her father's unknowing role in her lover's death. Paretsky deliberately challenges the bond between detective and client which narrows the issue to one of rights and obligations; she creates instead a character who is committed to relationships and sharing.

In *Deadlock,* Warshawski begins the pattern of investigating problems for family members and friends. These searches involve V.I. in a kind of active therapy as she confronts her own past—particularly the influence of her mother's life—through resolving a current case. Vic's active engagement with her own family is harshest in *Killing Orders* where her creation of an extended "family" is most revealing. Unlike the typical loner of the hard-boiled detective novels, Vic gathers a close circle of friends around her; throughout the six novels, their connections are explored, challenged, and re-defined. The effect of these familial clients and familial friends is to reinforce and legitimate the intensity of her emotional involvement with professional matters; the personal and the professional become inseparable but neither is sacrificed to the other.

In counterpoint to the personal attachment Warshawski has to her clients, Paretsky establishes the powerful social institutions which house, shield, and reward the criminals. Working for individuals against the corrupt power structure, Warshawski consciously takes on the role of "Dona Quixote," feeling that she can do more to redress imbalances by being an outsider herself. But, Warshawski doesn't ordinarily impose her personal or ideosyncratic code of morality; rather than creating a heroic individualistic detective, Paretsky has imagined her protagonist expanding the collective base of power through her inclusive style.

Paretsky's familiarity with other detective fiction is obvious; Warshawski contrasts herself with such famous characters as Mike Hammer, Lord Peter Wimsey, and Kinsey Milhone, usually to focus on her own apparent shortcomings. Paretsky herself is active with other women detective fiction writers through Sisters in Crime, an organization which is concerned with, among other matters, the underrepresentation of women authors among national reviews and annual prizes awarded by organizations such as Bouchercon or Mystery Writers of America. It is easy here to see author and character overlap in their concern for women's's issues.

Although all the criminals in these novels are individuals linked to institutional power and privilege, three of them are particularly insidious because the image they project is one of caring and protection. A reader might have low expectations of corporate business (*Deadlock, Blood Shot*), unions (*Indemnity Only*), and the local Chicago political system (*Blood Shot*); these are predictable villains. However, the Catholic Church (*Killing Orders*), the medical community (*Bitter Medicine*), and the police (*Burn Marks*) are less likely to provoke automatic suspicion. Yet, even here, Paretsky makes her criminals more than simply isolated individuals; they are entrenched within and protected by the system.

The novels are dense with the atmosphere of Chicago, a single woman's life amidst friends and family, the professional relationship of a detective with the police and other connections, and the difficulties of affecting more than a minute aspect of contemporary social injustice. Amidst a raft of new detective novelists focusing on women as private investigators, Sara Paretsky makes a unique and lasting contribution.

—Kathleen Gregory Klein

———

PARGETER, Edith. *See* **PETERS, Ellis.**

———

PARKER, Robert B(rown). American. Born in Springfield, Massachusetts, 17 September 1932. Educated at Colby College, Waterville, Maine, B.A. 1954; Boston University, M.A. 1957, Ph.D. 1971. Served in the United States Army, 1954–56. Married Joan Hall in 1956; two sons. Technical writer and group leader, Raytheon Company, 1957–59; copy writer and editor, Prudential Insurance Company, Boston, 1959–62; partner, Parker Farman Company, advertising, Boston, 1960–62; Teaching Fellow and Lecturer, Boston University, 1962–64; Instructor, Massachusetts State College, Lowell, 1964–66; Lecturer, Suffolk University, Boston, 1965–66; Instructor, Massachusetts State College, Bridgewater, 1964–68; Assistant Professor, 1968–74, Associate Professor, 1974–77, and Professor, 1977–79, Northeastern University, Boston. Recipient: Mystery Writers of America Edgar Allan Poe award, 1976. Lives in Cambridge, Massachusetts. Litt.D: Northeastern University, Boston, 1987. Agent: Helen L. Brann Agency, 94 Curtis Road, Bridgewater, Connecticut 06752, U.S.A.

CRIME PUBLICATIONS

Novels (series: Spenser in all books)

The Godwulf Manuscript. Boston, Houghton Mifflin, 1973; London, Deutsch, 1974.
God Save the Child. Boston, Houghton Mifflin, 1974; London, Deutsch, 1975.
Mortal Stakes. Boston, Houghton Mifflin, 1975; London, Deutsch, 1976.

Promised Land. Boston, Houghton Mifflin, 1976; London, Deutsch, 1977.
The Judas Goat. Boston, Houghton Mifflin, 1978; London, Deutsch, 1982.
Looking for Rachel Wallace. New York, Delacorte Press, 1980; Loughton, Essex, Piatkus, 1982.
A Savage Place. New York, Delacorte Press, 1981; Loughton, Essex, Piatkus, 1982.
Early Autumn. New York, Delacorte Press, 1981; London, Severn House, 1987.
Ceremony. New York, Delacorte Press, 1982; Loughton, Essex, Piatkus, 1983.
The Widening Gyre. New York, Delacorte Press, 1983.
Valediction. New York, Delacorte Press, 1984; London, Penguin, 1985.
A Catskill Eagle. New York, Delacorte Press, 1985; London, Viking, 1986.
Taming a Sea-Horse. New York, Delacorte Press, 1986; London, Viking, 1987.
Pale Kings and Princes. New York, Delacorte Press, 1987; London, Viking, 1988.
Crimson Joy. New York, Delacorte Press, 1988; London, Viking, 1989.
Playmates. New York, Putnam, 1989; London, Viking, 1990.
Poodle Springs (completion of novel by Raymond Chandler). New York, Putnam, 1989; London, Macdonald, 1990.
Stardust. New York, Putnam, 1990.

Short Story

Surrogate. Northridge, California, Lord John Press, 1982.

OTHER PUBLICATIONS

Novels

Wilderness. New York, Delacorte Press, 1979.
Love and Glory. New York, Delacorte Press, 1983.

Other

Sports Illustrated Training with Weights. Philadelphia, Lippincott, 1974.
"Marlowe's Moral Code," in *Popular Culture Scholar* (Frostburg, Maryland), 1976.
"Marxism and the Mystery," in *Murder Ink: The Mystery Reader's Companion,* edited by Dilys Winn. New York, Workman, 1977.
Three Weeks in Spring, with Joan H. Parker. Boston, Houghton Mifflin, and London, Deutsch, 1978.
The Private Eye in Hammett and Chandler. Northridge, California, Lord John Press, 1984.
Parker on Writing. Northridge, California, Lord John Press, 1985.

Editor, *The Personal Response to Literature.* Boston, Houghton Mifflin, 1971.
Editor, *Order and Diversity.* New York, Wiley, 1973.

*   *   *

Robert B. Parker's creditable completion of Raymond Chandler's *Poodle Springs* fragment only confirms his long-standing affiliation with Chandler. And if he has not surpassed his master, Parker has at least established himself as the preeminent contemporary writer in the hard-boiled tradition, a popular and critical success.

Spenser is, in several respects, a typical hard-boiled private investigator: a professional detective, proficient with guns and with his fists (formerly a professional boxer, he continues to train and never loses a fight), conveniently friendly with the official police. Though he is uncommonly literate (in *The Widening Gyre* alone he cites Tennyson, Arnold, Hopkins, Eliot, Frost, Stevens, and Kris Kristofferson), he relies primarily upon the hard-boiled virtues of persistence and toughness for his success. Uncommonly, he is an excellent cook.

Spenser's cases are also typical of the hard-boiled genre. They do not involve cerebral problems. Missing persons, blackmail, pornography, drugs, and bodyguard assignments provide familiar occasions for Spenser to act. He encounters organized crime, expresses his disapproval, but finds he can work with gangsters like Joe Broz (*The Godwulf Manuscript. The Widening Gyre, Valediction*) and Tony Marcus (*Ceremony, Crimson Joy*). In *Valediction,* he encounters that hard-boiled staple, the religious cult (the same novel also provides a rare example of Parker plotting a surprise ending). He frequently confronts another staple, the political conspiracy. In *The Godwulf Manuscript,* it is a left-wing conspiracy; in the later novels (*The Judas Goat Looking for Rachel Wallace, A Catskill Eagle*) it is a racist/sexist right-wing conspiracy. In *The Judas Goat,* Spenser accepts a rich man's charge to exterminate the conspirators; in *A Catskill Eagle* he accepts the government's charge to exterminate the rich mastermind of the conspiracy.

Spenser successfully revives the hard-boiled art of the wisecrack. But his repartee, though often as entertaining as Philip Marlowe's, reflects a different spirit. Marlowe's wit was the weapon of a vulnerable man; Spenser is never beaten; his is the exuberant humor of a confident man.

The Spenser series is notable for its concentration upon two themes—the troubled status of adolescents, and of women in contemporary society. Hard-boiled detectives have always drawn their clients from these categories of victims, but Spenser repeatedly finds himself engaged in freeing teenagers (*God Save the Child, Early Autumn, Ceremony, Taming a Seahorse, Playmates*) and women (*Mortal Stakes, Promised Land, The Widening Gyre, A Catskill Eagle*) and enabling them to make their own choices (with the women, he struggles mightily to avoid paternalism). The value of this freedom to choose becomes a central moral issue in the series.

Beginning with the introduction of Susan Silverman in *God Save the Child,* Parker has supplied Spenser with a complex network of personal relationships: with Susan; with his Black alter ego, Hawk (introduced in *Promised Land*); with his foster son, Paul Giacomin (*Early Autumn*); and with a number of more minor recurring characters such as the New York City madam, Patricia Utley, or the militant lesbian, Rachel Wallace. The evolution of these relationships has become a primary source of interest in the series.

The most important are certainly those with Susan and with Hawk. Susan's role in *God Save the Child* is an incidental one; she is an attractive guidance counsellor of a boy Spenser is looking for. In the course of the next seven novels, Spenser and Susan develop a mutual commitment. Then, beginning with *The Widening Gyre,* tensions within this relationship—derived in part from Susan's pursuit of her intellectual independence—take on a more and more central place until, in *A Catskill Eagle,* the entire plot of the novel concerns Spenser's melodramatic heroics in freeing Susan from captivity. (The more recent novels have returned the emphasis of the narrative to the investigation at hand.) The simplistic misogynies of the hard-boiled past no longer serve. However macho in his relationships with men (and he can be as brutal as Mike Hammer in his treatment of men; *A Catskill Eagle* also illustrates this quality), Spenser must come to new terms with contemporary womanhood.

Hawk first appears as a Black freelance mob enforcer in *Promised Land;* in *The Judas Goat* he emerges as Spenser's cold-blooded ally in the campaign to exterminate the gang of terrorists. A streetwise Chingachook/Queequeg/Jim, Hawk provides the occasion for humor (he frequently banters with Spenser in what Parker takes to be mock Black English) and, as Spenser's dark twin, he embodies what Spenser would be without his chivalric code (Hawk's conscienceless code evidently mandates only faultless proficiency in intimidation and two loyalties—to Spenser and to Susan).

The most interesting phase of Spenser's career is the initial one in which the very Chandleresque *The Godwulf Manuscript* is followed by three novels in which Parker discovers his own approach to the genre, placing less emphasis upon plot and sense of place and more upon action and moral judgement. The four novels which follow *The Judas Goat* are also interesting for their preoccupation with the themes of the status of women and children. The novels since *The Widening Gyre* have been competent, but have added little to the series (other than the mid-1980's obsession with Susan). Perhaps this recent return to his Chandler roots in *Poodle Springs* will signal a new stage in Parker's development.

—J.K. Van Dover

PARKHILL, John. *See* **COX, William R.**

PARRISH, Frank. Pseudonym for Roger Erskine Longrigg; also writes as Ivor Drummond; Rosalind Erskine; Domini Taylor. British. Born in Edinburgh, 1 May 1929. Educated privately and at Magdalen College, Oxford, B.A. in modern history 1952. Served in the British Army, 1947–49: Captain, Territorial and Army Volunteer Reserve. Married Jane Chichester in 1957; three daughters. Agent: Curtis Brown Ltd., 162–168 Regent Street, London W1R 5TB, England.

CRIME PUBLICATIONS

Novels (series: Dan Mallett in all books)

Fire in the Barley. London, Constable, 1977; New York, Dodd Mead, 1979.
Sting of the Honeybee. London, Constable, 1978; New York, Dodd Mead, 1979.
Snare in the Dark. London, Constable, 1982; New York, Dodd Mead 1983.
Bait on the Hook. London, Constable, and New York, Dodd Mead, 1983.
Face at the Window. London, Constable, 1984; as *Death in the Rain,* New York, Dodd Mead, 1985.
Fly in the Cobweb. London, Constable, and New York, Harper, 1986.
Caught in the Birdlime. London, Constable, 1987; as *Bird in the Net,* New York, Harper, 1988.

Novels as Ivor Drummond (series: Lady Jennifer Norrington, Count Alessandro di Ganzarello, and Coleridge Tucker III in all books)

The Man with the Tiny Head. London, Macmillan, 1969; New York, Harcourt Brace, 1970.
The Priests of the Abomination. London, Macmillan, 1970; New York, Harcourt Brace, 1971.
The Frog in the Moonflower. London, Macmillan, 1972; New York, St. Martin's Press, 1973.
The Jaws of the Watchdog. London, Macmillan, and New York, St. Martin's Press, 1973.
The Power of the Bug. London, Macmillan, and New York, St. Martin's Press, 1974.
The Tank of Sacred Eels. London, Joseph, and New York, St. Martin's Press, 1976.
The Necklace of Skulls. London, Joseph, and New York, St. Martin's Press, 1977.
A Stench of Poppies. London, Joseph, and New York, St. Martin's Press, 1978.
The Diamonds of Loreta. London, Constable, and New York, St. Martin's Press, 1980.

Uncollected Short Stories

"Death in the Private Dining Room," in *Compleat Imbiber 11* (London), 1970.
"The Five-Million-Dollar Baby," in *Winter's Crimes 2,* edited by George Hardinge. London, Macmillan, 1970.
"Lock-up," in *Woman's Journal* (London), June 1974.
"The Chair," in *Winter's Crimes 6,* edited by George Hardinge. London, Macmillan, 1974.
"Potterton's Particular," in *Winter's Crimes 11,* edited by George Hardinge. London, Macmillan, 1979.
"The Serpent Orchid" (as Roger Longrigg), in *Winter's Crimes 14,* edited by Hilary Watson. London, Macmillan, 1982.

OTHER PUBLICATIONS as Roger Longrigg

Novels

A High-Pitched Buzz. London, Faber, 1956.
Switchboard. London, Faber, 1957.
Wrong Number. London, Faber, 1959.
Daughters of Mulberry. London, Faber, 1961.
The Passion-Flower Hotel (as Rosalind Erskine). London, Cape, and New York, Simon and Schuster, 1962.
The Paper Boats. London, Faber, and New York, Harper, 1963.
Passion Flowers in Italy (as Rosalind Erskine). London, Cape, 1963; New York, Simon and Schuster, 1964.
Passion Flowers in Business (as Rosalind Erskine). London, Cape, 1965.
Love among the Bottles. London, Faber, 1967.
The Sun on the Water. London, Macmillan, 1969.
The Desperate Criminals. London, Macmillan, 1971.
The Jevington System. London, Macmillan, 1973.
Their Pleasing Sport. London, Macmillan, 1975.
Bad Bet. London, Hamish Hamilton, 1982; as *Outcross,* New York, Morrow, 1982.
Mother Love (as Domini Taylor). London, Hamish Hamilton, and New York, Putnam, 1983.
Gemini (as Domini Taylor). London, Hamish Hamilton, 1984; New York, Atheneum, 1985.
Suffer Little Children (as Domini Taylor). London, Hamish Hamilton, 1987; as *Teacher's Pet,* New York, Atheneum, 1987.

Praying Mantis (as Domini Taylor). London, Hamish Hamilton, 1988; New York, Atheneum, 1989.
Siege. London, Heinemann, 1989; New York, Harper, 1990.

Plays

Radio Play: *The Chair,* 1976.

Television Plays: *Arson,* 1974; *Firing Point,* 1974; *Dead Connection,* 1974; *Contempt of Court,* 1975.

Other

The Artless Gambler. London, Pelham, 1964.
The History of Horse Racing. London, Macmillan, and New York, Stein and Day, 1972.
The History of Foxhunting. London, Macmillan, and New York, Potter, 1975.
The Turf: Three Centuries of Horse Racing. London, Eyre Methuen, 1975.
The English Squire and His Sport. London, Joseph, and New York, St. Martin's Press, 1977.

*

Frank Parrish comments:
The late Ian Fleming was quoted as saying that his highest ambition as a writer of thrillers was to make the reader want to turn over the page to see what happened next. I disagreed with Fleming about many things (especially his dislike of Italy), but in this I wholly agree with him. The reader's curiosity is sharpened, I think, by credible and attractive characters—villains as well as heroes—and the escapism of exotic settings accurately described.

*   *   *

Roger Erskine Longrigg is best known for his series written under his pseudonyms of Ivor Drummond and Frank Parrish.

The series written as Ivor Drummond was written chiefly during the 1970's and features Lady Jennifer Norrington, Count Alessandro di Ganzarello, and Coleridge Tucker III, a team of wealthy adventurers who find themselves fighting against exotic villains indulging in sinister plots with all the fluff and panache of the James Bond books.

In *The Power of the Bug,* Jenny, Sandro, and Colly investigate the death of David Cordle, a rich and respected man, whose fear of blackmail forced him to take his own life. The settings—Vermont, the deep South, and finally the shattering conclusion in Mexico—results in the most American book in the series.

In *The Tank of Sacred Eels,* Colly and Sandro investigate the flow of drugs in the Middle East while Jenny falls in love with Mr. Wrong. The plot speeds along from Morocco to France, from London to the deserts of North Africa.

The Necklace of Skulls brings the trio to India to stop the ripoff of pharmaceuticals and the sale of contaminated drugs. Jenny, Sandro, and Colly discover the dreaded Thugs—a violent secret society believed to be extinct—are at work again. When Jenny disappears, Sandro and Colly race against the clock to save her from becoming a human sacrifice.

Jenny, Sandro, and Colly foil a kidnap plot involving a child, but the kidnappers decide to get their revenge at the trio's expense. Colly is kidnapped and the price of his release is the Diamonds of Loreta: the treasure kept under massive security in the museum in Prague. Jenny and Sandro have to find a way to steal the jewels from the impregnable fortress, and manage to turn the tables on the kidnappers before they kill Colly. This caper novel is the best in the series.

Longrigg's latest series, the Frank Parrish books, is the complete opposite of the Drummond books. Where the Drummond books are stylish and wacky with international settings, the Parrish books are homespun and simple with an English countryside setting.

The Frank Parrish series features poacher and petty thief Dan Mallett. Mallett lives outside the village of Medwell Fratorum with his aging, arthritic mother. He steals and poaches from the rich landowners who Mallett determines deserve the losses.

In *Fire in the Barley*, Mallett finds himself forced to defend his village when a protection racket limits Mallett's own freedom of operation. This unconventional plot and character hold readers' interest by their originality.

Another offbeat plot is evident in *Sting of the Honeybee*. An organized crime boss from London threatens life in Mallett's sleepy English village. The conclusion, with Mallett trapped in an old farmhouse with two spinsters and a young girl, is the most suspenseful in the series.

When gamekeeper Edgar Bland, Mallett's old adversary, is found murdered, Mallett is the chief suspect. In *Snare in the Dark* Mallett has to solve the murder in order to clear himself from the murder charge.

While Mallett is entertaining the pretty, young babysitter at Medwell Old Hall, an intruder is murdered. These events in *Bait on the Hook* lead Mallett to investigate the murder. Anna, the babysitter's charge, is a precocious child who plays a role in untangling the murder plot—and driving Mallett crazy.

When Mallett's elderly mother needs a hip replacement operation, Mallett decides to steal the silver from the new owner of Medwell Court, Harold Dartie. But during the robbery, Mallett sees something that could cost him his life as Dartie starts the hunt to get Mallett. The chase scenes in *Fly in the Cobweb* are the best of the Dan Mallett series.

—George Kelley

———

PARTRIDGE, Anthony. *See* **OPPENHEIM, E. Phillips.**

———

PATRICK, Q. *See* **QUENTIN, Patrick.**

———

PATTERSON, Henry. *See* **HIGGINS, Jack.**

———

PAUL, Elliot (Harold). Also wrote as Brett Rutledge. American. Born in Malden, Massachusetts, 11 February 1891. Educated at Malden High School; University of Maine, Orono, 1908–09. Served in 317th Field Signal Battalion in World War I: Sergeant. Had one son by first marriage, then married 2) Flora Thompson Brown in 1935; 3) Barbara Mayock in 1945; 4) Nancy Dolan. Surveyor and timekeeper on irrigation project in Idaho and Wyoming, 1909; worked on

Boston newspapers to 1914; Secretary, Massachusetts Soldiers' and Sailors' Commission, 1919–21; worked in Paris after the war for Associated Press, Chicago *Tribune*, 1925–26, and as literary editor on Paris edition of New York *Herald*, 1930. Founder, with Eugène Jolas, *Transition*, Paris 1927–28; lived in Santa Eulalia, Ibiza, in the 1930's *Died 7 April 1958.*

CRIME PUBLICATIONS

Novels (series: Homer Evans in all Paul books)

The Mysterious Mickey Finn; or, Murder at the Café du Dôme. New York, Modern Age, 1939; London, Penguin, 1952.
Hugger-Mugger in the Louvre. New York, Random House, 1940; London, Nicholson and Watson, 1949.
The Death of Lord Haw Haw (as Brett Rutledge). New York, Random House, 1940; London, Laurie, 1941.
Fracas in the Foothills. New York, Random House, 1940.
Mayhem in B-Flat. New York, Random House, 1940; London, Corgi, 1951.
I'll Hate Myself in the Morning, and Summer in December. New York, Random House, 1945; London, Nicholson and Watson, 1949.
Murder on the Left Bank. New York, Random House, and London, Corgi, 1951.
The Black Gardenia. New York, Random House, 1952.
Waylaid in Boston. New York, Random House, 1953.
The Black and the Red. New York, Random House, 1956.

OTHER PUBLICATIONS

Novels

Indelible. Boston, Houghton Mifflin, 1922; London, Jarrolds, 1924.
Impromptu. New York, Knopf, 1923.
Imperturbe. New York, Knopf, 1924.
Low Run Ride and Lava Rock. New York, Liveright, 1929.
The Governor of Massachusetts. New York, Liveright, 1930.
The Amazon. New York, Liveright, 1930.
Concert Pitch. New York, Random House, 1938.
The Stars and Stripes Forever. New York, Random House, 1939.

Plays

Screenplays: *A Woman's Face,* with Donald Ogden Stewart, 1941; *Our Russian Front,* 1942; *Rhapsody in Blue,* with Howard Koch and Sonya Levien, 1945; *It's a Pleasure,* with Lynn Starling, 1945; *London Town* (*My Heart Goes Crazy*), with others, 1946; *New Orleans,* with Dick Irving Hyland and Herbert J. Biberman, 1947.

Other

The Life and Death of a Spanish Town. New York, Random House, and London, Davies, 1937.
All the Brave, with Jay Allen. New York, Modern Age, 1939.
Intoxication Made Easy. New York, Modern Age, 1941.
The Last Time I Saw Paris. New York, Random House, 1942; as *A Narrow Street,* London, Cresset Press, 1942.
With a Hays Nonny Nonny. New York, Random House, 1942.
Paris, photographs by Fritz Henle. Chicago, Ziff Davis, 1947.

Linden on the Saugus Branch. New York, Random House, 1947; London, Cresset Press, 1948.

A Ghost Town on the Yellowstone. New York, Random House, 1948; London, Cresset Press, 1949.

My Old Kentucky Home. New York, Random House, 1949; London, Cresset Press, 1950.

Springtime in Paris. New York, Random House, 1950; London, Cresset Press, 1951.

Understanding the French. London, Muller, 1954; New York, Random House, 1955.

Desperate Scenery. New York, Random House, 1954; London, Cresset Press, 1955.

Flim Flam. London, Muller, 1956.

That Crazy American Music. Indianapolis, Bobbs Merrill, 1957; as *That Crazy Music,* London, Muller, 1957.

*   *   *

Elliot Paul, author, bon vivant, and boogie woogie pianist, cut his writing teeth as a newspaperman in Boston. His reflections on that city, and its Watch and Ward Society, have appeared in his later works. It is possible that Boston may never fully recover. Paul first came to wide notice with two non-crime books, *The Life and Death of a Spanish Town* and *The Last Time I Saw Paris,* an excellent account of pre-World War II Paris, deeply personal in nature, that quickly achieved something close to classic stature.

Like many another, Paul read the Philo Vance stories of S.S. Van Dine and found Vance himself an insufferable snob. His response to this was to parody Vance with his own creation, Homer Evans. An American living by choice in Paris, Evans outdoes Vance in almost every department: he speaks more languages, is capable of even more languid conduct, and is surrounded by a world of wild characters that would confound the Marx brothers. This ménage first appeared in *The Mysterious Mickey Finn* in 1939; perhaps mercifully Van Dine died the same year. Much to Paul's surprise, his cutting satire was taken seriously as a mystery story and there was a loud demand for more, particularly since the book's deft humor was enormously entertaining. The following year Paul obliged with *Hugger-Mugger in the Louvre* in which even more people met with fascinating, if violent, deaths. A fit companion and mate for Evans is his girlfriend, Miriam Leonard, a sharpshooting cowgirl from the American West who is in Paris to study the harpsichord. On one occasion when Homer failed to catch the eye of a gendarme on the far corner of a wide boulevard, Miriam drew, fired, and gently rang the bell on the officer's bicycle.

When Paris fell, Homer and Miriam returned to their homeland bringing with them many of their Parisian friends, including the Medical Examiner, Dr. Hyacinthe Toudoux. In the lower Yellowstone Valley of Montana, Miriam, at least, is fully at home and introduces Dr. Toudoux to his professional colleague, the Blackfoot medicine man, Trout-tail III. In addition to the two doctors, there are the Blackfoot Chief, Shot-on-Both-Sides, and the unforgettable Moritz, the Thinking Dog, whose mental powers are revealed as *Fracas in the Foothills* runs its mad course.

In all there are nine volumes in the Homer Evans canon, most of them filled with wild action and funny enough to make most readers laugh aloud in an empty room. In the whole field of mystery literature Paul is probably unique in his ability to blend far-out humor, satire, and the traditional detective story into a homogeneous whole. The author's knowledge of both classic and popular music adds spice, and few Bostonians will be able to read *Waylaid in Boston* unmoved. Some critics have

maintained that a detective story once read can never be as entertaining again. Paul has proved otherwise.

—John Ball

————

PAYNE, Laurence. British. Born in London, 5 June 1919. Educated at Tottenham Grammar School, London. Married Judith Mary Draper in 1973. Actor: numerous roles in stage, film, television, and radio productions. Drama teacher, Royal College of Music, London, and St. Catherine's School, Guildford, Surrey. Recipient: Old Vic Drama Scholarship, 1939. Address: West Bams, Low Cocklaw, Berwick upon Tweed, Northumberland TD15 1UY, England.

CRIME PUBLICATIONS

Novels (series: Chief Inspector Sam Birkett; Mark Savage; John Tibbet)

The Nose on My Face (Birkett). London, Hodder and Stoughton, and New York, Macmillan, 1962; as *The First Body,* New York, Avon, 1964.

Too Small for His Shoes (Birkett). London, Hodder and Stoughton, 1962; New York, Macmillan, 1963.

Deep and Crisp and Even (Birkett). London, Hodder and Stoughton, 1964.

Birds in the Belfry. London, Hodder and Stoughton, 1966: Philadelphia, Lippincott, 1967.

Spy for Sale (Tibbet). London, Hodder and Stoughton, 1969; New York, Doubleday, 1970.

Even My Foot's Asleep (Tibbet). London, Hodder and Stoughton, 1971.

Take the Money and Run (Savage). London, Hodder and Stoughton, 1982; New York, Doubleday, 1984.

Malice in Camera (Savage). London, Hodder and Stoughton, 1983; New York, Doubleday, 1985.

Vienna Blood (Savage). London, Hodder and Stoughton, 1984; New York, Doubleday, 1986.

Dead for a Ducat (Savage and Birkett). London, Hodder and Stoughton, and New York, Doubleday, 1986.

Late Knight (Savage). London, Hodder and Stoughton, 1987; as *Knight Fall,* New York, Doubleday, 1987.

*

Manuscript Collection: Mugar Memorial Library, Boston University.

Laurence Payne comments:

Having played a great number of "clever-dick" private eyes in films, who habitually pipped the police at the post, I decided to write a book in defence of the Metropolitan Police (*The Nose on My Face*) for whom I have a great deal of respect. This led to a trilogy with the same leading characters. My writing is greatly influenced, I think, by Raymond Chandler whose wry humour and abrasive style I appreciate, and Graham Greene whose economy and choice of words are, to me, a lesson. Charles Dickens too—for me the greatest of all novelists. Also of course, having lived in the glory of Shakespeare as an actor I have a great regard for the *sound* of words, and the beauty of the English language. In spite of being "just" a crime writer I consider it a duty therefore to choose the *right* word and will spend a considerable time finding it. For me writing must appeal to the ear as well as to the eye—another actor quirk.

I write crime not particularly because of choice—I dislike violence in all forms, vandalism and dishonesty I loathe—but because I have become "type-cast"—as indeed I became type-cast in the theatre as a romantic juvenile. I would, of course, prefer to write the Great Novel—wouldn't we all?—and I have a burning desire to write a book about Beethoven—the man not the musician. I have two gods: Beethoven and Shakespeare.

* * *

Laurence Payne, the creator of Inspector Sam Birkett and his assistant Sergeant Saunders, is one of the great humorists of the world of crime fiction. Faced by a murder in the opening pages of *The Nose on My Face,* Birkett looks at the hideously mutilated corpse and muses that Sherlock Holmes would doubtless make something of it as he cannot. That dry sense of self-mocking wit gained for Payne a small but select group of admirers among his readers when the first Birkett-Saunders novels began to appear in the 1960's. A professional actor himself, he brought to his novels a sense of fun and a mastery of comic dialogue, virtues that many writers who are also actors seem to achieve effortlessly. The police partnership provided by his two main heroes is an unlikely Holmes and Watson and their apparently frivolous behaviour makes it difficult to place Payne in the genre of realistic procedural novels, but beneath the fun and games and the verbal pyrotechnics Payne takes his craft very seriously. Logic is as important to him as maintaining a lightness of touch, and nothing occurs within the novels that cannot be proved by fact: at all times Birkett gives enough away about his methods to keep the reader involved in the intricacies of the plot.

Too Small for His Shoes, the second novel in the series, is subtitled "A Novel of Detection," an accurate description of its author's intentions. The wit employed by Birkett is of as high a standard as before but a new and unexpected seriousness underpins the comedy. The background is the world of film and entertainment, and, knowing it intimately, Payne is able to conjure up a background that is thoroughly believable. On the one hand there is the surface glamour of film studios and the hint of film-stars and producers leading lives of luxury; on the other is the hall-of-mirrors distortion created by their dreams and fantasies. It is into this world that Birkett must step to solve the murder of scriptwriter Karl Durer. (Payne usually has a good deal of fun in naming his characters.)

By the time of the publication of *Deep and Crisp and Even,* Birkett had begun to assume a greater presence in the scheme of Payne's writing, bearing more of the burden for taking forward the narrative while Saunders began to occupy a lesser role. By concentrating more on his fictional inspector, Payne was also able to bring a greater sense of cohesion to his plots, and what the novels lost in comic relief they made up with a harder edge to the characterisation and a greater emphasis on the patient police work involved in solving crimes. When Birkett describes his methods as being more Dixon of Dock Green than Starsky and Hutch he is not grasping for a joke but merely telling the truth. *Take the Money and Run,* in which Birkett makes a ghostly appearance as an "ex-inspector," is set in Wales against a background of private detectives involved with nationalist groups and ex-Nazis. As with the earlier novels it is notable for its easy flowing dialogue, the power of description (in this case a rural setting), and the good humour that permeates its pages.

—Trevor Royle

———

PENDLETON, Don(ald Eugene). Also writes as Dan Britain; Stephan Gregory. American. Born in Little Rock, Arkansas, 12 December 1927. Served in the United States Navy, 1942–47, 1952–54; Naval Commendation Medal, Iwo Jima, 1945. Married Marjorie Williamson in 1946; two daughters and four sons. Telegrapher, Southern Pacific Railroad, San Francisco, 1948–55; air traffic control specialist, Federal Aviation Administration, Western Region, 1957–61; engineering supervisor, Martin Company, Denver, 1961–64; engineering administrator, General Electric, NASA-Mississippi Test Facility, 1964–66, and Lockheed Corporation, Marietta, Georgia, 1966–67; participated in the Titan II project, NASA Moonshot, and United States Air Force C-5 Galaxy program. Senior editor and columnist, *Orion* magazine, 1967–70. Agent: Scott Meredith Literary Agency Inc., 845 Third Avenue, New York, New York 10022, U.S.A.

CRIME PUBLICATIONS

Novels (series: Mack Bolan, The Executioner; Joe Copp)

War Against the Mafia. New York, Pinnacle, 1969; London, Sphere, 1973.
Death Squad. New York, Pinnacle, 1969; London, Sphere, 1973.
Battle Mask. New York, Pinnacle, 1970; London, Sphere, 1973.
Miami Massacre. New York, Pinnacle, 1970; London, Corgi, 1973.
Continental Contract. New York, Pinnacle, 1971; London, Sphere, 1973.
Assault on Soho. New York, Pinnacle, 1971; London, Corgi, 1973.
Nightmare in New York. New York, Pinnacle, 1971; London, Corgi, 1973.
Chicago Wipe-Out. New York, Pinnacle, 1971; London, Corgi, 1973.
Vegas Vendetta. New York, Pinnacle, 1971; London, Corgi, 1973.
Caribbean Kill. New York, Pinnacle, 1972; London, Corgi, 1973.
California Hit. New York, Pinnacle, 1972; London, Corgi, 1974.
Boston Blitz. New York, Pinnacle, 1972; London, Corgi, 1974.
Washington IOU. New York, Pinnacle, 1972; London, Corgi, 1974.
San Diego Siege. New York, Pinnacle, 1972; London, Corgi, 1974.
Panic in Philly. New York, Pinnacle, 1973; London, Corgi, 1975.
Jersey Guns. New York, Pinnacle, 1974; London, Corgi, 1975.
Texas Storm. New York, Pinnacle, 1974; London, Corgi, 1975.
Detroit Deathwatch. New York, Pinnacle, 1974; London, Corgi, 1976.
New Orleans Knockout. New York, Pinnacle, 1974; London, Corgi, 1976.
Firebase Seattle. New York, Pinnacle, 1975; London, Corgi, 1976.
Hawaiian Hellground. New York, Pinnacle, 1975; London, Corgi, 1976.
St. Louis Showdown. New York, Pinnacle, 1975; London, Corgi, 1977.

Canadian Crisis. New York, Pinnacle, 1975; London, Corgi, 1977.

Colorado Kill-Zone. New York, Pinnacle, 1976; London, Corgi, 1977.

Acapulco Rampage. New York, Pinnacle, 1976; London, Corgi, 1977.

Dixie Convoy. New York, Pinnacle, 1976; London, Corgi, 1978.

Savage Fire. New York, Pinnacle, 1977; London, Corgi, 1978.

Command Strike, with Mike Newton and Stephen Mertz. New York, Pinnacle, 1977; London, Corgi, 1978.

Cleveland Pipeline, with Mike Newton and Stephen Mertz. Los Angeles, Pinnacle, 1977; London, Corgi, 1978.

Arizona Ambush, with Mike Newton. Los Angeles, Pinnacle, 1977; London, Corgi, 1979.

Tennessee Smash, with Mike Newton. Los Angeles, Pinnacle, 1978; London, Corgi, 1979.

Monday's Mob. Los Angeles, Pinnacle, 1978; London, Corgi, 1979.

Terrible Tuesday. Los Angeles, Pinnacle, 1979; London, Corgi, 1980.

Wednesday's Wrath. Los Angeles, Pinnacle, 1979; London, Corgi, 1980.

Thermal Thursday. Los Angeles, Pinnacle, 1979; London, Corgi, 1980.

Friday's Feast. Los Angeles, Pinnacle, 1979; London, Corgi, 1980.

Satan's Sabbath. Los Angeles, Pinnacle, 1980; London, Corgi, 1981.

Guerilla Games, with Gar Wilson. Toronto, Worldwide, 1982.

Argentina Scramble, with Gar Wilson. Toronto, Worldwide, 1982.

Argentina Deadline, with Gar Wilson. Toronto, Worldwide, 1982.

The Hostage Island, with Dick Stivers. Toronto, Worldwide, 1982.

Tower of Terror, with Dick Stivers. Toronto, Worldwide, 1982.

Ashes to Ashes. New York, Popular Library, 1986.

Copp for Hire. New York, Fine, 1987.

Copp on Fire. New York, Fine, 1988.

Copp in Deep. New York, Fine, 1989.

Haitian Hit. New York, Gold Eagle, 1989.

Copp in the Dark. New York, Fine, 1990.

Uncollected Short Story

"Willing to Kill," in *The Great American Detective,* edited by William Kittredge and Steven M. Krauzer. New York, New American Library, 1978.

OTHER PUBLICATIONS

Novels

Revolt. New York, Pinnacle, 1968; revised edition, as *Civil War II,* New York, Pinnacle, 1971.

The Olympians. San Diego, Greenleaf, 1969.

Cataclysm. New York, Pinnacle, 1969.

The Guns of Terra 10. New York, Pinnacle, 1970.

1989: Population Doomsday. New York, Pinnacle, 1970.

The Godmakers (as Dan Britain). New York, Pinnacle, 1970.

Novels as Stephan Gregory

Frame Up. Fresno, California, Vega, 1960.

All the Trimmings. New York, Tower, 1966.

The Huntress. New York, Pinnacle, 1966.

Color Her Adultress. North Hollywood, Brandon, 1967.

The Insatiables. New York, Pinnacle, 1967.

The Sex Goddess. New York, Pinnacle, 1967.

Madame Murder. Las Vegas, Neva, 1967.

The Sexy Saints. San Diego, PEC, 1967.

The Hot One. San Diego, PEC, 1967.

All Lovers Accepted. San Diego, Greenleaf, 1968.

Short Stories

All Heart. Lakemont, Georgia, Orion, 1968.

The Day God Appeared. Lakemont, Georgia, Orion, 1968.

Play

Screenplay: *The Executioner,* 1980.

Verse

The Search. Lakemont, Georgia, CSA Press, 1967.

The Place. Lakemont, Georgia, CSA Press, 1967.

Other as Stephan Gregory

How to Achieve Sexual Ecstasy. Los Angeles, Sherbourne Press, 1968; London, Running Man Press, 1969.

The Sexually Insatiable Female. Los Angeles, Sherbourne Press, 1968.

Hypnosis and the Sexual Life. San Diego, Greenleaf, 1968.

Religion and the Sexual Life. San Diego, Greenleaf, 1968.

Society and the Sexual Life. San Diego, Greenleaf, 1968.

Sex and the Supernatural, San Diego, Greenleaf, 1968.

ESP and the Sex Mystique. San Diego, Greenleaf, 1968.

Dialogues on Human Sexuality. San Diego, Greenleaf, 1968.

Secret Sex Desires. San Diego, Greenleaf, 1968.

The Sexuality Gap. San Diego, Greenleaf, 1968.

Hypnosis and the Free Female. San Diego, Greenleaf, 1969.

Other as Don Pendleton

The Truth about Sex. San Diego, Greenleaf, 1969.

The Executioner's War Book. New York, Pinnacle, 1977.

*

Manuscript Collection: Lilly Library, Indiana University, Bloomington.

Don Pendleton comments:

I am a "mystery writer" only by the broadest of definitions—and only, I fear, because there is no more acceptable genre of fiction under which my Executioner novels may travel. By the same sense and reasoning, I am a "romance writer" (*The Huntress,* etc.), a "SciFi writer" (*The Godmakers,* etc.), a "sex writer" (*The Truth About Sex,* etc.), a "metaphysical writer" (CSA Press and Orion Magazine), and a "futurist" (*Cataclysm,* etc.). Put all that together and what you have is a guy with no formal training as a writer, working entirely at the gut level within no particular genre, who blindly struck it lucky and thereafter found himself being shaped by forces beyond his direction and control. And although the Executioner series is far and away my most "significant" contribution to world literature, I still do not perceive myself as "belonging" to any particular literary niche. I am simply a storyteller, an entertainer who hopes to enthrall with visions of the reader's own incipient greatness. But go ahead: call me a mystery writer; I am proud to wear the label.

*   *   *

When a new paperback publishing house named Pinnacle released Don Pendleton's *The Executioner: War Against the Mafia* as its first book in 1969, a new genre was born: men's action-adventure novels starring a vigilante hero. At about the same time, Mario Puzo's *The Godfather* was a bestseller and the reading public's hunger for books about the Mafia and organized crime was growing. The Executioner series was the perfect vehicle to capitalize on this emerging market.

Pendleton's creation of Mack Bolan, a soldier who was a guerrilla warfare specialist and sniper in Vietnam, was inspired by the frustrations of the Vietnam War overseas and the lack of success of "the war on crime" on the home front. Bolan returns home to the funeral of his parents and sister and learns they were killed by the Mafia. He then launches a one-man war on organized crime, battling the Mafia from city to city—and more recently, international terrorists—for over 200 books in the continuing Executioner series and several spin-off series like Able Team and Phoenix Force.

Pendleton's Mack Bolan lives for revenge. Although Bolan has a couple of girlfriends in the series, they seldom live very long. Their deaths only serve to feed Bolan's lust for vengeance against the Mafia and fuel his city to city war of destruction.

This vengeance is strongest in *Detroit Deathwatch, Miami Massacre, Chicago Wipe-Out,* and *California Hit* which are little more than a series of graphically violent scenes held together by Bolan's need to avenge the deaths of his family. Bolan is a single-minded killing machine bent on destruction. It's this extremely focused, impossible objective of destroying the Mafia that proved so attractive to the millions of readers who related to Bolan's incredible quest for book after book.

Pendleton put his hero in an ambiguous situation: a vigilante operating outside the law—in fact, hunted by the very law enforcement agencies who were so impotent against the Mafia. Bolan finds himself constantly surrounded by enemies: the Mafia—and the forces of law and order Bolan is fighting his private war to preserve.

It was only with *Boston Blitz*, that Pendleton expands Bolan's character from being a mere killing machine to a man with some depth. The Mafia has kidnapped Bolan's only surviving family member: his brother Johnny. The plan is to trap Bolan once and for all. But Bolan has some surprises of his own and the violent confrontation at the book's conclusion sets the record for carnage in the series.

Pendleton also concentrated on arming Bolan for his war: Bolan's early armaments of handguns and sniper rifles were expanded with military-style rockets, anti-tank ordnance, and automatic weapons. Bolan's personal firearm—his legendary AutoMag—is a .44 Automatic Magnum, the world's most powerful handgun.

In 1973, Pendleton and Pinnacle fought over the financial aspects of the best-selling Executioner series. Pinnacle had *Sicilian Slaughter,* the sixteenth novel in the series, written by "Jim Peterson," a pseudonym of William Crawford. The book lacked Pendleton's intensity. In 1975, Pinnacle settled with Pendleton, who continued to write the series although the author was clearly tiring of his creation.

Pendleton decided to take his character into a new direction. Bolan is offered a position as head of a governmental counter-terrorist unit and a full pardon for his illegal activities in damaging organized crime. But first, Pendleton gets Bolan a six-day grace period to wipe out the remaining strongholds of the Mafia. Called "the last mile," this six book sequence starting with *Monday's Mob,* and continuing daily with *Terrible Tuesday, Wednesday's Wrath, Thermal Thursday,* and *Friday's Feast* to the final book, *Satan's Sabbath,* is clearly the high point of the Mack Bolan series. These are the last Mack Bolan books Pendleton would write.

Problems with Pinnacle surfaced again in 1981. Pendleton sued to get control of the series and a year later he won his lawsuit. Pendleton moved the series to Gold Eagle books—part of the Harlequin publishing company. In 1982, *The New War* appeared—it and all subsequent volumes in the series concentrating on international terrorism were ghostwritten by a stable of writers. Now the books in the "Mack Bolan" series appear without mention of Don Pendleton's name and without the Mafia connection that first created the genre.

In 1986, Pendleton introduced another paperback series featuring Ashton Ford, a former spy who turned adventurer who has psychic powers. *Ashes to Ashes,* the first book in the series, brings Ford together with a woman who wants Ford to cure her sexual problems. But Ford discovers his client is haunted by a spirit who has the power to kill. The novel is a mismash of clumsy writing and heavy-handed plotting. The Ashton Ford series failed to find an audience and was canceled.

Pendleton claims the writer who most influenced his style is Mickey Spillane. In fact, prior to his success with the Executioner series, Pendleton wrote hard-boiled private eye novels in the Mike Hammer style under the pseudonym of "Stephan Gregory."

Pendleton has come full circle: his latest series about private eye Joe Copp—Pendleton's first hardcover series—features a tough-as-nails character who investigates murders in Hollywood. Pendleton's writing style in these books is wooden and clumsy and Joe Copp doesn't have the charisma of Mack Bolan. Especially in *Copp for Hire,* Pendleton's razor-thin plot is held together by a string of fistfights and shootouts. The cardboard characters serve only as vehicles to set the stage for the next round of violent acts. The Copp series will probably have the short life-span of the Ashton Ford series.

Pendleton's fame will rest on the creation of Mack Bolan and the genre of men's action-adventure novels.

—George Kelley

————

PENTECOST, Hugh. Pseudonym for Judson (Pentecost) Philips; also writes as Philip Owen. American. Born in Northfield, Massachusetts, 10 August 1903. Educated in London; Mohegan Lake Military Academy; Columbia University, New York, A.B. 1925. Married Norma Burton in 1951; one son; one daughter and two sons by a former marriage. Sports reporter for New York *Tribune* while in high school; contributor to pulps and slicks in 1940's and 1950's. Co-owner and editor, Harlem Valley *Times,* 1949–56; founder and producer, Sharon Playhouse, Connecticut, 1950–77; political columnist and book reviewer, Lakeville *Journal;* radio talk show host, WTOR, Terrington, Connecticut, 1970–76. Past President, Mystery Writers of America. Recipient: Mystery Writers of America Grand Master Award, 1973; Nero Wolfe Award, 1982. *Died 7 March 1989.*

CRIME PUBLICATIONS

Novels (series: Luke Bradley; Pierre Chambrun; George Crowder; John Jericho; Lieutenant Pascal; Julian Quist; Grant Simon; Dr. John Smith)

Cancelled in Red (Bradley). New York, Dodd Mead, and London, Heinemann, 1939.
The 24th Horse (Bradley). New York, Dodd Mead, 1940; London, Hale, 1951.
I'll Sing at Your Funeral (Bradley). New York, Dodd Mead, 1942; London, Hale, 1945.
The Brass Chills (Bradley). New York, Dodd Mead, 1943; London, Hale, 1944.
Cat and Mouse. New York, Royce, 1945.
The Dead Man's Tale. New York, Royce, 1945.
Memory of Murder (novelets). New York, Ziff Davis, 1947.
Where the Snow Was Red (Smith). New York, Dodd Mead, 1949; London, Hale, 1951.
Shadow of Madness (Smith). New York, Dodd Mead, 1950.
Chinese Nightmare. New York, Dell, 1951.
Lieutenant Pascal's Tastes in Homicide. New York, Dodd Mead, 1954; London, Boardman, 1955.
The Assassins. New York, Dodd Mead, 1955.
The Obituary Club (Simon). New York, Dodd Mead, 1958; London, Boardman, 1959.
The Lonely Target (Simon). New York, Dodd Mead, 1959; London, Boardman, 1960.
The Kingdom of Death. New York, Dodd Mead, 1960; London, Boardman, 1961.
The Deadly Friend. New York, Dodd Mead, 1961; London, Boardman, 1962.
Choice of Violence (Crowder). New York, Dodd Mead, 1961; London, Boardman, 1962.
The Cannibal Who Overate (Chambrun). New York, Dodd Mead, 1962; London, Boardman, 1963.
The Tarnished Angel. New York, Dodd Mead, and London, Boardman, 1963.
Only the Rich Die Young (Pascal). New York, Dodd Mead, and London, Boardman, 1964.
The Shape of Fear (Chambrun). New York, Dodd Mead, and London, Boardman, 1964.
Sniper (Jericho). New York, Dodd Mead, 1965; London, Boardman, 1966.
The Evil That Men Do (Chambrun). New York, Dodd Mead, and London, Boardman, 1966.
Hide Her from Every Eye (Jericho). New York, Dodd Mead, and London, Boardman, 1966.
The Creeping Hours (Jericho). New York, Dodd Mead, 1966; London, Boardman, 1967.
Dead Woman of the Year (Jericho). New York, Dodd Mead, 1967; London, Macdonald, 1968.
The Golden Trap (Chambrun). New York, Dodd Mead, 1967; London, Macdonald, 1968.
The Gilded Nightmare (Chambrun). New York, Dodd Mead, 1968; London, Gollancz, 1969.
Girl Watcher's Funeral (Chambrun). New York, Dodd Mead, 1969; London, Gollancz, 1970.
The Girl with Six Fingers (Jericho). New York, Dodd Mead, 1969; London, Gollancz, 1970.
A Plague of Violence (Jericho). New York, Dodd Mead, 1970; London, Hale, 1972.
The Deadly Joke (Chambrun). New York, Dodd Mead, 1971; London, Hale, 1972.

Don't Drop Dead Tomorrow (Quist). New York, Dodd Mead, 1971; London, Hale, 1973.
The Champagne Killer (Quist). New York, Dodd Mead, 1972; London, Hale, 1974.
Birthday, Deathday (Chambrun). New York, Dodd Mead, 1972; London, Hale, 1975.
The Beautiful Dead (Quist). New York, Dodd Mead, 1973; London, Hale, 1975.
Walking Dead Man (Chambrun). New York, Dodd Mead, 1973; London, Hale, 1975.
Bargain with Death (Chambrun). New York, Dodd Mead, 1974; London, Hale, 1976.
The Judas Freak (Quist). New York, Dodd Mead, 1974; London, Hale, 1976.
Time of Terror (Chambrun). New York, Dodd Mead, 1975.
Honeymoon with Death (Quist). New York, Dodd Mead, 1975; London, Hale, 1976.
Die after Dark. New York, Dodd Mead, 1976; London, Hale, 1977.
The Fourteen Dilemma (Chambrun). New York, Dodd Mead, 1976; London, Hale, 1977.
The Day the Children Vanished. New York, Pocket Books, 1976; London, Hale, 1977.
The Steel Palace (Quist). New York, Dodd Mead, 1977; London, Hale, 1978.
Murder as Usual. New York, Dodd Mead, 1977; London, Hale, 1978.
Death after Breakfast (Chambrun). New York, Dodd Mead, 1978; London, Hale, 1979.
Deadly Trap (Quist). New York, Dodd Mead, 1978; London, Hale, 1979.
Random Killer (Chambrun). New York, Dodd Mead, 1979.
The Homicidal Horse (Quist). New York, Dodd Mead, 1979.
Mystery at a Country Inn (as Philip Owen). Pittsfield, Massachusetts, Berkshire, 1979; London, Hale, 1981.
Beware Young Lovers (Chambrun). New York, Dodd Mead, 1980; London, Hale, 1981.
Death Mask (Quist). New York, Dodd Mead, 1980; London, Hale, 1981.
Murder in Luxury (Chambrun). New York, Dodd Mead, and London, Hale, 1981.
Sow Death, Reap Death (Quist). New York, Dodd Mead, 1981; London, Hale, 1982.
With Intent to Kill (Chambrun). New York, Dodd Mead, 1982; London, Hale, 1983.
Past, Present, and Murder (Quist). New York, Dodd Mead, 1982; London, Hale, 1983.
Murder in High Places (Chambrun). New York, Dodd Mead, and London, Hale, 1983.
The Copycat Killers (Crowder). New York, Dodd Mead, 1983; London, Hale, 1984.
Murder Out of Wedlock (Quist). New York, Dodd Mead, 1983; London, Hale, 1984.
Remember to Kill Me (Chambrun). New York, Dodd Mead, 1984; London, Hale, 1985.
The Price of Silence. New York, Dodd Mead, 1984.
The Substitute Victim (Quist). New York, Dodd Mead, 1984; London, Hale, 1986.
Murder Sweet and Sour (Crowder). New York, Dodd Mead, 1985.
The Party Killer (Quist). New York, Dodd Mead, 1985; London, Hale, 1987.
Nightmare Time (Chambrun). New York, Dodd Mead, 1986; London, Hale, 1987.
Death by Fire (Crowder). New York, Dodd Mead, 1986.
Kill and Kill Again (Quist). New York, Dodd Mead, 1987; London, Hale, 1988.

Murder Goes Round and Round (Chambrun). New York, Dodd Mead, 1988; London, Hale, 1989.
Pattern for Terror. New York, Carroll and Graf, 1990.

Novels as Judson Philips (series: Coyle and Donovan; Peter Styles; Carole Trevor and Max Blythe)

Red War, with Thomas M. Johnson. New York, Doubleday, 1936.
The Death Syndicate (Trevor and Blythe). New York, Washburn, 1938; London, Hurst and Blackett, 1939.
Death Delivers a Postcard (Trevor and Blythe). New York, Washburn, 1939; London, Hurst and Blackett, 1940.
Murder in Marble. New York, Dodd Mead, 1940; London, Hale, 1950.
Odds on the Hot Seat (Coyle and Donovan). New York, Dodd Mead, 1941; London, Hale, 1946.
The Fourteenth Trump (Coyle and Donovan). New York, Dodd Mead, 1942; London, Hale, 1951.
Killer on the Catwalk. New York, Dodd Mead, 1959; London, Gollancz, 1960.
Whisper Town. New York, Dodd Mead, 1960; London, Gollancz, 1961.
Murder Clear, Track Fast. New York, Dodd Mead, 1961; London, Gollancz, 1962.
A Dead Ending. New York, Dodd Mead, 1962; London, Gollancz, 1963.
The Dead Can't Love. New York, Dodd Mead, and London, Gollancz, 1963.
The Laughter Trap (Styles). New York, Dodd Mead, 1964; London, Gollancz, 1965.
The Black Glass City (Styles). New York, Dodd Mead, and London, Gollancz, 1965.
The Twisted People (Styles). New York, Dodd Mead, and London, Gollancz, 1965.
The Wings of Madness (Styles). New York, Dodd Mead, 1966; London, Gollancz, 1967.
Thursday's Folly (Styles). New York, Dodd Mead, 1967; London, Gollancz, 1968.
Hot Summer Killing (Styles). New York, Dodd Mead, 1968; London, Gollancz, 1969.
Nightmare at Dawn (Styles). New York, Dodd Mead, 1970; London, Gollancz, 1971.
Escape a Killer (Styles). New York, Dodd Mead, 1971; London, Gollancz, 1972.
The Vanishing Senator (Styles). New York, Dodd Mead, 1972; London, Gollancz, 1973.
The Larkspur Conspiracy (Styles). New York, Dodd Mead, 1973; London, Gollancz, 1974.
The Power Killers (Styles). New York, Dodd Mead, 1974; London, Gollancz, 1975.
Walk a Crooked Mile (Styles). New York, Dodd Mead, 1975; London, Gollancz, 1976.
Backlash (Styles). New York, Dodd Mead, 1976; London, Gollancz, 1977.
Five Roads to Death (Styles). New York, Dodd Mead, 1977; London, Gollancz, 1978.
A Murder Arranged (Styles). New York, Dodd Mead, 1978; London, Gollancz, 1979.
Why Murder (Styles). New York, Dodd Mead, 1979; London, Hale, 1980.
Death Is a Dirty Trick (Styles). New York, Dodd Mead, 1980; London, Hale, 1981.
Death as the Curtain Rises (Styles). New York, Dodd Mead, 1981.
Target for Tragedy (Styles). New York, Dodd Mead, 1982; London, Hale, 1983.

Short Stories

Secret Corridors. New York, Century, 1945.
Death Wears a Copper Necktie and Other Stories. London, Edwards, 1946.
Around Dark Corners. New York, Dodd Mead, 1970.
Murder Round the Clock: Pierre Chambrun's Crime File. New York, Dodd Mead, 1985.

Uncollected Short Stories

"The Day the Children Vanished," in *Best Detective Stories of the Year,* edited by David C. Cooke. New York, Dutton, 1959.
"Pierre Chambrun and the Last Fling," in *Ellery Queen's Mystery Magazine* (New York), September 1971.
"Jericho and the Dead Clue," in *Ellery Queen's Mystery Magazine* (New York), December 1971.
"Pierre Chambrun Defends Himself," in *Ellery Queen's Mystery Magazine* (New York), November 1972.
"Jericho and the Two Ways to Die," in *Ellery Queen's Crookbook.* New York, Random House, 1974.
"Blood-Red in the Morning," in *Ellery Queen's Masters of Mystery.* New York, Davis, 1975.
"The Dark Plan," in *Ellery Queen's Mystery Magazine* (New York), February 1976.
"The Dark Gambit," in *Ellery Queen's Mystery Magazine* (New York), March 1976.
"The Dark Encounter," in *Ellery Queen's Mystery Magazine* (New York), April 1976.
"The Dark Maneuver," in *Ellery Queen's Mystery Magazine* (New York), August 1976.
"Jericho on Campus," in *Ellery Queen's Mystery Magazine* (New York), October 1976.
"The Dark Intuition," in *Ellery Queen's Mystery Magazine* (New York), December 1976.
"Chambrun and the Matter of Inches," in *Ellery Queen's Mystery Magazine* (New York), February 1977.
"The Show Must Go On," in *Ellery Queen's Mystery Magazine* (New York), July 1977.
"The Dark Gamble: End of the Trail," in *Ellery Queen's Mystery Magazine* (New York), October 1977.
"Jericho and the Unknown Lover," in *Ellery Queen's Searches and Seizures.* New York, Davis, 1977.
"Chambrun Plays It Cool," and "Jericho Plays It Cool," in *Ellery Queen's Who's Who of Whodunits.* New York, Davis, 1977.
"Chambrun Corrects an Imperfection," in *Ellery Queen's Mystery Magazine* (New York), October 1978.
"Jericho and the Deadly Errand," in *Ellery Queen's Masters of Mystery.* New York, Davis, 1978.
"Jericho and the Million-to-One Clue," in *Ellery Queen's Mystery Magazine* (New York), February 1979.
"The Man Who Stirred Champagne," in *Ellery Queen's Mystery Magazine* (New York), September 1979.
"The Dark Saga," in *Ellery Queen's Doors to Mystery.* New York, Davis, 1981.
"The Long Cry for Help," in *Ellery Queen's Eyes of Mystery.* New York, Davis, 1981.
"Pierre Chambrun's Dilemma," in *Ellery Queen's Mystery Magazine* (New York), 1 January 1981.
"Key Witness," in *Ellery Queen's Mystery Magazine* (New York), 22 April 1981.
"Paid in Full," in *Ellery Queen's Mystery Magazine* (New York), 4 November 1981.
"The Birthday Killer," in *Ellery Queen's Eyewitnesses.* New York, Davis, 1982.

"Chambrun Gets the Message," in *Ellery Queen's Mystery Magazine* (New York), 24 February 1982.

"Act of Violence," in *Ellery Queen's Mystery Magazine* (New York), Mid-July 1982.

"Bitter Secret," in *Ellery Queen's Mystery Magazine* (New York), October 1982.

"A Bad Influence," in *Ellery Queen's Mystery Magazine* (New York), April 1983.

"The Critical Time" (as Judson Philips), in *Ellery Queen's Mystery Magazine* (New York), February 1984.

"Chambrun and the 422 Names," in *Ellery Queen's Mystery Magazine* (New York), August 1984.

OTHER PUBLICATIONS

Plays

Lonely Boy (produced Sharon, Connecticut, 1954).
The Lame Duck Party (produced Sharon, Connecticut, 1977).

Radio Plays: *Suspense; Father Brown; The Whisper Men.*

Television Plays: *The Web; The Ray Milland Show; Studio One; Hallmark Hall of Fame.*

Other

Hold 'em Girls: The Intelligent Woman's Guide to Men and Football, with Robert W. Wood, Jr. New York, Putnam, 1936.

"The Short Story," in *How I Write,* with Robert Hayden and Lawson Carter. New York, Harcourt Brace, 1972.

Editor, *Cream of the Crime.* New York, Holt Rinehart, 1962; London, Harrap, 1964.

*

Hugh Pentecost commented (1984):

I suppose, after you have written more than a hundred mystery and suspense novels and hundreds of short stories, the most frequently asked question is, "Where do you get your plots?" It has been said that there are only 36 dramatic situations, only about half of which are not too raunchy to use. Those usable situations have been used by me and hundreds of other writers over and over again. The only variation any writer has is the people he writes about. There are endless variations in people. I once used to claim a deduction on my income tax for "saloon talk," explaining in a note that people were the source of my income and that I had to go where they were and listen to them. The IRS approved but insisted that I call it "research." The name of the game is people, and they are endlessly rewarding, never uninteresting, and where everything begins and ends.

* * *

"Professional" is a word critics often apply to Judson Pentecost Philips, whose writing career lasted over 60 years. It began in 1925 when, still a junior at Columbia University, he sold "Room Number Twenty-Three," a locked room mystery, his very first story, to *Flynn's.* He became a steady contributor to many magazines and even outlasted two markets for his work, "pulps" like *Blask Mask* and the "slicks," e.g., *Collier's.* Philips remained a contributor to the leading digest-sized magazine, *Ellery Queen's Mystery Magazine,* until his death.

By 1936 Philips turned to novels, showing the same narrative ability and sense of pace he had displayed in shorter fiction. This work demonstrated authenticity of subject matter and locale, evidence of his careful research and first-hand knowledge. Stamp collecting in *Cancelled in Red,* the Madison Square Garden Horse Show in *The 24th Horse,* and a submarine base in *The Brass Chills* were among the backgrounds he used effectively.

A long-time resident of Connecticut, Philips often described unusual New England settings, including a livestock auction in "The Talking Calf," a suburban development terrorized by a feral pack in "The Case of the Killer Dogs," and a town preparing for a hurricane in "In the Middle of Nowhere." He ran the Sharon Summer Playhouse and used this experience in "Murder in C Minor," reprinted as "The Show Must Go On," and *Murder Out of Wedlock,* in which the expense of financing a Broadway musical is important to the plot.

Philips created many series detectives, with the early ones tending to be bland. Luke Bradley is soft-spoken, and psychiatrist John Smith is as difficult to remember as his name. He was described as "a little gray man with a flat voice and a quiet unobtrusive manner." Lieutenant Pascal is casual and good-natured, even willing to apologize to a suspect to make his interrogation easier.

Later detectives are far more colorful, often larger-than-life. John Jericho was a painter whose stature (6'6" and 240 pounds), flaming red beard, and Viking-like appearance made him stand out. Julian Quist, head of one of New York's leading public relations firms, is blond and handsome, with "a profile that might have been carved on an ancient Greek coin." Though George Crowder was not unusual in appearance, his past history was distinctive. He was a Connecticut prosecutor with a brilliant political future, but he gave it all up when he found he had unknowingly sent an innocent man to the electric chair.

The most popular Pentecost sleuth, Pierre Chambrun, was a hero of the French Resistance during World War II who became manager of New York's luxurious Hotel Beaumont. Columnist Peter Styles not only lost his leg in an accident caused by a driver on drugs, but he later lost his wife who was killed by terrorists. Jason Dark lost his hand when he was tortured to stop his investigations.

What all recent Pentecost-Philips heroes have in common is a hatred, approaching obsession, for crime, violence, and terrorism. Dark crusaded against Quadrant International, the corporation responsible for his maiming as well as much of the world's crime. Though living in Greenwich village, Jericho travels throughout the world, painting "pictures of violence," while fighting terrorists. Peter Styles *wrote* about terror, having become a "crusader against senseless violence, a disease of the times." In *Hot Summer Killing,* one of the earliest and best mysteries to deal with terrorism, he battles against militants who threaten to destroy Grand Central Station during rush hour if their demands are not met.

Those of his heroes who did not travel to confront crime found it sought them out. They or those they loved were often kidnapped or held hostage. Crowder and his nephew Joey were kidnapped from a small town drug store in "In the Middle of Nowhere." In a posthumous Pentecost novel, *Pattern for Terror,* Joey is kidnapped to prevent Uncle George from investigating drug dealers who have invaded their small Connecticut town. Joey's relationship with Crowder, his "Uncle Sherlock," is only one example of the perceptive way Philips wrote about children and schools. Others are the novel, *Sniper,* and the short stories "Lonely Boy," "The Lame Duck House Party," and "A Kind of Murder."

Located near the United Nations' headquarters, Chambrun's Beaumont is a favorite hotel for world leaders and, thus, a prime target for terrorists. In *Remember to Kill Me,* in the confusion of an urban riot, terrorists seize four V.I.P's as hostages, demanding the release of a Central American political prisoner. First an Army officer who once saved Chambrun's life is kidnapped in *Nightmare Time,* and then the person closest to Chambrun, his secretary and lover, Betsy Ruysdale, is abducted.

Ruysdale combines the attributes of the two women closest to Julian Quist, his "perfect" secretary, Connie Parmalee, and Lydia Morton, his lover and the top researcher and writer for his business. In *Kill and Kill Again* Lydia is kidnapped to halt Quist's investigation of a munitions plant which sells "the tools of war and terror."

The ability of Chambrun and Quist to function effectively as crime-fighters depended on their having loyal teams of assistants. They constitute brain trusts which, in the case of Quist, "could anticipate what he wanted before he'd thought of it himself." These groups follow a pattern Philips established during his pulp days in a series about the Park Avenue Hunt Club, a secret organization formed for the purpose of capturing criminals: "In the underworld the very mention of Hunt Club brought fear in its wake."

Though many of his early mysteries depend upon clues and ratiocination for their resolution, in later years Philips usually posed the puzzle of how his heroes will rescue victims without cooperating with terrorists. Some of these "solutions" are very inventive, however. He also increasingly likened his characters to motion picture actors, though this was not entirely new. As far back as in the 1934 novelet "The Hawk Returns," the leading member of the Park Avenue Hunt Club, Geoffrey Saville, was described as looking "strikingly like Ronald Colman, the picture star." In recent examples of description by celebrity recognition, Chambrun is always described as looking like Claude Rains, and Quist's partner, Bobby Hilliard, is called a James Stewart look-alike.

Philips had occasionally used current news in his fiction but increased this tendency in the 1950's when he wrote short stories and a novel, *The Kingdom of Death,* about crime and corruption on New York's waterfront. A 1965 short story, "Jericho and the Silent Witnesses," was clearly derived from the case of Kitty Genovese of Queens, New York, a young woman murdered while 38 witnesses did nothing. The riot in *Remember to Kill Me* echoed the violence after a 1983 Diana Ross concert in Central Park. Sometimes, using current events can make a story seem prematurely dated, as in "Jericho and the à Go-Go Clue."

On one occasion newspaper headlines *followed* a Pentecost story. A Chowchilla, California schoolbus was hijacked in July 1976, and the F.B.I. was advised by a reader that Pentecost's short story, "The Day the Children Vanished," is about the disappearance of a school bus on its run between two small towns. When the California children were recovered, there was no evidence the kidnappers were aware of the story. Still, a publisher capitalized on the publicity value of this apparent example of life following art by having Pentecost expand his intriguing story into a novel. It was appropriate recognition for a writer whose outstanding work had sometimes been hidden behind his reliability and prolificity as the author of hundreds of short stories and more than a hundred novels.

—Marvin Lachman

———

PEROWNE, Barry. Pseudonym for Philip Atkey; also wrote as Pat Merriman. British. Born in Redlynch, Wiltshire, 25 June 1908. Educated at Central School, Oxford. Served in the Wiltshire Regiment of the British Army, 1940–43, and the Intelligence Corps, 1943–45: mentioned in despatches. Married Marjorie Florence Atkey in 1932 (divorced 1946); one daughter. Worked for a manufacturer of carnival equipment, and as a secretary to Bertram Atkey, 1922–25; assistant editor, George Newnes Ltd., publishers, London, 1925–27. *Died 24 December 1985.*

CRIME PUBLICATIONS

Novels (series: A.J. Raffles)

Arrest These Men! London, Cassell, 1932.
Enemy of Women. London, Cassell, 1934.
Ladies in Retreat. London, Cassell, 1935.
She Married Raffles. London, Cassell, 1936.
Raffles' Crime in Gibraltar. London, Amalgamated Press, 1937; as *They Hang Them in Gibraltar,* New York, Curl, 1939.
Raffles vs. Sexton Blake. London, Amalgamated Press, 1937.
Ask No Mercy. London, Cassell, 1937.
I'm No Murderer. London, Cassell, 1938; New York, Curl, 1939.
The Girl on Zero. London, Cassell, 1939.
The A.R.P. Mystery (Raffles). London, Amalgamated Press, 1939.
The Whispering Cracksman. London, Cassell, 1940; as *Ten Words of Poison,* New York, Arcadia House, 1941.
Blonde Without Escort. London, Cassell, 1940.
Raffles and the Key Man. Philadelphia, Lippincott, 1940.
Gibraltar Prisoner. London, Cassell, 1942; as *All Exits Blocked,* New York, Arcadia House, 1942.
The Tilted Moon. London, Cassell, 1949; as *Rogues' Island,* New York, Mill, 1950.
A Singular Conspiracy. Indianapolis, Bobbs Merrill, 1974.

Novels as Philip Atkey

Blue Water Murder. London, Cassell, 1935.
Heirs of Merlin. London, Cassell, 1945.
Juniper Rock. London, Cassell, 1953.

Short Stories (series character: A.J. Raffles)

Raffles after Dark. London, Cassell, 1933; revised edition, as *The Return of Raffles,* New York, Day, 1933.
Raffles in Pursuit. London, Cassell, 1934.
Raffles under Sentence. London, Cassell, 1936.
Raffles Revisited. New York, Harper, 1974; London, Hamish Hamilton, 1975.
Raffles of the Albany. London, Hamish Hamilton, and New York, St. Martin's Press, 1976.
Raffles of the M.C.C. New York, St. Martin's Press, and London, Macmillan, 1979.

OTHER PUBLICATIONS

Novel

Night Call (as Pat Merriman). London, Hutchinson, 1939.

Plays

Screenplay: *Walk a Crooked Path,* 1970.

Radio Plays: *Rescue from the Rock,* 1970; *Edgar and Charles,* 1970.

* * *

Although Barry Perowne has written other mystery novels, his reputation as a crime writer will probably be based ultimately on his revival, in a series of magazine stories and novels, of the character of Raffles, the celebrated turn-of-the-century Gentleman Crook. The original Raffles, as created by E.W. Hornung in *The Amateur Cracksman* (1899), is a gentleman and sportsman (a champion cricketer—"the finest slow bowler of his decade") who is also an expert burglar, a second calling which he takes to with all the ardor of the sportsman and the passion of the artist. In fact, in talking of the perfectly executed burglary, Hornung's Raffles evokes (and actually alludes to) the fin-de-siècle concern with art for art's sake. But he also steals in order to keep himself and his cohort Bunny Manders in elegant style at London's Albany and the various gentlemen's clubs which they frequent.

Perowne's Raffles is a changed man. While the ardor of the sportsman remains, it is tempered significantly by the addition of socially redeeming features: he still steals, but never simply for gain or thrills; his thefts are now motivated by desire to aid others. An aristocratic family fallen on hard times, a damsel in distress, an old friend unjustly menaced—in these cases and many like them, Raffles and Bunny put criminal skills to work for a higher purpose. Perowne has laundered his Raffles, made him more socially acceptable (and sentimentally romantic) than his morally ambiguous predecessor. But if Perowne's Raffles has something less of the fascination of the pure criminal, this deficiency is made up for in stories that are exciting, exotic, and frequently more richly evocative of the gaslit era of the 1890's than Hornung's originals.

—Frank Occhiogrosso

PERRY, Anne. British. Born in London, 28 October 1938. Privately educated. Has had a variety of jobs including airline stewardess, 1962–64; assistant buyer, Newcastle upon Tyne, 1964–66; property underwriter, Muldoon and Adams, Los Angeles. Lived in California, 1967–72. Agent: Meg Davis, MBA Literary Agency Ltd., 45 Fitzroy Street, London W1P 5HR, England. Address: 1 Seafield, Portmahomack, Ross-shire IY20 1YB, Scotland.

CRIME PUBLICATIONS

Novels (series: Charlotte and Thomas Pitt in all books)

The Cater Street Hangman. New York, St. Martin's Press, and London, Hale, 1979.
Callander Square. New York, St. Martin's Press, and London, Hale, 1980.
Paragon Walk. New York, St. Martin's Press, 1981.
Resurrection Row. New York, St. Martin's Press, 1981.
Rutland Place. New York, St. Martin's Press, 1983.
Bluegate Fields. New York, St. Martin's Press, 1984.
Death in the Devil's Acre. New York, St. Martin's Press, 1985.

Cardington Crescent. New York, St. Martin's Press, 1987; London, Souvenir Press, 1990.
Silence in Hanover Close. New York, St. Martin's Press, 1988; London, Souvenir Press, 1989.
Bethlehem Road. New York, St. Martin's Press, 1990.
Face of a Stranger. New York, Fawcett, 1990.

Uncollected Short Story

"Digby's First Case," in *Alfred Hitchcock's Mystery Magazine* (New York), February 1988.

*

Manuscript Collection: Mugar Memorial Library, Boston University.

Anne Perry comments:
I see mysteries as stories of what happens to people and communities under the pressure of fear and suspicion, especially the violent changes in perceptions and relationships brought about by investigation.
I enjoy the Victorian period because of its dramatic contrast between upstairs and downstairs, manners, morals, the splendour and squalor so close to each other, the value of reputation. There are so many understandable motives for crime, social ills, injustices, many of which are with us today, albeit in transmuted form. And I think long gowns, fog, hansom cabs, etc., the necessity of extraordinary manners, double standards etc. are fun! I hope my stories reflect expressions, emotion, social comment—and enjoyment.

* * *

Class differences and gender roles, the contrast and tensions between the working classes and the gentry, the wealthy, middle class, and very poor, servants and masters, women and men, color the Victorian London milieu in which Anne Perry places her engaging cast of characters. The nine novels follow in chronological sequence, centered on Charlotte Pitt, a woman of genteel upbringing who has married "below herself," and her husband, Inspector Thomas Pitt of the London police.

The Pitts are surrounded by a varied cast who reappear from one book to another, sometimes in major, sometimes in minor roles. The most important of these is Charlotte's younger sister Emily, who has married upward in society just as Charlotte has moved downward. Together the sisters pursue criminal investigations where Inspector Pitt cannot—in the drawing rooms of fashionable London. Their investigations shadow and parallel Pitt's, and often proceed without his knowledge or approval. This framework provides Perry with a realistic means of presenting a broader range of locations and characters than she could with a single detective.

The chronology allows characters to develop as they reappear from book to book, and provides continuity as the reader follows developments in their personal lives as well as events which further the plots. Thus one watches the Pitts adjust to marriage, produce children, move into larger quarters and acquire a maid. This is in contrast to, and in occasional conflict with, the more privileged lives of those among whom Charlotte and Emily pursue their investigations, and indeed of Emily herself. The relationship between Charlotte and Emily, with their vastly different lifestyles and shared interests, is wonderfully depicted. The books are generously sprinkled with the everyday concerns of 19th-century women's lives, from society gossip to household management and (in Charlotte's case) careful financial planning.

These are not light-hearted romps through Victorian rose gardens, however. Perry's interest lies in showing how individuals in a restrictive society with rigid notions of status and propriety may respond to pressures to conform, and how society in turn protects its interests in the face of deviation or rebellion. Nor are they for the ethically squeamish. Many of the deviations Perry examines are sexual in nature (this is Victorian England, after all) and, while not explicit in her descriptions, she handles such themes straightforwardly. Perry maintains a fine balance throughout, neither romanticizing nor condemning out of hand. Her depiction of Victorian London is rich and consistent in period detail. Her characters have depth and complexity, especially in the later books, and even the worst of them are generally presented with compassion. What is more, they never come across as moderns in a period play, but are firmly rooted in their own time and place.

If there is a drawback to Perry's fiction, it is its restriction to a narrow arena, with the result that a suspiciously large number of crimes plague a rather small number of people. Perry does her best to transcend such limitations, but her plots do tend to a certain sameness—Pitt's investigations, thwarted by considerations of class, are augmented by Charlotte and Emily's sleuthing, generally under some sort of false pretense. One wonders just how many lambs Perry can threaten to sacrifice for society's good, how many varieties of deviant behavior she can catalog, how many murders her fashionable little world can withstand. Still, her Victorian London is a lively and fascinating place, and her characters keep the reader coming back for more. Once hooked, one waits for each new volume as for a visit from old friends who call too infrequently.

Given Perry's stable cast and strict adherence to chronology, it is probably best to start with the first book in the series, *The Cater Street Hangman*. Here most of the ongoing characters are introduced and the basic framework set, including Pitt and Charlotte's courtship. *Cater Street* also sets the pattern for future plots, and gives the reader a good idea of what to expect. The quality of the subsequent books varies somewhat, but it is a fairly safe bet that the reader who enjoys the first will like the rest as well. Perry's portrayal of London is consistently fine, and her characters become deeper and more intriguing with each new adventure. Aside from *The Cater Street Hangman*, which is a good introduction, her best works are: *Cardington Crescent*, in which the theme of the outsider sacrificed for the good of the clan is particularly well handled when Emily is accused of her husband's murder; *Bluegate Fields*, an absorbing venture into the world of the Victorian lower classes and the ways in which the rich exploit the poor; and *Rutland Place*, with its insights into the kinds and degrees of rebellion against society, and their dangers. Also of particular interest are *Silence in Hanover Close*, which is about the isolation of widowhood and features the newly-widowed Emily masquerading as a lady's maid; and *Resurrection Row*, in which the murder of a blackmailing painter is masked by a series of peripatetic corpses.

—Helga Borck and GraceAnne A. DeCandido

———

PERRY, Ritchie (John Allen). Also writes as John Allen. British. Born in King's Lynn, Norfolk, 7 January 1942. Educated at King Edward VII School, King's Lynn; St. John's College, Oxford, B.A. (honours) in history 1964. Married Lynn Mary Charlotte Barton in 1976; two daughters. Trainee manager, Bank of London and South America, Brazil, 1964– 66; teacher, Docking, Norfolk, 1966, King's Lynn, 1967, Nottingham, 1967, and Ingoldisthorpe, Norfolk, 1967–74. Since 1975 teacher for the Bedfordshire County Council, Luton. Agent: Peters Fraser and Dunlop, 5th Floor, The Chambers, Chelsea Harbour, Lots Road, London, SW10 0XF, England.

CRIME PUBLICATIONS

Novels (series: MacAllister; Philis in all books except *MacAllister* and *Presumed Dead*)

The Fall Guy. London, Collins, and Boston, Houghton Mifflin, 1972.
Nowhere Man. London, Collins, 1973; as *A Hard Man to Kill*, Boston, Houghton Mifflin, 1973.
Ticket to Ride. London, Collins, 1973; Boston, Houghton Mifflin, 1974.
Holiday with a Vengeance. London, Collins, 1974; Boston, Houghton Mifflin, 1975.
Your Money and Your Wife. London, Collins, 1975; Boston, Houghton Mifflin, 1976.
One Good Death Deserves Another. London, Collins, 1976; Boston, Houghton Mifflin, 1977.
Dead End. London, Collins, 1977.
Dutch Courage. London, Collins, 1978; New York, Ballantine, 1982.
Bishop's Pawn. London, Collins, and New York, Pantheon, 1979.
Grand Slam. London, Collins, and New York, Pantheon, 1980.
Fool's Mate. London, Collins, and New York, Pantheon, 1981.
Foul Up. New York, Doubleday, 1982; London, Hale, 1985.
MacAllister. New York, Doubleday, 1984; London, Hale, 1986.
Kolwezi. New York, Doubleday, 1985; London, Hale, 1986.
Presumed Dead (MacAllister). New York, Doubleday, 1987.
The Creepy Tale. London, Hutchinson, 1989.

OTHER PUBLICATIONS

Novels as John Allen

Copacabana Stud. London, Hale, 1977.
Up Tight. London, Hale, 1979.

Other

Brazil: The Land and Its People. London, Macdonald, 1977; Morristown, New Jersey, Silver Burdett, 1978.
George H. Ghastly (for children). London, Hutchinson, 1981.
George H. Ghastly to the Rescue (for children). London, Hutchinson, 1981.
George H. Ghastly and the Little Horror (for children). London, Hutchinson, 1985.
Fenella Fang (for children). London, Hutchinson, 1986.
Fenella Fang and the Wicked Witch (for children). London, Hutchinson, 1989.

*

Manuscript Collection: Mugar Memorial Library, Boston University.

Ritchie Perry comments:

There was never any stage in my childhood or adolescence when my ambition was to become an author. None of my teachers ever said, "Young Perry has the fires of creative genius burning inside him." To the best of my knowledge nobody has said it since. As with most things in my life, I drifted into writing. The local library could no longer provide me with the dozen or so books I needed each week and it occurred to me that I ought to be able to produce fiction of my own. As such my books are self-indulgences, designed as much to entertain me as any potential readers. A shocking admission, but there it is. If I knew how one of my books was going to finish before I started on it, the book would never be typed out. It would bore me as much as it would to read a work by another author when I knew how the story was going to end. I suspect this may be one of the strengths of my stories—it must be very difficult for a reader to guess how a book will finish when the author isn't sure himself.

* * *

Ritchie Perry's best work is his Philis series. *The Fall Guy* introduces Philis, a small-time smuggler in Brazil. But a secret British Intelligence agency SR(2), headed by the enigmatic Pawson, decide to use Philis to smash an international drug-smuggling operation. Philis uses his luck and toughness to pull off the impossible operation.

In the second book of the series, *Nowhere Man,* Philis has been recruited as a fully-fledged agent of SR(2) but he remains a cynical, selfish character with little loyalty to Britain. Pawson assigns Philis to find and eliminate Schnellinger, a freelance agent who has left the free market to sell out completely to the CIA. Philis finds himself working with the KGB to find Schnellinger while the Israelis and Americans form the competition. This is the kind of underhanded spy novel that would make James Bond blanch.

Ticket to Ride features Philis masquerading as a private detective bodyguarding Catherine Zaferelli, a woman sought by the Mafia. To muddy the waters, Philis becomes a pawn between the FBI and the Mafia while Pawson plays his Machiavellian games in this nicely plotted thriller.

Holiday With a Vengeance opens with Philis trying to enjoy a vacation in the Caribbean. But when the British consul is kidnapped, Philis finds himself at the heart of the guerrilla movement about to topple the government.

With *Your Money and Your Wife,* Perry changes the pacing of the Philis series. The earlier books were face-paced and written in a droll style satirizing the notion that being a spy was glamorous. In this transitional book in the series, Philis and his new wife are enjoying their honeymoon when KGB agents kidnap Philis's wife and plunges Philis into a deadly game in which only the KGB enjoys all the advantages. The mood is darker and Perry starts exploring more substantial themes.

One Good Death Deserves Another brings Philis back to Brazil. But an assassin hired by a neo-Nazi group mistakenly assumes Philis is in Brazil to stop him and takes measures to eliminate Philis. They fail, but Philis is enraged by the assassination attempt and sets off on the assassin's trail. The South American manhunt which follows ends in a nifty duel of savage power.

Dutch Courage is set in Europe. Philis is trying to take the vacation he's been cheated out of the last couple of books. But vacations and Philis don't mix as Philis finds himself hunted by Israeli intelligence agents, the PLO, and a terrorist group called

the Hashishi who control a vast heroin pipeline. This is the most action-packed novel in the entire Philis series.

Bishop's Pawn is the cleverest of Philis's adventures. Pawson wants Philis to smuggle a defecting Polish Roman Catholic bishop out of East Germany. But the mission is complicated by the fact that the bishop turns out to have secretly been a mass murderer and war criminal in World War II. With that plotline and the hidden treasure looted from Italy during the German occupation, Philis has his hands full with this mission.

In *Grand Slam,* Philis gets to play private detective again. When the daughter of a powerful oil millionaire disappears, Pawson tricks Philis into investigating. The trail leads to a fanatic religious cult now operating in England. This is the most violent book of the series.

Fool's Mate was cited as one of the best books of 1981 by the *New York Times Book Review.* Pawson arranges a new cover for Philis: a mercenary. A very powerful English industrialist hires Philis to escort a mysterious woman across Europe—the woman has a fear of flying. The woman turns out to be the former dictator Idi Amin's mistress. And she holds the secret to a fortune in rubies. Rival groups try to stop Philis and his beautiful companion as they race across Europe leaving dead bodies in their wake.

Foul Up opens with Philis in the middle of a carefully organized "people's revolution" on a Caribbean island. Using a computer, Pawson and Philis discover a major increase in the number of carefully staged uprisings—too many for mere chance. The computer narrows the choices of suspects to one: SecAdCo., a security company charging large fees to protect companies and government installations. Now, it seems, they might actually be running a training school for terrorists. Philis is assigned the job of infiltrating the organization. This leads to an attempt on his life and a wild trip to Brussels where the KGB gets involved.

Perry's latest creation is a series featuring private detective Frank MacAllister. In the best book of the series, *Presumed Dead,* MacAllister is hired by a powerful Brazilian figure, Silvio Pinhal, to find his missing son. Eight months have passed since the disappearance and all the other Brazilian detectives Pinhal hired failed to find his son, Alvamir. MacAllister takes the case and is shot at by a sniper, encounters voodoo rituals, and discovers cocaine and slave trade smugglers operating in the Amazon. Furious action is the hallmark of the MacAllister series.

—George Kelley

———

PETERS, Bill. *See* **McGIVERN, William P.**

———

PETERS, Elizabeth. Pseudonym for Barbara (Louise) G(ross) Mertz: also writes as Barbara Michaels. American. Born in Canton, Illinois, 29 September 1927. Educated at the University of Chicago Oriental Institute, Ph.B. 1947, M.A. 1950, Ph.D. 1952. Married Richard R. Mertz in 1950 (divorced 1968); one daughter and one son. Agent: Dominick Abel, 146 West 82nd Avenue, New York, New York 10024, U.S.A.

CRIME PUBLICATIONS

Novels (series: Vicky Bliss; Amelia Peabody Emerson; Jacqueline Kirby)

The Jackal's Head. New York, Meredith, 1968; London, Jenkins, 1969.
The Camelot Caper. New York, Meredith, 1969; London, Cassell, 1976.
The Dead Sea Cipher. New York, Dodd Mead, 1970; London, Cassell, 1975.
The Night of Four Hundred Rabbits. New York, Dodd Mead, 1971; as *Shadows in the Moonlight,* London, Coronet, 1975.
The Seventh Sinner (Kirby). New York, Dodd Mead, 1972; London, Coronet, 1975.
Borrower of the Night (Bliss). New York, Dodd Mead, 1973; London, Cassell, 1974.
The Murders of Richard III (Kirby). New York, Dodd Mead, 1974; London, Piatkus, 1989.
Crocodile on the Sandbank (Emerson). New York, Dodd Mead, 1975; London, Cassell, 1976.
Legend in Green Velvet. New York, Dodd Mead, 1976; as *Ghost in Green Velvet,* London, Cassell, 1977.
Devil-May-Care. New York, Dodd Mead, 1977; London, Cassell, 1978.
Street of the Five Moons (Bliss). New York, Dodd Mead, 1978; London, Piatkus, 1988.
Summer of the Dragon. New York, Dodd Mead, 1979; London, Souvenir Press, 1980.
The Love Talker. New York, Dodd Mead, 1980; London, Souvenir Press, 1981.
The Curse of the Pharaohs (Emerson). New York, Dodd Mead, 1981; London, Souvenir Press, 1982.
The Copenhagen Connection. New York, Congdon and Lattès, 1982; London, Souvenir Press, 1983.
Silhouette in Scarlet (Bliss). New York, Congdon and Weed, 1983; London, Souvenir Press, 1984.
Die for Love (Kirby). New York, Congdon and Weed, 1984; London, Souvenir Press, 1985.
The Mummy Case (Emerson). New York, Congdon and Weed, 1985; London, Souvenir Press, 1986.
Lion in the Valley (Emerson). New York, Atheneum, 1986; London, Piatkus, 1987.
Trojan Gold (Bliss). New York, Atheneum, and London, Piatkus, 1987.
The Deeds of the Disturber (Emerson). New York, Atheneum, and London, Piatkus, 1988.
Naked Once More (Kirby). New York, Warner, 1989; London, Piatkus, 1990.

Novels as Barbara Michaels

The Master of Blacktower. New York, Appleton Century Crofts, 1966; London, Jenkins, 1967.
Sons of the Wolf. New York, Meredith, 1967; London, Jenkins, 1968; as *Mystery on the Moors,* New York, Paperback Library, 1968.
Ammie, Come Home. New York, Meredith, 1968; London, Jenkins, 1969.
Prince of Darkness. New York, Meredith, 1969; London, Hodder and Stoughton, 1971.
The Dark on the Other Side. New York, Dodd Mead, 1970; London, Souvenir Press, 1973.
Greygallows. New York, Dodd Mead, 1972; London, Souvenir Press, 1974.
The Crying Child. New York, Dodd Mead, and London, Souvenir Press, 1973.

Witch. New York, Dodd Mead, 1973; London, Souvenir Press, 1975.
House of Many Shadows. New York, Dodd Mead, 1974; London, Souvenir Press, 1976.
The Sea King's Daughter. New York, Dodd Mead, 1975; London, Souvenir Press, 1977.
Patriot's Dream. New York, Dodd Mead, 1976; London, Souvenir Press, 1978.
Wings of the Falcon. New York, Dodd Mead, 1977; London, Souvenir Press, 1979.
Wait for What Will Come. New York, Dodd Mead, 1978; London, Souvenir Press, 1980.
The Walker in Shadows. New York, Dodd Mead 1979; London, Souvenir Press, 1981.
The Wizard's Daughter. New York, Dodd Mead, 1980; London, Souvenir Press, 1982.
Someone in the House. New York, Dodd Mead, 1981; London, Souvenir Press, 1983.
Black Rainbow. New York, Congdon and Weed, 1982; London, Souvenir Press, 1983.
Here I Stay. New York, Congdon and Weed, 1983; London, Souvenir Press, 1985.
Dark Duet. New York, Congdon and Weed, 1983.
The Grey Beginning. New York, Congdon and Weed, 1984; London, Souvenir, 1986.
Be Buried in the Rain. New York, Atheneum, 1985; London, Piatkus, 1986.
Shattered Silk. New York, Atheneum, 1986; London, Piatkus, 1987.
Search the Shadows. New York, Atheneum, 1987; London, Piatkus, 1988.
Smoke and Mirrors. New York, Simon and Schuster, and London, Piatkus, 1989.
Into the Darkness. New York, Simon and Schuster, 1990.

Uncollected Short Stories

"The Locked Tomb Mystery," in *Sisters in Crime,* edited by Marilyn Wallace. New York, Berkley, 1989; London, Robinson, 1990.
"The Runaway" (as Barbara Michaels), in *Sisters in Crime,* edited by Marilyn Wallace. New York, Berkley, 1989; London, Robinson, 1990.

OTHER PUBLICATIONS

Other as Barbara G. Mertz

Temples, Tombs, and Hieroglyphs: The Story of Egyptology. New York, Coward McCann, and London, Gollancz, 1964; revised edition, New York, Dodd Mead, 1978.
Red Land, Black Land: The World of the Ancient Egyptians. New York, Coward McCann, 1966; London, Hodder and Stoughton, 1967; revised edition, New York, Dodd Mead, 1978.
Two Thousand Years in Rome, with Richard Mertz. New York, Coward McCann, 1968; London, Dent, 1969.

*

Manuscript Collections: Mugar Memorial Library, Boston University; University of Wyoming, Laramie.

Elizabeth Peters comments:
    Under my own name, I write popular non-fiction on Egyptology. Under two pseudonyms I write what are (in the United States) usually referred to as "gothics." I prefer the term "romantic suspense stories." "Barbara Michaels" concentrates

on historical suspense and on novels with a supernatural atmosphere; "Elizabeth Peters" prefers modern settings, often with archaeological backgrounds, and she is much more frivolous in her approach than is Michaels—in fact, she is sometimes rather giddy. Having been trained in historical research I try to make my books as accurate as possible, and I believe that precise, accurate detail is necessary in order to create an impression of authenticity.

*   *   *

Elizabeth Peters is a pseudonym for Barbara Mertz, an extraordinarily prolific writer who also publishes fiction as Barbara Michaels. Her Elizabeth Peters novels earn frequent praise from critics; *Naked Once More* won the award for best mystery novel of 1989 from the organization Malice Domestic, composed of both readers and writers of mystery fiction. An academically trained Egyptologist, the author regularly draws upon her knowledge and experience in archaeology and art history in constructing her plots. Peters's female protagonists are intelligent, strong, and intrepid. Never overtly feminist, all are nevertheless independent women who relate to men from a position of equality and respect. Most of her novels feature one of three recurring heroines: Dr. Victoria Bliss, Jacqueline Kirby, or Amelia Peabody.

Vicky Bliss, an American art historian, frequently finds herself on the trail of art thieves or smugglers. Self-reliant and intellectual, she describes herself in *Borrower of the Night* as having an "IQ as formidable as my height. ... If there is anything worse than being a tall girl, it is being a tall *smart* girl." Vicky insists she will never marry, but she is joined on many of her adventures by a scapegrace art thief who calls himself Sir John Smythe. Smythe drifts in and out of her life in such novels as *Trojan Gold, Street of the Five Moons,* and *Silhouette in Scarlet.* Vicky alternates between fury about his high-handed treatment of her and affectionate amusement at his antics. Although she is probably in love with him despite herself, his profession bars her from growing serious about him. The Vicky Bliss novels are usually set in exotic European locations such as Germany, where she works in a museum, Italy, or Sweden.

Jacqueline Kirby is a middle-aged American librarian who carries everything a sleuth could ever need in her capacious handbag. In *The Murders of Richard III* (Peters's homage to Josephine Tey's *Daughter of Time*), Kirby finds herself at an English country-house party in which all the guests act the parts of members of Richard III's court. As the villain attacks his victims, he uses methods that mimic the way the historical personages died. In *The Seventh Sinner,* Jacqueline solves a mystery set in Rome after a young scholar is murdered in the catacombs. In *Naked Once More,* Kirby—now a successful writer of romance novels—signs a contract to write a sequel for a blockbuster novel whose author has disappeared. Featuring characters named St. John Darcy and Hawkescliffe, the novel spoofs many of the conventions of romance fiction.

Amelia Peabody is Peters's most unusual creation. The Peabody stories are set in the Victorian era, in Britain or Egypt. Amelia and her husband Radcliff Emerson are archaeologists bent on saving the treasures of Egypt from the depredations of vandals and grave robbers. Their precocious son "Ramses" is featured in some novels. In *Crocodile on the Sandbank,* Peabody and Emerson—they refer to each other by their surnames even after their marriage—meet in Egypt where Emerson is excavating and Peabody is traveling with a female companion. The group is shadowed by someone who dresses up like a mummy to frighten them. *The Deeds of the Disturber,* set in London, features a murderer who disguises himself as an ancient Egyptian priest. Other Amelia Peabody novels include *Lion in the Valley* and *The Curse of the Pharaohs.*

Some Peters novels feature heroines that do not recur in other books. In *Legend in Green Velvet,* an American archaeologist flees from pursuers in the Scottish Highlands after she is suspected, along with the hero, of having murdered a man in Edinburgh. In *The Night of Four Hundred Rabbits,* the heroine travels to Mexico to search for her father.

All of Peters's novels exhibit a tone of humor and wit, particularly in the Vicky Bliss and Amelia Peabody books written in the first person. Often, her mysteries appear to mock the conventions of gothic or domestic mysteries without quite becoming full-blown parodies of the form. Despite her prolific output—more than 40 novels—Peters' work is fresh, engaging, and thoroughly professional.

—Kay Mussell

———

PETERS, Ellis. Pseudonym for Edith (Mary) Pargeter. Has also written as Peter Benedict; Jolyon Carr; John Redfern. British. Born in Horsehay, Shropshire, 28 September 1913. Educated at Dawley Church of England Elementary School, Shropshire; Coalbrookdale High School for Girls, Oxford School Certificate. Served in the Women's Royal Navy Service, 1940–45: British Empire Medal, 1944. Worked as a chemist's assistant, Dawley, 1933–40. Recipient: Mystery Writers of America Edgar Allan Poe award, 1963; Czechoslovak Society for International Relations Gold Medal, 1968; Crime Writers Association Silver Dagger award, 1981. Fellow, International Institute of Arts and Letters, 1961. Agent: Deborah Owen, 78 Narrow Street, London E14 8BP.

CRIME PUBLICATIONS

Novels (series: Brother Cadfael; members of the Felse family—Inspector George Felse, Bunty Felse, Dominic Felse)

The Victim Needs a Nurse (as John Redfern). London, Jarrolds, 1940.
Fallen into the Pit (Felse; as Edith Pargeter). London, Heinemann, 1951.
Death Mask. London, Collins, 1959; New York, Doubleday, 1960.
The Will and the Deed. London, Collins, 1960; as *Where There's a Will,* New York, Doubleday, 1960.
Death and the Joyful Woman (Felse). London, Collins, 1961; New York, Doubleday, 1962.
Funeral of Figaro. London, Collins, 1962; New York, Morrow, 1964.
Flight of a Witch (Felse). London, Collins, 1964.
A Nice Derangement of Epitaphs (Felse). London, Collins, 1965; as *Who Lies Here?,* New York, Morrow, 1965.
The Piper on the Mountain (Felse). London, Collins, and New York, Morrow, 1966.
Black Is the Colour of My True-Love's Heart (Felse). London, Collins, and New York, Morrow, 1967.
The Grass-Widow's Tale (Felse). London, Collins, and New York, Morrow, 1968.
The House of Green Turf (Felse). London, Collins, and New York, Morrow, 1969.
Mourning Raga (Felse). London, Macmillan, 1969; New York, Morrow, 1970.

The Knocker on Death's Door (Felse). London, Macmillan, 1970; New York, Morrow, 1971.

Death to the Landlords! (Felse). London, Macmillan, and New York, Morrow, 1972.

City of Gold and Shadows (Felse). London, Macmillan, 1973; New York, Morrow, 1974.

The Horn of Roland. London, Macmillan, and New York, Morrow, 1974.

Never Pick Up Hitch-Hikers! London, Macmillan, and New York, Morrow, 1976.

A Morbid Taste for Bones: A Mediaeval Whodunnit (Cadfael). London, Macmillan, 1977; New York, Morrow, 1978.

Rainbow's End (Felse). London, Macmillan, 1978; New York, Morrow, 1979.

One Corpse Too Many (Cadfael). London, Macmillan, 1979; New York, Morrow, 1980.

Monk's-Hood (Cadfael). London, Macmillan, 1980; New York, Morrow, 1981.

Saint Peter's Fair (Cadfael). London, Macmillan, and New York, Morrow, 1981.

The Leper of Saint Giles (Cadfael). London, Macmillan, 1981; New York, Morrow, 1982.

The Virgin in the Ice (Cadfael). London, Macmillan, 1982; New York, Morrow, 1983.

The Sanctuary Sparrow (Cadfael). London, Macmillan, and New York, Morrow, 1983.

The Devil's Novice (Cadfael). London, Macmillan, 1983; New York, Morrow, 1984.

Dead Man's Ransom (Cadfael). London, Macmillan, and New York, Morrow, 1984.

The Pilgrim of Hate (Cadfael). London, Macmillan, and New York, Morrow, 1984.

An Excellent Mystery (Cadfael). London, Macmillan, 1985; New York, Morrow, 1986.

The Raven in the Foregate (Cadfael). London, Macmillan, and New York, Morrow, 1986.

The Rose Rent (Cadfael). London, Macmillan, and New York, Morrow, 1986.

The Hermit of Eyton Forest (Cadfael). London, Headline, 1987; New York, Mysterious Press, 1988.

The Confession of Brother Haluin (Cadfael). London, Headline, 1988; New York, Mysterious Press, 1989.

The Heretic's Apprentice (Cadfael). London, Headline, 1989.

The Potter's Field (Cadfael). London, Headline, 1989.

Novels as Jolyon Carr

Murder in the Dispensary. London, Jenkins, 1938.
Death Comes by Post. London, Jenkins, 1940.

Short Stories

The Assize of the Dying (as Edith Pargeter). London, Heinemann, and New York, Doubleday, 1958.

A Rare Benedictine. London, Headline, 1988; New York, Mysterious Press, 1989.

Uncollected Short Stories as Ellis Peters

"The Chestnut Calf," in *This Week* (New York), December 1963.

"With Regrets," in *This Week* (New York), May 1965.

"Golden Girl," in *Alfred Hitchcock Presents: Stories Not for the Nervous.* New York, Random House, 1965; as "O Gold, O Girl!" (as Edith Pargeter), in *Argosy* (New York), January 1965.

"Villa for Sale," in *This Week* (New York), December 1965.

"A Grain of Mustard Seed," in *This Week* (New York), January 1966.

"Guide to Doom," in *Alfred Hitchcock Presents: Stories That Scared Even Me.* New York, Random House, 1967.

"Maiden Garland," in *Winter's Crimes 1,* edited by George Hardinge. London, Macmillan, and New York, St. Martin's Press, 1969.

"The Trinity Cat," in *Winter's Crimes 8,* edited by Hilary Watson. London, Macmillan, and New York, St. Martin's Press, 1976.

"Come to Dust," in *Winter's Crimes 16,* edited by Hilary Hale. London, Macmillan, 1984; New York, St. Martin's Press, 1985.

"Let Nothing You Dismay!," in *Winter's Crimes 21,* edited by Hilary Hale. London, Macmillan, 1989.

Uncollected Short Stories as Edith Pargeter

"The Face of Wax," in *Good Housekeeping* (London), December 1936.

"Change of Heart," in *Argosy* (New York), January 1959.

"Starcrossed," in *Argosy* (New York), April 1964.

"The Light Boy," in *Argosy* (New York), October 1964.

"Hostile Witness," in *Argosy* (New York), May 1965.

OTHER PUBLICATIONS as Edith Pargeter

Novels

Hortensius, Friend of Nero. London, Lovat Dickson, 1936; New York, Greystone Press, 1937.

Iron-Bound. London, Lovat Dickson, 1936.

Day Star (as Peter Benedict). London, Lovat Dickson, 1937.

The City Lies Foursquare. London, Heinemann, and New York, Reynal, 1939.

Freedom For Two (as Jolyon Carr). London, Jenkins, 1939.

Masters of the Parachute Mail (as Jolyon Carr). London, Jenkins, 1940.

Ordinary People. London, Heinemann, 1941; as *People of My Own,* New York, Reynal, 1942.

She Goes to War. London, Heinemann, 1942.

The Eighth Champion of Christendom. London, Heinemann, 1945.

Reluctant Odyssey. London, Heinemann, 1946.

Warfare Accomplished. London, Heinemann, 1947.

The Fair Young Phoenix. London, Heinemann, 1948.

By Firelight. London, Heinemann, 1948; as *By This Strange Fire,* New York, Reynal, 1948.

Lost Children. London, Heinemann, 1951.

Holiday with Violence. London, Heinemann, 1952.

This Rough Magic. London, Heinemann, 1953.

Most Loving Mere Folly. London, Heinemann, 1953.

The Soldier at the Door. London, Heinemann, 1954.

A Means of Grace. London, Heinemann, 1956.

The Heaven Tree. London, Heinemann, and New York, Doubleday, 1960.

The Green Branch. London, Heinemann, 1962.

The Scarlet Seed. London, Heinemann, 1963.

A Bloody Field by Shrewsbury. London, Macmillan, 1972; New York, Viking Press, 1973.

Sunrise in the West. London, Macmillan, 1974.

The Dragon at Noonday. London, Macmillan, 1975.

The Hounds of Sunset. London, Macmillan, 1976.

Afterglow and Nightfall. London, Macmillan, 1977.

The Marriage of Meggotta. London, Macmillan, and New York, Viking Press, 1979.

Short Stories

The Lily Hand and Other Stories. London, Heinemann, 1965.

Other

The Coast of Bohemia. London, Heinemann, 1950.
"The Thriller Is a Novel," in *Techniques of Novel-Writing,* edited by A.S. Burack. Boston, The Writer, 1973.

Translator, *Tales of the Little Quarter: Stories,* by Jan Neruda. London, Heinemann, 1957; New York, Greenwood Press, 1976.
Translator, *The Sorrowful and Heroic Life of John Amos Comenius,* by Frantisek Kosík. Prague, State Educational Publishing House, 1958.
Translator, *A Handful of Linden Leaves: An Anthology of Czech Poetry.* Prague, Artia, 1958.
Translator, *Don Juan,* by Josef Toman. London, Heinemann, and New York, Knopf, 1958.
Translator, *The Abortionists,* by Valja Stýblová. London, Secker and Warburg, 1961.
Translator, *Granny,* by Bozena Nemcová. Prague, Artia, 1962; New York, Greenwood Press, 1976.
Translator, with others, *The Linden Tree* (anthology). Prague, Artia, 1962.
Translator, *The Terezín Requiem,* by Josef Bor. London, Heinemann, and New York, Knopf, 1963.
Translator, *Legends of Old Bohemia,* by Alois Jirásek. London, Hamlyn, 1963.
Translator, *May,* by Karel Hynek Mácha. Prague, Artia, 1965.
Translator, *The End of the Old Times,* by Vladislav Vancura. Prague, Artia, 1965.
Translator, *A Close Watch on the Trains,* by Bohumil Hrabal. London, Cape, 1968.
Translator, *Report on My Husband,* by Josefa Slánská. London, Macmillan, 1969.
Translator, *A Ship Named Hope,* by Ivan Klíma. London, Gollancz, 1970.
Translator, *Mozart in Prague,* by Jaroslav Seifert. Prague, Orbis, 1970.

*

Ellis Peters comments:

I came to the field of the mystery after half a lifetime of novel-writing, and accepted the need to separate it from my previous work only because I discovered, having in the case of one book approached the detective story almost inadvertently, that though I refuse to categorise my books and like doing something different every time, the reading public likes to know just what to expect from an author, and resents being disconcerted. It's not, they said, a bit like your other books! In fact it was not very different, except that it included the act of murder; but I acknowledged, reluctantly, that a pseudonym might after all be more, not less, honest, and that those who wanted only one side of me had a right to some guidance as to where to find it. Naturally I have been influenced myself by the separation, and the categories have crystallised more and more since I began using two names.

But for me the thriller *is a novel.* My attitude to it is summed up in the article I wrote for *The Writer.* The pure puzzle, with a cast of characters kept deliberately two-dimensional and all equally expendable at the end, has no attraction for me. But the paradoxical puzzle, the impossible struggle to create a cast of genuine, rounded, knowable characters caught in conditions of stress, to let readers know everything about them, feel with them, like or dislike them, and still to try to preserve to the end the secret of which of these is a murderer—this is the attraction for me. The better a novel you write, the more you deploy characters realised and developed and consistently true to themselves, the more difficult you have made your own task of keeping the secret to the end. No use offering your readers as murderer a man they have got to know like their own kin, and whom, by that time, they know to be quite incapable of committing that particular crime, in those circumstances, and for that motive. They will rise up in wrath and give you the lie. But if just once you can provide them with a solution which is both startling and yet right and inevitable, the satisfaction is enormous. Does it ever happen? Now and again it may.

Apart from treating my characters with the same respect as in any other form of novel, I have one sacred rule about the thriller. It is, it ought to be, it must be, a morality. If it strays from the side of the angels, provokes total despair, wilfully destroys—without pressing need in the plot—the innocent and the good, takes pleasure in evil, that is unforgivable sin. I use the word deliberately and gravely.

It is probably true that I am not very good at villains. The good interest me so much more.

* * *

It is difficult to reduce a mystery-writing career spanning 40 years to a few paragraphs. Best known in more recent years for her lovingly detailed creation of a 12th-century Benedictine monk and his world, Ellis Peters wrote modern-day thrillers for nearly three decades before she found a way to meld her love of puzzles with her love of history. (And this ignores the several very early mysteries originally serialized in local newspapers, later published in book form under various pseudonyms.)

Peters's first thriller, written under her real name, echoed the sounds of the recently ended war which had occupied several years of her life and a good number of her previous books—and curiously hints at the future soldier-turned-monk Cadfael. "Understand me once and for all," a war hero-turned-teacher tells 13-year-old Dominic Felse and his sparring partner, "fighting is something not to be considered short of a life-and-death matter. . . . It proves nothing, it settles nothing, it solves nothing, except the problem of who has the most brawn and the least of any other qualities." And yet when Dominic finds the body of Peters's most evil villain, one feels that a great deal has been solved.

Peters waited a number of years before attempting another crime novel, this time choosing to separate her "new" writing career from her long-time mainstream one by assuming a pen-name (incidentally, using her much-loved brother's name, Ellis—his picture was later to appear as the cowled Cadfael on the back cover of several U.K. editions). As she would do so often in the future, in *Death Mask* she focused her attention on a young boy, troubled and in trouble. Having witnessed the death of his father in a suspicious accident, he is abruptly removed from his home by a mother he could barely remember; but he still cannot escape the evil intentions of someone who wants something badly enough to kill for it.

By the time of the Edgar-winning *Death and the Joyful Woman,* the returning Dominic is newly 16 and in the full bloom of his first love. Disaster strikes when the object of his affection is implicated in a murder, and perceptive but sometimes plodding George must simultaneously identify a killer and learn how to deal with a boy on the verge of manhood. The workings of the adolescent mind and heart is a theme which recurs in nearly all of her books.

A Nice Derangement of Epitaphs (*Who Lies Here?*), while

technically a Felse novel (the whole family is there, and George does solve a murder), is really the story of a 15-year-old Cornish boy who is about to find his world turned upside-down. In the midst of his turmoil, a hunt for the bones of some scandalous ancestors in the ancestral vault turns up not one, but two skeletons, neither of which was the expected one. In the companion vault there is another horrifying discovery, and the solution of a 200-year-old mystery is wonderfully satisfying. With the choice of a hiding place for the corpses, we once again see a hint of the future (*A Morbid Taste for Bones*).

Meanwhile, ever-unflappable wife and mother Bunty finds herself alone on her 41st birthday. With George in London on a case, and Dominic in Oxford, Bunty hurtles suddenly and headlong into the realization of her mortality and the ultimate definition of love. While on a long trip into the night with her would-be killer, it is early evident where they are headed, but not where they will end up. Essentially a *pas-de-deux* for the first half of the book, this unusual twist on the damsel-in-distress mystery finds Bunty extricating both of them from a very nasty situation.

A somewhat less successful solo adventure is *Mourning Raga*, which finds Dominic in India with his lady and a young girl to be delivered to her father. When they learn that the man has been missing for over a year, they feel obligated for the girl's safety. Peters's love of music and ambivalence towards Indian culture and society creates a most interesting backdrop, but Dominic, though nearly grown, seems less complete without the support of his family.

The little-known *Never Pick Up Hitch-Hikers!* was a departure for Peters in many ways. An immensely likeable young man, seeking to escape an overcontrolling mother, has told her some half-truths as he begins his first experience away from home. Luck (in the form of a bright and spunky young lady one wishes to have seen again) saves him from disaster, only to bring the pair into the vortex of a whirlwind criminal comedy of errors involving a lot of money and a variety of people who are all guilty of something—mostly stupidity and an abundance of blinding greed. More caper than mystery, more high camp than high drama, it was selected by the respected Garland Press as one of the "50 Classics of Crime Fiction 1950–75" and deserves much more notice from her fans.

In 1977 Peters, a life-long fan of the history of her small corner of the world, began thinking about an historical incident involving the translation of the bones of St. Winifred to the abbey in Shrewsbury. What if someone were to use this as an opportunity to hide another body? Who would do such a thing and why? Who would be able to detect such a crime? And so Brother Cadfael was born, a medieval renaissance man who can give Mr. Holmes a run for the money in a contest of the keenest and cleverest eyes. Soldier, sailor, Crusader and lover, come to the cloistered life late and of his own volition, the native Welshman joins a small company of monks going to Wales to secure Winifred's relics. Not quite convinced that the lady really wishes to be moved, he manages to solve a murder and help both the abbey and his countrymen in a delightfully ironic fashion.

Interestingly, Cadfael was not originally conceived of as a series character, and Peters had one further adventure with George Felse (*Rainbow's End*) before she discovered another historical event ripe for detection by a medieval Benedictine monk. In one of the more grisly battles between King Stephen and Empress Maud for the throne of England, 94 prisoners are taken and hung—but when Cadfael is called upon to prepare the bodies for burial he finds *One Corpse Too Many*. Cadfael took hold of his creator then and neither has looked back since.

One of the best entries in the Cadfael chronicles—certainly the most satisfying for those who want to know more about his life before the cowl—is *The Virgin in the Ice*, in which Cadfael's past confronts his present in an agonizingly bittersweet fashion as he seeks to identify the killer of a young nun.

The historically important "A Light on the Road to Woodstock," detailing Cadfael's decision to take the cowl, is included in *A Rare Benedictine*, a collection of three short stories. The other two ("The Price of Light" and "Eye Witness") are slight but charming vignettes of Cadfael, supported by magnificent color illustrations.

While sparing modern sensibilities most of the muck and mire of the 12th century, Peters manages to recreate various pieces of medieval life in each of her books. It isn't until the most recent chronicles, however, that the medieval mindset is put to its fullest use. The rebuttal of a charge of heresy is as important as the solution of a murder in *The Heretic's Apprentice*. The stunning conclusion of *The Potter's Field* is one which the modern mind will find completely incomprehensible, and yet totally justifiable in its context—which is an indication of just how powerful and evocative Peters' writing is.

Peters has always cared more about the people touched by a crime than the crime itself, more about the good than the bad, and most about the innate innocence and intelligence of the young. While there is no real pattern to plotline or setting, there is a commonality of theme that may make the stories sometimes seem a bit formulaic—but formula is not necessarily a bad thing. It is rather like sitting down with an old and much-loved friend—she may not have any news for you, but her very presence makes you feel all warm and good inside. So it is with Peters' mysteries—although you will rarely be kept guessing through the last page, her skilful and seemingly effortless pen paints a positive and basically friendly world which you will leave with a smile.

—Sue Feder

PETIEVICH, Gerald. American. Born in Los Angeles, California, 15 October 1944. Educated at California State University, Los Angeles, B.A. 1966. Served in the United States Army Intelligence Corps, 1967–70: sergeant. Married Pamela Lentz in 1968. Has been associated with the United States Secret Service. Address: c/o Simon and Schuster, 1230 Avenue of the Americas, New York, New York 10020, U.S.A.

CRIME PUBLICATIONS

Novels (series: Charles Carr; Jack Kelly)

Money Men (Carr, Kelly). New York, Pinnacle, 1981.
One Shot Deal (Carr, Kelly). New York, Pinnacle, 1983.
To Die in Beverly Hills (Carr, Kelly). New York, Arbor House, 1983; London, New English Library, 1987.
To Live and Die in L.A. New York, Arbor House, 1984.
The Quality of the Informant (Carr, Kelly). New York, Arbor House, 1985.

Shakedown. New York, Simon and Schuster, 1988; London, Chatto and Windus, 1989.
Earth Angels. New York, New American Library, 1989.

OTHER PUBLICATIONS

Plays

Screenplay: *To Live and Die in L.A.*, with William Friedkin, 1985.

Television Play: *C.A.T. Squad,* 1986.

*   *   *

Gerald Petievich has gained a certain amount of justly deserved praise for a series of novels which focus on the pursuit of professional counterfeiters by agents of the U.S. Treasury Department. It is an area about which Petievich has been able to write with assurance and authority, thanks in no small measure to his own long career as a T-Man.

Over half of his work thus far has detailed the exploits of Charlie Carr and Jack Kelly, a pair of aging, cynical Treasury agents who work out of the Los Angeles field office. Both men are similar to many of the tough, world-weary heroes who populate much of modern crime fiction but they are set apart from other such characters by the absolute single-mindedness and ruthlessness with which they pursue their quarry.

Petievich sees the criminal justice system as hopelessly choked with inept political appointees and double-talk artists who use their connections to rise to the top of law enforcement bureaucracy without any knowledge of crime or crime detection. These political hacks inevitably hobble the working agents with inane rules and regulations which prevent them from solving crimes and somehow work to penalize them even when they do score a victory.

Petievich's description of the fine line that these men must walk in order not to fall into criminal behavior themselves is brutally frank. The ease with which a lawman can slip over the edge into lawlessness is grimly and realistically depicted in Petiveich's best-known novel, *To Live and Die in L.A.*

In Petievich's world, the men who must deal with such an absurd system inevitably become cold-hearted, ruthless, and cruel in order to bring criminals to justice and simultaneously defeat the bureaucrats and liberal judges who would otherwise leave the criminals free to ply their trades.

Petievich is the only modern writer to examine the world of the counterfeiter and he brings a genuine sense of reality to his descriptions of both the art of counterfeiting and the underworld network which enables this crime to flourish. He makes it clear that the people who excel in this particular activity are of above-average intelligence, utterly without scruples, and willing to commit murder to further their own ends. Petievich seems to almost admire these criminal geniuses and the battles of wits he depicts between Charlie Carr and Paul LaMonica (*The Quality of the Informant*) or Travis Bailey (*To Die in Beverly Hills*) often take on the qualities of a chess match.

Petievich's heroes both hate and respect the men on the other side of the law. It is clear that the battle of wits and wills is what makes the game worth playing for Charlie Carr and Petievich's other protagonists. In some unexplainable way, playing the game with commitment and intensity makes it possible to endure in a system hopelessly fouled with nonsensical rules and bureaucratic bungling.

If there is a down side to Petievich's writing, it is in his misogynistic treatment of women. In large measure, he describes the girlfriends of both hero and criminal as crafty, selfish, and shallow. The love scenes he imagines with these women are seldom tender and resemble nothing so much as the brutal, lustful couplings of wild beasts.

The exemplar of this species is Sally Malone, the long-time girlfriend of Charlie Carr. She constantly seeks out his company but just as constantly nags him about his lack of commitment and his insistence on placing his job ahead of personal considerations. While it is true that Carr and Petievich's other protagonists are unable to discuss their fears or their motivations with their women, Petievich does not fault them for this. Rather he seems to be suggesting that women are essentially childish and therefore incapable of the realization that a law-enforcement career inevitably leads to both a deadening of a man's finer senses and an inability to focus on the ephemera that makes life bearable for women.

Petievich has done well with his work thus far. He has a genuine knack for projecting not only the intensity of the policeman's life but also the loneliness and emotional emptiness that accompanies it. He has successfully blended Elmore Leonard's colorful underworld milieu with Joseph Wambaugh's bleak picture of the cop's personal and professional life. Add to this his detailed picture of counterfeiting and the government's efforts to eliminate it and you have a unique and exciting body of writing which should endure far past Petievich's writing life.

—Robert E. Skinner

————

PETRIE, Rhona. *See* **CURZON, Clare.**

————

PHILIPS, Judson. *See* **PENTECOST, Hugh.**

————

PHILLIPS, Dennis. *See* **CHAMBERS, Peter.**

————

PHILLIPS, James Atlee. *See* **ATLEE, Philip.**

————

PHILLPOTTS, Eden. Also wrote as Harrington Hext. British. Born in Mount Aboo, India, 4 November 1862. Educated at Mannamead School, now Plymouth College. Married 1) Emily Topham in 1892 (died 1928); one son and one daughter; 2) Lucy Robina Webb in 1929. Clerk, Sun Fire Office, London, 1880–90; assistant editor, *Black and White,* London, for several years in the 1890's. Regular contributor to

The Idler, London. Lived in Devon from 1898. *Died 29 December 1960.*

CRIME PUBLICATIONS

Novels (series: Avis Bryden; John Ringrose)

The End of a Life. Bristol, Arrowsmith, 1891.
A Tiger's Cub. Bristol, Arrowsmith, 1892.
Doubloons, with Arnold Bennett. New York, McClure, 1906; as *The Sinews of War,* London, Laurie, 1906.
The Statue, with Arnold Bennett. London, Cassell, and New York, Moffat Yard, 1908.
The Three Knaves. London, Macmillan, 1912.
The Master of Merripit. London, Ward Lock, 1914.
Miser's Money. London, Heinemann, and New York, Macmillan, 1920.
The Grey Room. New York, Macmillan, and London, Hurst and Blackett, 1921.
The Red Redmaynes. New York, Macmillan, 1922; London, Hutchinson, 1923.
A Voice from the Dark (Ringrose). London, Hutchinson, and New York, Macmillan, 1925.
The Marylebone Miser (Ringrose). London, Hutchinson, 1926; as *Jig-Saw,* New York, Macmillan, 1926.
The Jury. London, Hutchinson, and New York, Macmillan, 1927.
"Found Drowned." London, Hutchinson, and New York, Macmillan, 1931.
A Clue from the Stars. London, Hutchinson, and New York, Macmillan, 1932.
Bred in the Bone (Bryden). London, Hutchinson, 1932; New York, Macmillan, 1933.
The Captain's Curio. London, Hutchinson, and New York, Macmillan, 1933.
Mr. Digweed and Mr. Lumb. London, Hutchinson, 1933; New York, Macmillan, 1934.
A Shadow Passes (Bryden). London, Hutchinson, 1933; New York, Macmillan, 1934.
Witch's Cauldron (Bryden). London, Hutchinson, and New York, Macmillan, 1933.
The Wife of Elias. London, Hutchinson, 1935; New York, Dutton, 1937.
Physician, Heal Thyself. London, Hutchinson, 1935; as *The Anniversary Murder,* New York, Dutton, 1936.
The Book of Avis (omnibus). London, Hutchinson, 1936.
A Close Call. London, Hutchinson, and New York, Macmillan, 1936.
Lycanthrope: The Mystery of Sir William Wolf. London, Butterworth, 1937; New York, Macmillan, 1938.
Portrait of a Scoundrel. London, Murray, and New York, Macmillan, 1938.
Monkshood. London, Methuen, and New York, Macmillan, 1939.
Awake Deborah! London, Methuen, 1940; New York, Macmillan, 1941.
A Deed Without a Name. London, Hutchinson, 1941; New York, Macmillan, 1942.
Ghostwater. London, Methuen, and New York, Macmillan, 1941.
Flower of the Gods. London, Hutchinson, 1942; New York, Macmillan, 1943.
They Were Seven. London, Hutchinson, 1944; New York, Macmillan, 1945.
The Changeling. London, Hutchinson, 1944.
There Was an Old Woman. London, Hutchinson, 1947.

Address Unknown. London, Hutchinson, 1949.
Dilemma. London, Hutchinson, 1949.
George and Georgina. London, Hutchinson, 1952.
The Hidden Hand. London, Hutchinson, 1952.
There Was an Old Man. London, Hutchinson, 1959.

Novels as Harrington Hext

Number 87. London, Butterworth, and New York, Macmillan, 1922.
The Thing at Their Heels. London, Butterworth, and New York, Macmillan, 1923.
Who Killed Diana? London, Butterworth, 1924; as *Who Killed Cock Robin?,* New York, Macmillan, 1924.
The Monster. New York, Macmillan, 1925.

Short Stories

My Adventure in the Flying Scotsman: A Romance of London and North-Western Railway Shares. London, Hogg, 1888; edited by Tom Schatz, Boulder, Colorado, Aspen Press, 1975.
Loup-Garou! London, Sands, 1899.
Fancy Free. London, Methuen, 1901.
The Transit of the Red Dragon and Other Tales. Bristol, Arrowsmith, 1903.
The Unlucky Number. London, Newnes, 1906.
Tales of the Tenements. London, Murray, and New York, Lane, 1910.
The Judge's Chair. London, Murray, 1914.
Black, White, and Brindled. London, Richards, and New York, Macmillan, 1923.
Peacock House and Other Mysteries. London, Hutchinson, 1926; New York, Macmillan, 1927; selection, as *The End of Count Rollo and Other Stories,* London, Todd, 1946
It Happened Like That. London, Hutchinson, and New York, Macmillan, 1928.
Once Upon a Time. London, Hutchinson, 1936.

OTHER PUBLICATIONS

Novels

Folly and Fresh Air. London, Trischler, 1891; New York, Harper, 1892; revised edition, London, Hurst and Blackett, 1899.
Some Every-Day Folks. London, Osgood, 3 vols., 1894; New York, Harper, 1895.
A Deal with the Devil. London, Bliss, 1895; New York, Warne, 1901.
Lying Prophets. London, Innes, and New York, Stokes, 1896.
Children of the Mist. London, Innes, 1898; New York, Putnam, 1899.
The Complete Human Boy. London, Hutchinson, 1930.
  The Human Boy. London, Methuen, 1899; New York, Harper, 1900.
  The Human Boy Again. London, Chapman and Hall, 1908.
  From the Angle of Seventeen. London, Murray, 1912; Boston, Little Brown, 1914.
  The Human Boy and the War. London, Methuen, and New York, Macmillan, 1916.
  The Human Boy's Diary. London, Heinemann, and New York, Macmillan, 1924.
Sons of Morning. London, Methuen, and New York, Putnam, 1900.
The Good Red Earth. Bristol, Arrowsmith, and New York, Doubleday, 1901; as *Johnny Fortnight,* Arrowsmith, 1904; revised edition, Arrowsmith, 1920.

The River. London, Methuen, and New York, Stokes, 1902.

The Golden Fetich. London, Harper, and New York, Dodd Mead, 1903.

The American Prisoner. New York, Macmillan, 1903; London, Methuen, 1904.

The Farm of the Dagger. London, Newnes, and New York, Dodd Mead, 1904.

The Secret Woman. London, Methuen, and New York, Macmillan, 1905.

The Portreeve. London, Methuen, and New York, Macmillan, 1906.

The Poacher's Wife. London, Methuen, 1906; as *Daniel Sweetland,* New York, Authors and Newspapers Association, 1906.

The Virgin in Judgment. New York, Reynolds, 1907; London, Cassell, 1908; abridged edition, as *A Fight to the Finish,* Cassell, 1911.

The Whirlwind. London, Chapman and Hall, and New York, McClure, 1907.

The Mother. London, Ward Lock, 1908; as *The Mother of the Man,* New York, Dodd Mead, 1908.

The Three Brothers. London, Hutchinson, and New York, Macmillan, 1909.

The Haven. London, Murray, and New York, Lane, 1909.

The Thief of Virtue. London, Murray, and New York, Lane, 1910.

The Flint Heart: A Fairy Story. London, Smith Elder, and New York, Dutton, 1910; revised edition, London, Chapman and Dodd, 1922.

Demeter's Daughter. London, Methuen, and New York, Lane, 1911.

The Beacon. London, Unwin, and New York, Lane, 1911.

The Forest on the Hill. London, Murray, and New York, Lane, 1912.

The Lovers: A Romance. London, Ward Lock, and Chicago, Rand McNally, 1912.

Widecombe Fair. London, Murray, and Boston, Little Brown, 1913.

The Joy of Youth: A Comedy. London, Chapman and Hall, and Boston, Little Brown, 1913.

Faith Tresillion. New York, Macmillan, 1914; London, Ward Lock, 1916.

Brunel's Tower. London, Heinemann, and New York, Macmillan, 1915.

Old Delabole. London, Heinemann, and New York, Macmillan, 1915.

The Green Alleys. London, Heinemann, and New York, Macmillan, 1916.

The Girl and the Faun. London, Palmer and Hayward, 1916; Philadelphia, Lippincott, 1917.

The Nursery (*Banks of Colne*). London, Heinemann, 1917; as *The Banks of Colne,* New York, Macmillan, 1917.

The Chronicles of St. Tid. London, Skeffington, 1917; New York, Macmillan, 1918.

The Spinners. London, Heinemann, and New York, Macmillan, 1918.

Storm in a Teacup. London, Heinemann, and New York, Macmillan, 1919.

Evander. London, Richards, and New York, Macmillan, 1919.

Orphan Dinah. London, Heinemann, 1920; New York, Macmillan, 1921.

The Bronze Venus. London, Richards, 1921.

Eudocia. London, Heinemann, and New York, Macmillan, 1921.

Pan and the Twins. London, Richards, and New York, Macmillan, 1922.

Children of Men. London, Heinemann, and New York, Macmillan, 1923.

The Lavender Dragon. London, Richards, and New York, Macmillan, 1923.

Cheat-the-Boys. London, Heinemann, and New York, Macmillan, 1924.

Redcliff. London, Hutchinson, and New York, Macmillan, 1924.

The Treasures of Typhon. London, Richards, 1924; New York, Macmillan, 1925.

George Westover. London, Hutchinson, 1925; New York, Macmillan, 1926.

Circé's Island, and The Girl and the Faun. London, Richards, and New York, Macmillan, 1926.

The Miniature. London, Watts, 1926; New York, Macmillan, 1927.

A Cornish Droll. London, Hutchinson, 1926; New York, Macmillan, 1928.

Arachne. London, Faber and Gwyer, 1927; New York, Macmillan, 1928.

Dartmoor Novels (Widecombe Edition: includes stories). New York, Macmillan, 20 vols., 1927–28.

The Ring Fence. London, Hutchinson, and New York, Macmillan, 1928.

Tryphena. London, Hutchinson, and New York, Macmillan, 1929.

The Apes. London, Faber, and New York, Macmillan, 1929.

The Three Maidens. London, Hutchinson, and New York, Smith, 1930.

Alcyone: A Fairy Story. London, Benn, 1930.

Stormbury. London, Hutchinson, 1931; New York, Macmillan, 1932.

The Broom Squires. London, Benn, and New York, Macmillan, 1932.

Nancy Owlett. London, Tuck, and New York, Macmillan, 1933.

Minions of the Moon. London, Hutchinson, 1934; New York, Macmillan, 1935.

The Oldest Inhabitant: A Comedy. London, Hutchinson, and New York, Macmillan, 1934.

Portrait of a Gentleman. London, Hutchinson, 1934.

Ned of the Caribbees. London, Hutchinson, 1935.

The Owl of Athene. London, Hutchinson, 1936.

Wood-Nymph. London, Hutchinson, 1936; New York, Dutton, 1937.

Farce in Three Acts. London, Hutchinson, 1937.

Dark Horses. London, Murray, 1938.

Saurus. London, Murray, 1938.

Tabletop. London, Macmillan, 1939.

Thorn in Her Flesh. London, Murray, 1939.

Chorus of Clowns. London, Methuen, 1940.

Goldcross. London, Methuen, 1940.

Pilgrims of the Night. London, Hutchinson, 1942.

A Museum Piece. London, Hutchinson, 1943.

The Drums of Dombali. London, Hutchinson, 1945.

Quartet. London, Hutchinson, 1946.

Fall of the House of Heron. London, Hutchinson, 1948.

The Waters of Walla. London, Hutchinson, 1950.

Through a Glass Darkly. London, Hutchinson, 1951.

His Brother's Keeper. London, Hutchinson, 1953.

The Widow Garland. London, Hutchinson, 1955.

Connie Woodland. London, Hutchinson, 1956.

Giglet Market. London, Methuen, 1957.

Short Stories

Summer Clouds and Other Stories. London, Tuck, 1893.
Down Dartmoor Way. London, Osgood McIlvaine, 1895.
The Striking Hours. London, Methuen, and New York, Stokes, 1901.
Knock at a Venture. London, Methuen, and New York, Macmillan, 1905.
The Folk Afield. London, Methuen, and New York, Putnam, 1907.
The Fun of the Fair. London, Murray, 1909.
The Old Time Before Them. London, Murray, 1913; revised edition, as *Told at The Plume,* London, Hurst and Blackett, 1921.
Up Hill, Down Dale. London, Hutchinson, and New York, Macmillan, 1925.
The Torch and Other Tales. London, Hutchinson, and New York, Macmillan, 1929.
(Selected Stories). London, Harrap, 1929.
Cherry Gambol and Other Stories. London, Hutchinson, 1930.
They Could Do No Other. London, Hutchinson, and New York, Macmillan, 1933.
The King of Kanga, and The Alliance. London, Todd, 1943.

Plays

The Policeman, with Walter Helmore (produced London, 1887).
A Platonic Attachment (produced London, 1889).
A Breezy Morning (produced Leeds and London, 1891). London, French, 1895.
The Councillor's Wife, with Jerome K. Jerome (produced New York, 1892); as *The Prude's Progress.* (produced Cambridge and London, 1895). London, Chatto and Windus, 1895.
Allendale, with G.B. Burgin (produced London, 1893).
The MacHaggis, with Jerome K. Jerome (produced Peterborough and London, 1897).
A Golden Wedding, with Charles Groves (produced London, 1898). London, French, 1899.
For Love of Prim (produced London, 1899).
A Pair of Knickerbockers (produced London, 1899). London and New York, French, 1900.
The Secret Woman, adaptation of his own novel (produced London, 1912). London, Duckworth, 1912, New York, Brentano's, 1914; revised version, Duckworth, 1935.
Curtain Raisers (includes *The Point of View, Hiatus, The Carrier-Pigeon*). London, Duckworth, 1912; New York, Brentano's, 1914.
The Carrier-Pigeon (produced Glasgow, 1913). Included in *Curtain Raisers,* 1912.
Hiatus (produced Manchester and London, 1913). Included in *Curtain Raisers,* 1912.
The Point of View (produced London, 1913). Included in *Curtain Raisers,* 1912.
The Shadow (produced Manchester and London, 1913; New York, 1922). London, Duckworth, 1913; New York, Brentano's, 1914.
The Mother, adaptation of his own novel (produced Liverpool, 1913; London, 1926). London, Duckworth, 1913; New York, Brentano's, 1914.
The Angel in the House, with Basil Macdonald Hastings (produced London and New York, 1915). London and New York, French, 1915.
Bed Rock, with Basil Macdonald Hastings (produced Manchester, 1916; London, 1924). London, The Stage, 1924.
The Farmer's Wife (produced Birmingham, 1916; London, and New York, 1924). London, Duckworth, and New York, Brentano's, 1916.

St. George and the Dragons (produced Birmingham, 1918; London, 1919). London, Duckworth, 1919; as *The Bishop's Night Out,* Boston, Baker, 1929.
The Market-Money (produced Liverpool, 1929). London, Gowans and Gray, and Boston, Phillips, 1923.
Devonshire Cream (produced Birmingham, 1924; London, 1926). London, Duckworth, and New York, Macmillan, 1925.
A Comedy Royal, adaptation of his novel *Eudocia.* London, Laurie, 1925; revised version, London, Duckworth, 1932.
Jane's Legacy: A Folk Play (produced Birmingham, 1925; London, 1930). London, Duckworth, 1931.
The Blue Comet (produced Birmingham, 1926; London, 1927). London, Duckworth, 1927.
Yellow Sands, with Adelaide Eden Phillpotts (produced London, 1926; New York, 1927). London, Duckworth, 1926; New York, French, 1927.
The Purple Bedroom (produced London, 1926). Included in *Three Short Plays,* 1928.
Devonshire Plays (includes *The Farmer's Wife, Devonshire Cream, Yellow Sands*). London, Duckworth, 1927.
Something to Talk About (produced London, 1927). Included in *Three Short Plays,* 1928.
Three Short Plays (includes *The Market-Money, Something to Talk About, The Purple Bedroom*). London, Duckworth, 1928.
My Lady's Mill, with Adelaide Eden Phillpotts (produced London, 1928).
The Runaways (produced Birmingham and London, 1928). London, Duckworth, 1928.
Buy a Broom. London, Duckworth, 1929.
Bert. London, French, 1932.
The Good Old Days, with Adelaide Eden Phillpotts (produced London, 1935). London, Duckworth, and New York, French, 1932.
A Cup of Happiness (produced London, 1932). London, Duckworth, 1933.
At the 'Bus Stop: A Duologue for Two Women. London, French, 1943.
The Orange Orchard, with Nancy Price, adaptation of the novel *The Waters of Walla* by Phillpotts (broadcast, 1949; produced London, 1950). London, French, 1951.

Radio Plays: *Old Bannerman,* 1938; *Witch's Cauldron,* from his novel, 1940; *The Tiger's Tail,* 1941; *The Gentle Hangman,* 1942; *Honest to Goodness Noah,* 1943; *The Poetical Gentleman,* 1944; *Brownberry,* 1944; *Hey-Diddle-Diddle,* 1946; *On the Night of the Fair,* 1947; *The Master Plumber,* 1947; *Hunter's Moon,* 1948; *The Orange Orchard,* 1949; *On Parole,* 1951; *Kitty Brown of Bristol,* 1953; *Quoth the Raven,* 1953; *The Laughing Widow,* 1954; *Aunt Betsey's Birthday,* 1955; *The Outward Show,* 1958; *The Red Dragon,* 1959; *Between the Deep Sea and the Devil,* 1960.

Verse

Up-Along and Down-Along. London, Methuen, 1905.
Wild Fruit. London, Lane, 1911.
The Iscariot. London, Murray, and New York, Lane, 1912.
Delight. London, Palmer and Hayward, 1916.
Plain Song 1914–1916. London, Heinemann, and New York, Macmillan, 1917.
As the Wind Blows. London, Elkin Mathews, and New York, Macmillan, 1920.
A Dish of Apples. London, Hodder and Stoughton, 1921.
Pixies' Plot. London, Richards, 1922.

Cherry-Stones. London, Richards, 1923; New York, Macmillan, 1924.

A Harvesting. London, Richards, 1924.

Brother Man. London, Richards, 1926.

(Selected Poems). London, Benn, 1926.

Brother Beast. London, Martin Secker, 1928.

Goodwill. London, Watts, 1928.

For Remembrance. Privately printed, 1929.

A Hundred Sonnets. London, Benn, 1929.

A Hundred Lyrics. London, Benn, and New York, Smith, 1930.

Becoming. London, Benn, 1932.

Song of a Sailor Man: Narrative Poem. London, Benn, 1933; New York, Macmillan, 1934.

Sonnets from Nature. London, Watts, 1935.

A Dartmoor Village. London, Watts, 1937.

Miniatures. London, Watts, 1942.

The Enchanted Wood. London, Watts, 1948.

Other

In Sugar-Cane Land (on the West Indies). New York, McClure, 1893.

My Laughing Philosopher (essays). London, Innes, 1896.

Little Silver Chronicles. Philadelphia, Biddle, 1900.

My Devon Year. London, Methuen, and New York, Macmillan, 1903.

My Garden. London, Country Life, and New York, Scribner, 1906.

The Mound by the Way. Philadelphia, Biddle, 1908.

Dance of the Months (sketches and verse). London, Gowans and Gray, 1911.

My Shrubs. London and New York, Lane, 1915.

The Eden Phillpotts Calendar, edited by H. Cecil Palmer. London, Palmer and Hayward, 1915.

A Shadow Passes (sketches and verse). London, Palmer and Hayward, 1918; New York, Macmillan, 1919.

One Hundred Pictures from Eden Phillpotts, edited by L.H. Brewitt. London, Methuen, 1919.

A West Country Pilgrimage (essays and verse). London, Parsons, and New York, Macmillan, 1920.

Thoughts in Prose and Verse. London, Watts, 1924.

A West Country Sketch Book. London, Hutchinson, 1928.

Essays in Little. London, Hutchinson, 1931.

A Year with Bisshe-Bantam (on rural life). London, Blackie, 1934.

The White Camel (for children). London, Country Life, 1936; New York, Dutton, 1938.

Golden Island (for children). London, Everett, 1938.

A Mixed Grill (essays). London, Watts, 1940.

From the Angle of 88 (autobiography). London, Hutchinson, 1951.

One Thing and Another. London Hutchinson, 1954.

Selected Letters, edited by James Y. Dayanda. Lanham, Maryland, University Press of America, 1984.

*

Bibliography: *Eden Phillpotts: A Bibliography of First Editions* by Percival Hinton, Birmingham, George Worthington, 1931.

Critical Studies: *Eden Phillpotts: An Assessment and a Tribute* edited by Waveney Girvan, London, Hutchinson, 1953; *Eden Phillpotts on Dartmoor* by K.F. Day, Newton Abbot, Devon, David and Charles, 1981.

*   *   *

In the course of his long productive life Eden Phillpotts wrote over one hundred novels, among them several mysteries. His weak points are his conventional characters, including his detectives, and his penchant for leisurely elaboration which could uncharitably be called padding; his strong points are his evocation of milieu and his ingenious situations. Phillpotts's gallery of characters is wide, but they are often stereotyped and romanticized, bluff honest countrymen and shrewd doctors and coroners abounding. His detectives fall into two classes, both conventional: the young and earnest who are apt to be misled by their feelings, and the old and cynical who solve the mysteries. John Ringrose, retired from Scotland Yard, is the very model of the latter type, penetrating, analytical, undeterred in his quest, as is Peter Ganns, the great American sleuth, whose slang (in Phillpotts's version) makes him a caricature until his creator forgets it while Ganns pursues the criminals. Other characters are similarly one-sided although in extenuation it may be said that Phillpotts does create a number of interesting eccentrics.

His tendency to pad out his stories is less forgivable. He seizes every opportunity to pursue the red herring of digression, reciting at length for the coroner's jury every detail of a case we have just been through, recounting in complete detail an interminable debate between a fanatic clergyman and a materialist detective concerning supernaturalism, dragging the story out over years with other events only tenuously related to the case. The result of this habit is, for the reader, simple boredom.

Because his stories often take off in these directions from some aspect of the milieu, one suspects that Phillpotts wrote mysteries only as an adjunct to his basic interest in his region, southwest England. Most of his novels are about Devon and Cornwall, done with the loving attention to detail of the regionalist, from topography to local attitudes and customs. These features of the mysteries are admittedly interesting for their own sake but they do get in the way of the tale itself. This tendency is true even of the stories where we are whisked off to the Italian lakes, of which Phillpotts was clearly very fond, and which he describes in rich evocative passages.

It is nevertheless true that he did contribute to the detective mystery some notably original situations, though they often are so bizarre as to call for indulgent willingness to suspend disbelief on the reader's part. *The Marylebone Miser,* for instance, is the locked-room case with a vengeance, the room lined with steel, the door double-bolted from the inside, and so on. Phillpotts solves the puzzle by having the old miser who lived in the room killed by a dagger suspended from the single light bulb the miser permitted himself, so that his meanness is partly the cause of his demise. And the murderer, a fine young chap, gets away scot-free. *The Grey Room* is intriguing mostly because the famous detective, Peter Hardcastle, called in to solve the problem of mysterious deaths in the room, becomes himself a victim—rather a disappointment after the build-up he has had. The dead turn out to be, of all things, victims of the Borgia's, for the bed is one of their infernal devices (still functioning after 400 years) which emits poisonous fumes when warmed by a body.

Stories like *A Voice from the Dark* and *The Red Redmaynes,* while unusual, are more credible. In *The Red Redmaynes* the plot turns on an initial deception, in which the murderer is thought to be murdered and his victim to be the murderer, whose role he plays by being seen in disguise from time to time. Many complications and another effective disguise elaborate the story which is eventually solved by Peter Ganns, who has seen through the whole thing, a younger detective having been bamboozled by the murderer's beautiful wife. *A Voice from the Dark* has John Ringrose tracking down a crime already a year old, when a sickly child was frightened to death for his inheritance. Ringrose figures out the perpetrator and the method; the rest of the story concerns his efforts to catch Lord Brooke for the murder both of his brother and the nephew. The twists of the plot are intriguing, especially the climax when Ringrose lays a trap for Brooke high on a mountain near Lake Lugano. Other original tales, though these are marred by padding, are *A Clue from the Stars* in which the weapon is a dangerous bull, and *Monkshood* in which a chef whose unfaithful wife tried to poison him with monkshood, instead poisons her and her lover with such patience and skillful role-playing that he is never even suspected until his own later suicide, which looks like murder. Dr. Thorne, amateur detective, explains the mystery by reconstruction long after the fact, in a lengthy account delivered to the murderer's foster father, another bizarre twist.

Phillpotts's mysteries, plodding, drawn-out, and conventional in characterization, are principally of historical interest. But a few of them, like *A Voice from the Dark, Monkshood,* and particularly *The Red Redmaynes,* can still hold the reader's attention.

—Richard C. Carpenter

PICKARD, Nancy. American. Born in Kansas City, Missouri, 19 September 1945. Educated at Missouri School of Journalism, bachelor of journalism 1967. Married Guy Pickard in 1976; one son. Reporter and editor, *The Squire,* Overland Park, Kansas, 1967–69; writer and supervisor, Western Auto, Kansas City, 1969–72; freelance writer, 1973–82; since 1982 full-time writer. President, Sisters in Crime, 1988–89. Recipient: Anthony award, 1985; Macavity award, for novel, 1987, for short story, 1989. Agent: Meredith Bernstein Literary Agency, 470 West End Avenue, New York, New York 10024. Address: 5740 Windsor Drive, Fairway, Kansas 66205, U.S.A.

CRIME PUBLICATIONS

Novels (series: Jenny Cain in all books)

Generous Death. New York, Avon, 1984.
Say No to Murder. New York, Avon, 1985.
No Body. New York, Scribner, 1986; London, Collins, 1987.
Marriage Is Murder. New York, Scribner, 1987; London, Collins, 1988.
Dead Crazy. New York, Scribner, and London, Collins, 1989.
Bum Steer. New York, Pocket Books, and London, Macmillan, 1990.

Uncollected Short Stories

"A Man Around the House," in *Ellery Qeen's Mystery Magazine* (New York), December 1982.
"Solo Flight," in *Woman's World* (Englewood, New Jersey), 24 May 1983.
"I, Witness," in *Alfred Hitchcock's Mystery Magazine* (New York), December 1987.
"Afraid All the Time," in *Sisters in Crime,* edited by Marilyn Wallace. New York, Berkley, 1989; London, Robinson, 1990.

"Storm Warnings," in *Sisters in Crime 2,* edited by Marilyn Wallace. New York, Berkley, 1990.
"Dust Devil," in *Armchair Detective* (New York), Winter 1990.

*

Nancy Pickard comments:
Jenny Cain, the amateur sleuth I created in 1983, has three jobs to do: one, to entertain her readers if she possibly can; two, to represent, as honestly as she can, the way it is and the way it feels *to her* to be a woman of her generation in the U.S. in these times; and three, to let me use her to honor, but also to experiment with, the amateur sleuth mystery tradition.

She gets involved with social and family issues perhaps more often and more deeply than her predecessors, but that's only because those are matters that interest her in much the same way that other sleuths are interested in banking or horses, theater or bells.

It pleases me very much if readers say they feel they could sit down and have a cup of coffee or a beer with Jenny; or if they say they laughed out loud or were moved to tears by something she does or says; or if they say, in regard to some issue presented in the novels (such as mental illness, racism, or domestic violence) that, according to their personal experiences, she got it right. Those are my aims, and I think, hers.

* * *

Nancy Pickard's novels provide outstanding examples of the new direction the traditional mystery has taken. Affectionate intimacy with the narrator, richness of characterization, and the judicious use of humor draw readers time and again to the Jennifer Cain series.

One of the major strengths of the six novels lies in Pickard's portrayal of Jennifer Cain, director of the Port Frederick Civic Foundation in a fictional Massachusetts small town. Jenny is appealing and even admirable—anyone who chooses to work rather than simply live off her own inherited trust fund is to be admired—but she doesn't suffer foolishness or pomposity gladly. Educated, compassionate, and gracious, Jenny is no one-dimensional "good girl," nor is she a loner stalking the mean streets. She's a competent, forthright business person who indulges in her share of worldly pleasures. Mistress of the clever aside, Jenny is cheerfully cynical.

Tempering the good fortune of her trust fund, Jenny must endure her share of personal tribulations, in the form of a family that would try anyone's patience. Her sister Sherry makes no bones about resenting her; her mother is in a mental institution and occasionally drifts into catatonia. And her father is a self-absorbed wanderer who threw the town of Port Frederick into a minor economic crisis when he ran the family fishing business into bankruptcy. Despite all this, Jenny manages her life with a minimum of self-pity. Jenny's personal difficulties allow readers to gain insight into the resources she brings to her dealings with people.

Written primarily in the first person from Jenny's point of view, the distinctive voice is one of the delights of reading a Pickard novel. A breezy personal narrator, Jenny exhibits a touching level of self-awareness without ever taking herself so seriously that she becomes ponderous. Occasional departures into third person nearly always are entertaining additions, and serve to increase suspense.

Generous Death introduces Jenny and the cast of series characters, including handsome, twice-divorced police officer Geoff Bushfield. Pickard deftly balances the whimsy of a villain who leaves behind doggerel-filled notes when prominent local philanthropists are murdered with the bittersweet sadness of Jenny's mother's illness. This balance is the hallmark of the series, and while the scales may tip one way or the other, all six books have both humor and poignancy.

In *Say No to Murder,* small town politics and special interests are explored. Jenny's father is one of the suspects in a series of incidents that seem designed to halt work on Liberty Harbor, an expensive and sometimes divisive waterfront restoration project. Jenny's relationship to Geoff Bushfield deepens as they try to determine the truth behind the murders.

No Body opens with one of the funniest scenes in Pickard's work. An example of the effective use of third person narrative, the scene recounts the discovery by Miss Lucille Grant, retired schoolteacher, that all the bodies buried in Union Hill Cemetery are missing. The ensuing investigation of the Union Hill plight, and the murders that follow, give Jenny opportunities to comment on the American funeral industry, as well as offering new insights into the people of Port Frederick.

Marriage Is Murder takes place while Jenny is considering marriage to Geoff Bushfield and reveals a side of Port Frederick clouded by the specter of domestic violence. The less frivolous tone of this book is appropriate to the topic. Here the scale is tipped in favor of a more serious examination of a contemporary social issue. This shift in balance adds dimension to a character who demonstrates that she can grow in response to the situations that confront her.

Continuing in a similar tone, *Dead Crazy* focuses on the plight of the homeless, particularly examining the consequences of early-release policies of institutions for the mentally ill. Sent into the mainstream of a society ill-prepared to handle their special needs, the former mental patients frighten some of Port Frederick's citizens. In waging the battle to provide a place for these people to go, Jenny learns about her own prejudices. Yet even in the midst of such serious matters, Pickard offers scenes that make readers chuckle and, in one case, laugh out loud.

Bum Steer brings Jenny to Kansas, where she attempts to understand a mysterious bequest to the Port Frederick Civic Foundation. Somone has bequeathed a cattle ranch to the Foundation, and complying with the complicated terms of the will makes demands on Jenny's ingenuity. Jenny proves equal to the task, but she must pass some challenging tests first. Vivid depictions of ranch life and of the prairie landscape add to the attraction of this sixth Jennifer Cain novel.

While Pickard's novels deal with the role of humor, courage, and love in everyday life, her short stories, including the Edgar nominee "Afraid All the Time," reveal a darker sensibility. This talented writer's body of work has earned numerous well-deserved awards—and the eager anticipation of readers who await her next mystery.

—Marilyn Wallace

———

PIKE, Robert L. *See* **FISH, Robert L.**

———

PIPER, Evelyn. Pseudonym for Merriam Modell. American. Born in New York City in 1908. Educated at Cornell University, Ithaca, New York, B.A. Worked as model, salesclerk, magazine editor.

CRIME PUBLICATIONS

Novels

The Innocent. New York, Simon and Schuster, 1949; London, Boardman, 1951.
The Motive. New York, Simon and Schuster, 1950; London, Boardman, 1951; as *Death of a Nymph,* New York, Spivak, 1951.
The Plot. New York, Simon and Schuster, 1951; London, Boardman, 1952.
The Lady and Her Doctor. New York, Doubleday, 1956.
Bunny Lake Is Missing. New York, Harper, 1957; London, Secker and Warburg, 1958.
Hanno's Doll. New York, Atheneum, 1961; London, Secker and Warburg, 1962.
The Naked Murderer. New York, Atheneum, 1962.
The Nanny. New York, Atheneum, 1964; London, Secker and Warburg, 1965.
The Stand-In. New York, McKay, 1970.

OTHER PUBLICATIONS

Novels as Merriam Modell

The Sound of Years. New York, Simon and Schuster, 1946; London, Cassell, 1947.
My Sister, My Bride. New York, Simon and Schuster, 1948; London, Cassell, 1949.

*

Manuscript Collection: Mugar Memorial Library, Boston University.

*   *   *

The Nanny and *Bunny Lake Is Missing* are the two novels, each a minor classic, that represent the thrust and focus of all Evelyn Piper's work. Specializing in suspense and development of character, from her first book, *The Innocent,* Piper has presented in each later work the theme of evil revealed in the destructiveness of possessive or overbearing love.

The stories start with someone who is blindly devoted to spouse or child. The object of that love (Charles in *The Innocent,* or Puppchen in *Hanno's Doll*) is a self-centered person whose amoral selfishness is apparent to everyone else, if not to the naive protagonist who gradually sees the truth and enters a desperate struggle to survive.

Piper is one of the few writers who effectively uses children in her suspense novels. Together with a mild domestic scene children are integrated into all her plots. *The Nanny,* for example, contrasts a child, a teenager, and an old woman. Each expresses an evil—the old woman acts out of self-justification, the teenager out of irresponsible mischievousness, and the child out of fear and ignorance. Piper depicts every shade and nuance, every effect and horrifying result of smothering overindulgent love. The effects of that grasping, protectively vicious love are, then, reflected in a small baby and the man who competes with that baby for attention.

Two of Piper's books are notable for departures from her usual pattern. *The Naked Murderer,* billed as her first "whodunit" rather than a suspense thriller, uses traditional detective elements to produce a form of a mystery, but the effect of the twist ending is spoiled by the reader's feeling of being tricked. In *The Stand-In* Piper leaves New York and uses a well-done English setting, and characters who are anything but domestic.

The plot involves the cast of a film crew on location; a more selfish profession has seldom been potrayed. A bitterly ironic ending rounds out the frustrations of all the major characters.

Piper's strong suspense and analysis of psychology in familiar situations produce a series of books that are fascinating despite their reworking of the same basic material.

—Fred Dueren

———

PLATTS, A. Monmouth. *See* **BERKELEY, Anthony.**

———

PORLOCK, Martin. *See* **MacDONALD, Philip.**

———

PORTER, Joyce. British. Born in Marple, Cheshire, 28 March 1924. Educated at the High School for Girls, Macclesfield, Cheshire, 1935–42; King's College, London, 1942–45, B.A. (honours) 1945. Served in the Women's Royal Air Force, 1949–63: Flight Officer. Agent: Curtis Brown Ltd., 162–168 Regent Street, London W1R 5TB. Address: 68 Sand Street, Longbridge Deverill, near Warminster, Wiltshire, England.

CRIME PUBLICATIONS

Novels (series: Inspector Wilfred Dover; Edmund Brown; Constance Ethel Morrison-Burke)

Dover One. London, Cape, and New York, Scribner, 1964.
Dover Two. London, Cape, and New York, Scribner, 1965.
Dover Three. London, Cape, 1965; New York, Scribner, 1966.
Sour Cream with Everything (Brown). London, Cape, and New York, Scribner, 1966.
Dover and the Unkindest Cut of All. London, Cape, and New York, Scribner, 1967.
The Chinks in the Curtain (Brown). London, Cape, 1967; New York, Scribner, 1968.
Dover Goes to Pott. London, Cape, and New York, Scribner, 1968.
Neither a Candle nor a Pitchfork (Brown). London, Weidenfeld and Nicolson, 1969; New York, McCall, 1970.
Rather a Common Sort of Crime (Morrison-Burke). London, Weidenfeld and Nicolson, and New York, McCall, 1970.
Dover Strikes Again. London, Weidenfeld and Nicolson, 1970; New York, McKay, 1973.
Only with a Bargepole (Brown). London, Weidenfeld and Nicolson, 1971; New York, McKay, 1974.
A Meddler and Her Murder (Morrison-Burke). London, Weidenfeld and Nicolson, 1972; New York, McKay, 1973.
It's Murder with Dover. London, Weidenfeld and Nicolson, and New York, McKay, 1973.
The Package Included Murder (Morrison-Burke). London, Weidenfeld and Nicolson, 1975; Indianapolis, Bobbs Merrill, 1976.

Dover and the Claret Tappers. London, Weidenfeld and Nicolson, 1977; Woodstock, Vermont, Countryman Press, 1989.
Who the Heck Is Sylvia (Morrison-Burke). London, Weidenfeld and Nicolson, 1977.
Dead Easy for Dover. London, Weidenfeld and Nicolson, 1978; New York, St. Martin's Press, 1979.
The Cart Before the Crime (Morrison-Burke). London, Weidenfeld and Nicolson, 1979.
Dover Beats the Band. London, Weidenfeld and Nicolson, 1980.

Uncollected Short Stories

"Dover Pulls a Rabbit," in *Ellery Queen's Mystery Magazine* (New York), February 1969.
"Dover Tangles with High Finance," in *Ellery Queen's Masters of Mystery.* New York, Davis, 1975; London, Gollancz, 1977.
"Dover Does Some Spadework," in *Best Detective Stories of the Year 1977,* edited by Edward D. Hoch. New York, Dutton, 1977.
"Dover and the Dark Lady," in *Ellery Queen's Masks of Mystery.* New York, Davis, 1978; London, Gollancz, 1979.
"A Gross Miscarriage of Justice," in *Alfred Hitchcock's Mystery Magazine* (New York), July 1978.
"A Case of Malicious Mischief," in *Alfred Hitchcock's Mystery Magazine* (New York), May 1979.
"Dover and the Smallest Room," in *Ellery Queen's Mystery Magazine* (New York), November 1979.
"Dover Goes to School," in *Ellery Queen's Circumstantial Evidence.* New York, Davis, 1980.
"The Mystery of the White Elephant," in *Alfred Hitchcock's Mystery Magazine* (New York), June 1980.
"Sweating It Out with Dover," in *John Creasey's Crime Collection 1981,* edited by Herbert Harris. London, Gollancz, 1981.
"Dover Without Perks," in *Ellery Queen's Eyewitnesses.* New York, Davis, 1982.
"The Stuff of Crime," in *Alfred Hitchcock's Mystery Magazine* (New York), February 1982.
"Dover Weighs the Evidence," in *Ellery Queen's Mystery Magazine* (New York), March 1982.
"Dover Sees the Trees," in *Ellery Queen's Mystery Magazine* (New York), September 1982.
"Stamping on Crime," in *Alfred Hitchcock's Mystery Magazine* (New York), September 1982.

OTHER PUBLICATIONS

Other

"The Solitary Life of the Writer," in *Murder Ink: The Mystery Reader's Companion,* edited by Dilys Winn. New York, Workman, 1977.

*

Joyce Porter comments:
I try to write books that will while away a couple of hours for the reader—and make as much money as possible for me!

*   *   *

Though occasionally outrageous in their exaggeration, Joyce Porter's comic variants of the international thriller with secret agent Eddie Brown, the police procedural novel with Detective-Inspector Dover, and the amateur-cum-private-eye novel with the Honourable Constance Ethel Morrison-Burke (the Hon-Con) ultimately play fair by observing the conventions of the three genres. The books delight in reducing human behavior to its lowest common denominator and then shocking the reader by descending further: anonymous letters in *Dover Three* hint at everything from "algolagnia to zoophilism." Unfortunately such exotic delights occur infrequently, and the reader must settle for quotidian activities like incest, lesbianism, and cannibalism. Typically, cold and rainy weather and muddy terrain worsen already unattractive tempers and appearances. Porter characters, driven by greed and malice, only rarely achieve the scientific detachment of the old man in *Dover Three* who coolly watches dangerous lorries threaten pedestrians on a lethal road.

The Eddie Brown books explore dangerous foreign locales, where the threat is as much his own ineptness and sex with unattractive females as the KGB: in *Neither a Candle nor a Pitchfork* a lesbian Russian official tries to seduce Eddie while he is in female disguise. Eddie's climactic attack on a prison which would be the high point of a conventional thriller is subsidiary to jokes about miscegenation. Russian officialdom is so corrupt and murderous, the Russian masses so bestial, especially the lethal children frequent in Porter, that Russia seems interchangeable with England.

Unlike the bland Eddie Brown, the Hon-Con and Dover, obese embarrassment to New Scotland Yard, are authentic grotesques who provide most of the humor in their books. Porter is ambivalent about Dover's intelligence, since he does, after all, solve the crimes the novels catalogue: "The fact that his career as a detective had endured, and even flourished in a mild way, was almost entirely due to the fact that most criminals, incredible as it may seem, were even more inept and stupid" (*Dover One*). Dover's forays into remote and inhospitable villages to aid the local police focus primarily on his quest for animal comfort (Porter dwells lovingly on his unhygienic habits and digestive malfunctions) and only secondarily on crime. Personal pique overrides professionalism: in *Dover Three* he delays solving a case until a hated sister-in-law ends her visit to his home; then rushing to wind up affairs, he allows everyone to believe an aggressive woman he dislikes guilty. When the real murderer commits suicide after confessing to Dover, he is too lazy or malicious to set the record straight (in a world where criminal is as nasty as victim, justice seems irrelevant). *Dover and the Unkindest Cut of All,* the only Porter novel which carries her view of humanity to its bizarre conclusion, plays with the comic horror of castration and leaves the guilty both unpunished and unrepentant. Like stereotyped rape victims, the mutilated roués who survive punishment at the hands of a civic-minded ladies group choose suicide or silence. As in the entire series, Dover's skirmishes with his elegant assistant Sgt. MacGregor, whom he almost sacrifices to these ladies, help define the solid police procedures supporting the grotesque façade of the novel.

The Hon-Con, a gentlewoman of independent means, turns to detection because vigorous calisthenics fail to satisfy her tremendous energy: "she went at everything like a bull at a gate" (*Rather a Common Sort of Crime*). Though protective of young girls, Con is "always the perfect gentleman" (*The Package Included Murder*) and remains true to her long-suffering companion, Miss Jones, and presumably innocent about elementary sexual facts and the unconventional behavior of other characters, like Mr. Welks, who supplies beauty advice. With characteristic equivocation Porter defines Con as not "as big a fool as many people thought her"; but her

tactlessness and police short-sightedness undermine her accomplishments and leave her frustrated enough to contemplate founding "the first ever Ladies' Rugby Football Club in the World" (*A Meddler and Her Murder*). In all three genres, despite inconsistencies about the wisdom of her protagonists, Porter balances her talent for straightforward thriller with the delight in spoofing the forms.

—Burton Kendle

POST, Melville Davisson. American. Born in Romines Mills, West Virginia, 19 April 1869. Educated at Buckhannon Academy, West Virginia, graduated 1885; West Virginia University, Morgantown, A.B. 1891, LL.B. 1892. Married Ann Bloomfield Gamble in 1903 (died 1919); one son. Practiced criminal and corporate law in Wheeling for 11 years, traveled extensively, and settled near Clarksburg, West Virginia, in 1914. Presidential elector-at-large, Democratic Party, and secretary, Electoral College, 1892; chairman, West Virginia Democratic Congressional Committee, 1898; Member, Advisory Committee of the National Economic League, 1914–15; headed group of writers supporting John W. Davis, Democratic candidate for President, 1924. *Died 23 June 1930.*

CRIME PUBLICATIONS

Short Stories (series Uncle Abner; Sir Henry Marquis; Randolph Mason)

The Strange Schemes of Randolph Mason. New York, Putnam, 1896.
The Man of Last Resort; or, The Clients of Randolph Mason. New York, Putnam, 1897.
The Corrector of Destinies (Mason). New York, Clode, 1908.
The Nameless Thing. New York, Appleton, 1912.
Uncle Abner, Master of Mysteries. New York, Appleton, 1918; London, Stacey, 1972.
The Mystery at the Blue Villa. New York, Appleton, 1919.
The Sleuth of St. James's Square (Marquis). New York, Appleton, 1920.
Monsieur Jonquelle, Prefect of Police of Paris. New York, Appleton, 1923.
Walker of the Secret Service. New York, Appleton, 1924.
The Bradmoor Murder (Marquis). New York, Sears, 1929; as *The Garden in Asia,* London, Brentano's, 1929.
The Silent Witness. New York, Farrar and Rinehart, 1930.
The Methods of Uncle Abner. Boulder, Colorado, Aspen Press, 1974.
The Complete Uncle Abner. San Diego, University of California Extension, 1977.

Uncollected Short Stories

"The Ventures of Mr. Clayvarden," in *Law Student's Helper* (Detroit), February 1898.
"The Plan of Malcolm Van Staak," in *Law Student's Helper* (Detroit), April 1898.
"The Marriage Contract," in *Pearson's Magazine* (New York), June 1908.
"The Unknown Disciple," in *Pictorial Review* (New York), December 1920.
"The Laughing Woman," in *Red Book* (Chicago), February 1923.

"The Miracle," in *Pictorial Review* (New York), December 1924.
"The Devil's Track," in *Country Gentleman* (Philadelphia), July 1927.
"The Mystery at the Mill," in *American Magazine* (Springfield, Ohio), August 1929.

OTHER PUBLICATIONS

Novels

Dwellers in the Hills. New York, Putnam, 1901.
The Gilded Chair. New York, Appleton, 1910.
The Mountain School-Teacher. New York, Appleton, 1922.
The Revolt of the Birds. New York, Appleton, 1927.

Other

"Mysteries of the Law . . . " (7 articles), in *Saturday Evening Post* (Philadelphia), 14 May–27 August 1910.
"Extraordinary Cases . . . " (6 articles), in *Saturday Evening Post* (Philadelphia), 23 September 1911–20 April 1912.
"The Blight," in *Saturday Evening Post* (Philadelphia), 20 December 1914.
"The Mystery Story," in *Saturday Evening Post* (Philadelphia), 27 February 1915.
"The Invisible Army," in *Saturday Evening Post* (Philadelphia), 10 April 1915.
"Secret Ciphers," in *Saturday Evening Post* (Philadelphia), 8 May 1915.
"Spy Methods in Europe," in *Saturday Evening Post* (Philadelphia), 15 May 1915.
"The Great Terror," in *Saturday Evening Post* (Philadelphia), 12 June 1915.
"Nick Carter, Realist," in *Saturday Evening Post* (Philadelphia), 3 March 1917.
"Spy Stories," in *Saturday Evening Post* (Philadelphia), 10 March 1917.
The Man Hunters. New York, Sears, 1926; London, Hutchinson, 1927.

*

Bibliography: in *The Complete Uncle Abner* by Allen J. Hubin, San Diego, University of California Extension, 1977.

Critical Study: *Melville Davisson Post, Man of Many Mysteries* by Charles A. Norton, Bowling Green, Ohio, Popular Press, 1973.

*   *   *

The lawyer Melville Davisson Post became involved early in his career in judicial reform and local politics and, for a brief period in the mid-1920's, in a national political campaign. But his greatest achievements were as an author, particularly as a short story writer.

After publishing two books of crime stories in 1896 and 1897, Post wrote almost exclusively for popular, wide-circulation magazines. His commercial success was unparalleled in his time. His forte was plotting and his stories invariably were constructed so as to capture and hold the reader's interest. While many of his tales reveal carelessness in style and details, their entertainment value was high.

Post's first book of crime stories was *The Strange Schemes of Randolph Mason* whose protagonist—like Post himself—was a

lawyer. Randolph Mason, however, was a strikingly new type of character: he was a skilled, unscrupulous lawyer who used his knowledge of the law to defeat the ends of justice. Mason assisted criminals by cynically employing his familiarity with legal loopholes. To complaints that these concepts might abet actual criminals, Post replied, in the preface to a second collection of Mason stories, *The Man of Last Resort,* that "nothing but good could come of exposing the law's defects." Some Post stories, in fact, did bring about changes in the criminal law codes. However, in the third and final book in the Mason series, *The Corrector of Destinies,* Post had his lawyer modify his attitude and decide to practice thereafter in the interest of the written law.

Post published several valuable articles on the theory of detective story plotting and structure. Brief excerpts from Post's own subsequent reworking of these pieces indicate the significant rethinking he was giving to the concept of the detective story. "The developing of the mystery and the developing toward its solution," Post proposed, "would go forward side by side; and when all the details of the mystery were uncovered, the solution also would be uncovered and the end of the story arrived at . . . This new formula, as will at once be seen, very markedly increases the rapidity of action in a story, holds the reader's interest throughout, and eliminates any impression of moving at any time over ground previously covered."

In the celebrated Uncle Abner tales one perceives a powerful sense of place—of the wild hills and lawless Virginia backlands where crimes against God and man were conceived and carried out and where God's and man's avenger could be impersonated only by the Old Testament moral grandeur of a man like Abner. If Post's early stories were novel in the protagonist's approach to the practice of law and the use (or misuse) of technical legal knowledge, his later stories, of which the Uncle Abner series is the best illustration, are striking (and intrinsically better) in their deliberate and effective blend (within the prescription of the detective tale itself) of character and place—dignity of character and dignity of place.

—Donald A. Yates

POSTGATE, Raymond (William). British. Born in Cambridge, 6 November 1896; brother of Margaret Postgate, i.e., Margaret Cole, *q.v.* Educated at Perse School, Cambridge; Liverpool College; St. John's College, Oxford. Married Daisy Lansbury in 1918; two sons. Journalist and writer from 1918: sub-editor, *Daily Herald;* assistant editor, *Lansbury's Weekly;* department editor, *Encyclopaedia Britannica,* 14th edition, 1927–28; European representative for Alfred A. Knopf, publishers, 1929–49; editor, *Tribune,* 1940–42; worked at the Board of Trade and Ministry of Supply, 1942–48. Founder, Good Food Club, 1950. Fellow, Trinity College, Cambridge. *Died 29 March 1971.*

CRIME PUBLICATIONS

Novels (series: Inspector Holly)

Verdict of Twelve. London, Collins, and New York, Double-day, 1940.

Somebody at the Door (Holly). London, Joseph, and New York, Knopf, 1943.
The Ledger Is Kept (Holly). London, Joseph, 1953.

Uncollected Short Story

"The Respectable Mr. Thompson," in *Murder Plain and Fanciful,* edited by James Sandoe. New York, Sheridan House, 1948.

OTHER PUBLICATIONS

Novel

No Epitaph. London, Hamish Hamilton, 1932; as *Felix and Anne,* New York, Vanguard Press, 1933.

Other

The International (Socialist Bureau) During the War. London, The Herald, 1918.
Doubts Concerning a League of Nations. London, The Herald, 1919.
The Bolshevik Theory. London, Richards, and New York, Dodd Mead, 1920.
The Workers' International. London, Swarthmore Press, and New York, Harcourt Brace, 1920.
Chartism and the "Trades Union." London, Labour Research Department, 1922.
Out of the Past: Some Revolutionary Sketches. London, Labour Publishing Company, 1922; Boston, Houghton Mifflin, 1923.
Revolutionary Biographies. Madras, Arka, 1922.
The Builders' History. London, Labour Publishing Company, 1923; New York, Garland, 1984.
A Short History of the British Workers. London, Plebs League, 1926.
A Workers' History of the Great Strike. London, Plebs League, 1927.
That Devil Wilkes. New York, Vanguard Press, 1929; London, Constable, 1930; revised edition, London, Dobson, 1956.
Robert Emmet. London, Secker and Warburg, 1931; as *Dear Robert Emmet,* New York, Vanguard Press, 1932.
Karl Marx. London, Hamish Hamilton, 1933.
How to Make a Revolution. London, Hogarth Press, and New York, Vanguard Press, 1934.
What to Do with the B.B.C. London, Hogarth Press, 1935.
A Pocket History of the British Workers to 1919. London, Fact, 1937.
Those Foreigners: The English People's Opinions on Foreign Affairs as Reflected in Their Newspapers since Waterloo, with Aylmer Vallance. London, Harrap, 1937; as *England Goes to Press,* Indianapolis, Bobbs Merrill, 1937.
The Common People 1746–1938, with G.D.H. Cole. London, Methuen, 1938; revised edition, 1946; as *The British Common People,* New York, Knopf, 1939; revised edition, as *The British People,* Knopf, 1947.
Let's Talk It Over: An Argument about Socialism. London, Fabian Society, 1942.
The Plain Man's Guide to Wine. London, Joseph, 1951; revised edition, 1957, 1965; New York, Taplinger, 1960.
The Life of George Lansbury. London, Longman, 1951.
An Alphabet of Choosing and Serving Wine. London, Jenkins, 1955.
Story of a Year, 1848. London, Cape, 1955; New York, Oxford University Press, 1956.

Every Man Is God. London, Joseph, 1959; New York, Simon and Schuster, 1960.
The Home Wine Cellar. London, Jenkins, 1960.
Story of a Year, 1798. London, Longman, and New York, Harcourt Brace, 1969.
Portuguese Wine. London, Dent, 1969.

Editor, *Revolution from 1789–1906: Documents.* London, Richards, 1920; Boston, Houghton Mifflin, 1921.
Editor and Translator, *Pervigilium Venus: The Eve of Venus.* London, Richards, and Boston, Houghton Mifflin, 1924.
Editor, *Murder, Piracy and Treason: A Selection of Notable English Trials.* London, Cape, and Boston, Houghton Mifflin, 1925.
Editor, *The Conversations of Dr. Johnson,* By James Boswell. London, Knopf, and New York, Vanguard Press, 1930.
Editor, *Detective Stories of Today.* London, Faber, 1940.
Editor, *"By Me . . .": A Report upon the Apparent Discovery of Some Working Notes by William Shakespeare,* by Moray MacLaren. London, Redington, 1949.
Editor, *The Outline of History,* by H.G. Wells. New York, Garden City Publishing Company, 1949; London, Cassell, 1956.
Editor, *The Good Food Guide 1951–52.* London, Cassell, 1951 (and later editions).

Translator, *Mitsou,* by Colette. London, Secker and Warburg, 1951.

*   *   *

Raymond Postgate, the noted social historian and close associate of the socialist leader George Lansbury, prefaced his best-known crime novel, *Verdict of Twelve,* with Marx's statement that man's social existence determines his consciousness. It could serve equally well to introduce *Somebody at the Door* or *The Ledger Is Kept.* Although all three novels are solidly plotted with sufficient detection to engage a reader of traditional detective fiction, Postgate's real concern is not with revealing the identity of the murderer but with analyzing the circumstances which shaped murderer, victim, or jury member and made their decisions and actions seemingly inevitable. While stressing the importance of early social and economic environment upon the development of personality and values, he understands that character formation is a dynamic process and that new experiences may modify or challenge existing attitudes. Although deterministic, Postgate's view of character does not negate individuality; rather, it enhances it. His novels are filled with fully realized, recognizable human beings who come alive as do few characters in detective fiction.

The technique used in the memorable *Verdict of Twelve* is typical of Postgate's approach to the detective novel. He gives detailed biographies of six of the 12 jurors who must decide whether a middle-aged woman has murdered her nephew. Each juror brings to his task a set of personal attitudes and problems which prevent his considering the evidence objectively; each responds emotionally rather than rationally to the crime. Because the reader understands the jurors, he is able to anticipate their reactions. Postgate's real skill, however, lies in his ability to show how these seemingly predictable reactions are modified or changed once discussion of the case begins, and subtle interplay of class distinctions and personality gradually causes the weaker jurors to side with the majority. The jury deliberations form the core of the novel, but they are buttressed by careful delineation of both accused and victim. Postgate also makes superb use of literary allusion and offers as neatly handled a twist ending as one could wish for.

A similar technique is less successful in *Somebody at the Door* because of diffusion of emphasis and a number of unconvincing suspects, but the novel does offer well-developed motivation in its central characters and an unusual method of murder. Sensitive to the nuances of romantic love, Postgate depicts an intense love affair between a woman approaching 40 and a man many years younger which gives substance and interest to a novel lacking structural coherence.

In *The Ledger Is Kept,* Postgate achieved what many detective novelists have dreamed of doing: he wrote a detective story which is also a first-rate realistic novel. Concentrating upon the life of the victim, Henry Proctor, he shows that the interaction of circumstance and character made Proctor's murder inevitable. Proctor is the child of an unsuccessful shoemaker and is brought up in an obscure and puritanical religious sect; his academic brilliance takes him to Oxford where he learns to appreciate the richness and variety of life but must also grapple with the conflict between his desire for social acceptance and the opposed values of his early training. Profoundly lonely in late middle age, he makes one last attempt at happiness through an affair with his teenaged housemaid. This brief and poignant love leads to his death. In this novel Postgate brings reality to the never-never land of detective fiction. Understanding of and respect for people of different educational, social, and intellectual levels, coupled with sure technical skill, have produced a detective novel which transcends the limitations of the genre.

—Jeanne F. Bedell

POTTS, Jean. American. Born in St. Paul, Nebraska, 17 November 1910. Educated at Nebraska Wesleyan University, Lincoln. Journalist in Nebraska; then freelance writer in New York. Recipient: Mystery Writers of America Edgar Allan Poe award, 1954. Agent: McIntosh and Otis Inc., 310 Madison Avenue, New York, New York 10017. Address: 53 Irving Place, Apartment 6D, New York, New York 10003, U.S.A.

CRIME PUBLICATIONS

Novels

Go, Lovely Rose. New York, Scribner, 1954; London, Gollancz, 1955.
Death of a Stray Cat. New York, Scribner, and London, Gollancz, 1955.
The Diehard. New York, Scribner, and London, Gollancz, 1956.
The Man with the Cane. New York, Scribner, 1957; London, Gollancz, 1958.
Lightning Strikes Twice. New York, Scribner, 1958; as *Blood Will Tell,* London, Gollancz, 1959.
Home Is the Prisoner. New York, Scribner, and London, Gollancz, 1960.
The Evil Wish. New York, Scribner, and London, Gollancz, 1962.
The Only Good Secretary. New York, Scribner, 1965; London, Gollancz, 1966.
The Footsteps on the Stairs. New York, Scribner, 1966; London, Gollancz, 1967.
The Trash Stealer. New York, Scribner, and London, Gollancz, 1968.
The Little Lie. New York, Scribner, 1968; London, Gollancz, 1969.
An Affair of the Heart. New York, Scribner, and London, Gollancz, 1970.
The Troublemaker. New York, Scribner, 1972; London, Gollancz, 1973.
My Brother's Killer. New York, Scribner, 1975; London, Gollancz, 1976.

Uncollected Short Stories

"The Withered Heart," in *Cream of the Crime.* New York, Holt Rinehart, 1962; London, Harrap, 1964.
"The Inner Voices," in *Ellery Queen's All-Star Lineup.* New York, New American Library, 1967; London, Gollancz, 1968.
"Murderer No. 2," in *Alfred Hitchcock's Tales to Keep You Spellbound,* edited by Eleanor Sullivan. New York, Davis, 1976.

OTHER PUBLICATIONS

Novel

Someone to Remember. Philadelphia, Westminster Press, 1943.

*   *   *

The mystery novel faced a period of change in the late 1940's and early 1950's. In a new push for realism, old masters (like Margery Allingham) and newcomers alike developed a "police procedural" approach. Others employed a more believable brand of private eye. Jean Potts took a more unusual approach. In her novels, realism stems, not from the professional sleuth or his investigation, but from the realistic portrayal of a small, inter-related group of people (i.e., the "suspects") confronted with unnatural death.

Potts's career began auspiciously with *Go, Lovely Rose,* which won an Edgar in 1954. More than most of her subsequent novels, it closely resembles a classic whodunit. There are official sleuths: Sheriff Jeffreys and Mr. Pigeon. But they can only get at part of the truth. The murder is finally solved by those most intimately involved—a cross-purpose collection of the major suspects. After her first mystery, Potts seldom bothered portraying police characters at all. Their part of the action occurs off-stage and is extraneous to the real process of tragic discovery for the central characters. Potts's style of domestic investigation is intense, if unorthodox. And since the law is unimportant, there is no stock-piling of evidence with a trial in view. Instead, a fortuitous bit of circumstantial evidence is often presented to the culprit by other suspects. A confession is often followed by suicide or mental collapse. All this is witnessed by the murderer's peers—as collective nemesis and mourner.

In addition to a healthy disrespect for legal procedures, Potts's novels also show a marked tendency to stray (much to the distaste of purist-critics) from the plot formulas of the traditional mystery. Her third novel, *The Diehard,* is the story of a small-town tyrant ego-muscling his way to an early grave. But as the tyrant dies at the end, and not at the beginning, of the novel, the question is not whodunit, but who (of the many candidates) *will* do it. The story is nicely suspenseful (complete with surprise ending) and almost allegorical. Love, we are shown, can be even more lethal than hatred. Potts continued to write mystery parables. *The Evil Wish* teaches that the intent to murder can be as morally destructive as the act. And *The Little*

Lie is an extremely macabre illustration of the old adage: "What a tangled web we weave. . . . "

Suspense or whodunit, the most important aspect of Potts's novels is character. The mystery plot, whatever its form, is but a means to that end. There are few absolute good guys or villains here. Characters are generally both unlovable and unhateable. They evoke, in the reader, and repeatedly in one another, only a sense of helpless pity. All are painfully human, and recognizable without being stereotypical. Take, for example, the passive antagonist—a character Potts carefully observes in such books as *Death of a Stray Cat* and *The Troublemaker.* These are born victims (both, not surprisingly, women) who unconsciously incite violence in others. Potts adds new, honest meaning to the old sexist concept of the girl "who asked for it." This is one author who doesn't trade in happily-ever-afters. Her characters, even the most blameless, cannot go unscathed by the violence around them. They carry their share of guilt and anguish. And it is a clear case of the survival of the fittest. Only those characters with sufficient mental and emotional strength will "survive." The murder (or death) and its investigation represent a crisis point for all involved. For some, like Martin Shipley in *The Footsteps on the Stairs,* the crisis provides the impetus to re-commit themselves to life. But these are the lucky few.

Potts does not, perhaps, write the most cheerful of mystery novels. But her exploration of the effects of violence on life-like characters is no mean accomplishment. Her steady eye, quiet wit, and unfailing compassion make her an important contributor to the modern mystery novel.

—Kathleen L. Maio

POWELL, James. Canadian. Born in Toronto, 12 June 1932. Educated at St. Michael's College, University of Toronto, B.A. 1955; University of Paris, 1955–56. Teacher in France, 1956–58; editor, Doubleday publishers, New York, 1958–60, *Catholic Messenger,* Davenport, Iowa, 1960–62, *Joel Satar's Antiques News,* Marietta, Pennsylvania, 1970–71. Address: 235 West Market Street, Marietta, Pennsylvania 17547, U.S.A.

CRIME PUBLICATIONS

Uncollected Short Stories

"Have You Heard the Latest," in *Caper* (New York), April 1967.
"The Friends of Hector Jouvet," in *Ellery Queen's All-Star Lineup.* New York, New American Library, 1967; London, Gollancz, 1968.
"The Stollmeyer Sonnets," in *Best Detective Stories of the Year,* edited by Anthony Boucher. New York, Dutton, 1967.
"The Daring Daylight Melon Robbery," in *Ellery Queen's Mystery Magazine* (New York), October 1968.
"The Great Paleontological Murder Mystery," in *Ellery Queen's Mystery Magazine* (New York), November 1968.
"The Beddoes Scheme," in *Best Detective Stories of the Year,* edited by Anthony Boucher. New York, Dutton, 1968.
"Maze in the Elevator," in *Ellery Queen's Murder Menu.* Cleveland, World, and London, Gollancz, 1969.
"The Altdorf Syndrome," in *Ellery Queen's Grand Slam.* Cleveland, World, 1970; London, Gollancz, 1971.

"Kleber on Murder in 30 Volumes," in *Best Detective Stories of the Year,* edited by Allen J. Hubin. New York, Dutton, 1970.
"The Plot Against Santa Claus," in *Ellery Queen's Mystery Magazine* (New York), January 1971.
"Three Men in a Tub," in *Ellery Queen's Mystery Magazine* (New York), September 1971.
"Coins in the Frascati Fountain," in *Best Detective Stories of the Year,* edited by Allen J. Hubin. New York, Dutton, 1971.
"Ganelon and the Master Thief," in *Ellery Queen's Mystery Magazine* (New York), October 1972.
"The Gobineau Necklace," in *Ellery Queen's Mystery Bag.* Cleveland, World, 1972; London, Gollancz, 1973.
"The Pomeranian's Whereabouts," in *Ellery Queen's Mystery Magazine* (New York), January 1973.
"The Ascent of the Grimselhorn," in *Ellery Queen's Mystery Magazine* (New York), April 1973.
"The Bee on the Finger," in *Playboy* (Chicago), September 1973.
"The Theft of the Fabulous Bird," in *Ellery Queen's Mystery Magazine* (New York), November 1973.
"The Oubliette Cipher," in *Ellery Queen's Mystery Magazine* (New York), November 1974.
"A Murder Coming," in *Best Detective Stories of the Year 1974,* edited by Allen J. Hubin. New York, Dutton, 1974.
"The Eye of Shafti," in *Every Crime in the Book,* edited by Robert L. Fish. New York, Putnam, 1975.
"The Trolls of God," in *Playboy* (Chicago), February 1977.
"Bianca and the Seven Sleuths," in *Ellery Queen's Searches and Seizures.* New York, Dial Press, 1977.
"Blind Man's Cuff," in *Ellery Queen's Mystery Magazine* (New York), July 1981.
"The Notorious Snowman," in *Ellery Queen's Mystery Magazine* (New York), October 1981.
"The Priest Without a Shadow," in *Ellery Queen's Mystery Magazine* (New York), January 1982.
"The Vigil of Death," in *Ellery Queen's Mystery Magazine* (New York), July 1982.
"The Haunted Bookcase," in *Ellery Queen's Mystery Magazine* (New York), August 1982.
"A Bagdad Reckoning," in *Ellery Queen's Mystery Magazine* (New York), November 1982.
"A Pocketful of Noses," in *The Year's Best Mystery and Suspense Stories,* edited by Edward D. Hoch. New York, Walker, 1983.
"Death in the Christmas Hour," in *Ellery Queen's Mystery Magazine* (New York), January 1983.
"The Scarlet Totem" in *Ellery Queen's Mystery Magazine* (New York), April 1983.
"The Bird-of-Paradise Man," in *Ellery Queen's Mystery Magazine* (New York), July 1983.
"The Phantom Haircut," in *Ellery Queen's Mystery Magazine* (New York), October 1983.
"The Meandering Pearl," in *Ellery Queen's Mystery Magazine* (New York), November 1983.
"The Dark Elf Master of Crack of Doom," in *Ellery Queen's Mystery Magazine* (New York), December 1983.
"The Labyrinth of Life," in *Ellery Queen's Mystery Magazine* (New York), February 1984.
"The Stranger at the Crossroads," in *Ellery Queen's Mystery Magazine* (New York), May 1984.
"The Polygon from Alpha Centauri," in *Ellery Queen's Mystery Magazine* (New York), July 1984.
"Under the Spangled Roger," in *Ellery Queen's Mystery Magazine* (New York), November 1984.
"The Mandalasian Garotte," in *Fingerprints,* edited by Beverly Beethan-Endersby. Toronto, Irwin, 1984.

"Death in the Christmas House," in *Sherlock Holmes Through Time and Space*, edited by Isaac Asimov, Martin H. Greenberg and Charles G. Waugh. New York, Bluejay, 1984; London, Severn House, 1985.

"The Verbatim Reply," in *Ellery Queen's Mystery Magazine* (New York), March 1985.

"The Dawn of Captain Sunset," in *Ellery Queen's Mystery Magazine* (New York), April 1985.

"The Brass Man," in *Ellery Queen's Mystery Magazine* (New York), June 1985.

"The Dunderhead Bus," in *Ellery Queen's Mystery Magazine* (New York), August 1985.

"The Hiccup Flask," in *Ellery Queen's Mystery Magazine* (New York), October 1985.

"The Bridge of Traded Dreams," in *Ellery Queen's Mystery Magazine* (New York), December 1985.

"Trophy Day at the Chateau Gai," in *Ellery Queen's More Lost Ladies*, edited by Eleanor Sullivan. New York, Davis, 1985.

"The Coffee-Table Book," in *Ellery Queen's Mystery Magazine* (New York), January 1986.

"The Singular Bird," in *Ellery Queen's Mystery Magazine* (New York), April 1986.

"The Origami Moose," in *Ellery Queen's Mystery Magazine* (New York), June 1986.

"Death's Sandwich Man," in *Ellery Queen's Mystery Magazine* (New York), August 1986.

"The Cannibal Gourmet," in *Ellery Queen's Mystery Magazine* (New York), December 1986.

"A Baksheesh from the North," in *Ellery Queen's Prime Crimes*, edited by Eleanor Sullivan. New York, Dial Press, 1986.

"The Brim Whistle," in *Ellery Queen's Mystery Magazine* (New York), February 1987.

"The Mad Scientist," in *Ellery Queen's Mystery Magazine* (New York), April 1987.

"Wingtips," in *Ellery Queen's Mystery Magazine* (New York), June 1987.

"The Tupil Juggernaut," in *Ellery Queen's Mystery Magazine* (New York), September 1987.

"The Talking Donkey," in *Ellery Queen's Mystery Magazine* (New York), Mid-December 1987.

"The Quick and the Dead," in *Ellery Queen's Mystery Magazine* (New York), February 1988.

"The Kidnap of the Bounding Mane," in *Ellery Queen's Mystery Magazine* (New York), June 1988.

"Midnight Pumpkins," in *Ellery Queen's Mystery Magazine* (New York), September 1988.

"The Cerebus Emerald," in *Ellery Queen's Mystery Magazine* (New York), October 1988.

"Still Life with Orioles," *Ellery Queen's Mystery Magazine* (New York), December 1988.

"A New Leaf," in *Ellery Queen's Mystery Magazine* (New York), January 1989.

"Burning Bridges," in *Ellery Queen's Mystery Magazine* (New York) February 1989.

"The Snood of Night," in *Ellery Queen's Mystery Magazine* (New York), March 1989.

"The Greenhouse Dogs," in *Ellery Queen's Mystery Magazine* (New York), June 1989.

"The Sting of the Hoop Snake," in *Ellery Queen's Mystery Magazine* (New York), July 1989.

"The Doors of Spring," in *Ellery Queen's Mystery Magazine* (New York), September 1989.

"The Hot-Stove League," in *Ellery Queen's Mystery Magazine* (New York), January 1990.

"Mrs. Brodie's Cow," in *Ellery Queen's Mystery Magazine* (New York), April 1990.

"A Dirge for Clowntown," in *The Year's Best Mystery and Suspense Stories 1990*, edited by Edward D. Hoch. New York, Walker, 1990.

*

Manuscript Collection: University of Wyoming, Laramie.

James Powell comments:

Since it may not come round again I mustn't let pass this chance to offer a few words of introduction to my modest body of work. I see myself as a writer of humorous fiction who is attracted to the mystery story. I don't find this strange. Both the funny story and the mystery travel down a strongly plotted road all the while preparing the reader for the punch line, the unexpected ending which he must instantly understand was the only ending there ever could have been.

Where they fall into groups my stories are currently of four kinds: those that relate the adventures of Acting Sergeant Maynard Bullock of the Royal Canadian Mounted Police, an earnest bungler of whom I am unashamedly fond; those fantasies of mystery and detection told in nursery story, fairy tale or Arabian nights settings; the adventures of Captain Sunset, my champion of the elderly; and stories about the Riviera principality of San Sebastiano. Among these can be found the cases of the Ambrose Ganelons, four generations of detectives with the same name whose activities span 125 years. Having fashioned a history for San Sebastiano worthy of any country in Europe, laid down its ample boulevards, set its buildings in place, and originated its many quaint customs I find myself replying sharply to those who suggest it is only Monaco under another name. In fact the truth is quite the other way around.

*   *   *

It is difficult to explain why the talents of James Powell have largely gone unappreciated and his stories uncollected and seldom anthologized. The S.J. Perelman of the mystery story, he specializes in outrageous, hilarious satires, dealing with international crime and surprise endings.

In "The Eye of Shafti" Powell dares to do a story about the theft of a jewel from an Asian temple. He includes a hilarious scene of temple priests pursuing the thief along the Street of Flowering Garbage. "The Beddoes Scheme" is a story about an incredible alternative to the atom bomb as a means of ending World War II. Many Powell stories are set in the fictional Riviera state of San Sebastiano. Stories such as "Coins in the Frascati Fountain," the longest and best of these, recount the adventures of Inspector Flanel, the Ambrose Ganelon Detective Agency, Warden Alfred Panache, and others. Another Powell series features the dim-witted Acting Sergeant Maynard Bullock of the Canadian mounties. In his first story, "The Stollmeyer Sonnets," Bullock explains, "for the last couple of years I've been guarding the flowerbeds in front of the Parliament Buildings in Ottawa ... It's exciting work in its own way. You never hear the bee that has your name on it." In "The Mandalasian Garotte" he parachutes into the jungles of Asia and ends up claiming territory in the name of Canada. Powell has even written a series of mysteries based on fairytales, including "The Plot Against Santa Claus," "Three Men in a Tub," "The Theft of the Fabulous Hen," and "Bianca and the Seven Sleuths," a Snow White take-off. One of his rare "serious" stories is "Maze in the Elevator," about two men trapped in an elevator. It is the kind of terror-filled urban situation most city dwellers dread—but told with a typically unusual, unguessable Powell finish.

—Marvin Lachman

———

POWELL, Talmage. Also writes as Robert Hart Davis; Robert Henry; Milton T. Lamb; Milton Land; Jack McCready; Ellery Queen; Dave Sands; Anne Talmage. American. Born in Hendersonville, North Carolina, 4 October 1920. Attended schools in North Carolina, Tennessee, New York, and California; studied creative writing at University of North Carolina, Chapel Hill. Married Mildred Morgan; one son. Agent: Scott Meredith Literary Agency, 845 Third Avenue, New York, New York 10022. Address: 33 Caledonia Road, Kenilworth, Asheville, North Carolina 28803, U.S.A.

CRIME PUBLICATIONS

Novels (series: Ed Rivers)

The Killer Is Mine (Rivers). New York, Pocket Books, 1959.
The Smasher. New York, Macmillan, 1959.
The Girl's Number Doesn't Answer (Rivers). New York, Pocket Books, 1960.
Man-Killer. New York, Ace, 1960.
The Girl Who Killed Things. N.p. Zenith, 1960.
With a Madman Behind Me (Rivers). New York, Pocket Books, 1962.
Start Screaming Murder (Rivers). New York, Pocket Books, 1962.
The Raper (as Jack McCready). Derby, Connecticut, Monarch, 1962.
Corpus Delectable (Rivers). New York, Pocket Books, 1965.

Novels as Ellery Queen (series: Tim Corrigan)

Murder with a Past. New York, Pocket Books, 1963.
Beware the Young Stranger. New York, Pocket Books, 1965.
Where Is Bianca? (Corrigan). New York, Popular Library, and London, New English Library, 1966.
Who Spies, Who Kills? (Corrigan). New York, Popular Library, 1966; London, New English Library, 1967.

Short Stories

Written for Hitchcock. Nashville, Tennessee, Rutledge Press, 1989.

Uncollected Short Stories

"Double-cross Work Puzzle," in *10-Story Detective* (Springfield, Massachusetts), January 1944.
"Another Man's Poison," in *Ten Detective Aces* (Springfield, Massachusetts), February 1944.
"Page Mr. Murder," in *Ten Detective Aces* (Springfield, Massachusetts), April 1944.
"I Bleed for You, Babe," in *Detective Tales* (Chicago), June 1944.
"Sunstroke at Midnight," in *The Shadow* (New York), August 1944.
"Murder Isn't Timid," in *The Shadow* (New York), September 1944.

"Death in Dirty Dishes," in *The Shadow* (New York), October 1944.
"Murder Reigns in Sunshine City," in *Ten Detective Aces* (Springfield, Massachusetts), November 1944.
"The Mouth Makes Murder," in *New Detective* (Chicago), November 1944.
"Homicide Hoax," in *10-Story Detective* (Springfield, Massachusetts), December 1944.
"Margin for Terror," in *Detective Tales* (Chicago), January 1945.
"Murder on the Expense Account," in *The Shadow* (New York), January 1945.
"An Occasional Rat," in *The Shadow* (New York), March 1945.
"Dead—But Still Knocking," in *Ten Detective Aces* (Springfield, Massachusetts), March 1945.
"Kill Once—Kill Twice," in *Dime Mystery* (Kokomo, Indiana), March 1945.
"All Things to Me," in *The Shadow* (New York), April 1945.
"Cain Had a Brother," in *Detective Tales* (Chicago), April 1945.
"Six Hours To Kill," in *Hollywood Detective* (Springfield, Massachusetts), April 1945.
"Early To Bed, Never To Rise," in *Crack Detective* (Holyoke, Massachusetts), May 1945.
"Remind Me to Kill You," in *New Detective* (Chicago), May 1945.
"The Dark Unfriendly Tide," in *Dime Mystery* (Kokomo, Indiana), May 1945.
"Need abody Cry?," in *Detective Tales* (Chicago), June 1945.
"When The Victim Dies," in *Hollywood Detective* (Springfield, Massachusetts), June 1945.
"Murder Bait," in *Dime Mystery* (Kokomo, Indiana), July 1945.
"To Fit The Crime," in *Crack Detective* (Holyoke, Massachusetts), July 1945.
"Uneasy Lies the Headstone," in *Ten Detective Aces* (Springfield, Massachusetts), September 1945.
"Scales and Blindfold," in *The Shadow* (New York), October 1945.
"The King of Hell," in *Detective Tales* (Chicago), October 1945.
"Back Door To Murder," in *Dime Mystery* (Kokomo, Indiana), November 1945.
"Johnny On The Spot," in *Crack Detective* (Holyoke, Massachusetts), November 1945.
"Keep My Picture There," in *Detective Tales* (Chicago), November 1945.
"Murder's Open House," in *10-Story Detective* (Springfield, Massachusetts), December 1945.
"Blood on His Hands," in *Detective Tales* (Chicago), January 1946.
"The Corpse Man," in *Dime Mystery* (Kokomo, Indiana), January 1946.
"Mystery of The Punctual Vulture," in *10-Story Detective* (Springfield, Massachusetts), February 1946.
"Stay as Dead as You Are," in *Dime Mystery* (Kokomo, Indiana), February 1946.
"Tab Me For The Kill," in *Private Detective Stories* (New York), February 1946.
"Barney Is the Hero," in *Doc Savage* (New York), March 1946.
"Nobody Knew The Corpse," in *Crack Detective* (Holyoke, Massachusetts), March 1946.
"The Corpse in the Crystal," in *Ten Detective Aces* (Springfield, Massachusetts), March 1946.
"Kill and Run Girl," in *Detective Tales* (Chicago), April 1946.
"The Impossible Godiva," in *The Shadow* (New York), April 1946.

"Each Man Kills," in *Dime Mystery* (Kokomo, Indiana), May 1946.

"Your Crime is My Crime," in *New Detective* (Chicago), May 1946.

"Blood On Her Hands," in *Thrilling Detective* (New York), July 1946.

"Make Your Kill," in *Private Detective Stories* (New York), July 1946.

"Murder Gets Easier," in *The Shadow* (New York), July 1946.

"Keep the Corpse in the Family," in *Detective Tales* (Chicago), August 1946.

"The Man from Six Feet Under," in *Ten Detective Aces* (Springfield, Massachusetts), August 1946.

"Show Them You're Tough," in *The Shadow* (New York), September 1946.

"A Gift for Jeannie," in *Detective Tales* (Chicago), November 1946.

"Death Is a Blonde," in *The Shadow* (New York), November 1946.

"Sin Sisters," in *Crack Detective* (Holyoke, Massachusetts), November 1946.

"Case of the Deadly Dream," in *Ten Detective Aces* (Springfield, Massachusetts), December 1946.

"Fury in the Family," in *The Shadow* (New York), December 1946.

"I Ain't So Dumb" (as Robert Henry), in *The Shadow* (New York), December 1946.

"Murder, Mamacita, Murder," in *Crack Detective* (Holyoke, Massachusetts), January 1947.

"Swamp Fever," in *Dime Mystery* (Kokomo, Indiana), January 1947.

"A Little on the Homicidal Side," in *Detective Tales* (Chicago), March 1947.

"Blood In Your Eye," in *Dime Mystery* (Kokomo, Indiana), March 1947.

"Clothes Make the Cop," in *Detective Tales* (Chicago), April 1947.

"The Killer Who Used His Skull," in *Ten Detective Aces* (Springfield, Massachusetts), April 1947.

"Cupid Packs a Pistol," in *10-Story Detective* (Springfield, Massachusetts), May 1947.

"The Guilty One," in *New Detective* (Chicago), May 1947.

"To Cross A Mountain," in *Dime Mystery* (Kokomo, Indiana), May 1947.

"Burn in Turn," in *Dime Detective* (Chicago), August 1947.

"The $64,000 Question," in *Detective Tales* (Chicago), August 1947.

"Undertake Murder," in *Crack Detective* (Holyoke, Massachusetts), August 1947.

"Crime of the Ancient Mariner," in *Dime Detective* (Chicago), September 1947.

"It Takes Two to Make a Kill," in *Ten Detective Aces* (Springfield, Massachusetts), September 1947.

"Rub-Out Inn," in *Detective Tales* (Chicago), October 1947.

"A Favor for Charlie," in *Detective Tales* (Chicago), November 1947.

"On Borrowed Crime," in *Ten Detective Aces* (Springfield, Massachusetts), November 1947.

"Time Out of Mind," in *Dime Mystery* (Kokomo, Indiana), November 1947.

"Slaughter's Daughter," in *10-Story Detective* (Springfield, Massachusetts), December 1947.

"You Got To Have A Corpse," in *Dime Mystery* (Kokomo, Indiana), January 1948.

"Last Laugh For The Dying," in *Crack Detective* (Holyoke, Massachusetts), February 1948.

"Murder On The Make," in *10-Story Detective* (Springfield, Massachusetts), February 1948.

"Jeannie with the Deep Red Scare," in *Ten Detective Aces* (Springfield, Massachusetts), March 1948.

"The Unsinkable Body," in *Detective Tales* (Chicago), March 1948.

"In My Coffin I Wait," in *Dime Mystery* (Kokomo, Indiana), April 1948.

"Orchids of Doom," in *10-Story Detective* (Springfield, Massachusetts), April 1948.

"Briers for Two," in *Ten Detective Aces* (Springfield, Massachusetts), May 1948.

"Barracuda!," in *Detective Tales* (Chicago), June 1948.

"The Last of Mrs. Satan," in *Dime Mystery* (Kokomo, Indiana), June 1948.

"The Screaming House," in *Dime Mystery* (Kokomo, Indiana), August 1948.

"Easy Kill," in *Detective Tales* (Chicago), September 1948.

"Deadly Memory," in *Detective Tales* (Chicago), November 1948.

"So Little Crime," in *New Detective* (Chicago), November 1948.

"Knock on any Grave," in *Detective Tales* (Chicago), December 1948.

"The Witness," in *Detective Tales* (Chicago), January 1949.

"Black Widow," in *Detective Tales* (Chicago), February 1949.

"Terror by Night," in *Detective Tales* (Chicago), March 1949.

"A Slight Taste of Murder," in *New Detective* (Chicago), May 1949.

"Hang the Man High," in *Ten Detective Aces* (Springfield, Massachusetts), May 1949.

"Dance, Little Devil-Doll," in *Dime Mystery* (Kokomo, Indiana), June 1949.

"Her Dagger Before Me," in *Black Mask* (New York), July 1949.

"A Head Off Her Shoulders," in *Dime Mystery* (Kokomo, Indiana), August 1949.

"Cry Murder," in *All-Story Detective* (Chicago), August 1949.

"Corpse For a Day," in *New Detective* (Chicago), September 1949.

"Midnight Pick-Up," in *Detective Tales* (Chicago), October 1949.

"Dead Man Up," in *Dime Mystery* (Kokomo, Indiana), December 1949.

"Belleef the Brawl," in *Detective Tales* (Chicago), January 1950.

"Murder's Merry Widows," in *15 Mystery Tales,* February 1950.

"A Woman's Job," in *Detective Tales* (Chicago), April 1950.

"Manhunt," in *Detective Tales* (Chicago), May 1950.

"So Near, So Dear, So Dead," in *Super Detective* (New York), May 1950.

"For Old Crime's Sake," in *Detective Tales* (Chicago), June 1950.

"Murder Paid in Advance," in *Dime Detective* (Chicago), June 1950.

"Forget-Me-Not Killer," in *Dime Detective* (Chicago), July 1950.

"The Wind Of Fear," in *15-Story Detective* (Kokomo, Indiana), August 1950.

"Lady On The Kill," in *15-Story Detective* (Kokomo, Indiana), October 1950.

"There Was a Crooked Man," in *Dime Detective* (Chicago), October 1950.

"Twin Kill," in *Smashing Detective* (Holyoke, Massachusetts), March 1951.

"Terror in the Sun," in *Suspense* (New York), Fall 1951.

"No Bodies, Darling," in *Dime Detective* (Chicago), February 1952.

"Murder Goes To The Dogs," in *Smashing Detective* (Holyoke, Massachusetts), March 1952.

"The Beautiful Miss Borgia," in *Dime Detective* (Chicago), August 1952.

"Man Sinister," in *5 Detective Novels* (Springfield, Massachusetts), Fall 1952.

"Deadliest Enemy," in *Detective Tales* (Chicago), October 1952.

"Nursery Crime," in *Popular Detective* (New York), November 1952.

"Killer Be Good," in *New Detective* (Chicago), December 1952.

"Gold-Plated Girl," in *Detective Tales* (Chicago), February 1953.

"The Murder Market," in *Detective Tales* (Chicago), April 1953.

"The Swamp Searchers," in *Detective Story* (New York), July 1953.

"Curtain Call," in *Detective Story* (New York), September 1953.

"The Third Revolutionary," in *G-Men Detective* (New York), Winter 1953.

"What Happened To Lisa?," in *5 Detective Novels* (Springfield, Massachusetts), Winter 1953.

"Shadow of Guilt," in *Smashing Detective* (Holyoke, Massachusetts), March 1956.

"The Nice Girl," in *Guilty* (New York), July 1956.

"Incubation Period," in *Hunted* (New York), August 1956.

"The Longest Shadow," in *Hunted* (New York), October 1956.

"Man on the Ledge," in *Guilty* (New York), November 1956.

"You Have a Vicious Mind," in *Trapped* (New York), December 1956.

"See No Evil," in *Double-Action Detective Stories 4* (New York), 1956.

"Somebody's Going to Die," in *Manhunt* (New York), January 1957

"He Won't Live Long," in *Sure Fire Detective Stories* (New York), February 1957.

"Next!," in *Manhunt* (New York), February 1957.

"Run, Carl, Run," in *Manhunt* (New York), February 1957.

"The Golden Kid," in *Guilty* (New York), March 1957.

"Midnight Blonde," in *Manhunt* (New York), May 1957.

"Inhuman Act," in *Trapped* (New York), June 1957.

"Boy with a Gun," in *Guilty* (New York), July 1957.

"Cold Steal," in *Murder* (New York), July 1957.

"Lead Cure," in *Manhunt* (New York), July 1957.

"Betrayal," in *Pursued* (New York), September–October 1957.

"On A Quiet Afternoon," in *Murder* (New York), September–October 1957.

"One Hell of a Night," in *Guilty* (New York), September 1957.

"The Favor," in *Manhunt* (New York), September 1957.

"A Beautiful Babe and Money," in *Manhunt* (New York), October 1957.

"The Big Thrill," in *Trapped* (New York), October 1957.

"Breaking Point," in *Double-Action Detective Stories* (New York), Winter 1957–58.

"Return No More," in *Manhunt* (New York), January 1958.

"Be a Man!," in *Manhunt* (New York), February 1958.

"The Crimson Trail" (as Dave Sands), in *Mike Shayne Mystery Magazine* (London), February 1958.

"The Dame Across the River," in *Manhunt* (New York), April 1958.

"Homecoming Party," in *Mike Shayne Mystery Magazine* (New York), October 1958.

"Rivals," in *Manhunt* (New York), October 1958.

"Dear Mr. Lonelyhearts," in *Ellery Queen's Mystery Magazine* (New York), November 1958.

"Salesmanship," in *Ellery Queen's Mystery Magazine* (New York), November 1958.

"Unholy Night" (as Dave Sands), in *15 Mystery Tales,* February 1959.

"Kill-Crazy Husband," in *Guilty* (New York), March 1959.

"Murderer's Gift," in *Mike Shayne Mystery Magazine* (New York), May 1959.

"Big Man in the Neighborhood," in *Trapped* (New York), June 1959.

"Demon of the Black," in *Two-Fisted Detective Stories* (New York), July 1959.

"I'll Never Tell," in *Guilty* (New York), July 1959.

"Accused of Rape," in *Trapped* (New York), August 1959.

"A Cell to Go Home To," in *Mystery Tales* (New York), August 1959.

"His Blood was Bad," in *Two-Fisted Detective Stories* (New York), September 1959.

"Your Husband's in the Morgue," in *Guilty* (New York), September 1959.

"Beast of Prey," in *Saint's Mystery Library* (New York), October 1959.

"Jury of One," in *Alfred Hitchcock's Mystery Magazine* (New York), October 1959.

"My Cousin Twice Removed," in *Mike Shayne Mystery Magazine* (New York), February 1960.

"Life Sentence," in *Manhunt* (New York), April 1960.

"A Man of Importance," in *Tightrope* (New York), May 1960.

"Death of a Daughter," in *Mike Shayne Mystery Magazine* (New York), May 1960.

"Twice Temptation," in *Sunset Strip* (New York), July 1960.

"The Big One," in *Mike Shayne Mystery Magazine* (New York), September 1960.

"30,000,000 Witnesses," in *Alfred Hitchcock's Mystery Magazine* (New York), November 1960.

"H-Man," in *Two-Fisted Detective Stories* (New York), December 1960.

"Passion's Fires Kill," in *Off Beat Detective Stories* (New York), January 1961.

"To the Last Drop!," in *Detective Tales* (London), March 1961.

"With a Madman Behind Me," in *Mike Shayne Mystery Magazine* (New York), April 1961.

"Fear Stalks the Shadows," in *Off Beat Detective Stories* (New York), May 1961.

"Money, Murder, or Love," in *Alfred Hitchcock's Mystery Magazine* (New York), June 1961.

"Dear Sir," in *Manhunt* (New York), October 1961.

"Family Affair," in *Alfred Hitchcock's Mystery Magazine* (New York), October 1961.

"The Blonde and the Patsy," in *Guilty* (New York), December 1961.

"Murder Method," in *Best Detective Stories of the Year 1961* edited by Brett Halliday. New York, Dutton, 1961.

"Death Will Find You," in *Keyhole* (New York), April 1962.

"Murderer's Role," in *Mike Shayne Mystery Magazine* (New York), April 1962.

"The Righteous," in *Manhunt* (New York), April 1962.

"Start Screaming, Murderer," in *Mike Shayne Mystery Magazine* (New York), August 1962.

"Winner Takes Nothing," in *The Saint* (New York), September 1962.

"Sister Pookie's Remedy," in *Mike Shayne Mystery Magazine* (New York), October 1962.

"Dead End Street Walker," in *Man's Magazine,* Spring 1963.

"Precious Pigeon," in *Manhunt* (New York), April 1963.

"A Break in the Weather," in *Ellery Queen's Mystery Magazine* (New York), August 1963.

"The Butler Didn't Do It," in *The Saint* (London), August 1963.

"Case of the Lewd Nude," in *Man's Magazine*, September 1963.

"The Belle Collector," in *Guy*, February 1964.

"Unnatural Death of a Natural Blonde," in *Man's Magazine*, April 1964.

"The Third Murderer," in *Mike Shayne Mystery Magazine* (New York), May 1964.

"False Start," in *Alfred Hitchcock's Mystery Magazine* (New York), October 1964.

"Corpus Delicti," in *Mink Is for Minx*. New York, Dell, 1964.

"Witness For The Prostitution," in *Man's Magazine*, 1964.

"Presentiment of Evil," in *Mike Shayne Mystery Magazine* (New York), March 1965.

"Mind the Posies," in *Alfred Hitchcock's Mystery Magazine* (New York), June 1965.

"The Five Year Caper," in *Alfred Hitchcock's Mystery Magazine* (New York), August 1965.

"Reward for Genius," in *Alfred Hitchcock's Mystery Magazine* (New York), November 1965.

"I Had a Hunch, and . . . . ," in *Alfred Hitchcock's Witches' Brew*. New York, Dell, 1965.

"The Bet," in *Bizarre* (Concord, New Hampshire), January 1966.

"The Self Defenders," in *Shell Scott Mystery Magazine* (New York), February 1966.

"Homicide Bride," in *Man's Magazine*, March 1966.

"Home Baked Cake," in *Mike Shayne Mystery Magazine* (New York), April 1966.

"Uncle Charlie's Wife," in *Shell Scott Mystery Magazine* (New York), April 1966.

"Fatherly Advice," in *Shell Scott Mystery Magazine* (New York), June 1966.

"Lorna's Back in Town," in *Ellery Queen's Mystery Magazine* (New York), June 1966.

"Every Possible Motive," in *Shell Scott Mystery Magazine* (New York), August 1966.

"The Seven Year Hitch," in *The Man from U.N.C.L.E.* (New York), August 1966.

"The Ripper and The Stripper," in *Guy*, October 1966.

"Last Run of the Night," in *Ellery Queen's Mystery Magazine* (New York), January 1967.

"The Hungry World Affair" (as Robert Davis), in *The Man from U.N.C.L.E.* (New York), March 1967.

"The Privilege of Crime," in *Alfred Hitchcock's Mystery Magazine* (New York), March 1967.

"The Death of Skipper Blake," in *Mike Shayne Mystery Magazine* (New York), July 1967.

"The Insured," in *Mike Shayne Mystery Magazine* (New York), August 1967.

"Counter Agent," in *The Girl from U.N.C.L.E.* (New York), December 1967.

"Heist in Pianisimo," in *Alfred Hitchcock's Games Killers Play*. New York, Dell, 1967.

"The Longest Trip," in *Alfred Hitchcock's Mystery Magazine* (New York), September 1968.

"Psycho Symptoms," in *Alfred Hitchcock's Mystery Magazine* (New York), November 1968.

"One Unnecessary Man," in *Alfred Hitchcock's Skull Session*. New York, Dell, 1968.

"Sudden, Sudden Death," in *Alfred Hitchcock's Coffin Corner*. New York, Dell, 1968.

"The Second Mrs. Randleman," in *Alfred Hitchcock's Mystery Magazine* (New York), February 1969.

"The Jury Caper," in *Mike Shayne Mystery Magazine* (New York), July 1969.

"The Way Out," in *Alfred Hitchcock's Mystery Magazine* (New York), July 1969.

"A Time for Triumph," in *Players Choice*. New York, Whitman, 1969.

"To Avoid a Scandal," in *Alfred Hitchcock's Death Bag*. New York, Dell, 1969.

"The Clueful Coffin," in *Alfred Hitchcock's Mystery Magazine* (New York), February 1970.

"To Spare a Life," in *Alfred Hitchcock's Mystery Magazine* (New York), March 1970.

"In the House of Rats," in *Ellery Queen's Mystery Magazine* (New York), September 1970.

"Old Man Emmons," in *Alfred Hitchcock's Get Them to Wake On Time*. New York, Dell, 1970.

"The Commune," in *Alfred Hitchcock's Mystery Magazine* (New York), January 1971.

"The Nylon Stocking Bandits," in *Ellery Queen's Mystery Magazine* (New York), February 1971.

"Gator Bait," in *Alfred Hitchcock's Mystery Magazine* (New 'York), March 1971.

"The Delicate Victim," in *Alfred Hitchcock's Mystery Magazine* (New York), July 1971.

"Trial Run," in *Alfred Hitchcock's Mystery Magazine* (New York), August 1971.

"Lone Witness," in *Alfred Hitchcock's Down By the Old Blood Stream*. New York, Dell, 1971.

"The Heir," in *Alfred Hitchcock's I Am Curious*. New York, Dell, 1971.

"The Man Downstairs," in *Mike Shayne Mystery Magazine* (Los Angeles), July 1972.

"A Truly Honest Man," in *Mike Shayne Mystery Magazine* (Los Angeles), September 1972.

"Welcome Home, Pal," in *Mike Shayne Mystery Magazine* (Los Angeles), October 1972.

"Drawer 14," in *Alfred Hitchcock's Happy Death Day*. New York, Dell, 1972.

"Parole Violation," in *Mike Shayne Mystery Magazine* (Los Angeles), May 1973.

"The Tip-Off," in *Alfred Hitchcock's Mystery Magazine* (New York), August 1973.

"An Interrogation," in *Alfred Hitchcock's Death Mate*. New York, Dell, 1973.

"Mac Without a Knife," in *Alfred Hitchcock's Let It All Bleed Out*. New York, Dell, 1973.

"The Deadly Taxicab," in *Mike Shayne Mystery Magazine* (Los Angeles), September 1974.

"Chimps Ain't Chumps," in *Alfred Hitchcock's Bleeding Hearts*. New York, Dell, 1974.

"A Change of Heart," in *Executioner* (Los Angeles), August 1975.

"New Neighbor," in *Alfred Hitchcock's Mystery Magazine* (North Palm Beach, Florida) October 1975.

"The Plunge," in *Mike Shayne Mystery Magazine* (Los Angeles), December 1975.

"A Time to Kill," in *Mike Shayne Mystery Magazine* (Los Angeles), May 1976.

"Death Pact," in *Mystery Monthly* (New York), July 1976.

"Hope Chest," in *Mike Shayne Mystery Magazine* (Los Angeles), August 1976.

"Easy Mark," in *Alfred Hitchcock's Stories That Go Bump in the Night*. New York, Random House, 1977.

"Proxy" in *Alfred Hitchcock's Tales to Make Your Blood Run Cold*, edited by Eleanor Sullivan. New York, Dial Press, 1978.

"The Vital Element," in *Alfred Hitchcock's Rogues' Gallery*. New York, Dell, 1978.

"The Holdup," in *Alfred Hitchcock's Mystery Magazine* (New York), May 1979.

"Charlie," in *Mummy*, edited by Bill Pronzini. New York, Arbor House, 1980.

"The Confident Killer," in *Alfred Hitchcock's Alive & Screaming*. New York, Dial Press, 1980.

"The Inspiration," in *Alfred Hitchcock's Alive & Screaming*. New York, Dial Press, 1980.

"Pigeon in an Iron Lung," and "The Ultimate Prey," in *Alfred Hitchcock's Tales to Make Your Hair Stand on End*, edited by Eleanor Sullivan. New York, Dial Press, 1981.

"Somebody Cares," in *The Arbor House Treasury of Mystery & Suspense*, edited by Bill Pronzini, Martin H. Greenberg and Barry N. Malzberg. New York, Arbor House, 1981.

"Survival Exercise," in *Creature!*, edited by Bill Pronzini. New York, Arbor House, 1981.

"The Swimmer," in *Pulpsmith*, Autumn 1983.

"Aftermath of Death," in *Alfred Hitchcock's A Choice of Evils*. edited by Elana Lore. New York, Dial Press, 1983.

"Night of the Goblins," in *13 Horrors of Halloween*. New York, Avon, 1983.

"Till Death Do Us Not Part," in *Alfred Hitchcock's Grave Suspicions*, edited by Cathleen Davis, New York, Dial Press, 1984.

"A Friendly Exorcise," in *Alfred Hitchcock's No Harm Done*. New York, Dial Press, 1985.

"Motive for Murder," in *The Wickedest Show on Earth*, edited by Bill Pronzini and Marcia Muller. New York, Macmillan, 1985.

"The Disappearance of Maggie," in *Dark Lessons*, edited by Bill Pronzini and Marcia Muller. New York, Macmillan, 1985.

"Stranger's Gift," in *Alfred Hitchcock's Words of Prey*. New York, Dial Press, 1986.

"To Avoid a Scandal," in *101 Mystery Stories*, edited by Bill Pronzini and Martin H. Greenberg. New York, Avenel, 1986.

"Bertillon's Odds," in *Alfred Hitchcock's A Brief Darkness*. New York, Dial Press, 1987.

"The Jabberwock Valentine," in *14 Vicious Valentines*, edited by Martin H. Greenberg. New York, Avon, 1988.

"A Hunger in the Blood," in *Curses!* New York, Signet, 1989.

"Time of the Demon," in *Le Monstre Ricanant*. Paris, Encrage, 1989.

"Harry's Ghost," in *Western Ghosts*. Nashville, Tennessee, Rutledge Hill Press, 1990.

"Spring Break," in *Lighthouse Horrors*. Wilmington, Delaware, Middle Atlantic Press, 1990.

Uncollected Short Stories as Milton T. Lamb

"Your Number Is Up," in *Ten Detective Aces* (Springfield, Massachusetts), June 1943.

"Crime Gets a Head," in *Ten Detective Aces* (Springfield, Massachusetts), September 1943.

"Crime Doesn't Play," in *10-Story Detective* (Springfield, Massachusetts), November 1943.

"Host to Homicide," in *10-Story Detective* (Springfield, Massachusetts), December 1947.

Uncollected Short Stories as Milton Land

"Blood-Money," in *Detective Tales* (Chicago), November 1945.

"Home to Kill," in *Dime Mystery* (Chicago), February 1946.

"Rhapsody in Blood," in *Ten Detective Aces* (Springfield, Massachusetts), September 1947.

"The Deadly Past," in *Detective Tales* (Chicago), October 1948.

"Dangerous Mission," in *Detective Tales* (Chicago), November 1948.

"Curtain Call for Roberto," in *Detective Tales* (Chicago), December 1948.

"Lady's Killer," in *Dime Mystery* (Chicago), December 1949.

"With This Blood," in *15 Mystery Tales*, February 1950.

OTHER PUBLICATIONS

Novels

The Girl from Big Pine. Derby, Connecticut, Monarch, 1961.

The Cage. New York, Avon, 1969.

Mission: Impossible—The Priceless Particle. Racine, Wisconsin, Whitman, 1969.

The Thing in B-3. Racine, Wisconsin, Whitman, 1969.

Mission: Impossible—The Money Explosion. Racine, Wisconsin, Whitman, 1970.

Dark over Arcadia (as Anne Talmage). N.p., Prestige, 1971.

Other

Cellar Team (for children). Racine, Wisconsin, Whitman, 1972.

*

Manuscript Collection: University of North Carolina Library, Chapel Hill.

Talmage Powell comments:

A wise Englishman is said to have said it: "No one but a blockhead ever wrote for anything except money." Or words to that effect. Despite the contrariness inherited from my Welsh forebears, I must agree.

The Englishman's indictment, at first glance as subtle as a broadaxe, was an exasperated re-statement of the realities facing the practicing writer in our western culture: How can a writing come before the judgment seat sans baptism in publisher's ink? And, with a few extremely rare exceptions, where is the publisher who will pay the bill for the ink in non-expectation of a profit?

Regardless of the plaints of the Artiste (whose work is usually deemed "too good" for the commercial press by the ego of the individual) and the dilettante, the sometimes-cruel state of affairs has bequeathed to us almost all of the writings we call classics, and produced a body of work hardly matched in any other culture.

For me, writing has been a way of life in which the checks had to equal or outweigh the bills reposing in the same mailbox. I have been a craftsman, respectful of professionalism, which has given me the freedom a goodly part of the time to write stories I wanted to write. As a result I've crafted for detective magazine editors stories in which there was no detective, stories sans mystery for mystery magazines.

I've always been more interested in the human being, the reflections in a situation or atmosphere than in the mechanics of a short story, although the mechanics had first to be absorbed, as in any profession. Above the mechanics lies another level, and I have not been entirely blind to a bi-level approach.

This is not to be construed as a denial of the far-too-many instances wherein I've clapped the flappers as a trained seal.

The professionals know what I'm talking about; the novice should refer once again to the statement by the wise Englishman. If the trained seal provides a moment of escape from cares and woes, who's to criticise the purpose served?

The passage of time separates not only wheat from chaff but trained-seal from the occasional glint of bi-level. Since we have not invented as yet a gadget to control time, we might as well put the matter of separation entirely aside—with a reminder to reprint editors and media producers that more and more of you seem to be dipping into my existing pool, and monetary bargains may be struck with my agent whose name and address are contained herein.

I close with an apology to my fellow professionals for breaking ranks and writing this brief piece with no promise of recompense whatever, a momentary truant from the school of the wise Englishman.

*   *   *

Like so many other writers of mystery and suspense fiction who began their careers during the period 1920–50, Talmage Powell learned his craft in the pulps. He made his first short story sale in 1943 and followed it with some 200 more to that voracious medium, as well as another 300 to a wide range of publications over the decades. Most of his short fiction, and most of his 20 novels (four of which were ghosted books for prominent figures), have been criminous in nature.

His best work is in the short-story—more than 30 of his stories have been anthologized—and in his series of five paperback originals about a Tampa private detective, Ed Rivers. Tough but human, a man with feelings and problems, Rivers is a far more memorable creation than the bulk of the paperback private eyes from the 1950's and 1960's. The Tampa scene is also vividly evoked; Ybor City, the Cuban *barrio* on the edge of which Rivers lives, and Gasparilla Week, Tampa's annual Mardi Gras celebration, are just two examples. The most accomplished of the five novels is *The Girl's Number Doesn't Answer,* which makes a strong racial statement in Rivers's search for the brutal murderer of three Japanese. In this and Powell's other work, the suspense is well maintained throughout, the characters are deftly drawn, and there is a richness of scene and incident.

Also notable is *The Smasher,* a tense story of a man named Steve Griffin and his relentless hunt for the deliberate hit-and-run murderer of his wife.

—Bill Pronzini

PRATHER, Richard S(cott). Also writes as David Knight; Douglas Ring. American. Born in Santa Ana, California, 9 September 1921. Educated at Riverside Junior College, California, 1940–41. Served as a fireman, oiler, and engineer in the United States Merchant Marine, 1942–45. Married Tina Hager in 1945. Civil Service clerk, March Air Force Base, Riverside, 1945–49. Since 1949, self-employed writer and avocado farmer. Twice Member of the Board of Directors, Mystery Writers of America.

CRIME PUBLICATIONS

Novels (series: Shell Scott)

Case of the Vanishing Beauty (Scott). New York, Fawcett, 1950; London, Fawcett, 1957.
Bodies in Bedlam (Scott). New York, Fawcett, 1951; London, Fawcett, 1957.
Everybody Had a Gun (Scott). New York, Fawcett, 1951; London, Muller, 1953.
Find This Woman (Scott). New York, Fawcett, 1951; London, Fawcett, 1957.
Way of a Wanton (Scott). New York, Fawcett, 1952; London, Fawcett, 1958.
Pattern for Murder (as David Knight). Hasbrouck Heights, New Jersey, Graphic, 1952; as *The Scrambled Yeggs,* New York, Fawcett, 1958; London, Muller, 1961.
Lie Down, Killer. New York, Lion, 1952; London, Fawcett, 1958.
Dagger of Flesh. New York, Falcon, 1952; London, Panther, 1961.
Darling, It's Death (Scott). New York, Fawcett, 1952; London, Fawcett, 1957.
The Peddler (as Douglas Ring). New York, Lion, 1952; (as Richard Prather) London, Muller, 1963.
Ride a High Horse (Scott). New York, Fawcett, 1953; as *Too Many Crooks,* New York, Fawcett, 1956; London, Fawcett, 1957.
Always Leave 'em Dying (Scott). New York, Fawcett, 1954; London, Fawcett, 1957.
Pattern for Panic. New York, Abelard Schuman, 1954; revised edition (Scott), New York, Fawcett, 1961; London, Muller, 1962.
Strip for Murder (Scott). New York, Fawcett, 1955; London, Fawcett, 1957.
Dragnet: Case No. 561 (as David Knight) New York, Pocket Books, 1956; London, Consul, 1957.
The Wailing Frail (Scott). New York, Fawcett, 1956; London, Fawcett, 1957.
Three's a Shroud (3 novelets; Scott). New York, Fawcett, 1957; London, Gold Lion, 1973.
Slab Happy (Scott). New York, Fawcett, 1958.
Take a Murder, Darling (Scott). New York, Fawcett, 1958; London, Muller, 1961.
Over Her Dead Body (Scott). New York, Fawcett, 1959; London, Panther, 1960.
Double in Trouble (Scott), with Stephen Marlowe. New York, Fawcett, 1959.
Dance with the Dead (Scott). New York, Fawcett, 1960; London, Muller, 1962.
Dig That Crazy Grave (Scott). New York, Fawcett, 1961; London, Muller, 1962.
Kill the Clown (Scott). New York, Fawcett, 1962; London, Muller, 1963.
Dead Heat (Scott). New York, Pocket Books, 1963.
Joker in the Deck (Scott). New York, Fawcett, 1964; London, Muller, 1965.
The Cockeyed Corpse (Scott). New York, Fawcett, 1964.
The Trojan Hearse (Scott). New York, Pocket Books, 1964; London, New English Library, 1967.
Kill Him Twice (Scott). New York, Pocket Books, 1965.
Dead Man's Walk (Scott). New York, Pocket Books, 1965; London, New English Library, 1968.
The Meandering Corpse (Scott). New York, Trident Press, 1965; London, New English Library, 1967.
The Kubla Khan Caper (Scott). New York, Trident Press, 1966.

Gat Heat (Scott). New York, Trident Press, 1967; London, New English Library, 1968.
The Cheim Manuscript (Scott). New York, Pocket Books, 1969.
Kill Me Tomorrow (Scott). New York, Pocket Books, 1969.
Shell Scott's Murder Mix (omnibus New York, Trident Press, 1970.
Dead-Bang (Scott). New York, Pocket Books, 1971.
The Sweet Ride (Scott). New York, Pocket Books, 1972.
The Sure Thing (Scott). New York, Pocket Books, 1975.
The Amber Effect (Scott). New York, Tor, 1986.
Shellshock (Scott). New York, Tor, 1987.

Short Stories

Have Gat—Will Travel. New York, Fawcett, 1957; London, Fawcett, 1958.
Shell Scott's Seven Slaughters. New York, Fawcett, 1961; London, Muller, 1962.
The Shell Scott Sampler. New York, Pocket Books, 1969.

OTHER PUBLICATIONS

Other

Editor, *The Comfortable Coffin: A Gold Medal Anthology.* New York, Fawcett, 1960.

* * *

Richard S. Prather published the *Case of the Vanishing Beauty* featuring his cocky detective Shell Scott in 1950 and so ushered in the decade of the Fawcett Gold Medal originals. Extremely popular, the Shell Scott series numbers 34 in all and spans over 25 years—Scott remaining throughout a healthy 30 year old. A cross between Spillane's Mike Hammer and Bellem's Dan Turner, Shell Scott is usually remembered for his happy-go-lucky attitude, wry and witty (if sexist) remarks, and his many cases of a not-too-serious nature. The Scott series presents entertaining escapist fiction with just enough gore, "dames," and jokes to keep the formula from growing stale.

Shell Scott is described as an ex-marine who, after serving in the South Pacific during World War II, turns detective inhabiting all the special haunts Hollywood has to offer. When not relaxing at the Spartan apartments and enjoying his tropical fish aquariums, Scott becomes entangled in all types of excessive antics. The most striking feature of Scott is his one-inch-tall white crewcut; some sour critics may argue it is his only feature. Along with his clipped ear, broken nose, and Spade-like V-shaped eyebrows he is a figure no reader can soon forget, especially if one notices first any one of the lovely nymphets that adorn the vintage paperback covers.

Unlike many of the fictional detectives currently being scrutinized by scholars, Shell Scott is no avenger or crusader against crime. He reminds one of Dick Powell's interpretation of Marlowe in the film *Murder, My Sweet,* a tough, hard-headed hero floundering in the chaos of the urban setting but enjoying the view all the same. His irreverence is what separates him from the angst-ridden *Black Mask*ers of note. It should be mentioned, however, that despite an occassional attack against "commies" and such, Scott's fun-loving lifestyle is what endeared him to decades of readers.

When Prather first penned the Shell Scott saga he produced a fairly conventional private eye. As the books continued, however, the typical Scott adventure was filled with risqué

surprises. In *Strip for Murder* Scott investigates a nudist colony and before long is leading a hundred enthusiasts in morning calisthenics *au naturel.* The story inevitably leads the newly nude detective on a daring escape via hot air balloon through downtown Los Angeles. A good Shell Scott novel has something for everyone. In *The Cockeyed Corpse* Scott travels to a film site in Arizona and disguises himself as a rock to—of all things—avoid suspicion. Imagine his surprise at finding that this particular Western involves an all-female cast . . . all nude. The reader meets voodoo-crazed zombies in *Dead Man's Walk* and one of the most violent and bloody detective stories in *Ride a High Horse.*

Scott is not the cop-hater that many a detective hero is. In fact, his best friend is Phil Sampson, the captain of the Los Angeles Police Departments central homicide division. With the help of Sampson and his own robin's-egg-blue Cadillac, Scott weaves his way through tale after tale ever dependent on his wits, strength, and an occasional crossbow (*Gat Heat*). Often Scott even turns down sexual favors from his female lady-friends, blaming a weak stomach. In *Gat Heat* he states: "I have looked upon death and destruction, blood and split brainboxes and disemboweled oxen. But I have seldom looked upon anything less appetizing than Aggie fluttering her bald lips at me."

Prather's primary accomplishment is of course the Shell Scott series, but he has also written as Douglas Ring, *The Peddler,* and as David Knight, *Pattern for Murder* and *Dragnet: Case No. 561.* He created ex-G.I. Mark Logan for his only appearance in *Dagger of Flesh.* Any one of these is of interest to the Prather purist, but above all the others Shell Scott still shines. To combat the naturalistic doom of the typical detective fiction anthology, Prather edited *The Comfortable Coffin,* a "feel-good" collection for those weary of sump-pump-corpses and thumb-sucking-psychos.

For the contemporary reader and scholar of detective fiction, Prather's work is a virtually unexplored gold mine of a popular literary type which has all but disappeared. Sadly, little remains in print of the Prather publications; let us hope that Shell Scott's retirement is only temporary.

—Michael Pettengell

———

PREEDY, George. *See* **SHEARING, Joseph.**

———

PRICE, Anthony. British. Born in Hertfordshire, 16 August 1928. Educated at the King's School, Canterbury, 1941–47; Merton College, Oxford (exhibitioner), 1949–52, B.A. (honours) in history 1952, M.A. Served in the British Army (national service), 1947–49: (Temporary) Captain. Married Ann Stone in 1953; two sons and one daughter. Has worked for the Westminster Press since 1952; since 1972, Editor, *Oxford Times.* Recipient: Crime Writers Association Silver Dagger award, 1971, and Gold Dagger award 1975; Swedish Academy of Detection award, 1979. Agent: Hilary Rubinstein, A.P. Watt and Son, 26–28 Bedford Row, London WC1R 4HL. Address: Wayside Cottage, Horton-cum-Studley, Oxford, OX9 1AW, England.

CRIME PUBLICATIONS

Novels (series: Dr. David Audley in all books)

The Labyrinth Makers. London, Gollancz, 1970; New York, Doubleday, 1971.
The Alamut Ambush. London, Gollancz, 1971; New York, Doubleday, 1972.
Colonel Butler's Wolf. London, Gollancz, 1972; New York, Doubleday, 1973.
October Men. London, Gollancz, 1973; New York, Doubleday, 1974.
Other Paths to Glory. London, Gollancz, 1974; New York, Doubleday, 1975.
Our Man in Camelot. London, Gollancz, 1975; New York, Doubleday, 1976.
War Game. London, Gollancz, 1976; New York, Doubleday, 1977.
The '44 Vintage. London, Gollancz, and New York, Doubleday, 1978.
Tomorrow's Ghost. London, Gollancz, and New York, Doubleday, 1979.
The Hour of the Donkey. London, Gollancz, 1980.
Soldier No More. London, Gollancz, 1981; New York, Doubleday, 1982.
The Old Vengeful. London, Gollancz, 1982; New York, Doubleday, 1983.
Gunner Kelly. London, Gollancz, 1983; New York, Doubleday, 1984.
Sion Crossing. London, Gollancz, and New York, Mysterious Press, 1985.
Here Be Monsters. London, Gollancz, and New York, Mysterious Press, 1985.
For the Good of the State. London, Gollancz, 1986; New York, Mysterious Press, 1987.
A New Kind of War. London, Gollancz, 1987; New York, Mysterious Press, 1988.
A Prospect of Vengeance. London, Gollancz, 1988.
The Memory Trap. London, Gollancz, 1989.

Uncollected Short Stories

"A Green Boy," in *Winter's Crimes 5,* edited by Virginia Whitaker. London, Macmillan, and New York, St. Martin's Press, 1973.
"The Boudicca Killing," in *Winter's Crimes 11,* edited by George Hardinge. London, Macmillan, and New York, St. Martin's Press, 1979.
"The Berzin Lecture," in *Winter's Crimes 15,* edited by George Hardinge. London, Macmillan, and New York, St. Martin's Press, 1983.

*

Anthony Price comments:

I started out with the aim of combining elements of the spy thriller with the detective mystery, through a group of characters who would appear and reappear in the series, taking it in turns to play the lead (though one character, David Audley, would have a linking role in all the stories). In addition—very obviously—the setting or background of each story reflects whatever piece of private research (or hobby) I am engaged in at the time—Roman history (*Colonel Butler's Wolf*), the 1914–18 war (*Other Paths to Glory*) and so on. It has been said (by one kind critic) that my obsession is with loyalty. That's fine—and I would hope to add all William Faulkner's "truths of the heart" to that. I take the (old-fashioned?) view, also, that "Our Side," with all its warts and all the character defects of my heroes and heroines, is Good, and "Their Side," whatever virtues they may have, is Bad. Of course, things are never quite as simple as that in practice. But that, for me, where it all begins and ends.

*   *   *

Anthony Price has brought the concept of history into his spy novels in quite a unique manner. Suspense fiction which takes place in historical time, often including real historical persons, is nothing new. The same goes for the concept of the "detective as historian," uncovering things in the past. But Price has brought the *real* meaning of history into his novels, as something that happened perhaps a long time ago, but still has significance for us today. In almost all of his novels the plot is based on a historical episode, and the knowledge of the historical truth is necessary for the solution of the mystery.

In *Other Paths to Glory* (perhaps his best novel) the knowledge of a forgotten battle in World War I is necessary for saving a summit meeting in the 1970's from being bombed. In *War Game* the background is the English Civil War, as enacted by modern cavaliers and roundheads. *Our Man in Camelot* is set at the time of King Arthur, and *Sion Crossing* deals with General Sherman's march through Georgia in the American Civil War. *A New Kind of War* takes place in Germany immediately after World War II, and concentrates on the "Herrmannschlacht" when Arminius (or Herrmann) ambushed and slaughtered the Roman legions under Varus in A.D. 9.

The historical dimensions of Price's novels are also apparent in another way. The novels do not follow chronologically, but move backwards and forwards in time from 1944 (when both his main characters Jack Butler and David Audley enter the war as very young men) to the present. As a classic archeologist meticuously glueing fragments of a Graecian urn together, eventually showing some wild ecstasy or mad pursuit, Price puts the two men's lives together piece by piece. You never know what the next fragment will reveal, what more sinister aspect will appear.

Thus he creates "The David Audley-Jack Butler Saga," about the specialist in medieval history, David Audley, who has a donnish appearance but the broken nose of a former rugby forward, and Jack Butler, a professional soldier of the Bulldog breed, who eventually becomes head of British Intelligence. In some novels they feature as the leading characters, while in others they play more subordinate supporting roles. They are often mirrored through other characters in the novels: former historian Paul Mitchell, ex-airman Hugh Roskill, the silly and vain Oliver St. John Latimer; female characters like Frances Fitzgibbons, killed off (and sadly missed) in *Tomorrow's Ghost,* and Elizabeth Loftus, who appears in *Here Be Monsters.*

Price has created a series with a couple of constant characters who guarantee an inner coherence, yet he also gives himself the opportunity to introduce new and interesting characters who can appear in the front line now and then and fade into the background when necessary.

He has suceeded in blending the intricacies of the spy novel with the plotting of the classical whodunnit. Apart from the moral riddles which always creep into the more serious British spy novels of the "after-Philby type" there is always a mystery to be solved, often with a historical dimension. This is not only achieved on a structural level, but is intricately blended into his literary style.

Price stands out as a unique contributor to a genre in which British authors have always excelled.

—Karl G. Fredriksson

PRIESTLEY, J(ohn) B(oynton). Also wrote as Peter Goldsmith. British. Born in Bradford, Yorkshire, 13 September 1894. Educated in Bradford schools, and at Trinity Hall, Cambridge, M.A. Served with the Duke of Wellington's and Devon Regiments, 1914–19. Married 1) Patricia Tempest (died 1925), two daughters; 2) Mary Wyndham Lewis (divorced 1952), two daughters and one son; 3) the writer Jacquetta Hawkes in 1953. Director, Mask Theatre, London, 1938–39; radio lecturer on BBC programme "Postscripts" during World War II; regular contributor, *New Statesman,* London. President, P.E.N., London, 1936–37; United Kingdom Delegate, and Chairman, Unesco International Theatre Conference, Paris, 1947, and Prague, 1948; chairman, British Theatre Conference, 1948; president, International Theatre Institute, 1949; member, National Theatre Board, London, 1966–67. Recipient: James Tait Black Memorial prize, 1930; Ellen Terry award, 1948. LL.D.: University of St. Andrews; D.Litt.: University of Birmingham; University of Bradford. Honorary Freeman, City of Bradford, 1973; Honorary Student, Trinity Hall, Cambridge, 1978. Order of Merit, 1977. *Died 14 August 1984.*

CRIME PUBLICATIONS

Novels

Benighted. London, Heinemann, 1927; as *The Old Dark House,* New York, Harper, 1928.
I'll Tell You Everything, with Gerald Bullett. New York, Macmillan, 1932; London, Heinemann, 1933.
The Doomsday Men. London, Heinemann, and New York, Harper, 1938.
Black-Out in Gretley: A Story of—and for—Wartime. London, Heinemann, and New York, Harper, 1942.
Saturn over the Water: An Account of His Adventures in London, South America and Australia by Tim Bedford, Painter: Edited, with Some Preliminary and Concluding Remarks, by Henry Sulgrave and Here Presented to the Reading Public. London, Heinemann, and New York, Doubleday, 1961.
The Shapes of Sleep: A Topical Tale. London, Heinemann, and New York, Doubleday, 1962.
Salt Is Leaving. London, Pan, 1966; New York, Harper, 1975.

OTHER PUBLICATIONS

Novels

Adam in Moonshine. London, Heinemann, and New York, Harper, 1927.
Farthing Hall, with Hugh Walpole. London, Macmillan, and New York, Doubleday, 1929.
The Good Companions. London, Heinemann, and New York, Harper, 1929.
Angel Pavement. London, Heinemann, and New York, Harper, 1930.
Faraway. London, Heinemann, and New York, Harper, 1932.

Wonder Hero. London, Heinemann, and New York, Harper, 1933.
They Walk in the City: The Lovers in the Stone Forest. London, Heinemann, and New York, Harper, 1936.
Let the People Sing. London, Heinemann, 1939; New York, Harper, 1940.
Daylight on Saturday: A Novel about an Aircraft Factory. London, Heinemann, and New York, Harper, 1943.
Three Men in New Suits. London, Heinemann, and New York, Harper, 1945.
Bright Day. London, Heinemann, and New York, Harper, 1946.
Jenny Villiers: A Story of the Theatre. London, Heinemann, and New York, Harper, 1947.
Festival at Farbridge. London, Heinemann, 1951; as *Festival,* New York, Harper, 1951.
The Magicians. London, Heinemann, and New York, Harper, 1954.
Low Notes on a High Level: A Frolic. London, Heinemann, and New York, Harper, 1954.
The Thirty-First of June. London, Heinemann, 1961; New York, Doubleday, 1962.
Sir Michael and Sir George. London, Heinemann, 1964; Boston, Little Brown, 1965.
Lost Empires. London, Heinemann, and Boston, Little Brown, 1965.
It's an Old Country. London, Heinemann, and Boston, Little Brown, 1967.
The Image Men: Out of Town, and London End. London, Heinemann, 2 vols., 1968; Boston, Little Brown, 1 vol., 1969.
Found, Lost, Found; or The English Way of Life. London, Heinemann, 1976; New York, Stein and Day, 1977.
Lost Empires. London, Heinemann, 1986.

Short Stories

The Town Major of Miraucourt. London, Heinemann, 1930.
Albert Goes Through. London, Heinemann, and New York, Harper, 1933.
Going Up: Stories and Sketches. London, Pan, 1950.
The Other Place and Other Stories of the Same Sort. London, Heinemann, and New York, Harper, 1953.
The Carfitt Crisis and Two Other Stories. London, Heinemann, 1975.

Plays

The Good Companions (book only) with Edward Knoblock, lyrics by Harry Graham and Frank Eyton, music by Richard Addinsell, adaptation of the novel by Priestley (produced London and New York, 1931). London and New York, French, 1935.
Dangerous Corner (produced London and New York, 1932). London, Heinemann, and New York, French, 1932.
The Roundabout (produced Liverpool, London, and New York, 1932). London, Heinemann, and New York, French, 1933.
Laburnum Grove: An Immoral Comedy (produced London, 1933; New York, 1935). London, Heinemann, 1934; New York, French, 1935.
Eden End (produced London, 1934; New York, 1935). London, Heinemann, 1934; in *Three Plays and a Preface,* 1935.
Cornelius: A Business Affair in Three Transactions (produced Birmingham and London, 1935). London, Heinemann, 1935; New York, French, 1936.
Duet in Floodlight (produced Liverpool and London, 1935). London, Heinemann, 1935.

Three Plays and a Preface (includes *Dangerous Corner, Eden End, Cornelius*). New York, Harper, 1935.

Bees on the Boat Deck: A Farcical Tragedy (produced London, 1936). London, Heinemann, and Boston, Baker, 1936.

Spring Tide (as Peter Goldsmith), with George Billam (produced London, 1936). London, Heinemann, and New York, French, 1936.

The Bad Samaritan (produced Liverpool, 1937).

Time and the Conways (produced London, 1937; New York, 1938). London, Heinemann, 1937; New York, Harper, 1938.

I Have Been Here Before (produced London, 1937; New York, 1938). London, Heinemann, 1937; New York, Harper, 1938.

Two Time Plays (includes *Time and the Conways* and *I Have Been Here Before*). London, Heinemann, 1937.

People at Sea (as *I Am a Stranger Here*, produced Bradford, 1937; as *People at Sea*, produced London, 1937). London, Heinemann, and New York, French, 1937.

Mystery at Greenfingers: A Comedy of Detection (produced London, 1938). London, French, 1937; New York, French, 1938.

The Rebels (produced Bradford, 1938).

When We Are Married: A Yorkshire Farcical Comedy (produced London, 1938; New York, 1939). London, Heinemann, 1938; New York, French, 1940.

Music at Night (produced Malvern, 1938; London, 1939). Included in *Three Plays*, 1943; in *Plays I*, 1948.

Johnson over Jordan (produced London, 1939). Published as *Johnson over Jordan: The Play, and All about It (An Essay)*, London, Heinemann, and New York, Harper, 1939.

The Long Mirror (produced Oxford, 1940; London, 1945). Included in *Three Plays*, 1943; in *Four Plays*, 1944.

Good Night Children: A Comedy of Broadcasting (produced London, 1942). Included in *Three Comedies*, 1945; in *Plays II*, 1949.

Desert Highway (produced Bristol, 1943; London, 1944). London, Heinemann, 1944; in *Four Plays*, 1944.

They Came to a City (produced London, 1943). Included in *Three Plays*, 1943; in *Four Plays*, 1944.

Three Plays (includes *Music at Night, The Long Mirror, They Came to a City*). London, Heinemann, 1943.

How Are They at Home? A Topical Comedy (produced London, 1944). Included in *Three Comedies*, 1945; in *Plays II*, 1949.

The Golden Fleece (as *The Bull Market*, produced Bradford, 1944). Included in *Three Comedies*, 1945.

Four Plays (includes *Music at Night, The Long Mirror, They Came to a City, Desert Highway*). London, Heinemann, and New York, Harper, 1944.

Three Comedies (includes *Good Night Children, The Golden Fleece, How Are They at Home?*). London, Heinemann, 1945.

An Inspector Calls (produced Moscow, 1945; London, 1946; New York, 1947). London, Heinemann, 1947; New York, Dramatists Play Service, 1948 (?).

Jenny Villiers (produced Bristol, 1946).

The Rose and Crown (televised, 1946). London, French, 1947.

Ever Since Paradise: An Entertainment, Chiefly Referring to Love and Marriage (also director: produced on tour, 1946; London, 1947). London and New York, French, 1949.

Three Time Plays (includes *Dangerous Corner, Time and the Conways, I Have Been Here Before*). London, Pan, 1947.

The Linden Tree (produced Sheffield and London, 1947; New York, 1948). London, Heinemann, and New York, French, 1948.

The Plays of J.B. Priestley:
I. *Dangerous Corner, I Have Been Here Before, Johnson over Jordan, Music at Night, The Linden Tree, Eden End, Time and the Conways*. London, Heinemann, 1948; as *Seven Plays*, New York, Harper, 1950.
II. *Laburnum Grove, Bees on the Boat Deck, When We Are Married, Good Night Children, The Good Companions, How Are They at Home?, Ever Since Paradise*. London, Heinemann, 1949; New York, Harper, 1951.
III. *Cornelius, People at Sea, They Came to a City, Desert Highway, An Inspector Calls, Home Is Tomorrow, Summer Day's Dream*. London, Heinemann, 1950; New York, Harper, 1952.

Home Is Tomorrow (produced Bradford and London, 1948). London, Heinemann, 1949; in *Plays III*, 1950.

The High Toby: A Play for the Toy Theatre (produced London, 1954). London, Penguin-Pollock, 1948.

Summer Day's Dream (produced Bradford and London, 1949). Included in *Plays III*, 1950.

The Olympians, music by Arthur Bliss (produced London, 1949). London, Novello, 1949.

Bright Shadow: A Play of Detection (produced Oldham and London, 1950). London, French, 1950.

Treasure on Pelican (as *Treasure on Pelican Island*, televised, 1951; as *Treasure on Pelican*, produced Cardiff and London, 1952). London, Evans, 1953.

Dragon's Mouth: A Dramatic Quartet, with Jacquetta Hawkes (also director: produced Malvern and London, 1952; New York, 1955). London, Heinemann, and New York, Harper, 1952.

Private Rooms: A One-Act Comedy in the Viennese Style. London, French, 1953.

Mother's Day. London, French, 1953.

Try It Again (produced London, 1965). London, French, 1953.

A Glass of Bitter. London, French, 1954.

The White Countess, with Jacquetta Hawkes (produced Dublin and London, 1954).

The Scandalous Affair of Mr. Kettle and Mrs. Moon (produced Folkestone and London, 1955). London, French, 1956.

Take the Fool Away (produced Vienna, 1955; Nottingham, 1959).

These Our Actors (produced Glasgow, 1956).

The Glass Cage (produced Toronto and London, 1957). London, French, 1958.

The Thirty-First of June (produced Toronto and London, 1957).

A Pavilion of Masks (produced Germany, 1961; Bristol, 1963). London, French, 1958.

A Severed Head, with Iris Murdoch, adaptation of the novel by Murdoch (produced Bristol and London, 1963; New York, 1964). London, Chatto and Windus, 1964.

Screenplays: *Sing As We Go*, with Gordon Wellesley, 1934; *Look Up and Laugh*, with Gordon Wellesley, 1935; *We Live in Two Worlds*, 1937; *Jamaica Inn*, with Sidney Gilliat and Joan Harrison, 1939; *Britain at Bay*, 1940; *Our Russian Allies*, 1941; *The Foreman Went to France (Somewhere in France)*, with others, 1942; *Last Holiday*, 1950.

Radio Plays: *The Return of Jess Oakroyd*, 1941; *The Golden Entry*, 1955; *End Game at the Dolphin*, 1956; *An Arabian Night in Park Lane*, 1965.

Television Plays: *The Rose and Crown*, 1946; *Whitehall Wonders*, 1949; *Treasure on Pelican Island*, 1951; *You Know What People Are*, 1953; *The Stone Faces*, 1957; *Now Let Him Go*, 1957; *Lost City* (documentary), 1958; *The Rack*, 1958;

Doomsday for Dyson, 1958; *The Fortrose Incident,* from his play *Home Is Tomorrow,* 1959; *Level Seven,* from the novel by Mordecai Roshwald, 1966; *The Lost Peace* series, 1966; *Anyone for Tennis,* 1968; *Linda at Pulteney's,* 1969.

Verse

The Chapman of Rhymes (for children). London, Moring, 1918.

Other

Brief Diversions, Being Tales, Travesties, and Epigrams. Cambridge, Bowes and Bowes, 1922.
Papers from Lilliput. Cambridge, Bowes and Bowes, 1922.
I for One. London, Lane, 1923; New York, Dodd Mead, 1924.
Figures in Modern Literature. London, Lane, and New York, Dodd Mead, 1924.
The English Comic Characters. London, Lane, and New York, Dodd Mead, 1925.
George Meredith. London and New York, Macmillan, 1926.
Talking. London, Jarrolds, and New York, Harper, 1926.
(Essays). London, Harrap, 1926.
Open House: A Book of Essays. London, Heinemann, and New York, Harper, 1927.
Thomas Love Peacock. London and New York, Macmillan, 1927.
The English Novel. London, Benn, 1927; revised edition, London and New York, Nelson, 1935.
Apes and Angels: A Book of Essays. London, Methuen, 1928; as *Too Many People and Other Reflections,* New York, Harper, 1928.
The Balconinny and Other Essays. London, Methuen, 1929; as *The Balconinny,* New York, Harper, 1930.
English Humour. London and New York, Longman, 1929.
Self-Selected Essays. London, Heinemann, 1932; New York, Harper, 1933.
Four-in-Hand (miscellany). London, Heinemann, 1934.
English Journey, Being a Rambling But Truthful Account of What One Man Saw and Heard and Felt and Thought During a Journey Through England During the Autumn of the Year 1933. London, Heinemann-Gollancz, and New York, Harper, 1934.
Midnight on the Desert: A Chapter of Autobiography. London, Heinemann, 1937; as *Midnight on the Desert, Being an Excursion into Autobiography During a Winter in America, 1935–36,* New York, Harper, 1937.
Rain upon Godshill: A Further Chapter of Autobiography. London, Heinemann, and New York, Harper, 1939.
Britain Speaks (radio talks). New York, Harper, 1940.
Postscripts (radio talks). London, Heinemann, 1940; as *All England Listened,* New York, Chilmark Press, 1968.
Out of the People. London, Collins-Heinemann, and New York, Harper, 1941.
Britain at War. New York, Harper, 1942.
British Women Go to War. London, Collins, 1943.
Manpower: The Story of Britain's Mobilisation for War. London, His Majesty's Stationery Office, 1944.
Here Are Your Answers. London, Socialist Book Centre, 1944.
Letter to a Returning Serviceman. London, Home and Van Thal, 1945.
The Secret Dream: An Essay on Britain, America, and Russia. London, Turnstile Press, 1946.
Russian Journey. London, Writers Group of the Society for Cultural Relations with the USSR, 1946.
The New Citizen (address). London, Council for Education in World Citizenship, 1946.

Theatre Outlook. London, Nicholson and Watson, 1947.
The Arts under Socialism (lecture). London, Turnstile Press, 1947.
Delight. London, Heinemann, and New York, Harper, 1949.
The Priestley Companion: A Selection from the Writings of J.B. Priestley. London, Penguin-Heinemann, 1951.
Journey down a Rainbow (travel), with Jacquetta Hawkes. London, Cresset Press-Heinemann, and New York, Harper, 1955.
All about Ourselves and Other Essays, edited by Eric Gillett. London, Heinemann, 1956.
The Writer in a Changing Society (lecture). Aldington, Kent, Hand and Flower Press, 1956.
Thoughts in the Wilderness (essays. London, Heinemann, and New York, Harper, 1957.
The Art of the Dramatist: A Lecture Together with Appendices and Discursive Notes. London, Heinemann, 1957; Boston, The Writer, 1958.
Topside; or, The Future of England: A Dialogue. London, Heinemann, 1958.
The Story of Theatre (for children). London, Rathbone, 1959; as *The Wonderful World of the Theatre,* New York, Doubleday, 1959.
Literature and Western Man. London, Heinemann, and New York, Harper, 1960.
William Hazlitt. London, Longman, 1960.
Charles Dickens: A Pictorial Biography. London, Thames and Hudson, 1961; New York, Viking Press, 1962; as *Charles Dickens and His World,* Thames and Hudson, and Viking Press, 1969.
Margin Released: A Writer's Reminiscences and Reflections. London, Heinemann, and New York, Harper, 1962.
Man and Time. London, Aldus, and New York, Doubleday, 1964.
The Moments and Other Pieces. London, Heinemann, 1966.
The World of J.B. Priestley, edited by Donald G. MacRae. London, Heinemann, 1967.
Essays of Five Decades, edited by Susan Cooper. Boston, Little Brown, 1968; London, Heinemann, 1969.
Trumpets over the Sea, Being a Rambling and Egotistical Account of the London Symphony Orchestra's Engagement at Daytona Beach, Florida, in July–August 1967. London, Heinemann, 1968.
The Prince of Pleasure and His Regency 1811–1820. London, Heinemann, and New York, Harper, 1969.
The Edwardians. London, Heinemann, and New York, Harper, 1970.
Anton Chekhov. London, International, Textbook, 1970.
Snoggle (for children). London, Heinemann, 1971; New York, Harcourt Brace, 1972.
Victoria's Heyday. London, Heinemann, and New York, Harcourt Brace, 1972.
Over the Long High Wall: Some Reflections and Speculations on Life, Death, and Time. London, Heinemann, 1972.
The English. London, Heinemann, and New York, Viking Press, 1973.
Outcries and Asides. London, Heinemann, 1974.
A Visit to New Zealand. London, Heinemann, 1974.
Particular Pleasures, Being a Personal Record of Some Varied Arts and Many Different Artists. London, Heinemann, 1975.
The Happy Dream: An Essay. Andoversford, Gloucestershire, Whittington Press, 1976.
English Humour (not the same as 1929 book). London, Heinemann, 1976.
Instead of the Trees: A Final Chapter of Autobiography. London, Heinemann, and New York, Stein and Day, 1977.

Seeing Straford, illustrated by Arthur Keene. Stratford-on-Avon, Warwickshire, Celandine Press, 1982.

Editor, *Essayists Past and Present: A Selection of English Essays.* London, Jenkins, and New York, Dial Press, 1925.
Editor, *Fools and Philosophers: A Gallery of Comic Figures from English Literature.* London, Lane, and New York, Dodd Mead, 1925.
Editor, *Tom Moore's Diary: A Selection.* London, Cambridge University Press, 1925.
Editor, *The Book of Bodley Head Verse.* London, Lane, and New York, Dodd Mead, 1926.
Editor, *Our Nation's Heritage.* London, Dent, 1939.
Editor, *Scenes from London Life, from Sketches by Boz,* by Dickens. London, Pan, 1947.
Editor, *The Best of Leacock.* Toronto, McClelland and Stewart, 1957; as *The Bodley Head Leacock,* London, Bodley Head, 1957.
Editor, with Josephine Spear, *Adventures in English Literature.* New York, Harcourt Brace, 1963.

*

Bibliography: *J.B. Priestley: An Annotated Bibliography* by Alan Edwin Day, New York, Garland, and Stroud, Gloucestershire, Hodgkins, 1980.

Manuscript Collection: University of Texas, Austin.

Critical Studies: *J.B. Priestley* by Ivor Brown, London, Longman, 1957, revised edition, 1964; *J.B. Priestley: An Informal Study of His Work* by David Hughes, London, Hart Davis, 1958, Freeport, New York, Books for Libraries, 1970; *J.B. Priestley the Dramatist* by Gareth Lloyd Evans, London, Heinemann, 1964; *J.B. Priestley: Portrait of an Author* by Susan Cooper, London, Heinemann, 1970, New York, Harper, 1971; *J.B. Priestley* by Kenneth Young, London, Longman, 1977; *J.B. Priestley* by John Braine, London, Weidenfeld and Nicolson, 1978, New York, Barnes and Noble, 1979; *J.B. Priestley* by A.A. De Vitis and Albert E. Kalson, Boston, Twayne, 1980; *J.B. Priestley: The Last of the Sages* by John Atkins, London, Calder, and New York, Riverrun Press, 1981; *The "Lost World" of J.B. Priestley* by Gary Firth, Lancaster, Dalesman, 1986; *J.B. Priestley* by Vincent Brome, London, Hamish Hamilton, 1988.

Theatrical Activities:

Director: **Plays**—*Ever Since Paradise,* tour, 1946, and London, 1947; *Dragon's Mouth,* London, 1952.

* * *

An enormously prolific and versatile writer, J.B. Priestley generously contributed also to the crime genre. In a wider sense this contribution embraces such divergent novels as *Adam in Moonshine* (his very first), *Benighted,* and *The Magicians,* stories like "The Grey Ones" (in eeriness akin to Dahl) and "The Carfitt Crisis" as well as *I'll Tell You Everything,* a hilarious early cloak-and-dagger yarn written with Gerald Bullett; in drama mainly *Mystery at Greenfingers,* a delightfully clever pastiche of the detective play, and also *Home Is Tomorrow and Treasure on Pelican.* There are no sharp dividing lines in Priestley's work. His late, quite differently angled novel *It's an Old Country* contains one of his satirical portraits of "private investigators," first-rate failures to a man. And *An Inspector Calls,* his most lasting international success in drama, uses the guise of the detective play for an excruciating analysis of pre-1914 industrialism. The characters on stage and in the audience take long to realise that Goole (an elder and more solid cousin of The Unidentified Guest in Eliot's *The Cocktail Party*) is no policeman. No one knows what he is, but it does not matter. He has done his job.

In a narrower sense, there are five long prose works one can call crime novels. They have no surface links; each is essentially an unrepeated experiment. They do share certain characteristics, however. Their central figures are not "professionals," but professional men. No longer young, they are good (and discerning) livers and good at their profession which they temporarily abandon to investigate the mysteries circumstances fling at them. There is a lot of humour and an "open" plot as opposed to the "closed-group-in-an-inaccessible-spot" (employed in *Benighted, Mystery at Greenfingers, Treasure on Pelican*). The ending is successful—crimes are elucidated or disasters averted, though the general outlook may remain bleak—and happy: no sequel being envisaged, the (strong) love interest can safely lead to marriage. These novels are remote from the intellectual puzzle and the story of massive, non-committal violence; their romantic albeit sober endings separate them also from the desolate alienation depicted in much recent British crime fiction (Deighton, Garve, le Carré, Symons). There are formal and conceptual links with Priestley's other writings, and the realism is coloured (though not impaired) by the strong commitment to human values of this ardent social critic, cultural historian, and philosopher.

Two are "global crime" stories. In *The Doomsday Men* pseudo-religious indoctrination (compare Hammett's *Dain Curse*) and advanced technology (compare Fleming's *You Only Live Twice*) are used by a despairing maniac for the (attempted) annihilation of all life on earth. This book, though set in the States, can nevertheless be seen as a shrewd (and thrilling) analysis of the Hitlerian death-drive. And in *Saturn over the Water* (structurally related to *Lost Empires,* thematically to *The Magicians*) an international set of powerful men conspire to drive mankind over the edge to self-destruction. *The Shapes of Sleep* is (like le Carré's *A Small Town in Germany*) a more thoughtful than violent cold war spy thriller concerning a psychological discovery equally useful for subliminal sales promotion, political propaganda, and enemy disorientation. It also (like Watson's *Hopjoy Was Here*) debunks our world of secret services. *Black-Out in Gretley* is a gripping counter-espionage story, authentically embedded in the life of a northern industrial city. One of Priestley's many contributions to the War Effort (and related to *Daylight on Saturday*) it compares favourably to corresponding works by Allingham, Blake, Christie, and Michael Innes. *Salt Is Leaving* (its title character gave something to Tuby and Saltana in *The Image Men*) is exactly what the publishers say on the cover: "a pungent novel of crime and detection." It is also a cheerfully biased, but uncomfortably close portrait of British society in the 1960's.

Viewed overall, Priestley was an exponent of the modern trend to dissolve the neatly isolated literature of crime in the more ambiguous, wider literature with a crime angle. Viewed as an occasional guest among "professional" crime writers, he has created five books with an unusual edge; all creditable, two outstanding. Not surprisingly, written as they are by so experienced a dramatist, all five novels would very easily make remarkable films.

—H.M. Klein

PRIOR, Allan. British. Born in Newcastle on Tyne, Northumberland. Educated at South Shore School, Blackpool, Lancashire. Served in the Royal Air Force, 1942–46. Married Edith Playford in 1944; one son and one daughter. Recipient: Crime Writers Association award, 1962, 1964; Writers Guild of Great Britain award, 1963, 1964; Grand Prix de Littérature Policière, 1961; British Academy award, 1974. Address: Summerhill, Waverley Road, St. Albans, Hertfordshire, England.

CRIME PUBLICATIONS

Novels

One Away. London, Eyre and Spottiswoode, 1961.
Z Cars Again (novelization of television series). London, Trust Books, 1963.
The Interrogators. London, Cassell, and New York, Simon and Schuster, 1965.
The Operators. London, Cassell, 1966; New York, Simon and Schuster, 1967.
His Majesty's Hit Man. London, Grafton, 1986; New York, Morrow, 1987.

OTHER PUBLICATIONS

Novels

A Flame in the Air. London, Joseph, 1951.
The Joy Ride. London, Joseph, 1952.
The One-Eyed Monster: A Novel about Television. London, Bodley Head, 1958.
The Loving Cup. London, Cassell, 1968; New York, Simon and Schuster, 1969.
The Contract. London, Cassell, 1970; New York, Simon and Schuster, 1971.
Paradiso. London, Cassell, 1972; New York, Simon and Schuster, 1973.
Affair. London, Cassell, and New York, Simon and Schuster, 1976.
Never Been Kissed in the Same Place Twice. London, Cassell, 1978; New York, Harper, 1979.
Theatre. London, Hamish Hamilton, 1982.
A Cast of Stars. New York, Holt, 1983.
The Big March. London, Hamish Hamilton, 1983.

Plays

The West Pier, adaptation of the novel by Patrick Hamilton, (produced Brighton, 1990).

Screenplays: *All Coppers Are . . . ,* 1972; *One Away,* 1974; *King Solomon's Treasure,* with Colin Turner, 1979.

Radio Plays: *The Prawn King,* 1951; *A Personal Affair,* 1952; *A Flame in the Air,* 1953; *Memo to Mr. Alexander,* 1953; *Worker in the Dawn,* 1953; *Missing from His Home,* 1953; *Power of the Press* (2 series), 1953–55; *The Running Man,* 1955; *Slack Water,* from a work by K. H. Thomas, 1955; *The Gorgio Girl,* 1956; *United Wives,* 1957; *Neighbours,* 1957; *Blind Orchid,* 1957; *The Gift Giver,* 1959; *A Young Affair,* 1959; *Family Business,* 1961; *The Girl Richards,* 1961; *Crack-Up,* 1964; *The Joy Ride,* 1966; *Paradiso,* 1975; *The One-Eyed Monster,* 1976; *Aaros in Winter,* 1977; *The Chief,* 1977; *Pity the Poor Potters,* 1979; *Girl at Risk,* 1980; *Never Been Kissed in the Same Place Twice,* from his own

novel, 1982; *Four Legs, One at Each Corner,* 1984; *The Big March* series, from his own novel, 1984; *Burglars,* 1984; *Muggers,* 1985; *The Chancer,* 1987; *Nosey!,* 1990.

Television Plays: *The Common Man,* 1956; *Bed, Board, and Romance,* from a play by Harry Jackson, 1957; *Starr and Company* (serial), 1958; *A Young Affair,* 1958; *Man at the Door* (serial), 1960; *Yorky* (serial), with Bill Naughton, 1960, 2nd series, 1961; *Town Vet* (documentary), 1961; *Magnolia Street,* from the novel by Louis Golding, 1961; *Deadline Midnight* series (3 episodes), 1961; *Top Secret* series (1 episode), 1962; *Z Cars* series (86 episodes), 1962–78; *Moonstrike* series (8 episodes), 1963; *Sergeant Cork* series (4 episodes), 1964–66; *The Case of Oscar Brodski,* and *Thorndyke* (serial), both from works by R. Austin Freeman; *Undercurrent,* from a work by Keith Watson, 1964; *They'll Throw It at You,* 1964; *The Girl in the Picture,* 1964; *I've Got a System,* 1965; *The Welcome,* 1965; *Four of Hearts,* 1965; *Knock on Any Door,* 1965; *Dr. Finlay's Casebook* series (2 episodes), 1965; *Old Mrs. Jones,* from a work by Mrs. J.H. Liddell, 1965 (USA), as *The Beckoning Window,* 1966; *Softly, Softly* series (37 episodes), 1966–76; *The Gold Robbers* series (1 episode), 1969; *Parkin's Patch* series (3 episodes), 1969; *The Borderers* series (1 episode), 1969; *Trespassers,* 1969; *Two-Way Traffic* 1969; *Ryan International* series (1 episode), 1970; *The Ten Commandments,* 1971; *The Onedin Line* series (4 episodes), 1972–77; *Marked Personal,* 1973; *Hawkeye the Pathfinder* (serial), with Alistair Bell, 1973; *Barlow at Large* series, and later series (7 episodes), 1973–75; *The Brave One,* 1973; *Crown Court* series (1 episode), 1974; *The Carnforth Practice* series (1 episode), 1974; *Sutherland's Law* series (1 episode), 1974; *One Pair of Eyes* (documentary), 1974; *Warship* series (3 episodes), 1974; *The Sweeney* series (2 episodes), 1975; *Ben Hall* series (1 episode), 1975; *The Expert* series (2 episodes), 1976; *General Hospital* series (2 episodes), 1976–79; *Blake's Seven* series (3 episodes), 1979; *Romany Rye,* from the work by George Borrow, 1979; *Spy!* (1 episode), 1980; *Juliet Bravo* series, 1982; *Bookie,* series, 1983–88; *Stookie* series, 1985; *Howard's Way* series, 1985–89; *The Charmer* series, 1987.

*

Manuscript Collection: Mugar Memorial Library, Boston University.

Allan Prior comments:

I have written only three original novels that can be considered "crime" books. On the other hand, I have written 150 hours of crime fiction on British television, in *Z Cars,* *Softly, Softly,* and *The Sweeney.* I write "police" novels rarely and have done only two: *The Interrogators* and *The Operators.* Julian Symons was kind enough to call me (in a broadcast) "the best police procedural writer we have." My defence rests!

* * *

An accomplished professional who, like many English writers, is less sensational but more polished than many of his American counterparts, Allan Prior has succeeded in several areas of popular fiction. Among other achievements in crime writing he was responsible for the British television police procedural series *Z Cars* and its follow-up, *Softly, Softly.* He has written a number of genre novels, including some interesting work in the mystery and detective field.

The Operators is a fine big caper novel, with a nicely assorted cast of characters and a well planned airport heist at its center;

in addition, it has an extremely successful sense of authenticity and atmosphere, whether in its scenes of prison and the life of a career criminal or in its picture of the actual daily work of a great airport. Exuding a strong and pungent flavor of the English criminal classes, showing their hatred for the system they inhabit, it's one of the few books that suggests the importance of class in English crime and English crime writing, where the fiction of gentlemanly or even comic criminals has been the rule.

Prior's best novel is probably *The Interrogators*, which may also be the best British police procedural of them all. The novel does everything that this sort of work should do but usually doesn't: instead of presenting the professional policemen as sturdy, hearts-of-oak yeomen in the great sentimental tradition of English fiction, it shows them as hard, tough, often corrupt men who are necessarily of the working classes (the titled Oxonian policeman is one of the most offensive inventions of detective fiction) and effectively representative of their society. Following the investigation of the rape and murder of a child—always the most reprehensible crime in English fiction—we see into the lives of Jack Eaves, a young detective, and his cynical, hard-bitten superior, Savage. In the process we witness the life of a smoky, gritty industrial city, the gray misery of working-class life, the immense discipline, patience, and boredom of police routine, the development of the qualities that go into the making of a good policeman. The novel presents a detailed and absolutely credible picture of the society in which such a crime can occur and the effect such an event can have on the lives of the investigators. It becomes, besides, a remarkable delineation of its locale and subject, a kind of horribly ironic *Bildungsroman;* Jack Eaves finds the murderer and demonstrates the combination of effort, thought, and intuition that makes up the good detective, but in the process he loses something of himself, whatever innocence he still possessed. He discovers, in fact, that to be a good cop he must abandon something of his own humanity; the powerful ending of the book precisely suggests the terrible ambiguity of his victory.

The fierce honesty of his other novels carries over into Prior's excursion into espionage of a sort, *Her Majesty's Hit Man,* a title that pretty much describes the protagonist, who kills people for his government, partly for money and partly out of a kind of patriotism. The protagonist has little faith in the people he works for—and is entirely correct in that judgment—but believes he is at least doing something that is good for his country. When his employers lend him to the Americans to do one of his jobs on a famous senator, he discovers new depths of corruption and betrayal both in his superiors and that favorite whipping boy of espionage, the CIA. The book's open ending implies that Prior may return to international intrigue and his professional killer. If he can lend to that sort of writing the professionalism and skill that his best work in fiction and television displays, he will continue to deserve enthusiastic attention.

—George Grella

PROCTER, Maurice. British. Born in Nelson, Lancashire, 4 February 1906. Educated at Nelson Grammar School. Served in the British Army, 1921–26. Married Winifred Blakey in 1933; one son. Constable, Halifax Borough Police, Yorkshire, 1927–46. *Died in 1973.*

CRIME PUBLICATIONS

Novels (series: Detective Superintendent Philip Hunter; Detective Chief Inspector Harry Martineau)

No Proud Chivalry. London, Longman, 1947.
Each Man's Destiny. London, Longman, 1947.
The End of the Street. London, Longman, 1949.
The Chief Inspector's Statement (Hunter). London, Hutchinson, 1951; as *The Pennycross Murders,* New York, Harper, 1953.
Hurry the Darkness. New York, Harper, 1951; London, Hutchinson, 1952.
Rich Is the Treasure. London, Hutchinson, 1952.
Hell Is a City (Martineau). London, Hutchinson, 1954; as *Somewhere in This City,* New York, Harper, 1954; as *Murder Somewhere in This City,* New York, Avon, 1956.
The Pub Crawler. London, Hutchinson, 1956; New York, Harper, 1957.
I Will Speak Daggers (Hunter). London, Hutchinson, 1956; as *The Ripper,* New York, Harper, 1956; as *The Ripper Murders,* New York, Avon, 1957.
The Midnight Plumber (Martineau). London, Hutchinson, 1957; New York, Harper, 1958.
Three at the Angel. London, Hutchinson, and New York, Harper, 1958.
Man in Ambush (Martineau). London, Hutchinson, 1958; New York, Harper, 1959.
Killer at Large (Martineau). London, Hutchinson, and New York, Harper, 1959.
Devil's Due (Martineau). London, Hutchinson, and New York, Harper, 1960.
The Spearhead Death. London, Hutchinson, 1960.
The Devil Was Handsome (Martineau). London, Hutchinson, and New York, Harper, 1961.
Devil in Moonlight. London, Hutchinson, 1962.
A Body to Spare (Martineau). London, Hutchinson, and New York, Harper, 1962.
Moonlight Flitting (Martineau). London, Hutchinson, 1963; as *The Graveyard Rolls,* New York, Harper, 1964.
Two Men in Twenty (Martineau). London, Hutchinson, and New York, Harper, 1964.
Death Has a Shadow (Martineau). London, Hutchinson, 1965; as *Homicide Blonde,* New York, Harper, 1965.
His Weight in Gold (Martineau). London, Hutchinson, and New York, Harper, 1966.
Rogue Running (Martineau). London, Hutchinson, and New York, Harper, 1967.
Exercise Hoodwink (Martineau). London, Hutchinson, and New York, Harper, 1967.
Hideaway (Martineau). London, Hutchinson, and New York, Harper, 1968.
The Dog Man. London, Hutchinson, 1969.

Uncollected Short Stories

"Fox in the Pennine Hills," in *Crook's Tour,* edited by Bruno Fischer. New York, Dodd Mead, 1953; London, Macdonald, 1954.
"No Place for Magic," in *Butcher, Baker, Murder-Maker,* edited by George Harmon Coxe. New York, Knopf, 1954.
"The Grasshopper Murder," in *Bestseller Mystery Magazine* (New York), November 1959.

"West Riding to Maryland," in *Tales for a Rainy Night,* edited by David Alexander. New York, Holt Rinehart, 1961.
"The Policeman and the Lamp," in *Ellery Queen's Mystery Magazine* (New York), July 1961.
"Diamonds for the Million," in *The Fourth Mystery Bedside Book,* edited by John Creasy. London, Hodder and Stoughton, 1963.
"The Million Dollar Mystery," in *Anthology 1968 Mid-Year,* edited by Ellery Queen. New York, Davis, 1968.

*

Manuscript Collection: Mugar Memorial Library, Boston University.

*   *   *

Maurice Procter is a transitional figure in the history of detective fiction. His main series character, Detective Chief Inspector Harry Martineau, has some of the qualities of the Great Policeman tradition represented by Ngaio Marsh's Inspector Alleyn and Josephine Tey's Inspector Grant, but he also belongs in the mode of the police procedural story, along with John Creasey's George Gideon. Some of this mixture in Martineau is undoubtedly the result of his chronological position in the development of the police procedural novel. The first story in which he appears, *Hell Is a City,* was published in December 1954, thus preceding the "pure" procedural series of Creasey by a few months and that of Ed McBain by a year.

In his first appearance Martineau shows several traits of the Gentleman Policeman. He loves to play the piano, and when a prostitute turns and flees after recognizing him he regrets "the social handicaps of being a prominent copper. The leper of the law." His reputation is already established as "the great Inspector Martineau." In later stories, however, Martineau comes to bear an increasing resemblance to George Gideon, particularly in his tendency to doubt his own abilities and motives; having killed a criminal in the process of capture, Martineau tells himself that he had been able to control his hatred right up until the last moment and them had given way to it. He shares another quality of Gideon, the ability to recognize promise in a young officer, and to build up a loyal following among such bright young men by using their talents and rewarding their good work with promotions.

Procter's other series protagonist, Detective Superintendent Philip Hunter, is as abrasive as Martineau is smooth. He badgers witnesses and suspects unmercifully, and he is harsh toward his subordinates, blaming them severely when they make a mistake, bawling them out in public and then telling them they needn't shout.

The police methods in Procter's stories are based somewhat less on modern forensic science than on common sense and an understanding of human nature. Martineau, for example, knows how to put pressure on an underworld type to force him to turn informer. Hunter passes on gossip from one suspect to another to set them at odds with each other and start them talking. There is some use of the police lab, but most of the results are obtained by careful investigation and painstaking questioning. The settings of the Procter stories are several imaginary cities in the North of England. In the Martineau series it is "Granchester," which might be Manchester or Liverpool, called the "Metropolis of the North," with a well-staffed police department that can do anything Scotland Yard can do. "Yoreborough" (York), the scene of the Philip Hunter stories, is a somewhat smaller town, having practically no

industry but, like "Granchester," boasting a highly efficient CID.

—George N. Dove

———

PRONZINI, Bill (William John Pronzini). Also writes as Robert Hart Davis; Jack Foxx; Brett Halliday; William Jeffrey; Alex Saxon; John Barry Williams. American. Born in Petaluma, California, 13 April 1943. Attended a junior college for 2 years. Married 1) Laura Patricia Adolphson in 1965 (divorced 1966); 2) Brunhilde Schier in 1972. Has worked as newsstand clerk, sports reporter, warehouseman, typist, salesman, civilian guard with U.S. Marshall's office. Since 1969, self-employed writer. Traveled extensively in Europe; lived in Majorca and West Germany, 1970–73. Recipient: Private Eye Writers of America award, 1981, 1983, Life Achievement award, 1987. Agent: Clyde Taylor, Curtis Brown Ltd., 10 Astor Place, New York, New York 10003. Address: P.O. Box 1349, Sonoma, California 95476, U.S.A.

CRIME PUBLICATIONS

Novels (series: Nameless Detective; Quincannon)

The Stalker. New York, Random House, 1971; London, Hale, 1974.
The Snatch (Nameless). New York, Random House, 1971; London, Hale, 1974.
Panic! New York, Random House, 1972; London, Hale, 1974.
A Run in Diamonds (as Alex Saxon). New York, Pocket Books, 1973.
The Vanished (Nameless). New York, Random House, 1973; London, Hale, 1974.
Undercurrent (Nameless). New York, Random House, 1973; London, Hale, 1975.
Snowbound. New York, Putnam, 1974; London, Weidenfeld and Nicolson, 1975.
Games. New York, Putnam, 1976; London, Hamlyn, 1978.
The Running of Beasts, with Barry N. Malzberg. New York, Putnam, 1976.
Blowback (Nameless). New York, Random House, 1977; London, Hale, 1978.
Acts of Mercy, with Barry N. Malzberg. New York, Putnam, 1977.
Twospot (Nameless), with Collin Wilcox. New York, Putnam, 1978.
Night Screams, with Barry N. Malzberg. Chicago, Playboy Press, 1979.
Labyrinth (Nameless). New York, St. Martin's Press, 1980; London, Hale, 1981.
Hoodwink (Nameless). New York, St. Martin's Press, and London, Hale, 1981.
Masques. New York, Arbor House, 1981.
Scattershot (Nameless). New York, St. Martin's Press, and London, Hale, 1982.
Dragonfire (Nameless). New York, St. Martin's Press, 1982; London, Hale, 1983.
Bindlestiff (Nameless). New York, St. Martin's Press, 1983; London, Severn House, 1984.
Day of the Moon (as William Jeffrey, with Jeff Wallmann). London, Hale, 1983.

Quicksilver (Nameless). New York, St. Martin's Press, 1984; London, Severn House, 1985.
The Eye, with John Lutz. New York, Mysterious Press, 1984.
Nightshades (Nameless). New York, St. Martin's Press, 1984; London, Severn House, 1986.
Double (Nameless) with Marcia Muller. New York, St. Martin's Press, 1984.
Bones (Nameless). New York, St. Martin's Press, 1985.
Quincannon. New York, Walker, 1985.
Deadfall (Nameless). New York, St. Martin's Press, 1986.
Beyond the Grave (Quincannon), with Marcia Muller. New York, Walker, 1986.
The Lighthouse, with Marcia Muller. New York, St. Martin's Press, 1987; London, Hale, 1988.
Shackles (Nameless) New York, St. Martin's Press, 1988.
Jackpot (Nameless) New York, Delacorte Press, 1990.

Novels as Jack Foxx (series: Dan Connell)

The Jade Figurine (Connell) Indianapolis, Bobbs Merrill, 1972.
Dead Run (Connell) Indianapolis, Bobbs Merrill, 1975.
Freebooty. Indianapolis, Bobbs Merrill, 1976.
Wildfire. Indianapolis, Bobbs Merrill, 1978.

Short Stories

A Killing in Xanadu. Richmond, Virginia, Waves Press, 1980.
Casefile: The Best of the "Nameless Detective" Stories. New York, St. Martin's Press, 1983.
Cat's-Paw. Richmond, Virginia, Waves Press, 1983.
Graveyard Plots. New York, St. Martin's Press, 1985.
Small Felonies: Fifty Mystery Short Stories. New York, St. Martin's Press, 1988.

Uncollected Short Stories

"You Don't Know What It's Like," in *Shell Scott Mystery Magazine* (New York), November 1966.
"Night Freight," in *Mike Shayne Mystery Magazine* (New York), May 1967.
"A Man Called Vinelli," in *Man from U.N.C.L.E.* (New York), May 1967.
"The Long Knives Wait," in *Mike Shayne Mystery Magazine* (New York), September 1967.
"The Pillars of Salt Affair" (as Robert Hart Davis), in *Man from U.N.C.L.E.* (New York), December 1967.
"The Swabbie and the Sexpot," in *Body Shop,* December 1967.
"Opportunity," in *Alfred Hitchcock's Mystery Magazine* (New York), December 1967.
"The Ethical Eye," in *Alfred Hitchcock's Mystery Magazine* (New York), February 1968.
"A Quiet Night," in *Alfred Hitchcock's Mystery Magazine* (New York), March 1968.
"Who's Afraid of Sherlock Holmes?," in *Mike Shayne Mystery Magazine* (New York), April 1968.
"The Bomb Expert," in *Mike Shayne Mystery Magazine* (New York), May 1968.
"The Perfect Crime," in *Mike Shayne Mystery Magazine* (New York), July 1968.
"You Can't Fight City Hall, Pete," in *Alfred Hitchcock's Mystery Magazine* (New York), July 1968.
"The Accident," in *Mike Shayne Mystery Magazine* (New York), September 1968.
"The Running Man," in *Alfred Hitchcock Presents: Murders I Fell In Love with.* New York, Dell, 1969.
"You Can Never Really Know," in *Mike Shayne Mystery Magazine* (New York), September 1969.

"The Almost Perfect Hiding Place," in *Mike Shayne Mystery Magazine* (New York), October 1969.
"A Nice Place to Visit, But . . . ," in *Mike Shayne Mystery Magazine* (New York), November 1969.
"The Crank," in *Mike Shayne Mystery Magazine* (New York), January 1970.
"The Snatch," in *Best Detective Stories of the Year 1970,* edited by Allen J. Hubin. New York, Dutton, 1970.
"The $50,000 Bosom," in *Adventure* (Glendale, California), December 1970.
"Beautiful Smuggler," in *Argosy* (New York), December 1970.
"Cain's Mark," in *Best Detective Stories of the Year 1971,* edited by Allen J. Hubin. New York, Dutton, 1971.
"Ice and Snow," in *Mike Shayne Mystery Magazine* (Los Angeles), March 1971.
"I Know a Way," in *Mike Shayne Mystery Magazine* (Los Angeles), September 1971.
"The Assignment," in *Alfred Hitchcock's Mystery Magazine* (New York), February 1972.
"Danger: Michael Shayne at Work!" (as Brett Halliday), with Jeff Wallmann, in *Mike Shayne Mystery Magazine* (Los Angeles), April 1972.
"The Amateur Touch," in *Alfred Hitchcock's Mystery Magazine* (New York), July 1972.
"Blowback," in *Argosy* (New York), September 1972.
"Majorcan Assignment," in *Mike Shayne Mystery Magazine* (Los Angeles), October 1972.
"The Web," in *Alfred Hitchcock's Mystery Magazine* (New York), January 1973.
"It's a Lousy World," in *Alfred Hitchcock Presents: Stories to Be Read with the Lights On.* New York, Random House, 1973.
"Sacrifice," in *Alfred Hitchcock's Mystery Magazine* (New York), February 1973.
"The Follower," in *Alfred Hitchcock's Mystery Magazine* (New York), March 1973.
"The Scales of Justice," in *Alfred Hitchcock's Mystery Magazine* (New York), July 1973.
"The Methodical Cop," in *Mike Shayne Mystery Magazine* (Los Angeles), July 1973.
"It's Not a Coffin," in *Mike Shayne Mystery Magazine* (Los Angeles), June 1974.
"A Matter of Life and Death," with Barry N. Malzberg, in *Mike Shayne Mystery Magazine* (Los Angeles), July 1974.
"The Pawns of Death" (as Robert Hart Davis), with Jeff Wallmann, in *Charlie Chan Mystery Magazine* (Los Angeles), August 1974.
"Up to Snuff," in *Alfred Hitchcock's Mystery Magazine* (North Palm Beach, Florida), October 1974.
"Free-Lance Operation," in *Alfred Hitchcock's Mystery Magazine* (North Palm Beach, Florida), May 1975.
"Quicker Than the Eye," with Michael Kurland, in *Alfred Hitchcock's Mystery Magazine* (North Palm Beach, Florida), September 1975.
"I Ought to Kill You," with Barry N. Malzberg, in *Every Crime in the Book,* edited by Robert L. Fish. New York, Putnam, 1975.
"Multiples," with Barry N. Malzberg, in *Tricks and Treats,* edited by Joe Gores and Bill Pronzini. New York, Doubleday, 1976.
"A Cold Day in November," in *Tales to Keep You Spellbound,* edited by Eleanor Sullivan. New York, Dial Press, 1976.
"Vanishing Act," with Michael Kurland, in *Alfred Hitchcock's Mystery Magazine* (New York), January 1976.
"If You Play with Fire . . . ," in *Mike Shayne Mystery Magazine* (Los Angeles), February 1976.
"A Matter of Survival," with Barry N. Malzberg, in *Alfred Hitchcock's Mystery Magazine* (New York), December 1976.

"What Kind of Person Are You?," with Barry N. Malzberg, in *Alfred Hitchcock's Mystery Magazine* (New York), April 1977.

"The Last Plagiarism," with Barry N. Malzberg, in *Alfred Hitchcock's Mystery Magazine* (New York), May 1977.

"The Dark Side," in *Mike Shayne Mystery Magazine* (Los Angeles), May 1977.

"Night Rider," with Barry N. Malzberg, in *Alfred Hitchcock's Mystery Magazine* (New York), June 1977.

"The Arrowmont Prison Riddle," in *Alfred Hitchcock's Tales to Take Your Breath Away*, edited by Eleanor Sullivan. New York, Dial Press, 1978.

"Deathlove," in *Shadows*, edited by Charles L. Grant. New York, Doubleday, 1978.

"The Half-Invisible Man," with Jeff Wallmann, in *Cop Cade*, edited by John Ball. New York, Doubleday, 1978.

"Birds of a Feather," with Barry N. Malzberg, in *Alfred Hitchcock's Mystery Magazine* (New York), April 1978.

"Bank Job," in *Ellery Queen's Mystery Magazine* (New York), August 1978.

"Cheeseburger" (as John Barry Williams), with Barry N. Malzberg and John Lutz, in *Alfred Hitchcock's Mystery Magazine* (New York), October 1978.

"Clocks," with Barry N. Malzberg, in *Shadows 2*, edited by Charles L. Grant. New York, Doubleday, 1979.

"Murder Is My Business," with Barry N. Malzberg, in *Mike Shayne Mystery Magazine* (Los Angeles), January 1979.

"Final Exam," with Barry N. Malzberg, in *Alfred Hitchcock's Mystery Magazine* (New York), February 1979.

"Million-to-One Shot," with Barry N. Malzberg, in *Ellery Queen's Mystery Magazine* (New York), July 1979.

"Problems Solved," in *Ellery Queen's Veils of Mystery*. New York, Davis, 1980.

"Connoisseur," in *Who Done It?*, edited by Alice Laurance and Issac Asimov. Boston, Houghton Mifflin, 1980.

"Opening a vein," with Barry N. Malzberg, in *Shadows 3*, edited by Charles L. Grant. New York, Doubleday, 1980.

"The Last One Left," with Barry N. Malzberg, in *Bug-Eyed Monsters*, edited by Bill Pronzini and Barry N. Malzberg. New York, Harcourt Brace, 1980.

"Blazing Guns of the Rio Rangers," with Barry N. Malzberg, in *Alfred Hitchcock's Mystery Magazine* (New York), 27 February 1980.

"The Lyran Case." with Barry N. Malzberg, in *Analog* (New York), March 1980.

"The Way the World Spins," in *Alfred Hitchcock's Tales to Make Your Hair Stand on End*, edited by Eleanor Sullivan. New York, Dial Press, 1981.

"Demolition, Inc.," in *Mike Shayne Mystery Magazine* (Los Angeles), February 1981.

"Coyote and Quarter-Moon," with Jeff Wallmann, in *The Year's Best Mystery and Suspense Stories 1982*, edited by Edward D. Hoch. New York, Walker, 1982.

"All the Same," in *Alfred Hitchcock's Death-Reach*, edited by Cathleen Jordan. New York, Dial Press, 1982.

"The Jade Figurine," in *Alfred Hitchcock's Tales to Make You Quake and Quiver*, edited by Cathleen Jordan. New York, Dial Press, 1982.

"Vanishing Point," with Barry N. Malzberg, in *Analog* (New York), 1 February 1982.

"Skeleton Rattle Your Mouldy Leg," in *The Eyes Have It*, edited by Robert J. Randisi. New York, Mysterious Press, 1984.

"Ace in the Hole," in *Mean Streets*, edited by Robert J. Randisi. New York, Mysterious Press, 1986.

"Stacked Deck," in *The New Black Mask No. 8*, edited by Richard Layman and Matthew J. Bruccoli. San Diego, Harcourt Brace, 1987.

"Incident in a Neighborhood Tavern," in *An Eye for Justice*, edited by Robert J. Randisi. New York, Mysterious Press, 1988.

"Wooden Indian," in *Alfred Hitchcock's Mystery Magazine* (New York), March 1989.

"Here Comes Santa Claus," in *Mistletoe Mysteries*, edited by Charlotte MacLeod. New York, Mysterious Press, 1989.

"Funeral Day," in *New Crimes*, edited by Maxim Jakubowksi. London, Robinson, 1989; New York, Carroll and Graf, 1990.

"Stakeout," in *Justice for Hire*, edited by Robert J. Randisi. New York, Mysterious Press, 1990.

Uncollected Short Stories as Jack Foxx

"Escape," in *Mike Shayne Mystery Magazine* (New York), May 1969.

"Little Old Ladies Can Be Dangerous," *Mike Shayne Mystery Magazine* (New York), September 1969.

"The Clincher," in *Alfred Hitchcock's Mystery Magazine* (New York), December 1969.

"The Right Move," in *Alfred Hitchcock's Mystery Magazine* (New York), March 1970.

"You're Safe Here," in *Mike Shayne Mystery Magazine* (Los Angeles), April 1970.

"Roadblock," in *Alfred Hitchcock's Mystery Magazine* (New York), May 1971.

"The Duel," in *Mike Shayne Mystery Magazine* (Los Angeles), April 1972.

"Suicide Note," in *Alfred Hitchcock's Mystery Magazine* (New York), May 1972.

"Incident in Three Crossings," in *Charlie Chan Mystery Magazine* (Los Angeles), May 1974.

"Your Choice," *Mike Shayne Mystery Magazine* (Los Angeles), April 1976.

Uncollected Short Stories as William Jeffrey

"Fire Hazaard," in *Alfred Hitchcock's Mystery Magazine* (New York), April 1970.

"The Day of the Moon," in *Alfred Hitchcock's Mystery Magazine* (New York), June 1970.

"Monday Is the Dullest Night of the Week," in *Mike Shayne Mystery Magazine* (Los Angeles), July 1970.

"Retribution," in *Mike Shayne Mystery Magazine* (Los Angeles), August 1970.

"Murder Is No Man's Friend," in *Mike Shayne Mystery Magazine* (Los Angeles), November 1970.

"The Ten Million Dollar Hijack," in *Alfred Hitchcock's Mystery Magazine* (New York), January 1972.

"A Run of Bad Luck," in *Alfred Hitchcock's Mystery Magazine* (New York), March 1972.

"The Island," in *Alfred Hitchcock's Mystery Magazine* (New York), August 1972.

"I Want a Lawyer." in *Mike Shayne Mystery Magazine* (Los Angeles), March 1973.

"A Slight Case of Suspicion," in *Alfred Hitchcock's Mystery Magazine* (New York), September 1973.

"O'Flaherty's Wake," in *Mike Shayne Mystery Magazine* (Los Angeles), September 1975.

OTHER PUBLICATIONS

Novels

Prose Bowl, with Barry N. Malzberg. New York, St. Martin's Press, 1980.
The Cambodia File, with Jack Anderson. New York, Doubleday, 1981; London, Sphere, 1983.
Duel at Gold Buttes (as William Jeffrey, with Jeffrey Wallmann). New York, Tower, 1981; London, Hale, 1982.
Border Fever (as William Jeffrey, with Jeffrey Wallmann). New York, Leisure, 1983; London, Hale, 1984.
The Gallows Land. New York, Walker, 1983; London, Hale, 1984.
Starvation Camp. New York, Walker, 1983; London, Hale, 1984.
The Last Days of Horse-Shy Halloran. New York, Evans, 1987.
The Hangings. New York, Walker, 1989.
Firewind. New York, Evans, 1989.

Short Stories

The Best Western Stories of Bill Pronzini, edited by Martin H. Greenberg. Athens, Ohio, Swallow Press, 1990.

Other

"The Mystery Career of Evan Hunter," in *Armchair Detective* (White Bear Lake, Minnesota), April 1972.
"The Saga of the Phoenix That Probably Should Never Have Arisen," in *Armchair Detective* (Del Mar, California), April 1977.
"Writing the Mystery Short-Short," in *The Writer* (Boston), December 1977.
"The Elements of Suspense," in *Writing Suspense and Mystery Fiction,* edited by A.S. Burack. Boston, The Writer, 1977.
"The Worst Mystery Novel of All Time," in *Armchair Detective* (White Bear Lake, Minnesota), Spring 1980.
"But That's Impossible!," in *The Writer* (Boston), November 1981.
Gun in Cheek: A Study of "Alternative" Crime. New York, Coward McCann, 1982.
"Should You Collaborate?" with Marcia Muller, in *The Writer* (Boston), March 1985.
Son of Gun in Cheek. New York, Mysterious Press, 1987.

Editor, with Joe Gores, *Tricks and Treats.* New York, Doubleday, 1976; as *Mystery Writers Choice,* London, Gollancz, 1977.
Editor, *Midnight Specials.* Indianapolis, Bobbs Merrill, 1977; London, Souvenir Press, 1978.
Editor, with Barry N. Malzberg, *Dark Sins, Dark Dreams.* New York, Doubleday, 1977.
Editor, *Werewolf!* New York, Arbor House, 1979.
Editor, with Barry N. Malzberg, *Shared Tomorrows: Collaboration in SF.* New York, St. Martin's Press, 1979.
Editor, with Barry N. Malzberg, *Bug-Eyed Monsters.* New York, Harcourt Brace, 1980.
Editor, *The Edgar Winners.* New York. Random House, 1980.
Editor, *Voodoo!* New York, Arbor House, 1980.
Editor *Mummy!* New York, Arbor House, 1980.
Editor, *Creature!* New York, Arbor House, 1981.
Editor, *The Arbor House Necropolis: Voodoo!, Mummy!, Ghoul!* New York, Arbor House, 1981; revised edition as *Tales of the Dead,* New York, Bonanza, 1982.

Editor, with Barry N. Malzberg and Martin H. Greenberg. *The Arbor House Treasure of Horror and the Supernatural* [*Mystery and Suspense*]. New York, Arbor House, 2 vols., 1981.
Editor, *Specter!* New York, Arbor House, 1982.
Editor, with Martin H. Greenberg, *The Arbor House Treasury of Great Western Stories.* New York, Arbor House, 1982.
Editor, *The Arbor House Treasury of Detective and Mystery Stories from the Great Pulps.* New York, Arbor House, 1983.
Editor, with Marcia Muller, *The Web She Weaves: An Anthology of Mysteries and Suspicious Stories by Women.* New York, Morrow, 1983.
Editor, with Charles G. Waugh and Martin H. Greenberg, *The Mystery Hall of Fame.* New York, Morrow, 1984.
Editor, with Marcia Muller, *Child's Ploy.* New York, Macmillan, 1984.
Editor, with Marcia Muller, *Witches' Brew: Horror and Supernatural Stories by Women.* New York, Macmillan, 1984.
Editor, with Martin H. Greenberg, *The Western Hall of Fame.* New York, Morrow, 1984.
Editor, with Martin H. Greenberg, *The Lawmen.* New York, Fawcett, 1984.
Editor, with Martin H. Greenberg, *The Outlaws.* New York, Fawcett, 1984.
Editor, with Martin H. Greenberg, *The Reel West.* New York, Doubleday, 1984.
Editor, with Martin H. Greenberg, *The Best Western Stories of Steve Frazee.* Carbondale, Southern Illinois University Press, 1984.
Editor, with Martin H. Greenberg, *The Best Western Stories of Wayne D. Overholser.* Carbondale, Southern Illinois University Press, 1984.
Editor, with Marcia Muller, *Chapter and Hearse.* New York, Morrow, 1985.
Editor, with Charles G. Waugh and Martin H. Greenberg, *Murder in the First Reel.* New York, Avon, 1985.
Editor, with Martin H. Greenberg, *13 Short Mystery Novels.* New York, Greenwich House, 1985.
Editor, with Martin H. Greenberg, *13 Short Espionage Novels.* New York, Bonanza, 1985.
Editor, with Marcia Muller, *Dark Lessons: Crime and Detection on Campus.* New York, Macmillan, 1985.
Editor, with Marcia Muller, *Kill or Cure.* New York, Macmillan, 1985.
Editor, with Martin H. Greenberg, *Women Sleuths.* Chicago, Academy, 1985.
Editor, with Martin H. Greenberg, *Police Procedurals,* Chicago, Academy, 1985.
Editor, with Marcia Muller, *The Wickedest Show on Earth: A Carnival of Circus Suspense.* New York, Morrow, 1985.
Editor, with Marcia Muller, *The Deadly Arts: A Collection of Artful Suspense.* New York, Arbor House, 1985.
Editor, with Marcia Muller, *She Won the West: An Anthology of Western and Frontier Stories by Women.* New York, Morrow, 1985.
Editor, with Martin H. Greenberg, *The Cowboys.* New York, Fawcett, 1985.
Editor, with Martin H. Greenberg, *The Warriors.* New York, Fawcett, 1985.
Editor, with Martin H. Greenberg, *The Second Reel West.* New York, Doubleday, 1985.
Editor, with Martin H. Greenberg, *A Treasury of Civil War Stories.* New York, Bonanza, 1985.
Editor, with Martin H. Greenberg, *A Treasury of World War II Stories.* New York, Bonanza, 1985.

Editor, with Marcia Muller, *1001 Midnights: The Aficionado's Guide to Mystery and Detective Fiction.* New York, Arbor House, 1986.

Editor, with Martin H. Greenberg, *Great Modern Police Stories.* New York, Walker, 1986; London, Severn House, 1987.

Editor, with Martin H. Greenberg, *101 Mystery Stories.* New York, Avenel, 1986.

Editor, with Martin H. Greenberg, *Locked Room Puzzles.* Chicago, Academy, 1986.

Editor, with Martin H. Greenberg, and Barry N. Malzberg, *Mystery in the Mainstream.* New York, Morrow, 1986.

Editor, with Martin H. Greenberg, *The Railroaders.* New York, Fawcett, 1986.

Editor, with Martin H. Greenberg, *The Third Reel West.* New York, Doubleday, 1986.

Editor, *Wild Westerns: Stories from the Grand Old Pulps,* New York, Walker, 1986.

Editor, with Martin H. Greenberg, *The Steamboaters.* New York, Fawcett, 1986.

Editor, with Martin H. Greenberg, *The Cattlemen.* New York, Fawcett, 1987.

Editor, with Martin H. Greenberg, *Prime Suspects.* New York, Ivy, 1987; London, Severn House, 1988.

Editor, with Martin H. Greenberg, *Uncollected Crimes.* New York, Walker, 1987.

Editor, with Martin H. Greenberg, *Suspicious Characters.* New York, Ivy, 1987. London, Severn House, 1988.

Editor, with Carol-Lynn Rössel Waugh and Martin H. Greenberg, *Manhattan Mysteries.* New York, Avenel, 1987.

Editor, with Martin H. Greenberg, *The Horse Soldiers.* New York, Fawcett, 1987.

Editor, with Martin H. Greenberg, *The Best Western Stories of Lewis B. Patten.* Carbondale, Southern Illinois University Press, 1987.

Editor, with Martin H. Greenberg, *Criminal Elements.* New York, Ivy, 1988.

Editor, with Martin H. Greenberg, *13 Short Detective Novels.* New York, Bonanza, 1988.

Editor, with Martin H. Greenberg, *Cloak and Dagger.* New York, Avenel, 1988.

Editor, with Marcia Muller and Martin H. Greenberg, *Lady on the Case.* New York, Bonanza, 1988.

Editor, with Martin H. Greenberg, *The Mammoth Book of Private Eye Stories.* New York, Carroll and Graf, and London, Robinson, 1988.

Editor, with Martin H. Greenberg, *The Gunfighters.* New York, Fawcett, 1988.

Editor, with Martin H. Greenberg, *The Texans.* New York, Fawcett, 1988.

Editor, with Martin H. Greenberg, *Homicidal Acts.* New York, Ivy, 1989.

Editor, with Martin H. Greenberg, *Felonious Assaults.* New York, Ivy, 1989.

Editor, with Martin H. Greenberg, *The Californians.* New York, Fawcett, 1989.

Editor, *More Wild Westerns.* New York, Walker, 1989.

Editor, with Martin H. Greenberg, *The Best Western Stories of Loren D. Estleman.* Athens, Ohio, Swallow Press, 1989.

Editor, with Martin H. Greenberg, *The Arizonans.* New York, Fawcett, 1989.

Editor, with Martin H. Greenberg, *The Best Western Stories of Frank Bonham.* Athens, Ohio, Swallow Press, 1989.

Editor, with Martin H. Greenberg, *New Frontiers,* New York, Tor, 2 vols., 1990.

Editor, with Martin H. Greenberg, *The Northerners,* New York, Fawcett, 1990.

Editor, with Martin H. Greenberg, *The Northwesterners.* New York, Fawcett, 1990.

Editor, with Martin H. Greenberg, *The Best Western Stories of Ryerson Johnson.* Athens, Ohio, Swallow Press, 1990.

*

Manuscript Collection: Mugar Memorial Library, Boston University.

Bill Pronzini comments:

I write mystery and suspense fiction because I enjoy reading it; because I find it challenging in terms of plot and construction; because it is one of the few remaining fictional categories which emphasizes *story* (i.e., it must have a beginning, a middle, and an end); and because in the fictional world, unlike the one in which we dwell, the villains almost always get their just deserts.

*   *   *

Some mystery writers start big, with an instant classic they are never able to surpass. Other, like Bill Pronzini, seem to improve from book to book, building a solid professional foundation. In Pronzini's early novels and short stories the influence of the pulp magazines he and his "Nameless Detective" protagonist collect seems especially noticeable. Certainly Nameless himself, operating out of San Francisco, owes something to Hammett's Continental Op, though at times his personality is more reminiscent of Thomas B. Dewey's "Mac."

The first of some 44 Pronzini novels published to date was *The Stalker,* dealing with six ex-servicemen who had successfully teamed up years before to rob an armored car. Now, as someone begins tracking them down and killing them one by one, terror and suspicion grow for the the survivors. It is a classic situation and Pronzini does well by it, deserving the Mystery Writers of America nomination the book received.

The Snatch, the first of his Nameless private eye series, was expanded from a 1969 short story, and works much better than this sort of expansion usually does. Nameless returned in 16 other novels to date, even surviving the author's apparent attempt to kill him off at the end of a short story, "Private Eye Blues." The best of the early Nameless novels is probably *Hoodwink,* winner of the best novel award for 1981 from the Private Eye Writers of America. Its locked-room puzzle set at a pulp collectors' convention in San Francisco has a broad appeal even to those mystery readers who might usually steer clear of private-eye fiction. A close second among the Nameless novels prior to 1985 is *Quicksilver,* in which the detective investigates a mystery with its roots in the internment of Japanese-Americans during World War II.

Quicksilver was followed by four more good Nameless novels, *Double, Nightshade, Bones,* and *Deadfall.* But nothing was to prepare the reader or Nameless for the revelation and insight of his next case, recounted in *Shackles.* Here the detective is kidnapped and shackled to the wall of a remote mountain cabin, facing a slow death once a small quantity of food has run out. The ski-masked villain, settling some mysterious score from the past, taunts him for a time and then leaves. The reader spends 90 days and nearly half the book with Nameless chained to that wall, and when he finally escapes and sets out to find his captor, he is a changed man in many ways. These changes continue to reveal themselves in *Jackpot,* the latest Nameless novel. Here a young man who has supposedly won $200,000 at a

Lake Tahoe casino is suddenly driven to commit suicide. The investigation leads Nameless into a mob-run world of high-stakes gambling, but it is a different Nameless—older, more serious and wiser in some ways—than the man the reader has known before. His prized collection of old pulp magazines has receded into the past, and when he is taunted by a younger, more powerful gang leader, the reader is full of sympathy for him. One knows that Nameless would like nothing better than to marry and settle down with his long-time girlfriend Kerry, but that is not to be.

With *Shackles* and *Jackpot* the reader is witnessing the metamorphosis of a character in a manner perhaps unique in detective fiction. If these two books lack some of the classic puzzle elements of earlier Nameless cases, they offer something more—something about the life of a man who has become very real to us, despite the fact that we never know his name.

Pronzini's other novels are both suspense and mystery, often built around a menace at some remote location. The best of these, *Snowbound,* has three robbers planning to loot an entire snowbound village in the Sierra Nevadas. *Games* follows a wealthy U.S. Senator to a remote Maine island for a terror-filled weekend. The suspense amounts throughout, though the final surprise can be forseen by clever readers. Pronzini has also published novels under the pseudonyms of Jack Foxx and Alex Saxon, usually mystery-adventure tales with exotic foreign settings.

A striking aspect of Pronzini's writing is his unmatched collaborative ability. Probably no other mystery writer has collaborated so successfully with so many different partners. He has written short stories with Jeff Wallmann, Michael Kurland, Barry N. Malzberg and John Lutz, the novel *Twospot* with Collin Wilcox, *The Cambodia File* with Jack Anderson, *The Eye* with Lutz, three western novels with Wallmann, and three mysteries and a science fiction novel with Malzberg. His most successful collaboration has been with Marcia Muller. Together they have produced the novels *Double, Beyond the Grave* and *The Lighthouse,* along with co-editing 10 anthologies, notably *The Web She Weaves* and *Lady on the Case,* the latter with Martin H. Greenberg.

At least two of Pronzini's collaborative novels deserve special mention. *The Running of Beasts,* written with Barry N. Malzberg, uses a shifting viewpoint among four men in an upstate New York town. One of the men is unaware that in another personality he is the Ripper-like killer terrorizing the region. The neat trick of limiting a mystery to only four suspects and still surprising the reader with a final twist is deftly and strikingly handled by Pronzini and Malzberg. In *Beyond the Grave,* written with Marcia Muller, Pronzini's 1890's sleuth Quincannon (hero of the novel by that name) fails to completely resolve a case involving stolen religious artefacts. It is left to Muller's modern detective Elena Oliverez to solve the case in the present.

Even with the publication of frequent novels and anthologies, Pronzini has always found time for short stories. The best of the early Nameless stories are collected in *Casefile,* while a few later ones appear together with excellent non-series tales in *Graveyard Plots* and *Small Felonies.* The reader should not overlook *The Best Western Stories of Bill Pronzini,* since most of the 13 stories are criminous. Still to be collected are such excellent stories as "Ace in the Hole," "Stacked Deck," "The Arrowmont Prison Riddle," and the collaborative efforts "Coyote and Quarter Moon" (with Jeff Wallmann) and "Vanishing Act" (with Michael Kurland).

In addition to his fiction, Pronzini has achieved growing fame in recent years as a mystery editor and critic. His numerous anthologies are notable for their careful selection and perceptive introductions. *Gun in Cheek* and *Son of Gun in Cheek*

are entertaining and knowledgeable looks at some less-than-memorable prose from crime novels and short stories. *1001 Midnights,* edited with Marcia Muller, is a massive volume containing 1001 new reviews of outstanding mystery novels and collections, the majority written by the editors. It brought Pronzini one of his five Edgar nominations to date.

—Edward D. Hoch

PROPPER, Milton (Morris). American. Born in Philadelphia, Pennsylvania, in 1906. Educated at Nazreth Hall Military Academy, Pennsylvania; University of Pennsylvania, Philadelphia (associate editor, *Law Review*), B.A. 1926, LL.B 1929; called to the Bar, 1929. Book and theatre critic for Philadelphia *Public Ledger* while an undergraduate; employed by the Social Security Adminstration in Philadelphia and Atlanta, Georgia; lived in Philadelphia after 1944. *Died (suicide) in 1962.*

CRIME PUBLICATIONS

Novels (series: Tommy Rankin in all books)

The Strange Disappearance of Mary Young. New York, Harper, 1929; London, Harrap, 1932.
The Ticker-Tape Murder. New York, Harper, 1930; London, Faber, 1932.
The Boudoir Murder. New York, Harper, 1931; as *And Then Silence,* London, Faber, 1932.
The Student Fraternity Murder. Indianapolis, Bobbs Merrill, 1932; as *Murder of an Initiate,* London, Faber 1933.
The Divorce Court Murder. New York, Harper, and London, Faber, 1934.
The Family Burial Murders. New York, Harper, 1934; London, Harrap, 1935.
The Election Booth Murder. New York, Harper, 1935; as *Murder at the Polls,* London, Harrap, 1937.
One Murdered, Two Dead. New York, Harper, 1936; London, Harrap, 1937.
The Great Insurance Murders. New York, Harper, 1937; London, Harrap, 1938.
The Case of the Cheating Bride. New York, Harper, 1938; London, Harrap, 1939.
Hide the Body! New York, Harper, 1939; London, Harrap, 1940.
The Station Wagon Murder. New York, Harper, 1940.
The Handwriting on the Wall. New York, Harper, 1941; as *You Can't Gag the Dead,* London, Jenkins, 1949.
The Blood Transfusion Murders. New York, Harper, 1943; as *Murders in Sequence,* London, Jenkins, 1947.

*   *   *

Milton Propper passed the Pennsylvania Bar exam in 1929, but he sold his first detective novel the same year and chose writing rather than law as his career. His 14 mysteries are set in Philadelphia and its suburbs and are solved by young Tommy Rankin, homicide specialist on that city's police force. Propper writes hopelessly dull prose, peoples his books with nonentities, flaunts his belief that the police and the powerful are above the law, and refuses to play fair with the reader. Yet paradoxically his best books, like *The Family Burial Murders* and *The Great*

Insurance Murders, hold some of the intellectual excitement of early Ellery Queen.

Propper generally begins with the discovery of a body in bizarre circumstances (on an amusement park's scenic railway, during a college fraternity initiation, in a voting booth) and then scatters suspicion among several characters with much to hide, all the while juggling clues and counterplots with dazzling nimbleness. His gifted detectives can make startlingly accurate deductions from a glance at a person's face, and casually commit burglary and other crimes while searching for evidence. His novels often involve varied forms of mass transportation and complex legal questions over the succession to a large estate. Near the end of his books, having established the innocence of all known suspects, Rankin invariably puts together some as yet unexplained pieces of the puzzle, concludes that the murderer was an avenger from the past who infiltrated the victim's milieu in disguise, and launches a breakneck chase to collar the killer before he or she escapes. Such is the Propper pattern, and despite their predictability and stylistic dullness his novels still interest aficionados. Unlike his books, Propper's life was wretched and messy. He alienated his family, lived in squalor, was picked up for homosexual activities by the police whose crimes he glorified, eventually lost all markets for his writing and, in 1962, killed himself.

—Francis M. Nevins, Jr.

———

PUNSHON, E(rnest) R(obertson). British. Born in London in 1872. Married Sarah Houghton. Office worker in London; wheat farmer in Canada. Contributed to many magazines including *Strand. Died in 1956.*

CRIME PUBLICATIONS

Novels (series Carter and Bell; Bobby Owen)

Earth's Great Lord. London, Ward Lock, 1901.
Constance West. Cleveland Ohio, and London, Lane, 1905.
Rhoda in Between. London, Lane, 1907.
The Mystery of Lady Isabel. London, Hurst and Blackett, 1907.
The Spin of the Coin. London, Hurst and Blackett, 1908.
The Choice. London, Ward Lock, 1908.
The Glittering Desire. London, Ward Lock, 1910.
The Wilderness Lovers. London, Houghton and Stoughton, 1912.
Hidden Lives. London, Ward Lock, 1913.
The Crowning Glory. London, Hodder and Stoughton, 1914.
Arrows of Chance. London, Ward Lock, 1917.
The Solitary House. New York, Knopf, 1918; London, Ward Lock, 1919.
The Woman's Footprint. London, Hodder and Stoughton, 1919.
Promise of Dawn. London, Ward Lock, 1921.
Old Fighting Days. New York, Knopf, 1921; London, Bale, 1923.
The Bittermeads Mystery. New York, Knopf, 1922; London, Withy Grove Press, 1946.
Dunslow. London, Ward Lock, 1922.
The Unexpected Legacy (Carter and Bell). London, Benn, 1929.

Proof, Counter Proof (Carter and Bell). London, Benn, 1931.
The Blue John Diamond. New York, Clode, 1929; London, (abridged) Cherry Tree, 1946.
The Cottage Murder (Carter and Bell). London, Benn, and Boston, Houghton Mifflin, 1932.
Truth Came Out (Carter and Bell). London, Benn, 1932; Boston, Houghton Mifflin, 1934.
Genius in Murder (Carter and Bell). London, Benn, 1932; Boston, Houghton Mifflin, 1933.
Information Received (Owen). London, Benn, 1933; Boston, Houghton Mifflin, 1934.
Crossword Mystery (Owen). London, Gollancz, 1934; as *The Crossword Murder,* New York, Knopf, 1934.
Death Among the Sunbathers. (Owen). London, Benn, 1934.
Mystery Villa. London, Gollancz, 1934.
Death of a Beauty Queen (Owen). London, Gollancz, 1935.
Death Comes to Cambers (Owen). London, Gollancz, 1935.
The Bath Mysteries (Owen). London, Gollancz, 1936; New York, Hillman Curl, 1938; as *The Bathtub Murder Case,* New York, Detective Novel Classics, 194?
The Dusky Hour (Owen). London, Gollancz, 1937; New York, Hillman Curl, 1938.
The Mystery of Mr. Jessop (Owen). London, Gollancz, and New York, Hillman Curl, 1937.
Dictator's Way (Owen). London, Gollancz, 1938; as *Death of a Tyrant,* New York, Hillman Curl, 1938.
Comes a Stranger (Owen). London, Gollancz, 1938.
Suspects-Nine (Owen). London, Gollancz, 1939.
Murder Abroad (Owen). London, Gollancz, 1939.
Four Strange Women (Owen). London, Gollancz, 1940.
The Dark Garden (Owen). London, Gollancz, 1941.
Ten Star Clues (Owen). London, Gollancz, 1941.
Diabolic Candelabra (Owen). London, Gollancz, 1942.
The Conqueror Inn (Owen). London, Gollancz, 1943; New York, Macmillan, 1944.
Night's Cloak (Owen). London, Gollancz, and New York, Macmillan, 1944.
Secrets Can't Be Helped (Owen). London, Gollancz, 1944; New York, Macmillan, 1946.
There's a Reason for Everything (Owen). London, Gollancz, 1945; New York, Macmillan, 1946.
It Might Lead Anywhere (Owen). London, Gollancz, 1946; New York, Macmillan, 1947.
Helen Passes By (Owen). London, Gollancz, 1947.
The House of Godwinsson (Owen). London, Gollancz, 1948.
Music Tells All (Owen). London, Gollancz, 1948.
So Many Doors (Owen). London, Gollancz, 1949; New York, Macmillan, 1950.
Death in the Chalkpit (Owen). New York, Mystery Novel of the Month, 194?
Everybody Always Tells (Owen). London, Gollancz, 1950.
The Golden Dagger (Owen). London, Gollancz, 1951.
The Secret Search (Owen). London, Gollancz, 1951.
The Attending Truth (Owen). London, Gollancz, 1952.
Strange Ending (Owen). London, Gollancz, 1953.
Brought to Light (Owen). London, Gollancz, 1954.
Triple Quest (Owen). London, Gollancz, 1955.
Dark Is the Clue! (Owen). London, Gollancz, 1955.
Six Were Present (Owen). London, Gollancz, 1956.

Uncollected Short Stories

"Blind Trails," in *Flynn's* (New York), parts 1–3, July–August 1925.
"Too Late for His Hat and Coat," in *Best Detective Magazine* (New York), November, 1934.

"Good Beginning," in *MacKill's Mystery Magazine* (London), October 1952.

"Dead Man's Hand," in *MacKill's Mystery Magazine* (London), April 1953.

"Find the Lady," in *MacKill's Mystery Magazine* (London), May 1953.

"The Tide Runs Strongly," in *MacKill's Mystery Magazine* (London), August 1954.

"Three Sovereigns for a Corpse," in *The Saint Detective Magazine* (New York), April 1955.

*   *   *

E.R. Punshon was writing mystery fiction before, during and after the Golden Age, in a career that spanned over half a century. His work in the field falls naturally into three distinct phases, a sporadic group of romantic melodramas, a brief detective series with two contrasting policemen, and a much longer series with a single police protagonist.

The first phase was launched in 1907 with *The Mystery of Lady Isobel,* an efficient exercise in formula melodrama that poses a still inviting question: is Lady Isobel a destructive "she-devil" or a blameless victim? This and its half-dozen successors met the demand of their time for lurid romances with a strong narrative drive. Victor Gollancz was right to list them as "thrillers," since their primary aim is excitement. Despite their evident vitality, they are too much of their time to appeal to any modern reader.

Punshon's later series are more accessible and continue to give pleasure to those who approach them with appropriate expectations. His second phase began in 1929 with *The Unexpected Legacy,* the first of five books known from their leading characters as the "Carter and Bell" novels. These are intricate and eventful narratives combining formal detection with action and atmosphere. They feature an incongruous pair of Scotland Yard detectives, whose relationship recalls that of the Hare and the Tortoise in Aesop's fable. Inspector Carter is essentially a hollow man, thrusting and showy, but seeing no more than the surface of things and easily led to false conclusions. His real gift is for self-promotion and he depends on his sergeant to solve their cases, though taking the credit himself. Sergeant Bell is astute but unassertive, a melancholy man who accepts the world as it is and resigns himself to his superior's need to bolster himself at the expense of a subordinate. He does eventually claim his due, however, in the last of the series, where Carter also encounters a drastic reversal of fortune.

In 1933, with *Information Received,* Punshon introduced a young policeman, Bobby Owen, who remained his series detective to the end of his life. There are 35 novels in the sequence and they follow Bobby's career from naive youth to experienced middle age. In his first case he gains the favour of Superintendent Mitchell, the shrewd and sparky veteran who oversees his early career. When war comes he is given charge of a rural C.I.D. and later, back at the Yard, he becomes a commander. An earl's nephew and Oxford graduate, he is very much in the decent, clean-limbed tradition, playing a straight bat and keeping his end up. Though brave, ambitious and resourceful, he is wholly without pretension and has no desire to be a hero. He shows endearing innocence as a young man but gains in authority and wisdom as the years pass. However bizarre the circumstances that involve him, he remains methodical, persistent and comfortingly sane.

The best of Punshon's work is in the Owen series, which, though uneven, has much to commend it. Given a sympathetic reading, he can still surprise, intrigue, and amuse. To some degree the books are conventional detective stories in the classic mould, with physical clues and familiar themes. The people are closely observed and continually assessed for their suspicious potential. Bobby takes stock from time to time, tabulating the evidence or talking things over with his accommodating wife, Olive. Implicit in all that occurs, however dreadful, is the reassurance that order will eventually be restored.

Beneath the traditional patterns of detective fiction, however, lies something altogether more disturbing. The series is shot through with an eerie intensity, a manic quality that seizes the author's imagination. He stretches the formal framework of detective fiction to accommodate driven personalities with "tumultuous, unrestrained passions." There are no half-measures in Punshon's novels: people don't experience dislike, they seethe with venomous hatred. He draws on the basic emotions, manipulating them to create havoc. Many of his characters are eccentric in one way or another, whether in mind or in body. They are set apart by a deformity, an obsession, a peculiar power: a turbulent religious fanatic, a one-eyed colonel with "excessive pride of birth," a young idealist with a club foot, a pianist whose playing unsettles those who hear it.

The novels also have their lighter side, apparent in the attractive presentation of Bobby's marriage and in caustic comments on aspects of contemporary life; and a mischievous humour surfaces on occasion, as when the text of a coded message is attributed to Gertrude Stein. But it is Punshon's intensity that distinguishes him and marks him as an original. He remained essentially a writer in the "dark secret" vein and he never entirely abandoned the themes and devices of his early career as a maker of melodrama. He brings off some amazing effects, not least the extraordinary suicide at the end of *Crossword Mystery,* when Bobby and his superiors are "held in utter stillness . . . by the horror and the greatness of the deed." His last novel, written in his eighties, is an astonishing work, unleashing all manner of hocus-pocus in a final mad dance of passion and obsession.

—B.A. Pike

———

PURSER, Philip. British. Born in Letchworth, Hertfordshire, 28 August 1925. Educated at Birkenhead School, Cheshire, 1938–43; King's College, Cambridge, 1943; St. Andrews University, Scotland, 1948–50, M.A. in English and history 1950. Served with the Royal Engineers, 1943–47. Married Ann Elizabeth Goodman in 1957; two daughters and one son. Television critic, *News Chronicle,* London, 1957–60, and *Sunday Telegraph,* London, 1961–87. Agent: David Higham Associates, 5–8 Lower John Street, London WIR 4HA. Address: 10 The Green, Blakesley, Towcester, Northamptonshire NN12 8RD, England.

CRIME PUBLICATIONS

Novels (series: Colin Panton)

Peregrination 22 (Panton). London, Cape, 1962.
Four Days to the Fireworks. London, Hodder and Stoughton, 1964; New York, Walker, 1965.
The Twentymen (Panton). London, Hodder and Stoughton, and New York, Walker, 1967.
Night of Glass. London, Hodder and Stoughton, 1968.

The Holy Father's Navy (Panton). London, Hodder and Stoughton, 1971.
Friedrich Harris: Shooting the Hero. London, Quartet, 1990.

Uncollected Short Story

"Rentakid," in *Sunday Telegraph Magazine* (London), 21 December 1980.

OTHER PUBLICATIONS

Novels

A Small Explosion. London, Secker and Warburg, 1979.

Short Stories

The Last Great Tram Race. London, Hodder and Stoughton, 1974.

Plays

Dr. Glas, adaptation of the novel by Hjalmar Soderberg (produced Derby, 1970).

Screenplay: *The One and Only Phyllis Dixey*, 1978.

Radio Plays: *Night of Glass*, 1971; *Ceremonies of War*, 1985.

Television Plays: *Calf Love*, 1966; *Hawkes and Doves*, 1967; *Hazard: A Family at War*, 1970; *Heydays Hotels*, 1976.

Other

Where Is He Now? (biography of Edward James). London, Quartet, 1978.
The One and Only Phyllis Dixey, with Jenny Wilkes (biography). London, Futura, 1978.

Editor, with Leslie Halliwell, *Halliwell's Television Companion*, 2nd and 3rd editions. London, Grafton, 1982–86.

*

Philip Purser comments:

I have never written a detective story as such (though it's never too late to start)! I write mysteries and adventure stories, the latest being *Shooting the Hero.* I have always been consumed by the need to make the historic or geographic circumstances of my fiction as faithful as possible to real history or geography, and have increasingly enjoyed working in a twilit area between fact and fiction. I love stories which could be absolutely true, and perhaps should have been!

*　　　*　　　*

On the face of it Philip Purser's collected works form an untidy and incongruous pile: political thrillers (sort of), a novel (sort of), a television guide (with the late Leslie Halliwell), a farrago of fantastic lies dressed up as autobiography (*The Last Great Tram Race*, which includes a description of the author being shackled to the Queen of England in a three-legged race

and caused a small flurry in the newspapers when it was published), and the odd volume of not quite categorizable non-fiction. Yet all are sharp and stylish and exhibit a strong sense of irony; and all are eminently readable.

Readability, too often, is viewed as something to be placed on the debit side of an author's account; readable writers, so the theory goes, are only readable because they have less to say, and what they do say is less than profound. Largely nonsense, of course; wholly so in Purser's case, for although most of his thrillers contain all the essential ingredients of the genre—suspense, tension, pursuit, resolution (more or less)—they contain, too, salient (and witty) observations on the human condition, skilful characterization, a good deal of compassion, and something of the bitter-sweet melancholy of the novelist Nigel Balchin, a writer Purser clearly much admires.

The majority of the thrillers were written in the 1960's and reflect, to an extent, the turmoil of those times, especially in the print and broadcasting media to which Purser himself has been attached in one way or another for most of his working life.

His series hero is Colin Panton who works chiefly in television and has a nose for things that are "not quite what they seem." This inevitably leads him into uncomfortable, indeed perilous, situations, only his innate stubbornness and the restless curiosity of the professional journalist getting him through to the (sometimes bitter) end.

In *Peregrination 22*, Purser's first book, Panton is having to work for an oddball travel agency after his previous employer, a television production company, went to the wall, and ends up investigating a scheme for developing a "youth camp" which bears an increasingly sinister resemblance to the pre-war *Hitlerjugend* movement. In a chilling finale a macabre mausoleum is unearthed in the icy wastes of the Arctic Circle, enshrining a not-so-ancient evil.

The Twentymen is set firmly in Britain and the brutal, wheeler-dealer world of politics and television. What seems at first to be a pirate television station, broadcasting only after normal closedown, turns out to be the only effective obstacle to a complete media takeover by the government of the day. This bald synopsis by no means does full justice to what is in fact a little masterpiece of controlled, and entirely non-violent, suspense. By contrast the final Panton book, *The Holy Father's Navy* (and Purser's last thriller for nearly 20 years), while entertaining enough, in the end suffers from a diffuseness of plot and a lack of obvious target, and thus tension.

Purser's non-Panton thrillers display strongly his talents as an original, indeed lateral, plotter. *Night of Glass* starts off as a prank or "rag" by four idealistic, and innocent, Cambridge students and ends horrifyingly—for the "rag" is to free a political prisoner from Dachau concentration camp in 1938. *Four Days to the Fireworks* is an extraordinary and riveting escape thriller describing the Buchanesque flight of a Cold War British spy whose cover has been blown—the ironic and un-Buchanesque twist is that the hero (a wholly sympathetic figure) has spied for Russia and is now desperate to flee Britain with his wife and children. The final third of the book, the actual escape, is a bravura performance of brilliantly sustained suspense, ending on a down-beat which is entirely realistic and, intellectually, deeply satisfying.

Purser's most recent book *Shooting The Hero* purports to be the memoirs of an elderly and Hollywood-based German film academic Friedrich Harris, who has a past. 45 years ago, in the final months of the War, he was ordered by the *Waffen-SS* to assassinate the actor Laurence Olivier, thus sabotaging his epic film of Shakespeare's *Henry V*. Of course, this kind of plot comes with its own inbuilt self-sabotage mechanism since we know (or we think we know) nothing like this ever happened. So where's the suspense?

The suspense is in getting Harris—latest in a line of slightly flawed, slightly furtive, rather less than charismatic heroes favoured by Purser—through a nightmarish and (to him) utterly alien landscape where just about every hand is against him and discovery seems certain at every turn. This Purser achieves faultlessly. *Shooting The Hero* is funny, taut and, at times, ugly (there are a couple of sudden, jolting, acts of violence); it is a superior product in every way and, like all of Purser's books, quite unputdownable.

—Jack Adrian

Q

QUARRY, Nick. *See* **ALBERT, Marvin.**

———

QUEEN, Ellery. *See* **DEMING, Richard; POWELL, Talmage; VANCE, John Holbrook.**

———

QUEEN, Ellery. Pseudonym for the cousins Frederic Dannay and Manfred B. Lee; also wrote as Barnaby Ross. Americans. **DANNAY, Frederic:** Born Daniel Nathan in Brooklyn, New York, 20 October 1905; grew up in Elmira, New York. Educated at Boys' High School, Brooklyn. Married 1) Mary Beck in 1926 (died), two sons; 2) Hilda Wisenthal in 1947 (died 1972), one son; 3) Rose Koppel in 1975. Writer and art director for a New York advertising agency prior to 1931; full-time writer, with Lee, 1931–71, and on his own from 1971. Visiting Professor, University of Texas, Austin, 1958–59. *Died 3 September 1982.* **LEE, Manfred B(ennington):** Born Manford Lepofsky in Brooklyn, New York, 11 January 1905. Educated at Boys' High School, Brooklyn; New York University. Married the actress Kaye Brinker (second wife), in 1942; four daughters and four sons. Publicity writer in New York for film companies prior to 1931; full-time writer, with Dannay, 1931 until his death. Justice of the Peace, Roxbury, Connecticut, 1957–58. *Died 3 April 1971.* Dannay and Lee were under contract to film companies in the 1930's; they edited *Mystery League* magazine, 1933–34, and *Ellery Queen's Mystery Magazine,* from 1941 (Dannay the active editor); they wrote the *Adventures of Ellery Queen* radio series, 1939–48. Co-founders and co-presidents, Mystery Writers of America. Recipients: Mystery Writers of America Edgar Allan Poe award, for radio play, 1945, for radio play, 1945, for story, 1947, 1949, special award, 1951, 1968, and Grand Master award, 1960.

Crime Publications

Novels (series: Ellery Queen and Inspector Richard Queen in all books except *The Glass Village* and *Cop Out*)

The Roman Hat Mystery. New York, Stokes, and London, Gollancz, 1929.
The French Powder Mystery. New York, Stokes, and London, Gollancz, 1930.
The Dutch Shoe Mystery. New York, Stokes, and London, Gollancz, 1931.
The Greek Coffin Mystery. New York, Stokes, and London, Gollancz, 1932.
The Egyptian Cross Mystery. New York, Stokes, 1932; London, Gollancz, 1933.

The American Gun Mystery. New York, Stokes, and London, Gollancz, 1933; as *Death at the Rodeo,* New York, Spivak, 1951.
The Siamese Twin Mystery. New York, Stokes, 1933; London, Gollancz, 1934.
The Chinese Orange Mystery. New York, Stokes, and London, Gollancz, 1934.
The Spanish Cape Mystery. New York, Stokes, and London, Gollancz, 1935.
Halfway House. New York, Stokes, and London, Gollancz, 1936.
The Door Between. New York, Stokes, and London, Gollancz, 1937.
The Devil to Pay. New York, Stokes, and London, Gollancz, 1938.
Ellery Queen's Big Book (omnibus). New York, Grosset and Dunlap, 1938.
The Four of Hearts. New York, Stokes, 1938; London, Gollancz, 1939.
The Dragon's Teeth. New York, Stokes, and London, Gollancz, 1939; as *The Virgin Heiresses,* New York, Pocket Books, 1954.
Calamity Town. Boston, Little Brown, and London, Gollancz, 1942.
There Was an Old Woman. Boston, Little Brown, 1943; London, Gollancz, 1944; as *The Quick and the Dead,* New York, Pocket Books, 1956.
Ellery Queen's Mystery Parade (omnibus). Cleveland, World, 1944.
The Murderer Is a Fox. Boston, Little Brown, and London, Gollancz, 1945.
Ten Days' Wonder. Boston, Little Brown, and London, Gollancz, 1948.
Cat of Many Tails. Boston, Little Brown, and London, Gollancz, 1949.
Double, Double. Boston, Little Brown, and London, Gollancz, 1950; as *The Case of the Seven Murders,* New York, Pocket Books, 1958.
The Origin of Evil. Boston, Little Brown, and London, Gollancz, 1951.
The King Is Dead. Boston, Little Brown, and London, Gollancz, 1952.
The Scarlet Letters. Boston, Little Brown, and London, Gollancz, 1953.
The Glass Village. Boston, Little Brown, and London, Gollancz, 1954.
Inspector Queen's Own Case. New York, Simon and Schuster, and London, Gollancz, 1956.
The Wrightsville Murders (omnibus). Boston, Little Brown, 1956.
The Hollywood Murders (omnibus). Philadelphia, Lippincott, 1957.
The Finishing Stroke. New York, Simon and Schuster, and London, Gollancz, 1958.
The New York Murders (omnibus). Boston, Little Brown, 1958.

The Bizarre Murders (omnibus). Philadelphia, Lippincott, 1962.

And on the Eighth Day. New York, Random House, and London, Gollancz, 1964.

The Fourth Side of the Triangle. New York, Random House, and London, Gollancz, 1965.

A Study in Terror (novelization of screenplay). New York, Lancer, 1966; as *Sherlock Holmes Versus Jack the Ripper*, London, Gollancz, 1967.

Face to Face. New York, New American Library, and London, Gollancz, 1967.

Cop Out. Cleveland, World, and London, Gollancz, 1969.

The Last Woman in His Life. Cleveland, World, and London, Gollancz, 1970.

A Fine and Private Place. Cleveland, World, and London, Gollancz, 1971.

Novels as Barnaby Ross (series: Drury Lane in all books)

The Tragedy of X. New York, Viking Press, and London, Cassell, 1932.

The Tragedy of Y. New York, Viking Press, and London, Cassell, 1932.

The Tragedy of Z. New York, Viking Press, and London, Cassell, 1933.

Drury Lane's Last Case. New York, Viking Press, and London, Cassell, 1933.

The XYZ Murders (omnibus). Philadelphia, Lippincott, 1961.

Short Stories

The Adventures of Ellery Queen. New York, Stokes, 1934; London, Gollancz, 1935.

The New Adventures of Ellery Queen. New York, Stokes, and London, Gollancz, 1940; with varied contents as *More Adventures of Ellery Queen*, New York, Spivak, 1940.

The Case Book of Ellery Queen. New York, Spivak, 1945.

The Case Book of Ellery Queen (omnibus). London, Gollancz, 1949.

Calendar of Crime. Boston, Little Brown, and London, Gollancz, 1952.

QBI: Queen's Bureau of Investigation. Boston, Little Brown, 1954; London, Gollancz, 1955.

Queens Full. New York, Random House, 1965; London, Gollancz, 1966.

QED: Queen's Experiments in Detection. New York, New American Library, 1968; London, Gollancz, 1969.

Uncollected Short Stories

"Terror Town," in *Best Detective Stories of the Year*, edited by David Coxe Cooke. New York, Dutton, 1957.

"Wedding Anniversary," in *Ellery Queen's Mystery Magazine* (New York), September 1967.

"Uncle from Australia," in *Ellery Queen's Mystery Magazine* (New York), November 1967.

"The Three Students," in *Playboy* (Chicago), March 1971.

"The Odd Man," in *Playboy* (Chicago), June 1971.

"The Honest Swindler," in *Saturday Evening Post* (Philadelphia), Summer 1971.

OTHER PUBLICATIONS

Novel

The Golden Summer (as Daniel Nathan; by Dannay). Boston, Little Brown, 1953.

Plays

Danger, Men Working, with Lowell Brentano (produced Baltimore and Philadelphia, c. 1936).

"The Adventure of the Frightened Star," in *Ellery Queen's Mystery Magazine* (New York), Spring 1942.

"The Adventure of the Meanest Man in the World," in *Ellery Queen's Mystery Magazine* (New York), July 1942.

"The Adventure of the Good Samaritan," in *Ellery Queen's Mystery Magazine* (New York), November 1942.

"The Adventure of the Mark of Cain," in *The Pocket Mystery Reader*, edited by Lee Wright. New York, Pocket Books, 1942.

"The Adventure of the Fire Bug," in *Ellery Queen's Mystery Magazine* (New York), March 1943.

"The Adventure of the Man Who Could Double the Size of Diamonds," in *Ellery Queen's Mystery Magazine* (New York), May 1943.

"The Adventure of the Blind Bullet," in *Ellery Queen's Mystery Magazine* (New York), September 1943.

"The Adventure of the One-Legged Man," in *Ellery Queen's Mystery Magazine* (New York), November 1943.

"The Adventure of the Wounded Lieutenant," in *Ellery Queen's Mystery Magazine* (New York), July 1944.

"The Disappearance of Mr. James Phillimore," in *The Misadventures of Sherlock Holmes*, edited by Ellery Queen. Boston, Little Brown, 1944.

"Ellery Queen, Swindler," in *Rogues' Gallery: The Great Criminals of Modern Fiction*, edited by Ellery Queen. Boston, Little Brown, 1945; London, Faber, 1947.

"The Double Triangle," and "The Invisible Clock," in *The Case Book of Ellery Queen*. New York, Spivak, 1945.

"The Invisible Clue," in *Adventures in Radio*, edited by Margaret Cuthbert. New York, Howell Soskin, 1945.

"The Adventure of the Murdered Ship," in *The Saint's Choice, Volume 7: Radio Thrillers*, edited by Leslie Charteris. Hollywood, Saint Enterprises, 1946.

"The Adventure of the Curious Thefts," in *Story Digest*, September 1946.

"The Adventure of the Mouse's Blood," in *Fireside Mystery Book*, edited by Frank Owen. New York, Lantern Press, 1947.

"The Adventure of the Last Man Club," and "The Adventure of the Murdered Millionaire," in *The Last Man Club*. New York, Pyramid, 1968.

Screenplay: *Ellery Queen, Master Detective*, with Eric Taylor, 1940.

Radio Plays: most scripts for *The Adventures of Ellery Queen*, 1939–48.

Other

The Detective Short Story: A Bibliography. Boston, Little Brown, 1942.

Queen's Quorum: A History of the Detective-Crime Short Story as Revealed by the 106 Most Important Books Published in This Field Since 1845. Boston, Little Brown, 1951; London, Gollancz, 1953; revised edition, New York, Biblo and Tannen, 1969.

In the Queen's Parlor, and Other Leaves from the Editors' Notebook. New York, Simon and Schuster, and London, Gollancz, 1957.

Ellery Queen's International Case Book (true crime). New York, Dell, 1964.

The Woman in the Case (true crime). New York, Bantam, 1966; as *Deadlier Than the Male*, London, Corgi, 1967.

Editor, *Challenge to the Reader.* New York, Stokes, 1938.

Editor, *101 Years' Entertainment: The Great Detective Stories, 1841–1941.* Boston, Little Brown, 1941; revised edition, New York, Modern Library, 1946.

Editor, *Sporting Blood: The Great Sports Detective Stories.* Boston, Little Brown, 1942; as *Sporting Detective Stories,* London, Faber, 1946.

Editor, *The Female of the Species: The Great Women Detectives and Criminals.* Boston, Little Brown, 1943; as *Ladies in Crime: A Collection of Detective Stories by English and American Writers,* London, Faber, 1947.

Editor, *The Misadventures of Sherlock Holmes.* Boston, Little Brown, 1944.

Editor, *Best Stories from Ellery Queen's Mystery Magazine.* Roslyn, New York, Detective Book Club, 1944.

Editor, *The Adventures of Sam Spade and Other Stories,* by Dashiell Hammett. New York, Spivak, 1944; as *They Can Only Hang You Once,* New York, Spivak, 1949; reprinted in part as *A Man Called Spade,* New York, Dell, 1945.

Editor, *Rogues' Gallery: The Great Criminals of Modern Fiction.* Boston, Little Brown, 1945; London, Faber, 1947.

Editor, *The Continental Op,* by Dashiell Hammett. New York, Spivak, 1945.

Editor, *The Return of the Continental Op,* by Dashiell Hammett. New York, Spivak, 1945.

Editor, *To the Queen's Taste: The First Supplement to 101 Years' Entertainment, Consisting of the Best Stories Published in the First Five Years of Ellery Queen's Mystery Magazine.* Boston, Little Brown, 1946; London, Faber 1949.

Editor, *Hammett Homicides,* by Dashiell Hammett. New York, Spivak, 1946.

Editor, *The Queen's Awards* (from *Ellery Queen's Mystery Magazine*). Boston, Little Brown, 10 vols, 1946–55; New York, Simon and Schuster, 2 vols., 1956–57; London, Gollancz, 8 vols., 1948–55; London, Collins, 4 vols., 1956–59; continued as *Mystery Annuals,* New York, Random House, 4 vols., 1958–61; Collins, 2 vols., 1960–61; Gollancz, 2 vols., 1961–62; then continued as anthologies:

To Be Read Before Midnight. New York, Random House, 1962; London, Gollancz, 1963.

Mystery Mix. New York, Random House, 1963; London, Gollancz, 1964.

Double Dozen. New York, Random House, 1964; London, Gollancz, 1965.

20th Anniversary Annual. New York, Random House, 1965; London, Gollancz, 1966.

Crime Carousel. New York, New American Library, 1966; London, Gollancz, 1967.

All-Star Lineup. New York, New American Library, 1966; London, Gollancz, 1968.

Mystery Parade. New York, New American Library, 1968; London, Gollancz, 1969.

Murder Menu. Cleveland, World, and London, Gollancz, 1969.

Grand Slam. Cleveland, World, 1970; London, Gollancz, 1971.

Headliners. Cleveland, World, 1971; London, Gollancz, 1972.

Mystery Bag. Cleveland, World, 1972; London, Gollancz, 1973.

Crookbook. New York, Random House, and London, Gollancz, 1974.

Murdercade. New York, Random House, 1975; London, Gollancz, 1976.

Crime Wave. New York, Putnam, and London, Gollancz, 1976.

Searches and Seizures. New York, Davis, 1977.

A Multitude of Sins. New York, Davis, 1978.

Circumstantial Evidence. New York, Davis, 1980.

Crime Cruise round the World. New York, Davis, 1981.

Editor, *Murder by Experts.* New York, Ziff Davis, 1947; London, Sampson Low, 1950.

Editor, *Dead Yellow Women,* by Dashiell Hammett. New York, Spivak, 1947.

Editor, *The Riddles of Hildegarde Withers,* by Stuart Palmer. New York, Spivak, 1947.

Editor, *Dr. Fell, Detective, and Other Stories,* by John Dickson Carr. New York, Spivak, 1947.

Editor, *The Department of Dead Ends,* by Roy Vickers. New York, Spivak, 1947.

Editor, *The Case Book of Mr. Campion,* by Margery Allingham. New York, Spivak, 1947.

Editor, *20th Century Detective Stories.* Cleveland, World, 1948; revised edition, New York, Popular Library, 1964.

Editor, *Nightmare Town,* by Dashiell Hammett. New York, Spivak, 1948.

Editor, *Cops and Robbers,* by O. Henry. New York, Spivak, 1948.

Editor, *The Literature of Crime: Stories by World-Famous Authors.* Boston, Little Brown, 1950; London, Cassell, 1952; as *Ellery Queen's Book of Mystery Stories,* London, Pan, 1957.

Editor, *The Creeping Siamese,* by Dashiell Hammett. New York, Spivak, 1950.

Editor, *The Monkey Murder and Other Hildegarde Withers Stories,* by Stuart Palmer. New York, Spivak, 1950.

Editor, *Woman in the Dark,* by Dashiell Hammett. New York, Spivak, 1952.

Editor, *Ellery Queen's 1960 Anthology,* and the later volumes. New York, Davis, 13 vols., 1959–71; later accompanied by *Mid-Year Editions,* 8 vols., 1963–70; continued as *Spring-Summer* and *Fall-Winter* editions, 6 vols., 1971–73; then continued as anthologies:

Christmas Hamper. New York, Davis, 1974; London, Gollancz, 1975.

Aces of Mystery. New York, Davis, 1975.

Masters of Mystery. New York, Davis, 1975; London, Gollancz, 1977.

Giants of Mystery. New York, Davis, 1976; London, Gollancz, 1977.

Magicians of Mystery. New York, Davis, 1976; London, Gollancz, 1978.

Champions of Mystery. New York, Davis, 1977; London, Gollancz, 1979.

Faces of Mystery. New York, Davis, 1977; London, Gollancz, 1978.

Who's Who of Whodunits. New York, Davis, 1977.

Masks of Mystery. New York, Davis, 1977; London, Gollancz, 1979.

Napoleons of Mystery. New York, Davis, 1978; London, Gollancz, 1981.

The Supersleuths. New York, Davis, 1978.

Wings of Mystery. New York, Davis, 1979.

Scenes of the Crime. New York, Davis, 1979; London, Hale, 1981.

Veils of Mystery. New York, Davis, 1980; London, Hale, 1981.

Windows of Mystery. New York, Davis, 1980.

Doors to Mystery. New York, Davis, 1981.

Editor, *A Man Named Thin and Other Stories,* by Dashiell Hammett. New York, Spivak, 1962.

Editor, *12.* New York, Dell, 1964.

Editor, *Lethal Black Book.* New York, Dell, 1965.

Editor, *Poetic Justice: 23 Stories of Crime, Mystery and Detection by World-Famous Poets from Geoffrey Chaucer to Dylan Thomas.* New York, New American Library, 1967.

Editor, *The Case of the Murderer's Bride and Other Stories,* by Erle Stanley Gardner. New York, Davis, 1969.

Editor, *Minimysteries: 70 Short-Short Stories of Crime, Mystery and Detection.* Cleveland, World, 1969.

Editor, *Murder—In Spades!* New York, Pyramid, 1969.

Editor, *Shoot the Works!* New York, Pyramid, 1969.

Editor, *Mystery Jackpot.* New York, Pyramid, 1970.

Editor, *P as in Police,* by Lawrence Treat. New York, Davis, 1970.

Editor, *The Golden 13: 13 First Prize Winners from Ellery Queen's Mystery Magazine.* Cleveland, World, 1971; London, Gollancz, 1972.

Editor, *The Spy and the Thief,* by Edward D. Hoch. New York, Davis, 1971.

Editor, *Ellery Queen's Best Bets.* New York, Pyramid, 1972.

Editor, *Amateur in Violence,* by Michael Gilbert. New York, Davis, 1973.

Editor, *Kindly Dig Your Grave and Other Stories,* by Stanley Ellin. New York, Davis, 1975.

Editor, *How to Trap a Crook and 12 Other Mysteries,* by Julian Symons. New York, Davis, 1977.

Editor, *Japanese Golden Dozen: The Detective Story World in Japan.* Rutland, Vermont, Charles Tuttle, 1978.

Editor, *Secrets of Mystery.* New York, Davis, 1979; London, Hale, 1981.

Editor, *Eyes of Mystery.* New York, Davis, 1981.

Editor, *Eyewitnesses.* New York, Davis, 1981.

Editor, *Maze of Mysteries.* New York, Davis, 1982.

Editor, with Eleanor Sullivan, *Book of First Appearances.* New York, Dial Press, 1982.

Editor, with Eleanor Sullivan, *Lost Ladies.* New York, Dial Press, 1983.

Editor, *The Best of Ellery Queen.* London, Hale, 1983.

Editor, with Eleanor Sullivan, *Lost Men.* New York, Dial Press, 1983.

Editor, with Eleanor Sullivan, *Prime Crimes.* New York, Dial Press, 1984.

Editor, with Eleanor Sullivan, *Memorable Characters.* New York, Dial Press, 1984.

Editor, with Eleanor Sullivan, *Crimes and Punishments.* New York, Dial Press 1984.

*

Manuscript Collection: Humanities Research Center, University of Texas, Austin.

Critical Studies: *Ellery Queen: A Double Profile* by Anthony Boucher, Boston, Little Brown, 1951; *Royal Bloodline: Ellery Queen, Author and Detective* by Francis M. Nevins, Jr., Bowling Green, Ohio, Popular Press, 1974 (includes bibliography).

*   *   *

Ellery Queen was both the pseudonym and the detective creation of two Brooklyn-born first cousins, Frederic Dannay and Manfred B. Lee. At the time they created Ellery, Dannay was a copywriter and art director for a Manhattan advertising agency and Lee a publicity writer for the New York office of a film studio. The anouncement of a $7500 prize contest for a detective novel catalyzed the cousins into literary action in 1928, and Ellery's first adventure was published the following year. Dannay's experience in advertising may have inspired the innovation of using the same name for the cousin's deductive protagonist and for their own joint byline—a device that, along with the excellence of the books themselves, turned Ellery Queen into a household name and his creators into wealthy men.

In the late 1920's the dominant figure in American detective fiction was S.S. Van Dine (Willard Huntington Wright), an erudite art critic whose novels about the impossibly intellectual aesthete-sleuth Philo Vance were consistent best-sellers of the time. The early Ellery Queen novels, with their patterned titles and their scholarly dilettante detective forever dropping classical quotations, were heavily influenced by Van Dine, though superior in plotting, characterization, and style. Ellery is a professional mystery writer and amateur sleuth who assists his father, Inspector Richard Queen, whenever a murder puzzle becomes too complex for ordinary police methods. His first-period cases, from *The Roman Hat Mystery* (1929) through *The Spanish Cape Mystery* (1935), are richly plotted specimens of the Golden Age deductive puzzle at its zenith, full of bizarre circumstances, conflicting testimony, enigmatic clues, alternative solutions, firework displays of virtuoso reasoning, and a constant crackle of intellectual excitement. All the facts are presented, trickily but fairly, and the reader is formally challenged to solve the puzzle ahead of Ellery. Most of Queen's distinctive story motifs—the negative clue, the dying message, the murderer as Iagoesque manipulator, the patterned series of clues deliberately left at crime scenes, the false answer followed by the true and devastating solution—originated in these early novels. Perhaps the best works of the first period are *The Greek Coffin Mystery* and *The Egyptian Cross Mystery,* which both appeared in 1932, the same year in which, under the second pseudonym of Barnaby Ross, Dannay and Lee published the first and best two novels in the tetralogy dealing with actor-detective Drury Lane: *The Tragedy of X* and *The Tragedy of Y.*

By 1936 the Van Dine touches had left Queen's work and were replaced by the influences of the slick-paper magazines and the movies, to both of which the cousins had begun to sell. In second-period Queen the patterned titles vanish and Ellery gradually becomes less priggish and more human. In several stories of the period he is seen working as a Hollywood screenwriter, reflecting the cousins' brief stints at Columbia, Paramount, and M-G-M. Most of Queen's work in the late 1930's is thinly plotted, overburdened with "love interest," and too obviously written with film sales in mind, but the best book of the period, *The Four of Hearts,* is an excellent detective story as well as a many-faceted evocation of Hollywood in its peak years.

At the start of the new decade most of the cousin's energies went into writing a script a week for the long-running *Adventures of Ellery Queen* radio series (1939–48) and accumulating a vast library of detective short stories. Out of this collection came Queen's *101 Years' Entertainment* (1941), the foremost anthology of the genre, and *Ellery Queen's Mystery Magazine,* which from its first issue in the fall of 1941 till shortly before his death in 1982 was edited personally by Fred Dannay. In 1942 the cousins returned to fiction with the superbly written and characterized *Calamity Town,* a semi-naturalistic detective novel in which Ellery solves a murder in the "typical small town," of Wrightsville, U.S.A. Their third and richest period as mystery writers lasted 16 years and embraced 12 novels, two short story collections, and Dannay's autobiographical novel, *The Golden Summer,* published as by Daniel Nathan. In third-period Queen the complex deductive puzzle is fused with in-depth character studies, magnificently detailed evocations of place and mood, occasional ventures into a topsy-turvy Alice in Wonderland otherworld reflecting Dannay's interest in Lewis Carroll, and explorations into historical, psychiatric, and religious dimensions. The best novels of this period are *Calamity Town* itself; *Ten Days' Wonder,* with its phantasmagoria of biblical symbolism; *Cat of Many Tails,* with its unforgettable images of New York City menaced by a heat wave, a mad strangler of what seem to be randomly chosen victims, and the threat of World War III; and *The Origin of Evil,* in which Darwinian motifs underlie the clues and deductions. Finally, in *The Finishing Stroke,* the cousins nostalgically recreated Ellery's young manhood in 1929, just after the publication of "his" first detective novel, *The Roman Hat Mystery.*

"In my end is my beginning," says Eliot; and the cousins apparently meant to retire as active writers after *The Finishing Stroke.* Five years later, however, they launched a fourth and final group of Ellery Queen novels, including *A Fine and Private Place,* which was published almost simultaneously with Manfred Lee's death of a heart attack. The novels and short stories of period four retreat from all semblance of naturalistic plausibility and rely on what Dannay liked to call "fun and games"—heavily stylized plots and characterizations and the repetition of dozens of motifs from the earlier periods.

No new novels appeared after Lee's death, although Dannay remained active and perceptive as ever in his capacity as editor of *EQMM* until his final illness. But the reputation of Ellery Queen, author and detective, has long been assured. Of all the American mystery writers Queen was the supreme practitioner of that noble but now dying genre, the classic formal detective story.

—Francis M. Nevins, Jr.

———————

QUENTIN, Patrick. Pseudonym for Hugh (Callingham) Wheeler; collaborated with Richard Wilson Webb to 1952; also wrote as Q. Patrick and Jonathan Stagge, both with Webb. American. Born in Northwood, Middlesex, England, 19 March 1912; naturalized American citizen, 1942. Educated at Claysmore School, Iwerne Minister, Dorset; University of London, B.A. in English 1932. Served in the United States Army Medical Corps during World War II. Recipient: Mystery Writers of America Edgar Allan Poe award, 1962; Tony award, for drama, 1973, 1979; New York Drama Critics Circle award, 1973, 1976, 1979; Vernon Rice award, 1973; Hull-Warriner award, 1981. *Died 26 July 1987.*

CRIME PUBLICATIONS

Novels (series: Peter Duluth; Lieutenant Timothy Trant)

A Puzzle for Fools (Duluth). New York, Simon and Schuster, and London, Gollancz, 1936.
Puzzle for Players (Duluth). New York, Simon and Schuster, 1938; London, Gollancz, 1939.
Puzzle for Puppets (Duluth). New York, Simon and Schuster, and London, Gollancz, 1944.
Puzzle for Wantons (Duluth). New York, Simon and Schuster, 1945; London, Gollancz, 1946; as *Slay the Loose Ladies,* New York, Pocket Books, 1948.
Puzzle for Fiends (Duluth). New York, Simon and Schuster, 1946; London, Gollancz, 1947; as *Love Is a Deadly Weapon,* New York, Pocket Books, 1949.

Puzzle for Pilgrims (Duluth). New York, Simon and Schuster, 1947; London, Gollancz, 1948; as *The Fate of the Immodest Blonde,* New York, Pocket Books, 1950.
Run to Death (Duluth). New York, Simon and Schuster, and London, Gollancz, 1948.
The Follower. New York, Simon and Schuster, and London, Gollancz, 1950.
Black Widow (Duluth). New York, Simon and Schuster, 1952; as *Fatal Woman,* London, Gollancz, 1953.
My Son, The Murderer (Trant). New York, Simon and Schuster, 1954; as *The Wife of Ronald Sheldon,* London, Gollancz, 1954.
The Man with Two Wives (Trant). New York, Simon and Schuster, and London, Gollancz, 1955.
The Man in the Net. New York, Simon and Schuster, and London, Gollancz, 1956.
Suspicious Circumstances. New York, Simon and Schuster, and London, Gollancz, 1957.
Shadow of Guilt (Trant). New York, Random House, and London, Gollancz, 1959.
The Green-Eyed Monster. New York, Random House, and London, Gollancz, 1960.
Family Skeletons (Trant). New York, Random House, and London, Gollancz, 1965.

Novels as Q. Patrick (series: Lieutenant Timothy Trant)

Death Goes to School. New York, Smith and Haas, and London, Cassell, 1936.
Death for Dear Clara (Trant). New York, Simon and Schuster, and London, Cassell, 1937.
The File on Fenton and Farr. New York, Morrow, 1937; London, Jarrolds, 1938.
The File on Claudia Cragge. New York, Morrow, and London, Jarrolds, 1938.
Death and the Maiden (Trant). New York, Simon and Schuster, and London, Cassell, 1939.
Return to the Scene. New York, Simon and Schuster, 1941; as *Death in Bermuda,* London, Cassell, 1941.
Danger Next Door. London, Cassell, 1952.

Novels as Jonathan Stagge (series: Dr. Hugh Westlake in all books)

Murder Gone to Earth. London, Joseph, 1936; as *The Dogs Do Bark,* New York, Doubleday, 1937.
Murder or Mercy. London, Joseph, 1937; as *Murder by Prescription,* New York, Doubleday, 1938.
The Stars Spell Death. New York, Doubleday, 1939; as *Murder in the Stars,* London, Joseph, 1940.
Turn of the Table. New York, Doubleday, 1940; as *Funeral for Five,* London, Joseph, 1940.
The Yellow Taxi. New York, Doubleday, 1942; as *Call a Hearse,* London, Joseph, 1942.
The Scarlet Circle. New York, Doubleday, 1943; as *Light from a Lantern,* London, Joseph, 1943.
Death My Darling Daughters. New York, Doubleday, 1945; as *Death and the Dear Girls,* London, Joseph, 1946.
Death's Old Sweet Song. New York, Doubleday, 1946; London, Joseph, 1947.
The Three Fears. New York, Doubleday, and London, Joseph, 1949.

Short Stories

The Ordeal of Mrs. Snow and Other Stories. London, Gollancz, 1961; New York, Random House, 1962.

Uncollected Short Stories as Q. Patrick

"Murder on New Year's Eve," in *American Magazine* (Springfield, Ohio), October 1937.
"Another Man's Poison," in *American Magazine* (Springfield, Ohio), January 1940.
"Witness for the Prosecution," in *Ellery Queen's Mystery Magazine* (New York), July 1946.
"The Plaster Cat," in *Mystery Book* (New York), July 1946.
"White Carnations," in *Best Detective Stories of the Year 1946*, edited by David Coxe Cooke. New York, Dutton, 1946.
"This Way Out," in *Mystery Book* (New York), March 1947.
"Little Boy Lost," in *Ellery Queen's Mystery Magazine* (New York), October 1947.
"The Corpse in the Closet," in *Ellery Queen's Mystery Magazine* (New York), January 1948.
"Farewell Performance," in *Ellery Queen's Mystery Magazine* (New York), September 1948.
"The Jack of Diamonds," in *Ellery Queen's Mystery Magazine* (New York), February 1949.
"Thou Lord Seest Me," in *Ellery Queen's Mystery Magazine* (New York), July 1949.
"Murder in One Scene," in *Best Detective Stories of the Year 1949*, edited by David Coxe Cooke. New York, Dutton, 1949.
"Girl Overboard," in *Four and Twenty Bloodhounds*, edited by Anthony Boucher. New York, Simon and Schuster, 1950; London, Hammond, 1951.
"Another Man's Poison," in *Ellery Queen's Mystery Magazine* (New York), January 1951.
"Death Fright," in *American Magazine* (Springfield, Ohio), January 1951.
"Who Killed the Mermaid?" in *Ellery Queen's Mystery Magazine* (New York), February 1951.
"Town Blonde, Country Blonde," in *Ellery Queen's Mystery Magazine* (New York), August 1951.
"All the Way to the Moon," in *Ellery Queen's Awards, 6th Series.* Boston, Little Brown, and London, Gollancz, 1951.
"This Looks Like Murder," in *Ellery Queen's Mystery Magazine* (New York), March 1952.
"The Pigeon Woman," in *Ellery Queen's Mystery Magazine* (New York), July 1952.
"Death on the Riviera," in *Ellery Queen's Mystery Magazine* (New York), September 1952.
"Death on Saturday Night," in *Ellery Queen's Mystery Magazine* (New York), January 1953.
"Woman of Ice," in *Ellery Queen's Mystery Magazine* (New York), February 1953.
"The Laughing Man," in *American Magazine* (Springfield, Ohio), March 1953.
"The Hated Woman," in *The Saint* (New York), August 1953.
"The Red Balloon," in *Weird Tales* (Chicago), November 1953.
"The Glamorous Opening," in *Ellery Queen's Mystery Magazine* (New York), January 1954.
"Death and Canasta," in *Ellery Queen's Mystery Magazine* (New York), April 1954.
"The Predestined," in *Weird Tales* (Chicago), May 1954.
"Death Before Breakfast," in *Crime for Two*, edited by Frances and Richard Lockridge. Philadelphia, Lippincott, 1955; London, Macdonald, 1957.
"On the Day of the Rose Show," in *Ellery Queen's Mystery Magazine* (New York), March 1956.

"Going, Going, Gone!" in *Ellery Queen's Mystery Magazine* (New York), October 1956.
"Murder in the Alps," in *"This Week's" Stories of Mystery and Suspense*, edited by Stewart Beach. New York, Random House, 1957.
"Lioness vs. Panther," in *Ellery Queen's Mystery Magazine* (New York), July 1958.
"This Will Kill You" (as Patrick Quentin), in *The Edgar Winners*, edited by Bill Pronzini. New York, Random House, 1980.

OTHER PUBLICATIONS as Hugh Wheeler

Novel

The Crippled Muse. London, Hart Davis, 1951; New York, Rinehart, 1952.

Plays

Big Fish, Little Fish (produced New York, 1961; London, 1962). New York, Random House, 1961; London, Hart Davis, 1962.
Look! We've Come Through! (produced New York, 1961). New York, Dramatists Play Service, 1963.
Rich Little Rich Girl, adaptation of a play by Miguel Mihura and Alvaro deLaiglesia (produced Philadelphia, 1964).
We Have Always Lived in the Castle, adaptation of the novel by Shirley Jackson (produced New York, 1966). New York, Dramatists Play Service, 1967.
A Little Night Music, music and lyrics by Stephen Sondheim, adaptation of a film by Ingmar Bergman (produced New York, 1973; London, 1975). New York, Applause, 1990.
Irene, with Joseph Stein, adaptation by Harry Rigby, music by Harry Tierney, lyrics by Joseph McCarthy, adaptation of the play by James Montgomery (produced New York, 1973; London, 1976).
Candide, music by Leonard Bernstein, lyrics by Richard Wilbur, adaptation of the novel by Voltaire (produced New York, 1973).
Truckload, music by Louis St. Louis, lyrics by Wes Harris (produced New York, 1975).
Pacific Overtures, with John Weidmann, music and lyrics by Stephen Sondheim (produced New York, 1976).
Sweeney Todd, The Demon Barber of Fleet Street, music and lyrics by Stephen Sondheim, adaptation of the play by C.G. Bond (produced New York, 1979; London, 1980). New York, Dodd Mead, 1979.
Silverlake, adaptation of a libretto by Georg Kaiser, music by Kurt Weill (produced New York, 1980).
The Student Prince, adaptation of the libretto by Dorothy Donelly, music by Sigmund Romberg (produced New York, 1980).

Screenplays: *Five Miles to Midnight,* with Peter Viertel, 1962; *Something for Everyone,* 1969; *Cabaret,* 1972; *Travels with My Aunt,* with Jay Presson Allen, 1973; *A Little Night Music,* 1977; *Nijinsky,* 1980.

Television Play: *The Snoop Sisters,* with Leonard B. Stern, 1972.

Other

"Who'd Do It?," in *Chimera* (Princeton, New Jersey), Summer 1947.

The Girl on the Gallows (as Q. Patrick). New York, Fawcett, 1954.

*

Patrick Quentin commented (1984):

Mystery novels are very tenacious of life. It amazes me that most of these novels are still in print somewhere or other all over the world—even though some of them were written almost 50 years ago. Apart from whatever merit they have as books, they have acquired an extra and quite unintended virtue—the preservation as in amber of a way of life as remote from 1984 as the Lambeth Walk is from punk rock.

* * *

With the publication in 1936 of the first of Simon and Schuster's "Inner Sanctum" mysteries, *A Puzzle for Fools,* mystery readers were presented with a new byline, Patrick Quentin, and a new detective, Peter Duluth. Both made an immediate impression on readers and critics alike, and the new mystery series was off to a flying start. When Q. Patrick's *Death for Dear Clara* was published in the same series a year later, the publishers took the unusual step of devoting the book's endpapers to a revelation that the already familiar Q. Patrick and the newly introduced Patrick Quentin were both pseudonyms for the same pair of Harvard-educated Englishmen. This was true enough as far as it went, but it was far from being the whole story.

The byline Q. Patrick was first used on *Cottage Sinister,* a well-crafted novel about a series of poisonings in a small English village. At this time, the byline hid the collaboration of two English writers, Richard Wilson Webb and Martha Mott Kelley. The second Q. Patrick novel, by the same pair, was less successful: *Murder at the Women's City Club* was nominally set in a small city near Philadelphia, but neither the setting nor the characters were convincingly American. With *S.S. Murder* Webb acquired a different collaborator, Mary Louise Aswell, while *Murder at Cambridge* was by Webb alone. A second collaboration with Mary Aswell, *The Grindle Nightmare,* a brooding study of sadism and child-murder, brought the first phase of the Q. Patrick career to a close.

Death Goes to School inaugurated a highly successful collaboration between Webb and Hugh Wheeler. All subsequent Q. Patrick stories were by this team. *Death for Dear Clara* introduced the New York police detective Lieutenant Timothy Trant, Princeton-educated and sartorially elegant, in whom "the impulsive human being and the shrewd detective always worked in harness." Trant also appeared in *Death and the Maiden,* perhaps the most memorable of his cases, and in a series of short stories. After *Return to the Scene,* set in Bermuda, the Q. Patrick byline appeared only on short stories during the 1940's. A final Q. Patrick novel, *Danger Next Door,* appeared in 1952. The last Q. Patrick book of all, however, was nonfiction: *The Girl on the Gallows,* a study of the Edith Thompson murder case.

Returning to 1936; the second Webb-Wheeler collaboration, after *Death Goes to School,* was a different type of mystery novel from those with which the Q. Patrick name had become associated. The publishers suggested that a new byline should be used, and so Patrick Quentin was born. *A Puzzle for Fools* takes place in a posh sanitarium ("just an expensive nuthouse for people . . . who had lost control") where Peter Duluth, once a successful Broadway producer, is drying out after a couple of alcoholic years. When murder strikes among the patients,

Duluth finds himself cast as detective, unraveling clues while battling post-alcoholic jitters. In *Puzzle for Players* Peter and his future wife, Iris, whom he had met in the sanitarium, are involved with a Broadway play being staged in an apparently jinxed theater. Peter and Iris go on to encounter crime in seven more novels and several shorter works. A distinguishing feature of the series is that Peter and Iris are not present merely to investigate murder among strangers; they are always the central characters in the books, and the plots revolve around crucial events in their own lives. For example, *Puzzle for Pilgrims* and *Run to Death* are concerned with the break-up and eventual repair of the Duluths' marriage, intermixed with intrigue and sudden death in Mexico.

In 1952, Richard Wilson Webb left the writing partnership, and subsequent Patrick Quentin novels were written by Hugh Wheeler alone. The first of these solo productions marked the final appearances of Peter and Iris Duluth, who serve as subsidiary characters along with Trant. The central figure in *My Son, The Murderer* is Peter's brother, Jake Duluth, with his unshakeable faith in the innocence of his son when he is accused of murder. Spurred by his faith, Peter and Trant together unmask the killer. Trant appears as the detective in three subsequent novels, *The Man with Two Wives, Shadow of Guilt,* and *Family Skeletons.* After the last book, Wheeler abandoned detective fiction and devoted himself most successfully to plays and film scripts.

Returning once more to that watershed year of 1936; two pen-names were not enough to cover the output of the Webb-Wheeler collaboration, so they adopted a third identity, Jonathan Stagge. Between 1936 and 1949, nine novels appeared under the Stagge byline, all featuring Dr. Hugh Westlake, general practitioner in a small country town in Pennsylvania. With remarkable frequency Westlake and his precocious daughter, Dawn, become involved with impersonations, mysterious deaths, and secrets out of the past.

In addition to the novels, Q. Patrick and Patrick Quentin were noted for their short stories. A collection of these shorter works, *The Ordeal of Mrs. Snow and Other Stories,* contains several stories that have established themselves as classics, notably "A Boy's Will," "Mother, May I Go Out to Swim?," and "Love Comes to Miss Lucy."

Anthony Boucher, in the *New York Times,* said, "Patrick Quentin is one of the truly great plotters in the field of suspense," and British critic Francis Iles (Anthony Berkeley) said, "To me he's the Number One of American crime novelists." All of the Q. Patrick/Patrick Quentin/Jonathan Stagge novels are characterized by intricate plots, cleverly planted clues, and endings which legitimately surprise the reader.

—R.E. Briney

———

QUILL, Monica. *See* **McINERY, Ralph.**

———

QUINN, Simon. *See* **SMITH, Martin Cruz.**

———

R

RABE, Peter. American.

CRIME PUBLICATIONS

Novels (series: Manny DeWitt; Daniel Port)

Benny Muscles In. New York, Fawcett, 1955; London, Fawcett, 1958.
A Shroud for Jesso. New York, Fawcett, 1955; London, Fawcett, 1956.
Stop This Man! New York, Fawcett, 1955; London, Fawcett, 1957.
Dig My Grave Deep (Port). New York, Fawcett, 1956; London, Fawcett, 1957.
A House in Naples. New York, Fawcett, 1956; London, Fawcett, 1958.
Kill the Boss Good-by. New York, Fawcett, 1956; London, Fawcett, 1957.
Agreement to Kill. New York, Fawcett, 1957; London, Fawcett, 1958.
It's My Funeral (Port). New York, Fawcett, 1957; London, Fawcett, 1959.
Journey into Terror. New York, Fawcett, 1957; London, Fawcett, 1959.
The Out Is Death (Port). New York, Fawcett, 1957; London, Fawcett, 1959.
Blood on the Desert. New York, Fawcett, 1958; London, Muller, 1960.
The Cut of the Whip. New York, Ace, 1958.
Mission for Vengeance. New York, Fawcett, 1958.
Bring Me Another Corpse (Port). New York, Fawcett, 1959; London, Muller, 1960.
Time Enough to Die (Port). New York, Fawcett, 1959; London, Muller, 1961.
Anatomy of a Killer. New York and London, Abelard Schuman, 1960.
Murder Me for Nickels. New York, Fawcett, 1960; London, Muller, 1961.
My Lovely Executioner. New York, Fawcett, 1960; London, Jenkins, 1967.
The Box. New York, Fawcett, 1962; London, Muller, 1963.
Girl in a Big Brass Bed (DeWitt). New York, Fawcett, 1965.
The Spy Who Was Three Feet Tall (DeWitt). New York, Fawcett, 1966.
Code Name Gadget (DeWitt). New York, Fawcett, 1967.
War of the Dons. New York, Fawcett, 1972; London, Coronet, 1973.
Black Mafia. New York, Fawcett, 1974.

Uncollected Short Story

"Hard Case Redhead," in *Mystery Tales* (New York), October 1959.

OTHER PUBLICATIONS

Novels

His Neighbor's Wife. New York, Universal, 1962.
Tobruk (novelization of screenplay). New York, Bantam, 1967.

Other

From Here to Maternity, illustrated by the author. New York, Vanguard Press, and London, Muller, 1955.
Psychotherapy from the Center: A Humanistic View of Change and of Growth, with Rahe B. Corlis. Scranton, Pennsylvania, International Textbook, 1969.

*   *   *

Peter Rabe came onto the crime-writing scene with a big push from his publisher (Fawcett Gold Medal), with his first three books appearing in consecutive months in 1955. He received enthusiastic cover endorsements from such popular authors as Mickey Spillane and Erskine Caldwell. He went on to write more than 20 novels, many of them works of considerable merit and interest, in a career that covered parts of three decades. Yet today his books are seldom read and studied, perhaps because only one of them was published in a hardback edition.

Rabe did not write mystery novels. He wrote crime and espionage fiction, and his best work, in books such as *Kill the Boss Good-by* and *Benny Muscles In,* recalls the great gangster novels of an earlier era (Hammett's *The Glass Key* or Burnett's *Little Caesar*). Rabe's style matches his subject matter perfectly in his gangster tales. He describes harsh brutality and violence, including sado-masochistic sexual encounters, with matter-of-fact objectivity and understatement. His dialogue is spare and elliptical. As a result, his novels attain an intensity and effectiveness seldom achieved by many better-known writers.

In his series of books about Daniel Port, beginning with *Dig My Grave Deep,* Rabe investigates the life of a man who severs his ties with a midwestern syndicate. Port is a hood who has become disgusted with his life, and in later books, such as *The Out Is Death* and *The Cut of the Whip,* he tries to help others escape the traps which their lives have become. He often reflects on how easy it is to slip back into the callousness of his former occupation, but the reader is aware that Port's toughness is more than mere callousness.

Rabe dabbled in espionage early in his career with *A Shroud for Jesso,* in which a gangster inadvertently becomes involved in spying activities, but *Blood on the Desert* was his first book fully devoted to international intrigue. Its Middle-Eastern setting is effective, and the story of ambiguous loyalties and shifting allegiances has not been outdated by current events. In the 1960's Rabe went on to develop an espionage series featuring Manny DeWitt, a lawyer for the multi-national firm of Lobbe Industriel. DeWitt's job often seems to get him involved in spying, but the three books in which he appears are written in a style different from most of Rabe's other works.

They are often quite funny, with extremely convoluted plot lines and a first-person narrator who never quite knows what is going on. Rabe's penchant for humor is also apparent in *Murder Me for Nickels,* a comic crime novel, and it crops up unexpectedly in more serious works like *The Box* and *Dig My Grave Deep.*

At the height of the "Godfather" craze in the early 1970's, Rabe produced two Mafia novels, *War of the Dons* and *Black Mafia.* His ability to describe the inner workings of a mob's power structure, as well as the inner working of his characters' minds, allows Rabe to achieve a level of intensity near to that of his early work.

Also worthy of mention is the atypical *Mission for Vengeance,* in which a paranoiac pursues three men he believes to have wronged him. His madness is strikingly depicted, and Rabe's use of alternating first- and third-person points of view adds to the story's suspense.

Unjustly neglected at present, Rabe's books will amply repay the effort required to locate them. Few writers are Rabe's equal in the field of the hardboiled gangster story, and all his works offer consistent and sometimes thought-provoking entertainment.

—Bill Crider

RADLEY, Sheila. Pseudonym for Sheila Robinson; also writes as Hester Rowan. British. Born in Cogenhoe, Northamptonshire, 18 November 1928. Educated at Cogenhoe village school, Northampton High School for Girls, 1940–48; Bedford College, University of London, 1948–51 B.A (honours) in history 1951. Served in the Women's Royal Air Force, 1951–60. Assistant Lecturer, Technical College, Northampton, 1960–61; district commissioner, National Savings, Shropshire, 1961–62; education officer, Institute of Practitioners in Advertising, London, 1962–64; assistant sub-postmistress, Banham, Norfolk, 1964–78. Since 1978 full-time writer. Agent: Curtis Brown, 162-168 Regent Street, London W1R 5TB. Address: Cyder Orchard, Church Lane, Banham, Norwich, Norfolk NR16 2HR, England.

CRIME PUBLICATIONS

Novels (series: Detective Chief Inspector Douglas Quantrill in all books)

Death and the Maiden. London, Hamish Hamilton, 1978; as *Death in the Morning,* New York, Scribner, 1979, London, Prior, 1981.
The Chief Inspector's Daughter. London, Constable, and New York, Scribner, 1981.
A Talent for Destruction. London, Constable, and New York, Scribner, 1982.
Blood on the Happy Highway. London, Constable, 1983; as *The Quiet Road to Death,* New York, Scribner, 1984.
Fate Worse Than Death. London, Constable, 1985; New York, Scribner, 1986.
Who Saw Him Die? London, Constable, 1987; New York, Scribner, 1988.
This Way Out. London, Constable, 1989; New York, Scribner, 1990.

Uncollected Short Story

"All in the Family," in *Reader, I Murdered Him,* edited by Jen Green. London, Women's Press, 1989.

OTHER PUBLICATIONS

Novels as Hester Rowan

Overture in Venice. London, Collins, 1975.
The Linden Tree. London, Collins, 1977.
Snowfall. London, Collins, 1978.

*

Sheila Radley comments:
Murder is essentially an amateur crime, committed for the most part not by psychopaths but by otherwise ordinary, decent people who would never dream of robbing a till. My concern in writing crime fiction is to explore the stresses and tensions that can drive such ordinary decent people to commit the ultimate crime of murder. I set my books in the English countryside because this is my own background, one that I understand and love.

*   *   *

Sheila Radley is one of the most distinctive of the new crime fiction writers who have emerged in the last decade or so. Her novels are placed firmly in the realistic tradition that has dominated crime writing since the 1960's. Less ambitious than P.D. James, less gothic than Ruth Rendell, her personal fingerprints are firm plotting, a vigorous style that can rise to brilliance when her emotions are involved, and a cunning eye for the minutiae of 20th-century living. Characterization is her other great strength, for she is both sharp-eyed and compassionate, and her novels are peppered with a gallery of believable people who are caught up in present-day dilemmas.

Radley served her apprenticeship as a romantic suspense writer, so her first detective novel, *Death and the Maiden,* was already a completely realized achievement. Set, like all her crime novels, in rural Suffolk, she gives a picture of village life that is neither sentimentalised nor condescended to. The characters are often inadequate to the challenge life has given them, sometimes are even shoddy, but they are not negligible, and they often have a real dignity. In a few scenes—such as the one at an intensive farming unit—the writing has virtuoso force. But "brilliance" is too vivid a word to describe the effect of her books, just as "solid" is too workaday a one. What principally strikes one is a probing, intense intelligence that gives the reader a sense that what is being written about is thoroughly understood. Only in the motive for the murder (and this is a problem in at least one of the later novels) is credulity stretched unduly.

The detective duo—Inspector Quantrill, late-promoted, rural, bogged down in a dull marriage, and Martin Tate, the young, university-educated high-flyer—is not an original combination, but it is sensitively and dramatically done, and it serves Radley well in most of the later books.

Perhaps Radley's most original and satisfying work to date is *A Talent for Destruction.* The talent of the title belongs to Janey Rolph, a gorgeous and ingratiating Australian student who specialises—like Iago—in wreaking havoc, particularly on apparently stable marriages. The marriage of the Aingers is superficially contented and fruitful, but in fact empty and ripe for shaking. He is a handsome clergyman whose greatest need is for admiration and psychological support. His plain wife's initial gratitude at being chosen by him has worn thin under the drudgery of parish work and a half-realization of the vacuity of the man she has married. It is the picture of this marriage and the horrendous cost in lives when Janey Rolph picks the pair as her targets that is the heart of the book. The detective element is compelling, but the real interest is not in who committed the murders but in how they came about. There is a feeling of spiritual and personal desolation in the novel that is extremely compelling.

Almost as impressive is *Who Saw Him Die?*, which has at its centre an extremely happy and successful second marriage. Jack Goodrum is a man transformed by marriage to a woman who is socially, intellectually, and morally above him. He is vigorous, chivalrous, and considerate—a new man. We are not left unaware of the fact that a new man has still within him the old man he has left behind: we hear enough about him from his first family and his ex-employees to see that there must be other sides to him than the ecstatically contented model husband. But his situation and its presentation to us ensure that we are emotionally on his side. Then Radley begins to unravel a series of causes and effects of great suggestiveness, in which class and character conflicts generate an exceptional tension. If the book just fails to be of the quality of *A Talent for Destruction* it is because its conclusion (with one thumping unlikelihood and a suddenly-produced murder in the past) does not have the satisfying feeling of inevitability that ideally a whodunnit's solution should have. But it stands as one of the most absorbing of recent crime novels.

Radley is not one of our prolific writers, yet in a handful of novels she has established herself as a writer of great distinction. Each novel has a different feel to it, due to the wide spectrum from which she draws her characters, her mastery of the specifics of differing life-styles, and her concern to make each plot slightly different from the run-of-the-mill whodunnit. She has an eye for detail, for the significant gesture, for symptoms of the times we live in, all at the service of a large and compassionate understanding of people and their personal crises.

—Robert Barnard

RAE, Hugh C(rauford). Also writes as James Albany; Robert Crawford; R.B. Houston; Stuart Stern; Jessica Stirling. British. Born in Glasgow, Scotland, 22 November 1935. Educated at Knightswood School, Glasgow, 1940–51. Served in the Royal Air Force (national service), 1953–54. Married Elizabeth McMillan Dunn in 1960; one daughter. Assistant, John Smith and Son, antiquarian bookseller, Glasgow, 1952–65; then full-time writer. Lecturer in creative writing, University of Glasgow. Founding member, Association of Scottish Writers. Address: Drumore Farm, Balfron Station, Stirlingshire, Scotland.

CRIME PUBLICATIONS

Novels (series: Inspector/Superintendent McCaig)

Skinner. London, Blond, and New York, Viking Press, 1965.
Night Pillow. London, Blond, and New York, Viking Press, 1967.
A Few Small Bones (McCaig). London, Blond, 1968; as *The House at Balnesmoor*, New York, Coward McCann, 1969.

The Interview. London, Blond, and New York, Coward McCann, 1969.
The Saturday Epic. London, Blond, and New York, Coward McCann, 1970.
The Marksman. London, Constable, and New York, Coward McCann, 1971.
The Shooting Gallery (McCaig). London, Constable, and New York, Coward McCann, 1972.
Two for the Grave (as R.B. Houston). London, Hale, 1972.
The Rock Harvest. London, Constable, 1973.
The Rookery. London, Constable, 1974; New York, St. Martin's Press, 1975.
The Minotaur Factor (as Stuart Stern). London, Futura, 1977; Chicago, Playboy Press, 1978.
The Poison Tree (as Stuart Stern). London, Futura, and Chicago, Playboy Press, 1978.
Sullivan. London, Constable, and Chicago, Playboy Press, 1978.
The Haunting at Waverley Falls. London, Constable, 1980.

Novels as Robert Crawford (series: Arthur Salisbury and Frank Shearer)

The Shroud Society. London, Constable, and New York, Putnam, 1969.
Cockleburr (Salisbury and Shearer). London, Constable, 1969; New York, Putnam, 1970; as *Pay as You Die,* New York, Berkley, 1971.
Kiss the Boss Goodbye (Salisbury and Shearer). London, Constable, 1970; New York, Putnam, 1971.
The Badger's Daughter. London, Constable, 1971.
Whip Hand. London, Constable, 1972.

OTHER PUBLICATIONS

Novels

Harkfast: The Making of a King. London, Constable, and New York, St. Martin's Press, 1976.
The Travelling Soul. New York, Avon, 1978.
Privileged Strangers. London, Hodder and Stoughton, 1982.

Novels (as Jessica Stirling, with Peggie Coghlan, until 1984)

The Spoiled Earth. London, Hodder and Stoughton, 1974; as *Strathmore,* New York, Delacorte Press, 1975.
The Hiring Fair. London, Hodder and Stoughton, 1976; as *Call Home the Heart,* New York, St. Martin's Press, 1977.
The Dresden Finch. New York, Delacorte Press, 1976; as *Beloved Sinner,* London, Pan, 1980.
The Dark Pasture. London, Hodder and Stoughton, 1977; New York, St. Martin's Press, 1978.
The Deep Well at Noon. London, Hodder and Stoughton, 1979; as *The Drums of Time,* New York, St. Martin's Press, 1980.
The Blue Evening Gone. London, Hodder and Stoughton, and New York, St. Martin's Press, 1981.
The Gates of Midnight. London, Hodder and Stoughton, and New York, St. Martin's Press, 1983.
Treasures on Earth. London, Hodder and Stoughton, and New York, St. Martin's Press, 1985.
Creature Comforts. London, Hodder and Stoughton, and New York, St. Martin's Press, 1986.
Hearts of Gold. London, Hodder and Stoughton, and New York, St. Martin's Press, 1987.
The Good Provider. London, Hodder and Stoughton, and New York, St. Martin's Press, 1988.

The Asking Price. London, Hodder and Stoughton, 1989;
    New York, St. Martin's Press, 1990.
The Wise Child. London, Hodder and Stoughton, 1990.

Novels as James Albany

Warrior Caste. London, Pan, 1982.
Mailed Fist. London, Pan, 1982.
Deacon's Dagger. London, Pan, 1982.
Close Combat. London, Pan, 1983.
Marching Fire. London, Pan, 1983.
Last Bastion. London, Pan, 1984.
Borneo Story. London, Pan, 1984.

Plays

The Freezer (broadcast, 1972; produced Leicester, 1973).

Radio Play: *The Freezer,* 1972.

Television Plays: *The Dear Ones,* 1966; *Swallowtale,* 1969.

Other

Editor, with Philip Ziegler and James Allen Ford, *Scottish
    Short Stories 1977.* London, Collins, 1977.
Editor, *Scottish Short Stories 1978.* London, Collins, 1978.

*

Hugh C. Rae comments:
    There can be little enough to say about a person who has
spent most of his life at a typewriter. Originally I made a
technical and subjective differentiation between my "crime
novels" and my "thrillers," publishing the latter titles under the
name Robert Crawford. It was my belief that it might be
possible, in Britain, to deliver material of some import—in
terms of theme and statement—within the confines of the
criminal *roman,* and my studies of the criminal and his victims
in the early Rae novels are in effect studies of fragments of the
Scottish environment and personality examined through the
medium of the police investigation. A common enough
technique but not one that goes down well either with serious
critics, or with the reading public.
    My "technique," if it can be so called, is based on the
synthesis of popularly available attitudes which I endeavour, to
some degree or another, to turn around by using a supercharged
and compacted language structure, a heightening of reality that
creates a serio-comic irony between "Mass Image" and
authentic historical fact, between popularly disseminated
"fictions" and how-it-is. At root, I'm interested in language
and, through language, in character. Plot, per se, kind of
follows on like a wooden duck on a string, though I am
generally—now—inventive enough to bridge the credibility
gap.

*   *   *

    Carefully utilizing the settings of suburban and slum
Glasgow, of the Hebrides, of Belfast, and of the Scottish
countryside, Hugh C. Rae creates an authentic color and
atmosphere. His use of the vernacular and the snarling gutter
language reinforces this authenticity in novels variously
categorized as thrillers or novels of psychological suspense.
    With his very first novel, *Skinner,* Rae began to investigate
the mind and manners of those living on the seamier side of life.
His pathological killer at large in a quiet Scottish community is
a portrait of an animal possessed. In *The Marksman* we find a

sensitive exploration of character as an underworld figure seeks
revenge on the killer of his illegitimate son. Many of Rae's
characters are perceptively well-rounded, and the novels'
actions grow out of these characters. Although there may be
unpleasant characters and violent plots, the complexity of both
makes for intelligent and convincing explorations of criminal
types.
    Rae's plots begin with an immediate impact and grow
organically. He maintains strict control, provides tension
throughout and often shattering conclusions. In *A Few Small
Bones,* a tale of dogged police investigation, each character is
believably suspect.
    Authentic language and locales, well-rounded characters, in-
depth portrayals, tight plotting, and satisfying conclusions
make Rae a writer whose novels should be better known.

—Frank Denton

———

RANDISI, Robert J(oseph). Also writes as Nick Carter; Tom
Cutter; W.B. Longley; Joseph Meek; Joshua Randall; J.R.
Roberts. American. Born in Brooklyn, New York, 24
August 1951. Educated at Canarsie High School, New York,
graduated 1968. Married Anna Y. Hom in 1972; two sons.
Worked as mailboy, mailroom manager, and collection clerk,
1968–72; administrative aide, New York City Police Depart-
ment, 1973–81. Since 1982 full-time writer. Founder, Private
Eye Writers of America, 1981; president, Private Eye Press;
co-founder, *Mystery Scene* Magazine, Cedar Rapids, Iowa.
Agent: Dominick Abel Literary Agency Inc., 146 West 82nd
Street, New York, New York 10024. Address: 1952 Hendrick-
son Street, Brooklyn, New York 11234, U.S.A.

CRIME PUBLICATIONS

Novels (series: Miles Jacoby)

The Disappearance of Penny. New York, Ace, 1980.
Dangerous Games, with Warren Murphy. Los Angeles,
    Pinnacle, 1980.
Midnight Man, with Warren Murphy. Los Angeles, Pinnacle,
    1981.
Eye in the Ring (Jacoby). New York, Avon, 1982.
Lucifer's Weekend, with Warren Murphy. New York, Pocket
    Books, 1982.
The Steinway Collection (Jacoby). New York, Avon, 1983.
Full Contact (Jacoby). New York, St. Martin's Press, 1984;
    London, Macmillan, 1986.
Total Recall, with Warren Murphy. New York, Pinnacle,
    1984.
The Ham Reporter. New York, Doubleday, 1986.
Once Upon a Murder. Lake Geneva, Wisconsin, TSR, 1987.
No Exit from Brooklyn. New York, St. Martin's Press, 1987.
Caribbean Blues, with others. New York, Paperjacks, 1988.
The Black Moon, with others. New York, Lynx, 1989.
Separate Cases (Jacoby). New York, Walker, 1990.

Novels as Nick Carter (series: Nick Carter in all books)

Pleasure Island. New York, Ace, 1981.
Chessmaster. New York, Ace, 1982.
The Mendoza Manuscript. New York, Ace, 1982.
The Greek Summit. New York, Ace, 1983.

The Decoy Hit. New York, Ace, 1983.
The Caribbean Coup. New York, Ace, 1984.

Uncollected Short Stories

"Murder among Witches," in *Mike Shayne Mystery Magazine*
   (Los Angeles), October 1974.
"Cop Without a Shield," in *Mystery Monthly* (New York),
   August 1976.
"Mirror Image," with John J. Mullen, in *Alfred Hitchcock's
   Mystery Magazine* (North Palm Beach, Florida), November
   1976.
"Nightwalker," in *Alfred Hitchcock's Mystery Magazine* (New
   York), January 1977.
"Deathlist," in *The Eyes Have It,* edited by Randisi.
   New York, Mysterious Press, 1984.
"The Snapchance," in *Harboiled* (Rockford, Illinois), 1985.
"The Equine Theft," in *Hardboiled* (Rockford, Illinois), 1986.
"The Vanishing Virgin," in *An Eye for Justice,* edited by
   Randisi. New York, Mysterious Press, 1986.
"The Nickel Derby," in *Hardboiled* (Rockford, Illinois), 1987.
"A Matter of Ethics," in *The Black Lizard Anthology of Crime
   Fiction,* edited by Ed Gorman. San Francisco, Black Lizard
   Press, 1987.
"Double Edge," in *Deadly Doings,* edited by Martin H.
   Greenberg. New York, Fawcett, 1989.
"Locker 246," in *Raymond Chandler's Philip Marlowe,* edited by
   Byron Preiss. New York, Knopf, 1989.
"Hardfall," in *Detective Story Magazine* (New York), 1990.
"Bad Day for a Hit," in *Hardboiled* (Rockford, Illinois), 1990.

OTHER PUBLICATIONS

Novels as J.R. Roberts

The Gunsmith series:
   1. *Macklin's Woman.* New York, Ace, 1982.
   2. *The Chinese Gunmen.* New York, Ace, 1982.
   3. *The Woman Hunt.* New York, Ace, 1982.
   4. *The Guns of Abilene.* New York, Ace, 1982.
   5. *Three Guns for Glory.* New York, Ace, 1982.
   6. *Leadtown.* New York, Ace, 1982.
   7. *The Longhorn War.* New York, Ace, 1982.
   8. *Quanah's Revenge.* New York, Ace, 1982.
   9. *Heavyweight Gun.* New York, Ace, 1982.
  10. *New Orleans Five.* New York, Ace, 1982.
  11. *One-Handed Gun.* New York, Ace, 1982.
  12. *The Canadian Payroll.* New York, Ace, 1983.
  13. *Draw to an Inside Death.* New York, Ace, 1983.
  14. *Dead Man's Hand.* New York, Ace, 1983.
  15. *Bandit Gold.* New York, Ace, 1983.
  16. *Buckskins and Sixguns.* New York, Ace, 1983.
  17. *Silver War.* New York, Ace, 1983.
  18. *High Noon at Lancaster.* New York, Ace, 1983.
  19. *Bandido Blood.* New York, Ace, 1983.
  20. *The Dodge City Gang.* New York, Ace, 1983.
  21. *Sasquatch Hunt.* New York, Ace, 1983.
  22. *Bullets and Ballots.* New York, Ace, 1983.
  23. *The Riverboat Gang.* New York, Ace, 1983.
  24. *Killer Grizzly.* New York, Ace, 1984.
  25. *North of the Border.* New York, Ace, 1984.
  26. *Eagle's Gap.* New York, Ace, 1984.

Novels as Tom Cutter

The Winning Hand. New York, Avon, 1983.
The Blue Cut Job. New York, Avon, 1983.

Lincoln County. New York, Avon, 1983.
Chinatown Chance. New York, Avon, 1983.
The Oklahoma Score. New York, Avon, 1985.
The Barbary Coast Tong. New York, Avon, 1985.
Huntsville Breakout. New York, Avon, 1985.

Novels as W.B. Longley

The Miracle of Revenge. New York, Paperjacks, 1985.
Death's Angel. New York, Paperjacks, 1985.
Wolf Pass. New York, Paperjacks, 1985.
Chinatown Justice. New York, Paperjacks, 1985.
Logan's Army. New York, Paperjacks, 1986.
Bullets and Bad Times. New York, Paperjacks, 1986.
Six Gun Angel. New York, Paperjacks, 1986.
Avenging Angel. New York, Paperjacks, 1986.
Angel for Hire. New York, Paperjacks, 1987.

Novels as Joshua Randall

Double the Bounty. New York, Paperjacks, 1987.
Bounty on a Lawman. New York, Paperjacks, 1987.
Beauty and the Bounty. New York, Paperjacks, 1988.
Bounty on a Baron. New York, Paperjacks, 1988.
Broadway Bounty. New York, Paperjacks, 1988.

Novels as Joseph Meek

Mountain Jack Pike. New York, Zebra, 1989.
Rocky Mountain Kill. New York, Zebra, 1989.
Crow Bait. New York, Zebra, 1989.
Green River Hunt. New York, Zebra, 1990.

Other

Editor, *The Eyes Have It* (anthology). New York, Mysterious
   Press, 1984; London, Severn House, 1988.
Editor, *Mean Streets* (anthology). New York, Mysterious
   Press, 1986.
Editor, *An Eye for Justice* (anthology). New York, Mysterious
   Press, 1988.
Editor, with Ed Gorman, *Under the Gun* (anthology).
   New York, New American Library, 1990.
Editor, *Justice for Hire* (anthology). New York, Mysterious
   Press, 1990.

*

Robert J. Randisi comments:
   Although the bulk of my writing has been in the Western
genre, my first love is the private eye story: and the books of
which I am most proud are my private eye novels. My Western
writing is done under pseudonyms so that my real name is
associated with my work in the private eye field. My aim has
been to elevate this field from a sub-genre of the mystery to a
genre of its own.

*   *   *

   One of the most prolific genre writers of the 1980's, Robert J.
Randisi continues on a strong roll into the final decade of the
century with no sign of letting up in either quantity or quality.
   While much of his writing falls outside the crime and mystery
field per se (primarily adult Westerns and men's action series)
he demonstrates with his latest novel *Separate Cases,* the fourth
novel in his popular Miles Jacoby series, that he hasn't lost a
step when it comes to delivering the goods on a complex,
entertaining private investigator yarn. Randisi's long-stated

personal preference has always been the private-eye story, an affection that caused him to found, in 1981, the Private Eye Writers of America and to remain at its helm through the present as executive director. Further evidence of his devotion to the private eye genre can be seen in the fact he has created four separate and distinct P.I. characters in ongoing series.

The first of these was Henry Po, in 1980's *The Disappearance of Penny*. Although an independently licensed P.I., Po works almost exclusively for the fictional New York State Racing Club and in *The Disappearance of Penny*, as a favor to his boss, he agrees to look for the missing daughter of one of Long Island Downs' most prominent horse owners. The plot quickly thickens to include murder and racing corruption and the flavor of the racetrack background is nicely maintained. Po is a breezy, likable character who deserves to return in more novel-length adventures. To date, however, he has reappeared only in short stories and cameo walk-ons in other Randisi novels. (Such "guest starring" bits have become something of a Randisi trade-mark; in addition to having his own detectives and supporting characters overlap into different series' books, he also uses popular detective creations of other contemporary writers as contacts and reference points in his story lines.)

Miles Jacoby first appears in *Eye in the Ring*, the title being a nod toward his emergence from the ranks of middleweight prize fighters to becoming a licensed private eye. This transition is one of the novel's many subplots, making Jacoby immediately endearing as a tough and competent individual, albeit a decidedly *un*-seasoned investigator as he attempts to solve the murder of his partner/mentor and clear his brother from being charged for the crime. This theme of Jacoby growing and learning in his detective craft is expanded in the following books (*The Steinway Collection*; *Full Contact*) of the series. It is an ironic developement that by *Separate Cases* we find Jacoby shouldering the mantle of veteran detective as he goes to the aid of Caroline McWilliams, novice private eye seeking help in solving the murder of *her* partner (and former husband). All of the Jacoby books are written in Randisi's fast-action, dialogue-driven style, featuring nifty plot twists and colorful secondary characters and a sprinkling of sexy encounters. Jacoby continues to evolve and, through the merit of four novel-length tales and a handful of short stories, stands as Randisi's most fully-realized series characters.

But rich as the Jacoby character may be, it is nevertheless *No Exit from Brooklyn*, the debut of Brooklyn private eye Nick Delvecchio, that stands out as one of Randisi's strongest works so far. The Delvecchio character is multi-layered and interesting, an ex-cop pressured off the force after suffering a terrible beating and then developing an overly aggressive attitude to avoid having the same ever happen again, a somewhat harder, more cynical individual than either Po or Jacoby. The plot of *No Exit from Brooklyn* is deliciously complex, including the Delvecchio family's personal conflicts, stolen artefacts, international terrorism, Mafia intervention, and murder. But it is Randisi's portrait of Brooklyn itself—its sights, sounds, smells, and attitudes; its *feel*—that lifts this book to a higher rung. More work featuring Delvecchio is promised.

The Black Moon, edited and co-authored by Randisi, is an ambitious undertaking that marks mysterydom's first attempt at the kind of "shared universe" efforts that are so popular in the science fiction field. In *The Black Moon* we are introduced to five different detectives in five different parts of the country who, each in a separate segment written by separate authors, take on smaller cases that are parts of a single, larger case. Randisi's Sal Carlucci, part-time private eye and owner of the Black Moon Saloon, is the orchestrator of these various undertakings and it is through him and the Black Moon that the whole exercise is "framed" and, ultimately, resolved. Each

individual episode is strong, so much so that the final wrap-up, while satisfying, is perhaps a bit strained. Carlucci is Randisi's oldest series character, a World War II veteran with a bum leg, gruff and crusty and savvy, a man comfortable with himself and not about to take any crap from anybody. As with Po, any reappearance by him would be welcome.

Randisi plots a good, solid mystery. Even many of his "non-mystery" works—particularly the Tracker series written under the pseudonym of Tom Cutter, and a number of titles in his Gunsmith series written as J.R. Roberts—are really whodunits in Western dress. It is noteworthy, however, that Randisi bylines his own name only to his straight mysteries because that is where his heart lies and where he hopes to leave his most lasting mark.

One Western on which he did not use a pseudonym, however, is *The Ham Reporter*. In fairness it must be pointed out that this is a Western largely only in the sense that that is how the publishers saw fit to package it. In fact, *The Ham Reporter* is an historical mystery, taking place around the turn of the century and featuring as its protagonist the legendary gunfighter and marshal, Bat Masterson, in his later days as a New York City sports reporter. This is an underappreciated book that unfortunately "fell between the cracks" of two genres. It is an ambitious undertaking, a carefully researched blend of fact and fiction that is satisfying both as a mystery and as an in-depth look at New York in the early 1900's. To say that it deserved better attention than it received is an understatement.

In any event, Randisi's place in the annals of popular fiction seems secure. He is a writer in the best sense of the word, and has demonstrated that he can apply his talent to any number of different areas. It seems safe to presume one of these will always be the mystery field.

—Wayne D. Dundee

* * *

RANSOME, Stephen. *See* **DAVID, Frederick C.**

* * *

RAPHAEL, Chaim. *See* **DAVEY, Jocelyn.**

* * *

RATHBONE, Julian. British. Born in London, 10 February 1935. Educated at Claysmore School, Iwerne Minister, Dorset, 1948–53; Magdalene College, Cambridge, B.A. (honours) in English 1958. Married; two children. Teacher of English in Turkey, 1959–62, and England, 1962–73. Since 1973 full-time writer. Agent: Margaret Hanbury, 27 Walcot Square, London SE11 4VB. Address: Sea View, School Road, Thorney Hill, Christchurch, BH23 8DS, England.

CRIME PUBLICATIONS

Novels (series: Jan Argand; Nur Bey)

Diamonds Bid (Bey). London, Joseph, 1966; New York, Walker, 1967.
Hand Out (Bey). London, Joseph, and New York, Walker, 1968.
With My Knives I Know I'm Good. London, Joseph, 1969; New York, Putnam, 1970.
Trip Trap (Bey). London, Joseph, and New York, St. Martin's Press, 1972.
Kill Cure. London, Joseph, and New York, St. Martin's Press, 1975.
Bloody Marvellous. London, Joseph, 1975; New York, St. Martin's Press, 1976.
Carnival! London, Joseph, and New York, St. Martin's Press, 1976.
A Raving Monarchist. London, Joseph, and New York, St. Martin's Press, 1978.
The Euro-Killers (Argand). London, Joseph, 1979; New York, Pantheon, 1980.
Base Case (Argand). London, Joseph, and New York, Pantheon, 1981.
A Spy of the Old School. London, Joseph, 1982; New York, Pantheon, 1983.
Watching the Detectives (Argand). London, Joseph, 1983; New York, Pantheon, 1984.
Lying in State. London, Heinemann, 1985; New York, Putnam, 1986.
Zdt. London, Heinemann, 1986; as *Greenfinger*, New York, Viking, 1987.
The Crystal Contract. London, Heinemann, 1988.
The Pandora Option. London, Heinemann, 1990.

OTHER PUBLICATIONS

Novels

King Fisher Lives. London, Joseph, and New York, St. Martin's Press, 1976.
The Princess, A Nun, with Hugh Ross Williamson. London, Joseph, 1978.
Joseph. London, Joseph, 1979.
A Last Resort—For These Times. London, Joseph, 1980.
Nasty, Very: A Mock Epic in Six Parts. London, Joseph, 1984.

Other

Editor, *Wellington's War: His Peninsular Dispatches.* London, Joseph, 1984.

*

Julian Rathbone comments:

My "detective" fiction has had very little detection in it and really not much mystery. The appeal has lain I think in suspense, very often the sort of ironical suspense arising from situations where the reader knows more than the characters, from realistic characterization allowing the interplay of real emotions, and from vivid descriptions of more or less exotic locales. For the last few years I have been trying to move out of the thriller "genre" into something more completely novelistic—the first successful attempt in this line was *King Fisher Lives,* followed by *A Last Resort* and *Nasty, Very.*

* * *

All of Julian Rathbone's thrillers are good, but three of them—*Lying in State, A Spy of the Old School,* and *Zdt*—are among the best that can be found. They give him a comfortable place in the tradition of Graham Greene and Eric Ambler, of the genre but transcending it, addressing major contemporary issues with political and social insights but no polemic.

The rest are intelligent, rewarding entertainment. Their hallmarks are intricate, well-paced plots, in which suspense rather than mystery is dominant, deft evocations of social ambience, the depiction of human flaws, a lacing of hard-edged humour. In these Rathbone is a polished practitioner of the thriller trade, but it is his novels outside the genre, especially the Booker short-listed *King Fisher Lives* and *Joseph,* which should have been fair warning that he was going to produce some really special thrillers.

His first five novels are set in Turkey, three of them featuring Colonel Nur Bey. The best is *Trip Trap:* Edward Amberley, visiting Turkey on business, is seduced into playing a not entirely innocent part in drug-smuggling. Amberley's character, his mood changing from impulsive confidence to corrosive misery at his mis-judgements, is a fine medium for the meeting of two worlds and the bursting of several bubbles of Anglocentric assumptions about foreigners, while Nur Bey—hitherto the incorruptible in a sea of corruption—must dicker with corruption himself for his investigation implicates his father.

The dilemmas of getting caught up in uncontrollable events are an archetypical Rathbone theme. In *Diamonds Bid,* the first Nur Bey novel, the unlikeable Jonathan Smollet gets trapped into an assassination plot after he has seen a bribe being passed. In *Kill Cure,* virulent toxins are among a batch of antibiotics being charitably sent to Bangladesh.

Bloody Marvellous—the first of three thrillers set in Spain—has the same theme, this time in a web of drug-smuggling, double-cross and treble-cross. Likewise in *Carnival!,* a television crew films a brutal murder. *A Raving Monarchist,* the most textured of this trio, explores the Spanish political undergrowth via a plot involving blackmail and assassination.

Having evoked in such sensitive detail the atmosphere of Spain and Turkey, Rathbone next created the fictional country of Brabt. Why he did so is a puzzle. The plots are as well-worked as ever and the central figure, the detective Jan Argand—perennially worried about his sanity in a world which inspires paranoia—is another fine creation. Argand's investigations all touch on the interface of crime and politics, involving big business (*The Euro-Killers*), the US military (*Base Case*) and European fascism (*Watching the Detectives*). But the artificial setting deprives them of some of the bite they might have had if set in a real country.

Perhaps Rathbone realised this for with *Lying in State, A Spy of the Old School* and *Zdt,* he not only returned to real settings but also spun his plots from actual events. The strength of the fiction comes in part from being put in a context which is not just realistic but real. They also experiment with narrative form. Straightforward, chronological story development co-exists with a melange of flashback and a shifting narrative viewpoint. That this is woven into a gripping tale in each case is testimony to Rathbone's story-telling skills.

A Spy of the Old School brings Rathbone for the first time to a British setting. Sir Richard Austen, renowned archaeologist, is the spy; William Cargill is the hunter—but why is he called off? A depiction of the ruthless manipulations of the powerful, a journey into the motives of the Philby generation of spies, a colourful portrayal of upper-class England before, during and after World War II, the book is also a masterfully plotted suspense novel with a sting in the tail.

Lying in State is set in Spain at the very moment of Franco's death, but the plot focuses on another dead dictator—Perón of Argentina. One set of tapes he made during exile in Spain has been discovered and sold. Now another set is on the market—indiscreet, lewd in places, embarrassing in others. Roberto Fairrie, Argentinian socialist and exile, is hired as a consultant to judge the tapes' authenticity. Shady far-right interests want their sale stopped at all costs. Fairrie comes under intense pressure and assassins loom. The tale contains a brilliant twist but its real strengths lie in the character of Fairrie and the atmosphere in Spain as the *ancien régime* is swept away by Franco's death.

Zdt is an education in central American politics and the role of multinational agri-business corporations. Zdt is an old variety of maize, believed to be extinct; its rediscovery could be extremely bad news for Associated Foods International. As the company acts to extinguish the problem, an idealistic agricultural expert working for the UN gets caught up and becomes a victim. His wife, their young baby with her, turns out to be too tough a nut for the company to crack. This is one of the few Rathbone novels in which the powerful criminals get a fully satisfying come-uppance.

By the standards of these three novels, *The Crystal Contract* is mildly disappointing. By any other criteria it is another success. It is a slam-bang, inter-continental tale of the cocaine trade, with high-powered European financiers, Colombian gangsters, English criminals of all sorts, an American detective who gets some of his men but not all, plenty of action, a splattering of mostly sordid sex and, again, that outstanding ability to evoke locale. *The Pandora Option* comes closer to Rathbone's best standards. Set like *Zdt* in agri-business, this time the problem is contaminated Iranian grain siloes. John Danby is given two flasks of contaminated grain to investigate. One is destroyed, the other is stolen, Danby's young wife and her younger lover disappear. The trail of intrigue—from Rome to Berlin via Vienna, Munich, and Warsaw—is studded with violence and peopled by Polish fascists, the CIA, an Iranian colonel, greedy businessmen and the old East German Stasi. The varied locales are again vivid, the characters are more strongly realised and engaging than in *The Crystal Contract* and the complex relationship between Danby, his wife and her amoral lover is sensitively explored. But when Rathbone opened this particular Pandora's box he let out a newly florid style which, for some readers, may blur what would otherwise have some very sharp edges.

—Dan Smith

———

RATTRAY, Simon. *See* **HALL, Adam.**

———

RAWSON, Clayton. Also wrote as The Great Merlini; Stuart Towne. American. Born in Elyria, Ohio, 15 August 1906. Educated at Ohio State University, Columbus, B.A. 1929; Chicago Art Institute. Married Catherine Stone in 1929; two daughters and two sons. Associate editor, *True Detective,* editor, *Master Detective,* New York, 1942–46; mystery editor, Ziff Davis, Chicago, 1946–47; director, Unicorn Mystery Book Club, 1948–52, and art director, Unicorn Books, New York, 1952–59; editor, Inner Sanctum Mystery series, Simon and Schuster, New York, 1959–62; managing editor, *Ellery Queen's*

Mystery Magazine, New York, 1963–70. Member, Society of American Magicians. *Died 1 March 1971.*

CRIME PUBLICATIONS

Novels (series: The Great Merlini in all Rawson books)

Death from a Top Hat. New York, Putnam, and London, Collins, 1938.
The Footprints on the Ceiling. New York, Putnam, and London, Collins, 1939.
The Headless Lady. New York, Putnam, and London, Collins, 1940.
Death Out of Thin Air (2 novelettes; as Stuart Towne). New York, Coward McCann, 1941; London, Cassell, 1947.
No Coffin for the Corpse. Boston, Little Brown, 1942; London, Stacey, 1972.
Death from Nowhere (2 novelettes; as Stuart Towne). N.p., Yogi, n.d.

Short Stories

The Great Merlini: The Complete Stories of the Magician Detective. Boston, Gregg Press, 1979.

OTHER PUBLICATIONS

Other

Scarne on Dice, with John Scarne. New York, Stackpole, 1945.
Al Baker's Pet Secrets. New York, Starke, 1951.
How to Entertain Children with Magic You Can Do (as The Great Merlini). New York, Simon and Schuster, 1962; London, Faber, 1964.
The Golden Book of Magic (for children; as The Great Merlini). New York, Golden Press, 1964.

*   *   *

Magic and mystery were intimately intertwined in the unique career of Clayton Rawson. After a stint as art director of several prominent business firms in the mid-1930's, he wrote his own professional stage identity as a magician called The Great Merlini into four mystery novels. In the first of these, *Death from a Top Hat,* the detective character named Merlini solves a series of New York City murders that occur in surroundings where magicians proliferate, bookish references to the occult accumulate on every hand, and the detective novel form itself is gently mocked. Rawson also wrote some pulp novelettes about another magician-sleuth called Don Diavolo, two of which were collected in *Death Out of Thin Air* and published under the pseudonym of Stuart Towne. As the real-life Merlini, Rawson created and marketed some 50 original tricks and wrote two books on magic.

Rawson's novels and stories are characteristically keyed to "impossible" situations, in the grand tradition of John Dickson Carr. In fact, the two writers carried out a series of challenges in the pages of the Queen magazine—with one proposing an "impossible" circumstance and the other inventing a solution and explanation. Characterization and setting were not usually well developed in Rawson's work; the plot was always pre eminent. In this sense, he belongs to a fondly remembered period of the past. He was not an innovator, but rather a clever and quick-witted cultivator of the genre to which he devoted his career.

—Donald A. Yates

———————

RAYMOND, Derek. Psuedonym for Robin (Robert William Arthur) Cook. Born in London, June 1931. Educated at Eton. Served in the British army for two years. Married 1) Eugenie Grossman in 1963, one son; 2) Rosemary Ann Reckitt in 1970, one daughter; 3) Agnès Bert in 1989. Lived in Spain in the 1950's; waiter, assistant editor for a Spanish language magazine, both New York, 1959–60; lived in Paris, two years, Tangiers, two years, taxi driver, London, two years. Lives in France. Recipient: Prix Mystère Etranger de la Critique de la Presse Français, 1984; Meilleur Roman Policier, 1986. Agent: Maxim Jakubowski, Murder One, 71–73 Charing Cross Road, London WC2, England. Address: Le Bourg, Rivière-sur-Tarn, France.

CRIME PUBLICATIONS

Novels (series: The Factory)

He Died with His Eyes Open. London, Secker and Warburg, 1984; New York, Ballantine, 1987.
The Devil's Home on Leave (Factory). London, Secker and Warburg, 1985; New York, Ballantine, 1987.
How the Dead Live (Factory). London, Secker and Warburg, 1986; New York, Ballantine, 1988.
I Was Dora Suarez. Paris, Rivages, London, Scribner, and New York, Ballantine, 1990.

OTHER PUBLICATIONS

Novels as Robin Cook

The Crust on Its Uppers. London, Hutchinson, 1962.
Bombe Surprise. London, Hutchinson, 1963.
The Legacy of the Stiff Upper Lip. London, Hutchinson, 1966.
Public Parts and Private Places. London, Hutchinson, 1967.
A State of Denmark, or, A Warning to the Incurious. London, Hutchinson, 1970.
The Tenants of Dirt Street. London, McGibbon and Kee, 1971.

*

Manuscript Collection: Mugar Memorial Library, Boston University.

Derek Raymond comments:

I finished writing *I Was Dora Suarez* on July 7th and feel as a result, and because of its predecessors, the previous Factory books, more than ever confirmed on certain points which I already held to be central in the writing of a black novel. There is nothing escapist about the black novel whatever. The writer cannot even escape himself in it; the black novel is the novel in which escape is shut off.

One thing is sure as far as black literature in contrast to white is concerned; in the construction of black writing all literary conventions have to be modified, recast, distorted (even invented); if the old rules resist these changes or snap in your hands there is no option but to drop them. Mood, action, penetration of—and osmosis with—the disturbed human psyche as contrasted to the everyday life around it is everything in the black novel; to this end, all generally accepted literary constructions have to be re-examined and analyzed one at a time, then changed to fit—or abandoned if they do not.

I have not generalized in *Suarez*. The book is based on three separate crimes taken from newspapers, life, and police records (they did not even all of them occur in the same country) which I geared, one into the other, to forge a single narrative. I transposed places, names, and even reasons for a given action, but not the facts; my overriding intention was, as it always is, to conjure evil out of its shadows and good out of its sky and put them face to face in a single situation, in a single flat. There is a chorus of secondary characters to comment, insofar as they are party to the main action, on what is happening and on their reaction to it—while the main characters, of course, comment on themselves too, just as everybody does.

The point I am making here, then, is that there can be nothing flimsy or superficial, let alone artificial, about black writing. As a genre, it exists to abolish the irrelevant and to show the wrong thing in the mirror; it can therefore afford to carry no excess fat on it whatever. The black novel is not just a good read; it is, when it succeeds, as much a social document as *Edwin Drood, The Trial, Thérèse Raquin, Erostrate, The Big Sleep, The Friends of Eddie Coyle,* or *Suicide Hill.* You cannot isolate murder, blackmail, and victimization from the rest of reality, as Chandler pointed out. If you do, the result may be a good read, but it is still a false, tinny, and contrived result, missing everything that the reader expects, because there is nothing superficial about murder, and such an approach strips terror, disease, and madness of its vital human dimension—the dimension in which a human being changes and becomes inhuman, a monster. But this monstrosity cannot be *seen* in literature unless it is placed in the context of society as a whole—the first rider being the social reason for the killer and the victim finding themselves cast in those fatal roles; the second, society's *real* (not pretend and mealy-mouthed) reaction to it.

For the truth of the matter is that murder crystallizes a society and shows it up; in a final and bloody way, as Shakespeare knew, for what it is; and if there is an increasing thirst on the reader's part for really black literature, it is because the public is, as a whole, even to a greater or lesser extent unconsciously, worried about what is going on.

*   *   *

Derek Raymond stands alone in contemporary crime fiction. He is not recognizably linked to the main British school, the country-house "cosy" tradition, yet, more surprisingly, as his main protagonist is a Detective-Sergeant, he has nothing in common with the police procedural tradition either. Raymond does not merely bend the rules of crime writing, he ignores them entirely. If he is comparable with any other crime writer it is perhaps Jim Thompson, with whom he shares an unsettling ability to evoke the mind of a psychopath. But where Thompson seduces you into an awful identification with the likes of Lou Ford in *The Killer Inside Me*, with Raymond there is not even that dubious pleasure; his psychopaths are entirely damned and *not good company.* Otherwise Raymond relates stylistically only perhaps to Patrick Hamilton, author of *Hangover Square,* but Raymond does not even have Hamilton's limited faith in Marxism, instead he seems to be ultimately a tortured moralist, obsessed with the twin questions—why do people suffer, and why does evil exist?

Raymond's first crime novel, *He Died with His Eyes Open,*

appeared in 1984. However it was scarcely a first novel. Derek Raymond is a pseudonym for Robin Cook, an old Etonian turned Soho character and minor villain, who wrote a series of novels in the 1960's under his own name. These include *The Crust on Its Uppers, Bombe Surprise, Public Parts and Private Places* and are generally black comedies of the English upper classes in terminal decline. Criminal activity tends to play a part but they are scarcely crime novels. A decline in fortunes in the 1970's found Cook driving a minicab around south London and then retreating to rural France. After some years working on the land in France he started writing again. A novel, *Les Mois D'Avril Sont Les Meurtriers,* which foreshadows the Raymond books, was published in France under his own name, but has yet to appear in English. He then wrote *He Died with His Eyes Open,* succeeded in finding a British publisher but was unable to use his own name due to the popularity at the time of the American medical-thriller writer also named Robin Cook.

He Died with His Eyes Open set the pattern for the novels to come. It is narrated by an unnamed Detective-Sergeant, based at "the Factory" in Poland Street, Soho, and working for Department A14—Unexplained Deaths. This is the department that gets to deal with the cases no one cares about, the killings that never make front pages—"Obscure, unimportant, apparently irrelevant deaths of people who don't matter and who never did." The book starts with the discovery of a body, a man in his fifties, one step up from vagrancy in appearance, beaten to death and dumped next to the North Circular. The case is swiftly dumped in the narrator's lap. By a typical Raymond contrivance the plot is advanced by the discovery of a series of cassette tapes on which the dead man has left a kind of fragmented autobiography, detailing his terminal decline into alcoholic and sexual self-abuse. The narrator then tracks down the killers by retracing the dead man's last months, in doing so almost taking on his personality and coming close to suffering the same fate.

In all the books there is a recurrent pattern of the detective witnessing a life of unbearable suffering ending in grisly death, identifying with it absolutely, to the considerable detriment of his career as a police officer. This is the strength of the books, the visceral nature of their obsessive search for morality. Certainly the books will not appeal to someone looking for a conventional account of policework, or even criminal activity. Raymond is cavalier with his plotting, shows little interest in recreating the day to day drudgery of police work, has his characters speak in a weird fusion of 1960's and 1980's slang, and paints south London as little short of Hades incarnate. At best, as in *He Died with His Eyes Open,* these failings do not matter a jot, they even strengthen the sense of being assailed by a very distinct world view. The second novel in the series, *The Devil's Home on Leave,* however, is weighed down by its somewhat contrived espionage plot and the third, *How the Dead Live* is considerably more coherent if taken as a prose poem of desolation than as a mystery novel. The fourth novel, *I Was Dora Suarez,* however, returns to the form of *He Died with His Eyes Open.* Once more it's a claustrophobic account of a murder investigation—this time into the horrific killing of a prostitute—revealing a ruined, tormented life.

Along the way *I Was Dora Suarez* contains this neat summary of its protagonist's world view, which in turn illuminates the author's singular fictional intention:

To work in A14 is to see everything that no one ever sees: the violence, misery and despair, the immeasurable distance in the mind of a human being that knows nothing but suffering between its dreams and its death.

—John Williams

REED, Eliot. *See* **AMBLER, Eric.**

REEVE, Arthur B(enjamin). American. Born in Patchogue, Long Island, New York, 15 October 1880. Educated in public schools in Brooklyn, New York; Princeton University, New Jersey, A.B. 1903 (phi beta kappa); New York Law School. Married Margaret Allen Wilson in 1906; one daughter and two sons. Assistant editor, *Public Opinion,* 1906; staff member, *Survey,* 1907; editor of annual *Our Own Times,* 1906–10. Invited to help establish detection laboratory in World War I. *Died 9 August 1936.*

CRIME PUBLICATIONS

Novels (series: Professor Craig Kennedy)

Guy Garrick. New York, Hearst's International Library, 1914; London, Hodder and Stoughton, 1916.
The Gold of the Gods (Kennedy). New York, Hearst's International Library, 1915; London, Hodder and Stoughton, 1916.
The Exploits of Elaine (Kennedy; novelization of screen-play). New York, Hearst's International Library, and London, Hodder and Stoughton, 1915.
The Romance of Elaine (Kennedy; novelization of screen-play). New York, Hearst's International Library, and London, Hodder and Stoughton, 1916.
The Triumph of Elaine (Kennedy; novelization of screenplay). London, Hodder and Stoughton, 1916.
The Ear in the Wall (Kennedy). New York, Hearst's International Library, 1916; London, Hodder and Stoughton, 1917.
The Adventures (Kennedy). New York, Harper, 1917; London, Collins, 1918.
The Master Mystery (novelization of screenplay), with John W. Grey. New York, Grosset and Dunlap, 1919.
The Soul Scar (Kennedy). New York, Harper, 1919.
The Film Mystery (Kennedy). New York, Harper, 1921; London, Hodder and Stoughton, 1922.
The Mystery Mind (novelization of screenplay). New York, Grosset and Dunlap, 1921.
Atavar (Kennedy). New York, Harper, 1924.
The Radio Detective (Kennedy; novelization of screen-play). New York, Grosset and Dunlap, 1926.
Pandora (Kennedy). New York, Harper, 1926.
The Kidnap Club (Kennedy). New York, Macaulay, 1932.
The Clutching Hand (Kennedy). Chicago, Reilly and Lee, 1934.
Enter Craig Kennedy (novelettes; adapted by Ashley Locke). New York, Macaulay, 1935.
The Stars Scream Murder. New York, Appleton, 1936.

Short Stories

The Poisoned Pen.   New York, Harper, 1911; London, Hodder and Stoughton, 1916.
The Silent Bullet: Adventures of Craig Kennedy, Scientific Detective.   New York, Dodd Mead, 1912; as *The Black Hand,* London, Nash, 1912.
Constance Dunlap, Woman Detective.   New York, Harper, 1913; London, Hodder and Stoughton, 1916.
The Dream Doctor.   New York, Hearst's International Library, 1914; London, Hodder and Stoughton, 1916.
The War Terror.   New York, Hearst's International Library, 1915; as *Craig Kennedy, Detective,* London, Simpkin Marshall, 1916.
The Social Gangster.   New York, Hearst's International Library, 1916; as *The Diamond Queen,* London, Hodder and Stoughton, 1917.
The Treasure Train.   New York, Harper, 1917; London, Collins, 1920.
The Panama Plot.   New York, Harper, 1918; London, Collins, 1920.
Craig Kennedy Listens In.   New York, Harper, 1923; London, Hodder and Stoughton, 1924.
The Fourteen Points: Tales of Craig Kennedy, Master of Mystery.   New York, Harper, 1925.
Craig Kennedy on the Farm.   New York, Harper, 1925.
The Boy Scouts' Craig Kennedy.   New York, Harper, 1925.

Uncollected Short Stories

"Kennedy Gets the Dope," in *Detective Story* (New York), 28 July 1928.
"Craig Kennedy and the Model," in *Detective Story* (New York), 11 August 1928.
"Craig Kennedy and the Ghost," in *Detective Story* (New York), 25 August 1928.
"Blood Will Pay," in *Detective Fiction Weekly* (New York), 22 September 1928.
"Radiant Doom," in *Detective Fiction Weekly* (New York), 6 October 1928.
"Craig Kennedy Splits Hairs," in *Detective Story* (New York), 27 October 1928.
"Craig Kennedy's Christmas Case," in *Detective Fiction Weekly* (New York), 22 December 1928.
"The Mystery Ray," in *Detective Fiction Weekly* (New York), 23 February–9 March 1929.
"The Beauty Wrecker," in *Detective Fiction Weekly* (New York), 16 March 1929.
"Poisoned Music," in *Detective Fiction Weekly* (New York), 31 August 1929.
"The Crime Student," in *Detective Fiction Weekly* (New York), 7 September 1929.
"The Mystery of the Bulawayo Diamond," in *Scientific Detective,* January 1930.
"The Junior League Murder," in *Complete Detective Novel Magazine* (New York), June 1932.
"Murder in the Tourist Camp," in *Complete Detective Novel Magazine* (New York), December 1932.
"The Golden Grave," in *Dime Detective* (New York), 1 October 1933.
"Doped," in *World Manhunters,* February 1934.
"The Royal Racket," in *Complete Detective Novel Magazine* (New York), January–February 1935.
"The Death Cry," in *Weird Tales* (Chicago), May 1935.

OTHER PUBLICATIONS

Novel

Tarzan the Mighty (novelization of screenplay).   Kansas City, Missouri, Vernell Coriell, 1974.

Plays

Screenplays (serials): *The Exploits of Elaine,* with Charles William Goddard, 1914; *The New Exploits of Elaine,* 1915; *The Romance of Elaine,* 1915; *The Hidden Hand,* with Charles A. Logue, 1917; *The House of Hate,* with Charles A. Logue, 1918; *The Master Mystery,* with Charles A. Logue, 1919; *The Carter Case,* with John W. Grey, 1919; *The Tiger's Trail,* with Charles A. Logue, 1919; *One Million Dollars Reward,* with John W. Grey, 1920; *The Mystery Mind,* with John W. Grey, 1920; *The Radio Detective,* 1926; *The Clutching Hand,* 1926; *The Return of the Riddle Rider,* 1927; (features): *The Grim Game,* with John W. Grey, 1919; *Terror Island,* with John W. Grey, 1920; *Unmasked,* with others, 1929.

Other

The Golden Age of Crime.   New York, Mohawk Press, 1931.

Editor, *The Best Ghost Stories.*   New York, Modern Library, 1930.

*

Bibliography: "Arthur B. Reeve and the American Sherlock Holmes" by John Harwood in *Armchair Detective* (Del Mar, California), October 1977; "A Chronological Bibliography of the Books of Arthur B. Reeve" by J. Randolph Cox in *Armchair Detective* (Del Mar, California), January 1978.

*   *   *

Arthur B. Reeve's creation, Professor Craig Kennedy, was sometimes referred to as "the American Sherlock Holmes." Like Holmes, Kennedy had his own Watson in the person of Walter Jameson, a newspaper reporter, who roomed with Kennedy and accompanied him on most of his cases.

A typical story started with a client arriving at the rooms of the two friends or at Kennedy's laboratory (he taught chemistry at Columbia University in New York). Many of Kennedy's cases ended with the gathering of all the persons concerned with the crime in the detective's laboratory. He would explain how a new scientific device worked and how it pointed to the identity of the criminal. Then he would expose the wrongdoer in much the same fashion as Nero Wolfe did many years later. Usually he acted as a private detective, but often he was brought into a case by the New York Police Department or one of the Federal Government's investigative organizations like the Secret Service. The high point of each mystery occurred when a new scientific device, adapted by Kennedy to crime investigation, revealed the identity of the criminal. Many much-used instruments of today first appeared in the works of Reeve when he showed Kennedy using the dictaphone, X-ray, blood sampling, handwriting or typing identification, and early versions of the lie detector.

Long before the FBI came into existence, Kennedy had files of tire tracks, types of paper, inks, and other materials. He also believed that in the future public places would use hidden cameras as deterrents to crime, much like the closed-circuit TV cameras of today's banks. Some people think these early stories led to the scientific investigation of crime by police laboratories in later years. During World War I Reeve was asked by the federal government to create a scientific crime lab for use against spies and saboteurs. This laboratory was supposed to have been the finest known in any nation up to that time.

Although the Craig Kennedy books aren't very popular today, they did have a huge following from 1912 into the 1920's. At one time during that period Reeve was the best-selling American mystery author in England. By 1914 the Craig Kennedy stories had become so popular that Reeve was asked to adapt stories of his famous sleuth for film. *The Exploits of Elaine*, featuring Pearl White, was so popular that two sequels were produced. He went on to write 16 movies in all, serials and features, about Kennedy and other characters. Several of the screenplays were later turned into book form.

Reeve was essentially a short story writer and many of his books were collections of short stories. Each novel was actually a series of interconnected short stories. At the end of each episode, instead of revealing the identity of the criminal, Kennedy showed how the villain committed the crime or the detective found a clue that led him further along the trail to the solution. Reeve is an almost forgotten author today and if he is read at all it is from a sense of nostalgia in an effort to bring back memories of the days when the American Sherlock Holmes was at the height of his popularity.

—John Harwood

REILLY, Helen (née Kieran). Also wrote as Kieran Abbey. American. Born in New York City in 1891. Married the artist Paul Reilly (died 1944); four daughters, including Ursula Curtiss L, *q.v.*, and Mary McMullen, *q.v.* Lived in Westport, Connecticut, New York City, 1944–60, and New Mexico after 1960. President, Mystery Writers of America, 1953. *Died 11 January 1962.*

CRIME PUBLICATIONS

Novels (series: Inspector Christopher McKee)

The Thirty-First Bullfinch. New York, Doubleday, 1930.
The Diamond Feather (McKee). New York, Doubleday, 1930.
Man with the Painted Head. New York, Farrar and Rinehart, 1931.
Murder in the Mews (McKee). New York, Doubleday, 1931.
The Doll's Trunk Murder. New York, Farrar and Rinehart, 1932; London, Hutchinson, 1933.
The Line-Up (McKee). New York, Doubleday, 1934; London, Cassell, 1935.
McKee of Centre Street. New York, Doubleday, 1934.
Mr. Smith's Hat (McKee). New York, Doubleday, and London, Cassell, 1936.
Dead Man Control (McKee). New York, Doubleday, 1936; London, Heinemann, 1937.
File on Rufus Ray. New York, Morrow, and London, Jarrolds, 1937.
All Concerned Notified (McKee). New York, Doubleday, and London, Heinemann, 1939.
Dead for a Ducat (McKee). New York, Doubleday, and London, Heinemann, 1939.
The Dead Can Tell (McKee). New York, Random House, 1940.

Death Demands an Audience (McKee). New York, Doubleday, 1940.
Murder in Shinbone Alley (McKee). New York, Doubleday, 1940.
Mourned on Sunday (McKee). New York, Random House, 1941.
Three Women in Black (McKee). New York, Random House, 1941.
Name Your Poison (McKee). New York, Random House, 1942.
The Opening Door (McKee). New York, Random House, 1944.
Murder on Angler's Island (McKee). New York, Random House, 1945; London, Hammond, 1948.
The Silver Leopard (McKee). New York, Random House, 1946; London, Hammond, 1949.
The Farmhouse (McKee). New York, Random House, 1947; London, Hammond, 1950.
Staircase 4 (McKee). New York, Random House, 1949; London, Hammond, 1950.
Murder at Arroways (McKee). New York, Random House, 1950; London, Museum Press, 1952.
Lament for the Bride (McKee). New York, Random House, 1951; London, Museum Press, 1954.
The Double Man (McKee). New York, Random House, 1952; London, Museum Press, 1954.
The Velvet Hand (McKee). New York, Random House, 1953; London, Museum Press, 1955.
Tell Her It's Murder (McKee). New York, Random House, 1954; London, Museum Press, 1955.
Compartment K (McKee). New York, Random House, 1955; as *Murder Rides the Express,* London, Hale, 1956.
The Canvas Dagger (McKee). New York, Random House, 1956; London, Hale, 1957.
Ding, Dong, Bell (McKee). New York, Random House, 1958; London, Hale, 1959.
Not Me, Inspector (McKee). New York, Random House, 1959; London, Hale, 1960.
Follow Me (McKee). New York, Random House, 1960; London, Hale, 1961.
Certain Sleep (McKee). New York, Random House, 1961; London, Hale, 1962.
The Day She Died (McKee). New York, Random House, 1962; London, Hale, 1963.

Novels as Kieran Abbey

Run with the Hare. New York, Scribner, 1941.
And Let the Coffin Pass. New York, Scribner, 1942.
Beyond the Dark. New York, Scribner, 1944.

Uncollected Short Stories

"The Perilous Journey," in *Mike Shayne Mystery Magazine* (New York), May 1962.
"The Phonograph Murder," in *Anthology 1965,* edited by Ellery Queen. New York, Davis, 1964.

* * *

In her famous detective series featuring Inspector Christopher McKee, Helen Reilly's most effective devices are point of view and characterization. The reader often shares McKee's viewpoint, searching with him to identify key clues; at other times, Reilly alternates the point of view between McKee and another sympathetic character. On other occasions, she indulges in a more Holmesian technique, and the Inspector keeps his own counsel until the dramatic disclosure scene. All these variations are deftly handled, and, combined with Reilly's ability to characterize swiftly and vividly, often using physical traits as symbols for personality, they produce brisk, readable, exciting fiction.

McKee, the Scotsman of the "short, thick eyelashes," well-worn tweeds, brown eyes, and lined face, is the head of the Manhattan Homicide Squad. It is instinct that focuses McKee's attention on key clues, hunches which often taunt him about an important observation hovering just outside his grasp, and hard perceptive detective work which brings him to his accurate and often amazing conclusions. Another of his tools is his keen ability to understand people; he trusts his judgments about suspects and is clear-headed in his evaluations. While he has an eye for a pretty woman, he finds beauty alone an empty trait and saves his sympathy for women whose physical charm is enhanced by vitality and intelligence. The Inspector is aided by a well-conceived and neatly developed cast of continuing characters: District Attorney Dwyer, stubborn and ambitious; Peirson, a good witness and an able officer; Dr. Fernandez, assistant medical examiner, in discussions with whom McKee tests his theories; and Lucy Sturm, nurse and undercover agent. One of Reilly's best strokes is Todhunter—unobtrusive, seemingly innocuous, but a clever detective—who is featured prominently in *Compartment K* while McKee detects long-distance.

Female characters are important throughout Reilly's work. Her portraits of older women are intriguing, for she frequently involves them in late romances, and they are generally attractive people of stamina and perception. The central characters are usually young women of sensitive consciences and high honor who feel bound to keep even impulsive or unwise promises. They tend to be independent and self-supporting and often know things, sometimes by chance, that place them in jeopardy either as chief suspects or crucial witnesses. Their tangled love affairs provide subplots; their well-meant allegiance to the wrong men and their struggle to subdue growing passion for other attractive males are made believable and interesting. Most of these suitors are suspects, and some are shrouded in mystery. The ill-chosen fiancés are handsome but weak; the true matches are strong and attractive but brusque; all conceal essential facts as well as their motives. All these factors lend a touch of the gothic to the novels.

Though the books stress tough, grim, realistic police procedure (some of which would no longer be acceptable methodology), they do not feature the mean streets, but rather focus upon closed circles of upper-class suspects, members of wealthy, extended families. The complex family relationships, the money, and often the false identities of some members are motives for duplicity and crime as well as for protectiveness and affection. Both sets of motives lend complication to the well-made plots whose melodramatic incidents are balanced by the even tone of the writing.

Reilly also wrote good, non-series mysteries such as the early *The Thirty-First Bullfinch*, which demonstrates that a local sheriff can be clever though unassuming. All told, her work makes a major contribution to the genre and reveals an able writer with an excellent grasp of police methods.

—Jane S. Bakerman

RENDELL, Ruth (Barbara, née Grasemann); also writes as Barbara Vine. British. Born in London, 17 February 1930. Educated at Loughton High School, Essex. Married Donald Rendell in 1950 (divorced 1975); remarried in 1977; one son. Reporter and sub-editor, Express and Independent Newspapers, West Essex, 1948–52. Recipient: Mystery Writers of America Edgar Allan Poe award, for short story, 1975, 1984; Crime Writers Association Silver Dagger award, 1984; Gold Dagger award, 1976, 1986, 1987; Arts Council National Book award, 1981; Arts Council bursary, 1981; Popular Culture Association award, 1983. Agent: Peters Fraser and Dunlop, 5th Floor, The Chambers, Chelsea Harbour, Lots Road, London SW10 0XF. Address: Nussteads, Polstead, Colchester CO6 5DN, England.

CRIME PUBLICATIONS

Novels (series: Detective Chief Inspector Reginald Wexford)

From Doon with Death (Wexford). London, Hutchinson, 1964; New York, Doubleday, 1965.
To Fear a Painted Devil. London, Long, and New York, Doubleday, 1965.
Vanity Dies Hard. London, Long, 1965; as *In Sickness and in Health,* New York, Doubleday, 1966; as *Vanity Dies Hard,* New York, Beagle, 1970.
A New Lease of Death (Wexford). London, Long, and New York, Doubleday, 1967; as *Sins of the Fathers,* New York, Ballantine, 1970.
Wolf to the Slaughter (Wexford). London, Long, 1967; New York, Doubleday, 1968.
The Secret House of Death. London, Long, 1968; New York, Doubleday, 1969.
The Best Man to Die (Wexford). London, Long, 1969; New York, Doubleday, 1970.
A Guilty Thing Surprised (Wexford). London, Hutchinson, and New York, Doubleday, 1970.
No More Dying Then (Wexford). London, Hutchinson, 1971; New York, Doubleday, 1972.
One Across, Two Down. London, Hutchinson, and New York, Doubleday, 1971.
Murder Being Done Once (Wexford). London, Hutchinson, and New York, Doubleday, 1972.
Some Lie and Some Die (Wexford). London, Hutchinson, and New York, Doubleday, 1973.
The Face of Trespass. London, Hutchinson, and New York, Doubleday, 1974.
Shake Hands for Ever (Wexford). London, Hutchinson, and New York, Doubleday, 1975.
A Demon in My View. London, Hutchinson, 1976; New York, Doubleday, 1977.
A Judgement in Stone. London, Hutchinson, 1977; New York, Doubleday, 1978.
A Sleeping Life (Wexford). London, Hutchinson, and New York, Doubleday, 1978.
Make Death Love Me. London, Hutchinson, and New York, Doubleday, 1979.
The Lake of Darkness. London, Hutchinson, and New York, Doubleday, 1980.
Put On by Cunning (Wexford). London, Hutchinson, 1981; as *Death Notes,* New York, Pantheon, 1981.
Master of the Moor. London, Hutchinson, and New York, Pantheon, 1982.
The Speaker of Mandarin (Wexford). London, Hutchinson, and New York, Pantheon, 1983.
The Killing Doll. London, Hutchinson, and New York, Pantheon, 1984.

The Tree of Hands.   London, Hutchinson, 1984; New York, Pantheon, 1985.
An Unkindness of Ravens (Wexford).   London, Hutchinson, and New York, Pantheon, 1985.
Live Flesh.   London, Hutchinson, and New York, Pantheon, 1986.
A Warning to the Curious.   London, Hutchinson, 1987.
Heartstones (with *Cuts* by Malcolm Bradbury).   London, Hutchinson, and New York, Harper, 1987.
Talking to Strange Men.   London, Hutchinson, and New York, Harper, 1987.
Wexford: An Omnibus.   London, Hutchinson, 1988.
The Veiled One (Wexford).   London, Hutchinson, and New York, Pantheon, 1988.
The Bridesmaid.   London, Hutchinson, and New York, Mysterious Press, 1989.
Going Wrong.   London, Hutchinson, 1990.

Novels as Barbara Vine

The Dark-Adapted Eye.   London, Viking, and New York, Bantam, 1986.
A Fatal Inversion.   London, Viking, and New York, Bantam, 1987.
The House of Stairs.   London, Viking, and New York, Crown, 1989.
Gallowglass.   London, Viking, and New York, Crown, 1990.

Short Stories

The Fallen Curtain and Other Stories.   London, Hutchinson, and New York, Doubleday, 1976.
Means of Evil and Other Stories.   London, Hutchinson, 1979; New York, Doubleday, 1980.
The Fever Tree and Other Stories.   London, Hutchinson, and New York, Pantheon, 1982.
The New Girl Friend.   London, Hutchinson, 1985; New York, Pantheon, 1986.
Collected Short Stories.   London, Hutchinson, 1987; New York, Pantheon, 1988.

OTHER PUBLICATIONS

Other

Ruth Rendell's Suffolk, photographs by Paul Bowden. London, Muller, 1989.

Editor, *A Warning to the Curious: The Ghost Stories of M.R. James.*   London, Century Hutchinson, 1987.
Editor, with Colin Ward, *Undermining the Central Line.*   London, Chatto and Windus, 1989.

*   *   *

Ruth Rendell has created three distinct groups of novels as well as a number of gripping short stories, earning warm praise from her peers as well as from an army of fans. Both prolific and artistically exacting, she has created a distinguished series of novels about Kingsmarkham police officers, an array of single novels which include some of her best work, and the short stories as Ruth Rendell. In the late 1980's she introduced the pseudonymous Barbara Vine, whose voice differs from the Ruth Rendell voice but whose standards of performance remain just as high.

Rendell first achieved fame with the series featuring Detective Chief Inspector Reg Wexford and his associate,

Mike Burden. The interplay between the central character, Wexford—senior in years and rank, pragmatic, yet imaginative—and Burden—straight-laced and somewhat inflexible—is an important attraction of these works. Their acerbic comradeship, both personally and professionally fulfilling, brings each man vividly to life, and their relationships with their families supply wide-ranging complications and subplots. The recently widowed Burden dominates the action of *No More Dying Then,* in which the mystery centers upon the second child to go missing from the area within a short time. Mike and Gemma Lawrence, single mother of the victim, both grieving profoundly, find comfort in one another's arms, despite Burden's extreme conventionality and Gemma's more "modern" lifestyle. A neat combination of solid detection and coincidence solves the kidnappings, and Burden's bittersweet romance is realistically resolved. *Murder Being Once Done* takes place in London, where Wexford goes to recover from a stroke. The body of a young woman found in Kenbourne Vale Cemetery lures the Chief Inspector into unofficial but intense involvement with several families whose dreams are sadly disrupted. Here, as in *No More Dying Then,* parents' attitudes toward their children are a central theme. Indeed, family interactions are a frequent theme in Rendell's work, and the Wexford and Burden families not only compare and contrast with one another but also with families of victims and criminals.

Parental influence is thematically important in a number of other Rendell novels as well. *A Demon in My View,* considers the burden of guilt and self-distrust borne by Arthur Johnson, "sold" by his mother and reared by a strict, cold aunt. A successful serial killer, Arthur constructs a narrow but safe routine which includes fanatic attention to the details of daily life—and the periodic strangulation of a shop-window mannequin he keeps at hand—until the innocent intrusion of Anthony Johnson, a neighbor, destroys Arthur's control. Rendell's trademark irony permeates the powerful conclusion.

Like Arthur Johnson, Eunice Parchman in *A Judgement in Stone* reveals effects of her upbringing throughout a disastrous adulthood. A handy dogsbody for her feckless parents, she grows up illiterate and without affection. Such extreme intellectual and emotional isolation makes Eunice profoundly suspicious of the lively, literate family for whom she keeps house and fairly easy prey for Joan Smith, amoral, mad, and dangerous. Here, Rendell compares Joan's manic religiosity with the dreamy mysticism of Giles Mont, teenaged son of Eunice's victims.

Giles, one of Rendell's most interesting characters, is a privileged youngster who exists worlds away from his mother and stepfather, even though he dwells in their household. Fascinated with language, religion, and his stepsister, Melinda Coverdale, Giles is preoccupied with his studies, his imagination, and his fantasies. Similarly, important young characters in *Talking to Strange Men* are at least theoretically close to their families but conduct wholly separate, secret lives. Mungo Cameron heads a gang of schoolboy "spies" taking part in a complex, absorbing game until John Creevy, divorced and asocial, and a traitorous gameplayer transform fun into disenchantment. Another player, Charles Mabledene, tests his courage by tempting a pederast. This study of the loss of innocence compares adult manipulations to children's imitative games with searing effect. In *The Bridesmaid,* a young woman's self-indulgent fantasies exact a terrible toll; like John Creevy, Senta is lost in love and too immature to grasp the difference between her attitudes and those of others.

The Barbara Vine novels examine the impact of past crimes upon a complex present. In *A Dark-Adapted Eye,* Faith Severn attempts to uncover the facts of the 30-year-old murder for which her aunt was executed. After 10 years of silence and concealment, Adam Verne-Smith learns that the crime which climaxed a youthful summer adventure is under investigation; in *A Fatal Inversion*, the details of that summer and of the lives of its survivors (some of whom cling willfully to childish passions) are revealed. In *The House of Stairs*, Elizabeth Vetch exploits her widowed aunt, Cosette, and soon, a number of hangers-on invade Cosette's home, capitalizing on her desire for youth, affection, and admiration. The open ending is tantalizing yet completely satisfying.

Clearly, obsessive love and an individual's failure or inability to mature are frequent motifs in the Rendell-Vine canon, always illuminated by detailed, absorbing characterization and enhanced with beautifully developed suspense.

—Jane S. Bakerman

RESNICOW, Herbert. American. Born in New York City, 28 May 1921. Educated at the Polytechnic Institute of Brooklyn, B.A. in civil engineering 1947, and post-graduate studies in structural engineering. Served in the United States Army Corps of Engineers in China, Burma, and India: sergeant. Married Melly E. Resnicow in 1946; two sons and two daughters. Architect and engineer on many buildings and projects in New York; Vice-President, Narco Construction Corporation, and Modular Technics Corporation; President, HBR Holding Corporation, Harbinger Development Corporation, and West-View Hill Corporation; partner, Resnicow and Kornfeld, Engineers and Consultants. Since 1986 full-time writer. Agent: Sharon Jarvis, 260 Willard Avenue, Staten Island, New York 10314. Address: 107 Weeks Road, East Williston, New York 11596, U.S.A.

CRIME PUBLICATIONS

Novels (series: Ed and Warren Baer; Crossword; Alexander Magnus and Norma Gold; Sport)

The Gold Solution. New York, St. Martin's Press, 1983.
The Gold Deadline. New York, St. Martin's Press, 1984.
The Gold Frame. New York, St. Martin's Press, 1984.
Murder Across and Down (Crossword). New York, Ballantine 1985.
The Seventh Crossword. New York, Ballantine, 1985.
The Gold Curse. New York, St. Martin's Press, 1986.
The Crossword Code. New York, Ballantine, 1986.
Murder at the Superbowl, with Fran Tarkenton (Sport). New York, Morrow, 1986.
The Crossword Legacy. New York, Ballantine, 1987.
The Crossword Hunt. New York, Ballantine, 1987.
The Dead Room (Baer). New York, Dodd Mead, 1987.
The Gold Gamble. New York, St. Martin's Press, 1988.
Bean Ball, with Tom Seaver (Sport). New York, Morrow, 1989.
The World Cup Murder, with Pele (Sport). New York, Wynwood Press, 1989.
The Hot Place (Baer). New York, St. Martin's Press, 1990.

Uncollected Short Stories

"Greater Love Than This," in *Distant Danger*, New York, Wynwood Press, 1988.
"Head up," in *Hardboiled* (Rockford, Illinois), Spring 1989.

"The Odds," "True Witness," "Sub Rosa," "Typecasting," "D.W.I.," all in *Detective Story Magazine* (New York), nos. 3–6, 7, n.d.
"The Christmas Bear," in *Alfred Hitchcock's Mystery Magazine* (New York), January 1990.
"Filial Gifts," in *Alfred Hitchcock's Mystery Magazine* (New York), April 1990.
"The Moonstone Earrings," in *Alfred Hitchcock's Mystery Magazine* (New York), May 1990.
"Head Up," in *New Detective* (New York), August 1990.
"Deconstruction," in *Crosscurrents* (Westlake Village, California), September 1990.

OTHER PUBLICATIONS

Other

"The Third Conflict," in *The Armchair Detective* (New York), Spring 1984.
"The Whodunnit List," in *The Armchair Detective* (New York), Fall 1985.
"How I Wrote *Murder at the Superbowl*," in *Mystery Readers of America Journal* (Berkeley, California), Summer 1987.
"The Birth of an Ethnic Detective," in *Mystery Readers of America Journal* (Berkeley, California), Fall 1987.
"By You, Zabars in Not a Region," in *Mystery Readers of America Journal* (Berkeley, California), Winter 1987.
"You Could Look It Up," in *Mystery Readers of America Journal* (Berkeley, California), Spring 1988.
". . . But I Know What I Like," in *Mystery Readers of America Journal* (Berkeley, California), Summer 1988.
"Fatal Oversights," in *The Armchair Detective* (New York), Summer 1988.
"It's a Jungle in There," in *Mystery Readers of America Journal* (Berkeley, California), Fall 1988.
"Smoke and Mirrors: Magic and Spells," in *Mystery Readers of America Journal* (Berkeley, California), Spring 1989.
"This Job Is Murder," in *Mystery Readers of America Journal* (Berkeley, California), Summer 1989.
"Why I Write What I Write the Way I Write It," in *Mystery Readers of America Annual* (Berkeley, California), 1989.
"Doing It the Hard Way," in *The Crime File* (Bonita, California), December 1989.
"Reason, Charm, and Wit," in *Mystery Writers Annual* (Berkeley, California), 1990.

*

Herbert Resnicow comments:
By definition, a mystery involves a puzzle, something made to be solved. A mystery story implies an ethic: that all the clues needed to solve the *fair* puzzle be presented openly, that the puzzle be soluble by deduction or by rational induction, and not by beating a confession out of a villain or shooting a blond bimbo through the belly button. There must be a unique solution that satisfies *all* the elements of the puzzle and leaves the world of the story orderly again, the good guys winning (it *is* fiction, after all), the bad guys punished, and justice triumphant.

A mystery must be a good story, with a puzzle as an essential element. I like a lean story, one not padded with descriptions of the streets the car chase takes us through, or of the sleazy bars the PI frequents, of lovingly detailed blood-spilling and bone-breaking, or digressions into detailed sexual fantasies. Rather than travelogue filler, I prefer, 'He sat at the bistro's outside table, breathing the smell of roasting chestnuts, slowly sipping

Pernod, and watching the pretty girls go by.' Does a reader need more to set the city, the season, the mood of the character? In my stories there is little sex (the protagonists are usually married) and only as much violence as is required to subdue the murderer.

* * *

Almost alone among the new writers to debut in the 1980's, Herbert Resnicow emphasizes the puzzle, focusing on analysis of a criminal problem as determinedly as the most formal products of the Golden Age 1920's–1930's. He has even gone to the extent of propounding rules for detective fiction in the manner of (and at greater length than) S.S. Van Dine and Father Ronald Knox. Resnicow is a specialized taste, but to the reader who shares his pleasure in the conventions that make the detective story unique, he can be recommended unreservedly.

Resnicow also emphasizes family relationships: his principal sleuthing teams are husband and wife (Alexander and Norma Gold) and father and son (Ed and Warren Baer). The author is clearly fascinated with how things work, resulting in a variety of detailed specialized backgrounds. In the two main series, the stories are told in conversational first person (by Norma Gold or Ed Baer), are set in a New York Jewish milieu, and are mostly driven by dialogue. Both the narrators and some of the characters are prone to garrulousness, and a detractor could justifiably call the books talkie. Much of the conversation concerns various interpretations of evidence. Standard features of the mystery as a game are used joyously and unapologetically. Suspense is often created by setting some kind of deadline for the detective.

The Edgar-nominated *The Gold Solution* sets the tone for what is to come. Engineer Alexander Gold has always been a problem solver, but he fears he lost brain cells in his recent near-fatal heart attack. When celebrated architect Roger Allen Talbott is murdered in circumstances that suggest only young Jonathan Candell (engaged to the daughter of family friends) could have done it, Gold takes up the practice of armchair detection with semi-reluctant assistance from wife Norma. The novel features not only a Carr-like impossible crime but an extremely elaborate dying message and a classical gathering of the suspects in which the whole room is Mirandized before Gold starts his summation. Along the way, there is also some pointed satire on the world of architecture.

Other arts are the subject in subsequent Gold cases: ballet in *The Gold Deadline*, painting in *The Gold Frame*, opera in *The Gold Curse*, and musical comedy in *The Gold Gamble*. The latter, involving a Broadway revival of *Guys and Dolls*, is an especially strong entry, with the timing of the entrances and exits of the various characters in the show vital to reconstructing the crime. The technical and financial side of the production is given greater connection than in most other theatrical mysteries.

Resnicow's second series, beginning with *Murder Across and Down*, is less notable but in its way just as ingenious. Each of the paperback originals about retired lawyer Giles Sullivan and college administrator Isabel Macintosh comes equipped with five crossword puzzles by Henry Hook, and one of the main interests of the series is seeing how many ways Resnicow can find of making a set of puzzles the crucial element in a murder mystery plot. That the gimmick unsurprisingly adds to the sense of artificiality does not reduce the enjoyability of the series.

The Baer series comes closest to equalling the Gold books in quality and human interest. Ed Baer's position as general partner in a venture-capital company gives him the potential to solve murders in commercial backgrounds as varied as Emma

Lathen's John Putnam Thatcher. *The Dead Room* involves a locked-room murder in a unique setting: an anechoic chamber used by a hi-fi company to test its equipment. *The Hot Place* concerns closed-circle murder in a country club steam room. Both are cleverly plotted, but the father-son relationship gives the books an extra resonance. The Baer novels may ultimately surpass the Golds as Resnicow's top line.

Resnicow's series of sports mysteries, ostensibly written in collaboration with famed athletes Fran Tarkenton, Pele, and Tom Seaver, set him another challenge: making the game action integral to the story and puzzle. The detective is sports reporter and former gymnastics champion Marcus Aurelius Burr, who constantly battles a typically irascible editor, Julius Witter. Resnicow's sports mysteries are more steeped in game strategy than any ever written: in fact, a frequent problem is the spectacle of players, coaches, sportswriters, and police telling each other things for the reader's benefit they clearly must already know. The mystery puzzles tend to be somewhat slighter than in Resnicow's other books, and it is doubtful a reader uninterested in the subject sport would be drawn to them.

The sports and crossword books are lesser series not because they are plotted any less meticulously—indeed, they present more difficult technical challenges—but because they seem one step farther removed from real life. However artificial the situations they find themselves in, the characters in the Gold and Baer books seem more real presumably because they come from a milieu the author knows well and feels comfortable in. The reader senses there is more of Resnicow in Gold or Baer than in Burr or Sullivan.

—Jon L. Breen

REYNOLDS, William J. American. Born in Omaha, Nebraska, 17 December 1956. Educated at Creighton University, Omaha, 1975–79, B.A. in political science 1979. Married Peggy Blankenfeld Reynolds in 1981; one daughter. Managing editor, *The Ambassador* magazine, St. Paul, Minnesota, 1979–84; vice president and creative director, Stafford Advertising, Sioux Falls, South Dakota, 1986–87. Agent: Robert Lescher, Lescher and Lescher Ltd., 67 Irving Place, New York, New York, 10003. Address: 1000 South Third Avenue, Sioux Falls, South Dakota 57105, U.S.A.

CRIME PUBLICATIONS

Novels (series: Nebraska in all books)

The Nebraska Quotient. New York, St. Martin's Press, 1984; London, Macmillan, 1986.
Moving Targets. New York, St. Martin's Press, 1986; London, Macmillan, 1987.
Money Trouble. New York, Putnam, and London, Macmillan, 1988.
Things Invisible. New York, Putnam, and London, Macmillan, 1989.
The Naked Eye. New York, Putnam, 1990.

Uncollected Short Stories

"The Two Ninety-Nine Alibi," in *Alfred Hitchcock's Mystery Magazine* (New York), February 1986.

"Guilt Enough to Go Round," in *Alfred Hitchcock's Mystery Magazine* (New York), September 1986.
"Hit and Run," in *Alfred Hitchcock's Mystery Magazine* (New York), December 1987.

*

William J. Reynolds comments:

While I hope my work speaks for itself, a brief explanation or introduction may be helpful. Especially to me.

Although I never considered myself a great devotee of detective or mystery fiction—I read mysteries along with everything else—I found myself, following my graduation from college, beginning a new job in an unfamiliar city and reading or rereading a great deal of Hammett, Chandler, et al.: I also came upon Robert B. Parker and other modern-day practitioners of the hardboiled private-eye novel. I decided, for some reason, to have a little fun with the genre—which tends to take itself pretty seriously—and the result was *The Nebraska Quotient*. which St. Martin's Press published in 1984 and which was nominated by the Private Eye Writers of America for a Shamus award as best first novel. *The Nebraska Quotient* introduced a private-eye protagonist known only as Nebraska, who operates in my hometown of Omaha in the American Midwest. The book was just short of parody: the not-quite hardboiled hero encounters monsters, pornographers, and blackmailers; gets hit over the head more often than Philip Marlowe could ever have hoped for; and doesn't have sense enough to keep his mouth shut whenever a wisecrack occurs to him. Good clean fun.

It had not occurred to me that this might be the first book in the series. If it had, I would have done some things differently—beginning with my hero's unusual name, the genesis of which I'm forced to explain in every book.

Because I was not thinking series, anyone who begins with *The Nebraska Quotient* and reads through to *The Naked Eye* will immediately see that *The Nebraska Quotient* stands apart. True, it introduces the hero and one or two other characters who appear again later. But the *series* doesn't really begin until the second book, *Moving Targets,* where I began unloading some of the baggage I encumbered myself with in the first book, and began to move away from the brink of parody. The books and the character (and perhaps their author) have matured and sobered somewhat since then, but Nebraska is and always will be only medium-hard boiled and the comic or parodic overtones will remain. They are essential to the character, who can never be merely a landlocked Travis McGee.

The books, I think, are best suited to readers who don't consider the detective genre (or life) deadly serious stuff.

*   *   *

Many years ago, in an article on writing detective fiction, someone (it might well have been Chandler) observed that only a few cities in the United States are good "story towns," that is, appropriate settings for crime novels. After all, this theory goes, the detective cannot operate in a vacuum. Sufficient population is required in order to provide the criminal with anonymity, and there must be enough interesting locales to relieve the tedium of the investigation. New York, Chicago, Los Angeles, and San Francisco are the most obvious examples. Although this observation is still true to a great extent, an increasing number of writers are using places within the "great fly-over" as settings for their novels. The reader will no doubt think of many others, but Tony Hillerman, K. C. Constantine, and Max Allan Collins will serve to make the point. William J. Reynolds is a worthy member of this group.

Although it does possess a certain charm, it is difficult to imagine many places less glamorous than Omaha, Nebraska, the setting for all five of Reynolds's books about a former private eye and present freelance writer known only as Nebraska. Lacking the instant glamor of place, Reynolds relies upon character development, meticulous plotting, interesting situations, and realistic, witty dialogue to provide the variety necessary to sustain the reader's interest.

As in every good series, Reynolds develops his central character by gradually revealing more about him in each successive book. In *The Nebraska Quotient,* for instance, we learn that he had given up his private detective agency six years previously and is now a struggling writer who survives by selling an occasional magazine article and by accepting infrequent investigative assignments while he works on The Book. Nebraska is deeply ambivalent about his choice of profession. Although devoted to his writing, he nevertheless enjoys the stimulation he receives from the danger associated with his work as a detective. Besides, as he points out on numerous occasions, he can always earn enough money on a case to satisfy his modest needs, and his chronic shortage of funds invariably leads him to accept the jobs that are referred to him, usually by his attorney friend, Mike Kennerly.

Nebraska enjoys a vivid fantasy life, and in *Money Trouble* expresses a desire to be "the Hammett of the Heartland, the Chandler of the Cornbelt, the Macdonald of the Midwest." Yet at the same time he admires and tries to emulate tough Sam Spade and compassionate Lew Archer. Thus, he is able to do both at once: write and be a detective. Lest we think him childish, however, it should be noted that these fantasies occur at whimsical moments when he is reflecting upon his life, and serve as a not-so-subtle reminder that we are witnessing the activities of a fictional character. Paradoxically, the mention of these authors and characters, among several others, lends a touch of verisimilitude. If Nebraska reads detective fiction then *he* must be "real." This is an ancient but successful device; neither Shakespeare in *Hamlet* nor Cervantes in *Don Quixote* was the first to use it.

Nebraska is separated, but not divorced, tough in the Chandler tradition, but not nearly so hardboiled as he would like to think. Just as ambivalent about his personal life as he is about his profession, he still cares for his wife and freely accepts her whenever she returns to Omaha after one of her frequent absences, understanding that she is "searching for her identity." Although he has an occasional sexual encounter with women he meets on his cases, such as with Carolyn Longo in *Money Trouble,* or Sharon Fahy in *The Naked Eye,* he does not exploit women. He is involved in an "exclusive" relationship with psychologist Koosje Van der Beek, although in *The Naked Eye* they are experiencing some problems, and it is unclear where the affair is headed. His love life is further complicated by the presence of Kim Banner, a detective on the Omaha Police Division, whom he meets in *Moving Targets.* She passes in and out of his life, and although there is always considerable sexual tension between them, it seldom leads to physical contact. Once again, his characteristic ambivalence comes to the surface and he is unable to decide between the two.

His writing is no less complex. Once The Book is accepted for publication, he plunges into The Next Book with fervor. But then disaster strikes: as soon as The Book is published, to decent reviews and with modest commercial success, he develops a horrible case of writer's block, "some kind of postpartum depression," that takes months to resolve. In fact, we learn in *The Naked Eye* that it is still only three-quarters finished, "or four-fifths, maybe."

Although the major strengths of this series are the main character and the sprightly dialogue, Reynolds is also adept at plot construction. They are complex, yet there are sufficient clues to enable the observant reader to arrive at the solution almost as soon as Nebraska. One of the most intriguing plot elements is the presence of the mafia. When one thinks about organized crime, neither Omaha, Nebraska, nor the the twin cities of Minneapolis/St. Paul, the setting for *The Naked Eye*, comes immediately to mind. But if Reynolds is to be believed (and he certainly makes it seem plausible), the mafia is alive and well in the Midwest.

The books are fast-paced, exciting, and with a humor that often borders on parody, yet never quite goes that far. Reynolds is a serious practitioner of the hard-boiled detective genre, and each of his books is better than the last. He has polished his craft to a fine sheen, and deserves all the critical praise that has come his way.

—Dale Carter

RHODE, John. Pseudonym for Cecil John Charles Street; also wrote as Miles Burton. British. Born in 1884. Career Army Officer: Major, Military Cross. O.B.E. (Officer, Order of the British Empire). *Died in January 1965.*

CRIME PUBLICATIONS

Novels (series: Dr. Lancelot Priestley)

A.S.F.: The Story of a Great Conspiracy. London, Bles, 1924; as *The White Menace,* New York, McBride, 1926.
The Double Florin. London, Bles, 1924.
The Alarm. London, Bles, 1925.
The Paddington Mystery (Priestley). London, Bles, 1925.
Dr. Priestley's Quest. London, Bles, 1926.
The Ellerby Case (Priestley). London, Bles, 1926; New York, Dodd Mead, 1927.
Mademoiselle from Armentières. London, Bles, 1927.
The Murders in Praed Street (Priestley). London, Bles, and New York, Dodd Mead, 1928.
Tragedy at the Unicorn (Priestley). London, Bles, and New York, Dodd Mead, 1928.
The House on Tollard Ridge (Priestley). London, Bles, and New York, Dodd Mead, 1929.
The Davidson Case (Priestley). London, Bles, 1929; as *Murder at Bratton Grange,* New York, Dodd Mead, 1929.
Peril at Cranbury Hall (Priestley). London, Bles, and New York, Dodd Mead, 1930.
Pinehurst. London, Bles, 1930; as *Dr. Priestley Investigates,* New York, Dodd Mead, 1930.
The Hanging Woman (Priestley). London, Collins, and New York, Dodd Mead, 1931.
The Floating Admiral, with others. London, Hodder and Stoughton, 1931; New York, Doubleday, 1932.
Tragedy on the Line (Priestley). London, Collins, and New York, Dodd Mead, 1931.
Mystery at Greycombe Farm (Priestley). London, Collins, 1932; as *The Fire at Greycombe Farm,* New York, Dodd Mead, 1932.
Dead Men at the Folly (Priestley). London, Collins, and New York, Dodd Mead, 1932.
The Claverton Mystery (Priestley). London, Collins, 1933; as *The Claverton Affair,* New York, Dodd Mead, 1933.

The Motor Rally Mystery. London, Collins, 1933; as *Dr. Priestley Lays a Trap,* New York, Dodd Mead, 1933.
Ask a Policeman, with others. London, Barker, and New York, Morrow, 1933.
The Venner Crime (Priestley). London, Odhams Press, 1933; New York, Dodd Mead, 1934.
Poison for One (Priestley). London, Collins, and New York, Dodd Mead, 1934.
The Robthorne Mystery (Priestley). London, Collins, and New York, Dodd Mead, 1934.
Shot at Dawn (Priestley). London, Collins, 1934; New York, Dodd Mead, 1935.
The Corpse in the Car (Priestley). London, Collins, and New York, Dodd Mead, 1935.
Hendon's First Case (Priestley). London, Collins, and New York, Dodd Mead, 1935.
Mystery at Olympia (Priestley). London, Collins, 1935; as *Murder at the Motor Show,* New York, Dodd Mead, 1936.
Death at Breakfast (Priestley). London, Collins, and New York, Dodd Mead, 1936.
In Face of the Verdict (Priestley). London, Collins, 1936; as *In the Face of the Verdict,* New York, Dodd Mead, 1940.
Death in the Hop Fields (Priestley). London, Collins, 1937; as *The Harvest Murder,* New York, Dodd Mead, 1937.
Death on the Board (Priestley). London, Collins, 1937; as *Death Sits on the Board,* New York, Dodd Mead, 1937.
Proceed with Caution (Priestley). London, Collins, 1937; as *Body Unidentified,* New York, Dodd Mead, 1938.
The Bloody Tower (Priestley). London, Collins, 1938; as *The Tower of Evil,* New York, Dodd Mead, 1938.
Invisible Weapons (Priestley). London, Collins, and New York, Dodd Mead, 1938.
Death on Sunday (Priestley). London, Collins, 1939; as *The Elm Tree Murder,* New York, Dodd Mead, 1939.
Death Pays a Dividend (Priestley). London, Collins, and New York, Dodd Mead, 1939.
Drop to His Death, with Carter Dickson. London, Heinemann, 1939; as *Fatal Descent,* New York, Dodd Mead, 1939.
Death on the Boat-Train (Priestley). London, Collins, and New York, Dodd Mead, 1940.
Murder at Lilac Cottage (Priestley). London, Collins, and New York, Dodd Mead, 1940.
Death at the Helm (Priestley). London, Collins, and New York, Dodd Mead, 1941.
They Watched by Night (Priestley). London, Collins, 1941; as *Signal for Death,* New York, Dodd Mead, 1941.
The Fourth Bomb (Priestley). London, Collins, and New York, Dodd Mead, 1942.
Night Exercise. London, Collins, 1942; as *Dead of the Night,* New York, Dodd Mead, 1942.
Dead on the Track (Priestley). London, Collins, and New York, Dodd Mead, 1943.
Men Die at Cyprus Lodge (Priestley). London, Collins, 1943; New York, Dodd Mead, 1944.
Vegetable Duck (Priestley). London, Collins, 1944; as *Too Many Suspects,* New York, Dodd Mead, 1945.
Death Invades the Meeting (Priestley). London, Collins, and New York, Dodd Mead, 1944.
The Bricklayer's Arms (Priestley). London, Collins, 1945; as *Shadow of a Crime,* New York, Dodd Mead, 1945.
Death in Harley Street (Priestley). London, Bles, and New York, Dodd Mead, 1946.
The Lake House (Priestley). London, Bles, 1946; as *The Secret of the Lake House,* New York, Dodd Mead, 1946.
Death of an Author (Priestley). London, Bles, 1947; New York, Dodd Mead, 1948.

Nothing But the Truth (Priestley). London, Bles, 1947; as *Experiment in Crime,* New York, Dodd Mead, 1947.

The Paper Bag (Priestley). London, Bles, 1948; as *The Links in the Chain,* New York, Dodd Mead, 1948.

The Telephone Call (Priestley). London, Bles, 1948; as *Shadows of an Alibi,* New York, Dodd Mead, 1949.

Blackthorn House (Priestley). London, Bles, and New York, Dodd Mead, 1949.

Up the Garden Path (Priestley). London, Bles, 1949; as *The Fatal Garden,* New York, Dodd Mead, 1949.

Family Affairs (Priestley). London, Bles, 1950; as *The Last Suspect,* New York, Dodd Mead, 1951.

The Two Graphs (Priestley). London, Bles, 1950; as *Double Identities,* New York, Dodd Mead, 1950.

The Secret Meeting (Priestley). London, Bles, 1951; New York, Dodd Mead, 1952.

Dr. Goodwood's Locum (Priestley). London, Bles, 1951; as *The Affair of the Substitute Doctor,* New York, Dodd Mead, 1951.

Death in Wellington Road (Priestley). London, Bles, and New York, Dodd Mead, 1952.

Death at the Dance (Priestley). London, Bles, 1952; New York, Dodd Mead, 1953.

By Registered Post (Priestley). London, Bles, 1953; as *The Mysterious Suspect,* New York, Dodd Mead, 1953.

Death at the Inn (Priestley). London, Bles, 1953; as *The Case of the Forty Thieves,* New York, Dodd Mead, 1954.

Death on the Lawn (Priestley). London, Bles, 1954; New York, Dodd Mead, 1955.

The Dovebury Murders (Priestley). London, Bles, and New York, Dodd Mead, 1954.

Death of a Godmother (Priestley). London, Bles, 1955; as *Delayed Payment,* New York, Dodd Mead, 1956.

The Domestic Agency (Priestley). London, Bles, 1955; as *Grave Matters,* New York, Dodd Mead, 1955.

An Artist Dies (Priestley). London, Bles, 1956; as *Death of an Artist,* New York, Dodd Mead, 1956.

Open Verdict (Priestley). London, Bles, 1956; New York, Dodd Mead, 1957.

Death of a Bridegroom (Priestley). London, Bles, 1957; New York, Dodd Mead, 1958.

Robbery with Violence (Priestley). London, Bles, and New York, Dodd Mead, 1957.

Death Takes a Partner (Priestley). London, Bles, 1958; New York, Dodd Mead, 1959.

Murder at Derivale (Priestley). London, Bles, and New York, Dodd Mead, 1958.

Licensed for Murder (Priestley). London, Bles, 1958; New York, Dodd Mead, 1959.

Three Cousins Die (Priestley). London, Bles, 1959; New York, Dodd Mead, 1960.

The Fatal Pool (Priestley). London, Bles, 1960; New York, Dodd Mead, 1961.

Twice Dead (Priestley). London, Bles, and New York, Dodd Mead, 1960.

The Vanishing Diary (Priestley). London, Bles, and New York, Dodd Mead, 1961.

Novels as Miles Burton (series: Inspector Arnold and Desmond Merrion in all books except *The Hardway Diamonds Mystery* and *Murder at the Moorings*)

The Hardway Diamonds Mystery. London, Collins, and New York, Mystery League, 1930.

The Secret of High Eldersham. London, Collins, 1930; New York, Mystery League, 1931; as *The Mystery of High Eldersham,* Collins, 1933.

The Menace on the Downs. London, Collins, 1931.

The Three Crimes. London, Collins, 1931.

Murder at the Moorings. London, Collins, 1932; New York, Sears, 1934.

Death of Mr. Gantley. London, Collins, 1932.

Death at the Cross-Roads. London, Collins, 1933.

Fate at the Fair. London, Collins, 1933.

Tragedy at the Thirteenth Hole. London, Collins, 1933.

The Charabanc Mystery. London, Collins, 1934.

To Catch a Thief. London, Collins, 1934.

The Devereux Court Mystery. London, Collins, 1935.

The Milk-Churn Murders. London, Collins, 1935; as *The Clue of the Silver Brush,* New York, Doubleday, 1936.

Death in the Tunnel. London, Collins, 1936; as *Dark Is the Tunnel,* New York, Doubleday, 1936.

Murder of a Chemist. London, Collins, 1936.

Where Is Barbara Prentice? London, Collins, 1936; as *The Clue of the Silver Cellar,* New York, Doubleday, 1937.

Death at the Club. London, Collins, 1937; as *The Clue of the Fourteen Keys,* New York, Doubleday, 1937.

Murder in Crown Passage. London, Collins, 1937; as *The Man with the Tattooed Face,* New York, Doubleday, 1937.

Death at Low Tide. London, Collins, 1938.

The Platinum Cat. London, Collins, and New York, Doubleday, 1938.

Death Leaves No Card. London, Collins, 1939.

Mr. Babbacombe Dies. London, Collins, 1939.

Death Takes a Flat. London, Collins, 1940; as *Vacancy with Corpse,* New York, Doubleday, 1941.

Mr. Westerby Missing. London, Collins, and New York, Doubleday, 1940.

Murder in the Coalhole. London, Collins, 1940; as *Written in Dust,* New York, Doubleday, 1940.

Death of Two Brothers. London, Collins, 1941.

Up the Garden Path. London, Collins, 1941; as *Death Visits Downspring,* New York, Doubleday, 1941.

This Undesirable Residence. London, Collins, 1942; as *Death at Ash House,* New York, Doubleday, 1942.

Murder, M.D. London, Collins, 1943; as *Who Killed the Doctor?,* New York, Doubleday, 1943.

Dead Stop. London, Collins, 1943.

Four-Ply Yarn. London, Collins, 1944; as *The Shadow on the Cliff,* New York, Doubleday, 1944.

The Three Corpse Trick. London, Collins, 1944.

Not a Leg to Stand On. London, Collins, and New York, Doubleday, 1945.

Early Morning Murder. London, Collins, 1945; as *Accidents Do Happen,* New York, Doubleday, 1946.

The Cat Jumps. London, Collins, 1946.

Situation Vacant. London, Collins, 1946.

Heir to Lucifer. London, Collins, 1947.

A Will in the Way. London, Collins, and New York, Doubleday, 1947.

Death in Shallow Water. London, Collins, 1948.

Devil's Reckoning. London, Collins, 1948; New York, Doubleday, 1949.

Death Takes the Living. London, Collins, 1949; as *The Disappearing Parson,* New York, Doubleday, 1949.

Look Alive. London, Collins, 1949; New York, Doubleday, 1950.

Ground for Suspicion. London, Collins, 1950.

A Village Afraid. London, Collins, 1950.

Murder Out of School. London, Collins, 1951.

Beware Your Neighbour. London, Collins, 1951.

Murder on Duty. London, Collins, 1952.

Heir to Murder. London, Collins, 1953.

Something to Hide. London, Collins, 1953.

Murder in Absence. London, Collins, 1954.

Unwanted Corpse. London, Collins, 1954.
Murder Unrecognized. London, Collins, 1955.
A Crime in Time. London, Collins, 1955.
Death in a Duffle Coat. London, Collins, 1956.
Found Drowned. London, Collins, 1956.
The Chinese Puzzle. London, Collins, 1957.
The Moth-Watch Murder. London, Collins, 1957.
Death Takes a Detour. London, Collins, 1958.
Bones in the Brickfield. London, Collins, 1958.
Return from the Dead. London, Collins, 1959.
A Smell of Smoke. London, Collins, 1959.
Legacy of Death. London, Collins, 1960.
Death Paints a Picture. London, Collins, 1960.

Uncollected Short Stories

"The Elusive Bullet," in *Great Short Stories of Detection, Mystery and Horror 2,* edited by Dorothy L. Sayers. London, Gollancz, 1931; as *The Second Omnibus of Crime,* New York, Coward McCann, 1932.
"The Vanishing Diamond," in *The Great Book of Thrillers,* edited by H. Douglas Thomson. London, Odhams Press, 1933.
"The Purple Line," in *The Evening Standard Detective Book.* London, Gollancz, 1950.

OTHER PUBLICATIONS as C.J.C. Street

Novel

The Worldly Hope (as F.O.O.). London, Nash, 1917.

Other

With the Guns (as F.O.O.). London, Nash, 1916.
The Making of a Gunner (as F.O.O.). London, Nash, 1916.
The Administration of Ireland (as I.O.). London, Philip Allan, 1921.
Ireland in 1921. London, Philip Allan, 1922.
Rhineland and Ruhr. London, Couldrey, 1923.
Hungary and Democracy. London, Unwin, 1923.
The Treachery of France. London, Philip Allan, 1924.
East of Prague. London, Bles, 1924.
A Hundred Years of Printing 1795–1895. Frome, Somerset, Butler and Tanner, 1927.
Lord Reading. London, Bles, and New York, Stokes, 1928.
Slovakia Past and Present. London, King, 1928.
The Case of Constance Kent. London, Bles, and New York, Scribner, 1928.
President Masaryk. London, Bles, 1930; as *Thomas Masaryk of Czechoslovakia,* New York, Dodd Mead, 1930.

Editor, *Detective Medley.* London, Hutchinson, 1939; shortened version, as *Line-up: A Collection of Crime Stories by Famous Mystery Writers,* New York, Dodd Mead, 1940; as *The Avon Book of Modern Crime Stories,* New York, Avon, 1942.

Translator, *Vauban, Builder of Fortresses,* by Daniel Halévy. London, Bles, 1924.
Translator, *French Headquarters 1915–1918,* by Jean de Pierrefeu. London, Bles, 1924.
Translator, *Captain Cook, Navigator and Discoverer,* by Maurice Thiéry. New York, McBride, 1930.

* * *

John Rhode's novels are of considerable technical competence. The first, *A.S.F.,* was a thriller concerning the cocaine traffic in England. It would be pretentious to suggest that it had any positive social purpose, although it dealt with a genuine problem. At the time, it must have given little promise of the author's successful career to come as a writer of pure detection, and still less of his imminent introduction of a series character of great importance in the field, Dr. Lancelot Priestley.

Priestley was in complete contrast to the urbane young men-about-town then so popular in detective fiction. He had some of the characteristics of Freeman's Dr. Thorndyke and of Professor Van Dusen, "The Thinking Machine" of Jacques Futrelle. An academic, in his later years, with little apparent sense of humour doing much of his detecting through various intermediaries, Priestley passes a comfortable existence in scientific research and in the application of his brilliantly logical mind to criminal problems. He does so with the scientist's lack of passion or emotional involvement, and with neither flair nor liking for the intuitional approach, propounding his solutions in after-dinner conversation with his friends, who gather round him as if in adoration of the Supreme Being. It would be an understatement, therefore, to describe Priestley as a larger-than-life character; he is, however, extremely well drawn by Rhode, whose ability in characterisation was normally limited indeed.

In *The Paddington Mystery* Priestley clears the name of Harold Merefield, who in later books is the Doctor's secretary and son-in-law. Although not recognised as among Rhode's best mysteries, it sets the scene for the series by presenting the biographical background of the regular characters. Of the long series of Priestley novels which followed, it is difficult to single out those of special merit; Rhode was a reliable writer, working to something of a pattern, and in such a case it is always easier to identify the few books which were disappointing or below standard. There are, nevertheless, some with special features that stand out from such a large and uniform output. *The Murders in Praed Street* is not only a good example of early Priestley before he became tied to his armchair in cerebral splendour, but also shows that the multi-murder story does not have to be monotonous and artificial. *The House on Tollard Ridge,* concerning the death of a rich eccentric, is perhaps the best technologically, has a good line of suspense, and (for Rhode) some surprisingly credible romantic interest.

Rhode was supreme in devising unusual methods of murder; one of the most unusual occurs in *The Claverton Mystery,* which also has spiritualism for good measure. He was excellent, too, when presenting murder against a transport or technical background, as in *The Motor Rally Mystery, Mystery at Olympia,* and *Death on the Boat-Train. Hendon's First Case* is not only a first-class story, but introduced Inspector Jimmy Waghorn who was to become Priestley's leg-man. One should not forget, also, that Rhode applied his own powers of reasoning most skilfully to the Julia Wallace murder in *The Telephone Call,* which was a fictionalised but impressive account, and further evidence of his analytical expertise is to be found in his non-fiction volume *The Case of Constance Kent.*

Street's novels under the Miles Burton pseudonym have not received the praise afforded to his work as John Rhode, although they are equally ingenious and carefully plotted. Perhaps Rhode had the advantage because of the presence of Dr. Priestley, a formidable force. Burton had his own series characters, Desmond Merrion and Inspector Arnold, but they never achieved the popularity of Priestley and his retinue. Merrion, regularly called upon to assist the police, does not possess the omnipotence of Priestley; Inspector Arnold, with whom Merrion enjoys a sometimes prickly relationship, is more than equal to the occasion in many of their joint cases. Merrion is a more imaginative and intuitive character than the scientific Priestley, and his manner permits the introduction of some lighter moments than one finds in the Priestley books. Although there is in the Burton books greater depth of characterisation, under neither name did Street permit this to interfere with the development of the plot; the story is everything, the solution of the mystery paramount.

The majority of Burton's novels fall within one of two categories. There are those set in the countryside or at the seaside, with murder of the domestic variety or associated with other crimes such as smuggling. Good examples are *The Secret of High Eldersham*, with witchcraft as the central theme; *The Chinese Puzzle*, with some unusual occurrences in an English port; and *Legacy of Death*, with its well-drawn setting of a convalescent home. In the second category are novels depicting Merrion's wartime adventures in counter-espionage. *Death Visits Downspring* and *Four-Ply Yarn* are both enthralling and have more activity than most of Burton's stories. It is difficult with Burton, as with Rhode, to name his best books. High on the list, however, are *Death in the Tunnel*, one of the best railway detective novels, and *Death Leaves No Card*, a nicely contrived solo case for Inspector Arnold.

The works of Rhode and Burton deserve to be remembered as good examples of the workmanlike and traditional type of detective fiction always so popular. Although unnecessarily pedantic at times, they gave readers what they wanted and what they expected. Some may now appear dated, particularly when an enlightened modern readership considers Priestley's pseudo-scientific utterances. Nevertheless, the inventiveness and direct style of Rhode/Burton have earned the lingering affection of many readers on both sides of the Atlantic.

—Melvyn Barnes

———

RICE, Craig. Pseudonym for Georgiana Ann Randolph; also wrote as Ruth Malone; Daphne Sanders; Michael Venning. American. Born in Chicago, Illinois, 5 June 1908. Educated privately. Marriages included: Lawrence Lipton in 1939 (divorced 1948); H.W. DeMott, Jr.; two daughters and one son. Journalist, 1925–30; radio writer and producer, 1931–38; freelance writer from 1938. *Died 28 August 1957.*

CRIME PUBLICATIONS

Novels (series: John J. Malone and the Justuses; Bingo Riggs and Handsome Kusak)

8 Faces at 3 (Malone and Justuses). New York, Simon and Schuster, and London, Eyre and Spottiswoode, 1939; as *Death at Three*, London, Cherry Tree, 1941.
The Corpse Steps Out (Malone and Justuses). New York, Simon and Schuster, and London, Eyre and Spottiswoode, 1940.
The Wrong Murder. New York, Simon and Schuster, 1940; London, Eyre and Spottiswoode, 1942.
The Right Murder (Malone and Justuses). New York, Simon and Schuster, 1941; London, Eyre and Spottiswoode, 1948.
Trial by Fury (Malone and Justuses). New York, Simon and Schuster, 1941; London, Hammond, 1950.
The Big Midget Murders (Malone and Justuses). New York, Simon and Schuster, 1942.

The Sunday Pigeon Murders (Riggs and Kusak). New York, Simon and Schuster, 1942; London, Nicholson and Watson, 1948.
Telefair. Indianapolis, Bobbs Merrill, 1942; as *Yesterday's Murder,* New York, Popular Library, 1950.
Having Wonderful Crime (Malone and Justuses). New York, Simon and Schuster, 1943; London, Nicholson and Watson, 1944.
To Catch a Thief (as Daphne Sanders). New York, Dial Press, 1943.
The Thursday Turkey Murders (Riggs and Kusak). New York, Simon and Schuster, 1943; London, Nicholson and Watson, 1946.
Home Sweet Homicide. New York, Simon and Schuster, 1944.
The Lucky Stiff (Malone and Justuses). New York, Simon and Schuster, 1945.
The Fourth Postman (Malone and Justuses). New York, Simon and Schuster, 1948; London, Hammond, 1951.
Innocent Bystander. New York, Simon and Schuster, 1949; London, Hammond, 1958.
Knocked for a Loop (Malone and Justuses). New York, Simon and Schuster, 1957; as *The Double Frame,* London, Hammond, 1958.
My Kingdom for a Hearse (Malone and Justuses). New York, Simon and Schuster, 1957; London, Hammond, 1959.
The April Robin Murders (Riggs and Kusak), completed by Ed McBain. New York, Random House, 1958; London, Hammond, 1959.
But the Doctor Died (Malone and Justuses). New York, Lancer, 1967.

Novels as Michael Venning (series: Melville Fairr in all books)

The Man Who Slept All Day. New York, Coward McCann, 1942.
Murder Through the Looking Glass. New York, Coward McCann, 1943; London, Nicholson and Watson, 1947.
Jethro Hammer. New York, Coward McCann, 1944; London, Nicholson and Watson, 1947.

Short Stories

The Name Is Malone. New York, Pyramid, 1958; London, Hammond, 1960.
People vs. Withers and Malone, with Stuart Palmer. New York, Simon and Schuster, 1963.
Once upon a Train and Other Stories, with Stuart Palmer, edited by Harold Straubing. Canoga Park, California, Gold Penny Press, 1981.

Uncollected Short Stories

"Dead Men's Shoes," in *Battling Detective,* July 1943.
"How Now, Ophelia" (as Michael Venning), in *Ellery Queen's Mystery Magazine* (New York), June 1947.
"Death in the Moonlight," in *Popular Detective* (New York), March 1953.
"Don't Go Near," in *Manhunt* (New York), May 1953.
"Hanged Him in the Mornin'," in *Verdict* (New York), June 1953.
"The Dead Mr. Duck," in *Verdict* (New York), August 1953.
"Motive," in *Verdict* (New York), September 1953.
"The Bells Are Ringing," in *Manhunt* (New York), November 1953.
"Murder Marches On," in *Manhunt* (New York), December 1953.
" . . . and Be Merry," in *Manhunt* (New York), January 1954.

"I'm a Stranger Here Myself," in *Manhunt* (New York), February 1954.

"The Little Knife That Wasn't There," in *Malcolm's* (New York), May 1954.

"I'll See You in My Dreams," in *Nero Wolfe Mystery Magazine* (Chicago), June 1954.

"No Vacancies," in *Manhunt* (New York), June 1954.

"Murder in the Family," in *The Saint* (New York), November 1954.

"Flowers to the Fair," in *Manhunt* (New York), 25 December 1954.

"The Last Man Alive," in *My Best Murder Story*, edited by David C. Cooke. New York, Merlini Press, 1955; London, Boardman, 1959.

"The Headless Hatbox," in *Double-Action Detective Stories 3* (New York), 1955.

"Mrs. Schultz Is Dead," in *The Saint* (New York), March 1955.

"No Motive for Murder," in *The Saint* (New York), July 1955.

"Shot in the Dark," in *Manhunt* (New York), August 1955.

"The Murdered Magdalen," in *Mercury* (New York), October 1955.

"The House of Missing Girls," in *Mercury* (New York), November 1955.

"Beyond the Shadow of a Dream," in *Best Detective Stories of the Year 1956*, edited by David C. Cooke. New York, Dutton, 1956.

"Breaking Point," "The Campfire Corpse," "Death in a Pick-Up Truck," "Do Not Disturb," "Frankie and Johnnie, M.D.," "House for Rent," "Identity Unknown," "No Motive," "No One Answers," "One Last Ride," "The Perfect Couple," "Small Footprints," "The TV Killer," "The Woman Hater," in *Detective Files 103* (New York), 1956.

"The Air-Tight Alibi," in *Mercury* (New York), February 1956.

"Dead Men Spend No Cash," in *Suspect* (New York), August 1956.

"The Quiet Life," in *Mike Shayne Mystery Magazine* (New York), September 1956.

"The Understanding Wife," in *Mercury* (New York), November 1956.

"The Deadly Deceiver," in *Pursuit* (New York), November 1956.

"No, Not Like Yesterday," in *Best Detective Stories of the Year 12*, edited by David C. Cooke. New York, Dutton, 1957.

"Sixty Cents Worth of Murder," in *Mercury* (New York), July 1957.

"Cheese It, The Corpse!," in *Manhunt* (New York), November 1957.

"Say It with Flowers," in *Best Detective Stories of the Year 13*, edited by David C. Cooke. New York, Dutton, 1958.

"Lady's Day at the Morgue," in *The Saint* (New York), May 1958.

"The Well-Liked Victim," in *Bestseller Mystery Magazine* (New York), July 1958.

"Wry Highball," in *Ellery Queen's 14th Mystery Annual*. New York, Random House, 1959.

"One More Clue," in *Best Detective Stories of the Year 14*, edited by David C. Cooke. New York, Dutton, 1959.

"They're Trying to Kill Me," in *The Saint* (New York), February 1959.

"The Very Groovy Corpse," in *Saint's Mystery Library 118* (New York), August 1959.

"Smoke Rings," in *Ellery Queen's Mystery Magazine* (New York), August 1959.

"The Frightened Millionaire," in *Saint's Mystery Library 121* (New York), September 1959.

"Murder in the Family," in *Saint's Mystery Library 123* (New York), October 1959.

"The Butler Who Didn't Do It," in *Alfred Hitchcock's Mystery Magazine* (New York), June 1960.

"The Fall of 'The House of Deuteronomy,'" in *The Saint* (London), April 1961.

"Hard Sell," in *Best Detective Stories of the Year 17*, edited by Brett Halliday. New York, Dutton, 1962.

"A Quiet Day in the County Jail," in *Cream of the Crime*, edited by Hugh Pentecost. New York, Holt Rinehart, 1962.

"Death in the Hills," in *The Saint* (New York), June 1962.

"The Man Who Swallowed a Horse," in *Ellery Queen's Anthology 1966*. New York, Davis, 1965.

"Alias: Trouble," in *Manhunt* (New York), July 1965.

"The Anniversary Murders," in *Manhunt* (New York), February–March 1966.

"A Weakness for Women," in *Manhunt* (New York), August–September 1966.

"The Dead Undertaker," in *Manhunt* (New York), April-May 1967.

Uncollected Short Stories as Ruth Malone

"Death of a Psychiatrist," in *Mike Shayne Mystery Magazine* (New York), August 1959.

"Death of a Light-Hearted Lady," in *Mike Shayne Mystery Magazine* (New York), November 1959.

"Deadly Insult," in *The Saint* (New York), January 1962.

OTHER PUBLICATIONS

Plays

Screenplays: *The Falcon's Brother*, with Stuart Palmer, 1942; *The Falcon in Danger*, with Fred Niblo, Jr., 1943; *Mrs. O'Malley and Mr. Malone*, with William Bowers and Stuart Palmer, 1951.

Radio Play: *Miracle at Midnight*.

Other

45 Murders: A Collection of True Crime Stories. New York, Simon and Schuster, 1952.

Editor, *Los Angeles Murders*. New York, Dell, 1947.

Ghostwriter: *The G-String Murders* by Gypsy Rose Lee, New York, Simon and Schuster, 1941, as *Lady of Burlesque*, New York, Tower, 1942, as *The Strip-Tease Murders*, London, Lane, 1943; *Mother Finds a Body* by Gypsy Rose Lee, New York, Simon and Schuster, 1942, London, Lane, 1944; (with Cleve Cartmill) *Crime on My Hands* by George Sanders, New York, Simon and Schuster, 1944, London, Edwards, 1948.

*   *   *

It is difficult to assess Craig Rice properly. Her complete canon has yet to be established. There are many short stories and novelettes from the 1950's which have never been collected and there are rumors about the authenticity of some of the later texts. She served as ghost writer for Gypsy Rose Lee and George Sanders, but there have been suggestions that she herself had substitute ghosts part of the time. Her readers, of course, never cared about such fine points: they just enjoyed the stories.

Few critics have ever tried to explain the reasons for her

popularity. If she can't be considered the first writer of humorous hard-boiled detective fiction, she can certainly be considered among the most successful. While not all of her work is intended to be enjoyed for its combination of mayhem and mirth, the majority of it is lighthearted: "screwball comedy"—part wisecrack and part comedy of situation. Her own brand of comedy can hardly be mistaken for that of anyone else; it is Damon Runyon without the idiomatic English, Thorne Smith without the fantasy. It is a difficult style to sustain and is perhaps best appreciated in small doses. Her introspective stories (such as those she wrote as Michael Venning) indicate a sensitivity sometimes lacking in her usual gangland romances.

Her most famous character is Chicago lawyer John J. Malone. He is no Perry Mason or Mr. Tutt except in his success in the courtroom, a setting we are never shown. It is said that his manner before a jury is "not so much technical as pyrotechnical" (*Trial by Fury*). Short and pudgy, with a red face and hair always in need of combing, Malone wears a suit with a perpetual slept-in look, his shirt front and vest covered with cigar ashes. His favourite drink is rye, but he also enjoys gin with a beer chaser. In a running parody of the standard hard-boiled detective cliché, he keeps his liquor in various drawers of his filing cabinet under labels like "Confidential," "Unanswered Correspondence," or "Emergency." Also like many of his hard-boiled colleagues in crime, Malone enjoys the company of beautiful women. It is rumored that someone named Louise meant something in his life once. Malone's compelling interest in life, however, is justice. He will reveal the guilty party in a story, then turn and offer to defend that person in the coming trial. His motto is "I've never lost a client yet." In an early novel, *The Wrong Murder*, he says: "I'm not an officer of the law . . . my profession has always put me on the other side of the fence. I've never served the cause of justice . . . but rather the cause of injustice."

A stock company of interesting secondary characters and the repetition of familiar scenes in a well-defined milieu help make the stories a real saga and not merely a series of episodes. The early novels are linked by events that carry over from book to book like variations on a theme. Jake and Helene Justus are central characters, along with Malone, in several novels. They are in the tradition of the husband and wife who stumble into problems that they can't solve entirely on their own. Jake, a press agent, does not have the steadiest job in town. His marriage to a beautiful blond heiress creates tension that provides a number of interesting story situations. Rice gave this trio equal parts of ineptitude, wit, and the ability to absorb liquor. That balance, plus some truly imaginative plot ideas, were enough to assure her of a large and devoted following. Other regulars in the series include Daniel von Flanagan, captain of homicide, who tries to play down his role as an Irish cop by adding the "von" to his name. He dreams of escaping Malone and the Justuses to a retirement raising mink or pecans in Georgia or running a weekly newspaper. Max Hook, the head of Chicago's gambling syndicate, is less trouble than the terrible trio. Many of the stories begin in Joe the Angel's City Hall Bar, run by Joe diAngelo, whose cousin, Rico, the undertaker, sometimes calls on Malone for help.

The basic format of a Rice novel involves a statement of the problem in an imaginative opening scene told from the point of view of the victim, chief suspect, or even the murderer. The scene then shifts to introduce von Flanagan, the Justuses, or Malone. Complications accumulate until the solution is found. Whether the characters or the problems are more appealing will depend on the individual reader. The victim is found in a room where the clocks have all stopped at three; a murder on a crowded street corner goes unnoticed; the murder victim's clothes all vanish on the way to the morgue; a reprieved murderess plans to haunt the people who sent her to jail. Her trilogy about street photographers Bingo Riggs and Handsome Kusak is in the comic tradition of the detective in spite of himself. *Home Sweet Homicide*, often ranked with *Trial by Fury* among her best novels, is the slightly autobiographical story of a mystery writer whose three children solve the murder of their next-door neighbor.

Those with a taste for strict realism in crime fiction may find fault with Rice's romantic version of Chicago's gangland, but the tone of some of her short stories and true crime articles could serve as a corrective. The warmth and humanity in her writing were matched by a sense of form and discipline all her own. She never forgot that the primary purpose of the detective story was entertainment.

—J. Randolph Cox

RICHARDS, Clay. *See* **CROSSEN, Ken.**

RICHARDS, Francis. *See* **LOCKRIDGE, Richard and Frances.**

RIDGWAY, Jason. *See* **MARLOWE, Stephen.**

RINEHART, Mary Roberts. American. Born in Pittsburgh, Pennsylvania, 12 August 1876. Educated in elementary and high schools in Pittsburgh; Pittsburgh Training School for nurses, graduated 1896. Married Dr. Stanley Marshall Rinehart in 1896 (died 1932); three sons. Full-time writer from 1903. Correspondent for *Saturday Evening Post*, Philadelphia, during World War I; reported Presidential nominating conventions. Lived in Pittsburgh until 1920, in Washington, D.C., 1920–32, and in New York City from 1932. Recipient: Mystery Writers of America Special award, 1953. Litt. D.: George Washington University, Washington, D.C., 1923. *Died 22 September 1958.*

CRIME PUBLICATIONS

Novels (series: Nurse Hilda Adams, "Miss Pinkerton")

The Circular Staircase. Indianapolis, Bobbs Merrill, 1908; London, Cassell, 1909.
The Man in Lower Ten. Indianapolis, Bobbs Merrill, and London, Cassell, 1909.
The Window at the White Cat. Indianapolis, Bobbs Merrill, 1910; London, Nash, 1911.
Where There's a Will. Indianapolis, Bobbs Merrill, 1912.
The Case of Jennie Brice. Indianapolis, Bobbs Merrill, 1913; London, Hodder and Stoughton, 1919.

The After House. Boston, Houghton Mifflin, 1914; London, Simpkin Marshall, 1915.

Dangerous Days. New York, Doran, and London, Hodder and Stoughton, 1919.

Sight Unseen, and The Confession. New York, Doran, and London, Hodder and Stoughton, 1921.

The Red Lamp. New York, Doran, 1925; as *The Mystery Lamp,* London, Hodder and Stoughton, 1925.

The Bat (novelization of play), with Avery Hopwood. New York, Doran, and London, Cassell, 1926.

Two Flights Up. New York, Doubleday, and London, Hodder and Stoughton, 1928.

The Door. New York, Farrar and Rinehart, and London, Hodder and Stoughton, 1930.

Miss Pinkerton. New York, Farrar and Rinehart, 1932; as *The Double Alibi,* London, Cassell, 1932.

Mary Roberts Rinehart's Crime Book (Adams; 2 novelettes). New York, Farrar and Rinehart, 1933; London, Cassell, 1958.

The Album. New York, Farrar and Rinehart, and London, Cassell, 1933.

The State Versus Elinor Norton. New York, Farrar and Rinehart, 1934; as *The Case of Elinor Norton,* London, Cassell, 1934.

The Wall. New York, Farrar and Rinehart, and London, Cassell, 1938.

The Great Mistake. New York, Farrar and Rinehart, 1940; London, Cassell, 1941.

Haunted Lady (Adams). New York, Farrar and Rinehart, and London, Cassell, 1942.

The Yellow Room. New York, Farrar and Rinehart, 1945; London, Cassell, 1949.

The Curve of the Catenary. New York, Royce, 1945.

Episode of the Wandering Knife: Three Mystery Tales. New York, Rinehart, 1950; as *The Wandering Knife,* London, Cassell, 1952.

The Swimming Pool. New York, Rinehart, 1952; as *The Pool,* London, Cassell, 1952.

Short Stories

The Amazing Adventures of Letitia Carberry. Indianapolis, Bobbs Merrill, 1911; London, Hodder and Stoughton, 1919.

Alibi for Isabel and Other Stories. New York, Farrar and Rinehart, 1944; London, Cassell, 1946.

The Frightened Wife and Other Murder Stories. New York, Rinehart, 1953; London, Cassell, 1954.

Uncollected Short Stories

"The Dog in the Orchard," in *The Second Mystery Book.* New York, Farrar and Rinehart, 1940.

"The Treasure Hunt," in *101 Years' Entertainment,* edited by Ellery Queen. Boston, Little Brown, 1941.

"The Splinter," in *Ellery Queen's Awards, 10th Series.* Boston, Little Brown, and London, Collins, 1955.

"Case Is Closed," in *"This Week's" Stories of Mystery and Suspense,* edited by Stewart Beach. New York, Random House, 1957.

"Four A.M.," in *Anthology 1962,* edited by Ellery Queen. New York, Davis, 1961.

OTHER PUBLICATIONS

Novels

When a Man Marries. Indianapolis, Bobbs Merrill, 1909; London, Hodder and Stoughton, 1920.

The Street of Seven Stars. Boston, Houghton Mifflin, 1914; London, Cassell, 1915.

K. Boston, Houghton Mifflin, and London, Smith Elder, 1915.

Bab, A Sub-Deb. New York, Doran, 1917; London, Hodder and Stoughton, 1920.

Long Live the King! Boston, Houghton Mifflin, and London, Murray, 1917.

Twenty-Three and a Half Hours' Leave. New York, Doran, 1918.

The Amazing Interlude. New York, Doran, and London, Murray, 1918.

A Poor Wise Man. New York, Doran, and London, Hodder and Stoughton, 1920.

The Truce of God. New York, Doran, 1920.

The Breaking Point. New York, Doran, and London, Hodder and Stoughton, 1922.

The Out Trail. New York, Doran, 1923.

Lost Ecstasy. New York, Doran, and London, Hodder and Stoughton, 1927; as *I Take This Woman,* New York, Grosset and Dunlap, 1927.

This Strange Adventure. New York, Doubleday, and London, Hodder and Stoughton, 1929.

Mr. Cohen Takes a Walk. New York, Farrar and Rinehart, 1934.

The Doctor. New York, Farrar and Rinehart, and London, Cassell, 1936.

A Light in the Window. New York, Rinehart, and London, Cassell, 1948.

Short Stories

Tish. Boston, Houghton Mifflin, 1916; London, Hodder and Stoughton, 1917.

Love Stories. New York, Doran, 1920.

Affinities and Other Stories. New York, Doran, and London, Hodder and Stoughton, 1920.

More Tish. New York, Doran, and London, Hodder and Stoughton, 1921.

Temperamental People. New York, Doran, and London, Hodder and Stoughton, 1924.

Tish Plays the Game. New York, Doran, 1926; London, Hodder and Stoughton, 1927.

Nomad's Land. New York, Doran, 1926.

The Romantics. New York, Farrar and Rinehart, 1929; London, Hodder and Stoughton, 1930.

Married People. New York, Farrar and Rinehart, and London, Cassell, 1937.

Tish Marches On. New York, Farrar and Rinehart, 1937; London, Cassell, 1938.

Familiar Faces: Stories of People You Know. New York, Farrar and Rinehart, 1941; London, Cassell, 1943.

The Best of Tish. New York, Rinehart, 1955; London, Cassell, 1956.

Plays

Seven Days, with Avery Hopwood (produced Trenton and New York, 1909; Harrogate, 1913; London, 1915). New York, French, 1931.

Cheer Up (produced New York, 1912).

Spanish Love, with Avery Hopwood (produced New York, 1920).

The Bat, with Avery Hopwood, adaptation of the novel *The Circular Staircase* by Rinehart (produced New York, 1920; London, 1921). New York, French, 1931.

The Breaking Point (produced New York, 1923).

Screenplay: *Aflame in the Sky,* with Ewart Anderson, 1927.

Other

Kings, Queens, and Pawns: An American Woman at the Front. New York, Doran, 1915.
Through Glacier Park: Seeing America First with Howard Eaton. Boston, Houghton Mifflin, 1916.
The Altar of Freedom. Boston, Houghton Mifflin, 1917.
Tenting Tonight: A Chronicle of Sport and Adventure in Glacier Park and the Cascade Mountians. Boston, Houghton Mifflin, 1918.
Isn't That Just Like a Man! New York, Doran, 1920.
My Story (autobiography). New York, Farrar and Rinehart, 1931; London, Cassell, 1932; revised edition, New York, Rinehart, 1948.
Writing Is Work. Boston, The Writer, 1939.

*

Manuscript Collection: University of Pittsburgh Library.

Critical Study: *Improbable Fiction: The Life of Mary Roberts Rinehart* by Jan Cohn, Pittsburgh, University of Pittsburgh Press, 1980.

*   *   *

Although she has recently come to be regarded, somewhat condescendingly, as a "woman's writer," Mary Roberts Rinehart was once the highest paid author in America, and the best of her work continues to entertain men and women alike. Although she wrote romances, adventure stories, and humorous sketches—of which the best-known are probably the "Tish" stories, chronicling the adventures of Miss Letitia Carberry—Rinehart is best known for inventing what has come to be called the "Had-I-But-Known" device, which has since been employed, with much less success, by myriads of mystery and gothic romance novelists.

Given the prevalence of the "Had-I-But-Known" school in subsequent years, it is easy to deprecate the originality of the invention. Rinehart is the spiritual descendant of Anna Katharine Green, but she differs from her predecessor in several important respects. First, Rinehart owes relatively little to the conventions of European detective fiction that influenced Green. Her novels tend to be mysteries or mystery/romances rather than novels of pure detection. Consequently, attention to forensic details, for example, is slight, since the object of the narrative is to arouse in the reader the same spine-chilling terror experienced by the central character. Similarly, the professional detective figures only sketchily in the typical Rinehart novel. The only continuing detective heroine is Nurse Hilda Adams, nicknamed "Miss Pinkerton" by Inspector Patton, for whom she does unofficial investigative duty. Implicit in what Julian Symons has called "The Rinehart Formula" is the complete emotional identification of the reader with the central character—usually the narrator—and no objective deduction or "professional" business is allowed to detract from that identification.

The now famous "Had-I-But-Known" device was probably invented in response to the requirements of serial publication. Given the necessity of maintaining a state of cozy terror between installments, it was appropriate for the narrator to remark at least once in each chapter, "If only we had left before it was too late!" or "Had I known then what I know now, I might have prevented the tragedy." The device raises our expectation of terrors to come, at the same time that it reassures us of the omniscience of the narrator, who, given a suitable number of chapters, will eventually explain all. Although this device is annoyingly redundant in a series of full-length novels, it was quite successful when occurring in serial installments. Logically, the reader might contend that foreknowledge on the part of the narrator would have changed nothing; however, one is rarely compelled to employ logic in a narrative which emphasizes forward action and suspense rather than deduction or ratiocination.

Another characteristic of "The Rinehart Formula," one which was subsequently exploited by such writers as Mignon G. Eberhart, is the predominance of romantic complications amidst murder and mayhem. Such love interest usually takes second place to the mystery, but it is inevitably present. When the narrator is a confirmed spinster, as in *The Circular Staircase,* the love interest is provided by a young niece and nephew. Nurse Hilda Adams is the object of admiration of Inspector Patton. In *The Man in Lower Ten,* the narrator himself becomes enamored of Miss Alison West, one of the suspects. These romantic interests, which tend to detract from the puzzles, also serve to soften the brutality of multiple murders, which are generally of a violent nature not usually associated with "women's novels." The lovers serve as symbols of normality amidst the extraordinary and sensational situations into which the principal characters are accidentally thrust.

The status quo which Rinehart's novels support is, as Julian Symons has pointed out, essentially agrarian rather than urban. Although some of her stories take place in town, or in New York City, their mood is that of an enclosed world—essentially the country house where pressures from the outside world of business or politics are rarely felt. Characters are classified as doctor, or lawyer, or chauffeur, or governess; but they are rarely shown at work. Nurse Adams, who is invariably hired by an unsuspecting family to nurse a sick relative or tend the children, when in fact she is on a "case" for Inspector Patton, has a great deal of time in which to investigate mysterious noises in the cellar or stealthy footsteps upon the back staircase; and when "Miss Pinkerton" is following the trail of a suspect, her patient never seems to miss her. In spite of the occurrence of innumerable criminal events, reporters never seem to obtrude into the closed world of the Rinehart story; and the official police are oblivious of attempts by the various characters to obstruct justice, so grateful are they for the help which the plucky narrators provide in the end. As in the classic detective story, legality is unimportant, so long as the cause of common-sense rough justice is served. In "Locked Doors," we are expected to believe that a potential outbreak of bubonic plague has been averted simply because Inspector Patton, with the aid of Nurse Adams, has solved the mystery of a locked basement laboratory which once contained infected rats (some of the rats are still missing, but Inspector Patton thinks that they have probably died without passing on the disease). Our sympathy is never diverted to the helpless victims of crime; it remains with the unofficial investigator, who must endure confusion after confusion, terror after terror, but whose common-sense and determination to unravel the mystery are ultimately rewarded

The Circular Staircase reveals all the characteristics of the

Rinehart formula at its best. The story captured the imagination of a wide public, and enshrined the formula in the public imagination. A middle-aged spinster, Rachel Innes, rents a summer house in the country with her niece and nephew, little dreaming that the house hides a guilty secret. Evidence that the house is "haunted" catapults Miss Innes into a series of eerie experiences which culminate in her being locked in a secret room with a multiple murderer: "There was someone else in the darkness, someone who breathed hard and was so close I could have touched him by the hand." Eventually, the "ghost" is revealed to be an embezzler, but only after five murders have been committed—"five lives were sacrificed in the course of this grim conspiracy." Repetitions of the original murder result largely from the reluctance of all the innocent parties to confide in the police. Nevertheless, the novel ends with the promise of two marriages; and Miss Innes, ruminating on the grisly events of the past, observes, "To be perfectly frank, I never really lived until that summer." We must conclude that, "had she but known" what was in store for her, she would have behaved in exactly the same way. Sensation is obviously its own reward. *The Circular Staircase* remains a success, in spite of the passage of time.

At their best, Rinehart's works are barely disguised adventure stories for adults, providing an opportunity for the reader to become, briefly, an accidental private eye. The effect is not unlike that which might be produced were Watson to solve cases without the direction of Holmes; hardly satisfying from a deductive point of view, but thoroughly justified from a sentimental one. In the later Rinehart novels (*The Album, The Great Mistake, The Yellow Room*), the reader's credulity is strained by a succession of increasingly implausible situations and bizarre motivations, as well as by the limitations of the self-enclosed worlds which are presented. Her early works, however, support Howard Haycraft's designation of Rinehart as America's "unquestioned dean of crime writing by and for women."

—Joanne Harack Hayne

RIPLEY, Jack. *See* **WAINRIGHT, John.**

RITCHIE, Jack (John George Reitci). American. Born 26 February 1922. Educated at Milwaukee State Teachers College, Wisconsin, 2 years. Served in the United States Army during World War II. Divorced; two daughters and two sons. *Died 23 April 1983.*

CRIME PUBLICATIONS

Short Stories

A New Leaf and Other Stories. New York, Dell, 1971.
The Adventures of Henry Turnbuckle: Detective Comedies of Jack Ritchie, edited by Francis M. Nevins Jr. and Martin H. Greenberg. Carbondale, Illinois, Southern Illinois University Press, 1987.
Little Boxes of Bewilderment, edited by Francis M. Nevins Jr. New York, St. Martin's Press, 1989.

Uncollected Short Stories

"My Game, My Rules," in *Manhunt* (New York), July 1954.
"Replacement," in *Manhunt* (New York), November 1954.
"Interrogation," in *Manhunt* (New York), June 1955.
"Solitary," in *Manhunt* (New York), July 1955.
"Try It My Way," in *Manhunt* (New York), August 1955.
"Devil Eyes," in *Manhunt* (New York), May 1956.
"The Canary," in *Manhunt* (New York), June 1956.
"A Touch for Tess," in *Mantrap* (New York), July 1956.
"The Partners," in *Manhunt* (New York), September 1956.
"Dead Cops Are Murder," in *Murder* (New York), September 1956.
"Death Rail," in *Mantrap* (New York), October 1956.
"Degree of Guilt," in *Manhunt* (New York), December 1956.
"Rainy Afternoon," in *Murder* (New York), December 1956.
"Bullet-Proof," in *Alfred Hitchcock's Mystery Magazine* (New York), January 1957.
"Divide and Conquer," in *Manhunt* (New York), February 1957.
"Bomb # 14," in *Alfred Hitchcock's Mystery Magazine* (New York), August 1957.
"Welcome to My Prison," in *Alfred Hitchcock's Mystery Magazine* (New York), October 1957.
"Kill Joy," in *Manhunt* (New York), November 1957.
"Hospitality Most Serene," in *Alfred Hitchcock's Mystery Magazine* (New York), January 1958.
"Don't Twist My Arm," in *Manhunt* (New York), April 1958.
"What Frightened You, Fred?," in *Alfred Hitchcock's Mystery Magazine* (New York), May 1958.
"Where the Wheel Stops," in *Alfred Hitchcock's Mystery Magazine* (New York), October 1958.
"Deadline Murder," in *Manhunt* (New York), October 1958.
"Man on a Leash," in *Alfred Hitchcock's Mystery Magazine* (New York), December 1958.
"22 Stories Up—and Down," in *Alfred Hitchcock's Mystery Magazine* (New York), January 1959.
"Frame-Up," in *Alfred Hitchcock's Mystery Magazine* (New York), April 1959.
"The $5,000 Getaway," in *Alfred Hitchcock's Mystery Magazine* (New York), May 1959.
"Such Things Happen at Night," in *Alfred Hitchcock's Mystery Magazine* (New York), July 1959.
"Good-By, World," in *Manhunt* (New York), August 1959.
"Between 4 and 12," in *Alfred Hitchcock's Mystery Magazine* (New York), October 1959.
"Painless Extraction," in *Alfred Hitchcock's Mystery Magazine* (New York), December 1959.
"Falcons Fly Far," in *Alfred Hitchcock's Mystery Magazine* (New York), January 1960.
"The Enormous $10," in *Alfred Hitchcock's Mystery Magazine* (New York), February 1960.
"Fragrant Puzzle," in *Alfred Hitchcock's Mystery Magazine* (New York), March 1960.
"You Should Live So Long," in *Manhunt* (New York), April 1960.
"Lily-White Town," in *Alfred Hitchcock's Mystery Magazine* (New York), May 1960.
"When Buying a Fine Murder," in *Alfred Hitchcock's Mystery Magazine* (New York), June 1960.
"The Fabulous Tunnel," in *Alfred Hitchcock's Mystery Magazine* (New York), August 1960.
"Politics Is Simply Murder," in *Alfred Hitchcock's Mystery Magazine* (New York), November 1960.
"Shatter Proof," in *Best Detective Stories of the Year 1961,* edited by Brett Halliday. New York, Dutton, 1961.

"The Killer with Red Hair," in *Suspense* (London), January 1961.

"The Crime Machine," in *Alfred Hitchcock's Mystery Magazine* (New York), January 1961.

"You Can Trust Me," in *Alfred Hitchcock's Mystery Magazine* (New York), February 1961.

"The Third Call," in *Alfred Hitchcock's Mystery Magazine* (New York), March 1961.

"Play a Game of Cyanide," in *Alfred Hitchcock's Mystery Magazine* (New York), May 1961.

"Under Dim Street Lights," in *Alfred Hitchcock's Mystery Magazine* (New York), July 1961.

"Goodbye Memory," in *Alfred Hitchcock's Mystery Magazine* (New York), August 1961.

"The Traveling Arm," in *Alfred Hitchcock's Mystery Magazine* (New York), November 1961.

"Punch Any Number," in *Alfred Hitchcock's Mystery Magazine* (New York), December 1961.

"The Queer Deal," in *Manhunt* (New York), December 1961.

"Holdout," in *Alfred Hitchcock's Mystery Magazine* (New York), March 1962.

"Upside Down World," in *Alfred Hitchcock's Mystery Magazine* (New York), May 1962.

"The Eyes Have It," in *Alfred Hitchcock's Mystery Magazine* (New York), November 1962.

"Travelers Check," in *Alfred Hitchcock's Mystery Magazine* (New York), December 1962.

"A Taste for Murder," in *Alfred Hitchcock's Mystery Magazine* (New York), January 1963.

"Just Between Us Dad," in *Alfred Hitchcock's Mystery Magazine* (New York), February 1963.

"Ripper Moon," in *Manhunt* (New York), February 1963.

"Ten Minutes from Now," in *Alfred Hitchcock's Mystery Magazine* (New York), October 1963.

"Anyone for Murder?," in *Alfred Hitchcock's Mystery Magazine* (New York), January 1964.

"Silence Is Gold," in *Alfred Hitchcock's Mystery Magazine* (New York), April 1964.

"Everybody Except Wilbur," in *Alfred Hitchcock's Mystery Magazine* (New York), June 1964.

"Captive Audience," in *Alfred Hitchcock's Mystery Magazine* (New York), August 1964.

"Who's Got the Lady?," in *Mike Shayne Mystery Magazine* (New York), September 1964.

"Mr. Policeman," in *Mike Shayne Mystery Magazine* (New York), April 1965.

"Sing a Song for Tony," in *Alfred Hitchcock's Mystery Magazine* (New York), April 1965.

"Swing High," in *Alfred Hitchcock's Mystery Magazine* (New York), May 1965.

"A Piece of the World," in *Alfred Hitchcock's Mystery Magazine* (New York), June 1965.

"Going Down?," in *Manhunt* (New York), July 1965.

"Memory Test," in *Alfred Hitchcock's Mystery Magazine* (New York), August 1965.

"Package Deal," in *Alfred Hitchcock's Mystery Magazine* (New York), September 1965.

"Queasy Does It Not," in *Alfred Hitchcock's Mystery Magazine* (New York), October 1965.

"The Pickup Man," in *Mike Shayne Mystery Magazine* (New York), January 1966.

"The Little Green Book," in *Intrigue* (New York), January 1966.

"Copy Cat," in *Alfred Hitchcock's Mystery Magazine* (New York), January 1966.

"Speaking of Murder," in *Mike Shayne Mystery Magazine* (New York), September 1966.

"Goodbye, Sweet Money," in *Alfred Hitchcock's Mystery Magazine* (New York), April 1967.

"The Fifty Cents Victims," in *Alfred Hitchcock's Mystery Magazine* (New York), May 1967.

"The Push Button," in *Alfred Hitchcock's Mystery Magazine* (New York), June 1967.

"With One Stone," in *Alfred Hitchcock's Mystery Magazine* (New York), July 1967.

"The $15,000 Shack," in *Alfred Hitchcock's Mystery Magazine* (New York), August 1967.

"The Best Driver in the Country," in *Alfred Hitchcock's Mystery Magazine* (New York), September 1967.

"Piggy Bank Killer," in *Alfred Hitchcock's Mystery Magazine* (New York), November 1967.

"By Child Undone," in *Best Detective Stories of the Year*, edited by Anthony Boucher. New York, Dutton, 1968.

"That Russian!," in *Alfred Hitchcock's Mystery Magazine* (New York), May 1968.

"The Killing Philosophy," in *Alfred Hitchcock's Mystery Magazine* (New York), June 1968.

"Pearls Before Wine," in *Mike Shayne Mystery Magazine* (New York), August 1968.

"Wearing of the Green," in *Mike Shayne Mystery Magazine* (New York), November 1968.

"Under a Cold Sun," in *Mike Shayne Mystery Magazine* (New York), January 1969.

"Dropout," in *Alfred Hitchcock's Mystery Magazine* (New York), January 1969.

"Welcome to the Club," in *Mike Shayne Mystery Magazine* (New York), April 1969.

"At Face Value," in *Alfred Hitchcock's Mystery Magazine* (New York), April 1969.

"Where Am I?," in *Mike Shayne Mystery Magazine* (New York), July 1969.

"Pardon My Death Ray," in *Alfred Hitchcock's Mystery Magazine* (New York), August 1969.

"You Got to Watch Ben," in *Mike Shayne Mystery Magazine* (New York), September 1969.

"A Finger Here ... a Finger There," in *Alfred Hitchcock's Mystery Magazine* (New York), December 1969.

"Plan Nineteen," in *Crimes and Misfortunes*, edited by J. Francis McComas. New York, Random House, 1970.

"The Havana Express," in *Alfred Hitchcock's Mystery Magazine* (New York), July 1970.

"For All the Rude People," in *Best of the Best Detective Stories*, edited by Allen J. Hubin. New York, Dutton, 1971.

"The Violet Business," in *Alfred Hitchcock's Mystery Magazine* (New York), September 1971.

"The Griggsby Papers," in *Mike Shayne Mystery Magazine* (Los Angeles), October 1971.

"Listen, Pigs, Listen," in *Alfred Hitchcock's Mystery Magazine* (New York), November 1971.

"Home-Town Boy," in *Alfred Hitchcock's Mystery Magazine* (New York), December 1971.

"Take Another Look," in *Best Detective Stories of the Year 1972*, edited by Allen J. Hubin. New York, Dutton, 1972.

"In Open Hiding," in *Alfred Hitchcock's Mystery Magazine* (New York), March 1972.

"Let Your Fingers Do the Walking," in *Alfred Hitchcock's Mystery Magazine* (New York), April 1972.

"Tight Little Town," in *Alfred Hitchcock's Mystery Magazine* (New York), May 1972.

"Rights and Wrongs," in *Alfred Hitchcock's Mystery Magazine* (New York), June 1972.

"Finger Man," in *Alfred Hitchcock's Mystery Magazine* (New York), July 1972.

"The Value of Privacy," in *Alfred Hitchcock's Mystery Magazine* (New York), August 1972.

"Four on an Alibi," in *Alfred Hitchcock's Mystery Magazine* (New York), April 1973.

"But Don't Tell Your Mother," in *Alfred Hitchcock's Mystery Magazine* (New York), August 1973.

"End of the Line," in *Alfred Hitchcock's Mystery Magazine* (New York), October 1973.

"The Wastebasket," in *Alfred Hitchcock's Mystery Magazine* (New York), December 1973.

"The Magnum," in *Alfred Hitchcock Presents: Stories to Be Read with the Door Locked.* New York, Random House, 1975.

"When the Sheriff Walked," in *Best Detective Stories of the Year 1975*, edited by Allen J. Hubin. New York, Dutton, 1975.

"To the Barricades," in *Alfred Hitchcock's Mystery Magazine* (North Palm Beach, Florida), April 1975.

"Bedlam at the Budgie," in *Alfred Hitchcock's Mystery Magazine* (North Palm Beach, Florida), May 1975.

"The Angler," in *Alfred Hitchcock's Mystery Magazine* (North Palm Beach, Florida), October 1975.

"The Many-Flavored Crime," in *Best Detective Stories of the Year 1976*, edited by Edward D. Hoch. New York, Dutton, 1976.

"The Deveraux Monster," in *Tricks and Treats*, edited by Joe Gores and Bill Pronzini. New York, Doubleday, 1976.

"To Kill a Man," in *Mystery Monthly* (New York), June 1976.

"Nobody Tells Me Anything," in *Ellery Queen's Mystery Magazine* (New York), October 1976.

"The Operator," in *Alfred Hitchcock Presents: Stories That Go Bump in the Night.* New York, Random House, 1977.

"Kid Cardula," in *Alfred Hitchcock's Tales to Take Your Breath Away*, edited by Eleanor Sullivan. New York, Davis, 1977.

"Next in Line," in *Best Detective Stories of the Year 1977*, edited by Edward D. Hoch. New York, Dutton, 1977.

"My Compliments to the Cook," in *Alfred Hitchcock's Mystery Magazine* (New York), January 1977.

"An Odd Pair of Socks," in *Alfred Hitchcock's Mystery Magazine* (New York), May 1977.

"The Canvas Caper," in *Alfred Hitchcock's Mystery Magazine* (New York), August 1977.

"Variations on the Scheme," in *Alfred Hitchcock's Mystery Magazine* (New York), September 1977.

"The Willinger Predicament," in *Ellery Queen's Mystery Magazine* (New York), October 1977.

"Cardula to the Rescue," in *Alfred Hitchcock's Mystery Magazine* (New York), December 1977.

"The Green Heart," in *Alfred Hitchcock's Tales to Scare You Stiff*, edited by Eleanor Sullivan. New York, Davis, 1978.

"Hung Jury," in *Best Detective Stories of the Year 1978*, edited by Edward D. Hoch. New York, Dutton, 1978.

"The School Bus Caper," in *Ellery Queen's Mystery Magazine* (New York), March 1978.

"The Scent of Camellias," in *Alfred Hitchcock's Mystery Magazine* (New York), March 1978.

"Cardula and the Kleptomaniac," in *Alfred Hitchcock's Mystery Magazine* (New York), April 1978.

"Cardula's Revenge," in *Alfred Hitchcock's Mystery Magazine* (New York), November 1978.

"The Return of Bridget," in *Alfred Hitchcock's Mystery Magazine* (New York), December 1978.

"Delayed Mail," in *Best Detective Stories of the Year 1979*, edited by Edward D. Hoch. New York, Dutton, 1979.

"Twenty-Two Cents a Day," in *Alfred Hitchcock Presents: The Master's Choice.* New York, Random House, 1979.

"The Seed Caper," in *Ellery Queen's Scenes of the Crime.* New York, Davis, 1979.

"The Little Room," in *Mike Shayne Mystery Magazine* (Los Angeles), January 1979.

"The Moonlighter," in *Ellery Queen's Mystery Magazine* (New York), January 1979.

"The Hanging Tree," in *Alfred Hitchcock's Mystery Magazine* (New York), January 1979.

"Stakeout," in *Alfred Hitchcock's Mystery Magazine* (New York), April 1979.

"Some Days Are Like That," in *Ellery Queen's Mystery Magazine* (New York), June 1979.

"You Could Get Killed," in *Alfred Hitchcock's Mystery Magazine* (New York), June 1979.

"Friend of the Family," in *Mike Shayne Mystery Magazine* (Los Angeles), August 1979.

"The Gourmet Kidnapper," in *Ellery Queen's Mystery Magazine* (New York), September 1979.

"The Sliver of Evidence," in *Ellery Queen's Mystery Magazine*, (New York), November 1979.

"Where the Finger Points," in *Alfred Hitchcock's Tales to Fill You with Fear and Trembling*, edited by Eleanor Sullivan. New York, Dial Press, 1980.

"The Davenport," in *A Chilling Collection*, edited by Helen Hoke. New York, Dutton, 1980.

"That Year's Victim," in *Alfred Hitchcock's Tales to Make Your Teeth Chatter*, edited by Eleanor Sullivan. New York, Dial Press, 1980.

"No Wider Than a Nickel," in *Ellery Queen's Circumstantial Evidence.* New York, Davis, 1980.

"The 23 Brown Paper Bags," in *Best Detective Stories of the Year 1980*, edited by Edward D. Hoch. New York, Dutton, 1980.

"The Alphabet Murders," in *Mike Shayne Mystery Magazine* (Los Angeles), February 1980.

"The Third-Floor Closet," in *Ellery Queen's Mystery Magazine* (New York), 30 June 1980.

"More Than Meets the Eye," in *Ellery Queen's Mystery Magazine* (New York), 10 September 1980.

"For the Good of Society," in *Mike Shayne Mystery Magazine* (Los Angeles), December 1980.

"The Last Journey," in *Alfred Hitchcock's Mystery Magazine* (New York), 15 December 1980.

"Too Solid Mildred," in *Alfred Hitchcock's Tales to Make Your Hair Stand on End*, edited by Eleanor Sullivan. New York, Dial Press, 1981.

"Box in a Box," in *All But Impossible!*, edited by Edward D. Hoch. New Haven, Connecticut, Ticknor and Fields, 1981.

"The Way to Do It," in *Best Detective Stories of the Year 1981*, edited by Edward D. Hoch. New York, Dutton, 1981.

"The Midnight Strangler," in *Ellery Queen's Crime Cruise round the World.* New York, Davis, 1981.

"Win Some, Lose Some," in *Ellery Queen's Mystery Magazine* (New York), 25 March 1981.

"Body Check," in *Ellery Queen's Mystery Magazine* (New York), 15 July 1981.

"The Connecting Link," in *Ellery Queen's Mystery Magazine* (New York), 7 October 1981.

"The Message in the Message," in *Ellery Queen's Mystery Magazine* (New York), 2 December 1981.

"Big Tony," in *Alfred Hitchcock's Tales to Make You Quake and Quiver*, edited by Cathleen Jordan. New York, Dial Press, 1982.

"The Absence of Emily," in *The Year's Best Mystery and Suspense Stories 1982*, edited by Edward D. Hoch. New York, Walker, 1982.

"Beauty Is as Beauty Does," in *Ellery Queen's Maze of Mysteries.* New York, Davis, 1982.
"A Case of Identity," in *Ellery Queen's Mystery Magazine* (New York), 27 January 1982.
"The Orange Murders," in *Ellery Queen's Mystery Magazine* (New York), 24 March 1982.
"Murder Off Limits," in *Ellery Queen's Mystery Magazine* (New York), June 1982.
"The Golden Goose," in *Ellery Queen's Mystery Magazine* (New York), Mid-July 1982.
"The Fifth Grave," in *Ellery Queen's Mystery Magazine* (New York), October 1982.

*   *   *

One hallmark of a mystery short story writer's success is the frequency with which his stories are reprinted in anthologies, especially in annual volumes like *Best Detective Stories of the Year.* By this standard Jack Ritchie has no equal. He appeared in *Best Detective Stories* 17 times since 1961, under four different editors, and he has also been reprinted in virtually all the hardcover Alfred Hitchcock anthologies. Ritchie never published a novel, and only one collection of his short stories has appeared, *A New Leaf and Other Stories.* Though he began publishing in 1953, his best work was the stories published during the 1960's and 1970's. One is tempted to generalize and say that the offbeat humor which is now Ritchie's trademark became more pronounced in the 1970's, though certainly an early story like "The Deveraux Monster" (1962) is tongue-in-cheek, to say the least.

Others from the early 1960's are in a more serious vein. "Shatter Proof" (1961) presents a man's confrontation with a hired killer sent by his wife. "For All the Rude People" (1961) has some humor but is mainly an angry tale of a man with only four months to live who sets out to murder those who have been rude to him. "The Operator" (1963) is about an undercover cop on the trail of a stolen car ring, and reveals something of Ritchie's debt to the best of the old medium-tough pulp writing.

But mainly Ritchie's world is a topsy-turvy creation full of bumbling detectives who occasionally stumble upon the right solution by accident, or who fail because no one told them some key fact everyone else knew. It is a world of bathtubs full of jello ("The Many-Flavored Crime"), or bungled prison breaks ("Plan Nineteen"), or the theft of flower seeds ("The Seed Caper"). It is even a world where, occasionally, the butler did it.

In recent years Ritchie's stories dealt more with detection, though here too his detectives are anything but orthodox. One series features Cardula, a vampire private eye. And a story aptly titled "By Child Undone" features a ten-year-old child who spots the single factor linking a series of baffling murders. Another series murder is solved by a Double-Crostics expert ("Hung Jury"). By its very nature the whimsy of Ritchie's plots works best in the short story length. "Next in Line" is a rare novelette where the humor—about the heirs to a large estate—is sustained for some 8500 words, helped by the author's usual deft characterizations.

—Edward D. Hoch

———

ROBBINS, Wayne. *See* **COX, William R.**

———

ROBERTS, James Hall. Pseudonym for Robert L(ipscomb) Duncan; also writes as W.R. Duncan. American. Born in Oklahoma City, 9 September 1927. Educated at the University of Oklahoma, Norman, B.A. 1950, M.A. 1972. Married Wanda Scott in 1949; one daughter and one son. Freelance writer; lecturer in television writing, University of California, Irvine, 1967–68; writer-in-residence, Chapman College, Orange, California, 1969–70; Associate Professor of Journalism, University of Oklahoma, 1972–80. Agent: John Hawkins Associates, 71 West 23rd Street, New York, New York 10010, U.S.A.

CRIME PUBLICATIONS

Novels

The Q Document. New York, Morrow, 1964; London, Cape, 1965.
The Burning Sky. New York, Morrow, 1966.
The February Plan. New York, Morrow, and London, Deutsch, 1967.

Novels as Robert L. Duncan

The Day the Sun Fell. New York, Morrow, 1970; London, Sphere, 1981.
The Dragons at the Gate. New York, Morrow, 1975; London, Joseph, 1976.
Temple Dogs. New York, Morrow, 1977; London, Joseph, 1978.
Fire Storm. New York, Morrow, 1978; London, Joseph, 1979.
Brimstone. New York, Morrow, and London, Joseph, 1980.
The Queen's Messenger (as W.R. Duncan, with Wanda Duncan). New York, Delacorte Press, and London, Joseph, 1982.
In the Blood. London, Sphere, 1985.
In the Enemy Camp. New York, Delacorte Press, 1985; London, Severn House, 1986.

OTHER PUBLICATIONS as Robert L. Duncan

Novels

The Voice of a Stranger. New York, Doubleday, 1961.
If It Moves Salute It. New York, Doubleday, 1961.
The General and the Coed. New York, Doubleday, 1962.
China Dawn. New York, Delacorte Press, and London, Collins, 1988.
The Serpent's Mark. New York, St. Martin's Press, 1989; London, Collins, 1990.

Short Stories

The Dicky Bird Was Singing. New York, Rinehart, 1952.
Buffalo Country. New York, Dutton, 1959.

Plays

Screenplay: *Black Gold,* 1962.

Television Plays: more than 100 scripts for *U.S. Steel Hour, NBC Matinee Theatre, G.E. Theatre,* and *Alcoa-Goodyear Theatre,* and for *Riverboat, One Step Beyond, Checkmate, Bonanza, Have Gun, Will Travel, Dr. Kildare, The Virginian, Lost in Space, The Young Lawyers, The Professionals,* and other series, 1956–70.

Other

Castles in the Air: The Memoirs of Irene Castle, with Wanda
    Duncan.   New York, Doubleday, 1958.
The Life and Times of Albert Pike.   New York, Dutton, 1961.

*

Manuscript Collection: Mugar Memorial Library, Boston
University.

*   *   *

Like many writers who employ pseudonyms, Robert Lipscomb Duncan/James Hall Roberts writes somewhat different
sorts of books under the two different names. As Roberts he
demonstrates the generally neglected potentiality of the thriller
to offer both factual and spiritual instruction; two of his novels
in that incarnation approach genuine excellence. His works as
Robert L. Duncan, though not without merit, lack the
individuality and power of the Roberts books; they generally
tend to be founded upon an interesting and unusual idea and
then founder upon the sorts of artificial tensions usually
associated with run-of-the-mill suspense novels.

In the Roberts books he combines the thriller's necessary plot
device of the search for a solution to a mystery or a problem
with other kinds of quests—the quest for knowledge and the
quest for faith. In the process his novels display a fascinating
erudition and grapple convincingly with the problem of
religious belief. In *The Q Document, The February Plan,* and *The
Burning Sky* his three protagonists are linked by the modernity
of their malaise, a hardening of the heart, a withdrawal and
detachment of the self from its humanity in reaction to some
personal catastrophe. Encountering a puzzle, the men also
encounter themselves; their search for particular facts becomes
the discovery of general truths. The two most important books
present puzzles intimately connected with beliefs—in *The Q
Document* a scholar has to authenticate some ostensibly ancient
manuscripts, one of which may have been written by Jesus; in
The Burning Sky an archaeologist and a priest, for different
reasons, investigate the survival of an ancient American Indian
culture. The protagonists discover not only the solutions to their
mysteries but also their own connections with humanity. Their
awakening derives from an objective search for truth but leads
to an intensely personal recognition of faith, redeeming them
from solitude and apostasy.

Aside from the intrinsic appeal of Roberts's theme of faith,
one of the most remarkable qualities of his two best novels is
their coherent and learned use of specialized scholarly
disciplines—archaeology and anthropology in *The Burning Sky*
and biblical linguistics and scholarship in *The Q Document;* the
clear and functional exposition of abstruse and utterly
absorbing kinds of knowledge is little short of brilliant. It has
been some time since the novel of suspense was prized as a
vehicle of information; Roberts's books revive that aspect of
the form, carrying it considerably further than the usual
instruction in technical details. Exploring more than mere
essential factual background, he sometimes demonstrates real
learning and real love of learning. The moral dimension of his
books enhances their instructional value—there is no reason
why the novel of suspense cannot, like other kinds of literature,
provide spiritual edification.

The Duncan books, unfortunately, retain the surface but not
the depth of those by Roberts. While they possess some of the
technical information—about computers, the Far East, government bureaucracy, etc.—they do not achieve the intellectual
and moral resonance of the others. There is a quantity of fact,

but not a good deal of truth in them. Like many thriller writers,
Duncan bases a good deal of his work on the climate of
paranoia that cloaks the contemporary world; he sees the
individual at the mercy of machinery, or big government, or
huge industrial cartels, all of which conspire against decent,
ordinary people everywhere. Typical of his works is *Brimstone,*
which begins with the perfectly wonderful notion of the
discovery of the notorious eighteen and one-half minutes of the
Watergate tapes, but too soon degenerates into one of those
familiar cross-country automobile chases one jump ahead of a
military-governmental conspiracy, exploding into a climactic
scene of violence and confusion.

Duncan/Roberts should probably be better known and more
highly regarded than he now seems to be. The spiritual and
scholarly side of his work, merged with the puzzles and
suspense, makes them, at their best, very good novels indeed.
At moments he seems capable of becoming an American
Graham Greene, which would place him among the highest
ranks of writers of thrillers, students of faith, or novelists of any
persuasion. He may not possess Greene's stylistic brilliance,
but he has some of Greene's balance of thought and action, of
moral engagement with suspense, of mystery with the Mystery
itself.

—George Grella

———————

ROBERTS, Les.   American.   Born in Chicago, Illinois, 18
July 1937. Educated at the University of Illinois, Champaign-
Urbana; Roosevelt University, Chicago, 1954–56. Served in
the United States Army, 1960–62. Married Gail Medland in
1957 (divorced 1980); one daughter and one son. Has had a
variety of jobs including actor, jazz pianist and singer,
songwriter; president, Roberts Two Production, 1971–79;
director, Delta Audio-Visual Services, 1984–85; restaurant
critic, *Today,* Los Angeles, 1984–86. Since 1989 mystery book
reviewer, Cleveland *Plain Dealer.* Recipient: Private Eye
Writers of America award, 1986. Agent: Dominick Abel, 146
West 82nd Street, New York, New York 10024. Address: 6701
Haskell Avenue, Van Nuys, California 91406, U.S.A.

CRIME PUBLICATIONS

Novels (series: Milan Jacovich; Saxon)

An Infinite Number of Monkeys (Saxon).   New York, St.
    Martin's Press, and London, Macmillan, 1987.
Not Enough Horses (Saxon).   New York, St. Martin's Press,
    and London, Macmillan, 1988.
Pepper Pike (Jacovich).   New York, St. Martin's Press, 1988;
    London, Coronet, 1990.
A Carrot for the Donkey (Saxon).   New York, St. Martin's
    Press, 1989.
Full Cleveland (Jacovich).   New York, St. Martin's Press,
    1989.
Snake Oil (Saxon).   New York, St. Martin's Press, 1990.
Deep Shaker (Jacovich).   New York, St. Martin's Press, 1991.

OTHER PUBLICATIONS

Plays

Screenplays: *Fox Bat,* 1977; *Solar Plexus,* 1981.

Television Plays: *The Lucy Show*, 1967; *The Man from U.N.C.L.E.*, 1967; *The Andy Griffith Show*, 1967; *When Things Were Rotten*, 1975.

*

Manuscript Collection: Bowling Green State University, Ohio.

Les Roberts comments:

I write two detective series at the moment. One features a Los Angeles-based private eye named Saxon (no first name) who also works occasionally as a film actor. Often (but not always) there is a "show business" connection in his cases.

The other series chronicles the adventures of Milan Jacovich (pronounced MY-lan YAK-o-vitch), who lives and works in Cleveland, Ohio. Although well-educated, Milan is ethnic (Slovenian), gritty and blue-collar like the city in which he lives.

All fiction writers deal with people in crisis of one sort or another, else there is no story. I choose to work in the mystery genre because there is no conflict more intense than the struggle for life. It is story-telling to the one-hundredth power. The form allows me to comment on what I think is wrong, and right, with the world today, and most of the subjects in my novels are those about which I feel passionately (i.e. artistic freedom, poverty, corruption, and most often, loyalty to friends). It also gives the reader the satisfaction of an ending in which justice is served and all is put to rights, a situation not always true in real life.

It also seems to me that the mystery is the modern-day equivalent of the medieval morality play, with the sleuth as Everyman. Working against time, the system, Big Money, and sometimes overwhelming odds, the little guy with guts and brains and the kind of smarts learned only on the "Mean Streets" proves himself more than equal to the task. And since the protagonist of any novel is the reader's surrogate, the success of the hero or heroine detective, whether a professional, a private eye, or an amateur, makes that reader feel just a little bit better about the world and about himself.

*   *   *

Les Roberts almost seems to be two people—in fact, he has said that his two series characters represent the two sides of himself. One is younger, hipper, and a modestly successful actor (who maintains solvency through his private investigation agency). He sometimes does things that aren't very nice (but always regrets them afterward). He lives in Los Angeles and has problems maintaining extended relationships with suitable women (although he might dispute this being a problem). He has, however, formed an unusual and loving bond with a young street child he met on his second adventure, thus showing himself to be a man of considerable substance.

The other man is an older ex-cop, well-educated but unhappily divorced and struggling to maintain a decent relationship with his sons. Born and raised in Cleveland, he epitomizes the solid ethnicity of the city.

The former is no-first-name Saxon, who made his first appearance in the award-winning *An Infinite Number of Monkeys*. It doesn't take him long to figure out that the bullet which almost struck his assistant's husband was really meant for pulp writer Buck Weldon, who has as many enemies as published works. He also has a beautiful daughter who quickly becomes one of Saxon's less suitable attachments. It is, in fact, Saxon's unreasoning infatuation with Tori which is the most unsatisfying aspect of the book—one expects better judgment from an intelligent man. There's some interesting background on publishing and pulp detective fiction collecting. One of the finer aspects of the book is the relationship between Saxon and his assistant Jo. Theirs is a loving friendship marked by mutual respect and no sex. Overall plotting is capable, although some major developments may be apparent sooner than Roberts intended. It is Saxon, however, who invites closer examination.

Not Enough Horses shows great strides in both plotting and character development, and Roberts convincingly shows Saxon to be a man to be reckoned with for the duration. Asked to look into the death of a gay actor by the man's lover ("Kevin, I told you I don't make any moral judgments. I'm sorry about Robbie and I'll do what I can to help, but you have to stop thinking of me as the enemy just because I like girls."), Saxon quickly learns more about life on the streets than he bargained for. He also learns a great deal about himself when he answers his own question ("Jo, sometimes you've got to decide whether you're really in the game or you're just going to be a spectator.") and adopts a street child who knew the dead man.

A Carrot for the Donkey once more brings to the fore his less admirable side. Set largely in violent and seamy Tijuana, Saxon contributes to the atmosphere of disregard for human dignity by almost unforgivably seducing a woman in order to find the man who might lead him to his client's missing daughter. Readers may again suspect certain plot developments earlier than they should, but Roberts's surer and more defined hand has created a dynamic sense of place along with a continually interesting and everchanging protagonist.

By *Snake Oil* Saxon has shown much growth as a character. Asked to obtain proof of a wife's infidelity, he is kept on to prove the lady innocent of murder. The supporting cast—his assistant Jo; his adopted son Marvel (who makes a significant reappearance); a wily old oilman and his beautiful and brilliant granddaughter—is excellent. Roberts's intimate knowledge of Los Angeles is felt in full force here; and while Saxon's observations have lost none of their sharp sense of irony ("'I'm a Christian, and I believe in the sanctity of human life [said Stack].' He took a pack of Marlboros from his shirt pocket and offered it to me. . . ."), it is in the context of the thoughtful and caring man we glimpsed in *Not Enough Horses*.

After the second Saxon book Roberts produced an entirely different character—the older, sadder and wiser Milan Jacovich. At loose ends after his divorce, feeling estranged from his Slavic roots, and running his own investigative agency after leaving the police department, he agrees to act as a temporary bodyguard for a wealthy advertising executive in *Pepper Pike*. ("I was a private cop with a temperament and personality more suited to teaching history; a blue-collar neighborhood guy with a master's degree; a devoted family man living alone in an apartment. I had yet to find the pigeonhole in which I'd be comfortable.") The man disappears before Milan gets there, and he is hired by the wife to locate him. It's a truism that people can never be too rich or too powerful, but while Milan uncovers evil behind the doors of suburban homes and country clubs he also finds that life and love go on.

Full Cleveland finds Milan hired to locate the con artists who successfully parted a hotel manager from a rather large sum of money. The local mob boss takes a great interest in the case and assigns Milan a partner. The development of the relationship between the two men is a cockeyed reflection of some other important developing relationships in Milan's life, and the book is successful on a variety of levels. Roberts also pokes fun at his "other half" when Milan calls Saxon for some information. ("He was a movie actor whenever anyone would hire him, and he had the ego to go with it, but he was a pretty engaging guy for all that, and we had spent much of our spare time between seminars and meetings drinking together and seeing the Las Vegas sights, including the two-legged blond variety, in which Saxon had shown inordinate interest. If he pursued his second career as relentlessly as he did leggy showgirls, he'd be a damn good investigator.")

Roberts is a classic example of a writer who learns from his mistakes. His ability to create complex and cohesive plots, fully developed characters and well-realized settings improves with each successive effort, and he is on course to becoming one of the more well-regarded writers of the 1990's.

—Sue Feder

ROBERTS, Willo Davis. American. Born in Grand Rapids, Michigan, 29 May 1928. Educated at a high school in Pontiac, Michigan, graduated 1946. Married David W. Roberts in 1949; two daughters and two sons. Worked in hospitals and doctors' offices, 1964–72; currently conducts a writers' workshop in Granite Falls, Washington. Founder, Mystery Writers of America Seattle Chapter. Recipient: Mystery Writers of America Edgar Allan Poe award, for children's book, 1989. Agent: Curtis Brown Associates Ltd., 10 Astor Place, New York, New York 10019. Address: 12020 Engebretson Road, Granite Falls, Washington 98252, U.S.A.

CRIME PUBLICATIONS

Novels

Murder at Grand Bay. New York, Arcadia House, 1955.
The Girl Who Wasn't There. New York, Arcadia House, 1957.
Murder Is So Easy. Fresno, California, Vega, 1961.
The Suspected Four. Fresno, California, Vega, 1962.
Return to Darkness. New York, Lancer, 1969.
Shroud of Fog. New York, Ace, 1970.
Devil Boy. New York, New American Library, 1970; London, New English Library, 1971.
The Waiting Darkness. New York, Lancer, 1970.
Shadow of a Past Love. New York, Lancer, 1970.
The House at Fern Canyon. New York, Lancer, 1970.
The Tarot Spell. New York, Lancer, 1970.
Invitation to Evil. New York, Lancer, 1970.
The Terror Trap. New York, Lancer, 1971.
King's Pawn. New York, Lancer, 1971.
The Gates of Montrain. New York, Lancer, 1971.
The Watchers. New York, Lancer, 1971.
The Ghosts of Harrel. New York, Lancer, 1971.
Inherit the Darkness. New York, Lancer, 1972.
Becca's Child. New York, Lancer, 1972.
Sing a Dark Song. New York, Lancer, 1972.
The Face of Danger. New York, Lancer, 1972.
Dangerous Legacy. New York, Lancer, 1972.
Sinister Gardens. New York, Lancer, 1972.
The Evil Children. New York, Lancer, 1973.
The Gods in Green. New York, Lancer, 1973.
Didn't Anybody Know My Wife? New York, Putnam, 1974; London, Hale, 1978.
White Jade. New York, Doubleday, 1975.
Key Witness. New York, Putnam, 1975; London, Hale, 1978.
Expendable. New York, Doubleday, 1976; London, Hale, 1979.
The Jaubert Ring. New York, Doubleday, 1976.
The House of Imposters. New York, Popular Library, 1977.
Cape of Black Sands. New York, Popular Library, 1977.

Act of Fear. New York, Doubleday, 1977; London, Hale, 1978.
The Black Pearl series:
   The Dark Dowry. New York, Popular Library, 1978.
   The Cade Curse. New York, Popular Library, 1978.
   The Stuart Stain. New York, Popular Library, 1978.
   The Devil's Double. New York, Popular Library, 1979.
   The Radkin Revenge. New York, Popular Library, 1979.
   The Hellfire Heritage. New York, Popular Library, 1979.
   The Macomber Menace. New York, Popular Library, 1979.
   The Gresham Ghost. New York, Popular Library, 1980.
The Search for Willie. New York, Popular Library, 1980.
The Face at the Window. Toronto, Harlequin, and New York, Raven Press, 1981; London, Hale, 1983.
A Long Time to Hate. New York, Avon, 1982.
The Sniper. New York, Doubleday, 1984.
The Annalise Experiment. New York, Doubleday, 1985.

OTHER PUBLICATIONS

Novels

Nurse Kay's Conquest. New York, Ace, 1966.
Once a Nurse. New York, Ace, 1966.
Nurse at Mystery Villa. New York, Ace, 1967.
Nurse in Danger. New York, Ace, 1972.
The Nurses. New York, Ace, 1972; as *The Secret Lives of the Nurses,* London, Pan, 1975.
The M.D. New York, Lancer, 1972.
Nurse Robin. New York, Lenox Hill Press, 1973.
Destiny's Women. New York, Popular Library, 1980.
The Gallant Spirit. New York, Popular Library, 1982.
Days of Valor. New York, Warner, 1983.
Keating's Landing. New York, Warner, 1984.
My Rebel, My Love. New York, Pocket Books, 1986.
To Share a Dream. Toronto, Worldwide, 1986.
Madawaska. Toronto, Worldwide, 1988.

Other (for children)

The View from the Cherry Tree. New York, Atheneum, 1975.
Don't Hurt Laurie! New York, Atheneum, 1977.
The Minden Curse. New York, Atheneum, 1978.
More Minden Curses. New York, Atheneum, 1980.
The Girl with the Silver Eyes. New York, Atheneum, 1980.
House of Fear. New York, Scholastic, 1983.
The Pet-Sitting Peril. New York, Atheneum, 1983.
No Monsters in the Closet. New York, Atheneum, 1983.
Eddie and the Fairy Godpuppy. New York, Atheneum, 1984.
Elizabeth. New York, Scholastic, 1984.
Caroline. New York, Scholastic, 1984.
Baby Sitting Is a Dangerous Job. New York, Atheneum, 1985.
Victoria. New York, Scholastic, 1985.
The Magic Book. New York, Atheneum, 1986.
Sugar Isn't Everything. New York, Atheneum, 1987.
Megan's Island. New York, Atheneum, 1988.
What Could Go Wrong? New York, Atheneum, 1989.
Nightmare. New York, Atheneum, 1989.
To Grandmother's House We Go. New York, Atheneum, 1990.

*

Manuscript Collections: Bowling Green University, Ohio; (children's books): de Grummond Collection, University of

Southern Mississippi, Hattiesburg; Central Missouri State University, Arrensburg.

* * *

Willo Davis Roberts has never achieved the success she deserves. She began as a writer of nurse romances, moved on to gothics when the boom in the 1960's occurred, then tried her hand at family sagas and mysteries. Roberts is one of those rare writers who seems capable of making any genre interesting. Her gothics, while limited by the commercial restrictions of the era, were shot through with traces of insight and humor virtually unknown to the form. *Inherit the Darkness,* for example, is a sturdy melodrama buttressed by a clean, quick-reading prose style and a definitely modern sensibility rare among this subgenre, even today. Various minority people appear in Roberts's gothics in interesting and enlightened roles. If you think that's of small value, try to read most of her peers of that time.

Of her mystery novels, *Act of Fear* is the most successfully realized. Here Roberts shows a particularly deft hand at the novel of "psychological suspense" (as blurb writers call them), balancing character studies with a central mystery. The book is notable also for Roberts's place description, her eye and feel for describing the outdoors as well as anybody since Rex Stout.

A second suspense novel, *Expendable,* got buried in a somewhat overlong and overwrought "I" narrative that nonetheless holds attention throughout. *The Face at the Window,* while occasionally sinking into the kind of sudsy prose of her lesser gothic efforts, holds up after two or three readings. Again, her sharp sense of character and her fondness for place description give the novel a permanence that eludes the somewhat familiar plot.

By the time Roberts published *A Long Time to Hate,* which is as much a polemic aimed at too-lenient judges as it is a novel, she had tried several routes to brand-name success, none of them notably successful.

The breakthrough novel seems to have eluded Roberts. One has to wonder why. Surely she is as skilled as Mary Higgins Clark; surely her world-view is as clearly defined as Phyllis Whitney's. Perhaps it is her almost dogged commitment to reality that holds her back. In a marketplace filled with "exotic" novels written by people who never venture further than their local library, Roberts's calm, considered dedication to reality may be too much for most bestseller readers. Roberts can give you a crowded supermarket and all its attendant complications with a skill the equal of Updike's. The world seems to want flashier virtues, and perhaps the brand-name level of achievement will never be hers. But that's ultimately a moot point. Her books are written with an ability, compassion, and warmth rare for the mystery genre or any other.

—Ed Gorman

———

ROBESON, Kenneth. *See* **DENT, Lester; GOULART, Ron.**

———

ROGERS, Joel Townsley. American. Born in Sedalia, Missouri, 22 November 1896. Educated at Harvard University, Cambridge, Massachusetts, B.A. 1917 (chairman of the editorial board, Harvard *Crimson*). Served in the United States Naval Air Force, 1917–19. Married Winifred Whitehouse. Worked in public relations and as editor of *Book Chat* for Brentano's, 1922–25; employed by Century Publishing Company. *Died 1 October 1984.*

CRIME PUBLICATIONS

Novels

Once in a Red Moon. New York, Brentano's, 1923.
The Red Right Hand. New York, Simon and Schuster, 1945.
Lady with the Dice. Kingston, New York, Quin, 1946.
The Stopped Clock. New York, Simon and Schuster, 1958; as *Never Leave My Bed*, Beacon, New York, Beacon Signal, 1960.

Uncollected Short Stories

"The Murderer," in *Best Detective Stories of the Year 1947,* edited by David Coxe Cooke. New York, Dutton, 1947.
"The Belated Corpse," in *Detective Fiction* (New York), May 1951.
"The Return of the Murderer," in *Detective Tales* (London), September 1960.

* * *

Joel Townsley Rogers, best known as the author of the classic mystery novel *The Red Right Hand*, was a freelance fiction writer for pulp and slick magazines for more than 40 years. In addition to his periodical fiction, Rogers published four book-length works, including *Once in a Red Moon*, described by him as "a hocus-pocus, semi-mystery novel"; *Lady with the Dice*, expanded from the 1938 pulp story "A Date with Lachesis"; and *The Stopped Clock*.

Rogers's best book is *The Red Right Hand*, the story of a young doctor, apparently implicated in a series of maniacal murders, who attempts to discover the identity of the real killer by painstakingly reviewing the details of the case while his own death is being planned. The nightmare setting of the story, its hallucinatory incidents, and its breathless prose all lend a kind of mythic grandeur to the events and help make the book one of the most distinguished in its genre.

—Elliot L. Gilbert

———

ROHMER, Sax. Pseudonym for Arthur Henry Sarsfield Ward; adopted name Sarsfield at the age of 18; later used Sax Rohmer even in personal life; also wrote as Michael Furey. British. Born in Birmingham, Warwickshire, 15 February 1883. Married Rose Elizabeth Knox in 1909. Journalist: covered the underworld in London's Limehouse; wrote songs and sketches for entertainers. Later lived in New York City. *Died 1 June 1959.*

CRIME PUBLICATIONS

Novels (series: Fu Manchu; Paul Harley; Daniel "Red" Kerry; Gaston Max; Sumuru)

The Mystery of Dr. Fu-Manchu. London, Methuen, 1913; as *The Insidious Dr. Fu-Manchu,* New York, McBride, 1913.

The Sins of Séverac Bablon. London, Cassell, 1914; New York, Bookfinger, 1967.

The Yellow Claw (Max). London, Methuen, and New York, McBride, 1915.

10.30 Folkstone Express. London, Lloyds, n.d.

The Devil Doctor. London, Methuen, 1916; as *The Return of Dr. Fu-Manchu,* New York, McBride, 1916.

The Si-Fan Mysteries. London, Methuen, 1917; as *The Hand of Fu-Manchu,* New York, McBride, 1917.

Brood of the Witch-Queen. London, Pearson, 1918; New York, Doubleday, 1924.

The Quest of the Sacred Slipper. London, Pearson, and New York, Doubleday, 1919.

Dope (Kerry). London, Cassell, and New York, McBride, 1919.

The Golden Scorpion (Fu Manchu; Max). London, Methuen, 1919; New York, McBride, 1920.

The Green Eyes of Bâst. London, Cassell, and New York, McBride, 1920.

Bat-Wing (Harley). London, Cassell, and New York, Doubleday, 1921.

Fire-Tongue (Harley). London, Cassell, 1921; New York, Doubleday, 1922.

Grey Face. London, Cassell, and New York, Doubleday, 1924.

Yellow Shadows (Kerry). London, Cassell, 1925; New York, Doubleday, 1926.

Moon of Madness. New York, Doubleday, and London, Cassell, 1927.

She Who Sleeps. New York, Doubleday, and London, Cassell, 1928.

The Emperor of America. New York, Doubleday, and London, Cassell, 1929.

The Day the World Ended (Max). New York, Doubleday, and London, Cassell, 1930.

Daughter of Fu Manchu. New York, Doubleday, and London, Cassell, 1931.

Yu'an Hee See Laughs. New York, Doubleday, and London, Cassell, 1932.

The Mask of Fu Manchu. New York, Doubleday, 1932; London, Cassell, 1933.

Fu Manchu's Bride. New York, Doubleday, 1933; as *The Bride of Fu Manchu,* London, Cassell, 1933.

The Trail of Fu Manchu. New York, Doubleday, and London, Cassell, 1934.

The Bat Flies Low. New York, Doubleday, and London, Cassell, 1935.

President Fu Manchu. New York, Doubleday, and London, Cassell, 1936.

White Velvet. New York, Doubleday, and London, Cassell, 1936.

The Drums of Fu Manchu. New York, Doubleday, and London, Cassell, 1939.

The Island of Fu Manchu. New York, Doubleday, and London, Cassell, 1941.

Seven Sins (Max). New York, McBride, 1943; London, Cassell, 1944.

Egyptian Nights. London, Hale, 1944; as *Bimbâshi Barûk of Egypt* (short stories version), New York, McBride, 1944.

Shadow of Fu Manchu. New York, Doubleday, 1948; London, Jenkins, 1949.

Hangover House. New York, Random House, 1949; London, Jenkins, 1950.

Nude in Mink. New York, Fawcett, 1950; as *Sins of Sumuru,* London, Jenkins, 1950; New York, Bookfinger, 1977.

Wulfheim (as Michael Furey). London, Jarrolds, 1950.

Sumuru. New York, Fawcett, 1951; as *Slaves of Sumuru,* London, Jenkins, 1952.

The Fire Goddess (Sumuru). New York, Fawcett, 1952; as *Virgin in Flames,* London, Jenkins, 1953.

The Moon Is Red. London, Jenkins, 1954.

Return of Sumuru. New York, Fawcett, 1954; as *Sand and Satin,* London, Jenkins, 1955.

Sinister Madonna (Sumuru). London, Jenkins, and New York, Fawcett, 1956.

Re-Enter Fu Manchu. New York, Fawcett, 1957; as *Re-Enter Dr. Fu Manchu,* London, Jenkins, 1957.

Emperor Fu Manchu. London, Jenkins, and New York, Fawcett, 1959.

Short Stories

The Exploits of Captain O'Hagan. London, Jarrolds, 1916; New York, Bookfinger, 1968.

Tales of Secret Egypt. London, Methuen, 1918; New York, McBride, 1919.

The Dream-Detective. London, Jarrolds, 1920; New York, Doubleday, 1925.

The Haunting of Low Fennel. London, Pearson, 1920.

Tales of Chinatown. London, Cassell, and New York, Doubleday, 1922.

Tales of East and West. London, Cassell, 1932; with different contents, New York, Doubleday, 1933.

Salute to Bazarada and Other Stories. London, Cassell, 1939; New York, Bookfinger, 1971.

The Secret of Holm Peel and Other Strange Stories. New York, Ace, 1970.

The Wrath of Fu Manchu and Other Stories. London, Stacey, 1973; New York, Daw, 1976.

Uncollected Short Stories

"The Oversized Trunk," in *This Week* (New York), 22 October 1944.

"The Stolen Peach Stone," in *This Week* (New York), 19 November 1944.

"Serpent Wind," in *Murder for the Millions,* edited by Frank Owen. New York, Fell, 1946.

"The Secret of the Ruins," in *Fourth Mystery Companion,* edited by Abraham Louis Furman. New York, Lantern Press, 1946.

"The Picture of Innocence," in *This Week* (New York), 9 May 1948.

"The Mysterious Harem," in *This Week* (New York), 26 September 1948.

"Seventeen Lotus Blossoms," in *National Home Weekly* (Winnipeg), March 1949.

"Jamaican Rose," in *To-day Magazine* (Philadelphia), 4 December 1949.

"Cease Play at Eleven," in *To-day Magazine* (Philadelphia), 22 January 1950.

"A Broken Blade," in *Blue Book* (Chicago), November 1950.

"X.Y.Z. Calls," in *Blue Book* (Chicago), January 1951.

"One Brother Was Evil," in *This Week* (New York), 29 April 1951.

"Kiss of the Scorpion," in *Blue Book* (Chicago), June 1951.

"Flee from Danger," in *This Week* (New York), 16 September 1951.

"Narky," in *Ellery Queen's Mystery Magazine* (New York), February 1952.

"The Bride's Dungeon," in *This Week* (New York), 7 November 1954.

"The Case of the Missing Heirloom" in *This Week* (New York), 22 April 1956.

"The Fugitive Celebrity," in *This Week* (New York), 22 April 1956.

"The Mystery of the Vanishing Treasure," in *"This Weeks'" Stories of Mystery and Suspense,* edited by Stewart Beach. New York, Random House, 1957.

"Deadly Blonde of Dartmoor," in *This Week* (New York), 19 October 1958.

"Death Is My Hostess," in *Spy in the Shadows,* edited by Marvin Allen Karp. New York, Popular Library, 1965.

"The Green Scarab," in *Edgar Wallace Mystery Magazine* (Oxford), June 1966.

"The Night of the Jackal," in *Edgar Wallace Mystery Magazine* (Oxford), November 1966.

OTHER PUBLICATIONS

Novel

The Orchard of Tears. London, Methuen, 1918; New York, Bookfinger, 1970.

Plays

Round in 50, with Julian and Lauri Wylie, music by H. Finck and J. Tate (produced Cardiff and London, 1922).
The Eye of Siva (produced London, 1923).
Secret Egypt (produced London, 1928).
The Nightingale, with Michael Martin-Harvey, music by Kennedy Russell (produced London, 1947).

Other

Pause! (published anonymously). London, Greening, 1910.
The Romance of Sorcery. London, Methuen, 1914; New York, Dutton, 1915.

Ghostwriter: *Little Tich: A Book of Travels and Wanderings,* by Harry Relph, London, Greening, 1911.

*

Bibliography: *Sax Rohmer: A Bibliography* by B.M. Day, Denver, New York, Science Fact and Fantasy, 1963.

Critical Study: *Master of Villainy,* by Cay Van Ash and Elizabeth Sax Rohmer, edited by R.E. Briney, Bowling Green, Ohio, Popular Press, 1972 (includes bibliography).

*   *   *

Nowadays the credit (or more often blame) for the "Yellow Peril" school of mystery thriller is placed firmly upon the shoulders of Sax Rohmer. Certainly Rohmer did not invent the concept, which was a staple of sensational journalism before the end of the 19th century. What he did was to find just the right variations on the theme, the proper ingredients for widespread popular success. First of all, Rohmer provided an assortment of vividly described and exotically appointed settings for his stories: perfumed apartments, strewn with cushions, furnished with carved teakwood tables and lacquer cabinets, and lit by brass lamps of strange design. Against such backgrounds the villains' whispered threats and the confidences of imperiled heroines seemed not at all out of place. These splashes of color alternated with set-pieces of familiar-made-mysterious: fog-shrouded London, streets, isolated ma-

nor houses, boats plying the darkened Thames. Next, Rohmer divorced the "Yellow Peril" story from the military context which most earlier writers had used. (M.P. Shiel's *The Yellow Danger* of 1898 is typical.) Rather than an invading army from the East, the reader was invited to shudder at a more personal menace: a paralyzing drug, a deadly insect searching out its prey, a Dacoit with his weird cry and strangler's kerchief. And finally, Rohmer had the talent and good fortune to create a near-mythic figure who embodied all the fancied villainy of the East combined with all the science of the West: "imagine a person, tall, lean and feline, high-shouldered, with a brow like Shakespeare and a face like Satan, a close-shaven skull, and long, magnetic eyes of the true cat-green . . . Imagine that awful being, and you have a mental picture of Dr. Fu-Manchu, the yellow peril incarnate in one man."

Fu Manchu was introduced in the story "The Zayat Kiss" in the October 1912 issue of the British magazine *The Story-Teller.* This was the first of a series of 10 adventures, gathered in book form as an episodic "novel," *The Mystery of Dr. Fu-Manchu.* During the next four years, two further series were published, each duly appearing in both magazine and book form. Although they were written and published during Britain's involvement in World War I, Rohmer allowed no hint of the war to intrude in the stories, which seem to take place in a sort of permanent 1912. At the end of the third book, *The Si-Fan Mysteries,* Fu Manchu was apparently killed, and readers may justifiably have thought they had seen the last of him. Rohmer probably intended this to be the case, since it was nine years before he planned another Fu Manchu adventure, and four years after that before it appeared in print: *Daughter of Fu Manchu.* With this novel, the series entered "real time" again, and subsequent volumes in the 1930's reflected, as in a distorting mirror, the political developments of the times. In *President Fu Manchu,* Fu Manchu was the power behind a U.S. presidential candidate, and disguised versions of Father Coughlin and Huey Long took part in the action. In *The Drums of Fu Manchu,* Fu Manchu fought Fascism, and disposed of a European dictator bearing the transparent pseudonym "Rudolph Adlon." After attempting to gain control of the Panama Canal in *The Island of Fu Manchu,* Rohmer's villain slumbered during World War II, only to return as an anti-Communist crusader in *Shadow of Fu Manchu.* In his final appearance, *Emperor Fu Manchu,* Fu Manchu was still plotting against "these unclean creatures [who] retain their hold upon China, my China."

In the early Fu Manchu stories, the thrills were intermixed with the casual xenophobia of the times, but Fu Manchu himself was always depicted as a man of impeccable integrity, an aristocrat, consistently more clever and resourceful than his opponents. His periodic defeats were caused by unforeseen accidents or, more often, by reliance on untrustworthy agents (usually women who had fallen in love with the hero/narrator). As the series progressed, Fu Manchu became less specifically Oriental and more of a generalized super-criminal. The peak of Fu Manchu's (and Sax Rohmer's) popularity was in the 1930's, when an enormous audience impatiently awaited each new serial. The books have seldom been out of print since their initial publication, and are still finding an audience today.

At the beginning of his writing career, there was no hint that Rohmer's greatest success would come from stories about a Chinese super-criminal. His main interest at that time (and indeed throughout much of his life) was the Near East, especially ancient Egypt. His first fiction sale, published while Rohmer was only 20 years old, was "The Mysterious Mummy" (*Pearson's Weekly,* 1903), a clever and amusing crime story about the theft of an Egyptian artefact from a London museum. During 1913 and 1914 he produced many stories and serials which would not see book publication for several years. The earliest of these were the stories about the psychic detective Moris Klaw (*The Dream-Detective*) who solved a series of bizarre crimes by his method of "odic photography." Klaw's cases included locked-room mysteries as well as hauntings and other supernatural manifestations. *The Quest of the Sacred Slipper,* the story of Hassan of Aleppo's attempts to recover a slipper of Mohammed which had been stolen from Mecca and taken to England, is also from this productive period. The serial version of *Brood of the Witch-Queen* appeared in 1914. This story of the survival of ancient Egyptian sorcery in the moden world is widely regarded as Rohmer's best book.

In 1915 Rohmer's detective character Gaston Max first appeared in *The Yellow Claw.* This was an "Oriental menace" story in the Fu Manchu vein, as was its successor *The Golden Scorpion,* in which Fu Manchu made a brief, anonymous appearance. Max next appeared in *The Day the World Ended* to battle a baroque scientific super-criminal called Anubis in Germany's Black Forest, and returned to combat Axis agents in wartime London in *Seven Sins.* Another of Rohmer's principal detectives is Paul Harley, who appeared in the novels *Bat-Wing* and *Fire-Tongue,* the stage play *The Eye of Siva,* and 11 shorter works published between 1920 and 1939. Chief Inspector Daniel "Red" Kerry appeared in *Dope, Yellow Shadows,* and in a few short stories.

In *Yu'an Hee See Laughs* Rohmer introduced an Oriental smuggler and white slaver with all of Fu Manchu's villainy but none of his imagination or nobility. The character did not prove popular, and was not used again. *White Velvet,* based on a film treatment intended as a vehicle for Marlene Dietrich, is a story of drug smuggling in the Mediterranean. *Egyptian Nights* is a collection of crime and espionage stories set in England and the Near East. *Hangover House* is a traditional "isolated house party" murder mystery, based on an unproduced play. *The Moon Is Red* is a bizarre murder mystery set in Florida, and is one of the best of Rohmer's later novels.

The series of five novels about Sumuru revived the Fu Manchu formula, but featured a carefully de-ethnicized female villain. The stories were popular in their U.S. paperback editions, but Rohmer did not think much of them. The series was dropped when Fu Manchu himself was revived in 1957, and Rohmer brought his writing career to a close by returning full-circle to the source of his greatest fame.

—R.E. Briney

———

ROME, Anthony. *See* **ALBERT, Marvin.**

———

RONNS, Edward. *See* **AARONS, Edward S.**

———

ROOS, Audrey and William. *See* **ROOS, Kelley.**

———

ROOS, Kelley. Joint pseudonym for Audrey Roos (née Kelley) and William Roos; William Roos also writes as William Rand. Americans. Audrey Roos was born in 1912 and died 11 December 1982; William Roos was born in 1911. Recipients: Mystery Writers of America Edgar Allan Poe award, for television play, 1961.

Crime Publications

Novels (series: Jeff and Haila Troy)

Made Up to Kill (Troy). New York, Dodd Mead, 1940; as *Made Up for Murder,* London, Jarrolds, 1941.
If the Shroud Fits (Troy). New York, Dodd Mead, 1941; as *Dangerous Blondes,* New York, Spivak, 1951.
The Frightened Stiff (Troy). New York, Dodd Mead, 1942; London, Hale, 1951.
Sailor, Take Warning! (Troy). New York, Dodd Mead, 1944; London, Hale, 1952.
There Was a Crooked Man (Troy). New York, Dodd Mead, 1945; London, Hale, 1953.
Ghost of a Chance (Troy). New York, Wyn, 1947.
Murder in Any Language (Troy). New York, Wyn, 1948.
Triple Threat (Troy; novelettes). New York, Wyn, 1949; reprinted in part as *Beauty Marks the Spot,* New York, Dell, 1951.
The Blonde Died Dancing. New York, Dodd Mead, 1956; as *She Died Dancing,* London, Eyre and Spottiswoode, 1957.
Requiem for a Blonde. New York, Dodd Mead, 1958; as *Murder Noon and Night,* London, Eyre and Spottiswoode, 1959.
Scent of Mystery (novelization of screenplay). New York, Dell, 1959.
Grave Danger. New York, Dodd Mead, 1965; London, Eyre and Spottiswoode, 1966.
Necessary Evil. New York, Dodd Mead, and London, Eyre and Spottiswoode, 1965.
A Few Days in Madrid (as Audrey and William Roos). New York, Scribner, 1965; London, Deutsch, 1966.
Cry in the Night. New York, Dodd Mead, 1966.
One False Move (Troy). New York, Dodd Mead, 1966.
Who Saw Maggie Brown? New York, Dodd Mead, 1967.
To Save His Life. New York, Dodd Mead, 1968; London, Cassell, 1969.
Suddenly One Night. New York, Dodd Mead, 1970.
What Did Hattie See? New York, Dodd Mead, and London, Cassell, 1970.
Bad Trip. New York, Dodd Mead, 1971.
Murder on Martha's Vineyard. New York, Walker, 1981; London, Hale, 1982.

Uncollected Short Stories

"Two over Par," in *Four and Twenty Bloodhounds,* edited by Anthony Boucher. New York, Simon and Schuster, 1950; London, Hammond, 1951.
"Murder among Ladies," in *American Magazine* (Springfield, Ohio), June 1950.
"Scream in the Night," in *American Magazine* (Springfield, Ohio), April 1953.
"One Victim Too Many," in *American Magazine* (Springfield, Ohio), September 1953.
"Case of the Hanging Gardens," in *American Magazine* (Springfield, Ohio), July 1954.
"Case of the Beautiful Body," in *Mike Shayne Mystery Magazine* (New York), July 1961.

"Death Waits in the Darkroom," in *Mike Shayne Mystery Magazine* (New York), April 1963.

"Murder Underground," in *Ellery Queen's Mystery Magazine* (New York), June 1966.

"The 'Watch Out!' Girls," in *Ellery Queen's Mystery Magazine* (New York), August 1968.

"Murder in the Antique Car Museum," in *Anthology 1971*, edited by Ellery Queen. New York, Davis, 1970.

"Death Is a Trooper," in *Ellery Queen's Mystery Magazine* (New York), 5 May 1980.

OTHER PUBLICATIONS by William Roos

Novel

The Hornet's Longboat. Boston, Houghton Mifflin, 1940.

Plays

Triple Play (produced Milford, Connecticut, 1937).

January Thaw (produced New York, 1946). Chicago, Dramatic Publishing Company, 1946.

Boy Wanted. New York, French, 1947.

Ellery Queen's The Four of Hearts Mystery (as William Rand). Chicago, Dramatic Publishing Company, 1948.

Belles on Their Toes. Chicago, Dramatic Publishing Company, 1952.

Speaking of Murder, with Audrey Roos. New York, Random House, 1957; London, French, 1959.

Television Play: *The Case of the Burning Court*, 1960.

*

Manuscript Collection: Mugar Memorial Library, Boston University.

*   *   *

Writing from 1940 to 1980, Kelley Roos is notable as an example of the changes in emphasis in mystery novels of that period. The first Jeff and Haila Troy books were typical of the light, breezy style practiced by Craig Rice, the Lockridges, Leslie Ford, and Stuart Palmer. Wit, sophistication, non-violent narration, and heroines in last-chapter-distress were hallmarks of the husband/wife detective teams. Roos let the Troys break no new ground in their eight early cases but used puzzle elements and likeable characters to entertain his audience. Throughout his career, Roos wrote for those who read for enjoyment, rather than aiming for the analytic or adventuresome reader.

Made Up to Kill began Roos's use of theatrical settings—a background to be repeated into the 1970's with *What Did Hattie See?* and the novelette "Death Is a Trooper." Jeff was the "detective," often hampering as well as helping the police, but Haila would spot an essential clue that would lead her to the killer one step ahead of Jeff. For the most part, Jeff and Haila were the only ones fully characterized (and we see Jeff through Haila's eyes) so there is little sympathy for the killer or the victim. In addition to the Troys' romance there were usually other young lovers torn by suspicion and a need to hide something. Lieutenant George Hankins maintained a friendly rivalry with Jeff—both ridiculing his amateur status, yet willing to accept an outsider's perspective. From *Murder in Any Language* in 1948 to *The Blonde Died Dancing* in 1956 there is a void. When it was filled it was the first step in Roos's conversion to modern suspense novels. *The Blonde Died*

Dancing was not about the Troys but about another young New York couple, making a small but significant break from the series formula. Connie and Steve Barton are very similar to the Troys, however, and their mystery is reminiscent of *Murder in Any Language*. A few years later Roos produced *Scent of Mystery,* the milestone in the evolution of his work from mysteries to intrigue/suspense. Roos took the plot elements of *Ghost of a Chance,* set it in Spain and replaced Jeff and Haila with another couple. The love interest and concentration on exotic locales superseded the priority of puzzle. These new emphases were continued in later works as the general trend to crime-suspense books became stronger. By the time of *Cry in the Night* and *Grave Danger* the culprit is known early on.

One False Move is a throwback to earlier work, bringing Jeff and Haila up to date (without aging them). Yet it is still a blend of old and new. There are the familiar elements of a theater background, naive lovers trying to hide a problem, and Haila's witty understatement and catty jealousy. But it's modern in that the scene is moved out of New York to a small Texas town and Jeff and Haila have been recently divorced (they are reconciled at the end).

Roos's last books reveal the final transition to a modern romance/suspense/intrigue formula. Although Jeff seldom explained his logic or his deductions, he gave an impression of detection by relating full details of the criminal's actions. These last books often take the reader inside the killer's mind, with no pretense of puzzle or "whodunit." In all cases Roos provided a substantial plot, good characters, and relief from the anxieties of a commonplace world.

—Fred Dueren

———

ROSEN, RICHARD (Dean). American. Born in Chicago, Illinois, 18 February 1949. Educated at Brown University, Providence, Rhode Island, 1967–68; Harvard University, Cambridge, Massachusetts, B.A. 1972. Assistant editor, *Playboy,* Chicago, 1968–69; chef, Peasant Stock Restaurant, Somerville, Massachusetts, 1972–77; teacher of expository writing, Harvard University, 1975–76; since 1977, staff writer and columnist, *Boston.* Address: Viking Books, 40 West 23rd Street, New York, New York 10001, U.S.A.

CRIME PUBLICATIONS

Novels (series: Harvey Blissberg in all books)

Strike Three You're Dead. New York, Walker, 1984.

Fadeaway. Southyarmouth, Massachusetts, Curley, 1986.

Saturday Night Dead. New York, Viking, 1988.

OTHER PUBLICATIONS

Other

Me and My Friends, We no Longer Profess any Graces: A Premature Memoir (essays). New York, Macmillan, 1971.

Psychobabble: Fast Talk and Quick Cure in the Era of Feeling. New York, Atheneum, 1977.

*   *   *

After a first mystery which was probably the finest to use baseball as a background, Richard Rosen wrote one equally good novel about basketball. His third book made use of his experience in television, effectively integrating 30 years of that broadcast medium's history into a mystery plot.

Once, mysteries, for example those by Cortland Fitzsimmons, presented a naive view of professional sports. Rosen's books are about greed, sex, crime, and violence, all the things which, according to the daily sports pages, are part of games. *Strike Three You're Dead* and *Fadeaway* authentically report those sensational aspects, especially the drug and alcohol addictions of young millionaire athletes. Yet, Rosen's technical knowledge of the sports about which he writes is impeccable, and baseball strategy, statistics, and the physical layout of stadiums become important to his first plot. There is little on-court basketball action in *Fadeaway,* except for a Boston Celtics game, but Rosen conveys the hypocrisy in college recruiting and the operation of lucrative professional franchises.

Rosen's series detective is Harvey Blissberg who in the first book is center fielder for the Providence Jewels, an American League expansion team, but becomes a reluctant detective when his roommate is murdered. Rosen handles particularly well the impact on a baseball team of the murder. Everyone professes to be shocked, but when attendance goes up, someone says sardonically about this last-place club, "We lead the league in murders." The decaying city of Providence, Rhode Island is an unhackneyed setting for the first two Blissberg books. Rosen explores the city in depth, sometimes treating it scathingly, as when he describes Harvey's dread of going there. "He felt like someone who has been fixed up on a blind date, only to discover, when he finally goes to pick the woman up, that it's his ex-wife." At other times the good features are presented, so that a real city comes to life. There is good use of local color, and New England accents are captured with accuracy and humor.

Even the title of the only Blissberg mystery without a sports background, *Saturday Night Dead,* indicates that its television program "Last Laughs," is based on "Saturday Night Live." Though its solution is overly melodramatic and identification of the murderer is not based on clues available to the reader, it has many strengths, notably its New York atmosphere and the behind-the-scenes look at television, especially its comedy programs.

Blissberg's early retirement from baseball at the start of *Fadeaway* is never sufficiently explained. His becoming a private detective seems fortuitous; he even obtains his next two cases because of his sports fame. He is a well-rounded hero, though at times he seems to be a Spenser clone, with his interest in cooking and his love affair with a woman who could be literary sister to Parker's Susan Silverman. Though Harvey is not a first-person narrator, it is from his viewpoint that Rosen's stories are told. His thoughts are usually interesting since he has been created as a complex combination of sophistication and earthiness. Even what he buys and eats are used to add to his characterization.

Fittingly for a series detective who batted 300 in his last season, his creator has an unusually high average for successful metaphors, that almost obligatory feature of the private-eye novel. A case suddenly comes to Blissberg like "a line drive to center field." Perplexed by clues, "He had the irritable feeling of someone who's gotten to the movie half an hour late."

Rosen has used two subjects enormously popular with millions of people, sports and television, and combined them with a vivid descriptions of how people talk and what they buy. The historians and sociologists of the future may turn to his books to find, in addition to the freshness and vigor of the

mysteries, graphic descriptions of life in New England and New York during the 1980's.

—Marvin Lachman

———

ROSS, Angus. Pseudonym for Kenneth Giggal. British. Born in Dewsbury, Yorkshire, 19 March 1927. Educated at grammar school. Served in the Fleet Air Arm of the Royal Navy, 1944–52. Married Alice Drummond in 1947; one daughter. Sales manager, D.C. Thomson, publishers, Dundee, 1952–59, and London, 1959–71. Agent: Andrew Mann Ltd., 1 Old Compton Street, London W1V 5PH. Address: Old Granary Mews, Bishop Monkton, Harrogate, North Yorkshire, England.

<small>CRIME PUBLICATIONS</small>

Novels (series: Marcus Aurelius Farrow in all books except *A Bad April*)

The Manchester Thing. London, Long, 1970; as *The Manchester Connection,* London, Severn House, 1984.
The Huddersfield Job. London, Long, 1971.
The London Assignment. London, Long, 1972.
The Dunfermline Affair. London, Long, 1973.
The Bradford Business. London, Long, 1974.
The Amsterdam Diversion. London, Long, 1974.
The Leeds Fiasco. London, Long, 1975.
The Edinburgh Exercise. London, Long, 1975.
The Ampurias Exchange. London, Long, 1976; New York, Walker, 1977.
The Aberdeen Conundrum. London, Long, 1977.
The Burgos Contract. London, Long, 1978; New York, Walker, 1979.
The Congleton Lark. London, Long, 1979.
The Hamburg Switch. London, Long, and New York, Walker, 1980.
The Menwith Tangle. London, Hale, 1982.
The Darlington Jaunt. London, Hale, 1983; New York, Walker, 1984.
A Bad April. London, Chivers, 1984.
The Luxembourg Run. Bath, Avon, Firecrest, 1985.
The Tyneside Ultimatum. Bath, Avon, Firecrest, 1988.

<small>OTHER PUBLICATIONS</small>

Plays

Dear Elsie (produced Wakefield, Yorkshire, 1977).

Television Play: *Runaround,* 1977.

Other as Kenneth Giggal

Classic Sailing Ships, with paintings by Cornelis de Vries. Exeter, Devon, Webb and Bower, and New York, Norton, 1988.

*

Bibliography: by Iwan Hedman-Morelius, in *DAST* (Strängnäs, Sweden), August 1977.

Manuscript Collection: University of Wyoming, Laramie.

Angus Ross comments:

My 12 years in Fleet Street taught me that acts of espionage do not happen only in cities like Bonn and Washington and London. Espionage happens everywhere, and often in the most unlikely places. It is also true to say that people engaged in espionage work are by no means always young and attractive and possessed of super powers. So it was, with these facts firmly in mind, that I set out in 1970 to write a series of espionage novels that would portray the whole business in a simple, down-to-earth manner. Every novel in the series has an absolutely authentic setting, and the espionage targets actually do exist. I do a great deal of research—although I might use only a fraction of it in the final draft of the book—and, so far, have set the action only in towns or cities I really do know well. Asked once by an interviewer why it was that so many people in so many countries were willing to go on buying books set in largely unheard-of British towns, I had to say I did not know. It might of course be that most people are interested in other people, rather than in abstract political principles. I hope it is because I write about real, fallible people caught up in situations which are sufficiently interesting in themselves to preclude any necessity of flights into fantasy.

The series is written around a central character, Marcus Aurelius (Mark) Farrow. He does, however, have a senior partner, Charles McGowan, and McGowan often features quite largely. Farrow is quite definitely a reluctant hero. He was drawn into the business almost inadvertently (see *The Manchester Thing*) and is frequently seen to be trying to get out of it. Basically he is a decent, humane man, and he does not have the mental stomach for some of the harsher contingencies forced upon him in the course of his Section duties. He is a political cynic, and bitterly resents the manipulation by faceless bureaucrats of ordinary people's lives. Most, though not all, of Farrow's attitudes represent my own. We are the same age, have much the same background, and like the same sort of things. This is a device to assist in the writing; it obviates the need to keep elaborate biographical notes. Farrow is not married, but although he is not a celibate man, his sexual encounters never take place within the context of the novels themselves. This, however, is largely because the term of action in any one book rarely exceeds five days. He simply doesn't have the time.

Charlie McGowan is a different man. He is totally bereft of compassion and completely pitiless in his pursuit of those who would do his country harm. He is cold and clever and calculating, and his life is dedicated utterly and unconditionally to the Service. Thus he is often infuriated by Farrow's respect for the human dignities and by Farrow's insistence that, sometimes, people are more important than principles. Theirs is a curious ambivalent association, but each has much unspoken respect for the other and they do in fact work exceptionally well as a team.

*   *   *

Mark (short for Marcus Aurelius!) Farrow is described by his author Angus Ross as a "reluctant hero," and indeed in several of the novels this seemingly tough investigative agent makes valiant, but ultimately thwarted, attempts to retire. His working conditions are far from ideal (frequently involving grave discomfort, not to mention severe damage to his person and his clothing), and his boss is a parsimonious, humourless teetotaller—making life hard for Farrow, who likes nothing more than a good meal accompanied by plentiful alcohol.

Farrow, former naval commando and ex-newspaper man,

enters this latest profession through his investigation of the girl victim of a hit and run killing. This unexpectedly leads to involvement in industrial espionage and drugs, and ultimately Farrow is recruited by MI6. In the second thriller, *The Huddersfield Job*, Farrow meets for the first time Charlie McGowan, his aforementioned boss; together they solve the identity of a Russian agent working at Fylingdales early warning system in Yorkshire. Many of these novels are set in Ross's (and Farrow's) native Yorkshire and the settings in these, and indeed in all the stories, are absolutely authentic. The descriptions of various cities in which action takes place, and more especially those of the Yorkshire countryside, add interest and an extra dimension to what could so easily be a run-of-the-mill series of spy thrillers.

The plots of these novels are (as is customary in this genre) complex, convoluted and confusing; somewhat in contrast to the authenticity of the backgrounds, they are not always terribly convincing. But with two characters as strong and as individual as McGowan and Farrow, the plotting can take a secondary role. The narration (the stories are all told in the first person by Farrow) is sharp and sardonic, the dialogue consists largely of verbal sparring, and the relationship between the two men is the excuse for much dry humor. This is well illustrated in *The Menwith Tangle*, in which Farrow, McGowan and a third agent, McKenzie, all inhabit Farrow's house for the duration of the investigation. The fastidious McGowan uses all the hot water for his frequent baths, rushes the other two through their infrequent and fervently-awaited meals, and generally makes the situation unpleasant for his colleagues and amusing for the reader. Running battles take place in all the novels over meals (their frequency, length, duration and component parts) and expenses—yet these more frivolous interludes do not preclude a lot of tough and fast-paced action, during which Farrow's frequent physical encounters with agents of other countries give him vast scope to acquire various items of clothing of a better quality than he might otherwise have purchased.

Farrow's character is seen to develop as the series progresses—he becomes tougher, more misanthropic, more sexist, racist, and xenophobic—but perhaps the latter can be seen as a professional hazard. Although always, when measured against Charlie McGowan, he appears humane, liberal and philanthropic. Interestingly, in those novels in which Farrow himself plays a superior role to another agent, he adopts some of McGowan's character traits—but never to the detriment of his expense account! Both Farrow and McGowan are extremely disparaging about all foreign agents, both the Russians ("the Others" or "the Ivans") and the Americans ("the Cousins"); in some of the later novels the Israeli Mossad assume the role of the "enemy" and amazingly are not the objects of quite so much scorn.

The Ampurias Exchange is one novel in which the roles of Farrow and McGowan are not so clearly defined. At the start of the book Farrow's current girlfriend Daisy (and the existence of such a person within the story is itself unusual) is murdered in an explosion intended for Farrow. He immediately contacts "the Man" (the seldom-encountered but omnipresent head of the section) who immediately diverts our hero to a rescue operation in Spain—and it is Charlie McGowan himself who is to be rescued, having been captured by a group of Basque terrorists. Here Farrow adopts the dominant role because of McGowan's inability to do so, and the reader is deprived of the customary acerbic exchanges between the two men; but compensation is provided in the form of full descriptions of Farrow's seafood meals—all the more frequent and lavish for McGowan's absence. Here again the descriptive element rings absolutely true, as does the portrayal of Mark Farrow as a man reluctantly enmeshed in a tough world which forces him to sacrifice the basic principles of humanity and compassion, which he struggles to maintain, in order to succeed and survive.

—Judith Rhodes

———

ROSS, Barnaby. *See* QUEEN, Ellery.

———

ROSS, Jonathan. Pseudonym for John Rossiter. British. Born in Staverton, Devon, 2 March 1916. Educated at military schools in Woolwich, London, and in Bulford, Wiltshire; Police College, Bramshill, Hampshire, 1949, 1959. Served in the Royal Air Force, 1943–45: Flight Lieutenant. Married Joan Gaisford in 1942; one daughter. Detective chief superintendent, Wiltshire Constabulary, 1939–69. Columnist, *Wiltshire Courier,* Swindon, 1963–64. Lived in Spain, 1969–76. Agent: Murray Pollinger Ltd., 222 Old Brompton Road, London SW5 0BZ. Address: 2 Church Close, Orcheston, near Salisbury, Wiltshire SP3 4RP, England.

CRIME PUBLICATIONS

Novels (series: Inspector/Detective Superintendent George Rogers in all books)

The Blood Running Cold. London, Cassell, 1968.
Diminished by Death. London, Cassell, 1968.
Dead at First Hand. London, Cassell, 1969.
The Deadest Thing You Ever Saw. London, Cassell, 1969; New York, McCall, 1970.
Here Lies Nancy Frail. London, Constable, and New York, Saturday Review Press, 1972.
The Burning of Billy Toober. London, Constable, 1974; New York, Walker, 1976.
I Know What It's Like to Die. London, Constable, 1976; New York, Walker, 1978.
A Rattling of Old Bones. London, Constable, 1979; New York, Scribner, 1982.
Dark Blue and Dangerous. London, Constable, and New York, Scribner, 1981.
Death's Head. London, Constable, 1982; New York, St. Martin's Press, 1983.
Dead Eye. London, Constable, 1983; New York, St. Martin's Press, 1984.
Dropped Dead. London, Constable, 1984; New York, St. Martin's Press, 1985.
Burial Deferred. London, Constable, 1985; New York, St. Martin's Press, 1986.
Fate Accomplished. London, Constable, and New York, St. Martin's Press, 1987.
Sudden Departures. London, Constable, and New York, St. Martin's Press, 1988.
A Time for Dying. London, Constable, and New York, St. Martin's Press, 1989.

Novels as John Rossiter (series: Roger Tallis)

The Murder Makers (Tallis). London, Cassell, 1970; New York, Walker, 1977.

The Deadly Green (Tallis). London, Cassell, 1970; New York, Walker, 1971.
The Victims. London, Cassell, 1971.
A Rope for General Dietz (Tallis). London, Constable, and New York, Walker, 1972.
The Manipulators. London, Cassell, 1973; New York, Simon and Schuster, 1974.
The Villains. London, Cassell, 1974; New York, Walker, 1976.
The Golden Virgin (Tallis). London, Constable, 1975; as *The Deadly Gold,* New York, Walker, 1975.

Uncollected Short Story

"Yes, Sir: No, Sir," in *John Creasey's Crime Collection 1978,* edited by Herbert Harris. London, Gollancz, 1978.

OTHER PUBLICATIONS as John Rossiter

Novels

The Man Who Came Back. London, Hamish Hamilton, 1978; Boston, Houghton Mifflin, 1979.
Dark Flight. London, Eyre Methuen, and New York, Atheneum, 1981.

*

Jonathan Ross comments:
Having been a policeman for 30 years, I intend that my novels should depict police work as it is, with a policeman's attitude towards crime and the criminal, toward the processes of law and justice (not always synonymous) and the mechanics of detection. Where there are warts, I have shown them. Where law and justice fail the police and society, I have shown it. I have shown policemen as men who sweat, who get tired and disillusioned, who are not necessarily good husbands and lovers, and who do, in fact, come from the same mould as the rest of *Homo sapiens.*

*   *   *

Jonathan Ross, with 30 years of police experience behind him, obviously brings a special perspective to his fiction. Except for a highly productive period in which he (under the name of John Rossiter) turned out a series of well-regarded suspense espionage novels, he has stayed with the police procedural novel and has come to occupy an honourable, and even eminent, place in that genre. The Rossiter novels, with Roger Tallis as the series hero, are very competently done, but their author's real forte has proved to be the novel of police action and detection.

Ross's series hero, Detective Superintendent George Rogers, is depicted as an impatient, often irascible, emotionally vulnerable policeman with few illusions about himself or about mankind generally. He is highly intelligent, having the sort of sensitive, flexible, imaginative, and inquisitive mind useful for solving the puzzles his creator sets him. However, Rogers wastes little time in elaborate and static ratiocination: the trail, the suspects, and the chase almost always draw him out of his office, and he has the scars to prove his personal involvement. He is highly susceptible to women but not very successful with any long-term relationship: sex (and a generous helping of violence) is usually a component in his adventures, though rarely to the detriment of the plot-line. His assistant and foil (the cool Lingard, elegant but in no way a twit) tends to point up, by contrast, Rogers's emotional and risk-taking nature.

Another frequently used form of contrast is seen in the pathology lab: the details of a necropsy performed on the victim, which the reader is not spared, give a scientific solidity behind the policeman's task of pursuing the guilty, and often add an unexpected fillip to the plot as well—as in *Fate Accomplished*, where a man "killed" by a train is shown to have died earlier, and turns out to be officially listed as dead in any case.

The Rogers novels are ingeniously and complexly plotted: switches in identity, false trails, and suspects who lie their heads off abound, and though Rogers says that he is "rarely taken for a ride by deceit and false cunning" (*A Rattling of Old Bones*) he, and the reader, usually have a wildly twisted path to follow. The author sometimes skirts, but never breaks, the fair play rule. His solutions are deft and convincing, if often accompanied by a crescendo of violence. Ross has also successfully used the device of having a later case (*A Rattling of Old Bones*) spring from the complications of an earlier (*Diminished by Death*).

Ross's style has improved with time and practice. His earlier novels tend toward the downright gaudy, heavy on the purple palette, but as Rogers—his main character—has mellowed, and (generally) stopped taking himself so seriously, the prose has settled down as well, and rarely intrudes. The earlier adventures also have a hard and even unpleasant edge of class-prejudice, where members of the lower orders seldom commit the key crimes, but are present as a violent, gormless (if male), sluttish (if female), unwashed and inarticulate fringe. Such a portrayal may affect different readers in different ways. But in sum, Ross has proven himself to be an increasingly skilled craftsman. His police experience has been successfully utilized in the creation of a three-dimensional protagonist, a nice balance of plot and characterization, and a series that stretches the reader's mind, not his credulity.

—D.A. Miller

———

ROSSITER, John. *See* **ROSS, Jonathan.**

———

ROTH, Holly. Also wrote as K.G. Ballard; P.J. Merrill. American. Born in Chicago, Illinois, in 1916; grew up in Brooklyn and London. Married Josef Franta. Worked as model, then held editorial jobs with *Cosmopolitan*, Dell Books, *Seventeen*, *American Journal of Surgery*, and New York Post. Formerly Secretary, Mystery Writers of America. *Died in 1964.*

CRIME PUBLICATIONS

Novels (series: Lieutenant Kelly; Inspector Medford)

The Content Assignment (Kelly). New York, Simon and Schuster, and London, Hamish Hamilton, 1954; as *The Shocking Secret,* New York, Dell, 1955.
The Mask of Glass. New York, Vanguard Press, 1954; London, Hamish Hamilton, 1955.
The Sleeper. New York, Simon and Schuster, and London, Hamish Hamilton, 1955.

The Crimson in the Purple. New York, Simon and Schuster, 1956; London, Hamish Hamilton, 1957.
Shadow of a Lady (Medford). New York, Simon and Schuster, and London, Hamish Hamilton, 1957.
The Slender Thread (as P.J. Merrill). New York, Harcourt Brace, 1959; London, Macdonald, 1960.
The Van Dreisen Affair. New York, Random House, and London, Hamish Hamilton, 1960.
Operation Doctors (Medford). London, Hamish Hamilton, 1962; as *Too Many Doctors,* New York, Random House, 1963.
Button, Button (Kelly). New York, Harcourt Brace, 1966; London, Hamish Hamilton, 1967.

Novels as K.G. Ballard

The Coast of Fear. New York, Doubleday, 1957; as *Five Roads to S'Agaro,* London, Boardman, 1958.
Bar Sinister. New York, Doubleday, 1960; London, Boardman, 1961.
Trial by Desire. London, Boardman, 1960.
Gauge of Deception. New York, Doubleday, 1963; London, Boardman, 1964.

Uncollected Short Stories

"The Fourth Man," in *Alfred Hitchcock's Mystery Magazine* (New York), January 1958.
"They Didn't Deserve Her Death," in *Alfred Hitchcock's Mystery Magazine* (New York), October 1958.
"The Cast-Iron Bachelor," in *Sleuth* (New York), October 1958.
"Vanishing Tricks," in *Suspense* (London), March 1959.
"Eye Witness," in *Suspense* (London), November 1959.
"The Pursuer," in *Alfred Hitchcock's Mystery Magazine* (New York), January 1960.
"The Six Mistakes," in *Ellery Queen's Mystery Magazine* (New York), June 1960.
"As with a Piece of Quartz," in *Ellery Queen's Mystery Magazine* (New York), April 1963.
"A Sense of Dynasty," in *Ellery Queen's Double Dozen.* New York, Random House, 1964; London, Gollancz, 1965.
"The Loves in George's Life," in *Ellery Queen's Mystery Magazine* (New York), February 1964.
"The Spy Who Was So Obvious," in *Ellery Queen's Twentieth Anniversary Annual.* New York, Random House, and London, Gollancz, 1965.
"Who Walks Behind?" in *Ellery Queen's Crime Carousel.* New York, New American Library, 1966; London, Gollancz, 1967.
"The Game's the Thing," in *Ellery Queen's All-Star Lineup.* New York, New American Library, 1967; London, Gollancz, 1968.
"The Girl Who Saw Too Much," in *Ellery Queen's Giants of Mystery.* New York, Davis, 1976; London, Gollancz, 1977.

*   *   *

Holly Roth deserted a modeling career to become a writer, first for newspapers and magazines, then as a successful author of mystery and espionage novels. Writing under the names of K.G. Ballard and P.J. Merrill as well as her own, she wrote 14 books in the 12 years of her short career as a mystery author.

One of Roth's earliest books, *The Content Assignment,* was also one of her most popular. Hailed by Barzun and Taylor in *A Catalogue of Crime* as "an excellent spy and counterspy story," *The Content Assignment* is based on the romantic premise of "love at first sight." When John Terrant, a 32-year-old English newspaper reporter assigned to Berlin, meets a female CIA agent, Ellen Content, one autumn evening in 1948, it is not only the start of a romance, but the beginning of a dangerous and fatal mission. The division of Berlin has placed The Russian Inn, a famous restaurant, in Communist territory although its proprietors are not Communists. A vital message concerning Russian warfare plans is overheard by the proprietor and Ellen Content is assigned to escort him and his family to safety. Unfortunately Ellen disappears while en route to New York, and is presumed dead. John Terrant, never ceasing in his efforts to locate Ellen, happens to read two years later that a dancer named Ellen Content is leaving London to tour the U.S. Knowing that the proprietor's daughter, Natasha, was an exotic dancer, Terrant persuades his editor to assign him to follow the dancer to New York in the hope of finding the real Ellen. His brash blundering methods prove an inadvertent aid to the CIA. A witty, entertaining, descriptive style makes this an appealing tale, even though the hinges of the plot sometimes creak.

Written when the fear of insidious Communist infiltration of the government was running high, *The Mask of Glass* is a chilling story of a plot to take over the United States by a well-organized and powerful Communist group. Well-respected and prominent citizens such as a United States Senator, the head of the Philadelphia branch of the FBI, and the head of the CIA are blackmailed into performing small tasks for the opposition, and are eventually replaced by well-rehearsed Communist look-alikes who have undergone plastic and dental surgery. When young James Kennemore, an inexperienced and brash private in the CIA, blunders into this desperate operation, he is practically blown to bits by what he thinks are members of his own organization. Rescued by a physician friend, he tries to fit together the pieces of his shattered body and the tatters of his reality. Good dialogue, fast-moving action-packed scenes, vivid description, and effective use of the flash-back are Roth's successful stylistic tools. *The Crimson in the Purple* takes on a Gothic character with a creepy mansion setting, hints of ghostly menace, and a playwright who is also a licensed private detective, all providing romance and drama to a haunting tale of blackmail and fraud combined with murder.

Roth's series character, Inspector Medford, appears first in *Shadow of a Lady*, a very well-written tale with a tight plausible plot, and interesting character studies. In *Operation Doctors* the combination of an amnesia case, a ship at sea, and murdered physicians provides an engaging challenge for the shrewd deduction of Inspector Medford.

—Mary Ann Grochowski

ROYCE, Kenneth. Pseudonym for Kenneth Royce Gandley; also writes as Oliver Jacks. British. Born in Croydon, Surrey, 11 December 1920. Served in the London Irish Rifles, Royal Ulster Rifles, 1st Northern Rhodesia Regiment, and King's African Rifles, 1939–46: Captain. Married Stella Amy Parker in 1946. Founder and managing director, Business and Holiday Travel Ltd., London, 1948–72. Agent: David Higham Associates Ltd., 5–8 Lower John Street, London W1R 4HA, England; or, Harold Ober Associates Inc., 40 East 49th Street, New York, New York 10017, U.S.A.

CRIME PUBLICATIONS

Novels (series: Spider Scott)

My Turn to Die. London, Barker, 1958.
The Soft-Footed Moor. London, Barker, 1959.
The Long Corridor. London, Cassell, 1960.
No Paradise. London, Cassell, 1961.
The Night Seekers. London, Cassell, 1962.
The Angry Island. London, Cassell, 1963.
The Day the Wind Dropped. London, Cassell, 1964.
Bones in the Sand. London, Cassell, 1967.
A Peck of Salt. London, Cassell, 1968.
A Single to Hong Kong. London, Hodder and Stoughton, 1969.
The XYY Man (Scott). London, Hodder and Stoughton, and New York, McKay, 1970.
The Concrete Boot (Scott). London, Hodder and Stoughton, and New York, McKay, 1971.
The Miniatures Frame (Scott). London, Hodder and Stoughton, and New York, Simon and Schuster, 1972.
Spider Underground. London, Hodder and Stoughton, 1973; as *The Masterpiece Affair*, New York, Simon and Schuster, 1973.
Trap Spider. London, Hodder and Stoughton, 1974.
The Woodcutter Operation (Scott). London, Hodder and Stoughton, and New York, Simon and Schuster, 1975.
Bustillo. London, Hodder and Stoughton, and New York, Coward McCann, 1976.
The Satan Touch. London, Hodder and Stoughton, 1978.
The Third Arm. London, Hodder and Stoughton, and New York, McGraw Hill, 1980.
10,000 Days. London, Hodder and Stoughton, and New York, McGraw Hill, 1981.
Channel Assault. London, Hodder and Stoughton, 1982; New York, McGraw Hill, 1983.
The Stalin Account. London, Hodder and Stoughton, 1983.
The Crypto Man. London, Hodder and Stoughton and New York, Stein and Day, 1984.
The Mosley Receipt (Scott). London, Hodder and Stoughton, and New York, Stein and Day, 1985.
No Way Back, London, Hodder and Stoughton, 1986; as *Hashimi's Revenge,* New York, Stein and Day, 1986.
The President Is Dead. London, Hodder and Stoughton, 1988; as *Patriots,* New York, Crown, 1988.
Fall-Out. London, Hodder and Stoughton, and New York, Crown, 1989.
Exchange of Doves. London, Hodder and Stoughton, 1990.

Novels as Oliver Jacks

Man on a Short Leash. London, Hodder and Stoughton, and New York, Stein and Day, 1974.
Assassination Day. London, Hodder and Stoughton, and New York, Stein and Day, 1976.
Autumn Heroes. London, Hodder and Stoughton, 1977; New York, St. Martin's Press, 1978.
Implant. London, Collins, 1980.

*

Kenneth Royce comments:
I always think the book I am writing is going to be my best, but as soon as I'm finished I am left in doubt. I put a great deal into each book and believe that revision plays the biggest part in success. I also believe in visiting those places I write about. I simply go on hoping to be better and go on believing that I am. Writing full time is a great help: the time is there, and acts as a

spur. I find it difficult to understand how some writers can publicly criticise others. Having said that I will add that I have no personal beef about reviewers—overall they have been quite kind to me. I am involved in my own fiction; involved to a point where I firmly believe that it can happen. Here and there in my experience it *has* happened. As I go on the themes seem to become more complex but never, I hope, too much so. With complexity come more sophisticated plots and presentation. I find structure comes instinctively. I never plan beyond a broad outline: only in this way can a sense of realism obviate manifest contrivance. In my view writing is a profession from which there is no retirement.

*   *   *

Kenneth Royce Gandley writing as Kenneth Royce is best known for his series featuring Willie "Spider" Scott, a former cat burglar, who's recruited by British Intelligence to work undercover for them.

One of the best Spider Scott novels is *The Mosley Receipt*. When Spider's friend, Tom Moody, dies in a freak accident, Spider investigates and finds a maze of political murders committed by a shadowy group within British Intelligence. It becomes a race whether Spider can expose the killers before the killers murder him. The book also contains a wonderful prison break-out scene.

Spider Scott's adventures have also been dramatized on British television; adaptations of *The XYY Man, The Concrete Boot, Spider Underground, The Miniatures Frame, Trap Spider,* and *The Woodcutter Operation* have all been popular with English audiences.

Under the Oliver Jacks pseudonym, Royce's best book is *Man on a Short Leash*. Todd, a former member of CID who now works for MI6, finds himself framed, convicted of treason, and put in prison. Todd finds that the only way to clear himself is to pretend to cooperate with the Russian group that framed him. The Russians help Todd escape from prison, but then the pressure is on for Todd to reveal all the secret information he learned conducting security checks for MI6. The book is riveting, with a fast and furious climax.

Of Royce's non-series books, *The Third Arm* stands out. Chosen as one of the best mysteries of 1980 by the *New York Times Book Review,* it's the story of Ross Gibbs whose mission is to infiltrate a group of international terrorists. Royce's depiction of the terrorists and their methods is frighteningly real.

In 1982, the London *Daily Mail* selected Royce's *10,000 Days* as one of the year's best books. The title refers to the estimate that the world supply of oil will run out in 37 years: 10,000 days. The Western powers mount a secret mission to gain Mideast oil: they use two pawns, Ray Wilson, a British agent, and Doug Shearer, an American agent. The mission is full of treachery and Royce brings the book to a startling conclusion.

Of Royce's more recent work, *The President Is Dead* and *Fall-Out* are topnotch thrillers. In *The President Is Dead,* the death of the President of the United States sets a mole for British Intelligence on the trail of a sinister plot. For years, Laurie Galvin has gained access to the most violent faction of the IRA. What he learns during his investigation leads Galvin to suspect a twisted scheme that would rock the governments of three countries if the truth comes out. Royce handles this book's complicated plot with deftness.

Fall-Out is even better. A man named Zotov finds himself wandering the streets of a Russian city, having lost his memory. He's managed to escape from a Soviet psychiatric "hospital" where he was subjected to "deprogramming" to erase the secret in his mind. However, with his escape, the KGB and British

Intelligence race to find him. Royce throws in another element: Zotov's hospital is very near the nuclear disaster that occurred at Chernobyl. This unusual mix of plot elements makes *Fall-Out* one of Royce's most satisfying books.

Royce is a world-class suspense and thriller writer whose work blends exotic locales and current events to produce highly entertaining novels.

—George Kelley

———

RUELL, Patrick. *See* **HILL, Reginald.**

———

RUSSELL, Martin (James). Also writes as James Arney; Mark Lester. British. Born in Bromley, Kent, 25 September 1934. Educated at Bromley Grammar School, 1946–51. Served in the Royal Air Force (national service) for two years. Reporter, *Kentish Times,* Bromley, 1951–58; reporter and sub-editor, *Croydon Advertiser,* Croydon, Surrey, and Beckenham, Kent, 1958–73. Editor, Crime Writers Association *Red Herrings,* 1979–81. Agent: Curtis Brown Ltd., 162–168 Regent Street, London W1R 5TA. Address: 15 Breckonmead, Wanstead Road, Bromley, Kent, England.

CRIME PUBLICATIONS

Novels (series: Jim Larkin)

No Through Road. London, Collins, 1965; New York, Coward MCann, 1966.
No Return Ticket. London, Collins, 1966.
Danger Money. London, Collins, 1968.
Hunt to a Kill. London, Collins, 1969.
Deadline (Larkin). London, Collins, 1971.
Advisory Service. London, Collins, 1971.
Concrete Evidence (Larkin). London, Collins, 1972.
Double Hit. London, Collins, 1973.
Crime Wave (Larkin). London, Collins, 1974.
Phantom Holiday (Larkin). London, Collins, 1974.
The Client. London, Collins, 1975.
Murder by the Mile (Larkin). London, Collins, 1975.
Double Deal. London, Collins, 1976.
Terror Trade (as Mark Lester). London, Hale, 1976.
Mr. T. London, Collins, 1977; as *The Man Without a Name,* New York, Coward McCann, 1977.
Dial Death. London, Collins, 1977.
Daylight Robbery. London, Collins, 1978.
A Dangerous Place to Dwell. London, Collins, 1978; as *Unwelcome Audience,* New York, Walker, 1986.
Touchdown. London, Collins, 1979.
Death Fuse. London, Collins, 1980; New York, St. Martin's Press, 1981.
Catspaw. London, Collins, 1980.
Backlash. London, Collins, 1981; New York, Walker, 1983.
All Part of the Service. London, Collins, 1982.
Rainblast. London, Collins, 1982.
The Search for Sara. London, Collins, 1983; New York, Walker, 1984.
A View to Ransom (as James Arney). London, Hale, 1983.

A Domestic Affair. London, Collins, 1984; New York, Walker 1985.
Censor. London, Collins, 1984.
The Darker Side of Death. London, Collins, 1985.
Prime Targets. London, Collins, 1985.
Dead Heat. London, Collins, 1986.
The Second Time Is Easy. London, Collins, 1987.
House Arrest. London, Collins, 1988.
Dummy Run. London, Collins, 1989.

*

Martin Russell comments:

In writing a crime novel my chief aim is to entertain, amuse, and intrigue the reader. If, in the bargain, I can baffle him until the final few pages, so much the better; if I bore anybody, I have failed. I should like to think that a few of my books also include an element of exploration into minds and motivations. Human psychology is an infinite jungle, and there is no end to the paths that can be pursued . . . or the dark destinations to which they can lead. To me there is more excitement in the mental processes of a schizophrenic than in a hundred pistol shots. If a percentage of crime fiction readers feel likewise, it is at them that much of my work is directed.

* * *

Martin Russell's fast-moving mysteries provide plenty of clues to his professional background. His writing is simple and clear and descriptions of people and places are always kept to a minimum: with Russell, as with all good newspaper reporters, the story is everything. His experience in journalism also provides him with material for several books. One of the best is *Deadline,* which introduces Jim Larkin, an enigmatic figure whose arrival on the staff of a seaside town's tri-weekly paper coincides with the start of a series of brutal murders. The casual cynicisms of the newsroom and the growing tensions within the community are conveyed with economy but also with conviction. The dialogue is witty and crisp and Russell's account of the behavior of vigilante groups set up by frightened members of the public adds an element of social comment which he seldom attempts elsewhere.

Larkin features in four later novels, but Russell specialises not in straightforward detection but in outlining a bizarre sequence of events and building suspense as his protagonists find themselves trapped in webs which are often of their own making. Russell can match Cornell Woolrich for ingenuity and is much better at tying up all the loose ends of his plots, although his books lack the emotional intensity and compelling metropolitan atmosphere of the American writer's celebrated thrillers.

All Part of the Service, for instance, is set in Glasgow but Russell makes little of that city's unique character. Instead the focus is on Barry Cribb, who edits an agony column under the name of Celia Sparke. Amiable on the surface, Barry is in fact neurotic about his inability to attract women. When he decides to pay a private visit to a disgruntled wife who has sought Celia's advice, he takes a first step towards becoming a serial murderer. Russell concentrates on offering a tense and well-paced thriller rather than an in-depth character study in the currently fashionable mode, and the novel is none the worse for that. A more ingenious story, although over-reliant on coincidence, is *Dead Heat.* Marvin Pike, the cuckolded shopkeeper is, like Barry, a weak individual whose loss of self-control leads to murder. *A Domestic Affair* recounts the misadventures of Colin Fletcher, a clerk in an estate agency whose ex-wife obstructs his right of access to their two children.

Complication piles upon complication as Colin tries to achieve justice and there is an excellent twist in the very last sentence.

The best Russell stories are those which offer the most intriguing puzzles. Because he knows his limitations as a writer and works within them, he hardly ever disappoints readers looking for entertainment unburdened with a finger-wagging message. Judged by his own standards, however, *Dummy Run* is something of a let-down. This is not due to the lack of a murder—the plot revolves around blackmail and drug-trafficking—but to the obviousness of the final twists. More complex and compelling is *Backlash.* Although this is not the only book in which Russell makes use of that old mystery writer's stand-by, the vanishing corpse, here the variations on a familiar theme are particularly fresh and enjoyable. From the outset, when Steven Cassell hears his business partner's confession to murder, the distinction between fact and fantasy is blurred. By the time of the final revelation, it is easy to believe that "the plot thickens" was a phrase coined to describe Russell's work.

—Martin Edwards

———

RUTHERFORD, Douglas. Pseudonym for James Douglas Rutherford McConnell; also wrote as Paul Temple. British. Born in Kilkenny, Ireland, 14 October 1915. Educated at Sedbergh School, Yorkshire; Clare College, Cambridge, 1934–37, M.A.; University of Reading, M.Phil. in education 1977. Served in the British Army Intelligence Corps in North Africa and Italy, 1940–46: mentioned in despatches. Married Margaret Laura Goodwin in 1953; one son. Language teacher and housemaster, Eton College, 1946–73. *Died 29 April 1988.*

CRIME PUBLICATIONS

Novels

Comes the Blind Fury. London, Faber, 1950.
Meet a Body. London, Faber, 1951.
Telling of Murder. London, Faber, 1952; as *Flight into Peril,* New York, Dodd Mead, 1952.
Grand Prix Murder. London, Collins, 1955.
The Perilous Sky. London, Collins, 1955.
The Chequered Flag. London, Collins, 1956.
The Long Echo. London, Collins, 1957; New York, Abelard Schuman, 1958.
A Shriek of Tyres. London, Collins, 1958; as *On the Track of Death,* New York, Abelard Schuman, 1959.
Murder Is Incidental. London, Collins, 1961.
The Creeping Flesh. London, Collins, 1963; New York, Walker, 1965.
The Black Leather Murders. London, Collins, and New York, Walker, 1966.
Skin for Skin. London, Collins, and New York, Walker, 1968.
The Gilt-Edged Cockpit. London, Collins, 1969; New York, Doubleday, 1971.
Clear the Fast Lane. London, Collins, 1971; New York, Holt Rinehart, 1972.
The Gunshot Grand Prix. London, Collins, 1972.
Killer on the Track. London, Collins, 1973; New York, Bradbury Press, 1974.
Kick Start. London, Collins, 1973; New York, Walker, 1974.
Rally to the Death. London, Collins, 1974; New York, Bradbury Press, 1974.

Race Against the Sun.   London, Collins, 1975.
Mystery Tour.   London, Collins, 1975; New York, Walker, 1976.
Return Load.   London, Collins, and New York, Walker, 1977.
Collision Course.   London, Macmillan, 1978; New York, State Mutual, 1982.
Turbo.   London, Macmillan, and New York, St. Martin's Press, 1980.
The Porcupine Basin.   London, Macmillan, 1981.
Stop at Nothing.   London, Macmillan, and New York, Walker, 1983.
A Game of Sudden Death.   London, Macmillan, 1987; New York, Doubleday, 1989.

Novels with Francis Durbridge as Paul Temple (series: Paul Temple in both books)

The Tyler Mystery.   London, Hodder and Stoughton, 1957.
East of Algiers.   London, Hodder and Stoughton, 1959.

OTHER PUBLICATIONS as James McConnell

Other

Learn Italian Quickly.   London, MacGibbon and Kee, 1960.
Learn Spanish Quickly.   London, MacGibbon and Kee, 1961; New York, Citadel Press, 1963.
Learn French Quickly.   London, MacGibbon and Kee, 1966.
Eton: How It Works.   London, Faber, 1967; New York, Humanities Press, 1968.
Eton Repointed: The New Structures of an Ancient Foundation.   London, Faber, 1970.
The Benedictine Commando.   London, Hamish Hamilton, 1981.

Editor (as Douglas Rutherford), *Best Motor Racing Stories.*   London, Faber, 1965.
Editor (as Douglas Rutherford), *Best Underworld Stories.*   London, Faber, 1969.
Editor, *Treasures of Eton.*   London, Chatto and Windus, 1976.

*

Douglas Rutherford commented (1984):
My novels deal more with speed and suspense than with crime. I started writing them as a relaxation and change from my more academic life. They had to be written during the short period of the holidays and at great speed. It was therefore suitable to write about fast vehicles and fast-moving situations, which is why many of my stories feature racing or sports cars, fast motorbikes, long-distance lorries, etc. Researching such subjects made a welcome change from teaching the young.
Since 1980 I have started working on novels based on personal experience, for example, Italy during World War II.

*   *   *

Douglas Rutherford spent part of his wartime service in counter-intelligence in Europe and his knowledge of the real life international crime scene gives the stamp of authenticity to all of his writings. Many of his most popular novels have a Grand Prix or motor racing background. I find the most absorbing of these are *The Long Echo* and *Meet a Body. The Perilous Sky* deals with the world of commercial flying and is portrayed as realistically as any of his motor racing stories. The pace of Rutherford's stories is fast, his plots are well worked out, and his skill as a story teller keeps his reader riding on a crest of excitement and tension right up unto the last page. His collaborations with Francis Durbridge, *East of Algiers* and *The Tyler Mystery,* both feature Paul Temple and are well worth reading.

—Donald C. Ireland

————

RUTLEDGE, Brett. *See* **PAUL, Elliot.**

————

RYDELL, Forbes. *See* **FORBES, Stanton.**

————

RYDER, Jonathan. *See* **LUDLUM, Robert.**

————

S

SADLER, Mark. *See* COLLINS, Michael.

———

SAGOLA, Mario J. *See* KANE, Henry.

———

ST. CLAIR, Dexter. *See* STERLING, Stewart.

———

ST. CLARE, Dexter. *See* STERLING, Stewart.

———

ST. JOHN, David. *See* HUNT, E. Howard.

———

SALE, Richard (Bernard). American. Born in New York City, 17 December 1911. Educated at Washington and Lee University, Lexington, Virginia, 1930–33. Married 2) Mary Anita Loos in 1946; 3) Irma Foster in 1971; three children. Freelance pulp magazine writer 1930–44; screen writer for Paramount, 1944, Republic, 1945–48, Twentieth Century-Fox, 1948–52, British Lion, 1953–54, United Artists, 1954, Columbia, 1956; television writer, director, and producer, Columbia Broadcasting System, 1958–59; film composer. Agent: H.N. Swanson, 8523 West Sunset Boulevard, Hollywood, California 90069. Address: 138 South Camden Drive, Beverly Hills, California 90212, U.S.A.

CRIME PUBLICATIONS

Novels (series: Daniel Webster)

Cardinal Rock. London, Cassell, 1940.
Lazarus No. 7 (Webster). New York, Simon and Schuster, 1942; as *Death Looks In,* London, Cassell, 1943; as *Lazarus Murder Seven,* Kingston, New York, Quin, 1943.
Sailor, Take Warning. London, Wells Gardner, 1942.
Passing Strange (Webster). New York, Simon and Schuster, 1942.
Destination Unknown. Kingswood, Surrey, World's Work, 1943; as *Death at Sea,* New York, Popular Library, 1948.

Benefit Performance (Webster). New York, Simon and Schuster, 1946.
Home Is the Hangman (novelettes). New York, Popular Library, 1949.
Murder at Midnight (novelettes). New York, Popular Library, 1950.
For the President's Eyes Only. New York, Simon and Schuster, 1971; as *The Man Who Raised Hell,* London, Cassell, 1971.

Uncollected Short Stories (series: Joe "Daffy" Dill, Bill Hanley, and Candid Jones in all stories)

"The Fifty Grand Brain," "A Nose for News," "The Ghost Wore Boots," "Cocked Dice," "A Slug for Cleopatra," "The Mute One," "The Bumper-Offer," "The Dancing Corpse," "Man Bites Dog!," "Green Mamba," "I Cover Crime," "Twenty-Three Million," "The Strangler Without Hands," "The Balinese Dagger," "Double Trouble," "Long Shot," "Neat But Not Gaudy," "The Dancing Rats," "The Cobra Is a Gentleman," "The Murderous Mr. Coon," "Murder on the Film," "One Herring—Very Red," "Ghost in C-Minor," "Flash!," "Hanley Has a Homicide," "Quoth the Raven, 'Nevermore,'" "Give Ghost Give," "The Big Top Murders," "Ghost of a Chance," "Make Way for a Dagger," "Guns for Spain," "Jim-jam," "Pictures in the Dark," "Exclusive!," "Chiller Diller," "The Mother Goose Murders," "No Nice Girl Kills," "Poke a Cobra in the Eye," "Nail Down the Lid," and "Ghosts Don't Make No Noise," all in *Detective Fiction Weekly* (New York), 1934–41; "Killer Takes All," in *Secret Agent X* (New York), 1935; "The Hot Ice Man," and "The Fifty Grand Payoff," both in *Clues* (New York), 1935; "The State Saves $230," in *Black Book Detective* (New York), 1936; "Spin Down, Spin In," and "A Short Voyage Home," both in *Argosy* (New York), 1937–40.

Uncollected Short Stories (series: Lieutenant Alec Mason in all stories)

"Where the Buffalo Roam," "Flash Fever," "Rendezvous with Sally," "Her Form Was Fair," "Avoid All Combat," "Heaven Is a Foxhole," "The Gentleman from Stalingrad," "A Ticket to Stateside," and "Always the Best Man," all in *Saturday Evening Post* (Philadelphia), 1942–44; "The Captain's Bill of Goods," in *Esquire* (Chicago), 1943; "Pickle Lugger," in *Collier's* (New York), 1943; "Me and My Bomb," in *Country Gentleman* (Philadelphia), 1943; "All Squared Away," in *Blue Book* (Chicago), 1944.

Uncollected Short Stories

"The White Cobra," in *The Shadow* (New York), 1932.
"The Black Mamba," in *Complete Detective* (New York), 1933.
"Terror Towers," "The House of Kaa," "The Grinning Ghoul," "The Headless Horseman," "Death at End House," "The Whispering Corpse," "The Bronze Casket," "Horror over Hollywood," in *10 Detective Aces* (New York), 1933–34.

"Terror Train," "Sting of the Scorpion," in *Secret Agent X* (New York), 1934.

"Vampire's Clutch," in *All Detective* (New York), 1934.

"The Reptile Murders," "Murder Eastbound," "Dead Man's Float," in *Thrilling Detective* (New York), 1934–38.

"House of the Praying Ghost," "The Egg," "The Museum Murders," in *Clues* (New York), 1934–35.

"A Breath of Murder," "Death on 1000 Legs," "The Guy from Superstition," "The Camera Kills," "Radio 67," "The Day I Die," "The Key," "Gaff!," "Backstage," "A Hearse for Hiawatha," "Perseus Had a Helmet," "Die Hamlet," "Banshee," "Contempt of Court," "Come Out of That Grave!," "Creeps by Night," "The Sinister Leaf," "The Scarlet Triangle," "One and One Makes One," "Dead Man's Dummy," "A Nice Quiet Place," "Eight Minutes to Live," "Dusty Death," "Alibi Ike," "Derringer," "Torio Had a Friend," "The Old Oaken 8-Ball," "Fifty Grand," "The Black Spot," "Ham on Wry," "High Voltage," "Washington Had Red Hair," "No Time for Mercy," in *Detective Fiction Weekly* (New York), 1934–41.

"Red Death Crawling," in *Super Detective* (New York), 1935.

"The Will," "He Who Makes Murder," "Dead Man's Theft," in *Popular Detective* (New York), 1935–36.

"The Murder Revue," "The Murder March," "A Knife Don't Shoot So Loud," "Whitemail," "G-Men Spotted," "The Chair That Judged," in *Black Book Detective* (New York), 1935–36.

"An Elegant Shot," in *Public Enemy* (New York), 1935.

"$50,000 Legs," in *Star Detective* (New York), 1937.

"Two at a Time," "Figure a Dame," "Heist," "A Place for the Night," "Lillies for the Lady," "Feet First," "Skeletons in the Closet," "Shoal Waters," "A Noose for Nicodemus," "The Head," "A Monkey in the Morgue," "Don't Crowd Your Luck," "Somebody Stole My Ghoul," "Three Wise Men of Babylon," "You Can't Live Forever," "Pardon My Ghoulish Laughter," "Jumped or Fell," "Crazy Night," in *Double Detective* (New York), 1937–39.

"Isle of Troubled Night," in *Thrilling Mystery* (New York), 1937.

"There's Money in Corpses," "A Killer's Book of Etiquette," "Death Is Where You Find It," "Big Game," in *Detective Tales*, 1938–41.

"Satan Made a Derringer," in *All American Fiction* (New York), 1938.

"Active Duty," in *Mystery Companion*, edited by Abraham Louis Furman. New York, Fawcett, 1943.

"Collar of Hercules," in *Baffling Detective* (New York), 1944.

"Ghosts Don't Make Noise," in *Second Mystery Companion*, edited by Abraham Louis Furman. New York, Fawcett, 1944.

"A Breath of Death," in *Mystery Book Magazine* (New York), October 1945.

"Death Had a Pencil," in *Third Mystery Companion*, edited by Abraham Louis Furman. New York, Fawcett, 1945.

"The Mad Brain," in *Giant Detective Annual*. New York, Best Books, 1950.

"The Lonely World," in *Mysterious Traveler* (New York), June 1952.

"Three Wise Men of Babylon," in *The Saint* (New York), September 1954.

"Death Flies High," in *The Saint* (New York), March 1955.

"The Ghost of a Dog," in *The Saint* (New York), January 1956.

"A Nose for News," in *The Hardboiled Dicks*, edited by Ron Goulart. Los Angeles, Sherbourne Press, 1965; London, Boardman, 1967.

OTHER PUBLICATIONS

Novels

Not Too Narrow, Not Too Deep. New York, Simon and Schuster, and London, Cassell, 1936.

Is a Ship Burning? London, Cassell, 1937; New York, Dodd Mead, 1938.

The Oscar. New York, Simon and Schuster, 1963.

The White Buffalo. New York, Simon and Schuster, 1975.

Plays

Screenplays: *Strange Cargo*, with others, 1937; *Find the Witness*, with Grace Neville and Fred Niblo, Jr., 1937; *The Dude Goes West*, with Mary Loos, 1938; *Shadows over Shanghai*, with Joseph Hoffman, 1938; *Rendezvous with Annie*, with Mary Loos, 1946; *Calendar Girl*, with Mary Loos and Lee Loeb, 1947; *Northwest Outpost*, with others, 1947; *Driftwood*, with Mary Loos, 1947; *The Inside Story*, with others, 1948; *Campus Honeymoon*, with Jerry Gruskin and Thomas R. St. George, 1948; *The Tender Years*, with others, 1948; *Lady at Midnight*, 1948; *Mother Is a Freshman*, with Mary Loos and Raphael Blau, 1949; *Mr. Belvedere Goes to College*, with Mary Loos and Mary C. McCall, 1949; *Father Was a Fullback*, with others, 1949; *When Willie Comes Marching Home*, with Mary Loos and Sy Gomberg, 1950; *A Ticket to Tomahawk*, with Mary Loos, 1950; *I'll Get By*, with others, 1950; *Meet Me after the Show*, with Mary Loos, 1951; *Let's Do It Again*, with Mary Loos, 1953; *The French Line*, with others, 1954; *Woman's World*, with others, 1954; *Suddenly*, 1954; *Gentlemen Marry Brunettes*, with Mary Loos, 1955; *Over-Exposed!*, with others, 1956; *Torpedo Run*, with William Wister Haines, 1958; *The White Buffalo*, 1977.

Television Plays: *Yancy Derringer, Bewitched, Wackiest Ship in the Army, FBI, Custer*, and *High Chapparal* series; *Assassination*, 1987.

*

Manuscript Collection: University of Southern California, Los Angeles.

Theatrical Activities:

Director: **Films**—*Spoilers of the North*, 1947; *Campus Honeymoon*, 1948; *A Ticket to Tomahawk*, 1950; *I'll Get By*, 1950; *Half Angel*, 1951; *Meet Me after the Show*, 1951; *Let's Make It Legal*, 1951; *My Wife's Best Friend*, 1952; *The Girl Next Door*, 1953; *Fire over Africa*, 1954; *Gentlemen Marry Brunettes*, 1955; *Abandon Ship*, 1957.

*   *   *

Richard Sale began his career in mystery writing in the early 1930's, selling stories to such pulp magazines as *Super Detective* and *Detective Fiction Weekly*. The latter publication featured Sale's reporter/detective Daffy Dill in a number of tales. Sale's first novel, *Not Too Narrow, Not Too Deep*, was not so much a mystery as an allegorical adventure about 10 convicts, their escape from a French penal colony much like Devil's Island, and the enigmatic stranger who accompanies them on their journey. This tour-de-force was followed in the 1940's by several mystery novels, the most interesting being *Lazarus No. 7* and *Passing Strange*, both of which have medical themes, are narrated by doctors, and feature a number of the same characters, the most notable of whom is a police detective named Daniel Webster. Both also demonstrate Sale's flair for the bizarre. *Lazarus No. 7* features a resurrectionist and Hollywood stars, writers, and producers, combined with murder and leprosy. *Passing Strange* includes a scene depicting the murder of a doctor who is shot while watching another doctor perform a Caesarean section on a famous actress. The two books contain well-drawn characters and bright dialogue as well as somewhat conventional love stories.

Sale's best book, *For the President's Eyes Only,* is a spy thriller that appeared a few years after the real vogue in such things had passed, probably the only reason it failed to become a bestseller. It has more action, adventure, intrigue, and glamor than any two or three similar novels, and a fine, tough hero besides. Reading it makes one wish that Sale had devoted less of his time to writing for movies and television and more to writing books like this.

—Bill Crider

———

SANBORN, B.X. *See* **BALLINGER, Bill S.**

———

SANDERS, Daphne. *See* **RICE, Craig.**

———

SANDERS, Lawrence. Also writes as Lesley Andress. American. Born in Brooklyn, New York, in 1920. Educated at Wabash College. Crawfordsville, Indiana, B.A. 1940. Served in the United States Marine Corps, 1943–46: Sergeant. Staff member, Macy's department store, New York, 1940–43; journalist: staff member, *Mechanix Illustrated;* Editor, *Science and Mechanics.* Recipient: Mystery Writers of America Edgar Allan Poe award, 1970. Address: c/o G.P. Putnam's Sons, 200 Madison Avenue, New York, New York 10016, U.S.A.

CRIME PUBLICATIONS

Novels (series: Timothy Cone; Edward X. Delaney; Peter Tangent)

The Anderson Tapes. New York, Putnam, and London, W.H. Allen, 1970.
The First Deadly Sin (Delaney). New York, Putnam, 1973; London, W.H. Allen, 1974.
The Tomorrow File. New York, Putnam, 1975; London, Corgi, 1977.
The Tangent Objective. New York, Putnam, 1976; London, Hart Davis, 1977.
The Second Deadly Sin (Delaney). New York, Putnam, 1977; London, Hart Davis, 1978.
The Tangent Factor. New York, Putnam, and London, Hart Davis, 1978.
The Sixth Commandment. New York, Putnam, and London, Granada, 1979.
Caper (as Lesley Andress). New York, Putnam, and London, Granada, 1980.

The Tenth Commandment. New York, Putnam, 1980; London, Granada, 1981.
The Third Deadly Sin (Delaney). New York, Putnam, and London, Granada, 1981.
The Case of Lucy Bending. New York, Putnam, 1982; London, New English Library, 1983.
The Seduction of Peter S. New York, Putnam, 1983; London, New English Library, 1984.
The Passion of Molly T. New York, Putnam, 1984; London, New English Library, 1985.
The Fourth Deadly Sin (Delaney). New York, Putnam, and London, New English Library, 1985.
The Loves of Harry Dancer. New York, Berkley, 1986; as *The Loves of Harry D.,* London, New English Library, 1986.
The Eighth Commandment. New York, Putnam, and London, New English Library, 1986.
Tales of the Wolf. New York, Avon, 1986; London, Severn House, 1988.
The Dream Lover. New York, Berkley, 1987.
The Timothy Files (Cone). New York, Putnam, 1987; London, New English Library, 1988.
Timothy's Game (Cone). New York, Putnam, and London, New English Library, 1988.
Love Songs. New York, Berkley, 1989.
Capital Crimes. New York, Putnam, and London, New English Library, 1989.
Stolen Blessings. New York, Berkley, 1989.
Sullivan's Sting. New York, Putnam, and London, New English Library, 1990.

OTHER PUBLICATIONS

Novels

The Pleasures of Helen. New York, Putnam, 1971.
Love Songs. New York, Putnam, 1972.
The Marlow Chronicles. New York, Putnam, 1977; Loughton, Essex, Piatkus, 1979.

Other

Handbook of Creative Crafts, with Richard Carol. New York, Pyramid, 1968.

Editor, *Thus Be Loved: A Book for Lovers.* New York, Arco, 1966.

*   *   *

One of the few authors of the "blockbuster" bestseller who works consistently within the crime and mystery tradition, Lawrence Sanders provides a good example of a writer whose work has steadily declined in interest as it has increased in sales. In his best work he combines with great adroitness the necessary ingredients for commercial success—sex, violence, and sensationalism, distinctive characterization, and sociological observation, all packaged with a slick and attractive wrapping of glossy style and suspenseful narrative. In several of his books he demonstrates enough skill to rank him among the more important and innovative contemporary writers of mystery and detective fiction. In recent years, however, as the books have issued forth at an alarming rate, it's become clear that his best work is behind him; the more he writes, the worse he gets.

His most valuable books occur early in his productive career—*The Anderson Tapes, The First Deadly Sin,* and *The Second Deadly Sin.* Although he has added more sins and several commandments and may well move on to the Beatitudes and the Boy Scout Oath, he has exhibited little development since those works, beyond a phenomenal ability to turn out large, popular novels. *The Anderson Tapes* is one of the most technically inventive thrillers of recent years, an outstanding big caper novel told entirely through documents, mostly the evidence of a variety of surveillance measures—wiretaps, listening devices, police reports—proving that a lot more than lyric poetry is the art of the overheard. The book's method meshes perfectly with its subject, since the big caper itself is a kind of technologically sophisticated crime, dependent on split-second timing, careful planning, clockwork routine, and so forth. The novel draws a powerful picture of a criminal world and a pervasively corrupt society; besides its unique narrative use of electronic eavesdropping, the book clearly indicates, long before Watergate, the threat to freedom and privacy posed by the enormous amount of technological advances in legal and illegal snooping in America carried on by a remarkable array of agencies, institutions, and individuals.

Taking a striking minor character from *The Anderson Tapes*—Edward X. "Iron Balls" Delaney—and employing some of that book's vision of society, Sanders crosses the police procedural with the crime novel in *The First Deadly Sin* and with the classic whodunit in *The Second Deadly Sin*; the later *Sins* tend toward the formula of the first book, showing both the criminal and the detective. A retired chief of detectives, Delaney hunts down a serial murderer in the first and best of those books, with both men motivated by the terrible sin of pride. In the second, based roughly on the Mark Rothko case, greed appears to cause the murder. Both books are distinguished by a fine feel for character, a mastery of narrative movement, and an intelligent use of unifying themes and devices. *The Third Deadly Sin*, which represents a considerable falling off from its predecessors, achieves some sort of a first by featuring a female killer motivated by premenstrual tension. Sanders is nothing if not trendy.

Sanders has ventured further into crime of all kinds, including a most unsatisfying caper novel called *Caper* under his pseudonym of Lesley Andress, a ridiculous novel about a male brothel, *The Seduction of Peter S.,* and *The Case of Lucy Bending,* a study in the sexual corruption of a Florida community which raises some troubling ideas about the children of affluence in America. He introduced a Wall Street financial detective in *The Timothy Files* and *Timothy's Games,* but the stories are so laborious and affected that it's hard to believe that an experienced and successful professional wrote them—even the slickness has worn off. Most of his books deal with some fairly uninteresting sexual activity from a rather juvenile and voyeuristic point of view, with occasional forays into unconvincing criminal investigation and his continuing interest in serial murder.

If he does go through all the sins and all the commandments, Sanders may find himself in some difficulty in further works. Lust, greed, and anger certainly provide plenty of fodder for the crime writer, but it must be rather difficult to build a novel around, say, sloth; some of the Ten Commandments are perfectly suitable for his books, but keeping holy the Sabbath day may prove tough to handle. Yet, as a crime novelist, he possesses one of the necessary qualities of any good writer—a sense of sin. Combined with his ability to write readable prose, his awareness of the evils of contemporary society, and his interest in technical innovation, that sense of sin should generate better novels than the astonishing number he has written in the last several years. He has probably missed the opportunity to be one of the major writers in his genre for our time; nevertheless, he has written a few quite important

documents in contemporary crime fiction and deserves some critical attention.

—George Grella

SANDS, Dave. *see* **POWELL, Talmage.**

SAPIR, Richard. *See* **MURPHY, Warren and SAPIR, Richard.**

SAPPER. Pseudonym for Herman Cyril McNeile. British. Born in Bodmin, Cornwall, 28 September 1888. Educated at Cheltenham College, Gloucestershire; Royal Military Academy, Woolwich. Served in the Royal Engineers, 1907–19: became Captain in 1914; retired as Lieutenant Colonel: Military Cross. Married Violet Douglas in 1914; two sons. *Died 14 August 1937.*

Crime Publications

Novels (series: Captain Hugh "Bulldog" Drummond; Ronald Standish; published as H.C. McNeile in US)

Bull-Dog Drummond: The Adventures of a Demobilized Officer Who Found Peace Dull. London, Hodder and Stoughton, and New York, Doran, 1920.
The Black Gang (Drummond). London, Hodder and Stoughton, and New York, Doran, 1922.
The Third Round. London, Hodder and Stoughton, 1924; as *Bulldog Drummond's Third Round,* New York, Doran, 1924.
The Final Count (Drummond). London, Hodder and Stoughton, and New York, Doran, 1926.
The Female of the Species. London, Hodder and Stoughton, and New York, Doubleday, 1928; as *Bulldog Drummond Meets the Female of the Species,* New York, Sun Dial Press, 1943; as *Bulldog Drummond Meets a Murderess,* New York, Thriller Novel Classic, n.d.
Temple Tower (Drummond). London, Hodder and Stoughton, and New York, Doubleday, 1929.
Tiny Carteret (Standish). London, Hodder and Stoughton, and New York, Doubleday, 1930.
The Island of Terror. London, Hodder and Stoughton, 1931; as *Guardians of the Treasure,* New York, Doubleday, 1931.
The Return of Bull-Dog Drummond. London, Hodder and Stoughton, 1932; as *Bulldog Drummond Returns,* New York, Doubleday, 1932.
Knock-Out (Standish). London, Hodder and Stoughton, 1933; as *Bulldog Drummond Strikes Back,* New York, Doubleday, 1933.
Bulldog Drummond at Bay (Standish). London, Hodder and Stoughton, and New York, Doubleday, 1935.
Challenge (Drummond; Standish). London, Hodder and Stoughton, and New York, Doubleday, 1937.

Short Stories (published as H.C. McNeile in US)

The Man in Ratcatcher and Other Stories. London, Hodder and Stoughton, and New York, Doran, 1921.
Jim Maitland. London, Hodder and Stoughton, 1923; New York, Doran, 1924.
The Dinner Club. London, Hodder and Stoughton, and New York, Doran, 1923.
Out of the Blue. London, Hodder and Stoughton, and New York, Doran, 1925.
Word of Honour. London, Hodder and Stoughton, and New York, Doran, 1926.
The Saving Clause. London, Hodder and Stoughton, 1927.
The Finger of Fate. London, Hodder and Stoughton, 1930; New York, Doubleday, 1931.
Ronald Standish. London, Hodder and Stoughton, 1933.
When Carruthers Laughed. London, Hodder and Stoughton, 1934.
51 Stories. London, Hodder and Stoughton, 1934.
Ask for Ronald Standish. London, Hodder and Stoughton, 1936.
Sapper: The Best Short Stories, edited by Jack Adrian. London, Dent, 1984.

Uncollected Short Stories

"The Man Who Ended the War," in *Pearson's Magazine* (London), September 1916.
"Pete Jobson, Criminal," in *Pearson's Magazine* (London), June 1918.
"When Mr. Wetheimer Hedged," in *Lloyds Magazine* (London), August 1918.
"The Ducking of Herbert Polton," in *Pearson's Magazine* (London), July 1924.
"An Act of Providence," in *Pearson's Magazine* (London), March 1927.
"Relative Values," in *Hutchinson's Magazine* (London), November 1927.
"The Three Numbers," in *The Legion Book,* edited by Captain H. Cotton Minchin. London, Cassell, 1929.

OTHER PUBLICATIONS

Novel

Mufti. London, Hodder and Stoughton, and New York, Doran, 1919.

Short Stories

The Lieutenant and Others. London, Hodder and Stoughton, 1915.
Sergeant Michael Cassidy, R.E. London, Hodder and Stoughton, 1915; as *Michael Cassidy, Sergeant.* New York, Doran, 1916.
Men, Women, and Guns. London, Hodder and Stoughton, and New York, Doran, 1916.
No Man's Land. London, Hodder and Stoughton, and New York, Doran, 1917.
The Human Touch. London, Hodder and Stoughton, and New York, Doran, 1918.
Jim Brent (selection). London, Hodder and Stoughton, 1926.
Shorty Bill (selection). London, Hodder and Stoughton, 1927.
John Walters (selection). London, Hodder and Stoughton, 1928.
Sapper's War Stories. London, Hodder and Stoughton, 1930.

Plays

Bulldog Drummond, with Gerald du Maurier, adaptation of the novel by Sapper (produced London and New York, 1921). London, French, 1925.
The Way Out (produced London, 1930).
Bulldog Drummond Hits Out, with Gerald Fairlie (produced Brighton and London, 1937).

Screenplay: *Bulldog Jack* (*Alias Bulldog Drummond*), with Gerard Fairlie and J.O.C. Orton, 1935.

Other

Uncle James's Golf Match. London, Hodder and Stoughton, 1932.

Editor, *The Best of O. Henry: One Hundred of His Stories.* London, Hodder and Stoughton, 1929.

*   *   *

Sapper, the creator of one of the most popular heroes of thriller fiction, is nonetheless an anomaly in the last quarter of the 20th century, for he is ineluctably locked into its second quarter. His characters talk (and he himself often writes) in that upper bourgeois language of Saki, P.G. Wodehouse, and Noël Coward: one's friends are addressed as "old lad," "old girl," "old thing," and one's enemies are "swine," "devils," "not human"—above all, not English and not public school. For Sapper's heroes are all of "the Breed," Dagoes begin at Calais, and the life of adventure so avidly sought is constantly characterized in playing field (or boxing ring) terms. Bulldog Drummond goes his "four rounds" with Carl Peterson, and the best of the Drummond novels, *The Female of the Species,* is actually plotted upon a paper chase, with each clue leading Drummond closer to his kidnapped wife, and, it is planned, his own death. Drummond begins his career, in fact, by advertising for "diversion"—"legitimate, if possible, but crime, if of a comparatively humorous description, no objection."

The motive power of all Sapper's heroes is that like Drummond they find peace "incredibly tedious," and in an age of deepening moral incertitude they find themselves justified in fighting England's enemies—the foreigners, especially of course the filthy Boche, and, increasingly in the 1920's, Bolshevists, "butcherers of women and children whose sole fault lay in the fact that they washed." Women especially are the objects of protection for these muscular public-school boys, who approach them, moreover, with great awe. Sapper's women, both good and bad, are an adolescent boy's dream: from Drummond's wife Phyllis, or the innumerable Mollys of the lesser fiction, all white to the core, all helpful in a tight corner while remaining properly feminine, to the immortal Irma, so often Drummond's antagonist after the death of her lover Carl Peterson, and still going strong in Gerard Fairlie's sequels. Particularly suggestive is the sixth Drummond book, *Temple Tower,* which ends as it begins, the heroes' bloodthirsty adventures framed by their wives' question, on departure and return: "Now mind you're both good while we're away./Have you both been good while we've been away?" These are Tom Sawyer games, with Aunt Polly, approving-reproving, watching from the proper distance.

These boys do not prize the life of the mind: Sapper's villains are almost always highly intelligent, even artistic. It is Drummond's practical straightforwardness—his bulldog quality—which defeats their guile. There is even something essentially feminine about them, and Drummond's relationship with Peterson (and Irma) is finally more sexually charged than is his relationship with Phyllis. (More than once, he "lovingly" strangles an antagonist.) Sapper's most intellectual hero is Ronald Standish, the private detective, his cases and his methods closely patterned after Holmes's, and he redeems himself by being a first-class cricketer, who takes only cases which "amuse" him, since he is independently wealthy. On the three occasions when he works with Drummond, it is Drummond's fists rather than Standish's brains that save the day. Sapper's other important hero, Jim Maitland, carries further what is in Drummond a mere suggestion of the Scarlet Pimpernel-Zorro figure—the public fool and the private hero. He is outwardly a "toff," and wears a monocle ("Rumour has it that once some man laughed at that eyeglass").

What makes Sapper finally an embarrassment in the post-atomic world is his sense of easy solution, his simple-minded chauvinism and even "racism," and his sadism. He remains, however, a real spellbinder on the level of story, and ought to retain his audience amongst the intelligent under-16's, preferably those who do not take too seriously the ethos of the playing fields.

—Barrie Hayne

SAUNDERS, Hilary Aiden St. George. *See* **BEEDING, Francis.**

SAUTER, Eric. American. Born in Bay City, Michigan, 1 November 1948. Educated at Michigan State University, East Lansing, B.A. 1971. Married Beth Olanoff in 1982. Freelance writer and editor, 1972–75; reporter, Trenton *Times,* New Jersey, 1975–77; freelance writer, 1977–79 and 1980–82; speech writer, U.S. Senate, Washington, D.C. 1979–80; publications manager, Squibb Corporation, Princeton, New Jersey, 1982–84. Address: c/o Pocket Books, 1230 Avenue of the Americas, New York, New York 10020, U.S.A.

CRIME PUBLICATIONS

Novels (series: Robert Lee Hunter in all books)

Hunter. New York, Avon, 1983.
Hunter and the Ikon. New York, Avon, 1984.
Hunter and Raven. New York, Avon, 1984.
Predators. New York, Pocket Books, 1987; London, Sphere, 1988.
Skeletons. New York, Dutton, 1990.

*   *   *

Eric Sauter, thus far, has a fine track-record for "getting it right." His Hunter novels appeared in the early 1980's, at the start of what may be described as the Second Coming of the Private Eye. His big blockbuster paperback original *Predators* came out in 1986, its basic plot incorporating a number of environmentalist themes not often found in similar supermarket checkout-rack doorstoppers. His most recent thriller *Skeletons* proves that serial-psychopaths are definitely on the up.

Collectively the Hunter series—three books in all—seems to have a pre-eminence over just about every other series of private investigator paperback originals (and a good many hardbacks, too) published in the past 20 years. Each book was better than the last and the first, *Hunter,* was so far superior to the rest of its year's output (1983) that it ought to have won an Edgar.

Hunter himself is thirty-something and independently wealthy (although this makes his investigations no less hazardous) through having written a book about his generation, which endured its rites of passage during the 1960's (tear-gassed and baton-beaten on campus, shot at in the jungles of Vietnam). He lives in an old Victorian pile on an island in the Delaware River, and has a mild obsession (akin to Mitch Tobin's preoccupation with his wall in Donald Westlake's "Tucker Coe" novels) about restoring and repairing it.

To a great extent Sauter deals in obsession, whether collector-dementia (as in *Hunter and the Ikon*), revenge (*Predators*), power (*Hunter*), or cat-and-mouse game-playing (*Skeletons*). In *Hunter and Raven,* the final volume in the trilogy, Hunter himself becomes obsessed with tracking down his own past, discovering inevitably that it's a quest best not embarked upon.

Like all the best PIs, reaching right back to Hammett's fat little unnamed Continental Op, Hunter does not search for clues (the bloodstained cigar butt, the thumb-printed shot-glass) but pokes his nose in where it's not wanted, manipulates, makes things happen. The plots are complex, all built intelligently on the "out of the past" principle and all containing convincingly rabid villains and, at times, outbursts of extraordinary violence.

In *Hunter* the past is represented, physically, by an illegitimate drifter whose search for his father involves Hunter in confrontations with a snakey Washington power-broker with a US Congressman in his pocket, a boonie colony which violently disencourages strangers from snooping, and a drug-dealer and his psychotic minion. While investigating possible art forgeries in *Hunter and the Ikon* Hunter, as he gloomily soliloquises at one stage, is beset by "insane Russians carrying a five-hundred-year-old grudge, a vicious millionaire and a handful of government geeks" (there is a muscular anti-Establishment thread running through all of Sauter's books).

The prose in his early novels is lean and wry and very funny, with just a touch of the contemporary lunacy of the deranged gonzo journalist Hunter (no coincidence?) S. Thompson in it to add extra spice to the pungent one-liners with which all are liberally stuffed. In *Hunter and Raven* post-1960's/post-Vietnam *angst* is at its most profound as Hunter tracks down a semi-demented radical who went underground a decade before, was reported dead, but who now seems to have resurfaced. His brother wants him found, others don't. *Hunter and Raven* touches on the ugliness of betrayal (of people; of ideals, however goofy), years-long hatreds, disastrous relationships. It is also a superb thriller.

After a three-year lay-off Sauter produced *Predators,* an engrossing and brilliantly crafted journey into the world of hunters and the hunted—this time literally, for the action is triggered off by the slaughter of a wolf-pack in Canada by Van Owen, a Vietnam-damaged professional hunter whose psyche is deteriorating fast. Equally unhinged is Dane, a zoologist and wolf-lover who tracks Van Owen through the dark canyons of Manhattan with the sole survivor of the pack massacre, a huge black wolf. Pitted against both is Yates, a New York Police Department detective desperately trying to make sense of what seems to be a series of bizarre mutilation murders. A large cast of characters is efficiently handled.

After *Predators,* and another three years, Sauter narrowed his sights in *Skeletons* to a one-to-one confrontation, a nail-bitingly tense battle between a flawed Philadelphia cop, Patrick Paige, and his nemesis, the psychopath Grant, a successful burglar turned sadistic killer.

Clearly Sauter is a writer to be watched. He could so easily have cranked out Hunter novels by the yard, thus in the end vitiating an enormously lively and original character. That he chooses to explore other avenues in the mystery/suspense genres is refreshing; that he deliberately threads dark and disturbing themes—obsession, betrayal, bitter disillusionment (as in *Hunter and Raven,* Paige in *Skeletons* finds that uncovering the past can have shattering consequences)—into his rarely less than riveting entertainments is wholly admirable.

—Jack Adrian

———

SAVAGE, Ernest. American. Born in Detroit, Michigan 25 March 1918. Attended Culver Military Academy, Indiana, 1934–36; University of Michigan, Ann Arbor, 1936–38. Served in the United States Army, 1940–44. Married 1) Elizabeth Bissell in 1941, one daughter; 2) Jean McMurray in 1964. Has worked as salesman, taxi driver, sailor and fisherman, advertising copywriter, builder; lived in Geneva and Madrid, 1958–62. Agent: Scott Meredith, 845 Third Avenue, New York, New York 10022. Address: 6104 Oliver Road, Paradise, California 95969, U.S.A.

CRIME PUBLICATIONS

Novel

Two If by Sea. New York, Scribner, 1982.

Uncollected Short Stories

"The Small Hours," in *Alfred Hitchcock's Mystery Magazine* (North Palm Beach, Florida), November 1976.
"Or Was She Pushed?," in *Mike Shayne Mystery Magazine* (Los Angeles), December 1976.
"Visitor from Bangladesh," in *Mike Shayne Mystery Magazine* (Los Angeles), March 1977.
"Doc Wharton's Legacy," in *Ellery Queen's Mystery Magazine* (New York), March 1977.
"Cleota," in *Mike Shayne Mystery Magazine* (Los Angeles), June 1977.
"It Must Be You, Harry," in *Mike Shayne Mystery Magazine* (Los Angeles), August 1977.
"The Man Who Liked Noise," in *Ellery Queen's Mystery Magazine* (New York), August 1977.
"Eight O'Clock Ferry," in *Ellery Queen's Mystery Magazine* (New York), November 1977.
"Aloha, Jenny Swire," in *Alfred Hitchcock's Mystery Magazine* (New York), February 1978.
"Get Rich Quick," in *Mike Shayne Mystery Magazine* (Los Angeles), March 1978.
"Your Move, Charlie," in *Alfred Hitchcock's Mystery Magazine* (New York), March 1978.
"The Patio," in *Alfred Hitchcock's Mystery Magazine* (New York), April 1978.

"The Park Plaza Thefts," in *Alfred Hitchcock's Mystery Magazine* (New York), June 1978.
"Count Me Out," in *Ellery Queen's Mystery Magazine* (New York), June 1978.
"Finders Weepers," in *Ellery Queen's Mystery Magazine* (New York), September 1978.
"The First of All Rules," in *Ellery Queen's Mystery Magazine* (New York), November 1978.
"The Man in the Lake," in *Alfred Hitchcock's Mystery Magazine* (New York), November 1978.
"Mr. Fixit," in *Ellery Queen's Mystery Magazine* (New York), February 1979.
"No Hard Evidence," in *Alfred Hitchcock's Mystery Magazine* (New York), February 1979.
"Murphy's Day," in *Alfred Hitchcock's Mystery Magazine* (New York), March 1979.
"The Quick and the Dead," in *Ellery Queen's Mystery Magazine* (New York), May 1979.
"Horse Player," in *Alfred Hitchcock's Mystery Magazine* (New York), June 1979.
"Coins at Large," in *Ellery Queen's Mystery Magazine* (New York), 17 December 1979.
"Assignment in Geneva," in *Alfred Hitchcock's Mystery Magazine* (New York), 2 January 1980.
"Sweetheart, I'm Dry!," in *Alfred Hitchcock's Mystery Magazine* (New York), 30 January 1980.
"Not Worth Flypaper," in *Alfred Hitchcock's Mystery Magazine* (New York), 27 February 1980.
"How Do I Kill Thee?," in *Alfred Hitchcock's Mystery Magazine* (New York), 26 March 1980.
"The Attaché Case," in *Alfred Hitchcock's Mystery Magazine* (New York), 23 April 1980.
"One of Those Things," in *Alfred Hitchcock's Mystery Magazine* (New York), 16 June 1980.
"A Time of Summing Up," in *Ellery Queen's Mystery Magazine* (New York), 30 June 1980.
"There Is No Tomorrow," in *Ellery Queen's Mystery Magazine* (New York), 23 July 1980.
"Companion Planting," in *Ellery Queen's Mystery Magazine* (New York), 10 September 1980.
"The Miracle Day," in *Ellery Queen's Mystery Magazine* (New York), 25 February 1981.
"Dangerous Ground," in *Ellery Queen's Mystery Magazine* (New York), 20 May 1981.
"The Best Man in Town," in *Ellery Queen's Mystery Magazine* (New York), 15 July 1981.

*

Ernest Savage comments:

As a writer of suspense fiction I consider myself an entertainer. As an entertainer I feel it's my duty to get on and off stage in a timely manner. If my audience is momentarily diverted, amused, or even moved to tears, I've done my job. But the great thing, sirs, is not to dawdle.

*   *   *

Fictional private eyes were born in short stories and novelettes, though Hammett and Chandler later combined or cannibalized these to produce their novels. Rogers, the Ross Macdonald prototype for Archer, appeared in a 1946 *EQMM* short story. From about 1955 to 1975 there was a dry period in the private detective short story, but Ernest Savage has been one of those changing that.

Having begun his writing career in his fifties, Savage appears to have a special understanding of those who change jobs late in life. His series character, the San Francisco private detective Sam Train, idealistically left the police after 19 years' service following an illegal police strike. Through his narrator, Train, Savage captures the essence of San Francisco. He is so aware of its beauty that he is able to convince one that owning an old mansion with a spectacular harbor view is a plausible murder motive. Male homosexuals, so large a part of the city's population, appear with believable regularity in the Train stories, but they are rendered realistically, not viciously as by Hammett and Chandler.

Yet Train speaks his creator's occasional disenchantment with the city. "I'd seen everything there is to see in this town that shows everything there is to show." In the best Train story, "Count Me Out," the detective is fishing in the woods, glad to be away from the city's noise, " . . . the rumble and squeal of traffic, . . . the screams of muggers' victims, and other not entirely imaginary sounds." But he demonstrates that urban settings have no monopoly on violence.

Train's methods are more instinctive than deductive. He is emotional and often smitten with the women he meets. A 19-year-old girl in "There Is No Tomorrow" is likened to a creation by Botticelli or Raphael. Tracing a kidnapped horse in "Horse Player" he is captivated by the 12-year-old who owned it. "In another year she would be ravishing." Then, he meets her mother and is even more awed. Ten minutes after Train meets a woman in "Assignment in Geneva," he admits he has fallen for one of his suspects. "I felt as objective as a bowl of mush." He is probably at his least convincing, though most human, as detective in "Visitor from Bangladesh" when a woman he loved comes back into his life, after seven years, and uses his love to make him find the buried spoils of a bank robbery.

Savage reveals a special understanding for the elderly, especially in his non-series stories. Grogarty, a 65 year-old watchman, is approaching his final years in "A Time of Summing Up," and "the arithmetic of his life was in low numbers." The retired, trying to make ends meet on fixed incomes, come in for special notice by Savage. In "Not Worth Flypaper" an old man is galvanized into action when his wife has been cheated after being forced to sell her beloved sewing machine. Tim Baker, unable to survive on his Social Security, takes a job, at age 66, selling on commission, until he finds the titular bag in "The Attaché Case," and it changes his life. A retired woman who has earned peace and quiet is beset by an impossible noisy neighbor in "Sweetheart, I'm Dry!" His best short story, "Mr. Fixit," shows great poignancy regarding the terminally ill, but also stands out because of its inventive ending.

Savage often writes of sailing, and his complex story "Aloha, Jenny Swire" tells of a man who loves the sea and yet is afraid of sailing. "Eighty Days at Sea" traces a Seattle-to-Greece freighter trip in a story so good that it permits suspension of disbelief regarding a ship with several murderers and a detective all coincidentally aboard. Savage's only novel to date, the very suspenseful *Two If by Sea,* reverses the route as a man tracks the hit-and-run driver who killed his son to a freighter bound from Genoa to Seattle. It earned Savage an Edgar nomination. Like his shorter work, it shows a mature writer who, in a short time, has brought new vitality to the hardboiled school.

—Marvin Lachman

———

SAXON, Alex. *See* **PRONZINI, Bill.**

———

SAXON, John A. *See* **BELLEM, Robert Leslie.**

———

SAYERS, Dorothy L(eigh). British. Born in Oxford, 13 July 1893. Educated at the Goldolphin School, Salisbury, Wiltshire, 1909–11; Somerville College, Oxford (Gilchrist Scholar), 1912–15, B.A. (honours) in French and M.A. 1920. Married Oswald Artherton Fleming in 1926 (died 1950); one illegitimate son. Taught modern languages at Hull High School for Girls, Yorkshire, 1915–17; Reader for Blackwell, publishers, Oxford, 1917–18; assistant at the Les Roches School, France, 1919–20; copywriter for Benson's advertising agency, London, 1922–29; full-time writer and broadcaster from 1931; editor, with Muriel St. Clare Byrne, Bridgeheads series, Methuen, London, 1941–46. Vicar's Warden, St. Thomas's, Regent Street, London, 1952–54, and St. Paul's, Covent Garden, London, from 1954. President, Modern Language Association, 1939–45, and the Detection Club, 1949–57. D.Litt., University of Durham, 1950. *Died 17 December 1957.*

CRIME PUBLICATIONS

Novels (series: Lord Peter Wimsey in all books except *The Documents in the Case* and collaborative works)

Whose Body? New York, Boni and Liveright, and London, Unwin, 1923.
Clouds of Witness. London, Unwin, 1926; New York, Dial Press, 1927.
Unnatural Death. London, Benn, 1927; as *The Dawson Pedigree,* New York, Dial Press, 1928.
The Unpleasantness at the Bellona Club. London, Benn, and New York, Payson and Clarke, 1928.
The Documents in the Case, with Robert Eustace. London, Benn, and New York, Brewer and Warren, 1930.
Strong Poison. London, Gollancz, and New York, Brewer and Warren, 1930.
The Five Red Herrings. London, Gollancz, 1931; as *Suspicious Characters,* New York, Brewer Warren and Putnam, 1931.
The Floating Admiral, with others. London, Hodder and Stoughton, 1931; New York, Doubleday, 1932.
Have His Carcase. London, Gollancz, and New York, Brewer Warren and Putnam, 1932.
Murder Must Advertise. London, Gollancz, and New York, Harcourt Brace, 1933.
Ask a Policeman, with others. London, Barker, and New York, Morrow, 1933.
The Nine Tailors: Changes Rung on an Old Theme in Two Short Touches and Two Full Peals. London, Gollancz, and New York, Harcourt Brace, 1934.
Gaudy Night. London, Gollancz, 1935; New York, Harcourt Brace, 1936.
Six Against the Yard, with others. London, Selwyn and Blount, 1936; as *Six Against Scotland Yard,* New York, Doubleday, 1936.
Busman's Honeymoon. London, Gollancz, and New York, Harcourt Brace, 1937.

Double Death: A Murder Story, with others.   London, Gollancz, 1939.

The Scoop, and Behind the Screen, with others.   London, Gollancz, 1983.

Crime on the Coast, and No Flowers by Request, with others.   London, Gollancz, 1984.

Short Stories

Lord Peter Views the Body.   London, Gollancz, 1928; New York, Payson and Clarke, 1929.

Hangman's Holiday.   London, Gollancz, and New York, Harcourt Brace, 1933.

In the Teeth of the Evidence and Other Stories.   London, Gollancz, 1939; New York, Harcourt Brace, 1940.

A Treasury of Sayers Stories.   London, Gollancz, 1958.

Lord Peter: A Collection of All the Lord Peter Wimsey Stories, edited by James Sandoe.   New York, Harper, 1972; augmented edition, 1972.

Striding Folly.   London, New English Library, 1972.

OTHER PUBLICATIONS

Plays

Busman's Honeymoon, with Muriel St. Clare Byrne (produced Birmingham and London, 1936; Mt. Kisco, New York, 1937).   London, Gollancz, 1937; New York, Dramatists Play Service, 1939.

The Zeal of Thy House (produced Canterbury, 1937; London, 1938).   London, Gollancz, and New York, Harcourt Brace, 1937.

He That Should Come: A Nativity Play (broadcast, 1938).   London, Gollancz, 1939.

The Devil to Pay, Being the Famous Play of John Faustus (produced Canterbury and London, 1939).   London, Gollancz, and New York, Harcourt Brace, 1939.

Love All (produced London, 1940).   In *Love All, and Busman's Honeymoon*, edited by Alzina Stone Dale.   Kent, Ohio, Kent State University Press, 1984.

The Man Born to Be King: A Play-Cycle on the Life of Our Lord and Saviour Jesus Christ (broadcast, 1941–42).   London, Gollancz, 1943; New York, Harper, 1949.

The Just Vengeance (produced Lichfield, 1946).   London, Gollancz, 1946.

The Emperor Constantine: A Chronicle (produced Colchester, 1951).   London, Gollancz, and New York, Harper, 1951; revised version, as *Christ's Emperor* (also co-director: produced London, 1952).

Screenplay: *The Silent Passenger*, with Basil Mason, 1935.

Radio Plays: *He That Should Come*, 1938; *The Golden Cockerel*, from the story by Pushkin, 1941; *The Man Born to Be King*, 1941–42; *Where Do We Go from Here?*, with others, 1948.

Verse

Op. 1.   Oxford, Blackwell, 1916.

Catholic Tales and Christian Songs.   Oxford, Blackwell, 1918.

Lord, I Thank Thee—.   Stamford, Connecticut, Overbrook Press, 1943.

The Story of Adam and Christ.   London, Hamish Hamilton, 1955.

Other

Papers Relating to the Family of Wimsey.   Privately printed, 1936.

An Account of Lord Mortimer Wimsey, The Hermit of the Wash.   Privately printed, 1937.

The Greatest Drama Ever Staged (on Easter).   London, Hodder and Stoughton, 1938.

Strong Meat.   London, Hodder and Stoughton, 1939.

Begin Here: A War-Time Essay.   London, Gollancz, 1940; New York, Harcourt Brace, 1941.

Creed or Chaos? (address).   London, Hodder and Stoughton, 1940.

The Mysterious English.   London, Macmillan, 1941.

The Mind of the Maker.   London, Methuen, and New York, Harcourt Brace, 1941.

Why Work? (address).   London, Methuen, 1942.

The Other Six Deadly Sins (address).   London, Methuen, 1943.

Even the Parrot: Exemplary Conversations for Enlightened Children.   London, Methuen, 1944.

Unpopular Opinions.   London, Gollancz, 1946; New York, Harcourt Brace, 1947.

Making Sense of the Universe (address).   London, St. Anne's Church House, 1946.

Creed or Chaos? and Other Essays in Popular Theology.   London, Methuen, 1947; New York, Harcourt Brace, 1949.

The Lost Tools of Learning (address).   London, Methuen, 1948.

The Days of Christ's Coming.   London, Hamish Hamilton, 1953; revised edition, 1960; New York, Harper, 1960.

Introductory Papers on Dante.   London, Methuen, 1954; New York, Harper, 1955.

The Story of Easter.   London, Hamish Hamilton, 1955.

The Story of Noah's Ark.   London, Hamish Hamilton, 1956.

Further Papers on Dante.   London, Methuen, and New York, Harper, 1957.

The Poetry of Search and the Poetry of Statement, and Other Posthumous Essays on Literature, Religion, and Language.   London, Gollancz, 1963.

Christian Letters to a Post-Christian World: A Selection of Essays, edited by Roderick Jellema.   Grand Rapids, Michigan, Eerdmans, 1969; as *The Whimsical Christian: 18 Essays*.   New York, Macmillan, 1978.

A Matter of Eternity: Selections from the Writings of Dorothy L. Sayers, edited by Rosamond Kent Sprague.   Grand Rapids, Michigan, Eerdmans, 1969; London, Mowbray, 1973.

Wilkie Collins: A Critical and Biographical Study, edited by E.R. Gregory.   Toledo, Ohio, Friends of the University of Toledo Libraries, 1977.

Editor, with Wilfred R. Childe and Thomas W. Earp, *Oxford Poetry 1917*.   Oxford, Blackwell, 1918.

Editor, with Thomas W. Earp and E.F.A. Geach, *Oxford Poetry 1918*.   Oxford, Blackwell, 1918.

Editor, with Thomas W. Earp and Siegfried Sassoon, *Oxford Poetry 1919*.   Oxford, Blackwell, 1919.

Editor, *Great Short Stories of Detection, Mystery, and Horror*.   London, Gollancz, 3 vols., 1928–34; as *The Omnibus of Crime*, New York, Payson and Clarke, 1929; *Second* and *Third Omnibus*, New York, Coward McCann, 1932–35.

Editor, *Tales of Detection*.   London, Dent, 1936.

Translator, *Tristan in Brittany*, by Thomas the Troubadour.   London, Benn, and New York, Payson and Clarke, 1929.

Translator, *The Heart of Stone, Being the Four Canzoni of the "Pietra" Group*, by Dante.   Witham, Essex, J.H. Clarke, 1946.

Translator, *Hell, Purgatory, Paradise* (the last volume with Barbara Reynolds), by Dante. London and Baltimore, Penguin, 3 vols., 1949–62.

Translator, *The Song of Roland*. London, Penguin, 1957.

*

Bibliography: *A Bibliography of the Works of Dorothy L. Sayers* by Colleen B. Gilbert, Hamden, Connecticut, Shoe String Press, 1978, London, Macmillan, 1979; *Dorothy L. Sayers: A Reference Guide* by Ruth Tanis Youngberg, Boston, Hall, 1982.

Manuscript Collections: Humanities Research Center, University of Texas, Austin; Marion E. Wade Collection, Wheaton College, Illinois.

Critical Studies: *Such a Strange Lady: An Introduction to Dorothy L. Sayers* by Janet Hitchman, London, New English Library, and New York, Harper, 1975; *An Annotated Guide to the Works of Dorothy L. Sayers* by Robert B. Harmon, New York, Garland, 1977; *Dorothy, L. Sayers: A Literary Biography* by Ralph E. Hone, Kent, Ohio, Kent State University Press, 1979; *As Her Whimsey Took Her: Critical Essays on the Work of Dorothy L. Sayers* edited by Margaret Hannay, Kent, Ohio, Kent State University Press, 1979; *Dorothy L. Sayers: Nine Literary Studies* by Trevor H. Hall, London, Duckworth, 1980; *Dorothy L. Sayers, A Pilgrim Soul* by Nancy M. Tischler, Atlanta, John Knox Press, 1980; *Dorothy L. Sayers: The Life of a Courageous Woman* by James Brabazon, London, Gollancz, and New York, Scribner, 1981; *Dorothy L. Sayers* by Dawson Gaillard, New York, Ungar, 1981; *Dorothy L. Sayers* by Mitzi Brunsdale, Oxford, Berg, 1989; *The Passionate Intellect: Dorothy L. Sayers' Encounter with Dante* by Barbara Reynolds, Kent, Ohio, Kent State University Press, 1989; *The Remarkable Case of Dorothy L. Sayers* by Catherine Kenney, Kent, Ohio, Kent State University Press, 1990.

Theatrical Activities:

Director: **Play**—*Christ's Emperor* (co-director, with Graham Suter), London, 1952.

*   *   *

In a 1939 essay entitled "Other People's Great Detectives," Dorothy L. Sayers pronounced: "Call no character great until the copyright has expired." She went on to say that a great fictional sleuth is not the same as a great real-life detective. She did not, she explained, "mean a man who displays unusual talent and ingenuity in his methods of detection, nor one who enjoys conspicuous success in bringing criminals to justice." Not ingenious problem-solving, not arduous legwork, but rather "the presentation of the character" is the criterion for affixing the highest superlative to a detective-in-fiction. So she believed.

At that time, with ornery modesty, Sayers added that a few hasty enthusiasts had asserted the greatness of her creation, Lord Peter Wimsey. For herself, she said, "I am obliged to them: but I shall feel more confidence if they are still saying it in fifty years." Even allowing for Wimseyphobes, there is no denying that Lord Peter is, by Sayers's own standards, great. And there is no more telling tribute to her (and Lord Peter's) success than that all of the Wimsey novels are currently in print and available. So, with her presentation of his character, she wrought an immortal of the genre. Her spectral reservations would be futile. Having introduced Wimsey in 1923 and having perceived his presence in her life as "ineluctable" as late as

1937, by 1940 she had experienced a change of heart. Preferring to pursue a course of religious writing, she closed the door on Lord Peter, leaving him forever in an arbitrary limbo of 11 novels and 21 stories.

Any regret that there are not more novels, more tales, is exceeded by the pleasure in knowing that what does exists. Like any special delight, perhaps the limitations of the Sayers-Wimsey canon enhance the satisfaction. Better to have Peter Wimsey stranded in time than to have him tottering through geriatric final adventures as did some of his peers in the pantheon of great detectives. He was in his prime and Sayers had been allowing him to evolve when she quit. Unlike Nero Wolfe he was not immutable; unlike Campion or Poirot he did not survive to become an anachronism. And unlike Sherlock Holmes he has not become a revenant. Authors are not immortal but characters can be. Fatalism did not inform Sayers; she simply changed her mind and in doing so left Lord Peter Wimsey intact for the ages.

When Wimsey is first seen, in *Whose Body?*, he is wearing a top hat. This is extremely appropriate to a discussion of what Wimsey's appeal stems from: style. It should not at all be an invidious comparison to say that the enduring popularity of Lord Peter Wimsey bears a notable resemblance to that of Fred Astaire. Fair, slender, well-groomed, and dapper, athletic without being brawny, graceful, dignified but able to behave with humor in bizarre situations, chivalrous, romantic: all of these traits are common to them both. Wimsey is a gentleman-scholar and a bibliophile and is depicted as having more of an electric intellectual curiosity than does Astaire, but, after all, Sayers had taken honours in medieval studies at Oxford and the demands of literature are different from those of film. What is more interesting is the notion of masculinity which Wimsey and Astaire alike present; they are sexless and sexy at the same time, underpoweringly sensuous, supremely attractive to women in ways that are inexplicable often to other men. Moreover, their peak periods coincided exactly; as heroes, both Wimsey and Astaire epitomize that golden era of effortless expertise and nonchalance and very high style.

And, just as Fred Astaire existed in a world peopled by distinctive personalities (Ginger Rogers, Eric Blore, Edward Everett Horton, Helen Broderick) so did Peter Wimsey: Harriet Vane, Bunter, Charles Parker, Miss Climpson, Mr. Murbles, Sir Impey Biggs, the Dowager Duchess. Though not all of these characters appear in all of the works still they are a repertory company supporting a leading man, except in such books as *Have His Carcase* or *Gaudy Night* in which Harriet Vane is far more than the love interest or the second banana. (Regarding the relationship between Peter and Harriet, it might be said that Sayers invented the latter so that she, Sayers, could consummate her, Sayers's, affair with the former. If an author desires a character she has created, is it incest? It could be argued that Wimsey's lengthy wooing period before Harriet capitulates is a result of Sayers's own unresolved feelings about "sinning" with the hero she has invented. But, this semi-facetious psychoanalyzing aside, Sayers herself does state that she first began *Strong Poison* "with the infanticidal intention of doing away with Peter; that is, of marrying him off and getting rid of him—for a lingering instinct of self-preservation.")

The perverseness of the relationship between Peter and Harriet catches the modern reader by surprise: there seems no rhyme or reason to it. But it must embrace the necessary changes in Wimsey (as Sayers explicates, in the 1937 essay "Gaudy Night," from which I've just quoted), *not* in Harriet, although it is the change in Harriet's attitude towards Peter which the reader is directed to notice rather than the metamorphosis in Peter himself. From a cliché idiot-aristocrat, charming in the manner of a Wodehouse or Saki character given to brightly delivered chatter Sayers transforms Lord Peter into a man with a past and a future; throughout this development, however, and even with added dimensions, he remains eccentric and elegant. The name Wimsey, in fact, is an inspired choice (family motto: *As my Whimsey takes me*) because it provides the right note of *esprit* between the "old" Peter and the "new" Peter.

Sayers also wrote 11 stories but no novels about Montague Egg, a commercial traveler in wines and spirits, but these are little more than pallid exercises in dropped clues and timetables. Her single non-Wimsey book of fiction, *The Documents in the Case*, is an epistolary novel about a tedious middlebrow illicit passion, and the toxological details contained therein are only slightly more interesting than the protagonists, which isn't saying much.

However, even if Sayers had not bestowed Lord Peter Wimsey upon the world, she would be an important figure in the history of the genre. Her introduction and her footnotes alone to the first book of her three-volume *Great Short Stories of Detection, Mystery, and Horror* are worth many another writer's entire career. In it, writing some of the earliest serious and scholarly interpretations, pronouncements, and recommendations about mystery fiction, she pays homage to her predecessors and her peers. In it, also, she refers to the detective as "the latest of the popular heroes, the true successor of Roland and Lancelot." If this was the light in which she created Lord Peter then, try as she would, she could never untie her colors from his sleeve.

—Michele Slung

————

SCANLON, C.K.M. *See* **DANIELS, Norman A.**

————

SCHERF, Margaret (Louise). American. Born in Fairmont, West Virginia, 1 April 1908. Educated in public schools in New Jersey, Wyoming, and Cascade, Montana; Antioch College, Yellow Springs, Ohio, 1925–28. Married Perry E. Beebe in 1965. Staff member, Robert M. McBride, publishers, New York, 1928–29; Camp Fire Girls national magazine, 1932–34; Wise Book Co., New York City, 1934–39; from 1939 a self-employed writer, except for a period as Secretary to the Naval Inspector, Bethlehem Steel Shipyard, Brooklyn, during World War II. Served in the House of the Montana State Legislature, 1965 session; active in Democratic Party. *Died 12 May 1979.*

CRIME PUBLICATIONS

Novels (series: Emily and Henry Bryce; the Reverend Martin Buell; Lieutenant Ryan; Grace Severance)

The Corpse Grows a Beard. New York, Putnam, 1940; London, Partridge, 1946.
The Case of the Kippered Corpse. New York, Putnam, 1941.
They Came to Kill. New York, Putnam, 1942.
The Owl in the Cellar (Ryan). New York, Doubleday, 1945; London, Nimmo, 1947.

Always Murder a Friend (Bryce). New York, Doubleday, 1948; London, Sampson Low, 1949.
Murder Makes Me Nervous (Ryan). New York, Doubleday, 1948; London, Sampson Low, 1952.
Gilbert's Last Toothache (Buell). New York, Doubleday, 1949; as *For the Love of Murder*, New York, Spivak, 1950.
The Gun in Daniel Webster's Bust (Bryce). New York, Doubleday, 1949.
The Curious Custard Pie (Buell). New York, Doubleday, 1950; as *Divine and Deadly,* New York, Spivak, 1953.
The Green Plaid Pants (Bryce). New York, Doubleday, 1951; as *The Corpse with One Shoe*, Roslyn, New York, Detective Book Club, 1951.
The Elk and the Evidence (Buell). New York, Doubleday, 1952.
Dead: Senate Office Building. New York, Doubleday, 1953; as *The Case of the Hated Senator*, New York, Ace, 1954.
Glass on the Stairs (Bryce). New York, Doubleday, 1954; London, Barker, 1955.
The Cautious Overshoes (Buell). New York, Doubleday, 1956.
Judicial Body. New York, Doubleday, 1957.
Never Turn Your Back (Buell). New York, Doubleday, 1959.
The Diplomat and the Gold Piano (Bryce). New York, Doubleday, 1963; as *Death and the Diplomat*, London, Hale, 1964.
The Corpse in the Flannel Nightgown (Buell). New York, Doubleday, 1965; London, Hale, 1966.
The Banker's Bones (Severance). New York, Doubleday, 1968; London, Hale, 1969.
The Beautiful Birthday Cake (Severance). New York, Doubleday, 1971.
To Cache a Millionaire (Severance). New York, Doubleday, 1972.
If You Want a Murder Well Done. New York, Doubleday, 1974.
Don't Wake Me Up While I'm Driving. New York, Doubleday, 1977; London, Hale, 1978.
The Beaded Banana (Severance). New York, Doubleday, 1978; London, Hale, 1979.

Uncollected Short Stories

"The Man with Nine Toes," in *American Magazine* (Springfield, Ohio), March 1952.
"The Man Who Liked Roquefort," in *Ellery Queen's Mystery Magazine* (New York), March 1960.

OTHER PUBLICATIONS

Novel

Wedding Train. New York, Doubleday, 1960.

Other (for children)

The Mystery of the Velvet Box. New York, Watts, 1963.
The Mystery of the Empty Trunk. New York, Watts, 1964.
The Mystery of the Shaky Staircase. New York, Watts, 1965.

*

Manuscript Collection: University of Oregon Library, Eugene.

Margaret Scherf commented (1979):
I began writing mysteries in the days of S.S. Van Dine, admired Agatha Christie very much, probably started reading Conan Doyle first. My idea was to write amusing books,

without too much gore but with sufficient suspense to carry the reader on. Small town characters, especially Episcopalians, were my delight, although I used two New York decorators in several books. Las Vegas and Howard Hughes were the material for *To Cache a Millionaire,* and the Arizona desert with its winter visitors figured in *The Banker's Bones.*

My theory is that mysteries appeal to people because the central problem is soluble, unlike most of the problems in the real world.

*   *   *

The variety of series and non-series detectives who inhabit Margaret Scherf's mystery novels range from a Prohibition rum-runner through a retired pathologist to an increasingly over-weight rural reverend. Always touched with humor, the works adhere to traditional means of detection, thoughtfully written and carefully plotted.

Set in Minot, North Dakota during Prohibition, *Don't Wake Me Up While I'm Driving* is the most exaggerated example of her unusual characters. Almost slapstick in the Laurel and Hardy vein, the plot is more concerned with whether Hal Brady will again postpone his luckless brother's wedding than with the investigation of a bank robbery in which he is accused. Scherf goes almost too far as the threads of detection are lost in local color, only to appear unexpectedly in the end. The characters are vividly drawn: even a dog, a blue chair, and Hal's car are thoroughly characterized.

With the Reverend Martin Buell, the most regular series detective, is retired pathologist Dr. Grace Severance whose wit and enjoyment are not diminished by age, only by her relatives. Her nephew Clarence is particularly officious, but in *To Cache a Millionaire,* set in Las Vegas in clear imitation of the Howard Hughes story, she outwits him and the security guards of multi-millionaire Arthur Acuff. The clever trick and bold determination with which she penetrates Acuff's hideaway capture the personality which she displays in all her investigations. Her background as a non-practising doctor and pathologist does not help with injured victims but rather in sniffing faint traces of formaldehyde or noticing similarities in skull shapes. Even so, her detecting is often intuitive.

Scherf combines typically traditional detective work with a touch of humor—usually surrounding the detective. While her novels include no startling new techniques, the characters are interesting and the plots, though somewhat predictable, are not dull.

—Kathleen Gregory Klein

———————

SCHORR, Mark. Also writes as Scott Ellis. American. Born in New York City, 6 September 1953. Educated at the State University of New York, Binghampton, graduated 1973. Married Sima Epstein in 1973; one daughter. Reporter, Los Angeles *Herald Examiner,* California 1980–82; producer in investigations unit, KNXT-TV, Los Angeles, 1983. Since 1983 Instructor in journalism, University of California, Los Angeles. Address: c/o St. Martin's Press, 175 Fifth Avenue, New York, New York 10010, U.S.A.

CRIME PUBLICATIONS

Novels (series: Red Diamond)

Red Diamond, Private Eye.   New York, St. Martin's Press, 1983.
Ace of Diamonds.   New York, St. Martin's Press, 1984.
Diamond Rock.   New York, St. Martin's Press, 1985.
Bully!   New York, St. Martin's Press, 1985.
The Borzoi Control (as Scott Ellis).   New York, St. Martin's Press, 1986.
Overkill.   New York, Pocket Books, 1987.
Seize the Dragon.   New York, Pocket Books, 1988.
An Eye for an Eye.   New York, St. Martin's Press, 1989.
Blindside.   New York, St. Martin's Press, 1989.
Gunpowder.   New York, Pocket Books, 1990.

*   *   *

Mark Schorr is best known for the innovations in the genre formula of his Red Diamond private-eye novels.

Red Diamond, Private Eye introduces cabby Simon Jaffe who lives in New York City with a nagging wife, an All-American son, and a promiscuous daughter. Simon Jaffe is a wimp. His only interest outside of his cab and his family is his hundreds of pulp magazines devoted to tough private-eye fiction. He's read each one a dozen times. Jaffe loves the adventures of the Continental Op and Race Williams and all the others. But his favorite private eye is rock-hard Red Diamond.

One day Jaffe's wife sells his beloved pulp collection without telling him. When Jaffe discovers what his wife has done, he goes into shock and wanders the streets in a daze. A prostitute picks the stunned Jaffe up and leads him to a hotel. Jaffe finds himself the victim of a badger game and loses all his money. Then he passes out. When he comes to, Jaffe thinks he's Red Diamond, private eye. Just like the stories in the pulps, Jaffe imagines himself forced to look for his girlfriend Fifi La Roche before his arch enemy Rocco Rico can find her.

Red Diamond, Private Eye broke new ground in many ways. It allowed Schorr to create a tough talking, macho private eye typical of the 1940's, but having to deal with the psychological problems of the 1980's. It showed readers that maybe what the 1980's needed was a few more guys like Red Diamond to take care of business. This innovative novel was nominated for the Edgar award for best first novel.

The next adventure, *Ace of Diamonds,* continues the story of Jaffe still in the persona of Red Diamond, private eye. A Las Vegas millionaire hires Red Diamond to find out who's trying to sabotage his casino and buy up most of Las Vegas cheaply. Jaffe, as Red Diamond, takes the case because " . . . He was destined to roam the underbellies of the tough towns searching for the lice that clung to the bottom."

Jaffe cracks the case in Vegas, leaving a pile of corpses behind him. This is another of Schorr's triumphs: he can take a basically comic situation and still create the mayhem of the typical private eye thriller.

In *Diamond Rock* Red Diamond is sued by his real wife, Milly Jaffe, whom he doesn't remember. His son arrives on the West Coast and tells Jaffe his daughter—whom he doesn't remember either—is missing. Red gives the kid a break and promises to look for the missing girl. Schorr takes some risks in *Diamond Rock* that pay off: he has Red Diamond revert back to Simon Jaffe for a while. The difference between the wimpy Jaffe and the dynamic Red Diamond is comic and a little sad. Jaffe wants to muddle along in the search for his daughter; Red Diamond wants to bust some heads.

What Schorr has done is to use the Clark Kent/Superman,

David Banner/The Incredible Hulk model and apply it to private-eye fiction. Take an average guy and give him superpowers. But what makes the Simon Jaffe/Red Diamond combination work is the sophistication and feeling Schorr gives his characters. Jaffe's a wimp, but he's also a good guy, a father who loves his kids, and a husband who loves his shrewish wife. Red Diamond is brutal but he's a good guy too—he's always willing to help the defenseless, the little people who can't defend themselves from the bullies and the thugs. The Red Diamond books are a refreshing addition to the private eye mythos.

Schorr's other work is less innovative. In *Bully!*, Schorr features President Teddy Roosevelt in a plot to topple the government. Someone is trying to blackmail the President. Roosevelt recruits one of his old Rough Rider friends, James White, to help him investigate the conspiracy. Based on much research and full of historical accuracy, *Bully!* is curiously flat and tedious.

Under the pseudonym Scott Ellis Schorr switched genres and produced *The Borzoi Control*, a conventional spy novel about the defection of a Soviet spy. Under his own name Schorr has recently published *Overkill*—a spy novel with geopolitical overtones, and *Seize the Dragon*—a spy novel set in the Orient. None of these books comes close to the ground-breaking impact of the innovative Red Diamond series.

—George Kelley

SCOTT, Jack S. Pseudonym for Jonathan Escott; also wrote as Jason Leonard. British. Born in London, 16 June 1922. Served in the British Army Film and Photographic Unit, 1941–46. Married Dorothy Oates; one daughter. Vaudeville actor, London, 1938–41; performer, 1946–67: actor, singer, and comedian in pantomimes, musicals, variety shows, cabaret, radio, and television, including a period as a singing cowboy, Silver Johnny Gray; Director of Entertainment, Canadian Pacific Ships, 1967–69. *Died in December 1987.*

CRIME PUBLICATIONS

Novels (series: Detective Inspector Alf Rosher)

The Poor Old Lady's Dead (Rosher). London, Hale, and New York, Harper, 1976.
A Better Class of Business. London, Hale, 1976; as *The Bastard's Name Was Bristow,* New York, Harper, 1977.
The Shallow Grave (Rosher). London, Hale, 1977; New York, Harper, 1978.
A Walk in Dead Man's Wood. London, W.H. Allen, 1978.
A Clutch of Vipers (Rosher). London, Collins, and New York, Harper, 1979.
The Gospel Lamb (Rosher). London, Collins, and New York, Harper, 1980.
A Distant View of Death (Rosher). London, Collins, 1981; as *The View from Deacon Hill,* New Haven, Connecticut, Ticknor and Fields, 1981.
An Uprush of Mayhem (Rosher). London, Collins, and New Haven, Connecticut, Ticknor and Fields, 1982.
The Local Lads (Rosher). London, Collins, 1982; New York, Dutton, 1983.
Corporal Smithers, Deceased. London, Collins, and New York, St. Martin's Press, 1983.

All the Pretty People (Rosher). London, Collins, 1983; New York, St. Martin's Press, 1984.
A Time of Fine Weather. London, Gollancz, 1984; New York, St. Martin's Press, 1985.
Death in Irish Town (Rosher). London, Collins, 1984; New York, St. Martin's Press, 1985.
A Little Darling, Dead. London, Collins, 1986; New York, St. Martin's Press, 1986.
A Knife Between the Ribs (Rosher). London, Collins, 1986; New York, St. Martin's Press, 1987.

OTHER PUBLICATIONS as Jonathan Escott

Novels

Landfall in Sefton Carey. London, Hale, 1976.
Shadow of Katie. London, Hale, 1977.
Moth to a Star. London, Hale, 1978.
A Little War in Sarawak (as Jason Leonard). London, Hale, 1982.

Short Stories as Jason Leonard

Meet Mrs. Piercey. London, Hale, 1981.

Play

Oh Dear (produced Bournemouth, Dorset, 1965).

*

Manuscript Collection: Mugar Memorial Library, Boston University.

Jack S. Scott commented (1984):
The writer is not, I think, the ideal person to comment upon his/her own work. He stands too close to it. By the time he has wrestled any book to some sort of groaning conclusion, probably he hates it and will never look at it again without sickness in the belly. Certainly this is true in my own case. I can't read the damn things.

Briefly, then: when I found I had written every possible short story and must advance to novels or perish, I looked around and found the police procedural genre debased into cliché. Lowly police inspectors seemed to solve utterly ridiculous cases all on their own and free of any supervision, in an utterly ridiculous manner. Nobody—but nobody—was writing credible policemen, warts and all, working as a fallible team. The warts-and-all school was in existence; but in over-reaction, perhaps, against the old-fashioned school of middle-class and jolly fantasy, particularly on television, all it presented was the warts. And old school or new school, nobody seemed to have explored the elements of black comedy present in crime, criminals, policemen and the cavorting between them, as it is in all branches of human activity.

I try, very hard, to create a credible world of accurately absurd cops and robbers, with the comedy shading sometimes into farce, as it has a wicked way of doing in real life. Whether I succeed is for other people to say. Me, I keep my head down to dodge the flak, and plod on.

One claim only I make: my investigating teams are accurately structured, and they pursue their investigations as the police do in reality. If a man—Rosher, in particular, my series Detective Inspector—goes it alone, at least he does it with a wary eye on the mailed fist upstairs.

* * *

It seems somehow wrong that a man whose career included a spell as Silver Johnny Gray, the Singing Cowboy, and who was also once a dance-band crooner, became not only a writer of successful crime novels but one who increasingly reached a high level of literary achievement. But such was the course of Jack S. Scott (published in Britain as Jack Scott).

True, his earliest books can be seen as being in the pattern of Singing Cowboy exploits. Chronicling the ups and downs of a provincial British police detective by the name of Rosher, they gave us a hero of, for the most part, caricature-like crudity. Rosher was set up as the antithesis of your clever and urbane investigator, whether amateur or as in more recent times police. Rosher wore heavy clothes dating in style, if not in fact, from some 20 years earlier than the contemporary date of his exploits. He carried a laughable bowler hat. He used crude language, made cruder jokes, lusted like an elephant, and, above all, frequently blew his nose into a drab cotton handkerchief with a noise ridiculously resounding and with farcical effect on all within hearing.

But even in his first appearance there were signs of a recognizable human being peeping through. Rosher's opinions (presumably shared often by his creator), though toughly uncompromising, were frequently truly shrewd and even sometimes cross-grainedly compassionate. Similar glimpses of subtler depths could be discerned, too, in the bouncingly engaging commentary of the books' author. Such "authorial intrusion" is generally held to be literary bad form, but it was practised in his day by a writer of the skill and achievement of Anthony Trollope and earned its bad reputation from a certain blind lack of understanding by high-priest critics. So Scott's use of it, whether deliberate or not, merits no down-marking.

Still retaining this unfashionable style and keeping his milieus strictly to the lower layers of British provincial society, Scott went on, however, to write increasingly effective books, gamier and gamier in flavour and step by step less caricature-like, more human. So that eventually he was achieving that difficult feat, writing fiction both entertaining and exciting but which also fulfils the function of the novel, to tell us about ourselves and our fellow human beings.

Then in 1983 Scott produced a book without Rosher and in a markedly human mode. Set in an army barracks in peace-time Britain, *Corporal Smithers, Deceased* evokes wonderfully the curious life of N.C.O. messes and army discipline and finagling. But it also contrives with very considerable skill to portray as hero an altogether unlikely figure, a Company Sergeant Major of limited outlook but strong natural intelligence. Scott moves him without signs of dislocation through episodes that vary from the robustly funny to the truly tender and include passages of genuine excitement as well. With much the same approach Scott followed this in 1984 with *A Time of Fine Weather*, another book in which tenderness—there are some finely written mature love passages—mingles with crime in the shape of a complex and credible contemporary murder plot. *A Little Darling, Dead* features Detective Chief Inspector Peter Parson and Sergeant Wammo Wimbush. A body is found in the turbulent waters under lover's leap and Parsons has to discover if the victim fell or if she was pushed. In the course of their investigation they uncover a web of nastiness spreading beyond the simple and routine matter of a young dead girl in a wood. Scott's last novel once again features Rosher. In *A Knife Between the Ribs* Rosher is mobilized into action after a fatal stabbing in a pub in his home town. The seriousness of the murder escalates and Rosher once more finds himself at odds with authority in a compelling and competent novel.

So the passage from Singing Cowboy to decidedly worthwhile writer is complete.

—H.R.F. Keating

SCOTT, Roney. *See* **GAULT, William Campbell.**

SCOTT, Warwick. *See* **HALL, Adam.**

SEELEY, Mabel (née Hodnefield). American. Born in Herman, Minnesota, 25 March 1903. Educated at schools in Illinois, Iowa, Wisconsin, and Minnesota; University of Minnesota, St. Paul, B.A. 1926. Married Kenneth Seeley in 1926; one son. Advertising copywriter in Chicago and Minneapolis, 1926–35.

CRIME PUBLICATIONS

Novels

The Listening House. New York, Doubleday, 1938; London, Collins, 1939.
The Crying Sisters. New York, Doubleday, 1939; London, Collins, 1940.
The Whispering Cup. New York, Doubleday, 1940; London, Collins, 1941.
The Chuckling Fingers. New York, Doubleday, 1941; London, Collins, 1942.
Eleven Came Back. New York, Doubleday, and London, Collins, 1943.
The Beckoning Door. New York, Doubleday, and London, Collins, 1950.
The Whistling Shadow. New York, Doubleday, 1954; London, Jenkins, 1958; as *The Blonde with the Deadly Past,* New York, Spivak, 1955.

Uncollected Short Stories

"The House That Nella Lived In," in *Queen's Awards, 7th Series.* Boston, Little Brown, 1952; London, Gollancz, 1954.
"Let Run, or Catch?" in *Ellery Queen's Mystery Magazine* (New York), December 1955.

OTHER PUBLICATIONS

Novels

Woman of Property. New York, Doubleday, 1947; London, Joseph, 1948.
The Stranger Beside Me. New York, Doubleday, 1951; London, Muller, 1953.

*   *   *

Mabel Seeley spent her formative years in the upper midwest. Her Norwegian ancestry and story-telling family circle influenced her development. Generous in praise of her mentors and filled with a self-confident pride in her origins, she was determined to portray the region and its people in her books. After several years writing advertising copy, much of it for department stores, she retired from a scene she claimed was too fast-paced and turned her attention to the creation of murder mysteries.

Unpretentious in regard to the "art" of writing, she meant to please the reader. She states as a premise of her mystery writing that "terror would be more terrible, horror more horrible, when visited on people the reader would feel were real, in places he would recognize as real." Her first suspense novel, *The Listening House,* was set in a squalid rooming house, presumably in St. Paul. The ladylike—though divorced—narrator establishes herself in what are surely unsuitable surroundings and becomes part of a sordid story involving white slavery, gangsters, and a disgustingly gruesome cadaver fed upon by hungry household pets. The plot is complicated and there are numerous characters to keep track of. Despite the evil landlady, her sluttish niece, and their down-and-out clientele, the heroine finds herself a presentable suitor, and the couple may live happily ever after on their dubiously acquired if not absolutely ill-gotten gains. The tale is a strange mixture of romantic thriller, some hard-boiled features, and a naturalism a bit reminiscent of Zola—all of this in an American city in the 1930's. It is a tale that can be read with some interest today.

The Whispering Cup takes place in a small Minnesota farming community and in its grain elevator. One victim, a monstrously greedy would-be opera star who sings solos at the local church, deserves to be murdered as much as any female personage in the annals of crime fiction; the heroine, in spite of her rather cloying spunkiness, deserves to win out in the end. Local color is well done, and small-town life in the midwest is shown at its most awful. This is probably Seeley's best mystery.

In *Eleven Came Back,* the Minnesota protagonists are transported to a ranch in the Teton Mountains of Wyoming. The landscape is endowed with "some vague, formless, imminent evil." The somewhat forced "horrors" and spuriously invoked menace notwithstanding, the story is fairly good. *The Chuckling Fingers,* in which Seeley is seen at her least convincing, is an overpopulated melodrama set in Minnesota on the shore of Lake Superior, a setting where nature is unfairly blamed for the shudders of the heroine who muses about "death walking hooded in the night, relentless and remorseless and successful." The author calls *Woman of Property* and *The Stranger Beside Me* "straight" novels. Both have small department stores as settings. In these books, where there is as much suspense as in her thrillers, Seeley felt freer to develop character and background and succeeds in depicting the struggles of immigrant families and of ambitious working-class characters to attain the "American dream."

Highly acclaimed when it first appeared, *The Listening House* is the 1938 entry in Howard Haycraft's "Cornerstones" list. In the 1941 edition of his *Murder for Pleasure,* Haycraft heaps lavish praise on Seeley, relishing her "drab" and "commonplace" settings, comparing her to Alfred Hitchcock (a comparison scarcely imaginable today), and calling her the "White Hope" of the American feminine detective story. Ben Hecht's delightful parody "The Whistling Corpse" (in *The Art of the Mystery Story,* edited by Haycraft, 1946), seems a more perceptive critique. Some three decades later Jacques Barzun declared in *A Catalogue of Crime* that "HIBK [Had I But Known] may be found at its best (i.e., worst) in *The Listening House . . . or The Chuckling Fingers.*"

Seeley wrote romantic thrillers which have much in common

with soap opera. In both *The Whispering Cup* and *The Beckoning Door,* for example, the heroines are in love with men married to their bitter enemies and rivals, in each case members—a stepsister, a cousin—of their own families. The Scandinavian-American characters are not made as interesting to the reader as they seem to be to the author, nor is there much detection. Seeley does not always find felicitous expression for her ideas, and her attempts to inject nameless terrors into everyday scenes detract from her narratives. Some readers will not care for these tales, others will become absorbed in a story, rapidly turn the pages as the heroine blunders through unspeakable dangers, and finally will arrive, along with the heroine, at the happy ending.

—Mary Helen Becker

SELWYN, Francis. British. Born in Brighton, Sussex, 20 August 1935. Educated at Taunton School, Somerset, 1948–54; Oxford University, 1956–60. Adult Education Organiser, 1961–65; research assistant, BBC, London, 1966–71. Since 1971 freelance translator and regular contributor to *Penthouse,* London. Address: c/o André Deutsch Ltd., 105 Great Russell Street, London WC1B 3LJ, England.

CRIME PUBLICATIONS

Novels (series: Sergeant William Verity in all books)

Cracksman on Velvet. London, Deutsch, and New York, Stein and Day, 1974; *as Sergeant Verity and the Cracksman,* London, Futura, 1975.
Sergeant Verity and the Imperial Diamond. London, Deutsch, 1975; New York, Stein and Day, 1976.
Sergeant Verity Presents His Compliments. London, Deutsch, and New York, Stein and Day, 1977.
Sergeant Verity and the Blood Royal. London, Deutsch, and New York, Stein and Day, 1979.
Sergeant Verity and the Swell Mob. New York, Stein and Day, 1980; London, Deutsch, 1981.

*   *   *

Francis Selwyn is a most historically-conscientious writer, using crime fiction as a way to portray history rather than using history as an interesting background for crime. He does such an excellent job of creating suspense in both areas, that the reader is as interested in the historical as the criminal outcome.

Sergeant William Clarence Verity is the portly, plodding investigator who leads us through the underworld slums of Victorian London in *Cracksman on Velvet.* Through his prudish, moralistic remarks and opinions the bull-headed sergeant represents the outward or public face of the times. But he moves in the slimy and hypocritical world that allows almost any behavior as long as the outward appearances are kept intact. Verity himself is a product of those morals and lets a gentleman villain kill himself rather than face the dishonor of public disgrace. Vigorously representing righteousness in *Sergeant Verity and the Imperial Diamond,* he faces the heathen society of mutinous India in the 1850's and comes out ahead. He is also an unacknowledged expert in the art of deduction—using details of one incident to find the objective logic behind it, and then applying that logic to another incident, thereby moving toward the solution of the crime.

Selwyn's sense of humor shouldn't be overlooked. It emerges in Verity's constant battle with higher authorities and less-perceptive co-workers. His later adventures seem a bit stretched in believability at times, but Verity's deductive mind finds escape routes and answers that few readers will anticipate. All elements from royalty to a meeting with Sergeant Cuff, from bawdy sex to a description of the abominable conditions of an insane asylum, contribute to suspenseful, educational entertainment.

—Fred Dueren

———

SERAFÍN, David. Pseudonym for Ian Michael. British. Alfonso XIII Professor of Spanish, University of Oxford. Recipient: Commander of the Order of Isabel the Catholic, Spain, 1986. Address: c/o Macmillan Publishers Ltd., 4 Little Essex Street, London WC2R 3LF, England.

CRIME PUBLICATIONS

Novels (series: Superintendent Luis Bernal in all books)

Saturday of Glory. London, Collins, 1979.
Madrid Underground. London, Collins, 1982.
Christmas Rising. London, Collins, 1982.
The Body in Cadiz Bay. London, Collins, 1985.
Port of Light. London, Collins, 1987.
The Angel of Torremolinos. London, Macmillan, 1988.

OTHER PUBLICATIONS as Ian Michael

Other

Gwyn Thomas. Cardiff, University of Wales Press, 1977.

Editor, *The Poem of the Cid.* Manchester, Manchester University Press, 1975.
Editor, with Richard A. Cardwell, *Medieval and Renaissance Studies in Honour of Robert Brian Tate.* Oxford, Dolphin, 1986.

*   *   *

There is something eminently comfortable about Superintendent Luis Bernal, hero of David Serafín's string of Spanish set thrillers. When we are first introduced to him in *Saturday of Glory,* the detective has a "thick-set body, with hairy chest and a slight paunch on short legs." Between this 1979 portrait and 1988's *The Angel of Torremolinos,* Bernal's figure grows a little stouter and, whilst he is still capable of "a considerable burst of speed" in evading a bomb blast, it is certainly true that the pace of his life becomes increasingly sedate.

Indeed, there are moments when Bernal looks to be only mildly curious about the crimes set before him and, habitually, they are resolved with a blend of gentle probing, indispensable assistance from a small band of expert minds at Bernal's disposal and flashes of his own brand of intuitive brilliance. Often, the real hero appears to be the pathologist, Dr. Palaez, who, drafted in at all hours of the night and day, performs feats of autopsy that, without fail, both unsettle Bernal's delicate

duodenum and provide vital clues—in every single plot. Only infrequently—*Port of Light* being an interesting example—does Bernal seem in danger of tearing out what remains of his own hair.

None of which should detract either from Serafín or his leading character, for a substantial part of Bernal's charm is his seeming imperturbability and a large component of the author's strength lies in his talent for engineering suspense, which is mainly achieved by the clever disruption of the leading character's peace of mind. In the better novels (*Saturday of Glory, Port of Light* and, perhaps, best of all, *Madrid Underground*), Serafín's movement towards a genuine and well-judged climax can seem almost effortless.

Bernal's brief is, ostensibly, to trace murderers, or at least this is how his career has been built. As promotion follows, however, and audiences with King Juan Carlos and senior members of the Government accrue, Bernal becomes a kind of criminological troubleshooter—uncovering a right-wing coup here, containing an E.T.A. campaign there, corralling an insurgent design on Spanish territory elsewhere, generally, in fact, fulfilling the role of "superpolicia" assigned to him.

Typically, a Bernal case involves a reasonably low corpse quota, an abduction—either of one of Bernal's team or a family member—a more or less complicated scheme to usurp some form of political power and a good number of stops for refreshment. Only *Madrid Underground* dispenses with the political aspect, being a relatively straightforward tale of a psychopath's murderous endeavours in the subterranean rail network of the capital city. Here, the crimes are more graphically rendered, the storyline is unencumbered by socio-political significance and, as previously suggested, the author probably gives us his best work, at least in terms of unadulterated tension and thrill factor. Whatever Serafín writes, though, is made readable, by and large, by his encyclopaedic knowledge of police procedure and his expert understanding of the volatile nature of contemporary Spanish politics.

And, if a fuller flavour of Spain is required, no-one could be a better guide than the hearty (notwithstanding the scar of his surgically removed gastric ulcer) Bernal. Those who relish the prospect of, say, "'sea-pike cooked in salt: the scales come away with the salt,'" will be especially happy.

A romantic thread runs through all the novels in the form of Bernal's inability to shake off his wife, the obsessive Eugenia (whose devotion to religion outstrips even Bernal's pursuit of justice and food) and replace her with his mistress, Consuelo Lazano. We come to appreciate the contrast between these two women in terms of the difference between the "cracked Manchegan cheese" from Eugenia's larder and the "fresh white Manchegan" that Bernal and Consuelo share in their *pied á terre* in suburban Madrid. Along with Elena Fernández and Ángel Gallardo, the two junior members of Bernal's staff, Consuelo brings some of the vibrancy of youth to the action and adds a more tingling dimension to Bernal's comfort. Further, her eventual pregnancy—and its outcome—is as good a surprise in a different way, as any of the gruesome cadavers (fake or otherwise) and various kidnappings with which Bernal is forced to contend.

Finally, we are offered proof that police work can take years off anyone's life, for, in *The Body in Cadiz Bay,* when Consuelo is well into her pregnancy, Bernal is emphatically 61. In the previous novel *Christmas Rising,* with the baby barely conceived, Bernal is a surprised father-to-be at 62. This, though, is the kind of thing one will only rarely find in Serafín's writing for the author's scrupulous regard for detail, alongside his ability to contrive well-structured, well-informed and generally plausible plots makes the Bernal series consistently enjoyable.

—Ian McMechan

SEYMOUR, Gerald (William Herschel Kean). British. Born in Surrey, 25 November 1941. Educated at Kelly College, Tavistock, Devon; University College, London, B.A. (honours) in modern history 1963. Married Gillian Mary Roberts in 1964; two sons. Reporter, Independent Television News, London, 1963–78. Recipient: Pye award, for television play, 1983. Agent: Michael Sissons, Peters Fraser and Dunlop, 5th Floor, The Chambers, Chelsea Harbour, Lots Road, London, England, SW10 0XF.

CRIME PUBLICATIONS

Novels

Harry's Game. London, Collins, and New York, Random House, 1975.
The Glory Boys. London, Collins, and New York, Random House, 1976.
Kingfisher. London, Collins, 1977; New York, Summit, 1978.
Red Fox. London, Collins, 1979; as *The Harrison Affair,* New York, Summit, 1980.
The Contract. London, Collins, 1980; New York, Holt Rinehart, 1981.
Archangel. London, Collins, and New York, Dutton, 1982.
In Honour Bound. London, Collins, and New York, Norton, 1984.
Field of Blood. London, Collins, and New York, Norton, 1985.
A Song in the Morning. London, Collins, 1986; New York, Norton, 1987.
At Close Quarters. London, Collins, 1987; as *An Eye for an Eye,* New York, Morrow, 1988.
Home Run. London, Collins, 1989; as *The Running Target,* New York, Morrow, 1990.

OTHER PUBLICATIONS

Plays

Television Plays (from his own novels): *Harry's Game,* 1982; *The Glory Boys,* 1984; *The Contract,* 1988.

*   *   *

It would be no exaggeration to say that Gerald Seymour's thrillers as a whole form a running commentary on world politics in the last decades.

In each of his novels he singles out one specific conflict and gives it a thorough and true representation: Northern Ireland in *Harry's Game* and *Field of Blood,* Italy of the Red Brigades in *Red Fox,* the Israeli-Palestinian conflict in the Middle East in *The Glory Boys,* Afghanistan in *In Honour Bound,* South Africa in *A Song in the Morning,* Iran of the Mullahs in *Home Run.* No doubt his experiences from his career as a television reporter have made it possible for Seymour to give such a strong feeling of reality to such a wide range of localities, such a vivid feeling of actually "being there."

Without this strong feeling of reality he couldn't possibly have succeeded with his very special conception of the basic conflicts in his novels, which he almost reduces to a "single combat" between two "champions," one from each side of the conflict. The prototype is there already in Seymour's first novel, *Harry's Game,* where British agent Harry Brown stalks IRA killer Billy Downs through the black streets and alleys of war-torn Belfast. More or less obviously this theme is repeated in all his other novels—the Palestinian terrorist Abdel-El-Famy versus the British agent Jimmy in *The Glory Boys,* the SAS Captain Barney Crispin, fighting with the Afghan guerillas, versus the Russian helicopter commander Medev in *In Honour Bound,* the young British diplomat Holt versus Abu Hamid, terrorist and killer of his girlfriend, in *At Close Quarters.*

Sometimes, especially in some of his later novels, he goes a bit too far, as in *A Song in the Morning,* when the son of the condemned Englishman almost takes on the whole of South Africa to save his father from imprisonment, and in *Home Run* where exiled Iranian Charlie Eshraq does the same with Iran to revenge the hanging of his sister. Novels like these lack the simplicity and integration of the single-combat-motive in the plot of *Harry's Game.* But generally it functions surprisingly well, and Seymour manages to make sometimes rather far-fetched plots seem plausible.

Seymour's special historical and philosophical vision—or perhaps even outlook on life—contributes to the sense of reality in the novels. These individuals are all fighting heroic combats for their countries, their political beliefs, their fellow human beings. But Seymour shows us that all their heroics are futile in the end. The "heroes" are only puppets, manipulated by puppet-masters, puppets in a cynically written play where they don't know the whole script or the whole cast. And they are all expendable, sacrificed by their supposed friends: Charlie Eshraq is cynically used by the British Intelligence, Michael Holly in *Archangel* is disavowed by his masters who without any visible struggle let him spend 14 years in Gulag; Harry Brown and Billy Downs in *Harry's Game* are driven harder and harder by their superiors, in the end to almost simultaneous deaths.

When the combat is over, nothing has really changed. The cynical manipulators of men—politicians, terrorist leaders et al—continue their game, a game with no winners and only losers. This may be Seymour's vision of the world, collected piecemeal from different parts of our planet—a vision of human courage sacrificed on the altar of cynicism and *Realpolitik.*

It is a rather pessimistic vision, which might seem reasonable considering the state of the world today. But against the grain of this vision goes another which speaks of the unconquerable human spirit.

—Karl G. Fredriksson

SHAFFER, Anthony. *See* **ANTONY, Peter.**

SHAFFER, Peter. *See.* **ANTONY, Peter.**

SHANNON, Dell. *See* **LININGTON, Elizabeth.**

SHANNON, Doris. *See* **GIROUX, E.X.**

SHEARING, Joseph. Pseudonym for Gabrielle Margaret Vere Campbell; also wrote as Marjorie Bowen; Robert Paye; George Preedy; John Winch. British. Born on Hayling Island, Hampshire, 29 October 1886. Married 1) Zeffrino Emilio Costanzo in 1912 (died 1916), one son 2) Arthur L. Long in 1917, two sons. *Died 23 December 1952.*

CRIME PUBLICATIONS

Novels

Withering Fires (as Marjorie Bowen). London, Collins, 1931.
The Shadow on Mockways (as Marjorie Bowen). London, Collins, 1932.
Forget-Me-Not. London, Heinemann, 1932; as *Lucile Cléry,* New York, Harper, 1932; as *The Strange Case of Lucile Cléry,* Harper, 1941.
Album Leaf. London, Heinemann, 1933; as *The Spider in the Cup* New York, Smith and Haas, 1934.
Moss Rose. London, Heinemann, 1934; New York, Smith and Haas, 1935.
The Golden Violet: The Story of a Lady Novelist. London, Heinemann, 1936; New York, Smith and Durrell, 1941; as *Night's Dark Secret* (as Margeret Campbell), New York, New American Library, 1975.
Blanche Fury; or, Fury's Ape. London, Heinemann, and New York, Harrison Hilton, 1939.
Aunt Beardie. London, Hutchinson, and New York, Harrison Hilton, 1940.
Laura Sarelle. London, Hutchinson, 1940; as *The Crime of Laura Sarelle,* New York, Smith and Durrell, 1941.
The Fetch. London, Hutchinson, 1942; as *The Spectral Bride,* New York, Smith and Durrell, 1942.
Airing in a Closed Carriage. London, Hutchinson, and New York, Harper, 1943.
The Abode of Love. London, Hutchinson, 1945.
For Her to See. London, Hutchinson, 1947; as *So Evil My Love,* New York, Harper, 1947.
Mignonette. New York, Harper, 1948; London, Heinemann, 1949.
Within the Bubble. London, Heinemann, 1950; as *The Heiress of Frascati,* New York, Berkley, 1966.
To Bed at Noon. London, Heinemann, 1951.

Novels as George Preedy

The Devil Snar'd. London, Benn, 1932.
Dr. Chaos, and The Devil Snar'd. London, Cassell, 1933.
The Poisoners. London, Hutchinson, 1936.
My Tattered Loving. London, Jenkins, 1937; as *The King's Favourite* (as Marjorie Bowen), London, Fontana, 1971.
Painted Angel. London, Jenkins, 1938.
The Fair Young Widow. London, Jenkins, 1939.

Short Stories

Orange Blossoms. London, Heinemann, 1938.
The Bishop of Hell and Other Stories (as Marjorie Bowen). London, Lane, 1949.

Uncollected Short Stories

"Supper with Madame Olhausen" (as George Preedy), in *World's Great Spy Stories.* Cleveland, World, 1944.
"Love-in-a-Mist," in *Ellery Queen's Mystery Magazine* (New York), November 1948.
"The Chinese Apple," in *Ellery Queen's Mystery Magazine* (New York), April 1949.

OTHER PUBLICATIONS as Marjorie Bowen

Novels

The Viper of Milan. London, Alston Rivers, and New York, McClure Phillips, 1906.
The Glen o' Weeping. London, Alston Rivers, 1907; as *The Master of Stair,* New York, McClure Phillips, 1907.
The Sword Decides! London, Alston Rivers, and New York, McClure, 1908.
Black Magic: A Tale of the Rise and Fall of Antichrist. London, Alston Rivers, 1909.
The Leopard and the Lily. New York, Doubleday, 1909; London, Methuen, 1920.
William III Trilogy:
    I Will Maintain. London, Methuen, 1910; New York, Dutton, 1911; revised edition, London, Penguin, 1943.
    Defender of the Faith. London, Methuen, and New York, Dutton, 1911.
    God and the King. London, Methuen, 1911; New York, Dutton, 1912.
Lover's Knots. London, Everett, 1912.
The Quest of Glory. London, Methuen, and New York, Dutton, 1912.
The Rake's Progress. London, Rider, 1912.
The Soldier from Virginia. New York, Appleton, 1912; as *Mister Washington,* London, Methuen, 1915.
The Governor of England. London, Methuen, 1913; New York, Dutton, 1914.
A Knight of Spain. London, Methuen, 1913.
The Two Carnations. London, Cassell, and New York, Reynolds, 1913.
Prince and Heretic. London, Methuen, 1914; New York, Dutton, 1915.
Because of These Things . . . London, Methuen, 1915.
The Carnival of Florence. London, Methuen, and New York, Dutton, 1915.
William, By the Grace of God—. London, Methuen, 1916; New York, Dutton, 1917; abridged edition, Methuen, 1928.
The Third Estate. London, Methuen, 1917; New York, Dutton, 1918; revised edition, as *Eugénie,* London, Fontana, 1971.
The Burning Glass. London, Collins, 1918; New York, Dutton, 1919.
Kings-at-Arms. London, Methuen, 1918; New York, Dutton, 1919.
Mr. Misfortunate. London, Collins, 1919.
The Cheats. London, Collins, 1920.
The Haunted Vintage. London, Odhams Press, 1921.
Rococo. London, Odhams Press, 1921.
The Jest. London, Odhams Press, 1922.

Affairs of Men (selections from novels). London, Cranton, 1922.

Stinging Nettles. London, Ward Lock, and Boston, Small Maynard, 1923.

The Presence and the Power. London, Ward Lock, 1924.

Five People. London, Ward Lock, 1925.

Boundless Water. London, Ward Lock, 1926.

Nell Gwyn: A Decoration. London, Hodder and Stoughton, 1926; as *Mistress Nell Gwyn,* New York, Appleton, 1926; London, Mellifont Press, 1949.

Five Winds. London, Hodder and Stoughton, 1927.

The Pagoda: Le Pagode de Chanteloup. London, Hodder and Stoughton, 1927.

The Countess Fanny. London, Hodder and Stoughton, 1928.

Renaissance Trilogy:

> *The Golden Roof.* London, Hodder and Stoughton, 1928.
> *The Triumphant Beast.* London, Lane, 1934.
> *Trumpets at Rome.* London, Hutchinson, 1936.

Dickon. London, Hodder and Stoughton, 1929.

The English Paragon. London, Hodder and Stoughton, 1930.

The Devil's Jig (as Robert Paye). London, Lane, 1930.

Brave Employments. London, Collins, 1931.

Dark Rosaleen. London, Collins, 1932; Boston, Houghton Mifflin, 1933.

Passion Flower. London, Collins, 1932; as *Beneath the Passion Flower* (as George Preedy), New York, McBride, 1932.

Idler's Gate (as John Winch). London, Collins, and New York, Morrow, 1932.

Julia Roseingrave (as Robert Paye). London, Benn, 1933.

I Dwelt in High Places. London, Collins, 1933.

Set with Green Herbs. London, Benn, 1933.

The Stolen Bride. London, Lovat Dickson, 1933; abridged edition, London, Mellifont Press, 1946.

The Veil'd Delight. London, Odhams Press, 1933.

A Giant in Chains: Prelude to Revolution—France 1775–1791. London, Hutchinson, 1938.

Trilogy:

> *God and the Wedding Dress.* London, Hutchinson, 1938.
> *Mr. Tyler's Saints.* London, Hutchinson, 1939.
> *The Circle in the Water.* London, Hutchinson, 1939.

Exchange Royal. London, Hutchinson, 1940.

Today Is Mine. London, Hutchinson, 1941.

The Man with the Scales. London, Hutchinson, 1954.

Novels as George Preedy

General Crack. London, Lane, and New York, Dodd Mead, 1928.

The Rocklitz. London, Lane, 1930; as *The Prince's Darling,* New York, Dodd Mead, 1930.

Tumult in the North. London, Lane, and New York, Dodd Mead, 1931.

The Pavilion of Honour. London, Lane, 1932.

Violante: Circe and Ermine. London, Cassell, 1932.

Double Dallilay. London, Cassell, 1933; as *Queen's Caprice,* New York, King, 1934.

The Autobiography of Cornelius Blake, 1773–1810, of Ditton See, Cambridgeshire. London, Cassell, 1934.

Laurell'd Captains. London, Hutchinson, 1935.

Dove in the Mulberry Tree. London, Jenkins, 1939.

Primula. London, Hodder and Stoughton, 1940.

Black Man—White Maiden. London, Hodder and Stoughton, 1941.

Findernes' Flowers. London, Hodder and Stoughton, 1941.

Lyndley Waters. London, Hodder and Stoughton, 1942.

Lady in a Veil. London, Hodder and Stoughton, 1943.

The Fourth Chamber. London, Hodder and Stoughton, 1944.

Nightcap and Plume. London, Hodder and Stoughton, 1945.

No Way Home. London, Hodder and Stoughton, 1947.

The Sacked City. London, Hodder and Stoughton, 1949.

Julia Ballantyne. London, Hodder and Stoughton, 1952.

Short Stories

God's Playthings. London, Smith Elder, 1912; New York, Dutton, 1913.

Shadows of Yesterday: Stories from an Old Catalogue. London, Smith Elder, and New York, Dutton, 1916.

Curious Happenings. London, Mills and Boon, 1917.

Crimes of Old London. London, Odhams Press, 1919.

The Pleasant Husband and Other Stories. London, Hurst and Blackett, 1921.

Seeing Life! and Other Stories. London, Hurst and Blackett, 1923.

The Seven Deadly Sins. London, Hurst and Blackett, 1926.

Dark Ann and Other Stories. London, Lane, 1927.

The Gorgeous Lover and Other Tales. London, Lane, 1929.

Sheep's-Head and Babylon, and Other Stories of Yesterday and Today. London, Lane, 1929.

Old Patch's Medley; or, A London Miscellany. London, Selwyn and Blount, 1930.

Bagatelle and Some Other Diversions (as George Preedy). London, Lane, 1930; New York, Dodd Mead, 1931.

Grace Latouche and the Warringtons: Some Nineteenth-Century Pieces, Mostly Victorian. London, Selwyn and Blount, 1931.

Fond Fancy and Other Stories. London, Selwyn and Blount, 1932.

The Last Bouquet: Some Twilight Tales. London, Lane, 1932.

The Knot Garden: Some Old Fancies Re-Set (as George Preedy). London, Lane, 1933.

Kecksies and Other Twilight Tales. Sauk City, Wisconsin, Arkham House, 1976.

Plays as George Preedy

Captain Banner (produced London, 1929). London, Lane, 1930.

A Family Comedy, 1840 (as Marjorie Bowen). London, French, 1930.

The Question. London, French, 1931.

The Rocklitz (produced London, 1931).

Rose Giralda (produced London, 1933).

Court Cards (produced London, 1934).

Royal Command (produced Wimbledon, Surrey, 1952).

Screenplay: *The Black Tulip* (as Marjorie Bowen), 1921.

Other

Luctor et Emergo, Being an Historical Essay on the State of England at the Peace of Ryswyck. Newcastle upon Tyne, Northumberland Press, 1925.

The Netherlands Display'd; or, The Delights of the Low Countries. London, Lane, 1926; New York, Dodd Mead, 1927.

Holland, Being a General Survey of the Netherlands. London, Harrap, 1928; New York, Doubleday, 1929.

The Winged Trees (for children). Oxford, Blackwell, 1928.

The Story of the Temple and Its Associations. London, Griffin Press, 1928.

Sundry Great Gentlemen: Some Essays in Historical Biography. London, Lane, and New York, Dodd Mead, 1928.

William, Prince of Orange, Afterwards King of England, Being an Account of His Early Life. London, Lane, and New York, Dodd Mead, 1928.

The Lady's Prisoner (for children). Oxford, Blackwell, 1929.

Mademoiselle Maria Gloria (for children). Oxford, Blackwell, 1929.

The Third Mary Stuart, Being a Character Study with Memoirs and Letters of Queen Mary II of England 1662–1694. London, Lane, 1929.

Exits and Farewells, Being Some Account of the Last Days of Certain Historical Characters. London, Selwyn and Blount, 1930.

Mary, Queen of Scots, Daughter of Debate. London, Lane, 1934; New York, Putnam, 1935.

The Scandal of Sophie Dawes. London, Lane, 1934; New York, Appleton Century, 1935.

Patriotic Lady: A Study of Emma, Lady Hamilton, and the Neapolitan Revolution of 1799. London, Lane, 1935; New York, Appleton Century, 1936.

The Angel of Assassination: Marie-Charlotte de Corday d'Armont, Jean-Paul Marat, Jean-Adam Lux: Three Disciples of Rousseau (as Joseph Shearing). London, Heinemann, and New York, Smith and Haas, 1935.

Peter Porcupine: A Study of William Cobbett, 1762–1835. London, Longman, 1935; New York, Longman, 1936.

William Hogarth, The Cockney's Mirror. London, Methuen, and New York, Appleton Century, 1936.

Crowns and Sceptres: The Romance and Pageantry of Coronations. London, Long, 1937.

The Lady and the Arsenic: The Life and Death of a Romantic, Marie Capelle, Madame Lafarge (as Joseph Shearing). London, Heinemann, 1937; New York, A.S. Barnes, 1944.

This Shining Woman: Mary Wollstonecraft Godwin 1759–1797 (as George Preedy). London, Collins, and New York, Appleton Century, 1937.

Wrestling Jacob: A Study of the Life of John Wesley and Some Members of His Family. London, Heinemann, 1937; abridged edition, London, Watts, 1948.

World's Wonder and Other Essays. London, Hutchinson, 1938.

The Trumpet and the Swan: An Adventure of the Civil War (for children). London, Pitman, 1938.

The Debate Continres, Being the Autobiography of Marjorie Bowen, by Margaret Campbell. London, Heinemann, 1939.

Ethichs in Modern Art (lecture). London, Watts, 1939.

Child of Chequer'd Fortune: The Life, Loves and Battles of Maurice de Saxe, Maréchal de France (as George Preedy). London, Jenkins, 1939.

Strangers to Freedom (for children). London, Dent, 1940.

The Life of John Knox (as George Preedy). London, Jenkins, 1940.

The Life of Rear-Admiral John Paul Jones, 1747–1792 (as George Preedy). London, Jenkins, 1940.

The Courtly Charlatan: The Enigmatic Comte de St. Germain (as George Preedy). London, Jenkins, 1942.

The Church and Social Progress: An Exposition of Rationalism and Reaction. London, Watts, 1945.

In the Steps of Mary, Queen of Scots. London, Rich and Cowan, 1952.

Editor, *Great Tales of Horror*. London, Lane, 1933.
Editor, *More Great Tales of Horror*. London, Lane, 1935.
Editor, *Some Famous Love Letters*. London, Jenkins, 1937.

*   *   *

Joseph Shearing's most successful novels are those which reconstruct famous 19th-century mysteries such as the Bravo case (*For Her to See*), the Maybrick poisoning (*Airing in a Closed Carriage*), and the murder of the Duchesse de Praslin

(*Forget-Me-Not*). Sometimes Shearing follows the known historical details closely, but interprets them anew; sometimes, as her foreword to *Moss Rose* tells us, "Nothing but the bare outline and a few unimportant details have been used"; sometimes, as in *Laura Sarelle,* the setting is authentically Victorian, but the crime and characters are largely imaginary. Shearing was obviously well-read in the cases she re-created, but retained the novelist's freedom of interpretation and invention, "to try to arrive at the truth not by study of actions alone, but by the study of the characters and events that produce those actions," as she said in *Airing in a Closed Carriage.*

In *For Her to See,* for instance, Shearing used not only the outline of the unsolved 1876 Charles Bravo case (husband supposedly poisoned by wife), but its secondary characters as well: Florence Bravo's dead first husband; her lover, the famous Dr. Gully (Sir John Curle in the novel); her antagonistic mother-in-law (but not her equally antagonistic father-in-law). The fiction even absorbs and reproduces portions of the two inquests. But the focus is no longer Florence Bravo, here called Susan Rue; instead, it is Mrs. Olivia Sacret, Shearing's version of Mrs. Cox, Florence's prim companion and, in popular opinion, her accomplice. It is Mrs. Sacret who provides Susan with drink, who blackmails her, who poisons Martin Rue, and is in turn punished by the avenging mother-in-law, too late aware of Susan's innocence.

Mrs. Sacret's motivation is partly her desire for comfort, fine clothes, and domestic power; partly her distorted sense that these things are her due; and partly her strange, will-less domination by a scoundrel and murderer, for whose benefit she victimizes Susan and of whom she is herself a victim. This attraction to a psychopath even against one's better judgment also motivates Belle, the otherwise cool and self-serving heroine of *Moss Rose,* based on an 1872 murder. Indeed, victimization of some sort is a recurrent motif in Shearing's novels, along with madness and religious fanaticism. Laura Sarelle, already over-excitable, slowly succumbs to the influence of Leppard Hall, haunted by the mysterious crime of her namesake. Under the spell of "the dreams of the dead," Laura, too, poisons her brother and falsely accuses her unloved husband. Accompanied by her ghostly predecessor, she drowns herself in the Avon.

In *The Abode of Love,* Rev. Stephen Finett, called "Beloved," and his devotees await the end of the world, with grotesque interludes of mass hysteria and love feasts in a fantastically decorated mansion. Finett's elderly wife is able to lead him safely back to anonymity just as his remaining disciples prepare to crucify "Beloved" in anticipation of a resurrection.

Shearing's plots generally begin slowly (*Moss Rose* is a notable exception) with careful establishment of a domestic status quo which will be broken either by the main character's desire to change her way of life or by some disturbing or dangerous external element, usually masculine, or by both as in *Forget-Me-Not.* Although these are not feminist novels, they often show Victorian women bored by narrow interests, incapable of self-preservation, held down by male authority, and Shearing is very successful in establishing a tone of brutal sexuality without recourse to explicit detail. Yet many of her "strong" women, although fascinating, are unsympathetic, calculating, manipulative: "Ah, it was delicious to be of such importance!" thinks the governess Lucile, feeling her power in a noble family.

Most physical violence takes place off-stage, and horror is usually reserved for the denouement, as when, for example, mad Lord Seagrove strikes Caroline Fenton dead in a reenactment of his ancestor's crime (*The Fetch*) or when Belle lies waiting for the embrace of Pastor Morl (*Moss Rose*), only to see him methodically preparing to cut her throat.

Between the quiet beginnings which draw the reader into the story and the shock of the strong endings, the novels frequently suffer from mid-plot repetition and lack of invention. Reversals become almost mechanical, as in *The Abode of Love,* or arbitrary, as in *For Her to See.* In *Forget-Me-Not* the heroine roams the streets of Paris ostensibly to satisfy "a restless, a brutal curiosity," but really to bring in atmosphere and historicity. We are too often led along a character's one-track mind, and are reminded too often of the symbols which give some of the novels their titles, e.g., *Moss Rose* and *The Golden Violet.* Shearing also uses symbols and similes as characterization (Mary Tyler is persistently identified with the ephemeral mayfly) and as clues (laurel leaves from which both Lauras distill poison). The reader, however, realizes and finds their significance exhausted long before the novelist ceases to call attention to them. In fact, Shearing's plots are not exercises in detection through the discovery and analysis of recondite clues, but are, rather, wanderings deeper into peril. Even in *Aunt Beardie,* the reader will very likely have guessed the main character's secret, but Shearing is always successful in depicting a character's stupefied or willing suspension of apprehension.

Like the "Silver Fork" novelists of the 1830's and 1840's, Shearing gives pleasure by detailed description of clothing, rooms, furnishings, possessions. The setting is almost always England, with occasional excursions to the Continent or America: *To Bed at Noon* is a version of the early 19th-century "Kentucky Tragedy." At times the author's pictures of London and Paris have a Dickensian scruffiness in the greasy backstage squalor of a music hall, the filthiness of gutters and slaughterhouses, the sordidness of mean streets. But she is adept at displaying luxurious upholstery and garments. Susan Rue, for instance, weeps in "a striped blue satin chair" and wears, "a loose rose-colored boudoir gown, edged with swan's-down," which Mrs. Sacret, "in pearl-gray color shot with lilac and azure tones," despises. The hallucinatory plot of *The Fetch* begins with "a pink bonnet with long satin strings . . . and two rosy-colored ostrich feathers, and a little wreath of velvet flowers inside the brim," and Laura Sarelle goes mad in yellow silk.

—Jane W. Stedman

———

SHEPARD, Neal. *See* **MORLAND, Nigel.**

———

SHEPHERD, John. *See* **BALLARD, Willis Todhunter.**

———

SHEPHERD, Michael. *See* **LUDLUM, Robert.**

———

SHERWOOD, John (Herman Mulso). British. Born in Cheltenham, Gloucestershire, 14 May 1913. Educated at Malborough College, Wiltshire, 1926–31; Oriel College, Oxford, 1931–35, Lit. Hum. 1935. Served in the British Army Intelligence Corps (signals intelligence), 1940–45: Major. Married Joan Yorke in 1953; one daughter. Teacher of Classics, Curcher's College, Petersfield and Blackpool Grammar School, 1935–39; worked in the control commission for Germany, 1945–46; held a variety of jobs in the British Broadcasting Corporation external services, 1946–63, and head of French Language services, 1963–73. Agent: A.P. Watt and Company, 20 John Street, London WC1N 2DR. Address: North End Cottage, 36 High Street, Charing Ashford, Kent TN27 0HX, England.

CRIME PUBLICATIONS

Novels (Charles Blessington; Celia Grant)

The Disappearance of Dr. Bruderstein (Blessington). London, Hodder and Stoughton, 1949; as *Dr. Bruderstein Vanishes,* New York, Doubleday, 1949.
Mr. Blessington's Plot. London, Hodder and Stoughton, 1951; as *Mr. Blessington's Imperialist,* New York, Doubleday, 1951.
Ambush for Anatole (Blessington). London, Hodder and Stoughton, and New York, Doubleday, 1952.
Two Died in Singapore (Blessington). London, Hodder and Stoughton, 1954.
Vote Against Poison. (Blessington). London, Hodder and Stoughton, 1956.
Undiplomatic Exit. London, Hodder and Stoughton, and New York, Doubleday, 1958.
The Half Hunter. London, Hodder and Stoughton, 1961; as *The Sleuth and the Liar,* New York, Doubleday, 1961.
Honesty Will Get You Nowhere. London, Gollancz, 1977.
The Limericks of Lachasse. London, Macmillan, 1978.
The Hour of the Hyenas. London, Macmillan, 1979.
A Shot in the Arm. London, Gollancz, 1982; as *Death at the BBC,* New York, Scribner, 1983.
Green Trigger Fingers (Grant). London, Gollancz, and New York, Scribner, 1984.
A Botanist at Bay (Grant). London, Gollancz, and New York, Scribner, 1985.
The Mantrap Garden (Grant). London, Gollancz, and New York, Scribner, 1986.
Flowers of Evil (Grant). London, Gollancz, and New York, Scribner, 1987.
Menacing Groves (Grant). London, Gollancz, 1988; New York, Scribner, 1989.
A Bouquet of Thorns (Grant). London, Macmillan, and New York, Scribner, 1989.

OTHER PUBLICATIONS

Other

No Golden Journey: A Biography of James Elroy Flecker. London, Heinemann, 1973.

*

John Sherwood comments:
My first mystery *The Disappearance of Dr. Bruderstein* arose from my experiences in the Control Commission during 1945–6 in chaotic spooky Germany, still reeling in the aftermath of war. Finding that the genre suited me, I wrote four more books with the same detective, an elderly civil servant called Charles Blessington. I dropped him because he belonged to the climate

of post-war shortages and regulations, and eventually became outdated.

After a few books without a series detective I was ordered by Livia Gollancz to provide myself with one. Rather than a policeman or a private eye, I favoured an amateur with a specialisation in a non-crime field which would provide insights denied to others when crime reared its head. Professional gardeners are taught to observe, and I know a bit about horticulture. So, I fixed on Celia Grant, a widow who runs a small nursery garden in a Sussex village. She does landscape gardening and maintenance on the side, and is easy to introduce into a variety of criminal contexts, so I hope to get a lot more mileage out of her.

* * *

Between 1945 and 1961 John Sherwood published a clutch of crime novels: the five Mr. Blessington novels were followed by a further four clever and amusing detective thrillers, which at the time were well received and well reviewed but which now appear a little dated. After a gap of some 10 years or so Sherwood produced another small handful of non-series mysteries before introducing his series amateur detective Celia Grant, a widowed horticulturalist who is physically in the Miss Marple mould.

Sherwood cheerfully admits the theft of the title of his book *The Hour of the Hyenas* from Frederick Forsyth but there all similarity ends. Sherwood's book is an entertaining if unbelievable tale of a couple forced into tax exile by the vast amounts of money earned by the wife, as she writes to order (and at one stage practically at gun point) an incredibly bad novel. The main characters are intelligent and sympathetic but, perhaps, slightly idiotic to have got caught up in the whole silly mess in the first place.

Far more complex a novel is *A Shot in the Arm,* set at the BBC in the 1930's at the time of Lord Reith's dictatorship. Sherwood's own experiences in the BBC External Services provides the authenticity in this vivid portrayal both of the hidden and overt tensions of Reith's regime, and of the plentiful technical detail. Some wonderful name-dropping is just one of the lighter touches: "'Who is this Mr. Olivier who queried his fee?' . . . 'He's an actor . . .'" And others whose names are resoundingly dropped include Bertrand Russell, Nevill Coghill, and Stephen Spender. The structure of this novel is highly unusual; it opens with the Features Organiser, Tony Chatham, having to cope not only with an acrimonious divorce suit which will ruin his career but also with an apparent attempt on his life. After some washing of dirty linen and an actual murder, we discover in a complete *volte face* that the person who has so far engaged our sympathies is in fact a murdering conniving villain in cahoots with his supposedly estranged wife.

A contrast to this intriguing novel is the earlier *The Limericks of Lachasse* in which improbable characters (not least the hero Peter Wiltshire) fail to function at all realistically in a complex, overdramatic, and somewhat dated plot.

It is in the Celia Grant mysteries that Sherwood demonstrates how skilfully he can characterize and plot. Celia is "small and fragile looking, with a china-doll complexion and prematurely silver hair, . . . permanently at risk from men whose protective urges overcome them then." At risk, too, from the various criminal elements who seem to infest her world as readily and as thoroughly as greenfly.

In *Green Trigger Fingers* Celia, in the course of staving off the local brothel owner's unsuccessful plot to run her out of business (unusual, one feels, to find a brothel in a Home Counties village), solves the twin crimes of murder and the forgery of a flower painting, and thus establishes her reputation as a gardener and as a sleuth. It is as an expert in both capacities that, in *The Mantrap Garden,* she is needed at Monk's Mead, an historical garden created by Gertrude Jekyll. While she is engaged upon the seemingly innocent task of revamping the herbaceous borders, her investigative talents are required to unravel the complex web which connects the intelligence machine of World War II, Shakespearian sonnets, auctions, blackmail, kidnapping, and the inevitable murder. In choosing the relatively narrow setting of horticulture for this series, Sherwood in no way prohibits himself or his sleuth from participating in far wider spheres of activity.

This activity ranges not only countrywide but worldwide. In *A Botanist at Bay* Celia travels to New Zealand where she becomes involved with a kidnapping by left-wing terrorists; in *Menacing Groves* her holiday tour of Italian gardens is rendered far from restful by murder and, once again, kidnapping. Despite all this mayhem her one recurring nightmare is, endearingly, that she is "a saxifrage and potbound, with her roots squeezed painfully into a three-inch pot."

Grant is aided and abetted in many of her alarms and excursions by Bill, former male model, excellent gardener, and somewhat aggressive henchman. Opinion in the village is divided as to his and Celia's sexual proclivities: they are viewed repectively as gay, lesbian, and as having an affair together, The truth of the matter is that Celia wears her widowhood sedately and Bill, while heterosexual, is forced to beat off the attentions of various local females. This all adds humour both verbal and circumstantial to interesting and unusual plots and situations.

The threads linking all three categories of Sherwood's books are action, humour, and sheer improbability. It is only in the Celia Grant books that these combine in such a way that the reader can readily swallow the last of these elements in enjoyment of these witty and interesting novels.

—Judith Rhodes

———

SHIEL, M(atthew) P(hipps). Also wrote as Gordon Holmes. British. Born on Montserrat Island, West Indies, 21 July 1865. Educated at Harrison College, Barbados; King's College, London; St. Bartholomew's Hospital Medical School, London. Married 1) Carolina García Gomez in 1898 (died), two daughters; 2) Mrs. Gerald Jewson c. 1918. Taught mathematics at a school in Derbyshire, two years. Granted Civil List pension, 1938. *Died 14 February 1947.*

CRIME PUBLICATIONS

Novels

The Rajah's Sapphire. London, Ward Lock, 1896.
The Yellow Danger. London, Richards, 1898; New York, Fenno, 1899.
The Weird o' It. London, Richards, 1902.
Unto the Third Generation. London, Chatto and Windus, 1903.
The Evil That Men Do. London, Ward Lock, 1904.
The Lost Viol. New York, Clode, 1905; London, Ward Lock, 1908.
The Late Tenant (as Gordon Holmes, with Louis Tracy). New York, Clode, 1906; London, Cassell, 1907.

By Force of Circumstances (as Gordon Holmes, with Louis Tracy). New York, Clode, 1909; London, Mills and Boon, 1910.
Dr. Krasinski's Secret. New York, Vanguard Press, 1929; London, Jarrolds, 1930.
The Black Box. New York, Vanguard Press, 1930; London, Richards, 1931.
Say Au R'Voir but Not Goodbye. London, Benn, 1933.

Short Stories

Prince Zaleski. London, Lane, and Boston, Roberts, 1895.
The Pale Ape and Other Pulses. London, Laurie, 1911.
How the Old Woman Got Home. London, Richards, 1927; New York, Vanguard Press, 1928.
Here Comes the Lady. London, Richards, 1928.
The Best Short Stories of M.P. Shiel, edited by John Gawsworth. London, Gollancz, 1948.
Xélucha and Others. Sauk City, Wisconsin, Arkham House, 1975.
Prince Zaleski and Cummings King Monk. Sauk City, Wisconsin, Arkham House, 1977.

OTHER PUBLICATIONS

Novels

An American Emperor (as Gordon Holmes, with Louis Tracy). New York, Putnam, and London, Pearson, 1897.
Contraband of War. London, Richards, 1899; revised edition, London, Pearson, 1914; Ridgewood, New Jersey, Gregg Press, 1968.
Cold Steel. London, Richards, 1899; New York, Brentano's, 1900; revised edition, London, Gollancz, and New York, Vanguard Press, 1929.
The Man-Stealers. London, Hutchinson, and Philadelphia, Lippincott, 1900; revised edition, Hutchinson, 1927.
The Purple Cloud. London, Chatto and Windus, 1901; revised edition, London, Gollancz, 1929; New York, Vanguard Press, 1930.
The Lord of the Sea. London, Richards, and New York, Stokes, 1901; revised edition, New York, Knopf, 1924; London, Gollancz, 1929.
The Yellow Wave. London, Ward Lock, 1905.
The Last Miracle. London, Laurie, 1907; revised edition, London, Gollancz, 1929.
The White Wedding. London, Laurie, 1908.
Children of the Wind. London, Laurie, 1908.
The Isle of Lies. London, Laurie, 1909.
This Knot of Life. London, Everett, 1909.
The House of Silence (as Gordon Holmes, with Louis Tracy). New York, Clode, 1911; as *The Silent House,* London, Nash, 1911.
The Dragon. London, Richards, 1913; New York, Clode, 1914; as *The Yellow Peril,* London, Gollancz, 1929.
This above All. New York, Vanguard Press, 1933; as *Above All Else,* London, Cole, 1943.
The Young Men Are Coming! London, Allen and Unwin, and New York, Vanguard Press, 1937.

Short Stories

Shapes in the Fire. London, Lane, and Boston, Roberts, 1896.
The Invisible Voices, with John Gawsworth. London, Richards, 1935; New York, Vanguard Press, 1936.

Verse

(Poems), edited by John Gawsworth. London, Richards, 1936.

Other

Science, Life, and Literature. London, Williams and Norgate, 1950.
The New King. Cleveland, Ohio, Reynolds Morse Foundation, 1980.

Translator, *The Hungarian Revolution: An Eyewitness's Account,* by Charles Henry Schmitt. London, Worker's Socialist Federation, 1919.

*

Bibliography: *The Works of M.P. Shiel: A Study in Bibliography* by A. Reynolds Morse, Los Angeles, Fantasy, 1948.

* * *

Shiel was undoubtedly one of English literature's eccentrics. So widely extravagant was his usual style that it bordered on the lunatic. To a reviewer who complained of his involuted obscurities he retorted that his aim was "the attainment of an elaborate simplicity that can be called biblical" and objected to being compared to George Meredith because he, "like Shakespeare, who influenced him, wrote very badly." Yet Shiel could, when he chose, restrain his exuberance and hold in check his Homeric love of metaphor to produce books that won him praise from the literati. Many of his best works are prophetic fantasies, notable among them being *The Purple Cloud,* which E.F. Bleiler has called the best of the "last man" novels.

Shiel left his native West Indies for an education in England, where he studied languages and, according to his own account, was for a time a medical student. His philosophical knowledge is evident in all his writings, but his vaunted scientific aptitude was shaky at best. He believed, for example, that it was possible to produce "an almost tasteless preparation out of pure black nicotine," an alkaloid which in pure form is a colorless liquid with a nauseating taste.

Most deserving of the mystery reader's attention are Shiel's handful of offbeat detective stories, beginning with the author's slim first volume, *Prince Zaleski,* which contains only three stories. Zaleski is an omniscient recluse, to whose exotic Welsh hideaway an admirer brings word of the world's puzzles. The last of the tales, "The S.S.," is the longest and best. In it the Prince is driven by curiosity into the world of men to test at first hand the conclusions he has deduced from hieroglyphic messages left under the tongues of a multitude of murder victims in various parts of Britain and Europe. In this story and in the first of the three, "The Race of Orven," the plot springs from the author's eugenic beliefs, his dreams of Superman, and his lifelong xenophobia.

The Zaleski stories are narrated in a manner heavily influenced by Edgar Allan Poe, with touches of Holmesian deduction at their most outrageous, yet the overall effect on the reader is one of rapt fascination. The collection of Shiel stories issued as a posthumous tribute by his friend and heir John Gawsworth in 1948 includes the three original Zaleski tales as well as, among others, an excellent narrative—for once plainly told—of vigilante justice, "The Primate of the Rose."

Prince Zaleski and Cummings King Monk adds to the three 1895 stories a short, disappointing sequel, "The Return of

Prince Zaleski," written by Shiel late in life and lost in the mail on the way to *Ellery Queen's Mystery Magazine*. The three Monk pieces reprinted in the volume are from Shiel's miscellany *Pale Ape*. Only in one, "He Wakes an Echo," does Monk show his detective skills, when he sniffs out at a distance skullduggery in the Scottish Highlands and races north to squelch it.

How the Old Woman Got Home is an eccentric thriller about the kidnapping of the hero's mother and his subsequent misfortunes. Those readers resolute enough to fight their way through its avalanche of words and images will find it unforgettable. *The Black Box* is an offbeat detective novel that chronicles, in often impenetrable poetics, the attempts of three sleuths, including the heroine, to fathom the deaths of four adults and a baby in a gloomy Gloucestershire milieu. *Dr. Krasinski's Secret* is an extravagant crime novel, the story of a Polish fanatic who is determined to possess a family fortune by successive murders of the male heirs and marriage to, or domination of, the female ones.

Shiel collaborated with Louis Tracy (1863–1928) in some of the mystery novels published under the pseudonym "Gordon Holmes," but here the characteristic Shiel style is sadly lacking. It is a style found to be admirable by some, exasperating, even incomprehensible, by others, but always startlingly original.

—Norman Donaldson

SIMON, Roger L(ichtenberg). American. Born in 1943. Educated at Dartmouth College, Hanover, New Hampshire, B.A.; Yale University Drama School, New Haven, Connecticut, M.F.A. Married; two sons. Self-employed writer. Recipient: Crime Writers Association John Creasey Memorial award, 1974.

CRIME PUBLICATIONS

Novels (series: Moses Wine in all books)

The Big Fix. New York, Simon and Schuster, 1973; London, Deutsch, 1974.
Wild Turkey. New York, Simon and Schuster, 1975; London, Deutsch, 1976.
Peking Duck. New York, Simon and Schuster, and London, Deutsch, 1979.
California Roll. New York, Villard, 1985.
The Straight Man. New York, Villard, 1986.
Raising the Dead. New York, Villard, 1988.
Dead Meet. Berkeley, California, Black Lizard, 1988.

OTHER PUBLICATIONS

Novels

Heir. New York, Macmillan, 1968.
The Mama Tass Manifesto. New York, Holt Rinehart, 1970.

Play

Screenplay: *Bustin' Loose,* with Lonne Elder III and Richard Pryor, 1981.

* * *

In a series of seven books, Roger L. Simon has steadily developed a distinctive version of the hard-boiled detective hero. Introduced in *The Big Fix,* Moses Wine is a thirtyish, dope-smoking divorced father of two young sons, living hand to mouth as a private investigator on the margins of Southern California society and nursing memories of his days as a 1960's student radical. Extravagantly praised by Ross Macdonald, and inviting comparison with Raymond Chandler's first novel *The Big Sleep, The Big Fix* has Wine uncovering and thwarting a conspiracy to discredit a Presidential candidate and threaten the outcome of a primary election. On the way to unmasking the smoothly menacing corporate manipulator at the heart of the conspiracy, Wine must contend with a Satanist cult, an aging abortionist, and assorted policemen.

Wine uncovers another form of right-wing conspiracy in *Peking Duck,* which finds him accompanying his aunt Sonya Lieberman, an unreconstructed Depression-era socialist, on one of the first American tours of the People's Republic of China. When the theft of a priceless antiquity jeopardizes the tour, Wine reluctantly investigates and uncovers a Taiwanese plot to sabotage the thaw in Chinese-American relations. *California Roll* finds Wine turning forty, clinging to what remains of the liberalism of his student days, but willing nonetheless to become head of corporate security for Tulip Computers when asked by its president, a computer whiz kid who began the business in a garage several years earlier. Temporarily a Yuppie, complete with BMW (supercharged) and an ambitious corporate executive for a girlfriend, Wine discovers a complicated plot to use Tulip to channel computer chips to the Soviets, chips that are designed to wreak havoc whatever their application. Not surprisingly, Wine discovers a murderous renegade CIA agent and electronics genius as the point man for the shadowy group responsible for the conspiracy.

Never one to remain in California long, Wine spends most of *Raising the Dead* in Israel, where for the first time in the series he is obliged to come to terms with his Jewishness, the most fundamental aspect of his identity, as he investigates the murder of an Arab leader. In the end, however, he returns to California, to his aging BMW, and his residual radicalism, declining an invitation to work for Israeli Intelligence. With Moses Wine, Simon has simultaneously enriched the conventions of the hard-boiled detective novel and used those conventions to explore the compromises, small and large, imposed on those who came of age in the turbulent, heady student activism of the 1960's but who had to find work and meaning in the very different decades that followed.

—R. Gordon Kelly

SIMPSON, Dorothy (née Preece). British. Born in Blaenavon, Monmouthshire, Wales, 20 June 1933. Educated at Bridgend Grammar School for Girls, Glamorganshire, 1944–51; University of Bristol, 1951–55, B.A. (honours) 1954, teaching diploma 1955. Married Keith Taylor Simpson in 1961; two sons and one daughter. Teacher of English and French, Dartford Grammar School for Girls, 1955–59, and Erith Grammar School, 1959–61, both Kent; teacher of English, Senacre School, Maidstone, Kent, 1961–62; marriage guidance counsellor, 1969–82. Lives in Leeds, Kent. Recipient: Crime Writers Association Silver Dagger award, 1985. Agent: Anne McDermid, Curtis Brown, 162–168 Regent Street, London W1R 5TB, England.

CRIME PUBLICATIONS

Novels (series: Detective-Inspector Luke Thanet in all books
  except *Harbingers of Fear*)

Harbingers of Fear. London, Macdonald and Jane's, 1977.
The Night She Died. London, Joseph, and New York,
  Scribner, 1981.
Six Feet Under. London, Joseph, and New York, Scribner,
  1982.
Puppet for a Corpse. London, Joseph, and New York,
  Scribner, 1983.
Close Her Eyes. London, Joseph, and New York, Scribner,
  1984.
Last Seen Alive. London, Joseph, and New York, Scribner,
  1985.
Dead on Arrival. London, Joseph, 1986; New York, Scribner,
  1987.
Element of Doubt. London, Joseph, 1987; New York,
  Scribner, 1988.
Suspicious Death. London, Joseph, and New York, Scribner,
  1988.
Dead by Morning. London, Joseph, and New York, Scribner,
  1989.

Uncollected Short Stories

"The Wisp of Sound," in *Ellery Queen's Mystery Magazine*
  (New York), November 1977.
"The Sanctuary," in *Alfred Hitchcock's Mystery Magazine*
  (New York), April 1978.
"Boxes Within Boxes," in *Ellery Queen's Mystery Magazine*
  (New York), 10 March 1980.

*

Dorothy Simpson comments:
    I began to write after a long illness in 1975. The success of my
first book, a suspense novel, gave me sufficient impetus to carry
me through the three rejections which followed—very disheartening at the time, but valuable in retrospect. It was during this
period that I realised that the crime novel is of such diversity
that it offers enormous scope to the writer, and I decided to
attempt to lay the foundation for a series of detective novels in
my next book. This was *The Night She Died.*
    The setting for the series is Sturrenden, an imaginary town in
Kent, and the lives and characters of Detective-Inspector Luke
Thanet and his Sergeant, Mike Lineham, do not remain static
but develop from book to book. Their personal lives and those
of their families are important elements in the stories,
sometimes reflecting the overall theme of the book, as in *Six
Feet Under,* or helping in the solution of the crime.
    Inspector Thanet works by delving deeply into the life and
relationships of the murder victim, and solves the crime by
reconstructing that victim's emotional past, a method which
sometimes has a profound effect on Thanet's personal life.
    My chief interest is in character, and these books might
perhaps be called Whydunnits. rather than Whodunnits. I try
to play fair with the reader and the mystery is solvable with the
information he is given, and for me that solution must be
psychologically sound. The reader must be able to look back at
the end and see that the murderer's behaviour is entirely
consistent with his having committed the crime.

*   *   *

Because she keeps murder to a minimum, and mayhem
generally occurs offstage, the impact of Dorothy Simpson's
neatly crafted mysteries is more of an aftershock than an initial
jolt. Even the gentrified grittiness of most English procedurals
is softened, for the cerebral quality of the investigations, like
Detective Inspector Luke Thanet's conversational interrogations and intuitive leaps, remind one of amateur detectives'
methods. In a sense, these qualities are the most sophisticated
red herrings Simpson creates, for, framed by the calm tone, the
decency of her continuing characters, and the attractiveness of
the Kentish setting, these crimes send a fearful message. If
murder occurs among these circumspect folk, it can—and very
likely will—happen anywhere. No raucous street scenes, ribald
squadroom humor, or wild car chases distract from this central
fact, and in their single-mindedness, Simpson's stories make a
deep impression.
    Though very directly focused, Simpson's puzzles are satisfy-
ingly knotty because the motives of criminal, witnesses, victim,
and sleuth are grounded in sound psychology. Victims' and
suspects' deceits, terrors, and secrets contrast sharply with the
generally open, honest relationships Inspector Luke Thanet,
the protagonist, enjoys with his wife, children, and aide.
Indeed, the continuing sagas of Thanet family life and that of
Mike Lineham, his associate, provide background and, by
implication, commentary on the lives of other characters, the
very homeliness of these details accounting for much reader-
identification. Being careful never to preach, Simpson portrays
Thanet as a Christian who works as conscientiously at being a
decent human being as he does at his job; thus, Luke Thanet
inhabits a world too often disrupted by criminality, but one
which can be restored to order through the efforts of good-
hearted, determined men and women.
    All this is not to say that Thanet is perfection itself; rather,
he's satisfyingly and humanly flawed—fearful of the upheaval
caused when his wife goes back to school, a bit jealous,
occasionally too protective of his daughter, sometimes perplexed by his lively son, plagued by vicious backaches, and
capable of impatience with Lineham. What makes Thanet a
good role model are the same characteristics which make him a
good police officer; he's imaginative, introspective, and
analytical, qualities which deepen his empathy, curb his faults,
and sharpen his intuition.
    In *The Night She Died,* the Inspector sorts out his relationship
with Mike Lineham, urging the latter to disagree with his chief
if necessary. This case also reveals Thanet's distinctive foible:
despite years of professional experience, he cannot view a
victim's body without feeling pity and regret for a life
unnaturally cut off, though, to be sure, he goes to great lengths
to conceal these emotions from the murder-scene crew. These
complications carry forward throughout the series; Thanet
never grows a fully protective shell, and Lineham always needs
a little assertiveness training.
    Initially, most of the victims appear to be fairly ordinary
people. Carrie Birch, for example, is an almost prototypical
spinster, but in *Six Feet Under,* Thanet discovers her hidden
delights and cruelties and hence the secrets of several residents
of Nettleton, a picturesque village. The plot of *Puppet for a
Corpse,* which deals with the suspicious suicide of Dr. Arnold
Pettifer, is, perhaps, the least persuasive of the series, yet the
characterizations of Pettifer and of his widow, a popular
actress, are powerful. *Close Her Eyes,* Simpson's strongest novel
to date, examines the impact of murder on a rigorously devout
family whose repressive beliefs complicate the investigation.
Good intentions gone terribly wrong trigger the plot of *Last
Seen Alive,* a compelling story. For Thanet, Lineham's absence
in *Dead on Arrival* is a personal complication in the
investigation as is daughter Bridget's preparation for a major

cooking contest which she sees as a step toward her career. The death of beautiful, self-absorbed Nerine Tarrant, another supposed suicide, forces the extensive array of people who have suffered at her hands to come to terms with themselves—and the law—in *Element of Doubt.* The inability to consider the rights of others (of which murder is, of course, the most excessive example) is also central to *Dead by Morning,* in which bad penny Leo Martindale's return resurrects a number of old grievances. In all these works, the revelations of family secrets, no matter how grim or hurtful, are informed by Luke Thanet's compassionate understanding of others and by his deepening understanding of himself.

—Jane S. Bakerman

SIMS, George (Frederick Robert). British. Born in Hammersmith, London, 3 August 1923. Educated at the Lower School of John Lyon, Harrow, Middlesex, 1934–40. Served in the British Army, 1942–47. Married Beryl Simcock in 1943; one daughter and two sons. Junior reporter, Press Association, London, 1940–42; worked for an antiquarian bookseller, Harrow, 1947–48. Since 1948 owner G.F. Sims (Rare Books), first in Harrow, and since 1952 in Hurst, Berkshire. Agent: Anthony Sheil Associates, 43 Doughty Street, London WC1N 2LF. Address: Peacocks, Hurst, Berkshire RG10 0DR, England.

CRIME PUBLICATIONS

Novels

The Terrible Door. London, Bodley Head, and New York, Horizon Press, 1964.
Sleep No More. London, Gollancz, and New York, Harcourt Brace, 1966.
The Last Best Friend. London, Gollancz, 1967; New York, Stein and Day, 1968.
The Sand Dollar. London, Gollancz, 1969.
Deadhand. London, Gollancz, 1971.
Hunters Point. London, Gollancz, 1973; New York, Penguin, 1977.
The End of the Web. London, Gollancz, and New York, Walker, 1976.
Rex Mundi. London, Gollancz, 1978.
Who Is Cato? London, Macmillan, 1981.
The Keys of Death. London, Macmillan, 1982.
Coat of Arms. London, Macmillan, 1984.

Uncollected Short Stories

"Experimental One," in *Points* (Paris), n.d.
"The Charlie Adams Affair," in *Pick of Today's Short Stories 7,* edited by John Pudney. London, Putnam, 1956.
"Collector's Piece," in *The Saturday Book 16,* edited by John Hadfield. London, Hutchinson, 1956.
"Family Butcher," in *Winter's Crimes 12,* edited by Hilary Watson. London, Macmillan, and New York, St. Martin's Press, 1980.
"Mrs. Fitz," in *John Creasey's Crime Collection 1987,* edited by Herbert Harris. London, Gollancz, 1987; New York, St. Martin's Press, 1988.
"He Should Have a medal," in *John Creasey's Crime Collection 1989,* edited by Herbert Harris. London, Gollancz, 1989.

OTHER PUBLICATIONS

Verse

The Swallow Lovers. Privately printed, 1942.
Poems. London, Fortune Press, 1944.
The Immanent Goddess. London, Fortune Press, 1944.
Some Cadences: Poems Written in 1945. Privately printed, 1960.

Other

A Catalogue of Letters, Manuscript Papers and Books of Frederick Rolfe, Baron Corvo. Harrow, Middlesex, G.F. Sims, 1949.
A Catalogue of Llewelyn Powys Manuscripts. Hurst, Berkshire, G.F. Sims, n.d.
Detective Inspector Chance. London, Ferret Fantasy, 1974.
The Rare Books Game. Philadelphia, Homes, 1985.

*

George Sims comments:

I think of my books as being "novels of suspense"; I am incapable of writing a straightforward detective story because I am primarily interested in describing characters and conveying atmosphere. My books are usually a mixture of fact and fiction; fictional stuff builds up gradually in my mind about something I've seen or experienced. I have been an admirer of Scott Fitzgerald's books for some forty years and a quotation from him, "the terrible door into the past," gave me the title for my first book. Another quotation from his book *The Crack-Up* I take as my motto: " . . . necessary to marry the futility of the effort with the urge to strive. . . . " I strive to write a book a quarter as good as *The Great Gatsby.*

*   *   *

Publishers' blurbs are not renowned for the strict accuracy with which they weigh up and describe their books. But a blurb writer for George Sims's British publisher once said that he never wrote "predictably, and never less predictably than here" (the book in question was *The End of the Web*), and though I might challenge the last part of that statement I must concede that its first part sums up Sims exactly. He is unpredictable, wildly unpredictable.

He is in fact an amateur writer, and that is by no means intended as a jibe. Like a good many other writers of crime stories, Sims is a part-timer. But with most of the others the amateur status either does not particularly show up at all, their books being as expert as any full-time writer's, or the amateurishness manifests itself in books that are frankly not awfully good. But Sims's books are awfully good. Yet he breaks, time and again, the rules. Often there is no harm in that, and the greatest writers have achieved some of their greatest successes in flouting the canons. But Sims breaks the rules with such splendid disregard, so wholeheartedly, that his willfulness does, alas, often affect the quality of the whole.

Look at one example, that 1976 book to which his publisher affixed the label "unpredictable." It begins as the story, told with fine skill, of a fiftyish London antiques dealer caught up in some mysterious, half-dubious transaction while at the same time, so as to reassure himself, embarking half-willingly, half-unwillingly, on an affair with a young girl. It makes you really feel you are this man, and this man is a representative sort of human being. Until page 50 when our hero is brutally killed.

You can't do it. But an amateur does. There's something else he wants to write about (while still keeping some sort of a story going) and he damn well writes about it. And he writes damn well about it. Which is the reason that over and over again one forgives Sims.

He has all the skill of many of the considerable novelists in the mainstream. As we have seen, he depicts a character marvellously. The man in middle age is one of his specialities. There is an excellent study in *Deadhand* of a hero facing—Sims uses the expressive German word—Torschusspanik (panic that all doors seem to be shutting in your face). Love is another of his successes, often the love of an older man for a younger girl. He describes the way it envelopes a person despite his better judgement, and the simultaneous sadness and unholy joy of it. He can even do that difficult thing, almost impossible in the narrow confines of a standard crime novel, of showing us a person changing, as he does wonderfully in *The Last Best Friend*. And he can do another more minor but very tricky thing: he can describe a fight and make you know just what went on.

Yet for all his achievement he has his faults, the faults of the amateur. He loves facts, all sorts of odd, inconsequent facts (London and its curiosities is one of his great delights) and he often pleases himself entirely to get a fact or two in. So sometimes there is in the books an air of knowingness which can only put off a considerable proportion of readers. On the other hand, the facts are often nuttily interesting and the books are the more enjoyable for their being in them.

—H.R.F. Keating

SKINNER, Ainslie. *See* **GOSLING, Paula.**

SLESAR, Henry. Also writes as O.H. Leslie. American Born in Brooklyn, New York, 12 June 1927. Educated in public schools; School of Industrial Art, New York. Served in the United States Army, 1946–47. Married 1) Oenone Scott in 1953 (divorced 1969); 2) Jan Maakestad in 1970 (divorced 1974); 3) Manuela Jone in 1974; one daughter and one son. Copywriter, Young and Rubicom Inc., New York, 1945–49; vice-president and creative director, Robert W. Orr Inc., New York, 1949–57; Fuller and Smith and Ross, New York, 1957–60; West Wir and Bartel, New York, 1960–64. President and creative director, Slesar and Kanzer, New York, 1964–69, and since 1974 Slesar and Manuela. Recipient: Mystery Writers of America Edgar Allan Poe award, for novel, 1960, for television serial, 1977; Emmy award, 1974. Agent: Jerome S. Siegel Associates, 8733 Sunset Boulevard, Hollywood, California 90069. Address: 125 East 72nd Street, New York, New York 10021, U.S.A.

CRIME PUBLICATIONS

Novels

The Gray Flannel Shroud. New York, Random House, 1959; London, Deutsch, 1960.
Enter Murderers. New York, Random House, 1960; London, Gollancz, 1961.

The Bridge of Lions. New York, Macmillan, 1963; London, Gollancz, 1964.
The Seventh Mask (novelization of television play). New York, Ace, 1969.
The Thing at the Door. New York, Random House, 1974; London, Hamish Hamilton, 1975.

Short Stories

A Bouquet of Clean Crimes and Neat Murders. New York, Avon, 1960.
A Crime for Mothers and Others. New York, Avon, 1962.
Death on Television: The Best of Henry Slesar's Alfred Hitchcock Stories, edited by Francis Nevins and Martin Greenberg. Southern Illinois University Press, 1989.

Uncollected Short Stories

"A Victim Must Be Found," in *Ellery Queen's Mystery Magazine* (New York), June 1956.
"The Man with Two Faces," in *Manhunt* (New York), August 1956.
"A Trip to Florida," in *Ellery Queen's Mystery Magazine* (New York), October 1956.
"We'll Open Your Skull," in *Trapped* (New York), October 1956.
"Cop for a Day," in *Manhunt* (New York), January 1957.
"Instrument of Torture," in *Terror* (New York), January 1957.
"The Second Jury," in *Killers* (New York), January 1957.
"The Trouble with Ruth," in *Alfred Hitchcock's Mystery Magazine* (New York), January 1957.
"The Right Kind of House," in *Mike Shayne Mystery Magazine* (New York), February 1957.
"Handcuffed Slayer," in *Terror* (New York), February 1957.
"The Gentleman from Boston," in *Crime and Justice* (New York), March 1957.
"M Is for the Many," in *Ellery Queen's Mystery Magazine* (New York), March 1957.
"Proposal of Marriage," in *Alfred Hitchcock's Mystery Magazine* (New York), March 1957.
"40 Detectives Later," in *Manhunt* (New York), May 1957.
"Symbol of Authority," in *Ellery Queen's Mystery Magazine* (New York), May 1957.
"The Day of the Execution," in *Alfred Hitchcock's Mystery Magazine* (New York), June 1957.
"The Mad Killer," in *Ellery Queen's Mystery Magazine* (New York), June 1957.
"The Substitute," in *Manhunt* (New York), July 1957.
"The First Crime of Ruby Martinson," in *Alfred Hitchcock's Mystery Magazine* (New York), September 1957.
"A Timely Reward," in *Mystery Digest* (New York), November 1957.
"Death of a Mistress," in *Trapped* (New York), December 1957.
"Fly Home to Betsy," in *Mike Shayne Mystery Magazine* (New York), December 1957.
"Personal Interview," in *Ellery Queen's Mystery Magazine* (New York), December 1957.
"Ruby Martinson, Confidence Man," in *Alfred Hitchcock's Mystery Magazine* (New York), December 1957.
"Lost Dog," in *Mike Shayne Mystery Magazine* (New York), February 1958.
"Sam's Heart," in *Alfred Hitchcock's Mystery Magazine* (New York), March 1958.
"Ruby Martinson, Ex-con," in *Alfred Hitchcock's Mystery Magazine* (New York), April 1958.
"The Love Nest," in *Mystery Digest* (New York), May 1958.

"Job for an Amateur," in *Alfred Hitchcock's Mystery Magazine* (New York), June 1958.

"The Love Song of Ruby Martinson," in *Alfred Hitchcock's Mystery Magazine* (New York), July 1958.

"Compliments to the Chef," in *Alfred Hitchcock's Mystery Magazine* (New York), August 1958.

"The Life You Lose," in *Alfred Hitchcock's Mystery Magazine* (New York), September 1958.

"Ten Per Cent of Murder," in *Ellery Queen's Mystery Magazine* (New York), September 1958.

"Case of the Kind Waitress," in *Alfred Hitchcock's Mystery Magazine* (New York), October 1958.

"Deadly Honeymoon," in *Sleuth* (New York), October 1958.

"My Name is Terror," in *Off Beat Detective Stories* (New York), November 1958.

"One Grave Too Many," in *Alfred Hitchcock's Mystery Magazine* (New York), November 1958.

"The Ordeal of Ruby Martinson," in *Alfred Hitchcock's Mystery Magazine* (New York), December 1958.

"Dear Mrs. Fenwick," in *Alfred Hitchcock's Mystery Magazine* (New York), January 1959.

"Not the Running Type," in *Ellery Queen's Mystery Magazine* (New York), January 1959.

"Something Borrowed," in *Mike Shayne Mystery Magazine* (New York), February 1959.

"Peephole," in *Alfred Hitchcock's Mystery Magazine* (New York), February 1959.

"The Only Thing to Do," in *Mercury* (New York), February 1959.

"Not So Sudden Death," in *Alfred Hitchcock's Mystery Magazine* (New York), March 1959.

"Masquerade," in *Mystery Digest* (New York), April 1959.

"Ruby Martinson, Cat Burglar," in *Alfred Hitchcock's Mystery Magazine* (New York), April 1959.

"Run, Willie, Run," in *Mike Shayne Mystery Magazine* (New York), May 1959.

"Homicide Only Knocks Once," in *Alfred Hitchcock's Mystery Magazine* (New York), May 1959.

"Dig You Later," in *Mystery Tales* (New York), June 1959.

"Say It Ain't So, Ruby Martinson," in *Alfred Hitchcock's Mystery Magazine* (New York), July 1959.

"To Save a Body," in *Mike Shayne Mystery Magazine* (New York), August 1959.

"The Case of M.J.H.," in *Alfred Hitchcock's Mystery Magazine* (New York), August 1959.

"A Blonde for Budo," in *Mystery Tales* (New York), October 1959.

"Ruby Martinson's Bank Job," in *Alfred Hitchcock's Mystery Magazine* (New York), October 1959.

"Hunt the Tiger," in *Alfred Hitchcock's Mystery Magazine* (New York), November 1959.

"Cop Without Medals," in *The Saint* (New York), January 1960.

"The Deadly Telephone," in *Alfred Hitchcock's Mystery Magazine* (New York), January 1960.

"Sleep Is for the Innocent," in *Alfred Hitchcock's Mystery Magazine* (New York), February 1960.

"Voodoo Doll—$1.98," in *Alfred Hitchcock's Mystery Magazine* (New York), April 1960.

"Ruby Martinson's Big Dentist Caper," in *Alfred Hitchcock's Mystery Magazine* (New York), May 1960.

"Joke on a Nice Old Lady," in *Alfred Hitchcock's Mystery Magazine* (New York), June 1960.

"More Than a Nightmare," in *Alfred Hitchcock's Mystery Magazine* (New York), July 1960.

"The Absent-Minded Professor," in *The Saint* (New York), August 1960.

"My Baby, The Embezzler," in *Alfred Hitchcock's Mystery Magazine* (New York), September 1960.

"The Crooked Road," in *Ellery Queen's Mystery Magazine* (New York), September 1960.

"With the Chef's Compliments," in *Suspense* (London), September 1960.

"Ruby Martinson's Poisoned Pen," in *Alfred Hitchcock's Mystery Magazine* (New York), November 1960.

"The Case of the Secret Sorrow," in *Alfred Hitchcock's Mystery Magazine* (New York), January 1961.

"The Man in the Next Cell," in *Ellery Queen's Mystery Magazine* (New York), February 1961.

"Mr. D. and Death," in *Alfred Hitchcock's Mystery Magazine* (New York), February 1961.

"Ruby Martinson and the Great Coffin Caper," in *Alfred Hitchcock's Mystery Magazine* (New York), March 1961.

"The Accomplice," in *Ellery Queen's Mystery Magazine* (New York), April 1961.

"You Can't Blame Me," in *Alfred Hitchcock's Mystery Magazine* (New York), May 1961.

"First Class Honeymoon," in *Mike Shayne Mystery Magazine* (New York), June 1961.

"I'm Better Than You!," in *Alfred Hitchcock's Mystery Magazine* (New York), June 1961.

"Murder Out of a Hat," in *Alfred Hitchcock's Mystery Magazine* (New York), July 1961.

"The Dirty Detail," in *Ellery Queen's Mystery Magazine* (New York), July 1961.

"The Mask of Ruby Martinson," in *Alfred Hitchcock's Mystery Magazine* (New York), September 1961.

"Beggars Can Be Choosers," in *Alfred Hitchcock's Mystery Magazine* (New York), October 1961.

"Thicker Than Water," in *Alfred Hitchcock's Mystery Magazine* (New York), November 1961.

"One Step to Hell," in *Keyhole* (New York), January 1962.

"Be My Valentine," in *Alfred Hitchcock's Mystery Magazine* (New York), January 1962.

"Museum Piece," in *Ellery Queen's Mystery Magazine* (New York), February 1962.

"Suicide Marathon," in *Trapped* (New York), February 1962.

"Item," in *Alfred Hitchcock's Mystery Magazine* (New York), July 1962.

"The Blackmailer," in *The Saint* (London), July 1962.

"Murder Delayed," in *Alfred Hitchcock's Mystery Magazine* (New York), August 1962.

"Blackmail," in *The Saint* (New York), August 1962.

"Mr. Justice," in *Ellery Queen's Mystery Magazine* (New York), September 1962.

"Whosits Disease," in *Alfred Hitchcock's Mystery Magazine* (New York), October 1962.

"Weep for the Guilty," in *Alfred Hitchcock's Mystery Magazine* (New York), November 1962.

"How to Stop Smoking," in *Alfred Hitchcock's Mystery Magazine* (New York), December 1962.

"Goodbye Charlie," in *Alfred Hitchcock's Mystery Magazine* (New York), January 1963.

"The Second Verdict," in *Alfred Hitchcock's Mystery Magazine* (New York), February 1963.

"Starring the Defense," in *Alfred Hitchcock's Mystery Magazine* (New York), April 1963.

"Sea of Troubles," in *Alfred Hitchcock's Mystery Magazine* (New York), May 1963.

"The Return of the Moresbys," in *Ellery Queen's Mystery Magazine* (New York), January 1964.

"Federal Offense," in *Ellery Queen's Mystery Magazine* (New York), April 1964.

"The Horse That Wasn't for Sale," in *Ellery Queen's Mystery Magazine* (New York), May 1964.

"Three Miles to Marylebone," in *Alfred Hitchcock's Mystery Magazine* (New York), September 1964.

"The Old Ones Are Hard to Kill," in *Mike Shayne Mystery Magazine* (New York), January 1965.

"The Ring of Truth," in *Mike Shayne Mystery Magazine* (New York), February 1965.

"Gomber's Army," in *Alfred Hitchcock's Mystery Magazine* (New York), April 1965.

"Cop in a Rocker," in *Alfred Hitchcock's Mystery Magazine* (New York), August 1965.

"The Rats of Dr. Picard," in *Bizarre* (Concord, New Hampshire), October 1965.

"One of Those Days," in *The Saint* (New York), October 1965.

"A Choice of Witnesses," in *Alfred Hitchcock's Mystery Magazine* (New York), March 1966.

"The Cop Who Loved Flowers," in *Ellery Queen's Mystery Magazine* (New York), November 1966.

"The Diagnosis," in *Alfred Hitchcock's Mystery Magazine* (New York), February 1967.

"The Bluff," in *Alfred Hitchcock's Mystery Magazine* (New York), April 1967.

"The House on Damn Street," in *Alfred Hitchcock's Mystery Magazine* (New York), June 1967.

"You Can Bet on Ruby Martinson," in *Alfred Hitchcock's Mystery Magazine* (New York), July 1967.

"Don't I Know You?," in *Ellery Queen's Mystery Magazine* (New York), September 1968.

"The Job," in *Alfred Hitchcock's Mystery Magazine* (New York), October 1968.

"An Affair of the Heart," in *Mike Shayne Mystery Magazine* (New York), November 1968.

"Death of the Kerry Blue," in *Alfred Hitchcock's Mystery Magazine* (New York), November 1968.

"Death of a General," in *Mike Shayne Mystery Magazine* (New York), February 1969.

"Bones," in *Mike Shayne Mystery Magazine* (New York), July 1969.

"Eulogy in a Phone Booth," in *Mike Shayne Mystery Magazine* (New York), September 1969.

"Cry, Baby, Cry," in *Startling Mystery Stories* (New York), Spring 1970.

"The Loan," in *Alfred Hitchcock's Mystery Magazine* (New York), December 1972.

"The Intruder," in *Alfred Hitchcock's Mystery Magazine* (New York), March 1973.

"Happiness Before Death," in *Alfred Hitchcock's Mystery Magazine* (New York), April 1973.

'The Girl Who Found Things," in *Alfred Hitchcock's Mystery Magazine* (New York), July 1973.

"The Memory Expert," in *Alfred Hitchcock's Mystery Magazine* (New York), August 1973.

"Thou Shalt Not," in *Charlie Chan Mystery Magazine* (Los Angeles), February 1974.

"The Seersucker Heart," in *Alfred Hitchcock's Mystery Magazine* (New York), February 1974.

"The Haunted Man," in *Ellery Queen's Mystery Magazine* (New York), April 1974.

"The Poisoned Pawn," in *Alfred Hitchcock's Mystery Magazine* (North Palm Beach, Florida), June 1974.

"The Kidnapping," in *Ellery Queen's Mystery Magazine* (New York), January 1975.

"The Bottom Dollar," in *Mike Shayne Mystery Magazine* (Los Angeles), April 1975.

"Hiding Out," in *Alfred Hitchcock's Mystery Magazine* (New York), March 1976.

"Sea Change," in *Alfred Hitchcock's Tales to Scare You Stiff,* edited by Eleanor Sullivan. New York, Davis, 1978.

"The Kindest Man in the World," in *Ellery Queen's Mystery Magazine* (New York), July 1979.

"The Candidate," in *Voodoo!,* edited by Bill Pronzini. New York, Arbor House, 1980.

"Light Fingers," in *Alfred Hitchcock's Tales to Fill You with Fear and Trembling,* edited by Eleanor Sullivan. New York, Dial Press, 1980.

"The Slave," in *Alfred Hitchcock's Tales to Make Your Teeth Chatter,* edited by Eleanor Sullivan. New York, Dial Press, 1980.

"The Game As It Is Played," in *Alfred Hitchcock's Mystery Magazine* (New York), 23 April 1980.

"The Witness," in *Alfred Hitchcock's Mystery Magazine* (New York), 13 August 1980.

"The Faded Photograph," in *Woman's World,* 5 January 1982.

"The Contessa Collection," in *Ellery Queen's Mystery Magazine* (New York), 24 March 1982.

"The Bracelet," in *Mike Shayne Mystery Magazine* (Los Angeles), September 1983.

"The Tin Man," in *Ellery Queen's Mystery Magazine* (New York), June 1984.

Uncollected Short Stories as O.H. Leslie

"Alibi on the Steve Allen Show," May 1956, "The Morning After," February 1957, "Kill the Umpire," May 1957, "A Foot in the Door," June 1957, "I'm Dead, Honey," September 1957, "Something Short of Murder," November 1957, "I Promise to Kill," April 1958, "Whodunit?," July 1958, "Ignore All Requests," September 1958, "Better Than Murder," December 1958, "Personal Challenge," January 1959, "You'll Be Sorry When I'm Dead," February 1959, "It Started Most Innocently," March 1959, "Coroner's Jury," May 1959, "Curiosity Killed a . . . ," June 1959, "Last Drink," July 1959, "Beware the Unloaded Weapon," August 1959, "Terror Requires Preparation," January 1960, "Key to a Skeleton Closet," May 1960, "Welcome to Our Bank," July 1960, "Faster Than an Honest Man," November 1960, "A Child Was Lost," December 1960, "Behind the Locked Door," January 1961, "Thoughts Before Murder," March 1961, "Dead Give-Away," November 1961, "Tony's Death," September 1963, all in *Alfred Hitchcock's Mystery Magazine* (New York).

OTHER PUBLICATIONS

Plays

Screenplays: *The Eyes of Annie Jones,* with Louis Vittes, 1963; *Two on a Guillotine,* with John Kneubuhl, 1965; *Murders in Rue Morgue,* with Christopher Wicking, 1970.

Radio Plays: *CBS Radio Mystery Theatre* (39 plays).

Television Plays: *Forty Detectives Later, Insomnia, Coming Home, The Hat Box, Keep Me Company, The Honey, The Man with Two Faces, The Last Escape, The Horseplayer, A Crime for Mothers, Incident in a Small Jail, A Woman's Help, The Throwback, Servant Problem, The Matched Pearl, First Class Honeymoon, The Right Kind of Medicine, Most Likely to Succeed, The Test, Burglar Proof, The Case of M.J.H.,* and *The Kerry Blue* (in *Alfred Hitchcock Presents* series), 1955–61; *The Self-Improvement of Salvatore Ross,* with Jerry McNeeley (in

Twilight Zone series), 1963; *The Edge of Night* series, 1968–79; *Honeymoon with a Stranger,* with David Harmon, from a novel by Robert Thomas, 1969; 100 scripts for other series.

*   *   *

Henry Slesar, when not creating ads at Slesar and Manuela Inc., writes fiction. Slesar's ability to delight his readers is exemplified throughout his work; in *Enter Murderers,* in which he concludes his story by littering the stage with corpses; in *The Bridge of Lions,* in which he cleverly combines foreign travel, espionage, chemical secrets, and beautiful women; and in his ingenious Janus Mystery Jigsaw Puzzle No. 1, *The Case of the Snoring Skinflint,* and No. 2, *The Case of the Shaky Showman,* a perplexing locked-room problem and a hilarious whodunit respectively, in which Slesar cunningly makes the puzzle-makers fit the pieces of the mysteries together. Moreover, Slesar has written at least 500 short stories, novelettes, and novels in magazines; several motion pictures; and many plays for radio and television.

Although it is his first novel, *The Gray Flannel Shroud* shows how Slesar typically entertains his readers: in this book Slesar combines the detective and the crime story with romance. The novel presents legitimate clues, colorless yet sympathetic suspects, and a puzzle—who killed Bob Bernstein, the friendly photographer, Anne Gander, the "voluptuous" model and Willie Shenk, the "pretty boy" thug. However, Dave Robbins, an adman turned amateur sleuth, is hardly detective fiction's stock brilliant bloodhound: sidetracked from the clues by his personal involvement in the Burke Baby Foods Account, Dave ponders what would make a silver-haired, paunchy business-man commit murder, but with the help of Max Theringer, a journalistic crime reporter, Dave stumbles into the real culprit. Even though the criminal's motive becomes an executive's moral (Dave says the real crime is loving money and never earning a cent of it), and the mystery is interspersed with somewhat irrelevant scenes of seduction, *The Gray Flannel Shroud* ends satisfactorily: Dave gets the murderer, and the girl.

Similarly, *The Thing at the Door,* Slesar's last and perhaps most popular mystery, is not without the typical trappings of crime fiction: a clue, a sinister murderer, a motive, and an investigator. Slesar quickly reveals the clue to "the thing," the murderer, and the motive. Slesar's self-employed private eye, Steve Tyner, works hard to solve the conspiracy, but in Slesar's fictional method the reader is usually one step ahead of the hero. The reader thus plays an active role in the book, beginning in the opening pages when Cousin Piers compels the horror-stricken child, Gail Gunnerson, to look upon the ugly man in black, the "thing." Slesar builds his story around Piers's terrorizing Gail with two staged suicides, one bloody murder, many cruel innuendos, and too many hallucinative drugs. And he concludes his mystery with Piers forcing his 24-year-old cousin into her bedroom for her to see "the thing at her door," in effect pushing her back into a mental institution. In *The Thing at the Door* Slesar skillfully unravels a psychological drama of suspense—will Gail, the pretty heiress, remain sane? Or will the villain drive her insane?

Slesar's mystery fiction may fail to appeal to readers looking for an intellectual solution to a complex puzzle; his is not the classical formula. But his works will please those who enjoy a mixture of detection, popular psychology, gothic horror, and romance.

—Frances McConachie

———

SLOVO, Gillian. South African. Born in Johannesburg, 15 March 1952. Daughter of the political activists Joe Slovo and Ruth First. Educated at Manchester University, B.A. in history and philosophy of science, 1974. Has one daughter. Has had a variety of research jobs and has worked as a producer of television documentaries. Lives in London. Agent: A.P. Watt Ltd., 20 John Street, London WC1N 2DL. Address: c/o Michael Joseph Ltd., 27 Wrights Lane, London W8 5TZ, England.

CRIME PUBLICATIONS

Novels (series: Kate Baeier in all books)

Morbid Symptoms. London, Pluto Press, 1984; New York, Dember, 1985.
Death by Analysis. London, Women's Press, 1986; New York, Doubleday, 1988.
Death Comes Staccato. London, Women's Press, 1987; New York, Doubleday, 1989.

OTHER PUBLICATIONS

Novel

Ties of Blood. London, Joseph, 1989; New York, Morrow, 1990.

*   *   *

"'What am I supposed to be—a detective?'" Ask a silly question ... Gillian Slovo has endowed her detective, Kate Baeier, with a healthy sense of curiosity, thus making the step from freelance journalist to private detective a relatively easy one. Baeier is very much a creation for the 1980's and 1990's, a socialist, feminist aged thirty-something who makes her debut in *Morbid Symptoms* when a researcher into African economics meets his death at the bottom of a conveniently empty lift shaft. The central question is the tried and tested one—did he jump or was he pushed? But that's where tradition ends. The real issue here is murder on a wider scale: the murky politics of apartheid and its supporters in London. This is a world in which a South African agent who steps out of line gets himself pushed under a passing train and Kate soon finds her own life in danger. Slovo uses her intimate knowledge of South African politics to deal out propaganda on a grand scale, and so deft is her touch she has you begging for more.

Slovo is one of the most exciting of the new breed of feminist crime writers, and although her work is set in Britain and catches its mood, she is closest in intention, and content, to writers like Mary Wings and Barbara Wilson from the United States.

Death by Analysis, the second of the Kate Baeier books, is also the slickest. It's 1981 in London and while there are fireworks on the streets to celebrate the wedding of Prince Charles to Lady Diana Spencer, the United Kingdom is actually disintegrating: IRA hunger strikers die in gaol, unemployment rockets. As an outsider Kate is in a particularly good position to appreciate this fact. Once again she becomes politically involved, although politics don't at first seem to have anything to do with the death of Paul Holland, a flamboyant psychoanalyst. The message here, however, is that politics are personal, and someone has taken Holland's probing into their political past very personally indeed: those with safe and successful careers in the 1980's can find themselves threatened by their radical personal histories. Kate, on the other hand, finds her recent past more disturbing—it is her ex-analyst who asks her to investigate this case, and the investigation becomes the last stage in therapy, she has to face up to the fact that her analyst doesn't have all the answers, that she too is human, fallible and flawed. *Death by Analysis* is about personal relationships, and Kate's own relationship with the man in her life, Sam, appears to be under threat in *Death Comes Staccato*. Here Kate discovers dangerous family secrets hidden in the cupboards of the famous and wealthy. She is employed to protect the 17-year-old Alicia, a musical prodigy, from a stranger who has been following her but Kate eventually realizes that the greatest threat to Alicia comes from within the family circle. Incest and child abuse have been hidden both from victim and public and when Kate comes too close to uncovering all this she finds herself at risk.

Played out against the background of a corrupt police force, high society drug dealing, industrial skulduggery and exploitation, *Death Comes Staccato* is racy and hard-hitting. Staccato is a word to apply to Slovo's own style—the pace is fast, the dialogue Chandleresque. Crime, however, is given a wide and challenging definition; if the political is to be found on a personal level, so too is crime—sexism, racism—these too constitute acts of violence. Class, race, and gender are the real issues for Slovo and in her hands the crime novel becomes a powerful political tool.

—Penny Smith

SMITH, Caesar. *See* **HALL, Adam.**

SMITH, Julie. American. Born in Annapolis, Maryland, 25 November 1944. Educated at the University of Mississippi, Lafayette County, B.A. in journalism 1965. Reporter, New Orleans *Times-Picayune*, 1965–66; copy editor, 1966–67, and reporter, 1968–79, San Francisco *Chronicle*; partner, Invisible Ink, California, 1979–83. Agent: Vicky Bijur, 333 West End Avenue, New York, New York 10023, or, Charlotte Sheedy, 41 King Street, New York, New York 10014, U.S.A.

CRIME PUBLICATIONS

Novels (series: Paul McDonald; Rebecca Schwartz)

Death Turns a Trick (Schwartz). New York, Walker, 1982.
The Sourdough Wars (Schwartz). New York, Walker, 1984.
True-Life Adventure (McDonald). New York, Mysterious Press, 1985.
Tourist Trap (Schwartz). New York, Mysterious Press, 1986.
Huckleberry Fiend (McDonald). New York, Mysterious Press, 1987.
New Orleans Mourning. New York, St. Martin's Press, 1990.

Uncollected Short Stories

"Grief Counselor," in *Mike Shayne Mystery Magazine* (California), September 1978.
"The Wrong Number," in *Mike Shayne Mystery Magazine* (California), September 1979.

"Crime Wave in Pinhole," in *Alfred Hitchcock's Mystery Magazine* (New York), May 1980.
"Project Mushroom," in *Ellery Queen's Mystery Magazine* (New York), 1983.
"Red Rock," in *Raymond Chandler's Philip Marlowe*, edited by Byron Priess; New York, Knopf, 1988.
"Blood Types," in *Sisters in Crime*, edited by Marilyn Wallace. New York Berkley, 1989; London, W.H. Allen, 1990.
"Cul-de-Sac," in *Sisters in Crime*, edited by Marilyn Wallace. New York, Berkley, 1990.
"Montezuma's Other Revenge," in *Justice for Hire*, edited by Robert Randisi, New York, Mysterious Press, 1990.

*

Julie Smith comments:
Rebecca Schwartz, Paul McDonald, and Skip Langdon—these are my heroes. (At any rate, my protagonists.) For a good time, call Rebecca or Paul. Rebecca's a San Francisco lawyer whose job gives her cases to investigate and whose calm, methodical (if slightly bemused) personality is sufficiently different from mine that she can do it without tripping over both feet. Paul is an ex-journalist trying to scratch out a living free-lancing to support his mystery-writing habit. He's a little more like me and I modestly admit that I'm crazy about him.

These two (Rebecca in *Death Turns a Trick, The Sourdough Wars,* and *Tourist Trap* and Paul in *True-Life Adventure* and *Huckleberry Fiend*) are meant to be fun for the reader. They're urban sleuths well tuned in to the absurdity of urban life, each full of sardonic opinions on the passing panorama.

But not everyone understands the deep seriousness of comedy—and besides Southerners at some time write about the South. So I also invented Officer Skip Langdon of the New Orleans Police Department.

Skip's a young woman from a social-climbing family who becomes a cop partly in the hopes of finally understanding the city where she's always felt like an outsider. She quickly learns that she understood all the time and just didn't want to look at it—her murderous townspeople (and perhaps Southerners in general and maybe most people) always hurt the one they love. It's her fate to encounter not mere mean streets but also mean rooms, which are meaner by far. Families live in them, tearing at each other with sharpened teeth, sharper tongues, and sometimes sharp instruments that end up in tagged in court.

That's the South for you—Faulkner and Tennessee Williams and Flannery O'Connor weren't kidding about that one. Skip's book, *New Orleans Mourning,* is dark and brooding, and so will any future ones be. Not pretty stories, but very real ones, molded from the miasma of peeling plaster and soggy "tradition."

* * *

In six novels, Julie Smith has proven her versatility as a crime writer. Her lighter mysteries are entertaining and fast-paced, enlivened by loveable characters who exhibit an engaging mix of flaws and strengths. Her latest book effectively builds suspense at the same time it offers a dark and provocative exploration of the lengths to which people will go to protect their secrets.

All her work demonstrates a keen eye for the special qualities that set one city apart from another—the landmarks, the language, the hopes and dreams of the inhabitants, and the unspoken rules, values, and customs that shape a place.

Rebecca Schwartz, an outspoken feminist lawyer who lives and works in San Francisco, is featured in three books. Especially cinematic, the Rebecca books offer vivid action scenes with such devices as careening car chases and diabolical dough machines serving as counterpoint to the clever dialogue and character interaction. The opening scene of *Death Turns a Trick* sets the tone of the book and, in fact, of the series. Rebecca, as a favor to a client, is playing the piano at a bordello when a police raid interrupts the activities. The ensuing hijinks are lively and unpredictable, and introduce a cast of characters including reporter/boyfriend Rob Burns, wisecracking secretary Alan Kruzick, sister Mickey, Rebecca's prominent Marin County attorney father, and her mother, the quintessential Jewish mama.

In *The Sourdough Wars,* the proprietary nature of sourdough recipes and the self-absorption of restaurant owners serve as the focus for a case that requires Rebecca's sleuthing. The entanglements give Smith opportunities to comment on San Francisco's preoccupation with things culinary, including the feuds of Italian food-families.

Tourist Trap finds Rebecca discovering that the biggest industry in San Francisco can be dangerous. A crucified corpse discovered at an Easter Sunday service is the first of a series of murders that tarnish the appeal of some of the city's tourist attractions. Shellfish poisoning at a Fisherman's Wharf restaurant and mortal injuries sustained on a cable car provide additional glimpses of the city, its attractions, and a host of typical denizens before Rebecca helps bring the perpetrator to justice.

The second series features the aptly-named San Francisco mystery writer/sleuth Paul McDonald. In *True-Life Adventure,* Paul turns to part-time detecting when his boss Jack Birnbaum, PI, is murdered in the middle of an investigation. Paul earns his stripes as he uses skills picked up as an investigative reporter to solve the crime—and to save his own life.

In *Huckleberry Fiend,* a bibliomystery concerning a newly-discovered Mark Twain manuscript, Paul gets help from Booker, a sometimes-burglar now in therapy. As Paul's relationship with advertising executive Sardis Kincannon, begun in *True-Life Adventure,* deepens, Paul also confronts his feelings when he realizes he's the victim of sexual harrassment. Plays on literary names help keep the reader amused while Paul hunts for the manuscript.

In *New Orleans Mourning,* Smith returns to her roots and offers a rich, textured examination of the contemporary South and its ongoing struggle to emerge from antebellum practices into the waning years of the 20th century. This novel moves in a new direction, offering a darker, more layered look at the inner lives of her characters. Through multiple viewpoints, Smith builds suspense at the same time she conveys the peculiarly Southern sense of collective guilt.

With the introduction in *New Orleans Mourning* of Skip Langdon, New Orleans Police Department rookie, Smith goes deep into the heart of a complex character. Skip's self-awareness, often unsettling and sometimes even painful, reflects her outsider status. This adds dimension to her observations, yet even at their darkest, Skip's comments are leavened by her endearing generosity of spirit.

Born into a socially prominent family, Skip is too tall, too big, and too straightforward to fit the Southern belle image. She harbors a distaste for many of the conventions of New Orleans society but that doesn't stop her from using her intimate knowledge of the city and its high society in her work.

New Orleans Mourning opens with a fascinating account of Mardi Gras and goes on to reveal the underside of a city that thrives, in part, because of the complicity of individuals trying to maintain a crumbling social structure. Danger crackles through the novel as Skip peels back layer after layer of lies in her search for truth.

In her earlier work, Smith applies her keen observation and wit to mystery fiction that is wickedly inventive and high-spirited. Her most recent work probes the dark heart of Southern families, and captures an atmosphere of decadence and danger in which secrets thrive. Whichever qualities she chooses to emphasize, Smith's mysteries reflect the fine talents of this versatile writer.

—Marilyn Wallace

———

SMITH, Kay Nolte.   American.   Born in Eveleth, Minnesota, 4 July 1932. Educated at the University of Minnesota, Minneapolis, B.A. (summa cum laude) 1952 (Phi Beta Kappa); University of Utah, Salt Lake City, M.A. 1955. Married Phillip J. Smith in 1958. Advertising copywriter, Stern Brothers, 1957–59, and Fletcher Richards Calkins and Holden, 1959–62, both New York; professional actress, under name Kay Gillian, New York and elsewhere, 1962–75. Adjunct Instructor, Brookdale College, Lincroft, New Jersey, 1975–82, and Instructor, Trenton State College, New Jersey. Since 1975 consultant, Bell Laboratories, New Jersey. Theatre and film reviewer, *The Objectivist,* New York, 1969–71. Recipient: Mystery Writers of America Edgar Allan Poe award, 1981. Agent: Meredith Bernstein, 2112 Broadway, New York, New York 10023. Address: 73 Hope Road, Tinton Falls, New Jersey 07724, U.S.A.

CRIME PUBLICATIONS

Novels

The Watcher.   New York, Coward McCann, 1980; London, Gollancz, 1981.
Catching Fire.   New York, Coward McCann, 1982.
Mindspell.   New York, Morrow, 1983; London, Hodder and Stoughton, 1984.
Elegy for a Soprano.   New York, Villard, 1985; London, Severn House, 1986.

Uncollected Short Stories

"Reflected Glory," in *Best Detective Stories of the Year 1975,* edited by Allen J. Hubin.   New York, Dutton, 1975.
"Theory of the Crime," in *Every Crime in the Book,* edited by Robert L. Fish.   New York, Putnam, 1975; London, Macmillan, 1976.
"The Secret Weapon," in *Ellery Queen's Mystery Magazine* (New York), April 1976.
"Caveat Emptor," in *Miniature Mysteries,* edited by Isaac Asimov, Martin H. Greenberg, and Joseph D. Olander. New York, Taplinger, 1981.

OTHER PUBLICATIONS

Novel

Country of the Heart.   New York, Villard, and London, Bodley Head, 1988.

Other

Translator, *Chanteder* by Edmond Rostand. Maryland, University Press of America, and London, Eurospan, 1988.

*

Kay Nolte Smith comments:

Several things characterize my work and are its goals: a strong plot, for I like suspense not only for its own sake but because it reflects the fact that human beings can be purposeful; the revelation and/or exploration of some aspect of psychology; and a style that is more stylized than journalistic—my books are not filled with naturalistic detail, though they are, I hope, grounded in reality. For me the challenge, and pleasure, is to devise something complex, involving unusual situations and motivations, and then present it as vividly but economically as possible. "Understated drama" is what I aim for.

My plots carry several levels of meaning; my books will always have a psychological theme and often will explore some sociological or political idea as well. In *The Watcher* I used the events of a police investigation and murder trial to dramatize the psychological phenomenon of repression and raise questions about the theory of egalitarianism. In *Catching Fire* I used a union-underworld attempt to destroy a man resisting union organization, to explore the psychologies of those who believe, and don't believe, in "earning one's way." In *Mindspell* I used the conventions of the occult story to challenge strongly belief in the occult and to show the psychological roots of accepting or rejecting the supernatural.

I wouldn't at all mind if a book of mine made the reader think, although if I had to choose between doing that and entertaining him, I would opt for the latter. I write my novels to be experienced first and foremost as suspenseful stories with intriguing characters. The detective in *The Watcher* who gave up the work and the woman he loved, only to find that she is the subject of his murder investigation. The actor-producer of *Catching Fire* who grew up with human and literal vermin but climbed out of his background to become a great classical-lyric actor. The woman president of the genetic-engineering firm in *Mindspell* who fought many private demons to become the advocate of reason and science. I dislike the heavy dose of cynicism in modern fiction, detective and otherwise, and enjoy inventing protagonists one can admire: people who have strong values, passions, and opinions and who can achieve something in the world. Such people are, to me, just as "realistic" as the helpless, the depraved, and the failures.

* * *

Kay Nolte Smith won a well-deserved Edgar for first mystery with her book, *The Watcher*. This novel and a story, "Reflected Glory," are her best work, with inventive plots, stimulating characters, and purposeful, enlightening ideas. *The Watcher* is a story of a woman charged with murder while attempting to save her husband's career. Astral Cain is a memorable heroine in the romantic mold and her adversary, Martin Granger, even in death is a villainous manipulator of fear and doubt, a ghost masked with altruism. The past and present come together in a dynamic courtroom scene which is as startling as some of the surprises in the work of the great writers in the mystery's golden era.

The second book, *Catching Fire,* dramatizes the murder and violence that result when a man of ability and individuality tries to operate an off-Broadway theater opposed by unions and critics. Mrs. Smith's knowledge and experience in theater give the milieu an interesting and meaningful reality. Neither plot

nor theme is as effective as in *The Watcher,* but there is suspense and intrigue both on and off the fictional stage.

Mindspell is an ambitious effort to take the occult mystery down a looking-glass path and subject it to astute detection, science and logic challenging mysticism. The heroine, head of a genetic engineering firm, probes the past of a visionary whose ghost is a psychological and life-threatening menace to scientific progress. Smith has acknowledged the influence upon her career of her early association with novelist-philosopher, Ayn Rand. Up to this point in Smith's fiction the integration of plot and theme was primary, as well as reason and happiness the dominant values of her characters, all tenets of Rand's aesthetics and overall philosophy. However, in *Mindspell,* she seems to close the door on philosophical absolutes. At the end of the novel, she adds an epilogue that shrouds the rational detective efforts of her heroine in relativism. Reader, take your choice, the epilogue says in effect; reason or faith, it's all the same.

The narrative in *Elegy for a Soprano* turns from the objective technique of the earlier work toward a more popular (and less challenging) subjective approach. The heroine, Dinah Mitchell, is a journalist attempting to find the truth about the death of an opera star, Vardis Wolf, by interviewing her husband and a coterie of minions. The latter's relationships with Vardis, beginning in childhood, in some cases reveal seemingly parasitical overtones of passivity which Dinah remains incognizant of to the end. Most are suspects in the murder and the singer's ghost haunts their reminiscences. This format, stressing emotion, is burdened by introspective musings, the effect compounded when Dinah begins to suspect that Vardis may have been the mother who abandoned her at birth. The soprano, unfortunately, emerges from this convoluted narrative as a grotesque, not the viable characterization of "universal genius" (if there is such a concept even in the relativistic sense) the author seems to want. Trauma and overtones of grand opera deteriorate into bathos, drama bordering on the intentions of soap opera, rather than any higher form of tragedy. Readers who compare the ghosts in the past of Christie, Allingham (at her best), or Smith's own *The Watcher* may realize the essentials lacking.

The first part of Smith's *Country of the Heart* is heavy with redundant introspection, making it the psychological part of this "novel of psychological suspense," as it is billed, and the ending (really only the climax) the suspense part. Hedy Lucas and her mother, defectors to America from Russia several years earlier, are haunted by the mystery of why Boris Nikolayev, a Soviet composer and their father and husband, did not succeed in joining them in their escape. Now, for the first time since, Nikolayev is granted a visit outside Russia to appear in Finland at the premiere of his new orchestral work. Hedy leaves her dying mother and politician-fiancé and travels to Finland in hopes of exorcising the family mystery and freeing her father. The book is an effort to incorporate ideas regarding censorship, individual and artistic freedom, and what the author sees as the "burden" of freedom on "the heart," with a "had-I-but known" entertainment. The plot is too thin and characters stereotyped overall to support or integrate serious ideas. *Country of the Heart* lacks the viability of Andrew Garve's novels on the same theme.

Smith seemed a promising writer, bucking the trend toward mediocrity in today's novel. For the time being at least, she places herself on the bank of mainstream conventions, neither better nor worse than the other workers in a difficult field.

—Newton Baird

SMITH, Martin Cruz. Has also written as Nick Carter; Jake Logan; Martin Quinn; Simon Quinn. American. Born Martin William Smith in Reading, Pennsylvania, 3 November 1942. Educated at the University of Pennsylvania, Philadelphia, B.A. 1964. Married Emily Stanton Arnold in 1968; two daughters and one son. Reporter, Philadelphia *Daily News*, 1965, and Magazine Management, 1966–69. Recipient: Crime Writers Association Gold Dagger, award, 1982. Agent: Knox Burger Associates, 39½ Washington Square South, New York, New York 10012, U.S.A. Address: 240 Cascade Drive, Mill Valley, California 94941, U.S.A.

CRIME PUBLICATIONS

Novels (series: Roman Grey; Arkady Renko)

Gypsy in Amber (Grey). New York, Putnam, 1971; London, Barker, 1975.
The Analog Bullet. New York, Belmont Tower, 1972; London, W.H. Allen, 1982.
Canto for a Gypsy (Grey). New York, Putnam, 1972; London, Barker, 1975.
Nightwing. New York, Norton, and London, Deutsch, 1977.
Gorky Park (Renko). New York, Random House, and London, Collins, 1981.
Stallion Gate. London, Collins Harvill, and New York, Random House, 1986.
Polar Star (Renko). London, Collins, and New York, Random House, 1989.

Novels as Nick Carter (series: Nick Carter in all books)

The Inca Death Squad. New York, Award, 1972; London, Tandem, 1973.
Code Name: Werewolf. New York, Award, and London, Tandem, 1973.
The Devil's Dozen. New York, Award, 1973; London, Tandem, 1974.

Novels as Simon Quinn (series: The Inquisitor [Francis Xavier Killy] in all books except *The Human Factor*)

His Eminence, Death. New York, Dell, 1974.
Nuplex Red. New York, Dell, 1974.
The Devil in Kansas. New York, Dell, 1974.
The Last Time I Saw Hell. New York, Dell, 1974.
The Midas Coffin. New York, Dell, 1975.
Last Rites for the Vulture. New York, Dell, 1975.
The Human Factor (novelization of screenplay). New York, Dell, and London, Futura, 1975.

OTHER PUBLICATIONS

Novels

The Indians Won (as Martin Smith). New York, Belmont Tower, 1970; London, Star, 1982.
The Adventures of the Wilderness Family (as Martin Quinn; novelization of screenplay). New York, Ballantine, 1976; London, Arrow, 1977.
North to Dakota (as Jake Logan). Chicago, Playboy Press, 1976.
Ride for Revenge (as Jake Logan). Chicago, Playboy Press, 1977.

Play

Screenplay: *Nightwing*, with Steve Shagan and Bud Shrake, 1981.

*   *   *

Martin Cruz Smith has taken three approaches to the writing of mysteries and thrillers. As Nick Carter and Simon Quinn, he wrote formula fiction; as Martin Smith and Martin Cruz Smith, he has written superior novels characterized by a command of uncommon material; and finally, as *the* Martin Cruz Smith, he wrote the celebrated *Gorky Park*.

Smith has said that he wishes to disassociate himself from the novels of the first approach. These include his contributions to the Nick Carter series and his own series of six Inquisitor novels, published under the name of Simon Quinn. The latter, featuring Francis Xavier Killy, a lay brother of the Vatican's Militia Christi and the nemesis of Communists and Satanists, possesses some originality.

The two "Gypsy" novels begin Smith's movement toward more substantial fiction. They still exploit an established formula—the ethnic detective—but Roman Grey's Gypsy heritage is more than a superficial hook. The narratives reflect Smith's substantial research into Gypsy history and lore (and into antiques). Carefully researched backgrounds are typical of Smith's fiction. Also typical is the outsider quality of the Gypsy hero, which complicates his relationships with his non-Gypsy girlfriend and his friend in the police force. Finally, the Gypsy lore adds an typical element of the paranormal to the action. The conclusion of *Gypsy in Amber*, for example, takes place on the fringes of a Woodstock-like festival. The leader of a small cult plans to kill Grey in part because he is a threat, but also in part because the leader hopes ritualistically to acquire the power of Grey's Gypsy wisdom.

The Analog Bullet is an interesting diversion. A young Congressman survives an assassination attempt, but then discovers he has become an unperson. The novel has a serious theme as it attempts to illustrate the dangers of assigning too much authority to powerful government computers.

Nightwing was a great popular success; it is a Stephen King-like horror story set in Tony Hillerman country. The vivid ethnographic details of Hopi (and Navaho) life are again the result of research (though Smith does possess an Indian heritage). Youngman Duran is a deputy investigating the deaths of an old medicine man and others; he is also a Hopi Indian who responds to the land and the myths of his people. Again Smith pairs his outsider hero with an Anglo colleague, Hayden Paine, and with an Anglo girlfriend, Anne Dillon. Paine is a scientist pursuing a vendetta against the flock of vampire bats which have invaded the Painted Desert. Smith's persistent fascination with the bonds between the searcher and the sought appears in minor details: the bats' fleas carry the deadly plague; the detective's Hopi name translates as Flea.

Gorky Park, the result of eight years of research and writing, was an enormous critical and popular success. Arkady Renko, Chief Homicide Investigator for the Moscow Prosecutor's Office, is a realistic Soviet policeman whose pursuit of the killer of three frozen faceless corpses in Gorky Park leads him into a labyrinth of confrontations with KGB officers, prosecutors, actresses, icon and sable smugglers, and New York City cops. All of these characters engage in deception, and many in violence; yet all are plausible. The recreation of the social details of Soviet life in the late 1970's has been highly praised for its accuracy. And Smith is especially effective in portraying modes of manipulation as the various characters mislead one another, particularly in the context of the pervasive and unrestrained Soviet bureaucratic system. Renko's relationships with his prosecutor, Iamskoy, with the KGB Major, Pribluda, and with the Americans in Moscow, Osborne and Kirwell, develop dramatically. The novel has a complicated plot and a large cast, yet builds clearly to its climax in Staten Island. In a central episode, the ethnographer Andreev scientifically sculpts a human face onto a skull; in *Gorky Park,* Smith artfully draws a portrait of Soviet life on the skeleton of a detective story.

It took Smith five years to produce his next novel. Again the product of extensive research, *Stallion Gate* is not really a mystery novel. It returns to the western terrain of *Nightwing,* but the hero is now a Pueblo Indian, Army Sergeant Joe Pena; the time is 1943–1945; and Joe's assignment is to provide security for Robert Oppenheimer as he supervises the construction of the first atomic bomb at Los Alamos. A minor plot line concerns the discovery of Klaus Fuchs's betrayal of atomic secrets, but the novel's primary concern lies in the contrast between the visions of the two tribes, the Indian and the scientific.

Gorky Park and *Stallion Gate* are ambitious novels that largely realize their ambitions. *Polar Star,* a sequel to *Gorky Park,* again illustrates Smith's brilliant integration of substantial research into his fiction, but though it is a very fine detective story and a very good account of an unusual environment, it lacks the thematic resonance of its two predecessors. Renko's exile in Siberia has ended in the lower depths of the "slime line" in the hold of a Soviet factory ship in the Bering Sea. But when a girl is murdered, he is called upon to investigate. Again he encounters a mixture of petty crimes and more serious issues of espionage and security. And in the end, he appears to be headed toward rehabilitation.

Smith's characteristic virtue lies in his ability to set his novels concretely in uncommon worlds: the world of a Gypsy or of a Hopi deputy, or, with increasing subtlety, of a Pueblo sergeant at Los Alamos in 1945, or of a chief homicide investigator in Cold War Moscow, or of an ex-investigator on a Bering Sea fishing ship. Though *Stallion Gate* and *Polar Star* are strong novels that exploit this strength, *Gorky Park* is justly celebrated for its brilliant integration of a fully observed world—its physical, institutional, and social realities—with an intriguing plot that reveals the ways the world operates.

—J.K. Van Dover

SMITH, Shelley. Pseudonym for Nancy Hermione Bodington, née Courlander. British. Born in Richmond, Surrey, 12 July 1912. Educated at Cours Maintenon, Cannes, 1926; College Femina, Paris, 1928; the Sorbonne, Paris, 1929–31. Married Stephen Bodington in 1933 (divorced 1938). Agent: McIntosh and Otis Inc., 475 Fifth Avenue, New York, New York 10017, U.S.A.; or A.M. Heath, 79 St. Martin's Lane, London WC2N 4AA. Address: Chequers Orchard, White Horse Square, Steyning, Sussex BN44 3GQ, England.

CRIME PUBLICATIONS

Novels (series: Jacob Chaos)

Background for Murder (Chaos). London, Swan, 1942.
Death Stalks a Lady. London, Swan, 1945.
This Is the House. London, Collins, 1945.

Come and Be Killed! London, Collins, 1946; New York, Harper, 1947.
He Died of Murder! (Chaos). London, Collins, 1947; New York, Harper, 1948.
The Woman in the Sea. London, Collins, and New York, Harper, 1948.
Man with a Calico Face. New York, Harper, 1950; London, Collins, 1951.
Man Alone. London, Collins, 1952; as *The Crooked Man,* New York, Harper, 1952.
An Afternoon to Kill. London, Collins, 1953; New York, Harper, 1954.
The Party at No. 5. London, Collins, 1954; as *The Cellar at No. 5,* New York, Harper, 1954; London, Constable, 1987.
The Lord Have Mercy. London, Hamish Hamilton, and New York, Harper, 1956; as *The Shrew Is Dead,* New York, Dell, 1959.
The Ballad of the Running Man. London, Hamish Hamilton, 1961; New York, Harper, 1962.
A Grave Affair. London, Hamish Hamilton, 1971; New York, Doubleday, 1973.
A Game of Consequences. London, Macmillan, 1978.

Short Stories

Rachel Weeping: A Triptych. London, Hamish Hamilton, and New York, Harper, 1957.

Uncollected Short Stories

"Did It Happen?," in *Ellery Queen's Mystery Magazine* (New York), November 1959.
"Sting of Death," in *Bestseller Mystery Magazine* (New York), July 1960.

OTHER PUBLICATIONS as Nancy Bodington

Short Stories

How Many Miles to Babylon? London and New York, Wingate, 1950.

Play

Screenplay: *Tiger Bay,* with John Hawkesworth, 1959.

*

Shelley Smith comments:
I began by writing whodunits but soon moved away from the formula to a type of story that was more a study of the psychology of the criminal and the situation which leads to crime. Even this sounds to me rather pretentious for what are really entertainments. I would add, for the benefit of those who have never come across my work, that I have never followed a pattern or formula and each book is quite distinct in form and story from the others. The reader who likes the same story repeated with variations (made recognisable by the same cosy protagonist) will, I fear, be disappointed with Shelley Smith. But I hope the books will satisfy those who look for something more penetrating.

*   *   *

The unattached, jobless, and friendless; these are some of the people used by Shelley Smith to populate her mysteries. Sometimes the individual is so completely alone or separated from family or friends that no one can be aware of his distress until it is far too late (*Come and Be Killed!*); and even when there is a family, it is often too far-removed or too unconcerned to provide any help. In *The Party at No. 5* a daughter's interference forces an elderly eccentric to take in a lodger that she does not want which leads to immediate and fatal troubles. In *The Ballad of the Running Man* it is the lack of social commitments, moral principles, and a sense of purpose in life that leads to insurance frauds and inevitable disaster. In *Man Alone,* Smith, like many other mystery writers, uses a true crime case. Thomas Bates has many of the qualities of George Joseph Smith and uses more-or-less the same methods.

Few of these characters, victims or murderers, are particularly attractive but all of them are interesting, perhaps in some of the cases due to their total lack of moral decay: if you are rotten how can you possibly deteriorate? The victims are sometimes so pathetic that they entirely fail to be likeable; in the Bates murders, the potential brides are so eager to run to their fates that it becomes impossible to sympathise with them. A great many of these mysteries are set at the end of World War II, when the age of the extended family was over forever and the new society of casual living conditions and transient renters started to take over many communities. The messes that the Smith characters make of their lives are nearly always entirely their own fault and the reader is able to enjoy watching them destroy themselves with a sense of excitement and enjoyment that is unencumbered by any regrets. Both the clever and the gullible are manipulated by the determined who, in their turn, are ruled either by other stronger minds or by circumstances.

Perhaps the most interesting of these novels is *An Afternoon to Kill* where the fraud is actually perpetrated upon the reader; even the most voracious mystery fan, relying on a lifetime of homicidal experiences, will fail to arrive at the true results beforehand. As in so many mystery novels, unhappy human relationships provide a greater part of the drama than does any craving for money or property. *Man with a Calico Face* and *The Lord Have Mercy* deal with situations that are repeated regularly in life; marriages that do not work, or greed for the possessions of someone else. Sometimes her characters seem to be totally detached from their guilt, not exactly amoral, but with a sense that anything is right so long as it is for their own advantage. In *Man Alone* Bates feels a tremendous sense of relief when he is cleared of causing the death of a mentally disturbed wife, without having any sense of guilt about marrying her to control her money. He feels it is most unjust when past murders are brought up against him and seems to feel that they should have been forgotten, having happened a while back.

In each of her books Smith produces a tense, interesting, and compact mystery. She well deserves the success she has achieved.

—Mary Groff

SOMERS, Paul. *See* **GARVE, Andrew.**

SPAIN, John. *See* **ADAMS, Cleve F.**

SPAIN, Nancy (Brooker). British. Born in Newcastle upon Tyne, Tyneside in 1917. Educated at Roedean School, Surrey. Served in the Women's Royal Navy Service, 1939–45. Journalist; assistant features editor *Empire News,* 1947. *Died in 1964.*

CRIME PUBLICATIONS

Novels (series: Miriam Birdseye; Johnny Duvivien)

Death Before Wicket (Duvivien). London, Hutchinson, 1946.
Poison in Play (Duvivien). London, Hutchinson, 1946.
Murder, Bless It! (Duvivien). London, Hutchinson, 1948.
Death Goes on Skis (Birdseye and Duvivien). London, Hutchinson, 1949.
Poison for Teacher (Birdseye and Duvivien). London, Hutchinson, 1949.
Cinderella Goes to the Morgue (Birdseye). London, Hutchinson, 1950; as *Minutes to Midnight,* London, Duckworth, 1978.
R. in the Month (Birdseye). London, Hutchinson, 1950.
Not Wanted on Voyage (Birdseye). London, Hutchinson, 1951.
Out, Damned Tot! (Birdseye). London, Hutchinson, 1952.
The Kat Strikes. London, Hutchinson, 1955.

OTHER PUBLICATIONS

Novels (for children)

The Tiger Who [*Couldn't Eat Meat, Went to the Moon, Won His Star, Saved the Train, Found the Treasure*]. London, Parrish, 5 vols., 1954–61.
My Boy Mo. London, Hutchinson, 1959.

Other

Thank You, Nelson (autobiography). London, Hutchinson, 1945.
Mrs. Beeton and Her Husband (biography). London, Collins, 1948; as *The Beeton Story,* London, Ward Lock, 1956.
Why I'm not a Millionaire (autobiography). London, Hutchinson, 1956.
"Teach" Tennant: The Story of Eleanor Tennant. London, Werner Laurie, 1953.
The Nancy Spain Colour Cookery Book. London, World, 1963.
A Funny Thing Happened on the Way (autobiography). London, Hutchinson, 1964.

Editor, *The Beaver Annual.* Manchester, Fairhaven, 1962.

* * *

The hackneyed phrase larger-than-life character can be used accurately in the case of Nancy Spain. Her career was a series of trails being blazed for the professional women who were to follow her. One of the first women journalists in "popular" newspapers when she wrote for Lord Beaverbrooks's *Daily Express;* one of the first presenters of *Woman's Hour,* a BBC radio magazine programme which still runs; a television personality in the early days of that medium as a regular panellist on *What's My Line?*; founder with her lover Joan Werner Laurie ('Johnnie') of the successful women's magazine *She.*

Spain's output as a writer of books was large. As well as 10 detective novels she published children's books, three volumes of autobiography—one published posthumously—two biographies and a cookbook which is a much sought-after rarity for Spain completists!

Nine of the 10 novels fall into the subgenre of "crime capers." They have much in common with the work of her contemporary Pamela Branch and share a sense of generic parody with Marion Mainwaring. They are also terribly dated and fixed in a particular English comic-world where all the girls' schools are like St. Trinians' and Bohemian types wear flowers and call each other "Daahling" a lot.

Despite their class and race stereotypes, these novels are remarkable; this is mainly because of the coded messages for her readers. For the novels which feature her series sleuth Miriam Birdseye can also be read as gay camp in the tradition of, for example, Compton Mackenzie's *Vestal Fire*. In *Poison in Play* the Wimbledon tennis fortnight becomes a hotbed of unnatural passions—Spain was herself a regular attender at the annual All-England Club Championships; sexually-ambiguous ballet dancers and gangsters abound; in *Poison for Teacher* female teachers develop odd relationships at a school called Radcliffe Hall.

Spain's own sexual preference was an open secret. She and fellow-gay television presenter Gilbert Harding flirted with the media about an engagement but her relationship with Johnnie was acknowledged. They died together when their private plane crashed while taking them to Aintree near Liverpool for the Grand National Steeplechase.

An oddity amongst her books is *The Kat Strikes*. This is an action-thriller which includes much autobiographical detail of her life immediately after World War II. The description of post-Blitz austerity in London is particularly fine. It is time her work was reprinted.

—Linda Semple

SPENCER, John. *See* **VICKERS, Roy.**

SPICER, Bart. Also writes as Jay Barbette (with Betty Coe Spicer). American. Born in Richmond, Virginia in 1918. Served in the United States Army in World War II: Captain. Journalist: worked for Scripps-Howard Syndicate and as a radio news writer; after the war worked in public relations for Universal Military Training, 3 years, and World Affairs Council, 1 year.

CRIME PUBLICATIONS

Novels (series: Benson Kellogg; Peregrine White; Carney Wilde)

The Dark Light (Wilde). New York, Dodd Mead, 1949; London, Collins, 1950.
Blues for the Prince (Wilde). New York, Dodd Mead, 1950; London, Collins, 1951.
The Golden Door (Wilde). New York, Dodd Mead, and London, Collins, 1951.
Black Sheep, Run (Wilde). New York, Dodd Mead, 1951; London, Collins, 1952.

The Long Green (Wilde). New York, Dodd Mead, 1952; as *Shadow of Fear*, London, Collins, 1953.
The Taming of Carney Wilde. New York, Dodd Mead, 1954; London, Hodder and Stoughton, 1955.
The Day of the Dead (White). New York, Dodd Mead, 1955; London, Hodder and Stoughton, 1956.
Exit, Running (Wilde). New York, Dodd Mead, 1959; London, Hodder and Stoughton, 1960.
Act of Anger (Kellogg). New York, Atheneum, 1962; London, Barker, 1963.
The Burned Man (White). New York, Atheneum, 1966; London, Hale, 1967.
Kellogg Junction. New York, Atheneum, 1969; London, Hodder and Stoughton, 1970.
The Adversary. New York, Putnam, and London, Hart Davis MacGibbon, 1974.

Novels as Jay Barbette (series: Harry Butten in all books)

Final Copy. London, Dodd Mead, 1950; London, Barker, 1952.
Dear Dead Days. New York, Dodd Mead, 1953; London, Barker, 1954; as *Death's Long Shadow*, New York, Bantam, 1955.
The Deadly Doll. New York, Dodd Mead, 1958; London, Long, 1959.
Look Behind You. New York, Dodd Mead, 1960; London, Long, 1961.

OTHER PUBLICATIONS

Novels

The Wild Ohio. New York, Dodd Mead, and London, Hodder and Stoughton, 1954.
The Tall Captains. New York, Dodd Mead, 1957.
Brother to the Enemy. New York, Dodd Mead, 1958; London, Hodder and Stoughton, 1959.
The Day Before Thunder. New York, Dodd Mead, 1960.
Festival. New York, Atheneum, 1970.

* * *

Bart Spicer has had two distinct writing careers. The first, beginning with *The Dark Light* in 1949, was as a hard-boiled series writer of great distinction. *Act of Anger*, published in 1962, marks the beginning of the second phase of his work, in which he abandoned strict genre material, and turned to writing books which, while strong in crime and suspense elements, are clearly aimed at the bestseller market rather than the specialized mystery readership.

The seven mysteries which feature Spicer's private-eye hero, Carney Wilde, neatly span the 1950's; and that period was the great decade of the series hard-boiled dick, with the paperback explosion and the Mickey Spillane phenomenon. Spicer's Wilde tales are among the very best private-eye novels of that or any decade, and it is regrettable that they have been largely ignored in the recent spate of private-eye criticism of what Michael Avallone has called the "Father, Son and Holy Ghost," school (i.e., concentration on the works of Hammett, Chandler, and Ross Macdonald to the exclusion of practically everyone else). The Wilde books are beautifully crafted. Spicer's plotting is coherent, with credible twists and surprises; his style strikes a satisfying balance between the telegraphic and the over-ripe; he writes convincing dialogue and makes imaginative use of the "hard-boiled simile." Wilde himself is an admirable, believable hero, not the formularized caricature that can be found in too many tough-guy series of the period. Wilde's first-person narration flows smoothly, steering clear of both excessive wisecrackery and windy philosophizing. The secondary characters, continuing and otherwise, are varied and interesting (Spicer's treatment of the cops, and Wilde's relations with them, is particularly good), and the settings are fresh. Wilde is based in Philadelphia (a welcome respite from Los Angeles and New York), but travels to Arizona in *The Long Green* and down the Mississippi in *The Taming of Carney Wilde*. *Blues for the Prince*, one of the best of the series, draws on Spicer's own passion for New Orleans jazz.

During the 1950's Spicer also wrote several non-Wilde mysteries; four collaborative works with his wife, Betty Coe Spicer, under the pseudonym Jay Barbette; and *The Day of the Dead*, a fast-paced spy novel set in Mexico. Spicer's books of the 1960's and 1970's mark a clear break with the insular world of straight genre fiction, reflecting the simultaneous decline in the popularity of the private-eye novel (he made the break decisive by gracefully "retiring" Carney Wilde to marriage and a less strenuous occupation in *Exit, Running*). *Act of Anger* and *The Adversary* are both courtroom dramas, powerfully written, rich in detail and characterization. *The Burned Man* is a vigorous, complex espionage novel, unmarred by post-Bondian cliché. *Kellogg Junction* concerns the effects of a campaign to legalize gambling in a corrupt town. These novels are fundamentally different from the Wilde books in market orientation, but they are nevertheless tales of crime and suspense; and they share with the earlier work the fine prose style, sharp eye for detail and characterization, and overall high marks as fictional entertainment.

—Art Scott

SPILLANE, Mickey (Frank Morrison Spillane). American. Born in Brooklyn, New York, 9 March 1918. Attended Kansas State University, Manhattan. Served in the United States Army Air Force during World War II. Married 1) Mary Ann Pearce in 1945 (divorced 1962); four children; 2) Sherri Malinou in 1965 (divorced). Began selling stories in 1935; wrote for the comic books *Captain Marvel, Captain America,* and others; trampoline artist, Ringling Brothers Barnum and Bailey Circus; Founder, with Robert Fellows, Spillane-Fellows Productions (films). Recipient: Private Eye Writers of American award, 1983. Lives in South Carolina. Address: c/o E.P. Dutton, 2 Park Avenue, New York, New York 10016, U.S.A.

CRIME PUBLICATIONS

Novels (series: Mike Hammer; Tiger Mann)

I, The Jury (Hammer). New York, Dutton, 1947; London, Barker, 1952.
My Gun Is Quick (Hammer). New York, Dutton, 1950; London, Barker, 1951.
Vengeance Is Mine! (Hammer). New York, Dutton, 1950; London, Barker, 1951.
The Big Kill (Hammer). New York, Dutton, 1951; London, Barker, 1952.
The Long Wait. New York, Dutton, 1951; London, Barker, 1953.

One Lonely Night (Hammer). New York, Dutton, 1951; London, Barker, 1952.
Kiss me, Deadly (Hammer). New York, Dutton, 1952; London, Barker, 1953.
The Deep. New York, Dutton, and London, Barker, 1961.
The Girl Hunters (Hammer). New York, Dutton, and London, Barker, 1962.
Me, Hood! (novelettes). London, Corgi, 1963.
Day of the Guns (Mann). New York, Dutton, 1964; London, Barker, 1965.
The Flier (novelettes). London, Corgi, 1964.
Return of the Hood (novelettes). London, Corgi, 1964.
The Snake (Hammer). New York, Dutton, and London, Barker, 1964.
Bloody Sunrise (Mann). New York, Dutton, and London, Barker, 1965.
The Death Dealers (Mann). New York, Dutton, 1965; London, Barker, 1966.
Killer Mine (novelettes). London, Corgi, 1965; New York, New American Library, 1968.
The By-Pass Control (Mann). New York, Dutton, 1966; London, Barker, 1967.
The Twisted Thing (Hammer). New York, Dutton, and London, Barker, 1966.
The Body Lovers (Hammer). New York, Dutton, and London, Barker, 1967.
The Delta Factor. New York, Dutton, 1967; London, Corgi, 1969.
Me, Hood! (novelettes; different book from previous title). New York, New American Library, 1969.
The Tough Guys (novelettes). New York, New American Library, 1969.
Survival ... Zero! (Hammer). New York, Dutton, and London, Corgi, 1970.
The Erection Set. New York, Dutton, and London, W.H. Allen, 1972.
The Last Cop Out. New York, Dutton, and London, W.H. Allen, 1973.
The Killing Man (Hammer). New York, Dutton, 1989.

Short Stories

Tomorrow I Die, edited by Max Allan Collins. New York, Mysterious Press, 1984; London, Heinemann, 1990.

OTHER PUBLICATIONS

Play

Screenplay: *The Girl Hunters,* with Roy Rowland and Robert Fellows, 1963.

Other

The Day the Sea Rolled Back (for children). New York, Windmill, 1979; London, Methuen, 1980.
The Ship That Never Was (for children). New York, Bantam, 1982.
Mike Hammer: The Comic Strip, edited by Max Allan Collins. Park Forest, Illinois, Pierce, 2 vols., 1982–84.

*

Critical Studies: *Murder in the Millions: Erle Stanley Gardner, Mickey Spillane, Ian Fleming* by J. Kenneth Van Dover, New York, Ungar, 1984; *One Lonely Knight: Mickey Spillane's Mike*

Hammer by Max Allan Collins and James L. Traylor, Bowling Green, Ohio, Popular Press, 1984.

Theatrical Activities:

Actor: **Films**—*Ring of Fear*, 1953; *The Girl Hunters*, 1963; **Television**—*Colombo* series, 1973.

* * *

Mickey Spillane is the acknowledged living master of the hard-boiled mystery story, having received the life achievement award from the PWA (Private Eye Writers of America) in 1983. No similar honor has yet emerged from the MWA (Mystery Writers of America), however, reflecting the fact that for years Spillane was the pariah of mystery fiction, despite having at one time written seven of the all-time 10 fiction (not just mystery) bestsellers. It has taken the more traditional mystery establishment over 30 years to begin appreciating Spillane's overwhelming contribution to the genre.

Spillane is a born storyteller. He wrote scripts for comics during the 1940s; *I, The Jury* (1947), perhaps his most famous Mike Hammer mystery, was originally conceived as a comic book entitled "Mike Danger." When it did not sell to the comics, Spillane rewrote it as a novel—in nine days, he says.

Spillane is the stylistic successor to Carroll John Daly, the most popular *Black Mask* writer. Mike Hammer is such a similar character to Daly's Race Williams that many have observed Hammer could well be Williams's literary son. Spillane's protagonists—Mike Hammer, Tiger Mann, The Deep, Morgan the Raider, Gill Burke—are direct pulp descendants of Daly's Williams (and Satan Hall). They are no-nonsense characters who act first and think second, without exception modern avengers. In turn, they influenced contemporary pulp series, particularly Don Pendleton's Executioner paperback saga and Clint Eastwood's Dirty Harry films.

Critics have always had problems with Hammer's seeming disregard for the law and his acting as judge and executioner. The reading public has had no such problem: they bought the Hammer novels by the millions—some 160 million copies through 1984.

Hammer, Spillane's most famous character, is often criticized for his supposed penchant for sex and sadism. Spillane's controversial subject matter led many into dismissing his work as having had no literary merit. Despite this, Hammer's saga—eleven novels from *I, The Jury* to *Survival . . . Zero!* (1970)—traces the development of a human psyche and a nation's self image, and does so in a remarkably original manner, through a vivid first-person technique.

In *I, The Jury* Hammer is a World War II veteran who is compelled to avenge the murder of his best friend, a man who lost an arm saving Hammer's life in the South Pacific. Trained as a policeman, honed to toughness by a brutal war, Hammer lives by a violent code. Nothing will stand in the way of his vengeance, even if the killer is someone he loves. Hammer executes the killer—fulfilling the novel's title—and spends his remaining years defending that action to himself and those around him. His psychological scar becomes a metaphor for the lost innocence of post-war America.

Spillane is a master craftsman whose characters live in the minds of millions. People know Mike Hammer and his secretary Velda as well as if they lived on some nearby—but meaner—street. If Hammer is a somewhat tarnished knight, Velda is a pristine lady knight, one who is equal to Hammer in both physical and mental toughness. Typical of the strong female characters in Spillane, Velda begins by playing Effie Perrine to Hammer's Sam Spade, but soon is the Jane to his Tarzan.

The quintessential Hammer is *One Lonely Night*. It, more than any other Spillane novel, is an emotional experience—combining the key elements of love, hate, and violence. A surreal nightmare, *One Lonely Night* deals with the very criticism Spillane's work had been attracting by giving Mike Hammer as an adversary a liberal judge who condemns him and his actions. Hammer comes to see himself as an angel of death sent by God to meet evil on its own terms. At the same time, Spillane flaunts his outrageously conservative politics in the face of the liberal critical establishment.

Spillane also created Tiger Mann, an attempt to capitalize on the James Bond phenomenon of the 1960's. The four Tiger Mann novels are of relatively minor interest in the Spillane canon, though the first, *Day of the Guns*, is an interesting variation of *I, The Jury*, providing an upbeat twist to the earlier book's famous striptease finale.

Spillane is not afraid to do the unexpected. Twice in his career he quit writing mysteries to concentrate on activities he considered more important—religion in the 1950's and "selling" Miller Lite beer in the 1970's and 1980's. *The Erection Set* and *The Last Cop Out*—have been unjustly ignored, critically. *The Last Cop Out*, written in the third person with shifting points-of-view (hence, unlike any Spillane novel before it), is perhaps technically the best novel Spillane has yet written. It is violent, tough, and yet sentimental in its classic approach to the American crime novel.

—Max Allan Collins and James L. Traylor

———

STAGGE, Jonathan. *See* **QUENTIN, Patrick.**

———

STANLEY, Bennett. *See* **HOUGH, S.B.**

———

STANTON, Vance. *See* **AVALLONE, Michael.**

———

STAPLETON, Katherine. *See* **KANE, Henry.**

———

STARK, Richard. *See* **WESTLAKE, Donald E.**

———

STARRETT, (Charles) Vincent (Emerson). American. Born in Toronto, Canada, 26 October 1886. Educated in public schools in Chicago. Journalist, Chicago *Inter-Ocean*, 1905–06, and Chicago *Daily News,* 1906–16 (war correspondent in Mexico 1914–15); editor, *The Wave* magazine, 1921–22; taught writing at Northwestern University, Evanston, Illinois; columnist, "Books Alive," Chicago *Tribune,* 1942–74. Co-founder, with Christopher Morley, Baker Street Irregulars; President, Society of Midland Authors; President, Mystery Writers of America, 1961. Recipient: Mystery Writers of America Grand Master award, 1957. *Died 4 January 1974.*

CRIME PUBLICATIONS

Novels (series: Riley Blackwood; Walter Ghost)

Murder on "B" Deck (Ghost). New York, Doubleday, 1929; Kingswood, Surrey, World's Work, 1936.
Dead Man Inside (Ghost). New York, Doubleday, 1931; Kingswood, Surrey, World's Work, 1935.
The End of Mr. Garment (Ghost). New York, Doubleday, 1932.
The Great Hotel Murder (Blackwood). New York, Doubleday, and London, Nicholson and Watson, 1935.
Midnight and Percy Jones (Blackwood). New York, Covici Friede, 1936; London, Nicholson and Watson, 1938.
The Laughing Buddha. Mount Morris, Illinois, Magna, 1937; as *Murder in Peking,* New York, Lantern Press, 1946; London, Edwards, 1947.

Short Stories (series: Jimmy Lavender)

The Unique Hamlet: A Hitherto Unchronicled Adventure of Mr. Sherlock Holmes. Privately printed, 1920.
Coffins for Two. Chicago, Covici McGee, 1924.
The Blue Door. New York, Doubleday, 1930.
The Case Book of Jimmie Lavender. New York, Fawcett, 1944.
The Quick and the Dead. Sauk City, Wisconsin, Arkham House, 1965.

Uncollected Short Stories

"Fog over Hong Kong," in *Fourth Mystery Companion,* edited by Abraham Louis Furman. New York, Lantern Press, 1946.
"The Day of the Cripples," in *The Saint* (New York), October 1956.
"The Tragedy of Papa Ponsard," in *Ellery Queen's Mystery Magazine* (New York), January 1959.
"Man in Hiding," in *Ellery Queen's Mystery Magazine* (New York), December 1964.
"Crazy Like a Fox," in *Anthology 1965,* edited by Ellery Queen. New York, Davis, 1964.
"The Eleventh Juror," in *Rogues' Gallery,* edited by Walter B. Gibson. New York, Doubleday, 1969.

OTHER PUBLICATIONS

Novel

Seaports in the Moon: A Fantasia on Romantic Themes. New York, Doubleday, 1928.

Short Stories

Snow for Christmas. Privately printed, 1935.

Verse

Rhymes for Collectors. Privately printed, 1921.
Ebony Flame. Chicago, Covici McGee, 1922.

Banners in the Dawn: Sixty-Four Sonnets. Chicago, Hill, 1923.
Flames and Dust. Chicago, Covici McGee, 1924.
Fifteen More Poems. Privately printed, 1927.
Autolycus in Limbo. New York, Dutton, 1943.
Sonnets and Other Verse. Chicago, Dierkes Press, 1949.

Other

Arthur Machen: A Novelist of Ecstasy and Sin. Chicago, Hill, 1918.
The Escape of Alice: A Christmas Fantasy. Privately printed, 1919.
Ambrose Bierce. Chicago, Hill, 1920.
A Student of Catalogues. Privately printed, 1921.
Stephen Crane: A Bibliography. Philadelphia, Centaur Book Shop, 1923.
Buried Caesars: Essays in Literary Appreciation. Chicago, Covici McGee, 1923.
Ambrose Bierce: A Bibliography. Philadelphia, Centaur Book Shop, 1929.
Penny Wise and Book Foolish. New York, Covici Friede, 1929.
All About Mother Goose. Privately printed, 1930.
The Private Life of Sherlock Holmes. New York, Macmillan, 1933; London, Nicholson and Watson, 1934; revised edition, Chicago, University of Chicago Press, 1960; London, Allen and Unwin, 1961.
Persons from Porlock (essays). Chicago, Normandie House, 1938.
Oriental Encounter: Two Essays in Bad Taste. Chicago, Normandie House, 1938.
Books Alive. New York, Random House, 1940.
Bookman's Holiday: The Private Satisfactions of an Incurable Collector. New York, Random House, 1942.
Books and Bipeds. New York, Argus, 1947.
Stephen Crane: A Bibliography, with Ames W. Williams. Glendale, California, J. Valentine, 1948.
Best Loved Books of the Twentieth Century. New York, Bantam, 1955.
The Great All-Star Animal League Ball Game (for children). New York, Dodd Mead, 1957.
Book Column. New York, Caxton Club, 1958.
Born in a Bookshop: Chapters from the Chicago Renascence (autobiography). Norman, University of Oklahoma Press, 1965.
Late, Later and Possibly Last: Essays. St. Louis, Autolycus Press, 1973.
Sincerely Tony/Faithfully Vincent: The Correspondence of Anthony Boucher and Vincent Starrett, edited by Robert W. Hahn. Chicago, Catullus Press, 1975.

Editor, *In Praise of Stevenson.* Chicago, Bookfellows, 1919.
Editor, *Men, Women, and Boats,* by Stephen Crane. New York, Boni and Liveright, 1921.
Editor, *The Shining Pyramids,* by Arthur Machen. Chicago, Covici McGee, 1923.
Editor, *The Glorious Mystery,* by Arthur Machen. Chicago, Covici McGee, 1924.
Editor, *Et Cetera: A Collector's Scrap Book.* Chicago, Covici McGee, 1924.
Editor, *Sins of the Fathers and Other Tales,* by George Gissing. Chicago, Pascal Covici, 1924.
Editor, *Fourteen Great Detective Stories.* New York, Modern Library, 1928.
Editor, *Maggie, A Girl of the Streets and Other Stories,* by Stephen Crane. New York, Modern Library, 1933.

Editor, *A Modern Book of Wonders: Amazing Facts in a Remarkable World*. Chicago, University of Knowledge, 1938.

Editor, with others, *221B: Studies in Sherlock Holmes*. New York, Macmillan, 1940.

Editor, *The Mystery of Edwin Drood*, by Charles Dickens. New York, Heritage Press, 1941.

Editor, *World's Great Spy Stories*. Cleveland, World, 1944.

Editor, *The Moonstone*, by Wilkie Collins. New York, Limited Editions Club, 1959.

* * *

Journalist, teacher, poet, scholar of detective fiction in general and Sherlock Holmes in particular, mystery writer, respected bibliophile—Vincent Starrett was among the more versatile talents to grace the world of detective fiction. His major contributions to the mystery genre are his Sherlock Holmes writings, with his remarkable *The Private Life of Sherlock Holmes*—the first biographical study of a fictional detective hero. This book collects many earlier Starrett essays on Holmes, adds a few new ones, and becomes a compendium of Sherlockiana. Starrett's written contributions go beyond his Holmes scholarship: he has also written what is generally considered the best Holmes pastiche, *The Unique Hamlet*. This story, detailing Holmes's search for a missing inscribed first edition of Shakespeare's famous tragedy, is not only a masterful Sherlockian burlesque—it is also an amusing satire on both book collecting and Shakespeare scholars. Starrett also advanced Sherlockiana significantly as a founding father of the Baker Street Irregulars.

For his own mystery fiction, Starrett enjoys a reputation as a deft creator of plots, often in the Holmes tradition of the intriguing puzzle and often showing Poe's influence as well. Starrett was neither a particularly effective nor a consistent creator of characters: his best-known series detective, Chicagoan Jimmie Lavender, was named for a fair-to-good Chicago Cubs pitcher of the 1910's, and in his earliest of about 50 appearances in print, Lavender is noteworthy chiefly for his two different colored eyes, a physical quirk which Starrett later eliminates altogether. The best of the Lavender stories were collected as the *Case Book* in 1944.

Murder on "B" Deck, his first longer mystery, was highly acclaimed critically; though it began as a Lavender book, it became in the writing process a vehicle for another series hero, the amateur sleuth Walter Ghost, who solves the murder of the exotic Countess Fogartini aboard the *Latakia* by awaiting the answers to several cablegrams; his companion Mollock, a Watson, seems simply inept—a good example both of the Holmes influence and of Starrett's comparative weakness at characterization. *The Great Hotel Murder* appeared first in serialized form, then as a novel, and finally as a film—although the movie is so unlike its source that Starrett admits (in his autobiography) that "Nobody was more surprised than the author by the revelation of the killer's identity." This story also follows the Holmes-Watson formula, as a hotel detective and a drama critic work together to solve the murder of a hotel guest.

Two other important Starrett publications are short-story collections, *The Blue Door* and *The Quick and the Dead*. The former is notable for the presence of Jimmie Lavender in two of its ten stories and for the introduction of the bibliophile and amateur sleuth G. Washington Troxell, who unfortunately appears in only a few scattered tales. This volume also includes a justly celebrated fictional rendering of the Oscar Slater case entitled "Too Many Sleuths." *The Quick and the Dead* reveals fully his debt to Poe: Poe's interest in popular pseudo-sciences is reflected in "The Elixir of Death" in which an undertaker

and his assistant discover a potion which will banish death and in "The Tattooed Man" in which a doctor tries to discover ways to eliminate some rather bizarre tattoos. Also derived from Poe are the device of burial alive and the repeated insistence on the greatest of all human fears—the inexplicable failure to perceive exactly what it is that so frightens. Throughout the book, irony and clever plotting provide strength: "The Head of Cromwell" follows the adventures of Cromwell's skull, which finally becomes an "excellent tobacco jar"; in "Footsteps of Fear" a man commits the perfect murder, but is pursued by fear of discovery, so when the police arrive he conceals himself in what proves to be a self-locking trunk—the policemen depart disappointed, unable to sell their benefit tickets, and the murderer suffocates.

Starrett's reading of Chinese fiction is also noteworthy; in his 1942 essay, "Some Chinese Detective Stories," Starrett introduced many Westerners to such famous figures as Judge Dee and Magistrate Pao. As always, Starrett's critical perceptions were acute and his judgments sound.

Starrett was a bookman's bookman: in his autobiography, Starrett borrows Eugene Field's neologism to label himself a "Dofab"—a "damned old fool about books." He was a studious critic and reviewer of detective literature. And he contributed substantively to the library of mystery fiction. But his greatest achievements and his ultimate reputation rest upon his eminence as an imaginative Sherlock Holmes reader and scholar.

—Elmer Pry

———

STEEL, Kurt. Pseudonym for Rudolf Hornaday Kagey. American. Born in Tuscola, Illinois, 5 September 1904. Educated at Columbia University, New York, Ph.D. 1931. Member of the Philosophy Department, New York University, from 1928. *Died 13 May 1946.*

CRIME PUBLICATIONS

Novels (series: Hank Hyer in all books except *The Impostor*)

Murder of a Dead Man. Indianapolis, Bobbs Merrill, 1935; abridged edition, as *The Traveling Corpses*, New York, Select, 1942.

Murder for What? Indianapolis, Bobbs Merrill, 1936.

Murder Goes to College. Indianapolis, Bobbs Merrill, 1936.

Murder in G-Sharp. Indianapolis, Bobbs Merrill, 1937; abridged edition, as *Strangler's Holiday,* New York, Select, 1942.

Crooked Shadow. Boston, Little Brown, 1939; London, Swan, 1945.

Judas, Incorporated. Boston, Little Brown, 1939.

Dead of Night. Boston, Little Brown, 1940; London, Swan, 1944.

Madman's Buff. Boston, Little Brown, 1941; London, Swan, 1945.

The Impostor. New York, Harcourt Brace, 1942; London, Gifford, 1945.

Ambush House. New York, Harcourt Brace, 1943.

Uncollected Short Stories

"With Intent to Kill," in *Mystery Book Magazine* (New York), November 1945.

"The Friendly Slayer," in *Detective Novel Magazine* (New York), September 1947.

"The Radio City Mystery," in *Popular Detective* (New York), November 1948.

"Change for Twenty," in *Murder Cavalcade*. New York, Harper, 1952.

"Under the Counter," in *Suspense* (London), June 1960.

OTHER PUBLICATIONS

Other

Noche oscura en Lima (Spanish reader), with Joseph W. Barlow. New York, Crofts, 1941.

*   *   *

It is difficult to account for the neglect suffered by writer Kurt Steel, the hard-boiled pseudonym of a New York University professor, Rudolf Kagey. An admirer of Hammett, Steel wrote nine of his ten novels featuring expensive New York private investigator Henry Hyer, who set himself up in business at the age of 25. He is first introduced in 1935 in *Murder of a Dead Man*, in which he is roped into investigating the disappearance of a dachshund named Markheim.

Heyer has an apartment on Bank Street in Greenwich Village, not far from Abingdon Square. The "off-Broadway" office mentioned in the first book seems to have vanished after that, with the apartment serving both functions. We learn the undistinguished-looking detective's age for the first time in *Judas, Incorporated*, where he is 38, 5'8", and shapely as the welterweight challenger he almost became 15 years earlier. Born in Iowa and raised in Chicago, he has an ongoing romance with New York City, where he chose to make his home and set up business. So enthralled is he with the big city that he almost turns down a case when it means investigating in a small Connecticut town. By the time of *Murder Goes to College*, he has been in New York five years with a growing reputation enabling him to demand exorbitant fees, 10 thousand dollars per case not being uncommon. One often disconcerting feature of the series, however, is the fact that the detective seems known by just about everyone he chances to run into in the course of his investigations.

The extremely fine series really gets off the ground with the fourth novel, *Murder in G-Sharp*, in which a cruel young heir is found strangled with a piano string in his opulent Bronx mansion. This is the first novel in which Steel seems to hit and maintain his stride. The fully developed characters, clearly delineated scenes, well-paced plot, and lively dialogue become the Steel hallmark and far outshine those of many more well-known practitioners of the private-eye sub-genre both of his own day and since. Theater, music, and voodoo share the stage in this novel, one of the earliest novels to make use of color-blindness.

In *Judas, Incorporated*, perhaps the finest in the series, the investigation of the murder of a factory owner revolves around the important issue of labor vs. management and the role of unions. Also in this novel Hyer meets for the first time youthful, freckled, redheaded Orson Quick, who will become his man Friday, to the point of later being arrested and indicted for murder while investigating an American pro-Nazi organization in *Crooked Shadow*.

The last three novels in the series continue in the same high caliber. In *Dead of Night* Hyer and Quick are involved in the murder of a wealthy publisher and amateur astrologer with the action ranging from New York to the Adirondacks and Long Island. *Madman's Buff* presents Hyer with a murder scene à la Ellery Queen when the sheet-shrouded corpse of a Broadway drama critic is discovered in his topsy-turvy bedroom. And *Ambush House*, the last novel before Kagey's untimely death in 1946, presents Henry Hyer playing nursemaid, *Little Miss Marker*-style, to a nine-year-old refugee named Angelica while two of his prospective clients are out to kill each other.

The one non-series book, *The Impostor*, is billed as "a modern spy novel," with a Nazi spy ring's attempt to sabotage American shores by creating a man who suddenly ceases to exist.

Challenging a few of Van Dine's rules on the detective story, Steel lays stress at this early date on the importance of character development, insisting on "characters equipped with full complements of the vital juices," including everything that goes into making a character, major or minor, truly human: "You must learn, first of all, to write a story, a yarn, fiction that is honest and true in its own right, about people who are real with that impelling reality that people in well-written fiction have always had since Homer's day" ("So You're Going to Write a Mystery," 1945). It is not surprising, then, that two of Henry Hyer's "chief aversions" are the amateur criminologist and the cerebrating detective of laboratory and fiction (*Murder Goes to College*).

A newspaperman himself at one time, Steel frequently makes use of reporters as characters, some of them recurrent (Corey Hilton, Mal Range), as are a few of his other characters; some of the language, too, is surprisingly earthy for the period. The novels are unfortunately sometimes marred by ethnic slurs, especially in the case of the Italians. This aside, Hyer is a highly likable guy, "cynical, realistic soul" that he is (*Murder for What?*).

—James R. McCahery

STEELE, Derwent. *See* VERNER, Gerald.

STEIN, Aaron Marc. Also wrote as George Bagby; Hampton Stone. American. Born in New York City, 15 November 1906. Educated at Ethical Culture School, New York, 1916–23; Princeton University, New Jersey, A.B. (Summa cum laude) 1927 (Phi Beta Kappa). Served in the Office of War Information, 1942–43, and the United States Army, 1943–45. Critic and columnist, New York *Evening Post*, 1927–38; contributing editor, *Time*, New York City, 1938. Freelance writer from 1939. Past President, Mystery Writers of America. Recipient: Mystery Writers of America Grand Master award, 1979. *Died in 1985.*

CRIME PUBLICATIONS

Novels (series: Matt Erridge; Tim Mulligan and Elsie Mae Hunt)

The Sun Is a Witness (Mulligan and Hunt). New York, Doubleday, 1940.

Up to No Good (Mulligan and Hunt). New York, Doubleday, 1941.

Only the Guilty (Mulligan and Hunt). New York, Doubleday, 1942.

The Case of the Absent-Minded Professor (Mulligan and Hunt). New York, Doubleday, 1943.

. . . and High Water (Mulligan and Hunt). New York, Doubleday, 1946.

We Saw Him Die (Mulligan and Hunt). New York, Doubleday, 1947.

Death Takes a Paying Guest (Mulligan and Hunt). New York, Doubleday, 1947.

The Cradle and the Grave (Mulligan and Hunt). New York, Doubleday, 1948.

The Second Burial (Mulligan and Hunt). New York, Doubleday, 1949.

Days of Misfortune (Mulligan and Hunt). New York, Doubleday, 1949.

Three—with Blood (Mulligan and Hunt). New York, Doubleday, 1950.

Frightened Amazon (Mulligan and Hunt). New York, Doubleday, 1950.

Shoot Me Dacent (Mulligan and Hunt). New York, Doubleday, 1951; London, Macdonald, 1957.

Pistols for Two (Mulligan and Hunt). New York, Doubleday, 1951.

Mask for Murder (Mulligan and Hunt). New York, Doubleday, 1952.

The Dead Thing in the Pool (Mulligan and Hunt). New York, Doubleday, 1952.

Death Meets 400 Rabbits (Mulligan and Hunt). New York, Doubleday, 1953.

Moonmilk and Murder (Mulligan and Hunt). New York, Doubleday, 1955; London, Macdonald, 1956.

Sitting Up Dead (Erridge). New York, Doubleday, 1958; London, Macdonald, 1959.

Never Need an Enemy (Erridge). New York, Doubleday, 1959; London, Boardman, 1960.

Home and Murder (Erridge). New York, Doubleday, 1962.

Blood on the Stars (Erridge). New York, Doubleday, and London, Hale, 1964.

I Fear the Greeks (Erridge). New York, Doubleday, 1966; as *Executioner's Rest*, London, Hale, 1967.

Deadly Delight (Erridge). New York, Doubleday, 1967; London, Hale, 1969.

Snare Andalucian (Erridge). New York, Doubleday, 1968; as *Faces of Death*, London, Hale, 1968.

Kill Is a Four-Letter Word (Erridge). New York, Doubleday, 1968; London, Hale, 1969.

Alp Murder (Erridge). New York, Doubleday, 1970; London, Hale, 1971.

The Finger (Erridge). New York, Doubleday, 1973; London, Hale, 1974.

Lock and Key. New York, Doubleday, 1973.

Coffin Country (Erridge). New York, Doubleday, and London, Hale, 1976.

Lend Me Your Ears (Erridge). New York, Doubleday, 1977.

Body Search (Erridge). New York, Doubleday, and London, Hale, 1978.

Nowhere? (Erridge). New York, Doubleday, and London, Hale, 1978.

Chill Factor (Erridge). New York, Doubleday, 1978; London, Hale, 1979.

The Rolling Heads (Erridge). New York, Doubleday, and London, Hale, 1979.

One Dip Dead (Erridge). New York, Doubleday, 1979; London, Hale, 1980.

The Cheating Butcher (Erridge). New York, Doubleday, 1980; London, Hale, 1981.

A Nose for It (Erridge). New York, Doubleday, 1980; London, Hale, 1981.

A Body for a Buddy (Erridge). New York, Doubleday, and London, Hale, 1981.

Hangman's Row (Erridge). New York, Doubleday, and London, Hale, 1982.

The Bombing Run (Erridge). New York, Doubleday, and London, Hale, 1983.

The Garbage Collector (Erridge). New York, Doubleday, and London, Hale, 1984.

Novels as George Bagby (series: Inspector Schmidt in all books)

Murder at the Piano. New York, Covici Friede, 1935; London, Sampson Low, 1936.

Ring Around a Murder. New York, Covici Friede, 1936.

Murder Half Baked. New York, Covici Friede, 1937; London, Cassell, 1938.

Murder on the Nose. New York, Doubleday, 1938; London, Cassell, 1939.

Bird Walking Weather. New York, Doubleday, 1939; London, Cassell, 1940.

The Corpse with the Purple Thighs. New York, Doubleday, 1939.

The Corpse Wore a Wig. New York, Doubleday, 1940; as *The Bloody Wig Murders*, n.p., Best Detective Selection, 1942.

Here Comes the Corpse. New York, Doubleday, 1941; London, Long, 1943.

Red Is for Killing. New York, Doubleday, 1941; London, Long, 1944.

Murder Calling "50". New York, Doubleday, 1942.

Dead on Arrival. New York, Doubleday, 1946.

The Original Carcase. New York, Doubleday, 1946; London, Aldor, 1947; as *A Body for the Bride*, New York, Spivak, 1954.

The Twin Killing. New York, Doubleday, 1947.

The Starting Gun. New York, Doubleday, 1948.

In Cold Blood. New York, Doubleday, 1948.

Drop Dead. New York, Doubleday, 1949.

Coffin Corner. New York, Doubleday, 1949.

Blood Will Tell. New York, Doubleday, 1950.

Death Ain't Commercial. New York, Doubleday, 1951.

Scared to Death. New York, Doubleday, 1952.

The Corpse with Sticky Fingers. New York, Doubleday, 1952.

Give the Little Corpse a Great Big Hand. New York, Doubleday, 1953; London, Macdonald, 1954; as *A Big Hand for the Corpse*, Roslyn, New York, Detective Book Club, 1953.

Dead Drunk. New York, Doubleday, 1953; London, Macdonald, 1954.

The Body in the Basket. New York, Doubleday, 1954; London, Macdonald, 1956.

A Dirty Way to Die. New York, Doubleday, 1955; London, Macdonald, 1956; as *Shadow on the Window*, Roslyn, New York, Detective Book Club, 1955.

Dead Storage. New York, Doubleday, 1956; London, Boardman, 1959.

Cop Killer. New York, Doubleday, 1956; London, Boardman, 1957.

Dead Wrong. New York, Doubleday, 1957; London, Boardman, 1958.

The Three-Time Losers. New York, Doubleday, and London, Boardman, 1958.

The Real Gone Goose. New York, Doubleday, 1959; London, Boardman, 1960.

Evil Genius. New York, Doubleday, 1961; London, Hammond, 1964.
Murder's Little Helper. New York, Doubleday, 1963; London, Hammond, 1964.
Mysteriouser and Mysteriouser. New York, Doubleday, 1965; as *Murder in Wonderland,* London, Hammond, 1965.
Dirty Pool. New York, Doubleday, 1966; as *Bait for Killer,* London, Hammond, 1967.
Corpse Candle. New York, Doubleday, 1967; London, Hale, 1968.
Another Day—Another Death. New York, Doubleday, and London, Hale, 1968.
Honest Reliable Corpse. New York, Doubleday, and London, Hale, 1969.
Killer Boy Was Here. New York, Doubleday, 1970; London, Hale, 1971.
Two in the Bush. New York, Doubleday, and London, Hale, 1976.
Innocent Bystander. New York, Doubleday, 1976; London, Hale, 1978.
My Dead Body. New York, Doubleday, 1976; London, Hale, 1978.
The Tough Get Going. New York, Doubleday, 1977; London, Hale, 1978.
Better Dead. New York, Doubleday, 1978; London, Hale, 1979.
Guaranteed to Fade. New York, Doubleday, 1978; London, Hale, 1979.
I Could Have Died. New York, Doubleday, 1979; London, Hale, 1980.
Mugger's Day. New York, Doubleday, 1979; London, Hale, 1980.
Country and Fatal. New York, Doubleday, 1980; London, Hale, 1981.
A Question of Quarry. New York, Doubleday, and London, Hale, 1981.
The Sitting Duck. New York, Doubleday, 1981; London, Hale, 1982.
The Golden Creep. New York, Doubleday, and London, Hale, 1982.
The Most Wanted. New York, Doubleday, 1983; London, Hale, 1984.

Novels as Hampton Stone (series: Jeremiah X. Gibson and Mac in all books)

The Corpse in the Corner Saloon. New York, Simon and Schuster, 1948.
The Girl with the Hole in Her Head. New York, Simon and Schuster, 1949; London, Boardman, 1958.
The Needle That Wouldn't Hold Still. New York, Simon and Schuster, 1950; London, Boardman, 1958.
The Murder That Wouldn't Stay Solved. New York, Simon and Schuster, 1951.
The Corpse That Refused to Stay Dead. New York, Simon and Schuster, 1952; London, Dobson, 1954.
The Corpse Who Had Too Many Friends. New York, Simon and Schuster, 1953; London, Foulsham, 1954.
The Man Who Had Too Much to Lose. New York, Simon and Schuster, and London, Foulsham, 1955.
The Strangler Who Couldn't Let Go. New York, Simon and Schuster, 1956; as *The Strangler,* London, Foulsham, 1957.
The Girl Who Kept Knocking Them Dead. New York, Simon and Schuster, and London, Foulsham, 1957.
The Man Who Was Three Jumps Ahead. New York, Simon and Schuster, 1959; London, Boardman, 1960.

The Man Who Looked Death in the Eye. New York, Simon and Schuster, 1961.
The Babe with the Twistable Arm. New York, Simon and Schuster, 1962; London, Hale, 1964.
The Real Serendipitous Kill. New York, Simon and Schuster, 1964.
The Kid Was Last Seen Hanging Ten. New York, Simon and Schuster, 1966.
The Funniest Killer in Town. New York, Simon and Schuster, 1967.
The Corpse Was No Bargain at All. New York, Simon and Schuster, 1968; London, Hale, 1969.
The Swinger Who Swung by the Neck. New York, Simon and Schuster, 1970.
The Kid Who Came Home with a Corpse. New York, Simon and Schuster, 1972.

Uncollected Short Stories

"He's Never Stopped Running," in *Manhunt* (New York), June 1957.
"Battle of Wits," in *The Saint* (New York), September 1957.
"This Was Willi's Day," in *Best Detective Stories of the Year,* edited by David Coxe Cooke. New York, Dutton, 1957.
"Togetherness," in *Manhunt* (New York), January 1958.
"The Mourners at the Bedside" (as Hampton Stone), in *Ed McBain's Mystery Book 3* (New York), 1961.
"Stamped and Self-Addressed," in *Ellery Queen's Mystery Magazine* (New York), April 1979.

Uncollected Short Stories as George Bagby

"Mugshot," in *Manhunt* (New York), April 1955.
"Body Snatcher," in *Manhunt* (New York), June 1955.
"The Wife-Beater," in *Manhunt* (New York), October 1957.
"A Few Dead Birds," in *Ed McBain's Mystery Book 2* (New York), 1960.

OTHER PUBLICATIONS

Novels

Spirals. New York, Covici Friede, 1930.
Her Body Speaks. New York, Covici Friede, 1931.
Bachelor's Wife (as George Bagby). New York, Covici Friede, 1932.

Other

"The Detective Story—How and Why," in *Princeton University Library Bulletin* (New Jersey), August 1974.
"Style," in *The Mystery Writer's Handbook,* edited by Lawrence Treat. Cincinnati, Writer's Digest, 1976.
"The Mystery Story in Cultural Perspective," in *The Mystery Story,* edited by John Ball. San Diego, University of California Extension, 1976.
"A Good Address," in *I, Witness,* edited by Brian Garfield. New York, Times Books, 1978.

*

Manuscript Collection: Firestone Library, Princeton University, New Jersey.

Aaron Marc Stein commented (1984):
I began by writing radical experiments in style, stream-of-consciousness novels. They were well received by the critics,

but they reached only a small audience. Pushed by my publishers to attempt something that might bring them and me a greater monetary return, I attempted a popular romance and it was published under the George Bagby pseudonym. I found no pleasure in writing it and, although its royalties were slightly better than those on the first two books, the difference was not great enough to induce me to go on with it. At that time I found myself developing a detective story plot. Why or how it came to me I don't know. One day it just was there. Published under the Bagby pseudonym, it was a critical and popular success. I found that I enjoyed writing detective stories and with them I could reach a larger audience that had an appreciation of what I was doing. It seems to me that, with the possible exception of science fiction, the mystery story is the only form of fiction which has more than a small, select audience with any interest in a novelist's technique.

*   *   *

While hospitalized in the 1930's, Aaron Marc Stein ran out of mysteries to read. Like fellow writers S.S. Van Dine and Margaret Millar during similar periods of illness, he became convinced that he could do as well as any author he had been reading. The record shows this was no idle boast on his part for he published over one hundred novels, beginning in 1932. He created three different types of mysteries under as many names. The common element has been the success of each.

As George Bagby, Stein wrote a long series of novels about Inspector Schmidt, Chief of Manhattan's Homicide Squad. The books are narrated by a "Watson" named, appropriately, "George Bagby" whom a publisher assigned to help Schmidt write a book about his career. They became friends, and Bagby continued to travel with Schmidt to gather material for additional books. Later, Bagby operates more independently but gets into trouble and has to be rescued by Schmidt.

Typical is *The Body in the Basket* in which Bagby becomes involved in the murder of a man in a policeman's uniform at a Spanish hotel. By acting in a less than sensible manner Bagby has contributed to his predicament. He interferes in the arrest of a teenage thief and then does not report a beating he receives to the police. Yet, this book, one of the most highly regarded of the Bagby series, also shows many of Stein's virtues, e.g., the excellent interweaving of Spanish customs (ranging from the fear of Franco's political police to dining habits) into the plot.

The Body in the Basket is the exception in the Bagby series, most of which is set in the New York City area, with unusual local settings. In *The Starting Gun* and *Coffin Corner* he used the local sports scene: a track meet at Madison Square Garden and a football game at Columbia's Baker Field respectively. *Mysteriouser and Mysteriouser* is about a corpse discovered near the Alice in Wonderland statue in Central Park.

Stein tried to keep Bagby and Schmidt involved in the changes taking place in the area. Schmidt, himself, is mugged in *A Dirty Way to Die*. He gets Bagby out of trouble in *Corpse Candle* when the latter becomes involved in a hippie commune in New Jersey. More recent cases have involved organized crime in *The Most Wanted* and criminal involvement in the "sexual revolution." Times Square pornography and homosexuality are integral to *Innocent Bystander*. In *The Golden Creep* Bagby is suspected of murdering a customer of the "Topless Towers."

The Hampton Stone series is as lively as that by Bagby and shares the use of unusual titles. (An early Bagby title was *The Corpse with the Purple Thighs*.) The heroes are two Manhattan Assistant District Attorneys, Jeremiah X. Gibson and his friend, "Mac," narrator of 18 books. As Stone, Stein also uses typical Manhattan settings. *The Corpse in the Corner Saloon* is

largely about the now defunct Third Avenue bars which were once in the shadow of the "El." Murder occurs at a Greenwich Village "happening" in *The Real Serendipitous Kill*. Other diverse settings such as the 42nd Street Library (*The Funniest Killer in Town*) and Madison Square Garden on boxing night (*The Swinger Who Swung by the Neck*) are used in this engaging series.

Under his own name, Stein created two series in which he made use of the extensive travelling he has always loved. In 18 books about archeologists Tim Mulligan and Elsie Mae Hunt, Stein placed them in such locations as France in *Moonmilk and Murder* and Yucatan in *Mask for Murder*. In 1958 Stein replaced the team with engineer Matt Erridge whose occupation causes him to be continuously on the move. The Erridge books are entertaining, though marred by the hero-narrator's labored attempts to use modern argot and his tendency to reach for a funny line. One of the best in the series is the atypical *A Body for a Buddy* in which Matt stays closer to home and begins to feel his age and a generation gap when he attends the 20th reunion of his college class. He also eschews his tendency to address the reader as "Charlie." *The Bombing Run* and *Hangman's Row* find Erridge travelling again, in Belgium and the Netherlands respectively.

Though a prolific novelist, Stein rarely wrote short stories, never having had a collection published. That is unfortunate because when constrained by the shorter form, as in "This Was Willi's Day" and "Stamped and Self-Addressed" he showed a talent for characterization and plotting that exceeded that shown in his novels.

—Marvin Lachman

STERLING, Stewart. Pseudonym for Prentice Winchell; also wrote as Spencer Dean; Jay de Bekker; Dexter St. Clair; Dexter St. Clare. American. Born in Illinois, in 1895. Worked as a journalist, editor of trade publications, and journalism lecturer; wrote and produced more than 500 radio programs; also wrote for films and television. Lived in Florida. *Died.*

CRIME PUBLICATIONS

Novels (series: Fire Marshall Ben Pedley; Gil Vine)

Five Alarm Funeral (Pedley). New York, Putnam, 1942.
Down among the Dead Men. New York, Putnam, 1943; Redhill, Surrey, Wells Gardner Darton, 1949.
Where There's Smoke (Pedley). Philadelphia, Lippincott, 1946.
Dead Wrong (Vine). Philadelphia, Lippincott, 1947.
Alarm in the Night (Pedley). New York, Dutton, 1949.
Dead Sure (Vine). New York, Dutton, 1949; London, Hennel Locke, 1951.
Dead of Night (Vine). New York, Dutton, 1950.
Nightmare at Noon (Pedley). New York, Dutton, 1951.
Saratoga Mantrap (as Dexter St. Clare). New York, Fawcett, 1951.
The Big Ear. New York, Dutton, 1953; London, Boardman, 1955.
Gutter Gang (as Jay de Bekker). New York, Beacon Publications, 1954.
Keyhole Peeper (as Jay de Bekker). New York, Beacon Publications, 1955.

Alibi Baby (Vine). New York, Washburn, and London, Boardman, 1955.

The Hinges of Hell (Pedley). New York, Washburn, 1955; London, Boardman, 1956.

Dead Right (Vine). Philadelphia, Lippincott, 1956; London, Boardman, 1957; as *The Hotel Murders,* New York, Avon, 1957.

Candle for a Corpse (Pedley). Philadelphia, Lippincott, 1957; London, Boardman, 1958; as *Too Hot to Kill,* New York, Avon, 1958.

Dead to the World (Vine). Philadelphia, Lippincott, 1958; London, Boardman, 1959; as *The Blonde in Suite 14,* New York, Avon, 1959.

Fire on Fear Street (Pedley). Philadelphia, Lippincott, 1958; London, Boardman, 1959.

The Body in the Bed (Vine). Philadelphia, Lippincott, 1959; London, Boardman, 1960.

Dead Certain (Vine; 2 novelettes). New York, Ace, 1960.

Dying Room Only (Pedley). New York, Ace, 1960.

Too Hot to Handle (Pedley). New York, Random House, 1961; London, Boardman, 1962.

The Lady's Not for Living (as Dexter St. Clair). New York, Fawcett, 1963; London, Muller, 1964.

Novels as Spencer Dean (series: Don Cadee in all books)

The Frightened Fingers. New York, Washburn, 1954; London, Boardman, 1955.

The Scent of Fear. New York, Washburn, 1954; London, Boardman, 1956; as *The Smell of Fear,* New York, Spivak, 1956.

Marked Down for Murder. New York, Doubleday, 1956; London, Boardman, 1957.

Murder on Delivery. New York, Doubleday, 1957; London, Boardman, 1958.

Dishonor among Thieves. New York, Doubleday, 1958; London, Boardman, 1959.

The Merchant of Murder. New York, Doubleday, 1959; London, Boardman, 1960.

Price Tag for Murder. New York, Doubleday, 1959; London, Boardman, 1960.

Murder after a Fashion. New York, Doubleday, 1960; London, Boardman, 1961.

Credit for a Murder. New York, Doubleday, 1961; London, Boardman, 1962.

Uncollected Short Stories

"Strictly for Suckers," May 1939, "Kill a Man Dead," July 1939, "Straight Across the Board," December 1939, "Ten Carats of Lead," August 1940, "Coat of Many Killers," December 1940, "The Platinum Pig," March 1941, "Over My Dead Body," June 1941, "Don't Bury Me at All," November 1941, "Kindly Omit Flowers," March 1942, "Blow the Man Down," July 1942, "Bullets, Back to Back," December 1942, "Dead as a Duck," July 1943, all in *Black Mask* (New York).

"Blood Feeds the Flames," in *Detective Tales 107* (London), 1948–49.

"Never Come Mourning," in *Four-and-Twenty Bloodhounds,* edited by Anthony Boucher. New York, Simon and Schuster, 1950; London, Hammond, 1951.

"Dead Right," in *Mercury* (New York), February 1956.

"The Well-Mannered Monster," in *The Saint* (New York), May 1957.

"Murder Comes to the Plaza Royal," in *Mike Shayne Mystery Magazine* (New York), August 1957.

"Frankie and Various Johnnies," in *The Saint* (London), December 1958.

"The Big Deal," in *The Saint Mystery Library 7* (New York), 1959.

"The Hinges of Hell," in *Mercury* (New York), February 1959.

"Corpse Doctor," in *The Saint* (London), January 1962.

"Dying Room Only," in *The Saint* (London), September 1962.

"Homicides—Hot Off the Griddle," in *The Saint* (New York), April 1964.

OTHER PUBLICATIONS

Other

I Was a House Detective, with Dev Collans. New York, Dutton, 1954.

Blaze Battlers (for children). New York, Prentice Hall, 1955.

Danger! Detectives Working (as Prentice Winchell). New York, Coward McCann, 1955.

Kick of the Wheel (for children). Englewood Cliffs, New Jersey, Prentice Hall, 1957.

Fifty Fathom Klondike (for children). New York, Funk and Wagnalls, 1959.

*   *   *

The prolific Prentice Winchell, writing most often as Stewart Sterling, created a unique niche for himself in the mass of crime fiction by specializing in unusual professional detectives: a fire marshal (the Ben Pedley series), a hotel detective (the Gil Vine series), a department store detective (the Don Cadee books, as by Spencer Dean), the New York harbor police (*Down among the Dead Men*).

Sterling wrote hundreds of short stories and novelettes for the detective pulps, most notably *Black Mask*. "Gimmick" detectives were a pulp staple, but Sterling was one of the few pulp professionals who was able to carry such characters over to the hardcover market successfully. His best-known series, with Chief Fire Marshal Pedley, began in the pulps, and carried over to nine novels. Ben Pedley is a humorless, hardbitten, veteran smoke-eater driven by an almost pathological hatred of arsonists. Novels such as *Where There's Smoke* and *Five Alarm Funeral* invariably begin with a major fire, with Pedley fearlessly charging into the teeth of it to salvage evidence. From that point the narrative takes off non-stop, as Pedley runs down leads and suspects, fighting injury, lack of sleep, and pressure from city hall. The headlong pace, complex plots, and snappy dialogue (a mixture of firefighter jargon and Broadway sharpie slang) are all hallmarks of pulp style, which Sterling had down pat. Sterling's evidently thorough research into the workings of fire departments and arson investigation lend interest and credibility to the stories.

The Gil Vine books are much the same in style and pace. Here the backstairs world of a large New York hotel, the "Plaza Royale," forms the backdrop. Vine is closer to the stereotypical private eye in character than is Pedley. He's younger, has an eye for the ladies, and is fond of wise-cracks. The stories are told in the first person, the narrative strongly spiced with slang of Walter Winchell variety ("Killercycle draymas" for radio detective shows, for instance). Vine's cases usually begin with a body in the bed (*The Body in the Bed,* obviously) or corpse in a hotel closet (*Dead of Night*), and proceed full speed from there. Vine invariably has to contend with pressure from the hotel's management, and from cops unsympathetic to his attempts to salvage the hotel's reputation while solving a murder or two.

Sterling's other major series, the Don Cadee store detective novels under the Spencer Dean pseudonym, are similar in structure but a bit different in style and tone. The pulpish elements are somewhat less evident, and the books seem to be slanted more to a female audience (the influence of the "slick" magazine market, apparently). There's usually a damsel-in-distress character, for instance (the "damsels" in the Gil Vine novels are usually cheating wives or Broadway bimbos). Cadee might nab her on a shoplifting charge at the outset—as in *Dishonor among Thieves,* or *Murder after a Fashion*—then find himself working to get her out of trouble for the rest of the novel. These books seem somewhat more routine than the Pedley and Vine novels, though again the behind-the-scenes look at the operation of a big department store ("Amblett's") provides novelty and interest.

Sterling was one of the best of the second-line pulp professionals—Frank Gruber and Frank Kane are other examples. They were not innovators or master stylists like Hammett and Chandler, nor were they wildly successful, like Erle Stanley Gardner. They were nuts-and-bolts writers, who could be relied upon to produce solid, entertaining detective stories, whether for the pulps, hardcover or paperback, radio or television. Sterling's novels seem somewhat dated now (even into the 1960's they were "pure forties" in character), but otherwise they hold up well—in part because of the fascinating background he created for his specialized detectives, principally because of his no-nonsense storytelling skill.

—Art Scott

STERN, Richard Martin. American. Born in Fresno, California, 17 March 1915. Educated at Harvard University, Cambridge, Massachusetts, 1933–36. Married Dorothy Helen Atherton in 1937; one adopted daughter. General Advertising, Hearst Corporation, 1936–37; dehydrator foreman, Boothe Fruit Company, Modesto, California, 1938–39; engineer, Lockheed Aircraft, Burbank, California, 1940–45. Self-employed writer. President, Mystery Writers of America, 1971; Member, Editorial Board, *The Writer,* Boston. Recipient: Mystery Writers of America Edgar Allan Poe Award, 1958. Agent: Brandt and Brandt, 1501 Broadway, New York, New York 10036; or, A.M. Health & Co. Inc., 40–42 King William IV Street, London WC2N 4DD, England. Address: Route 9, Box 55, Santa Fe, New Mexico 87501, U.S.A.

CRIME PUBLICATIONS

Novels (series: Johnny Ortiz)

The Bright Road to Fear. New York, Ballantine, 1958; London, Secker and Warburg, 1959.
Suspense: Four Short Novels. New York, Ballantine, 1959.
The Search for Tabitha Carr. New York, Scribner, and London, Secker and Warburg, 1960.
These Unlucky Deeds. New York, Scribner, 1961; as *Quidnunc County,* London, Eyre and Spottiswoode, 1961.
High Hazard. New York, Scribner, 1962.
Cry Havoc. New York, Scribner, 1963; London, Cassell, 1964.
Right Hand Opposite. New York, Scribner, 1964.
I Hide, We Seek. New York, Scribner, 1965; London, Deutsch, 1966.

The Kessler Legacy. New York, Scribner, 1967; London, Cassell, 1968.
Merry Go Round. New York, Scribner, 1969; London, Cassell, 1970.
Manuscript for Murder. New York, Scribner, 1970; London, Hale, 1973.
Murder in the Walls (Ortiz). New York, Scribner, 1971; London, Hale, 1973.
You Don't Need an Enemy (Ortiz). New York, Scribner, 1971; London, Hale, 1973.
Death in the Snow (Ortiz). New York, Scribner, 1973; London, Hale, 1974.
Wildfire. London, Secker and Warburg, 1985; New York, Norton, 1986.
Tsunami (Ortiz). London, Secker and Warburg, and New York, Norton, 1988.
Tangled Murders (Ortiz). New York, Pocket Books, 1989.
Missing Man (Ortiz). New York, Pocket Books, 1990.
Interloper (Ortiz). New York, Pocket Books, 1990.

Uncollected Short Story

"Present for Minna," in *Crime Without Murder,* edited by Dorothy Salisbury Davis. New York, Scribner, 1970.

OTHER PUBLICATIONS

Novels

Brood of Eagles. Cleveland, World, 1969; London, Secker and Warburg, 1976.
Stanfield Harvest. Cleveland, World, 1972; London, Secker and Warburg, 1974.
The Tower. New York, McKay, and London, Secker and Warburg, 1973.
Power. New York, McKay, and London, Secker and Warburg, 1975.
The Will. New York, Doubleday, and London, Secker and Warburg, 1976.
Snowbound Six. New York, Doubleday, 1977; London, Panther, 1979.
Flood. New York, Doubleday, and London, Secker and Warburg, 1979.
The Big Bridge. New York, Doubleday, 1982; London, Secker and Warburg, 1983.

*

Manuscript Collection: Mugar Memorial Library, Boston University.

Richard Martin Stern comments:
Personal statement? I can do no better than to quote Eric Ambler and John D. MacDonald. Ambler said on a panel in London in 1975, "I write for a living, and I write what I can." John D. wrote (I paraphrase), "When you do what you would rather do than anything else, tell stories, and people pay you for it—that is a license to steal." To both statements, Amen.

* * *

One of the most inventive and respected writers of the American mystery is Richard Martin Stern. Before becoming identified with the novel, he was a successful magazine writer, both in short and long stories. Regularly featured in *Good Housekeeping* and *The Saturday Evening Post,* he also wrote for most of the other top-ranking fiction magazines of the time. His first novel, *The Bright Road to Fear,* won an Edgar.

Stern continued writing mystery and suspense novels throughout the 1960's. Among the foremost of his works was *Cry Havoc,* a psychological suspense story of the effect of crime on a small town. His re-creation of the town and its people was exceptional. In the 1960's he also wrote a number of suspense-oriented espionage tales, such as *I Hide, We Seek,* with its background of the Scottish Highlands. Stern has traveled widely and has resided in many of the colorful places of which he has written. His backgrounds are as important as the story lines of his plots. After moving to Santa Fe, New Mexico in the mid-1960's, he soon developed a new series against the Spanish-Indian-Anglo background, with a detective indigenous to the scene.

In the 1970's Stern temporarily abandoned the mystery story to write *The Tower.* He did not, however, abandon suspense in this story of a skyscraper whose construction was flawed through business and political short cuts. In *Wildfire* a single bolt of lightning strikes a tree in Sanrio National Park starting the wildland fire known as *Backslope.* Stern, once again, writes a gripping suspenseful novel in which his characters are driven to a state of abject terror.

Stern's style is not influenced by fads and fancies. He writes the prose of an educated, intelligent man, who has a keen curiosity as to the whys of events, a curiosity only to be satisfied by solving the puzzles propounded.

—Dorothy B. Hughes

———

STERN, Stuart. *See* **RAE, Hugh C.**

———

STEVENS, R.L. *See* **HOCH, Edward D.**

———

STEWART, J.I.M. *See* **INNES, Michael.**

———

STEWART, Jay. *See* **PALMER, Stuart.**

———

STEWART, Mary (Florence Elinor, née Rainbow). British. Born in Sunderland, County Durham, 17 September 1916. Educated at Eden Hall, Penrith, Cumberland; Skellfield School, Ripon, Yorkshire; St. Hild's College, University of Durham, B.A. (honours) 1938, M.A. 1941. Served in the Royal Observer Corps during World War II. Married Sir Frederick Henry Stewart in 1945. Lecturer in English, Durham University, 1941-45; Part-time Lecturer in English, St. Hild's

Training College, Durham, and Durham University, 1948-56. Recipient: Crime Writers Association Silver Dagger award, 1961; Frederick Niven Award, 1971; Scottish Arts Council Award, 1975. Fellow, Royal Society of Arts, 1968; Fellow, Newnham College, Cambridge, 1986. Address: c/o Hodder and Stoughton Ltd., Mill Road, Dunton Green, Sevenoaks, Kent TN13 2YA, England.

CRIME PUBLICATIONS

Novels

Madam, Will You Talk? London, Hodder and Stoughton, 1955; New York, Mill, 1956.
Wildfire at Midnight. London, Hodder and Stoughton, and New York, Appleton Century Crofts, 1956.
Thunder on the Right. London, Hodder and Stoughton, 1957; New York, Mill, 1958.
Nine Coaches Waiting. London, Hodder and Stoughton, 1958; New York, Mill, 1959.
My Brother Michael. London, Hodder and Stoughton, and New York, Mill, 1960.
The Ivy Tree. London, Hodder and Stoughton, 1961; New York, Mill, 1962.
The Moon-Spinners. London, Hodder and Stoughton, 1962; New York, Mill, 1963.
This Rough Magic. London, Hodder and Stoughton, and New York, Mill, 1964.
Airs above the Ground. London, Hodder and Stoughton, and New York, Mill, 1965.
The Gabriel Hounds. London, Hodder and Stoughton, and New York, Mill, 1967.
Touch Not the Cat. London, Hodder and Stoughton, and New York, Morrow, 1976.
Thornyhold. London, Hodder and Stoughton, and New York, Morrow, 1988.

OTHER PUBLICATIONS

Novels

The Wind off the Small Isles. London, Hodder and Stoughton, 1968.
The Crystal Cave. London, Hodder and Stoughton, and New York, Morrow, 1970.
The Hollow Hills. London, Hodder and Stoughton, and New York, Morrow, 1973.
The Last Enchantment. London, Hodder and Stoughton, and New York, Morrow, 1979.
The Wicked Day. London, Hodder and Stoughton, and New York, Morrow, 1983.

Plays

Radio Plays: *Lift from a Stranger, Call Me at Ten-Thirty, The Crime of Mr. Merry,* and *The Lord of Langdale,* 1957-58.

Other (for children)

The Little Broomstick. Leicester, Brockhampton Press, 1971; New York, Morrow, 1972.
Ludo and the Star Horse. Leicester, Brockhampton Press, 1974; New York, Morrow, 1975.

A Walk in Wolf Wood. London, Hodder and Stoughton, and New York, Morrow, 1980.

*

Manuscript Collection: National Library of Scotland, Edinburgh.

* * *

Mary Stewart's long and successful career as a writer breaks into two parts. In her earlier period, she wrote a remarkable series of 10 popular novels of romantic suspense (*Madam, Will You Talk?, Wildfire at Midnight, Thunder on the Right, Nine Coaches Waiting, My Brother Michael, The Ivy Tree, The Moon-Spinners, This Rough Magic, Airs above the Ground*, and *The Gabriel Hounds*). In her later phase, beginning in the late 1960s, Stewart's novels have been concerned with history and frequently with the occult. Her best-known work from this period is her four-volume series about King Arthur and Merlin (*The Crystal Cave, The Hollow Hills, The Last Enchantment*, and *The Wicked Day*), but she has also published children's fiction and two mysteries (*Touch Not the Cat* and *Thornyhold*).

As a mystery writer, Stewart earns frequent praise from critics. "No one writes the damsel-in-distress tale with greater charm or urgency," wrote Anthony Boucher, reviewing *The Ivy Tree.* Unlike many other romantic suspense writers, she has an audience that includes male readers. Her mysteries are carefully crafted—a year or more in the writing of each—with particular attention to descriptive detail, intelligent plot development, and rich characterization.

Although Stewart's works may resemble the modern gothic formula, they clearly transcend it. Thoroughly contemporary, her heroines innocently embark on an adventure that quickly turns sinister. Most often, the terrifying events occur while the protagonists are cut off from safety in an exotic locale, such as Greece (*My Brother Michael*), Crete (*The Moon-Spinners*), the Pyrenees (*Thunder on the Right*), Lebanon (*The Gabriel Hounds*), or the Isle of Skye (*Wildfire at Midnight*). In *Nine Coaches Waiting,* Stewart employs a modern version of the classic governess tale; and in *The Ivy Tree* and *Touch Not the Cat,* her characters return to their ancestral English homes to find danger. In each book, the heroines must solve the mystery in order to save others as well as themselves. Often, the threatened victim is an adolescent or a young child, offering the heroine a strongly protective or maternal role to play. The novels usually conclude with a harrowing chase across unfamiliar terrain during which the villain is exposed and defeated. In the early phase, all Stewart's mysteries had rational solutions; the two from the later phase, however, feature heroines with mild powers of extrasensory perception. Although she draws on the traditions of genre fiction, Stewart almost always avoids cliché.

The love story is integral to Stewart's plots, for it is only through exposing the villain and vindicating the hero that the moral order of her fictional world can be revealed and restored. In *Nine Coaches Waiting* the heroine suspects the hero of attempting to murder her young charge. In *Airs above the Ground* the wife has reason to distrust her husband's honesty. In each case, the unmasking of the real villain allows the heroine to trust the hero as well as to love him. Without subservience, Stewart's heroines operate within a conventional value system. Confronted with someone else's trouble, each of them chooses to help rather than walk away.

One of Stewart's finest qualities as a writer is her extraordinary descriptive prose. Stewart's ability to evoke a highly specific time and place, through sensuous descriptions of locale, character, and food, provides an immediacy that is often lacking in mystery fiction. Her academic background in English literature lends thematic and dramatic elements in the epigrams to her chapters and the literary allusions within the works. *This Rough Magic* summons images from Shakespeare's *The Tempest*; *My Brother Michael*, set in Greece, draws on Greek tragedy; *Wildfire at Midnight* uses ancient pagan rites described in Frazer's *The Golden Bough*; *Nine Coaches Waiting* evokes both *Jane Eyre* and the Cinderella tale. Several of her heroes are named from British romantic poets.

Although Stewart's earliest novels were first published in 1956, most of her work remains in print, an unusual achievement for a genre writer.

—Kay Mussell

———

STONE, Hampton. *See* **STEIN, Aaron Marc.**

———

STONE, Lesley. *See* **HALL, Adam.**

———

STONE, Zachary. *See* **FOLLETT, Ken.**

———

STOUT, Rex (Todhunter). American. Born in Noblesville, Indiana, 1 December 1886. Educated at Topeka High School, Kansas; University of Kansas, Lawrence. Served in the United States Navy as a Yeoman on President Theodore Roosevelt's yacht, 1906–08. Married 1) Fay Kennedy in 1916 (divorced 1933); 2) Pola Hoffman in 1933; two daughters. Worked as an office boy, store clerk, bookkeeper, hotel manager, 1916–27; invented the banking system for school children; full-time writer from 1927. Founding director, Vanguard Press, New York; host, *Speaking of Liberty, Voice of Freedom,* and *Our Secret Weapon* radio programs, 1941–43. Chairman of the Writers' War Board, 1941–46, and the World Government Writers Board, 1949–75; President, Friends of Democracy, 1941–51, Authors' Guild, 1943–45, and Society for the Prevention of World War III, 1943–46; President, 1951–55, 1962–69, and Vice-President, 1956–61, Authors League of America; Treasurer, Freedom House, 1957–75; President, Mystery Writers of America, 1958. Recipient: Mystery Writers of America Grand Master award, 1959. *Died 27 October 1975.*

CRIME PUBLICATIONS

Novels (series: Tecumseh Fox; Nero Wolfe)

Fer-de-Lance (Wolfe). New York, Farrar and Rinehart, 1934; London, Cassell, 1935.

The President Vanishes (published anonymously). New York, Farrar and Rinehart, 1934.

The League of Frightened Men (Wolfe). New York, Farrar and Rinehart, and London, Cassell, 1935.

The Rubber Band (Wolfe). New York, Farrar and Rinehart, and London, Cassell, 1936; as *To Kill Again,* New York, Curl, 1960.

The Red Box (Wolfe). New York, Farrar and Rinehart, and London, Cassell, 1937.

The Hand in the Glove. New York, Farrar and Rinehart, 1937; as *Crime on Her Hands,* London, Collins, 1939.

Too Many Cooks (Wolfe). New York, Farrar and Rinehart, and London, Collins, 1938.

Some Buried Caesar (Wolfe). New York, Farrar and Rinehart, and London, Collins, 1938; as *The Red Bull,* New York, Dell, 1945.

Mountain Cat. New York, Farrar and Rinehart, 1939; London, Collins, 1940; as *The Mountain Cat Murders*, New York, Dell, 1943.

Double for Death (Fox). New York, Farrar and Rinehart, 1939; London, Collins, 1940.

Red Threads, in *The Mystery Book.* New York, Farrar and Rinehart, 1940; London, Collins, 1945.

Over My Dead Body (Wolfe). New York, Farrar and Rinehart, and London, Collins, 1940.

Bad for Business (Fox), in *The Second Mystery Book.* New York, Farrar and Rinehart, 1940; London, Collins, 1945.

Where There's a Will (Wolfe). New York, Farrar and Rinehart, 1940; London, Collins, 1941.

The Broken Vase (Fox). New York, Farrar and Rinehart, 1941; London, Collins, 1942.

Alphabet Hicks. New York, Farrar and Rinehart, 1941; London, Collins, 1942; as *The Sound of Murder,* New York, Pyramid, 1965.

Black Orchids (novelettes; Wolfe). New York, Farrar and Rinehart, 1942; London, Collins, 1943.

Not Quite Dead Enough (novelettes; Wolfe). New York, Farrar and Rinehart, 1944.

The Silent Speaker (Wolfe). New York, Viking Press, 1946; London, Collins, 1947.

Too Many Women (Wolfe). New York, Viking Press, 1947; London, Collins, 1948.

And Be a Villain (Wolfe). New York, Viking Press, 1948; as *More Deaths Than One,* London, Collins, 1949.

The Second Confession (Wolfe). New York, Viking Press, 1949; London, Collins, 1950.

Trouble in Triplicate (novelettes; Wolfe). New York, Viking Press, and London, Collins, 1949.

Three Doors to Death (novelettes; Wolfe). New York, Viking Press, and London, Collins, 1950.

In the Best Families (Wolfe). New York, Viking Press, 1950; as *Even in the Best Families,* London, Collins, 1951.

Curtains for Three (novelettes; Wolfe). New York, Viking Press, 1950; London, Collins, 1951.

Murder by the Book (Wolfe). New York, Viking Press, 1951; London, Collins, 1952.

Triple Jeopardy (novelettes; Wolfe). New York, Viking Press, 1951; London, Collins, 1952.

Prisoner's Base (Wolfe). New York, Viking Press, 1952; as *Out Goes She,* London, Collins, 1953.

The Golden Spiders (Wolfe). New York, Viking Press, 1953; London, Collins, 1954.

Three Men Out (novelettes; Wolfe). New York, Viking Press, 1954; London, Collins, 1955.

The Black Mountain (Wolfe). New York, Viking Press, 1954; London, Collins, 1955.

Before Midnight (Wolfe). New York, Viking Press, 1955; London, Collins, 1956.

Might As Well Be Dead (Wolfe). New York, Viking Press, 1956; London, Collins, 1957.

Three Witnesses (novelettes; Wolfe). New York, Viking Press, and London, Collins, 1956.

Three for the Chair (novelettes; Wolfe). New York, Viking Press, 1957; London, Collins, 1958.

If Death Ever Slept (Wolfe). New York, Viking Press, 1957; London, Collins, 1958.

Champagne for One (Wolfe). New York, Viking Press, 1958; London, Collins, 1959.

And Four to Go (novelettes; Wolfe). New York, Viking Press, 1958; as *Crime and Again,* London, Collins, 1959.

Plot It Yourself (Wolfe). New York, Viking Press, 1959; as *Murder in Style,* London, Collins, 1960.

Three at Wolfe's Door (novelettes; Wolfe). New York, Viking Press, 1960; London, Collins, 1961.

Too Many Clients (Wolfe). New York, Viking Press, 1960; London, Collins, 1961.

The Final Deduction (Wolfe). New York, Viking Press, 1961; London, Collins, 1962.

Gambit (Wolfe). New York, Viking Press, 1962; London, Collins, 1963.

Homicide Trinity (novelettes; Wolfe). New York, Viking Press, 1962; London, Collins, 1963.

The Mother Hunt (Wolfe). New York, Viking Press, 1963; London, Collins, 1964.

Trio for Blunt Instruments (novelettes; Wolfe). New York, Viking Press, 1964; London, Collins, 1965.

A Right to Die (Wolfe). New York, Viking 1964; London, Collins, 1965.

The Doorbell Rang (Wolfe). New York, Viking Press, 1965; London, Collins, 1966.

Death of a Doxy (Wolfe). New York, Viking Press, 1966; London, Collins, 1967.

The Father Hunt (Wolfe). New York, Viking Press, 1968; London, Collins, 1969.

Death of a Dude (Wolfe). New York, Viking Press, 1969; London, Collins, 1970.

Please Pass the Guilt (Wolfe). New York, Viking Press, 1973; London, Collins, 1974.

A Family Affair (Wolfe). New York, Viking Press, 1975; London, Collins, 1976.

Short Stories

Justice Ends at Home and Other Stories, edited by John McAleer. New York, Viking Press, 1977.

OTHER PUBLICATIONS

Novels

Her Forbidden Knight, in *All-Story Magazine* (New York), August–December 1913.

Under the Andes, in *All-Story Magazine* (New York), February 1914; New York, Mysterious Press, 1985.

A Prize for Princes, in *All-Story Weekly* (New York), 7 March–30 May 1914.

The Great Legend, in *All-Story Weekly* (New York), 1 January–29 January 1916.

How Like a God. New York, Vanguard Press, 1929.

Seed on the Wind. New York, Vanguard Press, 1930.

Golden Remedy. New York, Vanguard Press, 1931.

Forest Fire. New York, Farrar and Rinehart, 1933.
O Careless Love! New York, Farrar and Rinehart, 1935.
Mr. Cinderella. New York, Farrar and Rinehart, 1938.

Other

The Nero Wolfe Cook Book, with others. New York, Viking
Press, 1973.
Corsage (miscellany). N.p., Rock, 1977.

Editor, The Illustrious Dunderheads. New York, Knopf, 1942.
Editor, with Louis Greenfield, Rue Morgue No. 1. New York,
Creative Age Press, 1946.
Editor, Eat, Drink, and Be Buried. New York, Viking Press,
1956; as For Tomorrow We Die, London, Macdonald, 1958.

*

Bibliography: Rex Stout: An Annotated Primary and Secondary
Bibliography by Guy M. Townsend, New York, Garland, 1980.

Manuscript Collection: University of North Carolina Libraries, Chapel Hill.

Critical Studies: Nero Wolfe of West Thirty-Fifth Street: The
Life and Times of America's Largest Private Detective by William
S. Baring-Gould, New York, Viking Press, 1969; Rex Stout: A
Bibliography by John McAleer, Boston, Little Brown, 1977; The
Brownstone House of Nero Wolfe by Ken Darby, Boston, Little
Brown, 1983; Rex Stout by David R. Anderson, New York,
Ungar, 1984.

*   *   *

Rex Stout's writing covered a broad spectrum, from
mainstream novels to science fiction, but the bulk of his writing
was in the mystery field. Here his range was also broad,
covering a number of non-series and short series novels and
short stories. These items are not without merit, but neither do
they stand up to comparison with Stout's greatest achievement,
the Nero Wolfe series, nearly 40 each of novels and short stories
which comprise the most outstanding achievement in the
mystery field in the post-Holmes era.

Without doubt, 221B Baker Street is the most famous
fictional address in the history of literature. For all its fame,
however, the Baker Street address must yield pride of place in
matters of careful and loving delineation to Nero Wolfe's
Manhattan brownstone, uncertainly located somewhere on
West 35th Street. There, not just one room—as is the case with
the Baker Street flat—but the entire house becomes familiar as
the series progresses: the chef's quarters and the billiard room
in the basement; the office, front room, kitchen and dining
room on the ground floor; the bedrooms on the next two floors;
the plant rooms and gardener's quarters on the roof. And not
just the rooms themselves, but (with the exceptions of the chef's
and the gardener's quarters) their very contents and even the
arrangement of those contents becomes familiar to the follower
of the series, until he is as much at home in the brownstone as in
his own abode. Of course, like the Baker Street flat, the
brownstone achieves immortality not it its own right but as the
home and headquarters of a remarkable man, and as the focus
of many an interesting and entertaining tale. The stories are
memorable for their ingenuity, their well-drawn, substantial
characters, the wit and wisdom which Stout sprinkles liberally
throughout, and, to a very large degree, the relationship which
exists between its two principal characters.

Conan Doyle used Watson principally to shine light on
Holmes. No such lop-sidedness exists in the Saga. It is the Nero

Wolfe Saga, unquestionably; he is the eccentric genius, not
Archie. But their relationship is symbiotic—Wolfe could
continue to function without Archie (as he did before their
paths crossed), and Archie could make it on his own as a
private detective (as, indeed, he does at one point in the Saga).
But the two function most effectively together, which is part of
the reason why someone of Archie's capacities would be
content working for Wolfe rather than on his own. The rest of
the reason goes beyond professional considerations to what
may be the greatest charm of the series: Wolfe and Archie are
friends. What began as an employer/employee relationship
quickly developed beyond that; as each came to appreciate the
other's abilities and capacities, affection—though rarely
admitted—grew between them and developed at length into
that very rare thing, manly love. (The suggestion that their
relationship was a homosexual one rates mentioning only to be
dismissed.) They are very important parts of each other's lives,
and although their behavior toward each other is frequently
antagonistic it does not disguise the fact that the underlying
foundation of their relationship is respect and deep affection.

Wolfe is a polymath, a misogynist, and a man of great though
discerning appetite. Wolfe is in his fifties; his weight hovers
around a seventh of a ton, kept there by the consumption of
large quantities of the best food in North America, prepared by
the priceless Fritz Brenner, and by the downing of gallons of
beer daily. He is also an omnivorous reader, frequently reading
several books at the same time (and committing the appalling
barbarity of dog-earing their pages), and he is a passionate
orchid fancier, spending two hours every morning and
afternoon in the rooftop plant rooms among his 10,000 plants.
His various eccentricities include a reluctance to leave the
house on business and an aversion, almost a phobia, to
travelling in any mechanized vehicle. And he is a genius at
solving problems, usually murders, when he can overcome his
chronic laziness regarding matters of business.

Which is where Archie comes in. Tall, fit, handsome, and in
his early thirties, Archie Goodwin does Wolfe's leg work for
him, combining a respectable intelligence with considerable
cunning and native wit to produce results on even some of
Wolfe's more unreasonable instructions. But Archie does not
merely carry out Wolfe's instructions—he frequently has to
goad his employer into giving them. Whenever the bank
balance drops too low, or whenever Archie thinks Wolfe has
been loafing long enough, he goads and prods and generally
annoys Wolfe until at last the great man gives in and
undertakes—often with the worst possible grace—whatever
case Archie has decided he should tackle. And while Wolfe
supplies the genius which solves the case, there is no doubt that
he appreciates the talents and resources of his capable, if
frequently worrisome, assistant. As the narrator of the tales,
Archie supplies entertaining commentary and he contributes
substantially to the highly witty dialogue which is one of the
hallmarks of the series.

Wolfe and Archie are joined by a host of well-drawn minor
and not-so-minor regular characters. These include Inspector
Cramer, whose reaction to Wolfe's involvement in murder
cases ranges from mere impatience to outright rage; Saul
Panzer, an innocuous-looking but supremely effective freelance private detective; Lily Rowan, Archie's sometime
girlfriend, who achieved the remarkable feat of necking with
Wolfe in the back seat of an automobile; and Fritz Brenner,
Wolfe's majordomo and chef par excellence.

Stout had a wonderful gift for creating realistic characters
and interesting his readers in their lives. Indeed, these
characters and the dialogue between them really make the
Nero Wolfe tales. The story plots are usually more than
adequate and are sometimes very good indeed, but without

these incomparable characters they would not be especially memorable. With them, the Saga is not merely memorable, it is immortal.

—Guy M. Townsend

————

STRAKER, J(ohn) F(oster). Also writes as Ian Rosse. British. Born in Farnborough, Kent, 26 March 1904. Educated at Framlingham College, Suffolk (scholar). Served in the Buffs, British Army, 1940–45: Major. Married Margaret Brydon in 1935; one son. Senior mathematics master, Kingsland Grange School, Shrewsbury, Shropshire, 1927–35; headmaster, Blackheath Preparatory School, London, 1936–39; senior mathematics master, Cumnor House School, Danehill, Sussex, 1945–78. Agent: Michael Motley Ltd., 78 Gloucester Terrace, London W2 3HH. Address: Lincoln Cottage, Horsted Keynes, Sussex RH17 7AW, England.

CRIME PUBLICATIONS

Novels (series: Johnny Inch; Inspector Pitt; David Wright)

Postman's Knock (Pitt).   London, Harrap, 1954.
Pick Up the Pieces (Pitt).   London, Harrap, 1955.
The Ginger Horse (Pitt).   London, Harrap, 1956.
A Gun to Play With (Pitt).   London, Harrap, 1956.
Good-bye, Aunt Charlotte! (Pitt).   London, Harrap, 1958.
Hell Is Empty.   London, Harrap, 1958.
Death of a Good Woman (Pitt).   London, Harrap, 1961.
Murder for Missemily (Pitt).   London, Harrap, 1961.
A Coil of Rope (Wright).   London, Harrap, 1962.
Final Witness (Wright).   London, Harrap, 1963.
The Shape of Murder.   London, Harrap, 1964.
Ricochet.   London, Harrap, 1965.
Miscarriage of Murder.   London, Harrap, 1967.
Sin and Johnny Inch.   London, Harrap, 1968.
A Man Who Cannot Kill.   London, Harrap, 1969.
Tight Circle (Inch).   London, Harrap, 1970.
A Letter for Obi (Inch).   London, Harrap, 1971.
The Goat (Inch).   London, Harrap, 1972.
Arthur's Night.   London, Hale, 1976.
Swallow Them Up.   London, Hale, 1977.
Death on a Sunday Morning.   London, Hale, 1978.
A Pity It Wasn't George.   London, Hale, 1979.
Countersnatch.   London, Hale, 1980.
Another Man's Poison.   London, Hale, 1983.
A Choice of Victims.   London, Hale, 1984.

Uncollected Short Stories

"Advanced Judgment," and "Overdose of Vanity," in *Evening Standard* (London), December 1950.
"The Key," in *Evening News* (London), August 1961.

OTHER PUBLICATIONS

Novel

The Droop (as Ian Rosse).   London, New English Library, 1972.

Other

Southeast England: Kent, Sussex.   London, Travellers Realm, 1981.

*

J.F. Straker comments:
My books have been described by one reviewer as "typically English." They are strong on character and plot, and always have an unexpected twist in the tail.
May I, in all modesty, quote from an article on me by Bill Newton, another crime writer (Darlington *Evening Despatch,* 19 May 1973): "If a panel of experts on crime-writing was asked to list the top ten authors who consistently entertain with ingenious plots and sheer brilliance in their detectives' investigation, one of these would have to be John Foster Straker. Without hesitation, I name his book, *Postman's Knock,* as one of the top twenty detective stories ever written."

*   *   *

J.F. Straker had his first novel, *Postman's Knock,* published in 1954. It featured Inspector Pitt, an elderly, sympathetic policeman, who appeared in six more books. Straker then dropped Pitt, who was "cramping his style," and the next dozen or so books varied in pattern, some strong on detection, others straightforward thrillers. Sex featured in some, but only where it helped the plot.
In 1968 he invented a new central figure, a cheerful young detective attached to a special CID squad at the Yard. He appeared in *Sin and Johnny Inch* and *Tight Circle,* then went "private" in *A Letter for Obi* and *The Goat.* Straker turned to straight fiction for a time, then returned to crime with *Arthur's Night.*
A Pity It Wasn't George deals more with the effect of murder on boys and staff at a preparatory school than with actual police work. *Another Man's Poison* is concerned more with a man's love for his wife and his desire to shield her from the consequences of the crime than with the crime itself. Again, *A Choice of Victims* is set in a small Sussex village and is mainly concerned with the effects of a murder on the community and the contrast between the characters of the policemen involved.
Straker makes his police work authentic (seeking the help of his local Sussex police) and it sometimes has a documentary air. He avoids violence for the sake of violence and usually contrives a "twist in the tail."

—Herbert Harris

————

STRANGE, Elwin. *See* **LUTZ, John.**

————

STRANGE, John Stephen. Pseudonym for Dorothy Stockbridge Tillet. American. Born in 1896.

CRIME PUBLICATIONS

Novels (series: Barney Gantt; Lieutenant/Captain George Honegger; Van Dusen Ormsberry)

The Man Who Killed Fortescue (Ormsberry). New York, Doubleday, 1928; London, Collins, 1929.
The Clue of the Second Murder (Ormsberry). New York, Doubleday, and London, Collins, 1929.
The Strangler Fig. New York, Doubleday, 1930; London, Collins, 1931; as *Murder at World's End,* New York, Novel Selections, 1943.
Murder on the Ten-Yard Line (Ormsberry). New York, Doubleday, 1931; as *Murder Game,* London, Collins, 1931.
Black Hawthorn. New York, Doubleday, 1933; as *The Chinese Jar Mystery,* London, Collins, 1934.
For the Hangman. New York, Doubleday, 1934; London, Collins, 1935.
The Bell in the Fog (Gantt). New York, Doubleday, 1936; London, Collins, 1937.
Silent Witnesses (Gantt). New York, Doubleday, 1938; as *The Corpse and the Lady,* London, Collins, 1938.
Rope Enough (Gantt). New York, Doubleday, 1938; London, Collins, 1939; as *The Ballot Box Murders,* New York, Novel Selections, 1943.
A Picture of the Victim (Gantt). New York, Doubleday, and London, Collins, 1940.
Murder Gives a Lovely Light (Honegger). New York, Doubleday, 1941; London, Collins, 1942.
Look Your Last (Gantt). New York, Doubleday, 1943; London, Collins, 1944.
Make My Bed Soon (Gantt). New York, Doubleday, and London, Collins, 1948.
All Men Are Liars (Honegger). New York, Doubleday, 1948; as *Come to Judgment,* London, Collins, 1949.
Unquiet Grave. New York, Doubleday, 1949; as *Uneasy Is the Grave,* London, Collins, 1950.
Reasonable Doubt. New York, Doubleday, and London, Collins, 1951; as *The Fair and the Dead,* New York, Spivak, 1953.
Deadly Beloved (Gantt). New York, Doubleday, and London, Collins, 1952.
Let the Dead Past—. New York, Doubleday, 1953; as *Dead End,* London, Collins, 1953.
Catch the Gold Ring. New York, Doubleday, 1955; as *A Handful of Silver,* London, Collins, 1955.
Night of Reckoning. New York, Doubleday, 1958; London, Collins, 1959.
Eye Witness (Honegger). New York, Doubleday, 1961; London, Collins, 1962.
The House on 9th Street (Gantt). New York, Doubleday, 1976.

OTHER PUBLICATIONS as Dorothy Stockbridge

Novel

Angry Dust. New York, Doubleday, 1946.

Play

Jezebel, in *Contemporary One-Act Plays of 1921,* edited by Frank Shay. Cincinnati, Stewart Kid, 1922.

Verse

Paths of June. New York, Dutton, 1920.

* * *

Starting with *The Man Who Killed Fortescue* in 1928, Dorothy Stockbridge Tillett, under the pseudonym of John Stephen Strange, wrote more than 20 mystery novels primarily in the classic puzzler tradition. Although not very well known today, her books were very popular from the 1930's to the 1950's. In fact, her third book, *The Strangler Fig,* was selected by William Lyon Phelps as one of the 10 best detective stories published from 1928 to 1933. Her books reflect the times in which they were written. Earlier books, in the best classic puzzler style, had the murder taking place early in the book. Several suspects and much passion later, the murderer was revealed in a tense drawing-room scene. Plot line of later books varied to include courtroom scenes, gangsters, and even a hurricane.

In *The Man Who Killed Fortescue,* Strange provides a slightly different slant to the murder by having the victim killed while riding on the top of a double-decker bus. The victim is an author and criminologist who had been working on a solution to a two-year-old unsolved murder. The two murders are definitely linked and Detective Van Dusen Ormsberry, aided by a juvenile Sherlock Holmes, Bill Adams, follows a course of deductive reasoning which involves the members of an exclusive men's club, a relatively unnecessary third murder, and a few romantic twists to a successful and not readily anticipated conclusion.

Black Hawthorn displays the same careful plotting but adds an element of superstitious suspense. A family heirloom threatens the bodily safety and the sanity of a seafaring family which, though steeped in tradition, has wealth based on the opium trade. Several plot twists take place and the inevitable third murder occurs before Detective Sergeant Potter of the New London Police is able to piece together the psychological portrait of the ruthless family murderer.

Her series character Barney Gantt, a Pulitzer prize-winning photographer, is introduced in *The Bell in the Fog.* Barney is unlucky in love—until he meets Muriel, the *Globe's* lonely hearts columnist—but is extremely good at unravelling complicated intrigues. He is thin, of medium height, with a sharp face dominated by an aggressive nose, very keen blue eyes, and a wide mouth. In a crowd he is indistinguishable, which is just how he likes it. Barney appears in eight novels, including Strange's last one, *The House on 9th Street.* This is a modern novel of suspense and intrigue involving a violent revolutionary youth group and their bomb factory. Barney returns home from a tour of Africa (with insights into African revolutionaries) to find Muriel recovering from a car accident and his paper, *The Globe,* embroiled in an investigation of revolutionary activities in New England. A kidnapping, a murder, and an exciting climax polish off this fast-paced novel.

—Mary Ann Grochowski

———

STRIBLING, T(homas) S(igismund). American. Born in Clifton, Tennessee, 4 March 1881. Educated at Clifton Masonic Academy; Southern Normal College, Florence, Alabama, 1902–03, graduated 1903; studied law at the University of Alabama, Tuscaloo, LL.B. 1905. Married Lou

Ella Kloss in 1930. Editor, Clifton *News,* 1900–02; teacher, Tuscaloo High School, 1903–04; lawyer in Florence, 1906–07; staff member, *Taylor-Trotwood Magazine,* Nashville, Tennessee, 1907–08; full-time writer from 1908; wrote moral stories for Sunday school magazines; lived in South America and Europe, 1908–16; reporter, Chattanooga *News,* 1917; stenographer, Aviation Bureau, Washington, D.C., 1918; Instructor in Creative Writing, Columbia University, New York, 1936, 1940; lived in Clifton after 1959. Recipient: Pulitzer prize 1933. LL.D.: Oglethorpe University, Atlanta, 1936. *Died 10 July 1965.*

CRIME PUBLICATIONS

Short Stories (series: Dr. Poggioli)

Clues of the Caribbees, Being Certain Criminal Investigations of Henry Poggioli, Ph.D. New York, Doubleday, 1929; London, Heinemann, 1930.
Best Dr. Poggioli Detective Stories. New York, Dover, 1975; London, Dover, 1976.

Uncollected Short Stories

"A Pearl at Pampatar," in *Adventure,* 1 June 1929.
"Shadowed," in *Adventure,* 15 October 1930.
"Bullets," in *Adventure,* 1 May 1932.
"The Pink Colonnade," in *Adventure,* 1 February 1933.
"Private Jungle," in *Blue Book,* August 1933.
"The Resurrection of Chin Lee," in *101 Years' Entertainment,* edited by Ellery Queen. Boston, Little Brown, 1941.
"The Cablegram," in *Best Stories from Ellery Queen's Mystery Magazine.* Roslyn, New York, Detective Book Club, 1944.
"The Mystery of the Paper Wad," in *Ellery Queen's Mystery Magazine* (New York), July 1946.
"The Shadow," in *20th Century Detective Stories,* edited by Ellery Queen. Cleveland, World, 1948.
"Judge Lynch," in *Ellery Queen's Mystery Magazine* (New York), September 1950.
"The Mystery of the Choir Boy," in *Ellery Queen's Mystery Magazine* (New York), January 1951.
"Death Deals Diamonds," in *Famous Detective Stories,* November 1952.
"Figures Don't Die," in *Famous Detective Stories,* February 1953.
"Dead Wrong," in *Smashing Detective Stories,* March 1953.
"The Mystery of the Five Money Orders," in *Ellery Queen's Mystery Magazine* (New York), March 1954.
"Murder at Flowtide," in *The Saint* (New York), March 1955.
"Murder in the Hills," in *The Saint* (New York), February 1956.

OTHER PUBLICATIONS

Novels

The Cruise of the Dry Dock. Chicago, Reilly and Britton, 1917.
Birthright. New York, Century, 1922; London, Collins, 1925.
Fombombo. New York, Century, and London, Nisbet, 1923.
Red Sand. New York, Harcourt Brace, and London, Nisbet, 1924.
Teeftallow. New York, Doubleday, and London, Nisbet, 1926.
Bright Metal. New York, Doubleday, and London, Nisbet, 1928.
East Is East. New York, L. Harper Allen, 1928.

Strange Moon. New York, Doubleday, and London, Heinemann, 1929.
Backwater. New York, Doubleday, and London, Heinemann, 1930.
The Forge. New York, Doubleday, and London, Heinemann, 1931.
The Store. New York, Doubleday, and London, Heinemann, 1932.
Unfinished Cathedral. New York, Doubleday, and London, Heinemann, 1934.
The Sound Wagon. New York, Doubleday, 1935; London, Gollancz, 1936.
These Bars of Flesh. New York, Doubleday, 1938.

Play

Rope, with David Wallace, adaptation of the novel *Teeftallow* by Stribling (produced New York, 1928).

Other

Laughing Stock: The Posthumous Autobiography of T.S. Stribling, edited by Randy K. Cross and John T. McMillan. Memphis, Tennessee, St. Luke's Press, 1982.

*

Critical Study: *T.S. Stribling* by Wilton Eckley, Boston, Twayne, 1935.

* * *

T.S. Stribling, best known for his novels of Tennessee, also wrote a number of interesting stories featuring one of detective fiction's early psychologist-criminologists, Henry Poggioli, a psychology professor at Ohio State University. Poggioli is rarely seen in pursuit of his official profession in Ohio, but seems to spend most of his time in pursuit of his unofficial occupation in the Caribbean and Latin America. He is a slightly comical character, often scared but always curious, who initially gets involved in investigation by accident, and often, subsequently, against his will. His first case comes when he is staying in a hotel in Curaçao. The proprietor of the hotel dies and Poggioli is drawn into the investigation because he is interested in the psychological makeup of the main suspect, Pompalone, an ex-dictator from Venezuela. Poggioli solves the crime—the proprietor had intended to murder Pompalone, but in a mix-up of wine bottles (the identifying cobwebs had been accidentally wiped from the poisoned bottle) drinks the poisoned wine himself. The "detective" then goes to visit Haiti, and finds that his reputation has gone before him: he is virtually forced to help the government demonstrate that Voodooism is fraudulent. Ironically, he discovers that the Voodoo leaders are using truth drugs, his own detective tool, to read minds and enslave followers.

What ultimately attracts Poggioli to detection is his strong sense of social and racial justice. He longs for races to free themselves from superstition; he can't bear to see a poor man accused where a rich one is guilty. He develops an elaborate, compassionate philosophy of crime—it is a question of environmental conditioning. He believes that a Futuristic architecture will produce increasingly original criminals, and that the bizarre murals he observes in Martinique will lead to grotesque crimes. He believes also that certain races will commit certain kinds of crime—for instance, a criminal who has carried out his crime with a slow, deliberate perfection may well be of mixed French and Negro blood, the French in him accounting for the perfectionist, the Negro for the deliberation.

Poggioli is not free from a certain pride in his skill. He competes with local policemen, and in one instance goes so far as to make a wager with an informed stranger that he and not the stranger will be able to find the perpetrators of the next six crimes committed in the French town in which they are staying. But Poggioli's enthusiasm for the theory and science of crime and for his own skill are always sharply modified when his enthusiasm brings him into contact with gruesome facts. And his sense of triumph at solving a crime worries him; he may come to relish crime because it provides the opportunity for him to demonstrate his skill. "The detection of crime is a damnable occupation," he reflects; "a man who follows it will become a monster." Poggioli remains intensely human; his perception of the perverse dangers besetting the criminologist is one of the touches with which Stribling makes his thoughtful detective such an engaging character.

—Ann Massa

STUART, Donald. *See* **VERNER, Gerald.**

STUART, Ian. *See* **MacLEAN, Alistair.**

STUART, Ian. British. Also writes as Malcolm Gray. Born in Royston, Hertfordshire, 6 May 1927. Educated at Hitchin Boys' Grammar School, Hertfordshire, 1937–42. Married Audrey Joyce Allen in 1953; two sons. Staff member, Barclays Bank, 1943–84. Since 1984 full-time writer. Agent: Curtis Brown, 162–168 Regent Street, London W1R 5TB. Address: 218 Watford Road, Chiswell Green, St. Albans, Hertfordshire AL2 3EA, England.

CRIME PUBLICATIONS

Novels (series: David Grierson; Graham Lorimer)

The Snow on the Ben. London, Ward Lock, 1961.
Death from Disclosure (Grierson). London, Hale, 1976.
Flood Tide. London, Hale, 1977.
Sand Trap. London, Hale, 1977.
Fatal Switch. London, Hale, 1978.
A Weekend to Kill. London, Hale, 1978.
Pictures in the Dark. London, Hale, 1979; New York, Doubleday, 1986.
The Renshaw Strike. London, Hale, 1980.
End on the Rocks (Grierson). London, Hale, 1981.
The Garb of Truth (Grierson). London, Hale, 1982; New York, Doubleday, 1984.
Thrilling-Sweet and Rotten (Grierson). London, Hale, 1983.
A Growing Concern (Grierson). New York, Doubleday, 1985; London, Hale, 1987.
Sandscreen (Lorimer). New York, Doubleday, 1987.
The Margin (Lorimer). New York, Doubleday, 1988.
Master Plan (Lorimer). New York, Doubleday, 1990.

Novels as Malcolm Gray (series: Alan Craig)

Look Back on Murder (Craig). Bolton, Lancashire, Ross Anderson, 1985; New York, Doubleday, 1986.
Stab in the Back. New York, Doubleday, 1986.
A Matter of Record (Craig). New York, Doubleday, 1987.
An Unwelcome Presence (Craig). New York, Doubleday, 1989.

Uncollected Short Stories

"Second Honeymoon," in *Mystery Guild Anthology,* edited by John Waite. London, Constable, 1980.
"The Vanity of Martin Roscoe," in *John Creasey's Crime Collection 1981,* edited by Herbert Harris. London, Gollancz, 1981; New York, St. Martin's Press, 1982.
"Nobody's Told You, Have They?," in *Ellery Queen's Mystery Magazine* (New York), August 1982.
"The Steep, Dark Stairs," in *Ellery Queen's Mystery Magazine* (New York), June 1984.
"The Grotte of St. Simon," in *Ellery Queen's Mystery Magazine* (New York), September 1983.
"Justice and Sergeant Shardlow," in *Ellery Queen's Mystery Magazine* (New York), September 1984.
"Lorna's People," in *Ellery Queen's Mystery Magazine* (New York), May 1985.
"Dicker McLeish's Girl," in *Ellery Queen's Mystery Magazine* (New York), September 1985.
"The Approach of Winter," in *Ellery Queen's Mystery Magazine* (New York), December 1985.
"None of Us Is Perfect," in *Ellery Queen's Mystery Magazine* (New York), May 1986.
"Roberta," in *Ellery Queen's Prime Crimes 4.* New York, Dial Press, 1986.
"The Gilded Truth," in *Ellery Queen's Prime Crimes 5.* New York, Dial Press, 1987.
"The Night of the Storm," in *Ellery Queen's Mystery Magazine* (New York), January 1988.
"Francoise," in *Ellery Queen's Mystery Magazine* (New York), June 1988.
"Enter Miss Crindle" (as Malcolm Gray), in *Ellery Queen's Mystery Magazine* (New York), February 1990.

OTHER PUBLICATIONS

Other

Golf in Hertfordshire. Hitchin, Hertfordshire, Countryside, 1972.

*

Ian Stuart comments:
I started by writing books which, I hoped, contained more action than the conventional detective story and more rounded characters than the average thriller. At the same time I used realistic contemporary backgrounds, usually in commerce or industry. However, some years ago I came to the conclusion that I might be falling between two stools, and I began writing rather "tougher" books under my own name and "whodunnits" as Malcolm Gray. Lately the distinction seems to have become blurred again. None of my books so far has really satisfied me, and I doubt if one ever will.

*   *   *

A contemporary British mystery novelist of considerable diversity, Ian Stuart has shadowed a vast spectrum of interests in his fictional work, from variations on the locked-room murder situation, to more worldly scenarios involving British business concerns—within the U.K. and into the global market—often punctuated by highly placed malefactions.

Not to be confused with the pen name of the late Alistair MacLean, Stuart's writing is typified by a crisp authoritative style in detailing business-oriented topics, reflective of his own experience in the light engineering sector.

Stuart has also demonstrated an admirable talent in delineating the dark dimensions of multi-faceted business/financial structures. By contrast, under the pen name of Malcolm Gray, Stuart has published more traditional mystery novels albeit seasoned with haunting, ominous overtones.

Stuart has explored both the series and non-series arenas. The chronicles of bank inspector David Grierson offer fascinating accounts of intricate financial designs, defined by disturbing events and insidious motives. Stuart consistently depicts the London financial kingdom—the city—with chilling authenticity.

Far more ambitious are the exploits of Graham Lorimer, who investigates the infringements upon British business interests on foreign territory, usually of the most devastating adversity to national prestige or security.

Stuart's non-series novels, such as *Fatal Switch* and *The Renshaw Strike,* are executed with the same measured eye on characterization, motivation, and mystery as is exhibited in his series books.

In *The Garb of Truth,* bank inspector David Grierson investigates the cryptic past of the late Rosemary Sapsed (the victim of some savage knife-play), the wife of Britain's Minister of Defence, Gerald Sapsed. Stuart dexterously maneuvers his principal plot against a scandalous crisis which threatens the solidity of NATO and Gerald Sapsed's future within Whitehall. Here, Stuart strikes a somber level of authenticity rarely found in this type of fiction. In this respect *The Garb of Truth* might be regarded as a mainstream novel— with provocative mystery elements.

Stuart molds a meticulous, dark mosaic with *The Garb of Truth,* for the reader will encounter many shattered lives and malevolent motives before Grierson unmasks the mystery behind the enigmatic Rosemary Sapsed. The NATO segment of the plot is intensified so that Grierson faces highly-powered resistance within Whitehall to prevent Gerald Sapsed's domestic entanglements from blackening the NATO crisis.

A Growing Concern shifts in a new direction from *The Garb of Truth,* advancing into the high-stakes financial shocker concept. In this novel, Grierson discovers that the calculated movements of an avaricious investment consortium may have a shaded connection to the death of an attractive female bank teller. Stuart dramatically articulates the complex landscape of the British financial world without compromising the book's traditional mystery facets. In the latter area, Grierson links the teller's purported innocent background, several murders similar to that of the victim and a seemingly unrelated suicide before he is able to unravel the shadowy circumstances surrounding her death.

In terms of development, the progression of the Grierson books set the precedent for Stuart's later exploits involving Graham Lorimer. *Sandscreen* finds Lorimer, here a dedicated representative of the British Home Office, investigating the suicide of Michael O'Brien, the foreign manager of the Maxwell Shipping Syndicate in Shajiha, a small albeit prominent Arabic nation. Many of the supporting elements in the Grierson books are invoked in *Sandscreen,* but Stuart is so proficient in maintaining narrative movement that their appearance does not become repetitious. With *Sandscreen,* Stuart has conceived a compelling suspense novel from a seemingly transparent situation from which he shadows an apocalyptic terrorist network, its effect on the volatile Arabic landscape and the victim's mysterious interest in a desolate camp.

An intriguing facet of *Sandscreen* develops with the author's darkly accented depiction of the contemporary Arab world, from the cryptic dimensions of the Islamic faith to a more extensive portrait of a ravaged and troubled kingdom.

The Margin intensifies the precedent established in *Sandscreen,* although the emphasis of an aggressive British business group is dramatically altered to that of a more menacing image. Lorimer is called in to investigate printed allegations that Walker's Brewer, a subsidary outlet of United (a prominent British consortium), is involved in the sale and distribution of arms to South Africa. Stuart adroitly infuses into *The Margin* the inventive elements that punctuated the progression of suspense throughout *Sandscreen.* In this novel, Lorimer is confronted with an anti-Apartheid display, a perplexing incident on a football field, the savage demise of a Walker representative and the repercussions of his own involvement with Shelley van Rynveld, a South African national who figures critically in Stuart's complex maze.

Stuart's novels as Malcolm Gray are in a more traditional vein, often venturing into mystery spheres that generate ominous diversions. *Look Back on Murder* features Alan Craig, ex-Scotland Yard detective who becomes engaged in the private sector as an enquiry agent. Craig accepts an invitation from a school colleague, Miles Jordan, to spend a weekend at an exclusive country estate. It is revealed that some 30 years earlier and under similar circumstances, the murder of the smooth and urbane Nigel Randall occurred. Randall's wife, Susan, was convicted of the crime and subsequently died in prison. Jordan recreates the incident—in the company of several haunted guests, including veteran film star Lorrain Maxwell, and Simon and Gabriella Fenn, a controversial author and his wife. *Look Back on Murder* demonstrates Stuart's ability of conceiving insidious motives within a locked-room setting—while avoiding any suggestions of repetition in this tested mystery format.

In *Stab in the Back* Inspector Neil Lambert investigates the murder of an abrasive television comedian, Tommy Boston, in the home of television celebrity-mystery enthusiast Chester Logan. As in *Look Back on Murder,* Stuart devises the suspects and their motives effectively while providing the genesis of a consistent level of suspense throughout the narrative.

An Unwelcome Presence heightens Stuart's locked-room concept beyond traditional perimeters. Alan Craig investigates the disappearance of Keith Parkhouse, a liberal political activist. Stuart sets this facet against the classic village of Verbridge and the recent arrival of several gypsy factions in the area.

Stuart's provocative variation on the locked-room mystery, as exemplified by the Verbridge village in *An Unwelcome Presence,* signifies Stuart's talent as a mystery writer— accenting and puncuating traditional suspense designs with contemporary lines.

—Andy East

STUART, Sidney. *See* **AVALLONE, Michael.**

STUBBS, Jean. British. Born in Denton, Lancashire, 23 October 1926. Educated at Manchester High School for Girls, 1938–44; Manchester School of Art, 1944–47. Married; one daughter and one son. Reviewer, *Books and Bookmen,* London 1966–78. Recipient: Tom-Gallon Trust award, for short story, 1965. Agent: Macmillan London Ltd., 4 Little Essex Street, London WC2R 3LF. Address: Trewin, Nancegollan, near Helston, Cornwall TR13 OAJ, England.

CRIME PUBLICATIONS

Novels (series: Inspector John Joseph Lintott)

My Grand Enemy. London, Macmillan, 1967; New York, Stein and Day, 1968.
The Case of Kitty Ogilvie. London, Macmillan, 1970; New York, Walker, 1971.
Dear Laura (Lintott). London, Macmillan, and New York, Stein and Day, 1973.
The Painted Face (Lintott). London, Macmillan, and New York, Stein and Day, 1974.
The Golden Crucible (Lintott). New York, Stein and Day, 1976; London, Macmillan, 1977.

Uncollected Short Stories

"Question of Honour," in *Winter's Crimes 1,* edited by George Hardinge. London, Macmillan, 1969.
"The Belvedere," in *Winter's Crimes 3,* edited by George Hardinge. London, Macmillan, 1971.

OTHER PUBLICATIONS

Novels

The Rose-Grower. London, Macmillan, 1962; New York, St. Martin's Press, 1963.
The Travellers. London, Macmillan, and New York, St. Martin's Press, 1963.
Hanrahan's Colony. London, Macmillan, 1964.
The Straw Crown. London, Macmillan, 1966.
The Passing Star. London, Macmillan, 1970; as *Eleanora Duse,* New York, Stein and Day, 1970.
An Unknown Welshman. London, Macmillan, and New York, Stein and Day, 1972.
Kit's Hill. London, Macmillan, 1978; as *By Our Beginnings,* New York, St. Martin's Press, 1979.
The Ironmaster. London, Macmillan, 1981; as *An Imperfect Joy,* New York, St. Martin's Press, 1981.
The Vivian Inheritance. London, Macmillan, and New York, St. Martin's Press, 1982.
The Northern Correspondent. London, Macmillan, and New York, St. Martin's Press, 1984.
A Lasting Spring. London, Macmillan, and New York, St. Martin's Press, 1987.
Like We Used to Be. London, Macmillan, 1989; New York, St. Martin's Press, 1990.
Summer Secrets, London, Macmillan, 1990.

OTHER PUBLICATIONS

Play

Television Play: *Family Christmas,* 1965.

Other

100 Years Around the Lizard. Bodmin, Cornwall, Bossiney, 1985.
Great Houses of Cornwall. Bodmin, Cornwall, Bossiney, 1987.

*

Jean Stubbs comments (1980):
I became fascinated by crime-writing in 1966 when I found an old book on the library shelves called *Famous Trials.* Among the trials was the case of Mary Blandy, who was hanged for poisoning her father at Henley in 1752. I felt that Mary had received poor treatment and researched the case in the British Museum, producing my first crime documentary, *My Grand Enemy.* I based this, and *The Case of Kitty Ogilvie* (another 18th-century murder), on the facts and wrote it like a novel. Later someone created the word "faction" which seemed to describe what I was trying to achieve.

I write other books and it was 1972 before I again felt I should like to try another crime documentary, and to set it in the late-Victorian era. I enjoy researching history and such research has become a necessary factor in any book I contemplate. This time the Victorians were too well documented to be reproduced, so I composed my own "classic" plot for *Dear Laura.* The success, on both sides of the Atlantic, of this Victorian thriller brought along *The Painted Face* (set in Paris, 1902) and *The Golden Crucible* (set in San Francisco, 1906), all of them featuring Inspector Lintott, an elderly detective with mutton-chop whiskers. I am now engaged on "something completely different," but the "bones" of an early Lintott, set around 1860, are sitting on my bookshelf, waiting to be fleshed some day.

I always say I write *why-done-its* and not *who-done-its.*

* * *

Jean Stubbs is a welcome addition to the ranks of mystery fiction writers. *Dear Laura, The Painted Face,* and *The Golden Crucible* have style, complexity, wondrously believable female characters, and a delightful new detective-inspector—John Joseph Lintott.

Until a few years ago, Stubbs was writing historical and romantic fiction; she is thoroughly familiar with the sociology of her chosen Victorian period and her scene setting is vivid. She makes good sense of the psychology not only of her central characters, but also of many minor ones. And she takes the reader along a splendidly winding path at the end of which she manages to create surprise. Stubbs's books could be a good introduction to detective mysteries for a devoted reader of the modern psychological novel.

For the purists who want only ingenious plotting and detection, Stubbs's artful characterization and the echoes of Victorian literature could be disturbing. She uses the Victorian period to point to the beginning of our own times. The three Lintott mysteries are linked in their pictures of emerging modern women. The heroines are women of some depth. They grapple their ways to maturity in stages that make sense to other women. While their circumstances are unusual, the characters themselves, rather like Galsworthy's, are neither larger nor more glittering than life.

Neophyte or purist, all readers will agree that Inspector Lintott of Scotland Yard, retired, is a worthy character. Far from the hard-boiled private eye of American fiction, Lintott is sturdily British. As earthy as a character from Dickens, he is a family man and a guardian of Victorian values. He is a devoted husband to good, plain Bessie and bewildered father of the defiant young feminist, Lizzie. A representative of Scotland Yard, Lintott knows all that is seamy about 19th-century London. He speaks two languages—his own middle-class English and the patois of the gutter. When he questions the members of a household, he has them trusting, cowed, shaped-up, and comforted so quickly that you want to reread to see how it happened. And, when you do, it's clear! Having created Lintott, Stubbs appears to enjoy him as much as the reader. She pushes him into unlikely settings and we watch him struggle to grow. Before he retired, Lintott had never been more than 50 miles outside of London, but he agrees to follow a case to Paris. With no French to defend himself and with his staid English eye, Lintott learns to enjoy rural France and to survive an encounter with a wily courtesan in whose boudoir he must sit, uncomfortably massive, while he accounts for every penny he has spent in Paris. But the good old inspector is no superman. His gaffes are painful. His sensitivity to ordinary people is heartwarming, but he never understands the heroine of *The Painted Face* nor his own daughter.

In *The Golden Crucible* Stubbs sends her detective to America—to San Francisco tottering on the verge of the Great Quake. Lintott's daughter has failed to adapt to what appeared to be a suitable marriage, so the American mission includes a role for her. These two travel separately and Lizzie's very modern love story runs contrapuntally to her father's exploration of a sparkling, corrupt San Francisco at the turn of the century.

A major element in Stubbs's mystery novels is a concern for justice, less a legalistic matter than the workings of the gods. High prices are paid for failures in decent human interaction and love is the reward for giving and caring. Lintott says, "Justice is more than the law, sir, though the law administers justice. There are strange ways of bringing it about, and it happens in a way you couldn't have planned. It's personal, too, sir. Each man carries his own justice with him. I've done a few things in my time, I don't mind admitting, which ain't exactly the letter of the law. But they were always a form of justice." It is one of the pleasures of these books to watch the author devise a punishment that fits each crime.

Nevertheless, there are drawbacks to Stubbs's approach to mystery fiction. In *Dear Laura*, a stream of consciousness carries much of the richness of Laura's memory. Unfortunately, the device is often a nuisance to interpret—too much meditating is inappropriate for mysteries. Even more disconcerting is the author's tendency to stop at plot junctures and ruminate on her themes. Whenever this happens, something of the plot is given away. But *The Painted Face* is much more straightforward than *Dear Laura*, and *The Golden Crucible* is a fast-moving story from beginning to end.

Stubbs's work is genuinely in the art of the mystery novel—stylish, atmospherically accurate, and totally engrossing. You care about her people because it is quickly apparent that she cares. Along with the fine characterization and the well-drawn settings, Stubbs constructs a first-rate suspense story. Leading you through a maze of unfolding impressions and workable clues, she lets you bump time and again into the mirror of assumption before revealing her astonishing endings.

—Carol Washburne

———

STURROCK, Jeremy. Pseudonym for Benjamin James Healey; also writes as J.G. Jeffreys. British. Born in Birmingham, Warwickshire, 26 June 1908. Educated at Birmingham School of Art, 1922–23; Birmingham University, 1923–26. Served in the Royal Air Force 1940–45. Married Muriel Rose Herd in 1951. Scenic artist and stage designer, Birmingham Repertory Theatre, 1926–31; art designer, Decorative Crafts, Birmingham, 1935–40; scenic artist, Denham Film Studios, London, 1946–47; scenic artist and art director, Riverside Film Studios, London, 1947–50; freelance scenic artist and art director for various film companies, 1951–67. Agent: Dr. Jan Van Loewen Ltd., 21 Kingly Street, London, W1R 5LB; or, Barthold Fles Literary Agency, 501 Fifth Avenue, New York, New York 10017, U.S.A. Address: 19 Granard Avenue, London SW15 6HH, England.

CRIME PUBLICATIONS

Novels (series: Jeremy Sturrock in all books; published as J.G. Jeffreys in US)

The Village of Rogues. London, Macmillan, 1972; as *The Thieftaker,* New York, Walker, 1972.
A Wicked Way to Die. London, Macmillan, and New York, Walker, 1973.
The Wilful Lady. London, Macmillan, and New York, Walker, 1975.
A Conspiracy of Poisons. London, Hale, and New York, Walker, 1977.
Suicide Most Foul. London, Hale, and New York, Walker, 1981.
Captain Bolton's Corpse. London, Hale, and New York, Walker, 1982.
The Pangersbourne Murders. London, Hale, 1983; New York, Walker, 1984.
The Thistlewood Plot. New York, Walker, 1987.

Novels as Ben Healey (series: Harcourt d'Espinal; Paul Hedley)

Waiting for a Tiger (Hedley). London, Hale, and New York, Harper, 1965.
The Millstone Men (Hedley). London, Hale, 1966.
Death in Three Masks (Hedley). London, Hale, 1967; as *The Terrible Pictures,* New York, Harper, 1967.
Murder Without Crime (Hedley). London, Hale, 1968.
The Trouble with Penelope (Hedley). London, Hale, 1972.
The Vespucci Papers (d'Espinal). London, Hale, and Philadelphia, Lippincott, 1972.
The Stone Baby (d'Espinal). Philadelphia, Lippincott, 1973; London, Hale, 1974.
The Horstmann Inheritance (d'Espinal). London, Hale, 1975.
The Blanket of the Dark (Hedley). London, Hale, 1976.
The Snapdragon Murders (Hedley). London, Hale, 1978.
Last Ferry from the Lido (d'Espinal and Hedley). London, Hale, 1981; as *Midnight Ferry to Venice,* New York, Walker, 1982.

OTHER PUBLICATIONS

Novels as Ben Healey

The Red Head Herring. London, Hale, 1969.
Captain Havoc. London, Hale, 1977.
Havoc in the Indies. London, Hale, 1979.
The Most Wicked Bianca. London, Hamlyn, 1980.
The Week of the Scorpion. London, Hale, 1981.

Plays as Ben Healey

Television Series: *The Black Arrow,* 1972–73.

Other as B.J. Healey

A Gardener's Guide to Plant Names. New York, Scribner, 1972.
The Plant Hunters. New York, Scribner, 1975.

*

Manuscript Collection: Mugar Memorial Library, Boston University.

Jeremy Sturrock comments:

My novels are intended simply as light, entertaining reading. In the Jeremy Sturrock series, written with Sturrock's rather broad humour, as the memoirs of the chief of the Bow Street Runners (about 1805 to 1820), the basic plots and characters are fictional, but I try to present a socially and historically accurate background by research in the newspapers, periodicals, biographies, and gossip of the period. My main interests are art, books, history, and gardening, and in one way or another these are usually reflected in my work.

*   *   *

Following the recent trend of setting a plot in the past, the Jeremy Sturrock books go back to the beginnings of the English police force. In a note at the beginning of *The Village of Rogues* Sturrock states that his character is based generally on a real Bow Street Runner named Townsend. Combining that with frequent references to King George III, the playwright Sheridan, and conflict with Napoleon, Sturrock succeeds in removing the reader from the modern world. The historical elements blend in smoothly, however, and do not distract from the plot or immediate action. The bawdiness and roughness just beneath the thin surface of the upper classes comes through clearly. The dislike and contempt that people felt for the Bow Street Runners doesn't come through, however—people cooperate with Sturrock and readers find him likeable.

Sturrock is the narrator of the stories, presenting himself as almost all-knowing, boastful, humorous. He associates with and is aware of all the intrigue of the gentility, but he also knows the habits and coarseness of the working man (into whose class he was born). He claims to be the creator of the Art and Science of Detection—preceding Holmes by three-quarters of a century. Sturrock does come through with some actual detection, misleading his suspects by continually asking questions that seem irrelevant or inconsequential. The solution or plot behind all the mysterious activity tends to appear suddenly. Sturrock also anticipates Holmes by his use of Magsy, a street urchin used for shadowing, eavesdropping, and other various chores. Magsy also provides a large part of the humor as a foil for Sturrock's assumed suaveness.

—Fred Dueren

STYLES, Showell. *See* **CARR, Glyn.**

SYMONS, Julian (Gustave). British. Born in London, 30 May 1912. Educated in various state schools. Married Kathleen Clark in 1941; one son and one daughter (deceased). Has worked as a shorthand typist, secretary for an engineering company, and advertising copywriter. Founding editor, *Twentieth Century Verse,* London, 1937–39; reviewer, Manchester *Evening News,* 1947–56; editor, Penguin Mystery Series, 1974–77. Since 1958, reviewer for the *Sunday Times,* London. Visiting Professor, Amherst College, Massachusetts, 1975–76. Co-founder, 1953, and chairman, 1958–59, Crime Writers Association; chairman, Committee of Management, Society of Authors, 1969–71; member of the council, Westfield College, University of London, 1972–75. President, Detection Club 1976–85 and since 1989 President, Conan Doyle Society. Recipient: Crime Writers Association award, 1957, Special Merit award, 1966, Cartier Diamond Dagger award, 1990; Mystery Writers of America Edgar Allan Poe award, 1961, 1973, and Grand Master award, 1982; Swedish Academy of Detection Grand Master diploma, 1977. Fellow, Royal Society of Literature, 1975. Agent: Curtis Brown, Ltd., 162–168 Regent Street, London W1R 5TA. Address: Groton House, 330 Dover Road, Walmer, Deal, Kent CT14 7NX, England.

DiED: 21st NOVEMBER 1994

CRIME PUBLICATIONS

Novels (series: Inspector Bland)

The Immaterial Murder Case (Bland). London, Gollancz, 1945; New York, Macmillan, 1957.
A Man Called Jones (Bland). London, Gollancz, 1947.
Bland Beginning. London, Gollancz, and New York, Harper, 1949.
The Thirty-First of February. London, Gollancz, 1950; as *The 31st of February,* New York, Harper, 1950.
The Broken Penny. London, Gollancz, and New York, Harper, 1953.
The Narrowing Circle. London, Gollancz, and New York, Harper, 1954.
The Paper Chase. London, Collins, 1956; as *Bogue's Fortune,* New York, Harper, 1957.
The Colour of Murder. London, Collins, and New York, Harper, 1957.
The Gigantic Shadow. London, Collins, 1958; as *The Pipe Dream,* New York, Harper, 1959.
The Progress of a Crime. London, Collins, and New York, Harper, 1960.
The Killing of Francie Lake. London, Collins, 1962; as *The Plain Man,* and New York, Harper, 1962.
The End of Solomon Grundy. London, Collins, and New York, Harper, 1964.
The Belting Inheritance. London, Collins, and New York, Harper, 1965.
The Man Who Killed Himself. London, Collins, and New York, Harper, 1967.
The Man Whose Dreams Came True. London, Collins, 1968; New York, Harper, 1969.
The Man Who Lost His Wife. London, Collins, and New York, Harper, 1970.
The Players and the Game. London, Collins, and New York, Harper, 1972.
The Plot Against Roger Rider. London, Collins, and New York, Harper, 1973.
A Three-Pipe Problem. London, Collins, and New York, Harper, 1975.
The Blackheath Poisonings. London, Collins, and New York, Harper, 1978.
Sweet Adelaide. London, Collins, and New York, Harper, 1980.
The Detling Murders. London, Macmillan, 1982; as *The Detling Secret,* New York, Viking Press, 1983.

The Name of Annabel Lee. London, Macmillan, and New York, Viking Press, 1983.
The Criminal Comedy of the Contented Couple. London, Macmillan, 1985; as *A Criminal Comedy,* New York, Viking, 1985.
The Kentish Manor Murders. London, Macmillan, and New York, Viking, 1988.
Death's Darkest Face. London, Macmillan, and New York, Viking, 1990.

Short Stories (series: Francis Quarles)

Murder! Murder! (Quarles). London, Fontana, 1961.
Francis Quarles Investigates. London, Panther, 1965.
Ellery Queen Presents Julian Symons' How To Trap a Crook and Twelve Other Mysteries. New York, Davis, 1977.
The Great Detectives: Seven Original Investigations. London, Orbis, and New York, Abrams, 1981.
The Tigers of Subtopia and Other Stories. London, Macmillan, 1982; New York, Viking Press, 1983.

Uncollected Short Stories

"The Accident," in *The Evening Standard* (London), 17 September 1953.
"The Crime of Mr. Bonny," in *The Evening Standard* (London), 15 May 1954.
"The Cupboard Was Bare," in *The Evening Standard* (London), 6 July 1955.
"The What's My Line Murder," in *The Evening Standard* (London), 27 February–8 March 1956.
"James Mason Investigates," in *The Evening Standard* (London), 18–27 March 1957.
"Cup Final Kidnap," in *The Evening Standard* (London), 28 April–3 May 1958.
"Murder on Tour," in *The Evening Standard* (London), 25 July–3 August 1960.
"Castles in Spain," in *Crimes Across the Sea.* New York, Harper, 1964; London, Harrap, 1965.
"Waiting for Mr. McGregor," in *Verdict of Thirteen,* edited by Julian Symons. London, Faber, and New York, Harper, 1979.
"The Dream Is Better," in *Winter's Crimes 14,* edited by Hilary Watson. London, Macmillan, and New York, St. Martin's Press, 1982.
"The Birthmark," in *Winter's Crimes 17,* edited by Hilary Hale. London, Macmillan, 1985.
"Has Anybody Here Seen Me?," in *Winter's Crimes 19,* edited by Hilary Hale. London, Macmillan, 1987.
"The Borgia Heirloom," in *Ellery Queen's Mystery Magazine* (New York), November 1987.
"Did Sherlock Holmes Meet Hercule—?," in *Ellery Queen's Mystery Magazine* (New York), Mid-December 1987.
"The Affair of the Vanishing Diamonds," in *Daily Mail* (London), 24 December 1987.
"I, Too Lived in Arcadia," in *Ellery Queen's Mystery Magazine* (New York), September 1989.
"The Conjuring Trick," in *Ellery Queen's Mystery Magazine* (New York), March 1990.

OTHER PUBLICATIONS

Plays

Radio Plays: *Affection Unlimited,* 1968; *Night Ride to Dover,* 1969; *The Accident,* 1976.

Television Plays: *I Can't Bear Violence,* 1963; *Miranda and a Salesman,* 1963; *The Witnesses,* 1964; *The Finishing Touch,* 1965; *Curtains for Sheila,* 1965; *Tigers of Subtopia,* 1968; *The Pretenders,* 1970; *Whatever's Peter Playing At,* 1974.

Verse

Confusions about X. London, Fortune Press, 1939.
The Second Man. London, Routledge, 1943.
A Reflection on Auden. London, Poem-of-the-Month Club, 1973.
The Object of an Affair and Other Poems. Edinburgh, Tragara Press, 1974.
Seven Poems for Sarah. Edinburgh, Tragara Press, 1979.

Other

A.J.A. Symons: His Life and Speculations. London, Eyre and Spottiswoode, 1950.
Charles Dickens. London, Barker, and New York, Roy, 1951.
Thomas Carlyle: The Life and Ideas of a Prophet. London, Gollancz, and New York, Oxford University Press, 1952.
Horatio Bottomley. London, Cresset Press, 1955.
The General Strike: A Historical Portrait. London, Cresset Press, 1957; Chester Springs, Pennsylvania, Dufour, 1963.
The Thirties: A Dream Revolved. London, Cresset Press, 1960; Chester Springs, Pennsylvania, Dufour, 1963; revised edition, London, Faber, 1975.
A Reasonable Doubt: Some Criminal Cases Re-examined. London, Cresset Press, 1960.
The Detective Story in Britain. London, Longman, 1962.
Buller's Campaign. London, Cresset Press, 1963.
England's Pride: The Story of the Gordon Relief Expedition. London, Hamish Hamilton, 1965.
Crime and Detection: An Illustrated History from 1840. London, Studio Vista, 1966; as *A Pictorial History of Crime,* New York, Crown, 1966.
Critical Occasions. London, Hamish Hamilton, 1966.
Bloody Murder; From the Detective Story to the Crime Novel. London, Faber, 1972; as *Mortal Consequences,* New York, Harper, 1972 revised edition, as *Bloody Murder.* London and New York, Viking, 1985.
Between the Wars: Britain in Photographs. London, Batsford, 1972.
Notes from Another Country. London, London Magazine Editions, 1972.
"Dashiell Hammett: The Onlie Begetter," in *Crime Writers,* edited by H.R.F. Keating. London, BBC Publications, 1978.
The Tell-Tale Heart: The Life and Works of Edgar Allan Poe. London, Faber, and New York, Harper, 1978.
Conan Doyle: Portrait of an Artist. London, G. Whizzard, 1979; New York, Mysterious Press, 1988.
The Modern Crime Story. Edinburgh, Tragara Press, 1980.
Critical Observations. London, Faber, and New Haven, Connecticut, Ticknor and Fields, 1981.
Tom Adams' Agatha Christie Cover Story (paintings by Tom Adams). Limpsfield, Surrey, Dragon's World, 1981; as *Agatha Christie: The Art of Her Crimes,* New York, Everest House, 1981.
Crime and Detection Quiz. London, Weidenfeld and Nicolson, 1983.
1948 and 1984: The Second Orwell Memorial Lecture. Edinburgh, Tragara Press, 1984.

Two Brothers: Fragments of a Correspondence, with A.J. Symons. Edinburgh, Tragara Press, 1985.

Dashiell Hammett. San Diego, Harcourt Brace, 1985.

Makers of the New: The Revolution in Literature, 1912–39. London, Deutsch, and New York, Random House, 1987.

Oscar Wilde: A Problem in Biography (lecture). Council Bluffs, Yellow Barn Press, 1988.

Editor, *An Anthology of War Poetry.* London, Penguin, 1942.

Editor, *Selected Writings of Samuel Johnson.* London, Grey Walls Press, 1949.

Editor, *Selected Works, Reminiscences and Letters,* by Thomas Carlyle. London, Hart Davis, 1956; Cambridge, Massachusetts, Harvard University Press, 1957.

Editor, *Essays and Biographies,* by A.J.A. Symons. London, Cassell, 1969.

Editor, *The Woman in White,* by Wilkie Collins. London, Penguin, 1974.

Editor, *The Angry 30's.* London, Eyre Methuen, 1976.

Editor, *Selected Tales,* by Poe. London, Oxford University Press, 1976.

Editor, *Verdict of Thirteen: A Detection Club Anthology.* London, Faber, and New York, Harper, 1979.

Editor, *The Complete Sherlock Holmes,* by Arthur Conan Doyle. London, Secker and Warburg, and New York, Abrams, 1981.

Editor, *A.J.A. Symons to Wyndham Lewis: Twenty-Four Letters.* Edinburgh, Tragara Press, 1982.

Editor, *New Poetry 9.* London, Hutchinson, 1983.

Editor, *The Penguin Classic Crime Omnibus.* London, Penguin, 1984.

Editor, *The Essential Wyndham Lewis.* London, Deutsch, 1989.

*

Manuscript Collection: Humanities Research Center, University of Texas, Austin.

Critical Study: "Julian Symons and Civilization's Discontents," by Steven Carter in *Armchair Detective* (New York), January 1979.

Julian Symons comments:

I would still go along with the statement about my intentions made in my 1966 omnibus volume, with the qualification only that a crime writer is first of all an entertainer, and that if he fails as an entertainer his books won't succeed in any other way. Otherwise, let me repeat what I said in the omnibus:

The thing that absorbs me most in our age is the violence behind respectable faces, the civil servant planning how to kill Jews most efficiently, the judge speaking with passion about the need for capital punishment, the quiet obedient boy who kills for fun. These are extreme cases, but if you want to show the violence that lives behind the bland faces most of us present to the world, what better vehicle can you have than the crime novel?

*   *   *

Julian Symons published his first detective novel, *The Immaterial Murder Case,* in 1945, and its appearance marked, if it did not actually cause, an important turning point in his career as a writer. During the 1930's Symons was one of the leading members of the group of younger poets who, later in the decade, moved into prominence as successors to the Auden-Spender group. He edited *Twentieth Century Verse,* the rival of Geoffrey Grigson's historic *New Verse,* he published two volumes of his own sharply rational poems, and he began to emerge before the outbreak of World War II as an astute and sensitive literary critic. Today Symons is undoubtedly best known, on the basis of a score of novels, a couple of volumes of short stories, and an erudite account of crime literature, *Bloody Murder,* as one of our leading writers of mysteries, the nearest we have to an heir of Dorothy L. Sayers and Agatha Christie.

In his memoirs of his early days, *Notes from Another Country,* Symons has told how lightheartedly he entered the field of crime fiction, writing *The Immaterial Murder Case* during the 1930's as part of an elaborate joke shared with a fellow poet and leaving it six years in a drawer before he finally submitted it for publication. And in fact, though crime stories have become materially the most profitable side of Symons's writing life, he has not allowed them to deflect him from other types of writing. He is still a practising critic and book reviewer; he has written books on Charles Dickens and Thomas Carlyle, on Edgar Allan Poe and on his own brother A.J.A. Symons. He has also written historical studies of the 1926 General Strike, the 1930's, and the Gordon Relief Expedition, and he has dabbled in autobiography.

Yet over the years one is conscious that Symons's interest in the crime novel, which at first seemed peripheral to his ambition to become a serious writer, has steadily moved into the centre of his literary career. In other words, he has come to regard it also as a form of serious writing, of equal importance to his historical and critical writings, to his biographies and memoirs and poetry.

His detective novels, at least from *The Thirty-First of February* onwards, are strongly thematic works whose governing ideas might, as he admits, have been exemplified in other times and places more appropriately in the orthodox or "straight" novel. And certainly his way of approaching his subject has diverged markedly from that of earlier detective story writers. Usually, indeed, there is a crime to be considered, though this is not always the case; *The Thirty-First of February,* for instance, gains a great deal of its sinister force from the fact that there is no crime at all except in the mind of the detective who hounds an innocent man to his death.

In his best novels, like *The Broken Penny, The Narrowing Circle, The Colour of Murder, The End of Solomon Grundy,* and the recent *The Kentish Manor Murders,* Symons is not really concerned to create the well-made detective story which works itself out as the intellectually satisfying solution of a complex puzzle through the right manipulation of given clues. His plots are often loose rather than tight, sometimes they are disconcertingly open and obvious, and often the denouements are deliberately anti-climactic. There is more than a little irony in his attitude to such matters, and he is quite capable of leaving a little fog of mystery unresolved to annoy the meticulous reader.

In recent years he has been inclined to experiment with jesting forms, parody and pastiche. In a recent letter to me he described his 1975 novel, *A Three-Pipe Problem,* as "a sort of Sherlock Holmes pastiche which does not introduce Sherlock," while three later books, *The Blackheath Poisonings, Sweet Adelaide,* and *The Detling Murders,* are written as "period" novels, not only using Victorian settings, but parodying the Victorian literary manner in the service of crime detection.

What Symons does inject into his original and often disjointed variants on the classic crime-and-detection plot is the kind of content that comes from his own world view, that of a radical critic who looks on existing political and social orders with sardonic scepticism. Symons is concerned with how the crimes he portrays reflect the decay of society, with the pretences of the cultural world, with politics and power as corrupting elements and, in his "Victorian" novels, with the hypocrisies of self-consciously "moral" societies. A world he has peculiarly made his own is that Bohemian half-world where failed writers and hack artists and the calculating hangers-on of the arts combine to create a setting in which alienation encourages the emergence of crime; this is a world where the murderer and the victim seem to attract each other, a world dominated by frauds and hollow men whose presence suggests that Symons not merely knew Wyndham Lewis, as he did in his youth, but was also influenced by him. It is a world of ambiguous guilts, where the hunted man may be objectively innocent but subjectively culpable, and where the forces of law are unpredictable as defenders of true order. In the end, it is not for the way he solves the details of crimes that Symons's novels are interesting, but rather for the way he finds their causes in the minds of men and the shapes of societies.

—George Woodcock

T

TAPPLY, William G.   American.   Born in Waltham, Massachusetts, 16 July 1940. Educated at Amherst College, Massachusetts, 1958–62, B.A. in American Studies 1962; Harvard University, Cambridge, Massachusetts, 1962–63, MAT in social studies 1963; Tufts University, Medford, 1966–68. Travelli fellowship, Tufts University 1966–68. Married 1) Alice Sandra Knight in 1962 (divorced 1966); 2) Cynthia Ann Ehrgott in 1970, one son and two daughters. Teacher, Lexington High School, 1963–66; director of Economic Studies, Tufts University, Medford, 1968–69; housemaster, Lexington High School, 1972–87. Current contributing editor, *Field and Stream,* New York. Agent: Jed Mattes, 175 West 73rd Street, New York, New York 10023. Address: 187 Great Road, #C-5, Acton, Massachusetts 01720, U.S.A.

CRIME PUBLICATIONS

Novels (series: Brady Coyne in all books)

Death at Charity's Point.   New York, Scribner, 1984; London, Collins, 1985.
The Dutch Blue Error.   New York, Scribner, 1984; London, Collins, 1985.
Follow the Sharks.   New York, Scribner, 1985; London, Collins, 1986.
The Marine Corpse.   New York, Scribner, 1986; as *A Rodent of Doubt,* London, Collins, 1987.
Dead Meat.   New York, Scribner, 1987; London, Collins, 1988.
The Vulgar Boatman.   New York, Scribner, 1987; London, Collins, 1988.
A Void in Hearts.   New York, Scribner, 1988; London, Collins, 1989.
Dead Winter.   New York, Delacorte Press, 1989.
Client Privilege.   New York, Delacorte Press, 1990.

Uncollected Short Stories

"Partners," in *Ellery Queen's Prime Crimes* (New York), Fall 1986.
"A New Man," in *Ellery Queen's Mystery Magazine* (New York), August 1988.

OTHER PUBLICATIONS

Other

Those Hours Spent Outdoors (on hunting and fishing).   New York, Scribner, 1988.
Opening Day and Other Neuroses (on fishing).   New York, Lyons and Burford, 1990.

*

William G. Tapply comments:
In addition to crime fiction, I have written extensively for periodicals on subjects as various as gardening, education, nature, hunting and fishing, and sports. My work has appeared in *Sports Illustrated, Yankee, Better Homes and Gardens, Readers Digest, Newsweek, Outdoor Life, Field and Stream,* and others.

*   *   *

William G. Tapply's series character, Boston lawyer Brady Coyne, is a skillful blend of amateur versus professional, serious versus frivolous, and intellectual versus physical. He's an insider; his clients are the rich and powerful and he's capable of dealing with the police. At the same time, his legal practice isn't typical, and the work bores him. He keeps at it for two reasons. The first is that while he finds the work boring, he's selective about his clients and only works with interesting people. The second is that the substantial fees he collects buy him the opportunity to pursue his true love, fishing. In his forties, Brady Coyne hasn't quite grown up yet.

Coyne observes that "most rich people tend to be old, smart, and eccentric. I like them best when they're all those things. In fact, I specialize in the legal problems of old, smart, eccentric, rich people." The clients' problems frequently get complicated. A hunting lodge owner in *Dead Meat* faces a suit by Indians who claim that the lodge's grounds include a sacred burial site; a guest at the lodge is killed and a guide is arrested. The late author in *The Marine Corpse* for whom Coyne served as literary agent dies under mysterious circumstances. Sometimes, a case begins because a client needs help with a personal matter. In *The Vulgar Boatman,* a Massachusetts gubernatorial candidate's son is missing following the death of the son's girlfriend. Candidate Tom Baron must walk a fine line between concern for his son and fretting over the effect of a scandal on his campaign. Baron asks Coyne to look around quietly for his missing son; it's work for which Coyne may not be professionally suited—he knows that the police or a private detective would be more effective—but Coyne provides a commodity which, as he often reminds us, is surprisingly rare: discretion. Coyne's clients trust him to keep their business to himself.

Tapply is among the smoothest storytellers around—his books glide along quickly and effortlessly—but the plots tend towards the straightforward and they're not necessarily fair. He will introduce new elements in the closing chapters in order to facilitate a resolution. There's also a certain amount of repetition in the series: in two back-to-back novels, the villains occupy similar positions, for example. But only rarely do Tapply's stories really disappoint—*The Marine Corpse* is the one novel with substantial flaws. For the most part, the plots serve admirably in their main purpose, which is to give Tapply's loquacious characters plenty of time to tell their stories. This is where Tapply shines, painting each of these eccentric New Englanders vividly, colorfully and distinctly. They're worth meeting, and passing the time in their company is a pleasure.

If Tapply has a significant flaw, it's in Brady Coyne's peculiar reticence about his own life and feelings. Coyne tells us a few concrete things about his relationships with the regular supporting cast. But his explanations are rather facile, becoming convenient tags for repeated reintroductions over the course of the series. The one exception to this is in Coyne's relationship with his ex-wife—in the most recent Coyne novels, Tapply has introduced a tantalizing uncertainty into their interactions, and it'll be interesting to see how this develops in subsequent books.

The real problem is that the adventures leave no mark on Coyne. He reacts awfully calmly to nearly being killed in an explosion in *Dead Meat*. In *A Void in Hearts,* an accident leaves him without feeling in one hand; oddly enough, he never notes his recovery. Coyne ignores pointed requests for help from several people involved in helping homeless people in *The Marine Corpse*. He's committed to helping out one particular homeless man, but isn't prepared to go further.

In *Client Privilege,* the ninth book in the series, a judge asks Coyne to dissuade a blackmailer. The case gets messy when the blackmailer is murdered immediately after the meeting with Coyne; the police suspect him, but Coyne is bound by attorney/client privilege to keep quiet. The dilemma becomes acute when the police begin to suspect Coyne and Coyne begins to suspect the judge. Coyne occasionally mentions the tension of being in this situation, but that concern rarely comes through to us. The judge has been nominated for the federal bench, and he talks of this as a stepping stone to a Supreme Court appointment. From the first book in the series, Coyne has noted that his best friend, federal prosecutor Charlie McDevitt covets a seat on the Supreme Court. Yet Coyne never wonders how McDevitt, who also knows Popowski, feels about the situation. This is more than just a lapse in series continuity; it's characteristic of the way in which Coyne stays entirely focused on the person and case in front of him. On the other hand, Tapply makes those clients and their problems interesting. Brady Coyne's wry, good-humored narration reminds us not to take it all too seriously.

—Jim Huang

TARRANT, John. *See* **EGLETON, Clive.**

TAYLOR, Andrew (John Robert). British. Born in Hertfordshire, 14 October 1951. Educated at the King's School, Ely, Cambridgeshire, 1959–65; Woodbridge School, 1965–69; Emmanuel College, Cambridge, 1970–73, M.A. in English 1973; University College, London, 1978–79, M.A. and diploma in librarianship, archive and information science. Married Caroline Silverwood in 1979; one daughter and one son. Library assistant, 1976–78, and librarian, 1979–81, Brent Public Libraries, London. Since 1976 freelance writer. Recipient: Crime writers Association John Creasey Memorial award, 1982. Agent: Richard Scott Simon Ltd., 43 Doughty Street, London WC1N 2LF, England.

CRIME PUBLICATIONS

Novels (series: William Dougal)

Caroline Miniscule (Dougal). London, Gollancz, 1982; New York, Dodd Mead, 1983.

Waiting for the End of the World (Dougal). London, Gollancz, and New York, Dodd Mead, 1984.
Our Father's Lies (Dougal). London, Gollancz, and New York, Dodd Mead, 1985.
An Old School Tie (Dougal). London, Gollancz, and New York, Dodd Mead, 1986.
Freelance Death (Dougal). London, Gollancz, 1987; New York, Dodd Mead, 1988.
The Second Midnight. London, Collins, 1988.
Blacklist. London, Collins, 1988.
Toyshop. London, Collins, 1990.
Blood Relation (Dougal). London, Gollancz, 1990.

OTHER PUBLICATIONS

Novels (for children) as John Robert Taylor

Hairline Cracks. London, Collins, 1988; New York, Dutton, 1990.
Snapshot. London, Collins, 1988.
Double Exposure. London, Collins, 1989.
Private Nose. New York, Walker, 1990.

*

Andrew Taylor comments:
All my books, whether for adults or children, have the ingredients of crime and mystery in common; why this should be so I don't know—except that it reflects my own reading tastes, which of course begets the question. The flexibility of the genre is immensely attractive. I began by writing what are more or less straight crime novels—the Dougal series, which I hope will continue. At the time I was reading Patricia Highsmith and Gregory Macdonald, which perhaps influenced Dougal's ambivalence towards law and order. However, I do not agree with those critics and publishers who have labelled Dougal "amoral:" in practice, most people dilute their morals with squirts of pragmatism; Dougal merely carries this process a little further than most of us do. In the last few years I have also written a number of longer thrillers. Each, I think, belongs to a different sub-genre. Writing for children and teenagers has also been enormously enjoyable.

* * *

From the opening words of Andrew Taylor's *Caroline Miniscule* it was clear that a new and disturbing crime writer had arrived:

Typical, William Dougal thought. *How bloody inconvenient.* He was standing just inside the door of his supervisor's room in the History Department. Three yards away, a corpulent, tweed-covered shape sprawled on the oatmeal carpet, to the right of the desk. The eyes and the tongue protruded from its bloated face towards Dougal in the doorway.

His supervisor thus casually garotted, William Dougal, a poverty-stricken post-graduate student, discovers to his mild amazement that he is taking large sums of money to work for his supervisor's murderer. When the murderer is in turn apparently bumped off, William finds himself in possession of an incomplete set of clues which may or may not lead to a small fortune in illegally acquired diamonds.

What sets the book out of the ordinary is Taylor's ability to convince the reader that these baroque and unlikely events are entirely to be expected. Once William has taken the decision not to report his discovery of the body, everything that follows seems as foreordained as any tragedy. By not reporting the body he steps almost casually outside the law so that, when the murderer then approaches him, he hesitates, and hesitating, is lost. Each step further away from the unappealingly shabby world of 1980's academia, its pettiness and poverty, takes him into a seductively amoral world. Like William, the reader is drawn irresistably along, first by the urbane Hanbury—don-slayer—and then by William's discovery of his own amorality and that of his girlfriend Amanda.

Much of the appeal lies in the way that our everyday world so swiftly comes to seem so bizarre and richly comic. From the peculiar comedy of manners of life in a small hotel to the tortured delicacy of trying to ask two unwelcome guests if they will be sleeping together, from the labyrinths of parish politics to the mating habits of the staff room, Taylor's quick intelligent eye notes the comic oddities of a society from which William and Amanda become more and more detached until they are mere visitors, sharks drifting past, pursued by other, rather more experienced sharks.

Nominated for an Edgar and winner of the John Creasey award, *Caroline Miniscule* divided critics, some of whom found its amorality unlikely and disturbing. Taylor's next book, *Waiting for the End of the World,* was less satisfactory. Blackmailed by his old adversary Hanbury, William Dougal is drawn into the lunatic world of survivalist groups, arming for the Apocalypse. The social observation remains as sharp as ever—a splendidly awful Camden wine-bar is appallingly likely—but the plot lacks the clarity of the earlier book. Hanbury is no longer the omnipotent Machiavel. His machinations are exposed as mere stop-gaps, confused improvisations. This should lend the plot verisimilitude—this, after all, is how the world works—but in fact it deprives the plot of any logic. Undeniably entertaining and tightly written, the story nonetheless ends up an uncomfortable juxtaposition between the mundane and the extraordinary.

The most ominous sign in *Waiting for the End of the World* was the introduction of the world of spies. Spies are rarely a good sign in crime fiction, moving as they do in a world with a different logic and coherence. Spies, however, return in *Our Father's Lies* in which William is drawn into the apparent suicide of the father of his sometime girlfriend, Celia. The mystery takes in a framed court-martial and execution during World War I and a notorious poison trial during the 1930's and becomes inextricably embedded in William's father's own mysterious past in British Intelligence. The writing is as assured as ever, but the tone is very different to the almost facetious, mocking amorality of the earlier books. William is set in a family context; there is less ambiguity about his role. The earlier books escape comparison; this book is much more suggestive of the work of Anthony Price. Not a bad book, but an unexpected one.

Two further William Dougal books followed: *An Old School Tie* and *Freelance Death.* The first is the lesser of the two, with Hanbury married to a rich widow and then swiftly bereaved. In the face of what he himself sees as perfectly justifiable suspicion of Hanbury, William agrees to investigate to clear Hanbury's name. Although the description of the arcane and pompous rituals of minor public schools is cruelly accurate, the mystery itself is competent but mundane. *Freelance Death* is a more slapdash but energetic book. At points the writing is embarrassingly slack. But the repulsive Newleys and the world of Public Relations allow full exercise of Taylor's sardonic bent. William Dougal recovers some of his old vigour as the plot progresses from a pastiche of the classic Agatha Christie dinner party murder mystery to something close to an old-fashioned "caper" story. One event seems to lead naturally to the next, the

reader and William drawn on inexorably by events. Only towards the end are there signs of characters being changed so as to facilitate a tidy ending—one potentially inconvenient character simply leaves for foreign climes—and the book rather peters out. For all its faults, however, the sly social observation and the sheer verve of the writing indicate a return to form.

Following *Freelance Death,* however, Taylor pursued his interest in the spy story rather than crime. *The Second Midnight, Blacklist,* and *Toyshop* are competent, somewhat le Carré-esque novels, solidly written but without the distinctiveness of the earlier books. Only in their concern with the nature and effect of family ties in a secret and hidden world is there some suggestion in these books of the unsettling, almost father-son relationship between Hanbury and Dougal.

Taylor's most recent publication, *Blood Relation,* returns to this once-criminal partnership. Dougal is now Hanbury's occasional—and wary—employee; both of them are poachers turned gamekeepers in a large security company. Dougal is concerned with his recent fatherhood, Hanbury with the possibility of marrying into the company, when the death of a duplicitous publisher intrudes. The murder mystery is competent, and Taylor again turns his perceptive eye to the antics of publishing and public relations. Something, however, remains lacking. Perhaps it is that the new, domesticated Hanbury is now too much of a known quantity, lacking his earlier mystery and attraction. As a consequence, the sense of two parallel worlds, one mundane, the other murderous, which gave the earlier books their disconcerting quality, is lost. Hanbury and Dougal are back, which is to be welcomed, but perhaps they haven't yet recovered their full amoral energy.

—Philip Plowden

TAYLOR, H. Baldwin. *See* **WAUGH, Hillary.**

TAYLOR, Phoebe Atwood. Also wrote as Freeman Dana; Alice Tilton. American. Born in Boston, Massachusetts, 18 May 1909. Educated at Barnard College (Lucille Pulitzer Scholar), New York, B.A. 1930. Married Dr. Grantly Walden Taylor. Full-time writer from 1931. Lived in Weston, Massachusetts. *Died 9 January 1976.*

CRIME PUBLICATIONS

Novels (series: Asey Mayo in all books)

The Cape Cod Mystery. Indianapolis, Bobbs Merrill, 1931.
Death Lights a Candle. Indianapolis, Bobbs Merrill, 1932.
The Mystery of the Cape Cod Players. New York, Norton, 1933; London, Eyre and Spottiswoode, 1934.
The Mystery of the Cape Cod Tavern. New York, Norton, 1934; London, Eyre and Spottiswoode, 1935.
Sandbar Sinister. New York, Norton, 1934; London, Gollancz, 1936.
The Tinkling Symbol. New York, Norton, and London, Gollancz, 1935.
Deathblow Hill. New York, Norton, 1935; London, Gollancz, 1936.

The Crimson Patch. New York, Norton, and London, Gollancz, 1936.

Out of Order. New York, Norton, 1936; London, Gollancz, 1937.

Figure Away. New York, Norton, 1937; London, Collins, 1938.

Octagon House. New York, Norton, 1937; London, Collins, 1938.

The Annulet of Gilt. New York, Norton, 1938; London, Collins, 1939.

Banbury Bog. New York, Norton, 1938; London, Collins, 1939.

Murder at the New York World's Fair (as Freeman Dana). New York, Random House, 1938.

Spring Harrowing. New York, Norton, and London, Collins, 1939.

The Criminal C.O.D. New York, Norton, and London, Collins, 1940.

The Deadly Sunshade. New York, Norton, 1940; London, Collins, 1941.

The Perennial Boarder. New York, Norton, 1941; London, Collins, 1942.

The Six Iron Spiders. New York, Norton, 1942; London, Collins, 1943.

Three Plots for Asey Mayo (novelettes). New York, Norton, 1942.

Going, Going, Gone. New York, Norton, 1943; London, Collins, 1944.

Proof of the Pudding. New York, Norton, and London, Collins, 1945.

The Asey Mayo Trio (novelettes). New York, Messner, and London, Collins, 1946.

Punch with Care. New York, Farrar Straus, 1946; London, Collins, 1947.

Diplomatic Corpse. Boston, Little Brown, and London, Collins, 1951.

Novels as Alice Tilton (series: Leonidas Witherall in all books)

Beginning with a Bash. London, Collins, 1937; New York, Norton, 1972.

The Cut Direct. New York, Norton, and London, Collins, 1938.

Cold Steal. New York, Norton, 1939; London, Collins, 1940.

The Left Leg. New York, Norton, 1940; London, Collins, 1941.

The Hollow Chest. New York, Norton, 1941; London, Collins, 1942.

File for Record. New York, Norton, 1943; London, Collins, 1944.

Dead Ernest. New York, Norton, 1944; London, Collins, 1945.

The Iron Clew. New York, Farrar Straus, 1947; as *The Iron Hand*, London, Collins, 1947.

Uncollected Short Stories

"The Riddle of Volume Four," in *Mystery League Magazine* (Chicago), November 1933.

"The Disappearing Hermit," in *American Magazine* (Springfield, Ohio), April 1946.

"Swan-Boat Murders," in *Murder Cavalcade*, edited by Ken Crossen. New York, Duell, 1946; London, Hammond, 1953.

"Deadly Festival," in *American Magazine* (Springfield, Ohio), March 1948.

*

Manuscript Collection: Mugar Memorial Library, Boston University.

*   *   *

Phoebe Atwood Taylor, who also used the pseudonym Alice Tilton, produced some 30 mystery novels and a number of shorter tales, most of them written during the 1930's and 1940's. Though she was able to devise the plots and puzzles that were popular during that period, she was above all a humorist, sometimes understated and subtle, often wild and farcical, always witty and amusing. She created two major heroes, Asey Mayo and Leonidas Witherall, as well as a host of other well-drawn characters.

Asey Mayo of Wellfleet, on Cape Cod, is the quintessential Yankee. He thinks straight and talks plain, in a dialect masterfully recorded by his author. Independent, taciturn, tough, and extraordinarily clever, he embodies the traditional Yankee virtues. He went to sea as a boy and later became a mechanic and racing driver for an early automobile manufacturer. According to a newspaper article quoted in *Spring Harrowing*, "Sleuth Mayo pioneered Porter cars, made coast-to-coast tour in 1899 in two-cylindered Porter Century; drove Porter Bullet II in 1904 at Daytona Beach to beat fastest foreign racing car. . . . " Made famous by his exploits, he is "widely roto-gravured," and called, variously, the Codfish Sherlock, the Homespun Sleuth, and Jack-of-All-Trades; made rich by his ingenuity and hard work, he nevertheless relishes the simple life, preferring his old corduroys and ancient yachting cap to his good white flannels. The "Codfish Sherlock" does not lack a Watson—the local favourite "Doc" Cummings.

Asey's logic and clear-sightedness are indispensable in solving mysteries since the local lawmen, who are usually referred to as "combing" the area or "scouring" the underbrush, are none too bright. Details of Cape Cod atmosphere are interwoven with plot and character to provide gems like "Miss Curran of the dubious beachplum Currans" (*Proof of the Pudding*); a boarding house which seeks "Old fashioned boarders . . . for impossibly inconvenient house with no modern improvements whatsoever. Oil lamps, outhouse, pump. Prunes for breakfast, catch your own fish, dig your own clams!" (*Octagon House*); and Asey's views on a freshwater pond: "There's a pond up near the hollow where people do go . . . though I wouldn't give two cents for it myself. Tourists wash there, and cottages without any bathtubs take a cake of soap an' dabble with the outer layers, an' any number of dogs get washed there, too" (*Figure Away*). Cranberry bogs, old shipwrecks and legends of pirates' gold, summer visitors who descend on people lucky enough to have cottages, and natives who profit from every opportunity to make money from the tourists, all appear in these tales.

The Leonidas Witherall stories, by Alice Tilton, set in mythical suburbs of Boston, present such chaotic situations that ordinary suspense is superseded by curiosity about how the author can possibly extricate her protagonists from the shambles. Leonidas, who resembles well-known likenesses of Shakespeare and thus is called Will Shakespeare—or even Bill—by his cohorts, is first seen as a retired professor who hunts books for wealthy but lazy Boston collectors, later as owner of Meredith's Academy, a private school of venerable, if not always decorous, tradition. Unknown to other characters in the tales, Leonidas Witherall is the author of the "blood-and-thunder" thrillers featuring the intrepid Lieutenant Haseltine, whose adventures are invariably called to mind by those characters in the midst of their own problems. Witherall, cynic and intellectual, whose speech is stilted and pompous (and funny), and who appears to be a model of the dignified solid citizen, fails to report corpses (sometimes he even moves them), covers up burglaries, lies to the police, and behaves—it must be admitted—in a most irregular way. The reader, however, can scarcely fail to sympathize with "Bill Shakespeare," prevaricator and conspirator though he occasionally is, since he unfailingly pursues ultimate truth and justice.

Just as Witherall's companions in mischief see themselves as actors in thrillers within thrillers, other characters remark upon their own perplexities in contrast to those of the unlikely denizens of "fiction." In *Going, Going, Gone,* one fellow complains:

" 'I can always figure out book murders from the first page! I'm good at them!' 'It's a matter of extraneous odds an' ends,' Asey said. 'You run into more of 'em this way than you do in books. An' nobody presents you with printed descriptions. You got to figger out for yourself if the New York lawyer an' his fat sister an' his big-nosed nephew an' the antique lady an' the semi-antique man . . . an' the rich Madisons is all lyin' in whole, or in part, an' if so, which part.' " Taylor, in her game of mirrors, also has a Wellfleet woman comment on an outlander lady novelist: "She's mixed in with the women here in town, but I've always steered a little clear of her. I think her heartiness, like when she comes to the club, is just a put-on job. It's always been my opinion she was scratchin' up local color for one of her stories" (*Proof of the Pudding*).

The author was expert in depicting the everyday life of the times. Country auctions, local politics (including a mural containing malicious caricatures of local figures painted at government expense in a pork-barrel post office), opinion polls, lawn fêtes, cake sales and other fund-raisers, old home weeks, ladies' clubs, radio soap operas, and such wartime phenomena as blackouts, wardens, codes, and gasoline rationing, form the background of these stories. Her comic vision combined with a superb eye for detail enabled her to create tales that are period pieces in the best sense, never dated, but as fresh and full of fun as when they were written. Her works are a treasure for popular culture enthusiasts and connoisseurs of American humor. Taylor should find a new audience—even if not the masses—in each generation of crime fiction fans.

—Mary Helen Becker

TELFAIR, Richard. *See* **JESSUP, Richard.**

TEMPLE, Paul. *See* **DURBRIDGE, Francis; RUTHERFORD, Douglas.**

TEY, Josephine. Pseudonym for Elizabeth Mackintosh; also wrote as Gordon Daviot. British. Born in Inverness, Scotland, in 1897. Educated at the Royal Academy, Inverness; Anstey Physical Training College, Birmingham. Taught physical education in various schools in the 1920's. Lived in London. *Died 13 February 1952.*

CRIME PUBLICATIONS

Novels (series: Inspector Alan Grant)

The Man in the Queue (Grant; as Gordon Daviot). London, Methuen, and New York, Dutton, 1929; as *Killer in the Crowd,* New York, Spivak, 1954.
A Shilling for Candles: The Story of a Crime (Grant). London, Methuen, 1936; New York, Macmillan, 1954.
Miss Pym Disposes. London, Davies, 1946; New York, Macmillan, 1948.
The Franchise Affair. London, Davies, 1948; New York, Macmillan, 1949.
Brat Farrar. London, Davies, 1949; New York, Macmillan, 1950; as *Come and Kill Me,* New York, Pocket Books, 1951.
To Love and Be Wise (Grant). London, Davies, 1950; New York, Macmillan, 1951.
The Daughter of Time (Grant). London, Davies, 1951; New York, Macmillan, 1952.
The Singing Sands (Grant). London, Davies, 1952; New York, Macmillan, 1953.

OTHER PUBLICATIONS as Gordon Daviot

Novels

Kif: An Unvarnished History. London, Benn, and New York, Appleton, 1929.
The Expensive Halo. London, Benn, and New York, Appleton, 1931.
The Privateer. London, Davies, and New York, Macmillan, 1952.

Plays

Richard of Bordeaux (produced London, 1932). London, Gollancz, and Boston, Little Brown, 1933.
The Laughing Woman (produced London, 1934). London, Gollancz, 1934.
Queen of Scots (produced London, 1934). London, Gollancz, 1934.
The Stars Bow Down (produced Malvern, Worcestershire, 1939). London, Duckworth, 1939.
Leith Sands and Other Short Plays (includes *The Three Mrs. Madderleys, Mrs. Fry Has a Visitor, Remember Caesar, Rahab, The Mother of Masé, Sara, Clarion Call.*) London, Duckworth, 1946.
The Little Dry Thorn (produced London, 1947). Included in *Plays 1,* 1953.
Valerius (produced London, 1948). Included in *Plays 1,* 1953.
The Pen of My Aunt (broadcast, 1950). Included in *Plays 2,* 1954.
Plays. London, Davies, 3 vols., 1953–54.
Dickon (produced Salisbury, 1955). Included in *Plays 1,* 1953.
The Pomp of Mr. Pomfret (broadcast, 1954). Included in *Plays 2,* 1954.
Cornelia (broadcast, 1955). Included in *Plays 2,* 1954.
Sweet Coz (produced Farnham, Surrey, 1956). Included in *Plays 3,* 1954.

Radio Plays: *Leith Sands,* 1941; *The Three Mrs. Madderleys,* 1944; *Mrs. Fry Has a Visitor,* 1944; *Remember Caesar,* 1946; *The Pen of My Aunt,* 1950; *The Pomp of Mr. Pomfret,* 1954; *Cornelia,* 1955.

Other

Claverhouse (biography).   London, Collins, 1937.

*

Critical Study: *Josephine Tey* by Sandra Roy, Boston, Twayne, 1980.

*   *   *

Josephine Tey's novels of mystery and detection are often categorized with those of Dorothy L. Sayers and Ngaio Marsh. While her work differs from theirs in several respects, it undoubtedly belongs to the Golden Age of detective fiction. Her style is pure, her plots and characters carefully wrought, and her adherence to the classical traditions dependable. Tey wrote several non-series examples of detection and mystery in addition to her creation of the gentleman-police officer Alan Grant, whose shoes never revealed his status as CID investigator.

Tey's amateur detectives are each different from the other. In *Miss Pym Disposes* a former French teacher who has casually and flippantly written a popular psychology book begins to believe in her ability to understand the human psyche. At a girl's physical education college, which is described with fascinating details of programs of study, sport activities, and employment inquiries, Miss Pym undertakes the discovery of a murderer of an unpleasant student. The investigation gives Tey great opportunity to describe an improbable gathering of teen-aged physical education students: the independent and attractive Head Girl, "Beau" Nash; her pleasant, intelligent, competent friend, Mary Innes; and the fiery Latin American exchange student, far more sexually mature than her peers, who wants only to dance.

Miss Pym's faith in discovering people's guilt in crime by understanding their personalities is shared by lawyer Robert Blair who solves *The Franchise Affair* for his client Marion Sharpe. Unfortunately, Tey's adaptation of a true 18th-century crime is somewhat slow-paced and the tracking down of the accused seems too casually accomplished. The important developments in concluding the investigation appear later in the novel so that character study is the most significant activity: Tey draws vivid pictures of old Mrs. Sharpe and Blair's maiden Aunt Lin; even the girl Betty is clearly portrayed, her child's demure face and costume hiding a devious and self-centered core.

Deliberate detective work is minimized in Tey's only other non-Alan Grant mystery, *Brat Farrar.* A young man who closely resembles the dead son of a comfortable, horse-breeding English family, agrees to impersonate the young man, who is thought to have killed himself. The relationship between the imposter and his "family," including a young relative who begins to love him in a very unfamilial way, seems to provide the center of the story. However, the young man stumbles upon information about his new identity which could lead to murder. The difficulties of continuing the investigation and the imposture simultaneously are intertwined; the answer to one is the solution to both.

Although Alan Grant is a fairly fixed character throughout several novels, neither courting nor marrying (unlike Lord Peter Wimsey and Roderick Alleyn), he is clearly as significant a creation and as personal and human a character. His personality is defined in his first appearance in *The Man in the Queue* and while other characteristics are revealed subsequently, he is reliably predictable in his behavior. Recipient of a comfortable legacy, Grant chose to continue police work for the satisfaction he received in working out the puzzles of an investigation. He is a gentleman at the Yard (like Roderick Alleyn) and his manner and manners are intelligent and well-bred. Natty without looking like a tailor's dummy, he is more successful with the upper classes than his faithful Watson, Sergeant Williams; his unfailing courtesy makes him equally successful with the lower orders and the criminal class. His enjoyment of the sport and open spaces of the countryside is a common motif in the novels and is employed as a cure for his claustrophobia, induced by a severe injury. This "weakness," as Grant calls it in *The Singing Sands,* mortifies him; his investigations, requiring rides in closed cars, trains, and small aeroplanes, provide the motive to conquer rather than avoid this fear. When he finds a major clue to a mystery, he is suddenly able to make a return plane trip without this debilitating and demoralizing fear. This method of not concentrating on his most serious problem is also Grant's style of detection: while his chief "worries a case to death," Grant deliberately puts it from his mind when he reaches a stalemate to let his unconscious find the next move. Because of his good fortune in using this technique, he is credited by his colleagues with "flair." It should be acknowledged that Grant's flair often misleads him in his investigations; *The Man in the Queue* is the best example of perfect deduction being entirely wrong.

Grant's most famous case, in *The Daughter of Time,* is undertaken from a hospital bed as he re-examines the supposed murder by Richard III of his two nephews in the Tower of London in the 1480's. This famous crime, unchallenged in school texts and magnified by Shakespeare's successful portrayal of villainy personified, intrigues Grant who investigates contemporary sources to learn of Richard's innocence. When he and his assistant prove their case, both are shocked to discover their conclusions supported by similar claims since the 17th century; none has shaken the general public's belief. Grant's dismay and American Brent Carradine's crusade to educate are at the heart of the novel. Tey's introduction of similar episodes of belief opposing fact and her cast of characters ranged against Grant and Carradine's truth demonstrate the potency of "hearsay evidence." The intensity of Grant's search for accurate information mystifies his nurses, the porter, and sometimes even friends. Besides being a unique example of detection, the novel clearly presents the difficulty of establishing facts in the face of people's preference for what they believe to be the truth.

Because Tey writes so compelling a mystery novel, she is unquestionably one of the most significant authors in the genre. But her talent is not limited to the plotting and deducing of that form; in her detective and her characters she creates credible personalities whose individuality and relationships are realistic and complex. Beyond this, she is concerned, at the core of her work, with moral questions which go beyond the conventions of detective fiction without ever being extraneous to the carefully controlled structure and plot. The critical and popular success of her eight detective novels attests to the unmistakably fine quality of her work.

—Kathleen Gregory Klein

THAMES, C.A. *See* **MARLOWE, Stephen.**

THAYER, Lee (Emma Redington Thayer, née Lee). American. Born in Troy, Pennsylvania, 5 April 1874. Educated at Cooper Union and Pratt Institute, New York City. Married Henry W. Thayer in 1909. Artist and illustrator: paintings displayed at Chicago World's Fair, 1893; produced designs for book jackets. Interior decorator, Associated Artists, New York 1890–96; director, Decorative Designers, New York, 1896–1932. *Died 18 November 1973.*

CRIME PUBLICATIONS

Novels (series: Peter Clancy in all books except *Doctor S.O.S.*)

The Mystery of the Thirteenth Floor. New York, Century, 1919.
The Unlatched Door. New York, Century, 1920.
That Affair at "The Cedars." New York, Doubleday, 1921; London, Hurst and Blackett, 1924.
Q.E.D. New York, Doubleday, 1922; as *The Puzzle,* London, Hurst and Blackett, 1923.
The Sinister Mark. New York, Doubleday, and London, Hurst and Blackett, 1923.
The Key. New York, Doubleday, and London, Hurst and Blackett, 1924.
Doctor S.O.S. New York, Doubleday, and London, Hurst and Blackett, 1925.
Poison. New York, Doubleday, and London, Heinemann, 1926.
Alias Dr. Ely. New York, Doubleday, and London, Hurst and Blackett, 1927.
The Darkest Spot. New York, Sears, and London, Hurst and Blackett, 1928.
Dead Men's Shoes. New York, Sears, and London, Hurst and Blackett, 1929.
They Tell No Tales. New York, Sears, and London, Hurst and Blackett, 1930.
The Last Shot. New York, Sears, and London, Hurst and Blackett, 1931.
Set a Thief. New York, Sears, 1931; as *To Catch a Thief,* London, Hurst and Blackett, 1932.
The Glass Knife. New York, Sears, and London, Hurst and Blackett, 1932.
The Scrimshaw Millions. New York, Sears, 1932; London, Hurst and Blackett, 1933.
Counterfeit. New York, Sears, 1933; as *The Counterfeit Bill,* London, Hurst and Blackett, 1934.
Hell-Gate Tides. New York, Sears, and London, Hurst and Blackett, 1933.
The Second Bullet. New York, Sears, 1934; as *The Second Shot,* London, Hurst and Blackett, 1935.
Dead Storage. New York, Dodd Mead, 1935; as *The Death Weed,* London, Hurst and Blackett, 1935.
Sudden Death. New York, Dodd Mead, 1935; as *Red-Handed,* London, Hurst and Blackett, 1936.
Dark of the Moon. New York, Dodd Mead, 1936; as *Death in the Gorge,* London, Hurst and Blackett, 1937.
Dead End Street, No Outlet. New York, Dodd Mead, 1936; as *Murder in the Mirror,* London, Hurst and Blackett, 1936.
Last Trump. New York, Dodd Mead, and London, Hurst and Blackett, 1937.

A Man's Enemies. New York, Dodd Mead, 1937; as *This Man's Doom,* London, Hurst and Blackett, 1938.
Ransom Racket. New York, Dodd Mead, and London, Hurst and Blackett, 1938.
That Strange Sylvester Affair. New York, Dodd Mead, 1938; London, Hurst and Blackett, 1939.
Lightning Strikes Twice. New York, Dodd Mead, and London, Hurst and Blackett, 1939.
Stark Murder. New York, Dodd Mead, 1939; London, Hurst and Blackett, 1940.
Guilty. New York, Dodd Mead, 1940; London, Hurst and Blackett, 1941.
X Marks the Spot. New York, Dodd Mead, 1940; London, Hurst and Blackett, 1941.
Hallowe'en Homicide. New York, Dodd Mead, 1941; London, Hurst and Blackett, 1942.
Persons Unknown. New York, Dodd Mead, 1941; London, Hurst and Blackett, 1942.
Murder Is Out. New York, Dodd Mead, 1942; London, Hurst and Blackett, 1943.
Murder on Location. New York, Dodd Mead, 1942; London, Hurst and Blackett, 1944.
Accessory after the Fact. New York, Dodd Mead, 1943; London, Hurst and Blackett, 1944.
Hanging's Too Good. New York, Dodd Mead, 1943; London, Hurst and Blackett, 1945.
A Plain Case of Murder. New York, Dodd Mead, 1944; London, Hurst and Blackett, 1945.
Five Bullets. New York, Dodd Mead, 1944; London, Hurst and Blackett, 1947.
Accident, Manslaughter, or Murder? New York, Dodd Mead, 1945; London, Hurst and Blackett, 1946.
A Hair's Breadth. New York, Dodd Mead, 1946; London, Hurst and Blackett, 1947.
The Jaws of Death. New York, Dodd Mead, 1946; London, Hurst and Blackett, 1948.
Murder Stalks the Circle. New York, Dodd Mead, 1947; London, Hurst and Blackett, 1949.
Out, Brief Candle! New York, Dodd Mead, 1948; London, Hurst and Blackett, 1950.
Pig in a Poke. New York, Dodd Mead, 1948; as *A Clue for Clancy,* London, Hurst and Blackett, 1950.
Evil Root. New York, Dodd Mead, 1949; London, Hurst and Blackett, 1951.
Within the Vault. New York, Dodd Mead, 1950; as *Death Within the Vault,* London, Hurst and Blackett, 1951.
Too Long Endured. New York, Dodd Mead, 1950; London, Hurst and Blackett, 1952.
Do Not Disturb. New York, Dodd Mead, 1951; as *Clancy's Secret Mission,* London, Hurst and Blackett, 1952.
Guilt Edged. New York, Dodd Mead, 1951; as *Guilt-Edged Murder,* London, Hurst and Blackett, 1953.
Blood on the Knight. New York, Dodd Mead, 1952; London, Hurst and Blackett, 1953.
The Prisoner Pleads "Not Guilty." New York, Dodd Mead, 1953; London, Hurst and Blackett, 1954.
Dead Reckoning. New York, Dodd Mead, 1954; as *Murder on the Pacific,* London, Hurst and Blackett, 1955.
No Holiday for Death. New York, Dodd Mead, 1954; London, Hurst and Blackett, 1955.
Who Benefits? New York, Dodd Mead, 1955; as *Fatal Alibi,* London, Hurst and Blackett, 1956.
Guilt Is Where You Find It. New York, Dodd Mead, 1957; London, Long, 1958.
Still No Answer. New York, Dodd Mead, 1958; as *Web of Hate,* London, Long, 1959.

Two Ways to Die. New York, Dodd Mead, 1959; London, Long, 1961.
Dead on Arrival. New York, Dodd Mead, 1960; London, Long, 1962.
And One Cried Murder. New York, Dodd Mead, 1961; London, Long, 1962.
Dusty Death. New York, Dodd Mead, 1966; as *Death Walks in Shadow,* London, Long, 1966.

OTHER PUBLICATIONS

Other

Alice and the Wonderland People (stencil pictures). New York, Bungalow Book and Toy Company, 1914.
When Mother Lets Us Draw (for children). New York, Moffat Yard, 1916.

*   *   *

Perhaps the oldest-ever mystery novelist, Lee Thayer wrote her last book at the age of 92 and published some 60 novels during a career that began in 1919. Although Thayer considered herself an artist, not a writer, her prolific writing career could hardly be considered a mere hobby. Her artistic ability did prove useful, though, since she occasionally drew pictorial designs for book bindings and dust jackets, including many for her own books.

Except for *Doctor S.O.S.,* all of her mystery novels star a man-about-town private eye, Peter Clancy, and his very proper English valet, Wiggar. The atmosphere and charm of the Thayer novels depend heavily upon the relationship between Clancy and Wiggar, which is curiously reminiscent of P.G. Wodehouse's team of Bertie Wooster and Jeeves. Thayer's use of the master-butler relationship, however, is merely a diversion from the mystery plot, adding character and wit to the stories, whereas Wodehouse's use of Wooster and Jeeves is more a comic study of character interplay with less emphasis on plot. Although Wooster and Jeeves may, incidentally, solve a few mysteries, it is Wooster's comical bungling and Jeeves's masterful rescue of his master that are the essence of the Wodehouse novels. In contrast to Wooster, Peter Clancy is no common bungler, but a very adept private eye, aided and abetted by the extremely righteous Wiggar. Their humorous relationship, with Clancy often submitting to Wiggar's precise knowledge of correct behavior, adds richness and humor to their adventures.

Although fraught with dated devices of the "Had I But Known" school of mystery authors, Thayer's plots are nevertheless original, interesting, and credible. All of the plots contain some sort of damsel in distress, a dashing hero (usually wrongfully accused of the murder), a neurotic or at times even psychotic red herring of a character meant to mislead the reader, and, of course, the villain, motivated by passion.

The settings vary greatly, from New England to California to Europe. Usually each book features but one murder, although other crimes ranging from bank robbery to blackmail may also take place during the course of the story. In *Within the Vault* a bank's stockholder is found murdered within the safety deposit vault only a few days after the bank had been the scene of a daring daylight robbery. Of course Clancy and Wiggar happen casually upon the scene and are invited to participate in the investigation, much to the advantage of the local police. Even though the case appears to be a simple one, since everyone entering the vault, except bank employees, had to sign a card recording the time of their entrance, Clancy, Wiggar, and

Captain Michael Shannon have to work against time to prove that the most likely suspect was not the guilty party after all.

Too Long Endured and *Murder on Location,* as well as several other Thayer novels, feature actors or actresses as either victims or culprits. *Five Bullets* finds a college psychology experiment gone awry when a student is shot in a classroom by a gun supposedly filled with blanks.

Although Thayer's works are done primarily in the pre-war style, her unique characters and interesting settings make them worth sampling.

—Mary Ann Grochowski

———

THOMAS, Ross (Elmore). Also writes as Oliver Bleeck. American. Born in Oklahoma City, Oklahoma, 19 February 1926. Educated at the University of Oklahoma, Norman, B.A. 1949. Served in the United States Army Infantry in the Philippines, 1944–46. Married Rosalie Appleton in 1974. Reporter, *Daily Oklahoman,* 1943–44; public relations director, National Farmers Union, Denver, 1952–56; president, Stapp Thomas & Wade Inc., Denver, 1956–57; reporter, Bonn, Germany, 1958–59; representative for Dolan Associates, Ibadan, 1959–61; consultant, United States government, 1964–66. Recipient: Mystery Writers of America Edgar Allan Poe award, 1967, 1985. Agent: Robert Kent, STE Representation Ltd., 9301 Wilshire Boulevard, Suite 312, Beverly Hills, California 90210. Address: 3947 Rambla Orienta, Malibu, California 90265, U.S.A.

CRIME PUBLICATIONS

Novels (series: McCorkle and Padillo)

The Cold War Swap (McCorkle and Padillo). New York, Morrow, 1966; as *Spy in the Vodka,* London, Hodder and Stoughton, 1967.
Cast a Yellow Shadow (McCorkle and Padillo). New York, Morrow, 1967; London, Hodder and Stoughton, 1968.
The Seersucker Whipsaw. New York, Morrow, 1967; London, Hodder and Stoughton, 1968.
The Singapore Wink. New York, Morrow, and London, Hodder and Stoughton, 1969.
The Fools in Town Are on Our Side. London, Hodder and Stoughton, 1970; New York, Morrow, 1971.
The Backup Men (McCorkle and Padillo). New York, Morrow, and London, Hodder and Stoughton, 1971.
The Porkchoppers. New York, Morrow, 1972; London, Hamish Hamilton, 1974.
If You Can't Be Good. New York, Morrow, 1973; London, Hamish Hamilton, 1974.
The Money Harvest. New York, Morrow, and London, Hamish Hamilton, 1975.
Yellow-Dog Contract. New York, Morrow, 1976; London, Hamish Hamilton, 1977.
Chinaman's Chance. New York, Simon and Schuster, and London, Hamish Hamilton, 1978.
The Eighth Dwarf. New York, Simon and Schuster, and London, Hamish Hamilton, 1979.
The Mordida Man. New York, Simon and Schuster, and London, Hamish Hamilton, 1981.
Missionary Stew. New York, Simon and Schuster, 1983. London, Hamish Hamilton, 1984.

Briarpatch. New York, Simon and Schuster, 1984; London, Hamish Hamilton, 1985.
Out on the Rim. New York, Mysterious Press, 1987.
The Fourth Durango. New York, Mysterious Press, 1989; London, Mysterious Press, 1990.

Novels as Oliver Bleeck (series: Philip St. Ives in all books)

The Brass Go-Between. New York, Morrow, 1969; London, Hodder and Stoughton, 1970.
Protocol for a Kidnapping. New York, Morrow, and London, Hodder and Stoughton, 1971.
The Procane Chronicle. New York, Morrow, 1972; as *The Thief Who Painted Sunlight,* London, Hodder and Stoughton, 1972; as *St. Ives,* New York, Pocket Books, 1976.
The Highbinders. New York, Morrow, and London, Hamish Hamilton, 1974.
No Questions Asked. New York, Morrow, and London, Hamish Hamilton, 1976.

OTHER PUBLICATIONS

Play

Screenplay: *Hammett,* with Dennis O'Flaherty and Thomas Pope, 1983.

Other

Warriors for the Poor: The Story of VISTA, with William H. Crook. New York, Morrow, 1969.

*   *   *

As a writer of political thrillers, Ross Thomas is America's answer to Len Deighton and John Le Carré, except that Thomas is funnier than either. He assumes what some le Carré characters have still to learn—that no government or institution can be trusted, and that individuals are only slightly more reliable than institutions. His impressive first novel, *The Cold War Swap,* concerns an "amortized," or expendable, American agent, surveys governments' "recruitment" methods for spies, and suggests how important public image has become even in espionage. With Deighton, Thomas shares a fascination with how things work, although his field of interest is different. In *The Porkchoppers* the reader finds out how a union election campaign is managed, and rigged; in *The Money Harvest,* how the commodities market works, and how it could be rigged; and in *The Seersucker Whipsaw,* how a political campaign in an emerging African nation might be directed, and manipulated. Before turning to the novel, Thomas pursued careers in journalism and public relations, and nothing of what he learned was lost on him.

Each Thomas book runs like a well-oiled machine for entertaining readers who have good general intelligence and strong suspicions about the motives of the people in charge of things. As Thomas, he has written 17 books about reluctant spies and political skulduggery. As Oliver Bleeck, he has written five books about Philip St. Ives, a professional go-between who functions as the point of contact between people who own valuable things and thieves who steal them—these classes overlap fairly often, of course. The formula and major components in all these books are the same: a group of protagonists who are knowledgeable, likeable, and for whom heroism is a last resort; a collection of secondary characters as various and colorful as the protagonists are similar and conservative; convincing settings; a deceptively relaxed and always literate prose style; and plots as lucid as they are complicated. Thomas's heroes are cousins to Deighton's hero and lineal descendants of Bret Maverick; they are so laid back as to be almost supine. A few Thomas heroes are married, and those who are not are provided with companionship. Thomas's female characters deserve special mention: they are either coolly or warmly intelligent, have no more illusions than the men they work with, and take their sex like adults. Thomas never descends to overheated "Stud prose" in describing sex. And it may or may not be a comment on Travis McGee that one of the heroes of *Chinaman's Chance* has been suffering from a nasty case of psychologically based impotence until he is cured by the love of a good woman.

After the horrific insights into the way things work, the adult characters, and the beautifully paced plots, the major attraction of these books is their humor. Thomas prefers the kind that ambushes the reader, often in the dryly bemused narrative, or in the characters' understated dialogue. One of them, the redoubtable Park Tyler Wilson III from Bleeck's *Protocol for a Kidnapping,* has expected to be court martialled for a deed "of incredible pusillanimity" in Vietnam. Given a Silver Star instead, he chose to laugh rather than cry. Thomas's characters are often presented with similar dilemmas, and they always choose the path of wisdom. And Thomas is definitely not above a quiet literary joke. In *The Eighth Dwarf* one of the characters is a young woman whose prose and conversational styles were formed by unrelieved exposure to a library of Victorian literature. It is not until the hero takes her to bed that he discovers it was a complete Victorian library, and she had read everything in the locked case too.

In *The Mordida Man,* Thomas takes up the theme of international terrorism, and, in *Missionary Stew,* describes a C.I.A. plot of surpassing seaminess which goes badly awry in a Central American country not entirely unlike El Salvador. The considerable degree of poetic justice that emerges neatly from the conclusions of these novels is probably not a sign that Thomas is mellowing. In *Missionary Stew* the hero's willingness to lay the Central American mess at the door of the incumbent American president is apparently shared by the author.

—Carol Cleveland

———

THOMPSON, China. *See* **BRAND, Christianna.**

———

THOMPSON, Jim (James Myers Thompson). American. Born in Oklahoma in 1906. Educated at the University of Nebraska, B.A. Married Alberta Thompson in 1931; two children. Had a variety of jobs including oil pipeline worker, steeplejack, burlesque actor, and professional gambler. Journalist for the New York *Daily News* and the Los Angeles *Times Mirror.* Associated with the Federal Writers Project in Oklahoma in the 1930's. *Died 7 April 1977.*

CRIME PUBLICATIONS

Novels

Now and On Earth.   New York, Modern Age, 1942.
Heed the Thunder.   New York, Greenberg, 1946.
Nothing More Than Murder.   New York, Harper, 1949.
Cropper's Cabin.   New York, Lion, 1952.
The Killer Inside Me.   New York, Lion, 1952; London, Sphere, 1973.
The Alcoholics.   New York, Lion, 1953.
Bad Boy.   New York, Lion, 1953.
The Criminal.   New York, Lion, 1953.
Recoil.   New York, Lion, 1953; London, Corgi, 1988.
Savage Night.   New York, Lion, 1953; London, Corgi, 1988.
A Swell-Looking Babe.   New York, Lion, 1954.
The Golden Gizmo.   New York, Lion, 1954.
A Hell of a Woman.   New York, Lion, 1954; London, Corgi, 1988.
The Nothing Man.   New York, Dell, 1954.
Roughneck.   New York, Lion, 1954.
After Dark, My Sweet.   New York, Popular Library, 1955.
The Kill-Off.   New York, Lion, 1957; London, Corgi, 1988.
Wild Town.   New York, New American Library, 1957.
The Getaway.   New York, New American Library, 1959; London, Sphere, 1973.
The Transgressors.   New York, New American Library, 1961.
The Grifters.   Evanston, Illinois, Regency, 1963; London, Zomba, 1983.
Pop. 1280.   New York, Fawcett, 1964; London, Zomba, 1983.
Texas by the Tail.   New York, Fawcett, 1965.
Ironside (novelization of television series).   New York, Popular Library, 1967.
South of Heaven.   New York, Fawcett, 1967.
The Undefeated (novelization of screenplay).   New York, Popular Library, 1969.
Nothing But a Man (novelization of screenplay).   New York, Popular Library, 1970.
Child of Rage.   New York, Lancer, 1972.
King Blood.   London, Sphere, 1973.
Hard Core (omnibus).   New York, Fine, 1986.
More Hardcore (omnibus).   New York, Fine, 1987.

Uncollected Short Stories

"Bellboy," in *Mercury* (New York), February 1956.
"Prowlers in the Pear Trees," in *Mercury* (New York), March 1956.
"The Flaw in the System," in *Ellery Queen's Mystery Magazine* (New York), July 1956.
"Murder Came on the Mayflower," in *Mercury* (New York), November 1956.
"The Cellini Chalice," in *Alfred Hitchcock's Mystery Magazine* (New York), December 1956.
"The Frightening Frammis," in *Alfred Hitchcock's Mystery Magazine* (New York), February 1957.
"Forever After," in *Shock* (New York), May 1960.
"Exactly What Happened," in *Ellery Queen's Mystery Magazine* (New York), April 1967.
"This World—Then the Fireworks," in *Jim Thompson: The Killers Inside Him,* by Max Allan Collins and Ed Gorman. Cedar Rapids, Iowa, Fedora Press, 1983.

OTHER PUBLICATIONS

Play

Screenplay: *Paths of Glory,* with Stanley Kubrick and Calder Willingham, 1957.

Television Writing: scripts for *Dr. Kildare* series.

*

Critical Study: *Jim Thompson: The Killers Inside Him* by Max Allan Collins and Ed Gorman. Cedar Rapids, Iowa, Fedora Press, 1983.

Theatrical Activities:

Actor: **Film**—*Farewell, My Lovely,* 1975.

*   *   *

It might be said that, roughly, Jim Thompson is to James M. Cain as Raymond Chandler is to Dashiell Hammett. Like Chandler's, Thompson's talent and skills are worthy of his predecessor, but—like Chandler—he brings them to bear on areas his predecessor did not explore, in a voice uniquely his own.

Thompson co-wrote two of Stanley Kubrick's earliest (and best) films, *The Killing* and *Paths of Glory,* and a number of his books have themselves generated films, most recently in France, where most of his novels remain in print. But in the United States he is best known by the crime fiction fans who collect the now scarce and valuable original (and in most cases only) American paperback editions. With the exception of his one outright Cain imitation, the first-rate *Nothing More Than Murder,* all of Thompson's crime novels appeared as paperbacks and lack the legitimacy hardcover publication might have lent them—and him.

The subject matter of Thompson's best books is so disturbing as to make Cain, the master of the "tabloid murder," seem a friendly spinner of tales. Love as shabbily noble as Frank Chambers and Cora Papadakis's in Cain's *The Postman Always Rings Twice* is a rarity in Thompson, and the often quiet but all-pervasive madness of Thompson's protagonists is unrelenting—once it sneaks up on you. Thompson forces the reader into the tortured psyche of a soul whose "sickness" is cloaked in superficial normalcy. Intellectual and philosophical pretensions are common among Thompson narrators, and seem derived, in part, from the similar pretensions of Ralph Cotter, the college-educated narrator of Horace McCoy's 1948 novel, *Kiss Tomorrow Goodbye.*

Not all of Thompson's books have murderers of psychopaths as their protagonists—but the best ones, the most characteristic ones, do. Several of his novels are rather straightforward crime stories—often involving scams of one sort or another, as is the case in *Recoil; The Getaway* is a deftly plotted third-person crime novel with an ironic, bleak conclusion that the strangely sterile Peckinpah 1973 film adaptation omits. Among his other works are several modern-day Westerns (including *Wild Town* and *The Transgressors*). Several times he flirts with the mainstream by dealing with social concerns (alcoholism in *The Alcoholics,* racial tension in *Child of Rage*), but his quirky, surreal, blackly humorous treatment of such subjects relegates him to the paperback ghetto. Obviously, though, he had range, and could be a solid professional workhorse when necessary, as evidenced by the somewhat demeaning movie and television novelizations he turned to doing late in his career.

What served Thompson best was first-person narration, in

which he could follow his disturbed protagonists wherever their warped personalities and stream of consciousness happened to flow. First and most famous of these generally amiable psychopaths is Lou Ford, Deputy of Central City, the "hero" of *The Killer Inside Me.* Ford pretends to be a rather simple, cliché-spouting hick, the sort of dopey bore anybody hates to be cornered by; but Ford is actually a cunning, complex, even brilliant madman who is playing cat-and-mouse with the world. Thompson typically reveals Ford's madness a little at a time, allowing us to be fooled by him for a while ourselves.

While Ford is an untrustworthy narrator—though he doesn't lie to the reader so much as to himself—he (and most later Thompson psychopath/narrators) never becomes completely unsympathetic. In Thompson, the protagonist is driven to violent acts that seldom make the sort of "sense" of a Cain plot, with its motivations in greed and love, and its grounding in a vaguely religious "fate." Lou Ford kills because he has "the sickness." In Thompson "fate" is defined as environment and heredity ganging up on you. There is no master plan, no web of destiny, not even karma, to give sense to life; there are just "circumstances" beyond our control that form us. And some of us, like Lou Ford, are misshapen.

Thompson's psychopaths have much in common, but each is distinct. The closest Thompson comes to repeating himself is *Pop. 1280,* a re-working of *The Killer Inside Me* that surpasses the original, substituting black humor for bleak melodrama, as deputy Nick Corey indulges in self-serving murders while becoming deluded into thinking he's Jesus Christ Himself. Thompson's ever-present compassion for his troubled protagonists is most obvious in *The Nothing Man,* in which the "sickness" of the alcoholic reporter Clint Brown is a result of his having been castrated in the war. An outstanding, little-discussed Thompson novel is *Savage Night,* whose narrator—a diminutive, world-weary, dying hitman—is presented as just another victim of the human condition. *A Hell of a Woman* is perhaps the best example of Thompson's offhanded brilliance. Gradually, we become aware that this typical Thompson blue-collar "hero" isn't always telling us the truth; the self-pitying narrator whines and schemes and, eventually, kills—several times, cold-bloodedly. *After Dark, My Sweet* is the most accessible, best-crafted of Thompson's psychopath-as-narrator novels. The protagonist, Kid Collins, is a handsome, good-natured, simple soul—who can become violent under stress; unlike other Thompson protagonists, however, Kid actively tries to fight his "sickness," hoping to overcome it. Kid finally sacrifices himself for the welfare of the woman he loves and a kidnapped child with whom he identifies, and finds a nobility in his death—suicidal though it is—that no other Thompson "hero" achieves.

—Max Allan Collins

THOMSON, Basil (Home). British. Born 21 April 1861. Educated at Eton College; New College, Oxford; Inner Temple, London: called to the Bar. Married in 1889; three children. Worked in the Foreign Service: Prime Minister of Tonga in early 1890's; entered the Civil Service and became Governor of Dartmoor Prison, Devon, until 1907, and of Wormwood Scrubs Prison, London, 1907; Secretary to the Prison Commission, 1908; assistant commissioner, Metropolitan Police, London, 1913–19; Director of Intelligence, 1919–21. Recipient: Royal Humane Society Silver Medal. Companion, 1916, and Knight Commander of the Bath, 1919; Commander,

Crown of Italy; Member, Order of the Rising Sun, Japan; Member, Order of Leopold, and of the Crown, Belgium. *Died 26 March 1939.*

CRIME PUBLICATIONS

Novels (series: Peter Graham; Police Constable/Superintendent Richardson)

A Court Intrigue. London, Heinemann, 1896.
Carfax Abbey. London, Methuen, 1928.
The Metal Flask (Graham). London, Methuen, 1929.
The Prince from Overseas. London, Chapman and Hall, 1930.
P.C. Richardson's First Case. London, Eldon Press, and New York, Doubleday, 1933.
The Kidnapper (Graham). London, Eldon Press, 1933.
Richardson Scores Again. London, Eldon Press, 1934; as *Richardson's Second Case,* New York, Doubleday, 1934.
Inspector Richardson, C.I.D. London, Eldon Press, 1934; as *The Case of Naomi Clynes,* New York, Doubleday, 1934.
Richardson Goes Abroad. London, Eldon Press, 1935; as *The Case of the Dead Diplomat,* New York, Doubleday, 1935.
Richardson Solves a Dartmoor Mystery. London, Eldon Press, 1935; as *The Dartmoor Enigma,* New York, Doubleday, 1936.
Death in the Bathroom (Richardson). London, Eldon Press, 1936; as *Who Killed Stella Pomeroy?,* New York, Doubleday, 1936.
Milliner's Hat Mystery (Richardson). London, Eldon Press, 1937; as *The Mystery of The French Milliner,* New York, Doubleday, 1937.
A Murder Arranged (Richardson). London, Eldon Press, 1937; as *When Thieves Fall Out,* New York, Doubleday, 1937.

Short Stories

Mr. Pepper, Investigator. London, Castle, 1925.

OTHER PUBLICATIONS

Novel

The Indiscretions of Lady Asneath. London, Innes, 1898.

Play

The Elixir (produced London, 1917).

Other

The Diversions of a Prime Minister (history of Tonga). Edinburgh, Blackwood, 1894.
South Sea Yarns. Edinburgh, Blackwood, 1894.
Savage Island: An Account of a Sojourn in Niué and Tonga. London, Murray, 1902.
The Story of Dartmoor Prison. London, Heinemann, 1907.
The Fijians: A Study of the Decay of Custom. London, Heinemann, 1908.
Queer People. London, Hodder and Stoughton, 1922; as *My Experiences at Scotland Yard,* New York, Doubleday, 1923.
The Criminal. London, Hodder and Stoughton, 1925.
The Allied Secret Service in Greece. London, Hutchinson, 1930.
The Story of Scotland Yard. London, Grayson, 1935; New York, Doubleday, 1936.

The Gold Repeater: A Detective Story for Boys. London, A. and C. Black, 1936.
The Scene Changes (autobiography). New York, Doubleday, 1937; London, Collins, 1939.

Editor, with W.A.T. Amherst, *The Discovery of the Solomon Islands by Alvaro de Mendaña in 1568.* London, Bedford Press, 2 vols., 1901.
Editor, *The Skene Papers: Memories of Sir Walter Scott,* by James Skene. London, Murray, 1909.

* * *

Sir Basil Thomson served as colonial administrator, diplomat, governor of Dartmoor Prison, head of the CID of Scotland Yard during World War I, and director of intelligence in the postwar years. He also wrote numerous books, including Oceanic area studies, anthropology, historical criminology, memoirs, and fiction.

Thomson drew heavily upon his prison and police experiences in preparing eight detective novels that are set in Scotland Yard. Based on the career of Richardson, who rises from a probationer to the position of Chief Constable, they combine classical concepts of crime and narrative structure with an emphasis on procedural matters. Richardson, like his fellows at the Yard, is neither a superman nor an oaf; instead he is a conscientious, intelligent craftsman who must obtain permission from superiors, clear with the legal experts, fill out forms, and most of all bear the budget in mind. In the first six novels Richardson himself acts as detective; in the last two, because of his high position, he enters simply as instructor or coordinator. The Richardson novels are well-written and imaginative, with a wealth of detail about police operations, but there is little mystery per se in them, since the obvious suspect (as in life) is usually guilty. At its best—*P.C. Richardson's First Case, Richardson Solves a Dartmoor Mystery*—Thomson's work conveys a leisurely charm that is reminiscent of R. Austin Freeman's.

Thomson's other mystery-detective fiction includes a borderline romance, *A Court Intrigue,* which mingles Graustark, crime, and a spoof; *The Kidnapper* which abandons the realistic mode of the Richardson novels; and two minor works, *Carfax Abbey* and *The Metal Flask. Mr. Pepper, Investigator* is a collection of humorous short stories based upon a clownish American who poses as a great private detective. Pepper also appears in *The Kidnapper.* All these works are much inferior to the Richardson novels.

Criminology was also one of Thomson's interests. *The Criminal* is a social study based upon his prison experiences; *The Story of Dartmoor Prison* and *The Story of Scotland Yard* are anecdotal accounts stressing important crimes. His two volumes of memoirs say little about detective work or his writing experiences.

—E. F. Bleiler

THOMSON, June. British. Born in Kent, 24 June 1930. Educated at Chelmsford High School for Girls, Essex, 1941–49; Bedford College, University of London, 1949–52, B.A. (honours) in English 1952. Divorced; two sons. Teacher, Stoke-on-Trent and London, 1953–67, and St. Albans, 1967–73; lecturer, teacher training college, Watford, Hertfordshire,

1973–77. Agent: Tessa Sayle, 11 Jubilee Place, London SW3 3TE. Address: 177 Verulam Road, St. Albans, Hertfordshire AL3 4DW, England.

CRIME PUBLICATIONS

Novels (series: Inspector Finch in all books; in US Doubleday editions called Inspector Rudd)

Not One of Us. New York, Harper, 1971; London, Constable, 1972.
Death Cap. London, Constable, 1973; New York, Doubleday, 1977.
The Long Revenge. London, Constable, 1974; New York, Doubleday, 1975.
Case Closed. London, Constable, and New York, Doubleday, 1977.
A Question of Identity. New York, Doubleday, 1977; London, Constable, 1978.
Deadly Relations. London, Constable, 1979; as *The Habit of Loving,* New York, Doubleday, 1979.
Alibi in Time. London, Constable, and New York, Doubleday, 1980.
Shadow of a Doubt. London, Constable, 1981; New York, Doubleday, 1982.
To Make a Killing. London, Constable, 1982; as *Portrait of Lilith,* New York, Doubleday, 1983.
Sound Evidence. London, Constable, 1984; New York, Doubleday, 1985.
A Dying Fall. London, Constable, 1985; New York, Doubleday, 1986.
The Dark Stream. London, Constable and New York, Doubleday, 1986.
No Flowers, By Request. London, Constable, and New York, Doubleday, 1987.
Rosemary for Remembrance. London, Constable, and New York, Doubleday, 1988.
The Spoils of Time. London, Constable and New York, Doubleday, 1989.
Past Reckoning. London, Constable, 1990.

Uncollected Short Stories

"Crossing Bridges," in *Winter's Crimes 10,* edited by Hilary Watson. London, Macmillan, and New York, St. Martin's Press, 1978.
"Queen of Cups," in *Mystery Guild Anthology,* edited by John Waite. London, Constable, 1980.
"The Bait," in *Winter's Crimes 15,* edited by George Hardinge. London, Macmillan, and New York, St. Martin's Press, 1983.
"A Walk to the Paradise Garden," in *Ellery Queen's Mystery Magazine* (New York), December 1989.

*

June Thomson comments:
I have always enjoyed reading detective fiction: a mystery or a puzzle has its fascination. So has the process of unravelling. Writing detective fiction gives the opportunity to examine character and relationships in a very special way—pushed to the limit so to speak, and in jeopardy. I am interested in the personality of the outsider—the person who doesn't quite fit in with his environment. I use a country setting because I know it and feel I understand the kind of relationships, close and

closed, that can develop in a small community with its own special loyalties and tensions. Inspector Finch (Rudd in the US) can understand and sympathise with these loyalties and tensions, and sometimes exploit them.

* * *

Realism is the key note of June Thomson's novels: always careful to enlist a willing suspension of disbelief she finds no room for, nor need of, the surreal or bizarre. Despite being firmly rooted in the English tradition of detection, and despite her frequent use of country settings, she appears in little danger of being tempted by the potential for crime offered by the large country house, instead finding more than enough material in the lives of her middle- and working-class characters.

Thomson's emphasis is on the quotidian, everyday routines, and seemingly normal lives. Death by violence shatters this apparent normality. However it does so with an inevitability which is the result of scrupulous pacing and meticulous plotting: these texts disclose no gaps, in the end all the pieces do, quite carefully, fit.

Detective Chief Inspector Finch (Rudd in the United States), is as careful as his creator, solving each crime by painstakingly collecting together and studying every clue. A quiet man, careful to maintain a low profile, Finch does not hesitate to draw comparisons between his own life and that of the various suspects and victims. Indeed, like many of the latter, Finch's personal life is devoid of love—or, rather, the right sort of love. Living with his sister, his desire for a relationship with another woman seems futile and even treacherous. There are things which just can't be said or, when said, are not understood, and it is this failure of communication and the loneliness which results, which is also explored in *No Flowers*, *By Request*, and *Rosemary for Remembrance*.

Finch is trapped within the pattern of family, a theme which Thomson repeatedly comes back to and which also constitutes one of the most interesting aspects of her work. The dual title of *Deadly Relations*—published in the United States as *The Habit of Loving*—says it all. The pattern by which we love is set in childhood, within the family, and family relationships can be both deadening and deadly. In *Deadly Relations* the claustrophobic nature of his relationship with his mother results in a young man's outbursts of violence and subsequent breakdown and it takes insight and courage on the part of the lonely, middleaged Maggie Hearn to refuse to accept Chris as surrogate son/lover, thus breaking the pattern and offering him the chance of freedom. "'The more emotional the relationship,'" Finch realizes, "'the more violent the break.'" When self-knowledge is lacking the violence may manifest itself physically, but self-knowledge doesn't come easily, even for the professionals. In *Shadow of a Doubt* a psychologist's limited understanding of his own motives results in his preying on his vulnerable women patients.

The most vulnerable are often to be found closest to home and incest, the breaking of the final taboo, provides a motive for murder in *Deadly Relations* and in *To Make a Killing* (*Portrait of Lilith*), where an elderly artist, Max Gifford, tantalizes himself with the possibility that his younger lover is also his daughter.

Max and Nina have left London to become bohemian exiles in the country, so picking up on Thomson's interest in exile and isolation, an interest also demonstrated in *A Question of Identity,* and *Not One of Us.* In *The Long Revenge* Thomson steps outside her normal cast by introducing a secret service agent while in *Sound Evidence* she renders a sensitive portrait of a senior civil servant, caught by his love for a handsome but untrustworthy young man. Here Finch has not only to deal with the issue of scandal in the Foreign Office but also with his discovery of police corruption: delving into the past history of the victim reveals his connection with one of Finch's own men. In *Past Reckoning* Finch is granted a second meeting with Nina and once more the obsessive nature of family ties are revealed, this time against a backdrop of drug trafficking and blackmail.

This ability to deal with contemporary themes whilst not losing the suspense element of the traditional "whodunit" is what makes Thomson one of the most interesting of current British crime novelists: she manages to combine the best of both worlds.

—Penny Smith

THORNBURG, Newton (Kendall). American. Born in Harvey, Illinois, 13 May 1930. Educated at the University of Iowa, Iowa City, B.A. 1951; Writers' Workshop, New York, 1953. Married Karin Larson in 1954; one daughter and two sons. Advertising copywriter in various agencies, 1960–70. Address: c/o Arbor House, 105 Madison Avenue, New York, New York 10016, U.S.A.

CRIME PUBLICATIONS

Novels

Gentlemen Born.   New York, Fawcett, 1967.
The Knockover.   New York, Fawcett, and London, Coronet, 1968.
To Die in California.   Boston, Little Brown, 1973.
Cutter and Bone.   Boston, Little Brown, 1976; London, Heinemann, 1977.
Black Angus.   Boston, Little Brown, 1978; London, Heinemann, 1979.
Valhalla.   Boston, Little Brown, 1980.
Beautiful Kate.   Boston, Little Brown, 1982.
Dreamland.   New York, Arbor House, 1983.
The Lion at the Door.   New York, Morrow, 1990.

* * *

Newton Thornburg is pretty much the definitive crime writer as outsider. Nine books in 20 odd years obsessively work and rework the same themes. These are stories of loners with harsh, short names—Hook, Stone, Cutter, Bone, Crow, Cross—who have had their lives tipped out of their control—generally by fate, the government, or both.

Thornburg's first novel *Gentleman Born*, marked out one of his major themes, the family tragedy. Brandon Kendall is the last remnant of an old money Midwestern family; his father killed himself, his cousins died in a boating accident when they were children together, and golden boy Brandon is intent on going to the bad just as fast and as far as he can. Gambling and women are his chosen route to oblivion and along the way he entangles himself in small town corruption. When the end comes it is bleak and bloody and no surprise.

A relatively conventional caper novel, *The Knockover*, followed and Thornburg's subsequent literary career has tended to oscillate between these two poles. Family gone bad sagas like *Black Angus* or *Beautiful Kate* have alternated with seemingly more conventional crime novels like *Cutter and Bone* (his greatest success, filmed as *Cutter's Way*), *Dreamland*, or his most recent work, *The Lion At the Door*.

However, the contrast is superficial as all these books are driven by the same question of *how* one comes to terms with unbearable loss. Cutter in *Cutter and Bone* was crippled in Vietnam, Greg Kendall in *Beautiful Kate* tries to come to terms with his sister's death following their incestuous relationship, Blanchard in *Black Angus* is losing his dream, his farm in the Ozarks, Kohl in *The Lion at the Door* has lost both farm and family. This theme of loss takes flight as an echo of the American mood post-Vietnam; a sense that the whole country is losing control, losing sight of its dream.

In his strangest novel, *Valhalla*, this connection is made all to explicit. It's an apocalyptic novel of a near future in which America is gripped by race war, and in it Thornburg's terminal pessimism about the state of America leads him into territory uncomfortably close to that inhabited by the survivalist ultra-right.

Thornburg's pessimism is far more effective in his crime-based novels like *Cutter and Bone* and *Dreamland* whose pace prevents melancholic wallowing and whose cynicism is all too appropriate to the task of exposing the corporate roots of American crime. In these two novels particularly, Thornburg stands as a defiantly individual voice within the crime canon, bleak and true.

—John Williams

TIDYMAN, Ernest. American. Born in Cleveland, Ohio, 1 January 1928. Educated in public schools in Cleveland to the seventh grade. Served in the United States Army, 1945–46. Married Susan Gould in 1970; four sons, two by previous marriage. Staff member, Cleveland *News,* 1954–57, New York *Post,* 1957–60, and *New York Times,* 1960–66; magazine editor, 1966–69. After 1969, self-employed writer and film producer. Recipient: Writers Guild of America award, Mystery Writers of America Edgar Allan Poe award, and Academy award, all for screenplay, 1972; National Association for the Advancement of Colored People Image award. *Died 14 July 1984.*

CRIME PUBLICATIONS

Novels (series: John Shaft)

Shaft. New York, Macmillan 1970; London, Joseph, 1971.
Shaft among the Jews. New York, Dial Press, 1972; London, Weidenfeld and Nicolson, 1973.
Shaft's Big Score. New York, Bantam, and London, Corgi, 1972.
Shaft Has a Ball. New York, Bantam, and London, Corgi, 1973.
Goodbye, Mr. Shaft. New York, Dial Press, 1973; London, Weidenfeld and Nicolson, 1974.
Shaft's Carnival of Killers. New York, Bantam, 1974; London, Bantam, 1975.
Line of Duty. Boston, Little Brown, and London, W.H. Allen, 1974.
The Last Shaft. London, Weidenfeld and Nicolson, 1975.

OTHER PUBLICATIONS

Novels

Flower Power. New York, Paperback Library, 1968.
Absolute Zero. New York, Dial Press, 1971.
High Plains Drifter. New York, Bantam, and London, Corgi, 1973.
Starstruck. London, W.H. Allen, 1975.
Table Stakes. Boston, Little Brown, and London, Weidenfeld and Nicolson, 1978.

Plays

Screenplays: *The French Connection,* 1971; *Shaft,* with John D.F. Black, 1971; *Shaft's Big Score,* 1972; *High Plains Drifter,* 1973; *Report to the Commissioner (Operation Undercover),* with Abby Mann, 1975; *Street People,* 1976; *A Force of One,* with Pat Johnson, 1979; *Last Plane Out,* 1983.

Television Plays: *Shaft* series, 1974; *To Kill a Cop (Streets of Fear),* from a book by Robert Daley, 1978; *Dummy,* 1979; *Power: An American Saga,* 1979; *Alcatraz,* 1980; *Guyana Tragedy: The Story of Jim Jones,* 1980; *Power,* 1980; *Brotherly Love,* 1984; *Stark,* with Bill Stratton, 1985.

Other

The Anzio Death Trap. New York, Belmont, 1968.
Dummy. Boston, Little Brown, and London, W.H. Allen, 1974.
Big Bucks: The True, Outrageous Story of the Plymouth Mail Robbery and How They Got Away with It. New York, Norton, 1982.

*   *   *

Ernest Tidyman will no doubt always be known as the creator of Shaft, the black detective. He was high-styled, as violent in action as any of the descendants of Mike Hammer, but as intelligent as he was tough. Shaft became an even bigger star on the screen, important as a new type of detective, a sex symbol as well as a formidable fighter for good against evil. Nevertheless, Tidyman was not a one-theme writer. Though he produced some half dozen Shaft cases, he also wrote other police stories based on crimes besetting a modern city. One of these, *Line of Duty,* was a bestseller. Tidyman's city is Cleveland, where he worked as a reporter for 25 years before becoming a full-time writer. His style is less reportorial than it is out of *Black Mask;* it punches, is heavy on similes, and features odd characters.

—Dorothy B. Hughes

TILTON, Alice. *See* TAYLOR, Phoebe Atwood.

TINKER, Beamish. *See* **JESSE, F. Tennyson.**

———

TORRIE, Malcolm. *See* **MITCHELL, Gladys.**

———

TOWNE, Stuart. *See* **RAWSON, Clayton.**

———

TRAIN, Arthur (Cheney). American. Born in Boston, Massachusetts, 6 September 1875. Educated at Prince School, Boston; Boston Latin School; St. Paul's School, Concord, New Hampshire; Harvard University, Cambridge, Massachusetts, A.B. 1896, LL.B. 1899; admitted to the Massachusetts bar 1899. Married 1) Ethel Kissam in 1897 (died 1923); three daughters and one son; 2) Helen C. Gerard in 1926; one son. Lawyer: worked in firm of Robinson Biddle and Ward, 1900; assistant District Attorney for New York, 1901–08; in private practice (Train and Olney, later Perkins and Train) after 1908; Attorney General, Commonwealth of Massachusetts. Prolific story writer from 1904. President, National Institute of Arts and Letters, 1941–45. *Died 22 December 1945.*

CRIME PUBLICATIONS

Novels (series: Ephraim Tutt)

The Confessions of Artemas Quibble. New York, Scribner, 1911.
"C.Q."; or, In the Wireless House. New York, Century, 1912.
The Hermit of Turkey Hollow (Tutt). New York, Scribner, 1921.
The Blind Goddess. New York, Scribner, 1926.
The Adventures of Ephraim Tutt. New York, Scribner, 1930.
Manhattan Murder. New York, Scribner, 1936; as *Murderers' Medicine.* London, Constable, 1937.
Yankee Lawyer—Autobiography of Ephraim Tutt. New York, Scribner, 1943.

Short Stories

McAllister and His Double. New York, Scribner, and London, Newnes, 1905.
Mortmain. New York, Appleton, 1907.
Tutt and Mr. Tutt. New York, Scribner, 1920.
By Advice of Counsel. New York, Scribner, 1921.
Tut, Tut! Mr. Tutt. New York, Scribner, 1923; London, Nash, 1924.
Page Mr. Tutt. New York, Scribner, 1926.
When Tutt Meets Tutt. New York, Scribner, 1927.
Tutt for Tutt. New York, Scribner, 1934.
Mr. Tutt Takes the Stand. New York, Scribner, 1936.
Mr. Tutt's Case Book (omnibus). New York, Scribner, 1936.
Old Man Tutt. New York, Scribner, 1938.

Mr. Tutt Comes Home. New York, Scribner, 1941.
Mr. Tutt Finds a Way. New York, Scribner, 1945.
Mr. Tutt at His Best, edited by Harold R. Medina. New York, Scribner, 1961.

OTHER PUBLICATIONS

Novels

The Butler's Story. New York, Scribner, and London, Laurie, 1909.
The Man Who Rocked the Earth, with Robert William Wood. New York, Doubleday, 1915.
The World and Thomas Kelly. New York, Scribner, 1917.
As It Was in the Beginning. New York, Macmillan, 1921.
His Children's Children. New York, Scribner, and London, Nash, 1923.
The Needle's Eye. New York, Scribner, 1924.
The Lost Gospel. New York, Scribner, 1925.
High Winds. New York, Scribner, and London, Nash, 1927.
Ambition. New York, Scribner, and London, Nash, 1928.
The Horns of Ramadan. New York, Scribner, 1928; London, Nash, 1929.
Illusion. New York, Scribner, and London, Nash, 1929.
Paper Profits. New York, Liveright, and London, Mathews and Marrot, 1930.
Princess Pro Tem. New York, Scribner, 1932.
No Matter Where. New York, Scribner, 1933.
Jacob's Ladder. New York, Scribner, 1935.
Tassels on Her Boots. New York, Scribner, and London, Hutchinson, 1940.
The Moon Maker, with Robert William Wood. Hamburg, New York, Krueger, 1958.

Other

The Prisoner at the Bar. New York, Scribner, 1906; London, Laurie, 1907; revised edition, 1908; revised edition, as *From the District Attorney's Office,* 1939.
True Stories of Crime from the District Attorney's Office. New York, Scribner, and London, Laurie, 1908.
Courts, Criminals, and the Camorra. New York, Scribner, and London, Chapman and Hall, 1912.
The Earthquake. New York, Scribner, 1918.
Courts and Criminals (selection). New York, Scribner, 1921.
On the Trail of the Bad Men. New York, Scribner, 1925.
Puritan's Progress. New York, Scribner, 1931.
The Strange Attacks on Herbert Hoover. New York, Day, 1932.
My Day in Court (autobiography). New York, Scribner, 1939.

Editor, *The Goldfish, Being the Confessions of a Successful Man.* New York, Century, 1914.

* * *

As Assistant District Attorney for New York County, Arthur Train saw stories in the procession of human comedies and tragedies that passed through the criminal court building. His first book, *McAllister and His Double,* concerns a wealthy clubman whose look-alike valet is a known felon. It also contains four stories about a young Deputy District Attorney, John Dockbridge, who is a forerunner of Train's most famous character, Ephraim Tutt.

Though the bulk of Train's fiction deals with other characters, it is for Mr. Tutt that he is remembered. The

Lincolnesque lawyer with his frock coat, stove pipe hat, and fondness for stogies is a vivid character. The stories all follow a formula: the statement of the problem, the seeming impossibility of the triumph of justice over the technicalities of the law, and Mr. Tutt's solution to the problem. They are solid Americana, and Tutt is a figure from American folklore, the shrewd Yankee on the side of the underdog.

Most of Train's many other books do not deal with crime or the law, but with human nature. *His Children's Children* has been compared with *The Forsyte Saga*. *The Prisoner at the Bar* (non-fiction) and *The Blind Goddess* deal with the workings of the courts. *The Confessions of Artemas Quibble* is a genial satire on the legal profession, while *Manhattan Murder* is a vivid, if romantic, portrait of New York in the gangster era.

—J. Randolph Cox

———

TREAT, Lawrence. American. Born Lawrence Arthur Goldstone in New York City, 21 December 1903. Educated at Dartmouth College, Hanover, New Hampshire, B.A. (cum laude) 1924; Columbia University School of Law, New York, LL.B. (Phi Beta Kappa) 1927. Married Rose Ehrenfreund in 1943. Has taught mystery writing at Columbia University, New York, New York University, Adelphi College, Ditmas High School, Brooklyn, New York, and public schools in Westchester County, New York and Martha's Vineyard, Massachusetts, and elsewhere. Past President, Mystery Writers of America. Recipient: Mystery Writers of America Edgar Allan Poe award, 1965, 1978. Agent: Vicky Bijur, 333 West End Avenue, Apartment 5B, New York, New York 10023. Address: RFD Box 475A, Edgartown, Massachusetts 02539, U.S.A.

CRIME PUBLICATIONS

Novels (series: Bill Decker; Jub Freeman; Mitch Taylor; Carl Wayward)

Run Far, Run Fast (as Lawrence A. Goldstone). New York, Greystone Press, 1937.
B as in Banshee (Wayward). New York, Duell, 1940; as *Wail for the Corpses*, New York, Select, 1943.
D as in Dead (Wayward). New York, Duell, 1941.
H as in Hangman (Wayward). New York, Duell, 1942.
O as in Omen (Wayward). New York, Duell, 1943.
The Leather Man. New York, Duell, 1944; London, Rich and Cowan, 1947.
V as in Victim (Taylor; Freeman). New York, Duell, 1945; London, Rich and Cowan, 1950.
H as in Hunted (Freeman). New York, Duell, 1946; London, Boardman, 1950.
Q as in Quicksand (Taylor; Freeman). New York, Duell, 1947; as *Step into Quicksand*, London, Boardman, 1959.
T as in Trapped (Taylor; Freeman). New York, Morrow, 1947.
F as in Flight (Freeman; Decker). New York, Morrow, 1948; London, Boardman, 1949.
Over the Edge (Freeman; Decker). New York, Morrow, 1948; London, Boardman, 1958.
Trial and Terror. New York, Morrow, 1949; London, Boardman, 1958.

Big Shot (Taylor; Decker; Freeman). New York, Harper, 1951; London, Boardman, 1952.
Weep for a Wanton (Taylor; Freeman). New York, Ace, 1956; London, Boardman, 1957.
Lady, Drop Dead (Taylor; Freeman). New York and London, Abelard Schuman, 1960.
Venus Unarmed. New York, Doubleday, 1961.

Short Stories

P as in Police, edited by Ellery Queen. New York, Davis, 1970.

Uncollected Short Stories

"Snake in the Grass," in *Detective Fiction Weekly* (New York), 1937.
"The Murder of Katherine Scharn," in *New York Murders*, edited by Ted Collins. New York, Duell, 1944.
"The Squatters," in *Family Circle*, May 1945.
"Keep 'em Happy," in *Maclean's Magazine*, 1946.
"Twenty Dollar Debt," in *Murder Cavalcade*, edited by Ken Crossen. New York, Duell, 1946; London, Hammond, 1953.
"Four Bits for the Law," in *Giant Detective Annual*. New York, Best Books, 1950.
"Ring Around a Lady," in *Red Book*, 1950.
"The Cinderella Trick," in *Woman's Home Companion* (Springfield, Ohio), October 1951.
"Shoes for Breakfast," in *Maiden Murders*, edited by John Dickson Carr. New York, Harper, 1952.
"The Wire Brush," with Sidney Tarachow, in *Crooks Tour*. New York, Dodd Mead, 1953.
"Homicide Expert," in *Crime for Two*, edited by Frances and Richard Lockridge. Philadelphia, Lippincott, 1955; London, Macdonald, 1957.
"Proof of the Pudding," in *Eat, Drink, and Be Buried*, edited by Rex Stout. New York, Viking Press, 1956.
"A Man Named Smith," in *The Saint* (New York), November 1956.
"Murder Me Twice," in *For Love and Money*, edited by Dorothy Gardiner. New York, Doubleday, 1957; London, Macdonald, 1959.
"Exactly Five Thirty-Five," in *The Saint* (New York), May 1957.
"The Man Who Got Away with It," in *Alfred Hitchcock's Mystery Magazine* (New York), September 1957.
"Justice Magnifique," in *A Choice of Murders*, edited by Dorothy Salisbury Davis. New York, Scribner, 1958; London, Macdonald, 1960.
"Run into Trouble," in *Bestseller Mystery Magazine*, July 1958.
"Sing a Song of Murder," in *The Saint* (New York), March 1958.
"A Safe's Cracked in Brooklyn," in *Sleuth* (New York), October 1958.
"Reluctant Riot," in *The Saint* (New York), November 1958.
"Some Diamonds and I . . . ," in *Sleuth* (New York), December 1958.
"Ham on Toast," "Diamonds and Jazz," "The Devil May Care," all in *Sleuth* (New York), 1958.
"Dresden Alias Faraday," in *Alfred Hitchcock's Mystery Magazine* (New York), February 1959.
"Big Important Day," in *Alfred Hitchcock's Mystery Magazine* (New York), April 1959.
"Ice Cold Murder," in *The Saint* (New York), July 1959.
"Death in the Swamp," in *The Saint* (New York), August 1959.

"Perfect Shot," in *Alfred Hitchcock's Mystery Magazine* (New York), October 1959.

"Framed in Oil," in *The Saint* (New York), July 1960.

"Another Day, Another Murder," in *Alfred Hitchcock's Mystery Magazine* (New York), August 1961.

"The Helping Hand," in *The Saint* (London), October 1961.

"Family Code," in *Alfred Hitchcock's Mystery Magazine* (New York), March 1962.

"Friendly Murderer," in *Ellery Queen's Mystery Magazine* (New York), March 1962.

"Death Lives Here," in *The Saint* (London), June 1962.

"The Picture of Guilt," in *The Saint* (New York), June 1962.

"Murder Masquerade," in *The Saint* (New York), October 1962.

"Shoot a Friendly Bullet," in *Alfred Hitchcock's Mystery Magazine* (New York), November 1962.

"Run into Trouble," in *A Pride of Felons*, edited by the Gordons. New York, Macmillan, 1963; London, Dobson, 1964.

"Breathe Deep, Lady!," in *The Saint* (New York), February 1963.

"Instructions for Murder," in *The Saint* (New York), June 1963.

"Homicide, Maybe," in *Alfred Hitchcock's Mystery Magazine* (New York), August 1963.

"United Nations Murder Case," in *Crimes Across the Sea*, edited by John Creasey. New York, Harper, and London, Longman, 1964.

"Ugly Duckling," in *The Saint* (New York), October 1964.

"Some Other Time," in *The Saint* (New York), August 1965.

"Time and Tide," in *Masters of Mayhem*, edited by Edward D. Radin, New York, Morrow, 1965.

"Ask a Stupid Question," in *Sleuths and Consequences*, edited by Thomas B. Dewey. New York, Simon and Schuster, 1966.

"Bluebeard's Seventh Wife," in *The Saint* (New York), March 1966.

"Set a Thief," in *The Saint* (New York), August 1966.

"B as in Bloodstain," in *Ellery Queen's Mystery Magazine* (New York), October 1966.

"Music to Murder By," in *The Saint* (New York), October 1966.

"B as in Blackmail," in *Ellery Queen's Mystery Magazine* (New York), February 1968.

"S as in Shooting," in *Ellery Queen's Mystery Magazine* (New York), May 1968.

"Change of Heart," in *Ellery Queen's Mystery Magazine* (New York), August 1968.

"T as in Threat," in *Ellery Queen's Murder Menu*. Cleveland, World, 1969.

"The Inside Story," in *Ellery Queen's Mystery Magazine* (New York), March 1969.

"T as in Trespass," in *Ellery Queen's Mystery Magazine* (New York), December 1969.

"The Heart of the Case," in *Ellery Queen's Mystery Magazine* (New York), March 1970.

"Let's Have an Accident," in *Mike Shayne Mystery Magazine* (Los Angeles), July 1970.

"F as in Fake," in *Ellery Queen's Mystery Magazine* (New York), July 1970.

"The Suburban Tigress," in *Crime Without Murder*, edited by Dorothy Salisbury Davis. New York, Scribner, 1970.

"An Accident in Hudson Heights," in *Ellery Queen's Mystery Magazine* (New York), February 1971.

"Crime at Red Spit," in *Ellery Queen's Mystery Magazine* (New York), April 1971.

"Jackpot," in *Ellery Queen's Mystery Magazine* (New York), May 1971.

"The Mushroom Fanciers," in *Ellery Queen's Mystery Magazine* (New York), July 1971.

"The Verdict," in *Best Detective Stories of the Year*, edited by Allen J. Hubin. New York, Dutton, 1971.

"K as in Kidnapping," in *Ellery Queen's Mystery Magazine* (New York), December 1971.

"The Cautious Man," in *Murder Most Foul*, edited by Harold Q. Masur. New York, Walker, 1971.

"Wife Trouble," in *Ellery Queen's Mystery Magazine* (New York), March 1972.

"B as in Bandit," in *Ellery Queen's Mystery Magazine* (New York), April 1972.

"The Haunted Portrait," in *Ellery Queen's Mystery Magazine* (New York), July 1972.

"G as in Garrote," in *Ellery Queen's Mystery Magazine* (New York), August 1972.

"T as in Thief," in *Ellery Queen's Mystery Magazine* (New York), October 1972.

"C as in Cutthroat," in *Ellery Queen's Mystery Magazine* (New York), December 1972.

"R as in Riot," in *Ellery Queen's Mystery Magazine* (New York), August 1973.

"T as in Trap," in *Ellery Queen's Mystery Magazine* (New York), November 1973.

"The Innocent One," in *Charlie Chan Mystery Magazine* (Los Angeles), November 1973.

"Black Lace Gambit," in *Mike Shayne Mystery Magazine* (Los Angeles), February 1974.

"A Walk on the Beach," in *Charlie Chan Mystery Magazine* (Los Angeles), February 1974.

"Nice and Dead," in *Mike Shayne Mystery Magazine* (Los Angeles), April 1974.

"In Vino Veritas," in *Ellery Queen's Mystery Magazine* (New York), October 1974.

"The Motive," in *Every Crime in the Book*, edited by Robert L. Fish. New York, Putnam, 1975.

"Accuse Me Please," in *Mike Shayne Mystery Magazine* (Los Angeles), February 1975.

"B as in Bribe," in *Ellery Queen's Mystery Magazine* (New York), June 1975.

"V as in Vengeance," in *Ellery Queen's Mystery Magazine* (New York), August 1975.

"Before It's Too Late," in *Ellery Queen's Mystery Magazine* (New York), October 1975.

"G as in Gun," in *Ellery Queen's Mystery Magazine* (New York), November 1975.

"R as in Rookie," in *Ellery Queen's Magicians of Mystery*. New York, Davis, 1976.

"B as in Bludgeon," in *Ellery Queen's Crime Wave*. New York, Putnam, 1976.

"The Candle Flame," in *Best Detective Stories of the Year 1976*, edited by Edward D. Hoch. New York, Dutton, 1976.

"Moment of Truth," in *Ellery Queen's Mystery Magazine* (New York), January 1976.

"Shakespeare's Left Ear," in *Mike Shayne Mystery Magazine* (Los Angeles), February 1976.

"P as in Poison," in *Ellery Queen's Mystery Magazine* (New York), June 1976.

"The Second One," in *Alfred Hitchcock's Mystery Magazine* (North Palm Beach, Florida), November 1976.

"C as in Crooked," in *Ellery Queen's Mystery Magazine* (New York), January 1977.

"T as in Terror," in *Ellery Queen's Mystery Magazine* (New York), March 1977.

"The Killing of Wincoe Jones," in *Alfred Hitchcock's Mystery Magazine* (New York), May 1977.

"The Ginseng Root," in *Alfred Hitchcock's Mystery Magazine* (New York), July 1977.

"A Matter of Language," in *Alfred Hitchcock's Mystery Magazine* (New York), December 1977.

"M as in Missing," in *Ellery Queen's Masters of Mystery*. New York, Davis, 1978.

"From the Grass Roots Up," in *I Witness,* edited by Brian Garfield. New York, Times Books, 1978.

"Dead Duck," in *Alfred Hitchcock's Tales to Scare You Stiff,* edited by Eleanor Sullivan. New York, Davis, 1978.

"A Matter of Jurisdiction," in *Alfred Hitchcock's Mystery Magazine* (New York), January 1978.

"The Bottle of Wine," in *Mike Shayne Mystery Magazine* (Los Angeles), January 1978.

"The Two-Timer," in *Mike Shayne Mystery Magazine* (Los Angeles), February 1978.

"A Matter of Arson," in *Alfred Hitchcock's Mystery Magazine* (New York), April 1978.

"A Matter of Mushrooms," in *Alfred Hitchcock's Mystery Magazine* (New York), July 1978.

"Cop Goes the Weasel," in *Alfred Hitchcock's Mystery Magazine* (New York), October 1978.

"A Matter of Morality," in *Alfred Hitchcock's Mystery Magazine* (New York), January 1979.

"A Matter of Digging," in *Alfred Hitchcock's Mystery Magazine* (New York), February 1979.

"A Touch of Parmigiana," in *Mike Shayne Mystery Magazine* (Los Angeles), April 1979.

"The Miser," in *Mike Shayne Mystery Magazine* (Los Angeles), May 1979.

"To Love Thy Neighbor," in *Mike Shayne Mystery Magazine* (Los Angeles), September 1979.

"All in Good Taste," in *Crime Wave.* London, Collins, 1980.

"The Arabella Plot," in *Who Done It?,* edited by Alice Laurance and Isaac Asimov. Boston, Houghton Mifflin, 1980.

"A Matter of Witnesses," in *Alfred Hitchcock's Mystery Magazine* (New York), 13 August 1980.

"A Matter of Skating," in *Alfred Hitchcock's Mystery Magazine* (New York), 15 December 1980.

"Twice Around the Block," in *Miniature Mysteries,* edited by Isaac Asimov, Martin H. Greenberg and Joseph D. Olander, New York, Taplinger, 1980.

"C as in Crime," in *Ellery Queen's Eyes of Mystery.* New York, Davis, 1981.

"M as in Mayhem," in *Ellery Queen's Mystery Magazine* (New York), 17 June 1981.

"A Matter of Kicks," in *A Special Kind of Crime,* edited by Lawrence Treat. New York, Doubleday, 1982.

"Give the Devil His Due," in *The Crime of My Life,* edited by Brian Garfield. New York, Walker, 1984; London, Severn House, 1986.

"A Slip of the Lip," in *Murder on the Aisle,* edited by Mary Higgins Clark. New York, Simon and Schuster, 1987.

"A Matter of Arson," in *Alfred Hitchcock's Words of Prey,* edited by Lois Adams and Gail Hoyden. New York, Dial Press, 1986.

"Salt Free Bread," in *Plots and Pans,* edited by Nancy and Jean Francis Webb. New York, Wynwood Press, 1989.

OTHER PUBLICATIONS

Other

Bringing Sherlock Home (puzzle book). New York, Doubleday, 1930.

"Creating a Mystery Game," in *Murder Ink: The Mystery Reader's Companion,* edited by Dilys Winn. New York, Workman, 1977.

Crime and Puzzlement: 24 Solve-Them-Yourself Picture Mysteries. Boston, Godine, 3 vols., 1981–88; vol. 1 published London, Dorling Kindersley, 1982.

You're the Detective! (for children). Boston, Godine, 1983.

The Clue Armchair Detective. New York, Ballantine, 1983.

Editor, *Murder in Mind.* New York, Dutton, 1967.
Editor, *The Mystery Writer's Handbook* edited by Herbert Brean, revised edition. Cincinnati, Writer's Digest, 1976.
Editor, *A Special Kind of Crime.* New York, Doubleday, 1982.

*   *   *

Lawrence Treat is frequently called the "father" of the police procedural novel, but there are two reasons for questioning the appropriateness of the title. The first is that Treat himself disclaims any intention of creating a new form of detective fiction. The other is that the big impetus for the police procedural story came not from Treat's early books but a few years later from the radio and television show *Dragnet*, whose popularity created a climate for the beginning of successful series like Creasey's Gideon stories and McBain's 87th Precinct saga.

But whether he "invented" the procedural novel or not, Lawrence Treat set a pattern that has been rather consistently followed by writers in this sub-genre. The nine novels and numerous short stories featuring the police trio Mitch Taylor, Jub Freeman, and Bill Decker are different from the traditional detective story in that the work of crime detection is carried on not by a single masterful personality like Sherlock Holmes or Inspector Maigret but by a team of hard-working and believeable cops. Another important component of the Treat pattern is the use of such ordinary police methods as tailings, stakeouts, informants, and the principles of forensic science in the solution of crimes. It is, of course, this reliance on routines and procedures that gives the police procedural story its name. Treat not only set the narrative pattern of the procedural story but established a set of conventional situations that have been used repeatedly by writers of police fiction. There is the convention of the cop with family problems (Mitch Taylor worries about how he will support his beloved Amy), the hostile public ("People who aren't busy lying to you look at you as if you were a mechanical man"), the inter- and intra-departmental rivalries (detectives versus patrolmen, conventional cops versus the police lab), and the perennially under-staffed and over-worked squad (a policeman is never off duty). The formula has come to be as thoroughly established in the police procedural as the Poe conventions in the classic detective story and the *Black Mask* pattern in the hard-boiled school.

Treat made a particularly happy selection in his three series characters, because each of them plausibly represents an aspect of the police sub-culture. Mitch Taylor, the "veteran of an unjust world and experienced in warfare against his superiors," is the traditional flatfoot, inclined to cut corners and to goldbrick where work is involved. Mitch is not very intelligent, and sometimes worries a little because he does not read more. He is not above establishing a little "cushion" (graft on the side) for himself, and he considers himself fortunate in having a "rabbi," an influential relative who looks after his interests.

Mitch's basic attitude toward his job is, Get along, Stay out of trouble, Don't stick your neck out. It is significant that Treat relegated Mitch Taylor to a minor role, and gave an increasingly important part to Jub Freeman, the new-style scientific detective. Jub's field of operation is the police lab, and he has the qualities of the dedicated scientist, including meticulous analysis, suspension of judgment until all the data have been examined, and empirical support for every statement he makes on the witness stand. Jub knows his forensic science: he can identify a brand of ink by spectrophotometric analysis that breaks a substance up into color components, and he can prove that a suspect acted in self-defense by demonstrating that her hand-marks were on the barrel of a pistol only, not on the butt or trigger. Homicide Lieutenant Bill Decker, the third character, is a competent, business-like officer who runs a tight ship, who drives his men relentlessly and has to be extra-sure of his own men because he has not much use for the rest of the department. Decker can also be warm and understanding; he supports his men, and he does not hesitate to sit down and have a drink with them—after hours, of course. He encourages them to be unorthodox, to break minor rules or cut through red tape when necessary. As a result of his leadership, morale in Homicide is the highest in the department.

As a pioneer in police procedural fiction, Treat established one important precedent: a writer of police fiction must know the real-world cops, their methods and their attitudes. The reading public will tolerate a degree of fantasy in other types of detective fiction because very few people have ever seen a consulting detective or a private investigator, but everybody knows uniformed policemen and has at least some role-expectations for plainclothesmen. Treat's police detectives, with their politicking and their eye on the promotion-lists, their fallibility and their frequent reliance on sheer luck, have apparently satisfied those expectations. If Treat did not "invent" the police procedural novel, he certainly found an ideal medium when he began writing them. His novels before *V as in Victim* feature Carl Wayward, a devious, intuitive criminologist; the plots are conventional, the characters transparent and brittle as glass, the dialogue stiff and forced. When he turned to this world of policemen, however, Treat developed an easy natural prose and the ability to construct a narrative framework that is at once plausible and vivid.

—George N. Dove

TREE, Gregory. *See* BARDIN, John Franklin.

TRENCH, John (Chenevix). British. Born in Newick, Sussex, 17 October 1920. Educated at Wellington College, Berkshire, 1933–38; Royal Military Academy, Woolwich, London, 1939. Served in the Royal Signals in Africa and Europe, 1939–46. Married Ann Moore in 1944; one daughter and one son. Copywriter, 1945–56, copy group head, 1956–62, and creative group head, 1962–70, S. H. Benson Ltd., London. Since 1970, creative director, Foster Turner and Benson Ltd., London. Chairman of the council, Buckinghamshire Archaeological Society, 1977; parish councillor and churchwarden. Recipient: World's Press News Copywriting award, 1956, 1963; Advertising Creative Circle Essay prize, 1969. Agent:

Anthony Sheil Associates Ltd., 43 Doughty Street, London WCIN 2LF. Address: Windmill Farm, Coleshill, Amersham, Buckinghamshire, England.

CRIME PUBLICATIONS

Novels (series: Martin Cotterell in all books except *Beyond the Atlas*)

Docken Dead. London, Macdonald, 1953; New York, Macmillan, 1954.
Dishonoured Bones. London, Macdonald, 1954; New York, Macmillan, 1955.
What Rough Beast. London, Macdonald, and New York, Macmillan, 1957.
Beyond the Atlas. London, Macdonald, and New York, Macmillan, 1963.

OTHER PUBLICATIONS

Other

Archaeology Without a Spade. London, Newman Neame, 1960.
History for Postmen. London, Newman Neame, 1961.
The Bones of Britain. London, Newman Neame, 1962.

Editor, *The Harp Book of Graces.* London, Harp Lager, 1962.

*　*　*

Each of John Trench's series detective novels bears the hallmarks of the high English tradition: incisive wit, spirited invention, intricate and various action, frequent literary allusion, powerful feeling for locality, and pungent observation of character and customs, with an especially keen eye for the eccentric. As a stylist, Trench is comparable to any of his peers: even his detractors concede that he writes well.

The civil and military confusions of *Docken Dead* generate a continuous excitement, entangling an upper-crust family with a dead major, a secret weapon, and a lost Arthurian manuscript. It is a crowded, zestful book, as invigorating as its northern landscape, and lucid and shapely for all its teeming vitality. *Dishonoured Bones* is a rather wry book unfolding a complex deception against a background of local tensions in a Dorset quarrying community. A dig reveals a recent corpse; antiques vanish from the manor; a social solecism prompts a murder. By a neat poetic justice, the quarrymen encompass the murderer's destruction. *What Rough Beast* moves beyond its predecessors to heartfelt protest against the brutal ethos of modern times. A deep, fierce book, it lives up to its Yeatsian title, effective both as mystery and as statement of faith. Its vicious teenage gang is seen in a dual light: as destroyers of the peace and as victims of a ravaged environment. All three novels feature Martin Cotterell, an erudite archaeologist with an acutely "associative" mind. Tough, lean, exuberant, inquisitive, well-connected, one-handed, and chronically untidy, he deserves a wider fame.

—B.A. Pike

TRENHAILE, John (Stevens). British. Born in Hertford, 29 April 1949. Educated at Magdalen College, Oxford, B.A.

(honours) in jurisprudence 1971, M.A. 1975. Married Victoria Luisa Bayly in 1974; one daughter and one son. Barrister, London, 1973–76. Agent: Blake Friedman Literary Agency, 37–41 Gower Street, London WC1E 6HH, England.

CRIME PUBLICATIONS

Novels (series: General Povin; Simon Young)

Kyril (Povin).   London, Severn House, 1981; as *The Man Called Kyril*.   New York, Congdon and Weed, 1983.
A View from the Square (Povin).   London, Bodley Head, 1983; New York, Congdon and Weed, 1984.
Nocturne for the General (Povin).   London, Bodley Head, and New York, Congdon and Weed, 1985.
The Mah-Jongg Spies (Young).   London, Collins, and New York, Dutton, 1986.
The Gates of Exquisite View (Young).   London, Collins, 1987; New York, Dutton, 1988.
The Scroll of Benevolence (Young).   London, Collins, 1988.
Krysalis.   London, Collins, 1989.
Acts of Betrayal.   London, Collins, 1990.

*   *   *

The appearance of John Trenhaile's dramatic first novel heralded the arrival of a new espionage master. Like John le Carré, Trenhaile mines the psychological depths of personal and ideological betrayal by members of opposing governmental factions. Intricate subplots, character relationships, and finely researched cultural details contribute to suspenseful, captivating plots that naturally lead to sequels but stand alone equally as well. Thus far he has arranged his far-reaching stories in two trilogies.

The debut novel (*Kyril*) in Trenhaile's first trilogy, which features the Soviet point of view, pits the Russian KGB against British Intelligence in an entertaining and fast-paced, action-packed plot. Suspense builds rapidly as members of the KGB try to force a high-ranking spy in their midst to show his hand. While situations may appear larger than life, Trenhaile makes them realistic and intensely personal: attention focuses on the nerve-wracked "traitor" as attendant subplots exacerbate the overall tension. The author thus creates characters of depth, with unresolved emotional and moral ambiguities.

The next book in sequence, *A View from the Square,* offers another very real and possible scenario. The head of Soviet foreign intelligence (the same who earlier sympathized with the West) wishes to trade information about the Soviet capture of a newly developed American plane carrying ultra secret equipment for assistance in defecting. A strong personal element enters with the man's desire to help a pianist friend escape as well. The plot culminates in a lengthy trek across frozen Siberian wastelands by four mercenaries in search of the plane's location. This episode stands out as compelling, suspenseful, and memorable and heightens the psychological conflict, both within individuals and between characters, that plays an important role in the development of plot.

An intensely personal relationship also lies at the center of *Nocturne for the General.* Former KGB general Povin, now deposed and incarcerated in northern Russia, twists and turns to the questions of interrogator Inna, who wants to extract information from him concerning a secret escape route for defectors. The tension raised here and throughout the work shows itself in masterful dialog that is intelligent, witty, and precise, and in the dramatic juxtaposition of inherently opposed temperaments. Trenhaile again succeeds in captivating his readers with a high level of psychological complication and suspense.

Trenhaile's second trilogy, as yet incomplete, inherits the best qualities of his first, but maintains a lighter atmosphere, perhaps because of a change in venue. *The Mah-Jongg Spies* transports the politico-ideological conflict to Hong Kong, where Simon Young and family become the center of a power struggle between the KGB and Chinese Central Intelligence. In this work, the author exhibits a thoroughly researched knowledge of locality, language, and cultural lore that lends life and immediacy to the plot. As the KGB attempts to destroy Hong Kong's financial base before the city reverts to the Chinese in 1997, then, all actions occur in authentic and believable—albeit exotic—surroundings.

Both Simon Young and son Matthew reappear in *The Gates of Exquisite View,* where they become involved with the Apogee, an ultra-sensitive computer that can respond to the human voice, and with Red Chinese plans to invade Taiwan. Once again, Trenhaile shows a highly refined sense of character central to the plot.

A relative newcomer to the espionage novel, Trenhaile has nevertheless established a firm foothold among the ranks of his fellow writers. He owns the ability to plumb the depths of character, to analyze and animate political and moral struggle, to create a pervasive undercurrent of tension, and to establish a credible and exotic setting. His novels are eminently readable, highly involving, and thoroughly entertaining.

—Rex E. Klett

———

TREVANIAN. Pseudonym for Rodney Whitaker. Also writes as Nicholas Seare. American. Born in Granville, New York, 12 June 1931. Holds four university degrees, including Ph.D. in Communications. Formerly Professor, University of Texas, Austin. Agent: Michael V. Carlisle, William Morris Agency, 1350 Avenue of the Americas, New York, New York 10019, U.S.A.

CRIME PUBLICATIONS

Novels (series: Jonathan Hemlock)

The Eiger Sanction (Hemlock).   New York, Crown, 1972; London, Heinemann, 1973.
The Loo Sanction (Hemlock).   New York, Crown, 1973; London, Heinemann, 1974.
The Main.   New York, Harcourt Brace, 1976; London, Hart Davis, 1977.
Shibumi.   New York, Crown, and London, Granada, 1979.
The Summer of Katya.   New York, Crown, and London, Granada, 1983.

OTHER PUBLICATIONS

Play

Screenplay (as Rod Whitaker): *The Eiger Sanction,* with Hal Dresner and Warren Murphy, 1975.

Other

The Language of Film (as Rod Whitaker). Englewood Cliffs, New Jersey, Prentice Hall, 1970.
1332 or So, Being an Apology for a Pedlar (as Nicholas Seare). New York, Harcourt Brace, 1975.
Rude Tales and Glorious (as Nicholas Seare). New York, Potter, 1983; London, Granada, 1984.

*   *   *

Tough, unlikable, and unlikely, Trevanian's Jonathan Hemlock is a snob, art history professor, world-class mountain climber, and assassin for the CII, an American intelligence organization headed by Yurasis Dragon, an albino. Hemlock's $10,000 fee per "sanction" (counter-assassination) pays for his two passions, his home—a converted church—and his illegally purchased Impressionist paintings. Cold and self-consciously emotionless, Hemlock yet has a rigid code of friendship and love, constantly violated by others in *The Eiger Sanction.* That novel's plot involves Hemlock's attempt to discover and sanction one of three others during a climb of the Eigerwand, and the climbing scenes are particularly well-done, tense and exciting. In the second novel, the British equivalent of the CII, the Loo, blackmails Hemlock, forcing him out of a four-year retirement to sanction Maxmilian Strange, who means to auction films of governmental officials at their sexual play and thus to topple the British Empire. Hemlock here is a rather more sympathetic figure because of his love throughout of Maggie Coyne. The grim and convolute conclusion is again well-done. Hemlock's acerbic snobbery, Trevanian's snide narrative asides, and his bawdy naming of characters all suggest a Bondish derivation, but Trevanian's writing is more intelligent, witty, and stylish than Fleming's.

The Main, a very fine police procedural novel, is also a moving study of Claude LaPointe, the lonely, scruffy, tough-but-not-hard police lieutenant who is The Law in the Montreal district of the novel's title. As LaPointe investigates a murder, the contrast between his older methods and ideas and those of the forces of modernism—a college-educated policeman, a "liberal" police commissioner, and a young whore—provides additional tension and interest. The revelation of the murderer's identity is somewhat improbable, but otherwise the novel is strong.

Trevanian returns to the thriller with *Shibumi* and creates in its protagonist, Nicholai Hel, an intriguing variation of Jonathan Hemlock. Retired at the novel's opening, Hel is a professional assassin; a spelunker, he lives comfortably in a restored chateau in the Basque mountains. The novel's caving scenes, like the climbing scenes in *The Eiger Sanction,* are both authentic and nerve-wracking, and Hel's spelunking partner, Benat Le Cagot, is a wonderful comic creation. Fully half the novel traces Hel's maturation in Shanghai and Japan during World War II delineating reasons for his often-voiced sarcastic disgust with Western politics and cultural barbarism. Jolted from his retirement by the vengeful machinations of Mr. Diamond, one of the powers in the Mother Company, "a consortium of major international petroleum, communications, and transportation corporations that control the Western World's energy and information," Hel eventually neutralizes the Company and extracts his own vengeance against Diamond. Trevanian seldom describes here physical violence or details its gory results; instead, he concentrates attention either on Hel's preference for Eastern culture and cast of mind or on Diamond and the Mother Company as the emblems of the West and evidence that Hel's sarcastic views are accurate. The rare reader who is neither amused by Hel's sarcasm nor

intrigued and instructed by Trevanian's knowledge of the East may dismiss *Shibumi* as talky pseudo-philosophy, *Zen and the Art of Mayhem.* That would be a mistake, for the work is a significant variation of Trevanian's own earlier thrillers and a considerable novelistic achievement, Trevanian's finest book.

If one of Trevanian's concerns in *Shibumi* is with the characteristic identity of nations and with the differences between East and West, in *The Summer of Katya* his concern is with sexual identity and with the thin line between sanity and insanity. The I-narrator of the novel, Dr. Jean-Marc Montjean, a Basque, relates the story of his growing love for Katya Treville during the summer of 1914, while she, her twin brother Paul, and her father are living in Etcheverria, a rented villa near the small French village where Montjean is a physician's assistant. Writing 24 years after the event, Montjean is still trying to understand how his youthful affection precipitated the murder and double suicides with which the novel closes, horrors which adumbrate the larger ones of World War I and of modernism. The relationship between Katya and Paul may remind the reader of that between Poe's Ushers, and the novel, like Poe's short story, is both a psychological mystery and a Gothic thriller, very different from any of Trevanian's other works.

—David K. Jeffrey

TREVOR, Elleston. *See* **HALL, Adam.**

TRIPP, Miles (Barton). Also writes as Michael Brett. British. Born in Ganwick Corner, Hertfordshire, 5 May 1923. Educated at Queen Elizabeth's Grammar School, Barnet, Hertfordshire, 1933–41. Served in the Royal Air Force Bomber Command, 1942–46. Admitted as a solicitor, 1950; in private practice, Stamford, Lincolnshire, 1950–52; member of the legal staff, Charity Commission, London, 1953–83. Chairman, Crime Writers Association, 1968–69. Agent: Peters Fraser and Dunlop, 5th Floor, The Chambers, Chelsea Harbour, Lots Road, London SW10 0XF, England.

CRIME PUBLICATIONS

Novels (series: John Samson)

The Image of Man. London, Darwen Finlayson, 1955.
A Glass of Red Wine. London, Macdonald, 1960.
Kilo Forty. London, Macmillan, 1963; New York, Holt Rinehart, 1964.
A Quartet of Three. London, Macmillan, 1965.
The Chicken. London, Macmillan, 1966; with *Zilla,* London, Pan, 1968.
One Is One. London, Macmillan, 1968.
Malice and the Maternal Instinct. London, Macmillan, 1969.
A Man Without Friends. London, Macmillan, 1970.
Five Minutes with a Stranger. London, Macmillan, 1971.
The Claws of God. London, Macmillan, 1972.
Obsession (Samson). London, Macmillan, 1973.
Woman at Risk. London, Macmillan, 1974.

A Woman in Bed. London, Macmillan, 1976; New York, State Mutual, 1982.

The Once a Year Man (Samson). London, Macmillan, 1977.

The Wife-Smuggler (Samson). London, Macmillan, 1978.

Cruel Victim (Samson). London, Macmillan, 1979; New York, St. Martin's Press, 1985.

High Heels (Samson). London, Macmillan, 1980; New York, State Mutual, 1982.

Going Solo. London, Macmillan, 1981.

One Lover Too Many. (Samson). London, Macmillan, 1983.

A Charmed Death. London, Macmillan, 1984; New York, St. Martin's Press, 1985.

Some Predators Are Male (Samson). London, Macmillan, 1985; New York, St. Martin's Press, 1986.

Death of a Man-Tamer (Samson). London, Macmillan, and New York, St. Martin's Press, 1987.

The Frightened Wife (Samson). London, Macmillan, 1987; New York, St. Martin's Press, 1988.

The Cords of Vanity (Samson). London, Macmillan, 1989; New York, St. Martin's Press, 1990.

Novels as Michael Brett (series: Hugo Baron)

Diecast (Baron).   New York, Fawcett, 1963; London, Barker, 1964.

A Plague of Dragons (Baron). London, Barker, 1965.

A Cargo of Spent Evil (Baron; as John Michael Brett). London, Barker, 1966.

Uncollected Short Stories

"A Remedy for Nerves," in *Winter's Crimes 1,* edited by George Hardinge. London, Macmillan, and New York, St. Martin's Press, 1969.

"Fixation," in *Winter's Crimes 3,* edited by George Hardinge. London, Macmillan, and New York, St. Martin's Press, 1971.

"A Lady from the Jungle," in *John Creasey's Mystery Bedside Book 1972,* edited by Herbert Harris. London, Hodder and Stoughton, 1971.

"The Identity of His Father's Son," in *Winter's Crimes 6,* edited by George Hardinge. London, Macmillan, and New York, St. Martin's Press, 1974.

"Sister Nemesis," in *Winter's Crimes 8,* edited by Hilary Watson. London, Macmillan, and New York, St. Martin's Press, 1976.

"Ragsie's Mistress," in *Winter's Crimes 13,* edited by George Hardinge. London, Macmillan, and New York, St. Martin's Press, 1981.

"Form," in *Winter's Crimes 16,* edited by Hilary Hale. London, Macmillan, and New York, St. Martin's Press, 1984.

"The Casebook Casanova," in *Winter's Crimes 17,* edited by George Hardinge. London. Macmillan, and New York, St. Martin's Press, 1985.

OTHER PUBLICATIONS

Novels

Faith Is a Windsock. London, Davies, 1952.

The Skin Dealer. London, Macmillan, 1964; New York, Holt Rinehart, 1965.

The Fifth Point of the Compass. London, Macmillan, 1967.

Play

Television Play: *A Man Without Friends,* from his own novel, 1972.

Other

The Eighth Passenger: A Flight of Recollection and Discovery (autobiography). London, Heinemann, 1969.

*

Miles Tripp comments:

As someone who would rather plant characters than clues, and would prefer that the story evolves through the characters rather than by their being shaped to fit the structure of a plot, I naturally prefer psychology to technology and Simenon to either Christie or the imitators of Deighton. Although I write for my own pleasure, I also write in the hope that somewhere a reader will enjoy what I've written. I like to familiarize myself with a place before using it as a setting, but, apart from this, I have no rules, formulae, or special system.

*   *   *

Miles Tripp is an outstanding practitioner of the disturbing art of creating psychological suspense. Each novel features a different hero (or non-hero), but they are all flippant, cosmopolitan, British. In *A Man Without Friends* he writes about Marcus Wayne, a successful professional con-man who, among other things, practices graphology and enjoys high living. In *Woman at Risk* his protagonist is a barrister caught up in the murder of his mistress. The writing is brilliant and always witty; the reader does not so much ask himself "who done it?" as "who could have expected that to happen?" Of his recent books *High Heels* is the best, and follows the same formula that has worked so well for him in the past. *Going Solo* and *One Lover Too Many* are just average. His top books, and, by the way, Tripp himself agrees, are *Kilo Forty, A Man Without Friends, Woman at Risk,* and *High Heels.* He has also written the intriguing book *Five Minutes with a Stranger.* In reading Tripp's books you get the feeling that he could have been a regular contributor to the great Alfred Hitchcock movies: Tripp's style fits the old master to a T. Tripp retired from the legal profession in 1983, and since then has concentrated on his writing, publishing four more books featuring John Samson. Edmund Crispin called Tripp an excellent writer, and he certainly gets no disagreement from me.

—Don Cole

———

TROY, Simon. *See* **WARRINER, Thurman.**

———

TURNBULL, Peter. British. Born in Rotherham, Yorkshire, 23 October 1950. Educated at Cambridge College of Arts and Technology, 1971–74; Cardiff University, Wales, 1976–78, diploma in social work. Since 1978 social worker, Strathclyde Regional Council, Glasgow. Agent: Peters Fraser and Dunlop,

5th Floor, The Chambers, Chelsea Harbour, Lots Road, London SW10 0XF.

CRIME PUBLICATIONS

Novels (series: P Division in all books except *Claws of the Gryphon*)

Deep and Crisp and Even. London, Collins, 1981; New York, St. Martin's Press, 1982.
Dead Knock. London, Collins, 1982; New York, St. Martin's Press, 1983.
Fair Friday. London, Collins, and New York, St. Martin's Press, 1983.
Big Money. London, Collins, and New York, St. Martin's Press, 1984.
The Claws of the Gryphon. London, Collins, and New York, St. Martin's Press, 1986.
Two Way Cut. London, Collins, and New York, St. Martin's Press, 1988.
Condition Purple. London, Collins, 1989.

Uncollected Short Stories

"The Sort of Man He was," in *Ellery Queen's Mystery Magazine* (New York), 1986.
"McNaught's Obsession," "All in Scarlet When She Died," "Not at All Like the Scorpion," "The Surgeon's Daughter," "The Man Who Walked to Nowhere," all in *Ellery Queen's Mystery Magazine* (New York), 1987.
"Hugo Strillicom and the Killing Machine," "Aheunellyz Collar," both in *Ellery Queen's Mystery Magazine* (New York), 1988.
"A Story from a Dark Street," "The Man and the Jesus Lock," both in *Ellery Queen's Mystery Magazine* (New York), 1989.
"Perverse Judgement," in *Ellery Queen's Mystery Magazine* (New York), 1990.

OTHER PUBLICATIONS

Novel

The Justice Game: The Lady from Rome (novelization of television series). London, BBC Publications, 1990.

*

Peter Turnbull comments:
The "P" Division novels are stories of a fictional police station in the centre of Glasgow. The novels are fixed in time, i.e. the running characters never get older nor do their personal circumstances change. The time is the present and the novels are as much a social document of contemporary Glasgow as they are novels of detective fiction.

*   *   *

The crime novels of Peter Turnbull are reassuringly familiar in form, with satisfying surprises and twists in their plotting, and an interesting cast of characters. He consistently sets his investigations in Glasgow, a carefully delineated setting through which he expresses both a sense of the problems of modern urban experience, and a quizzical inflection of that experience. Without attempting any of the explicitly philosophical (and, it must be said, occasionally pretentious) ambitions of the Laidlaw novels of fellow Glasgow writer William McIlvanney, Turnbull has produced a string of easily-digestible and gripping detective stories, rich in local colour and diverse in characterisation. Like the highly influential American author Ed McBain, on whose 87th Precinct novels he draws heavily, Turnbull uses the cohort of a particular police division to populate and situate his stories. He deals with his policemen (and the occasional policewoman) in some depth, but without the sentimentality of his mentor, and without endorsing much of the American author's curious attitude towards women. And unlike some other contemporary British exponents of the police procedural style—notably John Penn, John Wainwright and R. D. Wingfield—Turnbull regularly manages to carry off the difficult feat of balancing the demands of detailed characterization with the need for fast-paced and compelling narrative.

His first novel, *Deep and Crisp and Even,* is probably his most wholly successful to date. Its initial evocation of a snow-covered wintry cityscape is extremely effective and memorable, and its plot—the urgent and quickening pursuit of a psychopathic serial killer—is compulsive and tense. The final scenes of the murderer stalking a policewoman through the streets at night are particularly thrilling and well-handled. His subsequent novels have appeared at regular intervals since then, and have followed similar patterns. *Dead Knock, Fair Friday,* and *Big Money* all contain many of the felicities of the first, but none entirely fulfils its promise. Although the local colour is consistently well-portrayed, and the Glasgow setting is evoked cleverly and economically, there are some awkwardnesses in the handling of narrative pace, and perhaps an overstrenuous reliance on the more pedestrian documentation of forensic practices.

However, his excellent 1988 novel, *Two Way Cut,* marks a genuine return to his best form, and makes him seem easily the most accomplished writer of the police procedural novel in Britain today. This book starts with the discovery of a mutilated body, freshly washed and dressed, on a plot of land in central Glasgow and the plot takes off in a splendidly serpentine investigation which takes in both the respectable, up-market side to Glasgow and the seamy underworld of violence and threat. The narrative involves an unusually varied cluster of locations, and the mystery is teased out with suspense and intelligently handled atmosphere. Anyone coming new to Turnbull's work might be advised to start with either this book or the first one. His most recent crime story, *Condition Purple,* continues this run of success, although the plot is somewhat more predictable. It is to be hoped that the author can continue to devise his taut variations on a relatively simple theme.

As well as his detective novels, Peter Turnbull has written a thriller, *The Claws of the Gryphon,* and a novelization of a popular television series set in Glasgow, *The Justice Game.* However, neither of these has the substance of his more orthodox crime writing.

—Ian A. Bell

TUROW, Scott. American. Born in Chicago, Illinois, 12 April 1949. Educated at Amherst College, Massachusetts, B.A. 1970; Stanford University, California, M.A. 1974; Harvard University, Cambridge, Massachusetts, J.D. 1978. Married Annette Weisberg in 1971. E.H. Jones lecturer in creative writing, Stanford University, 1972–75. Address; c/o

Farrar, Straus and Giroux Inc., 19 Union Square, New York, New York 10003, U.S.A.

CRIME PUBLICATIONS

Novels (Sandy Stern in both books)

Presumed Innocent.   New York, Farrar Straus, and London, Bloomsbury, 1987.
The Burden of Proof.   New York, Farrar Straus, and London, Bloomsbury, 1990.

OTHER PUBLICATIONS

Other

One L: An Inside Account of Life in the First Year at Harvard Law School.   New York, Putnam, 1977; London, Penguin, 1978; as *What They Really Teach You at Harvard Law School,*   London, Sceptre, 1988.

*   *   *

Scott Turow's Harvard Law School training, recorded in *One L,* a nonfiction description of his experiences as a first-year law student, has provided a solid legal foundation for his novels. So too has his practice as a Chicago lawyer. The result is two hard-hitting, thought-provoking novels that go beyond the limitations of the mystery genre to face the illusory nature of reality, what is meant by "justice" and the human soul, and to ask whether man and his institutions are really ever capable of finding even the simple truths. They form a diptych of darkness and light. Both are psychological studies of clever, cynical men, caught up in the justice system, made vulnerable by a death too close to home, unburdening their souls, their fears, their doubts: the one a devious political mind, manipulating and manipulated and never totally reliable, the other a basically decent honest man, driven, with a defense lawyer's idealism and skepticism, by a need to make sense of a seemingly senseless act. In the first, perceptions change rapidly and the final understanding is that there can be no final understanding; the second, in contrast, builds slowly and inexorably to a final awareness of act and motive. In both a host of "Kindle County" characters are fleshed out with a convincing complexity of detail—cops, judges, pathologists, prosecutors, defense attorneys, criminals of all sorts, ruthless social and political climbers, cynical jury members, abused children, black street toughs, lonely wives and angry sons and lovers. The first brings alive the behind-the-scene realities of the judicial scene; the second the complex interplay of love and hate, the misunderstandings, betrayals, abuses, and sacrifices of family life.

Despite its familiar plot idea—circumstantial evidence incriminating the "innocent" man—in Turow's first novel, *Presumed Innocent,* perceptions shift rapidly with each new piece of information. The result is not only a first-rate study of a metropolitan criminal-justice system from the inside, but a psychological study of a morose man seeking an ephemeral, beguiling illusion in a world of corruption, betrayal, and inescapable pain. Convincingly authentic and superbly crafted, *Presumed Innocent* captures the sights and smells, the intimacy and the clinical distance of the investigation scene, the drama, the suspense and the internal maneuverings of a headline trial, and the moral ambiguity of those who participate in and are touched by a case. Turow writes convincingly of daily routines, courtroom encounters, and trial procedures as well as of sexual obsessions and sexual pursuits.

The murder of an attractive, amoral young prosecuting attorney, sharp, competent, and corruptible, who cynically employs her erotic powers for political advantage, implicates 39-year-old Rusty Sabich, the chief deputy prosecuting attorney, colleague and once smitten lover of the dead woman, now presumed murderer. He narrates his own story.

His musings are the slow ruminations of a troubled man trying to puzzle out the significance of events, to come to terms with his past, to find meaning in act and innuendo. In doing so he provides capsule biographies of those around him, records the "tough-guy" exchanges of courtroom politicians, recalls the horror of past cases—whether the violation of innocence or the deserved retribution of tough against tough. His flesh-and-blood concerns leave him in an agony of psychic pain, betrayed by his boss and mentor of 12 years, obsessed by a woman who uses, abuses and jilts him, repulsed by and in need of his moody wife, awed by the wonder of his maladjusted son. He describes himself as "somebody everyone can depend on;" his wife calls him a "sap."

Sabich's style is polished, his voice philosophical. His story builds slowly but inexorably as he establishes characters and relationships, engages in introspective Dostoevsky-like monologues, and recites anecdotes that bring alive the human elements of the judicial system, and reveals unexpected twists and turns of character and event. His lawyer, Sandy Stern, surprises him in court, and the unexpected prevails as past "facts" require reevaluation and reinterpretation and new facets of the old "reality" become manifest. Characters prove base, exploitative, shameless, and even self-deluded. Sabich's images are bleak; he speaks of "the black forests" of his wife's moods, himself as a "shipwrecked survivor holding fast to the debris," his mistress as "a spider caught in her own web," and life as a constant struggle with darkness. He bares his soul to his readers, shows them the depths of his philosophical despair, and explores with them the roots of his anxieties. Consequently, his holding back information devastates. Though inured to the lies, half-truths, and deceits of the other characters, most readers come to know Sabich so intimately that it is painful to concede, as does his faithful friend and associate Lip, a doubt—a fear that we have been manipulated and at some deep level betrayed. This is perhaps why a number of critics are profoundly disturbed by Turow's ending. We are willing to accept a *Hamlet*-like world of seems, but in a mystery we expect the cloud of ignorance to be dispelled and the truth to shine brightly through. Instead, in *Presumed Innocent* nothing is what it seems and what truly is is ultimately impossible to know. Layer after layer is peeled away to reveal Byzantine complications, but the human heart remains hidden—sometimes even from itself. Rusty's "struggle to escape the darkness" leaves readers with "an idle doubt" and the question, "What is harder? Knowing the truth or finding it, telling it or being believed?" There are no real innocents—only a presumption of innocence.

Turow's second novel, *The Burden of Proof,* is equally well-written and equally compelling, but less showily dramatic because it focuses not on guilt or innocence but on human frailty, human need, and inescapable family ties. Therein Sabich's clever, enigmatic defense attorney, Jewish Argentine Alejandro "Sandy" Stern, ever the outsider, must deal with his wife's seemingly inexplicable suicide, a missing $850,000 check, an embarrassing social disease, and his maverick brother-in-law's grand jury indictment for business fraud in a commodity-futures firm. Psychologically and emotionally complicated, this book too involves interwoven plots and strong characters, succinctly brought to life, as Stern broods on his past and seeks to regain control and understanding of his present. The action turns on the conflict between unspoken family codes and the more formal legal codes, between loyalties and justice. Stern the lawyer must weigh the evidence, consider the options, plan the legal strategy, and judge the witnesses, but Stern the man must reevaluate his life and his relationships; he must reconcile dual obligations as well as contradictions and betrayals that call into question all past intimate relationships. His is a quest to come to terms with his dead wife and his alienated offspring, to make sense of acts that seem out-of-character, and to re-establish meaningful human relationships. The end result is more positive and upbeat than *Presumed Innocent* as Stern's burden of guilt is lifted, the human mysteries become clear, and Stern reasserts control over his life. Though *The Burden of Proof* is less satisfying as a mystery, it is as compelling in its portrait of alienation and the mystery of the human mind and as gripping in its final revelations.

Turow's psychological shrewdness, vivid detail, sense of courtroom finesse, and skill at misdirection capture the imagination, challenge the intellect, and produce unforgettable images of man's hidden darker self. Whether in first person (*Presumed Innocent*) or third (*The Burden of Proof*) his narrative voice provides a meticulous gloss on speech, testimony, and human behavior, with the analysis sometimes lawyerly explication of legal points and sometimes simply precise and careful observation of the interpretive possibilities of everyday communication. This prose is admirably precise, metaphorical, and elegantly classic in quality and structure; his characterizations are fully-rounded and fully believable. In other words, Turow combines mystery and suspense with style and vision not only to produce spellbinding plots but to provide a microcosm of the justice system on the one hand and of family life on the other.

—Gina Macdonald

TWOHY, Robert. American. Worked as a cab driver for 10 years. Address: c/o Ellery Queen's Mystery Magazine, Davis Publications Inc., 380 Lexington Avenue, New York, New York 10017, U.S.A.

CRIME PUBLICATIONS

Uncollected Short Stories

"Never Anything But Trouble," in *Ellery Queen's Mystery Magazine* (New York), June 1957.
"Out of This Nettle," in *To Be Read Before Midnight,* edited by Ellery Queen. New York, Random House, 1962; London, Gollancz, 1963.
"The Victim of Coincidence," in *Ellery Queen's Mystery Magazine* (New York), February 1964.
"Routine Investigations," in *Best Detective Stories of the Year 1965,* edited by Anthony Boucher. New York, Dutton, and London, Boardman, 1965.
"The Man on the Spot," in *Ellery Queen's Mystery Magazine* (New York), June 1968.
"McKevitt—100 Proof," in *Ellery Queen's Mystery Magazine* (New York), October 1968.
"Up Where the Air Is Clean," in *Ellery Queen's Mystery Magazine* (New York), February 1969.
"Mrs. Kendall's Trunk," in *Ellery Queen's Mystery Magazine* (New York), June 1969.

"The Gingham Dog and the Calico Cat," in *Ellery Queen's Mystery Magazine* (New York), August 1969.
"Passport to Freedom," in *Ellery Queen's Mystery Magazine* (New York), November 1969.
"Goodbye to Francie," in *Ellery Queen's Headliners.* Cleveland, World, 1971; London, Gollancz, 1972.
"The Man Who Could Only Write Things," in *Ellery Queen's Mystery Magazine* (New York), February 1974.
"Vengeance," in *Ellery Queen's Masks of Mystery.* New York, Davis, 1977; London, Gollancz, 1979.
"The Devil Inside," in *Alfred Hitchcock's Mystery Magazine* (New York), November 1977.
"The Woman on the Beach," in *Alfred Hitchcock's Mystery Magazine* (New York), December 1977.
"The Pistoleer," in *Alfred Hitchcock's Mystery Magazine* (New York), January 1978.
"Mouse," in *Alfred Hitchcock's Mystery Magazine* (New York), March 1978.
"Slime," in *Alfred Hitchcock's Mystery Magazine* (New York), June 1978.
"Installment Past Due," in *Ellery Queen's Mystery Magazine* (New York), September 1978.
"A Change in the Program," in *Ellery Queen's Mystery Magazine* (New York), January 1979.
"The Horse in the House," in *Ellery Queen's Mystery Magazine* (New York), April 1979.
"Crescent Rolls," in *Alfred Hitchcock's Mystery Magazine* (New York), May 1979.
"Dream Fragments," in *Alfred Hitchcock's Mystery Magazine* (New York), August 1979.
"Twang!," in *Alfred Hitchcock's Mystery Magazine* (New York), September 1979.
"Different Worlds," in *Alfred Hitchcock's Mystery Magazine* (New York), October 1979.
"The Slow Punch," in *Alfred Hitchcock's Mystery Magazine* (New York), December 1979.
"Down This Mean Street," in *Ellery Queen's Mystery Magazine* (New York), 14 January 1980.
"The System," in *Alfred Hitchcock's Mystery Magazine* (New York), 27 February 1980.
"A Very Ordinary Murder," in *Ellery Queen's Mystery Magazine* (New York), 5 May 1980.
"The Elegant Murders," in *Alfred Hitchcock's Mystery Magazine* (New York), 21 May 1980.
"Bottomed Out," in *Alfred Hitchcock's Mystery Magazine* (New York), 16 May 1980.
"Hooray for Hollywood," in *Ellery Queen's Mystery Magazine* (New York), 18 August 1980.
"A Masterpiece of Crime," in *Ellery Queen's Mystery Magazine* (New York), 6 October 1980.
"Tomorrow We Finish Ann," in *Ellery Queen's Mystery Magazine* (New York), 3 November 1980.
"Putting It on the Line," in *Alfred Hitchcock's Mystery Magazine* (New York), 19 November 1980.
"The Fix," in *Ellery Queen's Mystery Magazine* (New York), 1 January 1981.
"All the Hippies Are Dead," in *Ellery Queen's Mystery Magazine* (New York), 22 April 1981.
"Mousie," in *Ellery Queen's Mystery Magazine* (New York), 4 November 1981.
"The Man in the Ratty Overcoat," in *Ellery Queen's Mystery Magazine* (New York), 24 February 1982.
"The Bathtub Murders," in *Ellery Queen's Mystery Magazine* (New York), September 1982.
"A Somewhat Happy Ending," in *Ellery Queen's Mystery Magazine* (New York), January 1983.

"The End of What?," in *Ellery Queen's Mystery Magazine* (New York), April 1983.

"Seventeen," in *Ellery Queen's Mystery Magazine* (New York), May 1983.

"A New Feeling," in *Ellery Queen's Mystery Magazine* (New York), June 1983.

"Who's to Miss?," in *Ellery Queen's Mystery Magazine* (New York), August 1983.

"Teeth Like Little Radios," in *Ellery Queen's Mystery Magazine* (New York), 1984.

"Breakfast at Ojai," in *Ellery Queen's Mystery Magazine* (New York), September 1984.

"Philadelphia Story," in *Ellery Queen's Mystery Magazine* (New York), December 1984.

"Girl in a Dumpster," in *Ellery Queen's Mystery Magazine* (New York), February 1985.

"Yellow One-Eyed Cat," in *Ellery Queen's Mystery Magazine* (New York), May 1985.

"Narc in Love," in *Ellery Queen's Mystery Magazine* (New York), June 1985.

"TV Dope Show," in *Ellery Queen's Mystery Magazine* (New York), December 1985.

"Jinja the Cat," in *Ellery Queen's Mystery Magazine* (New York), March 1986.

"The Ten-Dollar Bill," in *Ellery Queen's Mystery Magazine* (New York), May 1987.

"Ojai Once Again," in *Ellery Queen's Mystery Magazine* (New York), December 1987.

"Maggie," in *Ellery Queen's Mystery Magazine* (New York), February 1988.

"Snapshots," in *Ellery Queen's Mystery Magazine* (New York), April 1988.

"Highway Girl," in *Ellery Queen's Mystery Magazine* (New York), July 1988.

"Everybody Goes Home," in *Ellery Queen's Mystery Magazine* (New York), Mid–December 1988.

"Sloat's Last Case," in *Ellery Queen's Mystery Magazine* (New York), May 1989.

"The Clean Place," in *Ellery Queen's Mystery Magazine* (New York), July 1989.

"At a Rest Stop South of Portland," in *Mystery Magazine* (New York), January 1990.

*

Robert Twohy comments:

First, I want to entertain. Second, I have no answers or statements, only questions. I like it that Mr. McSherry sees me as in the ballparks of Einstein, relativity, and Heisenberg, uncertainty. I don't know either of these gents and I am uninfluenced by them directly, but no doubt their influence has reached me through the works of other authors and philosophers, and novels and movies and tales and overheard conversations and a few comic strips maybe.

I never was much for moral judgements or opinions. Hammett was an early influence, and his view is generally of and from the two named ballparks. His Continental Op spoke of himself as a mancatcher, not as an agent of justice or morality. He didn't expect his work would improve society, he detected because he liked the job and was good at it.

I like writing crime stories and am as good at that as I am, and can't think of anything else I'd rather do.

*   *   *

A steady producer of above-average short fiction for mystery magazines, Robert Twohy was first classed as a hard-boiled writer—"crime . . . à la *Black Mask*"—but the bulk of his work is quite different from that of earlier writers in the genre.

His work is remarkably varied—puzzle stories like "A Masterpiece of Crime," in which a multiple murderer sends mocking notes to the police with clues to his name ("Her Highness has granted me the highest honor," which will delight Ellery Queen fans; indeed E.Q. is a character in the story); police procedurals; straight detection like "The Man in the Ratty Overcoat"; and even straight fantasy like "Bottomed Out" whose hero is a resurrected skeleton driving a cab in the grey limbo of small-town Lindenvale, California. But there's no series detective, the standby of most mystery writers. (There's Lt. Brickell, but his three cases are solved for him by citizens; a nameless cabdriver who appears in many more stories is more onlooker than detective. Once, after deciding who this killer is, he does nothing more; once, in "Coincidence," his probably false reasoning leads him straight to a murderer.) Nor are there any series criminals; Moorman, who tells absurd stories to the cops so he can sue them later for false arrest, is more a funny practical joker than a professional swindler.

Twohy's characteristics, both individually and as a modern writer, are best seen in two stories. An alcoholic hanger-on of the mob, Ben's beloved Uncle Al, who's been like a father to him, gets him an interview with the head of the mob in his skyscraper suite ("Up Where the Air Is Clean"). Ben is thrilled; this is his way out of the slum's smells, cockroaches, sickness, and poverty. But the head extorts a price: eliminate a man for us, to show you've got the right stuff, a too-talkative, alcoholic hanger-on of the mob. Unaware of the price, Uncle Al urges Ben to do it, whatever it is: you'll never get another chance like this again! Here Twohy stops. The power of the story, as in many Twohy stories, depends on what happens *after* it ends. It's as if the story was a snapshot of a river, whose flow goes on to the left and right of the photo scene. The story, probably Twohy's best, is unforgettable.

"The Flow" is a sad picture of a lonely misfit who turns to crime, not just because his low I.Q. makes it impossible for him to do anything else well, but because then he's "part of something. . . . It's like a flow—and if you go to jail, that's part of the flow. . . . I don't regret it. . . . It's a better life than I'd have had otherwise. . . . Better than standing alone, being alone, with everything flowing on by." In Limbo.

One of Twohy's two major themes is that for many Americans, lacking education and special gifts, crime is the only realistic way of rising above their status, their world, their flow. The second theme, the flow itself, marks Twohy as a modern writer living in the world of Einstein where all is relative and related, and of Heisenberg where all is uncertainty. If everything is related to every other, then no statement can be *entirely* false; the wrong reasoning can lead to the right conclusion. In an uncertain universe, morals will be uncertain too; Twohy's heroes lack the Victorian rigidity of the "right-is-right, crime-*must*-be-punished" morality of earlier detectives. His characters are lost losers, resigned rather than unhappy, living in a limbo, waiting for the bomb to drop.

Basically, Twohy seems not a genre writer at all, but a mainstream modern short-story writer who writes mystery and fantasy because those are the only major mass markets for short fiction now available.

—Frank D. McSherry, Jr.

TYRE, Nedra. American. Born in Offerman, Georgia. Educated in public schools in Georgia; correspondence and extension courses, B.A.; Emory University, Atlanta, M.A.; Richmond School of Social Work, Virginia. Worked as typist, sales clerk, library assistant, social worker, staff writer for social agencies, teacher of sociology at Richmond Professional Institute, Virginia. Book reviewer, Richmond *News Leader* and Atlanta *Journal.* Agent: Scott Meredith Literary Agency Inc., 845 Third Avenue, New York, New York 10022. Address: 1118 Grove Avenue, Apartment 34, Richmond, Virginia 23220, U.S.A.

CRIME PUBLICATIONS

Novels

Mouse in Eternity. New York, Knopf, 1952; London, Macdonald, 1953; as *Death Is a Lover,* New York, Spivak, 1953.
Death of an Intruder. New York, Knopf, 1953; London, Collins, 1954.
Journey to Nowhere. New York, Knopf, and London, Collins, 1954.
Hall of Death. New York, Simon and Schuster, 1960; as *Reformatory Girls,* New York, Ace, 1962.
Everyone Suspect. New York, Macmillan, 1964; London, Gollancz, 1965.
Twice So Fair. New York, Random House, 1971.

Uncollected Short Stories

"Murder at the Poe Shrine," in *Ellery Queen's Mystery Magazine* (New York), September 1955.
"Tour de Couleur," in *Ellery Queen's Mystery Magazine* (New York), August 1956.
"Carnival Day," in *Ellery Queen's Thirteenth Annual.* New York, Random House, 1958; London, Collins, 1960.
"Reflections on Murder," in *Sleuth* (New York), December 1958.
"The Delicate Murderer," in *Ellery Queen's Mystery Magazine* (New York), November 1959.
"What Is Going to Happen," in *The Lethal Sex.* New York, Dell, 1959.
"The Gentle Miss Bluebeard," in *Alfred Hitchcock's Mystery Magazine* (New York), November 1959.
"A Friendly Murder," in *Ellery Queen's Mystery Magazine* (New York), August 1961.
"Murder Between Friends," in *Alfred Hitchcock's Mystery Magazine* (New York), August 1963.
"A Neighborly Murder," in *Mike Shayne Mystery Magazine* (New York), March 1964.
"Typed for Murder," in *Signature* (New York), January 1967.
"A Case of Instant Detection," in *Ellery Queen's Mystery Magazine* (New York), May 1967.
"In the Fiction Alcove," in *Ellery Queen's Mystery Magazine* (New York), September 1967.
"Mrs. Sloan's Predicament," in *The Man from U.N.C.L.E.* (New York), September 1967.
"Beyond the Wall," in *Alfred Hitchcock's Mystery Magazine* (New York), June 1968.
"The Disappearance of Mrs. Standwick," in *Ellery Queen's Mystery Magazine* (New York), July 1968.
"The Attitude of Murder," in *Alfred Hitchcock's Mystery Magazine* (New York), October 1969.
"Another Turn of the Screw," in *Ellery Queen's Grand Slam.* Cleveland, World, 1970; London, Gollancz, 1971.
"Recipe for a Happy Marriage," in *Ellery Queen's Mystery Magazine* (New York), March 1971.

"An Act of Deliverance," in *Ellery Queen's Mystery Magazine* (New York), August 1971.
"The Stranger Who Came Knocking," in *Ellery Queen's Mystery Magazine* (New York), June 1972.
"You Can't Trust Anyone," in *Ellery Queen's Mystery Magazine* (New York), June 1973.
"The Murder Game," in *Ellery Queen's Masters of Mystery.* New York, Davis, 1975.
"A Murder Is Arranged," in *Alfred Hitchcock's Mystery Magazine* (North Palm Beach, Florida), March 1975.
"The Do-It-Yourself Solution," in *87th Precinct* (Los Angeles), May 1975.
"A Nice Place to Stay," in *Ellery Queen's Magicians of Mystery.* New York, Davis, 1976.
"Killed by Kindness," in *Alfred Hitchcock's Tales to Keep You Spellbound,* edited by Eleanor Sullivan. New York, Davis, 1976.
"On Little Cat Feet," in *Ellery Queen's Mystery Magazine* (New York), February 1976.
"The Web," in *Mystery Monthly* (New York), October 1976.
"Cousin Anne," *Mystery Monthly* (New York), February 1977.
"Accidental Widow," in *Alfred Hitchcock's Tales to Take Your Breath Away,* edited by Eleanor Sullivan. New York, Davis, 1977.
"The Dower Chest," in *Ellery Queen's Mystery Magazine* (New York), November 1977.
"Laughter Before Dying," in *Ellery Queen's Searches and Seizures.* New York, Davis, 1977.
"Daisies Deceive," in *Alfred Hitchcock's Tales to Scare You Stiff,* edited by Eleanor Sullivan. New York, Davis, 1978.
"Locks Won't Keep You Out," in *Ellery Queen's Napoleons of Mystery.* New York, Davis, 1978.
"Back for a Funeral," in *Ellery Queen's Mystery Magazine* (New York), October 1978.
"The More the Deadlier," in *Alfred Hitchcock's Mystery Magazine* (New York), October 1978.
"The Perfect Jewel," in *Ellery Queen's Mystery Magazine* (New York), June 1979.
"The Night Runner," in *Ellery Queen's Mystery Magazine* (New York), November 1979.
"The Same as Murder," in *Ellery Queen's Mystery Magazine* (New York), 18 August 1980.
"Mr. Smith and Myrtle," in *Ellery Queen's Mystery Magazine* (New York), 17 June 1981.
"They Shouldn't Uv Hung Willie," in *Ellery Queen's Mystery Magazine* (New York), 1 January 1982.
"Color Me Dead," in *Ellery Queen's Mystery Magazine* (New York), Mid-July 1983.

OTHER PUBLICATION

Short Stories

Red Wine First. New York, Simon and Schuster, 1947.

* * *

It is inevitable that writers will draw upon their own past geographical and vocational backgrounds. Having been a social worker, Nedra Tyre has a special understanding of disadvantaged people. They are often potential victims, and she portrays them realistically and with considerable poignancy. Tyre victims are never merely life's losers; they are people with considerable inner resources, though unlucky.

She is particularly adept at describing the terrors of the elderly and lonely. *Death of an Intruder* has a seemingly simple plot regarding an old woman, living alone, whose house is "invaded" by another woman whom she cannot evict. One either dismisses it as unbelievable or one suspends disbelief and is carried along, finishing the book in one sitting and agreeing with Frances Crane who called it "superbly handled suspense." Two excellent short stories regarding the elderly are "Locks Won't Keep You Out," in which the mystery revolves around *what* it is that her protagonist is afraid of, and "On Little Cat Feet," in which an elderly woman, alone in an apartment house, is in deathly fear of a cat: she is a typical Tyre heroine, alone, poor, on foot, inevitably loaded down with groceries and library books.

Her old women do not accept their reduced circumstances lightly. Mary Allthorpe in "You Can't Trust Anyone" saves all year for her only pleasure, spring house tours in the South. On one of these crime enters her life. Widow Ellen Williams in "The Disappearance of Mrs. Standwick" is travelling alone in Richmond when she calls a chance acquaintance and becomes involved in an unexpected adventure. Having lived most of her life in the South, Tyre is especially good at describing that area. While she doesn't write regional mysteries in the Faulknerian sense, she conveys how similar to the rest of the United States the new South has become, yet shows what it has retained to set it apart. A good example is "A Nice Place to Stay" regarding another character named Mrs. Williams.

Children are often as vulnerable as the old, and Tyre writes convincingly of them. Her novel *Hall of Death* is a fine mystery set at a Georgia reform school. "Carnival Day" is a heart-breaking story about a 12-year-old girl, whose parents are estranged, and her visit to an old-time Southern carnival. In "The Dower Chest" we see the terrors of apartment living and the city streets for Jenny, a bright little girl raised in the country, whose mother cannot meet her after school.

Tyre described the atmosphere and day-to-day operations of social work agencies in *Mouse in Eternity*. In "Another Turn of the Screw" she deals realistically with a work situation in a small bureaucracy, showing how a motive for murder can emerge from a supervisor-subordinate relationship. In "A Case of Instant Detection" a detective named Williams solves a murder committed while a film was shown in a sociology class.

Tyre's attachment to books (especially mysteries) is obvious. In "A Friendly Murder" Mary Williams (a name Tyre uses frequently) has her fateful meeting with a former Homicide Chief at the Public Library's Great Books Discussion Group. "In the Fiction Alcove" is set in a library in a large Georgia city while an ice storm paralyzes the city. Her devotion to literature (especially the work of Poe) is clear from one of her best short stories, the marvelously subtle "Tour de Couleur," and "Murder at the Poe Shrine" in which Miss Wilson, lecturer-guide-curator, solves a crime helped by knowledge of Poe.

In the appropriately named "Reflections on Murder" we have the archetypal Tyre heroine—an independent woman who lives alone and reads mysteries as a hobby. In fact, the opening of this story is a brief essay on the genre. What happens when the heroine lets her hobby lead her to think about committing a murder is the crux of a highly unusual story from a highly unusual author.

—Marvin Lachman

U

UHNAK, Dorothy. American. Born in the Bronx, New York, in 1933. Educated at City College of New York, three years; John Jay College of Criminal Justice, degree c. 1970. Married; one daughter. Joined New York City Transit Police Department in 1953: detective second grade, then assistant to the chief: Outstanding Police Duty Medal before leaving the force in 1967. Address: c/o Simon and Schuster, 1230 Avenue of the Americas, New York, New York 10020, U.S.A.

CRIME PUBLICATIONS

Novels (series: Christie Opara)

The Bait (Opara). New York, Simon and Schuster, and London, Hodder and Stoughton, 1968.
The Witness (Opara). New York, Simon and Schuster, 1969; London, Hodder and Stoughton, 1970.
The Ledger (Opara). New York, Simon and Schuster, 1970; London, Hodder and Stoughton, 1971.
Law and Order. New York, Simon and Schuster, and London, Hodder and Stoughton, 1973.
The Investigation. New York, Simon and Schuster, 1977; London, Hodder and Stoughton, 1978.
False Witness. New York, Simon and Schuster, 1981; London, Hutchinson, 1982.
Victims. New York, Simon and Schuster, and London, Century, 1986.

OTHER PUBLICATIONS

Other

Policewoman: A Young Woman's Initiation into the Realities of Justice. New York, Simon and Schuster, 1964; London, Star, 1978.

*

Manuscript Collection: Mugar Memorial Library, Boston University.

*   *   *

Dorothy Uhnak's credentials as a police novelist are impeccable. She served for 14 years with the New York City Transit Police, 12 of them as a detective. In 1964 she began to write of her experiences with a non-fiction account of her first years on the force. *Policewoman* has all Uhnak's strengths and weaknesses as a writer. Her strengths include a good eye for the scenes and characters that bring a subject to life for the reader, and a copious, pounding style that forces the reader to be involved. Her weaknesses include this same style, which is capable of making even the obvious points three times. Like her nearest literary relative, Joseph Wambaugh, Uhnak is at pains to dispel the myths about police work that have been propagated in literature and on film. She makes the real pressures of police work clear: the struggle to develop the emotional shell that is absolutely necessary protection against constant exposure to the worst in human behavior, and the struggle to keep compassion and a modified idealism alive inside the shell. In *Policewoman,* and in all of her novels, there are scenes that justify every insistent adjective lavished on them. There is, for example, a retarded six-year-old who has been beaten to death by his grandmother. Despite the fact that the neighbors characterize him as the Dumb One, an unresponsive burden, all of his fingernails are bitten bloody. A scene such as this stops the reader's preconceived judgments cold.

Uhnak has improved steadily as a writer; *Law and Order* is perhaps her best book, and *The Investigation* was a bestseller. *Law and Order* tells the story of three generations of the O'Malleys, an Irish Catholic family of policemen. Its argument is that New York's corrupt department cannot be reformed from the outside, only by insiders who know where all the bodies are buried and what happens if they are dug up and given a more appropriate funeral. Two episodes in the novel frame the inch-by-inch progress that Uhnak sees as the only kind of which humans are capable. At the beginning of the book, Sergeant O'Malley, violent and prejudiced, is killed in self-defense by a black prostitute whose pleas of illness he has ignored. She falls to her death moments afterward. O'Malley's grandson, 30 years later, has returned from Vietnam without prejudice, and with the knowledge of how to fight death. He gives the kiss of life to an injured black woman in the street. Both of these scenes ring with authenticity, as do Uhnak's portraits of the O'Malley wives and mothers, whose strength is narrow but very deep.

In all of Uhnak's work, there are impressive, unstereotyped portraits of women. *The Investigation* is held together by the slowly developed characterization of Kitty Keeler, a woman with beauty, intelligence, and Mafia connections, who may or may not have killed her two children. The character is based on a character from one of Uhnak's Christie Opara series, *The Ledger*. The earlier character, Elena Vargas, is presented as a woman trapped by her beauty, her innocence, and the color of her skin.

In *False Witness,* Uhnak returns to the theme of the talented dark-skinned woman battling overwhelming social odds: Sanderalee Dawson is a media celebrity whose underlying insecurity leaves her horribly vulnerable to manipulation. As counterpoint to Sanderalee's disintegration, we see the personal price that even the very talented white woman may have to pay for success in D.A. Lynne Jacobi's pursuit of Sanderalee's attacker. Both women have their considerable burdens increased by the amoral sensationalism of the press and television.

—Carol Cleveland

UNDERWOOD, Michael. Pseudonym for John Michael Evelyn. British. Born in Worthing, Sussex, 2 June 1916. Educated at Charterhouse School, Surrey; Christ Church, Oxford, 1935–38, M.A.; Grays Inn, London: called to the Bar, 1939. Served in the British Army, 1939–46: Major. Member of the Department of Public Prosecutions, London, 1946–76: assistant director, 1969–76; in grade Under-Secretary from 1972. Companion of the Bath, 1976. Agent: A.M. Heath and Company Ltd., 79 St. Martin's Lane, London WC2N 4AA.; or, Harriet Wasserman Literary Agency, 230 East 84th Street, New York, New York 10028, U.S.A. Address: 100 Ashdown, Eaton Road, Hove, Sussex BN3 3AR, England.

CRIME PUBLICATIONS

Novels (series: Nick Atwell; Rosa Epton; Inspector/Superintendent Simon Manton; Richard Monk)

Murder on Trial (Manton). London, Hammond, 1954; New York, Washburn, 1958.
Murder Made Absolute (Manton). London, Hammond, 1955; New York, Washburn, 1957.
Death on Remand (Manton). London, Hammond, 1956.
False Witness (Manton). London, Hammond, 1957; New York, Walker, 1961.
Lawful Pursuit (Manton). London, Hammond, and New York, Doubleday, 1958.
Arm of the Law (Manton). London, Hammond, 1959.
Cause of Death (Manton). London, Hammond, 1960.
Death by Misadventure (Manton). London, Hammond, 1960.
Adam's Case (Manton). London, Hammond, and New York, Doubleday, 1961.
The Case Against Phillip Quest (Manton). London, Macdonald, 1962.
Girl Found Dead (Manton). London, Macdonald, 1963.
The Crime of Colin Wise (Manton). London, Macdonald, and New York, Doubleday, 1964.
The Unprofessional Spy. London, Macdonald, and New York, Doubleday, 1964.
The Anxious Conspirator (Manton). London, Macdonald, and New York, Doubleday, 1965.
A Crime Apart. London, Macdonald, 1966.
The Man Who Died on Friday (Monk). London, Macdonald, 1967.
The Man Who Killed Too Soon (Monk). London, Macdonald, 1968.
The Shadow Game. London, Macdonald, 1969.
The Silent Liars. London, Macmillan, and New York, Doubleday, 1970.
Shem's Demise. London, Macmillan, 1970.
A Trout in the Milk. London, Macmillan, 1971; New York, Walker, 1972.
Reward for a Defector. London, Macmillan, 1973; New York, St. Martin's Press, 1974.
A Pinch of Snuff. London, Macmillan, and New York, St. Martin's Press, 1974.
The Juror (Atwell). London, Macmillan, and New York, St. Martin's Press, 1975.
Menaces, Menaces. London, Macmillan, and New York, St. Martin's Press, 1976.
Murder with Malice (Atwell). London, Macmillan, and New York, St. Martin's Press, 1977.
The Fatal Trip (Atwell). London, Macmillan, and New York, St. Martin's Press, 1977.

Crooked Wood (Atwell). London, Macmillan, and New York, St. Martin's Press, 1978.
Anything but the Truth. London, Macmillan, 1978; New York, St. Martin's Press, 1979.
Smooth Justice. London, Macmillan, and New York, St. Martin's Press, 1979.
Victim of Circumstance. London, Macmillan, and New York, St. Martin's Press, 1980.
A Clear Case of Suicide. London, Macmillan, and New York, St. Martin's Press, 1980.
Crime upon Crime (Epton). London, Macmillan, 1980; New York, St. Martin's Press, 1981.
Double Jeopardy (Epton). London, Macmillan, and New York, St. Martin's Press, 1981.
Hand of Fate. London, Macmillan, 1981; New York, St. Martin's Press, 1982.
Goddess of Death (Epton). London, Macmillan, and New York, St. Martin's Press, 1982.
A Party to Murder. London, Macmillan, 1983; New York, St. Martin's Press, 1984.
Death in Camera (Epton). London, Macmillan, and New York, St. Martin's Press, 1984.
The Hidden Man (Epton). London, Macmillan, and New York, St. Martin's Press, 1985.
Death at Deepwood Grange (Epton). London, Macmillan, and New York, St. Martin's Press, 1986.
The Uninvited Corpse (Epton). London, Macmillan, and New York, St. Martin's Press, 1987.
The Injudicious Judge (Epton). London, Macmillan, 1987; New York, St. Martin's Press, 1988.
Dual Enigma (Epton). London, Macmillan, and New York, St. Martin's Press, 1988.
A Compelling Case (Epton). London, Macmillan, and New York, St. Martin's Press, 1989.
Rosa's Dilemma (Epton). London, Macmillan, and New York, St. Martin's Press, 1990.

Uncollected Short Stories

"Coincidence," in *John Creasey Mystery Magazine* (London), March 1957.
"Operation Cash," in *Winter's Crimes 4,* edited by George Hardinge. London, Macmillan, and New York, St. Martin's Press, 1972.
"Murder at St. Oswalds," in *Verdict of Thirteen: A Detection Club Anthology,* edited by Julian Symons. London, Faber, and New York, Harper, 1979.
"Finale," in *Winter's Crimes 12,* edited by Hilary Watson. London, Macmillan, and New York, St. Martin's Press, 1980.
"O.K. for Murder," in *Winter's Crimes 15,* edited by George Hardinge. London, Macmillan, and New York, St. Martin's Press, 1983.
"The Man Who Nursed Grievances," in *Winter's Crimes 17,* edited by George Hardinge. London, Macmillan, 1985.
"Two's Company," in *Winter's Crimes 21,* edited by Hilary Hale. London, Macmillan, 1989.

*

Manuscript Collection: Mugar Memorial Library, Boston University.

Michael Underwood comments:
The common feature of all my books is a background of legal goings-on and court scenes and police (or private eye)

investigation. The ingredients vary in proportion according to the nature of the stories which range from detective novels to thrillers to spy books. All, however, are covered by the descriptive term of crime novel.

* * *

Michael Underwood is a crime writer who works largely by undramatic means. This might seem a contradiction. Crime, and especially murder, is at first blush a strongly dramatic affair. But it is so only at first blush. At the moment of a killing, though not always even then, there is drama. But often in real life it is momentary drama only. The whole process of a crime, both before that instant of drama and after it, is much more often tedious than high-coloured. And it is Underwood's great virtue—he is a lawyer and knows his facts—to convey, not perhaps the full tedium of a crime, but a good deal of its sober progress from point to point.

He does this whether he is describing the course of an investigation or, as he often does, the course of the legal process which is the true terminus of, say, an act of murder, though this is a part of the whole which in more crime books than not is simply omitted altogether. And Underwood's legal knowledge is used in such a way that his books differ even from those of that small section of the genre which does specialise in courtroom scenes. As often as not Underwood concentrates not on what happens in court, with all its slightly artificial dramatics, but on what happens outside the courtroom, in the Judge's chambers, in barristers' rooms, in public prosecutors' offices.

And to his undramatic, factually correct, yet always truly fictional stories (always written with the reader in mind and not the actual circumstances of some tortuous real-life situation) he brings the quality of craftsmanship. To say of a book that it is written "with old-fashioned craftsmanship" is generally thought to be praising with faint damns. But craftsmanship is something that can be employed in any sort of book, whether action-packed or quiet, and which when it is absent can spoil to greater or less degree any book but a work of roaring genius. It is the unobtrusive making sure that everything fits, that nothing jars, that what is promised is present. And this Underwood notably does.

It is a quality, too, which is likely to make an author's books progressively better as he learns what he does best, what it is sensible for him to eschew. And this, by and large, is true of the 45 books we have had from Underwood. One bonus of this steady achievement has been his increasing reliance on a young female investigator, Rosa Epton. She first appeared in 1964, in *The Unprofessional Spy,* in a minor role as a clerk in a solicitor's office. Since then she has risen to become a frequent heroine and a solicitor herself, i.e. a lawyer who deals with the day-to-day impact of legalities on life and can conduct cases in the lower courts. As such she is plausibly involved in all kinds of criminal activities, and Underwood convincingly shows, without plunging too deeply into her psychology, this young, with-it girl neatly triumphing, aided by no more heroic qualities than marked commonsense and simple determination.

From Underwood's steady level of high craftsmanship some novels have stood out, generally those in which the plot has been more than usually ingenious. In general all his plots are, as one might expect, sufficient to the subject. But every now and again he has hit on one that works especially well. There was the superb puzzle, in *Menaces, Menaces,* which gave us a professional blackmailer safely in the cells during his Old Bailey trial when a demand for money was received bearing all the hallmarks of his particular modus operandi. How could he

have been responsible? Or why was somebody imitating him so closely? And Underwood provided a thoroughly satisfactory explanation. Or, in *Hand of Fate* there is a logic-defying "perfect murder" plot which yet has its reasonable, and sting-in-the-tail comeuppance. These and others such are peaks in a long range of solid hills.

—H.R.F. Keating

———

UPFIELD, Arthur W(illiam). Australian. Born in Gosport, Hampshire, England, 1 September 1888. Educated in public school, then apprenticed to a surveyor and estate agent; shipped by his father to Australia in 1911, where he worked as a cook, boundary rider, and itinerant worker. Served in the Australian Imperial Force, 1914–19. Married in 1915; one son. Worked as a private secretary in England, then returned to Australia as an itinerant trapper and miner until becoming a full-time writer. Headed Australian Geological Society expedition to northern and western Australia, 1948. *Died 13 February 1964.*

CRIME PUBLICATIONS

Novels (series: Inspector Napoleon "Bony" Bonaparte)

The House of Cain. London, Hutchinson, 1928; New York, Dorrance, 1929.
The Barrakee Mystery (Bonaparte). London, Hutchinson, 1929; as *The Lure of the Bush,* New York, Doubleday, 1965.
The Beach of Atonement. London, Hutchinson, 1930.
The Sands of Windee (Bonaparte). London, Hutchinson, 1931.
A Royal Abduction. London, Hutchinson, 1932.
Gripped by Drought. London, Hutchinson, 1932.
Wings above the Diamantina (Bonaparte). Sydney, Angus and Robertson, 1936; as *Winged Mystery,* London, John Hamilton, 1937; as *Wings above the Claypan,* New York, Doubleday, 1943.
Mr. Jelly's Business (Bonaparte). Sydney, Angus and Robertson, 1937; London, John Hamilton, 1938; as *Murder Down Under,* New York, Doubleday, 1943.
Wind of Evil (Bonaparte). Sydney, Angus and Robertson, 1937; London, John Hamilton, 1939; New York, Doubleday, 1944.
The Bone Is Pointed (Bonaparte). Sydney, Angus and Robertson, 1938; London, John Hamilton, 1939; New York, Doubleday, 1947.
The Mystery of Swordfish Reef (Bonaparte). Sydney, Angus and Robertson, 1939; New York, Doubleday, 1943; London, Heinemann, 1960.
Bushranger of the Skies (Bonaparte). Sydney, Angus and Robertson, 1940; New York, British Book Centre, 1963; as *No Footprints in the Bush,* New York, Doubleday, 1944; London, Penguin, 1950.
Death of a Swagman (Bonaparte). New York, Doubleday, 1945; London, Aldor, 1946.
The Devil's Steps (Bonaparte). New York, Doubleday, 1946; London, Aldor, 1948.
An Author Bites the Dust (Bonaparte). Sydney, Angus and Robertson, and New York, Doubleday, 1948.

The Mountains Have a Secret (Bonaparte). New York, Doubleday, 1948; London, Heinemann, 1952.

The Widows of Broome (Bonaparte). New York, Doubleday, 1950; London, Heinemann, 1951.

The Bachelors of Broken Hill (Bonaparte). New York, Doubleday, 1950; London, Heinemann, 1958.

The New Shoe (Bonaparte). New York, Doubleday, 1951; London, Heinemann, 1952.

Venom House (Bonaparte). New York, Doubleday, 1952; London, Heinemann, 1953.

Murder Must Wait (Bonaparte). London, Heinemann, and New York, Doubleday, 1953.

Death of a Lake (Bonaparte). London, Heinemann, and New York, Doubleday, 1954.

Sinister Stones (Bonaparte). New York, Doubleday, 1954; as *Cake in the Hatbox,* London, Heinemann, 1955.

The Battling Prophet (Bonaparte). London, Heinemann, 1956.

The Man of Two Tribes (Bonaparte). London, Heinemann, and New York, Doubleday, 1956.

Bony Buys a Woman. London, Heinemann, 1957; as *The Bushman Who Came Back,* New York, Doubleday, 1957.

Bony and the Black Virgin. London, Heinemann, 1959; New York, Collier, 1965.

Bony and the Mouse. London, Heinemann, 1959; as *Journey to the Hangman,* New York, Doubleday, 1959.

Bony and the Kelly Gang. London, Heinemann, 1960; as *Valley of Smugglers,* New York, Doubleday, 1960.

Bony and the White Savage. London, Heinemann, 1961; as *The White Savage,* New York, Doubleday, 1961.

The Will of the Tribe (Bonaparte). New York, Doubleday, 1962; London, Heinemann, 1963.

Madman's Bend (Bonaparte). London, Heinemann, 1963; as *The Body at Madman's Bend,* New York, Doubleday, 1963.

The Lake Frome Monster (Bonaparte; completed by J. L. Price and Dorothy Strange). London, Heinemann, 1966.

*

Bibliography: "The Novels of Arthur Upfield" by Betty Donaldson in *Armchair Detective* (White Bear Lake, Minnesota), November 1974.

Critical Study: *Follow My Dust! A Biography of Arthur Upfield* by Jessica Hawke, London, Heinemann, 1957.

*   *   *

Arthur Upfield's retentive mind must have casually stored away thousands of images during the 20 years he roamed over Australia working at one job after another, from opal gouger to boundary rider. In England as a teenager he had scribbled incessantly at unpublishable "Yellow Peril" manuscripts. Now an older friend was prodding him to put his talents as a writer to good use. This was probably at the back of his mind when he accepted a job as cook at the isolated Wheeler's Well in New South Wales. Settling down in the little iron-roofed pine-log hut, he rediscovered the satisfaction of writing. He realized it would be foolish to compete with Edgar Wallace or S.S. Van Dine, and decided to use the background and people of Australia to form the basis of his stories. He did this so well that his fictional homesteads can be fairly accurately placed on a map of Australia.

The Barrakee Mystery did not satisfy him even after it was rewritten; he set it aside and wrote a straight thriller, *The House of Cain.* One day Tracker Leon rode by Wheeler's Well and stopped to reminisce with Upfield about the five months they had ridden the dog-proof fence together. The half-caste was a delightful companion, intelligent and knowledgeable. Upfield was aware Leon had been born in North Queensland; his father was known to be white, his mother an aborigine who had been killed for breaking tribal law. He had received a good education and was a valued tracker attached to the Queensland Police. Leon suggested they should exchange some books before he continued his journey to Ivanhoe. As Upfield watched him ride off he came to a sudden decision: he would change the white detective in *The Barrakee Mystery* to one based on the half-caste. But what to call him? One of the books Tracker Leon had left him was Abbot's *Life of Napoleon Bonaparte.* That was it!

Of the 33 novels ultimately published, 29 had as the crime investigator Detective Inspector Napoleon Bonaparte of the Queensland Police. Upfield had created a vivid, totally believable character. Bony, as he prefers to be called, is an attractive, slender man with unexpectedly blue eyes in a smooth, dark face. His hair is well brushed, his nose straight; when he smiles he reveals regular white teeth. Normally a fastidious dresser, he can assume a very different character, drifting onto the scene of the crime as a swagman or horse-trainer with elastic-sided boots, a slightly dirty shirt, and old gabardine trousers. Bony obtained an M.A. degree at Brisbane University and married an educated half-caste, grey-eyed Marie; they have three sons, Charles, Bob, and Ed. He does not like to be hurried when on an investigation; he refers to himself as a tortoise, and objects so strenuously when his superiors try to turn him into a hare that he often resigns. Of course, he is always reinstated. He is considerate of the local police and, perhaps because he puts himself in the criminal's shoes, is never vindictive towards him. The "blacks" (aborigines) are very impressed when they see the initiation marks that have been made with a sharp flint on Bony's back and chest. In *The Sands of Windee* old Moongalliti examines the welts and, with his black eyes bulging, comments, "My, you beeg feller chief Nor' Queensland!"

Time is often the only ally that Bony has. He likes tough cases, those on which he can exercise his peculiar talents. Often a crime will be weeks or months old; there may be no body; time and weather may have conspired to cover up the clues; people may have forgotten what has happened. But by observing clues visible only to his sharp eyes (a turned pebble, a single hair caught on the bark of a tree, the behavior of an ant), by using his inherited aboriginal instincts and Western intelligence, by patiently jogging people's memories and just as patiently listening to what they have to say, Bony always solves the problem. Only once, after a beautiful woman had pleaded with him, did he not conclude a case by naming the murderer.

Upfield had a remarkable ability to describe the land and the people he grew to love so well. Each of his books has a different setting which Upfield exploited to the full, giving the reader a first-rate adventure story running parallel to the detective plot. *The Mystery of Swordfish Reef* is an exciting tale of big-game fishing in the Tasman Sea where Bony, battling a huge swordfish, describes his pulse as beating "like Thor's great hammer." *The Man of Two Tribes* is a story of survival in the vast, desolate Nullarbor Plain, the treeless expanse of sand and saltbush in southern Australia. *Bony and the Mouse* tells of a man going mad in a totally silent West Australian forest where nothing moves—no birds, no rabbits, no jerboa rats, no banded anteaters. *The New Shoe* contains an extraordinary description of an old craftsman painstakingly making a red-gum casket, which all but becomes Bony's coffin. *The Bone Is Pointed* is a chilling psychological thriller; our hero has to fight hard against *mauia,* one of the most potent forms of magic employed by aborigines against their enemies. The *Lake Frome Monster* was finished by J.L. Price and Dorothy Strange, using the copious notes left by Upfield on his death in 1964. The books in which the half-caste detective appears have been reprinted several times; the remaining four have long been out of print.

—Betty Donaldson

V

VACHSS, Andrew (Henry). American. Born in New York City, 19 October 1942. Educated at Case-Western Reserve University, Cleveland, Ohio, B.A. 1965; United States Public Health Service Interviewing School, 1965; Industrial Areas Foundation Training Institute fellow, 1970–71; New England School of Law, Boston, Massachusetts, J.D. (magnum cum laude), 1975; John Hay Whitney Foundation Fellow, 1976–77. Married. Program representative, U.S. Public Health Service, Ohio, 1965–66; unit supervisor, Department of Social Services, New York City, 1966–69; urban coordinator, Community Development Foundation, Connecticut, 1969–70; organizer/coordinator, Calumet Community Congress, Indiana, 1970; Director, Uptown Community Organization, Illinois, 1970–71, and Libra, Inc., Massachusetts, 1971; Deputy Director, Medfield-Norfolk Prison Project, 1971–72; Director, Intensive Treatment Unit (ANDROS II), 1972–73; Project Director, Department of Youth Services, 1972–73, all Massachusetts; Director, Advocacy Associates, New York and New Jersey, 1973–75; Planner-Analyst, Crime Control Coordinator's Office, New York, 1974–75; Director, Juvenile Justice Planning Project, New York, 1975–85; Adjunct Professor, College of New Resources, New York, 1980–81. Since 1976 attorney, private practice, New York. Recipient: Grand Prix de Littérature Policière, 1988. Agent: Neal I. Gantcher, Leavy Rosenweig and Hyman, 11 East 44th Street, New York, New York 10017. Address: 299 Broadway, Suite 1803, New York, New York 10017-1901, U.S.A.

CRIME PUBLICATIONS

Novels (series: Burke in all books)

Flood. New York, Fine, 1985; London, Collins, 1986.
Strega. New York, Knopf, 1987; London, Collins, 1988.
Blue Belle. New York, Knopf, 1988; London, Knopf, Bodley Head, 1989.
Hard Candy. New York, Knopf, 1989; London, Bodley Head, 1990.
Blossom. New York, Knopf, 1990.

Uncollected Short Stories

"It's a Hard World," in *A Matter of Crime I*, edited by Matthew J. Bruccoli and Richard Layman. San Diego, Harcourt Brace, 1987.
"Dumping Ground," "The Promise," both in *A Matter of Crime 2*, edited by Matthew J. Bruccoli and Richard Layman. San Diego, Harcourt Brace, 1988.
"Placebo," in *Ellery Queen's Mystery Magazine* (New York), March 1989.
"Value Received," in *Hardboiled* (Rockford, Illinois), 1989.
"Cough," in *Ellery Queen's Mystery Magazine* (New York), August 1989.
"Exit," in *New Crimes*, edited by Maxim Jakubowski. London, Robinson, 1989; New York, Carroll and Graf, 1990.

"Family Resemblance," in *Ellery Queen's Mystery Magazine* (New York), January 1990.
"Mad Dog," in *Armchair Detective* (New York), Winter, 1990.
"White Alligator," in *Ellery Queen's Mystery Magazine* (New York), April 1990.

OTHER PUBLICATIONS

Other

The Life-Style Violent Juvenile: The Secure Treatment Approach. Lexington, Massachusetts, Lexington, 1979.
The Child Abuse-Delinquency Connection: A Lawyer's View. Lexington, Massachusetts, Lexington, 1989.

*

Andrew Vachss comments:

Writing isn't my work—it is an organic extension of that work. I see it as my opportunity to address a far wider audience than I might ever encounter in my professional life—a chance to increase the size of the congregation for my particular brand of gospel. I write about crimes, violence, and most particularly, the abuse of children—individually and commercially. While generally characterized as genre fiction, I believe it to be mainstream in that what I am writing about does happen. I wish it were fiction.

* * *

In the space of barely five years, Andrew Vachss, a New York attorney in criminal practice specializing in child abuse and delinquency, has firmly established himself as one of the leading exponents of the contemporary American hard-boiled genre.

Despite the repeated use of often distasteful subject matter used to relentless effect (some even accuse him of downright exploitation), Vachss is at heart a strong moralist, and an angry man who, through his renegade character Burke, summons up savage retribution against the society he perversely refuses to be a part of, a society which encourages child prostitution, sexual exploitation and other extreme vices, a society no longer deserving of the name, harbouring as it does in its dark heart the seeds of urban evil.

Burke fills a void; with his soiled white hat, he is a lone ranger of the 1990's who asks difficult questions while shining light into the darkest recesses. The universe in which Burke, the loner investigator and his colourful cronies, the Mole, Mama Wong, Immaculata, Michelle the transvestite whore, and Max the giant Mongol warrior all move swiftly and vengefully, is literally an urban jungle, where only the strongest survive (although Vachss's fifth and latest Burke novel, *Blossom*, does transplant some of the crew into a hitherto unfamiliar backroads country landscape).

There is nothing noble about Burke, an ex-con, an urban vigilante and angel of retribution who only takes on a case if his conscience is suitably alerted or given an emotional jump start by the acts of the criminals involved. Although it must be added that in deference to genre customs, somewhat ambiguous sexual relationships with some of the women closely involved in his current case can sometimes act as a useful reminder. Arrogant in his defiance of the system, Burke has isolated himself within the dark recesses of a beautifully depicted New York: he has no phone, no papers, pays no rent, conceals his whereabouts, and lives within the protection of his much-extended family of virtual outlaws.

Burke is a unique creation in modern crime fiction: a private investigator who is neither ex-cop or lone knight, but a reformed convict with strong born again convictions. His tactics are more often than not utterly illegal and the legal system is more enemy than aid. Vachss has admitted that he has no ambition to write novels without Burke, his illegal alter ego, and one can only hope that the anger in him does not diminish, or, perversely, that his real-life battle against crime keeps on furnishing him with further plots.

Vachss has also written a handful of short stories, in his usual sharp, staccato style, which do not feature Burke, but they are most often clever exercises in style with a nice touch in ironic endings.

—Maxim Jakubowski

VALENTINE, Douglas. *See* **WILLIAMS, Valentine.**

VALENTINE, Jo. *See* **ARMSTRONG, Charlotte.**

VALIN, Jonathan (Louis). American. Born in Cincinnati, Ohio, 23 November 1948. Educated at the University of Chicago, M.A. 1974; Washington University, St. Louis, 1976–79. Married Katherine Brockhaus in 1971. Lecturer in English, University of Cincinnati, 1974–76, and Washington University, 1976–79. Since 1979 freelance writer. Agent: Dominick Abel Literary Agency, 498 West End Avenue, New York, New York 10024. Address: c/o Delacorte Press, 666 Fifth Avenue, New York, New York 10103, U.S.A.

CRIME PUBLICATIONS

Novels (series: Harry Stoner in all books)

The Lime Pit. New York, Dodd Mead, 1980; London, Collins, 1981.
Final Notice. New York, Dodd Mead, 1980; London, Collins, 1981.
Dead Letter. New York, Dodd Mead, 1981; London, Collins, 1982.
Day of Wrath. New York, Congdon and Lattès, 1982; London, Collins, 1983.
Natural Causes. New York, Congdon and Weed, 1983; London, Collins, 1984.

Life's Work. New York, Delacorte Press, 1986; London, Century Hutchinson, 1988.
Fire Lake. New York, Delacorte Press, 1987; London, Century Hutchinson, 1989.
Extenuating Circumstances. New York, Delacorte Press, 1989.

*   *   *

Harry Stoner, Jonathan Valin's protagonist, has apparently maintained his Cincinnati office for several years, but only recently has he taken to discussing his work in print. Stoner is a private detective very much in the American hard-boiled tradition, but he is also (not untraditionally) very much his own man just as the tight, vigorous plots, crisply delineated characters, and precise settings are particularly Valin's despite the fact that his novels fit into a well-established, clearly defined subgenre. A loner like most of his colleagues, Stoner nevertheless tunes in his Zenith Globemaster constantly, just to be within sound of some human voice. This trick of shifting the formula a bit off center is typical of Valin's sophisticated manipulation of the form; it's also one of several ways in which Harry Stoner reveals his vulnerability rather more than do many of his counterparts.

Familial discord is central to Valin's plots. During each case, Stoner encounters a variety of families. Extended, family-like units which develop in the workplace—the slightly batty, supportive librarians who operate a small branch (*Final Notice*) or the predatory staff of a soap opera (*Natural Causes*)—appear, for example. Other extended families reflect their times (or times they *wish* were theirs) as do the youngsters surrounding musician-guru Theo Clinger (*Day of Wrath*) or Sarah Lovingwell's crowd of supposed environmentalists and political protestors (*Dead Letter*). Though a few of these relationships are worthy, all are flawed. Some, once healthy, are now decayed and damaging; still others, for instance the crime ring of *The Lime Pit*, are deadly from their inception. Chilling enough in themselves, such defects are even more alarming when they occur within blood-and-marriage families. And they always do occur, for Valin, like several of his contemporaries, takes social decay as symbolized by the ruin of the American family for his theme. By treating immediate families—husbands and wives, parents and children—against the backdrop of the extended families, Valin broadens his portrait of the contemporary scene. By concentrating primarily on ordinary folk (rather than on the rich) and by exploiting the Ohio Valley, an area he knows well, he suggests that corruption festers in America's heartland. These devices extend the symbolism and further alter the established elements of the formula.

Stoner often remarks upon the narrow, puritanical, distorted public morality of Cincinnatians which he believes he shares to some limited degree, and he fears it, for too frequently social convention conceals profound error, selfishness, irresponsibility, and guilt so patly that adults can evade proper responsibility for their actions—and for their children. Mothers so fixated upon propriety or fathers so defeated by life that they cannot really function as parents echo in Stoner's personal and professional memory. He knows those problems intimately, he reports, and he knows their cost, for he, himself, as is traditional among his peers, cannot sustain relationships well. Lovers appear and vanish; friends come and go; only his small apartment in the Delores, his radio music, his Pinto, and his caseload are constant.

Middle-class Americans in Mid-America are Valin's chief subject; dereliction of parental or filial duty, crime, appalling violence, abandonment, and rejection are the terms in which he discusses that subject. But so long as Harry Stoner, a big man with the face of a broken statue, can live decently and responsibly among his dolorous surroundings, there is, perhaps, a little hope. Stoner does what he can; that's as much as readers ask of most modern heroes.

—Jane S. Bakerman

———

VANCE, John Holbrook (Jack Vance). Also writes as Peter Held; John Holbrook; Ellery Queen; Alan Wade. American. Born in San Francisco, California, 28 August 1916. Educated at the University of California, Berkeley, B.A. 1942. Married Norma Ingold in 1946; one son. Self-employed writer. Recipient: Mystery Writers of America Edgar Allan Poe award, 1960; Hugo award, 1963, 1967; Nebula award, 1966; Jupiter award, 1974; World Fantasy Convention Life Achievement award, 1984. Agent: Ralph Vicinanza Ltd., 432 Park Avenue South, Suite 1205, New York, New York 10016. Address: 6383 Valley View Road, Oakland, California 94611, U.S.A.

CRIME PUBLICATIONS

Novels (series: Sheriff Joe Bain)

Isle of Peril (as Alan Wade). New York, Curl, 1957.
Take My Face (as Peter Held). New York, Curl, 1957.
The Man in the Cage. New York, Random House, 1960; London, Boardman, 1961.
The Fox Valley Murders (Bain). Indianapolis, Bobbs Merrill, 1966; London, Hale, 1967.
The Pleasant Grove Murders (Bain). Indianapolis, Bobbs Merrill, 1967; London, Hale, 1968.
The Deadly Isles. Indianapolis, Bobbs Merrill, 1969; London, Hale, 1970.
Bad Ronald. New York, Ballantine, 1973.

Novels as Jack Vance (series: Keith Gersen)

To Live Forever. New York, Ballantine, 1956; London, Sphere, 1976.
The Star King (Gersen). New York, Berkley, 1964; London, Dobson, 1966.
The Killing Machine (Gersen). New York, Berkley, 1964; London, Dobson, 1967.
The Palace of Love (Gersen). New York, Berkley, 1967; London, Dobson, 1968.
Marune: Alastor 993. New York, Ballantine, 1975; London, Coronet, 1978.
The Face (Gersen). New York, DAW, 1979; London, Dobson, 1980.
The House on Lily Street. San Francisco, Underwood Miller, 1979.
The View from Chickweed's Window. San Francisco, Underwood Miller, 1979.
The Book of Dreams (Gersen). New York, DAW, 1981; London, Coronet, 1982.
Strange Notions, and The Dark Ocean. Lancaster, Pennsylvania, Underwood Miller, 2 vols., 1985.

Novels as Ellery Queen

The Four Johns. New York, Pocket Books, 1964; as *Four Men Called John*, London, Gollancz, 1976.
A Room to Die In. New York, Pocket Books, 1965.
The Madman Theory. New York, Pocket Books, 1966.

Short Stories as Jack Vance

The Many Worlds of Magnus Ridolph. New York, Ace, 1966; London, Dobson, 1977.
Galactic Effectuator. Columbia, Pennsylvania, Underwood Miller, 1980; London, Coronet, 1983.

OTHER PUBLICATIONS as Jack Vance

Novels

The Space Pirate. New York, Toby Press, 1953; as *The Five Gold Bands*, New York, Ace, 1963; London, Granada, 1980.
Vandals of the Void (for children). Philadelphia, Winston, 1953.
Big Planet. New York, Avalon, 1957; London, Coronet, 1977.
The Languages of Pao. New York, Avalon, 1958.
Slaves of the Klau. New York, Ace, 1958.
The Dragon Masters. New York, Ace, 1963; London, Dobson, 1965.
The Houses of Iszm, Son of the Tree. New York, Ace, 1964; *Son of the Tree* published separately, London, Mayflower, 1974.
Monsters in Orbit. New York, Ace, 1965; London, Dobson, 1977.
Space Opera. New York, Pyramid, 1965.
The Blue World. New York, Ballantine, 1966; London, Mayflower, 1976.
The Brains of Earth. New York, Ace, 1966; London, Dobson, 1976.
City of the Chasch. New York, Ace, 1968; London, Dobson, 1975.
Emphyrio. New York, Doubleday, 1969.
Servants of the Wankh. New York, Ace, 1969; London, Dobson, 1975; as *Wankh*, New York, Bluejay, 1986.
The Dirdir. New York, Ace, 1969; London, Dobson, 1975.
The Pnume. New York, Ace, 1970; London, Dobson, 1975.
The Anome. New York, Dell, 1973; London, Hodder and Stoughton, 1975; as *The Faceless Man*, New York, Ace, 1978; London, Gollancz, 1987.
The Brave Free Men. New York, Dell, 1973; London, Hodder and Stoughton, 1975.
Trullion: Alastor 2262. New York, Ballantine, 1973; London, Mayflower, 1979.
The Asutra. New York, Dell, 1974; London, Hodder and Stoughton, 1975.
The Gray Prince. Indianapolis, Bobbs Merrill, 1974; London, Coronet, 1976.
Showboat World. New York, Pyramid, 1975; London, Coronet, 1977.
Maske: Thaery. New York, Berkley, 1976; London, Fontana, 1978.
Wyst: Alastor 1716. New York, DAW, 1978.
Nopalgarth. New York, DAW, 1980; London, Panther, 1984.
Lyonesse. I: Suldrum's Garden. New York, Berkley, 1983; London, Granada, 1984.
Cugel's Saga. New York, Pocket Books, 1983; London, Panther, 1985.
Rhialto the Marvellous. New York, Baen, and London, Panther, 1984.

Lyonesse II: The Green Pearl. Lancaster, Pennsylvania, Underwood Miller, 1985; London, Grafton, 1986.
Araminta Station. New York, Tor, and London, New English Library, 1988.
Lyonesse III: Madouc. Lancaster, Pennsylvania, Underwood Miller, 1989; London, Grafton, 1990.

Short Stories

The Dying Earth. New York, Curl, 1950; London, Mayflower, 1972.
Future Tense. New York, Ballantine, 1964.
The World Between and Other Stories. New York, Ace, 1965; as *The Moon Moth and Other Stories*, London, Dobson, 1975.
The Eyes of the Overworld. New York, Ace, 1966; London, Mayflower, 1972.
The Last Castle. New York, Ace, 1967.
Eight Fantasms and Magics. New York, Macmillan, 1969; as *Fantasms and Magics*, London, Mayflower, 1978.
The Worlds of Jack Vance. New York, Ace, 1973.
The Best of Jack Vance. New York, Pocket Books, 1976.
Green Magic. San Francisco, Underwood Miller, 1979.
Dust of Far Suns. New York, DAW, 1981.
The Narrow Land. New York, DAW, 1982.
Lost Moons. Columbia, Pennsylvania, Underwood Miller, 1982.
The Augmented Agent, edited by Steven Goedersky. Lancaster, Pennsylvania, Underwood Miller, 1986.
The Dark Side of the Moon. Lancaster, Pennsylvania, Underwood Miller, 1986.

Plays

Television Plays: *Captain Video* (6 episodes), 1952–53.

*

Bibliography: *Fantasms: A Bibliography of the Literature of Jack Vance* by Daniel J.H. Levack and Tim Underwood, San Francisco, Underwood Miller, 1978.

Manuscript Collection: Mugar Memorial Library, Boston University.

Critical Study: *Demon Prince: The Dissonant Worlds of Jack Vance* by Jack Rawlins. San Bernadino, Borgo Press, 1986.

John Holbrook Vance comments:

Most of my mystery/suspense fiction was written at the midpart of my career, even though two of these novels did not see publication until recently.

Mysteries have always been a favourite of mine. Long after I ceased to read science-fiction I continued to read in this field. Those who are acquainted with my science fiction know that mystery and suspense are often significant plot elements.

*   *   *

John Holbrook Vance was already famous as a writer of science fiction and fantastic adventure, under the shortened name Jack Vance, when he turned to mystery fiction. Much of his science fiction is built around pure crime story plots. Magnus Ridolph, created for a series of magazine stories in the late 1940's, is an interstellar trouble-shooter and con-man who redresses wrongs (for a fee) and even solves a murder. Six of his adventures were collected in book form as *The Many Worlds of Magnus Ridolph.* In *To Live Forever*, one of Vance's best novels, the murderer, Gavin Waylock, fights for survival in a highly

structured society of the future. And in the series beginning with the novel *The Star King* a man hunts the five disguised non-humans who murdered his parents. These and other Jack Vance books are worth the attention of any reader who enjoys exotic adventure and strange locales.

In 1957 Vance's first contemporary mystery novel, *Isle of Peril*, was published under the pseudonym Alan Wade. This is the story of the violent events that occur when the owner of a small island sells parcels of land to a group of buyers who are not what they seem. A second pseudonymous mystery, *Take My Face* (by Peter Held), also appeared in 1957. Three years later Vance felt ready to put his own name on a mystery novel, and his confidence was justified: *The Man in the Cage*, a tale of intrigue and smuggling in Tangier, won an Edgar. In 1966, he published the first of two novels featuring Sheriff Joe Bain of San Rodrigo County, California. About *The Fox Valley Murders*, the critic Anthony Boucher said that the setting "is wonderfully real, and so is Sheriff Bain. A fresh kind of procedural story." *The Pleasant Grove Murders* was equally good. In *The Deadly Isles* the setting shifted to Tahiti and the South Seas for a more artificial and much less satisfying story. Vance was back in top form with *Bad Ronald*, a fascinating study of a young psychopath which manages to make incredible events convincing.

—R.E. Briney

———

VANCE, Louis Joseph. American. Born in Washington, D.C., 19 September 1879. Educated at Brooklyn Polytechnic Institute; Art Students' League, New York City. Married Nance Elizabeth Hodges in 1898 (separated); one son. Worked for public service corporation, New York, before becoming full-time writer. Published hundreds of short stories in popular magazines before the success of his mystery novels. *Died 16 December 1933.*

CRIME PUBLICATIONS

Novels (series: Michael Lanyard, "The Lone Wolf")

Terrence O'Rourke, Gentleman Adventurer. New York, Wessels, 1905; London, Richards, 1906.
The Brass Bowl. Indianapolis, Bobbs Merrill, and London, Richards, 1907.
The Black Bag. Indianapolis, Bobbs Merrill, and London, Richards, 1908.
The Bronze Bell. New York, Dodd Mead, and London, Richards, 1909.
The Pool of Flame. New York, Dodd Mead, 1909; London, Richards, 1910.
No Man's Land. New York, Dodd Mead, and London, Stevens and Brown, 1910.
Cynthia-of-the-Minute. New York, Dodd Mead, and London, Richards, 1911.
The Bandbox. Boston, Little Brown, and London, Richards, 1912.
The Destroying Angel. Boston, Little Brown, 1912; London, Richards, 1913.
The Lone Wolf. Boston, Little Brown, 1914; London, Nash, 1915.
Nobody. New York, Doran, 1915; London, Hodder and Stoughton, 1916.

Sheep's Clothing. Boston, Little Brown, 1915.
The False Faces (Lanyard). New York, Doubleday, 1918; London, Skeffington, 1920.
Bean Revel. London, Nash, 1920.
The Dark Mirror. New York, Doubleday, 1920; London, Hurst and Blackett, 1921.
Alias the Lone Wolf. New York, Doubleday, and London, Hodder and Stoughton, 1921.
Red Masquerade (Lanyard). New York, Doubleday, and London, Hodder and Stoughton, 1921.
Baroque. New York, Dutton, and London, Hodder and Stoughton, 1923.
The Lone Wolf Returns. New York, Dutton, 1923; London, Hodder and Stoughton, 1924.
The Dark Power. London, Bles, 1925.
The Dead Ride Hard. Philadelphia, Lippincott, 1926; London, Bles, 1927.
Lip Service. London, Bles, 1928.
The Woman in the Shadow. Philadelphia, Lippincott, 1930; London, Jarrolds, 1931.
The Lone Wolf's Son. Philadelphia, Lippincott, 1931; London, Jarrolds, 1932.
The Trembling Flame. Philadelphia, Lippincott, 1931; London, Jarrolds, 1932.
Detective. Philadelphia, Lippincott, 1932; London, Jarrolds, 1933.
Encore the Lone Wolf. Philadelphia, Lippincott, 1933; London, Jarrolds, 1934.
The Lone Wolf's Last Prowl. Philadelphia, Lippincott, 1934; London, Jarrolds, 1935.
The Street of Strange Faces. Philadelphia, Lippincott, and London, Jarrolds, 1934.

Uncollected Short Stories

"Old Man Menace," in *The Saint* (New York), May 1965.
"The White Terror," in *The Saint* (New York), August 1965.
"The Gulp Stream," in *The Saint* (New York), April 1966.
"The Flash," in *The Saint* (New York), September 1966.

OTHER PUBLICATIONS

Novels

The Private War. New York, Appleton, and London, Richards, 1906.
The Fortune Hunter. New York, Dodd Mead, and London, Stevens and Brown, 1910.
Marrying Money (novelization of stage play *The Fortune Hunter*). London, Richards, 1911.
The Day of Days. Boston, Little Brown, 1913; London, Richards, 1914.
Joan Thursday. Boston, Little Brown, and London, Richards, 1913.
The Trey o' Hearts. New York, Grosset and Dunlap, 1914.
Linda Lee Incorporated. New York, Dutton, 1922.
Mrs. Paramour. New York, Dutton, 1924.
The Road to En-Dor. New York, Dutton, 1924.
White Fire. New York, Dutton, and London, Bles, 1926.
They Call It Love. Philadelphia, Lippincott, 1927.
Speaking of Women. Philadephia, Lippincott, 1930; London, Jarrolds, 1932.

Plays

Screenplays: *Patria*, 1917; *The Lone Wolf's Daughter*, with Sig Herzig and Harry Revier, 1929.

* * *

Had Louis Joseph Vance not created Michael Lanyard, alias the Lone Wolf, it may be doubted if his work would be remembered. Inspired by, and following in the tradition of, Arsène Lupin, Lanyard is more human and introspective. He is (in Robert Sampson's phrase) a "bent hero," one of that breed who rid society of criminals by working from outside the law. The ethical position of the bent hero is shaky, but it is also part of a venerable tradition which may be traced to Robin Hood.

Vance's style is one of subdued sensationalism peppered with arcane words, but the serious tone and the glimpses of the Lone Wolf's mind at work make the most preposterous situations seem plausible. The Lone Wolf's world is free of that social festering and inarticulate horror that underlie the *Black Mask* style. Lanyard's origins are a mystery. He became a criminal willingly and just as willingly rejected that profession to prove himself worthy of a woman's trust. In *The False Faces* he pursues the murderer of his wife while gathering intelligence information for the Allies. In *Red Masquerade* he works for the British Secret Service to prevent the assassination of the King and the members of the Cabinet.

Vance may have thought little of his creation for he wrote only eight novels about Lanyard. The tradition of the noble outlaw which he kept alive certainly had a great influence on writers like Sapper and Leslie Charteris, however differently they reflect it.

—J. Randolph Cox

---

van de WETERING, Janwillem. Dutch. Born in Rotterdam, 12 February 1931. Educated at Delft University, 1948; College for Service Abroad, 1949–51; Cambridge University, 1951; University of London, 1957–58. Married 1) Edyth Stewart-Wynne in 1954 (divorced); 2) Juanita Levy in 1960; one child. Salesman in South Africa, 1952–58; layman in Buddhist monastery, Kyoto, Japan, 1958–59, company director, Bogota, Colombia, 1959–62, and Lima, Peru, 1963; land salesman, Brisbane, Australia, 1964–65; director of textile company, Amsterdam, 1965–75; member of Buddhist group in Maine, 1975–80. Also member of Amsterdam Reserve Police from 1965. Lives in Maine. Recipient: Grand Prix de Littérature Policière, 1984. Address: c/o Smith Skolnik Literary Agents, 23 East 10th Street, New York, New York 10003.

CRIME PUBLICATIONS

Novels (series: Amsterdam Cop)

Outsider in Amsterdam (Amsterdam Cop). Boston, Houghton Mifflin, 1975; London, Heinemann, 1976.
Tumbleweed (Amsterdam Cop). Boston, Houghton Mifflin, and London, Heinemann, 1976.
The Corpse on the Dike (Amsterdam Cop). Boston, Houghton Mifflin, 1976; London, Heinemann, 1977.
Death of a Hawker (Amsterdam Cop). Boston, Houghton Mifflin, and London, Heinemann, 1977.

The Japanese Corpse (Amsterdam Cop). Boston, Houghton Mifflin, and London, Heinemann, 1977.

The Blond Baboon (Amsterdam Cop). Boston, Houghton Mifflin, and London, Heinemann, 1978.

The Maine Massacre (Amsterdam Cop). Boston, Houghton Mifflin, and London, Heinemann, 1979.

The Mind-Murders (Amsterdam Cop). Boston, Houghton Mifflin, and London, Heinemann, 1981.

The Butterfly Hunter. Boston, Houghton Mifflin, 1982; London, Severn House, 1983.

The Streetbird (Amsterdam Cop). New York, Putnam, 1983; London, Gollancz, 1984.

The Rattle-Rat (Amsterdam Cop). New York, Pantheon, 1985; London, Gollancz, 1986.

Hard Rain (Amsterdam Cop). New York, Pantheon, 1986; London, Gollancz, 1987.

Seesaw Millions. New York, Ballantine, 1988; London, Gollancz, 1989.

Short Stories

Inspector Saito's Small Satori. New York, Putnam, 1985.

The Sergeant's Cat and Other Stories. New York, Pantheon, 1987; London, Gollancz, 1988.

Uncollected Short Stories

"The Deadly Egg," in *Ellery Queen's Mystery Magazine* (New York), March 1979.

"The Machine Gun and the Mannequin," in *Ellery Queen's Mystery Magazine* (New York), Mid-July 1982.

OTHER PUBLICATIONS

Other

De Lege Spiegel. Amsterdam, Driehoek, 1971; as *The Empty Mirror: Experiences in a Japanese Monastery*, Boston, Houghton Mifflin, 1974; London, Routledge, 1987.

A Glimpse of Nothingness: Experiences in an American Zen Community. Boston, Houghton Mifflin, and London, Routledge, 1975.

Little Owl Boston, Houghton Mifflin, 1978.

Hugh Pine [*and the Good Place, and Something Else*] (for children). Boston, Houghton Mifflin, 3 vols., 1980–89.

Bliss and Bluster; or, How to Crack a Nut (for children). Boston, Houghton Mifflin, 1982.

Robert van Gulik: His Life, His Work. Palm Beach, California, McMillan, 1988.

Murder by Remote Control (cartoons). New York, Available Press, 1989.

* * *

Janwillem van de Wetering brings a singular background to his fiction. He served as a reserve policeman in Amsterdam, which, in part, supplies the element of authenticity to his stories; he also undertook a serious study of Zen Buddhism in Japan and in New England, which, in part, supplies the philosophical world view of the stories. From the beginning, van de Wetering, who has lived in Maine since 1975, wrote the novels in English and later rewrote them in Dutch. (The most recent novels have been published first in Dutch.)

Though his depiction of Amsterdam scenes and his construction of plausible mystery plots are strong points, the real virtue of the series lies in the development of his characters and their aesthetic and moral responses to their world. Adjutent Grijpstra and Sergeant de Gier are introduced in the first novel. The senior member of the team is a heavy, stolid Dutchman, unhappily married to a fat, stolid Dutchwoman, yet he is capable of original insights into events. De Gier, slim and attractive, is a more of a romantic; he pursues originality, yet he is capable of practical judgments and actions. The odd harmony between the two is epitomized in their regular drum-and-flute duets.

Though van de Wetering has said that the first four novels came to him in a single vision, the third principal member of the team, the commissaris (known only as Jan), only emerges in the second novel, *Tumbleweed*. Elderly, married, afflicted with rheumatism, devoted to a pet turtle, the commissaris functions as the spiritual center of the series. He enjoys passive observation of the spectacles of life; he is also committed to appropriate moral intervention in the situations that confront his murder brigade. (Cardozo, the young, eager, and most junior member of the brigade, is also introduced in *Tumbleweed*, but his importance develops more slowly.)

The best novels in the series are those set in Amsterdam. Van de Wetering offers a comprehensive view of the city—its streets, its canals, its 17th-century houses. He sets the action in various locales and draws upon all classes of people, yet every scene and every character is individualized. These novels offer the best mixture of realism, whimsy, and philosophy. All three elements are often embodied in a single character. In *Outsider in Amsterdam*, he is Jan Karel van Meteren, a Papuan ex-policeman whose name resembles that of the author and whose peculiar aesthetic approach to life fascinates Grijpstra and de Gier. Other such figures, often artists, who represent alternative visions include Louis Zilver (*Death of a Hawker*), Jan Vieuten (*The Blond Baboon*,) and the Fox (*The Maine Massacre.*) But all the novels raise questions concerning the meaning of moral action. The commissaris, Grijpstra, and de Gier repeatedly attempt to understand their experience through discussions of such concepts as "emptiness," "nothing," "zero," and "silence."

Several of the novels take the detectives outside Amsterdam. The best of these is *The Maine Massacre*, set on the wintry coast of Maine where the commissaris and de Gier help solve a series of murders. Though much of *The Japanese Corpse* is promisingly set in the home of Zen, there is insufficient opportunity to explore the nuances of the new world, and the commissaris and de Gier are caught up in a melodramatic plot involving Japanese organized crime, the yakusa. *The Rattle-Rat*, one of the oddest adventures, is set in Friesland (northeastern Holland); whimsical satire predominates, and only de Gier is spared.

Hard Rain is clearly a climax in the series. Van de Wetering splits his first name into two antagonists, Jan, the commissaris, and Willem, Amsterdam's Napoleon of Crime and the commissaris's look-alike second cousin. And in addition to defeating his nemesis, the commissaris must combat the deterioration and corruption in his own police force. In his triumph, the commissaris happily loses his best disciple: de Gier is denied his desire to engage in a death struggle with *his* mirror image, the evil Baron Bart de la Faille, but he proceeds to abandon Amsterdam in his pursuit of enlightenment. That his destination is New Guinea, home of van Meteren, the key figure in the first novel, draws a significant circle in the series. (Islands, as physical scenes and as metaphors for the human condition, are important in most of the novels).

Van de Wetering has also written crime novels outside his Amsterdam series. *The Butterfly Hunter* relates the adventures of Eddy Sachs as he pursues Nazi gold in Europe and Central and South America. *Murder by Remote Control* is a cartoon book with a slight mystery narrative by van de Wetering and effective drawings by Paul Kirchner. *Inspector Saito's Small Satori* consists of a series of short stories featuring young Inspector Saito of the Kyoto police. The book reflects van de Wetering's admiration of Robert van Gulik's Judge Dee stories; the 13th-century Chinese source to which Inspector Saito often refers—*Parallel Cases Under the Pear Tree*—was translated by van Gulik.

Van de Wetering's major achievement clearly lies in his Amsterdam series, a series distinguished by its unusually high quality. The novels are more than advertisements for Zen, but the qualities of humor and detachment give the investigations a peculiar perspective; aesthetic awareness seems to matter as much as moral judgement. Though there are biographical developments—such as de Gier losing one cat and gaining another, or Grijpstra finally losing his wife—the real pleasure in reading novels in sequence lies in the unfolding of this perspective.

—J.K. Van Dover

VAN DINE, S.S. Pseudonym for Willard Huntington Wright. American. Born in Charlottesville, Virginia, in 1888. Educated at St. Vincent College and Pomona College, California; Harvard University, Cambridge, Massachusetts; studied art in Munich and Paris. Married 1) Katharine Belle Boynton in 1907 (divorced 1930); one daughter; 2) Eleanor Pulapaugh. Literary and art critic, Los Angeles *Times*, 1907; editor-in-chief, *Smart Set*, New York, 1912–14; editor, *The International Studio*. Suffered a breakdown in 1923 and confined to bed for two years, when he began writing; screenwriter for Warner Brothers, 1931–32. *Died 11 April 1939.*

CRIME PUBLICATIONS

Novels (series: Philo Vance in all books except *The President's Mystery Story*)

The Benson Murder Case. New York, Scribner, and London, Benn, 1926.
The Canary Murder Case. New York, Scribner, and London, Benn, 1927.
The Greene Murder Case. New York, Scribner, and London, Benn, 1928.
The Bishop Murder Case. New York, Scribner, and London, Cassell, 1929.
The Scarab Murder Case. New York, Scribner, and London, Cassell, 1930.
The Kennel Murder Case. New York, Scribner, and London, Cassell, 1933.
The Dragon Murder Case. New York, Scribner, 1933; London, Cassell, 1934.
The Casino Murder Case. New York, Scribner, and London, Cassell, 1934.
The Garden Murder Case. New York, Scribner, and London, Cassell, 1935.
The President's Mystery Story, with others. New York, Farrar and Rinehart, 1935; London, Lane, 1936.
The Kidnap Murder Case. New York, Scribner, and London, Cassell, 1936.
The Gracie Allen Murder Case. New York, Scribner, and London, Cassell, 1938; as *The Smell of Murder*, New York, Bantam, 1950.

The Winter Murder Case. New York, Scribner, and London, Cassell, 1939.

Uncollected Short Stories

"The Scarlet Nemesis," in *Cosmopolitan* (New York), January 1929.
"A Murder in a Witches' Cauldron," in *Cosmopolitan* (New York), February 1929.
"The Man in the Blue Overcoat," in *Cosmopolitan* (New York), May 1929.
"Poison," in *Cosmopolitan* (New York), June 1929.
"The Almost Perfect Crime," in *Cosmopolitan* (New York), July 1929.
"The Inconvenient Husband," in *Cosmopolitan* (New York), August 1929.
"The Bonmartini Murder Case," in *Cosmopolitan* (New York), October 1929.
"Fool!" in *Cosmopolitan* (New York), January 1930.

OTHER PUBLICATIONS as Willard Huntington Wright

Novel

The Man of Promise. New York, Lane, 1916.

Play

Screenplay: *The Canary Murder Case*, with others, 1929.

Other

Europe after 8:15, with H.L. Mencken and George Jean Nathan. New York, Lane, 1914.
Modern Painting: Its Tendency and Meaning. New York, Lane, 1915.
What Nietzsche Taught. New York, Huebsch, 1915.
The Creative Will: Studies in the Philosophy and Syntax of Aesthetics. New York, Lane, 1916.
The Forum Exhibition of Modern American Painters, March Thirteenth to March Twenty-fifth, 1916. New York, Mitchell Kennerley, 1916.
Informing a Nation. New York, Dodd Mead, 1917.
Misinforming a Nation. New York, Huebsch, 1917.
The Future of Painting. New York, Huebsch, 1923.
"The Detective Novel," in *Scribner's* (New York), November 1926.
"Twenty Rules for Writing Detective Stories," in *American Magazine* (Springfield, Ohio), September 1928.
I Used to Be a Highbrow But Look at Me Now (as S.S. Van Dine). New York, Scribner, 1929.
"The Great Detective Stories," in *The Art of the Mystery Story: A Collection of Critical Essays*, edited by Howard Haycraft. New York, Simon and Schuster, 1946.

Editor, *The Great Modern French Stories.* New York, Boni and Liveright, 1917.
Editor, *The Great Detective Stories: A Chronological Anthology.* New York, Scribner, 1927.

*

Bibliography: "The Writings of Willard Huntington Wright" by Walter B. Crawford, in *Bulletin of Bibliography* (Westwood, Massachusetts), May–August 1963.

Manuscript Collection: Princeton University Library, New Jersey.

Critical Study: *Philo Vance: The Life and Times of S.S. Van Dine* by Jon Tuska and others, Bowling Green, Ohio, Popular Press, 1981.

*   *   *

Willard Huntington Wright was a distinguished art critic, an editor from 1912–14 of *The Smart Set* magazine, a collaborator with H.L. Mencken and George Jean Nathan, the author of several books—including a devastating attack on the *Encyclopaedia Britannica*, *Misinforming a Nation*—a study of Nietzsche, several works on modern painting, and a novel, *The Man of Promise*. He had shown little interest in detective fiction when he was forced by overwork to take a long rest, during which he was forbidden to do any "serious" reading. In his long convalescence he read over 2,000 volumes of detective fiction and works on criminology, and applied to them the analytical methods of an art and literary critic. Out of this analysis came a quite prescriptive theory of detective fiction, later expressed in his introduction to the anthology *The Great Detective Stories* and his famous "Twenty Rules for Writing Detective Stories." In both he insisted that "The detective story is a kind of intellectual game ... a sporting event," with definite laws dealing with fair play and concentration on the puzzle. He excluded "love interest," elaborate characterization and description, and conspiracies, spies, political plots, and professional criminals.

Wright set about creating a set of detective plots according to these rules, submitted three of them to a publisher, and was given a contract. The first, *The Benson Murder Case*, with the amateur detective Philo Vance, appeared in 1926. It and its successor, *The Canary Murder Case*, revitalized the moribund detective story in America, attracted a new audience, and launched in America what Howard Haycraft has called "The Golden Age." Nine more Philo Vance novels followed before Wright's death in 1939, and a final work, in abbreviated second-draft form, *The Winter Murder Case*, appeared posthumously. Except for the unfortunate *Gracie Allen Murder Case*, their titles all have six letters. Wright declared that he would write only six S.S. Van Dine novels, saying that no one "has more than six good detective novel ideas in his system," but the success of his first six Philo Vance novels with the critics, the reading public, and, above all, in motion picture versions, led him to continue. The last six, however, are markedly inferior to the first six, vindicating his initial judgment.

Despite the fact that the novels are written as though they were telling the inside story of actual celebrated cases—what Sutherland Scott calls "profound pseudo-realism"—and that the first two are, in fact, based on notorious murders (the Joseph Bowne Elwell case and the "Dot" King case), these stories are, as Van Dine's "Rules" would lead us to except, tales resting primarily on elaborate and intricate plots, that, as Nicholas Blake said of John Dickson Carr's, "possess the mad logic and extravagance of a dream." This extravagance, intricacy, and unreality reach perhaps their highest expression in *The Bishop Murder Case*, in which a series of murders is based on the Mother Goose rhymes—Johnny Sprigg is shot through his wig, Humpty Dumpty is pushed from a wall, Cock Robin is killed by an arrow—and the clues include such intellectual matters as Ibsen's plays, chess moves, and mathematical theories. *The Greene Murder Case*, with *The Bishop* and *The Scarab* one of Van Dine's best and his longest, revolves about a murderer who uses methods borrowed from—

and recognized by Vance as being from—a German work on criminology.

The *deus ex machina*, Vance's phrase for the detective in his "Rules," is Philo Vance, who is a "young social aristocrat," an aesthete, an art critic, an expert on a wide range of esoteric subjects, an Oxford graduate, a dilettante, and an inveterate dropper of terminal g's. Vance, the friend of the New York District Attorney Markham, is an American equivalent of Lord Peter Wimsey and with many characteristics that remind us of H.C. Bailey's Reggie Fortune (Vance's cigarettes are Régie's), but he is even more clearly an idealized portrait of his author. Van Dine, Vance's attorney and constant companion, is the narrator of these novels, and he approaches Vance with a gravity appropriate for a diety, thus, perhaps, completing Wright's wish-fulfillment.

Vance's method is to apply a psychological understanding of people, as well as a wide-ranging knowledge, to the solution of his "cases." In actual fact, the plots almost always involve a series of murders and in a sense solve themselves by elimination. Vance's proof often rests on psychological evidence too slight to be the basis for an arrest, but Wright's Nietzschean attitudes make it possible for Vance to be on occasion executioner as well as detective, himself killing the murderer, as in *The Bishop* and *The Scarab*, or more often, making the murderer's suicide possible. Although Vance aids his friend Markham in solving these cases, it is because they challenge him as intellectual puzzles; he has little interest in abstract justice and little respect for the law.

Two characteristic elements of the novels are extensive use of erudite footnotes and disquisitions on esoteric learning. In the early books, at least through *The Scarab Murder Case*, this learning and the footnotes, however pretentious, are integral to the plots and not only justified but entertaining. In the later books, like Vance's mannerisms, the erudition often seems added in undigested dollops and the pretensions of the notes become annoying. What once had amused and pleased became a source of irritation, resulting finally in Ogden Nash's couplet: "Philo Vance/Needs a kick in the pance."

Whether, had he lived, Wright could have adjusted to the changing tastes of his audience, no one knows. The early Ellery Queen novels, which certainly belong in the Van Dine tradition, gradually changed to very different kinds of books, but there is no evidence that Van Dine at the time of his death realized the need to change. These unchanged mannerisms and concepts have been costly to Van Dine's posthumous reputation, for they have prevented present-day readers from discovering works which are, as Julian Symons says, "models of construction." Van Dine's place in the history of the American detective story is secure and important, but his place with contemporary readers is far lower than it deserves to be. As John Dickson Carr, a master of the same kind of plotting, said, Van Dine "juggled suspects with such dexterity, like twirling Indian-clubs, that we could only stare in admiration." Van Dine's world was remote from real life, but it was the place of delightfully intricate and challenging make-believe.

—C. Hugh Holman

―――――――――

VANE, Nigel. *See* **VERNER, Gerald.**

―――――――――

VAN GREENAWAY, Peter. British. Born in London, in 1929. Former lawyer and full-time writer. *Died in 1988.*

CRIME PUBLICATIONS

Novels

The Man Who Held the Queen to Ransom and Sent Parliament Packing. London, Weidenfeld and Nicolson, 1968; New York, Atheneum, 1969.
Judas! London, Gollancz, 1972; as *The Judas Gospel*, New York, Atheneum, 1972.
The Medusa Touch. London, Gollancz, and New York, Stein and Day, 1973.
Take the War to Washington. London, Gollancz, 1974; New York, St. Martin's Press, 1975.
Doppelganger. London, Gollancz, 1975.
Suffer! Little Children. London, Gollancz, 1976.
The Destiny Man. London, Gollancz, 1977.
A Man Called Scavener. London, Gollancz, 1978.
The Dissident. London, Gollancz, 1980.
"Cassandra" Bell. London, Gollancz, 1981.
Edgar Allan Who—? London, Gollancz, 1981.
The Lazarus Lie. London, Gollancz, 1982.
Manrissa Man. London, Gollancz, 1982.
Graffiti. London, Gollancz, 1983.
Mutants. London, Gollancz, 1986.
The Killing Cup. London, Gollancz, 1987.

Short Stories

The Immortal Coil. London, Gollancz, 1985.

OTHER PUBLICATIONS

Novels

The Crucified City. London, New Authors, 1962.
The Evening Fool. London, Hutchinson, 1964.

*   *   *

Peter Van Greenaway's strange and eclectic work is a literature of ideas, and often not very comfortable ideas. Some true-blooded supporters of the British Establishment choked on their morning toast when he published *The Man Who Held the Queen to Ransom and Sent Parliament Packing*, about Captain Wyatt who makes a Tejeroesque *coup* and thoroughly changes everything. He abolishes the House of Lords, and introduces a Republic, he withdraws all British NATO forces as well as the support of the white minority regimes in South Africa and the Vietnam War. He takes on unemployment and housing problems. But the Establishment, reeling against the ropes, gathers its strength, fights back and kills Wyatt. "Order" is restored.

There is a strange dream-like atmosphere in *The Man Who Held the Queen to Ransom*, and even more so in Van Greenaway's other political novels *Take the War to Washington* and *Suffer! Little Children*. In the first a couple of veterans, shocked by the fate of innocent children in Vietnam, hijack a ship and set sail for Washington to end an unjust war; in the other two teachers in Northern Ireland—one Catholic, one Protestant—"kidnap" their pupils to put pressure on both sides of the conflict to end it. These novels, especially *Suffer! Little Children*, are dreams of the possibility of putting a stop to the seemingly unstoppable mechanisms of violence and cruelty.

But the dreams are crushed, there are too many vested interests in evil for good to prevail.

Van Greenaway's novels may seem to show a pessimistic vision of life (two novels, *The Crucified City* and *Graffiti*, depict a nuclear attack on London). They do, but they also show a glimmer of hope for there is also a strong conviction that ideas can change human conditions, or at least shake the foundations of the powers that be.

Somewhat similar in outlook to *The Man Who Held the Queen to Ransom* is *The Destiny Man*. In this novel, a hitherto unknown Shakespeare manuscript is found, dealing with "The Overbury Case," a well-known scandal from the court of James I. Shakespeare often attacked contemporary political conditions in a somewhat circumspect way, disguising them in Roman or Medieval costume or hiding them among the trees in the Forest of Arden. But this play is about conditions in the early 16th century, anti-royalist and anti-Establishment. The government of the day, facing many social and political problems, considers this play from the National Bard to be potentially dangerous. It must be proven a forgery, or be suppressed.

But Van Greenaway's strongest novel of ideas by far is *Judas!* During an archeological expedition in the Qumran area near the Dead Sea a strange scroll is found. It purports to be the Testament of Judas Iscariot, and the contents are dynamite; Jesus Christ is depicted as a common revolutionary, and Peter as a cheat and an informer. If these teachings are spread and believed the foundations of the Christian religion and especially of the Catholic Church are undermined. Western civilization is threatened. The manuscript must be destroyed, and all who know about it . . .

An author who strongly believes in the power of ideas is almost by necessity a strong believer in History. In several of Greenaway's novels historical events influence the present, often through documents. This is of course obvious in *The Destiny Man* and *Judas!* but the theme also appears in for example *"Cassandra" Bell*, the novel of the Victorian soothsayer whose predictions disturb the present, and *A Man Called Scavener*, in which murders in the last century cast their shadows over the present. In these novels, Van Greenaway's notion of time is reminiscent of T.S. Eliot's, "what might have been and what has been/ Point to one end, which is always present."

This historical dimension also gives Van Greenaway ample opportunities to show his versatility as a stylist; most succesfully in *The Destiny Man* with its astonishing Shakespeare pastiche.

But as Edgar Allan Poe stated, "There is no exquisite beauty without something strange in its proportions." And brilliant as he is in his best moments, Van Greenaway sometimes goes too far: his plots with their literary allusions become too farfetched, his psychology too subtle, his style over-elaborate as in the rather strange *Doppelganger*, with its variation on the Jedermann-theme.

There are many flaws in the strange and exiting work of Van Greenaway—but they are almost always the flaws of genius.

—Karl G. Fredriksson

———

VARDRE, Leslie. *See* **DAVIES, L.P.**

———

VEDDER, John K. *See* **GRUBER, Frank.**

———

VENABLES, Terry. *See* **YUILL, P.B.**

———

VENNING, Michael. *See* **RICE, Craig.**

———

VERNER, Gerald. Pseudonym for Donald William Steward (?); also wrote as Derwent Steele; Donald Stuart; Gerald Stuart; Nigel Vane. British. Born in London, 29 January 1896 (?). Writer and theatrical producer. *Died 16 September 1980.*

CRIME PUBLICATIONS

Novels (series: Superintendent Budd; Peter Chard; Michael Dene; Simon Gale; Felix Heron; Trevor Lowe; Paul Rivington)

The Embankment Murder. London, Wright and Brown, 1933.
Alias the Ghost. London, Wright and Brown, 1933.
Phantom Hollow (Lowe). London, Wright and Brown, 1933.
The Black Hunchback. London, Wright and Brown, 1933.
The Death Play. London, Wright and Brown, 1933.
The Next to Die (Lowe). London, Wright and Brown, 1934.
The Squealer. London, Wright and Brown, 1934.
The Lady of Doom (Lowe). London, Wright and Brown, 1934.
The Hangman (Lowe). London, Wright and Brown, 1934; New York, Godwin, 1935.
Green Mask (Budd). London, Wright and Brown, 1934.
The Con Man (Rivington). London, Wright and Brown, 1934.
White Wig (Rivington). London, Wright and Brown, 1935.
Terror Tower (Lowe). London, Wright and Brown, 1935.
Queer Face. London, Amalgamated Press, 1935.
The Crooked Circle (Budd). London, Wright and Brown, 1935; New York, Macaulay, 1937.
The "Q" Squad. London, Wright and Brown, 1935; New York, Macaulay, 1938.
The Ghost Man. London, Wright and Brown, and New York, Macaulay, 1936.
The Hand of Fear. London, Wright and Brown, 1936.
The Watcher (*Lowe*). London, Wright and Brown, 1936.
The River Men. London, Wright and Brown, 1936.
The Grim Joker (Budd). London, Wright and Brown, 1936.
The Seven Clues (Dene). London, Wright and Brown, 1936.
The Jockey (Budd). London, Wright and Brown, 1937.
The Token (Lowe). London, Wright and Brown, 1937.
The Frightened Man. London, Wright and Brown, 1937.
The Three Gnomes (Lowe). London, Wright and Brown, 1937.
The Glass Arrow (Lowe). London, Wright and Brown, 1937.
The Silver Horseshoe (Budd). London, Wright and Brown, 1938.
The River House Mystery (Lowe). London, Wright and Brown, 1938.
Witches' Moon (Budd). London, Wright and Brown, 1938.

The Clue of the Green Candle (Lowe). London, Wright and Brown, 1938.
The Angel. London, Wright and Brown, 1939.
The Football Pool Murders (Budd). London, Wright and Brown, 1939; as *The Coupon Crimes*, London, Mellifont, 1946.
The Huntsman (Budd). London, Wright and Brown, 1940.
The Poisoner. London, Wright and Brown, 1940.
The Heel of Achilles (Dene). London, Wright and Brown, 1946.
Thirsty Evil (Chard). London, Westhouse, 1946.
The Twelve Apostles (Budd). London, Wright and Brown, 1946.
The Seven Lamps (Budd). London, Wright and Brown, 1947.
They Walk in Darkness (Chard). London, Wright and Brown, 1947.
The Royal Flush Murders (Budd). London, Wright and Brown, 1948.
The Tipster (Budd). London, Wright and Brown, 1949.
The Whispering Woman (Budd). London, Wright and Brown, 1949.
The Show Must Go On (novelization of radio series). London, Wright and Brown, 1950.
Noose for a Lady (Gale; novelization of radio series). London, Wright and Brown, 1952.
Mr. Midnight (Budd). London, Wright and Brown, 1953.
Sorcerer's House (Gale). London, Hutchinson, 1956.
The Crimson Ramblers (novelization of television series). London, Wright and Brown, 1960.
The Nursery Rhyme Murders (Budd). London, Wright and Brown, 1960.
Grim Death. London, Wright and Brown, 1961.
The Third Key. London, Wright and Brown, 1961.
Ghost House. London, Wright and Brown, 1961.
The Shadow Men (Lowe). London, Wright and Brown, 1962.
The Red Tape Murders (Budd). London, Wright and Brown, 1962.
The Last Warning (Budd). London, Wright and Brown, 1962.
I Am Death. London, Wright and Brown, 1963.
The Ghost Squad. London, Wright and Brown, 1963.
Murder In Manuscript (Budd). London, Wright and Brown, 1963.
The Faceless Ones. London, Wright and Brown, 1964.
The Moor House Murders. London, Wright and Brown, 1964.
Six Men Died (Budd). London, Wright and Brown, 1965.
Death Set in Diamonds (Lowe). London, Wright and Brown, 1965.
The Tudor Garden Mystery (Heron). London, Wright and Brown, 1966.
Mister Big (Budd). London, Wright and Brown, 1966.
Dead Secret (Heron). London, Wright and Brown, 1967.

Novels as Donald Stuart (series: Sexton Blake; Lionel Crane); all novels anonymous up to and including *The Crime of Four*

The Clue of the Second Tooth (Blake). London, Amalgamated Press, 1927.
The Box of Doom (Blake). London, Amalgamated Press, 1928.
The Riddle of the Phantom Plague (Blake). London, Amalgamated Press, 1928.
The Mystery of Sherwood Towers (Blake). London, Amalgamated Press, 1928.
The Mystery of the Phantom Blackmailer (Blake). London, Amalgamated Press, 1928.
The Silent Slayer (Blake). London, Amalgamated Press, 1929.

The Fatal Manuscript (Blake). London, Amalgamated Press, 1929.
The Black Skull (Blake). London, Amalgamated Press, 1929.
The Secret of the Vault (Blake). London, Amalgamated Press, 1930.
The Crime of Four (Blake). London, Amalgamated Press, 1930.
The Hooded Terror. London, Amalgamated Press, 1930; as *Black Skull* (as Gerald Verner); London, Wright and Brown, 1933; as *The Hooded Stranger* (as Gerald Verner), London, Amalgamated Press, 1940.
The Death Card (Blake). London, Amalgamated Press, 1930.
The Fence's Victim (Blake). London, Amalgamated Press, 1930.
The Hooded Raider (Blake), London, Amalgamated Press, 1931.
The Next Victim (Blake). London, Amalgamated Press, 1931.
The Terror of Lonely Tor (Blake). London, Amalgamated Press, 1931.
The Garden City Crime (Blake). London, Amalgamated Press, 1931.
Dead Man's Secret (Blake). London, Amalgamated Press, 1932.
The Squealer's Secret (Blake). London, Amalgamated Press, 1932.
The Embankment Crime (Blake). London, Amalgamated Press, 1932.
The Case of the Missing Estate Agent (Blake). London, Amalgamated Press, 1932.
The Secret of Seven (Blake). London, Amalgamated Press, 1932.
The Empty House Murder (Blake). London, Amalgamated Press, 1933.
Guilty, But Insane (Blake). London, Amalgamated Press, 1933.
The £1,000,000 Film Murder Case (Blake). London, Amalgamated Press, 1933.
The Motor Bus Murder (Blake). London, Amalgamated Press, 1934.
The Man Outside. London, Wright and Brown, 1934.
The Village of Fear (Blake). London, Amalgamated Press, 1934.
The Shadow (novelization of his play). London, Wright and Brown, 1934.
The White Friar (Crane). London, Wright and Brown, 1934.
The Valley of Terror. London, Wright and Brown, 1935.
The Secret of the Sealed Room (Blake). London, Amalgamated Press, 1935.
The Cottage of Terror (Blake). London, Amalgamated Press, 1935.
The Man in the Dark. London, Wright and Brown, 1935.
The Truth About Lord Trench (Blake). London, Amalgamated Press, 1935.
Midnight Murder (Crane). London, Wright and Brown, 1935.
The Bells of Doom (Blake). London, Amalgamated Press, 1936.
The Unknown Menace (Blake). London, Amalgamated Press, 1937.
The Riddle of the Sunken Garden (Blake). London, Amalgamated Press, 1937.
The Time of the Crime (Blake). London, Amalgamated Press, 1938.
The Three Who Paid (Blake). London, Amalgamated Press, 1938.
The Secret of Moor House (Blake). London, Amalgamated Press, 1938.

Danger at Westways (Blake). London, Amalgamated Press, 1938.
The Third Victim (Blake). London, Amalgamated Press, 1939.
The Hidden Menace (Blake). London, Amalgamated Press, 1939.

Novels as Derwent Steele (series: John Blackmore)

The Black Gangster. London, Modern Publishing, 1934.
The Phantom Slayer (Blackmore). London, Modern Publishing, 1934.
The Purple Plague (Blackmore). London, Modern Publishing, 1934.
The Avengers (Blackmore). London, Modern Publishing, 1935.

Novels as Nigel Vane (series: James Hartley; Philip Quest)

The Menace of Li-Sin (Hartley). London, Modern Publishing, 1934.
The Vengeance of Li-Sin (Hartley). London, Modern Publishing, 1934.
The Devil's Dozen (Quest). London, Modern Publishing, 1934.
The Veils of Death (Quest). London, Modern Publishing, 1935.
The Midnight Gang (novelization of his play *Sexton Blake*). London, Smith, 1936.

Short Stories (series: Mr. Budd)

Sinister House. London, Wright and Brown, 1934.
The Cleverness of Mr. Budd. London, Wright and Brown, 1935; as *The Case of Mr. Budd*, New York, Macaulay, 1938.
Mr. Whipple Explains. London, Wright and Brown, 1936.
The Return of Mr. Budd. London, Wright and Brown, 1938.
Mr. Budd Again. London, Wright and Brown, 1939.
Mr. Budd Investigates. London, Wright and Brown, 1940.

Uncollected Short Stories

"River Rats," in *Thriller* (London), 26 September 1936.
"The Mystery of the Unfortunate Undertaker," in *Hutchinson's Christmas Pie* (London), September 1946.
"The Strange Affair of the Dancing Parson," in *Hutchinson's Spring Pie* (London), February, 1947.

Uncollected Short Stories as Donald Stuart

"Mr. Midnight," in *Union Jack* (London), 17 January 1931.
"The Witches' Moon," in *Union Jack* (London), 23 April 1932.
"The Unlikely Chance," in *Novel Magazine* (London), December 1932.
"The Crimson Smile," in *Union Jack* (London), 24 December 1932.
"The Clue of the Crimson Snow," in *Detective Weekly* (London), 23 December 1933.
"The Christmas Card Crime," in *Detective Weekly* (London), 22 December 1934.
"Murder at the Microphone," in *Detective Weekly* (London), 6 April 1935.
"The Fatal Hour," in *Thriller* (London), 26 September 1936.
"The Fatal 13th," in *Sexton Blake Annual* (London), September 1938.
"The Green Jester," in *Sexton Blake Wins*, edited by Jack Adrian. London, Dent, 1986.

OTHER PUBLICATIONS

Plays

Sexton Blake (as Donald Stuart; produced London, 1930).
The Shadow (as Donald Stuart; produced London, 1933).
Meet Mr. Callaghan, adaptation of *The Urgent Hangman* by
   Peter Cheyney (produced London, 1952).   London, French,
   1953.
Towards Zero, adaptation of the novel by Agatha Christie
   (produced Nottingham and London, 1956).   London,
   French, and New York, Dramatists Play Service, 1957.

Radio Plays: *The Show Must Go On*, 1949; *Noose for a Lady*,
1951; *There's No Escape* (as Gerald Stuart), 1964; *Sexton Blake*
series, 1967.

Screenplays: *Tread Softly*, 1952; *Noose for a Lady*, 1954.

Television writing: *The Crimson Ramblers* series, 1959.

Other

Editor, The Prince of Darkness.   London, Westhouse, 1946.

Recording: *Murder on the Portsmouth Road*, HMV, 1930.

*   *   *

Gerald Verner was surely, to borrow a classic Churchillism,
"a riddle wrapped in a mystery inside an enigma." To begin
with, it is highly unlikely that Verner was his real name (no
birth, at any rate, was registered in the relevant period, 1890–
1900), and although it's probable he was born Donald William
Steward, in Hackney, London, in 1896, it is by no means
certain. Nor can one be at all confident about his pre-writing
career. There are various colourful legends (pavement artist,
actor, Billingsgate fish-porter, and so on) which may well have
a thread of truth in them, but no more than that, Verner himself
having very good, indeed pressing, reasons for obfuscating the
issue. It is likely he spent some time in prison, although for
probably no more heinous crime than debt (arguably a natural
hazard of the pulp-writer's existence).

Then there is the thorny matter of his plagarisms. During his
lifetime he had over 130 books published under four
pseudonyms, an *oeuvre* which may be cut down as much as by
half because of recycling earlier material and, at times, outright
theft.

As Donald Stuart he broke into the Sexton Blake market in
1927 and quickly established himself as a highly popular writer
in the Edgar Wallace mould, his thrillers exhibiting all of
Wallace's weaknesses—the villain as least likely suspect (often
a doctor, banker, or solicitor), a certain casualness with
technological facts, and a tendency to end too many chapters
with a shot in the dark, a scream in the night, or a blunt
instrument pitching Blake into an abyss of Stygian blackness—
as well as many of his strengths (notably sardonic backchat
between petty crooks and worldly-wise desk-sergeants).

In 1933 Stuart became Verner by "de-Blakeanising" his
earlier paperback thrillers into hardbacks (a relatively simple
process utilised by many Blake authors and chiefly involving
changing the characters' names). Most of his Blake material
was later recycled, in some cases three or four times, Verner
having a horror of squandering a good plot on a single volume.
The Terror of Lonely Tor (1931), for instance, became *The Valley*

of Terror (1935), which was later drastically cut down into a
25,000-word novelette, "The Devil's Footprint" (1937), and
then collected in *The Return of Mr. Budd* (1938). This, though it
might be viewed as mildly unethical, showed sound business
sense, although the process of de-Blakeanisation itself often
transformed the re-named hero into a mere cypher who, though
performing precisely the same brilliant ratiocinatory feats and
deeds of derring-do, somehow lacked the essential charisma of
the original.

Yet Verner could create convincing, even attractive,
characters. His masterpiece was the fat and notably caustic
Superintendent Budd, modelled on Wallace's Superintendent
Minter but soon achieving a genuine originality largely due to
Verner's talent for expressive dialogue (a talent later used to
good effect in the plays he wrote for radio, television, and the
stage, including an impressive adaptation of Agatha Christie's
Towards Zero). Budd is at his best in the short story volumes
and thrillers of the late 1930's and 1940's (creatively speaking,
Verner's personal Golden Age), such as *Witches' Moon*, *The
Football Pool Murders*, *The Huntsman*, *The Twelve Apostles*, *The
Seven Lamps*, and *The Whispering Woman*, some demonstrating
Verner's penchant for bizarre plots and a hint of the strange, all
containing delightful bouts of verbal sparring between the
acidic Budd and his hapless subordinate Sergeant Leek.

Verner also had a fondness for the Impossible Crime,
particularly the John Dickson Carr model, although such
thrillers as *The Royal Flush Murders* and *They Walk in
Darkness*, moderately ingenious as their solutions are, showed
that he was indebted to Carr more for the latter's sense of
brooding atmosphere than the complexities of his plotting.

Verner's literary plunderings were on a fairly epic scale, the
transformation of Wallace's *The Terrible People* into a Blake,
Dead Man's Secret, Sax Rohmer's *Bat Wing* into *The Black
Skull*, undoubtedly his most audacious (the hardback *Black
Skull*, confusingly is a re-write of his own *The Hooded Terror*, in
turn a conflation of several of Wallace's J.G. Reeder stories).
His main source was Wallace, in large doses (*The Riddle of the
Phantom Plague* depends heavily on *The Green Rust*) or small (in
the middle of *The Menace of Li-Sin* up pops the opening pages
of *The Gaunt Stranger*).

Quite often he would knit two or three books together to
make one, although he was perfectly capable of grabbing an old
Blake by someone else, or even a sufficiently obscure
mainstream thriller, and simply publishing it under his own
name or one of his pseudonyms (in Verner's book-lists, above,
eight titles have not been included: although these titles
appeared under his names—three by Verner, three by Stuart,
one each by Steele and Vane—they were not in fact written by
Verner at all). Other depredations were rather more imaginative. *Noose for a Lady* (the novelization of his own radio serial)
is not at all a bad version of Christie's *Sad Cypress* but with a
hero who is a fusion of Carr's Sir Henry Marrivale and John
Newton Chance's DeHaviland.

It is difficult to condone outright theft; equally difficult (I
find) to be judgemental about one who, in later life, proved to
be an immensely likeable old scoundrel with a fund of
fascinating anecdotes about the Grub Street of 60 years ago.
When not looting other writers' work he wrote stories that
careered along (with thrill piled on thrill sensation) and were
extremely readable—far more so than those of his peers such as
Roland Daniel or Hugh Desmond. And there is an added bonus
for research-minded readers—the fun of spotting the swipes.

—Jack Adrian

VICKERS, Roy C. Also wrote as David Durham; Sefton Kyle; John Spencer. British. Born in 1888(?). Educated at Charterhouse School, Surrey; Brasenose College, Oxford. Married Mary van Rossem; one son. Worked as a journalist and court reporter; editor, *Novel Magazine*, London. *Died in 1965.*

CRIME PUBLICATIONS

Novels (series: Inspector J. Rason; James Segrove; Hugh Stanton)

The Mystery of the Scented Death (Rason). London, Jenkins, 1921.
The Vengeance of Henry Jarroman (Segrove). London, Jenkins, 1923.
Ishmael's Wife (Segrove). London, Jenkins, 1924.
A Murder for a Million. London, Jenkins, 1924.
Four Past Four (Segrove). London, Jenkins, 1925; New York, Jefferson House, 1945.
The Unforbidden Sin. London, Jenkins, 1926.
The Radingham Mystery. London, Jenkins, 1928.
The Gold Game. London, Jenkins, 1930.
The Deputy for Cain. London, Jenkins, 1931.
The Marriage for the Defence. London, Jenkins, 1932.
The Whispering Death (as John Spencer). London, Hodder and Stoughton, 1932; New York, Jefferson House, 1947.
Swell Garrick (as John Spencer). London, Hodder and Stoughton, 1933.
Bardelow's Heir (Rason). London, Jenkins, 1933.
Money Buys Everything (Rason). London, Jenkins, 1934.
Kidnap Island (Rason). London, Newnes, 1935.
Hide Those Diamonds! London, Newnes, 1935.
The Man in the Red Mask (Rason). London, Newnes, 1935.
Terror of Tongues! (Rason). London, Newnes, 1937.
The Girl in the News (Rason). London, Jenkins, 1937.
I'll Never Tell. London, Jenkins, 1937.
The Enemy Within. London, Jenkins, 1938.
The Life Between (Rason). London, Jenkins, 1938.
Playgirl Wanted. London, Jenkins, 1940.
She Walked in Fear (Rason). London, Jenkins, 1940.
Brenda Gets Married. London, Jenkins, 1941.
A Date with Danger. London, Jenkins, 1942; New York, Vanguard Press, 1944.
War Bride. London, Jenkins, 1942.
Six Came to Dinner (Stanton). London, Jenkins, 1948.
Gold and Wine (Stanton). London, Jenkins, 1949; New York, Walker, 1961.
Murder of a Snob. London, Jenkins, 1949; New York, British Book Centre, 1958.
Murdering Mr. Velfrage. London, Faber, 1950; as *Maid to Murder*, New York, Mill, 1950.
They Can't Hang Caroline (Stanton). London, Jenkins, 1950.
The Sole Survivor, and The Kynsard Affair. Roslyn, New York, Detective Book Club, 1951; London, Gollancz, 1952.
Murder in Two Flats (Stanton). London, Jenkins, and New York, Mill, 1952.
Find the Innocent. London, Jenkins, 1959; as *The Girl Who Wouldn't Talk*, Roslyn, New York, Detective Book Club, 1959.

Novels as David Durham

The Woman Accused. London, Hodder and Stoughton, 1923.
Hounded Down. London, Hodder and Stoughton, 1923.
The Pearl-Headed Pin. London, Hodder and Stoughton, 1925.
The Forgotten Honeymoon. London, Jenkins, 1935.
The Girl Who Dared. London, Jenkins, 1938.
Against the Law. London, Jenkins, 1939.

Novels as Sefton Kyle (series: Inspector J. Rason)

The Man in the Shadow (Rason). London, Jenkins, 1924.
Dead Man's Dower. London, Jenkins, 1925.
Guilty, But—. London, Jenkins, 1927.
The Hawk (Rason). London, Jenkins, and New York, Dial Press, 1930.
The Vengeance of Mrs. Danvers. London, Jenkins, 1932.
The Bloomsbury Treasure. London, Jenkins, 1932.
Red Hair (Rason). London, Jenkins, 1933.
The Life He Stole (Rason). London, Jenkins, 1934.
The Man Without a Name. London, Jenkins, 1935.
Silence (Rason). London, Jenkins, 1935.
The Durand Case. London, Jenkins, 1936.
Number Seventy-Three. London, Jenkins, 1936.
The Body in the Safe (Rason). London, Jenkins, 1937.
The Notorious Miss Walters. London, Jenkins, 1937.
During His Majesty's Pleasure (Rason). London, Jenkins, 1938.
Missing! London, Jenkins, 1938.
Miss X. London, Jenkins, 1939.
The Judge's Dilemma. London, Jenkins, 1939.
The Shadow over Fairholme. London, Jenkins, 1940.
The Girl Known as D 13. London, Jenkins, 1940.
The Price of Silence. London, Jenkins, 1942.
Love Was Married. London, Jenkins, 1943.

Short Stories (series: Department of Dead Ends; Inspector George Rason)

The Exploits of Fidelity Dove (Rason; as David Durham). London, Hodder and Stoughton, 1924.
The Department of Dead Ends. New York, Spivak, 1947; augmented edition, London, Faber, and Roslyn, New York, Detective Book Club, 1949.
Murder Will Out (Rason; Dead Ends). London, Faber, 1950; Roslyn, New York, Detective Book Club, 1954.
Eight Murders in the Suburbs. London, Jenkins, 1954; shortened version, as *Six Murders in the Suburbs*, Roslyn, New York, Detective Book Club, 1958.
Double Image and Other Stories. London, Jenkins, and Roslyn, New York, Detective Book Club, 1955.
Seven Chose Murder (Rason; Dead Ends). London, Jenkins, and Roslyn, New York, Detective Book Club, 1959.
Best Detective Stories (Rason; Dead Ends). London, Faber, 1965.

Uncollected Short Stories

"The Starting-Handle Murder," in *Pearson's Magazine* (London), October 1934.
"The Three-Foot Grave," in *Fiction Parade* (London), January 1936.
"Dinner for Two," in *A Century of Detective Stories.* London, Hutchinson, n.d.
"Molly the Marchioness," in *Fiction Parade* (London), February 1936.
"The Holborn Murder," in *Fiction Parade* (London), April 1936.
"Murder Through the Looking Glass," in *Mystery Book Magazine* (Chicago), Summer 1948.
"Murder at Bishops Runt," in *The Fifth Mystery Bedside Book.* London, Hodder and Stoughton, 1964.

OTHER PUBLICATIONS

Novels

His Other Wife. London, Jenkins, 1926.
The White Raven. London, Jenkins, 1927.
A Girl of These Days. London, Jenkins, 1929.
The Rose in the Dark. London, Jenkins, 1930.

Other

Lord Roberts: The Story of His Life. London, Pearson, 1914.

Editor, *Some Like Them Dead.* London, Hodder and Stoughton, 1960.
Editor, *Crime Writers' Choice: The Fifth Anthology of the Crime Writers' Association.* London, Hodder and Stoughton, 1964.
Editor, *Best Police Stories.* London, Faber, 1966.

*   *   *

The bibliography of Roy Vickers (who also wrote as Sefton Kyle, John Spencer, and David Durham) is not yet firm, since much of his work was pseudonymous and ephemeral, but he is known to have written more than 70 books of fiction.

Vickers's work up into World War II was primarily popular sensational fiction, occasionally topical (shopgirl romances, marital-law novels, depression stories, home-front novels), but more often concerned with crime, mystery, and/or detection. Most of this work attempted to follow market trends. His first novel in book form, *The Mystery of the Scented Death*, is in the manner of Sax Rohmer, while other novels are in the modes of Edgar Wallace, E.P. Oppenheim, and, occasionally, E.C. Bentley and Eric Ambler. Most of this earlier work is below the standard of his later short stories, but there are often rewarding elements that adumbrate his finer, more mature work. Sometimes there is a particularly intricate plot, as in *Hounded Down*, at other times highly imaginative "gimmicks" as in *The Exploits of Fidelity Dove*. More often, however, the outstanding element is in characterization, for example the Ant of *The Radingham Mystery* of the ancient criminal Jabez Winterbourne who appears in *The Gold Game* and *Hide Those Diamonds!* Winterbourne is one of the finest criminal masterminds in the literature.

In 1935 there appeared in *Fiction Parade* "The Rubber Trumpet," the first of the short stories concerning the Department of Dead Ends. After a year or two, however, Vickers temporarily abandoned the series, and did not resume work on it until after the war. It is these later tales which unexpectedly revealed Vickers to be one of the finest British short story writers. Indeed, it has often been stated, with much truth, that the Department of Dead Ends stories were the best detective short stories of the 1940's. There are 38 stories in the series, with several others loosely connected with them. They are based on a (fictional) section of Scotland Yard, a storage place for the detritus of unsolved crimes. From this collection— murder weapons, clothing, toys found near the crime— solutions often emerge by chance. In this concept, it should be noted, Vickers breaks with the older theories of emergent justice (purposive fate, as with Wilkie Collins; hyper-rationalism, despite undercurrents of irrationality, as with Poe and Doyle; the scientific method, as with R. Austin Freeman) and sets up blind chance as the avenger of wrongs. The Department of Dead Ends stories are formally unusual in combining the techniques of factual crime writing and fiction. In essence they are capsulated novels, in which scores of life patterns appear in brief, offering a *tragédie humaine* of British society.

Vickers's later novels, while superior to his earlier work, are still not on the same level as his best short stories. Among his better novels may be listed *Six Came to Dinner*, despite an annoyingly jaunty playboy detective, *Murdering Mr. Velfrage*, with exceedingly skilled intricacies, and *The Kynsard Affair*, with many of the effects of the Department of Dead Ends.

—E.F. Bleiler

———

VIDAL, Gore. *See* **BOX, Edgar.**

———

VINE, Barbara. *See* **RENDELL, Ruth.**

———

W

WADE, Alan. *See* **VANCE, John Holbrook.**

————

WADE, Henry. Pseudonym for Henry Lancelot Aubrey-Fletcher, 6th Baronet. British. Born in Leigh, Surrey, 10 September 1887. Educated at Eton College; New College, Oxford. Served in the First Battalion, Grenadier Guards, 1908–20, and fought in World War I: mentioned in despatches (twice); Distinguished Service Order; Croix de Guerre; also served in Grenadier Guards, 1940–45. Married 1) Mary Augusta Chilton in 1911 (died 1963); four sons and one daughter; 2) Nancy Cecil Reynolds in 1965. Succeeded to the baronetcy, 1937. Justice of the Peace and County Alderman for Buckinghamshire; High Sheriff of Buckinghamshire, 1925. Lieutenant in the Body Guard of the Honorable Corps of Gentlemen-at-Arms, 1956–57. Commander, Royal Victorian Order. *Died 30 May 1969.*

CRIME PUBLICATIONS

Novels (series: Chief Inspector Poole)

The Verdict of You All. London, Constable, 1926; New York, Payson and Clarke, 1927.
The Missing Partners. London, Constable, and New York, Payson and Clarke, 1928.
The Duke of York's Steps (Poole). London, Constable, and New York, Payson, and Clarke, 1929.
The Dying Alderman. London, Constable, and New York, Brewer and Warren, 1930.
The Floating Admiral, with others. London, Hodder and Stoughton, 1931; New York, Doubleday, 1932.
No Friendly Drop (Poole). London, Constable, 1931; New York, Brewer Warren and Putnam, 1932; revised edition, Constable, 1932.
The Hanging Captain. London, Constable, 1932; New York, Harcourt Brace, 1933.
Mist on the Saltings. London, Constable, 1933.
Constable, Guard Thyself! (Poole). London, Constable, 1934; Boston, Houghton Mifflin, 1935.
Heir Presumptive. London, Constable, 1935; New York, Macmillan, 1953.
Bury Him Darkly (Poole). London, Constable, 1936.
The High Sheriff. London, Constable, 1937.
Released for Death. London, Constable, 1938.
Lonely Magdalen (Poole). London, Constable, 1940; revised edition, 1946.
New Graves at Great Norne. London, Constable, 1947.
Diplomat's Folly. London, Constable, 1951; New York, Macmillan, 1952.
Be Kind to the Killer. London, Constable, 1952.
Too Soon to Die (Poole). London, Constable, 1953; New York, Macmillan, 1954.

Gold Was Our Grave (Poole). London, Constable, and New York, Macmillan, 1954.
A Dying Fall. London, Constable, and New York, Macmillan, 1955.
The Litmore Snatch. London, Constable, and New York, Macmillan, 1957.

Short Stories

Policeman's Lot. London, Constable, 1933.
Here Comes the Copper. London, Constable, 1938.

OTHER PUBLICATIONS

Other

A History of the Foot Guards to 1856 (as H.L. Aubrey-Fletcher). London, Constable, 1927.

*   *   *

Henry Wade was one of the really major figures of the Golden Age of the mystery story—and thereafter—but, unfortunately, too few of his better novels and neither of his historically important collections of short stories were published in America. This situation, combined with a long period of critical neglect, gave Wade the status of an unknown master until the late 1960's saw a long-overdue reassessment.

Wade was a practitioner of the school of modern British realism and a master of the police novel. A staunch advocate of the classical detective story in its purest form, Wade also had the ability to write inverted stories that bear comparison with the highest achievements in this genre. Wade can best be compared to Freeman Wills Crofts, in whose own demanding tradition Wade ranked second to none. His police novels and inverted tales never quite achieved the pinnacle of Crofts's *The Cask* or *The 12:30 from Croydon,* but his gifts for characterization were deeper—especially in the inverted stories. His personal experiences as Justice of the Peace lent depth to his depiction of the rural police. His strongly developed sense of irony and his criticism of the legal system anticipated and influenced such writers as Richard Hull, Cyril Hare, Henry Cecil, Raymond Postgate, Michael Underwood, and Roderic Jeffries. He observed with precision the changing values of post-World War II England—even more skilfully than did Agatha Christie—and he did more to explicate the psychology and mores of the British people than any other writer in this genre.

Wade's earliest novels question the British legal system and its traditions. One of them, *The Missing Partners,* details a potentially tragic miscarriage of justice. This novel is also Wade's closest approximation of Crofts's style and method. *The Duke of York's Steps* was among the most favorably reviewed books of the 1920's, and is usually cited in the older reference works devoted to the genre. *The Dying Alderman,* with its dying message clue, is an advance over his earlier work, and is written and plotted with great clarity and precision; it remains surprisingly fresh today. *Mist on the Saltings* is a completely unexpected and unprecedented work by Wade's or anyone else's standards. A partially inverted tale combined with a police novel, this masterpiece boasts penetrating characterization, superb East Anglian marshland atmosphere, and a powerful and deeply moving climax. Almost as good is *Heir Presumptive*—a fully inverted tale about a man's efforts to kill several relatives in order to inherit a fortune. Light in style and compulsively readable, its only drawback is that its ironic ending can be rather too easily anticipated. This book was one of Wade's personal favorites, and the deer-hunting scenes reflect his deep interest in the sport.

Wade stopped writing during the war and subsequent work indicates that this period and its aftermath had a profound effect on his outlook. Few major writers of the Golden Age ever staged a significant comeback as late as the 1950's. Wade did it by creating two masterpieces with all his old skill and cunning, enriched by experience. *Too Soon to Die* was another partially inverted murder tale about a family's attempt to evade exorbitant inheritance taxes. This gripping work shows that Wade continued to view his country's legal system with apprehension. *A Dying Fall* concerns the question of whether an unwanted wife's plunge from a balcony was suicide or murder. It combines Wade's best character delineation, a perceptive view of changing postwar values in England, and an ironic ending. This was Wade's last really major novel, a sublime and deeply personal work.

—Charles Shibuk

WADE, Robert. *See* **MILLER, Wade.**

WAINWRIGHT, John (William). Also writes as Jack Ripley. British. Born in Leeds, Yorkshire, 25 February 1921. Educated at elementary schools and studied at home; London University, external LL.B. 1956. Served as an Air Crew Gunner in the Royal Air Force, 1940–45. Married Avis Wainwright in 1942. Police Officer, West Riding Constabulary, Yorkshire, 1947–69. Since 1969 columnist, *Northern Echo,* Darlington, County Durham. Agent: Campbell Thomson and McLaughlin Ltd., 31 Newington Green, London N16 9PU, England.

CRIME PUBLICATIONS

Novels (series: Superintendent Gilliant; Chief Inspector Lennox; Inspector Lyle; Superintendent Charles Ripley)

Death in a Sleeping City. London, Collins, 1965.
Ten Steps to the Gallows. London, Collins, 1965.
Evil Intent (Ripley). London, Collins, 1966.
The Crystallised Carbon Pig (Gilliant). London, Collins, 1966; New York, Walker, 1967.
Talent for Murder. London, Collins, and New York, Walker, 1967.
The Worms Must Wait (Ripley). London, Collins, 1967.
Web of Silence. London, Collins, 1968.
Edge of Extinction. London, Collins, 1968.

The Darkening Glass. London, Collins, 1968.
The Take-Over Men. London, Collins, 1969.
The Big Tickle. London, Macmillan, 1969.
Freeze Thy Blood Less Coldly (Ripley). London, Macmillan, 1970.
Prynter's Devil. London, Macmillan, 1970.
The Last Buccaneer. London, Macmillan, 1971.
Dig the Grave and Let Him Lie. London, Macmillan, 1971.
Night Is a Time to Die. London, Macmillan, 1972.
Requiem for a Loser (Gilliant). London, Macmillan, 1972.
A Pride of Pigs. London, Macmillan, 1973.
High-Class Kill. London, Macmillan, 1973.
The Devil You Don't. London, Macmillan, 1973.
A Touch of Malice (Ripley). London, Macmillan, 1973.
The Evidence I Shall Give (Lennox). London, Macmillan, 1974.
Cause for a Killing. London, Macmillan, 1974.
Kill the Girls and Make Them Cry. London, Macmillan, 1974.
The Hard Hit (Ripley). London, Macmillan, 1974; New York, St. Martin's Press, 1975.
Square Dance (Lennox). London, Macmillan, and New York, St. Martin's Press, 1975.
Death of a Big Man (Ripley). London, Macmillan, and New York, St. Martin's Press, 1975.
Landscape with Violence (Gilliant). London, Macmillan, 1975; New York, St. Martin's Press, 1976.
Coppers Don't Cry. London, Macmillan, 1975.
Acquittal. London, Macmillan, and New York, St. Martin's Press, 1976.
Walther P.38. London, Macmillan, 1976; New York, State Mutual, 1982.
Who Goes Next? London, Macmillan, and New York, St. Martin's Press, 1976.
The Bastard. London, Macmillan, and New York, St. Martin's Press, 1976.
Pool of Tears (Lennox). London, Macmillan, and New York, St. Martin's Press, 1977.
A Nest of Rats. London, Macmillan, and New York, St. Martin's Press, 1977.
Do Nothin' till You Hear from Me. London, Macmillan, and New York, St. Martin's Press, 1977.
The Day of the Peppercorn Kill. London, Macmillan, 1977; New York, St. Martin's Press, 1981.
The Jury People. London, Macmillan, and New York, St. Martin's Press, 1978.
Thief of Time. London, Macmillan, and New York, St. Martin's Press, 1978.
Death Certificate. London, Macmillan, 1978; New York, State Mutual, 1982.
A Ripple of Murders (Gilliant). London, Macmillan, 1978; New York, St. Martin's Press, 1979.
Brainwash (Lyle). London, Macmillan, and New York, St. Martin's Press, 1979.
Duty Elsewhere (Lyle). London, Macmillan, and New York, St. Martin's Press, 1979.
Tension. London, Macmillan, 1979; New York, State Mutual, 1982.
The Reluctant Sleeper. London, Macmillan, 1979; New York, State Mutual, 1982.
Home Is the Hunter, and The Big Kayo. London, Macmillan, 1979.
Take Murder . . . (Lennox). London, Macmillan, 1979; New York, St. Martin's Press, 1981.
The Venus Fly-Trap. London, Macmillan, and New York, St. Martin's Press, 1980.
The Eye of the Beholder. London, Macmillan, and New York, St. Martin's Press, 1980.

Dominoes (Lyle). London, Macmillan, and New York, St. Martin's Press, 1980.
Man of Law. London, Macmillan, 1980; New York, St. Martin's Press, 1981.
A Kill of Small Consequence. London, Macmillan, 1980.
The Tainted Man. London, Macmillan, 1980.
All on a Summer's Day. London, Macmillan, and New York, St. Martin's Press, 1981.
An Urge for Justice. London, Macmillan, 1981; New York, St. Martin's Press, 1982.
Blayde R.I.P. London, Macmillan, and New York, St. Martin's Press, 1982.
Anatomy of a Riot. London, Macmillan, 1982.
The Distaff Factor. London, Macmillan, 1982.
Their Evil Ways. London, Macmillan, and New York, St. Martin's Press, 1983.
Spiral Staircase. London, Macmillan, and New York, St. Martin's Press, 1983.
Heroes No More. London, Macmillan, 1983.
Cul-de-Sac. London, Macmillan, and New York, St. Martin's Press, 1984.
The Forest. London, Macmillan, and New York, St. Martin's Press, 1984.
The Ride. London, Macmillan, 1984; New York, St. Martin's Press, 1985.
Clouds of Guilt. London, Macmillan, and New York, St. Martin's Press, 1985.
All Through the Night. London, Macmillan, and New York, St. Martin's Press, 1985.
Portrait in Shadows. London, Macmillan, and New York, St. Martin's Press, 1986.
The Tenth Interview. London, Macmillan, and New York, St. Martin's Press, 1986.
The Forgotten Murders. London, Macmillan, and New York, St. Martin's Press, 1987.
Blind Brag. London, Macmillan, and New York, St. Martin's Press, 1988.
A Very Parochial Murder. London, Macmillan, and New York, St. Martin's Press, 1988.
The Man Who Wasn't There (Lyle). London, Macmillan, and New York, St. Martin's Press, 1989.
The Gauntley Incident. London, Macmillan, 1990.

Novels as Jack Ripley (series: John George Davis in all books)

Davis Doesn't Live Here Any More. London, Hamish Hamilton, 1971; New York, Doubleday, 1972.
The Pig Got Up and Slowly Walked Away. London, Hamish Hamilton, 1971.
My Word You Should Have Seen Us. London, Hamish Hamilton, 1972.
My God How the Money Rolls In. London, Hamish Hamilton, 1972.

Uncollected Short Stories

"The Man Who Grassed," in *Winter's Crimes 1*, edited by George Hardinge. London, Macmillan, and New York, St. Martin's Press, 1969.
"Incident in Troletto," in *Winter's Crimes 4*, edited by George Hardinge. London, Macmillan, and New York, St. Martin's Press, 1972.
"You Are Not Obliged to Say Anything," in *Winter's Crimes 6*, edited by George Hardinge. London, Macmillan, and New York, St. Martin's Press, 1974.

"Rucker's New Year's Eve," in *Winter's Crimes 9*, edited by George Hardinge. London, Macmillan, and New York, St. Martin's Press, 1977.
"A Peal from the Past," in *Winter's Crimes 18*, edited by Hilary Hale. London, Macmillan, 1986.
"Who Needs Friends?," in *Winter's Crimes 21*, edited by Hilary Hale. London, Macmillan, 1989.

OTHER PUBLICATIONS

Plays

Radio Plays: *Death in a Sleeping City*, 1966; *Who Killed Emma Forcett?* (serial), 1967; *A Time for Despair*, 1967; *Hates Any Man?*, 1968; *Protection*, 1968; *Brainwash*, 1981; *Endangered Species*, 1985.

Other

Shall I Be a Policeman? Exeter, Wheaton, 1967.
Guard Your Castle: A Plain Man's Guide to the Protection of His Home. London, Gentry Books, 1973.
Tail-End Charlie (war memoirs). London, Macmillan, 1978.
Wainwright's Beat. London, Macmillan, 1987.

*

John Wainwright comments:
Despite this somewhat alarming list of books I find great difficulty in viewing myself as an "author." This, I think, is not unusual; for example, a bus driver rarely, if ever, consciously says to himself, "I'm a bus driver." The reality of authorship only comes home when an invitation is offered to attend some function *because* I happen to be an author. At that point a temporary world of unreality seems to take over, and it is a world of which I am not too fond. I like solitude and abhor any form of lionisation. The only product I (or any other writer of fiction) puts in the marketplace is an imagination. That I receive payment for that imagination never ceases to astound me. Of necessity I take my work seriously, but I never take myself seriously. I am a teller of tales. Nothing more.

*   *   *

John Wainwright's style is terse: he writes with short, almost elliptical sentences which serve to create a tense atmosphere. We get the message very quickly—this is a tough brutal world inhabited by tough brutal people, and every word spoken by one of them has a point to make.
The majority of Wainwright's vast output consists of police-procedural novels, written with all the insight of a man who spent a large part of his working life in the police force. The settings and characters have the ring of absolute authenticity, for all that the behaviour of the latter may give the reader some very uneasy moments. His policemen are working policemen—working coppers in fact, and the difference is not just one of terminology. The line between right and wrong is firmly and uncompromisingly drawn, but the characters cast on either side could in some cases be interchangeable. This portrayal of good and evil, of right and wrong, of lawbreaking and law enforcement finds echoes in the traditional Western; some of Wainwright's policemen would not look out of place wearing a tin star and a six-shooter.
These characteristics are evident in Wainwright's very first novel, *Death in a Sleeping City*, which is set (as are the vast majority of the books) in Yorkshire, and which introduces

several of the many policemen who people his work. Here we meet Lewis, Collins, Raff and Ripley, planning the capture of two Mafia killers who have murdered three people (including a policeman). Lewis, who is in charge of the case, pursues his quarry with a ruthless singlemindedness not endorsed by his colleagues. A trap is set and sprung, and Lewis finds himself at the mercy of the killers; at the climax of a rescue operation mounted by Lewis's colleagues, in what should be the tensest moment of the book, a genuinely humorous scene is enacted as Collins prepares the ground for the ultimate shoot-out. This element of a surprise or shock at the denouement was to become a feature of Wainwright's work.

These policemen and others appear again and again (albeit in different combinations) in Wainwright's books, but unlike the series characters in so many other crime novels (notably those of Ed McBain) we rarely see them functioning in a cohesive and consistent team. These men are individuals—they work together when necessity dictates, and indeed teamwork can be an important factor in the solution of individual cases, but one never senses that Wainwright's policemen share any common moral or philosophical goal. Friendships do spring up, and obviously there are individuals who feel great liking and respect for other individuals, but never to the extent that these personal relationships inhibit the purpose of the story.

Although Wainwright's stories are stark, brutal and above all ultrarealistic, he presents us with some surprisingly stylish plotting. In *Dominoes* he uses the symbolism of a series of falling dominoes in order to reveal a slow build up of seemingly unrelated crimes and crises. *The Day of the Peppercorn Kill* is the story of a man just released from jail, and bent on revenge against the policeman responsible for his totally unjust conviction. It is told in the form of several strands running apparently simultaneously, but in fact (as one gradually discerns) partly consecutively; the reader is faced here with the uncommon puzzle of deciphering the actual portrayal of events. Wainwright is unusual in using so deliberately abbreviated a style in order to describe such very complex and interlocking plots. It has to be admitted that the style does not vary a great deal, even in those books written in genres other than the police-procedural. Wainwright is treated somewhat dismissively by some critics—but could it be that they have not taken the trouble to look behind the ostensibly crude style and settings? These would appear, in fact, to be a deliberate contrast to the more refined atmosphere of many novels of detection.

Who Goes Next? is described as a "whodunnit," but in fact has much stronger elements of the customary police-procedural. The reader knows a fair amount about the killer (but not his name), and is more concerned to discover *why* the series murders have been committed; this particular device is very reminiscent of the works of Ed McBain, without in any way being derivative. This book does, however, contain some elements of the more traditional detective novel—in one fascinating scene Rucker (one of Wainwright's most repellent creations) conducts an interview, and evinces almost Holmesian powers of deduction from the crumbs of information drawn from the reluctant witness. And the denouement is an absolutely classic all-the-witnesses-gathered-together-in-one-room-while-the-detective-tells-us-whodunnit, to the extreme trepidation of the colleagues of the detective who sets the scene up. This is Lennox, a more cerebral policeman than many, and a complete contrast to the brutal and much-hated Rucker.

Death Certificate is rather more of a departure. This is told in the first person by Colin Hawkes, a thriller-writer who has just been told that he has inoperable lung cancer; his final novel is to be the true story, told as fiction, of underworld king Andrew Pollard. Hawkes, like most of Wainwright's major characters,

is a Yorkshireman and proud of it; in the internal conversations which feature largely in this story he analyses aspects of his character, and these musings would not be inappropriate had they come from one of the policemen who also feature in the novel. Hawkes co-operates with the police to set a trap for Pollard, and the knowledge that he does not have long to live enables him to be ruthless enough to engineer the criminal's death.

Even in those novels which depart entirely from his favourite format, Wainwright's policemen have an endearing habit of bobbing up on the periphery. Where they do not appear in person (as they do in the novels about Secret Service agent Dilton-Emmet) they are named and known by repute, and indeed in such circumstances seem like familiar friends. Although ruthless, these men are human and by no means invincible. As the novels and the years roll by we see them promoted and demoted, dismissed and retired, even imprisoned. They kill and maim, and they themselves are killed and maimed both physically and mentally.

—Judith Rhodes

WAKEFIELD, Hannah. Pseudonym for Sarah Burton and Judy Holland. Americans. **BURTON, Sarah:** Born in New York City. Educated at New York University, 1969–70. Moved to London in 1972. Qualified as a solicitor in 1972. Has worked for Seifert Sadeley Williams; since 1990 legal officer, Greenpeace, London. **HOLLAND, Judith:** Born in Boston, Massachusetts. Educated at Tufts University, Medford, Massachusetts; University of California, Berkley, B.A. 1970. Moved to London in 1971. Editor, Methuen publishers, London and Toronto, 1972–77; freelance editor, 1977–82; tenant housing co-operative campaigner and organizer, 1982–89; faculty adviser, Antioch master of arts in creative writing, London, 1987–89; since 1989 teacher of creative writing, Friends World College, Regents College, and Westminster Adult Education Institute, all London. Agent: Gregory and Radice, Riverside Studios, Crisp Road, London W6 9RL.

CRIME PUBLICATIONS

Novels (series: Dee Street in both books)

The Price You Pay. London, Women's Press, 1987; New York, St. Martin's Press, 1990.
A February Mourning. London, Women's Press, 1990; as *A Woman's Own Mystery*, New York, St. Martin's Press, 1991.

Play

Radio Play: *February Mourning*, 1991.

*   *   *

When writers have produced only two novels, it is difficult to accurately assess their output or to predict their future development. The two women who write as Hannah Wakefield have, it is fair to say, created one of the most interesting of the New Wave of feminist sleuths, certainly the most promising yet to come out of Great Britain.

Dee Street, their character in the two novels, is a solicitor working in an all-female, left-wing law firm. The novels are characterized by their first-person narration which draws the reader into a close relationship with Dee as she updates both her own state of mind and the state of play regularly. They contain a lot of action, cover a lot of different locations and look at a wide range of political issues. They are in fact much nearer in tone to espionage thrillers than to other feminist writing. If there is any criticism, it is that the leisurely, introspective voice of Dee is unsuited to the mass of action, chases and gunfights which happen at the end of both novels; loose ends are too rapidly tied up.

Politics of various kinds are central to both novels. *The Price You Pay* concerns murder, the CIA, ex-hippies and South American issues; *A February Mourning* is more explicitly feminist since it deals with issues such as lesbianism and the persecution of women at a peace camp as well as having a plotline concerning the IRA. But the clearest example of this feminism is the fact that throughout the novel, Dee also has to deal with her own pregnancy and her decision whether or not to have the baby. It is an accomplishment that by the end of the novel the reader is as gripped by the tension surrounding this as by the mystery being played out in a more traditional way.

Dee Street is a particularly appealing addition to the ranks of female sleuths; she is also unique—if we discount Sara Caudwell's gender-ambiguous Professor Hilary Tamar—in British mysteries as the only female solicitor/detective.

—Linda Semple

———

WALKER, Harry. *See* **WAUGH, Hillary.**

———

WALLACE, (Richard Horatio) Edgar. English. Born in Greenwich, London, 1 April 1875. Educated at St. Peter's School, London, Board School, Camberwell, London, to age 12. Served in the Royal West Kent Regiment in England, 1893–96, and in the Medical Staff Corps in South Africa, 1896–99; bought his discharge, 1899; served in the Lincoln's Inn branch of the Special Constabulary, and as a special interrogator for the War Office, during World War I. Married 1) Ivy Caldecott in 1901 (divorced 1919), two daughters and two sons; 2) Violet King in 1921, one daughter. Worked in a printing firm, shoe shop, rubber factory, and as a merchant seaman, plasterer, and milk delivery boy, in London, 1886–91; South African correspondent for Reuter's, 1899–1902, and the London *Daily Mail*, 1900–02; editor, *Rand Daily News*, Johannesburg, 1902–03; returned to London: reporter, *Daily Mail*, 1903–07, and *Standard*, 1910; racing editor, and later editor, *The Week-End*, later *The Week-End Racing Supplement*, 1910–12; racing editor and special writer, *Evening News*, 1910–12; founded *Bibury's Weekly* and *R.E. Walton's Weekly*, both racing papers; editor, *Ideas* and *The Story Journal*, 1913; writer, and later editor, *Town Topics*, 1913–16; regular contributor to the *Birmingham Post*, and *Thomson's Weekly News*, Dundee; racing columnist, *The Star*, 1927–32, and *Daily Mail*, 1930–32; drama critic, *Morning Post*, 1928; founder, *The Bucks Mail*, 1930; editor, *Sunday News*, 1931. Chairman of the board of directors, and film writer/director, British Lion Film Corporation. Chairman, Press Club, London, 1923–24. *Died 10 February 1932.*

CRIME PUBLICATIONS

Novels (series: Detective Sergeant/Inspector Elk; Four Just Men; Superintendent Minter, The Sooper; J.G. Reeder; T.B. Smith)

The Four Just Men. London, Tallis Press, 1906; revised edition, 1906; revised edition, Sheffield, Weekly Telegraph, 1908; Boston, Small Maynard, 1920.
Angel Esquire. Bristol, Arrowsmith, and New York, Holt, 1908.
The Council of Justice (Just Men). London, Ward Lock, 1908.
Captain Tatham of Tatham Island. London, Gale and Polden, 1909; revised edition, as *The Island of Galloping Gold*, London, Newnes, 1916; as *Eve's Island*, Newnes, 1926.
The Nine Bears (Smith; Elk). London, Ward Lock, 1910; revised edition as *The Other Man*, New York, Dodd Mead, 1911; as *Silinski, Master Criminal*, Cleveland, World, 1930; as *The Cheaters*, London, Digit, 1964.
The Fourth Plague. London, Ward Lock, 1913; New York, Doubleday, 1930.
Grey Timothy. London, Ward Lock, 1913; as *Pallard the Punter*, 1914.
The River of Stars. London, Ward Lock, 1913.
The Man Who Bought London. London, Ward Lock, 1915.
The Melody of Death. Bristol, Arrowsmith, 1915; New York, Dial Press, 1927.
The Clue of the Twisted Candle. Boston, Small Maynard, 1916; London, Newnes, 1917.
A Debt Discharged. London, Ward Lock, 1916.
The Tomb of Ts'in. London, Ward Lock, 1916.
The Just Men of Cordova. London, Ward Lock, 1917.
Kate Plus Ten (Smith). London, Ward Lock, and Boston, Small Maynard, 1917.
The Secret House (Smith). London, Ward Lock, 1917; Boston, Small Maynard, 1919.
Down under Donovan. London, Ward Lock, 1918.
The Man Who Knew. Boston, Small Maynard, 1918; London, Newnes, 1919.
The Green Rust. London, Ward Lock, 1919; Boston, Small Maynard, 1920.
The Daffodil Mystery. London, Ward Lock, 1920; as *The Daffodil Murder*, Boston, Small Maynard, 1921.
Jack o' Judgement. London, Ward Lock, 1920; Boston, Small Maynard, 1921.
The Book of All Power. London, Ward Lock, 1921.
The Angel of Terror. Boston, Small Maynard, and London, Hodder and Stoughton, 1922; as *The Destroying Angel*, London, Pan, 1959.
Captains of Souls. Boston, Small Maynard, 1922; London, Long, 1923.
The Crimson Circle. London, Hodder and Stoughton, 1922; New York, Doubleday, 1929.
The Flying Fifty-Five. London, Hutchinson, 1922.
Mr. Justice Maxell. London, Ward Lock, 1922.
The Valley of Ghosts. London, Odhams Press, 1922; Boston, Small Maynard, 1923.
The Clue of the New Pin. Boston, Small Maynard, and London, Hodder and Stoughton, 1923.
The Green Archer. London, Hodder and Stoughton, 1923; Boston, Small Maynard, 1924.
The Missing Million. London, Long, 1923; as *The Missing Millions*, Boston, Small Maynard, 1925.
The Dark Eyes of London. London, Ward Lock, 1924; New York, Doubleday, 1929.
Double Dan. London, Hodder and Stoughton, 1924; as *Diana of Kara-Kara*, Boston, Small Maynard, 1924.

The Face in the Night. London, Long, 1924; New York, Doubleday, 1929.

Room 13 (Reeder). London, Long, 1924.

Flat 2. New York, Garden City Publishing Company, 1924; revised edition, London, Long, 1927.

The Sinister Man. London, Hodder and Stoughton, 1924; Boston, Small Maynard, 1925.

The Three Oaks Mystery. London, Ward Lock, 1924.

Blue Hand. London, Ward Lock, 1925; Boston, Small Maynard, 1926.

The Daughters of the Night. London, Newnes, 1925.

The Fellowship of the Frog (Elk). London, Ward Lock, 1925; New York, Doubleday, 1928.

The Gaunt Stranger. London, Hodder and Stoughton, 1925; as *The Ringer*, New York, Doubleday, 1926.

The Hairy Arm. Boston, Small Maynard, 1925; as *The Avenger*, London, Long, 1926.

A King by Night. London, Long, 1925; New York, Doubleday, 1926.

The Strange Countess. London, Hodder and Stoughton, 1925; Boston, Small Maynard, 1926.

The Three Just Men. London, Hodder and Stoughton, 1925; New York, Doubleday, 1930.

Barbara on Her Own. London, Newnes, 1926.

The Black Abbot. London, Hodder and Stoughton, 1926; New York, Doubleday, 1927.

The Day of Uniting. London, Hodder and Stoughton, 1926; New York, Mystery League, 1930.

The Door with Seven Locks. London, Hodder and Stoughton, and New York, Doubleday, 1926.

The Joker (Elk). London, Hodder and Stoughton, 1926; as *The Colossus*, New York, Doubleday, 1932.

The Man from Morocco. London, Long, 1926; as *The Black*, New York, Doubleday, 1930.

The Million Dollar Story. London, Newnes, 1926.

The Northing Tramp. London, Hodder and Stoughton, 1926; New York, Doubleday, 1929; as *The Tramp*, London, Pan, 1965.

Penelope of the Polyantha. London, Hodder and Stoughton, 1926.

The Square Emerald. London, Hodder and Stoughton, 1926; as *The Girl from Scotland Yard*, New York, Doubleday, 1927.

The Terrible People. London, Hodder and Stoughton, and New York, Doubleday, 1926.

We Shall See! London, Hodder and Stoughton, 1926; as *The Gaol Breaker*, New York, Doubleday, 1931.

The Yellow Snake. London, Hodder and Stoughton, 1926.

Big Foot (Sooper). London, Long, 1927.

The Feathered Serpent. London, Hodder and Stoughton, 1927; New York, Doubleday, 1928.

The Forger. London, Hodder and Stoughton, 1927; as *The Clever One*, New York, Doubleday, 1928.

The Hand of Power. London, Long, 1927; New York, Mystery League, 1930.

The Man Who Was Nobody. London, Ward Lock, 1927.

The Ringer (novelization of stage play). London, Hodder and Stoughton, 1927.

The Squeaker. London, Hodder and Stoughton, 1927; as *The Squealer*, New York, Doubleday, 1928.

Terror Keep (Reeder). London, Hodder and Stoughton, and New York, Doubleday, 1927.

The Traitor's Gate. London, Hodder and Stoughton, and New York, Doubleday, 1927.

Number Six. London, Newnes, 1927.

The Double. London, Hodder and Stoughton, and New York, Doubleday, 1928.

The Thief in the Night. London, Readers Library, 1928; New York, World Wide, 1929.

The Flying Squad. London, Hodder and Stoughton, 1928; New York, Doubleday, 1929.

The Gunner. London, Long, 1928; as *Gunman's Bluff*, New York, Doubleday, 1929.

The Twister (Elk). London, Long, 1928; New York, Doubleday, 1929.

The Golden Hades. London, Collins, 1929.

The Green Ribbon. London, Hutchinson, 1929; New York, Doubleday, 1930.

The India-Rubber Men (Elk). London, Hodder and Stoughton, 1929; New York, Doubleday, 1930.

The Terror. London, Detective Story Club, 1929.

The Calendar. London, Collins, 1930; New York, Doubleday, 1931.

The Clue of the Silver Key. London, Hodder and Stoughton, 1930; as *The Silver Key*, New York, Doubleday, 1930.

The Lady of Ascot. London, Hutchinson, 1930.

White Face (Elk). London, Hodder and Stoughton, 1930; New York, Doubleday, 1931.

On the Spot. London, Long, and New York, Doubleday, 1931.

The Coat of Arms. London, Hutchinson, 1931; as *The Arranways Mystery*, New York, Doubleday, 1932.

The Devil Man. London, Collins, and New York, Doubleday, 1931; as *The Life and Death of Charles Peace*, 1932.

The Man at the Carlton. London, Hodder and Stoughton, 1931; New York, Doubleday, 1932.

The Frightened Lady. London, Hodder and Stoughton, 1932; New York, Doubleday, 1933.

When the Gangs Came to London. London, Long, and New York, Doubleday, 1932.

The Road to London, edited by Jack Adrian. London, Kimber, 1986.

Short Stories (series: Commissioner Sanders)

Sanders of the River. London, Ward Lock, 1911; New York, Doubleday, 1930.

The People of the River. London, Ward Lock, 1912.

The Admirable Carfew. London, Ward Lock, 1914.

Bosambo of the River. London, Ward Lock, 1914.

Bones, Being Further Adventures in Mr. Commissioner Sanders' Country. London, Ward Lock, 1915.

The Keepers of the King's Peace. London, Ward Lock, 1917.

Lieutenant Bones. London, Ward Lock, 1918.

The Adventures of Heine. London, Ward Lock, 1919.

Bones in London. London, Ward Lock, 1921.

The Law of the Four Just Men. London, Hodder and Stoughton, 1921; as *Again the Three Just Men*, New York, Doubleday, 1933.

Sandi, The King-Maker. London, Ward Lock, 1922.

Bones of the River. London, Newnes, 1923.

Chick. London, Ward Lock, 1923.

Educated Evans. London, Webster, 1924.

The Mind of Mr. J. G. Reeder. London, Hodder and Stoughton, 1925; as *The Murder Book of Mr. J. G. Reeder*, New York, Doubleday, 1929.

More Educated Evans. London, Webster, 1926.

Sanders. London, Hodder and Stoughton, 1926; as *Mr. Commissioner Sanders*, New York, Doubleday, 1930.

The Brigand. London, Hodder and Stoughton, 1927; Chicago, Academy, 1985.

Good Evans! London, Webster, 1927; as *The Educated Man—Good Evans!*, London, Collins, 1929.

The Mixer. London, Long, 1927.

Again Sanders. London, Hodder and Stoughton, 1928; New York, Doubleday, 1929.

Again the Three Just Men. London, Hodder and Stoughton, 1928; as *The Law of the Three Just Men*, New York, Doubleday, 1931; as *Again the Three*, London, Pan, 1968.

Elegant Edward. London, Readers Library, 1928.

The Orator. London, Hutchinson, 1928.

Again the Ringer. London, Hodder and Stoughton, 1929; as *The Ringer Returns*, New York, Doubleday, 1931.

Four Square Jane. London, Readers Library, and New York, World Wide, 1929.

The Big Four. London, Readers Library, 1929.

The Black. London, Readers Library 1929; augmented edition, London, Digit, 1962.

The Ghost of Down Hill (includes *The Queen of Sheba's Belt*). London, Readers Library, and New York, World Wide, 1929.

The Cat Burglar. London, Newnes, 1929.

Circumstantial Evidence. London, Newnes, 1929; Cleveland, World, 1934.

Fighting Snub Reilly. London, Newnes, 1929; Cleveland, World, 1934.

The Governor of Chi-Foo. London, Newnes, 1929; Cleveland, World, 1934.

The Little Green Man. London, Collins, 1929.

Planetoid 127 (includes *The Sweizer Pump*). London, Readers Library, 1929.

The Prison-Breakers. London, Newnes, 1929.

Forty-Eight Short Stories. London, Newnes, 1929.

For Information Received. London, Newnes, 1929.

The Lady of Little Hell. London, Newnes, 1929.

The Lone House Mystery (Sooper). London, Collins, 1929.

Red Aces (Reeder). London, Hodder and Stoughton, 1929; New York, Doubleday, 1930.

The Reporter. London, Readers Library, 1929.

The Iron Grip. London, Readers Library, 1929.

Mrs. William Jones and Bill. London, Newnes, 1930.

Killer Kay. London, Newnes, 1930.

The Stretelli Case and Other Mystery Stories (omnibus). Cleveland, World, 1930.

The Lady Called Nita. London, Newnes, 1930.

The Guv'nor and Other Stories (Reeder). London, Collins, 1932; as *Mr. Reeder Returns*, New York, Doubleday, 1932; as *The Guv'nor and Mr. J. G. Reeder Returns*, Collins, 2 vols., 1933–34.

Sergeant Sir Peter. London, Chapman and Hall, 1932; as *Sergeant Dunn C.I.D.*, London, Digit, 1962.

The Steward. London, Collins, 1932.

The Last Adventure. London, Hutchinson, 1934.

The Woman from the East and Other Stories. London, Hutchinson, 1934.

Nig-Nog (omnibus). Cleveland, World, 1934.

The Undisclosed Client. London, Digit, 1962.

The Man Who Married His Cook and Other Stories. London, White Lion, 1976.

Unexpected Endings. Oxford, Edgar Wallace Society, 1980.

Two Stories, and The Seventh Man. Oxford, Edgar Wallace Society, 1981.

The Sooper and Others, edited by Jack Adrian. London, Dent, 1984.

The Dead Room: Strange and Startling Stories, edited by Jack Adrian. London, Kimber 1986.

OTHER PUBLICATIONS

Novels

The Duke in the Suburbs. London, Ward Lock, 1909.

Private Selby. London, Ward Lock, 1912.

1925: The Story of a Fatal Peace. London, Newnes, 1915.

Those Folk of Bulboro. London, Ward Lock, 1918.

The Books of Bart. London, Ward Lock, 1923.

The Black Avons. London, Gill, 1925; as *How They Fared in the Times of the Tudors, Roundhead and Cavalier, From Waterloo to the the Mutiny, and Europe in the Melting Pot*, 4 vols., 1925.

Short Stories

Smithy. London, Tallis Press, 1905; revised edition, as *Smithy, Not to Mention Nobby Clark and Spud Murphy*, London, Newnes, 1914.

Smithy Abroad: Barrack Room Sketches. London, Hulton, 1909.

Smithy's Friend Nobby. London, Town Topics, 1914; as *Nobby*, London, Newnes, 1916.

Smithy and the Hun. London, Pearson, 1915.

Tam o' the Scouts. London, Newnes, 1918; as *Tam of the Scoots*, Boston, Small Maynard, 1919; as *Tam*, Newnes, 1928.

The Fighting Scouts. London, Pearson, 1919.

Plays

An African Millionaire (produced South Africa, 1904). London, Davis Poynter, 1972.

The Forest of Happy Dreams (produced London, 1910; New York, 1914). Published in *One-act Play Parade*, London, Allen and Unwin, 1935.

Dolly Cutting Herself (produced London, 1911).

Sketches, in *Hullo, Ragtime* (produced London, 1912).

Sketches, in *Hullo, Tango!* (produced London, 1912).

Hello, Exchange! (sketch; produced London, 1913; as *The Switchboard*, produced New York, 1915).

The Manager's Dream (sketch; produced London, 1913).

Sketches, in *Business as Usual* (produced London, 1914).

The Whirligig (revue), with Wal Pink and Albert de Courville, music by Frederick Chappelle (produced London, 1919; as *Pins and Needles*, produced New York, 1922).

M'Lady (produced London, 1921).

The Whirl of the World (revue), with Albert de Courville and William K. Wells, music by Frederick Chappelle (produced London, 1924).

The Looking Glass (revue), with Albert de Courville, music by Frederick Chappelle (produced London, 1924).

The Ringer, adaptation of his own novel *The Gaunt Stranger* (produced London, 1926). London, Hodder and Stoughton, and New York, French, 1929.

The Mystery of Room 45 (produced London, 1926).

Double Dan, adaptation of his own novel (produced Blackpool and London, 1926).

The Terror, adaptation of his own novel *Terror Keep* (produced Brighton and London, 1927). London, Hodder and Stoughton, 1929.

A Perfect Gentleman (produced London, 1927).

The Yellow Mask, music by Vernon Duke, lyrics by Desmond Carter (produced Birmingham, 1927; London, 1928).

The Flying Squad, adaptation of his own novel (produced Oxford and London, 1928). London, Hodder and Stoughton, 1929.

The Man Who Changed His Name (produced London, 1928; New York, 1932). London, Hodder and Stoughton, 1929.
The Squeaker, adaptation of his own novel (produced London, 1928; as *Sign of the Leopard*, produced New York, 1928). London, Hodder and Stoughton, 1929.
The Lad (produced Wimbledon, 1928; London, 1929).
Persons Unknown (produced London, 1929).
The Calendar (also director; produced Manchester and London, 1929). London, French, 1932.
On the Spot (produced London and New York, 1930).
The Mouthpiece (produced London, 1930).
Smoky Cell (produced London, 1930).
Charles III, adaptation of a play by Curt Götz (produced London, 1931).
The Old Man (produced London, 1931).
The Case of the Frightened Lady (produced London, 1931). London, French, 1932; as *Criminal at Large* (produced New York, 1932), New York, French, 1934.
The Green Pack (produced London, 1932). London, French, 1933.

Screenplays: *Nurse and Martyr*, 1915; *The Ringer*, 1928; *Valley of the Ghosts*, 1928; *The Forger*, 1928; *Red Aces*, 1929; *The Squeaker*, 1930; *Should a Doctor Tell?*, 1930; *The Hound of the Baskervilles*, with V. Gareth Gundrey, 1931; *The Old Man*, 1931; *King Kong*, with others, 1933.

Verse

The Mission That Failed! A Tale of the Raid and Other Poems. Cape Town, Maskew Miller, 1898.
Nicholson's Nek. Cape Town, Eastern Press, 1900.
War! and Other Poems. Cape Town, Eastern Press, 1900.
Writ in Barracks. London, Methuen, 1900.

Other

Unofficial Despatches. London, Hutchinson, 1901.
Famous Scottish Regiments. London, Newnes, 1914.
Fieldmarshall Sir John French and His Campaigns. London, Newnes, 1914.
Heroes All: Gallant Deeds of the War. London, Newnes, 1914.
The Standard History of the War. London, Newnes, 4 vols., 1914–16.
War of the Nations, vols. 2–11. London, Newnes, 1914–19.
Kitchener's Army and the Territorial Forces: The Full Story of a Great Achievement. London, Newnes, 6 vols., 1915.
The Real Shell-Man. London, Waddington, 1919.
People: A Short Autobiography. London, Hodder and Stoughton, 1926; New York, Doubleday, 1929.
This England. London, Hodder and Stoughton, 1927.
My Hollywood Diary. London, Hutchinson, 1932.

Ghostwriter: *My Life*, by Evelyn Thaw, London, Long, 1914.

Recording: *The Man in the Ditch*, Columbia, 1929.

*

Bibliography: *The British Bibliography of Edgar Wallace* by W.O.G. Lofts and Derek Adley, London, Barker, 1969; *A Guide to the First Editions of Edgar Wallace* by Charles Kiddle, Motcombe, Dorset, Ivory Head Press, 1981.

Critical Study: *Edgar Wallace: The Biography of a Phenomenon* by Margaret Lane, London, Heinemann, 1938; New York, Doubleday, 1939; revised edition, London, Hamish Hamilton, 1964.

Theatrical Activities:

Director: **Plays**—*The Calendar*, Manchester and London, 1929; *Brothers* by Herbert Ashton, Jr., London, 1929. **Films**—*Red Aces*, 1929; *The Squeaker*, 1930.

* * *

To this day the images conjured up by the name Edgar Wallace are of a frankly sensational nature—sinister cowled figures carrying swooning girls through shadowy corridors; bullets crashing through the windows of old manor houses; shrill cries of terror echoing through the murk of a dockside dawn—and it is often forgotten that this is merely the tip of a mammoth literary iceberg. He also wrote verse, essays, criticism, very good short stories, vast quantities of popular journalism, a 10-volume history of the Great War, various propaganda books, a number of highly successful plays, and ghosted at least three autobiographies—and it is this hugely diverse output that has undoubtedly done a great deal of harm to his latterday reputation. Nor has the frenetic pace at which he often worked helped matters. How could you take seriously a man who dashed off a play in four days and a novel over a weekend? Yet the play in question, *On the Spot*, is perhaps his most skillfully constructed drama, and the novel, *The Coat of Arms*, is certainly one of the tightest he ever plotted. Perhaps it is time, almost 60 years after his death, for a serious reappraisal of his work, for much of what he wrote is by no means as trivial or as flawed as more recent commentators have maintained.

Certainly the flaws are there. Yet careless writing (name-changes half-way through a book) and glaring factual errors (he invariably confused carbon monoxide with carbon dioxide) are largely dismissed by the reader caught up in the headlong rush of the narrative. And although Wallace's world seems cliché-ridden, it must be remembered that the majority of the "clichés" were invented by him and only turned into clichés by later writers. The element of pure detection in his books is minimal, but then he was far more interested in thrilling situations than in the slow planting of clues. Nevertheless *The Four Just Men, The Clue of the New Pin, We Shall See!* and *Big Foot* all contain ingenious locked-room mysteries, and the unmasking of the villain in *The Crimson Circle, The Valley of Ghosts, A King by Night* and *The India-Rubber Men* still comes as a nicely-contrived shock (as does the "unmasking" in *Room 13* and *The Squeaker* of the hero).

Wallace was never afraid of experimenting, and some of his most fascinating books are those well outside his normal field. *Captains of Souls*, for instance, concerns the transference of souls, and is one of his best stories; the eminently readable straight novel *Those Folk of Bulboro* attacks organised religion; the "twin worlds" theme of *Planetoid 127* still holds up well today; and his Sanders of the River series (11 books in all) is surely a unique contribution to popular literature.

A strong thread of comedy runs throughout his books, and he had an instinctive feel for such low-life characters as garrulous charwomen and small-time burglars which was undoubtedly fostered by his upbringing in the slums of south-east London (his soldier-sketches—the Smithy books—epitomise the broader aspect of his comic genius). Yet his humour—as in *Double Dan* and *Barbara on Her Own*—could often rival that of his friend P.G. Wodehouse in its lightness of touch, and even, on occasion, become pure satire, as in *The Man Who Knew*, a splendid joke at the expense of detective-story conventions (and indeed of his own plot techniques).

His grasp of character exhibits itself most strongly in the various second-string detectives (mainly from Scotland Yard) that people his books and comment, like sardonic choruses, on the hero, heroine, main villain, life in general, and the thousand natural shocks their own flesh is heir to (usually rheumatism). Sergeant Totty, in the excellent *The Frightened Lady*, is a noteworthy character in this respect, but perhaps the best-remembered are the laconic Sooper (*Big Foot* and *The Lone House Mystery*) and the lugubrious Elk, whose wit is at its most mordant in *The Fellowship of the Frog* and *The Joker*. But probably Wallace's most famous character is J.G. Reeder, that uniquely English detective (vaguely connected with the Public Prosecutor's office) whose mind is definitely devious and whose meekness hides a wolfish ferocity when aroused. In many ways the Reeder books—*The Mind of Mr. J.G. Reeder*, *Terror Keep*, *Red Aces*, and *The Guv'nor*—are Wallace's best endeavours in the field of pure detection, and undoubtedly the first book contains some of his best short stories.

To a certain extent Wallace was more convincing in the short story medium; certainly the compact format forced on him a self-discipline rarely to be found in the novels. His short stories are stunning examples of a lost art that flourished only during the inter-War years when there were so many fiction magazines to nourish it: pithy, tightly-plotted, neatly contrived, with twists in their tails even Ambrose Bierce and O. Henry would have applauded.

But it is still the thrillers—where nothing, except the hero (tough, tanned, and unfailingly cheerful) and the heroine (with her complexion of milk and roses, and nerves of steel), is as it seems to be—that grip the imagination and rivet the attention. How else could it be, when that sinister figure lurking just outside the street lamp's rays might possibly be a detective, and that benevolent old clergyman with the halo of white hair might well turn out to be a knife-wielding madman? In such a capricious world as this, it is surely satisfying to know, deep-down, that after astounding revelation piled upon astounding revelation (and a thrilling chase) good will at last triumph over evil.

And although there is far more to Wallace, if you look for it, than the genre for which he is best remembered (and which he himself, almost single-handed, created), still he was above all an entertainer. "I write to amuse," he once said in an interview. As a summing-up of his creative talent—indeed, as an epitaph—this surely cannot be bettered.

—Jack Adrian

WALLACE, Marilyn (née Weiss). American. Born in Brooklyn, New York, 21 September 1941. Educated at the City University of New York, B.A. in English, 1962; New School for Social Research, City University of New York, 1963–66; Golden Gate University, San Francisco, 1982. Married Bruce Wallace in 1964; two sons. English teacher, Brooklyn, 1962–66, and Philmont, New York, 1973–78; pastry chef, Albany, New York 1979; vice-president, Western Logic Corporation, San Anselmo, California, 1981–85. Recipient, Mystery Readers of America Macavity award, 1986. Agent: Molly Friedrich, Aaron Priest Literary Agency, 122 East 42nd Street, Suite 3902, New York, New York 10168.

CRIME PUBLICATIONS

Novels (series: Jay Goldstein and Carlos Cruz in both books)

A Case of Loyalties. New York, St. Martin's Press, 1986.
Primary Target. New York, Bantam, 1988.

Uncollected Short Stories

"The Sentence," in *Sisters in Crime*, edited by Marilyn Wallace. New York, Berkley, 1989: London, W.H. Allen, 1990.
"The Cutting Edge," in *Eye of a Woman*, edited by Sara Paretsky. New York, Delacorte Press, 1990.
"A Tale of Two Pretties," in *Sisters in Crime 3*, edited by Marilyn Wallace, New York, Berkley, 1990.

OTHER PUBLICATIONS

Other

Editor, *Sisters in Crime* [2, 3]. New York, Berkley, 3 vols., 1989–90; vol.1 published London, W.H. Allen, 1990.

*

Marilyn Wallace comments:

Even innocent acts have consequences that we can seldom predict—and when the act is murder, the consequences are even more far-reaching and compelling. In my novels, sergeants Goldstein and Cruz of the Oakland, California Police Department, share the spotlight with a character whose life is irrevocably affected by murder. In *A Case of Loyalties*, she's a painter who is the mother of a teenage girl who becomes a murder suspect. In *Primary Target*, she's the first woman to make a serious bid for the presidency of the United States. These people aren't victims in a classic sense; nevertheless, they must respond to their extraordinary circumstances. As Goldstein and Cruz sift through fact and interpretation and move closer to apprehending the criminal, the "guest narrator" follows her own path which intersects with Goldstein and Cruz at some critical point.

* * *

Marilyn Wallace has been described as one of our most promising new mystery writers. In just two novels her already considerable abilities show rapid expansion.

In *A Case of Loyalties*, Wallace makes use of an interesting trio of sleuths. The professionals are Oakland, California, police detectives Jay Goldstein and Carlos Cruz. Goldstein, a cultured, contemplative loner, provides a good counterpoint to Cruz, an emotional family man who struggles to balance the demands of his job with his personal life. The amateur sleuth is Carrie Rayborn, aspiring painter and single parent to 17-year-old Tricia. Rayborn's introduction to the police sergeants comes when Tricia is arrested for car theft and possession of marijuana; the car Tricia was driving has the same license plate as one used in a drive-by shooting on the same evening, thus bringing her under suspicion of murder. Wallace couples solid procedure with intelligent amateur detecting; she gives us characters we can care deeply about and a nice portrait of a troubled mother-daughter relationship. The book's only flaw is the inclusion of somewhat self-consciously arty passages of introspection on the part of Rayborn, which are distracting.

Goldstein and Cruz return in *Primary Target*. This time we see even more of their personal lives and conflicts, especially those of Cruz, who is a man trying to reconcile his Hispanic traditions with the realities of the modern world. The female protagonist is Jean Talbot, first woman to run for president and the target of a campaign of harrassment and, ultimately, terror by a mysterious group calling itself The Brotherhood of Men. Here, Wallace has abandoned the device of introspective passages in favor of a crisp, straightforward narrative from the viewpoint of the three principals.

The author's strengths are many, but her characters are particularly fresh and sympathetic, their believability enhanced by her avoidance of stereotypes (especially apparent in Jean Talbot). Her women are highly reflective of all modern women who struggle with new types of opportunities, responsibilities, and the attendant problems.

Wallace also demonstrates strong editorial skills with her series of *Sisters in Crime* anthologies. Numbering three volumes to date, these feature short stories by contemporary women mystery writers.

—Marcia Muller

———

WALLACE, Robert. *See* **DANIELS, Norman A.**

———

WALSH, Thomas (Francis Morgan). American. Born in New York City, 19 September 1908. Educated at Columbia University, New York, B.A. 1933. Reporter, Baltimore *Sun*. Self-employed writer. Recipient: Mystery Writers of America Edgar Allan Poe award, for novel, 1951, for short story, 1978. *Died 21 October 1984.*

CRIME PUBLICATIONS

Novels

Nightmare in Manhattan. Boston, Little Brown, 1950; London, Hamish Hamilton, 1951.
The Night Watch. Boston, Little Brown, and London, Hamish Hamilton, 1952.
The Dark Window. Boston, Little Brown, and London, Hamish Hamilton, 1956.
Dangerous Passenger. Boston, Little Brown, 1959.
The Eye of the Needle. New York, Simon and Schuster, 1961; London, Cassell, 1962.
A Thief in the Night. New York, Simon and Schuster, 1962; London, Cassell, 1963.
To Hide a Rogue. New York, Simon and Schuster, 1964; London, Cassell, 1965.
The Tenth Point. New York, Simon and Schuster, and London, Cassell, 1965.
The Resurrection Man. New York, Simon and Schuster, 1966; and London, Cassell, 1967.
The Face of the Enemy. New York, Simon and Schuster, 1966; London, Cassell, 1968.
The Action of the Tiger. New York, Simon and Schuster, 1968; London, Hale, 1969.

Uncollected Short Stories

"Double Check," in *Black Mask* (New York), July 1933.
"Tip on the Gallant," in *Black Mask* (New York), November 1933.
"Guns of Gannett," in *Mystery League Magazine* (Chicago), December 1933.
"Death Can Come Hard," in *Black Mask* (New York), July 1935.
"Diamonds Mean Death," in *Black Mask* (New York), March 1936.

"Alter Ego," in *A Century of Spy Stories*, edited by Dennis Wheatley. London, Hutchinson, 1938.
"Live Bait," in *My Best Spy Story*. London, Faber, 1938.
"Before the Act," in *Collier's* (Springfield, Ohio), 8 July 1939.
"Ed Mahoney's Boy," in *Collier's* (Springfield, Ohio), 10 February 1940.
"Mutton Dressed as Lamb," in *My Best Secret Service Story*, edited by A.D. Divine. London, Faber, 1940.
"In Line of Duty," in *Collier's* (Springfield, Ohio), 8 February 1941.
"Stranger in the Park," in *Collier's* (Springfield, Ohio), 27 December 1941.
"A Name for Baby," in *Collier's* (Springfield, Ohio), 18 December 1943.
"Peaceful in the Country," in *Collier's* (Springfield, Ohio), 13 April 1946.
"Best Man," in *The Hard-Boiled Omnibus: Early Stories from Black Mask*, edited by Joseph T. Shaw. New York, Simon and Schuster, 1946.
"Break-up," in *Murder: Plain and Fanciful*, edited by James Sandoe. New York, Sheridan House, 1948.
"Hard Guy," in *Ellery Queen's Mystery Magazine* (New York), September 1948.
"Getaway Money," in *Ellery Queen's Mystery Magazine* (New York), November 1948.
"Sentence of Death," in *Best Detective Stories of the Year 1949*, edited by David Coxe Cooke. New York, Dutton, 1949.
"Woman Expert," in *Ellery Queen's Mystery Magazine* (New York), May 1951.
"Girl in Car Thirty Two," in *Saturday Evening Post* (Philadelphia), 7 November 1953.
"The Night Calhoon Was Off Duty," in *Ellery Queen's Mystery Magazine* (New York), April 1954.
"The Blonde Nurse," in *Butcher, Baker, Murder-Maker*. New York, Knopf, 1954.
"You Can't Change Sides," in *Ellery Queen's Mystery Magazine* (New York), February 1955.
"Will You Always Be Helping Me?" in *Ellery Queen's Mystery Magazine* (New York), January 1956.
"Women—Pests or Poison," in *Ellery Queen's Mystery Magazine* (New York), November 1956.
"I Killed John Harrington," in *For Love or Money*, edited by Dorothy Gardiner. New York, Doubleday, 1957; London, Macdonald, 1959.
"Always Open and Shut," in *Ellery Queen's Mystery Magazine* (New York), February 1957.
"Murder on Order," in *Saturday Evening Post* (Philadelphia), 9 March 1957.
"Journey by Night," in *John Creasey Mystery Magazine* (London), May 1957.
"Cop on the Prowl," in *Ellery Queen's 13th Annual*. New York, Random House, 1958; London, Collins, 1960.
"Dear Lady," in *Ellery Queen's Mystery Magazine* (New York), March 1958.
"A Chump to Hold the Bag," in *Ellery Queen's Mystery Magazine* (New York), April 1958.
"Girl in Danger," in *Ellery Queen's Mystery Magazine* (New York), June 1958.
"Terror in His Heart," in *Ellery Queen's Mystery Magazine* (New York), August 1958.
"The Second Chance," in *Ellery Queen's Mystery Magazine* (New York), January 1959.
"Front Page Story," in *Suspense* (London), May 1959.
"The Harrington Case," in *The Saint* (New York), June 1959.
"Once Over, Not Too Lightly," in *Ellery Queen's Mystery Magazine* (New York), June 1959.

"Always a Stranger," in *Ellery Queen's Mystery Magazine* (New York), September 1959.

"Lady Cop," in *Ellery Queen's Mystery Magazine* (New York), December 1959.

"A Good Prospect," in *Anthology 1960*, edited by Ellery Queen. New York, Davis, 1960.

"Dangerous Bluff," in *Best Detective Stories of the Year*, edited by Brett Halliday. New York, Dutton, and London, Boardman, 1961.

"Three O'Clock Alarm" in *Ellery Queen's Mystery Magazine* (New York), December 1961.

"Homecoming," in *Ellery Queen's Mystery Magazine* (New York), December 1962.

"Callaghan in Buttons," in *Anthology 1964*, edited by Ellery Queen. New York, Davis, 1963.

"Danger in the Shadows," in *Anthology 1964 Mid-Year*, edited by Ellery Queen. New York, Davis, 1964.

"Enemy Agent," in *The Spy in the Shadows*, edited by Marvin Allen Karp. New York, Popular Library, 1965.

"Poor Little Rich Kid," in *Ellery Queen's Mystery Magazine* (New York), November 1967.

"Fall Guy," in *Ellery Queen's Mystery Magazine* (New York), September 1976.

"The Killer Instinct," in *Ellery Queen's Mystery Magazine* (New York), July 1977.

"Mr. Bountiful," in *Ellery Queen's Mystery Magazine* (New York), August 1977.

"Stakeout," in *Ellery Queen's Mystery Magazine* (New York), March 1978.

"The Closed Door," in *Ellery Queen's Mystery Magazine* (New York), May 1978.

"The Last of the Rossiters," in *Ellery Queen's Mystery Magazine* (New York), July 1978.

"Killer Bill," in *Ellery Queen's Mystery Magazine* (New York), September 1978.

"The Long Dark Street," in *Ellery Queen's Mystery Magazine* (New York), November 1978.

"Chance after Chance," in *Ellery Queen's Scenes of the Crime*. New York, Davis, 1979.

"The Stillness at 3:25," in *Ellery Queen's Mystery Magazine* (New York), February 1979.

"Paul Broderick's Man," in *Ellery Queen's Mystery Magazine* (New York), April 1979.

"The Mayhew Job," in *Alfred Hitchcock's Mystery Magazine* (New York), July 1979.

"A Hell of a Cop," in *Ellery Queen's Mystery Magazine* (New York), August 1979.

"Looking Out for Number One," in *Ellery Queen's Mystery Magazine* (New York), November 1979.

"The Sacrificial Goat," in *Ellery Queen's Circumstantial Evidence*. New York, Davis, 1980.

"Old Killeen's Promise," in *Ellery Queen's Mystery Magazine* (New York), 14 January 1980.

"The Way It Looks," in *Ellery Queen's Mystery Magazine* (New York), 23 July 1980.

"Born Gambler," in *Ellery Queen's Mystery Magazine* (New York), 10 September 1980.

"Leon's Last Job," in *Ellery Queen's Mystery Magazine* (New York), 7 October 1981.

"The Dead Past," in *Ellery Queen's Maze of Mysteries*. New York, Davis, 1982.

"Meek-as-a-Mouse McCabe," in *Ellery Queen's Mystery Magazine* (New York), 27 January 1982.

"Sitting Duck," in *Ellery Queen's Mystery Magazine* (New York), July 1982.

*

Bibliography: "Department of Unknown Mystery Writers: Thomas Walsh" by Marvin Lachman in *Poisoned Pen* (Brooklyn), January–February 1979.

* * *

Thomas Walsh won his first Edgar in 1951 for his first novel, *Nightmare in Manhattan*. In 1978, he won his second, for the short story "Chance after Chance." In the 27 years between, Walsh wrote steadily. There has been no better writer of the police story, and there has never been a better writer of the streets of New York.

Walsh was a prolific short story writer before turning to the novel, and his brief experience as a newspaperman shows up in his fiction. His books have the visual and action qualities which stem from good reporting, and make good motion pictures. *Nightmare in Manhattan* (filmed as *Union Station*) is still considered one of the most successful of mysteries transferred to film. What Walsh called "Manhattan Depot" was quite evidently Grand Central Station, and the author explored its many warrens, and utilized its multiple levels and the confusing exits and entrances. This book was also one of the most successful of deadline stories, the tension stretched to high wire tightness with all action taking place within a 48-hour span.

Walsh's later work is as bright and vital as his early writing, seasoned now with the maturity of long experience. His books stand the true test of expertness: they can be read today not as dated material but with the same zest as when first published.

—Dorothy B. Hughes

WAMBAUGH, Joseph (Aloysius, Jr.). American. Born in East Pittsburgh, Pennsylvania, 22 January 1937. Educated at Chaffey College, Alta Loma, California, A.A. 1958; California State College, Los Angeles, B.A. 1960, M.A. 1968. Served in the United States Marine Corps, 1954–57. Married Dee Allsup in 1955; two children. Worked in the Los Angeles Police Department, 1960–74: Detective Sergeant. Since 1974, self-employed writer: creator and consultant for *Police Story* and *The Blue Knight* television series. Recipient: Mystery Writers of America Special award, 1973, award for screenplay, 1980. Address: c/o William Morrow and Company, 105 Madison Avenue, New York, New York 10016, U.S.A.

CRIME PUBLICATIONS

Novels

The New Centurions. Boston, Little Brown, 1970; London, Joseph, 1971.

The Blue Knight. Boston, Little Brown, 1972; London, Joseph, 1973.

The Choirboys. New York, Delacorte Press, 1975; London, Weidenfeld and Nicolson, 1976.

The Black Marble. New York, Delacorte Press, and London, Weidenfeld and Nicolson, 1978.

The Glitter Dome. New York, Morrow, and London, Weidenfeld and Nicolson, 1981.

The Delta Star. New York, Morrow, and London, Macdonald, 1983.

The Secrets of Harry Bright. New York, Morrow, 1985; London, Joseph, 1986.

The Golden Orange. New York, Morrow, and London, Bantam, 1990.

OTHER PUBLICATIONS

Plays

Screenplays: *The Onion Field*, 1979; *The Black Marble*, 1980.

Television Play: *Echoes in the Darkness*, from his own book, 1987.

Other

The Onion Field. New York, Delacorte Press, 1973; London, Weidenfeld and Nicolson, 1974.
Lines and Shadows. New York, Morrow, 1983; London, Macdonald, 1984.
Echoes in the Darkness. New York, Morrow, and London, Bantam, 1987.
The Blooding: The True Story of the Marborough Village Murders. New York, Morrow, and London, Bantam Press, 1989.

* * *

Perhaps the first cop to write bestsellers, Joseph Wambaugh realistically portrays police activities in each of his works. *The New Centurions* and *The Blue Knight* adhere to the standard romance pattern, viewing man's environment dualistically as either paradisical or fallen, viewing man himself as either heroic or villainous. In *The Onion Field* and *The Choirboys* Wambaugh retains vestiges of the romance formula, but he treats that formula with tragic irony in the former work and with gradually darkening comic irony in the latter. *The Black Marble*, *The Glitter Dome*, *The Delta Star* and *The Secrets of Harry Bright* are essentially comic treatments of the police procedural, works which invert and subvert the procedural formula. *Lines and Shadows*, *Echoes in the Darkness*, and *The Blooding* are "non-fiction novels," accounts of, respectively, a San Diego police department experiment and murders on Philadelphia's Main Line and in Britain's Midlands.

The New Centurions traces the careers of three policemen from their beginnings in the Los Angeles police academy in 1960 to the Watts riot of 1965, which symbolizes the chaos on which the centurions must impose order. Wambaugh correctly points out the insularity inherent in police work; policemen reject the weak and villainous in order to cope psychologically with the horrors such people perpetrate. The novel bears the characteristic stamp of many first works; though Wambaugh is self-consciously serious and prone to lecture, he creates sympathetic and recognizably human characters. While his centurions define themselves as agents of the law, his Blue Knight, a 20-year veteran of the force, defines himself in terms of his own physical strength and his personal sense of what is good for the people on his beat. Unlike the new centurions, the Blue Knight sees himself as thwarted by the law. He will not allow himself any emotional involvement with others, choosing at the end of the novel not to retire, wed, and become a security officer but to remain on his beat. While he earns a measure of admiration for his courage, he seems primarily a pathetic figure, police work having isolated him from other people and also from the emotions of compassion and love.

Wambaugh carefully and with studied outrage examines the psychological effects of police work in *The Onion Field*, a "non-fiction novel" which delineates the mental collapse of Karl Hettinger after he and another policeman are surprised,

disarmed, and kidnapped by two petty thieves who eventually murder Hettinger's partner. Hettinger flees, "escaping" into continual nightmares, impotence, kleptomania, and a series of trials, for the conviction of the murderers occurred before the Escobedo, Dorado, and Miranda decisions, and their death sentences pronounced before the Anderson decision abolished capital punishment in California. Wambaugh recounts each new trial in horrified detail, manipulating ironic parallels between the two policemen and the two murderers throughout. Here the law seems not merely to thwart the policemen but actually to favor the criminals.

Wambaugh also examines the psychic cost of police work in *The Choirboys*, but he does so with a broad and bawdy comic technique reminiscent of *Catch-22*. The novel includes a series of hilarious episodes depicting incompetent, high-ranking officers and alcoholic, claustrophobic, masochistic, sadistic, and vampiric policemen. Wambaugh intersperses accounts of the patrolmen's desperate shenanigans in MacArthur Park with more and more brutal accounts of criminal inhumanity, which the patrolmen are forced by their job to witness. The juxtaposition suggests how and why police work taints a cop's vision of others and of himself; it suggests as well how some policemen try to cope with horror. Wambaugh's control here—of episode, of character, and especially of tone—is remarkable.

Wambaugh's focus shifts from patrolmen to detectives in *The Black Marble*, *The Glitter Dome*, and *The Delta Star*. Valnikov, the alcoholic hero of *The Black Marble*, is a former homicide detective, currently assigned to burglary. Like Hettinger and the choirboys, Valnikov has seen more than his share of cruelty and horror; the horror that causes him special anguish and that his partner, a policewoman/detective, helps him to purge, Wambaugh gradually reveals in the same way Joseph Heller reveals Snowden's secret in *Catch-22*. A dognapping provides the opportunity for some pointed satire of Pasadena, dogshows, and dogshow people. Valnikov's fight with the dognapper (whom he discovers accidentally) provides a realistic conclusion unlike most such fictional fare.

Wambaugh's satiric gifts are again evident in *The Glitter Dome*. In it four pairs of protagonists—detectives, narcotics officers, and patrolmen—are involved in an investigation into the murder of a movie mogul, and Wambaugh slams the Hollywood phonies his protagonists encounter everywhere in tinseltown. Wambaugh focuses here primarily on the two detective sergeants assigned to the case—one an alcoholic, the other so traumatized he ends a suicide—flaws which contribute to the dark edge of the novel's comic tone. Wambaugh makes clear that the detectives' adherence to police procedure only leads them *close* to the murderer; as in *The Black Marble*, accident, luck, and the detectives' inspired guesswork reveal the criminals' true identity. The novel's chopped, episodic structure, again like that of *Catch-22*, contributes to this ironic theme by mirroring the coincidental nature of events which lead to the discovery of that identity.

The Delta Star uses the same structure to make much the same point, the title being a chemical term for an excited state of pure creativity in which the detective sergeant who is the book's protagonist intuits the identity and motive of a scientist who has murdered a whore and a private detective. Only such an irrational, creative state helps the detective succeed; police procedure leads him only to questionable probabilities, not to provable answers. Again Wambaugh employs an episodic narrative structure and again he includes a group of wacky patrolmen as protagonists. Yet *The Delta Star* never seems to repeat earlier material and never bores the reader. Wambaugh's comic gifts and the apparently inexhaustible range of human stupidity and evil which is his subject combine here, too, to produce an original and exciting book.

With *Lines and Shadows* Wambaugh returns to the "non-fiction novel," chronicling the rise and fall of San Diego's experimental Border Alien Robbery Force (BARF), a group of ten mostly Mexican-American policemen who nightly patrolled the border between their city and Tijuana during 1976 and 1977, arresting the bandits who preyed on illegal aliens. The longer the experiment continued, the more the line between right and wrong, sanity and insanity, cop and bandit became shadowy. The experiment was terminated when two bandits were killed in a shootout; three Mexican policemen and three Barfers had been wounded in earlier shootouts *with each other*. Wambaugh studies the gradual deterioration of the Barfers sympathetically, recognizing that they were trapped by their *machismo*, by their view of themselves as Western gunslingers and by the media's adulation of them. This is a disturbing portrayal of police work.

The death of his own son in a traffic accident informs Wambaugh's next work, *The Secrets of Harry Bright*, a novel which, like the three preceding novels, treats the police procedural comically. Three of the novel's protagonists are men whose sons have been killed; the protagonists' anguished sense of how unnatural it is to bury one's child and Wambaugh's portrayals of his characters' strategies to cope with or deny their losses form poignant ironic contrasts with his comic characterizations of the msifits who comprise the Mineral Springs, California police department who have investigated the apparent murder of one of these sons. That the death is eventually discovered to be accidental rather than premeditated makes it no easier (indeed, makes it harder) to deal with. Here, as in his earlier novels, one of Wambaugh's points is that coincidence and accident, just as it may cause a victim's death, may also lead to the apprehension (the understanding) of that death, if not in this case to a villainous culprit.

Both *Echoes in the Darkness* and *The Blooding* are more or less straighforward journalistic accounts of murders, one on Philadelphia's Main Line and one in the British Midlands, accounts in which Wambaugh employs some of the techniques of the "non-fiction novel," as he had in two earlier books. *Echoes in the Darkness* recounts the events surrounding the trials of an English teacher and the principal of Upper Merion High School, both of whom were convicted of the murder of another teacher at the school. The case seems to be unique in the history of American law enforcement in that a team of police investigators was assigned to one case and worked on only it for seven years, from 1979 to 1986. *The Blooding* recounts the events surrounding the rapes and murders of two girls in Leicestershire and the apprehension of their killer by a technique known as genetic fingerprinting developed by a Leicester genticist named Alec Jeffreys; the technique enabled him to obtain X-ray patterns of DNA molecules in semen and blood, patterns which are unique to each individual and which, thus, may replace fingerprinting as a means of identification.

Wambaugh's "non-fiction novels," after *The Onion Field* lack its sense of outrage; constrained by the fact Wambuagh cannot give vent to his outrageous comic inventiveness in these works. His novels represent his best works to date and show his skills developing and undiminished.

—David K. Jeffrey

WARRINER, Thurman. Also wrote as John Kersey; Simon Troy. British. *Died.*

CRIME PUBLICATIONS

Novels (series: Mr. Scotter in all Warriner books except *The Golden Lantern*)

Method in His Murder. London, Hodder and Stoughton, and New York, Macmillan, 1950.
Ducats in Her Coffin. London, Hodder and Stoughton, 1951.
Death's Dateless Night. London, Hodder and Stoughton, 1952.
The Doors of Sleep. London, Hodder and Stoughton, 1955.
Death's Bright Angel. London, Hodder and Stoughton, 1956.
She Died, Of Course. London, Hodder and Stoughton, 1958.
The Golden Lantern. London, Hodder and Stoughton, 1958.
Heavenly Bodies. London, Hodder and Stoughton, 1960.
Night of the Wolf (as John Kersey). London, Cassell, 1968.

Novels as Simon Troy (series: Inspector Smith)

Road to Rhuine (Smith). London, Collins, and New York, Dodd Mead, 1952.
Half-Way to Murder (Smith). London, Gollancz, 1955.
Tonight and Tomorrow (Smith). London, Gollancz, 1957.
Drunkard's End. London, Gollancz, 1960; New York, Walker, 1961.
Second Cousin Removed (Smith). London, Gollancz, 1961; New York, Macmillan, 1962.
Waiting for Oliver. London, Gollancz, 1962; New York, Macmillan, 1963.
Don't Play with the Rough Boys (Smith). London, Gollancz, 1963; New York, Macmillan, 1964.
Cease upon the Midnight (Smith). London, Gollancz, 1964; New York, Macmillan, 1965.
No More A-Roving (Smith). London, Gollancz, 1965.
Sup with the Devil (Smith). London, Gollancz, 1967.
Swift to Its Close (Smith). London, Gollancz, and New York, Stein and Day, 1969.
Blind Man's Garden (Smith). London, Gollancz, 1970.

Uncollected Short Stories

"Wanted," in *The Evening Standard* (London), 27 July 1953.
"Edge of Terror" in *Suspense* (London), April 1961.
"Moment of Error," in *Argosy* (New York), March 1965.
"Pursuit," in *Argosy* (New York), December 1967.
"VIP," in *Argosy* (New York), October 1968.
"Once a Policeman" (as Simon Troy), in *Ellery Queen's Mystery Magazine* (New York), October 1969.
"The Liquidation File" (as Simon Troy), in *Ellery Queen's Giants of Mystery.* New York, Davis, 1976.

*   *   *

Good vs. evil and a seeming revolt against fundamentalist and fanatical religious groups are the sub-themes in many of the novels by Thurman Warriner. His hobbies—music, book collecting, ecclesiastical architecture—provide interesting diversions for the unique and passionate characters which inhabit the pages of his books. Warriner's first book, *Method in His Murder*, is a tense psychological thriller, rich in English background and ecclesiastical history. The series heroes are Mr. Ambo, a very proper wealthy bachelor, Scotter, an outspoken, brash, private detective, and Archdeacon Toft, a devil-fearing man. The interaction and mixed dialogue of these diametrically opposed do-gooders add an amusing element to the suspenseful tales in which they are featured.

The author's best work, however, is that published as Simon Troy and starring the compassionate, steady, and insightful Inspector Smith. Heavy in suspense, characters, local color, and psychology, the Troy novels involve characters from every walk of life, from prostitutes to deacons, concert musicians to automobile salesmen, none of whom escapes the watchful eye of the determined and just Inspector Smith. The characters are presented in depth, the motives, psychological or otherwise, of the crimes are thoroughly explored, and the tension builds to a suspenseful climax.

—Mary Ann Grochowski

* * *

WATSON, Colin. British. Born in Croydon, Surrey, 1 February 1920. Educated at Whitgift School, Croydon, 1930–36. Married 1) Peggy Swift; 2) Anne Watson; two daughters and one son. Worked in advertising, London, 1936–38; journalist, 1938–40; worked for an engineering firm, 1940–45; leader-writer, Thomson Newspapers, 1952–60; worked for the BBC, Newcastle upon Tyne, 1957–60. *Died 17 January 1982.*

CRIME PUBLICATIONS

Novels (series: Inspector Purbright in all books except *Bump in the Night* and *The Puritan*)

Coffin, Scarcely Used. London, Eyre and Spottiswoode, 1958; New York, Putnam, 1967.
Bump in the Night. London, Eyre and Spottiswoode, 1960; New York, Walker, 1962.
Hopjoy Was Here. London, Eyre and Spottiswoode, 1962; New York, Walker, 1963.
The Puritan. London, Eyre and Spottiswoode, 1966.
Lonelyheart 4122. London, Eyre and Spottiswoode, and New York, Putnam, 1967.
Charity Ends at Home. London, Eyre and Spottiswoode, and New York, Putnam, 1968.
The Flaxborough Crab. London, Eyre and Spottiswoode, 1969; as *Just What the Doctor Ordered*, New York, Putnam, 1969.
Broomsticks over Flaxborough. London, Eyre Methuen, 1972; as *Kissing Covens*, New York, Putnam, 1972.
The Naked Nuns. London, Eyre Methuen, 1975; as *Six Nuns and a Shotgun*, New York, Putnam, 1975.
One Man's Meat. London, Eyre Methuen, 1977; as *It Shouldn't Happen to a Dog*, New York, Putnam, 1977.
Blue Murder. London, Eyre Methuen, 1979.
Plaster Sinners. London, Eyre Methuen, 1980; New York, Doubleday, 1981.
Whatever's Been Going On at Mumblesby. London, Methuen, 1982; New York, Doubleday, 1983.

Uncollected Short Stories

"Return to Base," in *Ellery Queen's Mystery Magazine* (New York), June 1967.
"The Infallible Clock," in *Ellery Queen's Mystery Magazine* (New York), November 1967.
"The Harrowing of Henry Pygole," in *Winter's Crimes 6*, edited by George Hardinge. London, Macmillan, and New York, St. Martin's Press, 1974.

OTHER PUBLICATIONS

Other

Snobbery with Violence: Crime Stories and Their Audience. London, Eyre and Spottiswoode, 1971; New York, St. Martin's Press, 1972; revised edition, London, Eyre Methuen, 1979.
"Interview with a Character," in *Murder Ink: The Mystery Reader's Companion*, edited by Dilys Winn. New York, Workman, 1977.
"Mayhem Parva and Wicked Belgravia," in *Crime Writers*, edited by H.R.F. Keating. London, BBC Publications, 1978.

* * *

Snobbery with Violence, Colin Watson's study of 20th-century crime fiction, includes an acerbic chapter on the work of Agatha Christie; it is called "The Little World of Mayhem Parva" and it is sharply and wittily critical of those cloistered and sentimentalized villages in which Agatha Christie, like so many detective novelists of the 1920's and 1930's, loved to set her mysteries. Watson's own amiable and extremely funny novels can be read as a dramatized version of this objection to Christie and her generation. Flaxborough, the East Anglian town that has been the setting for all Watson's novels, is the opposite of Mayhem Parva; Christie's villages are genteel, chaste, and picturesque; Flaxborough is vulgar and lively. Even to the admiring gaze of a visiting New York policeman it does not seem entirely picturesque: "A little town with the oldest jumble of housetops you ever saw and a pub and a church every 20 yards, and girls like flowers and very, very slow-moving old men with brick-coloured faces who looked as if they'd have to be hit by lightning before they'd die." In the words of a knowledgeable inhabitant, Flaxborough is "A high-spirited town. . . . Like Gomorrah."

Colin Watson has published 11 novels in the series, and Flaxborough has become an elaborate and solid creation. It is depicted with a sharply satirical eye (and ear) for the unpicturesque aspects of contemporary English life. Flaxborough abounds in streets like Abdication Avenue and in charities called Our Dumb Companions, the Barkers' League, the Dogs at Sea Society, the Canine Law Alliance, and Four Foot Haven. Watson delights in describing overstuffed middle-class interiors and overtended middle-class gardens: "He admired the Nymph's Grotto and the Merry Fisher Lad and the big model windmill, painted bright blue and red, with sails that really went round whenever the wind blew from Wanstead, and he recognized Maisie's handiwork in the Lord's Prayer done in musselshell mosaic around the concrete base of the bird table." He catalogues the possessions of the newly affluent in loving detail: in *The Naked Nuns*, for example, Arnold Hatch is the proud owner of a gadget that automatically closes his bedroom curtains and switches the light on at sunset, and of a car, a "Fairway Executive," fitted with a refrigerator, telephone, and duplicating machine.

As this eye for consumer goods would suggest, Watson has a special interest in the activities, whether dishonest or merely comic, of modern business. *Broomsticks over Flaxborough*, for example, includes a campaign for the detergent Lucillite ("Only Lucillite has saponified granules") run by a group of advertising men whose professional jargon is deftly captured: "Folk-fond—that's an image situation. But first things first. Before product acceptance, product *presentation*, right?" *The Naked Nuns* has a superbly funny account of a medieval banquet for coach parties and American tourists organized by the Floradora Club, complete with "capons" (badly cooked chickens), "wassail" (cheap wine), waitresses dressed as Nell Gwynne, and music provided by Roy Hubbard and the Rockadours. The neatly titled *One Man's Meat* deals with the tribulations encountered by the makers of Woof, a popular dog food.

Watson's portrait of the tawdry side of English provincial life is saved from bitterness by something rare in detective novels: a dirty sense of humour. He has an innocent love of bawdy jokes, bedroom farce, and rude words. Flaxborough at times resembles an animated seaside postcard. *The Flaxborough Crab*, for example, deals with the alarming effects of an improperly tested drug being dispensed by a local doctor: it converts harmless elderly men into enthusiastic but incompetent sex maniacs. The plot of *Coffin, Scarcely Used* turns on an elaborate conspiracy by which a doctor's surgery is used as a brothel. It comes as no surprise to learn that the Floradora Club in *The Naked Nuns* has a brothel at the back (the girls are all named after flowers), and that the witches' coven in *Broomsticks over Flaxborough* is merely an excuse for various erotic goings-on.

In addition to the cast of sentimental animal lovers, drunken journalists, randy aldermen, and corrupt doctors, which changes from novel to novel, Watson uses a small group of recurrent characters. In this group the law is represented by Flaxborough's coroner, Mr. Albert Amblesby (once inadvertently described by a former mayor as one of "the venereal institutions of this ancient town"); his officer, Sergeant Malley; Dr. Heinemann, the pathologist; and Harcourt Chubb, the genteel and absent-minded Chief Constable. Most important are Inspector Purbright and his assistant, Detective Sergeant Sidney Love. Quiet, sensible, and with an air of deceptive amiability, Purbright is one of the more convincing detectives in recent fiction.

In his later work, though, Watson's interest seems to have been leaning more towards the criminals—more rogues than villains—who play minor but entertaining roles in his plots. The most important such figure—and probably Watson's best comic creation—is Lucilla Edith Cavell Teatime, the genteel confidence lady. Miss Teatime combines apparent respectability (she is Secretary of the Flaxborough and Eastern Counties Charities Alliance) with a love of fraudulent schemes (for example, her plan in *The Flaxborough Crab* for selling chopped dandelions as a sexual stimulant called Samson's Salad) and a disconcertingly racy line in conversation: "To tell the truth, it is regarding the physical side of marriage that I have always been apprehensive. . . . There so seldom seems to be enough of it."

What happens to detection amid all this comedy? Inevitably it receives short shrift. Watson's earliest books, *Coffin, Scarcely Used* and *Bump in the Night*, show his considerable skill in constructing intricate plots and allow Inspector Purbright to do some very creditable pieces of detection. But since then the comic element has predominated; the plots of the later novels are not slack or ill-constructed, but they are rarely the centre of either the reader's or the novelist's attention. There is no reason to regret this. There are many competent plotters among contemporary detective novelists, but there are few comic writers as energetic or entertaining as Watson.

—Ian Ousby

WAUGH, Hillary (Baldwin). Also writes as Elissa Grandower; H. Baldwin Taylor; Harry Walker. American. Born in New Haven, Connecticut, 22 June 1920. Educated at Hillhouse High School, New Haven; Yale University, New Haven, B.A. 1942. Served as a pilot in the United States Navy Air Corps, 1943–45: Lieutenant, J.G. Married 1) Diana M.A. Taylor in 1951 (divorced 1981), two daughters and one son; 2) Shannon O'Cork in 1983. Freelance cartoonist and song writer; teacher of mathematics and physics, Hamden Hall Country Day School, Connecticut, 1956–57; editor of Branford *Review*, weekly newspaper, Connecticut, 1961–62; First Selectman, Town of Guilford, Connecticut, 1971–73. Past President, Mystery Writers of America. Recipient: Swedish Academy of Detection Grand Master, 1981; Mystery Writers of American Grand Master award, 1989. Address: 9 Marshall Avenue, Guilford, Connecticut 06437, U.S.A.

CRIME PUBLICATIONS

Novels (series: Chief Fred Fellows; Simon Kaye; Detective Frank Sessions; Sheridan Wesley)

Madam Will Not Dine Tonight (Wesley). New York, Coward McCann, 1947; London, Boardman, 1949; as *If I Live to Dine*, Hasbrouck Heights, New Jersey, Graphic, 1949.
Hope to Die (Wesley). New York, Coward McCann, 1948; London, Boardman, 1949.
The Odds Run Out (Wesley). New York, Coward McCann, 1949; London, Boardman, 1950.
Last Seen Wearing . . . New York, Doubleday, 1952; London, Gollancz, 1953.
A Rag and a Bone. New York, Doubleday, 1954; London, Foulsham, 1955.
The Case of the Missing Gardener (as Harry Walker). New York, Arcadia House, 1954.
Rich Man, Dead Man. New York, Doubleday, 1956; as *Rich Man, Murder*, London, Foulsham, 1956; as *The Case of the Brunette Bombshell*, New York, Fawcett, 1957.
The Eighth Mrs. Bluebeard. New York, Doubleday, 1958; London, Foulsham, 1959.
The Girl Who Cried Wolf. New York, Doubleday, 1958; London, Foulsham, 1960.
Sleep Long, My Love (Fellows). New York, Doubleday, 1959; London, Gollancz, 1960; as *Jigsaw*, London, Pan, 1962.
Road Block (Fellows). New York, Doubleday, 1960; London, Gollancz, 1961.
That Night It Rained (Fellows). New York, Doubleday, and London, Gollancz, 1961.
Murder on the Terrace. London, Foulsham, 1961.
The Late Mrs. D. (Fellows). New York, Doubleday, and London, Gollancz, 1962.
Born Victim (Fellows). New York, Doubleday, 1962; London, Gollancz, 1963.
Death and Circumstance (Fellows). New York, Doubleday, and London, Gollancz, 1963.
Prisoner's Plea (Fellows). New York, Doubleday, 1963; London, Gollancz, 1964.
The Missing Man (Fellows). New York, Doubleday, and London, Gollancz, 1964.
End of a Party (Fellows). New York, Doubleday, and London, Gollancz, 1965.
Girl on the Run. New York, Doubleday, 1965; London, Gollancz, 1966.
Pure Poison (Fellows). New York, Doubleday, 1966; London, Gollancz, 1967.
The Con Game (Fellows). New York, Doubleday, and London, Gollancz, 1968.

"30" Manhattan East (Sessions). New York, Doubleday, 1968; London, Gollancz, 1969.

Run When I Say Go. New York, Doubleday, and London, Gollancz, 1969.

The Young Prey (Sessions). New York, Doubleday, 1969; London, Gollancz, 1970.

Finish Me Off (Sessions). New York, Doubleday, 1970; London, Gollancz, 1971.

The Shadow Guest. New York, Doubleday, and London, Gollancz, 1971.

Parrish for the Defense. New York, Doubleday, 1974; London, Gollancz, 1975; as *Doctor on Trial*, New York, Dell, 1977.

A Bride for Hampton House. New York, Doubleday, 1975; London, Gollancz, 1976.

Madman at My Door. New York, Doubleday, 1978; London, Gollancz, 1979.

The Glenna Powers Case (Kaye). Toronto, Raven, 1980; London, Gollancz, 1981.

The Doria Rafe Case (Kaye). Toronto, Raven, 1980; London, Gollancz, 1982.

The Billy Cantrell Case (Kaye). Toronto, Raven, 1981; London, Gollancz, 1982.

The Nerissa Claire Case (Kaye). London, Gollancz, 1983.

The Veronica Dean Case (Kaye). London, Gollancz, 1984.

The Priscilla Copperwaite Case (Kaye). London, Gollancz, 1986.

Murder on Safari. New York, Dodd Mead, 1987.

A Death in a Town. New York, Carroll and Graf, 1989.

Novels as H. Baldwin Taylor (series: David Halliday)

The Duplicate (Halliday). New York, Doubleday, 1964; London, Heinemann, 1965.

The Triumvirate (Halliday). New York, Doubleday, and London, Heinemann, 1966.

The Trouble with Tycoons. New York, Doubleday, 1967; as *The Missing Tycoon*, London, Hale, 1967.

Novels as Elissa Grandower (published as Hillary Waugh in UK)

Seaview Manor. New York, Doubleday, 1976; London, Gollancz, 1977.

The Summer at Raven's Roost. New York, Doubleday, 1976; London, Gollancz, 1978.

The Secret Room of Morgate House. New York, Doubleday, 1977; London, Gollancz, 1978.

Blackbourne Hall. New York, Doubleday, 1979; London, Gollancz, 1980.

Rivergate House. New York, Doubleday, 1980; London, Gollancz, 1981.

Uncollected Short Stories

"Nothing But Human Nature," in *Murder Most Foul*, edited by Harold Q. Masur. New York, Walker, 1971.

"Galton and the Yelling Boys," in *Alfred Hitchcock's Tales to Scare You Stiff*, edited by Eleanor Sullivan. New York, Davis, 1978.

"Some Explaining to Do," in *Ellery Queen's Mystery Magazine* (New York), April 1983.

"Death and the New Year," in *Woman's World* (Englewood, New Jersey), 1985.

OTHER PUBLICATIONS

Other

"Plots and People in Mystery Novels," in *Techniques of Novel Writing*, edited by A.S. Burack. Boston, The Writer, 1973.

"The Mystery Versus the Novel" and "The Police Procedural," in *The Mystery Story*, edited by John Ball. San Diego, University of California Extension, 1976.

Editor, *Merchants of Menace.* New York, Doubleday, 1969.

*

Manuscript Collection: Mugar Memorial Library, Boston University.

Hillary Waugh comments:

What does a writer say about his own work? I try to tell an interesting story about interesting people. I try to write it in such a way that the reader will forget he is reading and be totally unaware of my presence as the author. I try to put a little meat into my stories in hopes that the reader won't digest the book in a gulp and forget it, but will have something to chew on afterward. I would like my books to make the reader think, without the books telling him what to think. Lastly, I try to make sure that none of my books ever ends on an anti-climax. The tension should build to an explosion, not a let-down.

* * *

If Hillary Waugh had done nothing else than create the character of Chief Fred Fellows, he would hold an enviable place in the annals of detective fiction. Waugh has, however, another distinguished credit on his record: he wrote *Last Seen Wearing . . .* , widely recognized as one of the masterpieces of mystery-suspense fiction.

Unlike most writers of police fiction who set their stories in places like New York or Los Angeles, Waugh chose the small town of "Stockford," Connecticut as the setting of the Fred Fellows series. Stockford is a rather ordinary town inhabited by conventional people, though it does have a delightfully high homicide rate.

Chief Fellows, a tobacco-chewing, story-telling folksy type who has problems with keeping his chest measurement greater than his waist measurement, may give a first impression of being the stereotyped rube cop, but that he most decidedly is not. Fellows knows his police work, and although his methods are usually informal, they are well organized and consistent with forensic science. In *Road Block*, for example, he can get an approximate fix on the robbers' hangout by figuring the mileage on a car that has been driven to that point, and in *The Con Game* he uses publicity to determine the whereabouts of a fugitive. Fellows also has the abilities of the police expert, however, as in *The Late Mrs. D.*, where he identifies some typing on the basis of very competent analysis of the idiosyncracies of the typeface used.

Fellows is a strict chief (he chews out a patrolman for showing up with an unpolished button and chases a group of card-playing reporters out of headquarters), but he is a considerate officer who allows his men as much latitude as he can, and he is interested in justice to the extent that he once spent his vacation (in *Prisoner's Plea*) investigating the case of a condemned criminal who had appealed to him for help.

In some ways Fellows is closer to the Great Policeman tradition of Inspector Maigret than to that of the police procedural. He is a believer in police teamwork, but more often than not the solutions to his mysteries come from the workings of Fellows's intelligence rather than lucky breaks or the legwork of his subordinates. On more than one occasion Fellows has solved the case only two-thirds of the way into the story and spends the rest of the time searching for confirmatory proof.

Before he began the Fred Fellows series, Waugh wrote *Last Seen Wearing* . . . , which Julian Symons selected for his list of the 100 greatest crime novels. Aspiring writers of mystery fiction could profitably study the structure of this fine story, which is a model of sustained suspense. The tight form of *Last Seen Wearing* . . . is shaped by a pure, uncluttered story-line, with no sub-plots and no spinoffs, no distraction of attention from the consuming problem presented at the beginning, repeatedly analyzed, and finally resolved without having been diluted or distorted. The most remarkable feature of the novel, as far as its structure is concerned, is that all the relevant facts (including a reasonably accurate speculation regarding the solution) are presented in the original definition of the problem, which occupies the first fourth of the book. From there on, the suspense is sustained by means of re-examination of the mystery from different points of view and by the growing intensity of excitement as various explanations are tested. False leads and false clues are not allowed to stand for more than two or three pages, and periods of confusion are of short duration. One indication of the tight plotting of the story is that the first real break in the case does not come until halfway through the book.

Waugh is a practitioner of the well-made novel. Unlike many other writers of police procedurals, he avoids multiple plots, and the mystery presented at the beginning of a story is the one solved at the conclusion. The typical Waugh story fits the classic pattern of detective fiction: the Problem, the Initial Solution, the Complication, the Period of Confusion, the Dawning Light, the Solution, and the Explanation.

Waugh's other series policeman is Detective Second Grade Frank Sessions of Homicide, Manhattan North. Although his sphere of operation is quite different from Fred Fellows's Stockford, Sessions shares with Fellows the mold of the Genteel Policeman, in that he is more like Ngaio Marsh's Roderick Alleyn than most of the other roughnecks of police fiction: dining with a young woman at a good French restaurant, Sessions is annoyed by her apparent impression that a policeman is out of his depth anywhere else than at a lunch counter. He is, also like Fellows, a real professional who deplores the lack of pride and enthusiasm among young cops and who feels frustrated when a rapist-murderer gets off free. Society is all wrong, Sessions believes, but the police have to keep on trying.

Waugh has also written mysteries involving Sheridan Wesley and Philip Macadam, both standard private-eye types that might have come from the pages of Raymond Chandler, and he has produced a considerable body of non-series suspense stories, including ghostly tales and women's gothics.

Waugh has been a pioneer in the development of the police procedural story, along with Lawrence Treat in the United States and Maurice Procter in England. His main contribution to the craft has been his refusal to follow the formula adopted by most other writers with the result that his police stories are less conventional and harder to imitate, depending more on sharp definition than on multiplicity of involvements in the development of mystery and suspense.

—George N. Dove

WEBB, Jack. Also writes as John Farr; Tex Grady.

CRIME PUBLICATIONS

Novels (series: Father Joseph Shanley and Sammy Golden in all books except *One for My Dame* and *Make My Bed Soon*)

The Big Sin. New York, Rinehart, 1952; London, Boardman, 1953.
The Naked Angel. New York, Rinehart, 1953; as *Such Women Are Dangerous*, London, Boardman, 1954.
The Damned Lovely. New York, Rinehart, 1954; London, Boardman, 1955.
The Broken Doll. New York, Rinehart, 1955; London, Boardman, 1956.
The Bad Blonde. New York, Rinehart, 1956; London, Boardman, 1957.
The Brass Halo. New York, Rinehart, 1957; London, Boardman, 1958.
The Deadly Sex. New York, Rinehart, 1959; London, Boardman, 1960.
The Delicate Darling. New York, Rinehart, 1959; London, Boardman, 1960.
One for My Dame. New York, Holt Rinehart, 1961; London, Boardman, 1962.
The Gilded Witch. Evanston, Illinois, Regency, and London, Boardman, 1963.
Make My Bed Soon. New York, Holt Rinehart, 1963; London, Boardman, 1964.

Novels as John Farr

Don't Feed the Animals. New York, Abelard Schuman, 1955; as *The Zoo Murders*, London, Foulsham, 1956; as *Naked Fear*, New York, Spivak, 1955.
She Shark. New York, Ace, 1956.
The Lady and the Snake. New York, Ace, 1957.
The Deadly Combo. New York, Ace, 1958.

Uncollected Short Stories

"Broken Doll," in *Manhunt* (New York), May 1954.
"Getaway," in *Menace* (New York), November 1954.
"The First Fifty Thousand," in *Manhunt* (New York), March 1955.
"The Makeshift Martini," in *Manhunt* (New York), June 1955.
"Outside the Cages," in *Manhunt* (New York), December 1955.
"Moment of Truth," in *Accused* (New York), January 1956.
"The Mad Martini," in *Accused* (New York), March 1956.
"Time to Kill," in *Manhunt* (New York), December 1957.
"And Start with a Blonde," in *Ed McBain's Mystery Book 2* (New York), 1960.
"Day of the Tiger," in *Alfred Hitchcock's Mystery Magazine* (New York), December 1966.
"Murder Is My Host," in *Mike Shayne Mystery Magazine* (New York), May 1969.
"The Pandora Plan," in *Mike Shayne Mystery Magazine* (New York), June 1969.
"The Heart Givers," in *Mike Shayne Mystery Magazine* (Los Angeles), August 1972.
"This Man Must Die," in *Mike Shayne Mystery Magazine* (Los Angeles), February 1973.
"The Sensuous Corpse," in *Mike Shayne Mystery Magazine* (Los Angeles), October 1973.
"Love Letter," in *Best Detective Stories of the Year 1975*, edited by Allen J. Hubin. New York, Dutton, 1975.

OTHER PUBLICATIONS

Novel

High Mesa (as Tex Grady). New York, Dutton, 1952; London, Foulsham, 1954.

* * *

It is a remarkable coincidence that two men with the same name made their debut in crime fiction within three years of each other: Jack Webb (actor-director) in *Dragnet*, set in Los Angeles, and Jack Webb (writer) with his novels of Sammy Golden and Father Joseph Shanley, also set in Los Angeles. That they were no relation to each other was publicly stated when Webb's first short story in a brief series about the police on Airport Detail appeared in *Manhunt* (May 1954).

Critical reception to the nine Golden-Shanley novels was mixed, but that series may be the contribution to the genre for which Webb will be remembered. He took an unlikely combination of talents, a Jewish Detective-Sergeant and a Roman Catholic priest, and sent them forth down the mean streets of crime. Of the two, Sammy Golden plays the larger role in the novels, but events are not seen through his eyes exclusively. Webb keeps the story moving and builds suspense by swift changes of scene and point of view. He is not always successful, but when it works he gets under the skin of his characters in ways not usually associated with the hard-boiled school. These are tough stories, of tough events, and tough people, but told with sensitivity.

In *The Naked Angel* there is as much interest in character as in events. A dying derelict in the Church of St. Anne (Father Shanley's church), the murder of the wife of a television used-car pitchman, a missing stripper, and a frame-up against Sammy Golden seem like separate incidents in a kaleidoscope of police proceduralities, but Webb manages to link them before the last page. There are nice touches: Father Shanley as the wide-eyed innocent who stumbles into danger, Golden as the street-wise professional who is at bottom a very lonely man. Curiously, while Webb is able to make Shanley seem Roman Catholic, he never makes Golden appear really Jewish in anything but his name and references to his family. Father Shanley's hobby of cultivating roses surfaces in the stories just enough to make the reader accept it as a part of his characterization and to serve as a counterpoint to the content of Golden's conversation which focuses on the case at hand.

The same combination of several cases (homicide, robbery at a chemical company, the acid-blinding of the night watchman) come together in *The Bad Blonde*, with Father Shanley in jeopardy again in the last act. Of course, it's Sgt. Golden to the rescue once more. The mixture is not exactly the same in all of the books. A missing poet, a fire, a half-strangled girl lead to foreign intrigue and triple murder in *The Delicate Darling*. Additional ingredients include the daughter of Father Shanley's housekeeper and the poetry of John Donne. References to characters from the past who play no major roles in the current book and comments on earlier events serve to link the books into a true series. These are not disconnected cases. This device also adds verisimilitude without straining. There are enough references to topical matters (movie stars) and attitudes (Golden is irritated when his date tries to pay the check) to make them useful documents for social historians.

In spite of scenes told in vivid, short sentences to suggest significant events, Webb's short stories and novelettes are never quite up to the work in his best novels. Without the chemistry between Sammy Golden and Father Shanley there isn't always the humanity either.

At his best, Webb delivered a good story in which the characters walked the edge of terror. As such they do not deserve to be forgotten.

—J. Randolph Cox

WEBB, Richard Wilson. *See* **QUENTIN, Patrick.**

WEBSTER, Noah. *See* **KNOX, Bill.**

WELCOME, John. Pseudonym for John Needham Huggard Brennan. Irish. Born in Wexford, 22 June 1914. Educated at Sedbergh School, Yorkshire; Exeter College, Oxford, B.A. in law 1936. Served in the Royal Artillery, 1940–42: Captain. Married Stella Peart in 1944; four daughters. Since 1945 principal, Huggard and Brennan, solicitors, Wexford. Senior steward, Irish National Steeplechase Committee, 1970, 1978. Agent: Andrew Hewson, John Johnson Ltd., 45–47 Clerkenwell Green, London EC1R 0HT, England. Address: Hermitage, Drinagh, Wexford, Ireland.

CRIME PUBLICATIONS

Novels (series characters: Richard Graham; Simon Herald)

Run for Cover (Graham). London, Faber, 1958; New York, Knopf, 1959.
Stop at Nothing (Herald). London, Faber, 1959; New York, Knopf, 1960.
Beware of Midnight. London, Faber, and New York, Knopf, 1961.
Hard to Handle (Graham). London, Faber, 1964.
Wanted for Killing (Herald). London, Faber, 1965; New York, Holt Rinehart, 1967.
Hell Is Where You Find It (Graham). London, Faber, 1968.
On the Stretch (Graham). London, Faber, 1969.
Go for Broke (Graham). London, Faber, and New York, Walker, 1972.
A Painted Devil. London, Collins, 1988.
Reasons of Hate. London, Collins, 1990.

OTHER PUBLICATIONS

Novels

Red Coats Galloping. London, Constable, 1949.
Mr. Merston's Money. London, Constable, 1951.
Mr. Merston's Hounds. London, Jenkins, 1953.
Grand National. London, Hamish Hamilton, 1976.
Bellary Bay. London, Hamish Hamilton, and New York, Atheneum, 1979.
A Call to Arms. London, Hamish Hamilton, and New York, St. Martin's Press, 1985.

Other

The Cheltenham Gold Cup: The Story of a Great Steeplechase. London, Constable, 1957; revised edition, London, Pelham, 1973, 1984.
Cheating at Cards: The Cases in Court. London, Faber, 1963; as *Great Scandals of Cheating at Cards: Famous Court Cases,* New York, Horizon Press, 1964.
Fred Archer: His Life and Times. London, Faber, 1967.
Neck or Nothing: The Extraordinary Life and Times of Bob Sievier. London, Faber, 1970.
The Sporting Empress: The Story of Elizabeth of Austria and Bay Middleton. London, Joseph, 1975.
A Light-Hearted Guide to British Racing. London, Macdonald and Jane's, 1975.
Infamous Occasions (on racing scandals). London, Joseph, 1980.
The Sporting World of R.S. Surtees. Oxford and New York, Oxford University Press, 1982.
Irish Horse-Racing. London, Macmillan, and New York, State Mutual, 1982.
Great Racing Disasters. London, Weidenfeld and Nicolson, 1985.

Editor, with V.R. Orchard, *Best Hunting Stories.* London, Faber, 1954.
Editor, *Best Motoring Stories.* London, Faber, 1959.
Editor, *Best Secret Service Stories 1–2.* London, Faber, 2 vols., 1960–65.
Editor, *Best Gambling Stories.* London, Faber, 1961.
Editor, *Best Legal Stories 1–2.* London, Faber, 2 vols., 1962–70.
Editor, *Best Crime Stories 1–3.* London, Faber, 3 vols., 1964–68.
Editor, with Dick Francis, *Best Racing and Chasing Stories 1–2.* London, Faber, 2 vols., 1966–69.
Editor, *Best Smuggling Stories.* London, Faber, 1967.
Editor, *Best Spy Stories.* London, Faber, 1967.
Editor, with Dick Francis, *The Racing Man's Bedside Book.* London, Faber, 1969.
Editor, *Ten of the Best: Selected Short Stories.* London, Faber, 1969.
Editor, *The Welcome Collection: Fourteen Racing Stories.* London, Joseph, 1972.
Editor, with Dick Francis, *Great Racing Stories.* London, Bellew, 1989.

*   *   *

John Welcome lives and writes like the stereotypical British gentleman. He has been involved with fox-hunting, racing and horses—he was a senior steward of the Irish National Hunt Steeplechase Committee—throughout his life. Welcome has traveled widely—his descriptions of Irish, English, European, and Kenyan settings are detailed because he has lived in all the locales he uses in his books.

Welcome is best known for a series of suspense novels he wrote in the 1960's and early 1970's featuring sometime secret agent Richard Graham. Graham is the perfect English gentleman who just happens to bet on the wrong horse or love the wrong woman and consequently finds himself in need of money. At this point, British Intelligence personnel contact Graham and send him on his way into usually violent, bloody capers.

In the best book in the series, *Wanted for Killing,* Graham leaves England hurriedly and illegally because of a caper gone wrong. He needs a place to lay low and allow his bullet wounds to heal. He heads for Corsica where he finds his old friend Simon Herald—another former secret agent, now retired—and Simon's new young wife, Sue.

But Graham finds no rest as the Heralds' estate is besieged by violent beach bums, anonymous threats, and unsettling offers to buy the estate at several times its market value. Graham is also concerned about Simon and Sue—their relationship seems to mysteriously disintegrate before his eyes.

By the book's end, Graham has solved the secret behind the Heralds' marital problems and the reason why the Herald estate is so valuable—but only after he risks his life to get the evidence.

Run for Cover features Graham involved in a tangled plot when a manuscript he's reviewing is stolen. The manuscript was written by a man Graham thought was dead: Rupert Rawle, a former spy. But the dead man has come back to life. Graham finds himself on the trail of the man Graham once idolized—but that idolization turned to hatred when Rawle left Graham for dead during a daring World War II commando mission. Welcome's plotting is fastpaced, wild, and unpredictable.

Stop at Nothing features Welcome's other leading man: Simon Herald, another former spy. Herald, once a world class racing driver, faces turning 40 and a bitter divorce. He falls in love with a younger woman whose brother is hunted by a group of vicious thugs who want to gain the secret of a formula that makes horses race faster. Hairbreadth escape follows hairbreadth escape as Herald faces overwhelming odds, brutal beatings, a psychopathic killer, and an obsessed millionaire to save his lover's brother.

Go for Broke opens with Eric Vaughan, a wealthy financier, accusing Richard Graham of cheating at cards. Graham is mystified by the false charges, but finds himself drawn into a web of international intrigue. Graham finds himself a social outcast, discharged from his part-time espionage position, and forced to sell his meager land holdings to pay for his legal defense. But when Graham falls in love with a mysterious American woman, he finds an unexpected clue to the frame he's been put in. The only flaw in *Go for Broke* is the tedious courtroom proceedings; once outside the stuffy legal chambers, the pages fly by.

The formula of the Welcome books starring Graham and/or Herald begins with his hero reluctantly getting involved in a surprising plot involving a beautiful woman and then risking his life to reveal the secret. Welcome's villains are elegant, charming, and ruthlessly violent.

Since the 1970's, Welcome has abandoned his successful Richard Graham series and turned to writing bloated "adventure" novels in the mode of Wilbur Smith. The best of these—*Bellary Bay* and his latest novel, *A Call to Arms*—capture the excitement of World War II and set in Ireland and Kenya. While these novels are entertaining, they don't have the style and flare of the Richard Graham/Simon Herald books.

—George Kelley

_____

WELLS, Carolyn. Also wrote as Rowland Wright. American. Born in Rahway, New Jersey, 18 June 1869. Educated in public schools and privately. Married Hadwin Houghton in 1918 (died, 1919). Deaf from the age of six. Librarian; then freelance writer. Lived in New York City after 1919. *Died 26 March 1942.*

CRIME PUBLICATIONS

Novels (series: Kenneth Carlisle; Alan Ford; Lorimer Lane; Fleming Stone; Pennington Wise)

The Clue (Stone). Philadelphia, Lippincott, 1909; London, Hodder and Stoughton, 1920.
The Gold Bag (Stone). Philadelphia, Lippincott, 1911; London, Hodder and Stoughton, 1922.
A Chain of Evidence (Stone). Philadelphia, Lippincott, 1912.
The Maxwell Mystery (Stone). Philadelphia, Lippincott, 1913.
Anybody But Anne (Stone). Philadelphia, Lippincott, 1914; London, Thompson, 1929.
The White Alley (Stone). Philadelphia, Lippincott, 1915; London, Hodder and Stoughton, 1920.
The Bride of a Moment (Ford). New York, Doran, 1916; London, Hodder and Stoughton, 1920.
The Curved Blades (Stone). Philadelphia, Lippincott, 1916.
Faulkner's Folly (Ford). New York, Doran, 1917.
The Mark of Cain (Stone). Philadelphia, Lippincott, 1917; London, Hodder and Stoughton, 1920.
The Room with the Tassels (Ford). New York, Doran, 1918.
Vicky Van (Stone). Philadelphia, Lippincott, 1918; London, Hodder and Stoughton, 1920; as *The Elusive Vicky Van*, London, Mellifont Press, 1934.
The Diamond Pin (Stone). Philadelphia, Lippincott, 1919.
The Man Who Fell Through the Earth (Wise). New York, Doran, 1919; London, Harrap, 1924.
In the Onyx Lobby (Wise). New York, Doran, and London, Hodder and Stoughton, 1920.
The Disappearance of Kimball Webb (as Rowland Wright). New York, Dodd Mead, 1920.
Raspberry Jam (Stone). Philadelphia, Lippincott, 1920.
The Come Back (Wise). New York, Doran, and London, Hodder and Stoughton, 1921.
The Luminous Face (Wise). New York, Doran, 1921.
The Mystery of the Sycamore (Stone). Philadelphia, Lippincott, 1921.
The Mystery Girl (Stone). Philadelphia, Lippincott, 1922.
The Vanishing of Betty Varian (Wise). New York, Doran, 1922; London, Collins, 1924.
The Affair at Flower Acres (Wise). New York, Doran, 1923.
Feathers Left Around (Stone). Philadelphia, Lippincott, 1923.
More Lives Than One (Lane). New York, Boni, 1923; London, Hutchinson, 1924.
Spooky Hollow (Stone). Philadelphia, Lippincott, 1923.
Wheels Within Wheels (Wise). New York, Doran, 1923.
The Fourteenth Key (Lane). New York, Putnam, 1924.
The Furthest Fury (Stone). Philadelphia, Lippincott, 1924.
The Moss Mystery. New York, Garden City Publishing Company, 1924.
Prillilgirl (Stone). Philadelphia, Lippincott, 1924.
Anything But the Truth (Stone). Philadelphia, Lippincott, 1925.
The Daughter of the House (Stone). Philadelphia, Lippincott, 1925.
Face Cards. New York, Putnam, 1925.
The Bronze Hand (Stone). Philadelphia, Lippincott, 1926.
The Red-Haired Girl (Stone). Philadelphia, Lippincott, 1926.
The Vanity Case. New York, Putnam, 1926.
All at Sea (Stone). Philadelphia, Lippincott, 1927; London, Thompson, 1929.
The Sixth Commandment. New York, Doran, 1927.
Where's Emily? (Stone). Philadelphia, Lippincott, 1927.
The Crime in the Crypt (Stone). Philadelphia, Lippincott, 1928.
Deep-Lake Mystery. New York, Doubleday, 1928.

The Tannahill Tangle (Stone). Philadelphia, Lippincott, 1928.
Sleeping Dogs (Carlisle). New York, Doubleday, 1929.
The Tapestry Room Murder (Stone). Philadelphia, Lippincott, 1929.
Triple Murder (Stone). Philadelphia, Lippincott, 1929.
The Doomed Five (Stone). Philadelphia, Lippincott, 1930.
The Doorstep Murders (Carlisle). New York, Doubleday, 1930.
The Ghosts' High Noon (Stone). Philadelphia, Lippincott, 1930.
Horror House (Stone). Philadelphia, Lippincott, 1931.
The Skeleton at the Feast (Carlisle). New York, Doubleday, 1931.
The Umbrella Murder (Stone). Philadelphia, Lippincott, 1931.
Fuller's Earth (Stone). Philadelphia, Lippincott, 1932.
The Roll-Top Desk Mystery (Stone). Philadelphia, Lippincott, 1932.
The Broken O (Stone). Philadelphia, Lippincott, 1933.
The Clue of the Eyelash (Stone). Philadelphia, Lippincott, and London, Laurie, 1933.
The Master Murderer (Stone). Philadelphia, Lippincott, 1933.
Eyes in the Wall (Stone). Philadelphia, Lippincott, 1934.
In the Tiger's Cage (Stone). Philadelphia, Lippincott, 1934.
The Visiting Villain (Stone). Philadelphia, Lippincott, 1934.
The Beautiful Derelict (Stone). Philadelphia, Lippincott, 1935.
For Goodness' Sake (Stone). Philadelphia, Lippincott, 1935.
The Wooden Indian (Stone). Philadelphia, Lippincott, 1935.
The Huddle (Stone). Philadelphia, Lippincott, 1936.
Money Musk (Stone). Philadelphia, Lippincott, 1936.
Murder in the Bookshop (Stone). Philadelphia, Lippincott, 1936.
The Mystery of the Tarn (Stone). Philadelphia, Lippincott, 1937.
The Radio Studio Murder (Stone). Philadelphia, Lippincott, 1937.
Gilt-Edged Guilt (Stone). Philadelphia, Lippincott, 1938.
The Killer (Stone). Philadelphia, Lippincott, 1938.
The Missing Link (Stone). Philadelphia, Lippincott, 1938.
Calling All Suspects (Stone). Philadelphia, Lippincott, 1939.
Crime Tears On (Stone). Philadelphia, Lippincott, 1939.
The Importance of Being Murdered (Stone). Philadelphia, Lippincott, 1939.
Crime Incarnate (Stone). Philadelphia, Lippincott, 1940.
Devil's Work (Stone). Philadelphia, Lippincott, 1940.
Murder on Parade (Stone). Philadelphia, Lippincott, 1940.
Murder Plus (Stone). Philadelphia, Lippincott, 1940.
The Black Night Murders (Stone). Philadelphia, Lippincott, 1941.
Murder at the Casino (Stone). Philadelphia, Lippincott, 1941.
Murder Will In (Ford). Philadelphia, Lippincott, 1942.
Who Killed Caldwell? (Stone). Philadelphia, Lippincott, 1942.

Uncollected Short Stories

"Christabel's Crystal," in *The World's Best One Hundred Detective Stories*, edited by Eugene Thwing. New York, Funk and Wagnalls, 10 vols., 1929.
"A Point of Testimony," in *Ellery Queen's Mystery Magazine* (New York), November 1942.
"The Adventure of the Clothes Line," in *The Misadventures of Sherlock Holmes*, edited by Ellery Queen. Boston, Little Brown, 1944.
"The Shakespeare Title-Page Mystery," in *Ellery Queen's Mystery Magazine* (New York), September 1951.

OTHER PUBLICATIONS

Novels

Abeniki Caldwell. New York, Russell, 1902.
The Gordon Elopement, with Harry Persons Taber. New York, Doubleday, 1904.
Ptomaine Street: A Tale of Warble Petticoat. Philadelphia, Lippincott, 1921.

Plays

Maid of Athens, adaptation of the operetta by Victor Leon, music by Franz Lehár (produced New York, 1914).
Jolly Plays for Holidays. Boston, Baker, 1914.
The Meaning of Thanksgiving. Philadelphia, Penn, 1922.
Queen Christmas. Philadelphia, Penn, 1922.
The Sweet Girl Graduate. Philadelphia, Penn, 1922.

Verse

Children of Our Town. New York, Russell, 1902.
Folly for the Wise. Indianapolis, Bobbs Merrill, 1904.
Rubáiyát of a Motor Car. New York, Dodd Mead, 1906.
The Rubáiyát of a Bridge. New York, Harper, 1909.
The Seven Ages of Childhood. New York, Moffat Yard, 1909.

Other

The Story of Betty (for children). New York, Century, 1899.
The Jingle Book. New York, Macmillan, 1899.
Idle Idylls. New York, Dodd Mead, 1900.
Folly in Fairyland. Philadelphia, Altemus, and London, Kelly, 1901.
The Merry-Go-Round (for children). New York, Russell, 1901.
Mother Goose's Menagerie (for children). Boston, Noyes Platt, 1901.
Patty Fairfield (for children). New York, Dodd Mead, 1901.
The Pete and Polly Stories (for children). Chicago, McClurg, 1902.
A Phenomenal Fauna. New York, Russell, 1902.
Eight Girls and a Dog (for children). New York, Century, 1902.
Folly in the Forest. Philadelphia, Altemus, 1902.
Trotty's Trip. Philadelphia, Biddle, 1902.
The Bumblepuppy Book. London, Isbister, 1903.
Patty at Home (for children). New York, Dodd Mead, 1904.
In the Reign of Queen Dick (for children). New York, Appleton, 1904.
The Staying Guests (for children). New York, Century, 1904.
The Dorrance Domain (for children). Boston, Wilde, 1905.
The Matrimonial Bureau, with Harry Persons Taber. Boston, Houghton Mifflin, and London, Nash, 1905.
Patty in the City (for children). New York, Dodd Mead, 1905.
At the Sign of the Sphinx. New York, Duffield, 1906.
Dorrance Doings (for children). Boston, Wilde, 1906.
The Emily Emmins Papers. New York, Putnam, 1907.
Fluffy Ruffles (for children). New York, Appleton, 1907.
Marjorie's Vacation (for children). New York, Dodd Mead, 1907.
Rainy Day Diversions. New York, Moffat Yard, 1907.
Patty in Paris (for children). New York, Dodd Mead, 1907.
Patty's Friends (for children). New York, Dodd Mead, 1908.
Patty's Summer Days (for children). New York, Dodd Mead, 1908.
The Carolyn Wells Year Book of Old Favorites and New Fancies for 1909. New York, Holt, 1908.

The Happy Chaps. New York, Century, 1908.
Marjorie's Busy Days (for children). New York, Dodd Mead, 1908.
Dick and Dolly (for children). New York, Dodd Mead, 1909.
Marjorie's New Friend (for children). New York, Dodd Mead, 1909.
Patty's Pleasure Trip (for children). New York, Dodd Mead, 1909.
Pleasant Day Diversions. New York, Moffat Yard, 1909.
Betty's Happy Year (for children). New York, Century, 1910.
Dick and Dolly's Adventures (for children). New York, Dodd Mead, 1910.
Marjorie in Command (for children). New York, Dodd Mead, 1910.
Patty's Success (for children). New York, Dodd Mead, 1910.
Marjorie's Maytime (for children). New York, Dodd Mead, 1911.
Patty's Motor Car (for children). New York, Dodd Mead, 1911.
Patty's Butterfly Days (for children). New York, Dodd Mead, 1912.
The Lover's Baedeker and Guide to Arcady. New York, Stokes, 1912.
Marjorie at Seacote (for children). New York, Dodd Mead, 1912.
Christmas Carollin'. New York, Bigelow, 1913.
The Eternal Feminine. New York, Bigelow, 1913.
Girls and Gayety. New York, Bigelow, 1913.
The Technique of the Mystery Story. Springfield, Massachusetts, Home Correspondence School, 1913; revised edition, 1929.
Patty's Social Season (for children). New York, Dodd Mead, 1913.
Pleasing Prose. New York, Bigelow, 1913.
The Re-Echo Club. New York, Bigelow, 1913.
Patty's Suitors (for children). New York, Dodd Mead, 1914.
Two Little Women (for children). New York, Dodd Mead, 1915.
Patty's Romance (for children). New York, Dodd Mead, 1915.
Patty's Fortune (for children). New York, Dodd Mead, 1916.
Two Little Women and Treasure House (for children). New York, Dodd Mead, 1916.
Two Little Women on a Holiday (for children). New York, Dodd Mead, 1917.
Baubles. New York, Dodd Mead, 1917.
Doris of Dobbs Ferry (for children). New York, Doran, 1917.
Patty Blossom (for children). New York, Dodd Mead, 1917.
Patty-Bride (for children). New York, Dodd Mead, 1918.
Patty and Azalea (for children). New York, Dodd Mead, 1919.
A Concise Bibliography of the Works of Walt Whitman with Alfred Goldsmith. Boston, Houghton Mifflin, 1922.
Cross Word Puzzle Book. New York, Putnam, 1924.
Book of American Limericks. New York, Putnam, 1925.
A Book of Charades. New York, Doran, 1927.
All for Fun: Brain Teasers. New York, Day, 1933.
The Rest of My Life. Philadelphia, Lippincott, 1937.

Editor, *A Nonsense [Parody, Satire, Whimsey, Vers de Société] Anthology.* New York, Scribner, 5 vols., 1902–07.
Editor, *Such Nonsense.* New York, Doran, 1918.
Editor, *The Book of Humorous Verse.* New York, Doran, 1920; revised edition, 1936.
Editor, *An Outline of Humor.* New York, Putnam, 1923.
Editor, *Ask Me a Question.* Philadelphia, Winston, 1927.
Editor, *American Detective Stories.* New York, Oxford University Press, 1927.

Editor, *Best American Mystery Stories of the Year, Volume One* [and *Two*].   New York, Day, 2 vols., 1931–32.
Editor, *The World's Best Humor.*   New York, Boni, 1933.
Editor, *The Cat in Verse.*   Boston, Little Brown, 1935.

*   *   *

Of Carolyn Wells it must be very nearly true to say that she never had an unpublished thought. An accomplished parodist, an indefatigable anthologist, a bibliographer and collector of Whitman, the author of a number of "society" novels of the Edwardian period, and the author of the first important critical work on detective fiction, she found time at last even to write her autobiography.

Her detective novels, inevitably, since she produced three or four a year from about 1915 to 1940, are written to a formula: the characters are brought before us, the conflicts suggested and the suspicions cast; the crime, invariably murder, and usually only one, is committed; the police and the amateurs are baffled; some five chapters before the end the professional detective is summoned, often by the chief suspect, often by a personal friend of the detective, for he is quite *persona grata* in the upper-class circles in which the novel almost always takes place; the detective explicates the case, with all in attendance, and the criminal often confirms his guilt with his suicide; the juvenile leads (one of them often a prime suspect), whose love has been secondary to the murder story, come together.

While Wells's grasp of plot construction is considerable, her gift for characterization is not, and even her detectives are personally unmemorable, partly because their late arrival gives us little opportunity to see their ratiocinative methods at work. Four of her detectives are worth special mention. Lorimer Lane, whose shrewdness is not evident in his bland, middle-aged reserve, may be seen to best advantage in *The Fourteenth Key*. Pennington (Penny) Wise and his rather bizarre young female assistant Zizi, who is generally shrewder than he, are best seen in *The Luminous Face*. Kenneth Carlisle, a movie actor turned detective, uses his acting ability for easier entrapment of criminals, best seen in *The Doorstep Murders* or *The Skeleton at the Feast*. By far the most prominent, Fleming Stone, "the great man," appeared first in a short story in 1906, and stayed with her to the end. But even Stone lacks character; it is often easier, in retrospect, to recall the plot of one of Wells's novels than to place the right detective in it. Two novels, however, in which Stone appears early enough for us to see something of his methods are *The Broken O* and *The Wooden Indian*.

In her 80 novels Wells uses a variety of background—the world of the theatre (*Prillilgirl*), the world of politics (*The Mystery of the Sycamore*), the academic world (*The Mystery Girl*)—yet none of these novels widens our understanding of these worlds. Her range of murder method is not wide: stabbing and shooting account for most of the deaths. She returned several times (*Raspberry Jam, Face Cards, The Daughter of the House*) to the locked room as the scene for her murder, and at least once (*The Tannahill Tangle*) set a double murder behind locked doors.

The device that Wells used most often is the change of identity. Substitutions spin the plot of *The Daughter of the House* and *The Fourteenth Key*. Two of her novels turn on the murderer's having a twin or double to provide him with an alibi. The theme is rather egregiously used in *Vicky Van*, in which the central character leads two different existences in adjoining houses. Wells does not probe the theme of identity change for psychological penetration, but neither does she ever fall back on the supernatural as explanation.

Wells's novels make very entertaining reading, but they do not notably enlighten. *The Technique of the Mystery Story* deserves some homage as the first in its field, but its principal interest now is in its cataloguing of contemporary mystery writers, and its codification of rules for writing in the genre.

—Barrie Hayne

———

WELLS, Tobias. *See* **FORBES, Stanton.**

———

WENTWORTH, Patricia. Pseudonym for Dora Amy Elles. British. Born in Mussoorie, India, in 1878. Educated privately and at Blackheath High School, London. Married 1) George Dillon (died 1906), three stepsons; 2) George Oliver Turnbull in 1920, one daughter. Lived in Surrey after 1920. *Died 28 January 1961.*

C RIME P UBLICATIONS

Novels (series: Inspector Ernest Lamb; Maud Silver)

The Astonishing Adventure of Jane Smith.   London, Melrose, and Boston, Small Maynard, 1923.
The Red Lacquer Case.   London, Melrose, 1924; Boston, Small Maynard, 1925.
The Annam Jewel.   London, Melrose, 1924; Boston, Small Maynard, 1925.
The Black Cabinet.   London, Hodder and Stoughton, 1925; Boston, Small Maynard, 1926.
The Dower House Mystery.   London, Hodder and Stoughton, 1925; Boston, Small Maynard, 1926.
The Amazing Chance.   London, Hodder and Stoughton, 1926; Philadelphia, Lippincott, 1927.
Anne Belinda.   London, Hodder and Stoughton, 1927; Philadelphia, Lippincott, 1928.
Hue and Cry.   London, Hodder and Stoughton, and Philadelphia, Lippincott, 1927.
Grey Mask (Silver).   London, Hodder and Stoughton, 1928; Philadelphia, Lippincott, 1929.
Will-o'-the-Wisp.   London, Hodder and Stoughton, and Philadelphia, Lippincott, 1928.
Fool Errant.   London, Hodder and Stoughton, and Philadelphia, Lippincott, 1929.
Beggar's Choice.   London, Hodder and Stoughton, 1930; Philadelphia, Lippincott, 1931.
The Coldstone.   London, Hodder and Stoughton, and Philadelphia, Lippincott, 1930.
Kingdom Lost.   Philadelphia, Lippincott, 1930; London, Hodder and Stoughton, 1931.
Danger Calling.   London, Hodder and Stoughton, and Philadelphia, Lippincott, 1931.
Nothing Venture.   London, Cassell, and Philadelphia, Lippincott, 1932.
Red Danger.   London, Cassell, 1932; as *Red Shadow*, Philadelphia, Lippincott, 1932.
Seven Green Stones.   London, Cassell, 1933; as *Outrageous Fortune*, Philadelphia, Lippincott, 1933.

Walk with Care.   London, Cassell, and Philadelphia, Lippincott, 1933.

Fear by Night.   London, Hodder and Stoughton, and Philadelphia, Lippincott, 1934.

Devil-in-the-Dark.   London, Hodder and Stoughton, 1934; as *Touch and Go*, Philadelphia, Lippincott, 1934.

Blindfold. London, Hodder and Stoughton, and Philadelphia, Lippincott, 1935.

Red Stefan.   London, Hodder and Stoughton, and Philadelphia, Lippincott, 1935.

Hole and Corner.   London, Hodder and Stoughton, and Philadelphia, Lippincott, 1936.

Dead or Alive.   London, Hodder and Stoughton, and Philadelphia, Lippincott, 1936.

The Case Is Closed (Silver).   London, Hodder and Stoughton, and Philadelphia, Lippincott, 1937.

Down Under.   London, Hodder and Stoughton, and Philadelphia, Lippincott, 1937.

Mr. Zero.   London, Hodder and Stoughton, and Philadelphia, Lippincott, 1938.

Run!   London, Hodder and Stoughton, and Philadelphia, Lippincott, 1938.

The Blind Side (Lamb).   London, Hodder and Stoughton, and Philadelphia, Lippincott, 1939.

Lonesome Road (Silver).   London, Hodder and Stoughton, and Philadelphia, Lippincott, 1939.

Who Pays the Piper? (Lamb).   London, Hodder and Stoughton, 1940; as *Account Rendered*, Philadelphia, Lippincott, 1940.

Rolling Stone.   London, Hodder and Stoughton, and Philadelphia, Lippincott, 1940.

Unlawful Occasions.   London, Hodder and Stoughton, 1941; as *Weekend with Death*, Philadelphia, Lippincott, 1941.

In the Balance (Silver).   Philadelphia, Lippincott, 1941; as *Danger Point*, London, Hodder and Stoughton, 1942.

Pursuit of a Parcel (Lamb).   London, Hodder and Stoughton, and Philadelphia, Lippincott, 1942.

The Chinese Shawl (Silver).   London, Hodder and Stoughton, and Philadelphia, Lippincott, 1943.

Miss Silver Deals with Death. Philadelphia, Lippincott, 1943; as *Miss Silver Intervenes*, London, Hodder and Stoughton, 1944.

The Key (Silver).   Philadelphia, Lippincott, 1944; London, Hodder and Stoughton, 1946.

The Clock Strikes Twelve (Silver).   Philadelphia, Lippincott, 1944; London, Hodder and Stoughton, 1945.

She Came Back (Silver).   Philadelphia, Lippincott, 1945; as *The Traveller Returns*, London, Hodder and Stoughton, 1948.

Silence in Court.   Philadelphia, Lippincott, 1945; London, Hodder and Stoughton, 1947.

Pilgrim's Rest (Silver).   Philadelphia, Lippincott, 1946; London, Hodder and Stoughton, 1948; as *Dark Threat*, New York, Popular Library, 1951.

Latter End (Silver).   Philadelphia, Lippincott, 1947; London, Hodder and Stoughton, 1949.

Wicked Uncle (Silver).   Philadelphia, Lippincott, 1947; as *Spotlight*, London, Hodder and Stoughton, 1949.

The Case of William Smith (Silver).   Philadelphia, Lippincott, 1948; London, Hodder and Stoughton, 1950.

Eternity Ring (Silver).   Philadelphia, Lippincott, 1948; London, Hodder and Stoughton, 1950.

Miss Silver Comes to Stay.   Philadelphia, Lippincott, 1949; London, Hodder and Stoughton, 1951.

The Catherine Wheel (Silver).   Philadelphia, Lippincott, 1949; London, Hodder and Stoughton, 1951.

The Brading Collection (Silver).   Philadelphia, Lippincott, 1950; London, Hodder and Stoughton, 1952; as *Mr. Brading's Collection*, London Severn House, 1987.

Through the Wall (Silver).   Philadelphia, Lippincott, 1950; London, Hodder and Stoughton, 1952.

Anna, Where Are You? (Silver).   Philadelphia, Lippincott, 1951; London, Hodder and Stoughton, 1953; as *Death at Deep End*, New York, Pyramid, 1963.

The Ivory Dagger (Silver).   Philadelphia, Lippincott, 1951; London, Hodder and Stoughton, 1953.

The Watersplash (Silver).   Philadelphia, Lippincott, 1951; London, Hodder and Stoughton, 1954.

Ladies' Bane (Silver).   Philadelphia, Lippincott, 1952; London, Hodder and Stoughton, 1954.

Vanishing Point (Silver).   Philadelphia, Lippincott, 1953; London, Hodder and Stoughton, 1955.

Out of the Past (Silver).   Philadelphia, Lippincott, 1953; London, Hodder and Stoughton, 1955.

The Benevent Treasure (Silver).   Philadelphia, Lippincott, 1954; London, Hodder and Stoughton, 1956.

The Silent Pool (Silver).   Philadelphia, Lippincott, 1954; London, Hodder and Stoughton, 1956.

Poison in the Pen (Silver).   Philadelphia, Lippincott, 1955; London, Hodder and Stoughton, 1957.

The Listening Eye (Silver).   Philadelphia, Lippincott, 1955; London, Hodder and Stoughton, 1957.

The Gazebo (Silver).   Philadelphia, Lippincott, 1956; London, Hodder and Stoughton, 1958; as *The Summerhouse*, New York, Pyramid, 1967.

The Fingerprint (Silver).   Philadelphia, Lippincott, 1956; London, Hodder and Stoughton, 1959.

The Alington Inheritance (Silver).   Philadelphia, Lippincott, 1958; London, Hodder and Stoughton, 1960.

The Girl in the Cellar (Silver).   London, Hodder and Stoughton, 1961.

OTHER PUBLICATIONS

Novels

A Marriage under the Terror.   London, Melrose, and New York, Putnam, 1910.

A Little More Than Kin.   London, Melrose, 1911; as *More Than Kin*, New York, Putnam, 1911.

The Devil's Wind.   London, Melrose, 1912.

The Fire Within.   London, Melrose, 1913.

Simon Heriot.   London, Melrose, 1914.

Queen Anne Is Dead.   London, Melrose, 1915.

Verse

A Child's Rhyme Book.   London, Melrose, 1910.

Beneath the Hunter's Moon: Poems.   London, Hodder and Stoughton, 1945.

The Pool of Dreams: Poems.   London, Hodder and Stoughton, 1953; Philadelphia, Lippincott, 1954.

Other

Earl or Chieftain? The Romance of Hugh O'Neill.   Dublin, Catholic Truth Society of Ireland, 1919.

*   *   *

Although non-series mystery novels and a sequence of detective novels featuring the questionable competence of Inspector Lamb are included among Patrica Wentworth's dozens of contributions to the genre, she is best known for her enduring creation Miss Maud Silver whose career at a private detective agency after her retirement from the schoolroom spans 30 years.

Although Miss Silver is often compared with Christie's Miss Jane Marple, there is a major difference between the two. Unlike Miss Marple, whose knowledge of her village is unparalleled and whose understanding of human nature is keen but whose status is always amateur, Miss Silver is a professional detective. She uses her drawing room as an office, having furnished it with a sensible desk; she undertakes cases for both friends and strangers; she is efficient and workmanlike in her investigations; most significantly she is paid for her work. Generally Miss Silver's clients are recommended by friends whom she has assisted in the past; her acquaintances seem to populate most of the English countryside and almost every book mentions previous cases she has solved. Even Miss Silver's relationship with the police is socially rather than professionally based; Frank Abbott is both friend and, perhaps, surrogate nephew. Miss Silver's professional appearance is undercut by two features: her clothing and her knitting. In *The Gazebo* her dress is described as one forced upon undemanding elderly ladies by aggressive salewomen; her spinster's hats—black felt in winter and black straw in summer—are noted in most volumes. The small, delicately colored children's garments which Miss Silver is usually knitting serve to diminish her professional threat and seen to suggest domestic comfort and safety to frightened clients or old-maid foolishness to unperceptive suspects.

Despite appearances, this detective carefully investigates background facts, interviews witnesses, tails questionable suspects, sidesteps the law to enter a locked house. She uncovers the truth and saves the innocent before the police have solved the case. Her clients are usually doubly innocent: first, they have not committed any crime or, usually, even any social solecism; second, they are quite young, often in love, and through naivety leave their actions open to misinterpretation by the cynical or the official. Always, they are from nice families, and Miss Silver's investigation both demonstrates their innocence of the crime and ensures that they continue to be regarded as ladies or gentlemen.

While Lewis Brading's security precautions for his jewel collection are unusual, other elements of *The Brading Collection*, a typical Silver story, conform to traditional demands. Greed and sexual attraction motivate several obvious suspects; love and suspicion vibrate between the young couple; past mistakes haunt the falsely accused. Miss Silver's detection, always undertaken to discover the truth and protect the innocent rather than to save a client, is juxtaposed with her moral lectures and Tennyson quotations. As expected, the good are rewarded with marriage and financial security; the wicked are punished with death—here, murder and suicide.

Wentworth's plotting is straighforward and classical; no accusation of bad faith can be leveled at her. The writing is clear-cut and competent; the details are reasonable. It is true that the novels are not of equal value, and after 40 cases Miss Silver's appeal wanes; however, the best of them, like *The Fingerprint*, *Grey Mask*, *The Brading Collection*, and *Poison in the Pen*, are dependable and engaging tales of detection.

—Kathleen Gregory Klein

WESTLAKE, Donald E(dwin Edmund). Also writes as Curt Clark; Tucker Coe; Timothy J. Culver; Richard Stark. American. Born in New York City, 12 July 1933. Educated at State University of New York, Plattsburgh, 1949–50, and Binghamton, 1956–57. Served in the United States Air Force, 1954–56. Married 1) Nedra Henderson in 1957 (divorced 1966); 2) Sandra Kalb in 1967 (divorced 1975); 3) Abigail Adams in 1979; four sons. Recipient: Mystery Writers of America Edgar Allan Poe award, 1967. Agent: Knox Burger Associates, 39½ Washington Square South, New York, New York 10012. Address: 409 Bleecker Street, New York, New York 10014, U.S.A.

CRIME PUBLICATIONS

Novels (series: Dortmunder and others)

The Mercenaries. New York, Random House, 1960; London, Boardman, 1961; as *The Smashers*, New York, Dell, 1962.
Killing Time. New York, Random House, 1961; London, Boardman, 1962; as *The Operator*, New York, Dell, 1964.
361. New York, Random House, and London, Boardman, 1962.
Killy. New York, Random House, 1963; London, Boardman, 1964.
Pity Him Afterwards. New York, Random House, 1964; London, Boardman, 1965.
The Fugitive Pigeon. New York, Random House, 1965; London, Boardman, 1966.
The Busy Body. New York, Random House, and London, Boardman, 1966.
The Spy in the Ointment. New York, Random House, 1966; London, Boardman, 1967.
Anarchaos (as Curt Clark). New York, Ace, 1967.
God Save the Mark. New York, Random House, 1967; London, Joseph, 1968.
Who Stole Sassi Manoon? New York, Random House, 1969; London, Hodder and Stoughton, 1971.
Somebody Owes Me Money. New York, Random House, 1969; London, Hodder and Stoughton, 1970.
The Hot Rock (Dortmunder). New York, Simon and Schuster, 1970; London, Hodder and Stoughton, 1971.
Ex Officio (as Timothy J. Culver). New York, Evans, 1970; as *Power Play*, New York, Dell, 1971.
I Gave at the Office. New York, Simon and Schuster, 1971; London, Hodder and Stoughton, 1972.
Bank Shot (Dortmunder). New York, Simon and Schuster, and London, Hodder and Stoughton, 1972.
Cops and Robbers. New York, Evans, and London, Hodder and Stoughton, 1972.
Gangway, with Brian Garfield. New York, Evans, 1973; London, Barker, 1975.
Help I Am Being Held Prisoner. New York, Evans, 1974; London, Hodder and Stoughton, 1975.
Jimmy the Kid (Dortmunder). New York, Evans, 1974; London, Hodder and Stoughton, 1975.
Two Much! New York, Evans, 1975; London, Hodder and Stoughton, 1976.
Brothers Keepers. New York, Evans, 1975; London, Hodder and Stoughton, 1977.
Dancing Aztecs. New York, Evans, 1976; as *A New York Dance*, London, Hodder and Stoughton, 1979.
Enough. New York, Evans, 1977; London, Hodder and Stoughton, 1980.
Nobody's Perfect (Dortmunder). New York, Evans, 1977; London, Hodder and Stoughton, 1978.
Castle in the Air. New York, Evans, and London, Hodder and Stoughton, 1980.

Kahawa. New York, Viking Press, 1982; London, Allison and Busby, 1985.
Why Me? (Dortmunder). New York, Viking Press, 1983; London, Futura, 1984.
Levine. New York, Mysterious Press, 1984.
High Adventure. New York, Mysterious Press, 1985.
Good Behavior (Dortmunder). New York, Mysterious Press, 1985; London, Allison and Busby, 1987.
Trust Me on This. New York, Mysterious Press, 1988; London, Allison and Busby, 1989.
Sacred Monster. New York, Mysterious Press, 1989.
Drowned Hope (Dortmunder). New York, Mysterious Press, 1990.

Novels as Richard Stark (series: Alan Grofield; Parker)

The Hunter (Parker). New York, Pocket Books, 1962; as *Point Blank*, London, Hodder and Stoughton, 1967.
The Man with the Getaway Face (Parker). New York, Pocket Books, 1963; as *The Steel Hit*, London, Hodder and Stoughton, 1971.
The Outfit (Parker). New York, Pocket Books, 1963; London, Hodder and Stoughton, 1971.
The Mourner (Parker). New York, Pocket Books, 1963; London, Hodder and Stoughton, 1971.
The Score (Parker; Grofield). New York, Pocket Books, 1964; as *Killtown*, London, Hodder and Stoughton, 1971.
The Jugger (Parker). New York, Pocket Books, 1965; London, Hodder and Stoughton, 1971.
The Seventh (Parker). New York, Pocket Books, 1966; as *The Split*, London, Hodder and Stoughton, 1969.
The Handle (Parker; Grofield). New York Pocket Books, 1966; as *Run Lethal*, London, Hodder and Stoughton, 1972.
The Rare Coin Score (Parker). New York, Fawcett, 1967; London, Hodder and Stoughton, 1968.
The Damsel (Grofield). New York, Macmillan, 1967; London, Hodder and Stoughton, 1968.
The Green Eagle Score (Parker). New York, Fawcett, 1967; London, Hodder and Stoughton, 1968.
The Black Ice Score (Parker). New York, Fawcett, 1968; London, Hodder and Stoughton, 1969.
The Dame (Grofield). New York, Macmillan, and London, Hodder and Stoughton, 1969.
The Sour Lemon Score (Parker). New York, Fawcett, and London, Hodder and Stoughton, 1969.
The Blackbird (Grofield). New York, Macmillan, 1969; London, Hodder and Stoughton, 1970.
Deadly Edge (Parker). New York, Random House, 1971; London, Hodder and Stoughton, 1972.
Slayground (Parker). New York, Random House, 1971; London, Hodder and Stoughton, 1973.
Lemons Never Lie (Grofield). Cleveland, World, 1971.
Plunder Squad (Parker). New York, Random House, 1972; London, Hodder and Stoughton, 1974.
Butcher's Moon (Parker; Grofield). New York, Random House, 1974; London, Hodder and Stoughton, 1977.

Novels as Tucker Coe (series: Mitch Tobin in all books)

Kinds of Love, Kinds of Death. London, Random House, 1966; London, Souvenir Press, 1967.
Murder among Children. New York, Random House, and London, Souvenir Press, 1968.
Wax Apple. New York, Random House, 1970; London, Gollancz, 1973.
A Jade in Aries. New York, Random House, 1971; London, Gollancz, 1973.

Don't Lie to Me. New York, Random House, 1972; London, Gollancz, 1974.

Short Stories

The Curious Facts Preceding My Execution and Other Fictions. New York, Random House, 1968.
Tomorrow's Crimes. New York, Mysterious Press, 1989.

Uncollected Short Stories

"Arrest," in *Manhunt* (New York), January 1958.
"Everybody Killed Sylvia," in *Mystery Digest* (New York), May 1958.
"The Devil's Printer," in *Mystery Digest* (New York), September 1958.
"Sinner or Saint," in *Mystery Digest* (New York), December 1958.
"Decoy for Murder," in *Mystery Digest* (New York), March 1959.
"Death for Sale," in *Mystery Digest* (New York), April 1959.
"One on a Desert Island," in *Alfred Hitchcock's Mystery Magazine* (New York), June 1959.
"The Ledge Bit," in *Mystery Digest* (New York), September–October 1959.
"Knife Fighter," in *Guilty* (New York), November 1959.
"The Best-Friend Murder," in *Alfred Hitchcock's Mystery Magazine* (New York), December 1959.
"An Empty Threat," in *Manhunt* (New York), February 1960.
"Fresh Out of Prison," in *Guilty* (New York), June 1960.
"Friday Night," in *Tightrope* (New York), June 1960.
"Cat Killers," in *Shock* (New York), September 1960.
"Anatomy of an Anatomy," in *Alfred Hitchcock's Mystery Magazine* (New York), September 1960.
"Break-Out," in *Ed McBain's Mystery Book 3* (New York), 1961.
"The Feel of the Trigger," in *Alfred Hitchcock's Mystery Magazine* (New York), October 1961.
"A Time to Die," in *The Saint* (New York), January 1962.
"A Toast to the Damned," in *Off Beat Detective Stories* (New York), April 1962.
"Lock Your Room," in *Alfred Hitchcock's Mystery Magazine* (New York), August 1962.
"The Sound of Murder," in *Alfred Hitchcock's Mystery Magazine* (New York), December 1962.
"Nackles" as Curt Clark, in *Fantasy and Science Fiction* (New York), January 1964.
"The Death of a Bum," in *Mike Shayne Mystery Magazine* (New York), June 1965.
"The Letter," in *Mike Shayne Mystery Magazine* (New York), August 1965.
"Stage Fright," in *The Saint* (New York), September 1965.
"The Method," in *Alfred Hitchcock's Mystery Magazine* (New York), October 1965.
"The Spoils System," in *Alfred Hitchcock's Mystery Magazine* (New York), December 1965.
"Teamwork," in *Shell Scott Mystery Magazine* (New York), February 1966.
"Cool O'Toole," in *Alfred Hitchcock's Mystery Magazine* (New York), September 1966.
"Journey to Death," in *Alfred Hitchcock Presents: Stories That Scared Even Me*. New York, Random House, 1967.
"Come Back, Come Back," in *Alfred Hitchcock's Tales to Scare You Stiff*, edited by Eleanor Sullivan. New York, Davis, 1978.
"Heaven Help Us," in *Playboy* (Chicago). December 1983.

"Don't You Know There's a War On?," in *Playboy* (Chicago), December 1983.
"After I'm Gone," in *Ellery Queen's Mystery Magazine* (New York), June 1984.
"The World's a Stage," in *Playboy* (Chicago). July 1984.
"A Good Story," in *Playboy* (Chicago), October 1984.
"Breathe Deep," in *Playboy* (Chicago), July 1985.
"Hitch Your Spaceship to a Star," in *Playboy* (Chicago), December 1985.
"Horse Laugh," in *Playboy* (Chicago), June 1986.
"Here's Looking at You," in *Playboy* (Chicago), May 1989.
"Too Many Crooks," in *Playboy* (Chicago), August 1989.
"A Midsummer Daydream," in *Playboy* (Chicago), May 1990.

OTHER PUBLICATIONS

Novels

Up Your Banners. New York, Macmillan, 1969; London, Hodder and Stoughton, 1971.
Adios, Scheherazade. New York, Simon and Schuster, 1970; London, Hodder and Stoughton, 1971.
A Likely Story. New York, Penzler, 1984.

Plays

Screenplays: *Cops and Robbers*, 1972; *Hot Stuff*, with Michael Kane, 1975; *The Stepfather*, 1987; *The Grifters*, 1990.

Other

Philip (for children) New York, Crowell, 1967.
Under an English Heaven. New York, Simon and Schuster, and London, Hodder and Stoughton, 1972.
"Hearing Voices in My Head," in *Murder Ink: The Mystery Reader's Companion*, edited by Dilys Winn. New York, Workman, 1977.

Editor, with William Tenn, *Once Against the Law*. New York, Macmillan, 1968.

*

Manuscript Collection: Mugar Memorial Library, Boston University.

Donald E. Westlake comments:

Being prolific is at once both delightful and embarrassing. As I go along from day to day, it doesn't *seem* to me I'm getting much accomplished, but on those rare occasions (such as the present one) when I tot it all up, there is rather a mess here.

When I began, 25 years ago, I scattered my shots in a variety of directions, only very gradually focusing my fire enough to be recognizably the same person over a span of time—a week, say. As the pseudonyms and the other genres have sloughed off I do seem to have dug myself a very specific niche—or grave—here on the dim moor of mystery fiction. My subject (unless I'm wrong about this) seems to be Bewilderment. Or don't you agree?

*   *   *

If there's a common thread running through Donald E. Westlake's "serious" crime novels, it is that crime is just another business enterprise and the intelligent professional criminal simply an Organization Man. His earliest suspense novels under his own name, like *The Mercenaries* (1960), dealt with the world of organized crime as seen from within, and did so with a rigor and objectivity worthy of Dashiell Hammett, so that Westlake quickly established himself as a master of what Anthony Boucher called "sustained narrative and observation within the framework of a self-consistent world, alien to law and convention."

In 1962 Westlake adopted the byline of Richard Stark to launch a series of paperback originals about a cold-blooded professional thief known only as Parker. *The Hunter*, in which Parker seeks revenge after being betrayed and left for dead by his former associates, was described by Boucher as "a harsh and frightening story of criminal warfare and vengeance . . . written with economy, understatement and a deadly amoral objectivity." Five years later the book was freely adapted by director John Boorman into *Point Blank*, the finest *film noir* of the decade. In the same year Westlake took Alan Grofield, one of the recurring characters in earlier Parker capers, and gave him his own series under the Stark by-line. Grofield is not a full-time thief but robs banks and other institutions to support his less than scintillating career as a stage actor, and his adventures tend to be lighter in tone than Parker's. Westlake enjoys interweaving the exploits of his heist men in unusually striking ways. The first chapters of Grofield's third solo caper, *The Blackbird* (1969), and of a later Parker book, *Slayground* (1971), describe the exact same event—an armored car robbery that goes haywire—each from its protagonist's point of view, and the books go on to tell what happened to their respective viewpoint characters after the auto smash-up that ends their common experiences. Grofield and Parker are reunited in the last, longest and perhaps bloodiest of the Richard Stark novels, *Butcher's Moon* (1974).

During the late 1960's Westlake as Tucker Coe wrote five novels in the disillusioned, minimally violent private-eye tradition of Ross Macdonald. Protagonist of the quintet is Mitch Tobin, an ex-cop kicked off the NYPD in disgrace because of his squad-car partner's death while Tobin was in bed with a woman. Since then the guilt-wracked Tobin has buried himself in his Queens house, supported financially and emotionally by his forgiving wife, unable to relate to his teenage son or to function in the world outside. In the first four of the five novels about him, Tobin is interrupted in his self-imposed task of enclosing his house with a high wall and, in the role of unlicensed private investigator, is forced to enter the universe of some out-group which has constructed its own walls and bears other marked resemblances to himself. As he passes through the worlds of the professional criminal, the disaffected young, the mentally ill and the sexually different, he slowly comes to realize that he's not unique in his isolation and guilt and begins to accept himself and return to the real world. The best novel in the series is *Wax Apple*, in which a psychiatrist hires Tobin to pose as an ex-mental patient and find out which resident of a "halfway house" is responsible for a number of vicious pranks. In his fifth and last case, *Don't Lie to Me*, Tobin has obtained a private detective's license and is no longer obsessed with his wall.

Meanwhile, after his first few works in the Hammett tradition, Westlake's novels under his own name, beginning with *The Fugitive Pigeon* (1965), had mutated into wildly humorous farces populated by a parade of indolent young men, each wanting only to "do his own thing" but propelled willy nilly or nilly willy into unlikely criminous predicaments. In *The Spy in the Ointment* a Greenwich Village pacifist finds himself in a terrorist cell; in *God Save the Mark* the prime sucker for every con game in New York is sucked into a crime problem both funnier and nastier than bunco; and in *Somebody Owes Me Money* a Runyonesque cabbie is trapped in the middle of a gang war. The same comic spirit informs most of Westlake's later non-series books. *Two Much!*, with its good-hearted amateur con man posing as twin brothers in order to marry each of two lovely and fabulously wealthy twin sisters, is as hilarious a comedy of suspense as the genre has produced. And *Trust Me on This* and *Sacred Monster* miraculously manage to deliver the comedic goods while still making us cringe at the sleaziness of tabloid scandal-sheet employees and Hollywood deal-makers.

Westlake's brightest contribution to the literature of criminal lunacy is the series of novels beginning with *The Hot Rock* (1970) in which the inept John Dortmunder and his team of idiot accomplices dream up and attempt to pull off the ultimate in big capers, only to wind up flat on their prats. These adventures—like *Bank Shot* where they steal an entire bank located inside a mobile trailer home—are light-hearted inversions of the dead serious crime in the Richard Stark novels; indeed the kidnap scheme in *Jimmy the Kid* is inspired when one of those very novels is read by a mush-witted thief. As of this writing the Dortmunder crew's latest outing is *Good Behavior* (1985), in which the fighting legion of nincompoops set out to liberate a nun being held prisoner by her evil father and his deprogrammers on the 76th floor of an impregnable Manhattan bank tower and at the same time to clean out several wholesale jewelers' shops that happen to be in the same building. These books take place in a fairy-tale world where no one gets killed, raped, tortured or even bruised badly, probably the closest thing to the world of P.G. Wodehouse that any American has conjured up. And it's pure bliss to spend a few hours there.

Westlake is a skillful and prolific writer, at home in a variety of subgenres and committed to no formula but readability. When the history of contemporary suspense fiction is compiled, he'll be recognized as one of the masters of the past third of a century.

—Francis M. Nevins, Jr.

WHALLEY, Peter. British. Born in Colne, Lancashire, 12 March 1946. Educated at St. Mary's College, Blackburn, Lancashire; University of Lancaster. Married Ruth Whalley in 1970; one daughter and one son. School teacher, London and Yorkshire, 1968–77. Since 1977 full-time writer. Agent: Lemon Unna and Durbridge Ltd., 24 Pottery Lane, Holland Park, London W11 4LZ. Address: Holly House, Green Lane, Slyne-with-Hest, Lancaster, Lancashire.

CRIME PUBLICATIONS

Novels

Post Mortem. London, Macmillan, 1982; New York, Walker, 1988.
The Mortician's Birthday Party. London, Macmillan, 1983; New York, Walker, 1989.
Old Murders. London, Macmillan, 1984; New York, Doubleday, 1989.
Love and Murder. London, Macmillan, 1985; New York, Walker, 1989.
Robbers. London, Macmillan, 1986; New York, Walker, 1987.
Bandits. London, Macmillan, 1986; as *Rogues*, New York, Walker, 1988.
Villains. London, Macmillan, 1987; as *Crooks*, New York, Walker, 1988.
Blackmailer's Summer. New York, Doubleday, 1990.

Uncollected Short Story

"My Love, I Could Never Leave You," in *Winter's Crimes 14*, edited by Hilary Watson, London, Macmillan, and New York, St. Martin's Press, 1982.

OTHER PUBLICATIONS

Plays

The Maroon Cortina (produced Liverpool, 1984); as *Local Murder*, London, French, 1987.
Dead of Night (produced Liverpool, 1989).

Radio Plays: *The Hilton Boy, The Competitors, Happy Families, Poachers, Nearly Dead, Miracles, Nightingale's Defence, Scapegoat, Uncertain Angel, Bodies Beautiful, Maniacs, Telephone Calls, Getting Away, The Liverpool Match, Maintaining Standards, Albert's Quest, Crises, Driving Through, Not Cricket, Love of a Good Woman, Last Tango in Salford, Who Shot Ada Tansey?, Urbane Riots, Conversations Prior to Kick-Off, Hooligans, The Maroon Cortina, Neighbourhood Watch, Cromwell Mansion, Top Twenty.*

Television Plays: *Coronation Street* series, *Albion Market* series, *Angels* series, *Families, Jury, About Books, Man of Morality, Risking It, Jigsaw.*

*   *   *

The not-so-thin red line of Peter Whalley's work is moral ambivalence. In almost all his novels the leading character is a criminal or a person living in the twilight zone somewhere between crime and honesty. All these people are likeable characters, who through their likeability force us to reconsider our own moral values. This moral dilemma goes through a very definite development in Whalley's work.

In his first two novels—*Post Mortem* and *The Mortician's Birthday Party*—the leading characters are married men who want to get rid of their (at least to them) boring wives. Both novels are told from the point of view of the husband, resulting in the reader's sympathy naturally going with him. This is also enhanced by clever plotting, which forces the reader to identify with the killer, almost hoping he'll get away with it. When, for example, George Webster gets rid of his wife's body by cutting her up and putting the different parts of her body in other peoples' coffins, we can't condone such behaviour but in our hearts we admire him!

These novels form Whalley's first period as a crime writer—classic stuff in a way, although there is no classical detective to expose the murder.

In his second period—in novels such as *Old Murders* and *Love and Murder*—the theme appears in a slightly different form. In these books the setting is modern England, with gang warfare, drugs, blackmail, and other forms of "modern" callous crime, without the "personal" element prominent in classical crime novels. In *Old Murders* the leading character, architect Christian Lewis, starts by fighting his criminal father-in-law but in the end takes over his criminal empire. *Love and Murder* features young Martyn Culley, a drifting young man who appeared earlier in *The Mortician's Birthday Party*. Forever on his way to yet another unsuccessful job interview, Martyn gets involved in helping a young girl hide a man she has killed. Though not really a criminal, he almost haplessly drifts into a life of deception and violence, and then almost as haplessly steps out of it.

This dimension of a New England and a new crime, as compared to the old crime of the classical crime novel, is also enhanced by the settings of the plots. During Whalley's first period he "takes crime out of the Venetian vase" and places it not in the alley, which had already been done—but in the smoky and dirty Midlands. This dimension is much more obvious in *Old Murders* and *Love and Murder* with the more modern type of crime the novels depict. This is a society created by the forces of capitalism and industrialism and it is a society of moral ambivalence, to which the characters have to adapt.

This is taken one step further in Whalley's third period, characterized by his new "hero," Harry Sommers, ex-bouncer, ex-con man and now a somewhat reluctant private detective. Though not doing anything really criminal himself, Harry constantly finds himself doing "honest" work for slightly dishonest people.

In *Villains* a job in southern Spain gives Sommers and his teacher girlfriend Jill a free holiday in the sun. Jill is absolutely aghast when she discovers that their neighbours, friends of Harry's employer, are criminals and fugitives from British law. For Harry it's the usual balancing act on the border of the land of the angels and the land of the devils.

Whalley's *oeuvre* is not generally characterized by deep psychological portraits, but by rather successful psychological sketches of small-time crooks, hapless youths, bored housewives and even more bored husbands, and one or two really peculiar characters like the mortician George Webster. Harry Sommers is Whalley's most convincing character, his moral uncertainties and social and personal insecurities are well portrayed.

Whalley resists the temptation to moralize in his novels. Justice doesn't necessarily have to prevail and the reader is allowed to make up his/her own mind. While Whalley's novels may not be great novels of ideas, they are however the thinking person's crime novels.

—Karl G. and Lilian Fredriksson

WHEAT, Carolyn. American. Address: 307 President Street, Brooklyn, New York 11231, U.S.A.

CRIME PUBLICATIONS

Novels (series: Cass Jameson in both books)

Dead Man's Thoughts. New York, St. Martin's Press, 1983.
Where Nobody Dies. New York, St. Martin's Press, 1986.

Uncollected Short Stories

"Crime Scene," in *Sisters in Crime 1*, edited by Marilyn Wallace, New York, Berkley, 1989; London, W.H. Allen, 1990.
"Cousin Cora," in *Sisters in Crime 2*, edited by Marilyn Wallace. New York, Berkley, 1990.

"Flake Piece," in *City Sleuths and Tough Guys*, edited by David McCullough. Boston, Houghton Mifflin, 1990.
"Ghost Station," in *A Woman's Eye*, edited by Sara Paretsky. New York, Delacorte Press, 1990.

* * *

Frequently, a young writer, whose first book is a big success, will have difficulties with the second. That's what happened to Carolyn Wheat, a New York attorney who added crime writing to her career. Her first novel, *Dead Man's Thoughts*, was nominated for an Edgar as the best first mystery of 1983. Critics and fans alike eagerly awaited her second. When *Where Nobody Dies* appeared in 1986, it was an interesting and readable book on its own, but without the cohesiveness and authority of the first.

However, not all the books of even MWA Grand Masters nor Dames of the British Empire are of consistent quality. If you're serious about the genre, you persevere, and that's what Wheat has done. In the past two years, she has published four short stories and worked on her third novel.

In her first appearance in *Dead Man's Thoughts*, Brooklyn Legal Aid attorney, Cass Jameson, is a strong, vivid woman; a woman of her time, deeply involved in her environment, clients, and friends. Finding the body of her lover and colleague and refusing to believe the case as the police read it, Cass undertakes an independent investigation. Her investigation gives us a powerful and panoramic picture of legal processes and the people involved in them: lawyers, judges, criminals, cops, and the men and women in their personal lives in Brooklyn and Manhattan.

The language grabs you (We spun along the spaghetti strands of highways that connect the outer boroughs to Manhattan.... Jesse Winthrop [a reporter] would have given his left ball to be sitting where I was. In Del Parma's office ... with formerly locked-up cases spread out in front of me like a banquet.). The details worked (Roirdan sat at a window table ... from the chilly vantage point of Hudson Street, the scene was pure Hopper. A man in a bar, seen through a dirty window. Waiting ... "Look, Detective Button... can I be frank with you?" This was a little like saying "with all due respect" to a judge—whenever you hear a lawyer say that, you know he's about to come out with something highly disrespectful, if not totally outrageous.).

In *Where Nobody Dies*, the cohesiveness and authority are missing. One of the book's problems, in my estimation, was making it part of the projected series. On its own, with another name for the heroine, it might have held together better. Jameson is not the same woman here that she was in *Dead Man's Thoughts*. She has gone into private practice and gets involved in the crimes through her client in a nasty custody case. Thereafter confusion sets in, from Cass's characterization to the details of the book.

However, in the recent short stories, Wheat has recaptured her authority and is reaching for versatility. In "Flake Piece," she writes from a policeman's viewpoint; in "Ghost Station," from an Anglo woman sergeant's; in "Crime Scene," from a Hispanic woman rookie cop's; in "Cousin Cora," from an 11-year-old girl's. All but "Cousin Cora" are set in New York. "Cousin Cora" takes place in rural Ohio in the early 1900's. The girl dreamed of emulating Sherlock Holmes, but when she did, the results were disastrous. The results were also disastrous for the male narrator in "Flake Piece," but both the women in "Ghost Station" and "Crime Scene" grew from their experience. The language, details, and emotions in all their variety from story to story reflect the authority and cohesiveness of *Dead Man's Thoughts*.

If these stories are true indicators, we should see another book of high quality when her third novel is published.

—Pearl G. Aldrich

WHEATLEY, Dennis (Yates). British. Born in London, 8 January 1897. Educated at Dulwich College, London, 1908; H.M.S. Worcester, 1909–13; privately in Germany, 1913. Married 1) Nancy Robinson in 1923 (divorced 1931), one son; 2) Joan Gwendoline Johnstone in 1931. Served in the Royal Field Artillery, City of London Brigade, 1914–17; 36th Ulster Division, 1917–19 (invalided out); recommissioned in Royal Air Force Volunteer Reserve, 1939; member, National Recruiting Panel, 1940–41; member, Joint Planning Staff of War Cabinet, 1941–44; Wing Commander, 1944–45; United States Army Bronze Star. Joined his father's wine business, Wheatley & Son, London, 1914; worked in the business, 1919–26; sole owner, 1926–31. Editor, Dennis Wheatley's Library of the Occult, Sphere Books, London, from 1973 (over 40 volumes). Received Livery of Vintners' Company, 1918, and Distillers' Company, 1922. Fellow, Royal Society of Arts, and Royal Society of Literature. *Died 11 November 1977.*

CRIME PUBLICATIONS

Novels (series: Roger Brook; Julian Day; Molly Fountain; Duke de Richleau; Gregory Sallust)

The Forbidden Territory (Richleau). London, Hutchinson, and New York, Dutton, 1933.
Such Power Is Dangerous. London, Hutchinson, 1933.
Black August (Sallust). London, Hutchinson, and New York, Dutton, 1934.
The Fabulous Valley. London, Hutchinson, 1934.
The Devil Rides Out (Richleau). London, Hutchinson, 1934.
The Eunuch of Stamboul. London, Hutchinson, and Boston, Little Brown, 1935.
They Found Atlantis. London, Hutchinson, and Philadelphia, Lippincott, 1936.
Murder Off Miami with J.G. Links. London, Hutchinson, 1936; New York, Rutledge Press, 1981; as *File on Bolitho Blane*, New York, Morrow, 1936.
Contraband (Sallust). London, Hutchinson, 1936.
The Secret War. London, Hutchinson, 1937.
Who Killed Robert Prentice? with J.G. Links. London, Hutchinson, 1937; as *File on Robert Prentice*, New York, Greenberg, 1937.
Uncharted Seas. London, Hutchinson, 1938.
The Malinsay Massacre with J.G. Links. London, Hutchinson, 1938; New York, Rutledge Press, 1981.
The Golden Spaniard (Richleau). London, Hutchinson, 1938.
The Quest of Julian Day. London, Hutchinson, 1939.
Herewith the Clues! with J.G. Links. London, Hutchinson, 1939; New York, Mayflower, 1982.
Sixty Days to Live. London, Hutchinson, 1939.
The Scarlet Imposter (Sallust). London, Hutchinson, 1940; New York, Macmillan, 1942.
Three Inquisitive People (Richleau). London, Hutchinson, 1940; New York, Macmillan, 1942.
Faked Passports (Sallust). London, Hutchinson, 1940; New York, Macmillan, 1943.

The Black Baroness (Sallust). London, Hutchinson, 1940; New York, Macmillan, 1942.
Strange Conflict (Richleau). London, Hutchinson, 1941.
The Sword of Fate (Day). London, Hutchinson, 1941; New York, Macmillan, 1944.
"V" for Vengeance (Sallust). London, Hutchinson, and New York, Macmillan, 1942.
The Man Who Missed the War. London, Hutchinson, 1945.
Codeword—Golden Fleece (Richleau). London, Hutchinson, 1946.
Come into My Parlour (Sallust). London, Hutchinson, 1946.
The Launching of Roger Brook. London, Hutchinson, 1947.
The Shadow of Tyburn Tree (Brook). London, Hutchinson, 1948; New York, Ballantine, 1973.
The Haunting of Toby Jugg. London, Hutchinson, 1948.
The Rising Storm (Brook). London, Hutchinson, 1949.
The Second Seal (Richleau). London, Hutchinson, 1950.
The Man Who Killed the King (Brook). London, Hutchinson, 1951; New York, Putnam, 1965.
Star of Ill-Omen. London, Hutchinson, 1952.
To the Devil—A Daughter (Fountain). London, Hutchinson, 1953.
Curtain of Fear. London, Hutchinson, 1953.
The Island Where Time Stands Still (Sallust). London, Hutchinson, 1954.
The Dark Secret of Josephine (Brook). London, Hutchinson, 1955.
The Ka of Gifford Hillary. London, Hutchinson, 1956.
The Prisoner in the Mask (Richleau). London, Hutchinson, 1957.
Traitors' Gate (Sallust). London, Hutchinson, 1958.
The Rape of Venice (Brook). London, Hutchinson, 1959.
The Satanist (Fountain). London, Hutchinson, 1960; New York, Ballantine, 1974.
Vendetta in Spain (Richleau). London, Hutchinson, 1961.
Mayhem in Greece. London, Hutchinson, 1962.
The Sultan's Daughter (Brook). London, Hutchinson, 1963.
Bill for the Use of a Body (Day). London, Hutchinson, 1964.
They Used Dark Forces (Sallust). London, Hutchinson, 1964.
Dangerous Inheritance (Richleau). London, Hutchinson, 1965.
The Wanton Princess (Brook). London, Hutchinson, 1966.
Unholy Crusade. London, Hutchinson, 1967.
The White Witch of the South Seas (Sallust). London, Hutchinson, 1968.
Evil in a Mask (Brook). London, Hutchinson, 1969.
Gateway to Hell (Richleau). London, Hutchinson, 1970; New York, Ballantine, 1973.
The Ravishing of Lady Mary Ware (Brook). London, Hutchinson, 1971.
The Strange Story of Linda Lee. London, Hutchinson, 1972.
The Irish Witch (Brook). London, Hutchinson, 1973.
Desperate Measures (Brook). London, Hutchinson, 1974.

Short Stories

Mediterranean Nights. London, Hutchinson, 1942; revised edition, London, Arrow, 1963.
Gunmen, Gallants, and Ghosts. London, Hutchinson, 1943; revised edition, London, Arrow, 1963.

OTHER PUBLICATIONS

Play

Screenplay: *An Englishman's Home* (*Madmen of Europe*), with others, 1939.

Other

Old Rowley: A Private Life of Charles II. London, Hutchinson, 1933; as *A Private Life of Charles II*, 1938.
Red Eagle: A Life of Marshal Voroshilov. London, Hutchinson, 1937.
Invasion (war game). London, Hutchinson, 1938.
Blockade (war game). London, Hutchinson, 1939.
Total War. London, Hutchinson, 1941.
The Seven Ages of Justerini's. London, Riddle Books, 1949; revised edition, as *1749–1965: The Eight Ages of Justerini's*, Aylesbury, Buckinghamshire, Dolphin, 1965.
Alibi (war game). London, Geographia, 1951.
Stranger Than Fiction. London, Hutchinson, 1959.
Saturdays with Bricks and Other Days under Shell-Fire. London, Hutchinson, 1961.
The Devil and All His Works. London, Hutchinson, and New York, American Heritage Press, 1971.
The Time Has Come: The Memoirs of Dennis Wheatley. London, Arrow, 1981.
The Young Man Said 1897–1914. London, Hutchinson, 1977.
Officer and Temporary Gentleman 1914–1919. London, Hutchinson, 1978.
Drink and Ink 1919–1977, edited by Anthony Lejeune. London, Hutchinson, 1979.
The Deception Planners: My Secret War, edited by Anthony Lejeune. London, Hutchinson, 1980.

Editor, *A Century of Horror Stories.* London, Hutchinson, 1935; Freeport, New York, Books for Libraries, 1971; selection as *Quiver of Horror* and *Shafts of Fear*, London, Arrow, 2 vols., 1965; as *Tales of Strange Doings* and *Tales of Strange Happenings*, Hutchinson, 2 vols., 1968.
Editor, *A Century of Spy Stories.* London, Hutchinson, 1938.
Editor, *Uncanny Tales.* London, Sphere, 2 vols., 1974.

*

Bibliography: *Fyra Decennier med Dennis Wheatley: En Biografi & Bibliografi* by Iwan Hedman and Jan Alexandersson, privately printed, 1963; revised edition, Strägnäs, Sweden, DAST, 1973.

* * *

Dennis Wheatley was the master of the macabre to some, the creator (with Joe Links) of a series of detective games, the "Crime Dossiers," to others. These were but a small part of his output as the "Prince of Thriller Writers." In 40 years he produced over 60 books of detection, adventure, romance, and fantasy; they sold over 20 million copies.

His characters believe in Britain and regret the passing of the Empire. Women generally know their place, if not in the bed of the hero, then passing ammunition in battle. His heroes are of the upper class (like the Duke de Richleau) or upper middle class (like Gregory Sallust) or rise to the upper class (like Roger Brook). When in *Dangerous Inheritance* Fleur Eaton declares herself a Socialist and shows an enlightened attitude about race, sex, and the underprivileged it is only partially a comment on the class consciousness of her father's generation. It also demonstrates the changes that have taken place in the world since de Richleau and Simon Aron set off into Soviet Russia to rescue Rex Van Ryn in the author's first published novel, *The Forbidden Territory*.

Wheatley's earliest books are fast-moving stories filled with good old-fashioned British ideals of fair play and sportsmanship sometimes making way for common sense in the face of

death. His first written novel (not published for 10 years), *Three Inquisitive People* (1940), is actually a formal deductive story of murder. It is important because it is also the story of how his modern Musketeers (de Richleau, Simon Aron, Rex Van Ryn, and Richard Eaton) met. The murderer is obvious from the beginning, too many threads of the plot are inadequately tied together, and the last chapter is an anti-climax of maudlin sentiment, but there is a surprise or two.

As Wheatley developed he began to fill his books with digressions on economic theory, politics, and history, often in undigested helpings. Much of *They Used Dark Forces* is a combination of military strategy and Churchillian war memoirs and works to the detriment of the sweep of the plot. More interesting are the meals: details about what was served and with which wine, and descriptions of food down to the simplest meal of hot buttered toast and apple jelly. Wheatley's dialogue is often a sort of formal melodrama, not quite like ordinary speech. His Americans speak in the improbable accents found only in British fiction. Often his characters seem to be lecturing each other rather than responding, and Simon Aron's nasal negative, "ner," can be an irritant to the critical reader.

Though Wheatley became known for his stories of black magic (and followers of this subgenre sought out his books) fewer than a dozen of the novels deal with that theme. His supernatural manifestations are often described in too much detail for them to be truly frightening; they could just as well have been replaced by gunmen or exotic villains. He comes closest to success in *The Haunting of Toby Jugg* and some of the short stories in *Gunmen, Gallants, and Ghosts*. His novels may be divided into six categories: black magic novels, adventure novels, and four sets of books with series characters: the Duke de Richleau, Gregory Sallust, Roger Brook, and Julian Day. Some of these were influenced by one of his own favorite writers, Alexandre Dumas.

The Richleau books take the Duke from age 18 in 1894 to his death in 1960 at 85. They were purposely based on Dumas's Musketeers cycle with the exiled monarchist (and his fondness for Hoyo de Monterrey cigars) in the role of Athos, the conservative Richard Eaton as d'Artagnan, Simon Aron (the Liberal Jew) as Aramis, and the democratic American, Rex Van Ryn, as Porthos. Improbable as the stories may seem, they are entertaining and the characters are more vivid than others in the Wheatley world. *The Forbidden Territory* may have been inspired by John Buchan's *Greenmantle*, and almost matches that novel in excitement.

The first Gregory Sallust book, *Black August*, is a Wellsian view of England in the future during a Communist revolution. The Satanic-looking cynical egoist, Sallust, is at his best, however, in the seven volumes about his wartime service as a British agent. He is sent by Sir Pellinore Gwaine-Cust (think of C. Aubrey Smith) behind German lines to help the German masses throw off the Nazi yoke. His major opponent is the chief of the Gestapo Foreign Department, Gruppenführer Grauber, and his major assistant is the beautiful Erika von Epp whom he marries at the end of the war. In *The Black Baroness* he thwarts a plan to kidnap the King of Norway, and in the last volume (*They Used Dark Forces*) he tries to defeat Hitler by recourse to occult means.

The Roger Brook novels are historical espionage and take Brook (as a special agent for Prime Minister William Pitt) into adventures throughout Europe, Asia, and the Americas between 1783 and 1815. Virtually every major historical event and person in that era is used by Wheatley in the series. The thread of the plot that binds the books together is Roger's love for Georgina Thursby whom he wins and loses by turns. In the process he searches for the Dauphin, brings Napoleon and Josephine together, foils a plot to assassinate the Emperor, and saves his own daughter from being sacrificed in a Black Mass on Walpurgis Night. While the plots may be impossibly melodramatic, the historical details are accurate and may be one of the reasons critics have given this series so much praise. The stories are told with such vigor that the reader is swept along and kept turning the page. Wheatley is not without a sense of humor as the scene in which Roger's wife, Mary, finds him in bed with Georgina in the final volume, *Desperate Measures*, shows.

The Julian Day trilogy is Wheatley's *Count of Monte Cristo*: a hero whose career has been ruined seeks revenge against those responsible.

While it's easy to fault Wheatley for archaic mannerisms and padded writing, there is no denying he has had an enormous readership around the world. He found that what the public wanted was what he enjoyed writing. A study of public taste could be based on his work.

—J. Randolph Cox

———

WHEELER, Hugh. *See* **QUENTIN, Patrick.**

———

WHITE, Jon (Ewbank) Manchip. British. Born in Cardiff, Glamorganshire, 22 June 1924. Educated at St. Catharine's College, Cambridge, 1942–43, 1946–50 (Open Exhibitioner in English Literature), M.A. (honours) in English, prehistoric archaeology, and oriental languages (Egyptology), and University Diploma in anthropology 1950. Served in the Royal Navy and the Welsh Guards, 1942–46. Married Valerie Leighton in 1946; two daughters. Story editor, BBC, London, 1950–51; senior executive officer, British Foreign Service, London, 1952–56; freelance writer, 1956–67: scenario editor, Hammer Films, London, 1956–57; screenwriter, Samuel Bronston Productions, Paris and Madrid, 1960–64; Professor of English, University of Texas, El Paso, 1967–77. Since 1977 Lindsay Young Professor of Humanities and Professor of English, University of Tennessee, Knoxville. Address: Department of English, University of Tennessee, Knoxville, Tennessee 37916, U.S.A.

CRIME PUBLICATIONS

Novels (series: Colonel Rickman)

The Mercenaries. London, Long, 1958; Canoga Park, California, Major, 1979.
Nightclimber (Rickman). London, Chatto and Windus, and New York, Morrow, 1968.
The Game of Troy (Rickman). London, Chatto and Windus, and New York, McKay, 1971.
The Garden Game (Rickman). London, Chatto and Windus, 1973; Indianapolis, Bobbs Merrill, 1974.
Send for Mr. Robinson. London, Panther, 1974; New York, Pinnacle, 1975; as *The Robinson Factor.* London, Panther, 1976.
The Moscow Papers. Canoga Park, California, Major, 1979.
Death by Dreaming. Cambridge, Massachusetts, Apple-Wood, 1981.

Short Stories

Chills and Fevers: Three Extravagant Tales. Woodstock, Vermont, Foul Play Press, 1983.

OTHER PUBLICATIONS

Novels

Mask of Dust. London, Hodder and Stoughton, 1953; as *Last Race,* New York, Mill, 1953.
Build Us a Dam. London, Hodder and Stoughton, 1955.
The Girl from Indiana. London, Hodder and Stoughton, 1956.
No Home but Heaven. London, Hodder and Stoughton, 1957.
Hour of the Rat. London, Hutchinson, 1962.
The Rose in the Brandy Glass. London, Eyre and Spottiswoode, 1965.
The Last Grandmaster: A Novel of Revolution. Woodstock, Vermont, Countryman Press, 1985.

Plays

Screenplays: *Day of Grace,* with Francis Searle, 1957; *Man with a Dog,* 1958; *The Camp on Blood Island,* with Val Guest, 1958; *Mystery Submarine,* with Hugh Woodhouse and Bertram Ostrer, 1963; *Crack in the World,* with Julian Halevy, 1965.

Radio and Television Plays and Adaptations: *Chariot of Fire; Who Killed Menna Lorraine?; The Rose in the Brandy Glass,* from his own novel; *Hour of the Rat,* from his own novel; *Mustard Yellow; A Question of Honour; Wolf Pack; Musk and Amber.*

Verse

Dragon and Other Poems. London, Fortune Press, 1943.
Salamander. London, Fortune Press, 1946.
The Rout of San Ramano. Aldington, Kent, Hand and Flower Press, 1952.
The Mountain Lion. London, Chatto and Windus, 1971.

Other

Ancient Egypt. London, Wingate, 1952; New York, Crowell, 1953; revised edition, London, Allen and Unwin, and New York, Dover, 1970.
Anthropology. London, English Universities Press, 1954; New York, Philosophical Library, 1955.
Marshal of France: The Life and Times of Maurice, Comte de Saxe. London, Hamish Hamilton, and Chicago, Rand McNally, 1962.
Everyday Life in Ancient Egypt. London, Batsford, 1963; New York, Putnam, 1964.
Diego Velazquez, Painter and Courtier. London, Hamish Hamilton, and Chicago, Rand McNally, 1969.
The Land God Made in Anger: Reflections on a Journey Through South West Africa. London, Allen and Unwin, and Chicago, Rand McNally, 1969.
Cortés and the Downfall of the Aztec Empire. London, Hamish Hamilton, and New York, St. Martin's Press, 1971.
A World Elsewhere: One Man's Fascination with the American Southwest. New York, Crowell, 1975; as *The Great American Desert,* London, Allen and Unwin, 1977.
Everyday Life of the North American Indian. London, Batsford, and New York, Holmes and Meier, 1979.
What to Do When the Russians Come: A Survivor's Guide, with Robert Conquest. New York, Stein and Day, 1984.

Editor, *Life in Ancient Egypt*, by Adolf Erman. New York, Dover, 1971.

Editor, *The Tomb of Tutankhamen*, by Howard Carter. New York, Dover, 1971.

Editor, *Manners and Customs of the Modern Egyptians*, by E.W. Lane. New York, Dover, 1972.

Editor, *Egypt and the Holy Land: 77 Historic Photographs by Francis Frith*. New York, Dover, and London, Constable, 1980.

Translator, *The Glory of Egypt*, by Samivel. London, Thames and Hudson, 1955.

*

Jon Manchip White comments:

My early fiction fell into the category of the conventional novel (though even then many critics noted that it possessed a strong streak of the bizarre). My books were primarily narratives with a straightforward realistic and social flavour. My later fiction, however, from *Nightclimber* onwards, falls into the more venerable category of the romance. That is, my more recent books are stories with a non-realistic, surrealist, or supra-realist basis: dramatic, highly-coloured, rooted not in reality but in fantasy, dreams and nightmares.

What really occupies and amuses me nowadays is to devise an improbable or actually outrageous fundamental idea, and then, by treating it in a matter-of-fact manner, to induce my reader into being gripped by it and ultimately into accepting it, with an uneasy sensation, as something that might well have occurred. My masters in this field are such writers as Poe, Stevenson, d'Aurévilly, Kafka, Borges, Cortázar, Calvino, Mandiargues. For me, to speak purely personally, this oblique and equivocal genre is for some reason more exciting and compelling than the mystery or detective story *pur sang*, which are securely anchored in reality. Perhaps my later fictions might be classed under some such label as "psychological thrillers" or even "psychic thrillers."

At any event, I like to call my "romances," of which it would be interesting to write increasingly extreme examples, my "Extravagant Tales." As I have said, they owe much of their inspiration to Poe and to what Stevenson was fond of referring to as his "crawlers"—stories to make the hair rise on the back of your neck.

*   *   *

Jon Manchip White is the author of strange, frightening, and (especially in his later fiction) gothic adventures. The settings stretch across several continents, sometimes in the same story, and generally are staged against dreamlike, outlandish backgrounds; his plots are charged with exciting and usually fantastic events; and instead of intricate designs his mysteries abound in brooding terrors. However, the most characteristic feature of White's tales is the middle-aged, courageous protagonist who must confront extreme obstacles to achieve his goals.

Mask of Dust, White's first novel, takes place in northern Italy, the setting of a spectacular international automobile race. The plot involves the dangers and thrills of the competition; its hero, a past champion and World War II fighter pilot now seeking a final triumph, must ultimately decide between his wife and the race. In *Hour of the Rat*, a senior civil servant feels driven to kill a Japanese industrialist whom he identifies, tentatively, as his persecutor in a prisoner of war camp. This protagonist resembles the heroes of *No Home but Heaven* and

The Mercenaries, who must also conflict with their societies. In *The Rose in the Brandy Glass* the conflict is not so much the physical strife faced by most of White's protagonists, but the psychological and moral conflict of serious fiction: retired Colonel Morrigan, refusing to compromise his integrity, struggles against the opportunity to share, dishonestly, in an inheritance.

Though exploited by corrupt and exorbitantly wealthy men, the protagonists of White's next three grotesque adventures risk their lives by clinging to their convictions. The hero of *Nightclimber*, White's most thrilling adventure novel, is an art historian who impulsively practices climbing tall urban buildings, a skill he perfected as a youth at Cambridge. In need of money, the protagonist accepts an offer from a decadent millionaire art collector to practice climbing an unknown thing in an unknown place. The novel's action takes place in several European cities, but its world is blurred by fantasy. White begins his story with images of the hero's frightening dream. And throughout the novel White juxtaposes the same images against the reality of the hero's escapade. Finally the brave historian, although not compelled to do so, makes the impossible leap across a huge gulf in the Cave of the Cyclops high in a Greek mountain. Later he miraculously drops onto the roof of the millionaire's headquarters and saves himself and a sexy middle-aged opera singer from the clutches of the Merganser Corporation.

As bizarre as the sides of the buildings and the mountain in *Nightclimber*, the setting of the deadly encounter in *The Game of Troy* is a huge maze on a diabolical Texan's ranch. The hero, a successful architect, falls in love with and finally saves the life of a beautiful woman, the wife and the most valuable toy of the financial genius. Again White combines the actuality of the lovers' pending death with a nightmarish atmosphere: the vengeful husband traps, drugs, and finally hunts the protagonists through the winding corridors and the dead-ends of the architect's own elaborate contraption. In the last of his "extravagant tales," *The Garden Game*, White tells the story of how Major Morven Rickman, a "soldier-of-fortune," desperately tries to rescue men from an evil group of tycoons who secretly entertain themselves by gambling on 20th-century gladiatorial combats. More than any other of his tales, this story contains characteristics of the gothic novel—the location of the pernicious games is a medieval schloss, complete with gloomy underground passages, dark staircases, and a mysterious tropical garden. White's mysteries, particularly his later ones, are spellbinding adventures with seemingly super-human heroes who strive for their almost impossible conquests in progressively more ghastly situations.

—Frances D. McConachie

WHITE, Lionel. Also wrote as Nick Carter. American. Born in Buffalo, New York, 9 July 1905. Served in the United States Army during World War II. Married 1) Helaine Levy in 1947 (marriage dissolved); 2) Hedy Bergida in 1970; one son. Police reporter, Cleveland and Canton, Ohio, 1923–25; reporter and editor, New York, 1925–33; editor, *American Detective* magazine from 1933; executive editor, Hillman Periodicals, 1936–39; publisher of fact detective magazines *World, World Detective*, and *Homicide Detective*, 1940–51. Address: P.O. Box 1737, Cullowhee, North Carolina 28723, U.S.A.

CRIME PUBLICATIONS

Novels

The Snatchers. New York, Fawcett, 1953; London, Miller, 1958.
To Find a Killer. New York, Dutton, 1954; London, Boardman, 1956; as *Before I Die*, New York, Tower, 1964.
Love Trap. New York, New American Library, 1955.
The Big Caper. New York, Fawcett, 1955; London, Fawcett, 1956.
Clean Break. New York, Dutton, and London, Boardman, 1955; as *The Killing*, New York, New American Library, 1956.
Flight into Terror. New York, Dutton, 1955; London, Boardman, 1957.
Operation—Murder. New York, Fawcett, 1956; London, Fawcett, 1958.
The House Next Door. New York, Dutton, 1956; London, Boardman, 1958.
Right for Murder. London, Boardman, 1957.
Death Takes the Bus. New York, Fawcett, 1957; London, Fawcett, 1958.
Hostage for a Hood. New York, Fawcett, 1957; London, Fawcett, 1958.
Too Young to Die. New York, Fawcett, 1958; London, Fawcett, 1959.
Coffin for a Hood. New York, Fawcett, 1958; London, Fawcett, 1959.
Invitation to Violence. New York, Dutton, and London, Boardman, 1958.
The Merriweather File. New York, Dutton, 1959; London, Boardman, 1960.
Rafferty. New York, Dutton, 1959; London, Boardman, 1960.
Run, Killer, Run. New York, Avon, 1959.
Lament for a Virgin. New York, Fawcett, and London, Muller, 1960.
Steal Big. New York, Fawcett, 1960; London, Muller, 1961.
The Time of Terror. New York, Dutton, 1960; London, Boardman, 1961.
Marilyn K. Derby, Connecticut, Monarch, 1960.
A Grave Undertaking. New York, Dutton, 1961; London, Boardman, 1962.
A Death at Sea. New York, Dutton, 1961; London, Boardman, 1962.
Obsession. New York, Dutton, 1962; London, Boardman, 1963.
The Money Trap. New York, Dutton, 1963; London, Boardman, 1964.
The Ransomed Madonna. New York, Dutton, 1964; London, Boardman, 1965.
The House on K Street. New York, Dutton, 1965; London, Boardman, 1966.
A Party to Murder. New York, Fawcett, 1966; London, Jenkins, 1968.
The Mind Poisoners (as Nick Carter, with Valerie Moolman). New York, Award, 1966; London, Tandem, 1968.
The Night of the Rape. New York, Dutton, 1967; London, Hale, 1969.
The Crimshaw Memorandum. New York, Dutton, 1967; London, Macdonald, 1968.
Hijack. New York, Macfadden, 1969; London, Hale, 1970.
Death of a City. Indianapolis, Bobbs Merrill, 1970; London, Hale, 1972.
The Mexico Run. New York, Fawcett, 1974.
A Rich and Dangerous Game. New York, McKay, 1974.
Jailbreak. London, Hale, 1976.

Uncollected Short Stories

"To Kill a Wife," in *Murder* (New York), September 1956.
"Invitation to Violence," in *Alfred Hitchcock's Mystery Magazine* (New York), May 1957.

OTHER PUBLICATIONS

Other

Protect Yourself, Your Family, and Your Property in an Unsafe World. Chatsworth, California, Books for Better Living, 1974.
The Walked Yard. New York, Woodhill, 1978.

Editor, with Philip C. Blackburn, *Logical Nonsense: Works, Now, for the First Time, Complete*, by Lewis Carroll. New York, Putnam, 1934.

*

Lionel White comments:
It's one way to make a living if you are too lazy to work or too incompetent to hold a job.

* * *

"Caper" novels, those dealing with the planning and execution of large-scale crimes, are a recognized sub-genre of mystery fiction. Lionel White, if he did not invent the caper story, is certainly one of the ablest practitioners in the field. He is at his best detailing the step-by-step planning of a crime, the crime itself, and its aftermath. He does so in a harsh, spare style that is hardly literary but which is well-suited to his subjects. Though such stories are primarily action-oriented, White is often surprisingly acute in revealing the psychology of his criminal characters as well as in itemizing the minutiae of their lives. Always in these books there is the feeling of suppressed violence, but when the expected violence does occur it is often so shocking that it takes the reader unaware and achieves an unpredictable effect. An example of this is the stunning scene in *Death Takes the Bus* in which a young girl is raped with a pistol barrel. Such a scene might strike some readers as sordid, but it tells a great deal about the kinds of people who live in the world of White's books.

White usually deals with standard capers: kidnapping in *The Snatchers*, a train robbery in *Operation—Murder*, a bus hijacking in *Death Takes the Bus*, a diamond heist in *Too Young to Die*, and a bank robbery in what may well be the definitive White book, *The Big Caper*. Rarely are any of the criminals arrested; but there is always retribution, never as a result of poor planning, but because of accidents, the little things that no amount of planning can take into account. Or sometimes the characters discover a tiny core of decency (or sentimentality) within themselves and bring about their own downfalls.

White does not always adhere to the caper formula. In *Lament for a Virgin*, for instance, he presents the familiar story of a man framed for murder in a small southern town and tells how an individual in such a spot manages to save himself. In a much later book, *The Mexico Run*, he describes the predicament of a young man involved in dope smuggling and murder. These books are entertaining but do not really represent White at the top of his form. One of his best books, *The House Next*

Door, begins with a heist, but it is really a study of a small suburban community; the plot concerns an innocent man mistakenly jailed for murder. He can do nothing for himself, and even his lawyer believes him guilty. Only his wife comes to his defense and nearly loses her own life as one violent act begets another in what is almost a chain reaction. In *Rafferty* White tells the story of a Jimmy Hoffa-like labor leader and his rise to power. Such novels give White the opportunity to use a somewhat more refined style than in his paperback thrillers. He is also able to delve into the psychology of characters quite unlike the hardened criminals of his caper books.

White is rather neglected at present, but for unadorned action, suspense, and vigorous storytelling his novels have seldom been surpassed.

—Bill Crider

WHITE, Teri (née Honohan). American. Born in Topeka, Kansas, 30 October 1946. Educated at a variety of schools in the United States. Married James R. White in 1974; one daughter. Recipient: Mystery Writers of America Edgar Allan Poe award, 1983. Agent: Nat Sobel, 146 East 19th Street, New York, New York 10003. Address: 3280 Lansmere Road, Skajer Heights, Ohio 44122, U.S.A.

CRIME PUBLICATIONS

Novels (series: Blue Maguire and Spaceman Kowalski)

Triangle. New York, Charter, 1982.
Bleeding Hearts (Maguire and Kowalski). New York, Mysterious Press, 1984.
Tightrope (Maguire and Kowalski). New York, Mysterious Press, 1986.
Max Trueblood and the Jersey Desperado. New York, Mysterious Press, 1987.
Faultlines. New York, Mysterious Press, 1987; London, Mysterious Press, 1988.

Uncollected Short Stories

"Role Model," in *Sisters in Crime*, edited by Marilyn Wallace, Berkeley, California, 1989; London, W.H. Allen, 1990.
"Outlaw Blues," in *Sisters in Crime 3*, edited by Marilyn Wallace, Berkeley, California, 1990.

OTHER PUBLICATIONS

Novel as Stephen Lewis

Cowboy Blues. New York, Allison Press, 1985.

Play

Shootout on Topanga (produced Cleveland, Ohio, 1987)

*

Teri White comments:
As a writer, I have very little interest in doing "whodunnits". My primary interest is character and the relationship between people. For the most part, I prefer to create characters who live on the fringe of society, the outsiders. I also believe that the mystery/suspense genre is an ideal forum for discussions of current social problems—as long as the story and characters remain the primary focus. If I needed to sum up the general focus of my books, it would be the struggles of the outcast to find a place in society.

*　　*　　*

Edgar Award-winner Teri White's fast-moving thrillers are about male bonding. Whether it's police partners Blue Maguire and Spaceman Kowalski (*Bleeding Hearts, Tightrope*), a retired hit man and his inept apprentice (*Max Trueblood and the Jersey Desperado*) or two ex-cons in search of the big one (*Faultlines*), men and their relationships with each other are at the forefront.

Although these are men of the 1980's, facing crises in coping with a society that doesn't offer any breaks without strings attached, there is a flavour of the 1930's and 1940's in White's hard-boiled novels. The crooks and their molls bouncing through Los Angeles in beat-up cars waving illegally obtained guns could as easily be involved in the fight over the Maltese Falcon. These men are tough, but they learn, as Sam Spade did when he lost his partner due to the perfidy of Brigid O'Shaughnessy: you can't trust a dame.

Somewhat strangely for a woman writer, the female characters in White's books are all negative. In *Faultlines*, the story of Chris and Dwight—two men who were lovers in prison and are now robbing liquor stores trying to make enough money to go treasure hunting in Mexico—the villain is Kathryn Daily. Not only does she attempt to double-cross her partners in crime, she also corrupts her ex-lover Tray Detaglio who is trying to go straight after leaving prison. Kathryn is portrayed as a greedy, scheming bitch whose only interest is in money and who uses sex and coercion in equal parts to get what she wants. Her cold sexual relationship with Chris is contrasted with Dwight and Chris's homoerotic bonding and with the developing, quirky friendship between Detaglio and Bryan Murphy, an ex-cop. One of White's few sympathetic female characters, Ann Hamilton, is Bryan's neighbour and eventual girlfriend but even in this relationship, it is she who must do the chasing and Murphy almost resents her advances because he fears another heart attack if he has sex.

Max Trueblood and the Jersey Desperado also has two contrasting male buddy relationships, one threatened by another pushy bitch. Aaron Temple is a cop nearing retirement, trying to solve a series of mob killings but his daughter is pressing him to leave the job early and move in with her family. There is no warmth in the father/daughter relationship; all of Temple's paternal feelings are reserved for Cody Blaine, his younger partner. Their uneasy but ultimately rewarding bond is mirrored by that of Max and Jeremiah Donahue who also learn to live and work together after a fashion.

There is pair-bonding and a close-knit group of men in *Tightrope*, the story of an attempted diamond heist by a disturbed Vietnam veteran and his old army buddies. The two policemen, Spaceman Kowalski and Blue Maguire, who are trying to stop the action before it is too late, are also Vietnam vets and the villains and victims of the story are former boat-people who find the emnities of the war America lost have followed them to their new country. It's an exciting story, although it features lots of gunfire and a fair number of killings, as do White's other books. Again, the women in the book are untrustworthy and meet bad ends. Angel Tran and Marybeth Wexler are blamed for betraying their men in different ways and pay the ultimate price in the end.

There is a filmic quality that runs through White's work. Her sense of place, the back-alleys and barren suburbs of Los

Angeles, is wonderfully evocative of the city and it would not be surprising if her work ended up being adapted for television or the movies.

The books are certainly action-packed and although they won't appeal to the gun-control lobby and there is certainly no feminist analysis of relationships here, they are entertaining tales of a world where there isn't much to choose between the good guys and the bad guys, except that the good guys want justice a bit more than the bad guys want the loot. At the end of *Tightrope*, Maguire and Kowalski watch the sun come up over Los Angeles on New Year's Day and toast "the good guys," "a couple of tired, bloodied cops, watching the sun come up over their city. They cared more about the city than the city cared about them, that was for damned sure."

—Gillian Rodgerson

———————

WHITFIELD, Raoul. Also wrote as Ramon Decolta; Temple Field. American. Born in New York City, 22 November 1898; spent part of his youth in the Philippines. Served in the United States Army Air Corps in France during World War I. Newspaper reporter, then magazine writer. Traveled abroad and lived in France during the early 1930's; after 1935 illness curtailed his activity. *Died in January 1945.*

CRIME PUBLICATIONS

Novels

Green Ice. New York, Knopf, 1930; Harpenden, Hertfordshire, No Exit Press, 1988; as *The Green Ice Murders*, New York, Avon, 1947.
Death in a Bowl. New York, Knopf, 1931; Harpenden, Hertfordshire, No Exit Press, 1988.
Five (as Temple Field). New York, Farrar and Rinehart, 1931.
The Virgin Kills. New York, Knopf, 1932; Harpenden, Hertfordshire, No Exit Press, 1988.
Killer's Carnival (as Temple Field). New York, Farrar and Rinehart, 1932.

Uncollected Short Stories

"Scotty Troubles Trouble," in *Black Mask* (New York), March 1926.
"Scotty Scouts Around," in *Black Mask* (New York), April 1926.
"Jenny Meets the Boys," in *Black Mask* (New York), June 1926.
"Black Air," in *Black Mask* (New York), July 1926.
"Roaring Death," in *Black Mask* (New York), August 1926.
"Flying Gold," in *Black Mask* (New York), September 1926.
"Delivered Goods," in *Black Mask* (New York), November 1926.
"Ten Hours," in *Black Mask* (New York), December 1926.
"Uneasy Money," in *Black Mask* (New York), January 1927.
"White Murder," in *Black Mask* (New York), February 1927.
"Sky-High Odds," in *Black Mask* (New York), March 1927.
"South of Savannah," in *Black Mask* (New York), May 1927.
"Bottled Death," in *Black Mask* (New York), June 1927.
"Live Men's Gold," in *Black Mask* (New York), August 1927.
"Sixty Minutes," in *Black Mask* (New York), October 1927.

"Red Pearls," in *Black Mask* (New York), November 1927.
"The Sky's the Limit," in *Black Mask* (New York), January 1928.
"Soft Goods," in *Black Mask* (New York), February 1928.
"Little Guns," in *Black Mask* (New York), April 1928.
"Black Murder," in *Black Mask* (New York), May 1928.
"First Blood," in *Black Mask* (New York), June 1928.
"Blue Murder," in *Black Mask* (New York), July 1928.
"High Death," in *Black Mask* (New York), August 1928.
"Red Wings," in *Black Mask* (New York), September 1928.
"Ghost Guns," in *Black Mask* (New York), October 1928.
"The Sky Trap," in *Black Mask* (New York), November 1928.
"Outside," in *Black Mask* (New York), December 1929.
"Red Smoke," in *Black Mask* (New York), January 1930.
"Oval Face," in *Black Mask* (New York), March 1930.
"Killers' Show," in *Black Mask* (New York), April 1930.
"Murder by Mistake," in *Black Mask* (New York), August 1930.
"Murder in the Ring," in *Black Mask* (New York), December 1930.
"About Kid Deth," in *Black Mask* (New York), February 1931.
"Face Powder," in *Black Mask* (New York), April 1931.
"Soft City," in *Black Mask* (New York), May 1931.
"For Sale—Murder," in *Black Mask* (New York), June 1931.
"Mistral," in *Adventure* (New York), 15 December 1931.
"Man Killer," in *Black Mask* (New York), April 1932.
"Walking Dynamite," in *Black Mask* (New York), May 1932.
"Blue Murder," in *Black Mask* (New York), September 1932.
"Dead Men Tell Tales," in *Black Mask* (New York), November 1932.
"Murder by Request," in *Black Mask* (New York), January 1933.
"Dark Death," in *Black Mask* (New York), August 1933.
"A Woman Can Kill," in *Black Mask* (New York), September 1933.
"Money Talk," in *Black Mask* (New York), October 1933.
"Not Tomorrow," in *Black Mask* (New York), November 1933.
"Murder Again," in *Black Mask* (New York), December 1933.
"Cruise to Nowhere," in *Argosy* (New York), 23 December 1933.
"High Murder," in *Black Mask* (New York), January 1934.
"Death on Fifth Avenue," in *Black Mask* (New York), February 1934.
"The Mystery of the Fan-Backed Chair," in *Hearst's International-Cosmopolitan* (New York), February 1935.
"The Great Black," in *Hearst's International-Cosmopolitan* (New York), August 1937.
"Inside Job," in *The Hard-Boiled Omnibus: Early Stories from Black Mask*, edited by Joseph T. Shaw. New York, Simon and Schuster, 1946.
"Murder Is My Business," in *The Saint* (New York), March 1956.
"China Man," in *The Hardboiled Dicks*, edited by Ron Goulart. Los Angeles, Sherbourne Press, 1965; London, Boardman, 1967.

Uncollected Short Stories as Ramon Decolta

"West of Guam," in *Black Mask* (New York), February 1930.
"Red Hemp," in *Black Mask* (New York), April 1930.
"Signals of Storm," in *Black Mask* (New York), June 1930.
"Enough Rope," in *Black Mask* (New York), July 1930.
"Nagasaki Bound," in *Black Mask* (New York), September 1930.
"Nagasaki Knives," in *Black Mask* (New York), October 1930.

"The Caleso Murders," in *Black Mask* (New York), December 1930.
"Silence House," in *Black Mask* (New York), January 1931.
"Diamonds of Dread," in *Black Mask* (New York), February 1931.
"The Man in White," in *Black Mask* (New York), March 1931.
"The Blind Chinese," in *Black Mask* (New York), April 1931.
"Red Dawn," in *Black Mask* (New York) May 1931.
"Blue Glass," in *Black Mask* (New York), July 1931.
"Diamonds of Death," in *Black Mask* (New York), August 1931.
"Shooting Gallery," in *Black Mask* (New York), October 1931.
"The Javanese Mask," in *Black Mask* (New York), December 1931.
"The Siamese Cat," in *Black Mask* (New York), April 1932.
"The Black Sampan," in *Black Mask* (New York), June 1932.
"Climbing Death," in *Black Mask* (New York), July 1932.
"The Magician Murder," in *Black Mask* (New York), November 1932.
"The Man from Shanghai," in *Black Mask* (New York), May 1933.
"The Amber Fan," in *Black Mask* (New York), July 1933.
"Death in the Pasig," in *The Hard-Boiled Omnibus: Early Stories from Black Mask*, edited by Joseph T. Shaw. New York, Simon and Schuster, 1946.

OTHER PUBLICATIONS

Play

Screenplay: *Private Detective 62*, 1933.

Other (for children)

Wings of Gold. New York, Knopf, 1930.
Silver Wings. New York, Knopf, 1930.
Danger Zone. New York, Knopf, 1931.
Danger Circus. New York, Knopf, 1933.

*   *   *

At his best, Raoul Whitfield was very good; at his weakest, infuriatingly bad. Today he is little remembered. His short fiction is due a revival, especially the 24 stories in *Black Mask* featuring Jo Gar, a Filipino private detective in Manila, and written under the pseudonym Ramon Decolta (two stories about Gar also appeared in *Cosmopolitan*). For these stories Whitfield drew on his intimate knowledge of the islands. Six of them, forming a "serial," were reprinted in *Ellery Queen's Mystery Magazine*. His other *Black Mask* stories vary in quality, many of them stock action-pieces, the kind Joseph T. Shaw, the editor, was so fond of. However, upon occasion Whitfield did first-rate work, e.g., "Murder by Mistake" and "Murder in the Ring"; the latter is one of the best in the hard-boiled genre. Another memorable story, "Mistral," which appeared in *Adventure* (reprinted in *EQMM*, 22 April 1981), is set in the Riviera. Patently, Whitfield worked hard on this; it is a shame that he never did more in the same vein, for "Mistral" is something more than simply ambitious.

His novels fared well with critics and the public (he was at one time regarded as Hammett's peer), and still read well. *Green Ice* is a first-person narrative that concerns Mal Ourney, an ex-con just out of Sing Sing, who goes after what he calls The Crime Breeders, big-time hoods who prey on small-time crooks. In *Death in a Bowl* the Hollywood private dick Ben Jardinn solves the spectacular murder of conductor Hans

Reiner during a concert in Hollywood Bowl. The plot is complicated but the pacing is excellent, and it is Whitfield's best novel. *The Virgin Kills* is his latest satisfactory long work. *The Virgin* is a yacht; "kills" is a nominative plural as in murders; and the setting is the annual Poughkeepsie Regatta on the Hudson River. Al Connors, a newspaperman, narrates. The books by Temple Field are blessedly resting in oblivion.

In addition, Whitfield poured out at the very least half-a-hundred stories for *Boy's Life, Everybody's Adventure, Triple-X Magazine*, and *Battle Stories*. In the latter, for example, he concentrated on air-combat tales in World War I France, and thanks to his own experiences they have a verisimilitude about them not always found in the pulps. Whitfield, a pilot, knew his airplanes. Every once in a while in these pieces he was Temple Field.

Certainly there are additional stories by Whitfield somewhere out there buried in the rough-paper magazines, but they must await exhumation by collectors and aficionados.

—E.R. Hagemann

———

WHITNEY, Alec. *See* **FRASER, James.**

———

WHITNEY, Phyllis A(yame). American. Born in Yokohama, Japan, 9 September 1903. Educated at schools in Japan, China, the Philippines, California, and Texas; McKinley High School, Chicago, graduated 1924. Married 1) George A. Garner in 1925 (divorced 1945), one daughter; 2) Lovell F. Jahnke in 1950 (died 1973). Dance instructor, San Antonio, Texas, one year; children's books editor, Chicago *Sun*, 1942–46, and Philadephia *Inquirer*, 1947–48; instructor in children's fiction writing, Northwestern University, Evanston, Illinois, 1945, and New York University, 1947–58. Member, Board of Directors, 1959–62, and President, 1975, Mystery Writers of America. Recipient: Mystery Writers of America Edgar Allan Poe award, for children's book, 1961, 1964, and Grand Master award, 1988. Lives in Brookhaven, Long Island, New York. Agent: c/o McIntosh and Otis Inc., 310 Madison Avenue, New York, New York 10017, U.S.A.

CRIME PUBLICATIONS

Novels

Red Is for Murder. Chicago, Ziff Davis, 1943; as *Red Carnelian*, New York, Paperback Library, 1968; London, Coronet, 1976.
The Quicksilver Pool. New York, Appleton Century Crofts, 1955; London, Coronet, 1973.
The Trembling Hills. New York, Appleton Century Crofts, 1956; London, Coronet, 1974.
Skye Cameron. New York, Appleton Century Crofts, 1957; London, Hurst and Blackett, 1959.
The Moonflower. New York, Appleton Century Crofts, 1958; as *The Mask and the Moonflower*, London, Hurst and Blackett, 1960.
Thunder Heights. New York, Appleton Century Crofts, 1960; London, Coronet, 1973.

Blue Fire. New York, Appleton Century Crofts, 1961; London, Hodder and Stoughton, 1962.

Window on the Square. New York, Appleton Century Crofts, 1962; London, Coronet, 1969.

Seven Tears for Apollo. New York, Appleton Century Crofts, 1963; London, Coronet, 1969.

Black Amber. New York, Appleton Century Crofts, 1964; London, Hale, 1965.

Sea Jade. New York, Appleton Century Crofts, 1965; London, Hale, 1966.

Columbella. New York, Doubleday, 1966; London, Hale, 1967.

Silverhill. New York, Doubleday, 1967; London, Heinemann, 1968.

Hunter's Green. New York, Doubleday, 1968; London, Heinemann, 1969.

The Winter People. New York, Doubleday, 1969; London, Heinemann, 1970.

Lost Island. New York, Doubleday, 1970; London, Heinemann, 1971.

Listen for the Whisperer. New York, Doubleday, and London, Heinemann, 1972.

Snowfire. New York, Doubleday, and London, Heinemann, 1973.

The Turquoise Mask. New York, Doubleday, 1974; and London, Heinemann, 1975.

Spindrift. New York, Doubleday, and London, Heinemann, 1975.

The Golden Unicorn. New York, Doubleday, 1976; London, Heinemann, 1977.

The Stone Bull. New York, Doubleday, and London, Heinemann, 1977.

The Glass Flame. New York, Doubleday, 1978; London, Heinemann, 1979.

Domino. New York, Doubleday, 1979; London, Heinemann, 1980.

Poinciana. New York, Doubleday, 1980; London, Heinemann, 1981.

Vermilion. New York, Doubleday, 1981; London, Heinemann, 1982.

Emerald. New York, Doubleday, and London, Heinemann, 1983.

Rainsong. New York, Doubleday, and London, Heinemann, 1984.

Dream of Orchids. New York, Doubleday, and London, Hodder and Stoughton, 1985.

The Flaming Tree. New York, Doubleday, and London, Hodder and Stoughton, 1986.

Silversword. New York, Doubleday, and London, Hodder and Stoughton, 1987.

Feather on the Moon. New York, Doubleday, and London, Hodder and Stoughton, 1988.

Rainbow in the Mist. New York, Doubleday, and London, Hodder and Stoughton, 1989.

The Singing Stones. New York, Doubleday, and London, Hodder and Stoughton, 1990.

OTHER PUBLICATIONS

Fiction (for children)

A Place for Ann. Boston, Houghton Mifflin, 1941.
A Star for Ginny. Boston, Houghton Mifflin, 1942.
A Window for Julie. Boston, Houghton Mifflin, 1943.
The Silver Inkwell. Boston, Houghton Mifflin, 1945.
Willow Hill. New York, Reynal, 1947.

Ever After. Boston, Houghton Mifflin, 1948.
Mystery of the Gulls. Philadelphia, Westminster Press, 1949.
Linda's Homecoming. Philadelphia, McKay, 1950.
The Island of Dark Woods. Philadelphia, Westminster Press, 1951; as *Mystery of the Strange Traveler*, 1967.
Love Me, Love Me Not. Boston, Houghton Mifflin, 1952.
Step to the Music. New York, Crowell, 1953.
Mystery of the Black Diamonds. Philadelphia, Westminster Press, 1954; as *Black Diamonds*, Leicester, Brockhampton Press, 1957.
A Long Time Coming. Philadelphia, McKay, 1954.
Mystery on the Isle of Skye. Philadelphia, Westminster Press, 1955.
The Fire and the Gold. New York, Crowell, 1956.
The Highest Dream. Philadelphia, McKay, 1956.
Mystery of the Green Cat. Philadelphia, Westminster Press, 1957.
Secret of the Samurai Sword. Philadelphia, Westminster Press, 1958.
Creole Holiday. Philadelphia, Westminster Press, 1959.
Mystery of the Haunted Pool. Philadelphia, Westminster Press, 1960.
Secret of the Tiger's Eye. Philadelphia, Westminster Press, 1961.
Mystery of the Golden Horn. Philadelphia, Westminster Press, 1962.
Mystery of the Hidden Hand. Philadelphia, Westminster Press, 1963.
Secret of the Emerald Star. Philadelphia, Westminster Press, 1964.
Mystery of the Angry Idol. Philadelphia, Westminster Press, 1965.
Secret of the Spotted Shell. Philadelphia, Westminster Press, 1967.
Secret of Goblin Glen. Philadelphia, Westminster Press, 1968.
The Mystery of the Crimson Ghost. Philadelphia, Westminster Press, 1969.
Secret of the Missing Footprint. Philadelphia, Westminster Press, 1969.
The Vanishing Scarecrow. Philadelphia, Westminster Press, 1971.
Nobody Likes Trina. Philadelphia, Westminster Press, 1972.
Mystery of the Scowling Boy. Philadelphia, Westminster Press, 1973.
Secret of Haunted Mesa. Philadelphia, Westminster Press, 1975.
Secret of the Stone Face. Philadelphia, Westminster Press, 1977.

Other

Writing Juvenile Fiction. Boston, The Writer, 1947; revised edition, 1960.
Writing Juvenile Stories and Novels: How to Write and Sell Fiction for Young People. Boston, The Writer, 1976.
"Gothic Mysteries," in *The Mystery Story*, edited by John Ball. San Diego, University of California Extension, 1976.
"Good Little Girls and Boys," in *Murder Ink: The Mystery Reader's Companion*, edited by Dilys Winn. New York, Workman, 1977.
Guide to Fiction Writing. Boston, The Writer, 1982; London, Poplar Press, 1984.

*

Manuscript Collection: Mugar Memorial Library, Boston University.

Phyllis A. Whitney comments:

My interest lies in the field of romantic suspense. This doesn't mean detective stories. My characters never sit around adding up clues, and I try to keep the police offstage, except when needed.

I am interested in the relationships between characters. Conflicts and confrontations, all with a twist of mystery, are the story ingredients with which I like to deal. Murder is the ultimate in human passion, so there is a murder along the way—either past or present.

Settings are important in my novels, and there must be a new background for each book. The exotic appeals to me, and starts my imagination working—so I always look for beautiful and unusual places to write about. Background and characters affect each other and the action develops from both.

The game, of course, is to fool the reader, and sometimes I succeed.

*   *   *

Throughout the 1960's and 1970's, Phyllis A. Whitney was the best-known American writer of romantic suspense, a field that was dominated by British authors such as Mary Stewart, Victoria Holt, and Dorothy Eden. Whitney's long career of writing for young people and adults has produced more than 60 novels, a number of articles on the writing of fiction, and several textbooks for would-be writers of fiction. Although she wrote her first adult book, *Red Is for Murder*, in 1943, it was not until the publication of *The Quicksilver Pool* in 1955 that she began writing regularly for adults. Over the years, she evolved a particular form of romantic suspense novel, the family mystery, in which both the plot and the setting are thoroughly entwined in a complex history of sinister family feuds and secrets.

In most of Whitney's suspense novels, the crime has been committed some time before the beginning of the book, but it has never been solved. A young woman, perhaps a long-lost member of the family, returns home to find herself involved in events she does not understand. Often her parents have left the family home because of the hidden events that the heroine's presence brings forth once again. Alternatively, a young bride may find danger in her husband's family home. Over her career, Whitney has become more interested in crime and detection. The mystery element of *The Quicksilver Pool* or *The Trembling Hills* is not as central to the plot as it is in the later works.

For many years, Whitney took regular research trips to find settings for her novels; when she returned she would write a suspense novel and a children's book set in each locale. Her novels alternate between exotic foreign or American settings such as Turkey (*Black Amber*), Japan (*The Moonflower*), Great Britain (*Hunter's Green*), Norway (*Listen for the Whisperer*), the Caribbean (*Columbella*), the Blue Ridge mountains (*Rainbow in the Mist*), or the Catskills (*The Stone Bull*). A few of her novels are historical, although most have contemporary settings.

Whitney's typical young heroine is searching for her own past in order to understand her personal identity. Central to the heroine's quest is a mother-daughter relationship; many of the mothers in Whitney's work are beautiful women who are not nurturing toward their children. Some of them are villains. Competition between mother and daughter is frequently an important plot element. In *Columbella*, the protagonist works as a governess for a girl who feels inferior to her beautiful mother, as had the heroine during her own adolescence. *The Golden Unicorn* features an adopted child who wants to find her real parents. In *Rainbow in the Mist*, the heroine goes to her aunt's home for safety when the psychic powers she has inherited from her mother become too disturbing.

Whitney's villains are appropriate for family drama. They are usually motivated by a desire to avenge an imagined slight or settle an old grievance. The heroine is in danger because of something she knows or something she represents rather than for something she has done. Even when a family secret is not at the center of the novel, the solution to the mystery frequently lies in the past. Since the source of evil is so ambiguous in Whitney's novels, the atmosphere of suspense is both strong and diffuse. An aura of unease permeates her books, promising excitement and mystery that become clearly delineated only at the end when villain, method, motive, and reward are all revealed at once.

Whitney's published commentary on the writing of fiction reveals her seriousness about her art. Her work is formulaic, with an expected and anticipated pleasure for her wide audience, but through most of her career her work has been thoroughly professional. Only in the past few years—writing about such recent novels as *Rainsong*, *Silversword*, and *Feather on the Moon*—have reviewers begun to comment about "tired" plots and hackneyed characters. At her best, however, Whitney is superb at evoking and sustaining complex and sophisticated terrors in a small domestic circle. Winner of many honors from mystery fans and writers, Whitney recently received the Malice Domestic Teapot for lifetime achievement.

—Kay Mussell

WHITTINGTON, Harry (Benjamin). Also wrote as Ashley Carter; Robert Hart Davis; Tabor Evans; Whit Harrison; Kel Holland; Harriet Kathryn Myers; Blaine Stevens; Clay Stuart; Hondo Wells; Harry White; Hallam Whitney. American. Born in Ocala, Florida, 4 February 1915. Educated in Florida public schools and extension and night classes. Served in the United States Navy, 1945–46: Petty Officer. Married Kathryn Lavinia Odom in 1936; one daughter and one son. Copywriter, Griffith Advertising Agency, St. Petersburg, Florida, 1932–33; assistant manager and advertising manager, Capitol Theatre, St. Petersburg, 1933–34; post office clerk, St. Petersburg, 1934–45; editor, *Advocate*, St. Petersburg, 1938–45; freelance writer, 1946–68; editor, U.S. Department of Agriculture, 1968–75; from 1975 freelance writer: author of many stories for King Features Syndicate, 1948–57, and *Man from U.N.C.L.E.*, *Dime Detective*, *Manhunt*, *Bluebook*, *Mantrap*. Died.

CRIME PUBLICATIONS

Novels

Slay Ride for a Lady. Kingston, New York, Quin, 1950.
The Brass Monkey. Kingston, New York, Quin, 1951.
Call Me Killer. Hasbrouck Heights, New Jersey, Graphic, 1951.
Fires That Destroy. New York, Fawcett, 1951.
The Lady Was a Tramp. Kingston, New York, Quin, 1951.
Married to Murder. New York, Paperback Library, 1951.
Murder Is My Mistress. Hasbrouck Heights, New Jersey, Graphic, 1951.
Forever Evil. New York, Paperback Library, 1951.
Satan's Widow. New York, Phantom, 1952.
Drawn to Evil. New York, Ace, 1952.

Mourn the Hangman. Hasbrouck Heights, New Jersey, Graphic, 1952.

So Dead My Love! New York, Ace, 1953.

Vengeful Sinner. New York, Croydon, 1953; as *Die, Lover,* New York, Avon, 1960.

You'll Die Next! New York, Ace, 1954; London, Red Seal, 1959.

The Naked Jungle. New York, Ace, 1955.

One Got Away. New York, Ace, 1955.

Brute in Brass. New York, Fawcett, 1956; London, Red Seal, 1958.

Desire in the Dust. New York, Fawcett, 1956; London, Fawcett, 1957.

The Humming Box. New York, Ace, 1956.

Saturday Night Town. New York, Fawcett, 1956; London, Fawcett, 1958.

A Woman on the Place. New York, Ace, 1956; London, Red Seal, 1960.

Across That River. New York, Ace, 1957.

Man in the Shadow (novelization of screenplay). New York, Avon, 1957.

One Deadly Dawn. New York, Ace, 1957.

Play for Keeps. New York and London, Abelard Schuman, 1957.

Temptations of Valerie (novelization of screenplay). New York, Avon, 1957.

Teen-Age Jungle. New York, Avon, 1958.

Web of Murder. New York, Fawcett, 1958; London, Fawcett, 1959.

Backwoods Tramp. New York, Fawcett, 1959; London, Muller, 1961.

Halfway to Hell. New York, Avon, 1959.

Strange Bargain. New York, Avon, 1959.

Strangers on Friday. New York and London, Abelard Schuman, 1959.

A Ticket to Hell. New York, Fawcett, 1959; London, Muller, 1960.

Connolly's Woman. New York, Fawcett, 1960; London, Muller, 1962.

The Devil Wears Wings. New York and London, Abelard Schuman, 1960.

Heat of Night. New York, Fawcett, 1960; London, Muller, 1961.

Hell Can Wait. New York, Fawcett, 1960; London, Muller, 1962.

A Night for Screaming. New York, Ace, 1960.

Nita's Place. New York, Pyramid, 1960.

Rebel Woman. New York, Avon, 1960.

Guerrilla Girls. New York, Pyramid, 1960; London, New English Library, 1970.

God's Back Was Turned. New York, Fawcett, 1961; London, Muller, 1962.

Journey into Violence. New York, Pyramid, 1961.

A Haven for the Damned. New York, Fawcett, 1962; London, Muller, 1963.

Hot as Fire, Cold as Ice. New York, Belmont, 1962.

69 Babylon Park. New York, Avon, 1962.

Don't Speak to Strange Girls. New York, Fawcett, and London, Muller, 1963.

Cross the Red Creek. New York, Avon, 1964.

Wild Lonesome. New York, Ballantine, 1965.

The Doomsday Affair (novelization of television play). New York, Ace, and London, New English Library, 1965.

Doomsday Mission. New York, Banner, 1967.

Burden's Mission. New York, Avon, 1968.

Novels as Whit Harrison

Swamp Kill. New York, Phantom, 1951.

Violent Night. New York, Phantom, 1952.

Body and Passion. New York, Original Novels, 1952.

Uncollected Short Stories

"The Glass Alibi," in *Mantrap* (New York), July 1956.

"Preventative Medicine," in *Trapped* (New York), August 1956.

"Hole in Her Head," in *Guilty* (New York), September 1956.

"Night of Crisis," in *Manhunt* (New York), October 1956.

"Screaming Woman," in *Guilty* (New York), November 1956.

"You're Better Off Dead," in *Sure Fire Detective Stories* (New York), February 1957.

"The Velvet Fist," in *Shell Scott Mystery Magazine* (New York), May 1966.

"The Assassin," in *The Man from U.N.C.L.E.* (New York), June 1966.

"Please Don't Date the Easies," in *Shell Scott Mystery Magazine* (New York), August 1966.

"The Crooked Window," in *Shell Scott Mystery Magazine* (New York), November 1966.

"The Ship of Horror," in *Mike Shayne Mystery Magazine* (New York), February 1968.

OTHER PUBLICATIONS

Novels

Vengeance Valley. New York, Phoenix Press, 1945; London, Ward Lock, 1947.

Cracker Girl. Beacon, New York, Beacon Signal, 1953.

Wild Oats. Beacon, New York, Beacon Signal, 1953.

Prime Sucker. Beacon, New York, Beacon Signal, 1953.

This Woman Is Mine. New York, Fawcett, 1953.

Naked Island. New York, Ace, 1954.

Saddle the Storm. New York, Fawcett, 1954; London, Fawcett, 1955.

Shadow at Noon (as Harry White). New York, Pyramid, 1955; as Hondo Wells, London, Mews, 1977.

Mink. Paris, Gallimard, 1956.

Trouble Rides Tall. New York and London, Abelard Schuman, 1958.

Star Lust. N.p., B and B Library, 1958.

Strictly for the Boys. N.p., Stanley, 1959.

Native Girl. New York, Berkley, 1959.

Shack Road Girl. New York, Berkley, 1959.

Vengeance Is the Spur. New York and London, Abelard Schuman, 1960.

Desert Stake-Out. New York, Fawcett, 1961; London, Muller, 1963.

Searching Rider. New York, Ace, 1961.

The Young Nurses. New York, Pyramid, 1961.

Wild Sky. New York, Ace, 1962.

Small Town Nurse (as Harriet Kathryn Myers). New York, Ace, 1962.

A Trap for Sam Dodge. New York, Ace, 1962.

Dry Gulch Town. New York, Ace, 1963.

Prairie Raiders (as Hondo Wells). New York, Ace, 1963; London, New English Library, 1977.

Prodigal Nurse (as Harriet Kathryn Myers). New York, Ace, 1963.

The Fall of the Roman Empire (novelization of screenplay). New York, Fawcett, and London, Muller, 1964.

His Brother's Wife (as Clay Stuart). Beacon, New York, Beacon Signal, 1964.
The Tempted (as Kel Holland). Beacon, New York, Beacon Signal, 1964.
High Fury. New York, Ballantine, 1964; London, Mews, 1976.
Hangrope Town. New York, Ballantine, 1964.
Valley of the Savage Men. New York, Ace, 1965.
Treachery Trail. Racine, Wisconsin, Whitman, 1968.
Charro. New York, Fawcett, 1969.
The Outlanders (as Blaine Stevens). New York, Jove, 1979; as Ashley Carter, London, W.H. Allen, 1983.
Embrace the Wind (as Blaine Stevens). New York, Jove, 1982.

Novels as Whit Harrison

Nature Girl. New York, Popular Library, 1952.
Sailor's Weekend. New York, Popular Library, 1952.
Army Girl. New York, Popular Library, 1952.
Girl on Parole. New York, Popular Library, 1952.
Rapture Alley. New York, Popular Library, 1952.
Shanty Road. New York, Popular Library, 1953.
Strip the Town Naked. Beacon, New York, Beacon Signal, 1953.
Any Woman He Wanted. Beacon, New York, Beacon Signal, 1960.
A Woman Possessed. Beacon, New York, Beacon Signal, 1961.

Novels as Hallam Whitney

Backwoods Hussy. New York, Paperback Library, 1952; as Lisa, 1965.
Shack Road. New York, Paperback Library, 1953.
Sinners Club. New York, Paperback Library, 1953.
City Girl. New York, Paperback Library, 1953.
Backwoods Shack. New York, Paperback Library, 1954.
The Wild Seed. New York, Ace, 1956.

Novels as Ashley Carter

Golden Stud, with Lance Horner. New York, Fawcett, 1975.
Master of Black Oaks. New York, Fawcett, 1976; London, W.H. Allen, 1977.
The Sword of the Golden Stud. New York, Fawcett, 1977; London, W.H. Allen, 1978.
Secret of Blackoaks. New York, Fawcett, 1978; London, W.H. Allen, 1980.
Panama. New York, Fawcett, 1978; London, Pan, 1980.
Taproots of Falconhurst. New York, Fawcett, 1978; London, W.H. Allen, 1979.
Scandal of Falconhurst. New York, Fawcett, 1980; London, W.H. Allen, 1981.
Heritage of Blackoaks. New York, Fawcett, 1981; London, W.H. Allen, 1982.
Against All Gods. London, W.H. Allen, 1982.
Rogue of Falconhurst. New York, Fawcett, 1983.
Road to Falconhurst. London, W.H. Allen, 1983.
A Farewell to Blackoaks. London, W.H. Allen, 1984.
The Outlanders. London, W.H. Allen, 1983.
A Darkling Moon. London, W.H. Allen, 1985.
Embrace the Wind. London, W.H. Allen, 1985.
Falconhurst Fugitive. London, W.H. Allen, 1985.
Miz Lucretia of Falconhurst. London, W.H. Allen, 1985.
Mondingo Mansa. London, W.H. Allen, 1986.
Strange Harvest. London, W.H. Allen, 1986.

Novels as Tabor Evans

Longarm. New York, Jove, 1978; London, Magnum, 1979.
Longarm and the Avenging Angels. New York, Jove, 1978; London, Magnum, 1979.
Longarm on the Border. New York, Jove, 1978; London, Magnum, 1979.
Longarm and the Hatchett Men. New York, Jove, 1979; London, Methuen, 1981.
Longarm and the Highgragers. New York, Jove, 1979; London, Magnum, 1981.
Longarm and the Loggers. New York, Jove, 1979; London, Magnum, 1980.
Longarm and the Nesters. New York, Jove, 1979; London, Magnum, 1981.
Longarm and the Texas Rangers. New York, Jove, 1979; London, Magnum, 1982.
Longarm and the Wendigo. New York, Jove, and London, Magnum, 1979.
Longarm in the Indian Nation. New York, Jove, 1979; London, Magnum, 1980.
Longarm in Lincoln County. New York, Jove, 1979; London, Methuen, 1982.
Longarm on the Humboldt. New York, Jove, 1981.
Longarm and the Golden Lady. New York, Jove, 1981.
Longarm and the Blue Norther. New York, Jove, 1981.
Longarm in Silver City. New York, Jove, 1982.
Longarm in Boulder Canyon. New York, Jove, 1982.
Longarm in the Big Thicket. New York, Jove, 1982.
Longarm and the Lone Star Vengeance. New York, Jove, 1983.
Longarm and the Lone Star Rescue. New York, Jove, 1985.

Plays

Screenplays: *Face of the Phantom*, 1960; *Pain and Pleasure*, 1965; *Strange Desires*, 1967; *Fireball Jungle*, 1968; *Island of Lost Women*, 1973.

Television Plays: *Lawman*, *The Alaskans*, and *The Dakotas* series.

Other

"The Paperback Original," in *The Mystery Writer's Handbook*, edited by Herbert Brean. New York, Harper, 1956.
"The Lucky Henchman of Joseph Peel," in *Quality of Murder*, edited by Anthony Boucher. New York, Dutton, 1962.
"The Key to Plotting," in *Writer's Digest* (Cincinnati), November 1972.

*

Manuscript Collection: Florida State University, Tallahassee.

Theatrical Activities:

Director: **Film**—*Face of the Phantom*, 1960.

* * *

Of all the writers who specialized in soft-cover originals during the paperback boom of the 1950's, Harry Whittington was certainly the "King." Between 1951 and 1963 he published close to 50 crime novels in this medium, and at least 35 westerns and other genre fiction. Yet for all its prolificacy, Whittington's work is inventive and of consistently high quality. His writing is crisp, with a good deal of emotional impact, and his characters, unlike those in so many soft-cover mysteries, are three-dimensional human beings instead of cardboard stereo-types. No less a critic than Anthony Boucher, writing in the New York *Times*, praised him as "one of the most versatile and satisfactory creators" of paperback suspense fiction.

Among Whittington's best works are *Fires That Destroy*, *Desire in the Dust*, *A Ticket to Hell*, *A Night for Screaming*, and *The Devil Wears Wings*. The last combines straight suspense with an in-depth psychological character study, and features a knowledgeable flying background and (as is the case in most of his crime novels) a vividly drawn Florida setting. Whittington has also written an excellent article on his speciality, "The Paperback Original," in *The Mystery Writer's Handbook*.

—Bill Pronzini

———

WIBBERLEY, Leonard. *See* **HOLTON, Leonard.**

———

WICK, Carter. *See* **WILCOX, Collin.**

———

WICK, Stuart Mary. *See* **FITT, Mary.**

———

WILCOX, Collin. Also writes as Carter Wick. American. Born in Detroit, Michigan, 21 September 1924. Educated at Antioch College, Yellow Springs, Ohio, B.A. 1948. Served in the United States Air Force: Private. Married Beverly Buchman in 1954 (divorced, 1964); two sons. Merchandise Manager, San Francisco Progress, 1949–50; Teacher at Town School, San Francisco, 1950–53; Partner, Amthor and Company, furniture store, San Francisco, 1953–55; Owner, Collin Wilcox Lamps, San Francisco, 1955–70. Since 1970, self-employed writer. Regional Vice-President, 1975, and Member, Board of Directors, 1976, Mystery Writers of America. Agent: Dominick Abel, 1416 West 82nd Street, New York, New York 10024. Address: 4174 26th Street, San Francisco, California 94131, U.S.A.

CRIME PUBLICATIONS

Novels (series: Alan Bernhardt; Stephen Drake; Lieutenant Frank Hastings; Marshall McCloud)

The Black Door (Drake). New York, Dodd Mead, 1967; London, Cassell, 1968.
The Third Figure (Drake). New York, Dodd Mead, 1968; London, Hale, 1969.
The Lonely Hunter (Hastings). New York, Random House, 1969; London, Hale, 1971.
The Disappearance (Hastings). New York, Random House, 1970; London, Hale, 1971.

Dead Aim (Hastings). New York, Random House, 1971; London, Hale, 1973.
Hiding Place (Hastings). New York, Random House, 1973; London, Hale, 1974.
McCloud. New York, Award, 1973.
Long Way Down (Hastings). New York, Random House, 1974; New York, Hale, 1975.
The New Mexico Connection (McCloud). New York, Award, and London, Tandem, 1974.
Aftershock (Hastings). New York, Random House, 1975; London, Hale, 1976.
The Faceless Man (as Carter Wick). New York, Saturday Review Press, 1975; London, Hamish Hamilton, 1976.
The Third Victim. New York, Dell, 1976; London, Hale, 1977.
Doctor, Lawyer . . . (Hastings). New York, Random House, 1977; London, Hale, 1978.
The Watcher (Hastings). New York, Random House, 1978; London, Hale, 1979.
Twospot, with Bill Pronzini. New York, Putnam, 1978.
Night Games (Hastings). New York, Random House, 1979.
Power Plays. New York, Random House, 1979; London, Hale, 1982.
Mankiller (Hastings). New York, Random House, 1980; London, Hale, 1982.
Spellbinder. New York, Fawcett, 1981; London, W.H. Allen, 1988.
Stalking Horse. New York, Random House, 1982; London, Hale, 1987.
Swallow's Fall. Tokyo, Bungaishungu, 1983; London, Hale, 1987.
Victims (Hastings). New York, Mysterious Press, 1985; London, Hale, 1986.
Night Games (Hastings). New York, Mysterious Press, 1986; London, W.H. Allen, 1988.
The Pariah (Hastings). New York, Mysterious Press, 1988.
Bernhardt's Edge. New York, Tor, 1988.
A Death Before Dying (Hastings). New York, Holt, 1990.
Silent Witness (Bernhardt). New York, Tor, 1990.

OTHER PUBLICATIONS

Other

"Writing and Selling the Police Procedural Novel," in *The Writer* (Boston), January 1976.

*

Manuscript Collection: Mugar Memorial Library, Boston University.

Collin Wilcox comments:
Every game should have a gameplan. Since I published my first mystery novel, my plan has been to first establish an appealing detective hero, and then build a series around him. With that accomplished, my hero would be required to pay bills while I ventured farther afield, into the "straight suspense" novels that can offer more challenge than the more formulaic detective story. With that plan in mind, I created Stephen Drake, a clairvoyant crime reporter. After two books, it was apparent that Stephen Drake couldn't pay his own way, much less finance excursions into the literary pastures. So I created Frank Hastings, a stubborn, honest, hard-working San Francisco homicide lieutenant. With Pete Friedman, his irascible co-lieutenant in homicide, Hastings has just wrapped up his tenth case. I hope he'll solve many more cases before he retires. Meanwhile, I'm beginning a new private eye series

featuring Alan Bernhardt, who also acts and directs in theater. I've made two forays into straight suspense, one under the pseudonym Carter Wick. Neither of the two books has been very successful, but I'm glad I wrote them. I learned from the experience, and intend to continue learning. Like Hastings, I'm stubborn.

* * *

Since the first novel featuring Lieutenant Frank Hastings appeared in 1969, Collin Wilcox has achieved widespread recognition for his contemporary police procedural novels. He is one of the few writers (Ed McBain is another) who has been able to combine the portrayal of investigative police work with incisive psychological and sociological examinations of the people who live, love, and die in a major metropolitan city.

Wilcox's first two novels, however, feature a wholly different kind of detective: Stephen Drake, a San Francisco newspaper reporter who has the gift/curse of extrasensory perception. The first of these, *The Black Door*, relates the story of a double murder connected with a right-wing political group; the second and better of the two, *The Third Figure*, is about the slaying of an underworld crime czar. In both books Drake arrives at solutions through a nice balance of clue-gathering and clairvoyant insight.

But it was in *The Lonely Hunter* that Wilcox created Frank Hastings (then a sergeant on the San Francisco Homicide Squad) and began his climb into the front rank of procedural novelists. This is a tense and forceful story of murder and drug-dealing in the Haight-Ashbury hippie scene of the late 1960's, made intensely personal for Hastings by the fact that his own daughter, a runaway, is involved. Wilcox successfully uses this blend of straightforward police work and deep personal involvement in subsequent novels. *Aftershock*, for instance, deals with a sadistic youth's campaign of terror against Hastings's woman friend, Ann Haywood; and *The Watcher* places both the lieutenant and his teenage son in mortal danger in an isolated, rattlesnake-infested area of northern California—and offers in the bargain a probing look at a father and son trying to bridge the generation gap. Other early and mid-period novels in the series, such as *Dead Aim*, *The Disappearance*, and *Long Way Down*, feature two or more cases on which Hastings must work simultaneously. While each of these is well done, peopled with a rich cross-section of San Francisco's colorful and varied individuals and lifestyles, they are perhaps less successful than those books which focus on single cases. Particularly good among the single-case novels is *Doctor, Lawyer . . .*—a race-against-the-clock story about an extortion plot against the city in which the chief of police is marked for death.

With *Night Games*, Wilcox made a bold structural change which few writers of successful series would attempt. Whereas the earlier books were written in the first person, *Night Games*—and such subsequent titles as *The Pariah* and *A Death Before Dying*—are told in the third person from the viewpoints of other principal characters as well as that of Hastings. This allows the author to develop plot and explore complex relationships more freely and at greater depth, though the necessary deemphasizing of Hastings has served to make him and his personal life less absorbing. On balance, *Night Games*, a dark, moody tale of sexual ritualism, and especially *A Death Before Dying*, with its examination of obsession and physical and psychological abuse, are even more rewarding than the earlier Hastings novels.

Recently Wilcox has created yet another series character—Alan Bernhardt, an actor and playwright moonlighting as an operative for Herbert Dancer Limited, a San Francisco detective agency. *Bernhardt's Edge*, in which a simple skip-trace takes on complexities that include blackmail, art theft, and contract murder, and its sequel, *Silent Witness*, are also told in the third person from multiple points of view.

In addition to the Drake, Hastings, and Bernhardt books, Wilcox has written three excellent non-series suspense novels. These are *The Faceless Man* (as by Carter Wick), which concerns a plot by a criminal psychopathic to murder a small boy who witnessed a previous homicide; *The Third Victim*, a chilling and unnerving study of yet another kind of psychopathic personality; and *Spellbinder*, one of the first suspense novels to deal with the provocative milieu of television evangelism.

—Bill Pronzini

WILLIAMS, Charles. American. Born in San Angelo, Texas, 13 August 1909. Educated in Brownsville High School, Texas, through tenth grade. Married Lasca Foster in 1939; one daughter. Radio operator, United States Merchant Marine, 1929–39; radio inspector, Radiomarine Corporation, Galveston, Texas, 1939–42; electronics inspector, Puget Sound Navy Yard, Bremerton, Washington, 1942–46; radio inspector, Mackay Company, San Francisco, 1946–50. *Died in 1975.*

CRIME PUBLICATIONS

Novels (series: John Ingram)

Hill Girl. New York, Fawcett, 1951; London, Red Seal, 1958.
Big City Girl. New York, Fawcett, 1951; London, Fawcett, 1953.
River Girl. New York, Fawcett, 1951; as *The Catfish Tangle*, London, Cassell, 1963.
Hell Hath No Fury. New York, Fawcett, 1953; London, Red Seal, 1958; as *The Hot Spot*, London, Cassell, 1965.
Nothing in Her Way. New York, Fawcett, 1953; London, Fawcett, 1954.
A Touch of Death. New York, Fawcett, 1954; London, Fawcett, 1955; as *Mix Yourself a Redhead*, London, Cassell, 1965.
Go Home, Stranger. New York, Fawcett, 1954; London, Red Seal, 1957.
Scorpion Reef. New York, Macmillan, 1955; London, Cassell, 1956; as *Gulf Coast Girl*, London, Dell, 1956.
The Big Bite. New York, Dell, 1956; London, Cassell, 1957.
The Diamond Bikini. New York, Fawcett, 1956; London, Cassell, 1956.
Girl Out Back. New York, Dell, 1958; as *Operator*, London, Cassell, 1958.
Man on the Run. New York, Fawcett, 1958; as *Man in Motion*, London, Cassell, 1959.
Talk of the Town. New York, Dell, 1958; as *Stain of Suspicion*, London, Cassell, 1959.
All the Way. New York, Dell, 1958; as *The Concrete Flamingo*, London, Cassell, 1960.
Uncle Sagamore and His Girls. New York, Fawcett, 1959.
Aground (Ingram). New York, Viking Press, 1960; London, Cassell, 1961.
The Sailcloth Shroud. New York, Viking Press, and London, Cassell, 1960.
Nude on Thin Ice. New York, Avon, 1961.

The Long Saturday Night. New York, Fawcett, 1962; London, Cassell, 1964; as *Finally Sunday!: a.k.a. Confidentially Yours*, London, Penguin, 1988.
Dead Calm (Ingram). New York, Viking Press, 1963; London, Cassell, 1964.
The Wrong Venus. New York, New American Library, 1966; as *Don't Just Stand There*, London, Cassell, 1967.
And the Deep Blue Sea. New York, New American Library, 1971; London, Cassell, 1972.
Man on a Leash. New York, Putnam, 1973; London, Cassell, 1974.

Uncollected Short Stories

"And Share Alike," in *Manhunt* (New York), August 1954.
"Flight to Nowhere," in *Manhunt* (New York), September 1955.

OTHER PUBLICATIONS

Novel

Fires of Youth. New York, Magnet, 1960.

OTHER PUBLICATIONS

Plays

Screenplays: *Les Félins (Joy House)*, with René Clement and Pascal Jardin, 1964; *L'Arme à Gauche*, with Claude Sautet, 1965; *Don't Just Stand There*, 1968; *The Pink Jungle*, 1968.

* * *

The past and character constitute the mystery in the books of Charles Williams. For instance, the handsome young man in a dinghy, his boat adrift not far off, who seems mad with despair over the death of his fellow passengers, including his wife (*Dead Calm*); a good girl in town who seems as much a threat to the central character, a petty thief, as does a prostitute whose character and past are obvious (*Hell Hath No Fury*); the devastatingly beautiful Cathy Dunbar (central to Williams's plot) who is a clever bitch and a fallen angel besides (*Nothing in Her Way*); the strange girl first seen in a trance, apparent victim of a terrible plot, who blithely sets fire to the house and everything in it she owns (*A Touch of Death*).

His motto could be *cherchez la femme*, because most often the mystery is a woman. But sometimes the man who tells the story and runs into one of these amazing creatures has something to hide himself. The reader wants to know who did it, as well as what they'll do next, and that is not easy to predict. Williams rarely emphasizes detection, but is skilled at the conventions that make suspense, and a master at anticipating, outguessing, and surprising his reader. His most romantic novels are set at sea, for, like Conrad's, his characters handle themselves with more volition there than on land. The hero of two sea thrillers, *Aground* and *Dead Calm*, is the father of the more recent *Man on a Leash*, a tale set in Nevada and northern California. A man and a woman win out against the storms and waves, and best the human elements which take more than a compass to gauge. His best hero and heroine are in his sea thriller *Scorpion Reef*, with its compelling narrative, visual sensuality, and emulations of the plot twists of Joseph Conrad.

His novels include a series set in back-country bayou regions of the South. This recalls the characters of Erskine Caldwell and the milieus and style of some of the later books of James M. Cain. *Big City Girl* is about a scheming, profane villainess who manipulates the more naive hero and the more virtuous women with ease. More upbeat and entertaining than Caldwell's, the back-country novels are, nevertheless, sometimes more concerned with social forces than mystery and suspense.

In the 1980's after Williams's death, two of his thrillers were adapted by other screenwriters and made into films. The first was Francois Truffaut's last film, adapted by the director himself from *The Long Saturday Night*, and retitled *Confidentially Yours*. The other was an adaptation of *Dead Calm* (which had been filmed before by Orson Welles) which starred Sam Neill, and was very successful.

Williams abstained from formula. Though his plots are often ingeniously devised, and his characterizations remarkably realized, Williams never gained the rank of a first-class thriller writer. There is an inconsistency of quality, especially in the later work, and pragmatic unconcern for value or morality in some of his work, with plot-ideas based on immoral or amoral premises. But he is a writer who seems at home with any situation or idea. Every novel is different, from *And the Deep Blue Sea* with its large cast of characters seemingly bound for hell, held hostages aboard a ship with a burning cargo, to *Man on the Run* with the relationship of an innocent fugitive and the surprising owner of a house where he hides. His plots can take an astounding turn with the subtle wiggle of a walking girl's fingers, or the toss of a match when calm seems restored. Choosing one or another of Williams's books to read can be a highly unpredictable and entertaining experience.

—Newton Baird

———————

WILLIAMS, David. British. Born in Bridgend, Glamorganshire, 8 June 1926. Educated at Cathedral School, Hereford, 1938–43; St. John's College, Oxford, 1943–44, 1947–48, B.A. 1948, M.A. 1953. Served in the Royal Naval Volunteer Reserve, 1944–47: Sub-Lieutenant. Married Brenda Holmes in 1951; one son and one daughter. Director, Gordon and Gotch Advertising, London, 1950–58; managing director, David Williams and Partners, 1958–68, and chairman, David Williams and Ketchum, 1968–78, both London; director, Ketchum Communications, Pittsburgh, 1968–78; vice chairman, Ketchum Group Holdings, London, 1978–82. Honorary secretary, Institute of Practitioners in Advertising, 1972–74; council member, Advertising Standards Authority, 1976–80; vice chairman, Royal Commonwealth Society for the Blind, 1966–84. Since 1965 Governor, Pusey House, Oxford; since 1984 council member, Impact Foundation; London. Agent: John Farquharson Ltd., 162–168 Regent Street, London WIR 5TB. Address: Blandings, Pinewood Road, Virginia Water, Surrey GU25 4PA, England.

CRIME PUBLICATIONS

Novels (series: Mark Treasure in all books)

Unholy Writ. London, Collins, 1976; New York, St. Martin's Press, 1977.
Treasure by Degrees. London, Collins, and New York, St. Martin's Press, 1977.
Treasure Up in Smoke. London, Collins, and New York, St. Martin's Press, 1978.

Murder for Treasure. London, Collins, and New York, St. Martin's Press, 1980.

Copper, Gold and Treasure. London, Collins, and New York, St. Martin's Press, 1982.

Treasure Preserved. London, Collins, and New York, St. Martin's Press, 1983.

Advertise for Treasure. London, Collins, and New York, St. Martin's Press, 1984.

Wedding Treasure. London, Macmillan, and New York, St. Martin's Press, 1985.

Murder in Advent. London, Macmillan, and New York, St. Martin's Press, 1985.

Treasure in Roubles. London, Macmillan, and New York, St. Martin's Press, 1987.

Divided Treasure. London, Macmillan, and New York, St. Martin's Press, 1987.

Treasure in Oxford. London, Macmillan, and New York, St. Martin's Press, 1988.

Holy Treasure!. London, Macmillan, and New York, St. Martin's Press, 1989.

Prescription for Murder. London, Macmillan, and New York, St. Martin's Press, 1990.

Uncollected Short Stories

"Treasure Finds a Mistress," in *Winter's Crimes 12*, edited by Hilary Watson. London, Macmillan, and New York, St. Martin's Press, 1980.

"Uncle's Girl," in *Winter's Crimes 15*, edited by George Hardinge. London, Macmillan, and New York, St. Martin's Press, 1983.

"The Bully," in *Winter's Crimes 16*, edited by Hilary Hale. London, Macmillan, and New York, St. Martin's Press, 1984.

"Mr. Oliver," in *Ellery Queen's Prime Crimes 4*. New York, Dial Press, 1985, and in *John Creasey's Crime Collection 1988*, edited by Herbert Harris, London, Gollancz, 1988.

"Three's a Crowd," in *Winter's Crimes 18*, edited by Hilary Hale. London, Macmillan, and New York, St. Martin's Press, 1986.

"Something to Declare," in *Ellery Queen's Mystery Magazine* (New York), September 1988.

"The Other Woman," in *Winter's Crimes 20*, edited by Hilary Hale. London, Macmillan, 1988.

"Freeze Everybody," in *Winter's Crimes 21*, edited by Hilary Hale. London, Macmillan, 1989.

"Smoke Gets in . . . ," in *A Classic English Murder*, edited by Tim Heald. London, Pavilion, 1990.

OTHER PUBLICATIONS

Other

Advertising and Social Conscience: Exploiting Products—Not People. London, Foundation for Business Responsibilities, 1972; revised edition, 1976.

*

David Williams comments:

The Mark Treasure stories are "classic" whodunnits. I aim to make them above all credible, a touch incidentally informative (a characteristic of Welsh writers), and to lace them with humour. They ought to possess a certain spontaneity for the negative reason that I am totally unable to produce an advance scenario, and rarely know the identity of the murderer before

the penultimate chapter. Reviewers are sometimes complimentary about the plotting, so perhaps there is something to be said for the method which the author finds stimulating if often taxing.

*   *   *

The variety of situations into which David Williams places his series character Mark Treasure is precipitated in part by Treasure's occupation as a merchant banker and through familial associations. Similarities are constantly going to be drawn between Treasure and his American counterpart John Putnam Thatcher, the creation of Emma Latham, but the only resemblances between the two men are the banking backgrounds and the variety of companies that do business with their establishment. In addition to being a much younger man, Mark Treasure has a sense of humor, more imagination, and a personal life that leads to social encounters where crime seems to be prevalent. Williams's writing style is faster paced and he has avoided giving Treasure an air of portentousness.

Treasure is a sophisticated man with the polish acquired from a stable family background, intellect and a good education. He has a distinct flair for knowing what to learn and how to rely on others to be told and is disarmingly clever in an understated way. As vice-chairman of Greenwood, Phipps & Co., merchant bankers, his involvements with their enterprises are inevitably intertwined with devious activities, and high-powered corporations headed by persons with an intense need for achievement and satisfaction, often at any cost and under any circumstances. This invariably leads Treasure into situations where questionable actions take place and from which he must identify the prime culprits so as to preserve the bank's investments and maintain its reputation. The variety of companies that require financial backing for acquisition and expansion provides the diverse backgrounds into which Treasure must accommodate himself. The research into such subjects as Russian museums, candy making, unrest in the Middle East, or the effect of tobacco sales on the economy of a small island, is impeccable and integrated into the plots, conversations and unpredictable activities of characters to a degree that is wholly diverting and immensely satisfying.

Unholy Writ, Mark Treasure's debut, is one of the three titles of the series not to have Treasure's name in it. It is a bibliophilic excursion with the premise, known at first only to the reader, that a Shakespearean manuscript might be entombed in some property that belonged to a recently sold stately home. Treasure's intervention into the puzzle is somewhat accidental through his visit with the seller after he has changed his mind. The light humorous touch is evident here for the first time and Mark carefully draws his conclusions after a thorough study of the various activities, past and current, of the characters. A minor, semi-romantic subplot and even a genetic bit of history are all part of a well conceived and smoothly worked out set of circumstances.

Treasure by Degrees is fiduciarily related since it concerns an attempted purchase of a British agricultural university by an wealthy American widow who is being opposed by a Middle-Eastern Crown Prince. Williams stretches the eccentricities of his non-British characters into semi-caricature in most of the books more for effect than for slight. All the books are well conceived and intricate; however the send-up of the advertising business, its larger than life-size characters, their egos plus some short-sighted and long-winded projects, is perfectly presented in *Advertise for Treasure. Copper, Gold and Treasure*, a captivating title, introduces two elderly men, diverse and far from mellow, who are turned down for a residential establishment. Major Copper and ex-London cab driver Benny Gold decide to investigate with outstanding but unexpected results. As a director of the bank that has an interest in it, Treasure becomes involved with an aspect of the candy making industry in *Divided Treasure*.

Molly Treasure is one of the more successful members of a fictional husband/wife team, not as a sleuthing partner but with her trained command of observation and language she is an ideal sounding board and reporter. Her occupation as a successful actress who, on occasion, is "resting" between theatrical engagements allows her the freedom to accompany Mark on some of these excursions. She travels with him to the West Indies and she is the precipitating influence in an effort to save a church in a deteriorating section of London. Mark accompanies Molly and the Baroque Art Circle to Leningrad where a painting had been stolen the previous week. During their tour another painting disappears and a member of the tour group meets a spectacular death at the opera. *Treasure in Roubles* shows Mark working with a police officer and together they discern the motives for the crimes, disclose the murderer, discover the whereabouts of the paintings and build a degree of tolerant understanding.

Molly and Mark travel to the country to attend a wedding but the estranged father of the bride is found quite dead on a golf course while the groom's eccentric uncle is a suspect. The Treasure team is at its best in *Wedding Treasure*. *Murder in Advent* and *Holy Treasure!* exhibit Williams's knowledge of and association with the Anglican church as Mark Treasure participates in the solution of perplexing problems concerning the deteriorating fabric and increasing cost of maintenance of ancient buildings. The degree of research that Williams does to present an authentic background is obvious and is a major factor in the popularity of the series.

In *Prescription for Murder* Williams converts a newly discovered cure for migraine into murder as the drug company is blackmailed when one of their directors is kidnapped. The pharmaceutical information is smoothly interwoven into the plot, the character's conversations and certainly into the motive until all of this comes together in a smashing finish.

Humor pervades but never overwhelms the intricacies of the plots. The inventiveness with which Williams varies the locations and Mark's attitude toward the complex problems as they are presented account for the popularity of the series. This depth and flavor delight readers who follow the entire series and eagerly await the next book.

—Ellen A. Nehr

———

WILLIAMS, Gordon. *See* **YUILL, P.B.**

———

WILLIAMS, John Barry. *See* **LUTZ, John; MALZBERG, Barry N.; PRONZINI, Bill.**

———

WILLIAMS, (George) Valentine. Also wrote as Douglas Valentine. British. Born in London, 20 October 1883. Educated at Downside School; studied in Germany. Served as

a Lieutenant in the Irish Guards, 1915: Military Cross (twice wounded); with the Guards Division Staff, London, 1918–19; did confidential work for the Foreign Office, London, 1939–41, and at British Embassy, Washington, D.C., 1941–42; Member of the Political Warfare Department, Woburn Abbey, Bedfordshire, 1942–45. Married Alice Crawford. Sub-editor, 1902–03, and Berlin correspondent, 1904–09; Reuter's news agency; journalist for the *Daily Mail*, London, from 1909: Paris correspondent, 1909–13, special correspondent during Portuguese Revolution, 1910, reported Balkan War, 1913, first accredited correspondent to British General Headquarters, 1915, in charge of staff, Versailles Peace Conference, 1919, and later Foreign Editor; freelance journalist in North Africa and United States during 1930's and 1940's. Chevalier, Order of the Crown of Belgium. *Died 20 November 1946.*

CRIME PUBLICATIONS

Novels (series: Dr. Adolph Grundt [Clubfoot]; Detective Sergeant Trevor Dene)

The Man with the Clubfoot (as Douglas Valentine). London, Jenkins, 1918; as Valentine Williams, New York, McBride, 1918.
The Secret Hand: Some Further Adventures by Desmond Okewood of the British Secret Service (as Douglas Valentine). London, Jenkins, 1918; as *Okewood of the Secret Service*, New York, McBride, 1919.
The Return of Clubfoot. London, Jenkins, 1922; as *Island Gold*, Boston, Houghton Mifflin, 1923.
The Yellow Streak. London, Jenkins, and Boston, Houghton Mifflin, 1922.
The Orange Divan. London, Jenkins, and Boston, Houghton Mifflin, 1923.
Clubfoot the Avenger. London, Jenkins, and Boston, Houghton Mifflin, 1924.
The Three of Clubs. London, Hodder and Stoughton, and Boston, Houghton Mifflin, 1924.
The Red Mass. London, Hodder and Stoughton, and Boston, Houghton Mifflin, 1925.
Mr. Ramosi. London, Hodder and Stoughton, and Boston, Houghton Mifflin, 1926.
The Pigeon House. London, Hodder and Stoughton, 1926; as *The Key Man*, Boston, Houghton Mifflin, 1926.
The Eye in Attendance (Dene). London, Hodder and Stoughton, and Boston, Houghton Mifflin, 1927.
The Crouching Beast (Clubfoot). London, Hodder and Stoughton, and Boston, Houghton Mifflin, 1928.
Mannequin. London, Hodder and Stoughton, 1930; as *The Mysterious Miss Morrisot*, Boston, Houghton Mifflin, 1930.
Death Answers the Bell (Dene). London, Hodder and Stoughton, 1931; Boston, Houghton Mifflin, 1932.
The Gold Comfit Box (Clubfoot). London, Hodder and Stoughton, 1932; as *The Mystery of the Gold Box*, Boston, Houghton Mifflin, 1932.
The Clock Ticks On (Dene). London, Hodder and Stoughton, and Boston, Houghton Mifflin, 1933.
Fog, with Dorothy Rice Sims. London, Hodder and Stoughton, and Boston, Houghton Mifflin, 1933.
The Portcullis Room. London, Hodder and Stoughton, and Boston, Houghton Mifflin, 1934.
Masks Off at Midnight (Dene). London, Hodder and Stoughton, and Boston, Houghton Mifflin, 1934.
The Clue of the Rising Moon (Dene). London, Hodder and Stoughton, and Boston, Houghton Mifflin, 1935.

Dead Man Manor. London, Hodder and Stoughton, and Boston, Houghton Mifflin, 1936.
The Spider's Torch (Clubfoot). London, Hodder and Stoughton, and Boston, Houghton Mifflin, 1936.
The Fox Prowls. London, Hodder and Stoughton, and Boston, Houghton Mifflin, 1939.
Double Death, with others. London, Gollancz, 1939.
Courier to Marrakesh (Clubfoot). London, Hodder and Stoughton, 1944; Boston, Houghton Mifflin, 1946.
Skeleton Out of the Cupboard. London, Hodder and Stoughton, 1946.
The Scoop, and Behind the Screen, with others. London, Gollancz, 1983.

Short Stories

The Knife Behind the Curtain: Tales of Secret Service and Crime. London, Hodder and Stoughton, and Boston, Houghton Mifflin, 1930.
Mr. Treadgold Cuts In. London, Hodder and Stoughton, 1937; as *The Curiosity of Mr. Treadgold,* Boston, Houghton Mifflin, 1937.

OTHER PUBLICATIONS

Plays

Berlin, with Alice Crawford (produced New York, 1931; London, 1932).

Screenplay: *Land of Hope and Glory,* with Adrian Brunel, 1927.

Other

With Our Army in Flanders. London, Arnold, 1915.
Adventures of an Ensign (as Vedette). Edinburgh, Blackwood, 1917.
"Gaboriau: Father of Detective Novels," in *National Review* (London), December 1923.
The World of Action: The Autobiography of Valentine Williams. London, Hamish Hamilton, and Boston, Houghton Mifflin, 1938.

*   *   *

Journalist, actor, screenwriter, and mystery author, Valentine Williams produced more than 30 novels of espionage and suspense while also engaged in his many other occupations.

Noteworthy among his non-fiction works is his comprehensive biographical and critical account of Emile Gaboriau, the French mystery author who wrote 21 massive novels in 13 years.

Williams's fictional works are primarily suspense or spy novels rather than detective novels, although he did create several notable characters. Dr. Adolph Grundt, known as Clubfoot, is a tempestuous German spy, simian in appearance and villainous in performance, who first appeared in *The Man with the Clubfoot,* and appears in seven subsequent books. Trevor Dene, another series character, is a tawny-haired, bespectacled, young Detective Sergeant from Scotland Yard who has Holmesian powers of observation and deduction. He finds himself on a busman's holiday in the Adirondacks when a seeming suicide turns out to be murder in *The Clue of the Rising Moon* and again on Long Island in *Masks Off at Midnight* when a pageant is the scene of a homicide. Two other interesting characters are "The Fox," Baron Alexis De Bahl, in *The Fox*

Prowls and Mr. Treadgold, a West End tailor and amateur detective, in *Dead Man Manor.*

—Mary Ann Grochowski

————

WILLIS, Ted (Edward Henry Willis; Baron Willis of Chislehurst). Also writes as John Bishop. British. Born in Tottenham, Middlesex, 13 January 1918. Educated at state schools, including Tottenham Central School, 1923–33. Served in the Royal Fusiliers, 1940; writer for the War Office and Ministry of Information. Married Audrey Hale, in 1944; one son and one daughter. Artistic director, Unity Theatre, London, 1945–48. Director, World Wide Pictures since 1967, and Vitalcall since 1983. Executive member, League of Dramatists, London, 1948–74; chairman, 1958–63, and president, 1963–68 and 1976–79, Writers Guild of Great Britain; president, International Writers Guild, 1967–69. Since 1964 governor, Churchill Theatre Trust, Bromley, Kent; member of the Board of Governors, National Film School, London, 1970–73. Recipient: Berlin Festival award, for screenplay, 1957; Edingburgh Festival award; Writers Guild award, 1964, 1967; Royal Society of Arts Silver Medal, 1967; Variety Guild of Great Britain award, 1976; Willis Trophy, for television writing, 1983. Fellow, Royal Society of Arts. Life Peer, 1963. Agent: Elaine Greene Ltd., 31 Newington Green, London N16 9PU. Address: 5 Shepherds Green, Chislehurst, Kent BR7 6PB, England.

CRIME PUBLICATIONS

Novels (series: George Dixon)

The Blue Lamp (Dixon). London, Convoy, 1950.
Dixon of Dock Green: My Life, with Charles Hatton. London, Kimber, 1960.
Dixon of Dock Green: A Novel, with Paul Graham. London, Mayflower, 1961.
Death May Surprise Us. London, Macmillan, 1974; as *Westminster One,* New York, Putnam, 1975.
The Left-Handed Sleeper. London, Macmillan, 1975; New York, Putnam, 1976.
Man-Eater. London, Macmillan, 1976; New York, Morrow, 1977.
The Churchill Commando. London, Macmillan, and New York, Morrow, 1977.
The Buckingham Palace Connection. London, Macmillan, and New York, Morrow, 1977.
The Lions of Judah. London, Macmillan, 1979; New York, Holt Rinehart, 1980.
The Naked Sun. London, Macmillan, 1980.
The Most Beautiful Girl in the World. London, Macmillan, 1982.

Uncollected Short Stories

"The Man from the White Mountains," in *Winter's Crimes 7,* edited by George Hardinge. London, Macmillan, and New York, St. Martin's Press, 1975.
"Proof," in *Winter's Crimes 10,* edited by Hilary Watson. London, Macmillan, and New York, St. Martin's Press, 1978.

OTHER PUBLICATIONS

Novels

Black Beauty. London, Hamlyn, 1972.
Spring at the Winged Horse: The First Season of Rosie Carr. London, Macmillan, and New York, Morrow, 1983.
The Green Leaves of Summer: The Second Season of Rosie Carr. London, Macmillan, 1988; New York, St. Martin's Press, 1989.
The Bells of Autumn: The Third Season of Rosie Carr. London, Macmillan, 1990.

Plays

Sabotage (as John Bishop) (produced London, 1943).
Buster (produced London, 1943). London, Fore Publications, n.d.
All Change Here (produced London, 1944).
"God Bless the Guv'nor": A Moral Melodrama in Which the Twin Evils of Trades Unionism and Strong Drink are Exposed, "After Mrs. Henry Wood" (produced London, 1945). London, New Theatre Publications, 1945.
The Yellow Star (also director: produced London, 1945).
What Happened to Love? (produced London, 1947).
No Trees in the Street (produced London, 1948).
The Lady Purrs (produced London, 1950). London, Deane, and Boston, Baker, 1950.
The Magnificent Moodies (produced London, 1952).
The Blue Lamp, with Jan Read (produced London, 1952).
A Kiss for Adele, with Talbot Rothwell, adaptation of the play by Barillet and Grédy (produced London, 1952).
Kid Kenyon Rides Again, with Allan Mackinnon (produced Bromley, Kent, 1954).
George Comes Home. London, French, 1955.
Doctor in the House, adaptation of the novel by Richard Gordon (produced London, 1956). London, Evans, and New York, French, 1957.
Woman in a Dressing Gown (televised, 1956). Included in *Woman in a Dressing Gown and Other Television Plays*, 1959; (revised version, produced Bromley, Kent, 1963; London, 1964); London, Evans, 1964.
The Young and the Guilty (televised, 1956). Included in *Woman in a Dressing Gown and Other Television Plays*, 1959.
Look in Any Window (televised, 1958). Included in *Woman in a Dressing Gown and Other Television Plays*, 1959.
Hot Summer Night (produced Bournemouth and London, 1958). London, French, 1959.
Woman in a Dressing Gown and Other Television Plays (includes *The Young and the Guilty* and *Look in Any Window*). London, Barrie and Rockliff, 1959.
Brothers-in-Law, with Henry Cecil, adaptation of the novel by Cecil (produced Wimbledon, Surrey, 1959). London, French, 1959.
When in Rome, with Ken Ferry, music by Kramer, lyrics by Eric Shaw, adaptation of a play by Garinei and Giovannini (produced Oxford and London, 1959).
The Eyes of Youth, adaptation of the novel *A Dread of Burning* by Rosemary Timperley (as *Farewell Yesterday*, produced Worthing, Sussex, 1959; as *The Eyes of Youth*, produced Bournemouth, 1959). London, Evans, 1960.
Mother, adaptation of the novel by Gorky (produced Croydon, Surrey, 1961).
Doctor at Sea, adaptation of the novel by Richard Gordon (produced Bromley, Kent, 1961; London, 1966). London, Evans, and New York, French, 1961.
The Little Goldmine. London, French, 1962.

A Slow Roll of Drums (produced Bromley, Kent, 1964).
A Murder of Crows (produced Bromley, Kent, 1966).
The Ballad of Queenie Swann (televised, 1966; revised version, music by Dick Manning and Marvin Laird, lyrics by Willis, produced Guildford, Surrey, 1967; as *Queenie*, produced London, 1967).
Dead on Saturday (produced Leatherhead, Surrey, 1972).
Mr. Polly, music by Michael Begg and Ivor Slaney, lyrics by Willis, adaptation of the novel by H.G. Wells (produced Bromley, Kent, 1977).
Stardust (produced Bromley, Kent, and London, 1983).
Tommy Boy (produced Richmond, Surrey, 1988).
Intent to Kill (produced Bromley, Kent, 1990).

Screenplays: *The Waves Roll On* (documentary), 1945; *Holiday Camp*, with others, 1947; *Good Time Girl*, with Muriel and Sydney Box, 1948; *A Boy, A Girl, and a Bike*, 1949; *The Huggetts Abroad*, with others, 1949; *The Undefeated* (documentary), 1950; *The Blue Lamp*, with others, 1950; *The Wallet*, 1952; *Top of the Form*, with John Paddy Carstairs and Patrick Kirwan, 1953; *Trouble in Store*, with John Paddy Carstairs and Maurice Cowan, 1953; *The Large Rope*, 1953; *One Good Turn*, with John Paddy Carstairs and Maurice Cowan, 1954; *Burnt Evidence*, 1954; *Up to His Neck*, with others, 1954; *It's Great to Be Young*, 1956; *The Skywalkers*, 1956; *Woman in a Dressing Gown*, 1957; *The Young and the Guilty*, 1958; *No Trees in the Street*, 1959; *Six Men and a Nightingale*, 1961; *Flame in the Streets*, 1961; *The Horsemasters*, 1961; *Bitter Harvest*, 1963; *Last Bus to Banjo Creek*, 1968; *Our Miss Fred*, with Hugh Leonard, 1972; and other documentaries.

Radio Plays: *Big Bertha*, 1962; *And No Birds Sing*, 1979; *The Buckingham Palace Connection*, from his own novel, 1981; *The Left-Handed Sleeper*, from his own novel, 1982; *Obsession*, 1983; *Death May Surprise Us*, from his own novel, 1984.

Television Plays: *The Handlebar, The Pattern of Marriage, Big City, Dial 999, The Sullavan Brothers, Lifeline,* and *Taxi* series; *Dixon of Dock Green* series, 1954, and later series; *The Young and the Guilty*, 1956; *Woman in a Dressing Gown*, 1956; *Look in Any Window*, 1958; *Strictly for the Sparrows*, 1958; *Scent of Fear*, 1959; *Days of Vengeance*, with Edward J. Mason, 1960; *Flowers of Evil* series, with Mason, 1961; *Outbreak of Murder*, with Mason; *Sergeant Cork* series, 1963; *The Four Seasons of Rosie Carr*, 1964; *Dream of a Summer Night*, 1965; *Mrs. Thursday* series, 1966; *The Ballad of Queenie Swann*, 1966; *Virgin of the Secret Service* series, 1968; *Crimes of Passion* series, 1970–72; *Copper's End* series, 1971; *Hunter's Walk* series, 1973, 1976; *Black Beauty* series, 1975; *Barney's Last Battle*, 1976; *Street Party*, 1977; *Man-Eater*, from his own novel, 1980; *Einetleim für Tiere*, series (from 1984, Germany); *Mrs. Harris, M.P.*, 1985; *Mrs. Harris Goes to New York*, 1987; *The Iron Man*, 1987; *Mrs. Harris Goes to Moscow*, 1987; *Racecourse* series, 1987; *The Valley of Dream*, 1987; *Mrs. Harris Goes to Monte Carlo*, 1988; *Vincent Vincent*, 1989; *Mrs. Harris Goes to Majorca*, 1990.

Other

Fighting Youth of Russia. London, Russia Today Society, 1942.
The Devil's Churchyard (for children). London, Parrish, 1957.
Seven Gates to Nowhere (for children). London, Parrish, 1958.
Whatever Happened to Tom Mix? The Story of One of My Lives. London, Cassell, 1970.
A Problem for Mother Christmas (for children). London, Gollancz, 1986.

*

Theatrical Activities:

Director: **Plays**—Unity Theatre, London: *The Yellow Star*, 1945; *Boy Meets Girl* by Bella and Samuel Spewack, 1946; *All God's Chillun Got Wings* by Eugene O'Neill, 1946; *Golden Boy* by Clifford Odets, 1947; *Anna Christie* by Eugene O'Neill.

* * *

A late starter in the field of the crime novel, Ted Willis came to it with a considerable reputation in Britain both as a television writer (he was responsible for the creation of one of the best-loved characters on the small screen, the policeman Dixon of Dock Green) and as a playwright. The qualities he had shown in these pursuits, warmth, compassion, a feeling for the ordinary man, he brought to the crime novel. And it was this instinctive knowledge of what the average man or woman, the ordinary reader, wanted that accounted for Willis's increasing success as a writer of crime fiction.

But Ted Willis is also Lord Willis, a politically created Life Peer, a member of the Labour Party. And it was this aspect of his life that provided him with the setting for his first original novel, *Death May Surprise Us*, a story in which the Prime Minister of Great Britain is kidnapped. To it he brought his considerable knowledge of the everyday workings of politics, the little things, the day-to-day routine. And it was this accuracy of detail, a quality no doubt learnt in the making of television plays and series where in general an extremely lifelike surface is created, that gave to the book its distinctive quality. As a novel, however, it lacked the very quality spoken of in its title, surprise. Its people were inclined to behave in the expected way, lifelike though that was.

A year later he gave us *The Left-Handed Sleeper*, a novel on the fascinating subject of the sleeper spy, the man or woman left for years to build up a cover in a foreign country and then suddenly activated by a control in a distant and perhaps now largely forgotten homeland. To this he brought the same concentration on everyday detail that had given his first book its authenticity but now he seemingly felt more free to take risks with the characterisation, to create people who behaved occasionally in an unexpected way. And he concentrated a good deal of the book on the figure of the spy's wife (he has always been good at portraying women) with the result that you felt "Here is something that might have happened to me, or to my wife."

For his next book, *Man-Eater*, he deserted the world of Westminster and Whitehall to write something in the nature of a pure thriller. He took a very simple idea—two tigers escape into the English countryside—and he showed what the effects would be, in the likeliest manner. This was the "You are there" novel at its best. Subsequent books, though varying considerably in subject, increasingly hit on what was attractive to the taste of a wide public. *The Churchill Commando* was political fiction comparable to science fiction in that it was set in a future time and intended as a warning of possible consequences of present policies. *The Buckingham Palace Connection* plunged into the past with conjecture, always at a human level (the narrator of the present-day outer story was a certain Life Peer called Lord Willis) about the fate of the children of the last Tsar. *The Lions of Judah* imagined a situation in 1939, not without a strong lacing of facts, in which a terrible bargain is postulated over the fate of a number of Germany's Jews, and *The Naked Sun* took another very human piece of war history, the escape of Japanese prisoners from an Australian camp in 1944, to tell a strong story with simple and wide appeal.

In *The Most Beautiful Girl in the World*, however, the disadvantages of this appeal to a wide common denominator showed. A kidnap story moving from London to the Caribbean, it was crammed with adventurous episodes recalling at times the work of another author of huge popular appeal, Edgar Wallace. But in its simplicity of approach it tested, as did Wallace in his day, credibility to breaking-point and perhaps beyond.

—H.R.F. Keating

———

WILLS, (Maitland) Cecil M(elville). British. Born in 1891.

CRIME PUBLICATIONS

Novels (series: Geoffrey Boscobell; Roger Ellerdine; Sylvester Pinkney)

Author in Distress (Boscobell). London, Heritage, 1934; as *Number 18*, London, Lane, 1934.
Death at the Pelican (Boscobell). London, Heritage, 1934.
Death Treads—(Boscobell). London, Heritage, 1935.
Then Came the Police (Boscobell). London, Heritage, 1935.
The Chamois Murder (Boscobell). London, Heritage, 1935.
Fatal Accident (Boscobell). London, Hodder and Stoughton, 1936.
Defeat of a Detective (Boscobell). London, Hodder and Stoughton, 1936.
On the Night in Question (Boscobell). London, Hodder and Stoughton, 1937.
A Body in the Dawn (Boscobell). London, Hodder and Stoughton, 1938.
The Case of the Calabar Bean (Boscobell). London, Hodder and Stoughton, 1939.
The Case of the R.E. Pipe (Boscobell, Ellerdine). London, Hodder and Stoughton, 1940.
The Clue of the Lost Hour (Boscobell, Ellerdine). London, Hodder and Stoughton, 1949.
The Clue of the Golden Ear-Ring (Boscobell, Ellerdine). London, Hodder and Stoughton, 1950.
Who Killed Brother Treasurer? (Ellerdine). London, Hodder and Stoughton, 1951.
What Say the Jury? (Ellerdine). London, Hodder and Stoughton, 1951.
The Dead Voice (Ellerdine). London, Hodder and Stoughton, 1952.
It Pays to Die (Ellerdine). London, Hodder and Stoughton, 1953.
Death on the Line. London, Hutchinson, 1954.
Death in the Dark (Ellerline). London, Hutchinson, 1955.
Midsummer Murder London, Hutchinson, 1956.
The Tiger Strikes Again (Ellerdine). London, Hutchinson, 1957.
Mere Murder (Ellerdine). London, Hale, 1958.
The Case of the Empty Beehive (Pinkney). London, Hale, 1959.
Death of a Best Seller (Pinkney). London, Hale, 1959.
The Colonel's Foxhound (Pinkney). London, Hale, 1960.
Justice in Jeopardy (Ellerdine). London, Hale, 1961.

* * *

Cecil M. Wills wrote numerous detective novels most of them featuring series detectives Geoffrey Boscobell or Roger Ellerdine. The early novels experiment with the incomparable Boscobell, who develops from an inexperienced but perceptive police sergeant to a skillful Scotland Yard superintendent. In the later novels, Ellerdine and his colleague Cherry Blossom replace Boscobell and exhibit more sleuthing powers than their predecessor. Wills frequently laces the mystery with political intrigue, particularly in his later books.

Boscobell's cunning, like that of Ellerdine and Blossom, increases as Wills's handling of the genre improves. In *Death at the Pelican* Boscobell uses his wits to escape murder and arrest his arch enemy, Theodore Edwards. In *The Chamois Murder* Boscobell, now a superintendent at Scotland Yard, foils the same nemesis by discovering, in a maze of false clues, that Edwards's partner committed burglary and murder; the partner, in his haste to provide an alibi, broadcast the Big Ben chimes three minutes early. The mechanics and motives of the crime and the method of solution are smooth and credible in the Boscobell mysteries, because, with each book, Wills extends the greed and refines the cunning of the nemesis to keep pace with the sharpening talents of the detective. Edwards is a worthy opponent who skillfully eludes the authorities throughout the novels. In *Death at the Pelican*, he causes nine days of wonder in the newspapers with a sensational escape from a police van which was taking him to trial. His disappearance in *The Chamois Murder*, in which he escapes detection for months by adopting the disguise of a baron, is even more startling. Though Edwards's identity is suspected, he is not apprehended until Boscobell discovers the mistake of the criminal's partner.

Wills's use of worthy opponents, slick detection, intricate plots, and ingenious murders culminates in the Ellerdine and Blossom mysteries. *The Tiger Strikes Again* features the impressive victory of this pair over the bizarre murderer Dr. Floyd Huish, the creator of a snake venom that destroys the most influential drug peddlers in London. Horatio Pinckney, in *The Colonel's Foxhound*, exhibits the same sleuthing prowess as Ellerdine and Blossom. Commissioned by a count to find some stolen treaty papers, Pinckney unearths a murder, discovers smuggled rubies and, with the help of the colonel's foxhound, restores the stolen papers. The book features a very intricate murder: the murderer removes a bullet from the victim and replaces it with one from another gun. The tightly-knit plot closes with the detective's personal comments: Wills often used this classic device—the detective's lenthy explanation and the criminal's confession—in his later books.

In his 30-year career Wills developed into a skillful writer: the increasing talents of his detectives correspond to his growing technical mastery of the genre.

—Donna Casella-Kern

———

WILLS, Thomas. *See* **ARD, William.**

———

WILMER, Dale. *See* **MILLER, Wade.**

———

WILSON, Barbara (Ellen). American. Born in Long Beach, California, 17 October 1950. Publisher, Seal Press, Seattle, Washington. Address: c/o Seal Press, 3131 Western Avenue, Seattle, Washington 98121, U.S.A.

CRIME PUBLICATIONS

Novels (series: Pam Nilsen; Cassandra Reilly)

Murder in the Collective (Nilsen). Seattle, Washington, Seal Press, and London, Women's Press, 1984.
Sisters of the Road (Nilsen). Seattle, Washington, Seal Press, 1986; London, Women's Press, 1987.
The Dog Collar Murders (Nilsen). Seattle, Washington, Seal Press, and London, Virago, 1989.
Gaudi Afternoon (Reilly). Seattle, Washington, Seal Press, 1990; London, Virago Press, 1991.

Uncollected Short Stories

"Murder at the International Feminist Book Fair," in *Reader I Murdered Him*, edited by Jen Green. London, Women's Press, 1989; New York, St. Martin's Press, 1990.
"The Theft of the Poet," in *A Woman's Eye*, edited by Sara Paretsky and Martin H. Greenberg. New York, Delacorte Press, 1990.

OTHER PUBLICATIONS

Novels

Ambitious Women. Seattle, Washington, Seal Press, 1982; London, Women's Press, 1983.
Cows and Horses. Portland, Oregon, Eighth Mountain Press, 1988; London, Virago Press, 1989.

Short Stories

Talk and Contact. Seattle, Washington, Seal Press, 1978.
Thin Ice. Seattle, Washington, Seal Press, 1981.
Walking on the Moon. Seattle, Washington, Seal Press, 1983; London, Women's Press, 1986.
Miss Venezuela. Seattle, Washington, Seal Press, 1988.

Other

The Geography Lesson (for children). Seattle, Washington, Seal Press, 1977.

Editor, with Faith Conlon and Rachel de Silva, *The Things That Divide Us* (short stories). Seattle, Washington, Seal Press, 1985; London, Sheba, 1986.

Translator, *Cora Sandel: Collected Short Stories.* Seattle, Washington, Seal Press, 1985
Translator, *Nothing Happened*, by Ebba Haslund. Seattle, Washington, Seal Press, 1987.

*

Barbara Wilson comments:
My work is concerned with progressive and feminist issues such as collectives, Third World politics, juvenile prostitution, pornography, and transsexualism. The first three novels feature

Pam Nilsen; they deal with leftist and lesbian subcultures in Seattle. My fourth mystery novel introduces Irish-American Spanish translator Cassandra Reilly and is a comic crime novel set in Barcelona. Mystery fiction is a way for me to exercise my satiric bent as well as to question both society's conventions and those of the crime novel. I enjoy the idea of subverting the genre.

*   *   *

Barbara Wilson has been extremely visible in feminist publishing since the early 1980's. Her own background in women-run and/or feminist print cooperatives provides the settings of her crime novels. Like her later crime novels, Wilson's first novel—*Ambitious Women*, a political thriller—is set in Seattle. *Ambitious Women* focuses on women taking responsibility for their own lives. The complicated plot embraces the victims of domestic violence, the women who work with them, the politics of marriage and the family, and the world of political terrorism.

Many of these issues resurface in the Pam Nilsen books for which Wilson is most widely known and read. These have been widely hailed, if not universally enjoyed, as interesting contributions to the developing genre of feminist crime fiction. In the last decade there has been a rapid growth in the number of capable, competent, independent and, often, politically radical female sleuths on the crime fiction scene. It has been widely remarked that feminist writers have turned to detective fiction, and other popular genres, in an attempt to appropriate them for their own purposes. Genres which have often been considered to be conservative in form (like detective fiction) have taken on a new life as they have been made into the vehicles of a leftist politics and a radical sexual politics. Wilson is one of a number of lesbian/femininist writers who have played a particularly important part in this revamping of the detective novel.

As the part-owner of a left-wing printing press Wilson's Pam Nilsen is constantly embroiled in political discussion and political activism. In *Murder in the Collective* these issues take on a greater urgency when one of her male co-workers is murdered during merger discussions with another, lesbian-run, print collective. The ensuing investigation in which Pam becomes involved is presented as both an extension of her political activism and the means by which she comes to reassess both her politics and her activism. The denouement raises more political and ethical questions than it resolves. The motive for the murder, when it is revealed, raises broad political questions about American imperialism. The revelation of the identity of the murderer, and the question of what the "successful" amateur detectives should do with their knowledge raises important questions about the competing claims of legality, political solidarity and sisterhood. In this novel the detection process also involves the amateur detective in a reassessment of her own sexuality. The detection plot becomes a kind of metaphor for the heroine's discovery of her hitherto hidden sexual identity, as she becomes involved in a lesbian affair with Hadley, one of her co-detectives.

The issues of sexual politics come more to the fore in the second Nilsen adventure, *Sisters of the Road*. Nilsen's second case arises from a chance meeting with two teenage prostitutes, one of whom is actually dying of viciously inflicted head wounds. The second, Trish, immediately disappears, and Nilsen's subsequent journey through the Seattle streets in search of her, leads the investigator into the (to her) unfamiliar world of prostitutes, runaways, and sexual exploitation. Nilsen becomes involved in the search for Trish, partly from a sense of sisterhood, and partly from her own vulnerability and need as

the personal and political networks she has made for herself are in the process of change. Here, as in all the Nilsen novels, the investigator's personal life becomes part of, and is changed by, the investigation. The mystery plot focuses on sexual violence, on women as victims (and as survivors), and on attitudes to sexuality. Throughout this novel Wilson insistently places her detective inside the structures she investigates. Nilsen is not allowed to occupy the position of detached mastery which the investigative role (especially in the male hard-boiled detective novel) sometimes implies. Nilsen is forced (with the reader?) to see herself as part of the world and the structure of values which produces the wasted and tortured lives she observes on the mean streets of low-life Seattle, not least when Nilsen herself becomes a victim of the criminal she is seeking.

The latest Nilsen story, *The Dog Collar Murders*, focuses on recent feminist debates on pornography, and also on current controversies in lesbian sexual politics. The story is prefaced by an epigraph from Michel Foucault's *The History of Sexuality* which suggests that its author is, perhaps, more interested in polemics than in mystery plotting. Indeed the murder of Loie Marsh, a prominent anti-pornography activist, serves as a convenient peg on which to hang debates about the nature of sexual desire (especially lesbian desire), the values and dangers of pornography, the question of feminist involvement in the censorship of pornography and so on. The fact that Loie is found strangled by a dog collar immediately throws suspicion on the advocates of lesbian sado-masochism, and gives Wilson the opportunity of engaging in debates on this issue too. The mystery plot is also neatly tied to the complexities of Nilsen's evolving relationship with Hadley, a notable presence in all the Nilsen books. Despite a slight preachiness, this, like all the Nilsen books, is sharp, witty and streetwise.

—Lyn Pykett

———

WILSON, Colin (Henry). British. Born in Leicester, 26 June 1931. Educated at Gateway Secondary Technical School, Leicester, 1942–47. Served in the Royal Air Force, 1949–50. Married 1) Dorothy Betty Troop in 1951 (divorced 1952), one son; 2) Pamela Joy Stewart in 1960, two sons and one daughter. Laboratory assistant, Gateway School, 1948–49; tax collector, Leicester and Rugby, 1949–50; labourer and hospital porter in London, 1951–53; salesman for the magazines *Paris Review* and *Merlin*, Paris, 1953. Since 1954 full-time writer. British Council Lecturer in Germany, 1957; Writer-in-Residence, Hollins College, Virginia, 1966–67; Visiting Professor, University of Washington, Seattle, 1968; Professor, Institute of the Mediterranean (Dowling College, New York), Majorca, 1969; Visiting Professor, Rutgers University, New Brunswick, New Jersey, 1974. Agent: David Bolt Associates, 12 Heath Drive, Ripley, Surrey GV23 7EP; or, Al Zuckerman, Writers House Inc., 21 West 26 Street, New York, New York 10010, U.S.A. Address: Tetherdown, Trewallock Lane, Gorran Haven, Cornwall, England.

CRIME PUBLICATIONS

Novels

Ritual in the Dark. London, Gollancz, and Boston, Houghton Mifflin, 1960.

The World of Violence. London, Gollancz, 1963; as *The Violent World of Hugh Greene*, Boston, Houghton Mifflin, 1963.
Necessary Doubt. London, Barker, and New York, Simon and Schuster, 1964.
The Glass Cage: An Unconventional Detective Story. London, Barker, 1966; New York, Random House, 1967.
The Philosopher's Stone. London, Barker, 1969; New York, Crown, 1971.
The Killer. London, New English Library, 1970; as *Lingard*, New York, Crown, 1970.
The God of the Labyrinth. London, Hart Davis, 1970; as *The Hedonists*, New York, New American Library, 1971.
The Black Room. London, Weidenfeld and Nicolson, 1971; New York, Pyramid, 1975.
The Schoolgirl Murder Case. London, Hart Davis MacGibbon, and New York, Crown, 1974.
The Janus Murder Case. London, Granada, 1984.
The Personality Surgeon. London, New English Library, and San Francisco, Mercury, House, 1986.
The Magician from Siberia. London, Hale, 1988.

OTHER PUBLICATIONS

Novels

Adrift in Soho. London, Gollancz, and Boston, Houghton Mifflin, 1961.
Man Without a Shadow: The Diary of an Existentialist. London, Barker, 1963; as *The Sex Diary of Gerard Sorme*, New York, Dial Press, 1963.
The Mind Parasites. London, Barker, and Sauk City, Wisconsin, Arkham House, 1967.
The Space Vampires. London, Hart Davis MacGibbon, and New York, Random House, 1976.
Spider World: The Delta. London, Grafton, 1987.
Spider World: The Tower. London, Grafton, 1987.

Short Story

The Return of the Lloigor. London, Village Press, 1974.

Plays

Viennese Interlude (produced Scarborough, Yorkshire, and London, 1960).
Strindberg (as *Pictures in a Bath of Acid*, produced Leeds, Yorkshire, 1971; as *Strindberg: A Fool's Decision*, produced London, 1975). London, Calder and Boyars, 1970; New York, Random House, 1971.
Mysteries (produced Cardiff, 1979).

Other

The Outsider. London, Gollancz, and Boston, Houghton Mifflin, 1956.
Religion and the Rebel. London, Gollancz, and Boston, Houghton Mifflin, 1957.
The Age of Defeat. London, Gollancz, 1959; as *The Stature of Man*, Boston, Houghton Mifflin, 1959.
Encyclopaedia of Murder, with Patricia Pitman. London, Baker, 1961; New York, Putnam, 1962.
The Strength to Dream: Literature and the Imagination. London, Gollancz, and Boston, Houghton Mifflin, 1962.
Origins of the Sexual Impulse. London, Baker, and New York, Putnam, 1963.

Rasputin and the Fall of the Romanovs. London, Baker, and New York, Farrar Straus, 1964.
Brandy of the Damned: Discoveries of a Musical Eclectic. London, Baker, 1964; as *Chords and Discords: Purely Personal Opinions on Music*, New York, Crown, 1966; augmented edition as *Colin Wilson on Music*, London, Pan, 1967.
Beyond the Outsider: The Philosophy of the Future. London, Baker, and Boston, Houghton Mifflin, 1965.
Eagle and Earwig (essays). London, Baker, 1965.
Introduction to the New Existentialism. London, Hutchinson, 1966; Boston, Houghton Mifflin, 1967; as *The New Existentialism*, London, Wildwood House, 1980.
Sex and the Intelligent Teenager. London, Arrow, 1966; New York, Pyramid, 1968.
Voyage to a Beginning (autobiography). London, Cecil and Amelia Woolf, 1966; New York, Crown, 1969.
Bernard Shaw: A Reassessment. London, Hutchinson, and New York, Atheneum, 1969.
A Casebook of Murder. London, Frewin, 1969; New York, Cowles, 1970.
Poetry and Mysticism. San Francisco, City Lights, 1969; London, Hutchinson, 1970.
The Strange Genius of David Lindsay, with E.H. Visiak and J.B. Pick. London, Baker, 1970; as *The Haunted Man*, San Bernardino, California, Borgo Press, 1979.
The Occult. New York, Random House, and London, Hodder and Stoughton, 1971.
New Pathways in Psychology: Maslow and the Post-Freudian Revolution. New York, Taplinger, and London, Gollancz, 1972.
Order of Assassins: The Psychology of Murder. London, Hart Davis, 1972.
L'Amour: The Ways of Love, photographs by Piero Rimaldi. New York, Crown, 1972.
Strange Powers. London, Latimer New Dimensions, 1973; New York, Random House, 1975.
Tree by Tolkien. London, Covent Garden Press-Inca, 1973; Santa Barbara, California, Capra Press, 1974.
Hermann Hesse. London, Village Press, and Philadelphia, Leaves of Grass Press, 1974.
Wilhelm Reich. London, Village Press, and Philadelphia, Leaves of Grass Press, 1974.
Jorge Luis Borges. London, Village Press, and Philadelphia, Leaves of Grass Press, 1974.
A Book of Booze. London, Gollancz, 1974.
The Unexplained. Lake Oswego, Oregon, Lost Pleiade Press, 1975.
Mysterious Powers. London, Aldus, and Danbury, Connecticut, Danbury Press, 1975; as *They Had Strange Powers*, New York, Doubleday, 1975; revised edition, as *Mysteries of the Mind*, with Stuart Holroyd, London, Aldus, 1978.
The Craft of the Novel. London, Gollancz, 1975.
Enigmas and Mysteries. Danbury, Connecticut, Danbury Press, and London, Aldus, 1976.
The Geller Phenomenon. London, Aldus, 1976.
Mysteries: An Investigation into the Occult, The Paranormal, and the Supernatural. London, Hodder and Stoughton, and New York, Putnam, 1978.
Science Fiction as Existentialism. Hayes, Middlesex, Bran's Head, 1978.
The Search for the Real Arthur, with *King Arthur Country in Cornwall*, by Brenda Duxbury and Michael Williams. Bodmin, Cornwall, Bossiney, 1979.
Starseekers. London, Hodder and Stoughton, 1980; New York, Doubleday, 1981.

The War Against Sleep: The Philosophy of Gurdjieff. Wellingborough, Northamptonshire, Aquarian Press, and York Beach, Maine, Weiser, 1980; revised edition Aquarian Press, 1986.

Frankenstein's Castle. Sevenoaks, Kent, Ashgrove Press, 1980; Salem, New Hampshire, Salem House, 1982.

Anti-Sartre, with an Essay on Camus. San Bernardino, California, Borgo Press, 1981.

The Quest for Wilhelm Reich. London, Granada, and New York, Doubleday, 1981.

Witches. Limpsfield, Surrey, Dragon's World, 1981; New York, A and W, 1982.

Poltergeist! A Study in Destructive Haunting. London, New English Library, 1981; New York, Putnam, 1982.

Access to Inner Worlds: The Story of Brad Absetz. London, Rider, 1983.

Encyclopaedia of Modern Murder 1962–82, with Donald Seaman. London, Baker, 1983; New York, Putnam, 1985.

Psychic Detectives: The Story of Psychometry and the Paranormal in Crime Detection. London, Pan, 1984; San Francisco, Mercury House, 1985.

A Criminal History of Mankind. London, Granada, and New York, Putnam, 1984.

Lord of the Underworld: Jung and the Twentieth Century. Wellingborough, Northamptonshire, Aquarian Press, 1984.

The Essential Colin Wilson. London, Harrap, 1985.

The Bicameral Critic, edited by Howard F. Dossor. Bath, Avon, Ashgrove Press, 1985.

Rudolf Steiner: The Man and His Vision. Wellingborough, Northamptonshire, Aquarian Press, 1985.

Afterlife: An Investigation of the Evidence of Life After Death. London, Harrap, 1985; New York, Doubleday, 1987.

Scandal! An Encyclopaedia, with Donald Seaman. London, Weidenfeld and Nicolson, and New York, Stein and Day, 1986.

The Encyclopaedia of Unsolved Mysteries, with Damon Wilson. London, Harrap, 1987; Chicago, Contemporary Books, 1988.

Jack the Ripper: Summing Up and Verdict, with Robin Odell, edited by J.H.H. Gaute. London Bantam, 1987.

Aleister Crowley: The Nature of the Beast. Wellingborough, Northamptonshire, Aquarian Press, 1987.

The Musician as "Outsider". Nottingham, Pauper Press, 1987.

The Misfits: A Study of Sexual Outsiders. London, Grafton, 1988; New York, Carroll and Graf, 1989.

Beyond the Occult. London, Bantam, 1988; New York, Carroll and Graf, 1989.

Autobiographical Reflections. Nottingham, Pauper Press, 1988.

Lord Halifax's Ghost Book. London, Bellew, 1989.

Written in Blood: A History of Forensic Detection. Wellingborough, Northamptonshire, Equation, 1989.

Serial Killer, with Donald Seaman. London, W.H. Allen, 1990.

Editor, *Colin Wilson's Men of Mystery.* London, W.H. Allen, 1977.

Editor, *Dark Dimensions: A Celebration of the Occult.* London, Everest House, 1978.

Editor, with John Grant, *The Book of Time.* Newton Abbot, Devon, David and Charles, 1980.

Editor, with John Grant, *The Directory of Possibilities.* Exeter, Webb and Bower, and New York, Rutledge Press, 1981.

Editor, *The Book of Great Mysteries,* with Christopher Evans. London, Robinson, 1986.

Editor. *The Mammoth Book of True Crime,* London, Robinson, and New York, Carroll and Graf, 1988.

Editor, *The Mammoth Book of True Crime 2.* London, Robinson, and New York, Carroll and Graf, 1990.

*

Manuscript Collection: University of Texas, Austin.

Critical Studies: *The Angry Decade* by Kenneth Allsop, London, Peter Owen, 1958; *The World of Colin Wilson* by Sidney Campion, London, Muller, 1963; "The Novels of Colin Wilson" by Richard Dillard, in *Hollins Critic* (Hollins College, Virginia), October 1967; *Colin Wilson* by John A. Weigel, New York, Twayne, 1975; *The Novels of Colin Wilson* by Nicolas Tredell, London, Vision Press, 1982; *An Odyssey of Freedom: Four Themes in Colin Wilson's Novels* by K. Gunnar Bergström, Uppsala, University of Uppsala, 1983.

*   *   *

Colin Wilson is so much more than a writer of "mysteries" that his inclusion here might be equivocal if mystery writers had not recently become intellectually respectable. Wilson's first book, *The Outsider,* appeared in 1956 with a bang. Almost instantly an international bestseller, this compendium of learning later became controversial. Critics who at first had enthusiastically praised young Wilson as a prodigy of erudition reconsidered. After reading the work more carefully—or perhaps for the first time—many denounced him as a fraud.

Wilson, however, survived the attack on him and his first work. In fact, he flourished, establishing during the next two decades his professional competence as novelist, biographer, philosopher, and critic. In his crusade to defeat defeatism Wilson has not hesitated to mix genres, so that his novels are often didactic and his non-fiction anecdotal.

When read as Wilson intends them to be, his speculative fiction and so-called "crime novels" (Wilson's term) invite the reader to do much more than try to solve puzzles. Wilson makes no attempt to swindle the reader into vicarious thrills. He treats crime, for example, philosophically and esthetically. His killers are artists, and his detectives humanists. The "solution" is generally predictable because it is both logical and psychological. Wilson intends that killers, detectives, and readers all experience an epiphany. The victims, of course, are beyond redemption.

In *Ritual in the Dark* Wilson explores murder as a creative act. In *Necessary Doubt* the detective is an existentialist theologian who allows the criminal to escape at the end. In *The Glass Cage* the detective, an authority on the works of William Blake, is finally converted to the point of view of the killer. In *The Killer* the criminal is defended by the novelist as "not necessarily and completely wrong." In *The Schoolgirl Murder Case* the detective behaves much like a missionary. Wilson sees an affinity between detecting crimes and saving souls and thus Saltfleet in *The Schoolgirl Murder Case* is a new kind of detective, mixing mysticism and science. At one point he even consults a lady who specializes in psychic visions. Not surprisingly, her intuitions prove to be correct. It hardly seems to be playing the game fairly, however, to credit mystic events as equal to so-called real events in a hard-headed detective story. Yet Wilson may have found a new formula as viable for its genre as his new existentialism hopes to be for philosophy.

If Wilson shifts with the winds of opportunity it is because he is authentic enough to relate himself to humanity and its needs. Such awareness is indeed in danger of being mistrusted by skeptics not accustomed to dealing with a writer's work in terms of his intentions. Wilson addresses himself to strictly contemporary problems as he tries to penetrate the fog that for him obscures *real* reality. His methodology participates in his urgency, for his creed specifies that man is always more than any method. At times Wilson may be only absurdly heroic, in the sense of working against overwhelming odds; but he knows it more often than not and indulges in a minimum of despair and irony. Indeed, his urgency usually eradicates irony and discourages witty trivia as he fights the slackness which would follow an acceptance of despair as terminal. Determined to survive, he feels that, as the first new existentialist, he has earned the right to his optimism. Anyway, his ultimate wrongness or rightness may be insignificant when compared to the possible significance of his trust and impact in nontechnical contexts.

Balanced, then, at the edge of mysticism in a universe which is obviously not governed by any of the old Sunday School gods, Wilson asks, as earnestly as Julian Huxley has, for religion without revelation. He would also develop a science without limitations on freedom. He urges man toward salvation by exhorting and stimulating him to see more, to hear more, to feel more, to touch more—that is, to apprehend what is *really* out there and what is *really* inside oneself. The Outsider is invited to embrace the complete universe and to cure his outsiderism. Wilson would have us save our souls!

—John A. Weigel

WINGS, Mary. American. Born in Chicago, Illinois, 14 April 1949. Educated at San Francisco State University; Shimer College, Mount Cassoll, Illinois, 1988–90. Book designer, Transnational Institute, Amsterdam, 1983–86. Agent: Jane Gregory, Gregory and Radice, Riverside Studios, Crisp Road, London W6 9RL, England. Address: 678 Vermont Street, San Francisco, California 94107, U.S.A.

CRIME PUBLICATIONS

Novels (series: Emma Victor in both books)

She Came Too Late. London, Women's Press, 1986; Freedom, California, Crossing Press, 1987.
She Came in a Flash. London, Women's Press, and New York, New American Library, 1988.

Uncollected Short Stories

"Kill the Man for Me," in *A Woman's Eye,* edited by Sara Paretsky and Martin H. Greenberg, New York, Delacorte Press, 1990.
"Mars Bar," in *Outlook* (San Francisco), Summer 1990.

OTHER PUBLICATIONS

Other

Come Out Comix. Portland, Oregon, Portland Women's Resource Center, 1974.
Dyke Shorts. Privately printed, 1977.
Are Your Highs Getting You Down. Privately printed, 1980.

*

Mary Wings comments:
The conventions of the hard-boiled detective novel with its urban setting and disenfranchised heroine seem most appropriate for a lesbian detective story. I wanted to give my readers a heroine who took control, took action, but didn't take any lip.

* * *

There are books whose partial successes characterise a particular historical moment better than far more achieved texts; there are even books which do this through their crashing gallant failures. *She Came Too Late,* the first and more successful of Mary Wings's two thrillers, captures a particular moment of feminist radicalism, both in its background and in its serious attempt at the almost impossible—the reconciliation of the hard-boiled *noir* thriller with a particular impossibilist radical lesbian feminist agenda.

It fails partly because it tries to have its cake and eat it; where a more thorough-going book like Rebecca O'Rourke's *Between the Cracks* makes a feminist virtue out of the heroine's failure to understand what is going on except at a late stage, and laterally, Wings attempts to deconstruct the patriarchal notion of competence by having her heroine blunder around knuckling her forehead with impatience at herself, but getting the solution right in the end. This would work better at the ideological level, if it were not a standard device of the private eye thriller in any case. Wings is doing something a lot less unusual, and therefore less radical, than she seems to reckon.

Further, in the context in which it is placed, Emma's slow understanding of the plots in which she is enmeshed comes to seem less like the "I began to understand" of the private-eye novel and more like the "Had I but known" of the gothic woman in peril novel. The hidden crimes gradually revealed are particularly gothic in mode—the women whose avenger Emma Victor becomes have been the victim of almost fairy-tale treacheries. This is partly deliberate; part of Wings's agenda here is to discuss, sensationally, some of the grounds for concern which feminists have found in fertility research, and the use of myths of intrusion is a deliberate strategy. The trouble with the image of "woman in peril" is that it very easily slides into that of "woman as victim," as does the democratic refusal to make the heroine extraordinarily competent and the sense of betrayal around which the plot is arranged. If there is any point whatever in using the rhetoric of the private-eye novel to discuss a feminist agenda, it lies in the genre's myth of agenthood, of the detective as the avenger of victims.

These positions sit uneasily with the flirtations with the more traditional aspects of the *noir* thriller. At the climax, Emma tells the villainous Stacey "I'm sending you over," a sentence echoing in its anachronistic slang the final confrontation between Sam Spade and Bridget O'Shaughnessey in Hammett's *The Maltese Falcon;* where the individualistic ethos of Hammett's novel expresses refusal to compromise in the face of a personal appeal from someone loved but untrustworthy, here Emma refuses a political appeal from someone whose untrustworthiness has manifested at a political as well as at a personal level. The personal is political, of course, but somehow the echo and the extent to which it is also a refusal indicate what is wrong.

Where *She Came Too Late* is at least an interesting failure, *She Came in a Flash* is a rather dull one, taking various features of the Bhagwan scandal and shifting them to California. Here the sense of betrayal is rather more arbitrary; Emma has no particular reason save sexual attraction to trust the prosetylising Bumper in the first place, and the plot's resolution replaces what were at least real anxieties about reproductive technology with some stock drug dealing plot tropes, coincidences and disguises.

In all save plot, Wings is a competent writer—though her creation of local atmosphere tends towards, and sometimes reaches, travelogue—and her heroine is better than the books in which she finds herself. Emma Victor's insatiable capacity for getting sexually involved, though never distracted, in the middle of her investigations is agreeably raunchy, and the sense of the social milieu of her rather different Boston and West Coast activist environments is strong. Wings's popularity in that milieu and its equivalents has more to do with that than with her specifically thriller-writing skills.

—Roz Kaveney

WINSLOW, Pauline Glen. Also writes as Jane Sheridan. American. Born in London, England. Educated at Sybourn Street School, and Leyton County High School, both England; Hunter College, Columbia University, and New School for Social Research, all New York. Married Ray Winslow in 1964. Court reporter, New York City and State governments, and Federal Government, 1955–63; United Nations court reporter, New York, 1963–64; freelance court reporter, New York, 1964–73. Recipient: Yaddo grant; Huntington Hartford Foundation grant. Agent: Bleeker Street Associates, 88 Bleeker Street, New York, New York 10012, U.S.A.

CRIME PUBLICATIONS

Novels (series: Merle Capricorn in all books)

Death of an Angel. London, Macmillan, and New York, St. Martin's Press, 1975.
The Brandenburg Hotel. New York, St. Martin's Press, and London, Macmillan, 1976.
The Witch Hill Murder. New York, St. Martin's Press, and London, Collins, 1977.
Coppergold. New York, St. Martin's Press, and London, Collins, 1978.
The Counsellor Heart. New York, St. Martin's Press, and London, Collins, 1980; as *Sister Death*, London, Fontana, 1982.
The Rockefeller Gift. New York, St. Martin's Press, 1981; London, Collins, 1982.

OTHER PUBLICATIONS

Novels

The Strawberry Marten. London, Macmillan, 1973; as *Gallows Child*, New York, St. Martin's Press, 1978.
The Windsor Plot. London, Arlington, 1981; New York, St. Martin's Press, 1985.
I, Martha Adams. London, Arlington, 1982; New York, St. Martin's Press, 1984.
The Kindness of Strangers. London, Arlington, 1983.
Judgement Day. London, Arlington, 1984; New York, St. Martin's Press, 1986.
A Cry in the City. New York, St. Martin's Press, 1990.

Novels as Jane Sheridan

Damaris. New York, St. Martin's Press, 1978; London, Collins, 1979.
My Lady Hoyden. New York, St. Martin's Press, 1981.
Love at Sunset. New York, St. Martin's Press, 1982.

Other

"Anglo-American Conniving," in *Murderess Ink*, edited by Dilys Winn. New York, Workman, 1979.

*

Pauline Glen Winslow comments:

Many years ago I met a magician who had been famous in his time. His mental habit of always looking behind an effect for the mechanism which produced it struck me as being a useful one for a detective, who is every day required to ferret out truths that others are energetically hiding or disguising. So Merle Capricorn was born, conventional offspring of a flamboyant show-business family who, however he buries himself in his police work, never entirely escapes his background.

My work, like his, is touched by personal experience. My years in court directly inspired two novels: *The Strawberry Marten* (*Gallows Child*) and *The Kindness of Strangers*. *The Strawberry Marten* came from the observation that in a hard-fought trial a defendant is likely to hear more about himself than he wishes to know and that the recognition can be salutary; *The Kindness of Strangers*, from the belief held by some people who habitually work in courtrooms that they recognize the voice of truth. The first was set against the background of England just after the war; the second, New York at the present time, both well known to me.

Memories of the time of Dunkirk and the weeks that followed came back strongly when some of the hitherto secret documents of the war were released. How close we were to destruction then, yet how far from the thought of surrender! This was the basis of *The Windsor Plot*, set in Great Britain and Portugal. Now, in the 1980's, surrender to totalitarian power is no longer unthinkable. *I, Martha Adams*, set in the near future, is a story of the United States after such a surrender. Much of the action is set in New York at the United Nations and in the Connecticut countryside where one woman, the Martha Adams of the title, takes up arms against the conqueror.

My work at the UN also inspired one of the Capricorn novels, *The Rockefeller Gift*. A New York group of psychics were partly responsible for *Death of an Angel*, a story of the struggle of the great powers for psychic weapons, mostly prophetic then, fact later. *The Brandenburg Hotel*, the first in time of the Capricorn books, was set just after the war, a story of the aliens and Fascist sympathizers interned under the Regulation 18b.

The Witch Hill Murder, set in the English countryside, came from observing young people in a New Age cult, so easily carried on to excesses. This was written before the Manson case and before Jonestown. Another New Age cult, accompanied by various forms of the new atheism, has appeared in *Judgement Day*, a novel set in California, where it became embattled with the Judeo-Christian spirit. Religion is part of the theme of the Capricorn book *The Counsellor Heart* (*Sister Death*) where a warm, devout woman becomes a chance victim of a group of political terrorists. *The Counsellor Heart* is set in London, like *Coppergold*, another Capricorn novel. *Coppergold* is the story of Capricorn's young partner, who is suspected of corruption and murder at a time when Capricorn sees corruption all around him and despairs, almost, for England until he follows the course of the Thames to confront his villain at the shore. And he understands, for then and always, "That this was England, and his dwelling place."

* * *

Pauline Glen Winslow writes intelligent, often funny, sometimes sad books that belong to the tradition of the classic murder mystery while addressing contemporary concerns. Essentially, she places an old-fashioned detective in a modern world gone mad. Her recurring protagonist, Merle Capricorn of Scotland Yard, resembles the eccentric sleuth of the mystery novel's golden age. In fact, Winslow's Capricorn literalizes the familiar metaphor of detective as magician—for Capricorn is a trained magician. His father, the Great Capricornus, taught a reluctant son all the tricks of the stage illusionist's trade, and this patrimony serves Capricorn well. Sometimes specific conjuring skills prove valuable; more often, he relies on the professional magician's habit of seeing through another's tricks, of knowing inside out the arts of misdirection and illusion.

Capricorn also learned from his flamboyant aunts, "The Magic Merlinos" (frequent sources of manic comedy in the novels). After years of second billing in music halls, the Merlinos have become television stars, and thus provide their nephew with useful gossip about the more dubious sorts of celebrities: hoods and hangers-on, wayward scions of aristocratic families, fashionable psychics.

Despite the professional advantages his background offers, it embarrasses Capricorn; he wants to be a policeman, not a conjurer. Ironically, his first opportunity to prove himself mimics the most trite of theatrical legends: his superior officer becomes ill, and, like an understudy, the young Sergeant takes over and performs splendidly (*The Brandenburg Hotel*). A deeper irony, for Capricorn and the novels, accompanies his rise to Chief Superintendent. He became a policeman in reaction against the instability of his childhood; yet he finds himself both representing and longing for order in a collapsing world, one where the streets aren't safe and old notions of honor and decency are irrelevant.

Thematically, Winslow focuses on symptoms of society's decay. She is at her best on the danger of faith turned fanaticism, as in *The Witch Hill Murder* and *The Counsellor Heart*, and throughout her work one finds cults and the occult, betrayal, terrorism, threats to currencies (whose soundness requires faith). A degenerating world is suggested partly through characters' attitudes. Capricorn questions his official role as preserver of social order because he sees too clearly the near-collapse of his society, and he shares these doubts with his friends Manning of the Special Branch and Happy Delaney of the NYPD. Capricorn, Manning, and Delaney came of age during World War II, however, and the doubts they counterbalance with a sense of purpose are virtually articles of faith for Winslow's younger policemen, as typified by Inspector D.A. Copper (Capricorn's favorite associate who becomes a murder suspect in *Coppergold*). Honest himself, Copper takes corruption in others for granted; his private life is messy by the standards of Capricorn's generation; he had adopted police work as much for excitement as for any principle of order or justice.

So, too, Winslow's plots imply the exhaustion of old forms. We cannot rely on comforting expectations brought from traditional mysteries, whose conventions work to betray an essential order behind the apparent chaos of crime. (This is as true of Chandler as of Christie.) If Capricorn is simultaneously investigating multiple crimes, they may or may not turn out to be related. Frequently, murder that appears privately motivated turns out to have political causes; yet the reverse is also possible. And characters we have come to care for may be killed or be killers. In other words, these are thoroughly modern mysteries. Winslow's novels offer only tentative reassurance. As long as Capricorn can work his magic, the center will hold—but just barely, and we cannot know for how long.

—Susan Baker

———

WOOD, Ted (Edward John Wood). Also writes as Jack Barnao. Canadian. Born in England, 22 April 1931. Educated at Hartlebury Grammar School, Worcestershire, 1941–46. Served in the Royal Air Force, 1949–53. Married 1) Mary Gwendoline Wood in 1951 (died; 2) Mary Patricia Lawson in 1975; two daughters, one son, and three step-children. Salesman, London and Manchester Assurance, location 1953–54; Police Constable, Toronto City Police, Ontario, 1954–57; copy writer, MacLaren Advertising, 1957–66; creative director, Foster Advertising, 1966–69; and Cockfield Brown Advertising, 1969–74. Since 1974 freelance writer. Recipient: Ontario Arts Council grant, 1974; Scribner crime novel award, 1983. Agent: Richard Curtis Associates, 164 East 64th Street, New York, New York 10021, U.S.A. Address: 239 Wellington Street, Whitby, Ontario, L1N 5L7, Canada.

CRIME PUBLICATIONS

Novels (series: Reid Bennett; John Locke)

Dead in the Water (Bennett). New York, Scribner, 1983; London, Collins, 1984.
Murder on Ice (Bennett). New York, Scribner, 1984; as *The Killing Cold*, London, Collins, 1984.
Live Bait (Scribner). New York, Scribner, 1985; as *Dead Centre*, London, Collins, 1985.
Fool's Gold (Bennett). New York, Scribner, and London, Collins, 1986.
Corkscrew (Bennett). New York, Scribner, 1987; London, Collins, 1988.
Hammerlocke (as Jack Barnao). New York, Scribner, 1987.
Lockestep (as Jack Barnao). New York, Scribner, 1988.
When the Killing Starts (Bennett). New York, Scribner, and London, Collins, 1989.
On the Inside (Bennett). New York, Scribner, and London, Collins, 1990.

Uncollected Short Stories

"Pit Bull," in *Cold Blood*, Toronto, Mosaic Press, 1988.
"That Was no Lady," as Jack Barnao, in *Cold Blood*, Toronto, Mosaic Press, 1989.
"A Question of Proof," in *Cold Blood*, Toronto, Mosaic Press, 1989.

OTHER PUBLICATIONS

Play

Mister Scrooge, with others (produced Toronto, 1983).

Television Scripts: *It's not like Stealing* episode of *Sidestreet* series, 1974; *Susan* (from his own story "Somebody Else's Summer"), 1974; *The People You Never See*, 1976.

*

Ted Wood comments:

I hope nobody imputes a political motive to Reid Bennett's record of service with the US marines in Vietnam. He was conceived as a Canadian verteran of the Korean War. This was because the first book in the series, *Dead in the Water*, was written in 1969, when Reid and the writer were both in their thirties. However, the Canadian publishers to whom the book was submitted turned it down on the grounds that it was set in Canada and everybody knew that thrillers were just not set there. The book was laid aside for 12 years. By then, Reid would have had to be 50, a little old for the way he had been written.

I therefore made him one of the 20,000 or so young Canadians who volunteered for service with the Americans in Vietnam. This brought his age down to an acceptable level.

Similarly, he works in a one-man police department because the author's own police experience was gained in a pre-electronic time, under circumstances which are now found only in a small town. Setting him in a one-man department meant I was able to avoid talking about computers and other sophistications. It also let me indulge my own love of the Canadian outdoors.

I gave him Sam because I wanted to have backup available without having to load the book with superfluous conversation.

Reid is very Canadian, despite his American experience. He had an English father (because the author is English by birth) and a French-Canadian mother, from Clander, home of the Dionne quintets and close to my log cabin on Lake Nipissing, a Francophone area of Ontario. This heritage means that he can operate comfortably anywhere in Canada, being fluent in French. He has the same set of values as the policemen I have worked with and respect. He's straight arrow but has no love of lawyers or shrill activists.

The Jack Barnao character, John Locke, is Canadian born and lives in Toronto but has served in the Grenadier Guards and the SAS. The author's own father was a Grenadier. The Canadian armed forces have been emasculated by the old Trudeau government and it is quite understandable that a young man would look elsewhere for adventure.

He travels on assignment for two reasons. First, the readers like foreign settings; second, the author and his wife like to travel. Researching new locations for the books gives another reason both for travelling and for applying part of the cost against income taxes.

*   *   *

Ted Wood writes action-packed police procedurals which are not for the faint-hearted reader. The action centers around Reid Bennett, Chief of Police of Murphy's Harbour, Ontario, a fictional resort town north of Toronto. Bennett and his German Shepherd, Sam, are the entire police force of Murphy's Harbour.

Wood's own experiences in the Toronto police force and the fact that he lives in the same part of the country where his stories take place ensure the feel of authenticity in his novels. The clear-cut good against evil plots are well-developed and have satisfying conclusions. The crisp, direct dialogue moves the plots quickly causing suspense and tension.

Reid Bennett is the perfect hero: thirty-five, divorced, tall, dark, and rangy. Bennett was a Canadian volunteer who fought in Vietnam. After being with the Toronto police force for nine years, he resigned in disgust following harrassment from citizens, the media, and his own colleagues over an incident involving a gang of bikers. While off duty, Bennett had confronted the bikers raping a young girl. When he single-handedly killed two of them and seriously injured another, he was arrested by his own department. He was eventually acquitted of charges, but the controversy refused to die. After his wife left him because of the incident, he found the Chief's job in Murphy's Harbour, welcoming the prospect of a town where nothing violent ever happens. But, of course, things do happen, and each book is packed with adventure, violence, and murder.

Despite the macho image suggested by Bennett's background and physical appearance, he is a sensitive and caring person. Even though he has been trained to fight and kill, he does not enjoy or seek violence but neither does he walk away from it. Bennett uses only such force as is necessary to subdue the villains, but since some of them are extremely vicious, a good deal of force is often necessary. Another facet of Bennett's character is shown in his respect and affection for his dog, Sam. Bennett is also thoughtful and compassionate in his relationships with women whether victims, suspects, or lovers.

Since the action centers on Bennett, there is not a well-developed cast of secondary characters but this does not detract from the narrative. In fact, it serves to strengthen the role of the main character since at most times it is Bennett alone against the villains.

Wood makes use of the setting and the elements to adds atmosphere and suspense. Lakefront homes and adjacent waters are the focus of the search for a missing man in *Dead in the Water*. A deadly blizzard provides cover for the kidnappers of a winter carnival queen in *Murder on Ice*.

The memory of events from Bennett's past often adds dramatic tension to the plots. In *Live Bait*, old wounds are made painful again as Bennett takes on a short-term assignment for a security firm in Toronto and finds himself embroiled with the Toronto police force. An urban setting does not diminish the action as once again Bennett and Sam battle multiple villains in an exciting tale of deception. Bennett's old enemies, bikers, arrive on the scene in *Corkscrew* and he must keep the peace while treading lightly to avoid a repetition of the incident that brought him to Murphy's Harbour. Dealing with bikers on top of an investigation into tne death of a young tourist, Bennett once again proves himself a force to be reckoned with.

Bennett's adventures sometimes take him into the rugged wilderness areas outside of Murphy's Harbour. He is at the site of a gold strike in *Fool's Gold*. In *When the Killing Starts*, while on vacation from his job in Murphy's Harbour, Bennett is hired by a wealthy woman to track down and bring back her son who has joined a group of mercenaries. Tracking professional killers in the Canadian wilderness shows Reid Bennett at his very best.

For their strong series character, action and adventure in a rugged setting, and satisfying plots, Wood's mysteries are an exciting addition to the genre.

—Carol Barry

———

WOODS, Sara. Pseudonym for Sara Bowen-Judd, née Hutton; also wrote as Anne Burton; Mary Challis; Margaret Leek. British. Born in Bradford, Yorkshire, 7 March 1922. Educated privately and at Convent of the Sacred Heart, Filey,

Yorkshire, 1932–37. Married Anthony George Bowen-Judd in 1946. Worked in a bank and in a solicitor's office, London, during World War II; pig breeder, 1948–54; assistant to Company Secretary, Rotol Ltd., Gloucester, 1954–58; registrar, Saint Mary's University, Halifax, Nova Scotia, 1958–64. *Died 6 November 1985.*

CRIME PUBLICATIONS

Novels (series: Jeremy Locke; Antony Maitland in all Woods books; Stephen Marryat; Richard Trenton)

Bloody Instructions.   London, Collins, and New York, Harper, 1962.
Malice Domestic.   London, Collins, 1962.
The Taste of Fears.   London, Collins, 1963; as *The Third Encounter,* New York, Harper, 1963.
Error of the Moon.   London, Collins, 1963.
Trusted Like the Fox.   London, Collins, 1964; New York, Harper, 1965.
This Little Measure.   London, Collins, 1964.
The Windy Side of the Law.   London, Collins, and New York, Harper, 1965.
Though I Know She Lies.   London, Collins, 1965; New York, Holt Rinehart, 1972.
Enter Certain Murderers.   London, Collins, and New York, Harper, 1966.
Let's Choose Executors.   London, Collins, 1966; New York, Harper, 1967.
The Case Is Altered.   London, Collins, and New York, Harper, 1967.
And Shame the Devil.   London, Collins, 1967; New York, Holt Rinehart, 1972.
Knives Have Edges.   London, Collins, 1968; New York, Holt Rinehart, 1970.
Past Praying For.   London, Collins, and New York, Harper, 1968.
Tarry and Be Hanged.   London, Collins, 1969; New York, Holt Rinehart, 1971.
An Improbable Fiction.   London, Collins, 1970; New York, Holt Rinehart, 1971.
Serpent's Tooth.   London, Collins, 1971; New York, Holt Rinehart, 1973.
The Knavish Crows.   London, Collins, 1971.
They Love Not Poison.   London, Macmillan, and New York, Holt Rinehart, 1972.
Yet She Must Die.   London, Macmillan, 1973; New York, Holt Rinehart, 1974.
Enter the Corpse.   London, Macmillan, 1973; New York, Holt Rinehart, 1974.
Done to Death.   London, Macmillan, 1974; New York, Holt Rinehart, 1975.
A Show of Violence.   London, Macmillan, and New York, McKay, 1975.
My Life is Done.   London, Macmillan, 1975; New York, St. Martin's Press, 1976.
The Law's Delay.   London, Macmillan, and New York, St. Martin's Press, 1977.
A Thief or Two.   London, Macmillan, and New York, St. Martin's Press, 1977.
Exit Murderer.   London, Macmillan, and New York, St. Martin's Press, 1978.
The Fatal Writ.   London, Macmillan, and New York, St. Martin's Press, 1979.
Proceed to Judgment.   London, Macmillan, and New York, St. Martin's Press, 1979.

They Stay for Dinner.   London, Macmillan, and New York, St. Martin's Press, 1980.
The Dear Departed (Trenton; as Anne Burton).   Toronto, Raven, 1980.
Where There's a Will (Trenton; as Anne Burton).   Toronto, Raven, 1980.
Burden of Proof (Locke; as Mary Challis).   Toronto, Raven, 1980.
Crimes Past (Locke; as Mary Challis).   Toronto, Raven, 1980.
The Healthy Grave (Marryat; as Margaret Leek).   Toronto, Raven, 1980.
We Must Have a Trial (Marryat; as Margaret Leek).   Toronto, Raven, 1980.
Weep for Her.   London, Macmillan, 1980; New York, St. Martin's Press, 1981.
Cry Guilty.   London, Macmillan, and New York, St. Martin's Press, 1981.
Dearest Enemy.   London, Macmillan, and New York, St. Martin's Press, 1981.
Enter a Gentlewoman.   London, Macmillan, and New York, St. Martin's Press, 1982.
Villains by Necessity.   London, Macmillan, and New York, St. Martin's Press, 1982.
Most Grievous Murder.   London, Macmillan, and New York, St. Martin's Press, 1982.
Call Back Yesterday.   London, Macmillan, and New York, St. Martin's Press, 1983.
The Lie Direct.   London, Macmillan, and New York, St. Martin's Press, 1983.
Where Should He Die.   London, Macmillan, and New York, St. Martin's Press, 1983.
The Bloody Book of Law.   London, Macmillan, and New York, St. Martin's Press, 1984.
Murders Out of Tune.   London, Macmillan, and New York, St. Martin's Press, 1984.
Defy the Devil.   London, Macmillan, 1984; New York, St. Martin's Press, 1985.
An Obscure Grave.   London, Macmillan, and New York, St. Martin's Press, 1985.
Away with Them to Prison.   London, Macmillan, and New York, St. Martin's Press, 1985.
Most Deadly Hate.   London, Macmillan, and New York, St. Martin's Press, 1986.
Nor Live So Long.   London, Macmillan, and New York, St. Martin's Press, 1986.
Naked Villain.   London, Macmillan, and New York, St. Martin's Press, 1987.

Uncollected Short Story

"The Trouble with Some Policemen," in *The Saint* (London), July 1964.

*

Sara Woods commented (1984):
    I write crime novels with a legal background because the law has always interested me. To my great surprise, I have been complimented, occasionally, on my plots. This seems odd to me because my system is to take a situation, throw my characters in, and see what happens. You will gather from this that what I am most interested in is the development of character, and I expect that is why I have chosen to write a series, with a group of the characters appearing in every book, and others merely reappearing from time to time.

*   *   *

In more than 45 books written over a period of 25 years, Sarah Hutton Bowen-Judd writing as Sara Woods chronicled the cases of barrister Anthony Maitland and his uncle Sir Nicholas Harding. The books are a fascinating study of the English legal system and explore the ways that barristers, solicitors, and police try to see justice done within the sometimes frustrating boundaries of that system.

Despite the emphasis on legal procedures, Woods's books are more than Perry Mason-like accounts of trials. As Maitland builds his cases or attempts to demolish those of the prosecution he mercilessly examines his own feelings and motives and those of his clients. In *The Bloody Book of Law* Woods describes "the sensitivity that was perhaps the most dominant characteristic of the man ... which, combined with compassion and an instinctive distrust for his own judgement (uncomfortable bedfellows indeed) contributed, each in its own way, to the unconventional behaviour that some of his acquaintances were so ready to condemn." There is a similar description of Maitland in most of the books.

Each "case study" builds logically to a courtroom climax in which "the barrister who never loses a case" (a phrase Maitland is supposed to loathe) sees justice done. Because he has, as he says at least once a book, "unorthodox" methods and prefers to interview witnesses himself when possible, the narrative is able to move beyond the confines of courtroom and chambers and into the wider world: usually the city of London, but occasionally New York (*Most Grievous Murder*) or the village of Arkenshaw in Yorkshire.

Woods's writing is strongest in the area of plot. Her stories are a mixture of standard legal problems such as child custody battles (*Most Deadly Hate*), art theft (*Cry Guilty*) or libel (*Enter a Gentlewoman*) and more bizarre circumstances such as hypnotism and reincarnation (*Call Back Yesterday*) and convenient amnesia (*Defy the Devil*). The books are absorbing and Woods usually gives the reader ample opportunity to guess what really happened before Maitland solves the crime and sees the guilty one punished. Sometimes, however, the necessary revelations are quite late in the day and the twists can be a bit unlikely.

Where Woods falls down over the long course of the Maitland stories is in her drawing of characters, particularly the principal ones. Incidental characters such as Sergeant Mayhew (*Away with Them to Prison*) and the medium in *Weep for Her* are quite well done; the reader sympathises with their predicaments and cares what happens to them. But over the long haul, Woods doesn't sustain the recurring characters at all well. They do not really develop beyond certain characteristics which are described again and again. Maitland and his wife Jenny, Sir Nicholas and his wife Vera, Maitland's friend Roger Farrell and his actress wife Meg, Chief Inspector Sykes all have similar conversations with each other book after book. Sir Nicholas is usually bad tempered or critical of his nephew and although we are told of admiration and affection between them, this is not borne out by their interactions. Between Maitland and his long-suffering wife Jenny, again, although we're told of great affection and understanding, there is little evidence of a real relationship; Jenny is usually curled up in the same corner of the sofa, so "serene" as to be almost comatose. She seems to spend all her time at home mixing drinks and casseroles and although we're told she is famous for mixing up explanations, we don't hear her say much of anything, except to ask questions which help the narrative along. In *Most Deadly Hate*, however, Jenny does help her husband by questioning a child suspected of witnessing a murder and we learn that she is unable to have a child of her own, although she would have liked one.

Maitland himself is not a particularly sympathetic character. Again Woods uses narrative rather than example to tell us things about him: the narration says he is good humoured but he doesn't often say or do funny things. He is more often agonising over his psyche. We know he is insecure over his abilities and that he loathes being depended upon but because he refuses to talk about it we don't learn why. It seems to be connected with the war and a wound to his shoulder. Although in *Call Back Yesterday* he decides to have psychotherapy after he sees how it helped a client, he is still having crises of conscience in later books.

The books also lack a strong sense of place. We know the city where most of them take place is London but it's a curiously limited London, not really explored very fully. Most of the time it could be anywhere. This may be because Woods moved to Canada before the first Maitland book was published and she may have lacked confidence in describing a city she no longer lived in.

On the whole, the Anthony Maitland books are entertaining mysteries that provide pleasant puzzles and an insight into the law at work. They ought not to be read one after another as they can seem much alike after a while, but like most things as part of a mixed diet they are fine.

—Gillian Rodgerson

WOODS, Stockton. *See* **FORREST, Richard.**

WOOLF, F.X. *See* **ENGEL, Howard.**

WOOLRICH, Cornell (George Hopley-). Also wrote as George Hopley; William Irish. American. Born in New York City in 1903; grew up in South America and New York City. Educated at Columbia University, New York. Married and separated. Recipient: Mystery Writers of America Edgar Allan Poe award, for short story, 1948. *Died in 1968.*

CRIME PUBLICATIONS

Novels

The Bride Wore Black. New York, Simon and Schuster, 1940; London, Hale, 1942; as *Beware the Lady*, New York, Pyramid, 1953.
The Black Curtain. New York, Simon and Schuster, 1941; London, Macmillan, 1963.
Black Alibi. New York, Simon and Schuster, 1942; London, Hale, 1951.
The Black Angel. New York, Doubleday, 1943; London, Hale, 1949.
The Black Path of Fear. New York, Doubleday, 1944.
Night Has a Thousand Eyes (as George Hopley). New York, Farrar and Rinehart, 1945; London, Penguin, 1949.

Rendezvous in Black. New York, Rinehart, 1948; London, Hale, 1950.
Fright (as George Hopley). New York, Rinehart, and London, Foulsham, 1950.
Savage Bride. New York, Fawcett, 1950.
Death Is My Dancing Partner. New York, Pyramid, 1959.
The Doom Stone. New York, Avon, 1960.
Into the Night, completed by Lawrence Block. New York, Mysterious Press, 1987; London, Simon and Schuster, 1988.

Novels as William Irish

Phantom Lady. Philadelphia, Lippincott, 1942; London, Hale, 1945.
Deadline at Dawn. Philadelphia, Lippincott, 1944; London, Hutchinson, 1947.
Waltz into Darkness. Philadelphia, Lippincott, 1947; London, Hutchinson, 1948.
I Married a Dead Man. Philadelphia, Lippincott, 1948; London, Hutchinson, 1950.
You'll Never See Me Again. New York, Dell, 1951.
Strangler's Serenade. New York, Rinehart, 1951; London, Hale, 1952.

Short Stories

Nightmare. New York, Dodd Mead, 1956.
Violence. New York, Dodd Mead, 1958.
Hotel Room. New York, Random House, 1958.
Beyond the Night. New York, Avon, 1959.
The Ten Faces of Cornell Woolrich. New York, Simon and Schuster, 1965; London, Boardman, 1966.
The Dark Side of Love. New York, Walker, 1965.
Nightwebs, edited by Francis M. Nevins, Jr. New York, Harper, 1971; London, Gollancz, 1973.
Angels of Darkness. New York, Mysterious Press, 1979.
Darkness at Dawn: Early Suspense Classics, edited by Francis M. Nevins, Jr. and Martin H. Greenberg. Carbondale, Southern Illinois University Press, 1985; London, Xanadu, 1989.

Short Stories as William Irish

I Wouldn't Be in Your Shoes. Philadelphia, Lippincott, 1943; London, Hutchinson, 1946; as *And So to Death*, New York, Spivak, 1944; as *Nightmare*, New York, Reader's Choice Library, 1950.
After-Dinner Story. Philadelphia, Lippincott, 1944; London, Hutchinson, 1947; as *Six Times Death*, New York, Popular Library, 1948.
If I Should Die Before I Wake. New York, Avon, 1945.
The Dancing Detective. Philadelphia, Lippincott, 1946; London, Hutchinson, 1948.
Borrowed Crimes. New York, Avon, 1946.
Dead Man Blues. Philadelphia, Lippincott, 1948; London, Hutchinson, 1950.
The Blue Ribbon. Philadelphia, Lippincott, 1949; London, Hutchinson, 1950; as *Dilemma of the Dead Lady*, Hasbrouck Heights, New Jersey, Graphic, 1950.
Somebody on the Phone. Philadelphia, Lippincott, 1950; as *The Night I Died*, London, Hutchinson, 1951; as *Deadly Night Call*, Hasbrouck Heights, New Jersey, Graphic, 1951.
Six Nights of Mystery. New York, Popular Library, 1950.
Eyes That Watch You. New York, Rinehart, 1952.
Bluebeard's Seventh Wife. New York, Popular Library, 1952.
The Best of William Irish. Philadelphia, Lippincott, 1960.

Uncollected Short Stories

"Blonde Beauty Slain," in *Ellery Queen's Mystery Magazine* (New York), March 1959.
"Money Talks," in *Ellery Queen's Mystery Magazine* (New York), January 1962.
"The Poker Player's Wife," in *The Saint* (New York), October 1962.
"Story to Be Whispered," in *The Saint* (New York), May 1963.
"Steps . . . Coming Near" (as William Irish), in *Ellery Queen's Mystery Magazine* (New York), April 1964.
"When Love Turns," in *Ellery Queen's Mystery Magazine* (New York), June 1964.
"Murder after Death," in *Ellery Queen's Mystery Magazine* (New York), December 1964.
"It Only Takes a Minute to Die," in *Ellery Queen's Mystery Magazine* (New York), July 1966.
"Divorce—New York Style," in *Ellery Queen's Mystery Magazine* (New York), June and July 1967.
"Intent to Kill," in *The Saint* (New York), September 1967.
"New York Blues," in *Ellery Queen's Mystery Magazine* (New York), December 1970.
"Death Between Dances," in *Ellery Queen's Mystery Magazine* (New York), October 1978.

OTHER PUBLICATIONS

Novels

Cover Charge. New York, Boni and Liveright, 1926.
Children of the Ritz. New York, Boni and Liveright, 1927.
Times Square. New York, Liveright, 1929.
A Young Man's Heart. New York, Mason, 1930.
The Time of Her Life. New York, Liveright, 1931.
Manhattan Love Song. New York, Godwin, 1932.

Short Stories

The Fantastic Stories of Cornell Woolrich, edited by Charles G. Waugh and Martin H. Greenberg. Carbondale, Southern Illinois University Press, 1981.

*

Critical Study: *Cornell Woolrich: First You Dream, Then You Die* (biography) by Francis M. Nevins, Jr. New York, Mysterious Press, 1988.

*   *   *

Cornell Woolrich was born in 1903 to parents whose marriage collapsed in his youth. The experience of seeing Puccini's *Madame Butterfly* at age eight gave him a second intimation of tragedy, and from the night three years later that he understood fully that someday he too, like Cio-Cio-San, would have to die, he was haunted by a sense of doom that never left him. He began writing fiction while at Columbia University, quitting in his junior year to pursue his dream of becoming another F. Scott Fitzgerald, and his first novel, *Cover Charge*, chronicles the lives and loves of the Jazz Age's gilded youth in the manner of his then literary idol. Following five more mainstream novels, a stint in Hollywood, a brief marriage, and many homosexual encounters, he returned to Manhattan. For the next quarter century he lived with his mother in a succession of residential hotels, going out only when it was absolutely essential, trapped in a bizarre love-hate relationship which dominated his external world just as the inner world of his fiction reflected in its tortured patterns the strangler grip in which his mother held him.

From 1934 until his death he wrote dozens of haunting stories of suspense, despair, and lost love, set in a universe controlled by diabolical powers who delight in savaging us. During the 1930's he wrote only for pulp magazines like *Black Mask* and *Detective Fiction Weekly*. His first suspense novel, *The Bride Wore Black*, launched his so-called Black Series which inspired the French *roman noir* and *film noir*. During the early 1940's he published superb novels under his own name and the pseudonyms William Irish (*Phantom Lady* and *Deadline at Dawn*) and George Hopley (*Night Has a Thousand Eyes*). Throughout the 1940's and 1950's numerous hardcover and paperback collections of Woolrich's short stories were issued, and many of his tales were adapted into movies and radio and television dramas, perhaps the best known Woolrich-based film being Alfred Hitchcock's *Rear Window*. Despite his overwhelming financial and critical success his personal situation remained wretched, and when his mother died in 1957 he cracked. From then until his own death in 1968 he lived alone, completing only a handful of final "tales of love and despair" but still gifted with the magic touch that could chill the reader's heart. One of his titles for an unwritten story captures his bleak philosophy: "First You Dream, Then You Die."

Although he wrote many types of stories, including quasi-police procedural novels, rapid-action whizbangs, and tales of the occult, Woolrich is best known as the master of pure suspense, evoking with awesome power the desperation of those who walk the city's darkened streets and the terror that lurks at noonday in commonplace settings. In his hands even such clichéd storylines as the race to save the innocent man from the electric chair and the amnesiac's search for his lost self resonate with human anguish. Woolrich's world is a feverish place where the prevailing emotions are loneliness and fear and the prevailing action a race against time and death, as in his suspense classics "Three O'Clock" and "Guillotine." His most characteristic detective stories end with our realization that no rational account of events is possible, and his suspense stories tend to close not with the dissipation of the terror but with its omnipresence.

The typical Woolrich settings are the seedy hotel, the cheap dance hall, the rundown movie house, and the precinct station backroom. The dominant reality in his world is the Depression. Woolrich has no peers when it comes to describing a frightened little guy in a tiny apartment with no money, no job, a hungry wife and children, and anxiety eating him like a cancer. If a Woolrich protagonist is in love, the beloved is likely to vanish in such a way that the protagonist not only can't find her but can't convince anyone that she ever existed. Or, in another classic Woolrich situation, the protagonist comes to after a blackout (caused by amnesia, drugs, hypnosis, or whatever) and little by little becomes convinced that he committed a murder or other crime while out of himself. The police are rarely sympathetic, for they are the earthly counterparts of the malignant powers above and their primary function is to torment the helpless. All we can do about this nightmare world is to create, if we can, a few islands of love and trust to help us forget. But love dies while the lovers go on living, and Woolrich excels at showing the corrosion of a relationship between two people. Although he often wrote about the horrors both love and lovelessness can inspire, there are few irredeemably evil characters in his stories, for if any of his characters loves or needs love, or is at the brink of destruction, Woolrich identifies with him no matter what crimes he or she might also have

committed. Technically many of his stories are awful, but like the playwrights of the absurd Woolrich knew that a senseless tale best mirrors a senseless universe. Some of his tales indeed end quite happily (usually thanks to outlandish coincidence), but there are no series characters in his work, and the reader can never know in advance whether a particular story of his will be light or dark—which is one reason why his stories are so hauntingly suspenseful.

Woolrich was the Poe of the 20th century and the poet of its shadows. Trapped in a wretched psychological environment, understanding his own and everyone's trappedness, he took his decades of solitude and shaped them into the finest body of pure suspense literature ever written. He himself like Cio-Cio-San had to die, but the world he imagined will live.

—Francis M. Nevins, Jr.

————

WORMSER, Richard (Edward). Also wrote as Ed Friend. American. Born in 1908. Recipient: Western Writers of America Spur award, for children's book, 1965, 1972; Western Heritage Award, for children's book, 1972; Mystery Writers of America Edgar Allan Poe award, 1973. *Died in 1977.*

CRIME PUBLICATIONS

Novels (series: Lieutenant Andy Bastian; Sergeant Joe Dixon)

The Man with the Wax Face (Dixon). New York, Smith and Haas, 1934.
The Communist's Corpse (Dixon). New York, Smith and Haas, and London, Gollancz, 1935.
The Hanging Heiress. New York, Mill, 1949; as *The Widow Wore Red*, New York, Fawcett, 1958.
The Body Looks Familiar. New York, Dell, 1958.
The Late Mrs. Five. New York, Fawcett, 1960; London, Muller, 1962.
Drive East on 66 (Bastian). New York, Fawcett, 1962.
Perfect Pigeon. New York, Fawcett, 1962.
A Nice Girl Like You (Bastian). New York, Fawcett, and London, Muller, 1963.
Torn Curtain (novelization of screenplay). New York, Dell, and London, Mayflower, 1966.
The Takeover. New York, Fawcett, 1971; London, Coronet, 1972.
The Invader. New York, Fawcett, 1972.

Novels as Ed Friend

The Infernal Light (novelization of television series). New York, Dell, 1966.
The Most Deadly Game (novelization of television series). New York, Lancer, 1970.
The Corpse in the Castle. New York, Lancer, 1970.

Uncollected Short Stories

"Man with a Shiv," in *Manhunt* (New York), December 1956.
"Shadowed," in *Manhunt* (New York), March 1957.
"Locker 911," in *Manhunt* (New York), April 1957.
"Smart Sucker," in *Alfred Hitchcock Presents: Tales My Mother Never Told Me.* New York, Random House, 1963; London, Reinhardt, 1964.

OTHER PUBLICATIONS

Novels

All's Fair . . . New York, Modern Age, 1937.
Pass Through Manhattan. New York, Morrow, 1940.
The Lonesome Quarter. New York, Mill, 1951; London, Corgi, 1953.
The Longhorn Trail, with Dan Gordon. New York, Ace, 1955.
Slattery's Range. London, Abelard Schuman, 1957; New York, New American Library, 1959.
Battalion of Saints. New York, McKay, 1961.
Thief of Baghdad. New York, Dell, 1961.
The Last Days of Sodom and Gomorrah. New York, Fawcett, and London, Muller, 1962.
Three Cornered War. New York, Avon, 1962.
Pan Satyrus. New York, Avon, 1963.
McLintock. New York, Fawcett, 1963; London, Muller, 1964.
Bedtime Story (novelization of screenplay). London, Muller, 1964.
Operation Crossbow. New York, Dell, 1965.
Alvarez Kelly (as Ed Friend). New York, Fawcett, 1966.
The Wild Wild West. New York, New American Library, 1966.
The Scalphunters (as Ed Friend). New York, Fawcett, 1968; London, Gold Lion, 1974.
The Ranch by the Sea. New York, Doubleday, 1970; as *Double Decker*, New York, Manor, 1974.
On the Prod. New York, Fawcett, 1978.

Plays

Screenplays: *Start Cheering*, with Eugene Solow and Philip Rapp, 1937; *Let Them Live!*, with Bruce Manning and Lionel Houser, 1937; *Fugitives for a Night*, with Dalton Trumbo, 1938; *The Plainsman and the Lady* (*Drumbeats over Wyoming*), with Michael Uris and Ralph Spence, 1946; *The Phantom Thief*, with Richard Weil and G.A. Snow, 1946; *Perilous Waters*, with Francis Rosenwald, 1947; *Tulsa*, with others, 1949; *Powder River Rustlers*, 1950; *Vigilante Hideout*, 1950; *Rustlers on Horseback*, 1950; *Fort Dodge Stampede*, 1951; *Captive of Billy the Kid*, with Coates Webster, 1951; *The Half-Breed*, with others, 1952; *A Perilous Journey*, 1953; *Crime Wave*, with Crane Wilbur and Bernard Gordon, 1954; *The Outcast*, with John K. Butler, 1954.

Other

Trem McRae and the Golden Cinders (for children). Philadelphia, McKay, 1940.
Ride a Northbound Horse (for children). New York, Morrow, and London, Oxford University Press, 1964.
The Kidnapped Circus (for children). New York, Morrow, 1968.
Southwest Cookery; or, At Home on the Range. New York, Doubleday, 1969.
Gone to Texas (for children). New York, Morrow, 1970.
The Black Mustanger (for children). New York, Morrow, 1971.
Tubac. Tubac, Arizona, Tubac Historical Society, 1975.

* * *

Richard Wormser's first assignment at Street & Smith was to help in putting together a news magazine. When this venture did not succeed he began submitting short stories for the back pages of *The Shadow*. This in turn led to his being picked to write the lead novels for a new pulp magazine to feature a modern version of the dime novel detective, Nick Carter. While *Nick Carter Magazine* (1933–36) was not the success its publishers envisioned, the 17 novels Wormser contributed under the Nick Carter pseudonym proved a valuable training ground for the young writer. The restrictions imposed by the limitations of the medium on his creativity soon led him to cancel his contract with Street & Smith and take his talents elsewhere.

Wormser's pulp training was hard to shake and there are evidences of it in his first crime novels, *The Man with the Wax Face*, and *The Communist's Corpse*. Specific references to The Shadow and a "Master-of-Men" (meaning "The Spider") along with the staccato dialogue, rapid action, mini-climaxes, and some examples of over-writing betray their lineage. The mysteries and the detective (Sgt. Jocelyn—Joe—Dixon) are less memorable than the other characters and the local color. Erika Strindberg, the 6-foot-plus writer for a radical newspaper, perpetually in search of a crusade, appears in both novels. Her character as well as the remarks on communism in the 1930's and the attitudes of the other characters towards this social phenomenon are both original and entertaining.

Three decades later, both style and plot structure are more sophisticated in Wormser's novels. If it is formula, it is one of his own devising. There are both urbane dialogue and believably likeable characters in *The Late Mrs. Five*. When Paul Porter's ex-wife (now remarried to a man Porter has not met) is murdered, can Porter prove he is not the guilty party? Not easily since his fingerprints are all over the place. In *Perfect Pigeon* the reader gets an eerie sense of what it feels like to be an ex-con just freed, a man who still looks over his shoulder, and is likely to be drawn back to prison if he continues to keep bad company. It must have been like a dip into the pulp era again when he wrote novelizations based on movies or television plays. Those he wrote as Ed Friend (for *The Most Deadly Game* and *The Infernal Light*) are well-written but lack that depth of character and incident he used in the novels published under his own name.

During part of his life, Wormser lived in the southwest and it was natural for him to write about that area. His westerns have a feeling of reality about them and so do the crime novels he set in that same part of his country. Though advertised by Fawcett to emphasize a family resemblance to *The Godfather*, neither of Wormser's "mafia novels" follows the same formula. There is more political maneuvering than underworld in the Chicago story *The Takeover*, while *The Invader* tells a leisurely story of a small-town sheriff whose routine is disturbed when a suspicious fellow from back East buys the Angel Ranch. Dan Dominick is such a smooth character that Sheriff Craigie is almost ashamed of trying to run a check on him. Little things begin to add up (changes at the ranch—bullet-proof windows and a private army) and, like in a western a showdown is at hand.

Never a flashy talent, Wormser was a good storyteller and a solid craftsman.

—J. Randolph Cox

———

WRIGHT, Eric. Canadian. Born in London, 4 May 1929. Educated at Mitcham Grammar School, 1945; University of Manitoba, Winnipeg, 1952–57, B.A. (honors) 1957; University of Toronto, Ontario, 1958–60. Served in the Royal Air Force,

1947–49. Married Valerie Wright in 1958; two daughters. Recipient: Crime Writers Association John Creasey award, 1983; Crime Writers of Canada award, for novel, 1983, 1985, for short story, 1987. Agent: Bella Pomer, 22 Shallmar Boulevard, Toronto, Ontario. Address: 65 Gormley Avenue, Toronto, Ontario M4U 1Y9, Canada.

CRIME PUBLICATIONS

Novels (series: Inspector Charlie Salter in all books)

The Night the Gods Smiled. London, Collins, and New York, Scribner, 1983.
Smoke Detector. London, Collins, and New York, Scribner, 1984.
Death in the Old Country. London, Collins, and New York, Scribner, 1985.
A Single Death. London, Collins, 1986; as *The Man Who Changed His Name*, New York, Scribner, 1986.
A Body Surrounded by Water. London, Collins, and New York, Scribner, 1987.
A Question of Murder. London, Collins, and New York, Scribner, 1988.
A Sensitive Case. London, Collins, and New York, Scribner, 1990.

Uncollected Short Stories

"The Cure," in *Fingerprints.* Toronto, Irwin, 1984.
"Gothic Revival," in *Descant* (Toronto), Winter 1984–85.
"Looking for an Honest Man," in *Cold Blood.* Mosaic Press, Toronto, 1989.
"Haesphestus," in *Cold Blood 2.* Toronto, Mosaic Press, 1989.
"Kaput," in *Mistletoe Mysteries*, edited by Charlotte MacLeod. New York, Mysterious Press, 1989.
"Twins," in *A Suit of Diamonds.* London, Collins, 1990.

*   *   *

Eric Wright's Inspector Charlie Salter mysteries might best be described as soft-boiled procedurals. They involve murder investigations, but the victims are always middle class, the procedural details are low-tech, Salter is never in physical danger and family matters occupy a good deal of his time.

The Toronto policeman as we meet him in *The Night the Gods Smiled* is at a career low, having backed the wrong man for deputy chief and as a result receiving only chores no one else wants. He loves his second wife Annie (they have two sons, Seth and Angus), but he's not too enamored of her family, who come from Prince Edward Island's upper crust.

In the first mystery, the Montreal police ask a favor; they have on their hands the body of an English professor, murdered in a hotel room. Quebec Inspector Henri O'Brien asks Salter to interview the victim's Toronto work associates at Douglas College (he was killed while attending a convention). As he conducts his investigation, Salter sees a Conradian parallel; he's the same age and his marriage and job situation are much like the victim's. Peppering the description of Salter's police work are interludes involving the cop's misanthropic father and a sojourn at the race track.

Salter's success in this case brings him and assistant Sergeant Frank Gatenby better assignments. In *Smoke Detector*, he looks into the arson-related death of a less-than-scrupulous antiques dealer. At the same time the policeman is wrestling with doubts because his doctors want him to undergo tests. On top of that Annie has decided to take a job and he doesn't know how to deal with eldest son Angus who has taken an interest in skin magazines. In the course of his unraveling the crime, Salter becomes disgusted with himself for his tunnel vision— both professionally and personally.

The third and fifth novels in the series venture outside of Ontario. *Death in the Old Country* finds the Salters vacationing at a quaint country inn in England. There's a murder and Salter weasels his way into helping the constabulary sort things out. In this particularly gentle mystery, Wright's humor shines. Salter is repeatedly identified by the locals as having come from Canada. " 'Yes,' Salter said, faintly irritated. Did he smell of maple syrup?" Yet another facet of Salter's personality is explored; he enters into a bit of a one-upmanship game with the local police inspector—who knows what first? And who can solve the puzzle?

A Body Surrounded by Water picks up with the Salter clan vacationing in Prince Edward Island and assisting the Royal Canadian Mounted Police when a local historian is killed, apparently because he knows the whereabouts of the island's long lost great silver document seal.

A Single Death (*The Man Who Changed His Name*), brings yet a different torment to Salter; his ex-wife Gerry, whom he hasn't seen for 25 years (he was an avowed cop, she was a blossoming hippie, their moral standards didn't mesh), insists the police take a greater interest in the rape-murder of a social worker. She raises sufficient stink that Salter is assigned to the case. The investigation takes him into the world of singles dating and relationships—what he learns of others reveals more about himself.

A Question of Murder involves a hunt for a writer of threatening letters and protecting the Princess Royal as she tours Toronto while *A Sensitive Case* has Salter probing the affairs of a dead massage-therapist whose clients include high government officials. Family situations in the books—which by now have become predominant—are a son's new-found interest in family history and suspicions that Annie is having an affair.

The accent on subtle family psychology threatens to take precedence over the crimes in the books; in *A Single Death* in fact, after the murderer is revealed, the real mystery is answered: Will Salter's father and his girlfriend get along at Christmas with all the in-laws?

While perhaps short on innovation, the Wright novels (he has also written non-Salter short stories) are strong on character, setting and psychology, and are contributing to Canada's strong showing in the mystery genre.

—Bernard A. Drew

———

WRIGHT, L(aurali) R. American. Born in 1939. Recipient; Mystery Writers of America Edgar Allan Poe award, 1985. Address: c/o Viking, 40 West 23rd Street, New York, New York 10010, U.S.A.

CRIME PUBLICATIONS

Novels (series: Sergeant Karl Alberg)

Neighbours. Toronto, Macmillan, 1979.
The Favourite Toronto, Doubleday, 1982.
Among Friends. Toronto, and New York, Doubleday, 1984.

The Suspect (Alberg). New York, Viking Press, 1985; London, Hale, 1986.
Sleep While I Sing (Alberg). New York, Viking Press, 1986; London, Collins, 1987.
Love in the Temperate Zone (Alberg). New York, Viking Press, 1988; Bath, Avon, Firecrest, 1989.

* * *

L. R. Wright's mysteries are police procedural novels with strong undertones of psychological tension. They are expertly plotted and suspenseful. Equally important are the characters, the setting, and the elegantly-crafted narrative. The setting for Wright's mysteries is the "Sunshine Coast" of British Columbia with its contrast between bright sun and flowers and its gloomy fog and rain. These contrasts often add atmosphere and tension to the plots.

Wright's series character is Staff Sergeant Karl Alberg, head of the Sechelt detachment of the Royal Canadian Mounted Police. Alberg is tall, blond, in his mid forties, a solid, pleasant-looking but not exceedingly handsome man. From time to time he frets about his receding hairline and his expanding waistline. He misses his daughters and sometimes misses his ex-wife. These familiar emotions make Alberg real and likable.

Wright uses other continuing characters to add romantic interest or touches of humor. Cassandra Mitchell is the town librarian and Alberg's romantic interest. Alberg and Mitchell meet when he answers her ad for friendly dating in a personal column. Mitchell is single, in her early forties, tall, attractive, a few strands of gray beginning to show in her dark hair. The subplot of their on-again, off-again romance is a dimension readers expect and enjoy.

Another continuing character is Corporal Sanducci. Alberg is mildly jealous of the youthful Sanducci because of his thick dark hair, his sensual presence, and his success with women which adds a touch of humor and creates sympathy for Alberg.

There is little physical violence in the stories other than the murder itself. The plot follows Alberg's calm, methodical but persistent investigations, but the focus is more on the psychology behind the motive than on the identity of the murderer.

In *The Suspect*, the murder of an octogenarian, Carlyle Burke, by his long-time acquaintance and fellow-octogenarian, George Wilcox, is revealed in the opening scene. Alberg searches for a motive to prove his suspicion of Wilcox. Cassandra Mitchell is a friend of Wilcox and even though Alberg finds Wilcox likable and is fond of Mitchell, he is duty-bound to follow his instincts in the investigation, heartless as he may seem to Mitchell.

In *Sleep While I Sing*, a hitchhiker is found murdered on a dark, rainy night. Her identity is unknown and certain details of the murder scene are unusual. Alberg's objectivity in the investigation is threatened because Cassandra Mitchell, his romantic interest, is currently infatuated with one of the prime suspects.

In *Love in the Temperate Zone*, a beautiful recluse reports the accidental death of her brother. Alberg finds himself sexually attracted to the woman and once again struggling to maintain his objectivity. Meanwhile, an elderly woman escapes from a local nursing home and accidently stumbles into the strange environment of the recluse. The fog and rain add to the dramatic tension as the two plots intersect and reach a chilling conclusion.

Wright's series of mysteries are enjoyed not only by mystery fans but by anyone who appreciates elegantly-crafted stories of human relationships whether the good kind as between Karl Alberg and Cassandra Mitchell or the destructive kind as between the murderers and their victims.

—Carol Barry

––––––

WRIGHT, Rowland. *See* **WELLS, Carolyn.**

––––––

WRIGHT, Willard Huntington. *See* **VAN DINE, S.S.**

––––––

WYLIE, Philip. *See* **BALMER, Edwin.**

––––––

X, Mr. *See* **HOCH, Edward D.**

––––––

Y

YATES, Dornford. Pseudonym for Cecil William Mercer. British. Born in Upper Walmer, Kent, 7 August 1885. Educated at St. Clare, Walmer, 1894–99; Harrow School, 1899–1904; University College, Oxford (President, Dramatic Society, 1907), B.A. in jurisprudence 1907; Inner Temple, London: called to the Bar 1909. Served in the 3rd County of London Yeomanry in Egypt and Salonika during World War I: Captain; with the East Africa Command, 1942–43, then in Southern Rhodesia forces: Major. Married 1) Bettine Stokes Edwards in 1919 (marriage dissolved 1933), one son; 2) Elizabeth Lucy Bowie in 1934. Practicing solicitor from 1909: worked on the Crippen case, 1910; lived in France after World War I, and in Southern Rhodesia after World War II. *Died 5 March 1960.*

CRIME PUBLICATIONS

Novels (series: Berry; Richard Chandos; Chief Inspector/Superintendent Richard Falcon; Jonah Mansel)

Blind Corner (Mansel, Chandos). London, Hodder and Stoughton, and New York, Minton Balch, 1927.
Perishable Goods. (Mansel, Chandos, Berry). London, Hodder and Stoughton, and New York, Minton Balch, 1928.
Blood Royal (Chandos). London, Hodder and Stoughton, 1929; New York, Minton Balch, 1930.
Fire Below (Chandos). London, Hodder and Stoughton, 1930; as *By Royal Command*, New York, Minton Balch, 1931.
Adele & Co. (Berry, Mansel). New York, Minton Balch, 1931; London, Hodder and Stoughton, 1932.
Safe Custody. London, Hodder and Stoughton, and New York, Minton Balch, 1932.
Storm Music. London, Hodder and Stoughton, and New York, Minton Balch, 1934.
She Fell among Thieves (Mansel, Chandos). London, Hodder and Stoughton, and New York, Minton Balch, 1935.
She Painted Her Face. London, Ward Lock, and New York, Putnam, 1937.
Gale Warning (Mansel, Chandos). London, Ward Lock, 1939; New York, Putnam, 1940.
Shoal Water (Mansel). London, Ward Lock, 1940; New York, Putnam, 1941.
An Eye for a Tooth (Mansel, Chandos). London, Ward Lock, 1943; New York, Putnam, 1944.
The House That Berry Built (Berry, Mansel, Falcon). London, Ward Lock, and New York, Putnam, 1945.
Red in the Morning (Mansel, Chandos). London, Ward Lock, 1946; as *Were Death Denied*, New York, Putnam, 1946.
Cost Price (Mansel, Chandos). London, Ward Lock, 1949; as *The Laughing Bacchante*, New York, Putnam, 1949.
Ne'er-Do-Well (Mansel, Chandos, Falcon). London, Ward Lock, 1954.

Short Stories

Berry and Co. London, Ward Lock, 1921; New York, Minton Balch, 1928.
Jonah and Co. London, Ward Lock, 1922; New York, Minton Balch, 1927.
Maiden Stakes. London, Ward Lock, 1929.
And Berry Came Too. London, Ward Lock, and New York, Minton Balch, 1936.
Period Stuff. London, Ward Lock, 1942.
The Berry Scene. London, Ward Lock, and New York, Minton Balch, 1947.
The Best of Berry, edited by Jack Adrian. London, Dent, 1989.

Uncollected Short Stories

"Court Cards," in *Windsor Magazine* (London), December 1926.
"The Real Thing," in *Windsor Magazine* (London), April 1937.

OTHER PUBLICATIONS

Novels

Anthony Lyveden. London, Ward Lock, 1921.
Valerie French. London, Ward Lock, 1923.
This Publican. London, Ward Lock, 1938; as *The Devil in Satin*, New York, Doubleday, 1938.
Lower Than Vermin. London, Ward Lock, 1954.
Wife Apparent. London, Ward Lock, 1956.

Short Stories

The Brother of Daphne. London, Ward Lock, 1914.
The Courts of Idleness. London, Ward Lock, 1920.
And Five Were Foolish. London, Ward Lock, 1924.
As Other Men Are. London, Ward Lock, 1925.
The Stolen March. London, Ward Lock, 1926; New York, Minton Balch, 1933.

OTHER PUBLICATIONS

Play

Eastward Ho!, with Oscar Asche, music by Grace Torrens and John Ansell (produced London, 1919).

Other

As Berry and I Were Saying. London, Ward Lock, 1952.
B-Berry and I Look Back. London, Ward Lock, 1958.

Ghostwriter: *What I Know*, by C.W. Stamper. London, Mills and Boon, 1913.

*

Critical Study: *Dornford Yates: A Biography* by A.J. Smithers. London, Hodder and Stoughton, 1982.

* * *

Together with John Buchan and Sapper (H.C. McNeile), Dornford Yates formed the third in a triumvirate of high-adventure and essentially romantic (in the widest sense of the word) thriller writers which dominated the British literary scene during the inter-war years. All came from secure, semi-prosperous backgrounds, all held vaguely similar views on the role of their mother-country in the greater scheme of things, all were highly proficient at spinning the kind of yarns (what Buchan himself, in a faintly embarrassed throwaway, used to refer to as "shockers") that sold in their tens of thousands on first publication, their hundreds of thousands in reprint.

Buchan was perhaps the most original of the three, certainly the most patrician; Sapper, a man of generally odious opinions, the most thuggish. Yates slips neatly in between the two. His prose was stylish, his plotting meticulous, his pacing immaculate and above all else he had the priceless gift of being able at times to generate an almost unbearable tension in his thrillers, of a kind and quality not to be found in the books of either of his peers. And unlike them he could also often be hilariously funny.

Early in his career Yates gained a reputation as a writer of amusing trifles concerning amusing triflers: the Pleydell and the Mansel families—a carelessly wealthy blood-tied group from the middle echelons of High Society. The Berry series (after Bertram Pleydell, slothful but witty head of the house) ran to a number of short story volumes and a handful of novels, most of which were characterized by a heady mix of high farce and sparkling verbal wit wholly agreeable to his readers and still enjoyed today.

Yet if Yates had concentrated solely on comedy his books would doubtless be largely forgotten now, like those of other once-lauded humorists such as Denis Mackail, say, F.E. Bailly, Ian Hay; but he was called to the Bar in 1909 (and was involved on the fringes of the Crippen case) and this gave his work an extra dimension. Such real-life characters as "Cammy" Grizard, the biggest fence in London, and the shyster lawyer Arthur Newton (of whom it was reported that the entire staff of Marlborough Street police station had to be changed regularly in case he should have suborned any of them) appeared in his later novels and stories in one guise or another. Yates's main detective, Superintendent Falcon, too, was based on a CID man met in those pre-World War I days, Inspector Wensley, whose beat was the anarchist-infested East End. Falcon appears to good effect in *Period Stuff*, in the novel *The House That Berry Built* (which, though mainly a lively comedy, also features the breaking of a murderer's alibi), and triumphs in the oddly neglected *Ne'er-Do-Well*, a murder mystery set in the closed world of a convent hospice and related almost entirely in question-and-answer dialogue. A non-Falcon short story, "The Real Thing" (based on the shooting of PC Gutteridge in 1927 and the trial of his killers) also skilfully utilised the catechistic technique, this time in a courtroom setting.

Many of the Berry stories contain crime and mystery elements—confidence-trickery, robbery, kidnapping, murder—and a selection appeared in *The Best of Berry*, which also contains one of the most exhilarating car-chases Yates ever wrote (Ian Fleming much admired this aspect of his work), although Yates's best efforts at depicting car-drivers hurtling recklessly through the night or along dusty, poplar-lined roads as pursuers or pursued were reserved for his immensely popular thrillers, many of which feature a refugee from the Berry saga, that matchless motorist and champion of the Rolls Royce Jonah Mansel.

In most there is treasure to be found and fought over in desolate corners of Austria and south-west France, where, usefully, you could battle it out with a pair of Lewis guns uninterrupted. Often the treasure is booby-trapped (the Borgia jewels in *Safe Custody* and its sequel *Cost Price*; Axel the Red's booty hidden in the Great Well at Wagensberg Castle in *Blind Corner*); on occasion it is human (the beautiful Adele, for instance, held hostage as "perishable goods" in the novel of that name once recommended "without reservation" by no less a critic than Dashiell Hammett). But whatever it is and wherever it is, the hunt for it is invariably accomplished at an unflagging pace, each book featuring its full measure of dramatic set-pieces, sometimes of a chillingly macabre nature (the mass-poisoning at the end of *She Fell among Thieves*, the horrifying murder of his minions by the shepherd in *Shoal Water*).

All are more or less indebted to the romances of Anthony Hope and Maurice Hewlett and written in a prose that relies heavily on the language and rhythms of the law, the Bible, and Shakespeare. There is thus melodrama (no bad thing in itself) in abundance; and, too, allowances of an other-times-other-mores nature must be made at the odd hiccups of distinctly rascist and elitist comment from both author and characters.

An outstanding comedy-thriller (indeed, one of the very few genuinely to qualify in that notoriously difficult sub-genre) is *Adele & Co.*, which artfully combines the larks of the Berry series and the suspense and hectic pace of the Mansel novels.

—Jack Adrian

YORK, Andrew. Pseudonym for Christopher (Robin) Nicole; also writes as Leslie Arlen; Robin Cade; Peter Grange; Caroline Gray; Mark Logan; Simon Mckay C.R. Nicholson; Christina Nicholson; Robin Nicholson; Alan Savage; Alison York. British. Born in Georgetown, British Guiana, now Guyana, 7 December 1930. Educated at Harrison College, Barbados; Queen's College, Guyana. Married 1) Jean Barnett in 1951 (divorced), two sons and two daughters; 2) Diana Bachmann. Clerk, Royal Bank of Canada, in the West Indies, 1947–56. Lives in Guernsey. Agent: Curtis Brown and John Farquharson, 162–168 Regent Street, London W1R 5TB, England.

CRIME PUBLICATIONS

Novels (series: Colonel Munroe Tallant; Jonas Wilde)

The Eliminator (Wilde).   London, Hutchinson, 1966; Philadelphia, Lippincott, 1967.
The Co-Ordinator (Wilde).   London, Hutchinson, and Philadelphia, Lippincott, 1967.
The Predator (Wilde).   London, Hutchinson, and Philadelphia, Lippincott, 1968.
The Deviator (Wilde).   London, Hutchinson, and Philadelphia, Lippincott, 1969.
The Dominator (Wilde).   London, Hutchinson, 1969.
The Infiltrator (Wilde).   London, Hutchinson, and New York, Doubleday, 1971.
The Expurgator (Wilde).   London, Hutchinson, 1972; New York, Doubleday, 1973.
The Captivator (Wilde).   London, Hutchinson, 1973; New York, Doubleday, 1974.
The Fear Dealers (as Robin Cade).   London, Cassell, and New York, Simon and Schuster, 1974.
The Fascinator (Wilde).   London, Hutchinson, and New York, Doubleday, 1975.
Dark Passage.   New York, Doubleday, 1975; London, Hutchinson, 1976.

Tallant for Trouble. London, Hutchinson, and New York, Doubleday, 1977.

Tallant for Disaster. London, Hutchinson, and New York, Doubleday, 1978.

The Combination. New York, Doubleday, 1983; London, Severn House, 1984.

OTHER PUBLICATIONS as Christopher Nicole

Novels

Off White. London, Jarrolds, 1959.
Shadows in the Jungle. London, Jarrolds, 1961.
Ratoon. London, Jarrolds, and New York, St. Martin's Press, 1962.
Dark Noon. London, Jarrolds, 1963.
Amyot's Cay. London, Jarrolds, 1964.
Blood Amyot. London, Jarrolds, 1964.
The Amyot Crime. London, Jarrolds, 1965; New York, Bantam, 1974.
White Boy. London, Hutchinson, 1966.
The Self-Lovers. London, Hutchinson, 1968.
The Thunder and the Shouting. London, Hutchinson, and New York, Doubleday, 1969.
The Longest Pleasure. London, Hutchinson, 1970.
The Face of Evil. London, Hutchinson, 1971.
Lord of the Golden Fan. London, Cassell, 1973.
Heroes. London, Corgi, 1973.
Caribee. London, Cassell, and New York, St. Martin's Press, 1974.
The Devil's Own. London, Cassell, and New York, St. Martin's Press, 1975.
Mistress of Darkness. London, Cassell, and New York, St. Martin's Press, 1976.
Black Dawn. London, Cassell, and New York, St. Martin's Press, 1977.
Sunset. London, Cassell, and New York, St. Martin's Press, 1978.
The Secret Memoirs of Lord Byron. Philadelphia, Lippincott, and London, Joseph, 1978; as *Lord of Sin*, London, Corgi, 1980.
The Fire and the Rope (as Alison York). London, W.H. Allen, and New York, Berkley, 1979.
The Scented Sword (as Alison York). London, W.H. Allen, 1980.
Haggard. London, Joseph, and New York, New American Library, 1980.
The Friday Spy (as C.R. Nicholson). London, Corgi, 1980; as *A Passion for Treason* (as Robin Nicholson), New York, Jove, 1981.
Haggard's Inheritance. London, Joseph, 1981; as *The Inheritors*, New York, New American Library, 1981.
The New Americans:
  Brothers and Enemies. New York, Jove, 1982; London, Corgi, 1983.
  Lovers and Outlaws. New York, Jove, 1982.
The Young Haggards. London, Joseph, 1982.
The Crimson Pagoda. New York, New American Library, 1983; London, Joseph, 1984.
The Scarlet Princess. New York, New American Library, 1984; London, Joseph, 1985.
The Sun Rises. London, Hamlyn, 1984.
The Seas of Fortune (as Simon McKay). London, Severn House, 1984.
The Seeds of Rebellion. London, Severn House, 1984.
Red Dawn. London, Joseph, 1985.

The Sun and the Dragon. London, Hamlyn, 1985.
The Sun on Fire. London, Arrow, 1985.
The Rivals (as Simon Mckay). London, Severn House, 1985.
Wild Harvest. London, Severn House, 1985; New York, Severn House, 1987.
Old Glory. London, Severn House, 1986; New York, Severn House, 1988.
The Sea and the Sand. London, Severn House, 1986; New York, Severn House, 1988.
Iron Ships, Iron Men. London, Severn House, 1987.
The Wind of Destiny. London, Severn House, 1987.
The Ship with No Name. London, Severn House, 1987.
Raging Seas, Seering Skies. London, Severn House, 1988.
The Power and the Glory. London, Severn House, 1988.
The High Country. London, Century, 1988.
The Regiment. London, Century, 1988; New York, St. Martin's Press, 1989.
Pearl of the Orient. London, Century, 1988.
The Happy Valley. London, Century, 1989.
The Command. London, Century, 1989.
Dragon's Blood. London, Century, 1989.
The Triumph. London, Century, 1989.
Dark Sun. London, Century, 1990.
Ottoman (as Alan Savage). London, Macdonald Futura, 1990.

Novels as Peter Grange

King Creole. London, Jarrolds, 1966.
The Devil's Emissary. London, Jarrolds, 1968.
The Tumult at the Gate. London, Jarrolds, 1970.
The Golden Goddess. London, Jarrolds, 1973.

Novels as Mark Logan

Tricolour. London, Macmillan, and New York, St. Martin's Press, 1976; as *The Captain's Woman*, New York, New American Library, 1977.
Guillotine. London, Macmillan, and New York, St. Martin's Press, 1976; as *French Kiss*, New York, New American Library, 1978.
Brumaire. London, Wingate, and New York, St. Martin's Press, 1978; as *December Passion*, New York, New American Library, 1979.

Novels as Christina Nicholson

The Power and the Passion. London, Corgi, and New York, Coward McCann, 1977.
The Savage Sands. London, Corgi, and New York, Coward McCann, 1978.
The Queen of Paris. London, Corgi, 1979.

Novels as Leslie Arlen

The Borodins:
  Love and Honor. New York, Jove, and London, Futura, 1980.
  War and Passion. New York, Jove, and London, Futura, 1981.
  Fate and Dreams. New York, Jove, and London, Futura, 1981.
  Destiny and Desire. New York, Jove, 1982.
  Rage and Desire. New York, Jove, 1982.
  Hope and Glory. New York, Jove, 1984.

Novels as Caroline Gray

First Class. London, Joseph, 1984; as *Treasures*, New York, Fawcett, 1984.

Hotel De Luxe. London, Joseph, 1985; as *So Grand*, New York, Fawcett, 1985.
White Rani. London, Joseph, and New York, Fawcett, 1986.
Victoria's Walk. London, Joseph, 1986; New York, Fawcett, 1988.
Shadow of Death. London, Severn House, 1987.
The Third Life. London, Joseph, and New York, St. Martin's Press, 1988.

Other

West Indian Cricket. London, Phoenix House, 1957.
The West Indies: Their People and History. London, Hutchinson, 1965.
Introduction to Chess. London, Corgi, 1973.

Other (for children) as Andrew York

The Doom Fishermen. London, Hutchinson, 1969; as *Operation Destruct*, New York, Holt Rinehart, 1969.
Manhunt for a General. London, Hutchinson, 1970; as *Operation Manhunt*, New York, Holt Rinehart, 1970.
Where the Cavern Ends. London, Hutchinson, and New York, Holt Rinehart, 1971.
Appointment in Kiltone. London, Hutchinson, 1972; as *Operation Neptune*, New York, Holt Rinehart, 1972.

*   *   *

"He is the most dangerous man in the world." And the nine novels by Andrew York about this man, Jonas Wilde, the Eliminator, are to Ian Fleming's James Bond tales what a century ago the Martin Hewitt stories were to those about Sherlock Holmes: solid, if less spectacular, stories modeled on a more famous hero whose popularity gave new life to an old form—in this case, the spy-adventure tale. Lacking the bizarre villains, tricky gadgets, and exotic color of far-off lands, the Wilde series has all the other characteristics of the Fleming formula: the secret agent authorized to kill, immensely attractive to women, and a connoisseur of wine and food, appearing in melodramatic fast-action adventures filled with violence and sex. Nevertheless, Wilde is no mere carbon copy; for example, he does not use a gun, killing with a karate blow behind the ear. Large chunks of the books are as exciting as anything in Fleming: see the scene from *The Co-Ordinator* in which Wilde is recognized in the midst of his enemies and forced to flee onto an ice-coated skyscraper ledge in a snowstorm—and grimly tries to carry out his assassination attempt by smashing through his victim's reinforced window before the arctic wind topples him from the high ledge.

But the novels as a whole never rise above these individual scenes, flawed by a fault the author is probably unaware of: though the telling is deadly serious, the plot line is often parody, a wild black humor blowing through it, as if the author were unconsciously laughing at the Fleming form. A few examples: in one novel Wilde is told by his superior that the people the Elimination Section has been killing are traitors; reassured, Wilde goes on his next mission—and discovers that his superior is in the pay of the Russians and that the Elimination Section, without knowing it, has been killing Britain's best citizens for months. In a black way, that's funny—the British spend months and millions creating the Section; the Russians spend five minutes to bribe one man—and get the entire Section working for them. In another novel Wilde has a slipped disc that throws his back out of joint and knocks him to the floor every time he tries a killing karate blow. In a third he seeks a multiple murderer, but discovers that *everyone* he investigates

is guilty. In another, a group trying to assassinate an Arab prince orders Wilde to *protect* the prince in order to expose Wilde as an assassin—to make the prince's bodyguards so overconfident that perhaps the *next* attempt will succeed! A black mockery lies buried in these works. But that is the only major flaw in these well-written, suspenseful adventures; and Wilde remains, perhaps, the best of all the men modeled on Ian Fleming's James Bond.

In the late 1970's York struck out in a more original direction with a series of novels about Munroe Tallant, Police Chief of Grand Flamingo Island in the West Indies. Here his humor is conscious and intended, the native dialect authentic, and the setting so exotic—*Tallant for Disaster* deals with a tropical hurricane, sunken treasure ships centuries old, nude sunbathing beauties, and a vicious rape-murder—that it takes a while to realize that these works are really unusually colorful police procedural novels. Lighter in tone, better characterized, these novels are as a whole superior to the grimmer Wilde works and show a more individual future for York.

—Frank D. McSherry, Jr.

———————

YORK, Jeremy. *See* **CREASEY, John.**

———————

YORKE, Margaret. Pseudonym for Margaret Beda Nicholson, née Larminie. British. Born in Compton, Surrey, 30 January 1924. Educated at Prior's Field, Godalming, Surrey. Served in the Women's Royal Naval Service, 1942–45. Married Basil Nicholson in 1945 (divorced 1957); one daughter and one son. Assistant librarian, St. Hilda's College, Oxford, 1959–60; library assistant, Christ Church, Oxford, 1963–65. Vice-chairwoman, 1978, and chairwoman, 1979, Crime Writers Association. Recipient: Swedish Academy of Detection award, 1982. Agent: Curtis Brown Ltd., 162–168 Regent Street, London W1R 5TA. Address: Oriel Cottage, Long Crendon, Aylesbury, Buckinghamshire HP18 9AL, England.

CRIME PUBLICATIONS

Novels (series: Patrick Grant)

Dead in the Morning (Grant). London, Bles, 1970.
Silent Witness (Grant). London, Bles, 1972; New York, Walker, 1973.
Grave Matters (Grant). London, Bles, 1973; New York, Bantam, 1983.
Mortal Remains (Grant). London, Bles, 1974.
No Medals for the Major. London, Bles, 1974.
The Small Hours of the Morning. London, Bles, and New York, Walker, 1975.
Cast for Death (Grant). London, Hutchinson, and New York, Walker, 1976.
The Cost of Silence. London, Hutchinson, and New York, Walker, 1977.
The Point of Murder. London, Hutchinson, 1978; as *The Come-On*, New York, Harper 1979.
Death on Account. London, Hutchinson, 1979.

The Scent of Fear. London, Hutchinson, 1980; New York, St. Martin's Press, 1981.

The Hand of Death. London, Hutchinson, 1981; New York, St. Martin's Press, 1982.

Devil's Work. London, Hutchinson, and New York, St. Martin's Press, 1982.

Find Me a Villain. London, Hutchinson, and New York, St. Martin's Press, 1983.

The Smooth Face of Evil. London, Hutchinson, and New York, St. Martin's Press, 1984.

Intimate Kill. London, Hutchinson, and New York, St. Martin's Press, 1985.

Safely to the Grave. London, Hutchinson, and New York, St. Martin's Press, 1986.

Evidence to Destroy. London, Hutchinson, and New York, Viking, 1987.

Speak for the Dead. London, Mysterious Press, and New York, Viking, 1988.

Crime in Question. London, Mysterious Press, and New York, Viking, 1989.

Admit to Murder. London, Mysterious Press, 1990.

Uncollected Short Stories

"The Liberator," in *Winter's Crimes 9*, edited by George Hardinge. London, Macmillan, and New York, St. Martin's Press, 1977.

"Always Rather a Prig," in *John Creasey's Crime Collection 1978*, edited by Herbert Harris. London, Gollancz, 1978.

"Such a Gentleman," in *Mystery Guild Anthology*, edited by John Waite. London, Constable 1980.

"A Time for Indulgence," in *Winter's Crimes 13*, edited by George Hardinge. London, Macmillan, and New York, St. Martin's Press, 1981.

"The Reckoning," in *John Creasey's Crime Collection 1982*, edited by Herbert Harris. London, Gollancz, and New York, St. Martin's Press, 1982.

"Fair and Square," in *Ellery Queen's Mystery Magazine* (New York), August 1982.

"A Woman of Taste," in *Good Housekeeping* (London), June 1983.

"Bitter Harvest," in *Woman* (London), 18 June 1983.

"The Wrath of Zeus," in *John Creasey's Crime Collection 1986*, edited by Herbert Harris. London, Gollancz, 1986; New York, St. Martin's Press, 1987.

"Gifts for the Bridegroom," in *Winter's Crimes 18*, edited by Hilary Hale. London, Macmillan, 1986; New York, St. Martin's Press, 1987.

"Anniversary," in *Ellery Queen's Mystery Magazine* (New York), April 1986.

"The Mouse Will Play," in *Ladykillers*. London, Dent, 1987.

"The Breasts of Aphrodite," in *New Crimes*, edited by Maxim Jakubowski. London, Robinson, 1989; New York, Carroll and Graf, 1990.

"Luck of the Draw," in *Winter's Crimes 21*, edited by Hilary Hale. London, Macmillan, 1989.

OTHER PUBLICATIONS

Novels

Summer Flight. London, Hale, 1957.
Pray, Love, Remember. London, Hale, 1958.
Christopher. London, Hale, 1959.
Deceiving Mirror. London, Hale, 1960.
The China Doll. London, Hale, 1961.
Once a Stranger. London, Hurst and Blackett, 1962.

The Birthday. London, Hurst and Blackett, 1963.
Full Circle. London, Hurst and Blackett, 1965.
No Fury. London, Hurst and Blackett, 1967.
The Apricot Bed. London, Hurst and Blackett, 1968.
The Limbo Ladies. London, Hurst and Blackett, 1969.

Other

"St. Mary Mead and Other Troubled Villages" and "Oxford vs. Cambridge: The Dark Blues Have the Most," in *Murder Ink: The Mystery Reader's Companion*, edited by Dilys Winn. New York, Workman, 1977.

*

Margaret Yorke comments:

Writing about the hopes, fears, misunderstandings, and conflicts of ordinary people has always interested me. My first 11 novels were family problem novels, but I was always tempted to stir up their quiet plots with some violent action. With *Dead in the Morning* I turned to crime fiction and began with the whodunit form because of the pattern already set by successful women writers. The characters have always interested me more than the plots, though I have enjoyed devising the puzzles. The idea for *No Medals for the Major* came to me when I was thinking about how different we often feel inside from the face we present to the world, and how an action, slight in itself, can have profound effects on other people whom we may never meet. My recent novels have been about the victims of events over which they have had no control: whydunits, and how it happened.

*   *   *

"Miss Marple no longer lives in St. Mary Mead", says Margaret Yorke in her essay "St. Mary Mead and Other Troubled Villages" in Dilys Winn's *Murder Ink*, "but the village crime novel is still vigorous. Like rural life, however, it has changed and broadened."

The basic structure of the village or small town may be the same: the manor house, the thatched cottages, the Norman church with the eccentric vicar and his fussy wife, the inn with the quaint name, the close relations between the villagers, for better or for worse. But there might be a new supermarket in the High Street, the prettiest cottage might be inhabited by a commuting City stockbroker, there might be a block of council flats in the outskirts. This has also changed the family structures, and the relations between people in the village: divorces are much more common, as well as casual liaisons. A new and more cold-blooded and casual type of crime has also crept in: vandalism, muggings, juvenile delinquency, rape.

After having discarded the hero of her early, rather conventional detective novels, Oxford don Patrick Grant, Yorke has emerged as one of the foremost chroniclers of life in the "new" English village or small town and its crime scene, especially the kind of crime that springs from human relations, or the lack of them.

The scene is set already in her first non-Grant novel, *No Medals for the Major*, about the quiet, unassuming retired Major Johnson, who by chance gets involved in the death of a local girl, is destroyed by the villagers' ugly gossip and blows his brains out.

No Medals for the Major also introduces another of Yorke's major themes—juvenile delinquency. Yorke's novels are full of youths who haphazardly drift into crime. Ray Brett in *The Small Hours of the Morning* is a petty crook who dreams of the big hit and becomes a murderer almost by accident; Mick

Green in *The Cost of Silence* is a youngster of the same ilk, who "happens" to murder Emma Widness in a badly planned and badly executed burglary. Mick Harvey in *Safely to the Grave* likes to scare people, and woe betide the two ladies who have reported him for dangerous driving. All these and other murders are murders by mistake: careless, "unnecessary" murders.

But this theme is subordinate to the larger theme of relations between human beings as a motive for murder. And Yorke deals with *ordinary* human beings; there are neither real psychopaths nor criminal masterminds in her novels. Her thesis is that coincidence often decides who becomes a criminal—even a murderer. Book salesman Gary Browne in *The Point of Murder* likes to have "fun" with the ladies, but goes too far one day. The timid bank manager Robbie Robinson in *Death on Account* suddenly finds himself a bank robber; antique dealer Ronald Trimm in *The Hand of Death* has a sterile life which ultimately makes him a rapist.

As in the classic detective novel, marriage is a driving force in Yorke's novels. It's seldom *the* central force though, but rather some sort of catalyst. Ronald Trimm's loveless marriage makes him a rapist, but what is emphasized as the motive is not his frustrated lust as much as his lack of normal emotional relations to another human being. In *Intimate Kill* poor marital relations are the foundations of the story of how the innocent Stephen Dawes is convicted for the murder of his disappeared wife. Out of boredom with a marriage to an older man Carrie Matthews in *Speak for the Dead* starts a *belle du jour* life in London which leads to her death.

In almost all of Yorke's novels people commit small, seemingly insignificant mistakes, often sins of omission, with disastrous consequences. Major Johnson gets tangled in a web of his own making, when he lies abouts his whereabouts out of misguided chivalry. Alan Parker in *Devil's Work* can't face telling his strong, efficient wife that he has been made redundant and this ultimately makes him a suspect in the disappearence of little Tessa.

Maybe this motive is only a part of Yorke's main theme: how coincidence maketh criminal of us all. Many of these people commit no real crimes—but there are only shades of difference from the juvenile delinquents who commit hasty deeds with disastrous consequences.

This is ultimately the strength of Yorke's novels. The plots are based on the small human weaknesses that we all have, and would like to get rid of, but can't. "There but for the grace of God go you and I."

—Karl G. Fredriksson

———

YOUNG, Collier. *See* **BLOCH, Robert.**

———

YUILL, P.B. Pseudonym for Gordon Williams and Terry Venables. British. **WILLIAMS, Gordon (Maclean):** Born in Paisley, Renfrewshire, 20 June 1939. Educated at John Neilson Institution, Paisley, Scottish Higher Leaving Certificate 1951. Served in the Royal Air Force for two years (national service). Married to Claerweh Williams; two daughters and one son. Reporter, feature writer, and sub-editor on newspapers and magazines in the 1960's. Lives in London. Agent: Curtis Brown and John Farquharson, 162–168 Regent Street, London W1R 5TB, England. **VENABLES, Terry:** Born in Dagenham, Essex, 6 January 1943. Married in 1967 (divorced 1986); two daughters. Football player, for Chelsea, 1959–65, Tottenham Hotspur 1966–68, Queen's Park Rangers, 1969–74, and Crystal Palace, 1974; manager of the Crystal Palace football club, 1976–80, Queen's Park Rangers football club, 1980–84, Barcelona football club, Spain, 1984–87, and since 1987 Tottenham Hotspur.

CRIME PUBLICATIONS

Novels (series: James Hazell)

The Bornless Keeper (by Williams). London, Macmillan, 1974; New York, Walker, 1975.
Hazell Plays Solomon. London, Macmillan, 1974; New York, Walker, 1975.
Hazell and the Three Card Trick. London, Macmillan, 1975; New York, Walker, 1976.
Hazell and the Menacing Jester. London, Macmillan, 1976.

Uncollected Short Stories

"You Make Your Own Luck" (by Williams), in *Winter's Crimes 6*, edited by George Hardinge. London, Macmillan, and New York, St. Martin's Press, 1974.
"The Horseshoe Inn" (by Williams), in *Prevailing Spirits*, edited by Giles Gordon. London, Hamish Hamilton, 1976.
"Hazell and the Patriot," in *Winter's Crimes 9*, edited by George Hardinge. London, Macmillan, and New York, St. Martin's Press, 1977.

OTHER PUBLICATIONS by Gordon Williams

Novels

The Last Day of Lincoln Charles. London, Secker and Warburg, 1965; New York, Stein and Day, 1966.
The Camp. London, Secker and Warburg, and New York, Stein and Day, 1966.
The Man Who Had Power over Women. London, Secker and Warburg, 1966; New York, Stein and Day, 1967.
From Scenes Like These. London, Secker and Warburg, 1968; New York, Morrow, 1969.
The Siege of Trencher's Farm. London, Secker and Warburg, and New York, Morrow, 1969.
The Upper Pleasure Garden. London, Secker and Warburg, and New York, Morrow, 1970.
They Used to Play on Grass, with Terry Venables. London, Hodder and Stoughton, 1971.
Walk, Don't Walk. London, Hodder and Stoughton, and New York, St. Martin's Press, 1972.
Big Morning Blues. London, Hodder and Stoughton, 1974.
The Duellists (novelization of screenplay). London, Collins, 1977.
The Micronauts. New York, Bantam, 1978; London, New English Library, 1981.
The Microcolony. New York, Bantam, 1979; as *Micronaut World*, London, New English Library, 1981.
Revolt of the Micronauts. New York, Bantam, and London, New English Library, 1981.
Pomeroy. New York, Arbor House, 1981; London, Joseph, 1983.
Pomeroy Unleashed. New York, Arbor House, 1983.

Plays

Screenplay: *Tree of Hands*, 1989.

Television Script: *G4-Pay Hero: A Boxer's Tale*, 1986.

OTHER PUBLICATIONS by Terry Venables

Other

The Terry Venables Soccer Quiz Book. London, Scholastic, 1980.

*

Gordon Williams comments:

Hazell originated from an idea by Terry Venables for a story about switched babies, the private detective being only a useful story-teller. The character began to interest us while we were writing in tandem, and we began seeing Hazell as a suitable person to emulate in London terms the immortal Philip Marlowe. In general terms Hazell represented our own joint attitude to the wonderful world of British snobbery.

* * *

The name of P.B. Yuill, it is common knowledge, conceals two writers, the novelist Gordon Williams and the football club manager, Terry Venables. *The Bornless Keeper*, the first title to appear under the somewhat curious pseudonym, however, was exclusively a Williams work and as such, though it is an excellent crime story, full of genuine tension and one that looks at the world around it, really falls outside the canon.

The canonical Yuill is concerned entirely with the adventures of a London private eye, name of Hazell. Hazell is an East Ender, telling his stories in genuine East End argot with flicks of rhyming slang ("Apples and pears" stairs) and the hard rhythms that are typical of the area, and not all that easy to catch. He is tough, too, almost as much a criminal as the people he (on the whole) goes up against. And his knowledge of the dodges of the fly-boy world is extensive, as well as bearing all the signs of being accurate. But he is by no means a mere set of characteristics, surface true but stuck on to a dummy. He is underneath a recognisable human being, even a particularly warm one. Nor is the world in which Hazell operates simply a convenient setting for that particular sort of tale. It is the real world, the nerve-jangling metropolis of London where aspects of life that the Londoner daily experiences, not the romantic or seamy bits that are encountered by only a few, play their real parts. And since it is the real world we are shown, our world with its faults, there is in the books an undertow of moral comment, not forced, certainly not laid on, but definitely there.

When Hazell goes out on an investigation the sort of place he is likely to find himself at is "Herbert Morrison House . . . a twenty-storey block, shabby and rain-streaked, the walls thick with spray-on messages, nicknames, gang slogans, incurable optimism about West Ham football team." That's a real place where real people (and of the sort you don't too often find in crime books) live. In a similar way when Yuill portrays a bad man, such as "Moneybags" Beevers in *Hazell and the Menacing Jester*, although he is convincingly tough (as really tough and as really criminal as, on the other side of the Atlantic, are the hoods in the novels of George V. Higgins) he is also likely to be a person with whom in the end you sympathise, at least to the point of feeling you know what makes him tick.

It is, I suppose, no less than what one would expect of a novelist of the stature of Gordon Williams, author of *The Siege of Trencher's Farm* (filmed as *Straw Dogs*), itself a novel of suspense that only fails to qualify as a crime novel because it put what it had to say about violence before the mere build-up of tension. But the Yuill books are, quite definitely, as much written by the footballer as by the novel writer, and it is from the former, I suspect, that the unique flavour of Hazell comes, the sharply cheerful toughness.

—H.R.F. Keating

———

NINETEENTH-CENTURY
WRITERS

BRADDON, Mary Elizabeth (1835–1915). Also wrote as Babington White. British. Novels: *Lady Audley's Secret*, 1862; *Aurora Floyd*, 1863; *John Marchmont's Legacy*, 1863; *Eleanor's Victory*, 1863; *Henry Dunbar: The Story of an Outcast*, 1864; *Birds of Prey*, 1867; *Charlotte's Inheritance*, 1868; *Robert Ainsleigh*, 1872; *Lucius Davoren; or, Publicans and Sinners*, 1873; *The Cloven Foot*, 1879; *Wyllard's Weird*, 1885; *Thou Art the Man*, 1894; *Rough Justice*, 1898; *His Darling Sin*, 1899.

* * *

After deserting the stage, Miss Braddon in her twenties and thirties wrote popular fiction at frantic speed—under her own name and various pseudonyms—to save her lover, the Irish-born John Maxwell, from financial disaster. In later life the petite, cheerful author wrote in various genres, including novels of manners and historical fiction, and found time to edit Maxwell's magazine *Belgravia* and other publications. By far her most popular work, and one of her earliest, is *Lady Audley's Secret*. It is often deprecated as a "sensation novel," but Benjamin M. Nyberg remarks that in its depth of characterization and avoidance of a fairy-tale ending it is far superior to most works so designated. Nevertheless this eminently readable novel does include such features as bigamy, attempted murder, and madness. The amateur detective, Robert Audley, is particularly well drawn. Indeed, this work and the one that inspired it—Wilkie Collins's *The Woman in White*—are not only the earliest of all detective novels but two of the best. Her other good crime novels include *Aurora Floyd*, *John Marchmont's Legacy*, and the two-part story comprising *Birds of Prey* and *Charlotte's Inheritance*. Less recommended are *Henry Dunbar*, *Robert Ainsleigh*, and *Rough Justice*.

—Norman Donaldson

————

COLLINS, (William) Wilkie (1824–89). British. Novels: *Basil: A Story of Modern Life*, 1852; *Hide and Seek; or, The Mystery of Mary Grice*, 1854; *The Dead Secret*, 1857; *The Woman in White*, 1860; *No Name*, 1862; *Armadale*, 1866; *The Moonstone: A Romance*, 1868; *Man and Wife*, 1870; *The Law and the Lady*, 1875; *The Haunted Hotel: A Mystery of Modern Venice*, 1878; *I Say No*, 1884; *Little Novels*, 1887; *Blind Love*, completed by Walter Besant, 1890. Short Stories: *After Dark*, 1856; *The Queen of Hearts*, 1859; *Miss or Mrs.? And Other Stories in Outline*, 1873; *The Frozen Deep and Other Stories*, 1874; *Alicia Warlock, A Mystery and Other Stories*, 1875; *My Lady's Money*, 1878; *The Ghost's Touch and Other Stories*, 1885; *The Yellow Tiger and Other Tales*, 1924; *Tales of Suspense*, edited by Robert Ashley and Herbert van Thal, 1954. Plays: *No Name*, 1863; *Armadale*, 1886; *The Frozen Deep*, 1866; *The Woman in White*, 1871; *The Moonstone*, 1877.

* * *

Wilkie Collins is generally considered the greatest Victorian master of mystery fiction, and *The Moonstone* and *The Woman in White* are among the few works of the period that are still popularly read. Like most of the Victorians, however, Collins is now appreciated for only a small fragment of a very large corpus of work, and much of his better fiction lies unreprinted and unread. During his later years his reputation suffered greatly, and it is only recently that his greatness has been appreciated.

The Woman in White (serialized in Dickens's *All the Year Round* in 1859–60) made Collins a national figure. It was not only highly popular as fiction, but it became one of those odd works that have repercussions in the other arts. Collins's friends, if literary tradition is correct, recognized more than a story in the novel, for Collins is said to have met his longtime mistress, Caroline Graves, under the same circumstances as occur in the novel. This incident Collins combined with the history of a fraudulent inheritance, from Méjan's *Receuil des causes célebres*, a large collection of factual crimes that he had picked up in France.

Outstanding among Collins's other work are the two great novels *Armadale* and *The Moonstone*. *Armadale*, the story of a criminal fraud and an attempted murder, is told in the framework of an unfolding prophetic dream. *The Moonstone*, the first significant detective novel in English, covers a spectacular theft, accompanied by somnambulism, clever scheming, and a little Oriental magic.

While Collins wrote only a few stories that are detective fiction in the strict sense, many of his works describe crimes, upon which proto-detectives exercise themselves. In *Hide and Seek* Matt Marksman tries to find the seducer of his sister; in "The Diary of Anne Rodway" a working girl tries to identify the man who murdered her friend; in "The Yellow Tiger" a traveler becomes party to a scheme to force a confession from a murderer; and in *I Say No* and "The Story of the Sixth Poor Traveller" female proto-detectives perform elementary investigations. "The Girl at the Gate" is concerned with a poison plot, while "Miss or Mrs.?" tells of a hired assassination that miscarried. *Blind Love*, Collins's last, unfinished novel, returned to the theme of fraudulent death that he had used in *The Moonstone* and *The Haunted Hotel*, while *The Haunted Hotel* and "The Clergyman's Confession" combine crimes with supernatural manifestations.

Closer to the modern concept of a detective story (with reader participation in the mystery) are *The Moonstone*, *The Law and the Lady*, in which a female detective attempts to identify a murderer and break an alibi; and *My Lady's Money*, which features the eccentric private detective Old Sharon. In "A Marriage Tragedy" Mr. Dark first investigates a disappearance and then is confronted with one of the oldest crime plots, the blood-stained clothing without a corpse. "Who Killed Zebedee?" and "John Jasper's Ghost" are reminiscent of the form established by the writer known as "Waters," while "Who Is the Thief?" parodies that same form. "A Stolen Letter" is an obvious rehash of Poe's "Purloined Letter."

Collins's greatest strength lay in the technical skill with which he treated his involved plots. Probably no other author in English literature has been as skilled in manipulating complex material into a consistent story and in inventing suspense devices to maintain reader interest. His occasional prolixity is more than counterbalanced by the painterly detail, fine characterizations, and overall ingenuity of his writing. His gifts, however, required space for their development, with the result that most of his short stories are not on the same level of quality as his better novels. Many of his short stories, too, align themselves more with the traditional proto-detective story than with the avant-garde forms of his day. While Collins was aware of the work of Poe and Gaboriau, he paid little heed to their contributions and worked in the mainstream of Victorian domestic and social fiction.

Many of the novels that we read today for mystery elements were originally written as novels of purpose. *The Dead Secret*, with its long search, and *No Name*, with its wonderful plots and counterplots, are really concerned with illegitimacy, while *Man and Wife*, which contains an excellent sealed-room murder situation, is really focused upon the intricacies of the marriage laws of the British Isles. Even deeper than social purpose, however, was Collins's preoccupation with fate, not with the expected warp and weft, but with the strange lace knottings, crossed and tangled threads. Indeed, his interest did not lie in his characters themselves but in the cocoon around them. His fiction abounds with "coincidences," unusual parallelisms, and strange linkages. *Armadale*, "Percy and the Prophet," and *The Frozen Deep* are really stories of predestination, while the first version of *Basil* is obsessed with fate. Collins has often been criticized for such "illogical coincidence," but this is not a fair judgment. For Collins an involution of fate is not a cheap trick for effects, but is a study of the utterly unexpected, utterly irrational factor in life.

—E.F. Bleiler

———

DICKENS, Charles (John Huffam) (1812–70). British. Novels: *Oliver Twist; or, The Parish Boy's Progress*, 1838; *Barnaby Rudge: A Tale of the Riots of 'Eighty*, 1841; *Bleak House*, 1853; *Hunted Down*, 1859; *Great Expectations*, 1861; *Our Mutual Friend*, 1865; *The Mystery of Edwin Drood*, 1870. Sketches of police activity appear in *Household Words*, 1850–59, and *All the Year Round*, 1859–70, both edited by Dickens; *London Crimes* edited by Nadya Aisenberg, 1982.

*   *   *

Given his delight in complicated mysteries and startling denouements, his fascination with all forms of crime and punishment, and his love of novelty in an age when police detectives were still an innovation, it was inevitable that Dickens should have played an important role in shaping the development of the detective story in England.

Dickens made his first important contribution in a series of articles about the Detective Office in *Household Words*. Founded in 1842 and still employing only a small staff, the Office had received little attention and had, in fact, probably avoided publicity for fear of reawakening the traditional English antipathy to spies and detectives. But in Dickens it found an influential and energetic publicist. The policemen of Dickens's articles are ideal bureaucrats: efficient, resourceful, unflappable, and tireless in their service of the public good. At the same time they lead more raffish and adventurous lives than most bureaucrats do: they are expert at disguise and acting, and are ready to venture into those mysterious East End slums which most middle-class Victorians would have hesitated to enter.

Dickens's journalism about the police laid the groundwork for the portrait of Inspector Bucket in *Bleak House*. The book employs most of the familiar formulae of sensation fiction— missing wills, unacknowledged illegitimate children, mysterious pasts, violent deaths—and so affords considerable scope for the Inspector's activities. He crops up in most of the book's many plots and sub-plots before emerging, near the end, as a central figure in his investigation of the murder of the lawyer Tulkinghorn and his search for the missing Lady Dedlock. Like Inspector Field and the other policemen of the *Household Words* articles, Bucket conceals extraordinary qualities beneath an unassuming and respectable facade: he travels from place to place with an almost supernatural mobility, spans the social chasms that otherwise separate class from class, and sees with disturbing acuity into the hearts of his fellow-men.

Many of Bucket's qualities recur in the character of the imperturbable Inspector of *Our Mutual Friend* and in Sergeant Cuff of Wilkie Collins's *The Moonstone*. But Dickens's last contribution to detective fiction is of a different nature. *The Mystery of Edwin Drood*, the novel left half-finished at his death in 1870, concerns the disappearance of Edwin Drood (Dickens's projected titles carefully avoid mentioning the word "murder") amidst a host of sinister circumstances that seem to implicate his uncle, John Jasper. The book's fragmentary nature makes it tantalising and difficult to judge, but it still shows a careful dedication to the mechanics of the mystery plot and, in the figure of the complex and divided John Jasper, the beginnings of one of those studies in the tortured criminal that distinguish Dickens's later fiction.

—Ian Ousby

———

GODWIN, William (1756–1836). British. Novels: *Things as They Are; or, The Adventures of Caleb Williams*, 1794; *St. Leon: A Tale of the Sixteenth Century*, 1799.

*   *   *

William Godwin, pioneer anarchist and author of *Political Justice*, was also, in *Things as They Are; or, The Adventures of Caleb Williams*, the first British writer of consequence to use fiction as a vehicle for social criticism. *Caleb Williams*, as it is commonly known, was a popularization of ideas about the corrupting nature of power elaborated in *Political Justice*. It was also a political thriller and even a forerunner of the detective story in its strictest definition.

In *Caleb Williams* a wealthy and powerful landowner, Falkland, murders a neighbour and allows innocent men to be hanged because he cannot bear the shame of such a death. Falkland is a dual personality, a forerunner of Dr. Jekyll and Mr. Hyde, for he has endearing qualities of generosity and gentleness, and it is with horror that his devoted secretary, Caleb Williams, finds in an iron chest the evidence of his master's guilt. Caleb reveals his knowledge to Falkland, who threatens to accuse him of capital crimes if he reveals his discovery. Caleb flees, and, after many adventures, pursued by the law and subjected to relentless moral persecution by Falkland's agents, is driven to expose his master, who finally confesses. Here there is a Kafka-like inversion, for in confessing Falkland sheds his burden of guilt and Caleb assumes it, overwhelmed by remorse at having caused the downfall of a noble being culpable of a single great crime to which he was led by a false code of honour. *Caleb Williams* combines moral complexity, political lessons, and much suspenseful excitement.

The only other among Godwin's many novels that might be called a mystery is an occult tale, *St. Leon*, about an alchemist who gains wealth and immortality but finds that they bring him only sorrow and the world's enmity. The moral, close to Godwin's experience, is that whoever gains power through wisdom and uses it for the general good must expect misunderstanding and hatred. *St. Leon* is a less satisfying book than *Caleb Williams*, which, though its great popularity on publication has never revived, remains a minor classic.

—George Woodcock

———

LE FANU, (Joseph) Sheridan (1814–73). Irish. Novels: *The Cock and Anchor*, 1845; *The House by the Church-Yard*, 1863; *Wylder's Hand*, 1864; *Uncle Silas: A Tale of Bartram-Haugh*, 1864; *Guy Deverell*, 1865; *All in the Dark*, 1866; *The Tenants of Malory*, 1867; *A Lost Name*, 1868; *Haunted Lives*, 1868; *The Wyvern Mystery*, 1869; *Checkmate*, 1871; *The Rose and the Key*, 1871; *Willing to Die*, 1873; *The Purcell Papers*, 1880; *The Evil Guest*, 1895. Short Stories: *Ghost Stories and Tales of Mystery*, 1851; *Chronicles of Golden Friars*, 1871; *In a Glass Darkly*, 1872; *The Watcher and Other Weird Stories*, 1894; *Madam Crowl's Ghost and Other Tales of Mystery*, 1923.

* * *

"The Simenon of the peculiar"—properly qualified, this description (by V.S. Pritchett in *The Living Novel*) offers a useful corrective to the common misapprehension of Sheridan Le Fanu. This versatile writer, though justifiably esteemed for his ghost stories, is all too often unrecognised as one of the founders of the mystery/detective novel and a continuing influence upon the genre.

An awareness of the history of the machinery of justice is evident in Le Fanu's work from start to close. In his first novel, *The Cock and Anchor*, modelled on Sir Walter Scott, the action develops out of the obstacles to crime control in early 18th-century Dublin ("with a most notoriously ineffective police"), whereas in the somewhat analogously disturbed conditions of Restoration Paris, the foolhardy protagonist of "The Room in The Dragon Volant" (1872) owes his "resurrection" largely to the vigilance of the Sûreté. Indeed, all his major novels display a significant element of detective interest: in *The House by the Church-Yard* the distinctive features of a footprint near the corpse are recorded and followed up despite the difficulties (caused by the poor communications of the time) in tracking down a wanted man, and the vital evidence of the murder weapon is appreciated; in *Uncle Silas* the scrutiny by the trustees of "waste" as well as the heiress's attempt to solve an ancient locked-room mystery further provoke the murderer to self-disclosure; in *Wylder's Hand* a comparison of calligraphy and post-marks reveals forgery pointing to homicide, and additionally "the antiseptic properties of that sort of soil" function in the denouement; Le Fanu's most innovative use of forensic science appears in *Checkmate*, which deploys plastic surgery and medical records. Still further anticipation of developments in the genre is manifested by a characteristic of Le Fanu (predating Fortuné du Boisgobey's *Le Coup de Pouce* of 1875 by a decade) wherein the criminal mystery is not unravelled solely by the police or someone with particular skills in detection. There is a magistrate in *The House by the Church-Yard*, and an "ex-detective of the police office" in *Checkmate*, but generally solutions in Le Fanu's crime novels are the product of collective observation and reasoning, a plausible mixture of intelligence, miscalculation, and chance; women can be as alert as men, the search more intermittent than sustained.

Inevitably, with the swing of fashion such a realistic contribution came to be regarded as technically deficient by the standards of the classical detective story. Although in *Guy Deverell* readers are alerted to the possibility of secret passages, and the change in the appearance of a middle-aged man, insufficient warning about doubles is given in *Wylder's Hand*. Nor does Le Fanu concentrate upon the detective puzzle; the criminal is only one element in a complex social picture abundant with comedy, pathos, wisdom, and humanity. In all this Le Fanu resembles Simenon, yet the operative word in Pritchett's comparison is "peculiar"—the occult significance of which cannot be neglected.

"The mind is a different organ by night and by day," and Le Fanu's psychological tensions arise from the thrilling balance he maintains between the natural and supernatural explanation, a poise dependent partly on structure, partly on style. Frequently an inset ghost story foreshadows the crime; this structural play upon the legal, religious, mental, and bodily implications of "possession" is akin to the puns and literary allusions typical of this writer. Apparently limpid in style, the novels are suffused with references to *Robinson Crusoe*, Scripture and Swedenborg, the Elizabethan and Jacobean dramatists, Milton and Bunyan, *The Arabian Nights*, Celtic lore as well as Radcliffe, all of which impart supernatural meaning even to mysteries that prove open to rational explanation—Le Fanu's basic image seems to be "*Paradise Lost*" and precariously "*Regained*."

This spiritual message obviously distinguishes Le Fanu from Simenon. If they share a sombre understanding of the complexities that entrap not just the victim and bereaved but also the criminal, the ultimate enigma recognized by the Irishman lies beyond the Belgian's tragic destiny, in a sense of "how microscopic are the beginnings of the Kingdom of God or of the mystery of iniquity in a human being's heart." So finally Le Fanu relates less to Simenon than to Chesterton, and especially, as *The Nine Tailors* avows, to Dorothy L. Sayers.

—Peter Caracciolo

POE, Edgar Allan (1809–1849). American. Fiction: *The Narrative of Arthur Gordon Pym of Nantucket*, 1838; "William Wilson," in *Tales of the Grotesque and Arabesque*, 1840; "The Murder in the Rue Morgue," in *The Prose Romances of Edgar Allan Poe*, 1843; "The Mystery of Marie Roget," "The Gold Bug," "The Black Cat," "The Purloined Letter," in *Tales*, 1845; "Thou Art the Man," in *The Works of the Late Edgar Allan Poe*, edited by Rufus Griswold, 1850–56.

* * *

The modern detective story begins with Edgar Allan Poe's "The Murders in the Rue Morgue" which appeared in *Graham's Magazine* in April 1841. Poe's achievement, however, was based on several decades of fiction written in England, Ireland, America, France, and Germany, with much of which he was acquainted. Before Poe there were mystery and detective stories of various sorts, and many of the motifs that we now consider important were in fairly common use in dozens of pre-Poe stories. These include the concept of describing a crime and its detection in fictional form, the frame-up, the conflict between official and private investigators, the impossible crime, the red herring solution, bizarre subject matter, criminological technicalities, the fictionalization of historical crimes, the sealed room, and the concept of the self-limited case.

Poe added at least seven new elements of overwhelming importance. These are the stooge narrator, the eccentric detective, the complete outsider as detective, the armchair detective, reader participation in a puzzle, ratiocination or precise analytical reasoning, and a calculus of probabilities as a tool for cutting through conflicting evidence. It should be noted that the technique of ratiocination—interpreting minor clues to arrive at a large result—appeared in Voltaire's *Zadig* and other earlier literature, but Poe's analytic reasoning is much broader in scope and is now first applied by a detective to a murder case.

A listing of motifs, however, cannot convey the magnitude of Poe's achievement, for most of the earlier detective literature is bumbling and inconsequential. Poe not only improved on such elements as he borrowed, but with his remarkable structural sense worked out a viable form that served as model for thousands of successors. For the first time there was a clear and concise statement of the problem, tabulation of the evidence, and a solution based on this evidence. For these reasons "The Murders in the Rue Morgue" is the single most important story in the history of the genre. In terms of immediate sources, the murderous orang-utan was probably suggested by the similar ape, Sylvan, in Walter Scott's *Count Robert of Paris*, although it is possible that a couple of factual incidents may have contributed to the idea. Poe's Paris was probably derived from the popular image of the Paris of the day: a strange dichotomy between a wild and wooly crime center where anything might happen and a citadel of suave refinement and sophistication. Paris, too, had long been renowned for the efficiency of its police system. While Vidocq's Paris has often been suggested as the prototype for Poe's, a stronger case can be made for Eugene Sue's.

"The Mystery of Marie Roget" (*Snowden's Lady's Companion*, 1842–43) marked a new venture: the use of a fictional model to solve a historical crime. Poe based his somewhat rambling "story" on the contemporary case of Mary Rogers, a handsome but loose tobacconist's clerk, whose murdered corpse was found in the Hudson. Using his "calculus of probabilities" Dupin sifted the evidence, and, in the version published in *Snowden's*, came to the conclusion that her lover, a naval officer, had murdered her. (An interruption in the publication was probably caused by news reports that a break was near in the case, and Poe did not wish to be caught wrong.) In the revised version of 1845, however, Poe also admitted the possibility that Mary Rogers had died as the result of an abortion. This was the leading contemporary theory of the crime, which remains unsolved. In "The Purloined Letter" (*The Gift* for 1845, probably published in October 1844) Dupin once again demonstrates his faculty of analysis. The accusation, often made, that Poe erred in placing the seal and the address of a letter on the same side of the paper, leads one to think that the critics have never seen an early 19th century letter. In addition to the three Dupin stories, Poe wrote a fourth detective story, "Thou Art the Man!" (*Godey's Lady's Book*, November 1844). A parody of the crime story of the day, it fits the practice of William Leggett and William Gilmore Simms fairly closely, but Poe may well have had other authors in mind. It would be venturing too far to describe Poe's other stories that involve mystery in one form or another, but I might mention "The Gold Bug," in which the hero applies detectional anaylsis and cryptography; "William Wilson," murder and hypostatized personality fragments; "The Black Cat," murder and the irony of fate; and *The Narrative of Arthur Gordon Pym*, with cryptographic and mysterious elements that Poe left for the reader to work out for himself.

The recognition that Poe had created a new form was not immediate in the English-speaking world. In America his first disciple seems to have been John Babington Williams, M.D. (*Leaves from the Note-Book of a New York Detective*, 1864–65), and in England the probably pseudonymous Andrew Forrester, Jr. (The British short detective story of the day evolved independently of Poe). In France, however, Poe's work was recognized and rated highly, and Gaboriau, building upon Poe's foundation, created the modern detective novel.

—E.F. Bleiler

RICHMOND (anonymous author). British. Short Stories: *Richmond; or, Scenes from the Life of a Bow Street Runner*, 1827.

* * *

Richmond is the first collection of stories about a detective to be printed in the western world. It was published anonymously, and its authorship is unknown, although it has occasionally been attributed to either Thomas S. Surr or William Gaspey, popular novelists of the day. An analysis of its style, subject matter, and publishing circumstances, however, rules out both men as possible authors. (For details, see the edition by E.F. Bleiler, New York, Dover, 1976).

A rambling novel, *Richmond* first describes the picaresque youth of Thomas Richmond, in which he is associated with various criminal types. About one third of the way through the book Richmond tires of his haphazard existence and joins the Bow Street Court in London as a Runner. Five of his cases then follow. Sometimes interlocked, they are concerned with kidnapping, smuggling, resurrection men, swindling, and general police work. They are all solved by rational, procedural means. There is some attempt at realism in characterizations, crimes, and background. The sources for *Richmond* were probably contemporary journalistic accounts of the Bow Street Court and the exploits of historical Runners, but the author, who would seem to have been a young inexperienced writer, had no real knowledge of the Bow Street operation. Where literary form was concerned, the author did not use contemporary models for treating crime fictionally (Godwin's *Caleb Williams*, certain crime-Gothic novels, the "frame plot"), but was probably aware of the then-popular linked occupational stories.

While *Richmond* is not a great work of art, it anticipates later developments clearly. It went without recognition in its day, however, and was apparently without historical influence, unless its basic concept influenced the writer known as "Waters" some 20 years later.

—E.F. Bleiler

WATERS. Pseudonym for William Russell; also wrote as Inspector F; Lieutenant Robert Warneford, RN. British. Fiction: *Recollections of a Policeman*, 1852 (as *Recollections of a Detective Police-Officer*, 1856; *The Detective Officer and Other Tales*, 1878; *Recollections of a Detective*, 1887); *Leaves from the Diary of a Law Clerk*, 1857; *The Game of Life*, 1857 (as *Leonard Harlowe; or, The Game of Life*, 1862); *Recollections of a Sheriff's Officer*, 1860; *A Skeleton in Every House*, 1860; *The Experiences of a French Detective Officer Adapted from the Mss. of Theodore Duhamel*, 1861; *The Heir-at-Law and Other Tales*, 1861; *Experiences of a Real Detective* (as Inspector F.); 1862; *Undiscovered Crimes*, 1862; *Autobiography of an English Detective*, 1863; *Strange Stories of a Detective; or, Curiosities of Crime*, 1863; *Leaves from the Journal of a Custom-House Officer*, 1868; *The Valazy Family and Other Narratives*, 1869; *Mrs. Waldegrave's Will and Other Tales* (as Inspector F.), 1870.

* * *

Though there is no available biographical information on William Russell, who published most of his works under the pseudonym Waters, he is historically important as the first English writer of short detective fiction. In something of the manner of the pioneering French detective Eugène Vidocq, whose *Memoirs* (1829) presented as fact a considerably fictionalized version of his sensational career, Russell wrote in the first person a series of stories, the first of which appeared in 1849, purporting to deal with cases on which he had worked as a London police official. His first collection appeared in New York in 1852 under the title *Recollections of a Policeman*; it was reprinted in London in 1856 as *Recollections of a Detective Police-Officer*. The popularity of Waters's books in this period—Poe's detective stories had preceded them by only a few years, and Wilkie Collins's major detective novels were not to come until the 1860's—showed the English public's eager interest in detective tales, gave rise to many imitations, and helped create a climate favorable to the appearance of Doyle's Sherlock Holmes stories in a later generation. Most of the Waters's stories concentrate on the detective's often dangerous exploits in solving cases involving theft, forgery, murder, and the like, and thus exemplify, if in relatively crude ways, basic characteristics of detective fiction.

—Seymour Rudin

———

WOOD, Mrs. Henry (née Ellen Price) (1814–87). British. Novels: *East Lynne*, 1861; *The Channings*, 1862; *The Shadow of Ashlydyat*, 1863; *Trevlyn Hold; or, Squire Trevlyn's Heir*, 1864; *The Red Court Farm*, 1865; *Roland Yorke*, 1869; *Within the Maze*, 1872; *The Master of Greylands*, 1873. Short Stories: *Johnny Ludlow*, six series, 12 vols., 1874–99; *Told in the Twilight*, 1875.

* * *

In Mrs. Henry Wood's hundred or so stories (the count is not clear because of anonymous work and false attributions) murders, thefts, disappearances, and swindles appear frequently. They are often accompanied by detectives and detection. The second plot of her most famous work, *East Lynne*, for example, is an ingenious murder mystery superior to the sentimental first plot the Victorian stage treasured. Many of Wood's novels are concerned with crime: *Trevlyn Hold*, disappearance and suspected murder; *The Master of Greylands*, murder with Gothic elements; *Within the Maze*, an escaped felon and Scotland Yard; *The Channings* and *Roland Yorke*, theft or embezzlement; *The Red Court Farm*, murder. Her short stories, in addition, are even more strongly concerned with crime and detection. About half of the stories in the Johnny Ludlow series deal with matters criminal and mysterious, and here the crime is central, without the distraction of concurrent plots.

Wood was religious, a temperance enthusiast, and a moralist, and a strong element in her fiction is Victorian stability: rank, responsibility, harmony, morality. The life she evokes in well-plotted, detailed realism is now itself a fantasy world. This cosmos could be disturbed by the subtraction of a person, and much of Wood's fiction is concerned with mysterious revenants

(living or dead) who restore the original harmony. Crime, too, could shatter this crystalline world, but in a peculiar manner. Wood cared little about the crime, nor did the detective process interest her greatly. When professional detectives appear, they are usually wrong. What really concerned Wood was the impact of crime on the upper-middle-class social fabric and on the personalities of the suspects. These she analyzed in great detail.

Today Wood is undeservedly forgotten. She was a skilled craftsman, despite sentimental quirks common to the period, and could produce good work when she wished. Her contemporaries rated her Johnny Ludlow stories highest, and in this I would concur.

—E.F. Bleiler

———

ZANGWILL, Israel (1864–1926). British. Novel: *The Big Bow Mystery*, 1892.

* * *

Israel Zangwill, the English author, journalist, and Zionist, made but a single contribution to the literature of detection, but it was a considerable one. Urged by the *London Star* in 1891 to submit a somewhat "more original piece of fiction," he complied with a story he had sketched out some time before. It had occurred to him that it would be a sensational literary challenge to "murder a man in a room to which there was no possible access." The ingenious solution almost immediately suggested itself to him and it was this tale that he submitted, in installments, to the *Star*. *The Big Bow Mystery* stands today as the first "locked room" mystery novelet, second in historical importance only to Poe's ground-breaking short story, "The Murders in the Rue Morgue" (1841).

Zangwill's narrative recounts with the flavor and a goodly measure of the style of Dickens an "impossible" murder in the Bow district of London. Retired police inspector Grodman is centrally involved in the discovery of the crime and in its subsequent investigation. In his egotism and masterful grasp of the mystery and all of its ramifications he strikingly resembles Sherlock Holmes, who at almost the same moment was being fleshed out in stories appearing in the *Strand Magazine*. *The Big Bow Mystery* is still eminently readable today, although its good-natured but not entirely gentle satire now seems more picturesque than it must have nearly a century ago. Zangwill worked in some amusing jibes at British politics, literary fashions, and the detective genre itself. However, none of this in any way diminishes the effect of the masterful plot and its extraordinary denouement.

—Donald A. Yates

FOREIGN-LANGUAGE
WRITERS

BOILEAU, Pierre (Prosper) (1906–), and **Thomas NARCE-JAC** (pseudonym for Pierre Ayraud, 1908–). French. Novels: *The Woman Who Was*, 1954 (as *The Woman Who Was No More*, 1954; as *The Fiends*, 1965); *Faces in the Dark*, 1955; *The Living and the Dead*, 1956 (as *Vertigo*, 1958); *The Prisoner*, 1957; *The Evil Eye*, 1959; *Heart to Heart*, 1959; *Sleeping Beauty*, 1959; *The Tube*, 1960; *Spells of Evil*, 1961; *Who Was Clare Jallu?*, 1965 (as *The Victims*, 1967); *Choice Cuts*, 1966.

*   *   *

Within detective, crime and mystery fiction, writers in French have always held a position of importance second only to those writing in English—leaving all other languages, isolated lights notwithstanding, far, far behind. And among this dense crowd there has stood out, since the early 1950's, one author of the first magnitude: Georges Simenon, the creator of Maigret. Both Boileau and Narcejac had separately published creditable work; it was, however, when they combined their talents (we may surmise as primary components: inventive imagination in Boileau, theory-grounded detachment and stylistic acumen in Narcejac) that a new "author" arose, comparable in stature to (though fundamentally different from) Simenon. Since about 1950 they have produced a massive body of fiction enthralling a multitude of readers—translations soon adding an international resonance—not to forget the further multitude of viewers attracted by film and television versions which eminent producers evolved from Boileau-Narcejac texts. Moreover they share with a handful of practitioners the distinction of having made (especially with *Le Roman policier*) an incisive contribution to the history and theory of crime fiction.

Trying to delineate their chief concerns, their methods and scope, we may mention in passing the collections of short stories, the series of books for young readers centred on *Sans Atout*, and the loving, complimentary pastiches of Leblanc that have given a new, well-refurbished lease of life to Arsène Lupin, *La Poudrière* being perhaps the finest work in that group. Like the theoretical contributions these sidelines display great agility of mind, awareness of procedure, sureness of touch, and—paradoxically—originality.

The same characteristics mark the bulk of Boileau-Narcejac's work, the full-scale independent novels which are best described, adopting their own terminology and generalising one of their titles (*The Victims*), as centred on the victim (as opposed to the offender or the investigator); as sophisticated novels of suspense (rather than action), of internal, claustrophobic pressure, of subtle but overpowering terror as it grows in the individual consciousness, often in such a way as to merge with the existential *angst* of modern man fumbling about in a bleak hostile world, manipulated by forces beyond his control (and often even understanding) into a position of helplessness, of uncertainty and radical self-doubt; of man, in other words, as we see him frequently depicted also in other kinds of 20th-century fiction.

From these premises it follows that each novel exists on its own without antecedents or sequels; that most of them lead up to the main crime (save, for instance, *Les Eaux dormantes*) instead of starting from it as in the traditional detective story; and that they all work with a fixed (mainly male) perspective—or indeed more than one, as, for example, in that gripping interiorisation of the agent-and-manhunt story, *Maldonne*. Boileau-Narcejac's third-person narration is at times very "unreliable," notably in *Heart to Heart* and *Les Magiciennes*, both outstanding books. Occasionally their preferred mode, the first-person narration, entails some improbability, especially

where diaries, letters to the authorities, etc., are used; but even such means can be completely convincing, as in *Choice Cuts*. The main perspective is often followed by a brief epilogue that suddenly reveals an unexpected solution (thus already in *The Woman Who Was*, better known under the title of Clouzot's film, *Les Diaboliques*), or adds a final, sardonic twist—in the extreme pressed into a footnote (*The Evil Eye*).

Surprisingly enough, though we may register a jolt, we rarely mind such improbabilities of the narrative situation (a marked exception is the fanciful excursion into the early 19th-century, *Sleeping Beauty*) because we have become absorbed in these breathtakingly realistic fictional worlds, each of which is developed with perceptive empathy and sharp precision of external detail in a style coloured by strong and evocative images. Whether the central character—there are definitely no heroes—is chief steward of a restaurant car (*Terminus*) or a blinded industrialist (*Faces in the Dark*), a septuagenarian in an expensive old people's home (*Carte vermeil*), a country vet (*Spells of Evil*), or an alienated schoolboy (*L'Âge bête*), each is made intensely present, real in his own being and his environment.

Over the years Boileau-Narcejac have built up, each novel adding a new rural or urban landscape, social layer, level of education, profession, or job, set of circumstances and mental structure, a kind of grand if chilling mosaic of France and French people—indeed, by easily effected extrapolation, of Western life—in our time. Besides similarities in narrative technique there are similarities of underlying themes and atmosphere. Again and again the inexplicable slides into the uncanny, the extra-sensory and the supernatural (conspicuous in *The Living and the Dead*, world famous as Hitchcock's *Vertigo*) though at the end one discovers (a twinge of regret mixing in the relief) a solid, often sordid, at any rate all too human agency and motivation. Furthermore, although extremely clever, concentrated and ultimately impenetrable evil is sometimes at work, more often the concepts crime, guilt, and victim are multiply refracted if not disintegrated as we see accident leading to transgression, bad luck perverting planned action, machination arising from mute despair, and victims fighting for themselves, becoming progressively enmeshed in wrong-doing, as we experience ordinary (rather than extraordinary) human beings unable to cope.

If much crime fiction relates to melodrama, this particular brand has strong links to tragedy in the modern sense the theatre has evolved since Ibsen and Chekhov. "Naked, unaccommodated man" is shown as physically insecure and emotionally unstable, lacking any framework of moral (let alone spiritual) notions—and above all shown as weak. Regarding this latter aspect, however, "man" must here be understood as a sex distinction: the females in Boileau-Narcejac are the harder, stronger-willed personalities; with amazing regularity it is the males who are duped and nonplussed, are driven against a wall, crumble and succumb. *The Prisoner*, for example, combines these dominant themes in particular clarity, but they are pervasive. So is the theme of the individual's inescapable isolation and inability to communicate. Beyond shaping the action, this psychological entrapment assumes universal dimensions.

Owing to the presence and activity of the father-figure Maigret, the final effect in most Simenon novels could be called catharsis. There exists no guidance and no path towards such a release in Boileau-Narcejac; not by chance does the phrase *sans issue* recur. The "basic gesture" (Brecht), the fundamental situation of their characters, might be described as suffocation. It represents a major achievement of intelligence, craft, and art to keep wringing aesthetic pleasure from this for the reader, i.e., "pleasure" in the Aristotelian sense including, but often exceeding, the kind normally associated with leisure reading. This even though macabre fun is intermittently provided, most notably in *Choice Cuts*, which won the *Humour noir* prize in 1965. No doubt a well-deserved award, but one must insist that Boileau-Narcejac have produced better work still along the lines on which this brief account has been placing most emphasis.

—H.M. Klein

BORGES, Jorge Luis (1899–1986). Argentinian. Fiction: *Ficciones*, 1962 (as *Fictions*, 1965); *Labyrinths*, 1962; *The Aleph and Other Stories*, 1970.

* * *

Jorge Luis Borges began to experiment tentatively in the 1930's with the short narrative tale, the genre in which he was to gain international acclaim. In the 1940's he initiated the slow, steady flow of short prose pieces that continued for nearly 40 years, interrupted only briefly in the late 1950's when he became blind. His two most celebrated books—*Ficciones* (1944) and *El Aleph* (1949) were assembled from the earliest of these tales.

Borges's contributions to detective literature are extensive and—foreseeably—singular. Most significant are a handful of short stories—pre-eminent among them "Death and the Compass"—that have blended, in Borges's inimitable fashion, a popular form (the detective/crime short story) with perplexing metaphysical concepts. Borges's tale "The Garden of Forking Paths" has the form of a conventional spy story but in the end evokes a compelling metaphor of human existence. His fondness for detective fiction has been expressed in many ways. With his friend and collaborator Adolfo Bioy Casares, he published in 1942 a most unusual volume of detective short stories, *Seis problemas para don Isidro Parodi* [Six Problems for Don Isidro Parodi], and a short novelette, *Un modelo para la muerte* [A Model for Death] (1946). Also with Bioy Casares he established in the mid-1940's a series of English and American detective novels in translation that has continued unbroken for more than 35 years. Again with Bioy Casares he has edited and helped to translate two anthologies of largely English and American detective short stories, which appeared in 1943 and 1956. He has clearly done more to promote the merits of the detective story than any other writer in the Spanish language.

—Donald A. Yates

DÜRRENMATT, Friedrich (1921–1990). Swiss. Novels: *The Judge and His Hangman*, 1954 (as *End of the Game*, 1976); *The Pledge*, 1959; *A Dangerous Game*, 1960 (as *Traps*, 1960); *The Quarry*, 1961. Plays: *Fools Are Passing Through*, 1958 (as *The Marriage of Mr. Mississippi*, 1959); *The Visit*, 1958; *The Physicists*, 1963.

* * *

Inspired notably by Brecht, Kafka, and Wilder, but with an intellectual punch and theatrical drive altogether his own,

Dürrenmatt hit the post-war German-speaking stage like a meteor and has left an indelible mark on the whole of contemporary drama. Particularly *Fools Are Passing Through*, *The Visit*, and *The Physicists* include crimes dear to detectives. They are, however, incidental to perturbing explorations of the individual's helplessness and failure in uncontrollable conditions—of man in an environment governed by chance whose inexorable justice, if justice it is, is enigmatic. There are no solutions: "literature may not provide comfort" ("Conversation with Heinz Ludwig Arnold"). Yet the message of this brilliant and uncomfortable Swiss is not despair but humble persistence, tragi-comedy his natural medium. It is also basic to detective fiction, of which Dürrenmatt is the first German-writing exponent to achieve international resonance. His novels, already classics, show an amazing but probably—for him—inevitable sweep through the genre.

Poirot's Christian name may seem a laughable incongruity; yet in his way he *is* a Hercules, not just in the pre-retirement *Labours*. In characteristic contrast, Marlowe decides "It wasn't a game for knights" (*The Big Sleep*); nevertheless, he is one, an authentic hero of our time. Wildly different, both their worlds allow attitudes and actions whose structures suggest these associations. Such figures and their adventures satisfy strong psychological needs (among them that for comfort) and can, when masterfully presented, hardly die, though they may date. Of this kind is Dürrenmatt's first novel, *The Judge and His Hangman*. Here Bärlach, detective Komissar at Berne, looks like a successfully transplanted version of the old bear, a Maigret Helveticus. Introduced, like many detectives, with a telescoped background, Bärlach is, however, not just old and famous, but about to retire, and he suffers from terminal cancer. Nevertheless he dominates all and duly gets his murderer (one of his subordinates), using him to "execute" a life-long adversary and master-criminal (Lupin and Carlos rolled in one) before chasing him into exile. Bärlach thus, again like many predecessors, arrogates the functions of justice, anticipating the four horrific old men in Dürrenmatt's kafkaesque novella *A Dangerous Game* (originally a radio play), linked to Bärlach also through the motif of hectic gluttony.

Things change in the immediate sequel, *The Quarry*. Bärlach, operated upon and hospitalised, tries to unmask a devil: a Swiss doctor now in a luxury clinic torturing and killing (through operations without anesthetic) the rich as he did the Jews in a German extermination camp. Rumbling him by chance, Bärlach is recognised and destined to the same treatment. Utterly helpless, the weak old man awaits the hour of his martyrdom. He is saved (and the devil killed) by Gulliver, a new Ahasuerus, who tells him: "Today one cannot fight evil on one's own, as the knights of yore went forth to combat some dragon.... You fool of a detective, time itself has shown you to be absurd." Besides the horrors of Nazism, influences like Dostoevsky's "The Grand Inquisitor" and Kafka's "The Penal Colony" are visible. Bärlach, the hunter, has become the humiliated quarry whose supreme achievement is to meet with Christ-like silence the taunts of his tormentor, a voice of amoral, existential materialism. Bärlach had requested Dürer's picture "Knight, Death, and Devil" for his room. He is himself, Gulliver tells him, a "knight of the sad countenance"—a Don Quixote (and a staid variant of the grotesque Übelohe in *Fools Are Passing Through*). A later radio play, *An Evening's Hour in Late Autumn*, cruelly if farcically repeats this juxtaposition of devil and knight, casting a sensational author in the role of the mass murderer committing his crimes in order to write about them, egged on by his readers, and a miserable sod of a retired accountant who has investigated him (and duly becomes his next victim) in the role of a Don Quixote.

After the detective, the genre itself is dispatched in *The Pledge* (subtitled "Requiem for the Detective Novel") on the grounds that it falsifies reality by giving it pattern and meaning. Dürrenmatt, in this chilling story of miscarried justice and the thwarted chase of a sex killer, has his cake (or rather chocolate truffles) *and* eats it. Chance disposes of the maniac, the truth comes too late for Matthäi, the detective who has gone mad over the business—but not for the reader. He remains, like Mohammed in Dürrenmatt's parable "Lecture on Justice and Right," the instructed observer.

—H.M. Klein

GABORIAU, Émile (1833–1873). French. Novels: *The Mystery of Orcival*, 1871 (as *Crime at Orcival*, 1952); *The Widow Lerouge*, 1873 (as *The Lerouge Case*, 1925); *The Clique of Gold*, 1874; *Within an Inch of His Life*, 1874 (as *In Peril of His Life*, 1883; *In Deadly Peril*, 1888); *Other People's Money*, 1875; *Marriage at a Venture*, 1879; *The Men of the Bureau*, 1880; *Monsieur Lecoq*, 1880 (part one: *Monsieur Lecoq: The Detective's Dilemma*, and *Monsieur Lecoq: The Detective's Triumph*, 1888; part two: *The Honor of the Name*, 1900); *The Count's Secret*, 1881 (as *The Count's Millions*, 1913; *Baron Trigault's Vengeance*, 1913); *The Slaves of Paris*, 1882 (part one: *Caught in the Net*, 1891; part two: *The Champdoce Mystery*, 1891); *Promise of Marriage*, 1883 (with *Marriage at a Venture* in *Marriage of Adventure*, 1921); *The Downward Path*, 1883; *File No. 113*, 1883 (as *Warrant No. 113*, 1884; *The Blackmailers*, 1907); *The Catastrophe*, 1885; *The Intrigues of a Prisoner*, 1885; *The Marquise de Brinvilliers*, 1886 (as *Marie de Brinvilliers*, 1888); *Written in Cipher*, 1984. Short Stories: *The Little Old Man of the Batignolles: A Chapter from a Detective's Memoirs*, 1880 (various reprints, as *Max's Marriage*, 1880; *A Beautiful Scourge*, 1883; *A Thousand Francs Reward*, 1887).

* * *

Historically Émile Gaboriau is second in importance only to Edgar Allan Poe. Poe crystallized the detective short story, and Gaboriau was the first to see clearly what was required of a longer form. He wrote the first novels in which the nature of the crime, the introduction and role of the detective, the extenders, the misdirections, the reader participation, and the solution are all carried through in the modern manner. It is also important to note that when the mainstream of modern detective fiction arose in England, it followed not the mode of the British Victorians like Collins, but that of Gaboriau.

In September 1865 Gaboriau's first detective novel, *L'Affaire Lerouge* (*The Widow Lerouge*) began to appear serially. In a curious parallel to Sherlock Holmes, however, it attracted little attention on first publication, but on reprint made its author world famous. It offered the consultant detective Tabaret, who had studied the literature of crime and worked by ratiocination, an opportunity to solve a very deceptive murder that is said to have been based on a contemporary crime. Six other works by Gaboriau are detective stories in the puristic sense. Three of these are built upon the ebullient personality of Lecoq of the Sûreté: *The Mystery of Orcival*, *File No. 113*, and *Monsieur Lecoq*. Separate are the novella *The Little Old Man of the Batignolles*, the short story "A Disappearance," and the novel *In Deadly Peril*. Several other novels are sensational social novels, although they contain mystery and crime elements in varying degree: *Caught in the Net* and *The Champdoce Mystery*,

The Count's Secret and *Baron Trigault's Vengeance*, *The Clique of Gold*, and *Other People's Money*. A historical novel, *The Marquise de Brinvilliers*, is based loosely on the well-known factual crime.

Gaboriau considered himself a disciple of Poe's, and he united Poe's precision of form and concept of ratiocination with the sensational social novel of Balzac with its powerful emotional roots. Gaboriau, indeed, thought of himself as writing a new *comédie humaine*. Among the other sources which contributed to Gaboriau's crystallization were the French thriller of the day, particularly the work of his former employer, Paul Féval (who had previously unsuccessfully tried to imitate Poe); the strong French literature of factual crime; and the contemporary police blotter. Gaboriau attended the police courts and may have been the first writer of fiction to make a serious study of crime and criminology. As a result his work is a goldmine of information on legal and investigatory procedures.

From a literary point of view Gaboriau has been in eclipse for decades, but this is not just. He was a remarkable plotter, superior even to Collins, and a first-rate creator of criminalistic detail. His French is said to be brilliant stylistically, though he has been badly served in Victorian English translations. His largest weakness is in the creation of character; while the two detectives Tabaret and Lecoq are well drawn, the "romantic" characters, as has often been said, are cardboard. In terms of form perhaps his least valuable contribution has been the appending of second-rate historical romances to his detective stories to explain ultimate antecedents. In this he was followed by Doyle.

The individual novels have been variously estimated. Some critics have preferred *The Mystery of Orcival* or *File No. 113*, but this reviewer gives first preference to *Monsieur Lecoq*, Part One, and second to *The Widow Lerouge*.

—E.F. Bleiler

JAPRISOT, Sebastien (1931–). Pseudonym for Jean Baptiste Rossi. French. Novels: *The 10:30 from Marseilles*, 1963 (as *The Sleeping Car Murders*, 1967); *Trap for Cinderella*, 1964; *The Lady in the Car with Glasses and a Gun*, 1967; *Goodbye, Friend*, 1969; *One Deadly Summer*, 1980; *Woman in Evidence*, 1989.

* * *

Sebastien Japrisot's greatest talent lies in his ability to create fascinating, complex mysteries that keep the reader spellbound while trying to determine just what is going on. All four of his books are not merely escape stories but studies of personality and reality. The contradictions of what is and what appears to be are most blatant in *Trap for Cinderella* and *The Lady in the Car*. By carefully inflicting impossible situations and events on his characters, and telling their story by first-person narrative, he challenges the reader to find a way through the maze.

The 10:30 from Marseilles was Japrisot's first and most traditional novel. Using many of the techniques of the police procedural novel, he presents the problem of a girl found killed on a train after it arrives in Paris. Routine questioning and locating of the co-passengers is interspaced with episodes about the passengers themselves. Japrisot avoids stereotyping the passengers by concentrating on each one, showing his vanities and fears—and then letting the murderer get to them before the police do. His inexperience as a crime writer shows in the visibility of the villain, and by having a rather improbable young boy solve the crime. But suspense, forward thrust, and reader-involvement make it an excellent working of a now common device.

A purely psychological tale based on a crime, *Trap for Cinderella* won the Grand Prix de la Littérature Policière. The exceedingly complex plot shoves the reader back and forth (as Michelle Isola is) between thinking Mi is a murderer or a victim. After recovering from disfiguring burns, Mi has lost her memory and doesn't know if she has been trying to kill her friend Do, or if she is, in fact, Do, who had killed Mi and taken her place. Ironic twists and snaps reinforce the searching-for-reality theme; the same events are told several times from different viewpoints. Each time a new factor is added to change the significance. *Trap for Cinderella* is also a good example of Japrisot's ability to handle potentially sensational material (lesbianism, rampant sex) in a reasonable way. These elements figure in all his books but never dominate them.

The reality theme is again brought forward in *The Lady in the Car with Glasses and a Gun*, also a prize-winner. At the beginning of the book, Dany Longo is on her way to the sea. An act of nonsensical, meaningless violence by an unseen man results in her hand being injured. From that point on she repeatedly meets impossibilities and craziness—everything she does seems to be a repeat performance; others recognize her and say she's been there earlier in the day. But Dany knows she hasn't been there before. An explanation does come, carrying the conclusion that although the world seems unreliable, there is a pattern, determined by chance, self-choice, and the acts of others.

Goodbye, Friend is a departure in style though it keeps many of the earlier themes. Dr. Barran returns from Vietnam and is asked to help replace some embezzled bonds in a vault. Of course the scheme goes wrong and Barran and a mercenary are trapped in a building, accused of theft and murder. Women are again the primary villains (amid hints of lesbianism) and a sense of fantastic impossibility (the world gone wrong) is a strong factor. Intentionally written in a movie scenario form, the book moves quickly, giving no time for thought or analysis along the way. But the end provides a last-paragraph twist (as in *Cinderella*) that shows how some events in the book were predictable.

—Fred Dueren

KIRST, Hans Hellmut (1914–89). German. Novels: *The Officer Party*, 1962; *The Night of the Generals*, 1963; *Brothers in Arms*, 1965; *The Last Card*, 1967 (as *Death Plays the Last Card*, 1968); *Camp 7 Last Stop*, 1969; *Undercover Man*, 1970 (as *No Fatherland*, 1970); *Hero in the Tower*, 1972; *A Time for Scandal*, 1973 (as *Damned to Success*, 1973); *A Time for Truth*, 1974; *A Time for Payment*, 1976 (as *Everything Has Its Price*, 1976); *Nights of the Long Knives*, 1976.

* * *

One of the most successful of the post-war German novelists, Hans Hellmut Kirst is best known for his four "Gunner Asch" books, his novel *The Night of the Generals*, and for his satires of German army life. *The Night of the Generals* and *Nights of the Long Knives* might both be termed crime novels, particularly the former, which features an official detective. Both works

make exciting and terrifying reading and, in the cynical detachment of their narrative method, represent the best technical achievements of recent European crime fiction. However, Kirst's most significant contribution to the detective crime story is his "Munich Trilogy": *A Time for Scandal, A Time for Truth*, and *A Time for Payment*.

Featuring Detective-Inspector Keller of the Munich CID (who retires at the end of the first novel), the books are chronicles of crime, scandal, and corruption in high places in contemporary Germany. The novels are written with a kind of indifference; the narrative method involves the use of notebook and diary entries, newspaper reports, snatches of dialogue, and "straight" narration of events. The mood of the trilogy is thus starkly contemporary; the narration exposes the reader to a variety of interpretations or "filters" of events, while challenging him to put together a solution to the crime based upon "evidence" from a variety of predictable and unlikely sources. His stylistic originality places Kirst in the company of contemporary writers who have used the crime story to depict the paradoxes of modern urban life. Like the Swedes Sjöwall and Wahlöö, Kirst sees the official police as victims of the same mindless bureaucracy that has permeated civilian life, and like them, too, he is pessimistic about the possibility of social or legal reform. Finally, his passionate interest in social detail, and the combination of irony and compassion with which he records it, mark Kirst as a crime writer of a very high order.

Kirst has the distinction of having created perhaps the most memorable canine since *The Hound of the Baskervilles*. Anton the Newfoundland, who makes his appearance in *A Time for Scandal* and whose kidnapping is a central event in *A Time for Payment*, is one of the most endearing of fictional hounds. Endowed with a stoically loving personality, the dog is given to Detective-Inspector Keller by Harald Fein, an embattled but essentially decent architect-turned-businessman whom Keller saves from destruction. As Keller explains: "Anton has always known what it is to lead a dog's life—never abandoning hope of being loved unreservedly in spite of everything. Many people have never experienced such a hope and lots of them are forced to bury it still-born. They go on living, but what a life!" The first novel establishes the relationship between Keller and the dog, who becomes a symbol of integrity and hope in a sea of corruption. Keller's retirement from the CID allows him to employ methods, in the two subsequent novels, which would be unthinkable for the official force. Keller, then, forms a bridge between the professional detective of the *roman policier* and the more romantic private eye, with Anton as a combination partner and love interest.

A Time for Truth continues the examination of contemporary corruption by presenting the murder of journalist Heinz Horstmann. Predictably the murder starts a chain of other crimes, from which none of the principal characters escapes unscathed (although two rival newspapers, demonstrating the power of the press, are able to establish a merger which protects the vested interests of each). The observation of contemporary life and morals is acute, the irony superbly controlled. In *A Time for Payment*, Kirst concludes his contemporary epic with a story of kidnapping, murder, student unrest, and grand larceny. The narration of this final volume is somewhat more straightforward than the others, with the journalistic interpolations less frequent, particularly at the beginning. Keller has now become a force unto himself, a giver of advice and director of a private machine of justice: "If a stranger received orders to contact Keller, no personal description was ever attempted. 'You'll know him by his dog' was enough of a clue." Although he receives an offer to return to the force, Keller prefers to continue alone. Our last view of him is on a park bench, with Anton at his feet.

—Joanne Harack Hayne

———————

LEBLANC, Maurice (Marie Émile) (1864–1941). French. Arsène Lupin series (novels and short stories) from 1907. Novels: *813*, 1910; *The Hollow Needle*, 1910; *The Frontier*, 1912; *The Crystal Stopper*, 1913; *The Teeth of the Tiger*, 1914; *The Bomb-Shell*, 1916 (as *The Woman of Mystery*, 1916); *The Golden Triangle*, 1917; *Coffin Island*, 1920 (as *The Secret of Sarek*, 1920); *The Three Eyes*, 1921; *The Tremendous Event*, 1922; *Dorothy the Rope Dancer*, 1923 (as *The Secret Tomb*, 1923); *The Candlestick with Seven Branches*, 1925; *The Girl with the Green Eyes*, 1927; *The Melamare Mystery*, 1929; *Man of Miracles*, 1931; *The Double Smile*, 1933 (as *The Woman with Two Smiles*, 1933); *From Midnight to Morning*, 1933; *Wanton Venus*, 1935; Short Stories: *The Seven of Hearts*, 1908; *The Blonde Lady*, 1910; *The Eight Strokes of the Clock*, 1922; *Jim Barnett Intervenes*, 1928.

* * *

A law student, hack writer, crime reporter, and dramatist, Maurice Leblanc is best remembered as the author of the novels and stories featuring Arsène Lupin. Although he had enjoyed a prolific, if undistinguished, career as a writer for periodicals, it ws not until 1906, when he was asked to write a crime story for a new journal, *Je Sais Tout*, that he produced the first Lupin adventure. *Arsène Lupin: Gentleman-Cambrioleur* was published a year later, and soon Lupin became a household word, not only in France, but around the world.

The origins of Arsène Lupin lie, first of all, in the Sherlock Holmes adventures and their inversion, the Raffles stories; and, second, in the tradition of rogue literature, a popular French example of which was Ponson de Terrail's *Rocambole* (1866). As to the first influence, Holmes appears in *Arsène Lupin Versus Holmlock Shears* and is badly outwitted by the sprightly Frenchman; and the "Gentlemanly" Lupin is clearly a French version of the "amateur cracksman" who so alarmed Conan Doyle. Rocambole, the leader of a Paris street gang, a master of disguise and a flouter of bourgeois conventions (particularly as these are upheld by the police), was more a romantic adventurer than a detective/criminal. A further influence upon the creation of Lupin may be Gaboriau's Monsieur Lecoq; for, in his sardonic insistence that official detectives were merely thieves set to catch thieves, Gaboriau prepared the way for stories in which detective and criminal are one and the same. So clever is Lupin that he actually poses as Lenormand, chief of the Sûreté, and investigates the crimes committed by himself.

Most of the Lupin books cannot be considered detective fiction so much as burlesques of the form. Generally, the short stories are more successful than the full-length novels, in which the sense of frantic fun wears a bit thin. (Exceptions are *The Hollow Needle* and *813*, both of which contain some unusual features.) The rivalry between Lupin and Holmes is, to put it gently, sophomoric. The early short stories, however, can be read for sheer enjoyment of their farcical elements; and it is a tribute to Leblanc's creative energies that we are entirely engrossed by the "puzzles." We want to know how Lupin is going to escape from each new difficulty, and we side entirely with him because, unlike the fat bourgeois businessman from whom he steals works of art, or the dull-witted policemen who try to detect "by the book," Lupin exhibits a lively sense of the ridiculous, and so moves with ease from one cliff-hanging situation to another.

It is significant that murder rarely figures as the crime in a Lupin story. Lupin's criminal activities are almost never undertaken solely for personal gain. If he steals a painting, it is so that it may be genuinely appreciated. If he deliberately enchants a woman, it is because she is about to marry the wrong man. His disguises, so baffling to the police, are usually adopted for the sheer fun of the deception. Towards the end of his career, Lupin begins to work more and more in consort with the police—sometimes for reasons of his own, but often as a result of his idealism and sense of justice. Unfortunately, the feeling of fun so evident in the first volume of adventures is missing from those of the "reformed" Lupin.

Needless to say, deduction as a science plays little part in Lupin's methods; in this, he is at the opposite extreme from Gaboriau's Monsieur Lecoq. The mood of the stories is romantic, non-scientific, neo-gothic, and, above all, action-filled. They can, however, be read with enjoyment by the connoisseur of detective fiction—primarily as an antidote to those works which, in their insistence upon a rational explanation for all mysterious phenomena, take themselves—and the world—too seriously.

—Joanne Harack Hayne

———————

LEROUX, Gaston (1868–1927). French. Novels: Cheri-Bibi series from 1922; *The Mystery of the Yellow Room*, 1908 (as *Murder in the Bedroom*, 1945); *The Perfume of the Lady in Black*, 1909; *The Double Life*, 1909; *The Phantom of the Opera*, 1911; *The Man With the Black Feather*, 1912; *Balaoo*, 1913; *The Secret of the Night*, 1914; *The Bride of the Sun*, 1915; *The Man Who Came Back from the Dead*, 1916; *The Amazing Adventures of Carolus Herbert*, 1922; *The Floating Prison*, 1922 (as *Wolves of the Sea*, 1923); *Missing Men*, 1923; *The Veiled Prisoner*, 1923; *The Dark Road*, 1924; *The Dancing Girl*, 1924 (as *Nomads of the Night*, 1925); *The Kiss That Killed*, 1924; *The Burgled Heart*, 1925 (as *The New Terror*, 1926); *The Slave Bangle*, 1925 (as *The Phantom Clue*, 1926); *The Adventures of a Coquette*, 1926; *The Sleuth Hound*, 1926 (as *The Octopus of Paris*, 1927); *The Masked Man*, 1927; *The Son of Three Fathers*, 1927; *The New Idol*, 1928; *The Man of a Hundred Masks*, 1930 (as *The Man of a Hundred Faces*, 1930); *The Midnight Lady*, 1930; *The Haunted Chair*, 1931; *Lady Helena; or The Mysterious Lady*, 1931; *The Missing Archduke*, 1931; *The Machine to Kill*, 1935.

* * *

Gaston Leroux enjoyed an adventurous life as a newspaper correspondent, lawyer, drama critic, legal chronicler, writer on hygiene, playwright, and world traveler which he imaginatively transformed into over 30 popular novels of mystery and detection. Best known for his novel *The Phantom of the Opera*, Leroux was a *raconteur par excellence* who had a remarkable talent for telling a good—if somewhat incredible—story that engages and holds the reader's interest from first to last.

By general agreement, Leroux's *The Mystery of the Yellow Room* is considered the greatest masterpiece of French detective fiction. In this cleverly plotted novel, structured around a *crime passionel* and a much-admired variation of the locked-room puzzle, Leroux established for all time the Least-

Likely-Person element in detective fiction by making the "official" detective the culprit. To carry off his grand deception as well as to create rivalry between the professional detective and the amateur sleuth, Leroux introduced the 18-year-old Joseph Rouletabille, the first of the bright young reporters, who sees himself not as a policeman but as a journalist in the service of the truth. Rouletabille (so nicknamed for his bullet-shaped head) is blessed with ratiocinative powers and a devoted friend, Sainclair, who chronicles his adventures and serves as his perplexed Dr. Watson. Because it stretches coincidence beyond all credibility and has occasional moments of excessive melodrama, *The Mystery of the Yellow Room* ranks today among those classics of detective fiction that everyone "knows" but few have read.

—Arthur Nicholas Athanason

MATSUMOTO, Seicho (1909–). Japanese. Novels: *Points and Lines*, 1970; *Inspector Imanishi Investigates*, 1989. Short Stories: *The Voice and Other Stories*, 1989.

* * *

Japan's *ichiban*, or number one, mystery writer is Seicho Matsumoto. He has occupied this special status for many years, certainly since the death of Edogawa Rampo, "the father of the Japanese detective story," in 1965. Even in years when Matsumoto is not the top-selling mystery writer, he is still considered number one because of his enduring popularity and his outstanding contribution to the development of the mystery form in Japan.

Of humble origin and without a university degree, Matsumoto began writing at the age of 40. His early works, mainstream and historical novels, won for him an important writing contest and the prestigious Akutagawa Prize. It was with a short story, "The Stakeout," in 1955 that he first showed an interest in crime fiction. He continued to write short mysteries, six examples of which can be found in *The Voice and Other Stories*. The stories in this collection reveal that, although Matsumoto is capable of constructing a suspenseful plot, he is basically concerned with motivation, with the psychological factors leading to crime. Professional detectives are not featured in these stories. The main characters are usually ordinary people—a telephone operator, a bar hostess, a bank clerk—whose connection to the crime may be as the murderer, a suspect, or an amateur detective. In addition to entertaining the reader, these stories tell much about the problems and pressures faced by ordinary citizens in modern Japan, which is not at all the exotic Japan we see in travelogues.

Matsumoto's first mystery novel, *Points and Lines*, was an immediate success, it established him as a leading figure in the mystery field and helped to create the mystery fiction boom that continues in Japan to the present day. The plot involves the apparent double suicide of two lovers from Tokyo, whose bodies are found on a beach in Kyushu, the southernmost of Japan's four main islands. The detectives on the case are Kiichi Mihara of the Tokyo Metropolitan Police and Jutaro Torigai of the Fukuoka Police. In the course of working together, a strong bond develops between the young Mihara and the older Torigai. They conduct a lengthy investigation, finally arriving at a solution through hard work and careful study of the data, or "points and lines," on railroad timetables. Matsumoto has a fascination with his country's railway system, as do many Japanese, and references to trains often occur in his fiction.

Although it is difficult to explain the phenomenal success of *Points and Lines*, it is an admirable first novel that obviously had great appeal for Japanese readers. Matsumoto, who does not normally use series characters, brought back detectives Mihara and Torigai to solve another case in 1962.

Matsumoto has worked at a feverish pace since the late 1950's, producing over 450 books of fiction and nonfiction. Although well-known as a mystery writer, he has written many historical novels and a considerable number of essays on economics, archeology, and other subjects. One of his best mystery novels is *Inspector Imanishi Investigates*, a police procedural that begins with the discovery of the body of a murdered man on the tracks of a Tokyo railroad yard. The only clue is the word Kameda, perhaps a place name. Assigned to the case is Eitaro Imanishi, a respected homicide detective who is fond of gardening and writes haiku. Pursuing the investigation takes him across Japan and through the various strata of society. He learns that the victim is a retired cop. When the case is officially closed without a suspect being apprehended, the diligent Imanishi uses his vacation time to continue the hunt, finally uncovering the killer's identity and peculiarly Japanese motive.

Perhaps more important than the vast body of work Matsumoto has produced is his profound influence on the postwar generation of Japanese mystery writers. Urging his fellow authors to take a more serious approach to the genre, he championed what came to be known as the "social detective story" and attacked earlier mysteries, those written under the leadership of Edogawa Rampo, as nothing more than unrealistic puzzles. He called for mystery writers to use a more literate style, to reject the fantastic and strive for realism, to stress motivation, and to turn away from Poe and Doyle and toward Dostoevsky. Many Japanese authors responded to his message and accepted, at least in theory, *Crime and Punishment* as their model. In their fiction they began to delve into such matters as government corruption, industrial espionage, and the operations of the *yakuza*, Japan's organized crime alliance. While other types of mysteries continue to be written, Matsumoto and his colleagues have become the dominant faction among writers of crime fiction.

Anyone familiar with Japanese mainstream fiction or the films of Kurosawa, Mizoguchi, and Ozu knows of the strong emphasis on human values to be found in these works. Often the plot centers on the plight of ordinary human beings, their problems, their struggle for existence or for a better life. With Matsumoto providing inspiration and leadership, mystery fiction in Japan has joined the great humanistic stream that courses through the history of Japanese literature.

—John L. Apostolou

MONTEILHET, Hubert (1928–). French. Novels: *The Praying Mantises*, 1962 (as *Praying Mantis*, 1962); *Return from the Ashes*, 1963 (as *Phoenix from the Ashes*, 1963); *The Road to Hell*, 1964; *The Prisoner of Love*, 1965; *Cupid's Executioners*, 1967; *Murder at Leisure*, 1971; *A Perfect Crime, or Two*, 1971; *Murder at the Frankfurt Fair: A Wicked, Witty Novel about the Publishing of an International Bestseller*, 1976 (as *Dead Copy . . .* 1976).

* * *

Hubert Monteilhet, with no previous writing experience, chose to work in the detective novel where, according to his remarks in an interview published in the French edition of *Ellery Queen's Mystery Magazine* (No. 298), "the level was generally rather low and the slightest talent was more likely to be recognized."

His first novel, *The Praying Mantises*, was awarded the Grand Prix de Littérature Policière. A well-constructed and original plot based on the suspense novel, a pervasive, subtle humor, psychologically complex characters both cynical and detached, torn between greed and eroticism, were the ingredients which contributed to its success. In addition, the novel was distinguished by a consciously classical style which did not hesitate to use the imperfective subjunctive ostentatiously. These same elements, combined in similarly rigorous and virtuoso proportions, characterize all the early novels and, in particular, his masterpiece, *Return from the Ashes*. With his concern for approaching indirectly with a kind of mannered elegance and a taste for paradox certain moral and metaphysical problems, all these qualities were to make Monteilhet known as the Choderlos de Laclos of the detective novel. Subsequently, this subtle balance was very often disturbed either for eroticism, as the titles of certain novels suggest (*The Prisoner of Love, Cupid's Executioners*, and the untranslated *Pour Deux sous de Vertu*), or for an affected humor that becomes tedious (*The Road to Hell* and *Esprit, Es-Tu-La?*). Yet Monteilhet occasionally rediscovered the vein of his first novels (as in *Murder at the Frankfurt Fair*) and succeeded in proving with *A Perfect Crime, or Two* that the theses of Thomas De Quincey on the art of crime are not without substance.

Monteilhet has defined himself as a writer of classical tastes: "By classical, I mean a permanent tendency of the mind to give precedence to order and reason over feeling. But in a classicism which seeks to be harmonious, reason must only win against madness by a fraction." His conception of the detective novel is also worth quoting: "As I understand it, the 'detective' novel is for the modern public what the tragedy was for the contemporaries of Pericles or Louis XIV."

—Jacques Baudou, translated by Walter Albert

NATSUKI, Shizuko (1938–).   Japanese.   Novels: *Murder at Mt. Fuji*, 1984; *The Third Lady*, 1987; *Tragedy of M.*, 1987; *Woman at Border*, 1987; *Obituary Arrives at 2 O'Clock*, 1988; *Innocent Journey*, 1989; *Death From the Clouds*, 1989.

*   *   *

Shizuko Natsuki is one of the most popular mystery writers in Japan and has written more than 80 novels and short story collections over a period of 20 years.

In a collection of her own essays Natsuki commented, "I like to pursue the purposes and values of life in my mystery stories though they usually contain murder scenes. . . . I prefer to write about love rather than lust and affection rather than hatred." She further wrote, "Mysteries cannot be written without a unique idea. I think this unique idea, whether it be puzzles or motives, is the heart of mysteries. It makes mysteries what they are." These convictions are consistently reflected in her works.

Natsuki has evolved as a writer since she first started in 1969. Her evolution can be seen in three distinct stages. Stage one was marked by a preoccupation with family problems, stage two by an interest in social problems, and stage three by

experimentation with new techniques. As she progressed through each stage, her works have matured.

During her first stage as a writer, Natsuki wrote mysteries based largely on her own experiences as a mother, a wife, and as a woman. According to her, the most fascinating theme is motherhood. In fact, this theme is central to many of her works. In her first novel, *Tenshi ga Kiete Yuku* (*The Angel has Gone*), a prostitute's love for her baby is revealed after her death. Her hopeless maternal love made a strong impression on many readers.

In another novel, a woman disappears from an airplane during the flight, and her journalist lover begins his search for her. This is the main plot of her early masterpiece, *Johastu* (*Vanishing*). The impossible disappearance is dramatic but readers must never forget her motive for disappearing.

During her second stage, Natsuki expanded her view from her own personal world to encompass and challenge social problems. *Obituary Arrives at 2 O'Clock* is one of her best novels written during this stage. A professional golfer solves a lawsuit against her lover who is charged with a false accusation. Natsuki here switches her emphasis from the love between a man and a woman to expose the social problem—corruption in a golf club that accepts more members than its capacity allows purely to increase profits.

During her third stage, Natsuki polished her technique as a mystery writer. She further developed and expanded her areas of personal interest and experimented with new techniques. Mysteries have two faces: ordinariness which people can relate to and originality which keeps the novels exciting and unpredictable.

Murder at Mt. Fuji is an ambitious work which challenges the reader with a pure puzzle mystery. Natsuki sets the story in a traditional setting, an isolated snow-bound villa, and develops the story through a complex writing technique—a half-inverted story.

In *The Third Lady*, she criticizes the connection between the confectionary company and the professor who inspects the foods. But the central plot is the passionate love between a man and a woman who met in France. This novel is a story of suspense about exchanging murders, but the love story also features prominently.

Natsuki is a versatile writer who constantly challenges herself by moving her mysteries into new fields.

—Naomi Hoida

ØRUM, Poul (1919–).   Danish.   Novels: *The Whipping Boy*, 1975 (as *Scapegoat*, 1975); *Nothing But the Truth*, 1976.

*   *   *

Detective Inspector Jonas Morck and his assistant Einarsen are the detectives in both of the translated novels by Poul Ørum. Morck is a happily married man of 47 and Einarsen is miserably wed to a successful businesswoman a few years his senior. His life is spent worrying about her real or imaginary affairs with other men while he is working in remote parts of Denmark. While Morck is a thoughtful, kindly man, Einarsen is just the opposite and the weak, the foolish, and the confused have a tough time at his hands during investigations.

In *The Whipping Boy* the murder victim is a 33-year-old nurse in Vesterso, a small resort that is closed for a good part of the year. The prime suspect is a severely retarded kitchen hand, tall and strong but with the mind of a tiny child. He has been the butt of everybody's ill-humour since the day he was born, and it would seem quite natural that he might wish to wipe out a lifetime of bitterness by violence upon a woman. The boy also had a reputation of a peeping tom, but had never before tried sexually to molest anyone, except (possibly) a little slut also employed by the hotel. After the murderer has been arrested, it is still the scapegoat who suffers.

In *Nothing But the Truth* Jorgen Brehmer could be said to be the equal of Einarsen in both selfishness and cruelty. Possibly Brehmer might even be the more powerful in the small town that his family had controlled for so long; the local police did not care to be too openly critical of the man. A reporter on Brehmer's newspaper is murdered and the sordid personal lives of both the victim and the Brehmer family slowly emerges.

It is not just the themes that are so interesting in Poul Ørum's works. He also provides fascinating glimpses of a socialistic world that is not nearly so repressive as some of the spokesmen of capitalistic liberty wish us to believe.

—Mary Groff

ROBBE-GRILLET, Alain (1922–). French. Novels: *The Voyeur*, 1958; *Jealousy*, 1959; *In the Labyrinth*, 1960; *The Erasers*, 1964; *La Maison de rendez-vous*, 1966 (as *The House of Assignation*, 1970); *Project for a Revolution in New York*, 1972; *Topology of a Phantom City*, 1977. Short Stories: *Snapshots*, 1968. Screenplay: *Last Year at Marienbad*, 1962.

* * *

If every detective story is an abstraction from the mundane mechanics of crime and punishment, Alain Robbe-Grillet goes one step further, abstracting the abstraction by making the *style* of detection his subject. Yet because of this deflection of interest from the what to the how of mystery, Robbe-Grillet's best results are two novels almost totally unlike formula narratives. In *Jealousy* and *In the Labyrinth*, the reader is freed to engage in pure search, undistracted by the appetites stimulated by mystery-reading: for rational detectives, clock-time discrepancies, conclusive solutions.

In the Labyrinth is Robbe-Grillet's nearest approach to the effect of Kafka. We do not feel obliged to discover anything in particular: we easily adopt the position of the investigator's superior in *The Erasers*, who "has stopped believing in the existence of any solution whatsoever." Instead, we search along with the soldier-protagonist, "attend" in terror and pity, the way we track the figures of tragedy. Similarly, *Jealousy* requires us *to be* jealous: any possible material corroboration of the narrator's obsession would be as nothing compared with the experience of suspicion itself.

Robbe-Grillet thus, at times, can make aesthetic concern for detection style as mode and for point-of-view technique compatible with his phenomenology. According to his *For a New Novel*, words represent mental acts of reciprocity with external reality. Things are inviolably separate from the fictional self yet possibly, *only* possibly, correlative to emotions and thoughts. For Mathias, the controlling consciousness in *The Voyeur*, the environment can reflect and even trigger sexual compulsions; but just as frequently the author can wring his fictive context of sea and rocks completely dry of human significance. So, whether the reader is the detective tracing the putative crime and criminal (*The Voyeur*) or a "Tiresias"

accompanying the feverish searcher (*In the Labyrinth*, *Jealousy*), he must distinguish between described objects and events which mirror the central self's internal state, on the one hand— they will be "clues"—and, on the other, the novelistic "reality," which is always impermeably "objectal." Such an exercise in the form of detection, while not detection itself, is what Robbe-Grillet substitutes for the hunting of catchable culprits in detective fiction proper.

Of his other works, *The Erasers*, most like a conventional mystery, is a deadpan parody of classical French tragedy in form (Beckett) and, in content and effect, a travesty of Sophocles, with its pseudo-solemn Oedipus references (Joyce). Robbe-Grillet's first "ciné-roman" is an ironic attempt to discover what happened "last year at Marienbad" by inventing it. The most romantic of Robbe-Grillet's artefacts, *Last Year at Marienbad* denies the past as determinant; thus it is intrinsically anti-detection. After *La Maison de rendez-vous*, a neat parody of the 1960's spy novel, comes the anti-politics of *Project for a Revolution in New York*, which is either a Swiftian satire on contemporary madness (with oddball SLA-type terrorists who are also their own detectives) or a post-modernist parody of de Sade for its own aesthetico-pornographic sake. As always, Robbe-Grillet's style is impeccably matter-of-fact, leaving one with the discomforting thought that our 1970's world is one in which anything can be imagined—a logical extension of a world in which nearly everything has been perpetrated. The surreal *Topologie d'une cité fantôme* continues the sado-erotic emphasis of *The Voyeur* and *Project* and retains the Robbe-Grilletian Ackroydian narrator (now a ritual slayer of "blond virgins and semi-virgins"). This latest novel also realizes Robbe-Grillet's conception of "generative fiction," first broached in 1963, in which the interest is "no longer in the thing described, but in the very movement of the description" (*For a New Novel*).

—John Snyder

SCIASCIA, Leonardo (1921–89). Italian. Novels: *Mafia Vendetta*, 1963 (*The Day of the Owl*, 1984); *The Council of Egypt*, 1966; *A Man's Blessing*, 1968; *Death of the Inquisitor* in *Salt in the Wound*, 1969; *Equal Danger*, 1973; *One Way or Another*, 1977; *A Dream Dreamed in Sicily*, 1979; *The Wine-Dark Sea*, 1985; *Sicilian Uncles: Four Novellas*, 1986; *To Each His Own*, 1989.

* * *

Leonardo Sciascia was one of the most interesting 20th-century novelists working in the broadly-defined area of crime fiction. After publishing some thoughtful and polemical short pieces about peasant life and corruption in his native Sicily, he first achieved international celebrity with his 1961 novella *Il giorno della civetta* (translated under various titles, most recently as *The Day of the Owl*). This teasing, complex work starts with a murder: a bricklayer is brutally shot in broad daylight in a crowded square as he boards the morning bus for Palermo. Despite the many on-lookers, no-one seems to have heard or seen anything, and preliminary investigations quickly dry up. However, the officer in charge, a young policeman from the north of Italy, manages to persevere, and eventually gets beyond the barrier of silence, or "omerta," to discover that this particular murder is only a small, relatively insignificant part of a wider Mafia conspiracy to dominate the Sicilian building trade. As so often in Sciascia's tales, everyone in the community is implicated by fear and silence, making the investigator's task almost impossible. The conspiracy also involves prominent government officials, and though the investigation reveals how pervasive the corruption is, no single culprit is identified, and no trial can take place. Ironically, the government's official line is that the Mafia does not exist, so the book ends inconclusively and enigmatically, with the police inspector himself gradually losing interest, having discovered that his quarry is all around him, yet invisible. The initial crime is never solved, and justice remains wholly elusive.

Similar revelations distinguish a later crime work, *Il contesto* (translated as *Equal Danger*), wherein a dogged and intelligent officer of the law tries to identify the perpetrator of a series of apparently unrelated murders of judges. Although under pressure to find a personal vendetta behind these outrages, he finds, again, that no individual is to blame, and that the deaths are inspired by a group of wealthy establishment figures. Speaking of this book, Sciascia said, "The light, the color . . . the incidents, the details—all can be Sicilian, Italian, but the substance (if there is any) must be that of a fable about power anywhere in the world, about power that, in the impenetrable form of a concatenation that we can roughly term *mafioso*, works steadily greater degradation." Unlike many other popular authors, like Mario Puzo, therefore, Sciascia was not interested in glamourising or sensationalising his narratives, or engaging in "Mafia chic." Instead, he was more concerned to create fables or parables about power and corruption, using the form of the detective story in these two books and in *A ciascuno il suo* (*A Man's Blessing*) and *Todo Modo* (*One Way or Another*) to contemplate the eventually futile quest for knowledge and revelation.

Many of his other books display this metaphoric or philosophic quality vividly. *Il Consiglio d'Egitto* (*The Council of Egypt*) investigates a case of forgery in 18th-century Palermo, and *Candido* is an exuberant reworking and up-dating of Voltaire's fable in terms of post-war Sicilian history. Two historical reconstructions, *La scomparsa di Majorana* (*The Disappearance of Majorana*) and *I pugnalatori* (*The Knifers*), reinvestigate past mysteries in a journalistic style, and return to his perennial themes of personal integrity, injustice and conspiracies. More occasional works expressed his intimate involvement with contemporary Italian politics: he was at various times a member of the Italian and the European parliaments and a city councillor in Palermo. In *L'Affaire Moro*, (*The Moro Affair*), he produced a highly-charged and indignant piece of polemical writing, accusing the Italian state of lethargy and corruption in its handling of the kidnapping of Aldo Moro by the Red Brigade. For the remainder of his life, Sciascia wrote essays and literary criticism, specialising in "raconti-inchiesti," brief investigative and speculative tales, occasionally reminiscent of Borges.

Although his work has been turned into two excellent films—Francesco Rosi's *Illustrious Corpses* and Elio Petri's *Todo Modo*—and although he has attracted praise from eminent literary critics, including Frank Kermode, Sciascia has not as yet achieved the esteem in the English-speaking world that he certainly deserves. For Sciascia was not simply a crime writer. Rather, he is best understood as a chronicler of "metaphysical mysteries," featuring the complexities of individual life in a world where the operations of power are intricate and imperfectly understood. His writing is consistently cool and unimpassioned in tone, quizzically unveiling the absence of justice in the world and the incompetence of rationality in the face of human corruption and wickedness. It is to be hoped that his profoundly humane combination of indignation, commitment and the courage to be outspoken becomes better-known

and that his fables of crime and Sicilian life receive greater attention in the years to come.

—Ian A. Bell

SIMENON, Georges (1903–89). Belgian. Inspector Jules Maigret series from 1932; *The Death of Monsieur Gallet*, 1932; *The Strange Case of Peter the Lett*, 1933; *The Crime at Lock 14, and The Shadow on the Courtyard*, 1934; *The Disintegration of J.P.G.*, 1937; *In Two Latitudes*, 1942; *Affairs of Destiny*, 1942; *The Man Who Watched the Trains Go By*, 1942; *Escape in Vain*, 1943; *Havoc by Accident*, 1943; *On the Danger Line*, 1944; *The Shadow Falls*, 1945; *Blind Alley*, 1946; *Lost Moorings*, 1946; *Black Rain*, 1947; *Magnet of Doom*, 1948; *The First Born*, 1949; *A Wife at Sea, and The Murderer*, 1949; *A Chit of a Girl* (*The Girl in Waiting*, 1957), and *Justice*, 1949; *The Survivors, and Black Rain*, 1949; *Monsieur La Souris* (*The Mouse*, 1966), and *Poisoned Relations*, 1950; *Strange Inheritance*, 1950; *The Snow Was Black* (*The Stain on the Snow*, 1950), 1950; *At the Gai-Moulin and A Battle of Nerves*, 1951; *The Window over the Way, and The Gendarme's Report*, 1951; *Strangers in the House*, 1951; *The Heart of a Man*, 1951; *A Crime in Holland, and A Face for a Clue*, 1952; *The House by the Canal, and The Ostenders*, 1952; *The Burgomaster of Furnes*, 1952; *The Trial of Bebe Donge*, 1952; *Act of Passion*, 1952; *The Girl in His Past*, 1952; *Satan's Children*, 1953; *Aunt Jeanne*, 1953; *On Land and Sea*, 1954; *Ticket of Leave*, 1954; *Across the Street*, 1954; *Tidal Wave*, 1954; *Violent Ends*, 1954; *A Sense of Guilt*, 1955; *The Magician, and The Widow*, 1955; *Destinations*, 1955; *Danger Ahead*, 1955; *Fugitive* (*Account Unsettled*, 1962), 1955; *The Judge and the Hatter*, 1956; *The Witnesses, and the Watchmaker*, 1956; *The Stowaway*, 1957; *The Little Man from Arkangel*, 1957; *The Sacrifice*, 1958; *To Any Lengths*, 1958; *Inquest on Bouvet*, 1958; *In Case of Emergency*, 1958; *The Son*, 1958; *The Negro*, 1959; *Striptease*, 1959; *Sunday*, 1960; *The Premier*, 1961; *The Widower*, 1961; *The Fate of the Malous*, 1962; *A New Lease of Life*, 1963; *The Iron Staircase*, 1963; *The Patient* (*The Bells of Bicetre*, 1964), 1963; *Three Beds in Manhattan*, 1964; *The Accomplices, and the Blue Room*, 1964; *The Train*, 1964; *The Door*, 1964; *The Man with the Little Dog*, 1965; *The Little Saint*, 1965; *Monsieur Monde Vanishes*, 1967; *The Confessional*, 1967; *The Old Man Dies*, 1967; *The Cat*, 1967; *The Neighbours* (*The Move*, 1968), 1968; *The Prison*, 1969; *Big Bob*, 1969; *November*, 1970; *The Man on the Bench in the Barn*, 1970; *Teddy Bear*, 1971; *The Disappearance of Odile*, 1972; *The Glass Cage*, 1973; *The Innocents*, 1973; *The Venice Train*, 1974; *Betty*, 1975; *The Hatter's Phantoms*, 1976; *The Girl with a Squint*, 1978; *The Family Lie*, 1978; *The Little Doctor*, 1978; *The Night-Club*, 1979; *African Trio*, 1979; *The White Horse Inn*, 1980; *The Delivery*, 1981; *The Long Exile*, 1982; *The Reckoning*, 1984; *The Outlaw*, 1986; *Uncle Charles Has Locked Himself In*, 1987; *The Rules of the Game*, 1989.

* * *

Georges Simenon, one of the true giants of the novel, earned through the fecundity of his imagination and his devotion to his craft the right to be termed a genius. Apparently equally indifferent to critical scorn or praise, impervious to the shifting currents of literary fashion, disdainful of pretentious philosophizing or didacticism, Simenon resolutely went his own way, followed his unique vision, creating a body of work with the power and inevitability of life itself. Like Balzac or Dickens or

Faulkner, he staked out his own bleak territory of the human heart, a world of passion and violence, suffering and disorder, over which broods the massive presence of his detective, Jules Maigret. One of the most important novelists of his time, and certainly one of the major figures in French literature, Simenon must also be considered one of the major writers of detective fiction; his detective stories belong among the finest examples of the genre and, like other great detective stories, deserve serious critical study.

Simenon's detective fiction, naturally, is as original and individual within its form as his other kinds of fiction are within the traditions of the "straight" novel. One of the tired truisms of critical study of the form asserts that the detective story could only flourish in Anglo-Saxon countries because of their early traditions of constitutional democracy; whether this statement is entirely true is open to question, but certainly the works of Simenon demonstrate that great detective fiction outside of the English-speaking world takes an entirely different direction, departing radically from the established conventions of the genre. Aside from the obligatory pattern of crime, mystery, and investigation, Simenon's novels bear almost no apparent relationship to any particular sub-genre of detective and mystery fiction, including the police procedural novel, which they superficially resemble. They are truly *sui generis*, properly deserving their own generic name, the "Maigret," after their unique protagonist.

Although Maigret is an official detective, he never solves his cases by means of the machinery available to him, the usual business of fingerprints and laboratory reports and minute examinations that constitute the work of policemen everywhere. On the other hand, he possesses none of the eccentric genius of the famous great detectives in the Sherlockian mold. His methods are peculiarly his own—he immerses himself in the ambience of criminal action, soaking up, spongelike, the quality and "feel" of the geography, the social class, the habits, the sights and sounds and smells, the daily life of the place, the region, the people who inhabit it. In the process he comes to find himself a part of the action, almost a character in his own case, as much a suspect as anyone he is investigating. As he comes to live in the world he examines, so too he comes to understand it; with that understanding, in a way that the reader can never really duplicate, appears the solution.

The famous method of Maigret seems compounded mostly out of the sympathetic human imagination; working without a great deal in the way of facts, clues, chains of evidence, it succeeds infallibly and its success always seems, when it comes, absolutely inevitable. The Maigrets often end with the detective regretting in some way his victory over the recalcitrant facts of life; because of his vast understanding of humanity, his chief emotion in discovering guilt is not a feeling of triumph but of pity. The generally misshapen or sordid or wasted lives he confronts evoke from him sorrow and compassion; he rediscovers for all his readers, over and over again, the terrible sadness of human pain, violence, suffering, and guilt, the dreadful knowledge of the motives for murder that reside in every human heart. The mysteries he solves seldom engage him so much as the endless puzzle of life that he must continually penetrate; his profession is a constant initiation into man's capacity to sin.

One of the most remarkable aspects of Maigret's reactions to the crimes he investigates is his vision of his task, what motivates him to be a detective. He does not see himself as an avenging angel, a bringer of justice, an official agent of his society, but instead, as he says in *Maigret's First Case*, as "a repairer of destinies." Maigret understands that his great talent for criminal investigation derives from his ability to live other people's lives; he also recognizes that with this faculty comes the responsibility of caring about the lives he recreates within

himself. As he realizes, his task should really be like that of doctor or priest, to function as a sort of receptacle for the disease and corruption of humanity; like the doctor, he would like to cure his patients, like the priest, absolve them. In another book, he thinks of his ideal vocation as "a guide to the lost," and, like the psychoanalyst, he believes he can "bring a man face to face with his true self."

The unique quality of Maigret's character and the radical ideal of his detection indicate the originality of Simenon's work in mystery fiction. The conjunction of Simenon's sordid and frightening fictional world with the sympathetic omniscience of Maigret's methods has no parallel anywhere in the detective story. The absolute impersonality of the author in all of his novels helps to emphasize the importance of Maigret to the rest of his extraordinary body of work: the detective provides a view of the author and his attitudes toward his world and its people that appears nowhere else in Simenon. The detective seems to watch over the Simenon world, to act as guide, judge, even God for the people of that harsh continent that is everywhere and nowhere, except in the mind of its creator and within the human spirit—the country of sorrow that Simenon has made his own. The author's detective stories then, are important for themselves, for the genre, and for the rest of the Simenon canon; inevitably, they are important, too, for the study of literature anywhere.

—George Grella

TOGAWA, Masako (1933–). Japanese. Novels: *The Master Key*, 1984; *The Lady Killer*, 1985; *A Kiss of Fire*, 1988.

* * *

Masako Togawa has been called the P.D. James of Japan. To some extent, this nickname or label is an appropriate way to characterize Togawa. There are certain similarities between her fiction and that of James. Both authors approach the writing of mysteries seriously, and both write in a highly literate style. However, Togawa's unusual, almost bizarre novels of psychological suspense differ greatly from the more conventional detective stories of P.D. James.

Togawa's first novel, *The Master Key*, begins with a series of uncommon events. A young man, disguised as a woman, is killed in a traffic accident. A four-year-old child, the son of a U.S. Army major and his Japanese wife, is kidnapped. A dead child is secretly buried in the basement of an apartment house exclusively for women. Years later, a highway project makes it necessary for the apartment house to be moved, and the master key to every unit in the building is found to be missing. Togawa exposes the links between these events, relating a strange, complex story involving the elderly women who reside in the apartment house. The other major characters are the two ladies who are employed in the building as desk clerks. There is no professional detective, although one of the residents, a retired school teacher named Yoneko Kimura, acts as an amateur sleuth. She attempts to solve the novel's central mystery, the case of the kidnapped child. Important to the plot are a valuable Guarnerius violin and, of course, the master key. Writing in an exquisite, somewhat elliptical style, Togawa takes us into the minds of several characters, revealing their past experiences and intimate secrets. Although basically a crime novel, with an ending full of surprises, the book is also a penetrating study of loneliness and eccentricity.

The main character in Togawa's second novel, *The Lady Killer*, is Ichiro Honda, a Tokyo engineer in his late twenties. He is married but only sees his wife at weekends in Osaka. During his evenings after work, Honda prowls in bars and nightclubs searching for young women to seduce. He records his conquests in a journal he calls "The Huntsman's Log." When three of his former lovers are found raped and murdered, the police learn of his acquaintance with the victims and charge him with the crimes. The primary evidence against him are semen samples that match his blood type. As Togawa tells this dramatic tale, she shifts the reader's attention from one character to another. At the beginning the author follows a girl who has been seduced and made pregnant by Honda. When she commits suicide, the focus shifts to the girl's sister. Then Honda becomes the center of attention for a few chapters, and the last half of the novel features Hajime Shinji, a lawyer who diligently seeks information to prove Honda innocent.

In her first two novels, Togawa shows a great deal of sympathy for the many Japanese women who lead lonely and unfulfilled lives. Oddly enough, she does not seem to hold men responsible for the situation. Although Togawa is an active feminist, she recognizes that the low status of women is a generally accepted part of the Japanese social system and that women themselves are often their own worst enemies.

A Kiss of Fire is a recent work that differs markedly from Togawa's early mysteries. In the novel's opening pages, a prominent artist dies in a house fire. Three young boys, the artist's son and two of his classmates, are suspected of having caused the fire, but their guilt is not proven. 26 years later, the three classmates are brought together by another fire, an arson blaze in which a woman and a circus lion are killed. The former classmates have not seen each other for many years. One of them is Ryosaku Uno, the police detective assigned to tracking down an arsonist who is responsible for a series of fires. The other two, a fireman and the artist's son, are prime suspects.

Togawa has chosen to divide the novel into a great many short sections, most of which are titled "The Fireman," "The Arsonist," or "The Detective." The frequent shifting from one character to another, which might have been effective in a film, seems arbitrary and tends to confuse the reader who is already confused by the complex plot. Although Togawa may be trying to say something about the mother-son relationship in Japan, *A Kiss of Fire* seems little more than a very far-fetched puzzle. In fact, the final paragraph in the novel contains a hint that suggests the book was intended as a tribute to an author who championed the puzzle mystery, Edogawa Rampo.

—John L. Apostolou

* * *

van GULIK, Robert H(ans) (1910–67). Dutch. Novels and Novelets: *Dee Goong An*, 1949; *The Chinese Bell Murders*, 1958; *The Chinese Gold Murders*, 1959; *The Chinese Lake Murders*, 1960; *The Chinese Nail Murders*, 1961; *The Chinese Maze Murders*, 1962; *The Emperor's Pearl*, 1963; *The Haunted Monastery*, 1963; *The Lacquer Screen*, 1964; *The Red Pavilion*, 1964; *The Monkey and the Tiger*, 1965; *The Willow Pattern*, 1965; *Murder in Canton*, 1966; *The Phantom of the Temple*, 1966; *Necklace and Calabash*, 1967; *Poets and Murder*, 1968 (as *The Fox-Magic Murders*, 1973). Short Stories: *New Year's Eve in Lan-Fang*, 1958; *Judge Dee at Work*, 1967; *The Given Day*.

Robert H. van Gulik, the Netherlands diplomat and renowned Sinologist, has been the person most responsible for introducing the classical Chinese detective story to the West. His first contribution was the *Dee Goong An*, a translation into English of large portions of the anonymous 18th-century novel *Wu-ze-tian-si-da-qi-an*. This translation consisted of three interlocked cases of the famous detective-magistrate Dee Jen-djieh (transliterated in *pinyin* as Di Ren-jie). Although these cases were completely fictional, Di Ren-jie (630–700 A.D.) was a historical figure who rose through the ranks of the Chinese civil service to become the equivalent of Prime Minister to the Empress Wu. While Di had a significant place in Tang history, he lived, oddly enough, in popular memory as the ideal district magistrate: honest, fearless, righteous, highly intelligent, and remarkably gifted as a detective. Many folk plays and short stories narrate feats of detection attributed to Di. The *Dee Goong An* made a stir in many circles, for it was not only a fascinating work, but it revealed that China possessed a more advanced and more sophisticated detective literature than had been supposed from the rather trivial material that had hitherto been translated.

Van Gulik speculated that contemporary Chinese and Japanese readers might be interested in modern versions of the classical form, and he decided to continue the Judge Dee stories. He wrote two novels in English, *The Chinese Bell Murders* and *The Chinese Maze Murders*, which were then translated into Japanese and published. It was soon recognized, however, that the English texts had merits of their own and were too important to be used only as translation sources. Van Gulik thereupon began a new series of Judge Dee Mysteries aimed at the Western reader. All were first written in English, although some were first published in Dutch. (For Netherlands newspapers he prepared 12 scripts for a cartoon series based on Dee; the novel *The Phantom of the Temple* and several short stories were later adapted from these scripts.) Van Gulik also wrote a thriller set in Amsterdam (*Een gegeven Dag*, *The Given Day*), not published in English.

In his original fiction van Gulik took over the Judge Dee and associates (Ma Joong, Chiao Tai, Sergeant Hoong) of the *Dee Goong An* without too much regard for the historical Minister Di. While adhering to the common occidental practice of preparing a puzzle plot for the reader (a technique not commonly used in the orient), van Gulik drew upon the inexhaustible wealth of Chinese stories for special motifs. He also used certain Chinese structural devices in much of his work: a tripartite plot in which three seemingly independent cases move along simultaneously and at times interlace, story frames, and occasional mildly supernatural incidents. Dee was also portrayed as working within the historical circumstances of Chinese administrative and criminal law, using techniques taken from Chinese coroners' and magistrates' manuals. An erotic element in some of the novels, however, is less traditional and presumably reflects van Gulik's own interests.

The Judge Dee stories are certainly the finest ethnographic detective novels in English. They have been widely acclaimed for their originality, skilful plotting, and characterizations. They are also fascinating for the vivid pictures they give of Chinese life, the details of which are worked into the story without destroying narrative flow. This authentic China, however, is not the Tang China of Di Ren-jie, but is essentially a generalized medieval China, such as might have existed in Ming days, with an occasional Tang element. If van Gulik's work has a flaw, apart from occasional sensationalism, it is in the author's English, which is not always perfectly idiomatic; but this situation varies from text to text.

Van Gulik's books usually contain short essays explaining the peculiarly Chinese aspects of his stories, while the *Dee*

Goong An has extensive scholarly material on the Chinese detective story, criminology and jurisprudence. Van Gulik also translated a 13th-century collection of case histories and judicial decisions (*Parallel Cases from under the Peartree—Tang-yin-bi-shi*, 1956), which he occasionally used as a story source.

—E.F. Bleiler

WAHLÖÖ, Per (1926–75), and **Maj SJÖWALL** (1935–). Swedish. Novels in collaboration: *Roseanna*, 1967; *The Man on the Balcony*, 1968; *The Man Who Went Up in Smoke*, 1969; *The Laughing Policeman*, 1970; *The Fire Engine That Disappeared*, 1971; *Murder at the Savoy*, 1971; *The Abominable Man*, 1972; *The Locked Room*, 1973; *Cop Killer*, 1975; *The Terrorists*, 1976. Novels by Per Wahlöö: *The Assignment*, 1965; *Murder on the Thirty-First Floor*, 1966; (as *The Thirty-First Floor*, 1967); *The Lorry*, 1968 (as *A Necessary Action*, 1969); *The Steel Spring*, 1970; *The Generals*, 1974.

*   *   *

In a 1966 essay Per Wahlöö stated the basis for the Martin Beck series he and Maj Sjöwall had started a year earlier. The series would consist of only 10 novels. They chose the crime novel as a form because of its strong connection between people and society: it is impossible to be a lawbreaker—or a law enforcer—without a law, laid down and maintained by a society based upon certain political and economic realities and opinions. They wrote together, each writing alternate chapters after long research and detailed synopses. They were both communists, and the outspoken aim of their series was to "use the crime novel as a scalpel cutting open the belly of an ideologically pauperized and morally debatable so-called welfare state of the bourgeois type." The first two or three books would be almost totally apolitical; later ones would put down the mask and speak loud and clear.

Roseanna, The Man Who Went Up in Smoke, and *The Man on the Balcony,* thus, are straightforward police procedural novels: a hard-working police team solving murders committed for private, and in two cases even pathological, reasons holds center stage. They are better written, psychologically more complex, and more grimly realistic than most books in the type, but they keep inside the limits of good, serious entertainment.

Roseanna introduces Martin Beck, a laconic and competent detective with stomach pains, a failing marriage, and a quiet professionalism. He is surrounded by colleagues of the Stockholm Homicide Squad: the paunchy ex-paratrooper Lennart Kollberg, who hates violence and has a wider political, literary, and human outlook than his friend Beck; the big outspoken and impetuous Gunvald Larsson, a drop-out from high society; the small and careful Einar Rönn, who was born in, and forever longs to return to, the far north of Sweden; and last, but not least, the two patrolmen, Kristiansson and Kvant, recurrent comic characters with very little brain but quite a lot of brawn. *Roseanna* starts eight days after the nationalization of the Swedish police on 1 July 1964. The increasing replacement of common sense with weapons, gadgets, and a para-military organization following the take-over, the lack of backbone among the new, politically appointed leaders—these are prime targets for criticism throughout the series. The next two novels, *The Laughing Policeman* and *The Fire Engine That Disappeared*, begin to show the authors' intentions more clearly. In the first the motive for mass murder is the murderer's wish to keep his social position; in the second the Beck team confront professional crime, up to then a rare phenomenon both in Swedish crime novels and Swedish reality. If the first criminals in the series were pathological, these two are grimly rational. They have chosen crime as a way of living in Swedish society.

The later novels often deal with crime *as* punishment. The business tycoon in *Murder at the Savoy* and the police superintendent who provides the title for *The Abominable Man* are murder victims, but there is little doubt that they are the real criminals, protected by their society, much more than the poor devils who pulled the triggers. *The Locked Room* has a superb John Dickson Carr-type puzzle, and much wild farce, but also bitterly points out that crimes against capital—like bank robberies—are considered by the ruling authorities much more serious than crimes against persons. *Cop Killer* lashes the press for its biased news and contrasts the professional common sense of the old-timers in the Beck team with the para-military battles against scared, lonely, young lawbreakers preferred by Beck's superiors. *The Terrorist* is the bitter, logical conclusion of the scalpel cut through the welfare state, a state so little worthy of its name that the murder of its symbolically responsible Prime Minister seems quite fair, even to the still apolitical Beck—and probably to most of the readers around the world.

Unlike most procedural series the Beck novels allow the main characters to grow older; more important and even more rare—to grow wiser, to develop and change views. Lennart Killberg writes his resignation in *Cop Killer* because his qualities as a warm, thinking, feeling man are no longer of use to his society or his force. It is one of the authors' masterstrokes—and a proof of their ability to convince readers all over the world—when the resignation of a socialist detective for political reasons in a capitalistic state is a cause for regret both in Moscow and in New York, in Birmingham and in Belgrade. Beck stays on, but he has changed in the years since *Roseanna*. His career almost came to an end in *The Abominable Man* when he tried to carry the guilt of the whole force, and in *The Locked Room* he quietly and slowly reconsidered his life and his work. When we leave him in *The Terrorist* there is a Chairman Mao poster over his head. He didn't put it there, but he lets it stay up.

Wahlöö and Sjöwall's main contribution to the genre is their example of how a popular form can be used to distribute a new, complex—and in wide circles even unpopular—content. They have been misunderstood by some American critics with muddled politics who claimed that the series sharply criticized the socialist society of Sweden. They have been called simple communist propagandists. Both extremes are wrong. In writing a carefully planned and exceptionally well-executed series of police procedurals with socialist views, they have succeeded in a serious literary attempt to expand the borders of the detective story and use it to discuss and comment on a much wider and, in many ways, more criminal world.

—Bo Lundin

TITLE

INDEX

Affair at Royalties (Baxt), 1971
Affair at Thor's Head (Carnac, as Lorac), 1932
Affair in Death Valley (C. Knight), 1940
Affair of Sorcerers (Chesbro), 1979
Affair of the Black Sombrero (C. Knight), 1939
Affair of the Blood-Stained Egg Cosy (J. Anderson), 1975
Affair of the Circus Queen (C. Knight), 1940
Affair of the Corpse Escort (C. Knight), 1946
Affair of the Crimson Gull (C. Knight), 1941
Affair of the Dead Stranger (C. Knight), 1944
Affair of the Exotic Dancer (Benson), 1958
Affair of the Fainting Butler (C. Knight), 1943
Affair of the Ginger Lei (C. Knight), 1938
Affair of the Golden Buzzard (C. Knight), 1946
Affair of the Heart (Potts), 1970
Affair of the Heavenly Voice (C. Knight), 1937
Affair of the Jade Monkey (C. Knight), 1943
Affair of the Limping Sailor (C. Knight), 1942
Affair of the Mutilated Mink Coat (J. Anderson), 1982
Affair of the Scarlet Crab (C. Knight), 1937
Affair of the Sixth Button (C. Knight), 1947
Affair of the Skiing Clown (C. Knight), 1941
Affair of the Splintered Heart (C. Knight), 1942
Affair of the Substitute Doctor (Rhode), 1951
Affair on the Painted Desert (C. Knight), 1939
Affair with a Rich Girl (Chance), 1958
Affairs of Destiny (Simenon, trans), 1942
Affairs of O'Malley (s MacHarg), 1940
Afghan Onslaught (Caillou), 1971
Africa Flight (s Gielgud), 1940
African Poison Murders (Huxley), 1940
African Trio (Simenon, trans), 1979
After Dark (s Collins, appendix), 1856
After Dark, My Sweet (Thompson), 1955
After-Dinner Story (s Woolrich, as Irish), 1944
After House (Rinehart), 1914
After Midnight (Albrand), 1949
After Midnight (Nielsen), 1966
After the Act (W. Graham), 1965
After the Ball (Dewhurst), 1976
After the Fine Weather (M. Gilbert), 1963
After the First Death (Block), 1969
After the Funeral (Christie), 1953
After the Lady (Blackstock, as Allardyce), 1954
After the Last Race (Koontz), 1974
After the Verdict (A. Gilbert), 1961
After Things Fell Apart (Goulart), 1970
Aftermath of Murder (Fitt), 1941
Afternoon to Kill (S. Smith), 1953
Aftershock (L. O'Donnell), 1977
Aftershock (Wilcox), 1975
Afterwards (s Lowndes), 1925
Again the Ringer (s E. Wallace), 1929
Again the Three (s E. Wallace), 1968
Again the Three Just Men (s E. Wallace), 1928
Against the Evidence (Linington, as Egan), 1962
Against the Grain (O'Hagan), 1987
Against the Law (Vickers, as Durham), 1939
Agatha Webb (Green), 1899
Age of Death (Marshall), 1970
Age of the Junkman (Ballard, as P.D. Ballard), 1963
Agent in Place (MacInnes), 1976
Agent of Death (Demille), 1974
Agony Column (Biggers), 1916
Agreement to Kill (Rabe), 1957
Aground (C. Williams), 1960
Ah King (s Maugham), 1933

Air Apparent (J. Gardner), 1971
Air Bridge (H. Innes), 1951
Air Disaster (H. Innes), 1937
Air-Ship (s J. Fletcher), 1903
Air That Kills (Millar), 1957
Airing in a Closed Carriage (Shearing), 1943
Airline Pirates (J. Gardner), 1970
Airs above the Ground (Stewart), 1965
Akin to Murder (K. Knight), 1953
Aladdin in London (Hume), 1892
Alamut Ambush (Price), 1971
Alarm (Rhode), 1925
Alarm at Black Brake (Chance), 1960
Alarm in the Night (Sterling), 1949
Alarm of the Black Cat (Olsen), 1942
Alarming Clock (Avallone), 1961
Alas, For Her That Met Me! (Brand, as Ashe), 1976
Alas, Poor Father (J. Fleming), 1972
Albany, Jack series (Godey), from 1966
Albatross (Anthony), 1982
Albatross (s Armstrong), 1957
Alberg, Sergeant Karl series (L.R. Wright), from 1986
Album (Rinehart), 1933
Album Leaf (Shearing), 1933
Alcoholics (Thompson), 1953
Aleph (s Borges, trans), 1970
Aleutian Blue Mink (Fox), 1951
Alfred Hitchcock Murder Case (Baxt), 1986
Alias Basil Willing (McCloy), 1951
Alias Dr. Ely (Thayer), 1927
Alias His Wife (F. Davis, as Ransome), 1965
Alias the Dead (Coxe), 1943
Alias the Ghost (Verner), 1933
Alias the Victim (Gribble), 1971
Alias Uncle Hugo (Coles), 1952
Alibi (Carmichael), 1961
Alibi (Creasey), 1971
Alibi at Dusk (Benson), 1951
Alibi Baby (Sterling), 1955
Alibi for a Corpse (Lemarchand), 1969
Alibi for a Judge (Cecil), 1960
Alibi for a Witch (Ferrars), 1952
Alibi for Isabel (s Rinehart), 1944
Alibi for Murder (Armstrong), 1956
Alibi in Time (J. Thomson), 1980
Alibi of Guilt (Chambers, as Daniels), 1980
Alibi Too Soon (Ormerod), 1987
Alice (Cunningham), 1963
Alice in La-La Land (Campbell), 1987
Alicia Warlock (s Collins, appendix), 1875
Alien (Bell), 1964
Alien Virus (Caillou), 1957
Alington Inheritance (Wentworth), 1958
Alive and Dead (Ferrars), 1974
All About Women (s Greeley), 1990
All at Sea (Wells), 1927
All Concerned Notified (Reilly), 1939
All Exits Blocked (Perowne), 1942
All for One and One for Death (S. Forbes), 1971
All for the Love of a Lady (Ford), 1944
All God's Children (Lyons), 1975
All Grass Isn't Green (E. Gardner, as Fair), 1970
All I Can Get (Ard), 1959
All in the Dark (Le Fanu, appendix), 1866
All Is Discovered (Cannan), 1962
All Is Vanity (Bell), 1940
All Leads Negative (Jeffries, as Alding), 1967

All Men Are Liars (Strange), 1948
All Men are Lonely Now (Clifford), 1967
All Men Are Murderers (Blackstock), 1958
All on a Summer's Day (Wainwright), 1981
All Other Perils (B. Knox, as MacLeod), 1974
All Our Tomorrows (Allbeury), 1982
All Part of the Service (Russell), 1982
All-Purpose Bodies (McCutchan), 1969
All Roads Lead to Friday (H. Innes), 1939
All Roads to Sospel (Bellairs), 1981
All Shot Up (Himes), 1960
All That Glitters (Coles), 1954
All the Pretty People (Scott), 1983
All the Way (C. Williams), 1958
All the Way Down (Crossen, as Chaber), 1953
All These Condemned (J. MacDonald), 1954
All Through the Night (Miller, as Masterson), 1955
All Through the Night (Wainwright), 1985
All-White Elf (Dent, as Robeson), 1986
Alley Girl (Craig), 1954
Alleyn, Inspector Roderick series (Marsh), from 1934
Almost Murder (Jeffries), 1986
Almost Perfect Murder (s Footner), 1933
Almost Without Murder (Graeme), 1963
Aloha, Johnny series (Keene), from 1959
Along a Dark Path (Johnston), 1967
Alp Murder (Stein), 1970
Alpha List (Allbeury), 1979
Alpha List (J. Anderson), 1972
Alphabet Hicks (Stout), 1941
Alphabet Murders (Christie), 1966
Alpine Condo Cross Fire (Eberhart), 1984
Alscott Experiment (Hough, as Stanley), 1954
Alter Ego (Linington), 1987
Aluminum Turtle (Kendrick), 1960
Alvarez Journal (Burns), 1975
Alvarez, Enrique series (Jeffries), from 1974
Always a Body to Trade (Constantine), 1983
Always Expect the Unexpected (Graeme), 1965
Always Kill a Stranger (Fish), 1967
Always Leave 'em Dying (Prather), 1954
Always Murder a Friend (Scherf), 1948
Always Say Die (Ferrars), 1956
Always Take the Big Ones (Chambers), 1965
Amaranth Club (J. Fletcher), 1918
Amateur (Littell), 1981
Amateur City (K. Forrest), 1984
An Amateur Corpse (Brett), 1978
Amateur Cracksman (s Hornung), 1899
Amateur Crime (Berkeley, as Cox), 1928
Amateur in Violence (s M. Gilbert), 1973
Amateur Murderer (C. Daly), 1933
Amazing Adventures of Carolus Herbert (Leroux, trans), 1922
Amazing Adventures of Lester Leith (s E. Gardner), 1981
Amazing Adventures of Letitia Carberry (s Rinehart), 1911
Amazing Chance (Wentworth), 1926
Amazing Count (Le Queux), 1929
Amazing Judgment (Oppenheim), 1897
Amazing Partnership (s Oppenheim), 1914
Amazing Quest of Mr. Ernest Bliss (Oppenheim), 1922
Amazing Web (Keeler), 1929
Amber Effect (Prather), 1986
Amber Eyes (Crane), 1962
Amber Nine (J. Gardner), 1966
Ambitious Lady (J. Fletcher), 1923
Ambrose Lavendale, Diplomat (s Oppenheim), 1920
Ambrotox and Limping Dick (P. MacDonald, as Fleming), 1920

Ambush for Anatole (Sherwood), 1952
Ambush House (Steel), 1943
Ambushers (D. Hamilton), 1963
American Gothic (Bloch), 1974
American Gun Mystery (Queen), 1933
Amethyst Box (Green), 1905
Amethyst Cross (Hume), 1908
Amethyst Spectacles (Crane), 1944
Amiable Charlatan (s Oppenheim), 1916
Amigo, Amigo (Clifford), 1973
Ammie, Come Home (Elizabeth Peters, as Michaels), 1968
Amnesia Trap (Ormerod), 1979
Among Arabian Sands (J. Mitchell), 1962
Among Friends (L. R. Wright), 1984
Among Those Absent (Coles), 1948
Amorous Leander (Hunter), 1983
Ampersand Papers (M. Innes), 1978
Ampurias Exchange (A. Ross), 1976
Amsterdam Cops series (van de Wetering), from 1975
Amsterdam Diversion (A. Ross), 1974
Analog Bullet (M. Smith), 1972
Anarchaos (Westlake, as Clark), 1967
Anastasia Syndrome (s M. Clark), 1989
Anathema Stone (Hilton), 1980
Anatomy of a Killer (Rabe), 1960
Anatomy of a Riot (Wainwright), 1982
And a Bottle of Rum (Graeme), 1949
And Baby Will Fall (Lewin), 1988
And Be a Villain (Cannan), 1958
And Be a Villain (Meynell), 1939
And Be a Villain (Stout), 1948
And Being Dead (Erskine), 1938
And Call It Accident (Lowndes), 1936
And Dangerous to Know (E. Daly), 1949
And Death Came Too (A. Gilbert), 1956
And Death Came Too (Hull), 1939
And Died So? (Gielgud), 1961
And 47 Miles of Rope (Murphy), 1984
And Four to Go (Stout), 1958
. . . and High Water (Stein), 1946
And Left for Dead (Lockridge), 1962
And Let the Coffin Pass (Reilly, as Abbey), 1942
And No One Wept (Hocking), 1954
And on the Eighth Day (Queen), 1964
And One Cried Murder (Thayer), 1961
And One for the Dead (Audemars), 1975
. . . and Presumed Dead (L. Fletcher), 1963
And Shame the Devil (Woods), 1967
And So to Death (s Woolrich, as Irish), 1944
And So to Murder (J. Carr, as Dickson), 1940
And Sometimes Death (Armstrong), 1955
And Still I Cheat the Gallows (s Oppenheim), 1938
And Sudden Death (C. Adams), 1940
And Sudden Death (J. Fletcher), 1938
And the Deep Blue Sea (C. Williams), 1971
And the Girl Screamed (Brewer), 1956
And the Undead Sing (C. Brown), 1974
And Then Put Out the Light (Carnac, as Lorac), 1950
And Then Silence (Propper), 1932
And Then There Was Nun (McInerny, as Quill), 1984
And Then There Were None (Christie), 1940
And They Say You Can't Buy Happiness (McShane, as Lovell), 1979
And to My Beloved Husband— (Loraine), 1950
And Turned to Clay (Offord), 1950
And Where She Stops (Dewey), 1957
And Where's Mr. Bellamy? (Fitt, as Wick), 1948

Anders, Tad series (Allbeury), from 1974
Anderson Tapes (Sanders), 1970
Andrewlina (J. Fletcher), 1889
Andromeda Strain (Crichton), 1969
Angel (Brewer), 1960
Angel! (C. Brown), 1962
Angel (Verner), 1939
Angel and the Cuckoo (Kersh), 1966
Angel Death (Moyes), 1980
Angel Dust (A. Cohen), 1989
Angel Esquire (E. Wallace), 1908
Angel Eyes (Estleman), 1981
Angel Eyes (Hunt, as Dietrich), 1961
Angel Fire (Greeley), 1988
Angel in the Case (Kennedy, as Elder), 1932
Angel of Death (A. Cohen), 1983
Angel of Death (Ballard, as P.D. Ballard), 1974
Angel of Death (J. Anderson), 1978
Angel of Death (Loraine), 1961
Angel of Terror (E. Wallace), 1922
Angel of Torremolinos (Serafín), 1988
Angel of Vengeance (A. Cohen), 1983
Angel Without Mercy (A. Cohen), 1982
Angell, Pearl and Little God (W. Graham), 1970
Angels Fell (Fischer), 1950
Angels in the Snow (Lambert), 1969
Angels of Darkness (s Woolrich), 1979
Angels of Doom (Charteris), 1932
Angels of September (Greeley), 1986
Angel's Ransom (Dodge), 1956
Angel's Share (Irvine), 1989
Anger of Fear (Jeffries, as Ashford), 1978
Angle of Attack (Burns), 1979
Angry Amazons (C. Brown), 1972
Angry Battalion (H. Harris), 1976
Angry Canary (Dent, as Robeson), 1986
Angry Dream (Brewer), 1957
Angry Ghost (Dent, as Robeson), 1977
Angry Island (Royce), 1963
Angry Millionaire (Jepson), 1968
Angry Mountain (H. Innes), 1950
Anhalt, Mici series (L. O'Donnell), from 1977
Animal-Lover's Book of Beastly Murder (s Highsmith), 1975
Anna the Adventuress (Oppenheim), 1904
Anna, Where Are You? (Wentworth), 1951
Annalisa (S. Forbes, as Rydell), 1959
Annalise Experiment (W. Roberts), 1985
Annam Jewel (Wentworth), 1924
Anne Belinda (Wentworth), 1927
Annette of the Argonne (Le Queux), 1916
Annexation Society (J. Fletcher), 1916
Annihilators (D. Hamilton), 1983
Annihilist (Dent, as Robeson), 1968
Anniversary Murder (Phillpotts), 1936
Announcer's Holiday (s Gielgud), 1940
Annulet of Gilt (P. Taylor), 1938
Anodyne Necklace (Grimes), 1983
Another Day—Another Death (Stein, as Bagby), 1968
Another Death in Venice (Hill), 1976
Another Little Drink (Cheyney), 1940
Another Man's Life (Head), 1953
Another Man's Murder (Eberhart), 1957
Another Man's Poison (Straker), 1983
Another Man's Wife (Lowndes), 1934
Another Morgue Heard From (F. Davis), 1954
Another Part of the City (McBain), 1985
Another Way of Dying (Clifford), 1968

Another Way to Die (Michael Collins, as Crowe), 1972
Another Woman's House (Eberhart), 1947
Another Woman's Shoes (Durbridge), 1965
Answered (Hume), 1915
Antagonists (Haggard), 1964
Antidote to Venom (Crofts), 1938
Anxious Conspirator (Underwood), 1965
Any Man's Death (Estleman), 1986
Any Shape or Form (E. Daly), 1945
Anybody But Anne (Wells), 1914
Anybody's Pearls (Footner), 1929
Anything But Saintly (Deming), 1963
Anything but the Truth (Underwood), 1978
Anything But the Truth (Wells), 1925
Anything for a Quiet Life (s M. Gilbert), 1990
Anything to Declare? (Crofts), 1957
Ape, A Dog, and a Serpent (Kersh), 1945
Appearance of Evil (J. Anderson), 1977
Appearances of Death (Linington, as Shannon), 1977
Apple Tree (s du Maurier), 1952
Appleby, John series (M. Innes), from 1936
Applegreen Cat (Crane), 1943
Appointment at Nine (Doris Disney), 1947
Appointment in Cairo (Brewer), 1970
Appointment in Hell (Brewer), 1961
Appointment in Vienna (Gainham), 1958
Appointment with Death (Christie), 1938
Appointment with Yesterday (Fremlin), 1972
Apprehensive Dog (Bailey), 1942
April Evil (J. MacDonald), 1956
April Rainers (Anthea Fraser), 1989
April Robin Murders (McBain, Rice), 1958
April Shroud (Hill), 1975
Aquarius, My Evil (Avallone, as de Pre), 1972
Aquitaine Progression (Ludlum), 1984
Arabesque (Household), 1948
Arabian Nights Murder (J. Carr), 1936
Arafat Is Next! (L. Black), 1975
Aragon, Tom series (Millar), 1976
Araway Oath (Herbert Adams), 1942
Archangel (Seymour), 1982
Archer, Lew series (Macdonald), from 1949
Area of Suspicion (J. MacDonald), 1954
Arena (Haggard), 1961
Argand, Jan series (Rathbone), from 1979
Argentina Deadline (Pendleton), 1982
Argentina Scramble (Pendleton), 1982
Ariel (Block), 1980
Arigato (Condon), 1972
Aristo Autos series (Leasor), from 1969
Arizona Ambush (Pendleton), 1977
Arlette (Freeling), 1981
Arm of the Law (Underwood), 1959
Armadale (Collins, appendix), 1866
Armchair in Hell (H. Kane), 1948
Armitage Secret (Carmichael, as Howard), 1959
Arms for Adonis (Jay), 1960
Arms of Kali (Murphy), 1985
Armstrong (J. Fraser, as Whitney), 1973
Army of the Dead (F. Davis, as Steele), 1966
Around Dark Corners (s Pentecost), 1970
A.R.P. Mystery (Perowne), 1939
Arranways Mystery (E. Wallace), 1932
Arrest and Trial (Daniels), 1963
Arrest These Men! (Perowne), 1932
Arrival in Suspicion (Harvester), 1953
Arrow Pointing Nowhere (E. Daly), 1944

Arrows of Chance (Punshon), 1917
Arrows of Desire (Household), 1985
Arsenal Stadium Mystery (Gribble), 1939
Arsenic in Richmond (Ford, as Frome), 1934
Art Studio Murders (Aarons, as Ronns), 1950
Artful Egg (McClure), 1984
Arthur's Night (Straker), 1976
Artificial Man (Davies), 1965
Artist Dies (Rhode), 1956
Artists in Crime (Marsh), 1938
As a Favor (Dunlap), 1984
As a Man Lives (Oppenheim), 1898
As a Thief in the Night (Freeman), 1928
As Bad as I Am (Ard), 1959
As Empty as Hate (Creasey, as Halliday), 1972
As for the Woman (Berkeley, as Iles), 1939
As Good as Dead (Dewey), 1946
As I Was Going to St. Ives (Hocking), 1937
As Lonely as the Damned (Creasey, as Halliday), 1971
As Merry as Hell (Creasey, as Halliday), 1973
As October Dies (K. Davis), 1987
As Old as Cain (Crossen, as Chaber), 1954
As We Forgive Them (Le Queux), 1904
Ascent Into Hell (Greeley), 1983
Ascent of D-13 (Garve), 1969
Asch, Jacob series (Lyons), from 1974
Aseptic Murders (C. Brown), 1972
A.S.F. (Rhode), 1924
Ashenden (s Maugham), 1928
Ashes of Loda (Garve), 1965
Ashes to Ashes (Lathen), 1971
Ashes to Ashes (Pendleton), 1986
Ask a Policeman (Berkeley, Kennedy, G. Mitchell, Rhode,
    Sayers), 1933
Ask a Policeman (Carnac, as Lorac), 1955
Ask for Me Tomorrow (Millar), 1976
Ask Miss Mott (s Oppenheim), 1936
Ask No Mercy (Perowne), 1937
Ask the Cards a Question (Muller), 1982
Ask the Rattlesnake (Loraine), 1975
Ask the Right Question (Lewin), 1971
Asking for It (Coulter, as Mayo), 1971
Asking for Trouble (Meynell), 1931
Asking Price (Cecil), 1966
Asking Price (Hilton), 1983
Asphalt Jungle (Burnett), 1949
Assassin (Anthony), 1970
Assassin (J. Anderson), 1969
Assassin (Jepson), 1956
Assassin Who Gave Up His Gun (Cunningham), 1969
Assassination Brigade (Chastain), 1973
Assassination Bureau Ltd (Fish), 1963
Assassination Day (Royce, as Jacks), 1976
Assassination File (s J. Gardner), 1974
Assassins (Pentecost), 1955
Assassins Don't Die in Bed (Avallone), 1968
Assassins Have Starry Eyes (D. Hamilton), 1966
Assassins Play-Off (Murphy), 1975
Assassins Road (Harvester), 1965
Assault and Matrimony (J. Anderson), 1980
Assault on a Queen (Finney), 1959
Assault on Agathon (Caillou), 1972
Assault on Aimata (Caillou), 1975
Assault on Fellawi (Caillou), 1972
Assault on Kolchak (Caillou), 1969
Assault on Loveless (Caillou), 1969
Assault on Ming (Caillou), 1970

Assault on Soho (Pendleton), 1971
Assault with Intent (Kienzle), 1982
Assignment (Wahlöö, trans), 1965
Assignment Abacus (Davies), 1975
Assignment in Brittany (MacInnes), 1942
Assignment in Guiana (Coxe), 1942
Assignment K (Carmichael, as Howard), 1968
Assignment: Murder (D. Hamilton), 1956
Assignment series (Aarons), from 1955
Assignment series (McCutchan, as Galway), from 1963
Assignment to Vengeance (Cleeve), 1961
Assisi Murders (Holme), 1985
Assize of the Dying (s Ellis Peters, as Pargeter), 1958
Astonishing Adventure of Jane Smith (Wentworth), 1923
At a Farthing's Rate (Harvester, as Gibbs), 1943
At Bertram's Hotel (Christie), 1965
At Close Quarters (Seymour), 1987
At Death's Door (Barnard), 1988
At Death's Door (Bruce), 1955
At Large (Hornung), 1902
At One Fell Swoop (Palmer), 1951
At Sixty Miles an Hour (Chance, as Drummond), 1945
At Some Forgotten Door (Doris Disney), 1966
At the Cedars (Hocking), 1949
At the Gai-Moulin (Simenon, trans), 1951
At the Hands of Another (Lyons), 1983
At the Lake of Sudden Death (Holme), 1987
At the Sign of the Sword (Le Queux), 1915
At the Villa Rose (A. Mason), 1910
Atavar (Reeve), 1924
Athabasca (MacLean), 1980
Atlantic City (Murphy), 1979
Atlantic Fury (H. Innes), 1962
Atomic Murder (Gribble), 1947
Atoms and Evil (s Bloch), 1962
Atropos (DeAndrea), 1990
Attack Alarm (H. Innes), 1941
Attending Physician (Lathen, as Dominic), 1980
Attending Truth (Punshon), 1952
Attorney (Masur), 1973
Atwell, Nick series (Underwood), from 1975
Auber File (Bush, as Home), 1953
Audley, Dr. David series (Price), from 1970
Aunt Beardie (Shearing), 1940
Aunt Jeanne (Simenon, trans), 1953
Aunt Miranda's Murder (Chance), 1951
Auprès de ma Blonde (Freeling), 1972
Auriol (J. Anderson), 1982
Aurora Floyd (Braddon, appendix), 1863
Austen, Inspector William series (Hocking), from 1939
Author Bites the Dust (Upfield), 1948
Author in Distress (Wills), 1934
Authorized Murder (Asimov), 1976
Autobiography of an English Detective (Waters, appendix),
    1863
Autumn Dead (Gorman), 1987
Autumn Heroes (Royce, as Jacks), 1977
Avalanche Express (C. Forbes), 1976
Avenger (E. Wallace), 1926
Avenger (H. Kane), 1975
Avenger (Halliday, as Blood), 1952
Avenger (Oppenheim), 1908
Avengers (Verner, as Steele), 1935
Avenging Angel (Burns), 1983
Avenue of the Dead (Anthony), 1981
Aveyard, Inspector Bill series (J. Fraser), from 1968
Awake Deborah! (Phillpotts), 1940

Away Went the Little Fish (Bennett), 1946
Away with Them to Prison (Woods), 1985
Awful Dynasty (Dent, as Robeson), 1988
Awful Egg (Dent, as Robeson), 1978
Awkward Lie (M. Innes), 1971
Ax (McBain), 1964
Axe to Grind (E. Gardner, as Fair), 1951
Axwater (Butler, as Melville), 1978
Azrael (DeAndrea), 1987

B as in Banshee (Treat), 1940
"B" Is for Burglar (S. Grafton), 1985
Babe with the Twistable Arm (Stein, as Stone), 1962
Babes in the Woods (L. O'Donnell), 1965
Baby Blue Rip-Off (Max Collins), 1983
Baby Face (Gray), 1959
Baby in the Icebox (s J. Cain), 1981
Baby Merchants (L. O'Donnell), 1975
Baby, You're Guilt-Edged (C. Brown), 1956
Babylon South (Cleary), 1989
Babysitter (Coburn), 1979
Bachelors Get Lonely (E. Gardner, as Fair), 1961
Bachelors of Broken Hill (Upfield), 1950
Back in the Real World (Albert), 1986
Back of the North Wind (Freeling), 1983
Back Room Girl (Durbridge), 1950
Back Room in Somers Town (Malcolm), 1984
Backfire (Dan Marlowe), 1961
Backfire (Egleton), 1979
Background for Murder (S. Smith), 1942
Background to Danger (Ambler), 1937
Backing Winds (Bell), 1951
Backlash (Gosling), 1989
Backlash (Pentecost, as Philips), 1976
Backlash (Russell), 1981
Backstage Mystery (O. Cohen), 1930
Backtrack (Hansen), 1982
Backup Men (Thomas), 1971
Backwoods Teaser (Brewer), 1960
Backwoods Tramp (Whittington), 1959
Bad April (A. Ross), 1984
Bad Blonde (Webb), 1956
Bad Boy (Thompson), 1953
Bad Circle (Chance), 1985
Bad Company (Cody), 1982
Bad Die Young (Chambers), 1967
Bad Dream of Death (Chance), 1972
Bad for Business (Stout), 1940
Bad-News Man (McMullen), 1986
Bad Penny (Blackburn), 1985
Bad Ronald (J. Vance), 1973
Bad Samaritan (Gault), 1982
Bad Scene (Copper), 1987
Bad Trip (Roos), 1971
Badge of Evil (Miller, as Masterson), 1956
Badger's Daughter (Rae, as Crawford), 1971
Baeier, Kate series (Slovo), from 1984
Baer, Ed and Warren series (Resnicow), from 1987
Bag Man (McAuliffe), 1979
Bahama Crisis (Bagley), 1980
Bahamas Murder Case (Ford), 1952
Bain, Sherrif Joe series (J. Vance), from 1966
Bait (L. Black), 1966
Bait (Uhnak), 1968
Bait for Killer (Stein, as Bagby), 1967
Bait for Murder (K. Knight), 1948
Bait Money (Max Collins), 1973

Bait on the Hook (Parrish), 1983
Baker, Larry series (C. Brown), from 1963
Balance of Power (Murphy), 1981
Balaoo (Leroux, trans), 1913
Balcony (Dorothy Disney), 1940
Baley, Elijah series (Asimov), from 1954
Balkan Spy (B. Newman, as Betteridge), 1942
Ballad of Loving Jenny (C. Brown), 1963
Ballad of the Running Man (S. Smith), 1961
Balloon Man (Armstrong), 1968
Ballot Box Murders (Strange), 1943
Baltic Business (Corris), 1988
Balzic, Mario series (Constantine), from 1972
Bamboo Blonde (Hughes), 1941
Bamboo Prison (Harvester, as Gibbs), 1961
Bamboo Screen (Harvester), 1955
Banbury Bog (P. Taylor), 1938
Bandaged Nude (Finnegan), 1946
Bandbox (L. Vance), 1912
Bandicoot (Condon), 1978
Bandit (Charteris), 1929
Bandits (Leonard), 1987
Bandits (Whalley), 1986
Bang! Bang! You're Dead (Drummond), 1973
Banion, Dan series (Finnegan), from 1946
Bank Job (Fish, as Pike), 1974
Bank Manager (Oppenheim), 1934
Bank Shot (Westlake), 1972
Bank with the Bamboo Door (Olsen, as Hitchens), 1965
Banker (Francis), 1982
Banker's Bones (Scherf), 1968
Banking on Death (Lathen), 1961
Banner for Pegasus (Bonett), 1951
Banquet Ceases (Fitt), 1949
Banshee (Millar), 1983
Baptism for the Dead (Irvine), 1988
Bar Sinister (Roth, as Ballard), 1960
Barbara on Her Own (E. Wallace), 1926
Barbarous Coast (Macdonald), 1956
Barbed Wire Noose (Harold Adams), 1987
Barboza Credentials (Driscoll), 1976
Bardel's Murder (McGirr), 1973
Bardelow's Heir (Vickers), 1933
Bare Trap (F. Kane), 1952
Barely Seen (F. Kane), 1964
Bargain with Death (Pentecost), 1974
Barnaby, Detective Chief Inspector Tom series (C. Graham), from 1987
Barnaby Rudge (Dickens, appendix), 1841
Barney, Al series (Chase), from 1968
Baron series (Creasey, as Morton), from 1937
Baron, Bruce series (Daniels), from 1967
Baron, Hugo series (Tripp, as Brett), from 1963
Baron Trigault's Vengeance (Gaboriau, trans), 1913
Baroque (L. Vance), 1923
Barotique Mystery (Coxe), 1936
Barrakee Mystery (Upfield), 1929
Barrier Island (J. MacDonald), 1986
Bartenstein Case (J. Fletcher), 1913
Bartenstein Mystery (J. Fletcher), 1927
Bascombe, Carver series (K. Davis), from 1976
Base Case (Rathbone), 1981
Basement Room (s Greene), 1935
Basil (Collins, appendix), 1852
Basket Case (McInerny), 1987
Basle Express (Coles), 1956
Basnett, Andrew series (Ferrars), from 1983

Bass Derby Murder (K. Knight), 1949
Bastard (Wainwright), 1976
Bastard's Name Was Bristow (Scott), 1977
Bastian, Lieutenant Andy series (Wormser), from 1961
Bat (Rinehart), 1926
Bat Flies Low (Rohmer), 1935
Bat Out of Hell (Durbridge), 1972
Bat-Wing (Rohmer), 1921
Bath Mysteries (Punshon), 1936
Bathtub Murder Case (Punshon), 194?
Bats Fly at Dusk (E. Gardner, as Fair), 1942
Bats in the Belfry (Carnac, as Lorac), 1937
Battle Mask (Pendleton), 1970
Battle of Basinghall Street (Oppenheim), 1935
Battle of Nerves (Simenon, trans), 1951
Battle of the Singing Men (s Kersh), 1944
Battle Road (Harvester), 1967
Battle, Superintendent series (Christie), from 1925
Battling Prophet (Upfield), 1956
Batts, Singer series (Dewey), from 1944
Baxter Letters (Olsen, as Hitchens), 1971
Bay City Blast (Murphy), 1979
Bay Prowler (Malzberg, as Barry), 1973
Bayou Road (Eberhart), 1979
Be a Good Boy (J. Fleming), 1972
Be All and End All (Berckman), 1976
Be Buried in the Rain (Elizabeth Peters, as Michaels), 1985
Be Careful How You Live (Lacy), 1958
Be Kind to the Killer (Wade), 1952
Be My Victim (Hunt, as Dietrich), 1956
Be Shot for Sixpence (M. Gilbert), 1956
Beach Girls (J. MacDonald), 1959
Beach of Atonement (Upfield), 1930
Beacon in the Night (Ballinger), 1958
Beaded Banana (Scherf), 1978
Beagle, Otis series (Gruber), from 1941
Bean Ball (Resnicow), 1989
Bean Revel (L. Vance), 1920
Bear Island (MacLean), 1971
Bear Raid (Follett), 1976
Bearpit (Freemantle), 1988
Beast in View (Millar), 1955
Beast Must Die (Blake), 1938
Beast with Red Hands (Avallone, as Stuart), 1973
Beastly Business (Blackburn), 1982
Beasts of Valhalla (Chesbro), 1985
Beat Back the Tide (Olsen, as Hitchens), 1954
Beat Not the Bones (Jay), 1952
Beautiful Birthday Cake (Scherf), 1971
Beautiful But Dangerous (Hanshew), 1891
Beautiful Dead (Pentecost), 1973
Beautiful Derelict (Wells), 1935
Beautiful Golden Frame (Chambers), 1980
Beautiful Kate (Thornburg), 1982
Beautiful Scourge (Gaboriau, trans), 1883
Beautiful Trap (Ballinger), 1955
Beauty and the Beast (McBain), 1982
Beauty and the Policeman (s Horler), 1933
Beauty Is a Beast (K. Knight), 1959
Beauty Marks the Spot (Roos), 1951
Beauty Queen Killer (Creasey), 1956
Because of the Cats (Freeling), 1963
Because the Night (Ellroy), 1985
Becca's Child (W. Roberts), 1972
Beckoning Door (Seeley), 1950
Beckoning Dream (Berckman), 1955
Beckoning Lady (Allingham), 1955

Bed Disturbed (Holt, as Ford), 1952
Bedelia (Caspary), 1945
Bedford Row Mystery (J. Fletcher), 1925
Bedroom Bolero (Avallone), 1963
Bedrooms Have Windows (E. Gardner, as Fair), 1949
Beef, Sergeant William series (Bruce), from 1936
Before I Die (L. White), 1964
Before I Die (McCloy), 1963
Before I Wake (Halliday, as Debrett), 1949
Before It's Too Late (Palmer, as Stewart), 1950
Before Midnight (Stout), 1955
Before the Fact (Berkeley, as Iles), 1932
Before the Storm (Lowndes), 1941
Beggar's Choice (Branson), 1953
Beggar's Choice (Wentworth), 1930
Begin, Murderer! (Cory), 1951
Beginner's Luck (Garve, as Somers), 1958
Beginning with a Bash (P. Taylor, as Tilton), 1937
Behind Closed Doors (Green), 1888
Behind That Curtain (Biggers), 1928
Behind That Mask (Keeler), 1933
Behind the Bronze Door (Le Queux), 1923
Behind the Crimson Blind (J. Carr, as Dickson), 1952
Behind the German Lines (Le Queux), 1917
Behind the Monocle (s J. Fletcher), 1928
Behind the Panel (J. Fletcher), 1931
Behind the Throne (Le Queux), 1905
Behold, Here's Poison! (Heyer), 1936
Behold This Woman (Goodis), 1947
Bejewelled Death (Babson), 1981
Believe This, You'll Believe Anything (Chase), 1975
Believed Violent (Chase), 1968
Bell in the Fog (Strange), 1936
Bell of Death (A. Gilbert), 1939
Bella Donna Was Poison (C. Brown), 1957
Bellamy Trial (F. Hart), 1927
Bellamy, Sir Harker series (Horler), from 1932
Belle of Toorak (Hornung), 1900
Bells for the Dead (K. Knight), 1942
Bells of Bicetre (Simenon, trans), 1964
Bells of Doom (Verner, as Stuart), 1936
Beloved Enemy (Blackstock, as Allardyce), 1958
Below Suspicion (J. Carr), 1949
Belting Inheritance (Symons), 1965
Benasque, Mike series (Caillou), from 1960
Bencolin, Henri series (J. Carr), from 1930
Benedict, Jerry series (Aarons, as Ronns), from 1947
Benefit Performance (Sale), 1946
Benefits of Death (Jeffries), 1963
Benevent Treasure (Wentworth), 1954
Bengal Fire (Blochman), 1937
Benighted (Priestley), 1927
Benjamin, Derek series (Garfield), from 1972
Bennett (Cory), 1977
Bennett, Reid series (Wood), from 1983
Bennion, Major Roger series (Herbert Adams), from 1928
Benny Muscles In (Rabe), 1955
Benson Murder Case (Van Dine), 1926
Bent Copper (Jeffries, as Ashford), 1971
Bent, John series (Branson), from 1941
Bent Man (Maling), 1975
Berenice (Oppenheim), 1907
Beresford, Tuppence and Tommy series (Christie), from 1922
Berkley, George Stanhope series (Meynell), from 1928
Berkshire Mystery (Cole), 1930
Berlin Ending (Hunt), 1973
Berlin Game (Deighton), 1983

Berlin Memorandum (Hall), 1965
Bernal, Superintendant Luis series (Serafín), from 1979
Bernhardt, Alan series (Wilcox), from 1988
Bertie series (Lovesey), from 1987
Beryl of the Biplane (s Le Queux), 1917
Besides the Wench Is Dead (Erskine), 1973
Besserley, General series (s Oppenheim), from 1935
Best Laid Plans (Hocking), 1950
Best Man to Die (Rendell), 1969
Best of Her Sex (Hume), 1894
Best That Ever Did It (Lacy), 1955
Bethlehem Road (A. Perry), 1990
Betrayal (Oppenheim), 1904
Betrayals (Freemantle), 1989
Betrayed by Death (Jeffries, as Alding), 1982
Betrayers (D. Hamilton), 1966
Better Angels (McCarry), 1979
Better Class of Business (Scott), 1976
Better Corpses (C. Daly), 1940
Better Dead (Bonett), 1964
Better Dead (Stein, as Bagby), 1978
Better Mousetraps (s Lutz), 1988
Better Off Dead (Bonett), 1964
Better Off Dead (McCloy), 1951
Better Off Dead (McMullen), 1982
Better to Eat You (Armstrong), 1954
Better Wed Than Dead (H. Kane), 1970
Betty (Simenon, trans), 1975
Beverly Malibu (K. Forrest), 1989
Beware of Johnny Washington (Durbridge), 1951
Beware of Midnight (Welcome), 1961
Beware of the Banquet (Aiken), 1966
Beware of the Trains (s Crispin), 1953
Beware the Curves (E. Gardner, as Fair), 1956
Beware the Lady (Woolrich), 1953
Beware the Pale Horse (Benson), 1951
Beware the Young Stranger (Powell, as Queen), 1965
Beware Young Lovers (Pentecost), 1980
Beware Your Neighbour (Rhode, as Burton), 1951
Bey, Nur series (Rathbone), from 1966
Beyond a Reasonable Doubt (C. Grafton), 1950
Beyond Blame (Greenleaf), 1986
Beyond Dover (s Gielgud), 1940
Beyond Reasonable Doubt (Hull), 1941
Beyond the Atlas (Trench), 1963
Beyond the Dark (Reilly, as Abbey), 1944
Beyond the Grave (Muller, Pronzini), 1986
Beyond the Night (s Woolrich), 1959
Beyond This Point Are Monsters (Millar), 1970
Bid the Babe By-By (C. Brown), 1956
Bier for a Chaser (Crossen, as Foster), 1959
Big Apple (Follett, as Myles), 1975
Big Bedroom (Aarons, as Ronns), 1959
Big Bite (C. Williams), 1956
Big Black (Follett, as Myles), 1974
Big Bob (Simenon, trans), 1969
Big Bounce (Leonard), 1969
Big Bow Mystery (Zangwill, appendix), 1892
Big Business Murder (Cole), 1935
Big Bust (Lacy), 1969
Big Call (Creasey, as Ashe), 1964
Big Caper (L. White), 1955
Big Chill (Copper), 1972
Big City Girl (C. Williams), 1951
Big Clock (Fearing), 1946
Big Dive (Crossen), 1959
Big Dream (Fisher), 1970

Big Drop (s Corris), 1985
Big Ear (Sterling), 1953
Big Enchilada (Morse), 1982
Big Fear (Offord), 1953
Big Fear (Boucher, as Durrant), 1953
Big Fish (Beeding), 1938
Big Fix (Lacy), 1960
Big Fix (McBain, as Hunter), 1952
Big Fix (Simon), 1973
Big Foot (E. Wallace), 1927
Big Footprints (H. Innes), 1977
Big Four (Christie), 1927
Big Four (s E. Wallace), 1929
Big Frame (The Gordons), 1957
Big Gamble (Coxe), 1958
Big Gold Dream (Himes), 1960
Big Goodbye (Chambers), 1962
Big Greed (McGirr, as Giles), 1966
Big Grouse (D. Clark), 1986
Big Guy (Miller), 1953
Big Hand for the Corpse (Stein, as Bagby), 1953
Big Heat (McGivern), 1953
Big Hit (Follett, as Myles), 1975
Big Kayo (Wainwright), 1979
Big Kill (Spillane), 1951
Big Killing (s Morland), 1946
Big Kiss-Off (Keene), 1954
Big Knockover (s Hammett), 1966
Big Knock-Over (Hammett), 1948
Big Man (McBain, as Marsten), 1959
Big Man (McIlvanney), 1985
Big Midget Murders (Rice), 1942
Big Money (Masur), 1954
Big Money (Turnbull), 1984
Big Needle (Follett, as Myles), 1974
Big Night (Ellin), 1950
Big Nowhere (Ellroy), 1988
Big Pick-Up (Hall, as Trevor), 1955
Big Radium Mystery (Creasey, as Cooke), 1936
Big Rip-Off (Copper), 1979
Big Shot (Packard), 1929
Big Shot (Treat), 1951
Big Sin (Webb), 1952
Big Sleep (Chandler), 1939
Big Snatch (Carmichael, as Howard), 1958
Big Stan (Burnett, as Monahan), 1953
Big Stiffs (Avallone), 1977
Big Tickle (Wainwright), 1969
Big Wind for Summer (G. Black), 1975
Bigger They Are (D. Clark, as Ditton), 1973
Bigger They Come (E. Gardner, as Fair), 1939
Bilbao Looking Glass (MacLeod), 1983
Bill for the Use of a Body (Wheatley), 1964
Bill series (John Burke), from 1985
Billboard Madonna (Hall, as Trevor), 1960
Billingsate Shoal (Boyer), 1982
Billion-Dollar Brain (Deighton), 1966
Billion Dollar Killing (Erdman), 1973
Billion Dollar Sure Thing (Erdman), 1973
Billy Cantrell Case (Waugh), 1981
Bimbâshi Barûk of Egypt (Rohmer), 1944
Bimbo Heaven (Albert), 1990
Bimini Run (Hunt), 1949
Binary (Crichton, as Lange), 1972
Bind (Ellin), 1970
Bindlestiff (Pronzini), 1983
Bird in a Guilt-Edged Cage (C. Brown), 1963

Bird in the Hand (Cleeves), 1986
Bird in the Net (Parrish), 1988
Bird of Paradise (Oppenheim), 1936
Bird of Prey (Canning), 1951
Bird Walking Weather (Stein, as Bagby), 1939
Birdcage (Canning), 1978
Birds (s du Maurier), 1968
Birds in the Belfry (Payne), 1966
Birds of a Feather (Canning), 1985
Birds of a Feather Affair (Avallone), 1966
Birds of Death (Dent, as Robeson), 1989
Birds of Ill Omen (K. Knight), 1948
Birds of Prey (Braddon, appendix), 1867
Birds of Prey (Fairlie), 1932
Birdseye, Miriam series (Spain), from 1949
Birdwatcher's Quarry (Coles), 1956
Birkett, Chief Inspector Sam series (Payne), from 1962
Birth of a Dark Soul (Cleeve), 1953
Birthday Gift (Curtiss), 1975
Birthday Gifts (s Cole), 1946
Birthday, Deathday (Pentecost), 1972
Bishop as Pawn (McInerny), 1978
Bishop in Check (Hall, as Rattray), 1953
Bishop Murder Case (Van Dine), 1929
Bishop of Hell (s Shearing, Bowen), 1949
Bishop Pendle (Hume), 1900
Bishop, Robin series (Homes), from 1936
Bishop's Crime (Bailey), 1940
Bishop's Pawn (R. Perry), 1979
Bishop's Secret (Hume), 1900
Bismarck Herrings (G. Mitchell, as Torrie), 1971
Bit of a Shunt up the River (Cory), 1974
Bitch (Brewer), 1958
Bits and Pieces (s Masterman), 1961
Bitter Conquest (Blackstock), 1959
Bitter Finish (Barnes), 1983
Bitter Harvest (Haggard), 1971
Bitter Medicine (Paretsky), 1987
Bitter Path of Death (Audemars), 1982
Bitter Tea (G. Black), 1972
Bittermeads Mystery (Punshon), 1922
Bizarre Murders (Queen), 1962
Black (E. Wallace), 1930
Black (s E. Wallace), 1929
Black Abbot (E. Wallace), 1926
Black Alibi (Woolrich), 1942
Black Amber (Whitney), 1964
Black and the Red (Paul), 1956
Black Angel (Woolrich), 1943
Black Angus (Thornburg), 1978
Black Arrows (Beeding), 1938
Black as He's Painted (Marsh), 1974
Black August (Wheatley), 1934
Black Bag (L. Vance), 1908
Black Baroness (Wheatley), 1940
Black Beadle (Carnac, as Lorac), 1939
Black, Black Witch (Dent, as Robeson), 1981
Black Box (Oppenheim), 1915
Black Box (Shiel), 1930
Black Cabinet (Wentworth), 1925
Black Camel (Biggers), 1929
Black Camelot (Kyle), 1978
Black Carnation (Hume), 1892
Black Charade (John Burke), 1977
Black Chariots (Goulart, as Robeson), 1974
Black Cherry Blues (James Lee Burke), 1989
Black Curtain (Woolrich), 1941

Black Cypress (Crane), 1948
Black Dahlia (Ellroy), 1987
Black Death (A. Gilbert), 1953
Black Death (Herbert Adams), 1939
Black Doctor (s Doyle), 1925
Black Door (C. Adams), 1941
Black Door (Wilcox), 1967
Black Dudley Murder (Allingham), 1930
Black Envelope (Ford, as Frome), 1937
Black-Eyed Stranger (Armstrong), 1951
Black Flamingo (Canning), 1962
Black Fox (Heard), 1950
Black Friday (Goodis), 1954
Black Gang (Sapper), 1922
Black Gangster (Goines), 1972
Black Gangster (Verner, as Steele), 1934
Black Gardenia (Paul), 1952
Black Girl Lost (Goines), 1973
Black Girl, White Girl (Moyes), 1989
Black Glass City (Pentecost, as Philips), 1965
Black Hand (s Reeve), 1912
Black Hawthorn (Strange), 1933
Black Heart (Creasey, as Cooke), 1935
Black Heart (Horler), 1927
Black Hearts and Slow Dancing (Emerson), 1988
Black Hearts Murder (Deming, as Queen), 1970
Black Highway (Chance), 1947
Black House (s Highsmith), 1981
Black House in Harley Street (J. Fletcher), 1923
Black Hunchback (Verner), 1933
Black Ice Score (Westlake, as Stark), 1968
Black Image (Hume), 1918
Black Is the Colour of My True-Love's Heart (Ellis Peters),
    1967
Black Is the Fashion for Dying (Latimer), 1959
Black Italian (Jepson), 1954
Black Lace Hangover (C. Brown), 1966
Black Land, White Land (Bailey), 1937
Black Leather Murders (Rutherford), 1966
Black Mafia (Rabe), 1974
Black Mail (Doris Disney), 1958
Black Marble (Wambaugh), 1978
Black Market (B. Newman), 1942
Black Mask (s Hornung), 1901
Black Master (Gibson, as Grant), 1974
Black Mirror (Benson), 1957
Black Money (Macdonald), 1966
Black Moon (Randisi), 1989
Black Mountain (Stout), 1954
Black Night in Red Square (Kaminsky), 1983
Black Night Murders (Wells), 1941
Black Orchid (Aarons, as Ronns), 1959
Black Orchid (Meyer), 1977
Black Orchids (Stout), 1942
Black-Out Murders (Gribble, as Grex), 1940
Black Owl (Le Queux), 1926
Black Patch (Hume), 1906
Black Path of Fear (Woolrich), 1944
Black Plumes (Allingham), 1940
Black Rain (Simenon, trans), 1947
Black Rainbow (Elizabeth Peters, as Michaels), 1982
Black Room (C. Wilson), 1971
Black Rose Murder (McGuire), 1932
Black Sambo Affair (Gielgud), 1972
Black Satchel (Keeler), 1931
Black Seraphim (M. Gilbert), 1983
Black Sheep, Run (Spicer), 1951

Black Sheep, White Lamb (D. Davis), 1963
Black Shrike (MacLean), 1961
Black Skull (Verner), 1933
Black Skull (Verner, as Stuart), 1929
Black Spectacles (J. Carr), 1939
Black Spiders (Creasey), 1957
Black Stage (A. Gilbert), 1945
Black Sunday (Thomas Harris), 1975
Black Tide (H. Innes), 1982
Black Tower (James), 1975
Black Unicorn (Drummond), 1959
Black Venus Contract (Atlee), 1975
Black Watcher (Oppenheim), 1912
Black Widow (Chance), 1981
Black Widow (Quentin), 1952
Black Widow Weeps (C. Brown), 1953(?)
Black Widower (Moyes), 1975
Black Widowers series (s Asimov), from 1974
Black Windmill (Egleton), 1974
Black, Black Hearse (Ballinger, as Freyer), 1955
Black, Superintendent series (Chance), from 1935
Black, Thomas series (Emerson), from 1985
Black, White, and Brindled (s Phillpotts), 1923
Black-Out in Gretley (Priestley), 1942
Blackbird (Westlake, as Stark), 1969
Blackbirder (Hughes), 1943
Blackboard Jungle (McBain, as Hunter), 1954
Blackbourne Hall (Waugh, as Grandower), 1979
Blackheath Poisonings (Symons), 1978
Blacklight (B. Knox), 1967
Blacklist (A. Taylor), 1988
Blackmail North (McCutchan), 1978
Blackmailed (Le Queux), 1927
Blackmailers (Cecil), 1969
Blackmailers (Gaboriau, trans), 1907
Blackmailer's Summer (Whalley), 1990
Blackman's Wood (Oppenheim), 1929
Blackshirt series (Jeffries, as Graeme), from 1952
Blackshirt, Monsieur series (Graeme), from 1933
Blackstone, Edmund series (Lambert, as Falkirk), from 1972
Blackthorn House (Rhode), 1949
Blackwood, Riley series (Starrett), from 1935
Blade Is Bright (Horler), 1952
Blair, Margot series (K. Knight), from 1940
Blaise, Modesty series (P. O'Donnell), from 1965
Blake, Jonathan series (Chance), from 1966
Blake, Sexton series (Creasey), from 1939
Blake, Sexton series (Verner, as Stuart), from 1927
Blame the Dead (Lyall), 1972
Blanche Fury (Shearing), 1939
Blanco Case (Horler), 1950
Bland, Inspector series (Symons), from 1945
Blank Page (Constantine), 1974
Blank Wall (E. Holding), 1947
Blanket of the Dark (Sturrock, as Healey), 1976
Blast of Trumpets (Creasey, as Ashe), 1975
Blatchington, Everard series (Cole), from 1926
Blayde R.I.P (Wainwright), 1982
Blaze of Arms (Hall, as Fitzalan), 1967
Blaze of Roses (Hall, as Trevor), 1952
Blazing Affair (Avallone), 1966
Bleak House (Dickens, appendix), 1853
Bleeding Hearts (T. White), 1984
Bleeding House (Lawrence), 1950
Bleeding Scissors (Fischer), 1948
Bleke, The Butler (s Le Queux), 1924
Blessed Plot (Berckman), 1976

Blessing Way (Hillerman), 1970
Blessington Method (s Ellin), 1964
Blessington, Charles series (Sherwood), from 1949
Bleston Mystery (Kennedy), 1928
Blight (Creasey), 1968
Blind Alley (Simenon, trans), 1946
Blind Allies (Kendrick), 1954
Blind Barber (J. Carr), 1934
Blind Brag (Wainwright), 1988
Blind Corner (Yates), 1927
Blind Date for a Private Eye (Graeme), 1969
Blind Drifts (Clason), 1937
Blind Goddess (Train), 1926
Blind Hypnotist (McShane, as Lovell), 1976
Blind Love (Collins, appendix), 1890
Blind Man with a Pistol (Himes), 1969
Blind Man's Bluff (Johnson), 1987
Blind Man's Bluff (Kendrick), 1943
Blind Man's Buff (Futrelle), 1914
Blind Man's Eyes (Balmer), 1916
Blind Man's Garden (Warriner, as Troy), 1970
Blind Run (Freemantle), 1986
Blind Search (Linington, as Egan), 1977
Blind Side (Clifford), 1971
Blind Side (Wentworth), 1939
Blind Spot (Creasey), 1954
Blind Villain (Berckman), 1957
Blindfold (L. Fletcher), 1960
Blindfold (Wentworth), 1935
Blind-Girl's-Buff (Berckman), 1962
Blindside (Schorr), 1989
Bliss, Vicky series (Elizabeth Peters), from 1973
Blissberg, Harvey series (Rosen), from 1984
Blond Baboon (van de Wetering), 1978
Blonde (C. Brown), 1955
Blonde and Beautiful (Crossen, as Foster), 1955
Blonde and Johnny Malloy (Ard, as Kerr), 1958
Blonde Bait (Lacy), 1959
Blonde Bait (S. Marlowe), 1959
Blonde Betrayer (Godey), 1955
Blonde Cried Murder (Halliday), 1956
Blonde Died Dancing (Roos), 1956
Blonde for Murder (Gibson), 1948
Blonde in Black (Benson), 1958
Blonde in Suite 14 (Sterling), 1959
Blonde Lady (s Leblanc, trans), 1910
Blonde on a Broomstick (C. Brown), 1966
Blonde on Borrowed Time (Ballinger, as Sanborn), 1960
Blonde on the Rocks (C. Brown), 1963
Blonde on the Street Corner (Goodis), 1954
Blonde Verdict (C. Brown), 1956
Blonde with the Deadly Past (Seeley), 1955
Blonde Without Escort (Perowne), 1940
Blonde Wore Black (Chambers), 1968
Blonde, Bad, and Beautiful (C. Brown), 1957(?)
Blonde, Beautiful, and—Blam! (C. Brown), 1956
Blondes Die Young (McGivern, as Peters), 1952
Blondes' Requiem (Chase, as Marshall), 1945
Blondie Iscariot (Lustgarten), 1948
Blood and Judgement (M. Gilbert), 1959
Blood Brotherhood (Barnard), 1977
Blood Count (Linington, as Shannon), 1986
Blood Countess (Goulart, as Robeson), 1975
Blood Doesn't Tell (Barth), 1989
Blood Flies Upward (Ferrars), 1976
Blood Is a Beggar (Kyd), 1946
Blood Money (Hammett), 1943

Blood Money (Lewis), 1973
Blood Money (Max Collins), 1973
Blood of an Englishman (McClure), 1980
Blood of My Brother (S. Marlowe, as Thames), 1963
Blood of Poets (K. Davis), 1990
Blood of Vintage (Kyd), 1947
Blood on a Widow's Cross (J. Fraser), 1972
Blood on Baker Street (Boucher), 1953
Blood on Biscayne Bay (Halliday), 1946
Blood on Lake Louisa (Kendrick), 1934
Blood on the Black Market (Halliday), 1943
Blood on the Boards (Gault), 1953
Blood on the Bosom Devine (Kyd), 1948
Blood on the Desert (Rabe), 1958
Blood on the Happy Highway (Radley), 1983
Blood on the Knight (Thayer), 1952
Blood on the Moon (Copper), 1986
Blood on the Moon (Ellroy), 1984
Blood on the Stars (Halliday), 1948
Blood on the Stars (Morland), 1951
Blood on the Stars (Stein), 1964
Blood Red (Creasey, as Morton), 1960
Blood-Red Dream (Michael Collins), 1976
Blood Reign of the Dictator (F. Davis, as Steele), 1966
Blood Relation (A. Taylor), 1990
Blood Relatives (McBain), 1975
Blood Risk (Koontz, as Coffey), 1973
Blood Royal (Yates), 1929
Blood Run (Albert, as Al Conroy), 1973
Blood Run East (McCutchan), 1976
Blood Running Cold (J. Ross), 1968
Blood Runs Cold (s Bloch), 1961
Blood Shot (Paretsky), 1988
Blood Sky (s Nolan), 1990
Blood Sport (Francis), 1967
Blood Stone (Allegretto), 1988
Blood Test (J. Kellerman), 1986
Blood-Tie (Coulter), 1988
Blood Ties (Murphy), 1987
Blood Transfusion Murders (Propper), 1943
Blood upon the Snow (Lawrence), 1944
Blood Will Have Blood (Barnes), 1982
Blood Will Tell (Christie), 1952
Blood Will Tell (Potts), 1959
Blood Will Tell (Stein, as Bagby), 1950
Bloodspoor (Luard, as McVean), 1977
Bloodstain (Alexander), 1961
Bloodstained Bokhara (Gault), 1953
Bloodtide (B. Knox), 1982
Bloodwater (Michael Collins, as Crowe), 1974
Bloodworth, Leo and Serendipity Dahlquist series (Lochte), from 1985
Bloody Bokhara (Gault), 1952
Bloody Book of Law (Woods), 1984
Bloody Instructions (Woods), 1962
Bloody Marvellous (Rathbone), 1975
Bloody Medallion (Jessup, as Telfair), 1959
Bloody Moonlight (F. Brown), 1949
Bloody Passage (J. Higgins, as Graham), 1974
Bloody Sunrise (Spillane), 1965
Bloody Tower (Rhode), 1938
Bloody Wig Murders (Stein, as Bagby), 1942
Bloody Wood (M. Innes), 1966
Bloomer, Theo series (Hess, as Hadley), from 1986
Bloomsbury Treasure (Vickers, as Kyle), 1932
Bloomsbury Wonder (s T. Burke), 1929
Blossom (Vachss), 1990

Blow the House Down (Blackburn), 1970
Blow-Down (Blochman), 1939
Blowback (Pronzini), 1977
Blue Belle (Vachss), 1988
Blue Blood Will Out (Heald), 1974
Blue Bungalow (Le Queux), 1925
Blue City (Macdonald, as Millar), 1947
Blue Days and Fair (Harvester, as Gibbs), 1946
Blue Death (Michael Collins), 1975
Blue Diamond (Meade), 1901
Blue Door (s Starrett), 1930
Blue-Eyed Boy (Curzon), 1990
Blue Eyes (Charyn), 1975
Blue Fire (Whitney), 1961
Blue Geranium (Olsen, as Birkley), 1941
Blue Hammer (Macdonald), 1976
Blue Hand (E. Wallace), 1925
Blue Horse of Taxco (K. Knight), 1947
Blue Hour (Godey), 1948
Blue Ice (H. Innes), 1948
Blue Jay Summer (Hall, as Trevor), 1977
Blue John Diamond (Punshon), 1929
Blue Knight (Wambaugh), 1972
Blue Lamp (Willis), 1950
Blue Lenses (s du Maurier), 1970
Blue Mask series (Creasey, as Morton), 1937
Blue Movie Murders (Hoch, as Queen), 1972
Blue Murder (Bellem), 1938
Blue Murder (Watson), 1979
Blue Octavo (Blackburn), 1963
Blue Ribbon (s Woolrich, as Irish), 1949
Blue Room (Simenon, trans), 1964
Blue Scarab (s Freeman), 1924
Blue Smoke and Mirrors (Murphy), 1989
Blue Spectacles (Keeler), 1931
Blue Talisman (Hume), 1912
Blue Water Murder (Perowne, as Atkey), 1935
Blueback (B. Knox), 1969
Bluebeard's Seventh Wife (s Woolrich, as Irish), 1952
Bluebolt One (McCutchan), 1962
Bluefeather (Meynell), 1928
Bluegate Fields (A. Perry), 1984
Blueprint for Larceny (Chambers, as Chester), 1963
Blueprint for Murder (Garve, as Bax), 1948
Blues for the Prince (Spicer), 1950
Bluestocking (Drummond), 1985
Bluff (Herbert Adams), 1938
Blunderer (Highsmith), 1954
Blunt Darts (Healy), 1984
Blunt Instrument (Heyer), 1938
Blurred Reality (Lewis), 1985
Boat-House Riddle (Connington), 1931
Boat Off the Coast (Dobyns), 1987
Bodies (Barnard), 1986
Bodies Are Where You Find Them (Halliday), 1941
Bodies in Bedlam (Prather), 1951
Bodies of Water (Borthwick), 1990
Body (C. Brown), 1958
Body and Passion (Whittington, as Harrison), 1952
Body and Soul (McInerny), 1989
Body at Madman's Bend (Upfield), 1963
Body Beautiful (Ballinger), 1949
Body Beneath a Mandarin Tree (Crane), 1965
Body for a Buddy (Stein), 1981
Body for Sale (Deming), 1962
Body for the Bride (Stein, as Bagby), 1954
Body in Bedford Square (Ford, as Frome), 1935

Body in Cadiz Bay (Serafín), 1985
Body in the Basket (Stein, as Bagby), 1954
Body in the Beck (Cannan), 1952
Body in the Bed (Ballinger), 1948
Body in the Bed (Sterling), 1959
Body in the Billiard Room (Keating), 1987
Body in the Bonfire (Bush), 1936
Body in the Bunker (Herbert Adams), 1935
Body in the Dawn (Wills), 1938
Body in the Dumb River (Bellairs), 1961
Body in the Library (Christie), 1942
Body in the Safe (Vickers, as Kyle), 1937
Body in the Silo (R. Knox), 1934
Body in the Turl (Ford, as Frome), 1935
Body in the Volvo (Beck), 1987
Body Looks Familiar (Wormser), 1958
Body Lovers (Spillane), 1967
Body of a Girl (M. Gilbert), 1972
Body on Page One (Ames), 1951
Body on the Beam (A. Gilbert), 1932
Body on the Bench (Hughes), 1955
Body Politic (Aird), 1990
Body Search (Stein), 1978
Body Surrounded by Water (E. Wright), 1987
Body to Spare (Procter), 1962
Body Unidentified (Rhode), 1938
Body Unknown (Graeme), 1939
Bogart '48 (K. Davis), 1979
Bogey Men (s Bloch), 1963
Bognor, Simon series (Heald), from 1973
Bogue's Fortune (Symons), 1957
Bogus Buddha (Melville), 1990
Bohannon's Book (s Hansen), 1988
Bohemian Connection (Dunlap), 1985
Bolan, Mack series (Pendleton), from 1969
Bolero Murders (Avallone), 1972
Bolo, The Super-Spy (Le Queux), 1918
Bolt (Francis), 1986
Bomb Job (H. Kane), 1970
Bomb-Makers (s Le Queux), 1917
Bomb-Shell (Leblanc, trans), 1916
Bomb-Scare Flight 147 (Chambers), 1984
Bombay Mail (Blochman), 1934
Bombing Run (Stein), 1983
Bombshell (C. Brown), 1960
Bombship (B. Knox), 1980
Bonaparte, Inspector Napoleon "Bony" series (Upfield), from 1929
Bond of Black (Le Queux), 1899
Bond, James series (I. Fleming), from 1954
Bond, James series (J. Gardner), from 1981
Bonded Dead (Crossen, as Chaber), 1971
Bone (Chesbro), 1989
Bone and a Hank of Hair (Bruce), 1961
Bone Is Pointed (Upfield), 1938
Bonecrack (Francis), 1971
Bonegrinder (Lutz), 1977
Bones (Pronzini), 1985
Bones (s E. Wallace), 1915
Bones and Silence (Hill), 1990
Bones in London (s E. Wallace), 1921
Bones in the Barrow (Bell), 1953
Bones in the Brickfield (Rhode, as Burton), 1958
Bones in the Sand (Royce), 1967
Bones in the Wilderness (Bellairs), 1958
Bones of the River (s E. Wallace), 1923
Boodle (s Charteris), 1934

Book of All Power (E. Wallace), 1921
Book of Avis (Phillpotts), 1936
Book of Dreams (J. Vance), 1981
Book of Murder (s F. Anderson), 1930
Book of the Crime (E. Daly), 1951
Book of the Dead (Blackburn), 1984
Book of the Dead (E. Daly), 1944
Book of the Lion (E. Daly), 1948
Book with the Orange Leaves (Keeler), 1942
Boomerang (Garve), 1969
Boomerang (Graeme), 1959
Boomerang Clue (Christie), 1935
Boon Companions (Drummond), 1974
Booty for a Babe (C. Brown), 1956
Border Town Girl (J. MacDonald), 1956
Borderline Cases (C. Adams), 1952
Borderline Murder (K. Knight, as Amos), 1947
Borges, Inspector series (Bonett), from 1964
Borgia Cabinet (J. Fletcher), 1930
Bormann Brief (Egleton), 1974
Born Loser (C. Brown), 1973
Born to Be Hanged (Crossen, as Chaber), 1973
Born to Be Hanged (McGuire), 1935
Born Victim (Waugh), 1962
Bornless Keeper (Yuill), 1974
Borough Treasurer (J. Fletcher), 1919
Borrow the Night (Nielsen), 1957
Borrowed Alibi (Linington, as Egan), 1962
Borrowed Crimes (s Woolrich, as Irish), 1946
Borrower of the Night (Elizabeth Peters), 1973
Borzoi Control (Schorr, as Ellis), 1986
Bosambo of the River (s E. Wallace), 1914
Boscobell, Geoffrey series (Wills), from 1934
Boss of Taroomba (Hornung), 1894
Boss of Terror (Dent, as Robeson), 1976
Boston Avenger (Malzberg, as Barry), 1973
Boston Blitz (Pendleton), 1972
Botanist at Bay (Sherwood), 1985
Bottle with the Green Wax Seal (Keeler), 1942
Bottom Line (Murphy), 1979
Boudoir Murder (Propper), 1931
Bound to Kill (Blackburn), 1963
Bouquet Garni (D. Clark), 1984
Bouquet of Clean Crimes and Neat Murders (s Slesar), 1960
Bouquet of Thorns (Sherwood), 1989
Bourne series (Ludlum), from 1980
Bowering's Breakwater (McCutchan), 1964
Bowstring Murders (J. Carr, as Dickson), 1933
Box (Rabe), 1962
Box from Japan (Keeler), 1932
Box Hill Murder (J. Fletcher), 1929
Box of Doom (Verner, as Stuart), 1928
Box of Tricks (s Brett), 1985
Box Office Murders (Crofts), 1929
Box with Broken Seals (Oppenheim), 1919
Boy on Platform One (Canning), 1981
Boy Who Liked Monsters (McCutchan), 1989
Boyd, Danny series (C. Brown), from 1959
Boys from Brazil (Levin), 1976
Brace of Skeet (Hammond), 1989
Bradford Business (A. Ross), 1974
Brading Collection (Wentworth), 1950
Bradley, Luke series (Pentecost), from 1939
Bradley, Mrs. Beatrice Lestrange series (G. Mitchell), from 1929
Bradmoor Murder (Post), 1929
Bradshaw, Charlie series (Dobyns), from 1976

Bragg, Sergeant Joseph and Constable James Morton series (R. Harrison), from 1983
Brain and Ten Fingers (Kersh), 1943
Brain Drain (Murphy), 1976
Brain, Colonel series (Cecil), from 1952
Brainwash (Wainwright), 1979
Brand of the Werewolf (Dent, as Robeson), 1965
Brand X (s Brand), 1974
Brand, Mark series (Connington), from 1939
Branded Spy Murders (F. Mason), 1932
Branded Woman (Miller), 1952
Brandenburg Hotel (Winslow), 1976
Brandon Case (Connington), 1934
Brandstetter, Dave series (Hansen), from 1970
Brandy for a Hero (O'Farrell), 1948
Brandy Pole (Chance), 1949
Brass Bed (Flora), 1956
Brass Bowl (L. Vance), 1907
Brass Chills (Pentecost), 1943
Brass Cupcake (J. MacDonald), 1950
Brass Go-Between (Thomas, as Bleeck), 1969
Brass Halo (Webb), 1957
Brass Knuckle (Gribble, as Grex), 1964
Brass Knuckles (s Gruber), 1966
Brass Monkey (Whittington), 1951
Brass Rainbow (Michael Collins), 1969
Brat (Brewer), 1957
Brat Farrar (Tey), 1949
Brave, Bad Girls (Dewey), 1956
Bravo of London (Bramah), 1934
Brazen (C. Brown), 1960
Brazen Bull (s Kersh), 1952
Brazen Tongue (G. Mitchell), 1940
Brazilian Sleigh Ride (Fish), 1965
Bread (McBain), 1974
Bread of Deceit (s Lowndes), 1925
Break (Mather), 1970
Break In (Francis), 1986
Break in the Circle (Loraine), 1951
Break in the Line (Mather), 1970
Breakaway (Durbridge), 1981
Breakaway (L. Black), 1970
Breakfast with a Corpse (Murray), 1956
Breakheart Pass (MacLean), 1974
Breaking Point (Copper), 1973
Breaking Point (Meynell), 1957
Breaking Point (s du Maurier), 1959
Breastplate for Aaron (Harvester), 1949
Breath of Scandal (Balmer), 1922
Breath of Suspicion (Ferrars), 1972
Breath of Suspicion (Le Queux), 1917
Breathe No More, My Lady (Lacy), 1958
Bred in the Bone (Phillpotts), 1932
Bredder, Father Joseph series (Holton), from 1959
Bredon, Miles series (R. Knox), from 1927
Breed of the Beverleys (Horler), 1921
Breed, Barr series (Ballinger), from 1948
Brenda Gets Married (Vickers), 1941
Brenda's Murder (S. Forbes, as Wells), 1973
Brendel, Ernst series (Masterman), from 1933
Brentford, Inspector series (Hough), from 1959
Brewer, Charlie series (Hallahan), from 1986
Briar Patch (Blackstock), 1960
Briarpatch (Thomas), 1984
Bribe Was Beautiful (C. Brown), 1956
Bricklayer's Arms (Rhode), 1945
Bride for Hampton House (Waugh), 1975

Bride from the Bush (Hornung), 1890
Bride of a Moment (Wells), 1916
Bride of Death (Marsh), 1955
Bride of Newgate (J. Carr), 1950
Bride of Pendorric (Holt), 1963
Bride of the Sun (Leroux, trans), 1915
Bride of the Wilderness (McCarry), 1988
Bride Wore Black (Woolrich), 1940
Brides of Aberdar (Brand), 1982
Brides of Friedberg (Butler), 1977
Brides of Solomon (s Household), 1958
Bridesmaid (Rendell), 1989
Bridge of Lions (Slesar), 1963
Bridge of Sand (Gruber), 1963
Bridge That Went Nowhere (Fish), 1968
Bridge to Vengeance (W. Graham), 1957
Brief Candles (Coles, as Gaite), 1954
Brief for O'Leary (s Graeme), 1947
Brief Return (Eberhart), 1939
Brief Tales from the Bench (s Cecil), 1968
Brigand (s E. Wallace), 1927
Bright Face of Danger (Meynell), 1948
Bright Face of Danger (Ormerod), 1979
Bright Orange for the Shroud (J. MacDonald), 1965
Bright Red Businessmen (McCutchan), 1969
Bright Road to Fear (Stern), 1958
Bright Serpent (Fox), 1953
Brighter Buccaneer (s Charteris), 1933
Brighton Monster (s Kersh), 1953
Brighton Rock (Greene), 1938
Brimstone (J. Roberts, as Duncan), 1980
Brimstone Bed (Keene), 1960
Bring Him Back Dead (Keene), 1956
Bring Me Another Corpse (Rabe), 1959
Bring the Bride a Shroud (Olsen), 1945
Brink of Disaster (Cullingford), 1964
Brink of Murder (Nielsen), 1976
Brink of Silence (Jay), 1957
British Cross (Granger), 1983
Broadcast Mystery (Le Queux), 1925
Brock (Kersh), 1969
Brock series (Bingham), from 1981
Brogan, Jerry series (Breen), from 1983
Broken Blossoms (s T. Burke), 1920
Broken Boy (Blackburn), 1959
Broken Doll (Webb), 1955
Broken Jigsaw (Garve, as Somers), 1961
Broken Men (Gielgud), 1932
Broken O (Wells), 1933
Broken Penny (Symons), 1953
Broken Shield (Benson), 1955
Broken Thread (Le Queux), 1916
Broken Vase (Stout), 1941
Broken Waters (Packard), 1925
Brokenclaw (J. Gardner), 1990
Broker (Masur), 1981
Broker (Max Collins), 1976
Broker's Wife (Max Collins), 1976
Bronze Bell (L. Vance), 1909
Bronze Face (Le Queux), 1923
Bronze Hand (Wells), 1926
Bronze Perseus (Hough), 1959
Brood of Folly (Erskine), 1971
Brood of the Witch-Queen (Rohmer), 1918
Brook, Roger series (Wheatley), from 1947
Brooklyn Murders (Cole), 1923
Broom, Andrew series (McInerny), from 1987

By Frequent Anguish (Dean), 1982
By Hook or by Crook (Lathen), 1975
By Hook or Crook (A. Gilbert), 1947
By Horror Haunted (s Fremlin), 1974
By-Line for Murder (Garve), 1951
By Order of the Five (Herbert Adams), 1925
By-Pass Control (Spillane), 1966
By-Pass Murder (Ford, as Frome), 1932
By Persons Unknown (Creasey, as York), 1941
By Registered Post (Rhode), 1953
By Royal Command (Yates), 1931
By the Pricking of My Thumbs (Christie), 1968
By the Rivers of Babylon (Demille), 1978
By the Watchman's Clock (Ford), 1932
By Third Degree (Keeler), 1948
Bye, Baby Bunting (Keene), 1963

"C" Is for Corpse (S. Grafton), 1986
Cabin of Fear (Olsen, as Hitchens), 1968
Cabin 3033 (Clarke), 1986
Cabinda Affair (Head), 1949
Cable-Car (Drummond), 1965
Cade (Chase), 1966
Cade Curse (W. Roberts), 1978
Cadee, Don series (Sterling, as Dean), from 1954
Cadfael, Brother series (Ellis Peters), from 1977
Cage (Gadney), 1977
Cage (Horler), 1953
Cage Five Is Going to Break (Johnson), 1970
Cage of Ice (Kyle), 1970
Cain, Cabot series (Caillou), from 1969
Cain, Jenny series (Pickard), from 1984
Cairo Cabal (Caillou), 1974
Cairo Garter Murders (F. Mason), 1938
Cake in the Hatbox (Upfield), 1955
Calamity at Harwood (Bellairs), 1943
Calamity Fair (Miller), 1950
Calamity Town (Queen), 1942
Calder, Keith series (Hammond), from 1979
Calendar (E. Wallace), 1930
Calendar of Crime (s Queen), 1952
California Hit (Pendleton), 1972
California Roll (Simon), 1985
California Thriller (Byrd), 1981
Caligari Complex (Copper), 1980
Call a Hearse (Quentin, as Stagge), 1942
Call after Midnight (Eberhart), 1964
Call Back to Crime (Jeffries, as Alding), 1972
Call Back Yesterday (Woods), 1983
Call for the Dead (le Carré), 1961
Call from Austria (Albrand), 1963
Call Him Early for the Murder (Morland), 1952
Call It Coincidence (Lockridge), 1962
Call Me Killer (Whittington), 1951
Callaghan, Slim series (Cheney), from 1938
Callahan, Brock series (Gault), from 1955
Callan, David series (J. Mitchell), from 1973
Callander Square (A. Perry), 1980
Calling All Suspects (Wells), 1939
Calling Dr. Patchwork (Goulart), 1978
Calling Mr. Callaghan (s Cheyney), 1953
Calypso (McBain), 1979
Camberwell, Ronald series (J. Fletcher), from 1931
Came the Dawn (Garve, as Bax), 1949
Camelot Caper (Elizabeth Peters), 1969
Cameos (s O. Cohen), 1931
Camera Clue (Coxe), 1937

Camera Fiend (Hornung), 1911
Camouflage (Meynell), 1930
Camp 7 Last Stop (Kirst, trans), 1969
Campaign Train (The Gordons), 1952
Campbell's Kingdom (H. Innes), 1952
Campbell, Humphrey series (Homes), from 1938
Campion, Albert series (Allingham), from 1929
Can a Mermaid Kill? (Dewey), 1965
Can Ladies Kill? (Cheyney), 1938
Can of Worms (Chase), 1979
Cana Division (Gault), 1982
Canadian Bomber Contract (Atlee), 1971
Canadian Crisis (Pendleton), 1975
Canary Murder Case (Van Dine), 1927
Cancelled Czech (Block), 1966
Cancelled in Red (Pentecost), 1939
Candid Imposter (Coxe), 1968
Candidates for Murder (Hocking), 1961
Candle for a Corpse (Sterling), 1957
Candle for the Dead (J. Higgins, as Marlowe), 1966
Candle-Holders (Gielgud), 1970
Candle of the Wicked (Balmer), 1956
Candles for the Dead (Carmichael), 1973
Candleshoe (M. Innes), 1978
Candlestick with Seven Branches (Leblanc, trans), 1925
Candy Kid (Hughes), 1950
Cannibal (Demille), 1975
Cannibal Who Overate (Pentecost), 1962
Cannonball Run (Avallone), 1981
Canterbury Kilgrims (Chance), 1974
Canterbury Mystery (s J. Fletcher), 1933
Canto for a Gypsy (M. Smith), 1972
Canvas Coffin (Gault), 1953
Canvas Dagger (Reilly), 1956
Cape Cod Mystery (P. Taylor), 1931
Cape Fear (J. MacDonald), 1962
Cape of Black Sands (W. Roberts), 1977
Cape of Shadows (Harvester, as Gibbs), 1954
Caper (Sanders as Andress), 1980
Caper of the Golden Bulls (McGivern), 1966
Capital Crime (Ford), 1941
Capital Crimes (Sanders), 1989
Capitol Offense (Davey), 1956
Capricorn and Cancer (s Household), 1981
Capricorn One (Goulart), 1978
Capricorn, Merle series (Winslow), from 1975
Caprifoil (McGivern), 1972
Captain and the Enemy (Greene), 1988
Captain Bolton's Corpse (Sturrock), 1982
Captain Cut-Throat (J. Carr), 1955
Captain Gault (s Hodgson), 1917
Captain of the Polestar (s Doyle), 1890
Captain Tatham of Tatham Island (E. Wallace), 1909
Captain's Curio (Phillpotts), 1933
Captains of Souls (E. Wallace), 1922
Captivator (York), 1973
Captive (Daniels), 1959
Captive (Holt), 1989
Captive (The Gordons), 1957
Captive Audience (Mann), 1975
Captives of Mora Island (Canning), 1959
Carambola (Dodge), 1961
Caravan Mystery (Hume), 1926
Caravan of Night (Erskine), 1972
Caravan to Vaccarès (MacLean), 1970
Carbuncle Clue (Hume), 1896
Cardiff, Inspector series (Gray), from 1960

Cardinal of the Kremlin (Clancy), 1988
Cardinal Rock (Sale), 1940
Cardinal Sins (Greeley), 1981
Cardinal Virtues (Greeley), 1990
Cardinalli Contract (Johnson), 1975
Cardington Crescent (A. Perry), 1987
Cards on the Table (Christie), 1936
Cardyce for the Defence (Graeme), 1936
Care of Time (Ambler), 1981
Career in C Major (J. Cain), 1944
Careful Man (Deming), 1962
Careless Hangman (Morland), 1941
Caress Before Killing (C. Brown), 1956
Caretaker (Hume), 1915
Carfax Abbey (B. Thomson), 1928
Cargo Club (Corris), 1990
Cargo of Eagles (Allingham), 1968
Cargo of Spent Evil (Tripp, as Brett), 1966
Cargo Risk (B. Knox, as MacLeod), 1980
Cargo Unkown (Dent, as Robeson), 1980
Caribbean Conspiracy (Ford, as Conrad), 1942
Caribbean Coup (Randisi, as Carter), 1984
Caribbean Kill (Pendleton), 1972
Caribbean Mystery (Christie), 1964
Carlent Manor Crime (Gribble, as Grex), 1939
Carlisle, Kenneth series (Wells), from 1929
Carlyle, Carlotta series (Barnes), from 1987
Carmichael, Agnes series (A. Cohen), from 1982
Carnacki series (s Hodgson), from 1910
Carnal Island (Fuller), 1970
Carnival of Crime (s F. Brown), 1985
Carnival of Death (Keene), 1965
Carnival! (Rathbone), 1976
Caroline Miniscule (A. Taylor), 1982
Caroline Ormsby's Crime (Herbert Adams), 1929
Carr, Charles series (Petievich), from 1981
Carrados, Max series (Bramah), from 1914
Carrick, Chief Officer Webb series (B. Knox), from 1964
Carriers of Death (Creasey), 1937
Carrismore Ruby (s J. Fletcher), 1935
Carroll, David series (O. Cohen), from 1919
Carrot for the Donkey (L. Roberts), 1989
Carruthers, Simpson and Briggs series (Fish), from 1968
Carson's Conspiracy (M. Innes), 1984
Carstairs, Brett series (Horler), from 1931
Carstairs, "Apples" series (Follett, as Myles), from 1974
Cart Before the Crime (Porter), 1979
Cart Before the Hearse (Ormerod), 1979
Carter and Bell series (Punshon), from 1929
Carter, Inspector Neil series (Dewhurst), from 1977
Carter, Nick series (Michael Collins, as Carter), from 1974
Carter, Nick series (Randisi, as Carter), from 1981
Cartoon Crimes (Goulart, as Robeson), 1974
Cartwright Gardens Murder (J. Fletcher), 1924
Carvel, Kelly series (Daniels), from 1970
Carver, Fred series (Lutz), from 1986
Carver, Rex series (Canning), from 1965
Caryll, Victor series (Fairlie), from 1927
Casa Madrone (Eberhart), 1980
Case Against Andrew Fane (A. Gilbert), 1931
Case Against Butterfly (Bardin, as Tree), 1951
Case Against Myself (Bardin, as Tree), 1950
Case Against Phillip Quest (Underwood), 1962
Case Closed (J. Thomson), 1977
Case File: FBI (The Gordons), 1953
Case for Appeal (Linington, as Egan), 1961
Case for Solomon (Graeme), 1943

Case for the Defence (Fitt), 1958
Case for Three Detectives (Bruce), 1936
Case in Nullity (Berckman), 1967
Case in the Clinic (Carnac, as Lorac), 1941
Case Is Altered (Woods), 1967
Case Is Closed (Wentworth), 1937
Case Load—Maximum (Johnson), 1971
Case of Books (Graeme), 1946
Case of Colonel Marchand (Carnac, as Lorac), 1933
Case of Elinor Norton (Rinehart), 1934
Case of Jennie Brice (Rinehart), 1913
Case of Kitty Ogilvie (Stubbs), 1970
Case of L.A.C. Dickson (Chance, as Drummond), 1950
Case of Libel (Bingham), 1963
Case of Lone Star (Friedman), 1987
Case of Loyalties (M. Wallace), 1986
Case of Lucy Bending (Sanders), 1982
Case of Mary Fielding (Erskine), 1970
Case of Miss Elliott (s Orczy), 1905
Case of Naomi Clynes (B. Thomson), 1934
Case of Need (Crichton, as Hudson), 1968
Case of Robert Quarry (Garve), 1972
Case of Sonia Wayward (M. Innes), 1960
Case of Spirits (Lovesey), 1975
Case of the 100% Alibis (Bush), 1934
Case of the 16 Beans (Keeler), 1944
Case of the Abominable Snowman (Blake), 1941
Case of the Absent-Minded Professor (Stein), 1943
Case of the Acid Throwers (Creasey), 1960
Case of the Amateur Actor (Bush), 1955
Case of the Amorous Aunt (E. Gardner), 1963
Case of the Angry Actress (Cunningham), 1984
Case of the Angry Mourner (E. Gardner), 1951
Case of the April Fools (Bush), 1933
Case of the Backward Mule (E. Gardner), 1946
Case of the Baited Hook (E. Gardner), 1940
Case of the Baker Street Irregulars (Boucher), 1940
Case of the Barking Clock (Keeler), 1947
Case of the Beautiful Beggar (E. Gardner), 1965
Case of the Beautiful Body (Craig), 1957
Case of the Beckoning Dead (Morland, as Donavan), 1938
Case of the Benevolent Bookie (Bush), 1955
Case of the Berlin Spy (B. Newman, as Betteridge), 1954
Case of the Bigamous Spouse (E. Gardner), 1961
Case of the Black, Black Hearse (Ballinger, as Freyer), 1955
Case of the Black-Eyed Blonde (E. Gardner), 1944
Case of the Blonde Bonanza (E. Gardner), 1962
Case of the Bonfire Body (Bush), 1936
Case of the Borrowed Brunette (E. Gardner), 1946
Case of the Bouncing Betty (Avallone), 1957
Case of the Brazen Beauty (Craig), 1966
Case of the Brunette Bombshell (Waugh), 1957
Case of the Buried Clock (E. Gardner), 1943
Case of the Burning Bequest (Chastain), 1990
Case of the Burnt Bohemian (Bush), 1953
Case of the Calabar Bean (Wills), 1939
Case of the Calendar Girl (E. Gardner), 1958
Case of the Canny Killer (Keeler), 1946
Case of the Careless Cupid (E. Gardner), 1968
Case of the Careless Kitten (E. Gardner), 1942
Case of the Careless Thief (Bush), 1959
Case of the Caretaker's Cat (E. Gardner), 1935
Case of the Cautious Coquette (E. Gardner), 1949
Case of the Chased and the Unchaste (Dewey), 1959
Case of the Cheating Bride (Propper), 1938
Case of the Chinese Gong (Bush), 1935
Case of the Climbing Rat (Bush), 1940

Case of the Cold Coquette (Craig), 1957
Case of the Coloured Wind (Morland, as Donavan), 1939
Case of the Constant God (King), 1936
Case of the Constant Suicides (J. Carr), 1941
Case of the Corner Cottage (Bush), 1951
Case of the Corporal's Leave (Bush), 1945
Case of the Counterfeit Colonel (Bush), 1952
Case of the Counterfeit Eye (E. Gardner), 1935
Case of the Crimson Kiss (s E. Gardner), 1971
Case of the Crooked Candle (E. Gardner), 1944
Case of the Crumpled Knave (Boucher), 1939
Case of the Crying Swallow (s E. Gardner), 1971
Case of the Curious Bride (E. Gardner), 1934
Case of the Curious Client (Bush), 1947
Case of the Curious Heel (Crossen), 1944
Case of the Dancing Sandwiches (F. Brown), 1951
Case of the Dangerous Dowager (E. Gardner), 1937
Case of the Daring Decoy (E. Gardner), 1957
Case of the Daring Divorcee (E. Gardner), 1964
Case of the Dead Diplomat (B. Thomson), 1935
Case of the Dead Man Gone (Bush), 1962
Case of the Dead Shepherd (Bush), 1934
Case of the "Dead" Spy (Chance, as Drummond), 1949
Case of the Deadly Diamonds (Bush), 1967
Case of the Deadly Toy (E. Gardner), 1959
Case of the Death Computer (Chance), 1967
Case of the Demented Spiv (Bellairs), 1949
Case of the Demure Defendant (E. Gardner), 1956
Case of the Dowager's Etchings (King), 1944
Case of the Drowning Duck (E. Gardner), 1942
Case of the Drowsy Mosquito (E. Gardner), 1943
Case of the Dubious Bridegroom (E. Gardner), 1949
Case of the Duplicate Daughter (E. Gardner), 1960
Case of the Empty Beehive (Wills), 1959
Case of the Empty Tin (E. Gardner), 1941
Case of the Extra Grave (Bush), 1961
Case of the Extra Man (Bush), 1956
Case of the Fabulous Fake (E. Gardner), 1969
Case of the Famished Parson (Bellairs), 1949
Case of the Fan Dancer's Horse (E. Gardner), 1947
Case of the Fear Makers (Chance), 1967
Case of the Fenced-In Woman (E. Gardner), 1972
Case of the Fiery Fingers (E. Gardner), 1951
Case of the Fighting Soldier (Bush), 1942
Case of the First-Class Carriage (Carnac), 1939
Case of the Flowery Corpse (Bush), 1956
Case of the Flying Ass (Bush), 1939
Case of the Foot-Loose Doll (E. Gardner), 1958
Case of the Forty Thieves (Rhode), 1954
Case of the Four Friends (Masterman), 1957
Case of the Fourth Detective (Bush), 1951
Case of the Frightened Manequin (Bush), 1951
Case of the Fugitive Nurse (E. Gardner), 1954
Case of the Giant Killer (Branson), 1944
Case of the Gilded Fly (Crispin), 1944
Case of the Gilded Lily (E. Gardner), 1956
Case of the Glamorous Ghost (E. Gardner), 1955
Case of the Golddigger's Purse (E. Gardner), 1945
Case of the Good Employer (Bush), 1966
Case of the Grand Alliance (Bush), 1964
Case of the Green Felt Hat (Bush), 1939
Case of the Green-Eyed Sister (E. Gardner), 1953
Case of the Grinning Gorilla (E. Gardner), 1952
Case of the Half-Wakened Wife (E. Gardner), 1945
Case of the Hanging Rope (Bush), 1937
Case of the Happy Medium (Bush), 1952
Case of the Happy Warrior (Bush), 1950

Case of the Hated Senator (Scherf), 1954
Case of the Haunted Husband (E. Gardner), 1941
Case of the Haven Hotel (Bush), 1948
Case of the Headless Jesuit (Bellairs), 1950
Case of the Heavenly Twin (Bush), 1963
Case of the Hesitant Hostess (E. Gardner), 1953
Case of the Hook-Billed Kites (Borthwick), 1982
Case of the Horrified Heirs (E. Gardner), 1964
Case of the Housekeeper's Hair (Bush), 1948
Case of the Howling Dog (E. Gardner), 1934
Case of the Ice-Cold Hands (E. Gardner), 1962
Case of the Innocent Victims (Creasey), 1959
Case of the Innocent Wife (s Morland), 1947
Case of the Irate Witness (s E. Gardner), 1972
Case of the Ivory Arrow (Keeler), 1945
Case of the Jeweled Ragpicker (Keeler), 1948
Case of the Journeying Boy (M. Innes), 1949
Case of the Kidnapped Angel (Cunningham), 1982
Case of the Kidnapped Colonel (Bush), 1942
Case of the Kippered Corpse (Scherf), 1941
Case of the Lame Canary (E. Gardner), 1937
Case of the Late Pig (Allingham), 1937
Case of the Laughing Virgin (Craig), 1960
Case of the Lazy Lover (E. Gardner), 1947
Case of the Leaning Man (Bush), 1938
Case of the Lonely Heiress (E. Gardner), 1948
Case of the Lonely Lovers (Miller, as Daemer), 1951
Case of the Long-Legged Models (E. Gardner), 1958
Case of the Lucky Legs (E. Gardner), 1934
Case of the Lucky Loser (E. Gardner), 1957
Case of the Mad Inventor (Creasey), 1942
Case of the Magic Mirror (Bush), 1943
Case of the Malverne Diamonds (Gribble), 1936
Case of the Man with No Name (Chance, as Drummond), 1951
Case of the Marsden Rubies (Gribble), 1929
Case of the Mexican Knife (Homes), 1948
Case of the Mischievous Doll (E. Gardner), 1963
Case of the Missing Brontë (Barnard), 1983
Case of the Missing Estate Agent (Verner, as Stuart), 1932
Case of the Missing Gardener (Waugh, as Walker), 1954
Case of the Missing Men (Bush), 1946
Case of the Missing Minutes (Bush), 1937
Case of the Monday Murders (Bush), 1936
Case of the Moth-Eaten Mink (E. Gardner), 1952
Case of the Murdered Financier (Creasey), 1937
Case of the Murdered Mackenzie (Cunningham), 1984
Case of the Murdered Madame (s H. Kane), 1955
Case of the Murdered Major (Bush), 1941
Case of the Murdered Model (Dewey), 1955
Case of the Murdered Redhead (Lockridge), 1957
Case of the Murderer's Bride (s E. Gardner), 1969
Case of the Musical Cow (E. Gardner), 1950
Case of the Mysterious Moll (Keeler), 1945
Case of the Mythical Monkeys (E. Gardner), 1959
Case of the Negligent Nymph (E. Gardner), 1950
Case of the Nervous Accomplice (E. Gardner), 1955
Case of the Nervous Nude (Craig), 1959
Case of the One-Eyed Witness (E. Gardner), 1950
Case of the One-Penny Orange (Cunningham), 1977
Case of the Perjured Parrot (E. Gardner), 1939
Case of the Petticoat Murder (Craig), 1958
Case of the Phantom Fingerprints (Crossen), 1945
Case of the Phantom Fortune (E. Gardner), 1964
Case of the Plastic Man (Morland, as Donavan), 1940
Case of the Plastic Mask (Morland, as Donavan), 1941
Case of the Platinum Blonde (Bush), 1944
Case of the Poisoned Eclairs (Cunningham), 1979

Cat Saw Murder (Olsen), 1939
Cat series (The Gordons), from 1963
Cat Walk (Olsen), 1953
Cat Watchers (Chance), 1971
Cat Wears a Mask (Olsen), 1949
Cat Wears a Noose (Olsen), 1944
Cat Who Ate Danish Modern (Braun), 1967
Cat Who Could Read Backwards (Braun), 1966
Cat Who Had 14 Tales (s Braun), 1988
Cat Who Knew Shakespeare (Braun), 1988
Cat Who Lived High (Braun), 1990
Cat Who Played Brahms (Braun), 1987
Cat Who Played Post Office (Braun), 1987
Cat Who Saw Red (Braun), 1986
Cat Who Sniffed Glue (Braun), 1988
Cat Who Talked to Ghosts (Braun), 1990
Cat Who Turned On and Off (Braun), 1968
Cat Who Went Underground (Braun), 1989
Cat's Eye (Freeman), 1923
Cat's Meow (Campbell), 1988
Cat's Whisker (Bailey), 1944
Catalyst (Bell), 1966
Catastrophe (Gaboriau, trans), 1885
Catch a Falling Clown (Kaminsky), 1982
Catch a Falling Spy (Deighton), 1976
Catch a Killer (Curtiss), 1952
Catch and Kill (Blake), 1955
Catch as Catch Can (Lockridge), 1958
Catch-as-Catch-Can (Armstrong), 1952
Catch Me a Phoenix! (C. Brown), 1965
Catch Me If You Can (McGerr), 1948
Catch Me, Kill Me (Hallahan), 1977
Catch the Brass Ring (S. Marlowe), 1954
Catch the Gold Ring (Strange), 1955
Catching Fire (K. Smith), 1982
Cater Street Hangman (A. Perry), 1979
Caterpillar Cop (McClure), 1972
Catfish Tangle (C. Williams), 1963
Cathedral (Demille), 1981
Catherine Wheel (Wentworth), 1949
Catnapped (The Gordons), 1974
Cat's Claw (Olsen), 1943
Cat's Cradle (Harvester), 1952
Cats Don't Need Coffins (Olsen), 1946
Cats Don't Smile (Olsen), 1945
Cats Have Tall Shadows (Olsen), 1948
Cat's Paw (Hocking), 1933
Cat's-Paw (s Pronzini), 1983
Cats Prowl at Night (E. Gardner, as Fair), 1943
Catskill Eagle (Parker), 1985
Catspaw (Le Queux), 1918
Catspaw (Russell), 1980
Catspaw for Murder (Olsen), 1943
Catspaw Ordeal (Aarons, as Ronns), 1950
Caught at Last! (s Donovan), 1889
Caught in the Birdlime (Parrish), 1987
Caught in the Net (Gaboriau, trans), 1891
Cause and Effect (McInerny), 1987
Cause for a Killing (Wainwright), 1974
Cause for Alarm (Ambler), 1938
Cause of Death (Underwood), 1960
Causeway (Hubbard), 1976
Causeway to the Past (O'Farrell), 1950
Caution, Lemmy series (Cheyney), from 1936
Cautious Overshoes (Scherf), 1956
Cavalier Case (Antonia Fraser), 1990
Cavalier in White (Muller), 1986

Cavalier of Chance (Horler), 1931
Cavalier's Cup (J. Carr, as Dickson), 1953
Cavanaugh Quest (Gifford), 1976
Cave of Bats (B. Knox, as MacLeod), 1964
Caves of Steel (Asimov), 1954
Cawthorn Journals (S. Marlowe), 1975
CB Logbook of the White Knight (s Avallone), 1978
Cease upon the Midnight (Warriner, as Troy), 1964
Ceiling of Hell (Murphy), 1984
Celestial City (Orczy), 1962
Cell Car 54 (Fox), 1977
Cellar at No. 5 (S. Smith), 1954
Cellini, Dr. Emmanuel series (Creasey, as Halliday), from 1965
Censor (Russell), 1984
Centre Court Murder (B. Newman), 1951
Ceremony (Parker), 1982
Ceremony of Innocence (Dean), 1984
Certain Blindness (Lewis), 1980
Certain Sleep (Reilly), 1961
Chain of Evidence (Wells), 1912
Chain of Violence (Linington, as Egan), 1985
Chained Reaction (Murphy), 1978
Chairman of the Board (Freemantle, as Evans), 1982
Chalice Caper (MacKenzie), 1974
Challenge (Sapper), 1937
Challis, Bart series (Nielsen), from 1968
Chamber of Horrors (s Bloch), 1966
Chambers, Peter series (H. Kane), from 1947
Chambrun, Pierre series (Pentecost), from 1962
Chameleon (Keeler), 1939
Chameleon (Le Queux), 1927
Chamois Murder (Wills), 1935
Champagne for One (Stout), 1958
Champagne Killer (Pentecost), 1972
Champagne Marxist (Gadney), 1977
Champdoce Mystery (Gaboriau, trans), 1891
Champion, Kyle series (Harold Adams), from 1987
Chan, Charlie series (Biggers), from 1925
Chance Elson (Ballard), 1958
Chance to Die (L. Black), 1965
Chance to Kill (Linington, as Shannon), 1967
Chance, series (Chance), from 1944
Chancellor Manuscript (Ludlum), 1977
Chandler Policy (Doris Disney), 1971
Change for the Worse (Lemarchand), 1980
Change of Heart (McCloy), 1973
Change of Heir (M. Innes), 1966
Changeling (Phillpotts), 1944
Changeling Conspiracy (McCloy), 1976
Channay Syndicate (s Oppenheim), 1927
Channel Assault (Royce), 1982
Channings (Wood, appendix), 1862
Chaos of Crime (Linington, as Shannon), 1985
Chaos, Jacob series (S. Smith), from 1942
Charabanc Mystery (Rhode, as Burton), 1934
Chard, Peter series (Verner), from 1946
Charg, Monster (Gibson, as Grant), 1977
Charing Cross Mystery (J. Fletcher), 1923
Charitable End (Mann), 1971
Charity Ends at Home (Watson), 1968
Charity Killers (Creasey, as Manton), 1954
Charlatan (Horler), 1934
Charles and Elizabeth (Burley), 1979
Charlesworth, Inspector series (Brand), from 1941
Charlesworth, Sergeant series (J. Fletcher), from 1930
Charlie Chan and the Curse of the Dragon Queen (Avallone), 1981

Charlie Chan Returns (Michael Collins, as Lynds), 1974
Charlie Sent Me! (C. Brown), 1963
Charlotte's Inheritance (Braddon, appendix), 1868
Charm School (Demille), 1988
Charmed Death (Tripp), 1984
Charmer Chased (C. Brown), 1958(?)
Charred Witness (Coxe), 1942
Charter to Danger (Ambler, as Reed), 1954
Chase (Daniels), 1974
Chase (Koontz, as Dwyer), 1972
Chase (Lambert), 1987
Chase of the Golden Plate (Futrelle), 1906
Chase of the "Linda Belle." (Footner), 1925
Chasing Eights (Michael Collins), 1990
Chasm (Canning), 1947
Chateau of Mystery (Meade), 1907
Chateau of Wolves (C. Brown, as Farr), 1976
Cheat (Hunt, as Dietrich), 1954
Cheat the Hangman (Ferrars), 1946
Cheaters (E. Wallace), 1964
Cheating Butcher (Stein), 1980
Checkmate (Horler), 1930
Checkmate (Le Fanu, appendix), 1871
Checkmate to Murder (Carnac, as Lorac), 1944
Checkpoint Charlie (s Garfield), 1981
Chee, Sergeant Jim series (Hillerman), from 1980
Cheese from a Mousetrap (Fox), 1944
Cheim Manuscript (Prather), 1969
Chelsea Ghost (Hunter), 1985
Chelsea Murders (Davidson), 1978
Chequered Flag (Rutherford), 1956
Cherchez la Femme (Graeme), 1951
Cheri-Bibi series (Leroux, trans), from 1922
Cherry Blossom Corpse (Barnard), 1987
Cheshire Cat's Eye (Muller), 1983
Chessmaster (Randisi, as Carter), 1982
Chestermarke Instinct (J. Fletcher), 1918
Cheung, Detective (Keeler), 1938
Cheyne Mystery (Crofts), 1926
Chianti Flask (Lowndes), 1934
Chicago Girl (Kenrick), 1976
Chicago Princess (Barr), 1904
Chicago-7 (McGivern), 1970
Chicago Slaughter (Malzberg, as Barry), 1974
Chicago Wipe-Out (Pendleton), 1971
Chicane War (Gault), 1986
Chick (s E. Wallace), 1923
Chicken (Tripp), 1966
Chief Inspector's Daughter (Radley), 1981
Chief Inspector's Statement (Procter), 1951
Chief Legatee (Green), 1906
Chief Witness (Herbert Adams), 1940
Chiffon Scarf (Eberhart), 1939
Child Divided (Cecil), 1965
Child of Evil (O. Cohen), 1936
Child of Rage (Thompson), 1972
Child Proof (Lewin), 1988
Child's Play (Curtiss), 1965
Children of Despair (Creasey), 1958
Children of Hate (Creasey), 1952
Children of Tender Years (Allbeury), 1985
Children of the Mist (B. Knox), 1970
Children of the Night (Blackburn), 1966
Children of the Storm (Koontz, as Dwyer), 1972
Children's Overture (Harvester, as Gibbs), 1948
Children's Zoo (L. O'Donnell), 1981
Child's Garden of Death (R. Forrest), 1975

Child's Play (Hill), 1987
Child's Play (Murphy), 1976
Chill (Bentley), 1953
Chill (Macdonald), 1964
Chill and the Kill (J. Fleming), 1964
Chill Factor (Lambert, as Falkirk), 1971
Chill Factor (Stein), 1978
Chills and Fevers (s J. White), 1983
China Doll (Avallone, as Carter), 1964
China Gold (Egleton, as Tarrant), 1982
China Governess (Allingham), 1962
China Roundabout (Bell), 1956
China Sea Murders (F. Mason), 1959
China Seas (Hebden, as Harris), 1987
China White (Kenrick), 1986
Chinaman's Chance (Thomas), 1978
Chinese Bell Murders (van Gulik, trans), 1958
Chinese Gold Murders (van Gulik, trans), 1959
Chinese Hammer (Harvester), 1960
Chinese Jar (Hume), 1893
Chinese Jar Mystery (Strange), 1934
Chinese Lake Murders (van Gulik, trans), 1960
Chinese Mask (Ballinger), 1965
Chinese Maze Murders (van Gulik, trans), 1962
Chinese Nail Murders (van Gulik, trans), 1961
Chinese Nightmare (Pentecost), 1951
Chinese Orange Mystery (Queen), 1934
Chinese Parrot (Biggers), 1926
Chinese Puzzle (Murphy), 1972
Chinese Puzzle (Rhode, as Burton), 1957
Chinese Shawl (Wentworth), 1943
Chinese Widow (Leasor), 1975
Chink in the Armour (Lowndes), 1912
Chinks in the Curtain (Porter), 1967
Chipstead, Bunny series (Horler), from 1927
Chiselers (Albert, as Albert Conroy), 1953
Chit of a Girl (Simenon, trans), 1949
Chitterwick, Ambrose series (Berkeley), from 1929
Chocolate Cobweb (Armstrong), 1948
Choice (Allbeury), 1986
Choice (P. MacDonald), 1931
Choice (Punshon), 1908
Choice Cuts (Boileau, trans), 1966
Choice of Assassins (McGivern), 1963
Choice of Crimes (Linington, as Egan), 1980
Choice of Eddie Franks (Freemantle, as Winchester), 1986
Choice of Enemies (Allbeury), 1972
Choice of Enemies (G. Higgins), 1984
Choice of Victims (Straker), 1984
Choice of Violence (Pentecost), 1961
Choirboys (Wambaugh), 1975
Chorine Makes a Killing (C. Brown), 1957
Chorus of Echoes (Hall, as Trevor), 1950
Chosen Sparrow (Caspary), 1964
Christine Diamond (Lowndes), 1940
Christmas at Candleshoe (M. Innes), 1953
Christmas Bomber (Chastain), 1976
Christmas Egg (Kelly), 1958
Christmas Murder (Hare), 1953
Christmas Rising (Serafin), 1982
Christopher, James series (F. Davis, as Steele), from 1966
Christopher, Paul series (McCarry), from 1973
Christopher, Robert series (Irvine), from 1974
Chronicles of Golden Friars (s Le Fanu, appendix), 1871
Chronicles of Melhampton (s Oppenheim), 1928
Chronicles of Michael Danevitch of the Russian Secret Service (s Donovan), 1897

Chrysanthemum Chain (Melville), 1980
Chuckling Fingers (Seeley), 1941
Chucky, Inspector series (Brand), from 1948
Churchill Commando (Willis), 1977
Churchyard Salad (G. Mitchell, as Torrie), 1969
Cicely Disappears (Berkeley, as Platts), 1927
C.I.D. Room (Jeffries, as Alding), 1967
Cinderella (McBain), 1986
Cinderella Goes to the Morgue (Spain), 1950
Cinderella Spy (Chambers, as Daniels), 1984
"Cinders" of Harley Street (s Le Queux), 1916
Cinema Murder (Oppenheim), 1917
Cinnamon Murder (Crane), 1946
Cinnamon Skin (J. MacDonald), 1982
Cipher Six (Le Queux), 1919
Circe Complex (Cory), 1975
Circle of Danger (Jeffries, as Alding), 1968
Circle of Evil (Johnston), 1972
Circle of Fire (Michael Collins, as Sadler), 1973
Circle of Justice (Creasey, as Manton), 1938
Circular Staircase (Rinehart), 1908
Circular Study (Green), 1900
Circumstantial Evidence (Crofts), 1941
Circumstantial Evidence (s E. Wallace), 1929
Circus (MacLean), 1975
Circus Couronne (Campbell), 1977
Cities of the Dead (Barnes), 1986
City Called July (Engel), 1986
City in Heat (Murphy), 1973
City Limits (Deming, as Marino), 1958
City of Brass (s Hoch), 1971
City of Glass (Auster), 1985
City of Gold and Shadows (Ellis Peters), 1973
City of Kites (Cory, as Callas), 1955
City of Strangers (Barnard), 1990
City of the Soul (Bush, as Home), 1943
City of Whispering Stone (Chesbro), 1978
City Primeval (Leonard), 1980
City Solitary (Freeling), 1985
Clairvoyant Countess (Gilman), 1975
Clancy's Secret Mission (Thayer), 1952
Clancy, Lieutenant series (Fish, as Pike), from 1963
Clancy, Peter series (Thayer), from 1919
Clandestine (Ellroy), 1982
Clane, Terry series (E. Gardner), from 1937
Clash by Night (Bruce, as Croft-Cooke), 1962
Classics of the Macabre (s du Maurier), 1987
Clauberg Trigger (Egleton, as Tarrant), 1978
Claude Duval of Ninety-Five (Hume), 1897
Claverton Affair (Rhode), 1933
Claverton Mystery (Rhode), 1933
Claws of God (Tripp), 1972
Claws of Mercy (Hebden, as Harris), 1955
Claws of the Gryphon (Turnbull), 1986
Clay Assassin (Godey), 1959
Clay Hand (D. Davis), 1950
Clean Break (L. White), 1955
Clean, Bright, and Slightly Oiled (s Kersh), 1946
Clear and Present Danger (Clancy), 1989
Clear and Present Danger (Kendrick), 1958
Clear Case of Suicide (Underwood), 1980
Clear the Fast Lane (Rutherford), 1971
Cleek, Hamilton series (Hanshew), from 1910
Clemmie (J. MacDonald), 1958
Cleopatra Jones (Goulart), 1973
Cleopatra Jones and the Casino of Gold (Goulart), 1975
Cleopatra's Tears (Keeler), 1940

Cleveland Pipeline (Pendleton), 1977
Clever One (E. Wallace), 1928
Clew of the Forgotten Murder (E. Gardner, as Kendrake), 1935
Client (Russell), 1975
Client Is Cancelled (Lockridge), 1951
Client Privilege (Tapley), 1990
Climate of Courage (Cleary), 1954
Clique of Gold (Gaboriau, trans), 1874
Cloak of Darkness (MacInnes), 1982
Clock (s A. Mason), 1910
Clock in the Hat Box (A. Gilbert), 1939
Clock Strikes Thirteen (Brean), 1952
Clock Strikes Twelve (Wentworth), 1944
Clock Struck One (Hume), 1898
Clock That Wouldn't Stop (Ferrars), 1952
Clock Ticks On (V. Williams), 1933
Clock Without Hands (Kersh), 1949
Clocks (Christie), 1963
Clockwork's Pirates (s Goulart), 1971
Cloisonne Vase (Avallone, as Noone), 1970
Close All Roads to Sospel (Bellairs), 1976
Close Call (Phillpotts), 1936
Close Her Eyes (Simpson), 1984
Close Quarters (M. Gilbert), 1947
Close the Door on Murder (Creasey, as York), 1948
Close to Death (Michael Collins, as Crowe), 1979
Close to the Wind (Hebden, as Harris), 1956
Closed Book (Le Queux), 1904
Closed Circuit (Haggard), 1960
Closed Door (Horler), 1948
Cloud Nine (J. Cain), 1984
Clouds of Guilt (Wainwright), 1985
Clouds of Witness (Sayers), 1926
Cloven Foot (Braddon, appendix), 1879
Clown (C. Brown), 1972
Clowns and Criminals (s Oppenheim), 1931
Club of Queer Trades (s Chesterton), 1905
Club 17 (Ard, as Kerr), 1957
Clubb, Sergeant Caleb series (North), from 1960
Clubbable Woman (Hill), 1970
Clubfoot series (V. Williams), from 1918
Clue (Wells), 1909
Clue for Clancy (Thayer), 1950
Clue from the Stars (Phillpotts), 1932
Clue in the Clay (Olsen), 1938
Clue in the Mirror (Morland), 1937
Clue of the Artificial Eye (s J. Fletcher), 1939
Clue of the Bricklayer's Aunt (Morland), 1936
Clue of the Careless Hangman (Morland), 1940
Clue of the Eyelash (Wells), 1933
Clue of the Fourteen Keys (Rhode, as Burton), 1937
Clue of the Golden Ear-Ring (Wills), 1950
Clue of the Green Candle (Verner), 1938
Clue of the Judas Tree (Ford), 1933
Clue of the Lost Hour (Wills), 1949
Clue of the New Pin (E. Wallace), 1923
Clue of the Poor Man's Shilling (K. Knight), 1936
Clue of the Rising Moon (V. Williams), 1935
Clue of the Second Murder (Strange), 1929
Clue of the Second Tooth (Verner, as Stuart), 1927
Clue of the Silver Brush (Rhode, as Burton), 1936
Clue of the Silver Cellar (Rhode, as Burton), 1937
Clue of the Silver Key (E. Wallace), 1930
Clue of the Twisted Candle (E. Wallace), 1916
Clue Sinister (Carnac), 1947
Clue to the Labyrinth (Clason), 1939
Clues for Christabel (Fitt), 1944

Clues for Dr. Coffee (s Blochman), 1964
Clues of the Caribbees (s Stribling), 1929
Clues to Burn (Offord), 1942
Clunk, Joshua series (Bailey), from 1930
Cluster of Separate Sparks (Aiken), 1972
Clutch of Constables (Marsh), 1968
Clutch of Coppers (Creasey, as Ashe), 1967
Clutch of Vipers (Scott), 1979
Clutching Hand (Reeve), 1934
Coach North (McCutchan), 1974
Coast of Fear (Roth, as Ballard), 1957
Coat of Arms (E. Wallace), 1931
Coat of Arms (Sims), 1984
Cobb, Matt series (DeAndrea), from 1978
Cobweb Castle (J. Fletcher), 1928
Cock and Anchor (Le Fanu, appendix), 1845
Cock-Pit of Roses (J. Fraser), 1969
Cockatoo Crime (B. Knox), 1958
Cockeyed Corpse (Prather), 1964
Cockleburr (Rae, as Crawford), 1969
Cockpit (Hall, as Scott), 1953
Cockrill, Inspector series (Brand), from 1941
Cocktail for Cupid (s Cheyney), 1948
Cocktail Party (s Cheyney), 1948
Cocktails and the Killer (Cheyney), 1957
Coconut Killings (Moyes), 1977
Code Name Gadget (Rabe), 1967
Code Name: Werewolf (M. Smith, as Carter), 1973
Code Three (Fox), 1953
Codeword Cromwell (Allbeury, as Kelly), 1980
Codeword—Golden Fleece (Wheatley), 1946
Coffin Bird (C. Brown), 1970
Coffin Corner (Linington, as Shannon), 1966
Coffin Corner (Stein, as Bagby), 1949
Coffin Corner, U.S.A (Avallone, as Jason), 1981
Coffin Country (Stein), 1976
Coffin for a Hood (L. White), 1958
Coffin for Christopher (Ames), 1954
Coffin for Dimitrios (Ambler), 1939
Coffin for One (Beeding), 1943
Coffin for the Body (Morland), 1943
Coffin from Hong Kong (Chase), 1962
Coffin, Inspector John and Superintendent William Winter series (Butler), from 1957
Coffin Island (Leblanc, trans), 1920
Coffin, Scarcely Used (Watson), 1958
Coffin Things (Avallone), 1968
Coffins for Three (F. Davis), 1938
Coffins for Two (s Starrett), 1924
Cogan's Trade (G. Higgins), 1974
Coil of Rope (Straker), 1962
Coin of Edward VII (Hume), 1903
Coin of the Realm (Murphy), 1989
Colby, Al series (Dodge), from 1948
Cold Blood (Bruce), 1952
Cold-Blooded Murder (Crofts), 1947
Cold Chills (s Bloch), 1977
Cold Coming (Kelly), 1956
Cold Dark Night (Gainham), 1957
Cold Dog Soup (Dobyns), 1985
Cold Harbour (J. Higgins), 1990
Cold in July (Lansdale), 1989
Cold Iron (Freeling), 1986
Cold Jungle (G. Black), 1969
Cold, Lone, and Still (G. Mitchell), 1983
Cold Poison (Palmer), 1954
Cold Red Sunrise (Kaminsky), 1988

Cold Smell of Sacred Stone (Chesbro), 1988
Cold Steal (P. Taylor, as Tilton), 1939
Cold Trail (Linington, as Shannon), 1978
Cold War Swap (Thomas), 1966
Cold Waters (Hubbard), 1969
Coldstone (Wentworth), 1930
Cole, Schyler and Luke Speare series (F. Davis), from 1950
Collaborators (Hill), 1987
Collar for the Killer (Brean), 1957
Collection of Strangers (Olsen, as Hitchens), 1969
Collision Course (Rutherford), 1978
Colonel Bogus (Blackburn), 1964
Colonel Butler's Wolf (Price), 1972
Colonel's Foxhound (Wills), 1960
Color Him Guilty (Hensley), 1987
Color of Hate (Hensley), 1960
Colorado Kill-Zone (Pendleton), 1976
Colors for Murder (Dent, as Robeson), 1990
Colossus (E. Wallace), 1932
Colossus (S. Marlowe), 1972
Colossus of Arcadia (Oppenheim), 1938
Colour of Fear (Ormerod), 1976
Colour of Murder (Symons), 1957
Colour of Violence (Jeffries, as Ashford), 1974
Colour Scheme (Marsh), 1943
Columbella (Whitney), 1966
Comady, John and Larry Cohen series (Cunningham), from 1965
Combination (York), 1983
Come and Be Killed (Ferrars), 1987
Come and Be Killed! (S. Smith), 1946
Come and Go (Coles, as Gaite), 1958
Come and Kill Me (Tey), 1951
Come Away, Death (G. Mitchell), 1937
Come Back (Wells), 1921
Come Back Charleston Blue (Himes), 1970
Come Back to Murder (Courtier), 1957
Come Back, My Love (Aarons), 1953
Come Death and High Water (Cleeves), 1987
Come Die with Me (Gault), 1959
Come Easy—Go Easy (Chase), 1960
Come Hell and High Water (s Curzon, as Petrie), 1970
Come Here and Die (Creasey, as Halliday), 1959
Come Home and Be Killed (Butler, as Melville), 1962
Come Home to Crime (Creasey, as Deane), 1945
Come Home to Death (Creasey, as Ashe), 1958
Come into My Parlour (Wheatley), 1946
Come Kill with Me (H. Kane), 1972
Come Morning (Gores), 1986
Come Night, Come Evil (Craig), 1957
Come-On (Yorke), 1979
Come Over, Red Rover (S. Marlowe), 1968
Come See Me Die (Neville), 1963
Come, Thick Night (Neville), 1951
Come to Dust (Lathen), 1968
Come to Judgment (Strange), 1949
Comedian Dies (Brett), 1979
Comedians (Greene), 1966
Comedy of Terrors (M. Innes), 1940
Comes a Stranger (Punshon), 1938
Comes the Blind Fury (Rutherford), 1950
Comes the Dark Stranger (J. Higgins, as Patterson), 1962
Comfort Me with Spies (McShane, as Lovell), 1990
Coming of Carew (Graeme), 1945
Command Strike (Pendleton), 1977
Commission for Disaster (Chance), 1964
Common Sense Is All You Need (Connington), 1947

Corpse in Cold Storage (Kennedy), 1934
Corpse in My Bed (Alexander), 1954
Corpse in Oozak's Pond (MacLeod), 1986
Corpse in the Car (Rhode), 1935
Corpse in the Castle (Wormser, as Friend), 1970
Corpse in the Circus (s Morland), 1945
Corpse in the Constable's Garden (Cole), 1931
Corpse in the Corner Saloon (Stein, as Stone), 1948
Corpse in the Crevasse (G. Carr), 1952
Corpse in the Flannel Nightgown (Scherf), 1965
Corpse in the Snowman (Blake), 1941
Corpse in the Waxworks (J. Carr), 1932
Corpse Moved Upstairs (Gruber), 1964
Corpse on the Dike (van de Wetering), 1976
Corpse on the Flying Trapeze (Morland), 1941
Corpse on the Mat (Kennedy), 1929
Corpse Road (Moffat), 1974
Corpse Steps Out (Rice), 1940
Corpse That Refused to Stay Dead (Stein, as Stone), 1952
Corpse That Talked (Jessup, as Telfair), 1959
Corpse That Walked (O. Cohen), 1951
Corpse to Copenhagen (John Burke), 1957
Corpse Was No Bargain at All (Stein, as Stone), 1968
Corpse Was No Lady (Morland), 1950
Corpse Who Had Too Many Friends (Stein, as Stone), 1953
Corpse with One Shoe (Scherf), 1951
Corpse with Sticky Fingers (Stein, as Bagby), 1952
Corpse with the Purple Thighs (Stein, as Bagby), 1939
Corpse Won't Sing (Courtier), 1964
Corpse Wore a Wig (Stein, as Bagby), 1940
Corpses in Enderby (Bellairs), 1954
Corpus Delectable (Powell), 1965
Corrector of Destinies (Post), 1908
Corridor of Whispers (Avallone, as Noone), 1965
Corridors of Fear (Horler), 1947
Corridors of Guilt (Hilton), 1984
Corrigan, Brick-Top series (Chase, as Marshall), from 1950
Corrupt and Ensnare (Nevins), 1978
Corruption City (McCoy), 1959
Corsican (Ballinger), 1974
Cost of Silence (Yorke), 1977
Cost Price (Yates), 1949
Cottage Murder (Punshon), 1932
Cottage of Terror (Verner, as Stuart), 1935
Cotterell, Martin series (Trench), from 1953
Cotton Comes to Harlem (Himes), 1965
Couch (Bloch), 1962
Council of Egypt (Sciascia, trans), 1966
Council of Justice (E. Wallace), 1908
Counsel for the Defence (Jeffries, as Ashford), 1960
Counsellor (Connington), 1939
Counsellor Heart (Winslow), 1980
Count Down (Carmichael, as Howard), 1962
Count of Nine (E. Gardner, as Fair), 1958
Count the Cost (Ferrars), 1957
Count the Ways (Doris Disney), 1949
Counter Spy Murders (Cheyney), 1944
Counterfeit (Carmichael, as Howard), 1966
Counterfeit (Thayer), 1933
Counterfeit Bill (Thayer), 1934
Counterfeit Kill (Hunt, as Davis), 1963
Counterfeit of Murder (R. Harrison), 1986
Counterfeit Wife (Halliday), 1947
Counterpoint Murder (Cole), 1940
Countersnatch (Straker), 1980
Counterspy (Cleeve), 1966
Counterstroke (Garve), 1978

Country and Fatal (Stein, as Bagby), 1980
Country-House Burglar (M. Gilbert), 1955
Country Kind of Death (McMullen), 1975
Country of Again (Hubbard), 1968
Count's Chauffeur (s Le Queux), 1907
Count's Millions (Gaboriau, trans), 1913
Count's Secret (Gaboriau, trans), 1881
County Kill (Gault), 1962
Coupon Crimes (Verner), 1946
Courier to Marrakesh (V. Williams), 1944
Court Intrigue (B. Thomson), 1896
Court of Foxes (Brand), 1969
Court of Honour (Le Queux), 1901
Court of St. Simon (Oppenheim, as Partridge), 1912
Courtesy of Death (Household), 1967
Courtier to Death (A. Gilbert), 1936
Courtney Entry (Hebden, as Harris), 1970
Courts of the Morning (Buchan), 1929
Cousin Once Removed (Hammond), 1984
Coven (C. Brown), 1971
Coven (Hunt, as St. John), 1972
Coven Gibbet (Chance), 1948
Covenant with Death (Hebden, as Harris), 1961
Cover Her Face (James), 1962
Cover His Face (Kyd), 1949
Cover Story (C. Forbes), 1985
Cover-Up (Oliver), 1987
Cover-Up Story (Babson), 1971
Coward's Kiss (Block), 1987
Cowl of Doom (Aarons, as Ronns), 1946
Coyle and Donovan series (Pentecost, as Philips), from 1941
Coyne, Brady series (Tapply), from 1984
Coyote (Barnes), 1990
Coyote Connection (Crider, as Carter), 1981
Coyote Waits (Hillerman), 1990
Cozumel (Hunt), 1985
"C.Q." (Train), 1912
Crabtree Affair (M. Innes), 1962
Crack in the Sidewalk (Copper), 1976
Crack in the Teacup (M. Gilbert), 1966
Crack of Dawn (Ford), 1945
Crack of Doom (Bruce), 1963
Cracksman on Velvet (Selwyn), 1974
Crader, Carl and Earl Jazine series (Hoch), from 1971
Cradle and the Grave (Stein), 1948
Cradle Will Fall (M. Clark), 1980
Craghold series (Avallone, as Noone), from 1971
Craig, Alan series (Stuart, as Gray), from 1985
Crane, Bill series (Latimer), from 1935
Crane, Lionel series (Verner, as Stuart), from 1934
Crank in the Corner (Bush), 1933
Crash of '79 (Erdman), 1976
Crawford, Thea series (Mann), from 1973
Crawley, Ray series (Corris), from 1985
Crazy Joe (Albert, as Barone), 1974
Crazy Kill (Himes), 1959
Crazy Mixed-Up Corpse (Avallone), 1957
Crazy-Quilt (Hume), 1919
Creaking Chair (Meynell), 1941
Cream and Cider (Harvester, as Gibbs), 1952
Created (Murphy), 1971
Creative Murders (C. Brown), 1971
Creature of the Night (Hume), 1891
Creature Was Stirring (S. Forbes, as Wells), 1977
Credit for a Murder (Sterling, as Dean), 1961
Creeping Death (Gibson, as Grant), 1977
Creeping Flesh (Rutherford), 1963

Crowder, George series (Pentecost), from 1961
Crown Estate (Berckman), 1976
Crown of Night (Audemars), 1962
Crowned Skull (Hume), 1908
Crowning Glory (Punshon), 1914
Crows Can't Count (E. Gardner, as Fair), 1946
Crozart Story (Fearing), 1960
Crozier Pharaohs (G. Mitchell), 1984
Cruel as a Cat (Creasey, as Halliday), 1968
Cruel as the Grave (McCloy), 1977
Cruel Is the Night (Hunt), 1955
Cruel Victim (Tripp), 1979
Cruise of a Deathtime (Babson), 1983
Cruise of the Liza Jane (Hume), 1895
Crumpled Cup (H. Kane), 1961
Cry Aloud for Murder (McGuire), 1937
Cry at Dusk (Dent), 1952
Cry for Help (Doris Disney), 1975
Cry Guilty (Woods), 1981
Cry Hard, Cry Fast (J. MacDonald), 1955
Cry Havoc (Stern), 1963
Cry in the Jungle (K. Knight), 1958
Cry in the Night (M. Clark), 1982
Cry in the Night (Miller, as Masterson), 1956
Cry in the Night (Roos), 1966
Cry Killer! (Fearing), 1958
Cry of Shadows (Gorman), 1990
Cry of the Halidon (Ludlum, as Ryder), 1974
Cry of the Hunter (J. Higgins, as Patterson), 1960
Cry of the Owl (Highsmith), 1962
Cry on My Shoulder (Carmichael, as Howard), 1970
Cry Passion (Jessup), 1956
Cry Revenge! (Goines, as Clark), 1974
Cry Scandal (Ard), 1956
Crying Child (Elizabeth Peters, as Michaels), 1973
Crying Sisters (Seeley), 1939
Crypto Man (Royce), 1984
Crystal Cat (Johnston), 1985
Crystal Claw (Le Queux), 1924
Crystal Contract (Rathbone), 1988
Crystal Crow (Aiken), 1968
Crystal Stopper (Leblanc, trans), 1913
Crystallised Carbon Pig (Wainwright), 1966
Cuckoo Line Affair (Garve), 1953
Cuddy, John Francis series (Healy), from 1984
Cue for Murder (McCloy), 1942
Cul-de-Sac (Wainwright), 1984
Cummings, Chief Inspector series (McGuire), from 1931
Cunning and the Haunted (Jessup), 1954
Cunning as a Fox (Creasey, as Halliday), 1965
Cunning Serpent (Bloch), 1981
Cunningham, Captain John series (Hammond), from 1989
Cup and the Lip (Ferrars), 1975
Cup Final Murder (B. Newman), 1950
Cup of Cold Poison (J. Fleming), 1969
Cup, The Blade, or the Gun (Eberhart), 1961
Cupid's Executioners (Monteilhet, trans), 1967
Cure for Dying (Butler, as Melville), 1989
Curiosity of Etienne MacGregor (Cheyney), 1947
Curiosity of Mr. Treadgold (s V. Williams), 1937
Curious Affair of the Third Dog (Moyes), 1973
Curious Crime of Miss Julia Blossom (Meynell), 1970
Curious Custard Pie (Scherf), 1950
Curious Facts Preceding My Execution (s Westlake), 1968
Curious Happenings to the Rooke Legatees (s Oppenheim), 1937
Curious Quest (Oppenheim), 1919

Curse (Hume), 1913
Curse of Doone (Horler), 1928
Curse of the Bronze Lamp (J. Carr, as Dickson), 1945
Curse of the Giant Hogweed (MacLeod), 1985
Curse of the Kings (Holt), 1973
Curse of the Pharaohs (Elizabeth Peters), 1981
Curse the Darkness (Grant-Adamson), 1990
Cursed to Death (Crider), 1988
Curses! (Elkins), 1989
Cursing Stones Murder (Bellairs), 1954
Curtain (Christie), 1975
Curtain at Eight (O. Cohen), 1933
Curtain Call for a Corpse (Bell), 1965
Curtain Fall (Dewhurst), 1977
Curtain for a Jester (Lockridge), 1953
Curtain of Fear (Wheatley), 1953
Curtains for a Chorine (C. Brown), 1955
Curtains for a Lover (Hunt, as Dietrich), 1961
Curtains for Three (Stout), 1950
Curve of the Catenary (Rinehart), 1945
Curved Blades (Wells), 1916
Curves for the Coroner (C. Brown), 1955
Curzon Case (Durbridge), 1972
Custom of the Country (Hubbard), 1969
Cut Direct (P. Taylor, as Tilton), 1938
Cut Me In (McBain, as Collins), 1954
Cut of the Whip (Rabe), 1958
Cut Thin to Win (E. Gardner, as Fair), 1965
Cut Throat (Bush), 1932
Cutie Cashed His Chips (C. Brown), 1955
Cutie Takes the Count (C. Brown), 1958
Cutie Wins a Corpse (C. Brown), 1957
Cutter and Bone (Thornburg), 1976
Cyanide with Compliments (Lemarchand), 1972
Cyclops (Cussler), 1986
Cyclops Goblet (Blackburn), 1977
Cynthia (Cunningham), 1968
Cynthia Wakeham's Money (Green), 1892
Cynthia-of-the-Minute (L. Vance), 1911
Cypress Road (Bush, as Home), 1945
Czar of Fear (Dent, as Robeson), 1968
Czar's Spy (Le Queux), 1905

D as in Dead (Treat), 1941
"D" Is for Deadbeat (S. Grafton), 1987
D Notice (Graeme), 1974
D.A. series (E. Gardner), from 1937
Daddy Cool (Goines), 1974
Daddy's Girl (J. Milne), 1988
Daffodil Affair (M. Innes), 1942
Daffodil Blonde (Crane), 1950
Daffodil Murder (E. Wallace), 1921
Daffodil Mystery (E. Wallace), 1920
Dagger in the Sky (Dent, as Robeson), 1969
Dagger of Flesh (Prather), 1952
Dagger of the Mind (Fearing), 1941
Dain Curse (Hammett), 1929
Daisy-Chain for Satan (J. Fleming), 1950
Daisy Ducks (Boyer), 1986
Dale, Jimmie series (Packard), from 1917
Dalgliesh, Commander Adam series (James), from 1962
Dalziel, Superintendent Andrew and Sergeant Pascoe series (Hill), from 1970
Dame (C. Brown), 1959
Dame (Westlake, as Stark), 1969
Dame in Danger (Dewey), 1958
Dames Can Be Deadly (Chambers), 1963

Dames Don't Care (Cheyney), 1937
Dammed Spot (Herbert Adams), 1938
Damned (J. MacDonald), 1952
Damned If He Does (Ard, as Kerr), 1956
Damned Innocents (Neely), 1971
Damned Lovely (Webb), 1954
Damned to Success (Kirst, trans), 1973
Damocles Sword (Hall, as Trevor), 1981
Damsel (Westlake, as Stark), 1967
Dan Turner, Hollywood Detective (s Bellem), 1983
Dance Hall of the Dead (Hillerman), 1973
Dance of Death (C. Brown), 1964
Dance of Death (McCloy), 1938
Dance of the Dwarfs (Household), 1968
Dance to Your Daddy (G. Mitchell), 1969
Dance with the Dead (Prather), 1960
Dance with the Devil (Koontz, as Dwyer), 1973
Dance Without Music (Cheyney), 1947
Dance Without Music (s Cheyney), 1945
Dancer in Red (s Hume), 1906
Dancer with One Leg (Dobyns), 1983
Dancer, April series (Avallone), from 1966
Dancer's Debt (Lutz), 1988
Dancers in Mourning (Allingham), 1937
Dancing Aztecs (Westlake), 1976
Dancing Bear (Crumley), 1983
Dancing Death (Bush), 1931
Dancing Detective (s Woolrich, as Irish), 1946
Dancing Dodo (J. Gardner), 1978
Dancing Druids (G. Mitchell), 1948
Dancing Floor (Buchan), 1926
Dancing Girl (Leroux, trans), 1924
Dancing Man (Hubbard), 1971
Dancing Men (Kyle), 1985
Dandy (Meynell), 1938
Dandy in Aspic (Derek Marlowe), 1966
Dane, Timothy series (Ard), from 1951
Danger (Francis), 1983
Danger Ahead (Simenon, trans), 1955
Danger at Westways (Verner, as Stuart), 1938
Danger Calling (Wentworth), 1931
Danger—Death at Work (Morland, as Garnett), 1939
Danger: Hospital Zone (Curtiss), 1966
Danger in Paradise (O. Cohen), 1945
Danger in the Dark (Eberhart), 1937
Danger Is My Line (S. Marlowe), 1960
Danger Lies East (Dent, as Robeson), 1988
Danger Money (Eberhart), 1975
Danger Money (Russell), 1968
Danger Next Door (Quentin, as Patrick), 1952
Danger Point (Wentworth), 1942
Danger Preferred (Horler), 1942
Danger round the Corner (Meynell), 1952
Danger Within (M. Gilbert), 1952
Danger Woman (Creasey, as Mann), 1966
Danger! (s Doyle), 1918
Dangerfield Talisman (Connington), 1926
Dangerous Blondes (Roos), 1951
Dangerous Business (Balmer), 1927
Dangerous by Nature (Coles), 1950
Dangerous Cargo (Footner), 1934
Dangerous Curves (Cheyney), 1939
Dangerous Days (Rinehart), 1919
Dangerous Domicile (Carnac, as Lorac), 1957
Dangerous Funeral (McMullen), 1977
Dangerous Game (Dürrenmatt, trans), 1960
Dangerous Game (Le Queux), 1926

Dangerous Games (Murphy, Randisi), 1980
Dangerous Inheritance (Wheatley), 1965
Dangerous Journey (Creasey, as Deane), 1939
Dangerous Lady (O. Cohen), 1946
Dangerous Landing (McGerr), 1975
Dangerous Legacy (Coxe), 1946
Dangerous Legacy (W. Roberts), 1972
Dangerous Liaison (Davey), 1988
Dangerous Passenger (Walsh), 1959
Dangerous Pawn (W. Graham), 1937
Dangerous Place to Dwell (Russell), 1978
Dangerous Quest (Creasey), 1944
Dangerous Silence (MacKenzie), 1960
Dangerous to Know (Babson), 1980
Danger's Bright Eyes (Horler), 1930
Dangling Carrot (Keene), 1955
Dangling Man (H. Kane), 1959
D'Arblay Mystery (Freeman), 1926
Dardanelles Derelict (F. Mason), 1949
Daredevil (Charteris), 1929
Dark (Deming, as Franklin), 1978
Dark Abyss (C. Knight), 1949
Dark-Adapted Eye (Rendell, as Vine), 1986
Dark Avenue (Hume), 1920
Dark Bahama (Cheyney), 1950
Dark Blood, Dark Terror (Cleeve), 1965
Dark Blue and Dangerous (J. Ross), 1981
Dark Calypso (Gray), 1979
Dark Chase (Goodis), 1953
Dark Circle (Creasey, as Ashe), 1960
Dark Citadel (C. Brown, as Farr), 1971
Dark Crusade (Fox), 1954
Dark Crusader (MacLean, as Stuart), 1961
Dark Cypress (Avallone, as Noone), 1965
Dark Danger (Horler), 1945
Dark Death (A. Gilbert), 1963
Dark Deeds (s Donovan), 1895
Dark Destiny (Aarons, as Ronns), 1953
Dark Dowry (W. Roberts), 1978
Dark Duet (Cheyney), 1942
Dark Duet (Elizabeth Peters, as Michaels), 1983
Dark Encounter (Hunt), 1950
Dark Entry (Copper), 1981
Dark Eyes of London (E. Wallace), 1924
Dark Fantastic (Ellin), 1983
Dark Fantastic (Miller, as Masterson), 1959
Dark Frontier (Ambler), 1936
Dark Garden (Eberhart), 1933
Dark Garden (Punshon), 1941
Dark Goddess (Albert), 1978
Dark Harvest (Creasey), 1947
Dark Hazard (Burnett), 1933
Dark Hazard (G. Carr, as Styles), 1948
Dark Hero (Cheyney), 1946
Dark Hollow (Green), 1914
Dark Hostess (Horler), 1955
Dark Interlude (Cheyney), 1947
Dark Interval (Aiken), 1967
Dark Is the Clue! (Punshon), 1955
Dark Is the Tunnel (Rhode, as Burton), 1936
Dark Journey (Crofts), 1951
Dark Journey (Horler), 1938
Dark Lady (Doris Disney), 1960
Dark Light (Spicer), 1949
Dark Mansion (C. Brown, as Farr), 1974
Dark Memory (Aarons, as Ronns), 1950
Dark Mirror (Copper), 1966

Dark Mirror (L. Vance), 1920
Dark Mystery (Creasey, as Ashe), 1948
Dark Nantucket Noon (Langton), 1975
Dark Night (Horler), 1953
Dark Nights (s T. Burke), 1944
Dark Ocean (J. Vance), 1985
Dark of Summer (Koontz, as Dwyer), 1972
Dark of the Moon (J. Carr), 1967
Dark of the Moon (Thayer), 1936
Dark on Monday (Avallone), 1978
Dark on the Other Side (Elizabeth Peters, as Michaels), 1970
Dark Passage (Goodis), 1946
Dark Passage (York), 1975
Dark Peril (Creasey), 1944
Dark Place (Elkins), 1983
Dark Power (E. Holding), 1930
Dark Power (L. Vance), 1925
Dark Power (Michael Collins, as Arden), 1968
Dark Road (C. Knight), 1951
Dark Road (Doris Disney), 1946
Dark Road (Leroux, trans), 1924
Dark Saviour (Harling), 1952
Dark Secret of Josephine (Wheatley), 1955
Dark Shadow (Creasey, as Matheson)
Dark Ships (Footner), 1937
Dark Side (Hornig), 1986
Dark Side (K. Davis), 1976
Dark Side of Love (s Woolrich), 1965
Dark Side of the Island (Hebden), 1973
Dark Side of the Island (J. Higgins, as Patterson), 1963
Dark Side of the Street (J. Higgins, as Fallon), 1967
Dark Square (Meynell), 1941
Dark Star (Muller), 1989
Dark Stream (J. Thomson), 1986
Dark Street (Cheyney), 1944
Dark Street Murders (Cheyney), 1946
Dark Threat (Wentworth), 1951
Dark Trade (Lejeune), 1965
Dark Tunnel (Macdonald, as Millar), 1944
Dark Wanton (Cheyney), 1948
Dark Wheel (P. MacDonald), 1948
Dark Wind (Hillerman), 1982
Dark Window (Walsh), 1956
Darkened Room (Clarke), 1968
Darkened Room (M. Harrison), 1952
Darkening Door (Ballinger), 1952
Darkening Glass (Wainwright), 1968
Darkening Willows (Avallone, as Dalton), 1965
Darker Side of Death (Russell), 1985
Darker Than Amber (J. MacDonald), 1966
Darker the Night (Brean), 1949
Darkest Hour (McGivern), 1955
Darkest Hour (Nielsen), 1969
Darkest Spot (Thayer), 1928
Darkness at Dawn (s Woolrich), 1985
Darkness Within (Cunningham), 1953
Darling You're Doomed (C. Brown), 1956
Darling, It's Death (Prather), 1952
Darlington Jaunt (A. Ross), 1983
Darsham's Folly (John Burke, as Esmond), 1974
Darsham's Tower (John Burke, as Esmond), 1973
Dartmoor Enigma (B. Thomson), 1936
Darwin's Secret (Hoyt), 1989
da Silva, Captain José series (Fish), from 1962
Date after Dark (s Cheyney), 1946
Date with Danger (Vickers), 1942
Date with Darkness (D. Hamilton), 1947

Date with Death (Ford), 1949
Date with Death (Linington), 1966
Date with Death (Murphy), 1984
Daughter of Astrea (Oppenheim), 1898
Daughter of Darkness (Avallone, as Noone), 1966
Daughter of Darkness (McGerr), 1974
Daughter of the House (Wells), 1925
Daughter of the Marionis (Oppenheim), 1895
Daughter of Time (Tey), 1951
Daughters in Law (Cecil), 1961
Daughters of the Night (E. Wallace), 1925
Davidian Report (Hughes), 1952
Davidson Case (Rhode), 1929
Davie, R.E. series (Clinton-Baddeley), from 1967
Davies, John series (Bennett), from 1945
Davis, John George series (Wainwright, as Ripley), from 1971
Dawlish, Patrick series (Creasey, as Ashe), from 1939
Dawn of Darkness (Creasey), 1949
Dawson Pedigree (Sayers), 1928
Day and Night Stories (s Blackwood), 1917
Day in Monte Carlo (Albrand), 1959
Day It Rained Diamonds (Crossen, as Chaber), 1966
Day Miss Bessie Lewis Disappeared (Doris Disney), 1972
Day of Disaster (Creasey), 1942
Day of Fear (Creasey, as Ashe), 1956
Day of Judgement (J. Higgins), 1978
Day of Temptation (Le Queux), 1899
Day of Terror (Creasey, as Cooke), 1936
Day of the Arrow (Loraine), 1964
Day of the Big Dollar (Chambers), 1979
Day of the Coastwatch (McCutchan), 1968
Day of the Dead (Spicer), 1955
Day of the Donkey Derby (J. Fleming), 1978
Day of the Guns (Spillane), 1964
Day of the Jackal (Forsyth), 1971
Day of the Moon (Pronzini, as Jeffrey), 1983
Day of the Owl (Sciascia, trans), 1984
Day of the Peppercorn Kill (Wainwright), 1977
Day of the Ram (Gault), 1956
Day of Uniting (E. Wallace), 1926
Day of Wrath (Valin), 1982
Day She Died (Reilly), 1962
Day the Children Vanished (Pentecost), 1976
Day the Sun Fell (J. Roberts, as Duncan), 1970
Day the Thames Caught Fire (Chambers), 1989
Day the Wind Dropped (Royce), 1964
Day the World Ended (Rohmer), 1930
Day, Julian series (Wheatley), from 1939
Daylight Murder (McGuire), 1934
Daylight Robbery (Russell), 1978
Days of Danger (Creasey), 1937
Days of Misfortune (Stein), 1949
Days of Your Fathers (s Household), 1987
Deacon Brodie (Donovan), 1901
Deacon, William series (Brean), from 1960
Dead Against the Lawyers (Jeffries), 1965
Dead Aim (Wilcox), 1971
Dead and Alive (H. Innes), 1946
Dead and Buried (Engel), 1990
Dead and Dumb (Crispin), 1947
Dead Are Discreet (Lyons), 1974
Dead as a Dinosaur (Lockridge), 1952
Dead as a Dummy (Homes), 1949
Dead at First Hand (J. Ross), 1969
Dead at the Take-Off (Dent), 1946
Dead Babes in the Wood (Olsen), 1954
Dead-Bang (Prather), 1971

Dead Beat (Bloch), 1960
Dead Birds (J. Milne), 1986
Dead by Morning (Simpson), 1989
Dead by Now (Erskine), 1953
Dead by the Light of the Moon (S. Forbes, as Wells), 1967
Dead Calm (C. Williams), 1963
Dead Can Tell (Reilly), 1940
Dead Can't Love (Pentecost, as Philips), 1963
Dead Canary (Fox), 1979
Dead Centre (Wood), 1985
Dead Cert (Francis), 1962
Dead Certain (Sterling), 1960
Dead Circuit (Hall, as Rattray), 1955
Dead Clever (Jeffries), 1989
Dead Copy . . . (Monteilhet, trans), 1976
Dead Corse (Kelly), 1966
Dead Crazy (Pickard), 1989
Dead Darling (Craig), 1955
Dead Dolls Don't Talk (Keene), 1959
Dead Don't Care (Latimer), 1938
Dead Don't Scream (Gribble), 1983
Dead Don't Speak (Erskine), 1955
Dead Drunk (Carmichael, as Howard), 1974
Dead Drunk (Stein, as Bagby), 1953
Dead End (Lacy), 1960
Dead End (R. Perry), 1977
Dead End (Strange), 1953
Dead End in Mayfair (Gribble), 1981
Dead End Street (Murphy), 1973
Dead End Street, No Outlet (Thayer), 1936
Dead Ending (Pentecost, as Philips), 1962
Dead Ernest (J. Mitchell), 1986
Dead Ernest (P. Taylor, as Tilton), 1944
Dead Eye (J. Ross), 1983
Dead Fall (Miller, as Wilmer), 1954
Dead File (Copper), 1970
Dead Flowers (Johnson), 1990
Dead for a Ducat (Bruce), 1956
Dead for a Ducat (Payne), 1986
Dead for a Ducat (Reilly), 1939
Dead Game (Avallone), 1954
Dead Game (Hammond), 1979
Dead Give Away (Gray), 1974
Dead Giveaway (Brett), 1985
Dead Have No Friends (Morland, as Donavan), 1952
Dead Heat (Aarons, as Ayres), 1950
Dead Heat (Barnes), 1984
Dead Heat (Prather), 1963
Dead Heat (Russell), 1986
Dead Hero (Gault), 1963
Dead If I Remember (Courtier), 1972
Dead in a Row (Butler), 1957
Dead in Bed (H. Kane), 1961
Dead in Bed (Keene), 1959
Dead in the Morning (Yorke), 1970
Dead in the Water (Wood), 1983
Dead Knock (Turnbull), 1982
Dead Letter (D. Clark), 1984
Dead Letter (Murphy), 1982
Dead Letter (Valin), 1981
Dead Letters (John Burke, as George), 1972
Dead Liberty (Aird), 1986
Dead Line (McCutchan), 1966
Dead Lion (Bonett), 1949
Dead Look On (Kersh), 1943
Dead Loss (Curzon, as Petrie), 1966
Dead Low Tide (J. MacDonald), 1953

Dead Man Blues (s Woolrich, as Irish), 1948
Dead Man Calling (G. Black), 1962
Dead Man Control (Reilly), 1936
Dead Man Falling (Cory), 1953
Dead Man Inside (Starrett), 1931
Dead Man Manor (V. Williams), 1936
Dead Man Murder (B. Newman), 1946
Dead Man Running (Blackburn), 1960
Dead Man Twice (Bush), 1930
Dead Man's Bluff (Jeffries), 1970
Dead Man's Diary (Halliday), 1945
Dead Man's Dower (Vickers, as Kyle), 1925
Dead Man's Effects (Bailey), 1945
Dead Man's Folly (Christie), 1956
Dead Man's Handle (Blackburn), 1978
Dead Man's Handle (P. O'Donnell), 1985
Dead Man's Hat (Footner), 1932
Dead Man's Knock (Chance), 1957
Dead Man's Knock (J. Carr), 1948
Dead Man's Mirror (s Christie), 1937
Dead Man's Money (J. Fletcher), 1930
Dead Man's Mooring (B. Knox), 1987
Dead Man's Music (Bush), 1931
Dead Man's Ransom (Ellis Peters), 1984
Dead Man's Riddle (Kelly), 1957
Dead Man's Secret (Verner, as Stuart), 1932
Dead Man's Shoes (Bailey), 1942
Dead Man's Shoes (Bruce), 1958
Dead Man's Shoes (Chance), 1968
Dead Man's Shoes (s M. Innes), 1954
Dead Man's Tale (Pentecost), 1945
Dead Man's Tale (S. Marlowe, as Queen), 1961
Dead Man's Thoughts (Wheat), 1983
Dead Man's Walk (Prather), 1965
Dead Man's Watch (Cole), 1931
Dead March for Penelope (Bellairs), 1956
Dead March for Penelope Blow (Bellairs), 1951
Dead Meat (Tapley), 1987
Dead Meet (Simon), 1988
Dead Men Alive (Cory), 1969
Dead Men at the Folly (Rhode), 1932
Dead Men Don't Ski (Moyes), 1959
Dead Men Grin (Fischer), 1945
Dead Men of Sestos (Loraine), 1968
Dead Men Tell No Tales (Hornung), 1899
Dead Men's Letters (E. Gardner), 1990
Dead Men's Plans (Eberhart), 1952
Dead Men's Shoes (Thayer), 1929
Dead Men's Morris (G. Mitchell), 1936
Dead Mrs. Stratton (Berkeley), 1933
Dead-Nettle (Hilton), 1977
Dead of Jericho (Dexter), 1981
Dead of Night (Steel), 1940
Dead of Night (Sterling), 1950
Dead of Summer (Kelly), 1963
Dead of the Night (Carmichael), 1956
Dead of the Night (Rhode), 1942
Dead of Winter (Allegretto), 1989
Dead of Winter (Hallahan), 1972
Dead on Arrival (S. Marlowe), 1956
Dead on Arrival (Simpson), 1986
Dead on Arrival (Stein, as Bagby), 1946
Dead on Arrival (Thayer), 1960
Dead on Course (Hall, as Black), 1951
Dead on Cue (Morice), 1985
Dead on the Level (Nielsen), 1954
Dead on the Track (Rhode), 1943

Dead on Time (Keating), 1988
Dead or Alive (Creasey), 1951
Dead or Alive (Wentworth), 1936
Dead Pigeon (Fox), 1967
Dead Pigs at Hungry Farm (Graeme), 1951
Dead Reckoning (Thayer), 1954
Dead Ride Hard (L. Vance), 1926
Dead Right (Sterling), 1956
Dead Ringer (Chase), 1955
Dead Ringer (F. Brown), 1948
Dead Ringer (Lyons), 1977
Dead Ringer (Ormerod), 1985
Dead Rite (F. Kane), 1962
Dead Romantic (Brett), 1985
Dead Room (Resnicow), 1987
Dead Room (s E. Wallace), 1986
Dead Run (Lockridge), 1976
Dead Run (Pronzini, as Foxx), 1975
Dead Sea Cipher (Elizabeth Peters), 1970
Dead Sea Submarine (Caillou), 1971
Dead Secret (Verner), 1967
Dead Secret (Collins, appendix), 1857
Dead Seed (Gault), 1985
Dead: Senate Office Building (Scherf), 1953
Dead Sequence (Hall, as Rattray), 1957
Dead Shall Be Raised (Bellairs), 1942
Dead, She Was Beautiful (Miller, as Masterson), 1955
Dead Shot (Fox), 1979
Dead Side of the Mike (Brett), 1980
Dead Silence (Hall, as Rattray), 1954
Dead Skip (Gores), 1972
Dead Stay Dumb (Chase), 1939
Dead Stop (Doris Disney), 1956
Dead Stop (Rhode, as Burton), 1943
Dead Storage (Stein, as Bagby), 1956
Dead Storage (Thayer), 1935
Dead Straight (MacKenzie), 1969
Dead Sure (Brean), 1958
Dead Sure (Sterling), 1949
Dead Tale-Tellers (Chance), 1972
Dead Thing in the Pool (Stein), 1952
Dead to Rights (K. Davis), 1981
Dead to the World (Durbridge), 1967
Dead to the World (Sterling), 1958
Dead Voice (Wills), 1952
Dead Water (Marsh), 1963
Dead Weight (F. Kane), 1951
Dead Winter (Tapley), 1989
Dead with Sorrow (Audemars), 1965
Dead Woman of the Year (Pentecost), 1967
Dead Wrong (Stein, as Bagby), 1957
Dead Wrong (Sterling), 1947
Dead Yellow Women (s Hammett), 1947
Dead, Man, Dead (Alexander), 1959
Deader They Fall (Chambers), 1979
Deadest Thing You Ever Saw (J. Ross), 1969
Deadfall (Cory), 1965
Deadfall (Pronzini), 1986
Deadhand (Sims), 1971
Deadheads (Hill), 1983
Deadlier Sex (Ballinger), 1958
Deadline (Carmichael, as Howard), 1959
Deadline (Dewey), 1966
Deadline (Heald), 1975
Deadline (Russell), 1971
Deadline at Dawn (Woolrich, as Irish), 1944
Deadline for a Critic (Kienzle), 1987

Deadline for a Dream (B. Knox), 1957
Deadline 2 A.M (Fish, as Pike), 1976
Deadlock (Busby), 1971
Deadlock (C. Forbes), 1988
Deadlock (Paretsky), 1984
Deadly Ackee (Hess, as Hadley), 1988
Deadly Affair (Lacy), 1960
Deadly Affair (le Carré), 1966
Deadly Bedfellows (F. Davis), 1955
Deadly Beloved (Ard), 1958
Deadly Beloved (Strange), 1952
Deadly Climate (Barth), 1988
Deadly Climate (Curtiss), 1954
Deadly Combo (Webb, as Farr), 1958
Deadly Delight (Stein), 1967
Deadly Doll (H. Kane), 1959
Deadly Doll (Spicer, as Barbette), 1958
Deadly Dove (King), 1945
Deadly Downbeat (John Burke), 1962
Deadly Duo (Allingham), 1949
Deadly Duo (Jessup), 1959
Deadly Dwarf (Dent, as Robeson), 1968
Deadly Edge (Westlake, as Stark), 1971
Deadly Finger (H. Kane), 1957
Deadly Friend (Pentecost), 1961
Deadly Game (Daniels), 1959
Deadly Game (Jeffries, as Hastings), 1961
Deadly Gold (J. Ross, as Rossiter), 1975
Deadly Green (J. Ross, as Rossiter), 1970
Deadly Hall (J. Carr), 1971
Deadly Honeymoon (Block), 1967
Deadly Image (Coxe), 1964
Deadly Innocents (Michael Collins, as Sadler), 1986
Deadly Is the Diamond (s Eberhart), 1951
Deadly Is the Evil Tongue (Hocking), 1940
Deadly Isles (J. Vance), 1969
Deadly Joke (Pentecost), 1971
Deadly Joker (Blake), 1963
Deadly Kind of Lonely (S. Forbes), 1971
Deadly Kitten (C. Brown), 1967
Deadly Lampshade (Gray), 1971
Deadly Legacy (Michael Collins, as Arden), 1973
Deadly Marriage (Jeffries), 1967
Deadly Mermaid (Atlee, as Phillips), 1954
Deadly Miss (C. Brown), 1958
Deadly Miss Ashley (F. Davis), 1950
Deadly Night Call (s Woolrich, as Irish), 1951
Deadly Night-Cap (Carmichael), 1953
Deadly Nightshade (E. Daly), 1940
Deadly Nightshade (J. Fraser), 1970
Deadly Orbit Mission (F. Mason), 1968
Deadly Pattern (D. Clark), 1970
Deadly Pavilion (Lawrence), 1948
Deadly Percheron (Bardin), 1946
Deadly Petard (Jeffries), 1983
Deadly Picnic (Bingham), 1980
Deadly Place to Stay (Bell), 1983
Deadly Relations (J. Thomson), 1979
Deadly Seeds (Murphy), 1975
Deadly Sex (Webb), 1959
Deadly Shade of Gold (J. MacDonald), 1965
Deadly Sunshade (P. Taylor), 1940
Deadly Trap (Pentecost), 1978
Deadly Truth (McCloy), 1941
Deadly Valentine (C. Hart), 1990
Deadly Weapon (Miller), 1946
Deadly Welcome (J. MacDonald), 1959

Deaf, Dumb and Blonde (Creasey, as Morton), 1961
Deaken's War (Freemantle, as Winchester), 1985
Deal in Violence (Michael Collins, as Arden), 1969
Deal Me Out (Corris), 1986
Dealer (Max Collins), 1976
Dealing (Crichton, as Douglas), 1971
Dealing Out Death (Ballard), 1948
Dean's Daughters (Herbert Adams), 1950
Deane, Sarah series (Borthwick), from 1982
Dear Daughter Dead (Hough), 1965
Dear Dead Days (Spicer, as Barbette), 1953
Dear, Dead Girls (Morland), 1961
Dear Dead Woman (A. Gilbert), 1940
Dear Departed (Woods, as Burton), 1980
Dear Laura (Stubbs), 1973
Dear Miss Demeanor (Hess), 1987
Dear Mr. Right (Dewhurst), 1990
Dearest Enemy (Woods), 1981
Death About Face (F. Kane), 1948
Death after Breakfast (Pentecost), 1978
Death after Evensong (D. Clark), 1969
Death Against the Clock (A. Gilbert), 1958
Death Ain't Commercial (Stein, as Bagby), 1951
Death Among Friends (s Hare), 1984
Death among the Stars (McGirr, as Giles), 1968
Death Among the Sunbathers (Punshon), 1934
Death among the Tulips (Hocking), 1953
Death and a Madonna (O'Hagan), 1986
Death and Bright Water (J. Mitchell), 1974
Death and Chicanery (s P. MacDonald), 1962
Death and Circumstance (Waugh), 1963
Death and Daisy Bland (Blake), 1960
Death and Letters (E. Daly), 1950
Death and Little Brother (C. Knight), 1952
Death and Mary Dazill (Fitt), 1941
Death and Mr. Prettyman (McGirr, as Giles), 1967
Death and Taxes (Dewey), 1967
Death and Taxes (Dodge), 1941
Death and the Bright Day (Fitt), 1948
Death and the Chaste Apprentice (Barnard), 1989
Death and the Dancing Footman (Marsh), 1941
Death and the Dear Girls (Quentin, as Stagge), 1946
Death and the Diplomat (Scherf), 1964
Death and the Dutch Uncle (Moyes), 1968
Death and the Dutiful Daughter (Morice), 1973
Death and the Gentle Bull (Lockridge), 1954
Death and the Gilded Man (J. Carr, as Dickson), 1947
Death and the Golden Boy (Morland), 1958
Death and the Joyful Woman (Ellis Peters), 1961
Death and the Leaping Ladies (McGirr, as Drummond), 1968
Death and the Mad Heroine (Dean), 1985
Death and the Maiden (G. Mitchell), 1947
Death and the Maiden (Quentin, as Patrick), 1939
Death and the Maiden (Radley), 1978
Death and the Pleasant Voices (Fitt), 1946
Death and the Pregnant Virgin (Haymon), 1980
Death and the Princess (Barnard), 1982
Death and the Shortest Day (Fitt), 1952
Death and the Sky Above (Garve), 1953
Death and the Visiting Firemen (Keating), 1959
Death Angel (Clason), 1936
Death Answers the Bell (V. Williams), 1931
Death as the Curtain Rises (Pentecost, as Philips), 1981
Death at Ash House (Rhode, as Burton), 1942
Death at Breakfast (Rhode), 1936
Death at Broadcasting House (Gielgud), 1934
Death at Charity's Point (Tapley), 1984

Death at Court Lady (Horler), 1936
Death at Dancing Stones (Fitt), 1939
Death at Deep End (Wentworth), 1963
Death at Deepwood Grange (Underwood), 1986
Death at Dyke's Corner (Carnac, as Lorac), 1940
Death at Four Corners (A. Gilbert), 1929
Death at Half-Term (Bell), 1939
Death at Hallows End (Bruce), 1965
Death at Lord's (B. Newman), 1952
Death at Low Tide (Rhode, as Burton), 1938
Death at Sea (L. White), 1961
Death at Sea (Sale), 1948
Death at St. Asprey's School (Bruce), 1967
Death at Swaythling Court (Connington), 1926
Death at the Bar (Marsh), 1940
Death at the Bar (McGirr, as Drummond), 1972
Death at the BBC (Sherwood), 1983
Death at the Chase (M. Innes), 1970
Death at the Club (Rhode, as Burton), 1937
Death at the Cross-Roads (Rhode, as Burton), 1933
Death at the Dam (C. Adams), 1946
Death at the Dance (Rhode), 1952
Death at The Dog (Cannan), 1940
Death at the Dolphin (Marsh), 1967
Death at the Door (A. Gilbert), 1945
Death at the Furlong Post (McGirr, as Drummond), 1967
Death at the Helm (Rhode), 1941
Death at the Inn (Freeman), 1937
Death at the Inn (Rhode), 1953
Death at the Isthmus (Coxe), 1954
Death at the Medical Board (Bell), 1944
Death at the Opera (G. Mitchell), 1934
Death at the Pelican (Wills), 1934
Death at the President's Lodging (M. Innes), 1936
Death at the Rodeo (Queen), 1951
Death at the Wedding (Hocking), 1946
Death at Three (Rice), 1941
Death at Yew Corner (R. Forrest), 1981
Death Bed (Greenleaf), 1980
Death Before Bedtime (Box), 1953
Death Before Breakfast (Bellairs), 1962
Death Before Breakfast (C. Adams), 1942
Death Before Dinner (Carnac, as Lorac), 1948
Death Before Dying (Wilcox), 1990
Death Before Wicket (Spain), 1946
Death Beneath Jerusalem (Garve, as Bax), 1938
Death Beside the Sea (Babson), 1983
Death Beside the Seaside (Babson), 1982
Death Beyond the Go-Thru (Kendrick), 1938
Death Beyond the Nile (Mann), 1988
Death Bird Contract (Atlee), 1966
Death Blanks the Screen (L. O'Donnell), 1961
Death Blew Out the Match (K. Knight), 1935
Death-Bringers (Linington, as Shannon), 1965
Death Brings in the New Year (Bellairs), 1951
Death Brokers (Ballard, as P.D. Ballard), 1974
Death by Analysis (Slovo), 1986
Death by Arrangement (Meynell), 1972
Death by Association (Lockridge), 1952
Death by Bequest (McMullen), 1977
Death by Computer (Doris Disney), 1971
Death by Design (Derleth), 1953
Death by Dreaming (J. White), 1981
Death by Fire (Pentecost), 1986
Death by Hoax (L. Black), 1974
Death by Inches (Linington, as Shannon), 1965
Death by Misadventure (Underwood), 1960

Death by Moonlight (M. Innes), 1957
Death by Night (Creasey), 1940
Death by Sheer Torture (Barnard), 1982
Death By Surprise (C. Hart), 1983
Death by the Lake (Bruce), 1971
Death by Water (M. Innes), 1968
Death Calls the Shots (B. Knox), 1961
Death Came Dancing (K. Knight), 1940
Death Came Smiling (Dewhurst), 1975
Death Came Softly (Carnac, as Lorac), 1943
Death Cap (J. Thomson), 1973
Death-Cap Dancers (G. Mitchell), 1981
Death Card (Verner, as Stuart), 1930
Death Casts a Long Shadow (A. Gilbert), 1959
Death Ceremony (Melville), 1985
Death Certificate (Wainwright), 1978
Death Charge (Caillou), 1973
Death Check (Murphy), 1971
Death Checks In (F. Davis, as Ransome), 1939
Death Chemist (Chance), 1983
Death Chime (Gribble), 1934
Death Claims (Hansen), 1973
Death Comes as the End (Christie), 1944
Death Comes by Post (Ellis Peters, as Carr), 1940
Death Comes Early (Cox), 1961
Death Comes Staccato (Slovo), 1987
Death Comes to Cambers (Punshon), 1935
Death Commits Bigamy (Fox), 1948
Death Counts Three (Carmichael), 1954
Death Cracks a Bottle (McGirr, as Giles), 1969
Death Cuts a Silhouette (Olsen), 1939
Death Cuts the Deck (Fish), 1972
Death Dealers (Asimov), 1958
Death Dealers (Spillane), 1965
Death Deep Down (Dan Marlowe), 1965
Death Delivers a Postcard (Pentecost, as Philips), 1939
Death Demands an Audience (Reilly), 1940
Death Department (B. Knox), 1959
Death Disturbs Mr. Jefferson (Hocking), 1950
Death Dives Deep (Avallone), 1971
Death-Doctor (Le Queux), 1912
Death Drive (Creasey, as Cooke), 1935
Death Drop (B.M. Gill), 1979
Death Drops the Pilot (Bellairs), 1956
Death Duel (Hocking), 1933
Death Filled the Glass (Armstrong), 1945
Death Finds a Foothold (G. Carr), 1961
Death Finds a Target (Fitt), 1942
Death Flies Low (Morland, as Shepherd), 1938
Death for a Dancer (Giroux), 1985
Death for a Darling (Giroux), 1985
Death for a Dilettante (Giroux), 1987
Death for a Doctor (Giroux), 1986
Death for a Double (Giroux), 1990
Death for a Dreamer (Giroux), 1989
Death for a Playmate (Ball), 1972
Death for Adonis (Giroux), 1984
Death for Dear Clara (Quentin, as Patrick), 1937
Death for Dietitian (Giroux), 1988
Death for My Beloved (Doris Disney), 1949
Death for Sale (H. Kane), 1957
Death for Sale (Morland), 1957
Death from a Top Hat (Rawson), 1938
Death from Below (Creasey, as Ashe), 1963
Death from Disclosure (Stuart), 1976
Death from Nowhere (Rawson, as Towne)
Death From the Clouds (Natsuki, trans), 1989

Death Fugue (McGuire), 1933
Death Fuse (Russell), 1980
Death Giver (Gibson, as Grant), 1978
Death Goes on Skis (Spain), 1949
Death Goes to a Reunion (K. Knight), 1952
Death Goes to School (Quentin, as Patrick), 1936
Death Gong (Jepson), 1927
Death Grip! (Albert, as Al Conroy), 1972
Death Had Yellow Eyes (Dent, as Robeson), 1982
Death Has a Shadow (Procter), 1965
Death Has a Small Voice (Lockridge), 1953
Death Has Deep Roots (M. Gilbert), 1951
Death Has Four Hands (Lawrence), 1950
Death Has Green Fingers (L. Black), 1971
Death Has Many Doors (F. Brown), 1951
Death Has Three Lives (Halliday), 1955
Death House Doll (Keene), 1954
Death Importer (Chance), 1981
Death in a Bowl (Whitfield), 1931
Death in a Cold Climate (Barnard), 1980
Death in a Deck-Chair (Kennedy), 1930
Death in a Deckchair (Beck), 1984
Death in a Distant Land (Livingston), 1988
Death in a Duffle Coat (Rhode, as Burton), 1956
Death in a Hurry (Creasey, as Ashe), 1952
Death in a Lighthouse (Aarons, as Ronns), 1938
Death in a Million Living Rooms (McGerr), 1951
Death in a Pheasant's Eye (J. Fraser), 1971
Death in a Salubrious Place (Burley), 1973
Death in a Sleeping City (Wainwright), 1965
Death in a Sunny Place (Lockridge), 1972
Death in a Tenured Position (Cross), 1981
Death in a Town (Waugh), 1989
Death in a White Tie (Marsh), 1938
Death in Albert Park (Bruce), 1964
Death in Amsterdam (Freeling), 1964
Death in April (Greeley), 1980
Death in Autumn (Nabb), 1985
Death in Bermuda (Quentin, as Patrick), 1941
Death in Botanist's Bay (Ferrars), 1941
Death in Budapest (Gielgud), 1937
Death in Camera (Underwood), 1984
Death in Captivity (M. Gilbert), 1952
Death in China (Hiaasen), 1984
Death in Clairvoyance (Bell), 1949
Death in Close-Up (Livingston), 1989
Death in Cold Print (Creasey), 1961
Death in Dark Glasses (Bellairs), 1952
Death in Darkness (J. Fraser, as Whitney), 1975
Death in Deakins Wood (Curzon, as Petrie), 1963
Death in Desolation (Bellairs), 1957
Death in Despair (Bellairs), 1960
Death in Diamonds (Creasey, as Ashe), 1951
Death in Diamonds (McGirr, as Giles), 1967
Death in Donegal Bay (Gault), 1984
Death in Dream Time (Courtier), 1959
Death in Ecstasy (Marsh), 1936
Death in Fancy Dress (A. Gilbert), 1933
Death in Fashion (Babson), 1985
Death in Five Boxes (J. Carr, as Dickson), 1938
Death in Flames (Creasey, as Ashe), 1943
Death in Four Letters (Beeding), 1935
Death in Grease Paint (Palmer), 1956
Death in Harley Street (Rhode), 1946
Death in High Heels (Brand), 1941
Death in High Places (Creasey, as Ashe), 1942
Death in High Provence (Bellairs), 1957

Death-Riders (Beeding, as Cofyn), 1935
Death Rides Swiftly (Morland, as Shepherd), 1939
Death round the Corner (Creasey), 1935
Death Schuss (L. O'Donnell), 1963
Death Sends for the Doctor (Bellairs), 1957
Death Sentence (Garfield), 1975
Death Sentence (Murphy), 1990
Death Set in Diamonds (Verner), 1965
Death Set to Music (Hebden), 1979
Death Shall Overcome (Lathen), 1966
Death Sits on the Board (Rhode), 1937
Death Speaks Softly (Anthea Fraser), 1987
Death Spins the Platter (Deming, as Queen), 1962
Death Spins the Wheel (Bellairs), 1965
Death Spoke Sweetly (Morland, as Garnett), 1946
Death Squad (Copper), 1977
Death Squad (Demille), 1975
Death Squad (Pendleton), 1969
Death Stalk (Chastain), 1971
Death Stalks a Lady (S. Smith), 1945
Death Stalks the Cobbled Square (Chance), 1946
Death Stalks the Wakely Family (Derleth), 1937
Death Stands By (Creasey), 1938
Death Starts a Rumour (Fitt), 1940
Death Stops the Frolic (Bellairs), 1944
Death Swap (Babson), 1984
Death Syndicate (Pentecost, as Philips), 1938
Death Takes a Bow (Lockridge), 1943
Death Takes a Detour (Rhode, as Burton), 1958
Death Takes a Flat (Rhode, as Burton), 1940
Death Takes a Partner (Rhode), 1958
Death Takes a Paying Guest (Stein), 1947
Death Takes a Redhead (A. Gilbert), 1944
Death Takes a Star (s Morland), 1943
Death Takes a Wife (A. Gilbert), 1959
Death Takes an Editor (Morland), 1949
Death Takes an Option (Ballard, as MacNeil), 1958
Death Takes the Bus (L. White), 1957
Death Takes the Living (Rhode, as Burton), 1949
Death Takes the Low Road (Hill, as Ruell), 1974
Death That Lurks Unseen (s J. Fletcher), 1899
Death the Red Flower (G. Black, as Wynd), 1965
Death Therapy (Murphy), 1972
Death Through the Looking Glass (R. Forrest), 1978
Death Throws No Shadow (Gribble, as Grex), 1976
Death to a Downbeat (C. Brown), 1980
Death to My Beloved (Neely), 1969
Death to My Killer (Creasey, as York), 1950
Death to Remember (Ormerod), 1986
Death to Slow Music (Nichols), 1956
Death to the Fifth Column (B. Newman), 1941
Death to the Ladies (Morland), 1959
Death to the Landlords! (Ellis Peters), 1972
Death to the Rescue (Kennedy), 1931
Death to the Spy (B. Newman), 1939
Death Tolls the Bell (McGuire), 1933
Death Took a Greek God (Morland, as Forrest), 1937
Death Took a Publisher (Morland, as Forrest), 1936
Death Tower (Gibson, as Grant), 1969
Death Trap (Carmichael), 1970
Death Trap (J. MacDonald), 1957
Death Traps the Killer (Morland, as Dane), 1938
Death Treads (Wills), 1935
Death Treads Softly (Bellairs), 1956
Death Trick (Jeffries), 1988
Death Turns a Trick (J. Smith), 1982
Death Turns Right (Dewey), 1969

Death Turns the Tables (J. Carr), 1941
Death under Desolate (Chance), 1964
Death under Gibraltar (B. Newman), 1938
Death under Snowdon (G. Carr), 1952
Death Under the Lilacs (R. Forrest), 1985
Death Visits Downspring (Rhode, as Burton), 1941
Death Walks in Eastrepps (Beeding), 1931
Death Walks in Marble Halls (Blochman), 1951
Death Walks in Shadow (Thayer), 1966
Death Walks on Cat Feet (Olsen), 1956
Death Walks Softly (Morland, as Shepherd), 1938
Death Walks the Woods (Hare), 1954
Death Warmed Up (Babson), 1982
Death Watch (Hall, as Trevor), 1984
Death-Watch (J. Carr), 1935
Death Watch Ladies (Chance), 1980
Death Wears a Copper Necktie (s Pentecost), 1946
Death Wears a Mask (A. Gilbert), 1970
Death Wears a Red Hat (Kienzle), 1980
Death Wears a Veil (K. Knight)
Death Wears Cat's Eyes (Olsen), 1950
Death Weed (Thayer), 1935
Death When She Wakes (Morland), 1951
Death Wish (Caspary), 1951
Death Wish (E. Holding), 1934
Death Wish (Garfield), 1972
Death Wishes (Loraine), 1983
Death with Blue Ribbon (Bruce), 1969
Death Within the Vault (Thayer), 1951
Death Women (Chance), 1967
Death Won't Wait (A. Gilbert), 1954
Death's Bright Dart (Clinton-Baddeley), 1967
Death's Juggler (C. Daly), 1935
Death's Long Shadow (Spicer, as Barbette), 1955
Death, My Lover (Blackstock, as Allardyce), 1959
Death-Wish Green (Crane), 1960
Deathbed (Kienzle), 1986
Deathblow Hill (P. Taylor), 1935
Deathless and the Dead (Clarke), 1976
Death's Bright Angel (Warriner), 1956
Death's Darkest Face (Symons), 1990
Death's Dateless Night (Warriner), 1952
Death's Eye (Meynell), 1929
Death's Head (J. Ross), 1982
Death's Old Sweet Song (Quentin, as Stagge), 1946
Death's Sweet Music (s Morland), 1947
Deathwatch (R. Harrison), 1985
Deaves Affair (Footner), 1922
Deborah's Legacy (S. Marlowe), 1983
Debriefing (Littell), 1979
Debt Discharged (E. Wallace), 1916
Decayed Gentlewoman (Ferrars), 1963
Deceivers (J. MacDonald), 1958
Deceptive Clarity (Elkins), 1987
Decision (H. Kane), 1973
Decision at Delphi (MacInnes), 1961
Decker, Bill series (Treat), from 1948
Decker, Sergeant Peter series (F. Kellerman), from 1985
Decoy (Aarons, as Ronns), 1951
Decoy (C. Adams), 1941
Decoy (Maling), 1969
Decoy Hit (Randisi, as Carter), 1983
Decoys (Hoyt), 1980
Dee Goong An (van Gulik, trans), 1949
Dee, Mr. series (Cory), from 1961
Deed Without a Name (Phillpotts), 1941
Deeds of Dr. Deadcert (J. Fleming), 1955

Deeds of the Disturber (Elizabeth Peters), 1988
Deene, Carolus series (Bruce), from 1955
Deep (Spillane), 1961
Deep among the Dead Men (Blackburn), 1973
Deep and Crisp and Even (Payne), 1964
Deep and Crisp and Even (Turnbull), 1981
Deep Blue Cradle (Chambers), 1980
Deep Blue Goodby (J. MacDonald), 1964
Deep Cold Green (C. Brown), 1968
Deep Cover (Garfield), 1971
Deep Dive (Hornig), 1988
Deep End (F. Brown), 1952
Deep End (Hayes), 1967
Deep Fall (B. Knox), 1966
Deep-Lake Mystery (Wells), 1928
Deep Lay the Dead (F. Davis), 1942
Deep Pocket (Kenyon), 1978
Deep Purple (Allbeury), 1989
Deep Shaker (L. Roberts), 1991
Deep Six (Cussler), 1984
Deep Water (Highsmith), 1957
Deep, Dark and Dead (MacKenzie), 1978
Deer Leap (Grimes), 1985
Defeat of a Detective (Wills), 1936
Defection of A. J. Lewinter (Littell), 1973
Defector (Anthony), 1980
Defenders (Aarons), 1961
Defrauded Yeggman (Keeler), 1937
Defy the Devil (Woods), 1984
DeHavilland, Mr. series (Chance), from 1937
Delafield, Kate series (K. Forrest), from 1984
Delaney, Edward X series (Sanders), from 1973
Delaware, Alex series (J. Kellerman), from 1985
Delay in Danger (Harvester), 1954
Delay on Turtle (s Canning), 1962
Delayed Payment (Rhode), 1956
Delicate Ape (Hughes), 1944
Delicate Darling (Webb), 1959
Delicate Dust of Death (Audemars), 1973
Delilah Was Deadly (C. Brown), 1956
Deliver Us from Wolves (Holton), 1963
Deliver Us to Evil (Hensley), 1971
Delivery (Simenon, trans), 1981
Delivery of Furies (Canning), 1961
Delta Factor (Spillane), 1967
Delta Star (Wambaugh), 1983
Demise of a Louse (Ballard), 1962
Demolishers (D. Hamilton), 1987
Demon Child (Koontz, as Dwyer), 1971
Demon in My View (Rendell), 1976
Demon Island (Goulart, as Robeson), 1975
Demon Lover (Holt), 1982
Demoniacs (J. Carr), 1962
Dene, Detective Sergeant Trevor series (V. Williams), from 1927
Dene, Michael series (Verner), from 1936
Denis Dent (Hornung), 1903
Denson, John series (Hoyt), from 1980
Denton, Mickey series (Kane), from 1959
Depart This Life (Ferrars), 1958
Department K (Carmichael, as Howard), 1964
Department of Dead Ends series (s Vickers), from 1947
Department of Death (Creasey), 1949
Department of Queer Complaints (s J. Carr, as Dickson), 1940
Department Z series (Creasey), from 1933
Departure of Mr. Gaudette (Doris Disney), 1964
Depths (Creasey), 1963

Deputy for Cain (Vickers), 1931
Derelict of Skull Shoal (Dent, as Robeson), 1990
Derrick Devil (Dent, as Robeson), 1973
Desert Stalker (Malzberg, as Barry), 1974
Design for Dying (McCloy), 1938
Design for Dying (Morice), 1988
Design for Murder (C. Hart), 1988
Design for Murder (Durbridge), 1951
Design in Diamonds (K. Knight), 1944
Design in Evil (King), 1942
Designs on Life (s Ferrars), 1990
Desire in the Dust (Whittington), 1956
Desire to Kill (Clarke), 1982
Desired (C. Brown), 1959
Despatch of a Dove (Curzon, as Petrie), 1969.
Desperate Asylum (Flora), 1955
Desperate Hours (Hayes), 1954
Desperate Measures (Wheatley), 1974
Desperate Moment (Albrand), 1951
Desperate People (Durbridge), 1966
d'Espinal, Harcourt series (Sturrock, as Healey), from 1972
Despite the Evidence (Jeffries, as Alding), 1971
Destination Unknown (Christie), 1954
Destination Unknown (Sale), 1943
Destinations (Simenon, trans), 1955
Destiny Man (Van Greenaway), 1977
Destiny of Death (Linington, as Shannon), 1984
Destroyer (Horler), 1938
Destroyer series (Murphy and Sapir), from 1971
Destroying Angel (A. Cohen), 1988
Destroying Angel (E. Wallace), 1959
Destroying Angel (L. Vance), 1912
Destructors (Deming, as Franklin), 1974
Detection Unlimited (Heyer), 1953
Detective (L. Vance), 1932
Detective Officer (s Waters, appendix), 1878
Detective Wore Silk Drawers (Lovesey), 1971
Detective's Tale (G. Newman), 1977
Detective's Triumphs (s Donovan), 1891
Detectives (Daniels), 1962
Detective's Due (Linington, as Egan), 1965
Detling Murders (Symons), 1982
Detling Secret (Symons), 1983
Detonators (D. Hamilton), 1985
Detour (Nielsen), 1953
Detour to Death (Nielsen), 1955
Detour to Oblivion (F. Davis), 1947
Detours (s O. Cohen), 1927
Detroit Deathwatch (Pendleton), 1974
Detroit Massacre (Malzberg, as Barry), 1975
Deuces Wild (Linington, as Shannon), 1975
Devastators (D. Hamilton), 1965
Devereaux series (Granger), from 1979
Devereux Court Mystery (Rhode, as Burton), 1935
Deveron Hall (Johnston), 1976
Deviant Behaviour (Emerson), 1988
Deviant Death (Moffat), 1973
Deviator (York), 1969
Devices and Desires (James), 1989
Devil and All (s Collier), 1934
Devil and the C.I.D (Carnac, as Lorac), 1938
Devil and the Dolce Vita (Holme), 1982
Devil and X.Y.Z (Beeding, as Browne), 1931
Devil at Saxon Wall (G. Mitchell), 1935
Devil Boy (W. Roberts), 1970
Devil Comes to Bolobyn (Horler), 1951
Devil Daddy (Blackburn), 1972

Devil Doctor (Rohmer), 1916
Devil Drives (Chance), 1936
Devil for the Witch (Lacy), 1958
Devil Genghis (Dent, as Robeson), 1974
Devil His Due (O'Farrell), 1955
Devil in Davos (Brewer), 1969
Devil in Dungarees (Albert, as Albert Conroy), 1960
Devil in Greenlands (Chance), 1939
Devil in Kansas (M. Smith, as Quinn), 1974
Devil in Moonlight (Procter), 1962
Devil in the Bush (Head), 1945
Devil-in-the-Dark (Wentworth), 1934
Devil in Velvet (J. Carr), 1951
Devil Is Dead (Lewis), 1989
Devil Is Jones (Dent, as Robeson), 1990
Devil Kinsmere (J. Carr, as Fairbairn), 1934
Devil Loves Me (Millar), 1942
Devil Man (E. Wallace), 1931
Devil May Care (Miller), 1950
Devil-May-Care (Elizabeth Peters), 1977
Devil on the Moon (Dent, as Robeson), 1970
Devil on Two Sticks (Miller), 1949
Devil Rides Out (Wheatley), 1934
Devil Snar'd (Shearing, as Preedy), 1932
Devil-Stick (Hume), 1898
Devil Take the Blue-Tail Fly (Bardin), 1948
Devil to Pay (H. Kane), 1966
Devil to Pay (Queen), 1938
Devil to Play (Holton), 1974
Devil Was a Woman (Graeme), 1966
Devil Was Handsome (Procter), 1961
Devil Wears Wings (Whittington), 1960
Devil Wore Scarlet (Gray), 1964
Devil You Don't (Wainwright), 1973
Devil, Devil (Avallone), 1975
Devil's Ace (Hume), 1909
Devil's Alternative (Forsyth), 1979
Devil's Black Rock (Dent, as Robeson), 1989
Devil's Carnival (Le Queux), 1917
Devil's Dice (Le Queux), 1896
Devil's Double (W. Roberts), 1979
Devil's Dozen (M. Smith, as Carter), 1973
Devil's Dozen (Verner, as Vane), 1934
Devil's Due (Procter), 1960
Devil's Edge (Chance), 1975
Devil's Elbow (G. Mitchell), 1951
Devil's Footsteps (John Burke), 1976
Devil's Home on Leave (Raymond), 1985
Devil's Mantle (Packard), 1927
Devil's Novice (Ellis Peters), 1983
Devils of the Deep (Dent, as Robeson), 1984
Devil's Paw (Oppenheim), 1920
Devil's Pawn (Bruton), 1962
Devil's Reckoning (Rhode, as Burton), 1948
Devil's Steps (Upfield), 1946
Devil's Stronghold (Ford), 1948
Devil's Work (Yorke), 1982
Devil's Work (Wells), 1940
Devilweed (B. Knox), 1966
Devious Design (Olsen), 1948
Devious Murder (Bellairs), 1973
Devious Ones (Lockridge), 1964
Devlin, Liam series (J. Higgins), from 1975
Dewey Death (Blackstock), 1956
DeWitt, Manny series (Rabe), from 1965
Diabolic Candelabra (Punshon), 1942
Diabolus (Hunt, as St. John), 1971

Diagnosis (s King), 1941
Diagnosis: Homicide (s Blochman), 1950
Dial Death (Russell), 1977
Dial 577 R-A-P-E (L. O'Donnell), 1974
Diamond Bikini (C. Williams), 1956
Diamond Bubble (Fish), 1965
Diamond Exchange (Chastain), 1981
Diamond Feather (Reilly), 1930
Diamond in the Buff (Dunlap), 1990
Diamond Master (s Futrelle), 1909
Diamond Murders (J. Fletcher), 1929
Diamond Pin (Wells), 1919
Diamond Queen (s Reeve), 1917
Diamond, Red series (Schorr), from 1983
Diamonds (J. Fletcher), 1904
Diamonds Are Forever (I. Fleming), 1956
Diamonds Are Trumps (Herbert Adams), 1947
Diamonds Bid (Rathbone), 1966
Diamonds of Loreta (Parrish, as Drummond), 1980
Diamonds to Amsterdam (Coles), 1949
Diamonds Wild (Caillou), 1979
Diana of Kara-Kara (E. Wallace), 1924
Diary (Ard), 1952
Dick Tracy (Max Collins), 1990
Dictator's Destiny (B. Newman, as Betteridge), 1945
Dictator's Way (Punshon), 1938
Did She Fall or Was She Pushed? (Doris Disney), 1959
D.I. (Jeffries, as Ashford), 1962
Didn't Anybody Know My Wife? (W. Roberts), 1974
Die after Dark (Pentecost), 1976
Die All, Die Merrily (Bruce), 1961
Die Anytime, After Tuesday! (C. Brown), 1969
Die—as in Murder (Gribble, as Grex), 1974
Die by the Book (Meynell), 1966
Die for Big Betsy (B. Knox), 1961
Die for Love (Elizabeth Peters), 1984
Die in the Country (S. Forbes, as Wells), 1972
Die in the Dark (A. Gilbert), 1947
Die Laughing (Lockridge), 1969
Die Laughing (McGerr), 1952
Die Like a Dog (Gruber), 1957
Die Like a Dog (Moffat), 1982
Die Now, Live Later (Copper), 1968
Die Quickly, Dear Mother (S. Forbes, as Wells), 1969
Die Rich, Die Happy (J. Mitchell, as Munro), 1965
Die to a Distant Drum (Michael Collins, as Arden), 1972
Die, Darling, Die (Bruton), 1959
Die, Jessica, Die (Avallone, as de Pre), 1972
Die, Little Goose (Alexander), 1956
Die, Lover (Whittington), 1960
Diecast (Tripp, as Brett), 1963
Died in the Red (Gray), 1968
Died in the Wool (Marsh), 1945
Died on a Rainy Sunday (Aiken), 1972
Diehard (Potts), 1956
Diet to Die For (Hess), 1989
Different Drummer (Egleton), 1985
Different Kind of Summer (Butler, as Melville), 1967
Difficult Problem (s Green), 1900
Dig a Little Deeper (Curtiss), 1976
Dig Me a Grave (C. Adams, as Spain), 1942
Dig My Grave Deep (Rabe), 1956
Dig That Crazy Grave (Prather), 1961
Dig the Grave and Let Him Lie (Wainwright), 1971
Digger's Game (G. Higgins), 1973
Dilemma (Phillpotts), 1949
Dilemma of the Dead Lady (s Woolrich, as Irish), 1950

Dilemmas (s A. Mason), 1934
Dillinger (J. Higgins, as Patterson), 1983
DiMarco, Jeff series (Doris Disney), from 1946
Diminished by Death (J. Ross), 1968
Dine and Be Dead (Butler), 1960
Dine with Murder (Creasey, as Halliday), 1950
Ding, Dong, Bell (Reilly), 1958
Dingdong (Maling), 1974
Dinky Died (S. Forbes, as Wells), 1970
Dinner at Dupre's (Halliday), 1945
Dinner Club (s Sapper), 1923
Dinner to Die For (Dunlap), 1987
Dip into Murder (Ormerod), 1978
Diplomat and the Gold Piano (Scherf), 1963
Diplomat Dies (Gribble), 1969
Diplomat's Folly (Wade), 1951
Diplomatic Corpse (P. Taylor), 1951
Diplomatist (Haggard), 1987
Dirt Rich (Howard), 1986
Dirty Area (Luard), 1979
Dirty Butter for Servants (J. Fleming), 1972
Dirty Duck (Grimes), 1984
Dirty Gertie (H. Kane), 1963
Dirty Hands (Neely), 1976
Dirty Pool (Stein, as Bagby), 1966
Dirty Story (Ambler), 1967
Dirty Way to Die (Stein, as Bagby), 1955
Dirty White (Freemantle, as Evans), 1986
Disappearance (Derek Marlowe), 1977
Disappearance (Wilcox), 1970
Disappearance of Dr. Bruderstein (Sherwood), 1949
Disappearance of Kimball Webb (Wells, as Wright), 1920
Disappearance of Odile (Simenon, trans), 1972
Disappearance of Penny (Randisi), 1980
Disappearance of Roger Tremayne (Graeme), 1937
Disappearing Bridegroom (Erskine), 1950
Disappearing Eye (Hume), 1909
Disappearing Parson (Rhode, as Burton), 1949
Disgrace to the College (Cole), 1937
Dishonest Murderer (Lockridge), 1949
Dishonor among Thieves (Sterling, as Dean), 1958
Dishonour among Thieves (Carnac, as Lorac), 1959
Dishonoured Bones (Trench), 1954
Disintegration of J.P.G. (Simenon, trans), 1937
Dismal Ravens Crying (D. Fletcher), 1989
Dismal Thing to Do (MacLeod, as Craig), 1986
Displaced Persons (Hilton), 1987
Disposal of the Living (Barnard), 1985
Disposing of Henry (Garve, as Bax), 1946
Dispossessed (Linington, as Shannon), 1988
Disputed Barricade (Harvester, as Gibbs), 1952
Dissident (Van Greenaway), 1980
Distaff Factor (Wainwright), 1982
Distant Banner (Lewis), 1976
Distant Clue (Lockridge), 1963
Distant View of Death (Scott), 1981
Distributors (Oppenheim, as Partridge), 1908
Disturbance on Berry Hill (Fenwick), 1968
Dive into Darkness (L. O'Donnell), 1971
Dividend on Death (Halliday), 1939
Divine and Deadly (Scherf), 1953
Divining Rod for Murder (Neville), 1952
Divorce Court Murder (Propper), 1934
Dixie Convoy (Pendleton), 1976
Dixon, George series (Willis), from 1950
Dixon, Sergeant Joe series (Wormser), from 1934
DKA series (Gores), from 1972

Do Evil in Return (Millar), 1950
Do Me a Favour—Drop Dead (Chase), 1976
Do Not Disturb (McCloy), 1943
Do Not Disturb (Thayer), 1951
Do Not Fold, Spindle, or Mutilate (Doris Disney), 1970
Do Nothin' till You Hear from Me (Wainwright), 1977
Do unto Others (Doris Disney), 1953
Do You Know This Voice? (Berckman), 1960
Do You Remember England? (Derek Marlowe), 1972
Docken Dead (Trench), 1953
Doctor and the Corpse (Murray), 1952
Dr. Bruderstein Vanishes (Sherwood), 1949
Dr. Chaos (Shearing, as Preedy), 1933
Doctor Died at Dusk (Homes), 1936
Doctor Fischer of Geneva (Greene), 1980
Dr. Goodwood's Locum (Rhode), 1951
Doctor, His Wife, and the Clock (Green), 1895
Doctor Izard (Green), 1895
Dr. Jekyll and Mr. Holmes (Estleman), 1979
Doctor, Lawyer . . . (Wilcox), 1977
Doctor No (I. Fleming), 1958
Doctor of Pimlico (Le Queux), 1919
Doctor on Trial (Waugh), 1977
Dr. Quake (Murphy), 1972
Dr. Rumsey's Patient (Meade), 1896
Doctor S.O.S (Thayer), 1925
Dr. Time (Goulart, as Robeson), 1974
Doctor Who Held Hands (Footner), 1929
Doctor's Daughter (Blackstock, as Allardyce), 1955
Doctor's Wife (Avallone), 1963
Documents in the Case (Sayers), 1930
Dog (s Hansen), 1979
Dog Collar Murders (B. Wilson), 1989
Dog in the Dark (Hammond), 1989
Dog in the Manger (Curtiss), 1982
Dog It Was That Died (Carnac, as Lorac), 1952
Dog It Was That Died (Keating), 1962
Dog Man (Procter), 1969
Doghouse (Hammond), 1989
Dogs Do Bark (Quentin, as Stagge), 1937
Dogs of War (Forsyth), 1974
Dog's Ransom (Highsmith), 1972
Doings of Raffles Haw (Doyle), 1892
Dolan, Trixie and Evangeline Sinclair series (Babson), from 1986
Doldrum (Hammond, as Holden), 1987
Doll (Durbridge), 1982
Doll (McBain), 1965
Doll for the Big House (C. Brown), 1957
Doll's Bad News (Chase), 1970
Doll's Trunk Murder (Reilly), 1932
Dolly series (Dunnett), from 1965
Domesday Story (Hall, as Scott), 1952
Domestic Affair (Russell), 1984
Domestic Agency (Rhode), 1955
Dominator (York), 1969
Domino (Whitney), 1979
Dominoes (Wainwright), 1980
Don Is Dead (Albert, as Quarry), 1972
Don't Argue with Death (Gribble), 1959
Don't Ask Questions (Marquand), 1941
Don't Bleed on Me (Copper), 1968
Don't Bother to Knock (Chambers), 1966
Don't Call Me Madame (H. Kane), 1969
Don't Call Tonight (Gault), 1960

Double Trouble (Lacy), 1965
Double Turn (Carnac), 1956
Double Whammy (Hiaasen), 1987
Double Who Double Crossed (Hall, as Dudley-Smith), 1944
Double Z (Gibson, as Grant), 1975
Double, Double (Queen), 1950
Double, Double, Oil and Trouble (Lathen), 1978
Doubled in Diamonds (Canning), 1966
Doubles in Death (O'Farrell, as Grew), 1953
Doubloons (Phillpotts), 1906
Doubly Dead (Ferrars), 1963
Doubtful Disciple (Haggard), 1969
Dougal, William series (A. Taylor), from 1982
Dovebury Murders (Rhode), 1954
Dover Train Mystery (A. Gilbert), 1936
Dover, Inspector Wilfred series (Porter), from 1964
Dower House Mystery (Wentworth), 1925
Dowker—Detective (Hume), 1892
Dowling, Father Roger series (McInerny), from 1977
Down among the Dead Men (Moyes), 1961
Down among the Dead Men (Sterling), 1943
Down and Dirty (Murphy), 1974
Down-Beat Kill (Chambers), 1963
Down East Murders (Borthwick), 1985
Down for the Count (Kaminsky), 1985
Down I Go (Ard, as Kerr), 1955
Down There (Goodis), 1956
Down Under (Wentworth), 1937
Down under Donovan (E. Wallace), 1918
Downhill Ride of Leeman Popple (Bellairs), 1978
Downriver (Estleman), 1988
Downtown (McBain), 1989
Downward Path (Gaboriau, trans), 1883
Dracula Murders (Chambers, as Daniels), 1983
Drag the Dark (F. Davis), 1953
Dragnet: Case No. 561 (Prather, as Knight), 1956
Dragnet series (Deming), from 1958
Dragon (Cussler), 1990
Dragon for Christmas (G. Black), 1963
Dragon Murder Case (Van Dine), 1933
Dragon Portfolio (Hoyt), 1986
Dragon Road (Harvester), 1956
Dragon Tree (Canning), 1958
Dragon's Cave (Clason), 1939
Dragon's Claw (P. O'Donnell), 1978
Dragon's Eye (Butler, as Melville), 1976
Dragonfire (Pronzini), 1982
Dragonfly (Koontz, as Dwyer), 1975
Dragons at the Gate (J. Roberts, as Duncan), 1975
Dragons at the Party (Cleary), 1987
Dragons Can Be Dangerous (Chambers), 1983
Dragons Drive You (Balmer), 1934
Dragon's Jaws (Packard), 1937
Dragon's Teeth (Queen), 1939
Dragonship (B. Knox, as MacLeod), 1976
Drake, Earl series (Dan Marlowe), from 1962
Drake, Simon series (Nielsen), from 1951
Drake, Stephen series (Wilcox), from 1967
Dram of Poison (Armstrong), 1956
Draw Batons! (B. Knox), 1973
Draw the Curtain Close (Dewey), 1947
Draw the Dragon's Teeth (B. Newman), 1967
Drawn Blanc (Gadney), 1970
Drawn to Evil (Whittington), 1952
Dread and Water (D. Clark), 1976
Dread Journey (Hughes), 1945
Dreadful Hollow (Blake), 1953

Dreadful Lemon Sky (J. MacDonald), 1975
Dreadful Summit (Ellin), 1948
Dream and the Dead (Audemars), 1963
Dream Apart (Linington, as Egan), 1978
Dream-Detective (s Rohmer), 1920
Dream Doctor (s Reeve), 1914
Dream Dreamed in Sicily (Sciascia, trans), 1979
Dream Is Deadly (C. Brown), 1960
Dream Lover (Sanders), 1987
Dream Merchant (C. Brown), 1976
Dream of Darkness (Hill, as Ruell), 1989
Dream of Death (Hall, as Trevor), 1958
Dream of Fair Woman (Armstrong), 1966
Dream of Orchids (Whitney), 1985
Dream Walker (Armstrong), 1955
Dreamers in a Haunted House (McShane, as Lovell), 1975
Dreamland (Thornburg), 1983
Dreams and Swords (s K. Forrest), 1987
Dreemz of the Night (J. Harrington), 1987
Dresden Green (Freeling), 1966
Dress Her in Indigo (J. MacDonald), 1969
Dressed to Kill (Morland), 1947
Dressed to Kill (s Cheyney), 1952
Dressing of Diamond (Freeling), 1974
Dressing-Room Murder (J. Fletcher), 1930
Driffield, Sir Clinton series (Connington), from 1927
Drill Is Death (Lockridge), 1961
Drink This (Dewhurst), 1980
Drink to Yesterday (Coles), 1940
Driscoll, Clifford series (DeAndrea), from 1985
Driscoll's Diamonds (Albert, as MacAlister), 1973
Drive East on 66 (Wormser), 1962
Driven to Kill (Doris Disney), 1957
Droonin' Watter (J. Fletcher), 1919
Drop Dead (Creasey, as Ashe), 1954
Drop Dead (Drummond), 1976
Drop Dead (Neville), 1962
Drop Dead (Stein, as Bagby), 1949
Drop of Hot Gold (Chance), 1979
Drop to His Death (J. Carr, as Dickson), 1939
Dropped Dead (J. Ross), 1984
Drought (Creasey), 1959
Drowned Hope (Westlake), 1990
Drowned Rat (Ferrars), 1975
Drowner (J. MacDonald), 1963
Drowning Pool (Macdonald), 1950
Drug of Choice (Crichton, as Lange), 1970
Drug on the Market (Dodge), 1949
Drum Beat series (S. Marlowe), from 1964
Drum of Power (B. Knox), 1964
Drum of Ungara (B. Knox), 1963
Drum, Chester series (S. Marlowe), from 1955
Drummer in the Dark (Clifford), 1976
Drummond, Bulldog series (Fairlie), from 1938
Drummond, Captain Hugh "Bulldog" series (Sapper), from 1920
Drums Beat Red (Graeme), 1963
Drunkard's End (Warriner, as Troy), 1960
Drury Lane series (Queen, as Ross), from 1932
Drury Lane's Last Case (Queen, as Ross), 1933
Dry Spell (Creasey), 1967
Dual Enigma (Underwood), 1988
Dublin Nightmare (Loraine), 1952
Ducane series (Bingham), from 1967
Ducats in Her Coffin (Warriner), 1951
Ducrow Folly (Chance), 1978
Due or Die (F. Kane), 1961

Due to a Death (Kelly), 1962
Duel in the Shadows (Lejeune), 1962
Duenna to a Murder (King), 1951
Duet of Death (Lawrence), 1949
Duff, MacDougal series (Armstrong), from 1942
Duffy, Nick series (Kavanagh), from 1980
Duke of York's Steps (Wade), 1929
Dull Dead (Butler), 1958
Duluth, Peter series (Quentin), from 1936
Dumb Alibi (Morland), 1941
Dumb Gods Speak (Oppenheim), 1937
Dumb Witness (Christie), 1937
Dumdum Murder (C. Brown), 1962
Dummy Robberies (Creasey, as Cooke), 1936
Dummy Run (Russell), 1989
Dunfermline Affair (A. Ross), 1973
Dunslow (Punshon), 1922
Dupe (Cody), 1980
Duplicate (Waugh, as Taylor), 1964
Duplicate Death (Heyer), 1951
Dupuy, M. series (A. Gilbert), from 1934
Durand Case (Vickers, as Kyle), 1936
Durell, Sam series (Aarons), from 1955
During His Majesty's Pleasure (Vickers, as Kyle), 1938
Dusky Death (Morland, as Garnett), 1948
Dusky Hour (Punshon), 1937
Dust and the Heat (M. Gilbert), 1967
Dust in the Sun (Cleary), 1957
Dust of Death (Dent, as Robeson), 1969
Dusty Death (Thayer), 1966
Dutch Blue Error (Tapley), 1984
Dutch Courage (R. Perry), 1978
Dutch Shoe Mystery (Queen), 1931
Duty Elsewhere (Wainwright), 1979
Duty Free (Coles, as Gaite), 1959
Duvivien, Johnny series (Spain), from 1946
Dwarf's Chamber (s Hume), 1896
Dwell in Danger (Lewis), 1982
Dwyer, Jack series (Gorman), from 1985
Dying Alderman (Wade), 1930
Dying Day (J. Mitchell), 1988
Dying Echo (K. Knight), 1949
Dying Fall (J. Thomson), 1985
Dying Fall (Wade), 1955
Dying Room Only (Sterling), 1960
Dying Space (Murphy), 1982
Dying to Live (s Horler), 1935
Dying to Meet You (B.M. Gill), 1988
Dying Trade (Corris), 1980
Dying Voices (Crider), 1989
Dying Witnesses (Creasey, as Halliday), 1949
Dyke, Toby series (Ferrars), from 1940

"E" Is for Evidence (S. Grafton), 1988
Each Man's Destiny (Procter), 1947
Eagle Has Landed (J. Higgins), 1975
Ear in the Wall (Reeve), 1916
Ear to the Ground (Chase), 1968
Early Autumn (Parker), 1981
Early Graves (Hansen), 1987
Early Morning Murder (Rhode, as Burton), 1945
Earth Angels (Petievich), 1989
Earth's Great Lord (Punshon), 1901
East Lynne (Wood, appendix), 1861
East of Algiers (Durbridge, Rutherford, as Temple), 1959
East of Broadway (O. Cohen), 1938
East of Desolation (J. Higgins), 1968

East of Mansion House (s T. Burke), 1926
East, Mark series (Lawrence), from 1944
Easy Go (Crichton, as Lange), 1968
Easy Prey (Bell), 1959
Easy to Kill (Christie), 1939
Easy to Kill (Footner), 1931
Easy Way to Go (Coxe), 1969
Easy, John series (Goulart), from 1971
Eaters of the Dead (Crichton), 1976
Ebony Box (J. Fletcher), 1934
Echo in the Cave (Meynell), 1949
Echo of Barbara (John Burke), 1959
Echo of Treason (John Burke), 1966
Echoes from the Macabre (s du Maurier), 1976
Echoes of Celandine (Derek Marlowe), 1970
Echoing Strangers (G. Mitchell), 1952
Ecstasy Business (Condon), 1967
Ecstatic Thief (s Chesterton), 1930
Edgar Allan Who—? (Van Greenaway), 1981
Edge (Francis), 1988
Edge of Extinction (Wainwright), 1968
Edge of Panic (H. Kane), 1950
Edge of Terror (Creasey, as Halliday), 1961
Edge of the Law (Deming), 1960
Edinburgh Exercise (A. Ross), 1975
Edith's Diary (Highsmith), 1977
Educated Evans (s E. Wallace), 1924
Educated Man—Good Evans! (s E. Wallace), 1929
Education of Patrick Silver (Charyn), 1976
Edwin of the Iron Shoes (Muller), 1977
Eel Pie Murders (Ford, as Frome), 1933
Egerton, Scott series (A. Gilbert), from 1927
Egyptian Cross Mystery (Queen), 1932
Egyptian Nights (Rohmer), 1944
Eiger Sanction (Trevanian), 1972
Eight Black Horses (McBain), 1985
Eight Crooked Trenches (Beeding), 1936
8 Faces at 3 (Rice), 1939
Eight Million Ways to Die (Block), 1982
Eight Murders in the Suburbs (s Vickers, as Durham), 1954
Eight O'Clock Alibi (Bush), 1937
Eight of Swords (J. Carr), 1934
813 (Leblanc, trans), 1910
Eight Strokes of the Clock (s Leblanc, trans), 1922
Eighth Circle (Ellin), 1958
Eighth Commandment (Sanders), 1986
Eighth Deadly Sin (Mann), 1976
Eighth Dwarf (Thomas), 1979
Eighth Mrs. Bluebeard (Waugh), 1958
Eighty Dollars to Stamford (L. Fletcher), 1975
81st Site (Kenrick), 1980
Eighty Million Eyes (McBain), 1966
87th Precinct series (McBain), from 1956
Eisenhower Deception (Egleton), 1981
El Murders (Granger), 1987
El Rancho Rio (Eberhart), 1970
Elberg Collection (Oliver), 1985
Eldon, Sheriff Bill series (E. Gardner), from 1947
Eldorado Red (Goines), 1974
Eleanor's Victory (Braddon, appendix), 1863
Election Booth Murder (Propper), 1935
Elegant Edward (s E. Wallace), 1928
Elegy for a Soprano (K. Smith), 1985
Element of Doubt (Simpson), 1987
Elephant's Work (Bentley), 1950
Elephants Can Remember (Christie), 1972
Eleven (s Highsmith), 1970

Eleven Came Back (Seeley), 1943
11 Harrowhouse (G. Browne), 1972
Eleven of Diamonds (Kendrick), 1936
Eleven Thrilling Mysteries (s Morland, as McCall), 1945
Eleven Were Brave (Beeding), 1940
Eleventh Hour (J. Fletcher), 1935
Eleventh Hour (Murphy), 1987
Elgar Variations (Kenyon), 1981
Eliminator (York), 1966
Elizabeth Is Missing (de la Torre), 1945
Elizabeth X (Caspary), 1978
Elk and the Evidence (Scherf), 1952
Elk, Detective Sergeant series (E. Wallace), from 1910
Ellerby Case (Rhode), 1926
Ellerdine, Roger series (Wills), from 1940
Elm Tree Murder (Rhode), 1939
Elope to Death (Creasey, as Ashe), 1959
Elusive Four: Exciting Exploits of Four Thieves (s Le Queux), 1921
Elusive Isabel (Futrelle), 1909
Elusive Vicky Van (Wells), 1934
Embankment Crime (Verner, as Stuart), 1932
Embankment Murder (Verner), 1933
Embarrassing Death (Jeffries), 1964
Embassy (Coulter), 1969
Embezzler (J. Cain), 1944
Embroidered Sunset (Aiken), 1970
Emerald (Whitney), 1983
Emerald Clasp (Beeding), 1933
Emergency Exit (Carmichael), 1957
Emerson, Amelia Peabody series (Elizabeth Peters), from 1975
Emily Dickinson Is Dead (Langton), 1984
Eminence (Kienzle), 1989
Emp, H. series (Horler), from 1932
Emperor of America (Condon), 1990
Emperor of America (Rohmer), 1929
Emperor of Evil (C. Daly), 1936
Emperor's Snuffbox (J. Carr), 1942
Emperor's Pearl (van Gulik, trans), 1963
Empty Beach (Corris), 1983
Empty Bed (Herbert Adams), 1928
Empty Copper Sea (J. MacDonald), 1978
Empty Hours (s McBain), 1962
Empty House (M. Gilbert), 1978
Empty House Murder (Verner, as Stuart), 1933
Empty Silence (Copper), 1981
Empty Trap (J. MacDonald), 1957
Enchanted Isle (J. Cain), 1985
Encore Allain! (Graeme), 1941
Encore Murder (Babson), 1989
Encounter Darkness (S. Forbes), 1967
Encounter Group (Murphy), 1984
End of a Call Girl (Gault), 1958
End of a Life (Phillpotts), 1891
End of a Millionaire (Ballard, as P.D. Ballard), 1964
End of a Party (Waugh), 1965
End of a Shadow (Clarke), 1972
End of a Stripper (Hunt, as Dietrich), 1959
End of an Ancient Mariner (Cole), 1933
End of an Iron Man (Chance), 1978
End of Andrew Harrison (Crofts), 1938
End of Chapter (Blake), 1957
End of Count Rollo (s Phillpotts), 1946
End of Her Honeymoon (Lowndes), 1913
End of Mr. Garment (Starrett), 1932
End of Solomon Grundy (Symons), 1964
End of the Affair (Greene), 1951

End of the Game (Dürrenmatt, trans), 1976
End of the Game (Murphy), 1985
End of the Line (Olsen, as Hitchens), 1957
End of the Long Hot Summer (Meynell), 1972
End of the Night (J. MacDonald), 1960
End of the Street (Procter), 1949
End of the Tiger (s J. MacDonald), 1966
End of the Track (Garve), 1956
End of the Web (Sims), 1976
End of Violence (Benson), 1959
End on the Rocks (Stuart), 1981
End-Game (M. Gilbert), 1982
Endless Colonnade (Harling), 1958
Endless Night (Christie), 1967
Endure No Longer (Albrand), 1944
Enduring Old Charms (Doris Disney), 1947
Enemies Within (Lewin), 1974
Enemy (Bagley), 1977
Enemy and Brother (D. Davis), 1966
Enemy in the House (Eberhart), 1962
Enemy of Women (Perowne), 1934
Enemy Unseen (Crofts), 1945
Enemy Within (Creasey), 1950
Enemy Within (Vickers), 1938
Enemy Within the Gates (Horler), 1940
Engagement with Death (Creasey, as Ashe), 1948
England Made Me (Greene), 1935
England's Peril (Le Queux), 1899
English Lady (W. Harrington), 1982
English Murder (Hare), 1951
English Wife (Blackstock), 1964
Enoch Strone (Oppenheim), 1902
Enormous Hour Glass (Goulart), 1976
Enormous Shadow (Harling), 1955
Enough (Westlake), 1977
Enough to Kill a Horse (Ferrars), 1955
Enquiries Are Continuing (Jeffries, as Ashford), 1964
Enquiries Are Proceeding (Chambers, as Daniels), 1986
Enquiry (Francis), 1969
Enquiry into the Existence of Vampires (McShane, as Lovell), 1974
Enrollment Cancelled (Olsen), 1952
Ensign Knightley (s A. Mason), 1901
Enter a Gentlewoman (Woods), 1982
Enter a Murderer (Marsh), 1935
Enter Certain Murderers (Woods), 1966
Enter Murderers (Slesar), 1960
Enter the Corpse (Woods), 1973
Enter Three Witches (McGuire), 1940
Enter Without Desire (Lacy), 1954
Entry of Death (McGirr), 1969
Entwining (Condon), 1980
Envious Casca (Heyer), 1941
Envoy Extraordinary (Oppenheim), 1937
Envy of the Stranger (C. Graham), 1984
Epilogue (Graeme), 1933
Episode of the Wandering Knife (Rinehart), 1950
Epistle to a Friend (s Collier), 1931
Epitaph for a Dead Actor (Gray), 1960
Epitaph for a Lobbyist (Lathen, as Dominic), 1974
Epitaph for a Nurse (Hocking), 1958
Epitaph for a Spy (Ambler), 1938
Epitaph for Joanna (Carmichael, as Howard), 1972
Epitaphs for Lemmings (Harvester), 1943
Epton, Rosa series (Underwood), from 1980
Equal Danger (Sciascia, trans), 1973
Equal Opportunity Death (Dunlap), 1984

Erasers (Robbe-Grillet, trans), 1964
Erection Set (Spillane), 1972
Eros Affair (McCutchan), 1977
Errant Knights (Hebden), 1968
Erridge, Matt series (Stein), from 1958
Erring Under-Secretary (Beeding), 1937
Error of Judgement (Coxe), 1961
Error of Judgement (Lewis), 1971
Error of the Moon (Woods), 1963
Escape (P. MacDonald, as Porlock), 1932
Escape a Killer (Pentecost, as Philips), 1971
Escape for Sandra (s Cheyney), 1945
Escape from Prague (Cleeve), 1973
Escape in Vain (Simenon, trans), 1943
Escape of General Gerard (B. Newman, as Betteridge), 1943
Escape the Night (Eberhart), 1944
Escape to Athena (Egleton, as Blake), 1979
Escape to Fear (Hall, as Dudley-Smith), 1948
Escape to Love (Aarons), 1952
Escape to Quebec (Kennedy), 1946
Escapemanship (D. Clark, as Ditton), 1975
Escort Job (H. Kane), 1972
Esprit de Corpse (F. Kane), 1965
Essex Road Crime (Chance, as Drummond), 1944
Estate of the Beckoning Lady (Allingham), 1955
Eternity Ring (Wentworth), 1948
Ethel and the Naked Spy (McShane, as Lovell), 1989
Etruscan Bull (Gruber), 1969
Etruscan Net (M. Gilbert), 1969
Etruscan Smile (Johnston), 1977
Eugene Vidocq (Donovan), 1895
Eunuch of Stamboul (Wheatley), 1935
Euro-Killers (Rathbone), 1979
Evans, Homer series (Paul), from 1939
Eve (Chase), 1945
Eve Finds the Killer (s Morland, Garnett), 1947
Eve, It's Extortion (C. Brown), 1957
Eve of His Dying (C. Brown), 1956
Eve of the Wedding (L. Black), 1980
Even If You Run (Cory), 1972
Even in the Best Families (Stout), 1951
Even My Foot's Asleep (Payne), 1971
Even the Wicked (McBain, as Marsten), 1958
Evergreen Death (J. Fraser), 1968
Ever-Loving Blues (C. Brown), 1961
Every Bet's a Sure Thing (Dewey), 1953
Every Brilliant Eye (Estleman), 1986
Every Inch a Lady (J. Fleming), 1977
Every Little Crook and Nanny (McBain, as Hunter), 1972
Every Man Has His Price (J. Fraser, as Whitney), 1968
Everybody Always Tells (Punshon), 1950
Everybody Does It (J. Cain), 1949
Everybody Had a Gun (Prather), 1951
Everyone Suspect (Tyre), 1964
Everything Has Its Price (Kirst, trans), 1976
Eve's Island (E. Wallace), 1926
Evidence I Shall Give (Wainwright), 1974
Evidence Most Blind (Keene), 1950
Evidence of the Accused (Jeffries), 1961
Evidence of Things Seen (E. Daly), 1943
Evidence to Destroy (Yorke), 1987
Evil at the Root (Crider), 1990
Evil Chateau (Horler), 1930
Evil Children (W. Roberts), 1973
Evil Come, Evil Go (Miller, as Masterson), 1961
Evil Days (Fischer), 1974
Evil Eye (Boileau, trans), 1959

Evil Genius (Stein, as Bagby), 1961
Evil Gnome (Dent, as Robeson), 1976
Evil Guest (Le Fanu, appendix), 1895
Evil Hour (McGown), 1986
Evil Hour (Meynell), 1947
Evil in a Mask (Wheatley), 1969
Evil in the House (Holt, as Ford), 1954
Evil Intent (Wainwright), 1966
Evil Men Do (Avallone, as Nile), 1966
Evil Messenger (Horler), 1938
Evil of Time (Berckman), 1954
Evil Ones (J. Mitchell), 1982
Evil Phoenix (B. Newman), 1966
Evil Root (Thayer), 1949
Evil Shepherd (Oppenheim), 1922
Evil Sleep! (McBain, as Hunter), 1952
Evil Star (C. Adams, as Spain), 1944
Evil That Men Do (Hocking), 1953
Evil That Men Do (Pentecost), 1966
Evil That Men Do (Shiel), 1904
Evil under the Sun (Christie), 1941
Evil Wish (Potts), 1962
Evvie (Caspary), 1960
Ewe Lamb (Erskine), 1968
Ex-Detective (s Oppenheim), 1933
Ex-Duke (Oppenheim), 1927
Ex Officio (Westlake, as Culver), 1970
Excellent Intentions (Hull), 1938
Excellent Mystery (Ellis Peters), 1985
Exchange of Doves (Royce), 1990
Executioner series (Pendleton), from 1969
Executioner's Rest (Stein), 1967
Executioners (Creasey), 1967
Executioners (J. MacDonald), 1958
Executioners (McCutchan), 1986
Executor (Hammond), 1986
Exercise Hoodwink (Procter), 1967
Exercise in Terror (Kaminsky), 1985
Exeunt Murderers (s Boucher), 1983
Exhibit No. Thirteen (Jeffries), 1962
Exiled (Lutz, as Greene), 1982
Exit a Dictator (Oppenheim), 1939
Exit a Star (K. Knight), 1941
Exit from Prague (Cleeve), 1970
Exit Laughing (Palmer), 1954
Exit Lines (Hill), 1984
Exit Murderer (Woods), 1978
Exit, Running (Spicer), 1959
Exit the Disguiser (Horler), 1948
Exit the Skeleton (Herbert Adams), 1928
Exit to Music (Morland, as Shepherd), 1940
Exit to Music (s Morland), 1947
Exit with Intent (Loraine), 1950
Exocet (J. Higgins), 1983
Exorcism (Blackstock), 1961
Exotic (C. Brown), 1961
Expatriates (Haggard), 1989
Expected Death (Fitt), 1938
Expendable (W. Roberts), 1976
Expendable Man (Hughes), 1963
Expensive Place to Die (Deighton), 1967
Experience with Evil (Macdonald), 1954
Experiences of a French Detective Officer (Waters, appendix), 1861
Experiences of a Real Detective (Waters, appendix), 1862
Experiment in Crime (Rhode), 1947
Experiment in Terror (The Gordons), 1962

False Evidence (Oppenheim), 1896
False Face (Caspary), 1954
False Faces (L. Vance), 1918
False Inspector Dew (Lovesey), 1982
False Purple (Horler), 1932
False Scent (J. Fletcher), 1924
False Scent (Marsh), 1960
False to Any Man (Ford), 1939
False Witness (Nielsen), 1959
False Witness (Uhnak), 1981
False Witness (Underwood), 1957
False-Face (Horler), 1926
Families Repaired (J. Fletcher), 1916
Family Affair (Eberhart), 1981
Family Affair (M. Innes), 1969
Family Affair (Stout), 1975
Family Affairs (Rhode), 1950
Family at Tammerton (Erskine), 1966
Family Burial Murders (Propper), 1934
Family Fortune (Eberhart), 1976
Family Lie (Simenon, trans), 1978
Family Matter (Coles, as Gaite), 1956
Family Plot (Canning), 1976
Family Reunion (J. Harrington), 1982
Family Skeleton (Doris Disney), 1949
Family Skeletons (Quentin), 1965
Family Tomb (M. Gilbert), 1969
Family Vault (MacLeod), 1979
Famine (Creasey), 1967
Fancies and Goodnights (s Collier), 1951
Fancy Free (s Phillpotts), 1901
Fane, Martin and Richard series (Creasey, as Halliday), from
    1951
Fanks, Octavius series (Hume), from 1891
Fansler, Kate series (Cross), from 1964
Fantastic Island (Dent, as Robeson), 1966
Fantasy and Fugue (Fuller), 1954
Far Away Man (Marshall), 1984
Far Cry (F. Brown), 1951
Far Horizon (Copper), 1982
Far Sands (Garve), 1960
Far Side of Fear (Copper), 1985
Far Side of the Dollar (Macdonald), 1965
Far Traveller (Coles, as Gaite), 1956
Faraday's Flowers (Kenrick), 1984
Faraday, Mike series (Copper), from 1966
Farewell Crown and Good-Bye King (Bennett), 1953
Farewell, My Lovely (Chandler), 1940
Farewell Party (Drummond), 1971
Farewell to Passion (Keene), 1951
Farewell to the Admiral (Cheyney), 1943
Farm Villains (Chance), 1973
Farmhouse (Reilly), 1947
Farnsworth Score (Burns), 1977
Farrow, Marcus Aurelius series (A. Ross), from 1970
Fascinator (York), 1975
Fashion in Shrouds (Allingham), 1938
Fashioned for Murder (Coxe), 1947
Fast Buck (Chase), 1952
Fast Buck (Fischer), 1952
Fast Company (Page), 1938
Fast Fade (Lyons), 1987
Fast One (P. Cain), 1933
Fast Work (s Cheyney), 1948
Fast Work (s Cheyney), 1964
Fat and Skinny Murder Myster (Avallone, as Stanton), 1972
Fat Death (Avallone), 1966

Fat Man's Agony (G. Carr), 1969
Fat Tuesday (Emerson), 1987
Fatal Accident (Wills), 1936
Fatal Affair (Johnston), 1986
Fatal Alibi (Bellairs), 1968
Fatal Alibi (Thayer), 1956
Fatal Beauty (Godey), 1984
Fatal Choice (Doris Disney), 1970
Fatal Descent (J. Carr, as Dickson), 1939
Fatal Face (Le Queux), 1926
Fatal Fascination (Chance), 1959
Fatal Fingers (Le Queux), 1912
Fatal Flaw (Meynell), 1973
Fatal Flirt (Olsen, as Hitchens), 1956
Fatal Fortune (Babson), 1987
Fatal Foursome (F. Kane), 1958
Fatal Frails (Dan Marlowe), 1960
Fatal Garden (Rhode), 1949
Fatal Harvest (K. Knight, as Amos), 1957
Fatal in Furs (Fox), 1952
Fatal in My Fashion (McGerr), 1954
Fatal Inversion (Rendell, as Vine), 1987
Fatal Kiss Mystery (King), 1928
Fatal Manuscript (Verner, as Stuart), 1929
Fatal Obsession (Greenleaf), 1983
Fatal Pool (Rhode), 1960
Fatal Relations (Erskine), 1955
Fatal Ring (Donovan), 1905
Fatal Shadow (G. Black), 1983
Fatal Song (Hume), 1905
Fatal Step (Miller), 1948
Fatal Switch (Stuart), 1978
Fatal Thirteen (Le Queux), 1909
Fatal Trip (Underwood), 1977
Fatal Undertaking (F. Kane), 1964
Fatal Venture (Crofts), 1939
Fatal Woman (Donovan), 1911
Fatal Woman (Quentin), 1953
Fatal Writ (Woods), 1979
Fatality at Bath and Wells (Livingston), 1986
Fate Accomplished (J. Ross), 1987
Fate and Fernand (s Audemars), 1945
Fate and the Man (Hanshew), 1910
Fate at the Fair (Rhode, as Burton), 1933
Fate Laughs (Herbert Adams), 1935
Fate of the Immodest Blonde (Quentin), 1950
Fate of the Lying Jade (Chance), 1968
Fate of the Malous (Simenon, trans), 1962
Fate Worse Than Death (Radley), 1985
Fateful Departure (Doris Disney), 1965
Fateful Summer (Johnston), 1981
Father Hunt (Stout), 1968
Father's Comedy (Fuller), 1961
Fathers in Law (Cecil), 1965
Faulkner's Folly (Wells), 1917
Fault in the Structure (G. Mitchell), 1977
Faultlines (T. White), 1987
Favourite (L. R. Wright), 1982
FBI Story (The Gordons), 1950
Fear (Garfield), 1978
Fear and Trembling (s Bloch), 1989
Fear Around About (Bellairs), 1975
Fear by Instalments (John Burke), 1960
Fear by Night (Wentworth), 1934
Fear Cay (Dent, as Robeson), 1966
Fear Comes to Chalfont (Crofts), 1942
Fear Dealers (York, as Cade), 1974

Fine Night for Dying (J. Higgins, as Fallon), 1969
Fine Red Rain (Kaminsky), 1987
Finger (H. Kane), 1957
Finger (Stein), 1973
Finger! Finger! (Keeler), 1938
Finger Man (s Chandler), 1946
Finger of Fate (s Sapper), 1930
Finger of Saturn (Canning), 1973
Finger to Her Lips (Berckman), 1971
Fingered Man (Fischer), 1953
Fingerprint (A. Gilbert), 1964
Fingerprint (Wentworth), 1956
Fingers of Death (Gibson, as Grant), 1977
Fingers of Fear (s P. MacDonald), 1953
Finish Me Off (Waugh), 1970
Finishing Stroke (Queen), 1958
Finishing Touch (Hocking), 1948
Finnegan, John series (Morland, as Forrest), from 1936
Finney, Dr. Mary series (Head), from 1945
Finsbury Mob (Bruton), 1964
Fire and the Clay (Audemars), 1959
Fire at Greycombe Farm (Rhode), 1932
Fire at Will (Doris Disney), 1950
Fire Below (Yates), 1930
Fire Circle (Marshall), 1969
Fire Engine That Disappeared (Wahlöö, trans), 1971
Fire Goddess (Rohmer), 1952
Fire in the Barley (Parrish), 1977
Fire in the Flesh (Goodis), 1957
Fire in the Snow (H. Innes), 1947
Fire in the Thatch (Carnac, as Lorac), 1946
Fire Lake (Valin), 1987
Fire of Death (Creasey, as Cooke), 1934
Fire on Fear Street (Sterling), 1958
Fire-Raiser (Hall, as Trevor), 1970
Fire Storm (J. Roberts, as Duncan), 1978
Fire-Tongue (Rohmer), 1921
Fire Will Freeze (Millar), 1944
Fire, Burn! (J. Carr), 1957
Firebase Seattle (Pendleton), 1975
Firebug (Bloch), 1961
Firebug (Bruton), 1967
Firecrest (Canning), 1971
Firefly Gadroon (Gash), 1982
Fires at Fairlawn (Bell), 1954
Fires That Destroy (Whittington), 1951
Firing Line (Murphy), 1980
First a Murder (Creasey, as Halliday), 1948
First Body (Payne), 1964
First Born (Simenon, trans), 1949
First Came a Murder (Creasey), 1934
First Come, First Kill (Lockridge), 1962
First Deadly Sin (Sanders), 1973
First Team (Ball), 1971
First Television Murder (Gielgud), 1940
Fish Are So Trusting (Morland), 1948
Fish or Cut Bait (E. Gardner, as Fair), 1963
Fish Story (Hoyt), 1985
Fistful of Death (H. Kane), 1958
Fit of Shivers (Aiken), 1990
Five (Whitfield, as Field), 1931
Five Against the House (Finney), 1954
Five Alarm Funeral (Sterling), 1942
Five Bells and Bladebone (Grimes), 1987
Five Bullets (Thayer), 1944
Five Fatal Words (Balmer), 1932
Five Fathoms Dead (Dent, as Robeson), 1988

Five Flamboys (Beeding), 1929
Five-Leafed Clover (J. Fraser), 1973
Five Little Pigs (Christie), 1942
Five Little Rich Girls (Block), 1986
Five Minute Mysteries (s Avallone), 1978
Five Minutes with a Stranger (Tripp), 1971
Five Murders (s Chandler), 1944
Five O'Clock Lightning (DeAndrea), 1982
Five Passengers from Lisbon (Eberhart), 1946
Five Pieces of Jade (Ball), 1972
Five Red Herrings (Sayers), 1931
Five Roads to Death (Pentecost, as Philips), 1977
Five Roads to S'Agaro (Roth, as Ballard), 1958
Five Roundabouts to Heaven (Bingham), 1953
Five Silver Buddhas (Keeler), 1935
Five Sinister Characters (s Chandler), 1945
Five Star Fugitive (J. MacDonald), 1970
Five to Kill (Creasey, as Halliday), 1943
Five-Day Nightmare (F. Brown), 1962
Fix Like This (Constantine), 1975
Flagellator (C. Brown), 1969
Flagg, Webster series (Johns), from 1953
Flame (Lutz), 1990
Flame and the Wind (Blackburn), 1967
Flame in the Mist (Audemars), 1969
Flame of Evil (Doris Disney), 1968
Flame of Murder (Neville), 1958
Flaming Falcons (Dent, as Robeson), 1968
Flaming Man (Crossen, as Chaber), 1969
Flaming Tree (Whitney), 1986
Flamingo (J. Gardner), 1983
Flamstock Mystery (s J. Fletcher), 1932
Flannery, Jimmy series (Campbell), from 1986
Flash of Green (J. MacDonald), 1962
Flash Point (M. Gilbert), 1974
Flashback (Carmichael), 1964
Flashpoint (Dan Marlowe), 1970
Flat 2 (E. Wallace), 1924
Flat Tyre in Fulham (Bell), 1963
Flaw in the System (Lathen, as Dominic), 1983
Flaxborough Crab (Watson), 1969
Flee From the Past (C. Hart), 1975
Fleming, Roger series (Harvester), from 1942
Flesh and the Devil (Holt, as Ford), 1950
Flesh of the Orchid (Chase), 1948
Flesh Peddlers (F. Kane, as Boyd), 1959
Flesh Was Cold (Fischer), 1951
Fletcher, Irwin "Fletch" series (Mcdonald), from 1974
Fletcher, Johnny and Sam Cragg series (Gruber), from 1940
Flickering Death (B. Knox, as MacLeod), 1971
Flier (Spillane), 1964
Flies in the Web (Hume), 1907
Flight by Night (Keene), 1956
Flight from a Firing Wall (Kendrick), 1966
Flight from Paris (B. Knox, as MacLeod), 1987
Flight in Darkness (Harvester), 1964
Flight into Fear (Kyle), 1972
Flight into Peril (Rutherford), 1952
Flight into Terror (L. White), 1955
Flight of a Witch (Ellis Peters), 1964
Flight of Chariots (Cleary), 1963
Flight of the Falcon (du Maurier), 1965
Flight of the Phoenix (Hall, as Trevor), 1964
Flight to Darkness (Brewer), 1952
Flight to Yesterday (Johnston), 1990
Flip-Side (Copper), 1980

Frightened Wife (Tripp), 1987
Frightened Woman (Coxe), 1939
Frighteners (Busby), 1970
Frighteners (D. Hamilton), 1989
Frigor Mortis (McInerny), 1989
Frog in the Moonflower (Parrish, as Drummond), 1972
Frog in the Throat (Férrars), 1980
Frogmouth (Marshall), 1987
From a Surgeon's Diary (s Freeman, as Ashdown), 1975
From All Blindness (Harvester, as Gibbs), 1944
From Clue to Capture (s Donovan), 1893
From Doon with Death (Rendell), 1964
From Information Received (s Donovan), 1893
From London Far (M. Innes), 1946
From Midnight to Morning (Leblanc, trans), 1933
From Natural Causes (Bell), 1939
From Now On (Packard), 1919
From Russia, With Love (I. Fleming), 1957
From the Bosom of the Deep (Donovan, as Muddock), 1886
From the Hand of the Hunter (Meade), 1906
From This Dark Stairway (Eberhart), 1931
From Thunder Bay (Maling), 1981
From Whose Bourne? (s Barr), 1893
Frontier (Leblanc, trans), 1912
Frontier Incident (Hough), 1951
Frost, Dr. Henry series (Bell), from 1964
Frost, Gerald series (Horler), from 1937
Frozen Assets (Leasor), 1989
Frozen Deep (s Collins, appendix), 1874
Fu Manchu series (Rohmer), from 1913
Fugitive (Fish), 1962
Fugitive (Simenon, trans), 1955
Fugitive Eye (Jay), 1953
Fugitive Pigeon (Westlake), 1965
Fugitive Sleuth (Footner), 1918
Full Circle (s Cecil), 1948
Full Cleveland (L. Roberts), 1989
Full Contact (Randisi), 1984
Full Fury (Ormerod), 1975
Fuller's Earth (Wells), 1932
Funeral for Five (Quentin, as Stagge), 1940
Funeral in Berlin (Deighton), 1964
Funeral in Eden (McGuire), 1938
Funeral of Figaro (Ellis Peters), 1962
Funeral of Gondolas (Holme), 1981
Funeral Sites (Mann), 1981
Funeral Urn (Drummond), 1976
Funeral Was in Spain (McGirr), 1966
Funniest Killer in Town (Stein, as Stone), 1967
Funny, Jonas, You Don't Look Dead (McMullen), 1976
Funny Money (Murphy), 1975
Furious Old Women (Bruce), 1960
Furnished for Murder (Barth), 1990
Furnished for Murder (Ferrars), 1957
Further Secrets of Potsdam (s Le Queux), 1917
Further Side of Fear (McCloy), 1967
Furthest Fury (Wells), 1924
Fuse Time (Byrd), 1991
Futile Alibi (Crofts), 1938
Fuzz (McBain), 1968

"G" Is for Gumshoe (S. Grafton), 1990
G Man at the Yard (s Cheyney), 1946
Gabriel Hounds (Stewart), 1967
Gabriel Samara (Oppenheim), 1925
Gabrielle's Way (Hunter), 1981

Gadget (Freeling), 1977
Gail and Mitch series (The Gordons), from 1969
Galactic Effectuator (s J. Vance), 1980
Galatea (J. Cain), 1953
Gale Force (G. Black), 1978
Gale Force (Hall, as Trevor), 1956
Gale Warning (H. Innes), 1948
Gale Warning (Yates), 1939
Gale, Simon series (Verner), from 1952
Gall, Joe series (Atlee), from 1963
Gallant (Blackstock), 1962
Galloway Case (Garve), 1958
Gallowglass (Rendell, as Vine), 1990
Gallows Are Waiting (Creasey, as York), 1949
Gallows for the Groom (Olsen), 1947
Gallows Garden (Crossen, as Chaber), 1958
Gallows in My Garden (Deming), 1952
Gallows in My Garden (J. Fleming), 1951
Gallows of Chance (Oppenheim), 1934
Gallows' Foot (Gielgud), 1958
Galt, Jason series (McShane, as Lovell), from 1976
Galton Case (Macdonald), 1959
Gamadge, Henry series (E. Daly), from 1940
Gambit (Stout), 1962
Gamblers (Le Queux), 1901
Game (Hammond), 1982
Game Bet (R. Forrest, as Woods), 1981
Game for Heroes (J. Higgins, as Graham), 1970
Game for the Living (Highsmith), 1958
Game for Three Losers (Lustgarten), 1952
Game of Consequences (S. Smith), 1978
Game of Hazard (Blackstock, as Allardyce), 1955
Game of Liberty (s Oppenheim), 1915
Game of Life (Waters, appendix), 1857
Game of Murder (Durbridge), 1975
Game of Sudden Death (Rutherford), 1987
Game of Troy (J. White), 1971
Game Without Rules (s M. Gilbert), 1967
Game, Set, and Danger (Clarke), 1981
Game, Set and Match (Deighton), 1985
Gamecock Murders (Gruber), 1949
Gamekeeper's Gallows (Hilton), 1976
Games (Pronzini), 1976
Games to Keep the Dark Away (Muller), 1984
Gang Rumble (Aarons, as Ronns), 1958
Gangdom's Doom (Gibson, as Grant), 1970
Gangster's Glory (s Oppenheim), 1931
Gangway! (Garfield, Westlake), 1973
Gantry Episode (Drummond), 1968
Gantt, Barney series (Strange), from 1936
Gaol Breaker (E. Wallace), 1931
Gap in the Curtain (s Buchan), 1932
Garb of Truth (Stuart), 1982
Garbage Collector (Stein), 1984
Garden City Crime (Verner, as Stuart), 1931
Garden Game (J. White), 1973
Garden in Asia (Post), 1929
Garden Murder Case (Van Dine), 1935
Garden of Weapons (J. Gardner), 1980
Gargoyle Conspiracy (Albert), 1975
Garnett, David series (Egleton), from 1970
Garonsky Missile (Caillou), 1973
Garston Murder Case (Bailey), 1930
Garstons (Bailey), 1930
Garvey's Code (Busby), 1978
Gat Heat (Prather), 1967
Gates of Dawn (Hume), 1894

Girl in Cabin B54 (L. Fletcher), 1968
Girl in His Past (Simenon, trans), 1952
Girl in the Belfry (Offord), 1957
Girl in the Cage (Benson), 1954
Girl in the Case (Barr), 1910
Girl in the Cellar (Wentworth), 1961
Girl in the Cockpit (Avallone), 1972
Girl in the Crime Belt (Chance), 1974
Girl in the News (Vickers), 1937
Girl in the Plain Brown Wrapper (J. MacDonald), 1968
Girl in the Punchbowl (Dewey), 1964
Girl in Waiting (Simenon, trans), 1957
Girl Known as D 13 (Vickers, as Kyle), 1940
Girl Nobody Knows (McShane), 1965
Girl on the Beach (Johnston), 1987
Girl on the Run (Aarons), 1954
Girl on the Run (Waugh), 1965
Girl on Zero (Perowne), 1939
Girl Out Back (C. Williams), 1958
Girl, The Gold Watch, and Everything (J. MacDonald), 1962
Girl Watcher's Funeral (Pentecost), 1969
Girl Who Cried Wolf (Waugh), 1958
Girl Who Dared (Vickers, as Durham), 1938
Girl Who Had to Die (E. Holding), 1940
Girl Who Kept Knocking Them Dead (Stein, as Stone), 1957
Girl Who Killed Things (Powell), 1960
Girl Who Never Was (Dewey), 1962
Girl Who Was Possessed (C. Brown), 1963
Girl Who Wasn't There (Dewey), 1960
Girl Who Wasn't There (W. Roberts), 1957
Girl Who Wouldn't Talk (Vickers), 1959
Girl with a Golden Bar (Ford, as Conrad), 1944
Girl with a Secret (Armstrong), 1959
Girl with a Squint (Simenon, trans), 1978
Girl with No Place to Hide (Albert, as Quarry), 1959
Girl with Six Fingers (Pentecost), 1969
Girl with the Green Eyes (Leblanc, trans), 1927
Girl with the Hole in Her Head (Stein, as Stone), 1949
Girl with the Leopard-Skin Bag (Creasey, as Halliday), 1961
Girl With the Long Green Heart (Block), 1965
Girl with the Sweet Plump Knees (Dewey), 1963
Girland, Mark series (Chase), from 1965
Girl's Number Doesn't Answer (Powell), 1960
Giselle (Cooper), 1958
Give a Corpse a Bad Name (Ferrars), 1940
Give a Man a Gun (Creasey), 1954
Give Death a Name (A. Gilbert), 1957
Give 'em the Ax (E. Gardner, as Fair), 1944
Give Me Back Myself (Davies), 1971
Give Me Murder (Creasey, as Ashe), 1947
Give Me the Knife (Meynell), 1954
Give the Boys a Great Big Hand (McBain), 1960
Give the Girl a Gun (Deming), 1955
Give the Little Corpse a Great Big Hand (Stein, as Bagby), 1953
Give Up the Ghost (Erskine), 1949
Given Day (s van Gulik, trans)
Giveth This Woman? (Le Queux), 1905
Glade Manor Murder (Lemarchand), 1988
Gladstone Bag (MacLeod), 1989
Glass Alibi (Gribble), 1952
Glass Arrow (Verner), 1937
Glass Cage (Aarons, as Ronns), 1962
Glass Cage (C. Wilson), 1966
Glass Cage (Simenon, trans), 1973
Glass Cell (Highsmith), 1964
Glass Flame (Whitney), 1978

Glass Highway (Estleman), 1983
Glass Key (Hammett), 1931
Glass Knife (Thayer), 1932
Glass Man (Goulart, as Robeson), 1975
Glass Mask (Offord), 1944
Glass of Red Wine (Tripp), 1960
Glass on the Stairs (Scherf), 1954
Glass-Sided Ants' Nest (Dickinson), 1968
Glass Slipper (Eberhart), 1938
Glass Spear (Courtier), 1950
Glass Triangle (Coxe), 1940
Glass Village (Queen), 1954
Glendower Legacy (Gifford), 1978
Glenlitten Murder (Oppenheim), 1929
Glenna Powers Case (Waugh), 1980
Glenning, Paula series (Clarke), from 1985
Glimpse of Death (Ormerod), 1976
Glimpses of the Moon (Crispin), 1977
Glint of Spears (Lejeune), 1963
Glitter Dome (Wambaugh), 1981
Glittering Desire (Punshon), 1910
Glitz (Leonard), 1985
Glory Boys (Seymour), 1976
Glow Job (H. Kane), 1971
Glowrey series (Lejeune), from 1987
Go Ahead with Murder (Creasey, as Halliday), 1960
Go Away Death (Creasey), 1941
Go Die in Afghanistan (Avallone, as Jason), 1982
Go for Broke (Welcome), 1972
Go for the Body (Lacy), 1954
Go Gently, Gaijin (Melville), 1986
Go Home, Stranger (C. Williams), 1954
Go, Lovely Rose (Potts), 1954
Go to Sleep Jeannie (Dewey), 1959
Go to Thy Death Bed (S. Forbes), 1968
Go, Honeylou (Dewey), 1962
Go-Between (Maling), 1970
Goat (Straker), 1972
Goblin Market (McCloy), 1943
Goblins (Dent, as Robeson), 1984
God Keepers (Johnson), 1970
God of the Labyrinth (C. Wilson), 1970
God Save the Child (Parker), 1974
God Save the Mark (Westlake), 1967
God Speed the Night (D. Davis), 1968
God Squad Bod (Kenyon), 1982
God's Back Was Turned (Whittington), 1961
God's Defector (Bingham), 1976
Goddess Gone Bad (C. Brown), 1958
Goddess of Death (Underwood), 1982
Gods (Hammond, as Douglas), 1985
Gods in Green (W. Roberts), 1973
Godwin Sideboard (Malcolm), 1984
Godwulf Manuscript (Parker), 1973
Goggle-Box Affair (Gielgud), 1963
Going for the Gold (Lathen), 1981
Going It Alone (M. Innes), 1980
Going Solo (Tripp), 1981
Going to the Dogs (Kavanagh), 1987
Going Wrong (Rendell), 1990
Going, Going, Gone (P. Taylor), 1943
Gold and Wine (Vickers), 1949
Gold Bag (Wells), 1911
Gold Brick Island (Connington), 1933
Gold by Gemini (Gash), 1979
Gold Coast (Demille), 1990
Gold Coast (Leonard), 1980

Gold Coast Nocturne (Nielsen), 1951
Gold Comes in Bricks (E. Gardner, as Fair), 1940
Gold Comfit Box (V. Williams), 1932
Gold from Gemini (Gash), 1978
Gold Game (Vickers), 1930
Gold Gap (Gruber), 1968
Gold of Malabar (Mather), 1967
Gold of the Gods (Reeve), 1915
Gold of Troy (Fish), 1980
Gold Ogre (Dent, as Robeson), 1969
Gold Skull Murders (Packard), 1931
Gold-Spinner (Donovan), 1907
Gold Star Line (s Meade), 1899
Gold Was Our Grave (Wade), 1954
Gold, Alexander, Magnus and Norma series (Resnicow), from 1983
Gold, Max series (O. Cohen), from 1945
Golden Ape (Herbert Adams), 1930
Golden Ashes (Crofts), 1940
Golden Ball (s Christie), 1971
Golden Beast (Oppenheim), 1926
Golden Box (Crane), 1942
Golden Cockatrice (G. Black), 1974
Golden Creep (Stein, as Bagby), 1982
Golden Crucible (Stubbs), 1976
Golden Dagger (Punshon), 1951
Golden Dart (Jepson), 1949
Golden Death (Creasey, as Deane), 1952
Golden Deed (Garve), 1960
Golden Door (Spicer), 1951
Golden Express (Lambert), 1984
Golden-Eyes (Jepson), 1924
Golden Face (Le Queux), 1922
Golden Fear (Harvester), 1957
Golden Gate (MacLean), 1976
Golden Gizmo (Thompson), 1954
Golden Hades (E. Wallace), 1929
Golden Hoard (Balmer), 1934
Golden Hooligan (Dewey), 1961
Golden Keel (Bagley), 1963
Golden Key (O'Farrell), 1963
Golden Lantern (Warriner), 1958
Golden Man (Dent, as Robeson), 1984
Golden Man (Lockridge), 1960
Golden Orange (Wambaugh), 1990
Golden Pebble (Bennett), 1948
Golden Peril (Dent, as Robeson), 1970
Golden Rain (D. Clark), 1980
Golden Rendezvous (MacLean), 1962
Golden Salamander (Canning), 1949
Golden Scorpion (Rohmer), 1919
Golden Shadow (Meade), 1906
Golden Slipper (s Green), 1915
Golden Soak (H. Innes), 1973
Golden Spaniard (Wheatley), 1938
Golden Spiders (Stout), 1953
Golden Spur (J. Fletcher), 1901
Golden Swan Murder (Dorothy Disney), 1939
Golden Three (Le Queux), 1930
Golden Trap (Pentecost), 1967
Golden Triangle (Leblanc, trans), 1917
Golden Unicorn (Whitney), 1976
Golden Violet (Shearing), 1936
Golden Virgin (J. Ross, as Rossiter), 1975
Golden Wang-Ho (Hume), 1901
Golden Web (Oppenheim, as Partridge), 1910
Goldfinger (I. Fleming), 1959

Goldfish Have No Hiding Place (Chase), 1974
Goldilocks (Coburn), 1989
Goldilocks (McBain), 1977
Goldmine-London W1 (Chambers, as Daniels), 1979
Goldstein, Jay and Carlos Cruz series (M. Wallace), from 1986
Golf House Murder (Herbert Adams), 1933
Golgotha (J. Gardner), 1980
Goliath Scheme (Michael Collins, as Arden), 1971
Gondar (Luard), 1988
Gondola Scam (Gash), 1983
Gone Mi$$ing (Egleton), 1988
Gone to Earth (Boyer), 1990
Gone to Glory (Irvine), 1990
Gone to Her Death (Audemars), 1981
Gone to Her Death (McGown), 1990
Gone Tomorrow (F. Davis), 1948
Gone, No Forwarding (Gores), 1978
Good and Dead (Langton), 1986
Good and the Bad (J. Fleming), 1953
Good Behavior (Westlake), 1985
Good Evans! (s E. Wallace), 1927
Good Guys Wear Black (Deming, as Franklin), 1978
Good Luck to the Corpse (Murray), 1951
Good Luck, Sucker (Jessup, as Telfair), 1961
Good Men and True (Harvester), 1949
Good Morning, Mavis (C. Brown), 1957(?)
Good Night and Good-Bye (Timothy Harris), 1979
Good Night to Kill (L. O'Donnell), 1989
Good Old Anna (Lowndes), 1915
Good Old Charlie (Bingham), 1969
Good Old Stuff (s J. MacDonald), 1982
Good Place to Die (Copper), 1975
Good Policeman (Charyn), 1990
Good Spies Don't Grow on Trees (McShane, as Lovell), 1986
Good Year for Dwarfs? (C. Brown), 1970
Good-bye Chicago (Burnett), 1981
Good-bye, Aunt Charlotte! (Straker), 1958
Goodbye and Amen (Clifford), 1974
Goodbye California (MacLean), 1977
Goodbye Charlie (Albert), 1964
Goodbye, Friend (Japrisot, trans), 1969
Goodbye Look (Macdonald), 1969
Goodbye Mickey Mouse (Deighton), 1982
Goodbye to an Old Friend (Freemantle), 1973
Goodbye, Aunt Elva (Fenwick), 1968
Goodbye, Gillian (John Burke)
Goodnight Sweet Prince (Hunter), 1986
Gooseberry Fool (McClure), 1974
Gordon, Chet series (Macdonald, as Millar), from 1944
Gorky Park (M. Smith), 1981
Gorse, Ernest Ralph series (P. Hamilton), from 1951
Gory Dew (G. Mitchell), 1970
Gospel Lamb (Scott), 1980
Gospel of Death (W. Harrington), 1966
Gossip to the Grave (John Burke), 1967
Gossip Truth (John Burke), 1968
Gotham Gore (Avallone, as Jason), 1982
Gothic Pursuit (Malcolm), 1987
Goulburn, Richard series (J. Fletcher), from 1909
Governess (Keating, as Hervey), 1984
Government Contract (Hough, as Stanley), 1956
Governor of Chi-Foo (s E. Wallace), 1929
Governors (Oppenheim), 1908
Gownsman's Gallows (Farrer), 1957
Grab Bag (s MacLeod), 1987
Grab Operators (Chance), 1973
Gracie Allen Murder Case (Van Dine), 1938

Gracious Lily Affair (F. Mason), 1957
Graffiti (Van Greenaway), 1983
Graham, Davina series (Anthony), from 1980
Graham, Peter series (B. Thompson), from 1929
Graham, Richard series (Welcome), from 1958
Grail Tree (Gash), 1979
Granby, Colonel Alistair series (Beeding), from 1928
Grand Modena Murder (Gribble), 1930
Grand Prix Murder (Rutherford), 1955
Grand Slam (R. Perry), 1980
Granite Folly (C. Brown, as Farr), 1967
Grant, Celia series (Sherwood), from 1984
Grant, Inspector Alan series (Tey), from 1929
Grass Widow (McInerny), 1983
Grass-Widow's Tale (Ellis Peters), 1968
Grassleyes Mystery (Oppenheim), 1940
Grave Affair (S. Smith), 1971
Grave Case of Murder (Garve, as Bax), 1951
Grave Danger (F. Kane), 1954
Grave Danger (Roos), 1965
Grave Descend (Crichton, as Lange), 1970
Grave Error (Greenleaf), 1979
Grave for Two (Carmichael), 1977
Grave Goods (Mann), 1984
Grave Journey (Hebden), 1970
Grave Matter (Davies), 1968
Grave Matters (Rhode), 1955
Grave Matters (Yorke), 1973
Grave Mistake (Marsh), 1978
Grave of Truth (Anthony), 1979
Grave Undertaking (L. White), 1961
Grave Without Flowers (McMullen), 1983
Grave's Retreat (Gorman), 1989
Gravedigger (Hansen), 1982
Gravelhanger (Gielgud), 1934
Graves, I Dig! (C. Brown), 1960
Graveyard (Hubbard), 1975
Graveyard Never Closes (F. Davis), 1940
Graveyard of My Own (Goulart), 1985
Graveyard Plot (Erskine), 1959
Graveyard Plots (s Pronzini), 1985
Graveyard Rolls (Procter), 1964
Graveyard Shift (Curtiss), 1982
Graveyard Shift (J. Higgins, as Patterson), 1965
Graveyard to Let (J. Carr, as Dickson), 1949
Gravy Train (Miller, as Masterson), 1971
Gray Dusk (O. Cohen), 1920
Gray Fist (Gibson, as Grant), 1977
Gray Flannel Shroud (Slesar), 1959
Gray Stranger (Crane), 1958
Gray, Cordelia series (James), from 1972
Great Adventure (Horler), 1946
Great Affair (Canning), 1969
Great Air Swindle (Creasey), 1939
Great Awakening (Oppenheim), 1902
Great Bear (s Oppenheim), 1943
Great Brighton Mystery (J. Fletcher), 1925
Great California Game (Gash), 1990
Great Court Scandal (Le Queux), 1906
Great Deliverance (George), 1988
Great Detectives (s Symons), 1981
Great Expectations (Dickens, appendix), 1861
Great Fog (s Heard), 1944
Great Game (Bailey), 1939
Great God Gold (Le Queux), 1910
Great Hotel Murder (Starrett), 1935
Great Impersonation (Oppenheim), 1920

Great Insurance Murders (Propper), 1937
Great Keinplatz Experiment (s Doyle), 1894
Great Merlini series (Rawson), from 1938
Great Mistake (Rinehart), 1940
Great Plot (Le Queux), 1907
Great Portrait Mystery (s Freeman), 1918
Great Prince Shan (Oppenheim), 1922
Great Ruby (Hanshew), 1905
Great Secret (Oppenheim), 1907
Great Southern Mystery (Cole), 1931
Great Stories (s Doyle), 1959
Great Train HiJack (Miller, as Masterson), 1976
Great Train Robbery (Crichton), 1975
Great Turf Fraud (s Donovan), 1909
Great Wash (Kersh), 1953
Great White Queen (Le Queux), 1896
Great Year for Dying (Copper), 1973
Greaves, Emma series (L. Black), from 1965
Greek Affair (Gruber), 1964
Greek Coffin Mystery (Queen), 1932
Greek Fire (W. Graham), 1958
Greek Key (C. Forbes), 1989
Greek Summit (Randisi, as Carter), 1983
Greek Tragedy (Cole), 1939
Green Ace (Palmer), 1950
Green Archer (E. Wallace), 1923
Green Death (Dent, as Robeson), 1971
Green Diamond (s Morrison), 1904
Green Eagle (Dent, as Robeson), 1968
Green Eagle Score (Westlake, as Stark), 1967
Green Eye of Goona (s Morrison), 1904
Green-Eyed Monster (Quentin), 1960
Green Eyes (Gibson, as Grant), 1977
Green Eyes of Bâst (Rohmer), 1920
Green Fields of Eden (Clifford), 1963
Green Flag (s Doyle), 1900
Green for Danger (Brand), 1944
Green Frontier (Hilton), 1981
Green Gene (Dickinson), 1973
Green Grow the Dollars (Lathen), 1982
Green Grow the Graves (Crossen, as Chaber), 1970
Green Hazard (Coles), 1945
Green Hell Treasure (Fish), 1971
Green Ice (G. Browne), 1976
Green Ice (Whitfield), 1930
Green Ice Murders (Whitfield), 1947
Green Ink (s J. Fletcher), 1926
Green Jade Hand (Keeler), 1930
Green Light for Death (F. Kane), 1949
Green Mask (Verner), 1934
Green Master (Dent, as Robeson), 1990
Green Mummy (Hume), 1908
Green Plaid Pants (Scherf), 1951
Green Ray (Le Queux), 1934
Green Ribbon (E. Wallace), 1929
Green Ripper (J. MacDonald), 1979
Green River High (Kyle), 1979
Green Rope (J. Fletcher), 1927
Green Rust (E. Wallace), 1919
Green Shiver (Clason), 1941
Green Thoughts (s Collier), 1932
Green Trigger Fingers (Sherwood), 1984
Green Wolf Connection (Michael Collins, as Carter), 1976
Green Wound (Atlee), 1963
Green Wound Contract (Atlee), 1967.
Green, Horatio series (Nichols), from 1954
Greene Murder Case (Van Dine), 1928

Greenfield, C.B. series (Kallen), from 1979
Greenfinger (Rathbone), 1987
Greenfly (McCutchan), 1987
Greenmantle (Buchan), 1916
Greenmask! (Linington), 1964
Greenstone Griffins (G. Mitchell), 1983
Greenwell Mystery (Carnac, as Lorac), 1932
Greenwich Apartments (Corris), 1986
Greenwich Killing Time (Friedman), 1986
Gremlin's Grampa (Fish, as Pike), 1972
Gresham Ghost (W. Roberts), 1980
Grey Beginning (Elizabeth Peters, as Michaels), 1984
Grey Doctor (Hume), 1917
Grey Face (Rohmer), 1924
Grey Mask (Wentworth), 1928
Grey Room (Phillpotts), 1921
Grey Sentinels (B. Knox), 1963
Grey Timothy (E. Wallace), 1913
Grey, Lindy series (Cory), from 1951
Grey, Roman series (M. Smith), from 1971
Greygallows (Elizabeth Peters, as Michaels), 1972
Greyvale School Mystery (Creasey, as Manton), 1937
Grierson, David series (Stuart), from 1976
Grieve for the Past (S. Forbes), 1963
Grifters (Thompson), 1963
Grim Death (Verner), 1961
Grim Death and the Barrow Boys (J. Fleming), 1971
Grim Game (Horler), 1936
Grim Joker (Verner), 1936
Grim Vengeance (Connington), 1929
Gripped by Drought (Upfield), 1932
Grizzly Trail (Moffat), 1984
Groaning Spinney (G. Mitchell), 1950
Grofield, Alan series (Westlake, as Stark), from 1964
Grogan, Inspector series (Neville), from 1943
Groom Lay Dead (Coxe), 1944
Groote Park Murder (Crofts), 1924
Gross Carriage of Justice (Fish), 1979
Grosvenor Square Goodbye (Clifford), 1974
Ground for Suspicion (Rhode, as Burton), 1950
Ground Money (Burns), 1986
Grove of Doom (Gibson, as Grant), 1966
Grow Young and Die (O'Farrell), 1952
Growing Concern (Stuart), 1985
Grub-and-Stakers series (MacLeod, as Craig), from 1981
Grudge (Olsen, as Hitchens), 1963
Grundt, Dr. Adolph series (V. Williams), from 1918
Gryce, Ebenezer series (Green), from 1878
Guadalajara (Hunt), 1986
Guaranteed to Fade (Stein, as Bagby), 1978
Guarded Room (J. Fletcher), 1931
Guardian Angel (A. Cohen), 1985
Guardian Spectre (McShane, as Lovell), 1977
Guardians of the Prince (Hill), 1983
Guardians of the Treasure (Sapper), 1931
Guarnaccia, Marshal series (Nabb), from 1981
Guerilla Games (Pendleton), 1982
Guerrilla Girls (Whittington), 1960
Guest in the House (P. MacDonald), 1955
Guilt Edged (Burley), 1971
Guilt Edged (Thayer), 1951
Guilt-Edged Frame (F. Kane), 1964
Guilt Is Plain (Ford, as Frome), 1938
Guilt Is Where You Find It (Thayer), 1957
Guilt of Innocence (Creasey, as Halliday), 1964
Guilt on the Lily (Ormerod), 1989
Guilt with Honour (Jeffries, as Ashford), 1982

Guilt Without Proof (Jeffries, as Alding), 1970
Guilt-Edged Cage (C. Brown), 1962
Guilt-Edged Murder (Thayer), 1953
Guilty (Thayer), 1940
Guilty Are Afraid (Chase), 1957
Guilty Bonds (Le Queux), 1891
Guilty Bystander (Miller), 1947
Guilty House (Hume), 1903
Guilty Knowledge (Grant-Adamson), 1986
Guilty Party (Babson), 1988
Guilty Party (John Burke), 1963
Guilty Thing Surprised (Rendell), 1970
Guilty Witness (Chance), 1979
Guilty, But— (Vickers, as Kyle), 1927
Guilty, But Insane (Verner, as Stuart), 1933
Gulf Coast Girl (C. Williams), 1956
Gully of Bluemansdyke (s Doyle), 1892
Gun and Mr. Smith (Godey), 1947
Gun Before Butter (Freeling), 1963
Gun for a God (Morland), 1940
Gun for Sale (Greene), 1936
Gun in Daniel Webster's Bust (Scherf), 1949
Gun to Play With (Straker), 1956
Gunman's Bluff (E. Wallace), 1929
Gunmen, Gallants, and Ghosts (s Wheatley), 1943
Gunner (E. Wallace), 1928
Gunner Kelly (Price), 1983
Gunpowder (Schorr), 1990
Guns (McBain), 1976
Guns of Darkness (Clifford), 1962
Guns of Navarone (MacLean), 1957
Gunshot Grand Prix (Rutherford), 1972
Gutter Gang (Sterling, as Bekker), 1954
Guttersnipe (s Kersh), 1954
Guv'nor (s E. Wallace), 1932
Guvnor (G. Newman), 1977
Guy Deverell (Le Fanu, appendix), 1865
Guy Garrick (Reeve), 1914
Guy, Brian series (S. Marlowe, as Ridgway), from 1960
Gwen John Sculpture (Malcolm), 1985
Gypsy in Amber (M. Smith), 1971
Gypsy, Go Home (O'Farrell), 1961
Gyrth Chalice Mystery (Allingham), 1931

H as in Hangman (Treat), 1942
H as in Hunted (Treat), 1946
Habit of Fear (D. Davis), 1987
Habit of Loving (J. Thomson), 1979
Had I But Groaned (C. Brown), 1968
Hades and Hocus Pocus (Dent), 1979
Hadfield Mystery (Creasey, as Cooke), 1937
Hag's Nook (J. Carr), 1933
Hagar of the Pawn-Shop (s Hume), 1898
Ha-Ha Case (Connington), 1934
Haig, Inspector Digger series (Courtier), from 1957
Haig, Leo series (Block), from 1974
Haiku for Hanae (Melville), 1989
Hail, Hail, The Gang's All Here! (McBain), 1971
Hail to the Chief (McBain), 1973
Hair of the Sleuthhound (s Breen), 1982
Hair's Breadth (Thayer), 1946
Hairy Arm (E. Wallace), 1925
Haitian Hit (Pendleton), 1989
Halcyon Way (McShane), 1979
Hale, Max series (Coxe), from 1939
Half a Bag of Stringer (McCutchan), 1970
Half Hunter (Sherwood), 1961

Half-Mast for the Deemster (Bellairs), 1953
Half-Way to Murder (Warriner, as Troy), 1955
Half-Mast Murder (Kennedy), 1930
Half-Past Mortem (Bellem, as Saxon), 1947
Halfway House (Queen), 1936
Halfway to Hell (Whittington), 1959
Hall of Death (Tyre), 1960
Hall, Satan series (C. Daly), from 1935
Hallelujah Corner (Hebden, as Harris), 1952
Haller, Mike series (Byrd), from 1981
Halley, Sid series (Francis), from 1965
Halliday, Dave series (Waugh, as Taylor), from 1964
Hallowe'en Homicide (Thayer), 1941
Hallowe'en Party (Christie), 1969
Halloween Murder (Doris Disney), 1957
Halloween Murders (Chance), 1968
Halo for Nobody (H. Kane), 1947
Halo for Satan (H. Browne, as Evans), 1948
Halo in Blood (H. Browne, as Evans), 1946
Halo in Brass (H. Browne, as Evans), 1949
Ham Reporter (Randisi), 1986
Hambledon, Tommy series (Coles), from 1940
Hamburg Switch (A. Ross), 1980
Hamlet, Revenge! (M. Innes), 1937
Hammer in His Hand (Miller, as Masterson), 1960
Hammer Island (G. Carr, as Styles), 1947
Hammer of God (Demille), 1974
Hammer of Thor (C. Brown), 1965
Hammer, Mike series (Spillane), from 1947
Hammerhead (Cory), 1963
Hammerhead (Coulter, as Mayo), 1964
Hammerlocke (Wood, as Barnao), 1987
Hammersmith Murders (Ford, as Frome), 1930
Hammett (Gores), 1975
Hanaud, Inspector series (A. Mason), from 1910
Hand and Ring (Green), 1883
Hand in Glove (Eberhart), 1937
Hand in Glove (Marsh), 1962
Hand in the Glove (Stout), 1937
Hand Me a Fig-Leaf (Chase), 1981
Hand of Allah (Le Queux), 1914
Hand of Death (Yorke), 1981
Hand of Fate (Underwood), 1981
Hand of Fear (Verner), 1936
Hand of Glass (Butler, as Melville), 1983
Hand of Lazarus (Murphy), 1988
Hand of Power (E. Wallace), 1927
Hand Out (Rathbone), 1968
Hand over Mind (McShane, as Lovell), 1979
Hand to Burn (Cannan), 1936
Hand-Picked to Die (Deming), 1956
Handful of Silver (Canning), 1954
Handful of Silver (Strange), 1955
Handle (Westlake, as Stark), 1966
Handle with Fear (Dewey), 1951
Hands in the Dark (Gibson, as Grant), 1975
Hands of Eddy Loyd (Johnson), 1988
Hands of Innocence (Jeffries, as Ashford), 1965
Handwriting on the Wall (Propper), 1941
Handy Death (Fish), 1973
Hang by Your Neck (H. Kane), 1949
Hang Loose (Copper), 1982
Hang the Consequences (Meek), 1984
Hang the Little Man (Creasey), 1963
Hang the Man High (Household), 1957
Hanged for a Sheep (Lockridge), 1942
Hanged Man's House (Ferrars), 1974

Hanging Captain (Wade), 1932
Hanging Doll Murder (Ormerod), 1984
Hanging Heiress (Wormser), 1949
Hanging Tree (B. Knox), 1983
Hanging Woman (Rhode), 1931
Hanging's Too Good (Thayer), 1943
Hangman (Verner), 1934
Hangman's Choice (C. Knight), 1949
Hangman's Curfew (G. Mitchell), 1941
Hangman's Dozen (s Alexander), 1961
Hangman's Harvest (Crossen, as Chaber), 1952
Hangman's Holiday (s Sayers), 1933
Hangman's Moon (Gribble), 1950
Hangman's Noose (G. Mitchell), 1983
Hangman's Row (Stein), 1982
Hangman's Tide (Hilton), 1975
Hangman's Tree (Dorothy Disney), 1949
Hangman's Whip (Eberhart), 1940
Hangover House (Rohmer), 1949
Hangover Square (P. Hamilton), 1941
Hang-Up Kid (C. Brown), 1970
Hank of Hair (Jay), 1964
Hannasyde, Superintendent series (Heyer), from 1935
Hannay, Richard series (Buchan), from 1915
Hanno's Doll (Piper), 1961
Hanvey, Jim series (O. Cohen), from 1929
Happy Are the Clean of Heart (Greeley), 1986
Happy Are the Meek (Greeley), 1985
Happy Are Those Who Thirst for Justice (Greeley), 1987
Happy Highwayman (s Charteris), 1939
Happy New Year, Herbie (s McBain, as Hunter), 1963
Happy Returns (Coles, as Gaite), 1955
Happy Thieves (Condon), 1962
Harbingers of Fear (Simpson), 1977
Harbour (P. MacDonald, as Lawless), 1931
Hard Candy (Vachss), 1989
Hard Cash (Max Collins), 1981
Hard Contract (Copper), 1983
Hard Core (Thompson), 1986
Hard Hit (Wainwright), 1974
Hard Kill (Gribble, as Grex), 1969
Hard Line (Lewin), 1982
Hard Man to Kill (R. Perry), 1973
Hard Rain (van de Wetering), 1986
Hard Sell (Haggard), 1965
Hard to Handle (Welcome), 1964
Hard Trade (Lyons), 1982
Hardball (Hornig), 1985
Hardican's Hollow (J. Fletcher), 1910
Hardin, Bert series (Alexander), from 1954
Hardliners (Haggard), 1970
Hardly a Man Is Now Alive (Brean), 1950
Hardly a Man Is Now Alive (S. Marlowe, as Ridgway), 1962
Hardway Diamonds Mystery (Rhode, as Burton), 1930
Hardy, Cliff series (Corris), from 1980
Hare Sitting Up (M. Innes), 1959
Hargrave Deception (Hunt), 1980
Hark, Hark, The Watchdogs Bark (S. Forbes, as Wells), 1975
Harlem Showdown (Malzberg, as Barry), 1975
Harlem Underground (Lacy), 1965
Harlequin of Death (Horler), 1933
Harlequin Opal (Hume), 1893
Harley, Paul series (Rohmer), from 1921
Harm's Way (Aird), 1984
Harmas, Steve series (Chase), from 1952
Harper (Macdonald), 1966
Harpoon of Death (O'Farrell), 1953

Harriet Farewell (Erskine), 1975
Harris, Paul series (G. Black), from 1961
Harrison Affair (Seymour), 1980
Harrowing (Gosling), 1981
Harry's Game (Seymour), 1975
Hartinger's Mouse (McCutchan), 1970
Harvest Is Past (Bush, as Home), 1937
Harvest Moon (J. Fletcher), 1908
Harvest Murder (Rhode), 1937
Harvest of Death (R. Harrison), 1988
Harvester, Steve series (Fox), from 1954
Harvey Garrard's Crime (Oppenheim), 1926
Hashimi's Revenge (Royce), 1986
Haskell, Vejay series (Dunlap), from 1984
Hasting, Bill and Coco series (Offord), from 1938
Hastings, Lieutenant Frank series (Wilcox), from 1969
Hasty Wedding (Eberhart), 1938
Haswell, Jimmie series (Herbert Adams), from 1924
Hatch, Jake series (Campbell), from 1988
Hatch, Professor Cyrus series (F. Davis), from 1938
Hatchet Man (Marshall), 1976
Hatchet Murders (Morland), 1947
Hatchetman (Dodge), 1970
Hate Begins at Home (Aiken), 1967
Hate Genius (Dent, as Robeson), 1979
Hate Ship (Graeme), 1928
Hate to Kill (Creasey, as Halliday), 1962
Hated by All! (Chance, as Drummond), 1951
Hateful Voyage (Neville), 1956
Hatter's Phantoms (Simenon, trans), 1976
Haunted Bell (s Futrelle), 1915
Haunted Chair (Leroux, trans), 1931
Haunted Hotel (Collins, appendix), 1878
Haunted Lady (Rinehart), 1942
Haunted Lives (Le Fanu, appendix), 1868
Haunted Monastery (van Gulik, trans), 1963
Haunting at Waverley Falls (Rae), 1980
Haunting Me (Blackstock, as Allardyce), 1978
Haunting of Low Fennel (s Rohmer), 1920
Haunting of Toby Jugg (Wheatley), 1948
Havana Hit (Malzberg, as Barry), 1974
Have a Change of Scene (Chase), 1973
Have a Nice Night (Chase), 1982
Have Gat—Will Travel (s Prather), 1957
Have His Carcase (Sayers), 1932
Have Mercy upon Us (S. Forbes, as Wells), 1974
Have This One on Me (Chase), 1967
Haven for the Damned (Whittington), 1962
Havilland, Antony series (Gielgud), from 1934
Having Wonderful Crime (Rice), 1943
Havoc (Oppenheim), 1911
Havoc by Accident (Simenon, trans), 1943
Hawaii Five-O (Avallone), 1968
Hawaii Five-O: Terror in the Sun (Avallone), 1969
Hawaiian Hellground (Pendleton), 1975
Hawk (Vickers, as Kyle), 1930
Hawks, Joaquin series (Ballinger), from 1965
Hawkshaw (Goulart), 1972
Hayes, Julie series (D. Davis), from 1976
Hayes, Lee series (Lacy), from 1965
Hazard (G. Browne), 1973
Hazardous Duty (Hunt, as St. John), 1966
Hazelrigg, Inspector series (M. Gilbert), from 1947
He Came by Night (A. Gilbert), 1944
He Could Not Have Slipped (Beeding), 1939
He Could Stop the World (Dent, as Robeson), 1970
He Didn't Mind Danger (M. Gilbert), 1949

He Died of Murder! (S. Smith), 1947
He Died with His Eyes Open (Raymond), 1984
He Done Her Wrong (Kaminsky), 1983
He Found Himself Murdered (Ames), 1947
He Had to Die (Hocking), 1962
He Hanged His Mother on Monday (Morland), 1951
He Never Came Back (McCloy), 1954
He Ought to Be Shot (J. Fleming), 1955
He Should Have Died Hereafter (Hare), 1958
He Walked in Her Sleep (s Cheyney), 1946
He Who Hesitates (McBain), 1965
He Who Whispers (J. Carr), 1946
He Won't Need It Now (Chase, as Docherty), 1939
He Wouldn't Kill Patience (J. Carr, as Dickson), 1944
He Wouldn't Stay Dead (F. Davis), 1939
Head (Cory), 1960
Head First (Marshall), 1986
Head Men (Murphy), 1977
Head of a Traveller (Blake), 1949
Head of State (Hoyt), 1985
Head on the Sill (Neville), 1966
Headcase (Cody), 1985
Headed for a Hearse (Latimer), 1935
Headless Lady (Rawson), 1940
Headless Snowman (McShane), 1974
Heads and Tails (s Jepson), 1933
Heads I Win (M. Harrison, as Downes), 1953
Heads Off at Midnight (Beeding), 1938
Heads You Die (Gribble), 1964
Heads You Lose (Brand), 1941
Heads You Lose (Halliday), 1958
Healing Hands of Death (Audemars), 1977
Healthy Grave (Woods, as Leek), 1980
Healthy Way to Die (Kenyon), 1986
Healthy Way to Die (L. Black), 1976
Hear No Evil (F. Davis, as Ransome), 1953
Hearse Class Male (F. Kane), 1963
Hearse for Cinderella (Carmichael, as Howard), 1956
Hearse of Another Color (Crossen, as Chaber), 1958
Hearse on May-Day (G. Mitchell), 1972
Hearse with Horses (McGirr), 1967
Hearses Don't Hurry (F. Davis, as Ransome), 1941
Heart Cut Diamond (Horler), 1929
Heart of a Man (Simenon, trans), 1951
Heart of a Princess (Le Queux), 1920
Heart of Ice (Hume), 1918
Heart of Penelope (Lowndes), 1904
Heart of the Matter (Greene), 1948
Heart to Heart (Boileau, trans), 1959
Hearts Ease in Death (J. Fraser), 1977
Heartstones (Rendell), 1987
Heat (McBain), 1981
Heat of Night (Whittington), 1960
Heat Wave (Hall, as Smith), 1957
Heat Wave (Timothy Harris), 1979
Heat's On (Himes), 1966
Heaven-Kissed Hill (J. Fletcher), 1922
Heaven Ran Last (McGivern), 1949
Heaven-Sent Witness (s J. Fletcher), 1930
Heaven's Prisoners (James Lee Burke), 1988
Heavenly Bodies (Warriner), 1960
Heavy as Lead (G. Mitchell, as Torrie), 1966
Heavy Iron (Copper), 1987
Heavy, Heavy Hangs (Doris Disney), 1952
Heberden's Seat (D. Clark), 1979
Heckler (McBain), 1960
He'd Rather Be Dead (Bellairs), 1945

Hedley, Paul series (Sturrock, as Healey), from 1965
Hedonists (C. Wilson), 1971
Heed the Thunder (Thompson), 1946
Heel of Achilles (Verner), 1946
Hefferman, Hooky series (Meynell), from 1952
Height of Day (Cory), 1955
Heights of Zervos (C. Forbes), 1970
Heimrich, Captain Merton series (Lockridge), from 1947
Heir-at-Law (s Waters, appendix), 1861
Heir Hunters (Ballinger), 1966
Heir of Douglas (de la Torre), 1952
Heir of Starvelings (Berckman), 1967
Heir Presumptive (Wade), 1935
Heir to Lucifer (Rhode, as Burton), 1947
Heir to Murder (Creasey, as Halliday), 1940
Heir to Murder (Rhode, as Burton), 1953
Heiress of Fear (C. Brown, as Farr), 1978
Heiress of Frascati (Shearing), 1966
Heiress to Corsair Keep (C. Brown, as Farr), 1978
Heirloom (Haggard), 1983
Heirloom of Tragedy (Avallone, as Noone), 1965
Heirs of Merlin (Perowne, as Atkey), 1945
Heist Me Higher (Ballinger), 1969
Helen (Cunningham), 1966
Helen Passes By (Punshon), 1947
Helen Vardon's Confession (Freeman), 1922
Helen, Sister Mary series (O'Marie), from 1984
Helga's Web (Cleary), 1970
Hell Below (Dent, as Robeson), 1980
Hell-Black Night (Fisher), 1970
Hell Can Wait (Whittington), 1960
Hell-Gate Tides (Thayer), 1933
Hell Hath No Fury (C. Williams), 1953
Hell Is a City (Ard), 1955
Hell Is a City (Procter), 1954
Hell Is Always Today (J. Higgins, as Patterson), 1968
Hell Is Empty (Straker), 1958
Hell Is Too Crowded (J. Higgins, as Patterson), 1962
Hell Is Where You Find It (Welcome), 1968
Hell Let Loose (Beeding), 1937
Hell of a Woman (Thompson), 1954
Hell on the Way (Fox), 1943
Hell Street (Deming, as Franklin), 1954
Hell to Eternity (Aarons), 1960
Hell to Pay (Cox), 1958
Hellcat (C. Brown), 1962
Heller, Nathan series (Max Collins), from 1983
Hellfire Heritage (W. Roberts), 1979
Hell's Angel (A. Cohen), 1986
Hell's Belle (J. Fleming), 1968
Hell's Brew (Horler), 1952
Hell's Our Destination (Brewer), 1953
Hellspout (B. Knox), 1976
Helltracks (Nolan), 1990
Helm, Ben series (Fischer), from 1945
Helm, Matt series (D. Hamilton), from 1960
Help I Am Being Held Prisoner (Westlake), 1974
Help the Poor Struggler (Grimes), 1985
Hemingway's Notebook (Granger), 1986
Hemingway, Inspector series (Heyer), from 1941
Hemlock, Jonathan series (Trevanian), from 1972
Hendon's First Case (Rhode), 1935
Hennessy (Deming, as Franklin), 1975
Hennings, Rachel series (Breen), from 1984
Henrietta Who? (Aird), 1968
Henry Dunbar (Braddon, appendix), 1864
Henry MaGee Is Not Dead (Granger), 1988

Henry, Gil series (C. Grafton), from 1943
Her Death of Cold (McInerny), 1977
Her Great Moment (Balmer), 1921
Her Majesty's Minister (Le Queux), 1901
Her Royal Highness (Le Queux), 1914
Herald of Doom (Creasey, as Ashe), 1974
Herald, Simon series (Welcome), from 1959
Herapath Property (J. Fletcher), 1920
Here Be Monsters (Price), 1985
Here Comes a Candle (F. Brown), 1950
Here Comes a Chopper (G. Mitchell), 1946
Here Comes a Hero (Block), 1968
Here Comes the Copper (s Wade), 1938
Here Comes the Corpse (Stein, as Bagby), 1941
Here Comes the Lady (s Shiel), 1928
Here I Stay (Elizabeth Peters, as Michaels), 1983
Here Is an S.O.S. (Horler), 1939
Here Is Danger! (Creasey, as Ashe), 1946
Here Lies (Doris Disney), 1963
Here Lies Gloria Mundy (G. Mitchell), 1982
Here Lies My Wife (McGirr), 1967
Here Lies Nancy Frail (J. Ross), 1972
Here to Die (Michael Collins, as Sadler), 1971
Here's a Villain! (J. Mitchell), 1957
Heretic's Apprentice (Ellis Peters), 1989
Herewith the Clues! (Wheatley), 1939
Heritage (Driscoll), 1982
Hermit of Eyton Forest (Ellis Peters), 1987
Hermit of Turkey Hollow (Train), 1921
Hero for Leanda (Garve), 1959
Hero in the Tower (Kirst, trans), 1972
Heroes No More (Wainwright), 1983
Heroin Annie (s Corris), 1984
Heron, Felix series (Verner), from 1966
Hex (Dent, as Robeson), 1968
Hickory, Dickory, Death (Christie), 1955
Hickory, Dickory, Dock (Christie), 1955
Hidden Death (Gibson, as Grant), 1970
Hidden Door (Packard), 1933
Hidden Face (Canning), 1956
Hidden Hand (C. Daly), 1929
Hidden Hand (Horler), 1937
Hidden Hand (Phillpotts), 1952
Hidden Hands (Le Queux), 1926
Hidden Hour (F. Davis, as Ransome), 1966
Hidden Key (Coxe), 1963
Hidden Kingdom (Beeding), 1927
Hidden Lives (Albert), 1981
Hidden Lives (Punshon), 1913
Hidden Malice (Berckman)
Hidden Man (Underwood), 1985
Hidden Menace (Verner, as Stuart), 1939
Hidden Target (MacInnes), 1980
Hide and Go Seek (Garve), 1966
Hide and Kill (Creasey, as York), 1959
Hide and Seek (Collins, appendix), 1854
Hide Her from Every Eye (Pentecost), 1966
Hide in the Dark (F. Hart), 1929
Hide My Eyes (Allingham), 1958
Hide the Body! (Propper), 1939
Hide Those Diamonds! (Vickers), 1935
Hideaway (Procter), 1968
Hideaway (s J. Gardner), 1968
Hiding Place (Wilcox), 1973
Hi-Fi Fadeout (C. Brown), 1958
High Adventure (Westlake), 1985
High Citadel (Bagley), 1965

High-Class Kill (Wainwright), 1973
High Commissioner (Cleary), 1966
High Corniche (Dodge), 1961
High Fashion in Homicide (C. Brown), 1958
High Game (Horler), 1950
High Hand (Futrelle), 1911
High Hazard (Horler), 1943
High Hazard (Stern), 1962
High Heel Homicide (F. Davis), 1961
High Heels (Tripp), 1980
High Jinx (Buckley), 1986
High Jump (Gielgud), 1953
High Midnight (Kaminsky), 1981
High Pavement (Bonett, as Carter), 1944
High Place (Household), 1950
High Priest (Murphy), 1987
High Rendezvous (K. Knight), 1954
High Requiem (Cory), 1956
High Road to China (Cleary), 1977
High Sheriff (Wade), 1937
High Sierra (Burnett), 1940
High Stakes (Dent), 1953
High Stakes (Francis), 1975
High Stakes (Horler), 1932
High Stand (H. Innes), 1985
High Tide (Hubbard), 1970
High Voltage (Chastain), 1979
High Wall (Copper), 1975
High Water Mark (Hume), 1910
High Window (Chandler), 1942
High Wire (Haggard), 1963
Highbinders (Thomas, as Bleeck), 1974
Highly Explosive Case (Chambers), 1982
Highway to Murder (Carmichael, as Howard), 1973
Hijack (L. White), 1969
Hi-Jack for a Jill (C. Brown), 1956
Hilda Wade (s Doyle), 1900
Hilda, Take Heed (Creasey, as Halliday), 1957
Hildegarde Withers Makes the Scene (Flora), 1969
Hill Fog (Chance), 1975
Hill Girl (C. Williams), 1951
Hill of the Terrified Monk (Homes), 1943
Hiller Weapon (Chance), 1987
Hillman (Oppenheim), 1917
Himalayan Assignment (F. Mason), 1952
Hindsight (Dickinson), 1983
Hinges of Hell (Sterling), 1955
Hip-Deep in Alligators (Campbell), 1987
His Aunt Came Late (Meynell), 1939
His Bones Are Coral (Canning), 1955
His Burial Too (Aird), 1973
His Darling Sin (Braddon, appendix), 1899
His Eminence, Death (M. Smith, as Quinn), 1974
His Father's Crime (Oppenheim), 1929
His Last Bow (s Doyle), 1917
His Majesty's Hit Man (Prior), 1986
His Name Was Death (F. Brown), 1954
His Weight in Gold (Procter), 1966
Hit (Garfield), 1970
Hit and Run (Chase, as Marshall), 1958
Hit and Run (Creasey), 1959
Hit and Run (Deming), 1960
Hit and Run (Jeffries, as Ashford), 1966
Hit Man (Chance), 1987
Hit Them Where It Hurts (Chase), 1984
Hitler Diamonds (Cory), 1979
Hive of Glass (Hubbard), 1965

Hobbema Prospect (Hilton), 1984
Hochmann Miniatures (Fish), 1967
HOG Murders (DeAndrea), 1979
Hog's Back Mystery (Crofts), 1933
Hogget, Ron series (J. Mitchell), from 1985
Holcroft Covenant (Ludlum), 1978
Hold Out (Bruton), 1961
Hold the Four Aces (Chase), 1977
Hole and Corner (Wentworth), 1936
Hole in the Ground (Bell), 1971
Hole in the Ground (Garve), 1952
Hole in the Wall (Morrison), 1902
Holiday for a Spy (Graeme), 1963
Holiday for Murder (Christie), 1947
Holiday Homicide (King), 1940
Holiday with a Vengeance (R. Perry), 1974
Holiday with Murder (G. Carr), 1960
Hollow (Christie), 1946
Hollow Chest (P. Taylor, as Tilton), 1941
Hollow House (Curtiss), 1951
Hollow Man (J. Carr), 1935
Hollow Needle (Coxe), 1948
Hollow Needle (Leblanc, trans), 1910
Hollow Sunday (Harling), 1967
Hollow Vengeance (Morice), 1982
Holly, Inspector series (Postgate), from 1943
Hollywood Gothic (Gifford), 1979
Hollywood Hoax (Creasey, as Frazer), 1961
Hollywood Murders (Queen), 1957
Holm Oaks (Hubbard), 1965
Holman, Rick series (C. Brown), from 1961
Holmes, Sherlock series (Doyle), from 1888
Holmes, Sherlock series (Estleman), from 1978
Holocaust (H. Kane, as McCall), 1967
Holy Disorders (Crispin), 1945
Holy Father's Navy (Purser), 1971
Holy Terror (Charteris), 1932
Holy Terror (Murphy), 1975
Home and Murder (Stein), 1962
Home Is the Hangman (Sale), 1949
Home Is the Heart (A. Gilbert), 1942
Home Is the Hunter (Wainwright), 1979
Home Is the Prisoner (Potts), 1960
Home Is the Sailor (Keene), 1952
Home of Silence (Meade), 1907
Home Run (Seymour), 1989
Home Sweet Homicide (Rice), 1944
Home to Roost (Garve), 1976
Homes, Schlock series (s Fish), from 1966
Homicidal Horse (Pentecost), 1979
Homicidal Lady (Keene), 1954
Homicide at Yuletide (H. Kane), 1966
Homicide Blonde (Procter), 1965
Homicide Harem (C. Brown), 1965
Homicide House (Ford, as Frome), 1950
Homicide Hoyden (C. Brown), 1954
Homicide Is My Game (S. Marlowe), 1959
Homicide Johnny (Fisher, as Gould), 1940
Homicide Trinity (Stout), 1962
Honegger, Lieutenant series (Strange), from 1941
Honest Dealer (Gruber), 1947
Honest Reliable Corpse (Stein, as Bagby), 1969
Honesty Will Get You Nowhere (Sherwood), 1977
Honey Ant (Kyle), 1988
Honey Harlot (Brand), 1978
Honey, Here's Your Hearse! (C. Brown), 1955
Honeybath, Charles series (M. Innes), from 1974

Honeymoon with Death (Pentecost), 1975
Honeymoon with Murder (C. Hart), 1989
Honfleur Decision (Hunter), 1980
Hong Kong Airbase Murders (F. Mason), 1937
Hong Kong Caper (C. Brown), 1962
Honolulu Murder Story (Ford), 1947
Honolulu Murders (Ford), 1967
Honolulu Story (Ford), 1946
Honor (Campbell), 1987
Honor of the Name (Gaboriau, trans), 1900
Honorary Consul (Greene), 1973
Honour among Thieves (Bailey), 1947
Honourable Algernon Knox, Detective (s Oppenheim), 1920
Honourable Detective (Jeffries, as Ashford), 1988
Honourable Schoolboy (le Carré), 1977
Hooded Raider (Verner, as Stuart), 1931
Hooded Stranger (Verner), 1940
Hooded Terror (Verner, as Stuart), 1930
Hoodlum Was a Honey (C. Brown), 1956
Hoodoo Horror (Avallone, as Jason), 1981
Hoods Come Calling (Albert, as Quarry), 1958
Hoodwink (Gosling), 1988
Hoodwink (Pronzini), 1981
Hoof (McCutchan), 1983
Hook (Copper), 1984
Hooligan (Dodge), 1969
Hooray for Homicide (J. Anderson), 1985
Hope to Die (Waugh), 1948
Hope, Matthew series (McBain), from 1977
Hopjoy Was Here (Watson), 1962
Hopkinson and the Devil of Hate (McCutchan), 1961
Hopscotch (Garfield), 1975
Horizon (MacInnes), 1945
Horizontal Hold (Irvine), 1978
Horizontal Man (Eustis), 1946
Horn of Roland (Ellis Peters), 1974
Hornet's Nest (Fischer), 1944
Horrible Dummy (s Kersh), 1944
Horrible Man (Avallone), 1968
Horror House (Wells), 1931
Horror on the Ruby X (Crane), 1956
Horror's Head (Horler), 1932
Horror-7 (s Bloch), 1963
Horse under Water (Deighton), 1963
Horse's Head (McBain, as Hunter), 1967
Horstmann Inheritance (Sturrock, as Healey), 1975
Horton Mystery (Hanshew), 1905
Hospitality of Miss Tolliver (s Kersh), 1965
Hospitality of the House (Doris Disney), 1964
Host for Dying (Audemars), 1970
Host of Extras (Leasor), 1973
Hostage (Horler), 1943
Hostage for a Hood (L. White), 1957
Hostage Game (McShane), 1979
Hostage Island (Pendleton), 1982
Hostage to Death (Jeffries, as Ashford), 1977
Hostage—London (Household), 1977
Hostess to Murder (E. Holding), 1943
Hosts of the Flaming Death (F. Davis, as Steele), 1966
Hot as Fire, Cold as Ice (Whittington), 1962
Hot Body (Avallone), 1973
Hot Dam (Ballard, as MacNeil), 1960
Hot Day, Hot Night (Himes), 1970
Hot Ice (Gribble, as Grex), 1983
Hot Money (Francis), 1987
Hot Place (Resnicow), 1990
Hot Red Money (Kendrick), 1959

Hot Rock (Westlake), 1970
Hot Seat for a Honey (C. Brown), 1956
Hot Shot (Flora), 1956
Hot Spot (C. Williams), 1965
Hot Summer Killing (Pentecost, as Philips), 1968
Hot Times (Cox), 1973
Hotel Murders (Sterling), 1957
Hotel Room (s Woolrich), 1958
Hotel X (s Le Queux), 1919
Hound of Death (s Christie), 1933
Hound of the Baskervilles (Doyle), 1902
Hounded Down (Vickers, as Durham), 1923
Hounds of Vengeance (Creasey), 1945
Hour Before Midnight (Johnston), 1978
Hour Before Zero (Harvester), 1959
Hour of Reckoning (s Oppenheim), 1944
Hour of the Dog (Mather), 1982
Hour of the Donkey (Price), 1980
Hour of the Hyenas (Sherwood), 1979
Hours after Midnight (Hayes), 1958
Hours Before Dawn (Fremlin), 1958
Hours to Kill (Curtiss), 1961
House above Hollywood (Johnston), 1968
House above the River (Bell), 1959
House Arrest (Russell), 1988
House at Balnesmoor (Rae), 1969
House at Fern Canyon (W. Roberts), 1970
House at Landsdowne (C. Brown, as Farr), 1977
House at Pluck's Gutter (Coles), 1963
House at Satan's Elbow (J. Carr), 1965
House by the Canal (Simenon, trans), 1952
House by the Church-Yard (Le Fanu, appendix), 1863
House by the Sea (Eberhart), 1972
House by the Sea (Lowndes), 1937
House Dick (Hunt, as Davis), 1961
House in Belmont Square (Erskine), 1963
House in Greek Street (s Horler), 1935
House in Hook Street (Erskine), 1977
House in Lordship Lane (A. Mason), 1946
House in Marsh Road (Meynell), 1960
House in Naples (Rabe), 1956
House in the Hills (Meynell), 1937
House in the Mist (s Green), 1905
House in the Woods (Chance, as Drummond), 1950
House in Tuesday Market (J. Fletcher), 1929
House Next Door (L. White), 1956
House of a Thousand Lanterns (Holt), 1974
House of Alexandrine (Dobyns), 1990
House of Assignation (Robbe-Grillet, trans), 1970
House of Cain (Upfield), 1928
House of Cards (Ellin), 1967
House of Care (Burley), 1981
House of Dark Illusions (C. Brown, as Farr), 1973
House of Destiny (C. Brown, as Farr), 1970
House of Dr. Edwardes (Beeding), 1927
House of En-Dor (Hocking), 1936
House of Evil (Le Queux), 1927
House of Ferrars (Creasey, as Mattheson)
House of Flesh (Fischer), 1950
House of Ghosts (Gibson, as Grant), 1981
House of Godwinsson (Punshon), 1948
House of Green Turf (Ellis Peters), 1969
House of Imposters (W. Roberts), 1977
House of Jackals (Horler), 1951
House of Many Shadows (Elizabeth Peters, as Michaels), 1974
House of Numbers (Finney), 1957
House of Peril (Lowndes), 1935

House of Secrets (C. Brown, as Farr), 1973
House of Secrets (Horler), 1926
House of Soldiers (Garve), 1961
House of Sorcery (C. Brown), 1967
House of Stairs (Rendell, as Vine), 1989
House of Storm (Eberhart), 1949
House of Terror (Berckman), 1960
House of the Arrow (A. Mason), 1924
House of the Bears (Creasey), 1946
House of the Black Magic (Meade), 1912
House of the Dead Ones (Chance), 1977
House of the Enchantress (Erskine), 1959
House of the Four Winds (Buchan), 1935
House of the Hatchet (s Bloch), 1965
House of the Seven Flies (Canning), 1952
House of the Uneasy Dead (Horler), 1950
House of the Whispering Pines (Green), 1910
House of the Wicked (Le Queux), 1906
House of Tomba (C. Brown, as Farr), 1966
House of Treachery (C. Brown, as Farr), 1977
House of Valhalla (C. Brown, as Farr), 1978
House of Whispers (Le Queux), 1909
House on Bostwick Square (Johnston), 1987
House on K Street (L. White), 1965
House on Lily Street (J. Vance), 1979
House on 9th Street (Strange), 1976
House on Plymouth Street (s Curtiss), 1985
House on Q Street (Hunt, as Dietrich), 1959
House on the Cliff (Meynell), 1932
House on the Cliffs (C. Brown, as Farr), 1974
House on the Hill (Chance, as Drummond), 1945
House on the Left Bank (Johnston), 1975
House on the River (Chance, as Drummond), 1952
House on the Roof (Eberhart), 1935
House on the Strand (du Maurier), 1969
House on Tollard Ridge (Rhode), 1929
House Possessed (Blackstock), 1962
House That Jack Built (Dewhurst), 1983
House That Jack Built (McBain), 1988
House with Crooked Walls (Graeme), 1942
House with the Blue Door (Footner), 1942
House with the Light (Horler), 1948
House with the Stained-Glass Windows (W. Graham), 1934
House Without a Key (Biggers), 1925
House Without the Door (E. Daly), 1942
House-Dick (Copper), 1988
Household Traitors (Blackburn), 1971
Hovering Darkness (Berckman), 1957
How Doth the Little Crocodile? (Antony), 1952
How Goes the Murder? (Deming, as Queen), 1967
How Hard to Kill (Dewey), 1962
How Like an Angel (Millar), 1962
How Many Coupons for a Shroud? (s Morland), 1946
How Many to Kill? (Creasey, as Halliday), 1960
How the Dead Live (Raymond), 1986
How the Old Woman Got Home (s Shiel), 1927
How to Kill a Man (S. Forbes, as Wells), 1972
How to Live Dangerously (J. Fleming), 1974
How To Trap a Crook (s Symons), 1977
Howard Hughes Affair (Kaminsky), 1979
Howling in the Woods (Johnston), 1968
Huckleberry Fiend (J. Smith), 1987
Huddersfield Job (A. Ross), 1971
Huddle (Wells), 1936
Hue and Cry (Dewey), 1944
Hue and Cry (Wentworth), 1927
Hugger-Mugger in the Louvre (Paul), 1940

Human Chase (s Oppenheim), 1929
Human Factor (Greene), 1978
Human Factor (M. Smith, as Quinn), 1975
Humming Box (Whittington), 1956
Hunchback of Westminister (Le Queux), 1904
Hundred-Dollar Girl (Gault), 1961
Hungry Dog (Gruber), 1941
Hungry Dog Murders (Gruber), 1943
Hungry Goblin (J. Carr), 1972
Hungry One (Brewer), 1966
Hungry Spider (Jepson), 1950
Hunt Ball Murder (s Crofts), 1943
Hunt Club (Daniels), 1964
Hunt for Red October (Clancy), 1984
Hunt Is Up (Hocking), 1934
Hunt the Killer (Keene), 1952
Hunt the Slipper (Cecil), 1977
Hunt the Tortoise (Ferrars), 1950
Hunt to a Kill (Russell), 1969
Hunt with the Hounds (Eberhart), 1950
Hunted (Leonard), 1977
Hunted Down (Dickens, appendix), 1859
Hunted Woman (Albrand), 1952
Hunter (Busby), 1985
Hunter (Westlake, as Stark), 1962
Hunter and the Hunted (Linington, as Egan), 1979
Hunter and the Trapped (Bell), 1963
Hunter at Large (Dewey), 1961
Hunter in the Shadows (Butler, as Melville), 1969
Hunter of the Blood (Miller, as Masterson), 1977
Hunter's Green (Whitney), 1968
Hunter, Detective Superintendent Philip series (Procter), from 1951
Hunter, Ed and Am series (F. Brown), from 1947
Hunter, Lieutenant Max series (Ballard), from 1961
Hunter, Robert Lee series (Sauter), from 1983
Hunter, Sam series (Morse), from 1982
Hunters (Howard), 1976
Hunters Point (Sims), 1973
Hunting of Mr. Exe (Chance), 1982
Hunting of Mr. Gloves (Chambers, as Daniels), 1986
Hunting-Ground (Clifford), 1964
Huntington, Captain Colin series (Condon), from 1972
Huntingtower (Buchan), 1922
Huntress Is Dead (Benson), 1960
Huntress of Death (Horler), 1933
Huntsman (Verner), 1940
Hurricane (J. MacDonald), 1957
Hurricane Drift (Chance), 1967
Hurry the Darkness (Procter), 1951
Hurton Treasure Mystery (Hume), 1937
Husband (Caspary), 1957
Hush Money (Max Collins), 1981
Hush, Gabriel! (Johns), 1941
Hush-a-Bye Murder (Alexander), 1957
Hushed Up at German Headquarters (s Le Queux), 1917
Hushed Up! (Le Queux), 1911
Hut (Meynell), 1938
Huuygens, Kek series (Fish), from 1967
Hydra with Six Heads (Bell), 1970
Hyer, Hank series (Steel), from 1935
Hypnotic Demon (Creasey, as Cooke), 1936

I Am Death (Verner), 1963
I Am the Only Running Footman (Grimes), 1986
I Am the Withered Man (Creasey, as Deane), 1941
I and My True Love (MacInnes), 1953

I Came to Kill (Hunt, as Davis), 1953
I Came to the Castle (Johnston), 1969
I Came to the Highlands (Johnston), 1974
I Can't Stop Running (Aarons, as Ronns), 1951
I Could Be Good to You (Blackstock, as Keppel), 1980
I Could Have Died (Stein, as Bagby), 1979
I Could Murder Her (Carnac, as Lorac), 1951
I Die Slowly (Macdonald, as Millar), 1955
I Died Yesterday (Dent, as Robeson), 1988
I Fear the Greeks (Stein), 1966
I Fear You Not (Ard, as Kerr), 1956
I Gave at the Office (Westlake), 1971
I Give You Five Days (Curzon), 1983
I Hide, We Seek (Stern), 1965
I Knew MacBean (Erskine), 1948
I Know What It's Like to Die (J. Ross), 1976
I Like 'em Tough (s McBain, as Cannon), 1958
I Love You Again (O. Cohen), 1937
I Love, I Kill (Bingham), 1968
I, Lucifer (P. O'Donnell), 1967
I Married a Dead Man (Woolrich, as Irish), 1948
I Met Murder (Ferrars), 1985
I Met Murder (Jepson), 1930
I Met Murder on the Way (Blackstock), 1977
"I!" Said the Demon (Baxt), 1969
I, Said the Fly (Ferrars), 1945
I, Said the Spy (Lambert), 1980
I Saw Him Die (Drummond), 1979
I Say No (Collins, appendix), 1884
I See You (s Armstrong), 1966
I Should Have Stayed Home (McCoy), 1938
I Spy (MacKenzie), 1964
I, The Executioner (F. Davis, as Ransome), 1953
I, The Jury (Spillane), 1947
I Wake Up Screaming (Fisher), 1941
I Want to Go Home (Lockridge), 1948
I Was Dora Suarez (Raymond), 1990
I Will Speak Daggers (Procter), 1956
I Would Rather Stay Poor (Chase), 1962
I Wouldn't Be in Your Shoes (s Woolrich, as Irish), 1943
Icarus Agenda (Ludlum), 1988
Ice (McBain), 1983
Ice Axe Murders (G. Carr), 1958
Ice Maidens (Chance), 1969
Ice Station Zebra (MacLean), 1963
Iceberg (Cussler), 1975
Icebreaker (J. Gardner), 1983
Ice-Cold in Ermine (C. Brown), 1958
Ice-Cold Nude (C. Brown), 1962
Iciest Sin (Keating), 1990
Icy Clutches (Elkins), 1990
Ideal Crime (Jeffries, as Ashford), 1985
Idol of the Town (Le Queux), 1905
If Anything Happens to Hester (Creasey, as Morton), 1962
If Death Ever Slept (Stout), 1957
If Dying Was All (Goulart), 1971
If I Live to Dine (Waugh), 1949
If I Should Die Before I Wake (s Woolrich, as Irish), 1945
If Laurel Shot Hardy the World Would End (S. Forbes), 1970
If She Should Die (S. Forbes, as Rydell), 1961
If Sinners Entice Thee (Le Queux), 1898
If the Coffin Fits (Keene), 1952
If the Shroud Fits (Roos), 1941
If Two of Them Are Dead (S. Forbes), 1968
If Wishes Were Hearses (Cullingford), 1952
If You Can't Be Good (Thomas), 1973
If You Have Tears (H. Browne, as Evans), 1947

If You Want a Murder Well Done (Scherf), 1974
Ilion Like a Mist (J. Mitchell), 1969
I'll Be Judge, I'll Be Jury (Kennedy), 1937
I'll Bring Her Back (Cheyney), 1952
I'll Bury My Dead (Chase), 1953
I'll Die for You (F. Davis, as Ransome), 1959
I'll Eat You Last (Branson), 1941
I'll Get You for This (Chase), 1946
I'll Hate Myself in the Morning (Paul), 1945
I'll Kill You Last (Branson), 1942
I'll Never Leave You (Lustgarten), 1971
I'll Never Tell (Vickers), 1937
I'll Say She Does! (Cheyney), 1945
I'll Sing at Your Funeral (Pentecost), 1942
I'll Tell You Everything (Priestley), 1932
Ill Deeds Done (Hocking), 1938
Ill Met by a Fish Shop on George Street (McShane), 1968
Ill Met by Moonlight (Ford), 1937
Ill Wind (Fitt), 1951
Ill Wind Contract (Atlee), 1969
Illustrious Prince (Oppenheim), 1910
I'm Cannon—For Hire (McBain, as Cannon), 1958
I'm No Hero (Carmichael, as Howard), 1961
I'm No Murderer (Perowne), 1938
Image in the Dust (Hall, as Scott), 1951
Image of a Society (Fuller), 1956
Image of Hell (Fisher), 1961
Image of Man (Tripp), 1955
Imago (McClure), 1988
Imitation Thieves (McShane, as Lovell), 1971
Immaterial Murder Case (Symons), 1945
Immortal Coil (s Van Greenaway), 1985
Immortal Error (Hall, as Trevor), 1946
Impact (Copper), 1975
Impact of Evidence (Carnac), 1954
Impact-20 (s Nolan), 1963
Impeached! (Graeme), 1933
Impeccable People (Fenwick), 1971
Imperfect Crime (Graeme), 1932
Imperial Treasure (Gielgud), 1931
Impetuous Mistress (Coxe), 1958
Implacable Hunter (Kersh), 1961
Implant (Royce, as Jacks), 1980
Import of Evil (Chance), 1961
Importance of Being Murdered (Wells), 1939
Impossible Virgin (P. O'Donnell), 1971
Imposter (McCloy), 1977
Imposters (G. Higgins), 1986
Impostor (Steel), 1942
Improbable Fiction (Woods), 1970
In a Deadly Vein (Halliday), 1956
In a Glass Darkly (s Le Fanu, appendix), 1872
In a House Unknown (Olsen, as Hitchens), 1973
In a Lonely Place (Hughes), 1947
In a Vain Shadow (Chase, as Marshall), 1951
In at the Death (Ford, as Frome), 1929
In at the Kill (B. Knox), 1961
In at the Kill (Ferrars), 1978
In Black and Whitey (Lacy), 1967
In Case of Emergency (Simenon, trans), 1958
In Chinatown (s T. Burke), 1921
In Cold Blood (Stein, as Bagby), 1948
In Cold Pursuit (Curtiss), 1977
In Connection with Kilshaw (Driscoll), 1974
In Deadly Peril (Gaboriau, trans), 1888
In Deep (Kyle), 1976
In Enemy Hands (Murphy), 1977

Invader (Wormser), 1972
Invasion of Privacy (Page, as Kurnitz), 1955
Invasion of the Yellow Warlords (F. Davis, as Steele), 1966
Inverted Crime (Gribble), 1954
Investigation (Uhnak), 1977
Investigations Are Proceeding (Jeffries, as Ashford), 1961
Investigators (J. Fletcher), 1902
Invisible Empire (F. Davis, as Steele), 1966
Invisible Flamini (C. Brown), 1971
Invisible Man Murders (Crossen, as Foster), 1945
Invisible Weapons (Rhode), 1938
Invisible Worm (Millar), 1941
Invisible-Box Murders (Dent, as Robeson), 1989
Invitation to a Dynamite Party (Lovesey), 1974
Invitation to Adventure (Creasey, as Ashe), 1945
Invitation to an Inquest (Hull), 1950
Invitation to Evil (W. Roberts), 1970
Invitation to Murder (Ford), 1954
Invitation to Vengeance (K. Knight), 1960
Invitation to Violence (L. White), 1958
Involvement in Austria (Chance), 1969
I.O.U. Murder (Dewey), 1958
Ipcress File (Deighton), 1962
Irish Beauty Contract (Atlee), 1966
Irish Witch (Wheatley), 1973
Iron Chalice (O. Cohen), 1925
Iron Clew (P. Taylor, as Tilton), 1947
Iron Cobweb (Curtiss), 1953
Iron Gates (Millar), 1945
Iron Grip (s E. Wallace), 1929
Iron Hand (P. Taylor, as Tilton), 1947
Iron Maiden (C. Brown), 1975
Iron Ring (Keeler), 1944
Iron Sanctuary (B. Knox, as MacLeod), 1968
Iron Skull (Goulart, as Robeson), 1974
Iron Spiders (Kendrick), 1936
Iron Staircase (Simenon, trans), 1963
Iron Tiger (J. Higgins, as Patterson), 1966
Iron Virgin (Fox), 1951
Ironside (Thompson), 1967
Ironwood (Butler, as Melville), 1972
Irralie's Bushranger (Hornung), 1896
Irrepressible Peccadillo (Flora), 1962
Is She Dead Too? (A. Gilbert), 1956
Is Skin-Deep, Is Fatal (Keating), 1965
Is There a Traitor in the House? (McGerr), 1964
Is This Revenge? (Gribble), 1931
Ishmael's Wife (Vickers), 1924
Iskirlak, Nuri series (J. Fleming), from 1962
Island Gold (V. Williams), 1923
Island of Evil (C. Brown, as Farr), 1978
Island of Fear (Footner), 1936
Island of Galloping Gold (E. Wallace), 1916
Island of Peril (Creasey), 1940
Island of Sheep (Buchan), 1936
Island of Terror (Sapper), 1931
Island Where Time Stands Still (Wheatley), 1954
Isle of Dragons (B. Knox, as MacLeod), 1967
Isle of Peril (J. Vance, as Wade), 1957
Isle of the Snakes (Fish), 1963
It Ain't Hay (Dodge), 1946
It Began in New York (Kennedy), 1943
It Can't Be My Grave (Dean), 1983
It Couldn't Matter Less (Cheyney), 1941
It Happened Like That (s Phillpotts), 1928
It Might Lead Anywhere (Punshon), 1946
It Pays to Die (Wills), 1953

It Shouldn't Happen to a Dog (Watson), 1977
It Walks by Night (J. Carr), 1930
It's a Sin to Kill (Keene), 1958
It's Her Own Funeral (Carnac), 1951
It's Loaded, Mr. Bauer (Marquand), 1949
It's Murder with Dover (Porter), 1973
It's My Funeral (Rabe), 1957
Italian Assets (Allbeury, as Butler), 1976
It's a Battlefield (Greene), 1934
Ivory Dagger (Wentworth), 1951
Ivory God (s J. Fletcher), 1907
Ivory Grin (Macdonald), 1952
Ivy Tree (Stewart), 1961

Jack and the Beanstalk (McBain), 1984
Jack-in-the-Box (Connington), 1944
Jack o' Judgement (E. Wallace), 1920
Jack on the Gallows Tree (Bruce), 1960
Jackal's Head (Elizabeth Peters), 1968
Jackpot (Pronzini), 1990
Jackson, Kane series (Michael Collins, as Arden), from 1968
Jacob Street Mystery (Freeman), 1942
Jacob's Ladder (Oppenheim), 1921
Jacoby, Miles series (Randisi), from 1982
Jacovich, Milan series (L. Roberts), from 1988
Jade Dragon (Gibson, as Grant), 1981
Jade Eye (Hume), 1903
Jade Figurine (Pronzini, as Foxx), 1972
Jade for a Lady (Crossen, as Chaber), 1962
Jade in Aries (Westlake, as Coe), 1971
Jade Venus (Coxe), 1945
Jade Wind (Hebden, as Harris), 1969
Jade Woman (Gash), 1988
Jade-Eyed Jinx (C. Brown), 1963
Jade-Eyed Jungle (C. Brown), 1963
Jail Bait (Chambers), 1983
Jail-Breakers (B. Newman), 1968
Jailbreak (L. White), 1976
Jamaica Inn (du Maurier), 1936
James Joyce Murder (Cross), 1967
James Knowland, Deceased (Carmichael), 1958
James Tarrant, Adventurer (Crofts), 1941
Jameson, Cass series (Wheat), from 1983
Jantry, Auguste series (Graeme), from 1946
January Zone (Corris), 1987
Janus Imperative (Anthony), 1980
Janus Man (C. Forbes), 1988
Janus Murder Case (C. Wilson), 1984
Japanese Corpse (van de Wetering), 1977
Japanese Girl (s W. Graham), 1971
Japanese Mistress (Neely), 1972
Jason series (Chance), from 1953
Jaubert Ring (W. Roberts), 1976
Javelin for Jonah (G. Mitchell), 1974
Jaws of Death (Thayer), 1946
Jaws of the Watchdog (Parrish, as Drummond), 1973
Jealous One (Fremlin), 1965
Jealous Woman (J. Cain), 1950
Jealousy (Robbe-Grillet, trans), 1959
Jeanne of the Marshes (Oppenheim), 1908
Jekyll Legacy (Bloch), 1990
Jenner, James series (Milne), from 1986
Jennerton & Co (s Oppenheim), 1929
Jennie Baxter, Journalist (Barr), 1899
Jenny Newstead (Lowndes), 1932
Jeopardy Is My Job (S. Marlowe), 1962
Jeremiah and the Princess (Oppenheim), 1933

Jericho Day (Murphy), 1989
Jericho Man (Lutz), 1980
Jericho, John series (Pentecost), from 1965
Jersey Guns (Pendleton), 1974
Jerusalem Inn (Grimes), 1984
Jet-Lag (Copper), 1986
Jethro Hammer (Rice, as Venning), 1944
Jewel of Death (Berckman), 1968
Jewelled Eye (D. Clark), 1985
Jew's House (Hume), 1911
Jews Without Jehovah (Kersh), 1934
Jig-Saw (Phillpotts), 1926
Jigsaw (McBain), 1970
Jigsaw (Waugh), 1962
Jim Barnett Intervenes (s Leblanc, trans), 1928
Jim Maitland (s Sapper), 1923
Jim the Penman (Donovan), 1901
Jimmy the Kid (Westlake), 1974
Jiu San (Dent, as Robeson), 1981
Job of Murder (Gruber), 1950
Jockey (Verner), 1937
Joey's Case (Constantine), 1988
John Brand's Will (Herbert Adams), 1933
John Brown's Body (Carnac, as Lorac), 1939
John Doe—Murderer (Daniels, as Dale), 1942
John Jenkin, Public Enemy (Graeme), 1935
John Macnab (Buchan), 1925
John Marchmont's Legacy (Braddon, appendix), 1863
Johnnie (Hughes), 1944
Johnny Come Lately (F. Kane), 1963
Johnny Danger (Blackstock, as Allardyce), 1960
Johnny Get Your Gun (Ball), 1969
Johnny Goes East (Cory), 1958
Johnny Goes North (Cory), 1956
Johnny Goes South (Cory), 1959
Johnny Goes West (Cory), 1959
Johnny Ludlow (s Wood, appendix), 1874–99
Johnny Staccato (F. Kane, as Boyd), 1960
Johnny under Ground (Moyes), 1965
Johnson, Coffin Ed and Grave Digger Jones series (Himes),
    from 1957
Johnson, Helen Markham series (Dewhurst), from 1982
Johnson, Johnson series (Dunnett), from 1968
Joker (E. Wallace), 1926
Joker in the Deck (Prather), 1964
Joker in the Pack (Chase), 1975
Jonah and Co (s Yates), 1922
Jonah's Luck (Hume), 1906
Jones, Jason and Necessary Smith series (Crossen), from 1944
Jordan, Scott series (Masur), from 1947
Journey into Danger (Fox), 1943
Journey into Fear (Ambler), 1940
Journey into Terror (Rabe), 1957
Journey into Violence (Whittington), 1961
Journey to Nowhere (Tyre), 1954
Journey to Orassia (Caillou), 1965
Journey to the Hangman (Upfield), 1959
Journey with a Stranger (The Gordons), 1963
Journey's End (Berckman), 1977
Journeying Boy (M. Innes), 1949
Joy House (Keene), 1954
Judah Lion Contract (Atlee), 1972
Judas (Johnson), 1971
Judas Cat (D. Davis), 1949
Judas Code (Lambert), 1983
Judas Country (Lyall), 1975
Judas Factor (Allbeury), 1984

Judas Freak (Pentecost), 1974
Judas Goat (Cleeve), 1966
Judas Goat (Parker), 1978
Judas Gospel (Van Greenaway), 1972
Judas Hour (Hunt), 1951
Judas Judge (Avallone, as Jason), 1979
Judas Kiss (Herbert Adams), 1955
Judas Kiss (Holt), 1981
Judas Mandate (Egleton), 1972
Judas Pair (Gash), 1977
Judas Window (J. Carr, as Dickson), 1938
Judas! (Van Greenaway), 1972
Judas, Incorporated (Steel), 1939
Judd, Inspector George series (Bruton), from 1963
Judge and His Hangman (Dürrenmatt, trans), 1954
Judge and the Hatter (Simenon, trans), 1956
Judge Dee at Work (s van Gulik, trans), 1967
Judge Is Reversed (Lockridge), 1960
Judge Me Not (J. MacDonald), 1951
Judge's Dilemma (Vickers, as Kyle), 1939
Judgement in Stone (Rendell), 1977
Judge's Chair (s Phillpotts), 1914
Judges of Hades (s Hoch), 1971
Judgment Day (Murphy), 1974
Judgment of Deke Hunter (G. Higgins), 1976
Judgment on Deltchev (Ambler), 1951
Judicial Body (Scherf), 1957
Judy of Bunter's Buildings (Oppenheim), 1936
Jugger (Westlake, as Stark), 1965
Juggernaut (Bagley), 1985
Juice (Campbell), 1989
Juke Box King (F. Kane), 1959
July at Fritham (Bush, as Home), 1938
Jump Cut (Irvine), 1974
Jumping Jenny (Berkeley), 1933
Jungle Heat (Miller, as Wilmer), 1954
Jungle Kids (s McBain, as Hunter), 1956
Jungle Murder (K. Knight, as Amos), 1947
Juniper Rock (Perowne, as Atkey), 1953
Junkyard Dog (Campbell), 1986
Junta (Drummond), 1989
Jupiter Crisis (W. Harrington), 1971
Jurnet, Ben series (Haymon), from 1980
Juror (Underwood), 1975
Juror in Waiting (Cecil), 1970
Jury (Phillpotts), 1927
Jury of One (Eberhart), 1960
Jury People (Wainwright), 1978
Jury, Inspector Richard series (Grimes), from 1981
Juryman (MacKenzie), 1957
Just a Face in the Dark (McShane), 1987
Just a Matter of Time (Chase), 1972
Just an Ordinary Case (Graeme), 1956
Just Another Sucker (Chase), 1961
Just Desserts (Heald), 1977
Just Desserts (Jeffries), 1980
Just Let Me Be (Cleary), 1950
Just Men of Cordova (E. Wallace), 1917
Just the Way It Is (Chase, as Marshall), 1944
Just What the Doctor Ordered (Watson), 1969
Justice (Simenon, trans), 1949
Justice Ends at Home (s Stout), 1977
Justice Enough (Carmichael), 1956
Justice Has No Sword (Deming, as Franklin), 1953
Justice in Jeopardy (Wills), 1961
Justice on the Rocks (B. Knox), 1967
Justin Bayard (Cleary), 1955

Juvenile Delinquent (Deming), 1958

Ka of Gifford Hillary (Wheatley), 1956
Kahawa (Westlake), 1982
Kaleidoscope (Avallone), 1966
Kane, Andy series (C. Brown), from 1962
Kang-He Vase (J. Fletcher), 1924
Karma (Dunlap), 1984
Kat Strikes (Spain), 1955
Kate Plus Ten (E. Wallace), 1917
Kauffman, Inspector Max series (Chastain), from 1974
Kaye, Simon series (Waugh), from 1980
Keate, Sarah and Lance O'Leary series (Eberhart), from 1929
Keeban (Balmer), 1923
Keep It Quiet (Hull), 1935
Keep Murder Quiet (Jepson), 1940
Keep the Baby, Faith (DeAndrea, as DeGrave), 1986
Keeper of the Children (Hallahan), 1978
Keeper of the Keys (Biggers), 1932
Keepers of the King's Peace (s E. Wallace), 1917
Keith Partridge, Master Spy (Avallone, as Stanton), 1971
Keith, John series (Daniels), from 1964
Keller, Joe series (Demille), from 1975
Kelley, Lieutenant Joseph series (Ford), from 1932
Kelley, Professor Neil series (Dean), from 1982
Kelling, Sarah series (MacLeod), from 1979
Kellogg, Benson series (Spicer), from 1962
Kells, Michael series (Cheyney), from 1945
Kelly, Homer series (Langton), from 1964
Kelly, Jack series (Petievich), from 1981
Kelly, Lieutenant series (Roth), from 1954
Kemp, Lennox series (Meek), from 1983
Kennedy series (G. Higgins), from 1980
Kennedy, Professor Craig series (Reeve), from 1915
Kennel Murder Case (Van Dine), 1933
Kentish Manor Murders (Symons), 1988
Kenton, Malcolm series (Harvester), from 1955
Kenworthy, Superintendent Simon series (Hilton), from 1968
Kenyatta series (Goines, as Clark), from 1974
Kept Women Can't Quit (E. Gardner, as Fair), 1960
Kerr, Constable and Inspector Fusil series (Jeffries, as Alding),
   from 1967
Kerry, Detective Inspector Don series (Jeffries, as Ashford),
   from 1961
Kessler Legacy (Stern), 1967
Key (Thayer), 1924
Key (Wentworth), 1944
Key Man (V. Williams), 1926
Key to Death (Lockridge), 1954
Key to Nicholas Street (Ellin), 1952
Key to Rebecca (Follett), 1980
Key to the Morgue (Carmichael, as Howard), 1957
Key to the Suite (J. MacDonald), 1962
Key Without a Door (Lejeune), 1988
Key Witness (F. Kane), 1956
Key Witness (W. Roberts), 1975
Keyhole Peeper (Sterling, as Bekker), 1955
Keys from a Window (Berckman), 1965
Keys of Chance (W. Graham), 1939
Keys of Death (Sims), 1982
Keys of Hell (J. Higgins, as Fallon), 1965
Keys to Crime (Creasey, as Martin), 1947
Keystone (Lovesey), 1983
Keziah Dane (S. Grafton), 1967
KGB Kill (J. Mitchell), 1987
Khufra Run (J. Higgins, as Graham), 1972
Kick Start (Rutherford), 1973

Kid (McCutchan), 1958
Kid Was Last Seen Hanging Ten (Stein, as Stone), 1966
Kid Who Came Home with a Corpse (Stein, as Stone), 1972
Kidnap Castle (G. Carr, as Styles), 1947
Kidnap Club (Reeve), 1932
Kidnap Island (Vickers), 1935
Kidnap Kid (Kenrick), 1975
Kidnap Murder Case (Van Dine), 1936
Kidnapped Child (Creasey, as Ashe), 1955
Kidnapper (B. Thomson), 1933
Kidnapper (Bloch), 1954
Kill a Wicked Man (Creasey, as Hunt), 1957
Kill and Kill Again (Pentecost), 1987
Kill and Tell (Kienzle), 1984
Kill Claudio (Hubbard), 1979
Kill Cure (Rathbone), 1975
Kill for the Millions (H. Kane), 1972
Kill Her—You'll Like It! (Avallone), 1973
Kill Him Twice (Prather), 1965
Kill Is a Four-Letter Word (Stein), 1968
Kill Joy (E. Holding), 1942
Kill Me Tomorrow (Prather), 1969
Kill My Love (Creasey, as Hunt), 1958
Kill Now—Pay Later (Gribble, as Grex), 1971
Kill of Small Consequence (Wainwright), 1980
Kill-Off (Thompson), 1957
Kill Once, Kill Twice (Creasey, as Hunt), 1956
Kill or Be Killed (Creasey, as Ashe), 1949
Kill or Cure (Ferrars), 1956
Kill or Cure (J. Fleming), 1968
Kill or Cure (Murphy), 1973
Kill the Boss Good-by (Rabe), 1956
Kill the Clown (Prather), 1962
Kill the Girls and Make Them Cry (Wainwright), 1974
Kill Them Silently (Avallone, as Jason), 1980
Kill to Fit (Fischer), 1946
Kill with Kindness (Linington, as Shannon), 1968
Kill Your Darlings (Max Collins), 1984
Kill Zone (Estleman), 1984
Killain, Johnny series (Dan Marlowe), from 1959
Killdog (John Burke, as George), 1970
Killed in Paradise (DeAndrea), 1988
Killed in the Act (DeAndrea), 1981
Killed in the Ratings (DeAndrea), 1978
Killed on the Ice (DeAndrea), 1984
Killed on the Rocks (DeAndrea), 1990
Killed with a Passion (DeAndrea), 1983
Killer (C. Wilson), 1970
Killer (Miller), 1951
Killer (Wells), 1938
Killer at His Back (Godey), 1955
Killer at Large (Procter), 1959
Killer Boy Was Here (Stein, as Bagby), 1970
Killer by Proxy (Jepson), 1950
Killer Chromosomes (Murphy), 1978
Killer Dolphin (Marsh), 1966
Killer for a Song (J. Gardner), 1975
Killer for the Chairman (Hebden), 1972
Killer in the Crowd (Tey, as Daviot), 1954
Killer in the Rain (s Chandler), 1964
Killer in the Straw (Lockridge), 1955
Killer in the Street (Nielsen), 1967
Killer Inside Me (Thompson), 1952
Killer Is Kissable (C. Brown), 1955
Killer Is Loose (Brewer), 1954
Killer Is Mine (Powell), 1959
Killer Kay (s E. Wallace), 1930

Kiwi Target (Ball), 1988
Kleine Geschichten für Weiberfeinde (s Highsmith), 1974
Klondyker (B. Knox), 1968
Knave of Eagles (Miller, as Wade), 1969
Knave of Hearts (Linington, as Shannon), 1962
Knave Takes Queen (s Cheyney), 1939
Knaves & Co (s Horler), 1938
Knavish Crows (Woods), 1971
Knee-Deep in Death (Fischer), 1956
Knife (Herbert Adams), 1934
Knife Behind the Curtain (s V. Williams), 1930
Knife Between the Ribs (Scott), 1986
Knife Edge (MacKenzie), 1961
Knife for Harry Dodd (Bellairs), 1953
Knife for the Juggler (Coles), 1953
Knife for the Killer (Morland), 1939
Knife in the Dark (Cole), 1941
Knife Is Feminine (Jay), 1951
Knight and the Castle (Chance), 1946
Knight Fall (Payne), 1987
Knight of Evil (Donovan), 1905
Knight Sinister (Hall, as Rattray), 1951
Knives Have Edges (Woods), 1968
Knock at Midnight (Blackstock), 1966
Knock-Down (Francis), 1974
Knock-Out (Sapper), 1933
Knock Three-One-Two (F. Brown), 1959
Knock, Knock! Who's There? (Chase), 1973
Knock, Knock, Who's There? (A. Gilbert), 1964
Knocked for a Loop (Rice), 1957
Knocker on Death's Door (Ellis Peters), 1970
Knockover (Thornburg), 1968
Know Then Thyself (Harvester, as Gibbs), 1947
Knutsford Mystery (Donovan), 1906
Koberg Link (Maling), 1979
Kobra Manifesto (Hall), 1976
Koesler, Father Robert series (Kienzle), from 1979
Kolchak's Gold (Garfield), 1974
Kolwezi (R. Perry), 1985
Kono Diamond (Daniels), 1969
Kosygin Is Coming (Ardies), 1974
Kowloon Contract (Atlee), 1974
Kozminski series (M. Harrison, as Downes), from 1952
Kramer, Lieutenant and Sergeant Zondi series (McClure),
    from 1971
Kremlin Conspiracy (Hunt), 1985
Kremlin File (Ballard, as Carter), 1973
Kremlin Kiss (Freemantle), 1986
Kremlin Letter (Behn), 1966
Kreutzemark, Professor (Beeding), from 1925
Krim, Harvey series (Cunningham), from 1964
Kruger, Herbie series (J. Gardner), from 1979
Krysalis (Trenhaile), 1989
Kubla Khan Caper (Prather), 1966
Kyd, Thomas series (Timothy Harris), from 1977
Kyle Contract (MacKenzie), 1970
Kynsard Affair (Vickers), 1951
Kyril (Trenhaile), 1981

La Belle Laurine (Graeme), 1926
L.A. Confidential (Ellroy), 1990
La-La-Land series (Campbell), from 1986
La Maison de rendez-vous (Robbe-Grillet, trans), 1966
Laboratory Murder (s Morland), 1944
Labour of Hercules (s Lowndes), 1943
Labours of Hercules (s Christie), 1947
LaBrava (Leonard), 1983

Labyrinth (Pronzini), 1980
Labyrinth Makers (Price), 1970
Labyrinthine Ways (Greene), 1940
Labyrinths (Borges, trans), 1962
Lacquer Screen (van Gulik, trans), 1964
Ladies' Bane (Wentworth), 1952
Ladies in Retreat (Perowne), 1935
Ladies in the Dark (Neville), 1965
Ladies Won't Wait (Cheyney), 1951
Lady Afraid (Dent), 1948
Lady and Her Doctor (Piper), 1956
Lady and the Pirate (Blackstock, as Allardyce), 1957
Lady and the Snake (Webb, as Farr), 1957
Lady Audley's Secret (Braddon, appendix), 1862
Lady Beware (Cheyney), 1950
Lady Called Nita (s E. Wallace), 1930
Lady Came by Night (Halliday), 1954
Lady Came to Kill (Crossen, as Chaber), 1959
Lady Doctor—Woman Spy (B. Newman), 1937
Lady Doth Protest (Graeme), 1971
Lady Eleanor, Lawbreaker (Barr), 1911
Lady Electra (s Barr), 1904
Lady for Sale (Daniels), 1960
Lady from Nowhere (Hume), 1900
Lady Had a Gun (Morland), 1951
Lady Has No Convictions (C. Brown), 1956
Lady Helena (Leroux, trans), 1931
Lady—Here's Your Wreath (Chase, as Marshall), 1940
Lady in a Frame (Chance), 1960
Lady in Armor (O. Cohen), 1941
Lady in Black (Clarke), 1977
Lady in Black (Graeme), 1952
Lady in Cement (Albert, as Rome), 1961
Lady in Green (s Cheyney), 1947
Lady in Mink (Caspary), 1946
Lady in Peril (Dent), 1959
Lady in Tears (s Cheyney), 1949
Lady in the Car (s Le Queux), 1908
Lady in the Car with Glasses and a Gun (Japrisot, trans), 1967
Lady in the Case (Futrelle), 1910
Lady in the Lake (Chandler), 1943
Lady in the Morgue (Latimer), 1936
Lady-in-Waiting (Le Queux), 1921
Lady Is a Spy (L. Black), 1969
Lady Is Afraid (Coxe), 1940
Lady Is Available (C. Brown), 1963
Lady Is Chased (C. Brown), 1953
Lady Is Not Available (C. Brown), 1963
Lady Is Transparent (C. Brown), 1962
Lady Is Waiting (J. Mitchell), 1958
Lady Jezebel (Hume), 1898
Lady Jim of Curzon Street (Hume), 1905
Lady Killer (Coxe), 1949
Lady Killer (E. Holding), 1942
Lady Killer (McBain), 1958
Lady Killer (Togawa, trans), 1985
Lady-Killer (A. Gilbert), 1951
Lady Kills (Fischer), 1951
Lady, Lady, I Did It! (McBain), 1961
Lady Lost (Cory), 1953
Lady Macbeth (Freeling), 1988
Lady Molly of Scotland Yard (s Orczy), 1910
Lady of a Thousand Sorrows (Malzberg, as Mason), 1977
Lady of Ascot (E. Wallace), 1930
Lady of Doom (Verner), 1934
Lady of Little Hell (s E. Wallace), 1929
Lady of the Night (Horler), 1929

Lady on a Train (Charteris), 1945
Lady on Platform One (Meynell), 1950
Lady Regrets (Fox), 1947
Lady so Innocent (Herbert Adams), 1929
Lady So Silent (Dent), 1951
Lady Takes a Flyer (Aarons, as Ronns), 1958
Lady to Kill (Dent), 1946
Lady Was a Tramp (Whittington), 1951
Lady Who Never Was (Chambers), 1981
Lady with a Cool Eye (Moffat), 1973
Lady with the Dice (Rogers), 1946
Lady with the Limp (Horler), 1944
Lady Yesterday (Estleman), 1987
Lady, Behave! (Cheyney), 1950
Lady, Drop Dead (Treat), 1960
Lady, The Guy Is Dead (Aarons, as Ronns), 1950
Lady, This Is Murder (Chambers), 1963
Lady, You're Killing Me (Chambers), 1979
Ladygrove (John Burke), 1978
Ladykiller (L. O'Donnell), 1984
Lady's Not for Living (Sterling, as St. Clair), 1963
Laidlaw, Detective Inspector Jack series (McIlvanney), from 1977
Laird, Andrew series (B. Knox, as MacLeod), from 1974
Lake Frome Monster (Upfield), 1966
Lake House (Rhode), 1946
Lake Isle (Freeling), 1976
Lake of Darkness (Rendell), 1980
Lake of Fury (B. Knox, as MacLeod), 1966
Lamb, Inspector Ernest series (Wentworth), from 1939
Lambert's Son (Maling), 1972
Lame Dog Murder (Creasey, as Halliday), 1952
Lament for a Lousy Lover (C. Brown), 1960
Lament for a Lover (Highsmith), 1956
Lament for a Maker (M. Innes), 1938
Lament for a Virgin (L. White), 1960
Lament for Four Brides (Berckman), 1959
Lament for Leto (G. Mitchell), 1971
Lament for the Bride (Reilly), 1951
Lampton Dreamers (Davies), 1966
Land God Gave to Cain (H. Innes), 1958
Land of Always-Night (Dent, as Robeson), 1966
Land of Fear (Dent, as Robeson), 1973
Land of Leys (Davies), 1979
Land of Terror (Dent, as Robeson), 1935
Land, Marty series (Alexander), from 1960
Landower Legacy (Holt), 1984
Landscape with Corpse (Ames), 1955
Landscape with Violence (Wainwright), 1975
Landslide (Bagley), 1967
Lane, Lorimer series (Wells), from 1923
Lane, Paul series (Lockridge), from 1962
Language of Cannibals (Chesbro), 1990
Lantern for Diogenes (Harvester), 1946
Lantern Network (Allbeury), 1978
Lanyard, Michael series (L. Vance), from 1914
Larceny in Her Heart (Gribble, as Grex), 1959
Largo, Lou series (Ard), from 1959
Larkin, Jim series (Russell), from 1971
Larkspur Conspiracy (Pentecost, as Philips), 1973
Lash, Simon series (Gruber), from 1941
Lashed But Not Leashed (McShane), 1976
Last Adventure (s E. Wallace), 1934
Last Alchemist (Murphy), 1986
Last Annual Slugfest (Dunlap), 1986
Last Appointment (Carmichael, as Howard), 1951
Last Best Friend (Sims), 1967

Last Breath (Masur), 1958
Last Bridge (Garfield), 1966
Last Buccaneer (Wainwright), 1971
Last Bus to Woodstock (Dexter), 1975
Last Call (Murphy), 1978
Last Card (Kirst, trans), 1967
Last Chance Country (Moffat), 1983
Last Commandment (Coxe), 1960
Last Contract (Howard), 1973
Last Cop Out (Spillane), 1973
Last Day in Limbo (P. O'Donnell), 1976
Last Days of America (Erdman), 1981
Last Deception (Carmichael, as Howard), 1951
Last Ditch (Marsh), 1977
Last Domino Contract (Atlee), 1976
Last Doorbell (Gruber, as Vedder), 1941
Last Drop (Murphy), 1983
Last Escape (Carnac, as Lorac), 1959
Last Express (Kendrick), 1937
Last Ferry from the Lido (Sturrock, as Healey), 1981
Last First (Hull), 1947
Last Frontier (MacLean), 1959
Last Galley (s Doyle), 1911
Last Gamble (Masur), 1958
Last Good Kiss (Crumley), 1978
Last Great Death Stunt (Howard), 1977
Last Hero (Charteris), 1930
Last Hours Before Dawn (Gadney), 1975
Last House-Party (Dickinson), 1982
Last Judgement (Clarke), 1985
Last Movement (Aiken), 1977
Last Note for a Lovely (C. Brown), 1957
Last of Lysandra (Fenwick), 1973
Last of Philip Banter (Bardin), 1947
Last One Kills (Miller, as Masterson), 1969
Last One Left (J. MacDonald), 1967
Last Place God Made (J. Higgins), 1971
Last Post for a Partisan (Egleton), 1971
Last Respects (Aird), 1982
Last Rights (Hammond, as Douglas), 1986
Last Rites for the Vulture (M. Smith, as Quinn), 1975
Last Seance (McShane, as Lovell), 1982
Last Seen Alive (Simpson), 1985
Last Seen in London (Clarke), 1987
Last Seen Wearing . . . (Waugh), 1952
Last Seen Wearing (Dexter), 1976
Last Seven Hours (Chance), 1956
Last Sherlock Holmes Story (Dibdin), 1978
Last Shot (Loraine), 1986
Last Shot (Thayer), 1931
Last Smile (Albert), 1988
Last Spin (s McBain, as Hunter), 1960
Last Straw (Doris Disney), 1954
Last Straw (Hume), 1932
Last Supper (McCarry), 1983
Last Suspect (Rhode), 1951
Last Temple (Murphy), 1977
Last Time I Saw Hell (M. Smith, as Quinn), 1974
Last Tomb (Crichton, as Lange), 1974
Last Train Out (Oppenheim), 1940
Last Train to Limbo (Chance), 1972
Last Trump (J. Gardner), 1980
Last Trump (Thayer), 1937
Last Two Weeks of Georges Rivac (Household), 1978
Last Vanity (Carmichael, as Howard), 1952
Last Voyage (Clarke), 1980
Last War Dance (Murphy), 1974

Last Warning (Verner), 1962
Last Will and Testament (Cole), 1936
Last Will and Testament (Ferrars), 1978
Last Woman in His Life (Queen), 1970
Last Year's Blood (Branson), 1947
Late and Cold (G. Mitchell, as Torrie), 1967
Late Bill Smith (Garve), 1971
Late Knight (Payne), 1987
Late Lamented (F. Brown), 1959
Late, Late in the Evening (G. Mitchell), 1976
Late Miss Trimming (Carnac), 1957
Late Mrs. D. (Waugh), 1962
Late Mrs. Five (Wormser), 1960
Late Mrs. Fonsell (Johnston), 1972
Late Payments (Lewin), 1986
Late Phoenix (Aird), 1971
Late Tenant (Shiel, as Holmes), 1906
Late Uncle Max (Fitt), 1957
Late Unlamented (Carmichael), 1961
Latham, Grace series (Ford), from 1937
Latter End (Wentworth), 1947
Laugh of Death (Dent, as Robeson), 1984
Laughing Bacchante (Yates), 1949
Laughing Buddha (Starrett), 1937
Laughing Buddha Murders (Crossen, as Foster), 1944
Laughing Dog (Lochte), 1988
Laughing Fish (Jepson), 1960
Laughing Fox (Gruber), 1940
Laughing Man (R. Forrest, as Woods), 1980
Laughing Policeman (Bruton), 1963
Laughing Policeman (Wahlöö, trans), 1970
Laughter Came Screaming (H. Kane), 1953
Laughter in the Alehouse (H. Kane), 1968
Laughter Trap (Pentecost, as Philips), 1964
Laundryman (Freemantle, as Evans), 1985
Laura (Caspary), 1943
Laura Sarelle (Shearing), 1940
Laurels Are Poison (G. Mitchell), 1942
Laurence, Annie and Max Darling series (C. Hart), from 1987
Laurine (Graeme), 1935
Lavender Gripsack (Keeler), 1941
Law (Ballinger), 1975
Law and Order (G. Newman), 1983
Law and Order (Uhnak), 1973
Law and the Lady (Collins, appendix), 1875
Law of the Four Just Men (s E. Wallace), 1921
Law of the Three Just Men (s E. Wallace), 1931
Law's Delay (Woods), 1977
Lawful Pursuit (Underwood), 1958
Lawless Hand (Le Queux), 1927
Laxham Haunting (Chance, as Lymington), 1976
Lay Her among the Lilies (Chase), 1950
Lay On, Mac Duff! (Armstrong), 1942
Layers of Deceit (Jeffries), 1985
Layton Court Mystery (Berkeley), 1925
Lazarus Lie (Van Greenaway), 1982
Lazarus Man (Lutz), 1979
Lazarus Murder Seven (Sale), 1943
Lazarus No. 7 (Sale), 1942
Lead Astray (C. Brown), 1955
Lead-Lined Coffin (McGirr), 1968
Lead with Your Left (Lacy), 1957
Leaden Bubble (Branson), 1949
Leader and the Damned (C. Forbes), 1983
League of Dark Men (Creasey), 1947
League of Discontent (Beeding), 1930
League of 89 (Hebden), 1977

League of Frightened Men (Stout), 1935
League of Light (Creasey), 1949
Leaning Man (Bush), 1938
Leaphorn, Lieutenant Joe series (Hillerman), from 1970
Leather Duke (Gruber), 1949
Leather Man (Treat), 1944
Leave a Message for Willie (Muller), 1984
Leave Her to Hell (Flora), 1958
Leave It to the Hangman (B. Knox), 1960
Leave the Dead Behind Us (McCutchan), 1962
Leaven of Malice (Curzon), 1979
Leavenworth Case (Green), 1878
Leaves from the Diary of a Law Clerk (Waters, appendix), 1857
Leaves from the Journal of a Custom-House Officer (Waters, appendix), 1868
Ledger (Uhnak), 1970
Ledger Is Kept (Postgate), 1953
Lee, Anna series (Cody), from 1980
Leeds Fiasco (A. Ross), 1975
Left-Handed Death (Hull), 1946
Left-Handed Sleeper (Willis), 1975
Left Leg (P. Taylor, as Tilton), 1940
Legacy (Bagley), 1982
Legacy from Tenerife (B. Knox, as MacLeod), 1984
Legacy in Blood (Allingham), 1949
Legacy Lenders (Masur), 1967
Legacy of Danger (McGerr), 1970
Legacy of Death (Rhode, as Burton), 1960
Legacy of Evil (Clarke), 1976
Legacy of Pride (Blackstock, as Allardyce), 1975
Legacy of Terror (Koontz, as Dwyer), 1971
Legal Fiction (Ferrars), 1964
Legend (Anthony), 1969
Legend in Green Velvet (Elizabeth Peters), 1976
Legend of the Seventh Virgin (Holt), 1965
Legend of the Slain Soldiers (Muller), 1985
Legion of the Living Dead (C. Daly), 1947
Legion of the Lost (Creasey), 1943
Legions of the Death Master (F. Davis, as Steele), 1966
Legislative Body (Hensley), 1972
Leisure Dying (L. O'Donnell), 1976
Leithen, Sir Edward series (Buchan), from 1916
Lemmings (Blackstock), 1969
Lemon in the Basket (Armstrong), 1967
Lemons Never Lie (Westlake, as Stark), 1971
Lena Hates Men (Neville), 1943
Lend a Hand to Murder (Creasey, as Halliday), 1947
Lend Me Your Ears (Stein), 1977
Lenient Beast (F. Brown), 1956
Lennox, Bill series (Ballard), from 1942
Lennox, Chief Inspector series (Wainwright), from 1974
Leonardo's Law (Murphy), 1978
Leopold's Way (s Hoch), 1985
Leper of Saint Giles (Ellis Peters), 1981
Leric, Detective Inspector series (Busby), from 1969
Lerouge Case (Gaboriau, trans), 1925
Lesser Antilles Case (King), 1934
Lessing Murder Case (Horler), 1935
Lesson in Crime (s Cole), 1933
Lesson in Dying (Cleeves), 1990
Lester Affair (Garve), 1974
Let Dead Enough Alone (Lockridge), 1956
Let Me Kill You, Sweetheart (Flora), 1958
Let or Hindrance (Lemarchand), 1973
Let Sleeping Dogs Die (Heald), 1976
Let Sleeping Girls Lie (Coulter, as Mayo), 1965

Let the Dead Past— (Strange), 1953
Let the Man Die (Courtier), 1961
Let the Skeletons Rattle (F. Davis), 1944
Let the Tiger Die (Coles), 1947
Let Them Prey (Harvester), 1942
Let Us Prey (Hammond), 1990
Let Us Prey (McInerny, as Quill), 1982
Let Well Alone (Carnac, as Lorac), 1954
Lethal in Love (C. Brown), 1953(?)
Lethal Lady (King), 1947
Let's Choose Executors (Woods), 1966
Let's Hear It for the Deaf Man (McBain), 1973
Let's Kill Ames (Dent, as Robeson), 1987
Let's Kill Uncle Lionel (Creasey, as York), 1947
Letter (s Maugham), 1930
Letter E (Le Queux), 1926
Letter for Obi (Straker), 1971
Letter from the Dead (Clarke), 1977
Letter of Intent (Curtiss), 1971
Letter to a Dead Girl (Jepson), 1971
Letty Lynton (Lowndes), 1931
Levanter (Ambler), 1972
Levine (Westlake), 1984
Levkas Man (H. Innes), 1971
Levy, Lieutenant series (Holding), from 1947
Lewker, Sir Abercrombie series (G. Carr), from 1951
Liberator series (Creasey, as Deane), from 1939
Liberators (Cleary), 1971
Libertines (D. Clark), 1978
Licence Renewed (J. Gardner), 1981
License to Kill (Daniels), 1972
Licensed for Murder (Rhode), 1958
Liddell, Johnny series (F. Kane), from 1947
Lie Direct (Woods), 1983
Lie Down, I Want to Talk to You (McGivern), 1967
Lie Down, Killer (Prather), 1952
Lie Down with Lions (Follett), 1985
Lies (Neely), 1978
Lieutenant Bones (s E. Wallace), 1918
Lieutenant What's-His-Name (Futrelle), 1915
Life and Death of Charles Peace (E. Wallace), 1932
Life and Death of Peter Wade (L. Black), 1973
Life Between (Vickers), 1938
Life Cycle (Carmichael), 1978
Life for a Death (Creasey, as Ashe), 1973
Life for Sale (Horler), 1928
Life He Stole (Vickers, as Kyle), 1934
Life Sentence (Bailey), 1946
Life's Work (Valin), 1986
Lifetime (McShane), 1977
Lift Up the Lid (A. Gilbert), 1948
Light Beyond (Oppenheim), 1928
Light Cavalry Action (Hebden, as Harris), 1967
Light from a Lantern (Quentin, as Stagge), 1943
Light in the Swamp (Johnston), 1970
Light of Day (Ambler), 1962
Light Thickens (Marsh), 1982
Light Through Glass (Lemarchand), 1984
Lighted Way (Oppenheim), 1912
Lighthouse (Muller, Pronzini), 1987
Lightning (Koontz), 1988
Lightning (McBain), 1984
Lightning Strikes Twice (Potts), 1958
Lightning Strikes Twice (Thayer), 1939
Lights of Skaro (Dodge), 1954
Lights, Camera, Murder (Ballard, as Shepherd), 1960
Ligny's Lake (Courtier), 1971

Like a Hole in the Head (Chase), 1970
Like a Lamb to the Slaughter (s Block), 1984
Like Any Other Fugitive (Hayes), 1971
Like Ice She Was (Ard), 1960
Like Love (McBain), 1962
Lil of the Slums (Donovan), 1909
Lilies in Her Garden Grew (F. Davis), 1951
Lily in Her Coffin (Benson), 1952
Limbo Line (Canning), 1963
Lime Pit (Valin), 1980
Limehouse Nights (s T. Burke), 1916
Limericks of Lachasse (Sherwood), 1978
Limited Vision (Lewis), 1983
Limping Goose (Gruber), 1954
Limping Man (Erskine), 1939
Lincoln, John Abraham series (Dodge), from 1969
Linden Affair (Albrand), 1956
Lindsay, Trooper Ralph series (Benson), from 1953
Line of Duty (Tidyman), 1974
Line of Fire (D. Hamilton), 1955
Line of Succession (Garfield), 1972
Line of Succession (Murphy), 1988
Line Up for Murder (Babson), 1981
Line-Up (F. Kane), 1959
Line-Up (Reilly), 1934
Lingard (C. Wilson), 1970
Link (Carmichael), 1962
Link (P. MacDonald), 1930
Link by Link (s Donovan), 1893
Links in the Chain (Rhode), 1948
Lintott, Inspector John Joseph series (Stubbs), from 1973
Lion and the Lamb (Oppenheim), 1930
Lion at the Door (Thornburg), 1990
Lion in the Cellar (Branch), 1951
Lion in the Valley (Elizabeth Peters), 1986
Lion Triumphant (Holt, as Carr), 1974
Lions of Judah (Willis), 1979
Lions' Ransom (Loraine), 1980
Lip Service (L. Vance), 1928
Lipstick Larceny (C. Brown), 1955
Liquidator (J. Gardner), 1964
Lissendale, Gerald series (Horler), from 1929
List (G. Newman), 1979
List of Adrian Messenger (P. MacDonald), 1959
Listen for the Click (Breen), 1983
Listen for the Whisperer (Whitney), 1972
Listen to the Children (Butler, as Melville), 1986
Listener (s Blackwood), 1907
Listening Eye (Wentworth), 1955
Listening House (Seeley), 1938
Listening in the Dusk (Fremlin), 1990
Listening to the Mocking Bird (Courtier), 1974
Listening Walls (Millar), 1959
Listening Woman (Hillerman), 1978
Listerdale Mystery (s Christie), 1934
Litmore Snatch (Wade), 1957
Little Blue Goddess (Le Queux), 1918
Little Boy Lost (Linington, as Egan), 1983
Little Brothers (D. Davis), 1973
Little Caesar (Burnett), 1929
Little Captain (Bailey), 1941
Little Class on Murder (C. Hart), 1989
Little Crime (Chance), 1957
Little Darling, Dead (Scott), 1986
Little Doctor (Simenon, trans), 1978
Little Dog Laughed (Hansen), 1986
Little Drops of Blood (B. Knox), 1962

Little Drummer Girl (le Carré), 1983
Little Gentleman from Okehampstead (s Oppenheim), 1926
Little Green Man (s E. Wallace), 1929
Little Hercules (Gruber), 1965
Little Less Than Kind (Armstrong), 1963
Little Lie (Potts), 1968
Little Local Murder (Barnard), 1976
Little Madness (Kallen), 1986
Little Man from Arkangel (Simenon, trans), 1957
Little Man Who Wasn't There (The Gordons), 1946
Little Matter of Arson (Meynell), 1972
Little Men, Big World (Burnett), 1951
Little Miss Murder (Avallone), 1971
Little Novels (Collins, appendix), 1887
Little Old Man of the Batignolles (Gaboriau, trans), 1880
Little Red Phone (H. Kane), 1982
Little Saint (Simenon, trans), 1965
Little Sister (Chandler), 1949
Little Tales of Misogyny (s Highsmith), 1977
Little Tramp (Brewer), 1957
Little Victims (Barnard), 1983
Little Victims Play (Hocking), 1938
Little Walls (W. Graham), 1955
Little White Hag (Beeding), 1926
Littlejohn, Thomas series (Bellairs), from 1941
Live and Let Die (I. Fleming), 1954
Live Bait (B. Knox), 1978
Live Bait (Wood), 1985
Live Flesh (Rendell), 1986
Lively Corpse (Millar), 1956
Lively Dead (Dickinson), 1975
Lives and Times of Bernardo Brown (Household), 1973
Living and the Dead (Boileau, trans), 1956
Living Bomb (Avallone), 1963
Living Daylights (s I. Fleming), 1966
Living Demons (s Bloch), 1967
Living End (F. Kane), 1957
Living Fire Menace (Dent, as Robeson), 1971
Liz (F. Kane), 1958
Lizard in the Cup (Dickinson), 1972
Lizzie (McBain, as Hunter), 1984
Lizzie Borden (Lowndes), 1939
Llorca, Juan series (Ames), from 1960
Lloyd, Chief Inspector and Sergeant Judy Hill series
    (McGown), from 1983
Loaded Questions (Loraine), 1985
Local Lads (Scott), 1982
Lock and Key (Stein), 1973
Lock and the Key (Gruber), 1948
Locke, Jeremy series (Woods, as Challis), from 1980
Locke, John series (Wood, as Barnao), from 1987
Locke, Kim series (Crossen), from 1957
Locked Book (Packard), 1924
Locked Room (Auster), 1987
Locked Room (Wahlöö, trans), 1973
Lockestep (Wood, as Barnao), 1988
Lodger (Lowndes), 1913
Lolly-Madonna War (S. Grafton), 1969
Lomax, Jacob series (Allegretto), from 1987
Lona (H. Browne, as Evans), 1952
London Assignment (A. Ross), 1972
London, Bloody London (Avallone), 1972
London Calling (Gielgud), 1934
London Fields (J. Milne), 1983
London Match (Deighton), 1985
London Particular (Brand), 1952
London Spy Murders (Cheyney), 1944

Lone House Mystery (s E. Wallace), 1929
Lone Inn (Hume), 1894
Lone Wolf series (L. Vance), from 1914
Lone Wolf series (Malzberg, as Barry), from 1973
Loneliest Girl in the World (Fearing), 1951
Lonely Church (Hume), 1904
Lonely Graves (Crossen, as Monig), 1960
Lonely House (Lowndes), 1920
Lonely Hunter (Wilcox), 1969
Lonely Inn Mystery (Gribble, as Grex), 1933
Lonely Magdalen (Wade), 1940
Lonely Margins (Allbeury, as Kelly), 1981
Lonely Place (Copper), 1976
Lonely Side of the River (MacKenzie), 1965
Lonely Silver Rain (J. MacDonald), 1985
Lonely Skier (H. Innes), 1947
Lonely Subaltern (Hume), 1910
Lonely Target (Pentecost), 1959
Lonely Voyage (Hebden, as Harris), 1951
Lonely Walk (Crossen, as Chaber), 1956
Lonely Way to Die (Halliday, as Debrett), 1950
Lonelyheart 4122 (Watson), 1967
Lonesome Badger (Gruber), 1954
Lonesome Road (Wentworth), 1939
Long Arm (Cecil), 1957
Long Arm (s Oppenheim), 1909
Long Arm of Mannister (s Oppenheim), 1908
Long Arm of Murder (Gruber), 1956
Long Arm of the Prince (Berckman), 1968
Long Body (McCloy), 1955
Long Cool Day in Hell (Kersh), 1965
Long Corridor (Royce), 1960
Long Dark Night (Hayes), 1974
Long Divorce (Crispin), 1951
Long Echo (Rutherford), 1957
Long Escape (Dodge), 1948
Long Exile (Simenon, trans), 1982
Long Farewell (M. Innes), 1958
Long Goodbye (Chandler), 1953
Long Green (Spicer), 1952
Long Hate (S. Forbes), 1966
Long Journey Home (M. Gilbert), 1985
Long Kill (Hill, as Ruell), 1986
Long Lavender Look (J. MacDonald), 1970
Long Night (Carmichael, as Howard), 1957
Long Night (Graeme), 1958
Long Pursuit (Cleary), 1967
Long Rest (Copper), 1981
Long Revenge (J. Thomson), 1974
Long Saturday Night (C. Williams), 1962
Long Search (Creasey, as Ashe), 1953
Long Shadow (A. Gilbert), 1932
Long Shadow (Cleary), 1949
Long Shadow (Fremlin), 1975
Long Shadows (Cannan), 1955
Long Shadows (Carnac), 1958
Long Short Cut (Garve), 1968
Long Silence (Freeling), 1972
Long Skeleton (Lockridge), 1958
Long Teeth (Albert), 1987
Long Time Dead (Chambers), 1981
Long Time No See (McBain), 1977
Long Time to Hate (W. Roberts), 1982
Long Wait (Spillane), 1951
Long Way Down (Fenwick), 1959
Long Way Down (Wilcox), 1974
Long Way to Shiloh (Davidson), 1966

Luciano's Luck (J. Higgins), 1981
Lucifer at Sunset (Harvester), 1953
Lucifer's Weekend (Murphy, Randisi), 1982
Lucile Cléry (Shearing), 1932
Lucius Davoren (Braddon, appendix), 1873
Luck of the Secret Service (s Le Queux), 1921
Luck Runs Out (MacLeod), 1979
Luck Was No Lady (C. Brown), 1958(?)
Lucky Devil (Maling), 1978
Lucky Jane (Ames), 1959
Lucky Stiff (Rice), 1945
Lullaby (McBain), 1989
Lullaby of Murder (D. Davis), 1984
Luminous Face (Wells), 1921
Lunatic Fringe (DeAndrea), 1980
Lure of Love (Le Queux), 1919
Lure of the Bush (Upfield), 1965
Lust Is No Lady (Avallone), 1964
Lust of Power (H. Kane), 1975
Lustful Ape (Fischer, as Gray), 1950
Luxembourg Run (A. Ross), 1985
Luxembourg Run (Ellin), 1977
Lycanthrope (Phillpotts), 1937
Lydia (Cunningham), 1964
Lying in State (Rathbone), 1985
Lying Jade (Ford), 1953
Lying Ladies (Finnegan), 1946
Lying Lips (Le Queux), 1910
Lying Three (McInerny), 1979
Lying Voices (Ferrars), 1954
Lyle, Inspector series (Wainwright), from 1979
Lynch Town (Murphy), 1974
Lynley, Inspector Thomas and Sergeant Barbara Havers series
    (George), from 1988
Lynne Court Spinney (J. Fletcher), 1916

Mac series (Dewey), from 1947
Macall, Johnny series (Fairlie), from 1953
MacAllister series (R. Perry), from 1984
MacArthur, Ian series (Jepson), from 1922
Machine to Kill (Leroux, trans), 1935
Mackintosh Man (Bagley), 1973
Macklin, Peter series (Estleman), from 1984
Maclain, Captain Duncan series (Kendrick), from 1937
MacLurg Goes West (Curzon, as Petrie), 1968
Macomber Menace (W. Roberts), 1979
Macomber, Elisha series (K. Knight), from 1935
MacWhorter, Angus series (Keeler), from 1941
Mad Baxter (Miller), 1955
Mad Eyes (Dent, as Robeson), 1969
Mad Hatter Mystery (J. Carr), 1933
Mad Hatter's Holiday (Lovesey), 1973
Mad Mesa (Dent, as Robeson), 1972
Madam Crowl's Ghost (s Le Fanu, appendix), 1923
Madam Will Not Dine Tonight (Waugh), 1947
Madam, Will You Talk? (Stewart), 1955
Madam, You Must Die (Blackstock, as Keppel), 1975
Madam, You're Mayhem (C. Brown), 1957
Madame (s Oppenheim), 1927
Madame and Her Twelve Virgins (s Oppenheim), 1927
Madame Midas (Hume), 1888
Madame Spy (Graeme), 1935
Madame X (Avallone), 1966
Madball (F. Brown), 1953
Madden, David series (Doris Disney), from 1956
Maddon's Rock (H. Innes), 1948
Maddox, Sergeant Ivor series (Linnington), from 1964

Made Up for Murder (Roos), 1941
Made Up to Kill (Roos), 1940
Mademoiselle from Armentières (Rhode), 1927
Mademoiselle of Monte Carlo (Le Queux), 1921
Madero, Jose Manuel series (Homes), from 1942
Madhouse in Washington Square (Alexander), 1958
Madison Murder (Gribble, as Grex), 1933
Madman at My Door (Waugh), 1978
Madman Theory (J. Vance, as Queen), 1966
Madman's Bend (Upfield), 1963
Madman's Buff (Steel), 1941
Madman's Will (Chance), 1982
Madness in Maggody (Hess), 1990
Madness of the Heart (Neely), 1976
Madonna of the Music Halls (Le Queux), 1897
Madrid Underground (Serafín), 1982
Madrigal (J. Gardner), 1967
Maelstrom (Hunt), 1948
Mafia Fix (Murphy), 1972
Mafia Kiss (Loraine), 1969
Mafia Vendetta (Sciascia, trans), 1963
Magic Casket (s Freeman), 1927
Magic Eardrums (Keeler), 1939
Magic Forest (Dent, as Robeson), 1988
Magic Grandfather (Doris Disney), 1966
Magic Island (Dent, as Robeson), 1977
Magic Lantern Murders (J. Carr, as Dickson), 1936
Magician (Simenon, trans), 1955
Magician from Siberia (C. Wilson), 1988
Magician's Wife (J. Cain), 1965
Maginot Line Murder (B. Newman), 1939
Magnet of Doom (Simenon, trans), 1948
Magnetic Man (Daniels), 1968
Magnificent Hoax (Oppenheim), 1936
Magnum for Schneider (J. Mitchell), 1969
Maguire, Blue and Spaceman Kowalski series (T. White), from
    1984
Mah-Jongg Spies (Trenhaile), 1986
Mahon, Ambrose series (Courtier), from 1950
Maid for Murder (C. Brown), 1954
Maid in Paris (F. Kane), 1966
Maid to Murder (Vickers), 1950
Maiden Possessed (Chance), 1937
Maiden Stakes (s Yates), 1929
Maiden's Prayer (J. Fleming), 1957
Maigret, Inspector Jules series (Simenon, trans), from 1932
Main (Trevanian), 1976
Main Attraction (Avallone, as Michaels), 1963
Main Line Kill (Busby), 1968
Maine Massacre (van de Wetering), 1979
Maitland, Anthony series (Woods), from 1962
Majii (Dent, as Robeson), 1971
Makassar Strait Contract (Atlee), 1976
Make a Killing (Masur), 1964
Make Death Love Me (Rendell), 1979
Make Do with Spring (Bonett, as Carter), 1941
Make Haste to Live (The Gordons), 1950
Make Me a Murderer (Butler), 1961
Make Me Rich (Corris), 1985
Make Mine Maclain (Kendrick), 1947
Make My Bed Soon (Strange), 1948
Make My Bed Soon (Webb), 1963
Make My Coffin Strong (Cox), 1954
Make Out With Murder (Block, as Harrison), 1974
Make the Corpse Walk (Chase, as Marshall), 1946
Make-Believe Man (Fenwick), 1963
Maker of History (Oppenheim), 1905

Maker of Secrets (Le Queux), 1914
Making Good Again (Davidson), 1968
Making Good Blood (Butler, as Melville), 1990
Malachite Jar (s J. Fletcher), 1930
Malaspiga Exit (Anthony), 1974
Malcolm, Mr. series (Fairlie), from 1932
Malefactor (Oppenheim), 1906
Malice Aforethought (Berkeley, as Iles), 1931
Malice and the Maternal Instinct (Tripp), 1969
Malice Domestic (Woods), 1962
Malice in Camera (Payne), 1983
Malice in Maggody (Hess), 1987
Malice in Wonderland (Blake), 1940
Malice in Wonderland (s King), 1958
Malice Matrimonial (J. Fleming), 1959
Malice with Murder (Blake), 1964
Malicious Mischief (Linington, as Egan), 1971
Malinsay Massacre (Wheatley), 1938
Mallett, Dan series (Parrish), from 1977
Mallett, Inspector series (Hare), from 1937
Mallett, Superintendent series (Fitt), from 1938
Mallin, David series (Ormerod), from 1974
Mallison Mystery (Hanshew), 1903
Mallory (Chase, as Marshall), 1950
Mallory series (Max Collins), from 1983
Mallory, Captain series (MacLean), from 1957
Malloy's Subway (Campbell), 1981
Malloy, Chance series (Dent), from 1946
Malloy, Claire series (Hess), from 1986
Malloy, Vic series (Chase), from 1949
Malone, John J. and the Justuses series (Rice), from 1939
Malone, Scobie series (Cleary), from 1966
Malone, Steven series (Morland), from 1946
Maltese Falcon (Hammett), 1930
Malvery Hold (J. Fletcher), 1917
Man about Town (Le Queux), 1916
Man above Suspicion (Coulter, as Mayo), 1969
Man Alone (S. Smith), 1952
Man and His Kingdom (Oppenheim), 1899
Man and Wife (Collins, appendix), 1870
Man at the Carlton (E. Wallace), 1931
Man at the Wheel (Kenyon), 1982
Man at Windermere (Johnston), 1988
Man Behind Me (Chance), 1963
Man Called Harry Brent (Durbridge), 1970
Man Called Jones (Symons), 1947
Man Called Kyril (Trenhaile), 1983
Man Called Scavener (Van Greenaway), 1978
Man Condemned (Jeffries, as Alding), 1981
Man Dead (Jepson), 1951
Man Died Talking (Morland, as Garnett), 1943
Man-Eater (Willis), 1976
Man Everybody Was Afraid Of (Hansen), 1978
Man from Atlantis (Goulart, as Robeson), 1974
Man from AVON (Avallone), 1967
Man from Downing Street (Le Queux), 1904
Man from Fleet Street (Creasey), 1940
Man from G-2 (F. Mason)
Man from Lisbon (Gifford), 1977
Man from Manchester (Donovan), 1890
Man from Manhattan (Gribble, as Grex), 1934
Man from Michigan (Graeme), 1938
Man from Morocco (E. Wallace), 1926
Man from Moscow (McCutchan), 1963
Man from Nowhere (Ellin), 1970
Man from Nowhere (J. Fleming), 1960
Man from Scotland Yard (Ford, as Frome), 1932

Man from Scotland Yard (Horler), 1934
Man from Sing Sing (Oppenheim), 1932
Man from St. Petersburg (Follett), 1982
Man from the Norlands (Buchan), 1936
Man from the River (Cole), 1928
Man from the Sea (M. Innes), 1955
Man from the "Turkish Slave." (Canning), 1954
Man from Tibet (Clason), 1938
Man from White Hat (Avallone, as Jason), 1982
Man Hunt (Household), 1942
Man-Hunter (s Donovan), 1888
Man I Didn't Kill (Creasey, as Deane), 1950
Man I Killed (Creasey, as Halliday), 1961
Man in Ambush (Procter), 1958
Man in Button Boots (A. Gilbert), 1934
Man in Charge (Jessup), 1957
Man in Gray (Crane), 1958
Man in Grey (s Orczy), 1918
Man in Lower Ten (Rinehart), 1909
Man in Motion (C. Williams), 1959
Man in My Shoes (Chance), 1952
Man in No. 3 (s J. Fletcher), 1931
Man in Question (Godey), 1951
Man in Ratcatcher (s Sapper), 1921
Man in the Bottle (B. Knox), 1963
Man in the Brown Suit (Christie), 1924
Man in the Cage (J. Vance), 1960
Man in the Cape (Bailey), 1933
Man in the Cloak (Horler), 1951
Man in the Dark (Verner, as Stuart), 1935
Man in the Fur Coat (s J. Fletcher), 1932
Man in the Green Hat (Coles), 1955
Man in the Hood (Horler), 1955
Man in the Middle (Crossen, as Chaber), 1967.
Man in the Moonlight (McCloy), 1940
Man in the Net (Quentin), 1956
Man in the Purple Gown (Beeding, as Haddon), 1939
Man in the Queue (Tey, as Daviot), 1929
Man in the Red Mask (Vickers), 1935
Man in the Shadow (Vickers, as Kyle), 1924
Man in the Shadow (Whittington), 1957
Man in the Shadows (C. Daly), 1928
Man in the Shadows (Horler), 1955
Man in the Shadows (s Corris), 1988
Man in the Tricorn Hat (Ames), 1960
Man in White (Horler), 1942
Man Inside (Crossen, as Chaber), 1954
Man-Killer (Powell), 1960
Man Lay Dead (Marsh), 1934
Man, Let's Go On (McCutchan), 1970
Man Missing (Eberhart), 1954
Man Named Thin (s Hammett), 1962
Man Next Door (Eberhart), 1943
Man No One Knew (Meynell), 1951
Man Nobody Saw (Cheyney), 1949
Man of a Hundred Faces (Leroux, trans), 1930
Man of a Hundred Masks (Leroux, trans), 1930
Man of Affairs (Horler), 1949
Man of Affairs (J. MacDonald), 1957
Man of Bronze (Dent, as Robeson), 1935
Man of Dangerous Secrets (Allingham, as March), 1933
Man of Evil (Horler), 1951
Man of Gold (Keating, as Hervey), 1985
Man of Last Resort (Post), 1897
Man of Law (Wainwright), 1980
Man of Little Evils (Dobyns), 1973
Man of Miracles (Leblanc, trans), 1931

Man of the Forty Faces (s Hanshew), 1910
Man of Two Tribes (Upfield), 1956
Man of Wrath (Blackstock, as Allardyce), 1956
Man on a Leash (C. Williams), 1973
Man on a Nylon String (Miller, as Masterson), 1963
Man on a Rope (Coxe), 1956
Man on a Short Leash (Royce, as Jacks), 1974
Man on All Fours (Derleth), 1934
Man on the Balcony (Wahlöö, trans), 1968
Man on the Bench in the Barn (Simenon, trans), 1970
Man on the Cliff (Chance), 1988
Man on the Run (C. Williams), 1958
Man Out of Nowhere (Davies), 1965
Man Out of the Rain (s P. MacDonald), 1955
Man Outside (Verner, as Stuart), 1934
Man Overboard! (Crofts), 1936
Man Returns (Fairlie), 1934
Man Running (Jepson), 1948
Man-Trap (J. MacDonald), 1961
Man Who Bought London (E. Wallace), 1915
Man Who Came Back from the Dead (Leroux, trans), 1916
Man Who Cannot Kill (Straker), 1969
Man Who Changed His Name (E. Wright), 1986
Man Who Changed His Plea (Oppenheim), 1942
Man Who Could Not Shudder (J. Carr), 1940
Man Who Cried All the Way Home (Olsen, as Hitchens), 1966
Man Who Did Not Hang (Horler), 1948
Man Who Didn't Exist (Homes), 1937
Man Who Didn't Fly (Bennett), 1955
Man Who Died on Friday (Underwood), 1967
Man Who Died Too Soon (Coxe), 1962
Man Who Died Twice (Coxe), 1951
Man Who Died Twice (Horler), 1939
Man Who Fell Through the Earth (Wells), 1919
Man Who Fell Up (Dent, as Robeson), 1982
Man Who Finally Died (John Burke), 1963
Man Who Followed Women (Olsen, as Hitchens), 1959
Man Who Grew Tomatoes (G. Mitchell), 1959
Man Who Had Too Much to Lose (Stein, as Stone), 1955
Man Who Heard Too Much (Granger), 1989
Man Who Heard Too Much (R. Forrest, as Woods), 1983
Man Who Held the Queen to Ransom and Sent Parliament Packing (Van Greenaway), 1968
Man Who Killed Fortescue (Strange), 1928
Man Who Killed Himself (Symons), 1967
Man Who Killed the King (Wheatley), 1951
Man Who Killed Too Soon (Underwood), 1968
Man Who Knew (E. Wallace), 1918
Man Who Knew Too Much (s Chesterton), 1922
Man Who Laughed (Fairlie), 1928
Man Who Laughed at Murder (Creasey, as Ashe), 1960
Man Who Left Well Enough (McShane), 1971
Man Who Liked Slow Tomatoes (Constantine), 1982
Man Who Liked to Look at Himself (Constantine), 1973
Man Who Looked Back (J. Fleming), 1951
Man Who Looked Death in the Eye (Stein, as Stone), 1961
Man Who Lost His Wife (Symons), 1970
Man Who Loved His Wife (Caspary), 1966
Man Who Loved Spiders (Horler), 1949
Man Who Married His Cook (s E. Wallace), 1976
Man Who Met the Train (Harold Adams), 1988
Man Who Missed the Party (Harold Adams), 1989
Man Who Missed the War (Wheatley), 1945
Man Who Murdered Goliath (Homes), 1938
Man Who Murdered Himself (Homes), 1936
Man Who Preferred Cocktails (Horler), 1943
Man Who Raised Hell (Sale), 1971

Man Who Rang the Bell (Kennedy), 1929
Man Who Shook the Earth (Dent, as Robeson), 1969
Man Who Shook the Earth (s Horler), 1933
Man Who Shook the World (Creasey), 1950
Man Who Shot Birds (s Fitt), 1954
Man Who Shot Lewis Vance (Kaminsky), 1986
Man Who Slept All Day (Rice, as Venning), 1942
Man Who Sold Death (J. Mitchell, as Munro), 1964
Man Who Stayed Alive (Creasey, as Ashe), 1955
Man Who Stayed at Home (Jesse, as Tinker), 1915
Man Who Thought He Was a Pauper (s Oppenheim), 1943
Man Who Used Perfume (Horler), 1952
Man Who Vanished (Hume), 1892
Man Who Walked Away (Jay), 1958
Man Who Walked Like a Bear (Kaminsky), 1990
Man Who Walked with Death (Horler), 1931
Man Who Wanted Tomorrow (Freemantle), 1975
Man Who Was London (A. Gilbert, as Keith), 1925
Man Who Was Nobody (E. Wallace), 1927
Man Who Was Not Himself (Creasey, as Halliday), 1976
Man Who Was Saturday (Lambert), 1985
Man Who Was Scared (Dent, as Robeson), 1981
Man Who Was Three Jumps Ahead (Stein, as Stone), 1959
Man Who Was Thursday (Chesterton), 1908
Man Who Was Too Clever (A. Gilbert), 1935
Man Who Wasn't There (A. Gilbert), 1937
Man Who Wasn't There (Wainwright), 1989
Man Who Watched the Trains Go By (Simenon, trans), 1942
Man Who Went Up in Smoke (Wahlöö, trans), 1969
Man Whose Dreams Came True (Symons), 1968
Man Will Be Kidnapped Tomorrow (Jeffries, as Ashford), 1972
Man with a Calico Face (S. Smith), 1950
Man with a Load of Mischief (Grimes), 1981
Man with a Secret (Hume), 1890
Man with Dry Hands (Horler), 1944
Man with Fifty Complaints (McMullen), 1978
Man with No Face (Chance), 1959
Man with No Shadow (S. Marlowe), 1974
Man with Talent (Fairlie), 1931
Man With the Black Feather (Leroux, trans), 1912
Man with the Cane (Potts), 1957
Man with the Clubfoot (V. Williams, as Valentine), 1918
Man with the Crimson Box (Keeler), 1940
Man with the Getaway Face (Westlake, as Stark), 1963
Man with the Golden Gun (I. Fleming), 1965
Man with the Little Dog (Simenon, trans), 1965
Man with the Magic Eardrums (Keeler), 1939
Man with the Painted Head (Reilly), 1931
Man with the President's Mind (Allbeury), 1977
Man with the Tattooed Face (Rhode, as Burton), 1937
Man with the Tiny Head (Parrish, as Drummond), 1969
Man with the Wax Face (Wormser), 1934
Man with the Wooden Spectacles (Keeler), 1941
Man with Three Chins (Ames), 1965
Man with Three Jaguars (Ames), 1961
Man with Three Passports (Ames), 1967
Man with Three Witches (Chance), 1958
Man with Two Clocks (Miller, as Masterson), 1974
Man with Two Faces (Horler), 1934
Man with Two Heads (Chance), 1972
Man with Two Names (Beeding), 1940
Man with Two Wives (Quentin), 1955
Man with Two Wives (s Cheyney), 1946
Man Within (Greene), 1929
Man Without a Name (Russell), 1977
Man Without a Name (Vickers, as Kyle), 1935

Man Without Friends (Tripp), 1970
Man Without Nerves (Oppenheim), 1934
Man's Blessing (Sciascia, trans), 1968
Manacle (H. Kane as Sagola), 1978
Manasco Road (Canning), 1957
Manchester Connection (A. Ross), 1984
Manchester Thing (A. Ross), 1970
Manchu Jade (Jepson), 1935
Manchurian Candidate (Condon), 1959
Mandarin Cypher (Hall), 1975
Mandarin's Fan (Hume), 1904
Mandragora (Beeding), 1940
Mandrake, Professor series (Bonett), from 1949
Mandrell, Augustus series (s McAuliffe), from 1965
Manhattan Cowboy (C. Brown), 1973
Manhattan Murder (Train), 1936
Manhattan North (Albrand), 1971
Manhunt (MacKenzie), 1957
Manhunt Is My Mission (S. Marlowe), 1961
Manhunter (Thomas Harris), 1986
Manifest Destiny (Garfield), 1989
Manila Bay (Marshall), 1986
Manipulators (J. Ross, as Rossiter), 1973
Mankiller (Wilcox), 1980
Mann, Tiger series (Spillane), from 1964
Manna Enzyme (Hoyt), 1982
Mannequin (V. Williams), 1930
Mannering, John series (Creasey, as Morton), from 1937
Mannix (Avallone), 1968
Manor House Menace (Chance, as Drummond), 1944
Manor House Mystery (s J. Fletcher), 1933
Manrissa Man (Van Greenaway), 1982
Man's Enemies (Thayer), 1937
Mansion Malevolent (C. Brown, as Farr), 1974
Mansion of Evil (C. Brown, as Farr), 1966
Mansion of Menace (C. Brown, as Farr), 1976
Mansion of Peril (C. Brown, as Farr), 1966
Mantle of Ishmael (J. Fletcher), 1909
Manton, Inspector Simon series (Underwood), from 1954
Mantrap (Chance), 1968
Mantrap Garden (Sherwood), 1986
Manuscript for Murder (Stern), 1970
Many a Monster (Finnegan), 1948
Many a Slip (s Crofts), 1955
Many Deadly Returns (Moyes), 1970
Many Engagements (s J. Fletcher), 1923
Many Worlds of Magnus Ridolph (s J. Vance), 1966
Mappin, Amos Lee series (Footner), from 1930
Maracaibo Mission (F. Mason), 1965
Maras Affair (Ambler, as Reed), 1953
Marble Forest (Boucher, Offord, as Durrant), 1951
Marble Jungle (Crossen, as Richards), 1961
Marble Orchard (Copper), 1969
Marceau Case (Keeler), 1936
March Hare Murders (Ferrars), 1949
March of the Flame Marauders (F. Davis, as Steele), 1966
March to the Gallows (Kelly), 1964
Marchand Woman (Garfield, as Ives), 1979
Marchester Royal (J. Fletcher), 1909
Marco Polo, If You Can (Buckley), 1982
Margie (Cunningham), 1966
Margin (Stuart), 1988
Margin for Terror (F. Kane), 1967
Margin of Terror (McGivern), 1953
Maria (Cooper), 1956
Marie de Brinvilliers (Gaboriau, trans), 1888
Marijuana Mob (Chase), 1952

Marilyn K (L. White), 1960
Marilyn the Wild (Charyn), 1976
Marine Corpse (Tapley), 1986
Marion (Bingham), 1958
Mark of Cain (Wells), 1917
Mark of Murder (Linington, as Shannon), 1964
Mark of the Crescent (Creasey), 1935
Mark of the Hand (Armstrong), 1963
Mark One—The Dummy (Ball), 1974
Mark the Sparrow (Howard), 1975
Marked Down for Murder (Sterling, as Dean), 1956
Marked for Murder (Halliday), 1945
Marked for Murder (Kienzle), 1988
Marked for Murder (Macdonald), 1953
Marked Man (Carmichael), 1959
Marked Man (Le Queux), 1925
Marked "Personal" (Green), 1893
Markenmore Mystery (J. Fletcher), 1921
Market for Murder (Gruber), 1947
Marksman (Rae), 1971
Marley's Empire (McCutchan), 1963
Marlow, Peter series (Hone), from 1971
Marlowe, Philip series (Chandler), from 1939
Marnie (W. Graham), 1961
Maroc 7 (John Burke, as Sands), 1967
Marple, Jane series (Christie), from 1930
Marquis, Sir Henry series (Post), from 1920
Marquise de Brinvilliers (Gaboriau, trans), 1886
Marrendon Mystery (s J. Fletcher), 1930
Marriage at a Venture (Gaboriau, trans), 1879
Marriage-Broker (Lowndes), 1937
Marriage Bureau Murders (Bingham), 1977
Marriage for the Defence (Vickers), 1932
Marriage Has Been Arranged (Blackstock, as Allardyce), 1959
Marriage Is Murder (Pickard), 1987
Marriage Lines (J. Fletcher), 1914
Marriage Mystery (Hume), 1896
Married to Murder (Whittington), 1951
Marryat, Stephen series (Woods, as Leek), from 1980
Marseilles (Caillou), 1964
Marsh, John series (Chance), from 1967
Marshal and the Madwoman (Nabb), 1988
Marshal and the Murderer (Nabb), 1987
Marshal's Own Case (Nabb), 1990
Marshall, John and Suzy series (Fox), from 1943
Marshall, Sergeant series (B. Newman), from 1935
Martello Tower (Haggard), 1986
Martin, Inspector George series (Beeding), from 1935
Martineau Murders (Hull), 1953
Martineau, Detective Chief Inspector Harry series (Procter), from 1954
Martinis and Murder (H. Kane), 1956
Martiny, Paul series (Haggard), from 1972
Marune: Alastor 993 (J. Vance), 1975
Marvellous Boy (Corris), 1982
Mary Deare (H. Innes), 1956
Marylebone Miser (Phillpotts), 1926
Mask (Le Queux), 1905
Mask and the Moonflower (Whitney), 1960
Mask for Murder (H. Kane), 1957
Mask for Murder (Stein), 1952
Mask of Alexander (Albrand), 1955
Mask of Dimitrios (Ambler), 1939
Mask of Evil (Doris Disney), 1967
Mask of Evil (s Armstrong), 1958
Mask of Glass (Roth), 1954
Mask of Memory (Canning), 1974

Mask of Mephisto (Gibson, as Grant), 1975
Mask of Pursuit (Chance), 1967
Mask of the Andes (Cleary), 1971
Mask of the Enchantress (Holt), 1980
Mask of Violence (Hebden), 1970
Masked Invasion (F. Davis, as Steele), 1974
Masked Man (Leroux, trans), 1927
Masks and Faces (Curzon), 1984
Masks Off at Midnight (V. Williams), 1934
Mason, Perry series (Chastain), from 1989
Mason, Perry series (E. Gardner), from 1933
Mason, Randolph series (Post), from 1896
Masquerade (Kienzle), 1990
Masquerade in Venice (Johnston), 1973
Masquerade Mystery (Hume), 1895
Masques (Pronzini), 1981
Massingham Affair (Grierson), 1962
Massingham Butterfly (s J. Fletcher), 1926
Master (C. Brown), 1973
Master Hand (Futrelle), 1914
Master Key (Togawa, trans), 1984
Master-Mind (Hume), 1919
Master Mummer (Oppenheim), 1904
Master Murderer (Wells), 1933
Master Mystery (Reeve), 1919
Master of Blacktower (Elizabeth Peters, as Michaels), 1966
Master of Broken Men (F. Davis, as Steele), 1966
Master of Greylands (Wood, appendix), 1873
Master of Men (Oppenheim), 1901
Master of Merripit (Phillpotts), 1914
Master of Mysteries (s Meade), 1898
Master of the Moor (Rendell), 1982
Master of Venom (Horler), 1949
Master Plan (Stuart), 1990
Masterpiece Affair (Royce), 1973
Masterpieces of Mystery (s Green), 1913
Masters and Green series (D. Clark), from 1969
Master's Challenge (Murphy), 1984
Masters of Bow Street (Creasey), 1972
Masterstroke (Heald), 1982
Masuto, Masao series (Cunningham), from 1967
Matarese Circle (Ludlum), 1979
Match for a Murderer (Dunnett), 1971
Mather, Detective Sergeant Robert series (Graeme), from 1970
Matheson Formula (J. Fletcher), 1929
Matilda Hunter Murder (Keeler), 1931
Matlock Paper (Ludlum), 1973
Matorni's Vineyard (Oppenheim), 1928
Matter of Conviction (McBain, as Hunter), 1959
Matter of Fact (Brean), 1956
Matter of Honor (McGivern), 1984
Matter of Love and Death (S. Forbes, as Wells), 1966
Matter of Luck (s Cheyney), 1947
Matter of Millions (Green), 1890
Matter of Nerves (Hull), 1950
Matter of Record (Stuart, as Gray), 1987
Matter of Taste (Lockridge), 1949
Mausoleum Key (Daniels), 1942
Mauve Front Door (Meynell), 1967
Max's Marriage (Gaboriau, trans), 1880
Max Trueblood and the Jersey Desperado (T. White), 1987
Maxim, Harry series (Lyall), from 1980
Maxwell Mystery (Wells), 1913
May Day Mystery (O. Cohen), 1929
May You Die in Ireland (Kenyon), 1965
Maybe a Trumpet (Harvester), 1945

Maybridge, Detective Chief Inspector Tom series (B.M. Gill), from 1981
Mayday from Malaga (B. Knox, as MacLeod), 1983
Mayday! (Cussler), 1977
Mayhem in B-Flat (Paul), 1940
Mayhem in Greece (Wheatley), 1962
Mayhem in Parva (Livingston), 1990
Mayhem Madchen (Chance), 1980
Mayhew, Lieutenant Stephen series (Olsen), from 1938
Mayo, Asey series (P. Taylor), from 1931
Mayor of Ballydaghan (s Oppenheim), 1944
Mayor on Horseback (Oppenheim), 1937
Mayor's Wife (Green), 1907
Mazaroff Murder (J. Fletcher), 1922
Mazaroff Mystery (J. Fletcher), 1924
Mazatlan (Hunt), 1987
Maze (P. MacDonald), 1932
McAllister and His Double (s Train), 1905
McBride, Rex series (C. Adams), from 1940
McCaig, Inspector series (Rae), from 1968
McCone, Sharon series (Muller), from 1977
McCorkle and Padillo series (Thomas), from 1966
Mc'Cunn, Dickson series (Buchan), from 1922
McDonald, Paul series (J. Smith), from 1985
McGarr, Inspector Peter series (Bartholomew), from 1977
McGee, Travis series (J. MacDonald), from 1964
McGregor, Inspector series (H. Kane), from 1965
McKee, Inspector Christopher series (Reilly), from 1930
McKinnon, Todd series (Offord), from 1942
McMurdo, Chief Inspector Andy series (Morland), from 1948
McTavish, Alonzo series (s Cheyney), from 1943
Me, Hood! (Spillane), 1963
Mead, Selena series (McGerr), from 1964
Meadowsweet (Butler), 1977
Mean Streets (Dewey), 1955
Meandering Corpse (Prather), 1965
Means of Evil (s Rendell), 1979
Meanwhile Back at the Morgue (Avallone), 1960
Measures for a Coffin (Dent, as Robeson), 1987
Meatyard, Chief Constable series (Horler), from 1939
Mecca for Murder (S. Marlowe), 1956
Meddler and Her Murder (Porter), 1972
Medford, Inspector series (Roth), from 1957
Median Line (Haggard), 1979
Mediterranean Caper (Brewer), 1969
Mediterranean Caper (Cussler), 1973
Mediterranean Murder (Hocking), 1951
Mediterranean Nights (s Wheatley), 1942
Medusa (H. Innes), 1988
Medusa Complex (Albert), 1981
Medusa Touch (Van Greenaway), 1973
Meet a Body (Rutherford), 1951
Meet in Darkness (F. Davis, as Ransome), 1964
Meet Mark Girland (Chase), 1977
Meet Me at the Morgue (Macdonald), 1953
Meet Me Tonight (Albrand), 1960
Meet Murder, My Angel (C. Brown), 1956
Meet the Smiths (Daniels), 1971
Meet the Tiger (Charteris), 1928
Megstone Plot (Garve), 1956
Melamare Mystery (Leblanc, trans), 1929
Melody of Death (E. Wallace), 1915
Melody of Terror (S. Forbes), 1967
Melon in the Cornfield (Blackstock), 1969
Melora (Eberhart), 1959
Melting Man (Canning), 1968
Melting Point (K. Davis), 1984

Memo for Murder (Miller, as Wilmer), 1951
Memoirs of a Dance Hall Romeo (J. Higgins), 1989
Memorial Hall Murder (Langton), 1978
Memory Boy (Canning), 1981
Memory Man (Lambert), 1979
Memory of Megan (McShane, as Lovell), 1970
Memory of Murder (Pentecost), 1947
Memory of Passion (Brewer), 1963
Memory Trap (Price), 1989
Memsahib (Mather), 1977
Men Are So Ardent (Kersh), 1935
Men Die at Cyprus Lodge (Rhode), 1943
Men for Counters (Fairlie), 1933
Men from the Boys (Lacy), 1956
Men in Her Death (F. Davis, as Ransome), 1956
Men in Her Death (Morice), 1981
Men of Fear (Dent, as Robeson), 1987
Men of Subtle Craft (Lewis), 1987
Men of the Bureau (Gaboriau, trans), 1880
Men Vanished (Dent, as Robeson), 1988
Men Who Explained Miracles (s J. Carr, as Dickson), 1963
Men with the Guns (G. Newman), 1982
Men Without Bones (s Kersh), 1955
Men, Maids, and Murder (Creasey), 1933
Menace (Horler), 1933
Menace (P. MacDonald), 1933
Menace (The Gordons), 1962
Menace! (Creasey), 1938
Menace (Blochman), 1951
Menace of Li-Sin (Verner, as Vane), 1934
Menace on the Downs (Rhode, as Burton), 1931
Menace Within (Curtiss), 1979
Menacers (D. Hamilton), 1968
Menaces, Menaces (Underwood), 1976
Menacing Groves (Sherwood), 1988
Mendoza Manuscript (Randisi, as Carter), 1982
Mendoza, Lieutenant Luis series (Linnington, as Shannon),
   from 1960
Menfreya (Holt), 1966
Menfreya in the Morning (Holt), 1966
Menorah Men (Davidson), 1966
Mensing, Loren series (Nevins), from 1975
Mental Monster (Dent, as Robeson), 1973
Mental Wizard (Dent, as Robeson), 1970
Menwith Tangle (A. Ross), 1982
Mercenaries (Hebden, as Harris), 1969
Mercenaries (J. White), 1958
Mercenaries (Westlake), 1960
Merchant of Murder (Sterling, as Dean), 1959
Merchants of Disaster (Dent, as Robeson), 1969
Merciless Ladies (W. Graham), 1944
Mere Murder (Wills), 1958
Merely Murder (Heyer), 1935
Meritocrats (Haggard), 1985
Merlin's Furlong (G. Mitchell), 1953
Mermaid (Millar), 1982
Mermaid Murmurs Murder (C. Brown), 1953
Mermaids on the Golf Course (s Highsmith), 1985
Merriman, Mike series (John Burke), from 1960
Merrion, Inspector Arnold and Desmond series (Rhode, as
   Burton), from 1930
Merrivale, Sir Henry series (J. Carr, as Dickson), from 1934
Merriweather File (L. White), 1959
Merry Go Round (Stern), 1969
Merry Hippo (Huxley), 1963
Merry Widower (J. Fleming), 1975
Message from Hong Kong (Eberhart), 1969

Message from Málaga (MacInnes), 1972
Messiter's Dream (Cooper), 1990
Metal Flask (B. Thomson), 1929
Meteor Menace (Dent, as Robeson), 1964
Method in His Murder (Warriner), 1950
Method in Madness (Doris Disney), 1957
Metropolitan Opera Murders (Masur), 1951
Mexican Slay Ride (Ballard, as MacNeil), 1962
Mexican Slayride (Dewey), 1961
Mexico Run (L. White), 1974
Mexico Set (Deighton), 1984
Miami 59 (Keene), 1959
Miami Marauder (Malzberg, as Barry), 1974
Miami Massacre (Pendleton), 1970
Miami Mayhem (Albert, as Rome), 1960
Miami Mob (Creasey, as Frazer), 1965
Miasma (E. Holding), 1929
Micah Faraday, Adventurer (s Meade), 1910
Michael's Evil Deeds (s Oppenheim), 1923
Micklem, Don series (Chase, as Marshall), from 1954
Midas Coffin (M. Smith, as Quinn), 1975
Midas Man (Dent, as Robeson), 1970
Midas Men (Freemantle, as Evans), 1981
Middle Kingdom (Marshall), 1971
Middle of Things (J. Fletcher), 1922
Middle Temple Murder (J. Fletcher), 1919
Midget Marvel (Creasey, as Manton), 1940
Midnight (Koontz), 1989
Midnight (O. Cohen), 1922
Midnight and Percy Jones (Starrett), 1936
Midnight Ferry to Venice (Sturrock, as Healey), 1982
Midnight Gang (Verner, as Vane), 1936
Midnight Gun (Mather), 1981
Midnight Hag (J. Fleming), 1966
Midnight Have I (Max Collins), 1986
Midnight Lady (Leroux, trans), 1930
Midnight Man (Estleman), 1982
Midnight Man (H. Kane), 1965
Midnight Man (Murphy, Randisi), 1981
Midnight Murder (Verner, as Stuart), 1935
Midnight Mystery (Hume), 1894
Midnight Never Comes (J. Higgins, as Fallon), 1966
Midnight Pleasures (s Bloch), 1987
Midnight Plumber (Procter), 1957
Midnight Plus One (Lyall), 1965
Midnight Sailing (Blochman), 1938
Midnight Sister (Albert), 1989
Midsummer Murder (Wills), 1956
Midsummer Slay Ride (Gribble), 1976
Miernik Dossier (McCarry), 1973
Might As Well Be Dead (Stout), 1956
Mighty Blockhead (Gruber), 1942
Mignon (J. Cain), 1962
Mignonette (Shearing), 1948
Mikado Jewel (Hume), 1910
Milan Grill Room (s Oppenheim), 1940
Milano, John series (Ellin), from 1979
Mildred Pierce (J. Cain), 1941
Mile High (Condon), 1969
Military Intelligence (F. Mason), 1941
Milk and Honey (F. Kellerman), 1990
Milk-Churn Murders (Rhode, as Burton), 1935
Milk of Human Kindness (Ferrars), 1950
Mill House Murder (J. Fletcher), 1937
Mill Mystery (Green), 1886
Mill of Many Windows (J. Fletcher), 1925
Millhone, Kinsey series (S. Grafton), from 1982

Millie (Cunningham), 1973
Milliner's Hat Mystery (B. Thomson), 1937
Million Dollar Babe (C. Brown), 1961
Million-Dollar Diamond (J. Fletcher), 1923
Million Dollar Murder (Aarons, as Ronns), 1950
Million Dollar Snapshot (Carmichael, as Howard), 1971
Million Dollar Story (E. Wallace), 1926
Million Dollar Tramp (Gault), 1960
Million Pound Deposit (Oppenheim), 1930
Million-Dollar Wound (Max Collins), 1986
Millionaire Baby (Green), 1905
Millionaire Mystery (Hume), 1901
Millionaire of Yesterday (Oppenheim), 1900
Mills Bomb (Egleton), 1978
Millstone Men (Sturrock, as Healey), 1966
Milodragovitch series (Crumley), from 1975
Mimic a Murderer (Courtier), 1964
Mind-Murders (van de Wetering), 1981
Mind of Max Duvine (Hall, as Trevor), 1960
Mind of Mr. J. G. Reeder (s E. Wallace), 1925
Mind over Murder (Kienzle), 1981
Mind Poisoners (L. White, as Carter), 1966
Mind Readers (Allingham), 1965
Mind to Murder (Clarke), 1971
Mind to Murder (James), 1963
Mind's Eye (Gosling, as Skinner), 1980
Mindanao Pearl (Caillou), 1959
Mindspell (K. Smith), 1983
Mine to Avenge (Ard, as Wills), 1955
Ming Yellow (Marquand), 1935
Mingled with Venom (G. Mitchell), 1978
Mini-Murders (C. Brown), 1968
Miniature Murder Mystery (Chambers), 1982
Miniatures Frame (Royce), 1972
Minister of Evil (Le Queux), 1918
Ministering Angel (A. Cohen), 1987
Ministry of Death (Bingham), 1977
Ministry of Fear (Greene), 1943
Mink-Lined Coffin (Latimer), 1960
Minnesota Strip (Michael Collins), 1987
Minor Murders (Hensley), 1979
Minor Operation (Connington), 1937
Minotaur Country (McCloy), 1975
Minotaur Factor (Rae, as Stern), 1977
Minter, Superintendent series (E. Wallace), from 1927
Minute for Murder (Blake), 1947
Minute Man Murder (Langton), 1976
Minutes to Midnight (Spain), 1978
Minx Is Murder (C. Brown), 1957
Miracle at St. Bruno's (Holt, as Carr), 1972
Miracle Man (Packard), 1914
Mirage (Cunningham, as Fast), 1965
Mirror Crack'd (Christie), 1963
Mirror Crack'd from Side to Side (Christie), 1962
Mirror Image (L. Fletcher), 1988
Mirror Image (Michael Collins, as Sadler), 1972
Mirror, Mirror on the Wall (Ellin), 1972
Mirror of Hell (Holton), 1972
Mirror Train (Chance), 1970
Miscarriage of Murder (Straker), 1967
Mischief (Armstrong), 1950
Mischief in Maggody (Hess), 1988
Mischief in the Lane (Derleth), 1944
Mischief-Maker (Oppenheim), 1912
Mischief-Makers (Haggard), 1982
Miser (Linington, as Egan), 1981
Miser of Maida Vale (s Orczy), 1925

Miser's Money (Phillpotts), 1920
Miser's Will (Hume), 1903
Misfire (Freemantle, as Evans), 1980
Misfortunes of Mr. Teal (Charteris), 1934
Miss Bones (J. Fleming), 1959
Miss Brown of X.Y.O. (Oppenheim), 1927
Miss Callaghan Comes to Grief (Chase), 1941
Miss Called Murder (C. Brown), 1955
Miss Charley (Blackstock), 1979
Miss Fenny (Blackstock), 1957
Miss Hurd (Green), 1894
Miss Mephistopheles (Hume), 1890
Miss Milverton (Hocking), 1941
Miss Mystery (Horler), 1928
Miss or Mrs.? (s Collins, appendix), 1873
Miss Pinnegar Disappears (A. Gilbert), 1952
Miss Pym Disposes (Tey), 1946
Miss Shumway Waves a Wand (Chase), 1944
Miss X (Vickers, as Kyle), 1939
Missing (Creasey, as Halliday), 1960
Missing! (Avallone), 1969
Missing! (Vickers, as Kyle), 1938
Missing . . . and Presumed Dead (Hayes), 1975
Missing Archduke (Leroux, trans), 1931
Missing Aunt (Cole), 1937
Missing Brontë (Barnard), 1983
Missing Chancellor (J. Fletcher), 1927
Missing Delora (Oppenheim), 1910
Missing from Her Home (A. Gilbert), 1969
Missing from Home (Creasey, as Halliday), 1959
Missing from the Record (Egleton), 1988
Missing Link (Farrer), 1952
Missing Link (Murphy), 1980
Missing Link (Wells), 1938
Missing Madonna (O'Marie), 1989
Missing Man (Stern), 1990
Missing Man (Waugh), 1964
Missing Men (Leroux, trans), 1923
Missing Million (E. Wallace), 1923
Missing Millions (E. Wallace), 1925
Missing Moon (Harold Adams), 1983
Missing or Dead? (Creasey, as Ashe), 1951
Missing Partners (Wade), 1928
Missing Rope (Carnac), 1937
Missing Tycoon (Waugh, as Taylor), 1967
Missing Widow (A. Gilbert), 1948
Missing Witness (Daniels), 1964
Missing Woman (Lewin), 1981
Mission Berlin (Allbeury), 1986
Mission for Betty Smith (Cooper), 1967
Mission for Vengeance (Rabe), 1958
Mission in Guemo (Hough), 1953
Mission of Fear (Coxe), 1962
Mission to Malaspiga (Anthony), 1974
Mission to Siena (Chase, as Marshall), 1955
Mission to Venice (Chase, as Marshall), 1954
Missionary Stew (Thomas), 1983
Missioner (Oppenheim), 1907
Mrs. Craggs (s Keating), 1985
Mrs. Homicide (Keene), 1953
Mrs. Knox's Profession (Mann), 1972
Mrs. McGinty's Dead (Christie), 1952
Mrs. Meeker's Money (Doris Disney), 1961
Mrs. Murphy's Underpants (F. Brown), 1963
Mrs. Presumed Dead (Brett), 1988
Mrs. Pym (s Morland), 1976
Mrs. Pym of Scotland Yard (s Morland), 1946

Moon in the Gutter (Goodis), 1953
Moon Is Red (Rohmer), 1954
Moon Murders (Morland), 1935
Moon of Madness (Rohmer), 1927
Moon-Spinners (Stewart), 1962
Moon Was Made for Murder (Morland), 1953
Moon, Manville "Manny" series (Deming), from 1952
Moondrop to Murder (Hilton), 1986
Moonflower (Nichols), 1955
Moonflower (Whitney), 1958
Moonflower Murder (Nichols), 1955
Moonlight Flitting (Procter), 1963
Moonlighter (H. Kane), 1971
Moonmilk and Murder (Stein), 1955
Moonraker (I. Fleming), 1955
Moonshine Momma (C. Brown), 1960
Moonshine War (Leonard), 1969
Moonspender (Gash), 1986
Moonstone (Collins, appendix), 1868
Moonstone Jungle (Harvester), 1961
Moor House Murders (Verner), 1964
Moore, Troussaint series (Lacy), from 1957
Moran Chambers Smiled (Oppenheim), 1932
Moran's Woman (Keene), 1959
Morbid Symptoms (Slovo), 1984
Morbid Taste for Bones (Ellis Peters), 1977
Mordida Man (Thomas), 1981
More Beautiful Than Murder (O. Cohen), 1948
More Dead Than Alive (Ormerod), 1980
More Deadly Than the Male (Chase, as Grant), 1946
More Deadly Than the Male (Meynell), 1964
More Deaths Than One (Fischer), 1947
More Deaths Than One (Stout), 1949
More Educated Evans (s E. Wallace), 1926
More Hardcore (Thompson), 1987
More Knaves Than One (s Packard), 1938
More Limehouse Nights (s T. Burke), 1921
More Lives Than One (Wells), 1923
More Nightmares (s Bloch), 1962
More Secrets of Potsdam (s Le Queux), 1917
More Than Once upon a Time (s Kersh), 1964
More Work for the Undertaker (Allingham), 1948
Morgan, Rain series (Grant-Adamson), from 1985
Morgue Amour (C. Brown), 1954
Morgue for Venus (Craig), 1956
Moriarty, Professor series (J. Gardner), from 1974
Morning after Death (Blake), 1966
Morning for Flamingoes (James Lee Burke), 1990
Morning Walk (Davies), 1983
Morrison-Burke, Constance Ethel series (Porter), from 1970
Morse, Inspector series (Dexter), from 1975
Mortal Fire (Harvester, as Gibbs), 1963
Mortal Remains (Yorke), 1974
Mortal Ruin (Malcolm), 1988
Mortal Stakes (Parker), 1975
Mortician's Birthday Party (Whalley), 1983
Mortmain (s Train), 1907
Mortover Grange Affair (J. Fletcher), 1927
Mortover Grange Mystery (J. Fletcher), 1926
Moscow Coach (McCutchan), 1964
Moscow Metal (Boyer), 1987
Moscow Murder (B. Newman), 1948
Moscow Papers (J. White), 1979
Moscow Quadrille (Allbeury), 1976
Moscow Road (Harvester), 1970
Mosley Receipt (Royce), 1985
Mosley, Inspector series (Hilton, as Greenwood), from 1983

Moss Mystery (Wells), 1924
Moss Rose (Shearing), 1934
Most Beautiful Girl in the World (Willis), 1982
Most Contagious Game (Aird), 1967
Most Cunning Workmen (Lewis), 1984
Most Dangerous Game (Lyall), 1963
Most Deadly Game (Wormser, as Friend), 1970
Most Deadly Hate (Carmichael), 1971
Most Deadly Hate (Woods), 1986
Most Grievous Murder (Woods), 1982
Most Likely to Love (Flora), 1960
Most Men Don't Kill (Alexander), 1951
Most Secret (J. Carr, as Fairbairn), 1964
Most Wanted (Stein, as Bagby), 1983
Mostly Murder (s F. Brown), 1953
Mostyn, Colonel series (Hebden), from 1970
Moth (J. Cain), 1948
Moth-Watch Murder (Rhode, as Burton), 1957
Moth-Woman (Hume), 1923
Mother Goose Murders (Gibson, as Grant), 1979
Mother Hunt (Stout), 1963
Mother Mandarin (Hume), 1912
Mother Russia (Littell), 1978
Mother's Boys (Barnard), 1981
Motion Menace (Dent, as Robeson), 1971
Motive (Carmichael), 1974
Motive (Lowndes), 1938
Motive (Piper), 1950
Motive for a Kill (Chance), 1977
Motive in Shadow (Linington, as Egan), 1980
Motive on Record (Linington, as Shannon), 1982
Moto, Mr. series (Marquand), from 1935
Motor Bus Murder (Verner, as Stuart), 1934
Motor City Blue (Estleman), 1980
Motor Rally Mystery (Rhode), 1933
Mountain Cat (Stout), 1939
Mountain Cat Murders (Stout), 1943
Mountain Madness (Ford), 1935
Mountain Meadow (Buchan), 1941
Mountain Monster (Dent, as Robeson), 1976
Mountain of the Blind (Creasey), 1960
Mountain Terror (Creasey, as Cooke), 1938
Mountainhead (Cory), 1966
Mountains Have a Secret (Upfield), 1948
Mourn the Hangman (Whittington), 1952
Mourned on Sunday (Reilly), 1941
Mourner (Westlake, as Stark), 1963
Mourning After (Dewey), 1950
Mourning After (F. Kane), 1961
Mourning After (Masur), 1983
Mourning Raga (Ellis Peters), 1969
Mourning Trees (Johnston), 1972
Mouse (Simenon, trans), 1966
Mouse in Eternity (Tyre), 1952
Mouse Trap (Hocking, as Messer), 1931
Mouse Who Wouldn't Play Ball (A. Gilbert), 1943
Mousetrap (s Christie), 1949
Mouthful of Sand (Meek), 1988
Move (Simenon, trans), 1968
Movement Toward Eden (Howard), 1969
Moving Eye (Creasey, as Cooke), 1937
Moving Finger (Christie), 1942
Moving Finger (Oppenheim), 1910
Moving Graveyard (Avallone), 1973
Moving Picture Writes (Chambers), 1984
Moving Target (Macdonald), 1949
Moving Targets (Reynolds), 1986

Moving Toyshop (Crispin), 1946
Mox (Gibson, as Grant), 1975
Much Ado about Something (Graeme), 1967
Much Ado in Maggody (Hess), 1989
Much in Evidence (Cecil), 1957
Mud in His Eye (Hammond), 1967
Mudflats of the Dead (G. Mitchell), 1979
Muffin, Charlie series (Freemantle), from 1977
Mugger (McBain), 1956
Mugger Blood (Murphy), 1977
Mugger's Day (Stein, as Bagby), 1979
Mulcahaney, Norah series (L. O'Donnell), from 1972
Mulligan, Tim and Elsie Mae Hunt series (Stein), from 1940
Multi-Million Dollar Murders (F. Mason), 1960
Mummy Case (Elizabeth Peters), 1985
Mum's the Word for Murder (Halliday, as Baker), 1938
Mundy, Al series (Brewer), from 1969
Munitions Master (Dent, as Robeson), 1971
Munro, Brigadier Dougal and Captain Jack Carter series (J. Higgins), from 1987
Murder (Harold Adams), 1981
Murder à la Mode (Moyes), 1963
Murder Abroad (Punshon), 1939
Murder Across and Down (Resnicow), 1985
Murder Adrift (Bellairs), 1972
Murder after a Fashion (Sterling, as Dean), 1960
Murder after Hours (Christie), 1954
Murder Against the Grain (Lathen), 1967
Murder Ahead (Creasey, as Deane), 1953
Murder All Over (C. Adams), 1950
Murder among Children (Westlake, as Coe), 1968
Murder among Friends (Ferrars), 1946
Murder among Members (Carnac), 1955
Murder among Thieves (Jeffries, as Alding), 1969
Murder among Us (C. Brown), 1962
Murder and Blueberry Pie (Lockridge), 1959
Murder and Gardenias (Neville), 1946
Murder and Poor Jenny (Neville), 1954
Murder and the Married Virgin (Halliday), 1944
Murder and the Wanton Bride (Halliday), 1958
Murder Anonymous (A. Gilbert), 1968
Murder Arranged (B. Thomson), 1937
Murder Arranged (Pentecost, as Philips), 1978
Murder as a Fine Art (Carnac), 1953
Murder as Usual (Pentecost), 1977
Murder Assured (Creasey, as Halliday), 1958
Murder at Arroways (Reilly), 1950
Murder at Bratton Grange (Rhode), 1929
Murder at Crome House (Cole), 1927
Murder at Derivale (Rhode), 1958
Murder at Elstree (T. Burke), 1936
Murder at End House (Creasey, as Halliday), 1955
Murder at Fenwold (Bush), 1930
Murder at Government House (Huxley), 1937
Murder at Grand Bay (W. Roberts), 1955
Murder at Hazelmoor (Christie), 1931
Murder at High Noon (McGuire), 1935
Murder at King's Kitchen (Creasey, as Halliday), 1943
Murder at Leisure (Monteilhet, trans), 1971
Murder at Lilac Cottage (Rhode), 1940
Murder at Madingley Grange (C. Graham), 1990
Murder at Mid-Day (Hocking), 1956
Murder at Midnight (Blackburn), 1964
Murder at Midnight (Sale), 1950
Murder at Monte Carlo (Oppenheim), 1933
Murder at Moose Jaw (Heald), 1981
Murder at Mornington (Carnac), 1937

Murder at Mt. Fuji (Natsuki, trans), 1984
Murder at Our House (C. Daly), 1950
Murder at Radio City (Morland), 1939
Murder at the ABA (Asimov), 1976
Murder at the Casino (Wells), 1941
Murder at the Cat Show (Babson), 1989
Murder at the Flea Club (Head), 1955
Murder at the Frankfurt Fair (Monteilhet, trans), 1976
Murder at the Gallop (Christie), 1963
Murder at the Gardner (Langton), 1988
Murder at the Mimosa Inn (Hess), 1986
Murder at the Moorings (Rhode, as Burton), 1932
Murder at the Motor Show (Rhode), 1936
Murder at the Munition Works (Cole), 1940
Murder at the New York World's Fair (P. Taylor, as Dana), 1938
Murder at the Nightwood Bar (K. Forrest), 1987
Murder at the Old Vicarage (McGown), 1989
Murder at the Piano (Stein, as Bagby), 1935
Murder at the Polls (Propper), 1937
Murder at the Savoy (Wahlöö, trans), 1971
Murder at the Superbowl (Resnicow), 1986
Murder at the Vicarage (Christie), 1930
Murder at World's End (Strange), 1943
Murder at Wrides Park (J. Fletcher), 1931
Murder Before Breakfast (Offord), 1938
Murder Before Marriage (Neville), 1951
Murder Begets Murder (Jeffries), 1979
Murder Begins at Home (Ames), 1949
Murder Beyond the Pale (Neville), 1961
Murder, Bless It! (Spain), 1948
Murder Book of Mr. J. G. Reeder (s E. Wallace), 1929
Murder by an Aristocrat (Eberhart), 1932
Murder by Experts (A. Gilbert), 1936
Murder by Latitude (King), 1930
Murder by Magic (Gibson, as Grant), 1975
Murder by Matchlight (Carnac, as Lorac), 1945
Murder by Miss-Demeanor (C. Brown), 1956
Murder by Moonlight (Gibson, as Grant), 1966
Murder by Precedent (Curzon, as Petrie), 1964
Murder by Prescription (Quentin, as Stagge), 1938
Murder by Proxy (Carmichael), 1967
Murder by Proxy (Morice), 1978
Murder by Proxy (Nielsen), 1952
Murder by Reflection (Heard), 1942
Murder by Request (Nichols), 1960
Murder by the Book (Lockridge), 1963
Murder by the Book (Stout), 1951
Murder by the Clock (King), 1929
Murder by the Day (Johns), 1953
Murder by the Law (McGuire), 1932
Murder by the Mile (Russell), 1975
Murder by the Tale (s Linington, as Shannon), 1987
Murder by the Way (Creasey, as Halliday), 1941
Murder Calling "50" (Stein, as Bagby), 1942
Murder Came Late (Creasey, as York), 1946
Murder Can Be Fun (F. Brown), 1948
Murder Can't Stop (Ballard), 1946
Murder Can't Wait (Lockridge), 1964
Murder Charge (Miller), 1950
Murder Cheats the Bride (A. Gilbert), 1948
Murder Children (Ball), 1979
Murder Clear, Track Fast (Pentecost, as Philips), 1961
Murder Comes First (Lockridge), 1951
Murder Comes Home (A. Gilbert), 1950
Murder Comes Home (Creasey, as Halliday), 1940

Murder Comes to Eden (Ford), 1955
Murder Cries Out (Hocking), 1968
Murder De Luxe (King), 1927
Murder Doesn't Always Out (F. Davis), 1939
Murder Down South (Ford), 1943
Murder Down Under (Upfield), 1943
Murder Every Monday (Branch), 1954
Murder Fantastical (Moyes), 1967
Murder for a Million (Vickers), 1924
Murder for Art's Sake (Lockridge), 1967
Murder for Christmas (Christie), 1939
Murder for Empire (K. Knight)
Murder for Missemily (Straker), 1961
Murder for Sale (s Horler), 1945
Murder for the Asking (Coxe), 1939
Murder for the Bride (J. MacDonald), 1951
Murder for the Millions (H. Kane), 1964
Murder for Two (Coxe), 1943
Murder for What? (Steel), 1936
Murder Forestalled (Chambers, as Chester), 1960
Murder from the East (C. Daly), 1935
Murder Game (Strange), 1931
Murder Games (Davidson), 1978
Murder Gives a Lovely Light (Strange), 1941
Murder Goes Mumming (MacLeod, as Craig), 1981
Murder Goes Round and Round (Pentecost), 1988
Murder Goes to College (Steel), 1936
Murder Gone Mad (Bellairs), 1968
Murder Gone Mad (P. MacDonald), 1931
Murder Gone Minoan (Clason), 1939
Murder Gone to Earth (Quentin, as Stagge), 1936
Murder Greets Jean Holton (K. Knight)
Murder Half Baked (Stein, as Bagby), 1937
Murder Has a Pretty Face (Butler, as Melville), 1981
Murder Has Its Points (Lockridge), 1961
Murder Has Many Faces (O'Farrell, as Grew), 1955
Murder Has No Tongue (A. Gilbert), 1937
Murder in a Blue Moon (Neville), 1948
Murder in a Hurry (Lockridge), 1950
Murder in a Mummy Case (Beck), 1986
Murder in Absence (Rhode, as Burton), 1954
Murder in Advent (D. Williams), 1985
Murder in Any Language (Roos), 1948
Murder in Black and White (Alexander), 1951
Murder in Black and White (Kennedy, as Elder), 1931
Murder in Blue Street (Crane), 1951
Murder in Bostall (McGuire), 1931
Murder in Bright Red (Crane), 1953
Murder in Canton (van Gulik, trans), 1966
Murder in Chelsea (Carnac, as Lorac), 1934
Murder in Crown Passage (Rhode, as Burton), 1937
Murder in False-Face (Lockridge), 1968
Murder in Focus (Dunnett), 1973
Murder in Four Degrees (J. Fletcher), 1931
Murder in Four Parts (Cole), 1934
Murder in G-Sharp (Steel), 1937
Murder in Haste (Fenwick), 1944
Murder in Haste (McGuire), 1934
Murder in Havana (Coxe), 1943
Murder in High Place (Lathen, as Dominic), 1969
Murder in High Places (Pentecost), 1983
Murder in Highlands (Creasey, as Manton), 1939
Murder in Hospital (Bell), 1937
Murder in Luxury (Pentecost), 1981
Murder in Manuscript (Verner), 1963
Murder in Marble (Pentecost, as Philips), 1940
Murder in Married Life (Morice), 1971

Murder in Maryland (Ford), 1932
Murder in Medora Mansions (s J. Fletcher), 1933
Murder in Melbourne (Gray), 1958
Murder in Mesopotamia (Christie), 1936
Murder in Mimicry (Morice), 1977
Murder in Mind (Fuller), 1986
Murder in Mind (Gray), 1963
Murder in Moonlight (F. Brown), 1950
Murder in Moscow (Garve), 1951
Murder in Oils (Chance), 1935
Murder in Outline (Morice), 1979
Murder in Paradise (Cleeves), 1988
Murder in Paradise (Davey), 1982
Murder in Peking (Starrett), 1946
Murder in Retrospect (Christie), 1942
Murder in Rockwater (Neville), 1944
Murder in Room 13 (Albert, as Albert Conroy), 1958
Murder in St. John's Wood (Carnac, as Lorac), 1934
Murder in Season (O. Cohen), 1946
Murder in Shinbone Alley (Reilly), 1940
Murder in Space (Engel, as Woolf), 1985
Murder in State (Hunt), 1990
Murder in Style (Stout), 1960
Murder in the Atlantic (J. Carr, as Dickson), 1959
Murder in the Basement (Berkeley), 1932
Murder in the Bedroom (Leroux, trans), 1945
Murder in the Bookshop (Wells), 1936
Murder in the Calais Coach (Christie), 1934
Murder in the Coalhole (Rhode, as Burton), 1940
Murder in the Collective (B. Wilson), 1984
Murder in the Dispensary (Ellis Peters, as Carr), 1938
Murder in the Family (Creasey, as York), 1944
Murder in the Family Way (C. Brown), 1971
Murder in the Garden (Butler, as Melville), 1990
Murder in the Harem Club (C. Brown), 1962
Murder in the Key Club (C. Brown), 1962
Murder in the Madhouse (Latimer), 1935
Murder in the Maze (Connington), 1927
Murder in the Mews (Reilly), 1931
Murder in the Mews (s Christie), 1937
Murder in the Mill-Race (Carnac, as Lorac), 1952
Murder in the Mills (Keeler), 1946
Murder in the Mirror (Thayer), 1936
Murder in the Navy (McBain, as Marsten), 1955
Murder in the O.P.M (Ford), 1942
Murder in the Pallant (J. Fletcher), 1927
Murder in the Queen's Armes (Elkins), 1985
Murder in the Raw (Fischer), 1957
Murder in the Raw (Gault), 1956
Murder in the Round (Dunnett), 1970
Murder in the Rue Royale (s M. Harrison), 1972
Murder in the Sanctuary (Gribble, as Grex), 1934
Murder in the Senate (F. Mason, as Coffin), 1935
Murder in the Squire's Pew (J. Fletcher), 1932
Murder in the Stars (Creasey, as Halliday), 1953
Murder in the Stars (Quentin, as Stagge), 1940
Murder in the Stork Club (Caspary), 1946
Murder in the Submarine Zone (J. Carr, as Dickson), 1950
Murder in the Sun (Footner), 1938
Murder in the Title (Brett), 1983
Murder in the Walls (Stern), 1971
Murder in the Willett Family (King), 1931
Murder in the Wind (J. MacDonald), 1956
Murder in the Wings (Gorman), 1986
Murder in Three Acts (Christie), 1934
Murder in Time (Ferrars), 1953
Murder in Two Flats (Vickers), 1952

Murder in Vegas (Cox), 1960
Murder in Vienna (Carnac, as Lorac), 1956
Murder in Waiting (Eberhart), 1973
Murder in Wardour Street (Morland), 1940
Murder in Wonderland (Stein, as Bagby), 1965
Murder in Writing (Clarke), 1988
Murder Included (Cannan), 1950
Murder Intended (Beeding), 1932
Murder Is a Habit (Halliday), 1951
Murder Is a Kill-Joy (E. Holding), 1946
Murder Is a Package Deal (C. Brown), 1964
Murder Is a Witch (Bingham), 1957
Murder Is Absurd (McGerr), 1967
Murder Is an Art (M. Innes), 1959
Murder Is Announced (Christie), 1950
Murder Is Cheap (A. Gilbert), 1949
Murder Is Easy (Christie), 1939
Murder Is for Keeps (Chambers), 1961
Murder Is Incidental (Rutherford), 1961
Murder Is Its Own Reward (Chambers), 1982
Murder Is My Business (Halliday), 1945
Murder Is My Dish (S. Marlowe), 1957
Murder Is My Mistress (C. Brown), 1954
Murder Is My Mistress (Whittington), 1951
Murder Is Out (Thayer), 1942
Murder Is Served (Lockridge), 1948
Murder Is So Easy (W. Roberts), 1961
Murder Is So Nostalgic (C. Brown), 1972
Murder Is So Simple (Horler), 1943
Murder Is Suggested (Lockridge), 1959
Murder Is Suspected (Jeffries, as Alding), 1977
Murder Is the Message (C. Brown), 1969
Murder Is the Pay-Off (Ford), 1951
Murder Isn't Easy (Hull), 1936
Murder Las Vegas Style (Ballard), 1967
Murder League (Fish), 1968
Murder Line (Jeffries, as Alding), 1974
Murder Listens In (E. Daly), 1949
Murder, London—Australia (Creasey), 1965
Murder, London—Miami (Creasey), 1969
Murder, London—New York (Creasey), 1958
Murder, London—South Africa (Creasey), 1966
Murder Made Absolute (Underwood), 1955
Murder, Maestro, Please (Ames), 1952
Murder Maker (Chance), 1976
Murder Makers (J. Ross, as Rossiter), 1970
Murder Makes Haste (Creasey)
Murder Makes Me Nervous (Scherf), 1948
Murder Makes Mistakes (Bellairs), 1958
Murder Makes Murder (Creasey, as Halliday), 1946
Murder Makes the Wheels Go Round (Lathen), 1966
Murder Manor (Creasey, as Manton), 1937
Murder Mars the Tour (Fitt), 1936
Murder Mask (Horler), 1930
Murder Masks Miami (King), 1939
Murder Masquerade (Bellairs), 1981
Murder, M.D. (Rhode, as Burton), 1943
Murder Me for Nickels (Rabe), 1960
Murder Mission! (Albert, as Al Conroy), 1973
Murder Mistaken (Gribble), 1953
Murder Money (Aarons, as Ronns), 1938
Murder Most Foul (Creasey, as Ashe), 1942
Murder Most Fouled Up (S. Forbes, as Wells), 1968
Murder Most Strange (Linington, as Shannon), 1981
Murder Motive (Creasey, as Halliday), 1947
Murder Moves In (Ferrars), 1956
Murder Movie (McGown), 1990

Murder! Murder! (s Symons), 1961
Murder, Murder, Little Star (Babson), 1977
Murder! Murder! Murder! (Lockridge), 1956
Murder Muscles In (Deming, as Franklin), 1956
Murder Must Advertise (Sayers), 1933
Murder Must Wait (Creasey), 1939
Murder Must Wait (Upfield), 1953
Murder '97 (Gruber), 1948
Murder Noon and Night (Roos), 1959
Murder Now and Then (Brean), 1965
Murder of a Bad Man (Footner), 1935
Murder of a Banker (J. Fletcher), 1933
Murder of a Chemist (Rhode, as Burton), 1936
Murder of a Dead Man (Steel), 1935
Murder of a Fifth Columnist (Ford), 1941
Murder of a Martinet (Carnac, as Lorac), 1951
Murder of a Mouse (Fitt), 1939
Murder of a Nymph (Neville), 1949
Murder of a Quack (Bellairs), 1943
Murder of a Snob (Vickers), 1949
Murder of a Suicide (Ferrars), 1941
Murder of Alonzo (s Cheyney), 1943
Murder of an Initiate (Propper), 1933
Murder of an Old Man (Ford, as Frome), 1929
Murder of an Owl (G. Carr), 1956
Murder of Busy Lizzie (G. Mitchell), 1973
Murder of London Lew (Keeler), 1952
Murder of Love (Gray), 1967
Murder of Marion Mason (Dewey), 1951
Murder of Mary Steers (Cooper), 1966
Murder of Miranda (Millar), 1979
Murder of Mrs. Davenport (A. Gilbert), 1928
Murder of My Aunt (Hull), 1934
Murder of My Patient (Eberhart), 1934
Murder of Olympia (Neville), 1956
Murder of Quality (le Carré), 1962
Murder of Roger Ackroyd (Christie), 1926
Murder of Sherlock Holmes (J. Anderson), 1985
Murder of Some Importance (Graeme), 1931
Murder of the Admiral (Fisher, as Gould), 1936
Murder of the Lawyer's Clerk (J. Fletcher), 1933
Murder of the Maharajah (Keating), 1980
Murder of the Ninth Baronet (J. Fletcher), 1932
Murder of the Only Witness (J. Fletcher), 1933
Murder of the Park Avenue Playgirl (s H. Kane), 1957
Murder of the Pigboat Skipper (Fisher), 1937
Murder of the Secret Agent (J. Fletcher), 1934
Murder of the Well-Beloved (Neville), 1953
Murder of Whistler's Brother (Alexander), 1956
Murder Off Miami (Wheatley), 1936
Murder off the Record (Bingham), 1957
Murder on a Bad Trip (Drummond), 1968
Murder on a Monument (Carnac, as Lorac), 1958
Murder on a Mystery Tour (Babson), 1987
Murder on a Saturday (Gray), 1961
Murder on a Tangent (Doris Disney), 1945
Murder on Angler's Island (Reilly), 1945
Murder on "B" Deck (Starrett), 1929
Murder on Broadway (Masur), 1959
Murder on Delivery (Sterling, as Dean), 1957
Murder on Duty (Rhode, as Burton), 1952
Murder on French Leave (Morice), 1972
Murder on Her Mind (Hunt, as Dietrich), 1960
Murder on High (C. Brown), 1973
Murder on Honeymoon (Gray), 1969
Murder on Ice (Wood), 1984
Murder on Largo Island (Creasey, as Hogarth), 1944

Murder's a Waiting Game (A. Gilbert), 1972
Murders Anonymous (Ferrars), 1977
Murder's Burning (Courtier), 1967
Murders in Praed Street (Rhode), 1928
Murders in Sequence (Propper), 1947
Murders in Volume 2 (E. Daly), 1941
Murder's Little Helper (Stein, as Bagby), 1963
Murder's Little Sister (Branch), 1959
Murder's Nest (Armstrong), 1955
Murders of Richard III (Elizabeth Peters), 1974
Murders' Out of Tune (Woods), 1984
Murder's Shield (Murphy), 1973
Murdoch, Bruce series (Creasey, as Deane), from 1939
Murdock, Kent series (Coxe), from 1935
Murdock, Rachel and Jennifer series (Olsen), from 1939
Murmur, Heron series (Harvester), from 1960
Museum Piece No. 13 (King), 1946
Music Tells All (Punshon), 1948
Musical Comedy Crime (A. Gilbert), 1933
Mussolini Murder Plot (B. Newman), 1939
Muster of Vultures (Fairlie), 1929
Mustering of the Hawks (Hebden, as Harris), 1972
Mutable Many (Barr), 1896
Mutants (Van Greenaway), 1986
Mute Witness (Fish, as Pike), 1963
My Adventure in the Flying Scotsman (s Phillpotts), 1888
My Bad Boy (Neville), 1964
My Body (Hunt, as Dietrich), 1962
My Bones Will Keep (G. Mitchell), 1962
My Brother Michael (Stewart), 1960
My Brother's Killer (Creasey, as York), 1958
My Brother's Killer (Potts), 1975
My Business Is Murder (H. Kane), 1954
My Child, My Sister (Fuller), 1965
My Cousin Death (McMullen), 1980
My Cousin Rachel (du Maurier), 1951
My Darlin' Evangeline (H. Kane), 1961
My Darling Is Deadpan (C. Brown), 1956
My Dead Body (Stein, as Bagby), 1976
My Dear Miss Emma (Blackstock, as Allardyce), 1958
My Father Sleeps (G. Mitchell), 1944
My Flesh Is Sweet (Keene), 1951
My Foe Outstretch'd Beneath the Tree (Clinton-Baddeley), 1968
My Friend Charles (Durbridge), 1963
My Friend the Murderer (s Doyle), 1893
My God How the Money Rolls In (Wainwright, as Ripley), 1972
My Grand Enemy (Stubbs), 1967
My Gun Is Quick (Spillane), 1950
My Kind of Game (Albert, as Rome), 1962
My Kingdom for a Hearse (Rice), 1957
My Lady Dangerous (Horler), 1932
My Lady's Garter (Futrelle), 1912
My Lady's Money (s Collins, appendix), 1878
My Late Wives (J. Carr, as Dickson), 1946
My Laugh Comes Last (Chase), 1977
My Life is Done (Woods), 1975
My Lord Duke (Hornung), 1897
My Love Is Violent (Dewey), 1956
My Love Wears Black (O. Cohen), 1948
My Lovely Executioner (Rabe), 1960
My Name Is Clary Brown (Blackstock, as Keppel), 1976
My Name Is Death (Linington, as Egan), 1965
My Name Is Michael Sibley (Bingham), 1952
My Neighbor's Wife (Doris Disney), 1957
My Own Murderer (Hull), 1940

My Search for Ruth (Clarke), 1975
My Son, The Murderer (Quentin), 1954
My Tattered Loving (Shearing, as Preedy), 1937
. . . My True Love Lies (Offord), 1947
My Turn Next (W. Graham), 1942
My Turn to Die (Royce), 1958
My Wife Melissa (Durbridge), 1967
My Word You Should Have Seen Us (Wainwright, as Ripley), 1972
Mycroft, Mr. series (Heard), from 1941
Myopic Mermaid (C. Brown), 1961
Mysteries (s Le Queux), 1913
Mysteries and Adventures (s Doyle), 1889
Mysteries of the Great City (s Le Queux), 1919
Mysteries of the Riviera (s Oppenheim), 1916
Mysterious Affair at Styles (Christie), 1920
Mysterious Chinaman (J. Fletcher), 1923
Mysterious Commission (M. Innes), 1974
Mysterious Mickey Finn (Paul), 1939
Mysterious Miss Morrisot (V. Williams), 1930
Mysterious Mr. I (Keeler), 1937
Mysterious Mr. Miller (Le Queux), 1906
Mysterious Mr. Sabin (Oppenheim), 1898
Mysterious Mr. Quin (s Christie), 1930
Mysterious Suspect (Rhode), 1953
Mysterious Three (Le Queux), 1915
Mysteriouser and Mysteriouser (Stein, as Bagby), 1965
Mystery and Minette (Herbert Adams), 1934
Mystery at a Country Inn (Pentecost, as Owen), 1979
Mystery at Friar's Pardon (P. MacDonald, as Porlock), 1931
Mystery at Greycombe Farm (Rhode), 1932
Mystery at Landy Court (Hume), 1894
Mystery at Lovers' Cave (Berkeley), 1927
Mystery at Lynden Sands (Connington), 1928
Mystery at Newton Ferry (Meynell), 1930
Mystery at Olympia (Rhode), 1935
Mystery at Ramshackle House (Footner), 1932
Mystery at the Blue Villa (Post), 1919
Mystery at Tudor Arches (Gribble), 1935
Mystery Blues (s Cheyney), 1954
Mystery De Luxe (King), 1927
Mystery Girl (Wells), 1922
Mystery in Kensington Gore (P. MacDonald, as Porlock), 1932
Mystery in the Channel (Crofts), 1931
Mystery in the English Channel (Crofts), 1931
Mystery in the Woodshed (A. Gilbert), 1942
Mystery Island (Dent, as Robeson), 1987
Mystery Lady (Clarke), 1986
Mystery Lamp (Rinehart), 1925
Mystery Manor (Gribble), 1951
Mystery Mile (Allingham), 1930
Mystery Mind (Reeve), 1921
Mystery Mission (s Horler), 1931
Mystery of a Butcher's Shop (G. Mitchell), 1929
Mystery of a Hansom Cab (Hume), 1886
Mystery of a Motor Cab (Hume), 1908
Mystery of a Motor-Car (Le Queux), 1906
Mystery of Angelina Frood (Freeman), 1924
Mystery of Cloomber (Doyle), 1888
Mystery of Edwin Drood (Dickens, appendix), 1870
Mystery of Enda Favell (Chance), 1981
Mystery of High Eldersham (Rhode, as Burton), 1933
Mystery of Hunting's End (Eberhart), 1930
Mystery of Jamaica Terrace (Donovan), 1896
Mystery of Lady Isabel (Punshon), 1907
Mystery of Lynne Court (J. Fletcher), 1923
Mystery of Mademoiselle (Le Queux), 1926

Mystery of Mr. Bernard Brown (Oppenheim), 1896
Mystery of Mr. Jessop (Punshon), 1937
Mystery of Mr. X (Horler), 1951
Mystery of Mr. X (P. MacDonald, as Porlock), 1934
Mystery of Nine (Le Queux), 1912
Mystery of No. 1 (Horler), 1925
Mystery of Orcival (Gaboriau, trans), 1871
Mystery of Sherwood Towers (Verner, as Stuart), 1928
Mystery of Swordfish Reef (Upfield), 1939
Mystery of the Baghdad Chest (s Christie), 1943
Mystery of the Blue Geranium (s Christie), 1940
Mystery of the Blue Train (Christie), 1928
Mystery of the Cape Cod Players (P. Taylor), 1933
Mystery of the Crime in Cabin 66 (s Christie), 1943
Mystery of the Dead Police (P. MacDonald, as Porlock), 1933
Mystery of the Deserted Camp (Chance, as Drummond), 1948
Mystery of the Fiddling Cracksman (Keeler), 1934
Mystery of the Five Guilty Men (Chance, as Drummond), 1954
Mystery of the Folded Paper (Footner), 1930
Mystery of The French Milliner (B. Thomson), 1937
Mystery of the Gold Box (V. Williams), 1932
Mystery of the Green Ray (Le Queux), 1915
Mystery of the Hasty Arrow (Green), 1917
Mystery of the Haunted Square (Chance, as Drummond), 1950
Mystery of the Hushing Pool (J. Fletcher), 1938
Mystery of the London Banker (J. Fletcher), 1933
Mystery of the Missing Book (Hall, as Burgess), 1950
Mystery of the Open Window (A. Gilbert), 1929
Mystery of the Phantom Blackmailer (Verner, as Stuart), 1928
Mystery of the Rabbit's Paw (Jepson), 1932
Mystery of the Sabotaged Jet (Chance, as Drummond), 1951
Mystery of the Scented Death (Vickers), 1921
Mystery of the Seven Cafés (Horler), 1935
Mystery of the Shadow (Hume), 1906
Mystery of the Sleeping Car Express (s Crofts), 1956
Mystery of the Smoking Gun (C. Daly), 1936
Mystery of the Stolen Hats (Graeme), 1939
Mystery of the Stolen Plans (Coles), 1960
Mystery of the Sycamore (Wells), 1921
Mystery of the Tarn (Wells), 1937
Mystery of the Thirteenth Floor (Thayer), 1919
Mystery of the White Knight (MacLeod), 1964
Mystery of the Woman in Red (A. Gilbert), 1944
Mystery of the Yellow Room (Leroux, trans), 1908
Mystery of 31, New Inn (Freeman), 1912
Mystery on Happy Bones (Dent, as Robeson), 1979
Mystery on Southampton Water (Crofts), 1934
Mystery on the Moors (Elizabeth Peters, as Michaels), 1968
Mystery on the Queen Mary (Graeme), 1937
Mystery on the Snow (Dent, as Robeson), 1972
Mystery Queen (Hume), 1912
Mystery Road (Oppenheim), 1923
Mystery Stories (s Ellin), 1956
Mystery Tour (Rutherford), 1975
Mystery under the Sea (Dent, as Robeson), 1968
Mystery Villa (Punshon), 1934
Mystic Mullah (Dent, as Robeson), 1965
Mythmaker (Gainham), 1957

N or M? (Christie), 1941
N3 Conspiracy (Michael Collins, as Carter), 1974
Naked and the Innocent (Ard), 1960
Naked Angel (Webb), 1953
Naked Bishop (H. Kane, as Sagola), 1980
Naked Canvas (Hall, as Scott), 1954
Naked Eye (Reynolds), 1990
Naked Fear (Webb, as Farr), 1955

Naked Fury (Keene), 1952
Naked in the Night (Cleary), 1955
Naked Jungle (Whittington), 1955
Naked Land (H. Innes), 1954
Naked Liar (Harold Adams), 1985
Naked Murderer (Piper), 1962
Naked Nuns (Watson), 1975
Naked Once More (Elizabeth Peters), 1989
Naked Runner (Clifford), 1966
Naked Sun (Asimov), 1957
Naked Sun (Willis), 1980
Naked Tide (Graeme, as Hastings), 1958
Naked to the Grave (Carmichael), 1972
Naked Villain (Woods), 1987
Naked Villainy (Davey), 1958
Name Is Archer (s Macdonald), 1955
Name Is Chambers (s H. Kane), 1957
Name Is Jordan (s Masur), 1962
Name of Action (Greene), 1930
Name of Annabel Lee (Symons), 1983
Name of the Game (Cory), 1964
Name of the Game Is Death (Dan Marlowe), 1962
Name Your Poison (Reilly), 1942
Nameless Detective series (Pronzini), from 1971
Nameless Ones (Davies, as Vardre), 1967
Nameless Ones (Linington, as Egan), 1967
Nameless Road (Harvester), 1969
Nameless Thing (Post), 1912
Name's Death, Remember Me? (S. Forbes), 1969
Names Make Clues (Carnac, as Lorac), 1937
Nanny (Piper), 1964
Nantucket Soap Opera (Dean), 1987
Napalm Bugle (Lacy), 1968
Narracong Riddle (Derleth), 1940
Narrative of Arthur Gordon Pym of Nantucket (Poe, appendix), 1838
Narrow Corner (Copper), 1983
Narrow Search (Garve), 1957
Narrowing Circle (Symons), 1954
Narrowing Lust (H. Kane), 1956
Nash, Monty series (Jessup, as Telfair), from 1959
Nasty Piece of Work (Bruce, as Croft-Cooke), 1973
Nation's Missing Guest (Footner), 1939
Natural Causes (Cecil), 1953
Natural Causes (Valin), 1983
Natural Enemy (Langton), 1982
Naughty Maid of Mitcham (Donovan), 1910
Navy Colt (Gruber), 1941
Nazi Assassins (Cory), 1970
Neapolitan Streak (Holme), 1980
Neat Little Corpse (Murray), 1950
Nebraska series (Reynolds), from 1984
Necessary Action (Wahlöö, trans), 1969
Necessary Dealing (Lewis), 1989
Necessary Doubt (C. Wilson), 1964
Necessary End (Anthea Fraser), 1985
Necessary End (Gielgud), 1969
Necessary Evil (Roos), 1965
Necessity (Garfield), 1984
Neck and Neck (Bruce), 1951
Neck in a Noose (Ferrars), 1943
Necklace and Calabash (van Gulik, trans), 1967
Necklace of Parmona (Meade), 1909
Necklace of Skulls (Parrish, as Drummond), 1977
Need to Know (Haggard), 1984
Needle That Wouldn't Hold Still (Stein, as Stone), 1950
Ne'er-Do-Well (Yates), 1954

Negative in Blue (C. Brown), 1974
Negative Man (McCutchan, as Galway), 1971
Negotiator (Busby), 1984
Negotiator (Forsyth), 1989
Negro (Simenon, trans), 1959
Neighbours (L. R. Wright), 1979
Neighbours (Simenon, trans), 1968
Neither a Candle nor a Pitchfork (Porter), 1969
Neither Five Nor Three (MacInnes), 1951
Neither Man nor Dog (s Kersh), 1946
Nell Alone (Butler, as Melville), 1966
Nella (Godey), 1981
Nemesis (Christie), 1971
Nemesis at Raynham Parva (Connington), 1929
Nemesis Wore Nylons (C. Brown), 1954
Neon Graveyard (Baxt), 1979
Neon Jungle (J. MacDonald), 1953
Neon Mirage (Max Collins), 1988
Neon Rain (James Lee Burke), 1987
Neon Tough (Kenrick), 1988
Nerissa Claire Case (Waugh), 1983
Nerve (Francis), 1964
Nervous Laughter (Emerson), 1986
Nest of Rats (Wainwright), 1977
Nest of Traitors (Creasey, as Ashe), 1970
Nest of Vipers (G. Mitchell), 1979
Nest of Vultures (B. Knox, as MacLeod), 1973
Net (Aarons, as Ronns), 1953
Net of Cobwebs (E. Holding), 1945
Nets to Catch the Wind (Olsen, as Hitchens), 1952
Never a Dull Moment (Cheyney), 1942
Never Bet Your Life (Coxe), 1952
Never Cross a Vampire (Kaminsky), 1980
Never Die Alone (Goines), 1974
Never Give a Millionaire an Even Break (H. Kane), 1963
Never Go Dark (Bonett, as Carter), 1940
Never Had a Spanner on Her (Leasor), 1970
Never Leave My Bed (Rogers), 1960
Never Live Twice (Dan Marlowe), 1964
Never Look Back (Eberhart), 1951
Never Mix Business with Pleasure (Graeme), 1968
Never Need an Enemy (Stein), 1959
Never Pick Up Hitch-Hikers! (Ellis Peters), 1976
Never Put Off till Tomorrow What You Can Kill Today (Godey), 1970
Never Trust a Woman (Chase, as Marshall), 1957
Never Turn Your Back (Scherf), 1959
Never Walk Alone (King), 1951
Never-Was Girl (C. Brown), 1964
New Centurions (Wambaugh), 1970
New Face in Hell (Busby), 1976
New Girl Friend (s Rendell), 1985
New Graves at Great Norne (Wade), 1947
New Idol (Leroux, trans), 1928
New, Improved Murder (Gorman), 1986
New Kind of Killer, An Old Kind of Death (Butler, as Melville), 1970
New Kind of War (Price), 1987
New Leaf (s Ritchie), 1971
New Lease of Death (Rendell), 1967
New Lease of Life (Simenon, trans), 1963
New Made Grave (Footner), 1935
New Mexico Connection (Wilcox), 1974
New Orleans Knockout (Pendleton), 1974
New Orleans Mourning (J. Smith), 1990
New People at the Hollies (Bell), 1961
New Shoe (Upfield), 1951

New Sonia Wayward (M. Innes), 1960
New Tenant (Oppenheim), 1912
New Terror (Leroux, trans), 1926
New Year's Eve in Lan-Fang (s van Gulik, trans), 1958
New York Dance (Westlake), 1979
New York Detective (Marshall), 1989
New York Murders (Queen), 1958
New York series (Auster), from 1985
News of Murder (Lejeune), 1961
News Travels by Night (Graeme), 1943
Newspaper Murders (Granger, as Gash), 1985
Next Door (Hume), 1918
Next Door to Danger (MacLeod), 1965
Next Man (Lewin), 1976
Next of Kin (Eberhart), 1982
Next of Kin (Murphy), 1981
Next to Die (Godey), 1975
Next to Die (Verner), 1934
Next Victim (Verner, as Stuart), 1931
Nice Class of Corpse (Brett), 1986
Nice Cup of Tea (A. Gilbert), 1950
Nice Day for a Funeral (Carmichael, as Howard), 1972
Nice Derangement of Epitaphs (Ellis Peters), 1965
Nice Girl Like You (Wormser), 1963
Nice Guys Finish Dead (Albert, as Albert Conroy), 1957
Nice Knight for Murder (Chambers, as Daniels), 1982
Nice Little Business (Dewhurst), 1987
Nice Little Killing (A. Gilbert), 1974
Nice Quiet Girl (Chambers, as Daniels), 1980
Nice Weekend for a Murder (Max Collins), 1986
Nicholas Goade, Detective (s Oppenheim), 1927
Nicholson series (Kelly), from 1961
Nig-Nog (s E. Wallace), 1934
Night after the Wedding (The Gordons), 1979
Night and the City (Kersh), 1938
Night at the Mocking Widow (J. Carr, as Dickson), 1950
Night at the Vulcan (Marsh), 1951
Night Before Chaos (Avallone), 1971
Night Before Murder (Fisher), 1939
Night Before the Wedding (The Gordons), 1969
Night-Blooming Cereus (Hess, as Hadley), 1986
Night Boat from Puerto Vedra (MacKenzie), 1970
Night Boat to Paris (Jessup), 1956
Night Chills (Koontz), 1976
Night Club (s Cheyney), 1945
Night-Club (Simenon, trans), 1979
Night-Comers (Ambler), 1956
Night Cover (Lewin), 1976
Night Drop (F. Davis), 1955
Night Encounter (A. Gilbert), 1968
Night Exercise (Rhode), 1942
Night Extra (McGivern), 1957
Night Ferry to Death (Moyes), 1985
Night for Screaming (Whittington), 1960
Night Frost (Copper), 1966
Night Games (Wilcox), 1979
Night Has a Thousand Eyes (Woolrich, as Hopley), 1945
Night Hawk (Cory), 1969
Night I Died (s Woolrich, as Irish), 1951
Night Is a Time to Die (Wainwright), 1972
Night Journey (W. Graham), 1941
Night Judgment at Sinos (J. Higgins), 1970
Night Lady (Gault), 1958
Night Lords (Freeling), 1978
Night of Clear Choice (Doris Disney), 1967
Night of Error (Bagley), 1984
Night of Errors (M. Innes), 1947

Night of Four Hundred Rabbits (Elizabeth Peters), 1971
Night of Glass (Purser), 1968
Night of Morningstar (P. O'Donnell), 1982
Night of Reckoning (Horler), 1942
Night of Reckoning (Strange), 1958
Night of Reunion (Allegretto), 1990
Night of Shadows (Gorman), 1990
Night of Shadows (Lockridge), 1962
Night of the Bowstring (Olsen), 1963
Night of the Fog (A. Gilbert), 1930
Night of the Fox (J. Higgins), 1986
Night of the Full Moon (Chance), 1950
Night of the Generals (Kirst, trans), 1963
Night of the Jabberwock (F. Brown), 1951
Night of the Juggler (McGivern), 1975
Night of the Phoenix (Demille), 1975
Night of the Rape (L. White), 1967
Night of the Ripper (Bloch), 1984
Night of the Settlement (Chance), 1961
Night of the Toads (Michael Collins), 1970
Night of the Twelfth (M. Gilbert), 1976
Night of the Watchman (Creasey)
Night of the Wolf (Warriner, as Kersey), 1968
Night of Wenceslas (Davidson), 1960
Night People (Finney), 1977
Night Pieces (s T. Burke), 1935
Night Pillow (Rae), 1967
Night Probe! (Cussler), 1981
Night Raider (Malzberg, as Barry), 1973
Night Run (Fenwick), 1961
Night Run from Java (G. Black), 1979
Night Screams (Malzberg, Pronzini), 1979
Night Seekers (Royce), 1962
Night She Died (Simpson), 1981
Night Squad (Goodis), 1961
Night Stop (Hall, as Trevor), 1975
Night the Gods Smiled (E. Wright), 1983
Night, The Woman (F. Davis, as Ransome), 1963
Night They Killed Joss Varran (Bellairs), 1970
Night Train (Macdonald, as Millar), 1955
Night Train to Paris (Coles), 1952
Night Walk (E. Daly), 1947
Night Walker (Avallone, as Stuart), 1964
Night Walker (D. Hamilton), 1954
Night Watch (Walsh), 1952
Night-Watchman's Friend (Fitt), 1953
Night Wheeler (C. Brown), 1974
Night Winds (Cleeve), 1954
Night Without End (MacLean), 1960
Night Without Stars (W. Graham), 1950
Night-World (Bloch), 1972
Nightborn (Gribble, as Grex), 1931
Nightclimber (J. White), 1968
Nightfall (Goodis), 1947
Nighthawk series (Horler), from 1937
Nightingale, Inspector Brett series (Kelly), from 1956
Nightlines (Lutz), 1985
Nightmare (Aarons), 1948
Nightmare (Linington, as Blaisdell), 1961
Nightmare (s Woolrich), 1956
Nightmare (s Woolrich, as Irish), 1950
Nightmare at Dawn (Pentecost, as Philips), 1970
Nightmare at Noon (Sterling), 1951
Nightmare Chase (Berckman), 1975
Nightmare Cruise (Miller), 1961
Nightmare in Copenhagen (Albrand), 1954
Nightmare in Dublin (Loraine), 1952

Nightmare in Manhattan (Walsh), 1950
Nightmare in New York (Pendleton), 1971
Nightmare in Pink (J. MacDonald), 1964
Nightmare in Rust (Audemars), 1975
Nightmare Time (Pentecost), 1986
Nightmare Town (s Hammett), 1948
Nightmares (Bloch), 1961
Nightmares and Geezenstacks (s F. Brown), 1961
Nightrunners (Lansdale), 1987
Nightrunners (Michael Collins), 1978
Night's Black Agent (Bingham), 1961
Night's Candles (Hocking), 1941
Night's Cloak (Punshon), 1944
Night's Dark Secret (Shearing, as Campbell), 1975
Night's Evil (McShane), 1966
Nights of the Long Knives (Kirst, trans), 1976
Nightscape (Chastain), 1982
Nightshade (Derek Marlowe), 1975
Nightshade (Gadney), 1987
Nightshade and Damnations (s Kersh), 1968
Nightshades (Pronzini), 1984
Nighttime Guy (Kenrick), 1979
Nightwebs (s Woolrich), 1971
Nightwing (M. Smith), 1977
Nightwitch Devil (Goulart, as Robeson), 1974
Nightwork (Hansen), 1984
Nijinsky Is Dead (K. Davis), 1987
Nile Green (Hocking), 1943
Nilsen, Pam series (B. Wilson), from 1984
Nine—and Death Makes Ten (J. Carr, as Dickson), 1940
Nine Bears (E. Wallace), 1910
Nine Bright Shiners (Anthea Fraser), 1987
Nine Coaches Waiting (Stewart), 1958
9 Dark Hours (Offord), 1941
911 (Chastain), 1976
Nine Lives of Bill Nelson (Kersh), 1942
Nine Mile Walk (s Kemelman), 1967
Nine O'Clock Tide (Eberhart), 1978
Nine Tailors (Sayers), 1934
Nine Times Nine (Boucher, as Holmes), 1940
Nine Waxed Faces (Beeding), 1936
Nine Wrong Answers (J. Carr), 1952
1956 (S. Marlowe), 1981
Nineteen Stories (s Greene), 1947
19 Purchase Street (G. Browne), 1982
Nineteenth Hole Mystery (Herbert Adams), 1939
90 Gramercy Park (Avallone, as Dalton), 1965
Ninety-Million Dollar Mouse (Nevins), 1987
99 44/100% Dead (Deming, as Franklin), 1974
Ninety-Second Tiger (M. Gilbert), 1973
9th Directive (Hall), 1966
Ninth Hour (Benson), 1956
Ninth Life (Ferrars), 1965
Ninth Netsuke (Melville), 1982
Nipped in the Bud (Palmer), 1951
Nirvana Can Also Mean Death (H. Kane), 1959
Nita's Place (Whittington), 1960
No Alibi (Creasey, as York), 1943
No Angels for Me (Ard), 1954
No Bail for the Judge (Cecil), 1952
No Better Fiend (McGirr), 1971
No Birds Sang (Hilton), 1975
No Blonde Is an Island (C. Brown), 1965
No Body (Pickard), 1986
No Body She Knows (C. Brown), 1958
No Bones about It (J. Fleming), 1967
No Business Being a Cop (L. O'Donnell), 1979

No Business of Mine (Chase, as Marshall), 1947
No Case for the Police (Clinton-Baddeley), 1970
No Certain Life (Neely), 1978
No Chance in Hell (Albert, as Quarry), 1960
No Clues for Dexter (Graeme), 1948
No Coffin for the Corpse (Rawson), 1942
No Comebacks (s Forsyth), 1982
No Coupons for a Shroud (Morland), 1949
No Crime More Cruel (Creasey, as Halliday), 1944
No Cure for Death (Max Collins), 1983
No Darker Crime (Creasey), 1943
No Dignity in Death (Lockridge), 1962
No Dust in the Attic (A. Gilbert), 1962
No Duty on a Corpse (Murray), 1950
No End to Danger (Creasey, as Halliday), 1948
No Enemy But Time (Anthony), 1987
No Entry (Coles), 1958
No Escape (Bell), 1965
No Escape (Hayes), 1982
No Escape from Murder (Creasey, as Manton), 1953
No Evil Angel (Linington), 1964
No Exit (W. Graham), 1940
No Exit from Brooklyn (Randisi), 1987
No Fatherland (Kirst, trans), 1970
No Fear or Favour (Cecil), 1968
No Flowers by Request (Palmer), 1937
No Flowers, By Request (J. Thomson), 1987
No Flowers for the General (Copper), 1967
No Footprints in the Bush (Upfield), 1944
No Friendly Drop (Wade), 1931
No Fury (Beeding), 1937
No Future for Luana (Derleth), 1945
No Future, Fair Lady (C. Brown), 1958
No Gold When You Go (Chambers), 1966
No Good from a Corpse (Brackett), 1944
No Grave for a Lady (Bonett), 1959
No Grave for March (Crossen, as Chaber), 1953
No Greater Love (Le Queux), 1917
No Halo for Hedy (C. Brown), 1956
No Hands on the Clock (Homes), 1939
No Harm Intended (E. Holding), 1939
No Harp for My Angel (C. Brown), 1956
No Hero (Marquand), 1935
No Holiday for Crime (Linington, as Shannon), 1973
No Holiday for Death (Thayer), 1954
No House Limit (Fisher), 1958
No Hurry to Kill (Creasey, as Deane), 1950
No Known Grave (Berckman), 1958
No Lady in the House (Kallen), 1982
No Law Against Angels (C. Brown), 1957
No Letters from the Grave (Copper), 1971
No Light to Die By (Dent, as Robeson), 1988
No Love Lost (Allingham), 1954
No Man's Island (Mann), 1983
No Man's Land (Hill), 1985
No Man's Land (L. Vance), 1910
No Man's Street (Nichols), 1954
No Mask for Murder (Garve), 1950
No Medals for the Major (Yorke), 1974
No More A-Roving (Warriner, as Troy), 1965
No More Dying Then (Rendell), 1971
No Mourning for the Matador (Ames), 1953
No Murder (Bailey), 1942
No Name (Collins, appendix), 1862
No Need to Die (Creasey, as Ashe), 1956
No Next of Kin (Doris Disney), 1959
No Obelisk for Emily (Courtier), 1970

No One Knows My Name (J. Harrington), 1980
No Orchids for Miss Blandish (Chase), 1939
No Other Tiger (A. Mason), 1927
No Paradise (Royce), 1961
No Part in Your Death (Freeling), 1984
No Past Is Dead (Connington), 1942
No Peace for the Wicked (Chambers), 1968
No Peace for the Wicked (Ferrars), 1966
No Place for Murder (Coxe), 1975
No Place to Hide (Allbeury), 1984
No Place to Live (Aarons, as Ronns), 1947
No Pockets in a Shroud (McCoy), 1937
No Proud Chivalry (Procter), 1947
No Quarter for a Star (Gray), 1964
No Questions Asked (S. Forbes, as Rydell), 1963
No Questions Asked (Thomas, as Bleeck), 1976
No Return Ticket (Russell), 1966
No Sign of Life (Ormerod), 1990
No Smoke, No Flame (M. Harrison, as Downes), 1952
No Snow in Latching (Bush, as Home), 1949
No Surrender (Albrand), 1942
No Tears for Hilda (Garve), 1950
No Tears for the Dead (Audemars), 1974
No Tears from the Widow (C. Brown), 1966
No Through Road (Russell), 1965
No Time for Leola (C. Brown), 1967
No Time for Terror (P. MacDonald), 1956
No Time to Kill (Bonett), 1972
No Time to Kill (Coxe), 1941
No Traveller Returns (Ames), 1934
No Traveller Returns (s Collier), 1931
No Vacation from Murder (Lemarchand), 1974
No Villain Need Be (Linington), 1979
No Walls of Jasper (Cannan), 1930
No Way Back (Royce), 1986
No Way Out (Fearing), 1980
No Wind of Blame (Heyer), 1939
No Winding Sheet (G. Mitchell), 1984
No Wings on a Cop (Bellem), 1950
No Wings on a Cop (C. Adams), 1950
No Word from Winifred (Cross), 1986
Nobody (L. Vance), 1915
Nobody Here by That Name (MacKenzie), 1986
Nobody Knew They Were There (McBain, as Hunter), 1971
Nobody Lives Forever (Burnett), 1943
Nobody Lives Forever (Chambers), 1964
Nobody Lives Forever (J. Gardner), 1986
Nobody Loves a Loser (H. Kane), 1963
Nobody Wore Black (Ames), 1951
Nobody's Perfect (D. Clark), 1969
Nobody's Perfect (Westlake), 1977
Nobody's Supposed to Murder the Butler (Chance), 1984
Nobody's Vineyard (Bailey), 1942
Nobody's Man (Oppenheim), 1921
Nocturne for the General (Trenhaile), 1985
Nodding Canaries (G. Mitchell), 1961
Noise in the Night (Jepson), 1957
Nolan series (Max Collins), from 1973
Nomads of the Night (Leroux, trans), 1925
None But the Lethal Heart (C. Brown), 1959
None Shall Know (Albrand), 1945
Noon, Ed series (Avallone), from 1953
Noonday and Night (G. Mitchell), 1977
Noonday Devil (Curtiss), 1951
Noose (P. MacDonald), 1930
Noose for a Lady (Carmichael), 1955
Noose for a Lady (Verner), 1952

Noose for Her (Crispin), 1952
Nor Live So Long (Woods), 1986
Norgil series (s Gibson), from 1976
Norrington, Ganzarello and Tucker series (Parrish, as Drummond), from 1969
Norris, Mrs. and Jaspar Tully series (D. Davis), from 1957
North from Rome (MacInnes), 1958
North from Thursday (Cleary), 1960
North Star (H. Innes), 1974
North, Hugh series (F. Mason), from 1930
North, Mr. and Mrs. and Bill Wiegand series (Lockridge), from 1941
Northeast, Inspector Guy series (Cannan), from 1939
Northing Tramp (E. Wallace), 1926
Northlight (Hall), 1985
Norwich Victims (Beeding), 1935
Nose for It (Stein), 1980
Nose on My Face (Payne), 1962
Nostradamus Traitor (J. Gardner), 1979
Not a Bad Show (Beeding), 1940
Not a Blessed Thing! (McInerny, as Quill), 1981
Not a Leg to Stand On (Rhode, as Burton), 1945
Not after Midnight (s du Maurier), 1971
Not as Far as Velma (Freeling), 1989
Not Comin' Home to You (Block, as Kavanagh), 1974
Not Dead, Only Resting (Brett), 1984
Not Enough Horses (L. Roberts), 1988
Not Exactly a Brahmin (Dunlap), 1985
Not for Export (Coles), 1954
Not I, Said the Sparrow (Lockridge), 1973
Not I, Said the Vixen (Ballinger), 1965
Not in the Script (Bonett), 1951
Not in Utter Nakedness (Ames), 1932
Not Me, Inspector (Reilly), 1959
Not My Thing (Chase), 1983
Not Negotiable (Coles), 1949
Not One of Us (J. Thomson), 1971
Not Proven (Graeme), 1935
Not Quite Dead Enough (Stout), 1944
Not Safe to Be Free (Chase), 1958
Not Single Spies (B. Newman, as Betteridge), 1951
Not to Be Taken (Berkeley), 1938
Not to the Swift (Harvester, as Gibbs), 1944
Not Wanted (Hume), 1914
Not Wanted on Voyage (Spain), 1951
Notch on the Knife (Haggard), 1973
Notched Hairpin (Heard), 1949
Nothing But a Man (Thompson), 1970
Nothing but Foxes (Lewis), 1977
Nothing But the Night (Blackburn), 1968
Nothing But the Truth (Rhode), 1947
Nothing But the Truth (Ørum, trans), 1976
Nothing Can Rescue Me (E. Daly), 1943
Nothing in Her Way (C. Williams), 1953
Nothing Is the Number When You Die (J. Fleming), 1965
Nothing Like Blood (Bruce), 1962
Nothing Man (Thompson), 1954
Nothing More Than Murder (Thompson), 1949
Nothing Personal (Chambers), 1980
Nothing to Declare (s Coles), 1960
Nothing to Do with the Case (Lemarchand), 1981
Nothing Venture (Wentworth), 1932
Notorious (Keene), 1954
Notorious Miss Walters (Vickers, as Kyle), 1937
Notorious Sophie Lang (F. Anderson), 1925
Novak, Jack series (Hunt), from 1985
November (Simenon, trans), 1970

November Man (Freemantle), 1976
November Man (Granger), 1979
Novena for Murder (O'Marie), 1984
Now and On Earth (Thompson), 1942
Now and Then, Amen (Cleary), 1988
Now Dead Is Any Man (Audemars), 1978
Now It's My Turn (Crossen, as Chaber), 1954
Now or Never (Coles), 1951
Now Seek My Bones (Courtier), 1957
Now Try the Morgue (Hall, as Dudley-Smith), 1948
Nowhere Man (R. Perry), 1973
Nowhere to Go (MacKenzie), 1956
Nowhere? (Stein), 1978
Nude in Mink (Rohmer), 1950
Nude in Nevada (Dewey), 1965
Nude on Thin Ice (Brewer), 1960
Nude on Thin Ice (C. Williams), 1961
Nude—with a View (C. Brown), 1965
Nudger, Alo series (Lutz), from 1976
Number 18 (Wills), 1934
Number 87 (Phillpotts, as Hext), 1922
No. 9 Belmont Square (Erskine), 1963
Number One's Last Crime (Creasey, as Cooke), 1935
No. 7, Saville Square (Le Queux), 1920
Number 70, Berlin (Le Queux), 1916
Number Seventy-Three (Vickers, as Kyle), 1936
Number Six (E. Wallace), 1927
Nun in the Closet (Gilman), 1975
Nun in the Cupboard (Gilman), 1976
Nun of the Above (McInerny, as Quill), 1985
Nun's Castle (Butler, as Melville), 1973
Nuplex Red (M. Smith, as Quinn), 1974
Nursemaid Who Disappeared (P. MacDonald), 1938
Nursery Crimes (B.M. Gill), 1986
Nursery Rhyme Murders (Verner), 1960
Nursery Tea and Poison (Morice), 1975
Nursing-Home Murder (Marsh), 1935
Nymph to the Slaughter (C. Brown), 1963

O as in Omen (Treat), 1943
Oakes, Blackford series (Buckley), from 1976
Oakes, Boysie series (J. Gardner), from 1964
Oasis (Creasey), 1969
Oasis Nine (s Canning), 1959
Obeah Murders (Footner), 1937
Obedience (Hansen), 1988
Oberst (W. Harrington), 1987
Obit Delayed (Nielsen), 1952
Obituary Arrives at 2 O'Clock (Natsuki, trans), 1988
Obituary Club (Pentecost), 1958
Obligation (Neely), 1979
Obols for Charon (Harvester), 1951
O'Breen, Fergus series (Boucher), from 1939
Obscure Grave (Woods), 1985
Obsequies at Oxford (Crispin), 1945
Obsession (L. White), 1962
Obsession (Tripp), 1973
Obstinate Murderer (E. Holding), 1938
Occupying Power (Anthony), 1973
Octagon House (P. Taylor), 1937
October Circle (Littell), 1976
October Men (Price), 1973
October Plot (Egleton), 1974
Octopus of Paris (Leroux, trans), 1927
Octopussy (s I. Fleming), 1966
Odd Job No. 101 (s Goulart), 1975
Oddkins (Koontz), 1988

Odds Against (Francis), 1965
Odds Against Tomorrow (McGivern), 1957
Odds On (Crichton, as Lange), 1966
Odds on Bluefeather (Meynell), 1934
Odds on Death (McGirr, as Drummond), 1969
Odds on the Hot Seat (Pentecost, as Philips), 1941
Odds Run Out (Waugh), 1949
Oddways (Herbert Adams), 1929
O'Dea, Rita Gardella series (Coburn), from 1985
Odessa File (Forsyth), 1972
Odor of Violets (Kendrick), 1941
Of All the Bloody Cheek (s McAuliffe), 1965
Of Demons and Darkness (s Collier), 1965
O'Fear (Corris), 1990
Of Malicious Intent (Meynell), 1969
Of Missing Persons (Goodis), 1950
Of Royal Blood (Le Queux), 1900
Of Singular Purpose (Lewis), 1973
Of Tender Sin (Goodis), 1952
Of Unsound Mind (Carmichael), 1962
O'Farrell's Law (Freemantle), 1990
Off Duty (Coburn), 1980
Off With Her Head! (Cole), 1938
Off with His Head (Marsh), 1957
Office Secret (Le Queux), 1927
Officer Party (Kirst, trans), 1962
Officer! (Footner), 1924
Offshore Conspiracy (Chance), 1988
Offshore! (Coulter), 1965
Oil Bastards (McCutchan), 1972
Oil Slick (Murphy), 1974
Okewood of the Secret Service (V. Williams), 1919
Oklahoma Punk (Estleman), 1976
Old Battle Ax (E. Holding), 1943
Old Bones (Elkins), 1987
Old Dark House (Priestley), 1928
Old Dick (Morse), 1981
Old Die Young (Lockridge), 1980
Old English Peep Show (Dickinson), 1969
Old-Fashioned Mystery (Morse, as Fairleigh), 1983
Old-Fashioned War (Murphy), 1987
Old Fighting Days (Punshon), 1921
Old Fox Deceiv'd (Grimes), 1982
Old Hall, New Hall (M. Innes), 1956
Old Jew Mystery (Herbert Adams), 1936
Old Lady Dies (A. Gilbert), 1934
Old Lattimer's Legacy (J. Fletcher), 1892
Old Lover's Ghost (Ford), 1940
Old Man Dies (Bellairs), 1980
Old Man Dies (Simenon, trans), 1967
Old Man in the Corner series (s Orczy), from 1909
Old Masters (Haggard), 1973
Old Mrs. Camelot (Bonett, as Carter), 1944
Old Mrs. Fitzgerald (Hocking), 1939
Old Mrs. Ommanney Is Dead (Erskine), 1955
Old Murders (Whalley), 1984
Old Offenders and a Few Old Scores (s Hornung), 1923
Old School Tie (A. Taylor), 1986
Old Silent (Grimes), 1989
Old Sinners Never Die (D. Davis), 1959
Old Stone House (s Green), 1891
Old Trade of Killing (Hebden, as Harris), 1966
Old Vengeful (Price), 1982
Oldest Confession (Condon), 1958
Oliver Twist (Dickens, appendix), 1838
Oliver, Gideon series (Elkins), from 1982
Oliverez, Elena series (Muller), from 1985

Olura (Household), 1965
O'Malley, Superintendent series (Kenyon), from 1970
Omega Minus (Allbeury), 1975
Omit Flowers (Palmer), 1937
On an Odd Note (s Kersh), 1958
On Hazardous Duty (Hunt, as St. John), 1965
On Her Majesty's Secret Service (I. Fleming), 1963
On Land and Sea (Simenon, trans), 1954
On Suspicion (D. Fletcher), 1985
On the Brink of a Chasm (Meade), 1899
On the Danger Line (Simenon, trans), 1944
On the Edge (Lovesey), 1989
On the Inside (Wood), 1990
On the Make (J. MacDonald), 1960
On the Night in Question (Wills), 1937
On the Night of the 18th . . . (Meynell), 1936
On the Night of the Seventh Moon (Holt), 1972
On the Run (J. MacDonald), 1963
On the Spot (E. Wallace), 1931
On the Stretch (Welcome), 1969
On the Track of Death (Rutherford), 1959
Once a Mutt (Murphy), 1986
Once a Prostitute (Hunter), 1984
Once a Year Man (Tripp), 1977
Once and Future Spy (Littell), 1990
Once Dying, Twice Dead (Lewis), 1984
Once in a Lifetime (Coulter, as Mayo), 1968
Once in a Red Moon (Rogers), 1923
Once Over Deadly (Gruber), 1956
Once Over Lightly (Dent, as Robeson), 1987
Once upon a Crime (Crossen, as Monig), 1959
Once Upon a Fairy Tale (McShane), 1990
Once Upon a Murder (Randisi), 1987
Once Upon a Time (s Phillpotts), 1936
Once upon a Train (s Palmer, Rice), 1981
One Across, Two Down (Rendell), 1971
One Against the Earth (Homes, as Mainwaring), 1933
One Angry Man (Daniels), 1971
One Away (Prior), 1961
One Bright Summer Morning (Chase), 1963
One Corpse Too Many (Ellis Peters), 1979
One Cried Murder (Courtier), 1954
One Damn Thing after Another (Freeling), 1981
One Dead Dean (Crider), 1988
One Deadly Dawn (Whittington), 1957
One Deadly Summer (Japrisot, trans), 1980
One Deathless Hour (Ormerod), 1981
One Dip Dead (Stein), 1979
One Dollar Death (Barth), 1982
One Endless Hour (Dan Marlowe), 1969
One-Eyed Mystic (Dent, as Robeson), 1982
One-Faced Girl (Armstrong), 1963
One False Move (Roos), 1966
One Fearful Yellow Eye (J. MacDonald), 1966
One Fine Day the Rabbi Bought a Cross (Kemelman), 1987
One Foot in the Grave (Dickinson), 1979
One for My Dame (Webb), 1961
One for the Road (F. Brown), 1958
One for the Road (Hunt, as Dietrich), 1954
One Good Death Deserves Another (R. Perry), 1976
One Got Away (Whittington), 1955
One Grave Too Many (Goulart), 1974
One Hour to Kill (Coxe), 1963
$106,000 Blood Money (Hammett), 1943
153 Oakland Street (Avallone, as Highland), 1973
120-Hour Clock (Nevins), 1986
100,000 Welcomes (Kenyon), 1970

One Is One (Tripp), 1968
One Lonely Night (Spillane), 1951
One Lover Too Many (Tripp), 1983
One-Man Show (M. Innes), 1952
One Man's Justice (Jeffries, as Alding), 1983
One Man's Meat (Watson), 1977
£1,000,000 Film Murder Case (Verner, as Stuart), 1933
$1,000,000 in Corpses (Aarons, as Ronns), 1943
One Minute Past Eight (Coxe), 1957
One Monday We Killed Them All (J. MacDonald), 1961
One More Sunday (J. MacDonald), 1984
One More Time (Avallone), 1970
One More Unfortunate (Lustgarten), 1947
One Murder Too Many (Coxe), 1969
One Murder Too Many (F. Davis), 1938
One Murdered, Two Dead (Propper), 1936
One Night Stand (Murphy), 1973
One Night with Nora (Halliday), 1953
One of My Sons (Green), 1901
One of Our Agents Is Missing (Hunt, as St. John), 1967
One of Those Things (Cheyney), 1949
One of Those Ways (Lowndes), 1929
One of Us Must Die (Clarke), 1977
One Sane Man (Beeding), 1934
One Shall Be Taken (Hocking), 1942
One Shot Deal (Petievich), 1983
One Step from Murder (Meynell), 1958
One That Got Away (McCloy), 1945
One to Play (Herbert Adams), 1949
One Way or Another (Sciascia, trans), 1977
One Way Out (Coxe), 1960
One-Way Ticket (Olsen, as Hitchens), 1956
One, Two, Buckle My Shoe (Christie), 1940
One-Man Jury (F. Davis, as Ransome), 1964
One-Way Ticket (Carmichael, as Howard), 1978
O'Neill, Jim series (Doris Disney), from 1943
Only a Matter of Time (Clinton-Baddeley), 1969
Only Children (D. Fletcher), 1976
Only Couples Need Apply (Doris Disney), 1973
Only Girl in the Game (J. MacDonald), 1960
Only Good Body's a Dead One (Kenrick), 1970
Only Good German (Allbeury), 1976
Only Good Secretary (Potts), 1965
Only on Tuesdays (Dewey), 1964
Only One More Miracle (Avallone), 1975
Only Security (Mann), 1973
Only the Guilty (Stein), 1942
Only the Rich Die Young (Pentecost), 1964
Only the Ruthless Can Play (John Burke), 1965
Only the Very Rich? (C. Brown), 1969
Only with a Bargepole (Porter), 1971
Opal Serpent (Hume), 1905
Opara, Christie series (Uhnak), from 1968
Open Door (Meynell), 1984
Open House (M. Innes), 1972
Open Secret (Leasor), 1982
Open Verdict (Le Queux), 1921
Open Verdict (Rhode), 1956
Open Window (Ormerod), 1988
Opener of the Way (s Bloch), 1945
Opening Door (Reilly), 1944
Opening Night (Marsh), 1951
Operation Barbarossa (B. Newman), 1956
Operation series (Dan Marlowe), from 1969
Operation Dancing Dog (Fox), 1974
Operation Delta (H. Kane), 1966
Operation Doctors (Roth), 1962

Operation Lila (Albert), 1983
Operation Manhunt (Coles), 1954
Operation Pax (M. Innes), 1951
Operation Piracy (Garve, as Somers), 1958
Operation series (Daniels), from 1965
Operation Terror (The Gordons), 1961
Operation—Murder (L. White), 1956
Operator (C. Williams), 1958
Operator (Westlake), 1964
Operator No. 5 series (F. Davis, as Steele), from 1966
Operators (Prior), 1966
...Or Be He Dead (Carmichael), 1958
Or Was He Pushed? (Lockridge), 1975
Oracle of Maddox Street (s Meade), 1904
Orange Blossoms (s Shearing), 1938
Orange Divan (V. Williams), 1923
Orange-Yellow Diamond (J. Fletcher), 1920
Orator (s E. Wallace), 1928
Orchids to Murder (Footner), 1945
Ordeal (The Gordons), 1976
Ordeal by Innocence (Christie), 1958
Ordeal of Mrs. Snow (s Quentin), 1961
Order of the Octopus (Horler), 1926
Organ Speaks (Carnac, as Lorac), 1935
Orient Express (Greene), 1933
Oriental Division G-2 (F. Mason)
Origin of Evil (Queen), 1951
Original Carcase (Stein, as Bagby), 1946
Orion Line (Luard), 1976
Ormsberry, Van Dusen series (Strange), from 1928
Orphan Ann (Bailey), 1941
Orphan of Mars (Cannan), 1930
Ortiz, Johnny series (Stern), from 1971
Ostenders (Simenon, trans), 1952
Osterman Weekend (Ludlum), 1972
Ostrekoff Jewels (Oppenheim), 1932
Otan Plot (B. Newman), 1957
Otani, Superintendent Tetsuo series (Melville), from 1979
Othello Complex (McShane), 1974
Other Devil's Name (Ferrars), 1986
Other Karen (Johnston), 1983
Other Kinds of Treason (s Allbeury), 1990
Other Man (Durbridge), 1958
Other Man (E. Wallace), 1911
Other Man's Danger (Allingham, as March), 1933
Other Paths to Glory (Price), 1974
Other People's Money (Gaboriau, trans), 1875
Other People's Money (Lyons), 1989
Other Person (Hume), 1920
Other Romilly (Oppenheim), 1918
Other Shoe (McMullen), 1981
Other Side of Silence (Allbeury), 1981
Other Side of the Door (Carmichael, as Howard), 1953
Other Side of the Door (L. O'Donnell), 1987
Other Sins Only Speak (H. Kane), 1965
Other Woman (O. Cohen), 1917
Other World (Dent, as Robeson), 1968
Our Father's Lies (A. Taylor), 1985
Our Jubilee Is Death (Bruce), 1959
Our Lady of Pain (Blackburn), 1974
Our Man in Camelot (Price), 1975
Our Man in Havana (Greene), 1958
Our Mutual Friend (Dickens, appendix), 1865
Out, Brief Candle! (Thayer), 1948
Out, Damned Tot! (Spain), 1952
Out for the Kill (A. Gilbert), 1960
Out Goes She (Stout), 1953

Out Is Death (Rabe), 1957
Out of a Dark Sky (Horler), 1946
Out of Control (Kendrick), 1945
Out of Nowhere (Marshall), 1988
Out of Order (P. Taylor), 1936
Out of Season (Kenyon), 1968
Out of Season (Lewin), 1984
Out of the Blackout (Barnard), 1985
Out of the Blue (J. Milne), 1985
Out of the Blue (s Sapper), 1925
Out of the Dark (Curtiss), 1964
Out of the Depths (Holton), 1966
Out of the Fire (Carmichael, as Howard), 1965
Out of the Mouths of Graves (s Bloch), 1979
Out of the Past (Wentworth), 1953
Out of the Shadows (Creasey, as Halliday), 1954
Out of the War? (Lowndes), 1918
Out of Time (Lewin), 1984
Out on the Cutting Edge (Block), 1989
Out on the Rim (Thomas), 1987
Out There (Donovan), 1922
Outbreak (L. Black), 1968
Outcasts (Hensley), 1981
Outer Gate (O. Cohen), 1927
Outfit (Westlake, as Stark), 1963
Outlaw (Simenon, trans), 1986
Outlaws (G. Higgins), 1987
Outrage in Manchukuo (Gielgud), 1937
Outrage on Gallows Hill (Bellairs), 1948
Outrageous Fortune (Wentworth), 1933
Outrun the Constable (Jepson), 1948
Outside In (Lewin), 1980
Outside the Law (Loraine), 1953
Outsider in Amsterdam (van de Wetering), 1975
Over Her Dead Body (Prather), 1959
Over My Dead Body (Stout), 1940
Over the Border (Barr), 1903
Over the Edge (J. Kellerman), 1987
Over the Edge (Treat), 1948
Over the Garden Wall (Carnac), 1948
Over the High Side (Freeling), 1971
Over the Hump (s E. Gardner), 1945
Over the Sea to Death (Moffat), 1976
Over the Wall (Hall, as Dudley-Smith), 1943
Overdose of Death (Christie), 1953
Overdrive (M. Gilbert), 1968
Overdue (Clifford), 1957
Overkill (Crichton, as Lange), 1972
Overkill (Daniels), 1964
Overkill (Schorr), 1987
Overload (Cory), 1964
Overture to Death (Marsh), 1939
Owen, Bill series (s Orczy), from 1909
Owen, Bobby series (Punshon), from 1933
Owl (Herbert Adams, as Gray), 1937
Owl in the Cellar (Scherf), 1945
Owl Taxi (Footner), 1921
Owls Don't Blink (E. Gardner, as Fair), 1942
Oxford Blood (Antonia Fraser), 1985
Oxford Gambit (Hone), 1980
Oxford Tragedy (Masterman), 1933
Ozark series (Hess), from 1987

P as in Police (s Treat), 1970
P Division series (Turnbull), from 1981
Pacific Vortex! (Cussler), 1983
Pack of Lies (Creasey, as Ashe), 1959

Package Holiday Spy Case (B. Newman, as Betteridge), 1962
Package Included Murder (Porter), 1975
Packed for Murder (Blackburn), 1964
Pact with Satan (Holton), 1960
Paddington Mystery (Rhode), 1925
Pagan's Cup (Hume), 1902
Pageant of Murder (G. Mitchell), 1965
Pagoda (Atlee, as Phillips), 1951
Pagoda Tree (Mather), 1979
Paid in Full (Meynell), 1933
Painswick Line (Cecil), 1951
Paint Gold and Blood (M. Gilbert), 1989
Paint the Town Black (Alexander), 1954
Paint the Town Red (Harold Adams), 1983
Painted Angel (Shearing, as Preedy), 1938
Painted Castle (Butler, as Melville), 1982
Painted Dagger (Chance, as Drummond), 1944
Painted Devil (Welcome), 1988
Painted Face (Stubbs), 1974
Painted in Blood (H. Harris), 1972
Painted Mask (Erskine), 1972
Palace (Erdman), 1987
Palace Guard (MacLeod), 1981
Palace of Love (J. Vance), 1967
Paladin (Garfield), 1980
Pale Ape and Other Pulses (s Shiel), 1911
Pale Betrayer (D. Davis), 1965
Pale Gray for Guilt (J. MacDonald), 1968
Pale Horse (Christie), 1961
Pale Kings and Princes (Parker), 1987
Palermo Ambush (C. Forbes), 1972
Palfrey, Dr. series (Creasey), from 1942
Pall for a Painter (Carnac, as Lorac), 1936
Pallard the Punter (E. Wallace), 1914
Palm Springs (Ardies), 1978
Palmer-Jones, George series (Cleeves), from 1986
Palomino Blonde (Allbeury), 1975
Panama Plot (s Reeve), 1918
Panama Portrait (Ellin), 1962
Pandemic (Ardies), 1973
Pandora (Reeve), 1926
Pandora Option (Rathbone), 1990
Pandora's Box (Chastain), 1974
Pangersbourne Murders (Sturrock), 1983
Pangolin (Driscoll), 1979
Panic (McCloy), 1944
Panic! (Creasey), 1939
Panic! (Pronzini), 1972
Panic in Box C (J. Carr), 1966
Panic in Paradise (K. Knight, as Amos), 1951
Panic in Philly (Pendleton), 1973
Panic of '89 (Erdman), 1986
Panic Party (Berkeley), 1934
Panthers' Moon (Canning), 1948
Panton, Colin series (Purser), from 1962
Papa La-Bas (J. Carr), 1968
Papa Pontivy and the Maginot Murder (B. Newman), 1940
Paper Albatross (Bruce, as Croft-Cooke), 1965
Paper Bag (Rhode), 1948
Paper Chase (Linington, as Egan), 1972
Paper Chase (Symons), 1956
Paper Circle (Fischer), 1951
Paper Dolls (Davies), 1964
Paper Gun (H. Browne, as Evans), 1985
Paper Money (Follett, as Stone), 1977
Paper Palace (Harling), 1951
Paper Pistol Contract (Atlee), 1966

Paper Thunderbolt (M. Innes), 1951
Papers of Tony Veitch (McIlvanney), 1983
Papersnake (Meynell), 1978
Parade of Cockeyed Creatures (Baxt), 1967
Paradise Court (J. Fletcher), 1908
Paradise Man (Charyn), 1987
Paradise Men (Harvester), 1956
Paradise Mystery (J. Fletcher), 1920
Paradise Party (McBain, as Hunter), 1968
Paradise Row (Blackstock, as Allardyce), 1976
Paradoxes of Mr. Pond (s Chesterton), 1936
Paragon (Hall, as Trevor), 1975
Paragon Walk (A. Perry), 1981
Parasite Person (Fremlin), 1982
Pargeter, Mrs. series (Brett), from 1986
Pariah (Wilcox), 1988
Paris Trap (Hone), 1977
Paris, Charles series (Brett), from 1975
Paris, Detective Inspector Wade series (Benson), from 1951
Park Avenue Tramp (Flora), 1958
Parker Pyne Investigates (s Christie), 1934
Parker series (Westlake, as Stark), from 1962
Parrish for the Defense (Waugh), 1974
Parsifal Mosaic (Ludlum), 1982
Part for a Poisoner (Carnac, as Lorac), 1948
Part for a Policeman (Creasey), 1970
Part of Virtue (Lewis), 1975
Parting Breath (Aird), 1977
Partisans (MacLean), 1982
Partners (W. Harrington), 1980
Partners in Crime (s Christie), 1929
Party at No. 5 (S. Smith), 1954
Party Girl (Albert), 1958
Party in Dolly Creek (Blackstock), 1967
Party Killer (Pentecost), 1985
Party of Eight (Meynell), 1950
Party to Murder (L. White), 1966
Party to Murder (Underwood), 1983
Party Was the Pay-Off (E. Holding), 1952
Pasang Run (Hall, as Trevor), 1962
Pascal, Lieutenant series (Pentecost), from 1954
Pascoe's Ghost (s Hill), 1979
Pasquinado (s J. Fletcher), 1898
Pass Beyond Kashmir (Mather), 1960
Pass the Gravy (E. Gardner, as Fair), 1959
Passage by Night (J. Higgins, as Marlowe), 1964
Passage for One (s Ford, as Frome), 1945
Passage of Arms (Ambler), 1959
Passage to Samoa (Keene), 1958
Passage to Terror (Aarons, as Ronns), 1952
Passenger (Durbridge), 1977
Passenger (Fenwick), 1967
Passenger to Folkestone (J. Fletcher), 1927
Passenger to Frankfurt (Christie), 1970
Passenger to Nowhere (A. Gilbert), 1965
Passers-By (Oppenheim, as Partridge), 1910
Passing of Evil (McShane), 1961
Passing Strange (Aird), 1980
Passing Strange (Sale), 1942
Passion and the Pity (Hall, as Trevor), 1953
Passion in the Park (Hilton), 1986
Passion Murders (Keene), 1955
Passion of Molly T (Sanders), 1984
Passionate (C. Brown), 1959
Passionate Pagan (C. Brown), 1963
Passionate Quest (Oppenheim), 1924
Passport for a Pilgrim (Leasor), 1968

Passport in Suspense (Leasor), 1967
Passport to Oblivion (Leasor), 1964
Passport to Panic (Ambler, as Reed), 1958
Passport to Peril (Leasor), 1966
Passport to Peril (S. Marlowe), 1959
Past All Dishonor (J. Cain), 1946
Past Praying For (Woods), 1968
Past, Present, and Murder (Pentecost), 1982
Past Reckoning (J. Thomson), 1990
Path of Ghosts (B. Knox, as MacLeod), 1971
Path to the Bridge (Cooper), 1958
Patience of a Saint (Greeley), 1987
Patient (Simenon, trans), 1963
Patient in Cabin C (Eberhart), 1983
Patient in Room 18 (Eberhart), 1929
Paton Street Case (Bingham), 1955
Patriot Game (G. Higgins), 1982
Patriot Games (Clancy), 1987
Patriot's Dream (Elizabeth Peters, as Michaels), 1976
Patriotic Murders (Christie), 1941
Patriots (Drummond), 1979
Patriots (Royce), 1988
Pattern (Eberhart), 1937
Pattern for Murder (Prather, as Knight), 1952
Pattern for Panic (Prather), 1954
Pattern for Terror (Pentecost), 1990
Pattern of Murder (Eberhart), 1948
Pattern of Violence (Busby), 1973
Patterns in the Dust (Grant-Adamson), 1985
Patton, Richard series (Ormerod), from 1986
Paul Campenhaye, Specialist in Criminology (s J. Fletcher), 1918
Paulton Plot (Herbert Adams), 1931
Pauper of Park Lane (Le Queux), 1908
Pavilion (Lawrence), 1946
Paw in the Bottle (Chase, as Marshall), 1949
Pawn in Jeopardy (Hall, as Rattray), 1971
Pawned (Packard), 1921
Pawns Count (Oppenheim), 1918
Pay Any Price (Allbeury), 1983
Pay as You Die (Rae, as Crawford), 1971
Pay-Off in Switzerland (B. Knox, as MacLeod), 1977
Pay the Devil (J. Higgins, as Patterson), 1963
Pay-Grab Murders (Chambers, as Chester), 1962
Payment in Blood (George), 1989
Payoff (Carmichael, as Howard), 1976
Payoff for the Banker (Lockridge), 1945
Payola (Keene), 1960
Peace, Charlie series (Barnard), from 1986
Peacock Fan (Keeler), 1941
Peacock Feather Murders (J. Carr, as Dickson), 1937
Peacock House (s Phillpotts), 1926
Peacock of Jewels (Hume), 1910
Pearl-Headed Pin (Vickers, as Durham), 1925
Pearlhanger (Gash), 1985
Pearls Are a Nuisance (s Chandler), 1953
Pearls Before Swine (Allingham), 1945
Peccavi (Hornung), 1900
Peck of Salt (Royce), 1968
Peck, Judge Ephraim series (Derleth), from 1934
Peddler (Prather, as Ring), 1952
Pedigreed Murder Case (J. Fletcher)
Pedley, Fire Marshal Ben series (Sterling), from 1942
Peeper (Estleman), 1989
Peer and the Woman (Oppenheim), 1892
Pekin Target (Hall), 1981
Peking Duck (Simon), 1979

Peking Target (Hall), 1982
Pel, Inspector Clovis series (Hebden), from 1979
Pellew, Inspector Gregory and Viscount Clymping (Gielgud), from 1958
Penance of Brother Alaric (Graeme), 1930
Penelope (Cunningham), 1965
Penelope of the Polyantha (E. Wallace), 1926
Penguin Pool Murder (Palmer), 1931
Penhallow (Heyer), 1942
Penknife in My Heart (Blake), 1958
Pennies from Hell (Alexander), 1960
Penny Ferry (Boyer), 1984
Penny Murders (L. Black), 1979
Penny series (Moody), from 1984
Pennycross Murders (Procter), 1953
Pennyfeather, Professor A. series (Olsen), from 1945
Penrose Mystery (Freeman), 1936
Penthouse (Hall, as Trevor), 1983
Penthouse Passout (C. Brown), 1953(?)
People from the Sea (Johnston), 1979
People in Glass House (Drummond), 1969
People in Glass Houses (S. Marlowe, as Ridgway), 1961
People of Darkness (Hillerman), 1980
People of the River (s E. Wallace), 1912
People on the Hill (Johnston), 1971
People vs. Withers and Malone (s Palmer, Rice), 1963
People Who Knock on the Door (Highsmith), 1983
People Will Talk (Carnac, as Lorac), 1958
People's Man (Oppenheim), 1914
Pepper Pike (L. Roberts), 1988
Perchance of Death (Linington), 1977
Peregrination 22 (Purser), 1962
Perennial Boarder (P. Taylor), 1941
Perfect Crime (H. Kane), 1961
Perfect Crime, or Two (Monteilhet, trans), 1971
Perfect End (Marshall), 1981
Perfect Fool (Fuller), 1963
Perfect Frame (Ard), 1951
Perfect Gallows (Dickinson), 1988
Perfect Match (McGown), 1983
Perfect Murder (Keating), 1964
Perfect Murder Case (Bush), 1929
Perfect Pigeon (Wormser), 1962
Perfect Spy (le Carré), 1986
Performance (D. Clark), 1985
Perfume of the Lady in Black (Leroux, trans), 1909
Peril! (Horler), 1930
Peril Ahead (Creasey), 1946
Peril at Cranbury Hall (Rhode), 1930
Peril at End House (Christie), 1932
Peril in the North (Dent, as Robeson), 1984
Peril Is My Pay (S. Marlowe), 1960
Peril of Helen Marklove (s Le Queux), 1928
Peril Under the Palms (Beck), 1989
Perilous Country (Creasey), 1949
Perilous Crossways (J. Fletcher), 1917
Perilous Sky (Rutherford), 1955
Period of Evil (Creasey, as Halliday), 1970
Period Stuff (s Yates), 1942
Perish the Thought (Bonett), 1984
Perishable Goods (Yates), 1928
Perkins, Douglas series (Babson), from 1971
Peroni, Achille series (Holme), from 1980
Perris of the Cherry-Trees (J. Fletcher), 1913
Persian Price (Anthony), 1975
Persian Ransom (Anthony), 1975
Personality Surgeon (C. Wilson), 1986

Persons Unknown (Moffat), 1978
Persons Unknown (P. MacDonald), 1931
Persons Unknown (Thayer), 1941
Peruvian Nightmare (Malzberg, as Barry), 1974
Peter Gunn (H. Kane), 1960
Peter's Pence (Cleary), 1974
Peters, Toby series (Kaminsky), from 1977
Pettigrew, Francis series (Hare), from 1942
Pew Group (Oliver), 1980
Phantom City (Dent, as Robeson), 1966
Phantom Clue (Leroux, trans), 1926
Phantom Cottage (Johnston), 1970
Phantom Forward (Horler), 1939
Phantom Gunman (Morland), 1935
Phantom Holiday (Russell), 1974
Phantom Hollow (Verner), 1933
Phantom Lady (C. Brown), 1980
Phantom Lady (Woolrich, as Irish), 1942
Phantom of the Opera (Leroux, trans), 1911
Phantom of the Temple (van Gulik, trans), 1966
Phantom Slayer (Verner, as Steele), 1934
Pharaoh and His Waggons (s Bruce, as Croft-Cooke), 1937
Pharaoh's Ghost (Dent, as Robeson), 1981
Phelan, Sam series (Kyd), from 1946
Philadelphia Blowup (Malzberg, as Barry), 1975
Philadelphia Murder Story (Ford), 1945
Philis series (R. Perry), from 1972
Philosopher's Stone (C. Wilson), 1969
Phoenix from the Ashes (Monteilhet, trans), 1963
Phoenix in the Blood (J. Higgins, as Patterson), 1964
Phoenix Inferno (Malzberg, as Barry), 1975
Phoenix Sings (Cory), 1955
Phone Calls (L. O'Donnell), 1972
Photo-Finish (Marsh), 1980
Photogenic Soprano (Dunnett), 1968
Photographs Have Been Sent to Your Wife (Loraine), 1971
Phreak-Out! (C. Brown), 1973
Phyllis (Cunningham), 1962
Physician, Heal Thyself (Phillpotts), 1935
Pianist Shoots First (Fairlie), 1938
Piano Bird (Kallen), 1984
Pibble, Superintendent James series (Dickinson), from 1968
Piccadilly Murder (Berkeley), 1929
Piccadilly Puzzle (s Hume), 1889
Pick Up Sticks (Lathen), 1970
Pick Up the Pieces (Straker), 1955
Pick Your Victim (McGerr), 1946
Pick-Up on Noon Street (s Chandler), 1952
Pickup (Chase, as Marshall), 1955
Pickup Alley (Aarons, as Ronns), 1957
Picture of Death (Carnac, as Lorac), 1957
Picture of Death (McGirr, as Giles), 1970
Picture of Guilt (M. Innes), 1969
Picture of Millie (Hubbard), 1964
Picture of the Victim (Strange), 1940
Picture of the Year (Egleton), 1987
Picture-Perfect Murders (Chastain), 1987
Pictures in the Dark (Stuart), 1979
Pictures in the Fire (s Collier), 1958
Piece of Resistance (Egleton), 1970
Pieces of Modesty (s P. O'Donnell), 1972
Pig Got Up and Slowly Walked Away (Wainwright, as Ripley), 1971
Pig in a Poke (Thayer), 1948
Pig-Tail Murder (Durbridge), 1969
Pigeon among the Cats (Bell), 1974
Pigeon House (V. Williams), 1926

Pigs Get Fat (Murphy), 1985
Pigskin Bag (Fischer), 1946
Pilgrim of Hate (Ellis Peters), 1984
Pilgrim, Mr. series (Cory), from 1957
Pilgrims Meet Murder (Gribble, as Muir), 1948.
Pilgrim's Rest (Wentworth), 1946
Pillars of Midnight (Hall, as Trevor), 1957
Pilot Error (B. Knox), 1977
Pimlico Plot (McMullen), 1975
Pin to See the Peepshow (Jesse), 1934
Pinaud, Monsieur (Audemars), from 1958
Pinch of Poison (Lockridge), 1941
Pinch of Snuff (Hill), 1978
Pinch of Snuff (Underwood), 1974
Pine, Paul series (Browne), from 1957
Pinehurst (Rhode), 1930
Pink Lady (Dent, as Robeson), 1989
Pink Panther (Albert), 1964
Pink Shop (Hume), 1911
Pink Umbrella (Crane), 1943
Pink, ex-Detective Sergeant Norman series (McShane), from 1965
Pink, Melinda series (Moffat), from 1973
Pinkerton, Miss series (Rinehart), from 1932
Pinkney, Sylvester series (Wills), from 1959
Pint of Murder (MacLeod, as Craig), 1980
Pious Deception (Dunlap), 1989
Pipe Dream (Symons), 1959
Piper on the Mountain (Ellis Peters), 1966
Piper, John series (Carmichael), from 1952
Pipes Are Calling (C. Brown), 1976
Pirate Isle (Dent, as Robeson), 1983
Pirate of the Pacific (Dent, as Robeson), 1967
Pirate's Ghost (Dent, as Robeson), 1971
Piron series (McGirr), from 1966
Pistols for Two (Stein), 1951
Pit in the Garden (Meynell), 1961
Pit-prop Syndicate (Crofts), 1922
Pitt, Charlotte and Thomas series (A. Perry), from 1979
Pitt, Dirk series (Cussler), from 1975
Pitt, Inspector series (Straker), from 1954
Pity for Pamela (Fitt), 1950
Pity Him Afterwards (Westlake), 1964
Pity It Wasn't George (Straker), 1979
Pity the Honest (Lacy), 1964
Place Called Skull (Chance), 1980
Place for a Poisoner (Carnac, as Lorac), 1949
Place for Murder (Lathen), 1963
Place for the Wicked (Hall, as Trevor), 1968
Place of Dragons (Le Queux), 1916
Place of Mists (B. Knox, as MacLeod), 1969
Place to Hide (Anthony), 1987
Plague Court Murders (J. Carr, as Dickson), 1934
Plague of Demons (Creasey, as Ashe), 1976
Plague of Dragons (Tripp, as Brett), 1965
Plague of Silence (Creasey), 1958
Plague of Violence (Pentecost), 1970
Plain Case of Murder (Thayer), 1944
Plain Man (Symons), 1962
Plain Old Man (MacLeod), 1985
Plain Sailing (D. Clark), 1987
Plan B (Himes), 1983
Planetoid 127 (s E. Wallace), 1929
Planning for Murder (Morice), 1990
Plaster Sinners (Watson), 1980
Plastic Nightmare (Neely), 1969
Plate of Red Herrings (Lockridge), 1968

Platinum Cat (Rhode, as Burton), 1938
Play for Keeps (Whittington), 1957
Play for Murder (Creasey, as Deane), 1946
Play It Hard (Brewer), 1964
Play Like You're Dead (Miller, as Masterson), 1967
Play Now—Kill Later (C. Brown), 1966
Playback (Chandler), 1958
Playback (The Gordons), 1955
Players and the Game (Symons), 1972
Players in a Dark Game (Coulter), 1968
Playgirl Wanted (Vickers), 1940
Playground of Death (Hilton), 1981
Playing Safe (Dewhurst), 1985
Playing with Fire (Moody), 1989
Playmates (Parker), 1989
Pleasant Dreams—Nightmares (s Bloch), 1960
Pleasant Grove Murders (J. Vance), 1967
Pleasantries of Old Quong (s T. Burke), 1931
Please Kill My Cousin (Fairlie), 1961
Please Pass the Guilt (Stout), 1973
Pleasure Island (Randisi, as Carter), 1981
Pledge (Dürrenmatt, trans), 1959
Plot (Piper), 1951
Plot Against Roger Rider (Symons), 1973
Plot Counter-Plot (Clarke), 1974
A Plot for Murder (F. Brown), 1949
Plot It Yourself (Stout), 1959
Plotkin, Sylvia and Max Van Larsen series (Baxt), from 1967
Plotters (Caillou), 1960
Plugged Nickle (Campbell), 1988
Plumley Inheritance (Bush), 1926
Plunder of the Sun (Dodge), 1949
Plunder Squad (Westlake, as Stark), 1972
Plunderers (Oppenheim, as Partridge), 1916
Plush-Lined Coffin (C. Brown), 1967
Poacher's Bag (D. Clark), 1980
Pocket Full of Rye (Christie), 1953
Poellenberg Inheritance (Anthony), 1972
Poet and the Lunatic (s Chesterton), 1929
Poetic Justice (Cross), 1970
Poets and Murder (van Gulik, trans), 1968
Poggioli, Dr. series (Stribling), from 1929
Poinciana (Whitney), 1980
Point Blank (Westlake, as Stark), 1967
Point of Murder (Yorke), 1978
Point of Peril (Aarons, as Ronns), 1956
Points and Lines (Matsumoto, trans), 1970
Poirot, Hercule series (Christie), from 1920
Poison (McBain), 1987
Poison (Thayer), 1926
Poison Cupboard (John Burke), 1956
Poison for One (Rhode), 1934
Poison for Teacher (Spain), 1949
Poison in Jest (J. Carr), 1932
Poison in Paradise (Hocking), 1955
Poison in Pimlico (Holt, as Ford), 1950
Poison in Play (Spain), 1946
Poison in the Garden Suburb (Cole), 1929
Poison in the Parish (Kennedy), 1935
Poison in the Pen (Wentworth), 1955
Poison Is a Bitter Brew (Hocking), 1942
Poison Island (Dent, as Robeson), 1971
Poison Ivy (C. Brown), 1965
Poison Ivy (Cheyney), 1937
Poison Jasmine (Clason), 1940
Poison Oracle (Dickinson), 1974
Poison Parsley (Clarke), 1979

Poison People (Haggard), 1978
Poison Shadows (Le Queux), 1927
Poison Summer (Hensley), 1974
Poison Tree (Rae, as Stern), 1978
Poisoned Chalice (Hocking), 1959
Poisoned Chocolates Case (Berkeley), 1929
Poisoned Orchard (Curtiss), 1980
Poisoned Pen (s Reeve), 1911
Poisoned Relations (Simenon, trans), 1950
Poisoned Sleep (Graeme), 1939
Poisoned Web (Clarke), 1979
Poisoner (Verner), 1940
Poisoners (D. Hamilton), 1971
Poisoners (Shearing, as Preedy), 1936
Poisonous Relations (Cannan), 1950
Poisons Unknown (F. Kane), 1953
Pokerface (Corris), 1985
Polar Star (M. Smith), 1989
Polar Treasure (Dent, as Robeson), 1965
Polferry Mystery (P. MacDonald), 1932
Polferry Riddle (P. MacDonald), 1931
Police at the Funeral (Allingham), 1931
Police Blotter (Fish, as Pike), 1965
Police Chief (Ball), 1977
Police Special (McGivern), 1962
Policeman at the Door (Carnac), 1953
Policeman in the Precinct (Carnac, as Lorac), 1949
Policeman's Dread (Creasey), 1962
Policeman's Lot (Linington), 1968
Policeman's Lot (s Wade), 1933
Policeman's Triumph (Creasey, as Manton), 1948
Political Suicide (Barnard), 1986
Polkadot Murder (Crane), 1951
Pollard, Detective Superintendent Tom series (Lemarchand),
    from 1967
Pollifax, Mrs. Emily series (Gilman), from 1966
Polly Put the Kettle On (J. Fleming), 1952
Pomeroy, Deceased (Bellairs), 1971
Pons, Solar series (Derleth), from 1945
Ponson Case (Crofts), 1921
Pontivy, Papa series (B. Newman), from 1939
Poodle Springs (Chandler, Parker), 1962
Pool (Rinehart), 1952
Pool of Flame (L. Vance), 1909
Pool of Tears (Wainwright), 1977
Poole, Chief Inspector series (Wade), from 1929
Poor Butterfly (Kaminsky), 1990
Poor Harriet (Fenwick), 1957
Poor Man's Shilling (K. Knight), 1947
Poor Old Lady's Dead (Scott), 1976
Poor, Poor Yorick (F. Davis), 1939
Pop Goes the Queen (Miller), 1947
Pop. 1280 (Thompson), 1964
Porcupine Basin (Rutherford), 1981
Pork City (H. Browne), 1988
Porkchoppers (Thomas), 1972
Pornbroker (C. Brown), 1972
Port Angelique (Jessup), 1961
Port of Light (Serafin), 1987
Port of London Murders (Bell), 1938
Port of Seven Strangers (K. Knight), 1945
Port, Daniel series (Rabe), from 1956
Portcullis Room (V. Williams), 1934
Porter, Appleton "Apple" series (McShane, as Lovell), from
    1980
Portrait in a Dusty Frame (Hebden), 1969
Portrait in Shadows (Wainwright), 1986

Portrait in Smoke (Ballinger), 1950
Portrait of a Beautiful Harlot (Carmichael, as Howard), 1966
Portrait of a Dead Heiress (Dewey), 1965
Portrait of a Judge (s Cecil), 1964
Portrait of a Murderer (A. Gilbert, as Meredith), 1933
Portrait of a Scoundrel (Phillpotts), 1938
Portrait of Alison (Durbridge), 1962
Portrait of Jirjohn Cobb (Keeler), 1940
Portrait of Lilith (J. Thomson), 1983
Possessed (C. Brown, as Farr), 1973
Possession (Davies), 1976
Possession (Fremlin), 1969
Post after Post-Mortem (Carnac, as Lorac), 1936
Post Mortem (Carmichael), 1965
Post Mortem (Cullingford), 1953
Post Mortem (Whalley), 1982
Post Office Case (Doris Disney), 1957
Postern of Fate (Christie), 1973
Posthumous Papers (Barnard), 1979
Postman Always Rings Twice (J. Cain), 1934
Postman's Knock (Straker), 1954
Postmark Murder (Eberhart), 1956
Postmaster of Market Deignton (Oppenheim), 1896(?)
Postscript to a Dead Letter (MacKenzie), 1973
Postscript to Nightmare (Olsen, as Hitchens), 1967
Potsdam Murder Plot (B. Newman, as Betteridge), 1947
Potter's Field (Ellis Peters), 1989
Potter, Brock series (Maling), from 1976
Poulter's Passage (McCutchan), 1967
Poverty Bay (Emerson), 1985
Povin, General series (Trenhaile), from 1981
Powder Barrel (Haggard), 1965
Powder Burn (Hiaasen), 1981
Powder, Lieutenant Leroy series (Lewin), from 1976
Power (W. Harrington), 1964
Power and the Glory (Greene), 1940
Power House (Haggard), 1966
Power Killers (Pentecost, as Philips), 1974
Power of the Borgias (Le Queux), 1921
Power of the Bug (Parrish, as Drummond), 1974
Power Play (Murphy), 1979
Power Play (The Gordons), 1965
Power Play (Westlake), 1971
Power Plays (Wilcox), 1979
Power-House (Buchan), 1916
Practice to Deceive (Linington), 1971
Practice to Deceive (Lockridge), 1957
Praed Street Dossier (s Derleth), 1968
Praed Street Papers (s Derleth), 1965
Pray for a Brave Heart (MacInnes), 1955
Pray for a Miracle (K. Knight, as Amos), 1941
Pray Silence (Coles), 1940
Prayer for the Dying (J. Higgins), 1973
Praying Mantis (Monteilhet, trans), 1962
Praying Mantises (Monteilhet, trans), 1962
Preach No More (Lockridge), 1971
Preaching Jim (Donovan), 1919
Predator (York), 1968
Predators (Sauter), 1987
Prelude for War (Charteris), 1938
Prelude to a Certain Midnight (Kersh), 1947
Prelude to Murder (A. Gilbert), 1959
Prelude to Terror (MacInnes), 1978
Premedicated Murder (D. Clark), 1975
Premeditated Murder (Cheyney), 1943
Premier (Simenon, trans), 1961
Premium on Death (Lewis), 1986

Prepare for Action (Creasey), 1942
Prescription for Murder (D. Williams), 1990
Prescription: Murder (Doris Disney), 1953
Presence in an Empty Room (Johnston), 1980
Presence in the House (McShane, as Lovell), 1972
Presenting Moonshine (s Collier), 1941
President Is Dead (Royce), 1988
President Vanishes (Stout), 1934
President's Mystery Story (Van Dine), 1935
Press of Suspects (Garve), 1951
Pressure-Point (Copper), 1983
Preston, Mark series (Chambers), from 1961
Presumed Dead (R. Perry), 1987
Presumed Innocent (Turow), 1987
Presumption of Guilt (Jeffries, as Ashford), 1984
Pretty Lady (Babson), 1973
Pretty Maids all in a Row (Anthea Fraser), 1986
Pretty Miss Murder (Ballard), 1961
Pretty Pink Shroud (Ferrars), 1977
Pretty Sinister (Beeding), 1929
Prey by Dawn (H. Kane), 1965
Prey for Me (Dewey), 1954
Prey to Murder (Cleeves), 1989
Price (G. Newman), 1974
Price of Admiralty (Lowndes), 1915
Price of Murder (J. MacDonald), 1957
Price of Power (Le Queux), 1913
Price of Silence (Pentecost), 1984
Price of Silence (Vickers, as Kyle), 1942
Price Tag for Murder (Sterling, as Dean), 1959
Price You Pay (Wakefield), 1987
Price, Inspector Ronald series (Cannan), from 1950
Price, Tessa Crichton series (Morice), from 1970
Pricking Thumb (Branson), 1942
Pride of Dolphins (Hebden), 1974
Pride of Heroes (Dickinson), 1969
Pride of Pigs (Wainwright), 1973
Pride of Place (McGivern), 1962
Pride of the Peacock (Holt), 1976
Priestly Murders (Granger, as Gash), 1984
Priestly, Dr. Lancelot series (Rhode), from 1926
Priests of the Abomination (Parrish, as Drummond), 1970
Prike, Inspector Leonidas series (Blochman), from 1934
Prillilgirl (Wells), 1924
Primary Target (M. Wallace), 1988
Primary Target (Max Collins), 1987
Prime Targets (Russell), 1985
Primrose, Colonel John series (Ford), from 1934
Prince from Overseas (B. Thomson), 1930
Prince of Darkness (Elizabeth Peters, as Michaels), 1969
Prince of Good Fellows (Barr), 1902
Prince of Plunder (Horler), 1934
Prince of Sinners (Oppenheim), 1903
Prince of the Captivity (Buchan), 1933
Prince Zaleski (s Shiel), 1895
Prince Zaleski and Cummings King Monk (s Shiel), 1977
Princess after Dark (Horler), 1931
Pringle, G.D.H. series (Livingston), from 1985
Print-Out (Copper), 1988
Printer's Error (G. Mitchell), 1939
Prinvest-London (Gielgud), 1965
Priority Murder (Ford), 1943
Priscilla Copperwaite Case (Waugh), 1986
Prison (Simenon, trans), 1969
Prison of Ice (Koontz, as Axton), 1976
Prison-Breakers (s E. Wallace), 1929

Prisoner (Boileau, trans), 1957
Prisoner at the Bar (Jeffries, as Ashford), 1969
Prisoner in the Mask (Wheatley), 1957
Prisoner in the Opal (A. Mason), 1928
Prisoner of Love (Monteilhet, trans), 1965
Prisoner Pleads "Not Guilty" (Thayer), 1953
Prisoner's Base (Fremlin), 1967
Prisoner's Base (Stout), 1952
Prisoner's Friend (Garve), 1962
Prisoner's Plea (Waugh), 1963
Prisoner's Tale (G. Newman), 1977
Private Carter's Crime (Creasey), 1943
Private Eye (C. Adams), 1942
Private Eyeful (H. Kane), 1959
Private Face of Murder (Bonett), 1966
Private Party (Ard), 1953
Private Prosecution (Dewhurst), 1986
Private Sector (Hone), 1971
Private View (M. Innes), 1952
Private Wound (Blake), 1968
Prizzi series (Condon), from 1982
Problem at Pollensa Bay (s Christie), 1943
Problem in Angels (Holton), 1970
Problem in Prague (B. Knox, as MacLeod), 1981
Problem of Cell 13 (s Futrelle), 1918
Problem of the Green Capsule (J. Carr), 1939
Problem of the Wire Cage (J. Carr), 1939
Procane Chronicle (Thomas, as Bleeck), 1972
Proceed to Judgment (Woods), 1979
Proceed with Caution (Rhode), 1937
Process of Elimination (Baxt), 1984
Prodigals of Monte Carlo (Oppenheim), 1926
Professor in Peril (Lejeune), 1987
Professor on the Case (s Futrelle), 1909
Profile of a Murder (King), 1935
Profit Motive (Murphy), 1982
Profiteers (Oppenheim), 1921
Programmed for Death (Gribble), 1973
Progress of a Crime (Symons), 1960
Project for a Revolution in New York (Robbe-Grillet, trans), 1972
Prologue to the Gallows (McGuire), 1936
Promise of Dawn (Punshon), 1921
Promise of Diamonds (Creasey, as Ashe), 1964
Promise of Marriage (Gaboriau, trans), 1883
Promise of Murder (Eberhart), 1961
Promised Land (Parker), 1976
Proof (Francis), 1984
Proof, Counter Proof (Punshon), 1931
Proof of the Pudding (P. Taylor), 1945
Property in Cyprus (B. Knox, as MacLeod), 1970
Property of a Lady (Oliver), 1983
Prophet of Fire (Creasey), 1951
Proposition (McBain), 1955
Prosecutor (Nabb), 1986
Prospect of Vengeance (Price), 1988
Protectors (Haggard), 1972
Protégé (Armstrong), 1970
Protocol for a Kidnapping (Thomas, as Bleeck), 1971
Provenance of Death (McGirr, as Giles), 1966
Provincial Crime (L. Black), 1960
Prudence Be Damned (McMullen), 1978
Prussian Blue (Hocking), 1947
Prye, Dr. Paul series (Millar), from 1941
Prynter's Devil (Wainwright), 1970
Psychic Trap (Chance), 1986
Psycho (Bloch), 1959

Psycho House (Bloch), 1990
Psycho II (Bloch), 1982
Pub Crawler (Procter), 1956
Public Enemy—No. 1 (Graeme), 1934
Public Murders (Granger), 1980
Publish and Be Killed (Morice), 1986
Publish and Perish (Nevins), 1975
Pull My String (McCutchan), 1973
Pulpit in the Grill Room (s Oppenheim), 1938
Pulse of Danger (Cleary), 1966
Puma, Joe series (Gault), from 1953
Punch and Judy Murder (J. Carr, as Dickson), 1937
Punch with Care (P. Taylor), 1946
Puppet for a Corpse (Simpson), 1983
Puppet on a Chain (MacLean), 1969
Puppets of Fate (Jepson), 1922
Purbright, Inspector series (Watson), from 1958
Purcell Papers (Le Fanu, appendix), 1880
Pure Evil (Dent, as Robeson), 1987
Pure Poison (Waugh), 1966
Puritan (Watson), 1966
Purloining Tiny (Bardin), 1978
Purple Ball (Packard), 1933
Purple Dragon (Dent, as Robeson), 1978
Purple Fern (Hume), 1907
Purple Parrot (Clason), 1937
Purple Place for Dying (J. MacDonald), 1964
Purple Plague (Verner, as Steele), 1934
Purple Sickle Murders (Crofts), 1929
Purple Zombie (Goulart, as Robeson), 1974
Pursuit (Blochman), 1951
Pursuit (Fish), 1978
Pursuit of a Parcel (Wentworth), 1942
Pursuit of Arms (Hammond), 1985
Pusher (McBain), 1956
Puss in Boots (McBain), 1987
Put On by Cunning (Rendell), 1981
Put Out That Star (Carmichael), 1957
Putting the Boot In (Kavanagh), 1985
Puzzle (Thayer), 1923
Puzzle for Fiends (Quentin), 1946
Puzzle for Fools (Quentin), 1936
Puzzle for Pilgrims (Quentin), 1947
Puzzle for Players (Quentin), 1938
Puzzle for Puppets (Quentin), 1944
Puzzle for Wantons (Quentin), 1945
Puzzle in Pearls (Creasey, as Ashe), 1949
Puzzle in Poison (Berkeley), 1938
Puzzle Lock (s Freeman), 1925
Puzzle of the Blue Banderilla (Palmer), 1937
Puzzle of the Briar Pipe (Palmer), 1936
Puzzle of the Happy Hooligan (Palmer), 1941
Puzzle of the Pepper Tree (Palmer), 1933
Puzzle of the Red Stallion (Palmer), 1936
Puzzle of the Silver Persian (Palmer), 1934
Pym, Henry series (Burley), from 1966
Pym, Mrs. Palmyra series (Morland), from 1935
Python Project (Canning), 1967

Q as in Quicksand (Treat), 1947
Q Document (J. Roberts), 1964
"Q" Squad (Verner), 1935
Q.E.D (Thayer), 1922
Qualified Adventurer (Jepson), 1922
Quality of the Informant (Petievich), 1985
Quantrill, Detective Chief Inspector Douglas series (Radley), from 1978

Quarrel with Murder (Creasey, as Halliday), 1951
Quarry (Dürrenmatt, trans), 1961
Quarry (Fish, as Pike), 1964
Quarry series (Max Collins), from 1976
Quarter of Eight (Gibson, as Grant), 1978
Quartet of Three (Tripp), 1965
Quayle, Peter series (Cheyney), from 1943
Queen and the Corpse (Murray), 1949
Queen in Danger (Hall, as Rattray), 1952
Queen of a Day (J. Fletcher), 1907
Queen of Clubs (Footner), 1927
Queen of Hearts (s Collins, appendix), 1859
Queen of Spades (Bailey), 1944
Queen, Ellery and Inspector Richard Queen series (Queen), from 1929
Queen's Crossing (Granger), 1982
Queen's Gate Mystery (Herbert Adams), 1927
Queen's Mate (Herbert Adams), 1931
Queen's Messenger (J. Roberts, as Duncan), 1982
Queen's Pawn (Canning), 1969
Queen's Treasure (s Freeman, as Ashdown), 1975
Queer Face (Verner), 1935
Queer Kind of Death (Baxt), 1966
Quest for K (Curzon), 1986
Quest for the Bogeyman (Lockridge), 1964
Quest of Qui (Dent, as Robeson), 1965
Quest of the Sacred Slipper (Rohmer), 1919
Quest of the Spider (Dent, as Robeson), 1935
Questing Man (Bush, as Home), 1936
Question of Degree (Lewis), 1974
Question of Identity (J. Thomson), 1977
Question of Inheritance (Bell), 1980
Question of Loyalty (Freeling), 1963
Question of Max (Cross), 1976
Question of Murder (A. Gilbert), 1955
Question of Murder (E. Wright), 1988
Question of Principle (Jeffries, as Ashford), 1986
Question of Proof (Blake), 1935
Question of Quarry (Stein, as Bagby), 1981
Question of Queens (M. Innes), 1956
Question of Time (Carmichael), 1958
Question of Time (McCloy), 1971
Queue Here for Murder (Babson), 1980
Quick and the Dead (Queen), 1956
Quick and the Dead (s Starrett), 1965
Quick Brown Fox (Burnett), 1942
Quick Red Fox (J. MacDonald), 1964
Quick Silver (Howard), 1988
Quickness of the Hand (Coulter, as Mayo), 1952
Quicksilver (Pronzini), 1984
Quicksilver Pool (Whitney), 1955
Quidnunc County (Stern), 1961
Quiet American (Greene), 1955
Quiet as a Nun (Antonia Fraser), 1977
Quiet Dogs (J. Gardner), 1982
Quiet Fear (Creasey, as Halliday), 1963
Quiet Horror (s Ellin), 1959
Quiet Killer (MacKenzie), 1968
Quiet Ones (Graeme), 1970
Quiet River (Hubbard), 1978
Quiet Road to Death (Radley), 1984
Quiet Room in Hell (Copper), 1979
Quiet Stranger (Hilton), 1985
Quiet Violence (Doris Disney), 1959
Quiet Woman (Carmichael), 1971
Quiller series (Hall), from 1965
Quin, Sebastian series (Horler), from 1938

St. Ives, Philip series (Thomas, as Bleeck), from 1969
St. Leon (Godwin, appendix), 1799
St. Louis Showdown (Pendleton), 1975
Saint Maker (Holton), 1959
Saint Peter's Fair (Ellis Peters), 1981
St. Peter's Finger (G. Mitchell), 1938
Saint Peter's Plot (Lambert), 1978
Saint series (Charteris), from 1928
Salamander Chill (Lewis), 1988
Salisbury, Arthur and Frank Shearer series (Rae, as Crawford), from 1969
Sallust, Gregory series (Wheatley), from 1934
Sally (Cunningham), 1967
Sally of Scotland Yard (Gribble), 1954
Salt Is Leaving (Priestley), 1966
Salter, Inspector Charlie series (E. Wright), from 1983
Saltmarsh Murders (G. Mitchell), 1932
Salute from a Dead Man (MacKenzie), 1966
Salute to Bazarada (s Rohmer), 1939
Salvage Job (B. Knox, as MacLeod), 1978
Salvation of Pisco Gabar (s Household), 1938
Salzburg Connection (MacInnes), 1968
Samantha (Cunningham), 1967
Same Lie Twice (Goulart), 1973
Samson, Albert series (Lewin), from 1971
Samson, John series (Tripp), from 1973
San Andreas (MacLean), 1984
San Diego Siege (Pendleton), 1972
Sanctuary Club (s Meade), 1900
Sanctuary Isle (B. Knox), 1962
Sanctuary Sparrow (Ellis Peters), 1983
Sand and Satin (Rohmer), 1955
Sand Castles (Freeling), 1989
Sand Dollar (Sims), 1969
Sand Trap (Stuart), 1977
Sandbar Sinister (P. Taylor), 1934
Sanders, Commissioner series (s E. Wallace), from 1911
Sandi, The King-Maker (s E. Wallace), 1922
Sands of Windee (Upfield), 1931
Sands, Inspector series (Millar), from 1942
Sandscreen (Stuart), 1987
Sant of the Secret Service (s Le Queux), 1918
Santorini (MacLean), 1986
Sapphire (A. Mason), 1933
Saratoga Bestiary (Dobyns), 1988
Saratoga Headhunter (Dobyns), 1985
Saratoga Hexameter (Dobyns), 1990
Saratoga Longshot (Dobyns), 1976
Saratoga Mantrap (Sterling, as St. Clare), 1951
Saratoga Snapper (Dobyns), 1986
Saratoga Swimmer (Dobyns), 1983
Sargasso Ogre (Dent, as Robeson), 1967
Sargasso People (Miller), 1961
Satan Black (Dent, as Robeson), 1980
Satan Bug (MacLean, as Stuart), 1962
Satan Comes Across (Crossen, as Barlay), 1945
Satan Is a Woman (Baxt), 1987
Satan Is a Woman (Brewer), 1951
Satan Sampler (Canning), 1979
Satan Touch (Royce), 1978
Satan's Widow (Whittington), 1952
Satanist (Wheatley), 1960
Satan's Angel (Fisher), 1935
Satan's Children (Simenon, trans), 1953
Satan's Mistress (Graeme), 1935
Satan's Sabbath (Pendleton), 1980
Saturday Epic (Rae), 1970

Saturday Night Dead (Rosen), 1988
Saturday Night Town (Whittington), 1956
Saturday of Glory (Serafin), 1979
Saturday Out (Meynell), 1956
Saturday the Rabbi Went Hungry (Kemelman), 1966
Saturn over the Water (Priestley), 1961
Sauce for the Pigeon (Hammond), 1984
Savage Bride (Woolrich), 1950
Savage Day (J. Higgins), 1972
Savage Fire (Pendleton), 1977
Savage Night (Thompson), 1953
Savage Place (Parker), 1981
Savage Salome (C. Brown), 1961
Savage Season (Lansdale), 1990
Savage Sisters (C. Brown), 1976
Savage State of Grace (MacKenzie), 1988
Savage Streets (McGivern), 1959
Savage, Doc series (Dent, as Robeson), from 1935
Savage, Mark series (Payne), from 1982
Savage, Myra series (McShane), from 1961
Savant's Vendetta (Freeman), 1920
Save a Rope (Bailey), 1948
Save the Witness (McGerr), 1949
Save Them for Violence (Fox), 1959
Saving a Rope (Bailey), 1948
Saving Clause (s Sapper), 1927
Saving the Queen (Buckley), 1976
Savings and Loan (McInerny), 1990
Sawyer, Pierre-Ange series (Albert), from 1986
Saxon series (L. Roberts), from 1987
Saxon's Ghost (Fisher), 1969
Say Au R'Voir but Not Goodbye (Shiel), 1933
Say It with Flowers (G. Mitchell), 1960
Say It with Murder (Aarons, as Ronns), 1954
Say No to Murder (Pickard), 1985
Say Yes to Murder (Ballard), 1942
Sayonara, Sweet Amaryllis (Melville), 1983
Scales of Justice (Marsh), 1955
Scalpel (McCoy), 1952
Scandal at High Chimneys (J. Carr), 1959
Scandal at School (Cole), 1935
Scandal-Monger (s Le Queux), 1917
Scapegoat (du Maurier), 1957
Scapegoat (Ørum, trans), 1975
Scarab Murder Case (Van Dine), 1930
Scared to Death (Morice), 1977
Scared to Death (Stein, as Bagby), 1952
Scarf (Bloch), 1947
Scarf (Durbridge), 1960
Scarf of Passion (Bloch), 1948
Scarhaven Keep (J. Fletcher), 1920
Scarlatti Inheritance (Ludlum), 1971
Scarlet and Black (s Green), 1916
Scarlet Bat (Hume), 1905
Scarlet Button (A. Gilbert), 1944
Scarlet Circle (Quentin, as Stagge), 1943
Scarlet Feather (Gruber), 1948
Scarlet Feather (Herbert Adams), 1943
Scarlet Flush (C. Brown), 1963
Scarlet Imperial (Hughes), 1946
Scarlet Imposter (Wheatley), 1940
Scarlet Letters (Queen), 1953
Scarlet Night (D. Davis), 1980
Scarlet Ruse (J. MacDonald), 1973
Scarlet Scissors (Fischer), 1950
Scarlet Seal (Donovan), 1902
Scarlet Sign (Le Queux), 1926

Secret Beyond the Door (King), 1947
Secret Cargo (J. Fletcher), 1913
Secret Corridors (s Pentecost), 1945
Secret Errand (Creasey, as Deane), 1939
Secret Families (J. Gardner), 1989
Secret Fear (O'Farrell), 1954
Secret Fear (s A. Mason), 1940
Secret for a Nightingale (Holt), 1986
Secret Formula (Creasey, as Cooke), 1936
Secret Formula (Le Queux), 1928
Secret Generations (J. Gardner), 1985
Secret Hand (Horler), 1954
Secret Hand (V. Williams, as Valentine), 1918
Secret House (E. Wallace), 1917
Secret House of Death (Rendell), 1968
Secret Houses (J. Gardner), 1987
Secret Isaac (Charyn), 1978
Secret Life of the Ex-Tsaritza (Le Queux), 1918
Secret Lovers (McCarry), 1977
Secret Masters (Kersh), 1953
Secret Meeting (Rhode), 1951
Secret Ministry (Cory), 1951
Secret Mission to Bangkok (F. Mason), 1960
Secret Murder (Creasey, as Ashe), 1940
Secret of Annexe 3 (Dexter), 1986
Secret of Castle Ferrara (C. Brown, as Farr), 1971
Secret of Chimneys (Christie), 1925
Secret of Elizabeth (Caspary), 1979
Secret of High Eldersham (Rhode, as Burton), 1930
Secret of Holm Peel (s Rohmer), 1970
Secret of Moor House (Verner, as Stuart), 1938
Secret of Sarek (Leblanc, trans), 1920
Secret of Secrets (J. Fletcher), 1929
Secret of Seven (Verner, as Stuart), 1932
Secret of Simon Cornell (Carmichael, as Howard), 1969
Secret of Tangles (Gribble), 1933
Secret of the Barbican (s J. Fletcher), 1924
Secret of the Bogey House (Herbert Adams), 1924
Secret of the Chateau (C. Brown, as Farr), 1967
Secret of the Chinese Jar (Hume), 1928
Secret of the Dead (Meade), 1901
Secret of the Doubting Saint (Holton), 1961
Secret of the Lake House (Rhode), 1946
Secret of the Living Skeleton (Chance, as Drummond), 1949
Secret of the Night (Leroux, trans), 1914
Secret of the Pit (Meynell), 1982
Secret of the Sealed Room (Verner, as Stuart), 1935
Secret of the Sixty Steps (Chance, as Drummond), 1951
Secret of the Sky (Dent, as Robeson), 1967
Secret of the Square (Le Queux), 1907
Secret of the Su (Dent, as Robeson), 1984
Secret of the Vault (Verner, as Stuart), 1930
Secret Passage (Hume), 1905
Secret Room of Morgate House (Waugh, as Grandower), 1977
Secret Search (Punshon), 1951
Secret Servant (B. Newman), 1935
Secret Servant (Lyall), 1980
Secret Service (s Le Queux), 1896
Secret Service Man (Horler), 1929
Secret Shame of the Kaiser (Le Queux), 1919
Secret Sin (Le Queux), 1913
Secret Singing (Lewis), 1972
Secret Telephone (s Le Queux), 1920
Secret Tomb (Leblanc, trans), 1923
Secret Vanguard (M. Innes), 1940
Secret War (Daniels), 1964
Secret War (Wheatley), 1937

Secret Way (J. Fletcher), 1903
Secret Ways (MacLean), 1959
Secret Weapon (B. Newman), 1941
Secret Weapon (Beeding), 1940
Secret Whispers (Allbeury), 1981
Secret Woman (Holt), 1970
Secrets Can't Be Helped (Punshon), 1944
Secrets of Harry Bright (Wambaugh), 1985
Secrets of Monte Carlo (s Le Queux), 1899
Secrets of Potsdam (s Le Queux), 1917
Secrets of the Foriegn Office (s Le Queux), 1903
Secrets of the White Tsar (Le Queux), 1919
Seducer (Flora), 1961
Seduction of a Tall Man (Gadney), 1972
Seduction of Peter S (Sanders), 1983
Seductress (C. Brown), 1961
See It Again, Sam (C. Brown), 1979
See-Pah-Poo (Dent, as Robeson), 1990
See Them Die (McBain), 1960
See Who's Dying (Courtier), 1967
See You at the Morgue (Blochman), 1941
See You Later, Alligator (Buckley), 1985
Seed of Doubt (Keene), 1961
Seeds of Hate (Carmichael), 1959
Seeds of Murder (Creasey, as York), 1956
Seeds of Murder (F. Mason), 1930
Seeds of Treason (Allbeury), 1986
Seeing Double (Ferrars), 1962
Seeing Eye (Bell), 1958
Seeing Is Believing (J. Carr, as Dickson), 1941
Seeing Life (Oppenheim, as Partridge), 1919
Seeing Red (Ormerod), 1984
Seek for Justice (Lewis), 1981
Seen in the Shadow (Hume), 1913
Seersucker Whipsaw (Thomas), 1967
Seesaw Millions (van de Wetering), 1988
Segrove, James series (Vickers), from 1923
Seidlitz, Mavis series (C. Brown), from 1955
Seige (Hoyt), 1987
Seize the Dragon (Schorr), 1988
Selby, Doug series (E. Gardner), from 1937
Selby, Pete series (Craig), from 1955
Self-Made Thief (Footner), 1929
Seminar for Murder (B.M. Gill), 1985
Semonov Impulse (Kyle as Meldrum), 1975
Send Another Hearse (Masur), 1960
Send for Mr. Robinson (J. White), 1974
Send No More Roses (Ambler), 1977
Sending (Household), 1980
Sense of Guilt (Simenon, trans), 1955
Sense of Loyalty (Jeffries, as Ashford), 1983
Sense of Reality (s Greene), 1963
Sensitive Case (E. Wright), 1990
Sentence Deferred (Derleth), 1939
Sentence of Death (Creasey, as York), 1950
Sentries (McBain), 1965
Separate Cases (Randisi), 1990
Sequins Lost Their Lustre (Harvester), 1948
Serenade (J. Cain), 1937
Sergeant Death (Coulter, as Mayo), 1968
Sergeant Dunn C.I.D. (s E. Wallace), 1962
Sergeant Nelson of the Guards (Kersh), 1945
Sergeant Sir Peter (s E. Wallace), 1932
Sergeant's Cat (s van de Wetering), 1987
Sergeant, Peter Cutler series (Box), from 1952
Series of Murders (Brett), 1989
Serious Investigation (Linington, as Egan), 1968

Serpent's Tooth (Woods), 1971
Serpentine Murder (Gribble), 1932
Serpents in Paradise (H. Harris), 1975
Servant's Problem (Johns), 1958
Service of All the Dead (Dexter), 1979
Session, Detective Frank series (Waugh), from 1968
Set a Thief (G. Newman), 1986
Set a Thief (Thayer), 1931
Set-Up for Murder (Cheyney), 1950
Settled Out of Court (Cecil), 1959
Settled Out of Court (R. Knox), 1934
Settling of Accounts (C. Hart), 1976
Seven (s J. MacDonald), 1971
Seven Agate Devils (Dent, as Robeson), 1973
Seven Chose Murder (s Vickers, as Durham), 1959
Seven Clues (Verner), 1936
Seven Clues in Search of a Crime (Graeme), 1941
Seven Conundrums (s Oppenheim), 1923
Seven Day Soldiers (Kenrick), 1976
Seven Days Before Dying (Nielsen), 1958
Seven Days to a Killing (Egleton), 1973
Seven Days' Secret (J. Fletcher), 1919
Seven Deadly Sisters (McGerr), 1947
Seven Dials Mystery (Christie), 1929
Seven Died (Homes), 1943
711—Officer Needs Help (Miller, as Masterson), 1965
Seven File (McGivern), 1956
Seven Green Stones (Wentworth), 1933
Seven Keys to Baldpate (Biggers), 1913
Seven Lamps (Verner), 1947
Seven Lean Years (Fremlin), 1961
Seven Lies South (McGivern), 1960
Seven of Hearts (s Leblanc, trans), 1908
Seven-Per-Cent Solution (Meyer), 1974
Seven Pillars to Hell (J. Higgins, as Marlowe), 1963
Seven Seas Murders (F. Mason), 1936
Seven Seats to the Moon (Armstrong), 1969
Seven Secrets (Le Queux), 1903
Seven Silent Men (Behn), 1984
Seven Sins (Rohmer), 1943
Seven Sirens (C. Brown), 1972
Seven Sisters (Ballard), 1962
Seven Slayers (s P. Cain), 1946
Seven Sleepers (Beeding), 1925
Seven Sleepers (Ferrars), 1970
Seven Steps East (Benson), 1959
Seven Suspects (M. Innes), 1937
Seven Tears for Apollo (Whitney), 1963
7.30 Victoria (McGuire), 1935
Seven Thunders (Bruce, as Croft-Cooke), 1955
Seven Times Seven (Creasey), 1932
7 to 12 (Green), 1887
Seven Were Suspect (K. Knight), 1942
Seven Were Veiled (K. Knight), 1937
Seven Who Waited (Derleth), 1943
Seven Witnesses (Hall, as Trevor), 1977
Seventeen Widows of Sans Souci (Armstrong), 1959
Seventeenth Letter (Dorothy Disney), 1945
Seventh (Westlake, as Stark), 1966
Seventh Mask (Slesar), 1969
Seventh Sinner (Elizabeth Peters), 1972
Seventh Station (McInerny), 1977
Seventh Stone (Murphy), 1985
77 Rue Paradis (Brewer), 1955
Several Deaths Later (Gorman), 1988
Severance, Grace series (Scherf), from 1968
Severed Key (Nielsen), 1973

Sex Castle (Lacy), 1963
Sex Clinic (C. Brown), 1971
Sex Marks the Spot (Gribble, as Browning), 1954
Sex Trap (C. Brown), 1975
Sexton Women (Neely), 1972
Shackles (Pronzini), 1988
Shades of Darkness (G. Mitchell, as Torrie), 1970
Shadow (Verner, as Stuart), 1934
Shadow series (Gibson, as Grant), from 1931
Shadow series (Michael Collins, as Grant), from 1964
Shadow and the Stone (Meynell), 1929
Shadow Before (Chance), 1988
Shadow Before (Davies), 1970
Shadow Behind the Curtain (Johnston), 1985
Shadow Called Janet (Chance), 1956
Shadow Falls (Simenon, trans), 1945
Shadow Game (Underwood), 1969
Shadow Guest (Waugh), 1971
Shadow in Pursuit (Chance), 1982
Shadow in the House (Allingham, as March), 1936
Shadow in the Wild (Miller, as Masterson), 1957
Shadow Man (Lutz), 1981
Shadow, Men (Verner), 1962
Shadow of a Broken Man (Chesbro), 1977
Shadow of a Crime (Rhode), 1945
Shadow of a Dead Man (Hanshew), 1906
Shadow of a Doubt (Daniels, as Judd), 1961
Shadow of a Doubt (J. Thomson), 1981
Shadow of a Lady (Roth), 1957
Shadow of a Man (Doris Disney), 1965
Shadow of a Man (Hornung), 1901
Shadow of a Past Love (W. Roberts), 1970
Shadow of a Tiger (Michael Collins), 1972
Shadow of Ashlydyat (Wood, appendix), 1863
Shadow of Death (Creasey, as Ashe), 1968
Shadow of Death (Kienzle), 1983
Shadow of Doom (Creasey), 1946
Shadow of Evil (Donovan), 1907
Shadow of Evil (Hall, as Black), 1953
Shadow of Fear (Spicer), 1953
Shadow of Guilt (Quentin), 1959
Shadow of Madness (Pentecost), 1950
Shadow of Murder (Blackstock), 1959
Shadow of Ravenscliffe (J. Fletcher), 1914
Shadow of Shadows (Allbeury), 1982
Shadow of the Killer (Chance), 1974
Shadow of the Knife (H. Kane, as McKay), 1978
Shadow of the Lynx (Holt), 1971
Shadow of the Rope (s Hornung), 1902
Shadow of the Wolf (Freeman), 1925
Shadow of Tyburn Tree (Wheatley), 1948
Shadow on Mockways (Shearing, as Bowen), 1932
Shadow on the Cliff (Rhode, as Burton), 1944
Shadow on the Courtyard (Simenon, trans), 1934
Shadow on the Wall (Bailey), 1934
Shadow on the Window (Stein, as Bagby), 1955
Shadow over Fairholme (Vickers, as Kyle), 1940
Shadow Passes (Phillpotts), 1933
Shadow Play (J. Milne), 1987
Shadow Spy (Luard), 1979
Shadowboxer (Behn), 1969
Shadowed Love (Blackstock, as Allardyce), 1977
Shadowed Millions (Gibson, as Grant), 1976
Shadowed Porch (Deming, as Moor), 1972
Shadowers (D. Hamilton), 1964
Shadows and Dark Places (McShane, as Lovell), 1980
Shadows from the Past (Neely), 1983

Shadows in a Hidden Land (Harvester), 1966
Shadows in the Moonlight (Elizabeth Peters), 1975
Shadows of an Alibi (Rhode), 1949
Shadowtown (Lutz), 1988
Shadowy Third (Page), 1946
Shady Doings (Johns), 1941
Shady Lady (C. Adams), 1955
Shady Lady (C. Brown), 1953(?)
Shaft, John series (Tidyman), from 1970
Shaggy Dog (s F. Brown), 1963
Shake a Crooked Town (Dan Marlowe), 1961
Shake Hands for Ever (Rendell), 1975
Shakedown (Ard, as Kerr), 1952
Shakedown (Gault, as Scott), 1953
Shakedown (Petievich), 1988
Shakedown for Murder (Lacy), 1958
Shaken Leaf (Cory), 1955
Shakeout (Follett), 1975
Shallow Grave (Scott), 1977
Shamelady (Coulter, as Mayo), 1966
Shameless (J. Cain), 1958
Shamus, Your Slip Is Showing (C. Brown), 1955
Shandy, Peter series (MacLeod), from 1978
Shanghai (Marshall), 1979
Shanghai Bund Murders (F. Mason), 1933
Shanghai Jim (s Packard), 1928
Shanghai Surprise (Kenrick), 1986
Shankhill Road Contract (Atlee), 1973
Shanley, Father Joseph and Sammy Golde series (Webb), from 1952
Shannon, John J. series (C. Adams), from 1942
Shape of a Stain (Ferrars), 1942
Shape of Dread (Muller), 1989
Shape of Fear (Pentecost), 1964
Shape of Murder (Straker), 1964
Shape of Terror (Dent, as Robeson), 1982
Shapes of Sleep (Priestley), 1962
Shapiro, Nathan series (Lockridge), from 1956
Shard, Detective Chief Inspector Simon series (McCutchan), from 1974
Shark Run (Canning), 1968
Sharkskin Book (Keeler), 1941
Sharp Rise in Crime (Creasey), 1978
Shattered (Koontz, as Dwyer), 1973
Shattered Eye (Granger), 1982
Shattered Raven (Hoch), 1969
Shattered Silk (Elizabeth Peters, as Michaels), 1986
Shaw, Commander Esmonde series (McCutchan), from 1960
Shaw, Paul series (Michael Collins, as Sadler), from 1970
Shayne, Mike series (Halliday), from 1940
She Asked for It (Berckman), 1969
She Came Back (Wentworth), 1945
She Came in a Flash (Wings), 1988
She Came Too Late (Wings), 1986
She Didn't Like Dying (Morland), 1948
She Died a Lady (J. Carr, as Dickson), 1943
She Died Dancing (Roos), 1957
She Died Laughing (Gribble), 1953
She Died, Of Course (Warriner), 1958
She Fell among Thieves (Yates), 1935
She Painted Her Face (Yates), 1937
She Shall Die (A. Gilbert), 1961
She Shall Have Murder (Ames), 1948
She Shark (Webb, as Farr), 1956
She Vanished in the Dawn (A. Gilbert), 1941
She Walked in Fear (Vickers), 1940
She Walks Alone (McCloy), 1948

She Was a Lady (Charteris), 1931
She Was Only the Sheriff's Daughter (S. Forbes), 1970
She Who Sleeps (Rohmer), 1928
She Woke to Darkness (Halliday), 1954
She Wouldn't Say Who (Ames), 1957
Shear the Black Sheep (Dodge), 1942
Sheep May Safely Graze (Harvester), 1950
Sheep's Clothing (L. Vance), 1915
Sheer Torture (Barnard), 1981
Sheiks and Adders (M. Innes), 1982
She'll Hate Me Tomorrow (Deming), 1963
Shelf Life (D. Clark), 1982
Shell of Death (Blake), 1936
Shellshock (Prather), 1987
Shelter (Meynell), 1970
Sheltering Night (Fisher), 1952
Shem's Demise (Underwood), 1970
Shepherd's Crook (Carnac, as Lorac), 1953
Sheriff of Bombay (Keating), 1984
Sheringham, Roger series (Berkeley), from 1925
Sherlock Holmes Versus Jack the Ripper (Queen), 1967
Shibumi (Trevanian), 1979
Shield for Murder (McGivern), 1951
Shield of Silence (Balmer), 1936
Shilling for Candles (Tey), 1936
Shills Can't Cash Chips (E. Gardner, as Fair), 1961
Ship of Death (Murphy), 1977
Ship of Gold (Leasor), 1984
Shipwrecked (Greene), 1953
Shirley (Cunningham), 1964
Shirt Front (Blackstock), 1977
Shivering Bough (Olsen, as Burke), 1942
Shivering Mountain (Garve, as Somers), 1959
Shivering Sands (Holt), 1969
Shoal Water (Yates), 1940
Shock Corridor (Avallone), 1963
Shock to the System (Brett), 1984
Shock to the System (Brett), 1987
Shock Treatment (Chase), 1959
Shock Value (Murphy), 1983
Shock Wave (D. Davis), 1972
Shock-Wave (Copper), 1973
Shocking Pink Hat (Crane), 1946
Shocking Secret (Roth), 1955
Shockwave (C. Forbes), 1990
Shockwave (Cory), 1964
Shoot (Hall, as Trevor), 1966
Shoot! (B. Newman), 1949
Shoot a Sitting Duck (Alexander), 1955
Shoot It Again (Lacy), 1969
Shoot It Again, Sam (Avallone), 1972
Shoot Me Dacent (Stein), 1951
Shoot the Piano Player (Goodis), 1962
Shoot the Scene (Deming, as Queen), 1966
Shoot the Works (Halliday), 1957
Shoot to Kill (Miller), 1951
Shoot-Out (Copper), 1982
Shooting Gallery (Rae), 1972
Shooting of Dan McGrew (Kenyon), 1972
Shooting Schedule (Murphy), 1989
Shooting Script (Lyall), 1966
Shooting Star (Bloch), 1958
Shore, Jemima series (Antonia Fraser), from 1977
Short Bier (F. Kane), 1960
Short Time to Live (Moffat), 1976
Shortest Way to Hades (Caudwell), 1984
Shot at Dawn (Rhode), 1934

Shot Bolt (Curzon), 1988
Shot in the Arm (Sherwood), 1982
Shot in the Dark (Fairlie), 1932
Shot in the Dark (Ford), 1949
Shot on Location (Nielsen), 1971
Shotgun (McBain), 1969
Shotgun Saturday Night (Crider), 1987
Should Auld Acquaintance (Doris Disney), 1962
Show Must Go On (Verner), 1950
Show of Violence (Woods), 1975
Show Red for Danger (Lockridge), 1960
Shrew Is Dead (S. Smith), 1959
Shriek of Tyres (Rutherford), 1958
Shroud for a Lady (E. Daly), 1956
Shroud for a Nightingale (James), 1971
Shroud for Aquarius (Max Collins), 1985
Shroud for Delilah (Anthea Fraser), 1984
Shroud for Grandmama (Bardin, as Ashe), 1951
Shroud for Jesso (Rabe), 1955
Shroud for Mr. Bundy (Fox), 1952
Shroud for My Sugar (C. Brown), 1955
Shroud for Shylock (F. Davis, as Ransome), 1939
Shroud for Unlac (Courtier), 1958
Shroud of Darkness (Carnac, as Lorac), 1954
Shroud of Fog (W. Roberts), 1970
Shroud Off Her Back (F. Davis, as Ransome), 1953
Shroud Society (Rae, as Crawford), 1969
Shrouded Death (Bailey), 1950
Shrunken Head (Fish), 1963
Shrunken Heads (J. Kellerman), 1985
Shudders and Thrills (s Oppenheim), 1932
Shy Plutocrat (Oppenheim), 1941
Shylock of the River (Hume), 1900
Si-Fan Mysteries (Rohmer), 1917
Siamese Twin Mystery (Queen), 1933
Siberian Road (Harvester), 1976
Sibling (Hall), 1979
Sic Transit Gloria (Kennedy), 1936
Sicilian Heritage (J. Higgins), 1970
Sicilian Uncles (Sciascia, trans), 1986
Sick Heart River (Buchan), 1941
Sick to Death (D. Clark), 1971
Sidel, Isaac series (Charyn), from 1975
Siege of the Villa Lipp (Ambler), 1977
Siegfried Spy (B. Newman), 1940
Sight of Death (Creasey, as York), 1956
Sight Unseen (Rinehart), 1921
Sign of Fear (Derleth), 1935
Sign of Four (Doyle), 1890
Sign of Silence (Le Queux), 1915
Sign of the Seven Sins (Le Queux), 1901
Sign of the Stranger (Le Queux), 1904
Signal for Death (Rhode), 1941
Signal for Invasion (Herbert Adams), 1942
Signet of Death (Gribble), 1934
Silence (Vickers, as Kyle), 1935
Silence for the Murderer (Crofts), 1948
Silence in Court (Wentworth), 1945
Silence in Hanover Close (A. Perry), 1988
Silence Observed (M. Innes), 1961
Silence of Herondale (Aiken), 1964
Silence of the Lambs (Thomas Harris), 1988
Silence of the Night (Ormerod), 1974
Silence, John series (Blackwood), from 1908
Silenced (s Meade), 1904
Silencers (D. Hamilton), 1962
Silent Are the Dead (Coxe), 1942

Silent Bullet (s Reeve), 1912
Silent Cousin (Fenwick), 1962
Silent Death (Gibson, as Grant), 1978
Silent Dust (Fischer), 1950
Silent Hostage (Gainham), 1960
Silent House (Creasey, as Deane), 1947
Silent House (Hume), 1907
Silent House in Pimlico (Hume), 1899
Silent Liars (Underwood), 1970
Silent Partner (Brackett), 1969
Silent Partner (J. Kellerman), 1989
Silent Partner (K. Knight), 1950
Silent Pool (Wentworth), 1954
Silent Salesman (Lewin), 1978
Silent Scream (Michael Collins), 1973
Silent Seven (Gibson, as Grant), 1975
Silent Signal (Hume), 1917
Silent, Silken Shadows (Avallone, as Dalton), 1965
Silent Slayer (Verner, as Stuart), 1929
Silent Speaker (Stout), 1946
Silent Terror (Ellroy), 1986
Silent Thunder (Estleman), 1989
Silent Witness (Coxe), 1973
Silent Witness (Freeman), 1914
Silent Witness (Post), 1930
Silent Witness (Wilcox), 1990
Silent Witness (Yorke), 1972
Silent Witnesses (Strange), 1938
Silent World of Nicholas Quinn (Dexter), 1977
Silhouette (Hall, as Trevor), 1959
Silhouette in Scarlet (Elizabeth Peters), 1983
Silinski, Master Criminal (E. Wallace), 1930
Silk Road (Harvester), 1962
Silk Stocking Murders (Berkeley), 1928
Silk Vendetta (Holt), 1987
Silk, Dorian series (Harvester), from 1956
Silk, Lu series (Chase), from 1968
Silken Baroness (Atlee), 1963
Silken Baroness Contract (Atlee), 1966
Silken Nightmare (C. Brown), 1963
Silver Bears (Erdman), 1975
Silver Bullet (Hume), 1903
Silver City Scandal (Hammond), 1986
Silver Cobweb (Benson), 1955
Silver Dolphin (Johnston), 1979
Silver Eagle (Burnett), 1931
Silver Falcon (Anthony), 1977
Silver Ghost (MacLeod), 1987
Silver Greyhound (B. Newman), 1960
Silver Guilt (Meynell), 1983
Silver Horseshoe (Verner), 1938
Silver Jackass (Gruber, as Boston), 1941
Silver Key (E. Wallace), 1930
Silver Ladies (Erskine), 1951
Silver Leopard (Reilly), 1946
Silver Mistress (P. O'Donnell), 1973
Silver Street (Johnson), 1968
Silver Street Killer (Johnson), 1969
Silver Tombstone (Gruber), 1945
Silver Tombstone Mystery (Gruber), 1959
Silver, Maud series (Wentworth), from 1928
Silverhill (Whitney), 1967
Silversword (Whitney), 1987
Simmons, Bernard series (Lockridge), from 1962
Simon, Grant series (Pentecost), from 1958
Simple Art of Murder (s Chandler), 1950
Simple Case of Ill-Will (Berckman), 1964

Simple Case of Susan (Futrelle), 1908
Simple Pass On (Cannan), 1929
Simple Peter Cradd (Oppenheim), 1931
Simple Way of Poison (Ford), 1937
Simple Way of Poison (Hocking), 1957
Simpson, Arthur Abdel series (Ambler), from 1962
Simpson, Tim series (Malcolm), from 1984
Sin File (F. Davis, as Ransome), 1965
Sin for Me (Brewer), 1967
Sin in Their Blood (Lacy), 1952
Sin of Preaching Jim (Donovan), 1908
Sin That Was His (Packard), 1917
Sine Qua Nun (McInerny, as Quill), 1986
Sinews of War (Phillpotts), 1906
Sinful Stones (Dickinson), 1970
Sinful Woman (J. Cain), 1948
Sinfully Rich (Footner), 1940
Sinfully Yours (C. Brown), 1958(?)
Sing a Dark Song (W. Roberts), 1972
Sing a Song of Cyanide (Morland), 1953
Sing Me a Murder (Nielsen), 1960
Sing Sing Nights (Keeler), 1927
Singapore (Ball), 1986
Singapore Exile Murders (F. Mason), 1939
Singapore Wink (Thomas), 1969
Singing Bone (s Freeman), 1912
Singing Diamonds (s McCloy), 1965
Singing Head (Hume), 1920
Singing in the Shrouds (Marsh), 1958
Singing Sands (Tey), 1952
Singing Stones (Whitney), 1990
Singing Widow (Johns), 1941
Single Death (E. Wright), 1986
Single Hair (Herbert Adams), 1937
Single Ticket to Death (Bellairs), 1967
Single to Hong Kong (Royce), 1969
Singular Case of the Multiple Dead (McShane), 1969
Singular Conspiracy (Perowne), 1974
Sinister Cargo (Hall, as Black), 1951
Sinister Errand (Cheyney), 1945
Sinister Gardens (W. Roberts), 1972
Sinister House (C. Brown, as Farr), 1978
Sinister House (s Verner), 1934
Sinister Lady (Doris Disney), 1962
Sinister Madonna (Rohmer), 1956
Sinister Man (E. Wallace), 1924
Sinister Mark (Thayer), 1923
Sinister Murders (Cheyney), 1957
Sinister Ray (s Dent), 1987
Sinister Stones (Upfield), 1954
Sinkiang Executive (Hall), 1978
Sinner Take All (Miller), 1960
Sinner, You Slay Me! (C. Brown), 1957
Sinners (Aarons), 1953
Sinners (C. Brown), 1963
Sinners and Shrouds (Latimer), 1955
Sinners Beware (s Oppenheim), 1931
Sins of Billy Serene (Ard), 1960
Sins of Séverac Bablon (Rohmer), 1914
Sins of the City (Le Queux), 1905
Sins of the Father (Blackburn), 1979
Sins of the Fathers (Block), 1976
Sins of the Fathers (Rendell), 1970
Sins of Their Father (G. Higgins), 1988
Sion Crossing (Price), 1985
Sir Adam Disappeared (Oppenheim), 1939
Sir John Magill's Last Journey (Crofts), 1930

Sir, You Bastard (G. Newman), 1970
Siren in the Night (Ford), 1943
Siren Song (Hall, as Stone), 1985
Siren Sounds Off (C. Brown), 1958
Sirens Sang of Murder (Caudwell), 1989
Siskiyou (Hoyt), 1984
Siskiyou Two-Step (Hoyt), 1983
Sister Death (Winslow), 1982
Sister Disciple (Le Queux), 1918
Sisters (Littell), 1986
Sisters of the Road (B. Wilson), 1986
Sittaford Mystery (Christie), 1931
Sitting Duck (Stein, as Bagby), 1981
Sitting Ducks (Meek), 1984
Sitting Up Dead (Stein), 1958
Situation Tragedy (Brett), 1981
Situation Vacant (Rhode, as Burton), 1946
Six Against Scotland Yard (Allingham, Berkeley, Crofts, R. Knox, Sayers), 1936
Six Against the Yard (Allingham, Berkeley, Crofts, R. Knox, Sayers), 1936
Six Came to Dinner (Vickers), 1948
Six Days to Death (Jeffries, as Alding), 1975
Six Deadly Dames (s Nebel), 1950
Six Feet Under (Simpson), 1982
Six Green Bottles (Hocking), 1943
600-Pound Gorilla (Campbell), 1987
Six Iron Spiders (P. Taylor), 1942
Six-Letter Word for Death (Moyes), 1983
Six Men Died (Verner), 1965
Six-Mile Face (Harvester, as Gibbs), 1952
Six Murders in the Suburbs (s Vickers, as Durham), 1958
Six Nights of Mystery (s Woolrich, as Irish), 1950
Six Nuns and a Shotgun (Watson), 1975
Six Proud Walkers (Anthea Fraser), 1988
Six Proud Walkers (Beeding), 1928
Six Seconds of Darkness (O. Cohen), 1921
Six Silver Handles (Homes), 1944
Six Times Death (s Woolrich, as Irish), 1948
Six Were Present (Punshon), 1956
Six Who Ran (Crossen, as Chaber), 1964
Sixteenth Stair (Carnac, as Lorac), 1942
Sixth Commandment (Sanders), 1979
Sixth Commandment (Wells), 1927
Sixth Directorate (Hone), 1975
Sixty Days to Live (Wheatley), 1939
69 Babylon Park (Whittington), 1962
Skarratt, Inspector series (J. Fletcher), from 1909
Skeleton at the Feast (Wells), 1931
Skeleton Coast Contract (Atlee), 1968
Skeleton in Every House (Waters, appendix), 1860
Skeleton in Search of a Closet (Ferrars), 1982
Skeleton in Search of a Cupboard (Ferrars), 1982
Skeleton in the Clock (J. Carr, as Dickson), 1948
Skeleton in the Grass (Barnard), 1987
Skeleton Island (G. Mitchell), 1967
Skeleton Key (Offord), 1943
Skeleton Out of the Cupboard (V. Williams), 1946
Skeleton Staff (Ferrars), 1969
Skeleton-in-Waiting (Dickinson), 1989
Skeletons (Sauter), 1990
Skeletons in the Closet (Linington), 1982
Skin Deep (Dickinson), 1968
Skin Deep (Murphy), 1982
Skin Deep (W. Harrington), 1983
Skin for Skin (Rutherford), 1968
Skin o' My Tooth (s Orczy), 1928

Skin Tight (Hiaasen), 1989
Skinflick (Hansen), 1979
Skinner (Rae), 1965
Skinwalkers (Hillerman), 1987
Skirmish (Egleton), 1975
Skuldoggery (Flora), 1967
Skulduggery (C. Hart), 1984
Skulduggery (Marshall), 1979
Skull Beneath the Skin (James), 1982
Skull of the Marquis de Sade (s Bloch), 1965
Skull of the Waltzing Clown (Keeler), 1935
Sky High (M. Gilbert), 1955
Sky Is Falling (Murphy), 1986
Sky-Rocket (Fitt), 1938
Skye Cameron (Whitney), 1957
Skylark Mission (Albert, as MacAlister), 1973
Skyprobe (McCutchan), 1966
Skyrocket Steele (Goulart), 1980
Skytip (Ambler, as Reed), 1950
Slab Happy (Prather), 1958
Slack Tide (Coxe), 1959
Sladd's Evil (McCutchan), 1965
Slade series (Bagley), from 1970
Slade, Superintendent Anthony series (Gribble), from 1929
Slam the Big Door (J. MacDonald), 1960
Slane's Long Shots (s Oppenheim), 1930
Slappey, Forian series (s O. Cohen), from 1928
Slasher (Max Collins), 1977
Slasher (Michael Collins), 1980
Slaughter in Satin (C. Brown), 1960
Slaughter in September (Avallone, as Jason), 1979
Slave Bangle (Leroux, trans), 1925
Slave Junk (Packard), 1927
Slave Safari (Murphy), 1973
Slavers (Jessup, as Telfair), 1961
Slaves of Paris (Gaboriau, trans), 1882
Slay Me a Sinner (Audemars), 1979
Slay Ride (F. Kane), 1950
Slay Ride for a Lady (Whittington), 1950
Slay-Ride (Francis), 1973
Slay the Loose Ladies (Quentin), 1948
Slayer and the Slain (McCloy), 1957
Slayground (Westlake, as Stark), 1971
Sleaze (Morse), 1985
Sleep! (Creasey), 1964
Sleep and His Brother (Dickinson), 1971
Sleep for the Wicked (Carmichael, as Howard), 1955
Sleep Is for the Rich (MacKenzie), 1971
Sleep Long, My Love (Waugh), 1959
Sleep No More (Erskine), 1958
Sleep No More (Sims), 1966
Sleep of Death (Morice), 1982
Sleep of the Unjust (Meynell), 1963
Sleep While I Sing (L. R. Wright), 1986
Sleep with Slander (Olsen, as Hitchens), 1960
Sleep with Strangers (Olsen, as Hitchens), 1955
Sleep with the Devil (Keene), 1954
Sleep Without Dreams (H. Kane), 1958
Sleep, My Pretty One (Carmichael, as Howard), 1958
Sleeper (Dewhurst), 1988
Sleeper (Roth), 1955
Sleepers East (Nebel), 1933
Sleepers of Erin (Gash), 1983
Sleeping Bacchus (Beeding), 1951
Sleeping Beauty (Boileau, trans), 1959
Sleeping Beauty (Macdonald), 1973
Sleeping Beauty Murders (L. O'Donnell), 1967

Sleeping Car Murders (Japrisot, trans), 1967
Sleeping Death (Cole), 1936
Sleeping Dog (Lochte), 1985
Sleeping Dogs (Ferrars), 1960
Sleeping Dogs (Wells), 1929
Sleeping Draught (Herbert Adams), 1951
Sleeping Life (Rendell), 1978
Sleeping Memory (Oppenheim), 1902
Sleeping Mountain (Hebden, as Harris), 1958
Sleeping Murder (Christie), 1976
Sleeping Partner (W. Graham), 1956
Sleeping Sphinx (J. Carr), 1947
Sleepwalker (McCloy), 1974
Sleepy Death (Creasey, as Ashe), 1953
Sleight of Body (McInerny), 1989
Slender Thread (Roth, as Merrill), 1959
Sleuth and the Liar (Sherwood), 1961
Sleuth Hound (Leroux, trans), 1926
Sleuth of St. James's Square (Post), 1920
Sleuth, Satan series (Avallone), from 1974
Slickensides (Hilton), 1987
Slight Mourning (Aird), 1975
Slightly Bitter Taste (Carmichael), 1968
Slippery Ann (Bailey), 1944
Slippery Dick (Herbert Adams), 1954
Slippery Staircase (Carnac, as Lorac), 1938
Sloan, Inspector series (Aird), from 1966
Sloane Square Mystery (Herbert Adams), 1925
Slow Burner (Haggard), 1958
Slow Down the World (Jeffries, as Ashford), 1976
Slow Gallows (Miller, as Masterson), 1979
Slowly, Slowly in the Wind (s Highsmith), 1979
Slowly the Poison (Drummond), 1975
Sly as a Serpent (Creasey, as Halliday), 1967
Smack Man (Demille), 1975
Small Felonies (s Pronzini), 1988
Small Hours of the Morning (Yorke), 1975
Small Masterpiece (Heald), 1982
Small Slain Body (Audemars), 1985
Small Town in Germany (le Carré), 1968
Small World of Murder (Ferrars), 1973
Small, Rabbi David series (Kemelman), from 1964
Smallbone Deceased (M. Gilbert), 1950
Smart Aleck Kill (s Chandler), 1953
Smart Guy (s MacHarg), 1951
Smart Moves (Kaminsky), 1987
Smash and Grab (Morland, as McCall), 1946
Smasher (Powell), 1959
Smashers (Westlake), 1962
Smear Job (J. Mitchell), 1975
Smell of Fear (s Chandler), 1965
Smell of Fear (Sterling, as Dean), 1956
Smell of Money (Head), 1943
Smell of Murder (Van Dine), 1950
Smell of Smoke (Rhode, as Burton), 1959
Smiler with the Knife (Blake), 1938
Smiley, George series (le Carré), from 1961
Smiling Cadaver (Chance), 1987
Smiling Tiger (Offord), 1949
Smiling Willie and the Tiger (Hebden, as Harris), 1974
Smith Conspiracy (Neely), 1972
Smith, Dr. John series (Pentecost), from 1949
Smith, Inspector series (Warriner, as Troy), from 1952
Smith, Jill series (Dunlap), from 1984
Smith, T.B. series (E. Wallace), from 1924
Smith, William Wilbeforce series (Haggard), from 1986
Smithfield Slayer (Bruton), 1965

Smog (Creasey), 1970
Smoke and Mirrors (Elizabeth Peters, as Michaels), 1989
Smoke Detector (E. Wright), 1984
Smoke Without Fire (Ferrars), 1990
Smoked Out (Murphy), 1982
Smokescreen (Francis), 1972
Smokescreen (Allbeury), 1986.
Smoking Mirror (McCloy), 1979
Smooth Face of Evil (Yorke), 1984
Smooth Justice (Underwood), 1979
Snaggletooth (Jepson), 1926
Snail-Watcher (s Highsmith), 1970
Snake (Godey), 1978
Snake (McClure), 1975
Snake (Spillane), 1964
Snake in the Grass (A. Gilbert), 1954
Snake Oil (L. Roberts), 1990
Snake Tattoo (Barnes), 1989
Snakes of St. Cyr (O'Farrell), 1951
Snapdragon Murders (Sturrock, as Healey), 1978
Snapshots (s Robbe-Grillet, trans), 1968
Snare (Moffat), 1987
Snare Andalucian (Stein), 1968
Snare in the Dark (Parrish), 1982
Snare of Serpents (Holt), 1990
Snare of the Hunter (MacInnes), 1974
Snark (DeAndrea), 1985
Snarl of the Beast (C. Daly), 1926
Snatch (Creasey, as Ashe), 1965
Snatch (Graeme), 1976
Snatch (Pronzini), 1971
Snatch an Eye (H. Kane), 1963
Snatched (Mcdonald), 1980
Snatchers (L. White), 1953
Sneed, Inspector Terry series (G. Newman), from 1970
Sniper (Demille), 1974
Sniper (Pentecost), 1965
Sniper (W. Roberts), 1984
Snow Man (Busby), 1987
Snow on the Ben (Stuart), 1961
Snow Tiger (Bagley), 1975
Snow Was Black (Simenon, trans), 1950
Snow White and Rose Red (McBain), 1985
Snow-White Murder (Ford), 1940
Snow-Job (Copper), 1986
Snowball (Allbeury), 1974
Snowbound (Pronzini), 1974
Snowfire (Whitney), 1973
Snowline (Mather), 1973
Snowman (Maling), 1973
So Blue Marble (Hughes), 1940
So Dead My Love! (Whittington), 1953
So Dead My Lovely (Keene), 1959
So Dead the Rose (Crossen, as Chaber), 1959
So Deadly My Love (F. Davis, as Ransome), 1957
So Deadly, Sinner! (C. Brown), 1959
So Dies the Dreamer (Curtiss), 1960
So Evil My Love (Shearing), 1947
So Like Sleep (Healy), 1987
So Long as You Both Shall Live (McBain), 1976
So Lovely She Lies (C. Brown), 1958
So Many Doors (Hocking), 1939
So Many Doors (Meynell), 1933
So Many Doors (Punshon), 1949
So Many Steps to Death (Christie), 1955
So Move the Body (C. Brown), 1973
So Much Blood (Brett), 1976

So Much Blood (Fischer), 1939
So Near and Yet (C. Brown, as Farr), 1967
So Nude, So Dead (McBain, as Marsten), 1956
So Quiet a Death (Morland), 1960
So Rich, So Dead (Brewer), 1951
So Rich, So Lovely, and So Dead (Masur), 1952
So Sharp the Razor (Graeme), 1955
So Soon Done For (Babson), 1979
So Soon to Die (Creasey, as York), 1955
So What Happens To Me? (Chase), 1974
So What Killed the Vampire? (C. Brown), 1966
So Wicked My Love (Fischer), 1954
So Wild a Heart (Johnston, as Jason), 1981
So Young to Burn (Creasey), 1968
So Young to Die (Bardin, as Tree), 1953
So Young, So Cold, So Fair (Creasey), 1958
So Young, So Wicked (Craig), 1957
Sob-Sister Cries Murder (C. Brown), 1955
Sober as a Judge (Cecil), 1958
Social Gangster (s Reeve), 1916
Society Intrigues I Have Known (s Le Queux), 1920
Soft Arms of Death (Kendrick, as Hayward), 1955
Soft Centre (Chase), 1964
Soft-Footed Moor (Royce), 1959
Soft Talkers (Millar), 1957
Soft Touch (J. MacDonald), 1958
Softly Dust the Corpse (Courtier), 1961
Softly in the Night (Crossen, as Chaber), 1963
Solange Stories (s Jesse), 1931
Soldato! (Albert, as Al Conroy), 1972
Soldier No More (Price), 1981
Sole Survivor (Murphy), 1988
Sole Survivor (Vickers), 1951
Solitary Farm (Hume), 1909
Solitary House (Punshon), 1918
Solitary Man (Freemantle, as Winchester), 1980
Solo (J. Higgins), 1980
Solo Blues (Gosling), 1981
Solomon's Vineyard (Latimer), 1941
Solomons Seal (H. Innes), 1980
Solution of a Mystery (J. Fletcher), 1932
Some Avenger, Rise! (Linington, as Egan), 1966
Some Beasts No More (McGirr, as Giles), 1965
Some Buried Caesar (Stout), 1938
Some Dames Are Deadly (Latimer), 1955
Some Die Hard (Albert, as Quarry), 1961
Some Die Running (Daniels), 1960
Some Died Eloquent (Aird), 1979
Some Geese Lay Golden Eggs (Graeme), 1968
Some Lie and Some Die (Rendell), 1973
Some Men and Women (s Lowndes), 1925
Some Must Die (Brewer), 1954
Some Must Watch (F. Davis, as Ransome), 1961
Some Persons Unknown (s Hornung), 1898
Some Poisoned by Their Wives (S. Forbes), 1974
Some Predators Are Male (Tripp), 1985
Some Run Crooked (Hilton), 1978
Some Slips Don't Show (E. Gardner, as Fair), 1957
Some Village Borgia (Courtier), 1971
Some Women Won't Wait (E. Gardner, as Fair), 1953
Somebody at the Door (Postgate), 1943
Somebody Has to Lose (Chambers), 1975
Somebody on the Phone (s Woolrich, as Irish), 1950
Somebody Owes Me Money (Westlake), 1969
Somebody's Done For (Goodis), 1967
Somebody's Sister (Derek Marlowe), 1974
Someday the Rabbi Will Leave (Kemelman), 1985

Someone from the Past (Bennett), 1958
Someone in the House (Elizabeth Peters, as Michaels), 1981
Someone Lying, Someone Dying (John Burke), 1968
Something about Midnight (Olsen), 1950
Something Blue (Armstrong), 1962
Something Burning (Daniels), 1963
Something in the Air (Lathen), 1988
Something Nasty in the Woodshed (A. Gilbert), 1942
Something of the Night (McMullen), 1980
Something the Cat Dragged In (MacLeod), 1983
Something to Hide (Rhode, as Burton), 1953
Something to Hide (s P. MacDonald), 1952
Something up a Sleeve (Lockridge), 1972
Something Wicked (C. Hart), 1988
Something Wicked (Ferrars), 1983
Something Worth Fighting For (Gadney), 1974
Something Wrong (Linington), 1967
Sometime Wife (C. Brown), 1965
Sometimes They Bite (s Block), 1983
Sometimes You Could Die (J. Mitchell), 1985
Somewhere in England (Gadney), 1971
Somewhere in the House (E. Daly), 1946
Somewhere in This City (Procter), 1954
Somewhere in This House (King), 1930
Son (Simenon, trans), 1958
Son of Ishmael (Meade), 1896
Son of Three Fathers (Leroux, trans), 1927
Song in the Morning (Seymour), 1986
Song of Corpus Juris (Hensley), 1974
Song of the Flea (Kersh), 1948
Sons of Satan (Creasey), 1948
Sons of Satan (Le Queux), 1914
Sons of the Wolf (Elizabeth Peters, as Michaels), 1967
Soon She Must Die (Clarke), 1984
Sooper (s E. Wallace), 1984
Sooper series (E. Wallace), from 1927
Sooper's Cases (s Morland), 1943
Sorcerer's House (Verner), 1956
Sorcerers (Hunt, as St. John), 1969
Sorceress of the Strand (s Meade), 1903
Sorry State (Kenyon), 1974
Sorry You've Been Troubled (Cheyney), 1942
Sort of Samurai (Melville), 1981
S.O.S. (Horler), 1934
Soul Scar (Reeve), 1919
Sound Evidence (J. Thomson), 1984
Sound of Dying Roses (Avallone, as de Pre), 1971
Sound of Footsteps (Ford), 1931
Sound of Lightning (Cleary), 1976
Sound of Murder (Bonett), 1970
Sound of Murder (Fearing), 1952
Sound of Murder (Stout), 1965
Sound of Revelry (O. Cohen), 1943
Soundless Years (Bush, as Home), 1951
Sour Apple Tree (Blackburn), 1958
Sour Cream with Everything (Porter), 1966
Sour Lemon Score (Westlake, as Stark), 1969
Source of Fear (Ballinger), 1968
Sourdough Wars (J. Smith), 1984
South by Java Head (MacLean), 1958
South Coast Mystery (Chance, as Drummond), 1949
South Foreland Murder (J. Fletcher), 1930
South of Heaven (Thompson), 1967
South of the Sun (Miller), 1953
South Pacific Affair (Lacy), 1961
South Pole Terror (Dent, as Robeson), 1974
Southarn Folly (Blackstock, as Allardyce), 1957

Sow Death, Reap Death (Pentecost), 1981
Sow the Wind (Doris Disney), 1948
Soyuz Affair (Coulter), 1977
Space, Sam series (Nielsen), from 1971
Spacehawk, Inc (Goulart), 1974
Spade, Sam series (s Hammett), from 1944
Spandau Quid (P. MacDonald, as Fleming), 1923
Spanish Blood (s Chandler), 1946
Spanish Cape Mystery (Queen), 1935
Spanish Duet (Clifford), 1966
Spanish Prisoner (Gruber), 1969
Spanish Steps (McGuire), 1940
Spanking Girls (C. Brown), 1979
Spanner, J.T. series (Chastain), from 1974
Sparkling Cyanide (Christie), 1945
Sparrow, Charlie series (Ardies), from 1971
Spatchcock Plan (McCutchan), 1990
Speak for the Dead (Burns), 1978
Speak for the Dead (Yorke), 1988
Speak Ill of the Dead (Chambers), 1968
Speak Justly of the Dead (Carnac, as Lorac), 1953
Speak No Evil (Eberhart), 1941
Speak of the Devil (E. Holding), 1941
Speaker (Creasey, as Ashe), 1939
Speaker of Mandarin (Rendell), 1983
Speaking Stone (Dent, as Robeson), 1983
Spear Gun Murders (Kendrick), 1961
Spearhead (Driscoll), 1988
Spearhead Death (Procter), 1960
Spears, Inspector Simon series (Gielgud), from 1934
Special Collection (Allbeury), 1975
Special Delivery (Gielgud), 1950
Special Occasions (Curzon), 1981
Specialists (Block), 1969
Speciality of the House (s Ellin), 1967
Specimen Case (s Bramah), 1924
Speck of the Motley (Hume), 1893
Speckled Swan (Gribble, as Muir), 1949
Spectacles of Mr. Cagliostro (Keeler), 1926
Spectral Bride (Shearing), 1942
Spectre in Brown (Herbert Adams), 1953
Speedy Death (G. Mitchell), 1929
Spellbinder (Wilcox), 1981
Spellbound (Beeding), 1945
Spells of Evil (Boileau, trans), 1961
Spend Game (Gash), 1980
Spend the Night (Fisher, as Lane), 1935
Spenser series (Parker), from 1973
Sphere (Crichton), 1987
Spice Route Contract (Atlee), 1973
Spider (Hume), 1910
Spider House (F. Mason), 1932
Spider in the Cup (Shearing), 1934
Spider Lily (Fischer), 1946
Spider-Orchid (Fremlin), 1977
Spider Strikes (M. Innes), 1939
Spider Underground (Royce), 1973
Spider Webs (Millar), 1986
Spider's Eye (Le Queux), 1905
Spider's Torch (V. Williams), 1936
Spiders' Web (Harvester), 1953
Spiderweb (Bloch), 1954
Spies Left! (B. Newman, as Betteridge), 1950
Spies of Peenemünde (B. Newman, as Betteridge), 1958
Spies of the Kaiser (s Le Queux), 1909
Spiked Heel (McBain, as Marsten), 1956
Spill the Jackpot (E. Gardner, as Fair), 1941

Star-Crossed Lover (C. Brown), 1974
Stardust (Parker), 1990
Starfish Affair (Chance), 1974
Staring Man (s Lovesey), 1989
Stark Murder (Thayer), 1939
Stark, Joanna series (Muller), from 1986
Starr Bedford Dies (Morland, as Garnett), 1937
Starrbelow (Brand, as Thompson), 1958
Stars Are Dark (Cheyney), 1943
Stars Give Warning (Ford, as Conrad), 1941
Stars Scream Murder (Reeve), 1936
Stars Spell Death (Quentin, as Stagge), 1939
Start Screaming Murder (Powell), 1962
Starting Gun (Stein, as Bagby), 1948
Startling Crimes and Notorious Criminals (s Donovan), 1908
Starvel Hollow Tragedy (Crofts), 1927
State Department Murders (Aarons, as Ronns), 1950
State of Siege (Ambler), 1956
State Versus Elinor Norton (Rinehart), 1934
State Visit (Egleton), 1976
Stately Home Murder (Aird), 1970
Stately Homicide (Haymon), 1984
State's Evidence (Greenleaf), 1982
Station Wagon Murder (Propper), 1940
Statue (Phillpotts), 1908
Statue and the Lady (Fitt, as Wick), 1950
Stay of Execution (s M. Gilbert), 1971
Steady Boys, Steady (J. Mitchell), 1960
Steaked-Blonde Slave (C. Brown), 1969
Steal Big (L. White), 1960
Stealing Lillian (Kenrick), 1975
Steam Pig (McClure), 1971
Steel Crown (Hume), 1911
Steel Hit (Westlake, as Stark), 1971
Steel Mirror (D. Hamilton), 1948
Steel Palace (Pentecost), 1977
Steel Spring (Wahlöö, trans), 1970
Steeltown Strangler (Keeler), 1950
Steelyard Blues (Timothy Harris), 1972
Steinway Collection (Randisi), 1983
Stench of Poppies (Parrish, as Drummond), 1978
Step in the Dark (Lemarchand), 1976
Step into Quicksand (Treat), 1959
Step on the Stair (Green), 1923
Stepfather (Jay), 1958
Stepford Wives (Levin), 1972
Steps Going Down (Hansen), 1985
Steps in the Dark (Hall, as Black), 1954
Steps to Murder (s King), 1960
Stern, Sandy series (Turow), from 1987
Stevens, Superintendent William and Inspector Pierre Allain series (Graeme), from 1931
Steward (s E. Wallace), 1932
Stick (Leonard), 1983
Sticking Place (Mann), 1974
Stiffs Don't Vote (Homes), 1947
Still Dead (R. Knox), 1934
Still Life with Pistol (Ormerod), 1986
Still No Answer (Thayer), 1958
Still Waters (Carnac, as Lorac), 1949
Stillwatch (M. Clark), 1984
Sting (Le Queux), 1928
Sting of Death (Mann), 1978
Sting of the Honeybee (Parrish), 1978
Stingaree (s Hornung), 1905
Stinger (Hornig), 1990
Stitch in Time (Lathen), 1968

Stockholm Syndicate (C. Forbes), 1981
Stolen Blessings (Sanders), 1989
Stolen Budget (J. Fletcher), 1926
Stolen Death (Gribble, as Grex), 1936
Stolen Formula Mystery (Creasey, as Cooke), 1935
Stolen Home Secretary (Gribble), 1932
Stolen Idols (Oppenheim), 1925
Stolen Like Magic Away (Audemars), 1971
Stolen Souls (s Le Queux), 1895
Stolen Statesman (Gribble), 1932
Stolen Statesman (Le Queux), 1918
Stolen Sweets (Le Queux), 1908
Stolen Woman (Miller), 1950
Stone Angel (Albert), 1986
Stone Baby (Sturrock, as Healey), 1973
Stone Blunts Scissors (Fairlie), 1928
Stone Bull (Whitney), 1977
Stone 588 (G. Browne), 1985
Stone Hawk (Moffat), 1989
Stone Killer (J. Gardner), 1973
Stone Leopard (C. Forbes), 1975
Stone Maiden (Johnston), 1980
Stone Man (Dent, as Robeson), 1976
Stone Roses (Gainham), 1959
Stone, Fleming series (Wells), from 1909
Stoner, Harry series (Valin), from 1980
Stoneware Monkey (Freeman), 1938
Stop at Nothing (Rutherford), 1983
Stop at Nothing (Welcome), 1959
Stop at the Red Light (E. Gardner, as Fair), 1962
Stop Press (M. Innes), 1939
Stop This Man! (Rabe), 1955
Stopover: Tokyo (Marquand), 1957
Stopped Clock (Rogers), 1958
Storey, Rosika series (Footner), from 1925
Stories from the Diary of a Doctor (s Meade), 1894
Storm Against the Wall (Meynell), 1931
Storm Centre (D. Clark), 1986
Storm Island (Follett), 1978
Storm Music (Yates), 1934
Storm South (McCutchan), 1959
Storm Warning (J. Higgins), 1976
Stormlight (Chance), 1966
Stormtide (B. Knox), 1972
Story of Henri Tod (Buckley), 1984
Story of Ivy (Lowndes), 1927
Story That Could Not Be Told (Albrand), 1956.
Story-Teller (Highsmith), 1965
Stowaway (Simenon, trans), 1957
Straight (Francis), 1989
Straight and the Crooked (McShane), 1960
Straight Man (Simon), 1986
Strange and Private War (Lejeune), 1986
Strange Bargain (Whittington), 1959
Strange Bedfellow (Berckman), 1956
Strange Blue Yawl (L. Fletcher), 1964
Strange Boarders of Palace Crescent (Oppenheim), 1934
Strange Case of Dr. Earle (Crofts), 1933
Strange Case of Lucile Cléry (Shearing), 1941
Strange Case of Mr. Jocelyn Thew (Oppenheim), 1919
Strange Case of Mr. Henry Marchmont (J. Fletcher), 1927
Strange Case of Peter the Lett (Simenon, trans), 1933
Strange Conflict (Wheatley), 1941
Strange Countess (E. Wallace), 1925
Strange Crime in Bermuda (E. Holding), 1937
Strange Death of Martin Green (Ford, as Frome), 1931
Strange Disappearance (Green), 1880

Suddenly a Corpse (Masur), 1949
Suddenly a Widow (Coxe), 1956
Suddenly at His Residence (Brand), 1947
Suddenly, At Singapore. . . (G. Black), 1961
Suddenly by Shotgun (Daniels), 1961
Suddenly by Violence (C. Brown), 1959
Suddenly One Night (Roos), 1970
Suddenly While Gardening (Lemarchand), 1978
Sue Me (Murphy), 1986
Suffer! Little Children (Van Greenaway), 1976
Sugar (Brewer), 1959
Sugartown (Estleman), 1984
Suicide Clause (Carmichael), 1966
Suicide Excepted (Hare), 1939
Suicide Kill (Ellroy), 1986
Suicide Most Foul (Sturrock), 1981
Suicide Murders (Engel), 1980
Suicide Notice (Engel), 1980
Suicide Season (Burns), 1987
Suitable for Framing (Atlee, as Phillips), 1949
Sullen Sky Mystery (Bailey), 1935
Sullivan (Rae), 1978
Sullivan's Sting (Sanders), 1990
Sultan's Daughter (Wheatley), 1963
Sulu Sea Murders (F. Mason), 1933
Sumatra Seven Zero (G. Black, as Wynd), 1968
Summer Assassin (Butler, as Melville), 1971
Summer at Raven's Roost (Waugh, as Grandower), 1976
Summer Camp Mystery (Blake), 1940
Summer in December (Paul), 1945
Summer in the Twenties (Dickinson), 1981
Summer of Katya (Trevanian), 1983
Summer of the Dragon (Elizabeth Peters), 1979
Summer School Mystery (Bell), 1950
Summerhouse (Wentworth), 1967
Summit (S. Marlowe), 1970
Summit Chase (Murphy), 1973
Summit Kill (Howard), 1975
Summitt (McGivern), 1982
Summon the Bright Water (Household), 1981
Summons (A. Mason), 1920
Sun Chemist (Davidson), 1976
Sun Is a Witness (Stein), 1940
Sunburst (Cory), 1971
Sunday (Simenon, trans), 1960
Sunday Hangman (McClure), 1977
Sunday Pigeon Murders (Rice), 1942
Sunday the Rabbi Stayed Home (Kemelman), 1969
Sunken Sailor (Moyes), 1961
Sunningdale Mystery (s Christie), 1933
Sunset at Sheba (Hebden, as Harris), 1960
Sunset Law (Hilton), 1982
Sunset over Soho (G. Mitchell), 1943
Sunshine Corpse (Murray), 1954
Sunshine Enemies (Constantine), 1990
Sunstrike (McCutchan), 1979
Sup with the Devil (Warriner, as Troy), 1967
Superintendent's Room (Jeffries, as Ashford), 1965
Surabaya (Fox, as Holmes), 1956
Surakarta (Balmer), 1913
Sure Thing (Murphy), 1988
Sure Thing (Prather), 1975
Surfeit of Lampreys (Marsh), 1941
Surfeit of Suspects (Bellairs), 1966
Surprise, Surprise (s McCloy), 1965
Surprise! Surprise! (s Christie), 1965
Surrender Value (Hilton), 1981

Surrogate (s Parker), 1982
Surrounded (Koontz, as Coffey), 1974
Survival . . . Zero! (Spillane), 1970
Survivor (Oppenheim), 1901
Survivors (H. Innes), 1950
Survivors (Simenon, trans), 1949
Suspect (B.M. Gill), 1981
Suspect (Fairlie), 1930
Suspect (L. R. Wright), 1985
Suspected Four (W. Roberts), 1962
Suspects All (Page), 1948
Suspects-Nine (Punshon), 1939
Suspense (Graeme), 1953
Suspense (Stern), 1959
Suspension of Mercy (Highsmith), 1965
Suspicion Aroused (s Donovan), 1893
Suspicious (Chambers, as Daniels), 1981
Suspicious Characters (Sayers), 1931
Suspicious Circumstances (Quentin), 1957
Suspicious Death (Simpson), 1988
Sutton Papers (Jepson), 1924
Suvarov' Adventure (Kyle), 1974
Swag (Leonard), 1976
Swallow Them Up (Straker), 1977
Swallow's Fall (Wilcox), 1983
Swamp Kill (Whittington, as Harrison), 1951
Swamp Man (Goines), 1974
Swamp War (Caillou), 1973
Swan Dive (Healy), 1988
Swan Song (Crispin), 1947
Swan Song for a Siren (C. Brown), 1955
Swan-Song Betrayed (Bell), 1978
Swastika Hunt (Cory), 1969
S.W.A.T.—Crossfire (Michael Collins, as Lynds), 1975
Swaying Pillars (Ferrars), 1968
Sweeps (Granger), 1980
Sweepstake Murders (Connington), 1931
Sweet Adelaide (Symons), 1980
Sweet and Deadly (P. MacDonald), 1959
Sweet and Low (Lathen), 1974
Sweet Blond Trap (Gault), 1959
Sweet Charlie (H. Kane), 1957
Sweet Danger (Allingham), 1933
Sweet Death, Kind Death (Cross), 1984
Sweet Dreams (Murphy), 1976
Sweet La-la Land (Campbell), 1990
Sweet Night for Murder (Neville), 1959
Sweet Poison (D. Clark), 1970
Sweet Poison (Fitt), 1956
Sweet Reason (Littell), 1974
Sweet Ride (Prather), 1972
Sweet Sister Seduced (Hough), 1968
Sweet Wild Wench (Gault), 1959
Sweet Women Lie (Estleman), 1990
Sweetheart (Coburn), 1985
Sweetheart of the Razors (Cheyney), 1962
Sweetheart, This Is Homicide (C. Brown), 1956
Sweetwater, Caleb series (Green), from 1899
Swell Garrick (Vickers, as Spencer), 1933
Swell-Looking Babe (Thompson), 1954
Swift to Its Close (Warriner, as Troy), 1969
Swift, Loren series (Hornig), from 1984
Swimming Pool (Rinehart), 1952
Swing Away, Climber (G. Carr), 1959
Swing, Brother, Swing (Marsh), 1949
Swing High, Sweet Murder (Courtier), 1962
Swing Low Swing Dead (Gruber), 1964

Swing Low, Sweet Harriet (Baxt), 1967
Swing, Swing Together (Lovesey), 1976
Swinger Who Swung by the Neck (Stein, as Stone), 1970
Swingers (C. Brown), 1980
Swinging Murder (L. Black, as Matthews), 1969
Switch (Leonard), 1978
Swooning Lady (Dent, as Robeson), 1986
Sword of Damocles (Green), 1881
Sword of Fate (Wheatley), 1941
Sword of Harlequin (A. Gilbert, as Keith), 1927
Sword Swallower (Goulart), 1968
Sylvia (Cunningham), 1960
Symbols at Your Door (Anthea Fraser), 1990
Syndicate Girl (F. Kane), 1958

T as in Trapped (Treat), 1947
Table d'Hote (D. Clark), 1977
Table near the Band (s A. Milne), 1950
Table Number Seven (Canning), 1987
Tachí Tree (L. O'Donnell), 1968
Tag Murders (C. Daly), 1930
Tail Job (H. Kane), 1971
Tailor, Soldier, Spy (le Carré), 1974
Taine, Roger series (Household), from 1951
Tainted Man (Wainwright), 1980
Tainted Power (C. Daly), 1931
Tainted Token (K. Knight), 1938
Take a Body (Creasey, as Halliday), 1951
Take a Dark Journey (Erskine), 1965
Take a Murder, Darling (Prather), 1958
Take a Step to Murder (Keene), 1959
Take All You Can Get (Fisher), 1955
Take It Crooked (Beeding), 1932
Take Me Home (Flora), 1959
Take Murder . . . (Wainwright), 1979
Take My Drum to England (Cory), 1971
Take My Face (J. Vance, as Held), 1957
Take My Life (W. Graham), 1947
Take One for Murder (Crossen, as Chaber), 1955
Take the Money and Run (Payne), 1982
Take the War to Washington (Van Greenaway), 1974
Take Two at Bedtime (Allingham), 1950
Take-Over Men (Wainwright), 1969
Taken at the Flood (B. Newman), 1958
Taken at the Flood (Christie), 1948
Takeover (Freemantle, as Evans), 1982
Takeover (Wormser), 1971
Taking of Pelham One Two Three (Godey), 1973
Talbot Odyssey (Demille), 1984
Tale of Tangled Ladies (Chance), 1989
Tale of Two Murders (Ferrars), 1959
Talent for Destruction (Radley), 1982
Talent for Murder (Wainwright), 1967
Tales for a Stormy Night (s D. Davis), 1984
Tales in a Jugular Vein (s Bloch), 1965
Tales of Adventurers (s Household), 1952
Tales of Chinatown (s Rohmer), 1922
Tales of East and West (s Rohmer), 1932
Tales of Espionage (s Hoch), 1989
Tales of Natural and Unnatural Catastrophes (s Highsmith), 1987
Tales of Secret Egypt (s Rohmer), 1918
Tales of Suspense (s Collins, appendix), 1954
Tales of Terror (s Donovan), 1899
Tales of Terror and Mystery (s Doyle), 1922
Tales of the Frightened (s Avallone), 1963
Tales of the Mysterious and Macabre (s Blackwood), 1968

Tales of the Tenements (s Phillpotts), 1910
Tales of the Wolf (Sanders), 1986
Tales of Two Continents (s Barr), 1920
Talisman (Godey), 1976
Talk of the Town (C. Williams), 1958
Talking Clock (Gruber), 1941
Talking Devil (Dent, as Robeson), 1982
Talking God (Hillerman), 1989
Talking to Strange Men (Rendell), 1987
Tall Dolores (Avallone), 1953
Tall, Dark, and Deadly (Masur), 1956
Talleyrand Maxim (J. Fletcher), 1919
Tallis, Roger series (J. Ross, as Rossiter), from 1970
Tallon, Jack series (Ball), from 1977
Tallulah Bankhead Murder Case (Baxt), 1987
Tallyman (B. Knox), 1969
Tamar, Hilary series (Caudwell), from 1981
Tamarind Seed (Anthony), 1971
Taming a Sea-Horse (Parker), 1986
Tan and Sandy Silence (J. MacDonald), 1972
Tancred, Benjamin series (Cole), from 1935
Tangent, Peter series (Sanders), from 1976
Tangled Cord (Lockridge), 1957
Tangled Destinies (Donovan), 1908
Tangled Murders (Stern), 1989
Tangled Web (Blake), 1956
Tanglewood Murder (Kallen), 1980
Tango Briefing (Hall), 1973
Tank of Sacred Eels (Parrish, as Drummond), 1976
Tank of Serpents (Leasor), 1986
Tannahill Tangle (Wells), 1928
Tanner, Evan series (Block), from 1966
Tanner, John Marshall series (Greenleaf), from 1979
Tapestry Room Murder (Wells), 1929
Taps, Colonel Roberts (Harvester, as Gibbs), 1951
Target Five (C. Forbes), 1973
Target for Their Dark Desire (C. Brown), 1966
Target for Tonight (Jessup, as Telfair), 1962
Target for Tragedy (Pentecost, as Philips), 1982
Target in Taffeta (Benson), 1953
Target Manhattan (Garfield, as Mallory), 1975
Target of Opportunity (Byrd), 1988
Target Practice (Meyer), 1974
Target Westminster (B.M. Gill), 1977
Tarnished Angel (Pentecost), 1963
Tarot Spell (W. Roberts), 1970
Tarot's Tower (Butler, as Melville), 1978
Tarry and Be Hanged (Woods), 1969
Tartan Ringers (Gash), 1986
Tartan Sell (Gash), 1986
Taste for Death (James), 1986
Taste for Death (P. O'Donnell), 1969
Taste for Honey (Heard), 1941
Taste for Murder (Heard), 1955
Taste for Violence (Halliday), 1949
Taste of Ashes (H. Browne), 1957
Taste of Fears (Millar), 1950
Taste of Fears (Woods), 1963
Taste of Murder (Cannan), 1951
Taste of Power (Burley), 1966
Taste of Proof (B. Knox), 1965
Taste of Sin (Brewer), 1961
Taste of Terror (Albrand), 1976
Taste of Treason (Maling), 1983
Taste of Treasure (Creasey, as Ashe), 1966
Tattoo Mystery (Le Queux), 1927
Tau Cross Mystery (Connington), 1935

Taurus Trip (Dewey), 1970
Taylor, Mitch series (Treat), from 1945
Tea Tray Murders (Bush), 1934
Tea-Shop in Limehouse (s T. Burke), 1931
Teach Yourself Treachery (John Burke), 1962
Tears of Autumn (McCarry), 1975
Tease (Brewer), 1967
Teddy Bear (Simenon, trans), 1971
Teddy-Boy Mystery (Chance, as Drummond), 1955
Teen-Age Jungle (Whittington), 1958
Teeth of the Dragon (Gibson, as Grant), 1975
Teeth of the Tiger (Leblanc, trans), 1914
Tefuga (Dickinson), 1986
Telefair (Rice), 1942
Telemann Touch (Haggard), 1958
Telephone Call (Rhode), 1948
Tell Her It's Murder (Reilly), 1954
Tell It to the Birds (Chase), 1963
Tell It to the Dead (Davies, as Vardre), 1966
Tell You What I'll Do (Cecil), 1969
Telling of Murder (Rutherford), 1952
Tempering Steel (Jepson), 1949
Tempestuous Petticoat (Barr), 1905
Templar, Simon series (Charteris), from 1928
Temple Dogs (J. Roberts, as Duncan), 1977
Temple Dogs (Murphy), 1989
Temple Tower (Sapper), 1929
Temple, Paul series (Durbridge), from 1938
Tempt a Tigress (C. Brown), 1958(?)
Temptation of Mary Gordon (Horler), 1931
Temptation of Tavernake (Oppenheim), 1913
Temptations of Valerie (Whittington), 1957
Tempting of Tavernake (Oppenheim), 1911
Temptress (C. Brown), 1960
Temptress (Le Queux), 1895
Ten Days' Wonder (Queen), 1948
Ten Grand Tallulah and Temptation (C. Brown), 1957
Ten Holy Terrors (Beeding), 1939
Ten Hours (Keeler), 1934
Ten Little Indians (Christie), 1965
Ten Little Niggers (Christie), 1939
Ten Minutes on a June Morning (s Clifford), 1977
Ten Plus One (McBain), 1963
Ten Star Clues (Punshon), 1941
Ten Steps to the Gallows (Wainwright), 1965
Ten Teacups (J. Carr, as Dickson), 1937
10.30 Folkstone Express (Rohmer)
10:30 from Marseilles (Japrisot, trans), 1963
Ten-Thirty Sharp (Harvester, as Gibbs), 1949
10,000 Days (Royce), 1981
Ten Ton Snake (Dent, as Robeson), 1982
Ten Trails to Tyburn (Graeme), 1944
Ten Were Missing (Allingham), 1959
Ten Words of Poison (Perowne), 1941
Tenant for Death (Hare), 1937
Tenant for the Tomb (A. Gilbert), 1971
Tenants of Malory (Le Fanu, appendix), 1867
Tender Killer (Hough), 1963
Tender Poisoner (Bingham), 1953
Tender to Danger (Ambler, as Reed), 1951
Tender to Moonlight (Ambler, as Reed), 1952
Tennessee Smash (Pendleton), 1978
Tension (Wainwright), 1979
Tenth Commandment (Sanders), 1980
Tenth Interview (Wainwright), 1986
Tenth Life (Lockridge), 1977
Tenth Man (Greene), 1985

Tenth Point (Walsh), 1965
Terhune, Theodore I. series (Graeme), from 1941
Terminal (C. Forbes), 1984
Terminal Man (Crichton), 1972
Terminators (D. Hamilton), 1975
Terminators (Mather), 1971
Terrace Suicide Mystery (Gribble), 1929
Terrell, Frank series (Chase), from 1964
Terrence O'Rourke (L. Vance), 1905
Terrible Door (Sims), 1964
Terrible Hobby of Sir Joseph Londe, Bt (s Oppenheim), 1924
Terrible Night (Cheyney), 1959
Terrible People (E. Wallace), 1926
Terrible Pictures (Sturrock, as Healey), 1967
Terrible Stork (Dent, as Robeson), 1988
Terrible Tide (MacLeod, as Craig), 1983
Terrible Tuesday (Pendleton), 1979
Terribly Wild Flowers (s Kersh), 1962
Terriford Mystery (Lowndes), 1924
Terror (Bloch), 1962
Terror (Creasey), 1962
Terror (E. Wallace), 1929
Terror and the Lonely Widow (Dent, as Robeson), 1989
Terror at Deepcliff (Avallone, as Nile), 1966
Terror by Day (Creasey, as Ashe), 1940
Terror by Twilight (K. Knight), 1942
Terror Comes Creeping (C. Brown), 1959
Terror Comes to Twelvetrees (Horler), 1945
Terror in Rio (Caillou), 1971
Terror in the Navy (Dent, as Robeson), 1969
Terror in the Night (s Bloch), 1958
Terror in the Town (Aarons, as Ronns), 1947
Terror Is My Trade (S. Marlowe), 1958
Terror Keep (E. Wallace), 1927
Terror Lurks in Darkness (Olsen, as Hitchens), 1953
Terror of Lonely Tor (Verner, as Stuart), 1931
Terror of the Air (Le Queux), 1920
Terror of Tongues! (Vickers), 1937
Terror on Broadway (Alexander), 1954
Terror on Duncan Island (C. Brown, as Farr), 1971
Terror on Tip-Toe (Horler), 1939
Terror Squad (Murphy), 1973
Terror Takes 7 (Dent, as Robeson), 1989
Terror Touches Me (S. Forbes), 1966
Terror Tower (Verner), 1935
Terror Trade (Russell, as Lester), 1976
Terror Train (Chance), 1983
Terror Trap (Creasey), 1936
Terror Trap (W. Roberts), 1971
Terror Wears a Smile (Gribble, as Grex), 1962
Terror Wears No Shoes (Dent, as Robeson), 1990
Terrorists (Wahlöö, trans), 1976
Terrorizers (D. Hamilton), 1977
Terror's Cradle (Kyle), 1974
Terrors of the Earth (S. Forbes), 1964
Testament of Caspar Schultz (J. Higgins, as Fallon), 1962
Testimony by Silence (Doris Disney), 1948
Testing Ground (G. Newman), 1987
Tether's End (Allingham), 1958
Tethered Goat (Healy), 1986
Texas by the Tail (Thompson), 1965
Texas Storm (Pendleton), 1974
Thane, Detective Chief Inspector Colin and Phil Moss series (B. Knox), from 1957
Thanet, Detective Inspector Luke series (Simpson), from 1981
Thanks for the Felony (Gribble, as Grex), 1958
That Affair at "The Cedars" (Thayer), 1921

That Affair Next Door (Green), 1897
That Darn Cat (The Gordons), 1966
That Distant Afternoon (Fuller), 1959
That Girl in the Alley (Kelly), 1974
That Great Big Trench Coat in the Sky (McShane, as Lovell), 1988
That Night It Rained (Waugh), 1961
That Royle Girl (Balmer), 1925
That Strange Sylvester Affair (Thayer), 1938
That Summer's Earthquake (Bennett), 1964
That Was Yesterday (Bush, as Home), 1955
That Which Is Crooked (Doris Disney), 1948
That Yew Tree's Shade (Hare), 1954
That's Piracy, My Pet (C. Brown), 1957
That's Your Man, Inspector! (Ford, as Frome), 1934
Thatcher, John Putnam series (Lathen), from 1961
Theban Mysteries (Cross), 1971
Theft of Magna Carta (Creasey), 1973
Theft of the Iron Dogs (Carnac, as Lorac), 1946
Thefts of Nick Velvet (s Hoch), 1978
Their Evil Ways (Wainwright), 1983
Their Man in the White House (Ardies), 1971
Thelma (Caspary), 1952
Then Came the Police (Wills), 1935
Then Came Two Women (Armstrong), 1962
Then Came Violence (Ball), 1980
Then There Were Three (Homes), 1938
Theobald, Kate series (L. Black), from 1969
There Are More Ways of Killing.... (Fitt), 1960
There Are No Ghosts in the Soviet Union (s Hill), 1987
There Are No Spies (Granger), 1986
There Are Thirteen (Beeding), 1946
There Came Both Mist and Snow (M. Innes), 1940
There Goes Death (Creasey, as Ashe), 1942
There Hangs the Knife (Muller), 1988
There Is a Serpent in Eden (Bloch), 1979
There Is a Tide.. (Christie), 1948
There Is No Justice (Lathen, as Dominic), 1971
There Is Something about a Dame (Avallone), 1963
There Lies Your Love (Butler, as Melville), 1965
There Must Be Some Mistake (Babson), 1975
There Sits Death (McGuire), 1933
There Was a Crooked Man (Keene), 1954
There Was a Crooked Man (Roos), 1945
There Was a Little Girl (Dewhurst), 1984
There Was an Old Man (Phillpotts), 1959
There Was an Old Woman (Phillpotts), 1947
There Was an Old Woman (Queen), 1943
There's a Hippie on the Highway (Chase), 1970
There's a Reason for Everything (Punshon), 1945
There's Always a Price Tag (Chase), 1956
There's Always Time to Die (O. Cohen), 1949
There's Always Tomorrow (A. Gilbert, as Meredith), 1941
There's Death in the Cup (Hocking), 1952
There's Nothing to Be Afraid Of (Muller), 1985
There's Something in a Sunday (Muller), 1989
There's Trouble Brewing (Blake), 1937
Thermal Thursday (Pendleton), 1979
These Arrows Point to Death (O'Farrell), 1951
These Men and Women (Horler), 1951
These Small Glories (s Cleary), 1946
These Unlucky Deeds (Stern), 1961
Theta Syndrome (Hall, as Trevor), 1977
They All Ran Away (Aarons, as Ronns), 1955
They Call It Murder (Chambers), 1973
They Came to Baghdad (Christie), 1951
They Came to Kill (Scherf), 1942

They Can Only Hang You Once (s Hammett), 1949
They Can't Hang Caroline (Vickers), 1950
They Die with Their Boots Clean (Kersh), 1941
They Died Twice (Dent, as Robeson), 1981
They Do It with Mirrors (Christie), 1952
They Don't Make Them Like That Any More (Leasor), 1969
They Found Atlantis (Wheatley), 1936
They Found Each Other (Fairlie), 1946
They Found Him Dead (Heyer), 1937
They Hadn't a Clue (M. Harrison, as Downes), 1954
They Hang Them in Gibraltar (Perowne), 1939
They Journey by Night (Ames), 1932
They Kidnapped Stanley Matthews (Gribble), 1950
They Love Not Poison (Woods), 1972
They Never Looked Inside (M. Gilbert), 1948
They Never Say When (Cheyney), 1944
They Rang Up the Police (Cannan), 1939
They Shoot Horses, Don't They? (McCoy), 1935
They Stay for Dinner (Woods), 1980
They Tell No Tales (Coles), 1941
They Tell No Tales (Thayer), 1930
They Thought He Was Dead (Horler), 1949
They Used Dark Forces (Wheatley), 1964
They Walk in Darkness (Verner), 1947
They Watched by Night (Rhode), 1941
They Were Seven (Phillpotts), 1944
They Wouldn't Be Chessmen (A. Mason), 1935
They're Going to Kill Me (K. Knight), 1955
They're Not Home Yet (S. Forbes, as Rydell), 1962
Thicker Than Water (Creasey, as Halliday), 1959
Thicker Than Water (McInerny), 1981
Thief (Bruce, as Croft-Cooke), 1960
Thief in the Night (Creasey, as Manton), 1950
Thief in the Night (E. Wallace), 1928
Thief in the Night (s Hornung), 1905
Thief in the Night (Walsh), 1962
Thief of Time (Hillerman), 1988
Thief of Time (Wainwright), 1978
Thief or Two (Woods), 1977
Thief Who Couldn't Sleep (Block), 1966
Thief Who Painted Sunlight (Thomas, as Bleeck), 1972
Thieftaker (Sturrock), 1972
Thieves' Kitchen (Chance), 1979
Thieves' Nights (Keeler), 1929
Thieves of Enchantment (Audemars), 1956
Thieves' Picnic (Charteris), 1937
Thieves' Wit (Footner), 1918
Thin Air (H. Browne), 1954
Thin Air (Marshall), 1977
Thin Edge of Violence (O'Farrell), 1949
Thin Man (Hammett), 1934
Thin-Spun Life (Hocking), 1960
Thing at the Door (Slesar), 1974
Thing at Their Heels (Phillpotts, as Hext), 1923
Thing That Happens to You (Berckman), 1964
Thing That Pursued (Dent, as Robeson), 1987
Thing to Love (Household), 1963
Things as They Are (Godwin, appendix), 1794
Things Beyond Midnight (s Nolan), 1984
Things Invisible (Reynolds), 1989
Things Men Do (Chase, as Marshall), 1953
Think Fast, Mr. Peters (Kaminsky), 1988
Think of Death (Lockridge), 1947
Thinking Machine series (Futrelle), from 1907
Thinner Than Water (Ferrars), 1981
Thinning the Turkey Herd (Campbell), 1988
Third Arm (Royce), 1980

Third Bullet (J. Carr, as Dickson), 1937
Third Crime Lucky (A. Gilbert), 1959
Third Day (Hayes), 1964
Third Deadly Sin (Sanders), 1981
Third Encounter (Woods), 1963
Third Figure (Wilcox), 1968
Third Girl (Christie), 1966
Third Hour (Household), 1937
Third Key (Verner), 1961
Third Lady (Natsuki, trans), 1987
Third Man (Greene), 1950
Third Murderer (C. Daly), 1931
Third on a Seesaw (Ballard, as MacNeil), 1959
Third Party Risk (Cullingford), 1962
Third Possibility (Jepson), 1965
Third Round (Sapper), 1924
Third Shadow (Avallone, as Nile), 1973
Third Side of the Coin (Clifford), 1965
Third Skin (Bingham), 1954
Third Time Unlucky! (Meynell), 1935
Third Victim (Verner, as Stuart), 1939
Third Victim (Wilcox), 1976
Third Volume (Hume), 1895
Third Woman (Avallone, as de Pre), 1971
Thirsty Evil (Hubbard), 1974
Thirsty Evil (Verner), 1946
13 (Loraine), 1966
Thirteen at Dinner (Christie), 1933
Thirteen Detectives (s Chesterton), 1987
13 for Luck! (s Christie), 1961
13 French Street (Brewer), 1951
Thirteen in a Fog (Graeme), 1940
Thirteen Problems (s Christie), 1932
Thirteen Trumpeters (Meynell), 1973
13 West Street (Brackett), 1962
13 White Tulips (Crane), 1953
Thirteenth Guest (Hume), 1913
13th Hour (Horler), 1928
Thirty Days Hath September (Dorothy Disney), 1942
Thirty Days to Live (A. Gilbert), 1944
Thirty Days' War (Hebden, as Harris), 1986
.38 (Ard), 1952
Thirty-First Bullfinch (Reilly), 1930
Thirty-First Floor (Wahlöö, trans), 1967
31st of February (Symons), 1950
Thirty-First of February (Symons), 1950
30 for a Harry (Hoyt), 1981
"30" Manhattan East (Waugh), 1968
Thirty-Nine Steps (Buchan), 1915
This Crowded Earth, and Ladies' Day (s Bloch), 1968
This Downhill Path (Clarke), 1977
This Drakotny (McCutchan), 1971
This Fortress (Coles), 1942
This Game of Murder (Deming), 1964
This Gun for Hire (Greene), 1936
This House to Let (Le Queux), 1921
This Is for Real (Chase), 1965
This Is Jezebel (Cory), 1952
This Is Murder (Ard), 1954
This Is Murder (E. Gardner, as Kenny), 1935
This Is Murder (Keene), 1948
This Is My Night (Deming), 1961
This Is the Castle (Freeling), 1968
This Is the House (S. Smith), 1945
This Is Your Life (B. Newman), 1963
This Little Measure (Woods), 1964
This Man Did I Kill? (Creasey, as Halliday), 1974

This Man Is Dangerous (Cheyney), 1936
This Man's Doom (Thayer), 1938
This Murder Come to Mind (Ormerod), 1977
This Rough Magic (Stewart), 1964
This Side Murder? (Bonett), 1967
This Suitcase Is Going to Explode (Ardies), 1972
This Sweet Sickness (Highsmith), 1960
This Traitor, Death (Cory), 1952
This Troublesome World (Meade), 1893
This Undesirable Residence (Rhode, as Burton), 1942
This Way for a Shroud (Chase), 1953
This Way Out (Radley), 1989
This Year's Death (Godey), 1953
This'll Kill You (Chambers), 1964
Thistlewood Plot (Sturrock), 1987
Thomas, Mrs. and ex-Detective Inspector John Webber series
    (Oliver), from 1980
Thorn in the Dust (Audemars), 1967
Thorndyke, Dr. John Evelyn series (Freeman), from 1907
Thorne in the Flesh (Curzon, as Petrie), 1971
Thornyhold (Stewart), 1988
Those in Peril (Freeling), 1990
Those Other Days (s Oppenheim), 1912
Those Who Walk Away (Highsmith), 1967
Thou Art the Man (Braddon, appendix), 1894
Thou Shalt Not Kill (Lowndes), 1927
Thou Shell of Death (Blake), 1936
Though I Know She Lies (Woods), 1965
Thousand Coffins Affair (Avallone), 1965
Thousand Deaths of Mr. Small (Kersh), 1950
Thousand Faces of Night (J. Higgins, as Patterson), 1961
Thousand Francs Reward (Gaboriau, trans), 1887
Thousand-Headed Man (Dent, as Robeson), 1964
Thousandth Woman (Hornung), 1913
Threat (Jessup), 1981
Threatening Eye (Grant-Adamson), 1988
Three (Hume), 1921
Three Act Tragedy (Christie), 1935
Three and One Make Five (Jeffries), 1984
Three at the Angel (Procter), 1958
Three at Wolfe's Door (Stout), 1960
Three Beans (Coles), 1957
Three Beds in Manhattan (Simenon, trans), 1964
Three Blind Mice (McBain), 1990
Three Blind Mice (s Christie), 1950
Three Bright Pebbles (Ford), 1938
Three Coffins (J. Carr), 1935
Three-Core Lead (Curzon), 1988
Three-Cornered Halo (Brand), 1957
Three Corpse Trick (Rhode, as Burton), 1944
Three Cousins Die (Rhode), 1959
Three Crimes (Rhode, as Burton), 1931
Three Days for Emeralds (Eberhart), 1988
Three Days in Hong Kong (Crane), 1965
Three Days' Terror (Creasey, as Manton), 1938
Three Days' Terror (J. Fletcher), 1901
Three Dead Men (McGuire), 1931
Three Devils (Dent, as Robeson), 1987
Three Doors to Death (Stout), 1950
Three Eyes (Leblanc, trans), 1921
Three Fears (Quentin, as Stagge), 1949
Three Fishers (Beeding), 1931
Three For Adventure (Creasey, as Halliday), 1937
Three for the Chair (Stout), 1957
Three for the Money (Ballard), 1963
Three Glass Eyes (Le Queux), 1903
Three Gnomes (Verner), 1937

Three Hostages (Buchan), 1924
Three Hunting Horns (Fitt), 1937
Three in a Cell (Bruce, as Croft-Cooke), 1968
Three Inquisitive People (Wheatley), 1940
Three Just Men (E. Wallace), 1925
Three Knaves (Phillpotts), 1912
Three Knots (Le Queux), 1922
Three Layers of Guilt (Jeffries, as Ashford), 1975
Three Masks of Death (Chance), 1970
Three Men Out (Stout), 1954
Three Minus Two (MacKenzie), 1968
Three Oaks Mystery (E. Wallace), 1924
Three of a Kind (J. Cain), 1944
Three of Clubs (V. Williams), 1924
Three of Diamonds (K. Knight), 1953
Three of Hearts (J. Cain), 1949
Three of Spades (Chase), 1974
Three-Pipe Problem (Symons), 1975
Three Quick and Five Dead (G. Mitchell), 1968
Three Roads (Macdonald, as Millar), 1948
Three Sentinels (Household), 1972
Three Sisters Flew Home (Fitt), 1936
361 (Westlake), 1962
Three Taps (R. Knox), 1927
Three Thousand Dollars (Green), 1910
Three-Time Losers (Stein, as Bagby), 1958
Three Times a Corpse (Dent, as Robeson), 1990
Three-Toed Pussy (Burley), 1968
Three-Way Split (Brewer), 1960
Three Who Died (Derleth), 1935
Three Who Paid (Verner, as Stuart), 1938
Three Wild Men (Dent, as Robeson), 1984
Three with a Bullet (Lyons), 1985
Three—with Blood (Stein), 1950
Three Witnesses (Stout), 1956
Three Women and a Mystery (Green), 1902
Three Women in Black (Reilly), 1941
Three Worlds of Johnny Handsome (Godey), 1972
Threepence to Marble Arch (McGuire), 1936
Threepersons Hunt (Garfield), 1974
Three's a Crowd (Doris Disney), 1971
Three's a Shroud (Prather), 1957
Threshing-Floor (J. Fletcher), 1905
Threshold (Coulter), 1964
Thrilling-Sweet and Rotten (Stuart), 1983
Through a Glass Darkly (Gielgud), 1963
Through a Glass, Darkly (McCloy), 1950
Through the Eyes of the Judge (Graeme), 1930
Through the Wall (Wentworth), 1950
Thug Executive (Chance), 1967
Thunder at Dawn (Harvester, as Gibbs), 1957
Thunder at Noon (J. Higgins, as Patterson), 1964
Thunder Heights (Whitney), 1960
Thunder in Europe (Creasey), 1936
Thunder on the Right (Stewart), 1957
Thunder-Maker (Creasey), 1976
Thunderball (I. Fleming), 1961
Thursby, Roger series (Cecil), from 1955
Thursday the Rabbi Walked Out (Kemelman), 1978
Thursday Turkey Murders (Rice), 1943
Thursday, Max series (Miller), from 1947
Thursday's Blade (F. Davis), 1947
Thursday's Folly (Pentecost, as Philips), 1967
Thurtell's Crime (Donovan), 1906
Thus Was Adonis Murdered (Caudwell), 1981
Thy Brother's Wife (Greeley), 1982
Tibbet, John series (Payne), from 1969

Tibbett, Henry and Emmy series (Moyes), from 1959
Tibbs, Virgil series (Ball), from 1965
Tick of Death (Lovesey), 1974
Tickencote Treasure (Le Queux), 1903
Ticker-Tape Murder (Propper), 1930
Ticket of Leave (Simenon, trans), 1954
Ticket to Hell (Whittington), 1959
Ticket to Ride (R. Perry), 1973
Ticket to the Boneyard (Block), 1990
Tickets for Death (Halliday), 1941
Ticking Clock (Lockridge), 1962
Ticking Heart (Olsen), 1940
Tickled to Death (s Brett), 1985
Tidal Wave (Simenon, trans), 1954
Tied Up in Tinsel (Marsh), 1972
Tiger among Us (Brackett), 1957
Tiger by the Tail (Chase), 1954
Tiger Claws (Packard), 1928
Tiger Dawn (Jepson), 1929
Tiger in the North (Harvester), 1955
Tiger in the Smoke (Allingham), 1952
Tiger on My Back (The Gordons), 1960
Tiger Snake (Keeler), 1931
Tiger Street (Hall, as Trevor), 1951
Tiger Strikes Again (Wills), 1957
Tiger's Cub (Phillpotts), 1892
Tigers Have Claws (Graeme), 1949
Tigers of Subtopia (s Symons), 1982
Tiger's Wife (Miller), 1951
Tight Circle (Straker), 1970
Tight Corner (Copper), 1976
Tightrope (T. White), 1986
Tightrope for Three (Babson), 1978
Tightrope Men (Bagley), 1973
Tightrope Walker (Gilman), 1979
Tigress (C. Brown), 1961
Tijuana Bible (Goulart), 1990
'Til Death (McBain), 1959
Till Death Do Us Part (J. Carr), 1944
Till It Hurts (Albert, as Quarry), 1960
Tilted Moon (Perowne), 1949
Timber Line (Murphy), 1980
Time and Time Again (B.M. Gill), 1989
Time Bomb (Carmichael, as Howard), 1961
Time Bomb (Chance), 1985
Time Bomb (J. Kellerman), 1990
Time Enough to Die (Rabe), 1959
Time Exposure (Lutz), 1989
Time for Caution (s Cheyney), 1946
Time for Dying (J. Ross), 1989
Time for Frankie Coolin (Granger, as Griffith), 1982
Time for Payment (Kirst, trans), 1976
Time for Pirates (G. Black), 1971
Time for Scandal (Kirst, trans), 1973
Time for Survival (McCutchan), 1966
Time for Truth (Kirst, trans), 1974
Time Is an Ambush (Clifford), 1962
Time of Day (Durbridge), 1959
Time of Fine Weather (Scott), 1984
Time of Predators (Gores), 1969
Time of Temptation (Audemars), 1966
Time of Terror (L. White), 1960
Time of Terror (Pentecost), 1975
Time of the Crime (Verner, as Stuart), 1938
Time of the Hunter's Moon (Holt), 1983
Time Right Deadly (Gainham), 1956
Time Terror (Dent, as Robeson), 1981

Time to Change Hats (Bennett), 1945
Time to Die (Lawrence), 1945
Time to Kill (Household), 1951
Time to Kill (Ormerod), 1974
Time to Murder and Create (Block), 1977
Time to Prey (F. Kane), 1960
Time to Retreat (Cooper), 1963
Time Trial (Murphy), 1983
Time Without Shadows (Allbeury), 1990
Time-Worn Town (J. Fletcher), 1924
Timelock (Cory), 1967
Timid Tycoon (Creasey, as Frazer), 1966
Timothy Files (Sanders), 1987
Timothy's Game (Sanders), 1988
Tin Cop (Campbell, as Clinton), 1983
Tincture of Death (R. Harrison), 1989
Tinkling Symbol (P. Taylor), 1935
Tiny Carteret (Sapper), 1930
Tiny Luttrell (Hornung), 1893
Tipster (Verner), 1949
Titan (Luard, as McVean), 1984
To Any Lengths (Simenon, trans), 1958
To Bed at Noon (Gielgud), 1960
To Bed at Noon (Shearing), 1951
To Cache a Millionaire (Scherf), 1972
To Catch a King (J. Higgins, as Patterson), 1979
To Catch a Thief (Dodge), 1952
To Catch a Thief (Rhode, as Burton), 1934
To Catch a Thief (Rice, as Sanders), 1943
To Catch a Thief (Thayer), 1932
To Cease upon the Midnight (Hocking), 1959
To Die in Beverly Hills (Petievich), 1983
To Die in California (Thornburg), 1973
To Die or Not to Die (H. Kane), 1964
To Each His Own (Sciascia, trans), 1989
To Fear a Painted Devil (Rendell), 1965
To Find a Killer (L. White), 1954
To Hide a Rogue (Walsh), 1964
To Kill a Cat (Burley), 1970
To Kill a Coconut (Moyes), 1977
To Kill a Killer (Creasey, as Hunt), 1960
To Kill a Witch (B. Knox), 1971
To Kill Again (Stout), 1960
To Kill or to Die (Creasey, as York), 1960
To Kiss or Kill (Keene), 1951
To Let, Furnished (Bell), 1952
To Live and Die in L.A. (Petievich), 1984
To Live Forever (J. Vance), 1956
To Love and Be Wise (Tey), 1950
To Make a Killing (J. Thomson), 1982
... To Make an Underworld (J. Fleming), 1976
To Protect the Guilty (Jeffries, as Ashford), 1970
To Run a Little Faster (J. Gardner), 1976
To Save His Life (Roos), 1968
To Study a Long Silence (Clinton-Baddeley), 1972
To the Devil—A Daughter (Wheatley), 1953
To the Minute (s Green), 1916
To Wake the Dead (J. Carr), 1937
To Win the Love He Sought (Oppenheim), 1915
Toast for Tomorrow (Coles), 1941
Tobin series (Gorman), from 1987
Tobin, Colonel series (Caillou), from 1971
Tobin, Inspector series (Hughes), from 1940
Tobin, Mitch series (Westlake, as Coe), from 1966
Todd Dossier (Bloch, as Young), 1969
Todmanhawe Grange (J. Fletcher), 1937
Toff series (Creasey), from 1938

Token (Verner), 1937
Told in the Twilight (s Wood, appendix), 1875
Toll Call (Greenleaf), 1987
Toll for the Brave (J. Higgins, as Patterson), 1971
Toll the Bell for Murder (Bellairs), 1959
Tom Brown's Body (G. Mitchell), 1949
Tom Tiddler's Island (Connington), 1933
Tomb of Ts'in (E. Wallace), 1916
Tombstone Treasure (Hume), 1897
Tomorrow File (Sanders), 1975
Tomorrow I Die (s Spillane), 1984
Tomorrow Is Murder (C. Brown), 1960
Tomorrow's Another Day (Burnett), 1945
Tomorrow's Crimes (s Westlake), 1989
Tomorrow's Ghost (Price), 1979
Tomorrow's Yesterday (Graeme), 1972
Tonight and Tomorrow (Warriner, as Troy), 1957
Too Black for Heaven (Keene), 1959
Too Clever by Half (Jeffries), 1990
Too Clever by Half (Meynell), 1953
Too Close to the Edge (Dunlap), 1987
Too Dangerous to Be Free (Chase), 1951
Too French and Too Deadly (H. Kane), 1955
Too Good to Be True (Creasey, as Halliday), 1969
Too Hot for Hawaii (Dewey), 1960
Too Hot to Handle (I. Fleming), 1957
Too Hot to Handle (Sterling), 1961
Too Hot to Hold (Keene), 1959
Too Hot to Kill (Sterling), 1958
Too Innocent to Kill (Doris Disney), 1957
Too Late for Morning (Crossen, as Foster), 1960
Too Late for Tears (Carmichael), 1973
Too Late for the Funeral (Ormerod), 1977
Too Late to Die (Crider), 1986
Too Late! Too Late! the Maiden Cried (J. Fleming), 1975
Too Long Endured (Thayer), 1950
Too Many Bottles (E. Holding), 1951
Too Many Chiefs (S. Marlowe), 1977
Too Many Clients (Stout), 1960
Too Many Cooks (Stout), 1938
Too Many Crooks (Prather), 1956
Too Many Doctors (Roth), 1963
Too Many Enemies (Haggard), 1972
Too Many Suspects (Rhode), 1945
Too Many Women (Stout), 1947
Too Old a Cat (Murphy), 1987
Too Small for His Shoes (Payne), 1962
Too Soon to Die (Wade), 1953
Too Sweet to Die (Goulart), 1972
Too Tough to Die (Gruber), 1954
Too Young to Die (L. White), 1958
Tooth and the Nail (Ballinger), 1955
Top Assignment (Coxe), 1955
Top Boot (Kennedy), 1950
Top Dog (Hume), 1909
Top of the Heap (E. Gardner, as Fair), 1952
Top Storey Murder (Berkeley), 1931
Toper's End (Cole), 1942
Topkapi (Ambler), 1964
Topless Tulip Caper (Block), 1975
Topology of a Phantom City (Robbe-Grillet, trans), 1977
Topsy and Evil (Baxt), 1968
Tormentors (Bellairs), 1962
Torn Curtain (Wormser), 1966
Torn Letter (Balmer), 1941
Torry, Derek series (J. Gardner), from 1969
Tortuous Trails (s Footner), 1937

Tortured Path (Crossen), 1957
Total Recall (Murphy, Randisi), 1984
Touch (Leonard), 1987
Touch and Go (Wentworth), 1934
Touch Not the Cat (Stewart), 1976
Touch of Darkness (Michael Collins, as Crowe), 1972
Touch of Death (C. Williams), 1954
Touch of Death (Creasey), 1954
Touch of Death (Michael Collins, as Sadler), 1983
Touch of Drama (Cullingford), 1960
Touch of Evil (Miller, as Masterson), 1958
Touch of Jonah (Holton), 1968
Touch of Malice (Wainwright), 1973
Touch of Nutmeg (s Collier), 1943
Touch of Stagefright (Davey), 1960
Touch of the Past (Breen), 1988
Touch of Thunder (Cooper), 1961
Touch the Devil (J. Higgins), 1982
Touch the Lion's Paw (Lambert), 1975
Touchdown (Russell), 1979
Tough Get Going (Stein, as Bagby), 1977
Tough Guys (Spillane), 1969
Tough One to Lose (Kenrick), 1972
Tough Spot for Cupid (s Cheyney), 1945
Tour de Force (Brand), 1955
Tourist Season (Hiaasen), 1986
Tourist Trap (J. Smith), 1986
Tourists Are for Trapping (Babson), 1989
Towards Zero (Christie), 1944
Tower (Hubbard), 1967
Tower Mystery (McGuire), 1932
Tower of Evil (Rhode), 1938
Tower of Terror (Pendleton), 1982
Towers of Fear (C. Brown, as Farr), 1972
Towers of Silence (Hunt, as St. John), 1966
Town Cried Murder (Ford), 1939
Town of Masks (D. Davis), 1952
Town of Shadows (Chance, as Drummond), 1948
Townsend Murder Mystery (O. Cohen), 1933
Toxic Shock (Paretsky), 1988
Toyshop (A. Taylor), 1990
Traces of Brillhart (Brean), 1960
Traces of Mercury (Howard), 1980
Traces of Merrilee (Brean), 1966
Tracked and Taken (s Donovan), 1890
Tracked by a Tattoo (Hume), 1896
Tracked by Wireless (s Le Queux), 1922
Tracked to Doom (Donovan), 1891
Trade (Hallahan), 1981
Trade-Off (G. Newman), 1979
Trademark of a Traitor (K. Knight), 1943
Traditional Murders (Chance), 1983
Tragedy at Draythorpe (Gribble, as Grex), 1931
Tragedy at Freyne (A. Gilbert), 1927
Tragedy at Law (Hare), 1942
Tragedy at Ravensthorpe (Connington), 1927
Tragedy at the Thirteenth Hole (Rhode, as Burton), 1933
Tragedy at the Unicorn (Rhode), 1928
Tragedy in E Flat (Gribble), 1938
Tragedy in the Hollow (Crofts), 1939
Tragedy of Andrea (Oppenheim), 1906
Tragedy of M. (Natsuki, trans), 1987
Tragedy of X (Queen, as Ross), 1932
Tragedy of Y (Queen, as Ross), 1932
Tragedy of Z (Queen, as Ross), 1933
Tragedy on the Line (Rhode), 1931

Tragic Case of the Station Master's Legacy (Chance, as Drummond), 1944
Trail of a Tramp (Albert, as Quarry), 1958
Trail of Ashes (Babson), 1984
Trail of Fire (Curzon), 1987
Trail of the White Knight (Graeme), 1926
Train (Simenon, trans), 1964
Train, Rick series (Fischer), from 1944
Traitor (Horler), 1936
Traitor in London (Hume), 1900
Traitors (Chambers, as Chester), 1964
Traitors (Oppenheim), 1902
Traitor's Blood (Hill), 1983
Traitor's Crime (Jeffries), 1968
Traitors' Doom (Creasey), 1942
Traitor's End (Hunter), 1988
Traitor's Exit (J. Gardner), 1970
Traitor's Gate (E. Wallace), 1927
Traitor's Gate (Harvester), 1952
Traitors' Gate (Wheatley), 1958
Traitor's Mountain (G. Carr, as Styles), 1945
Traitor's Purse (Allingham), 1941
Tramp (E. Wallace), 1965
Tramp in Armour (C. Forbes), 1969
Trance (Lambert), 1981
Transatlantic Trouble (Gribble, as Grex), 1937
Transcendental Murder (Langton), 1964
Transgressors (Thompson), 1961
Transit of the Red Dragon (s Phillpotts), 1903
Translation (S. Marlowe), 1976
Transvection Machine (Hoch), 1971
Trant, Lieutenant Timothy series (Quentin, as Patrick), from 1937
Trap (Donovan), 1911
Trap for a Redhead (Palmer), 1955
Trap for Bellamy (Cheyney), 1941
Trap for Cinderella (Japrisot, trans), 1964
Trap for Fools (Cross), 1989
Trap Line (Hiaasen), 1982
Trap No. 6 (F. Davis, as Ransome), 1971
Trap Spider (Royce), 1974
Trapped (H. Innes), 1940
Trapped (Kendrick, as Hayward), 1952
Traps (Dürrenmatt, trans), 1960
Traps Need Fresh Bait (E. Gardner, as Fair), 1967
Trash Stealer (Potts), 1968
Traveler, Moroni series (Irvine), from 1988
Traveling Corpses (Steel), 1942
Traveller Returns (Wentworth), 1948
Travelling Executioners (B. Newman), 1964
Travelling Horseman (Luard), 1975
Travels (Crichton), 1988
Travels with My Aunt (Greene), 1969
Travers, Ludovic series (Bush), from 1926
Treacherous Road (Harvester), 1966
Treachery in Type (Bell), 1980
Tread Lightly, Angel (F. Davis), 1952
Tread Softly in This Place (Cleeve), 1972
Treason in My Breast (A. Gilbert), 1938
Treasure (Cussler), 1988
Treasure House of Martin Hews (Oppenheim), 1929
Treasure Nets (Fairlie), 1933
Treasure of Israel (Le Queux), 1910
Treasure of the Cosa Nostra (S. Marlowe, as Ridgway), 1966
Treasure Train (s Reeve), 1917
Treasure, Mark series (D. Williams), from 1976
Treasury Alarm (Davey), 1976

Treble Cross (Carmichael, as Howard), 1975
Treble Exposure (Morice), 1987
Tree of Death (Muller), 1983
Tree of Hands (Rendell), 1984
Trembling Earth (Clifford), 1955
Trembling Earth Contract (Atlee), 1969
Trembling Flame (L. Vance), 1931
Trembling Hills (Whitney), 1956
Tremendous Event (Leblanc, trans), 1922
Tremor of Forgery (Highsmith), 1969
Trent, Marla series (H. Kane), from 1959
Trent, Philip series (Bentley), from 1913
Trenton, Richard series (Wood, as Burton), from 1980
Trespassers (Coburn), 1974
Trethowan, Perry series (Barnard), from 1981
Trevayne (Ludlum, as Ryder), 1973
Trevlyn Hold (Wood, appendix), 1864
Trevor, Carole and Max Blythe series (Pentecost, as Philips),
    from 1938
Triad (Lambert), 1987
Trial (W. Harrington), 1970
Trial and Error (Berkeley), 1937
Trial and Terror (Treat), 1949
Trial by Ambush (Ford), 1962
Trial by Desire (Roth, as Ballard), 1960
Trial by Fury (Ferrars), 1989
Trial by Fury (Rice), 1941
Trial by Murder (E. Holding)
Trial by Terror (Lockridge), 1954
Trial by Water (Footner), 1930
Trial from Ambush (Ford), 1962
Trial of Bebe Donge (Simenon, trans), 1952
Trial Run (Francis), 1978
Trials of O'Brien (Fish), 1965
Triangle (T. White), 1982
Triangle of Fear (Chance), 1962
Trick of Time (Hume), 1922
Trick or Treat (Doris Disney), 1955
Tricks (McBain), 1987
Tricks of the Trade (Fish), 1972
Trieste (Cory), 1968
Trigger Mortis (F. Kane), 1958
Trigger-Man (Copper), 1983
Trilogy in Jeopardy (H. Kane), 1955
Trinity in Violence (H. Kane), 1954
Trio for Blunt Instruments (Stout), 1964
Trio in Three Flats (Dewhurst), 1981
Trip Trap (Rathbone), 1972
Triple (Follett), 1979
Triple Cross (Michael Collins, as Carter), 1976
Triple Crown (Breen), 1985
Triple Death (Carnac), 1936
Triple Exposure (Coxe), 1959
Triple Jeopardy (Stout), 1951
Triple Murder (Creasey), 1940
Triple Murder (Wells), 1929
Triple Quest (Punshon), 1955
Triple Terror (s H. Kane), 1958
Triple Threat (Roos), 1949
Triple Zero (J. Fraser, as Whitney), 1971
Tripletrap (Hallahan), 1989
Tripoli Documents (H. Kane), 1976
Triptych (Ballinger), 1971
Tripwire (Garfield), 1973
Triumph of Elaine (Reeve), 1916
Triumph of Evil (Block, as Kavanagh), 1971
Triumphs of Eugène Valmont (s Barr), 1906

Triumphs of Fabian Field, Criminologist (s Donovan), 1912
Triumvirate (Waugh, as Taylor), 1966
Troika (Egleton), 1984
Troika (Harvester), 1962
Trojan Gold (Elizabeth Peters), 1987
Trojan Hearse (Curzon), 1985
Trojan Hearse (Prather), 1964
Trojan Horse (H. Innes), 1940
Trojan Mule (Drummond), 1982
Tropical Heat (Lutz), 1986
Trotsky's Run (Hoyt), 1982
Trotter, Tuddleton series (Keeler), from 1931
Trouble (M. Gilbert), 1987
Trouble! (Graeme), 1929
Trouble at Aquitaine (Livingston), 1985
Trouble at Saxby's (Creasey), 1959
Trouble at Turkey Hill (K. Knight), 1946
Trouble at Wrekin Farm (Bell), 1942
Trouble Follows Me (Macdonald, as Millar), 1946
Trouble in Burma (F. Mason), 1962
Trouble in Hunter Ward (Bell), 1976
Trouble in Paradise (Fish), 1975
Trouble in the Brasses (MacLeod, as Craig), 1989
Trouble in Thor (Armstrong, as Valentine), 1953
Trouble in Triplicate (Stout), 1949
Trouble Is a Dame (C. Brown), 1953(?)
Trouble Is My Business (s Chandler), 1951
Trouble Is My Name (S. Marlowe), 1957
Trouble of Fools (Barnes), 1987
Trouble on Parade (Dent, as Robeson), 1989
Trouble with Murder (Garve, as Bax), 1948
Trouble with Penelope (Sturrock, as Healey), 1972
Trouble with Product X (Aiken), 1966
Trouble with Series Three (Kenyon), 1967
Trouble with Tycoons (Waugh, as Taylor), 1967
Troublecross (Mann), 1973
Troubled Deaths (Jeffries), 1977
Troubled Journey (Lockridge), 1970
Troubled Waters (Lemarchand), 1982
Troublemaker (Hansen), 1975
Troublemaker (Potts), 1972
Trouble-Makers (Fremlin), 1963
Troubleshooter (Dodge), 1971
Trout in the Milk (Lewis), 1986
Trout in the Milk (Underwood), 1971
Troy, Jeff and Haila series (Roos), from 1940
True Crime (Max Collins), 1985
True Detective (Max Collins), 1983
True-Life Adventure (J. Smith), 1985
True Son of the Beast! (C. Brown), 1970
Trust (G. Higgins), 1989
Trust Me on This (Westlake), 1988
Trusted Like the Fox (Chase, as Marshall), 1948
Trusted Like the Fox (Woods), 1964
Truth about Belle Gunness (de la Torre), 1955
Truth About Lord Trench (Verner, as Stuart), 1935
Truth Came Out (Punshon), 1932
Truth Comes Limping (Connington), 1938
Truth of the Matter (Lutz), 1971
Truth with Her Boots On (Cecil), 1974
Try Anything Once (E. Gardner, as Fair), 1962
Try Anything Twice (Cheyney), 1948
Try This One for Size (Chase), 1980
Tryst (Dibdin), 1989
Tryst for a Tragedy (Carnac, as Lorac), 1940
Tsing-Boom! (Freeling), 1969
Tsing-Boum (Freeling), 1969

Uncharted Seas (Wheatley), 1938
Uncle Abner series (Post), from 1918
Uncle Charles Has Locked Himself In (Simenon, trans), 1987
Uncle Paul (Fremlin), 1959
Uncle Sagamore and His Girls (C. Williams), 1959
Uncle Silas (Le Fanu, appendix), 1864
Uncle Target (Lyall), 1988
Uncoffin'd Clay (G. Mitchell), 1980
Uncommon Danger (Ambler), 1937
Uncomplaining Corpses (Halliday), 1940
Unconquerable (MacInnes), 1944
Unconscious Witness (Freeman), 1942
Undaunted (Hebden, as Harris), 1953
Undefeated (Thompson), 1969
Under a Monsoon Cloud (Keating), 1986
Under Contract (Cody), 1986
Under-Cover Man (s Creasey), 1953
Under Dog (s Christie), 1929
Under Dogs (Footner), 1925
Under London (Gielgud), 1933
Under Proof (Cannan), 1934
Under-Secretary (Le Queux), 1902
Under the Dragon Throne (s Meade), 1897
Under the Long Barrow (Beeding, as Haddon), 1939
Under Twelve Stars (Keeler), 1933
Under Two Skies (s Hornung), 1892
Under World (Hill), 1988
Undercover Cat (The Gordons), 1963
Undercover Cat Prowls Again (The Gordons), 1966
Undercover Man (Kirst, trans), 1970
Undercurrent (Pronzini), 1973
Underdog (Burnett), 1957
Underground Cities Contract (Atlee), 1974
Underground Man (Macdonald), 1971
Understrike (J. Gardner), 1965
Understudy to Murder (Gray), 1972
Undertaker Wind (Miller, as Masterson), 1973
Undertow (Cory), 1962
Undetective (Graeme), 1962
Undiplomatic Exit (Sherwood), 1958
Undisclosed Client (s E. Wallace), 1962
Undiscovered Crimes (Waters, appendix), 1862
Undoubted Deed (Davey), 1956
Undressed to Kill (Cheyney), 1959
Une Affaire de Viol (Himes), 1968
Uneasy Is the Grave (Strange), 1950
Uneasy Lies the Dead (Crossen, as Chaber), 1964
Uneasy Street (Miller), 1948
Uneasy Terms (Cheyney), 1946
Unexpected (Hume), 1921
Unexpected Death (Linington, as Shannon), 1970
Unexpected Developments (Lathen, as Dominic), 1984
Unexpected Endings (s E. Wallace), 1980
Unexpected Legacy (Punshon), 1929
Unexpected Night (E. Daly), 1940
Unfair Exchange (Babson), 1974
Unfair Lady (Fairlie), 1931
Unfinished Clue (Heyer), 1934
Unfinished Crime (E. Holding), 1935
Unfinshed Crime (McCloy), 1954
Unforbidden Sin (Vickers), 1926
Unforgiving Wind (Hebden, as Harris), 1963
Unfortunate Murderer (Hull), 1941
Unhanged Man (Hunter), 1984
Unhappy Hooligan (Palmer), 1956
Unhappy Lady (s Cheyney), 1948
Unhappy Returns (Lemarchand), 1977

Unholy Crusade (Wheatley), 1967
Unholy Moses (DeAndrea, as DeGrave), 1985
Unholy Trio (H. Kane), 1967
Unholy Writ (D. Williams), 1976
Unhung Man (Hunter), 1984
Unicorn Murders (J. Carr, as Dickson), 1935
Unidentified Woman (Eberhart), 1943
Uninvited Corpse (Underwood), 1987
Uninvited Guest (Coxe), 1953
Union Bust (Murphy), 1973
Union Club Mysteries (s Asimov), 1983
Unique Hamlet (s Starrett), 1920
Unkindness of Ravens (Rendell), 1985
Unknown Assailant (P. Hamilton), 1955
Unknown Man No. 89 (Leonard), 1977
Unknown Menace (Verner, as Stuart), 1937
Unknown Mission (Creasey, as Deane), 1940
Unknown Quantity (Eberhart), 1953
Unknown Tomorrow (Le Queux), 1910
Unlatched Door (Thayer), 1920
Unlawful Occasions (Cecil), 1962
Unlawful Occasions (Wentworth), 1941
Unloved (Olsen, as Birkley), 1965
Unlucky Number (s Phillpotts), 1906
Unnamed (Le Queux), 1902
Unnatural Causes (James), 1967
Unnatural Causes (Lyons), 1988
Unnatural Death (Sayers), 1927
Unneutral Murder (Footner), 1944
Unorthodox Corpse (C. Brown), 1957
Unpleasantness at the Bellona Club (Sayers), 1928
Unprofessional Spy (Underwood), 1964
Unquiet Grave (Strange), 1949
Unquiet Sleep (Haggard), 1962
Unravelled Knots (s Orczy), 1925
Unreasonable Doubt (Ferrars), 1958
Unruly Son (Barnard), 1978
Unseemly End (Jeffries), 1981
Unsolved (Graeme), 1931
Unspeakable (F. Davis, as Ransome), 1960
Unsuitable Job for a Woman (James), 1972
Unsuitable Miss Pelham (Drummond), 1990
Unsung Road (Harvester), 1960
Unsuspected (Armstrong), 1946
Unsuspected Chasm (M. Innes), 1946
Unsuspected Evil (Doris Disney), 1965
Untidy Murder (Lockridge), 1947
Until Death Do Us Part (McMullen), 1982
Until She Was Dead (Hull), 1949
Until Temptation Do Us Part (C. Brown), 1967
Until You Are Dead (H. Kane), 1951
Untimely Death (Hare), 1958
Untimely Guest (Babson), 1976
Untimely Ripped (McShane), 1962
Untitled (Dunnett), 1990
Unto the Third Generation (Shiel), 1903
Untouchables (Albert), 1987
Unwanted Attentions (Beck), 1988
Unwanted Corpse (Rhode, as Burton), 1954
Unwelcome Audience (Russell), 1986
Unwelcome Presence (Stuart, as Gray), 1989
Unwilling Bride (Hume), 1895
Up for Grabs (E. Gardner, as Fair), 1964
Up from Earth's Center (Dent, as Robeson), 1990
Up Jumped the Devil (C. Adams), 1943
Up the Garden Path (Rhode, as Burton), 1941
Up the Ladder of Gold (Oppenheim), 1931

Up to Her Neck (Chance), 1955
Up to No Good (Stein), 1941
Up-Tight Blonde (C. Brown), 1969
Upfold Witch (Bell), 1964
Upon Some Midnights Clear (Constantine), 1985
Upright Corpse (s Ball), 1979
Uprush of Mayhem (Scott), 1982
Upstairs and Downstairs (Carnac), 1950
Upstairs, Downstairs (Carnac), 1950
Urge for Justice (Wainwright), 1981
Urgent Hangman (Cheyney), 1938
Urn Burial (Hill, as Ruell), 1975
Usher, Ambrose series (Davey), from 1956
Uttermost Farthing (Freeman), 1914
Uttermost Farthing (Lowndes), 1908

V as in Victim (Treat), 1945
"V" for Vengeance (Wheatley), 1942
Vacancy with Corpse (Rhode, as Burton), 1941
Vachell, Inspector series (Huxley), from 1937
Valazy Family (Waters, appendix), 1869
Valcour, Lieutenant series (King), from 1929
Valediction (Parker), 1984
Valentine Estate (Ellin), 1968
Valhalla (Thornburg), 1980
Valhalla Exchange (J. Higgins, as Patterson), 1976
Valkyrie Encounter (S. Marlowe), 1978
Valley of Fear (Creasey), 1943
Valley of Fear (Doyle), 1914
Valley of Ghosts (E. Wallace), 1922
Valley of Headstrong Men (J. Fletcher), 1919
Valley of Smugglers (Upfield), 1960
Valley of Terror (Verner, as Stuart), 1935
Valley of the Assassins (Albert, as MacAlister), 1975
Valley of the Fox (Hone), 1982
Valley of the Shadow (Le Queux), 1905
Vallon, Johnny series (Cheney), from 1950
Valparaiso (Freeling, as Nicolas), 1964
Valrose Mystery (Le Queux), 1925
Valse Macabre (K. Knight), 1952
Vampire (Horler), 1935
Vampire Cameo (Avallone, as Nile), 1968
Vampire of the Village (s Chesterton), 1947
Vampires in the Shadows (McShane, as Lovell), 1976
Van (Ball), 1989
Van der Valk series (Freeling), from 1962
Van Dreisen Affair (Roth), 1960
Van Dusen, Professor Augustus S.F.X. series (Futrelle), from 1906
Van Langeren Girl (Cooper), 1960
Vance, Philo series (Van Dine), from 1926
Vanderlyn's Adventure (Lowndes), 1931
Vane Pursuit (MacLeod), 1989
Vanish in an Instant (Millar), 1952
Vanished (Pronzini), 1973
Vanished Messenger (Oppenheim), 1914
Vanisher (Dent, as Robeson), 1970
Vanishers (D. Hamilton), 1986
Vanishing Corpse (A. Gilbert), 1941
Vanishing Diary (Rhode), 1961
Vanishing Gold Truck (Keeler), 1941
Vanishing Holes Murders (Chambers), 1985
Vanishing Ladies (McBain, as Marsten), 1957
Vanishing Man (Freeman), 1912
Vanishing of Betty Varian (Wells), 1922
Vanishing of Tera (Hume), 1900

Vanishing Point (Canning), 1982
Vanishing Point (Wentworth), 1953
Vanishing Senator (Pentecost, as Philips), 1972
Vanishing Track (Carmichael), 1952
Vanity Case (Wells), 1926
Vanity Dies Hard (Rendell), 1965
Vanity Row (Burnett), 1952
Varallo, Vic series (Linnington, as Egan), from 1961
Vardy (Hebden, as Harris), 1964
Variation on a Theme (s Collier), 1935
Variety of Weapons (King), 1943
Vatican Rip (Gash), 1981
Vega$ (Deming, as Franklin), 1978
Vegas Vendetta (Pendleton), 1971
Vegetable Duck (Rhode), 1944
Veil of Ignorance (McInerny, as Quill), 1988
Veiled Lady (s Christie), 1944
Veiled Man (Le Queux), 1899
Veiled One (Rendell), 1988
Veiled Prisoner (Leroux, trans), 1923
Veils of Death (Verner, as Vane), 1935
Vein of Violence (Gault), 1961
Veins of Compassion (Audemars), 1967
Velvet Hand (Reilly), 1953
Velvet Hand (s Footner), 1928
Velvet Johnnie (s Cheyney), 1952
Velvet Mask (s Gribble), 1952
Velvet Vixen (C. Brown), 1964
Vendetta (Albert, as Quarry), 1972
Vendetta (Carmichael), 1963
Vendetta (Dibdin), 1990
Vendetta (Lambert), 1986
Vendetta in Spain (Wheatley), 1961
Vendettists (Haggard), 1990
Venetian Affair (MacInnes), 1963
Venetian Bird (Canning), 1951
Venetian Blind (Haggard), 1959
Vengeance Is Mine! (Spillane), 1950
Vengeance Man (Coles), 1967
Vengeance Man (Dan Marlowe), 1966
Vengeance of Henry Jarroman (Vickers), 1923
Vengeance of Li-Sin (Verner, as Vane), 1934
Vengeance of Mrs. Danvers (Vickers, as Kyle), 1932
Vengeance with a Twist (s Cheyney), 1946
Vengeful Sinner (Whittington), 1953
Vengeful Virgin (Brewer), 1958
Venice Train (Simenon, trans), 1974
Venner Crime (Rhode), 1933
Venom Business (Crichton, as Lange), 1969
Venom House (Upfield), 1952
Venturous Lady (Coxe), 1948
Venus Death (Benson), 1953
Venus Fly-Trap (Wainwright), 1980
Venus in Plastic (J. Mitchell), 1970
Venus Probe (Hunt, as St. John), 1966
Venus Unarmed (C. Brown), 1953
Venus Unarmed (Treat), 1961
Venus with Pistol (Lyall), 1969
Verdict in Question (Jepson), 1960
Verdict of Twelve (Postgate), 1940
Verdict of You All (Wade), 1926
Verdict Suspended (Nielsen), 1964
Verity, Mr. series (Antony), from 1951
Verity, Sergeant William series (Selwyn), from 1974
Vermilion (Whitney), 1981
Veron Mystery (Bailey), 1939
Veronica Dean Case (Waugh), 1984

Verrall Street Affair (Creasey, as Cooke), 1940
Vertigo (Boileau, trans), 1958
Very Big Bang (McCutchan), 1975
Very Cold for May (McGivern), 1950
Very Good Hater (Hill), 1974
Very Last Gambado (Gash), 1989
Very Old Money (Ellin), 1984
Very Parochial Murder (Wainwright), 1988
Very Particular Murder (Haymon), 1989
Very Quiet Murder (Crane), 1966
Very Quiet Place (Garve), 1967
Very Wrong Number (Hammond, as Douglas), 1987
Veseloffsky, Baron series (Horler), from 1926
Vesey Inheritance (Butler), 1975
Vesper Service Murders (F. Mason), 1931
Vespers (McBain), 1990
Vespucci Papers (Sturrock, as Healey), 1972
Vessel May Carry Explosives (Harvester), 1951
Viaduct Murder (R. Knox), 1925
Vicar's Roses (Breen), 1984
Vice Cop (Deming), 1961
Vice Czar Murders (C. Adams and Bellam, as Charles), 1941
Vice Isn't Private (Cleeve), 1966
Vicious Circle (D. Clark), 1983
Vicky Van (Wells), 1918
Victim (Bell), 1975
Victim (C. Brown), 1959
Victim Must Be Found (Engel), 1988
Victim Must Be Found (Hocking), 1959
Victim Needs a Nurse (Ellis Peters, as Redfern), 1940
Victim of Circumstance (Underwood), 1980
Victims (B.M. Gill), 1981
Victims (Boileau, trans), 1967
Victims (J. Ross, as Rossiter), 1971
Victims (Uhnak), 1986
Victims (Wilcox), 1985
Victor, Emma series (Wings), from 1986
Victoria (Gadney), 1975
Victorian Album (Berckman), 1973
Victorian Crown (Avallone, as Noone), 1966
Victory Song (Herbert Adams), 1943
Vienna Blood (Payne), 1984
Vietnam Legacy (Freemantle), 1984
View from Chickweed's Window (J. Vance), 1979
View from Daniel Pike (s B. Knox), 1974
View from Deacon Hill (Scott), 1981
View from the Square (Trenhaile), 1983
View from the Terrace (Meynell), 1972
View to Ransom (Russell, as Arney), 1983
Villa of Shadow (C. Brown, as Farr), 1966
Village Afraid (Rhode, as Burton), 1950
Village of Fear (Verner, as Stuart), 1934
Village of Rogues (Sturrock), 1972
Villain and the Virgin (Chase), 1948
Villains (Blackstock, as Keppel), 1980
Villains (J. Ross, as Rossiter), 1974
Villains (Whalley), 1987
Villains by Necessity (Woods), 1982
Villain's Tale (G. Newman), 1977
Villiers Touch (Garfield), 1970
Vindicator (Oppenheim), 1907
Vine, Gil series (Sterling), from 1947
Vintage Murder (Marsh), 1937
Violator (H. Kane), 1974
Violence (s Woolrich), 1958
Violence in Velvet (Avallone), 1956
Violence Is Golden (S. Marlowe, as Thames), 1956

Violence Is My Business (S. Marlowe), 1958
Violent Brothers (Bruton), 1960
Violent Dark (Gribble), 1965
Violent Death (Lewis), 1979
Violent Death of a Bitter Englishman (Cleeve), 1967
Violent Ends (Simenon, trans), 1954
Violent Enemy (J. Higgins, as Marlowe), 1969
Violent Keepsake (Gribble, as Grex), 1967
Violent Midnight (Gribble), 1986
Violent Night (Whittington, as Harrison), 1952
Violent Ones (Hunt), 1950
Violent World of Hugh Greene (C. Wilson), 1963
V.I.P. (Hall, as Trevor), 1959
Viper (s Footner), 1930
Virgin and Martyr (Greeley), 1985
Virgin Heiresses (Queen), 1954
Virgin Huntress (E. Holding), 1951
Virgin in Flames (Rohmer), 1953
Virgin in the Ice (Ellis Peters), 1982
Virgin Kills (Whitfield), 1932
Virgin Luck (Meynell), 1963
Virility Factor (H. Kane), 1971
Virus (Hornig, as Caine), 1989
Virus X (Horler), 1945
Visa to Death (Lacy), 1956
Visa to Limbo (Haggard), 1978
Vision (Koontz), 1977
Visiting Villain (Wells), 1934
Visitor (A. Gilbert), 1967
Vital Statistics (Chastain), 1977
Vivanti, Paul series (Horler), from 1925
Vivero Letter (Bagley), 1968
Vixen (C. Brown), 1964
Vixen Zero Three (Cussler), 1979
Vixen 03 (Cussler), 1978
Voice (A. Gilbert), 1965
Voice (s Matsumoto, trans), 1989
Voice from the Dark (Phillpotts), 1925
Voice from the Dead (Copper), 1974
Voice from the Grave (Doris Disney), 1968
Voice from the Living (McShane, as Lovell), 1978
Voice from the Void (Le Queux), 1922
Voice of Air (Berckman), 1970
Voice of Murder (Erskine), 1956
Voice of the Charmer (Meade), 1895
Voice of the Corpse (Murray), 1947
Voice of the Crab (Jay, as Halls), 1974
Voice of the House (Erskine), 1947
Voice of the Night (Koontz, as Coffey), 1980
Voice of the Seven Sparrows (Keeler), 1924
Voice Out of Darkness (Curtiss), 1948
Voiceless Ones (Creasey), 1973
Voices in an Empty Room (Loraine), 1973
Voices in the Night (Johnston), 1984
Voices on the Wind (Anthony), 1985
Void in Hearts (Tapley), 1988
Volcanoes of San Domingo (Hall), 1963
Voodoo Death (Gibson, as Grant), 1966
Voodoo Die (Murphy), 1978
Voodoo Murders (Avallone), 1957
Vortex (Cleary), 1977
Vote Against Poison (Sherwood), 1956
Vote for Murder (Creasey, as Martin), 1948
Vote X for Treason (Cleeve), 1964
Voyage into Violence (Lockridge), 1956
Voyage with Murder (Creasey, as York), 1952
Voyeur (Robbe-Grillet, trans), 1958

Vulgar Boatman (Tapley), 1987
Vulture in the Sun (Bingham), 1971
Vulture Is a Patient Bird (Chase), 1969
Vultures Gather (Hocking), 1945

Wabush Factor (Cunningham), 1986
Wager (Fish), 1974
Wager, Gabriel series (Burns), from 1975
Wages of Zen (Melville), 1979
Wagon-Load of Monkeys (D. Fletcher), 1988
Wail for the Corpses (Treat), 1943
Wailing Frail (Prather), 1956
Wainwright, James series (Mather), from 1968
Wait (Berckman), 1973
Wait for a Corpse (Murray), 1957
Wait for Death (Creasey, as Ashe), 1957
Wait for the Dawn (Albrand), 1950
Wait for the Wedding (Fremlin), 1961
Wait for What Will Come (Elizabeth Peters, as Michaels), 1978
Wait, Just You Wait (Berckman), 1973
Waiting Darkness (W. Roberts), 1970
Waiting for a Tiger (Sturrock, as Healey), 1965
Waiting for Oliver (Warriner, as Troy), 1962
Waiting for Orders (s Ambler), 1990
Waiting for the End of the World (A. Taylor), 1984
Wake Up to Murder (Keene), 1952
Wake Up with a Stranger (Flora), 1959
Walk a Black Wind (Michael Collins), 1971
Walk a Crooked Mile (Deming), 1959
Walk a Crooked Mile (Pentecost, as Philips), 1975
Walk in Dead Man's Wood (Scott), 1978
Walk in Fear (Ballard), 1952
Walk into My Parlour (Hocking), 1934
Walk Out on Death (Armstrong), 1954
Walk Softly, Men Praying (G. Black, as Wynd), 1967
Walk Softly Witch! (C. Brown), 1959
Walk the Dark Bridge (O'Farrell), 1952
Walk with Care (Wentworth), 1933
Walker in Shadows (Elizabeth Peters, as Michaels), 1979
Walker of the Secret Service (Post), 1924
Walker, Amos series (Estleman), from 1980
Walking Corpse (Cole), 1931
Walking Dead (Dickinson), 1977
Walking Dead Man (Pentecost), 1973
Walking Fingers (Avallone, as Stanton), 1972
Walking Shadow (Offord), 1959
Walking Stick (W. Graham), 1967
Walking Wounded (Murphy), 1988
Wall (Rinehart), 1938
Wall of Eyes (Millar), 1943
Wall of Masks (Koontz, as Coffey), 1975
Walsh, Marty series (O. Cohen), from 1948
Walter Syndrome (Neely), 1970
Walther P.38 (Wainwright), 1976
Waltz into Darkness (Woolrich, as Irish), 1947
Wanawake, Penny series (Moody), from 1984
Wandering Knife (Rinehart), 1952
Wandering Widows (Ferrars), 1962
Want to Stay Alive? (Chase), 1971
Wanted! (s Donovan), 1892
Wanted: Danny Fontaine (Ard), 1960
Wanted: Dead Men (Crossen, as Chaber), 1965
Wanted for Killing (Welcome), 1965
Wanted for Murder (Charteris), 1931
Wanted Man (Cecil), 1972
Wanted: Someone Innocent (s Allingham), 1946
Wanton (C. Brown), 1959

Wanton Princess (Wheatley), 1966
Wanton Venus (Leblanc, trans), 1935
Wantons Die Hard (Gribble), 1961
War Against the Mafia (Pendleton), 1969
War Bride (Vickers), 1942
War Cries Over Avenue C (Charyn), 1985
War Game (Price), 1976
War Machine (Marshall), 1982
War of the Dons (Rabe), 1972
War Terror (s Reeve), 1915
Ward, Eric series (Lewis), from 1980
Wardens (Howard), 1979
'Ware Danger! (Creasey, as Ashe), 1941
Warlock's Woman (Avallone, as de Pre), 1973
Warm and Golden War (Luard), 1967
Warmaster (McCutchan), 1963
Warning Bell (F. Davis, as Ransome), 1960
Warning Shot (Miller, as Masterson), 1967
Warning to the Curious (Rendell), 1987
Warrant for X (P. MacDonald), 1938
Warrant No. 113 (Gaboriau, trans), 1884
Warren, Malcolm series (Kitchin), from 1929
Warrington-Reeve, Claude series (Bell), from 1959
Warsaw Document (Hall), 1970
Warshawski, V.I. series (Paretsky), from 1982
Wary Transgressor (Chase, as Marshall), 1952
Washington IOU (Pendleton), 1972
Washington Legation Murders (F. Mason), 1935
Washington Payoff (Hunt), 1975
Washington Square Enigma (Keeler), 1933
Washington Whispers Murder (Ford), 1953
Wasp (Curtiss), 1963
Watch the Wall (Meynell), 1933
Watcher (K. Smith), 1980
Watcher (Verner), 1936
Watcher (Olsen, as Hitchens), 1959
Watcher (s Le Fanu, appendix), 1894
Watcher (Wilcox), 1978
Watcher by the Threshold (s Buchan), 1902
Watcher in the Shadows (Household), 1960
Watchers (A. Mason), 1899
Watchers (Koontz), 1987
Watchers (W. Roberts), 1971
Watching the Detectives (Rathbone), 1983
Watchmaker (Simenon, trans), 1956
Watchman, Sam series (Garfield), from 1972
Waterfront Cop (McGivern), 1956
Waterman (Hornig), 1987
Watermead Affair (Barr), 1906
Watersplash (Wentworth), 1951
Watson's Choice (G. Mitchell), 1955
Wavecrest (B. Knox), 1985
Waves of Death (Dent, as Robeson), 1989
Wax Apple (Westlake, as Coe), 1970
Waxwork (Lovesey), 1978
Waxworks Murder (J. Carr), 1932
Way Back (J. Mitchell), 1959
Way of a Wanton (Prather), 1952
Way of These Women (Oppenheim), 1913
Way Out (Graeme), 1954
Way Some People Die (Macdonald), 1951
Way the Cookie Crumbles (Chase), 1965
Way to Dusty Death (MacLean), 1973
Way to Go, Doll Baby! (Cox), 1967
Way to Nowhere (McShane), 1967
Way We Die Now (Lewin), 1973
Waylaid by Wireless (Balmer), 1909.

Waylaid in Boston (Paul), 1953
Wayne, Morgan series (Halliday, as Blood), from 1952
Ways and Means (Cecil), 1952
Ways of Darkness (Hayes), 1985
Wayward (C. Brown), 1962
Wayward Wahine (C. Brown), 1960
Wayward Widow (Gault), 1959
Wayward, Carl series (Treat), from 1940
We All Killed Grandma (F. Brown), 1952
We Haven't Seen Her Lately (Ferrars), 1956
We Must Have a Trial (Woods, as Leek), 1980
We Saw Him Die (Stein), 1947
We Shall See! (E. Wallace), 1926
We the Bereaved (Clarke), 1982
We'll Share a Double Funeral (Chase), 1982
Weak and the Strong (Kersh), 1945
Weak-Eyed Bat (Millar), 1942
Wealth Seeker (Gibson, as Grant), 1978
Weave a Rope of Sand (Hall, as Trevor), 1965
Web (Horler), 1952
Web of Hate (Thayer), 1959
Web of Horror (C. Brown, as Farr), 1966
Web of Murder (Whittington), 1958
Web of Silence (Wainwright), 1968
Webb, Detective Chief Inspector David and Sergeant Ken
    Jackson series (Anthea Fraser), from 1984
Webster, Daniel series (Sale), from 1942
Wedding Night Murder (Bush), 1937
Wednesday the Rabbi Got Wet (Kemelman), 1976
Wednesday's Wrath (Pendleton), 1979
Wee Ones (Dent, as Robeson), 1989
Week of Love (s Leasor), 1969
Weekend for Murder (Babson), 1985
Weekend Girls (John Burke), 1966
Weekend to Kill (Stuart), 1978
Weekend with Death (Wentworth), 1941
Weep for a Blonde (Halliday), 1957
Weep for a Wanton (Treat), 1956
Weep for Her (Woods), 1980
Weep for Me (J. MacDonald), 1951
Weep No More, My Lady (M. Clark), 1987
Weeping and the Laughter (Caspary), 1950
Weight of Evidence (Ormerod), 1978
Weight of the Evidence (M. Innes), 1943
Weird o' It (Shiel), 1902
Weird Tales of Terror and Detection (s Heard), 1946
Weird Valley (Dent, as Robeson), 1989
Welch, Agatha series (Johns), from 1941
Welcome Home! (Herbert Adams), 1946
Welcome, My Dear, to Belfrey House (S. Forbes), 1973
Welcome, Proud Lady (Drummond), 1964
Welcome to the Grave (McMullen), 1979
Well Now, My Pretty— (Chase), 1967
Well-Known Face (Bell), 1960
Well-Schooled in Murder (George), 1990
Wench Is Dead (Dexter), 1989
Wench Is Dead (F. Brown), 1955
Wench Is Wicked (C. Brown), 1955
Wentworth, Lyon and Bea series (R. Forrest), from 1975
Were Death Denied (Yates), 1946
Werewolf (McCutchan), 1982
Werewolf Trace (J. Gardner), 1977
Werewolf Walks Tonight (Avallone), 1974
Wesley, Sheridan series (Waugh), from 1947
West End Horror (Meyer), 1976
West Pier (P. Hamilton), 1951
West Side Jungle (S. Marlowe, as Ridgway), 1958

West, Inspector Roger (Creasey), from 1942
Westborough, Theocritus Lucius series (Clason), from 1936
Westland Case (Latimer), 1938
Westminster One (Willis), 1975
Westworld (Crichton), 1975
Wetback (O'Farrell), 1956
Wexford, Detective Chief Inspector Reginald series (Rendell),
    from 1964
Whale's Footprint (Boyer), 1988
What a Tangled Web (Hocking), 1937
What Are the Bugles Blowing For? (Freeling), 1975
What Bloody Man Is That? (Brett), 1987
What Changed Charley Farthing (Hebden), 1965
What Did Hattie See? (Roos), 1970.
What Did I Do Tomorrow? (Davies), 1972
What Dread Hand? (s Brand), 1968
What Happened at Hazelwood? (M. Innes), 1946
What Happened to Forester (s Oppenheim), 1929
What Mrs. McGillicuddy Saw! (Christie), 1957
What of Terry Coniston? (Garfield), 1971
What Price Murder (C. Adams), 1942
What Really Happened (Halliday), 1952
What Really Happened (Lowndes), 1926
What Rough Beast (Trench), 1957
What Say the Jury? (Wills), 1951
What Should You Know of Dying? (S. Forbes, as Wells), 1967
What to Do Until the Undertaker Comes (S. Forbes, as Wells),
    1971
Whatever Happened to Aunt Alice? (Curtiss), 1969
Whatever's Been Going On at Mumblesby (Watson), 1982
What's Become of Screwloose? (s Goulart), 1971
What's Better Than Money? (Chase), 1960
What's in the Dark? (Deming, as Queen), 1968
What's the Matter with Helen? (Deming), 1971
Whatsoever a Man Soweth (Le Queux), 1906
Whatsoever Loveth (Le Queux), 1907
Whatsoever Things Are True (Harvester), 1947
Wheatstack (s J. Fletcher), 1909
Wheel Is Fixed (Fox), 1951
Wheel That Turned (K. Knight), 1936
Wheel Turns (Lemarchand), 1983
Wheeler, Al series (C. Brown), from 1955
Wheeling Light (Hume), 1904
Wheels in the Forest (Chance), 1935
Wheels Within Wheels (Wells), 1923
When Carruthers Laughed (s Sapper), 1934
When Dorinda Dances (Halliday), 1951
When Eight Bells Toll (MacLean), 1966
When Elephants Forget (Murphy), 1984
When Fell the Night (Deming, as Queen), 1970
When I Grow Rich (J. Fleming), 1962
When I Say Goodbye, I'm Clary Brown (Blackstock, as
    Keppel), 1977
When in Greece (Lathen), 1969
When in Rome (Marsh), 1970
When Last I Died (G. Mitchell), 1941
When No Man Pursueth (Lowndes), 1910
When Rich Men Die (Harold Adams), 1987
When Rogues Fall Out (Freeman), 1932
When She Was Bad (Ard), 1960
When the Bough Breaks (J. Kellerman), 1985
When the Cat's Away (Friedman), 1980
When the Dark Man Calls (Kaminsky), 1983
When the Devil Was Sick (Carnac), 1939
When the Gangs Came to London (E. Wallace), 1932
When the Gods Laughed (Audemars), 1946
When the Killing Starts (Wood), 1989

When the Sacred Ginmill Closes (Block), 1986
When the Sun Goes Down (Blackstock), 1965
When the Wind Blows (Hare), 1949
When They Kill Your Wife (Michael Collins, as Crowe), 1977
When Thief Meets Thief (Keeler), 1938
When Thieves Fall Out (B. Thomson), 1937
When Were You Born? (Avallone), 1971
Where All the Girls Are Sweeter (Allbeury, as Butler), 1975
Where Are the Children? (M. Clark), 1975
Where Did Charity Go? (C. Brown), 1970
Where Eagles Dare (MacLean), 1967
Where Is Barbara Prentice? (Rhode, as Burton), 1936
Where Is Bianca? (Powell, as Queen), 1966
Where Is Janice Gantry? (J. MacDonald), 1961
Where Is She Now? (Meynell), 1955
Where Is the Withered Man? (Creasey, as Deane), 1942
Where Monsters Walk (s Avallone), 1978
Where Murder Waits (Hunt, as Davis), 1965
Where Nobody Dies (Wheat), 1986
Where Should He Die (Woods), 1983
Where the Dark Streets Go (D. Davis), 1969
Where the Desert Ends (Le Queux), 1923
Where the Fresh Grass Grows (Cooper), 1955
Where the Shoe Pinches (s Meade), 1900
Where the Snow Was Red (Pentecost), 1949
Where the Spies Are (Leasor), 1965
Where the Truth Lies (Chastain), 1988
Where There's a Will (Ellis Peters), 1960
Where There's a Will (Rinehart), 1912
Where There's a Will (Stout), 1940
Where There's a Will (Woods, as Burton), 1980
Where There's Smoke (McBain), 1975
Where There's Smoke (Sterling), 1946
Where's Emily? (Wells), 1927
Which the Justice, Which the Thief (W. Harrington), 1963
Which Way to Die? (Deming, as Queen), 1967
Whiff of Death (Asimov), 1968
Whiff of Money (Chase), 1969
While Love Lay Sleeping (Neely), 1969
While My Pretty One Sleeps (M. Clark), 1989
While Still We Live (MacInnes), 1944
While the Patient Slept (Eberhart), 1930
Whilst the Crowd Roared (Horler), 1949
Whim to Kill (Linington, as Shannon), 1971
Whip Hand (Canning), 1965
Whip Hand (Francis), 1979
Whip Hand (Rae, as Crawford), 1972
Whipping Boy (Ørum, trans), 1975
Whipping Boys (Cullingford), 1958
Whip-Poor-Will Mystery (Footner), 1935
Whirligig (Fish), 1970
Whirlpool (C. Forbes), 1991
Whirlwind (Creasey), 1979
Whisker of Hercules (Dent, as Robeson), 1981
Whisper (Marshall), 1988
Whisper Her Name (Hunt), 1952
Whisper in the Gloom (Blake), 1954
Whisper of Love (Flora), 1959
Whisper of the Axe (Condon), 1976
Whisper of the Glen (Hubbard), 1972
Whisper Town (Pentecost, as Philips), 1960
Whispering Corpse (McGivern), 1950
Whispering Cracksman (Perowne), 1940
Whispering Cup (Seeley), 1940
Whispering Death (Vickers, as Spencer), 1932
Whispering Ear (Clason), 1938
Whispering Hill (Albrand), 1947

Whispering House (Erskine), 1947
Whispering Knights (G. Mitchell), 1980
Whispering Lane (Hume), 1924
Whispering Master (Gruber), 1947
Whispering Windows (s T. Burke), 1921
Whispering Woman (Verner), 1949
Whispers (Koontz), 1980
Whispers of the Flesh (Flora), 1958
Whistle and I'll Come (McCutchan), 1957
Whistle Past the Graveyard (Deming), 1954
Whistler in the Dark (Malcolm), 1986
Whistler, series (Campbell), from 1986
Whistling Hangman (Kendrick), 1937
Whistling Shadow (Seeley), 1954
White Alley (Wells), 1915
White Bikini (C. Brown), 1963
White Cad Cross-Up (Nolan), 1969
White Circle (C. Daly), 1926
White Cockatoo (Eberhart), 1933
White Cottage Mystery (Allingham), 1928
White Crow (P. MacDonald), 1928
White Dacoit (Mather), 1974
White Dress (Eberhart), 1946
White Face (E. Wallace), 1930
White Friar (Verner, as Stuart), 1934
White Glove (Le Queux), 1915
White Horse Inn (Simenon, trans), 1980
White Jade (W. Roberts), 1975
White Leaves of Death (Audemars), 1968
White Lie (Le Queux), 1914
White Lie Assignment (Driscoll), 1971
White Lie the Dead (Loraine), 1950
White Man's Justice, Black Man's Grief (Goines), 1973
White Meat (Corris), 1981
White Menace (Rhode), 1926
White Moll (Packard), 1920
White Pavilion (Johnston), 1973
White Prior (Hume), 1895
White Priory Murders (J. Carr, as Dickson), 1934
White Rider (Charteris), 1928
White Room (Davies), 1969
White Savage (Upfield), 1961
White South (H. Innes), 1949
White Velvet (Rohmer), 1936
White Wig (Verner), 1935
White Witch of the South Seas (Wheatley), 1968
White Wolverine Contract (Atlee), 1971
White, Peregrine series (Spicer), from 1955
Whitelands Affair (Clarke), 1989
Whiteout! (Kyle), 1976
Whitewater (B. Knox), 1974
Whither Thou Goest (Le Queux), 1920
Whitney, Whit series (Dodge), from 1941
Who Benefits? (Thayer), 1955
Who Died at the Grange? (Creasey, as Halliday), 1942
Who Dies for Me? (Courtier), 1962
Who Dies There? (H. Kane), 1969
Who Goes Home? (Lemarchand), 1986
Who Goes Next? (Wainwright), 1976
Who Guards a Prince? (Hill), 1982
Who Guards the Prince? (Hill), 1982
Who Has Wilma Lathrop? (Keene), 1955
Who Is Cato? (Sims), 1981
Who Is Lewis Pinder? (Davies), 1966
Who Is Simon Warwick? (Moyes), 1978
Who Kill to Live (H. Harris), 1962
Who Killed Alfred Snowe? (J. Fletcher), 1933

Who Killed Brother Treasurer? (Wills), 1951
Who Killed Caldwell? (Wells), 1942
Who Killed Chloe? (Allingham), 1943
Who Killed Cock Robin? (Phillpotts, as Hext), 1924
Who Killed Diana? (Phillpotts, as Hext), 1924
Who Killed Dr. Sex? (C. Brown), 1964
Who Killed Mr. Garland's Mistress? (R. Forrest), 1974
Who Killed Oliver Cromwell? (Gribble), 1937
Who Killed Rebecca? (Creasey, as Halliday), 1949
Who Killed Robert Prentice? (Wheatley), 1937
Who Killed Stella Pomeroy? (B. Thomson), 1936
Who Killed Sweet Sue? (H. Kane), 1956
Who Killed the Doctor? (Rhode, as Burton), 1943
Who Killed the Husband? (Footner), 1941
Who Killed the Robins Family? (Chastain), 1983
Who Lies Here? (Ellis Peters), 1965
Who Pays the Piper? (Wentworth), 1940
Who Poisoned Hetty Duncan? (s Donovan), 1890
Who Rides a Tiger (Doris Disney), 1946
Who Rides on a Tiger (Lowndes), 1935
Who Said Murder? (Creasey, as Halliday), 1944
Who Saw Her Die? (Moyes), 1970
Who Saw Him Die? (Creasey, as Halliday), 1941
Who Saw Him Die? (Radley), 1987
Who Saw Maggie Brown? (Roos), 1967
Who Shot the Bull? (B. Knox), 1970
Who Spies, Who Kills? (Powell, as Queen), 1966
Who Steals My Name? (Crossen, as Richards), 1964
Who Steals My Name? (J. Fraser), 1974
Who Stole Sassi Manoon? (Westlake), 1969
Who the Heck Is Sylvia (Porter), 1977
Who Took Toby Rinaldi? (Mcdonald), 1980
Who Was Clare Jallu? (Boileau, trans), 1965
Who Was the Jester? (Creasey, as Ashe), 1940
Whoever I Am (Dewhurst), 1982
Whole Hog (Kenyon), 1967
Who'll Buy My Evil? (Caillou), 1966
Whom God Hath Joined (Hume), 1891
W.H.O.R.E (C. Brown), 1971
Whoreson (Goines), 1972
Who's Afraid? (E. Holding), 1940
Who's Been Sitting in My Chair? (Armstrong), 1963
Who's Calling (McCloy), 1942
Who's Next? (Baxt), 1988
Who's on First? (Buckley), 1980
Who's That Laughing in the Grave? (Avallone, as
  Stanton), 1972
Whose Body? (Sayers), 1923
Whose Corpse? (F. Davis, as Ransome), 1939
Whose Dog Are You? (Hammond), 1990
Whose Was the Hand? (Donovan, as Muddock), 1901
Whoso Findeth a Wife (Le Queux), 1897
Why Didn't They Ask Evans? (Christie), 1934
Why It Happened (Lowndes), 1938
Why Kill Arthur Potter (R. Harrison), 1984
Why Kill Johnny? (Carmichael), 1954
Why Me? (Westlake), 1983
Why Murder (Pentecost, as Philips), 1979
Why Murder? (Creasey, as Deane), 1948
Why Pick on Me? (Chase, as Marshall), 1951
Why She Cries, I Do Not Know (Miller, as Masterson), 1972
Why Shoot a Butler? (Heyer), 1933
Why So Dead? (Deming, as Queen), 1966
Why They Married (s Lowndes), 1923
W.I. (McGuire), 1937
Wicked as the Devil (Creasey, as Halliday), 1966
Wicked Designs (L. O'Donnell), 1980

Wicked Flee (Hocking), 1940
Wicked Marquis (Oppenheim), 1919
Wicked Saint (Bruton), 1965
Wicked Slice (Elkins), 1989
Wicked Uncle (Wentworth), 1947
Wicked Way to Die (Sturrock), 1973
Wicked Widow (C. Brown), 1981
Widening Gyre (Parker), 1983
Widow (Blackstock), 1967
Widow (Freeling), 1979
Widow (Simenon, trans), 1955
Widow Barony (Burnett), 1962
Widow Bewitched (C. Brown), 1958
Widow Had a Gun (Coxe), 1951
Widow Lerouge (Gaboriau, trans), 1873
Widow of Bath (Bennett), 1952
Widow Wore Red (Wormser), 1958
Widow's Cruise (Blake), 1959
Widow's Walk (Coburn), 1984
Widow's Web (Curtiss), 1956
Widower (Simenon, trans), 1961
Widow's Mite (E. Holding), 1953
Widows of Broome (Upfield), 1950
Widows Ought to Weep (Olsen), 1947
Widows Wear Weeds (E. Gardner, as Fair), 1966
Wife at Sea (Simenon, trans), 1949
Wife of Elias (Phillpotts), 1935
Wife of Ronald Sheldon (Quentin), 1954
Wife of the Red-Haired Man (Ballinger), 1957
Wife or Death (Deming, as Queen), 1963
Wife-Smuggler (Tripp), 1978
Wiggins, Gramps series (E. Gardner), from 1941
W.I.L. One to Curtis (Loraine), 1967
Wilberforce Legacy (Bell), 1969
Wilby Conspiracy (Driscoll), 1972
Wilcox, Carl series (Harold Adams), from 1981
Wild (Brewer), 1958
Wild Beauty (Donovan), 1909
Wild Island (Antonia Fraser), 1978
Wild Justice (Clifford), 1972
Wild Justice (Grant-Adamson), 1987
Wild Lonesome (Whittington), 1965
Wild Midnight Falls (Crossen, as Chaber), 1968
Wild to Possess (Brewer), 1959
Wild Town (Thompson), 1957
Wild Turkey (Simon), 1975
Wildcat (C. Brown), 1962
Wilde, Carney series (Spicer), from 1949
Wilderness Lovers (Punshon), 1912
Wilderness of Mirrors (Allbeury), 1988
Wilders Walk Away (Brean), 1948
Wildfire (Pronzini, as Foxx), 1978
Wildfire (Stern), 1985
Wildfire at Midnight (Stewart), 1956
Wiles of the Wicked (Le Queux), 1899
Wilful and Premeditated (Crofts), 1934
Wilful Lady (Sturrock), 1975
Wilful Murder (Creasey, as York), 1946
Will and Last Testament of Constance Cobble (S. Forbes), 1980
Will and the Deed (Ellis Peters), 1960
Will Anyone Who Saw the Accident . . . (Jeffries, as Ashford),
  1963
Will in the Way (Rhode, as Burton), 1947
Will-o'-the-Wisp (Wentworth), 1928
Will of the Tribe (Upfield), 1962
Will to Kill (Bloch), 1954
Williams, Race series (C. Daly), from 1927

Williams, Reno series (Murphy and Sapir), from 1971
Willing to Die (Le Fanu, appendix), 1873
Willing, Dr. Basil series (McCloy), from 1938
Willow Pattern (van Gulik, trans), 1965
Wilson, Superintendent Henry series (Cole), from 1923
Wimsey, Lord Peter series (Sayers), from 1923
Win, Lose, or Die (J. Gardner), 1989
Wind Blows Death (Hare), 1950
Wind Chill Factor (Gifford), 1975
Wind of Death (G. Black), 1967
Wind of Evil (Upfield), 1937
Wind-Up Doll (C. Brown), 1963
Windfall (Bagley), 1982
Winding Stair (A. Mason), 1923
Winding Way (J. Fletcher), 1890
Window at the White Cat (Rinehart), 1910
Window in Chungking (Courtier), 1975
Window on the Square (Whitney), 1962
Window over the Way (Simenon, trans), 1951
Window with the Sleeping Nude (Bellem), 1950
Windows Won't Wait (Olsen, as Hitchens), 1954
Winds of Midnight (Blackburn), 1964
Winds of Time (Harvester, as Gibbs), 1956
Windscreen Weepers (s Aiken), 1969
Windsor Red (Butler, as Melville), 1988
Windy Side of the Law (Woods), 1965
Wine of Life (Linington, as Egan), 1985
Wine of Violence (Linington, as Egan), 1969
Wine, Moses series (Simon), from 1973
Wine-Dark Sea (Sciascia, trans), 1985
Winged Mystery (Upfield), 1937
Wings above the Claypan (Upfield), 1943
Wings above the Diamantina (Upfield), 1936
Wings of Darkness (Audemars), 1963
Wings of Fear (Eberhart), 1945
Wings of Madness (Pentecost, as Philips), 1966
Wings of Peace (Creasey), 1948
Wings of the Falcon (Elizabeth Peters, as Michaels), 1977
Winifred (Doris Disney), 1976
Winking at the Brim (G. Mitchell), 1974
Winner Take All (Fairlie), 1953
Winner's Circle (Hayes), 1980
Winners (J. Mitchell), 1970
Winston Affair (Cunningham, as Fast), 1959
Winter (Deighton), 1987
Winter after This Summer (Ellin), 1960
Winter Kill (Fisher), 1946
Winter Kills (Condon), 1974
Winter Murder Case (Van Dine), 1939
Winter People (Whitney), 1969
Winter Touch (Egleton), 1981
Wintino, Dave series (Lacy), from 1957
Wintringham, Dr. David series (Bell), from 1937
Wire Devils (Packard), 1918
Wise Fool (Jepson), 1934
Wise, Pennington series (Wells), from 1919
Wisemann Originals (Goulart), 1989
Wish You Were Dead (McCloy), 1958
Wishful Think (B. Newman), 1954
Witch (Elizabeth Peters, as Michaels), 1973
Witch from the Sea (Holt, as Carr), 1975
Witch Hill Murder (Winslow), 1977
Witch Hunt (Harvester), 1951
Witch of the Lowtide (J. Carr), 1961
Witch's Hammer (C. Brown, as Farr), 1967
Witch's House (Armstrong), 1963
Witch's Money (s Collier), 1940

Witchdance in Bavaria (B. Knox, as MacLeod), 1975
Witches (C. Brown), 1969
Witches' Moon (Verner), 1938
Witches' Sabbath (Blackstock, as Allardyce), 1961
Witching Hill (s Hornung), 1913
Witching Murder (Butler, as Melville), 1990
Witchline (B. Knox, as MacLeod), 1988
Witchrock (B. Knox), 1977
Witch's Cauldron (Phillpotts), 1933
With a Bare Bodkin (Hare), 1946
With a Madman Behind Me (Powell), 1962
With a Vengeance (Linington, as Shannon), 1966
With Extreme Prejudice (Mather), 1975
With Flowers that Fell (Meek), 1983
With Fondest Thoughts (Blackstock), 1980
With Intent to Deceive (Coles), 1947
With Intent to Kill (Coxe), 1965
With Intent to Kill (Linington, as Shannon), 1972
With Intent to Kill (Pentecost), 1982
With Murder in Mind (Ferrars), 1948
With My Knives I Know I'm Good (Rathbone), 1969
With No Crying (Fremlin), 1980
With One Stone (Lockridge), 1961
With Option to Die (Lockridge), 1967
With This Ring (Eberhart), 1941
Withdrawing Room (MacLeod), 1980
Wither, Hildegarde series (Palmer), from 1947
Withered Garland (Harvester, as Gibbs), 1950
Withered Man (Creasey, as Deane), 1940
Withered Murder (Antony), 1955
Withering Fires (Shearing, as Bowen), 1931
Within an Inch of His Life (Gaboriau, trans), 1874
Within the Bubble (Shearing), 1950
Within the Maze (Wood, appendix), 1872
Within the Vault (Thayer), 1950
Without a Trace (F. Davis, as Ransome), 1962
Without Lawful Authority (Coles), 1943
Without Malice (Graeme), 1946
Without Motive (W. Graham), 1936
Without Orders (Albrand), 1943
Without Sin among You (H. Kane, as Stapleton), 1979
Without the Option (Hocking), 1935
Without Trace (Le Queux), 1912
Witness (Uhnak), 1969
Witness at Large (Eberhart), 1966
Witness Before the Fact (Ferrars), 1979
Witness for the Defence (A. Mason), 1913
Witness for the Prosecution (s Christie), 1948
Witness My Death (Lewis), 1976
Witnesses (Simenon, trans), 1956
Wives to Burn (Blochman), 1940
Wizard of Death (R. Forrest), 1977
Wizard's Daughter (Elizabeth Peters, as Michaels), 1980
Wobble to Death (Lovesey), 1970
Wolf by the Ears (Lewis), 1970
Wolf Cop (Jessup), 1961
Wolf in Man's Clothing (Eberhart), 1942
Wolf Time (Gores), 1989
Wolf to the Slaughter (Rendell), 1967
Wolf! Wolf! (Bell), 1979
Wolfe, Nero series (Stout), from 1934
Wolfnight (Freeling), 1982
Wolves and the Lamb (J. Fletcher), 1914
Wolves of the Night (Horler), 1931
Wolves of the Sea (Leroux, trans), 1923
Woman Accused (Vickers, as Durham), 1923
Woman Aroused (Lacy), 1951

Xélucha (s Shiel), 1975
XPD (Deighton), 1981
XYY Man (Royce), 1970
XYZ (Green), 1883
XYZ Murders (Queen, as Ross), 1961

Yang Meridian (Leasor), 1968
Yankee Lawyer (Train), 1943
Y. Cheung, Business Detective (Keeler), 1939
Yeadings, Inspector Mike and Sergeant Angus Mott series
    (Curzon), from 1983
Year of the Dragon (Copper), 1977
Year of the Golden Ape (C. Forbes), 1974
Year of the Tiger (J. Higgins, as Fallon), 1963
Year or So with Edgar (G. Higgins), 1979
Yellow Arrow Murders (F. Mason), 1932
Yellow Bungalow Mystery (Gribble), 1933
Yellow Cat (C. Knight), 1950
Yellow Claw (Rohmer), 1915
Yellow Cloud (Dent, as Robeson), 1971
Yellow Crayon (Oppenheim), 1903
Yellow Danger (Shiel), 1898
Yellow-Dog Contract (Thomas), 1976
Yellow Holly (Hume), 1903
Yellow House (Oppenheim), 1908
Yellow Hunchback (Hume), 1907
Yellow Munro (Fairlie), 1929
Yellow Overcoat (Gruber, as Acre), 1942
Yellow Ribbon (Le Queux), 1918
Yellow Room (Rinehart), 1945
Yellow Scourge (F. Davis, as Steele), 1974
Yellow Shadows (Rohmer), 1925
Yellow Snake (E. Wallace), 1926
Yellow Streak (V. Williams), 1922
Yellow Taxi (Quentin, as Stagge), 1942
Yellow Tiger (s Collins, appendix), 1924
Yellow Turban (Jay), 1955
Yellow Violet (Crane), 1942
Yellowthread Street (Marshall), 1975
Yermakov Transfer (Lambert), 1974
Yesterday Walkers (Harvester), 1958
Yesterday's Enemy (Haggard), 1976
Yesterday's Murder (Creasey, as York), 1945
Yesterday's Murder (Rice), 1950
Yesterday's News (Healy), 1989
Yesterday's Spy (Deighton), 1975
Yet She Must Die (Woods), 1973
Yogi Shrouds Yolanda (C. Brown), 1965
Yorkshire Moorland Murder (J. Fletcher), 1930
Yoshar the Soldier (W. Harrington), 1966
You Asked for It (I. Fleming), 1955
You Bet Your Life (Kaminsky), 1979
You Can Always Duck (Cheyney), 1943
You Can Call It a Day (Cheyney), 1949
You Can Die Laughing (E. Gardner, as Fair), 1957
You Can Say That Again (Chase), 1980
You Can't Believe Your Eyes (J. Fleming), 1957
You Can't Die Tomorrow (Gribble), 1975
You Can't Gag the Dead (Propper), 1949
You Can't Hit a Woman (s Cheyney), 1937
You Can't Keep the Change (Cheyney), 1940
You Can't Live Forever (Masur), 1950
You Can't See Around Corners (Cleary), 1947
You Can't Stop Me (Ard), 1953
You Can't Trust Duchesses (s Cheyney), 1945
You Could Call it Murder (Block), 1987
You Die Today (Kendrick), 1952

You Don't Need an Enemy (Stern), 1971
You Find Him—I'll Fix Him (Chase, as Marshall), 1956
You Have Yourself a Deal (Chase), 1966
You Kill Me (J. MacDonald), 1961
You Live Once (J. MacDonald), 1956
You Must Be Kidding (Chase), 1979
You Must Never Go Back (Cleeve), 1968
You Never Know with Women (Chase), 1949
You Nice Bastard (G. Newman), 1972
You Only Die Once (Copper), 1984
You Only Live Twice (I. Fleming), 1964
You Want to Die, Johnny? (G. Black), 1966
You Won't Let Me Finish (J. Fleming), 1973
You'd Be Surprised (Cheyney), 1940
You'll Die Next! (Whittington), 1954
You'll Get Yours (Ard, as Wills), 1952
You'll Never See Me Again (Woolrich, as Irish), 1951
You're Better Off Dead (Chambers), 1965
You're Dead Without Money (Chase), 1972
You're Lonely When You're Dead (Chase), 1949
You've Got Him Cold (Dewey), 1958
You've Got It Coming (Chase), 1955
Young Archduchess (Le Queux), 1922.
Young Blood (Hornung), 1898
Young Can Die Protesting (S. Forbes, as Wells), 1969
Young Dillinger (Avallone, as Stuart), 1965
Young Don't Cry (Jessup), 1957
Young Lucifer (Blackstock), 1960
Young Man from Lima (Blackburn), 1968
Young Man, I Think You're Dying (J. Fleming), 1970
Young Man on a Bicycle (s Canning), 1958
Young Mrs. Cavendish and the Kaiser's Men (Beck), 1987
Young Prey (Waugh), 1969
Young Savages (McBain, as Hunter), 1966
Young, Simon series (Trenhaile), from 1986
Your Deal, My Lovely (Cheyney), 1941
Your Loving Victim (McGerr), 1951
Your Money and Your Wife (R. Perry), 1975
Your Neck in a Noose (Ferrars), 1942
Your Royal Hostage (Antonia Fraser), 1987
Your Secret Friend (G. Mitchell, as Torrie), 1968
You're Fairly Welcome (D. Clark, as Ditton), 1973
Yours Truly, Jack the Ripper (s Bloch), 1962
Youth Hostel Murders (G. Carr), 1952
Yu'an Hee See Laughs (Rohmer), 1932

Z Cars Again (Prior), 1963
Zaleski's Percentage (MacKenzie), 1974
Zanzibar Intrigue (F. Mason), 1963
Zdt (Rathbone), 1986
Zebra-Striped Hearse (Macdonald), 1962
Zelda (C. Brown), 1961
Zemba (Gibson, as Grant), 1977
Zen There Was Murder (Keating), 1960
Zen, Aurelio series (Dibdin), from 1988
Zeppelin Destroyer (Le Queux), 1916
Zeppelin's Passenger (Oppenheim), 1918
Zero at the Bone (Ferrars), 1967
Zero Cool (Crichton, as Lange), 1969
Zero Trap (Gosling), 1979
Zigzag (Kenyon), 1981
Zilla (Tripp), 1968
Zion Road (Harvester), 1968
Zoo Murders (Webb, as Farr), 1956
Zoraida (Le Queux), 1895
Zürich AZ/900 (Albrand), 1974
Zurich Numbers (Granger), 1984

NOTES
ON
ADVISERS
AND
CONTRIBUTORS

ADEY, Robert C. S. Customs officer. Author of reviews for *Cloak and Dagger* and *The Poisoned Pen*; "Behind a Victorian Locked Door," in *Antiquarian Book Monthly Review*, April 1975; and the bibliography, *Locked Rooms and Other Impossible Crimes*, 1979. Editor of *The Art of the Impossible* (with Jack Adrian), 1990. **Essay:** Peter Antony.

ADRIAN, Jack. Freelance writer, researcher, and editor; author of pulp fiction and comic books under a variety of pseudonyms, and of critical articles on popular and genre fiction. Editor of *Sapper: The Best Short Stories*, 1984, *The Sooper and Others*, 1984, *The Road to London*, 1986, and *The Death Room: Strange and Startling Stories*, 1986, all by Edgar Wallace; *Section Blake Wins*, 1986; *The Flint Knife: Further Spook Stories*, 1988, and *The Diversions of Amy Bondham and Other Entertainments*, 1991, both by E.F. Benson; *Warning Whispers*, 1988, and *Un-Paying Guests*, 1989, both by A.M. Burrage; *Crime at Christmas*, 1988; *The Best of Berry* by Dornford Yates, 1989; and *The Art of the Impossible* (with Robert C. S. Adey), 1990. A short story appeared in *The Year's Best Mystery and Suspense Stories 1990*, 1990. **Essays:** John Newton Chance; John Gardner; Dan Kavanagh; L. A. Morse; Philip Purser; Eric Sauter; Gerald Verner; Edgar Wallace; Dornford Yates.

ALBERT, Walter. Associate Professor of French, University of Pittsburgh. Editor of *International Bibliography of Secondary Sources on Crime Literature*, 1985; author of articles and reviews in *Armchair Detective*, *Europe*, *Mystery Fancier*, *Science Fiction* and *Fantasy Book Review*; contributor to *Mystery, Detective and Espionage Magazines*, 1984 and to *Fantasy Literature*, 1990, and to *Horror Literature*, 1990. **Essays:** James Anderson; K.C. Constantine; Timothy Harris; translator of essay Hubert Monteilhet (appendix).

ALDERSON, Martha. Editorial Director, Ligature, Inc. Author of articles in *Clues*, *Mystery Fancier*, and *Reading in Virginia*; contributor to *Adolescent Female Portraits in the American Novel 1961–1981*, 1983; and contributor (with Neysa Chouteau) of chapters on Anne Morice and Lillian O'Donnell in *And Then There Were Nine*, 1984. **Essays** (with Neysa Chouteau): Dorothy Cameron Disney; Jonathan Gash; Alistair MacLean.

ALDRICH, Pearl G. Freelance writer and editor in Washington, D.C. Member of the board of directors, Washington EdPress; founder, Washington Mystery Writers. Author of numerous textbooks including *The Impact of Mass Media*, *How to Plan and Organize Your Writing*, a crime novel, *Frosty Death*, and articles in professional journals including *English Journal*, *Research in the Teaching of English*, and *Journal of Popular Culture*. Contributor to *The Washington Post*, *The Philadelphia Inquirer*, *Armchair Detective*, and *Ellery Queen's Mystery Magazine*. **Essays:** Catherine Aird; John Buxton Hilton; Carolyn Wheat.

ALLEY, Kenneth D. Associate Professor of English, Western Illinois University, Macomb. Author of articles on film and literature. **Essay:** E. Richard Johnson.

APOSTOLOU, John L. Audiovisual manager, U.S. Air Force Space Systems Division, Los Angeles, California. Co-editor of *Murder and Japan*, and *The Best Japanese Science Fiction Stories*. Contributor to *Armchair Detective*, *Mystery Fancier*, *Extrapolation* and other periodicals. **Essays:** Seicho Matsumoto (appendix); Masaka Togawa (appendix).

ATHANASON, Arthur Nicholas. Associate Professor of English, Michigan State University, East Lansing. Author of entries on Agatha Christie and John Osborne in *British Dramatists Since World War II*, 1982; contributor to *Armchair Detective*; drama reviewer for *World Literature Today*, *The Shaw Review*, and *Modern Drama*. **Essays:** Francis Beeding; Thomas Burke; Gaston Leroux (appendix).

BAIRD, Newton. Partner in Talisman Press, Georgetown, California. Author of *A Key to Fredric Brown's Wonderland: A Study and An Annotated Bibliographical Checklist*, 1981; co-editor, *An Annotated Bibliography of California Fiction 1664–1970*. Author of numerous articles, including a study of Fredric Brown, in *Armchair Detective*. Contributor of introduction to Black Box Thriller series reprinting four novels of Charles Williams. **Essays:** Fredric Brown; Michael Crichton; Joseph Hansen; Kay Nolte Smith; Charles Williams.

BAKER, Susan. Associate Professor of English, University of Nevada, Reno. Contributor of essay on E.X. Ferrars to *And Then There Were Nine*, 1984. Author of articles on Shakespeare, John Webster, and Walter Van Tilburg Clark. Teaches a course in murder mysteries. **Essays:** Richard Forrest; The Gordons; Leonard Holton; Pauline Glen Winslow.

BAKERMAN, Jane S. Professor of English, Indiana State University, Terre Haute. Author of critical articles, interviews, and regular reviews. Contributor of essay on Ruth Rendell to *Ten Women of Mystery*, 1981. Editor of *Adolescent Female Portraits in the American Novel 1961–1981* (with Mary Jean DeMarr), 1983; *And Then There Were Nine; More Women of Mystery*, 1984. **Essays:** Vera Caspary; Liza Cody; Ursula Curtiss; Daphne du Maurier; Ken Follett; Elizabeth George; Anthony Gilbert; Paula Gosling; Elisabeth Sanxay Holding; Lucille Kallen; Jane Langton; Emma Lathen; Charlotte MacLeod; Mary McMullen; Helen Reilly; Ruth Rendell; Dorothy Simpson; Jonathan Valin.

BALL, John. See his own entry. **Essay:** Elliot Paul.

BANKS, Jeff. Associate Professor of English, Stephen F. Austin State University, Nacogdoches, Texas. Regular contributor to *Poisoned Pen*. *The Not-So-Private Eye*, and *Mystery Fancier*. **Essays:** Philip Atlee; George Baxt; Stephen Marlow.

BARNARD, Robert. See his own entry. **Essay:** Sheila Radley.

BARNES, Melvyn. Director of Libraries and Art Galleries, City of London. Author of *Best Detective Fiction: A Guide from Godwin to the Present*, 1975; *Dick Francis*, 1986, and *Murder in Print: A Guide to Two Centuries of Crime Fiction*, 1986. Editor of the Remploy "Deerstalker" series of reprints of classic crime fiction, 1977–82. **Essays:** Margot Bennett; Evelyn Berckman; Anthony Berkeley; J. J. Connington; John Creasey; Freeman Wills Crofts; Francis Durbridge; Robert Finnegan; J.S. Fletcher; Leonard Gribble; Edward Grierson; Philip MacDonald; Gil North; John Rhode.

BARRY, Carol. Freelance publisher, formerly, senior production supervisor, School Division, McGraw-Hill Book Company. **Essays:** Lilian Jackson Braun; Ted Wood; L.R. Wright.

BAUDOU, Jacques. Film animator; editor-in-chief of *Enigmatika* (Paris). Has written on le roman policier, Jules Verne, Jorge Luis Borges, and Maurice Renard. **Essay:** Hubert Monteilhet (appendix).

BECKER, Jens Peter. Assistant Professor of English, Kiel University, Germany. Author of *Der englische Spionageroman*, 1973, and *Sherlock Holmes & Co.*, 1975, and co-author of *Der Detektivroman*, 1973 (revised 1978); *Literatur und Film*, 1985, co-editor of *Der Detektiverzählung auf der Spur*, 1977, and *Filmphilologie*, 1982. Author of many essays on English and American literature and a study of popular culture, *Das Automobil und die amerikanische Kultur*. **Essay:** Chester Himes.

BECKER, Mary Helen. Instructor in French, Madison Area Technical College, Wisconsin. Editor of *BREFF* (Bulletin de Récherches et d'Etudes Feministes Francophones). Author of essays on Proust, French women authors, and art, and translations from the Latin and French; co-author, *Ecrits de Femmes*, 1979. **Essays:** Pierre Audemars; Herbert Brean; Desmond Cory; L.P. Davies; Margaret Erskine; Elizabeth Ferrars; Andrew Garve; Dorothy Gilman; P.M. Hubbard; Elizabeth Lemarchand; Mabel Seeley; Phoebe Atwood Taylor.

BEDELL, Jeanne F. Assistant Professor of English, Wentworth Institute of Technology, Boston. Author of essays on Wilkie Collins in *Twelve Englishmen of Mystery*, 1984, Emma Lathen in *Ten Women of Mystery*, 1981, Mary Elizabeth Braddon in *Clues*, Anthony Price and Rudyard Kipling in *Armchair Detective*, Peter Lovesey in *Cops and Constables*, and W. Somerset Maugham in *Studies in Popular Culture*. **Essays:** G.D.H. and Margaret Cole; S.F.X. Dean; Bill Knox; Raymond Postgate.

BELL, Ian A. Lecturer in English, University College of Wales, Aberystwyth. Author of *Defoe's Fiction*, 1985; co-editor of *Watching the Detectives*, 1990. **Essays:** Michael Dibdin; Patricia Highsmith; William McIlvanney; Leonardo Sciascia (appendix); Peter Turnbull.

BERGMANN, Carol Ann. Editor, Follett Publishing Company, Chicago. Contributor to *Contemporary Poets*. **Essay:** Brian Garfield.

BERTRAM, Manfred A. Senior English master and librarian, Christ's Church College, Christchurch, New Zealand. Formerly, Lecturer at Canterbury University.

BINYON, T.J. Lecturer in Russian, Oxford University. Author of *Murder Will Out: The Detective in Fiction*, 1989, and of two novels, *Swan Song*, 1982, and *Greek Gifts*, 1988.

BLEILER, E.F. Freelance writer. Former executive vice-president, Dover Publications; editorial consultant, Scribner's. Author of *The Checklist of Science-Fiction and Supernatural Fiction*, 1978. Editor of *A Treasury of Victorian Detective Stories*, *A Treasury of Victorian Ghost Stories*, *Science Fiction Writers*, *Supernatural Fiction Writers*, and of works by Ernest Bramah, R. Austin Freeman, Émile Gaboriau, Robert H. van Gulik, and Roy Vickers, and anthologies of dime novelists and Victorian sensational novelists. **Essays:** Frederick Irving Anderson; Robert Barr; Algernon Blackwood; Wilkie Collins (appendix); Dick Donovan; Jacques Futrelle; Émile Gaboriau (appendix); H.F. Heard; William Hope Hodgson; L.T. Meade; Arthur Morrison; Baroness Orczy; Edgar Allan Poe (appendix); Richmond (appendix); Basil Thomson; Robert H. van Gulik (appendix); Roy Vickers; Mrs. Henry Wood (appendix).

BLEILER, Ellen H. Editor, *Medical Economics Magazine* and freelance writer. Author of *Verdi's Aida*, 1983, *Verdi's Rigoletto*,

1983, *Mozart's Don Giovanni*, 1985, and other books on opera. **Essay:** Jessica Mann.

BORCK, Helga. Chief of reprographic services, New York Public Library, Research Libraries. Author of numerous professional articles. **Essays** (with GraceAnne A. DeCandido): Sarah Caudwell; Anne Perry.

BOWMAN, David A. Freelance writer. **Essay** (with E.R. Hagemann): Paul Cain.

BREEN, Jon L. See his own entry. **Essays:** Robert Barnard; Clyde B. Clason; Max Allan Collins; William DeAndrea; C.W. Grafton; William Harrington; Robert Irvine; Clifford Knight; Richard Neely; Herbert Resnicow.

BRINEY, R.E. Professor of computer science and formerly departmental chair, Salem State College, Massachusetts. Editor and publisher of *The Rohmer Review*. Co-author of *SF Bibliographies*, 1972. Contributor to *The Mystery Writer's Art*, 1971, *The Conan Grimoire*, 1971, *The Mystery Story*, 1976, *The Spell of Conan*, 1980, *Twentieth-Century Science-Fiction Writers*, 1981, *Twentieth-Century Western Writers*, 1982, and *1001 Midnights*, 1986. Editor of *Master of Villainy: A Biography of Sax Rohmer*, 1972, and co-editor of *Multiplying Villainies: Selected Mystery Criticism* by Anthony Boucher, 1973. Contributing editor of *Encyclopedia of Mystery and Detection*, 1976, and *Encyclopedia of Frontier and Western Fiction*, 1983. Contributor of introductions to books by John Dickson Carr, Sax Rohmer, Christianna Brand, Bill Pronzini, Frances and Richard Lockridge, Robert E. Howard, and Lewis B. Patten. Member of the editorial board of The Mystery Library. **Essays:** Robert Bloch; Anthony Boucher; John Dickson Carr; S.H. Courtier; August Derleth; Patrick Quentin; Sax Rohmer; John Holbrook Vance.

BROBERG, Jan. Teacher and writer. Author in Swedish of six books about detective fiction, 15 anthologies of mystery short stories, and books about World War II and archaeological and historical problems. Editor of *Spektra Crime Fiction*, 1973-82. A founder of Swedish Academy of Detection. **Essays:** Francis Clifford; James McClure.

BROWN, Richard. Lecturer of English, University of Leeds. Author of *James Joyce and Sexuality*, 1985; editor of *The James Joyce Broadsheet*. **Essay:** John Milne.

CAMPENNI, Frank. Associate Professor of English, University of Wisconsin, Milwaukee. Author of reviews and articles for a number of periodicals.

CARACCIOLO, Peter. Lecturer, Royal Holloway College, London University. Author of studies of Wilkie Collins, Arthur Conan Doyle, and *Wuthering Heights*. Editor of *The Arabian Nights in Literature: Studies in the Reception of the Thousand and One Nights into British Culture*, 1988. **Essay:** Sheridan Le Fanu (appendix).

CARPENTER, Richard C. Professor Emeritus of English, Bowling Green State University, Ohio. Author of *Thomas Hardy*, 1964, and articles on Hawthorne, Conrad, Kay Boyle, and others. **Essays:** Michael Collins; Martha Grimes; Eden Phillpotts.

CARTER, Dale. Professor of Spanish and chair, Department of Foreign Languages and Literatures, California State University, Los Angeles. Co-editor of *Cuentos argentinos de misterio*, 1966, and editor of *Antologiá del realismo mágico*, 1970.

Author of *Julio Cortázar: Life, Work, and Criticism*, 1986, and *Otro round: ensayos sobre la obra de Julio Cortázar*, 1988. Has translated several stories and one novel by Spanish-American writers, and published numerous articles on Latin-American fiction. **Essays:** Aaron J. Elkins; Jonathan Kellerman; William J. Reynolds.

CARTER, Steven. Assistant Professor of English, University of Puerto Rico, Rio Piedras. Author of essay on Amanda Cross in *Ten Women of Mystery*, 1981, a study of Ross Macdonald in *Mystery and Detection Annual*, of Ishmael Reed in *Dimensions of Detective Fiction*, 1976, and *Hansberry's Drama: Commitment amid Complexity*, 1990. **Essays:** Arthur Lyons; Mark McShane.

CASSELLA-KERN, Donna. Associate Professor of Popular Culture, Mankato State University. Contributor to *Clues, Journal of Mystery and Detection, Journal of American Culture, Journal of Popular Literature*, and *Ball State Forum*. **Essays:** Bernard Newman; Cecil M. Wills.

CAWELTI, John G. Professor of English, University of Kentucky, Lexington. Author of *Apostles of the Self-Made Man*, 1965, *The Six-Gun Mystique*, 1971, *Adventure, Mystery, Romance: Formula Stories as Art and Popular Culture*, 1976; *The Spy Story* (with Bruce A. Rosenberg), 1987, and many essays on popular literature and culture.

CHOUTEAU, Neysa. Director, Sub-Scripts. Contributor (with Martha Alderson) of chapters on Anne Morice and Lillian O'Donnell in *And Then There Were Nine*, 1984, and "Joseph Harrington's Francis X. Kerrigan," in *Cops and Constables*, 1986, and "The Little Old Ladies," in *Comic Crime*, 1987. Author of articles in *Mystery Fancier* and *Clues*. **Essays** (with Martha Alderson): Dorothy Cameron Disney; Jonathan Gash; Alistair MacLean.

CLEVELAND, Carol. Instructor in Writing and Reading Program, Ithaca College, New York; freelance writer. Contributor to *American Women Writers* and *The Academic American Encyclopedia*. **Essays:** Joan Aiken; Charlotte Armstrong; Amanda Cross; Dorothy Dunnett; Elizabeth Fenwick; Anne Morice; Ross Thomas; Dorothy Uhnak.

COLE, Don. Radio and television personality at KFAB in Omaha, Nebraska. Author of television documentaries and training films. Contributor of articles on high adventure to magazines. Winner of 1983 Communication Achievement award from the University of Nebraska for outstanding service to the community. **Essays:** Brian Cooper; William H. Hallahan; Miles Tripp.

COLLINS, Max Allan. See his own entry. **Essays:** Mickey Spillane (with James L. Traylor); Jim Thompson.

COLLINS, Michael. See his own entry. **Essays:** Brett Halliday.

COX, J. Randolph. Reference and government documents librarian, Saint Olaf College, Northfield, Minnesota. Author of bibliographies and studies of John Buchan, the Nick Carter authors, George Harmon Coxe, Arthur Conan Doyle, and others for *Dime Novel Roundup, Baker Street Journal, Edgar Wallace Newsletter, English Literature in Transition, Xenophile, Armchair Detective*, and other journals. Contributor to *Mystery, Detective and Espionage Magazines*, 1983, *Dictionary of Literary Biography*, 1988, *Critical Survey of Mystery and Detective Fiction*, 1989. Editor of *H.G. Wells: A Reference*

Guide (with William J. Scheick) 1988, and *Magill's Bibliography of Masters of Mystery and Detective Fiction*, 1989. Author of *Man of Magic and Mystery: A Guide to the Work of Walter G. Gibson*, 1989. **Essays:** George Harmon Coxe; Ron Goulart; Thomas W. Hanshew; Gavin Lyall: F. Van Wyck Mason; Craig Rice; Arthur Train; Louis Joseph Vance; Jack Webb; Dennis Wheatley; Richard Wormser.

CRAIG, Patricia. Literary critic and reviewer. Author of *You're a Brick, Angela!*, 1976. *Women and Children First*, 1978, and *The Lady Investigates: Women Detectives and Spies in Fiction*, 1981, all with Mary Cadogan, and of *Elizabeth Bowen*, 1986. Editor of *The Oxford Book of Detective Stories*, 1990, and *The Penguin Book of British Comic Stories*, 1990. Contributor to *Times Literary Supplement, New Statesman, Guardian, Books and Bookmen*, and *Irish Press*. **Essays:** Gwendoline Butler; Joanna Cannan.

CRIDER, Bill. See his own entry. **Essays:** Alan Caillou; Richard Jessup; Peter Rabe; Richard Sale; Lionel White.

DANIEL, Kathy B. Editor of *Armchair Detective*.

DeCANDIDO, GraceAnne A. Senior editor, *Library Journal*. Contributor to *New York Times Book Review, American Book Collector*, and *Bookwhiz*. **Essays** (with Helga Borck): Sarah Caudwell; Anne Perry.

DeMARR, Mary Jean. Professor of English, Indiana State University, Terre Haute. Editor of *Adolescent Female Portraits in the American Novel 1961–1981* (with Jane S. Bakerman), 1983; American editor, *Annual Bibliography of English Language and Literature* (M H R A). Member of editorial advisory board and contributor to *Clues*. **Essays:** Marian Babson; Joan Hess; Velda Johnston; Carol Ann O'Marie.

DENTON, Frank. Retired after 30 years in education; now a freelance writer; reviewer for Seattle *Times*; author of short stories. **Essays:** John Blackburn: Victor Canning; Michael Gilbert; Hugh C. Rae.

DONALDSON, Betty. Formerly freelance writer. Author of "The Novels of Arthur Upfield" (bibliography) in *Armchair Detective*, 1974; and *How Did They Die?* (with Norman Donaldson), 1980. Contributor to *The Annual Obituary*, 1981, 1982. Died. **Essays:** Stephen Coulter; John Mortimer; Arthur W. Upfield.

DONALDSON, Norman. Formerly senior editor, Chemical Abstracts Service, Columbus, Ohio. Author of *Chemistry and Technology of Naphthalene Compounds*, 1958, *In Search of Dr. Thorndyke*, 1971; and *How Did They Die?* (with Betty Donaldson), 1980. Contributor to *Armchair Detective, Thorndyke File*, and *Supernatural Fiction Writers; Fantasy and Horror*, 1984. **Essays:** Mary Elizabeth Braddon (appendix); Ernest Bramah; R. Austin Freeman; Ronald A. Knox; M.P. Shiel.

DOVE, George N. Dean (retired), College of Arts and Sciences, East Tennessee State University, Johnson City. Author of *The Police Procedural*, 1982, editor of *Cops and Constables: American and British Fictional Policemen* (with Earl F. Bargainnier), 1986. Member of editorial advisory board for *Clues*. Contributor to *Armchair Detective* and the revised edition of *The Reader's Encyclopedia*. **Essays:** Rex Burns; Ed McBain; Maurice Procter; Lawrence Treat; Hilary Waugh.

DREW, Bernard A. Managing editor, *The Berkshire Courier*, Great Barrington. Editor of *Hard-Boiled Dames: Stories Featuring Women Detectives, Reporters, Adventurers, and Criminals from the Pulp Fiction Magazines of the 1930's*, 1986. Author of *Western Series and Sequels: A Reference Guide* (with Martin H. Greenberg and Charles G. Waugh), 1986, *Action Series and Sequels: A Bibliography of Espionage, Vigilante, and Soldier of Fortune Novels*, 1988, *Heroines: A Bibliography of Women Series Characters in Mystery, Police Procedural, Private Detective, Espionage, Science Fiction, Fantasy, Horror, Western, Romance, Juvenile and Action Novels*, 1989, *Lawmen in Scarlet: An Annotated Bibliography of Royal Canadian Mounted Police in Fiction and Films*, 1990, and *Motion Picture Series and Sequels: A Reference Guide*, 1990. **Essays:** Jeremiah Healy; Eric Wright.

DUEREN, Fred. Insurance claims supervisor; contributor to *Armchair Detective*. **Essays:** Harry Carmichael; Frances Crane; Sebastien Japrisot (appendix); Arthur Maling; Lenore Glen Offord; D.B. Olsen; Evelyn Piper; Kelley Roos; Francis Selwyn; Jeremy Sturrock.

DUKE, Elizabeth F. Member of English Department, Virginia Commonwealth University, Richmond; editor of Sunday book page in the Richmond *Times-Dispatch*. **Essays:** Manning Coles; Elizabeth Linington.

DUNDEE, Wayne D. Author; advisory staff member, *Detective Store Magazine;* founder and editor, *Hardboiled* 1985–90. Author of numerous short stories and two crime novels, *The Burning Season*, 1988, and *The Skintight Shroud*, 1989. **Essay:** Robert J. Randisi.

EAST, Andy. Parts manager, Fetzer company. Author of *The Agatha Christie Quizbook*, 1975, and *The Cold War File*, 1983. Contributor to *Mystery Magazine, Armchair Detective*. **Essays:** James Leasor; Philip McCutchan; Ian Stuart.

EDWARDS, Martin. Solicitor. Author of five non-fiction books and many articles for newspapers and magazines; crime fiction reviewer for *The Criminologist*. **Essays:** Eileen Dewhurst; David Fletcher; B.M. Gill; Lesley Grant-Adamson; Reginald Hill; Martin Russell.

EMMONS, Jeanne Carter. Assistant Professor of English, Briar Cliff College, Sioux City, Iowa. **Essay:** Winston Graham.

EVANS, Elizabeth. Professor of English, Georgia Institute of Technology, Atlanta. **Essay:** Helen MacInnes.

FEDER, Sue. Insurance claims investigator. Founder of the Ellis Peters Appreciation Society; editor and publisher of the Ellis Peters Appreciation Society's journal, *Most Loving Mere Folly*. Contributor to *Mystery Readers International Journal, Mystery and Detective Monthly, Mystery Scene*, and *Armchair Detective*. **Essays:** Richard Barth; Ellis Peters; Les Roberts.

FREDRIKSSON, Karl G. Publishing consultant, translator, and critic. Editor of *Jury-tidskrift för deckarvänner*. Author of a collection of essays on crime fiction *Intryck & Uttryck* (with Lilian Fredriksson), and many books in other fields. Member of the Swedish Academy of Detection. **Essays:** Tony Hillerman (with Lilian Fredriksson); Anthony Price; Gerald Seymour; Peter Van Greenaway; Peter Whalley (with Lilian Fredriksson); Margaret Yorke.

FREDRIKSSON, Lilian. Teacher, translator, and critic. Editor of *Jury-tidskrift för deckarvänner* (with Karl G. Fredriksson). Author of a collection of essays on crime fiction, *Intryck & Uttryck* (with Karl G. Fredriksson). President of the Swedish Academy of Detection. **Essays** (with Karl G. Fredriksson): Tony Hillerman; Peter Whalley.

FRENCH, Larry L. Formerly general counsel, Southern Illinois University. Edwardsville. Author of eight books on education law; reviewer and contributor to journals on mystery fiction. Died in 1978. **Essays:** Lawrence G. Blochman; Nicholas Meyer.

GEHERIN, David. Professor of English, Eastern Michigan University, Ypsilanti. Author of *Sons of Sam Spade*, 1980, *John D. MacDonald*, 1982, *The American Private Eye*, 1984 and *Elmore Leonard*, 1989. **Essay:** Robert Leslie Bellem; Max Byrd; Howard Engel; Sue Grafton.

GIBSON, Curtis S. Mystery buff. **Essays:** John Ball; Richard Hoyt.

GILBERT, Elliot L. Professor of English. University of California, Davis. Editor of *The World of Mystery Fiction*, 1978, and *"O Beloved kids": Rudyard Kipling's Letters to His Children*, 1983. Short story writer. **Essay:** Joel Townsley Rogers.

GINDIN, James. Professor of English. University of Michigan. Ann Arbor. Author of *Postwar British Fiction*, 1962, *Harvest of a Quiet Eye: The Novel of Compassion*, 1971, *The English Climate: An Excursion into a Biography of John Galsworthy*, 1979, *John Galsworthy's Life and Art: An Alien's Fortress*, 1987, and *William Golding*, 1988. **Essays:** Lionel Black; Nicholas Blake; John D. MacDonald.

GOODE, Greg. Computer consultant, University of Rochester, New York. Associate editor and film reviewer for Syndicated News Service, and action/adventure columnist for *Mystery Scene*. Author of five-part series, "The Oriental in Mystery Fiction," in *Armchair Detective* and reviews, articles, and bibliographies for *Mystery Fancier, Poisoned Pen, MELUS*, and other journals. Contributor to *International Bibliography of Secondary Sources on Crime Literature*, 1984, and *Afro-American Novelists since 1955*. **Essays:** Ted Allbeury; Nelson DeMille; Colin Forbes; Donald Goines; Duncan Kyle.

GORMAN, Ed. See his own entry. **Essays:** Dean R. Koontz; Joe R. Lansdale; Willo Davis Roberts.

GOTTSCHALK, Jane. Professor of English. University of Wisconsin, Oshkosh. Author of articles on Afro-American literature for *Wisconsin Review, Phylon, Renascence*, and on themes and types of mystery fiction for *Armchair Detective*. Contributor to *Twentieth-Century Romance and Gothic Writers*, 1982, and *Mystery, Detective, and Espionage Magazines*, 1983. Frequent lecturer on detective fiction. **Essays:** H.C. Bailey; William X. Kienzle.

GREEN, Jen. Senior editor, Aladdin Books, formerly crime editor, The Women's Press. Editor of *Reader, I Murdered Him*. 1989, and co-editor of *Despatches from the Frontiers of the Female Mind*, 1985.

GRELLA, George. Associate Professor of English, University of Rochester, New York. Author of the well-known essays, "Murder and Manners: The Formal Detective Novel" (1970) and "Murder and the Mean Streets: The Hard-Boiled

Detective Novel" (1970), and studies of Simenon, John le Carré, Ross Macdonald, the Colonial film, and images of popular culture. **Essays:** W.R. Burnett; Len Deighton; Stephen Dobyns; Ian Fleming; Thomas Harris; Joseph Hone; Elmore Leonard; Charles McCarry; Allan Prior; James Hall Roberts; Lawrence Sanders; Georges Simenon (appendix).

GRIMES, Larry E. Head of the English department and Perry Epler Gresham chair in humanities, Bethany College, West Virginia. Author of *The Fifth Dimension: The Religious Dimension of Hemingway's Early Fiction*, 1985, the chapter on Julian Symons for *Thirteen English Gentlemen of Mystery*, 1984, and *Dictionary of Literary Biography: British Mystery and Thriller Writers Since 1940*, 1989, and articles for *Modern Fiction Studies, Studies in Short Fiction*, and *Clues*. **Essays:** Anna Clarke; S.B. Hough; Michael Z. Lewin.

GROCHOWSKI, Mary Ann. Psychiatric social worker and owner of Suspense Unlimited Bookstore, West Allis, Wisconsin. Frequent contributor to journals. **Essays:** Carol Carnac; James Hadley Chase; Octavus Roy Cohen; Robert L. Fish; Hulbert Footner; John Godey; Simon Harvester; Holly Roth; John Stephen Strange; Lee Thayer; Thurman Warriner; Valentine Williams.

GROFF, Mary. Freelance writer; specializes in articles on the English mystery and on adaptation of true crime to fiction. Contributor to *Armchair Detective, Poisoned Pen*, and *Murderess Ink*, 1979. **Essays:** Guy Cullingford; Helen Nielsen; Poul Ørum (appendix); Shelley Smith.

HAGEMANN, E.R. Formerly Professor of Humanities, University of Louisville, Kentucky. Author of *A Comprehensive Index to Black Mask 1920–1951*, 1982. Editor of special issue of *Clues* on pulp detective fiction, 1981. Has written extensively on American authors and history. **Essays:** Paul Cain (with David A. Bowman); Raoul Whitfield.

HARPER, Carol M. Instructor in biological sciences, Houston Community College System, Houston. Associate editor of *Mystery Readers International Journal*. Reviewer for "Booked and Printed" column in *Alfred Hitchcock's Mystery Magazine*. **Essays:** Susan Dunlap; E.X. Giroux; Carolyn Hart; S.T. Haymon; Mark Hebden.

HARRIS, Herbert. See his own entry. **Essays:** John Burke; Margot Neville; J.F. Straker.

HARWOOD, John. Retired textile worker. Contributor to *Armchair Detective, Rohmer Review*. **Essay:** Arthur B. Reeve.

HAYNE, Barrie. Professor of English, St. Michael's College, Toronto. Author of numerous papers for the Popular Culture Association. **Essays:** John Buchan; Gerard Fairlie; Frances Noyes Hart; Fergus Hume; Thomas Kyd; E. Phillips Oppenheim; Sapper; Carolyn Wells.

HAYNE, Joanne Harack. Teacher of courses on detective literature in continuing studies programs. Author of many professional papers on the genre. **Essays:** Christianna Brand; Lillian de la Torre; Mignon G. Eberhart; Helen Eustis; Hans Hellmut Kirst (appendix); Maurice Leblanc (appendix); Mary Roberts Rinehart.

HERGENHAN, L.T. Professor of English, University of Queensland, Brisbane; editor, *Australian Literary Studies*.

HILL, Reginald. See his own entry. **Essays:** Desmond Bagley; H. R. F. Keating, Michael Kenyon: Berkely Mather.

HINCKLEY, Barbara. Freelance writer and author of *American Best Sellers: A Reader's Guide to Popular Fiction* (with Karen Hinckley), 1989. **Essays:** William F. Buckley, Jr.; Harry Kemelman.

HINCKLEY, Karen. Freelance writer and author of *American Best Sellers: A Reader's Guide to Popular Fiction* (with Barbara Hinckley), 1989. **Essays:** Clive Cussler; Victoria Holt; Robert Ludlum.

HOCH, Edward D. See his own entry. **Essays:** William Brittain; Mary Higgins Clark; John Collier; Dorothy Salisbury Davis; Stanley Ellin; Joyce Harrington; Michael Harrison; Clark Howard; Ira Levin; Margaret Millar; Wade Miller; Bill Pronzini; Jack Ritchie.

HOIDA, Naomi. Freelance writer and reviewer for numerous journals and magazines in Japan. **Essay:** Shizuko Natsuki (appendix).

HOLMAN, C. Hugh. Formerly Professor of English at the University of North Carolina. Author of studies on Southern American fiction. Under his own name and as Clarence Hunt he wrote six detective novels, four of them featuring Sheriff Macready, between 1942 and 1951. Died. **Essay:** S.S. Van Dine.

HUANG, Jim. Editor and publisher of *The Drood Review of Mystery*. **Essays:** Rick Boyer; Carl Hiaasen; M.R.D. Meek; William G. Tapply.

HUBIN, Allen J. Manager, 3M Company; founding editor, *Armchair Detective*. Author of *Crime Fiction 1749–1980: A Comprehensive Bibliography*, 1984, the revision of *The Bibliography of Crime Fiction*, 1979, and of *1981–1985 Supplement to Crime Fiction 1749–1980*, 1988. Editor of six volumes of *Best Detective Stories of the Year*, 1970–75, and *Best of the Best Detective Stories*, 1971. Conducted the weekly "Criminals at Large" column in the New York *Times*, 1968–71, and wrote "The Jury Box" for *Ellery Queen's Mystery Magazine*, 1983–88. Now writes "AJH Reviews" for *Armchair Detective* and "The Armchair Review" for *Mystery Fancier*. Received a special Edgar Allan Poe award from the Mystery Writers of America in 1977 for a decade of work editing *Armchair Detective*, and another Edgar in 1980 for *The Bibliography of Crime Fiction*.

HUGHES, Dorothy B. See her own entry. **Essays:** Gavin Black; Paul E. Erdman; Stanton Forbes; Sarah Gainham; Matthew Head; Hammond Innes; Charlotte Jay; Richard Martin Stern; Ernest Tidyman; Thomas Walsh.

IRELAND, Donald C. Assistant headmaster of a boys' preparatory school and proprietor of A1 Crime Fiction in Sherborne, Dorset. **Essays:** Roger Busby; Douglas Rutherford.

JAKUBOWSKI, Maxim. Publisher, writer, and owner of Murder One crime bookshop, London. Series editor of Blue Murder crime imprint; editor of *New Crimes, The Detective Directory* (forthcoming), and many other books on crime fiction, science fiction, fantasy, film, and music. Contributor of reviews and articles to many journals and newspapers including *The Times, Time Out* and *The Observer*. **Essays:** Paul Auster; Peter Corris; Andrew Vachss.

JAMES, Trevor. Senior Lecturer in English Literature, Darwin Community College, Northern Territory, Australia. Author of *English Literature in the Third World*, 1984; editor of *The Word Within the Word*, 1984, and *The Metaphysical Poets*, 1988. Member, editorial board, *Studies in Mystical Literature* and other journals. Contributor to academic and literary quarterlies. **Essays:** Charity Blackstock; Basil Copper; Derek Lambert.

JEFFARES, A. Norman. Professor Emeritus of English Studies, University of Stirling, Scotland; past editor of *Ariel: A Review of International English Literature* and general editor of the Writers and Critics series and the New Oxford English series. Past editor of *A Review of English Studies.* Author of *Yeats: Man and Poet*, 1949, *Seven Centuries of Poetry*, 1956, *A Commentary on the Collected Poems* (1958) and *Collected Plays* (1957) *of Yeats*, *Anglo-Irish Literature*, 1982, *A New Commentary on the Poems of W.B. Yeats*, 1984, and *W.B. Yeats: A New Biography*, 1988. Editor of *Restoration Comedy*, 1974, *Yeats: The Critical Heritage*, 1977, *Poems of W.B. Yeats: A New Selection*, 1984, *Yeats's Poems*, 1989, and *Yeats's Vision*, 1990. Formerly chairman of the Literature Section of the Scottish Arts Council; life president, the International Association for the Study of Anglo-Irish Literature. **Essay:** Nicolas Freeling.

JEFFREY, David K. Professor and Head, Department of English, James Madison University, Harrisonburg. Editor, *A Grit's Triumph: Essays on the Works of Harry Crews*, 1983. Author of essays on the mythology of crime and violence and on various writers of police and detective fiction in *Denver Quarterly* and *Midwest Quarterly*. Formerly co-editor, *Southern Humanities Review*. **Essays:** Edward S. Aarons; James Lee Burke; Stephen Greenleaf; Trevanian; Joseph Wambaugh.

JOYNER, Nancy C. Member of the Department of English, Western Carolina University, Cullowhee, North Carolina. Author of *Edwin Arlington Robinson: A Reference Guide*, 1978, and articles on modern poetry and fiction in numerous scholarly journals and books, including a chapter on P.D. James in *Ten Women of Mystery*, 1981, and an interview with Amanda McKay in *Arts Journal*, 1983. Contributor to *Great Writers of the English Language*. **Essays:** Dorothy B. Hughes; Helen McCloy.

KAVENEY, Roz. Freelance writer. **Essays:** Gregory Macdonald; Mary Wings.

KEATING, H.R.F. See his own entry. **Essays:** Margery Allingham; G.K. Chesterton; Agatha Christie; Lionel Davidson; Peter Dickinson; Arthur Conan Doyle; Mary Fitt; Dick Francis; Reg Gadney; Dulcie Gray; William Haggard; Herbert Harris; E.W. Hornung; Mary Kelly; Philip Loraine; Laurence Meynell; Jack S. Scott; George Sims; Michael Underwood; Ted Willis; P.B. Yuill.

KELLEY, George. Professor of business administration, Erie Community College, Buffalo, New York. Contributor to *Twentieth-Century Science-Fiction Writers*, *Twentieth-Century Western Writers*, *Mass Market Publishing in America*, and *Poisoned Pen*. **Essays:** Marvin Albert; George Bellairs; Robert Bloch; Thomas Chastain; Steve Fisher; James M. Fox; Bill Granger; Jack Higgins; Tony Kendrick; Gerald Kersh; Robert Littell; Dan J. Marlowe, James Mitchell; Frank Parrish; Don Pendleton; Ritchie Perry; Kenneth Royce; Mark Schorr; John Welcome.

KELLY, R. Gordon. Chair, Department of American Studies, University of Maryland, College Park. Editor of *Children's*

Periodicals of the United States, 1984. Author of *Mother Was a Lady: Self and Society in Selected American Children's Periodicals 1865–1890*, 1974. Contributor to *Twentieth-Century Children's Writers*. **Essays:** Noel Behn; John Bingham; Peter Driscoll; Adam Hall; Roger L. Simon.

KENDLE, Burton. Professor of English, Roosevelt University, Chicago. Author of articles on D.H. Lawrence, John Cheever, William March, Tennessee Williams, and others, and on screenwriting. Contributor to *Contemporary Novelists, Contemporary Poets, Contemporary Dramatists*, and *Great Writers of the English Language*. **Essay:** Joyce Porter.

KING, Daniel P. Professor and writer. Regular reviewer for *World Literature Today*; contributor of articles on criminal law and criminology to international journals. **Essays:** William Le Queux; Edgar Lustgarten; A.E.W. Mason; Nigel Morland.

KING, Margaret J. Researcher. Has written on the detective genre for *Antioch Review, Armchair Detective*, and *MELUS*. **Essay:** Earl Derr Biggers.

KLEIN, H.M. Reader in English and Comparative Literature, University of East Anglia, Norwich. Author of *Das weibliche Porträt in der Versdichtung der englischen Renaissance* (2 vols.), 1970, and *J. B. Priestley's Plays*, 1988. Editor, *The First World War in Fiction*, 1976, *The Second World War in Fiction*, 1984, *English and Scottish Sonnet Sequences of the Renaissance* (2 vols.), 1984; editor and translator, *William Wycherly, The Country Wife /Die Unschuld vom Lande*, 1972, and *Hamlet* (2 vols.), 1984. General editor, Gerstenberg English Reprints, 1977–81. **Essays:** Pierre Boileau and Thomas Narcejac (appendix); Friedrich Dürrenmatt (appendix); J. B. Priestley.

KLEIN, Kathleen Gregory. Professor and chairperson, English Department, Southern Connecticut State University, New Haven. Author of *The Woman Detective: Gender and Genre*, 1988, and numerous articles on women writers. **Essays:** Joan Fleming; Lucille Fletcher; Georgette Heyer; Lillian O'Donnell; Sara Paretsky; Margaret Scherf, Josephine Tey; Patricia Wentworth.

KLETT, Rex E. Library Director, Hampton B. Allen Library, Wadesboro, North Carolina. Regular crime fiction reviewer for *Library Journal*. **Essays:** Jon Cleary; Anthea Fraser; John Stevens Trenhaile.

LACHMAN, Marvin. Freelance writer. Co-author and co-editor of *Detectionary*, 1971 (revised 1977), and *Encyclopedia of Mystery and Detection*, 1976. Author of "Tennis and the Mystery Story" in *World Tennis*, "Murder at the Opera" in *Opera News*, and "The President and the Mystery Story" in *Mystery*. Contributes quarterly columns "Original Sins" to *Armchair Detective*, and "It's about Crime" to *Mystery Fancier*. **Essays:** William Bankier; Ben Benson; Doris Miles Disney; Leslie Ford; James Holding; Sydney Horler; E. Howard Hunt; Ed Lacy; William O'Farrell; Hugh Pentecost; James Powell; Ernest Savage; Aaron Marc Stein; Nedra Tyre.

LANDRUM, Larry N. Associate Professor of English, Michigan State University, East Lansing. Co-editor, *Dimensions of Detective Fiction*, 1976; contributed "Guide to Detective Fiction" to *Handbook of American Popular Culture*, 1978. **Essays:** Frank Gruber; Ross Macdonald.

LA PORTE, Richard G. Conservator, The Silver Door, Redondo Beach, California. Regular reviwer for *Mystery*

Scene. **Essays:** Michael Allegretto; Kenn Davis; William F. Nolan.

LEWIS, Margaret B. Biographer. Author of *Ngaio Marsh: A Life Divided*, 1991. **Essay:** Ngaio Marsh.

LEWIS, Peter. Reader in English, University of Durham. Author of *John Gay: The Beggar's Opera*, 1976, *Radio Drama*, 1981, *John le Carré*, 1985, *Fielding's Burlesque Drama*, 1987, *John Gay and the Scriblerians*, 1988, and *Eric Ambler*, 1990. **Essay:** Eric Ambler.

LOWENKOPF, Shelly. Adjunct Professor, Professional Writing Program, Graduate Division, University of Southern California, Los Angeles. Former Regional President of Southern California Chapter of Mystery Writers of America. Former director, Dell Publishing California Office, and former editor-in-chief of the Book Division, American Bibliographical Center—Clio Press, and of Sherbourne Press and Ross-Erikson Publishers. Author of over 40 novels and the critical work, "Who Cares Who Agatha Christie Killed?" **Essays:** Richard Condon; George V. Higgins.

LUNDIN, Bo. Journalist and critic. Author of three studies of detective fiction; *Salongsbödlarna*, 1971, *Spårhundarna*, 1973, and *Svenska deckare/The Swedish Crime Story*, 1981. Member of Swedish Academy of Detection and an editor of *Jury*. **Essays:** Leslie Charteris; Peter O'Donnell; Per Wahlöö and Maj Sjöwall (appendix).

MACDONALD, Andrew. Assistant Professor, Loyola University, New Orleans. Author of articles on Jonson, Shakespeare, English as a second language, science fiction, and popular culture. Contributor to *Twentieth-Century Western Writers*, 1982, *Twentieth-Century Science-Fiction Writers*, 1986, and *Twentieth-Century Romance and Historical Writers*, 1990. **Essay:** Frederick Forsyth.

MACDONALD, Gina. Assistant Professor, Loyola University, New Orleans. Author of articles on southwestern writers, Shakespeare, English as a second language, science fiction, and popular culture. Contributor to *Twentieth-Century Western Writers*, 1982, *Twentieth-Century Romance and Gothic Writers*, 1982, *Twentieth-Century Science-Fiction Writers*, 1986, and *Twentieth-Century Romance and Historical Writers*, 1990. **Essays:** Douglas Clark; Brian Cleeve; Clive Egleton; Robert Harling; Alan Hunter; Marie Belloc Lowndes; Scott Turow.

MAIO, Kathleen L. Book editor, *Sojourner: The Women's Forum.* Author of monthly mystery review column, "Murder in Print," in *Wilson Library Bulletin.* Contributor to *Murderess Ink*, 1979, *American Women Writers*, 1981, *The Female Gothic*, 1983, and to various journals and fan magazines. **Essays:** John and Emery Bonett; Anne Hocking; Jean Potts.

MALLOY, William. Editor-in-chief, Mysterious Press. **Essays:** Harold Adams; Jerome Charyn; George C. Chesbro; James Ellroy.

MASSA, Ann. Lecturer in American Literature, University of Leeds. Author of *Vachel Lindsay: Fieldworker for the American Dream*, 1970, *The American Novel Since 1945*, 1975, *American Literature in Context 1900–1930*, 1982, co-author, *American Literature, Nineteenth and Twentieth Centuries*, 1978. Editor: *Declarations of Love*, 1990. **Essays:** Elspeth Huxley; T.S. Stribling.

McCAHERY, James R. Teacher of French language and literature at Xavier High School in New York City; chairman of the Foreign Language Department, and past teacher of Romanian and Italian languages. Fulbright Scholar, 1956–1957. Author of a novel, *Grave Undertaking*, 1990, and of short stories published in *Detective Story Magazine.* Adviser and contributor to *Mystery, Detective, and Espionage Magazines*, 1983. **Essays:** Patricia McGerr; Ralph McInerny; Kurt Steel.

McCONACHIE, Frances D. Teacher of composition and literature. **Essays:** Henry Slesar; Jon Manchip White.

McMECHAN, Ian. Freelance writer. **Essays:** Joan O'Hagan; David Serafin.

McSHERRY, Frank D., Jr. Commercial artist and writer. Editor of *Treasury of American Horror Stories*, 1985, *Studies in Scarlet: Essays on Murder and Detective Fiction*, 1985, and *Treasury of American Mystery Stories*, 1989; co-editor of *Sunshine Crime*, 1987. An example of his design work appears as the dustjacket for the Mysterious Press edition of Cornell Woolrich's *Angels of Darkness.* **Essays:** Robert Twohy; Andrew York.

MEIER, Robert H. Criminal defense attorney, Minneapolis. Co-author of 18 legal texts; contributor to *Armchair Detective.* **Essay:** Warren Murphy and Richard Sapir.

MELLING, John Kennedy. Editor, Chivers Crime Writers Association Black Dagger series of crime classics. Past crime fiction reviewer for BBC, Radio London and Radio Essex. **Essays:** Gwendoline Butler; Patrick Hamilton; Milward Kennedy.

MERTZ, Stephen. Freelance writer. Contributor to *Armchair Detective* and *Mystery Fancier.* **Essays:** Peter Cheyney; Frank Kane.

MEYERSON, Jeffrey. Editor and publisher, *Poisoned Pen*, and mail-order book dealer. Has written for many other publications in the field. **Essay:** Thomas Gifford.

MILLER, D.A. Professor of History and Comparative Religion, University of Rochester, New York. Author of *The Byzantine Tradition*, 1966, *Imperial Constantinople*, 1969, and *The Book of the Hero* (forthcoming); co-editor of *Incognita.* **Essays:** Bartholomew Gill; Donald MacKenzie; Jonathan Ross.

MORRISON, Roda M. Works for Macmillan Educational Ltd.; freelance writer. **Essay:** Edmund Crispin.

MULLER, Marcia. See her own entry. **Essay:** Marilyn Wallace.

MURRAY, Will. Freelance writer and editorial director, Odyssey Publications. Author of *Doc Savage: Reflections in Bronze*, 1978. *The Duende History of The Shadow Magazine*, 1980, *Secrets of Doc Savage*, 1981, and *The Assassin's Handbook*, 1982. Co-author, *The Man Behind Doc Savage*, 1974, and *Secret Agent X*, 1980. Edited the journals *Duende*, 1975–1977, and *Skullduggery*, 1981–82. Contributor to *Armchair Detective, Clues, Starlog, Fangoria, Destroyer, Ellery Queen Mystery Magazine*, and other journals. Scriptwriter of *The Adventures of Doc Savage* radio series. **Essays:** Ken Crossen; Carroll John Daly; Norman A. Daniels; Lester Dent; Walter B. Gibson; Frank McAuliffe; Frederick Nebel; Frank L. Packard.

MUSSELL, Kay. Professor of Literature and American studies, chair of the Department of Literature, American University, Washington, D.C. Author of *Women's Gothic and Romantic Fiction: A Reference Guide*, 1981, and *Fantasy and Reconciliation: Contemporary Formulas of Women's Romance Fiction*, 1984. Co-editor, *Ethnic and Regional Foodways in the United States: The Performance of Group Identity*, 1984. **Essays:** Martha Albrand; Evelyn Anthony; Elizabeth Peters; Mary Stewart; Phyllis A. Whitney.

MUSTE, John M. Professor Emeritus of English, Ohio State University, Columbus. Author of *Say That We Saw Spain Die*, 1966, and numerous essays on modern fiction. **Essays:** Bill S. Ballinger; Thomas B. Dewey; Earl W. Emerson.

NEHR, Ellen A. Formerly senior contributing editor to *Mystery Scene;* contributor to *1001 Midnights*, 1986, and reviewer for *Columbus Dispatch* and *The Bloomsbury Review.* **Essays:** Delano Ames; K.K. Beck; Veronica Parker Johns; Kathleen Moore Knight; Marcia Muller; Max Murray; David Williams.

NEVINS, Francis M., Jr. See his own entry. **Essays:** Cleve F. Adams; William Ard; Michael Avallone; Edgar Box; Jon L. Breen; James Crumley; Erle Stanley Gardner; David Goodis; Joe L. Hensley; Edward D. Hoch; Harry Stephen Keeler; John Lutz; Barry N. Malzberg; Milton Propper; Ellery Queen; Donald E. Westlake; Cornell Woolrich.

OCCHIOGROSSO, Frank. Professor of English, Drew University, Madison, New Jersey. Member of the staff of *Shakespeare Bulletin.* Author of "Murder in the Dark: Dashiell Hammett," for *The New Republic*; a study of John Fowles. Stanislaw Lem, and the detective story for *Armchair Detective*; and an analysis of Peter Hall's Shakespearean productions in *Literature/Film Quarterly.* **Essays:** Kenneth Fearing; Barry Perowne.

OLESKIW, Susan. Freelance writer and editor; Instructor, Graphic Arts Program, Northeastern University. Author of *A Reader's Guide to the Classic British Mystery*, 1988; contributor of articles and reviews to *The Drood Review of Mystery* and journals in other fields. **Essays:** Herbert Adams; James Anderson; W.J. Burley; Ray Harrison; John Masterman; Gwen Moffat.

OUSBY, Ian. Author of *Bloodhounds of Heaven: The Detective in English Fiction from Godwin to Doyle*, 1976. Editor of *An Introduction to Fifty American Novels*, 1979, *Literary Britain and Ireland*, 1985, *The Correspondence of John Ruskin and Charles Eliot Norton* (with J.L. Bradley), 1987, *The Cambridge Guide to Literature in English*, 1988, and *The Englishman's England: Taste, Travel and the Rise of Tourism*, 1990. **Essays:** Charles Dickens (appendix); Geoffrey Household; Colin Watson.

PARKER, Robert B. See his own entry. **Essay:** Dashiell Hammett.

PATTOW, Donald J. Professor of English, University of Wisconsin, Stevens Point. Teaches courses in mystery literature. **Essay:** Henry Cecil.

PENZLER, Otto. President and publisher, Mysterious Press, New York. Editor of *Whodunit? Houdini?: Thirteen Tales of Magic, Murder, Mystery*, 1976, *The Great Detectives*, 1978; co-editor of *Encyclopedia of Mystery and Detection*, 1976.

PETTENGELL, Michael. Assistant Professor, Department of English, Mankato State University, Minnesota. **Essays:** Kinky Friedman; Richard S. Prather.

PIKE, B.A. Formerly teacher in London; occasional lecturer on crime fiction and sometime crossword-setter for *The Listener* and *Opera.* Author of *Campion's Career*, 1987, and *Detective Fiction: The Collector's Guide* (with John Cooper), 1988. Contributor to *A Review of English Literature, Books and Bookmen, Armchair Detective*, and *Dictionary of Literary Biography.* **Essays:** J.S. Borthwick; Christopher Bush; Ann Cleeves; James Fraser; Jill McGown; James Melville; Beverley Nichols; Anthony Oliver; E.R. Punshon; John Trench.

PLOWDEN, Philip. Lawyer. Editor of *Penny Sumner: Poems and Prose*, 1984. **Essays:** William Marshall; Andrew Taylor.

PRONZINI, Bill. See his own entry. **Essays:** David Alexander; Gil Brewer; Howard Browne; Frederick C. Davis; Bruno Fischer; Fletcher Flora; Ed Gorman; Geoffrey Homes; Day Keene; Talmage Powell; Harry Whittington; Collin Wilcox.

PRY, Elmer. Late Professor of English, De Paul University, Chicago. **Essay:** Vincent Starrett.

PYKETT, Lyn. Member of the English Department, University College of Wales, Aberystwyth. Author of *Emily Brontë*, 1989. **Essays:** Antonia Fraser; Katherine V. Forrest; Barbara Wilson.

QUINN, L. M. Bookseller and freelance writer. Contributor to *Twentieth-Century Romance and Historical Writers*, 1990. **Essay:** Anthea Cohen.

REILLY, John M. Professor of English, State University of New York at Albany. Editor of *Richard Wright: The Critical Reception*, 1978; author of bibliographical essays on Black literature in *American Literary Scholarship/An Annual.* Member of the board of advisers, *Contemporary Novelists.* Editor of *Twentieth-Century Crime and Mystery Writers*, first edition 1980, second edition 1985.

RESTAINO, Katherine M. Dean, Saint Peter's College, Englewood Cliffs, New Jersey. Teacher of detective fiction. Delivers lecture series on mystery and crime writers in public libraries of northern New Jersey. Author of papers for Popular Culture Association. **Essays:** Leigh Brackett; Andrew M. Greeley; Joseph Hayes; Stuart M. Kaminsky; William P. McGivern.

RHODES, Judith. Librarian, Leeds City Libraries, West Yorkshire. Contributor to *Twentieth-Century Romance and Historical Writers*, 1990. **Essays:** Claire Curzon; Gerald Hammond; Tim Heald; John Malcolm; Susan Moody; Angus Ross; John Sherwood; John Wainwright.

RODGERSON, Gillian. Freelance writer. Regular contributor to *Gay Times, Capital Gay* and *Rouge.* **Essays:** Pamela Branch; Faye Kellerman; Teri White; Sara Woods.

ROYLE, Trevor. Literary editor of *Scotland on Sunday.* Author of *Precipitous City: The Story of Literary Edinburgh*, 1980. *Death Before Dishonour: The True Story of Fighting Mac*, 1982, *James and Jim: A Biography of James Kennaway*, 1983, *The Macmillan Companion to Scottish Literature*, 1983, *The Kitchener Enigma*, 1985, *The Best Years of Their Lives*, 1986,

War Report, 1987, *The Last Days of the Raj*, 1989, *Dictionary of Military Quotations*, 1989, and *Anatomy of a Regiment*, 1990. **Essays:** Eric Bruton; Andrew Coburn; Nicholas Luard; Roger Ormerod; Laurence Payne.

RUDIN, Seymour. Professor of English, University of Massachusetts, Amherst. Performing arts critic, *Massachusetts Review*, 1969–1975, and member of the editorial board. Author of essays and reviews in *Hudson Review*, *Commentary*, *Educational Theatre Journal*, and *York Dance Review*. **Essays:** Jack Finney; Waters (appendix).

RUDOLPH, Janet A. Founder of Mystery Readers International.

RUSSELL, Sharon A. Professor of communication, Indiana State University, Terre Haute. Author of many articles on mystery and horror fiction and films. Editor of *Animals in Mysteries* (forthcoming). **Essay:** Dick Lochte.

SALISKAS, Joan M. Programmer/analyst in the Information Systems Division of the Marriott Corporation. **Essay:** Brian Freemantle.

SCOTT, Art. Senior research engineer, Kaiser Aluminum and Chemical Corporation. Editor of *Elementary, My Dear APA*, bi-monthly collection of mystery fan magazines, and publisher of *Shot Scott's Rap Sheet* for the series. Contributor to *Mystery Fancier*, *Mystery Nook*, *Poisoned Pen*, and other magazines. **Essays:** Carter Brown; Jonathan Craig; Richard Deming; David Dodge; William Campbell Gault; Henry Kane; Jonathan Latimer; Harold Q. Masur; Stuart Palmer; Bart Spicer; Stewart Sterling.

SEMPLE, Linda. Writer, and owner of Silver Moon Women's Bookshop, London. Author of *A Suitable Job for a Woman: Women Mystery Writers*, 1990, and many articles and reviews on women writers. **Essays:** Linda Barnes; Celia Fremlin; Katherine Farrer; Nancy Spain; Hannah Wakefield.

SHIBUK, Charles. Freelance writer. Senior editor of *Encyclopedia of Mystery and Detection*, 1976; co-author of *Detectionary*, 1971 (revised 1977); columnist for *Armchair Detective*. **Essays:** E.C. Bentley; Leo Bruce; Glyn Carr; Elizabeth Daly; Val Gielgud; Bruce Graeme; Cyril Hare; Richard Hull; Selwyn Jepson; Baynard H. Kendrick; C.H.B. Kitchin; Paul McGuire; Patricia Moyes; Henry Wade.

SKINNER, Robert E. Librarian, Xavier University, New Orleans. Author of *The Hard-Boiled Explicator; A Guide to the Study of Dashiell Hammett, Raymond Chandler, and Ross Macdonald*, 1984; *The New Hard-Boiled Dicks: A Personal Checklist*, 1987, and *Two Guns from Harlem: The Detective Fiction of Chester Himes*, 1989. Regular crime fiction critic for the New Orleans *Times-Picayune*. **Essays:** Robert Campbell; Donald Hamilton; Doug Hornig; Gerald Petievich.

SLUNG, Michele. Freelance writer. Editor of *Crime on Her Mind*, 1975, McKay-Washburn novels of suspense, 1975–77, and *Mother Knows Best: A Timeless Collection of Maternal Wisdom*, 1986. Author of *Momilies: As My Mother Used to Say*, 1985, *Momilies and More Momilies*, 1987, and *Only Child Book*, 1989. Contributor to *The Mystery Story*, 1976, and to many magazines; columnist for the Washington Post *Book World*. **Essays:** Anna Katharine Green; Michael Innes; Hilda Lawrence; Gladys Mitchell; Dorothy L. Sayers.

SMITH, Christopher. Senior Lecturer, School of Modern Languages and European History, University of East Anglia, Norwich; editor of *Seventeenth-Century French Studies*. Author of *Alabaster, Bikinis, and Calvados: An A.B.C. of Toponymous Words*, 1985, and *Jean Anouilh: Life, Work and Criticism*. Editor of continental emblem books, and of works by Prévost, Betham-Edwards, and Balzac. **Essays:** Erskine Childers; Timothy Holme; A.A. Milne.

SMITH, Dan. Associate director, Transnational Institute, Amsterdam. Author of three novels—*Fathers' Law*, 1986, *Serious Crimes*, 1987, and *The Fourth Crow*, 1989, and of *The Defence of the Realm in the 1980's*, 1980, *Pressure: How America Runs NATO*, 1989; co-editor of *Protest and Survive*, 1980, editor of *European Security in the 1990's*, 1989. **Essay:** Julian Rathbone.

SMITH, Penny. Member of the Department of Historical and Critical Studies, Newcastle upon Tyne Polytechnic. **Essays:** Gillian Slovo; June Thomson.

SNYDER, John. Associate Professor of Humanities, University of Houston, Clear Lake City. Author of *The Dear Love of Man: Tragic and Lyric Communion in Walt Whitman*, 1975, and "The Spy Story as Modern Tragedy" and "Film and Classical Genre" in *Literature/Film Quarterly*. **Essays:** John le Carré; Alain Robbe-Grillet (appendix).

SPURRIER, Ralph. Owner of Post Mortem Books, Hassocks, Sussex. **Essays:** Colin Dexter; Peter Lovesey.

STAPLES, Katherine. Head of Department of Technical Communications, Austin Community College, Texas. Translator of works by Henri Rousseau and of Arthur Rimbaud's *Les Illuminations*. **Essays:** Edwin Balmer and William McHarg; Jocelyn Davey; John P. Marquand.

STEDMAN, Jane W. Professor Emerita of English, Roosevelt University, Chicago. Editor of *W. S. Gilbert: Six Comic Plays*. 1967; author of *Gilbert Before Sullivan*, 1967, "From Dame to Woman: W. S. Gilbert and Theatrical Transvestitism," 1972, "The Victorian After-Image of Dr. Samuel Johnson," 1983, "Victorian Imitations of and variations on *A Midsummer Night's Dream* and *The Tempest*," in *Shakespeare and the Victorian Stage*, 1986, and many scholarly articles in *Modern Philology*, *Victorian Studies*, *Nineteenth Century Theatre Research*, *Theatre Notebook*, *American Speech* and other journals. In 1975, she added a new play to the Gilbert canon; member of the advisory board of *Victorian Studies* and *Nineteenth Century Theatre*. **Essays:** P.D. James; F. Tennyson Jesse; Joseph Shearing.

STEINER, T. R. Associate Professor of English, University of California, Santa Barbara. Author of *English Translation Theory 1650–1800*, 1975, "Stanislaw Lern's Detective Stories," 1983, "Ross Macdonald and Mind of the Hardboiled," 1986, and many articles and reviews on 18th and 20th century literature and detective fiction. **Essays:** Simon Brett; Raymond Chandler.

STERN, Carol Simpson. Professor and Chairperson of the Department of Performance Studies, Northwestern University, Evanston, Illinois; member of the advisory board, *Text and Performance Quarterly*. Contributor to *Contemporary Poets*, *Contemporary Novelists*, and *Contemporary Dramatists*, *Dictionary of Literary Biography: British Mystery and Thriller Writers Since 1940*, and to *Communication Quarterly*, *Victorian*

Studies, English Literature in Transition, Literature in Performance, and other journals. Co-author of *Texts and Context: Advanced Performance Studies* (forthcoming). **Essays:** Tom Ardies; Gerald Browne; Tom Clancy; June Drummond; Roderic Jeffries; Anthony Lejeune; Edmund McGirr.

STILWELL, Steven A. Owner of Murder for Pleasure Mystery Books, Minneapolis. **Essay:** Bill Crider.

TALBURT, Nancy Ellen. Assistant Vice-Chancellor for Academic Affairs and Professor of English, University of Arkansas, Fayetteville. Co-editor of *A Mystery Reader*, 1975, and *The American Experience*, 1978. Author of articles on Josephine Tey, H.C. Bailey, Michael Innes, and "Fetishes in Detective Fiction." Has delivered numerous papers to Popular Culture Association. **Essays:** Isaac Asimov; Josephine Bell; W. Somerset Maugham.

TAYLOR, Anna-Marie. Lecturer in Drama, University College of Wales, Aberystwyth; freelance theatre critic. Has published numerous articles on crime fiction and on educational research. **Essays:** Caroline Graham; Magdalen Nabb.

THOMPSON, George J. Member of English Department, Emporia State University, Kansas. Contributor to *Armchair Detective* and author of papers for Popular Culture Association. **Essays:** Francis M. Nevins, Jr.

THOMSON, June. See her own entry. **Essay:** Peter Chambers.

TOWNSEND, Guy M. Chief probation officer, Jefferson and Switzerland Counties, Indiana. Former History Professor, journalist, and newspaper editor, now part-time law student. Founder and publisher of *Mystery Fancier* and Brownstone Books. Senior editor, *Rex Stout: An Annotated Primary and Secondary Bibliography*, 1982; author of *To Prove a Villain*, 1985. **Essays:** V.C. Clinton-Baddeley; Richard and Frances Lockridge; Marco Page; Rex Stout.

TRAYLOR, James L. Manager, Contract Development, Blue Cross and Blue Shield of Atlanta. Editor, *Hollywood Troubleshooter: W. T. Ballard's Bill Lennox*, 1984; co-author, *One Lovely Knight: Mickey Spillane's Mike Hammer*, 1984; author of numerous articles on hard-boiled writers in *Armchair Detective, Mystery Fancier*, and *Thieftaker Journal*. Contributor of book reviews to Atlanta *Journal-Constitution*. **Essays:** Willis Todhunter Ballard; William R. Cox; Mickey Spillane (with Max Allan Collins).

VAN Dover, J.K. Professor of English, Lincoln University, Jefferson City. Author of *Murder in the Millions: Erle Stanley Gardner, Mickey Spillane, Ian Fleming*, 1984. **Essays:** Robert B. Parker; Martin Cruz Smith; Janwillen van de Wetering.

WALL, Donald C. Professor of English, Eastern Washington University, Cheney. Author of two stories in *Mike Shayne's Mystery Magazine*, one in *Skullduggery*, and a soccer novel, *Best Foot Forward*. Former program chair for mystery and detective writing for Popular Culture Association. **Essays:** Joe Gores; G.F. Newman.

WALLACE, Marilyn. See her own entry. **Essays:** Nancy Pickard; Julie Smith.

WASHBURNE, Carol. Senior editor, Elementary Language Arts, Webster Division, McGraw-Hill Book Company. Writes professionally for *Elementary English*. **Essay:** Jean Stubbs.

WEAVER, William. Critic and translator. Recipient of the National Book award in the United States and the John Florio prize in Great Britain, twice, for translations of contemporary Italian fiction. Author of *Duse: A Biography*, 1985, and *The Golden Century of Italian Opera: From Rossini to Puccini*, 1988. Chief reviewer of crime fiction and music critic for *Financial Times*, London; critic for *International Herald Tribune*. **Essay:** Roy Lewis.

WEIGEL, John A. Professor of English, Miami University, Ohio. Author of *Lawrence Durrell*, 1965, *Colin Wilson*, 1975, and *Patrick White*, 1984. **Essay:** Colin Wilson.

WHITLEY, John S. Dean, School of English and American Studies, University of Sussex, Brighton. Author of *William Golding: Lord of the Flies*, 1970, *F. Scott Fitzgerald: The Great Gatsby*, 1970, and *Detectives and Friends: Dashiell Hammett's The Glass Key and Raymond Chandler's The Long Goodbye*, 1981. **Essays:** John Franklin Bardin; James M. Cain; Derek Marlowe; Horace McCoy.

WILLIAMS, John. Freelance writer and journalist. Author of *Into the Badlands*, 1991. Regular columnist for *The Face*. **Essays:** James Hall, Derek Raymond; Newton Thornburg.

WOOD, Neville W. Retired. Collector of major Golden Age authors and Boys Weekly Publications. **Essay:** Rufus King.

WOODCOCK, George. Freelance writer, lecturer, and editor. Author of verse, plays, travel books, biographies, and works on history and politics; critical works include *William Godwin*, 1946, *The Paradox of Oscar Wilde*, 1949, *The Crystal Spirit* (on Orwell), 1966, *Hugh MacLennan*, 1969, *Odysseus Ever Returning: Canadian Writers and Writing*, 1970, *Mordecai Richler*, 1970, *Herbert Read*, 1972, *Thomas Merton*, 1978, *Orwell's Message*, 1984, and *Northern Spring: The Flowering of Canadian Literature*, 1987. **Essays:** Roy Fuller; William Godwin (appendix); Graham Greene; Julian Symons.

YATES, Donald A. Professor Emeritus, Michigan State University, East Lansing, poet and author. Co-editor of *Tales for a Rainy Night*, 1961; editor and translator of *Latin Blood*, 1972. Collaborated in translating and editing *Labyrinths* by Jorge Luis Borges, 1962; has translated several Argentine detective novels and many detective short stories, and published widely on Latin American fiction, the locked-room puzzle, and other literary topics. **Essays:** Jorge Luis Borges (appendix); H.C. Branson; Loren D. Estleman; Melville Davisson Post; Clayton Rawson; Israel Zangwill (appendix).